D1588778

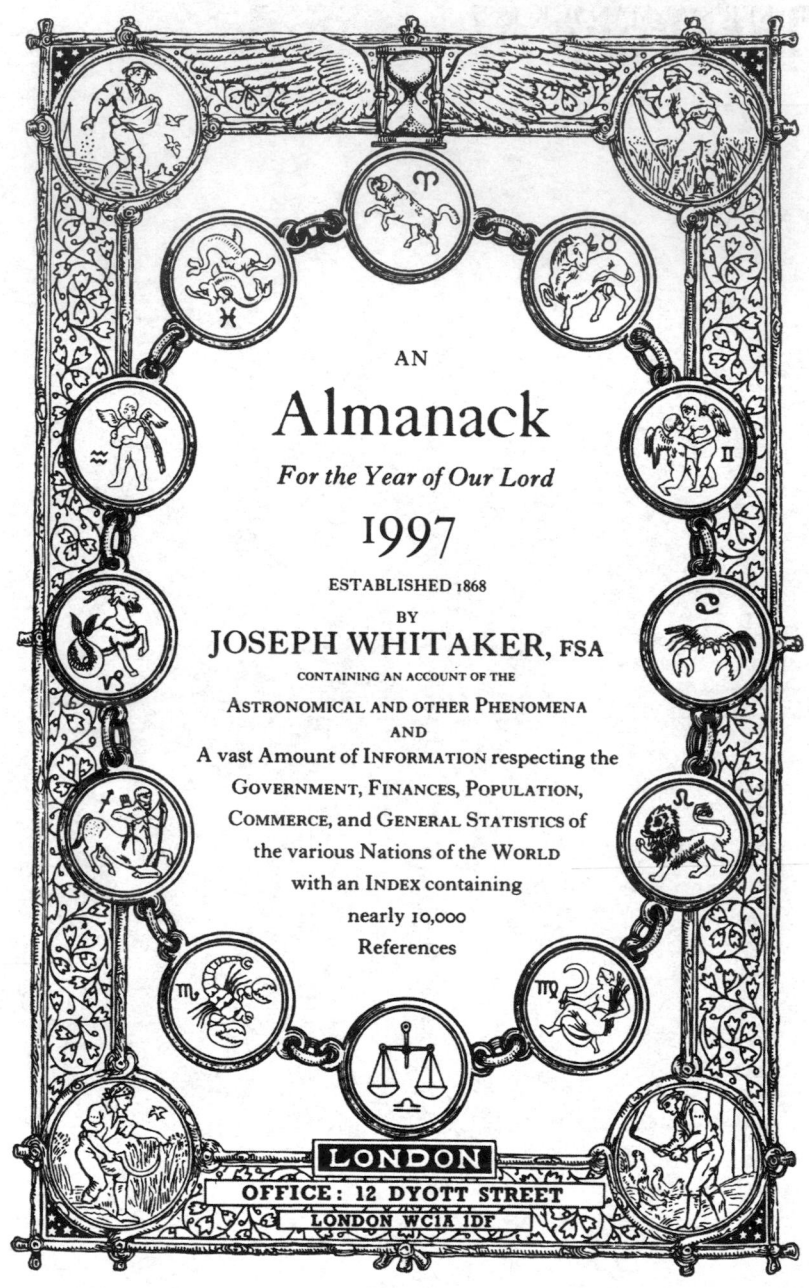

AN

Almanack

For the Year of Our Lord

1997

ESTABLISHED 1868

BY

JOSEPH WHITAKER, FSA

CONTAINING AN ACCOUNT OF THE

ASTRONOMICAL AND OTHER PHENOMENA

AND

A vast Amount of INFORMATION respecting the
GOVERNMENT, FINANCES, POPULATION,
COMMERCE, and GENERAL STATISTICS of
the various Nations of the WORLD
with an INDEX containing
nearly 10,000
References

LONDON

OFFICE: 12 DYOTT STREET
LONDON WC1A 1DF

The traditional design of the title page for Whitaker's Almanack which has appeared in each edition since 1868

Whitaker's Almanack

1997

J. WHITAKER & SONS LTD

12 DYOTT STREET · LONDON WC1A 1DF

J. Whitaker and Sons Ltd
12 Dyott Street, London wc1a 1df

Whitaker's Almanack published annually since 1868
© 129th edition J. Whitaker and Sons Ltd 1996

Standard edition (1,280 pages)
Cloth covers
0 85021 260 X

Leather binding
0 85021 261 8

Designed by Douglas Martin
Typeset by Page Bros (Norwich) Ltd
Printed and bound in Great Britain by
Clays Ltd, part of St Ives plc, Bungay, Suffolk

All rights reserved. No part of this publication may be
reproduced, stored in a retrieval system, or transmitted in
any form or by any means – electronic, mechanical,
photocopying, recording or otherwise – without prior written
permission of the publisher

SCOTTISH BORDERS LIBRARY SERVICE

ACCESSION No.	CLASS No.
116973	032·02

Contents

CONTENTS CONTINUED

Preface

SCOTTISH
BORDERS
LIBRARY
SERVICE

TO THE 129TH ANNUAL VOLUME 1997

As the last edition of Whitaker was published, the future of the peace process in the Middle East looked uncertain following the assassination of Yitzhak Rabin, the prime minister of Israel. Progress towards peace has indeed faltered in the past year, and as this edition of Whitaker goes to press, violence between Israeli and Palestinian has left over 50 dead. Nearer home, the Northern Ireland peace process has also failed to live up to the hopes invested in it, expressed in the reception accorded President Clinton when he visited Ireland at the end of 1995, and this year has seen the return of terrorism and sectarian violence. However, the year has also seen an end to fighting in Bosnia-Hercegovina, where the establishment of stable government continues. Developments throughout the year in these areas are recorded in this edition.

By the time Whitaker 1997 is published, the National Lottery will have reached its second anniversary. Its impact on the social and cultural life of Britain has been phenomenal. Details of the amounts spent on the Lottery and of the grants made with the proceeds are summarized in this edition. Statistics about other forms of gambling provide a wider context, and the articles on the year in the arts, conservation, etc., record the effect of the grants.

A summer of high-profile sporting events included the Olympic Games and Euro '96; the highlights of both are recorded and illustrated. Coverage of local government and education reflects the local government changes in Wales, Scotland and parts of England in April 1996, and details are included of proposed changes in England in 1997 and 1998.

A significant revision is the rewriting of the Legal Notes in less legalistic language. We hope readers will find the information more clearly presented and easier to use.

As ever, I must thank my staff and our specialist contributors, and the many individuals and organizations who provide us with information; without their efforts, Whitaker's Almanack could not sustain its high standards of accuracy, comprehensiveness and topicality each year.

12 DYOTT STREET   HILARY MARSDEN
LONDON WCIA IDF   *Editor*
TEL 0171-420 6000

OCTOBER 1996

The Year 1997

CHRONOLOGICAL CYCLES AND ERAS

Dominical Letter	E
Epact	21
Golden Number (Lunar Cycle)	III
Julian Period	6710
Roman Indiction	5
Solar Cycle	18

	Beginning
Japanese year Heisei 9	1 January
Regnal year 46	6 February
Chinese year of the Ox	7 February
Indian (Saka) year 1919	22 March
Hindu new year	8 April
Sikh new year	13 April
Muslim year AH 1418	9 May
Jewish year AM 5758	2 October
Roman year 2750 AUC	

RELIGIOUS CALENDARS

Epiphany	6 January
Ramadan, first day	10 January
Makara Sankranti	14 January
Birthday of Guru Gobind Singh Ji	15 January
Vasant Panchami (Sarasvati-puja)	11 February
Ash Wednesday	12 February
Mahashivaratri	7 March
Holi	23 March
Good Friday	28 March
Easter Day (western churches)	30 March
Baisakhi Mela (Sikh new year)	13 April
Ramanavami	16 April
Idu-l-adha	18 April
Passover, first day	22 April
Easter Day (Greek Orthodox)	27 April
Rogation Sunday	4 May
Ascension Day	8 May
Pentecost (Whit Sunday)	18 May
Trinity Sunday	25 May
Corpus Christi	29 May
Martyrdom of Guru Arjan Dev Ji	9 June
Feast of Weeks, first day	11 June
Raksha-bandhan	18 August
Janmashtami	24 August
Ganesh Chaturthi, first day	6 September
Ganesh festival, last day	15 September
Navaratri festival, first day	2 October
Durga-puja	2 October
Sarasvati-puja	9 October
Dasara	11 October
Yom Kippur (Day of Atonement)	11 October
Feast of Tabernacles, first day	16 October
Diwali (Hindu), first day	28 October
Diwali (Hindu), last day	2 November
Birthday of Guru Nanak Dev Ji	14 November
First Sunday in Advent	30 November
Martyrdom of Guru Tegh Bahadur Ji	4 December
Chanucah, first day	24 December
Christmas Day	25 December
Ramadan	31 December

CIVIL CALENDAR

Accession of Queen Elizabeth II	6 February
Duke of York's birthday	19 February
St David's Day	1 March
Prince Edward's birthday	10 March
Commonwealth Day	10 March
St Patrick's Day	17 March
Birthday of Queen Elizabeth II	21 April
St George's Day	23 April
Coronation of Queen Elizabeth II	2 June
Duke of Edinburgh's birthday	10 June
The Queen's Official Birthday	14 June
Diana, Princess of Wales' birthday	1 July
Queen Elizabeth the Queen Mother's birthday	4 August
Princess Royal's birthday	15 August
Princess Margaret's birthday	21 August
Lord Mayor's Day	8 November
Remembrance Sunday	9 November
Prince of Wales's birthday	14 November
Wedding Day of Queen Elizabeth II	20 November
St Andrew's Day	30 November

LEGAL CALENDAR

LAW TERMS

Hilary Term	11 January to 26 March
Easter Term	8 April to 23 May
Trinity Term	3 June to 31 July
Michaelmas Term	1 October to 20 December

QUARTER DAYS

England, Wales and Northern Ireland

Lady	25 March
Midsummer	24 June
Michaelmas	29 September
Christmas	25 December

TERM DAYS

Scotland

Candlemas	28 February
Whitsunday	28 May
Lammas	28 August
Martinmas	28 November
Removal Terms	28 May, 28 November

1997

JANUARY

Sunday		5	12	19	26
Monday		6	13	20	27
Tuesday		7	14	21	28
Wednesday	1	8	15	22	29
Thursday	2	9	16	23	30
Friday	3	10	17	24	31
Saturday	4	11	18	25	

FEBRUARY

Sunday		2	9	16	23
Monday		3	10	17	24
Tuesday		4	11	18	25
Wednesday		5	12	19	26
Thursday		6	13	20	27
Friday		7	14	21	28
Saturday	1	8	15	22	

MARCH

Sunday		2	9	16	23	30
Monday		3	10	17	24	31
Tuesday		4	11	18	25	
Wednesday		5	12	19	26	
Thursday		6	13	20	27	
Friday		7	14	21	28	
Saturday	1	8	15	22	29	

APRIL

Sunday		6	13	20	27
Monday		7	14	21	28
Tuesday	1	8	15	22	29
Wednesday	2	9	16	23	30
Thursday	3	10	17	24	
Friday	4	11	18	25	
Saturday	5	12	19	26	

MAY

Sunday		4	11	18	25
Monday		5	12	19	26
Tuesday		6	13	20	27
Wednesday		7	14	21	28
Thursday	1	8	15	22	29
Friday	2	9	16	23	30
Saturday	3	10	17	24	31

JUNE

Sunday	1	8	15	22	29
Monday	2	9	16	23	30
Tuesday	3	10	17	24	
Wednesday	4	11	18	25	
Thursday	5	12	19	26	
Friday	6	13	20	27	
Saturday	7	14	21	28	

JULY

Sunday		6	13	20	27
Monday		7	14	21	28
Tuesday	1	8	15	22	29
Wednesday	2	9	16	23	30
Thursday	3	10	17	24	31
Friday	4	11	18	25	
Saturday	5	12	19	26	

AUGUST

Sunday		3	10	17	24	31
Monday		4	11	18	25	
Tuesday		5	12	19	26	
Wednesday		6	13	20	27	
Thursday		7	14	21	28	
Friday	1	8	15	22	29	
Saturday	2	9	16	23	30	

SEPTEMBER

Sunday		7	14	21	28
Monday	1	8	15	22	29
Tuesday	2	9	16	23	30
Wednesday	3	10	17	24	
Thursday	4	11	18	25	
Friday	5	12	19	26	
Saturday	6	13	20	27	

OCTOBER

Sunday		5	12	19	26
Monday		6	13	20	27
Tuesday		7	14	21	28
Wednesday	1	8	15	22	29
Thursday	2	9	16	23	30
Friday	3	10	17	24	31
Saturday	4	11	18	25	

NOVEMBER

Sunday		2	9	16	23	30
Monday		3	10	17	24	
Tuesday		4	11	18	25	
Wednesday		5	12	19	26	
Thursday		6	13	20	27	
Friday		7	14	21	28	
Saturday	1	8	15	22	29	

DECEMBER

Sunday		7	14	21	28
Monday	1	8	15	22	29
Tuesday	2	9	16	23	30
Wednesday	3	10	17	24	31
Thursday	4	11	18	25	
Friday	5	12	19	26	
Saturday	6	13	20	27	

PUBLIC HOLIDAYS

	England and Wales	Scotland	Northern Ireland
New Year	1 January	1, 2 January	1 January
St Patrick's Day	—	—	17 March
*Good Friday	28 March	28 March	28 March
Easter Monday	31 March	—	31 March
May Day	5 May	26 May	5 May
Spring	26 May	5 May	26 May
Battle of the Boyne	—	—	14 July
Summer	25 August	4 August	25 August
*Christmas	25, 26 December	25, 26 December	25, 26 December

* In England, Wales, and Northern Ireland, Christmas Day and Good Friday are common law holidays
In the Channel Islands, Liberation Day (9 May) is a bank and public holiday

1998

JANUARY

Sunday		4	11	18	25
Monday		5	12	19	26
Tuesday		6	13	20	27
Wednesday		7	14	21	28
Thursday	1	8	15	22	29
Friday	2	9	16	23	30
Saturday	3	10	17	24	31

FEBRUARY

Sunday	1	8	15	22
Monday	2	9	16	23
Tuesday	3	10	17	24
Wednesday	4	11	18	25
Thursday	5	12	19	26
Friday	6	13	20	27
Saturday	7	14	21	28

MARCH

Sunday	1	8	15	22	29
Monday	2	9	16	23	30
Tuesday	3	10	17	24	31
Wednesday	4	11	18	25
Thursday	5	12	19	26
Friday	6	13	20	27
Saturday	7	14	21	28

APRIL

Sunday		5	12	19	26
Monday		6	13	20	27
Tuesday		7	14	21	28
Wednesday	1	8	15	22	29
Thursday	2	9	16	23	30
Friday	3	10	17	24
Saturday	4	11	18	25

MAY

Sunday		3	10	17	24	31
Monday		4	11	18	25
Tuesday		5	12	19	26
Wednesday		6	13	20	27
Thursday		7	14	21	28
Friday	1	8	15	22	29
Saturday	2	9	16	23	30

JUNE

Sunday		7	14	21	28
Monday	1	8	15	22	29
Tuesday	2	9	16	23	30
Wednesday	3	10	17	24
Thursday	4	11	18	25
Friday	5	12	19	26
Saturday	6	13	20	27

JULY

Sunday		5	12	19	26
Monday		6	13	20	27
Tuesday		7	14	21	28
Wednesday	1	8	15	22	29
Thursday	2	9	16	23	30
Friday	3	10	17	24	31
Saturday	4	11	18	25

AUGUST

Sunday		2	9	16	23	30
Monday		3	10	17	24	31
Tuesday		4	11	18	25
Wednesday		5	12	19	26
Thursday		6	13	20	27
Friday		7	14	21	28
Saturday	1	8	15	22	29

SEPTEMBER

Sunday		6	13	20	27
Monday		7	14	21	28
Tuesday	1	8	15	22	29
Wednesday	2	9	16	23	30
Thursday	3	10	17	24
Friday	4	11	18	25
Saturday	5	12	19	26

OCTOBER

Sunday		4	11	18	25
Monday		5	12	19	26
Tuesday		6	13	20	27
Wednesday		7	14	21	28
Thursday	1	8	15	22	29
Friday	2	9	16	23	30
Saturday	3	10	17	24	31

NOVEMBER

Sunday	1	8	15	22	29
Monday	2	9	16	23	30
Tuesday	3	10	17	24
Wednesday	4	11	18	25
Thursday	5	12	19	26
Friday	6	13	20	27
Saturday	7	14	21	28

DECEMBER

Sunday		6	13	20	27
Monday		7	14	21	28
Tuesday	1	8	15	22	29
Wednesday	2	9	16	23	30
Thursday	3	10	17	24	31
Friday	4	11	18	25
Saturday	5	12	19	26

PUBLIC HOLIDAYS

	England and Wales	Scotland	Northern Ireland
New Year	1 January	1, 2 January	1 January
St Patrick's Day	—	—	17 March
*Good Friday	10 April	10 April	10 April
Easter Monday	13 April	—	13 April
May Day	4 May	25 May	4 May
Spring	25 May	4 May	25 May
Battle of the Boyne	—	—	13 July†
Summer	31 August	3 August	31 August
*Christmas	25, 28 December	25, 28 December	25, 28 December

†provisional date

FORTHCOMING EVENTS 1997

This is the European Year Against Racism, and the Arts Council Year for Opera and Musical Theatre
The European City of Culture is Thessaloniki
* Provisional dates

3 – 12 January	London International Boat Show Earls Court, London
6 – 9 March	Cruft's Dog Show National Exhibition Centre, Birmingham
13 March – 6 April	Ideal Home Exhibition Earls Court, London
16 – 18 March	London International Book Fair Olympia, London
April – October	Chichester Festival Theatre season
*1 – 24 May	Mayfest 1997 Glasgow
2 May – 11 October	Pitlochry Festival Theatre season Tayside
16 May – 1 June	Bath International Music Festival
18 May – 24 August	Glyndebourne Festival Opera season Lewes, E. Sussex
22 – 23 May	Chelsea Flower Show Royal Hospital, Chelsea
23 May – 1 June	Hay Festival of Literature Hay-on-Wye, Hereford
*1 June – 10 August	Royal Academy Summer Exhibition Piccadilly, London
13 – 29 June	Aldeburgh Festival of Music and Arts Suffolk
14 June	Trooping the Colour Horse Guards Parade, London
30 June – 3 July	The Royal Show Stoneleigh Park, Kenilworth, Warks
4 – 13 July	York Early Music Festival
5 – 20 July	Cheltenham International Festival of Music
10 – 13 July	Hampton Court Palace Flower Show East Molesey, Surrey
*11 – 27 July	Buxton Festival Derbyshire
15 – 26 July	Royal Tournament Earls Court, London
17 – 26 July	Welsh Proms 1997 St David's Hall, Cardiff
17 July – 3 August	Buxton Festival Derbyshire
18 July – 13 September	Promenade Concerts season Royal Albert Hall, London
1 – 23 August	Edinburgh Military Tattoo Edinburgh Castle
2 – 9 August	Royal National Eisteddfod of Wales Bala
10 – 30 August	Edinburgh International Festival
14 – 15 August	Wisley Flower Show RHS Garden, Wisley, Surrey
14 – 15 August	Battle of the Flowers Jersey
17 – 22 August	Three Choirs Festival Hereford
24 – 25 August	Notting Hill Carnival Notting Hill, London
29 August – 2 November	Blackpool Illuminations
6 September	Braemar Royal Highland Gathering Aberdeenshire

8 – 12 September	TUC Annual Congress Blackpool
13 – 21 September	Southampton International Boat Show, Western Esplanade, Southampton
21 – 25 September	Liberal Democrat Party Conference Eastbourne
29 September – 3 October	Labour Party Conference Brighton
7 – 10 October	Conservative Party Conference Blackpool
24 – 27 October	Commonwealth Heads of Government meeting Edinburgh
November	London International Film Festival
2 November	London to Brighton Veteran Car Run
8 November	Lord Mayor's Procession and Show City of London
9 – 11 November	CBI Annual Conference Birmingham
19 – 30 November	Huddersfield Contemporary Music Festival

SPORTS EVENTS

18 January	Rugby Union: Ireland v. France Lansdowne Road, Dublin Scotland v. Wales Murrayfield, Edinburgh
1 February	Rugby Union: England v. Scotland Twickenham, London Wales v. Ireland Cardiff Arms Park
15 February	Rugby Union: Ireland v. England Lansdowne Road, Dublin France v. Wales Parc des Princes, Paris
1 March	Rugby Union: England v. France Twickenham, London Scotland v. Ireland Murrayfield, Edinburgh
7 – 9 March	Athletics: World Indoor Championships Paris
15 March	Rugby Union: Wales v. England Cardiff Arms Park France v. Scotland Parc des Princes
29 March	Oxford and Cambridge Boat Race Putney to Mortlake, London
*13 April	Athletics: London Marathon
19 April	Rugby Union: County Championship finals Twickenham, London
*19 April – 5 May	Snooker: World Professional Championship Crucible Theatre, Sheffield
3 May	Rugby League: Challenge Cup final Wembley Stadium, London
8 – 11 May	Badminton Horse Trials Badminton
*10 May	Rugby Union: Pilkington Cup final Twickenham, London
14 – 18 May	Royal Windsor Horse Show Home Park, Windsor

17 May	Football: FA Cup final
	Wembley Stadium, London
*17 May	Football: Welsh FA Cup final
	Cardiff Arms Park
*22 May	Cricket: One-day International
	England v. Australia
	Headingley, Leeds
24 May	Football: Scottish FA Cup final
	Hampden Park, Glasgow
*24 May	Cricket: One-day International
	England v. Australia
	The Oval, London
*25 May	Cricket: One-day International
	England v. Australia
	Lord's, London
1 June	TT Motorcycle Races
	Isle of Man
2 – 7 June	Golf: British Amateur Championship
	Royal St George's, Sandwich
*5 – 9 June	Cricket: 1st Test Match
	England v. Australia
	Edgbaston, Birmingham
*19 – 23 June	Cricket: 2nd Test Match
	England v. Australia
	Lord's, London
23 June – 6 July	Lawn Tennis Championships
	Wimbledon, London
2 – 6 July	Henley Royal Regatta
	Henley-on-Thames
*3 – 8 July	Cricket: 3rd Test Match
	England v. Australia
	Old Trafford, Manchester
13 July	British Formula 1 Grand Prix
	Silverstone, Northants
*12 July	Cricket: Benson and Hedges Cup
	final
	Lord's, London
12 – 26 July	Shooting: NRA Imperial Meeting
	Bisley Camp, Woking, Surrey
*24 – 28 July	Cricket: 4th Test Match
	England v. Australia
	Headingley, Leeds
28 July –	Yachting: Admiral's Cup
14 August	Cowes, Isle of Wight
1 – 10 August	Athletics: World Championships
	Athens
2 – 9 August	Yachting: Cowes Week
	Isle of Wight
*7 – 11 August	Cricket: 5th Test Match
	England v. Australia
	Trent Bridge, Nottingham
9 August	Yachting: Fastnet Race
	Cowes/Plymouth
9 – 10 August	Golf: Walker Cup
	Quaker Ridge, NY State, USA
14 – 24 August	Swimming: European
	Championships
	Seville
*21 – 25 August	Cricket: 6th Test Match
	England v. Australia
	The Oval, London
27 – 31 August	Show Jumping: European
	Championships
	Mannheim, Germany
*6 September	Cricket: NatWest Trophy Final
	Lord's, London
11 – 14 September	Eventing: Burghley Horse Trials
	Burghley, Lincs

26 – 28 September	Golf: Ryder Cup
	Valderrama, Sotogrande, Spain
October	Rugby League: World Cup
	Wembley Stadium, London
1 – 5 October	Horse of the Year Show
	Wembley Arena, London

HORSE RACING

*13 March	Cheltenham Gold Cup
*22 March	Lincoln Handicap
	Doncaster
*5 April	Grand National
	Aintree
*3 May	Two Thousand Guineas
	Newmarket
*4 May	One Thousand Guineas
	Newmarket
*6 June	The Oaks
	Epsom
*7 June	The Derby
	Epsom
*7 June	Coronation Cup
	Epsom
*17 – 20 June	Royal Ascot
*26 July	King George VI and Queen
	Elizabeth Diamond Stakes
	Ascot
*13 September	St Leger
	Doncaster
*4 October	Cambridgeshire Handicap
	Newmarket
*18 October	Cesarewitch
	Newmarket

The horse-racing fixtures are the copyright of the British Horse-racing Board

CENTENARIES OF 1997

597

*   St Augustine landed in England and converted the kingdom of Kent to Christianity

1497

24 June   John Cabot, Italian explorer, discovered Newfoundland

1697

18 October   Antonio Canaletto, Venetian artist, born
10 November   William Hogarth, painter and pictorial satirist, born
2 December   The rebuilt St Paul's Cathedral opened

1797

31 January   Franz Schubert, Austrian composer, born
14 February   Battle of Cape St Vincent
2 March   Horace Walpole, politician and man of letters, died
27 March   Alfred, Comte de Vigny, French poet, born
8 July   Edmund Burke, statesman and political writer, died
30 August   Mary Wollstonecraft Shelley, novelist, born
10 September   Mary Wollstonecraft Godwin, writer, died
11 October   Battle of Camperdown
16 October   Earl of Cardigan, commander of the charge of the Light Brigade in the Crimean War, born

* exact date not known

13 December   Heinrich Heine, German poet and journalist, born

1897

8 January   Dennis Wheatley, novelist, born
12 January   Sir Isaac Pitman, inventor of phonetic shorthand system, died
19 February   Charles Blondin, tightrope walker famous for crossing Niagara Falls, died
3 April   Johannes Brahms, German composer, died
17 April   Thornton Wilder, American novelist and playwright, born
22 May   Blackwall Tunnel opened in London
27 May   Sir John Cockcroft, nuclear physicist and Nobel Prize winner, born
12 June   Leon Goossens, musician, born
12 June   Anthony Eden, Prime Minister 1955–7, born
21 July   Tate Gallery opened on Millbank
11 August   Enid Blyton, children's author and educationalist, born
3 September   Cecil Parker, film actor, born
25 September   William Faulkner, American novelist and Nobel Prize winner, born
29 October   Joseph Goebbels, Nazi leader, born
15 November   Aneurin Bevan, politician and Labour party leader, born
12 December   Royal Automobile Club founded under the name The Automobile Club of Great Britain

CENTENARIES OF 1998

1498

23 May   Girolamo Savonarola, Italian religious and political reformer, martyred

1598

13 April   Edict of Nantes, ending civil war in France
19 July   Gilbert Sheldon, Archbishop of Canterbury 1663–78, born

1798

19 January   Auguste Comte, French philosopher, born
26 April   Eugène Delacroix, French romantic painter, born
10 May   George Vancouver, British explorer, died
4 June   Giovanni Casanova, Italian adventurer and spy, died
1 August   Battle of The Nile
4 December   Luigi Galvani, Italian scientist and anatomist, died

1898

9 January   Dame Gracie Fields, singer and comedienne, born
14 January   Lewis Carroll, novelist, died
15 January   Uffa Fox, yachtsman, born
15 March   Sir Henry Bessemer, inventor and engineer, died

16 March   Aubrey Beardsley, illustrator, died
9 April   Paul Robeson, American singer and black activist, born
3 May   Golda Meir, Prime Minister of Israel 1969–74, born
19 May   William Gladstone, statesman and Prime Minister 1868–74, 1880–5, 1886 and 1892–4, died
3 June   Samuel Plimsoll, social reformer and inventor of the 'Plimsoll line' for the safe loading of ships, died
6 June   Dame Ninette de Valois, Irish dancer and choreographer, founder of the Royal Ballet, born
9 June   Hong Kong leased by Britain from China for 99 years
17 June   Sir Edward Burne-Jones, painter, died
30 July   Otto von Bismarck, Prusso-German statesman, died
    Henry Moore, sculptor, born
8 August   Waterloo and City Line on London Underground opened
2 September   Battle of Omdurman
26 September   George Gershwin, American composer, born
20 November   Sir John Fowler, civil engineer and co-designer of the Forth Bridge, died
26 December   Radium discovered by Pierre and Marie Curie

Astronomy

The following pages give astronomical data for each month of the year 1997. There are four pages of data for each month. All data are given for 0h Greenwich Mean Time (GMT), i.e. at the midnight at the beginning of the day named. This applies also to data for the months when British Summer Time is in operation (for dates, *see* below).

The astronomical data are given in a form suitable for observation with the naked eye or with a small telescope. These data do not attempt to replace the *Astronomical Almanac* for professional astronomers.

A fuller explanation of how to use the astronomical data is given on pages 71–3.

CALENDAR FOR EACH MONTH

The calendar for each month shows dates of religious, civil and legal significance for the year 1997.

The days in bold type are the principal holy days and the festivals and greater holy days of the Church of England as set out in the calendar of the Alternative Service Book 1980, and the calendar of Sundays set out in the Book of Common Prayer. Observance of certain festivals and greater holy days is transferred if the day falls on a principal holy day. The calendar shows the date on which holy days and festivals are to be observed in 1997.

The days in small capitals are dates of significance in the calendars of non-Anglican denominations and non-Christian religions.

The days in italic type are dates of civil and legal significance. The royal anniversaries shown in italic type are the days on which the Union flag is to be flown.

The rest of the calendar comprises days of general interest and the dates of birth or death of well-known people.

Fuller explanations of the various calendars can be found under Time Measurement and Calendars (pages 81–9).

The zodiacal signs through which the Sun is passing during each month are illustrated. The date of transition from one sign to the next, to the nearest hour, is given under Astronomical Phenomena.

JULIAN DATE

The Julian date on 1997 January 0.0 is 2450448.5. To find the Julian date for any other date in 1997 (at 0h GMT), add the day-of-the-year number on the extreme right of the calendar for each month to the Julian date for January 0.0.

SEASONS

The seasons are defined astronomically as follows:

Spring from the vernal equinox to the summer solstice
Summer from the summer solstice to the autumnal equinox
Autumn from the autumnal equinox to the winter solstice
Winter from the winter solstice to the vernal equinox

The seasons in 1997 are:

Northern hemisphere

Vernal equinox	March 20d 14h GMT
Summer solstice	June 21d 08h GMT
Autumnal equinox	September 23d 00h GMT
Winter solstice	December 21d 20h GMT

Southern hemisphere

Autumnal equinox	March 20d 14h GMT
Winter solstice	June 21d 08h GMT
Vernal equinox	September 23d 00h GMT
Summer solstice	December 21d 20h GMT

The longest day of the year, measured from sunrise to sunset, is at the summer solstice. For the remainder of this century the longest day in the United Kingdom will fall each year on 21 June. *See also* page 81.

The shortest day of the year is at the winter solstice. For the remainder of this century the shortest day in the United Kingdom will fall on 21 December in 1997 and 2000, and on 22 December in 1998 and 1999. *See also* page 81.

The equinox is the point at which day and night are of equal length all over the world. *See also* page 81.

In popular parlance, the seasons in the northern hemisphere comprise the following months:

Spring	March, April, May
Summer	June, July, August
Autumn	September, October, November
Winter	December, January, February

BRITISH SUMMER TIME

British Summer Time is the legal time for general purposes during the period in which it is in operation (*see also* page 75). During this period, clocks are kept one hour ahead of Greenwich Mean Time. The hour of changeover is 01h Greenwich Mean Time. The duration of Summer Time in 1997 is:

March 30 01h GMT to October 26 01h GMT

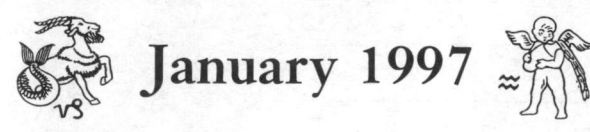

January 1997

FIRST MONTH, 31 DAYS. *Janus*, god of the portal, facing two ways, past and future

1	*Wednesday*	**The Naming of Jesus.** *Bank Holiday in the UK*	*week 52 day* 1
2	*Thursday*	*Bank Holiday in Scotland.* Sir Michael Tippett b. 1905	2
3	*Friday*	J. R. R. Tolkien b. 1892. Marshal Joffre d. 1931	3
4	*Saturday*	Augustus John b. 1878. Donald Campbell d. 1967	4
5	*Sunday*	**2nd S. after Christmas.** Twelfth Night	*week* 1 *day* 5
6	*Monday*	**The Epiphany.** Fanny Burney d. 1840	6
7	*Tuesday*	Francis Poulenc b. 1899. Trevor Howard d. 1988	7
8	*Wednesday*	Sir Lawrence Alma-Tadema b. 1836	8
9	*Thursday*	Simone de Beauvoir b. 1908. Ruskin Spear d. 1990	9
10	*Friday*	RAMADAN begins. Dashiel Hammett d. 1961	10
11	*Saturday*	*Hilary Law Sittings begin.* Fred Archer b. 1857	11
12	*Sunday*	**1st S. after Epiphany.** Charles Perrault b. 1628	*week* 2 *day* 12
13	*Monday*	Jan van Goyen b. 1596. James Joyce d. 1941.	13
14	*Tuesday*	Fantin-Latour b. 1836. Harold Abrahams d. 1978	14
15	*Wednesday*	British Museum opened 1759. Karl Liebknecht d. 1919	15
16	*Thursday*	Amilcare Ponchielli d. 1886. Laura Riding b. 1901	16
17	*Friday*	Gen. Thomas Fairfax b. 1612. David Lloyd George b. 1863	17
18	*Saturday*	Capt. Scott reaches the South Pole 1912	18
19	*Sunday*	**2nd S. after Epiphany.** Paul Cézanne b. 1839	*week* 3 *day* 19
20	*Monday*	David Garrick d. 1779. Audrey Hepburn d. 1993	20
21	*Tuesday*	Christian Dior b. 1905. Lytton Strachey d. 1932	21
22	*Wednesday*	Lord Byron b. 1788. Walter Sickert d. 1942	22
23	*Thursday*	Thomas Peacock d. 1866. Charles Kingsley d. 1875	23
24	*Friday*	Pierre de Beaumarchais b. 1732. ⚔ Battle of Dogger Bank 1915	24
25	*Saturday*	**Conversion of St Paul.** Somerset Maugham b. 1874	25
26	*Sunday*	**9th S. before Easter/Septuagesima**	*week* 4 *day* 26
27	*Monday*	Samuel Palmer b. 1805. Jerome Kern b. 1885	27
28	*Tuesday*	Gen. Charles Gordon b. 1833. W. B. Yeats d. 1939	28
29	*Wednesday*	Emanuel Swedenborg b. 1688. Fritz Kreisler d. 1962	29
30	*Thursday*	Walter Savage Landor b. 1775. Stanley Holloway d. 1982	30
31	*Friday*	Bonnie Prince Charlie d. 1788. A. A. Milne d. 1956	31

ASTRONOMICAL PHENOMENA

d	h	
1	01	Mars in conjunction with Moon. Mars 3° N.
2	00	Earth at perihelion (147 million km)
2	01	Mercury in inferior conjunction
7	17	Venus in conjunction with Moon. Venus 5° S.
8	05	Mercury in conjunction with Moon. Mercury 2° S.
9	18	Jupiter in conjunction with Moon. Jupiter 5° S.
12	15	Venus in conjunction with Mercury. Venus 3° S.
12	21	Mercury at stationary point
14	03	Saturn in conjunction with Moon. Saturn 2° S.
17	13	Neptune in conjunction
19	13	Jupiter in conjunction
20	01	Sun's longitude 300° ≋
24	05	Mercury at greatest elongation W.25°
24	14	Uranus in conjunction
28	20	Mars in conjunction with Moon. Mars 3° N.

MINIMA OF ALGOL

d	h	d	h	d	h
1	12.1	12	23.4	24	10.7
4	09.0	15	20.2	27	07.5
7	05.8	18	17.1	30	04.3
10	02.6	21	13.9		

CONSTELLATIONS

The following constellations are near the meridian at

	d	h		d	h
December	1	24	January	16	21
December	16	23	February	1	20
January	1	22	February	15	19

Draco (below the Pole), Ursa Minor (below the Pole), Camelopardus, Perseus, Auriga, Taurus, Orion, Eridanus and Lepus

THE MOON

Phases, Apsides and Node	d	h	m
☾ Last Quarter	2	01	45
● New Moon	9	04	26
☽ First Quarter	15	20	02
○ Full Moon	23	15	11
☾ Last Quarter	31	19	40
Perigee (359,227 km)	10	08	43
Apogee (406,218 km)	25	16	31

Mean longitude of ascending node on January 1, 183°

THE SUN

s.d. 16′.3

Day	Right Ascension	Dec. —	Equation of time	Rise 52°	Rise 56°	Transit	Set 52°	Set 56°	Sidereal time	Transit of First Point of Aries
	h m s	° ′	m s	h m	h m	h m	h m	h m	h m s	h m s
1	18 46 09	23 01	− 3 24	8 08	8 31	12 04	15 59	15 36	6 42 44	17 14 26
2	18 50 33	22 56	− 3 53	8 08	8 31	12 04	16 00	15 38	6 46 41	17 10 30
3	18 54 58	22 50	− 4 21	8 08	8 31	12 05	16 02	15 39	6 50 37	17 06 34
4	18 59 22	22 44	− 4 48	8 08	8 30	12 05	16 03	15 40	6 54 34	17 02 38
5	19 03 46	22 38	− 5 15	8 07	8 30	12 05	16 04	15 42	6 58 30	16 58 42
6	19 08 09	22 31	− 5 42	8 07	8 29	12 06	16 05	15 43	7 02 27	16 54 46
7	19 12 32	22 23	− 6 08	8 06	8 28	12 06	16 07	15 45	7 06 24	16 50 50
8	19 16 54	22 16	− 6 34	8 06	8 28	12 07	16 08	15 46	7 10 20	16 46 55
9	19 21 16	22 07	− 7 00	8 05	8 27	12 07	16 09	15 48	7 14 17	16 42 59
10	19 25 38	21 59	− 7 24	8 05	8 26	12 08	16 11	15 49	7 18 13	16 39 03
11	19 29 58	21 50	− 7 49	8 04	8 25	12 08	16 12	15 51	7 22 10	16 35 07
12	19 34 18	21 40	− 8 12	8 04	8 24	12 08	16 14	15 53	7 26 06	16 31 11
13	19 38 38	21 30	− 8 35	8 03	8 23	12 09	16 15	15 55	7 30 03	16 27 15
14	19 42 57	21 20	− 8 58	8 02	8 22	12 09	16 17	15 56	7 33 59	16 23 19
15	19 47 15	21 09	− 9 19	8 01	8 21	12 09	16 18	15 58	7 37 56	16 19 23
16	19 51 33	20 58	− 9 40	8 00	8 20	12 10	16 20	16 00	7 41 53	16 15 27
17	19 55 50	20 46	−10 00	7 59	8 19	12 10	16 22	16 02	7 45 49	16 11 31
18	20 00 06	20 34	−10 20	7 58	8 18	12 10	16 23	16 04	7 49 46	16 07 35
19	20 04 21	20 22	−10 39	7 57	8 16	12 11	16 25	16 06	7 53 42	16 03 39
20	20 08 36	20 09	−10 57	7 56	8 15	12 11	16 27	16 08	7 57 39	15 59 44
21	20 12 50	19 56	−11 14	7 55	8 13	12 11	16 28	16 10	8 01 35	15 55 48
22	20 17 03	19 43	−11 31	7 54	8 12	12 12	16 30	16 12	8 05 32	15 51 52
23	20 21 15	19 29	−11 47	7 53	8 10	12 12	16 32	16 14	8 09 28	15 47 56
24	20 25 27	19 15	−12 02	7 51	8 09	12 12	16 33	16 16	8 13 25	15 44 00
25	20 29 37	19 00	−12 16	7 50	8 07	12 12	16 35	16 18	8 17 22	15 40 04
26	20 33 47	18 45	−12 29	7 49	8 06	12 13	16 37	16 20	8 21 18	15 36 08
27	20 37 57	18 30	−12 42	7 47	8 04	12 13	16 39	16 22	8 25 15	15 32 12
28	20 42 05	18 14	−12 54	7 46	8 02	12 13	16 41	16 24	8 29 11	15 28 16
29	20 46 13	17 58	−13 05	7 45	8 00	12 13	16 42	16 27	8 33 08	15 24 20
30	20 50 19	17 42	−13 15	7 43	7 59	12 13	16 44	16 29	8 37 04	15 20 24
31	20 54 25	17 26	−13 24	7 42	7 57	12 13	16 46	16 31	8 41 01	15 16 29

DURATION OF TWILIGHT (in minutes)

Latitude	52°	56°	52°	56°	52°	56°	52°	56°
	1 January		11 January		21 January		31 January	
Civil	41	47	40	45	38	43	37	41
Nautical	84	96	82	93	80	90	78	87
Astronomical	125	141	123	138	120	134	117	130

THE NIGHT SKY

Mercury is visible in the mornings around the middle of the month, as it reaches greatest western elongation (25°) on the 24th. Even from England and Wales it will be difficult to detect, low above the south-eastern horizon around the beginning of morning civil twilight, between about the 12th to the 23rd. On the morning of the 13th Venus could be a useful guide to finding Mercury as Mercury will then be seen 3° above Venus. During its period of visibility its magnitude ranges from + 0.6 to − 0.1. Because of its considerable southerly declination, observers in Scotland are unlikely to see Mercury at all.

Venus is a brilliant object in the morning sky, magnitude − 3.9, and at the beginning of the month is visible low in the east-south-eastern sky for nearly an hour before dawn. On the morning of the 7th the old crescent Moon, only two days before New, will be seen about 6° above the planet. For the last week of the month Venus is too close to the Sun for observation.

Mars, although technically a morning object, is becoming visible low in the eastern sky shortly before midnight. During January its magnitude increases in brightness from +0.5 to − 0.2. Mars is moving slowly eastwards in the western part of Virgo. The Moon, near Last Quarter, passes about 3° S. of Mars on the mornings of the 1st and 29th.

Jupiter passes through conjunction on the 19th and is therefore too close to the Sun for observation.

Saturn magnitude +1.0, is an evening object in the south-western sky. Saturn is in the southern part of the constellation of Pisces. With a minor axis of only three arcseconds, the rings will be very difficult to detect with small telescopes.

THE MOON

Day	RA h m	Dec °	Hor. par. '	Semi-diam. '	Sun's co-long. °	PA of Bright Limb °	Phase %	Age d	Rise 52° h m	Rise 56° h m	Transit h m	Set 52° h m	Set 56° h m
1	11 55	+ 0.2	54.7	14.9	173	113	60	21.3	—	—	5 21	11 23	11 22
2	12 41	− 3.6	55.2	15.0	185	113	51	22.3	0 14	0 17	6 05	11 47	11 42
3	13 28	− 7.3	55.9	15.2	197	112	41	23.3	1 20	1 27	6 51	12 12	12 04
4	14 18	−10.8	56.7	15.4	209	110	31	24.3	2 28	2 38	7 38	12 42	12 30
5	15 10	−13.9	57.6	15.7	221	108	22	25.3	3 37	3 50	8 30	13 16	13 02
6	16 06	−16.4	58.5	15.9	234	106	14	26.3	4 46	5 02	9 24	13 59	13 42
7	17 04	−17.9	59.4	16.2	246	104	7	27.3	5 52	6 10	10 22	14 51	14 33
8	18 05	−18.4	60.2	16.4	258	106	2	28.3	6 53	7 11	11 23	15 54	15 36
9	19 08	−17.6	60.7	16.6	270	145	0	29.3	7 46	8 03	12 24	17 06	16 50
10	20 10	−15.6	61.0	16.6	282	237	1	0.8	8 31	8 45	13 24	18 24	18 11
11	21 11	−12.5	61.0	16.6	295	245	5	1.8	9 09	9 19	14 22	19 44	19 36
12	22 10	− 8.6	60.6	16.5	307	246	12	2.8	9 42	9 48	15 18	21 04	21 00
13	23 06	− 4.3	60.1	16.4	319	246	20	3.8	10 11	10 13	16 11	22 22	22 22
14	0 01	+ 0.2	59.4	16.2	331	247	30	4.8	10 39	10 37	17 02	23 38	23 42
15	0 55	+ 4.6	58.6	16.0	343	247	41	5.8	11 07	11 01	17 53	—	—
16	1 47	+ 8.6	57.8	15.8	355	249	52	6.8	11 35	11 26	18 43	0 51	0 59
17	2 39	+12.1	57.1	15.6	8	251	62	7.8	12 07	11 55	19 33	2 02	2 13
18	3 31	+14.9	56.4	15.4	20	254	72	8.8	12 42	12 27	20 23	3 09	3 23
19	4 24	+16.9	55.8	15.2	32	257	81	9.8	13 21	13 05	21 13	4 11	4 27
20	5 16	+18.1	55.3	15.1	44	260	88	10.8	14 07	13 49	22 02	5 07	5 25
21	6 08	+18.4	54.9	15.0	56	262	94	11.8	14 57	14 40	22 51	5 57	6 15
22	6 59	+17.8	54.6	14.9	68	261	97	12.8	15 52	15 36	23 39	6 41	6 57
23	7 49	+16.4	54.3	14.8	80	247	99	13.8	16 51	16 37	—	7 18	7 32
24	8 38	+14.4	54.1	14.7	93	150	100	14.8	17 52	17 41	0 25	7 50	8 02
25	9 25	+11.7	54.0	14.7	105	120	98	15.8	18 54	18 45	1 10	8 18	8 27
26	10 12	+ 8.6	54.0	14.7	117	116	95	16.8	19 56	19 51	1 54	8 43	8 49
27	10 57	+ 5.1	54.1	14.7	129	114	90	17.8	20 59	20 57	2 36	9 06	9 09
28	11 42	+ 1.5	54.3	14.8	141	114	84	18.8	22 02	22 04	3 19	9 29	9 29
29	12 28	− 2.3	54.6	14.9	153	113	76	19.8	23 06	23 11	4 02	9 52	9 49
30	13 14	− 6.0	55.1	15.0	165	112	68	20.8	—	—	4 46	10 16	10 10
31	14 02	− 9.5	55.7	15.2	178	110	58	21.8	0 11	0 20	5 31	10 43	10 33

MERCURY

Day	RA h m	Dec °	Diam. "	Phase %	Transit h m	5° high 52° h m	5° high 56° h m
1	18 56	−20.5	10	1	12 08	15 32	15 04
3	18 44	−20.2	10	1	11 49	8 24	8 52
5	18 33	−20.1	10	4	11 31	8 05	8 32
7	18 24	−20.0	10	10	11 14	7 48	8 15
9	18 18	−20.1	9	17	11 00	7 34	8 02
11	18 14	−20.2	9	24	10 49	7 24	7 52
13	18 13	−20.5	8	32	10 41	7 18	7 46
15	18 14	−20.7	8	39	10 35	7 13	7 42
17	18 17	−21.0	8	45	10 31	7 11	7 41
19	18 23	−21.3	7	51	10 28	7 11	7 42
21	18 29	−21.5	7	56	10 27	7 12	7 43
23	18 37	−21.8	7	61	10 27	7 14	7 46
25	18 46	−22.0	7	65	10 28	7 17	7 49
27	18 55	−22.1	6	68	10 30	7 19	7 52
29	19 05	−22.2	6	71	10 33	7 22	7 55
31	19 16	−22.2	6	74	10 35	7 25	7 58

VENUS

Day	RA h m	Dec °	Diam. "	Phase %	Transit h m	5° high 52° h m	5° high 56° h m
1	17 10	−22.2	11	93	10 28	7 18	7 50
6	17 37	−22.8	11	94	10 35	7 30	8 05
11	18 04	−23.1	11	94	10 43	7 40	8 16
16	18 31	−23.1	11	95	10 50	7 48	8 23
21	18 59	−22.8	10	96	10 58	7 53	8 27
26	19 26	−22.3	10	96	11 05	7 55	8 28
31	19 52	−21.4	10	97	11 12	7 55	8 25

MARS

Day	RA h m	Dec °	Diam. "	Phase %	Transit h m	5° high 52° h m	5° high 56° h m
1	12 01	+ 2.7	8	91	5 18	23 35	23 36
6	12 07	+ 2.2	8	91	5 04	23 24	23 26
11	12 13	+ 1.7	9	91	4 50	23 12	23 14
16	12 17	+ 1.4	9	92	4 35	22 58	23 01
21	12 21	+ 1.1	10	92	4 19	22 44	22 46
26	12 24	+ 0.9	10	93	4 02	22 28	22 30
31	12 26	+ 0.8	11	94	3 45	22 10	22 13

SUNRISE AND SUNSET

	London		Bristol		Birmingham		Manchester		Newcastle		Glasgow		Belfast	
	0°05′	51°30′	2°35′	51°28′	1°55′	52°28′	2°15′	53°28′	1°37′	54°59′	4°14′	55°52′	5°56′	54°35′
	h m	h m	h m	h m	h m	h m	h m	h m	h m	h m	h m	h m	h m	h m
1	8 06	16 02	8 16	16 12	8 18	16 05	8 25	16 01	8 31	15 49	8 47	15 54	8 46	16 09
2	8 06	16 03	8 16	16 13	8 18	16 06	8 25	16 02	8 31	15 50	8 47	15 55	8 46	16 10
3	8 06	16 04	8 16	16 15	8 18	16 07	8 24	16 03	8 31	15 52	8 47	15 57	8 46	16 11
4	8 05	16 06	8 15	16 16	8 18	16 08	8 24	16 04	8 30	15 53	8 46	15 58	8 45	16 13
5	8 05	16 07	8 15	16 17	8 17	16 09	8 24	16 05	8 30	15 54	8 46	15 59	8 45	16 14
6	8 05	16 08	8 15	16 18	8 17	16 11	8 23	16 07	8 29	15 56	8 45	16 01	8 44	16 15
7	8 04	16 09	8 14	16 19	8 16	16 12	8 23	16 08	8 29	15 57	8 45	16 02	8 44	16 17
8	8 04	16 11	8 14	16 21	8 16	16 13	8 22	16 10	8 28	15 59	8 44	16 04	8 43	16 18
9	8 03	16 12	8 13	16 22	8 15	16 15	8 22	16 11	8 27	16 00	8 43	16 06	8 42	16 20
10	8 03	16 13	8 13	16 24	8 15	16 16	8 21	16 13	8 27	16 02	8 42	16 07	8 42	16 21
11	8 02	16 15	8 12	16 25	8 14	16 18	8 20	16 14	8 26	16 03	8 41	16 09	8 41	16 23
12	8 02	16 16	8 11	16 26	8 13	16 19	8 20	16 16	8 25	16 05	8 41	16 11	8 40	16 25
13	8 01	16 18	8 11	16 28	8 13	16 21	8 19	16 17	8 24	16 07	8 40	16 12	8 39	16 26
14	8 00	16 19	8 10	16 29	8 12	16 22	8 18	16 19	8 23	16 09	8 38	16 14	8 38	16 28
15	7 59	16 21	8 09	16 31	8 11	16 24	8 17	16 21	8 22	16 10	8 37	16 16	8 37	16 30
16	7 58	16 22	8 08	16 33	8 10	16 25	8 16	16 22	8 21	16 12	8 36	16 18	8 36	16 31
17	7 57	16 24	8 07	16 34	8 09	16 27	8 15	16 24	8 20	16 14	8 35	16 20	8 35	16 33
18	7 57	16 26	8 06	16 36	8 08	16 29	8 14	16 26	8 19	16 16	8 34	16 22	8 34	16 35
19	7 56	16 27	8 05	16 37	8 07	16 31	8 13	16 27	8 17	16 18	8 32	16 24	8 33	16 37
20	7 54	16 29	8 04	16 39	8 06	16 32	8 12	16 29	8 16	16 20	8 31	16 26	8 31	16 39
21	7 53	16 31	8 03	16 41	8 05	16 34	8 10	16 31	8 15	16 21	8 30	16 28	8 30	16 41
22	7 52	16 32	8 02	16 42	8 03	16 36	8 09	16 33	8 13	16 23	8 28	16 30	8 29	16 43
23	7 51	16 34	8 01	16 44	8 02	16 37	8 08	16 35	8 12	16 25	8 27	16 32	8 27	16 44
24	7 50	16 36	8 00	16 46	8 01	16 39	8 06	16 37	8 10	16 27	8 25	16 34	8 26	16 46
25	7 49	16 37	7 58	16 48	8 00	16 41	8 05	16 38	8 09	16 29	8 24	16 36	8 24	16 48
26	7 47	16 39	7 57	16 49	7 58	16 43	8 03	16 40	8 07	16 31	8 22	16 38	8 23	16 50
27	7 46	16 41	7 56	16 51	7 57	16 45	8 02	16 42	8 06	16 33	8 20	16 40	8 21	16 52
28	7 45	16 43	7 54	16 53	7 55	16 47	8 00	16 44	8 04	16 35	8 18	16 42	8 20	16 54
29	7 43	16 45	7 53	16 55	7 54	16 48	7 59	16 46	8 02	16 37	8 17	16 44	8 18	16 56
30	7 42	16 46	7 52	16 56	7 52	16 50	7 57	16 48	8 01	16 40	8 15	16 46	8 16	16 58
31	7 40	16 48	7 50	16 58	7 51	16 52	7 56	16 50	7 59	16 42	8 13	16 48	8 15	17 00

JUPITER

Day	RA	Dec.	Transit	5° high	
				52°	56°
	h m	° ′	h m	h m	h m
1	19 48.7	−21 25	13 04	16 21	15 50
11	19 58.6	−21 00	12 35	15 55	15 25
21	20 08.4	−20 32	12 05	15 29	15 01
31	20 18.2	−20 02	11 36	15 03	14 36

Diameters – equatorial 32″ polar 30″

SATURN

Day	RA	Dec.	Transit	5° high	
				52°	56°
	h m	° ′	h m	h m	h m
1	0 08.7	− 1 38	17 23	22 41	22 37
11	0 10.7	− 1 22	16 46	22 06	22 01
21	0 13.4	− 1 03	16 09	21 31	21 27
31	0 16.5	− 0 41	15 33	20 56	20 53

Diameters – equatorial 17″ polar 15″
Rings – major axis 38″ minor axis 3″

URANUS

Day	RA	Dec.	Transit	10° high	
				52°	56°
	h m	° ′	h m	h m	h m
1	20 22.8	−19 59	13 38	16 18	15 36
11	20 25.2	−19 51	13 01	15 42	15 01
21	20 27.6	−19 42	12 24	15 07	14 26
31	20 30.0	−19 34	11 47	14 31	13 51

Diameter 4″

NEPTUNE

Day	RA	Dec.	Transit	10° high	
				52°	56°
	h m	° ′	h m	h m	h m
1	19 55.1	−20 22	13 10	10 34	11 18
11	19 56.7	−20 18	12 33	9 56	10 39
21	19 58.3	−20 14	11 55	9 17	10 00
31	19 59.8	−20 09	11 17	8 39	9 21

Diameter 2″

 # February 1997

SECOND MONTH, 28 or 29 DAYS. *Februa*, Roman festival of Purification

1	*Saturday*	Clark Gable b. 1901. Piet Mondrian d. 1944	*week 4 day* 32
2	*Sunday*	**Presentation of Christ. 8th S. before Easter/Sexagesima**	*week 5 day* 33
3	*Monday*	Felix Mendelssohn b. 1809. Marquess of Salisbury b. 1830	34
4	*Tuesday*	Thomas Carlyle d. 1881. Charles Lindbergh b.1902	35
5	*Wednesday*	Sir Robert Peel b. 1788. Sir John Pritchard b. 1921	36
6	*Thursday*	*Queen's Accession 1952.* Charles II d. 1685	37
7	*Friday*	Sir Thomas More b. 1478. Charles Dickens b. 1812	38
8	*Saturday*	*Chinese Year of the Ox.* Sir Giles Gilbert Scott d. 1960	39
9	*Sunday*	**7th S. before Easter/Quinquagesima**	*week 6 day* 40
10	*Monday*	Charles Lamb b. 1775. Boris Pasternak b. 1890 (NS)	41
11	*Tuesday*	Shrove Tuesday. Thomas Edison b. 1847	42
12	*Wednesday*	**Ash Wednesday.** Lady Jane Grey exec. 1554	43
13	*Thursday*	Dame Christabel Pankhurst d. 1958	44
14	*Friday*	St Valentine's Day. Benvenuto Cellini d. 1571	45
15	*Saturday*	Galileo Galilei b. 1564. Mikhail Glinka d. 1857 (NS)	46
16	*Sunday*	**1st S. in Lent.** Angela Carter d. 1992	*week 7 day* 47
17	*Monday*	Johann Pestalozzi d. 1827. Heinrich Heine d. 1856	48
18	*Tuesday*	Martin Luther d. 1546. Dame Ngaio Marsh d. 1982	49
19	*Wednesday*	*Duke of York b. 1960.* Nicolas Copernicus b. 1473	50
20	*Thursday*	Dame Marie Rambert b. 1888. Ferruccio Lamborghini d. 1993	51
21	*Friday*	Léo Delibes b. 1836. Dame Margot Fonteyn d. 1991	52
22	*Saturday*	Arthur Schopenhauer b. 1788. Hugo Wolf d. 1903	53
23	*Sunday*	**2nd S. in Lent.** Samuel Pepys b. 1633	*week 8 day* 54
24	*Monday*	Wilhelm Grimm b. 1786. Dinah Shore d. 1994	55
25	*Tuesday*	Sir Christopher Wren d. 1723	56
26	*Wednesday*	Maj.-Gen. Orde Wingate b. 1903	57
27	*Thursday*	John Evelyn d. 1706. Henry Longfellow b. 1807	58
28	*Friday*	Sir Stephen Spender b. 1909. Sir Peter Medawar b. 1915	59

ASTRONOMICAL PHENOMENA

d	h	
6	01	Mars at stationary point
6	02	Jupiter in conjunction with Venus. Jupiter 0°.3 N.
6	02	Mercury in conjunction with Moon. Mercury 5° S.
6	15	Jupiter in conjunction with Moon. Jupiter 5° S.
6	16	Venus in conjunction with Moon. Venus 5° S.
10	16	Saturn in conjunction with Moon. Saturn 2° S.
12	18	Jupiter in conjunction with Mercury. Jupiter 1° N.
18	15	Sun's longitude 330° ♓
24	23	Mars in conjunction with Moon. Mars 3° N.

MINIMA OF ALGOL

d	h	d	h	d	h
2	01.2	13	12.5	24	23.7
4	22.0	16	09.3	27	20.6
7	18.8	19	06.1		
10	15.6	22	02.9		

CONSTELLATIONS

The following constellations are near the meridian at

	d	h		d	h
January	1	24	February	15	21
January	16	23	March	1	20
February	1	22	March	16	19

Draco (below the Pole), Camelopardus, Auriga, Taurus, Gemini, Orion, Canis Minor, Monoceros, Lepus, Canis Major and Puppis

THE MOON

Phases, Apsides and Node	d	h	m
● New Moon	7	15	06
☽ First Quarter	14	08	58
○ Full Moon	22	10	27
Perigee (356,848 km)	7	20	33
Apogee (406,395 km)	21	16	51

Mean longitude of ascending node on February 1, 181°

THE SUN

s.d. 16'.2

Day	Right Ascension	Dec. —	Equation of time	Rise 52°	Rise 56°	Transit	Set 52°	Set 56°	Sidereal time	Transit of First Point of Aries
	h m s	° '	m s	h m	h m	h m	h m	h m	h m s	h m s
1	20 58 30	17 09	−13 33	7 40	7 55	12 14	16 48	16 33	8 44 57	15 12 33
2	21 02 35	16 52	−13 41	7 38	7 53	12 14	16 50	16 35	8 48 54	15 08 37
3	21 06 38	16 34	−13 48	7 37	7 51	12 14	16 52	16 37	8 52 51	15 04 41
4	21 10 41	16 16	−13 54	7 35	7 49	12 14	16 53	16 40	8 56 47	15 00 45
5	21 14 43	15 58	−14 00	7 33	7 47	12 14	16 55	16 42	9 00 44	14 56 49
6	21 18 45	15 40	−14 04	7 32	7 45	12 14	16 57	16 44	9 04 40	14 52 53
7	21 22 45	15 21	−14 08	7 30	7 43	12 14	16 59	16 46	9 08 37	14 48 57
8	21 26 45	15 03	−14 11	7 28	7 41	12 14	17 01	16 48	9 12 33	14 45 01
9	21 30 43	14 44	−14 14	7 26	7 39	12 14	17 03	16 51	9 16 30	14 41 05
10	21 34 41	14 24	−14 15	7 25	7 36	12 14	17 05	16 53	9 20 26	14 37 09
11	21 38 39	14 05	−14 16	7 23	7 34	12 14	17 07	16 55	9 24 23	14 33 14
12	21 42 35	13 45	−14 16	7 21	7 32	12 14	17 08	16 57	9 28 20	14 29 18
13	21 46 31	13 25	−14 15	7 19	7 30	12 14	17 10	16 59	9 32 16	14 25 22
14	21 50 26	13 04	−14 13	7 17	7 28	12 14	17 12	17 02	9 36 13	14 21 26
15	21 54 20	12 44	−14 11	7 15	7 25	12 14	17 14	17 04	9 40 09	14 17 30
16	21 58 13	12 23	−14 08	7 13	7 23	12 14	17 16	17 06	9 44 06	14 13 34
17	22 02 06	12 02	−14 04	7 11	7 21	12 14	17 18	17 08	9 48 02	14 09 38
18	22 05 58	11 41	−13 59	7 09	7 18	12 14	17 20	17 10	9 51 59	14 05 42
19	22 09 49	11 20	−13 54	7 07	7 16	12 14	17 21	17 13	9 55 55	14 01 46
20	22 13 40	10 59	−13 48	7 05	7 14	12 14	17 23	17 15	9 59 52	13 57 50
21	22 17 30	10 37	−13 41	7 03	7 11	12 14	17 25	17 17	10 03 48	13 53 55
22	22 21 19	10 15	−13 34	7 01	7 09	12 14	17 27	17 19	10 07 45	13 49 59
23	22 25 08	9 53	−13 26	6 59	7 06	12 13	17 29	17 21	10 11 42	13 46 03
24	22 28 56	9 31	−13 17	6 57	7 04	12 13	17 31	17 23	10 15 38	13 42 07
25	22 32 43	9 09	−13 08	6 55	7 02	12 13	17 32	17 26	10 19 35	13 38 11
26	22 36 30	8 47	−12 59	6 52	6 59	12 13	17 34	17 28	10 23 31	13 34 15
27	22 40 16	8 24	−12 48	6 50	6 57	12 13	17 36	17 30	10 27 28	13 30 19
28	22 44 02	8 02	−12 38	6 48	6 54	12 13	17 38	17 32	10 31 24	13 26 23

DURATION OF TWILIGHT (in minutes)

Latitude	52°	56°	52°	56°	52°	56°	52°	56°
	1 February		11 February		21 February		28 February	
Civil	37	41	35	39	34	38	34	38
Nautical	77	86	75	83	74	81	73	81
Astronomical	117	130	114	126	113	125	112	124

THE NIGHT SKY

Mercury is unsuitably placed for observation.

Venus is also unsuitably placed for observation.

Mars, its magnitude brightening during the month from −0.2 to −0.9, becomes an increasingly conspicuous object in the night sky, visible low in the eastern sky shortly after 22h at the beginning of February and shortly before 20h at the end. The gibbous Moon passes about 4°S. of the planet in the early hours of the 25th. Mars is in Virgo, reaching its first stationary point on the 6th, whereupon its motion becomes retrograde.

Jupiter is unsuitably placed for observation.

Saturn continues to be visible as an evening object in the south-western sky, magnitude +1.0, though by the end of the month it will be a difficult object to detect in the gathering twilight. On the evening of the 10th the thin crescent Moon, only three days old, will be seen only 1° above the planet.

Zodiacal Light. The evening cone may be observed stretching up from the western horizon, along the ecliptic after the end of twilight, from the beginning of the month to the 8th and again after the 22nd. This faint phenomenon is only visible under good conditions and in the absence of both moonlight and artificial lighting.

THE MOON

Day	RA h m	Dec. °	Hor. par. '	Semi-diam. '	Sun's co-long. °	PA of Bright Limb °	Phase %	Age d	Rise 52° h m	Rise 56° h m	Transit h m	Set 52° h m	Set 56° h m
1	14 52	−12.7	56.5	15.4	190	107	48	22.8	1 18	1 30	6 19	11 14	11 01
2	15 44	−15.3	57.3	15.6	202	104	38	23.8	2 25	2 40	7 10	11 51	11 36
3	16 40	−17.2	58.3	15.9	214	100	28	24.8	3 31	3 48	8 05	12 37	12 19
4	17 38	−18.2	59.3	16.1	226	96	18	25.8	4 33	4 51	9 02	13 32	13 14
5	18 39	−18.0	60.2	16.4	238	93	10	26.8	5 30	5 47	10 02	14 38	14 21
6	19 41	−16.7	60.9	16.6	251	91	4	27.8	6 19	6 34	11 03	15 52	15 38
7	20 42	−14.1	61.3	16.7	263	99	1	28.8	7 02	7 13	12 03	17 13	17 02
8	21 43	−10.6	61.4	16.7	275	222	0	0.4	7 38	7 46	13 01	18 35	18 28
9	22 43	− 6.3	61.2	16.7	287	243	3	1.4	8 10	8 14	13 58	19 57	19 55
10	23 40	− 1.7	60.7	16.5	299	246	8	2.4	8 40	8 40	14 52	21 17	21 19
11	0 36	+ 2.9	59.9	16.3	312	248	16	3.4	9 09	9 05	15 45	22 34	22 40
12	1 31	+ 7.2	59.0	16.1	324	250	25	4.4	9 38	9 31	16 37	23 48	23 58
13	2 25	+10.9	58.1	15.8	336	252	36	5.4	10 09	9 59	17 28	—	—
14	3 18	+14.0	57.2	15.6	348	255	46	6.4	10 44	10 30	18 19	0 58	1 11
15	4 11	+16.3	56.4	15.4	0	259	57	7.4	11 22	11 06	19 10	2 03	2 18
16	5 03	+17.7	55.7	15.2	12	263	66	8.4	12 06	11 48	19 59	3 02	3 19
17	5 55	+18.2	55.1	15.0	25	266	75	9.4	12 54	12 37	20 48	3 54	4 12
18	6 46	+17.9	54.6	14.9	37	270	83	10.4	13 47	13 31	21 36	4 39	4 56
19	7 36	+16.8	54.3	14.8	49	273	90	11.4	14 44	14 30	22 22	5 18	5 34
20	8 25	+14.9	54.1	14.7	61	275	95	12.4	15 44	15 32	23 08	5 52	6 05
21	9 13	+12.4	54.0	14.7	73	275	98	13.4	16 45	16 36	23 52	6 21	6 32
22	10 00	+ 9.5	54.0	14.7	85	261	100	14.4	17 47	17 42	—	6 48	6 55
23	10 46	+ 6.1	54.0	14.7	97	127	100	15.4	18 50	18 47	0 35	7 12	7 16
24	11 31	+ 2.5	54.2	14.8	110	115	98	16.4	19 53	19 54	1 18	7 35	7 36
25	12 17	− 1.2	54.4	14.8	122	112	94	17.4	20 57	21 01	2 00	7 58	7 55
26	13 03	− 4.9	54.7	14.9	134	111	89	18.4	22 02	22 09	2 44	8 21	8 16
27	13 50	− 8.5	55.2	15.0	146	109	82	19.4	23 07	23 17	3 29	8 47	8 39
28	14 38	−11.7	55.7	15.2	158	106	74	20.4	—	—	4 15	9 16	9 05

MERCURY

Day	RA h m	Dec. °	Diam. "	Phase %	Transit h m	5° high 52° h m	5° high 56° h m
1	19 21	−22.2	6	75	10 37	7 26	7 59
3	19 33	−22.0	6	77	10 41	7 29	8 01
5	19 44	−21.9	6	80	10 44	7 31	8 02
7	19 56	−21.6	6	82	10 48	7 32	8 03
9	20 08	−21.2	5	83	10 53	7 34	8 04
11	20 21	−20.8	5	85	10 57	7 35	8 04
13	20 33	−20.3	5	86	11 02	7 35	8 03
15	20 46	−19.7	5	88	11 07	7 35	8 02
17	20 58	−19.0	5	89	11 12	7 35	8 00
19	21 11	−18.2	5	91	11 17	7 34	7 58
21	21 24	−17.3	5	92	11 22	7 33	7 55
23	21 37	−16.4	5	93	11 27	7 32	7 52
25	21 50	−15.3	5	94	11 32	7 30	7 49
27	22 04	−14.2	5	95	11 38	7 28	7 45
29	22 17	−13.0	5	96	11 43	7 26	7 41
31	22 30	−11.6	5	97	11 49	7 23	7 37

VENUS

Day	RA h m	Dec. °	Diam. "	Phase %	Transit h m	5° high 52° h m	5° high 56° h m
1	19 58	−21.2	10	97	11 13	7 54	8 24
6	20 24	−20.1	10	97	11 20	7 52	8 19
11	20 50	−18.6	10	98	11 26	7 47	8 12
16	21 15	−17.0	10	98	11 32	7 41	8 03
21	21 40	−15.2	10	99	11 37	7 34	7 53
26	22 05	−13.2	10	99	11 41	7 26	7 42
31	22 29	−11.0	10	99	11 46	7 17	7 31

MARS

Day	RA h m	Dec. °	Diam. "	Phase %	Transit h m	5° high 52° h m	5° high 56° h m
1	12 26	+ 0.8	11	94	3 41	22 07	22 09
6	12 27	+ 0.8	11	95	3 22	21 47	21 50
11	12 27	+ 1.0	12	96	3 02	21 26	21 29
16	12 25	+ 1.2	12	97	2 41	21 03	21 05
21	12 22	+ 1.6	13	97	2 18	20 38	20 40
26	12 18	+ 2.1	13	98	1 54	20 12	20 13
31	12 13	+ 2.7	13	99	1 30	19 44	19 45

SUNRISE AND SUNSET

	London		Bristol		Birmingham		Manchester		Newcastle		Glasgow		Belfast	
	0°05'	51°30'	2°35'	51°28'	1°55'	52°28'	2°15'	53°28'	1°37'	54°59'	4°14'	55°52'	5°56'	54°35'
	h m	h m	h m	h m	h m	h m	h m	h m	h m	h m	h m	h m	h m	h m
1	7 39	16 50	7 49	17 00	7 49	16 54	7 54	16 52	7 57	16 44	8 11	16 51	8 13	17 03
2	7 37	16 52	7 47	17 02	7 48	16 56	7 52	16 54	7 55	16 46	8 09	16 53	8 11	17 05
3	7 35	16 54	7 45	17 04	7 46	16 58	7 51	16 56	7 54	16 48	8 07	16 55	8 09	17 07
4	7 34	16 55	7 44	17 05	7 44	17 00	7 49	16 58	7 52	16 50	8 05	16 57	8 07	17 09
5	7 32	16 57	7 42	17 07	7 42	17 02	7 47	17 00	7 50	16 52	8 03	16 59	8 06	17 11
6	7 31	16 59	7 40	17 09	7 41	17 04	7 45	17 02	7 48	16 54	8 01	17 02	8 04	17 13
7	7 29	17 01	7 39	17 11	7 39	17 05	7 43	17 04	7 46	16 56	7 59	17 04	8 02	17 15
8	7 27	17 03	7 37	17 13	7 37	17 07	7 41	17 06	7 44	16 58	7 57	17 06	8 00	17 17
9	7 25	17 05	7 35	17 15	7 35	17 09	7 40	17 08	7 42	17 01	7 55	17 08	7 58	17 19
10	7 24	17 06	7 33	17 16	7 33	17 11	7 38	17 10	7 40	17 03	7 53	17 10	7 56	17 21
11	7 22	17 08	7 32	17 18	7 32	17 13	7 36	17 12	7 38	17 05	7 51	17 12	7 54	17 23
12	7 20	17 10	7 30	17 20	7 30	17 15	7 34	17 14	7 35	17 07	7 49	17 15	7 52	17 25
13	7 18	17 12	7 28	17 22	7 28	17 17	7 32	17 16	7 33	17 09	7 46	17 17	7 49	17 27
14	7 16	17 14	7 26	17 24	7 26	17 19	7 30	17 18	7 31	17 11	7 44	17 19	7 47	17 29
15	7 14	17 16	7 24	17 26	7 24	17 21	7 28	17 20	7 29	17 13	7 42	17 21	7 45	17 31
16	7 12	17 17	7 22	17 27	7 22	17 23	7 25	17 22	7 27	17 15	7 40	17 23	7 43	17 34
17	7 10	17 19	7 20	17 29	7 20	17 24	7 23	17 24	7 25	17 17	7 37	17 26	7 41	17 36
18	7 08	17 21	7 18	17 31	7 18	17 26	7 21	17 25	7 22	17 19	7 35	17 28	7 39	17 38
19	7 06	17 23	7 16	17 33	7 16	17 28	7 19	17 27	7 20	17 22	7 33	17 30	7 36	17 40
20	7 04	17 25	7 14	17 35	7 14	17 30	7 17	17 29	7 18	17 24	7 30	17 32	7 34	17 42
21	7 02	17 26	7 12	17 36	7 12	17 32	7 15	17 31	7 15	17 26	7 28	17 34	7 32	17 44
22	7 00	17 28	7 10	17 38	7 09	17 34	7 13	17 33	7 13	17 28	7 25	17 36	7 30	17 46
23	6 58	17 30	7 08	17 40	7 07	17 36	7 10	17 35	7 11	17 30	7 23	17 39	7 27	17 48
24	6 56	17 32	7 06	17 42	7 05	17 38	7 08	17 37	7 08	17 32	7 21	17 41	7 25	17 50
25	6 54	17 34	7 04	17 44	7 03	17 39	7 06	17 39	7 06	17 34	7 18	17 43	7 23	17 52
26	6 52	17 35	7 02	17 45	7 01	17 41	7 04	17 41	7 04	17 36	7 16	17 45	7 20	17 54
27	6 50	17 37	7 00	17 47	6 59	17 43	7 01	17 43	7 01	17 38	7 13	17 47	7 18	17 56
28	6 48	17 39	6 58	17 49	6 56	17 45	6 59	17 45	6 59	17 40	7 11	17 49	7 15	17 58

JUPITER

Day	RA	Dec.	Transit	5° high	
				52°	56°
	h m	° '	h m	h m	h m
1	20 19.2	−19 59	11 33	8 05	8 32
11	20 28.8	−19 27	11 03	7 32	7 57
21	20 38.2	−18 55	10 33	6 57	7 22
31	20 47.2	−18 22	10 03	6 23	6 47

Diameters – equatorial 33″ polar 31″

SATURN

Day	RA	Dec.	Transit	5° high	
				52°	56°
	h m	° '	h m	h m	h m
1	0 16.8	− 0 39	15 30	20 53	20 49
11	0 20.4	− 0 14	14 54	20 19	20 16
21	0 24.3	+ 0 13	14 18	19 46	19 43
31	0 28.5	+ 0 41	13 43	19 14	19 11

Diameters – equatorial 16″ polar 15″
Rings – major axis 37″ minor axis 3″

URANUS

Day	RA	Dec.	Transit	10° high	
				52°	56°
	h m	° '	h m	h m	h m
1	20 30.2	−19 33	11 43	9 00	9 39
11	20 32.6	−19 25	11 07	8 21	9 00
21	20 34.9	−19 17	10 29	7 43	8 22
31	20 37.0	−19 09	9 52	7 05	7 43

Diameter 4″

NEPTUNE

Day	RA	Dec.	Transit	10° high	
				52°	56°
	h m	° '	h m	h m	h m
1	20 00.0	−20 09	11 13	8 35	9 18
11	20 01.5	−20 05	10 35	7 57	8 39
21	20 02.9	−20 00	9 58	7 18	8 00
31	20 04.2	−19 57	9 20	6 39	7 21

Diameter 2″

March 1997

THIRD MONTH, 31 DAYS. *Mars*, Roman god of battle

1	*Saturday*	St David's Day. Robert Lowell b. 1917	*week* 8 *day* 60
2	*Sunday*	**3rd S. in Lent.** Cardinal Archbishop Hume b. 1923	*week* 9 *day* 61
3	*Monday*	Alexander Graham Bell b. 1847. Jean Harlow b. 1911	62
4	*Tuesday*	Opening of the Forth Railway Bridge 1890	63
5	*Wednesday*	Gerardus Mercator b. 1512. Flora Macdonald d. 1790	64
6	*Thursday*	Valentina Tereshkova b. 1937. Zoltán Kodály d. 1967	65
7	*Friday*	Maurice Ravel b. 1875. Viv Richards b. 1952	66
8	*Saturday*	William III d. 1702. Sir William Walton d. 1983	67
9	*Sunday*	**4th S. in Lent.** Mothering Sunday	*week* 10 *day* 68
10	*Monday*	*Prince Edward b. 1964.* Commonwealth Day	69
11	*Tuesday*	Harold Wilson b. 1916. Haydn Wood d. 1959	70
12	*Wednesday*	Bishop George Berkeley b. 1685	71
13	*Thursday*	Angela Brazil d. 1947. Sir Frank Worrell d. 1967	72
14	*Friday*	Johann Strauss (the elder) b. 1804. Sir Huw Wheldon d. 1986	73
15	*Saturday*	Salvator Rosa d. 1673. Dame Rebecca West d. 1983	74
16	*Sunday*	**5th S. in Lent.** Georg Ohm b. 1787	*week* 11 *day* 75
17	*Monday*	St Patrick's Day. *Bank Holiday in Northern Ireland*	76
18	*Tuesday*	Grover Cleveland b. 1837. Rudolf Diesel b. 1858	77
19	*Wednesday*	**St Joseph of Nazareth.** A. J. Balfour d. 1930	78
20	*Thursday*	Sir Isaac Newton d. 1727. Dame Vera Lynn b. 1917.	79
21	*Friday*	Modest Mussorgsky b. 1839 (NS). Paul Tortelier b. 1914	80
22	*Saturday*	Johann Wolfgang von Goethe d. 1832	81
23	*Sunday*	**Palm Sunday.** Princess Eugenie of York b. 1990	*week* 12 *day* 82
24	*Monday*	Walter Bagehot d. 1877. J. M. Synge d. 1909	83
25	*Tuesday*	Joachim Murat b. 1767. Treaty of Rome signed 1957	84
26	*Wednesday*	*Hilary Law Sittings end.* Ludwig van Beethoven d. 1827	85
27	*Thursday*	**Maundy Thursday.** Alfred, Comte de Vigny b. 1797	86
28	*Friday*	**Good Friday.** *Public Holiday in the UK*	87
29	*Saturday*	**Easter Eve.** John Major b. 1943	88
30	*Sunday*	**Easter Day** (Western churches)	*week* 13 *day* 89
31	*Monday*	*Bank Holiday in England, Wales and Northern Ireland*	90

ASTRONOMICAL PHENOMENA

d h
2 15 Venus in conjunction with Mercury. Venus 0°.8 N.
6 12 Jupiter in conjunction with Moon. Jupiter 4° S.
8 13 Pluto at stationary point
8 15 Venus in conjunction with Moon. Venus 3° S.
8 21 Mercury in conjunction with Moon. Mercury 3° S.
9 01 Total eclipse of Sun (*see* page 66).
10 08 Saturn in conjunction with Moon. Saturn 1° S.
11 16 Mercury in superior conjunction
17 08 Mars at opposition
20 14 Sun's longitude 0° ♈
20 16 Saturn in conjunction with Mercury. Saturn 2° S.
23 10 Mars in conjunction with Moon. Mars 4° N.
24 05 Partial eclipse of Moon (*see* page 66)
30 22 Saturn in conjunction
31 13 Saturn in conjunction with Venus. Saturn 0°.9 S.

MINIMA OF ALGOL

d	h	d	h	d	h
2	17.4	14	04.7	25	16.0
5	14.2	17	01.5	28	12.8
8	11.0	19	22.3	31	09.6
11	07.9	22	19.1		

CONSTELLATIONS

The following constellations are near the meridian at

	d	h		d	h
February	1	24	March	16	21
February	15	23	April	1	20
March	1	22	April	15	19

Cepheus (below the Pole), Camelopardus, Lynx, Gemini, Cancer, Leo, Canis Minor, Hydra, Monoceros, Canis Major and Puppis

THE MOON

Phases, Apsides and Node

	d	h	m
☾ Last Quarter	2	09	38
● New Moon	9	01	15
☽ First Quarter	16	00	06
○ Full Moon	24	04	45
☾ Last Quarter	31	19	38

Perigee (357,763 km)	8	08	54
Apogee (405,964 km)	20	23	29

Mean longitude of ascending node on March 1, 180°

THE SUN

s.d. 16'.1

Day	Right Ascension	Dec.	Equation of time	Rise 52°	Rise 56°	Transit	Set 52°	Set 56°	Sidereal time	Transit of First Point of Aries
	h m s	° '	m s	h m	h m	h m	h m	h m	h m s	h m s
1	22 47 47	− 7 39	− 12 26	6 46	6 52	12 12	17 40	17 34	10 35 21	13 22 27
2	22 51 32	− 7 16	− 12 15	6 44	6 49	12 12	17 41	17 36	10 39 17	13 18 31
3	22 55 16	− 6 53	− 12 02	6 41	6 47	12 12	17 43	17 38	10 43 14	13 14 35
4	22 59 00	− 6 30	− 11 50	6 39	6 44	12 12	17 45	17 41	10 47 11	13 10 40
5	23 02 44	− 6 07	− 11 36	6 37	6 41	12 11	17 47	17 43	10 51 07	13 06 44
6	23 06 26	− 5 44	− 11 23	6 35	6 39	12 11	17 49	17 45	10 55 04	13 02 48
7	23 10 09	− 5 21	− 11 09	6 33	6 36	12 11	17 50	17 47	10 59 00	12 58 52
8	23 13 51	− 4 57	− 10 54	6 30	6 34	12 11	17 52	17 49	11 02 57	12 54 56
9	23 17 33	− 4 34	− 10 40	6 28	6 31	12 11	17 54	17 51	11 06 53	12 51 00
10	23 21 15	− 4 10	− 10 25	6 26	6 29	12 10	17 56	17 53	11 10 50	12 47 04
11	23 24 56	− 3 47	− 10 09	6 24	6 26	12 10	17 57	17 55	11 14 46	12 43 08
12	23 28 36	− 3 23	− 9 53	6 21	6 23	12 10	17 59	17 57	11 18 43	12 39 12
13	23 32 17	− 3 00	− 9 37	6 19	6 21	12 09	18 01	17 59	11 22 40	12 35 16
14	23 35 57	− 2 36	− 9 21	6 17	6 18	12 09	18 03	18 01	11 26 36	12 31 20
15	23 39 37	− 2 12	− 9 04	6 14	6 16	12 09	18 05	18 03	11 30 33	12 27 25
16	23 43 17	− 1 49	− 8 47	6 12	6 13	12 09	18 06	18 06	11 34 29	12 23 29
17	23 46 56	− 1 25	− 8 30	6 10	6 10	12 08	18 08	18 08	11 38 26	12 19 33
18	23 50 35	− 1 01	− 8 13	6 07	6 08	12 08	18 10	18 10	11 42 22	12 15 37
19	23 54 14	− 0 37	− 7 55	6 05	6 05	12 08	18 11	18 12	11 46 19	12 11 41
20	23 57 53	− 0 14	− 7 38	6 03	6 02	12 07	18 13	18 14	11 50 15	12 07 45
21	0 01 32	+ 0 10	− 7 20	6 00	6 00	12 07	18 15	18 16	11 54 12	12 03 49
22	0 05 10	+ 0 34	− 7 02	5 58	5 57	12 07	18 17	18 18	11 58 09	11 59 53
23	0 08 49	+ 0 57	− 6 44	5 56	5 54	12 07	18 18	18 20	12 02 05	11 55 57
24	0 12 27	+ 1 21	− 6 26	5 54	5 52	12 06	18 20	18 22	12 06 02	11 52 01
25	0 16 05	+ 1 45	− 6 07	5 51	5 49	12 06	18 22	18 24	12 09 58	11 48 06
26	0 19 44	+ 2 08	− 5 49	5 49	5 47	12 06	18 23	18 26	12 13 55	11 44 10
27	0 23 22	+ 2 32	− 5 31	5 47	5 44	12 05	18 25	18 28	12 17 51	11 40 14
28	0 27 00	+ 2 55	− 5 13	5 44	5 41	12 05	18 27	18 30	12 21 48	11 36 18
29	0 30 39	+ 3 18	− 4 54	5 42	5 39	12 05	18 29	18 32	12 25 44	11 32 22
30	0 34 17	+ 3 42	− 4 36	5 40	5 36	12 04	18 30	18 34	12 29 41	11 28 26
31	0 37 56	+ 4 05	− 4 18	5 37	5 33	12 04	18 32	18 36	12 33 37	11 24 30

DURATION OF TWILIGHT (in minutes)

Latitude	52°	56°	52°	56°	52°	56°	52°	56°
	1 March		11 March		21 March		31 March	
Civil	34	38	34	37	34	37	34	38
Nautical	73	81	73	80	74	82	76	84
Astronomical	112	124	113	125	116	129	120	136

THE NIGHT SKY

Mercury is unsuitably placed for observation at first, superior conjunction occurring on the 11th. It then moves rapidly eastwards from the Sun and for the last week of the month it is an evening object, magnitude − 1.2 to − 0.7. It is visible low above the western horizon about the end of evening civil twilight. This is the most favourable apparition of the year for observers in the northern hemisphere.

Venus continues to be unsuitably placed for observation.

Mars, magnitude − 1.3, is at opposition on the 17th and therefore visible throughout the hours of darkness. It is a prominent object with a slightly reddish tinge, which is a useful aid to identification. Mars is retrograding in Virgo and moves back into Leo at the end of the month. The Full Moon will be seen about 6° below Mars on the evening of the 23rd.

Jupiter is too close to the Sun for observation at first but shortly after the middle of March it should be possible to see it as a morning object, low above the south-eastern horizon for a short time before dawn. Its magnitude is − 2.0.

Saturn, magnitude + 0.8 is only visible for a short time, low in the west-south-western sky in the early evenings for the early part of the month. Thereafter it is lost in the gathering twilight.

Zodiacal Light. The evening cone may be observed stretching up from the western horizon, after the end of twilight, from the beginning of the month to the 10th and again after the 24th.

THE MOON

Day	RA	Dec.	Hor. par.	Semi- diam.	Sun's co- long.	PA of Bright Limb	Phase	Age	Rise 52°	Rise 56°	Transit	Set 52°	Set 56°
	h m	°	′	′	°	°	%	d	h m	h m	h m	h m	h m
1	15 29	−14.5	56.4	15.4	170	103	65	21.4	0 12	0 26	5 04	9 50	9 36
2	16 22	−16.6	57.1	15.6	183	99	54	22.4	1 17	1 33	5 55	10 31	10 14
3	17 18	−17.9	58.0	15.8	195	95	44	23.4	2 18	2 36	6 50	11 20	11 02
4	18 15	−18.1	58.8	16.0	207	90	33	24.4	3 16	3 33	7 46	12 18	12 01
5	19 15	−17.3	59.7	16.3	219	86	23	25.4	4 07	4 23	8 44	13 26	13 10
6	20 15	−15.3	60.4	16.5	231	82	14	26.4	4 52	5 05	9 43	14 41	14 29
7	21 15	−12.3	61.0	16.6	244	79	6	27.4	5 30	5 40	10 41	16 01	15 53
8	22 15	− 8.4	61.3	16.7	256	78	2	28.4	6 05	6 11	11 38	17 24	17 19
9	23 13	− 3.9	61.2	16.7	268	121	0	29.4	6 36	6 38	12 35	18 46	18 46
10	0 11	+ 0.8	60.9	16.6	280	248	1	0.9	7 06	7 04	13 30	20 07	20 11
11	1 07	+ 5.3	60.2	16.4	292	251	6	1.9	7 36	7 30	14 24	21 25	21 33
12	2 03	+ 9.4	59.4	16.2	305	253	12	2.9	8 07	7 58	15 18	22 39	22 51
13	2 59	+12.9	58.4	15.9	317	256	20	3.9	8 41	8 29	16 10	23 49	—
14	3 53	+15.5	57.5	15.7	329	260	30	4.9	9 19	9 04	17 03	—	0 03
15	4 48	+17.3	56.5	15.4	341	264	40	5.9	10 02	9 45	17 54	0 52	1 09
16	5 41	+18.1	55.8	15.2	353	268	50	6.9	10 50	10 32	18 44	1 48	2 05
17	6 33	+18.0	55.1	15.0	6	272	60	7.9	11 42	11 25	19 32	2 36	2 54
18	7 23	+17.1	54.6	14.9	18	276	69	8.9	12 38	12 23	20 19	3 18	3 34
19	8 13	+15.4	54.3	14.8	30	280	78	9.9	13 37	13 24	21 05	3 53	4 07
20	9 01	+13.1	54.1	14.7	42	283	85	10.9	14 37	14 27	21 49	4 24	4 35
21	9 47	+10.3	54.0	14.7	54	285	91	11.9	15 39	15 32	22 33	4 51	4 59
22	10 33	+ 7.0	54.1	14.7	66	287	96	12.9	16 42	16 38	23 16	5 16	5 21
23	11 19	+ 3.4	54.2	14.8	78	289	99	13.9	17 45	17 44	23 59	5 39	5 41
24	12 05	− 0.3	54.5	14.8	91	299	100	14.9	18 49	18 52	—	6 02	6 01
25	12 51	− 4.0	54.8	14.9	103	104	99	15.9	19 54	20 00	0 42	6 26	6 22
26	13 38	− 7.6	55.1	15.0	115	105	97	16.9	20 59	21 09	1 27	6 51	6 44
27	14 27	−11.0	55.6	15.1	127	103	93	17.9	22 05	22 17	2 13	7 19	7 09
28	15 17	−13.9	56.1	15.3	139	101	86	18.9	23 09	23 25	3 01	7 52	7 38
29	16 09	−16.1	56.6	15.4	151	97	79	19.9	—	—	3 52	8 30	8 14
30	17 04	−17.6	57.2	15.6	164	93	69	20.9	0 11	0 29	4 44	9 15	8 57
31	18 00	−18.2	57.9	15.8	176	89	59	21.9	1 09	1 27	5 39	10 09	9 51

MERCURY

Day	RA	Dec.	Diam.	Phase	Transit	5° high 52°	5° high 56°
	h m	°	″	%	h m	h m	h m
1	22 17	−13.0	5	96	11 43	7 26	7 41
3	22 30	−11.6	5	97	11 49	7 23	7 37
5	22 44	−10.2	5	98	11 54	7 21	7 33
7	22 58	− 8.7	5	99	12 00	16 44	16 33
9	23 11	− 7.2	5	100	12 06	16 59	16 50
11	23 25	− 5.5	5	100	12 12	17 14	17 07
13	23 39	− 3.8	5	100	12 18	17 30	17 24
15	23 53	− 2.0	5	99	12 24	17 46	17 41
17	0 07	− 0.2	5	98	12 31	18 01	17 59
19	0 22	+ 1.7	5	96	12 37	18 17	18 16
21	0 36	+ 3.6	5	93	12 43	18 33	18 33
23	0 50	+ 5.4	5	89	12 49	18 49	18 51
25	1 03	+ 7.3	6	84	12 55	19 04	19 07
27	1 16	+ 9.0	6	78	13 00	19 18	19 22
29	1 29	+10.7	6	72	13 04	19 30	19 36
31	1 40	+12.2	6	64	13 08	19 41	19 49

VENUS

Day	RA	Dec.	Diam.	Phase	Transit	5° high 52°	5° high 56°
	h m	°	″	%	h m	h m	h m
1	22 19	−11.9	10	99	11 44	7 21	7 35
6	22 43	− 9.7	10	99	11 48	7 12	7 24
11	23 06	− 7.3	10	100	11 52	7 02	7 12
16	23 29	− 4.9	10	100	11 55	6 52	7 00
21	23 52	− 2.4	10	100	11 58	6 42	6 48
26	0 15	+ 0.1	10	100	12 01	6 32	6 36
31	0 38	+ 2.6	10	100	12 04	6 23	6 24

MARS

Day	RA	Dec.	Diam.	Phase	Transit	5° high 52°	5° high 56°
1	12 15	+ 2.5	13	99	1 40	19 55	19 56
6	12 10	+ 3.1	14	99	1 14	19 26	19 27
11	12 03	+ 3.8	14	100	0 48	18 57	18 57
16	11 56	+ 4.5	14	100	0 21	18 26	18 26
21	11 49	+ 5.2	14	100	23 49	17 56	17 55
26	11 41	+ 5.8	14	100	23 22	17 26	17 24
31	11 35	+ 6.4	14	99	22 56	16 57	16 55

SUNRISE AND SUNSET

	London		Bristol		Birmingham		Manchester		Newcastle		Glasgow		Belfast	
	0°05′	51°30′	2°35′	51°28′	1°55′	52°28′	2°15′	53°28′	1°37′	54°59′	4°14′	55°52′	5°56′	54°35′
	h m	h m	h m	h m	h m	h m	h m	h m	h m	h m	h m	h m	h m	h m
1	6 46	17 41	6 56	17 51	6 54	17 47	6 57	17 47	6 56	17 42	7 08	17 51	7 13	18 00
2	6 43	17 42	6 53	17 52	6 52	17 49	6 55	17 49	6 54	17 44	7 06	17 53	7 11	18 02
3	6 41	17 44	6 51	17 54	6 50	17 50	6 52	17 51	6 52	17 46	7 03	17 56	7 08	18 04
4	6 39	17 46	6 49	17 56	6 47	17 52	6 50	17 53	6 49	17 48	7 01	17 58	7 06	18 06
5	6 37	17 48	6 47	17 58	6 45	17 54	6 48	17 54	6 47	17 50	6 58	18 00	7 03	18 08
6	6 35	17 49	6 45	17 59	6 43	17 56	6 45	17 56	6 44	17 52	6 56	18 02	7 01	18 10
7	6 32	17 51	6 42	18 01	6 41	17 58	6 43	17 58	6 42	17 54	6 53	18 04	6 59	18 12
8	6 30	17 53	6 40	18 03	6 38	18 00	6 40	18 00	6 39	17 56	6 51	18 06	6 56	18 14
9	6 28	17 55	6 38	18 05	6 36	18 01	6 38	18 02	6 37	17 58	6 48	18 08	6 54	18 16
10	6 26	17 56	6 36	18 06	6 34	18 03	6 36	18 04	6 34	18 00	6 45	18 10	6 51	18 18
11	6 24	17 58	6 34	18 08	6 31	18 05	6 33	18 06	6 32	18 02	6 43	18 12	6 49	18 20
12	6 21	18 00	6 31	18 10	6 29	18 07	6 31	18 08	6 29	18 04	6 40	18 14	6 46	18 22
13	6 19	18 02	6 29	18 12	6 27	18 09	6 29	18 09	6 27	18 06	6 38	18 16	6 44	18 24
14	6 17	18 03	6 27	18 13	6 24	18 10	6 26	18 11	6 24	18 08	6 35	18 18	6 41	18 26
15	6 15	18 05	6 25	18 15	6 22	18 12	6 24	18 13	6 22	18 10	6 32	18 20	6 39	18 28
16	6 12	18 07	6 22	18 17	6 20	18 14	6 21	18 15	6 19	18 12	6 30	18 23	6 36	18 30
17	6 10	18 08	6 20	18 18	6 17	18 16	6 19	18 17	6 17	18 14	6 27	18 25	6 34	18 32
18	6 08	18 10	6 18	18 20	6 15	18 17	6 16	18 19	6 14	18 16	6 25	18 27	6 31	18 33
19	6 05	18 12	6 15	18 22	6 13	18 19	6 14	18 21	6 11	18 18	6 22	18 29	6 29	18 35
20	6 03	18 13	6 13	18 23	6 10	18 21	6 12	18 22	6 09	18 20	6 19	18 31	6 26	18 37
21	6 01	18 15	6 11	18 25	6 08	18 23	6 09	18 24	6 06	18 22	6 17	18 33	6 24	18 39
22	5 59	18 17	6 09	18 27	6 06	18 24	6 07	18 26	6 04	18 24	6 14	18 35	6 21	18 41
23	5 56	18 19	6 06	18 29	6 03	18 26	6 04	18 28	6 01	18 26	6 11	18 37	6 19	18 43
24	5 54	18 20	6 04	18 30	6 01	18 28	6 02	18 30	5 59	18 28	6 09	18 39	6 16	18 45
25	5 52	18 22	6 02	18 32	5 59	18 30	5 59	18 32	5 56	18 30	6 06	18 41	6 14	18 47
26	5 49	18 24	5 59	18 34	5 56	18 31	5 57	18 33	5 54	18 32	6 04	18 43	6 11	18 49
27	5 47	18 25	5 57	18 35	5 54	18 33	5 55	18 35	5 51	18 34	6 01	18 45	6 09	18 51
28	5 45	18 27	5 55	18 37	5 52	18 35	5 52	18 37	5 49	18 36	5 58	18 47	6 06	18 53
29	5 43	18 29	5 53	18 39	5 49	18 37	5 50	18 39	5 46	18 38	5 56	18 49	6 04	18 55
30	5 40	18 30	5 50	18 40	5 47	18 38	5 47	18 41	5 43	18 40	5 53	18 51	6 01	18 56
31	5 38	18 32	5 48	18 42	5 45	18 40	5 45	18 42	5 41	18 42	5 50	18 53	5 59	18 58

JUPITER

Day	RA	Dec.	Transit	5° high	
				52°	56°
	h m	° ′	h m	h m	h m
1	20 45.4	−18 28	10 09	6 30	6 54
11	20 54.1	−17 55	9 38	5 55	6 19
21	21 02.2	−17 23	9 07	5 20	5 43
31	21 09.8	−16 52	8 35	4 45	5 06

Diameters – equatorial 34″ polar 32″

SATURN

Day	RA	Dec.	Transit	5° high	
				52°	56°
	h m	° ′	h m	h m	h m
1	0 27.6	+ 0 35	13 50	19 20	19 17
11	0 32.0	+ 1 04	13 15	18 48	18 45
21	0 36.5	+ 1 34	12 41	18 15	18 13
31	0 41.1	+ 2 03	12 06	17 43	17 42

Diameters – equatorial 16″ polar 14″
Rings – major axis 36″ minor axis 4″

URANUS

Day	RA	Dec.	Transit	10° high	
				52°	56°
	h m	° ′	h m	h m	h m
1	20 36.6	−19 11	10 00	7 12	7 50
11	20 38.6	−19 03	9 22	6 34	7 12
21	20 40.4	−18 57	8 45	5 55	6 33
31	20 42.0	−18 51	8 07	5 17	5 54

Diameter 4″

NEPTUNE

Day	RA	Dec.	Transit	10° high	
				52°	56°
	h m	° ′	h m	h m	h m
1	20 04.0	−19 57	9 27	6 47	7 29
11	20 05.2	−19 54	8 49	6 08	6 50
21	20 06.2	−19 51	8 11	5 30	6 11
31	20 07.0	−19 48	7 32	4 51	5 32

Diameter 2″

 # April 1997

FOURTH MONTH, 30 DAYS. *Asperire*, to open; Earth opens to receive seed

1	Tuesday	Ferruccio Busoni b. 1866. Cosima Wagner d. 1930	*week* 13 *day* 91
2	Wednesday	Hans Christian Andersen b. 1805	92
3	Thursday	Richard D'Oyly Carte d. 1901. Kurt Weill d. 1950	93
4	Friday	Oliver Goldsmith d. 1774. Gloria Swanson d. 1983	94
5	Saturday	Joseph Lister b. 1827. A. C. Swinburne b. 1837	95
6	Sunday	**1st. S. after Easter.** Raphael d. 1520	*week* 14 *day* 96
7	Monday	**The Annunciation.** Henry Ford d. 1947	97
8	Tuesday	HINDU NEW YEAR. *Easter Law Sittings begin*	98
9	Wednesday	Sir Francis Bacon d. 1626. Sir Robert Helpmann b. 1909	99
10	Thursday	Joseph Pulitzer b. 1847. A. C. Swinburne d. 1909	100
11	Friday	Treaty of Utrecht 1713. Sir Charles Hallé b. 1819	101
12	Saturday	Feodor Chaliapin d. 1938. Alan Paton d. 1988	102
13	Sunday	**2nd S. after Easter.** SIKH NEW YEAR	*week* 15 *day* 103
14	Monday	Sir John Gielgud b. 1904. Ernest Bevin d. 1951	104
15	Tuesday	Henry James b. 1843. Matthew Arnold d. 1888	105
16	Wednesday	Anatole France b. 1844. Wilbur Wright b. 1867	106
17	Thursday	Benjamin Franklin d. 1790. Nikita Khrushchev b. 1894 (NS)	107
18	Friday	Judge Jeffreys d. 1689. Albert Einstein d. 1955	108
19	Saturday	Benjamin Disraeli d. 1881. Charles Darwin d. 1882	109
20	Sunday	**3rd S. after Easter.** Joan Miró b. 1893	*week* 16 *day* 110
21	Monday	*Queen Elizabeth II b. 1926.* Charlotte Brontë b. 1816	111
22	Tuesday	PASSOVER begins. Henry Fielding b. 1707	112
23	Wednesday	St George's Day. Viscount Allenby b. 1861	113
24	Thursday	Anthony Trollope b. 1815. Sir Stafford Cripps b. 1889	114
25	Friday	**St Mark.** Oliver Cromwell b. 1599	115
26	Saturday	David Hume b. 1711. Eugene Delacroix b. 1798	116
27	Sunday	**4th S. after Easter.** EASTER DAY (Greek Orthodox)	*week* 17 *day* 117
28	Monday	Lionel Barrymore b. 1878. Olivier Messiaen d. 1992	118
29	Tuesday	Sir Thomas Beecham b. 1879	119
30	Wednesday	Mary II b. 1662. Franz Lehár b. 1870	120

ASTRONOMICAL PHENOMENA

d h
2 14 Venus in superior conjunction
3 06 Jupiter in conjunction with Moon. Jupiter 4° S.
6 01 Mercury at greatest elongation E.19°
7 00 Saturn in conjunction with Moon. Saturn 1° S.
7 13 Venus in conjunction with Moon. Venus 0°.7 N.
8 20 Mercury in conjunction with Moon. Mercury 6° N.
15 00 Mercury at stationary point
19 03 Mars in conjunction with Moon. Mars 4° N.
20 01 Sun's longitude 30° ♉
22 07 Venus in conjunction with Mercury. Venus 3° S.
25 11 Mercury in inferior conjunction
27 19 Mars at stationary point
30 19 Jupiter in conjunction with Moon. Jupiter 4° S.

MINIMA OF ALGOL

d	h	d	h	d	h
3	06.4	14	17.7	26	05.0
6	03.2	17	14.5	29	01.8
9	00.1	20	11.3		
11	20.9	23	08.2		

CONSTELLATIONS

The following constellations are near the meridian at

	d	h		d	h
March	1	24	April	15	21
March	16	23	May	1	20
April	1	22	May	16	19

Cepheus (below the Pole), Cassiopeia (below the Pole), Ursa Major, Leo Minor, Leo, Sextans, Hydra and Crater

THE MOON

Phases, Apsides and Node	d	h	m
● New Moon	7	11	02
☽ First Quarter	14	17	00
○ Full Moon	22	20	33
☾ Last Quarter	30	02	37

Perigee (361,497 km) 5 16 42
Apogee (405,003 km) 17 15 20

Mean longitude of ascending node on April 1, 178°

THE SUN

s.d. 16'.0

Day	Right Ascension h m s	Dec. + ° '	Equation of time m s	Rise 52° h m	Rise 56° h m	Transit h m	Set 52° h m	Set 56° h m	Sidereal time h m s	Transit of First Point of Aries h m s
1	0 41 34	4 28	−4 00	5 35	5 31	12 04	18 34	18 38	12 37 34	11 20 34
2	0 45 13	4 51	−3 42	5 33	5 28	12 04	18 35	18 40	12 41 31	11 16 38
3	0 48 52	5 14	−3 25	5 30	5 25	12 03	18 37	18 42	12 45 27	11 12 42
4	0 52 31	5 37	−3 07	5 28	5 23	12 03	18 39	18 44	12 49 24	11 08 46
5	0 56 10	6 00	−2 50	5 26	5 20	12 03	18 41	18 46	12 53 20	11 04 51
6	0 59 49	6 23	−2 33	5 24	5 18	12 02	18 42	18 48	12 57 17	11 00 55
7	1 03 29	6 46	−2 16	5 21	5 15	12 02	18 44	18 50	13 01 13	10 56 59
8	1 07 09	7 08	−1 59	5 19	5 13	12 02	18 46	18 52	13 05 10	10 53 03
9	1 10 49	7 31	−1 42	5 17	5 10	12 02	18 47	18 55	13 09 06	10 49 07
10	1 14 29	7 53	−1 26	5 15	5 07	12 01	18 49	18 57	13 13 03	10 45 11
11	1 18 10	8 15	−1 10	5 12	5 05	12 01	18 51	18 59	13 17 00	10 41 15
12	1 21 51	8 37	−0 54	5 10	5 02	12 01	18 53	19 01	13 20 56	10 37 19
13	1 25 32	8 59	−0 39	5 08	5 00	12 01	18 54	19 03	13 24 53	10 33 23
14	1 29 13	9 21	−0 24	5 06	4 57	12 00	18 56	19 05	13 28 49	10 29 27
15	1 32 55	9 42	−0 09	5 03	4 55	12 00	18 58	19 07	13 32 46	10 25 31
16	1 36 37	10 04	+0 05	5 01	4 52	12 00	18 59	19 09	13 36 42	10 21 36
17	1 40 19	10 25	+0 20	4 59	4 50	12 00	19 01	19 11	13 40 39	10 17 40
18	1 44 02	10 46	+0 33	4 57	4 47	11 59	19 03	19 13	13 44 35	10 13 44
19	1 47 45	11 07	+0 47	4 55	4 45	11 59	19 05	19 15	13 48 32	10 09 48
20	1 51 29	11 27	+1 00	4 53	4 42	11 59	19 06	19 17	13 52 29	10 05 52
21	1 55 13	11 48	+1 12	4 51	4 40	11 59	19 08	19 19	13 56 25	10 01 56
22	1 58 57	12 08	+1 25	4 48	4 37	11 58	19 10	19 21	14 00 22	9 58 00
23	2 02 42	12 28	+1 36	4 46	4 35	11 58	19 11	19 23	14 04 18	9 54 04
24	2 06 27	12 48	+1 48	4 44	4 32	11 58	19 13	19 25	14 08 15	9 50 08
25	2 10 13	13 08	+1 58	4 42	4 30	11 58	19 15	19 27	14 12 11	9 46 12
26	2 13 59	13 27	+2 09	4 40	4 28	11 58	19 16	19 29	14 16 08	9 42 17
27	2 17 46	13 47	+2 19	4 38	4 25	11 58	19 18	19 31	14 20 04	9 38 21
28	2 21 33	14 06	+2 28	4 36	4 23	11 57	19 20	19 33	14 24 01	9 34 25
29	2 25 21	14 24	+2 37	4 34	4 21	11 57	19 21	19 35	14 27 57	9 30 29
30	2 29 09	11 43	+2 45	4 32	4 18	11 57	19 23	19 37	14 31 54	9 26 33

DURATION OF TWILIGHT (in minutes)

Latitude	52°	56°	52°	56°	52°	56°	52°	56°
	1 April		11 April		21 April		30 April	
Civil	34	38	35	40	37	42	39	44
Nautical	76	85	79	90	84	96	89	105
Astronomical	121	137	128	148	138	167	152	200

THE NIGHT SKY

Mercury continues to be visible in the evenings, magnitude −0.6 to +1.0, for the first ten days of the month. It may be detected low above the western horizon around the end of evening civil twilight. Mercury passes through inferior conjunction on the 25th.

Venus passes through superior conjunction on the 2nd and is therefore too close to the Sun for observation throughout April.

Mars is just past opposition and therefore still available for observation during the greater part of the night, though by the end of the month it has sunk too low in the western sky to be visible after 03h. Its magnitude fades from −1.1 to −0.5 during April. On the 29th Mars reaches its second stationary point in the eastern part of Leo and then resumes its direct motion. The gibbous Moon will be seen 4° below Mars in the early hours of the 19th.

Jupiter, magnitude −2.1, is a brilliant object in the south-eastern sky for a short time in the mornings before dawn, though being so far south of the equator its altitude is always less than 20°. On the morning of the 3rd the old crescent Moon will be seen about 4° above the planet about an hour before sunrise.

Saturn is unsuitably placed for observation.

THE MOON

Day	RA	Dec.	Hor. par.	Semi-diam.	Sun's co-long.	PA of Bright Limb	Phase	Age	Rise 52°	Rise 56°	Transit	Set 52°	Set 56°
	h m	°	'	'	°	°	%	d	h m	h m	h m	h m	h m
1	18 57	−17.7	58.6	16.0	188	85	48	22.9	2 01	2 18	6 34	11 11	10 54
2	19 55	−16.1	59.2	16.1	200	80	37	23.9	2 46	3 01	7 31	12 21	12 07
3	20 53	−13.5	59.8	16.3	212	76	26	24.9	3 26	3 37	8 27	13 36	13 26
4	21 51	−10.0	60.3	16.4	225	73	16	25.9	4 01	4 09	9 23	14 55	14 48
5	22 48	− 5.9	60.6	16.5	237	70	9	26.9	4 32	4 36	10 18	16 15	16 13
6	23 45	− 1.3	60.6	16.5	249	67	3	27.9	5 02	5 02	11 13	17 36	17 38
7	0 42	+ 3.3	60.4	16.5	261	57	0	28.9	5 32	5 28	12 07	18 56	19 02
8	1 38	+ 7.7	60.0	16.3	273	267	0	0.5	6 02	5 55	13 02	20 14	20 23
9	2 35	+11.5	59.3	16.1	286	261	3	1.5	6 35	6 25	13 56	21 27	21 41
10	3 31	+14.6	58.4	15.9	298	262	9	2.5	7 12	6 58	14 50	22 36	22 52
11	4 27	+16.7	57.6	15.7	310	266	16	3.5	7 54	7 38	15 43	23 37	23 54
12	5 22	+17.9	56.7	15.4	322	269	24	4.5	8 41	8 23	16 35	—	—
13	6 15	+18.2	55.9	15.2	335	273	34	5.5	9 32	9 15	17 26	0 30	0 47
14	7 07	+17.5	55.2	15.0	347	277	43	6.5	10 28	10 12	18 14	1 15	1 32
15	7 58	+16.0	54.7	14.9	359	281	53	7.5	11 27	11 13	19 01	1 53	2 08
16	8 47	+13.9	54.3	14.8	11	284	62	8.5	12 27	12 16	19 46	2 26	2 38
17	9 34	+11.2	54.2	14.8	23	287	71	9.5	13 28	13 20	20 29	2 54	3 04
18	10 20	+ 8.0	54.1	14.8	36	290	79	10.5	14 31	14 26	21 12	3 20	3 26
19	11 06	+ 4.5	54.3	14.8	48	292	86	11.5	15 34	15 32	21 55	3 44	3 47
20	11 51	+ 0.8	54.5	14.9	60	293	92	12.5	16 38	16 39	22 39	4 06	4 07
21	12 38	− 2.9	54.9	14.9	72	296	97	13.5	17 43	17 48	23 23	4 30	4 27
22	13 25	− 6.7	55.3	15.1	84	304	99	14.5	18 49	18 57	—	4 54	4 48
23	14 13	−10.1	55.7	15.2	96	48	100	15.5	19 56	20 07	0 09	5 22	5 12
24	15 04	−13.2	56.2	15.3	109	90	99	16.5	21 02	21 16	0 57	5 53	5 40
25	15 56	−15.7	56.7	15.5	121	92	95	17.5	22 06	22 23	1 48	6 29	6 14
26	16 51	−17.4	57.2	15.6	133	90	89	18.5	23 05	23 23	2 40	7 12	6 55
27	17 47	−18.2	57.7	15.7	145	87	82	19.5	23 59	—	3 35	8 04	7 46
28	18 44	−18.0	58.2	15.8	157	83	73	20.5	—	0 17	4 30	9 03	8 46
29	19 41	−16.7	58.6	16.0	170	79	63	21.5	0 46	1 02	5 25	10 10	9 55
30	20 38	−14.4	59.0	16.1	182	75	51	22.5	1 26	1 39	6 21	11 22	11 10

MERCURY

Day	RA	Dec.	Diam.	Phase	Transit	5° high 52°	5° high 56°
	h m	°	"	%	h m	h m	h m
1	1 46	+12.9	7	60	13 09	19 46	19 54
3	1 56	+14.2	7	52	13 11	19 54	20 03
5	2 04	+15.3	7	45	13 11	20 00	20 10
7	2 12	+16.2	8	37	13 10	20 03	20 14
9	2 17	+16.9	8	30	13 07	20 04	20 15
11	2 22	+17.3	9	24	13 03	20 01	20 13
13	2 24	+17.6	9	18	12 57	19 56	20 08
15	2 25	+17.6	10	13	12 50	19 48	20 00
17	2 24	+17.4	10	9	12 41	19 37	19 49
19	2 22	+16.9	11	5	12 31	19 24	19 35
21	2 19	+16.3	11	3	12 20	19 09	19 19
23	2 16	+15.5	12	1	12 08	18 53	19 02
25	2 11	+14.6	12	0	11 56	5 15	5 06
27	2 07	+13.7	12	0	11 44	5 08	5 00
29	2 02	+12.7	12	1	11 32	5 01	4 54
31	1 59	+11.7	12	3	11 20	4 54	4 48

VENUS

Day	RA	Dec.	Diam.	Phase	Transit	5° high 52°	5° high 56°
	h m	°	"	%	h m	h m	h m
1	0 42	+ 3.1	10	100	12 05	17 50	17 50
6	1 05	+ 5.6	10	100	12 08	18 06	18 08
11	1 28	+ 8.0	10	100	12 11	18 22	18 26
16	1 51	+10.4	10	100	12 15	18 38	18 43
21	2 15	+12.7	10	100	12 19	18 53	19 01
26	2 38	+14.8	10	100	12 23	19 09	19 18
31	3 03	+16.8	10	99	12 27	19 24	19 36

MARS

Day	RA	Dec.	Diam.	Phase	Transit	5° high 52°	5° high 56°
1	11 33	+ 6.5	14	99	22 51	4 55	4 57
6	11 27	+ 6.9	14	98	22 25	4 32	4 34
11	11 22	+ 7.2	13	97	22 01	4 09	4 11
16	11 19	+ 7.3	13	96	21 38	3 46	3 49
21	11 16	+ 7.4	12	95	21 16	3 24	3 27
26	11 15	+ 7.3	12	94	20 55	3 03	3 05
31	11 15	+ 7.1	12	93	20 35	2 42	2 44

SUNRISE AND SUNSET

	London 0°05' 51°30'		Bristol 2°35' 51°28'		Birmingham 1°55' 52°28'		Manchester 2°15' 53°28'		Newcastle 1°37' 54°59'		Glasgow 4°14' 55°52'		Belfast 5°56' 54°35'	
	h m	h m	h m	h m	h m	h m	h m	h m	h m	h m	h m	h m	h m	h m
1	5 36	18 34	5 46	18 44	5 42	18 42	5 43	18 44	5 38	18 43	5 48	18 55	5 56	19 00
2	5 34	18 35	5 44	18 45	5 40	18 44	5 40	18 46	5 36	18 45	5 45	18 57	5 54	19 02
3	5 31	18 37	5 41	18 47	5 38	18 45	5 38	18 48	5 33	18 47	5 43	18 59	5 51	19 04
4	5 29	18 39	5 39	18 49	5 35	18 47	5 35	18 50	5 31	18 49	5 40	19 01	5 49	19 06
5	5 27	18 40	5 37	18 50	5 33	18 49	5 33	18 52	5 28	18 51	5 37	19 03	5 46	19 08
6	5 25	18 42	5 35	18 52	5 31	18 51	5 31	18 53	5 26	18 53	5 35	19 05	5 44	19 10
7	5 22	18 44	5 32	18 54	5 28	18 52	5 28	18 55	5 23	18 55	5 32	19 07	5 41	19 12
8	5 20	18 45	5 30	18 55	5 26	18 54	5 26	18 57	5 21	18 57	5 30	19 09	5 39	19 14
9	5 18	18 47	5 28	18 57	5 24	18 56	5 23	18 59	5 18	18 59	5 27	19 11	5 36	19 16
10	5 16	18 49	5 26	18 59	5 21	18 58	5 21	19 01	5 16	19 01	5 25	19 13	5 34	19 18
11	5 13	18 50	5 24	19 00	5 19	18 59	5 19	19 03	5 13	19 03	5 22	19 15	5 31	19 19
12	5 11	18 52	5 21	19 02	5 17	19 01	5 16	19 04	5 11	19 05	5 19	19 17	5 29	19 21
13	5 09	18 54	5 19	19 04	5 15	19 03	5 14	19 06	5 08	19 07	5 17	19 19	5 26	19 23
14	5 07	18 55	5 17	19 05	5 12	19 05	5 12	19 08	5 06	19 09	5 14	19 21	5 24	19 25
15	5 05	18 57	5 15	19 07	5 10	19 06	5 09	19 10	5 04	19 11	5 12	19 23	5 22	19 27
16	5 03	18 59	5 13	19 09	5 08	19 08	5 07	19 12	5 01	19 13	5 09	19 25	5 19	19 29
17	5 01	19 00	5 11	19 10	5 06	19 10	5 05	19 13	4 59	19 15	5 07	19 27	5 17	19 31
18	4 58	19 02	5 08	19 12	5 04	19 12	5 03	19 15	4 56	19 17	5 04	19 29	5 15	19 33
19	4 56	19 04	5 06	19 14	5 01	19 13	5 00	19 17	4 54	19 19	5 02	19 32	5 12	19 35
20	4 54	19 05	5 04	19 15	4 59	19 15	4 58	19 19	4 52	19 21	4 59	19 34	5 10	19 37
21	4 52	19 07	5 02	19 17	4 57	19 17	4 56	19 21	4 49	19 22	4 57	19 36	5 08	19 39
22	4 50	19 09	5 00	19 19	4 55	19 19	4 54	19 23	4 47	19 24	4 55	19 38	5 05	19 40
23	4 48	19 10	4 58	19 20	4 53	19 20	4 51	19 24	4 44	19 26	4 52	19 40	5 03	19 42
24	4 46	19 12	4 56	19 22	4 51	19 22	4 49	19 26	4 42	19 28	4 50	19 42	5 01	19 44
25	4 44	19 14	4 54	19 24	4 49	19 24	4 47	19 28	4 40	19 30	4 47	19 44	4 58	19 46
26	4 42	19 15	4 52	19 25	4 47	19 25	4 45	19 30	4 38	19 32	4 45	19 46	4 56	19 48
27	4 40	19 17	4 50	19 27	4 45	19 27	4 43	19 32	4 35	19 34	4 43	19 48	4 54	19 50
28	4 38	19 19	4 48	19 29	4 43	19 29	4 41	19 33	4 33	19 36	4 40	19 50	4 52	19 52
29	4 36	19 20	4 46	19 30	4 41	19 31	4 39	19 35	4 31	19 38	4 38	19 52	4 50	19 54
30	4 34	19 22	4 44	19 32	4 39	19 32	4 37	19 37	4 29	19 40	4 36	19 54	4 47	19 56

JUPITER

Day	RA	Dec.	Transit	5° high 52°	5° high 56°
	h m	° '	h m	h m	h m
1	21 10.5	−16 49	8 32	4 42	5 03
11	21 17.3	−16 20	7 59	4 06	4 26
21	21 23.3	−15 55	7 26	3 30	3 49
31	21 28.5	−15 32	6 52	2 53	3 12

Diameters – equatorial 37" polar 34"

SATURN

Day	RA	Dec.	Transit	5° high 52°	5° high 56°
	h m	° '	h m	h m	h m
1	0 41.6	+ 2 06	12 02	6 25	6 26
11	0 46.2	+ 2 35	11 28	5 48	5 49
21	0 50.8	+ 3 03	10 53	5 10	5 11
31	0 55.2	+ 3 30	10 18	4 33	4 34

Diameters – equatorial 16" polar 14"
Rings – major axis 36" minor axis 5"

URANUS

Day	RA	Dec.	Transit	10° high 52°	10° high 56°
	h m	° '	h m	h m	h m
1	20 42.1	−18 51	8 03	5 13	5 50
11	20 43.3	−18 47	7 25	4 34	5 11
21	20 44.2	−18 44	6 47	3 55	4 32
31	20 44.8	−18 42	6 08	3 16	3 53

Diameter 4"

NEPTUNE

Day	RA	Dec.	Transit	10° high 52°	10° high 56°
	h m	° '	h m	h m	h m
1	20 07.1	−19 48	7 28	4 47	5 28
11	20 07.7	−19 46	6 50	4 08	4 48
21	20 08.0	−19 45	6 11	3 29	4 09
31	20 08.2	−19 45	5 31	2 49	3 30

Diameter 2"

May 1997 ♊

FIFTH MONTH, 31 DAYS. *Maia*, goddess of growth and increase

1	*Thursday*	**SS Philip and James.** Joseph Addison b. 1672	*week* 17 *day* 121
2	*Friday*	Joseph McCarthy d. 1957. Nancy Astor d. 1964	122
3	*Saturday*	Niccolò Machiavelli b. 1469. Dodie Smith b. 1896	123
4	*Sunday*	**5th S. after Easter.** Audrey Hepburn b. 1929	*week* 18 *day* 124
5	*Monday*	*Bank Holiday in the UK.* Søren Kierkegaard b. 1813	125
6	*Tuesday*	Sigmund Freud b. 1856. Tony Blair b. 1953	126
7	*Wednesday*	Antonio Salieri d. 1825. Earl of Rosebery b. 1847	127
8	*Thursday*	**Ascension Day.** Harry Gordon Selfridge d. 1947	128
9	*Friday*	MUSLIM NEW YEAR (1418). Sir James Barrie b. 1860	129
10	*Saturday*	Karl Barth b. 1886. Sir Henry Stanley d. 1904	130
11	*Sunday*	**S. after Ascension Day.** Salvador Dali b. 1904	*week* 19 *day* 131
12	*Monday*	Sir Lennox Berkeley b. 1903. John Masefield d. 1967	132
13	*Tuesday*	Fridtjof Nansen d. 1930. Gary Cooper d. 1961	133
14	*Wednesday*	**St Matthias.** August Strindberg d. 1912	134
15	*Thursday*	Daniel O'Connell d. 1847. Edwin Muir b. 1887	135
16	*Friday*	Sir John Hare b. 1844. H. E. Bates d. 1905	136
17	*Saturday*	Sandro Botticelli d. 1510. Paul Dukas d. 1935	137
18	*Sunday*	**Pentecost/Whit Sunday.** Pope John Paul II b. 1920	*week* 20 *day* 138
19	*Monday*	Dame Nellie Melba b. 1861. Nathaniel Hawthorne d. 1864	139
20	*Tuesday*	John Stuart Mill b. 1806. Dame Barbara Hepworth d. 1975	140
21	*Wednesday*	Alexander Pope b. 1688. Elizabeth Fry b. 1780	141
22	*Thursday*	Blackwall Tunnel opened 1897	142
23	*Friday*	*Easter Law Sittings end.* Carl Linnaeus b. 1707	143
24	*Saturday*	George III b. 1738. Jean-Paul Marat b. 1743	144
25	*Sunday*	**Trinity Sunday.** Lord Beaverbrook b. 1879	*week* 21 *day* 145
26	*Monday*	*Bank Holiday in the UK.* Sir Matt Busby b. 1909	146
27	*Tuesday*	John Calvin d. 1564. Arnold Bennett b. 1867	147
28	*Wednesday*	William Pitt (the younger) b. 1759	148
29	*Thursday*	**Corpus Christi.** John F. Kennedy b. 1917	149
30	*Friday*	Rubens d. 1640. Alexander Pope d. 1744	150
31	*Saturday*	Joseph Grimaldi d. 1837. Walter Sickert b. 1860	151

ASTRONOMICAL PHENOMENA

d	h	
1	23	Neptune at stationary point
4	15	Saturn in conjunction with Moon. Saturn 0°.8 S.
5	17	Mercury in conjunction with Moon. Mercury 1° N.
7	14	Venus in conjunction with Moon. Venus 4° N.
8	18	Mercury at stationary point
13	04	Uranus at stationary point
16	14	Mars in conjunction with Moon. Mars 2° N.
21	00	Sun's longitude 60° ♊
22	23	Mercury at greatest elongation W. 25°
25	10	Pluto at opposition
28	04	Jupiter in conjunction with Moon. Jupiter 4° S.

MINIMA OF ALGOL

Algol is inconveniently situated for observation during May.

CONSTELLATIONS

The following constellations are near the meridian at

	d	h		d	h
April	1	24	May	16	21
April	15	23	June	1	20
May	1	22	June	15	19

Cepheus (below the Pole), Cassiopeia (below the Pole), Ursa Minor, Ursa Major, Canes Venatici, Coma Berenices, Bootes, Leo, Virgo, Crater, Corvus and Hydra

THE MOON

Phases, Apsides and Node	d	h	m
● New Moon	6	20	47
☽ First Quarter	14	10	55
○ Full Moon	22	09	13
☾ Last Quarter	29	07	51
Perigee (366,619 km)	3	11	06
Apogee (404,216 km)	15	10	09
Perigee (369,791 km)	29	06	58

Mean longitude of ascending node on May 1, 177°

THE SUN   s.d. 15'.8

Day	Right Ascension	Dec. +	Equation of time	Rise 52°	Rise 56°	Transit	Set 52°	Set 56°	Sidereal time	Transit of First Point of Aries
	h m s	° '	m s	h m	h m	h m	h m	h m	h m s	h m s
1	2 32 58	15 01	+2 52	4 30	4 16	11 57	19 25	19 39	14 35 51	9 22 37
2	2 36 48	15 19	+3 00	4 29	4 14	11 57	19 26	19 41	14 39 47	9 18 41
3	2 40 38	15 37	+3 06	4 27	4 12	11 57	19 28	19 43	14 43 44	9 14 45
4	2 44 28	15 55	+3 12	4 25	4 10	11 57	19 30	19 45	14 47 40	9 10 49
5	2 48 19	16 12	+3 18	4 23	4 07	11 57	19 31	19 47	14 51 37	9 06 53
6	2 52 11	16 29	+3 22	4 21	4 05	11 57	19 33	19 49	14 55 33	9 02 57
7	2 56 03	16 46	+3 27	4 19	4 03	11 57	19 35	19 51	14 59 30	8 59 02
8	2 59 56	17 02	+3 30	4 18	4 01	11 56	19 36	19 53	15 03 26	8 55 06
9	3 03 49	17 18	+3 34	4 16	3 59	11 56	19 38	19 55	15 07 23	8 51 10
10	3 07 43	17 34	+3 36	4 14	3 57	11 56	19 40	19 57	15 11 20	8 47 14
11	3 11 38	17 50	+3 38	4 13	3 55	11 56	19 41	19 59	15 15 16	8 43 18
12	3 15 33	18 05	+3 40	4 11	3 53	11 56	19 43	20 01	15 19 13	8 39 22
13	3 19 29	18 20	+3 41	4 09	3 51	11 56	19 44	20 03	15 23 09	8 35 26
14	3 23 25	18 35	+3 41	4 08	3 49	11 56	19 46	20 05	15 27 06	8 31 30
15	3 27 22	18 49	+3 41	4 06	3 47	11 56	19 47	20 07	15 31 02	8 27 34
16	3 31 19	19 03	+3 40	4 05	3 45	11 56	19 49	20 09	15 34 59	8 23 38
17	3 35 17	19 17	+3 39	4 03	3 44	11 56	19 50	20 10	15 38 55	8 19 42
18	3 39 15	19 31	+3 37	4 02	3 42	11 56	19 52	20 12	15 42 52	8 15 47
19	3 43 14	19 44	+3 35	4 00	3 40	11 56	19 53	20 14	15 46 49	8 11 51
20	3 47 13	19 56	+3 32	3 59	3 38	11 57	19 55	20 16	15 50 45	8 07 55
21	3 51 13	20 09	+3 28	3 58	3 37	11 57	19 56	20 17	15 54 42	8 03 59
22	3 55 14	20 21	+3 24	3 56	3 35	11 57	19 58	20 19	15 58 38	8 00 03
23	3 59 15	20 33	+3 20	3 55	3 34	11 57	19 59	20 21	16 02 35	7 56 07
24	4 03 17	20 44	+3 15	3 54	3 32	11 57	20 00	20 22	16 06 31	7 52 11
25	4 07 19	20 55	+3 09	3 53	3 31	11 57	20 02	20 24	16 10 28	7 48 15
26	4 11 21	21 06	+3 03	3 52	3 29	11 57	20 03	20 26	16 14 24	7 44 19
27	4 15 24	21 16	+2 57	3 51	3 28	11 57	20 04	20 27	16 18 21	7 40 23
28	4 19 28	21 26	+2 50	3 50	3 27	11 57	20 06	20 29	16 22 18	7 36 27
29	4 23 32	21 35	+2 42	3 49	3 25	11 57	20 07	20 30	16 26 14	7 32 32
30	4 27 36	21 44	+2 34	3 48	3 24	11 57	20 08	20 32	16 30 11	7 28 36
31	4 31 41	21 53	+2 26	3 47	3 23	11 58	20 09	20 33	16 34 07	7 24 40

DURATION OF TWILIGHT (in minutes)

Latitude	52°	56°	52°	56°	52°	56°	52°	56°
	1 May		11 May		21 May		31 May	
Civil	39	45	41	49	44	53	46	57
Nautical	90	106	97	121	106	143	116	TAN
Astronomical	154	209	179	TAN	TAN	TAN	TAN	TAN

THE NIGHT SKY

Mercury, although at greatest western elongation on the 22nd, is unsuitably placed for observation.

Venus is beginning to move out of the long evening twilight, becoming a brilliant object in the evening sky, magnitude −3.9. It may be seen low above the western horizon for a short time after sunset.

Mars continues to move away from opposition and its magnitude fades during the month from −0.4 to +0.2. Mars is moving slowly eastwards in Virgo and is still a conspicuous object in the south-western skies in the evenings, though by the end of May it is not observable for long after midnight. During the evening of the 16th the waxing gibbous Moon will be seen about 5° to the left of Mars.

Jupiter continues to be visible as a brilliant object in the south-eastern sky in the mornings, magnitude −2.3. Jupiter is in the constellation of Capricornus. The Moon, near Last Quarter, will be seen to the left of Jupiter on the morning of the 1st, while on the morning of the 28th it will be seen 4° above the planet. The four Galilean satellites are readily observable with a small telescope, or a good pair of binoculars provided that they are held rigidly. Times of eclipses and shadow transits of these satellites are given on page 70.

Saturn remains too close to the Sun for observation.

THE MOON

Day	RA h m	Dec. °	Hor. par. '	Semi- diam. '	Sun's co- long. °	PA of Bright Limb °	Phase %	Age d	Rise 52° h m	Rise 56° h m	Transit h m	Set 52° h m	Set 56° h m
1	21 35	−11.2	59.4	16.2	194	72	40	23.5	2 02	2 11	7 15	12 37	12 29
2	22 31	− 7.3	59.6	16.3	206	69	29	24.5	2 33	2 39	8 08	13 55	13 50
3	23 26	− 3.0	59.8	16.3	218	67	19	25.5	3 02	3 04	9 01	15 13	15 13
4	0 21	+ 1.5	59.8	16.3	231	66	11	26.5	3 30	3 29	9 54	16 31	16 35
5	1 16	+ 6.0	59.6	16.2	243	64	5	27.5	4 00	3 54	10 48	17 49	17 56
6	2 12	+10.0	59.2	16.1	255	56	1	28.5	4 31	4 22	11 41	19 04	19 16
7	3 08	+13.4	58.7	16.0	267	320	0	0.1	5 05	4 53	12 36	20 16	20 30
8	4 04	+16.0	58.0	15.8	280	276	2	1.1	5 45	5 29	13 30	21 21	21 38
9	5 00	+17.7	57.3	15.6	292	274	6	2.1	6 29	6 12	14 23	22 19	22 37
10	5 55	+18.3	56.6	15.4	304	276	12	3.1	7 20	7 02	15 15	23 09	23 27
11	6 49	+18.0	55.8	15.2	316	279	19	4.1	8 15	7 58	16 06	23 51	—
12	7 41	+16.8	55.2	15.0	328	282	27	5.1	9 13	8 58	16 54	—	0 07
13	8 31	+14.8	54.7	14.9	341	285	36	6.1	10 14	10 01	17 40	0 27	0 40
14	9 19	+12.3	54.4	14.8	353	288	46	7.1	11 15	11 06	18 25	0 57	1 07
15	10 06	+ 9.2	54.3	14.8	5	290	55	8.1	12 18	12 11	19 08	1 23	1 31
16	10 51	+ 5.8	54.3	14.8	17	292	65	9.1	13 20	13 17	19 51	1 48	1 52
17	11 37	+ 2.2	54.4	14.8	30	293	73	10.1	14 24	14 24	20 34	2 10	2 12
18	12 22	− 1.6	54.8	14.9	42	294	81	11.1	15 28	15 32	21 17	2 33	2 32
19	13 09	− 5.4	55.2	15.0	54	294	88	12.1	16 34	16 41	22 03	2 57	2 52
20	13 57	− 9.0	55.8	15.2	66	295	94	13.1	17 41	17 52	22 50	3 23	3 15
21	14 47	−12.3	56.4	15.4	78	299	98	14.1	18 49	19 02	23 41	3 52	3 41
22	15 40	−15.1	57.0	15.5	90	326	100	15.1	19 55	20 12	—	4 26	4 12
23	16 35	−17.1	57.5	15.7	103	66	99	16.1	20 58	21 16	0 33	5 08	4 51
24	17 31	−18.2	58.1	15.8	115	79	97	17.1	21 56	22 14	1 28	5 57	5 39
25	18 29	−18.3	58.5	15.9	127	80	92	18.1	22 46	23 03	2 24	6 55	6 37
26	19 28	−17.3	58.8	16.0	139	77	85	19.1	23 29	23 43	3 21	8 00	7 44
27	20 26	−15.2	59.1	16.1	151	74	76	20.1	—	—	4 17	9 12	8 58
28	21 23	−12.2	59.2	16.1	164	71	65	21.1	0 06	0 17	5 12	10 26	10 17
29	22 18	− 8.5	59.3	16.2	176	69	54	22.1	0 38	0 45	6 05	11 42	11 37
30	23 13	− 4.3	59.3	16.2	188	67	42	23.1	1 07	1 10	6 57	12 59	12 57
31	0 07	+ 0.2	59.2	16.1	200	66	31	24.1	1 34	1 34	7 49	14 15	14 18

MERCURY

Day	RA h m	Dec. °	Diam. "	Phase %	Transit h m	5° high 52° h m	5° high 56° h m
1	1 59	+11.7	12	3	11 20	4 54	4 48
3	1 56	+10.9	12	5	11 10	4 48	4 42
5	1 54	+10.2	11	8	11 00	4 42	4 37
7	1 53	+ 9.6	11	11	10 51	4 36	4 32
9	1 53	+ 9.1	11	15	10 44	4 31	4 27
11	1 54	+ 8.9	10	18	10 38	4 25	4 21
13	1 56	+ 8.8	10	22	10 32	4 20	4 16
15	2 00	+ 8.9	10	25	10 28	4 15	4 12
17	2 04	+ 9.1	9	29	10 25	4 11	4 07
19	2 09	+ 9.4	9	32	10 22	4 06	4 02
21	2 15	+ 9.9	9	36	10 20	4 02	3 57
23	2 22	+10.5	8	39	10 20	3 58	3 53
25	2 30	+11.2	8	43	10 20	3 54	3 48
27	2 39	+12.0	8	47	10 20	3 51	3 44
29	2 48	+12.9	7	50	10 22	3 48	3 40
31	2 58	+13.8	7	54	10 24	3 45	3 37

VENUS

Day	RA h m	Dec. °	Diam. "	Phase %	Transit h m	5° high 52° h m	5° high 56° h m
1	3 03	+16.8	10	99	12 27	19 24	19 36
6	3 28	+18.6	10	99	12 33	19 40	19 53
11	3 53	+20.2	10	99	12 38	19 54	20 09
16	4 18	+21.5	10	98	12 44	20 08	20 25
21	4 44	+22.7	10	98	12 50	20 21	20 39
26	5 11	+23.5	10	97	12 57	20 33	20 52
31	5 38	+24.1	10	96	13 04	20 44	21 03

MARS

Day	RA h m	Dec. °	Diam. "	Phase %	Transit h m	52° h m	56° h m
1	11 15	+ 7.1	12	93	20 35	2 42	2 44
6	11 16	+ 6.7	11	92	20 17	2 22	2 24
11	11 18	+ 6.3	11	92	19 59	2 02	2 04
16	11 20	+ 5.8	10	91	19 43	1 42	1 44
21	11 24	+ 5.2	10	90	19 27	1 24	1 24
26	11 29	+ 4.5	9	90	19 12	1 05	1 05
31	11 34	+ 3.8	9	89	18 58	0 47	0 47

SUNRISE AND SUNSET

	London		Bristol		Birmingham		Manchester		Newcastle		Glasgow		Belfast	
	0°05′	51°30′	2°35′	51°28′	1°55′	52°28′	2°15′	53°28′	1°37′	54°59′	4°14′	55°52′	5°56′	54°35′
	h m	h m	h m	h m	h m	h m	h m	h m	h m	h m	h m	h m	h m	h m
1	4 32	19 24	4 42	19 33	4 37	19 34	4 35	19 39	4 27	19 42	4 34	19 56	4 45	19 58
2	4 30	19 25	4 41	19 35	4 35	19 36	4 33	19 41	4 24	19 44	4 31	19 58	4 43	19 59
3	4 29	19 27	4 39	19 37	4 33	19 37	4 31	19 42	4 22	19 46	4 29	20 00	4 41	20 01
4	4 27	19 28	4 37	19 38	4 31	19 39	4 29	19 44	4 20	19 48	4 27	20 02	4 39	20 03
5	4 25	19 30	4 35	19 40	4 29	19 41	4 27	19 46	4 18	19 49	4 25	20 04	4 37	20 05
6	4 23	19 32	4 33	19 42	4 27	19 43	4 25	19 48	4 16	19 51	4 23	20 06	4 35	20 07
7	4 21	19 33	4 32	19 43	4 25	19 44	4 23	19 49	4 14	19 53	4 21	20 08	4 33	20 09
8	4 20	19 35	4 30	19 45	4 24	19 46	4 21	19 51	4 12	19 55	4 19	20 10	4 31	20 11
9	4 18	19 36	4 28	19 46	4 22	19 47	4 19	19 53	4 10	19 57	4 16	20 12	4 29	20 12
10	4 16	19 38	4 27	19 48	4 20	19 49	4 17	19 55	4 08	19 59	4 14	20 13	4 27	20 14
11	4 15	19 40	4 25	19 49	4 18	19 51	4 16	19 56	4 06	20 01	4 12	20 15	4 25	20 16
12	4 13	19 41	4 23	19 51	4 17	19 52	4 14	19 58	4 04	20 02	4 11	20 17	4 23	20 18
13	4 12	19 43	4 22	19 53	4 15	19 54	4 12	20 00	4 03	20 04	4 09	20 19	4 22	20 20
14	4 10	19 44	4 20	19 54	4 13	19 56	4 10	20 01	4 01	20 06	4 07	20 21	4 20	20 21
15	4 09	19 46	4 19	19 56	4 12	19 57	4 09	20 03	3 59	20 08	4 05	20 23	4 18	20 23
16	4 07	19 47	4 17	19 57	4 10	19 59	4 07	20 05	3 57	20 10	4 03	20 25	4 17	20 25
17	4 06	19 49	4 16	19 59	4 09	20 00	4 06	20 06	3 56	20 11	4 01	20 27	4 15	20 26
18	4 04	19 50	4 14	20 00	4 07	20 02	4 04	20 08	3 54	20 13	4 00	20 28	4 13	20 28
19	4 03	19 52	4 13	20 01	4 06	20 03	4 03	20 09	3 52	20 15	3 58	20 30	4 12	20 30
20	4 02	19 53	4 12	20 03	4 05	20 05	4 01	20 11	3 51	20 16	3 56	20 32	4 10	20 31
21	4 00	19 54	4 10	20 04	4 03	20 06	4 00	20 12	3 49	20 18	3 55	20 34	4 09	20 33
22	3 59	19 56	4 09	20 06	4 02	20 08	3 58	20 14	3 48	20 20	3 53	20 35	4 07	20 35
23	3 58	19 57	4 08	20 07	4 01	20 09	3 57	20 15	3 46	20 21	3 51	20 37	4 06	20 36
24	3 57	19 58	4 07	20 08	3 59	20 10	3 56	20 17	3 45	20 23	3 50	20 39	4 04	20 38
25	3 56	20 00	4 06	20 10	3 58	20 12	3 54	20 18	3 43	20 24	3 49	20 40	4 03	20 39
26	3 54	20 01	4 05	20 11	3 57	20 13	3 53	20 20	3 42	20 26	3 47	20 42	4 02	20 41
27	3 53	20 02	4 04	20 12	3 56	20 14	3 52	20 21	3 41	20 27	3 46	20 43	4 00	20 42
28	3 52	20 03	4 03	20 13	3 55	20 16	3 51	20 22	3 40	20 29	3 44	20 45	3 59	20 44
29	3 51	20 05	4 02	20 14	3 54	20 17	3 50	20 24	3 38	20 30	3 43	20 46	3 58	20 45
30	3 51	20 06	4 01	20 16	3 53	20 18	3 49	20 25	3 37	20 32	3 42	20 48	3 57	20 46
31	3 50	20 07	4 00	20 17	3 52	20 19	3 48	20 26	3 36	20 33	3 41	20 49	3 56	20 48

JUPITER

Day	RA	Dec.	Transit	5° high 52°	5° high 56°
	h m	° ′	h m	h m	h m
1	21 28.5	−15 32	6 52	2 53	3 12
11	21 32.6	−15 15	6 16	2 16	2 35
21	21 35.7	−15 02	5 40	1 38	1 57
31	21 37.6	−14 55	5 03	1 00	1 18

Diameters – equatorial 40″ polar 38″

SATURN

Day	RA	Dec.	Transit	5° high 52°	5° high 56°
	h m	° ′	h m	h m	h m
1	0 55.2	+ 3 30	10 18	4 33	4 34
11	0 59.4	+ 3 55	9 43	3 56	3 56
21	1 03.4	+ 4 18	9 07	3 19	3 18
31	1 07.1	+ 4 39	8 32	2 41	2 41

Diameters – equatorial 16″ polar 15″
Rings – major axis 37″ minor axis 6″

URANUS

Day	RA	Dec.	Transit	10° high 52°	10° high 56°
	h m	° ′	h m	h m	h m
1	20 44.8	−18 42	6 08	3 16	3 53
11	20 45.1	−18 41	5 29	2 37	3 13
21	20 45.0	−18 42	4 49	1 58	2 34
31	20 44.6	−18 44	4 10	1 18	1 55

Diameter 4″

NEPTUNE

Day	RA	Dec.	Transit	10° high 52°	10° high 56°
	h m	° ′	h m	h m	h m
1	20 08.2	−19 45	5 31	2 49	3 30
11	20 08.1	−19 45	4 52	2 10	2 51
21	20 07.8	−19 46	4 12	1 31	2 11
31	20 07.3	−19 47	3 33	0 51	1 32

Diameter 2″

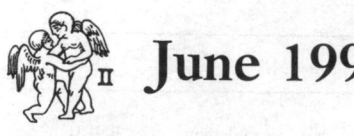 # June 1997

SIXTH MONTH, 30 DAYS. *Junius*, Roman *gens* (family)

1	*Sunday*	**2nd S. after Pentecost/1st S. after Trinity**	*week 22 day* 152
2	*Monday*	*Coronation Day 1953.* Sir Edward Elgar b. 1857	153
3	*Tuesday*	*Trinity Law Sittings begin.* Arthur Ransome d. 1967	154
4	*Wednesday*	⚔ Battle of Magenta 1859. Lord Thorneycroft d. 1994	155
5	*Thursday*	Sir Robert Mayer b. 1879. John Maynard Keynes b. 1883	156
6	*Friday*	Pierre Corneille b. 1606. Thomas Mann b. 1875	157
7	*Saturday*	Beau Brummell b. 1778. Jean Harlow d. 1937	158
8	*Sunday*	**3rd S. after Pentecost/2nd S. after Trinity**	*week 23 day* 159
9	*Monday*	Charles Dickens d. 1870. Robert Donat d. 1958	160
10	*Tuesday*	*Duke of Edinburgh b. 1921.* Frederick Loewe b. 1901	161
11	*Wednesday*	**St Barnabas.** FEAST OF WEEKS begins	162
12	*Thursday*	Leon Goossens b. 1897. John Ireland d. 1962	163
13	*Friday*	Dorothy L. Sayers b. 1893. Sir Henry Segrave d. 1930	164
14	*Saturday*	*Queen's Official Birthday.* Jerome K. Jerome d. 1927	165
15	*Sunday*	**4th S. after Pentecost/3rd S. after Trinity**	*week 24 day* 166
16	*Monday*	Margaret Bondfield d. 1953. Lord Reith d. 1971	167
17	*Tuesday*	John Wesley b. 1703. ⚔ Battle of Bunker Hill 1775	168
18	*Wednesday*	⚔ Battle of Waterloo 1815. Douglas Jardine d. 1958	169
19	*Thursday*	James I b. 1566. Walter Hammond b. 1903	170
20	*Friday*	Jacques Offenbach b. 1819. William IV d. 1837	171
21	*Saturday*	Prince William of Wales b. 1982.	172
22	*Sunday*	**5th S. after Pentecost/4th S. after Trinity**	*week 25 day* 173
23	*Monday*	Jean Anouilh b. 1910. Cecil James Sharp d. 1924	174
24	*Tuesday*	**St John the Baptist.** Grover Cleveland d. 1908	175
25	*Wednesday*	Col. George Custer d. 1876. Lady Baden-Powell d. 1977	176
26	*Thursday*	Samuel Crompton d. 1827. George IV d. 1830	177
27	*Friday*	Charles Stewart Parnell b. 1846	178
28	*Saturday*	Henry VIII b. 1491. Luigi Pirandello b. 1867	179
29	*Sunday*	**St Peter. 6th S. after Pentecost/5th S. after Trinity**	*week 26 day* 180
30	*Monday*	Tower Bridge opened 1894. Margery Allingham d. 1966	181

ASTRONOMICAL PHENOMENA

d	h	
1	03	Saturn in conjunction with Moon. Saturn 0°.4 S.
3	13	Mercury in conjunction with Moon. Mercury 2° N.
6	17	Venus in conjunction with Moon. Venus 6° N.
10	00	Jupiter at stationary point
13	16	Mars in conjunction with Moon. Mars 0°.3 N.
21	08	Sun's longitude 90° ♋.
24	10	Jupiter in conjunction with Moon. Jupiter 3° S.
25	19	Mercury in superior conjunction
28	12	Saturn in conjunction with Moon. Saturn 0°.2 S.

MINIMA OF ALGOL

Algol is inconveniently situated for observation during June.

CONSTELLATIONS

The following constellations are near the meridian at

	d	h		d	h
May	1	24	June	15	21
May	16	23	July	1	20
June	1	22	July	16	19

Cassiopeia (below the Pole), Ursa Minor, Draco, Ursa Major, Canes Venatici, Bootes, Corona, Serpens, Virgo and Libra

THE MOON

Phases, Apsides and Node	d	h	m
● New Moon	5	07	04
☽ First Quarter	13	04	51
○ Full Moon	20	19	09
☾ Last Quarter	27	12	42
Apogee (404,186 km)	12	05	07
Perigee (366,490 km)	24	05	07

Mean longitude of ascending node on June 1, 175°

THE SUN

s.d. 15'.8

Day	Right Ascension	Dec. +	Equation of time	Rise 52°	Rise 56°	Transit	Set 52°	Set 56°	Sidereal time	Transit of First Point of Aries
	h m s	° '	m s	h m	h m	h m	h m	h m	h m s	h m s
1	4 35 47	22 02	+ 2 17	3 46	3 22	11 58	20 10	20 34	16 38 04	7 20 44
2	4 39 53	22 10	+ 2 08	3 45	3 21	11 58	20 11	20 36	16 42 00	7 16 48
3	4 43 59	22 17	+ 1 58	3 44	3 20	11 58	20 12	20 37	16 45 57	7 12 52
4	4 48 06	22 24	+ 1 48	3 44	3 19	11 58	20 13	20 38	16 49 53	7 08 56
5	4 52 12	22 31	+ 1 38	3 43	3 18	11 58	20 14	20 39	16 53 50	7 05 00
6	4 56 20	22 38	+ 1 27	3 42	3 17	11 59	20 15	20 41	16 57 47	7 01 04
7	5 00 27	22 44	+ 1 16	3 42	3 17	11 59	20 16	20 42	17 01 43	6 57 08
8	5 04 35	22 50	+ 1 04	3 41	3 16	11 59	20 17	20 43	17 05 40	6 53 12
9	5 08 43	22 55	+ 0 53	3 41	3 15	11 59	20 18	20 44	17 09 36	6 49 16
10	5 12 52	23 00	+ 0 41	3 41	3 15	11 59	20 19	20 44	17 13 33	6 45 21
11	5 17 00	23 04	+ 0 29	3 40	3 14	12 00	20 19	20 45	17 17 29	6 41 25
12	5 21 09	23 08	+ 0 17	3 40	3 14	12 00	20 20	20 46	17 21 26	6 37 29
13	5 25 18	23 12	+ 0 04	3 40	3 14	12 00	20 21	20 47	17 25 22	6 33 33
14	5 29 27	23 15	− 0 08	3 40	3 13	12 00	20 21	20 48	17 29 19	6 29 37
15	5 33 36	23 18	− 0 21	3 39	3 13	12 00	20 22	20 48	17 33 16	6 25 41
16	5 37 46	23 20	− 0 34	3 39	3 13	12 01	20 22	20 49	17 37 12	6 21 45
17	5 41 55	23 22	− 0 46	3 39	3 13	12 01	20 23	20 49	17 41 09	6 17 49
18	5 46 05	23 24	− 0 59	3 39	3 13	12 01	20 23	20 50	17 45 05	6 13 53
19	5 50 14	23 25	− 1 12	3 39	3 13	12 01	20 23	20 50	17 49 02	6 09 57
20	5 54 24	23 26	− 1 25	3 40	3 13	12 02	20 24	20 50	17 52 58	6 06 01
21	5 58 33	23 26	− 1 38	3 40	3 13	12 02	20 24	20 50	17 56 55	6 02 06
22	6 02 43	23 26	− 1 51	3 40	3 13	12 02	20 24	20 51	18 00 52	5 58 10
23	6 06 52	23 26	− 2 04	3 40	3 14	12 02	20 24	20 51	18 04 48	5 54 14
24	6 11 02	23 25	− 2 17	3 41	3 14	12 02	20 24	20 51	18 08 45	5 50 18
25	6 15 11	23 23	− 2 30	3 41	3 14	12 03	20 24	20 51	18 12 41	5 46 22
26	6 19 20	23 22	− 2 42	3 41	3 15	12 03	20 24	20 50	18 16 38	5 42 26
27	6 23 29	23 20	− 2 55	3 42	3 15	12 03	20 24	20 50	18 20 34	5 38 30
28	6 27 38	23 17	− 3 07	3 42	3 16	12 03	20 24	20 50	18 24 31	5 34 34
29	6 31 47	23 14	− 3 19	3 43	3 17	12 03	20 24	20 50	18 28 27	5 30 38
30	6 35 55	23 11	− 3 31	3 44	3 17	12 04	20 23	20 49	18 32 24	5 26 42

DURATION OF TWILIGHT (in minutes)

Latitude	52°	56°	52°	56°	52°	56°	52°	56°
	1 June		11 June		21 June		30 June	
Civil	47	58	48	61	49	63	49	62
Nautical	117	TAN	125	TAN	128	TAN	125	TAN
Astronomical	TAN	TAN	TAN	TAN	TAN	TAN	TAN	TAN

THE NIGHT SKY

Mercury is too close to the Sun for observation, superior conjunction occurring on the 25th.

Venus is a brilliant object in the evening skies, magnitude −3.9, but only visible low above the west-north-west horizon for about half an hour after sunset.

Mars is an evening object in the south-western skies, in Virgo, though by the end of June it is no longer observable after 23h. During the month its magnitude fades from +0.2 to +0.6. The Moon, at First Quarter, will be seen about 3° to the left of Mars on the evening of the 13th.

Jupiter, magnitude −2.6, is a brilliant object in the south-eastern sky in the mornings and becomes visible before midnight towards the end of the month. On the morning of the 24th the waning gibbous Moon will be seen about 6° to the right of Jupiter.

Saturn, magnitude +0.7, becomes a morning object early in the month, low above the east-south-east horizon before twilight inhibits observation. On the morning of the 28th the Moon, at Last Quarter, will be seen about 6° to the right of Jupiter.

Twilight. Reference to the section above shows that astronomical twilight lasts all night for a period around the summer solstice (i.e. in June and July), even in southern England. Under these conditions the sky never gets completely dark since the Sun is always less than 18° below the horizon.

THE MOON

Day	RA h m	Dec. °	Hor. par. '	Semi-diam. '	Sun's co-long. °	PA of Bright Limb °	Phase %	Age d	Rise 52° h m	Rise 56° h m	Transit h m	Set 52° h m	Set 56° h m
1	1 00	+ 4.6	59.0	16.1	213	66	21	25.1	2 02	1 58	8 40	15 31	15 37
2	1 54	+ 8.7	58.7	16.0	225	66	13	26.1	2 31	2 23	9 32	16 46	16 56
3	2 49	+12.3	58.3	15.9	237	66	6	27.1	3 03	2 52	10 25	17 58	18 11
4	3 44	+15.2	57.9	15.8	249	62	2	28.1	3 39	3 25	11 18	19 06	19 22
5	4 39	+17.2	57.3	15.6	262	29	0	29.1	4 21	4 04	12 12	20 07	20 25
6	5 35	+18.3	56.7	15.5	274	297	1	0.7	5 08	4 50	13 05	21 01	21 19
7	6 29	+18.4	56.1	15.3	286	286	3	1.7	6 01	5 44	13 56	21 47	22 04
8	7 22	+17.5	55.6	15.1	298	285	8	2.7	6 59	6 43	14 46	22 26	22 41
9	8 14	+15.8	55.0	15.0	311	287	14	3.7	7 59	7 45	15 34	22 59	23 11
10	9 03	+13.4	54.6	14.9	323	289	21	4.7	9 01	8 50	16 19	23 27	23 36
11	9 50	+10.5	54.4	14.8	335	291	30	5.7	10 04	9 56	17 03	23 52	23 58
12	10 37	+ 7.2	54.2	14.8	347	292	39	6.7	11 06	11 01	17 46	—	—
13	11 22	+ 3.7	54.3	14.8	359	293	48	7.7	12 09	12 08	18 28	0 15	0 18
14	12 07	− 0.1	54.5	14.9	12	294	58	8.7	13 13	13 14	19 11	0 37	0 37
15	12 53	− 3.9	54.9	15.0	24	293	67	9.7	14 17	14 22	19 55	1 00	0 57
16	13 40	− 7.5	55.4	15.1	36	293	76	10.7	15 23	15 32	20 41	1 25	1 18
17	14 29	−11.0	56.1	15.3	48	292	84	11.7	16 30	16 43	21 30	1 52	1 42
18	15 20	−14.0	56.8	15.5	60	291	91	12.7	17 38	17 53	22 22	2 23	2 10
19	16 14	−16.4	57.6	15.7	73	291	96	13.7	18 44	19 01	23 16	3 01	2 45
20	17 11	−18.0	58.3	15.9	85	300	99	14.7	19 45	20 04	—	3 47	3 29
21	18 10	−18.5	58.9	16.1	97	27	100	15.7	20 40	20 58	0 13	4 42	4 23
22	19 10	−17.8	59.4	16.2	109	67	98	16.7	21 28	21 43	1 11	5 46	5 29
23	20 09	−16.0	59.7	16.3	121	71	93	17.7	22 08	22 20	2 09	6 57	6 43
24	21 08	−13.2	59.8	16.3	134	70	87	18.7	22 42	22 51	3 06	8 13	8 02
25	22 05	− 9.6	59.8	16.3	146	68	78	19.7	23 12	23 17	4 01	9 30	9 23
26	23 01	− 5.5	59.6	16.2	158	67	67	20.7	23 40	23 41	4 54	10 48	10 45
27	23 55	− 1.1	59.3	16.2	170	67	56	21.7	—	—	5 46	12 05	12 05
28	0 49	+ 3.4	58.9	16.1	182	67	45	22.7	0 08	0 05	6 38	13 20	13 25
29	1 42	+ 7.6	58.5	15.9	195	68	34	23.7	0 36	0 29	7 29	14 34	14 43
30	2 35	+11.3	58.0	15.8	207	70	24	24.7	1 06	0 56	8 20	15 46	15 58

MERCURY

Day	RA h m	Dec. °	Diam. "	Phase %	Transit h m	5° high 52° h m	5° high 56° h m
1	3 03	+14.3	7	56	10 26	3 44	3 35
3	3 14	+15.3	7	60	10 29	3 41	3 32
5	3 26	+16.3	6	64	10 34	3 40	3 29
7	3 39	+17.4	6	69	10 39	3 39	3 27
9	3 53	+18.5	6	73	10 45	3 39	3 26
11	4 08	+19.5	6	78	10 52	3 39	3 26
13	4 23	+20.5	6	82	10 59	3 41	3 26
15	4 39	+21.5	5	87	11 08	3 44	3 28
17	4 56	+22.4	5	91	11 18	3 48	3 31
19	5 14	+23.1	5	94	11 28	3 53	3 35
21	5 33	+23.7	5	97	11 39	4 00	3 41
23	5 52	+24.2	5	99	11 50	4 08	3 49
25	6 11	+24.5	5	100	12 01	19 45	20 05
27	6 30	+24.6	5	100	12 13	19 56	20 16
29	6 49	+24.5	5	99	12 24	20 06	20 26
31	7 08	+24.2	5	97	12 34	20 14	20 34

VENUS

Day	RA h m	Dec. °	Diam. "	Phase %	Transit h m	5° high 52° h m	5° high 56° h m
1	5 43	+24.2	10	96	13 06	20 46	21 05
6	6 10	+24.4	10	96	13 13	20 54	21 14
11	6 37	+24.3	10	95	13 20	21 00	21 20
16	7 03	+23.9	11	94	13 27	21 04	21 23
21	7 30	+23.3	11	93	13 34	21 06	21 24
26	7 56	+22.3	11	92	13 40	21 06	21 23
31	8 21	+21.1	11	91	13 46	21 05	21 20

MARS

Day	RA h m	Dec. °	Diam. "	Phase %	Transit h m	5° high 52° h m	5° high 56° h m
1	11 35	+ 3.6	9	89	18 55	0 43	0 43
6	11 42	+ 2.8	9	89	18 42	0 26	0 25
11	11 48	+ 1.9	8	89	18 29	0 08	0 07
16	11 56	+ 1.0	8	88	18 16	23 48	23 45
21	12 03	+ 0.1	8	88	18 05	23 31	23 27
26	12 11	− 1.0	8	88	17 53	23 14	23 10
31	12 20	− 2.0	7	88	17 42	22 57	22 52

SUNRISE AND SUNSET

	London		Bristol		Birmingham		Manchester		Newcastle		Glasgow		Belfast	
	0°05′	51°30′	2°35′	51°28′	1°55′	52°28′	2°15′	53°28′	1°37′	54°59′	4°14′	55°52′	5°56′	54°35′
	h m	h m	h m	h m	h m	h m	h m	h m	h m	h m	h m	h m	h m	h m
1	3 49	20 08	3 59	20 18	3 51	20 20	3 47	20 27	3 35	20 34	3 40	20 50	3 55	20 49
2	3 48	20 09	3 58	20 19	3 50	20 22	3 46	20 29	3 34	20 35	3 39	20 52	3 54	20 50
3	3 47	20 10	3 58	20 20	3 50	20 23	3 45	20 30	3 33	20 37	3 38	20 53	3 53	20 51
4	3 47	20 11	3 57	20 21	3 49	20 24	3 44	20 31	3 32	20 38	3 37	20 54	3 52	20 52
5	3 46	20 12	3 56	20 22	3 48	20 25	3 44	20 32	3 32	20 39	3 36	20 55	3 52	20 53
6	3 45	20 13	3 56	20 23	3 48	20 26	3 43	20 33	3 31	20 40	3 35	20 57	3 51	20 55
7	3 45	20 14	3 55	20 24	3 47	20 27	3 42	20 34	3 30	20 41	3 35	20 58	3 50	20 56
8	3 45	20 15	3 55	20 24	3 46	20 27	3 42	20 35	3 30	20 42	3 34	20 59	3 50	20 56
9	3 44	20 15	3 54	20 25	3 46	20 28	3 41	20 35	3 29	20 43	3 33	21 00	3 49	20 57
10	3 44	20 16	3 54	20 26	3 46	20 29	3 41	20 36	3 29	20 44	3 33	21 00	3 49	20 58
11	3 43	20 17	3 54	20 27	3 45	20 30	3 41	20 37	3 28	20 44	3 32	21 01	3 48	20 59
12	3 43	20 18	3 53	20 27	3 45	20 30	3 40	20 38	3 28	20 45	3 32	21 02	3 48	21 00
13	3 43	20 18	3 53	20 28	3 45	20 31	3 40	20 38	3 27	20 46	3 31	21 03	3 47	21 00
14	3 43	20 19	3 53	20 29	3 44	20 32	3 40	20 39	3 27	20 47	3 31	21 03	3 47	21 01
15	3 43	20 19	3 53	20 29	3 44	20 32	3 40	20 40	3 27	20 47	3 31	21 04	3 47	21 02
16	3 42	20 20	3 53	20 29	3 44	20 33	3 39	20 40	3 27	20 48	3 31	21 05	3 47	21 02
17	3 42	20 20	3 53	20 30	3 44	20 33	3 39	20 40	3 27	20 48	3 31	21 05	3 47	21 03
18	3 42	20 20	3 53	20 30	3 44	20 33	3 39	20 41	3 27	20 49	3 31	21 05	3 47	21 03
19	3 43	20 21	3 53	20 31	3 44	20 34	3 40	20 41	3 27	20 49	3 31	21 06	3 47	21 03
20	3 43	20 21	3 53	20 31	3 44	20 34	3 40	20 41	3 27	20 49	3 31	21 06	3 47	21 04
21	3 43	20 21	3 53	20 31	3 45	20 34	3 40	20 42	3 27	20 49	3 31	21 06	3 47	21 04
22	3 43	20 21	3 53	20 31	3 45	20 34	3 40	20 42	3 27	20 49	3 31	21 06	3 47	21 04
23	3 43	20 22	3 54	20 31	3 45	20 34	3 40	20 42	3 28	20 50	3 32	21 07	3 48	21 04
24	3 44	20 22	3 54	20 31	3 45	20 35	3 41	20 42	3 28	20 50	3 32	21 07	3 48	21 04
25	3 44	20 22	3 54	20 31	3 46	20 35	3 41	20 42	3 28	20 50	3 32	21 07	3 48	21 04
26	3 45	20 22	3 55	20 31	3 46	20 34	3 42	20 42	3 29	20 49	3 33	21 06	3 49	21 04
27	3 45	20 21	3 55	20 31	3 47	20 34	3 42	20 42	3 29	20 49	3 33	21 06	3 49	21 04
28	3 46	20 21	3 56	20 31	3 47	20 34	3 43	20 42	3 30	20 49	3 34	21 06	3 50	21 04
29	3 46	20 21	3 56	20 31	3 48	20 34	3 43	20 41	3 31	20 49	3 35	21 06	3 51	21 03
30	3 47	20 21	3 57	20 31	3 49	20 34	3 44	20 41	3 31	20 48	3 35	21 05	3 51	21 03

JUPITER

Day	RA	Dec.	Transit	5° high	
				52°	56°
	h m	° ′	h m	h m	h m
1	21 37.7	−14 55	4 59	0 56	1 15
11	21 38.2	−14 55	4 20	0 17	0 36
21	21 37.6	−15 01	3 40	23 34	23 53
31	21 35.6	−15 13	2 59	22 54	23 13

Diameters – equatorial 44″ polar 42″

SATURN

Day	RA	Dec.	Transit	5° high	
				52°	56°
	h m	° ′	h m	h m	h m
1	1 07.4	+ 4 41	8 28	2 38	2 37
11	1 10.6	+ 4 58	7 52	2 00	1 59
21	1 13.4	+ 5 13	7 15	1 22	1 21
31	1 15.7	+ 5 24	6 38	0 44	0 43

Diameters – equatorial 17″ polar 15″
Rings – major axis 38″ minor axis 7″

URANUS

Day	RA	Dec.	Transit	10° high	
				52°	56°
	h m	° ′	h m	h m	h m
1	20 44.5	−18 44	4 06	1 14	1 51
11	20 43.8	−18 47	3 26	0 35	1 11
21	20 42.7	−18 51	2 45	23 51	0 32
31	20 41.5	−18 56	2 05	23 11	23 49

Diameter 4″

NEPTUNE

Day	RA	Dec.	Transit	10° high	
				52°	56°
	h m	° ′	h m	h m	h m
1	20 07.2	−19 48	3 29	0 47	1 28
11	20 06.5	−19 50	2 49	0 07	0 48
21	20 05.6	−19 52	2 08	23 24	0 09
31	20 04.6	−19 55	1 28	22 44	23 25

Diameter 2″

July 1997

SEVENTH MONTH, 31 DAYS. *Julius* Caesar, formerly *Quintilis*, fifth month of Roman pre-Julian calendar

1	*Tuesday*	*Princess of Wales b. 1961.* George Sand b. 1804	*week* 26 *day* 182
2	*Wednesday*	Hermann Hesse b. 1877. Sir Herbert Beerbohm Tree d. 1917	183
3	*Thursday*	**St Thomas.** Tom Stoppard b. 1937	184
4	*Friday*	Alec Bedser b. 1918. Suzanne Lenglen d. 1938	185
5	*Saturday*	Mrs Sarah Siddons b. 1755. George Borrow b. 1803	186
6	*Sunday*	**7th S. after Pentecost/6th S. after Trinity**	*week* 27 *day* 187
7	*Monday*	Joseph Jacquard b. 1752. Marc Chagall b. 1887	188
8	*Tuesday*	Joseph Chamberlain b. 1836. Vivien Leigh d. 1967	189
9	*Wednesday*	Mrs Ann Radcliffe b. 1764. David Hockney b. 1937	190
10	*Thursday*	George Stubbs d. 1806. Camille Pissarro b. 1830	191
11	*Friday*	George Gershwin d. 1937. Paul Nash d. 1946	192
12	*Saturday*	Josiah Wedgwood bapt. 1730. Kirsten Flagstad b. 1895	193
13	*Sunday*	**8th S. after Pentecost/7th S. after Trinity**	*week* 28 *day* 194
14	*Monday*	*Bank Holiday in Northern Ireland*	195
15	*Tuesday*	St Swithin's Day. Ernest Bloch d. 1959	196
16	*Wednesday*	Sir Joshua Reynolds b. 1723. Hilaire Belloc d. 1953	197
17	*Thursday*	James Whistler d. 1903. Jules Henri Poincaré d. 1912	198
18	*Friday*	Jane Austen d. 1817. Thomas Sturge Moore d. 1944	199
19	*Saturday*	*Mary Rose* sank 1545. Edgar Degas b. 1834	200
20	*Sunday*	**9th S. after Pentecost/8th S. after Trinity**	*week* 29 *day* 201
21	*Monday*	Robert Burns d. 1796. Henry Longhurst d. 1978	202
22	*Tuesday*	**St Mary Magdalen.** Tate Gallery opened 1897	203
23	*Wednesday*	Raymond Chandler b. 1888. Olivia Manning d. 1980	204
24	*Thursday*	John Sell Cotman d. 1842. E. F. Benson b. 1867	205
25	*Friday*	**St James.** A. J. Balfour b. 1848	206
26	*Saturday*	George Bernard Shaw b. 1856. Carl Jung b. 1875	207
27	*Sunday*	**10th S. after Pentecost/9th S. after Trinity**	*week* 30 *day* 208
28	*Monday*	Thomas Cromwell exec. 1540. Sir Garfield Sobers b. 1936	209
29	*Tuesday*	Defeat of the Spanish Armada 1588	210
30	*Wednesday*	William Penn d. 1718. Henry Ford b. 1863	211
31	*Thursday*	*Trinity Law Sittings end.* Franz Liszt d. 1886	212

ASTRONOMICAL PHENOMENA

d	h	
4	19	Earth at aphelion (152 milion km)
5	18	Mercury in conjunction with Moon. Mercury 6° N.
6	23	Venus in conjunction with Moon. Venus 5° N.
12	03	Mars in conjunction with Moon. Mars 2° S.
21	07	Neptune at opposition
21	15	Jupiter in conjunction with Moon. Jupiter 4° S.
22	19	Sun's longitude 120° Ω
25	19	Saturn in conjunction with Moon. Saturn 0°.08 N.
29	19	Uranus at opposition

MINIMA OF ALGOL

d	h	d	h	d	h
1	03.7	12	14.9	24	02.2
4	00.5	15	11.8	26	23.0
6	21.3	18	08.6	29	19.8
9	18.1	21	05.4		

CONSTELLATIONS

The following constellations are near the meridian at

	d	h		d	h
June	1	24	July	16	21
June	15	23	August	1	20
July	1	22	August	16	19

Ursa Minor, Draco, Corona, Hercules, Lyra, Serpens, Ophiuchus, Libra, Scorpius and Sagittarius

THE MOON

Phases, Apsides and Node	d	h	m
● New Moon	4	18	40
☽ First Quarter	12	21	44
○ Full Moon	20	03	20
☾ Last Quarter	26	18	28
Apogee (404,947 km)	9	22	55
Perigee (361,577 km)	21	23	07

Mean longitude of ascending node on July 1, 173°

THE SUN

s.d. 15'.8

Day	Right Ascension	Dec. +	Equation of time	Rise 52°	Rise 56°	Transit	Set 52°	Set 56°	Sidereal time	Transit of First Point of Aries
	h m s	° '	m s	h m	h m	h m	h m	h m	h m s	h m s
1	6 40 04	23 07	− 3 43	3 44	3 18	12 04	20 23	20 49	18 36 21	5 22 46
2	6 44 12	23 03	− 3 55	3 45	3 19	12 04	20 23	20 48	18 40 17	5 18 51
3	6 48 20	22 58	−4 06	3 46	3 20	12 04	20 22	20 48	18 44 14	5 14 55
4	6 52 27	22 53	−4 17	3 47	3 21	12 04	20 22	20 47	18 48 10	5 10 59
5	6 56 35	22 48	−4 28	3 47	3 22	12 05	20 21	20 46	18 52 07	5 07 03
6	7 00 42	22 42	−4 38	3 48	3 23	12 05	20 21	20 46	18 56 03	5 03 07
7	7 04 48	22 36	−4 48	3 49	3 24	12 05	20 20	20 45	19 00 00	4 59 11
8	7 08 55	22 30	−4 58	3 50	3 25	12 05	20 19	20 44	19 03 56	4 55 15
9	7 13 00	22 23	−5 07	3 51	3 27	12 05	20 19	20 43	19 07 53	4 51 19
10	7 17 06	22 15	−5 16	3 52	3 28	12 05	20 18	20 42	19 11 50	4 47 23
11	7 21 11	22 08	−5 25	3 53	3 29	12 05	20 17	20 41	19 15 46	4 43 27
12	7 25 15	22 00	−5 32	3 54	3 30	12 06	20 16	20 40	19 19 43	4 39 31
13	7 29 19	21 51	−5 40	3 55	3 32	12 06	20 15	20 39	19 23 39	4 35 36
14	7 33 23	21 42	−5 47	3 57	3 33	12 06	20 14	20 37	19 27 36	4 31 40
15	7 37 26	21 33	−5 53	3 58	3 35	12 06	20 13	20 36	19 31 32	4 27 44
16	7 41 28	21 23	−5 59	3 59	3 36	12 06	20 12	20 35	19 35 29	4 23 48
17	7 45 30	21 14	−6 05	4 00	3 38	12 06	20 11	20 33	19 39 25	4 19 52
18	7 49 32	21 03	−6 10	4 02	3 39	12 06	20 10	20 32	19 43 22	4 15 56
19	7 53 32	20 53	−6 14	4 03	3 41	12 06	20 09	20 31	19 47 19	4 12 00
20	7 57 33	20 42	−6 18	4 04	3 43	12 06	20 08	20 29	19 51 15	4 08 04
21	8 01 32	20 30	−6 21	4 06	3 44	12 06	20 06	20 27	19 55 12	4 04 08
22	8 05 32	20 19	−6 23	4 07	3 46	12 06	20 05	20 26	19 59 08	4 00 12
23	8 09 30	20 07	−6 26	4 08	3 48	12 06	20 04	20 24	20 03 05	3 56 16
24	8 13 28	19 54	−6 27	4 10	3 49	12 06	20 02	20 22	20 07 01	3 52 21
25	8 17 26	19 41	−6 28	4 11	3 51	12 06	20 01	20 21	20 10 58	3 48 25
26	8 21 23	19 28	−6 28	4 13	3 53	12 06	19 59	20 19	20 14 54	3 44 29
27	8 25 19	19 15	−6 28	4 14	3 55	12 06	19 58	20 17	20 18 51	3 40 33
28	8 29 15	19 01	−6 27	4 16	3 56	12 06	19 56	20 15	20 22 48	3 36 37
29	8 33 10	18 47	−6 26	4 17	3 58	12 06	19 55	20 13	20 26 44	3 32 41
30	8 37 05	18 33	−6 24	4 19	4 00	12 06	19 53	20 11	20 30 41	3 28 45
31	8 40 59	18 19	−6 22	4 20	4 02	12 06	19 52	20 09	20 34 37	3 24 49

DURATION OF TWILIGHT (in minutes)

Latitude	52°	56°	52°	56°	52°	56°	52°	56°
	1 July		11 July		21 July		31 July	
Civil	48	61	46	58	44	53	41	49
Nautical	124	TAN	116	TAN	107	144	98	122
Astronomical	TAN	TAN	TAN	TAN	TAN	TAN	180	TAN

THE NIGHT SKY

Mercury is still unsuitably placed for observation.

Venus, magnitude − 3.9, is a brilliant object in the evening sky, but only visible low above the western horizon for about half an hour after sunset.

Mars, magnitude +0.7, is still visible in the evenings but no longer the prominent object that it was during the spring. It is moving rapidly towards the Sun and by the end of the month is only visible for a short time low in the west-south-western sky. The Moon, approaching First Quarter, is near the planet on the evening of the 11th.

Jupiter is now visible low above the south-eastern horizon well before midnight. Its magtnitude is −2.8. On the evening of the 21st the Moon, just after Full, will be seen about 6° to the left of the planet.

Saturn is a morning object, magnitude +0.6, visible low in the south-eastern sky before it pales to invisibility in the morning twilight. By the end of the month it is visible well before midnight. On the morning of the 26th the waning gibbous Moon will be seen moving eastwards from the planet.

Uranus is at opposition on the 29th, in Capricornus. It is barely visible to the naked eye as its magnitude is only +5.7 but it is readily located with only small optical aid.

Neptune is at opposition on the 21st, on the borders of Sagittarius and Capricornus. It is not visible to the naked eye as its magnitude is +7.8.

THE MOON

Day	RA	Dec.	Hor. par.	Semi-diam.	Sun's co-long.	PA of Bright Limb	Phase	Age	Rise 52°	Rise 56°	Transit	Set 52°	Set 56°
	h m	°	'	'	°	°	%	d	h m	h m	h m	h m	h m
1	3 29	+14.4	57.5	15.7	219	72	15	25.7	1 39	1 26	9 12	16 54	17 09
2	4 23	+16.7	57.0	15.5	231	73	8	26.7	2 18	2 02	10 04	17 57	18 14
3	5 18	+18.0	56.5	15.4	244	73	4	27.7	3 02	2 44	10 57	18 54	19 12
4	6 12	+18.5	56.0	15.3	256	63	1	28.7	3 52	3 34	11 48	19 43	20 00
5	7 05	+17.9	55.6	15.1	268	337	0	0.2	4 47	4 30	12 39	20 24	20 40
6	7 57	+16.5	55.1	15.0	280	297	2	1.2	5 47	5 31	13 27	20 59	21 13
7	8 47	+14.4	54.7	14.9	293	292	5	2.2	6 48	6 36	14 14	21 30	21 40
8	9 36	+11.7	54.4	14.8	305	292	10	3.2	7 50	7 41	14 58	21 56	22 03
9	10 22	+ 8.5	54.2	14.8	317	293	16	4.2	8 53	8 47	15 42	22 20	22 24
10	11 08	+ 5.0	54.1	14.8	329	293	24	5.2	9 56	9 53	16 24	22 42	22 44
11	11 53	+ 1.4	54.2	14.8	342	293	32	6.2	10 58	10 59	17 07	23 05	23 03
12	12 38	− 2.4	54.5	14.8	354	293	41	7.2	12 02	12 05	17 49	23 28	23 23
13	13 24	− 6.1	54.9	15.0	6	292	51	8.2	13 06	13 13	18 34	23 53	23 45
14	14 11	− 9.6	55.5	15.1	18	290	61	9.2	14 12	14 22	19 20	—	—
15	15 01	−12.8	56.2	15.3	31	288	70	10.2	15 18	15 32	20 10	0 22	0 10
16	15 53	−15.4	57.0	15.5	43	286	79	11.2	16 24	16 40	21 02	0 56	0 41
17	16 48	−17.3	57.9	15.8	55	283	87	12.2	17 28	17 46	21 58	1 36	1 20
18	17 46	−18.3	58.7	16.0	67	281	94	13.2	18 27	18 45	22 56	2 26	2 08
19	18 46	−18.2	59.5	16.2	79	282	98	14.2	19 19	19 35	23 55	3 26	3 08
20	19 46	−16.9	60.1	16.4	92	325	100	15.2	20 03	20 17	—	4 35	4 19
21	20 47	−14.5	60.5	16.5	104	59	99	16.2	20 42	20 52	0 54	5 51	5 38
22	21 46	−11.1	60.6	16.5	116	66	95	17.2	21 15	21 21	1 51	7 11	7 02
23	22 44	− 7.0	60.5	16.5	128	67	89	18.2	21 45	21 47	2 47	8 31	8 26
24	23 40	− 2.5	60.2	16.4	140	67	80	19.2	22 13	22 11	3 41	9 50	9 50
25	0 35	+ 2.1	59.6	16.2	153	68	70	20.2	22 41	22 36	4 34	11 08	11 11
26	1 30	+ 6.4	59.0	16.1	165	69	59	21.2	23 11	23 02	5 26	12 24	12 31
27	2 23	+10.3	58.3	15.9	177	71	48	22.2	23 43	23 31	6 18	13 36	13 47
28	3 17	+13.6	57.7	15.7	189	74	37	23.2	—	—	7 09	14 46	15 00
29	4 11	+16.1	57.0	15.5	201	77	27	24.2	0 19	0 04	8 01	15 50	16 06
30	5 05	+17.7	56.4	15.4	214	80	18	25.2	1 01	0 44	8 53	16 48	17 06
31	5 59	+18.3	55.9	15.2	226	83	11	26.2	1 48	1 30	9 44	17 39	17 57

MERCURY

Day	RA	Dec.	Diam.	Phase	Transit	5° high 52°	5° high 56°
	h m	°	"	%	h m	h m	h m
1	7 08	+24.2	5	97	12 34	20 14	20 34
3	7 26	+23.8	5	94	12 45	20 21	20 40
5	7 44	+23.2	5	92	12 54	20 26	20 44
7	8 00	+22.5	5	89	13 03	20 30	20 47
9	8 17	+21.6	5	86	13 11	20 33	20 48
11	8 32	+20.7	6	83	13 18	20 34	20 49
13	8 46	+19.7	6	80	13 24	20 34	20 48
15	9 00	+18.6	6	77	13 30	20 33	20 46
17	9 13	+17.5	6	74	13 35	20 32	20 43
19	9 26	+16.3	6	71	13 39	20 29	20 39
21	9 37	+15.1	6	68	13 43	20 26	20 35
23	9 48	+13.9	6	65	13 46	20 23	20 30
25	9 58	+12.7	7	62	13 48	20 18	20 25
27	10 08	+11.4	7	60	13 50	20 14	20 19
29	10 17	+10.3	7	57	13 51	20 08	20 13
31	10 25	+ 9.1	7	54	13 51	20 02	20 06

VENUS

Day	RA	Dec.	Diam.	Phase	Transit	5° high 52°	5° high 56°
	h m	°	"	%	h m	h m	h m
1	8 21	+21.1	11	91	13 46	21 05	21 20
6	8 47	+19.6	11	90	13 51	21 01	21 15
11	9 11	+18.0	11	89	13 56	20 56	21 08
16	9 35	+16.1	12	88	14 00	20 50	21 00
21	9 59	+14.0	12	87	14 04	20 42	20 50
26	10 22	+11.8	12	86	14 07	20 34	20 40
31	10 44	+ 9.5	12	84	14 10	20 24	20 28

MARS

Day	RA	Dec.	Diam.	Phase	Transit	5° high 52°	5° high 56°
1	12 20	− 2.0	7	88	17 42	22 57	22 52
6	12 29	− 3.1	7	88	17 31	22 41	22 35
11	12 38	− 4.2	7	88	17 21	22 25	22 18
16	12 48	− 5.3	7	88	17 11	22 09	22 01
21	12 58	− 6.4	7	88	17 01	21 53	21 44
26	13 08	− 7.6	7	88	16 52	21 37	21 27
31	13 19	− 8.7	6	88	16 43	21 22	21 10

SUNRISE AND SUNSET

	London		Bristol		Birmingham		Manchester		Newcastle		Glasgow		Belfast	
	0°05′	51°30′	2°35′	51°28′	1°55′	52°28′	2°15′	53°28′	1°37′	54°59′	4°14′	55°52′	5°56′	54°35′
	h m	h m	h m	h m	h m	h m	h m	h m	h m	h m	h m	h m	h m	h m
1	3 47	20 21	3 58	20 30	3 49	20 33	3 45	20 41	3 32	20 48	3 36	21 05	3 52	21 03
2	3 48	20 20	3 58	20 30	3 50	20 33	3 45	20 40	3 33	20 48	3 37	21 04	3 53	21 02
3	3 49	20 20	3 59	20 30	3 51	20 33	3 46	20 40	3 34	20 47	3 38	21 04	3 54	21 02
4	3 50	20 19	4 00	20 29	3 52	20 32	3 47	20 39	3 35	20 46	3 39	21 03	3 55	21 01
5	3 50	20 19	4 01	20 29	3 52	20 32	3 48	20 39	3 36	20 46	3 40	21 02	3 56	21 00
6	3 51	20 18	4 01	20 28	3 53	20 31	3 49	20 38	3 37	20 45	3 41	21 02	3 57	21 00
7	3 52	20 18	4 02	20 28	3 54	20 30	3 50	20 37	3 38	20 44	3 42	21 01	3 58	20 59
8	3 53	20 17	4 03	20 27	3 55	20 30	3 51	20 37	3 39	20 44	3 43	21 00	3 59	20 58
9	3 54	20 16	4 04	20 26	3 56	20 29	3 52	20 36	3 40	20 43	3 44	20 59	4 00	20 57
10	3 55	20 16	4 05	20 25	3 57	20 28	3 53	20 35	3 41	20 42	3 46	20 58	4 01	20 56
11	3 56	20 15	4 06	20 25	3 58	20 27	3 54	20 34	3 42	20 41	3 47	20 57	4 02	20 55
12	3 57	20 14	4 07	20 24	4 00	20 26	3 55	20 33	3 44	20 40	3 48	20 56	4 03	20 54
13	3 58	20 13	4 09	20 23	4 01	20 25	3 57	20 32	3 45	20 39	3 50	20 55	4 05	20 53
14	4 00	20 12	4 10	20 22	4 02	20 24	3 58	20 31	3 46	20 37	3 51	20 53	4 06	20 52
15	4 01	20 11	4 11	20 21	4 03	20 23	3 59	20 30	3 48	20 36	3 53	20 52	4 07	20 51
16	4 02	20 10	4 12	20 20	4 04	20 22	4 00	20 29	3 49	20 35	3 54	20 51	4 09	20 50
17	4 03	20 09	4 13	20 19	4 06	20 21	4 02	20 28	3 51	20 34	3 56	20 50	4 10	20 49
18	4 04	20 08	4 14	20 18	4 07	20 20	4 03	20 26	3 52	20 32	3 57	20 48	4 12	20 47
19	4 06	20 07	4 16	20 17	4 08	20 19	4 04	20 25	3 54	20 31	3 59	20 47	4 13	20 46
20	4 07	20 06	4 17	20 15	4 10	20 17	4 06	20 24	3 55	20 29	4 00	20 45	4 15	20 44
21	4 08	20 04	4 18	20 14	4 11	20 16	4 07	20 22	3 57	20 28	4 02	20 44	4 16	20 43
22	4 10	20 03	4 20	20 13	4 12	20 15	4 09	20 21	3 58	20 26	4 04	20 42	4 18	20 42
23	4 11	20 02	4 21	20 12	4 14	20 13	4 10	20 20	4 00	20 25	4 05	20 40	4 19	20 40
24	4 12	20 00	4 22	20 10	4 15	20 12	4 12	20 18	4 01	20 23	4 07	20 39	4 21	20 38
25	4 14	19 59	4 24	20 09	4 17	20 11	4 13	20 17	4 03	20 22	4 09	20 37	4 23	20 37
26	4 15	19 58	4 25	20 07	4 18	20 09	4 15	20 15	4 05	20 20	4 11	20 35	4 24	20 35
27	4 17	19 56	4 27	20 06	4 20	20 08	4 16	20 13	4 06	20 18	4 12	20 33	4 26	20 33
28	4 18	19 55	4 28	20 04	4 21	20 06	4 18	20 12	4 08	20 16	4 14	20 31	4 27	20 32
29	4 19	19 53	4 30	20 03	4 23	20 04	4 20	20 10	4 10	20 15	4 16	20 30	4 29	20 30
30	4 21	19 52	4 31	20 01	4 24	20 03	4 21	20 08	4 12	20 13	4 18	20 28	4 31	20 28
31	4 22	19 50	4 33	20 00	4 26	20 01	4 23	20 07	4 13	20 11	4 20	20 26	4 33	20 26

JUPITER

Day	RA	Dec.	Transit	5° high	
				52°	56°
	h m	° ′	h m	h m	h m
1	21 35.6	−15 13	2 59	22 54	23 13
11	21 32.6	−15 30	2 16	22 14	22 33
21	21 28.6	−15 52	1 33	21 33	21 52
31	21 23.9	−16 16	0 49	20 51	21 12

Diameters – equatorial 48″ polar 45″

SATURN

Day	RA	Dec.	Transit	5° high	
				52°	56°
	h m	° ′	h m	h m	h m
1	1 15.7	+ 5 24	6 38	0 44	0 43
11	1 17.4	+ 5 32	6 01	0 06	0 05
21	1 18.6	+ 5 35	5 23	23 23	23 22
31	1 19.1	+ 5 35	4 44	22 45	22 43

Diameters – equatorial 18″ polar 16″
Rings – major axis 41″ minor axis 8″

URANUS

Day	RA	Dec.	Transit	10° high	
				52°	56°
	h m	° ′	h m	h m	h m
1	20 41.5	−18 56	2 05	23 11	23 49
11	20 40.0	−19 02	1 24	22 31	23 09
21	20 38.5	−19 08	0 43	21 51	22 29
31	20 36.8	−19 14	0 02	21 11	21 50

Diameter 4″

NEPTUNE

Day	RA	Dec.	Transit	10° high	
				52°	56°
	h m	° ′	h m	h m	h m
1	20 04.6	−19 55	1 28	22 44	23 25
11	20 03.5	−19 59	0 48	22 04	22 46
21	20 02.4	−20 02	0 07	21 24	22 06
31	20 01.3	−20 05	23 23	20 44	21 26

Diameter 2″

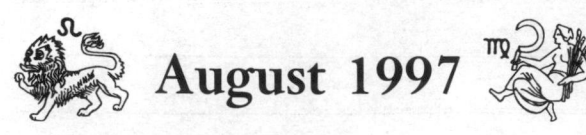

August 1997

EIGHTH MONTH, 31 DAYS. Julius, Caesar *Augustus*, formerly *Sextilis*, sixth month of Roman pre-Julian calendar

1	*Friday*	Queen Anne d. 1714. Herman Melville b. 1819	*week 30 day* 213
2	*Saturday*	William II d. 1100. Gen. von Hindenburg d. 1934	214
3	*Sunday*	**11th S. after Pentecost/10th S. after Trinity**	*week 31 day* 215
4	*Monday*	*Bank Holiday in Scotland. Queen Elizabeth the Queen Mother b. 1900*	216
5	*Tuesday*	Guy de Maupassant b. 1850. Marilyn Monroe d. 1962	217
6	*Wednesday*	**The Transfiguration.** Anne Hathaway d. 1623	218
7	*Thursday*	Joseph Jacquard d. 1834. Oliver Hardy d. 1957	219
8	*Friday*	Princess Beatrice of York b. 1988	220
9	*Saturday*	Thomas Telford b. 1757. Capt. Frederick Marryat d. 1848	221
10	*Sunday*	**12th S. after Pentecost/11th S. after Trinity**	*week 32 day* 222
11	*Monday*	Charlotte Yonge b. 1823. Edith Wharton d. 1937	223
12	*Tuesday*	George IV b. 1762. William Blake d. 1827	224
13	*Wednesday*	Sir Basil Spence b. 1907. Ben Hogan b. 1912	225
14	*Thursday*	Ira Sankey d. 1908. William Randolph Hearst d. 1951	226
15	*Friday*	*Princess Royal b. 1950.* Sir Walter Scott b. 1771	227
16	*Saturday*	Ted Hughes b. 1930. Stewart Granger d. 1993	228
17	*Sunday*	**13th S. after Pentecost/12th S. after Trinity**	*week 33 day* 229
18	*Monday*	Earl Russell b. 1792. Sir Frederick Ashton d. 1988	230
19	*Tuesday*	President Bill Clinton b. 1946. Groucho Marx d. 1977	231
20	*Wednesday*	Raymond Poincaré b. 1860. Gen. William Booth d. 1912	232
21	*Thursday*	*Princess Margaret b. 1930.* Elie Halévy d. 1937	233
22	*Friday*	⚔Battle of Bosworth Field 1485. Dr Jacob Bronowski d. 1974	234
23	*Saturday*	William Wallace exec. 1305. Rudolf Valentino d. 1926	235
24	*Sunday*	**St Bartholomew. 14th S. after Pentecost/13th S. after Trinity**	*week 34 day* 236
25	*Monday*	*Bank Holiday in England, Wales and Northern Ireland*	237
26	*Tuesday*	Sir Robert Walpole b. 1676. William James d. 1910	238
27	*Wednesday*	Umberto Giordano b. 1867. Eric Coates b. 1886	239
28	*Thursday*	Count Leo Tolstoy b. 1828 (os). Leigh Hunt d. 1859	240
29	*Friday*	Edward Carpenter b. 1844. Lady Diana Cooper b. 1892	241
30	*Saturday*	Mary Wollstonecraft Shelley b. 1797. Denis Healey b. 1917	242
31	*Sunday*	**15th S. after Pentecost/14th S. after Trinity**	*week 35 day* 243

ASTRONOMICAL PHENOMENA

d	h	
1	17	Saturn at stationary point
4	00	Mercury at greatest elongation E.27°
5	20	Mercury in conjunction with Moon. Mercury 1° S.
6	08	Venus in conjunction with Moon. Venus 2° N.
9	14	Jupiter at opposition
9	18	Mars in conjunction with Moon. Mars 4° S.
13	09	Pluto at stationary point
17	20	Jupiter in conjunction with Moon. Jupiter 4° S.
17	20	Mercury at stationary point
22	02	Saturn in conjunction with Moon. Saturn 0°.09 N.
23	02	Sun's longitude 150° ♍
31	14	Mercury in inferior conjunction

MINIMA OF ALGOL

d	h	d	h	d	h
1	16.6	13	03.9	24	15.1
4	13.4	16	00.7	27	11.9
7	10.2	18	21.5	30	08.7
10	07.0	21	18.3		

CONSTELLATIONS

The following constellations are near the meridian at

	d	h		d	h
July	1	24	August	16	21
July	16	23	September	1	20
August	1	22	September	15	19

Draco, Hercules, Lyra, Cygnus, Sagitta, Ophiuchus, Serpens, Aquila and Sagittarius

THE MOON

Phases, Apsides and Node	d	h	m
● New Moon	3	08	14
☽ First Quarter	11	12	42
○ Full Moon	18	10	55
☾ Last Quarter	25	02	24
Apogee (405,935 km)	6	13	42
Perigee (358,017 km)	19	05	09

Mean longitude of ascending node on August 1, 172°

THE SUN   s.d. 15′.8

Day	Right Ascension	Dec. +	Equation of time	Rise 52°	Rise 56°	Transit	Set 52°	Set 56°	Sidereal time	Transit of First Point of Aries
	h m s	° ′	m s	h m	h m	h m	h m	h m	h m s	h m s
1	8 44 52	18 04	−6 19	4 22	4 04	12 06	19 50	20 07	20 38 34	3 20 53
2	8 48 45	17 48	−6 15	4 23	4 06	12 06	19 48	20 05	20 42 30	3 16 57
3	8 52 37	17 33	−6 10	4 25	4 08	12 06	19 46	20 03	20 46 27	3 13 01
4	8 56 29	17 17	−6 06	4 26	4 09	12 06	19 45	20 01	20 50 23	3 09 06
5	9 00 20	17 01	−6 00	4 28	4 11	12 06	19 43	19 59	20 54 20	3 05 10
6	9 04 10	16 45	−5 54	4 29	4 13	12 06	19 41	19 57	20 58 17	3 01 14
7	9 08 00	16 28	−5 47	4 31	4 15	12 06	19 39	19 55	21 02 13	2 57 18
8	9 11 49	16 11	−5 40	4 33	4 17	12 06	19 37	19 53	21 06 10	2 53 22
9	9 15 38	15 54	−5 32	4 34	4 19	12 05	19 36	19 51	21 10 06	2 49 26
10	9 19 26	15 37	−5 23	4 36	4 21	12 05	19 34	19 48	21 14 03	2 45 30
11	9 23 13	15 19	−5 14	4 37	4 23	12 05	19 32	19 46	21 17 59	2 41 34
12	9 27 00	15 01	−5 04	4 39	4 25	12 05	19 30	19 44	21 21 56	2 37 38
13	9 30 47	14 43	−4 54	4 41	4 27	12 05	19 28	19 41	21 25 52	2 33 42
14	9 34 32	14 25	−4 43	4 42	4 29	12 05	19 26	19 39	21 29 49	2 29 46
15	9 38 17	14 06	−4 32	4 44	4 31	12 04	19 24	19 37	21 33 46	2 25 51
16	9 42 02	13 48	−4 20	4 45	4 33	12 04	19 22	19 34	21 37 42	2 21 55
17	9 45 46	13 29	−4 07	4 47	4 35	12 04	19 20	19 32	21 41 39	2 17 59
18	9 49 30	13 09	−3 54	4 49	4 37	12 04	19 18	19 30	21 45 35	2 14 03
19	9 53 13	12 50	−3 41	4 50	4 39	12 04	19 16	19 27	21 49 32	2 10 07
20	9 56 55	12 30	−3 27	4 52	4 41	12 03	19 14	19 25	21 53 28	2 06 11
21	10 00 37	12 10	−3 12	4 54	4 43	12 03	19 11	19 22	21 57 25	2 02 15
22	10 04 19	11 50	−2 57	4 55	4 44	12 03	19 09	19 20	22 01 21	1 58 19
23	10 08 00	11 30	−2 42	4 57	4 46	12 03	19 07	19 17	22 05 18	1 54 23
24	10 11 41	11 10	−2 26	4 59	4 48	12 02	19 05	19 15	22 09 15	1 50 27
25	10 15 21	10 49	−2 10	5 00	4 50	12 02	19 03	19 12	22 13 11	1 46 31
26	10 19 01	10 29	−1 53	5 02	4 52	12 02	19 01	19 10	22 17 08	1 42 36
27	10 22 40	10 08	−1 36	5 03	4 54	12 01	18 58	19 07	22 21 04	1 38 40
28	10 26 20	9 47	−1 19	5 05	4 56	12 01	18 56	19 05	22 25 01	1 34 44
29	10 29 59	9 25	−1 01	5 07	4 58	12 01	18 54	19 02	22 28 57	1 30 48
30	10 33 37	9 04	−0 43	5 08	5 00	12 01	18 52	19 00	22 32 54	1 26 52
31	10 37 15	8 42	−0 25	5 10	5 02	12 00	18 49	18 57	22 36 50	1 22 56

DURATION OF TWILIGHT (in minutes)

Latitude	52°	56°	52°	56°	52°	56°	52°	56°
	1 August		11 August		21 August		31 August	
Civil	41	48	39	45	37	42	35	40
Nautical	97	120	89	106	83	96	79	89
Astronomical	177	TAN	153	205	138	166	127	147

THE NIGHT SKY

Mercury is at greatest eastern elongation on the 4th and at inferior conjunction on the last day of the month, but remains too close to the Sun for observation.

Venus continues to be visible as a brilliant object in the evening skies, magnitude −4.0, but only visible for about half an hour after sunset, low above the western horizon.

Mars, magnitude +0.9, passes 2° N. of Spica, magnitude +1.0, on the evening of the 2nd, but is not visible after the middle of the month as it moves closer to the Sun. The crescent Moon will be seen 4° above Mars on the evening of the 9th. Mars has the longest period of invisibility of any of the major planets as seen from the Earth. It will be almost a year before it reappears in the morning skies again.

Jupiter, magnitude −2.8, is at opposition on the 9th, and thus visible throughout the hours of darkness. Jupiter is in Capricornus. On the evening of the 17th the Full Moon passes 3° N. of the planet. An unusual event occurs on the evening of the 27th: none of the Galilean satellites is visible between 21h 39m and 21h 59m.

Saturn, magnitude +0.5, is becoming a more prominent object in the night sky and by the end of the month is rising in the eastern sky as soon as the sky is really dark. Saturn is in Pisces. On the night of the 21st to 22nd, the waning gibbous Moon passes 1° S. of the planet.

Meteors. The maximum of the famous Perseid meteor shower occurs on the 12th. A gibbous Moon will interfere with observations before midnight.

THE MOON

Day	RA h m	Dec °	Hor. par. ′	Semi-diam. ′	Sun's co-long. °	PA of Bright Limb °	Phase %	Age d	Rise 52° h m	Rise 56° h m	Transit h m	Set 52° h m	Set 56° h m
1	6 51	+18.1	55.4	15.1	238	86	5	27.2	2 41	2 23	10 34	18 23	18 39
2	7 43	+17.0	55.0	15.0	250	85	2	28.2	3 38	3 22	11 23	19 00	19 14
3	8 33	+15.1	54.6	14.9	263	62	0	29.2	4 38	4 25	12 10	19 32	19 44
4	9 22	+12.6	54.4	14.8	275	308	0	0.7	5 40	5 29	12 55	20 00	20 08
5	10 09	+ 9.6	54.1	14.8	287	296	3	1.7	6 42	6 35	13 39	20 25	20 30
6	10 55	+ 6.2	54.0	14.7	299	294	6	2.7	7 45	7 41	14 22	20 48	20 50
7	11 40	+ 2.6	54.0	14.7	312	293	12	3.7	8 47	8 46	15 04	21 10	21 09
8	12 25	− 1.1	54.1	14.8	324	292	18	4.7	9 50	9 52	15 46	21 33	21 29
9	13 10	− 4.8	54.4	14.8	336	291	26	5.7	10 53	10 59	16 29	21 57	21 50
10	13 57	− 8.3	54.8	14.9	348	289	35	6.7	11 57	12 06	17 14	22 23	22 13
11	14 45	−11.6	55.4	15.1	1	287	45	7.7	13 02	13 14	18 01	22 54	22 41
12	15 35	−14.4	56.1	15.3	13	284	55	8.7	14 06	14 21	18 51	23 30	23 15
13	16 27	−16.5	56.9	15.5	25	281	65	9.7	15 10	15 27	19 43	—	23 57
14	17 22	−17.9	57.9	15.8	37	277	75	10.7	16 10	16 28	20 39	0 14	—
15	18 20	−18.3	58.8	16.0	49	273	84	11.7	17 05	17 22	21 37	1 08	0 50
16	19 20	−17.5	59.7	16.3	62	269	91	12.7	17 53	18 08	22 35	2 11	1 54
17	20 20	−15.6	60.5	16.5	74	267	97	13.7	18 35	18 47	23 34	3 24	3 09
18	21 21	−12.6	61.0	16.6	86	275	100	14.7	19 11	19 19	—	4 42	4 31
19	22 21	− 8.8	61.2	16.7	98	58	100	15.7	19 43	19 48	0 32	6 04	5 57
20	23 19	− 4.3	61.1	16.7	110	67	96	16.7	20 14	20 14	1 29	7 26	7 24
21	0 16	+ 0.4	60.8	16.6	122	68	91	17.7	20 43	20 39	2 24	8 48	8 49
22	1 13	+ 4.9	60.1	16.4	135	70	82	18.7	21 13	21 06	3 18	10 07	10 13
23	2 08	+ 9.1	59.3	16.2	147	72	73	19.7	21 45	21 34	4 12	11 23	11 33
24	3 03	+12.7	58.5	15.9	159	75	62	20.7	22 21	22 07	5 05	12 35	12 48
25	3 58	+15.4	57.6	15.7	171	78	51	21.7	23 01	22 45	5 57	13 42	13 58
26	4 52	+17.2	56.8	15.5	183	82	41	22.7	23 46	23 29	6 50	14 43	15 00
27	5 46	+18.2	56.1	15.3	196	86	31	23.7	—	—	7 41	15 36	15 54
28	6 39	+18.1	55.5	15.1	208	90	22	24.7	0 37	0 19	8 31	16 22	16 39
29	7 31	+17.3	55.0	15.0	220	94	14	25.7	1 32	1 16	9 20	17 01	17 16
30	8 21	+15.6	54.6	14.9	232	97	8	26.7	2 31	2 17	10 07	17 35	17 47
31	9 10	+13.3	54.3	14.8	245	100	4	27.7	3 32	3 21	10 53	18 03	18 13

MERCURY

Day	RA h m	Dec °	Diam. ″	Phase %	Transit h m	5° high 52° h m	5° high 56° h m
1	10 29	+ 8.5	7	52	13 51	19 59	20 03
3	10 37	+ 7.4	8	49	13 50	19 53	19 55
5	10 43	+ 6.3	8	46	13 48	19 46	19 47
7	10 49	+ 5.3	8	43	13 46	19 38	19 39
9	10 54	+ 4.4	8	40	13 43	19 31	19 31
11	10 58	+ 3.6	9	36	13 38	19 22	19 22
13	11 01	+ 2.9	9	32	13 33	19 13	19 12
15	11 03	+ 2.3	9	28	13 27	19 04	19 03
17	11 03	+ 1.9	10	24	13 19	18 55	18 53
19	11 03	+ 1.6	10	20	13 11	18 45	18 43
21	11 01	+ 1.6	10	16	13 00	18 35	18 33
23	10 58	+ 1.7	10	12	12 49	18 25	18 23
25	10 53	+ 2.1	11	8	12 37	18 14	18 13
27	10 48	+ 2.7	11	5	12 23	18 04	18 03
29	10 42	+ 3.5	11	2	12 09	17 55	17 54
31	10 35	+ 4.5	11	1	11 55	6 05	6 05

VENUS

Day	RA h m	Dec °	Diam. ″	Phase %	Transit h m	5° high 52° h m	5° high 56° h m
1	10 49	+ 9.0	12	84	14 11	20 22	20 26
6	11 11	+ 6.6	13	83	14 13	20 12	20 14
11	11 33	+ 4.1	13	81	14 15	20 01	20 01
16	11 54	+ 1.5	13	80	14 17	19 50	19 48
21	12 16	− 1.1	14	79	14 19	19 38	19 34
26	12 37	− 3.6	14	77	14 20	19 26	19 20
31	12 58	− 6.2	14	76	14 22	19 14	19 05

MARS

Day	RA h m	Dec °	Diam. ″	Phase %	Transit h m	5° high 52° h m	5° high 56° h m
1	13 21	− 8.9	6	89	16 41	21 19	21 07
6	13 32	−10.1	6	89	16 32	21 03	20 51
11	13 43	−11.3	6	89	16 24	20 48	20 34
16	13 55	−12.4	6	89	16 16	20 33	20 18
21	14 07	−13.5	6	89	16 08	20 19	20 02
26	14 19	−14.6	6	90	16 01	20 04	19 46
31	14 31	−15.7	6	90	15 54	19 50	19 30

SUNRISE AND SUNSET

	London		Bristol		Birmingham		Manchester		Newcastle		Glasgow		Belfast	
	0°05'	51°30'	2°35'	51°28'	1°55'	52°28'	2°15'	53°28'	1°37'	54°59'	4°14'	55°52'	5°56'	54°35'
	h m	h m	h m	h m	h m	h m	h m	h m	h m	h m	h m	h m	h m	h m
1	4 24	19 48	4 34	19 58	4 27	19 59	4 25	20 05	4 15	20 09	4 21	20 24	4 34	20 24
2	4 25	19 47	4 36	19 57	4 29	19 58	4 26	20 03	4 17	20 07	4 23	20 22	4 36	20 23
3	4 27	19 45	4 37	19 55	4 31	19 56	4 28	20 01	4 19	20 05	4 25	20 20	4 38	20 21
4	4 28	19 43	4 39	19 53	4 32	19 54	4 30	19 59	4 21	20 03	4 27	20 18	4 40	20 19
5	4 30	19 42	4 40	19 51	4 34	19 52	4 31	19 58	4 22	20 01	4 29	20 16	4 41	20 17
6	4 32	19 40	4 42	19 50	4 35	19 51	4 33	19 56	4 24	19 59	4 31	20 13	4 43	20 15
7	4 33	19 38	4 43	19 48	4 37	19 49	4 35	19 54	4 26	19 57	4 33	20 11	4 45	20 13
8	4 35	19 36	4 45	19 46	4 39	19 47	4 36	19 52	4 28	19 55	4 35	20 09	4 47	20 11
9	4 36	19 34	4 46	19 44	4 40	19 45	4 38	19 50	4 30	19 53	4 37	20 07	4 49	20 09
10	4 38	19 32	4 48	19 42	4 42	19 43	4 40	19 48	4 32	19 51	4 38	20 05	4 50	20 06
11	4 39	19 31	4 49	19 40	4 44	19 41	4 41	19 46	4 33	19 49	4 40	20 02	4 52	20 04
12	4 41	19 29	4 51	19 39	4 45	19 39	4 43	19 44	4 35	19 46	4 42	20 00	4 54	20 02
13	4 43	19 27	4 53	19 37	4 47	19 37	4 45	19 41	4 37	19 44	4 44	19 58	4 56	20 00
14	4 44	19 25	4 54	19 35	4 49	19 35	4 47	19 39	4 39	19 42	4 46	19 56	4 58	19 58
15	4 46	19 23	4 56	19 33	4 50	19 33	4 48	19 37	4 41	19 40	4 48	19 53	5 00	19 56
16	4 47	19 21	4 57	19 31	4 52	19 31	4 50	19 35	4 43	19 37	4 50	19 51	5 01	19 53
17	4 49	19 19	4 59	19 29	4 53	19 29	4 52	19 33	4 45	19 35	4 52	19 48	5 03	19 51
18	4 50	19 17	5 01	19 27	4 55	19 27	4 54	19 31	4 46	19 33	4 54	19 46	5 05	19 49
19	4 52	19 15	5 02	19 25	4 57	19 25	4 55	19 29	4 48	19 30	4 56	19 44	5 07	19 46
20	4 54	19 13	5 04	19 23	4 58	19 22	4 57	19 26	4 50	19 28	4 58	19 41	5 09	19 44
21	4 55	19 11	5 05	19 20	5 00	19 20	4 59	19 24	4 52	19 26	5 00	19 39	5 10	19 42
22	4 57	19 08	5 07	19 18	5 02	19 18	5 01	19 22	4 54	19 23	5 02	19 36	5 12	19 40
23	4 58	19 06	5 08	19 16	5 03	19 16	5 02	19 20	4 56	19 21	5 04	19 34	5 14	19 37
24	5 00	19 04	5 10	19 14	5 05	19 14	5 04	19 17	4 58	19 19	5 06	19 31	5 16	19 35
25	5 02	19 02	5 12	19 12	5 07	19 11	5 06	19 15	5 00	19 16	5 08	19 29	5 18	19 32
26	5 03	19 00	5 13	19 10	5 08	19 09	5 08	19 13	5 01	19 14	5 10	19 26	5 20	19 30
27	5 05	18 58	5 15	19 08	5 10	19 07	5 09	19 10	5 03	19 11	5 12	19 24	5 21	19 28
28	5 06	18 56	5 16	19 05	5 12	19 05	5 11	19 08	5 05	19 09	5 14	19 21	5 23	19 25
29	5 08	18 53	5 18	19 03	5 13	19 02	5 13	19 06	5 07	19 06	5 15	19 19	5 25	19 23
30	5 10	18 51	5 20	19 01	5 15	19 00	5 15	19 03	5 09	19 04	5 17	19 16	5 27	19 20
31	5 11	18 49	5 21	18 59	5 17	18 58	5 16	19 01	5 11	19 01	5 19	19 14	5 29	19 18

JUPITER

Day	RA	Dec.	Transit	5° high	
				52°	56°
	h m	° '	h m	h m	h m
1	21 23.4	−16 18	0 45	4 38	4 18
11	21 18.3	−16 43	0 00	3 51	3 30
21	21 13.2	−17 07	23 12	3 04	2 42
31	21 08.5	−17 29	22 28	2 17	1 55

Diameters – equatorial 49" polar 46"

SATURN

Day	RA	Dec.	Transit	5° high	
				52°	56°
	h m	° '	h m	h m	h m
1	1 19.1	+ 5 35	4 40	22 41	22 39
11	1 18.9	+ 5 31	4 00	22 02	22 00
21	1 18.0	+ 5 23	3 20	21 22	21 21
31	1 16.6	+ 5 12	2 39	20 42	20 41

Diameters – equatorial 19" polar 17"
Rings – major axis 43" minor axis 9"

URANUS

Day	RA	Dec.	Transit	10° high	
				52°	56°
	h m	° '	h m	h m	h m
1	20 36.7	−19 15	23 54	2 45	2 06
11	20 35.1	−19 21	23 13	2 03	1 24
21	20 33.5	−19 26	22 32	1 21	0 42
31	20 32.1	−19 31	21 52	0 40	0 00

Diameter 4"

NEPTUNE

Day	RA	Dec.	Transit	10° high	
				52°	56°
	h m	° '	h m	h m	h m
1	20 01.2	−20 06	23 19	2 01	1 19
11	20 00.1	−20 09	22 38	1 20	0 38
21	19 59.1	−20 12	21 58	0 40	23 53
31	19 58.3	−20 15	21 18	23 55	23 12

Diameter 2"

September 1997

NINTH MONTH, 30 DAYS. *Septem* (seven), seventh month of Roman pre-Julian calendar

1	*Monday*	Amilcare Ponchielli b. 1834. Siegfried Sassoon d. 1967	*week 35 day* 244
2	*Tuesday*	Thomas Telford d. 1834. Frederick Soddy b. 1877	245
3	*Wednesday*	✗ Battle of Dunbar 1650. Oliver Cromwell d. 1658	246
4	*Thursday*	Darius Milhaud b. 1892. Albert Schweitzer d. 1965	247
5	*Friday*	Jesse James b. 1847. Arthur Koestler b. 1905	248
6	*Saturday*	Marquis de Lafayette b. 1757. Austin Reed b. 1873	249
7	*Sunday*	**16th S. after Pentecost/15th S. after Trinity**	*week 36 day* 250
8	*Monday*	**Blessed Virgin Mary.** Antonin Dvořák b. 1841	251
9	*Tuesday*	Capt. William Bligh b. 1754. Mao Tse-tung d. 1976	252
10	*Wednesday*	Treaty of St Germain signed 1919. Arnold Palmer b. 1929	253
11	*Thursday*	✗ Battle of Malplaquet 1709. David Ricardo b. 1823	254
12	*Friday*	Jean-Philippe Rameau d. 1764. Marshal von Blücher d. 1819	255
13	*Saturday*	Andrea Mantegna d. 1506. Leopold Stokowski d. 1977	256
14	*Sunday*	**17th S. after Pentecost/16th S. after Trinity**	*week 37 day* 257
15	*Monday*	Prince Henry of Wales b. 1984. Battle of Britain Day	258
16	*Tuesday*	Gabriel Fahrenheit d. 1736. John McCormack d. 1945	259
17	*Wednesday*	Comte de Vigny d. 1863. Fox Talbot d. 1877	260
18	*Thursday*	Dr Samuel Johnson b. 1709. Sean O'Casey d. 1964	261
19	*Friday*	Sir William Golding b. 1911. Sir Geraint Evans d. 1992	262
20	*Saturday*	✗ Battle of the Alma 1854. Jean Sibelius d. 1957	263
21	*Sunday*	**St Matthew. 18th S. after Pentecost/17th S. after Trinity**	*week 38 day* 264
22	*Monday*	Michael Faraday b. 1791. Irving Berlin d. 1989	265
23	*Tuesday*	Vincenzo Bellini b. 1835. Baroness Orczy b. 1865	266
24	*Wednesday*	George Cross introduced 1940. Dame Isobel Baillie d. 1983	267
25	*Thursday*	William Faulkner b. 1897. Erich Maria Remarque d. 1970	268
26	*Friday*	Daniel Boone d. 1820. Charles Bradlaugh b. 1833	269
27	*Saturday*	Edgar Degas d. 1917. Adelina Patti d. 1919	270
28	*Sunday*	**19th S. after Pentecost/18th S. after Trinity**	*week 39 day* 271
29	*Monday*	**St Michael and All Angels.** Lord Nelson b. 1758	272
30	*Tuesday*	Truman Capote b. 1924. Storm Jameson d. 1986	273

ASTRONOMICAL PHENOMENA

d	h	
1	19	Mercury in conjunction with Moon. Mercury 3° S.
2	00	Partial eclipse of Sun (*see* page 66)
5	15	Venus in conjunction with Moon. Venus 3° S.
7	13	Mars in conjunction with Moon. Mars 5° S.
10	02	Mercury at stationary point
14	02	Jupiter in conjunction with Moon. Jupiter 4° S.
16	19	Total eclipse of Moon (*see* page 66)
16	22	Mercury at geatest elongation W.18°
18	10	Saturn in conjunction with Moon. Saturn 0°.2 S.
23	00	Sun's longitude 180° ♎
30	18	Mercury in conjunction with Moon. Mercury 1° N.

MINIMA OF ALGOL

d	h	d	h	d	h
2	05.5	13	16.8	25	04.0
5	02.3	16	13.6	28	00.8
7	23.1	19	10.4	30	21.6
10	19.9	22	07.2		

CONSTELLATIONS

The following constellations are near the meridian at

	d	h		d	h
August	1	24	September	15	21
August	16	23	October	1	20
September	1	22	October	16	19

Draco, Cepheus, Lyra, Cygnus, Vulpecula, Sagitta, Delphinus, Equuleus, Aquila, Aquarius and Capricornus

THE MOON

Phases, Apsides and Node	d	h	m
● New Moon	1	23	52
☽ First Quarter	10	01	31
○ Full Moon	16	18	50
☾ Last Quarter	23	13	35
Apogee (406,476 km)	2	21	33
Perigee (356,964 km)	16	15	28
Apogee (406,323 km)	29	23	44

Mean longitude of ascending node on September 1, 170°

THE SUN   s.d. 15′.9

Day	Right Ascension	Dec.	Equation of time	Rise 52°	Rise 56°	Transit	Set 52°	Set 56°	Sidereal time	Transit of First Point of Aries
	h m s	° ′	m s	h m	h m	h m	h m	h m	h m s	h m s
1	10 40 53	+8 21	−0 06	5 12	5 04	12 00	18 47	18 54	22 40 47	1 19 00
2	10 44 31	+7 59	+0 13	5 13	5 06	12 00	18 45	18 52	22 44 43	1 15 04
3	10 48 08	+7 37	+0 32	5 15	5 08	11 59	18 43	18 49	22 48 40	1 11 08
4	10 51 45	+7 15	+0 52	5 16	5 10	11 59	18 40	18 47	22 52 37	1 07 12
5	10 55 22	+6 53	+1 11	5 18	5 12	11 59	18 38	18 44	22 56 33	1 03 16
6	10 58 58	+6 30	+1 31	5 20	5 14	11 58	18 36	18 41	23 00 30	0 59 21
7	11 02 35	+6 08	+1 52	5 21	5 16	11 58	18 33	18 39	23 04 26	0 55 25
8	11 06 11	+5 46	+2 12	5 23	5 18	11 58	18 31	18 36	23 08 23	0 51 29
9	11 09 47	+5 23	+2 33	5 25	5 20	11 57	18 29	18 34	23 12 19	0 47 33
10	11 13 22	+5 00	+2 54	5 26	5 22	11 57	18 27	18 31	23 16 16	0 43 37
11	11 16 58	+4 38	+3 15	5 28	5 24	11 57	18 24	18 28	23 20 12	0 39 41
12	11 20 33	+4 15	+3 36	5 29	5 26	11 56	18 22	18 26	23 24 09	0 35 45
13	11 24 09	+3 52	+3 57	5 31	5 27	11 56	18 20	18 23	23 28 06	0 31 49
14	11 27 44	+3 29	+4 18	5 33	5 29	11 56	18 17	18 20	23 32 02	0 27 53
15	11 31 19	+3 06	+4 40	5 34	5 31	11 55	18 15	18 18	23 35 59	0 23 57
16	11 34 54	+2 43	+5 01	5 36	5 33	11 55	18 13	18 15	23 39 55	0 20 02
17	11 38 29	+2 20	+5 23	5 38	5 35	11 54	18 10	18 12	23 43 52	0 16 06
18	11 42 04	+1 56	+5 44	5 39	5 37	11 54	18 08	18 10	23 47 48	0 12 10
19	11 45 39	+1 33	+6 05	5 41	5 39	11 54	18 05	18 07	23 51 45	0 08 14
20	11 49 14	+1 10	+6 27	5 43	5 41	11 53	18 03	18 04	23 55 41	0 04 18
21	11 52 50	+0 47	+6 48	5 44	5 43	11 53	18 01	18 02	23 59 38	{ 0 00 22 ⁄ 23 56 26
22	11 56 25	+0 23	+7 09	5 46	5 45	11 53	17 58	17 59	0 03 35	23 52 30
23	12 00 00	0 00	+7 31	5 47	5 47	11 52	17 56	17 56	0 07 31	23 48 34
24	12 03 36	−0 23	+7 52	5 49	5 49	11 52	17 54	17 54	0 11 28	23 44 38
25	12 07 12	−0 47	+8 12	5 51	5 51	11 52	17 51	17 51	0 15 24	23 40 42
26	12 10 48	−1 10	+8 33	5 52	5 53	11 51	17 49	17 49	0 19 21	23 36 47
27	12 14 24	−1 34	+8 53	5 54	5 55	11 51	17 47	17 46	0 23 17	23 32 51
28	12 18 00	−1 57	+9 14	5 56	5 57	11 51	17 44	17 43	0 27 14	23 28 55
29	12 21 37	−2 20	19 34	5 57	5 59	11 50	17 42	17 41	0 31 10	23 24 59
30	12 25 13	−2 44	+9 53	5 59	6 01	11 50	17 40	17 38	0 35 07	23 21 03

DURATION OF TWILIGHT (in minutes)

Latitude	52°	56°	52°	56°	52°	56°	52°	56°
	1 September		11 September		21 September		30 September	
Civil	35	39	34	38	34	37	34	37
Nautical	79	89	76	84	74	82	73	80
Astronomical	127	146	120	135	115	129	113	126

THE NIGHT SKY

Mercury is too close to the Sun to be observed early in the month but after the first twelve days of the month it is visible low above the eastern horizon about the beginning of morning civil twilight. Mercury is then visible until almost the end of the month. This is the most favourable morning apparition of the year for observers in the northern hemisphere. During its period of visibility its magnitude ranges from +0.8 to −1.2.

Venus, magnitude −4.1, is a brilliant object in the early evening sky but only visible for about half an hour after sunset, low above the south-western horizon.

Mars is unsuitably placed for observation.

Jupiter continues to be visible as a brilliant object in the night sky, magnitude −2.7, though by the end of the month it is no longer visible after midnight. On the evening of the 13th the waxing gibbous Moon will be seen above and to the right of the planet.

Saturn continues to be visible in the southern skies during the greater part of the night, magnitude +0.3. On the morning of the 18th the gibbous Moon will be seen approaching the planet.

Zodiacal Light. The morning cone may be seen stretching up from the eastern horizon before the beginning of twilight from the beginning of the month until the 15th.

THE MOON

Day	RA	Dec.	Hor. par.	Semi-diam.	Sun's co-long.	PA of Bright Limb	Phase	Age	Rise 52°	Rise 56°	Transit	Set 52°	Set 56°
	h m	°	'	'	°	°	%	d	h m	h m	h m	h m	h m
1	9 57	+10.4	54.1	14.7	257	100	1	28.7	4 34	4 26	11 37	18 29	18 36
2	10 43	+ 7.1	54.0	14.7	269	19	0	0.0	5 36	5 31	12 20	18 53	18 56
3	11 29	+ 3.6	53.9	14.7	281	292	1	1.0	6 39	6 37	13 02	19 15	19 16
4	12 14	− 0.1	54.0	14.7	294	290	4	2.0	7 42	7 43	13 45	19 38	19 35
5	12 59	− 3.8	54.2	14.8	306	289	8	3.0	8 44	8 49	14 27	20 01	19 56
6	13 45	− 7.4	54.4	14.8	318	288	14	4.0	9 48	9 55	15 11	20 27	20 18
7	14 32	−10.7	54.8	14.9	330	285	21	5.0	10 51	11 02	15 57	20 55	20 43
8	15 20	−13.6	55.3	15.1	342	283	30	6.0	11 54	12 08	16 44	21 29	21 14
9	16 11	−15.9	56.0	15.3	355	279	39	7.0	12 57	13 13	17 34	22 08	21 51
10	17 04	−17.5	56.8	15.5	7	275	49	8.0	13 57	14 14	18 27	22 56	22 38
11	17 59	−18.2	57.6	15.7	19	271	60	9.0	14 52	15 10	19 22	23 53	23 35
12	18 56	−17.9	58.6	16.0	31	267	70	10.0	15 42	15 58	20 18	—	—
13	19 55	−16.5	59.5	16.2	43	262	80	11.0	16 26	16 40	21 16	0 59	0 43
14	20 54	−14.1	60.3	16.4	56	258	89	12.0	17 04	17 15	22 13	2 13	2 00
15	21 53	−10.6	61.0	16.6	68	255	95	13.0	17 38	17 45	23 11	3 32	3 23
16	22 52	− 6.4	61.4	16.7	80	251	99	14.0	18 10	18 12	—	4 54	4 49
17	23 51	− 1.7	61.4	16.7	92	79	100	15.0	18 40	18 38	0 07	6 17	6 17
18	0 49	+ 3.0	61.1	16.7	104	74	98	16.0	19 10	19 05	1 03	7 40	7 44
19	1 46	+ 7.5	60.5	16.5	116	74	93	17.0	19 43	19 34	1 59	9 00	9 08
20	2 43	+11.4	59.7	16.3	129	77	85	18.0	20 18	20 05	2 54	10 17	10 29
21	3 40	+14.6	58.8	16.0	141	80	76	19.0	20 58	20 42	3 49	11 29	11 44
22	4 36	+16.8	57.9	15.8	153	84	66	20.0	21 42	21 25	4 43	12 34	12 51
23	5 32	+18.0	56.9	15.5	165	88	56	21.0	22 32	22 15	5 36	13 31	13 49
24	6 26	+18.2	56.1	15.3	177	92	46	22.0	23 27	23 10	6 27	14 20	14 38
25	7 18	+17.5	55.4	15.1	190	96	36	23.0	—	—	7 17	15 02	15 17
26	8 09	+16.1	54.9	14.9	202	100	27	24.0	0 25	0 10	8 05	15 37	15 50
27	8 58	+13.9	54.5	14.8	214	104	19	25.0	1 25	1 12	8 51	16 07	16 18
28	9 45	+11.1	54.2	14.8	226	107	12	26.0	2 27	2 17	9 35	16 34	16 41
29	10 32	+ 8.0	54.0	14.7	238	109	6	27.0	3 29	3 22	10 18	16 58	17 02
30	11 17	+ 4.5	54.0	14.7	251	113	3	28.0	4 31	4 28	11 01	17 21	17 22

MERCURY

Day	RA	Dec.	Diam.	Phase	Transit	5° high 52°	5° high 56°
	h m	°	"	%	h m	h m	h m
1	10 32	+ 5.0	11	1	11 48	5 56	5 55
3	10 26	+ 6.1	10	2	11 34	5 37	5 35
5	10 21	+ 7.2	10	5	11 22	5 19	5 16
7	10 18	+ 8.1	10	9	11 11	5 03	4 59
9	10 17	+ 9.0	9	15	11 02	4 50	4 46
11	10 17	+ 9.6	9	22	10 56	4 40	4 35
13	10 21	+ 9.9	8	30	10 52	4 34	4 29
15	10 26	+10.0	8	39	10 50	4 31	4 26
17	10 33	+ 9.8	7	48	10 49	4 32	4 27
19	10 42	+ 9.3	7	57	10 51	4 35	4 31
21	10 52	+ 8.6	6	66	10 54	4 42	4 38
23	11 04	+ 7.7	6	73	10 57	4 50	4 47
25	11 16	+ 6.6	6	80	11 02	5 00	4 58
27	11 29	+ 5.4	6	85	11 07	5 12	5 11
29	11 42	+ 4.0	5	90	11 12	5 24	5 24
31	11 55	+ 2.6	5	93	11 17	5 36	5 38

VENUS

Day	RA	Dec.	Diam.	Phase	Transit	5° high 52°	5° high 56°
	h m	°	"	%	h m	h m	h m
1	13 03	− 6.7	14	75	14 22	19 12	19 02
6	13 24	− 9.2	15	74	14 24	19 00	18 48
11	13 46	−11.6	15	72	14 26	18 48	18 33
16	14 08	−13.9	16	70	14 28	18 36	18 18
21	14 30	−16.1	16	69	14 31	18 24	18 03
26	14 52	−18.2	17	67	14 33	18 12	17 48
31	15 15	−20.1	18	65	14 36	18 02	17 34

MARS

Day	RA	Dec.	Diam.	Phase	Transit	5° high 52°	5° high 56°
1	14 34	−15.9	6	90	15 52	19 47	19 27
6	14 47	−17.0	6	90	15 45	19 34	19 12
11	15 00	−18.0	6	90	15 39	19 20	18 57
16	15 14	−19.0	5	91	15 33	19 07	18 42
21	15 28	−19.9	5	91	15 27	18 55	18 28
26	15 42	−20.7	5	91	15 22	18 43	18 14
31	15 56	−21.5	5	92	15 17	18 32	18 01

SUNRISE AND SUNSET

	London		Bristol		Birmingham		Manchester		Newcastle		Glasgow		Belfast	
	0°05'	51°30'	2°35'	51°28'	1°55'	52°28'	2°15'	53°28'	1°37'	54°59'	4°14'	55°52'	5°56'	54°35'
	h m	h m	h m	h m	h m	h m	h m	h m	h m	h m	h m	h m	h m	h m
1	5 13	18 47	5 23	18 57	5 18	18 56	5 18	18 59	5 13	18 59	5 21	19 11	5 31	19 15
2	5 14	18 44	5 24	18 54	5 20	18 53	5 20	18 56	5 14	18 56	5 23	19 09	5 33	19 13
3	5 16	18 42	5 26	18 52	5 22	18 51	5 21	18 54	5 16	18 54	5 25	19 06	5 34	19 10
4	5 18	18 40	5 28	18 50	5 23	18 49	5 23	18 52	5 18	18 51	5 27	19 03	5 36	19 08
5	5 19	18 38	5 29	18 48	5 25	18 46	5 25	18 49	5 20	18 49	5 29	19 01	5 38	19 06
6	5 21	18 35	5 31	18 45	5 27	18 44	5 27	18 47	5 22	18 46	5 31	18 58	5 40	19 03
7	5 22	18 33	5 32	18 43	5 28	18 42	5 28	18 44	5 24	18 44	5 33	18 56	5 42	19 01
8	5 24	18 31	5 34	18 41	5 30	18 39	5 30	18 42	5 26	18 41	5 35	18 53	5 43	18 58
9	5 25	18 29	5 36	18 39	5 32	18 37	5 32	18 39	5 28	18 39	5 37	18 50	5 45	18 55
10	5 27	18 26	5 37	18 36	5 33	18 35	5 34	18 37	5 29	18 36	5 39	18 48	5 47	18 53
11	5 29	18 24	5 39	18 34	5 35	18 32	5 35	18 35	5 31	18 34	5 41	18 45	5 49	18 50
12	5 30	18 22	5 40	18 32	5 37	18 30	5 37	18 32	5 33	18 31	5 43	18 42	5 51	18 48
13	5 32	18 19	5 42	18 29	5 38	18 28	5 39	18 30	5 35	18 29	5 45	18 40	5 53	18 45
14	5 33	18 17	5 43	18 27	5 40	18 25	5 41	18 27	5 37	18 26	5 47	18 37	5 54	18 43
15	5 35	18 15	5 45	18 25	5 42	18 23	5 42	18 25	5 39	18 23	5 48	18 35	5 56	18 40
16	5 37	18 13	5 47	18 23	5 43	18 20	5 44	18 22	5 41	18 21	5 50	18 32	5 58	18 38
17	5 38	18 10	5 48	18 20	5 45	18 18	5 46	18 20	5 42	18 18	5 52	18 29	6 00	18 35
18	5 40	18 08	5 50	18 18	5 47	18 16	5 48	18 17	5 44	18 16	5 54	18 27	6 02	18 33
19	5 41	18 06	5 51	18 16	5 48	18 13	5 49	18 15	5 46	18 13	5 56	18 24	6 04	18 30
20	5 43	18 03	5 53	18 13	5 50	18 11	5 51	18 13	5 48	18 11	5 58	18 21	6 05	18 28
21	5 45	18 01	5 55	18 11	5 52	18 09	5 53	18 10	5 50	18 08	6 00	18 19	6 07	18 25
22	5 46	17 59	5 56	18 09	5 53	18 06	5 55	18 08	5 52	18 05	6 02	18 16	6 09	18 23
23	5 48	17 56	5 58	18 06	5 55	18 04	5 56	18 05	5 54	18 03	6 04	18 13	6 11	18 20
24	5 49	17 54	5 59	18 04	5 57	18 01	5 58	18 03	5 55	18 00	6 06	18 11	6 13	18 17
25	5 51	17 52	6 01	18 02	5 58	17 59	6 00	18 00	5 57	17 58	6 08	18 08	6 15	18 15
26	5 53	17 50	6 03	18 00	6 00	17 57	6 02	17 58	5 59	17 55	6 10	18 05	6 17	18 12
27	5 54	17 47	6 04	17 57	6 02	17 54	6 03	17 55	6 01	17 53	6 12	18 03	6 18	18 10
28	5 56	17 45	6 06	17 55	6 04	17 52	6 05	17 53	6 03	17 50	6 14	18 00	6 20	18 07
29	5 58	17 43	6 08	17 53	6 05	17 50	6 07	17 51	6 05	17 47	6 16	17 58	6 22	18 05
30	5 59	17 40	6 09	17 50	6 07	17 47	6 09	17 48	6 07	17 45	6 18	17 55	6 24	18 02

JUPITER

Day	RA	Dec.	Transit	5° high	
				52°	56°
	h m	° '	h m	h m	h m
1	21 08.1	−17 31	22 23	2 13	1 50
11	21 04.2	−17 47	21 40	1 28	1 05
21	21 01.3	−17 59	20 58	0 44	0 21
31	20 59.7	−18 05	20 17	0 03	23 35

Diameters – equatorial 46″ polar 44″

SATURN

Day	RA	Dec.	Transit	5° high	
				52°	56°
	h m	° '	h m	h m	h m
1	1 16.4	+ 5 11	2 35	20 38	20 37
11	1 14.4	+ 4 56	1 54	19 58	19 57
21	1 12.0	+ 4 40	1 12	19 18	19 17
31	1 09.2	+ 4 22	0 30	18 37	18 37

Diameters – equatorial 20″ polar 18″
Rings – major axis 44″ minor axis 8″

URANUS

Day	RA	Dec.	Transit	10° high	
				52°	56°
	h m	° '	h m	h m	h m
1	20 32.0	−19 32	21 48	0 36	23 52
11	20 30.8	−19 36	21 07	23 50	23 11
21	20 29.9	−19 39	20 27	23 10	22 30
31	20 29.3	−19 41	19 47	22 30	21 49

Diameter 4″

NEPTUNE

Day	RA	Dec.	Transit	10° high	
				52°	56°
	h m	° '	h m	h m	h m
1	19 58.2	−20 15	21 14	23 51	23 08
11	19 57.5	−20 17	20 34	23 11	22 27
21	19 57.0	−20 19	19 54	22 31	21 47
31	19 56.7	−20 20	19 14	21 51	21 07

Diameter 2″

 # October 1997

TENTH MONTH, 31 DAYS. *Octo* (eight), eighth month of Roman pre-Julian calendar

1	Wednesday	Michaelmas Law Sittings begin. Stanley Holloway b. 1890	week 39 day 274
2	Thursday	JEWISH NEW YEAR (5758). Gen. von Hindenberg b. 1847	275
3	Friday	Sir Malcolm Sargent d. 1967. Jean Anouilh d. 1987	276
4	Saturday	Sputnik I launched 1957. Max Planck d. 1947	277
5	Sunday	**20th S. after Pentecost/19th S. after Trinity**	week 40 day 278
6	Monday	Charles Stewart Parnell d. 1891. Helen Wills-Moody b. 1905	279
7	Tuesday	Archbishop William Laud b. 1573. Marie Lloyd d. 1922	280
8	Wednesday	Henry Fielding d. 1754. Clement Attlee d. 1967	281
9	Thursday	John Lennon b. 1940. André Maurois d. 1967	282
10	Friday	Jean Watteau b. 1684. Viscount Nuffield b. 1877	283
11	Saturday	YOM KIPPUR. Anton Bruckner d. 1896	284
12	Sunday	**21st S. after Pentecost/20th S. after Trinity**	week 41 day 285
13	Monday	Joachim Murat d. 1815. Lady Thatcher b. 1925	286
14	Tuesday	George Grenville b. 1712. Eamon de Valera b. 1882	287
15	Wednesday	Friedrich Nietzsche b. 1844. Dr Marie Stopes b. 1880	288
16	Thursday	FEAST OF TABERNACLES begins. Earl of Cardigan b. 1797	289
17	Friday	Sir Philip Sidney d. 1586. Arthur Miller b. 1915	290
18	Saturday	**St Luke.** Viscount Palmerston d. 1865	291
19	Sunday	**22nd S. after Pentecost/21st S. after Trinity**	week 42 day 292
20	Monday	Sir Christopher Wren b. 1632. Jack Buchanan d. 1957	293
21	Tuesday	Samuel Taylor Coleridge b. 1772. Sir Georg Solti b. 1912	294
22	Wednesday	Paul Cézanne d. 1906. Pablo Casals d. 1973	295
23	Thursday	Earl of Derby d. 1869. Pélé b. 1940	296
24	Friday	Alessandro Scarlatti d. 1725. Franz Lehár d. 1948	297
25	Saturday	Lord Grenville b. 1759. George II d. 1760	298
26	Sunday	**9th S. before Christmas/22nd S. after Trinity**	week 43 day 299
27	Monday	Theodore Roosevelt b. 1858. Dylan Thomas b. 1914	300
28	Tuesday	**SS Simon and Jude.** John Locke d. 1704	301
29	Wednesday	James Boswell b. 1740. Wilfred Rhodes b. 1877	302
30	Thursday	R. B. Sheridan bapt. 1751. Ezra Pound b. 1885	303
31	Friday	Hallowmass Eve. Jan Vermeer b. 1632	304

ASTRONOMICAL PHENOMENA

d	h	
5	17	Venus in conjunction with Moon. Venus 7° S.
6	09	Mars in conjunction with Moon. Mars 6° S.
8	05	Jupiter at stationary point
9	01	Neptune at stationary point
10	04	Saturn at opposition
11	09	Jupiter in conjunction with Moon. Jupiter 4° S.
13	21	Mercury in superior conjunction
14	11	Uranus at stationary point
15	18	Saturn in conjunction with Moon. Saturn 0°.4 S.
23	09	Sun's longitude 210° ♏
26	12	Mars in conjunction with Venus. Mars 2° N.

MINIMA OF ALGOL

d	h		d	h		d	h
3	18.4		15	05.7		26	16.9
6	15.2		18	02.5		29	13.7
9	12.1		20	23.3			
12	08.9		23	20.1			

CONSTELLATIONS

The following constellations are near the meridian at

	d	h			d	h
September	1	24		October	16	21
September	15	23		November	1	20
October	1	22		November	15	19

Ursa Major (below the Pole), Cepheus, Cassiopeia, Cygnus, Lacerta, Andromeda, Pegasus, Capricornus, Aquarius and Piscis Austrinus

THE MOON

Phases, Apsides and Node	d	h	m
● New Moon	1	16	52
☽ First Quarter	9	12	22
○ Full Moon	16	03	46
☾ Last Quarter	23	04	48
● New Moon	31	10	01
Perigee (358,864 km)	15	02	09
Apogee (405,597 km)	27	09	12

Mean longitude of ascending node on October 1, 169°

THE SUN

s.d. 16'.1

Day	Right Ascension	Dec. −	Equation of time	Rise 52°	Rise 56°	Transit	Set 52°	Set 56°	Sidereal time	Transit of First Point of Aries
	h m s	° ′	m s	h m	h m	h m	h m	h m	h m s	h m s
1	12 28 51	3 07	+10 13	6 01	6 03	11 50	17 38	17 35	0 39 03	23 17 07
2	12 32 28	3 30	+10 32	6 02	6 05	11 49	17 35	17 33	0 43 00	23 13 11
3	12 36 06	3 53	+10 51	6 04	6 07	11 49	17 33	17 30	0 46 57	23 09 15
4	12 39 43	4 17	+11 10	6 06	6 09	11 49	17 31	17 27	0 50 53	23 05 19
5	12 43 22	4 40	+11 28	6 07	6 11	11 48	17 28	17 25	0 54 50	23 01 23
6	12 47 00	5 03	+11 46	6 09	6 13	11 48	17 26	17 22	0 58 46	22 57 27
7	12 50 40	5 26	+12 03	6 11	6 15	11 48	17 24	17 20	1 02 43	22 53 32
8	12 54 19	5 49	+12 20	6 13	6 17	11 48	17 22	17 17	1 06 39	22 49 36
9	12 57 59	6 12	+12 37	6 14	6 19	11 47	17 19	17 15	1 10 36	22 45 40
10	13 01 39	6 34	+12 53	6 16	6 21	11 47	17 17	17 12	1 14 32	22 41 44
11	13 05 20	6 57	+13 09	6 18	6 23	11 47	17 15	17 09	1 18 29	22 37 48
12	13 09 01	7 20	+13 25	6 19	6 25	11 46	17 13	17 07	1 22 26	22 33 52
13	13 12 43	7 42	+13 39	6 21	6 27	11 46	17 10	17 04	1 26 22	22 29 56
14	13 16 25	8 05	+13 54	6 23	6 29	11 46	17 08	17 02	1 30 19	22 26 00
15	13 20 07	8 27	+14 08	6 25	6 31	11 46	17 06	16 59	1 34 15	22 22 04
16	13 23 51	8 49	+14 21	6 26	6 33	11 46	17 04	16 57	1 38 12	22 18 08
17	13 27 34	9 11	+14 33	6 28	6 35	11 45	17 02	16 54	1 42 08	22 14 13
18	13 31 19	9 33	+14 46	6 30	6 37	11 45	17 00	16 52	1 46 05	22 10 17
19	13 35 04	9 55	+14 58	6 32	6 39	11 45	16 57	16 50	1 50 01	22 06 21
20	13 38 50	10 16	+15 08	6 33	6 42	11 45	16 55	16 47	1 53 58	22 02 25
21	13 42 36	10 38	+15 19	6 35	6 44	11 45	16 53	16 45	1 57 55	21 58 29
22	13 46 23	10 59	+15 28	6 37	6 46	11 44	16 51	16 42	2 01 51	21 54 33
23	13 50 11	11 20	+15 37	6 39	6 48	11 44	16 49	16 40	2 05 48	21 50 37
24	13 53 59	11 41	+15 45	6 40	6 50	11 44	16 47	16 38	2 09 44	21 46 41
25	13 57 48	12 02	+15 53	6 42	6 52	11 44	16 45	16 35	2 13 41	21 42 45
26	14 01 38	12 23	+15 59	6 44	6 54	11 44	16 43	16 33	2 17 37	21 38 49
27	14 05 28	12 43	+16 05	6 46	6 56	11 44	16 41	16 31	2 21 34	21 34 53
28	14 09 20	13 03	+16 11	6 48	6 58	11 44	16 39	16 28	2 25 30	21 30 58
29	14 13 12	13 23	+16 15	6 49	7 00	11 44	16 37	16 26	2 29 27	21 27 02
30	14 17 05	13 43	+16 19	6 51	7 03	11 44	16 35	16 24	2 33 24	21 23 06
31	14 20 58	14 03	+16 22	6 53	7 05	11 44	16 34	16 22	2 37 20	21 19 10

DURATION OF TWILIGHT (in minutes)

Latitude	52°	56°	52°	56°	52°	56°	52°	56°
	1 October		11 October		21 October		31 October	
Civil	34	37	34	37	34	38	36	40
Nautical	73	80	73	80	74	81	75	83
Astronomical	113	125	112	124	113	124	114	126

THE NIGHT SKY

Mercury is unsuitably placed for observation, superior conjunction occurring on the 13th.

Venus continues to be visible as a brilliant object in the early evenings, magnitude −4.2, low above the south-western horizon after sunset. Although not visible for long after sunset, this interval increases slightly during October so that by the end of the month Venus is visible for nearly an hour. On the early evening of the 5th the waxing crescent Moon will be seen about 7° above Venus.

Mars is too close to the Sun for observation.

Jupiter, magnitude −2.5, is a splendid evening object in the south-western sky in the evenings. On the evenings of the 10th and 11th the gibbous Moon will be seen in the vicinity of the planet.

Saturn, magnitude +0.2, reaches opposition on the 10th and is therefore visible throughout the hours of darkness. On the evening of the 15th the Full Moon will be seen a few degrees to the left of Saturn. Titan, Saturn's largest satellite is of magnitude +8.5, and visible in small telescopes. The rings of Saturn present a beautiful spectacle to the observer, even with only a small telescope. However, the minor axis is only 8 arcseconds, as compared with Saturn's polar diameter of 18 arcseconds.

THE MOON

Day	RA	Dec.	Hor. par.	Semi-diam.	Sun's co-long.	PA of Bright Limb	Phase	Age	Rise 52°	Rise 56°	Transit	Set 52°	Set 56°
	h m	°	'	'	°	°	%	d	h m	h m	h m	h m	h m
1	12 02	+ 0.8	54.0	14.7	263	121	0	29.0	5 34	5 34	11 43	17 43	17 41
2	12 48	− 2.9	54.1	14.8	275	261	0	0.3	6 37	6 40	12 26	18 06	18 01
3	13 33	− 6.6	54.4	14.8	287	280	2	1.3	7 40	7 47	13 10	18 31	18 23
4	14 20	− 9.9	54.7	14.9	300	281	5	2.3	8 44	8 54	13 55	18 58	18 47
5	15 08	−13.0	55.0	15.0	312	280	10	3.3	9 47	10 00	14 41	19 30	19 16
6	15 58	−15.4	55.5	15.1	324	277	17	4.3	10 50	11 05	15 30	20 07	19 51
7	16 50	−17.2	56.1	15.3	336	274	25	5.3	11 50	12 07	16 21	20 51	20 33
8	17 44	−18.2	56.7	15.5	348	270	34	6.3	12 45	13 04	17 14	21 43	21 25
9	18 39	−18.2	57.5	15.7	1	266	45	7.3	13 36	13 53	18 08	22 43	22 27
10	19 36	−17.2	58.2	15.9	13	261	55	8.3	14 20	14 36	19 03	23 52	23 37
11	20 33	−15.1	59.1	16.1	25	257	66	9.3	14 59	15 12	19 59	—	—
12	21 30	−12.1	59.8	16.3	37	253	77	10.3	15 34	15 43	20 54	1 06	0 55
13	22 27	− 8.3	60.5	16.5	49	250	86	11.3	16 06	16 10	21 49	2 24	2 17
14	23 25	− 3.9	60.9	16.6	61	247	93	12.3	16 36	16 36	22 45	3 45	3 42
15	0 22	+ 0.8	61.1	16.6	74	242	98	13.3	17 06	17 02	23 41	5 07	5 09
16	1 20	+ 5.5	61.0	16.6	86	197	100	14.3	17 37	17 30	—	6 30	6 35
17	2 18	+ 9.8	60.5	16.5	98	88	99	15.3	18 11	18 00	0 37	7 50	8 00
18	3 16	+13.4	59.9	16.3	110	84	95	16.3	18 50	18 35	1 33	9 07	9 20
19	4 14	+16.1	59.0	16.1	122	86	89	17.3	19 33	19 17	2 29	10 18	10 34
20	5 11	+17.8	58.1	15.8	134	89	81	18.3	20 22	20 05	3 25	11 21	11 38
21	6 07	+18.4	57.1	15.6	147	93	72	19.3	21 17	20 59	4 19	12 15	12 32
22	7 02	+18.0	56.3	15.3	159	97	62	20.3	22 15	21 59	5 11	13 00	13 17
23	7 54	+16.7	55.5	15.1	171	101	52	21.3	23 15	23 02	6 00	13 38	13 52
24	8 44	+14.7	54.9	15.0	183	105	42	22.3	—	—	6 47	14 10	14 22
25	9 33	+12.0	54.5	14.8	195	108	33	23.3	0 17	0 06	7 33	14 38	14 47
26	10 19	+ 8.9	54.2	14.8	207	110	24	24.3	1 19	1 12	8 16	15 03	15 08
27	11 05	+ 5.5	54.1	14.7	220	112	17	25.3	2 22	2 17	8 59	15 26	15 28
28	11 50	+ 1.9	54.1	14.7	232	114	10	26.3	3 24	3 23	9 41	15 48	15 47
29	12 35	− 1.9	54.2	14.8	244	117	5	27.3	4 27	4 30	10 24	16 11	16 07
30	13 21	− 5.6	54.4	14.8	256	121	2	28.3	5 31	5 37	11 07	16 35	16 28
31	14 08	− 9.1	54.8	14.9	268	147	0	29.3	6 35	6 44	11 52	17 01	16 51

MERCURY

Day	RA	Dec.	Diam.	Phase	Transit	5° high 52°	5° high 56°
	h m	°	"	%	h m	h m	h m
1	11 55	+ 2.6	5	93	11 17	5 36	5 38
3	12 08	+ 1.1	5	95	11 22	5 49	5 52
5	12 21	− 0.4	5	97	11 27	6 02	6 06
7	12 34	− 1.9	5	98	11 32	6 16	6 21
9	12 47	− 3.5	5	99	11 37	6 29	6 35
11	12 59	− 5.0	5	100	11 42	6 42	6 49
13	13 12	− 6.5	5	100	11 47	6 54	7 04
15	13 24	− 8.0	5	100	11 51	7 07	7 18
17	13 37	− 9.4	5	100	11 56	7 20	7 32
19	13 49	−10.8	5	100	12 00	16 26	16 13
21	14 01	−12.1	5	99	12 04	16 23	16 07
23	14 13	−13.4	5	99	12 09	16 19	16 02
25	14 26	−14.7	5	98	12 13	16 15	15 57
27	14 38	−15.9	5	97	12 17	16 12	15 51
29	14 50	−17.1	5	97	12 22	16 08	15 46
31	15 02	−18.2	5	96	12 26	16 05	15 41

VENUS

Day	RA	Dec.	Diam.	Phase	Transit	5° high 52°	5° high 56°
	h m	°	"	%	h m	h m	h m
1	15 15	−20.1	18	65	14 36	18 02	17 34
6	15 38	−21.8	18	63	14 40	17 52	17 20
11	16 01	−23.2	19	61	14 43	17 43	17 06
16	16 25	−24.5	20	59	14 47	17 35	16 54
21	16 49	−25.5	21	57	14 51	17 29	16 43
26	17 12	−26.3	22	55	14 55	17 25	16 34
31	17 35	−26.8	23	53	14 59	17 24	16 29

MARS

Day	RA	Dec.	Diam.	Phase	Transit	5° high 52°	5° high 56°
1	15 56	−21.5	5	92	15 17	18 32	18 01
6	16 11	−22.2	5	92	15 12	18 21	17 48
11	16 26	−22.8	5	92	15 07	18 11	17 36
16	16 42	−23.4	5	92	15 03	18 02	17 25
21	16 58	−23.9	5	93	14 59	17 54	17 16
26	17 14	−24.2	5	93	14 55	17 47	17 07
31	17 30	−24.5	5	93	14 52	17 41	17 00

SUNRISE AND SUNSET

	London 0°05' 51°30'		Bristol 2°35' 51°28'		Birmingham 1°55' 52°28'		Manchester 2°15' 53°28'		Newcastle 1°37' 54°59'		Glasgow 4°14' 55°52'		Belfast 5°56' 54°35'	
	h m	h m	h m	h m	h m	h m	h m	h m	h m	h m	h m	h m	h m	h m
1	6 01	17 38	6 11	17 48	6 09	17 45	6 10	17 46	6 09	17 42	6 20	17 52	6 26	18 00
2	6 02	17 36	6 12	17 46	6 10	17 43	6 12	17 43	6 11	17 40	6 22	17 50	6 28	17 57
3	6 04	17 34	6 14	17 44	6 12	17 40	6 14	17 41	6 13	17 37	6 24	17 47	6 30	17 55
4	6 06	17 31	6 16	17 41	6 14	17 38	6 16	17 39	6 14	17 35	6 26	17 45	6 31	17 52
5	6 07	17 29	6 17	17 39	6 16	17 36	6 18	17 36	6 16	17 32	6 28	17 42	6 33	17 50
6	6 09	17 27	6 19	17 37	6 17	17 33	6 19	17 34	6 18	17 30	6 30	17 39	6 35	17 47
7	6 11	17 25	6 21	17 35	6 19	17 31	6 21	17 31	6 20	17 27	6 32	17 37	6 37	17 45
8	6 12	17 22	6 22	17 32	6 21	17 29	6 23	17 29	6 22	17 25	6 34	17 34	6 39	17 42
9	6 14	17 20	6 24	17 30	6 22	17 26	6 25	17 27	6 24	17 22	6 36	17 32	6 41	17 40
10	6 16	17 18	6 26	17 28	6 24	17 24	6 27	17 24	6 26	17 20	6 38	17 29	6 43	17 38
11	6 17	17 16	6 27	17 26	6 26	17 22	6 29	17 22	6 28	17 17	6 40	17 27	6 45	17 35
12	6 19	17 14	6 29	17 24	6 28	17 20	6 30	17 20	6 30	17 15	6 42	17 24	6 47	17 33
13	6 21	17 11	6 31	17 21	6 29	17 17	6 32	17 17	6 32	17 13	6 44	17 22	6 49	17 30
14	6 22	17 09	6 32	17 19	6 31	17 15	6 34	17 15	6 34	17 10	6 46	17 19	6 50	17 28
15	6 24	17 07	6 34	17 17	6 33	17 13	6 36	17 13	6 36	17 08	6 48	17 17	6 52	17 26
16	6 26	17 05	6 36	17 15	6 35	17 11	6 38	17 10	6 38	17 05	6 50	17 14	6 54	17 23
17	6 28	17 03	6 38	17 13	6 37	17 09	6 40	17 08	6 40	17 03	6 52	17 12	6 56	17 21
18	6 29	17 01	6 39	17 11	6 38	17 06	6 41	17 06	6 42	17 01	6 54	17 09	6 58	17 19
19	6 31	16 59	6 41	17 09	6 40	17 04	6 43	17 04	6 44	16 58	6 56	17 07	7 00	17 16
20	6 33	16 57	6 43	17 07	6 42	17 02	6 45	17 02	6 46	16 56	6 58	17 04	7 02	17 14
21	6 34	16 55	6 44	17 05	6 44	17 00	6 47	16 59	6 48	16 53	7 00	17 02	7 04	17 12
22	6 36	16 53	6 46	17 03	6 45	16 58	6 49	16 57	6 50	16 51	7 02	17 00	7 06	17 09
23	6 38	16 51	6 48	17 01	6 47	16 56	6 51	16 55	6 52	16 49	7 04	16 57	7 08	17 07
24	6 40	16 49	6 50	16 59	6 49	16 54	6 53	16 53	6 54	16 47	7 07	16 55	7 10	17 05
25	6 41	16 47	6 51	16 57	6 51	16 52	6 55	16 51	6 56	16 44	7 09	16 52	7 12	17 03
26	6 43	16 45	6 53	16 55	6 53	16 50	6 56	16 49	6 58	16 42	7 11	16 50	7 14	17 00
27	6 45	16 43	6 55	16 53	6 55	16 48	6 58	16 47	7 00	16 40	7 13	16 48	7 16	16 58
28	6 47	16 41	6 57	16 51	6 56	16 46	7 00	16 44	7 02	16 38	7 15	16 46	7 18	16 56
29	6 48	16 39	6 58	16 49	6 58	16 44	7 02	16 42	7 04	16 36	7 17	16 43	7 20	16 54
30	6 50	16 37	7 00	16 47	7 00	16 42	7 04	16 40	7 06	16 33	7 19	16 41	7 22	16 52
31	6 52	16 35	7 02	16 45	7 02	16 40	7 06	16 38	7 08	16 31	7 21	16 39	7 24	16 50

JUPITER

Day	RA	Dec.	Transit	5° high 52°	56°
	h m	° '	h m	h m	h m
1	20 59.7	−18 05	20 17	0 03	23 35
11	20 59.4	−18 06	19 38	23 19	22 56
21	21 00.4	−18 00	19 00	22 41	22 18
31	21 02.7	−17 50	18 23	22 06	21 43

Diameters – equatorial 43″ polar 40″

SATURN

Day	RA	Dec.	Transit	5° high 52°	56°
	h m	° '	h m	h m	h m
1	1 09.2	+ 4 22	0 30	6 19	6 19
11	1 06.3	+ 4 04	23 44	5 35	5 35
21	1 03.4	+ 3 46	23 02	4 52	4 51
31	1 00.7	+ 3 30	22 19	4 08	4 08

Diameters – equatorial 20″ polar 18″
Rings – major axis 45″ minor axis 8″

URANUS

Day	RA	Dec.	Transit	10° high 52°	56°
	h m	° '	h m	h m	h m
1	20 29.3	−19 41	19 47	22 30	21 49
11	20 29.0	−19 41	19 07	21 50	21 10
21	20 29.0	−19 41	18 28	21 11	20 30
31	20 29.4	−19 39	17 49	20 32	19 52

Diameter 4″

NEPTUNE

Day	RA	Dec.	Transit	10° high 52°	56°
	h m	° '	h m	h m	h m
1	19 56.7	−20 20	19 14	21 51	21 07
11	19 56.6	−20 20	18 35	21 11	20 28
21	19 56.8	−20 20	17 56	20 32	19 49
31	19 57.2	−20 19	17 17	19 54	19 10

Diameter 2″

November 1997

ELEVENTH MONTH, 30 DAYS. *Novem* (nine), ninth month of Roman pre-Julian calendar

1	Saturday	All Saints. L. S. Lowry b. 1887. Gary Player b. 1935	*week* 43 *day* 305
2	Sunday	8th S. before Christmas/23rd S. after Trinity	*week* 44 *day* 306
3	Monday	Vincenzo Bellini b. 1801. Henri Matisse d. 1954	307
4	Tuesday	William III b. 1650. Wilfred Owen d. 1918	308
5	Wednesday	✗Battle of Inkerman 1854. Vladimir Horowitz d. 1989	309
6	Thursday	Colley Cibber b. 1671. Sir John Alcock b. 1892	310
7	Friday	Marie Curie b. 1867. Alexander Dubcek d. 1992	311
8	Saturday	John Milton d. 1674. Thomas Bewick d. 1828	312
9	Sunday	7th S. before Christmas/24th S. after Trinity	*week* 45 *day* 313
10	Monday	William Hogarth b. 1697. Kamâl Atatürk d. 1938	314
11	Tuesday	Armistice Day 1918. Sir Edward German d. 1936	315
12	Wednesday	Harry Haldeman d. 1993. Umberto Giordano d. 1948	316
13	Thursday	Robert Louis Stevenson b. 1850. Archbishop Carey b. 1935	317
14	Friday	*Prince of Wales b. 1948.* Claude Monet b. 1840	318
15	Saturday	Johann Kepler d. 1630. Aneurin Bevan b. 1897	319
16	Sunday	6th S. before Christmas/25th S. after Trinity	*week* 46 *day* 320
17	Monday	Robert Owen d. 1858. Heitor Villa-Lobos d. 1959	321
18	Tuesday	Francis Thompson d. 1907. Niels Bohr d. 1962	322
19	Wednesday	Gettysburg address 1863. Indira Gandhi b. 1917	323
20	Thursday	*Queen's Wedding Day 1947.* Thomas Chatterton b. 1752	324
21	Friday	Sir Arthur Quiller Couch b. 1863	325
22	Saturday	Martin Frobisher d. 1594. Benjamin Britten b. 1913	326
23	Sunday	5th S. before Christmas/26th S. after Trinity	*week* 47 *day* 327
24	Monday	John Knox d. 1572. Frances Hodgson Burnett b. 1849	328
25	Tuesday	Harley Granville-Barker b. 1877. Lilian Baylis d. 1937	329
26	Wednesday	William Cowper b. 1731. John McAdam d. 1836	330
27	Thursday	Anders Celsius b. 1701. Eugene O'Neill d. 1953	331
28	Friday	William Blake b. 1757. Friedrich Engels b. 1820	332
29	Saturday	Christian Doppler b. 1803. Giacomo Puccini d. 1924	333
30	Sunday	Advent Sunday. Sir Philip Sidney b. 1554	*week* 48 *day* 334

Astronomical Phenomena

d	h	
1	10	Mercury in conjunction with Moon. Mercury 6° S.
4	06	Mars in conjunction with Moon. Mars 6° S.
4	11	Venus in conjunction with Moon. Venus 9° S.
6	07	Venus at greatest elongation E.47°
7	18	Jupiter in conjunction with Moon. Jupiter 4° S.
12	01	Saturn in conjunction with Moon. Saturn 0°.4 S.
22	07	Sun's longitude 240° ♐
27	17	Pluto in conjunction
28	16	Mercury at greatest elongation E.22°

Minima of Algol

d	h		d	h		d	h
1	10.6		12	21.8		24	09.1
4	07.4		15	18.6		27	05.9
7	04.2		18	15.4		30	02.7
10	01.0		21	12.3			

Constellations

The following constellations are near the meridian at

	d	h		d	h
October	1	24	November	15	21
October	16	23	December	1	20
November	1	22	December	16	19

Ursa Major (below the Pole), Cepheus, Cassiopeia, Andromeda, Pegasus, Pisces, Aquarius and Cetus

The Moon

Phases, Apsides and Node	d	h	m
☽ First Quarter	7	21	43
○ Full Moon	14	14	12
☾ Last Quarter	21	23	58
● New Moon	30	02	14

	d	h	m
Perigee (363,384 km)	12	08	02
Apogee (404,699 km)	24	02	30

Mean longitude of ascending node on November 1, 167°

THE SUN

s.d. 16′.2

Day	Right Ascension	Dec. −	Equation of time	Rise 52°	Rise 56°	Transit	Set 52°	Set 56°	Sidereal time	Transit of First Point of Aries
	h m s	° ′	m s	h m	h m	h m	h m	h m	h m s	h m s
1	14 24 53	14 22	+16 24	6 55	7 07	11 44	16 32	16 19	2 41 17	21 15 14
2	14 28 48	14 41	+16 25	6 57	7 09	11 44	16 30	16 17	2 45 13	21 11 18
3	14 32 44	15 00	+16 26	6 58	7 11	11 44	16 28	16 15	2 49 10	21 07 22
4	14 36 41	15 19	+16 25	7 00	7 13	11 44	16 26	16 13	2 53 06	21 03 26
5	14 40 38	15 37	+16 24	7 02	7 15	11 44	16 25	16 11	2 57 03	20 59 30
6	14 44 37	15 55	+16 22	7 04	7 18	11 44	16 23	16 09	3 00 59	20 55 34
7	14 48 36	16 13	+16 20	7 06	7 20	11 44	16 21	16 07	3 04 56	20 51 38
8	14 52 36	16 31	+16 16	7 07	7 22	11 44	16 19	16 05	3 08 52	20 47 43
9	14 56 37	16 48	+16 12	7 09	7 24	11 44	16 18	16 03	3 12 49	20 43 47
10	15 00 39	17 05	+16 07	7 11	7 26	11 44	16 16	16 01	3 16 46	20 39 51
11	15 04 41	17 22	+16 01	7 13	7 28	11 44	16 15	15 59	3 20 42	20 35 55
12	15 08 45	17 38	+15 54	7 15	7 30	11 44	16 13	15 57	3 24 39	20 31 59
13	15 12 49	17 55	+15 46	7 16	7 32	11 44	16 12	15 56	3 28 35	20 28 03
14	15 16 54	18 10	+15 38	7 18	7 34	11 44	16 10	15 54	3 32 32	20 24 07
15	15 21 00	18 26	+15 28	7 20	7 36	11 45	16 09	15 52	3 36 28	20 20 11
16	15 25 07	18 41	+15 18	7 22	7 39	11 45	16 07	15 50	3 40 25	20 16 15
17	15 29 14	18 56	+15 07	7 23	7 41	11 45	16 06	15 49	3 44 21	20 12 19
18	15 33 23	19 11	+14 55	7 25	7 43	11 45	16 05	15 47	3 48 18	20 08 23
19	15 37 32	19 25	+14 42	7 27	7 45	11 45	16 04	15 46	3 52 15	20 04 28
20	15 41 42	19 39	+14 29	7 28	7 47	11 46	16 02	15 44	3 56 11	20 00 32
21	15 45 53	19 52	+14 15	7 30	7 49	11 46	16 01	15 43	4 00 08	19 56 36
22	15 50 05	20 05	+13 59	7 32	7 51	11 46	16 00	15 41	4 04 04	19 52 40
23	15 54 18	20 18	+13 43	7 33	7 52	11 46	15 59	15 40	4 08 01	19 48 44
24	15 58 31	20 30	+13 26	7 35	7 54	11 47	15 58	15 39	4 11 57	19 44 48
25	16 02 45	20 42	+13 09	7 37	7 56	11 47	15 57	15 37	4 15 54	19 40 52
26	16 07 00	20 54	+12 50	7 38	7 58	11 47	15 56	15 36	4 19 50	19 36 56
27	16 11 16	21 05	+12 31	7 40	8 00	11 48	15 55	15 35	4 23 47	19 33 00
28	16 15 32	21 16	+12 11	7 41	8 02	11 48	15 54	15 34	4 27 44	19 29 04
29	16 19 50	21 27	+11 51	7 43	8 03	11 48	15 54	15 33	4 31 40	19 25 08
30	16 24 07	21 37	+11 29	7 44	8 05	11 49	15 53	15 32	4 35 37	19 21 13

DURATION OF TWILIGHT (in minutes)

Latitude	52°	56°	52°	56°	52°	56°	52°	56°
	1 November		11 November		21 November		30 November	
Civil	36	40	37	41	38	43	39	45
Nautical	75	84	78	87	80	90	82	93
Astronomical	115	127	117	130	120	134	123	137

THE NIGHT SKY

Mercury, although at greatest eastern elongation on the 28th, is not suitably placed for observation.

Venus, magnitude −4.5, is still visible as a brilliant object in the early evenings, low above the south-western horizon. The planet is at greatest eastern elongation (47°) on the 6th and during the month is gradually becoming visible for a little longer each evening, until by the end of November it may be seen for almost two hours after sunset. On the early evening of the 4th the crescent Moon will be seen about 9° N. of the planet.

Mars remains too close to the Sun for observation.

Jupiter continues to be visible as a splendid evening object, magnitude −2.3, low in the south-western sky. By the end of the month it is unlikely to be visible for

long after 20h. On the evening of the 7th the Moon, at First Quarter, passes 3° N. of the planet.

Saturn is still visible for the greater part of the night, magnitude +0.4, but by the end of the month it is not visible after 02h. The waxing gibbous Moon occults the planet in the early hours of the 12th (see page 67 for details).

THE MOON

Day	RA	Dec.	Hor. par.	Semi- diam.	Sun's co- long.	PA of Bright Limb	Phase	Age	Rise 52°	Rise 56°	Transit	Set 52°	Set 56°
	h m	°	′	′	°	°	%	d	h m	h m	h m	h m	h m
1	14 56	−12.3	55.1	15.0	281	254	0	0.6	7 40	7 52	12 39	17 31	17 18
2	15 46	−15.0	55.5	15.1	293	268	3	1.6	8 44	8 59	13 27	18 06	17 51
3	16 38	−17.0	56.0	15.3	305	269	7	2.6	9 45	10 02	14 18	18 48	18 31
4	17 31	−18.2	56.5	15.4	317	267	13	3.6	10 43	11 01	15 10	19 38	19 20
5	18 26	−18.4	57.0	15.5	329	264	21	4.6	11 35	11 53	16 04	20 35	20 18
6	19 22	−17.7	57.6	15.7	342	260	30	5.6	12 20	12 37	16 58	21 40	21 24
7	20 18	−16.0	58.2	15.8	354	256	40	6.6	13 00	13 14	17 52	22 50	22 38
8	21 14	−13.3	58.7	16.0	6	253	51	7.6	13 35	13 45	18 45	—	23 56
9	22 09	− 9.8	59.3	16.2	18	250	62	8.6	14 06	14 12	19 39	0 05	—
10	23 05	− 5.6	59.8	16.3	30	247	73	9.6	14 35	14 38	20 32	1 22	1 17
11	0 00	− 1.1	60.1	16.4	42	246	83	10.6	15 04	15 02	21 25	2 41	2 40
12	0 56	+ 3.5	60.3	16.4	55	244	91	11.6	15 33	15 28	22 20	4 01	4 04
13	1 52	+ 8.0	60.3	16.4	67	241	96	12.6	16 05	15 56	23 16	5 21	5 28
14	2 50	+11.9	60.0	16.3	79	225	99	13.6	16 40	16 28	—	6 39	6 51
15	3 48	+15.1	59.5	16.2	91	118	100	14.6	17 21	17 06	0 12	7 54	8 09
16	4 46	+17.3	58.8	16.0	103	97	97	15.6	18 08	17 51	1 09	9 03	9 20
17	5 44	+18.4	58.0	15.8	115	96	92	16.6	19 01	18 43	2 05	10 03	10 21
18	6 41	+18.4	57.2	15.6	127	99	86	17.6	19 59	19 42	2 59	10 54	11 11
19	7 36	+17.5	56.3	15.4	140	102	78	18.6	21 01	20 46	3 51	11 36	11 52
20	8 28	+15.7	55.6	15.2	152	105	69	19.6	22 03	21 51	4 41	12 11	12 24
21	9 17	+13.2	55.0	15.0	164	108	60	20.6	23 06	22 57	5 27	12 41	12 51
22	10 05	+10.2	54.6	14.9	176	110	50	21.6	—	—	6 12	13 07	13 14
23	10 51	+ 6.8	54.3	14.8	188	112	41	22.6	0 09	0 03	6 55	13 31	13 34
24	11 37	+ 3.2	54.2	14.8	200	114	32	23.6	1 12	1 09	7 38	13 53	13 54
25	12 22	− 0.6	54.2	14.8	213	114	23	24.6	2 15	2 16	8 20	14 15	14 13
26	13 07	− 4.3	54.5	14.8	225	115	16	25.6	3 18	3 23	9 03	14 38	14 32
27	13 53	− 8.0	54.8	14.9	237	115	9	26.6	4 23	4 30	9 47	15 03	14 54
28	14 41	−11.3	55.2	15.0	249	117	5	27.6	5 28	5 39	10 33	15 32	15 20
29	15 31	−14.3	55.7	15.2	261	123	1	28.6	6 33	6 47	11 22	16 05	15 50
30	16 23	−16.6	56.2	15.3	274	177	0	29.6	7 37	7 53	12 12	16 45	16 28

MERCURY

Day	RA	Dec.	Diam.	Phase	Transit	5° high 52°	5° high 56°
	h m	°	″	%	h m	h m	h m
1	15 08	−18.7	5	96	12 28	16 04	15 38
3	15 21	−19.7	5	95	12 33	16 01	15 33
5	15 33	−20.6	5	94	12 37	15 58	15 29
7	15 45	−21.5	5	92	12 41	15 55	15 24
9	15 58	−22.3	5	91	12 46	15 53	15 20
11	16 10	−23.0	5	90	12 50	15 52	15 16
13	16 22	−23.7	5	88	12 55	15 50	15 12
15	16 34	−24.3	5	86	12 59	15 50	15 09
17	16 47	−24.7	5	84	13 03	15 49	15 07
19	16 59	−25.1	6	82	13 08	15 50	15 05
21	17 10	−25.5	6	79	13 11	15 51	15 04
23	17 22	−25.7	6	76	13 15	15 52	15 05
25	17 33	−25.8	6	72	13 18	15 54	15 06
27	17 43	−25.8	6	67	13 20	15 56	15 08
29	17 53	−25.8	7	62	13 21	15 58	15 11
31	18 01	−25.6	7	56	13 21	16 00	15 14

VENUS

Day	RA	Dec.	Diam.	Phase	Transit	5° high 52°	5° high 56°
	h m	°	″	%	h m	h m	h m
1	17 40	−26.8	24	52	14 59	17 24	16 28
6	18 03	−27.0	25	50	15 02	17 25	16 28
11	18 25	−26.9	26	47	15 05	17 29	16 33
16	18 46	−26.6	28	44	15 06	17 34	16 41
21	19 06	−26.1	30	41	15 06	17 41	16 52
26	19 25	−25.3	32	38	15 04	17 47	17 03
31	19 41	−24.4	35	35	15 01	17 53	17 13

MARS

Day	RA	Dec.	Diam.	Phase	Transit	5° high 52°	5° high 56°
1	17 33	−24.5	5	93	14 51	17 40	16 59
6	17 49	−24.7	5	94	14 48	17 36	16 54
11	18 06	−24.7	5	94	14 45	17 33	16 51
16	18 22	−24.6	5	94	14 42	17 30	16 49
21	18 39	−24.4	5	95	14 39	17 29	16 49
26	18 56	−24.1	5	95	14 36	17 30	16 51
31	19 13	−23.7	5	95	14 33	17 31	16 53

SUNRISE AND SUNSET

	London		Bristol		Birmingham		Manchester		Newcastle		Glasgow		Belfast	
	0°05'	51°30'	2°35'	51°28'	1°55'	52°28'	2°15'	53°28'	1°37'	54°59'	4°14'	55°52'	5°56'	54°35'
	h m	h m	h m	h m	h m	h m	h m	h m	h m	h m	h m	h m	h m	h m
1	6 54	16 33	7 04	16 43	7 04	16 38	7 08	16 36	7 10	16 29	7 23	16 37	7 26	16 48
2	6 56	16 32	7 05	16 42	7 06	16 36	7 10	16 35	7 12	16 27	7 26	16 35	7 28	16 46
3	6 57	16 30	7 07	16 40	7 07	16 34	7 12	16 33	7 14	16 25	7 28	16 33	7 30	16 44
4	6 59	16 28	7 09	16 38	7 09	16 33	7 14	16 31	7 16	16 23	7 30	16 30	7 32	16 42
5	7 01	16 26	7 11	16 36	7 11	16 31	7 16	16 29	7 18	16 21	7 32	16 28	7 34	16 40
6	7 03	16 25	7 13	16 35	7 13	16 29	7 18	16 27	7 20	16 19	7 34	16 26	7 36	16 38
7	7 04	16 23	7 14	16 33	7 15	16 27	7 19	16 25	7 22	16 17	7 36	16 24	7 38	16 36
8	7 06	16 21	7 16	16 32	7 17	16 26	7 21	16 24	7 24	16 15	7 38	16 22	7 40	16 34
9	7 08	16 20	7 18	16 30	7 18	16 24	7 23	16 22	7 26	16 14	7 40	16 20	7 42	16 32
10	7 10	16 18	7 20	16 28	7 20	16 22	7 25	16 20	7 28	16 12	7 42	16 19	7 44	16 31
11	7 11	16 17	7 21	16 27	7 22	16 21	7 27	16 18	7 30	16 10	7 45	16 17	7 46	16 29
12	7 13	16 15	7 23	16 25	7 24	16 19	7 29	16 17	7 32	16 08	7 47	16 15	7 48	16 27
13	7 15	16 14	7 25	16 24	7 26	16 18	7 31	16 15	7 34	16 07	7 49	16 13	7 50	16 25
14	7 17	16 12	7 26	16 23	7 27	16 16	7 33	16 14	7 36	16 05	7 51	16 11	7 52	16 24
15	7 18	16 11	7 28	16 21	7 29	16 15	7 34	16 12	7 38	16 03	7 53	16 10	7 54	16 22
16	7 20	16 10	7 30	16 20	7 31	16 13	7 36	16 11	7 40	16 02	7 55	16 08	7 56	16 21
17	7 22	16 08	7 32	16 19	7 33	16 12	7 38	16 09	7 42	16 00	7 57	16 06	7 58	16 19
18	7 23	16 07	7 33	16 17	7 35	16 11	7 40	16 08	7 44	15 59	7 59	16 05	8 00	16 18
19	7 25	16 06	7 35	16 16	7 36	16 09	7 42	16 06	7 46	15 57	8 01	16 03	8 02	16 16
20	7 27	16 05	7 37	16 15	7 38	16 08	7 44	16 05	7 48	15 56	8 03	16 02	8 03	16 15
21	7 28	16 04	7 38	16 14	7 40	16 07	7 45	16 04	7 50	15 54	8 05	16 00	8 05	16 13
22	7 30	16 03	7 40	16 13	7 41	16 06	7 47	16 03	7 52	15 53	8 07	15 59	8 07	16 12
23	7 32	16 02	7 41	16 12	7 43	16 05	7 49	16 02	7 54	15 52	8 09	15 58	8 09	16 11
24	7 33	16 00	7 43	16 11	7 45	16 04	7 51	16 00	7 55	15 50	8 11	15 56	8 11	16 10
25	7 35	16 00	7 45	16 10	7 46	16 03	7 52	15 59	7 57	15 49	8 12	15 55	8 12	16 09
26	7 36	15 59	7 46	16 09	7 48	16 02	7 54	15 58	7 59	15 48	8 14	15 54	8 14	16 07
27	7 38	15 58	7 48	16 08	7 49	16 01	7 56	15 57	8 01	15 47	8 16	15 53	8 16	16 06
28	7 39	15 57	7 49	16 07	7 51	16 00	7 57	15 56	8 02	15 46	8 18	15 52	8 18	16 05
29	7 41	15 56	7 51	16 06	7 52	15 59	7 59	15 56	8 04	15 45	8 20	15 51	8 19	16 04
30	7 42	15 56	7 52	16 06	7 54	15 58	8 00	15 55	8 06	15 44	8 21	15 50	8 21	16 04

JUPITER

Day	RA	Dec.	Transit	5° high	
				52°	56°
	h m	° '	h m	h m	h m
1	21 03.0	−17 48	18 19	22 02	21 40
11	21 06.7	−17 32	17 43	21 29	21 06
21	21 11.4	−17 10	17 09	20 57	20 35
31	21 17.1	−16 44	16 35	20 26	20 05

Diameters – equatorial 39″ polar 36″

SATURN

Day	RA	Dec.	Transit	5° high	
				52°	56°
	h m	° '	h m	h m	h m
1	1 00.4	+ 3 29	22 15	4 04	4 03
11	0 58.1	+ 3 15	21 34	3 21	3 20
21	0 56.1	+ 3 05	20 52	2 39	2 38
31	0 54.7	+ 2 59	20 12	1 58	1 57

Diameters – equatorial 19″ polar 17″
Rings – major axis 44″ minor axis 7″

URANUS

Day	RA	Dec.	Transit	10° high	
				52°	56°
	h m	° '	h m	h m	h m
1	20 29.5	−19 39	17 45	20 28	19 48
11	20 30.3	−19 36	17 07	19 50	19 10
21	20 31.4	−19 32	16 29	19 13	18 33
31	20 32.8	−19 27	15 51	18 36	17 57

Diameter 4″

NEPTUNE

Day	RA	Dec.	Transit	10° high	
				52°	56°
	h m	° '	h m	h m	h m
1	19 57.2	−20 19	17 13	19 50	19 06
11	19 57.9	−20 17	16 35	19 11	18 28
21	19 58.7	−20 15	15 56	18 33	17 50
31	19 59.8	−20 12	15 18	17 55	17 13

Diameter 2″

December 1997

TWELFTH MONTH, 31 DAYS. *Decem* (ten), tenth month of Roman pre-Julian calendar

1	*Monday*	**St Andrew.** Edmund Campion exec. 1581	*week* 48 *day* 335
2	*Tuesday*	Hernando Cortés d. 1547. ⚔Battle of Austerlitz 1805	336
3	*Wednesday*	Robert Louis Stephenson d. 1894. Renoir d. 1919	337
4	*Thursday*	Thomas Hobbes d. 1679. Edith Cavell b. 1865	338
5	*Friday*	Christina Rossetti b. 1830. Earl Jellicoe b. 1859	339
6	*Saturday*	Finland declared its independence 1917	340
7	*Sunday*	**2nd S. in Advent.** Ferdinand de Lesseps d. 1894	*week* 49 *day* 341
8	*Monday*	Jean Sibelius b. 1865. Golda Meir d. 1978	342
9	*Tuesday*	Sir Anthony van Dyck d. 1641. R. A. Butler b. 1902	343
10	*Wednesday*	Royal Academy of Arts founded 1768. Melvil Dewey b. 1851	344
11	*Thursday*	Hector Berlioz b. 1803. Alexander Solzhenitsyn b. 1918	345
12	*Friday*	Edward G. Robinson b. 1893. Frank Sinatra b. 1915	346
13	*Saturday*	Glen Byam Shaw b. 1904. Vassily Kandinsky d. 1944	347
14	*Sunday*	**3rd S. in Advent.** Stanley Baldwin d. 1947	*week* 50 *day* 348
15	*Monday*	Jan Vermeer d. 1675. Walt Disney d. 1966	349
16	*Tuesday*	Sir Jack Hobbs b. 1882. Zoltán Kodály b. 1882	350
17	*Wednesday*	Simón Bolívar d. 1830. Ford Madox Ford b. 1873	351
18	*Thursday*	Christopher Fry b. 1907. Sir John Alcock d. 1919	352
19	*Friday*	J. M. W. Turner d. 1851. Leonid Brezhnev b. 1906	353
20	*Saturday*	*Michaelmas Law Sittings end.* Artur Rubinstein d. 1982	354
21	*Sunday*	**4th S. in Advent.** Boccaccio d. 1375. Heinrich Böll b. 1917	*week* 51 *day* 355
22	*Monday*	Dame Peggy Ashcroft b. 1907. Beatrix Potter d. 1943	356
23	*Tuesday*	Richard Arkwright b. 1732. Thomas Malthus d. 1834	357
24	*Wednesday*	CHANUCAH begins. Vasco de Gama d. 1524	358
25	*Thursday*	**Christmas Day.** *Public Holiday in the UK*	359
26	*Friday*	**St Stephen.** *Bank Holiday in the UK*	360
27	*Saturday*	**St John the Evangelist.** Louis Pasteur b. 1822	361
28	*Sunday*	**1st S. after Christmas.** Paul Hindemith d. 1963	*week* 52 *day* 362
29	*Monday*	**Holy Innocents.** William Gladstone b. 1809	363
30	*Tuesday*	Amelia Bloomer b. 1894. L. P. Hartley b. 1895	364
31	*Wednesday*	RAMADAN begins. John Flamsteed d. 1719	365

ASTRONOMICAL PHENOMENA

d	h	
1	20	Mercury in conjunction with Moon. Mercury 7° S.
3	03	Mars in conjunction with Moon. Mars 5° S.
3	15	Venus in conjunction with Moon. Venus 7° S.
5	06	Jupiter in conjunction with Moon. Jupiter 3° S.
7	17	Mercury at stationary point
9	06	Saturn in conjunction with Moon. Saturn 0°.2 S.
11	23	Venus at greatest brilliancy
16	10	Saturn at stationary point
17	08	Mercury in inferior conjunction
21	20	Sun's longitude 270° ♑
22	22	Mars in conjunction with Venus. Mars 1° S.
26	21	Venus at stationary point
27	12	Mercury at stationary point
28	04	Mercury in conjunction with Moon. Mercury 2° S.
31	13	Venus in conjunction with Moon. Venus 1° S.

MINIMA OF ALGOL

d	h	d	h	d	h
2	23.5	14	10.8	25	22.1
5	20.3	17	07.6	28	18.9
8	17.2	20	04.4	31	15.7
11	14.0	23	01.3		

CONSTELLATIONS

The following constellations are near the meridian at

	d	h		d	h
November	1	24	December	16	21
November	15	23	January	1	20
December	1	22	January	16	19

Ursa Major (below the Pole), Ursa Minor (below the Pole), Cassiopeia, Andromeda, Perseus, Triangulum, Aries, Taurus, Cetus and Eridanus

THE MOON

Phases, Apsides and Node	d	h	m
☽ First Quarter	7	06	09
○ Full Moon	14	02	37
☾ Last Quarter	21	21	43
● New Moon	29	16	57

	d	h	m
Perigee (368,878 km)	9	17	03
Apogee (404,259 km)	21	23	24

Mean longitude of ascending node on December 1, 165°

THE SUN

s.d. 16'.3

Day	Right Ascension	Dec. −	Equation of time	Rise 52°	Rise 56°	Transit	Set 52°	Set 56°	Sidereal time	Transit of First Point of Aries
	h m s	° '	m s	h m	h m	h m	h m	h m	h m s	h m s
1	16 28 26	21 46	+11 07	7 46	8 07	11 49	15 52	15 31	4 39 33	19 17 17
2	16 32 45	21 55	+10 45	7 47	8 08	11 49	15 52	15 30	4 43 30	19 13 21
3	16 37 05	22 04	+10 21	7 48	8 10	11 50	15 51	15 29	4 47 26	19 09 25
4	16 41 25	22 13	+ 9 58	7 50	8 12	11 50	15 50	15 29	4 51 23	19 05 29
5	16 45 46	22 20	+ 9 33	7 51	8 13	11 51	15 50	15 28	4 55 19	19 01 33
6	16 50 08	22 28	+ 9 08	7 52	8 15	11 51	15 50	15 27	4 59 16	18 57 37
7	16 54 30	22 35	+ 8 43	7 54	8 16	11 52	15 49	15 27	5 03 13	18 53 41
8	16 58 52	22 42	+ 8 17	7 55	8 17	11 52	15 49	15 26	5 07 09	18 49 45
9	17 03 15	22 48	+ 7 50	7 56	8 19	11 52	15 49	15 26	5 11 06	18 45 49
10	17 07 39	22 54	+ 7 24	7 57	8 20	11 53	15 49	15 26	5 15 02	18 41 53
11	17 12 02	22 59	+ 6 56	7 58	8 21	11 53	15 48	15 25	5 18 59	18 37 58
12	17 16 27	23 04	+ 6 29	7 59	8 22	11 54	15 48	15 25	5 22 55	18 34 02
13	17 20 51	23 08	+ 6 01	8 00	8 23	11 54	15 48	15 25	5 26 52	18 30 06
14	17 25 16	23 12	+ 5 33	8 01	8 24	11 55	15 48	15 25	5 30 49	18 26 10
15	17 29 41	23 15	+ 5 04	8 02	8 25	11 55	15 49	15 25	5 34 45	18 22 14
16	17 34 07	23 18	+ 4 35	8 03	8 26	11 56	15 49	15 25	5 38 42	18 18 18
17	17 38 32	23 21	+ 4 06	8 03	8 27	11 56	15 49	15 25	5 42 38	18 14 22
18	17 42 58	23 23	+ 3 37	8 04	8 28	11 57	15 49	15 25	5 46 35	18 10 26
19	17 47 24	23 24	+ 3 07	8 05	8 28	11 57	15 50	15 26	5 50 31	18 06 30
20	17 51 50	23 25	+ 2 38	8 05	8 29	11 58	15 50	15 26	5 54 28	18 02 34
21	17 56 17	23 26	+ 2 08	8 06	8 30	11 58	15 50	15 27	5 58 24	17 58 38
22	18 00 43	23 26	+ 1 38	8 06	8 30	11 59	15 51	15 27	6 02 21	17 54 42
23	18 05 09	23 26	+ 1 08	8 07	8 31	11 59	15 52	15 28	6 06 18	17 50 47
24	18 09 36	23 25	I 0 38	8 07	8 31	12 00	15 52	15 28	6 10 14	17 46 51
25	18 14 02	23 24	+ 0 08	8 07	8 31	12 00	15 53	15 29	6 14 11	17 42 55
26	18 18 29	23 22	− 0 21	8 08	8 31	12 01	15 54	15 30	6 18 07	17 38 59
27	18 22 55	23 20	− 0 51	8 08	8 32	12 01	15 54	15 31	6 22 04	17 35 03
28	18 27 21	23 17	− 1 21	8 08	8 32	12 02	15 55	15 32	6 26 00	17 31 07
29	18 31 47	23 14	− 1 50	8 08	8 32	12 02	15 56	15 33	6 29 57	17 27 11
30	18 36 13	23 11	− 2 19	8 08	8 32	12 03	15 57	15 34	6 33 53	17 23 15
31	18 40 38	23 06	− 2 48	8 08	8 31	12 03	15 58	15 35	6 37 50	17 19 19

DURATION OF TWILIGHT (in minutes)

Latitude	52°	56°	52°	56°	52°	56°	52°	56°
	1 December		11 December		21 December		31 December	
Civil	40	45	41	47	41	47	41	47
Nautical	82	93	84	96	85	97	84	96
Astronomical	123	138	125	141	126	142	125	141

THE NIGHT SKY

Mercury is unsuitably placed for observation at first, inferior conjunction occurring on the 17th. For the last week of the month Mercury is visible as a morning object, magnitude +0.9 to 0.0, low above the south-eastern horizon around the beginning of morning civil twilight. On the morning of the 28th the thin sliver of the crescent Moon, little more than one day before New, may be detected with Mercury about 1° below and to the right.

Venus is still a magnificent object in the early evening sky, attaining its greatest brilliancy (magnitude −4.7) on the 11th. It is visible low above the south-western horizon for about two hours after sunset. Observers with telescopes can witness the decreasing crescent phase during the month (falling from 35 per cent to 9 per cent illuminated)

while the diameter increases from 35" to 55". On the evening of the 3rd the crescent Moon is near Venus, but some 6° higher in altitude.

Mars continues to be too close to the Sun for observation.

Jupiter, magnitude −2.2, is still visible as a splendid early evening object, low in the south-western sky. On the evenings of the 4th and 5th the crescent Moon will be seen in the vicinity of the planet.

Saturn, magnitude +0.6, is an evening object in the south-western sky. The Moon, just after First Quarter, is in the vicinity of the planet on the evenings of the 8th and 9th.

Meteors. The maximum of the well-known Geminid meteor showers occurs on the night of the 13th to 14th. The Full Moon will cause serious interference with observations.

THE MOON

Day	RA	Dec.	Hor. par.	Semi-diam.	Sun's co-long.	PA of Bright Limb	Phase	Age	Rise 52°	Rise 56°	Transit	Set 52°	Set 56°
	h m	°	'	'	°	°	%	d	h m	h m	h m	h m	h m
1	17 17	−18.1	56.8	15.5	286	250	1	0.9	8 37	8 56	13 05	17 32	17 14
2	18 12	−18.6	57.2	15.6	298	258	4	1.9	9 33	9 51	14 00	18 28	18 10
3	19 09	−18.2	57.7	15.7	310	257	9	2.9	10 21	10 38	14 54	19 31	19 15
4	20 06	−16.7	58.1	15.8	322	255	17	3.9	11 03	11 18	15 49	20 40	20 27
5	21 02	−14.2	58.5	15.9	334	252	26	4.9	11 39	11 51	16 42	21 54	21 43
6	21 57	−10.9	58.8	16.0	347	250	36	5.9	12 11	12 19	17 35	23 09	23 03
7	22 51	− 6.9	59.1	16.1	359	248	47	6.9	12 40	12 44	18 27	—	—
8	23 45	− 2.6	59.3	16.2	11	246	59	7.9	13 07	13 07	19 18	0 25	0 23
9	0 39	+ 1.9	59.4	16.2	23	246	70	8.9	13 35	13 31	20 11	1 42	1 44
10	1 34	+ 6.4	59.4	16.2	35	246	79	9.9	14 04	13 56	21 04	3 00	3 06
11	2 29	+10.5	59.3	16.2	47	247	88	10.9	14 36	14 25	21 58	4 17	4 27
12	3 25	+13.9	59.1	16.1	60	247	94	11.9	15 13	14 59	22 54	5 32	5 45
13	4 23	+16.5	58.7	16.0	72	242	98	12.9	15 56	15 39	23 49	6 43	6 59
14	5 21	+18.1	58.2	15.8	84	192	100	13.9	16 46	16 28	—	7 47	8 05
15	6 18	+18.7	57.5	15.7	96	114	99	14.9	17 42	17 24	0 45	8 43	9 01
16	7 14	+18.1	56.9	15.5	108	107	96	15.9	18 43	18 26	1 39	9 31	9 47
17	8 08	+16.7	56.2	15.3	120	107	91	16.9	19 46	19 32	2 30	10 10	10 24
18	8 59	+14.4	55.5	15.1	132	109	84	17.9	20 50	20 39	3 19	10 42	10 54
19	9 49	+11.5	55.0	15.0	144	111	76	18.9	21 54	21 47	4 06	11 10	11 19
20	10 36	+ 8.3	54.6	14.9	157	112	68	19.9	22 57	22 53	4 50	11 35	11 40
21	11 22	+ 4.7	54.3	14.8	169	113	59	20.9	—	23 59	5 33	11 58	12 00
22	12 07	+ 0.9	54.2	14.8	181	113	49	21.9	0 00	—	6 15	12 20	12 19
23	12 52	− 2.8	54.3	14.8	193	113	40	22.9	1 03	1 06	6 57	12 42	12 38
24	13 37	− 6.5	54.6	14.9	205	113	31	23.9	2 07	2 13	7 41	13 06	12 58
25	14 24	−10.0	55.0	15.0	217	112	22	24.9	3 11	3 20	8 25	13 32	13 22
26	15 13	−13.1	55.6	15.1	230	110	15	25.9	4 16	4 29	9 13	14 03	13 49
27	16 04	−15.7	56.2	15.3	242	109	8	26.9	5 21	5 36	10 02	14 39	14 23
28	16 58	−17.6	56.9	15.5	254	109	4	27.9	6 24	6 42	10 55	15 23	15 05
29	17 53	−18.6	57.5	15.7	266	119	1	28.9	7 23	7 42	11 50	16 16	15 58
30	18 51	−18.5	58.1	15.8	278	215	0	0.3	8 16	8 34	12 46	17 18	17 00
31	19 49	−17.3	58.7	16.0	291	247	2	1.3	9 02	9 18	13 42	18 27	18 12

MERCURY

Day	RA	Dec.	Diam.	Phase	Transit	5° high 52°	5° high 56°
	h m	°	"	%	h m	h m	h m
1	18 01	−25.6	7	56	13 21	16 00	15 14
3	18 07	−25.4	7	49	13 19	16 01	15 17
5	18 12	−25.0	8	42	13 16	16 01	15 18
7	18 15	−24.6	8	33	13 09	15 59	15 18
9	18 14	−24.1	9	24	13 00	15 54	15 16
11	18 10	−23.5	9	16	12 48	15 47	15 11
13	18 03	−22.9	9	8	12 32	15 37	15 03
15	17 54	−22.2	10	3	12 14	15 25	14 53
17	17 42	−21.5	10	0	11 55	8 40	9 10
19	17 31	−20.9	10	2	11 36	8 15	8 44
21	17 20	−20.4	10	6	11 18	7 54	8 21
23	17 12	−20.0	9	13	11 03	7 36	8 03
25	17 07	−19.8	9	21	10 51	7 22	7 49
27	17 05	−19.8	8	29	10 41	7 13	7 40
29	17 06	−20.0	8	38	10 34	7 07	7 34
31	17 09	−20.2	8	45	10 30	7 05	7 33

VENUS

Day	RA	Dec.	Diam.	Phase	Transit	5° high 52°	5° high 56°
	h m	°	"	%	h m	h m	h m
1	19 41	−24.4	35	35	15 01	17 53	17 13
6	19 56	−23.4	37	31	14 56	17 57	17 21
11	20 08	−22.2	40	27	14 48	17 59	17 27
16	20 17	−21.0	44	22	14 37	17 58	17 29
21	20 23	−19.8	48	18	14 22	17 52	17 26
26	20 24	−18.7	52	13	14 04	17 42	17 18
31	20 22	−17.6	55	9	13 41	17 27	17 04

MARS

Day	RA	Dec.	Diam.	Phase	Transit	5° high 52°	5° high 56°
1	19 13	−23.7	5	95	14 33	17 31	16 53
6	19 29	−23.1	5	95	14 30	17 33	16 57
11	19 46	−22.5	5	96	14 27	17 35	17 02
16	20 02	−21.7	4	96	14 23	17 38	17 07
21	20 19	−20.9	4	96	14 20	17 42	17 13
26	20 35	−19.9	4	96	14 16	17 46	17 19
31	20 51	−18.9	4	97	14 13	17 50	17 25

SUNRISE AND SUNSET

	London		Bristol		Birmingham		Manchester		Newcastle		Glasgow		Belfast	
	0°05′	51°30′	2°35′	51°28′	1°55′	52°28′	2°15′	53°28′	1°37′	54°59′	4°14′	55°52′	5°56′	54°35′
	h m	h m	h m	h m	h m	h m	h m	h m	h m	h m	h m	h m	h m	h m
1	7 44	15 55	7 53	16 05	7 55	15 58	8 02	15 54	8 07	15 43	8 23	15 49	8 22	16 03
2	7 45	15 54	7 55	16 04	7 57	15 57	8 03	15 53	8 09	15 43	8 25	15 48	8 24	16 02
3	7 46	15 54	7 56	16 04	7 58	15 56	8 05	15 53	8 10	15 42	8 26	15 47	8 25	16 01
4	7 48	15 53	7 57	16 03	8 00	15 56	8 06	15 52	8 12	15 41	8 28	15 46	8 27	16 01
5	7 49	15 53	7 59	16 03	8 01	15 55	8 07	15 52	8 13	15 41	8 29	15 46	8 28	16 00
6	7 50	15 52	8 00	16 03	8 02	15 55	8 09	15 51	8 15	15 40	8 31	15 45	8 30	16 00
7	7 51	15 52	8 01	16 02	8 04	15 55	8 10	15 51	8 16	15 40	8 32	15 45	8 31	15 59
8	7 53	15 52	8 02	16 02	8 05	15 54	8 11	15 50	8 17	15 39	8 33	15 44	8 32	15 59
9	7 54	15 52	8 04	16 02	8 06	15 54	8 13	15 50	8 19	15 39	8 35	15 44	8 34	15 58
10	7 55	15 51	8 05	16 02	8 07	15 54	8 14	15 50	8 20	15 38	8 36	15 43	8 35	15 58
11	7 56	15 51	8 06	16 01	8 08	15 54	8 15	15 50	8 21	15 38	8 37	15 43	8 36	15 58
12	7 57	15 51	8 07	16 01	8 09	15 54	8 16	15 50	8 22	15 38	8 38	15 43	8 37	15 58
13	7 58	15 51	8 08	16 01	8 10	15 54	8 17	15 49	8 23	15 38	8 39	15 43	8 38	15 58
14	7 59	15 51	8 08	16 01	8 11	15 54	8 18	15 49	8 24	15 38	8 40	15 43	8 39	15 58
15	7 59	15 51	8 09	16 02	8 12	15 54	8 19	15 50	8 25	15 38	8 41	15 43	8 40	15 58
16	8 00	15 52	8 10	16 02	8 13	15 54	8 19	15 50	8 26	15 38	8 42	15 43	8 41	15 58
17	8 01	15 52	8 11	16 02	8 13	15 54	8 20	15 50	8 27	15 38	8 43	15 43	8 42	15 58
18	8 02	15 52	8 12	16 02	8 14	15 54	8 21	15 50	8 28	15 39	8 44	15 43	8 42	15 58
19	8 02	15 52	8 12	16 03	8 15	15 55	8 22	15 51	8 28	15 39	8 45	15 44	8 43	15 59
20	8 03	15 53	8 13	16 03	8 15	15 55	8 22	15 51	8 29	15 39	8 45	15 44	8 44	15 59
21	8 04	15 53	8 13	16 03	8 16	15 56	8 23	15 51	8 29	15 40	8 46	15 44	8 44	15 59
22	8 04	15 54	8 14	16 04	8 16	15 56	8 23	15 52	8 30	15 40	8 46	15 45	8 45	16 00
23	8 05	15 54	8 14	16 05	8 17	15 57	8 24	15 52	8 30	15 41	8 47	15 46	8 45	16 01
24	8 05	15 55	8 15	16 05	8 17	15 57	8 24	15 53	8 31	15 41	8 47	15 46	8 45	16 01
25	8 05	15 56	8 15	16 06	8 18	15 58	8 24	15 54	8 31	15 42	8 47	15 47	8 46	16 02
26	8 06	15 56	8 15	16 07	8 18	15 59	8 25	15 55	8 31	15 43	8 47	15 48	8 46	16 03
27	8 06	15 57	8 16	16 07	8 18	16 00	8 25	15 55	8 31	15 44	8 48	15 49	8 46	16 04
28	8 06	15 58	8 16	16 08	8 18	16 00	8 25	15 56	8 32	15 45	8 48	15 49	8 46	16 04
29	8 06	15 59	8 16	16 09	8 18	16 01	8 25	15 57	8 32	15 46	8 48	15 50	8 46	16 05
30	8 06	16 00	8 16	16 10	8 18	16 02	8 25	15 58	8 32	15 47	8 48	15 52	8 46	16 06
31	8 06	16 01	8 16	16 11	8 18	16 03	8 25	15 59	8 31	15 48	8 47	15 53	8 46	16 07

JUPITER

Day	RA	Dec.	Transit	5° high	
				52°	56°
	h m	° ′	h m	h m	h m
1	21 17.1	−16 44	16 35	20 26	20 05
11	21 23.7	−16 13	16 03	19 57	19 37
21	21 30.9	−15 38	15 30	19 29	19 10
31	21 38.8	−14 59	14 59	19 02	18 43

Diameters – equatorial 36″ polar 33″

SATURN

Day	RA	Dec.	Transit	5° high	
				52°	56°
	h m	° ′	h m	h m	h m
1	0 54.7	+ 2 59	20 12	1 58	1 57
11	0 54.0	+ 2 57	19 32	1 17	1 17
21	0 53.9	+ 2 59	18 52	0 38	0 37
31	0 54.4	+ 3 06	18 14	0 00	23 55

Diameters – equatorial 18″ polar 17″
Rings – major axis 42″ minor axis 6″

URANUS

Day	RA	Dec.	Transit	10° high	
				52°	56°
	h m	° ′	h m	h m	h m
1	20 32.8	−19 27	15 51	18 36	17 57
11	20 34.5	−19 20	15 13	17 59	17 20
21	20 36.4	−19 13	14 36	17 23	16 45
31	20 38.5	−19 05	13 59	16 47	16 09

Diameter 4″

NEPTUNE

Day	RA	Dec.	Transit	10° high	
				52°	56°
	h m	° ′	h m	h m	h m
1	19 59.8	−20 12	15 18	17 55	17 13
11	20 01.0	−20 09	14 40	17 18	16 35
21	20 02.4	−20 05	14 02	16 41	15 58
31	20 03.8	−20 01	13 24	16 03	15 22

Diameter 2″

RISING AND SETTING TIMES

TABLE 1. SEMI-DIURNAL ARCS (HOUR ANGLES AT RISING/SETTING)

Dec.	Latitude												Dec.
	0°	10°	20°	30°	40°	45°	50°	52°	54°	56°	58°	60°	
	h m	h m	h m	h m	h m	h m	h m	h m	h m	h m	h m	h m	
0°	6 00	6 00	6 00	6 00	6 00	6 00	6 00	6 00	6 00	6 00	6 00	6 00	0°
1°	6 00	6 01	6 01	6 02	6 03	6 04	6 05	6 05	6 06	6 06	6 06	6 07	1°
2°	6 00	6 01	6 03	6 05	6 07	6 08	6 10	6 10	6 11	6 12	6 13	6 14	2°
3°	6 00	6 02	6 04	6 07	6 10	6 12	6 14	6 15	6 17	6 18	6 19	6 21	3°
4°	6 00	6 03	6 06	6 09	6 13	6 16	6 19	6 21	6 22	6 24	6 26	6 28	4°
5°	6 00	6 04	6 07	6 12	6 17	6 20	6 24	6 26	6 28	6 30	6 32	6 35	5°
6°	6 00	6 04	6 09	6 14	6 20	6 24	6 29	6 31	6 33	6 36	6 39	6 42	6°
7°	6 00	6 05	6 10	6 16	6 24	6 28	6 34	6 36	6 39	6 42	6 45	6 49	7°
8°	6 00	6 06	6 12	6 19	6 27	6 32	6 39	6 41	6 45	6 48	6 52	6 56	8°
9°	6 00	6 06	6 13	6 21	6 31	6 36	6 44	6 47	6 50	6 54	6 59	7 04	9°
10°	6 00	6 07	6 15	6 23	6 34	6 41	6 49	6 52	6 56	7 01	7 06	7 11	10°
11°	6 00	6 08	6 16	6 26	6 38	6 45	6 54	6 58	7 02	7 07	7 12	7 19	11°
12°	6 00	6 09	6 18	6 28	6 41	6 49	6 59	7 03	7 08	7 13	7 20	7 26	12°
13°	6 00	6 09	6 19	6 31	6 45	6 53	7 04	7 09	7 14	7 20	7 27	7 34	13°
14°	6 00	6 10	6 21	6 33	6 48	6 58	7 09	7 14	7 20	7 27	7 34	7 42	14°
15°	6 00	6 11	6 22	6 36	6 52	7 02	7 14	7 20	7 27	7 34	7 42	7 51	15°
16°	6 00	6 12	6 24	6 38	6 56	7 07	7 20	7 26	7 33	7 41	7 49	7 59	16°
17°	6 00	6 12	6 26	6 41	6 59	7 11	7 25	7 32	7 40	7 48	7 57	8 08	17°
18°	6 00	6 13	6 27	6 43	7 03	7 16	7 31	7 38	7 46	7 55	8 05	8 17	18°
19°	6 00	6 14	6 29	6 46	7 07	7 21	7 37	7 45	7 53	8 03	8 14	8 26	19°
20°	6 00	6 15	6 30	6 49	7 11	7 25	7 43	7 51	8 00	8 11	8 22	8 36	20°
21°	6 00	6 16	6 32	6 51	7 15	7 30	7 49	7 58	8 08	8 19	8 32	8 47	21°
22°	6 00	6 16	6 34	6 54	7 19	7 35	7 55	8 05	8 15	8 27	8 41	8 58	22°
23°	6 00	6 17	6 36	6 57	7 23	7 40	8 02	8 12	8 23	8 36	8 51	9 09	23°
24°	6 00	6 18	6 37	7 00	7 28	7 46	8 08	8 19	8 31	8 45	9 02	9 22	24°
25°	6 00	6 19	6 39	7 02	7 32	7 51	8 15	8 27	8 40	8 55	9 13	9 35	25°
26°	6 00	6 20	6 41	7 05	7 37	7 57	8 22	8 35	8 49	9 05	9 25	9 51	26°
27°	6 00	6 21	6 43	7 08	7 41	8 03	8 30	8 43	8 58	9 16	9 39	10 08	27°
28°	6 00	6 22	6 45	7 12	7 46	8 08	8 37	8 52	9 08	9 28	9 53	10 28	28°
29°	6 00	6 22	6 47	7 15	7 51	8 15	8 45	9 01	9 19	9 41	10 10	10 55	29°
30°	6 00	6 23	6 49	7 18	7 56	8 21	8 54	9 11	9 30	9 55	10 30	12 00	30°
35°	6 00	6 28	6 59	7 35	8 24	8 58	9 46	10 15	10 58	12 00	12 00	12 00	35°
40°	6 00	6 34	7 11	7 56	8 59	9 48	12 00	12 00	12 00	12 00	12 00	12 00	40°
45°	6 00	6 41	7 25	8 21	9 48	12 00	12 00	12 00	12 00	12 00	12 00	12 00	45°
50°	6 00	6 49	7 43	8 54	12 00	12 00	12 00	12 00	12 00	12 00	12 00	12 00	50°
55°	6 00	6 58	8 05	9 42	12 00	12 00	12 00	12 00	12 00	12 00	12 00	12 00	55°
60°	6 00	7 11	8 36	12 00	12 00	12 00	12 00	12 00	12 00	12 00	12 00	12 00	60°
65°	6 00	7 29	9 25	12 00	12 00	12 00	12 00	12 00	12 00	12 00	12 00	12 00	65°
70°	6 00	7 56	12 00	12 00	12 00	12 00	12 00	12 00	12 00	12 00	12 00	12 00	70°
75°	6 00	8 45	12 00	12 00	12 00	12 00	12 00	12 00	12 00	12 00	12 00	12 00	75°
80°	6 00	12 00	12 00	12 00	12 00	12 00	12 00	12 00	12 00	12 00	12 00	12 00	80°

TABLE 2. CORRECTION FOR REFRACTION AND SEMI-DIAMETER

	m	m	m	m	m	m	m	m	m	m	m	m	
0°	3	3	4	4	4	5	5	5	6	6	6	7	0°
10°	3	3	4	4	4	5	5	6	6	6	7	7	10°
20°	4	4	4	4	5	5	6	7	7	8	8	9	20°
25°	4	4	4	4	5	6	7	8	8	9	11	13	25°
30°	4	4	4	5	6	7	8	9	11	14	21	—	30°

NB: Regarding Table 1. If latitude and declination are of the same sign, take out the respondent directly. If they are of opposite signs, subtract the respondent from 12h.
Example:

Lat.	Dec.	Semi-diurnal arc
+52°	+20°	7h 51m
+52°	−20°	4h 09m

SUNRISE AND SUNSET

The local mean time of sunrise or sunset may be found by obtaining the hour angle from Table 1 and applying it to the time of transit. The hour angle is negative for sunrise and positive for sunset. A small correction to the hour angle, which always has the effect of increasing it numerically, is necessary to allow for the Sun's semi-diameter (16′) and for refraction (34′); it is obtained from Table 2. The resulting local mean time may be converted into the standard time of the country by taking the difference between the longitude of the standard meridian of the country and that of the place, adding it to the local mean time if the place is west of the standard meridian, and subtracting it if the place is east.

Example – Required the New Zealand Mean Time (12h fast on GMT) of sunset on May 23 at Auckland, latitude 36° 50′ S. (or minus), longitude 11h 39m E. Taking the declination as $+20°.6$ (page 33), we find

	h	m
Tabular entry for 30° Lat. and Dec. 20°, opposite signs	+ 5	11
Proportional part for 6° 50′ of Lat.	–	15
Proportional part for 0°.6 of Dec.	–	2
Correction (Table 2)	+	4
Hour angle	4	58
Sun transits (page 33)	11	57
Longitudinal correction	+	21
New Zealand Mean Time	17	16

MOONRISE AND MOONSET

It is possible to calculate the times of moonrise and moonset using Table 1, though the method is more complicated because the apparent motion of the Moon is much more rapid and also more variable than that of the Sun.

The parallax of the Moon, about 57′, is near to the sum of the semi-diameter and refraction but has the opposite effect on these times. It is thus convenient to neglect all three quantities in the method outlined below.

TABLE 3. LONGITUDE CORRECTION

X A h	40m m	45m m	50m m	55m m	60m m	65m m	70m m
1	2	2	2	2	3	3	3
2	3	4	4	5	5	5	6
3	5	6	6	7	8	8	9
4	7	8	8	9	10	11	12
5	8	9	10	11	13	14	15
6	10	11	13	14	15	16	18
7	12	13	15	16	18	19	20
8	13	15	17	18	20	22	23
9	15	17	19	21	23	24	26
10	17	19	21	23	25	27	29
11	18	21	23	25	28	30	32
12	20	23	25	28	30	33	35
13	22	24	27	30	33	35	38
14	23	26	29	32	35	38	41
15	25	28	31	34	38	41	44
16	27	30	33	37	40	43	47
17	28	32	35	39	43	46	50
18	30	34	38	41	45	49	53
19	32	36	40	44	48	51	55
20	33	38	42	46	50	54	58
21	35	39	44	48	53	57	61
22	37	41	46	50	55	60	64
23	38	43	48	53	58	62	67
24	40	45	50	55	60	65	70

Notation

φ = latitude of observer
λ = longitude of observer (measured positively towards the west)
T_{-1} = time of transit of Moon on previous day
T_0 = time of transit of Moon on day in question
T_1 = time of transit of Moon on following day
δ_0 = approximate declination of Moon
δ_R = declination of Moon at moonrise
δ_S = declination of Moon at moonset
h_0 = approximate hour angle of Moon
h_R = hour angle of Moon at moonrise
h_S = hour angle of Moon at moonset
t_R = time of moonrise
t_S = time of moonset

Method

1. With arguments φ, δ_0 enter Table 1 on page 64 to determine h_0 where h_0 is negative for moonrise and positive for moonset.

2. Form approximate times from
$$t_R = T_0 + \lambda + h_0$$
$$t_S = T_0 + \lambda + h_0$$

3. Determine δ_R, δ_S for times t_R, t_S respectively.

4. Re-enter Table 1 on page 64 with
   (*a*) arguments φ, δ_R to determine h_R
   (*b*) arguments φ, δ_S to determine h_S

5. Form $t_R = T_0 + \lambda + h_R + AX$
   $t_S = T_0 + \lambda + h_S + AX$

   where $A = (\lambda + h)$

   and $X = (T_0 - T_{-1})$ if $(\lambda + h)$ is negative
   $X = (T_1 - T_0)$ if $(\lambda + h)$ is positive

   AX is the respondent in Table 3.

Example – To find the times of moonrise and moonset at Vancouver ($\varphi = +49°$, $\lambda = +8h\ 12m$) on 1997 January 7. The starting data (page 18) are

T_{-1} = 9h 24m
T_0 = 10h 22m
T_1 = 11h 23m
δ_0 = $-18°$

1. h_0 = 4h 32m
2. Approximate values
   t_R = 7d 10h 22m + 8h 12m + (−4h 32m)
   = 7d 14h 02m
   t_S = 7d 10h 22m + 8h 12m + (+4h 32m)
   = 7d 23h 06m
3. δ_R = $-18°.2$
   δ_S = $-18°.4$
4. h_R = −4h 31m
   h_S = +4h 30m
5. t_R = 7d 10h 22m + 8h 12m + (−4h 31m) + 9m
   = 7d 14h 12m
   t_S = 7d 10h 22m + 8h 12m + (+4h 30m) + 32m
   = 7d 23h 36m

To get the LMT of the phenomenon the longitude is subtracted from the GMT thus:
Moonrise = 7d 14h 12m − 8h 12m = 7d 06h 00m
Moonset = 7d 23h 36m − 8h 12m = 7d 15h 24m

ECLIPSES AND OCCULTATIONS 1997

ECLIPSES

There will be four eclipses in 1997, two of the Sun and two of the Moon. (Penumbral eclipses are not mentioned in this section as they are too difficult to observe.)

1. A total eclipse of the Sun on March 8–9 is visible as a partial eclipse from Asia, the Philippine Islands, the north-western part of the Pacific Ocean, Alaska, north-western Canada and the Arctic Ocean. The eclipse begins at 8d 23h 17m and ends at 9d 03h 31m. The track of the total phase starts on the borders of the CIS, Sinkiang (China) and Mongolia and then sweeps north-eastwards through the eastern part of the CIS before ending in the Arctic Ocean. The total phase begins at 9d 00h 41m and ends at 9d 02h 06m: the maximum duration is 2m 50s.

2. A partial eclipse of the Moon on March 24 is visible from Africa, the western part of Madagascar, western Asia Minor and western Asia, Europe, the Atlantic Ocean, Iceland, Greenland, the Americas, the eastern Pacific Ocean, and part of Antarctica. The eclipse begins at 2h 58m and ends at 6h 21m. At maximum eclipse 92 per cent of the Moon's diameter is obscured.

3. A partial eclipse of the Sun on September 1–2 is visible from Australasia, the south Pacific Ocean (including New Caledonia and Vanuatu), and part of Antarctica. The eclipse begins at 1d 21h 44m and ends at 2d 23h 23m.

4. A total eclipse of the Moon on September 16 is visible from the western Pacific Ocean, Australasia, Asia, the Indian Ocean, Africa, Europe, Iceland, eastern Greenland, the Atlantic Ocean, the eastern part of South America and Antarctica. The eclipse begins at 17h 08m and ends at 20h 25m. Totality begins at 18h 16m and ends at 19h 18m.

LUNAR OCCULTATIONS

Observations of the times of occultations are made by both amateur and professional astronomers. Such observations are later analysed to yield accurate positions of the Moon; this is one method of determining the difference between ephemeris time and universal time.

Many of the observations made by amateurs are obtained with the use of a stop-watch which is compared with a time-signal immediately after the observation. Thus an accuracy of about one-fifth of a second is obtainable, though the observer's personal equation may amount to one-third or one-half of a second.

The list on page 67 includes most of the occultations visible under favourable conditions in the British Isles. No occultation is included unless the star is at least 10° above the horizon and the Sun sufficiently far below the horizon to permit the star to be seen with the naked eye or with a small telescope. The altitude limit is reduced from 10° to 2° for stars and planets brighter than magnitude 2.0 and such occultations are also predicted in daylight.

The column Phase shows (i) whether a disappearance (D) or reappearance (R) is to be observed; and (ii) whether it is at the dark limb (D) or bright limb (B). The column headed 'El. of Moon' gives the elongation of the Moon from the Sun, in degrees. The elongation increases from 0° at New Moon to 180° at Full Moon and on to 360° (or 0°) at New Moon again. Times and position angles (P), reckoned from the north point in the direction north, east, south, west, are given for Greenwich (lat. 51° 30′, long. 0°) and Edinburgh (lat. 56° 00′, long. 3° 12′ west).

The coefficients a and b are the variations in the GMT for each degree of longitude (positive to the west) and latitude (positive to the north) respectively; they enable approximate times (to within about 1m generally) to be found for any point in the British Isles. If the point of observation is $\Delta\lambda$ degrees west and $\Delta\phi$ degrees north, the approximate time is found by adding $a.\Delta\lambda + b.\Delta\phi$ to the given GMT.

Example: the reappearance of ZC 692 on May 8 at Liverpool, found from both Greenwich and Edinburgh.

	Greenwich	Edinburgh
	°	°
Longitude	0.0	+ 3.2
Long. of Liverpool	+ 3.0	+ 3.0
$\Delta\lambda$	+ 3.0	− 0.2
Latitude	+ 51.5	+ 56.0
Lat. of Liverpool	+ 53.4	+ 53.4
$\Delta\phi$	+ 1.9	− 2.6
	h m	h m
GMT	14 19.0	14 15.0
$a.\Delta\lambda$	− 4.5	+ 0.3
$b.\Delta\phi$	+ 0.6	+ 0.3
	14 15.1	14 15.6

If the occultation is given for one station but not the other, the reason for the suppression is given by the following code:

N = star not occulted
A = star's altitude less than 10° (2° for bright stars and planets)
S = Sun not sufficiently below the horizon
G = occultation is of very short duration

In some cases the coefficients a and b are not given; this is because the occultation is so short that prediction for other places by means of these coefficients would not be reliable.

Observers may like to note that ZC 692 = *Aldebaran* (occulted on March 14, May 8, July 2, July 29 and December 13).

LUNAR OCCULTATIONS 1997

Date		ZC No.	Mag.	Phase	El. of Moon	GREENWICH UT	a	b	P	EDINBURGH UT	a	b	P
					°	h m	m	m	°	h m	m	m	°
January	11	3205	6.8	D.D.	36	17 14.8	−0.9	−0.8	74	17 9.4	−0.8	−0.5	61
	11	3208	6.5	D.D.	36	17 46.0	−0.4	0.2	35	17 47.4	−0.1	0.9	16
	12	3357	6.8	D.D.	50	18 41.9	−0.8	−0.8	72	18 36.8	−0.6	−0.5	58
	16	360	6.8	D.D.	101	17 14.6	−1.5	0.8	87	17 15.2	−1.1	1.2	75
	18	627	6.8	D.D.	126	20 19.8	−1.5	0.8	68	20 20.5	−1.2	1.4	53
	18	636	6.9	D.D.	127	22 52.3	G		2	N			
	19	667	5.3	D.D.	129	2 46.5	0.1	−1.5	95	2 39.6	0.0	−1.5	87
	19	672	6.6	D.D.	129	A				3 6.0	0.5	−2.9	142
	19	677	4.8	D.D.	130	A				3 45.2	0.5	−2.4	136
	20	806	5.1	D.D.	141	A				4 26.0	0.3	−1.6	102
February	12	344	8.4	D.D.	72	A				22 43.8	−0.1	−1.5	87
	13	464	6.4	D.D.	84	21 22.4	−0.7	−1.7	96	21 13.5	−0.8	−1.2	83
	15	741	5.7	D.D.	108	21 18.8	−1.4	0.0	63	21 15.9	−1.3	0.7	48
	16	878	5.5	D.D.	118	19 43.4	−1.6	0.5	80	19 42.4	−1.4	1.2	66
	17	1029	5.1	D.D.	131	22 13.3	G		30	N			
	20	1271	5.9	D.D.	154	2 4.2	−1.2	−0.9	66	1 57.0	−1.2	−0.6	59
March	14	692	1.1	D.D.	76	18 43.2	−1.4	0.0	69	18 40.1	−1.3	0.6	54
	14	692	1.1	R.B.	76	19 55.8	−1.0	−1.6	281	19 44.5	−1.0	−2.0	294
	16	975	6.8	D.D.	99	18 53.0	−1.7	0.0	88	S			
	17	1106	3.7	D.D.	111	21 32.0	−1.2	−1.9	117	21 21.0	−1.2	−1.4	108
	18	1234	6.1	D.D.	123	23 43.7	−0.4	−2.8	144	23 30.4	−0.6	−2.5	137
	20	1428	3.8	D.D.	143	20 7.1	G		170	19 54.1	−0.9	−1.3	151
April	10	635	3.9	D.D.	46	21 42.2	0.6	−2.8	143	21 32.0	0.3	−2.4	130
	13	1073	6.0	D.D.	81	22 33.0	G		162	22 19.0	0.1	−3.1	151
May	8	692	1.1	D.D.	22	13 3.1	−1.6	0.2	92	13 0.7	−1.3	0.7	78
	8	692	1.1	R.B.	23	14 19.0	−1.5	0.3	250	14 15.0	−1.3	−0.1	264
	9	878	5.5	D.D.	38	21 18.5	−0.1	−0.6	51	21 15.6	−0.2	−0.5	42
	12	1271	5.9	D.D.	74	23 35.2	0.1	−1.3	80	23 29.2	0.0	−1.4	76
June	16	2060	6.3	D.D.	131	21 18.1	−0.8	−2.0	164	S			
	16	2064	6.5	D.D.	131	21 45.2	−1.4	−1.1	124	S			
July	2	692	1.1	D.B.	328	4 3.9	0.4	2.5	28	4 18.4	G		12
	2	692	1.1	R.D.	329	4 41.3	−0.6	0.6	308	4 40.8	G		325
	29	635	3.9	R.D.	299	3 14.9	−0.4	1.7	257	S			
	29	692	1.1	D.B.	304	11 26.6	−1.1	−0.1	53	11 24.3	−1.1	0.6	37
	29	692	1.1	R.D.	304	12 23.4	−0.4	−2.4	299	12 10.0	−0.4	−3.0	313
August	5	Mercury	0.4	D.D.	27	A				19 38.2	0.0	−2.3	133
	23	327	4.5	R.D.	244	1 55.2	−1.5	0.4	291	1 51.5	−1.6	0.0	307
September	8	2291	5.5	D.D.	75	19 27.6	−1.3	−2.2	144	19 15.0	−1.2	−1.7	137
	11	2733	6.4	D.D.	113	21 35.8	G		162	21 16.0	−1.6	−1.8	141
	22	699	5.8	R.D.	251	0 13.2	−0.4	1.9	246	0 20.3	−0.4	1.8	256
	22	704	4.9	R.D.	251	0 27.5	0.2	3.4	200	0 40.5	−0.1	2.6	216
October	9	2846	6.9	D.D.	95	21 7.7	−1.4	−2.2	124	A			
	13	3430	5.7	D.D.	148	21 9.6	−1.2	0.9	59	21 10.6	−1.0	1.1	49
	19	635	3.9	R.D.	221	2 54.8	−1.4	1.1	234	2 54.2	−1.2	0.6	249
November	5	2787	6.4	D.D.	63	17 30.0	−1.2	−0.1	56	17 26.3	−1.1	0.0	47
	5	2794	6.7	D.D.	63	18 22.6	−1.5	−1.7	118	18 11.8	−1.3	−1.2	108
	9	3353	3.8	D.D.	114	17 43.5	−1.3	1.0	87	17 44.4	−1.1	1.1	79
	9	3360	6.3	D.D.	115	19 0.7	−1.2	1.0	52	19 2.2	−0.9	1.1	42
	9	3383	6.5	D.D.	117	23 26.9	−0.8	−1.6	97	23 18.1	−0.7	−1.2	82
	12	Saturn	0.4	D.D.	145	1 28.2	−0.5	0.0	43	1 28.0	−0.4	0.7	25
	12	Saturn	0.4	R.B.	146	2 21.2	−0.4	−1.7	278	2 10.4	−0.5	−2.5	295
December	4	3029	6.9	D.D.	57	16 38.2	−1.3	0.1	63	16 35.1	−1.1	0.2	55
	6	3333	6.9	D.D.	85	20 27.1	−1.0	−0.9	79	20 20.9	−0.8	−0.6	65
	8	55	6.4	D.D.	109	17 15.4	−1.2	1.1	82	17 17.4	−1.0	1.3	73
	12	635	3.9	D.D.	164	22 4.2	−1.9	−1.4	128	21 56.1	−1.4	−0.1	110
	13	692	1.1	D.D.	168	A				6 11.3	G		13
	22	1772	4.0	R.D.	274	7 7.9	G		10	N			

MEAN PLACES OF STARS 1997.5

Name	Mag.	RA h m	Dec. ° '	Spectrum	Name	Mag.	RA h m	Dec. ° '	Spectrum
α And *Alpheratz*	2.1	0 08.3	+29 05	A0p	γ Corvi	2.6	12 15.7	−17 32	B8
β Cassiopeiae *Caph*	2.3	0 09.0	+59 08	F5	α Crucis	1.0	12 26.5	−63 05	B1
γ Pegasi *Algenib*	2.8	0 13.1	+15 10	B2	γ Crucis	1.6	12 31.0	−57 06	M3
β Mensae	2.9	0 25.7	−77 16	G0	γ Centauri	2.2	12 41.4	−48 57	A0
α Phoenicis	2.4	0 26.2	−42 19	K0	γ Virginis	2.7	12 41.5	− 1 26	F0
α Cassiopeiae *Schedar*	2.2	0 40.4	+56 31	K0	β Crucis	1.3	12 47.6	−59 41	B1
β Ceti *Diphda*	2.0	0 43.5	−18 00	K0	ε Ursae Majoris *Alioth*	1.8	12 53.9	+55 58	A0p
γ Cassiopeiae*	Var.	0 56.6	+60 42	B0p	α Canum Venaticorum	2.9	12 55.9	+38 20	A0p
β Andromedae *Mirach*	2.1	1 09.6	+35 36	M0	ζ Ursae Majoris *Mizar*	2.1	13 23.8	+54 56	A2p
δ Cassiopeiae	2.7	1 25.7	+60 13	A5	α Virginis *Spica*	1.0	13 25.1	−11 09	B2
α Eridani *Achernar*	0.5	1 37.6	−57 15	B5	ε Centauri	2.6	13 39.7	−53 27	B1
β Arietis *Sheratan*	2.6	1 54.5	+20 48	A5	η Ursae Majoris *Alkaid*	1.9	13 47.4	+49 20	B3
γ Andromedae *Almak*	2.3	2 03.7	+42 19	K0	β Centauri *Hadar*	0.6	14 03.6	−60 22	B1
α Arietis *Hamal*	2.0	2 07.0	+23 27	K2	θ Centauri	2.1	14 06.5	−36 21	K0
α Ursae Minoris *Polaris*	2.0	2 29.1	+89 15	F8	α Bootis *Arcturus*	0.0	14 15.5	+19 12	K0
β Persei *Algol*	Var.	3 08.0	+40 57	B8	α Centauri *Rigil Kent*	0.1	14 39.4	−60 49	G0
α Persei *Mirfak*	1.8	3 24.1	+49 51	F5	ε Bootis	2.4	14 44.9	+27 05	K0
η Tauri *Alcyone*	2.9	3 47.3	+24 06	B5p	β UMi *Kochab*	2.1	14 50.7	+74 10	K5
α Tauri *Aldebaran*	0.9	4 35.8	+16 30	K5	γ Ursae Minoris	3.1	15 20.7	+71 51	A2
β Orionis *Rigel*	0.1	5 14.4	− 8 12	B8p	α CrB *Alphecca*	2.2	15 34.6	+26 43	A0
α Aurigae *Capella*	0.1	5 16.5	+46 00	G0	β Trianguli Australis	3.0	15 54.9	−63 25	F0
γ Orionis *Bellatrix*	1.6	5 25.0	+ 6 21	B2	δ Scorpii	2.3	16 00.2	−22 37	B0
β Tauri *Elnath*	1.7	5 26.1	+28 36	B8	β Scorpii	2.6	16 05.3	−19 48	B1
δ Orionis	2.2	5 31.9	− 0 18	B0	α Scorpii *Antares*	1.0	16 29.3	−26 26	M0
α Leporis	2.6	5 32.6	−17 49	F0	α Trianguli Australis	1.9	16 48.4	−69 01	K2
ε Orionis	1.7	5 36.1	− 1 12	B0	ε Scorpii	2.3	16 50.0	−34 17	K0
ζ Orionis	1.8	5 40.6	− 1 57	B0	α Herculis†	Var.	17 14.5	+14 24	M3
κ Orionis	2.1	5 47.6	− 9 40	B0	λ Scorpii	1.6	17 33.4	−37 06	B2
α Orionis *Betelgeuse*	Var.	5 55.0	+ 7 24	M0	α Ophiuchi *Rasalhague*	2.1	17 34.8	+12 34	A5
β Aurigae *Menkalinan*	1.9	5 59.3	+44 57	A0p	θ Scorpii	1.9	17 37.1	−43 00	F0
β CMa *Mirzam*	2.0	6 22.6	−17 57	B1	κ Scorpii	2.4	17 42.3	−39 02	B2
α Carinae *Canopus*	−0.7	6 23.9	−52 42	F0	γ Draconis	2.2	17 56.5	+51 29	K5
γ Geminorum *Alhena*	1.9	6 37.6	+16 24	A0	ε Sgr *Kaus Australis*	1.9	18 24.0	−34 23	A0
α Canis Majoris *Sirius*	−1.5	6 45.0	−16 43	A0	α Lyrae *Vega*	0.0	18 36.9	+38 47	A0
ε Canis Majoris	1.5	6 58.5	−28 58	B1	σ Sagittarii	2.0	18 55.1	−26 18	B3
δ Canis Majoris	1.9	7 08.3	−26 23	F8p	β Cygni *Albireo*	3.1	19 30.6	+27 57	K0
α Geminorum *Castor*	1.6	7 34.4	+31 54	A0	α Aquilae *Altair*	0.8	19 50.7	+ 8 52	A5
α CMi *Procyon*	0.4	7 39.2	+ 5 14	F5	α Capricorni	3.8	20 17.9	−12 33	G5
β Geminorum *Pollux*	1.1	7 45.2	+28 02	K0	γ Cygni	2.2	20 22.1	+40 15	F8p
ζ Puppis	2.3	8 03.5	−40 00	Od	α Pavonis	1.9	20 25.5	−56 45	B3
γ Velorum	1.8	8 09.5	−47 20	Oap	α Cygni *Deneb*	1.3	20 41.3	+45 16	A2p
ε Carinae	1.9	8 22.5	−59 30	K0	α Cephei *Alderamin*	2.4	21 18.5	+62 35	A5
δ Velorum	2.0	8 44.6	−54 42	A0	ε Pegasi	2.4	21 44.1	+ 9 52	K0
λ Velorum *Suhail*	2.2	9 07.9	−43 25	K5	δ Capricorni	2.9	21 46.9	−16 08	A5
β Carinae	1.7	9 13.2	−69 42	A0	α Gruis	1.7	22 08.1	−46 58	B5
ι Carinae	2.2	9 17.0	−59 16	F0	δ Cephei†	3.7	22 29.1	+58 24	†
κ Velorum	2.6	9 22.0	−55 00	B3	β Gruis	2.1	22 42.5	−46 54	M3
α Hydrae *Alphard*	2.0	9 27.5	− 8 39	K2	α PsA *Fomalhaut*	1.2	22 57.5	−29 38	A3
α Leonis *Regulus*	1.3	10 08.2	+11 59	B8	β Pegasi *Scheat*	2.4	23 03.7	+28 04	M0
γ Leonis *Algeiba*	1.9	10 19.8	+19 51	K0	α Pegasi *Markab*	2.5	23 04.6	+15 12	A0
β Ursae Majoris *Merak*	2.4	11 01.7	+56 24	A0					
α Ursae Majoris *Dubhe*	1.8	11 03.6	+61 46	K0	*γ Cassiopeiae, 1996 mag. 2.5. β Persei, mag. 2.1 to 3.4.				
δ Leonis	2.6	11 14.0	+20 32	A3	α Orionis, mag. 0.1 to 1.2.				
β Leonis *Denebola*	2.1	11 48.9	+14 35	A2	†α Herculis, mag. 3.1 to 3.9. δ Cephei, mag. 3.7 to 4.4,				
γ Ursae Majoris *Phecda*	2.4	11 53.7	+53 43	A0	Spectrum F5 to G0.				

The positions of heavenly bodies on the celestial sphere are defined by two co-ordinates, right ascension and declination, which are analogous to longitude and latitude on the surface of the Earth. If we imagine the plane of the terrestrial equator extended indefinitely, it will cut the celestial sphere in a great circle known as the celestial equator. Similarly the plane of the Earth's orbit, when extended, cuts in the great circle called the ecliptic. The two intersections of these circles are known as the First Point of Aries and the First Point of Libra. If from any star a perpendicular be drawn to the celestial equator, the length of this perpendicular is the star's declination. The arc, measured eastwards along the equator from the First Point of Aries to the foot of this perpendicular, is the right ascension. An alternative definition of right ascension is that it is the angle at the celestial pole (where the Earth's axis, if prolonged, would meet the sphere) between the great circles to the First Point of Aries and to the star.

The plane of the Earth's equator has a slow movement, so that our reference system for right ascension and declination is not fixed. The consequent alteration in these quantities from year to year is called precession. In right ascension it is an increase of about 3 seconds a year for equatorial stars, and larger or smaller changes in either direction for stars near the poles, depending on the right ascension of the star. In declination it varies between $+20''$ and $-20''$ according to the right ascension of the star.

A star or other body crosses the meridian when the sidereal time is equal to its right ascension. The altitude is then a maximum, and may be deduced by remembering that the altitude of the elevated pole is numerically equal to the latitude, while that of the equator at its intersection with the meridian is equal to the co-latitude, or complement of the latitude.

Thus in London (lat. 51° 30′) the meridian altitude of Sirius is found as follows:

	°	′
Altitude of equator	38	30
Declination south	16	43
Difference	21	47

The altitude of Capella (Dec. $+46°\ 00'$) at lower transit is:

	°	′
Altitude of pole	51	30
Polar distance of star	44	00
Difference	7	30

The brightness of a heavenly body is denoted by its magnitude. Omitting the exceptionally bright stars Sirius and Canopus, the twenty brightest stars are of the first magnitude, while the faintest stars visible to the naked eye are of the sixth magnitude. The magnitude scale is a precise one, as a difference of five magnitudes represents a ratio of 100 to 1 in brightness. Typical second magnitude stars are Polaris and the stars in the belt of Orion. The scale is most easily fixed in memory by comparing the stars with Norton's *Star Atlas* (*see* page 71). The stars Sirius and Canopus and the planets Venus and Jupiter are so bright that their magnitudes are expressed by negative numbers. A small telescope will show stars down to the ninth or tenth magnitude, while stars fainter than the twentieth magnitude may be photographed by long exposures with the largest telescopes.

MEAN AND SIDEREAL TIME

Acceleration

h	m s	m s	s
1	0 10	0 00	
2	0 20	3 02	0
3	0 30	9 07	1
4	0 39	15 13	2
5	0 49	21 18	3
6	0 59	27 23	4
7	1 09	33 28	5
8	1 19	39 34	6
9	1 29	45 39	7
10	1 39	51 44	8
11	1 48	57 49	9
12	1 58	60 00	10
13	2 08		
14	2 18		
15	2 28		
16	2 38		
17	2 48		
18	2 57		
19	3 07		
20	3 17		
21	3 27		
22	3 37		
23	3 47		
24	3 57		

Retardation

h	m s	m s	s
1	0 10	0 00	
2	0 20	3 03	0
3	0 29	9 09	1
4	0 39	15 15	2
5	0 49	21 21	3
6	0 59	27 28	4
7	1 09	33 34	5
8	1 19	39 40	6
9	1 28	45 46	7
10	1 38	51 53	8
11	1 48	57 59	9
12	1 58	60 00	10
13	2 08		
14	2 18		
15	2 27		
16	2 37		
17	2 47		
18	2 57		
19	3 07		
20	3 17		
21	3 26		
22	3 36		
23	3 46		
24	3 56		

The length of a sidereal day in mean time is 23h 56m 04s.09. Hence 1h MT = 1h + 9s.86 ST and 1h ST = 1h − 9s.83 MT.

To convert an interval of mean time to the corresponding interval of sidereal time, enter the acceleration table with the given mean time (taking the hours and the minutes and seconds separately) and add the acceleration obtained to the given mean time. To convert an interval of sidereal time to the corresponding interval of mean time, take out the retardation for the given sidereal time and subtract.

The columns for the minutes and seconds of the argument are in the form known as critical tables. To use these tables, find in the appropriate left-hand column the two entries between which the given number of minutes and seconds lies; the quantity in the right-hand column between these two entries is the required acceleration or retardation. Thus the acceleration for 11m 26s (which lies between the entries 9m 07s and 15m 13s) is 2s. If the given number of minutes and seconds is a tabular entry, the required acceleration or retardation is the entry in the right-hand column above the given tabular entry, e.g. the retardation for 45m 46s is 7s.

Example – Convert 14h 27m 35s from ST to MT

	h	m	s
Given ST	14	27	35
Retardation for 14h		2	18
Retardation for 27m 35s			5
Corresponding MT	14	25	12

For further explanation, *see* pages 73–4.

ECLIPSES AND SHADOW TRANSITS OF JUPITER'S SATELLITES 1997

GMT d h m	Sat.	Phen.
APRIL		
9 05 17	I	Sh.I
20 03 58	II	Ec.D
24 04 42	IV	Sh.E
25 03 33	I	Sh.I
28 04 17	III	Ec.R
29 04 35	II	Sh.E
MAY		
6 04 19	II	Sh.I
11 04 05	I	Sh.E
16 02 16	III	Sh.E
18 03 42	I	Sh.I
22 03 35	II	Ec.D
23 02 42	III	Sh.I
26 02 55	I	Ec.D
27 02 20	I	Sh.E
31 01 21	II	Sh.I
JUNE		
3 01 57	I	Sh.I
5 03 15	IV	Ec.R
11 01 10	I	Ec.D
12 00 37	I	Sh.E
16 00 40	II	Ec.D
18 03 04	I	Ec.D
19 00 13	I	Sh.I
19 02 31	I	Sh.E
23 03 16	II	Ec.D
25 01 14	I	Sh.E
26 02 07	I	Sh.I
28 02 15	III	Sh.E
30 00 28	IV	Sh.I
JULY		
2 00 57	II	Sh.I
4 01 20	I	Ec.D
5 00 47	I	Sh.E
5 02 38	III	Sh.I
9 03 32	II	Sh.I
11 03 14	I	Ec.D
12 00 24	I	Sh.I
12 02 42	I	Sh.E
16 23 28	IV	Sh.E
18 00 24	II	Ec.D
19 02 18	I	Sh.I
19 22 15	II	Sh.E
19 23 36	I	Ec.D
20 23 05	I	Sh.E
23 00 33	III	Ec.D
25 03 01	II	Ec.D
26 04 13	I	Sh.I
26 21 58	II	Sh.I
27 00 49	II	Sh.E
27 01 30	I	Ec.D
27 22 41	I	Sh.I
28 00 59	I	Sh.E
AUGUST		
2 22 17	III	Sh.E
3 00 32	II	Sh.I
3 03 24	II	Sh.E

GMT d h m	Sat.	Phen.
AUGUST		
3 03 24	I	Ec.D
4 00 36	I	Sh.I
4 02 54	I	Sh.E
4 21 53	I	Ec.D
5 21 23	I	Sh.E
9 22 39	III	Sh.I
10 02 18	III	Sh.E
10 03 07	II	Sh.I
11 02 31	I	Sh.I
11 03 46	IV	Ec.R
12 00 30	II	Ec.R
12 02 05	I	Ec.R
12 20 59	I	Sh.I
12 23 18	I	Sh.E
13 20 33	I	Ec.R
17 02 39	III	Sh.I
19 03 08	II	Ec.R
19 22 55	I	Sh.I
20 01 13	I	Sh.E
20 20 14	II	Ec.R
20 21 51	II	Sh.E
20 22 28	I	Ec.R
21 19 42	I	Sh.E
27 00 50	I	Sh.I
27 21 34	II	Sh.I
27 21 55	IV	Ec.R
28 00 14	III	Ec.R
28 00 22	I	Ec.R
28 00 25	II	Sh.E
28 21 37	I	Sh.E
SEPTEMBER		
4 00 09	II	Sh.I
4 21 14	I	Sh.I
4 23 32	I	Sh.E
5 01 10	IV	Sh.I
5 20 46	I	Ec.R
5 21 43	II	Ec.R
11 23 09	I	Sh.I
12 01 27	I	Sh.E
12 22 40	I	Ec.R
13 00 21	II	Ec.R
13 19 56	I	Sh.E
14 18 45	III	Sh.I
14 18 53	II	Sh.E
14 22 23	III	Sh.E
19 01 05	I	Sh.I
20 00 35	I	Ec.R
20 19 34	I	Sh.I
20 21 52	I	Sh.E
21 18 38	II	Sh.I
21 19 04	I	Ec.R
21 19 24	IV	Sh.I
21 21 28	II	Sh.E
21 22 46	III	Sh.I
22 00 12	IV	Sh.E
27 21 30	I	Sh.I
27 23 47	I	Sh.E
28 20 59	I	Ec.R
28 21 13	II	Sh.I
29 00 03	II	Sh.E
29 18 16	I	Sh.E
30 18 57	II	Ec.R

GMT d h m	Sat.	Phen.
OCTOBER		
2 20 19	III	Ec.R
4 23 25	I	Sh.I
5 22 54	I	Ec.R
5 23 49	II	Sh.I
6 20 11	I	Sh.E
7 21 35	II	Ec.R
8 18 25	IV	Sh.E
9 20 41	III	Ec.D
13 19 50	I	Sh.I
13 22 07	I	Sh.E
14 19 18	I	Ec.R
16 18 32	II	Sh.E
20 18 30	III	Sh.E
20 21 46	I	Sh.I
21 21 13	I	Ec.R
22 18 32	I	Sh.E
23 18 19	II	Sh.I
23 21 08	II	Sh.E
27 18 55	III	Sh.I
27 22 32	III	Sh.E
29 18 11	I	Sh.I
29 20 27	I	Sh.E
30 17 38	I	Ec.R
30 20 55	II	Sh.I
NOVEMBER		
1 18 48	II	Ec.R
2 17 53	IV	Ec.D
5 20 06	I	Sh.I
6 19 33	I	Ec.R
8 21 26	II	Ec.R
13 21 28	I	Ec.R

GMT d h m	Sat.	Phen.
NOVEMBER		
14 16 49	III	Ec.D
14 18 48	I	Sh.E
14 20 28	III	Ec.R
17 18 15	II	Sh.E
19 16 48	IV	Ec.R
21 18 27	I	Sh.I
21 20 44	I	Sh.E
21 20 50	III	Ec.D
22 17 53	I	Ec.R
24 18 02	II	Sh.I
24 20 52	II	Sh.E
27 20 25	IV	Sh.I
28 20 23	I	Sh.I
29 19 48	I	Ec.R
30 17 08	I	Sh.E
DECEMBER		
1 20 39	II	Sh.I
2 18 40	III	Sh.E
3 18 38	II	Ec.R
7 16 47	I	Sh.I
7 19 04	I	Sh.E
9 19 06	III	Sh.I
14 18 43	I	Sh.I
14 19 18	IV	Sh.E
15 18 08	I	Ec.R
19 18 01	II	Sh.E
20 16 34	III	Ec.R
23 17 24	I	Sh.E
26 17 49	II	Sh.I
27 16 58	III	Ec.D
30 17 02	I	Sh.I

Jupiter's satellites transit across the disk from east to west, and pass behind the disk from west to east. The shadows that they cast also transit across the disk. With the exception at times of Satellite IV, the satellites also pass through the shadow of the planet, i.e. they are eclipsed. Just before opposition the satellite disappears in the shadow to the west of the planet and reappears from occultation on the east limb. Immediately after opposition the satellite is occulted at the west limb and reappears from eclipse to the east of the planet. At times approximately two to four months before and after opposition, both phases of eclipses of Satellite III may be seen. When Satellite IV is eclipsed, both phases may be seen.

The times given refer to the centre of the satellite. As the satellite is of considerable size, the immersion and emersion phases are not instantaneous. Even when the satellite enters or leaves the shadow along a radius of the shadow, the phase can last for several minutes. With Satellite IV, grazing phenomena can occur so that the light from the satellite may fade and brighten again without a complete eclipse taking place.

The list of phenomena gives most of the eclipses and shadow transits visible in the British Isles under favourable conditions.

Ec. = Eclipse	R. = Reappearance
Sh. = Shadow transit	I. = Ingress
D. = Disappearance	E. = Egress

EXPLANATION OF ASTRONOMICAL DATA

Positions of the heavenly bodies are given only to the degree of accuracy required by amateur astronomers for setting telescopes, or for plotting on celestial globes or star atlases. Where intermediate positions are required, linear interpolation may be employed.

Definitions of the terms used cannot be given here. They must be sought in astronomical literature and textbooks. Probably the best source for the amateur is Norton's *Star Atlas and Reference Handbook* (Longman, 18th edition, 1989; £25.00), which contains an introduction to observational astronomy, and a series of star maps for showing stars visible to the naked eye. Certain more extended ephemerides are available in the British Astronomical Association Handbook, an annual popular among amateur astronomers (Secretary: Burlington House, Piccadilly, London WIV 9AG).

A special feature has been made of the times when the various heavenly bodies are visible in the British Isles. Since two columns, calculated for latitudes 52° and 56°, are devoted to risings and settings, the range 50° to 58° can be covered by interpolation and extrapolation. The times given in these columns are Greenwich Mean Times for the meridian of Greenwich. An observer west of this meridian must add his/her longitude (in time) and vice versa.

In accordance with the usual convention in astronomy, + and − indicate respectively north and south latitudes or declinations.

All data are, unless otherwise stated, for 0h Greenwich Mean Time (GMT), i.e. at the midnight at the beginning of the day named. Allowance must be made for British Summer Time during the period that this is in operation (*see* pages 15 and 75).

PAGE ONE OF EACH MONTH

The calendar for each month is explained on page 15.

Under the heading Astronomical Phenomena will be found particulars of the more important conjunctions of the Sun, Moon and planets with each other, and also the dates of other astronomical phenomena of special interest.

Times of Minima of Algol are approximate times of the middle of the period of diminished light.

The Constellations listed each month are those that are near the meridian at the beginning of the month at 22h local mean time. Allowance must be made for British Summer Time if necessary. The fact that any star crosses the meridian 4m earlier each night or 2h earlier each month may be used, in conjunction with the lists given each month, to find what constellations are favourably placed at any moment. The table preceding the list of constellations may be extended indefinitely at the rate just quoted.

The principal phases of the Moon are the GMTs when the difference between the longitude of the Moon and that of the Sun is 0°, 90°, 180° or 270°. The times of perigee and apogee are those when the Moon is nearest to, and farthest from, the Earth, respectively. The nodes or points of intersection of the Moon's orbit and the ecliptic make a complete retrograde circuit of the ecliptic in about 19 years. From a knowledge of the longitude of the ascending node and the inclination, whose value does not vary much from 5°, the path of the Moon among the stars may be plotted on a celestial globe or star atlas.

PAGE TWO OF EACH MONTH

The Sun's semi-diameter, in arc, is given once a month.

The right ascension and declination (Dec.) is that of the true Sun. The right ascension of the mean Sun is obtained by applying the equation of time, with the sign given, to the right ascension of the true Sun, or, more easily, by applying 12h to the Sidereal Time. The direction in which the equation of time has to be applied in different problems is a frequent source of confusion and error. Apparent Solar Time is equal to the Mean Solar Time plus the Equation of Time. For example at noon on August 8 the Equation of Time is −5m 36s and thus at 12h Mean Time on that day the Apparent Time is 12h −5m 36s = 11h 54m 24s.

The Greenwich Sidereal Time at 0h and the Transit of the First Point of Aries (which is really the mean time when the sidereal time is 0h) are used for converting mean time to sidereal time and vice versa.

The GMT of transit of the Sun at Greenwich may also be taken as the local mean time (LMT) of transit in any longitude. It is independent of latitude. The GMT of transit in any longitude is obtained by adding the longitude to the time given if west, and vice versa.

LIGHTING-UP TIME

The legal importance of sunrise and sunset is that the Road Vehicles Lighting Regulations 1989 (SI 1989 No. 1796) make the use of front and rear position lamps on vehicles compulsory during the period between sunset and sunrise. Headlamps on vehicles are required to be used during the hours of darkness on unlit roads or whenever visibility is seriously reduced. The hours of darkness are defined in these regulations as the period between half an hour after sunset and half an hour before sunrise.

In all laws and regulations 'sunset' refers to the local sunset, i.e. the time at which the Sun sets at the place in question. This common-sense interpretation has been upheld by legal tribunals. Thus the necessity for providing for different latitudes and longitudes, as already described, is evident.

SUNRISE AND SUNSET

The times of sunrise and sunset are those when the Sun's upper limb, as affected by refraction, is on the true horizon of an observer at sea-level. Assuming the mean refraction to be 34′, and the Sun's semi-diameter to be 16′, the time given is that when the true zenith distance of the Sun's centre is 90° + 34′ + 16′ or 90° 50′, or, in other words, when the depression of the Sun's centre below the true horizon is 50′. The upper limb is then 34′ below the true horizon, but is brought there by refraction. It is true, of course, that an observer on a ship might see the Sun for a minute or so longer, because of the dip of the horizon, while another viewing the sunset over hills or mountains would record an earlier time. Nevertheless, the moment when the true zenith distance of the Sun's centre is 90° 50′ is a precise time dependent only on the latitude and longitude of the place, and independent of its altitude above sea-level, the contour of its horizon, the vagaries of refraction or the small seasonal change in the Sun's semi-diameter; this moment is suitable in every way as a definition of sunset (or sunrise) for all statutory purposes. (For further information, *see* footnote on page 72.)

TWILIGHT

Light reaches us before sunrise and continues to reach us for some time after sunset. The interval between darkness and sunrise or sunset and darkness is called twilight. Astronomically speaking, twilight is considered to begin or end when the Sun's centre is 18° below the horizon, as no light from the Sun can then reach the observer. As thus defined twilight may last several hours; in high latitudes at the summer solstice the depression of 18° is not reached, and twilight lasts from sunset to sunrise.

The need for some sub-division of twilight is met by dividing the gathering darkness into four stages.

(1) *Sunrise or Sunset*, defined as above
(2) *Civil twilight*, which begins or ends when the Sun's centre is 6° below the horizon. This marks the time when operations requiring daylight may commence or must cease. In England it varies from about 30 to 60 minutes after sunset and the same interval before sunrise
(3) *Nautical twilight*, which begins or ends when the Sun's centre is 12° below the horizon. This marks the time when it is, to all intents and purposes, completely dark
(4) *Astronomical twilight*, which begins or ends when the Sun's centre is 18° below the horizon. This marks theoretical perfect darkness. It is of little practical importance, especially if nautical twilight is tabulated

To assist observers the durations of civil, nautical and astronomical twilights are given at intervals of ten days. The beginning of a particular twilight is found by subtracting the duration from the time of sunrise, while the end is found by adding the duration to the time of sunset. Thus the beginning of astronomical twilight in latitude 52°, on the Greenwich meridian, on March 11 is found as 06h 24m − 113m = 04h 31m and similarly the end of civil twilight as 17h 57m + 34m = 18h 31m. The letters TAN (twilight all night) are printed when twilight lasts all night.

Under the heading The Night Sky will be found notes describing the position and visibility of the planets and other phenomena.

PAGE THREE OF EACH MONTH

The Moon moves so rapidly among the stars that its position is given only to the degree of accuracy that permits linear interpolation. The right ascension (RA) and declination (Dec.) are geocentric, i.e. for an imaginary observer at the centre of the Earth. To an observer on the surface of the Earth the position is always different, as the altitude is always less on account of parallax, which may reach 1°.

The lunar terminator is the line separating the bright from the dark part of the Moon's disk. Apart from irregularities of the lunar surface, the terminator is elliptical, because it is a circle seen in projection. It becomes the full circle forming the limb, or edge, of the Moon at New and Full Moon. The selenographic longitude of the terminator is measured from the mean centre of the visible disk, which may differ from the visible centre by as much as 8°, because of libration.

Instead of the longitude of the terminator the Sun's selenographic co-longitude (Sun's co-long.) is tabulated. It is numerically equal to the selenographic longitude of the morning terminator, measured eastwards from the mean centre of the disk. Thus its value is approximately 270° at New Moon, 360° at First Quarter, 90° at Full Moon and 180° at Last Quarter.

The Position Angle (PA) of the Bright Limb is the position angle of the midpoint of the illuminated limb, measured eastwards from the north point on the disk. The Phase column shows the percentage of the area of the Moon's disk illuminated; this is also the illuminated percentage of the diameter at right angles to the line of cusps. The terminator is a semi-ellipse whose major axis is the line of cusps, and whose semi-minor axis is determined by the tabulated percentage; from New Moon to Full Moon the east limb is dark, and vice versa.

The times given as moonrise and moonset are those when the upper limb of the Moon is on the horizon of an observer at sea-level. The Sun's horizontal parallax (Hor. par.) is about 9″, and is negligible when considering sunrise and sunset, but that of the Moon averages about 57′. Hence the computed time represents the moment when the true zenith distance of the Moon is 90° 50′ (as for the Sun) minus the horizontal parallax. The time required for the Sun or Moon to rise or set is about four minutes (except in high latitudes). *See also* page 65 and footnote below.

The GMT of transit of the Moon over the meridian of Greenwich is given; these times are independent of latitude but must be corrected for longitude. For places in the British Isles it suffices to add the longitude if west, and vice versa. For other places a further correction is necessary because of the rapid movement of the Moon relative to the stars. The entire correction is conveniently determined by first finding the west longitude λ of the place. If the place is in west longitude, λ is the ordinary west longitude; if the place is in east longitude λ is the complement to 24h (or 360°) of the longitude and will be greater than 12h (or 180°). The correction then consists of two positive portions, namely λ and the fraction λ/24 (or λ°/360) multiplied by the difference between consecutive transits. Thus for Sydney, New South Wales, the longitude is 10h 05m east, so λ=13h 55m and the fraction λ/24 is 0.58. The transit on the local date 1997 January 15 is found as follows:

		d	h	m
GMT of transit at Greenwich	Jan.	15	17	53
λ			13	55
0.58×(18h 43m−17h 53m)				29
GMT of transit at Sydney		16	08	17
Corr. to NSW Standard Time			10	00
Local standard time of transit		16	18	17

As is evident, for any given place the quantities λ and the correction to local standard time may be combined permanently, being here 23h 55m.

Positions of Mercury are given for every second day, and those of Venus and Mars for every fifth day; they may be interpolated linearly. The diameter (Diam.) is given in seconds of arc. The phase is the illuminated percentage of the disk. In the case of the inner planets this approaches 100 at superior conjunction and 0 at inferior conjunction. When the phase is less than 50 the planet is crescent-shaped or horned; for greater phases it is gibbous. In the case of the exterior planet Mars, the phase approaches 100 at conjunction and opposition, and is a minimum at the quadratures.

Since the planets cannot be seen when on the horizon, the actual times of rising and setting are not given; instead, the time when the planet has an apparent altitude of 5° has

---

SUNRISE, SUNSET AND MOONRISE, MOONSET

The tables have been constructed for the meridian of Greenwich, and for latitudes 52° and 56°. They give Greenwich Mean Time (GMT) throughout the year. To obtain the GMT of the phenomenon as seen from any other latitude and longitude in the British Isles, first interpolate or extrapolate for latitude by the usual rules of proportion. To the time thus found, the longitude (expressed in time) is to be added if west (as it usually is in Great Britain) or subtracted if east. If the longitude is expressed in degrees and minutes of arc, it must be converted to time at the rate of 1° = 4m and 15′ = 1m.

A method of calculating rise and set times for other places in the world is given on pages 64 and 65

been tabulated. If the time of transit is between 00h and 12h the time refers to an altitude of 5° above the eastern horizon; if between 12h and 24h, to the western horizon. The phenomenon tabulated is the one that occurs between sunset and sunrise. The times given may be interpolated for latitude and corrected for longitude, as in the case of the Sun and Moon.

The GMT at which the planet transits the Greenwich meridian is also given. The times of transit are to be corrected to local meridians in the usual way, as already described.

PAGE FOUR OF EACH MONTH

The GMTs of sunrise and sunset for seven cities, whose adopted positions in longitude (W.) and latitude (N.) are given immediately below the name, may be used not only for these phenomena, but also for lighting-up times (*see* page 71 for a fuller explanation).

The particulars for the four outer planets resemble those for the planets on Page Three of each month, except that, under Uranus and Neptune, times when the planet is 10° high instead of 5° high are given; this is because of the inferior brightness of these planets. The diameters given for the rings of Saturn are those of the major axis (in the plane of the planet's equator) and the minor axis respectively. The former has a small seasonal change due to the slightly varying distance of the Earth from Saturn, but the latter varies from zero when the Earth passes through the ring plane every 15 years to its maximum opening half-way between these periods. The rings were last open at their widest extent in 1988.

TIME

From the earliest ages, the natural division of time into recurring periods of day and night has provided the practical time-scale for the everyday activities of the human race. Indeed, if any alternative means of time measurement is adopted, it must be capable of adjustment so as to remain in general agreement with the natural time-scale defined by the diurnal rotation of the Earth on its axis. Ideally the rotation should be measured against a fixed frame of reference; in practice it must be measured against the background provided by the celestial bodies. If the Sun is chosen as the reference point, we obtain Apparent Solar Time, which is the time indicated by a sundial. It is not a uniform time but is subject to variations which amount to as much as a quarter of an hour in each direction. Such wide variations cannot be tolerated in a practical time-scale, and this has led to the concept of Mean Solar Time in which all the days are exactly the same length and equal to the average length of the Apparent Solar Day.

The positions of the stars in the sky are specified in relation to a fictitious reference point in the sky known as the First Point of Aries (or the Vernal Equinox). It is therefore convenient to adopt this same reference point when considering the rotation of the Earth against the background of the stars. The time-scale so obtained is known as Apparent Sidereal Time.

GREENWICH MEAN TIME

The daily rotation of the Earth on its axis causes the Sun and the other heavenly bodies to appear to cross the sky from east to west. It is convenient to represent this relative motion as if the Sun really performed a daily circuit around a fixed Earth. Noon in Apparent Solar Time may then be defined as the time at which the Sun transits across the observer's meridian. In Mean Solar Time, noon is similarly defined by the meridian transit of a fictitious Mean Sun moving uniformly in the sky with the same average speed as the true Sun. Mean Solar Time observed on the meridian of the transit circle telescope of the Old Royal Observatory at Greenwich is called Greenwich Mean Time (GMT). The mean solar day is divided into 24 hours and, for astronomical and other scientific purposes, these are numbered 0 to 23, commencing at midnight. Civil time is usually reckoned in two periods of 12 hours, designated a.m. (*ante meridiem*, i.e. before noon) and p.m. (*post meridiem*, i.e. after noon).

UNIVERSAL TIME

Before 1925 January 1, GMT was reckoned in 24 hours commencing at noon; since that date it has been reckoned from midnight. To avoid confusion in the use of the designation GMT before and after 1925, since 1928 astronomers have tended to use the term Universal Time (UT) or Weltzeit (WZ) to denote GMT measured from Greenwich Mean Midnight.

In precision work it is necessary to take account of small variations in Universal Time. These arise from small irregularities in the rotation of the Earth. Observed astronomical time is designated UT0. Observed time corrected for the effects of the motion of the poles (giving rise to a 'wandering' in longitude) is designated UT1. There is also a seasonal fluctuation in the rate of rotation of the Earth arising from meteorological causes, often called the annual fluctuation. UT1 corrected for this effect is designated UT2 and provides a time-scale free from short-period fluctuations. It is still subject to small secular and irregular changes.

APPARENT SOLAR TIME

As mentioned above, the time shown by a sundial is called Apparent Solar Time. It differs from Mean Solar Time by an amount known as the Equation of Time, which is the total effect of two causes which make the length of the apparent solar day non-uniform. One cause of variation is that the orbit of the Earth is not a circle but an ellipse, having the Sun at one focus. As a consequence, the angular speed of the Earth in its orbit is not constant; it is greatest at the beginning of January when the Earth is nearest the Sun.

The other cause is due to the obliquity of the ecliptic; the plane of the equator (which is at right angles to the axis of rotation of the Earth) does not coincide with the ecliptic (the plane defined by the apparent annual motion of the Sun around the celestial sphere) but is inclined to it at an angle of 23° 26'. As a result, the apparent solar day is shorter than average at the equinoxes and longer at the solstices. From the combined effects of the components due to obliquity and eccentricity, the equation of time reaches its maximum values in February (−14 minutes) and early November (+16 minutes). It has a zero value on four dates during the year, and it is only on these dates (approximately April 15, June 14, September 1, and December 25) that a sundial shows Mean Solar Time.

SIDEREAL TIME

A sidereal day is the duration of a complete rotation of the Earth with reference to the First Point of Aries. The term sidereal (or 'star') time is a little misleading since the time-scale so defined is not exactly the same as that which would be defined by successive transits of a selected star, as there is a small progressive motion between the stars and the First Point of Aries due to the precession of the Earth's axis. This makes the length of the sidereal day shorter than the true period of rotation by 0.008 seconds. Superimposed on this steady precessional motion are small oscillations (nutation), giving rise to fluctuations in apparent sidereal time amounting to as much as 1.2 seconds. It is therefore customary to employ Mean Sidereal Time, from which these fluctuations have been removed. The conversion of GMT to Greenwich sidereal time (GST) may be performed by adding the value of the GST at 0h on the day in question (Page Two of each month) to the GMT converted to sidereal time using the table on page 69.

Example – To find the GST at August 8d 02h 41m 11s GMT

	h	m	s
GST at 0h	21	07	07
GMT	2	41	11
Acceleration for 2h			20
Acceleration for 41m 11s			7
Sum = GST =	23	48	45

If the observer is not on the Greenwich meridian then his/her longitude, measured positively westwards from Greenwich, must be subtracted from the GST to obtain Local Sidereal Time (LST). Thus, in the above example, an observer 5h east of Greenwich, or 19h west, would find the LST as 4h 48m 45s.

Ephemeris Time

An analysis of observations of the positions of the Sun, Moon and planets taken over an extended period is used in preparing ephemerides. (An ephemeris is a table giving the apparent position of a heavenly body at regular intervals of time, e.g. one day or ten days, and may be used to compare current observations with tabulated positions.) Discrepancies between the positions of heavenly bodies observed over a 300-year period and their predicted positions arose because the time-scale to which the observations were related was based on the assumption that the rate of rotation of the Earth is uniform. It is now known that this rate of rotation is variable. A revised time-scale, Ephemeris Time (ET), was devised to bring the ephemerides into agreement with the observations.

The second of ET is defined in terms of the annual motion of the Earth in its orbit around the Sun (1/31556925.9747 of the tropical year for 1900 January 0d 12h ET). The precise determination of ET from astronomical observations is a lengthy process as the requisite standard of accuracy can only be achieved by averaging over a number of years.

In 1976 the International Astronomical Union adopted a new dynamical time-scale for general use whose scale unit is the SI second (*see* Atomic Time). ET is now of little more than historical interest.

Terrestrial Dynamical Time

The uniform time system used in computing the ephemerides of the solar system is Terrestrial Dynamical Time (TDT), which has replaced ET for this purpose. Except for the most rigorous astronomical calculations, it may be assumed to be the same as ET. During 1997 the estimated difference TDT – UT is about 63 seconds.

Atomic Time

The fundamental standards of time and frequency must be defined in terms of a periodic motion adequately uniform, enduring and measurable. Progress has made it possible to use natural standards, such as atomic or molecular oscillations. Continuous oscillations are generated in an electrical circuit, the frequency of which is then compared or brought into coincidence with the frequency characteristic of the absorption or emission by the atoms or molecules when they change between two selected energy levels. The

National Physical Laboratory (NPL) routinely uses clocks of high stability produced by locking a quartz oscillator to the frequencies defined by caesium or hydrogen atoms.

International Atomic Time (TAI), established through international collaboration, is formed by combining the readings of many caesium clocks and was set close to the astronomically-based Universal Time (UT) near the beginning of 1958. It was formally recognized in 1971 and since 1988 January 1 has been maintained by the International Bureau of Weights and Measures (BIPM). The second markers are generated according to the International System (SI) definition adopted in 1967 at the 13th General Conference of Weights and Measures: 'The second is the duration of 9 192 631 770 periods of the radiation corresponding to the transition between the two hyperfine levels of the ground state of the caesium-133 atom.'

Civil time in almost all countries is now based on Co-ordinated Universal Time (UTC), which was adopted for scientific purposes on 1972 January 1. UTC differs from TAI by an integer number of seconds (determined from studies of the rate of rotation of the Earth) and was designed to make both atomic time and UT accessible with accuracies appropriate for most users. The UTC time-scale is adjusted by the insertion (or, in principle, omission) of leap seconds in order to keep it within ±0.9 s of UT. These leap seconds are introduced, when necessary, at the same instant throughout the world, either at the end of December or at the end of June. So, for example, the 20th leap second occurred at 0h GMT on 1996 January 1. All leap seconds so far have been positive, with 61 seconds in the final minute of the UTC month. The time 23h 59m 60s UTC is followed one second later by 0h 0m 00s of the first day of the following month. Notices concerning the insertion of leap seconds are issued by the International Earth Rotation Service (IERS) at the Observatoire de Paris.

Radio Time-Signals

UTC is made generally available through time-signals and standard frequency broadcasts such as MSF in the UK, CHU in Canada and WWV and WWVH in the USA. These are based on national time-scales that are maintained in close agreement with UTC and provide traceability to the national time-scale and to UTC. The markers of seconds in the UTC scale coincide with those of TAI.

To disseminate the national time-scale in the UK, special signals are broadcast on behalf of the National Physical Laboratory from the BT (British Telecom) radio station at Rugby (call-sign MSF). The signals are controlled from a caesium beam atomic frequency standard and consist of a precise frequency carrier of 60 kHz which is switched off, after being on for at least half a second, to mark every second. In part of the first second of each minute the carrier may be switched on and off to carry data at 100 bits/second. In the other seconds the carrier is always off for at least one tenth of a second at the start and then it carries an on-off code giving similar information for British clock time and date, together with information identifying the start of the next minute. Changes to and from summer time are made following government announcements. Leap seconds are inserted as announced by the IERS and information provided by them on the difference between UTC and UT is also signalled. Other broadcast signals in the UK include the BBC six pips signal, the BT Timeline ('speaking clock'), the NPL Truetime service for computers, and a coded time-signal on the BBC 198 kHz transmitters which is used for timing in the electricity supply industry. From 1972 January 1 the six pips on the BBC have consisted of five short pips from second 55 to second 59 (six pips in the case of a leap second) followed by one lengthened pip, the start of which indicates the exact minute. From 1990 February 5 these signals have been controlled by the BBC with seconds markers referenced to the satellite-based US navigation system GPS (Global Positioning System) and time and day referenced to the MSF transmitter. Formerly they were generated by the Royal Greenwich Observatory. The BT Timeline is compared daily with the National Physical Laboratory caesium beam atomic frequency standard at the Rugby radio station. The NPL Truetime service is directly connected to the national time scale.

Accurate timing may also be obtained from the signals of international navigation systems such as the ground-based Loran-C or Omega, or the satellite-based American GPS or Russian GLONASS systems.

Standard Time

Since 1880 the standard time in Britain has been Greenwich Mean Time (GMT); a statute that year enacted that the word 'time' when used in any legal document relating to Britain meant, unless otherwise specifically stated, the mean time of the Greenwich meridian. Greenwich was adopted as the universal meridian on 13 October 1884. A system of standard time by zones is used world-wide, standard time in each zone differing from that of the Greenwich meridian by an integral number of hours, either fast or slow. The large territories of the USA and Canada are divided into zones approximately 7.5° on either side of central meridians. (For time zones of countries of the world, see Index.)

Variations from the standard time of some countries occur during part of the year; they are decided annually and are usually referred to as Summer Time or Daylight Saving Time.

At the 180th meridian the time can be either 12 hours fast on Greenwich Mean Time or 12 hours slow, and a change of date occurs. The internationally-recognized date or calendar line is a modification of the 180th meridian, drawn so as to include islands of any one group on the same side of the line, or for political reasons. The line is indicated by joining up the following co-ordinates:

Lat.	Long.	Lat.	Long.
60° S.	180°	48° N.	180°
51° S.	180°	53° N.	170° E.
45° S.	172.5° W.	65.5° N.	169° W.
15° S.	172.5° W.	75° N.	180°
5° S.	180°		

British Summer Time

In 1916 an Act ordained that during a defined period of that year the legal time for general purposes in Great Britain should be one hour in advance of Greenwich Mean Time. The Summer Time Acts 1922 to 1925 defined the period during which Summer Time was to be in force, stabilizing practice until the Second World War.

During the war the duration of Summer Time was extended and in the years 1941 to 1945 and in 1947 Double Summer Time (two hours in advance of Greenwich Mean Time) was in force. After the war, Summer Time was extended each year in 1948–52 and 1961–4 by Order in Council.

Between 1968 October 27 and 1971 October 31 clocks were kept one hour ahead of Greenwich Mean Time throughout the year. This was known as British Standard Time.

The most recent legislation is the Summer Time Act 1972, which enacted that 'the period of summer time for the purposes of this Act is the period beginning at two o'clock, Greenwich mean time, in the morning of the day after the third Saturday in March or, if that day is Easter Day, the day

after the second Saturday in March, and ending at two o'clock, Greenwich mean time, in the morning of the day after the fourth Saturday in October.'

The duration of Summer Time can be varied by Order in Council and in recent years alterations have been made to bring the operation of Summer Time in Britain closer to similar provisions in other countries of the European Union; for instance, since 1981 the hour of changeover has been 01h Greenwich Mean Time.

The duration of Summer Time in 1997 will be 30 March to 26 October.

MEAN REFRACTION

Alt.	Ref.		Alt.	Ref.		Alt.	Ref.	
° ′	′		° ′	′		° ′	′	
1 20		21	3 12		13	7 54		6
1 30		20	3 34		12	9 27		5
1 41		19	4 00		11	11 39		4
1 52		18	4 30		10	15 00		3
2 05		17	5 06		9	20 42		2
2 19		16	5 50		8	32 20		1
2 35		15	6 44		7	62 17		0
2 52		14	7 54			90 00		
3 12								

The refraction table is in the form of a critical table (see page 69)

ASTRONOMICAL CONSTANTS

Solar parallax	8″.794
Astronomical unit	149597870 km
Precession for the year 1997	50″.291
Precession in right ascension	3s.075
Precession in declination	20″.043
Constant of nutation	9″.202
Constant of aberration	20″.496
Mean obliquity of ecliptic (1997)	23° 26′ 23″
Moon's equatorial hor. parallax	57′ 02″.70
Velocity of light in vacuo per second	299792.5 km
Solar motion per second	20.0 km
Equatorial radius of the Earth	6378.140 km
Polar radius of the Earth	6356.755 km

North galactic pole (IAU standard)
RA 12h 49m (1950.0). Dec. 27°.4 N.
Solar apex   RA 18h 06m Dec.+30°

Length of year (in mean solar days)	
Tropical	365.24219
Sidereal	365.25636
Anomalistic (perihelion to perihelion)	365.25964
Eclipse	346.6200

Length of month (mean values)	d	h	m	s
New Moon to New	29	12	44	02.9
Sidereal	27	07	43	11.5
Anomalistic (perigee to perigee)	27	13	18	33.2

ELEMENTS OF THE SOLAR SYSTEM

Orb	Mean distance from Sun (Earth = 1)	km 10⁶	Sidereal period days	Synodic period days	Incl. of orbit to ecliptic ° '	Diameter km	Mass (Earth = 1)	Period of rotation on axis days
Sun	—	—	—	—	—	1,392,530	332,946	25–35*
Mercury	0.39	58	88.0	116	7 00	4,879	0.0553	58.646
Venus	0.72	108	224.7	584	3 24	12,104	0.8150	243.017r
Earth	1.00	150	365.3	—	—	12,756e	1.0000	0.997
Mars	1.52	228	687.0	780	1 51	6,794e	0.1074	1.026
Jupiter	5.20	778	4,332.6	399	1 18	{142,984e / 133,708p}	317.89	{0.410e}
Saturn	9.54	1427	10,759.2	378	2 29	{120,536e / 108,728p}	95.18	{0.426e}
Uranus	19.18	2870	30,684.6	370	0 46	51,118e	14.54	0.718r
Neptune	30.06	4497	60,191.0	367	1 46	49,528e	17.15	0.671
Pluto	39.80	5954	91,708.2	367	17 09	2,302	0.002	6.387

e equatorial, p polar, r retrograde, * depending on latitude

THE SATELLITES

Name	Star mag.	Mean distance from primary km	Sidereal period of revolution d
EARTH			
I Moon	—	384,400	27.322
MARS			
I Phobos	12	9,380	0.319
II Deimos	13	23,460	1.262
JUPITER			
XVI Metis	17	127,960	0.295
XV Adrastea	19	128,980	0.298
V Amalthea	14	181,300	0.498
XIV Thebe	16	221,900	0.675
I Io	5	421,600	1.769
II Europa	5	670,900	3.551
III Ganymede	5	1,070,000	7.155
IV Callisto	6	1,880,000	16.689
XIII Leda	20	11,094,000	239
VI Himalia	15	11,480,000	251
X Lysithea	18	11,720,000	259
VII Elara	17	11,737,000	260
XII Ananke	19	21,200,000	631r
XI Carme	17	22,600,000	692r
VIII Pasiphae	17	23,500,000	735r
IX Sinope	18	23,700,000	758r
SATURN			
XVIII Pan	—	133,600	0.575
XV Atlas	18	137,640	0.602
XVI Prometheus	16	139,350	0.613
XVII Pandora	16	141,700	0.629
XI Epimetheus	15	151,420	0.694
X Janus	14	151,470	0.695
I Mimas	13	185,520	0.942
II Enceladus	12	238,020	1.370
III Tethys	10	294,660	1.888
XIII Telesto	19	294,660	1.888
XIV Calypso	19	294,660	1.888
IV Dione	10	377,400	2.737
XII Helene	18	377,400	2.737
V Rhea	10	527,040	4.518
VI Titan	8	1,221,850	15.945

Name	Star mag.	Mean distance from primary km	Sidereal period of revolution d
SATURN			
VII Hyperion	14	1,481,000	21.277
VIII Iapetus	11	3,561,300	79.330
IX Phoebe	16	12,952,000	550.5r
URANUS			
VI Cordelia	—	49,770	0.335
VII Ophelia	—	53,790	0.376
VIII Bianca	—	59,170	0.435
IX Cressida	—	61,780	0.464
X Desdemona	—	62,660	0.474
XI Juliet	—	64,350	0.493
XII Portia	—	66,090	0.513
XIII Rosalind	—	69,940	0.558
XIV Belinda	—	75,260	0.624
XV Puck	—	86,010	0.762
V Miranda	17	129,390	1.413
I Ariel	14	191,020	2.520
II Umbriel	15	266,300	4.144
III Titania	14	435,910	8.706
IV Oberon	14	583,520	13.463
NEPTUNE			
III Naiad	25	48,230	0.294
IV Thalassa	24	50,070	0.311
V Despina	23	52,530	0.335
VI Galatea	22	61,950	0.429
VII Larissa	22	73,550	0.555
VIII Proteus	20	117,650	1.122
I Triton	13	354,760	5.877
II Nereid	19	5,513,400	360.136
PLUTO			
I Charon	17	19,700	6.387

THE EARTH

The shape of the Earth is that of an oblate spheroid or solid of revolution whose meridian sections are ellipses not differing much from circles, whilst the sections at right angles are circles. The length of the equatorial axis is about 12,756 km, and that of the polar axis is 12,714 km. The mean density of the Earth is 5.5 times that of water, although that of the surface layer is less. The Earth and Moon revolve about their common centre of gravity in a lunar month; this centre in turn revolves round the Sun in a plane known as the ecliptic, that passes through the Sun's centre. The Earth's equator is inclined to this plane at an angle of 23.4°. This tilt is the cause of the seasons. In mid-latitudes, when the Sun is high above the Equator, not only does the high noon altitude make the days longer, but the Sun's rays fall more directly on the Earth's surface; these effects combine to produce summer. In equatorial regions the noon altitude is large throughout the year, and there is little variation in the length of the day. In higher latitudes the noon altitude is lower, and the days in summer are appreciably longer than those in winter.

The average velocity of the Earth in its orbit is 30 km a second. It makes a complete rotation on its axis in about 23h 56m of mean time, which is the sidereal day. Because of its annual revolution round the Sun, the rotation with respect to the Sun, or the solar day, is more than this by about four minutes (see page 73). The extremity of the axis of rotation, or the North Pole of the Earth, is not rigidly fixed, but wanders over an area roughly 20 metres in diameter.

TERRESTRIAL MAGNETISM

A magnetic compass points along the horizontal component of a magnetic line of force. These lines of force converge on the 'magnetic dip-poles', the places where a freely suspended magnetized needle would become vertical. Not only do these poles move with time, but their exact locations are ill-defined, particularly so in the case of the north dip-pole where the lines of force on the north side of it, instead of converging radially, tend to bunch into a channel. Although it is therefore unrealistic to attempt to specify the locations of the dip-poles exactly, the present approximate adopted positions are 79°.0 N., 105°.1 W. and 64°.7 S., 138°.6 E. The two magnetic dip-poles are thus not antipodal, the line joining them passing the centre of the Earth at a distance of about 1,250 km. The distances of the magnetic dip-poles from the north and south geographical poles are about 1,200 km and 2,800 km respectively.

There is also a 'magnetic equator', at all points of which the vertical component of the Earth's magnetic field is zero and a magnetized needle remains horizontal. This line runs between 2° and 10° north of the geographical equator in Asia and Africa, turns sharply south off the west African coast, and crosses South America through Brazil, Bolivia and Peru; it recrosses the geographical equator in mid-Pacific.

Reference has already been made to secular changes in the Earth's field. The following table indicates the changes in magnetic declination (or variation of the compass). Declination is the angle in the horizontal plane between the direction of true north and that in which a magnetic compass points. Similar, though much smaller, changes have occurred in 'dip' or magnetic inclination. Secular changes differ throughout the world. Although the London observations strongly suggest a cycle with a period of several hundred years, an exact repetition is unlikely.

London		Greenwich	
1580	11° 15' E.	1850	22° 24' W.
1622	5° 56' E.	1900	16° 29' W.
1665	1° 22' W.	1925	13° 10' W.
1730	13° 00' W.	1950	9° 07' W.
1773	21° 09' W.	1975	6° 39' W.

In order that up-to-date information on declination may be available, many governments publish magnetic charts on which there are lines (isogonic lines) passing through all places at which specified values of declination will be found at the date of the chart.

In the British Isles, isogonic lines now run approximately north-east to south-west. Though there are considerable local deviations due to geological causes, a rough value of magnetic declination may be obtained by assuming that at 50° N. on the meridian of Greenwich, the value in 1997 is 3° 06' west and allowing an increase of 15' for each degree of latitude northwards and an increase of 28' for each degree of longitude westwards. For example, at 53° N., 5° W., declination will be about 3° 06' + 45' + 140', i.e. 6° 11' west. The average annual change at the present time is about 9' decrease.

The number of magnetic observatories is about 200, irregularly distributed over the globe. There are three in Great Britain, run by the British Geological Survey: at Hartland, north Devon; at Eskdalemuir, Dumfriesshire; and at Lerwick, Shetland Islands. The following are some recent annual mean values of the magnetic elements for Hartland.

Year	Declination West ° '	Dip or inclination ° '	Horizontal force gauss	Vertical force gauss
1955	10 30	66 49	0.1859	0.4340
1960	9 59	66 44	0.1871	0.4350
1965	9 30	66 34	0.1887	0.4354
1970	9 06	66 26	0.1903	0.4364
1975	8 32	66 17	0.1921	0.4373
1980	7 44	66 10	0.1933	0.4377
1985	6 56	66 08	0.1938	0.4380
1990	6 15	66 10	0.1939	0.4388
1995	5 33	66 07	0.1946	0.4395

The normal world-wide terrestrial magnetic field corresponds approximately to that of a very strong small bar magnet near the centre of the Earth, but with appreciable smooth spatial departures. The origin and the slow secular change of the normal field are not fully understood but are generally ascribed to electric currents associated with fluid motions in the Earth's core. Superimposed on the normal field are local and regional anomalies whose magnitudes may in places approach that of the normal field; these are due to the influence of mineral deposits in the Earth's crust. A small proportion of the field is of external origin, mostly associated with electric currents in the ionosphere. The configuration of the external field and the ionization of the atmosphere depend on the incident particle and radiation flux from the Sun. There are, therefore, short-term and non-periodic as well as diurnal, 27-day, seasonal and 11-year periodic changes in the magnetic field, dependent upon the position of the Sun and the degree of solar activity.

MAGNETIC STORMS

Occasionally, sometimes with great suddenness, the Earth's magnetic field is subject for several hours to marked disturbance. During a severe storm in 1989 the declination at Lerwick changed by almost 8° in less than an hour. In many instances such disturbances are accompanied by widespread displays of aurorae, marked changes in the incidence of cosmic rays, an increase in the reception of 'noise' from the Sun at radio frequencies, and rapid changes in the ionosphere and induced electric currents within the Earth which adversely affect radio and telegraphic communications. The disturbances are caused by changes in the stream of ionized particles which emanates from the Sun and through which the Earth is continuously passing. Some of these changes are associated with visible eruptions on the Sun, usually in the region of sun-spots. There is a marked tendency for disturbances to recur after intervals of about 27 days, the apparent period of rotation of the Sun on its axis, which is consistent with the sources being located on particular areas of the Sun.

ARTIFICIAL SATELLITES

To consider the orbit of an artificial satellite, it is best to imagine that one is looking at the Earth from a distant point in space. The Earth would then be seen to be rotating about its axis inside the orbit described by the rapidly revolving satellite. The inclination of a satellite orbit to the Earth's equator (which generally remains almost constant throughout the satellite's lifetime) gives at once the maximum range of latitudes over which the satellite passes. Thus a satellite whose orbit has an inclination of 53° will pass overhead all latitudes between 53° S. and 53° N., but would never be seen in the zenith of any place nearer the poles than these latitudes. If we consider a particular place on the earth, whose latitude is less than the inclination of the satellite's orbit, then the Earth's rotation carries this place first under the northbound part of the orbit and then under the southbound portion of the orbit, these two occurrences being always less than 12 hours apart for satellites moving in direct orbits (i.e. to the east). (For satellites in retrograde orbits, the words 'northbound' and 'southbound' should be interchanged in the preceding statement.) As the value of the latitude of the observer increases and approaches the value of the inclination of the orbit, so this interval gets shorter until (when the latitude is equal to the inclination) only one overhead passage occurs each day.

OBSERVATION OF SATELLITES
The regression of the orbit around the Earth causes alternate periods of visibility and invisibility, though this is of little concern to the radio or radar observer. To the visual observer the following cycle of events normally occurs (though the cycle may start in any position): invisibility, morning observations before dawn, invisibility, evening observations after dusk, invisibility, morning observations before dawn, and so on. With reasonably high satellites and for observers in high latitudes around the summer solstice, the evening observations follow the morning observations without interruption as sunlight passing over the polar regions can still illuminate satellites which are passing over temperate latitudes at local midnight. At the moment all satellites rely on sunlight to make them visible, though a satellite with a flashing light has been suggested for a future launching. The observer must be in darkness or twilight in order to make any useful observations and the durations of twilight and the sunrise, sunset times given on Page Two of each month will be a useful guide.

Some of the satellites are visible to the naked eye and much interest has been aroused by the spectacle of a bright

satellite disappearing into the Earth's shadow. The event is even more interesting telescopically as the disappearance occurs gradually as the satellite traverses the Earth's penumbral shadow, and during the last few seconds before the eclipse is complete the satellite may change colour (in suitable atmospheric conditions) from yellow to red. This is because the last rays of sunlight are refracted through the denser layers of our atmosphere before striking the satellite.

Some satellites rotate about one or more axes so that a periodic variation in brightness is observed. This was particularly noticeable in several of the Soviet satellites.

Satellite research has provided some interesting results, including a revised value of the Earth's oblateness (1/298.2), and the discovery of the Van Allen radiation belts.

LAUNCHINGS
Apart from their names, e.g. Cosmos 6 Rocket, the satellites are also classified according to their date of launch. Thus 1961 α refers to the first satellite launching of 1961. A number following the Greek letter indicated the relative brightness of the satellites put in orbit. From the beginning of 1963 the Greek letters were replaced by numbers and the numbers by roman letters e.g. 1963−01A. For all satellites successfully injected into orbit the following table gives the designation and names of the main objects, the launch date and some initial orbital data. These are the inclination to the equator (i), the nodal period of revolution (P), the eccentricity (e), and the perigee height.

Although most of the satellites launched are injected into orbits less than 1,000 km high, there are an increasing number of satellites in geostationary orbits, i.e. where the orbital inclination is zero, the eccentricity close to zero, and the period of revolution is 1436.1 minutes. Thus the satellite is permanently situated over the equator at one selected longitude at a mean height of 35,786 km. This geostationary band is crowded. In one case there are four television satellites (Astra 1A, Astra 1B, Astra 1C and Astra 1D) orbiting within a few tens of kilometres of each other. In the sky they appear to be separated by only a few arc minutes.

ARTIFICIAL SATELLITE LAUNCHES 1995–6

Designation	Satellite	Launch date	i	P	e	Perigee height
1995–			°	m		km
011	Himawari 5, GMS 5	March 18	0.6	1436.1	0.000	35786
012	Cosmos 2310, rocket	March 22	82.9	104.5	0.002	987
013	Intelsat 7-05	March 22	26.5	720.0	0.727	333
014	Cosmos 2311, Hotbird 1, rocket	March 22	67.0	88.8	0.001	190
015	DMSP 2-08	March 24	98.8	102.0	0.001	845
016	Brazilsat B2, Hotbird 1 Eutelsat	March 28	0.0	1436.0	0.000	35782
017	Orbcomm 1 & 2, Microlab 1	April 3	70.0	91.0	0.002	450
018	Offeq 3, rocket	April 5	143.0	102.7	0.095	200
019	AMSC 1	April 8	0.0	1436.0	0.000	35781
020	Progress M27, rocket	April 9	51.6	88.5	0.001	190
021	ERS2, rocket	April 20	98.7	102.0	0.002	860
022	USA 110	May 14	–	–	–	–
023	ARIANE	May 17	0.0	1436.0	0.000	35774
024	Spektr	May 20	51.6	89.4	0.001	190
025	GOES 9	May 23	0.1	1439.7	0.001	35807
026	Cosmos 2312, rocket	May 24	62.7	91.0	0.017	222
027	UHF5	May 31	4.8	1435.9	0.000	35774
028	Cosmos 2313	May 31	65.0	89.0	0.001	190
029	DBS3	May 31	0.0	1436.0	0.000	35765
030	STS71	June 23	51.6	91.5	0.161	302
031	Cosmos 2314	June 28	67.0	89.5	0.002	200
032	Cosmos 2315	July 5	82.9	104.0	0.001	987
033	Helios 1A, UPM LBSAT 1	July 7	98.0	100.0	0.001	833
034	USA112, Sigint	July 10	–	–	–	–
035	Shuttle 70, TDRS7	July 13	0.3	1436.1	0.000	35774
036	Progress M28	July 20	–	–	–	–
037	Cosmos 2317, 2316, rocket	July 24	65.0	674.0	0.002	19010
038	DSCS3	July 31	–	–	–	–
039	Interball 1, Magion 4	August 3	67.1	5463.0	0.881	5833
040	PAS 4	August 3	7.0	700.0	0.711	768
041	Muhungha	August 5	0.0	1436.1	0.000	35778
042	Molniya 3-47, platform	August 9	63.0	710.0	0.745	400
043	JCSAT 3	August 29	0.0	1436.0	0.000	35780
044	NSTAR 1	August 29	0.0	1436.0	0.007	36000
045	Cosmos 2319	August 30	0.0	1436.0	0.007	36000
046	SICH-1 Okean, rocket	August 31	82.5	97.8	0.003	632
047	Soyuz TM22	September 3	51.6	88.9	0.002	170
048	Spartan 201	September 7	28.5	90.0	0.001	290
049	Telstar 402	September 24	4.0	1436.0	0.004	36666
050	Resurs F2	September 26	82.2	89.0	0.000	230
051	Cosmos 2320	September 29	64.9	89.9	0.008	179
052	Cosmos 2321	October 6	82.9	95.1	0.039	257
053	Progress M29	October 8	51.6	91.5	0.004	194
054	Luch 1, platform	October 11	2.8	1436.0	0.001	35750
055	Astra 1E	October 19	0.1	1436.0	0.000	35777
056	STS73	October 20	39.0	90.0	0.001	267
057	UHF F6	October 22	5.0	1436.0	0.000	35779
058	Cosmos 2322	October 31	71.0	102.0	0.000	800
059	Radarsat	November 4	100.5	109.9	0.037	935
060	USA 115	November 6	–	–	–	–
061	STS74	November 12	51.6	90.9	0.108	300
062	ISO	November 17	4.8	1436.0	0.823	1097
063	GALS 2, rocket	November 17	0.1	1436.0	0.000	35771
064	Asiasat LMRB	November 28	0.2	1435.9	0.000	35780
065	Soho	December 2	–	–	–	–

Desig-nation	Satellite	Launch date	i	P	e	Perigee height
066	USA 116	December 5	–	–	–	–
067	Telecom 2C, rocket	December 6	0.0	1436.0	0.001	35666
068	Cosmos 2324, rocket	December 14	64.7	675.0	0.000	19111
069	GALAXY 3R	December 15	26.8	690.0	0.728	250
070	Progress M30	December 18	51.6	88.4	0.001	180
071	Cosmos 2326	December 20	65.0	88.4	0.001	180
072	Skipper	December 28	98.5	101.2	0.001	806
073	Echostar 1	December 28	0.1	1436.0	0.001	35764
074	XTE	December 30	23.0	95.9	0.001	562
1996–						
001	STS 72, OAST	January 11	28.5	90.4	0.000	310
002	Panamsat 3R, Measat 1	January 12	0.1	1435.4	0.000	35886
003	KOREASAT 2, rocket	January 14	0.2	1448.5	0.000	36343
004	COSMOS 2327, rocket	January 16	83.0	104.9	0.005	952
005	Gorizont, rocket	January 25	1.5	1477.5	0.002	36524
006	PALAPA C-1, rocket	February 1	0.1	1436.1	0.000	36000
007	N-STAR B	February 5	0.1	1436.0	0.001	35753
008	NEAR	February 17	(Heliocentric	orbit)		
009	Cosmos 2328-2330, rocket	February 19	82.5	113.9	0.001	1400
010	Raduga 33, rocket	February 19	48.6	645.5	0.733	241
011	SOYUZ TM23, rocket	February 21	51.6	88.7	0.001	180
012	STS75, TSS 1R	February 22	28.5	91.0	0.001	280
013	POLAR, rocket	February 24	86.0	937.2	0.793	186
014	REX II, rocket	March 9	89.9	100.0	0.000	768
015	Intelsat 707	March 14	0.0	1436.1	0.000	35780
016	Cosmos 2331, rocket	March 14	67.0	88.5	0.001	180
017	PSLV D3, rocket	March 21	98.7	101.4	0.003	802
018	STS76	March 22	51.6	92.3	0.001	388
019	GPS NAVSTAR, rocket	March 28	54.7	726.8	0.006	20252
020	Inmarsat 3	April 3	0.1	1436.0	0.001	35600

Time Measurement and Calendars

MEASUREMENTS OF TIME

Measurements of time are based on the time taken by the earth to rotate on its axis (day); by the moon to revolve round the earth (month); and by the earth to revolve round the sun (year). From these, which are not commensurable, certain average or mean intervals have been adopted for ordinary use.

THE DAY

The day begins at midnight and is divided into 24 hours of 60 minutes, each of 60 seconds. The hours are counted from midnight up to 12 noon (when the sun crosses the meridian), and these hours are designated a.m. (*ante meridiem*); and again from noon up to 12 midnight, which hours are designated p.m. (*post meridiem*), except when the 24-hour reckoning is employed. The 24-hour reckoning ignores a.m. and p.m., numbering the hours 0 to 23 from midnight.

Colloquially the 24 hours are divided into day and night, day being the time while the sun is above the horizon (including the four stages of twilight defined on page 72). Day is subdivided into morning, the early part of daytime, ending at noon; afternoon, from noon to about 6 p.m.; and evening, which may be said to extend from 6 p.m. until midnight. Night, the dark period between day and day, begins at the close of astronomical twilight (*see* page 72) and extends beyond midnight to sunrise the next day.

The names of the days are derived from Old English translations or adaptations of the Roman titles.

Sunday	Sun	Sol
Monday	Moon	Luna
Tuesday	Tiw/Tyr (god of war)	Mars
Wednesday	Woden/Odin	Mercury
Thursday	Thor	Jupiter
Friday	Frigga/Freyja (goddess of love)	Venus
Saturday	Saeternes	Saturn

THE MONTH

The month in the ordinary calendar is approximately the twelfth part of a year, but the lengths of the different months vary from 28 (or 29) days to 31.

THE YEAR

The equinoctial or tropical year is the time that the earth takes to revolve round the sun from equinox to equinox, i.e. 365.24219 mean solar days, or 365 days 5 hours 48 minutes and 45 seconds.

The calendar year usually consists of 365 days but a year containing 366 days is called bissextile (*see* Roman calendar, page 89) or leap year, one day being added to the month of February so that a date 'leaps over' a day of the week. In the Roman calendar the day that was repeated was the sixth day before the beginning of March, the equivalent of 24 February.

A year is a leap year if the date of the year is divisible by four without remainder, unless it is the last year of a century. The last year of a century is a leap year only if its number is divisible by 400 without remainder, e.g. the years 1800 and 1900 had only 365 days but the year 2000 will have 366 days.

THE SOLSTICE

A solstice is the point in the tropical year at which the sun attains its greatest distance, north or south, from the Equator. In the northern hemisphere the furthest point north of the Equator marks the summer solstice and the furthest point south the winter solstice.

The date of the solstice varies according to locality. For example, if the summer solstice falls on 21 June late in the day by Greenwich time, that day will be the longest of the year at Greenwich though it may be by only a second, but it will fall on 22 June, local date, in Japan, and so 22 June will be the longest day there. The date of the solstice is also affected by the length of the tropical year, which is 365 days 6 hours less about 11 minutes 15 seconds. If a solstice happens late on 21 June in one year, it will be nearly six hours later in the next (unless the next year is a leap year), i.e. early on 22 June, and that will be the longest day.

This delay of the solstice does not continue because the extra day in leap year brings it back a day in the calendar. However, because of the 11 minutes 15 seconds mentioned above, the additional day in leap year brings the solstice back too far by 45 minutes, and the time of the solstice in the calendar is earlier, in a four-year pattern, as the century progresses. The last year of a century is in most cases not a leap year, and the omission of the extra day puts the date of the solstice later by about six hours too much. Compensation for this is made by the fourth centennial year being a leap year. The solstice has become earlier in date throughout this century and, because the year 2000 is a leap year, the solstice will get earlier still throughout the 21st century.

The date of the winter solstice, the shortest day of the year, is affected by the same factors as the longest day.

At Greenwich the sun sets at its earliest by the clock about ten days before the shortest day. The daily change in the time of sunset is due in the first place to the sun's movement southwards at this time of the year, which diminishes the interval between the sun's transit and its setting. However, the daily decrease of the Equation of Time causes the time of apparent noon to be continuously later day by day, which to some extent counteracts the first effect. The rates of the change of these two quantities are not equal or uniform; their combination causes the date of earliest sunset to be 12 or 13 December at Greenwich. In more southerly latitudes the effect of the movement of the sun is less, and the change in the time of sunset depends on that of the Equation of Time to a greater degree, and the date of earliest sunset is earlier than it is at Greenwich, e.g. on the Equator it is about 1 November.

THE EQUINOX

The equinox is the point at which the sun crosses the Equator and day and night are of equal length all over the world. This occurs in March and September.

DOG DAYS

The days about the heliacal rising of the Dog Star, noted from ancient times as the hottest period of the year in the northern hemisphere, are called the Dog Days. Their incidence has been variously calculated as depending on the Greater or Lesser Dog Star (Sirius or Procyon) and their duration has been reckoned as from 30 to 54 days. A generally accepted period is from 3 July to 15 August.

CHRISTIAN CALENDAR

In the Christian chronological system the years are distinguished by cardinal numbers before or after the birth of Christ, the period being denoted by the letters BC (Before Christ) or, more rarely, AC (*Ante Christum*), and AD (*Anno Domini* – In the Year of Our Lord). The correlative dates of the epoch are the fourth year of the 194th Olympiad, the 753rd year from the foundation of Rome, AM 3761 (Jewish chronology), and the 4714th year of the Julian period. The actual date of the birth of Christ is somewhat uncertain.

The system was introduced into Italy in the sixth century. Though first used in France in the seventh century, it was not universally established there until about the eighth century. It has been said that the system was introduced into England by St Augustine (AD 596), but it was probably not generally used until some centuries later. It was ordered to be used by the Bishops at the Council of Chelsea (AD 816).

THE JULIAN CALENDAR

In the Julian calendar (adopted by the Roman Empire in 45 BC, *see* page 89) all the centennial years were leap years, and for this reason towards the close of the 16th century there was a difference of ten days between the tropical and calendar years; the equinox fell on 11 March of the calendar, whereas at the time of the Council of Nicaea (AD 325), it had fallen on 21 March. In 1582 Pope Gregory ordained that 5 October should be called 15 October and that of the end-century years only the fourth should be a leap year (*see* page 81).

THE GREGORIAN CALENDAR

The Gregorian calendar was adopted by Italy, France, Spain and Portugal in 1582, by Prussia, the Roman Catholic German states, Switzerland, Holland and Flanders on 1 January 1583, by Poland in 1586, Hungary in 1587, the Protestant German and Netherland states and Denmark in 1700, and by Great Britain and Dominions (including the North American colonies) in 1752, by the omission of eleven days (3 September being reckoned as 14 September). Sweden omitted the leap day in 1700 but observed leap days in 1704 and 1708, and reverted to the Julian calendar by having two leap days in 1712; the Gregorian calendar was adopted in 1753 by the omission of eleven days (18 February being reckoned as 1 March). Japan adopted the calendar in 1872, China in 1912, Bulgaria in 1915, Turkey and Soviet Russia in 1918, Yugoslavia and Romania in 1919, and Greece in 1923.

In the same year that the change was made in England from the Julian to the Gregorian calendar, the beginning of the new year was also changed from 25 March to 1 January (*see* page 86).

THE ORTHODOX CHURCHES

Some Orthodox Churches still use the Julian reckoning but the majority of Greek Orthodox Churches and the Romanian Orthodox Church have adopted a modified 'New Calendar', observing the Gregorian calendar for fixed feasts and the Julian for movable feasts.

The Orthodox Church year begins on 1 September. There are four fast periods and, in addition to Pascha (Easter), twelve great feasts, as well as numerous commemorations of the saints of the Old and New Testaments throughout the year.

THE DOMINICAL LETTER

The dominical letter is one of the letters A–G which are used to denote the Sundays in successive years. If the first day of the year is a Sunday the letter is A; if the second, B; the third, C; and so on. A leap year requires two letters, the first for 1 January to 29 February, the second for 1 March to 31 December (*see* page 84).

EPIPHANY

The feast of the Epiphany, commemorating the manifestation of Christ, later became associated with the offering of gifts by the Magi. The day was of great importance from the time of the Council of Nicaea (AD 325), as the primate of Alexandria was charged at every Epiphany feast with the announcement in a letter to the churches of the date of the forthcoming Easter. The day was also of importance in Britain as it influenced dates, ecclesiastical and lay, e.g. Plough Monday, when work was resumed in the fields, fell on the Monday in the first full week after Epiphany.

LENT

The Teutonic word *Lent*, which denotes the fast preceding Easter, originally meant no more than the spring season; but from Anglo-Saxon times at least it has been used as the equivalent of the more significant Latin term Quadragesima, meaning the 'forty days' or, more literally, the fortieth day. Ash Wednesday is the first day of Lent, which ends at midnight before Easter Day.

PALM SUNDAY

Palm Sunday, the Sunday before Easter and the beginning of Holy Week, commemorates the triumphal entry of Christ into Jerusalem and is celebrated in Britain (when palm is not available) by branches of willow gathered for use in the decoration of churches on that day.

MAUNDY THURSDAY

Maundy Thursday is the day before Good Friday, the name itself being a corruption of *dies mandati* (day of the mandate) when Christ washed the feet of the disciples and gave them the mandate to love one another.

EASTER DAY

Easter Day is the first Sunday after the full moon which happens on, or next after, the 21st day of March; if the full moon happens on a Sunday, Easter Day is the Sunday after.

This definition is contained in an Act of Parliament (24 Geo. II c. 23) and explanation is given in the preamble to the Act that the day of full moon depends on certain tables that have been prepared. These tables are summarized in the early pages of the Book of Common Prayer. The moon referred to is not the real moon of the heavens, but a hypothetical moon on whose 'full' the date of Easter depends, and the lunations of this 'calendar' moon consist of twenty-nine and thirty days alternately, with certain necessary modifications to make the date of its full agree as nearly as possible with that of the real moon, which is known as the Paschal Full Moon. At present, Easter falls on one of 35 days (22 March to 25 April).

A FIXED EASTER

In 1928 the House of Commons agreed to a motion for the third reading of a bill proposing that Easter Day shall, in the calendar year next but one after the commencement of the Act and in all subsequent years, be the first Sunday after the second Saturday in April. Easter would thus fall on the second or third Sunday in April, i.e. between 9 and 15 April (inclusive). A clause in the Bill provided that before it shall come into operation, regard shall be had to any opinion expressed officially by the various Christian churches.

Efforts by the World Council of Churches to secure a unanimous choice of date for Easter by its member churches have so far been unsuccessful.

ROGATION DAYS

Rogation Days are the Monday, Tuesday and Wednesday preceding Ascension Day and from the fifth century were observed as public fasts with solemn processions and supplications. The processions were discontinued as religious observances at the Reformation, but survive in the ceremony known as 'beating the parish bounds'. Rogation Sunday is the Sunday before Ascension Day.

EMBER DAYS

The Ember Days at the four seasons are the Wednesday, Friday and Saturday (a) before the third Sunday in Advent, (b) before the second Sunday in Lent, and (c) before the Sundays nearest to the festivals of St Peter and of St Michael and All Angels.

TRINITY SUNDAY

Trinity Sunday is eight weeks after Easter Day, on the Sunday following Pentecost (Whit Sunday). Subsequent Sundays are reckoned in the Book of Common Prayer calendar of the Church of England as 'after Trinity'.

Thomas Becket (1118–70) was consecrated Archbishop of Canterbury on the Sunday after Whit Sunday and his first act was to ordain that the day of his consecration should be held as a new festival in honour of the Holy Trinity. This observance spread from Canterbury throughout the whole of Christendom.

MOVABLE FEASTS TO THE YEAR 2029

Year	Ash Wednesday	Easter	Ascension	Pentecost (Whit Sunday)	Sundays after Pentecost	Advent Sunday
1997	12 February	30 March	8 May	18 May	22	30 November
1998	25 February	12 April	21 May	31 May	20	29 November
1999	17 February	4 April	13 May	23 May	21	28 November
2000	8 March	23 April	1 June	11 June	19	3 December
2001	28 February	15 April	24 May	3 June	20	2 December
2002	13 February	31 March	9 May	19 May	22	1 December
2003	5 March	20 April	29 May	8 June	19	30 November
2004	25 February	11 April	20 May	30 May	20	28 November
2005	9 February	27 March	5 May	15 May	22	27 November
2006	1 March	16 April	25 May	4 June	20	3 December
2007	21 February	8 April	17 May	27 May	21	2 December
2008	6 February	23 March	1 May	11 May	23	30 November
2009	25 February	12 April	21 May	31 May	20	29 November
2010	17 February	4 April	13 May	23 May	21	28 November
2011	9 March	24 April	2 June	12 June	18	27 November
2012	22 February	8 April	17 May	27 May	21	2 December
2013	13 February	31 March	9 May	19 May	22	1 December
2014	5 March	20 April	29 May	8 June	19	30 November
2015	18 February	5 April	14 May	24 May	21	29 November
2016	10 February	27 March	5 May	15 May	22	27 November
2017	1 March	16 April	25 May	4 June	20	3 December
2018	14 February	1 April	10 May	20 May	22	2 December
2019	6 March	21 April	30 May	9 June	19	1 December
2020	26 February	12 April	21 May	31 May	20	29 November
2021	17 February	4 April	13 May	23 May	21	28 November
2022	2 March	17 April	26 May	5 June	19	27 November
2023	22 February	9 April	18 May	28 May	21	3 December
2024	14 February	31 March	9 May	19 May	22	1 December
2025	5 March	20 April	29 May	8 June	19	30 November
2026	18 February	5 April	14 May	24 May	21	29 November
2027	10 February	28 March	6 May	16 May	22	28 November
2028	1 March	16 April	25 May	4 June	20	3 December
2029	14 February	1 April	10 May	20 May	22	2 December

NOTES

Ash Wednesday (first day in Lent) can fall at earliest on 4 February and at latest on 10 March

Mothering Sunday (fourth Sunday in Lent) can fall at earliest on 1 March and at latest on 4 April

Easter Day can fall at earliest on 22 March and at latest on 25 April

Ascension Day is forty days after Easter Day and can fall at earliest on 30 April and at latest on 3 June

Pentecost (Whit Sunday) is seven weeks after Easter and can fall at earliest on 10 May and at latest on 13 June

Trinity Sunday is the Sunday after Whit Sunday

Corpus Christi falls on the Thursday after Trinity Sunday

Sundays after Pentecost – there are not less than 18 and not more than 23

Advent Sunday is the Sunday nearest to 30 November

EASTER DAYS AND DOMINICAL LETTERS 1500 TO 2033

Dates up to and including 1752 are according to the Julian calendar

	1500–1599	1600–1699	1700–1799	1800–1899	1900–1999	2000–2033
March						
d 22	1573	1668	1761	1818		
e 23	1505/16	1600	1788	1845/56	1913	2008
f 24		1611/95	1706/99		1940	
g 25	1543/54	1627/38/49	1722/33/44	1883/94	1951	
A 26	1559/70/81/92	1654/65/76	1749/58/69/80	1815/26/37	1967/78/89	
b 27	1502/13/24/97	1608/87/92	1785/96	1842/53/64	1910/21/32	2005/16
c 28	1529/35/40	1619/24/30	1703/14/25	1869/75/80	1937/48	2027/32
d 29	1551/62	1635/46/57	1719/30/41/52	1807/12/91	1959/64/70	
e 30	1567/78/89	1651/62/73/84	1746/55/66/77	1823/34	1902/75/86/97	
f 31	1510/21/32/83/94	1605/16/78/89	1700/71/82/93	1839/50/61/72	1907/18/29/91	2002/13/24
April						
g 1	1526/37/48	1621/32	1711/16	1804/66/77/88	1923/34/45/56	2018/29
A 2	1553/64	1643/48	1727/38	1809/20/93/99	1961/72	
b 3	1575/80/86	1659/70/81	1743/63/68/74	1825/31/36	1904/83/88/94	
c 4	1507/18/91	1602/13/75/86/97	1708/79/90	1847/58	1915/20/26/99	2010/21
d 5	1523/34/45/56	1607/18/29/40	1702/13/24/95	1801/63/74/85/96	1931/42/53	2015/26
e 6	1539/50/61/72	1634/45/56	1729/35/40/60	1806/17/28/90	1947/58/69/80	
f 7	1504/77/88	1667/72	1751/65/76	1822/33/44	1901/12/85/96	
g 8	1509/15/20/99	1604/10/83/94	1705/87/92/98	1849/55/60	1917/28	2007/12
A 9	1531/42	1615/26/37/99	1710/21/32	1871/82	1939/44/50	2023
b 10	1547/58/69	1631/42/53/64	1726/37/48/57	1803/14/87/98	1955/66/77	
c 11	1501/12/63/74/85/96	1658/69/80	1762/73/84	1819/30/41/52	1909/71/82/93	2004
d 12	1506/17/28	1601/12/91/96	1789	1846/57/68	1903/14/25/36/98	2009/20
e 13	1533/44	1623/28	1707/18	1800/73/79/84	1941/52	2031
f 14	1555/60/66	1639/50/61	1723/34/45/54	1805/11/16/95	1963/68/74	
g 15	1571/82/93	1655/66/77/88	1750/59/70/81	1827/38	1900/06/79/90	2001
A 16	1503/14/25/36/87/98	1609/20/82/93	1704/75/86/97	1843/54/65/76	1911/22/33/95	2006/17/28
b 17	1530/41/52	1625/36	1715/20	1808/70/81/92	1927/38/49/60	2022/33
c 18	1557/68	1647/52	1731/42/56	1802/13/24/97	1954/65/76	
d 19	1500/79/84/90	1663/74/85	1747/67/72/78	1829/35/40	1908/81/87/92	
e 20	1511/22/95	1606/17/79/90	1701/12/83/94	1851/62	1919/24/30	2003/14/25
f 21	1527/38/49	1622/33/44	1717/28	1867/78/89	1935/46/57	2019/30
g 22	1565/76	1660	1739/53/64	1810/21/32	1962/73/84	
A 23	1508	1671		1848	1905/16	2000
b 24	1519	1603/14/98	1709/91	1859		2011
c 25	1546	1641	1736	1886	1943	

HINDU CALENDAR

The Hindu calendar is a luni-solar calendar of twelve months, each containing 29 days, 12 hours. Each month is divided into a light fortnight (Shukla or Shuddha) and a dark fortnight (Krishna or Vadya) based on the waxing and waning of the moon. In most parts of India the month starts with the light fortnight, i.e. the day after the new moon, although in some regions it begins with the dark fortnight, i.e. the day after the full moon.

The new year begins in the month of Chaitra (March/April) and ends in the month of Phalgun (March). The twelve months, Chaitra, Vaishakh, Jyeshtha, Ashadh, Shravan, Bhadrapad, Ashvin, Kartik, Margashirsh, Paush, Magh and Phalgun, have Sanskrit names derived from twelve asterisms (constellations). There are regional variations to the names of the months but the Sanskrit names are understood throughout India.

Every lunar month must have a solar transit and is termed pure (shuddha). The lunar month without a solar transit is impure (mala) and called an intercalary month. An intercalary month occurs approximately every 32 lunar months, whenever the difference between the Hindu year of 360 lunar days (354 days 8 hours solar time) and the 365 days 6 hours of the solar year reaches the length of one Hindu lunar month (29 days 12 hours).

The leap month may be added at any point in the Hindu year. The name given to the month varies according to when it occurs but is taken from the month immediately following it. Leap months occur in 1996–7 (Ashadh) and 1999–2000 (Jyeshtha).

The days of the week are called Raviwar (Sunday), Somawar (Monday), Mangalwar (Tuesday), Budhawar (Wednesday), Guruwar (Thursday), Shukrawar (Friday) and Shaniwar (Saturday). The names are derived from the Sanskrit names of the Sun, the Moon and five planets, Mars, Mercury, Jupiter, Venus and Saturn.

Most fasts and festivals are based on the lunar calendar but a few are determined by the apparent movement of the Sun, e.g. Sankranti, which is celebrated on 14/15 January to mark the start of the Sun's apparent journey northwards and a change of season.

Festivals celebrated throughout India are Chaitra (the New Year), Raksha-bandhan (the renewal of the kinship bond between brothers and sisters), Navaratri (a nine-night festival dedicated to the goddess Parvati), Dasara (the victory of Rama over the demon army), Diwali (a festival of lights), Makara Sankranti, Shivaratri (dedicated to Shiva), and Holi (a spring festival).

Regional festivals are Durga-puja (dedicated to the goddess Durga (Parvati)), Sarasvati-puja (dedicated to the goddess Sarasvati), Ganesh Chaturthi (worship of Ganesh on the fourth day (Chaturthi) of the light half of Bhadrapad), Ramanavami (the birth festival of the god Rama) and Janmashtami (the birth festival of the god Krishna).

The main festivals celebrated in Britain are Navaratri, Dasara, Durga-puja, Diwali, Holi, Sarasvati-puja, Ganesh Chaturthi, Raksha-bandhan, Ramanavami and Janmashtami.

The dates of the main festivals in 1997 are given on page 9.

JEWISH CALENDAR

The story of the Flood in the Book of Genesis indicates the use of a calendar of some kind and that the writers recognized thirty days as the length of a lunation. However, after the diaspora, Jewish communities were left in considerable doubt as to the times of fasts and festivals. This led to the formation of the Jewish calendar as used today. It is said that this was done in AD 358 by Rabbi Hillel II, though some assert that it did not happen until much later.

The calendar is luni-solar, and is based on the lengths of the lunation and of the tropical year as found by Hipparchus (c.120 BC), which differ little from those adopted at the present day. The year AM 5757 (1996–7) is the 19th year of the 303rd Metonic (Minor or Lunar) cycle of 19 years and the 17th year of the 206th Solar (or Major) cycle of 28 years since the Era of the Creation. Jews hold that the Creation occurred at the time of the autumnal equinox in the year known in the Christian calendar as 3760 BC (954 of the Julian period). The epoch or starting point of Jewish chronology corresponds to 7 October 3761 BC. At the beginning of each solar cycle, the Tekufah of Nisan (the vernal equinox) returns to the same day and to the same hour.

The hour is divided into 1080 minims, and the month between one new moon and the next is reckoned as 29 days, 12 hours, 793 minims. The normal calendar year, called a Regular Common year, consists of 12 months of 30 days and 29 days alternately. Since twelve months such as these comprise only 354 days, in order that each of them shall not diverge greatly from an average place in the solar year, a thirteenth month is occasionally added after the fifth month of the civil year (which commences on the first day of the month Tishri), or as the penultimate month of the ecclesiastical year (which commences on the first day of the month Nisan). The years when this happens are called Embolismic or leap years.

Of the 19 years that form a Metonic cycle, seven are leap years; they occur at places in the cycle indicated by the numbers 3, 6, 8, 11, 14, 17 and 19, these places being chosen so that the accumulated excesses of the solar years should be as small as possible.

A Jewish year is of one of the following six types:

Minimal Common	353 days
Regular Common	354 days
Full Common	355 days
Minimal Leap	383 days
Regular Leap	384 days
Full Leap	385 days.

The Regular year has alternate months of 30 and 29 days. In a Full year, whether common or leap, Marcheshvan, the second month of the civil year, has 30 days instead of 29; in Minimal years Kislev, the third month, has 29 instead of 30. The additional month in leap years is called Adar I and precedes the month called Adar in Common years. Adar II is called Adar Sheni in leap years, and the usual Adar festivals are kept in Adar Sheni. Adar I and Adar II always have 30 days, but neither this, nor the other variations mentioned, is allowed to change the number of days in the other months, which still follow the alternation of the normal twelve.

These are the main features of the Jewish calendar, which must be considered permanent because as a Jewish law it cannot be altered except by a great Sanhedrin.

The Jewish day begins between sunset and nightfall. The time used is that of the meridian of Jerusalem, which is 2h 21m in advance of Greenwich Mean Time. Rules for the beginning of sabbaths and festivals were laid down for the latitude of London in the 18th century and hours for nightfall are now fixed annually by the Chief Rabbi.

JEWISH CALENDAR 5757–8

AM 5757 (757) is a Minimal Leap year of 13 months, 55 sabbaths and 383 days. AM 5758 (758) is a Regular Common year of 12 months, 51 sabbaths and 354 days.

Jewish Month	AM 5757	AM 5758
Tishri 1	14 September 1996	2 October 1997
Marcheshvan 1	14 October	1 November
Kislev 1	12 November	30 November
Tebet 1	11 December	30 December
Shebat 1	9 January 1997	28 January 1998
*Adar 1	8 February	27 February
†Adar II	10 March	
Nisan 1	8 April	28 March
Iyar 1	8 May	27 April
Sivan 1	6 June	26 May
Tammuz 1	6 July	25 June
Ab 1	4 August	24 July
Elul 1	3 September	23 August

*Known as Adar Rishon in leap years
†Known as Adar Sheni in leap years

JEWISH FASTS AND FESTIVALS

For dates of principal festivals in 1997, see page 9

Tishri 1–2	Rosh Hashanah (New Year)
Tishri 3	*Fast of Gedaliah
Tishri 10	Yom Kippur (Day of Atonement)
Tishri 15–21	Succoth (Feast of Tabernacles)
Tishri 21	Hoshana Rabba
Tishri 22	Shemini Atseret (Solemn Assembly)
Tishri 23	Simchat Torah (Rejoicing of the Law)
Kislev 25	Chanucah (Dedication of the Temple) begins
Tebet 10	Fast of Tebet
†Adar 13	§Fast of Esther
†Adar 14	Purim
†Adar 15	Shushan Purim
Nisan 15–22	Pesach (Passover)
Sivan 6–7	Shavuot (Feast of Weeks)
Tammuz 17	*Fast of Tammuz
Ab 9	*Fast of Ab

*If these dates fall on the sabbath the fast is kept on the following day
†Adar Sheni in leap years
§This fast is observed on Adar 11 (or Adar Sheni 11 in leap years) if Adar 13 falls on a sabbath

THE MUSLIM CALENDAR

The Muslim era is dated from the *Hijrah*, or flight of the Prophet Muhammad from Mecca to Medina, the corresponding date of which in the Julian calendar is 16 July AD 622. Hijrah years (AH) are used principally in Iran, Turkey, Egypt, Malaysia, various Arab states and certain parts of India. The dating system was adopted about AD 639, commencing with the first day of the month Muharram. Muharram precedes the month in which the Hijrah took place and was recognized as the beginning of the year because it followed the month of pilgrimage.

The calendar is a lunar calendar and consists of twelve months containing an alternate sequence of 30 and 29 days, with the intercalation of one day at the end of the twelfth month at stated intervals in each cycle of 30 years. The object of the intercalation is to reconcile the date of the first day of the month with the date of the actual new moon.

Some adherents still take the date of the evening of the first physical sighting of the crescent of the new moon as that of the first of the month. For this reason, the beginning of a new month and the date of religious festivals can vary by a few days from the published calendars.

In each cycle of 30 years, 19 years are common and contain 354 days, and 11 years are intercalary (leap years) of 355 days, the latter being called *kabishah*. The mean length of the Hijrah years is 354 days 8 hours 48 minutes and the period of mean lunation is 29 days 12 hours 44 minutes.

To ascertain if a year is common or kabishah, divide it by 30: the quotient gives the number of completed cycles and the remainder shows the place of the year in the current cycle. If the remainder is 2, 5, 7, 10, 13, 16, 18, 21, 24, 26 or 29, the year is kabishah and consists of 355 days.

MUSLIM CALENDAR 1417–18

Hijrah year 1417 AH (remainder 7) is a kabishah year; 1418 AH (remainder 8) is a common year.

Month (length)	1417 AH	1418 AH
Muharram (30)	19 May 1996	9 May 1997
Safar (29)	18 June	8 June
Rabi' I (30)	17 July	7 July
Rabi' II (29)	16 August	6 August
Jumada I (30)	14 September	4 September
Jumada II (29)	14 October	4 October
Rajab (30)	12 November	2 November
Shaabân (29)	12 December	2 December
Ramadân (30)	10 January 1997	31 December
Shawwâl (29)	9 February	30 January 1998
Dhû'l-Qa'da (30)	10 March	28 February
Dhû'l-Hijjah (29 or 30)	9 April	30 March

MUSLIM FESTIVALS

Ramadan is a month of fasting for all Muslims because it is the month in which the revelation of the *Qur'an* (Koran) began. During Ramadan Muslims abstain from food, drink and sexual pleasure from dawn until after sunset throughout the month.

The two major festivals are *Idu-l-fitr* and *Idu-l-adha*. Idu-l-fitr marks the end of the Ramadan fast and is celebrated on the day after the sighting of the new moon of the following month. Idu-l-adha, the festival of sacrifice (also known as the great festival), celebrates the submission of the Prophet

Ibrahim (Abraham) to Allah. Idu-l-adha falls on the tenth day of Dhul-Hijjah, coinciding with the day when those on *hajj* (pilgrimage to Mecca) sacrifice animals.

Other days accorded special recognition are:

Muharram 1	New Year's Day
Muharram 10	Ashura (the day Prophet Nuh left the Ark and Prophet Musa was saved from Pharaoh (Sunni), the death of the Prophet's grandson Husain (Shi'ite))
Rabi'u-l-Awwal (Rabi' I) 12	Mawlidu-n-Nabiyy (birthday of the Prophet Muhammad)
Rajab 27	Laylatu-l-Isra wa l-Miraj (Night of the Journey and Ascension)
Ramadân Odd-numbered nights in the last 10 of the month	Laylatu-l-Qadr (Night of Power)
Dhû'l-Hijjah 10	Idu-l-adha (Festival of Sacrifice)

THE SIKH CALENDAR

The Sikh calendar is a lunar calendar of 365 days divided into 12 months. The length of the months varies between 29 and 32 days.

There are no prescribed feast days and no fasting periods. The main celebrations are Baisakhi Mela (the new year and the anniversary of the founding of the Khalsa), Diwali Mela (festival of light), Hola Mohalla Mela (a spring festival held in the Punjab), and the Gurpurbs (anniversaries associated with the ten Gurus).

The dates of the major celebrations in 1997 are given on page 9.

CIVIL AND LEGAL CALENDAR

THE HISTORICAL YEAR

Before the year 1752, two calendar systems were in use in England. The civil or legal year began on 25 March and the historical year on 1 January. Thus the civil or legal date 24 March 1658 was the same day as the historical date 24 March 1659; and a date in that portion of the year is written as 24 March 165⁸⁄₉ the lower figure showing the historical year.

THE NEW YEAR

In England in the seventh century, and as late as the 13th, the year was reckoned from Christmas Day, but in the 12th century the Church in England began the year with the feast of the Annunciation of the Blessed Virgin ('Lady Day') on 25 March and this practice was adopted generally in the 14th century. The civil or legal year in the British Dominions (exclusive of Scotland) began with Lady Day until 1751. But in and since 1752 the civil year has begun with 1 January. New Year's Day in Scotland was changed from 25 March to 1 January in 1600.

Elsewhere in Europe, 1 January was adopted as the first day of the year by Venice in 1522, German states in 1544, Spain, Portugal, and the Roman Catholic Netherlands in 1556, Prussia, Denmark and Sweden in 1559, France in 1564, Lorraine in 1579, the Protestant Netherlands in 1583, Russia in 1725, and Tuscany in 1751.

REGNAL YEARS

Regnal years are the years of a sovereign's reign and each begins on the anniversary of his or her accession, e.g. regnal year 46 of the present Queen begins on 6 February 1997.

The system was used for dating Acts of Parliament until 1962. The Summer Time Act 1925, for example, is quoted as 15 and 16 Geo. V c. 64, because it became law in the parliamentary session which extended over part of both of these regnal years. Acts of a parliamentary session during which a sovereign died were usually given two year numbers, the regnal year of the deceased sovereign and the regnal year of his or her successor, e.g. those passed in 1952 were dated 16 Geo. VI and 1 Elizabeth II. Since 1962 Acts of Parliament have been dated by the calendar year.

QUARTER AND TERM DAYS

Holy days and saints days were the usual means in early times for setting the dates of future and recurrent appointments. The quarter days in England and Wales are the feast of the Nativity (25 December), the feast of the Annunciation (25 March), the feast of St John the Baptist (24 June) and the feast of St Michael and All Angels (29 September).

The term days in Scotland are Candlemas (the feast of the Purification), Whitsunday, Lammas (Loaf Mass), and Martinmas (St Martin's Day). These fell on 2 February, 15 May, 1 August and 11 November respectively. However, by the Term and Quarter Days (Scotland) Act 1990, the dates of the term days were changed to 28 February (Candlemas), 28 May (Whitsunday), 28 August (Lammas) and 28 November (Martinmas).

RED-LETTER DAYS

Red-letter days were originally the holy days and saints days indicated in early ecclesiastical calendars by letters printed in red ink. The days to be distinguished in this way were approved at the Council of Nicaea in AD 325.

These days still have a legal significance, as judges of the Queen's Bench Division wear scarlet robes on red-letter days falling during the law sittings. The days designated as red-letter days for this purpose are:

Holy and saints days
The Conversion of St Paul, the Purification, Ash Wednesday, the Annunciation, the Ascension, the feasts of St Mark, SS Philip and James, St Matthias, St Barnabas, St John the Baptist, St Peter, St Thomas, St James, St Luke, SS Simon and Jude, All Saints, St Andrew

Civil calendar
The anniversaries of The Queen's accession, The Queen's birthday and The Queen's coronation, The Queen's official birthday, the birthday of the Duke of Edinburgh, the birthday of Queen Elizabeth the Queen Mother, the birthday of the Prince of Wales, St David's Day and Lord Mayor's Day

PUBLIC HOLIDAYS

Public holidays are divided into two categories, common law and statutory. Common law holidays are holidays 'by habit and custom'; in England, Wales and Northern Ireland these are Good Friday and Christmas Day.

Statutory public holidays, known as bank holidays, were first established by the Bank Holidays Act 1871. They were, literally, days on which the banks (and other public institutions) were closed and financial obligations due on that day were payable the following day. The legislation currently governing public holidays in the United Kingdom is the Banking and Financial Dealings Act 1971. It

stipulates which days are to be public holidays in England, Wales, Scotland and Northern Ireland.

Certain holidays (indicated by * below) are granted annually by royal proclamation, either throughout the United Kingdom or in any place in the United Kingdom. The public holidays are:

England and Wales
*New Year's Day
Easter Monday
*The first Monday in May
The last Monday in May
The last Monday in August
26 December, if it is not a Sunday
27 December when 25 or 26 December is a Sunday

Scotland
New Year's Day, or if it is a Sunday, 2 January
2 January, or if it is a Sunday, 3 January
Good Friday
The first Monday in May
*The last Monday in May
The first Monday in August
Christmas Day, or if it is a Sunday, 26 December
*Boxing Day − if Christmas Day falls on a Sunday, 26 December is given in lieu and an alternative day is given for Boxing Day

Northern Ireland
*New Year's Day
17 March, or if it is a Sunday, 18 March
Easter Monday
*The first Monday in May
The last Monday in May
*12 July, or if it is a Sunday, 13 July
The last Monday in August
26 December, if it is not a Sunday
27 December if 25 or 26 December is a Sunday

For dates of public holidays in 1997 and 1998, see pages 10−11.

CHRONOLOGICAL CYCLES AND ERAS

SOLAR (OR MAJOR) CYCLE
The solar cycle is a period of twenty-eight years in any corresponding year of which the days of the week recur on the same day of the month.

METONIC (LUNAR, OR MINOR) CYCLE
In 432 BC, Meton, an Athenian astronomer, found that 235 lunations are very nearly, though not exactly, equal in duration to 19 solar years and so after 19 years the phases of the Moon recur on the same days of the month (nearly). The dates of full moon in a cycle of 19 years were inscribed in figures of gold on public monuments in Athens, and the number showing the position of a year in the cycle is called the golden number of that year.

JULIAN PERIOD
The Julian period was proposed by Joseph Scaliger in 1582. The period is 7980 Julian years, and its first year coincides with the year 4713 BC. The figure of 7980 is the product of the number of years in the solar cycle, the Metonic cycle and the cycle of the Roman indiction (28 × 19 × 15).

ROMAN INDICTION

The Roman indiction is a period of fifteen years, instituted for fiscal purposes about AD 300.

EPACT

The epact is the age of the calendar Moon, diminished by one day, on 1 January, in the ecclesiastical lunar calendar.

CHINESE CALENDAR

A lunar calendar was the sole calendar in use in China until 1911, when the government adopted the new (Gregorian) calendar for official and most business activities. The Chinese tend to follow both calendars, the lunar calendar playing an important part in personal life, e.g. birth celebrations, festivals, marriages; and in rural villages the lunar calendar dictates the cycle of activities, denoting the change of weather and farming activities.

The lunar calendar is used in Hong Kong, Singapore, Malaysia, Tibet and elsewhere in south-east Asia. The calendar has a cycle of 60 years. The new year begins at the first new moon after the sun enters the sign of Aquarius, i.e. the new year falls between 21 January and 19 February in the Gregorian calendar.

Each year in the Chinese calendar is associated with one of 12 animals: the rat, the ox, the tiger, the rabbit, the dragon, the snake, the horse, the goat or sheep, the monkey, the chicken or rooster, the dog, and the pig.

The date of the Chinese new year and the astrological sign for the years 1997–2000 are:

1997	7 February	Ox
1998	28 January	Tiger
1999	16 February	Rabbit
2000	5 February	Dragon

COPTIC CALENDAR

In the Coptic calendar, which is used by part of the population of Egypt and Ethiopia, the year is made up of 12 months of 30 days each, followed, in general, by five complementary days. Every fourth year is an intercalary or leap year and in these years there are six complementary days. The intercalary year of the Coptic calendar immediately precedes the leap year of the Julian calendar. The era is that of Diocletian or the Martyrs, the origin of which is fixed at 29 August AD 284 (Julian date).

INDIAN ERAS

In addition to the Muslim reckoning, other eras are used in India. The Saka era of southern India, dating from 3 March AD 78, was declared the national calendar of the Republic of India with effect from 22 March 1957, to be used concurrently with the Gregorian calendar. As revised, the year of the new Saka era begins at the spring equinox, with five successive months of 31 days and seven of 30 days in ordinary years, and six months of each length in leap years. The year AD 1997 is 1919 of the revised Saka era.

The year AD 1997 corresponds to the following years in other eras:

Year 2054 of the Vikram Samvat era
Year 1404 of the Bengali San era
Year 1173 of the Kollam era
Jovian year (Barhaspatya varsa or 60-year cycle of Jupiter) 25 Vikrta (North Indian usage) and 11 Dhatri (South Indian usage)
Vedanga Jyotisa year 3 Parivatsara of the five-yearly cycle (384th cycle of Paitamah Siddhanta)
Year 5098 of the Kaliyuga era
Year 2541 of the Buddha Nirvana era

JAPANESE CALENDAR

The Japanese calendar is essentially the same as the Gregorian calendar, the years, months and weeks being of the same length and beginning on the same days as those of the Gregorian calendar. The numeration of the years is different, for Japanese chronology is based on a system of epochs or periods, each of which begins at the accession of an Emperor or other important occurrence. The method is not unlike the former British system of regnal years, except that each year of a period closes on 31 December. The Japanese chronology begins about AD 650 and the three latest epochs are defined by the reigns of Emperors, whose actual names are not necessarily used:

Epoch

Taishō   1 August 1912 to 25 December 1926
Shōwa   26 December 1926 to 7 January 1989
Heisei   8 January 1989

The year Heisei 9 begins on 1 January 1997.

The months are not named. They are known as First Month, Second Month, etc., First Month being equivalent to January. The days of the week are Nichiyōbi (Sun-day), Getsuyōbi (Moon-day), Kayōbi (Fire-day), Suiyōbi (Water-day), Mokuyōbi (Wood-day), Kinyōbi (Metal-day), Doyōbi (Earth-day).

THE MASONIC YEAR

Two dates are quoted in warrants, dispensations, etc., issued by the United Grand Lodge of England, those for the current year being expressed as *Anno Domini* 1997 – *Anno Lucis* 5997. This *Anno Lucis* (year of light) is based on the Book of Genesis 1:3, the 4000-year difference being derived, in modified form, from *Ussher's Notation*, published in 1654, which places the Creation of the World in 4004 BC.

OLYMPIADS

Ancient Greek chronology was reckoned in Olympiads, cycles of four years corresponding with the periodic Olympic Games held on the plain of Olympia in Elis once every four years. The intervening years were the first, second, etc., of the Olympiad, which received the name of the victor at the Games. The first recorded Olympiad is that of Choroebus, 776 BC.

ZOROASTRIAN CALENDAR

Zoroastrians, followers of the Iranian prophet Zarathushtra (known to the Greeks as Zoroaster) are mostly to be found in Iran and in India, where they are known as Parsees.

The Zoroastrian era dates from the coronation of the last Zoroastrian Sasanian king in AD 631. The Zoroastrian calendar is divided into twelve months, each comprising 30 days, followed by five holy days of the Gathas at the end of each year to make the year consist of 365 days.

In order to synchronize the calendar with the solar year of 365 days, an extra month was intercalated once every 120 years. However, this intercalation ceased in the 12th century and the New Year, which had fallen in the spring, slipped back until it now falls in August. Because intercalation ceased at different times in Iran and India, there was one month's difference between the calendar followed in Iran (Kadmi calendar) and by the Parsees (Shenshai calendar).

In 1906 a group of Zoroastrians decided to bring the calendar back in line with the seasons again and restore the New Year to 21 March each year (Fasli calendar).

The Shenshai calendar (New Year in August) is mainly used by Parsees. The Fasli calendar (New Year, 21 March) is mainly used by Zoroastrians living in Iran, in the Indian subcontinent, or away from Iran.

THE ROMAN CALENDAR

Roman historians adopted as an epoch the foundation of Rome, which is believed to have happened in the year 753 BC. The ordinal number of the years in Roman reckoning is followed by the letters AUC (*ab urbe condita*), so that the year 1997 is 2750 AUC (MMDCCL). The calendar that we know has developed from one said to have been established by Romulus using a year of 304 days divided into ten months, beginning with March. To this Numa added January and February, making the year consist of 12 months of 30 and 29 days alternately, with an additional day so that the total was 355. It is also said that Numa ordered an intercalary month of 22 or 23 days in alternate years, making 90 days in eight years, to be inserted after 23 February.

However, there is some doubt as to the origination and the details of the intercalation in the Roman calendar. It is certain that some scheme of this kind was inaugurated and not fully carried out, for in the year 46 BC Julius Caesar found that the calendar had been allowed to fall into some confusion. He sought the help of the Egyptian astronomer Sosigenes, which led to the construction and adoption (45 BC) of the Julian calendar, and, by a slight alteration, to the Gregorian calendar now in use. The year 46 BC was made to consist of 445 days and is called the Year of Confusion.

In the Roman (Julian) calendar the days of the month were counted backwards from three fixed points, or days, and an intervening day was said to be so many days before the next coming point, the first and last being counted. These three points were the Kalends, the Nones, and the Ides. Their positions in the months and the method of counting from them will be seen in the table below. The year containing 366 days was called *bissextilis annus*, as it had a doubled sixth day (*bissextus dies*) before the March Kalends on 24 February – *ante diem sextum Kalendas Martias*, or a.d. VI Kal. Mart.

Present days of the month	March, May, July, October have thirty-one days		January, August, December have thirty-one days		April, June, September, November have thirty days		February has twenty-eight days, and in leap year twenty-nine	
1	Kalendis		Kalendis		Kalendis		Kalendis	
2	VI		IV ⎱ ante		IV ⎱ ante		IV ⎱ ante	
3	V	ante	III ⎰ Nonas		III ⎰ Nonas		III ⎰ Nonas	
4	IV	Nonas	pridie Nonas		pridie Nonas		pridie Nonas	
5	III		Nonis		Nonis		Nonis	
6	pridie Nonas		VIII		VIII		VIII	
7	Nonis		VII		VII		VII	
8	VIII		VI ⎱ ante		VI ⎱ ante		VI ⎱ ante	
9	VII		V ⎰ Idus		V ⎰ Idus		V ⎰ Idus	
10	VI	ante	IV		IV		IV	
11	V	Idus	III		III		III	
12	IV		pridie Idus		pridie Idus		pridie Idus	
13	III		Idibus		Idibus		Idibus	
14	pridie Idus		XIX		XVIII		XVI	
15	Idibus		XVIII		XVII		XV	
16	XVII		XVII		XVI		XIV	
17	XVI		XVI		XV		XIII	
18	XV		XV		XIV		XII	
19	XIV		XIV		XIII		XI	
20	XIII		XIII		XII	ante Kalendas	X	ante Kalendas
21	XII		XII	ante Kalendas	XI	(of the month	IX	Martias
22	XI	ante Kalendas	XI	(of the month	X	following)	VIII	
23	X	(of the month	X	following)	IX		VII	
24	IX	following)	IX		VIII		*VI	
25	VIII		VIII		VII		V	
26	VII		VII		VI		IV	
27	VI		VI		V		III	
28	V		V		IV		pridie Kalendas	
29	IV		IV		III		Martias	
30	III		III		pridie Kalendas			
31	pridie Kalendas (Aprilis, Iunias, Sextilis, Novembris)		pridie Kalendas (Februarias, Septembris, Ianuarias)		(Maias, Quinctilis, Octobris, Decembris)		* (repeated in leap year)	

Calendar for Any Year 1780–2040

To select the correct calendar for any year between 1780 and 2040, consult the index below
* leap year

Year		Year		Year		Year		Year		Year		Year		Year	
1780	N*	1813	K	1846	I	1879	G	1912	D*	1945	C	1978	A	2011	M
1781	C	1814	M	1847	K	1880	J*	1913	G	1946	E	1979	C	2012	B*
1782	E	1815	A	1848	N*	1881	M	1914	I	1947	G	1980	F*	2013	E
1783	G	1816	D*	1849	C	1882	A	1915	K	1948	J*	1981	I	2014	G
1784	J*	1817	G	1850	E	1883	C	1916	N*	1949	M	1982	K	2015	I
1785	M	1818	I	1851	G	1884	F*	1917	C	1950	A	1983	M	2016	L*
1786	A	1819	K	1852	J*	1885	I	1918	E	1951	C	1984	B*	2017	A
1787	C	1820	N*	1853	M	1886	K	1919	G	1952	F*	1985	E	2018	C
1788	F*	1821	C	1854	A	1887	M	1920	J*	1953	I	1986	G	2019	E
1789	I	1822	E	1855	C	1888	B*	1921	M	1954	K	1987	I	2020	H*
1790	K	1823	G	1856	F*	1889	E	1922	A	1955	M	1988	L*	2021	K
1791	M	1824	J*	1857	I	1890	G	1923	C	1956	B*	1989	A	2022	M
1792	B*	1825	M	1858	K	1891	I	1924	F*	1957	E	1990	C	2023	A
1793	E	1826	A	1859	M	1892	L*	1925	I	1958	G	1991	E	2024	D*
1794	G	1827	C	1860	B*	1893	A	1926	K	1959	I	1992	H*	2025	G
1795	I	1828	F*	1861	E	1894	C	1927	M	1960	L*	1993	K	2026	I
1796	L*	1829	I	1862	G	1895	E	1928	B*	1961	A	1994	M	2027	K
1797	A	1830	K	1863	I	1896	H*	1929	E	1962	C	1995	A	2028	N*
1798	C	1831	M	1864	L*	1897	K	1930	G	1963	E	1996	D*	2029	C
1799	E	1832	B*	1865	A	1898	M	1931	I	1964	H*	1997	G	2030	E
1800	E	1833	E	1866	C	1899	A	1932	L*	1965	K	1998	I	2031	G
1801	I	1834	G	1867	E	1900	C	1933	A	1966	M	1999	K	2032	J*
1802	K	1835	I	1868	H*	1901	E	1934	C	1967	A	2000	N*	2033	M
1803	M	1836	L*	1869	K	1902	G	1935	E	1968	D*	2001	E	2034	A
1804	B*	1837	A	1870	M	1903	I	1936	H*	1969	G	2002	E	2035	C
1805	E	1838	C	1871	A	1904	L*	1937	K	1970	I	2003	G	2036	F*
1806	G	1839	E	1872	D*	1905	A	1938	M	1971	K	2004	J*	2037	I
1807	I	1840	H*	1873	G	1906	C	1939	A	1972	N*	2005	M	2038	K
1808	L*	1841	K	1874	I	1907	E	1940	D*	1973	C	2006	A	2039	M
1809	A	1842	M	1875	K	1908	H*	1941	G	1974	E	2007	C	2040	B*
1810	C	1843	A	1876	N*	1909	K	1942	I	1975	G	2008	F*		
1811	E	1844	D*	1877	C	1910	M	1943	K	1976	J*	2009	I		
1812	H*	1845	G	1878	E	1911	A	1944	N*	1977	M	2010	K		

A

	January	*February*	*March*
Sun.	1 8 15 22 29	5 12 19 26	5 12 19 26
Mon.	2 9 16 23 30	6 13 20 27	6 13 20 27
Tue.	3 10 17 24 31	7 14 21 28	7 14 21 28
Wed.	4 11 18 25	1 8 15 22	1 8 15 22 29
Thur.	5 12 19 26	2 9 16 23	2 9 16 23 30
Fri.	6 13 20 27	3 10 17 24	3 10 17 24 31
Sat.	7 14 21 28	4 11 18 25	4 11 18 25

	April	*May*	*June*
Sun.	2 9 16 23 30	7 14 21 28	4 11 18 25
Mon.	3 10 17 24	1 8 15 22 29	5 12 19 26
Tue.	4 11 18 25	2 9 16 23 30	6 13 20 27
Wed.	5 12 19 26	3 10 17 24 31	7 14 21 28
Thur.	6 13 20 27	4 11 18 25	1 8 15 22 29
Fri.	7 14 21 28	5 12 19 26	2 9 16 23 30
Sat.	1 8 15 22 29	6 13 20 27	3 10 17 24

	July	*August*	*September*
Sun.	2 9 16 23 30	6 13 20 27	3 10 17 24
Mon.	3 10 17 24 31	7 14 21 28	4 11 18 25
Tue.	4 11 18 25	1 8 15 22 29	5 12 19 26
Wed.	5 12 19 26	2 9 16 23 30	6 13 20 27
Thur.	6 13 20 27	3 10 17 24 31	7 14 21 28
Fri.	7 14 21 28	4 11 18 25	1 8 15 22 29
Sat.	1 8 15 22 29	5 12 19 26	2 9 16 23 30

	October	*November*	*December*
Sun.	1 8 15 22 29	5 12 19 26	3 10 17 24 31
Mon.	2 9 16 23 30	6 13 20 27	4 11 18 25
Tue.	3 10 17 24 31	7 14 21 28	5 12 19 26
Wed.	4 11 18 25	1 8 15 22 29	6 13 20 27
Thur.	5 12 19 26	2 9 16 23 30	7 14 21 28
Fri.	6 13 20 27	3 10 17 24	1 8 15 22 29
Sat.	7 14 21 28	4 11 18 25	2 9 16 23 30

EASTER DAYS

March 26	1815, 1826, 1837, 1967, 1978, 1989
April 2	1809, 1893, 1899, 1961
April 9	1871, 1882, 1939, 1950, 2023, 2034
April 16	1786, 1797, 1843, 1854, 1865, 1911 1922, 1933, 1995, 2006, 2017
April 23	1905

B (LEAP YEAR)

	January	*February*	*March*
Sun.	1 8 15 22 29	5 12 19 26	4 11 18 25
Mon.	2 9 16 23 30	6 13 20 27	5 12 19 26
Tue.	3 10 17 24 31	7 14 21 28	6 13 20 27
Wed.	4 11 18 25	1 8 15 22 29	7 14 21 28
Thur.	5 12 19 26	2 9 16 23	1 8 15 22 29
Fri.	6 13 20 27	3 10 17 24	2 9 16 23 30
Sat.	7 14 21 28	4 11 18 25	3 10 17 24 31

	April	*May*	*June*
Sun.	1 8 15 22 29	6 13 20 27	3 10 17 24
Mon.	2 9 16 23 30	7 14 21 28	4 11 18 25
Tue.	3 10 17 24	1 8 15 22 29	5 12 19 26
Wed.	4 11 18 25	2 9 16 23 30	6 13 20 27
Thur.	5 12 19 26	3 10 17 24 31	7 14 21 28
Fri.	6 13 20 27	4 11 18 25	1 8 15 22 29
Sat.	7 14 21 28	5 12 19 26	2 9 16 23 30

	July	*August*	*September*
Sun.	1 8 15 22 29	5 12 19 26	2 9 16 23 30
Mon.	2 9 16 23 30	6 13 20 27	3 10 17 24
Tue.	3 10 17 24 31	7 14 21 28	4 11 18 25
Wed.	4 11 18 25	1 8 15 22 29	5 12 19 26
Thur.	5 12 19 26	2 9 16 23 30	6 13 20 27
Fri.	6 13 20 27	3 10 17 24 31	7 14 21 28
Sat.	7 14 21 28	4 11 18 25	1 8 15 22 29

	October	*November*	*December*
Sun.	7 14 21 28	4 11 18 25	2 9 16 23 30
Mon.	1 8 15 22 29	5 12 19 26	3 10 17 24 31
Tue.	2 9 16 23 30	6 13 20 27	4 11 18 25
Wed.	3 10 17 24 31	7 14 21 28	5 12 19 26
Thur.	4 11 18 25	1 8 15 22 29	6 13 20 27
Fri.	5 12 19 26	2 9 16 23 30	7 14 21 28
Sat.	6 13 20 27	3 10 17 24	1 8 15 22 29

EASTER DAYS

April 1	1804, 1888, 1956, 2040
April 8	1792, 1860, 1928, 2012
April 22	1832, 1984

C

	January	February	March
Sun.	7 14 21 28	4 11 18 25	4 11 18 25
Mon.	1 8 15 22 29	5 12 19 26	5 12 19 26
Tue.	2 9 16 23 30	6 13 20 27	6 13 20 27
Wed.	3 10 17 24 31	7 14 21 28	7 14 21 28
Thur.	4 11 18 25	1 8 15 22	1 8 15 22 29
Fri.	5 12 19 26	2 9 16 23	2 9 16 23 30
Sat.	6 13 20 27	3 10 17 24	3 10 17 24 31

	April	May	June
Sun.	1 8 15 22 29	6 13 20 27	3 10 17 24
Mon.	2 9 16 23 30	7 14 21 28	4 11 18 25
Tue.	3 10 17 24	1 8 15 22 29	5 12 19 26
Wed.	4 11 18 25	2 9 16 23 30	6 13 20 27
Thur.	5 12 19 26	3 10 17 24 31	7 14 21 28
Fri.	6 13 20 27	4 11 18 25	1 8 15 22 29
Sat.	7 14 21 28	5 12 19 26	2 9 16 23 30

	July	August	September
Sun.	1 8 15 22 29	5 12 19 26	2 9 16 23 30
Mon.	2 9 16 23 30	6 13 20 27	3 10 17 24
Tue.	3 10 17 24 31	7 14 21 28	4 11 18 25
Wed.	4 11 18 25	1 8 15 22 29	5 12 19 26
Thur.	5 12 19 26	2 9 16 23 30	6 13 20 27
Fri.	6 13 20 27	3 10 17 24 31	7 14 21 28
Sat.	7 14 21 28	4 11 18 25	1 8 15 22 29

	October	November	December
Sun.	7 14 21 28	4 11 18 25	2 9 16 23 30
Mon.	1 8 15 22 29	5 12 19 26	3 10 17 24 31
Tue.	2 9 16 23 30	6 13 20 27	4 11 18 25
Wed.	3 10 17 24 31	7 14 21 28	5 12 19 26
Thur.	4 11 18 25	1 8 15 22 29	6 13 20 27
Fri.	5 12 19 26	2 9 16 23 30	7 14 21 28
Sat.	6 13 20 27	3 10 17 24	1 8 15 22 29

Easter Days

March 25	1883, 1894, 1951, 2035
April 1	1866, 1877, 1923, 1934, 1945, 2018, 2029
April 8	1787, 1798, 1849, 1855, 1917, 2007
April 15	1781, 1827, 1838, 1900, 1906, 1979, 1990, 2001
April 22	1810, 1821, 1962, 1973

E

	January	February	March
Sun.	6 13 20 27	3 10 17 24	3 10 17 24 31
Mon.	7 14 21 28	4 11 18 25	4 11 18 25
Tue.	1 8 15 22 29	5 12 19 26	5 12 19 26
Wed.	2 9 16 23 30	6 13 20 27	6 13 20 27
Thur.	3 10 17 24 31	7 14 21 28	7 14 21 28
Fri.	4 11 18 25	1 8 15 22	1 8 15 22 29
Sat.	5 12 19 26	2 9 16 23	2 9 16 23 30

	April	May	June
Sun.	7 14 21 28	5 12 19 26	2 9 16 23 30
Mon.	1 8 15 22 29	6 13 20 27	3 10 17 24
Tue.	2 9 16 23 30	7 14 21 28	4 11 18 25
Wed.	3 10 17 24	1 8 15 22 29	5 12 19 26
Thur.	4 11 18 25	2 9 16 23 30	6 13 20 27
Fri.	5 12 19 26	3 10 17 24 31	7 14 21 28
Sat.	6 13 20 27	4 11 18 25	1 8 15 22 29

	July	August	September
Sun.	7 14 21 28	4 11 18 25	1 8 15 22 29
Mon.	1 8 15 22 29	5 12 19 26	2 9 16 23 30
Tue.	2 9 16 23 30	6 13 20 27	3 10 17 24
Wed.	3 10 17 24 31	7 14 21 28	4 11 18 25
Thur.	4 11 18 25	1 8 15 22 29	5 12 19 26
Fri.	5 12 19 26	2 9 16 23 30	6 13 20 27
Sat.	6 13 20 27	3 10 17 24 31	7 14 21 28

	October	November	December
Sun.	6 13 20 27	3 10 17 24	1 8 15 22 29
Mon.	7 14 21 28	4 11 18 25	2 9 16 23 30
Tue.	1 8 15 22 29	5 12 19 26	3 10 17 24 31
Wed.	2 9 16 23 30	6 13 20 27	4 11 18 25
Thur.	3 10 17 24 31	7 14 21 28	5 12 19 26
Fri.	4 11 18 25	1 8 15 22 29	6 13 20 27
Sat.	5 12 19 26	2 9 16 23 30	7 14 21 28

Easter Days

March 24	1799
March 31	1782, 1793, 1839, 1850, 1861, 1907, 1918, 1929, 1991, 2002, 2013
April 7	1822, 1833, 1901, 1985
April 14	1805, 1811, 1895, 1963, 1974
April 21	1867, 1878, 1889, 1935, 1946, 1957, 2019, 2030

D (LEAP YEAR)

	January	February	March
Sun.	7 14 21 28	4 11 18 25	3 10 17 24 31
Mon.	1 8 15 22 29	5 12 19 26	4 11 18 25
Tue.	2 9 16 23 30	6 13 20 27	5 12 19 26
Wed.	3 10 17 24 31	7 14 21 28	6 13 20 27
Thur.	4 11 18 25	1 8 15 22 29	7 14 21 28
Fri.	5 12 19 26	2 9 16 23	1 8 15 22 29
Sat.	6 13 20 27	3 10 17 24	2 9 16 23 30

	April	May	June
Sun.	7 14 21 28	5 12 19 26	2 9 16 23 30
Mon.	1 8 15 22 29	6 13 20 27	3 10 17 24
Tue.	2 9 16 23 30	7 14 21 28	4 11 18 25
Wed.	3 10 17 24	1 8 15 22 29	5 12 19 26
Thur.	4 11 18 25	2 9 16 23 30	6 13 20 27
Fri.	5 12 19 26	3 10 17 24 31	7 14 21 28
Sat.	6 13 20 27	4 11 18 25	1 8 15 22 29

	July	August	September
Sun.	7 14 21 28	4 11 18 25	1 8 15 22 29
Mon.	1 8 15 22 29	5 12 19 26	2 9 16 23 30
Tue.	2 9 16 23 30	6 13 20 27	3 10 17 24
Wed.	3 10 17 24 31	7 14 21 28	4 11 18 25
Thur.	4 11 18 25	1 8 15 22 29	5 12 19 26
Fri.	5 12 19 26	2 9 16 23 30	6 13 20 27
Sat.	6 13 20 27	3 10 17 24 31	7 14 21 28

	October	November	December
Sun.	6 13 20 27	3 10 17 24	1 8 15 22 29
Mon.	7 14 21 28	4 11 18 25	2 9 16 23 30
Tue.	1 8 15 22 29	5 12 19 26	3 10 17 24 31
Wed.	2 9 16 23 30	6 13 20 27	4 11 18 25
Thur.	3 10 17 24 31	7 14 21 28	5 12 19 26
Fri.	4 11 18 25	1 8 15 22 29	6 13 20 27
Sat.	5 12 19 26	2 9 16 23 30	7 14 21 28

Easter Days

March 24	1940
March 31	1872, 2024
April 7	1844, 1912, 1996
April 14	1816, 1968

F (LEAP YEAR)

	January	February	March
Sun.	6 13 20 27	3 10 17 24	2 9 16 23 30
Mon.	7 14 21 28	4 11 18 25	3 10 17 24 31
Tue.	1 8 15 22 29	5 12 19 26	4 11 18 25
Wed.	2 9 16 23 30	6 13 20 27	5 12 19 26
Thur.	3 10 17 24 31	7 14 21 28	6 13 20 27
Fri.	4 11 18 25	1 8 15 22 29	7 14 21 28
Sat.	5 12 19 26	2 9 16 23	1 8 15 22 29

	April	May	June
Sun.	6 13 20 27	4 11 18 25	1 8 15 22 29
Mon.	7 14 21 28	5 12 19 26	2 9 16 23 30
Tue.	1 8 15 22 29	6 13 20 27	3 10 17 24
Wed.	2 9 16 23 30	7 14 21 28	4 11 18 25
Thur.	3 10 17 24	1 8 15 22 29	5 12 19 26
Fri.	4 11 18 25	2 9 16 23 30	6 13 20 27
Sat.	5 12 19 26	3 10 17 24 31	7 14 21 28

	July	August	September
Sun.	6 13 20 27	3 10 17 24 31	7 14 21 28
Mon.	7 14 21 28	4 11 18 25	1 8 15 22 29
Tue.	1 8 15 22 29	5 12 19 26	2 9 16 23 30
Wed.	2 9 16 23 30	6 13 20 27	3 10 17 24
Thur.	3 10 17 24 31	7 14 21 28	4 11 18 25
Fri.	4 11 18 25	1 8 15 22 29	5 12 19 26
Sat.	5 12 19 26	2 9 16 23 30	6 13 20 27

	October	November	December
Sun.	5 12 19 26	2 9 16 23 30	7 14 21 28
Mon.	6 13 20 27	3 10 17 24	1 8 15 22 29
Tue.	7 14 21 28	4 11 18 25	2 9 16 23 30
Wed.	1 8 15 22 29	5 12 19 26	3 10 17 24 31
Thur.	2 9 16 23 30	6 13 20 27	4 11 18 25
Fri.	3 10 17 24 31	7 14 21 28	5 12 19 26
Sat.	4 11 18 25	1 8 15 22 29	6 13 20 27

Easter Days

March 23	1788, 1856, 2008
April 6	1828, 1980
April 13	1884, 1952, 2036
April 20	1924

G

	January	February	March
Sun.	5 12 19 26	2 9 16 23	2 9 16 23 30
Mon.	6 13 20 27	3 10 17 24	3 10 17 24 31
Tue.	7 14 21 28	4 11 18 25	4 11 18 25
Wed.	1 8 15 22 29	5 12 19 26	5 12 19 26
Thur.	2 9 16 23 30	6 13 20 27	6 13 20 27
Fri.	3 10 17 24 31	7 14 21 28	7 14 21 28
Sat.	4 11 18 25	1 8 15 22	1 8 15 22 29

	April	May	June
Sun.	6 13 20 27	4 11 18 25	1 8 15 22 29
Mon.	7 14 21 28	5 12 19 26	2 9 16 23 30
Tue.	1 8 15 22 29	6 13 20 27	3 10 17 24
Wed.	2 9 16 23 30	7 14 21 28	4 11 18 25
Thur.	3 10 17 24	1 8 15 22 29	5 12 19 26
Fri.	4 11 18 25	2 9 16 23 30	6 13 20 27
Sat.	5 12 19 26	3 10 17 24 31	7 14 21 28

	July	August	September
Sun.	6 13 20 27	3 10 17 24 31	7 14 21 28
Mon.	7 14 21 28	4 11 18 25	1 8 15 22 29
Tue.	1 8 15 22 29	5 12 19 26	2 9 16 23 30
Wed.	2 9 16 23 30	6 13 20 27	3 10 17 24
Thur.	3 10 17 24 31	7 14 21 28	4 11 18 25
Fri.	4 11 18 25	1 8 15 22 29	5 12 19 26
Sat.	5 12 19 26	2 9 16 23 30	6 13 20 27

	October	November	December
Sun.	5 12 19 26	2 9 16 23 30	7 14 21 28
Mon.	6 13 20 27	3 10 17 24	1 8 15 22 29
Tue.	7 14 21 28	4 11 18 25	2 9 16 23 30
Wed.	1 8 15 22 29	5 12 19 26	3 10 17 24 31
Thur.	2 9 16 23 30	6 13 20 27	4 11 18 25
Fri.	3 10 17 24 31	7 14 21 28	5 12 19 26
Sat.	4 11 18 25	1 8 15 22 29	6 13 20 27

EASTER DAYS

March 23	1845, 1913
March 30	1823, 1834, 1902, 1975, 1986, 1997
April 6	1806, 1817, 1890, 1947, 1958, 1969
April 13	1800, 1873, 1879, 1941, 2031
April 20	1783, 1794, 1851, 1862, 1919, 1930, 2003, 2014, 2025

I

	January	February	March
Sun.	4 11 18 25	1 8 15 22	1 8 15 22 29
Mon.	5 12 19 26	2 9 16 23	2 9 16 23 30
Tue.	6 13 20 27	3 10 17 24	3 10 17 24 31
Wed.	7 14 21 28	4 11 18 25	4 11 18 25
Thur.	1 8 15 22 29	5 12 19 26	5 12 19 26
Fri.	2 9 16 23 30	6 13 20 27	6 13 20 27
Sat.	3 10 17 24 31	7 14 21 28	7 14 21 28

	April	May	June
Sun.	5 12 19 26	3 10 17 24 31	7 14 21 28
Mon.	6 13 20 27	4 11 18 25	1 8 15 22 29
Tue.	7 14 21 28	5 12 19 26	2 9 16 23 30
Wed.	1 8 15 22 29	6 13 20 27	3 10 17 24
Thur.	2 9 16 23 30	7 14 21 28	4 11 18 25
Fri.	3 10 17 24	1 8 15 22 29	5 12 19 26
Sat.	4 11 18 25	2 9 16 23 30	6 13 20 27

	July	August	September
Sun.	5 12 19 26	2 9 16 23 30	6 13 20 27
Mon.	6 13 20 27	3 10 17 24 31	7 14 21 28
Tue.	7 14 21 28	4 11 18 25	1 8 15 22 29
Wed.	1 8 15 22 29	5 12 19 26	2 9 16 23 30
Thur.	2 9 16 23 30	6 13 20 27	3 10 17 24
Fri.	3 10 17 24 31	7 14 21 28	4 11 18 25
Sat.	4 11 18 25	1 8 15 22 29	5 12 19 26

	October	November	December
Sun.	4 11 18 25	1 8 15 22 29	6 13 20 27
Mon.	5 12 19 26	2 9 16 23 30	7 14 21 28
Tue.	6 13 20 27	3 10 17 24	1 8 15 22 29
Wed.	7 14 21 28	4 11 18 25	2 9 16 23 30
Thur.	1 8 15 22 29	5 12 19 26	3 10 17 24 31
Fri.	2 9 16 23 30	6 13 20 27	4 11 18 25
Sat.	3 10 17 24 31	7 14 21 28	5 12 19 26

EASTER DAYS

March 22	1818
March 29	1807, 1891, 1959, 1970
April 5	1795, 1801, 1863, 1874, 1885, 1931, 1942, 1953, 2015, 2026, 2037
April 12	1789, 1846, 1857, 1903, 1914, 1925, 1998, 2009
April 19	1829, 1835, 1981, 1987

H (LEAP YEAR)

	January	February	March
Sun.	5 12 19 26	2 9 16 23	1 8 15 22 29
Mon.	6 13 20 27	3 10 17 24	2 9 16 23 30
Tue.	7 14 21 28	4 11 18 25	3 10 17 24 31
Wed.	1 8 15 22 29	5 12 19 26	4 11 18 25
Thur.	2 9 16 23 30	6 13 20 27	5 12 19 26
Fri.	3 10 17 24 31	7 14 21 28	6 13 20 27
Sat.	4 11 18 25	1 8 15 22 29	7 14 21 28

	April	May	June
Sun.	5 12 19 26	3 10 17 24 31	7 14 21 28
Mon.	6 13 20 27	4 11 18 25	1 8 15 22 29
Tue.	7 14 21 28	5 12 19 26	2 9 16 23 30
Wed.	1 8 15 22 29	6 13 20 27	3 10 17 24
Thur.	2 9 16 23 30	7 14 21 28	4 11 18 25
Fri.	3 10 17 24	1 8 15 22 29	5 12 19 26
Sat.	4 11 18 25	2 9 16 23 30	6 13 20 27

	July	August	September
Sun.	5 12 19 26	2 9 16 23 30	6 13 20 27
Mon.	6 13 20 27	3 10 17 24 31	7 14 21 28
Tue.	7 14 21 28	4 11 18 25	1 8 15 22 29
Wed.	1 8 15 22 29	5 12 19 26	2 9 16 23 30
Thur.	2 9 16 23 30	6 13 20 27	3 10 17 24
Fri.	3 10 17 24 31	7 14 21 28	4 11 18 25
Sat.	4 11 18 25	1 8 15 22 29	5 12 19 26

	October	November	December
Sun.	4 11 18 25	1 8 15 22 29	6 13 20 27
Mon.	5 12 19 26	2 9 16 23 30	7 14 21 28
Tue.	6 13 20 27	3 10 17 24	1 8 15 22 29
Wed.	7 14 21 28	4 11 18 25	2 9 16 23 30
Thur.	1 8 15 22 29	5 12 19 26	3 10 17 24 31
Fri.	2 9 16 23 30	6 13 20 27	4 11 18 25
Sat.	3 10 17 24 31	7 14 21 28	5 12 19 26

EASTER DAYS

March 29	1812, 1964
April 5	1896
April 12	1868, 1936, 2020
April 19	1840, 1908, 1992

J (LEAP YEAR)

	January	February	March
Sun.	4 11 18 25	1 8 15 22 29	7 14 21 28
Mon.	5 12 19 26	2 9 16 23	1 8 15 22 29
Tue.	6 13 20 27	3 10 17 24	2 9 16 23 30
Wed.	7 14 21 28	4 11 18 25	3 10 17 24 31
Thur.	1 8 15 22 29	5 12 19 26	4 11 18 25
Fri.	2 9 16 23 30	6 13 20 27	5 12 19 26
Sat.	3 10 17 24 31	7 14 21 28	6 13 20 27

	April	May	June
Sun.	4 11 18 25	2 9 16 23 30	6 13 20 27
Mon.	5 12 19 26	3 10 17 24 31	7 14 21 28
Tue.	6 13 20 27	4 11 18 25	1 8 15 22 29
Wed.	7 14 21 28	5 12 19 26	2 9 16 23 30
Thur.	1 8 15 22 29	6 13 20 27	3 10 17 24
Fri.	2 9 16 23 30	7 14 21 28	4 11 18 25
Sat.	3 10 17 24	1 8 15 22 29	5 12 19 26

	July	August	September
Sun.	4 11 18 25	1 8 15 22 29	5 12 19 26
Mon.	5 12 19 26	2 9 16 23 30	6 13 20 27
Tue.	6 13 20 27	3 10 17 24 31	7 14 21 28
Wed.	7 14 21 28	4 11 18 25	1 8 15 22 29
Thur.	1 8 15 22 29	5 12 19 26	2 9 16 23 30
Fri.	2 9 16 23 30	6 13 20 27	3 10 17 24
Sat.	3 10 17 24 31	7 14 21 28	4 11 18 25

	October	November	December
Sun.	3 10 17 24 31	7 14 21 28	5 12 19 26
Mon.	4 11 18 25	1 8 15 22 29	6 13 20 27
Tue.	5 12 19 26	2 9 16 23 30	7 14 21 28
Wed.	6 13 20 27	3 10 17 24	1 8 15 22 29
Thur.	7 14 21 28	4 11 18 25	2 9 16 23 30
Fri.	1 8 15 22 29	5 12 19 26	3 10 17 24 31
Sat.	2 9 16 23 30	6 13 20 27	4 11 18 25

EASTER DAYS

March 28	1880, 1948, 2032
April 4	1920
April 11	1784, 1852, 2004
April 18	1824, 1976

K

	January	February	March
Sun.	3 10 17 24 31	7 14 21 28	7 14 21 28
Mon.	4 11 18 25	1 8 15 22	1 8 15 22 29
Tue.	5 12 19 26	2 9 16 23	2 9 16 23 30
Wed.	6 13 20 27	3 10 17 24	3 10 17 24 31
Thur.	7 14 21 28	4 11 18 25	4 11 18 25
Fri.	1 8 15 22 29	5 12 19 26	5 12 19 26
Sat.	2 9 16 23 30	6 13 20 27	6 13 20 27

	April	May	June
Sun.	4 11 18 25	2 9 16 23 30	6 13 20 27
Mon.	5 12 19 26	3 10 17 24 31	7 14 21 28
Tue.	6 13 20 27	4 11 18 25	1 8 15 22 29
Wed.	7 14 21 28	5 12 19 26	2 9 16 23 30
Thur.	1 8 15 22 29	6 13 20 27	3 10 17 24
Fri.	2 9 16 23 30	7 14 21 28	4 11 18 25
Sat.	3 10 17 24	1 8 15 22 29	5 12 19 26

	July	August	September
Sun.	4 11 18 25	1 8 15 22 29	5 12 19 26
Mon.	5 12 19 26	2 9 16 23 30	6 13 20 27
Tue.	6 13 20 27	3 10 17 24 31	7 14 21 28
Wed.	7 14 21 28	4 11 18 25	1 8 15 22 29
Thur.	1 8 15 22 29	5 12 19 26	2 9 16 23 30
Fri.	2 9 16 23 30	6 13 20 27	3 10 17 24
Sat.	3 10 17 24 31	7 14 21 28	4 11 18 25

	October	November	December
Sun.	3 10 17 24 31	7 14 21 28	5 12 19 26
Mon.	4 11 18 25	1 8 15 22 29	6 13 20 27
Tue.	5 12 19 26	2 9 16 23 30	7 14 21 28
Wed.	6 13 20 27	3 10 17 24	1 8 15 22 29
Thur.	7 14 21 28	4 11 18 25	2 9 16 23 30
Fri.	1 8 15 22 29	5 12 19 26	3 10 17 24 31
Sat.	2 9 16 23 30	6 13 20 27	4 11 18 25

EASTER DAYS
March 28   1869, 1875, 1937, 2027
April 4   1790, 1847, 1858, 1915, 1926, 1999, 2010, 2021
April 11   1819, 1830, 1841, 1909, 1971, 1982, 1993
April 18   1802, 1813, 1897, 1954, 1965
April 25   1886, 1943, 2038

M

	January	February	March
Sun.	2 9 16 23 30	6 13 20 27	6 13 20 27
Mon.	3 10 17 24 31	7 14 21 28	7 14 21 28
Tue.	4 11 18 25	1 8 15 22	1 8 15 22 29
Wed.	5 12 19 26	2 9 16 23	2 9 16 23 30
Thur.	6 13 20 27	3 10 17 24	3 10 17 24 31
Fri.	7 14 21 28	4 11 18 25	4 11 18 25
Sat.	1 8 15 22 29	5 12 19 26	5 12 19 26

	April	May	June
Sun.	3 10 17 24	1 8 15 22 29	5 12 19 26
Mon.	4 11 18 25	2 9 16 23 30	6 13 20 27
Tue.	5 12 19 26	3 10 17 24 31	7 14 21 28
Wed.	6 13 20 27	4 11 18 25	1 8 15 22 29
Thur.	7 14 21 28	5 12 19 26	2 9 16 23 30
Fri.	1 8 15 22 29	6 13 20 27	3 10 17 24
Sat.	2 9 16 23 30	7 14 21 28	4 11 18 25

	July	August	September
Sun.	3 10 17 24 31	7 14 21 28	4 11 18 25
Mon.	4 11 18 25	1 8 15 22 29	5 12 19 26
Tue.	5 12 19 26	2 9 16 23 30	6 13 20 27
Wed.	6 13 20 27	3 10 17 24 31	7 14 21 28
Thur.	7 14 21 28	4 11 18 25	1 8 15 22 29
Fri.	1 8 15 22 29	5 12 19 26	2 9 16 23 30
Sat.	2 9 16 23 30	6 13 20 27	3 10 17 24

	October	November	December
Sun.	2 9 16 23 30	6 13 20 27	4 11 18 25
Mon.	3 10 17 24 31	7 14 21 28	5 12 19 26
Tue.	4 11 18 25	1 8 15 22 29	6 13 20 27
Wed.	5 12 19 26	2 9 16 23 30	7 14 21 28
Thur.	6 13 20 27	3 10 17 24	1 8 15 22 29
Fri.	7 14 21 28	4 11 18 25	2 9 16 23 30
Sat.	1 8 15 22 29	5 12 19 26	3 10 17 24 31

EASTER DAYS
March 27   1785, 1842, 1853, 1910, 1921, 2005
April 3   1825, 1831, 1983, 1994
April 10   1803, 1814, 1887, 1898, 1955, 1966, 1977, 2039
April 17   1870, 1881, 1927, 1938, 1949, 2022, 2033
April 24   1791, 1859, 2011

L (LEAP YEAR)

	January	February	March
Sun.	3 10 17 24 31	7 14 21 28	6 13 20 27
Mon.	4 11 18 25	1 8 15 22 29	7 14 21 28
Tue.	5 12 19 26	2 9 16 23	1 8 15 22 29
Wed.	6 13 20 27	3 10 17 24	2 9 16 23 30
Thur.	7 14 21 28	4 11 18 25	3 10 17 24 31
Fri.	1 8 15 22 29	5 12 19 26	4 11 18 25
Sat.	2 9 16 23 30	6 13 20 27	5 12 19 26

	April	May	June
Sun.	3 10 17 24	1 8 15 22 29	5 12 19 26
Mon.	4 11 18 25	2 9 16 23 30	6 13 20 27
Tue.	5 12 19 26	3 10 17 24 31	7 14 21 28
Wed.	6 13 20 27	4 11 18 25	1 8 15 22 29
Thur.	7 14 21 28	5 12 19 26	2 9 16 23 30
Fri.	1 8 15 22 29	6 13 20 27	3 10 17 24
Sat.	2 9 16 23 30	7 14 21 28	4 11 18 25

	July	August	September
Sun.	3 10 17 24 31	7 14 21 28	4 11 18 25
Mon.	4 11 18 25	1 8 15 22 29	5 12 19 26
Tue.	5 12 19 26	2 9 16 23 30	6 13 20 27
Wed.	6 13 20 27	3 10 17 24 31	7 14 21 28
Thur.	7 14 21 28	4 11 18 25	1 8 15 22 29
Fri.	1 8 15 22 29	5 12 19 26	2 9 16 23 30
Sat.	2 9 16 23 30	6 13 20 27	3 10 17 24

	October	November	December
Sun.	2 9 16 23 30	6 13 20 27	4 11 18 25
Mon.	3 10 17 24 31	7 14 21 28	5 12 19 26
Tue.	4 11 18 25	1 8 15 22 29	6 13 20 27
Wed.	5 12 19 26	2 9 16 23 30	7 14 21 28
Thur.	6 13 20 27	3 10 17 24	1 8 15 22 29
Fri.	7 14 21 28	4 11 18 25	2 9 16 23 30
Sat.	1 8 15 22 29	5 12 19 26	3 10 17 24 31

EASTER DAYS
March 27   1796, 1864, 1932, 2016
April 3   1836, 1904, 1988
April 17   1808, 1892, 1960

N (LEAP YEAR)

	January	February	March
Sun.	2 9 16 23 30	6 13 20 27	5 12 19 26
Mon.	3 10 17 24 31	7 14 21 28	6 13 20 27
Tue.	4 11 18 25	1 8 15 22 29	7 14 21 28
Wed.	5 12 19 26	2 9 16 23	1 8 15 22 29
Thur.	6 13 20 27	3 10 17 24	2 9 16 23 30
Fri.	7 14 21 28	4 11 18 25	3 10 17 24 31
Sat.	1 8 15 22 29	5 12 19 26	4 11 18 25

	April	May	June
Sun.	2 9 16 23 30	7 14 21 28	4 11 18 25
Mon.	3 10 17 24	1 8 15 22 29	5 12 19 26
Tue.	4 11 18 25	2 9 16 23 30	6 13 20 27
Wed.	5 12 19 26	3 10 17 24 31	7 14 21 28
Thur.	6 13 20 27	4 11 18 25	1 8 15 22 29
Fri.	7 14 21 28	5 12 19 26	2 9 16 23 30
Sat.	1 8 15 22 29	6 13 20 27	3 10 17 24

	July	August	September
Sun.	2 9 16 23 30	6 13 20 27	3 10 17 24
Mon.	3 10 17 24 31	7 14 21 28	4 11 18 25
Tue.	4 11 18 25	1 8 15 22 29	5 12 19 26
Wed.	5 12 19 26	2 9 16 23 30	6 13 20 27
Thur.	6 13 20 27	3 10 17 24 31	7 14 21 28
Fri.	7 14 21 28	4 11 18 25	1 8 15 22 29
Sat.	1 8 15 22 29	5 12 19 26	2 9 16 23 30

	October	November	December
Sun.	1 8 15 22 29	5 12 19 26	3 10 17 24 31
Mon.	2 9 16 23 30	6 13 20 27	4 11 18 25
Tue.	3 10 17 24 31	7 14 21 28	5 12 19 26
Wed.	4 11 18 25	1 8 15 22 29	6 13 20 27
Thur.	5 12 19 26	2 9 16 23 30	7 14 21 28
Fri.	6 13 20 27	3 10 17 24	1 8 15 22 29
Sat.	7 14 21 28	4 11 18 25	2 9 16 23 30

EASTER DAYS
March 26   1780
April 2   1820, 1972
April 9   1944
April 16   2028
April 23   1848, 1916, 2000

GEOLOGICAL TIME

The earth is thought to have come into existence approximately 4,600 million years ago, but for nearly half this time, the Archean era, it was uninhabited. Life is generally believed to have emerged in the succeeding Proterozoic era. The Archean and the Proterozoic eras are often together referred to as the Precambrian.

Although primitive forms of life, e.g. algae and bacteria, existed during the Proterozoic era, it is not until the strata of Palaeozoic rocks is reached that abundant fossilized remains appear.

Since the Precambrian, there have been three great geological eras:

PALAEOZOIC ('ancient life')
c.570–c.245 million years ago

Cambrian – Mainly sandstones, slate and shales; limestones in Scotland. Shelled fossils and invertebrates, e.g. trilobites and brachiopods appear
Ordovician – Mainly shales and mudstones, e.g. in north Wales; limestones in Scotland. First fishes
Silurian – Shales, mudstones and some limestones, found mostly in Wales and southern Scotland
Devonian – Old red sandstone, shale, limestone and slate, e.g. in south Wales and the West Country
Carboniferous – Coal-bearing rocks, millstone grit, limestone and shale. First traces of land-living life
Permian – Marls, sandstones and clays. First reptile fossils

There were two great phases of mountain building in the Palaeozoic era: the Caledonian, characterized in Britain by NE–SW lines of hills and valleys; and the later Hercyian, widespread in west Germany and adjacent areas, and in Britain exemplified in E.–W. lines of hills and valleys.

The end of the Palaeozoic era was marked by the extensive glaciations of the Permian period in the southern continents and the decline of amphibians. It was succeeded by an era of warm conditions.

MESOZOIC ('middle forms of life')
c.245–c.65 million years ago

Triassic – Mostly sandstone, e.g. in the West Midlands
Jurassic – Mainly limestones and clays, typically displayed in the Jura mountains, and in England in a NE–SW belt from Lincolnshire and the Wash to the Severn and the Dorset coast
Cretaceous – Mainly chalk, clay and sands, e.g. in Kent and Sussex

Giant reptiles were dominant during the Mesozoic era, but it was at this time that marsupial mammals first appeared, as well as *Archaeopteryx lithographica*, the earliest known species of bird. Coniferous trees and flowering plants also developed during the era, and, with the birds and the mammals, were the main species to survive into the Cenozoic era. The giant reptiles became extinct.

CENOZOIC ('recent life')
from c.65 million years ago

Palaeocene ⎱ The emergence of new forms of life, includ-
Eocene ⎰ ing existing species
Oligocene – Fossils of a few still existing species
Miocene – Fossil remains show a balance of existing and extinct species
Pliocene – Fossil remains show a majority of still existing species
Pleistocene – The majority of remains are those of still existing species

Holocene – The present, post-glacial period. Existing species only, except for a few exterminated by man

In the last 25 million years, from the Miocene through the Pliocene periods, the Alpine-Himalayan and the circum-Pacific phases of mountain building reached their climax. During the Pleistocene period ice-sheets repeatedly locked up masses of water as land ice; its weight depressed the land, but the locking-up of the water lowered the sea-level by 100–200 metres. The glaciations and interglacials of the Ice Age are difficult to date and classify, but recent scientific opinion considers the Pleistocene period to have begun approximately 1.64 million years ago. The last glacial retreat, merging into the Holocene period, was 10,000 years ago.

HUMAN DEVELOPMENT

Any consideration of the history of mankind must start with the fact that all members of the human race belong to one species of animal, i.e. *Homo sapiens*, the definition of a species being in biological terms that all its members can interbreed. As a species of mammal it is possible to group man with other similar types, known as the primates. Amongst these is found a sub-group, the apes, which includes, in addition to man, the chimpanzees, gorillas, orang-utans and gibbons. All lack a tail, have shoulder blades at the back, and a Y-shaped chewing pattern on the surface of their molars, as well as showing the more general primate characteristics of four incisors, a thumb which is able to touch the fingers of the same hand, and finger and toe nails instead of claws. The factors available to scientific study suggest that human beings have chimpanzees and gorillas as their nearest relatives in the animal world. However, there remains the possibility that there once lived creatures, now extinct, which were closer to modern man than the chimpanzees and gorillas, and which shared with modern man the characteristics of having flat faces (i.e. the absence of a pronounced muzzle), being bipedal, and possessing large brains.

There are two broad groups of extinct apes recognized by specialists. The ramapithecines, the remains of which, mainly jaw fragments, have been found in east Africa, Asia, and Turkey. They lived about 14 to 8 million years ago, and from the evidence of their teeth it seems they chewed more in the manner of modern man than the other presently living apes. The second group, the australopithecines, have left more numerous remains amongst which sub-groups may be detected, although the geographic spread is limited to south and east Africa. Living between 5 and 1.5 million years ago, they were closer relatives of modern man to the extent that they walked upright, did not have an extensive muzzle and had similar types of pre-molars. The first australopithecine remains were recognized at Taung in South Africa in 1924 and subsequent discoveries include those at the Olduvai Gorge in Tanzania. The most impressive discovery was made at Hadar, Ethiopia, in 1974 when about half a skeleton, known as 'Lucy', was found.

Also in east Africa, between 2 million and 1.5 million years ago, lived a hominid group which not only walked upright, had a flat face, and a large brain case, but also made simple pebble and flake stone tools. On present evidence these habilines seem to have been the first people to make tools, however crude. This facility is related to the larger brain size and human beings are the only animals to make implements to be used in other processes. These early pebble tool users, because of their distinctive

GEOLOGICAL TIME

Era	Period	Epoch	Date began*	Evolutionary stages
Cenozoic	Quaternary	Holocene	0.01	Man
Cenozoic	Quaternary	Pleistocene	1.64	Man
Cenozoic	Tertiary	Pliocene	5.2	
Cenozoic	Tertiary	Miocene	23.3	
Cenozoic	Tertiary	Oligocene	35.4	
Cenozoic	Tertiary	Eocene	56.5	
Cenozoic	Tertiary	Palaeocene	65.0	
Mesozoic	Cretaceous		145.6	
Mesozoic	Jurassic		208.0	First birds
Mesozoic	Triassic		245.0	First mammals
Palaeozoic	Permian		290.0	First reptiles
Palaeozoic	Carboniferous		362.5	First amphibians and insects
Palaeozoic	Devonian		408.5	
Palaeozoic	Silurian		439.0	
Palaeozoic	Ordovician		510.0	First fishes
Palaeozoic	Cambrian		570.0	First invertebrates
Precambrian			4,600.0	First primitive life forms, e.g. algae and bacteria

*millions of years ago

characteristics, have been grouped as a separate sub-species, now extinct, of the genus *Homo* and are known as *Homo habilis*.

The use of fire, again a human characteristic, is associated with another group of extinct hominids whose remains, about a million years old, are found in south and east Africa, China, Indonesia, north Africa and Europe. Mastery of the techniques of making fire probably helped the colonization of the colder northern areas and in this respect the site of Vertesszollos in Hungary is of particular importance. *Homo erectus* is the name given to this group of fossils and it includes a number of famous individual discoveries, e.g. Solo Man, Heidelberg Man, and especially Peking Man who lived at the cave site at Choukoutien which has yielded evidence of fire and burnt bone.

The well-known group Neanderthal Man, or *Homo sapiens neandertalensis*, is an extinct form of modern man who lived between about 100,000 and 40,000 years ago, thus spanning the last Ice Age. Indeed, its ability to adapt to the cold climate on the edge of the ice-sheets is one of its characteristic features, the remains being found only in Europe, Asia and the Middle East. Complete neanderthal skeletons were found during excavations at Tabun in Israel, together with evidence of tool-making and the use of fire. Distinguished by very large brains, it seems that neanderthal man was the first to develop recognizable social customs, especially deliberate burial rites. Why the neanderthalers became extinct is not clear but it may be connected with the climatic changes at the end of the Ice Ages, which would have seriously affected their food supplies; possibly they became too specialized for their own good.

The Swanscombe skull is the only known human fossil remains found in England. Some specialists see Swanscombe Man (or, more probably, woman) as a neanderthaler. Others group these remains together with the Steinheim skull from Germany, seeing both as a separate sub-species. There is too little evidence as yet on which to form a final judgement.

Modern Man, *Homo sapiens sapiens*, the surviving sub-species of *Homo sapiens*, had evolved to our present physical condition and had colonized much of the world by about 30,000 years ago. There are many previously distinguished individual specimens, e.g. Cromagnon Man, which may now be grouped together as *Homo sapiens sapiens*. It was modern man who spread to the American continent by crossing the landbridge between Siberia and Alaska and thence moved south through North America and into South America. Equally it is modern man who over the last 30,000 years has been responsible for the major developments in technology, art and civilization generally.

One of the problems for those studying fossil man is the lack in many cases of sufficient quantities of fossil bone for analysis. It is important that theories should be tested against evidence, rather than the evidence being made to fit the theory. The Piltdown hoax is a well-known example of 'fossils' being forged to fit what was seen in some quarters as the correct theory of man's evolution.

CULTURAL DEVELOPMENT

The Eurocentric bias of early archaeologists meant that the search for a starting point for the development and transmission of cultural ideas, especially by migration, trade and warfare, concentrated unduly on Europe and the Near East. The Three Age system, whereby pre-history was divided into a Stone Age, a Bronze Age and an Iron Age, was devised by Christian Thomsen, curator of the National Museum of Denmark in the early 19th century, to facilitate the classification of the museum's collections.

The descriptive adjectives referred to the materials from which the implements and weapons were made and came to be regarded as the dominant features of the societies to which they related. The refinement of the Three Age system once dominated archaeological thought and remains a generally accepted concept in the popular mind. However, it is now seen by archaeologists as an inadequate model for human development.

Common sense suggests that there were no complete breaks between one so-called Age and another, any more than contemporaries would have regarded 1485 as a complete break between medieval and modern English history. Nor can the Three Age system be applied universally. In some areas it is necessary to insert a Copper Age, while in Africa south of the Sahara there would seem to be no Bronze Age at all; in Australia, Old Stone Age societies survived, while in South America, New Stone Age communities existed into modern times. The civilizations in other parts of the world clearly invalidate a Eurocentric theory of human development.

The concept of the 'Neolithic revolution', associated with the domestication of plants and animals, was a development of particular importance in the human cultural pattern. It reflected change from the primitive hunter/gatherer economies to a more settled agricultural way of life and therefore, so the argument goes, made possible the development of urban civilization. However, it can no longer be argued that this 'revolution' took place only in one area from which all development stemmed. Though it appears that the cultivation of wheat and barley was first undertaken, together with the domestication of cattle and goats/sheep in the Fertile Crescent (the area bounded by the rivers Tigris and Euphrates), there is evidence that rice was first deliberately planted and pigs domesticated in south-east Asia, maize first cultivated in Central America and llamas first domesticated in South America. It has been recognized in recent years that cultural changes can take place independently of each other in different parts of the world at different rates and different times. There is no need for a general diffusionist theory.

Although scholars will continue to study the particular societies which interest them, it may be possible to obtain a reliable chronological framework, in absolute terms of years, against which the cultural development of any particular area may be set. The development and refinement of radio-carbon dating and other scientific methods of producing absolute chronologies is enabling the cross-referencing of societies to be undertaken. As the techniques of dating become more rigorous in application and the number of scientifically obtained dates increases, the attainment of an absolute chronology for prehistoric societies throughout the world comes closer to being achieved.

Tidal Tables

CONSTANTS

The constant tidal difference may be used in conjunction with the time of high water at a standard port shown in the predictions data (pages 98–103) to find the time of high water at any of the ports or places listed below.

These tidal differences are very approximate and should be used only as a guide to the time of high water at the places below. More precise local data should be obtained for navigational and other nautical purposes.

All data allow high water time to be found in Greenwich Mean Time; this applies also to data for the months when British Summer Time is in operation and the hour's time difference should also be allowed for. Ports marked * are in a different time zone and the standard time zone difference also needs to be added/subtracted to give local time.

EXAMPLE

Required time of high water at Stranraer at 2 January 1997
Appropriate time of high water at Greenock

Morning tide 2 January	0556 hrs
Tidal difference	−0020 hrs
High water at Stranraer	0536 hrs

The columns headed 'Springs' and 'Neaps' show the height, in metres, of the tide above datum for mean high water springs and mean high water neaps respectively.

Port	Diff.		Springs	Neaps
		h m	m	m
Aberdeen	Leith	−1 19	4.3	3.4
*Antwerp (Prosperpolder)	London	+0 50	5.8	4.8
Ardrossan	Greenock	−0 15	3.2	2.6
Avonmouth	London	−6 45	13.2	9.8
Ayr	Greenock	−0 25	3.0	2.5
Barrow (Docks)	Liverpool	0 00	9.3	7.1
Belfast	London	−2 47	3.5	3.0
Blackpool	Liverpool	−0 10	8.9	7.0
*Boulogne	London	−2 44	8.9	7.2
*Calais	London	−2 04	7.2	5.9
*Cherbourg	London	−6 00	6.4	5.0
Cobh	Liverpool	−5 55	4.2	3.2
Cowes	London	−2 38	4.2	3.5
Dartmouth	London	+4 25	4.9	3.8
*Dieppe	London	−3 03	9.3	7.3
Douglas, IOM	Liverpool	−0 04	6.9	5.4
Dover	London	−2 52	6.7	5.3
Dublin	London	−2 05	4.1	3.4
Dun Laoghaire	London	−2 10	4.1	3.4
*Dunkirk	London	−1 54	6.0	4.9
Fishguard	Liverpool	−4 01	4.8	3.4
Fleetwood	Liverpool	0 00	9.2	7.3
*Flushing	London	−0 15	4.7	3.9
Folkestone	London	−3 04	7.1	5.7
Galway	Liverpool	−6 08	5.1	3.9
Glasgow	Greenock	+0 26	4.7	4.0
Harwich	London	−2 06	4.0	3.4
*Havre, Le	London	−3 55	7.9	6.6
Heysham	Liverpool	+0 05	9.4	7.4
Holyhead	Liverpool	−0 50	5.6	4.4
*Hook of Holland	London	−0 01	2.1	1.7
Hull (Albert Dock)	London	−7 40	7.5	5.8
Immingham	London	−8 00	7.3	5.8
Larne	London	−2 40	2.8	2.5
Lerwick	Leith	−3 48	2.2	1.6
Londonderry	London	−5 37	2.7	2.1
Lowestoft	London	−4 25	2.4	2.1
Margate	London	−1 53	4.8	3.9
Milford Haven	Liverpool	−5 08	7.0	5.2
Morecambe	Liverpool	+0 07	9.5	7.4
Newhaven	London	−2 46	6.7	5.1
Oban	Greenock	+5 43	4.0	2.9
*Ostend	London	−1 32	5.1	4.2
Plymouth (Devonport)	London	+4 05	5.5	4.4
Portland	London	+5 09	2.1	1.4
Portsmouth	London	−2 38	4.7	3.8
Ramsgate	London	−2 32	5.2	4.1
Richmond Lock	London	+1 00	4.9	3.7
Rosslare Harbour	Liverpool	−5 24	1.9	1.4
Rosyth	Leith	+0 09	5.8	4.7
*Rotterdam	London	+1 45	2.0	1.7
St Helier	London	+4 48	11.0	8.1
St Malo	London	+4 27	12.2	9.2
St Peter Port	London	+4 54	9.3	7.0
Scrabster	Leith	−6 06	5.0	4.0
Sheerness	London	−1 19	5.8	4.7
Shoreham	London	−2 44	6.3	4.9
Southampton (1st high water)	London	−2 54	4.5	3.7
Spurn Head	London	−8 25	6.9	5.5
Stornoway	Liverpool	−4 16	4.8	3.7
Stranraer	Greenock	−0 20	3.0	2.4
Stromness	Leith	−5 26	3.6	2.7
Swansea	London	−7 35	9.5	7.2
Tees, River Entrance	Leith	+1 09	5.5	4.3
Tilbury	London	−0 49	6.4	5.4
Tobermory	Liverpool	−5 11	4.4	3.3
Tyne River (North Shields)	London	−10 30	5.0	3.9
Ullapool	Leith	−7 40	5.2	3.9
Walton-on-the-Naze	London	−2 10	4.2	3.4
Wick	Leith	−3 26	3.5	2.8
*Zeebrugge	London	−0 55	4.8	3.9

PREDICTIONS

The tidal predictions for London Bridge, Liverpool, Greenock and Leith on pages 98–103 are reproduced with the permission of the UK Hydrographic Office and the Controller of HMSO. Crown copyright reserved.
*Datum of predictions for each port shows the difference of height, in metres, from Ordnance data (Newlyn).

JANUARY 1997   *High water*   GMT

		LONDON BRIDGE *Datum of predictions 3.20 m below				LIVERPOOL *Datum of predictions 4.93 m below				GREENOCK *Datum of predictions 1.62 m below				LEITH *Datum of predictions 2.90 m below			
		hr	ht m	hr	ht m	hr	ht m	hr	ht m	hr	ht m	hr	ht m	hr	ht m	hr	ht m
1	Wednesday	05 50	6.3	18 31	6.4	03 27	8.0	15 47	8.1	05 08	3.1	17 04	3.3	07 15	4.7	19 29	4.7
2	Thursday	06 37	6.2	19 20	6.2	04 17	7.7	16 41	7.8	05 56	3.0	17 53	3.2	08 05	4.6	20 23	4.6
3	Friday	07 32	6.0	20 17	6.1	05 18	7.5	17 43	7.7	06 50	2.9	18 49	3.1	09 01	4.5	21 24	4.5
4	Saturday	08 36	5.9	21 21	6.1	06 28	7.5	18 50	7.7	07 52	2.9	19 53	3.0	10 03	4.6	22 31	4.6
5	Sunday	09 47	6.0	22 29	6.2	07 36	7.8	19 56	8.1	09 06	2.9	21 07	3.0	11 07	4.7	23 38	4.8
6	Monday	10 57	6.2	23 34	6.5	08 36	8.4	20 56	8.5	10 14	3.1	22 14	3.2	12 09	5.0	—	—
7	Tuesday	12 01	6.5	—	—	09 28	8.9	21 50	9.0	11 05	3.3	23 10	3.3	00 38	5.1	13 04	5.2
8	Wednesday	00 32	6.8	12 59	6.9	10 17	9.4	22 40	9.4	11 50	3.5	—	—	01 31	5.3	13 51	5.5
9	Thursday	01 24	7.0	13 51	7.2	11 04	9.8	23 29	9.7	00 02	3.4	12 35	3.6	02 18	5.6	14 35	5.7
10	Friday	02 13	7.2	14 40	7.4	11 52	10.0	—	—	00 52	3.4	13 18	3.7	03 03	5.8	15 18	5.9
11	Saturday	02 59	7.3	15 28	7.5	00 17	9.8	12 40	10.2	01 42	3.5	14 02	3.8	03 49	5.9	16 03	5.9
12	Sunday	03 43	7.3	16 14	7.5	01 06	9.8	13 29	10.1	02 29	3.5	14 45	3.9	04 36	5.9	16 50	5.9
13	Monday	04 27	7.3	17 00	7.4	01 54	9.7	14 17	9.9	03 15	3.5	15 29	3.9	05 25	5.7	17 40	5.7
14	Tuesday	05 10	7.1	17 47	7.1	02 42	9.3	15 06	9.6	04 00	3.5	16 14	3.8	06 17	5.5	18 34	5.5
15	Wednesday	05 56	6.9	18 38	6.8	03 32	8.9	15 57	9.0	04 46	3.4	17 02	3.6	07 12	5.2	19 33	5.3
16	Thursday	06 47	6.6	19 35	6.5	04 26	8.4	16 55	8.5	05 35	3.3	17 55	3.4	08 12	5.0	20 38	5.0
17	Friday	07 51	6.3	20 40	6.2	05 31	7.9	18 03	8.0	06 28	3.1	18 59	3.2	09 16	4.8	21 47	4.9
18	Saturday	09 06	6.1	21 47	6.2	06 47	7.7	19 18	7.9	07 33	3.0	20 37	3.0	10 24	4.8	22 57	4.8
19	Sunday	10 16	6.2	22 50	6.3	07 59	7.9	20 27	8.0	09 09	3.0	21 59	3.1	11 33	4.8	—	—
20	Monday	11 19	6.4	23 47	6.5	08 59	8.2	21 23	8.4	10 17	3.2	22 58	3.1	00 05	4.8	12 37	5.0
21	Tuesday	12 16	6.6	—	—	09 48	8.6	22 11	8.7	11 07	3.3	23 47	3.2	01 04	5.0	13 28	5.1
22	Wednesday	00 40	6.7	13 08	6.8	10 31	9.0	22 52	8.9	11 51	3.4	—	—	01 52	5.1	14 12	5.3
23	Thursday	01 28	6.8	13 54	6.9	11 09	9.1	23 29	9.0	00 31	3.2	12 31	3.5	02 32	5.2	14 49	5.3
24	Friday	02 10	6.8	14 35	6.9	11 44	9.2	—	—	01 11	3.2	13 07	3.5	03 07	5.3	15 23	5.4
25	Saturday	02 46	6.7	15 10	6.7	00 03	9.0	12 18	9.2	01 46	3.2	13 40	3.6	03 39	5.3	15 54	5.4
26	Sunday	03 15	6.6	15 40	6.6	00 36	9.0	12 51	9.2	02 18	3.1	14 11	3.6	04 11	5.3	16 26	5.3
27	Monday	03 42	6.5	16 09	6.6	01 09	8.9	13 24	9.1	02 48	3.2	14 43	3.6	04 44	5.2	16 58	5.3
28	Tuesday	04 12	6.5	16 42	6.7	01 42	8.8	13 58	9.0	03 19	3.2	15 17	3.5	05 20	5.1	17 32	5.2
29	Wednesday	04 46	6.6	17 19	6.7	02 17	8.6	14 34	8.8	03 53	3.1	15 53	3.5	05 57	5.0	18 07	5.0
30	Thursday	05 24	6.5	18 00	6.6	02 53	8.4	15 13	8.5	04 29	3.0	16 32	3.4	06 37	4.8	18 47	4.8
31	Friday	06 07	6.4	18 46	6.5	03 36	8.1	15 59	8.1	05 10	3.0	17 15	3.2	07 22	4.7	19 34	4.7

FEBRUARY 1997   *High water*   GMT

		LONDON BRIDGE				LIVERPOOL				GREENOCK				LEITH			
1	Saturday	06 57	6.2	19 39	6.3	04 29	7.7	16 58	7.8	05 57	2.9	18 05	3.0	08 14	4.6	20 33	4.5
2	Sunday	07 56	6.0	20 39	6.1	05 37	7.5	18 07	7.6	06 55	2.8	19 05	2.9	09 15	4.5	21 44	4.5
3	Monday	09 04	5.9	21 48	6.1	06 51	7.6	19 20	7.8	08 12	2.8	20 25	2.9	10 25	4.6	23 02	4.6
4	Tuesday	10 19	6.0	23 01	6.2	08 04	8.1	20 31	8.3	09 37	2.9	21 48	3.0	11 37	4.8	—	—
5	Wednesday	11 35	6.3	—	—	09 06	8.8	21 33	8.9	10 41	3.1	22 54	3.1	00 13	4.9	12 39	5.1
6	Thursday	00 07	6.6	12 40	6.7	10 00	9.4	22 26	9.4	11 31	3.4	23 49	3.3	01 12	5.3	13 31	5.4
7	Friday	01 04	6.9	13 35	7.1	10 49	9.9	23 15	9.8	12 18	3.6	—	—	02 01	5.6	14 16	5.7
8	Saturday	01 55	7.2	14 25	7.4	11 37	10.3	—	—	00 40	3.4	13 04	3.7	02 47	5.9	15 00	6.0
9	Sunday	02 42	7.4	15 12	7.6	00 03	10.0	12 25	10.4	01 29	3.4	13 49	3.8	03 32	6.0	15 45	6.1
10	Monday	03 27	7.5	15 57	7.7	00 50	10.1	13 11	10.4	02 15	3.5	14 32	3.9	04 18	5.9	16 32	6.1
11	Tuesday	04 09	7.5	16 41	7.6	01 35	9.9	13 57	10.2	02 57	3.5	15 14	3.9	05 05	5.8	17 21	5.9
12	Wednesday	04 51	7.4	17 24	7.3	02 20	9.6	14 42	9.7	03 37	3.5	15 55	3.8	05 54	5.5	18 13	5.6
13	Thursday	05 32	7.2	18 08	6.9	03 04	9.1	15 28	9.1	04 18	3.4	16 38	3.6	06 45	5.2	19 07	5.3
14	Friday	06 17	6.8	18 55	6.5	03 51	8.5	16 20	8.4	05 00	3.3	17 24	3.4	07 40	4.9	20 08	4.9
15	Saturday	07 10	6.3	19 55	6.0	04 49	7.8	17 25	7.7	05 47	3.2	18 17	3.1	08 40	4.7	21 15	4.7
16	Sunday	08 27	5.9	21 12	5.8	06 06	7.4	18 49	7.4	06 41	3.0	19 31	2.8	09 48	4.5	22 28	4.5
17	Monday	09 50	5.8	22 22	5.8	07 31	7.5	20 05	7.6	07 58	2.9	21 44	2.8	11 03	4.6	23 45	4.6
18	Tuesday	10 58	6.0	23 23	6.1	08 37	7.9	21 04	8.0	09 51	3.0	22 45	2.9	12 15	4.7	—	—
19	Wednesday	11 56	6.3	—	—	09 29	8.4	21 52	8.4	10 47	3.2	23 32	3.0	00 49	4.8	13 12	4.9
20	Thursday	00 17	6.4	12 48	6.7	10 12	8.8	22 34	8.7	11 32	3.3	—	—	01 37	5.0	13 55	5.1
21	Friday	01 06	6.7	13 33	6.8	10 51	9.1	23 10	8.9	00 14	3.1	12 13	3.4	02 15	5.1	14 31	5.3
22	Saturday	01 49	6.8	14 13	6.8	11 25	9.2	23 43	9.0	00 53	3.1	12 48	3.4	02 47	5.2	15 03	5.3
23	Sunday	02 26	6.7	14 48	6.8	11 58	9.2	—	—	01 27	3.1	13 19	3.4	03 16	5.3	15 33	5.4
24	Monday	02 56	6.6	15 17	6.7	00 15	9.0	12 29	9.2	01 56	3.1	13 48	3.4	03 47	5.3	16 03	5.4
25	Tuesday	03 24	6.6	15 46	6.7	00 46	9.0	13 01	9.1	02 22	3.1	14 18	3.4	04 19	5.3	16 34	5.3
26	Wednesday	03 52	6.6	16 17	6.8	01 17	9.0	13 33	9.1	02 49	3.1	14 52	3.4	04 53	5.2	17 06	5.2
27	Thursday	04 24	6.7	16 52	6.8	01 49	8.9	14 07	8.9	03 20	3.1	15 27	3.4	05 27	5.1	17 39	5.1
28	Friday	05 00	6.7	17 31	6.7	02 23	8.7	14 43	8.6	03 53	3.1	16 04	3.3	06 05	5.0	18 17	4.9

MARCH 1997 *High water* GMT

		London Bridge *Datum of predictions 3.20 m below*				Liverpool *Datum of predictions 4.93 m below*				Greenock *Datum of predictions 1.62 m below*				Leith *Datum of predictions 2.90 m below*			
		hr	ht m	hr	ht m	hr	ht m	hr	ht m	hr	ht m	hr	ht m	hr	ht m	hr	ht m
1	Saturday	05 42	6.6	18 16	6.5	03 02	8.4	15 27	8.3	04 30	3.0	16 44	3.2	06 46	4.8	19 03	4.8
2	Sunday	06 31	6.4	19 06	6.3	03 51	8.0	16 23	7.8	05 11	2.9	17 30	3.0	07 35	4.6	19 59	4.6
3	Monday	07 28	6.1	20 05	6.0	04 57	7.6	17 34	7.5	06 04	2.7	18 28	2.8	08 36	4.5	21 11	4.5
4	Tuesday	08 34	5.9	21 14	5.9	06 16	7.5	18 53	7.6	07 22	2.7	19 49	2.8	09 49	4.5	22 33	4.6
5	Wednesday	09 52	5.9	22 32	6.0	07 37	7.9	20 12	8.1	09 05	2.8	21 28	2.8	11 07	4.7	23 51	4.9
6	Thursday	11 15	6.2	23 44	6.4	08 45	8.6	21 17	8.8	10 18	3.0	22 40	3.0	12 15	5.0	—	—
7	Friday	12 22	6.7	—	—	09 42	9.3	22 10	9.4	11 11	3.3	23 36	3.2	00 52	5.3	13 10	5.4
8	Saturday	00 43	6.8	13 17	7.1	10 32	9.9	22 58	9.9	12 00	3.5	—	—	01 42	5.6	13 56	5.7
9	Sunday	01 35	7.2	14 07	7.5	11 19	10.3	23 44	10.1	00 25	3.3	12 47	3.7	02 27	5.8	14 41	6.0
10	Monday	02 22	7.5	14 53	7.7	12 05	10.5	—	—	01 12	3.4	13 32	3.8	03 12	6.0	15 26	6.1
11	Tuesday	03 06	7.6	15 36	7.7	00 28	10.1	12 50	10.4	01 54	3.5	14 15	3.8	03 56	5.9	16 13	6.1
12	Wednesday	03 48	7.7	16 18	7.6	01 12	10.0	13 34	10.1	02 33	3.5	14 56	3.8	04 42	5.8	17 01	5.9
13	Thursday	04 29	7.6	16 57	7.3	01 54	9.6	14 17	9.6	03 11	3.6	15 35	3.7	05 29	5.5	17 50	5.6
14	Friday	05 09	7.3	17 36	6.9	02 35	9.1	15 00	9.0	03 49	3.5	16 16	3.5	06 17	5.2	18 43	5.2
15	Saturday	05 50	6.9	18 16	6.5	03 18	8.5	15 47	8.2	04 29	3.4	16 59	3.3	07 08	4.9	19 39	4.8
16	Sunday	06 36	6.4	19 01	6.0	04 08	7.8	16 46	7.5	05 13	3.2	17 48	3.0	08 04	4.6	20 41	4.5
17	Monday	07 41	5.8	20 14	5.6	05 20	7.3	18 13	7.1	06 04	3.0	18 50	2.7	09 09	4.4	21 51	4.4
18	Tuesday	09 20	5.6	21 47	5.5	06 54	7.2	19 36	7.2	07 08	2.8	21 19	2.6	10 23	4.3	23 11	4.4
19	Wednesday	10 31	5.8	22 52	5.8	08 07	7.6	20 37	7.7	09 07	2.8	22 22	2.8	11 42	4.5	—	—
20	Thursday	11 29	6.1	23 48	6.2	09 01	8.1	21 26	8.2	10 19	3.0	23 08	2.9	00 22	4.6	12 44	4.7
21	Friday	12 20	6.5	—	—	09 46	8.5	22 07	8.6	11 06	3.2	23 49	3.0	01 11	4.8	13 28	4.9
22	Saturday	00 37	6.5	13 06	6.7	10 25	8.9	22 44	8.8	11 46	3.2	—	—	01 49	5.0	14 04	5.1
23	Sunday	01 21	6.7	13 46	6.8	11 00	9.0	23 17	9.0	00 26	3.1	12 22	3.2	02 20	5.1	14 36	5.3
24	Monday	01 59	6.7	14 20	6.8	11 33	9.1	23 49	9.0	01 00	3.1	12 52	3.2	02 49	5.2	15 07	5.4
25	Tuesday	02 32	6.7	14 51	6.8	12 04	9.1	—	—	01 28	3.1	13 20	3.3	03 20	5.3	15 39	5.4
26	Wednesday	03 03	6.7	15 22	6.8	00 19	9.1	12 35	9.1	01 52	3.1	13 52	3.3	03 53	5.3	16 10	5.4
27	Thursday	03 32	6.7	15 53	6.8	00 51	9.0	13 08	9.0	02 19	3.1	14 27	3.3	04 26	5.3	16 43	5.3
28	Friday	04 05	6.8	16 28	6.8	01 23	9.0	13 43	8.9	02 49	3.2	15 03	3.3	05 01	5.2	17 18	5.2
29	Saturday	04 41	6.8	17 07	6.7	01 58	8.8	14 21	8.7	03 23	3.2	15 41	3.3	05 37	5.1	17 57	5.0
30	Sunday	05 24	6.7	17 50	6.5	02 38	8.5	15 05	8.3	03 58	3.1	16 21	3.1	06 19	4.9	18 44	4.8
31	Monday	06 13	6.4	18 40	6.2	03 27	8.1	16 02	7.9	04 37	3.0	17 08	3.0	07 08	4.7	19 41	4.6

APRIL 1997 *High water* GMT

		London Bridge				Liverpool				Greenock				Leith			
1	Tuesday	07 09	6.1	19 38	6.0	04 32	7.8	17 13	7.5	05 29	2.8	18 08	2.8	08 08	4.5	20 52	4.5
2	Wednesday	08 16	5.9	20 49	5.8	05 52	7.6	18 35	7.6	06 47	2.7	19 31	2.7	09 22	4.5	22 13	4.6
3	Thursday	09 36	5.9	22 09	6.0	07 14	7.9	19 54	8.0	08 36	2.8	21 12	2.8	10 42	4.7	23 29	4.9
4	Friday	10 57	6.3	23 20	6.3	08 24	8.6	20 58	8.7	09 54	3.0	22 24	3.0	11 51	5.0	—	—
5	Saturday	12 01	6.8	—	—	09 22	9.2	21 51	9.3	10 50	3.3	23 18	3.2	00 31	5.2	12 47	5.4
6	Sunday	00 20	6.8	12 57	7.2	10 12	9.8	22 38	9.8	11 39	3.5	—	—	01 22	5.5	13 35	5.7
7	Monday	01 12	7.2	13 46	7.5	10 59	10.1	23 22	10.0	00 06	3.3	12 26	3.6	02 07	5.8	14 20	5.9
8	Tuesday	02 00	7.4	14 31	7.6	11 44	10.2	—	—	00 50	3.4	13 12	3.7	02 50	6.0	15 06	6.0
9	Wednesday	02 44	7.6	15 14	7.6	00 05	9.9	12 28	10.1	01 30	3.5	13 55	3.7	03 34	5.8	15 53	5.9
10	Thursday	03 27	7.6	15 54	7.5	00 47	9.8	13 10	9.8	02 08	3.6	14 36	3.7	04 19	5.7	16 41	5.7
11	Friday	04 08	7.5	16 32	7.2	01 28	9.4	13 52	9.3	02 45	3.6	15 16	3.6	05 04	5.4	17 29	5.4
12	Saturday	04 48	7.2	17 07	6.9	02 07	9.0	14 33	8.8	03 22	3.6	15 56	3.4	05 50	5.2	18 18	5.1
13	Sunday	05 28	6.8	17 43	6.5	02 48	8.5	15 17	8.1	04 02	3.4	16 39	3.2	06 38	4.9	19 10	4.8
14	Monday	06 12	6.4	18 23	6.1	03 34	7.9	16 09	7.5	04 45	3.3	17 27	2.9	07 30	4.6	20 06	4.5
15	Tuesday	07 06	5.9	19 15	5.7	04 33	7.4	17 23	7.0	05 34	3.1	18 26	2.7	08 30	4.4	21 09	4.3
16	Wednesday	08 32	5.6	20 49	5.4	06 02	7.1	18 52	7.0	06 33	2.9	19 51	2.6	09 38	4.3	22 20	4.3
17	Thursday	09 52	5.6	22 10	5.6	07 24	7.3	19 59	7.4	07 50	2.8	21 43	2.7	10 52	4.3	23 33	4.4
18	Friday	10 52	5.9	23 09	5.9	08 23	7.8	20 50	7.9	09 32	2.9	22 33	2.9	11 59	4.5	—	—
19	Saturday	11 44	6.3	—	—	09 11	8.2	21 33	8.3	10 28	3.0	23 15	3.0	00 29	4.6	12 49	4.8
20	Sunday	00 00	6.3	12 31	6.6	09 52	8.6	22 11	8.7	11 10	3.1	23 53	3.0	01 10	4.9	13 29	5.0
21	Monday	00 46	6.5	13 12	6.8	10 29	8.8	22 46	8.9	11 45	3.1	—	—	01 45	5.0	14 04	5.1
22	Tuesday	01 27	6.7	13 49	6.9	11 03	8.9	23 19	9.0	00 27	3.1	12 17	3.1	02 18	5.2	14 38	5.3
23	Wednesday	02 04	6.8	14 24	6.9	11 36	9.0	23 52	9.1	00 57	3.1	12 49	3.2	02 52	5.3	15 12	5.3
24	Thursday	02 39	6.8	14 58	6.9	12 09	9.0	—	—	01 23	3.1	13 25	3.2	03 27	5.3	15 47	5.3
25	Friday	03 13	6.8	15 32	6.9	00 25	9.1	12 46	9.0	01 52	3.2	14 04	3.3	04 02	5.3	16 22	5.3
26	Saturday	03 49	6.9	16 09	6.9	01 01	9.1	13 24	8.9	02 25	3.3	14 43	3.3	04 38	5.3	17 00	5.2
27	Sunday	04 28	6.8	16 48	6.7	01 40	8.9	14 06	8.7	03 00	3.3	15 24	3.2	05 16	5.1	17 43	5.1
28	Monday	05 12	6.7	17 32	6.5	02 24	8.7	14 54	8.4	03 37	3.2	16 08	3.1	05 59	5.0	18 32	4.9
29	Tuesday	06 01	6.5	18 21	6.2	03 15	8.4	15 50	8.0	04 18	3.1	16 58	2.9	06 50	4.8	19 30	4.8
30	Wednesday	06 59	6.2	19 20	6.0	04 19	8.0	16 59	7.7	05 12	2.9	18 02	2.8	07 50	4.7	20 38	4.7

MAY 1997 *High water* GMT

		London Bridge *Datum of predictions 3.20 m below				Liverpool *Datum of predictions 4.93 m below				Greenock *Datum of predictions 1.62 m below				Leith *Datum of predictions 2.90 m below			
		hr	ht m	hr	ht m	hr	ht m	hr	ht m	hr	ht m	hr	ht m	hr	ht m	hr	ht m
1	Thursday	08 07	6.1	20 32	5.9	05 34	7.9	18 17	7.7	06 30	2.8	19 23	2.8	09 03	4.6	21 54	4.7
2	Friday	09 25	6.2	21 49	6.1	06 51	8.1	19 32	8.1	08 10	2.8	20 52	2.8	10 19	4.7	23 06	4.9
3	Saturday	10 36	6.5	22 55	6.4	08 00	8.5	20 35	8.6	09 28	3.0	22 02	3.0	11 27	5.0	—	—
4	Sunday	11 38	6.9	23 54	6.8	08 59	9.1	21 28	9.1	10 26	3.3	22 56	3.1	00 08	5.2	12 25	5.3
5	Monday	12 32	7.2	—	—	09 51	9.5	22 16	9.5	11 17	3.4	23 43	3.3	01 00	5.4	13 15	5.5
6	Tuesday	00 48	7.1	13 22	7.4	10 38	9.7	23 00	9.6	12 05	3.5	—	—	01 46	5.6	14 02	5.7
7	Wednesday	01 37	7.4	14 09	7.5	11 23	9.8	23 42	9.6	00 26	3.4	12 52	3.5	02 30	5.7	14 49	5.7
8	Thursday	02 24	7.5	14 52	7.5	12 06	9.7	—	—	01 07	3.4	13 36	3.5	03 14	5.7	15 36	5.7
9	Friday	03 08	7.4	15 32	7.3	00 23	9.5	12 49	9.4	01 45	3.5	14 18	3.5	03 58	5.5	16 23	5.5
10	Saturday	03 50	7.3	16 08	7.0	01 03	9.2	13 29	9.1	02 22	3.6	14 58	3.4	04 42	5.4	17 09	5.3
11	Sunday	04 30	7.1	16 42	6.8	01 42	8.9	14 09	8.6	03 00	3.6	15 39	3.3	05 25	5.1	17 54	5.0
12	Monday	05 10	6.7	17 16	6.5	02 22	8.5	14 50	8.2	03 39	3.5	16 21	3.1	06 10	4.9	18 41	4.8
13	Tuesday	05 51	6.4	17 55	6.2	03 05	8.1	15 36	7.7	04 20	3.3	17 09	2.9	06 58	4.6	19 31	4.5
14	Wednesday	06 37	6.0	18 42	5.9	03 35	7.7	16 33	7.3	05 06	3.1	18 03	2.8	07 51	4.4	20 25	4.4
15	Thursday	07 35	5.8	19 43	5.7	05 00	7.3	17 49	7.1	06 00	3.0	19 04	2.7	08 50	4.3	21 24	4.3
16	Friday	08 47	5.7	21 01	5.6	06 20	7.3	19 04	7.2	07 02	2.8	20 19	2.7	09 54	4.3	22 27	4.3
17	Saturday	09 56	5.8	22 13	5.8	07 31	7.5	20 03	7.6	08 13	2.8	21 40	2.8	10 59	4.4	23 28	4.5
18	Sunday	10 54	6.1	23 12	6.1	08 26	7.9	20 52	8.1	09 27	2.9	22 32	2.9	11 57	4.6	—	—
19	Monday	11 46	6.4	—	—	09 12	8.2	21 34	8.5	10 21	3.0	23 15	3.0	00 20	4.7	12 46	4.8
20	Tuesday	00 03	6.4	12 33	6.7	09 52	8.6	22 12	8.8	11 02	3.0	23 52	3.0	01 05	4.9	13 28	5.0
21	Wednesday	00 51	6.6	13 16	6.9	10 30	8.8	22 48	9.0	11 40	3.1	—	—	01 45	5.1	14 08	5.2
22	Thursday	01 34	6.8	13 56	7.0	11 07	8.9	23 25	9.1	00 24	3.1	12 20	3.1	02 24	5.3	14 47	5.3
23	Friday	02 15	6.9	14 36	7.0	11 46	9.0	—	—	00 57	3.2	13 02	3.2	03 02	5.4	15 25	5.4
24	Saturday	02 55	7.0	15 15	7.0	00 03	9.2	12 28	9.1	01 31	3.3	13 45	3.2	03 40	5.4	16 04	5.4
25	Sunday	03 36	7.0	15 54	6.9	00 44	9.2	13 11	9.0	02 07	3.3	14 29	3.2	04 18	5.4	16 46	5.4
26	Monday	04 19	7.0	16 36	6.8	01 28	9.1	13 57	8.9	02 45	3.4	15 14	3.2	05 00	5.3	17 31	5.3
27	Tuesday	05 04	6.9	17 20	6.6	02 16	9.0	14 46	8.7	03 25	3.3	16 01	3.1	05 45	5.2	18 22	5.1
28	Wednesday	05 55	6.7	18 10	6.4	03 08	8.7	15 41	8.4	04 10	3.2	16 55	3.0	06 36	5.0	19 18	5.0
29	Thursday	06 51	6.5	19 08	6.2	04 08	8.4	16 44	8.1	05 05	3.1	17 57	2.9	07 36	4.9	20 23	4.9
30	Friday	07 57	6.3	20 17	6.2	05 16	8.2	17 55	8.0	06 15	3.0	19 07	2.9	08 45	4.8	21 33	4.8
31	Saturday	09 07	6.4	21 26	6.3	06 26	8.3	19 05	8.1	07 41	3.0	20 23	2.9	09 57	4.9	22 41	4.9

JUNE 1997 *High water* GMT

		London Bridge				Liverpool				Greenock				Leith			
1	Sunday	10 13	6.6	22 31	6.5	07 34	8.5	20 10	8.4	09 01	3.1	21 35	3.0	11 04	5.0	23 44	5.1
2	Monday	11 13	6.8	23 30	6.8	08 36	8.8	21 06	8.8	10 04	3.2	22 32	3.1	12 04	5.2	—	—
3	Tuesday	12 08	7.1	—	—	09 31	9.1	21 55	9.1	10 58	3.3	23 22	3.2	00 39	5.3	12 59	5.3
4	Wednesday	00 26	7.0	13 00	7.3	10 20	9.3	22 40	9.3	11 47	3.3	—	—	01 28	5.4	13 49	5.4
5	Thursday	01 18	7.2	13 48	7.3	11 06	9.3	23 22	9.3	00 06	3.3	12 35	3.3	02 14	5.5	14 36	5.5
6	Friday	02 06	7.3	14 32	7.3	11 48	9.3	—	—	00 47	3.4	13 20	3.3	02 58	5.5	15 22	5.5
7	Saturday	02 52	7.2	15 12	7.1	00 02	9.2	12 30	9.1	01 26	3.5	14 03	3.2	03 41	5.4	16 06	5.4
8	Sunday	03 34	7.1	15 48	6.9	00 42	9.1	13 09	8.9	02 03	3.5	14 43	3.2	04 23	5.3	16 48	5.2
9	Monday	04 14	6.9	16 21	6.7	01 20	8.9	13 47	8.6	02 40	3.5	15 22	3.1	05 03	5.1	17 29	5.1
10	Tuesday	04 50	6.7	16 53	6.5	01 59	8.7	14 25	8.4	03 18	3.5	16 03	3.1	05 43	5.0	18 11	4.9
11	Wednesday	05 28	6.4	17 31	6.4	02 39	8.4	15 06	8.0	03 56	3.4	16 47	3.0	06 26	4.8	18 55	4.7
12	Thursday	06 09	6.2	18 14	6.2	03 22	8.1	15 52	7.7	04 38	3.2	17 34	2.9	07 12	4.6	19 42	4.5
13	Friday	06 55	6.1	19 05	6.0	04 12	7.7	16 47	7.4	05 25	3.1	18 24	2.8	08 04	4.5	20 34	4.4
14	Saturday	07 49	5.9	20 05	5.9	05 11	7.5	17 54	7.3	06 17	2.9	19 18	2.7	08 59	4.4	21 30	4.4
15	Sunday	08 50	5.9	21 10	5.8	06 19	7.4	19 03	7.5	07 16	2.8	20 21	2.7	09 59	4.4	22 28	4.4
16	Monday	09 54	6.0	22 16	6.0	07 25	7.6	20 02	7.8	08 21	2.8	21 32	2.8	11 00	4.5	23 28	4.6
17	Tuesday	10 56	6.3	23 17	6.2	08 23	7.9	20 53	8.3	09 25	2.9	22 30	2.9	11 59	4.7	—	—
18	Wednesday	11 52	6.6	—	—	09 13	8.3	21 37	8.7	10 21	3.0	23 16	3.0	00 23	4.8	12 52	4.9
19	Thursday	00 13	6.5	12 43	6.8	09 58	8.7	22 19	9.0	11 10	3.1	23 55	3.1	01 13	5.1	13 39	5.1
20	Friday	01 04	6.8	13 31	7.0	10 42	8.9	23 01	9.3	11 55	3.1	—	—	01 58	5.3	14 23	5.3
21	Saturday	01 52	7.0	14 16	7.1	11 27	9.1	23 45	9.4	00 34	3.2	12 42	3.2	02 40	5.4	15 05	5.5
22	Sunday	02 38	7.2	14 59	7.1	12 12	9.2	—	—	01 14	3.4	13 30	3.2	03 20	5.5	15 47	5.5
23	Monday	03 23	7.2	15 42	7.1	00 30	9.5	13 00	9.3	01 54	3.4	14 18	3.2	04 01	5.6	16 31	5.6
24	Tuesday	04 09	7.2	16 25	7.0	01 18	9.5	13 48	9.2	02 35	3.5	15 06	3.2	04 45	5.5	17 18	5.5
25	Wednesday	04 55	7.1	17 09	6.9	02 07	9.4	14 37	9.1	03 17	3.5	15 55	3.2	05 32	5.5	18 09	5.4
26	Thursday	05 44	7.0	17 57	6.7	02 58	9.2	15 28	8.8	04 03	3.4	16 46	3.1	06 23	5.3	19 03	5.2
27	Friday	06 38	6.7	18 51	6.5	03 53	8.9	16 24	8.4	04 54	3.3	17 41	3.0	07 21	5.2	20 04	5.0
28	Saturday	07 38	6.5	19 54	6.4	04 53	8.6	17 28	8.2	05 54	3.2	18 39	3.0	08 26	5.0	21 08	4.9
29	Sunday	08 43	6.4	21 01	6.3	05 59	8.3	18 37	8.0	07 07	3.0	19 45	2.9	09 34	4.9	22 15	4.9
30	Monday	09 48	6.5	22 06	6.4	07 08	8.3	19 45	8.2	08 32	3.0	21 03	2.9	10 43	4.9	23 21	5.0

JULY 1997 *High water* GMT

		London Bridge* Datum of predictions 3.20 m below				Liverpool* Datum of predictions 4.93 m below				Greenock* Datum of predictions 1.62 m below				Leith* Datum of predictions 2.90 m below			
		hr	m	hr	m	hr	m	hr	m	hr	m	hr	m	hr	m	hr	m
1	Tuesday	10 49	6.6	23 09	6.6	08 15	8.4	20 46	8.4	09 44	3.1	22 09	3.0	11 48	5.0	—	—
2	Wednesday	11 46	6.9	—	—	09 14	8.6	21 39	8.8	10 44	3.1	23 02	3.1	00 21	5.1	12 48	5.1
3	Thursday	00 07	6.8	12 40	7.0	10 05	8.8	22 25	9.0	11 35	3.2	23 49	3.3	01 15	5.2	13 40	5.2
4	Friday	01 01	7.0	13 29	7.1	10 51	9.0	23 07	9.1	12 24	3.2	—	—	02 03	5.3	14 26	5.3
5	Saturday	01 51	7.1	14 14	7.1	11 33	9.0	23 46	9.1	00 30	3.3	13 09	3.1	02 46	5.4	15 09	5.3
6	Sunday	02 37	7.1	14 55	7.0	12 12	8.9			01 10	3.4	13 50	3.1	03 26	5.4	15 48	5.3
7	Monday	03 19	7.0	15 30	6.8	00 23	9.1	12 49	8.8	01 46	3.4	14 28	3.1	04 04	5.3	16 25	5.2
8	Tuesday	03 55	6.8	16 01	6.6	00 59	9.0	13 25	8.7	02 22	3.5	15 04	3.1	04 40	5.2	17 02	5.1
9	Wednesday	04 28	6.7	16 31	6.5	01 35	8.8	14 00	8.6	02 56	3.5	15 41	3.0	05 16	5.1	17 40	5.0
10	Thursday	05 01	6.6	17 06	6.5	02 12	8.7	14 37	8.3	03 32	3.4	16 19	3.0	05 54	5.0	18 20	4.9
11	Friday	05 38	6.5	17 45	6.4	02 50	8.4	15 16	8.1	04 09	3.3	16 59	3.0	06 35	4.8	19 03	4.7
12	Saturday	06 20	6.4	18 30	6.3	03 32	8.1	16 01	7.8	04 49	3.2	17 43	2.9	07 18	4.7	19 49	4.6
13	Sunday	07 07	6.2	19 21	6.1	04 21	7.8	16 55	7.5	05 36	3.0	18 31	2.8	08 08	4.5	20 40	4.5
14	Monday	08 02	6.1	20 20	6.0	05 19	7.6	18 00	7.4	06 29	2.9	19 25	2.7	09 04	4.4	21 38	4.5
15	Tuesday	09 04	6.1	21 25	6.0	06 24	7.5	19 08	7.6	07 31	2.8	20 30	2.7	10 07	4.4	22 40	4.5
16	Wednesday	10 10	6.2	22 32	6.1	07 32	7.7	20 11	8.0	08 40	2.8	21 43	2.8	11 14	4.6	23 44	4.7
17	Thursday	11 15	6.4	23 38	6.4	08 35	8.1	21 06	8.6	09 48	2.9	22 43	3.0	12 18	4.8	—	—
18	Friday	12 13	6.7	—	—	09 30	8.5	21 55	9.0	10 46	3.0	23 31	3.2	00 42	5.0	13 13	5.1
19	Saturday	00 38	6.7	13 07	7.0	10 21	9.0	22 41	9.4	11 38	3.1			01 33	5.3	14 01	5.4
20	Sunday	01 32	7.1	13 56	7.2	11 09	9.3	23 28	9.7	00 15	3.3	12 28	3.2	02 18	5.5	14 45	5.6
21	Monday	02 21	7.3	14 43	7.3	11 57	9.5	—	—	00 58	3.4	13 18	3.2	03 00	5.7	15 29	5.8
22	Tuesday	03 09	7.4	15 27	7.3	00 15	9.9	12 46	9.6	01 41	3.6	14 08	3.3	03 43	5.8	16 14	5.8
23	Wednesday	03 55	7.5	16 10	7.3	01 04	9.9	13 33	9.6	02 24	3.6	14 55	3.3	04 28	5.8	17 01	5.7
24	Thursday	04 40	7.4	16 53	7.2	01 52	9.8	14 21	9.4	03 07	3.7	15 41	3.3	05 16	5.8	17 51	5.6
25	Friday	05 27	7.2	17 38	7.1	02 41	9.6	15 08	9.1	03 50	3.6	16 27	3.3	06 07	5.6	18 43	5.3
26	Saturday	06 15	6.9	18 26	6.8	03 31	9.2	15 59	8.7	04 37	3.5	17 13	3.2	07 02	5.4	19 40	5.1
27	Sunday	07 10	6.6	19 23	6.5	04 26	8.7	16 58	8.2	05 28	3.3	18 04	3.1	08 04	5.1	20 42	4.9
28	Monday	08 13	6.3	20 31	6.3	05 31	8.2	18 08	7.8	06 29	3.1	19 00	3.0	09 11	4.9	21 48	4.8
29	Tuesday	09 21	6.2	21 42	6.2	06 44	7.9	19 22	7.8	07 57	2.9	20 19	2.9	10 22	4.8	22 58	4.8
30	Wednesday	10 25	6.3	22 50	6.3	07 57	8.0	20 29	8.1	09 31	2.9	21 47	3.0	11 33	4.8	—	—
31	Thursday	11 25	6.5	23 50	6.6	08 59	8.2	21 24	8.5	10 35	3.0	22 45	3.1	00 05	4.9	12 38	4.9

AUGUST 1997 *High water* GMT

		London Bridge				Liverpool				Greenock				Leith			
1	Friday	12 20	6.8	—	—	09 51	8.5	22 11	8.8	11 27	3.1	23 33	3.2	01 04	5.1	13 32	5.1
2	Saturday	00 45	6.9	13 10	7.0	10 37	8.8	22 52	9.0	12 14	3.1	—	—	01 52	5.2	14 16	5.2
3	Sunday	01 36	7.1	13 56	7.0	11 17	8.9	23 30	9.1	00 15	3.3	12 57	3.1	02 33	5.3	14 54	5.3
4	Monday	02 20	7.1	14 36	6.9	11 54	8.9			00 54	3.4	13 35	3.1	03 10	5.4	15 28	5.3
5	Tuesday	03 00	7.0	15 11	6.8	00 04	9.1	12 28	8.9	01 29	3.4	14 10	3.1	03 44	5.4	16 01	5.3
6	Wednesday	03 33	6.8	15 39	6.6	00 37	9.1	13 00	8.8	02 01	3.4	14 41	3.1	04 16	5.3	16 34	5.2
7	Thursday	04 02	6.7	16 08	6.6	01 10	9.0	13 33	8.7	02 32	3.4	15 12	3.1	04 48	5.3	17 09	5.1
8	Friday	04 32	6.7	16 39	6.6	01 44	8.8	14 07	8.6	03 05	3.4	15 45	3.1	05 23	5.2	17 46	5.0
9	Saturday	05 06	6.7	17 15	6.5	02 18	8.6	14 42	8.4	03 39	3.4	16 20	3.0	05 59	5.0	18 25	4.9
10	Sunday	05 44	6.6	17 55	6.4	02 56	8.4	15 21	8.1	04 17	3.3	17 00	3.0	06 38	4.8	19 08	4.7
11	Monday	06 28	6.4	18 42	6.2	03 40	8.0	16 09	7.8	04 58	3.1	17 44	2.9	07 22	4.7	19 56	4.6
12	Tuesday	07 19	6.2	19 37	6.1	04 34	7.7	17 09	7.5	05 47	2.9	18 37	2.8	08 16	4.5	20 53	4.5
13	Wednesday	08 18	6.0	20 41	5.9	05 39	7.5	18 21	7.5	06 48	2.8	19 42	2.7	09 21	4.4	21 58	4.5
14	Thursday	09 27	6.0	21 52	6.0	06 51	7.5	19 33	7.9	08 02	2.8	21 02	2.8	10 34	4.5	23 08	4.7
15	Friday	10 40	6.2	23 07	6.2	08 04	7.9	20 38	8.4	09 22	2.9	22 15	3.0	11 48	4.8	—	—
16	Saturday	11 46	6.5	—	—	09 08	8.5	21 33	9.1	10 30	3.0	23 09	3.2	00 14	5.0	12 50	5.1
17	Sunday	00 15	6.6	12 44	6.9	10 02	9.0	22 23	9.6	11 25	3.2	23 56	3.4	01 09	5.3	13 40	5.5
18	Monday	01 12	7.0	13 35	7.2	10 52	9.5	23 10	10.0	12 16	3.3	—	—	01 55	5.6	14 26	5.8
19	Tuesday	02 03	7.4	14 23	7.4	11 40	9.8	23 57	10.2	00 41	3.6	13 05	3.4	02 38	5.9	15 10	5.9
20	Wednesday	02 51	7.6	15 07	7.5	12 27	9.9	—	—	01 26	3.7	13 52	3.4	03 22	6.1	15 54	6.0
21	Thursday	03 36	7.7	15 50	7.5	00 44	10.2	13 13	9.8	02 09	3.8	14 37	3.5	04 08	6.1	16 41	5.9
22	Friday	04 20	7.6	16 32	7.5	01 31	10.1	13 58	9.6	02 52	3.8	15 18	3.5	04 55	6.0	17 29	5.7
23	Saturday	05 03	7.4	17 14	7.3	02 18	9.7	14 44	9.2	03 33	3.7	15 59	3.5	05 46	5.8	18 19	5.4
24	Sunday	05 47	7.0	17 58	7.0	03 05	9.2	15 31	8.7	04 15	3.6	16 41	3.4	06 40	5.5	19 14	5.1
25	Monday	06 34	6.6	18 49	6.5	03 57	8.5	16 25	8.1	05 01	3.4	17 27	3.2	07 41	5.1	20 14	4.9
26	Tuesday	07 34	6.1	19 57	6.1	05 00	7.9	17 36	7.6	05 54	3.1	18 19	3.1	08 48	4.8	21 20	4.7
27	Wednesday	08 50	5.9	21 19	5.9	06 21	7.5	19 00	7.5	07 09	2.8	19 26	2.9	10 00	4.7	22 32	4.7
28	Thursday	10 00	5.9	22 30	6.1	07 40	7.6	20 11	7.8	09 22	2.8	21 21	3.0	11 16	4.7	23 46	4.8
29	Friday	11 02	6.2	23 32	6.4	08 42	7.9	21 06	8.3	10 26	3.0	22 25	3.1	12 25	4.8	—	—
30	Saturday	11 58	6.6	—	—	09 34	8.3	21 53	8.7	11 15	3.1	23 14	3.3	00 47	5.0	13 18	5.0
31	Sunday	00 26	6.8	12 48	6.9	10 17	8.7	22 33	9.0	11 58	3.2	23 56	3.4	01 35	5.2	14 00	5.2

SEPTEMBER 1997   *High water*   GMT

		London Bridge *Datum of predictions 3.20 m below*				Liverpool *Datum of predictions 4.93 m below*				Greenock *Datum of predictions 1.62 m below*				Leith *Datum of predictions 2.90 m below*			
		hr	ht m	hr	ht m	hr	ht m	hr	ht m	hr	ht m	hr	ht m	hr	ht m	hr	ht m
1	Monday	01 15	7.0	13 33	7.0	10 56	8.9	23 09	9.1	12 37	3.2	———	—	02 14	5.3	14 34	5.3
2	Tuesday	01 58	7.1	14 13	7.0	11 31	8.9	23 42	9.2	00 33	3.4	13 13	3.2	02 48	5.4	15 04	5.3
3	Wednesday	02 36	7.0	14 47	6.8	12 03	8.9			01 07	3.4	13 45	3.1	03 19	5.4	15 34	5.3
4	Thursday	03 07	6.9	15 16	6.7	00 12	9.1	12 34	8.9	01 37	3.4	14 13	3.1	03 49	5.4	16 05	5.3
5	Friday	03 35	6.8	15 43	6.6	00 43	9.0	13 04	8.8	02 06	3.4	14 40	3.2	04 20	5.4	16 39	5.3
6	Saturday	04 03	6.8	16 12	6.6	01 14	8.9	13 36	8.7	02 37	3.4	15 09	3.2	04 53	5.3	17 14	5.2
7	Sunday	04 35	6.8	16 46	6.6	01 47	8.7	14 09	8.6	03 11	3.4	15 43	3.2	05 27	5.1	17 51	5.0
8	Monday	05 11	6.7	17 25	6.5	02 23	8.5	14 46	8.3	03 47	3.3	16 19	3.1	06 05	5.0	18 31	4.9
9	Tuesday	05 52	6.5	18 10	6.3	03 05	8.1	15 31	8.0	04 26	3.2	17 00	3.0	06 48	4.8	19 18	4.7
10	Wednesday	06 40	6.3	19 04	6.1	03 57	7.7	16 30	7.6	05 12	3.0	17 51	2.9	07 41	4.6	20 14	4.6
11	Thursday	07 37	6.0	20 07	5.9	05 05	7.4	17 44	7.5	06 11	2.8	18 59	2.8	08 47	4.5	21 21	4.6
12	Friday	08 46	5.8	21 19	5.9	06 22	7.4	19 02	7.8	07 30	2.8	20 27	2.8	10 04	4.5	22 36	4.7
13	Saturday	10 05	6.0	22 40	6.1	07 41	7.8	20 14	8.4	09 02	2.9	21 48	3.0	11 22	4.8	23 46	5.0
14	Sunday	11 19	6.3	23 52	6.6	08 49	8.5	21 13	9.1	10 16	3.1	22 46	3.3	12 27	5.2		
15	Monday	12 19	6.8	———	—	09 44	9.1	22 03	9.7	11 12	3.3	23 35	3.5	00 43	5.4	13 19	5.6
16	Tuesday	00 51	7.1	13 11	7.1	10 32	9.6	22 51	10.2	12 00	3.4	———	—	01 31	5.7	14 04	5.9
17	Wednesday	01 42	7.4	13 59	7.4	11 19	9.9	23 37	10.4	00 21	3.7	12 47	3.5	02 15	6.0	14 48	6.0
18	Thursday	02 29	7.7	14 43	7.6	12 04	10.0			01 07	3.8	13 31	3.6	03 00	6.2	15 32	6.1
19	Friday	03 13	7.8	15 26	7.7	00 22	10.3	12 49	9.9	01 51	3.9	14 12	3.6	03 46	6.2	16 17	6.0
20	Saturday	03 56	7.7	16 08	7.6	01 08	10.1	13 33	9.7	02 33	3.9	14 51	3.7	04 34	6.1	17 05	5.8
21	Sunday	04 36	7.4	16 49	7.4	01 53	9.7	14 16	9.2	03 13	3.8	15 30	3.6	05 25	5.8	17 54	5.5
22	Monday	05 17	7.1	17 32	7.0	02 38	9.1	15 00	8.7	03 54	3.6	16 10	3.6	06 18	5.4	18 47	5.1
23	Tuesday	05 57	6.6	18 19	6.5	03 27	8.4	15 51	8.0	04 37	3.4	16 54	3.4	07 17	5.0	19 44	4.8
24	Wednesday	06 44	6.1	19 21	6.0	04 28	7.7	16 59	7.5	05 28	3.1	17 45	3.2	08 21	4.7	20 50	4.6
25	Thursday	08 05	5.7	20 52	5.8	05 54	7.2	18 30	7.3	06 34	2.8	18 47	3.0	09 31	4.5	22 01	4.6
26	Friday	09 31	5.7	22 05	5.9	07 16	7.3	19 44	7.6	09 05	2.8	20 32	3.0	10 48	4.5	23 17	4.7
27	Saturday	10 34	6.0	23 06	6.2	08 18	7.7	20 41	8.1	10 08	3.0	21 57	3.1	12 00	4.7		
28	Sunday	11 30	6.3	23 59	6.6	09 09	8.2	21 27	8.6	10 53	3.1	22 47	3.3	00 21	4.9	12 54	4.9
29	Monday	12 20	6.7	———	—	09 51	8.6	22 07	8.9	11 33	3.2	23 30	3.4	01 09	5.1	13 34	5.1
30	Tuesday	00 47	6.9	13 05	6.9	10 29	8.8	22 43	9.1	12 10	3.3	———	—	01 47	5.3	14 06	5.3

OCTOBER 1997   *High water*   GMT

		London Bridge				Liverpool				Greenock				Leith			
1	Wednesday	01 30	7.0	13 45	6.9	11 03	9.0	23 15	9.1	00 07	3.4	12 45	3.3	02 20	5.4	14 35	5.4
2	Thursday	02 06	7.0	14 20	6.9	11 34	9.0	23 45	9.1	00 40	3.4	13 16	3.3	02 51	5.5	15 05	5.4
3	Friday	02 38	6.9	14 50	6.7	12 05	9.0			01 08	3.4	13 43	3.3	03 21	5.5	15 37	5.4
4	Saturday	03 06	6.9	15 19	6.7	00 15	9.0	12 35	8.9	01 37	3.4	14 08	3.3	03 54	5.4	16 11	5.4
5	Sunday	03 35	6.9	15 48	6.7	00 47	8.9	13 07	8.8	02 10	3.4	14 37	3.4	04 27	5.3	16 45	5.3
6	Monday	04 06	6.8	16 22	6.7	01 20	8.8	13 40	8.7	02 46	3.4	15 10	3.3	05 02	5.2	17 21	5.2
7	Tuesday	04 42	6.8	17 01	6.6	01 57	8.6	14 18	8.5	03 23	3.4	15 46	3.3	05 40	5.1	18 01	5.0
8	Wednesday	05 22	6.6	17 47	6.4	02 39	8.2	15 03	8.1	04 02	3.2	16 24	3.2	06 25	4.9	18 47	4.8
9	Thursday	06 09	6.3	18 41	6.2	03 32	7.8	16 02	7.8	04 46	3.1	17 12	3.0	07 18	4.7	19 44	4.7
10	Friday	07 04	6.0	19 43	6.0	04 40	7.5	17 16	7.6	05 44	2.9	18 21	2.9	08 24	4.6	20 52	4.6
11	Saturday	08 12	5.8	20 56	5.9	05 59	7.4	18 36	7.8	07 07	2.8	19 55	2.9	09 40	4.6	22 09	4.8
12	Sunday	09 35	5.9	22 18	6.2	07 20	7.8	19 50	8.4	08 43	2.9	21 21	3.1	10 58	4.9	23 20	5.1
13	Monday	10 50	6.3	23 28	6.6	08 28	8.5	20 50	9.1	09 59	3.1	22 22	3.4	12 03	5.3		
14	Tuesday	11 52	6.7	———	—	09 23	9.2	21 42	9.7	10 54	3.3	23 13	3.6	00 18	5.4	12 56	5.6
15	Wednesday	00 26	7.1	12 45	7.1	10 11	9.7	22 30	10.1	11 41	3.5	———	—	01 08	5.8	13 41	5.9
16	Thursday	01 18	7.5	13 34	7.4	10 56	10.0	23 15	10.3	00 00	3.7	12 25	3.6	01 53	6.0	14 25	6.0
17	Friday	02 05	7.7	14 19	7.6	11 40	10.0			00 47	3.8	13 07	3.7	02 39	6.2	15 09	6.0
18	Saturday	02 49	7.7	15 03	7.7	00 00	10.2	12 24	9.9	01 31	3.9	13 47	3.8	03 26	6.1	15 55	5.9
19	Sunday	03 31	7.6	15 46	7.6	00 45	9.9	13 07	9.6	02 13	3.8	14 25	3.8	04 14	6.0	16 41	5.7
20	Monday	04 11	7.4	16 28	7.4	01 29	9.5	13 49	9.2	02 54	3.8	15 04	3.8	05 05	5.7	17 29	5.4
21	Tuesday	04 48	7.0	17 10	7.0	02 13	8.9	14 32	8.7	03 35	3.6	15 44	3.7	05 57	5.3	18 19	5.1
22	Wednesday	05 25	6.6	17 55	6.6	02 59	8.3	15 19	8.1	04 18	3.4	16 27	3.6	06 52	5.0	19 15	4.8
23	Thursday	06 02	6.2	18 49	6.1	03 53	7.6	16 17	7.6	05 08	3.1	17 16	3.4	07 51	4.7	20 16	4.6
24	Friday	06 52	5.7	20 12	5.7	05 10	7.2	17 42	7.3	06 09	2.9	18 15	3.2	08 54	4.5	21 22	4.5
25	Saturday	08 46	5.5	21 29	5.8	06 37	7.1	19 03	7.4	07 56	2.8	19 27	3.1	10 04	4.5	22 33	4.6
26	Sunday	09 57	5.7	22 30	6.0	07 43	7.5	20 05	7.8	09 32	3.0	21 09	3.1	11 16	4.6	23 40	4.7
27	Monday	10 54	6.1	23 24	6.3	08 35	7.9	20 54	8.3	10 20	3.1	22 11	3.3	12 14	4.8		
28	Tuesday	11 45	6.4	———	—	09 19	8.4	21 36	8.6	11 01	3.3	22 56	3.3	00 32	4.9	12 57	5.0
29	Wednesday	00 12	6.6	12 31	6.7	09 57	8.7	22 13	8.9	11 39	3.4	23 35	3.4	01 13	5.1	13 32	5.2
30	Thursday	00 55	6.9	13 13	6.8	10 32	9.0	22 46	9.0	12 14	3.4	———	—	01 48	5.3	14 04	5.3
31	Friday	01 33	6.9	13 50	6.8	11 05	9.0	23 17	9.0	00 07	3.4	12 46	3.4	02 22	5.4	14 37	5.4

NOVEMBER 1997 *High water* GMT

		London Bridge *Datum of predictions 3.20 m below*				Liverpool *Datum of predictions 4.93 m below*				Greenock *Datum of predictions 1.62 m below*				Leith *Datum of predictions 2.90 m below*			
		hr	m	hr	ht m	hr	m	hr	ht m	hr	m	hr	ht m	hr	m	hr	ht m
1	Saturday	02 07	7.0	14 23	6.8	11 36	9.1	23 49	9.0	00 38	3.4	13 13	3.4	02 55	5.5	15 11	5.5
2	Sunday	02 39	6.9	14 56	6.8	12 08	9.1	—	—	01 10	3.4	13 40	3.5	03 30	5.5	15 45	5.4
3	Monday	03 11	6.9	15 29	6.8	00 23	9.0	12 43	9.0	01 46	3.4	14 11	3.5	04 05	5.4	16 20	5.4
4	Tuesday	03 44	6.9	16 05	6.8	01 00	8.9	13 19	8.9	02 24	3.4	14 45	3.5	04 42	5.3	16 57	5.3
5	Wednesday	04 20	6.8	16 46	6.7	01 39	8.7	14 00	8.7	03 04	3.4	15 22	3.5	05 22	5.2	17 37	5.1
6	Thursday	05 00	6.6	17 32	6.5	02 24	8.4	14 48	8.4	03 45	3.3	16 01	3.3	06 08	5.0	18 25	5.0
7	Friday	05 46	6.3	18 25	6.3	03 17	8.0	15 45	8.1	04 31	3.1	16 49	3.2	07 02	4.9	19 21	4.8
8	Saturday	06 40	6.1	19 27	6.1	04 22	7.7	16 55	7.9	05 30	3.0	17 54	3.1	08 05	4.8	20 28	4.8
9	Sunday	07 46	5.9	20 39	6.1	05 38	7.6	18 11	8.0	06 48	2.9	19 23	3.1	09 18	4.8	21 43	4.8
10	Monday	09 08	6.0	21 55	6.3	06 56	7.9	19 23	8.4	08 17	3.0	20 51	3.2	10 32	5.0	22 54	5.1
11	Tuesday	10 22	6.3	23 02	6.7	08 04	8.5	20 26	9.0	09 34	3.2	21 57	3.4	11 37	5.3	23 54	5.4
12	Wednesday	11 24	6.7	—	—	09 00	9.1	21 20	9.5	10 31	3.4	22 50	3.6	12 32	5.5	—	—
13	Thursday	00 01	7.0	12 20	7.1	09 49	9.5	22 10	9.8	11 19	3.5	23 40	3.7	00 46	5.7	13 20	5.7
14	Friday	00 53	7.4	13 10	7.4	10 35	9.8	22 56	10.0	12 03	3.6	—	—	01 35	5.9	14 05	5.9
15	Saturday	01 42	7.5	13 58	7.5	11 19	9.8	23 41	9.9	00 27	3.8	12 45	3.7	02 22	6.0	14 49	5.9
16	Sunday	02 27	7.6	14 44	7.6	12 02	9.7	—	—	01 13	3.8	13 25	3.8	03 09	5.9	15 34	5.8
17	Monday	03 09	7.4	15 28	7.5	00 24	9.7	12 44	9.5	01 57	3.7	14 04	3.9	03 58	5.8	16 20	5.6
18	Tuesday	03 49	7.2	16 11	7.3	01 08	9.3	13 26	9.2	02 38	3.7	14 43	3.9	04 46	5.6	17 06	5.4
19	Wednesday	04 25	6.9	16 53	7.0	01 50	8.8	14 07	8.8	03 19	3.5	15 22	3.8	05 35	5.3	17 53	5.2
20	Thursday	04 59	6.6	17 35	6.6	02 33	8.4	14 50	8.4	04 02	3.4	16 04	3.7	06 24	5.0	18 43	4.9
21	Friday	05 34	6.3	18 21	6.2	03 19	7.8	15 39	7.9	04 49	3.2	16 50	3.5	07 16	4.7	19 38	4.7
22	Saturday	06 17	6.0	19 16	5.9	04 16	7.4	16 40	7.5	05 44	3.0	17 42	3.3	08 11	4.6	20 37	4.5
23	Sunday	07 15	5.7	20 27	5.7	05 31	7.1	17 58	7.4	06 46	2.9	18 41	3.2	09 10	4.5	21 40	4.5
24	Monday	08 51	5.6	21 37	5.8	06 49	7.2	19 11	7.5	08 08	2.9	19 50	3.1	10 12	4.5	22 43	4.6
25	Tuesday	10 02	5.7	22 35	6.0	07 50	7.6	20 10	7.9	09 29	3.0	21 10	3.1	11 14	4.6	23 42	4.7
26	Wednesday	11 00	6.0	23 27	6.3	08 40	8.1	20 57	8.3	10 21	3.2	22 11	3.2	12 08	4.8	—	—
27	Thursday	11 50	6.3	—	—	09 22	8.5	21 38	8.6	11 04	3.3	22 55	3.3	00 32	4.9	12 52	5.0
28	Friday	00 14	6.6	12 36	6.6	10 00	8.8	22 15	8.8	11 42	3.4	23 32	3.3	01 14	5.1	13 32	5.2
29	Saturday	00 57	6.8	13 18	6.8	10 36	9.0	22 50	9.0	12 15	3.4	—	—	01 53	5.3	14 10	5.4
30	Sunday	01 37	6.9	13 57	6.9	11 11	9.2	23 26	9.1	00 08	3.3	12 46	3.5	02 31	5.4	14 47	5.5

DECEMBER 1997 *High water* GMT

		London Bridge				Liverpool				Greenock				Leith			
1	Monday	02 15	7.0	14 35	6.9	11 47	9.2	—	—	00 46	3.4	13 17	3.5	03 09	5.4	15 23	5.5
2	Tuesday	02 51	7.0	15 13	6.9	00 04	9.1	12 25	9.2	01 26	3.4	13 51	3.6	03 46	5.5	16 00	5.5
3	Wednesday	03 28	6.9	15 53	6.9	00 45	9.0	13 06	9.2	02 08	3.4	14 28	3.6	04 25	5.4	16 38	5.4
4	Thursday	04 06	6.8	16 36	6.9	01 28	8.9	13 50	9.1	02 50	3.4	15 07	3.6	05 07	5.3	17 20	5.3
5	Friday	04 46	6.7	17 23	6.7	02 15	8.7	14 39	8.9	03 34	3.3	15 48	3.5	05 54	5.2	18 08	5.2
6	Saturday	05 32	6.5	18 15	6.5	03 06	8.4	15 33	8.6	04 22	3.2	16 36	3.4	06 47	5.1	19 02	5.1
7	Sunday	06 23	6.3	19 13	6.4	04 05	8.1	16 35	8.4	05 18	3.1	17 35	3.3	07 47	5.0	20 06	5.0
8	Monday	07 26	6.1	20 21	6.3	05 14	7.9	17 44	8.3	06 25	3.0	18 49	3.2	08 54	4.9	21 17	5.0
9	Tuesday	08 42	6.1	21 31	6.4	06 27	8.0	18 54	8.4	07 41	3.0	20 16	3.2	10 05	5.0	22 28	5.1
10	Wednesday	09 55	6.3	22 37	6.6	07 37	8.3	20 01	8.7	09 01	3.1	21 30	3.3	11 11	5.1	23 32	5.2
11	Thursday	10 59	6.6	23 36	6.9	08 38	8.7	21 01	9.1	10 05	3.3	22 30	3.4	12 10	5.3	—	—
12	Friday	11 57	6.9	—	—	09 31	9.2	21 53	9.4	10 57	3.4	23 23	3.5	00 29	5.4	13 02	5.5
13	Saturday	00 30	7.1	12 52	7.2	10 19	9.5	22 41	9.5	11 43	3.6	—	—	01 22	5.6	13 50	5.6
14	Sunday	01 21	7.3	13 42	7.3	11 03	9.6	23 26	9.6	00 12	3.6	12 26	3.7	02 11	5.7	14 35	5.7
15	Monday	02 08	7.3	14 29	7.4	11 45	9.6	—	—	01 00	3.6	13 07	3.8	02 58	5.7	15 19	5.7
16	Tuesday	02 51	7.2	15 14	7.3	00 09	9.4	12 27	9.5	01 45	3.6	13 46	3.8	03 44	5.6	16 03	5.6
17	Wednesday	03 30	7.0	15 56	7.1	00 50	9.2	13 06	9.3	02 25	3.5	14 25	3.8	04 28	5.5	16 45	5.4
18	Thursday	04 05	6.8	16 35	6.9	01 29	8.9	13 46	9.0	03 05	3.4	15 04	3.8	05 12	5.3	17 27	5.2
19	Friday	04 37	6.6	17 13	6.6	02 08	8.6	14 25	8.7	03 45	3.3	15 43	3.7	05 55	5.1	18 10	5.0
20	Saturday	05 10	6.4	17 51	6.4	02 49	8.2	15 06	8.4	04 28	3.2	16 24	3.6	06 39	4.9	18 57	4.8
21	Sunday	05 50	6.2	18 34	6.2	03 33	7.8	15 53	8.0	05 13	3.1	17 08	3.4	07 26	4.7	19 47	4.7
22	Monday	06 36	6.0	19 23	6.0	04 25	7.5	16 47	7.7	06 03	3.0	17 57	3.3	08 17	4.5	20 43	4.5
23	Tuesday	07 33	5.8	20 20	5.9	05 31	7.3	17 54	7.5	06 57	3.0	18 51	3.1	09 12	4.5	21 41	4.5
24	Wednesday	08 41	5.7	21 24	5.9	06 45	7.3	19 05	7.5	08 02	2.9	19 53	3.0	10 10	4.5	22 43	4.5
25	Thursday	09 54	5.7	22 29	6.0	07 50	7.7	20 08	7.8	09 21	3.0	21 03	3.0	11 11	4.6	23 44	4.7
26	Friday	10 59	6.0	23 28	6.3	08 43	8.1	21 00	8.2	10 22	3.1	22 08	3.1	12 08	4.8	—	—
27	Saturday	11 56	6.3	—	—	09 28	8.6	21 45	8.6	11 08	3.3	22 58	3.2	00 38	4.9	12 59	5.1
28	Sunday	00 21	6.6	12 47	6.6	10 09	8.9	22 26	8.9	11 46	3.4	23 43	3.3	01 26	5.1	13 44	5.3
29	Monday	01 09	6.8	13 33	6.8	10 49	9.2	23 07	9.1	12 22	3.5	—	—	02 09	5.3	14 25	5.4
30	Tuesday	01 53	7.0	14 17	7.0	11 29	9.4	23 50	9.3	00 26	3.3	12 58	3.5	02 49	5.4	15 04	5.6
31	Wednesday	02 35	7.0	15 00	7.1	12 11	9.5	—	—	01 11	3.3	13 36	3.6	03 29	5.5	15 42	5.6

World Geographical Statistics

THE EARTH

The shape of the Earth is that of an oblate spheroid or solid of revolution whose meridian sections are ellipses, whilst the sections at right angles are circles.

DIMENSIONS

Equatorial diameter = 12,756.27 km (7,926.38 miles)
Polar diameter = 12,713.50 km (7,899.80 miles)
Equatorial circumference = 40,075.01 km (24,901.46 miles)
Polar circumference = 40,007.86 km (24,859.73 miles)

The equatorial circumference is divided into 360 degrees of longitude, which is measured in degrees, minutes and seconds east or west of the Greenwich meridian (0°) to 180°, the meridian 180° E. coinciding with 180° W. This was internationally ratified in 1884.

Distance north and south of the Equator is measured in degrees, minutes and seconds of latitude. The Equator is 0°, the North Pole is 90° N. and the South Pole is 90° S. The Tropics lie at 23° 26′ N. (Tropic of Cancer) and 23° 26′ S. (Tropic of Capricorn). The Arctic Circle lies at 66° 34′ N. and the Antarctic Circle at 66° 34′ S. (NB The Tropics and the Arctic and Antarctic circles are of variable latitude due to the mean obliquity of the Ecliptic; the values given are for 1997.5.)

AREA, ETC.

The surface area of the Earth is 510,069,120 km^2 (196,938,800 miles^2), of which the water area is 70.92 per cent and the land area is 29.08 per cent.

The velocity of a given point of the Earth's surface at the Equator exceeds 1,000 miles an hour (24,901.45 miles in 24 hours, viz 1,037.56 m.p.h.); the Earth's velocity in its orbit round the Sun averages 66,629 m.p.h. (584,081.400 miles in 365.256363 days). The Earth is distant from the Sun 92,955,900 miles, on average.

Source: Royal Greenwich Observatory

OCEANS

AREA

	km^2	miles^2
Pacific	166,240,000	64,186,300
Atlantic	86,550,000	33,420,000
Indian	73,427,000	28,350,500
Arctic	13,223,700	5,105,700

GREATEST DEPTHS

Greatest depth location	metres	feet
Mariana Trench (Pacific)	10,924	35,840
Puerto Rico Trench (Atlantic)	8,605	28,232
Java Trench (Indian)	7,125	23,376
Eurasian Basin (Arctic)	5,450	17,880

SEAS

AREA

	km^2	miles^2
South China	2,974,600	1,148,500
Caribbean	2,515,900	971,400
Mediterranean	2,509,900	969,100
Bering	2,226,100	873,000
Gulf of Mexico	1,507,600	582,100
Okhotsk	1,392,000	537,500
Japan	1,015,000	391,100
Hudson Bay	730,100	281,900
East China	664,600	256,600
Andaman	564,880	218,100
Black Sea	507,900	196,100
Red Sea	453,000	174,900
North Sea	427,100	164,900
Baltic Sea	382,000	147,500
Yellow Sea	294,000	113,500
Persian Gulf	230,000	88,800

GREATEST DEPTHS

	Maximum depth metres	feet
Caribbean	8,605	28,232
East China	7,507	24,629
South China	7,258	23,812
Mediterranean	5,150	16,896
Andaman	4,267	14,000
Bering	3,936	12,913
Gulf of Mexico	3,504	11,496
Okhotsk	3,365	11,040
Japan	3,053	10,016
Red Sea	2,266	7,434
Black Sea	2,212	7,257
North Sea	439	1,440
Hudson Bay	111	364
Baltic Sea	90	295
Yellow Sea	73	240
Persian Gulf	73	240

THE CONTINENTS

There are six geographic continents, though America is often divided politically into North and Central America, and South America.

AFRICA is surrounded by sea except for the narrow isthmus of Suez in the north-east, through which is cut the Suez Canal. Its extreme longitudes are 17° 20′ W. at Cape Verde, Senegal, and 51° 24′ E. at Ras Hafun, Somalia. The extreme latitudes are 37° 20′ N. at Cape Blanc, Tunisia, and 34° 50′ S. at Cape Agulhas, South Africa, about 4,400 miles apart. The Equator passes through the middle of the continent.

NORTH AMERICA, including Mexico, is surrounded by ocean except in the south, where the isthmian states of CENTRAL AMERICA link North America with South America. Its extreme longitudes are 168° 5′ W. at Cape Prince of Wales, Alaska, and 55° 40′ W. at Cape Charles,

Newfoundland. The extreme continental latitudes are the tip of the Boothia peninsula, NW Territories, Canada (71° 51' N.) and 14° 22' N. at Ocós in the south of Mexico.

SOUTH AMERICA lies mostly in the southern hemisphere; the Equator passes through the north of the continent. It is surrounded by ocean except where it is joined to Central America in the north by the narrow isthmus through which is cut the Panama Canal. Its extreme longitudes are 34° 47' W. at Cape Branco in Brazil and 81° 20' W. at Punta Pariña, Peru. The extreme continental latitudes are 12° 25' N. at Punta Gallinas, Colombia, and 53° 54' S. at the southernmost tip of the Brunswick peninsula, Chile. Cape Horn, on Cape Island, Chile, lies at 55° 59' S.

ANTARCTICA lies almost entirely within the Antarctic Circle (66° 34' S.) and is the largest of the world's glaciated areas. The continent has an area of about 5.5 million square miles, 99 per cent of which is permanently ice-covered. The ice amounts to some 7.2 million cubic miles and represents more than 90 per cent of the world's fresh water. The environment is too hostile for unsupported human habitation. See also pages 782–3

ASIA is the largest continent and occupies 30 per cent of the world's land surface. The extreme longitudes are 26° 05' E. at Baba Buran, Turkey and 169° 40' W. at Mys Dežneva (East Cape), Russia, a distance of about 6,000 miles. Its extreme northern latitude is 77° 45' N. at Cape Čeljuskin, Russia, and it extends over 5,000 miles south to about 1° 15' N. of the Equator.

AUSTRALIA is the smallest of the continents and lies in the southern hemisphere. It is entirely surrounded by ocean. Its extreme longitudes are 113° 11' E. at Steep Point and 153° 11' E. at Cape Byron. The extreme latitudes are 10° 42' S. at Cape York and 39° S. at South East Point, Tasmania.

EUROPE, including European Russia, is the smallest continent in the northern hemisphere. Its extreme latitudes are 71° 11' N. at North Cape in Norway, and 36° 23' N. at Cape Matapan in southern Greece, a distance of about 2,400 miles. Its breadth from Cabo Carvoeiro in Portugal (9° 34' W.) in the west to the Kara River, north of the Urals (66° 30' E.) in the east is about 3,300 miles. The division between Europe and Asia is generally regarded as the watershed of the Ural Mountains; down the Ural river to Gur'yev, Kazakhstan; across the Caspian Sea to Apsheronskiy Poluostrov, near Baku; along the watershed of the Caucasus Mountains to Anapa and thence across the Black Sea to the Bosporus in Turkey; across the Sea of Marmara to Çanakkale Boğazi (Dardanelles).

	Area km²	miles²
Asia	43,998,000	16,988,000
*America	41,918,000	16,185,000
Africa	29,800,000	11,506,000
Antarctica	c.13,600,000	c.5,500,000
†Europe	9,699,000	3,745,000
Australia	7,618,493	2,941,526

*North and Central America has an area of 24,255,000 km² (9,365,000 miles²)

†Includes 5,571,000 km² (2,151,000 miles²) of former USSR territory, including the Baltic states, Belarus, Moldova, the Ukraine, that part of Russia west of the Ural Mountains and Kazakhstan west of the Ural river. European Turkey (24,378 km²/9,412 miles²) comprises territory to the west and north of the Bosporus and the Dardanelles

GLACIATED AREAS

It is estimated that 15,600,000 km² (6,020,000 miles²) or 10.51 per cent of the world's land surface is permanently covered with ice.

	Area km²	miles²
South Polar regions	13,597,000	5,250,000
North Polar regions (incl. Greenland or Kalaallit Nunaat)	1,965,000	758,500
Alaska-Canada	58,800	22,700
Asia	37,800	14,600
South America	11,900	4,600
Europe	10,700	4,128
New Zealand	984	380
Africa	238	92

PENINSULAS

	Area km²	miles²
Arabian	3,250,000	1,250,000
Southern Indian	2,072,000	800,000
Alaskan	1,500,000	580,000
Labradorian	1,300,000	500,000
Scandinavian	800,300	309,000
Iberian	584,000	225,500

LARGEST ISLANDS

Island (and Ocean)	Area km²	miles²
Greenland (Kalaallit Nunaat) (Arctic)	2,175,500	840,000
New Guinea (Pacific)	792,500	306,000
Borneo (Pacific)	725,450	280,100
Madagascar (Indian)	587,040	226,658
Baffin Island (Arctic)	507,451	195,928
Sumatra (Indian)	427,350	165,000
Honshu (Pacific)	227,413	87,805
*Great Britain (Atlantic)	218,040	84,186
Victoria Island (Arctic)	217,292	83,897
Ellesmere Island (Arctic)	196,236	75,767
Sulawesi (Celebes) (Indian)	178,700	69,000
South Island, NZ (Pacific)	151,010	58,305
Java (Indian)	126,650	48,900
Cuba (Atlantic)	114,525	44,218
North Island, NZ (Pacific)	114,050	44,035
Newfoundland (Atlantic)	108,855	42,030
Luzon (Pacific)	105,880	40,880
Iceland (Atlantic)	103,000	39,770
Mindanao (Pacific)	95,247	36,775
Ireland (Atlantic)	82,462	31,839

*Mainland only

LARGEST DESERTS

	Area (approx.)	
	km²	miles²
The Sahara (N. Africa)	9,000,000	3,500,000
Australian Desert	1,550,000	600,000
Arabian Desert	1,300,000	500,000
*The Gobi (Mongolia/China)	1,300,000	500,000
Kalahari Desert (Botswana/		
Namibia/S. Africa)	583,000	225,000
Sonoran Desert (USA/		
Mexico)	310,000	120,000
Namib Desert (Namibia)	310,000	120,000
†Kara Kum (Turkmenistan)	310,000	120,000
Thar Desert (India/		
Pakistan)	260,000	100,000
Somali Desert (Somalia)	260,000	100,000
†Kyzyl Kum (Kazakhstan/		
Uzbekistan)	260,000	100,000
Atacama Desert (Chile)	180,000	70,000
Dasht-e Lut (Iran)	52,000	20,000
Mojave Desert (USA)	35,000	13,500
Desierto de Sechura (Peru)	26,000	10,000

*Including the Takla Makan – 320,000 km² (125,000 miles²)
†Together known as the Turkestan Desert

DEEPEST DEPRESSIONS

	Maximum depth below sea level	
	metres	feet
Dead Sea (Jordan/Israel)	395	1,296
Turfan Depression (Sinkiang, China)	153	505
Qattara Depression (Egypt)	132	436
Mangyshlak peninsula (Kazakhstan)	131	433
Danakil Depression (Ethiopia)	116	383
Death Valley (California, USA)	86	282
Salton Sink (California, USA)	71	235
W. of Ustyurt plateau (Kazakhstan)	70	230
Prikaspiyskaya Nizmennost' (Russia/Kazakhstan)	67	220
Lake Sarykamysh (Uzbekistan/ Turkmenistan)	45	148
El Faiyûm (Egypt)	44	147
Valdies peninsula, Lago Enriquillo (Dominican Republic)	40	131

The world's largest exposed depression is the
Prikaspiyskaya Nizmennost' covering the hinterland of the
northern third of the Caspian Sea, which is itself 28 m
(92 ft) below sea level
Western Antarctica and Central Greenland largely
comprise crypto-depressions under ice burdens. The
Antarctic Wilkes subglacial basin has a bedrock 2,341 m
(7,680 ft) below sea-level. In Greenland (lat. 73° N., long.
39° W.) the bedrock is 365 m (1,197 ft) below sea-level

LONGEST MOUNTAIN RANGES

Range (location)	Length	
	km	miles
Cordillera de Los Andes (W. South America)	7,200	4,500
Rocky Mountains (W. North America)	4,800	3,000
Himalaya-Karakoram-Hindu Kush (S. Central Asia)	3,800	2,400
Great Dividing Range (E. Australia)	3,600	2,250
Trans-Antarctic Mts (Antarctica)	3,500	2,200
Atlantic Coast Range (E. Brazil)	3,000	1,900
West Sumatran-Javan Range (Indonesia)	2,900	1,800
Aleutian Range (Alaska and NW Pacific)	2,650	1,650
Tien Shan (S. Central Asia)	2,250	1,400
Central New Guinea Range (Irian Jaya/Papua New Guinea)	2,000	1,250

HIGHEST MOUNTAINS

The world's 8,000-metre mountains (with six subsidiary
peaks) are all in the Himalaya-Karakoram-Hindu Kush
range.

Mountain	Height	
	metres	feet
Mt Everest*	8,848	29,028
K2 (Chogori)†	8,607	28,238
Kangchenjunga	8,597	28,208
Lhotse	8,511	27,923
Makalu I	8,481	27,824
Lhotse Shar (II)	8,400	27,560
Dhaulagiri I	8,171	26,810
Manaslu I (Kutang I)	8,156	26,760
Cho Oyu	8,153	26,750
Nanga Parbat (Diamir)	8,125	26,660
Annapurna I	8,078	26,504
Gasherbrum I (Hidden Peak)	8,068	26,470
Broad Peak I	8,046	26,400
Gasherbrum II	8,034	26,360
Shisha Pangma (Gosainthan)	8,012	26,287
Makalu South-East	8,010	26,280
Broad Peak Central	8,000	26,246

*Named after Sir George Everest (1790–1866), Surveyor-General of
India 1830–43, in 1863. He pronounced his name Eve-rest
†Formerly Godwin-Austin

The culminating summits in the other major mountain
ranges are:

Mountain (by range or country)	Height	
	metres	feet
Pik Pobedy (Tien Shan)	7,439	24,406
Cerro Aconcagua (Cordillera de Los Andes)	6,960	22,834
Mt McKinley, S. Peak (Alaska Range)	6,194	20,320
Kilimanjaro (Kibo) (Tanzania)	5,894	19,340
Hkakabo Razi (Myanmar)	5,881	19,296
Citlaltépetl (Orizaba) (Sierra Madre Oriental, Mexico)	5,699	18,700

Mountain (by range or country)	Height metres	feet
El'brus, *W. Peak* (Caucasus)	5,641	18,510
Vinson Massif (E. Antarctica)	4,897	16,067
Puncak Jaya (Central New Guinea Range)	4,884	16,023
Mt Blanc (Alps)	4,807	15,771
Klyuchevskaya Sopka (Kamchatka peninsula, Russia)	4,750	15,584
Ras Dashan (Ethiopian Highlands)	4,620	15,158
Zard Kūh (Zagros Mts, Iran)	4,547	14,921
Mt Kirkpatrick (Trans Antarctic)	4,529	14,860
Mt Belukha (Altai Mts, Russia/ Kazakhstan)	4,505	14,783
Mt Elbert (Rocky Mountains)	4,400	14,433
Mt Rainier (Cascade Range, N. America)	4,392	14,410
Nevado de Colima (Sierra Madre Occidental, Mexico)	4,268	14,003
Jebel Toubkal (Atlas Mts, N. Africa)	4,165	13,665
Kinabalu (Crocker Range, Borneo)	4,101	13,455
Kerinci (West Sumatran-Javan Range, Indonesia)	3,800	12,467
Jabal an Nabī Shu'ayb (N. Tihāmat, Yemen)	3,760	12,336
Teotepec (Sierra Madre del Sur, Mexico)	3,703	12,149
Thaban Ntlenyana (Drakensberg, South Africa)	3,482	11,425
Pico de Bandeira (Atlantic Coast Range)	2,890	9,482
Shishaldin (Aleutian Range)	2,861	9,387
Kosciusko (Great Dividing Range)	2,228	7,310

HIGHEST VOLCANOES

Volcano (last major eruption) and location	Height metres	feet
Guallatiri (1993), Andes, Chile	6,060	19,882
Lascar (1991), Andes, Chile	5,990	19,652
Cotopaxi (1975), Andes, Ecuador	5,897	19,347
Tupungatito (1986), Andes, Chile	5,640	18,504
Nevado del Ruiz (1985, 1992), Colombia	5,400	17,716
Sangay (1988), Andes, Ecuador	5,230	17,159
Guagua Pichincha (1988), Andes, Ecuador	4,784	15,696
Purace (1977), Colombia	4,756	15,601
Klyuchevskaya Sopka (1995), Kamchatka peninsula, Russia	4,750	15,584
Nevado de Colima (1991), Mexico	4,268	14,003
Galeras (1991), Colombia	4,266	13,996
Mauna Loa (1987), Hawaii Is.	4,170	13,680
Cameroon (1982), Cameroon	4,070	13,354
Acatenango (1972), Guatemala	3,960	12,992
Fuego (1991), Guatemala	3,835	12,582
Kerinci (1987), Sumatra, Indonesia	3,800	12,467
Erebus (1995), Ross Island, Antarctica	3,794	12,450
Tacana (1988), Guatemala	3,780	12,400
Fuji (1708), Honshu, Japan	3,775	12,388
Santiaguito (1902, 1991), Guatemala	3,768	12,362
Rindjani (1966), Lombok, Indonesia	3,726	12,224
Semeru (1995), Java, Indonesia	3,675	12,060
Nyirgongo (1994), Zaïre	3,475	11,400

Volcano (last major eruption) and location	Height metres	feet
Koryakskaya (1957), Kamchatka, Russia	3,456	11,339
Irazú (1992), Costa Rica	3,432	11,260
Slamet (1988), Java, Indonesia	3,428	11,247
Spurr (1953), Alaska, USA	3,374	11,069
Mt Etna (1169, 1669, 1993, 1995), Sicily, Italy	3,369	11,053
Raung, Java, Indonesia (1993)	3,322	10,932
Shiveluch (1964), Kamchatka, Russia	3,283	10,771
Turrialba (1992), Costa Rica	3,246	10,650
Agung (1964), Bali, Indonesia	3,142	10,308
Llaima (1990), Chile	3,128	10,239
Redoubt (1991), Alaska, USA	3,108	10,197
Tjareme (1938), Java, Indonesia	3,078	10,098
On-Taka (1991), Japan	3,063	10,049
Nyamuragira (1991), Zaïre	3,056	10,028
Iliamna (1978), Alaska, USA	3,052	10,016

OTHER NOTABLE VOLCANOES

	Height metres	feet
Tambora (1815), Sumbawa, Indonesia	2,850	9,353
Mt St Helens (1980, 1986, 1991), Washington State, USA	2,530	8,300
Pinatubo (1991), Philippines	1,758	5,770
Hekla (1981, 1991), Iceland	1,491	4,892
Mt Pelée (1902), Martinique	1,397	4,583
Mt Unzen (1792, 1991), Kyushu, Japan	1,360	4,462
Vesuvius (AD 79, 1944), Italy	1,280	4,198
Kilauea (1995), Hawaii, USA	1,242	4,077
Stromboli (1995), Lipari Is., Italy	926	3,038
Krakatau (1883, 1995), Sunda Strait, Indonesia	813	2,667
Santoriní (Thíra) (1628 BC), Aegean Sea, Greece	566	1,857
Vulcano (Monte Aria), Lipari Is., Italy	499	1,637
Tristan da Cunha (1961), South Atlantic	243	800
Surtsey (1963–7), off Iceland	173	568

LARGEST LAKES

The areas of some of these lakes are subject to seasonal variation.

	Area km^2	miles^2	Length km	miles
Caspian Sea, Iran/ Azerbaijan/Russia/ Turkmenistan/ Kazakhstan	371,000	143,000	1,171	728
*Michigan–Huron, USA/Canada	117,610	45,300	1,010	627
Superior, Canada/ USA	82,100	31,700	563	350

*Lakes Michigan and Huron are regarded as lobes of the same lake. The Michigan lobe has an area of 57,750 km^2 (22,300 miles^2) and the Huron lobe an area of 59,570 km^2 (23,000 miles^2)

	Area km²	miles²	Length km	miles
Victoria, Uganda/Tanzania/Kenya	69,500	26,828	362	225
Aral Sea, Kazakhstan/Uzbekistan	40,400	15,600	331	235
Tanganyika, Zaïre/Tanzania/Zambia/Burundi	32,900	12,700	675	420
†Baykal (*Baikal*), Russia	31,500	12,162	635	395
Great Bear, Canada	31,328	12,096	309	192
Malawi (Nyasa), Tanzania/Malawi/Mozambique	28,880	11,150	580	360
Great Slave, Canada	28,570	11,031	480	298
Erie, Canada/USA	25,670	9,910	388	241
Winnipeg, Canada	24,390	9,417	428	266
Ontario, Canada/USA	19,550	7,550	310	193
Balkhash, Kazakhstan	18,427	7,115	605	376
Ladozhskoye (*Ladoga*), Russia	17,700	6,835	200	124

†World's deepest lake (1,940 m/6,365 ft)

UNITED KINGDOM (BY COUNTRY)

	Area km²	miles²	Length km	miles
Lough Neagh, Northern Ireland	381.73	147.39	28.90	18.00
Loch Lomond, Scotland	71.12	27.46	36.44	22.64
Windermere, England	14.74	5.69	16.90	10.50
Lake Vyrnwy, Wales (artificial)	4.53	1.75	7.56	4.70
Llyn Tegid (*Bala*), Wales (natural)	4.38	1.69	5.80	3.65

LONGEST RIVERS

River (source and outflow)	Length km	miles
Nile (*Bahr-el-Nil*) (R. Luvironza, Burundi – E. Mediterranean Sea)	6,670	4,145
Amazon (*Amazonas*) (Lago Villafro, Peru – S. Atlantic Ocean)	6,448	4,007
Mississippi-Missouri-Red Rock (Montana – Gulf of Mexico)	5,970	3,710
Yenisey-Angara (W. Mongolia – Kara Sea)	5,540	3,442
Yangtze-Kiang (*Chang Jiang*) (Kunlun Mts, W. China – Yellow Sea)	5,530	3,436
Huang He (*Yellow River*) (Bayan Har Shan range, central China – Yellow Sea)	5,463	3,395
Ob'-Irtysh (W. Mongolia – Kara Sea)	5,410	3,362
Zaïre (*Congo*) (R. Lualaba, Zaïre-Zambia – S. Atlantic Ocean)	4,700	2,920
Amur-Argun (R. Argun, Khingan Mts, N. China – Sea of Okhotsk)	4,670	2,903
Lena-Kirenga (R. Kirenga, W. of Lake Baykal – Arctic Ocean)	4,400	2,734
Mackenzie-Peace (Tatlatui Lake, British Columbia – Beaufort Sea)	4,240	2,635
Mekong (Lants'ang, Tibet – South China Sea)	4,184	2,600
Niger (Loma Mts, Guinea – Gulf of Guinea, E. Atlantic Ocean)	4,168	2,590

River (source and outflow)	Length km	miles
Río de la Plata-Paraná (R. Paranáiba, central Brazil – S. Atlantic Ocean)	4,000	2,485
Murray-Darling (SE Queensland – Lake Alexandrina, S. Australia)	3,750	2,330
Volga (Valdai plateau – Caspian Sea)	3,690	2,293
Zambezi (NW Zambia – S. Indian Ocean)	3,540	2,200

OTHER NOTABLE RIVERS

	Length km	miles
St Lawrence (Minnesota, USA – Gulf of St Lawrence)	3,130	1,945
Ganges-Brahmaputra (R. Matsang, SW Tibet – Bay of Bengal)	2,900	1,800
Indus (R. Sengge, SW Tibet – N. Arabian Sea)	2,880	1,790
Danube (*Donau*) (Black Forest, SW Germany – Black Sea)	2,856	1,775
Tigris-Euphrates (R. Murat, E. Turkey – Persian Gulf)	2,740	1,700
Irrawaddy (R. Mali Hka, Myanmar – Andaman Sea)	2,151	1,337
Don (SE of Novomoskovsk – Sea of Azov)	1,969	1,224

BRITISH ISLES

	Length km	miles
Shannon (Co. Cavan, Rep. of Ireland – Atlantic Ocean)	386	240
Severn (Powys, Wales – Bristol Channel)	354	220
Thames (Gloucestershire, England – North Sea)	346	215
Tay (Perthshire, Scotland – North Sea)	188	117
Clyde (Lanarkshire, Scotland – Firth of Clyde)	158	98½
Tweed (Peeblesshire, Scotland – North Sea)	155	96½
Bann (Upper and Lower) (Co. Down, N. Ireland – Atlantic Ocean)	122	76

GREATEST WATERFALLS – BY HEIGHT

Waterfall (river and location)	Total drop metres	feet	Greatest single leap metres	feet
Angel (Carrao, Venezuela)	979	3,212	807	2,648
Tugela (Tugela, S. Africa)	947	3,110	410	1,350
Utigård (Jostedal Glacier, Norway)	800	2,625	600	1,970
Mongefossen (Monge, Norway)	774	2,540	—	—
Yosemite (Yosemite Creek, USA)	739	2,425	435	1,430
Østre Mardøla Foss (Mardals, Norway)	656	2,154	296	974
Tyssestrengane (Tysso, Norway)	646	2,120	289	948
Cuquenán (Arabopó, Venezuela)	610	2,000	—	—
Sutherland (Arthur, NZ)	580	1,904	248	815
*Kjellfossen (Naeröfjord, Norway)	561	1,841	149	490

*Volume often so low the fall atomizes into a 'bridal veil'

Waterfall (river and location)	Total drop		Greatest single leap	
	metres	feet	metres	feet
BRITISH ISLES (BY COUNTRY)				
Eas a' Chuàl Aluinn (Glas Bheinn, Sutherland, Scotland)	200	658		
Powerscourt Falls (Dargle, Co. Wicklow, Rep. of Ireland)	106	350		
Pistyll-y-Llyn (Powys/ Dyfed border, Wales)	c.73	230– 240	(cascades)	
Pistyll Rhyadr (Clwyd/ Powys border, Wales)	71.5	235	(single leap)	
Caldron Snout (R. Tees, Cumbria/Durham, England)	61	200	(cascades)	

GREATEST WATERFALLS – BY VOLUME

Waterfall (river and location)	Mean annual flow	
	m³/sec	galls/sec
Boyoma (R. Lualaba, Zaïre)	c.17,000	
	c.3,750,000	
Khône (Mekong, Laos)	11,500	2,530,000
Niagara (Horseshoe) (R. Niagara/Lake Erie–Lake Ontario)	3,000	670,000
Paulo Afonso (R. São Francisco, Brazil)	2,800	625,000
Urubupunga (Alto Paraná, Brazil)	2,800	625,000
Cataratas del Iguazú (R. Iguaçu, Brazil/Argentina)	1,725	380,000
Patos-Maribando (Rio Grande, Brazil)	1,500	330,000
Victoria (Mosi-oa-tunya) (R. Zambezi, Zambia/ Zimbabwe)	1,000	220,000
Churchill (R. Churchill, Canada)	975	215,000
Kaieteur (R. Potaro, Guyana)	660	145,000

TALLEST DAMS

	metres	feet
Rogun, Tajikistan	335	1,098
Nurek, Russia	300	984
Grand Dixance, Switzerland	285	935
*Longtan, China	285	935
Inguri, Russia	272	892
Chicoasén, Mexico	261	856
*Tehri, India	261	856

*Under construction

The world's most massive dam is the Syncrude Tailings dam in Alberta, Canada, which will have a volume of 540 million cubic metres/706 million cubic yards

TALLEST INHABITED BUILDINGS

Building and city	Height	
	metres	feet
Petronas Towers I and II, Kuala Lumpur	450	1,476
Sears Tower, Chicago[1]	443	1,454
One World Trade Center Tower, New York[2]	417	1,368
Empire State Building, New York[3]	381	1,250
Amoco Building, Chicago	346	1,136
John Hancock Center, Chicago	343	1,127
Chrysler Building, New York	319	1,046
Bank of China, Hong Kong[4]	315	1,033
Nation's Bank Tower, Atlanta	312	1,023
First Interstate World Center, Los Angeles	310	1,017
Vegas World Tower	308	1,012
Central Plaza, Hong Kong[5]	306.5	1,005
Texas Commerce Tower, Houston	305	1,002

[1] With TV antennae 520 m/1,707 ft
[2] With TV antennae, 521.2 m/1,710 ft; Two World Trade Center Tower, 415 m/1,362 ft
[3] With TV tower (added 1950–1), 430.9 m/1,414 ft
[4] With steel mast, 367.4 m/1,205 ft
[5] With steel mast, 374 m/1,227 ft

TALLEST STRUCTURES

Structure and location	Height	
	metres	feet
*Warszawa Radio Mast, Konstantynow, Poland	646	2,120
KTHI-TV Mast, Fargo, North Dakota (guyed)	629	2,063
CN Tower, Metro Centre, Toronto, Canada	555	1,822
Ostankino Tower, Moscow	537	1,762

*Collapsed during renovation, August 1991

LONGEST BRIDGES – BY SPAN

Bridge and location	Length	
	metres	feet
SUSPENSION SPANS		
Humber Estuary, Humberside, England	1,410	4,626
Verrazano Narrows, Brooklyn–Staten I, USA	1,298	4,260
Golden Gate, San Francisco Bay, USA	1,280	4,200
Mackinac Straits, Michigan, USA	1,158	3,800
Minami Bisan-Seto, Japan	1,100	3,609
Bosporus I, Istanbul, Turkey	1,089	3,576
Bosporus II, Istanbul, Turkey	1,074	3,524
George Washington, Hudson River, New York City, USA	1,067	3,500
Ponte 25 Abril (Tagus), Lisbon, Portugal	1,013	3,323
Firth of Forth (road), nr Edinburgh, Scotland	1,006	3,300
Severn River, Severn Estuary, England	988	3,240

The Akashi-Kaikyo road bridge (1988–98) will have a main span of 1,990 m/6,528 ft and the Store Baelt East Bridge, Denmark (due for completion 1997) will have a span of 1,624 m/5,328 ft

Bridge and location	Length	
	metres	feet

CANTILEVER SPANS

	metres	feet
Pont de Québec (rail-road), St Lawrence, Canada	548.6	1,800
Ravenswood, W. Virginia, USA	525.1	1,723
Firth of Forth (rail), nr Edinburgh, Scotland	521.2	1,710
Nanko, Osaka, Japan	510.0	1,673
Commodore Barry, Chester, Pennsylvania, USA	494.3	1,622
Greater New Orleans, Louisiana, USA	480.0	1,575
Howrah (rail-road), Calcutta, India	457.2	1,500

STEEL ARCH SPANS

	metres	feet
New River Gorge, Fayetteville, W. Virginia, USA	553.8	1,817
Bayonne (Kill van Kull), Bayonne, NJ – Staten I, USA	503.5	1,652
Sydney Harbour, Sydney, Australia	502.9	1,650

The 'floating' bridging at Evergreen, Seattle, Washington State, USA, is 3,839 m/12,596 ft long
The longest stretch of bridgings of any kind are those between Mandeville and Jefferson, Louisiana, USA; the Lake Pontchartrain Causeway II 38.422 km/23.87 miles and Causeway I 38.352 km/23.83 miles

LONGEST VEHICULAR TUNNELS

Tunnel and location	Length	
	km	miles
*Seikan (rail), Tsugaru Channel, Japan	53.90	33.49
*Channel Tunnel, Cheriton, Kent – Sangatte, Calais	49.94	31.03
Moscow metro, Belyaevo – Bittsevsky, Moscow, Russia	37.90	23.50
Northern line tube, East Finchley – Morden, London	27.84	17.30
Oshimizu, Honshū, Japan	22.17	13.78
Simplon II (rail), Brigue, Switzerland – Iselle, Italy	19.82	12.31
Simplon I (rail), Brigue, Switzerland – Iselle, Italy	19.80	12.30
*Shin-Kanmon (rail), Kanmon Strait, Japan	18.68	11.61
Great Appennine (rail), Vernio, Italy	18.49	11.49
St Gotthard (road), Göschenen – Airolo, Switzerland	16.32	10.14
Rokko (rail), Ōsaka – Kōbe, Japan	16.09	10.00

*Sub-aqueous

The longest non-vehicular tunnelling in the world is the Delaware Aqueduct in New York State, USA, constructed in 1937–44 to a length of 168.9 km/105 miles

BRITAIN – RAIL TUNNELS

	miles	yards
Severn, Bristol – Newport	4	484
Totley, Manchester – Sheffield	3	950
Standedge, Manchester – Huddersfield	3	66
Sodbury, Swindon – Bristol	2	924
Disley, Stockport – Sheffield	2	346

	miles	yards
Ffestiniog, Llandudno – Blaenau Ffestiniog	2	338
Bramhope, Leeds – Harrogate	2	241
Cowburn, Manchester – Sheffield	2	182

The longest road tunnel in Britain is the Mersey Road Tunnel, 2 miles 228 yards long. The longest canal tunnel, at Standedge, W. Yorks, is 3 miles 330 yards long; it was closed in 1944 but is currently being restored

LONGEST SHIP CANALS

Canal (opening date)	Length		Min. depth	
	km	miles	metres	feet
White Sea-Baltic (formerly Stalin) (1933) Canalized river; canal	227	141.00	5.0	16.5
51.5 km/32 miles				
*Suez (1869) Links Red and Mediterranean Seas	162	100.60	12.9	42.3
V. I. Lenin Volga-Don (1952) Links Black and Caspian Seas	100	62.20	n/a	n/a
Kiel (or North Sea) (1895) Links North and Baltic Seas	98	60.90	13.7	45.0
*Houston (1940) Links inland city with sea	91	56.70	10.4	34.0
Alphonse XIII (1926) Gives Seville access to sea	85	53.00	7.6	25.0
Panama (1914) Links Pacific Ocean and Caribbean Sea; lake chain, 78.9 km/49 miles dug	82	50.71	12.5	41.0
Manchester Ship (1894) Links city with Irish Channel	64	39.70	8.5	28.0
Welland (1931) Circumvents Niagara Falls and Rapids	45	28.00	8.8	29.0
Brussels (Rupel Sea) (1922) Renders Brussels an inland port	32	19.80	6.4	21.0

*Has no locks

The first section of China's Grand Canal, running 1,780 km/1,107 miles from Beijing to Hangchou, was opened AD 610
The longest boat canal in the world is the Volga-Baltic canal from Astrakhan to St Petersburg with 2,300 route km/1,850 miles

Distances from London by Air

The list of the distances in statute miles from London, Heathrow, to various cities (airport) abroad has been supplied by the publishers of *IATA/Serco-IAL Ltd Air Distances Manual*, Southall, Middx.

To	Miles
Abidjan	3,197
Abu Dhabi (International)	3,425
Addis Ababa	3,675
Adelaide (International)	10,111
Aden	3,670
Algiers	1,035
Amman (Queen Alia)	2,287
Amsterdam	230
Ankara (Esenboga)	1,770
Athens	1,500
Atlanta	4,198
Auckland	11,404
Baghdad (Saddam)	2,551
Bahrain	3,163
Baku	2,485
Bangkok	5,928
Barbados	4,193
Barcelona (Muntadas)	712
Basle	447
Beijing (Capital)	5,063
Beirut	2,161
Belfast (Aldergrove)	325
Belgrade	1,056
Berlin (Tegel)	588
Bermuda	3,428
Berne	476
Bogota	5,262
Bombay (Mumbai)	4,478
Boston	3,255
Brasilia	5,452
Bratislava	817
Brisbane (Eagle Farm)	10,273
Brussels	217
Bucharest (Otopeni)	1,307
Budapest	923
Buenos Aires	6,915
Cairo (International)	2,194
Calcutta	4,958
Calgary	4,357
Canberra	10,563
Cape Town	6,011
Caracas	4,639
Casablanca (Mohamed V)	1,300
Chicago (O'Hare)	3,941
Cologne	331
Colombo (Katunayake)	5,411
Copenhagen	608
Dakar	2,706
Dallas (Fort Worth)	4,736
Dallas (Lovefield)	4,732
Damascus (International)	2,223
Dar-es-Salaam	4,662
Darwin	8,613
Delhi	4,180
Denver	4,655

To	Miles
Detroit (Metropolitan)	3,754
Dhahran	3,143
Dhaka	4,976
Doha	3,253
Dubai	3,414
Dublin	279
Durban	5,937
Düsseldorf	310
Entebbe	4,033
Frankfurt (Main)	406
Freetown	3,046
Geneva	468
Gibraltar	1,084
Gothenburg (Landvetter)	664
Hamburg	463
Harare	5,156
Havana	4,647
Helsinki (Vantaa)	1,148
Hobart	10,826
Ho Chi Minh City	6,345
Hong Kong	5,990
Honolulu	7,220
Houston (Intercontinental)	4,821
Houston (William P. Hobby)	4,837
Islamabad	3,767
Istanbul	1,560
Jakarta (Halim Perdanakusuma)	7,295
Jeddah	2,947
Johannesburg	5,634
Kabul	3,558
Karachi	3,935
Kathmandu	4,570
Khartoum	3,071
Kiev (Borispol)	1,357
Kiev (Julyany)	1,337
Kingston, Jamaica	4,668
Kuala Lumpur (Subang)	6,557
Kuwait	2,903
Lagos	3,107
Larnaca	2,036
Lima	6,303
Lisbon	972
Lomé	3,129
Los Angeles (International)	5,439
Madras	5,113
Madrid	773
Malta	1,305
Manila	6,685
Marseille	614
Mauritius	6,075
Melbourne (Essendon)	10,504
Melbourne (Tullamarine)	10,499
Mexico City	5,529
Miami	4,414
Milan (Linate)	609
Minsk	1,176
Montego Bay	4,687
Montevideo	6,841
Montreal (Mirabel)	3,241
Moscow (Sheremetievo)	1,557
Munich (Franz Josef Strauss)	584

To	Miles
Muscat	3,621
Nairobi (Jomo Kenyatta)	4,248
Naples	1,011
Nassau	4,333
New York (J. F. Kennedy)	3,440
Nice	645
Oporto	806
Oslo (Fornebu)	722
Ottawa	3,321
Palma, Majorca (Son San Juan)	836
Paris (Charles de Gaulle)	215
Paris (Le Bourget)	215
Paris (Orly)	227
Perth, Australia	9,008
Port of Spain	4,404
Prague	649
Pretoria	5,602
Reykjavik (Domestic)	1,167
Reykjavik (Keflavik)	1,177
Rhodes	1,743
Rio de Janeiro	5,745
Riyadh	3,067
Rome (Fiumicino)	895
St John's, Newfoundland	2,308
St Petersburg	1,314
Salzburg	651
San Francisco	5,351
São Paulo	5,892
Sarajevo	1,017
Seoul (Kimpo)	5,507
Shanghai	5,725
Shannon	369
Singapore (Changi)	6,756
Sofia	1,266
Stockholm (Arlanda)	908
Suva	10,119
Sydney (Kingsford Smith)	10,568
Tangier	1,120
Tehran	2,741
Tel Aviv	2,227
Tokyo (Narita)	5,956
Toronto	3,544
Tripoli (International)	1,468
Tunis	1,137
Turin (Caselle)	570
Ulan Bator	4,340
Valencia	826
Vancouver	4,707
Venice (Tessera)	715
Vienna (Schwechat)	790
Vladivostok	5,298
Warsaw	912
Washington (Dulles)	3,665
Wellington	11,692
Yangon/Rangoon	5,582
Yokohama (Aomori)	5,647
Zagreb	848
Zürich	490

The United Kingdom

The United Kingdom comprises Great Britain (England, Wales and Scotland) and Northern Ireland. The Isle of Man and the Channel Islands are Crown dependencies with their own legislative systems, and not a part of the United Kingdom.

AREA AS AT 31 MARCH 1981

	Land miles²	km²	*Inland water miles²	km²	Total miles²	km²
United Kingdom	93,006	240,883	1,242	3,218	94,248	244,101
England	50,058	129,652	293	758	50,351	130,410
Wales	7,965	20,628	50	130	8,015	20,758
Scotland	29,767	77,097	653	1,692	30,420	78,789
†Northern Ireland	5,215	13,506	246	638	5,461	14,144
Isle of Man	221	572	—	—	221	572
Channel Islands	75	194	—	—	75	194

*Excluding tidal water
†Excluding certain tidal waters that are parts of statutory areas in Northern Ireland

POPULATION

The first official census of population in England, Wales and Scotland was taken in 1801 and a census has been taken every ten years since, except in 1941 when there was no census because of war. The last official census in the United Kingdom was taken on 21 April 1991 and the next is due in April 2001.

The first official census of population in Ireland was taken in 1841. However, all figures given below refer only to the area which is now Northern Ireland. Figures for Northern Ireland in 1921 and 1931 are estimates based on the censuses taken in 1926 and 1937 respectively.

Estimates of the population of England before 1801, calculated from the number of baptisms, burials and marriages, are:

1570	4,160,221	1670	5,773,646
1600	4,811,718	1700	6,045,008
1630	5,600,517	1750	6,517,035

Thousands	United Kingdom Total	Male	Female	England and Wales Total	Male	Female	Scotland Total	Male	Female	Northern Ireland Total	Male	Female
CENSUS RESULTS 1801–1991												
1801	—	—	—	8,893	4,255	4,638	1,608	739	869	—	—	—
1811	13,368	6,368	7,000	10,165	4,874	5,291	1,806	826	980	—	—	—
1821	15,472	7,498	7,974	12,000	5,850	6,150	2,092	983	1,109	—	—	—
1831	17,835	8,647	9,188	13,897	6,771	7,126	2,364	1,114	1,250	—	—	—
1841	20,183	9,819	10,364	15,914	7,778	8,137	2,620	1,242	1,378	1,649	800	849
1851	22,259	10,855	11,404	17,928	8,781	9,146	2,889	1,376	1,513	1,443	698	745
1861	24,525	11,894	12,631	20,066	9,776	10,290	3,062	1,450	1,612	1,396	668	728
1871	27,431	13,309	14,122	22,712	11,059	11,653	3,360	1,603	1,757	1,359	647	712
1881	31,015	15,060	15,955	25,974	12,640	13,335	3,736	1,799	1,936	1,305	621	684
1891	34,264	16,593	17,671	29,003	14,060	14,942	4,026	1,943	2,083	1,236	590	646
1901	38,237	18,492	19,745	32,528	15,729	16,799	4,472	2,174	2,298	1,237	590	647
1911	42,082	20,357	21,725	36,070	17,446	18,625	4,761	2,309	2,452	1,251	603	648
1921	44,027	21,033	22,994	37,887	18,075	19,811	4,882	2,348	2,535	1,258	610	648
1931	46,038	22,060	23,978	39,952	19,133	20,819	4,843	2,326	2,517	1,243	601	642
1951	50,225	24,118	26,107	43,758	21,016	22,742	5,096	2,434	2,662	1,371	668	703
1961	52,709	25,481	27,228	46,105	22,304	23,801	5,179	2,483	2,697	1,425	694	731
1971	55,515	26,952	28,562	48,750	23,683	25,067	5,229	2,515	2,714	1,536	755	781
1981	55,848	27,104	28,742	49,155	23,873	25,281	5,131	2,466	2,664	*1,533	750	783
1991	56,467	27,344	29,123	49,890	24,182	25,707	4,999	2,392	2,606	1,578	769	809
†RESIDENT POPULATION: PROJECTIONS (MID-YEAR)												
2001	59,800	29,475	30,325	52,989	26,148	26,841	5,143	2,508	2,636	1,667	819	848
2011	61,257	30,380	30,878	54,471	27,045	27,426	5,077	2,490	2,587	1,709	844	865
2021	62,146	30,883	31,263	55,320	27,518	27,802	5,051	2,486	2,565	1,775	879	896
2031	62,241	30,900	31,341	55,412	27,530	27,882	4,998	2,462	2,536	1,831	908	923

*Figures include 44,500 non-enumerated persons
† Projections are 1992 based

Source: HMSO – *Annual Abstract 1996*; OPCS – Census reports

ISLANDS: Census Results 1901–91

	Isle of Man			Jersey			*Guernsey		
	Total	Male	Female	Total	Male	Female	Total	Male	Female
1901	54,752	25,496	29,256	52,576	23,940	28,636	40,446	19,652	20,794
1911	52,016	23,937	28,079	51,898	24,014	27,884	41,858	20,661	21,197
1921	60,284	27,329	32,955	49,701	22,438	27,263	38,315	18,246	20,069
1931	49,308	22,443	26,865	50,462	23,424	27,038	40,643	19,659	20,984
1951	55,123	25,749	29,464	57,296	27,282	30,014	43,652	21,221	22,431
1961	48,151	22,060	26,091	57,200	27,200	30,000	45,068	21,671	23,397
1971	56,289	26,461	29,828	72,532	35,423	37,109	51,458	24,792	26,666
1981	64,679	30,901	33,778	77,000	37,000	40,000	53,313	25,701	27,612
1991	69,788	33,693	36,095	84,082	40,862	43,220	58,867	28,297	30,570

* Population of Guernsey, Herm, Jethou and Lithou. Figures for 1901–71 record all persons present on census night; census figures for 1981 and 1991 record all persons resident in the islands on census night
Source: 1991 Census

RESIDENT POPULATION

Mid-Year Estimate

	1984	1994
United Kingdom	56,506,000	58,395,000
England	47,004,000	48,708,000
Wales	2,806,000	2,913,000
Scotland	5,146,000	5,132,000
Northern Ireland	1,550,000	1,642,000

Source: HMSO – *Annual Abstract of Statistics 1996*

By Age and Sex 1994

Males	Under 16	65 and over
United Kingdom	6,194,000	3,710,000
England	5,137,000	3,119,000
Wales	311,000	204,000
Scotland	531,000	304,000
Northern Ireland	214,000	83,000

Females	Under 16	60 and over
United Kingdom	5,881,000	6,920,000
England	4,874,000	5,774,000
Wales	295,000	376,000
Scotland	507,000	607,000
Northern Ireland	205,000	163,000

Source: HMSO – *Population Trends 84*

By Ethnic Group (1991 Census (Great Britain))

Ethnic group	Estimated population	Percentage
Caribbean	500,000	16.6
African	212,000	7
Other black	178,000	5.9
Indian	840,000	27.9
Pakistani	477,000	15.8
Bangladeshi	163,000	5.4
Chinese	157,000	5.2
Other Asian	198,000	6.6
Other	290,000	9.6
Total ethnic minority groups	3,015,000	100
White	51,874,000	—
All ethnic groups	54,889,000	—

Source: HMSO – *Population Trends 72*

Average Density *Persons per hectare*

	1981	1991
England	3.55	3.61
Wales	1.34	1.36
Scotland	0.66	0.65
Northern Ireland	1.12	1.11

Sources: OPCS – Census reports

IMMIGRATION 1994
Acceptances for settlement in the UK by nationality

Region	Number of persons
Europe: total	4,650
European Economic Area	620
Remainder of Europe	4,040
Americas: total	7,890
USA	3,990
Canada	810
Africa: total	11,920
Asia: total	25,900
Indian sub-continent	14,070
Middle East	2,620
Oceania: total	2,850
British Overseas Citizens	710
Stateless	1,180
Total	55,110

Source: HMSO – *Annual Abstract of Statistics 1996*

LIVE BIRTHS AND BIRTH RATES 1994

	Live births	Birth rate*
United Kingdom	751,000	12.9
England and Wales	665,000	12.9
Scotland	62,000	12.0
Northern Ireland	24,000	14.9

*Live births per 1,000 population
Source: HMSO – *Annual Abstract of Statistics 1996*

LEGAL ABORTIONS 1994 (England and Wales)

Age group	Number
Under 16	3,250
16–19	25,200
20–34	108,500
35–44	19,200
45 and over	440
Age not stated	10
Total	156,500

Source: HMSO – Population Trends 84

BIRTHS OUTSIDE MARRIAGE (UK)

Age group	1981	1994
Under 20	30,000	41,000
20–24	33,000	80,000
25–29	16,000	65,000
Over 30	13,000	55,000
Total	91,000	240,000

Source: HMSO – Annual Abstract of Statistics 1996

MARRIAGE AND DIVORCE 1993

	Marriages	Divorces*
United Kingdom	341,246	—
England and Wales	299,197	165,018
Scotland	33,366	12,787
Northern Ireland	8,683	2,206

*Decrees absolute granted
Source: HMSO – Annual Abstract of Statistics 1996; Annual Report of the Registrar-General for Northern Ireland 1994

DEATHS AND DEATH RATES 1994

Males	Deaths	Death rate*
United Kingdom	303,333	10.6
England and Wales	267,555	—
Scotland	28,416	—
Northern Ireland	7,362	—
Females		
United Kingdom	324,303	10.9
England and Wales	285,639	—
Scotland	30,912	—
Northern Ireland	7,752	—

* Deaths per 1,000 population
Sources: OPCS; Annual Report of the Registrar-General for Scotland 1994; Annual Report of the Registrar-General for Northern Ireland 1994

INFANT MORTALITY 1994
Deaths of infants under 1 year of age per 1,000 live births

	Number
United Kingdom	6.2
England and Wales	6.2
Scotland	6.2
Northern Ireland	6.1

Source: HMSO – Annual Abstract of Statistics 1996

EXPECTATION OF LIFE LIFE TABLES 1991–93 (INTERIM FIGURES)

Age	England and Wales Male	Female	Scotland Male	Female	Northern Ireland Male	Female
0	73.7	79.1	71.5	77.1	72.5	78.3
5	69.3	74.6	67.2	72.6	68.2	73.9
10	64.4	69.7	62.3	67.7	63.2	68.9
15	59.4	64.7	57.3	62.8	58.3	64.0
20	54.6	59.8	52.5	57.9	53.6	59.1
25	49.8	54.9	47.8	52.9	48.9	54.2
30	45.0	50.0	43.1	48.1	44.1	49.3
35	40.2	45.1	38.3	43.2	39.3	44.4
40	35.5	40.3	33.6	38.4	34.6	39.6
45	30.8	35.5	29.0	33.7	29.9	34.8
50	26.3	30.9	24.6	29.1	25.4	30.2
55	22.0	26.4	20.5	24.8	21.2	25.7
60	18.0	22.1	16.7	20.6	17.2	21.5
65	14.3	18.1	13.3	16.8	13.7	17.6
70	11.2	14.5	10.4	13.4	10.7	13.9
75	8.6	11.2	8.0	10.3	8.2	10.7
80	6.5	8.4	6.0	7.7	6.1	8.0
85	4.8	6.1	4.5	5.6	4.5	5.7

Source: HMSO – Annual Abstract of Statistics 1996

DEATHS ANALYSED BY CAUSE 1994

	England & Wales	Scotland	N. Ireland
TOTAL DEATHS	553,194	59,328	15,114
Infectious and parasitic diseases	3,318	306	39
Neoplasms	141,747	15,394	3,665
Malignant neoplasm of stomach	7,590	754	201
Malignant neoplasm of colon	10,899	1,139	324
Malignant neoplasm of rectum, rectosigmoid junction and anus	5,022	602	114
Malignant neoplasm of trachea, bronchus and lung	32,143	4,237	768
Malignant neoplasm of female breast	12,830	1,275	338
Leukaemia	3,507	290	94
Endocrine, nutritional and metabolic diseases and immunity disorders	7,430	754	73
Diabetes mellitus	5,938	503	45
Diseases of blood and blood-forming organs	1,898	121	29
Mental disorders	8,042	1,306	91
Diseases of the nervous system and sense organs	9,010	853	187
Meningitis	170	24	21
Diseases of the circulatory system	242,213	27,138	7,011
Chronic rheumatic heart disease	1,719	175	30
Hypertensive disease	2,800	312	79
Ischaemic heart disease	135,440	15,234	4,168
Diseases of pulmonary circulation and other forms of heart disease	25,795	2,200	633
Cerebrovascular disease	58,768	7,684	1,738
Atherosclerosis	2,480	281	49
Diseases of the respiratory system	81,484	6,981	2,398
Pneumonia	48,917	3,757	1,595
Diseases of the digestive system	18,635	2,192	424
Ulcer of stomach and duodenum	4,111	380	100
Chronic liver disease and cirrhosis	3,244	555	66
Diseases of the genitourinary system	6,812	816	220
Complications of pregnancy, childbirth and the puerperium	50	9	—
Diseases of the skin, musculoskeletal system and connective tissue	4,513	380	58
Congenital anomalies	1,301	170	131
Certain conditions originating in the perinatal period	147	191	69
Signs, symptoms and ill-defined conditions	7,754	331	44
Injury and Poisoning	16,091	2,372	688
Motor vehicle traffic accidents	3,232	352	158
Suicide and self-inflicted injury	3,619	624	138

Sources: OPCS; General Register Office for Scotland; *Annual Report of the Registrar General for Northern Ireland 1994*

The National Flag

The national flag of the United Kingdom is the Union Flag, generally known as the Union Jack. (The name 'Union Jack' derives from the use of the Union Flag on the jack-staff of naval vessels.)

The Union Flag is a combination of the cross of St George, patron saint of England, the cross of St Andrew, patron saint of Scotland, and a cross similar to that of St Patrick, patron saint of Ireland.

Cross of St George: cross Gules in a field Argent (red cross on a white ground).

Cross of St Andrew: saltire Argent in a field Azure (white diagonal cross on a blue ground).

Cross of St Patrick: saltire Gules in a field Argent (red diagonal cross on a white ground).

The Union Flag was first introduced in 1606 after the union of the kingdoms of England and Scotland under one sovereign. The cross of St Patrick was added in 1801 after the union of Great Britain and Ireland.

DAYS FOR FLYING FLAGS

The correct orientation of the Union Flag when flying is with the broader diagonal band of white uppermost in the hoist (i.e. near the pole) and the narrower diagonal band of white uppermost in the fly (i.e. furthest from the pole).

It is the practice to fly the Union Flag daily on some customs houses. In all other cases, flags are flown on government buildings by command of The Queen.

Days for hoisting the Union Flag are notified to the Department of National Heritage by The Queen's command and communicated by the department to the other government departments. On the days appointed, the Union Flag is flown on government buildings in the United Kingdom from 8 a.m. to sunset.

The Queen's Accession	6 February
Birthday of The Duke of York	19 February
*St David's Day (in Wales only)	1 March
Birthday of The Prince Edward	10 March
Commonwealth Day (1997)	10 March
Birthday of The Queen	21 April
*St George's Day (in England only)	23 April
Coronation Day	2 June
Birthday of The Duke of Edinburgh	10 June
The Queen's Official Birthday (1997)	14 June
Birthday of Diana, Princess of Wales	1 July
Birthday of Queen Elizabeth the Queen Mother	4 August
Birthday of The Princess Royal	15 August
Birthday of The Princess Margaret	21 August
Remembrance Sunday (1997)	9 November
Birthday of The Prince of Wales	14 November
The Queen's Wedding Day	20 November
*St Andrew's Day (in Scotland only)	30 November
†The opening of Parliament by The Queen	
†The prorogation of Parliament by The Queen	

*Where a building has two or more flagstaffs, the appropriate national flag may be flown in addition to the Union Flag, but not in a superior position
†Flags are flown whether or not The Queen performs the ceremony in person. Flags are flown only in the Greater London area

FLAGS AT HALF-MAST

Flags are flown at half-mast on the following occasions:

(a) From the announcement of the death up to the funeral of the Sovereign, except on Proclamation Day, when flags are hoisted right up from 11 a.m. to sunset
(b) The funerals of members of the Royal Family, subject to special commands from The Queen in each case
(c) The funerals of foreign rulers, subject to special commands from The Queen in each case
(d) The funerals of Prime Ministers and ex-Prime Ministers of the United Kingdom, subject to special commands from The Queen in each case
(e) Other occasions by special command of The Queen

On occasions when days for flying flags coincide with days for flying flags at half-mast, the following rules are observed. Flags are flown:

(a) although a member of the Royal Family, or a near relative of the Royal Family, may be lying dead, unless special commands be received from The Queen to the contrary
(b) although it may be the day of the funeral of a foreign ruler

If the body of a very distinguished subject is lying at a government office, the flag may fly at half-mast on that office until the body has left (provided it is a day on which the flag would fly) and then the flag is to be hoisted right up. On all other government buildings the flag will fly as usual.

THE ROYAL STANDARD

The Royal Standard is hoisted only when The Queen is actually present in the building, and never when Her Majesty is passing in procession.

The Royal Family

ELIZABETH II, by the Grace of God, of the United Kingdom of Great Britain and Northern Ireland and of her other Realms and Territories Queen, Head of the Commonwealth, Defender of the Faith

Her Majesty Elizabeth Alexandra Mary of Windsor, elder daughter of King George VI and of HM Queen Elizabeth the Queen Mother
Born 21 April 1926, at 17 Bruton Street, London W1
Ascended the throne 6 February 1952
Crowned 2 June 1953, at Westminster Abbey
Married 20 November 1947, in Westminster Abbey, HRH The Duke of Edinburgh
Official residences: Buckingham Palace, London SW1; Windsor Castle, Berks; Palace of Holyroodhouse, Edinburgh
Private residences: Sandringham, Norfolk; Balmoral Castle, Aberdeenshire
Office: Buckingham Palace, London SW1A 1AA. Tel: 0171-930 4832

HUSBAND OF HM THE QUEEN

HRH THE PRINCE PHILIP, DUKE OF EDINBURGH, KG, KT, OM, GBE, AC, QSO, PC, Ranger of Windsor Park
Born 10 June 1921, son of Prince and Princess Andrew of Greece and Denmark (*see* page 129), naturalized a British subject 1947, created Duke of Edinburgh, Earl of Merioneth and Baron Greenwich 1947

CHILDREN OF HM THE QUEEN

HRH THE PRINCE OF WALES (Prince Charles Philip Arthur George), KG, KT, GCB and Great Master of the Order of the Bath, AK, QSO, PC, ADC(P)
Born 14 November 1948, created Prince of Wales and Earl of Chester 1958, succeeded as Duke of Cornwall, Duke of Rothesay, Earl of Carrick and Baron Renfrew, Lord of the Isles and Prince and Great Steward of Scotland 1952
Married 29 July 1981 Lady Diana Frances Spencer, now Diana, Princess of Wales (*born* 1 July 1961, youngest daughter of the 8th Earl Spencer and the Hon. Mrs Shand Kydd), marriage dissolved 1996
Issue:
(1) HRH Prince William of Wales (Prince William Arthur Philip Louis), *born* 21 June 1982
(2) HRH Prince Henry of Wales (Prince Henry Charles Albert David), *born* 15 September 1984
Residences of the Prince of Wales: St James's Palace, London SW1A 1BS; Highgrove, Doughton, Tetbury, Glos.
Office of the Prince of Wales: St James's Palace, London SW1A 1BS. Tel: 0171-930 4832
Residence of Diana, Princess of Wales: Kensington Palace, London W8 4PU
Office of Diana, Princess of Wales, St James's Palace, London SW1A 1BS. Tel: 0171-930 4832

HRH THE PRINCESS ROYAL (Princess Anne Elizabeth Alice Louise), KG, GCVO

Born 15 August 1950, declared The Princess Royal 1987
Married (1) 14 November 1973 Captain Mark Anthony Peter Phillips, CVO (*born* 22 September 1948); marriage dissolved 1992; (2) 12 December 1992 Captain Timothy James Hamilton Laurence, MVO (*born* 1 March 1955)
Issue:
(1) Peter Mark Andrew Phillips, *born* 15 November 1977
(2) Zara Anne Elizabeth Phillips, *born* 15 May 1981
Residence: Gatcombe Park, Minchinhampton, Glos.
Office: Buckingham Palace, London SW1A 1AA. Tel: 0171-930 4832

HRH THE DUKE OF YORK (Prince Andrew Albert Christian Edward), CVO, ADC(P)
Born 19 February 1960, created Duke of York, Earl of Inverness and Baron Killyleagh 1986
Married 23 July 1986 Sarah Margaret Ferguson, now The Duchess of York (*born* 15 October 1959, younger daughter of Major Ronald Ferguson and Mrs Hector Barrantes), marriage dissolved 1996
Issue:
(1) HRH Princess Beatrice of York (Princess Beatrice Elizabeth Mary), *born* 8 August 1988
(2) HRH Princess Eugenie of York (Princess Eugenie Victoria Helena), *born* 23 March 1990
Residences: Buckingham Palace, London SW1; Sunninghill Park, Ascot, Berks.
Office: Buckingham Palace, London SW1 1AA. Tel: 0171-930 4832

HRH THE PRINCE EDWARD (Prince Edward Antony Richard Louis), CVO
Born 10 March 1964
Residence and Office: Buckingham Palace, London SW1A 1AA. Tel: 0171-930 4832

SISTER OF HM THE QUEEN

HRH THE PRINCESS MARGARET, COUNTESS OF SNOWDON, CI, GCVO, Royal Victorian Chain, Dame Grand Cross of the Order of St John of Jerusalem
Born 21 August 1930, younger daughter of King George VI and HM Queen Elizabeth the Queen Mother
Married 6 May 1960 Antony Charles Robert Armstrong-Jones, GCVO (*born* 7 March 1930, created Earl of Snowdon 1961, Constable of Caernarvon Castle); marriage dissolved 1978
Issue:
(1) David Albert Charles, Viscount Linley, *born* 3 November 1961, *married* 8 October 1993 the Hon. Serena Stanhope
(2) Lady Sarah Chatto (Sarah Frances Elizabeth), *born* 1 May 1964, *married* 14 July 1994 Daniel Chatto, and has issue, Samuel David Benedict Chatto, *born* 28 July 1996
Residence and Office: Kensington Palace, London W8 4PU. Tel: 0171-930 3141

MOTHER OF HM THE QUEEN

HM QUEEN ELIZABETH THE QUEEN MOTHER (Elizabeth Angela Marguerite), Lady of the Garter, Lady of the Thistle, CI, GCVO, GBE, Dame Grand Cross of the Order of

St John, Royal Victorian Chain, Lord Warden and Admiral of the Cinque Ports and Constable of Dover Castle
Born 4 August 1900, youngest daughter of the 14th Earl of Strathmore and Kinghorne
Married 26 April 1923 (as Lady Elizabeth Bowes-Lyon) Prince Albert, Duke of York, afterwards King George VI (*see* page 128)
Residences: Clarence House, St James's Palace, London SW1; Royal Lodge, Windsor Great Park, Berks; Castle of Mey, Caithness
Office: Clarence House, St James's Palace, London SW1A 1BA. Tel: 0171-930 3141

AUNT OF HM THE QUEEN

HRH PRINCESS ALICE, DUCHESS OF GLOUCESTER (Alice Christabel), GCB, CI, GCVO, GBE, Grand Cordon of Al Kamal
Born 25 December 1901, third daughter of the 7th Duke of Buccleuch and Queensberry
Married 6 November 1935 (as Lady Alice Montagu-Douglas-Scott) Prince Henry, Duke of Gloucester, third son of King George V (*see* page 128)
Residence and Office: Kensington Palace, London W8 4PU. Tel: 0171-937 6374

COUSINS OF HM THE QUEEN

HRH THE DUKE OF GLOUCESTER (Prince Richard Alexander Walter George), GCVO, Grand Prior of the Order of St John of Jerusalem
Born 26 August 1944
Married 8 July 1972 Birgitte Eva van Deurs, now HRH The Duchess of Gloucester, GCVO (*born* 20 June 1946, daughter of Asger Henriksen and Vivian van Deurs)
Issue:
(1)   Earl of Ulster (Alexander Patrick Gregers Richard), *born* 24 October 1974
(2)   Lady Davina Windsor (Davina Elizabeth Alice Benedikte), *born* 19 November 1977
(3)   Lady Rose Windsor (Rose Victoria Birgitte Louise), *born* 1 March 1980
Residence and Office: Kensington Palace, London W8 4PU. Tel: 0171-937 6374

HRH THE DUKE OF KENT (Prince Edward George Nicholas Paul Patrick), KG, GCMG, GCVO, ADC(P)
Born 9 October 1935
Married 8 June 1961 Katharine Lucy Mary Worsley, now HRH The Duchess of Kent, GCVO (*born* 22 February 1933, daughter of Sir William Worsley, Bt.)
Issue:
(1)   Earl of St Andrews (George Philip Nicholas), *born* 26 June 1962, *married* 9 January 1988 Sylvana Tomaselli, and has issue, Edward Edmund Maximilian George, Baron Downpatrick, *born* 2 December 1988; Lady Marina Charlotte Alexandra Katharine Windsor, *born* 30 September 1992; Lady Amelia Sophia Theodora Mary Margaret Windsor, *born* 24 August 1995
(2)   Lady Helen Taylor (Helen Marina Lucy), *born* 28 April 1964, *married* 18 July 1992 Timothy Taylor, and has issue, Columbus George Donald Taylor, *born* 6 August 1994
(3)   Lord Nicholas Windsor (Nicholas Charles Edward Jonathan), *born* 25 July 1970
Residence and Office: York House, St James's Palace, London SW1 1BQ. Tel: 0171-930 4872

HRH PRINCESS ALEXANDRA, THE HON. LADY OGILVY (Princess Alexandra Helen Elizabeth Olga Christabel), GCVO *Born* 25 December 1936
Married 24 April 1963 The Hon. Sir Angus Ogilvy, KCVO (*born* 14 September 1928, second son of 12th Earl of Airlie)
Issue:
(1)   James Robert Bruce Ogilvy, *born* 29 February 1964, *married* 30 July 1988 Julia Rawlinson, and has issue, Flora Alexandra Ogilvy, *born* 15 December 1994
(2)   Marina Victoria Alexandra, Mrs Mowatt, *born* 31 July 1966, *married* 2 February 1990 Paul Mowatt (separated 1996), and has issue, Zenouska May Mowatt, *born* 26 May 1990; Christian Alexander Mowatt, *born* 4 June 1993
Residence: Thatched House Lodge, Richmond Park, Surrey
Office: Buckingham Palace, London SW1A 1AA. Tel: 0171-930 1860

HRH PRINCE MICHAEL OF KENT (Prince Michael George Charles Franklin), KCVO
Born 4 July 1942
Married 30 June 1978 Baroness Marie-Christine Agnes Hedwig Ida von Reibnitz, now HRH Princess Michael of Kent (*born* 15 January 1945, daughter of Baron Gunther von Reibnitz)
Issue:
(1)   Lord Frederick Windsor (Frederick Michael George David Louis), *born* 6 April 1979
(2)   Lady Gabriella Windsor (Gabriella Marina Alexandra Ophelia), *born* 23 April 1981
Residences: Kensington Palace, London W8 4PU; Nether Lypiatt Manor, Stroud, Glos.
Office: Kensington Palace, London W8 4PU. Tel: 0171-938 3519

ORDER OF SUCCESSION

1   HRH The Prince of Wales
2   HRH Prince William of Wales
3   HRH Prince Henry of Wales
4   HRH The Duke of York
5   HRH Princess Beatrice of York
6   HRH Princess Eugenie of York
7   HRH The Prince Edward
8   HRH The Princess Royal
9   Peter Phillips
10   Zara Phillips
11   HRH The Princess Margaret, Countess of Snowdon
12   Viscount Linley
13   Lady Sarah Chatto
14   Samuel Chatto
15   HRH The Duke of Gloucester
16   Earl of Ulster
17   Lady Davina Windsor
18   Lady Rose Windsor
19   HRH The Duke of Kent
20   Baron Downpatrick
21   Lady Marina Charlotte Windsor
22   Lady Amelia Windsor
23   Lord Nicholas Windsor
24   Lady Helen Taylor
25   Columbus Taylor
26   Lord Frederick Windsor
27   Lady Gabriella Windsor
28   HRH Princess Alexandra, the Hon. Lady Ogilvy
29   James Ogilvy
30   Flora Ogilvy
31   Marina, Mrs Paul Mowatt

Royal Households

THE QUEEN'S HOUSEHOLD

Lord Chamberlain, The Earl of Airlie, KT, GCVO, PC
Lord Steward, The Viscount Ridley, KG, GCVO, TD
Master of the Horse, The Lord Somerleyton, KCVO
Treasurer of the Household, A. Mackay, MP
Comptroller of the Household, T. Wood, MP
Vice-Chamberlain, D. Conway, MP

Gold Sticks, Maj.-Gen. Lord Michael Fitzalan-Howard, GCVO, CB, CBE, MC; Gen. Sir Desmond Fitzpatrick, GCB, DSO, MBE, MC
Vice-Adm. of the United Kingdom, Adm. Sir James Eberle, GCB
Rear-Adm. of the United Kingdom, Adm. Sir Nicholas Hunt, GCB, LVO
First and Principal Naval Aide-de-Camp, Adm. Sir Jock Slater, GCB, LVO
Flag Aide-de-Camp, Adm. Sir Michael Boyce, KCB, OBE
Aides-de-Camp-General, Gen. Sir Charles Guthrie, GCB, LVO, OBE; Gen. Sir John Wilsey, GCB, CBE; Gen. Sir Michael Rose, KCB, CBE, DSO, QGM
Air Aides-de-Camp, Air Chief Marshal Sir Michael Graydon, GCB, CBE; Air Chief Marshal Sir William Wratten, KBE, CB, AFC

Mistress of the Robes, The Duchess of Grafton, GCVO
Ladies of the Bedchamber, The Countess of Airlie, DCVO; The Lady Farnham
Extra Lady of the Bedchamber, The Marchioness of Abergavenny, DCVO
Women of the Bedchamber, Hon. Mary Morrison, DCVO; Lady Susan Hussey, DCVO; Lady Dugdale, DCVO; The Lady Elton
Extra Women of the Bedchamber, The Hon. Mrs Van der Woude, CVO; Mrs John Woodroffe, CVO; Mrs Michael Wall, DCVO; Lady Abel Smith, DCVO; Mrs Robert de Pass
Equerries, Lt. Col. Sir Guy Acland, Bt., MVO; Lt.-Cdr. T. Williamson; Capt. C. Winter (temp.)
Extra Equerries, Vice-Adm. Sir Peter Ashmore, KCB, KCVO, DSC; Maj. Sir Shane Blewitt, GCVO; Lt.-Col. The Lord Charteris of Amisfield, GCB, GCVO,QSO, OBE, PC; Maj.-Gen. Sir Simon Cooper, KCVO; Air Cdre the Hon. T. Elworthy, CVO, CBE; The Rt Hon. Sir Robert Fellowes, GCVO, KCB; Sir Edward Ford, KCB, KCVO, ERD; Rear-Adm. Sir John Garnier, KCVO, CBE; Rear-Adm. Sir Paul Greening, GCVO; Brig. Sir Geoffrey Hardy-Roberts, KCVO, CB, CBE; The Rt. Hon. Sir William Heseltine, GCB, GCVO, AC, QSO; Lt.-Col. Sir John Johnston, GCVO, MC; Lt.-Col. A. Mather, OBE; Sir Peter Miles, KCVO; Lt.-Col. Sir John Miller, GCVO, DSO, MC; Air Cdre Sir Dennis Mitchell, KBE, CVO, DFC, AFC; The Lord Moore of Wolvercote, GCB, GCVO, CMG, QSO; Lt.-Gen. Sir John Richards, KCB, KCVO; Lt.-Col. W. H. M. Ross, CVO, OBE; Sir Kenneth Scott, KCVO, CMG; Air Vice-Marshal Sir John Severne, KCVO, OBE, AFC; Lt.-Col. Sir Blair Stewart-Wilson, KCVO; Rear-Adm. Sir Richard Trowbridge, KCVO; Lt.-Col. G. West, CVO; Air Cdre Sir Archie Winskill, KCVO, CBE, DFC, AE; Rear-Adm. Sir Robert Woodard, KCVO

THE PRIVATE SECRETARY'S OFFICE

Buckingham Palace, London SWIA IAA

Private Secretary to The Queen, The Rt Hon. Sir Robert Fellowes, GCVO, KCB

Deputy Private Secretary, R. B. Janvrin, CVO
Assistant Private Secretary, Mrs M. Francis
Special Assistant to the Private Secretary, S. Gimson
Press Secretary, C. V. Anson, CVO
Deputy Press Secretary, G. Crawford, LVO
Assistant Press Secretary, Miss P. Russell-Smith
Chief Clerk, Mrs G. S. Coulson, LVO
Secretary to the Private Secretary, Miss E. Ash

THE QUEEN'S ARCHIVES

Round Tower, Windsor Castle, Berks

Keeper of The Queen's Archives, The Rt Hon. Sir Robert Fellowes, GCVO, KCB
Assistant Keeper, O. Everett, CVO
Registrar, Lady de Bellaigue, MVO

THE PRIVY PURSE AND TREASURER'S OFFICE

Buckingham Palace, London SWIA IAA

Keeper of the Privy Purse and Treasurer to The Queen, M. Peat, CVO
Deputy Keeper of the Privy Purse and Deputy Treasurer, J. Parsons, LVO
Chief Accountant and Paymaster, I. McGregor
Personnel Officer, Miss P. Lloyd
Land Agent, Sandringham, J. Major, FRICS
Resident Factor, Balmoral, P. Ord, FRICS
Master of The Queen's Music, M. Williamson, CBE, AO
Poet Laureate, Ted Hughes, OBE
Keeper of the Royal Philatelic Collection, C. Goodwyn

PROPERTY SERVICES

Director of Property Services, J. Tiltman
Superintending Architect, G. Sharpe

ROYAL ALMONRY

High Almoner, The Rt. Revd John Taylor
Hereditary Grand Almoner, The Marquess of Exeter
Sub-Almoner, Revd W. Booth
Secretary, C. Williams, RVM
Assistant Secretary, P. Hartley, LVO

THE LORD CHAMBERLAIN'S OFFICE

Buckingham Palace, London SWIA IAA

Comptroller, Lt.-Col. W. H. M. Ross, CVO, OBE
Assistant Comptroller, Lt.-Col. A. Mather, OBE
Secretary, J. Spencer, MVO
State Invitations Assistant, J. O. Hope
Permanent Lords-in-Waiting, Lt.-Col. the Lord Charteris of Amisfield, GCB, GCVO, OBE, QSO, PC; The Lord Moore of Wolvercote, GCB, GCVO, CMG, QSO
Lords-in-Waiting, The Lord Camoys; The Viscount Long, CBE; The Lord Lucas of Crudwell; The Earl of Courtown
Baronesses-in-Waiting, The Baroness Trumpington; The Baroness Miller of Hendon, MBE
Gentlemen Ushers, Maj. N. Chamberlayne-Macdonald, LVO, OBE; Capt. M. Barrow, DSO, RN; Capt. M. Fulford-Dobson, RN; Lt.-Gen. Sir Richard Vickers, KCB, LVO, OBE; Air Vice-Marshal B. Newton, CB, OBE; Col. M. Havergal, OBE; Rear Adm. C. H. D. Cooke-Priest, CB; Air Vice-Marshal D. Hawkins, CB, MBE; Maj.-Gen. B. Pennicott, CVO; Gp Capt. H. Rolfe, CVO, CBE

Extra Gentlemen Ushers, Maj. T. Harvey, CVO, DSO, ERD; Lt.-Col. Sir John Hugo, KCVO, OBE; Vice-Adm. Sir Ronald Brockman, KCB, CSI, CIE, CVO, CBE; Air Marshal Sir Maurice Heath, KBE, CB, CVO; Sir James Scholtens, KCVO; Sir Patrick O'Dea, KCVO; Adm. Sir David Williams, GCB; H. Davis, CVO, CM; Maj.-Gen. R. Reid, CVO, MC, CD; Lt.-Cdr. J. Holdsworth, CVO, OBE, RN; Col. G. Leigh, CVO, CBE; Lt.-Cdr. Sir Russell Wood, KCVO, VRD; Maj.-Gen. Sir Desmond Rice, KCVO, CBE; Lt.-Col. Sir Julian Paget, Bt., CVO; S. W. F. Martin, CVO; J. Haslam, CVO; Prof. Sir Norman Blacklock, KCVO, OBE, FRCS; Air Marshal Sir Roy Austin-Smith, KBE, CB, CVO, DFC; Vice-Adm. Sir David Loram, KCB, CVO; Sir Carron Greig, KCVO, CBE; Gp Capt J. Slessor, CVO
Gentleman Usher to the Sword of State, Gen. Sir Edward Burgess, KCB, OBE
Gentleman Usher of the Black Rod, Gen. Sir Edward Jones, KCB, CBE
Serjeants-at-Arms, Maj. B. Eastwood, LVO, MBE; M. Jephson, MVO
Marshal of the Diplomatic Corps, Vice-Adm. Sir James Weatherall, KBE
Vice-Marshal, P. Astley, LVO
Constable and Governor of Windsor Castle, Gen. Sir Patrick Palmer, KBE
Bargemaster, R. Crouch
Swan Warden, Prof. C. Perrins, LVO
Swan Marker, D. Barber
Superintendent of the State Apartments, St James's Palace, B. Andrews, BEM

ECCLESIASTICAL HOUSEHOLD

THE COLLEGE OF CHAPLAINS
Clerk of the Closet, Rt. Revd J. Waine
Deputy Clerk of the Closet, Revd W. Booth
Chaplains to The Queen, Ven. D. N. Griffiths, RD; Revd Canon J. V. Bean; Revd K. Huxley; Ven. P. Ashford; Revd Canon D. C. Gray, TD; Revd Canon J. Hester; Revd S. Pedley; Revd Canon M. A. Moxon; Revd Canon G. Murphy, LVO; Revd D. J. Burgess; Revd E. R. Ayerst; Revd R. S. Clarke; Revd Canon K. Pound; Revd J. Haslam; Revd Canon G. Hall; Revd Canon A. C. Hill; Revd J. C. Priestley; Revd Canon J. O. Colling; Revd Canon G. Jones; Revd Canon D. G. Palmer; Revd Canon D. H. Wheaton; Revd Canon P. Boulton; Revd Canon R. A. Bowden; Revd Canon E. Buchanan; Revd J. Robson; Revd Canon J. Stanley; Revd Canon I. Hardaker; Revd Canon L. F. Webber; Ven. F. Bentley; Revd D. Adams; Revd Canon J. Sykes; Revd Canon I. Smith-Cameron; Revd Canon A. Craig; Ven. D. Fleming; Revd Canon R. Gilbert; Ven. D. Bartles-Smith; Revd Canon I. Knox; Revd Canon M. Mingins
Extra Chaplains, Preb. S. A. Williams, CVO; Ven. E. J. G. Ward, LVO; Revd J. R W. Stott; Revd Canon A. D. Caesar, CVO; Revd Canon E. James; Revd Canon J. G. M. W. Murphy, LVO

CHAPELS ROYAL
Dean of the Chapels Royal, The Bishop of London
Sub-Dean of Chapels Royal, Revd W. Booth
Priests in Ordinary, Revd S. E. Young; Revd R. Bolton; Revd P. Hunt
Organist, Choirmaster and Composer, R. J. Popplewell, MVO, FRCO, FRCM
Domestic Chaplain, Buckingham Palace, Revd W. Booth
Domestic Chaplain, Windsor Castle, The Dean of Windsor
Domestic Chaplain, Sandringham, Revd Canon G. R. Hall

Chaplain, Royal Chapel, Windsor Great Park, Revd Canon M. Moxon
Chaplain, Hampton Court Palace, Revd Canon M. Moore
Chaplain, Tower of London, Revd P. Abram
Organist and Choirmaster, Hampton Court Palace, C. Jackson

MEDICAL HOUSEHOLD

Head of the Medical Household and Physician to The Queen, R. Thompson, DM, FRCP
Physician, R. W. Davey, MB, BS
Serjeant Surgeon, B. T. Jackson, MS, FRCS
Surgeon Oculist, P. Holmes Sellors, LVO, FRCS, FRCophth.
Surgeon Gynaecologist, M. E. Setchell, FRCS, FRCOG
Surgeon Dentist, N. A. Sturridge, CVO, LDS, BDS, DDS
Orthopaedic Surgeon, R. H. Vickers, BM, B.ch., FRCS
Physician to the Household, J. Cunningham, DM, FRCP
Surgeon to the Household, A. A. M. Lewis, MB, FRCS
Surgeon Oculist to the Household, T. J. ffytche, MB, FRCS, FRCophth.
Apothecary to The Queen and to the Household, N. R. Southward, CVO, MB, B.chir.
Apothecary to the Household at Windsor, J. H. D. Briscoe, MB, B.chir., D.obst., FRCGP
Apothecary to the Household at Sandringham, I. K. Campbell, MB, BS, D.obst., FRCGP
Coroner of The Queen's Household, J. Burton, CBE, MB, BS

CENTRAL CHANCERY OF THE ORDERS OF KNIGHTHOOD
St James's Palace, London SW1A 1BS
Secretary, Lt.-Col. A. Mather, OBE
Assistant Secretary, Miss R. Wells, MVO

THE HONOURABLE CORPS OF GENTLEMEN-AT-ARMS
St James's Palace, London SW1A 1BS
Captain, The Lord Strathclyde, PC
Lieutenant, Col. T. A. Hall, OBE
Standard Bearer, Maj. Sir Fergus Matheson of Matheson, Bt.
Clerk of the Cheque and Adjutant, Lt.-Col. R. Mayfield, DSO
Harbinger, Maj. Sir Philip Duncombe, Bt.

Gentlemen of the Corps
Colonels, Sir Piers Bengough, KCVO, OBE; Hon. N. Crossley, TD; T. Wilson; D. Fanshawe, OBE; J. Baker; R. ffrench Blake; Sir William Mahon, Bt.; Sir Brian Barttelot, Bt., OBE; M. J. C. Robertson, MC
Lieutenant-Colonels, Hon. P. H. Lewis; R. Macfarlane; Hon. G. B. Norrie; J. H. Fisher, OBE; R. Ker, MC; P. Chamberlin
Majors, J. A. J. Nunn; I. B. Ramsden, MBE; M. J. Drummond-Brady; A. Arkwright; G. M. B. Colenso-Jones; T. Gooch, MBE; J. B. B. Cockcroft; C. J. H. Gurney; P. D. Johnson; R. M. O. Webster; Maj. J. Warren; Maj. E. Crofton

THE QUEEN'S BODY GUARD OF THE YEOMEN OF THE GUARD
St James's Palace, London SW1A 1BS
Captain, The Lord Chesham
Lieutenant, Col. G. W. Tufnell
Clerk of the Cheque and Adjutant, Col. S. Longsdon
Ensign, Maj. C. Marriott
Exons, Maj. C. Enderby; Maj. M. T. N. H. Wills

MASTER OF THE HOUSEHOLD'S DEPARTMENT

BOARD OF GREEN CLOTH
Buckingham Palace, London SW1A 1AA
Master of the Household, Maj.-Gen. Sir Simon Cooper, KCVO
Deputy Master of the Household, Lt.-Col. Sir Guy Acland, Bt., MVO
Assistants to the Master of the Household, M. T. Parker, MVO; A. Jarman
Chief Clerk, M. C. W. N. Jephson, MVO
Chief Housekeeper, Miss H. Colebrook, MVO
Palace Steward, P. S. Croasdale, RVM
Royal Chef, L. Mann, RVM
Superintendent, Windsor Castle, Maj. B. Eastwood, LVO, MBE
Superintendent, The Palace of Holyroodhouse, Lt.-Col. D. Anderson, OBE

ROYAL MEWS DEPARTMENT
Buckingham Palace, London SW1W 0QH
Crown Equerry, Lt.-Col. S. Gilbart-Denham, CVO
Veterinary Surgeon, P. Scott Dunn, LVO, MRCVS
Superintendent Royal Mews, Buckingham Palace, Maj. A. Smith, MVO, MBE

THE ROYAL COLLECTION TRUST
St James's Palace, London SW1A 1BS
Director of Royal Collection and Surveyor of The Queen's Works of Art, H. Roberts, LVO, FSA
Surveyor of The Queen's Pictures, C. Lloyd, LVO
Surveyor Emeritus of The Queen's Pictures, Sir Oliver Millar, GCVO, FBA, FSA
Surveyor Emeritus of The Queen's Works of Art, Sir Geoffrey de Bellaigue, GCVO, FBA, FSA
Librarian, The Royal Library, Windsor Castle, O. Everett, CVO
Deputy Surveyor of The Queen's Works of Art, J. Marsden
Librarian Emeritus, Sir Robin Mackworth-Young, GCVO, FSA
Director of Media Affairs, R. Arbiter, LVO
Curator of the Print Room, The Hon. Mrs Roberts, LVO
Financial Director, M. Stevens
Financial Controller, Mrs G. Johnson
Administrator and Assistant to The Surveyors, D. Rankin-Hunt, MVO, TD
Senior Picture Restorer, Miss V. Pemberton-Pigott, MVO
Chief Restorer, Old Master Drawings, A. Donnithorne
Senior Furniture Restorer, E. Fancourt, MVO, RVM
Armourer, J. Jackson, RVM
Chief Binder, R. Day, MVO, RVM

ROYAL COLLECTION ENTERPRISES LTD
Managing Director, M. E. K. Hewlett, LVO

ASCOT OFFICE
St James's Palace, London SW1A 1BS
Tel 0171-930 9882
Her Majesty's Representative at Ascot, Col. Sir Piers Bengough, KCVO, OBE
Secretary, Miss L. Thompson-Royds, MVO

THE QUEEN'S HOUSEHOLD IN SCOTLAND

Hereditary Lord High Constable, The Earl of Erroll
Hereditary Master of the Household, The Duke of Argyll
Lord Lyon King of Arms, Sir Malcolm Innes of Edingight, KCVO, WS

Hereditary Bearer of the Royal Banner of Scotland, The Earl of Dundee
Hereditary Bearer of the Scottish National Flag, The Earl of Lauderdale
Hereditary Keepers:
  Palace of Holyroodhouse, The Duke of Hamilton and Brandon
  Falkland Palace, N. Crichton-Stuart
  Stirling Castle, The Earl of Mar and Kellie
  Dunstaffnage Castle, The Duke of Argyll
  Dunconnel Castle, Sir Charles Maclean, Bt.
Hereditary Carver, Maj. Sir Ralph Anstruther, Bt., GCVO, MC
Keeper of Dumbarton Castle, vacant
Governor of Edinburgh Castle, Maj.-Gen. J. Hall, OBE
Historiographer, Prof. T. C. Smout, CBE, FBA, FRSE, FSA SCOT.
Botanist, Prof. D. Henderson, CBE, FRSE
Painter and Limner, vacant
Sculptor in Ordinary, Prof. Sir Eduardo Paolozzi, CBE, RA
Astronomer, Prof. J. Brown, PH.D., FRSE
Heralds and Pursuivants, see page 281

ECCLESIASTICAL HOUSEHOLD
Dean of the Chapel Royal, Very Revd J. Harkness, CB, OBE
Dean of the Order of the Thistle, Very Revd G. I. Macmillan
Chaplains in Ordinary, Very Revd J. Harkness, CB, OBE; Revd J. McLeod; Very Revd G. I. Macmillan; Revd M. D. Craig; Very Revd W. B. R. Macmillan, LL.D, DD.; Very Revd J. L. Weatherhead, DD; Revd C. Robertson; Very Revd J. A. Simpson; Revd N. W. Drummond; Revd J. Paterson; Revd A. Symington
Extra Chaplains, Very Revd W. R. Sanderson, DD; Revd T. J. T. Nicol, LVO, MBE, MC, TD; Very Revd Prof. J. McIntyre, CVO, DD, FRSE; Revd C. Forrester-Paton; Revd H. W. M. Cant; Very Revd R. A. S. Barbour, KCVO, MC, DD; Revd K. MacVicar, MBE, DFC, TD; Very Revd W. B. Johnston, DD; Revd A. J. C. Macfarlane; Revd M. I. Levison, DD; Revd J. K. Angus, LVO, TD; Revd J. McLeod; Very Revd W. J. Morris, KCVO, DD; Revd A. S. Todd, DD
Domestic Chaplain, Balmoral, Revd R. P. Sloan

MEDICAL HOUSEHOLD
Physicians in Scotland, P. Brunt, OBE, MD, FRCP; A. Toft, CBE, FRCPE
Surgeons in Scotland, J. Engeset, CH.M., FRCS; Prof. Sir David Carter MD, FRCS
Apothecary to the Household at Balmoral, D. J. A. Glass, MB, CH.B.
Apothecary to the Household at the Palace of Holyroodhouse, Dr J. Cormack, MD, FRCPE, FRCGP

THE QUEEN'S BODY GUARD FOR SCOTLAND

ROYAL COMPANY OF ARCHERS
Archers' Hall, Buccleuch Street, Edinburgh EH8 9LR
Captain-General and Gold Stick for Scotland, Maj. Sir Hew Hamilton-Dalrymple, Bt., KCVO
Captains, The Duke of Buccleuch and Queensberry, KT, VRD; Maj. the Earl of Wemyss and March, KT; The Earl of Airlie, KT, GCVO
Lieutenants, Capt. Sir Iain Tennant, KT; The Marquess of Lothian, KCVO; Cdre Sir John Clerk of Penicuik, Bt., CBE, VRD; The Earl of Elgin and Kincardine, KT
Ensigns, Col. G. R. Simpson, DSO, LVO, TD; Maj. Sir David Butter, KCVO, MC; The Earl of Minto, OBE; Maj.-Gen. Sir John Swinton, KCVO, OBE

Brigadiers, Gen. Sir Michael Gow, GCB; The Hon. Lord
Elliott, MC; Maj. the Hon. Sir Lachlan Maclean, Bt.; The
Rt. Hon. Lord Younger of Prestwick, KT, KCVO, TD;
Capt. G. Burnet, LVO; The Duke of Montrose; Lt.-Gen.
Sir Norman Arthur, KCB; The Hon. Sir William
Macpherson of Cluny, TD; The Lord Nickson, KBE; Maj.
the Lord Glenarthur; Earl of Dalkeith; Maj. R. Y.
Henderson, TD; H. F. O. Bewsher, LVO, OBE
Adjutant, Maj. the Hon. Sir Lachlan Maclean, Bt.
Surgeon, Dr P. A. P. Mackenzie, TD
Chaplain, Very Revd W. J. Morris, KCVO, DD
President of the Council and Silver Stick for Scotland, vacant
Vice-President, Capt. Sir Iain Tennant, KT
Secretary, Capt. J. D. B. Younger
Treasurer, J. M. Haldane of Gleneagles

HOUSEHOLD OF THE PRINCE PHILIP, DUKE OF EDINBURGH

Treasurer, Sir Brian McGrath, KCVO
Private Secretary, Brig. M. G. Hunt-Davis, CBE
Equerry, Lt.-Col. A. C. Richards
Extra Equerries, J. B. V. Orr, CVO; The Lord Buxton of Alsa;
Brig. C. Robertson, CVO; Sir Brian McGrath, KCVO
Temporary Equerries, Maj. J. Cosby; Capt. R. Goodfellow;
Capt. the Hon. J. Geddes
Chief Clerk and Accountant, G. D. Partington

HOUSEHOLD OF QUEEN ELIZABETH THE QUEEN MOTHER

Lord Chamberlain, The Earl of Crawford and Balcarres, PC
Private Secretary, Comptroller and Equerry, Capt. Sir Alastair
Aird, KCVO
Assistant Private Secretary and Equerry, Maj. R. Seymour, CVO
Treasurer and Equerry, Maj. Sir Ralph Anstruther, Bt., GCVO,
MC
Equerry, Maj. A. C. B. MacEwan (*temp.*)
Extra Equerries, Maj. Sir John Griffin, KCVO; The Lord
Sinclair, CVO; Maj. W. Richardson, LVO; Maj. D.
McMicking, LVO; Capt. A. Windham, LVO
Apothecary to the Household, Dr N. Southward, CVO, MB,
B.chir.
Surgeon-Apothecary to the Household (Royal Lodge, Windsor), Dr
J. Briscoe, D.obst.
Mistress of the Robes, vacant
Ladies of the Bedchamber, The Lady Grimthorpe, DCVO; The
Countess of Scarbrough
Women of the Bedchamber, Dame Frances Campbell-Preston,
DCVO; Lady Angela Oswald, LVO; The Hon. Mrs
Rhodes; Mrs Michael Gordon-Lennox
Extra Women of the Bedchamber, Lady Jean Rankin, DCVO;
Miss Jane Walker-Okeover, LVO; Lady Margaret
Colville, CVO; Lady Elizabeth Basset, DCVO
Clerk Comptroller, M. Blanch, CVO
Information Officer, Mrs R. Murphy, LVO
Clerks, Miss F. Fletcher, LVO; Mrs W. Stevens

HOUSEHOLD OF THE PRINCE OF WALES

Private Secretary and Treasurer to the Prince of Wales, Cdr. R. J.
Aylard, CVO, RN
Deputy Private Secretary to the Prince of Wales, S. Lamport

Assistant Private Secretaries to the Prince of Wales, Dr M.
Williams; J. Skan
Press Secretary to the Prince of Wales, Miss S. Henney
Assistant Press Secretary to the Prince of Wales, M. Bolland
Equerry to the Prince of Wales, Lt. Cdr. J. Lavery, RN
Extra Equerries to the Prince of Wales, The Hon. Edward
Adeane, CVO; Maj.-Gen. Sir Christopher Airy, KCVO,
CBE; Sqn. Ldr. Sir David Checketts, KCVO; Sir David
Landale, KCVO; Sir John Riddell, Bt., CVO; G. J. Ward,
CBE; Brig. J. Q. Winter, LVO; M. Butler
Secretary to the Duchy of Cornwall and Keeper of the Records,
J. N. C. James, CBE

HOUSEHOLD OF DIANA, PRINCESS OF WALES

Private Secretary, M. Gibbins
Ladies-in-Waiting, Miss Anne Beckwith-Smith, LVO;
Viscountess Campden, LVO; Mrs Max Pike; Mrs Duncan
Byatt; Mrs James Lonsdale
Extra Lady-in-Waiting, Lady Sarah McCorquodale

HOUSEHOLD OF THE DUKE OF YORK

*Private Secretary, Treasurer and Extra Equerry to the Duke of
York*, Capt. R. N. Blair, RN
Comptroller and Assistant Private Secretary to the Duke of York,
Cdr. C. Manley, OBE
Equerry to The Duke of York, Capt. T. E. D. Allan

HOUSEHOLD OF THE PRINCE EDWARD

Private Secretary, Lt.-Col. S. G. O'Dwyer, LVO
Assistant Private Secretary, Mrs R. Warburton, MVO
Clerk, Miss L. Buggé

HOUSEHOLD OF THE PRINCESS ROYAL

Private Secretary, Lt.-Col. P. Gibbs, CVO
Assistant Private Secretary, The Hon. Mrs Louloudis
Ladies-in-Waiting, Lady Carew Pole, LVO; Mrs Andrew
Feilden, LVO; The Hon. Mrs Legge-Bourke, LVO; Mrs
William Nunneley; Mrs Timothy Holderness-
Roddam; Mrs Charles Ritchie; Mrs David Bowes Lyon
Extra Ladies-in-Waiting, Miss Victoria Legge-Bourke, LVO;
Mrs Malcolm Innes, LVO; The Countess of Lichfield

HOUSEHOLD OF THE PRINCESS MARGARET, COUNTESS OF SNOWDON

Private Secretary and Comptroller, The Lord Napier and
Ettrick, KCVO
Lady-in-Waiting, The Hon. Mrs Whitehead, LVO
Extra Ladies-in-Waiting, Lady Elizabeth Cavendish, LVO;
Lady Aird, LVO; Mrs Robin Benson, LVO, OBE; Lady
Juliet Townsend, LVO; Mrs Jane Stevens, LVO; The
Hon. Mrs Wills, LVO; The Lady Glenconner, LVO; The
Countess Alexander of Tunis, LVO; Mrs Charles
Vyvyan

HOUSEHOLD OF THE DUKE AND DUCHESS OF GLOUCESTER

Private Secretary, Comptroller and Equerry, Maj.
  N. M. L. Barne, LVO
Assistant Private Secretary to the Duchess of Gloucester, Miss S.
  Marland, LVO
Extra Equerry, Lt.-Col. Sir Simon Bland, KCVO
Ladies-in-Waiting, Mrs Michael Wigley, CVO; Mrs Euan
  McCorquodale, LVO; Mrs Howard Page, LVO
Extra Ladies-in-Waiting, Miss Jennifer Thomson; The
  Lady Camoys

HOUSEHOLD OF PRINCESS ALICE, DUCHESS OF GLOUCESTER

Private Secretary, Comptroller and Equerry, Maj.
  N. M. L. Barne, LVO
Extra Equerry, Lt.-Col. Sir Simon Bland, KCVO
Ladies-in-Waiting, Dame Jean Maxwell-Scott, DCVO; Mrs
  Michael Harvey, LVO
Extra Ladies-in-Waiting, Miss Diana Harrison; The Hon.
  Jane Walsh, LVO; Miss Jane Egerton-Warburton, LVO

HOUSEHOLD OF THE DUKE AND DUCHESS OF KENT

Private Secretary, N. C. Adamson, OBE
Extra Equerries, Lt.-Cdr. Sir Richard Buckley, KCVO; Maj. J.
  Stewart; A. Palmer, CVO, CMG
Temporary Equerry, Capt. M. Barnett
Ladies-in-Waiting, Mrs Fiona Henderson, CVO; Mrs Colin
  Marsh, LVO; Mrs Julian Tomkins; Mrs Peter Troughton;
  Mrs Richard Beckett

HOUSEHOLD OF PRINCE AND PRINCESS MICHAEL OF KENT

Personal Secretary, Ms P. Goldspink
Ladies-in-Waiting, The Hon. Mrs Sanders; Miss Anne
  Frost; Mrs J. Fellowes

HOUSEHOLD OF PRINCESS ALEXANDRA, THE HON. LADY OGILVY

Comptroller and Private Secretary, Capt. N. Blair, RN
Extra Equerry, Maj. Sir Peter Clarke, KCVO
Lady-in-Waiting, Lady Mary Mumford, DCVO
Extra Ladies-in-Waiting, Mrs Peter Afia; Lady Mary
  Colman; Lady Nicholas Gordon Lennox; The Hon.
  Lady Rowley; Dame Mona Mitchell, DCVO

Royal Salutes

ENGLAND
A salute of 62 guns is fired on the wharf at the Tower of
London on the following occasions:
(a) the anniversaries of the birth, accession and
    coronation of the Sovereign
(b) the anniversary of the birth of HM Queen Elizabeth
    the Queen Mother
(c) the anniversary of the birth of HRH Prince Philip,
    Duke of Edinburgh
A salute of 41 guns only is fired on extraordinary and
triumphal occasions, e.g. on the occasion of the Sovereign
opening, proroguing or dissolving Parliament in person, or
when passing through London in procession, except when
otherwise ordered.
A salute of 41 guns is fired from the two saluting stations
in London (the Tower of London and Hyde Park) on the
occasion of the birth of a Royal infant.
Constable of the Royal Palace and Fortress of London, Field
  Marshal Sir Peter Inge, GCB
Lieutenant of the Tower of London, Lt.-Gen. Sir Michael Gray,
  KCB, OBE
Resident Governor and Keeper of the Jewel House, Maj.-Gen. G.
  Field, CB, OBE

Master Gunner of St James's Park, Gen. Sir Martin Farndale,
  KCB
Master Gunner within the Tower, Col. S. Lalor

SCOTLAND
Royal salutes are authorized at Edinburgh Castle and
Stirling Castle, although in practice Edinburgh Castle is
the only operating saluting station in Scotland.
A salute of 21 guns is fired on the following occasions:
(a) the anniversaries of the birth, accession and coronation
    of the Sovereign
(b) the anniversary of the birth of HM Queen Elizabeth
    the Queen Mother
(c) the anniversary of the birth of HRH Prince Philip,
    Duke of Edinburgh
A salute of 21 guns is fired in Edinburgh on the occasion
of the opening of the General Assembly of the Church of
Scotland.
A salute of 21 guns may also be fired in Edinburgh on the
arrival of HM The Queen, HM Queen Elizabeth the
Queen Mother, or a member of the Royal Family who is a
Royal Highness on an official visit.

Royal Finances

FUNDING

THE CIVIL LIST

The Civil List dates back to the late 17th century. It was originally used by the sovereign to pay the salaries of judges, ambassadors and other government offices as well as the expenses of the royal household. In 1760 on the accession of George III it was decided that the Civil List would be provided by Parliament in return for the King surrendering the hereditary revenues of the Crown. At that time Parliament undertook to pay the salaries of judges, ambassadors, etc. In 1831 Parliament agreed also to meet the costs of the royal palaces. Each sovereign has agreed to continue this arrangement.

The Civil List paid to The Queen is charged on the Consolidated Fund. Until 1972, the amount of money allocated annually under the Civil List was set for the duration of a reign. The system was then altered to a fixed annual payment for ten years but from 1975 high inflation made an annual review necessary. The system of payments reverted to the practice of a fixed annual payment for ten years from 1 January 1991.

The Civil List Acts provide for other members of the royal family to receive parliamentary annuities from government funds to meet the expenses of carrying out their official duties. Since 1975 The Queen has reimbursed the Treasury for the annuities paid to the Duke of Gloucester, the Duke of Kent and Princess Alexandra. Since April 1993 The Queen has reimbursed all the annuities except those paid to herself, Queen Elizabeth the Queen Mother and the Duke of Edinburgh.

The Prince of Wales does not receive a parliamentary annuity. He derives his income from the revenues of the Duchy of Cornwall and these monies meet the official and private expenses of the Prince of Wales and his family.

The annual payments for the years 1991–2000 are:

The Queen	£7,900,000
Queen Elizabeth the Queen Mother	643,000
The Duke of Edinburgh	359,000
*The Duke of York	249,000
*The Prince Edward	96,000
*The Princess Royal	228,000
*The Princess Margaret, Countess of Snowdon	219,000
*Princess Alice, Duchess of Gloucester	87,000
*The Duke of Gloucester	175,000
*The Duke of Kent	236,000
*Princess Alexandra	225,000
	10,417,000
*Refunded to the Treasury	1,515,000
Total	8,902,000

GRANT-IN-AID

Grant-in-aid from the Department of National Heritage is voted annually by Parliament to pay for the upkeep of the occupied royal palaces which are used as royal residences or for official or ceremonial purposes.

THE PRIVY PURSE

The funds received by the Privy Purse pay for official expenses incurred by The Queen as head of state and for some of The Queen's private expenditure. The revenues of the Duchy of Lancaster are the principal source of income for the Privy Purse. The revenues of the Duchy were retained by George III in 1760 when the hereditary revenues were surrendered in exchange for the Civil List.

PERSONAL INCOME

The Queen's personal income derives mostly from investments, and is used to meet private expenditure.

DEPARTMENTAL VOTES

Items of expenditure connected with the official duties of the royal family which fall on votes of government departments include:

Ministry of Defence – The Royal Yacht; The Queen's Flight
Foreign and Commonwealth Office – Marshal of the Diplomatic Corps; overseas visits at the request of government departments
Department of National Heritage – Royal palaces
Department of Transport – The Royal Train
HM Treasury – Central Chancery of the Orders of Knighthood

TAXATION

The sovereign is not legally liable to pay income tax, capital gains tax or inheritance tax. After income tax was reintroduced in 1842 some income tax was paid voluntarily by the sovereign but over a long period these payments were phased out. In 1992 the Prime Minister announced that The Queen had offered to pay tax on a voluntary basis from 6 April 1993, and that the Prince of Wales also wished to pay tax on a voluntary basis on his income from the Duchy of Cornwall. (He was already taxed in all other respects.)

The provisions for The Queen and the Prince of Wales to pay tax were set out in a Memorandum of Understanding on Royal Taxation presented to Parliament on 11 February 1993. The main provisions are that The Queen will pay income tax and capital gains tax in respect of her private income and assets, and on the proportion of the income and capital gains of the Privy Purse used for private purposes. Inheritance tax will be paid on The Queen's assets, except for those which pass to the next sovereign, whether automatically or by gift or bequest. The Prince of Wales will pay income tax on income from the Duchy of Cornwall used for private purposes.

The Prince of Wales has confirmed that he intends to pay tax on the same basis following his accession to the throne.

Other members of the royal family are subject to tax as for any taxpayer.

Military Ranks and Titles

THE QUEEN

Lord High Admiral of the United Kingdom

Colonel-in-Chief
The Life Guards; The Blues and Royals (Royal Horse Guards and 1st Dragoons); The Royal Scots Dragoon Guards (Carabiniers and Greys); The Queen's Royal Lancers; Royal Tank Regiment; Corps of Royal Engineers; Grenadier Guards; Coldstream Guards; Scots Guards; Irish Guards; Welsh Guards; The Royal Welch Fusiliers; The Queen's Lancashire Regiment; The Argyll and Sutherland Highlanders (Princess Louise's); The Royal Green Jackets; Adjutant General's Corps; The Royal Mercian and Lancastrian Yeomanry; The Governor General's Horse Guards (of Canada); The King's Own Calgary Regiment; Canadian Forces Military Engineers Branch; Royal 22e Regiment (of Canada); Governor-General's Foot Guards (of Canada); The Canadian Grenadier Guards; Le Regiment de la Chaudiere (of Canada); 2nd Bn Royal New Brunswick Regiment (North Shore); The 48th Highlanders of Canada; The Argyll and Sutherland Highlanders of Canada (Princess Louise's); The Calgary Highlanders; Royal Australian Engineers; Royal Australian Infantry Corps; Royal Australian Army Ordnance Corps; Royal Australian Army Nursing Corps; The Corps of Royal New Zealand Engineers; Royal New Zealand Infantry Regiment; Royal New Zealand Army Ordnance Corps; Royal Malta Artillery; The Malawi Rifles

Affiliated Colonel-in-Chief
The Queen's Gurkha Engineers

Captain-General
Royal Regiment of Artillery; The Honourable Artillery Company; Combined Cadet Force; Royal Regiment of Canadian Artillery; Royal Regiment of Australian Artillery; Royal Regiment of New Zealand Artillery; Royal New Zealand Armoured Corps

Patron
Royal Army Chaplains' Department

Air Commodore-in-Chief
Royal Auxiliary Air Force; Royal Air Force Regiment; Royal Observer Corps; Air Reserve (of Canada); Royal Australian Air Force Reserve; Territorial Air Force (of New Zealand)

Commandant-in-Chief
Royal Air Force College, Cranwell

Hon. Air Commodore
RAF Marham

HM QUEEN ELIZABETH THE QUEEN MOTHER

Colonel-in-Chief
1st The Queen's Dragoon Guards; The Queen's Royal Hussars (Queen's Own and Royal Irish); 9th/12th Royal Lancers (Prince of Wales's); The King's Regiment; The Royal Anglian Regiment; The Light Infantry; The Black Watch (Royal Highland Regiment); Royal Army Medical Corps; The Black Watch (Royal Highland Regiment) of Canada; The Toronto Scottish Regiment; Canadian Forces Medical Services; Royal Australian Army Medical Corps; Royal New Zealand Army Medical Corps

Hon. Colonel
The Royal Yeomanry; The London Scottish; Inns of Court and City Yeomanry

Commandant-in-Chief
Women in the Royal Navy; Women, Royal Air Force; Royal Air Force Central Flying School

HRH THE PRINCE PHILIP, DUKE OF EDINBURGH

Admiral of the Fleet
Field Marshal
Marshal of the Royal Air Force

Admiral of the Fleet, Royal Australian Navy
Field Marshal, Australian Military Forces
Marshal of the Royal Australian Air Force

Admiral of the Fleet, Royal New Zealand Navy
Field Marshal, New Zealand Army
Marshal of the Royal New Zealand Air Force

Captain-General, Royal Marines

Admiral
Royal Canadian Sea Cadets

Colonel-in-Chief
The Royal Gloucestershire, Berkshire and Wiltshire Regiment; The Highlanders (Seaforth, Gordons and Camerons); Corps of Royal Electrical and Mechanical Engineers; Intelligence Corps; Army Cadet Force; The Royal Canadian Regiment; The Royal Hamilton Light Infantry (Wentworth Regiment) (of Canada); The Cameron Highlanders of Ottawa; The Queen's Own Cameron Highlanders of Canada; The Seaforth Highlanders of Canada; The Royal Canadian Army Cadets; The Royal Australian Electrical and Mechanical Engineers; The Australian Cadet Corps; The Royal New Zealand Corps of Electrical and Mechanical Engineers

Deputy Colonel-in-Chief
The Queen's Royal Hussars (Queen's Own and Royal Irish)

Colonel
Grenadier Guards

Hon. Colonel
The King's Own Yorkshire Yeomanry (Light Infantry); City of Edinburgh Universities Officers' Training Corps; The Trinidad and Tobago Regiment

Air Commodore-in-Chief
Air Training Corps; Royal Canadian Air Cadets

Hon. Air Commodore
RAF Kinloss

HRH THE PRINCE OF WALES

Captain, Royal Navy
Group Captain, Royal Air Force

Colonel-in-Chief
The Royal Dragoon Guards; The Cheshire Regiment; The Royal Regiment of Wales (24th/41st Foot); The Parachute Regiment; The Royal Gurkha Rifles; Army Air Corps; The Royal Canadian Dragoons; Lord Strathcona's Horse (Royal Canadians); Royal Regiment of Canada; Royal Winnipeg Rifles; Air Reserve Group of Air Command (of Canada); Royal Australian Armoured Corps; The Royal Pacific Islands Regiment

Deputy Colonel-in-Chief
The Highlanders (Seaforth, Gordons and Camerons)

Colonel
Welsh Guards

Air Commodore-in-Chief
Royal New Zealand Air Force

Hon. Air Commodore
RAF Valley

HRH THE DUKE OF YORK

Lieutenant-Commander, Royal Navy

Admiral
Sea Cadet Corps

Colonel-in-Chief
The Staffordshire Regiment (The Prince of Wales's); The Royal Irish Regiment (27th (Inniskilling), 83rd, 87th and The Ulster Defence Regiment)

HRH THE PRINCESS ROYAL

Rear Admiral
Chief Commandant for Women in the Royal Navy

Colonel-in-Chief
The King's Royal Hussars; Royal Corps of Signals; The Royal Scots (The Royal Regiment); The Worcestershire and Sherwood Foresters Regiment (29th/45th Foot); The Royal Logistic Corps; 8th Canadian Hussars (Princess Louise's); Canadian Forces Communications and Electronics Branch; The Grey and Simcoe Foresters; The Royal Regina Rifle Regiment; Royal Newfoundland Regiment; Royal Australian Corps of Signals; Royal New Zealand Corps of Signals; Royal New Zealand Nursing Corps

Affiliated Colonel-in-Chief
The Queen's Gurkha Signals; The Queen's Own Gurkha Transport Regiment

Hon. Colonel
University of London Officers' Training Corps

Hon. Air Commodore
RAF Lyneham; University of London Air Squadron

Commandant-in-Chief
Women's Transport Service (FANY)

HRH THE PRINCESS MARGARET, COUNTESS OF SNOWDON

Colonel-in-Chief
The Royal Highland Fusiliers (Princess Margaret's Own Glasgow and Ayrshire Regiment); Queen Alexandra's Royal Army Nursing Corps; The Highland Fusiliers of Canada; The Princess Louise Fusiliers (of Canada); The Bermuda Regiment

Deputy Colonel-in-Chief
The Royal Anglian Regiment

Hon. Air Commodore
RAF Coningsby

HRH PRINCESS ALICE, DUCHESS OF GLOUCESTER

Air Chief Marshal

Colonel-in-Chief
The King's Own Scottish Borderers; Royal Australian Corps of Transport; Royal New Zealand Corps of Transport

Deputy Colonel-in-Chief
The King's Royal Hussars; The Royal Anglian Regiment

Air Chief Commandant
Women, Royal Air Force

HRH THE DUKE OF GLOUCESTER

Deputy Colonel-in-Chief
The Royal Gloucestershire, Berkshire and Wiltshire Regiment; The Royal Logistic Corps

Hon. Colonel
Royal Monmouthshire Royal Engineers (Militia)

Hon. Air Commodore
RAF Odiham

HRH THE DUCHESS OF GLOUCESTER

Colonel-in-Chief
Royal Australian Army Educational Corps; Royal New Zealand Army Educational Corps

Deputy Colonel-in-Chief
Adjutant-General's Corps

HRH THE DUKE OF KENT

Field Marshal
Hon. Air Vice-Marshal

Colonel-in-Chief
The Royal Regiment of Fusiliers; The Devonshire and Dorset Regiment; The Lorne Scots (Peel, Dufferin and Hamilton Regiment)

Deputy Colonel-in-Chief
  The Royal Scots Dragoon Guards (Carabiniers and
  Greys)

Colonel
  Scots Guards

Hon. Air Commodore
  RAF Leuchars

HRH THE DUCHESS OF KENT

Hon. Major-General

Colonel-in-Chief
  The Prince of Wales's Own Regiment of Yorkshire

Deputy Colonel-in-Chief
  The Royal Dragoon Guards; Adjutant-General's Corps;
  The Royal Logistic Corps

HRH PRINCE MICHAEL OF KENT

Major (retd), The Royal Hussars (Prince of Wales's Own)

Hon. Commodore
  Royal Naval Reserve

HRH PRINCESS ALEXANDRA, THE HON. LADY OGILVY

Patron
  Queen Alexandra's Royal Naval Nursing Service

Colonel-in-Chief
  The King's Own Royal Border Regiment; The Queen's
  Own Rifles of Canada; The Canadian Scottish
  Regiment (Princess Mary's)

Deputy Colonel-in-Chief
  The Queen's Royal Lancers; The Light Infantry

Deputy Hon. Colonel
  The Royal Yeomanry

Patron and Air Chief Commandant
  Princess Mary's Royal Air Force Nursing Service

The Royal Arms

ENGLAND

1st and 4th quarters (representing England) – Gules, three
  lions passant guardant in pale Or
2nd quarter (representing Scotland) – Or, a lion rampant
  within a double tressure flory counterflory Gules
3rd quarter (representing Ireland) – Azure, a harp Or,
  stringed Argent
The whole shield is encircled with the Garter

SCOTLAND

The Royal Arms shown with the Lion of Scotland in the 1st
and 4th quarters, and the Lions of England in the 2nd
quarter
The whole shield is encircled with the Thistle

SUPPORTERS (ENGLAND)

Dexter (right) – a lion rampant guardant Or, imperially
  crowned (shown in Scotland on the sinister)
Sinister (left) – a unicorn Argent, armed, crined, and
  unguled Or, gorged with a coronet composed of crosses
  patées and fleurs-de-lis, a chain affixed, passing
  between the forelegs, and reflexed over the back (shown
  in Scotland on the dexter and imperially crowned)

CRESTS

England – the Royal Crown Proper thereon a lion statant
  guardant Or imperially crowned also Proper
Scotland – upon an imperial crown Proper a lion sejant
  affrontée Gules imperially crowned Or, holding in the
  dexter paw a sword and in the sinister a sceptre erect,
  also Proper
Ireland – a tower triple-towered of the First, from the
  portal a hart springing Argent, attired and hooved Or

BADGES

England – the red and white rose united, slipped and
  leaved proper
Scotland – a thistle, slipped and leaved proper
Ireland – a shamrock leaf slipped Vert; also a harp Or,
  stringed Argent
United Kingdom – the rose of England, the thistle of
  Scotland, and the shamrock of Ireland engrafted on the
  same stem proper, and an escutcheon charged as the
  Union Flag (all ensigned with the Royal Crown)
Wales – upon a mount Vert a dragon passant, wings
  elevated Gules

The House of Windsor

King George V assumed by royal proclamation (17 June 1917) for his House and family, as well as for all descendants in the male line of Queen Victoria who are subjects of these realms, the name of Windsor.

KING GEORGE V (George Frederick Ernest Albert), second son of King Edward VII, *born* 3 June 1865; *married* 6 July 1893 HSH Princess Victoria Mary Augusta Louise Olga Pauline Claudine Agnes of Teck (Queen Mary, *born* 26 May 1867; *died* 24 March 1953); *succeeded* to the throne 6 May 1910; *died* 20 January 1936. *Issue:*

1. HRH PRINCE EDWARD Albert Christian George Andrew Patrick David, *born* 23 June 1894, *succeeded* to the throne as King Edward VIII, 20 January 1936; *abdicated* 11 December 1936; created *Duke of Windsor*, 1937; *married* 3 June 1937, Mrs Wallis Warfield (Her Grace The Duchess of Windsor, *born* 19 June 1896; *died* 24 April 1986), *died* 28 May 1972

2. HRH PRINCE ALBERT Frederick Arthur George, *born* 14 December 1895, *created* Duke of York 1920; *married* 26 April 1923, Lady Elizabeth Bowes-Lyon, youngest daughter of the 14th Earl of Strathmore and Kinghorne (HM Queen Elizabeth the Queen Mother, *see* pages 117–8), *succeeded* to the throne as King George VI, 11 December 1936; *died* 6 February 1952, having had issue (*see* page 117)

3. HRH PRINCESS (Victoria Alexandra Alice) MARY (*Princess Royal*), *born* 25 April 1897, *married* 28 February 1922, Viscount Lascelles, later the 6th Earl of Harewood (1882–1947), *died* 28 March 1965. *Issue:*

(1) George Henry Hubert Lascelles, 7th Earl of Harewood, KBE, *born* 7 February 1923; *married* (1) 1949, Maria (Marion) Stein (marriage dissolved 1967); *issue*, (*a*) David Henry George, Viscount Lascelles, *born* 1950; (*b*) James Edward, *born* 1953; (*c*)

(Robert) Jeremy Hugh, *born* 1955; (2) 1967, Mrs Patricia Tuckwell; *issue*, (*d*) Mark Hubert, *born* 1964
(2) Gerald David Lascelles, *born* 21 August 1924, *married* (1) 1952, Miss Angela Dowding (marriage dissolved 1978); *issue*, (*a*) Henry Ulick, *born* 1953; (2) 1978, Mrs Elizabeth Colvin; *issue*, (*b*) Martin David, *born* 1962

4. HRH PRINCE HENRY William Frederick Albert, *born* 31 March 1900, *created* Duke of Gloucester, Earl of Ulster and Baron Culloden 1928, *married* 6 November 1935, Lady Alice Christabel Montagu-Douglas-Scott, daughter of the 7th Duke of Buccleuch (HRH Princess Alice, Duchess of Gloucester, *see* page 118); *died* 10 June 1974. *Issue:*
(1) HRH Prince William Henry Andrew Frederick, *born* 18 December 1941; *accidentally killed* 28 August 1972
(2) HRH Prince Richard Alexander Walter George (HRH The Duke of Gloucester), *see* page 118

5. HRH PRINCE GEORGE Edward Alexander Edmund, *born* 20 December 1902, *created* Duke of Kent, Earl of St Andrews and Baron Downpatrick 1934, *married* 29 November 1934, HRH Princess Marina of Greece and Denmark (*born* 30 November OS, 1906; *died* 27 August 1968); *killed on active service*, 25 August 1942. *Issue:*
(1) HRH Prince Edward George Nicholas Paul Patrick (HRH The Duke of Kent), *see* page 118
(2) HRH Princess Alexandra Helen Elizabeth Olga Christabel (HRH Princess Alexandra, the Hon. Lady Ogilvy), *see* page 118
(3) HRH Prince Michael George Charles Franklin (HRH Prince Michael of Kent), *see* page 118

6. HRH PRINCE JOHN Charles Francis, *born* 12 July 1905; *died* 18 January 1919

Descendants of Queen Victoria

QUEEN VICTORIA (Alexandrina Victoria), *born* 24 May 1819; *succeeded* to the throne 20 June 1837; *married* 10 February 1840 (Francis) Albert Augustus Charles Emmanuel, Duke of Saxony, Prince of Saxe-Coburg and Gotha (HRH Albert, Prince Consort, *born* 26 August 1819, *died* 14 December 1861); *died* 22 January 1901. *Issue:*

1. HRH PRINCESS VICTORIA Adelaide Mary Louisa (Princess Royal) (1840–1901), *m.* 1858, Frederic (1831–88), Emperor of Germany March–June 1888. *Issue:*
(1) HIM Wilhelm II (1859–1941), Emperor of Germany 1888–1918, *m.* (1) 1881 Princess Augusta Victoria of Schleswig-Holstein-Sonderburg-Augustenburg (1858–1921); (2) 1922 Princess Hermine of Reuss (1887–1947). *Issue:*
(*a*) Prince Wilhelm (1882–1951), *Crown Prince* 1888–1918, *m.* 1905 Duchess Cecilie of Mecklenburg-Schwerin; *issue:* Prince Wilhelm (1906–40); Prince Louis Ferdinand (1907–94), *m.* 1938 Grand Duchess Kira (*see* page 129); Prince Hubertus (1909–50); Prince Friedrich Georg (1911–66); Princess Alexandrine Irene (1915–80); Princess Cecilie (1917–75)
(*b*) Prince Eitel-Friedrich (1883–1942), *m.* 1906 Duchess Sophie of Oldenburg (marriage dissolved 1926)
(*c*) Prince Adalbert (1884–1948), *m.* 1914 Duchess Adelheid of Saxe-Meiningen; *issue:* Princess Victoria Marina (1917–81); Prince Wilhelm Victor (1919–89)
(*d*) Prince August Wilhelm (1887–1949), *m.* 1908 Princess Alexandra of Schleswig-Holstein-Sonderburg-Glücksburg (marriage dissolved 1920); *issue:* Prince Alexander (1912–85)
(*e*) Prince Oskar (1888–1958), *m.* 1914 Countess von Ruppin; *issue:* Prince Oskar (1915–39); Prince Burchard (1917–88); Princess Herzeleide (1918–89); Prince Wilhelm (*b.* 1922)
(*f*) Prince Joachim (1890–1920), *m.* 1916 Princess Marie of Anhalt; *issue:* Prince Karl Franz Joseph (1916–75)

(*g*) Princess Viktoria Luise (1892–1980), *m.* 1913 Ernst, Duke of Brunswick 1913–18 (1887–1953); *issue:* Prince Ernst (1914–87); Prince Georg (*b.* 1915), *m.* 1946 Princess Sophie of Greece (*see* page 129) and has issue (two sons, one daughter); Princess Frederika (1917–81), *m.* 1938 Paul I, King of the Hellenes (*see* page 129); Prince Christian (1919–81); Prince Welf Heinrich (*b.* 1923)
(2) Princess Charlotte (1860–1919), *m.* 1878 Bernhard, Duke of Saxe-Meiningen 1914 (1851–1914). *Issue:*
Princess Feodora (1879–1945), *m.* 1898 Prince Heinrich XXX of Reuss
(3) Prince Heinrich (1862–1929), *m.* 1888 Princess Irene of Hesse (*see* page 129). *Issue:*
(*a*) Prince Waldemar (1889–1945), *m.* Princess Calixsta of Lippe
(*b*) Prince Sigismund (1896–1978), *m.* 1919 Princess Charlotte of Saxe-Altenburg; *issue:* Princess Barbara (*b.* 1920); Prince Alfred (*b.* 1924)
(*c*) Prince Heinrich (1900–4)
(4) Prince Sigismund (1864–6)
(5) Princess Victoria (1866–1929), *m.* (1) 1890, Prince Adolf of Schaumburg-Lippe (1859–1916); (2) 1927 Alexander Zubkov
(6) Prince Joachim Waldemar (1868–79)
(7) Princess Sophie (1870–1932), *m.* 1889 Constantine I (1868–1923), King of the Hellenes 1913–17, 1920–3. *Issue:*
(*a*) George II (1890–1947), King of the Hellenes 1923–4 and 1935–47, *m.* 1921 Princess Elisabeth of Roumania (marriage dissolved 1935) (*see* page 129)
(*b*) Alexander I (1893–1920), King of the Hellenes 1917–20, *m.* 1919 Aspasia Manos; *issue:* Princess Alexandra (1921–93), *m.* 1944 King Petar II of Yugoslavia (*see* page 129)
(*c*) Princess Helena (1896–1982), *m.* 1921 King Carol of Roumania (*see* page 129), (marriage dissolved 1928)

(d) Paul I (1901–64), King of the Hellenes 1947–64, m. 1938 Princess Frederika of Brunswick (see page 128); issue: King Constantine II (b. 1940), m. 1964 Princess Anne-Marie of Denmark (see page 130), and has issue (three sons, two daughters); Princess Sophie (b. 1938), m. 1962 Juan Carlos I of Spain (see page 130); Princess Irene (b. 1942)
(e) Princess Irene (1904–74), m. 1939 4th Duke of Aosta; issue: Prince Amedeo (b. 1943)
(f) Princess Katherine (Lady Katherine Brandram) (b. 1913), m. 1947 Major R. C. A. Brandram, MC, TD; issue: R. Paul G. A. Brandram (b. 1948)
(8) Princess Margarethe (1872–1954), m. 1893 Prince Friedrich Karl of Hesse (1868–1940). Issue:
(a) Prince Friedrich Wilhelm (1893–1916)
(b) Prince Maximilian (1894–1914)
(c) Prince Philipp (1896–1980), m. 1925 Princess Mafalda of Italy; issue: Prince Moritz (b. 1926); Prince Heinrich (b. 1927); Prince Otto (b. 1937); Princess Elisabeth (b. 1940)
(d) Prince Wolfgang (b. 1896), m. (1) 1924 Princess Marie Alexandra of Baden; (2) 1948 Ottilie Möller
(e) Prince Richard (1901–69)
(f) Prince Christoph (1901–43), m. 1930 Princess Sophie of Greece (see below) and has issue (two sons, three daughters)

2. HRH PRINCE ALBERT EDWARD (HM KING EDWARD VII), b. 9 November 1841, m. 1863 HRH Princess Alexandra of Denmark (1844–1925), succeeded to the throne 22 January 1901, d. 6 May 1910. Issue:
(1) Albert Victor, Duke of Clarence and Avondale (1864–92)
(2) George (HM KING GEORGE V) (see page 128)
(3) Louise (1867–1931) Princess Royal 1905–31, m. 1889 1st Duke of Fife (1849–1912). Issue:
(a) Princess Alexandra, Duchess of Fife (1891–1959), m. 1913 Prince Arthur of Connaught (see page 130)
(b) Princess Maud (1893–1945), m. 1923 11th Earl of Southesk (1893–1992); issue: The Duke of Fife (b. 1929)
(4) Victoria (1868–1935)
(5) Maud (1869–1938), m. 1896 Prince Carl of Denmark (1872–1957), later King Haakon VII of Norway 1905–57. Issue:
(a) Olav V (1903–91), King of Norway 1957–91, m. 1929 Princess Märtha of Sweden (1901–54); issue: Princess Ragnhild (b. 1930); Princess Astrid (b. 1932); Harald V, King of Norway (b. 1937)
(6) Alexander (6–7 April 1871)

3. HRH PRINCESS ALICE Maud Mary (1843–78), m. 1862 Prince Ludwig (1837–92), Grand Duke of Hesse 1877–92. Issue:
(1) Victoria (1863–1950), m. 1884 Admiral of the Fleet Prince Louis of Battenberg (1854–1921), cr. 1st Marquess of Milford Haven 1917. Issue:
(a) Alice (1885–1969), m. 1903 Prince Andrew of Greece (1882–1944); issue: Princess Margarita (1905–81) m. 1931 Prince Gottfried of Hohenlohe-Langenburg (see below); Princess Theodora (1906–69), m. Prince Berthold of Baden (1906–63) and has issue (two sons, one daughter); Princess Cecilie (1911–37), m. George, Grand Duke of Hesse (see below); Princess Sophie (b. 1914), m. (1) 1930 Prince Christoph of Hesse (see above); (2) 1946 Prince Georg of Hanover (see page 128); Prince Philip, Duke of Edinburgh (b. 1921) (see page 117)
(b) Louise (1889–1965), m. 1923 Gustaf VI Adolf (1882–1973), King of Sweden 1950–73
(c) George, 2nd Marquess of Milford Haven (1892–1938), m. 1916 Countess Nadejda, daughter of Grand Duke Michael of Russia; issue: Lady Tatiana (1917–88); David Michael, 3rd Marquess (1919–70)
(d) Louis, 1st Earl Mountbatten of Burma (1900–79), m. 1922 Edwina Ashley, daughter of Lord Mount Temple; issue: Patricia, Countess Mountbatten of Burma (b. 1924), Pamela (b. 1929)
(2) Elizabeth (1864–1918), m. 1884 Grand Duke Sergius of Russia (1857–1905)
(3) Irene (1866–1953), m. 1888 Prince Heinrich of Prussia (see page 128)
(4) Ernst Ludwig (1868–1937), Grand Duke of Hesse 1892–1918, m. (1) 1894 Princess Victoria Melita of Saxe-Coburg (see below) (marriage dissolved 1901); (2) 1905 Princess Eleonore of Solms-Hohensolmslich. Issue:
(a) Princess Elizabeth (1895–1903)

(b) George, Grand Duke of Hesse (1906–37), m. Princess Cecilie of Greece (see above), and had issue, two sons, accidentally killed with parents 1937
(c) Ludwig, Grand Duke of Hesse (1908–68), m. 1937 Margaret, daughter of 1st Lord Geddes
(5) Frederick William (1870–3)
(6) Alix (Tsaritsa of Russia) (1872–1918), m. 1894 Nicholas II (1868–1918) Tsar of All the Russias 1894–1917, assassinated 16 July 1918. Issue:
(a) Grand Duchess Olga (1895–1918)
(b) Grand Duchess Tatiana (1897–1918)
(c) Grand Duchess Marie (1899–1918)
(d) Grand Duchess Anastasia (1901–18)
(e) Alexis, Tsarevich of Russia (1904–18)
(7) Marie (1874–8)

4. HRH PRINCE ALFRED Ernest Albert, Duke of Edinburgh, Admiral of the Fleet (1844–1900), m. 1874 Grand Duchess Marie Alexandrovna of Russia (1853–1920); succeeded as Duke of Saxe-Coburg and Gotha 22 August 1893. Issue:
(1) Alfred (Prince of Saxe-Coburg) (1874–99)
(2) Marie (1875–1938), m. 1893 Ferdinand (1865–1927), King of Roumania 1914–27. Issue:
(a) Carol II (1893–1953), King of Roumania 1930–40, m. (2) 1921 Princess Helena of Greece (see page 128) (marriage dissolved 1928); issue: Michael (b. 1921), King of Roumania 1927–30, 1940–7, m. 1948 Princess Anne of Bourbon-Parma, and has issue (five daughters)
(b) Elisabeth (1894–1956), m. 1921 George II, King of the Hellenes (see page 128)
(c) Marie (1900–61), m. 1922 Alexander (1888–1934), King of Yugoslavia 1921–34; issue: Petar II (1923–70), King of Yugoslavia 1934–45, m. 1944 Princess Alexandra of Greece (see page 128) and has issue (Crown Prince Alexander, b. 1945); Prince Tomislav (b. 1928), m. (1) 1957 Princess Margarita of Baden (daughter of Princess Theodora of Greece and Prince Berthold of Baden, see above); (2) 1982 Linda Bonney; and has issue (three sons, one daughter); Prince Andrej (1929–90), m. (1) 1956 Princess Christina of Hesse (daughter of Prince Christoph of Hesse and Princess Sophie of Greece, see above); (2) 1963 Princess Kira-Melita of Leiningen (see below) and has issue (three sons, two daughters)
(d) Prince Nicolas (1903–78)
(e) Princess Ileana (1909–91), m. (1) 1931 Archduke Anton of Austria; (2) 1954 Dr Stefan Issarescu; issue: Archduke Stefan (b. 1932); Archduchess Maria Ileana (1933–59); Archduchess Alexandra (b. 1935); Archduke Dominic (b. 1937); Archduchess Maria Magdalena (b. 1939); Archduchess Elisabeth (b. 1942)
(f) Prince Mircea (1913–16)
(3) Victoria Melita (1876–1936), m. (1) 1894 Grand Duke Ernst Ludwig of Hesse (see above) (marriage dissolved 1901); (2) 1905 the Grand Duke Kirill of Russia (1876–1938). Issue:
(a) Marie Kirillovna (1907–51), m. 1925 Prince Friedrich Karl of Leiningen; issue: Prince Emich (b. 1926); Prince Karl (b. 1928); Princess Kira-Melita (b. 1930), m. Prince Andrej of Yugoslavia (see above); Princess Margarita (b. 1932); Princess Mechtilde (b. 1936); Prince Friedrich (b. 1938)
(b) Kira Kirillovna (1909–67), m. 1938 Prince Louis Ferdinand of Prussia (see page 128); issue: Prince Friedrich Wilhelm (b. 1939); Prince Michael (b. 1940); Princess Marie (b. 1942); Princess Kira (b. 1943); Prince Louis Ferdinand (1944–77); Prince Christian (b. 1946); Princess Xenia (1949–92)
(c) Vladimir Kirillovich (1917–92), m. 1948 Princess Leonida Bagration-Mukhransky; issue: Grand Duchess Maria (b. 1953), and has issue
(4) Alexandra (1878–1942), m. 1896 Ernst, Prince of Hohenlohe Langenburg. Issue:
(a) Gottfried (1897–1960), m. 1931 Princess Margarita of Greece (see above); issue: Prince Kraft (b. 1935), Princess Beatrix (b. 1936), Prince Georg Andreas (b. 1938), Prince Ruprecht (1944–); Prince Albrecht (1944–92)
(b) Maria (1899–1967), m. 1916 Prince Friedrich of Schleswig-Holstein-Sonderburg-Glücksburg; issue: Prince Peter (1922–80); Princess Marie (b. 1927)
(c) Princess Alexandra (1901–63)
(d) Princess Irma (1902–86)
(5) Princess Beatrice (1884–1966), m. 1909 Alfonso of Orleans, Infante of Spain. Issue:

(a) Prince Alvaro (b. 1910), m. 1937 Carla Parodi-Delfino;
issue: Doña Gerarda (b. 1939); Don Alonso (1941–75); Doña
Beatriz (b. 1943); Don Alvaro (b. 1947)
(b) Prince Alonso (1912–36)
(c) Prince Ataulfo (1913–74)

5. HRH Princess Helena Augusta Victoria (1846–1923), m. 1866
Prince Christian of Schleswig-Holstein-Sonderburg-Augustenburg (1831–1917). Issue:
(1) Prince Christian Victor (1867–1900)
(2) Prince Albert (1869–1931), Duke of Schleswig-Holstein
1921–31
(3) Princess Helena (1870–1948)
(4) Princess Marie Louise (1872–1956), m. 1891 Prince Aribert
of Anhalt (marriage dissolved 1900)
(5) Prince Harold (12–20 May 1876)

6. HRH Princess Louise Caroline Alberta (1848–1939), m. 1871
the Marquess of Lorne, afterwards 9th Duke of Argyll (1845–1914);
without issue

7. HRH Prince Arthur William Patrick Albert, Duke of
Connaught, Field Marshal (1850–1942), m. 1879 Princess Louisa of
Prussia (1860–1917). Issue:
(1) Margaret (1882–1920), m. 1905 Crown Prince Gustaf Adolf
(1882–1973), afterwards King of Sweden 1950–73. Issue:
(a) Gustaf Adolf, Duke of Västerbotten (1906–47), m. 1932
Princess Sibylla of Saxe-Coburg-Gotha (see below); issue:
Princess Margaretha (b. 1934); Princess Birgitta (b. 1937);
Princess Désirée (b. 1938); Princess Christina (b. 1943); Carl
XVI Gustaf, King of Sweden (b. 1946)
(b) Count Sigvard Bernadotte (b. 1907), m.; issue: Count
Michael (b. 1944)
(c) Princess Ingrid (Queen Mother of Denmark) (b. 1910), m.
1935 Frederick IX (1899–72), King of Denmark 1947–72;
issue: Margrethe II, Queen of Denmark (b. 1940); Princess
Benedikte (b. 1944); Princess Anne-Marie (b. 1946), m. 1964
Constantine II of Greece (see page 129)
(d) Prince Bertil, Duke of Halland (b. 1912), m. 1976 Mrs
Lilian Craig
(e) Count Carl Bernadotte (b. 1916), m. (1) 1946 Mrs Kerstin
Johnson; (2) 1988 Countess Gunnila Bussler
(2) Arthur (1883–1938), m. 1913 HH the Duchess of Fife (see
page 129). Issue:
Alastair Arthur, 2nd Duke of Connaught (1914–43)
(3) (Victoria) Patricia (1886–1974), m. 1919 Adm. Hon. Sir
Alexander Ramsay. Issue:

Alexander Ramsay of Mar (b. 1919), m. 1956 Hon. Flora
Fraser (Lady Saltoun)

8. HRH Prince Leopold George Duncan Albert, Duke of Albany
(1853–84), m. 1882 Princess Helena of Waldeck (1861–1922). Issue:
(1) Alice (1883–1981), m. 1904 Prince Alexander of Teck
(1874–1957), cr. 1st Earl of Athlone 1917. Issue:
(a) Lady May (1906–94), m. 1931 Sir Henry Abel-Smith,
KCMG, KCVO, DSO; issue: Anne (b. 1932); Richard (b. 1933);
Elizabeth (b. 1936)
(b) Rupert, Viscount Trematon (1907–28)
(c) Prince Maurice (March–September 1910)
(2) Charles Edward (1884–1954), Duke of Albany 1884 until
title suspended 1917, Duke of Saxe-Coburg-Gotha 1900–18, m.
1905 Princess Victoria Adelheid of Schleswig-Holstein-
Sonderburg-Glücksburg. Issue:
(a) Prince Johann Leopold (1906–72), and has issue, including Ernst-Leopold (b. 1935) in whom is vested the right to
petition for restoration of the Dukedom of Albany
(b) Princess Sibylla (1908–72) m. 1932 Prince Gustav Adolf
of Sweden (see above)
(c) Prince Dietmar Hubertus (1909–43)
(d) Princess Caroline (1912–83), and has issue
(e) Prince Friedrich Josias (b. 1918), and has issue

9. HRH Princess Beatrice Mary Victoria Feodore (1857–1944),
m. 1885 Prince Henry of Battenberg (1858–96). Issue:
(1) Alexander, 1st Marquess of Carisbrooke (1886–1960), m.
1917 Lady Irene Denison. Issue:
Lady Iris Mountbatten (1920–82), m.; issue: Robin A. Bryan (b.
1957)
(2) Victoria Eugénie (1887–1969), m. 1906 Alfonso XIII
(1886–1941) King of Spain 1886–1931. Issue:
(a) Prince Alfonso (1907–38)
(b) Prince Jaime (1908–75), and has issue
(c) Princess Beatrice (b. 1909), and has issue
(d) Princess Maria (b. 1911), and has issue
(e) Prince Juan (1913–93), Count of Barcelona, and has issue:
Princess Maria (b. 1936); Juan Carlos I, King of Spain (b.
1938), m. 1962 Princess Sophie of Greece (see page 129)
and has issue (one son, two daughters); Princess Margarita
(b. 1939)
(f) Prince Gonzalo (1914–34)
(3) Major Lord Leopold Mountbatten (1889–1922)
(4) Maurice (1891–1914), died of wounds received in action

Kings and Queens

ENGLISH KINGS AND QUEENS 927 to 1603

HOUSES OF CERDIC AND DENMARK

Reign

927–939   Æthelstan
Son of Edward the Elder, by Ecgwynn, and
grandson of Alfred
Acceded to Wessex and Mercia c.924, established
direct rule over Northumbria 927, effectively
creating the Kingdom of England
Reigned 15 years

939–946   Edmund I
Born 921, son of Edward the Elder, by Eadgifu
Married (1) Ælfgifu (2) Æthelflæd
Killed aged 25, *reigned* 6 years

946–955   Eadred
Son of Edward the Elder, by Eadgifu
Reigned 9 years

955–959   Eadwig
Born before 943, son of Edmund and Ælfgifu
Married Ælfgifu
Reigned 3 years

959–975   Edgar I
Born 943, son of Edmund and Ælfgifu
Married (1) Æthelflæd (2) Wulfthryth (3) Ælfthryth
Died aged 32, *reigned* 15 years

975–978   Edward I (the Martyr)
Born c.962, son of Edgar and Æthelflæd
Assassinated aged c.16, *reigned* 2 years

978–1016   Æthelred (the Unready)
Born c.968/969, son of Edgar and Ælfthryth
Married (1) Ælfgifu (2) Emma, daughter of
Richard I, count of Normandy
1013–14 dispossessed of kingdom by Swegn
Forkbeard (king of Denmark 987–1014)
Died aged c.47, *reigned* 38 years

1016   Edmund II (Ironside)
Born before 993, son of Æthelred and Ælfgifu
Married Ealdgyth
Died aged over 23, *reigned* 7 months
(April–November)

1016–1035   Cnut (Canute)
Born c.995, son of Swegn Forkbeard, king of
Denmark, and Gunhild
Married (1) Ælfgifu (2) Emma, widow of
Æthelred the Unready
Gained submission of West Saxons 1015,
Northumbrians 1016, Mercia 1016, king of all
England after Edmund's death

	King of Denmark 1019–35, king of Norway 1028–35
	Died aged *c.*40, *reigned* 19 years
1035–1040	HAROLD I (Harefoot)
	*Born c.*1016/17, son of Cnut and Ælfgifu
	Married Ælfgifu
	1035 recognized as regent for himself and his brother Harthacnut; 1037 recognized as king
	Died aged *c.*23, *reigned* 4 years
1040–1042	HARTHACNUT
	*Born c.*1018, son of Cnut and Emma
	Titular king of Denmark from 1028
	Acknowledged king of England 1035–7 with Harold I as regent; effective king after Harold's death
	Died aged *c.*24, *reigned* 2 years
1042–1066	EDWARD II (the Confessor)
	Born between 1002 and 1005, son of Æthelred the Unready and Emma
	Married Eadgyth, daughter of Godwine, earl of Wessex
	Died aged over 60, *reigned* 23 years
1066	HAROLD II (Godwinesson)
	*Born c.*1020, son of Godwine, earl of Wessex, and Gytha
	Married (1) Eadgyth (2) Ealdgyth
	Killed in battle aged *c.*46, *reigned* 10 months (January–October)

THE HOUSE OF NORMANDY

1066–1087	WILLIAM I (the Conqueror)
	Born 1027/8, son of Robert I, duke of Normandy; obtained the Crown by conquest
	Married Matilda, daughter of Baldwin, count of Flanders
	Died aged *c.*60, *reigned* 20 years
1087–1100	WILLIAM II (Rufus)
	Born between 1056 and 1060, third son of William I; succeeded his father in England only
	Killed aged *c.*40, *reigned* 12 years
1100–1135	HENRY I (Beauclerk)
	Born 1068, fourth son of William I
	Married (1) Edith or Matilda, daughter of Malcolm III of Scotland (2) Adela, daughter of Godfrey, count of Louvain
	Died aged 67, *reigned* 35 years
1135–1154	STEPHEN
	Born not later than 1100, third son of Adela, daughter of William I, and Stephen, count of Blois
	Married Matilda, daughter of Eustace, count of Boulogne
	1141 (February–November) held captive by adherents of Matilda, daughter of Henry I, who contested the crown until 1153
	Died aged over 53, *reigned* 18 years

THE HOUSE OF ANJOU (PLANTAGENETS)

1154–1189	HENRY II (Curtmantle)
	Born 1133, son of Matilda, daughter of Henry I, and Geoffrey, count of Anjou
	Married Eleanor, daughter of William, duke of Aquitaine, and divorced queen of Louis VII of France
	Died aged 56, *reigned* 34 years
1189–1199	RICHARD I (Coeur de Lion)
	Born 1157, third son of Henry II
	Married Berengaria, daughter of Sancho VI, king of Navarre
	Died aged 42, *reigned* 9 years
1199–1216	JOHN (Lackland)
	Born 1167, fifth son of Henry II
	Married (1) Isabella or Avisa, daughter of William, earl of Gloucester (divorced) (2) Isabella, daughter of Aymer, count of Angoulême
	Died aged 48, *reigned* 17 years

1216–1272	HENRY III
	Born 1207, son of John and Isabella of Angoulême
	Married Eleanor, daughter of Raymond, count of Provence
	Died aged 65, *reigned* 56 years
1272–1307	EDWARD I (Longshanks)
	Born 1239, eldest son of Henry III
	Married (1) Eleanor, daughter of Ferdinand III, king of Castile (2) Margaret, daughter of Philip III of France
	Died aged 68, *reigned* 34 years
1307–1327	EDWARD II
	Born 1284, eldest surviving son of Edward I and Eleanor
	Married Isabella, daughter of Philip IV of France
	Deposed January 1327, *killed* September 1327 aged 43, *reigned* 19 years
1327–1377	EDWARD III
	Born 1312, eldest son of Edward II
	Married Philippa, daughter of William, count of Hainault
	Died aged 64, *reigned* 50 years
1377–1399	RICHARD II
	Born 1367, son of Edward (the Black Prince), eldest son of Edward III
	Married (1) Anne, daughter of Emperor Charles IV (2) Isabelle, daughter of Charles VI of France
	Deposed September 1399, *killed* February 1400 aged 33, *reigned* 22 years

THE HOUSE OF LANCASTER

1399–1413	HENRY IV
	Born 1366, son of John of Gaunt, fourth son of Edward III, and Blanche, daughter of Henry, duke of Lancaster
	Married (1) Mary, daughter of Humphrey, earl of Hereford (2) Joan, daughter of Charles, king of Navarre, and widow of John, duke of Brittany
	Died aged *c.*47, *reigned* 13 years
1413–1422	HENRY V
	Born 1387, eldest surviving son of Henry IV and Mary
	Married Catherine, daughter of Charles VI of France
	Died aged 34, *reigned* 9 years
1422–1471	HENRY VI
	Born 1421, son of Henry V
	Married Margaret, daughter of René, duke of Anjou and count of Provence
	Deposed March 1461, *restored* October 1470
	Deposed April 1471, *killed* May 1471 aged 49, *reigned* 39 years

THE HOUSE OF YORK

1461–1483	EDWARD IV
	Born 1442, eldest son of Richard of York, who was the grandson of Edmund, fifth son of Edward III, and the son of Anne, great-granddaughter of Lionel, third son of Edward III
	Married Elizabeth Woodville, daughter of Richard, Lord Rivers, and widow of Sir John Grey
	Acceded March 1461, *deposed* October 1470, *restored* April 1471
	Died aged 40, *reigned* 21 years
1483	EDWARD V
	Born 1470, eldest son of Edward IV
	Deposed June 1483, *died* probably July–September 1483, aged 12, *reigned* 2 months (April–June)
1483–1485	RICHARD III
	Born 1452, fourth son of Richard of York and brother of Edward IV
	Married Anne Neville, daughter of Richard, earl of Warwick, and widow of Edward, Prince of Wales, son of Henry VI
	Killed in battle aged 32, *reigned* 2 years

THE HOUSE OF TUDOR

1485–1509   HENRY VII
Born 1457, son of Margaret Beaufort, great-granddaughter of John of Gaunt, fourth son of Edward III, and Edmund Tudor, earl of Richmond
Married Elizabeth, daughter of Edward IV
Died aged 52, reigned 23 years

1509–1547   HENRY VIII
Born 1491, second son of Henry VII
Married (1) Catherine, daughter of Ferdinand II, king of Aragon, and widow of his elder brother Arthur (divorced) (2) Anne, daughter of Sir Thomas Boleyn (executed) (3) Jane, daughter of Sir John Seymour (died in childbirth) (4) Anne, daughter of John, duke of Cleves (divorced) (5) Catherine Howard, niece of the Duke of Norfolk (executed) (6) Catherine, daughter of Sir Thomas Parr and widow of Lord Latimer
Died aged 55, reigned 37 years

1547–1553   EDWARD VI
Born 1537, son of Henry VIII and Jane Seymour
Died aged 15, reigned 6 years

1553   JANE
Born 1537, daughter of Frances, daughter of Mary Tudor, the younger sister of Henry VIII, and Henry Grey, duke of Suffolk
Married Lord Guildford Dudley, son of the Duke of Northumberland
Deposed July 1553, executed February 1554 aged 16, reigned 14 days

1553–1558   MARY I
Born 1516, daughter of Henry VIII and Catherine of Aragon
Married Philip II of Spain
Died aged 42, reigned 5 years

1558–1603   ELIZABETH I
Born 1533, daughter of Henry VIII and Anne Boleyn
Died aged 69, reigned 44 years

BRITISH KINGS AND QUEENS SINCE 1603

THE HOUSE OF STUART

Reign
1603–1625   JAMES I (VI OF SCOTLAND)
Born 1566, son of Mary, queen of Scots and granddaughter of Margaret Tudor, elder daughter of Henry VII, and Henry Stewart, Lord Darnley
Married Anne, daughter of Frederick II of Denmark
Died aged 58, reigned 22 years
(see also page 134)

1625–1649   CHARLES I
Born 1600, second son of James I
Married Henrietta Maria, daughter of Henry IV of France
Executed 1649 aged 48, reigned 23 years

COMMONWEALTH DECLARED 19 May 1649
1649–53 Government by a council of state
1653–8 Oliver Cromwell, Lord Protector
1658–9 Richard Cromwell, Lord Protector

1660–1685   CHARLES II
Born 1630, eldest son of Charles I
Married Catherine, daughter of John IV of Portugal
Died aged 54, reigned 24 years

1685–1688   JAMES II (VII of Scotland)
Born 1633, second son of Charles I
Married (1) Lady Anne Hyde, daughter of Edward, earl of Clarendon (2) Mary, daughter of Alphonso, duke of Modena
Reign ended with flight from kingdom December 1688
Died 1701 aged 67, reigned 3 years

INTERREGNUM 11 December 1688 to 12 February 1689

1689–1702   WILLIAM III
Born 1650, son of William II, prince of Orange, and Mary Stuart, daughter of Charles I
Married Mary, elder daughter of James II
Died aged 51, reigned 13 years

and
1689–1694   MARY II
Born 1662, elder daughter of James II and Anne
Died aged 32, reigned 5 years

1702–1714   ANNE
Born 1665, younger daughter of James II and Anne
Married Prince George of Denmark, son of Frederick III of Denmark
Died aged 49, reigned 12 years

THE HOUSE OF HANOVER

1714–1727   GEORGE I (Elector of Hanover)
Born 1660, son of Sophia (daughter of Frederick, elector palatine, and Elizabeth Stuart, daughter of James I) and Ernest Augustus, elector of Hanover
Married Sophia Dorothea, daughter of George William, duke of Lüneburg-Celle
Died aged 67, reigned 12 years

1727–1760   GEORGE II
Born 1683, son of George I
Married Caroline, daughter of John Frederick, margrave of Brandenburg-Anspach
Died aged 76, reigned 33 years

1760–1820   GEORGE III
Born 1738, son of Frederick, eldest son of George II
Married Charlotte, daughter of Charles Louis, duke of Mecklenburg-Strelitz
Died aged 81, reigned 59 years

REGENCY 1811–20
Prince of Wales regent owing to the insanity of George III

1820–1830   GEORGE IV
Born 1762, eldest son of George III
Married Caroline, daughter of Charles, duke of Brunswick-Wolfenbüttel
Died aged 67, reigned 10 years

1830–1837   WILLIAM IV
Born 1765, third son of George III
Married Adelaide, daughter of George, duke of Saxe-Meiningen
Died aged 71, reigned 7 years

1837–1901   VICTORIA
Born 1819, daughter of Edward, fourth son of George III
Married Prince Albert of Saxe-Coburg and Gotha
Died aged 81, reigned 63 years

THE HOUSE OF SAXE-COBURG AND GOTHA

1901–1910   EDWARD VII
Born 1841, eldest son of Victoria and Albert
Married Alexandra, daughter of Christian IX of Denmark
Died aged 68, reigned 9 years

THE HOUSE OF WINDSOR

1910–1936   GEORGE V
Born 1865, second son of Edward VII
Married Victoria Mary, daughter of Francis, duke of Teck
Died aged 70, reigned 25 years

1936   EDWARD VIII
Born 1894, eldest son of George V
Married (1937) Mrs Wallis Warfield
Abdicated 1936, died 1972 aged 77, reigned 10 months (20 January to 11 December)

1936–1952   GEORGE VI
Born 1895, second son of George V
Married Lady Elizabeth Bowes-Lyon, daughter of 14th Earl of Strathmore and Kinghorne (see also pages 117–8)
Died aged 56, reigned 15 years

1952–   ELIZABETH II
Born 1926, elder daughter of George VI
Married Philip, son of Prince Andrew of Greece
(see also page 117)
WHOM GOD PRESERVE

KINGS AND QUEENS OF SCOTS 1016 TO 1603

Reign
1016–1034   MALCOLM II
Born c.954, son of Kenneth II
Acceded to Alba 1005, secured Lothian c.1016,
obtained Strathclyde for his grandson Duncan
c.1016, thus forming the Kingdom of Scotland
Died aged c.80, reigned 18 years
1034–1040   DUNCAN I
Son of Bethoc, daughter of Malcolm II, and
Crinan
Married a cousin of Siward, earl of Northumbria
Reigned 5 years
1040–1057   MACBETH
Born c.1005, son of a daughter of Malcolm II and
Finlaec, mormaer of Moray
Married Gruoch, granddaughter of Kenneth III
Killed aged c.52, reigned 17 years
1057–1058   LULACH
Born c. 1032, son of Gillacomgan, mormaer of
Moray, and Gruoch (and stepson of Macbeth)
Died aged c.26, reigned 7 months (August–March)
1058–1093   MALCOLM III (Canmore)
Born c.1031, elder son of Duncan I
Married (1) Ingibiorg (2) Margaret (St Margaret),
granddaughter of Edmund II of England
Killed in battle aged c.62, reigned 35 years
1093–1097   DONALD III BÁN
Born c. 1033, second son of Duncan I
Deposed May 1094, restored November 1094, deposed
October 1097, reigned 3 years
1094   DUNCAN II
Born c.1060, elder son of Malcolm III and Ingibiorg
Married Octreda of Dunbar
Killed aged c.34, reigned 6 months
(May–November)
1097–1107   EDGAR
Born c.1074, second son of Malcolm III and
Margaret
Died aged c.32, reigned 9 years
1107–1124   ALEXANDER I (The Fierce)
Born c.1077, fifth son of Malcolm III and Margaret
Married Sybilla, illegitimate daughter of Henry I
of England
Died aged c.47, reigned 17 years
1124–1153   DAVID I (The Saint)
Born c.1085, sixth son of Malcolm III and Margaret
Married Matilda, daughter of Waltheof, earl of
Huntingdon
Died aged c.68, reigned 29 years
1153–1165   MALCOLM IV (The Maiden)
Born c.1141, son of Henry, earl of Huntingdon,
second son of David I
Died aged c.24, reigned 12 years
1165–1214   WILLIAM I (The Lion)
Born c.1142, brother of Malcolm IV
Married Ermengarde, daughter of Richard,
viscount of Beaumont
Died aged c.72, reigned 49 years
1214–1249   ALEXANDER II
Born 1198, son of William I
Married (1) Joan, daughter of John, king of
England (2) Marie, daughter of Ingelram de Coucy
Died aged 50, reigned 34 years

1249–1286   ALEXANDER III
Born 1241, son of Alexander II and Marie
Married (1) Margaret, daughter of Henry III of
England (2) Yolande, daughter of the Count of
Dreux
Killed accidentally aged 44, reigned 36 years
1286–1290   MARGARET (The Maid of Norway)
Born 1283, daughter of Margaret (daughter of
Alexander III) and Eric II of Norway
Died aged 7, reigned 4 years

FIRST INTERREGNUM 1290–2
Throne disputed by 13 competitors. Crown
awarded to John Balliol by adjudication of Edward
I of England

THE HOUSE OF BALLIOL

1292–1296   JOHN (Balliol)
Born c.1250, son of Dervorguilla, great-great-
granddaughter of David I, and John de Balliol
Married Isabella, daughter of John, earl of Surrey
Abdicated 1296, died 1313 aged c.63, reigned 3 years

SECOND INTERREGNUM 1296–1306
Edward I of England declared John Balliol to have
forfeited the throne for contumacy in 1296 and
took the government of Scotland into his own
hands

THE HOUSE OF BRUCE

1306–1329   ROBERT I (Bruce)
Born 1274, son of Robert Bruce and Marjorie,
countess of Carrick, and great-grandson of the
second daughter of David, earl of Huntingdon,
brother of William I
Married (1) Isabella, daughter of Donald, earl of
Mar (2) Elizabeth, daughter of Richard, earl of
Ulster
Died aged 54, reigned 23 years
1329–1371   DAVID II
Born 1324, son of Robert I and Elizabeth
Married (1) Joanna, daughter of Edward II of
England (2) Margaret Drummond, widow of Sir
John Logie (divorced)
Died aged 46, reigned 41 years

1332 Edward Balliol, son of John Balliol, crowned
King of Scots September, expelled December
1333–6 Edward Balliol restored as King of Scots

THE HOUSE OF STEWART

1371–1390   ROBERT II (Stewart)
Born 1316, son of Marjorie, daughter of Robert I,
and Walter, High Steward of Scotland
Married (1) Elizabeth, daughter of Sir Robert
Mure of Rowallan (2) Euphemia, daughter of
Hugh, earl of Ross
Died aged 74, reigned 19 years
1390–1406   ROBERT III
Born c.1337, son of Robert II and Elizabeth
Married Annabella, daughter of Sir John
Drummond of Stobhall
Died aged c.69, reigned 16 years
1406–1437   JAMES I
Born 1394, son of Robert III
Married Joan Beaufort, daughter of John, earl of
Somerset
Assassinated aged 42, reigned 30 years
1437–1460   JAMES II
Born 1430, son of James I
Married Mary, daughter of Arnold, duke of
Gueldres
Killed accidentally aged 29, reigned 23 years
1460–1488   JAMES III
Born 1452, son of James II
Married Margaret, daughter of Christian I of
Denmark
Assassinated aged 36, reigned 27 years

1488–1513	JAMES IV *Born* 1473, son of James III *Married* Margaret Tudor, daughter of Henry VII of England *Killed* in battle aged 40, *reigned* 25 years
1513–1542	JAMES V *Born* 1512, son of James IV *Married* (1) Madeleine, daughter of Francis I of France (2) Mary of Lorraine, daughter of the Duc de Guise *Died* aged 30, *reigned* 29 years
1542–1567	MARY *Born* 1542, daughter of James V and Mary *Married* (1) the Dauphin, afterwards Francis II of France (2) Henry Stewart, Lord Darnley (3) James Hepburn, earl of Bothwell *Abdicated* 1567, prisoner in England from 1568, executed 1587, *reigned* 24 years
1567–1625	JAMES VI (and I of England) *Born* 1566, son of Mary, queen of Scots, and Henry, Lord Darnley Acceded 1567 to the Scottish throne, *reigned* 58 years Succeeded 1603 to the English throne, so joining the English and Scottish crowns in one person. The two kingdoms remained distinct until 1707 when the parliaments of the kingdoms became conjoined For British Kings and Queens since 1603, *see* pages 132–3

WELSH SOVEREIGNS AND PRINCES

Wales was ruled by sovereign princes from the earliest times until the death of Llywelyn in 1282. The first English Prince of Wales was the son of Edward I, who was born in Caernarvon town on 25 April 1284. According to a discredited legend, he was presented to the Welsh chieftains as their prince, in fulfilment of a promise that they should have a prince who 'could not speak a word of English' and should be native born. This son, who afterwards became Edward II, was created 'Prince of Wales and Earl of Chester' at the Lincoln Parliament on 7 February 1301.

The title Prince of Wales is borne after individual conferment and is not inherited at birth, though some Princes have been declared and styled Prince of Wales but never formally so created (*s.*). The title was conferred on Prince Charles by The Queen on 26 July 1958. He was invested at Caernarvon on 1 July 1969.

INDEPENDENT PRINCES AD 844 TO 1282

844–878	Rhodri the Great
878–916	Anarawd, son of Rhodri
916–950	Hywel Dda, the Good
950–979	Iago ab Idwal (or Ieuaf)
979–985	Hywel ab Ieuaf, the Bad
985–986	Cadwallon, his brother
986–999	Maredudd ab Owain ap Hywel Dda
999–1008	Cynan ap Hywel ab Ieuaf
1018–1023	Llywelyn ap Seisyll
1023–1039	Iago ab Idwal ap Meurig
1039–1063	Gruffydd ap Llywelyn ap Seisyll
1063–1075	Bleddyn ap Cynfyn
1075–1081	Trahaern ap Caradog
1081–1137	Gruffydd ap Cynan ab Iago
1137–1170	Owain Gwynedd
1170–1194	Dafydd ab Owain Gwynedd
1194–1240	Llywelyn Fawr, the Great
1240–1246	Dafydd ap Llywelyn
1246–1282	Llywelyn ap Gruffydd ap Llywelyn

ENGLISH PRINCES SINCE 1301

1301	Edward (Edward II)
1343	Edward the Black Prince, s. of Edward III
1376	Richard (Richard II), s. of the Black Prince
1399	Henry of Monmouth (Henry V)
1454	Edward of Westminster, son of Henry VI

1471	Edward of Westminster (Edward V)
1483	Edward, son of Richard III (d. 1484)
1489	Arthur Tudor, son of Henry VII
1504	Henry Tudor (Henry VIII)
1610	Henry Stuart, son of James I (d. 1612)
1616	Charles Stuart (Charles I)
*c.*1638 (*s.*)	Charles (Charles II)
1688 (*s.*)	James Francis Edward (The Old Pretender) (d. 1766)
1714	George Augustus (George II)
1729	Frederick Lewis, s. of George II (d. 1751)
1751	George William Frederick (George III)
1762	George Augustus Frederick (George IV)
1841	Albert Edward (Edward VII)
1901	George (George V)
1910	Edward (Edward VIII)
1958	Charles Philip Arthur George

PRINCESSES ROYAL

The style Princess Royal is conferred at the Sovereign's discretion on his or her eldest daughter. It is an honorary title, held for life, and cannot be inherited or passed on. It was first conferred on Princess Mary, daughter of Charles I, in approximately 1642.

*c.*1642	Princess Mary (1631–60), daughter of Charles I
1727	Princess Anne (1709–59), daughter of George II
1766	Princess Charlotte (1766–1828), daughter of George III
1840	Princess Victoria (1840–1901), daughter of Victoria
1905	Princess Louise (1867–1931), daughter of Edward VII
1932	Princess Mary (1897–1965), daughter of George V
1987	Princess Anne (b. 1950), daughter of Elizabeth II

Precedence

ENGLAND AND WALES

The Sovereign
The Prince Philip, Duke of
  Edinburgh
The Prince of Wales
The Sovereign's younger sons
The Sovereign's grandsons
The Sovereign's cousins
Archbishop of Canterbury
Lord High Chancellor
Archbishop of York
The Prime Minister
Lord President of the Council
Speaker of the House of Commons
Lord Privy Seal
Ambassadors and High
  Commissioners
Lord Great Chamberlain
Earl Marshal
Lord Steward of the Household
Lord Chamberlain of the Household
Master of the Horse
Dukes, according to their patent of
  creation:
  (1) of England
  (2) of Scotland
  (3) of Great Britain
  (4) of Ireland
  (5) those created since the Union
Ministers and Envoys
Eldest sons of Dukes of Blood Royal
Marquesses, according to their
  patent of creation:
  (1) of England
  (2) of Scotland
  (3) of Great Britain
  (4) of Ireland
  (5) those created since the Union
Dukes' eldest sons
Earls, according to their patent of
  creation:
  (1) of England
  (2) of Scotland
  (3) of Great Britain
  (4) of Ireland
  (5) those created since the Union
Younger sons of Dukes of Blood
  Royal
Marquesses' eldest sons
Dukes' younger sons
Viscounts, according to their patent
  of creation:
  (1) of England
  (2) of Scotland
  (3) of Great Britain
  (4) of Ireland
  (5) those created since the Union
Earls' eldest sons
Marquesses' younger sons
Bishops of London, Durham and
  Winchester

Other English Diocesan Bishops,
  according to seniority of
  consecration
Suffragan Bishops, according to
  seniority of consecration
Secretaries of State, if of the degree
  of a Baron
Barons, according to their patent of
  creation:
  (1) of England
  (2) of Scotland
  (3) of Great Britain
  (4) of Ireland
  (5) those created since the Union
Treasurer of the Household
Comptroller of the Household
Vice-Chamberlain of the Household
Secretaries of State under the degree
  of Baron
Viscounts' eldest sons
Earls' younger sons
Barons' eldest sons
Knights of the Garter
Privy Counsellors
Chancellor of the Exchequer
Chancellor of the Duchy of
  Lancaster
Lord Chief Justice of England
Master of the Rolls
President of the Family Division
Vice-Chancellor
Lords Justices of Appeal
Judges of the High Court
Viscounts' younger sons
Barons' younger sons
Sons of Life Peers
Baronets, according to date of patent
Knights of the Thistle
Knights Grand Cross of the Bath
Members of the Order of Merit
Knights Grand Commanders of the
  Star of India
Knights Grand Cross of St Michael
  and St George
Knights Grand Commanders of the
  Indian Empire
Knights Grand Cross of the Royal
  Victorian Order
Knights Grand Cross of the British
  Empire
Companions of Honour
Knights Commanders of the Bath
Knights Commanders of the Star of
  India
Knights Commanders of St Michael
  and St George
Knights Commanders of the Indian
  Empire
Knights Commanders of the Royal
  Victorian Order
Knights Commanders of the British
  Empire
Knights Bachelor
Vice-Chancellor of the County
  Palatine of Lancaster

Official Referees of the Supreme
  Court
Circuit judges and judges of the
  Mayor's and City of London
  Court
Companions of the Bath
Companions of the Star of India
Companions of St Michael and St
  George
Companions of the Indian Empire
Commanders of the Royal Victorian
  Order
Commanders of the British Empire
Companions of the Distinguished
  Service Order
Lieutenants of the Royal Victorian
  Order
Officers of the British Empire
Companions of the Imperial Service
  Order
Eldest sons of younger sons of Peers
Baronets' eldest sons
Eldest sons of Knights, in the same
  order as their fathers
Members of the Royal Victorian
  Order
Members of the British Empire
Younger sons of the younger sons of
  Peers
Baronets' younger sons
Younger sons of Knights, in the same
  order as their fathers
Naval, Military, Air, and other
  Esquires by office

WOMEN

Women take the same rank as their
husbands or as their brothers; but the
daughter of a peer marrying a commoner retains her title as Lady or
Honourable. Daughters of peers rank
next immediately after the wives of
their elder brothers, and before their
younger brothers' wives. Daughters
of peers marrying peers of lower
degree take the same order of precedence as that of their husbands;
thus the daughter of a Duke marrying
a Baron becomes of the rank of
Baroness only, while her sisters
married to commoners retain their
rank and take precedence of the
Baroness. Merely official rank on the
husband's part does not give any
similar precedence to the wife.

  Peeresses in their own right take
the same precedence as peers of the
same rank, i.e. from their date of
creation.

Forms of address

It is only possible to cover here the forms of address for peers, baronets and knights, their wife and children, and Privy Counsellors. Greater detail should be sought in one of the publications devoted to the subject.

Both formal and social forms of address are given where usage differs; nowadays, the social form is generally preferred to the formal, which increasingly is used only for official documents and on very formal occasions.

F— represents forename
S— represents surname

BARON – *Envelope (formal)*, The Right Hon. Lord —; *(social)*, The Lord —. *Letter (formal)*, My Lord; *(social)*, Dear Lord —. *Spoken*, Lord —.

BARON'S WIFE – *Envelope (formal)*, The Right Hon. Lady —; *(social)*, The Lady —. *Letter (formal)*, My Lady; *(social)*, Dear Lady —. *Spoken*, Lady —.

BARON'S CHILDREN – *Envelope*, The Hon. F—S—. *Letter*, Dear Mr/Miss/Mrs S—. *Spoken*, Mr/Miss/Mrs S—.

BARONESS IN OWN RIGHT – *Envelope*, may be addressed in same way as a Baron's wife or, if she prefers *(formal)*, The Right Hon. the Baroness —; *(social)*, The Baroness —. Otherwise as for a Baron's wife.

BARONET – *Envelope*, Sir F—S—, Bt. *Letter (formal)*, Dear Sir; *(social)*, Dear Sir F—. *Spoken*, Sir F—.

BARONET'S WIFE – *Envelope*, Lady S—. *Letter (formal)*, Dear Madam; *(social)*, Dear Lady S—. *Spoken*, Lady S—.

COUNTESS IN OWN RIGHT – As for an Earl's wife.

COURTESY TITLES – The heir apparent to a Duke, Marquess or Earl uses the highest of his father's other titles as a courtesy title. (For list, *see* pages 165–6.) The holder of a courtesy title is not styled The Most Hon. or The Right Hon., and in correspondence 'The' is omitted before the title. The heir apparent to a Scottish title may use the title 'Master' (*see* below).

DAME – *Envelope*, Dame F—S—, followed by appropriate post-nominal letters. *Letter (formal)*, Dear Madam; *(social)*, Dear Dame F—. *Spoken*, Dame F—.

DUKE – *Envelope (formal)*, His Grace the Duke of —; *(social)*, The Duke of —. *Letter (formal)*, My Lord Duke; *(social)*, Dear Duke. *Spoken (formal)*, Your Grace; *(social)*, Duke.

DUKE'S WIFE – *Envelope (formal)*, Her Grace the Duchess of —; *(social)*, The Duchess of —. *Letter (formal)*, Dear Madam; *(social)*, Dear Duchess. *Spoken*, Duchess.

DUKE'S ELDEST SON – *see* Courtesy titles.

DUKE'S YOUNGER SONS – *Envelope*, Lord F—S—. *Letter (formal)*, My Lord; *(social)*, Dear Lord F—. *Spoken (formal)*, My Lord; *(social)*, Lord F—.

DUKE'S DAUGHTER – *Envelope*, Lady F—S—. *Letter (formal)*, Dear Madam; *(social)*, Dear Lady F—. *Spoken*, Lady F—.

EARL – *Envelope (formal)*, The Right Hon. the Earl (of) —; *(social)*, The Earl (of) —. *Letter (formal)*, My Lord; *(social)*, Dear Lord —. *Spoken (formal)*, My Lord; *(social)*, Lord —.

EARL'S WIFE – *Envelope (formal)*, The Right Hon. the Countess (of) —; *(social)*, The Countess (of) —. *Letter (formal)*, Madam; *(social)*, Lady —. *Spoken (formal)*, Madam; *(social)*, Lady —.

EARL'S CHILDREN – *Eldest son, see* Courtesy titles. *Younger sons*, The Hon. F—S— (for forms of address, *see* Baron's children). *Daughters*, Lady F—S— (for forms of address, *see* Duke's daughter).

KNIGHT (BACHELOR) – *Envelope*, Sir F—S—. *Letter (formal)*, Dear Sir; *(social)*, Dear Sir F—. *Spoken*, Sir F—.

KNIGHT (ORDERS OF CHIVALRY) – *Envelope*, Sir F—S—, followed by appropriate post-nominal letters. Otherwise as for Knight Bachelor.

KNIGHT'S WIFE – As for Baronet's wife.

LIFE PEER – As for Baron or for Baroness in own right.

LIFE PEER'S WIFE – As for Baron's wife.

LIFE PEER'S CHILDREN – As for Baron's children.

MARQUESS – *Envelope (formal)*, The Most Hon. the Marquess of —; *(social)*, The Marquess of —. *Letter (formal)*, My Lord; *(social)*, Dear Lord —. *Spoken (formal)*, My Lord; *(social)*, Lord —.

MARQUESS'S WIFE – *Envelope (formal)*, The Most Hon. the Marchioness of —; *(social)*, The Marchioness of —. *Letter (formal)*, Madam; *(social)*, Dear Lady —. *Spoken*, Lady —.

MARQUESS'S CHILDREN – *Eldest son, see* Courtesy titles. *Younger sons*, Lord F—S— (for forms of address, *see* Duke's younger sons). *Daughters*, Lady F—S— (for forms of address, *see* Duke's daughter).

MASTER – The title is used by the heir apparent to a Scottish peerage, though usually the heir apparent to a Duke, Marquess or Earl uses his courtesy title rather than 'Master'. *Envelope*, The Master of —. *Letter (formal)*, Dear Sir; *(social)*, Dear Master of —. *Spoken (formal)*, Master, or Sir; *(social)*, Master, or Mr S—.

MASTER'S WIFE – Addressed as for the wife of the appropriate peerage style, otherwise as Mrs S—.

PRIVY COUNSELLOR – *Envelope*, The Right (or Rt.) Hon. F—S—. *Letter*, Dear Mr/Miss/Mrs S—. *Spoken*, Mr/Miss/Mrs S—. It is incorrect to use the letters PC after the name in conjunction with the prefix The Right Hon., unless the Privy Counsellor is a peer below the rank of Marquess and so is styled The Right Hon. because of his rank. In this case only, the post-nominal letters may be used in conjunction with the prefix The Right Hon.

VISCOUNT – *Envelope (formal)*, The Right Hon. the Viscount —; *(social)*, The Viscount —. *Letter (formal)*, My Lord; *(social)*, Dear Lord —. *Spoken*, Lord —.

VISCOUNT'S WIFE – *Envelope (formal)*, The Right Hon. the Viscountess —; *(social)*, The Viscountess —. *Letter (formal)*, Madam; *(social)*, Dear Lady —. *Spoken*, Lady —.

VISCOUNT'S CHILDREN – As for Baron's children.

The Peerage

and Members of the House of Lords

The rules which govern the creation and succession of peerages are extremely complicated. There are, technically, five separate peerages, the Peerage of England, of Scotland, of Ireland, of Great Britain, and of the United Kingdom. The Peerage of Great Britain dates from 1707 when an Act of Union combined the two kingdoms of England and Scotland and separate peerages were discontinued. The Peerage of the United Kingdom dates from 1801 when Great Britain and Ireland were combined under an Act of Union. Some Scottish peers have received additional peerages of Great Britain or of the United Kingdom since 1707, and some Irish peers additional peerages of the United Kingdom since 1801.

The Peerage of Ireland was not entirely discontinued from 1801 but holders of Irish peerages, whether pre-dating or created subsequent to the Union of 1801, are not entitled to sit in the House of Lords if they have no additional English, Scottish, Great Britain or United Kingdom peerage. However, they are eligible for election to the House of Commons and to vote in parliamentary elections, which other peers are not. An Irish peer holding a peerage of a lower grade which enables him to sit in the House of Lords is introduced there by the title which enables him to sit, though for all other purposes he is known by his higher title.

In the Peerage of Scotland there is no rank of Baron; the equivalent rank is Lord of Parliament, abbreviated to 'Lord' (the female equivalent is 'Lady'). All peers of England, Scotland, Great Britain or the United Kingdom who are 21 years or over, and of British, Irish or Commonwealth nationality are entitled to sit in the House of Lords.

No fees for dignities have been payable since 1937. The House of Lords surrendered the ancient right of peers to be tried for treason or felony by their peers in 1948.

HEREDITARY WOMEN PEERS

Most hereditary peerages pass on death to the nearest male heir, but there are exceptions, and several are held by women (*see* pages 145 and 157–8).

A woman peer in her own right retains her title after marriage, and if her husband's rank is the superior she is designated by the two titles jointly, the inferior one second. Her hereditary claim still holds good in spite of any marriage whether higher or lower. No rank held by a woman can confer any title or even precedence upon her husband but the rank of a hereditary woman peer in her own right is inherited by her eldest son (or in some cases daughter).

Since the Peerage Act 1963, hereditary women peers in their own right have been entitled to sit in the House of Lords, subject to the same qualifications as men.

LIFE PEERS

Since 1876 non-hereditary or life peerages have been conferred on certain eminent judges to enable the judicial functions of the House of Lords to be carried out. These Lords are known as Lords of Appeal or law lords and, to date, such appointments have all been male.

Since 1958 life peerages have been conferred upon distinguished men and women from all walks of life, giving them seats in the House of Lords in the degree of Baron or Baroness. They are addressed in the same way as heredi-

tary Lords and Barons, and their children have similar courtesy titles.

PEERAGES EXTINCT SINCE THE LAST EDITION

VISCOUNTCIES: Watkinson (*cr.* 1964)
BARONIES: Airedale (*cr.* 1907)
LIFE PEERAGES: Bottomley (*cr.* 1984), Collison (*cr.* 1964), Faithfull (*cr.* 1975), Fraser of Kilmorack (*cr.* 1974), Home of the Hirsel (*cr.* 1974), Houghton of Sowerby (*cr.* 1974), Jacques (*cr.* 1968), Jay (*cr.* 1987), McFadzean (*cr.* 1966), Marshall of Goring (*cr.* 1985), Matthews (*cr.* 1980), O'Brien of Lothbury (*cr.* 1973), Pritchard (*cr.* 1975), Stedman (*cr.* 1974)

DISCLAIMER OF PEERAGES

The Peerage Act 1963 enables peers to disclaim their peerages for life. Peers alive in 1963 could disclaim within twelve months after the passing of the Act (31 July 1963); a person subsequently succeeding to a peerage may disclaim within twelve months (one month if an MP) after the date of succession, or of reaching 21, if later. The disclaimer is irrevocable but does not affect the descent of the peerage after the disclaimant's death, and children of a disclaimed peer may, if they wish, retain their precedence and any courtesy titles and styles borne as children of a peer. The disclaimer permits the disclaimant to sit in the House of Commons if elected as an MP.

The following peerages are currently disclaimed:

EARLDOMS: Durham (1970); Selkirk (1994)
VISCOUNTCIES: Camrose (1995); Hailsham (1963); Stansgate (1963)
BARONIES: Altrincham (1963); Archibald (1975); Merthyr (1977); Reith (1972); Sanderson of Ayot (1971); Silkin (1972)

PEERS WHO ARE MINORS (i.e. under 21 years of age)
EARLS: Craven (*b.* 1989)
BARONS: Elphinstone (*b.* 1980); Lovat (*b.* 1977)

CONTRACTIONS AND SYMBOLS

s.   Scottish title
i.   Irish title
*   The peer holds also an Imperial title, specified after the name by Engl., Brit. or UK
°   there is no 'of' in the title
b. born
s. succeeded
m. married
w. widower or widow
M. minor
†   heir not ascertained at time of going to press

Hereditary Peers

ROYAL DUKES

Style, His Royal Highness The Duke of —
Style of address (*formal*) May it please your Royal Highness; (*informal*) Sir

Created	Title, order of succession, name, etc.	Heir
1947	*Edinburgh* (1st), The Prince Philip, Duke of Edinburgh, (*see* page 117)	The Prince of Wales
1337	*Cornwall,* Charles, Prince of Wales, *s.* 1952 (*see* page 117)	‡
1398	*Rothesay,* Charles, Prince of Wales, *s.* 1952 (*see* page 117)	‡
1986	*York* (1st), The Prince Andrew, Duke of York (*see* page 117)	None
1928	*Gloucester* (2nd), Prince Richard, Duke of Gloucester, *s.* 1974 (*see* page 118)	Earl of Ulster (*see* page 118)
1934	*Kent* (2nd), Prince Edward, Duke of Kent, *s.* 1942 (*see* page 118)	Earl of St Andrews (*see* page 118)

‡ The title is not hereditary but is held by the Sovereign's eldest son from the moment of his birth or the Sovereign's accession

DUKES

Coronet, Eight strawberry leaves
Style, His Grace the Duke of —
Wife's style, Her Grace the Duchess of —
Eldest son's style, Takes his father's second title as a courtesy title
Younger sons' style, 'Lord' before forename and family name
Daughters' style, 'Lady' before forename and family name
For forms of address, *see* page 136

Created	Title, order of succession, name, etc.	Heir
1868 ɪ.*	*Abercorn* (5th), James Hamilton (6th *Brit. Marq.,* 1790, and 14th *Scott. Earl,* 1606, both *Abercorn*), *b.* 1934, *s.* 1979, *m.*	Marquess of Hamilton, *b.* 1969.
1701 s.*	*Argyll* (12th), Ian Campbell (5th *UK Duke Argyll,* 1892), *b.* 1937, *s.* 1973, *m.*	Marquess of Lorne, *b.* 1968.
1703 s.	*Atholl* (11th), John Murray, *b.* 1929, *s.* 1996, *m.*	Marquess of Tullibardine, *b.* 1960.
1682	*Beaufort* (11th), David Robert Somerset, *b.* 1928, *s.* 1984, *w.*	Marquess of Worcester, *b.* 1952.
1694	*Bedford* (13th), John Robert Russell, *b.* 1917, *s.* 1953, *m.*	Marquess of Tavistock, *b.* 1940.
1663 s.*	*Buccleuch* (9th) & *Queensberry* (11th) (1684), Walter Francis John Montagu Douglas Scott, ᴋᴛ, ᴠʀᴅ (8th *Engl. Earl, Doncaster,* 1662), *b.* 1923, *s.* 1973, *m.*	Earl of Dalkeith, *b.* 1954.
1694	*Devonshire* (11th), Andrew Robert Buxton Cavendish, ᴋɢ, ᴍᴄ, ᴘᴄ, *b.* 1920, *s.* 1950, *m.*	Marquess of Hartington, *b.* 1944.
1900	*Fife* (3rd), James George Alexander Bannerman Carnegie (12th *Scott. Earl, Southesk,* 1633, *s.* 1992), *b.* 1929, *s.* 1959. (*see* page 129)	Earl of Southesk, *b.* 1961.
1675	*Grafton* (11th), Hugh Denis Charles FitzRoy, ᴋɢ, *b.* 1919, *s.* 1970, *m.*	Earl of Euston, *b.* 1947.
1643 s.*	*Hamilton* (15th) & *Brandon* (12th) (*Brit.* 1711), Angus Alan Douglas Douglas-Hamilton (*Premier Peer of Scotland*), *b.* 1938, *s.* 1973	Marquess of Douglas and Clydesdale, *b.* 1978.
1766 ɪ.*	*Leinster* (8th), Gerald FitzGerald (*Premier Duke and Marquess of Ireland*; 8th *Brit. Visct., Leinster,* 1747), *b.* 1914, *s.* 1976, *m.*	Marquess of Kildare, *b.* 1948.
1719	*Manchester* (12th), Angus Charles Drogo Montagu, *b.* 1938, *s.* 1985, *m.*	Viscount Mandeville, *b.* 1962.
1702	*Marlborough* (11th), John George Vanderbilt Henry Spencer-Churchill, *b.* 1926, *s.* 1972, *m.*	Marquess of Blandford, *b.* 1955.
1707 s.*	*Montrose* (8th), James Graham (6th *Brit. Earl, Graham,* 1722), *b.* 1935, *s.* 1992, *m.*	Marquess of Graham, *b.* 1973.
1483	*Norfolk* (17th), Miles Francis Stapleton Fitzalan-Howard, ᴋɢ, ɢᴄᴠᴏ, ᴄʙ, ᴄʙᴇ, ᴍᴄ (*Premier Duke*; 12th *Eng. Baron Beaumont,* 1309, *s.* 1971; 4th *UK Baron Howard of Glossop,* 1869, *s.* 1972), *b.* 1915, *s.* 1975, *m.* *Earl Marshal*	Earl of Arundel and Surrey, *b.* 1956.
1766	*Northumberland* (12th), Ralph George Algernon Percy, *b.* 1956, *s.* 1995, *m.*	Earl Percy, *b.* 1984.
1675	*Richmond* (10th) & *Gordon* (5th) (*UK* 1876), Charles Henry Gordon Lennox (10th *Scott. Duke, Lennox,* 1675), *b.* 1929, *s.* 1989, *m.*	Earl of March and Kinrara, *b.* 1955.

Created	Title, order of succession, name, etc.	Heir
1707 s.*	*Roxburghe* (10th), Guy David Innes-Ker (5th *UK Earl, Innes*, 1837), *b.* 1954, *s.* 1974, *m.* (*Premier Baronet of Scotland*)	Marquess of Bowmont and Cessford, *b.* 1981.
1703	*Rutland* (10th), Charles John Robert Manners, CBE, *b.* 1919, *s.* 1940, *m.*	Marquess of Granby, *b.* 1959.
1684	*St Albans* (14th), Murray de Vere Beauclerk, *b.* 1939, *s.* 1988, *m.*	Earl of Burford, *b.* 1965.
1547	*Somerset* (19th), John Michael Edward Seymour, *b.* 1952, *s.* 1984, *m.*	Lord Seymour, *b.* 1982.
1833	*Sutherland* (6th), John Sutherland Egerton, TD (5th *UK Earl, Ellesmere*, 1846, *s.* 1944), *b.* 1915, *s.* 1963, *m.*	Francis R. E., *b.* 1940.
1814	*Wellington* (8th), Arthur Valerian Wellesley, KG, LVO, OBE, MC (9th *Irish Earl, Mornington*, 1760), *b.* 1915, *s.* 1972, *m.*	Marquess of Douro, *b.* 1945.
1874	*Westminster* (6th), Gerald Cavendish Grosvenor, OBE, *b.* 1951, *s.* 1979, *m.*	Earl Grosvenor, *b.* 1991.

MARQUESSES

Coronet, Four strawberry leaves alternating with four silver balls
Style, The Most Hon. the Marquess (of) ___ . In Scotland the spelling 'Marquis' is preferred for pre-Union creations
Wife's style, The Most Hon. the Marchioness (of) ___
Eldest son's style, Takes his father's second title as a courtesy title
Younger sons' style, 'Lord' before forename and family name
Daughters' style, 'Lady' before forename and family name
For forms of address, *see* page 136

Created	Title, order of succession, name, etc.	Heir
1916	*Aberdeen and Temair* (6th), Alastair Ninian John Gordon (12th *Scott. Earl, Aberdeen*, 1682), *b.* 1920, *s.* 1984, *m.*	Earl of Haddo, *b.* 1955.
1876	*Abergavenny* (5th), John Henry Guy Nevill, KG, OBE, *b.* 1914, *s.* 1954, *m.*	Christopher G. C. N., *b.* 1955.
1821	*Ailesbury* (8th), Michael Sidney Cedric Brudenell-Bruce, *b.* 1926, *s.* 1974	Earl of Cardigan, *b.* 1952.
1831	*Ailsa* (8th), Archibald Angus Charles Kennedy (20th *Scott. Earl, Cassillis*, 1509), *b.* 1956, *s.* 1994	Lord David Kennedy, *b.* 1958.
1815	*Anglesey* (7th), George Charles Henry Victor Paget, *b.* 1922, *s.* 1947, *m.*	Earl of Uxbridge, *b.* 1950.
1789	*Bath* (7th), Alexander George Thynn, *b.* 1932, *s.* 1992, *m.*	Viscount Weymouth, *b.* 1974.
1826	*Bristol* (7th), (Frederick William) John Augustus Hervey, *b.* 1954, *s.* 1985	Lord F. W. C. Nicholas W. H., *b.* 1961.
1796	*Bute* (7th), John Colum Crichton-Stuart (12th *Scott. Earl, Dumfries*, 1633), *b.* 1958, *s.* 1993, *m.*	Earl of Dumfries, *b.* 1989.
1812	°*Camden* (6th), David George Edward Henry Pratt, *b.* 1930, *s.* 1983	Earl of Brecknock, *b.* 1965.
1815	*Cholmondeley* (7th), David George Philip Cholmondeley (11th *Irish Viscount, Cholmondeley*, 1661), *b.* 1960, *s.* 1990. *Lord Great Chamberlain*	Charles G. C., *b.* 1959.
1816 I.*	°*Conyngham* (7th), Frederick William Henry Francis Conyngham (7th *UK Baron, Minster*, 1821), *b.* 1924, *s.* 1974, *m.*	Earl of Mount Charles, *b.* 1951.
1791 I.*	*Donegall* (7th), Dermot Richard Claud Chichester, LVO (7th *Brit. Baron, Fisherwick*, 1790, 6th *Brit. Baron, Templemore*, 1831, *s.* 1953), *b.* 1916, *s.* 1975, *m.*	Earl of Belfast, *b.* 1952.
1789 I.*	*Downshire* (8th), (Arthur) Robin Ian Hill (8th *Brit. Earl, Hillsborough*, 1772), *b.* 1929, *s.* 1989, *m.*	Earl of Hillsborough, *b.* 1959.
1801 I.*	*Ely* (8th) Charles John Tottenham (8th *UK Baron, Loftus*, 1801), *b.* 1913, *s.* 1969, *m.*	Viscount Loftus, *b.* 1943.
1801	*Exeter* (8th), (William) Michael Anthony Cecil, *b.* 1935, *s.* 1988, *m.*	Lord Burghley, *b.* 1970.
1800 I.*	*Headfort* (6th), Thomas Geoffrey Charles Michael Taylour (4th *UK Baron, Kenlis*, 1831), *b.* 1932, *s.* 1960, *m.*	Earl of Bective, *b.* 1959.
1793	*Hertford* (8th), Hugh Edward Conway Seymour (9th *Irish Baron, Conway*, 1712), *b.* 1930, *s.* 1940, *m.*	Earl of Yarmouth, *b.* 1958.
1599 s.*	*Huntly* (13th), Granville Charles Gomer Gordon (*Premier Marquess of Scotland*) (5th *UK Baron, Meldrum*, 1815), *b.* 1944, *s.* 1987, *m.*	Earl of Aboyne, *b.* 1973.
1784	*Lansdowne* (8th), George John Charles Mercer Nairne Petty-Fitzmaurice, PC (8th *Irish Earl, Kerry*, 1723), *b.* 1912, *s.* 1944, *m.*	Earl of Shelburne, *b.* 1941.
1902	*Linlithgow* (4th), Adrian John Charles Hope (10th *Scott. Earl, Hopetoun*, 1703), *b.* 1946, *s.* 1987, *m.*	Earl of Hopetoun, *b.* 1969.
1816 I.*	*Londonderry* (9th), Alexander Charles Robert Vane-Tempest-Stewart (6th *UK Earl, Vane*, 1823), *b.* 1937, *s.* 1955, *m.*	Viscount Castlereagh, *b.* 1972.
1701 s.*	*Lothian* (12th), Peter Francis Walter Kerr, KCVO (6th *UK Baron, Kerr*, 1821), *b.* 1922, *s.* 1940, *m.*	Earl of Ancram, PC, MP, *b.* 1945.

Created	Title, order of succession, name, etc.	Heir
1917	*Milford Haven* (4th), George Ivar Louis Mountbatten, *b.* 1961, *s.* 1970, *m.*	Earl of Medina, *b.* 1991.
1838	*Normanby* (5th), Constantine Edmund Walter Phipps, (9th *Irish Baron, Mulgrave*, 1767), *b.* 1954, *s.* 1994, *m.*	Lord Justin, C. *P., b.* 1958.
1812	*Northampton* (7th), Spencer Douglas David Compton, *b.* 1946, *s.* 1978, *m.*	Earl Compton, *b.* 1973.
1825 I.*	*Ormonde* (7th), James Hubert Theobald Charles Butler, MBE (7th *UK Baron, Ormonde*, 1821), *b.* 1899, *s.* 1971, *w.*	None to Marquessate. To Earldoms of Ormonde and Ossory, Viscount Mountgarret, *b.* 1936 (*see* page 147).
1682 s.	*Queensberry* (12th), David Harrington Angus Douglas, *b.* 1929, *s.* 1954	Viscount Drumlanrig, *b.* 1967.
1926	*Reading* (4th), Simon Charles Henry Rufus Isaacs, *b.* 1942, *s.* 1980, *m.*	Viscount Erleigh, *b.* 1986.
1789	*Salisbury* (6th), Robert Edward Peter Cecil, *b.* 1916, *s.* 1972, *m.*	Viscount Cranborne, PC, *b.* 1946 (*see also* Baron Cecil, page 150).
1800 I.*	*Sligo* (11th), Jeremy Ulick Browne (11th *UK Baron, Monteagle*, 1806), *b.* 1939, *s.* 1991, *m.*	Sebastian U. *B., b.* 1964.
1787	°*Townshend* (7th), George John Patrick Dominic Townshend, *b.* 1916, *s.* 1921, *w.*	Viscount Raynham, *b.* 1945.
1694 s.*	*Tweeddale* (13th), Edward Douglas John Hay (4th *UK Baron, Tweeddale*, 1881), *b.* 1947, *s.* 1979	Lord Charles D. M. *H., b.* 1947.
1789 I.*	*Waterford* (8th), John Hubert de la Poer Beresford (8th *Brit. Baron, Tyrone*, 1786), *b.* 1933, *s.* 1934, *m.*	Earl of Tyrone, *b.* 1958.
1551	*Winchester* (18th), Nigel George Paulet (*Premier Marquess of England*), *b.* 1941, *s.* 1968, *m.*	Earl of Wiltshire, *b.* 1969.
1892	*Zetland* (4th), Lawrence Mark Dundas (6th *UK Earl of Zetland*, 1838, 7th *Brit. Baron Dundas*, 1794), *b.* 1937, *s.* 1989, *m.*	Earl of Ronaldshay, *b.* 1965.

EARLS

Coronet, Eight silver balls on stalks alternating with eight gold strawberry leaves
Style, The Right Hon. the Earl (of) —
Wife's style, The Right Hon. the Countess (of) —
Eldest son's style, Takes his father's second title as a courtesy title
Younger sons' style, 'The Hon.' before forename and family name
Daughters' style, 'Lady' before forename and family name
For forms of address, *see* page 136

Created	Title, order of succession, name, etc.	Heir
1639 s.	*Airlie* (13th), David George Coke Patrick Ogilvy, KT, GCVO, PC, *b.* 1926, *s.* 1968, *m. Lord Chamberlain*	Lord Ogilvy, *b.* 1958.
1696	*Albemarle* (10th), Rufus Arnold Alexis Keppel, *b.* 1965, *s.* 1979	Crispian W. J. *K., b.* 1948.
1952	°*Alexander of Tunis* (2nd), Shane William Desmond Alexander, *b.* 1935, *s.* 1969, *m.*	Hon. Brian J. *A., b.* 1939.
1662 s.	*Annandale and Hartfell* (11th), Patrick Andrew Wentworth Hope Johnstone, *b.* 1941, *claim established* 1985, *m.*	Lord Johnstone, *b.* 1971.
1789 I.	°*Annesley* (10th), Patrick Annesley, *b.* 1924, *s.* 1979, *m.*	Hon. Philip H. *A., b.* 1927.
1785 I.	*Antrim* (9th), Alexander Randal Mark McDonnell, *b.* 1935, *s.* 1977, *m.* (*Viscount Dunluce*)	Hon. Randal A. St J. *M., b.* 1967.
1762 I.*	*Arran* (9th), Arthur Desmond Colquhoun Gore (5th *UK Baron Sudley*, 1884), *b.* 1938, *s.* 1983, *m.*	Paul A. *G.*, CMG, CVO, *b.* 1921.
1955	°*Attlee* (3rd), John Richard Attlee, *b.* 1956, *s.* 1991, *m.*	None.
1714	*Aylesford* (11th), Charles Ian Finch-Knightley, *b.* 1918, *s.* 1958, *w.*	Lord Guernsey, *b.* 1947.
1937	°*Baldwin of Bewdley* (4th), Edward Alfred Alexander Baldwin, *b.* 1938, *s.* 1976, *m.*	Viscount Corvedale, *b.* 1973.
1922	*Balfour* (4th), Gerald Arthur James Balfour, *b.* 1925, *s.* 1968, *m.*	Eustace A. G. *B., b.* 1921.
1772	°*Bathurst* (8th), Henry Allen John Bathurst, *b.* 1927, *s.* 1943, *m.*	Lord Apsley, *b.* 1961.
1919	°*Beatty* (3rd), David Beatty, *b.* 1946, *s.* 1972, *m.*	Viscount Borodale, *b.* 1973.
1797 I.	*Belmore* (8th), John Armar Lowry-Corry, *b.* 1951, *s.* 1960, *m.*	Viscount Corry, *b.* 1985.
1739 I.*	*Bessborough* (11th), Arthur Mountifort Longfield Ponsonby (8th *UK Baron, Duncannon*, 1834), *b.* 1912, *s.* 1993, *m.*	Hon. Myles F. L. *P., b.* 1941.
1815	*Bradford* (7th), Richard Thomas Orlando Bridgeman, *b.* 1947, *s.* 1981, *m.*	Viscount Newport, *b.* 1980.
1677 s.	*Breadalbane and Holland* (10th), John Romer Boreland Campbell, *b.* 1919, *s.* 1959	None.

Created	Title, order of succession, name, etc.	Heir

1469 s.*   *Buchan* (17th), Malcolm Harry Erskine, (8th *UK Baron Erskine* 1806), *b.*   Lord Cardross, *b.* 1960.
1930, *s.* 1984, *m.*

1746   *Buckinghamshire* (10th), (George) Miles Hobart-Hampden, *b.* 1944, *s.*   Sir John Hobart, Bt., *b.* 1945.
1983, *m.*

1800   °*Cadogan* (7th), William Gerald Charles Cadogan, MC, *b.* 1914, *s.* 1933,   Viscount Chelsea, *b.* 1937.
m.

1878   °*Cairns* (6th), Simon Dallas Cairns, CBE, *b.* 1939, *s.* 1989, *m.*   Viscount Garmoyle, *b.* 1965.

1455 s.   *Caithness* (20th), Malcolm Ian Sinclair, PC, *b.* 1948, *s.* 1965, *w.*   Lord Berriedale, *b.* 1981.

1800 I.   *Caledon* (7th), Nicholas James Alexander, *b.* 1955, *s.* 1980, *m.*   Viscount Alexander, *b.* 1990.

1661   *Carlisle* (13th), George William Beaumont Howard (13th *Scott. Baron,*   Hon. Philip C. W. H., *b.* 1963.
Ruthven of Freeland, 1651), *b.* 1949, *s.* 1994

1793   *Carnarvon* (7th), Henry George Reginald Molyneux Herbert, KCVO,   Lord Porchester, *b.* 1956.
KBE, *b.* 1924, *s.* 1987, *m.*

1748 I.*   *Carrick* (10th), David James Theobald Somerset Butler (4th *UK Baron,*   Viscount Ikerrin, *b.* 1975.
Butler, 1912), *b.* 1953, *s.* 1992, *m.*

1800 I.   °*Castle Stewart* (8th), Arthur Patrick Avondale Stuart, *b.* 1928, *s.* 1961,   Viscount Stuart, *b.* 1953.
m.

1814   °*Cathcart* (6th), Alan Cathcart, CB, DSO, MC (15th *Scott. Baron, Cathcart,*   Lord Greenock, *b.* 1952.
1447), *b.* 1919, *s.* 1927, *m.*

1647 I.   *Cavan.* The 12th Earl died in 1988. Heir had not established his claim   Roger C. Lambart, *b.* 1944.
to the title at the time of going to press

1827   °*Cawdor* (7th), Colin Robert Vaughan Campbell, *b.* 1962, *s.* 1993, *m.*   Hon. Frederick W. C., *b.* 1965.

1801   *Chichester* (9th), John Nicholas Pelham, *b.* 1944, *s.* 1944, *m.*   Richard A. H. P., *b.* 1952.

1803 I.*   *Clancarty* (9th), Nicholas Power Richard Le Poer Trench (8th *UK*   None.
Visct. Clancarty, 1823), *b.* 1952, *s.* 1995

1776 I.*   *Clanwilliam* (7th), John Herbert Meade (5th *UK Baron Clanwilliam,*   Lord Gillford, *b.* 1960.
1828), *b.* 1919, *s.* 1989, *m.*

1776   *Clarendon* (7th), George Frederick Laurence Hyde Villiers, *b.* 1933, *s.*   Lord Hyde, *b.* 1976.
1955, *m.*

1620 I.*   *Cork* (14th) & *Orrery* (14th) (I. 1660), John William Boyle, DSC (10th   Hon. John R. B., *b.* 1945.
Brit. Baron, Boyle of Marston, 1711), *b.* 1916, *s.* 1995, *m.*

1850   *Cottenham* (8th), Kenelm Charles Everard Digby Pepys, *b.* 1948, *s.*   Viscount Crowhurst, *b.* 1983.
1968, *m.*

1762 I.*   *Courtown* (9th), James Patrick Montagu Burgoyne Winthrop Stopford   Viscount Stopford, *b.* 1988.
(8th *Brit. Baron, Saltersford,* 1796), *b.* 1954, *s.* 1975, *m.*

1697   *Coventry* (11th), George William Coventry, *b.* 1934, *s.* 1940, *m.*   Viscount Deerhurst, *b.* 1957.

1857   °*Cowley* (7th), Garret Graham Wellesley, *b.* 1934, *s.* 1975, *m.*   Viscount Dangan, *b.* 1965.

1892   *Cranbrook* (5th), Gathorne Gathorne-Hardy, *b.* 1933, *s.* 1978, *m.*   Lord Medway, *b.* 1968.

1801   *Craven* (9th), Benjamin Robert Joseph Craven, *b.* 1989, *s.* 1990, *M.*   Rupert J. E. C., *b.* 1926.

1398 s.*   *Crawford* (29th) & *Balcarres* (12th) (s. 1651), Robert Alexander   Lord Balniel, *b.* 1958.
Lindsay, PC (*Premier Earl on Union Roll,* 5th *UK Baron, Wigan,* 1826,
and *Baron Balniel* (life peerage), 1974, *b.* 1927, *s.* 1975, *m.*

1861   *Cromartie* (5th), John Ruaridh Blunt Grant Mackenzie, *b.* 1948, *s.*   Viscount Tarbat, *b.* 1987.
1989, *m.*

1901   *Cromer* (4th), Evelyn Rowland Esmond Baring, *b.* 1946, *s.* 1991, *m.*   Viscount Errington, *b* 1994.

1633 s.*   *Dalhousie* (16th), Simon Ramsay, KT, GCVO, GBE, MC (4th *UK Baron,*   Lord Ramsay, *b.* 1948.
Ramsay, 1875), *b.* 1914, *s.* 1950, *m.*

1725 I.*   *Darnley* (11th), Adam Ivo Stuart Bligh (20th *Engl. Baron, Clifton of*   Lord Clifton, *b.* 1968.
Leighton Bromswold, 1608), *b.* 1941, *s.* 1980, *m.*

1711   *Dartmouth* (9th), Gerald Humphry Legge, *b.* 1924, *s.* 1962, *m.*   Viscount Lewisham, *b.* 1949.

1761   °*De La Warr* (11th), William Herbrand Sackville, *b.* 1948, *s.* 1988, *m.*   Lord Buckhurst, *b.* 1979.

1622   *Denbigh* (12th) & *Desmond* (11th) (I. 1622), Alexander Stephen   William D. F, *b.* 1939.
Rudolph Feilding, *b.* 1970, *s.* 1995, *m.*

1485   *Derby* (19th), Edward Richard William Stanley, *b.* 1962, *s.* 1994, *m.*   Hon. Peter H. C. S., *b.* 1964.

1553   *Devon* (17th), Charles Christopher Courtenay, *b.* 1916, *s.* 1935, *m.*   Lord Courtenay, *b.* 1942.

1800 I.*   *Donoughmore* (8th), Richard Michael John Hely-Hutchinson (8th *UK*   Viscount Suirdale, *b.* 1952.
Visct., Hutchinson, 1821), *b.* 1927, *s.* 1981, *m.*

1661 I.*   *Drogheda* (12th), Henry Dermot Ponsonby Moore (3rd *UK Baron,*   Viscount Moore, *b.* 1983.
Moore, 1954), *b.* 1937, *s.* 1989, *m.*

1837   *Ducie* (7th), David Leslie Moreton, *b.* 1951, *s.* 1991, *m.*   Lord Moreton, *b.* 1981.

1860   *Dudley* (4th), William Humble David Ward, *b.* 1920, *s.* 1969, *m.*   Viscount Ednam, *b.* 1947.

1660 s.*   *Dundee* (12th), Alexander Henry Scrymgeour (2nd *UK Baron, Glassary,*   Lord Scrymgeour, *b.* 1982.
1954), *b.* 1949, *s.* 1983, *m.*

1669 s.   *Dundonald* (15th), Iain Alexander Douglas Blair Cochrane, *b.* 1961, *s.*   Lord Cochrane, *b.* 1991.
1986, *m.*

1686 s.   *Dunmore* (12th), Malcolm Kenneth Murray, *b.* 1946, *s.* 1995, *m.*   †

1822 I.   *Dunraven and Mount-Earl* (7th), Thady Windham Thomas   None.
Wyndham-Quin, *b.* 1939, *s.* 1965, *m.*

Created	Title, order of succession, name, etc.	Heir
1833	Durham. Disclaimed for life 1970 (*Antony Claud Frederick Lambton, b.* 1922, *s.* 1970, *m.*)	Hon. Edward R. *L.* (Baron Durham), *b.* 1961.
1837	*Effingham* (7th), David Mowbray Algernon Howard (17th *Engl. Baron, Howard of Effingham,* 1554), *b.* 1939, *s.* 1996, *m.*	Lord Howard of Effingham, *b.* 1971.
1507 s.*	*Eglinton* (18th) & *Winton* (9th) (1600), Archibald George Montgomerie (6th *UK Earl, Winton,* 1859), *b.* 1939, *s.* 1966, *m.*	Lord Montgomerie, *b.* 1966.
1733 I.*	*Egmont* (11th), Frederick George Moore Perceval (9th *Brit. Baron, Lovel & Holland,* 1762), *b.* 1914, *s.* 1932, *m.*	Viscount Perceval, *b.* 1934.
1821	*Eldon* (5th), John Joseph Nicholas Scott, *b.* 1937, *s.* 1976, *m.*	Viscount Encombe, *b.* 1962.
1633 s.*	*Elgin* (11th), & *Kincardine* (15th) (s. 1647), Andrew Douglas Alexander Thomas Bruce (4th *UK Baron, Elgin,* 1849), KT, *b.* 1924, *s.* 1968, *m.*	Lord Bruce, *b.* 1961.
1789 I.*	*Enniskillen* (7th), Andrew John Galbraith Cole (5th *UK Baron, Grinstead,* 1815) *b.* 1942, *s.* 1989, *m.*	Arthur G. *C., b.* 1920.
1789 I.*	*Erne* (6th), Henry George Victor John Crichton (3rd *UK Baron, Fermanagh,* 1876), *b.* 1937, *s.* 1940, *m.*	Viscount Crichton, *b.* 1971.
1452 s.	*Erroll* (24th), Merlin Sereld Victor Gilbert Hay, *b.* 1948, *s.* 1978, *m.* Hereditary Lord High Constable and Knight Marischal of Scotland	Lord Hay, *b.* 1984.
1661	*Essex* (10th), Robert Edward de Vere Capell, *b.* 1920, *s.* 1981, *m.*	Viscount Malden, *b.* 1944.
1711	°*Ferrers* (13th), Robert Washington Shirley, PC, *b.* 1929, *s.* 1954, *m.*	Viscount Tamworth, *b.* 1952.
1789	°*Fortescue* (8th), Charles Hugh Richard Fortescue, *b.* 1951, *s.* 1993, *m.*	Hon. Martin D. *F., b.* 1924.
1841	*Gainsborough* (5th), Anthony Gerard Edward Noel, *b.* 1923, *s.* 1927, *m.*	Viscount Campden, *b.* 1950.
1623 s.*	*Galloway* (13th), Randolph Keith Reginald Stewart (6th *Brit. Baron, Stewart of Garlies,* 1796), *b.* 1928, *s.* 1978, *m.*	Andrew C. *S., b.* 1949.
1703 s.*	*Glasgow* (10th), Patrick Robin Archibald Boyle (4th *UK Baron, Fairlie,* 1897), *b.* 1939, *s.* 1984, *m.*	Viscount of Kelburn, *b.* 1978.
1806 I.*	°*Gosford* (7th), Charles David Nicholas Alexander John Sparrow Acheson (5th *UK Baron, Worlingham,* 1835), *b.* 1942, *s.* 1966, *m.*	Hon. Patrick B. V. M. *A., b.* 1915.
1945	*Gowrie* (2nd), Alexander Patric Greysteil Hore-Ruthven, PC (3rd *UK Baron, Ruthven of Gowrie,* 1919), *b.* 1939, *s.* 1955, *m.*	Viscount Ruthven of Canberra, *b.* 1964.
1684 I.*	*Granard* (10th), Peter Arthur Edward Hastings Forbes, (5th *UK Baron, Granard,* 1806), *b.* 1957, *s.* 1992, *m.*	Viscount Forbes, *b.* 1981.
1833	°*Granville* (5th), Granville James Leveson-Gower, MC, *b.* 1918, *s.* 1953, *m.*	Lord Leveson, *b.* 1959.
1806	°*Grey* (6th), Richard Fleming George Charles Grey, *b.* 1939, *s.* 1963, *m.*	Philip K. *G., b.* 1940.
1752	*Guilford* (9th), Edward Francis North, *b.* 1933, *s.* 1949, *w.*	Lord North, *b.* 1971.
1619 s.	*Haddington* (13th), John George Baillie-Hamilton, *b.* 1941, *s.* 1986, *m.*	Lord Binning, *b.* 1985.
1919	°*Haig* (2nd), George Alexander Eugene Douglas Haig, OBE, *b.* 1918, *s.* 1928, *m.*	Viscount Dawick, *b.* 1961.
1944	*Halifax* (3rd), Charles Edward Peter Neil Wood (5th *UK Viscount, Halifax,* 1866), *b.* 1944, *s.* 1980, *m.*	Lord Irwin, *b.* 1977.
1898	*Halsbury* (3rd), John Anthony Hardinge Giffard, FRS, FEng., *b.* 1908, *s.* 1943, *w.*	Adam E. *G., b.* 1934.
1754	*Hardwicke* (10th), Joseph Philip Sebastian Yorke, *b.* 1971, *s.* 1974	Richard C. J. *Y., b.* 1916.
1812	*Harewood* (7th), George Henry Hubert Lascelles, KBE, *b.* 1923, *s.* 1947, *m.* (*see also* page 128)	Viscount Lascelles, *b.* 1950.
1742	*Harrington* (11th), William Henry Leicester Stanhope (8th *Brit. Viscount, Stanhope of Mahon,* 1717), *b.* 1922, *s.* 1929, *m.*	Viscount Petersham, *b.* 1945.
1809	*Harrowby* (7th), Dudley Danvers Granville Coutts Ryder, TD, *b.* 1922, *s.* 1987, *m.*	Viscount Sandon, *b.* 1951.
1605 s.	*Home* (15th) David Alexander Cospatrick Douglas-Home, *b.* 1943, *s.* 1995, *m.*	Lord Dunglass, *b.* 1987.
1821	°*Howe* (7th), Frederick Richard Penn Curzon, *b.* 1951, *s.* 1984, *m.*	Viscount Curzon, *b.* 1994.
1529	*Huntingdon* (16th), William Edward Robin Hood Hastings Bass, *b.* 1948, *s.* 1990, *m.*	Hon. Simon A. R. H. *H. B., b.* 1950.
1885	*Iddesleigh* (4th), Stafford Henry Northcote, *b.* 1932, *s.* 1970, *m.*	Viscount St Cyres, *b.* 1957.
1756	*Ilchester* (9th), Maurice Vivian de Touffreville Fox-Strangways, *b.* 1920, *s.* 1970, *m.*	Hon. Raymond G. *F.-S., b.* 1921.
1929	*Inchcape* (4th), (Kenneth) Peter (Lyle) Mackay, *b.* 1943, *s.* 1994, *m.*	Viscount Glenapp, *b.* 1979.
1919	*Iveagh* (4th), Arthur Edward Rory Guinness, *b.* 1969, *s.* 1992	Hon. Rory M. B. *G., b.* 1974.
1925	°*Jellicoe* (2nd), George Patrick John Rushworth Jellicoe, KBE, DSO, MC, PC, FRS, *b.* 1918, *s.* 1935, *m.*	Viscount Brocas, *b.* 1950.
1697	*Jersey* (9th), George Francis Child Villiers (12th *Irish Visct., Grandison,* 1620), *b.* 1910, *s.* 1923, *m.*	Viscount Villiers, *b.* 1948.
1822 I.	*Kilmorey* (6th), Richard Francis Needham, PC, MP, *b.* 1942, *s.* 1977, *m.*	Viscount Newry and Morne, *b.* 1966.
1866	*Kimberley* (4th), John Wodehouse, *b.* 1924, *s.* 1941, *m.*	Lord Wodehouse, *b.* 1951.
1768 I.	*Kingston* (11th), Barclay Robert Edwin King-Tenison, *b.* 1943, *s.* 1948, *m.*	Viscount Kingsborough, *b.* 1969.

Created	Title, order of succession, name, etc.	Heir
1633 s.*	*Kinnoull* (15th), Arthur William George Patrick Hay (9th *Brit. Baron, Hay of Pedwardine*, 1711), *b.* 1935, *s.* 1938, *m.*	Viscount Dupplin, *b.* 1962.
1677 s.*	*Kintore* (13th), Michael Canning William John Keith (3rd *UK Viscount Stonehaven*, 1938), *b.* 1939, *s.* 1989, *m.*	Lord Inverurie, *b.* 1976.
1914	°*Kitchener of Khartoum* (3rd), Henry Herbert Kitchener, TD, *b.* 1919, *s.* 1937	None.
1756 I.	*Lanesborough* (9th), Denis Anthony Brian Butler, TD, *b.* 1918, *s.* 1950, *m.*	None.
1624 s.	*Lauderdale* (17th), Patrick Francis Maitland, *b.* 1911, *s.* 1968, *m.*	Viscount Maitland, *b.* 1937.
1837	*Leicester* (7th), Edward Douglas Coke, *b.* 1936, *s.* 1994, *m.*	Viscount Coke, *b.* 1965.
1641 s.	*Leven* (14th) & *Melville* (13th) (s. 1690), Alexander Robert Leslie Melville, *b.* 1924, *s.* 1947, *m.*	Lord Balgonie, *b.* 1954.
1831	*Lichfield* (5th), Thomas Patrick John Anson, *b.* 1939, *s.* 1960	Viscount Anson, *b.* 1978.
1803 I.*	*Limerick* (6th), Patrick Edmund Pery, KBE (6th *UK Baron, Foxford*, 1815), *b.* 1930, *s.* 1967, *m.*	Viscount Glentworth, *b.* 1963.
1572	*Lincoln* (18th), Edward Horace Fiennes-Clinton, *b.* 1913, *s.* 1988, *m.*	Hon. Edward G. *F.-C., b.* 1943.
1633 s.	*Lindsay* (16th), James Randolph Lindesay-Bethune, *b.* 1955, *s.* 1989, *m.*	Viscount Garnock, *b.* 1990.
1626	*Lindsey* (14th) *and Abingdon* (9th) (1682), Richard Henry Rupert Bertie, *b.* 1931, *s.* 1963, *m.*	Lord Norreys, *b.* 1958.
1776 I.	*Lisburne* (8th), John David Malet Vaughan, *b.* 1918, *s.* 1965, *m.*	Viscount Vaughan, *b.* 1945.
1822 I.*	*Listowel* (5th), William Francis Hare, GCMG, PC, (3rd *UK Baron, Hare*, 1869), *b.* 1906, *s.* 1931, *m.*	Viscount Ennismore, *b.* 1964.
1905	*Liverpool* (5th), Edward Peter Bertram Savile Foljambe, *b.* 1944, *s.* 1969	Viscount Hawkesbury, *b.* 1972.
1945	°*Lloyd George of Dwyfor* (3rd), Owen Lloyd George, *b.* 1924, *s.* 1968, *m.*	Viscount Gwynedd, *b.* 1951.
1785 I.*	*Longford* (7th), Francis Aungier Pakenham, KG, PC (6th *UK Baron, Silchester*, 1821; 1st *UK Baron, Pakenham*, 1945), *b.* 1905, *s.* 1961, *m.*	Thomas F. D. *P., b.* 1933.
1807	*Lonsdale* (7th), James Hugh William Lowther, *b.* 1922, *s.* 1953, *m.*	Viscount Lowther, *b.* 1949.
1838	*Lovelace* (5th), Peter Axel William Locke King (12th *Brit. Baron, King*, 1725), *b.* 1951, *s.* 1964, *m.*	None.
1795 I.*	*Lucan* (7th), Richard John Bingham (3rd *UK Baron, Bingham*, 1934), *b.* 1934, *s.* 1964, *m.*	Lord Bingham, *b.* 1967.
1880	*Lytton* (5th), John Peter Michael Scawen Lytton (18th *Engl. Baron, Wentworth*, 1529), *b.* 1950, *s.* 1985, *m.*	Viscount Knebworth, *b.* 1989.
1721	*Macclesfield* (9th), Richard Timothy George Mansfield Parker, *b.* 1943, *s.* 1992, *m.*	Hon. J. David G. *P., b.* 1945.
1800	*Malmesbury* (6th), William James Harris, TD, *b.* 1907, *s.* 1950, *w.*	Viscount FitzHarris, *b.* 1946.
1776 & 1792	*Mansfield and Mansfield* (8th), William David Mungo James Murray (14th *Scott. Visct., Stormont*, 1621), *b.* 1930, *s.* 1971, *m.*	Viscount Stormont, *b.* 1956.
1565 s.	*Mar* (14th) & *Kellie* (16th) (s. 1616), James Thorne Erskine, *b.* 1949, *s.* 1994, *m.*	Hon. Alexander D. *E., b.* 1952.
1785 I.	*Mayo* (10th), Terence Patrick Bourke, *b.* 1929, *s.* 1962	Lord Naas, *b.* 1953.
1627 I.*	*Meath* (14th), Anthony Windham Normand Brabazon (5th *UK Baron, Chaworth*, 1831), *b.* 1910, *s.* 1949, *m.*	Lord Ardee, *b.* 1941.
1766 I.	*Mexborough* (8th), John Christopher George Savile, *b.* 1931, *s.* 1980, *m.*	Viscount Pollington, *b.* 1959.
1813	*Minto* (6th), Gilbert Edward George Lariston Elliot-Murray-Kynynmound, OBE, *b.* 1928, *s.* 1975, *m.*	Viscount Melgund, *b.* 1953.
1562 s.*	*Moray* (20th) Douglas John Moray Stuart (12th *Brit. Baron, Stuart* of *Castle Stuart*, 1796), *b.* 1928, *s.* 1974, *m.*	Lord Doune, *b.* 1966.
1815	*Morley* (6th), John St Aubyn Parker, *b.* 1923, *s.* 1962, *m.*	Viscount Boringdon, *b.* 1956.
1458 s.	*Morton* (22nd), John Charles Sholto Douglas, *b.* 1927, *s.* 1976, *m.*	Lord Aberdour, *b.* 1952.
1789	*Mount Edgcumbe* (8th), Robert Charles Edgcumbe, *b.* 1939, *s.* 1982	Piers V. *E., b.* 1946.
1831	*Munster* (7th), Anthony Charles FitzClarence, *b.* 1926, *s.* 1983, *w.*	None.
1805	°*Nelson* (9th), Peter John Horatio Nelson, *b.* 1941, *s.* 1981, *m.*	Viscount Merton, *b.* 1971.
1660 s.	*Newburgh* (12th), Don Filippo Giambattista Camillo Francesco Aldo Maria Rospigliosi, *b.* 1942, *s.* 1986, *m.*	Princess Donna Benedetta F. M. *R., b.* 1974.
1827 I.	*Norbury* (6th), Noel Terence Graham-Toler, *b.* 1939, *s.* 1955, *m.*	Viscount Glandine, *b.* 1967.
1806 I.*	*Normanton* (6th), Shaun James Christian Welbore Ellis Agar (9th *Brit. Baron, Mendip*, 1794, 4th *UK Baron, Somerton*, 1873), *b.* 1945, *s.* 1967, *m.*	Viscount Somerton, *b.* 1982.
1647 s.	*Northesk* (14th), David John MacRae Carnegie, *b.* 1954, *s.* 1994, *m.*	Lord Rosehill, *b.* 1980.
1801	*Onslow* (7th), Michael William Coplestone Dillon Onslow, *b.* 1938, *s.* 1971, *m.*	Viscount Cranley, *b.* 1967.
1696 s.	*Orkney* (8th), Cecil O'Bryen Fitz-Maurice, *b.* 1919, *s.* 1951, *w.*	O. Peter *St John, b.* 1938.
1925	*Oxford and Asquith* (2nd), Julian Edward George Asquith, KCMG, *b.* 1916, *s.* 1928, *m.*	Viscount Asquith, OBE, *b.* 1952.
1929	°*Peel* (3rd), William James Robert Peel (4th *UK Viscount Peel*, 1895), *b.* 1947, *s.* 1969, *m.*	Viscount Clanfield, *b.* 1976.

Created	Title, order of succession, name, etc.	Heir
1551	*Pembroke* (17th) & *Montgomery* (14th) (1605), Henry George Charles Alexander Herbert, *b.* 1939, *s.* 1969	Lord Herbert, *b.* 1978.
1605 s.	*Perth* (17th), John David Drummond, PC, *b.* 1907, *s.* 1951, *w.*	Viscount Strathallan, *b.* 1935.
1905	*Plymouth* (3rd), Other Robert Ivor Windsor-Clive (15th *Engl. Baron, Windsor,* 1529), *b.* 1923, *s.* 1943, *m.*	Viscount Windsor, *b.* 1951.
1785 I.	*Portarlington* (7th), George Lionel Yuill Seymour Dawson-Damer, *b.* 1938, *s.* 1959, *m.*	Viscount Carlow, *b.* 1965.
1689	*Portland* (11th), Count Henry Noel Bentinck, *b.* 1919, *s.* 1990, *m.*	Viscount Woodstock, *b.* 1953.
1743	*Portsmouth* (10th), Quentin Gerard Carew Wallop, *b.* 1954, *s.* 1984, *m.*	Viscount Lymington, *b.* 1981.
1804	*Powis* (8th), John George Herbert (9th *Irish Baron, Clive,* 1762), *b.* 1952, *s.* 1993, *m.*	Viscount Clive, *b.* 1979.
1765	*Radnor* (8th), Jacob Pleydell-Bouverie, *b.* 1927, *s.* 1968, *m.*	Viscount Folkestone, *b.* 1955.
1831 I.*	*Ranfurly* (7th), Gerald Françoys Needham Knox (8th *UK Baron, Ranfurly,* 1826), *b.* 1929, *s.* 1988, *m.*	Edward J. K., *b.* 1957.
1771 I.	*Roden* (10th), Robert John Jocelyn, *b.* 1938, *s.* 1993, *m.*	Viscount Jocelyn, *b.* 1989.
1801	*Romney* (7th), Michael Henry Marsham, *b.* 1910, *s.* 1975, *m.*	Julian C. M., *b.* 1948.
1703 s.*	*Rosebery* (7th), Neil Archibald Primrose (3rd *UK Earl, Midlothian,* 1911), *b.* 1929, *s.* 1974, *m.*	Lord Dalmeny, *b.* 1967.
1806 I.	*Rosse* (7th), William Brendan Parsons, *b.* 1936, *s.* 1979, *m.*	Lord Oxmantown, *b.* 1969.
1801	*Rosslyn* (7th), Peter St Clair-Erskine, *b.* 1958, *s.* 1977, *m.*	Lord Loughborough, *b.* 1986.
1457 s.	*Rothes* (21st), Ian Lionel Malcolm Leslie, *b.* 1932, *s.* 1975, *m.*	Lord Leslie, *b.* 1958.
1861	°*Russell* (5th), Conrad Sebastian Robert Russell, FBA, *b.* 1937, *s.* 1987, *m.*	Viscount Amberley, *b.* 1968.
1915	°*St Aldwyn* (3rd), Michael Henry Hicks Beach, *b.* 1950, *s.* 1992, *m.*	Hon. David S. H. B., *b.* 1955.
1815	*St Germans* (10th), Peregrine Nicholas Eliot, *b.* 1941, *s.* 1988	Lord Eliot, *b.* 1966.
1660	*Sandwich* (11th), John Edward Hollister Montagu, *b.* 1943, *s.* 1995, *m.*	Viscount Hinchingbrooke, *b.* 1969.
1690	*Scarbrough* (12th), Richard Aldred Lumley (13th *Irish Visct., Lumley,* 1628), *b.* 1932, *s.* 1969, *m.*	Viscount Lumley, *b.* 1973.
1701 s.	*Seafield* (13th), Ian Derek Francis Ogilvie-Grant, *b.* 1939, *s.* 1969, *m.*	Viscount Reidhaven, *b.* 1963.
1882	*Selborne* (4th), John Roundell Palmer, KBE, FRS, *b.* 1940, *s.* 1971, *m.*	Viscount Wolmer, *b.* 1971.
1646 s.	*Selkirk.* Disclaimed for life 1994. (*Rt. Hon. Lord James Douglas-Hamilton,* MP, *b.* 1942, *succession decided in his favour* 1996, *m.*)	Hon. John A. D.-H., *b.* 1978
1672	*Shaftesbury* (10th), Anthony Ashley-Cooper, *b.* 1938, *s.* 1961, *m.*	Lord Ashley, *b.* 1977.
1756 I.*	*Shannon* (9th), Richard Bentinck Boyle (8th *Brit. Baron Carleton,* 1786), *b.* 1924, *s.* 1963	Viscount Boyle, *b.* 1960.
1442	*Shrewsbury* & *Waterford* (22nd) (I. 1446), Charles Henry John Benedict Crofton Chetwynd Chetwynd-Talbot (*Premier Earl of England and Ireland;* 7th *Earl Talbot,* 1784), *b.* 1952, *s.* 1980, *m.*	Viscount Ingestre, *b.* 1978.
1961	*Snowdon* (1st), Antony Charles Robert Armstrong-Jones, GCVO, *b.* 1930, *m.* (*see also* page 117)	Viscount Linley, *b.* 1961 (*see also* page 117).
1880	°*Sondes* (5th), Henry George Herbert Milles-Lade, *b.* 1940, *s.* 1970, *m.*	None.
1765	°*Spencer* (9th), Charles Edward Maurice Spencer, *b.* 1964, *s.* 1992, *m.*	Viscount Althorp, *b.* 1994.
1703 s.*	*Stair* (14th), John David James Dalrymple (7th *UK Baron, Oxenfoord,* 1841), *b.* 1961, *s.* 1996	Hon. David H. D., *b.* 1963
1984	*Stockton* (2nd), Alexander Daniel Alan Macmillan, *b.* 1943, *s.* 1986, *m.*	Viscount Macmillan of Ovenden, *b.* 1974.
1821	*Stradbroke* (6th), Robert Keith Rous, *b.* 1937, *s.* 1983, *m.*	Viscount Dunwich, *b.* 1961.
1847	*Strafford* (8th), Thomas Edmund Byng, *b.* 1936, *s.* 1984, *m.*	Viscount Enfield, *b.* 1964.
1606 s.*	*Strathmore* & *Kinghorne* (18th), Michael Fergus Bowes Lyon (16th *Scottish Earl, Strathmore,* 1677, & 18th *Kinghorne,* 1606; 5th *UK Earl, Strathmore* & *Kinghorne,* 1937), *b.* 1957, *s.* 1987, *m.*	Lord Glamis, *b.* 1986.
1603	*Suffolk* (21st) & *Berkshire* (14th) (1626), Michael John James George Robert Howard, *b.* 1935, *s.* 1941, *m.*	Viscount Andover, *b.* 1974.
1955	*Swinton* (2nd), David Yarburgh Cunliffe-Lister, *b.* 1937, *s.* 1972, *m.*	Hon. Nicholas J. C.-L., *b.* 1939.
1714	*Tankerville* (10th), Peter Grey Bennet, *b.* 1956, *s.* 1980	Revd the Hon. George A. G. B., *b.* 1925.
1822	°*Temple of Stowe* (8th), (Walter) Grenville Algernon Temple-Gore-Langton, *b.* 1924, *s.* 1988, *m.*	Lord Langton, *b.* 1955.
1815	*Verulam* (7th), John Duncan Grimston (11th *Irish Visct., Grimston,* 1719; 16th *Scott. Baron, Forrester of Corstorphine,* 1633), *b.* 1951, *s.* 1973, *m.*	Viscount Grimston, *b.* 1978.
1729	°*Waldegrave* (13th), James Sherbrooke Waldegrave, *b.* 1940, *s.* 1995, *m.*	Viscount Chewton, *b.* 1986.
1759	*Warwick* (9th) & °*Brooke* (9th) (*Brit.* 1746), Guy David Greville, *b.* 1957, *s.* 1996, *m.*	Lord Brooke, *b.* 1982.
1633 s.*	*Wemyss* (12th) & *March* (8th) (s. 1697), Francis David Charteris, KT (5th *UK Baron, Wemyss,* 1821), *b.* 1912, *s.* 1937, *m.*	Lord Neidpath, *b.* 1948.
1621 I.	*Westmeath* (13th), William Anthony Nugent, *b.* 1928, *s.* 1971, *m.*	Hon. Sean C. W. N., *b.* 1965.
1624	*Westmorland* (16th), Anthony David Francis Henry Fane, *b.* 1951, *s.* 1993, *m.*	Hon. Harry St C. F., *b.* 1953.

Created	Title, order of succession, name, etc.	Heir
1876	*Wharncliffe* (5th), Richard Alan Montagu Stuart Wortley, *b.* 1953, *s.* 1987, *m.*	Viscount Carlton, *b.* 1980.
1801	*Wilton* (7th), Seymour William Arthur John Egerton, *b.* 1921, *s.* 1927, *m.*	Baron Ebury, *b.* 1934 (*see* page 151).
1628	*Winchilsea* (16th) & *Nottingham* (11th) (1681), Christopher Denys Stormont Finch Hatton, *b.* 1936, *s.* 1950, *m.*	Viscount Maidstone, *b.* 1967.
1766 I.	°*Winterton* (8th), (Donald) David Turnour, *b.* 1943, *s.* 1991, *m.*	Robert C. T., *b.* 1950.
1956	*Woolton* (3rd), Simon Frederick Marquis, *b.* 1958, *s.* 1969, *m.*	None.
1837	*Yarborough* (8th), Charles John Pelham, *b.* 1963, *s.* 1991, *m.*	Lord Worsley, *b.* 1990.

COUNTESSES IN THEIR OWN RIGHT

Style, The Right Hon. the Countess (of) ___
Husband, Untitled
Children's style, As for children of an Earl
For forms of address, *see* page 136

Created	Title, order of succession, name, etc.	Heir
1643 s.	*Dysart* (11th in line), Rosamund Agnes Greaves, *b.* 1914, *s.* 1975	Lady Katherine *Grant of Rothiemurchus, b.* 1918.
1633 s.	*Loudoun* (13th in line), Barbara Huddleston Abney-Hastings, *b.* 1919, *s.* 1960, *m.*	Lord Mauchline, *b.* 1942.
c.1115 s.	*Mar* (31st in line), Margaret of Mar (*Premier Earldom of Scotland*), *b.* 1940, *s.* 1975, *m.*	Mistress of Mar, *b.* 1963.
1947	°*Mountbatten of Burma* (2nd in line), Patricia Edwina Victoria Knatchbull, CBE, *b.* 1924, *s.* 1979, *m.*	Lord Romsey, *b.* 1947 (*see also* page 149).
c.1235 s.	*Sutherland* (24th in line), Elizabeth Millicent Sutherland, *b.* 1921, *s.* 1963, *m.*	Lord Strathnaver, *b.* 1947.

VISCOUNTS

Coronet, Sixteen silver balls
Style, The Right Hon. the Viscount ___
Wife's style, The Right Hon. the Viscountess ___
Children's style, 'The Hon.' before forename and family name
In Scotland, the heir apparent to a Viscount may be styled 'The Master of ___ (title of peer)'
For forms of address, *see* page 136

Created	Title, order of succession, name, etc.	Heir
1945	*Addison* (4th), William Matthew Wand Addison, *b.* 1945, *s.* 1992, *m.*	Hon. Paul W. A., *b.* 1973.
1946	*Alanbrooke* (3rd), Alan Victor Harold Brooke, *b.* 1932, *s.* 1972	None.
1919	*Allenby* (3rd), Lt.-Col. Michael Jaffray Hynman Allenby, *b.* 1931, *s.* 1984, *m.*	Hon. Henry J. H. A., *b.* 1968.
1911	*Allendale* (3rd), Wentworth Hubert Charles Beaumont, *b.* 1922, *s.* 1956	Hon. Wentworth P. I. B., *b.* 1948.
1642 s.	*of Arbuthnott* (16th), John Campbell Arbuthnott, CBE, DSC, FRSE, *b.* 1924, *s.* 1966, *m.*	Master of Arbuthnott, *b.* 1950.
1751 I.	*Ashbrook* (11th), Michael Llowarch Warburton Flower, *b.* 1935, *s.* 1995, *m.*	Hon. Rowland F. W. F., *b.* 1975.
1917	*Astor* (4th), William Waldorf Astor, *b.* 1951, *s.* 1966, *m.*	Hon. William W. A., *b.* 1979.
1781 I.	*Bangor* (8th), William Maxwell David Ward, *b.* 1948, *s.* 1993, *m.*	Hon. E. Nicholas W., *b.* 1953.
1925	*Bearsted* (5th), Nicholas Alan Samuel, *b.* 1950, *s.* 1996, *m.*	Hon. Harry R. S., *b.* 1988.
1963	*Blakenham* (2nd), Michael John Hare, *b.* 1938, *s.* 1982, *m.*	Hon. Caspar J. H., *b.* 1972.
1935	*Bledisloe* (3rd), Christopher Hiley Ludlow Bathurst, QC, *b.* 1934, *s.* 1979	Hon. Rupert E. L. B., *b.* 1964.
1712	*Bolingbroke* (7th) & *St John* (8th) (1716), Kenneth Oliver Musgrave St John, *b.* 1927, *s.* 1974	Hon. Henry F. *St J., b.* 1957.
1960	*Boyd of Merton* (2nd), Simon Donald Rupert Neville Lennox-Boyd, *b.* 1939, *s.* 1983, *m.*	Hon. Benjamin A. *L.-B., b.* 1964.

Created	Title, order of succession, name, etc.	Heir

1717 ɪ.* *Boyne* (11th), Gustavus Michael Stucley Hamilton-Russell (5th *UK Baron, Brancepeth*, 1866), *b.* 1965, *s.* 1995, *m.* — Hon. Richard G. *H.-R.*, DSO, LVO, *b.* 1909.

1929 *Brentford* (4th), Crispin William Joynson-Hicks, *b.* 1933, *s.* 1983, *m.* — Hon. Paul W. *J.-H.*, *b.* 1971.

1929 *Bridgeman* (3rd), Robin John Orlando Bridgeman, *b.* 1930, *s.* 1982, *m.* — Hon. William O. C. *B.*, *b.* 1968.

1868 *Bridport* (4th), Alexander Nelson Hood (7th *Duke of Brontë in Sicily*, 1799, *and* 6th *Irish Baron Bridport*, 1794), *b.* 1948, *s.* 1969, *m.* — Hon. Peregrine A. N. *H.*, *b.* 1974.

1952 *Brookeborough* (3rd), Alan Henry Brooke, *b.* 1952, *s.* 1987, *m.* — Hon. Christopher A. *B.*, *b.* 1954.

1933 *Buckmaster* (3rd), Martin Stanley Buckmaster, OBE, *b.* 1921, *s.* 1974 — Hon. Colin J. *B.*, *b.* 1923.

1939 *Caldecote* (2nd), Robert Andrew Inskip, KBE, DSC, FE ng., *b.* 1917, *s.* 1947, *m.* — Hon. Piers J. H. *I.*, *b.* 1947.

1941 *Camrose*. Disclaimed for life 1995 (*see* Baron Hartwell, page 160) — Hon. Adrian M. *Berry*, *b.* 1937.

1954 *Chandos* (3rd), Thomas Orlando Lyttelton, *b.* 1953, *s.* 1980, *m.* — Hon. Oliver A. *L.*, *b.* 1986.

1665 ɪ. *Charlemont* (14th), John Day Caulfeild (18th *Irish Baron, Caulfeild of Charlemont*, 1620), *b.*1934, *s.*1985, *m.* — Hon. John D. *C.*, *b.* 1966.

1921 *Chelmsford* (3rd), Frederic Jan Thesiger, *b.* 1931, *s.*1970, *m.* — Hon. Frederic C. P. *T.*, *b.* 1962.

1717 ɪ. *Chetwynd* (10th), Adam Richard John Casson Chetwynd, *b.* 1935, *s.* 1965, *m.* — Hon. Adam D. *C.*, *b.* 1969.

1911 *Chilston* (4th), Alastair George Akers-Douglas, *b.* 1946, *s.* 1982, *m.* — Hon. Oliver I. *A.-D.*, *b.* 1973.

1902 *Churchill* (3rd), Victor George Spencer (5th *UK Baron Churchill*, 1815), *b.* 1934, *s.* 1973 — None to Viscountcy. To Barony, Richard H. R. *S.*, *b.* 1926.

1718 *Cobham* (11th), John William Leonard Lyttelton (8th *Irish Baron, Westcote*, 1776), *b.* 1943, *s.* 1977 — Hon. Christopher C. *L.*, *b.* 1947.

1902 *Colville of Culross* (4th), John Mark Alexander Colville, QC (13th *Scott. Baron, Colville of Culross*, 1604), *b.* 1933, *s.* 1945, *m.* — Master of Colville, *b.* 1959.

1826 *Combermere* (5th), Michael Wellington Stapleton-Cotton, *b.* 1929, *s.* 1969, *m.* — Hon. Thomas R. W. *S.-C.*, *b.* 1969.

1917 *Cowdray* (4th), Michael Orlando Weetman Pearson (4th *UK Baron, Cowdray*, 1910), *b.* 1944, *s.* 1995, *m.* — Hon. Charles A. *P.*, *b.* 1956.

1927 *Craigavon* (3rd), Janric Fraser Craig, *b.* 1944, *s.* 1974 — None.

1886 *Cross* (3rd), Assheton Henry Cross, *b.* 1920, *s.* 1932 — None.

1943 *Daventry* (3rd), Francis Humphrey Maurice FitzRoy Newdegate, *b.* 1921, *s.* 1986, *m.* — Hon. James E. *F. N.*, *b.* 1960.

1937 *Davidson* (2nd), John Andrew Davidson, *b.* 1928, *s.* 1970, *m.* — Hon. Malcolm W. M. *D.*, *b.* 1934.

1956 *De L'Isle* (2nd), Philip John Algernon Sidney, MBE, (7th *Baron De L'Isle and Dudley*, 1835), *b.* 1945, *s.* 1991, *m.* — Hon. Philip W. E. *S.*, *b.* 1985.

1776 ɪ. *De Vesci* (7th), Thomas Eustace Vesey (8th *Irish Baron, Knapton*, 1750), *b.* 1955, *s.* 1983, *m.* — Hon. Oliver I. *V.*, *b.* 1991.

1917 *Devonport* (3rd), Terence Kearley, *b.* 1944, *s.* 1973 — Chester D. H. *K.*, *b.* 1932.

1964 *Dilhorne* (2nd), John Mervyn Manningham-Buller, *b.* 1932, *s.* 1980, *m.* — Hon. James E. *M.-B.*, *b.* 1956.

1622 ɪ. *Dillon* (22nd), Henry Benedict Charles Dillon, *b.* 1973, *s.* 1982 — Hon. Richard A. L. *D.*, *b.* 1948.

1785 ɪ. *Doneraile* (10th), Richard Allen St Leger, *b.* 1946, *s.* 1983, *m.* — Hon. Nathaniel W. R. St J. *St L.*, *b.* 1971.

1680 ɪ.* *Downe* (11th), John Christian George Dawnay (4th *UK Baron, Dawnay*, 1897), *b.* 1935, *s.* 1965, *m.* — Hon. Richard H. *D.*, *b.* 1967.

1959 *Dunrossil* (2nd), John William Morrison, CMG, *b.* 1926, *s.* 1961, *m.* — Hon. Andrew W. R. *M.*, *b.* 1953.

1964 *Eccles* (1st), David McAdam Eccles, CH, KCVO, PC, *b.* 1904, *m.* — Hon. John D. *E.*, CBE, *b.* 1931.

1897 *Esher* (4th), Lionel Gordon Baliol Brett, CBE, *b.* 1913. *s.* 1963, *m.* — Hon. Christopher L. B. *B.*, *b.* 1936.

1816 *Exmouth* (10th), Paul Edward Pellew, *b.* 1940, *s.* 1970, *m.* — Hon. Edward F. *P.*, *b.* 1978.

1620 s. *Falkland* (15th), Lucius Edward William Plantagenet Cary (*Premier Scottish Viscount on the Roll*), *b.* 1935, *s.* 1984, *m.* — Master of Falkland, *b.* 1963.

1720 *Falmouth* (9th), George Hugh Boscawen (26th *Eng. Baron, Le Despencer*, 1264), *b.* 1919, *s.* 1962, *m.* — Hon. Evelyn A. H. *B.*, *b.* 1955.

1720 ɪ.* *Gage* (8th), (Henry) Nicolas Gage, (7th *Brit. Baron, Gage*, 1790), *b.* 1934, *s.* 1993, *m.* — Hon. Henry W. *G.*, *b.* 1975.

1727 ɪ. *Galway* (12th), George Rupert Monckton-Arundell, *b.* 1922, *s.* 1980, *m.* — Hon. J. Philip *M.*, *b.* 1952.

1478 ɪ.* *Gormanston* (17th), Jenico Nicholas Dudley Preston (*Premier Viscount of Ireland*; 5th *UK Baron, Gormanston*, 1868), *b.* 1939, *s.* 1940, *w.* — Hon. Jenico F. T. *P.*, *b.* 1974.

1816 ɪ. *Gort* (9th), Foley Robert Standish Prendergast Vereker, *b.* 1951, *s.* 1995, *m.* — Hon. Nicholas L. P. *V.*, *b.* 1954.

1900 *Goschen* (4th), Giles John Harry Goschen, *b.* 1965, *s.* 1977, *m.* — None.

1849 *Gough* (5th), Shane Hugh Maryon Gough, *b.* 1941, *s.* 1951 — None.

1937 *Greenwood* (2nd), David Henry Hamar Greenwood, *b.* 1914, *s.* 1948 — Hon. Michael G. H. *G.*, *b.* 1923.

1929 *Hailsham*. Disclaimed for life 1963 (*see* Lord Hailsham of St Marylebone, page 160) — Rt. Hon. Douglas M. *Hogg*, QC, MP, *b.* 1945.

1891 *Hambleden* (4th), William Herbert Smith, *b.* 1930, *s.* 1948, *m.* — Hon. William H. B. *S.*, *b.* 1955.

1884 *Hampden* (6th), Anthony David Brand, *b.* 1937, *s.* 1975, *m.* — Hon. Francis A. *B.*, *b.* 1970.

1936 *Hanworth* (2nd), David Bertram Pollock, *b.* 1916, *s.* 1936, *m.* — Hon. David S. G. *P.*, *b.* 1946.

1791 ɪ. *Harberton* (10th), Thomas de Vautort Pomeroy, *b.* 1910, *s.* 1980, *m.* — Hon. Robert W. *P.*, *b.* 1916.

Created	Title, order of succession, name, etc.	Heir
1846	*Hardinge* (6th), Charles Henry Nicholas Hardinge, *b.* 1956, *s.* 1984, *m.*	Hon. Andrew H. *H., b.* 1960.
1791 I.	*Hawarden* (9th), (Robert) Connan Wyndham Leslie Maude, *b.* 1961, *s.* 1991, *m.*	Hon. Thomas P. C. *M., b.* 1964.
1960	*Head* (2nd), Richard Antony Head, *b.* 1937, *s.* 1983, *m.*	Hon. Henry J. *H., b.* 1980.
1550	*Hereford* (18th), Robert Milo Leicester Devereux (*Premier Viscount of England*), *b.* 1932, *s.* 1952	Hon. Charles R. de B. *D., b.* 1975.
1842	*Hill* (8th), Antony Rowland Clegg-Hill, *b.* 1931, *s.* 1974, *m.*	Peter D. R. C. *C.-H., b.* 1945.
1796	*Hood* (7th), Alexander Lambert Hood (7th *Irish Baron, Hood,* 1782), *b.* 1914, *s.* 1981, *m.*	Hon. Henry L. A. *H., b.* 1958.
1956	*Ingleby* (2nd), Martin Raymond Peake, *b.* 1926, *s.* 1966, *w.*	None.
1945	*Kemsley* (2nd), (Geoffrey) Lionel Berry, *b.* 1909, *s.* 1968, *m.*	Richard G. *B., b.* 1951.
1911	*Knollys* (3rd), David Francis Dudley Knollys, *b.* 1931, *s.* 1966, *m.*	Hon. Patrick N. M. *K., b.* 1962.
1895	*Knutsford* (6th), Michael Holland-Hibbert, *b.* 1926, *s.* 1986, *m.*	Hon. Henry T. *H.-H., b.* 1959.
1945	*Lambert* (3rd), Michael John Lambert, *b.* 1912, *s.* 1989, *m.*	None.
1954	*Leathers* (3rd), Christopher Graeme Leathers, *b.* 1941, *s.* 1996, *m.*	Hon. James F. *L., b.* 1969.
1922	*Leverhulme* (3rd), Philip William Bryce Lever, KG, TD, *b.* 1915, *s.* 1949, *w.*	None.
1781 I.	*Lifford* (9th), (Edward) James Wingfield Hewitt, *b.* 1949, *s.* 1987, *m.*	Hon. James T. W. *H., b.* 1979.
1921	*Long* (4th), Richard Gerard Long, CBE, *b.* 1929, *s.* 1967, *m.*	Hon. James R. *L., b.* 1960.
1957	*Mackintosh of Halifax* (3rd), (John) Clive Mackintosh, *b.* 1958, *s.* 1980, *m.*	Hon. Thomas H. G. *M., b.* 1985.
1955	*Malvern* (3rd), Ashley Kevin Godfrey Huggins, *b.* 1949, *s.* 1978	Hon. M. James *H., b.* 1928.
1945	*Marchwood* (3rd), David George Staveley Penny, *b.* 1936, *s.* 1979, *m.*	Hon. Peter G. W. *P., b.* 1965.
1942	*Margesson* (2nd), Francis Vere Hampden Margesson, *b.* 1922, *s.* 1965, *m.*	Capt. Hon. Richard F. D. *M., b.* 1960.
1660 I.*	*Massereene* (14th) & *Ferrard* (7th) (1797), John David Clotworthy Whyte-Melville Foster Skeffington (7th *UK Baron, Oriel,* 1821), *b.* 1940, *s.* 1992, *m.*	Hon. Charles J. C. W.-M. F. *S., b.* 1973.
1802	*Melville* (9th), Robert David Ross Dundas, *b.* 1937, *s.* 1971, *m.*	Hon. Robert H. K. *D., b.* 1984.
1916	*Mersey* (4th), Richard Maurice Clive Bigham (13th *Scott. Lord Nairne,* 1681, *s.* 1995), *b.* 1934, *s.* 1979, *m.*	Hon. Edward J. H. *B., b.* 1966.
1717 I.*	*Midleton* (12th), Alan Henry Brodrick (9th *Brit. Baron, Brodrick of Peper Harow,* 1796), *b.* 1949, *s.* 1988, *m.*	Hon. Ashley R. *B., b.* 1980.
1962	*Mills* (3rd), Christopher Philip Roger Mills, *b.* 1956, *s.* 1988, *m.*	None.
1716 I.	*Molesworth* (11th), Richard Gosset Molesworth, *b.* 1907, *s.* 1961, *w.*	Hon. Robert B. K. *M., b.* 1959.
1801 I.*	*Monck* (7th), Charles Stanley Monck (4th *UK Baron, Monck,* 1866), *b.* 1953, *s.* 1982 (does not use title)	Hon. George S. *M., b.* 1957.
1957	*Monckton of Brenchley* (2nd), Maj.-Gen. Gilbert Walter Riversdale Monckton, CB, OBE, MC, *b.* 1915, *s.* 1965, *m.*	Hon Christopher W. *M., b.* 1952.
1946	*Montgomery of Alamein* (2nd), David Bernard Montgomery, CBE, *b.* 1928, *s.* 1976, *m.*	Hon. Henry D. *M., b.* 1954.
1550 I.*	*Mountgarret* (17th), Richard Henry Piers Butler (4th *UK Baron, Mountgarret,* 1911), *b.* 1936, *s.* 1966, *m.*	Hon. Piers J. R. *B., b.* 1961.
1952	*Norwich* (2nd), John Julius Cooper, CVO, *b.* 1929, *s.* 1954, *m.*	Hon. Jason C. D. B. *C., b.* 1959.
1651 S.	*of Oxfuird* (13th), George Hubbard Makgill, *b.* 1934, *s.* 1986, *m.*	Master of Oxfuird, *b.* 1969.
1873	*Portman,* (9th), Edward Henry Berkeley Portman, *b.* 1934, *s.* 1967, *m.*	Hon. Christopher E. B. *P., b.* 1958.
1743 I.*	*Powerscourt* (10th), Mervyn Niall Wingfield (4th *UK Baron, Powerscourt,* 1885), *b.* 1935, *s.* 1973, *m.*	Hon. Mervyn A. *W., b.* 1963.
1900	*Ridley* (4th), Matthew White Ridley, KG, GCVO, TD, *b.* 1925, *s.* 1964, *m.* Lord Steward	Hon. Matthew W. *R., b.* 1958.
1960	*Rochdale* (2nd), St John Durival Kemp, *b.* 1938, *s.* 1993, *m.*	Hon. Jonathan H. D. *K., b.* 1961.
1919	*Rothermere* (3rd), Vere Harold Esmond Harmsworth, *b.* 1925, *s.* 1978, *m.*	Hon. H. Jonathan E. V. *H., b.* 1967.
1937	*Runciman of Doxford* (3rd), Walter Garrison Runciman (Garry), CBE, FBA (4th *UK Baron, Runciman,* 1933), *b.* 1934, *s.* 1989, *m.*	Hon. David W. *R., b.* 1967.
1918	*St Davids* (3rd), Colwyn Jestyn John Philipps (20th *Engl. Baron Strange of Knokin,* 1299, 8th *Engl. Baron Hungerford,* 1426, and *De Moleyns,* 1445), *b.* 1939, *s.* 1991, *m.*	Hon. Rhodri C. *P., b.* 1966.
1801	*St Vincent* (7th), Ronald George James Jervis, *b.* 1905, *s.* 1940, *m.*	Hon. Edward R. J. *J., b.* 1951.
1937	*Samuel* (3rd), David Herbert Samuel, OBE, PH.D., *b.* 1922, *s.* 1978, *m.*	Hon. Dan J. *S., b.* 1925.
1911	*Scarsdale* (3rd), Francis John Nathaniel Curzon (7th *Brit. Baron, Scarsdale,* 1761), *b.* 1924, *s.* 1977, *m.*	Hon. Peter G. N. *C., b.* 1949.
1905	*Selby* (4th), Michael Guy John Gully, *b.* 1942, *s.* 1959, *m.*	Hon. Edward T. W. *G., b.* 1967.
1805	*Sidmouth* (7th), John Tonge Anthony Pellew Addington, *b.* 1914, *s.* 1976, *m.*	Hon. Jeremy F. *A., b.* 1947.
1940	*Simon* (3rd), Jan David Simon, *b.* 1940, *s.* 1993, *m.*	None.
1960	*Slim* (2nd), John Douglas Slim, OBE, *b.* 1927, *s.* 1970, *m.*	Hon. Mark W. R. *S., b.* 1960.

Created	*Title, order of succession, name, etc.*	*Heir*
1954	*Soulbury* (2nd), James Herwald Ramsbotham, *b.* 1915, *s.* 1971, *w.*	Hon. Sir Peter E. *R.*, GCMG, GCVO, *b.* 1919.
1776 I.	*Southwell* (7th), Pyers Anthony Joseph Southwell, *b.* 1930, *s.* 1960, *m.*	Hon. Richard A. P. *S.*, *b.* 1956.
1942	*Stansgate.* Disclaimed for life 1963 (*Rt. Hon. Anthony Neil Wedgwood Benn*, MP, *b.* 1925, *s.* 1960, *m.*)	Stephen M. W. *B.*, *b.* 1951.
1959	*Stuart of Findhorn* (2nd), David Randolph Moray Stuart, *b.* 1924, *s.* 1971, *m.*	Hon. J. Dominic *S.*, *b.* 1948.
1957	*Tenby* (3rd), William Lloyd George, *b.* 1927, *s.* 1983, *m.*	Hon. Timothy H. G. *L. G.*, *b.* 1962.
1952	*Thurso* (3rd), John Archibald Sinclair, *b.* 1953, *s.* 1995, *m.*	Hon. James A. R. *S.*, *b.* 1984.
1983	*Tonypandy* (1st), (Thomas) George Thomas, PC, *b.* 1909	None.
1721	*Torrington* (11th), Timothy Howard St George Byng, *b.* 1943, *s.* 1961, *m.*	John L. *B.*, MC, *b.* 1919.
1936	*Trenchard* (3rd), Hugh Trenchard, *b.* 1951, *s.* 1987, *m.*	Hon. Alexander T. *T.*, *b.* 1978.
1921	*Ullswater* (2nd), Nicholas James Christopher Lowther, PC, *b.* 1942, *s.* 1949, *m.*	Hon. Benjamin J. *L.*, *b.* 1975.
1621 I.	*Valentia* (15th), Richard John Dighton Annesley, *b.* 1929, *s.* 1983, *m.*	Hon. Francis W. D. *A.*, *b.* 1959.
1952	*Waverley* (3rd), John Desmond Forbes Anderson, *b.* 1949, *s.* 1990	None.
1938	*Weir* (3rd), William Kenneth James Weir, *b.* 1933, *s.* 1975, *m.*	Hon. James W. H. *W.*, *b.* 1965.
1983	*Whitelaw* (1st), William Stephen Ian Whitelaw, KT, CH, MC, PC, *b.* 1918, *m.*	None.
1918	*Wimborne* (4th), Ivor Mervyn Vigors Guest (5th *UK Baron, Wimborne,* 1880), *b.* 1968, *s.* 1993	Hon. Julian J. *G.*, *b.* 1945.
1923	*Younger of Leckie* (3rd), Edward George Younger, OBE, TD, *b.* 1906, *s.* 1946, *w.*	Baron Younger of Prestwick, KT, KCVO, TD, PC, *b.* 1931 (*see* page 162).

BARONS/LORDS

Coronet, Six silver balls
Style, The Right Hon. the Lord ___ . In the Peerage of Scotland there is no rank of Baron; the equivalent rank is Lord of Parliament (*see* page 137) and Scottish peers should always be styled 'Lord', never 'Baron'
Wife's style, The Right Hon. the Lady ___
Children's style, 'The Hon.' before forename and family name
In Scotland, the heir apparent to a Lord may be styled 'The Master of ___ (title of peer)'
For forms of address, *see* page 136

Created	*Title, order of succession, name, etc.*	*Heir*
1911	*Aberconway* (3rd), Charles Melville McLaren, *b.* 1913, *s.* 1953, *m.*	Hon. H. Charles *M.*, *b.* 1948.
1873	*Aberdare* (4th), Morys George Lyndhurst Bruce, KBE, PC, *b.* 1919, *s.* 1957, *m.*	Hon. Alastair J. L. *B.*, *b.* 1947.
1835	*Abinger* (8th), James Richard Scarlett, *b.* 1914, *s.* 1943, *m.*	Hon. James H. *S.*, *b.* 1959.
1869	*Acton* (4th), Richard Gerald Lyon-Dalberg-Acton, *b.* 1941, *s.* 1989, *m.*	Hon. John C. F. H. *L.-D.-A.*, *b.* 1966.
1887	*Addington* (6th), Dominic Bryce Hubbard, *b.* 1963, *s.* 1982	Hon. Michael W. L. *H.*, *b.* 1965.
1896	*Aldenham* (6th), and *Hunsdon of Hunsdon* (4th) (1923), Vicary Tyser Gibbs, *b.* 1948, *s.* 1986, *m.*	Hon. Humphrey W. F. *G.*, *b.* 1989.
1962	*Aldington* (1st), Toby Austin Richard William Low, KCMG, CBE, DSO, TD, PC, *b.* 1914, *m.*	Hon Charles H. S. *L.*, *b.* 1948.
1945	*Altrincham.* Disclaimed for life 1963 (*John Edward Poynder Grigg*, *b.* 1924, *s.* 1955, *m.*)	Hon. Anthony U. D. D. *G..*, *b.* 1934.
1929	*Alvingham* (2nd), Maj.-Gen. Robert Guy Eardley Yerburgh, CBE, *b.* 1926, *s.* 1955, *m.*	Capt. Hon. Robert R. G. *Y.*, *b.* 1956.
1892	*Amherst of Hackney* (4th), William Hugh Amherst Cecil, *b.* 1940, *s.* 1980, *m.*	Hon. H. William A. *C.*, *b.* 1968.
1881	*Ampthill* (4th), Geoffrey Denis Erskine Russell, CBE, PC, *b.* 1921, *s.* 1973	Hon. David W. E. *R.*, *b.* 1947.
1947	*Amwell* (3rd), Keith Norman Montague, *b.* 1943, *s.* 1990, *m.*	Hon. Ian K. *M.*, *b.* 1973.
1863	*Annaly* (6th), Luke Richard White, *b.* 1954, *s.* 1990, *m.*	Hon. Luke H. *W.*, *b.* 1990.
1949	*Archibald.* Disclaimed for life 1975 (*George Christopher Archibald*, *b.* 1926, *s.* 1975, *m.*)	None.
1885	*Ashbourne* (4th), Edward Barry Greynville Gibson, *b.* 1933, *s.* 1983, *m.*	Hon. Edward C. d'O. *G.*, *b.* 1967.

Created	Title, order of succession, name, etc.	Heir
1835	*Ashburton* (7th), John Francis Harcourt Baring, KG, KCVO, b. 1928, s. 1991, m.	Hon. Mark F. R. B., b. 1958.
1892	*Ashcombe* (4th), Henry Edward Cubitt, b. 1924, s. 1962, m.	Mark E. C., b. 1964.
1911	*Ashton of Hyde* (3rd), Thomas John Ashton, TD, b. 1926, s. 1983, m.	Hon. Thomas H. A., b. 1958.
1800 I.	*Ashtown* (7th), Nigel Clive Crosby Trench, KCMG, b. 1916, s. 1990, w.	Hon. Roderick N. G. T., b. 1944.
1956	*Astor of Hever* (3rd), John Jacob Astor, b. 1946, s. 1984, m.	Hon. Charles G. J. A., b. 1990.
1789 I.*	*Auckland* (9th), Ian George Eden (9th *Brit. Baron, Auckland*, 1793), b. 1926, s. 1957, m.	Hon. Robert I. B. E., b. 1962.
1313	*Audley* (25th), Richard Michael Thomas Souter, b. 1914, s. 1973, m.	Three co-heiresses.
1900	*Avebury* (4th), Eric Reginald Lubbock, b. 1928, s. 1971, m.	Hon. Lyulph A. J. L., b. 1954.
1718 I.	*Aylmer* (13th), Michael Anthony Aylmer, b. 1923, s. 1982, m.	Hon. A. Julian A., b. 1951.
1929	*Baden-Powell* (3rd), Robert Crause Baden-Powell, b. 1936, s. 1962, m.	Hon. David M. B.-P., b. 1940.
1780	*Bagot* (9th), Heneage Charles Bagot, b. 1914, s. 1979, m.	Hon. C. H. Shaun B., b. 1944.
1953	*Baillieu* (3rd), James William Latham Baillieu, b. 1950, s. 1973, m.	Hon. Robert L. B., b. 1979.
1607 S.	*Balfour of Burleigh* (8th), Robert Bruce, FRSE, b. 1927, s. 1967, m.	Hon. Victoria B., b. 1973.
1945	*Balfour of Inchrye* (2nd), Ian Balfour, b. 1924, s. 1988, m.	None.
1924	*Banbury of Southam* (3rd), Charles William Banbury, b. 1953, s. 1981, m.	None.
1698	*Barnard* (11th), Harry John Neville Vane, TD, b. 1923, s. 1964	Hon. Henry F. C. V., b. 1959.
1887	*Basing* (5th), Neil Lutley Sclater-Booth, b. 1939, s. 1983, m.	Hon. Stuart W. S.-B., b. 1969.
1917	*Beaverbrook* (3rd), Maxwell William Humphrey Aitken, b. 1951, s. 1985, m.	Hon. Maxwell F. A, b. 1977.
1647 S.	*Belhaven and Stenton* (13th), Robert Anthony Carmichael Hamilton, b. 1927, s. 1961, m.	Master of Belhaven, b. 1953.
1848 I.	*Bellew* (7th), James Bryan Bellew, b. 1920, s. 1981, m.	Hon. Bryan E. B., b. 1943.
1856	*Belper* (4th), (Alexander) Ronald George Strutt, b. 1912, s. 1956	Hon. Richard H. S., b. 1941.
1938	*Belstead* (2nd), John Julian Ganzoni, PC, b. 1932, s. 1958	None.
1421	*Berkeley* (18th), Anthony Fitzhardinge Gueterbock, OBE, b. 1939, s. 1992, m.	Hon. Thomas F. G., b. 1969.
1922	*Bethell* (4th), Nicholas William Bethell, b. 1938, s. 1967, m.	Hon. James N. B., b. 1967.
1938	*Bicester* (3rd), Angus Edward Vivian Smith, b. 1932, s. 1968	Hugh C. V. S., b. 1934.
1903	*Biddulph* (5th), (Anthony) Nicholas Colin Maitland Biddulph, b. 1959, s. 1988, m.	Hon. William I. R. M. B., b. 1963.
1938	*Birdwood* (3rd), Mark William Ogilvie Birdwood, b. 1938, s. 1962, m.	None.
1958	*Birkett* (2nd), Michael Birkett, b. 1929, s. 1962, m.	Hon. Thomas B., b. 1982.
1907	*Blyth* (4th), Anthony Audley Rupert Blyth, b. 1931, s. 1977, m.	Hon. Riley A. J. B., b. 1955.
1797	*Bolton* (7th), Richard William Algar Orde-Powlett, b. 1929, s. 1963, m.	Hon. Harry A. N. O.-P., b. 1954.
1452 S.	*Borthwick* (23rd), John Henry Stuart Borthwick, TD, b. 1905, *claim succeeded* 1986, w.	Master of Borthwick, b. 1940.
1922	*Borwick* (4th), James Hugh Myles Borwick, MC, b. 1917, s. 1961, m.	Hon. George S. B., b. 1922.
1761	*Boston* (10th), Timothy George Frank Boteler Irby, b. 1939, s. 1978, m.	Hon. George W. E. B. I., b. 1971.
1942	*Brabazon of Tara* (3rd), Ivon Anthony Moore-Brabazon, b. 1946, s. 1974, m.	Hon. Benjamin R. M.-B., b. 1983.
1880	*Brabourne* (7th), John Ulick Knatchbull, CBE, b. 1924, s. 1943, m.	Lord Romsey, b. 1947 (*see* page 145).
1925	*Bradbury* (3rd), John Bradbury, b. 1940, s. 1994, m.	Hon. John B., b. 1973.
1962	*Brain* (2nd), Christopher Langdon Brain, b. 1926, s. 1966, m.	Hon. Michael C. B., DM, FRCP, b. 1928.
1938	*Brassey of Apethorpe* (3rd), David Henry Brassey, OBE, b. 1932, s. 1967, m.	Hon. Edward B., b. 1964.
1788	*Braybrooke* (10th), Robin Henry Charles Neville, b. 1932, s. 1990, m.	George N., b. 1943.
1957	*Bridges* (2nd), Thomas Edward Bridges, GCMG, b. 1927, s. 1969, m.	Hon. Mark T. B., b. 1954.
1945	*Broadbridge* (3rd), Peter Hewett Broadbridge, b. 1938, s. 1972, m.	Martin H. B., b. 1929.
1933	*Brocket* (3rd), Charles Ronald George Nall-Cain, b. 1952, s. 1967, m.	Hon. Alexander C. C. N.-C., b. 1984.
1860	*Brougham and Vaux* (5th), Michael John Brougham, CBE, b. 1938, s. 1967	Hon. Charles W. B., b. 1971.
1945	*Broughshane* (3rd), (William) Kensington Davison, DSO, DFC, b. 1914, s. 1995	None.
1776	*Brownlow* (7th), Edward John Peregrine Cust, b. 1936, s. 1978, m.	Hon. Peregrine E. Q. C., b. 1974.
1942	*Bruntisfield* (2nd), John Robert Warrender, OBE, MC, TD, b. 1921, s. 1993, m.	Hon. Michael J. V. W., b. 1949.
1950	*Burden* (3rd), Andrew Philip Burden, b. 1959, s. 1995	Hon. Fraser W. E. B., b. 1964.
1529	*Burgh* (7th), Alexander Peter Willoughby Leith, b. 1935, s. 1959, m.	Hon. A. Gregory D. L., b. 1958.
1903	*Burnham* (6th), Hugh John Frederick Lawson, b. 1931, s. 1993, m.	Hon. Harry F. A. L., b. 1968.
1897	*Burton* (3rd), Michael Evan Victor Baillie, b. 1924, s. 1962, m.	Hon. Evan M. R. B., b. 1949.
1643	*Byron* (13th), Robert James Byron, b. 1950, s. 1989, m.	Hon. Charles R. G. B., b. 1990.
1937	*Cadman* (3rd), John Anthony Cadman, b. 1938, s. 1966, m.	Hon. Nicholas A. J. C., b. 1977.
1796	*Calthorpe* (10th), Peter Waldo Somerset Gough-Calthorpe, b. 1927, s. 1945, m.	None.
1945	*Calverley* (3rd), Charles Rodney Muff, b. 1946, s. 1971, m.	Hon. Jonathan E. M., b. 1975.

Created	Title, order of succession, name, etc.	Heir
1383	*Camoys* (7th), (Ralph) Thomas Campion George Sherman Stonor, *b.* 1940, *s.* 1976, *m.*	Hon. R. William R. T. *S., b.* 1974.
1715 I.	*Carbery* (11th), Peter Ralfe Harrington Evans-Freke, *b.* 1920, *s.* 1970, *m.*	Hon. Michael P. *E.-F., b.* 1942.
1834 I.*	*Carew* (7th), Patrick Thomas Conolly-Carew (7th *UK Baron, Carew,* 1838), *b.* 1938, *s.* 1994, *m.*	Hon. William P. *C.-C., b.* 1973.
1916	*Carnock* (4th), David Henry Arthur Nicolson, *b.* 1920, *s.* 1982	Nigel *N.,* MBE, *b.* 1917.
1796 I.*	*Carrington* (6th), Peter Alexander Rupert Carington, KG, GCMG, CH, MC, PC (6th *Brit. Baron, Carrington,* 1797), *b.* 1919, *s.* 1938, *m.*	Hon. Rupert F. J. *C., b.* 1948.
1812 I.	*Castlemaine* (8th), Roland Thomas John Handcock, MBE, *b.* 1943, *s.* 1973, *m.*	Hon. Ronan M. E. *H., b.* 1989.
1936	*Catto* (2nd), Stephen Gordon Catto, *b.* 1923, *s.* 1959, *m.*	Hon. Innes G. *C., b.* 1950.
1918	*Cawley* (3rd), Frederick Lee Cawley, *b.* 1913, *s.* 1954, *m.*	Hon. John F. *C., b.* 1946.
1603	*Cecil,* a subsidiary title of the Marquess of Salisbury. His heir Viscount Cranborne, PC, was given a Writ in Acceleration in this title to enable him to sit in the House of Lords whilst his father is still alive (*see also* page 140)	
1937	*Chatfield* (2nd), Ernle David Lewis Chatfield, *b.* 1917, *s.* 1967, *m.*	None.
1858	*Chesham* (6th), Nicholas Charles Cavendish, *b.* 1941, *s.* 1989, *m.*	Hon. Charles G. C. *C., b.* 1974.
1945	*Chetwode* (2nd), Philip Chetwode, *b.* 1937, *s.* 1950, *m.*	Hon. Roger *C., b.* 1968.
1945	*Chorley* (2nd), Roger Richard Edward Chorley, *b.* 1930, *s.* 1978, *m.*	Hon. Nicholas R. D. *C., b.* 1966.
1858	*Churston* (5th), John Francis Yarde-Buller, *b.* 1934, *s.* 1991, *m.*	Hon. Benjamin F. A. *Y.-B., b.* 1974.
1946	*Citrine* (2nd), Norman Arthur Citrine, *b.* 1914, *s.* 1983, *w.*	Hon. Ronald E. *C., b.* 1919.
1800 I.	*Clanmorris* (8th), Simon John Ward Bingham, *b.* 1937, *s.* 1988, *m.*	Robert D. de B. *B., b.* 1942.
1672	*Clifford of Chudleigh* (14th), Thomas Hugh Clifford, *b.* 1948, *s.* 1988, *m.*	Hon. Alexander T. H. *C., b.* 1985.
1299	*Clinton* (22nd), Gerard Nevile Mark Fane Trefusis, *b.* 1934, *title called out of abeyance* 1965, *m.*	Hon. Charles P. R. F. *T., b.* 1962.
1955	*Clitheroe* (2nd), Ralph John Assheton, *b.* 1929, *s.* 1984, *m.*	Hon. Ralph C. *A., b.* 1962.
1919	*Clwyd* (3rd), (John) Anthony Roberts, *b.* 1935, *s.* 1987, *m.*	Hon. J. Murray *R., b.* 1971.
1948	*Clydesmuir* (2nd), Ronald John Bilsland Colville, KT, CB, MBE, TD, *b.* 1917, *s.* 1954, *m.*	Hon. David R. *C., b.* 1949.
1960	*Cobbold* (2nd), David Antony Fromanteel Lytton Cobbold, *b.* 1937, *s.* 1987, *m.*	Hon. Henry F. *L. C., b.* 1962.
1919	*Cochrane of Cults* (4th), (Ralph Henry) Vere Cochrane, *b.* 1926, *s.* 1990, *m.*	Hon. Thomas H. V. *C., b.* 1957.
1954	*Coleraine* (2nd), (James) Martin (Bonar) Law, *b.* 1931, *s.* 1980, *w.*	Hon. James P. B. *L., b.* 1975.
1873	*Coleridge* (5th), William Duke Coleridge, *b.* 1937, *s.* 1984, *m.*	Hon. James D. *C., b.* 1967.
1946	*Colgrain* (3rd), David Colin Campbell, *b.* 1920, *s.* 1973, *m.*	Hon. Alastair C. L. *C., b.* 1951.
1917	*Colwyn* (3rd), (Ian) Anthony Hamilton-Smith, CBE, *b.* 1942, *s.* 1966, *m.*	Hon. Craig P. *H.-S., b.* 1968.
1956	*Colyton* (2nd), Alisdair John Munro Hopkinson, *b.* 1958, *s.* 1996, *m.*	Hon. James P. M. *H., b.* 1983.
1841	*Congleton* (8th), Christopher Patrick Parnell, *b.* 1930, *s.* 1967, *m.*	Hon. John P. C. *P., b.* 1959.
1927	*Cornwallis* (3rd), Fiennes Neil Wykeham Cornwallis, OBE, *b.* 1921, *s.* 1982, *m.*	Hon. F. W. Jeremy *C., b.* 1946.
1874	*Cottesloe* (5th), Cdr. John Tapling Fremantle, *b.* 1927, *s.* 1994, *m.*	Hon. Thomas F. H. *F., b.* 1966.
1929	*Craigmyle* (3rd), Thomas Donald Mackay Shaw, *b.* 1923, *s.* 1944, *m.*	Hon. Thomas C. *S., b.* 1960.
1899	*Cranworth* (3rd), Philip Bertram Gurdon, *b.* 1940, *s.* 1964, *m.*	Hon. Sacha W. R. *G., b.* 1970.
1959	*Crathorne* (2nd), Charles James Dugdale, *b.* 1939, *s.* 1977, *m.*	Hon. Thomas A. J. *D., b.* 1977.
1892	*Crawshaw* (4th), William Michael Clifton Brooks, *b.* 1933, *s.* 1946	Hon. David G. *B., b.* 1934.
1940	*Croft* (2nd), Michael Henry Glendower Page Croft, *b.* 1916, *s.* 1947, *w.*	Hon. Bernard W. H. P. *C., b.* 1949.
1797 I.	*Crofton* (7th), Guy Patrick Gilbert Crofton, *b.* 1951, *s.* 1989, *m.*	Hon. E. Harry P. *C., b.* 1988.
1375	*Cromwell* (7th), Godfrey John Bewicke-Copley, *b.* 1960, *s.* 1982, *m.*	Hon. Thomas D. *B.-C., b.* 1964.
1947	*Crook* (2nd), Douglas Edwin Crook, *b.* 1926, *s* 1989, *m.*	Hon. Robert D. E. *C., b.* 1955.
1920	*Cullen of Ashbourne* (2nd), Charles Borlase Marsham Cokayne, MBE, *b.* 1912, *s.* 1932, *w.*	Hon. Edmund W. M. *C., b.* 1916.
1914	*Cunliffe* (3rd), Roger Cunliffe, *b.* 1932, *s.* 1963, *m.*	Hon. Henry *C., b.* 1962.
1927	*Daresbury* (3rd), Edward Gilbert Greenall, *b.* 1928, *s.* 1990, *m.*	Hon. Peter G. *G., b.* 1953.
1924	*Darling* (2nd), Robert Charles Henry Darling, *b.* 1919, *s.* 1936, *m.*	Hon. R. Julian H. *D., b.* 1944.
1946	*Darwen* (3rd), Roger Michael Davies, *b.* 1938, *s.* 1988, *m.*	Hon. Paul *D., b.* 1962.
1932	*Davies* (3rd), David Davies, *b.* 1940, *s.* 1944, *m.*	Hon. David D. *D., b.* 1975.
1812 I.	*Decies* (7th), Marcus Hugh Tristram de la Poer Beresford, *b.* 1948, *s.* 1992, *m.*	Hon. Robert M. D. *de la P. B., b.* 1988.
1299	*de Clifford* (27th), John Edward Southwell Russell, *b.* 1928, *s.* 1982, *m.*	Hon. William S. *R., b.* 1930.
1851	*De Freyne* (7th), Francis Arthur John French, *b.* 1927, *s.* 1935, *m.*	Hon. Fulke C. A. J. *F., b.* 1957.
1821	*Delamere* (5th), Hugh George Cholmondeley, *b.* 1934, *s.* 1979, *m.*	Hon. Thomas P. G. *C., b.* 1968.
1838	*de Mauley* (6th), Gerald John Ponsonby, *b.* 1921, *s.* 1962, *m.*	Col. Hon. Thomas M. *P.,* TD, *b.* 1930.
1937	*Denham* (2nd), Bertram Stanley Mitford Bowyer, KBE, PC, *b.* 1927, *s.* 1948, *m.*	Hon. Richard G. G. *B., b.* 1959.

Created	Title, order of succession, name, etc.	Heir
1834	*Denman* (5th), Charles Spencer Denman, CBE, MC, TD, *b.* 1916, *s.* 1971, *w.*	Hon. Richard T. S. *D.*, *b.* 1946.
1885	*Deramore* (6th), Richard Arthur de Yarburgh-Bateson, *b.* 1911, *s.* 1964, *m.*	None.
1887	*De Ramsey* (4th), John Ailwyn Fellowes, *b.* 1942, *s.* 1993, *m.*	Hon. Freddie J. *F.*, *b.* 1978.
1264	*de Ros* (28th), Peter Trevor Maxwell, *b.* 1958, *s.* 1983, *m.* (*Premier Baron of England*)	Hon. Finbar J. *M.*, *b.* 1988.
1881	*Derwent* (5th), Robin Evelyn Leo Vanden-Bempde-Johnstone, I.VO, *b.* 1930, *s.* 1986, *m.*	Hon. Francis P. H. *V.-B.-J.*, *b.* 1965.
1831	*de Saumarez* (7th), Eric Douglas Saumarez, *b.* 1956, *s.* 1991, *m.*	Hon. Victor T. *S.*, *b.* 1956.
1910	*de Villiers* (3rd), Arthur Percy de Villiers, *b.* 1911, *s.* 1934	Hon. Alexander C. *de V.*, *b.* 1940.
1930	*Dickinson* (2nd), Richard Clavering Hyett Dickinson, *b.* 1926, *s.* 1943, *m.*	Hon. Martin H. *D.*, *b.* 1961.
1620 I.*	*Digby* (12th), Edward Henry Kenelm Digby (6th *Brit. Baron, Digby*, 1765), *b.* 1924, *s.* 1964, *m.*	Hon. Henry N. K. *D.*, *b.* 1954.
1615	*Dormer* (17th), Geoffrey Henry Dormer, *b.* 1920, *s.* 1995, *m.*	Hon. William R. *D.*, *b.* 1960.
1943	*Dowding* (3rd), Piers Hugh Tremenheere Dowding, *b.* 1948, *s.* 1992	Hon. Mark D. J. *D.*, *b.* 1949.
1800 I.	*Dufferin and Clandeboye.* The 10th Baron died in 1991. Heir had not established his claim to the title at the time of going to press	Sir John Blackwood, Bt., *b.* 1944.
1929	*Dulverton* (3rd), (Gilbert) Michael Hamilton Wills, *b.* 1944, *s.* 1992, *m.*	Hon. Robert A. H. *W.*, *b.* 1983.
1800 I.	*Dunalley* (7th), Henry Francis Cornelius Prittie, *b.* 1948, *s.* 1992, *m.*	Hon. Joel H. *P.*, *b.* 1981.
1324 I.	*Dunboyne* (28th), Patrick Theobald Tower Butler, VRD, *b.* 1917, *s.* 1945, *m.*	Hon. John F. *B.*, *b.* 1951.
1802	*Dunleath* (5th), Michael Henry Mulholland, *b.* 1915, *s.* 1993, *w.*	Hon. Brian H. *M.*, *b.* 1950.
1439 I.	*Dunsany* (19th), Randal Arthur Henry Plunkett, *b.* 1906, *s.* 1957, *m.*	Hon. Edward J. C. *P.*, *b.* 1939.
1780	*Dynevor* (9th), Richard Charles Uryan Rhys, *b.* 1935, *s.* 1962	Hon. Hugo G. U. *R.*, *b.* 1966.
1857	*Ebury* (6th), Francis Egerton Grosvenor, *b.* 1934, *s.* 1957, *m.*	Hon. Julian F. M. *G.*, *b.* 1959.
1963	*Egremont* (2nd), & *Leconfield* (7th) (1859), John Max Henry Scawen Wyndham, *b.* 1948, *s.* 1972, *m.*	Hon. George R. V. *W.*, *b.* 1983.
1643	*Elibank* (14th), Alan D'Ardis Erskine-Murray, *b.* 1923, *s.* 1973, *m.*	Master of Elibank, *b.* 1964.
1802	*Ellenborough* (8th), Richard Edward Cecil Law, *b.* 1926, *s.* 1945, *m.*	Maj. Hon. Rupert E. H. *L.*, *b.* 1955.
1509 S.*	*Elphinstone* (19th), Alexander Mountstuart Elphinstone (5th *UK Baron Elphinstone*, 1885), *b.* 1980, *s.* 1994, *M.*	Hon. Angus J. *E.*, *b.* 1982.
1934	*Elton* (2nd), Rodney Elton, TD, *b.* 1930, *s.* 1973, *m.*	Hon. Edward P. *E.*, *b.* 1966.
1964	*Erroll of Hale* (1st), Frederick James Erroll, TD, PC, *b.* 1914, *m.*	None.
1627 S.	*Fairfax of Cameron* (14th), Nicholas John Albert Fairfax, *b.* 1956, *s.* 1964, *m.*	Hon. Edward N. T. *F.*, *b.* 1984.
1961	*Fairhaven* (3rd), Ailwyn Henry George Broughton, *b.* 1936, *s.* 1973, *m.*	Maj. Hon. James H. A. *B.*, *b.* 1963.
1916	*Faringdon* (3rd), Charles Michael Henderson, *b.* 1937, *s.* 1977, *m.*	Hon. James H. *H.*, *b.* 1961.
1756 I.	*Farnham* (12th), Barry Owen Somerset Maxwell, *b.* 1931, *s.* 1957, *m.*	Hon. Simon K. *M.*, *b.* 1933.
1856 I.	*Fermoy* (6th), Patrick Maurice Burke Roche, *b.* 1967, *s.* 1984	Hon. E. Hugh B. *R.*, *b.* 1972.
1826	*Feversham* (6th), Charles Antony Peter Duncombe, *b.* 1945, *s.* 1963, *m.*	Hon. Jasper O. S. *D.*, *b.* 1968.
1798 I.	*ffrench* (8th), Robuck John Peter Charles Mario ffrench, *b.* 1956, *s.* 1986, *m.*	Hon. John C. M. J. F. *ff.*, *b.* 1928.
1909	*Fisher* (3rd), John Vavasseur Fisher, DSC, *b.* 1921, *s.* 1955, *m.*	Hon. Patrick V. *F.*, *b.* 1953.
1295	*Fitzwalter* (21st), (Fitzwalter) Brook Plumptre, *b.* 1914, *title called out of abeyance*, 1953, *m.*	Hon. Julian B. *P.*, *b.* 1952.
1776	*Foley* (8th), Adrian Gerald Foley, *b.* 1923, *s.* 1927, *m.*	Hon. Thomas H. *F.*, *b.* 1961.
1445 S.	*Forbes* (22nd), Nigel Ivan Forbes, KBE (*Premier Lord of Scotland*), *b.* 1918, *s.* 1953, *m.*	Master of Forbes, *b.* 1946.
1821	*Forester* (8th), (George Cecil) Brooke Weld-Forester, *b.* 1938, *s.* 1977, *m.*	Hon. C. R. George *W.-F.*, *b.* 1975.
1922	*Forres* (4th), Alastair Stephen Grant Williamson, *b.* 1946, *s.* 1978, *m.*	Hon. George A. M. *W.*, *b.* 1972.
1917	*Forteviot* (4th), John James Evelyn Dewar, *b.* 1938, *s.* 1993, *m.*	Hon. Alexander J. E. *D.*, *b.* 1971.
1951	*Freyberg* (3rd), Valerian Bernard Freyberg, *b.* 1970, *s.* 1993	None.
1917	*Gainford* (3rd), Joseph Edward Pease, *b.* 1921, *s.* 1971, *m.*	Hon. George *P.*, *b.* 1926.
1818 I.	*Garvagh* (5th), (Alexander Leopold Ivor) George Canning, *b.* 1920, *s.* 1956, *m.*	Hon. Spencer G. S. de R. *C.*, *b.* 1953.
1942	*Geddes* (3rd), Euan Michael Ross Geddes, *b.* 1937, *s.* 1975, *m.*	Hon. James G. N. *G.*, *b.* 1969.
1876	*Gerard* (5th), Anthony Robert Hugo Gerard, *b.* 1949, *s.* 1992, *m.*	Hon. Rupert B. C. *G.*, *b.* 1981.
1824	*Gifford* (6th), Anthony Maurice Gifford, QC, *b.* 1940, *s.* 1961, *m.*	Hon. Thomas A. *G.*, *b.* 1967.
1917	*Gisborough* (3rd), Thomas Richard John Long Chaloner, *b.* 1927, *s.* 1951, *m.*	Hon. T. Peregrine L. *C.*, *b.* 1961.
1960	*Gladwyn* (1st), (Hubert Miles) Gladwyn Jebb, GCMG, GCVO, CB, *b.* 1900, *w.*	Hon. Miles A. G. *J.*, *b.* 1930.
1899	*Glanusk* (4th), David Russell Bailey, *b.* 1917, *s.* 1948, *m.*	Hon. Christopher R. *B.*, *b.* 1942.
1918	*Glenarthur* (4th), Simon Mark Arthur, *b.* 1944, *s.* 1976, *m.*	Hon. Edward A. *A.*, *b.* 1973.
1911	*Glenconner* (3rd), Colin Christopher Paget Tennant, *b.* 1926, *s.* 1983, *m.*	Hon. Charles E. P. *T.*, *b.* 1957.

Created	Title, order of succession, name, etc.	Heir
1964	Glendevon (2nd), Julian John Somerset Hope, b. 1950, s. 1996	Hon. Jonathan C. H., b. 1952.
1922	Glendyne (3rd), Robert Nivison, b. 1926, s. 1967, m.	Hon. John N., b. 1960.
1939	Glentoran (3rd), (Thomas) Robin (Valerian) Dixon, CBE, b. 1935, s. 1995, m.	Hon. Daniel G. D., b. 1959.
1909	Gorell (4th), Timothy John Radcliffe Barnes, b. 1927, s. 1963, m.	Hon. Ronald A. H. B., b. 1931.
1953	Grantchester (3rd), Christopher John Suenson-Taylor, b. 1951, s. 1995, m.	Hon. Jesse D. S.-T., b. 1977.
1782	Grantley (8th), Richard William Brinsley Norton, b. 1956, s. 1995	Hon. Francis J. H. N., b. 1960.
1794 I.	Graves (9th), Evelyn Paget Graves, b. 1926, s. 1994, m.	Hon. Timothy E. G., b. 1960.
1445 S.	Gray (22nd), Angus Diarmid Ian Campbell-Gray, b. 1931, s. 1946, m.	Master of Gray, b. 1964.
1950	Greenhill (3rd), Malcolm Greenhill, b. 1924, s. 1989	None.
1927	Greenway (4th), Ambrose Charles Drexel Greenway, b. 1941, s. 1975, m.	Hon. Mervyn S. K. G., b. 1942.
1902	Grenfell (3rd), Julian Pascoe Francis St Leger Grenfell, b. 1935, s. 1976, m.	Francis P. J. G., b. 1938.
1944	Gretton (4th), John Lysander Gretton, b. 1975, s. 1989	None.
1397	Grey of Codnor (5th), Charles Legh Shuldham Cornwall-Legh, CBE, AE, b. 1903, title called out of abeyance 1989, w.	Hon. Richard H. C.-L., b. 1936.
1955	Gridley (3rd), Richard David Arnold Gridley, b. 1956, s. 1996, m.	Hon. Carl R. G., b. 1981.
1964	Grimston of Westbury (2nd), Robert Walter Sigismund Grimston, b. 1925, s. 1979, m.	Hon. Robert J. S. G., b. 1951.
1886	Grimthorpe (4th), Christopher John Beckett, OBE, b. 1915, s. 1963, m.	Hon. Edward J. B., b. 1954.
1945	Hacking (3rd), Douglas David Hacking, b. 1938, s. 1971, m.	Hon. Douglas F. H., b. 1968.
1950	Haden-Guest (5th), Christopher Haden-Guest, b. 1948, s. 1996, m.	Hon. Nicholas H.-G., b. 1951.
1886	Hamilton of Dalzell (4th), James Leslie Hamilton, b. 1938, s. 1990, m.	Hon. Gavin G. H., b. 1968.
1874	Hampton (6th), Richard Humphrey Russell Pakington, b. 1925, s. 1974, m.	Hon. John H. A. P., b. 1964.
1939	Hankey (2nd), Robert Maurice Alers Hankey, KCMG, KCVO, b. 1905, s. 1963, m.	Hon. Donald R. A. H., b. 1938.
1958	Harding of Petherton (2nd), John Charles Harding, b. 1928, s. 1989, m.	Hon. William A. J. H., b. 1969.
1910	Hardinge of Penshurst (3rd), George Edward Charles Hardinge, b. 1921, s. 1960, m.	Hon. Julian A. H., b. 1945.
1876	Harlech (6th), Francis David Ormsby-Gore, b. 1954, s. 1985, m.	Hon. Jasset D. C. O.-G., b. 1986.
1939	Harmsworth (3rd), Thomas Harold Raymond Harmsworth, b. 1939, s. 1990, m.	Hon. Dominic M. E. H., b. 1973.
1815	Harris (8th), Anthony Harris, b. 1942, s. 1996, m.	†
1954	Harvey of Tasburgh (2nd), Peter Charles Oliver Harvey, b. 1921, s. 1968, w.	Charles J. G. H., b. 1951.
1295	Hastings (22nd), Edward Delaval Henry Astley, b. 1912, s. 1956, m.	Hon. Delaval T. H. A., b. 1960.
1835	Hatherton (8th), Edward Charles Littleton, b. 1950, s. 1985, m.	Hon. Thomas E. L., b. 1977.
1776	Hawke (11th), Edward George Hawke, TD, b. 1950, s. 1992, m.	None.
1927	Hayter (3rd), George Charles Hayter Chubb, KCVO, CBE, b. 1911, s. 1967, m.	Hon. G. William M. C., b. 1943.
1945	Hazlerigg (2nd), Arthur Grey Hazlerigg, MC, TD, b. 1910, s. 1949, w.	Hon. Arthur G. H., b. 1951.
1943	Hemingford (3rd), (Dennis) Nicholas Herbert, b. 1934, s. 1982, m.	Hon. Christopher D. C. H., b. 1973.
1906	Hemphill (5th), Peter Patrick Fitzroy Martyn Martyn-Hemphill, b. 1928, s. 1957, m.	Hon. Charles A. M. M.-H., b. 1954.
1799 I.*	Henley (8th), Oliver Michael Robert Eden (6th UK Baron, Northington, 1885), b. 1953, s. 1977, m.	Hon. John W. O. E., b. 1988.
1800 I.*	Henniker (8th), John Patrick Edward Chandos Henniker-Major, KCMG, CVO, MC (4th UK Baron, Hartismere, 1866), b. 1916, s. 1980, m.	Hon. Mark I. P. C. H.-M., b. 1947.
1886	Herschell (3rd), Rognvald Richard Farrer Herschell, b. 1923, s. 1929, m.	None.
1935	Hesketh (3rd), Thomas Alexander Fermor-Hesketh, PC, b. 1950, s. 1955, m.	Hon. Frederick H. F.-H., b. 1988.
1828	Heytesbury (6th), Francis William Holmes à Court, b. 1931, s. 1971, m.	Hon. James W. H. à C., b. 1967.
1886	Hindlip (6th), Charles Henry Allsopp, b. 1940, s. 1993, m.	Hon. Henry W. A., b. 1973.
1950	Hives (2nd), John Warwick Hives, CBE, b. 1913, s. 1965, m.	Matthew P. H., b. 1971.
1912	Hollenden (3rd), Gordon Hope Hope-Morley, b. 1914, s. 1977, m.	Hon. Ian H. H.-M., b. 1946.
1897	HolmPatrick (4th), Hans James David Hamilton, b. 1955, s. 1991, m.	Hon. Ion H. J. H., b. 1956.
1933	Horder (2nd), Thomas Mervyn Horder, b. 1910, s. 1955	None.
1797 I.	Hotham (8th), Henry Durand Hotham, b. 1940, s. 1967, m.	Hon. William B. H., b. 1972.
1881	Hothfield (6th), Anthony Charles Sackville Tufton, b. 1939, s. 1991, m.	Hon. William S. T., b. 1977.
1597	Howard de Walden (9th), John Osmael Scott-Ellis, TD (5th UK Baron, Seaford, 1826), b. 1912, s. 1946, m.	To Barony of Howard de Walden, four co-heiresses. To Barony of Seaford, Colin H. F. Ellis, b. 1946.
1930	Howard of Penrith (2nd), Francis Philip Howard, b. 1905, s. 1939, m.	Hon. Philip E. H., b. 1945.
1960	Howick of Glendale (2nd), Charles Evelyn Baring, b. 1937, s. 1973, m.	Hon. David E. C. B., b. 1975.
1796 I.	Huntingfield (7th), Joshua Charles Vanneck, b. 1954, s. 1994, m.	Hon. Gerard C. A. V., b. 1985.

Created	Title, order of succession, name, etc.	Heir
1866	Hylton (5th), Raymond Hervey Jolliffe, b. 1932, s. 1967, m.	Hon. William H. M. J., b. 1967.
1933	Iliffe (3rd), Robert Peter Richard Iliffe, b. 1944, s. 1996, m.	Hon. Edward R. I., b. 1968.
1543 I.	Inchiquin (18th), Conor Myles John O'Brien, b. 1943, s. 1982, m.	Murrough R. O'B., b. 1910.
1962	Inchyra (2nd), Robert Charles Reneke Hoyer Millar, b. 1935, s. 1989, m.	Hon. C. James C. H. M., b. 1962.
1964	Inglewood (2nd), (William) Richard Fletcher-Vane, b. 1951, s. 1989, m.	Hon. Henry W. F. F.-V., b. 1990.
1919	Inverforth (4th), Andrew Peter Weir, b. 1966, s. 1982	Hon. John V. W., b. 1935.
1941	Ironside (2nd), Edmund Oslac Ironside, b. 1924, s. 1959, m.	Hon. Charles E. G. I., b. 1956.
1952	Jeffreys (3rd), Christopher Henry Mark Jeffreys, b. 1957, s. 1986, m.	Hon. Arthur M. H. J., b. 1989.
1906	Joicey (5th), James Michael Joicey, b. 1953, s. 1993, m.	Hon. William J. J., b. 1990.
1937	Kenilworth (4th), (John) Randle Siddeley, b. 1954, s. 1981, m.	Hon. William R. J. S., b. 1992.
1935	Kennet (2nd), Wayland Hilton Young, b. 1923, s. 1960, m.	Hon. W. A. Thoby Y., b. 1957.
1776 I.*	Kensington (8th), Hugh Ivor Edwardes (5th UK Baron, Kensington, 1886), b. 1933, s. 1981, m.	Hon. W. Owen A. E., b. 1964.
1951	Kenswood (2nd), John Michael Howard Whitfield, b. 1930, s. 1963, m.	Hon. Michael C. W., b. 1955.
1788	Kenyon (6th), Lloyd Tyrell-Kenyon, b. 1947, s. 1993, m.	Hon. Lloyd N. T.-K., b. 1972.
1947	Kershaw (4th), Edward John Kershaw, b. 1936, s. 1962, m.	Hon. John C. E. K., b. 1971.
1943	Keyes (2nd), Roger George Bowlby Keyes, b. 1919, s. 1945, m.	Hon. Charles W. P. K., b. 1951.
1909	Kilbracken (3rd), John Raymond Godley, DSC, b. 1920, s. 1950	Hon. Christopher J. G., b. 1945.
1900	Killanin (3rd), Michael Morris, MBE, TD, b. 1914, s. 1927, m.	Hon. G. Redmond F. M., b. 1947.
1943	Killearn (3rd), Victor Miles George Aldous Lampson, b. 1941, s. 1996, m.	Hon. Miles H. M. L., b. 1977.
1789 I.	Kilmaine (7th), John David Henry Browne, b. 1948, s. 1978, m.	Hon. John F. S. B., b. 1983.
1831	Kilmarnock (7th), Alastair Ivor Gilbert Boyd, b. 1927, s. 1975, m.	Hon. Robin J. B., b. 1941.
1941	Kindersley (3rd), Robert Hugh Molesworth Kindersley, b. 1929, s. 1976, m.	Hon. Rupert J. M. K., b. 1955.
1223 I.	Kingsale (35th), John de Courcy (Premier Baron of Ireland), b. 1941, s. 1969	Nevinson R. de C., b. 1920.
1682 s.*	Kinnaird (13th), Graham Charles Kinnaird (5th UK Baron, Kinnaird, 1860), b. 1912, s. 1972, m.	None.
1902	Kinross (5th), Christopher Patrick Balfour, b. 1949, s. 1985, m.	Hon. Alan I. B., b. 1978.
1951	Kirkwood (3rd), David Harvie Kirkwood, PH.D., b. 1931, s. 1970, m.	Hon. James S. K., b. 1937.
1800 I.	Langford (9th), Col. Geoffrey Alexander Rowley-Conwy, OBE, b. 1912, s. 1953, m.	Hon. Owain G. R.-C., b. 1958.
1942	Latham (2nd), Dominic Charles Latham, b. 1954, s. 1970	Anthony M. L., b. 1954.
1431	Latymer (8th), Hugo Nevill Money-Coutts, b. 1926, s. 1987, m.	Hon. Crispin J. A. N. M.-C., b. 1955.
1869	Lawrence (5th), David John Downer Lawrence, b. 1937, s. 1968	None.
1947	Layton (3rd), Geoffrey Michael Layton, b. 1947, s. 1989, m.	Hon. David L., MBE, b. 1914.
1839	Leigh (5th), John Piers Leigh, b. 1935, s. 1979, m.	Hon. Christopher D. P. L., b. 1960.
1962	Leighton of St Mellons (2nd), (John) Leighton Seager, b. 1922, s. 1963, m.	Hon. Robert W. H. L. S., b. 1955.
1797	Lilford (7th), George Vernon Powys, b. 1931, s. 1949, m.	Hon. Mark V. P., b. 1975.
1945	Lindsay of Birker (3rd), James Francis Lindsay, b. 1945, s. 1994, m.	Hon. Thomas M. L., b. 1915.
1758 I.	Lisle (7th), John Nicholas Horace Lysaght, b. 1903, s. 1919, m.	Patrick J. L., b. 1931.
1850	Londesborough (9th), Richard John Denison, b. 1959, s. 1968, m.	Hon. James F. D., b. 1990.
1541 I.	Louth (16th), Otway Michael James Oliver Plunkett, b. 1929, s. 1950, m.	Hon. Jonathan O. P., b. 1952.
1458 s.*	Lovat (16th), Simon Fraser (5th UK Baron, Lovat, 1837), b. 1977, s. 1995, M.	Jack F., b. 1984.
1946	Lucas of Chilworth (2nd), Michael William George Lucas, b. 1926, s. 1967, m.	Hon. Simon W. L., b. 1957.
1663	Lucas (11th) & Dingwall (8th) (Scottish Lordship, 1609), Ralph Matthew Palmer, b. 1951, s. 1991, m.	Hon. Lewis E. P., b. 1987
1929	Luke (3rd), Arthur Charles St John Lawson-Johnston, b. 1933, s. 1996, m.	Hon. Ian J. St J. L.-J., b. 1963.
1914	Lyell (3rd), Charles Lyell, b. 1939, s. 1943	None.
1859	Lyveden (6th), Ronald Cecil Vernon, b. 1915, s. 1973, m.	Hon. Jack L. V., b. 1938.
1959	MacAndrew (3rd), Christopher Anthony Colin MacAndrew, b. 1945, s. 1989, m.	Hon. Oliver C. J. M., b. 1983.
1776 I.	Macdonald (8th), Godfrey James Macdonald of Macdonald, b. 1947, s. 1970, m.	Hon. Godfrey E. H. T. M., b. 1982.
1949	Macdonald of Gwaenysgor (2nd), Gordon Ramsay Macdonald, b. 1915, s. 1966, m.	None.
1937	McGowan (3rd), Harry Duncan Cory McGowan, b. 1938, s. 1966, m.	Hon. Harry J. C. M., b. 1971.
1922	Maclay (3rd), Joseph Paton Maclay, b. 1942, s. 1969, m.	Hon. Joseph P. M., b. 1977.
1955	McNair (3rd), Duncan James McNair, b. 1947, s. 1989, m.	Hon. Thomas J. M., b. 1990.
1951	Macpherson of Drumochter (2nd), (James) Gordon Macpherson, b. 1924, s. 1965, m.	Hon. James A. M., b. 1979.

Created	Title, order of succession, name, etc.	Heir
1937	*Mancroft* (3rd), Benjamin Lloyd Stormont Mancroft, *b.* 1957, *s.* 1987, *m.*	None.
1807	*Manners* (5th), John Robert Cecil Manners, *b.* 1923, *s.* 1972, *m.*	Hon. John H. R. *M.*, *b.* 1956.
1922	*Manton* (3rd), Joseph Rupert Eric Robert Watson, *b.* 1924, *s.* 1968, *m.*	Maj. Hon. Miles R. M. *W.*, *b.* 1958.
1908	*Marchamley* (4th), William Francis Whiteley, *b.* 1968, *s.* 1994	None.
1964	*Margadale* (2nd), James Ian Morrison, TD, *b.* 1930, *s.* 1996, *m.*	Hon. Alastair J. *M.*, *b.* 1958.
1961	*Marks of Broughton* (2nd), Michael Marks, *b.* 1920, *s.* 1964	Hon. Simon R. *M.*, *b.* 1950.
1964	*Martonmere* (2nd), John Stephen Robinson, *b.* 1963, *s.* 1989	David A. *R.*, *b.* 1965.
1776 I.	*Massy* (9th), Hugh Hamon John Somerset Massy, *b.* 1921, *s.* 1958, *m.*	Hon. David H. S. *M.*, *b.* 1947.
1935	*May* (3rd), Michael St John May, *b.* 1931, *s.* 1950, *m.*	Hon. Jasper B. St J. *M.*, *b.* 1965.
1928	*Melchett* (4th), Peter Robert Henry Mond, *b.* 1948, *s.* 1973	None.
1925	*Merrivale* (3rd), Jack Henry Edmond Duke, *b.* 1917, *s.* 1951, *m.*	Hon. Derek J. P. *D.*, *b.* 1948.
1911	*Merthyr.* Disclaimed for life 1977 (*Trevor Oswin Lewis, Bt.*, CBE, *b.* 1935, *s.* 1977, *m.*)	David T. *L.*, *b.* 1977.
1919	*Meston* (3rd), James Meston, *b.* 1950, *s.* 1984, *m.*	Hon. Thomas J. D. *M.*, *b.* 1977.
1838	*Methuen* (7th), Robert Alexander Holt Methuen, *b.* 1931, *s.* 1994, *m.*	Christopher P. M. C. *Methuen-Campbell*, *b.* 1928.
1711	*Middleton* (12th), (Digby) Michael Godfrey John Willoughby, MC, *b.* 1921, *s.* 1970, *m.*	Hon. Michael C. J. *W.*, *b.* 1948.
1939	*Milford* (3rd), Hugo John Laurence Philipps, *b.* 1929, *s.* 1993, *m.*	Hon. Guy W. *P.*, *b.* 1961.
1933	*Milne* (2nd), George Douglass Milne, TD, *b.* 1909, *s.* 1948, *m.*	Hon. George A. *M.*, *b.* 1941.
1951	*Milner of Leeds* (2nd), Arthur James Michael Milner, AE, *b.* 1923, *s.* 1967, *m.*	Hon. Richard J. *M.*, *b.* 1959.
1947	*Milverton* (2nd), Revd Fraser Arthur Richard Richards, *b.* 1930, *s.* 1978, *m.*	Hon. Michael H. *R.*, *b.* 1936.
1873	*Moncreiff* (5th), Harry Robert Wellwood Moncreiff, *b.* 1915, *s.* 1942, *w.*	Hon. Rhoderick H. W. *M.*, *b.* 1954.
1884	*Monk Bretton* (3rd), John Charles Dodson, *b.* 1924, *s.* 1933, *m.*	Hon. Christopher M. *D.*, *b.* 1958.
1885	*Monkswell* (5th), Gerard Collier, *b.* 1947, *s.* 1984, *m.*	Hon. James A. *C.*, *b.* 1977.
1728	*Monson* (11th), John Monson, *b.* 1932, *s.* 1958, *m.*	Hon. Nicholas J. *M.*, *b.* 1955.
1885	*Montagu of Beaulieu* (3rd), Edward John Barrington Douglas-Scott-Montagu, *b.* 1926, *s.* 1929, *m.*	Hon. Ralph *D.-S.-M.*, *b.* 1961.
1839	*Monteagle of Brandon* (6th), Gerald Spring Rice, *b.* 1926, *s.* 1946, *m.*	Hon. Charles J. S. *R.*, *b.* 1953.
1943	*Moran* (2nd), (Richard) John (McMoran) Wilson, KCMG, *b.* 1924, *s.* 1977, *m.*	Hon. James M. *W.*, *b.* 1952.
1918	*Morris* (3rd), Michael David Morris, *b.* 1937, *s.* 1975, *m.*	Hon. Thomas A. S. *M.*, *b.* 1982.
1950	*Morris of Kenwood* (2nd), Philip Geoffrey Morris, *b.* 1928, *s.* 1954, *m.*	Hon. Jonathan D. *M.*, *b.* 1968.
1945	*Morrison* (2nd), Dennis Morrison, *b.* 1914, *s.* 1953	None.
1831	*Mostyn* (5th), Roger Edward Lloyd Lloyd-Mostyn, MC, *b.* 1920, *s.* 1965, *m.*	Hon. Llewellyn R. L. *L.-M.*, *b.* 1948.
1933	*Mottistone* (4th), David Peter Seely, CBE, *b.* 1920, *s.* 1966, *m.*	Hon. Peter J. P. *S.*, *b.* 1949.
1945	*Mountevans* (3rd), Edward Patrick Broke Evans, *b.* 1943, *s.* 1974, *m.*	Hon. Jeffrey de C. R. *E.*, *b.* 1948.
1283	*Mowbray* (26th), *Segrave* (27th) (1283), & *Stourton* (23rd) (1448), Charles Edward Stourton, CBE, *b.* 1923, *s.* 1965, *m.*	Hon. Edward W. S. *S.*, *b.* 1953.
1932	*Moyne* (3rd), Jonathan Bryan Guinness, *b.* 1930, *s.* 1992, *m.*	Hon. Jasper J. R. *G.*, *b.* 1954.
1929	*Moynihan.* Barony dormant since the 3rd Baron died in November 1991. A High Court case in July 1996 cleared the way for the 3rd Baron's half-brother Colin Moynihan to petition the House of Lords to consider his claim to the title. At the time of going to press a petition had not been submitted	
1781 I.	*Muskerry* (9th), Robert Fitzmaurice Deane, *b.* 1948, *s.* 1988, *m.*	Hon. Jonathan F. *D.*, *b.* 1986.
1627 S.	*Napier* (14th) & *Ettrick* (5th) (*UK* 1872), Francis Nigel Napier, KCVO, *b.* 1930, *s.* 1954, *m.*	Master of Napier, *b.* 1962.
1868	*Napier of Magdala* (6th), Robert Alan Napier, *b.* 1940, *s.* 1987, *m.*	Hon. James R. *N.*, *b.* 1966.
1940	*Nathan* (2nd), Roger Carol Michael Nathan, *b.* 1922, *s.* 1963, *m.*	Hon. Rupert H. B. *N.*, *b.* 1957.
1960	*Nelson of Stafford* (3rd), Henry Roy George Nelson, *b.* 1943, *s.* 1995, *m.*	Hon. Alastair W. H. *N.*, *b.* 1973.
1959	*Netherthorpe* (3rd), James Frederick Turner, *b.* 1964, *s.* 1982, *m.*	Hon. Andrew J. E. *T.*, *b.* 1993.
1946	*Newall* (2nd), Francis Storer Eaton Newall, *b.* 1930, *s.* 1963, *m.*	Hon. Richard H. E. *N.*, *b.* 1961.
1776 I.	*Newborough* (7th), Robert Charles Michael Vaughan Wynn, DSC, *b.* 1917, *s.* 1965, *m.*	Hon. Robert V. *W.*, *b.* 1949.
1892	*Newton* (5th), Richard Thomas Legh, *b.* 1950, *s.* 1992, *m.*	Hon. Piers R. *L.*, *b.* 1979.
1930	*Noel-Buxton* (3rd), Martin Connal Noel-Buxton, *b.* 1940, *s.* 1980, *m.*	Hon. Charles C. *N.-B*, *b.* 1975.
1957	*Norrie* (2nd), (George) Willoughby Moke Norrie, *b.* 1936, *s.* 1977, *m.*	Hon. Mark W. J. *N.*, *b.* 1972.
1884	*Northbourne* (5th), Christopher George Walter James, *b.* 1926, *s.* 1982, *m.*	Hon. Charles W. H. *J.*, *b.* 1960.
1866	*Northbrook* (6th), Francis Thomas Baring, *b.* 1954, *s.* 1990, *m.*	None.
1878	*Norton* (8th), James Nigel Arden Adderley, *b.* 1947, *s.* 1993, *m.*	Hon. Edward J. A. *A.*, *b.* 1982.
1906	*Nunburnholme* (4th), Ben Charles Wilson, *b.* 1928, *s.* 1974	Hon. Charles T. *W.*, *b.* 1935.
	Oaksey, see *Trevethin and Oaksey*	

Created	Title, order of succession, name, etc.	Heir
1950	*Ogmore* (2nd), Gwilym Rees Rees-Williams, *b.* 1931, *s.* 1976, *m.*	Hon. Morgan *R.-W., b.* 1937.
1870	*O'Hagan* (4th), Charles Towneley Strachey, *b.* 1945, *s.* 1961	Hon. Richard T. *S., b.* 1950.
1868	*O'Neill* (4th), Raymond Arthur Clanaboy O'Neill, TD, *b.* 1933, *s.* 1944, *m.*	Hon. Shane S. C. *O'N., b.* 1965.
1836 I.*	*Oranmore and Browne* (4th), Dominick Geoffrey Edward Browne (2nd UK Baron Mereworth, 1926), *b.* 1901, *s.* 1927, *m.*	Hon. Dominick G. T. *B., b.* 1929.
1933	*Palmer* (4th), Adrian Bailie Nottage Palmer, *b.* 1951, *s.* 1990, *m.*	Hon. Hugo B. R. *P., b.* 1980.
1914	*Parmoor* (4th), (Frederick Alfred) Milo Cripps, *b.* 1929, *s.* 1977	M. Anthony L. *C.,* CBE, DSO, TD, QC, *b.* 1913.
1937	*Pender* (3rd), John Willoughby Denison-Pender, *b.* 1933, *s.* 1965, *m.*	Hon. Henry J. R. *D.-P., b.* 1968.
1866	*Penrhyn* (6th), Malcolm Frank Douglas-Pennant, DSO, MBE, *b.* 1908, *s.* 1967, *m.*	Hon. Nigel *D.-P., b.* 1909.
1603	*Petre* (18th), John Patrick Lionel Petre, *b.* 1942, *s.* 1989, *m.*	Hon. Dominic W. *P., b.* 1966.
1918	*Phillimore* (5th), Francis Stephen Phillimore, *b.* 1944, *s.* 1994, *m.*	Hon. Tristan A. S. *P., b.* 1977.
1945	*Piercy* (3rd), James William Piercy, *b.* 1946, *s.* 1981	Hon. Mark E. P. *P., b.* 1953.
1827	*Plunket* (8th), Robin Rathmore Plunket, *b.* 1925, *s.* 1975, *m.*	Hon. Shaun A. F. S. *P., b.* 1931.
1831	*Poltimore* (7th), Mark Coplestone Bampfylde, *b.* 1957, *s.* 1978, *m.*	Hon. Henry A. W. *B., b.* 1985.
1690 s.	*Polwarth* (10th), Henry Alexander Hepburne-Scott, TD, *b.* 1916, *s.* 1944, *m.*	Master of Polwarth, *b.* 1947.
1930	*Ponsonby of Shulbrede* (4th), Frederick Matthew Thomas Ponsonby, *b.* 1958, *s.* 1990	None.
1958	*Poole* (2nd), David Charles Poole, *b.* 1945, *s.* 1993, *m.*	Hon. Oliver J. *P., b.* 1972.
1852	*Raglan* (5th), FitzRoy John Somerset, *b.* 1927, *s.* 1964	Hon. Geoffrey *S., b.* 1932.
1932	*Rankeillour* (4th), Peter St Thomas More Henry Hope, *b.* 1935, *s.* 1967	Michael R. *H., b.* 1940.
1953	*Rathcavan* (3rd), Hugh Detmar Torrens O'Neill, *b.* 1939, *s.* 1994, *m.*	Hon. François H. N. *O'N., b.* 1984.
1916	*Rathcreedan* (3rd), Christopher John Norton, *b.* 1949, *s.* 1990, *m.*	Hon. Adam G. *N., b.* 1952.
1868 I.	*Rathdonnell* (5th), Thomas Benjamin McClintock-Bunbury, *b.* 1938, *s.* 1959, *m.*	Hon. William L. *M.-B., b.* 1966.
1911	*Ravensdale* (3rd), Nicholas Mosley, MC, *b.* 1923, *s.* 1966, *m.*	Hon. Shaun N. *M., b.* 1949.
1821	*Ravensworth* (8th), Arthur Waller Liddell, *b.* 1924, *s.* 1950, *m.*	Hon. Thomas A. H. *L., b.* 1954.
1821	*Rayleigh* (6th), John Gerald Strutt, *b.* 1960, *s.* 1988, *m.*	Hon. John F. *S., b.* 1993.
1937	*Rea* (3rd), John Nicolas Rea, MD, *b.* 1928, *s.* 1981, *m.*	Hon. Matthew J. *R., b.* 1956.
1628 s.	*Reay* (14th), Hugh William Mackay, *b.* 1937, *s.* 1963, *m.*	Master of Reay, *b.* 1965.
1902	*Redesdale* (6th), Rupert Bertram Mitford, *b.* 1967, *s.* 1991	None.
1940	*Reith.* Disclaimed for life 1972 (*Christopher John Reith, b.* 1928, *s.* 1971, *m.*)	Hon. James H. J. *R., b.* 1971.
1928	*Remnant* (3rd), James Wogan Remnant, CVO, *b.* 1930, *s.* 1967, *m.*	Hon. Philip J. *R., b.* 1954.
1806 I.	*Rendlesham* (8th), Charles Anthony Hugh Thellusson, *b.* 1915, *s.* 1943, *w.*	Hon. Charles W. B. *T., b.* 1954.
1933	*Rennell* (3rd), (John Adrian) Tremayne Rodd, *b.* 1935, *s.* 1978, *m.*	Hon. James R. D. T. *R., b.* 1978.
1964	*Renwick* (2nd), Harry Andrew Renwick, *b.* 1935, *s.* 1973, *m.*	Hon. Robert J. *R., b.* 1966.
1885	*Revelstoke* (5th), John Baring, *b.* 1934, *s.* 1994	Hon. James C. *B., b.* 1938.
1905	*Ritchie of Dundee* (5th), (Harold) Malcolm Ritchie, *b.* 1919, *s.* 1978, *m.*	Hon. C. Rupert R. *R., b.* 1958.
1935	*Riverdale* (2nd), Robert Arthur Balfour, *b.* 1901, *s.* 1957, *w.*	Hon. Mark R. *B., b.* 1927.
1961	*Robertson of Oakridge* (2nd), William Ronald Robertson, *b.* 1930, *s.* 1974, *m.*	Hon. William B. E. *R., b.* 1975.
1938	*Roborough* (3rd), Henry Massey Lopes, *b.* 1940, *s.* 1992, *m.*	Hon. Massey J. H. *L., b.* 1969.
1931	*Rochester* (2nd), Foster Charles Lowry Lamb, *b.* 1916, *s.* 1955, *m.*	Hon. David C. *L., b.* 1944.
1934	*Rockley* (3rd), James Hugh Cecil, *b.* 1934, *s.* 1976, *m.*	Hon. Anthony R. *C., b.* 1961.
1782	*Rodney* (10th), George Brydges Rodney, *b.* 1953, *s.* 1992, *m.*	Nicholas S. H. *R., b.* 1947.
1651 s.*	*Rollo* (13th), Eric John Stapylton Rollo (4th UK Baron, Dunning, 1869), *b.* 1915, *s.* 1947, *m.*	Master of Rollo, *b.* 1943.
1959	*Rootes* (3rd), Nicholas Geoffrey Rootes, *b.* 1951, *s.* 1992, *m.*	William B. *R., b.* 1944.
1796 I.*	*Rossmore* (7th), William Warner Westenra (6th UK Baron, Rossmore, 1838), *b.* 1931, *s.* 1958, *m.*	Hon. Benedict W. *W., b.* 1983.
1939	*Rotherwick* (3rd), (Herbert) Robin Cayzer, *b.* 1954, *s.* 1996, *m.*	Hon. H. Robin *C., b.* 1989.
1885	*Rothschild* (4th), (Nathaniel Charles) Jacob Rothschild, *b.* 1936, *s.* 1990, *m.*	Hon. Nathaniel P. V. J. *R., b.* 1971.
1911	*Rowallan* (4th), John Polson Cameron Corbett, *b.* 1947, *s.* 1993, *m.*	Hon. Jason W. P. C. *C., b.* 1972.
1947	*Rugby* (3rd), Robert Charles Maffey, *b.* 1951, *s.* 1990, *m.*	Hon. Timothy J. H. *M., b.* 1975.
1919	*Russell of Liverpool* (3rd), Simon Gordon Jared Russell, *b.* 1952, *s.* 1981, *m.*	Hon. Edward C. S. *R., b.* 1985.
1876	*Sackville* (6th), Lionel Bertrand Sackville-West, *b.* 1913, *s.* 1965, *m.*	Hugh R. I. *S.-W.,* MC, *b.* 1919.
1964	*St Helens* (2nd), Richard Francis Hughes-Young, *b.* 1945, *s.* 1980, *m.*	Hon. Henry T. *H.-Y., b.* 1986.
1559	*St John of Bletso* (21st), Anthony Tudor St John, *b.* 1957, *s.* 1978, *m.*	Hon. Oliver B. *St J., b.* 1995.
1887	*St Levan* (4th), John Francis Arthur St Aubyn, DSC, *b.* 1919, *s.* 1978, *m.*	Hon. O. Piers *St A.,* MC, *b.* 1920.
1885	*St Oswald* (5th), Derek Edward Anthony Winn, *b.* 1919, *s.* 1984, *m.*	Hon. Charles R. A. *W., b.* 1959.

Created	Title, order of succession, name, etc.	Heir
1960	*Sanderson of Ayot.* Disclaimed for life 1971 (*Alan Lindsay Sanderson, b.* 1931, *s.* 1971, *m.*)	Hon. Michael S., *b.* 1959.
1945	*Sandford* (2nd), Revd John Cyril Edmondson, DSC, *b.* 1920, *s.* 1959, *m.*	Hon. James J. M. *E., b.* 1949.
1871	*Sandhurst* (5th), (John Edward) Terence Mansfield, DFC, *b.* 1920, *s.* 1964, *m.*	Hon. Guy R. J. *M., b.* 1949.
1802	*Sandys* (7th), Richard Michael Oliver Hill, *b.* 1931, *s.* 1961, *m.*	The Marquess of Downshire (*see* page 139).
1888	*Savile* (3rd), George Halifax Lumley-Savile, *b.* 1919, *s.* 1931	Hon. Henry L. T. *L.-S., b.* 1923.
1447	*Saye and Sele* (21st), Nathaniel Thomas Allen Fiennes, *b.* 1920, *s.* 1968, *m.*	Hon. Richard I. *F., b.* 1959.
1932	*Selsdon* (3rd), Malcolm McEacharn Mitchell-Thomson, *b.* 1937, *s.* 1963, *m.*	Hon. Callum M. M. *M.-T., b.* 1969.
1489 s.	*Sempill* (21st), James William Stuart Whitemore Sempill, *b.* 1949, *s.* 1995, *m.*	Master of Sempill, *b.* 1979.
1916	*Shaughnessy* (3rd), William Graham Shaughnessy, *b.* 1922, *s.* 1938, *m.*	Hon. Michael J. S., *b.* 1946.
1946	*Shepherd* (2nd), Malcolm Newton Shepherd, PC, *b.* 1918, *s.* 1954, *m.*	Hon. Graeme G. S., *b.* 1949.
1964	*Sherfield* (1st), Roger Mellor Makins, GCB, GCMG, FRS, *b.* 1904, *w.*	Hon. Christopher J. *M., b.* 1942.
1902	*Shuttleworth* (5th), Charles Geoffrey Nicholas Kay-Shuttleworth, *b.* 1948, *s.* 1975, *m.*	Hon. Thomas E. *K.-S., b.* 1976.
1950	*Silkin.* Disclaimed for life 1972 (*Arthur Silkin, b.* 1916, *s.* 1972, *m.*)	Hon. Christopher L. S., *b.* 1947.
1963	*Silsoe* (2nd), David Malcolm Trustram Eve, QC, *b.* 1930, *s.* 1976, *m.*	Hon. Simon R. T. *E., b.* 1966.
1947	*Simon of Wythenshawe* (2nd), Roger Simon, *b.* 1913, *s.* 1960, *m.*	Hon. Matthew S., *b.* 1955.
1449 s.	*Sinclair* (17th), Charles Murray Kennedy St Clair, CVO, *b.* 1914, *s.* 1957, *m.*	Master of Sinclair, *b.* 1968.
1957	*Sinclair of Cleeve* (3rd), John Lawrence Robert Sinclair, *b.* 1953, *s.* 1985	None.
1919	*Sinha* (5th), Anindo Kumar Sinha, *b.* 1930, *s.* 1992	†
1828	*Skelmersdale* (7th), Roger Bootle-Wilbraham, *b.* 1945, *s.* 1973, *m.*	Hon. Andrew *B.-W., b.* 1977.
1916	*Somerleyton* (3rd), Savile William Francis Crossley, KCVO, *b.* 1928, *s.* 1959, *m. Master of the Horse*	Hon. Hugh F. S. C., *b.* 1971.
1784	*Somers* (9th), Philip Sebastian Somers Cocks, *b.* 1948, *s.* 1995	Alan B. C., *b.* 1930
1780	*Southampton* (6th), Charles James FitzRoy, *b.* 1928, *s.* 1989, *m.*	Hon. Edward C. *F., b.* 1955.
1959	*Spens* (3rd), Patrick Michael Rex Spens, *b.* 1942, *s.* 1984, *m.*	Hon. Patrick N. G. S., *b.* 1968.
1640	*Stafford* (15th), Francis Melfort William Fitzherbert, *b.* 1954, *s.* 1986, *m.*	Hon. Benjamin J. B. *F., b.* 1983.
1938	*Stamp* (4th), Trevor Charles Bosworth Stamp, MD, FRCP, *b.* 1935, *s.* 1987, *m.*	Hon. Nicholas C. T. S., *b.* 1978.
1839	*Stanley of Alderley* (8th) & *Sheffield* (8th) (1738 I.), Thomas Henry Oliver Stanley (7th *UK Baron Eddisbury*, 1848), *b.* 1927, *s.* 1971, *m.*	Hon. Richard O. S., *b.* 1956.
1318	*Strabolgi* (11th), David Montague de Burgh Kenworthy, *b.* 1914, *s.* 1953, *m.*	Andrew D. W. *K., b.* 1967.
1954	*Strang* (2nd), Colin Strang, *b.* 1922, *s.* 1978, *m.*	None.
1955	*Strathalmond* (3rd), William Roberton Fraser, *b.* 1947, *s.* 1976, *m.*	Hon. William G. *F., b.* 1976.
1936	*Strathcarron* (2nd), David William Anthony Blyth Macpherson, *b.* 1924, *s.* 1937, *m.*	Hon. Ian D. P. *M., b.* 1949.
1955	*Strathclyde* (2nd), Thomas Galloway Dunlop du Roy de Blicquy Galbraith, PC, *b.* 1960, *s.* 1985, *m.*	Hon. Charles W. du R. de B. G., *b.* 1962.
1900	*Strathcona and Mount Royal* (4th), Donald Euan Palmer Howard, *b.* 1923, *s.* 1959, *m.*	Hon. D. Alexander S. *H., b.* 1961.
1836	*Stratheden* (6th) & *Campbell* (6th) (1841), Donald Campbell, *b.* 1934, *s.* 1987, *m.*	Hon. David A. C., *b.* 1963.
1884	*Strathspey* (6th), James Patrick Trevor Grant of Grant, *b.* 1943, *s.* 1992, *m.*	Hon. Michael P. F. G., *b.* 1953.
1838	*Sudeley* (7th), Merlin Charles Sainthill Hanbury-Tracy, *b.* 1939, *s.* 1941	D. Andrew J. *H-T., b.* 1928.
1786	*Suffield* (11th), Anthony Philip Harbord-Hamond, MC, *b.* 1922, *s.* 1951, *m.*	Hon. Charles A. A. *H.-H., b.* 1953.
1893	*Swansea* (4th), John Hussey Hamilton Vivian, *b.* 1925, *s.* 1934, *m.*	Hon. Richard A. H. *V., b.* 1957.
1907	*Swaythling* (4th), David Charles Samuel Montagu, *b.* 1928, *s.* 1990, *m.*	Hon. Charles E. S. *M., b.* 1954.
1919	*Swinfen* (3rd), Roger Mynors Swinfen Eady, *b.* 1938, *s.* 1977, *m.*	Hon. Charles R. P. S. *E., b.* 1971.
1935	*Sysonby* (3rd), John Frederick Ponsonby, *b.* 1945, *s.* 1956	None.
1831 I.	*Talbot of Malahide* (10th), Reginald John Richard Arundell, *b.* 1931, *s.* 1987, *m.*	Hon. Richard J. T. *A., b.* 1957.
1946	*Tedder* (3rd), Robin John Tedder, *b.* 1955, *s.* 1994, *m.*	Hon. Benjamin J. *T., b.* 1985.
1884	*Tennyson* (5th), Cdr. Mark Aubrey Tennyson, DSC, *b.* 1920, *s.* 1991, *m.*	Lt.-Cdr. James A. *T.,* DSC, *b.* 1913.
1918	*Terrington* (4th), (James Allen) David Woodhouse, *b.* 1915, *s.* 1961, *m.*	Hon. C. Montague *W.,* DSO, OBE, *b.* 1917.
1940	*Teviot* (2nd), Charles John Kerr, *b.* 1934, *s.* 1968, *m.*	Hon. Charles R. *K., b.* 1971.

Created	Title, order of succession, name, etc.	Heir
1616	Teynham (20th), John Christopher Ingham Roper-Curzon, b. 1928, s. 1972, m.	Hon. David J. H. I. R.-C., b. 1965.
1964	Thomson of Fleet (2nd), Kenneth Roy Thomson, b. 1923, s. 1976, m.	Hon. David K. R. T., b. 1957.
1792	Thurlow (8th), Francis Edward Hovell-Thurlow-Cumming-Bruce, KCMG, b. 1912, s. 1971, w.	Hon. Roualeyn R. H.-T.-C.-B., b. 1952.
1876	Tollemache (5th), Timothy John Edward Tollemache, b. 1939, s. 1975, m.	Hon. Edward J. H. T., b. 1976.
1564 s.	Torphichen (15th), James Andrew Douglas Sandilands, b. 1946, s. 1975, m.	Douglas R. A. S., b. 1926.
1947	Trefgarne (2nd), David Garro Trefgarne, PC, b. 1941, s. 1960, m.	Hon. George G. T., b. 1970.
1921	Trevethin (4th), and Oaksey (2nd) (1947), John Geoffrey Tristram Lawrence, OBE, b. 1929, s. 1971, m.	Hon. Patrick J. T. L., b. 1960.
1880	Trevor (4th), Charles Edwin Hill-Trevor, b. 1928, s. 1950, m.	Hon. Marke C. H.-T., b. 1970.
1461 I.	Trimlestown (20th), Anthony Edward Barnewall, b. 1928, s. 1990, m.	Hon. Raymond C. B., b. 1930.
1940	Tryon (3rd), Anthony George Merrik Tryon, b. 1940, s. 1976, m.	Hon. Charles G. B. T., b. 1976.
1935	Tweedsmuir (3rd), William de l'Aigle Buchan, b. 1916, s. 1996, m.	Hon. John W. H. de l'A. B., b. 1950.
1523	Vaux of Harrowden (10th), John Hugh Philip Gilbey, b. 1915, s. 1977, m.	Hon. Anthony W. G., b. 1940.
1800 I.	Ventry (8th), Andrew Wesley Daubeny de Moleyns, b. 1943, s. 1987, m.	Hon. Francis W. D. de M., b. 1965.
1762	Vernon (10th), John Lawrance Vernon, b. 1923, s. 1963, m.	Col. William R. D. Vernon-Harcourt, OBE, b. 1909.
1922	Vestey (3rd), Samuel George Armstrong Vestey, b. 1941, s. 1954, m.	Hon. William G. V., b. 1983.
1841	Vivian (6th), Nicholas Crespigny Laurence Vivian, b. 1935, s. 1991, m.	Hon. Charles H. C. V., b. 1966.
1934	Wakehurst (3rd), (John) Christopher Loder, b. 1925, s. 1970, m.	Hon. Timothy W. L., b. 1958.
1723	Walpole (10th), Robert Horatio Walpole (8th Brit. Baron Walpole of Wolterton, 1756), b. 1938, s. 1989, m.	Hon. Jonathan R. H. W., b. 1967.
1780	Walsingham (9th), John de Grey, MC, b. 1925, s. 1965, m.	Hon. Robert de G., b. 1969.
1936	Wardington (2nd), Christopher Henry Beaumont Pease, b. 1924, s. 1950, m.	Hon. William S. P., b. 1925.
1792 I.	Waterpark (7th), Frederick Caryll Philip Cavendish, b. 1926, s. 1948, m.	Hon. Roderick A. C., b. 1959.
1942	Wedgwood (4th), Piers Anthony Weymouth Wedgwood, b. 1954, s. 1970, m.	John W., CBE, MD, FRCP, b. 1919.
1861	Westbury (5th), David Alan Bethell, CBE, MC, b. 1922, s. 1961, m.	Hon. Richard N. B., MBE, b. 1950.
1944	Westwood (3rd), (William) Gavin Westwood, b. 1944, s. 1991, m.	Hon. W. Fergus W., b. 1972.
1935	Wigram (2nd), (George) Neville (Clive) Wigram, MC, b. 1915, s. 1960, w.	Maj. Hon. Andrew F. C. W., MVO, b. 1949.
1491	Willoughby de Broke (21st), Leopold David Verney, b. 1938, s. 1986, m.	Hon. Rupert G. V., b. 1966.
1946	Wilson (2nd), Patrick Maitland Wilson, b. 1915, s. 1964, w.	None.
1937	Windlesham (3rd), David James George Hennessy, CVO, PC, b. 1932, s. 1962, w.	Hon. James R. H., b. 1968.
1951	Wise (2nd), John Clayton Wise, b. 1923, s. 1968, m.	Hon. Christopher J. C. W., PH.D., b. 1949.
1869	Wolverton (7th), Christopher Richard Glyn, b. 1938, s. 1988	Hon. Andrew J. G., b. 1943.
1928	Wraxall (2nd), George Richard Lawley Gibbs, b. 1928, s. 1931	Hon. Sir Eustace H. B. G., KCVO, CMG, b. 1929.
1915	Wrenbury (3rd), Revd John Burton Buckley, b. 1927, s. 1940, m.	Hon. William E. B., b. 1966.
1838	Wrottesley (6th), Clifton Hugh Lancelot de Verdon Wrottesley, b. 1968, s. 1977	Hon. Stephen J. W., b. 1955.
1919	Wyfold (3rd), Hermon Robert Fleming Hermon-Hodge, ERD, b. 1915, s. 1942	None.
1829	Wynford (8th), Robert Samuel Best, MBE, b. 1917, s. 1943, m.	Hon. John P. R. B., b. 1950.
1308	Zouche (18th), James Assheton Frankland, b. 1943, s. 1965, m.	Hon. William T. A. F., b. 1984.

BARONESSES/LADIES IN THEIR OWN RIGHT

Style, The Right Hon. the Lady ___ , *or* The Right Hon. the Baroness ___ , according to her preference. Either style may be used, except in the case of Scottish titles (indicated by s.), which are not baronies (*see* page 137) and whose holders are always addressed as Lady
Husband, Untitled
Children's style, As for children of a Baron
For forms of address, *see* page 136

Created	Title, order of succession, name, etc.	Heir
1455	*Berners* (16th in line), Pamela Vivien Kirkham, *b.* 1929, *title called out of abeyance* 1995, *m.*	Hon. Rupert W. T. *K.*, *b.* 1953.
1529	*Braye* (8th in line), Mary Penelope Aubrey-Fletcher, *b.* 1941, *s.* 1985, *m.*	Two co-heiresses.
1321	*Dacre* (27th in line), Rachel Leila Douglas-Home, *b.* 1929, *title called out of abeyance*, 1970, *w.*	Hon. James T. A. *D.-H.*, *b.* 1952.
1332	*Darcy de Knayth* (18th in line), Davina Marcia Ingrams, DBE, *b.* 1938, *s.* 1943, *w.*	Hon. Caspar D. *I.*, *b.* 1962.
1439	*Dudley* (14th in line), Barbara Amy Felicity Hamilton, *b.* 1907, *s.* 1972, *m.*	Hon. Jim A. H. *Wallace*, *b.* 1930.
1490 s.	*Herries of Terregles* (14th in line), Anne Elizabeth Fitzalan-Howard, *b.* 1938, *s.* 1975, *m.*	Lady Mary *Mumford*, CVO, *b.* 1940.
1602 s.	*Kinloss* (12th in line), Beatrice Mary Grenville Freeman-Grenville, *b.* 1922, *s.* 1944, *m.*	Master of Kinloss, *b.* 1953.
1445 s.	*Saltoun* (20th in line), Flora Marjory Fraser, *b.* 1930, *s.* 1979, *m.*	Hon. Katharine I. M. I. *F.*, *b.* 1957.
1628	*Strange* (16th in line), (Jean) Cherry Drummond of Megginch, *b.* 1928, *title called out of abeyance*, 1986, *m.*	Hon. Adam H. *D. of M.*, *b.* 1953.
1544/5	*Wharton* (11th in line), Myrtle Olive Felix Robertson, *b.* 1934, *title called out of abeyance*, 1990, *m.*	Hon. Myles C. D. *R.*, *b.* 1964.
1313	*Willoughby de Eresby* (27th in line), (Nancy) Jane Marie Heathcote-Drummond-Willoughby, *b.* 1934, *s.* 1983	Two co-heiresses.

Life Peers

Between 1 September 1995 and 31 August 1996, the conferment of 33 life peerages was announced:

LAW LORDS: (27 November 1995) the Rt. Hon. Sir Robin Cook, KBE; (4 June 1996) the Rt. Hon. Sir Thomas Bingham
'WORKING' PEERS (17 November 1995): Sir Gordon Borrie, QC; Sir Peter Bowness, CBE; Sir Basil Feldman; Sir Philip Harris; Helene Hayman; Tom McNally; Canon Peter Pilkington; John Sewel; Dr William Wallace; Lady Wilcox; Prof. Robert Winston; (21 August 1996) *John Alderdice; *Dame Joyce Anelay, DBE; *Dame Hazel Byford, DBE; *Prof. David Currie; *Peter Gummer; *Sir Ian MacLaurin; *Swraj Paul; *Ms Meta Ramsay; *Sir Richard Rogers, RA; *Maurice Saatchi; *Ms Elizabeth Symonds; *John Taylor; *Martin Thomas; *Larry Whitty
NEW YEAR'S HONOURS (29 December 1995): Sir David Gillmore, GCMG; Sir Robert Kilpatrick, CBE; Dick Taverne, QC
QUEEN'S BIRTHDAY HONOURS (7 June 1996): Prof. Dame June Lloyd, DBE; *Marmaduke Hussey; *Field Marshal Sir Richard Vincent, GBE, DSO

*No title gazetted at time of going to press

CREATED UNDER THE APPELLATE JURISDICTION ACT 1876 (AS AMENDED)

BARONS

Created	
1986	*Ackner*, Desmond James Conrad Ackner, PC, *b.* 1920, *m.*
1981	*Brandon of Oakbrook*, Henry Vivian Brandon, MC, PC, *b.* 1920, *m.*
1980	*Bridge of Harwich*, Nigel Cyprian Bridge, PC, *b.* 1917, *m.*
1982	*Brightman*, John Anson Brightman, PC, *b.* 1911, *m.*
1991	*Browne-Wilkinson*, Nicolas Christopher Henry Browne-Wilkinson, PC, *b.* 1930, *m.* Lord of Appeal in Ordinary
1957	*Denning*, Alfred Thompson Denning, PC, *b.* 1899, *w.*
1986	*Goff of Chieveley*, Robert Lionel Archibald Goff, PC, *b.* 1926, *m.* Lord of Appeal in Ordinary
1985	*Griffiths*, (William) Hugh Griffiths, MC, PC, *b.* 1923, *m.*
1995	*Hoffmann*, Leonard Hubert Hoffmann, PC, *b.* 1934, *m.*
1988	*Jauncey of Tullichettle*, Charles Eliot Jauncey, PC, *b.* 1925, *m.* Lord of Appeal in Ordinary

1977   *Keith of Kinkel*, Henry Shanks Keith, PC, *b.* 1922, *m.* Lord of Appeal in Ordinary
1979   *Lane*, Geoffrey Dawson Lane, AFC, PC, *b.* 1918, *m.*
1993   *Lloyd of Berwick*, Anthony John Leslie Lloyd, PC, *b.* 1929, *m.* Lord of Appeal in Ordinary
1992   *Mustill*, Michael John Mustill, PC, *b.* 1931, *m.* Lord of Appeal in Ordinary
1994   *Nicholls of Birkenhead*, Donald James Nicholls, PC, *b.* 1933, *m.*
1994   *Nolan*, Michael Patrick Nolan, PC, *b.* 1928, *m.* Lord of Appeal in Ordinary
1986   *Oliver of Aylmerton*, Peter Raymond Oliver, PC, *b.* 1921, *m.*
1980   *Roskill*, Eustace Wentworth Roskill, PC, *b.* 1911, *m.*
1977   *Scarman*, Leslie George Scarman, OBE, PC, *b.* 1911, *m.*
1992   *Slynn of Hadley*, Gordon Slynn, PC, *b.* 1930, *m.* Lord of Appeal in Ordinary
1995   *Steyn*, Johan van Zyl Steyn, PC, *b.* 1932, *m.*
1982   *Templeman*, Sydney William Templeman, MBE, PC, *b.* 1920, *w.*
1964   *Wilberforce*, Richard Orme Wilberforce, CMG, OBE, PC, *b.* 1907, *m.*
1992   *Woolf*, Harry Kenneth Woolf, PC, *b.* 1933, *m.* Master of the Rolls

CREATED UNDER THE LIFE PEERAGES ACT 1958

BARONS

Created
1988   *Alexander of Weedon*, Robert Scott Alexander, QC, *b.* 1936, *m.*
1976   *Allen of Abbeydale*, Philip Allen, GCB, *b.* 1912, *m.*
1961   *Alport*, Cuthbert James McCall Alport, TD, PC, *b.* 1912, *w.*
1992   *Amery of Lustleigh*, Julian Amery, PC, *b.* 1919, *w.*
1965   *Annan*, Noël Gilroy Annan, OBE, *b.* 1916, *m.*
1992   *Archer of Sandwell*, Peter Kingsley Archer, PC, QC, *b.* 1926, *m.*
1992   *Archer of Weston-super-Mare*, Jeffrey Howard Archer, *b.* 1940, *m.*
1988   *Armstrong of Ilminster*, Robert Temple Armstrong, GCB, CVO, *b.* 1927, *m.*
1992   *Ashley of Stoke*, Jack Ashley, CH, PC, *b.* 1922, *m.*
1993   *Attenborough*, Richard Samuel Attenborough, CBE, *b.* 1923, *m.*
1974   *Balniel*, The Earl of Crawford and Balcarres, *see* page 141
1982   *Bancroft*, Ian Powell Bancroft, GCB, *b.* 1922, *m.*
1974   *Banks*, Desmond Anderson Harvie Banks, CBE, *b.* 1918, *m.*
1974   *Barber*, Anthony Perrinott Lysberg Barber, TD, PC, *b.* 1920, *m.*
1992   *Barber of Tewkesbury*, Derek Coates Barber, *b.* 1918, *m.*
1983   *Barnett*, Joel Barnett, PC, *b.* 1923, *m.*
1982   *Bauer*, Prof. Peter Thomas Bauer, D.SC., FBA, *b.* 1915
1967   *Beaumont of Whitley*, Revd Timothy Wentworth Beaumont, *b.* 1928, *m.*
1979   *Bellwin*, Irwin Norman Bellow, *b.* 1923, *m.*
1981   *Beloff*, Max Beloff, FBA, *b.* 1913, *m.*
1996   *Bingham of Cornhill*, Thomas Henry Bingham, PC, *b.* 1933, *m., Lord Chief Justice of England*
1971   *Blake*, Robert Norman William Blake, FBA, *b.* 1916, *w.*

1994   *Blaker*, Peter Allan Renshaw Blaker, KCMG, PC, *b.* 1922, *m.*
1978   *Blease*, William John Blease, *b.* 1914, *m.*
1995   *Blyth of Rowington*, James Blyth, *b.* 1940, *m.*
1980   *Boardman*, Thomas Gray Boardman, MC, TD, *b.* 1919, *m.*
1996   *Borrie*, Gordon Johnson Borrie, QC, *b.* 1931, *m.*
1976   *Boston of Faversham*, Terence George Boston, QC, *b.* 1930, *m.*
1996   *Bowness*, Peter Spencer Bowness, CBE, *b.* 1943, *m.*
1972   *Boyd-Carpenter*, John Archibald Boyd-Carpenter, PC, *b.* 1908, *m.*
1992   *Braine of Wheatley*, Bernard Richard Braine, PC, *b.* 1914, *w.*
1987   *Bramall*, Edwin Noel Westby Bramall, KG, GCB, OBE, MC, *Field Marshal*, *b.* 1923, *m.*
1976   *Briggs*, Asa Briggs, FBA, *b.* 1921, *m.*
1975   *Brookes*, Raymond Percival Brookes, *b.* 1909, *m.*
1979   *Brooks of Tremorfa*, John Edward Brooks, *b.* 1927, *m.*
1974   *Bruce of Donington*, Donald William Trevor Bruce, *b.* 1912, *m.*
1976   *Bullock*, Alan Louis Charles Bullock, FBA, *b.* 1914, *m.*
1988   *Butterfield*, (William) John (Hughes) Butterfield, OBE, DM, FRCP, *b.* 1920, *m.*
1985   *Butterworth*, John Blackstock Butterworth, CBE, *b.* 1918, *m.*
1978   *Buxton of Alsa*, Aubrey Leland Oakes Buxton, MC, *b.* 1918, *m.*
1987   *Callaghan of Cardiff*, (Leonard) James Callaghan, KG, PC, *b.* 1912, *m.*
1979   *Dacre of Glanton*, Hugh Redwald Trevor-Roper, *b.* 1914, *m.*
1993   *Dahrendorf*, Ralf Dahrendorf, KBE, PH.D., D.PHIL., FBA, *b.* 1929, *m.*
1986   *Dainton*, Frederick Sydney Dainton, PH.D., SC.D., FRS, *b.* 1914, *m.*
1983   *Dean of Beswick*, Joseph Jabez Dean, *b.* 1922
1993   *Dean of Harptree*, (Arthur) Paul Dean, PC, *b.* 1924, *m.*
1986   *Deedes*, William Francis Deedes, MC, *b.* 1913, *m.*
1991   *Desai*, Prof. Meghnad Jagdishchandra Desai, PH.D., *b.* 1940, *m.*
1970   *Diamond*, John Diamond, PC, *b.* 1907, *m.*
1993   *Dixon-Smith*, Robert William Dixon-Smith, *b.* 1934, *m.*
1967   *Donaldson of Kingsbridge*, John George Stuart Donaldson, OBE, *b.* 1907, *w.*
1988   *Donaldson of Lymington*, John Francis Donaldson, PC, *b.* 1920, *m.*
1985   *Donoughue*, Bernard Donoughue, D.PHIL., *b.* 1934.
1987   *Dormand of Easington*, John Donkin Dormand, *b.* 1919, *m.*
1994   *Dubs*, Alfred Dubs, *b.* 1932, *m.*
1995   *Eames*, Robert Henry Alexander Eames, PH.D., *b.* 1937, *m.*
1992   *Eatwell*, John Leonard Eatwell, *b.* 1945, *m.*
1983   *Eden of Winton*, John Benedict Eden, PC, *b.* 1925, *m.*
1992   *Elis-Thomas*, Dafydd Elis Elis-Thomas, *b.* 1946, *m.*
1985   *Elliott of Morpeth*, Robert William Elliott, *b.* 1920, *m.*
1981   *Elystan-Morgan*, Dafydd Elystan Elystan-Morgan, *b.* 1932, *m.*
1980   *Emslie*, George Carlyle Emslie, MBE, PC, FRSE, *b.* 1919, *m.*

1992   *Ewing of Kirkford*, Harry Ewing, *b.* 1931, *m.*
1983   *Ezra*, Derek Ezra, MBE, *b.* 1919, *m.*
1983   *Fanshawe of Richmond*, Anthony Henry Fanshawe Royle, KCMG, *b.* 1927, *m.*
1996   *Feldman*, Basil Feldman, *b.* 1926, *m.*
1992   *Finsberg*, Geoffrey Finsberg, MBE, *b.* 1926, *w.*
1983   *Fitt*, Gerard Fitt, *b.* 1926, *w.*
1979   *Flowers*, Brian Hilton Flowers, FRS, *b.* 1924, *m.*
1967   *Foot*, John Mackintosh Foot, *b.* 1909, *m.*
1982   *Forte*, Charles Forte, *b.* 1908, *m.*
1989   *Fraser of Carmyllie*, Peter Lovat Fraser, PC, QC, *b.* 1945, *m.*
1982   *Gallacher*, John Gallacher, *b.* 1920, *m.*
1992   *Geraint*, Geraint Wyn Howells, *b.* 1925, *m.*
1975   *Gibson*, (Richard) Patrick (Tallentyre) Gibson, *b.* 1916, *m.*
1979   *Gibson-Watt*, (James) David Gibson-Watt, MC, PC, *b.* 1918, *m.*
1996   *Gillmore of Thamesfield*, David Howe Gillmore, GCMG, *b.* 1934, *m.*
1992   *Gilmour of Craigmillar*, Ian Hedworth John Little Gilmour, PC, *b.* 1926, *m.*
1994   *Gladwin of Clee*, Derek Oliver Gladwin, CBE, *b.* 1930, *m.*
1977   *Glenamara*, Edward Watson Short, CH, PC, *b.* 1912, *m.*
1987   *Goold*, James Duncan Goold, *b.* 1934, *w.*
1976   *Grade*, Lew Grade, *b.* 1906, *m.*
1983   *Graham of Edmonton*, (Thomas) Edward Graham, *b.* 1925, *m.*
1967   *Granville of Eye*, Edgar Louis Granville, *b.* 1899, *m.*
1983   *Gray of Contin*, James (Hamish) Hector Northey Gray, PC, *b.* 1927, *m.*
1974   *Greene of Harrow Weald*, Sidney Francis Greene, CBE, *b.* 1910, *m.*
1974   *Greenhill of Harrow*, Denis Arthur Greenhill, GCMG, OBE, *b.* 1913, *m.*
1975   *Gregson*, John Gregson, *b.* 1924
1968   *Grey of Naunton*, Ralph Francis Alnwick Grey, GCMG, GCVO, OBE, *b.* 1910, *w.*
1991   *Griffiths of Fforestfach*, Brian Griffiths, *b.* 1941, *m.*
1995   *Habgood*, Rt. Revd John Stapylton Habgood, PC, PH.D., *b.* 1927, *m.*
1970   *Hailsham of St Marylebone*, Quintin McGarel Hogg, KG, CH, PC, FRS, *b.* 1907, *m.*
1994   *Hambro*, Charles Eric Alexander Hambro, *b.* 1930, *m.*
1983   *Hanson*, James Edward Hanson, *b.* 1922, *m.*
1974   *Harmar-Nicholls*, Harmar Harmar-Nicholls, *b.* 1912, *m.*
1974   *Harris of Greenwich*, John Henry Harris, *b.* 1930, *m.*
1979   *Harris of High Cross*, Ralph Harris, *b.* 1924, *m.*
1996   *Harris of Peckham*, Philip Charles Harris, *b.* 1942, *m.*
1968   *Hartwell*, (William) Michael Berry, MBE, TD, *b.* 1911, *w.*
1974   *Harvington*, Robert Grant Grant-Ferris, AE, PC, *b.* 1907, *m.*
1993   *Haskel*, Simon Haskel, *b.* 1934, *m.*
1990   *Haslam*, Robert Haslam, *b.* 1923, *m.*
1992   *Hayhoe*, Bernard John (Barney) Hayhoe, PC, *b.* 1925, *m.*
1992   *Healey*, Denis Winston Healey, CH, MBE, PC, *b.* 1917, *m.*
1984   *Henderson of Brompton*, Peter Gordon Henderson, KCB, *b.* 1922, *m.*
1979   *Hill-Norton*, Peter John Hill-Norton, GCB, *Admiral of the Fleet*, *b.* 1915, *m.*

1979   *Holderness*, Richard Frederick Wood, PC, *b.* 1920, *m.*
1991   *Hollick*, Clive Richard Hollick, *b.* 1945, *m.*
1990   *Holme of Cheltenham*, Richard Gordon Holme, CBE, *b.* 1936, *m.*
1979   *Hooson*, (Hugh) Emlyn Hooson, QC, *b.* 1925, *m.*
1995   *Hope of Craighead*, (James Arthur) David Hope, PC, *b.* 1938, *m.*
1992   *Howe of Aberavon*, (Richard Edward) Geoffrey Howe, CH, PC, QC, *b.* 1926, *m.*
1992   *Howell*, Denis Herbert Howell, PC, *b.* 1923, *m.*
1978   *Howie of Troon*, William Howie, *b.* 1924, *m.*
1961   *Hughes*, William Hughes, CBE, PC, *b.* 1911, *w.*
1966   *Hunt*, (Henry Cecil) John Hunt, KG, CBE, DSO, *b.* 1910, *m.*
1980   *Hunt of Tanworth*, John Joseph Benedict Hunt, GCB, *b.* 1919, *m.*
1978   *Hutchinson of Lullington*, Jeremy Nicolas Hutchinson, QC, *b.* 1915, *m.*
1982   *Ingrow*, John Aked Taylor, OBE, TD, *b.* 1917, *m.*
1987   *Irvine of Lairg*, Alexander Andrew Mackay Irvine, QC, *b.* 1940, *m.*
1988   *Jakobovits*, Immanuel Jakobovits, *b.* 1921, *m.*
1987   *Jenkin of Roding*, (Charles) Patrick (Fleeming) Jenkin, PC, *b.* 1926, *m.*
1987   *Jenkins of Hillhead*, Roy Harris Jenkins, OM, PC, *b.* 1920, *m.*
1981   *Jenkins of Putney*, Hugh Gater Jenkins, *b.* 1908, *w.*
1987   *Johnston of Rockport*, Charles Collier Johnston, TD, *b.* 1915, *m.*
1991   *Judd*, Frank Ashcroft Judd, *b.* 1935, *m.*
1980   *Keith of Castleacre*, Kenneth Alexander Keith, *b.* 1916, *m.*
1996   *Kilpatrick of Kincraig*, Robert Kilpatrick, CBE, *b.* 1926, *m.*
1985   *Kimball*, Marcus Richard Kimball, *b.* 1928, *m.*
1983   *King of Wartnaby*, John Leonard King, *b.* 1918, *m.*
1993   *Kingsdown*, Robert (Robin) Leigh-Pemberton, KG, PC, *b.* 1927, *m.*
1994   *Kingsland*, Christopher James Prout, TD, PC, QC, *b.* 1942
1965   *Kings Norton*, Harold Roxbee Cox, PH.D., FENG., *b.* 1902, *m.*
1975   *Kirkhill*, John Farquharson Smith, *b.* 1930, *m.*
1974   *Kissin*, Harry Kissin, *b.* 1912, *m.*
1987   *Knights*, Philip Douglas Knights, CBE, QPM, *b.* 1920, *m.*
1991   *Laing of Dunphail*, Hector Laing, *b.* 1923, *m.*
1990   *Lane of Horsell*, Peter Stewart Lane, *b.* 1925, *w.*
1992   *Lawson of Blaby*, Nigel Lawson, PC, *b.* 1932, *m.*
1993   *Lester of Herne Hill*, Anthony Paul Lester, QC, *b.* 1936, *m.*
1982   *Lewin*, Terence Thornton Lewin, KG, GCB, LVO, DSC, *Admiral of the Fleet*, *b.* 1920, *m.*
1989   *Lewis of Newnham*, Jack Lewis, FRS, *b.* 1928, *m.*
1974   *Lovell-Davis*, Peter Lovell Lovell-Davis, *b.* 1924, *m.*
1979   *Lowry*, Robert Lynd Erskine Lowry, PC, PC (NI), *b.* 1919, *m.*
1984   *McAlpine of West Green*, (Robert) Alistair McAlpine, *b.* 1942, *m.*
1988   *Macaulay of Bragar*, Donald Macaulay, QC, *b.* 1933, *m.*
1975   *McCarthy*, William Edward John McCarthy, D.PHIL., *b.* 1925, *m.*
1976   *McCluskey*, John Herbert McCluskey, *b.* 1929, *m.*
1989   *McColl of Dulwich*, Ian McColl, FRCS, FRCSE, *b.* 1933, *m.*
1995   *McConnell*, Robert William Brian McConnell, PC (NI), *b.* 1922, *m.*

1991   *Macfarlane of Bearsden*, Norman Somerville Macfarlane, FRSE, *b.* 1926, *m.*

1978   *McGregor of Durris*, Oliver Ross McGregor, *b.* 1921, *m.*

1982   *McIntosh of Haringey*, Andrew Robert McIntosh, *b.* 1933, *m.*

1991   *Mackay of Ardbrecknish*, John Jackson Mackay, PC, *b.* 1938, *m.*

1979   *Mackay of Clashfern*, James Peter Hymers Mackay, PC, FRSE, *b.* 1927, *m. Lord High Chancellor*

1995   *Mackay of Drumadoon*, Donald Sage Mackay, *b.* 1946, *m.*

1988   *Mackenzie-Stuart*, Alexander John Mackenzie Stuart, *b.* 1924, *m.*

1974   *Mackie of Benshie*, George Yull Mackie, CBE, DSO, DFC, *b.* 1919, *m.*

1982   *MacLehose of Beoch*, (Crawford) Murray MacLehose, KT, GBE, KCMG, KCVO, *b.* 1917, *m.*

1995   *McNally*, Tom McNally, *b.* 1943, *m.*

1991   *Marlesford*, Mark Shuldham Schreiber, *b.* 1931, *m.*

1981   *Marsh*, Richard William Marsh, PC, *b.* 1928, *m.*

1987   *Mason of Barnsley*, Roy Mason, PC, *b.* 1924, *m.*

1981   *Mayhew*, Christopher Paget Mayhew, *b.* 1915, *m.*

1985   *Mellish*, Robert Joseph Mellish, PC, *b.* 1913, *m.*

1993   *Menuhin*, Yehudi Menuhin, OM, KBE, *b.* 1916, *m.*

1992   *Merlyn-Rees*, Merlyn Merlyn-Rees, PC, *b.* 1920, *m.*

1978   *Mishcon*, Victor Mishcon, *b.* 1915, *m.*

1981   *Molloy*, William John Molloy, *b.* 1918

1992   *Moore of Lower Marsh*, John Edward Michael Moore, PC, *b.* 1937, *m.*

1986   *Moore of Wolvercote*, Philip Brian Cecil Moore, GCB, GCVO, CMG, PC, *b.* 1921, *m.*

1990   *Morris of Castle Morris*, Brian Robert Morris, D.Phil., *b.* 1930, *m.*

1971   *Moyola*, James Dawson Chichester-Clark, PC (NI), *b.* 1923, *m.*

1985   *Murray of Epping Forest*, Lionel Murray, OBE, PC, *b.* 1922, *m.*

1979   *Murton of Lindisfarne*, (Henry) Oscar Murton, OBE, TD, PC, *b.* 1914, *m.*

1994   *Nickson*, David Wigley Nickson, KBE, FRSE, *b.* 1929, *m.*

1975   *Northfield*, (William) Donald Chapman, *b.* 1923

1976   *Oram*, Albert Edward Oram, *b.* 1913, *m.*

1971   *Orr-Ewing*, (Charles) Ian Orr-Ewing, OBE, *b.* 1912, *m.*

1992   *Owen*, David Anthony Llewellyn Owen, CH, PC, *b.* 1938, *m.*

1991   *Palumbo*, Peter Garth Palumbo, *b.* 1935, *m.*

1992   *Parkinson*, Cecil Edward Parkinson, PC, *b.* 1931, *m.*

1975   *Parry*, Gordon Samuel David Parry, *b.* 1925, *m.*

1990   *Pearson of Rannoch*, Malcolm Everard MacLaren Pearson, *b.* 1942, *m.*

1979   *Perry of Walton*, Walter Laing Macdonald Perry, OBE, FRS, FRSE, *b.* 1921, *m.*

1987   *Peston*, Maurice Harry Peston, *b.* 1931, *m.*

1983   *Peyton of Yeovil*, John Wynne William Peyton, PC, *b.* 1919, *m.*

1994   *Phillips of Ellesmere*, Prof. David Chilton Phillips, KBE, FRS, *b.* 1924, *m.*

1996   *Pilkington of Oxenford*, Revd Canon Peter Pilkington, *b.* 1933, *m.*

1992   *Plant of Highfield*, Prof. Raymond Plant, PH.D., *b.* 1945, *m.*

1959   *Plowden*, Edwin Noel Plowden, GBE, KCB, *b.* 1907, *m.*

1987   *Plumb*, (Charles) Henry Plumb, MEP, *b.* 1925, *m.*

1981   *Plummer of St Marylebone*, (Arthur) Desmond (Herne) Plummer, TD, *b.* 1914, *m.*

1990   *Porter of Luddenham*, George Porter, OM, FRS, *b.* 1920, *m.*

1992   *Prentice*, Reginald Ernest Prentice, PC, *b.* 1923, *m.*

1987   *Prior*, James Michael Leathes Prior, PC, *b.* 1927, *m.*

1982   *Prys-Davies*, Gwilym Prys Prys-Davies, *b.* 1923, *m.*

1987   *Pym*, Francis Leslie Pym, MC, PC, *b.* 1922, *m.*

1982   *Quinton*, Anthony Meredith Quinton, FBA, *b.* 1925, *m.*

1994   *Quirk*, Prof. (Charles) Randolph Quirk, CBE, FBA, *b.* 1920, *m.*

1978   *Rawlinson of Ewell*, Peter Anthony Grayson Rawlinson, PC, QC, *b.* 1919, *m.*

1976   *Rayne*, Max Rayne, *b.* 1918, *m.*

1983   *Rayner*, Derek George Rayner, *b.* 1926

1987   *Rees*, Peter Wynford Innes Rees, PC, QC, *b.* 1926, *m.*

1988   *Rees-Mogg*, William Rees-Mogg, *b.* 1928, *m.*

1991   *Renfrew of Kaimsthorn*, (Andrew) Colin Renfrew, FBA, *b.* 1937, *m.*

1979   *Renton*, David Lockhart-Mure Renton, KBE, TD, PC, QC, *b.* 1908, *w.*

1990   *Richard*, Ivor Seward Richard, PC, QC, *b.* 1932, *m.*

1979   *Richardson*, John Samuel Richardson, LVO, MD, FRCP, *b.* 1910, *w.*

1983   *Richardson of Duntisbourne*, Gordon William Humphreys Richardson, KG, MBE, TD, PC, *b.* 1915, *m.*

1987   *Rippon of Hexham*, (Aubrey) Geoffrey (Frederick) Rippon, PC, QC, *b.* 1924, *m.*

1992   *Rix*, Brian Norman Roger Rix, CBE, *b.* 1924, *m.*

1961   *Robens of Woldingham*, Alfred Robens, PC, *b.* 1910, *m.*

1992   *Rodger of Earlsferry*, Alan Ferguson Rodger, PC, QC, FBA, *b.* 1944, *Lord Advocate*

1992   *Rodgers of Quarry Bank*, William Thomas Rodgers, PC, *b.* 1928, *m.*

1977   *Roll of Ipsden*, Eric Roll, KCMG, CB, *b.* 1907, *m.*

1991   *Runcie*, Rt Revd Robert Alexander Kennedy Runcie, MC, PC, Royal Victoria Chain, *b.* 1921, *m.*

1975   *Ryder of Eaton Hastings*, Sydney Thomas Franklin (Don) Ryder, *b.* 1916, *m.*

1962   *Sainsbury*, Alan John Sainsbury, *b.* 1902, *w.*

1989   *Sainsbury of Preston Candover*, John Davan Sainsbury, KG, *b.* 1927, *m.*

1987   *St John of Fawsley*, Norman Antony Francis St John-Stevas, PC, *b.* 1929

1985   *Sanderson of Bowden*, Charles Russell Sanderson, *b.* 1933, *m.*

1979   *Scanlon*, Hugh Parr Scanlon, *b.* 1913, *m.*

1978   *Sefton of Garston*, William Henry Sefton, *b.* 1915, *m.*

1996   *Sewel*, John Buttifant Sewel, CBE, *b.* 19–

1994   *Shaw of Northstead*, Michael Norman Shaw, *b.* 1920, *m.*

1959   *Shawcross*, Hartley William Shawcross, GBE, PC, QC, *b.* 1902, *w.*

1994   *Sheppard of Didgemere*, Allan John George Sheppard, *b.* 1932, *m.*

1980   *Sieff of Brimpton*, Marcus Joseph Sieff, OBE, *b.* 1913, *m.*

1971   *Simon of Glaisdale*, Jocelyn Edward Salis Simon, PC, *b.* 1911, *m.*

1991   *Skidelsky*, Robert Jacob Alexander Skidelsky, D.Phil., *b.* 1939, *m.*

1978   *Smith*, Rodney Smith, KBE, FRCS, *b.* 1914, *m.*

1965   *Soper*, Revd Donald Oliver Soper, PH.D., *b.* 1903, *m.*

1990   *Soulsby of Swaffham Prior*, Ernest Jackson Lawson
Soulsby, PH.D., *b.* 1926, *m.*

1983   *Stallard*, Albert William Stallard, *b.* 1921, *m.*

1991   *Sterling of Plaistow*, Jeffrey Maurice Sterling, CBE,
b. 1934, *m.*

1987   *Stevens of Ludgate*, David Robert Stevens, *b.* 1936,
m.

1992   *Stewartby*, (Bernard Harold) Ian (Halley) Stewart,
RD, PC, FBA, FRSE, *b.* 1935, *m.*

1981   *Stodart of Leaston*, James Anthony Stodart, PC, *b.*
1916, *w.*

1983   *Stoddart of Swindon*, David Leonard Stoddart, *b.*
1926, *m.*

1969   *Stokes*, Donald Gresham Stokes, TD, FENG., *b.*
1914, *w.*

1971   *Tanlaw*, Simon Brooke Mackay, *b.* 1934, *m.*

1996   *Taverne*, Dick Taverne, QC, *b.* 1928, *m.*

1978   *Taylor of Blackburn*, Thomas Taylor, CBE, *b.* 1929,
m.

1992   *Taylor of Gosforth*, Peter Murray Taylor, PC, *b.*
1930, *w.*

1968   *Taylor of Gryfe*, Thomas Johnston Taylor, FRSE, *b.*
1912, *m.*

1992   *Tebbit*, Norman Beresford Tebbit, CH, PC, *b.* 1931,
m.

1987   *Thomas of Gwydir*, Peter John Mitchell Thomas,
PC, QC, *b.* 1920, *w.*

1981   *Thomas of Swynnerton*, Hugh Swynnerton
Thomas, *b.* 1931, *m.*

1977   *Thomson of Monifieth*, George Morgan Thomson,
KT, PC, *b.* 1921, *m.*

1962   *Todd*, Alexander Robertus Todd, OM, D.SC.,
D.Phil., FRS, *b.* 1907, *w.*

1990   *Tombs*, Francis Leonard Tombs, FENG., *b.* 1924, *m.*

1994   *Tope*, Graham Norman Tope, CBE, *b.* 1943, *m.*

1981   *Tordoff*, Geoffrey Johnson Tordoff, *b.* 1928, *m.*

1993   *Tugendhat*, Christopher Samuel Tugendhat, *b.*
1937, *m.*

1990   *Varley*, Eric Graham Varley, PC, *b.* 1932, *m.*

1985   *Vinson*, Nigel Vinson, LVO, *b.* 1931, *m.*

1990   *Waddington*, David Charles Waddington, GCVO,
PC, QC, *b.* 1929, *m.*

1990   *Wade of Chorlton*, (William) Oulton Wade, *b.* 1932,
m.

1992   *Wakeham*, John Wakeham, PC, *b.* 1932, *m.*

1992   *Walker of Worcester*, Peter Edward Walker, MBE,
PC, *b.* 1932, *m.*

1974   *Wallace of Campsie*, George Wallace, *b.* 1915, *m.*

1974   *Wallace of Coslany*, George Douglas Wallace, *b.*
1906, *m.*

1995   *Wallace of Saltaire*, William John Lawrence
Wallace, PH.D., *b.* 1941, *m.*

1989   *Walton of Detchant*, John Nicholas Walton, TD,
FRCP, *b.* 1922, *m.*

1992   *Weatherill*, (Bruce) Bernard Weatherill, PC, *b.*
1920, *m.*

1977   *Wedderburn of Charlton*, (Kenneth) William
Wedderburn, FBA, QC, *b.* 1927, *m.*

1976   *Weidenfeld*, (Arthur) George Weidenfeld, *b.* 1919,
m.

1980   *Weinstock*, Arnold Weinstock, *b.* 1924, *m.*

1978   *Whaddon*, (John) Derek Page, *b.* 1927, *m.*

1974   *Wigoder*, Basil Thomas Wigoder, QC, *b.* 1921, *m.*

1985   *Williams of Elvel*, Charles Cuthbert Powell
Williams, CBE, *b.* 1933, *m.*

1992   *Williams of Mostyn*, Gareth Wyn Williams, QC, *b.*
1941, *m.*

1969   *Wilson of Langside*, Henry Stephen Wilson, PC,
QC, *b.* 1916, *m.*

1992   *Wilson of Tillyorn*, David Clive Wilson, GCMG,
PH.D., *b.* 1935, *m.*

1995   *Winston*, Robert Maurice Lipson Winston,
FRCOG, *b.* 1940, *m.*

1985   *Wolfson*, Leonard Gordon Wolfson, *b.* 1927, *m.*

1991   *Wolfson of Sunningdale*, David Wolfson, *b.* 1935, *m.*

1994   *Wright of Richmond*, Patrick Richard Henry
Wright, GCMG, *b.* 1931, *m.*

1987   *Wyatt of Weeford*, Woodrow Lyle Wyatt, *b.* 1918,
m.

1978   *Young of Dartington*, Michael Young, PH.D., *b.* 1915,
m.

1984   *Young of Graffham*, David Ivor Young, PC, *b.* 1932,
m.

1992   *Younger of Prestwick*, George Kenneth Hotson
Younger, KT, KCVO, TD, PC, *b.* 1931, *m.*

BARONESSES

Created

1967   *Birk*, Alma Birk, *b.* 1921, *m.*

1987   *Blackstone*, Tessa Ann Vosper Blackstone, PH.D., *b.*
1942

1987   *Blatch*, Emily May Blatch, CBE, PC, *b.* 1937, *m.*

1990   *Brigstocke*, Heather Renwick Brigstocke, *b.* 1929,
w.

1964   *Brooke of Ystradfellte*, Barbara Muriel Brooke, DBE,
b. 1908, *w.*

1982   *Carnegy of Lour*, Elizabeth Patricia Carnegy of
Lour, *b.* 1925

1990   *Castle of Blackburn*, Barbara Anne Castle, PC, *b.*
1910, *w.*

1992   *Chalker of Wallasey*, Lynda Chalker, PC, *b.* 1942, *m.*

1982   *Cox*, Caroline Anne Cox, *b.* 1937, *m.*

1990   *Cumberlege*, Julia Frances Cumberlege, CBE, *b.*
1943, *m.*

1978   *David*, Nora Ratcliff David, *b.* 1913, *w.*

1993   *Dean of Thornton-le-Fylde*, Brenda Dean, *b.* 1943,
m.

1974   *Delacourt-Smith of Alteryn*, Margaret Rosalind
Delacourt-Smith, *b.* 1916, *m.*

1978   *Denington*, Evelyn Joyce Denington, DBE, *b.* 1907,
m.

1991   *Denton of Wakefield*, Jean Denton, CBE, *b.* 1935

1990   *Dunn*, Lydia Selina Dunn, DBE, *b.* 1940, *m.*

1990   *Eccles of Moulton*, Diana Catherine Eccles, *b.* 1933,
m.

1972   *Elles*, Diana Louie Elles, *b.* 1921, *m.*

1974   *Falkender*, Marcia Matilda Falkender, CBE, *b.* 1932

1994   *Farrington of Ribbleton*, Josephine Farrington, *b.*
19–, *m.*

1974   *Fisher of Rednal*, Doris Mary Gertrude Fisher, *b.*
1919, *w.*

1990   *Flather*, Shreela Flather, *b.* 19–, *m.*

1981   *Gardner of Parkes*, (Rachel) Trixie (Anne)
Gardner, *b.* 1927, *m.*

1993   *Gould of Potternewton*, Joyce Brenda Gould, *b.*
1932, *m.*

1991   *Hamwee*, Sally Rachel Hamwee, *b.* 1947

1996   *Hayman*, Helene Valerie Hayman, *b.* 1949, *m.*

1991   *Hilton of Eggardon*, Jennifer Hilton, QPM, *b.* 1936

1995   *Hogg*, Sarah Elizabeth Mary Hogg, *b.* 1946, *m.*

1990   *Hollis of Heigham*, Patricia Lesley Hollis, D.Phil., *b.*
1941, *m.*

1985   *Hooper*, Gloria Dorothy Hooper, *b.* 1939

1965   *Hylton-Foster*, Audrey Pellew Hylton-Foster, DBE,
b. 1908, *w.*

1991   *James of Holland Park*, Phyllis Dorothy White (P.
D. James), OBE, *b.* 1920, *w.*

1992   *Jay of Paddington*, Margaret Ann Jay, *b.* 1939

1979   *Jeger*, Lena May Jeger, *b.* 1915, *w.*
1967   *Llewelyn-Davies of Hastoe*, (Annie) Patricia
       Llewelyn-Davies, PC, *b.* 1915, *w.*
1996   *Lloyd of Highbury*, Prof. June Kathleen Lloyd, DBE,
       FRCP, FRCPE, FRCGP, *b.* 1928
1978   *Lockwood*, Betty Lockwood, *b.* 1924, *w.*
1979   *McFarlane of Llandaff*, Jean Kennedy McFarlane,
       b. 1926
1971   *Macleod of Borve*, Evelyn Hester Macleod, *b.* 1915,
       w.
1991   *Mallalieu*, Ann Mallalieu, QC, *b.* 1945, *m.*
1970   *Masham of Ilton*, Susan Lilian Primrose Cunliffe-
       Lister, *b.* 1935, *m.* (*Countess of Swinton*)
1993   *Miller of Hendon*, Doreen Miller, MBE, *b.* 1933, *m.*
1982   *Nicol*, Olive Mary Wendy Nicol, *b.* 1923, *m.*
1991   *O'Cathain*, Detta O'Cathain, OBE, *b.* 1938, *m.*
1989   *Oppenheim-Barnes*, Sally Oppenheim-Barnes, PC,
       b. 1930, *m.*
1990   *Park of Monmouth*, Daphne Margaret Sybil
       Désirée Park, CMG, OBE, *b.* 1921
1991   *Perry of Southwark*, Pauline Perry, *b.* 1931, *m.*
1974   *Pike*, (Irene) Mervyn (Parnicott) Pike, DBE, *b.*
       1918
1981   *Platt of Writtle*, Beryl Catherine Platt, CBE, FEng.,
       b. 1923, *m.*
1994   *Rawlings*, Patricia Elizabeth Rawlings, *b.* 1939

1974   *Robson of Kiddington*, Inga-Stina Robson, *b.* 1919,
       w.
1979   *Ryder of Warsaw*, Margaret Susan Cheshire (Sue
       Ryder), CMG, OBE, *b.* 1923, *w.*
1991   *Seccombe*, Joan Anna Dalziel Seccombe, DBE, *b.*
       1930, *m.*
1971   *Seear*, (Beatrice) Nancy Seear, PC, *b.* 1913
1967   *Serota*, Beatrice Serota, DBE, *b.* 1919, *m.*
1973   *Sharples*, Pamela Sharples, *b.* 1923, *m.*
1995   *Smith of Gilmorehill*, Elizabeth Margaret Smith, *b.*
       19–, *w.*
1992   *Thatcher*, Margaret Hilda Thatcher, OM, PC, FRS,
       b. 1925, *m.*
1994   *Thomas of Walliswood*, Susan Petronella Thomas,
       OBE, *b.* 19–, *m.*
1980   *Trumpington*, Jean Alys Barker, PC, *b.* 1922, *w.*
1985   *Turner of Camden*, Muriel Winifred Turner, *b.*
       1927, *m.*
1985   *Warnock*, Helen Mary Warnock, DBE, *b.* 1924, *w.*
1970   *White*, Eirene Lloyd White, *b.* 1909, *w.*
1996   *Wilcox*, Judith Ann Wilcox, *b.* 19–, *w.*
1993   *Williams of Crosby*, Shirley Vivien Teresa Brittain
       Williams, PC, *b.* 1930, *m.*
1971   *Young*, Janet Mary Young, PC, *b.* 1926, *m.*

Lords Spiritual

The Lords Spiritual are the Archbishops of Canterbury and York and 24 diocesan bishops of the Church of England. The Bishops of London, Durham and Winchester always have seats in the House of Lords; the other 21 seats are filled by the remaining diocesan bishops in order of seniority. The Bishop of Sodor and Man and the Bishop of Gibraltar are not eligible to sit in the House of Lords.

ARCHBISHOPS

Style, The Most Revd and Right Hon. the Lord Archbishop
of —
Addressed as Archbishop, *or* Your Grace

Introduced to House of Lords
1991   *Canterbury* (103rd), George Leonard Carey, PC,
       PH.D., *b.* 1935, *m. Consecrated Bishop of Bath and
       Wells* 1987, *trans.* 1991
1990   *York* (96th), David Michael Hope, KCVO, PC,
       D.Phil., *b.* 1940, *cons.* 1985, *elected* 1985, *trans.*
       1991, 1995

BISHOPS

Style, The Right Revd the Lord Bishop of —
Addressed as My Lord
elected = date of election as diocesan bishop

Introduced to House of Lords
1995   *London* (132nd), Richard John Carew Chartres, *b.*
       1947, *m., cons.* 1992

1994   *Durham* (93rd), (Anthony) Michael (Arnold)
       Turnbull, *b.* 1935, *m., cons.* 1988, *elected* 1988,
       trans. 1994
1995   *Winchester* (96th), Michael Charles Scott-Joynt, *b.*
       1943, *m., cons.* 1987
1979   *Chichester* (102nd), Eric Waldram Kemp, DD, *b.*
       1915, *m., cons.* 1974, *elected* 1974
1980   *Liverpool* (6th), David Stuart Sheppard, *b.* 1929,
       m., cons. 1969, *elected* 1975
1984   *Ripon* (11th), David Nigel de Lorentz Young, *b.*
       1931, *m., cons.* 1977, *elected* 1977
1985   *Sheffield* (5th), David Ramsay Lunn, *b.* 1930, *cons.*
       1980, *elected* 1980
1985   *Newcastle* (10th), Andrew Alexander Kenny
       Graham, *b.* 1929, *cons.* 1977, *elected* 1981
1988   *Southwark* (7th), Robert Kerr Williamson, *b.* 1932,
       m., cons. 1984, *elected* 1984, *trans.* 1991
1989   *Lichfield* (97th), Keith Norman Sutton, *b.* 1934,
       m., cons. 1978, *elected* 1984
1989   *Exeter* (69th), (Geoffrey) Hewlett Thompson, *b.*
       1929, *m., cons.* 1974, *elected* 1985
1990   *Bristol* (54th), Barry Rogerson, *b.* 1936, *m., cons.*
       1979, *elected* 1985
1991   *Coventry* (7th), Simon Barrington-Ward, *b.* 1930,
       m., cons. 1985, *elected* 1985
1991   *Norwich* (70th), Peter John Nott, *b.* 1933, *m., cons.*
       1977, *elected* 1985
1993   *Lincoln* (70th), Robert Maynard Hardy, *b.* 1936,
       m., cons. 1980, *elected* 1986
1993   *Oxford* (41st), Richard Douglas Harries, *b.* 1936,
       m., cons. 1987, *elected* 1987
1994   *Birmingham* (7th), Mark Santer, *b.* 1936, *w., cons.*
       1981, *elected* 1987
1995   *Southwell* (9th), Patrick Burnet Harris, *b.* 1934, *m.,
       cons.* 1973, *elected* 1988

1995   *Blackburn* (7th), Alan David Chesters, *b.* 1937, *m.*, cons. 1989, *elected* 1989

1996   *Carlisle* (65th), Ian Harland, *b.* 1932, *m.*, cons. 1985, *elected* 1989

Bishops awaiting seats, in order of seniority

Truro (13th), Michael Thomas Ball, *b.* 1932, *cons.* 1980, *elected* 1990

Ely (67th), Stephen Whitefield Sykes, *b.* 1939, *m.*, cons. 1990, *elected* 1990

Hereford (103rd), John Keith Oliver, *b.* 1935, *m.*, cons. 1990, *elected* 1990

Leicester (5th), Thomas Frederick Butler, *b.* 1940, *m.*, cons. 1985, *elected* 1991

Bath and Wells (77th), James Lawton Thompson, *b.* 1936, *m.*, cons. 1978, *elected* 1991

Wakefield (11th), Nigel Simeon McCulloch, *b.* 1942, *m.*, cons. 1986, *elected* 1992

Bradford (8th), David James Smith, *b.* 1935, *m.*, cons. 1987, *elected* 1992

Manchester (10th), Christopher John Mayfield, *b.* 1935, *m.*, cons. 1985, *elected* 1993

Salisbury (77th), David Staffurth Stancliffe, *b.* 1942, *m.*, cons. 1993, *elected* 1993

Gloucester (39th), David Edward Bentley, *b.* 1935, *m.*, cons. 1986, *elected* 1993

Rochester (106th), Michael James Nazir-Ali, ph.d., *b.* 1949, *m.*, cons. 1984, *elected* 1995

Guildford (8th), John Warren Gladwin, *b.* 1942, *m.*, cons. 1994, *elected* 1994

Derby (6th), Jonathan Sansbury Bailey, *b.* 1940, *m.*, cons. 1992, *elected* 1995

St Albans (9th), Christopher William Herbert, *b.* 1944, *m.*, cons. 1995, *elected* 1995

Portsmouth (8th), Kenneth William Stevenson, *b.* 1949, *m.*, cons. 1995, *elected* 1995

Peterborough (37th), Ian Cundy, *b.* 1945, *m.*, cons. 1992, *elected* 1996

Chelmsford (8th), John Freeman Perry, *b.* 1935, *m.*, cons. 1989, *elected* 1996

Chester (40th), Peter Robert Forster, ph.d., *b.* 1950, *cons.* 1996, *elected* 1996

The sees of St Edmundsbury and Ipswich and Worcester were vacant at the time of going to press

The Order of St John

THE MOST VENERABLE ORDER OF THE HOSPITAL OF ST JOHN OF JERUSALEM (1888)

GCStJ   Bailiff/Dame Grand Cross
KStJ   Knight of Justice/Grace
DStJ   Dame of Justice/Grace
ChStJ   Chaplain
CStJ   Commander
OStJ,   Officer
SBStJ   Serving Brother
SSStJ   Serving Sister
EsqStJ   Esquire

Mottoes, Pro Fide *and* Pro Utilitate Hominum

The Order of St John, founded in the early 12th century in Jerusalem, was a religious order with a particular duty to care for the sick. In Britain the Order was dissolved by Henry VIII in 1540 but the British branch was revived in the early 19th century. The branch was not accepted by the Grand Magistracy of the Order in Rome but its search for a role in the tradition of the Hospitallers led to the founding of the St John Ambulance Association in 1877 and later the St John Ambulance Brigade; in 1882 the St

John Ophthalmic Hospital was founded in Jerusalem. A royal charter was granted in 1888 establishing the British Order of St John as a British Order of Chivalry with the Sovereign as its head.

Admission to the Order is conferred in recognition of service, usually in St John Ambulance. Membership does not confer any rank, style, title or precedence on a recipient.

SOVEREIGN HEAD OF THE ORDER
HM The Queen

GRAND PRIOR
HRH The Duke of Gloucester, GCVO

Lord Prior, The Lord Vestey
Prelate, The Rt. Revd M. A. Mann, KCVO
Chancellor, Prof. A. R. Mellows, TD
Bailiff of Egle, The Lord Remnant
Headquarters, St John's Gate, Clerkenwell, London ECIM 4DA. Tel: 0171-253 6644

COURTESY TITLES

From this list it will be seen that, for example, the Marquess of Blandford is heir to the Dukedom of Marlborough, and Viscount Amberley to the Earldom of Russell. Titles of second heirs are also given, and the courtesy title of the father of a second heir is indicated by *; e.g. Earl of Burlington, eldest son of *Marquess of Hartington
For forms of address, *see* page 136

MARQUESSES
*Blandford – *Marlborough, D.*
Bowmont and Cessford – *Roxburghe, D.*
Douglas and Clydesdale – *Hamilton, D.*
*Douro – *Wellington, D.*
Graham – *Montrose, D.*
Granby – *Rutland, D.*
Hamilton – *Abercorn, D.*
*Hartington – *Devonshire, D.*
*Kildare – *Leinster, D.*
Lorne – *Argyll, D.*
*Tavistock – *Bedford, D.*
Tullibardine – *Atholl, D.*
*Worcester – *Beaufort, D.*

EARLS
Aboyne – *Huntly, M.*
Altamont – *Sligo, M.*
Ancram – *Lothian, M.*
Arundel and Surrey – *Norfolk, D.*
*Bective – *Headfort, M.*
*Belfast – *Donegall, M.*
Brecknock – *Camden, M.*
Burford – *St Albans, D.*
Burlington – *Hartington, M.*
*Cardigan – *Ailesbury, M.*
Compton – *Northampton, M.*
*Dalkeith – *Buccleuch, D.*
Dumfries – *Bute, M.*
*Euston – *Grafton, D.*
Glamorgan – *Worcester, M.*
Grosvenor – *Westminster, D.*
*Haddo – *Aberdeen and Temair, M.*
*Hillsborough – *Downshire, M.*
Hopetoun – *Linlithgow, M.*
March and Kinrara – *Richmond, D.*
*Mount Charles – *Conyngham, M.*
Mornington – *Douro, M.*
Offaly – *Kildare, M.*
Percy – *Northumberland, D.*
Ronaldshay – *Zetland, M.*
*St Andrews – *Kent, D.*
*Shelburne – *Lansdowne, M.*
*Southesk – *Fife, D.*

Sunderland – *Blandford, M.*
*Tyrone – *Waterford, M.*
Ulster – *Gloucester, D.*
*Uxbridge – *Anglesey, M.*
Wiltshire – *Winchester, M.*
Yarmouth – *Hertford, M.*

VISCOUNTS
Althorp – *Spencer, E.*
Amberley – *Russell, E.*
Andover – *Suffolk and Berkshire, E.*
Anson – *Lichfield, E.*
Asquith – *Oxford & Asquith, E.*
Boringdon – *Morley, E.*
Borodale – *Beatty, E.*
Boyle – *Shannon, E.*
Brocas – *Jellicoe, E.*
Calne and Calstone – *Shelburne, E.*
Campden – *Gainsborough, E.*
Carlow – *Portarlington, E.*
Carlton – *Wharncliffe, E.*
Castlereagh – *Londonderry, M.*
Chelsea – *Cadogan, E.*
Chewton – *Waldegrave, E.*
Chichester – *Belfast, E.*
Clanfield – *Peel, E.*
Clive – *Powis, E.*
Coke – *Leicester, E.*
Corry – *Belmore, E.*
Corvedale – *Baldwin of Bewdley, E.*
Cranborne – *Salisbury, M.*
Cranley – *Onslow, E.*
Crichton – *Erne, E.*
Crowhurst – *Cottenham, E.*
Curzon – *Howe, E.*
Dangan – *Cowley, E.*
Dawick – *Haig, E.*
Deerhurst – *Coventry, E.*
Drumlanrig – *Queensberry, M.*
Dunwich – *Stradbroke, E.*
Dupplin – *Kinnoull, E.*
Ebrington – *Fortescue, E.*
Ednam – *Dudley, E.*
Emlyn – *Cawdor, E.*
Encombe – *Eldon, E.*
Ennismore – *Listowel, E.*
Enfield – *Strafford, E.*
Erleigh – *Reading, M.*
Errington – *Cromer, E.*

FitzHarris – *Malmesbury, E.*
Folkestone – *Radnor, E.*
Forbes – *Granard, E.*
Garmoyle – *Cairns, E.*
Garnock – *Lindsay, E.*
Glandine – *Norbury, E.*
Glenapp – *Inchcape, E.*
Glentworth – *Limerick, E.*
Grimstone – *Verulam, E.*
Gwynedd – *Lloyd George of Dwyfor, E.*
Hawkesbury – *Liverpool, E.*
Hinchingbrooke – *Sandwich, E.*
Ikerrin – *Carrick, E.*
Ingestre – *Shrewsbury, E.*
Ipswich – *Euston, E.*
Jocelyn – *Roden, E.*
Kelburn – *Glasgow, E.*
Kilwarlin – *Hillsborough, E.*
Kingsborough – *Kingston, E.*
Knebworth – *Lytton, E.*
Lascelles – *Harewood, E.*
Lewisham – *Dartmouth, E.*
Linley – *Snowdon, E.*
Loftus – *Ely, M.*
Lowther – *Lonsdale, E.*
Lumley – *Scarbrough, E.*
Lymington – *Portsmouth, E.*
Macmillan of Ovenden – *Stockton, E.*
Maidstone – *Winchilsea and Nottingham, E.*
Maitland – *Lauderdale, E.*
Malden – *Essex, E.*
Mandeville – *Manchester, D.*
Medina – *Milford Haven, M.*
Melgund – *Minto, E.*
Merton – *Nelson, E.*
Moore – *Drogheda, E.*
Newport – *Bradford, E.*
Newry and Mourne – *Kilmorey, E.*
Parker – *Macclesfield, E.*
Perceval – *Egmont, E.*
Petersham – *Harrington, E.*
Pollington – *Mexborough, E.*
Raynham – *Townshend, M.*
Reidhaven – *Seafield, E.*
Ruthven of Canberra – *Gowrie, E.*
St Cyres – *Iddesleigh, E.*
Sandon – *Harrowby, E.*
Savernake – *Cardigan, E.*
Slane – *Mount Charles, E.*
Somerton – *Normanton, E.*

Stopford – *Courtown, E.*
Stormont – *Mansfield, E.*
Strathallan – *Perth, E.*
Stuart – *Castle Stewart, E.*
Suirdale – *Donoughmore, E.*
Tamworth – *Ferrers, E.*
Tarbat – *Cromartie, E.*
Vaughan – *Lisburne, E.*
Villiers – *Jersey, E.*
Weymouth – *Bath, M.*
Windsor – *Plymouth, E.*
Wolmer – *Selborne, E.*
Woodstock – *Portland, E.*

BARONS (LORD —)
Aberdour – *Morton, E.*
Apsley – *Bathurst, E.*
Ardee – *Meath, E.*
Ashley – *Shaftesbury, E.*
Balgonie – *Leven & Melville, E.*
Balniel – *Crawford and Balcarres, E.*
Berriedale – *Caithness, E.*
Bingham – *Lucan, E.*
Binning – *Haddington, E.*
Brooke – *Warwick, E.*
Bruce – *Elgin, E.*
Buckhurst – *De La Warr, E.*
Burghley – *Exeter, M.*
Cardross – *Buchan, E.*
Carnegie – *Southesk, E.*
Clifton – *Darnley, E.*
Cochrane – *Dundonald, E.*
Courtenay – *Devon, E.*
Dalmeny – *Rosebery, E.*
Doune – *Moray, E.*
Downpatrick – *St Andrews, E.*
Dunglass – *Home, E.*
Eliot – *St Germans, E.*
Eskdail – *Dalkeith, E.*
Formartine – *Haddo, E.*
Gillford – *Clanwilliam, E.*
Glamis – *Strathmore, E.*
Greenock – *Cathcart, E.*
Guernsey – *Aylesford, E.*
Hay – *Erroll, E.*
Herbert – *Pembroke, E.*
Howard of Effingham – *Effingham, E.*
Howland – *Tavistock, M.*
Hyde – *Clarendon, E.*
Inverurie – *Kintore, E.*
Irwin – *Halifax, E.*
Johnstone – *Annandale and Hartfell, E.*
Kenlis – *Bective, E.*
Langton – *Temple of Stowe, E.*
La Poer – *Tyrone, E.*

Leslie – *Rothes, E.*
Leveson – *Granville, E.*
Loughborough – *Rosslyn, E.*
Maltravers – **Arundel and Surrey, E.*
Mauchline – *Loudoun, C.*
Medway – *Cranbrook, E.*
Montgomerie – *Eglinton and Winton, E.*

Moreton – *Ducie, E.*
Naas – *Mayo, E.*
Neidpath – *Wemyss & March, E.*
Norreys – *Lindsey & Abingdon, E.*
North – *Guilford, E.*
Ogilvy – *Airlie, E.*
Oxmantown – *Rosse, E.*

Paget de Beaudesert – **Uxbridge, E.*
Porchester – *Carnarvon, E.*
Ramsay – *Dalhousie, E.*
Romsey – *Mountbatten of Burma, C.*
Rosehill – *Northesk, E.*
Scrymgeour – *Dundee, E.*
Seymour – *Somerset, D.*

Strathnaver – *Sutherland, C.*
Wodehouse – *Kimberley, E.*
Worsley – *Yarborough, E.*

PEERS' SURNAMES WHICH DIFFER FROM THEIR TITLES

The following symbols indicate the rank of the peer holding each title:

C. Countess
D. Duke
E. Earl
M. Marquess
V. Viscount
* Life Peer

Where no designation is given, the title is that of an hereditary Baron or Baroness

Abney-Hastings – *Loudoun, C.*
Acheson – *Gosford, E.*
Adderley – *Norton*
Addington – *Sidmouth, V.*
Agar – *Normanton, E.*
Aitken – *Beaverbrook*
Akers-Douglas – *Chilston, V.*
Alexander – *A. of Tunis, E.*
Alexander – *A. of Weedon**
Alexander – *Caledon, E.*
Allen – *A. of Abbeydale**
Allen – *Croham**
Allsopp – *Hindlip*
Amery – *A. of Lustleigh**
Anderson – *Waverley, V.*
Annesley – *Valentia, V.*
Anson – *Lichfield, E.*
Archer – *A. of Sandwell**
Archer – *A. of Weston-super-Mare**
Armstrong – *A. of Ilminster**
Armstrong-Jones – *Snowdon, E.*
Arthur – *Glenarthur*
Arundell – *Talbot of Malahide*
Ashley – *A. of Stoke**
Ashley-Cooper – *Shaftesbury, E.*
Ashton – *A. of Hyde*
Asquith – *Oxford & Asquith, E.*
Assheton – *Clitheroe*
Astley – *Hastings*
Astor – *A. of Hever*
Atkins – *Colnbrook**
Aubrey-Fletcher – *Braye*
Bailey – *Glanusk*
Baillie – *Burton*

Baillie Hamilton – *Haddington, E.*
Baldwin – *B. of Bewdley, E.*
Balfour – *B. of Inchrye*
Balfour – *Kinross*
Balfour – *Riverdale*
Bampfylde – *Poltimore*
Banbury – *B. of Southam*
Barber – *B. of Tewkesbury**
Baring – *Ashburton*
Baring – *Cromer, E.*
Baring – *Howick of Glendale*
Baring – *Northbrook*
Baring – *Revelstoke*
Barker – *Trumpington**
Barnes – *Gorell*
Barnewall – *Trimlestown*
Bathurst – *Bledisloe, V.*
Beauclerk – *St Albans, D.*
Beaumont – *Allendale, V.*
Beaumont – *B. of Whitley**
Beckett – *Grimthorpe*
Bellow – *Bellwin**
Benn – *Stansgate, V.*
Bennet – *Tankerville, E.*
Bentinck – *Portland, E.*
Beresford – *Decies*
Beresford – *Waterford, M.*
Berry – *Camrose, V.*
Berry – *Hartwell**
Berry – *Kemsley, V.*
Bertie – *Lindsey, E.*
Best – *Wynford*
Bethell – *Westbury*
Bewicke-Copley – *Cromwell*
Bigham – *Mersey, V.*
Bingham – *Clanmorris*
Bingham – *Lucan, E.*
Bingham – *B. of Cornhill**
Blackwood – *Dufferin & Clandeboye*
Bligh – *Darnley, E.*
Blyth – *B. of Rowington**
Bootle-Wilbraham – *Skelmersdale*
Boscawen – *Falmouth, V.*
Boston – *B. of Faversham**
Bourke – *Mayo, E.*
Bowes Lyon – *Strathmore, E.*
Bowyer – *Denham*
Boyd – *Kilmarnock*
Boyle – *Cork & Orrery, E.*
Boyle – *Glasgow, E.*
Boyle – *Shannon, E.*

Brabazon – *Meath, E.*
Braine – *B. of Wheatley**
Brand – *Hampden, V.*
Brandon – *B. of Oakbrook**
Brassey – *B. of Apethorpe*
Brett – *Esher, V.*
Bridge – *B. of Harwich**
Bridgeman – *Bradford, E.*
Brodrick – *Midleton, V.*
Brooke – *Alanbrooke, V.*
Brooke – *Brookeborough, V.*
Brooke – *B. of Ystradfellte**
Brooks – *B. of Tremorfa**
Brooks – *Crawshaw*
Brougham – *Brougham and Vaux*
Broughton – *Fairhaven*
Browne – *Kilmaine*
Browne – *Oranmore and Browne*
Browne – *Sligo, M.*
Bruce – *Aberdare*
Bruce – *Balfour of Burleigh*
Bruce – *B. of Donington**
Bruce – *Elgin and Kincardine, E.*
Brudenell-Bruce – *Ailesbury, M.*
Buchan – *Tweedsmuir*
Buckley – *Wrenbury*
Butler – *Carrick, E.*
Butler – *Dunboyne*
Butler – *Lanesborough, E.*
Butler – *Mountgarret, V.*
Butler – *Ormonde, M.*
Buxton – *B. of Alsa**
Byng – *Strafford, E.*
Byng – *Torrington, V.*
Callaghan – *C. of Cardiff**
Cameron – *C. of Lochbroom**
Campbell – *Argyll, D.*
Campbell – *Breadalbane and Holland, E.*
Campbell – *C. of Alloway**
Campbell – *C. of Croy**
Campbell – *Cawdor, E.*
Campbell – *Colgrain*
Campbell – *Stratheden and Campbell*
Campbell-Gray – *Gray*
Canning – *Garvagh*
Capell – *Essex, E.*
Carington – *Carrington*
Carlisle – *C. of Bucklow**
Carmichael – *C. of Kelvingrove**

Carnegie – *Fife, D.*
Carnegie – *Northesk, E.*
Carr – *C. of Hadley**
Cary – *Falkland, V.*
Castle – *C. of Blackburn**
Caulfeild – *Charlemont, V.*
Cavendish – *C. of Furness**
Cavendish – *Chesham*
Cavendish – *Devonshire, D.*
Cavendish – *Waterpark*
Cayzer – *Rotherwick*
Cecil – *Amherst of Hackney*
Cecil – *Exeter, M.*
Cecil – *Rockley*
Cecil – *Salisbury, M.*
Chalker – *C. of Wallasey**
Chaloner – *Gisborough*
Chapman – *Northfield**
Charteris – *C. of Amisfield**
Charteris – *Wemyss and March, E.*
Cheshire – *Ryder of Warsaw**
Chetwynd-Talbot – *Shrewsbury, E.*
Chichester – *Donegall, M.*
Chichester-Clark – *Moyola**
Child Villiers – *Jersey, E.*
Cholmondeley – *Delamere*
Chubb – *Hayter*
Clark – *C. of Kempston**
Clegg-Hill – *Hill, V.*
Clifford – *C. of Chudleigh*
Cochrane – *C. of Cults*
Cochrane – *Dundonald, E.*
Cocks – *C. of Hartcliffe**
Cocks – *Somers*
Cokayne – *Cullen of Ashbourne*
Coke – *Leicester, E.*
Cole – *Enniskillen, E.*
Collier – *Monkswell*
Colville – *Clydesmuir*
Colville – *C. of Culross, V.*
Compton – *Northampton, M.*
Conolly-Carew – *Carew*
Constantine – *C. of Stanmore**
Cooke – *C. of Islandreagh**
Cooke – *C. of Thorndon**
Cooper – *Norwich, V.*
Corbett – *Rowallan*
Courtenay – *Devon, E.*
Cox – *Kings Norton**

Craig – *C. of Radley**
Craig – *Craigavon, V.*
Crichton – *Erne, E.*
Crichton-Stuart – *Bute, M.*
Cripps – *Parmoor*
Crossley – *Somerleyton*
Cubitt – *Ashcombe*
Cunliffe-Lister – *Masham of Ilton**
Cunliffe-Lister – *Swinton, E.*
Curzon – *Howe, E.*
Curzon – *Scarsdale, V.*
Cust – *Brownlow*
Dalrymple – *Stair, E.*
Daubeny de Moleyns – *Ventry*
Davies – *Darwen*
Davison – *Broughshane*
Dawnay – *Downe, V.*
Dawson-Damer – *Portarlington, E.*
Dean – *D. of Beswick**
Dean – *D. of Harptree**
Dean – *D. of Thornton-le-Fylde**
Deane – *Muskerry*
de Courcy – *Kingsale*
de Grey – *Walsingham*
Delacourt-Smith – *Delacourt Smith of Alteryn**
Denison – *Londesborough*
Denison-Pender – *Pender*
Denton – *D. of Wakefield**
Devereux – *Hereford, V.*
Dewar – *Forteviot*
De Yarburgh-Bateson – *Deramore*
Dixon – *Glentoran*
Dodson – *Monk Bretton*
Donaldson – *D. of Kingsbridge**
Donaldson – *D. of Lymington**
Dormand – *D. of Easington**
Douglas – *Morton, E.*
Douglas – *Queensberry, M.*
Douglas-Hamilton – *Hamilton, D.*
Douglas-Hamilton – *Selkirk, E.*
Douglas-Home – *Dacre*
Douglas-Home – *Home, E.*
Douglas-Pennant – *Penrhyn*
Douglas-Scott-Montagu – *Montagu of Beaulieu*
Drummond – *Perth, E.*
Drummond of Megginch – *Strange*
Dugdale – *Crathorne*
Duke – *Merrivale*
Duncombe – *Feversham*
Dundas – *Melville, V.*
Dundas – *Zetland, M.*
Eady – *Swinfen*
Eccles – *E. of Moulton**
Eden – *Auckland*
Eden – *E. of Winton**
Eden – *Henley*

Edgcumbe – *Mount Edgcumbe, E.*
Edmondson – *Sandford*
Edwardes – *Kensington*
Edwards – *Chelmer**
Edwards – *Crickhowell**
Egerton – *Sutherland, D.*
Egerton – *Wilton, E.*
Eliot – *St Germans, E.*
Elliot-Murray-Kynynmound – *Minto, E.*
Elliott – *E. of Morpeth**
Erroll – *E. of Hale*
Erskine – *Buchan, E.*
Erskine – *Mar* & *Kellie, E.*
Erskine-Murray – *Elibank*
Evans – *Mountevans*
Evans-Freke – *Carbery*
Eve – *Silsoe*
Ewing – *E. of Kirkford**
Fairfax – *F. of Cameron*
Fane – *Westmorland, E.*
Farrington – *F. of Ribbleton**
Feilding – *Denbigh, E.*
Fellowes – *De Ramsey*
Fermor-Hesketh – *Hesketh*
Fiennes – *Saye* & *Sele*
Fiennes-Clinton – *Lincoln, E.*
Finch Hatton – *Winchilsea, E.*
Finch-Knightley – *Aylesford, E.*
Fisher – *F. of Rednal**
Fitzalan-Howard – *Herries of Terregles*
Fitzalan-Howard – *Norfolk, D.*
FitzClarence – *Munster, E.*
FitzGerald – *Leinster, D.*
Fitzherbert – *Stafford*
Fitz-Maurice – *Orkney, E.*
FitzRoy – *Grafton, D.*
FitzRoy – *Southampton*
FitzRoy Newdegate – *Daventry, V.*
Fletcher-Vane – *Inglewood*
Flower – *Ashbrook, V.*
Foljambe – *Liverpool, E.*
Forbes – *Granard, E.*
Fox-Strangways – *Ilchester, E.*
Frankland – *Zouche*
Fraser – *F. of Carmyllie**
Fraser – *F. of Kilmorack**
Fraser – *Lovat*
Fraser – *Saltoun*
Fraser – *Strathalmond*
Freeman-Grenville – *Kinloss*
Fremantle – *Cottesloe*
French – *De Freyne*
Galbraith – *Strathclyde*
Ganzoni – *Belstead*
Gardner – *G. of Parkes**
Gathorne-Hardy – *Cranbrook, E.*
Gibbs – *Aldenham*
Gibbs – *Wraxall*
Gibson – *Ashbourne*

Giffard – *Halsbury, E.*
Gilbey – *Vaux of Harrowden*
Gillmore – *G. of Thamesfield**
Gilmour – *G. of Craigmillar**
Gladwin – *G. of Clee**
Glyn – *Wolverton*
Godley – *Kilbracken*
Goff – *G. of Chieveley**
Gordon – *Aberdeen, M.*
Gordon – *Huntly, M.*
Gordon Lennox – *Richmond, D.*
Gore – *Arran, E.*
Gough-Calthorpe – *Calthorpe*
Gould – *G. of Potternewton**
Graham – *G. of Edmonton**
Graham – *Montrose, D.*
Graham-Toler – *Norbury, E.*
Grant of Grant – *Strathspey*
Grant-Ferris – *Harvington**
Granville – *G. of Eye**
Gray – *G. of Contin**
Greaves – *Dysart, C.*
Greenall – *Daresbury*
Greene – *G. of Harrow Weald**
Greenhill – *G. of Harrow**
Greville – *Warwick, E.*
Grey – *G. of Naunton**
Griffiths – *G. of Fforestfach**
Grigg – *Altrincham*
Grimston – *G. of Westbury*
Grimston – *Verulam, E.*
Grosvenor – *Ebury*
Grosvenor – *Westminster, D.*
Gueterbock – *Berkeley*
Guest – *Wimborne, V.*
Guinness – *Iveagh, E.*
Guinness – *Moyne*
Gully – *Selby, V.*
Gurdon – *Cranworth*
Gwynne Jones – *Chalfont**
Hamilton – *Abercorn, D.*
Hamilton – *Belhaven and Stenton*
Hamilton – *Dudley*
Hamilton – *H. of Dalzell*
Hamilton – *Holm Patrick*
Hamilton-Russell – *Boyne, V.*
Hamilton-Smith – *Colwyn*
Hanbury-Tracy – *Sudeley*
Handcock – *Castlemaine*
Harbord-Hamond – *Suffield*
Harding – *H. of Petherton*
Hardinge – *H. of Penshurst*
Hare – *Blakenham, V.*
Hare – *Listowel, E.*
Harmsworth – *Rothermere, V.*
Harris – *H. of Greenwich**
Harris – *H. of High Cross**
Harris – *H. of Peckham**
Harris – *Malmesbury, E.*
Harvey – *H. of Tasburgh*

Hastings Bass – *Huntingdon, E.*
Hay – *Erroll, E.*
Hay – *Kinnoull, E.*
Hay – *Tweeddale, M.*
Heathcote-Drummond-Willoughby – *Willoughby de Eresby*
Hely-Hutchinson – *Donoughmore, E.*
Henderson – *Faringdon*
Henderson – *H. of Brompton**
Hennessy – *Windlesham*
Henniker-Major – *Henniker*
Hepburne-Scott – *Polwarth*
Herbert – *Carnarvon, E.*
Herbert – *Hemingford*
Herbert – *Pembroke, E.*
Herbert – *Powis, E.*
Hermon-Hodge – *Wyfold*
Hervey – *Bristol, M.*
Hewitt – *Lifford, V.*
Hicks Beach – *St Aldwyn, E.*
Hill – *Downshire, M.*
Hill – *Sandys*
Hill-Trevor – *Trevor*
Hilton – *H. of Eggardon**
Hobart-Hampden – *Buckinghamshire, E.*
Hogg – *Hailsham of St Marylebone**
Holland-Hibbert – *Knutsford, V.*
Hollis – *H. of Heigham**
Holme – *H. of Cheltenham**
Holmes à Court – *Heytesbury*
Hood – *Bridport, V.*
Hope – *Glendevon*
Hope – *H. of Craighead**
Hope – *Linlithgow, M.*
Hope – *Rankeillour*
Hope Johnstone – *Annandale and Hartfell, E.*
Hope-Morley – *Hollenden*
Hopkinson – *Colyton*
Hore Ruthven – *Gowrie, E.*
Houghton – *H. of Sowerby**
Hovell-Thurlow-Cumming-Bruce – *Thurlow*
Howard – *Carlisle, E.*
Howard – *Effingham, E.*
Howard – *H. of Penrith*
Howard – *Strathcona*
Howard – *Suffolk and Berkshire, E.*
Howe – *H. of Aberavon**
Howells – *Geraint**
Howie – *H. of Troon**
Hubbard – *Addington*
Huggins – *Malvern, V.*
Hughes – *Cledwyn of Penrhos**
Hughes-Young – *St Helens*
Hunt – *H. of Tanworth**
Hutchinson – *H. of Lullington**

Ponsonby – *Sysonby*
Porter – *P. of Luddenham**
Powys – *Lilford*
Pratt – *Camden, M.*
Preston – *Gormanston, V.*
Primrose – *Rosebery, E.*
Prittie – *Dunalley*
Prout – *Kingsland**
Ramsay – *Dalhousie, E.*
Ramsbotham – *Soulbury, V.*
Rawlinson – *R. of Ewell**
Rees-Williams – *Ogmore*
Renfrew – *R. of Kaimsthorn**
Rhys – *Dynevor*
Richards – *Milverton*
Richardson – *R. of Duntisbourne**
Rippon – *R. of Hexham**
Ritchie – *R. of Dundee*
Robens – *R. of Woldingham**
Roberts – *Clwyd*
Robertson – *R. of Oakridge*
Robertson – *Wharton*
Robinson – *Martonmere*
Robson – *R. of Kiddington**
Roche – *Fermoy*
Rodd – *Rennell*
Rodger – *R. of Earlsferry**
Rodgers – *R. of Quarry Bank**
Roll – *R. of Ipsden**
Roper-Curzon – *Teynham*
Rospigliosi – *Newburgh, E.*
Rous – *Stradbroke, E.*
Rowley-Conwy – *Langford*
Royle – *Fanshawe of Richmond**
Runciman – *R. of Doxford, V.*
Russell – *Ampthill*
Russell – *Bedford, D.*
Russell – *de Clifford*
Russell – *R. of Liverpool*
Ryder – *Harrowby, E.*
Ryder – *R. of Eaton Hastings**
Ryder – *R. of Warsaw**
Sackville – *De La Warr, E.*
Sackville-West – *Sackville*
Sainsbury – *S. of Preston Candover**
St Aubyn – *St Levan*
St Clair – *Sinclair*
St Clair-Erskine – *Rosslyn, E.*
St John – *Bolingbroke and St John, V.*
St John – *St John of Blesto*
St John-Stevas – *St John of Fawsley**
St Leger – *Doneraile, V.*
Samuel – *Bearsted, V.*
Sanderson – *S. of Ayot*
Sanderson – *S. of Bowden**
Sandilands – *Torphichen*
Saumarez – *De Saumarez*
Savile – *Mexborough, E.*
Scarlett – *Abinger*
Schreiber – *Marlesford**
Sclater-Booth – *Basing*
Scott – *Eldon, E.*

Scott-Ellis – *Howard de Walden*
Scrymgeour – *Dundee, E.*
Seager – *Leighton of St Mellons*
Seely – *Mottistone*
Sefton – *S. of Garston**
Seymour – *Hertford, M.*
Seymour – *Somerset, D.*
Shaw – *Craigmyle*
Shaw – *S. of Northstead**
Sheppard – *S. of Didgemere**
Shirley – *Ferrers, E.*
Short – *Glenamara**
Siddeley – *Kenilworth*
Sidney – *De L'Isle, V.*
Sieff – *S. of Brimpton**
Simon – *S. of Glaisdale**
Simon – *S. of Wythenshawe*
Sinclair – *Caithness, E.*
Sinclair – *S. of Cleeve*
Sinclair – *Thurso, V.*
Skeffington – *Massereene, V.*
Slynn – *S. of Hadley**
Smith – *Bicester*
Smith – *Hambleden, V.*
Smith – *Kirkhill**
Smith – *S. of Gilmorehill**
Somerset – *Beaufort, D.*
Somerset – *Raglan*
Souter – *Audley*
Spencer – *Churchill, V.*
Spencer-Churchill – *Marlborough, D.*
Spring Rice – *Monteagle of Brandon*
Stanhope – *Harrington, E.*
Stanley – *Derby, E.*
Stanley – *Stanley of Alderley & Sheffield*
Stapleton-Cotton – *Combermere, V.*
Sterling – *S. of Plaistow**
Stevens – *S. of Ludgate**
Stewart – *Galloway, E.*
Stewart – *Stewartby**
Stodart – *S. of Leaston**
Stoddart – *S. of Swindon**
Stonor – *Camoys*
Stopford – *Courtown, E.*
Stourton – *Mowbray*
Strachey – *O'Hagan*
Strutt – *Belper*
Strutt – *Rayleigh*
Stuart – *Castle Stewart, E.*
Stuart – *Moray, E.*
Stuart – *S. of Findhorn, V.*
Suenson-Taylor – *Grantchester*
Taylor – *Ingrow**
Taylor – *T. of Blackburn**
Taylor – *T. of Gosforth**
Taylor – *T. of Gryfe**
Taylour – *Headfort, M.*
Temple-Gore-Langton – *Temple of Stowe, E.*
Tennant – *Glenconner*
Thellusson – *Rendlesham*
Thesiger – *Chelmsford, V.*

Thomas – *T. of Gwydir**
Thomas – *T. of Swynnerton**
Thomas – *T. of Walliswood**
Thomas – *Tonypandy, V.*
Thomson – *T. of Fleet*
Thomson – *T. of Monifieth**
Thynn – *Bath, M.*
Thynne – *Bath, M.*
Tottenham – *Ely, M.*
Trefusis – *Clinton*
Trench – *Ashtown*
Trevor-Roper – *Dacre of Glanton**
Tufton – *Hothfield*
Turner – *Netherthorpe*
Turner – *T. of Camden**
Turnour – *Winterton, E.*
Tyrell-Kenyon – *Kenyon*
Vanden-Bempde-Johnstone – *Derwent*
Vane – *Barnard*
Vane – *Inglewood*
Vane-Tempest-Stewart – *Londonderry, M.*
Vanneck – *Huntingfield*
Vaughan – *Lisburne, E.*
Vereker – *Gort, V.*
Verney – *Willoughby de Broke*
Vernon – *Lyveden*
Vesey – *De Vesci, V.*
Villiers – *Clarendon, E.*
Vivian – *Swansea*
Wade – *W. of Chorlton**
Walker – *W. of Worcester**
Wallace – *W. of Campsie**
Wallace – *W. of Coslany**
Wallace – *W. of Saltaire**
Wallop – *Portsmouth, E.*
Walton – *W. of Detchant**
Ward – *Bangor, V.*
Ward – *Dudley, E.*
Warrender – *Bruntisfield*
Watson – *Manton*
Wedderburn – *W. of Charlton**
Weir – *Inverforth*
Weld-Forester – *Forester*
Wellesley – *Cowley, E.*
Wellesley – *Wellington, D.*
Westenra – *Rossmore*
White – *Annaly*
White – *James of Holland Park**
Whiteley – *Marchamley*
Whitfield – *Kenswood*
Williams – *W. of Crosby**
Williams – *W. of Elvel**
Williams – *W. of Mostyn**
Williamson – *Forres*
Willoughby – *Middleton*
Wills – *Dulverton*
Wilson – *Moran*
Wilson – *Nunburnholme*
Wilson – *W. of Langside**
Wilson – *W. of Tillyorn**
Windsor – *Gloucester, D.*
Windsor – *Kent, D.*
Windsor-Clive – *Plymouth, E.*

Wingfield – *Powerscourt, V.*
Winn – *St Oswald*
Wodehouse – *Kimberley, E.*
Wolfson – *W. of Sunningdale**
Wood – *Halifax, E.*
Wood – *Holderness**
Woodhouse – *Terrington*
Wright – *W. of Richmond**
Wyatt – *W. of Weeford**
Wyndham – *Egremont & Leconfield*
Wyndham-Quin – *Dunraven, E.*
Wynn – *Newborough*
Yarde-Buller – *Churston*
Yerburgh – *Alvingham*
Yorke – *Hardwicke, E.*
Young – *Kennet*
Young – *Y. of Dartington**
Young – *Y. of Graffham**
Younger – *Y. of Leckie, V.*
Younger – *Y. of Prestwick**

Orders of Chivalry

THE MOST NOBLE ORDER OF THE GARTER (1348)

KG

Ribbon, Blue
Motto, Honi soit qui mal y pense
(*Shame on him who thinks evil of it*)
The number of Knights Companions is limited to 24

SOVEREIGN OF THE ORDER
The Queen

LADIES OF THE ORDER
HM Queen Elizabeth the Queen
Mother, 1936
HRH The Princess Royal, 1994

ROYAL KNIGHTS
HRH The Prince Philip, Duke of
Edinburgh, 1947
HRH The Prince of Wales, 1958
HRH The Duke of Kent, 1985

EXTRA KNIGHTS COMPANIONS AND
LADIES
HRH Princess Juliana of the
Netherlands, 1958
HRH The Grand Duke of
Luxembourg, 1972
HM The Queen of Denmark, 1979
HM The King of Sweden, 1983
HM The King of Spain, 1988
HM The Queen of the Netherlands,
1989

KNIGHTS AND LADY COMPANIONS
The Earl of Longford, 1971
The Marquess of Abergavenny, 1974
The Duke of Grafton, 1976
The Lord Hunt, 1979
The Duke of Norfolk, 1983
The Lord Lewin, 1983
The Lord Richardson of
Duntisbourne, 1983
The Lord Carrington, 1985
The Lord Callaghan of Cardiff, 1987
The Viscount Leverhulme, 1988
The Lord Hailsham of St
Marylebone, 1988
The Duke of Wellington, 1990
Field Marshall the Lord Bramall,
1990
Sir Edward Heath, 1992
The Viscount Ridley, 1992
The Lord Sainsbury of Preston
Candover, 1992
The Lord Ashburton, 1994
The Lord Kingsdown, 1994

Sir Ninian Stephen, 1994
The Baroness Thatcher, 1995
Sir Edmund Hillary, 1995
The Duke of Devonshire, 1996
Sir Timothy Coleman, 1996

Prelate, The Bishop of Winchester
Chancellor, The Lord Carrington, KG,
GCMG, CH, MC
Register, The Dean of Windsor
Garter King of Arms, P. Gwynn-Jones,
LVO
Gentleman Usher of the Black Rod, Gen.
Sir Edward Jones, KCB, CBE
Secretary, D. H. B. Chesshyre, LVO

THE MOST ANCIENT AND MOST NOBLE ORDER OF THE THISTLE (REVIVED 1687)

KT

Ribbon, Green
Motto, Nemo me impune lacessit (*No
one provokes me with impunity*)
The number of Knights is limited to 16

SOVEREIGN OF THE ORDER
The Queen

LADY OF THE THISTLE
HM Queen Elizabeth the Queen
Mother, 1937

ROYAL KNIGHTS
HRH The Prince Philip, Duke of
Edinburgh, 1952
HRH The Prince of Wales, Duke of
Rothesay, 1977

KNIGHTS
The Earl of Wemyss and March, 1966
The Earl of Dalhousie, 1971
The Lord Clydesmuir, 1972
Sir Donald Cameron of Lochiel, 1973
The Duke of Buccleuch and
Queensberry, 1978
The Earl of Elgin and Kincardine,
1981
The Lord Thomson of Monifieth,
1981
The Lord MacLehose of Beoch, 1983
The Earl of Airlie, 1985
Capt. Sir Iain Tennant, 1986
The Viscount Whitelaw, 1990
The Lord Younger of Prestwick, 1995

Chancellor, The Duke of Buccleuch
and Queensberry, KT, VRD
Dean, The Very Revd G. I. Macmillan

Secretary and Lord Lyon King of Arms, Sir
Malcolm Innes of Edingight, KCVO,
WS
Usher of the Green Rod, Rear-Adm. D.A.
Dunbar-Nasmith, CB, DSC

THE MOST HONOURABLE ORDER OF THE BATH (1725)

GCB *Military*   GCB *Civil*

GCB Knight (or Dame) Grand
     Cross
KCB Knight Commander
DCB Dame Commander
CB   Companion
Ribbon, Crimson
Motto, Tria juncta in uno (*Three joined
in one*)
Remodelled 1815, and enlarged many
times since. The Order is divided into
civil and military divisions. Women
became eligible for the Order from 1
January 1971

THE SOVEREIGN

GREAT MASTER AND FIRST OR
PRINCIPAL KNIGHT GRAND
CROSS
HRH The Prince of Wales, KG, KT,
GCB

Dean of the Order, The Dean of
Westminster
Bath King of Arms, Air Chief Marshal
Sir David Evans, GCB, CBE
Registrar and Secretary, Rear-Adm.
D. E. Macey, CB
Genealogist, P. Gwynn-Jones, LVO
Gentleman Usher of the Scarlet Rod, Air
Vice-Marshal Sir Richard Peirse,
KCVO, CB
Deputy Secretary, The Secretary of the
Central Chancery of the Orders of
Knighthood
Chancery, Central Chancery of the
Orders of Knighthood, St James's
Palace, London SW1A 1BH

THE ORDER OF MERIT
(1902)

OM *Military*   OM *Civil*

OM

Ribbon, Blue and crimson

This Order is designed as a special distinction for eminent men and women without conferring a knighthood upon them. The Order is limited in numbers to 24, with the addition of foreign honorary members. Membership is of two kinds, military and civil, the badge of the former having crossed swords, and the latter oak leaves

THE SOVEREIGN

HRH The Prince Philip, Duke of Edinburgh, 1968
Dame Veronica Wedgwood, 1969
Sir Isaiah Berlin, 1971
Sir George Edwards, 1971
Sir Alan Hodgkin, 1973
The Lord Todd, 1977
Revd Prof. Owen Chadwick, KBE, 1983
Sir Andrew Huxley, 1983
Sir Michael Tippett, 1983
Frederick Sanger, 1986
The Lord Menuhin, 1987
Prof. Sir Ernst Gombrich, 1988
Dr Max Perutz, 1988
Dame Cicely Saunders, 1989
The Lord Porter of Luddenham, 1989
The Baroness Thatcher, 1990
Dame Joan Sutherland, 1991
Prof. Francis Crick, 1991
Dame Ninette de Valois, 1992
Sir Michael Atiyah, 1992
Lucian Freud, 1993
The Lord Jenkins of Hillhead, 1993
Sir Aaron Klug, 1995
Honorary Members, Mother Teresa, 1983; Nelson Mandela, 1995

Secretary and Registrar, Sir Edward Ford, KCB, KCVO, ERD
Chancery, Central Chancery of the Orders of Knighthood, St James's Palace, London SW1A 1BH

THE MOST EXALTED ORDER OF THE STAR OF INDIA (1861)

GCSI   Knight Grand Commander
KCSI   Knight Commander
CSI   Companion
Ribbon, Light blue, with white edges
Motto, Heaven's Light our Guide

THE SOVEREIGN
Registrar, The Secretary of the Central Chancery of the Orders of Knighthood
No conferments have been made since 1947

THE MOST DISTINGUISHED ORDER OF ST MICHAEL AND ST GEORGE (1818)

GCMG   KCMG

GCMG   Knight (or Dame) Grand Cross
KCMG   Knight Commander
DCMG   Dame Commander
CMG   Companion

Ribbon, Saxon blue, with scarlet centre
Motto, Auspicium melioris aevi (*Token of a better age*)

THE SOVEREIGN

GRAND MASTER
HRH The Duke of Kent, KG, GCMG, GCVO, ADC

Prelate, The Rt. Revd the Bishop of Coventry
Chancellor, Sir Antony Acland, GCMG, GCVO
Secretary, Sir John Coles, KCMG
Registrar, Sir John Graham, Bt., GCMG
King of Arms, Sir Ewen Fergusson, GCMG, GCVO
Gentleman Usher of the Blue Rod, Sir John Margetson, KCMG
Dean, The Dean of St Paul's
Deputy Secretary, The Secretary of the Central Chancery of the Orders of Knighthood
Chancery, Central Chancery of the Orders of Knighthood, St James's Palace, London SW1A 1BH

THE MOST EMINENT ORDER OF THE INDIAN EMPIRE (1868)

GCIE   Knight Grand Commander
KCIE   Knight Commander
CIE   Companion

Ribbon, Imperial purple
Motto, Imperatricis auspiciis (*Under the auspices of the Empress*)

THE SOVEREIGN
Registrar, The Secretary of the Central Chancery of the Orders of Knighthood

No conferments have been made since 1947

THE IMPERIAL ORDER OF THE CROWN OF INDIA
(1877) FOR LADIES

CI

Badge, the royal cipher in jewels within an oval, surmounted by an heraldic crown and attached to a bow of light blue watered ribbon, edged white
The honour does not confer any rank or title upon the recipient
No conferments have been made since 1947

HM The Queen, 1947
HM Queen Elizabeth the Queen Mother, 1931
HRH The Princess Margaret, Countess of Snowdon, 1947
HRH Princess Alice, Duchess of Gloucester, 1937

THE ROYAL VICTORIAN ORDER (1896)

GCVO   KCVO

GCVO   Knight or Dame Grand Cross
KCVO   Knight Commander
DCVO   Dame Commander
CVO   Commander
LVO   Lieutenant
MVO   Member

Ribbon, Blue, with red and white edges
Motto, Victoria

THE SOVEREIGN
GRAND MASTER
HM Queen Elizabeth the Queen Mother

Chancellor, The Lord Chamberlain
Secretary, The Keeper of the Privy Purse
Registrar, The Secretary of the Central Chancery of the Orders of Knighthood
Chaplain, The Revd J. Robson
Hon. Genealogist, D. H. B. Chesshyre, LVO

THE MOST EXCELLENT ORDER OF THE BRITISH EMPIRE (1917)

GBE   KBE

The Order was divided into military and civil divisions in December 1918

GBE   Knight or Dame Grand Cross
KBE   Knight Commander
DBE   Dame Commander
CBE   Commander
OBE   Officer
MBE   Member

Ribbon, Rose pink edged with pearl grey with vertical pearl stripe in centre (military division); without vertical pearl stripe (civil division)
Motto, For God and the Empire

THE SOVEREIGN
GRAND MASTER
HRH The Prince Philip, Duke of Edinburgh, KG, KT, OM, GBE, PC, FRS

Prelate, The Bishop of London
King of Arms, Adm. Sir Anthony Morton, GBE, KCB
Registrar, The Secretary of the Central Chancery of the Orders of Knighthood
Secretary, Sir Robin Butler, GCB, CVO
Dean, The Dean of St Paul's
Gentleman Usher of the Purple Rod, Sir Robin Gillett, Bt., GBE, RD
Chancery, Central Chancery of the Orders of Knighthood, St James's Palace, London SW1A 1BH

ORDER OF THE COMPANIONS OF HONOUR (1917)

CH

Ribbon, Carmine, with gold edges
This Order consists of one class only and carries with it no title. The number of awards is limited to 65 (excluding honorary members)

Anthony, Rt. Hon. John, 1981
Ashley of Stoke, The Lord, 1975
Astor, Hon. David, 1993
Attenborough, Sir David, 1995
Baker, Dame Janet, 1993
Baker, Rt. Hon. Kenneth, 1992
Brenner, Sydney, 1986
Brooke, Rt. Hon. Peter, 1992

Carrington, The Lord, 1983
Casson, Sir Hugh, 1984
Cledwyn of Penrhos, The Lord, 1976
de Valois, Dame Ninette, 1981
Doll, Sir Richard, 1995
Eccles, The Viscount, 1984
Fraser, Rt. Hon. Malcolm, 1977
Freud, Lucian, 1983
Gielgud, Sir John, 1977
Glenamara, The Lord, 1976
Gorton, Rt. Hon. Sir John, 1971
Guinness, Sir Alec, 1994
Hailsham of St Marylebone, The Lord, 1974
Hawking, Prof. Stephen, 1989
Healey, The Lord, 1979
Howe of Aberavon, The Lord, 1996
Hurd, Rt. Hon. Douglas, 1995
Jones, James, 1977
Jones, Prof. Reginald, 1994
King, Rt. Hon. Tom, 1992
Lange, Rt. Hon. David, 1989
Lasdun, Sir Denys, 1995
Milstein, César, 1994
Owen, The Lord, 1994
Pasmore, Victor, 1980
Perutz, Prof. Max, 1975
Powell, Anthony, 1987
Powell, Sir Philip, 1984
Pritchett, Sir Victor, 1992
Runciman, Hon. Sir Steven, 1984
Rylands, George, 1987
Sanger, Frederick, 1981
Sisson, Charles, 1993
Smith, Sir John, 1993
Somare, Rt. Hon. Sir Michael, 1978
Talboys, Rt. Hon. Sir Brian, 1981
Tebbit, The Lord, 1987
Tippett, Sir Michael, 1979
Trudeau, Rt. Hon. Pierre, 1984
Weight, Prof. Carel, 1994
Whitelaw, The Viscount, 1974
Widdowson, Dr Elsie, 1993
Worlock, Most Revd Derek, 1995
Honorary Members, Lee Kuan Yew, 1970; Dr Joseph Luns, 1971

Secretary and Registrar, The Secretary of the Central Chancery of the Orders of Knighthood

THE DISTINGUISHED SERVICE ORDER (1886)

DSO

Ribbon, Red, with blue edges
Bestowed in recognition of especial services in action of commissioned officers in the Navy, Army and Royal Air Force and (since 1942) Mercantile Marine. The members are Companions only. A Bar may be awarded for any additional act of service

THE IMPERIAL SERVICE ORDER (1902)

ISO
Ribbon, Crimson, with blue centre

Appointment as Companion of this Order is open to members of the Civil Services whose eligibility is determined by the grade they hold. The Order consists of The Sovereign and Companions to a number not exceeding 1,900, of whom 1,300 may belong to the Home Civil Services and 600 to Overseas Civil Services. The Prime Minister announced in March 1993 that he would make no further recommendations for appointments to the Order.

Secretary, Sir Robin Butler, GCB, CVO
Registrar, The Secretary of the Central Chancery of the Orders of Knighthood, St James's Palace, London SW1A 1BH

THE ROYAL VICTORIAN CHAIN (1902)

It confers no precedence on its holders

HM THE QUEEN
HM Queen Elizabeth the Queen Mother, 1937
HRH Princess Juliana of the Netherlands, 1950
HM The King of Thailand, 1960
HIH The Crown Prince of Ethiopia, 1965
HM The King of Jordan, 1966
HM King Zahir Shah of Afghanistan, 1971
HM The Queen of Denmark, 1974
HM The King of Nepal, 1975
HM The King of Sweden, 1975
The Lord Coggan, 1980
HM The Queen of the Netherlands, 1982
Gen. Antonio Eanes, 1985
HM The King of Spain, 1986
HM The King of Saudi Arabia, 1987
HRH The Princess Margaret, Countess of Snowdon, 1990
The Lord Runcie, 1991
The Lord Charteris of Amisfield, 1992
HE Richard von Weizsäcker, 1992
HM The King of Norway, 1994

Baronetage and Knightage

BARONETS

Style, 'Sir' before forename and surname, followed by 'Bt.'
Wife's style, 'Lady' followed by surname
For forms of address, *see* page 136

There are five different creations of baronetcies: Baronets of England (creations dating from 1611); Baronets of Ireland (creations dating from 1619); Baronets of Scotland or Nova Scotia (creations dating from 1625); Baronets of Great Britain (creations after the Act of Union 1707 which combined the kingdoms of England and Scotland); and Baronets of the United Kingdom (creations after the union of Great Britain and Ireland in 1801).

Badge of Baronets of the   *Badge of Baronets of Nova Scotia*
United Kingdom

Badge of Ulster

The patent of creation limits the destination of a baronetcy, usually to male descendants of the first baronet, although special remainders allow the baronetcy to pass, if the male issue of sons fail, to the male issue of daughters of the first baronet. In the case of baronetcies of Scotland or Nova Scotia, a special remainder of 'heirs male and of tailzie' allows the baronetcy to descend to heirs general, including women. There are four existing Scottish baronets with such a remainder, one of whom, the holder of the Dunbar of Hempriggs creation, is a Baronetess.

The Official Roll of Baronets is kept at the Home Office by the Registrar of the Baronetage. Anyone who considers that he is entitled to be entered on the Roll may petition the Crown through the Home Secretary. Every person succeeding to a baronetcy must exhibit proofs of succession to the Home Secretary. A person whose name is not entered on the Official Roll will not be addressed or mentioned by the title of baronet in any official document, nor will he be accorded precedence as a baronet.

BARONETCIES EXTINCT SINCE THE LAST EDITION
Corbet (*cr.* 1808); Kitson (*cr.* 1886), by the death of Lord Airedale; Levy (*cr.* 1913); Neville (*cr.* 1927); Vaughan-Morgan (*cr.* 1960), by the death of Lord Reigate

Registrar of the Baronetage, Miss C. E. C. Sinclair
Assistant Registrar, Mrs F. G. Bright
Office, Home Office, 50 Queen Anne's Gate, London SW1H 9AT. Tel: 0171-273 3498

KNIGHTS

Style, 'Sir' before forename and surname, followed by appropriate post-nominal initials if a Knight Grand Cross, Knight Grand Commander or Knight Commander
Wife's style, 'Lady' followed by surname
For forms of address, *see* page 136

The prefix 'Sir' is not used by knights who are clerics of the Church of England, who do not receive the accolade. Their wives are entitled to precedence as the wife of a knight but not to the style of 'Lady'.

ORDERS OF KNIGHTHOOD
Knight Grand Cross, Knight Grand Commander, and Knight Commander are the higher classes of the Orders of Chivalry (*see* pages 170–2). Honorary knighthoods of these Orders may be conferred on men who are citizens of countries of which The Queen is not head of state. As a rule, the prefix 'Sir' is not used by honorary knights.

KNIGHTS BACHELOR

The Knights Bachelor do not constitute a Royal Order, but comprise the surviving representation of the ancient State Orders of Knighthood. The Register of Knights Bachelor, instituted by James I in the 17th century, lapsed, and in 1908 a voluntary association under the title of The Society of Knights (now The Imperial Society of Knights Bachelor by Royal Command) was formed with the primary objects of continuing the various registers dating from 1257 and obtaining the uniform registration of every created Knight Bachelor. In 1926 a design for a badge to be worn by Knights Bachelor was approved and adopted; in 1974 a neck badge and miniature were added.

Knight Principal, Sir Conrad Swan, KCVO
Chairman of Council, The Lord Lane of Horsell
Prelate, Rt. Revd and Rt. Hon. The Bishop of London
Hon. Registrar, Sir Kenneth Newman, GBE, QPM
Hon. Treasurer, Sir Douglas Morpeth, TD
Clerk to the Council, R. M. Esden
Office, 21 Old Buildings, Lincoln's Inn, London WC2A 3UJ

LIST OF BARONETS AND KNIGHTS
Revised to 31 August 1996

Peers are not included in this list

†	Not registered on the Official Roll of the Baronetage at the time of going to press
( )	The date of creation of the baronetcy is given in parenthesis
I	Baronet of Ireland
NS	Baronet of Nova Scotia
S	Baronet of Scotland

If a baronet or knight has a double barrelled or hyphenated surname, he is listed under the final element of the name
A full entry in italic type indicates that the recipient of a knighthood died during the year in which the honour was conferred. The name is included for purposes of record

Abal, Sir Tei, Kt., CBE

Abbott, Sir Albert Francis, Kt., CBE

Abbott, *Vice-Adm.* Sir Peter Charles, KCB

Abdy, Sir Valentine Robert Duff, Bt. (1850)

Abel, Sir Seselo (Cecil) Charles Geoffrey, Kt., OBE

Abeles, Sir (Emil Herbert) Peter, Kt.

Abercromby, Sir Ian George, Bt. (s. 1636)

Abraham, Sir Edward Penley, Kt., CBE, FRS

Acheson, *Prof.* Sir (Ernest) Donald, KBE

Ackers, Sir James George, Kt.

†Ackroyd, Sir Timothy Robert Whyte, Bt. (1956)

Acland, Sir Antony Arthur, GCMG, GCVO

Acland, *Lt.-Col.* Sir (Christopher) Guy (Dyke), Bt., MVO (1890)

Acland, Sir John Dyke, Bt. (1644)

Acland, *Maj.-Gen.* Sir John Hugh Bevil, KCB, CBE

Adam, Sir Christopher Eric Forbes, Bt. (1917)

Adams, Sir Philip George Doyne, KCMG

Adams, Sir William James, KCMG

Adamson, Sir (William Owen) Campbell, Kt.

Adrien, *Hon.* Sir Maurice Latour-, Kt.

Adye, Sir John Anthony, KCMG

Agnew, Sir Crispin Hamlyn, Bt. (s. 1629)

Agnew, Sir John Keith, Bt. (1895)

Aiken, *Air Chief Marshal* Sir John Alexander Carlisle, KCB

Ainsworth, Sir (Thomas) David, Bt. (1916)

Aird, *Capt.* Sir Alastair Sturgis, KCVO

Aird, Sir (George) John, Bt. (1901)

Airey, Sir Lawrence, KCB

Airy, *Maj.-Gen.* Sir Christopher John, KCVO, CBE

Aitchison, Sir Charles Walter de Lancey, Bt. (1938)

Aitken, Sir Robert Stevenson, Kt., MD, D.Phil.

Akehurst, *Gen.* Sir John Bryan, KCB, CBE

Albert, Sir Alexis François, Kt., CMG, VRD

Albu, Sir George, Bt. (1912)

Alcock, *Air Chief Marshal* Sir (Robert James) Michael, GCB, KBE

Aldous, *Rt. Hon.* Sir William, Kt.

Alexander, Sir Charles Gundry, Bt. (1945)

Alexander, Sir Claud Hagart-, Bt. (1886)

Alexander, Sir Douglas, Bt. (1921)

Alexander, Sir (John) Lindsay, Kt.

Alexander, *Prof.* Sir Kenneth John Wilson, Kt.

Alexander, Sir Michael O'Donal Bjarne, GCMG

Alexander, Sir Norman Stanley, Kt., CBE

†Alexander, Sir Patrick Desmond William Cable-, Bt. (1809)

Allan, Sir Anthony James Allan Havelock-, Bt. (1858)

Allen, *Prof.* Sir Geoffrey, Kt., Ph.D., FRS

Allen, Sir John Derek, Kt., CBE

Allen, *Hon.* Sir Peter Austin Philip Jermyn, Kt.

Allen, Sir William Guilford, Kt.

Allen, Sir (William) Kenneth (Gwynne), Kt.

Alleyne, Sir George Allanmoore Ogarren, Kt.

Alleyne, *Revd* Sir John Olpherts Campbell, Bt. (1769)

Alliance, Sir David, Kt., CBE

Allinson, Sir (Walter) Leonard, KCVO, CMG

Alliott, *Hon.* Sir John Downes, Kt.

Allison, *Air Chief Marshal* Sir John Shakespeare, KCB, CBE

Alment, Sir (Edward) Anthony John, Kt.

Althaus, Sir Nigel Frederick, Kt.

Ambo, *Rt. Revd* George, KBE

Amet, *Hon.* Sir Arnold Karibone, Kt.

Amies, Sir (Edwin) Hardy, KCVO

Amory, Sir Ian Heathcoat, Bt. (1874)

Anderson, Sir John Anthony, KBE

Anderson, *Maj.-Gen.* Sir John Evelyn, KBE

Anderson, Sir John Muir, Kt., CMG

Anderson, *Hon.* Sir Kevin Victor, Kt.

Anderson, *Vice-Adm.* Sir Neil Dudley, KBE, CB

Anderson, *Prof.* Sir (William) Ferguson, Kt., OBE

Anderton, Sir (Cyril) James, Kt., CBE, QPM

Andrew, Sir Robert John, KCB

Andrews, Sir Derek Henry, KCB, CBE

Andrews, *Hon.* Sir Dormer George, Kt.

Angus, Sir Michael Richardson, Kt.

Annesley, Sir Hugh Norman, Kt., QPM

Anson, *Vice-Adm.* Sir Edward Rosebery, KCB

Anson, Sir John, KCB

Anson, *Rear-Adm.* Sir Peter, Bt., CB (1831)

Anstey, *Brig.* Sir John, Kt., CBE, TD

Anstruther, *Maj.* Sir Ralph Hugo, Bt., GCVO, MC (s. 1694)

Antico, Sir Tristan Venus, Kt.

†Antrobus, Sir Edward Philip, Bt. (1815)

Appleyard, Sir Leonard Vincent, KCMG

Appleyard, Sir Raymond Kenelm, KBE

Arbuthnot, Sir Keith Robert Charles, Bt. (1823)

Arbuthnot, Sir William Reierson, Bt. (1964)

Archdale, *Capt.* Sir Edward Folmer, Bt., DSC, RN (1928)

Archer, *Gen.* Sir (Arthur) John, KCB, OBE

Arculus, Sir Ronald, KCMG, KCVO

Armitage, *Air Chief Marshal* Sir Michael John, KCB, CBE

Armour, *Prof.* Sir James, Kt., CBE

Armstrong, Sir Andrew Clarence Francis, Bt., CMG (1841)

Armytage, Sir John Martin, Bt. (1738)

Arnold, *Rt. Hon.* Sir John Lewis, Kt.

Arnold, Sir Malcolm Henry, Kt., CBE

Arnold, Sir Thomas Richard, Kt., MP

Arnott, Sir Alexander John Maxwell, Bt. (1896)

Arnott, *Prof.* Sir (William) Melville, Kt., TD, MD

Arrindell, Sir Clement Athelston, GCMG, GCVO, QC

Arthur, *Lt.-Gen.* Sir (John) Norman Stewart, KCB

Arthur, Sir Stephen John, Bt. (1841)

Ash, *Prof.* Sir Eric Albert, Kt., CBE, FRS, FEng.

Ashburnham, Sir Denny Reginald, Bt. (1661)

Ashe, Sir Derick Rosslyn, KCMG

Ashley, Sir Bernard Albert, Kt.

Ashmore, *Admiral of the Fleet* Sir Edward Beckwith, GCB, DSC

Ashmore, *Vice-Adm.* Sir Peter William Beckwith, KCB, KCVO, DSC

Ashworth, Sir Herbert, Kt.

Aske, *Revd* Sir Conan, Bt. (1922)

Askew, Sir Bryan, Kt.

Asscher, *Prof.* (Adolf) William, Kt., MD, FRCP

Astill, *Hon.* Sir Michael John, Kt.

Aston, Sir Harold George, Kt., CBE

Aston, *Hon.* Sir William John, KCMG

Astor, *Hon.* Sir John Jacob, Kt., MBE

Astwood, *Hon.* Sir James Rufus, KBE

Astwood, *Lt.-Col.* Sir Jeffrey Carlton, Kt., CBE, ED

Atcherley, Sir Harold Winter, Kt.

Atiyah, Sir Michael Francis, Kt., OM, Ph.D., FRS

Atkinson, *Air Marshal* Sir David William, KBE

Atkinson, Sir Frederick John, KCB

Atkinson, Sir John Alexander, KCB, DFC

Atkinson, Sir Robert, Kt., DSC, FEng.

Attenborough, Sir David Frederick, Kt., CH, CVO, CBE, FRS

Atwell, Sir John William, Kt., CBE, FRSE, FEng.

Atwill, Sir (Milton) John (Napier), Kt.

Audland, Sir Christopher John, KCMG

Audley, Sir George Bernard, Kt.

Augier, *Prof.* Sir Fitz-Roy Richard, Kt.

Auld, *Rt. Hon.* Sir Robin Ernest, Kt.

†Austin, Sir Anthony Leonard, Bt. (1894)

Austin, *Vice-Adm.* Sir Peter Murray, KCB

Austin, *Air Marshal* Sir Roger Mark, KCB, AFC

Axford, Sir William Ian, Kt.

Aykroyd, Sir James Alexander Frederic, Bt. (1929)

Aykroyd, Sir William Miles, Bt., MC (1920)

Aylmer, Sir Richard John, Bt. (I. 1622)

Bacha, Sir Bhinod, Kt., CMG

Backhouse, Sir Jonathan Roger, Bt. (1901)

Bacon, Sir Nicholas Hickman Ponsonby, Bt. *Premier Baronet of England* (1611 and 1627)

Bacon, Sir Sidney Charles, Kt., CB, FEng.

Baddeley, Sir John Wolsey Beresford, Bt. (1922)

Baddiley, *Prof.* Sir James, Kt., Ph.D., D.Sc., FRS, FRSE

Badger, Sir Geoffrey Malcolm, Kt.

Bagge, Sir (John) Jeremy Picton, Bt. (1867)

Bagnall, *Field Marshal* Sir Nigel Thomas, GCB, CVO, MC

Bailey, Sir Alan Marshall, KCB

Bailey, Sir Brian Harry, Kt., OBE

Bailey, Sir Derrick Thomas Louis, Bt., DFC (1919)

Bailey, Sir John Bilsland, KCB

Bailey, Sir Richard John, Kt., CBE

Bailey, Sir Stanley Ernest, Kt., CBE, QPM

Bailhache, Sir Philip Martin, Kt.

Baillie, Sir Gawaine George Hope, Bt. (1823)

Baines, *Prof.* Sir George Grenfell-, Kt., OBE

Baird, Sir David Charles, Bt. (1809)

Baird, *Lt.-Gen.* Sir James Parlane, KBE, MD

Baird, Sir James Richard Gardiner, Bt., MC (s. 1695)

Baird, *Vice-Adm.* Sir Thomas Henry Eustace, KCB

Bairsto, *Air Marshal* Sir Peter Edward, KBE, CB

Baker, Sir Robert George Humphrey Sherston-, Bt. (1796)

Baker, *Hon.* Sir (Thomas) Scott (Gillespie), Kt.

Balchin, Sir Robert George Alexander, Kt.

Balcombe, *Rt. Hon.* Sir (Alfred) John, Kt.

Balderstone, Sir James Schofield, Kt.

Baldwin, Sir Peter Robert, KCB

Ball, *Air Marshal* Sir Alfred Henry Wynne, KCB, DSO, DFC

Ball, Sir Charles Irwin, Bt. (1911)

Ball, Sir Christopher John Elinger, Kt.

Ball, *Prof.* Sir Robert James, Kt., Ph.D.

Bamford, Sir Anthony Paul, Kt.

Banham, Sir John Michael Middlecott, Kt.

Bannerman, Sir David Gordon, Bt., OBE (s. 1682)

Bannister, Sir Roger Gilbert, Kt., CBE, DM, FRCP

Barber, Sir (Thomas) David, Bt., (1960)

Barbour, *Very Revd* Sir Robert Alexander Stewart, KCVO, MC

Barclay, Sir Colville Herbert Sanford, Bt. (s. 1668)

Barclay, Sir Peter Maurice, Kt., CBE

Barclay, Sir Roderick Edward, GCVO, KCMG

Barder, Sir Brian Leon, KCMG

Barker, Sir Alwyn Bowman, Kt., CMG

Barker, Sir Colin, Kt.

Barker, *Hon.* Sir (Richard) Ian, Kt.

Barlow, Sir Christopher Hilaro, Bt. (1803)

Barlow, Sir (George) William, Kt., FEng.

Barlow, Sir John Kemp, Bt. (1907)

Barlow, Sir Thomas Erasmus, Bt., DSC (1902)

Barnard, Sir Joseph Brian, Kt.

Barnes, Sir (James) David (Francis), Kt., CBE

Barnes, Sir James George, Kt., MBE

Barnes, Sir Kenneth, KCB

Barnewall, Sir Reginald Robert, Bt. (I. 1623)

Baron, Sir Thomas, Kt., CBE

Barraclough, *Air Chief Marshal* Sir John, KCB, CBE, DFC, AFC

Barraclough, Sir Kenneth James Priestley, Kt., CBE, TD

Barran, Sir David Haven, Kt.

Barran, Sir John Napoleon Ruthven, Bt. (1895)

Barratt, Sir Lawrence Arthur, Kt.

Barratt, Sir Richard Stanley, Kt., CBE, QPM

Barrett, *Lt.-Gen.* Sir David William Scott-, KBE, MC

Barrett, *Lt.-Col.* Sir Dennis Charles Titchener, Kt., TD

Barrett, Sir Stephen Jeremy, KCMG

Barrington, Sir Alexander (Fitzwilliam Croker), Bt. (1831)

Barrington, Sir Nicholas John, KCMG, CVO

Barron, Sir Donald James, Kt.

Barrow, *Capt.* Sir Richard John Uniacke, Bt. (1835)

Barrowclough, Sir Anthony Richard, Kt., QC

Barry, Sir (Lawrence) Edward (Anthony Tress), Bt. (1899)

Bartlett, Sir John Hardington, Bt. (1913)

Barton, *Prof.* Sir Derek Harold Richard, Kt., FRS, FRSE

Barttelot, *Col.* Sir Brian Walter de Stopham, Bt., OBE (1875)

Barwick, *Rt. Hon.* Sir Garfield Edward John, GCMG

Batchelor, Sir Ivor Ralph Campbell, Kt., CBE

Bate, Sir David Lindsay, KBE

Bate, Sir (Walter) Edwin, Kt., OBE

Bateman, Sir Cecil Joseph, KBE

Bateman, Sir Geoffrey Hirst, Kt., FRCS

Bates, Sir Geoffrey Voltelin, Bt., MC (1880)

Bates, Sir (John) Dawson, Bt., MC (1937)

Batho, Sir Peter Ghislain, Bt. (1928)

Bathurst, *Admiral of the Fleet* Sir (David) Benjamin, GCB

Bathurst, Sir Frederick John Charles Gordon Hervey-, Bt. (1818)

Bathurst, Sir Maurice Edward, Kt., CMG, CBE, QC

Batten, Sir John Charles, KCVO

Battersby, *Prof.* Sir Alan Rushton, Kt., FRS

Battishill, Sir Anthony Michael William, KCB

Batty, Sir William Bradshaw, Kt., TD

Baxendell, Sir Peter Brian, Kt., CBE, FEng.

Bayliss, *Prof.* Sir Noel Stanley, Kt., CBE

Bayliss, Sir Richard Ian Samuel, KCVO, MD, FRCP

Bayly, *Vice-Adm.* Sir Patrick Uniacke, KBE, CB, DSC

Bayne, Sir Nicholas Peter, KCMG

Baynes, Sir John Christopher Malcolm, Bt. (1801)

Bazley, Sir Thomas Stafford, Bt. (1869)

Beach, *Gen.* Sir (William Gerald) Hugh, GBE, KCB, MC

Beale, *Lt.-Gen.* Sir Peter John, KBE, FRCP

Beament, Sir James William Longman, Kt., SC.D., FRS

Beattie, *Hon.* Sir Alexander Craig, Kt.

Beattie, *Hon.* Sir David Stuart, GCMG, GCVO

Beauchamp, Sir Christopher Radstock Proctor-, Bt. (1745)

Beaumont, *Capt.* the Hon. Sir (Edward) Nicholas (Canning), KCVO

Beaumont, Sir George (Howland Francis), Bt. (1661)

Beaumont, Sir Richard Ashton, KCMG, OBE

Beavis, *Air Chief Marshal* Sir Michael Gordon, KCB, CBE, AFC

Becher, Sir William Fane Wrixon, Bt., MC (1831)

Beck, Sir Edgar Charles, Kt., CBE, FEng.

Beck, Sir Edgar Philip, Kt.

Beckett, *Capt.* Sir (Martyn) Gervase, Bt., MC (1921)

Beckett, Sir Terence Norman, KBE, FEng.

Bedingfeld, *Capt.* Sir Edmund George Felix Paston-, Bt. (1661)

Beecham, Sir Jeremy Hugh, Kt.

Beecham, Sir John Stratford Roland, Bt. (1914)

Beeley, Sir Harold, KCMG, CBE

Beetham, *Marshal of the Royal Air Force* Sir Michael James, GCB, CBE, DFC, AFC

Bonfield, Sir Peter Leahy, Kt., CBE, FENg.

Bonham, *Maj.* Sir Antony Lionel Thomas, Bt. (1852)

Bonington, Sir Christian John Storey, Kt., CBE

Bonsall, Sir Arthur Wilfred, KCMG, CBE

Bonsor, Sir Nicholas Cosmo, Bt., MP (1925)

Boolell, Sir Satcam, Kt.

Boon, Sir Peter Coleman, Kt.

Boord, Sir Nicolas John Charles, Bt. (1896)

Boorman, *Lt.-Gen.* Sir Derek, KCB

Booth, Sir Christopher Charles, Kt., MD, FRCP

Booth, Sir Douglas Allen, Bt. (1916)

Booth, Sir Gordon, KCMG, CVO

†Booth, Sir Josslyn Henry Robert Gore-, Bt. (I. 1760)

Booth, Sir Michael Addison John Wheeler-, KCB

Booth, Sir Robert Camm, Kt., CBE, TD

Boothby, Sir Brooke Charles, Bt. (1660)

Boreel, Sir Francis David, Bt. (1645)

Boreham, *Hon.* Sir Leslie Kenneth Edward, Kt.

Bornu, The Waziri of, KCMG, CBE

Borthwick, Sir John Thomas, Bt., MBE (1908)

Bossom, *Hon.* Sir Clive, Bt. (1953)

Boswall, Sir (Thomas) Alford Houstoun-, Bt. (1836)

Boswell, *Lt.-Gen.* Sir Alexander Crawford Simpson, KCB, CBE

Bosworth, Sir Neville Bruce Alfred, Kt., CBE

Bottomley, Sir James Reginald Alfred, KCMG

Boughey, Sir John George Fletcher, Bt. (1798)

Boulton, Sir Clifford John, GCB

Boulton, Sir (Harold Hugh) Christian, Bt. (1905)

Boulton, Sir William Whytehead, Bt., CBE, TD (1944)

Bourn, Sir John Bryant, KCB

Bourne, Sir (John) Wilfrid, KCB

Bovell, *Hon.* Sir (William) Stewart, Kt.

Bowater, Sir Euan David Vansittart, Bt. (1939)

Bowater, Sir (John) Vansittart, Bt. (1914)

Bowden, Sir Andrew, Kt., MBE, MP

Bowden, Sir Frank, Bt. (1915)

Bowen, Sir Geoffrey Fraser, Kt.

Bowen, Sir Mark Edward Mortimer, Bt. (1921)

†Bowlby, Sir Richard Peregrine Longstaff, Bt. (1923)

Bowman, Sir Jeffery Haverstock, Kt.

Bowman, Sir Paul Humphrey Armytage, Bt. (1884)

Bowmar, Sir Charles Erskine, Kt.

Bowness, Sir Alan, Kt., CBE

Boxer, *Air Vice-Marshal* Sir Alan Hunter Cachemaille, KCVO, CB, DSO, DFC

Boyce, *Vice-Adm.* Sir Michael Cecil, KCB, OBE

Boyce, Sir Robert Charles Leslie, Bt. (1952)

Boyd, Sir Alexander Walter, Bt. (1916)

Boyd, Sir John Dixon Iklé, KCMG

Boyd, The Hon. Sir Mark Alexander Lennox-, Kt., MP

Boyd, *Prof.* Sir Robert Lewis Fullarton, Kt., CBE, D.SC., FRS

Boyes, Sir Brian Gerald Barratt-, KBE

Boyle, Sir Stephen Gurney, Bt. (1904)

Boyne, Sir Henry Brian, Kt., CBE

Boynton, Sir John Keyworth, Kt., MC

Boys, *Rt. Hon.* Sir Michael Hardie, GCMG

Boyson, *Rt. Hon.* Sir Rhodes, Kt., MP

Brabham, Sir John Arthur, Kt., OBE

Bradbeer, Sir John Derek Richardson, Kt., OBE, TD

Bradbury, *Surgeon Vice-Adm.* Sir Eric Blackburn, KBE, CB

Bradford, Sir Edward Alexander Slade, Bt. (1902)

Bradley, Sir Burton Gyrth Burton-, Kt., OBE

Bradman, Sir Donald George, Kt.

Bradshaw, Sir Kenneth Anthony, KCB

Bradshaw, *Lt.-Gen.* Sir Richard Phillip, KBE

Brain, Sir (Henry) Norman, KBE, CMG

Braithwaite, Sir (Joseph) Franklin Madders, Kt.

Braithwaite, *Rt. Hon.* Sir Nicholas Alexander, Kt., OBE

Braithwaite, Sir Rodric Quentin, GCMG

Bramall, Sir (Ernest) Ashley, Kt.

Bramley, *Prof.* Sir Paul Anthony, Kt.

Branigan, Sir Patrick Francis, Kt., QC

Bray, Sir Theodor Charles, Kt., CBE

Brennan, *Hon.* Sir (Francis) Gerard, KBE

Brett, Sir Charles Edward Bainbridge, Kt., CBE

Brickwood, Sir Basil Greame, Bt. (1927)

Bridges, *Hon.* Sir Phillip Rodney, Kt., CMG

Brierley, Sir Ronald Alfred, Kt.

Bright, Sir Graham Frank James, Kt., MP

Bright, Sir Keith, Kt.

Brinckman, Sir Theodore George Roderick, Bt. (1831)

Brisco, Sir Donald Gilfrid, Bt. (1782)

Briscoe, Sir John Geoffrey James, Bt. (1910)

Brise, Sir John Archibald Ruggles-, Bt., CB, OBE, TD (1935)

Bristow, *Hon.* Sir Peter Henry Rowley, Kt.

Brittan, *Rt. Hon.* Sir Leon, Kt., QC

Brittan, Sir Samuel, Kt.

Britton, Sir Edward Louis, Kt., CBE

Broackes, Sir Nigel, Kt.

†Broadbent, Sir Andrew George, Bt. (1893)

Brocklebank, Sir Aubrey Thomas, Bt. (1885)

Brockman, *Vice-Adm.* Sir Ronald Vernon, KCB, CSI, CIE, CVO, CBE

Brodie, Sir Benjamin David Ross, Bt. (1834)

Bromhead, Sir John Desmond Gonville, Bt. (1806)

Bromley, Sir Rupert Charles, Bt. (1757)

Bromley, Sir Thomas Eardley, KCMG

Brook, Sir Robin, Kt., CMG, OBE

†Brooke, Sir Alistair Weston, Bt. (1919)

Brooke, Sir Francis George Windham, Bt. (1903)

Brooke, *Rt. Hon.* Sir Henry, Kt.

Brooke, Sir Richard Neville, Bt. (1662)

Brookes, Sir Wilfred Deakin, Kt., CBE, DSO

Brooksbank, Sir (Edward) Nicholas, Bt. (1919)

Broom, *Air Marshal* Sir Ivor Gordon, KCB, CBE, DSO, DFC, AFC

Broomfield, Sir Nigel Hugh Robert Allen, KCMG

Broughton, *Air Marshal* Sir Charles, KBE, CB

†Broughton, Sir David Delves, Bt. (1661)

Broun, Sir William Windsor, Bt. (s. 1686)

Brown, Sir Allen Stanley, Kt., CBE

Brown, Sir (Arthur James) Stephen, KBE

Brown, Sir (Austen) Patrick, KCB

Brown, *Adm.* Sir Brian Thomas, KCB, CBE

Brown, *Lt.-Col.* Sir Charles Frederick Richmond, Bt. (1863)

Brown, Sir (Cyril) Maxwell Palmer, KCB, CMG

Brown, *Vice-Adm.* Sir David Worthington, KCB

Brown, Sir Derrick Holden-, Kt.

Brown, Sir Douglas Denison, Kt.

Brown, *Hon.* Sir Douglas Dunlop, Kt.

Brown, Sir (Frederick Herbert) Stanley, Kt., CBE, FENg.

Brown, *Prof.* Sir (George) Malcolm, Kt., FRS

Brown, Sir George Noel, Kt.

Brown, Sir John Douglas Keith, Kt.

Brown, Sir John Gilbert Newton, Kt., CBE

Brown, Sir Mervyn, KCMG, OBE

Brown, *Hon.* Sir Ralph Kilner, Kt., OBE, TD

Brown, Sir Robert Crichton-, KCMG, CBE, TD

Brown, *Rt. Hon.* Sir Simon Denis, Kt.

Brown, *Rt. Hon.* Sir Stephen, Kt.

Brown, Sir Thomas, Kt.

Brown, Sir William, Kt., CBE

Brown, Sir William Brian Piggott-, Bt. (1903)

Browne, *Rt. Hon.* Sir Patrick Reginald Evelyn, Kt., OBE, TD

Brownrigg, Sir Nicholas (Gawen), Bt. (1816)

Browse, *Prof.* Sir Norman Leslie, Kt., MD, FRCS

Bruce, Sir (Francis) Michael Ian, Bt. (s. 1628)

Bruce, Sir Hervey James Hugh, Bt. (1804)

Bruce, *Rt. Hon.* Sir (James) Roualeyn Hovell-Thurlow-Cumming-, Kt.

Brunner, Sir John Henry Kilian, Bt. (1895)

Brunton, Sir (Edward Francis) Lauder, Bt. (1908)

Brunton, Sir Gordon Charles, Kt.

Bryan, Sir Arthur, Kt.

Bryan, Sir Paul Elmore Oliver, Kt., DSO, MC

Bryce, *Hon.* Sir (William) Gordon, Kt., CBE

Bryson, *Adm.* Sir Lindsay Sutherland, KCB, FEng.

Buchan, Sir John, Kt., CMG

Buchanan, Sir Andrew George, Bt. (1878)

Buchanan, Sir Charles Alexander James Leith-, Bt. (1775)

Buchanan, *Prof.* Sir Colin Douglas, Kt., CBE

Buchanan, *Vice-Adm.* Sir Peter William, KBE

Buchanan, Sir Robert Wilson (Robin), Kt.

Buchanan, Sir (Ranald) Dennis, Kt., MBE

Buck, Sir (Philip) Antony (Fyson), Kt., QC

Buckley, *Rt. Hon.* Sir Denys Burton, Kt., MBE

Buckley, Sir John William, Kt.

Buckley, *Lt.-Cdr.* Sir (Peter) Richard, KCVO

Buckley, *Hon.* Sir Roger John, Kt.

Bulkeley, Sir Richard Thomas Williams-, Bt. (1661)

Bull, Sir Simeon George, Bt. (1922)

Bullard, Sir Julian Leonard, GCMG

Bullus, Sir Eric Edward, Kt.

Bulmer, Sir William Peter, Kt.

Bultin, Sir Bato, Kt., MBE

Bunbury, Sir Michael William, Bt. (1681)

Bunbury, Sir (Richard David) Michael Richardson-, Bt. (I. 1787)

Bunch, Sir Austin Wyeth, Kt., CBE

Bunyard, Sir Robert Sidney, Kt., CBE, QPM

Burbidge, Sir Herbert Dudley, Bt. (1916)

Burbury, *Hon.* Sir Stanley Charles, KCMG, KCVO, KBE

Burdett, Sir Savile Aylmer, Bt. (1665)

Burgen, Sir Arnold Stanley Vincent, Kt., FRS

Burgess, *Gen.* Sir Edward Arthur, KCB, OBE

Burgess, Sir (Joseph) Stuart, Kt., CBE, Ph.D., FRSC

Burgh, Sir John Charles, KCMG, CB

Burke, Sir James Stanley Gilbert, Bt. (I. 1797)

Burke, Sir (Thomas) Kerry, Kt.

Burley, Sir Victor George, Kt., CBE

Burman, Sir (John) Charles, Kt.

Burnet, Sir James William Alexander (Sir Alastair Burnet), Kt.

Burnett, *Air Chief Marshal* Sir Brian Kenyon, GCB, DFC, AFC

Burnett, Sir David Humphery, Bt., MBE, TD (1913)

Burnett, Sir John Harrison, Kt.

Burnett, Sir Walter John, Kt.

Burney, Sir Cecil Denniston, Bt. (1921)

Burns, Sir Terence, GCB

Burns, *Maj.-Gen.* Sir (Walter Arthur) George, GCVO, CB, DSO, OBE, MC

Burrell, Sir John Raymond, Bt. (1774)

Burrenchobay, Sir Dayendranath, KBE, CMG, CVO

Burrows, Sir Bernard Alexander Brocas, GCMG

Burston, Sir Samuel Gerald Wood, Kt., OBE

Burt, *Hon.* Sir Francis Theodore Page, KCMG

Burton, Sir Carlisle Archibald, Kt., OBE

Burton, Sir George Vernon Kennedy, Kt., CBE

Burton, Sir Michael St Edmund, KCVO, CMG

Bush, *Adm.* Sir John Fitzroy Duyland, GCB, DSC

Butler, *Rt. Hon.* Sir Adam Courtauld, Kt.

Butler, *Hon.* Sir Arlington Griffith, KCMG

Butler, Sir Clifford Charles, Kt., ph.D., FRS

Butler, Sir (Frederick) (Edward) Robin, GCB, GCVO

Butler, Sir Michael Dacres, GCMG

Butler, Sir (Reginald) Michael (Thomas), Bt. (1922)

Butler, *Hon.* Sir Richard Clive, Kt.

†Butler, Sir Richard Pierce, Bt. (1628)

Butt, Sir (Alfred) Kenneth Dudley, Bt. (1929)

Butter, *Maj.* Sir David Henry, KCVO, MC

Butterfield, *Hon.* Sir Alexander Neil Logie, Kt.

Buxton, *Hon.* Sir Richard Joseph, Kt.

Buxton, Sir Thomas Fowell Victor, Bt. (1840)

Buzzard, Sir Anthony Farquhar, Bt. (1929)

Byatt, Sir Hugh Campbell, KCVO, CMG

Byers, Sir Maurice Hearne, Kt., CBE, QC

Byford, Sir Lawrence, Kt., CBE, QPM

Cable, Sir James Eric, KCVO, CMG

Cadbury, Sir (George) Adrian (Hayhurst), Kt.

Cadell, *Vice-Adm.* Sir John Frederick, KBE

Cadogan, *Prof.* Sir John Ivan George, Kt., CBE, FRS, FRSE

Cahn, Sir Albert Jonas, Bt. (1934)

Cain, Sir Edward Thomas, Kt., CBE

Cain, Sir Henry Edney Conrad, Kt.

Caine, Sir Michael Harris, Kt.

Caines, Sir John, KCB

Cairncross, Sir Alexander Kirkland, KCMG

Calcutt, Sir David Charles, Kt., QC

Calderwood, Sir Robert, Kt.

Caldwell, *Surgeon Vice-Adm.* Sir (Eric) Dick, KBE, CB

Callard, Sir Eric John, Kt., FEng.

Callaway, *Prof.* Sir Frank Adams, Kt., CMG, OBE

Calley, Sir Henry Algernon, Kt., DSO, DFC

Calman, *Prof.* Sir Kenneth Charles, KCB, MD, FRCP, FRCS, FRSE

Calne, *Prof.* Sir Roy Yorke, Kt., FRS

Calthorpe, Sir Euan Hamilton Anstruther-Gough-, Bt. (1929)

Cameron of Lochiel, Sir Donald Hamish, KT, CVO, TD

Cameron, Sir (Eustace) John, Kt., CBE

Cameron, Sir John Watson, Kt., OBE

Campbell, Sir Alan Hugh, GCMG

Campbell, Sir Colin Moffat, Bt., MC (s. 1668)

Campbell, *Prof.* Sir Colin Murray, Kt.

Campbell, *Prof.* Sir Donald, Kt., CBE, FRCS, FRCPGlas.

Campbell, Sir Ian Tofts, Kt., CBE, VRD

Campbell, Sir Ilay Mark, Bt. (1808)

Campbell, Sir Lachlan Philip Kemeys, Bt. (1815)

Campbell, Sir Matthew, KBE, CB, FRSE

Campbell, Sir Niall Alexander Hamilton, Bt. (1831)

Campbell, Sir Robin Auchinbreck, Bt. (s. 1628)

Campbell, Sir Thomas Cockburn-, Bt. (1821)

Campbell, *Hon.* Sir Walter Benjamin, Kt.

Campbell, *Hon.* Sir William Anthony, Kt.

†Carden, Sir Christopher Robert, Bt. (1887)

Carden, Sir John Craven, Bt. (I. 1787)

Carew, Sir Rivers Verain, Bt. (1661)

Carey, Sir Peter Willoughby, GCB

Carlisle, Sir James Beethoven, GCMG

Carlisle, Sir John Michael, Kt.

Carlisle, Sir Kenneth Melville, Kt., MP

Carmichael, Sir David Peter William Gibson-Craig-, Bt. (s. 1702 and 1831)

Carnac, *Revd Canon* Sir (Thomas) Nicholas Rivett-, Bt. (1836)

Carnegie, *Lt.-Gen.* Sir Robin Macdonald, KCB, OBE

Carnegie, Sir Roderick Howard, Kt.

Carnwath, Sir Robert John Anderson, Kt., CVO

Caro, Sir Anthony Alfred, Kt., CBE

Carpenter, *Very Revd* Edward Frederick, KCVO

Carpenter, *Lt.-Gen.* the Hon. Sir Thomas Patrick John Boyd-, KBE

Carr, Sir (Albert) Raymond (Maillard), Kt.

Carr, *Air Marshal* Sir John Darcy Baker-, KBE, CB, AFC

Carrick, *Hon.* Sir John Leslie, KCMG

Carrick, Sir Roger John, KCMG, LVO

Carsberg, *Prof.* Sir Bryan Victor, Kt.

Carswell, *Rt. Hon.* Sir Robert Douglas, Kt.

Carter, Sir Charles Frederick, Kt., FBA

Carter, *Prof.* Sir David Craig, Kt., FRCSE, FRCSGlas., FRCPE

Carter, Sir Derrick Hunton, Kt., TD

Carter, Sir John, Kt., QC

Carter, Sir John Alexander, Kt.

Carter, Sir Philip David, Kt., CBE

Carter, Sir Richard Henry Alwyn, Kt.

Carter, Sir William Oscar, Kt.

Cartland, Sir George Barrington, Kt., CMG

Cartledge, Sir Bryan George, KCMG

Cary, Sir Roger Hugh, Bt. (1955)

Casey, *Rt. Hon.* Sir Maurice Eugene, Kt.

Cash, Sir Gerald Christopher, GCMG, GCVO, OBE

Cass, Sir Geoffrey Arthur, Kt.

Cass, Sir John Patrick, Kt., OBE

Cassel, Sir Harold Felix, Bt., TD, QC (1920)

Cassels, *Field Marshal* Sir (Archibald) James Halkett, GCB, KBE, DSO

Cassels, Sir John Seton, Kt., CB

Cassels, *Adm.* Sir Simon Alastair Cassillis, KCB, CBE

Cassidi, *Adm.* Sir (Arthur) Desmond, GCB

Casson, Sir Hugh Maxwell, CH, KCVO, PPRA, FRIBA

Cater, Sir Jack, KBE

Cater, Sir John Robert, Kt.

Catford, Sir (John) Robin, KCVO, CBE

Catherwood, Sir (Henry) Frederick (Ross), Kt., MEP

Catling, Sir Richard Charles, Kt., CMG, OBE

Cato, *Hon.* Sir Arnott Samuel, KCMG

Cave, Sir Charles Edward Coleridge, Bt. (1896)

Cave, Sir (Charles) Philip Haddon-, KBE, CMG

Cave, Sir Robert Cave-Browne-, Bt. (1641)

Cawley, Sir Charles Mills, Kt., CBE, ph.D.

Cayley, Sir Digby William David, Bt. (1661)

Cayzer, Sir James Arthur, Bt. (1904)

Cazalet, *Hon.* Sir Edward Stephen, Kt.

Cazalet, Sir Peter Grenville, Kt.

Cecil, *Rear-Adm.* Sir (Oswald) Nigel Amherst, KBE, CB

Chacksfield, *Air Vice-Marshal* Sir Bernard Albert, KBE, CB

Chadwick, *Revd Prof.* Henry, KBE

Chadwick, *Hon.* Sir John Murray, Kt., ED

Chadwick, Sir Joshua Kenneth Burton, Bt. (1935)

Chadwick, *Revd Prof.* (William) Owen, OM, KBE, FBA

Chalstrey, Sir (Leonard) John, Kt., MD, FRCS

Chan, *Rt. Hon.* Sir Julius, GCMG, KBE

Chance, Sir (George) Jeremy ffolliott, Bt. (1900)

Chandler, Sir Colin Michael, Kt.

Chandler, Sir Geoffrey, Kt., CBE

Chaney, *Hon.* Sir Frederick Charles, KBE, AFC

Chantler, *Prof.* Sir Cyril, Kt., MD, FRCP

Chaplin, Sir Malcolm Hilbery, Kt., CBE

Chapman, Sir David Robert Macgowan, Bt. (1958)

Chapman, Sir George Alan, Kt.

Chapman, Sir Sidney Brookes, Kt., MP

Chapple, *Field Marshal* Sir John Lyon, GCB, CBE

Charlton, Sir Robert (Bobby), Kt., CBE

Charnley, Sir (William) John, Kt., CB, FEng.

Chataway, *Rt. Hon.* Sir Christopher, Kt.

Chatfield, Sir John Freeman, Kt., CBE

Chaytor, Sir George Reginald, Bt. (1831)

Checketts, *Sqn. Ldr.* Sir David John, KCVO

Checkland, Sir Michael, Kt.

Cheetham, Sir Nicolas John Alexander, KCMG

Cheshire, *Air Marshal* Sir John Anthony, KBE, CB

Chessells, Sir Arthur David (Tim), Kt.

Chesterman, Sir (Dudley) Ross, Kt., ph.D.

Chesterton, Sir Oliver Sidney, Kt., MC

Chetwood, Sir Clifford Jack, Kt.

Chetwynd, Sir Arthur Ralph Talbot, Bt. (1795)

Cheung, Sir Oswald Victor, Kt., CBE

Cheyne, Sir Joseph Lister Watson, Bt., OBE (1908)

Chichester, Sir (Edward) John, Bt. (1641)

Chilcot, Sir John Anthony, KCB

Child, Sir (Coles John) Jeremy, Bt. (1919)

Chilton, *Brig.* Sir Frederick Oliver, Kt., CBE, DSO

Chilwell, *Hon.* Sir Muir Fitzherbert, Kt.

Chinn, Sir Trevor Edwin, Kt., CVO

Chipperfield, Sir Geoffrey Howes, KCB

Chitty, Sir Thomas Willes, Bt. (1924)

Cholmeley, Sir Montague John, Bt. (1806)

Christie, Sir George William Langham, Kt.

Christie, Sir William, Kt., MBE

Christopherson, Sir Derman Guy, Kt., OBE, D.phil., FRS, FEng.

Chung, Sir Sze-yuen, GBE, FEng.

Clapham, Sir Michael John Sinclair, KBE

Clark, Sir Francis Drake, Bt. (1886)

Clark, Sir John Allen, Kt.

Clark, Sir John Stewart-, Bt., MEP (1918)

†Clark, Sir Jonathan George, Bt. (1917)

Clark, Sir Robert Anthony, Kt., DSC

Clark, Sir Robin Chichester-, Kt.

Clark, Sir Terence Joseph, KBE, CMG, CVO

Clark, Sir Thomas Edwin, Kt.

Clarke, *Hon.* Sir Anthony Peter, Kt.

Clarke, Sir (Charles Mansfield) Tobias, Bt. (1831)

Clarke, *Prof.* Sir Cyril Astley, KBE, MD, SC.D., FRS, FRCP

Clarke, Sir Ellis Emmanuel Innocent, GCMG

Clarke, Sir Jonathan Dennis, Kt.

Clarke, *Maj.* Sir Peter Cecil, KCVO

Clarke, Sir Robert Cyril, Kt.

Clarke, Sir Rupert William John, Bt., MBE (1882)

Clay, Sir Richard Henry, Bt. (1841)

Clayton, Sir David Robert, Bt. (1732)

Clayton, Sir Robert James, Kt., CBE, FEng.

Cleaver, Sir Anthony Brian, Kt.

Cleminson, Sir James Arnold Stacey, KBE, MC

Clerk, Sir John Dutton, Bt., CBE, VRD (s. 1679)

Clerke, Sir John Edward Longueville, Bt. (1660)

Clifford, Sir Roger Joseph, Bt. (1887)

Clothier, Sir Cecil Montacute, KCB, QC

Clucas, Sir Kenneth Henry, KCB

Clutterbuck, *Vice-Adm.* Sir David Granville, KBE, CB

Coates, Sir David Frederick Charlton, Bt. (1921)

Coats, Sir Alastair Francis Stuart, Bt. (1905)

Coats, Sir William David, Kt.

Cobban, Sir James Macdonald, Kt., CBE, TD

Cobham, Sir Michael John, Kt., CBE

Cochrane, Sir (Henry) Marc (Sursock), Bt. (1903)

Cockburn, Sir John Elliot, Bt. (s. 1671)

Cockcroft, Sir Wilfred Halliday, Kt., D.phil.

Cockerell, Sir Christopher Sydney, Kt., CBE, FRS

Cockram, Sir John, Kt.

Cockshaw, Sir Alan, Kt., FEng.

Codrington, Sir Simon Francis Bethell, Bt. (1876)

Codrington, Sir William Alexander, Bt. (1721)

Coghill, Sir Egerton James Nevill Tobias, Bt. (1778)

Cohen, Sir Edward, Kt.

Cohen, Sir Ivor Harold, Kt., CBE, TD

Cohen, Sir Stephen Harry Waley-, Bt. (1961)

Coldstream, Sir George Phillips, KCB, KCVO, QC

Cole, Sir (Alexander) Colin, KCB, KCVO, TD

Cole, Sir David Lee, KCMG, MC

Cole, Sir (Robert) William, Kt.

Coleman, Sir Timothy, KG

Coles, Sir (Arthur) John, KCMG

Colfox, Sir (William) John, Bt. (1939)

Collett, Sir Christopher, GBE

Collett, Sir Ian Seymour, Bt. (1934)

Collins, Hon. Sir Andrew David, Kt.

Collins, Sir Arthur James Robert, KCVO

Collins, Sir John Alexander, Kt.

Collyear, Sir John Gowen, Kt., FEng.

Colman, Hon. Sir Anthony David, Kt.

Colman, Sir Michael Jeremiah, Bt. (1907)

Colquhoun of Luss, Sir Ivar Iain, Bt. (1786)

Colt, Sir Edward William Dutton Bt. (1694)

Colthurst, Sir Richard La Touche, Bt. (1744)

Colvin, Sir Howard Montagu, Kt., CVO, CBE, FBA

Compston, Vice-Adm. Sir Peter Maxwell, KCB

Comyn, Hon. Sir James, Kt.

Conant, Sir John Ernest Michael, Bt. (1954)

Condon, Sir Paul Leslie, Kt., QPM

Connell, Hon. Sir Michael Bryan, Kt.

Conran, Sir Terence Orby, Kt.

Cons, Hon. Sir Derek, Kt.

Constable, Sir Frederic Strickland-, Bt. (1641)

Cook, Prof. Sir Alan Hugh, Kt.

Cook, Sir Christopher Wymondham Rayner Herbert, Bt. (1886)

Cooke, Sir Charles Fletcher-, Kt., QC

Cooke, Lt.-Col. Sir David William Perceval, Bt. (1661)

Cooke, Sir Howard Felix Hanlan, ON, GCMG, GCVO, CD

Cooksey, Sir David James Scott, Kt.

Cooley, Sir Alan Sydenham, Kt., CBE

Cooper, Rt. Hon. Sir Frank, GCB, CMG

Cooper, Sir (Frederick Howard) Michael Craig-, Kt., CBE, TD

Cooper, Gen. Sir George Leslie Conroy, GCB, MC

Cooper, Sir Louis Jacques Blom-, Kt., QC

Cooper, Sir Patrick Graham Astley, Bt. (1821)

Cooper, Sir Richard Powell, Bt. (1905)

Cooper, Maj.-Gen. Sir Simon Christie, KCVO

Cooper, Sir William Daniel Charles, Bt. (1863)

Coote, Sir Christopher John, Bt., Premier Baronet of Ireland (I. 1621)

Copas, Most Revd Virgil, KBE, DD

Cope, Rt. Hon. Sir John Ambrose, Kt., MP

Copisarow, Sir Alcon Charles, Kt.

Corbett, Maj.-Gen. Sir Robert John Swan, KCVO, CB

Corby, Sir (Frederick) Brian, Kt.

Corfield, Rt. Hon. Sir Frederick Vernon, Kt., QC

Corfield, Sir Kenneth George, Kt., FEng.

Corley, Sir Kenneth Sholl Ferrand, Kt.

Cormack, Sir Magnus Cameron, KBE

Cormack, Sir Patrick Thomas, Kt., MP

Corness, Sir Colin Ross, Kt.

Cornford, Sir (Edward) Clifford, KCB, FEng.

Cornforth, Sir John Warcup, Kt., CBE, D.phil., FRS

Corry, Sir William James, Bt. (1885)

Cortazzi, Sir (Henry Arthur) Hugh, GCMG

Cory, Sir (Clinton Charles) Donald, Bt. (1919)

Cossons, Sir Neil, Kt., OBE

Cotter, Lt.-Col. Sir Delaval James Alfred, Bt., DSO (I. 1763)

Cotterell, Sir John Henry Geers, Bt. (1805)

Cotton, Sir John Richard, KCMG, OBE

Cotton, Hon. Sir Robert Carrington, KCMG

Cottrell, Sir Alan Howard, Kt., ph.D., FRS, FEng.

†Cotts, Sir Richard Crichton Mitchell, Bt. (1921)

Coulson, Sir John Eltringham, KCMG

Couper, Sir (Robert) Nicholas (Oliver), Bt. (1841)

Court, Hon. Sir Charles Walter Michael, KCMG, OBE

Cousins, Air Marshal Sir David, KCB, AFC

Coutts, Sir David Burdett Money-, KCVO

Couzens, Sir Kenneth Edward, KCB

Covacevich, Sir (Anthony) Thomas, Kt., DFC

Coward, Vice-Adm. Sir John Francis, KCB, DSO

Cowdrey, Sir (Michael) Colin, Kt., CBE

Cowen, Rt. Hon. Prof. Sir Zelman, GCMG, GCVO, QC

Cowie, Sir Thomas (Tom), Kt., OBE

Cowperthwaite, Sir John James, KBE, CMG

Cox, Sir Alan George, Kt., CBE

Cox, Prof. Sir David Roxbee, Kt., FRS

Cox, Sir Geoffrey Sandford, Kt., CBE

Cox, Vice-Adm. Sir John Michael Holland, KCB

Cradock, Rt. Hon. Sir Percy, GCMG

Craig, Sir (Albert) James (Macqueen), GCMG

Craufurd, Sir Robert James, Bt. (1781)

Craven, Sir John Anthony, Kt.

Craven, Air Marshal Sir Robert Edward, KBE, CB, DFC

Crawford, Prof. Sir Frederick William, Kt., FEng.

Crawford, Sir (Robert) Stewart, GCMG, CVO

Crawford, Vice-Adm. Sir William Godfrey, KBE, CB, DSC

Crawshay, Col. Sir William Robert, Kt., DSO, ERD, TD

Creagh, Maj.-Gen. Sir (Kilner) Rupert Brazier-, KBE, CB, DSO

Cresswell, Hon. Sir Peter John, Kt.

Crill, Sir Peter Leslie, KBE

Cripps, Sir Cyril Humphrey, Kt.

Crisp, Sir (John) Peter, Bt. (1913)

Critchett, Sir Ian (George Lorraine), Bt. (1908)

Critchley, Sir Julian Michael Gordon, Kt., MP

Croft, Sir Owen Glendower, Bt. (1671)

Croft, Sir Thomas Stephen Hutton, Bt. (1818)

†Crofton, Sir Hugh Denis, Bt. (1801)

Crofton, Prof. Sir John Wenman, Kt.

Crofton, Sir Malby Sturges, Bt. (1838)

Croker, Sir Walter Russell, KBE

Crookenden, Lt.-Gen. Sir Napier, KCB, DSO, OBE

Cross, Air Chief Marshal Sir Kenneth Brian Boyd, KCB, CBE, DSO, DFC

Crossland, Prof. Sir Bernard, Kt., CBE, FEng.

Crossland, Sir Leonard, Kt.

Crossley, Sir Nicholas John, Bt. (1909)

Crouch, Sir David Lance, Kt.

Cruthers, Sir James Winter, Kt.

Cubbon, Sir Brian Crossland, GCB

Cubitt, Sir Hugh Guy, Kt., CBE

Cullen, Sir (Edward) John, Kt., F.Eng.

Cumming, Sir William Gordon Gordon-, Bt. (1804)

Cuninghame, Sir John Christopher Foggo Montgomery-, Bt. (NS 1672)

†Cuninghame, Sir William Henry Fairlie-, Bt. (s. 1630)

Cunliffe, Sir David Ellis, Bt. (1759)

Cunningham, Sir Charles Craik, GCB, KBE, CVO

Cunningham, Lt.-Gen. Sir Hugh Patrick, KBE

Cunynghame, Sir Andrew David Francis, Bt. (s. 1702)

Curle, Sir John Noel Ormiston, KCVO, CMG

Curran, Sir Samuel Crowe, Kt., D.SC., ph.D., FRS, FRSE, FEng.

†Currie, Sir Donald Scott, Bt. (1847)

Currie, Sir Neil Smith, Kt., CBE

Curtis, Sir Barry John, Kt.

Curtis, Sir (Edward) Leo, Kt.
Curtis, *Hon.* Sir Richard Herbert, Kt.
Curtis, Sir William Peter, Bt. (1802)
Curtiss, *Air Marshal* Sir John Bagot, KCB, KBE
Curwen, Sir Christopher Keith, KCMG
Cutler, Sir (Arthur) Roden, VC, KCMG, KCVO, CBE
Cutler, Sir Charles Benjamin, KBE, ED
Cutler, Sir Horace Walter, Kt., OBE
Dacie, *Prof.* Sir John Vivian, Kt., MD, FRS
Dale, Sir William Leonard, KCMG
Dalrymple, *Maj.* Sir Hew Fleetwood Hamilton-, Bt., KCVO (s. 1697)
Dalton, Sir Alan Nugent Goring, Kt., CBE
Dalton, *Vice-Adm.* Sir Geoffrey Thomas James Oliver, KCB
Daly, *Lt.-Gen.* Sir Thomas Joseph, KBE, CB, DSO
Dalyell, Sir Tam, Bt., MP (NS 1685)
Daniel, Sir Goronwy Hopkin, KCVO, CB, D.Phil.
Daniel, Sir John Sagar, Kt., D.SC.
Daniell, Sir Peter Averell, Kt., TD
Danks, Sir Alan John, KBE
Darby, Sir Peter Howard, Kt., CBE, QFSM
Darell, Sir Jeffrey Lionel, Bt., MC (1795)
Dargie, Sir William Alexander, Kt., CBE
Dark, Sir Anthony Michael Beaumont-, Kt.
Darling, Sir Clifford, GCVO
Darling, *Gen.* Sir Kenneth Thomas, GBE, KCB, DSO
Darlington, *Rear-Adm.* Sir Charles Roy, Kt.
Darvall, Sir (Charles) Roger, Kt., CBE
Dashwood, Sir Francis John Vernon Hereward, Bt., *Premier Baronet of Great Britain* (1707)
Dashwood, Sir Richard James, Bt. (1684)
Daunt, Sir Timothy Lewis Achilles, KCMG
David, Sir Jean Marc, Kt., CBE, QC
David, *His Hon.* Sir Robin (Robert) Daniel George, Kt., QC
Davidson, Sir Robert James, Kt., FEng.
Davie, Sir Antony Francis Ferguson-, Bt. (1847)
Davies, *Air Marshal* Sir Alan Cyril, KCB, CBE
Davies, *Hon.* Sir (Alfred William) Michael, Kt.
Davies, Sir Alun Talfan, Kt., QC
Davies, Sir Charles Noel, Kt.
Davies, *Prof.* Sir David Evan Naughton, Kt., CBE, FRS, FEng.
Davies, Sir David Henry, Kt.
Davies, *Hon.* Sir (David Herbert) Mervyn, Kt., MC, TD
Davies, *Prof.* Sir Graeme John, Kt., FEng.

Davies, *Vice-Adm.* Sir Lancelot Richard Bell, KBE
Davies, Sir Peter Maxwell, Kt., CBE
Davies, Sir Victor Caddy, Kt., OBE
Davis, Sir Charles Sigmund, Kt., CB
Davis, Sir Colin Rex, Kt., CBE
Davis, *Hon.* Sir (Dermot) Renn, Kt., OBE
Davis, Sir (Ernest) Howard, Kt., CMG, OBE
Davis, Sir John Gilbert, Bt. (1946)
Davis, Sir Rupert Charles Hart-, Kt.
Davis, *Hon.* Sir Thomas Robert Alexander Harries, KBE
Davison, *Rt. Hon.* Sir Ronald Keith, GBE, CMG
Dawbarn, Sir Simon Yelverton, KCVO, CMG
Dawson, Sir Anthony Michael, KCVO, MD, FRCP
Dawson, *Hon.* Sir Daryl Michael, KBE, CB
Dawson, Sir Hugh Michael Trevor, Bt. (1920)
Dawtry, Sir Alan (Graham), Kt., CBE, TD
Day, Sir Derek Malcolm, KCMG
Day, Sir (Judson) Graham, Kt.
Day, Sir Michael John, Kt., OBE
Day, Sir Robin, Kt.
Deakin, Sir (Frederick) William (Dampier), Kt., DSO
Deane, *Hon.* Sir William Patrick, KBE
Dear, *Hon.* Sir John Stanley Bruce, KCMG
Dearing, Sir Ronald Ernest, Kt., CB
de Bellaigue, Sir Geoffrey, GCVO
Debenham, Sir Gilbert Ridley, Bt. (1931)
de Deney, Sir Geoffrey Ivor, KCVO
de Hoghton, Sir (Richard) Bernard (Cuthbert), Bt. (1611)
De la Bère, Sir Cameron, Bt. (1953)
de la Rue, Sir Andrew George Ilay, Bt. (1898)
Dellow, Sir John Albert, Kt., CBE
de Montmorency, Sir Arnold Geoffroy, Bt. (I. 1631)
Denholm, Sir John Ferguson (Ian), Kt., CBE
Denman, Sir (George) Roy, KCB, CMG
Denny, Sir Anthony Coningham de Waltham, Bt. (I. 1782)
Denny, Sir Charles Alistair Maurice, Bt. (1913)
Dent, Sir John, Kt., CBE, FEng.
Dent, Sir Robin John, KCVO
Denton, *Prof.* Sir Eric James, Kt., CBE, FRS
Derbyshire, Sir Andrew George, Kt.
Derham, Sir Peter John, Kt.
de Trafford, Sir Dermot Humphrey, Bt. (1841)
Devesi, Sir Baddeley, GCMG, GCVO
De Ville, Sir Harold Godfrey Oscar, Kt., CBE
†Devitt, Sir James Hugh Thomas, Bt. (1916)
de Waal, Sir (Constant Henrik) Henry, KCB, QC

Dewey, Sir Anthony Hugh, Bt. (1917)
Dewhurst, *Prof.* Sir (Christopher) John, Kt.
d'Eyncourt, Sir Mark Gervais Tennyson-, Bt. (1930)
Dhenin, *Air Marshal* Sir Geoffrey Howard, KBE, AFC, GM, MD
Dhrangadhra, HH the Maharaja Raj Saheb of, KCIE
Dibela, *Hon.* Sir Kingsford, GCMG
Dickenson, Sir Aubrey Fiennes Trotman-, Kt.
Dickinson, Sir Harold Herbert, Kt.
Dickinson, Sir Samuel Benson, Kt.
Dilbertson, Sir Geoffrey, Kt., CBE
Dilke, Sir John Fisher Wentworth, Bt. (1862)
Dillon, *Rt. Hon.* Sir (George) Brian (Hugh), Kt.
Dillon, Sir Max, Kt.
Diver, *Hon.* Sir Leslie Charles, Kt.
Dixon, Sir Ian Leonard, Kt., CBE
Dixon, Sir Jonathan Mark, Bt. (1919)
Djanogly, Sir Harry Ari Simon, Kt., CBE
Dobbs, *Capt.* Sir Richard Arthur Frederick, KCVO
Dobson, *Vice-Adm.* Sir David Stuart, KBE
Dobson, *Gen.* Sir Patrick John Howard-, GCB
Dodds, Sir Ralph Jordan, Bt. (1964)
Dodson, Sir Derek Sherborne Lindsell, KCMG, MC
Dodsworth, Sir John Christopher Smith-, Bt. (1784)
Doll, *Prof.* Sir (William) Richard (Shaboe), Kt., CH, OBE, FRS, DM, MD, D.SC.
Dollery, Sir Colin Terence, Kt.
Donald, Sir Alan Ewen, KCMG
Donald, *Air Marshal* Sir John George, KBE
Donne, *Hon.* Sir Gaven John, KBE
Donne, Sir John Christopher, Kt.
Dookun, Sir Dewoonarain, Kt.
Dorey, Sir Graham Martyn, Kt.
Dorman, *Lt.-Col.* Sir Charles Geoffrey, Bt., MC (1923)
Dougherty, *Maj.-Gen.* Sir Ivan Noel, Kt., CBE, DSO, ED
Doughty, Sir William Roland, Kt.
Douglas, Sir (Edward) Sholto, Kt.
Douglas, Sir Robert McCallum, Kt., OBE
Douglas, *Hon.* Sir Roger Owen, Kt.
Douglas, *Rt. Hon.* Sir William Randolph, KCMG
Dover, *Prof.* Sir Kenneth James, Kt., D.Litt., FBA, FRSE
Dowell, Sir Anthony James, Kt., CBE
Down, Sir Alastair Frederick, Kt., OBE, MC, TD
Downes, Sir Edward Thomas, Kt., CBE
Downey, Sir Gordon Stanley, KCB
Downs, Sir Diarmuid, Kt., CBE, FEng.
Downward, Sir William Atkinson, Kt.

Dowson, Sir Philip Manning, Kt., CBE, ARA

Doyle, Sir Reginald Derek Henry, Kt., CBE

D'Oyly, Sir Nigel Hadley Miller, Bt. (1663)

Drake, Sir (Arthur) Eric (Courtney), Kt., CBE

Drake, *Hon.* Sir (Frederick) Maurice, Kt., DFC

Dreyer, *Adm.* Sir Desmond Parry, GCB, CBE, DSC

Drinkwater, Sir John Muir, Kt., QC

Driver, Sir Antony Victor, Kt.

Driver, Sir Eric William, Kt.

Drummond, Sir John Richard Gray, Kt., CBE

Drury, Sir (Victor William) Michael, Kt., OBE

Dryden, Sir John Stephen Gyles, Bt. (1733 and 1795)

du Cann, *Rt. Hon.* Sir Edward Dillon Lott, KBE

Duckworth, *Maj.* Sir Richard Dyce, Bt. (1909)

du Cros, Sir Claude Philip Arthur Mallet, Bt. (1916)

Duff, *Rt. Hon.* Sir (Arthur) Antony, GCMG, CVO, DSO, DSC

Duffell, *Lt.-Gen.* Sir Peter Royson, KCB, CBE, MC

Duffus, *Hon.* Sir William Algernon Holwell, Kt.

Duffy, Sir (Albert) (Edward) Patrick, Kt., ph.D.

Dugdale, Sir William Stratford, Bt., MC (1936)

Dunbar, Sir Archibald Ranulph, Bt. (s. 1700)

Dunbar, Sir David Hope-, Bt. (s. 1664)

Dunbar, Sir Drummond Cospatrick Ninian, Bt., MC (s. 1698)

Dunbar, Sir James Michael, Bt. (s. 1694)

Dunbar of Hempriggs, Dame Maureen Daisy Helen (Lady Dunbar of Hempriggs), Btss. (s. 1706)

Duncan, Sir James Blair, Kt.

Duncombe, Sir Philip Digby Pauncefort-, Bt. (1859)

Dunham, Sir Kingsley Charles, Kt., ph.D., FRS, FRSE, FEng.

Dunlop, Sir Thomas, Bt. (1916)

Dunlop, Sir William Norman Gough, Kt.

Dunn, *Air Marshal* Sir Eric Clive, KBE, CB, BEM

Dunn, *Air Marshal* Sir Patrick Hunter, KBE, CB, DFC

Dunn, *Rt. Hon.* Sir Robin Horace Walford, Kt., MC

Dunne, Sir Thomas Raymond, KCVO

Dunnett, Sir Alastair MacTavish, Kt.

Dunnett, Sir (Ludovic) James, GCB, CMG

Dunning, Sir Simon William Patrick, Bt. (1930)

Dunphie, *Maj.-Gen.* Sir Charles Anderson Lane, Kt., CB, CBE, DSO

Dunstan, *Lt.-Gen.* Sir Donald Beaumont, KBE, CB

†Duntze, Sir Daniel Evans, Bt. (1774)

Dupre, Sir Tumun, Kt., MBE

Dupree, Sir Peter, Bt. (1921)

Durand, Sir Edward Alan Christopher David Percy, Bt. (1892)

Durant, Sir (Robert) Anthony (Bevis), Kt., MP

Durham, Sir Kenneth, Kt.

Durie, Sir Alexander Charles, Kt., CBE

Durkin, *Air Marshal* Sir Herbert, KBE, CB

Durrant, Sir William Alexander Estridge, Bt. (1784)

Duthie, *Prof.* Sir Herbert Livingston, Kt.

Duthie, Sir Robert Grieve (Robin), Kt., CBE

Duxbury, *Air Marshal* Sir (John) Barry, KCB, CBE

Dyer, *Prof.* Sir (Henry) Peter (Francis) Swinnerton-, Bt., KBE, FRS (1678)

Dyke, Sir David William Hart, Bt. (1677)

Dyson, *Hon.* Sir John Anthony, Kt.

Earle, Sir (Hardman) George (Algernon), Bt. (1869)

East, Sir (Lewis) Ronald, Kt., CBE

Easton, Sir Robert William Simpson, Kt., CBE

Eaton, *Adm.* Sir Kenneth John, GBE, KCB

Eberle, *Adm.* Sir James Henry Fuller, GCB

Ebrahim, Sir (Mahomed) Currimbhoy, Bt. (1910)

Eccles, Sir John Carew, Kt., D.Phil., FRS

Echlin, Sir Norman David Fenton, Bt. (I. 1721)

Eckersley, Sir Donald Payze, Kt., OBE

Edge, *Capt.* Sir (Philip) Malcolm, KCVO

†Edge, Sir William, Bt. (1937)

Edmonstone, Sir Archibald Bruce Charles, Bt. (1774)

Edwardes, Sir Michael Owen, Kt.

Edwards, Sir Christopher John Churchill, Bt. (1866)

Edwards, Sir George Robert, Kt., OM, CBE, FRS, FEng.

Edwards, Sir (John) Clive (Leighton), Bt. (1921)

Edwards, Sir Llewellyn Roy, Kt.

Edwards, *Prof.* Sir Samuel Frederick, Kt., FRS

Egan, Sir John Leopold, Kt.

Egerton, Sir John Alfred Roy, Kt.

Egerton, Sir (Philip) John (Caledon) Grey-, Bt. (1617)

Egerton, Sir Seymour John Louis, GCVO

Egerton, Sir Stephen Loftus, KCMG

Eggleston, *Hon.* Sir Richard Moulton, Kt.

Eichelbaum, *Rt. Hon.* Sir Thomas, GBE

Eliott of Stobs, Sir Charles Joseph Alexander, Bt. (s. 1666)

Ellerton, Sir Geoffrey James, Kt., CMG, MBE

Elliot, Sir Gerald Henry, Kt.

Elliott, Sir Clive Christopher Hugh, Bt. (1917)

Elliott, Sir David Murray, KCMG, CB

Elliott, *Prof.* Sir John Huxtable, Kt., FBA

Elliott, Sir Randal Forbes, KBE

Elliott, *Prof.* Sir Roger James, Kt., FRS

Elliott, Sir Ronald Stuart, Kt.

Ellis, Sir John Rogers, Kt., MBE, MD, FRCP

Ellis, Sir Ronald, Kt., FEng.

Ellison, *Col.* Sir Ralph Harry Carr-, Kt., TD

Elphinstone, Sir John, Bt. (s. 1701)

Elphinstone, Sir (Maurice) Douglas (Warburton), Bt., TD (1816)

Elton, Sir Arnold, Kt., CBE

Elton, Sir Charles Abraham Grierson, Bt. (1717)

Elwes, Sir Jeremy Vernon, Kt., CBE

Elwood, Sir Brian George Conway, Kt., CBE

Elworthy, Sir Peter Herbert, Kt.

Elyan, Sir (Isadore) Victor, Kt.

Emery, *Rt. Hon.* Sir Peter Frank Hannibal, Kt., MP

Empson, *Adm.* Sir (Leslie) Derek, GBE, KCB

Engineer, Sir Noshirwan Phirozshah, Kt.

Engle, Sir George Lawrence Jose, KCB, QC

English, Sir Cyril Rupert, Kt.

English, Sir David, Kt.

English, Sir Terence Alexander Hawthorne, KBE, FRCS

Epstein, *Prof.* Sir (Michael) Anthony, Kt., CBE, FRS

Ereaut, Sir (Herbert) Frank Cobbold, Kt.

Errington, *Col.* Sir Geoffrey Frederick, Bt. (1963)

Errington, Sir Lancelot, KCB

Erskine, Sir (Thomas) David, Bt. (1821)

Esmonde, Sir Thomas Francis Grattan, Bt. (I. 1629)

Espie, Sir Frank Fletcher, Kt., OBE

Esplen, Sir John Graham, Bt. (1921)

Eustace, Sir Joseph Lambert, GCMG, GCVO

Evans, Sir Anthony Adney, Bt. (1920)

Evans, *Rt. Hon.* Sir Anthony Howell Meurig, Kt., RD

Evans, *Air Chief Marshal* Sir David George, GCB, CBE

Evans, *Air Chief Marshal* Sir David Parry-, GCB, CBE

Evans, *Hon.* Sir Haydn Tudor, Kt.

Evans, Sir Richard Harry, Kt., CBE

Evans, Sir Richard Mark, KCMG, KCVO

Evans, Sir Robert, Kt., CBE, FEng.

Evans, Very Revd (Thomas) Eric, KCVO

Evans, Sir (William) Vincent (John), GCMG, MBE, QC

Eveleigh, *Rt. Hon.* Sir Edward Walter, Kt., ERD

Everard, Sir Robin Charles, Bt. (1911)

Everson, Sir Frederick Charles, KCMG

Every, Sir Henry John Michael, Bt. (1641)

Ewans, Sir Martin Kenneth, KCMG

Ewart, Sir William Michael, Bt. (1887)

Ewbank, *Hon.* Sir Anthony Bruce, Kt.

Ewin, Sir (David) Ernest Thomas Floyd, Kt., OBE, LVO

Ewing, *Vice-Adm.* Sir (Robert) Alastair, KBE, CB, DSC

Ewing, Sir Ronald Archibald Orr-, Bt. (1886)

Eyre, Sir Graham Newman, Kt., QC

Eyre, *Maj.-Gen.* Sir James Ainsworth Campden Gabriel, KCVO, CBE

Eyre, Sir Reginald Edwin, Kt.

Faber, Sir Richard Stanley, KCVO, CMG

Fadahunsi, Sir Joseph Odeleye, KCMG

Fagge, Sir John William Frederick, Bt. (1660)

Fairbairn, *Hon.* Sir David Eric, KBE, DFC

Fairbairn, Sir (James) Brooke, Bt. (1869)

Fairclough, Sir John Whitaker, Kt., FEng.

Fairgrieve, Sir (Thomas) Russell, Kt., CBE, TD

Fairhall, *Hon.* Sir Allen, KBE

Fairweather, Sir Patrick Stanislaus, KCMG

Falconer, *Hon.* Sir Douglas William, Kt., MBE

Falk, Sir Roger Salis, Kt., OBE

Falkiner, Sir Edmond Charles, Bt. (I. 1778)

Fall, Sir Brian James Proetel, GCVO, KCMG

Falle, Sir Samuel, KCMG, KCVO, DSC

Fareed, Sir Djamil Sheik, Kt.

Farmer, Sir (Lovedin) George Thomas, Kt.

Farndale, *Gen.* Sir Martin Baker, KCB

Farquhar, Sir Michael Fitzroy Henry, Bt. (1796)

Farquharson, *Rt. Hon.* Sir Donald Henry, Kt.

Farquharson, Sir James Robbie, KBE

Farr, Sir John Arnold, Kt.

Farrer, Sir (Charles) Matthew, GCVO

Farrington, Sir Henry Francis Colden, Bt. (1818)

Fat, Sir (Maxime) Edouard (Lim Man) Lim, Kt.

Faulkner, Sir (James) Dennis (Compton), Kt., CBE, VRD

Fawcus, Sir (Robert) Peter, KBE, CMG

Fawkes, Sir Randol Francis, Kt.

Fay, Sir (Humphrey) Michael Gerard, Kt.

Fayrer, Sir John Lang Macpherson, Bt. (1896)

Fearn, Sir (Patrick) Robin, KCMG

Feilden, Sir Bernard Melchior, Kt., CBE

Feilden, Sir Henry Wemyss, Bt., (1846)

Fell, Sir Anthony, Kt.

Fell, Sir David, KCB

Fellowes, *Rt. Hon.* Sir Robert, GCVO, KCB

Fenn, Sir Nicholas Maxted, GCMG

Fennell, *Hon.* Sir (John) Desmond Augustine, Kt., OBE

Fennessy, Sir Edward, Kt., CBE

Ferguson, Sir Ian Edward Johnson-, Bt. (1906)

Fergusson of Kilkerran, Sir Charles, Bt. (s. 1703)

Fergusson, Sir Ewan Alastair John, GCMG, GCVO

Fergusson, Sir James Herbert Hamilton Colyer-, Bt. (1866)

Feroze, Sir Rustam Moolan, Kt., FRCS

Ferris, *Hon.* Sir Francis Mursell, Kt., TD

ffolkes, Sir Robert Francis Alexander, Bt, OBE (1774)

Field, Sir Malcolm David, Kt.

Fielding, Sir Colin Cunningham, Kt., CB

Fielding, Sir Leslie, KCMG

Fiennes, Sir Ranulph Twisleton-Wykeham-, Bt., OBE (1916)

Figg, Sir Leonard Clifford William, KCMG

Figgess, Sir John George, KBE, CMG

Figgis, Sir Anthony St John Howard, KCVO, CMG

Figures, Sir Colin Frederick, KCMG, OBE

Fingland, Sir Stanley James Gunn, KCMG

Finlay, Sir David Ronald James Bell, Bt. (1964)

Firth, *Prof.* Sir Raymond William, Kt., PH.D., FBA

Fish, Sir Hugh, Kt., CBE

Fisher, Sir George Read, Kt., CMG

Fisher, *Hon.* Sir Henry Arthur Pears, Kt.

Fisher, Sir Nigel Thomas Loveridge, Kt., MC

Fison, Sir (Richard) Guy, Bt., DSC (1905)

†Fitzgerald, *Revd* (Sir) Daniel Patrick, Bt. (1903)

FitzGerald, Sir George Peter Maurice, Bt., MC (*The Knight of Kerry*) (1880)

FitzHerbert, Sir Richard Ranulph, Bt. (1784)

Fitzpatrick, *Gen.* Sir (Geoffrey Richard) Desmond, GCB, DSO, MBE, MC

Fitzpatrick, *Air Marshal* Sir John Bernard, KBE, CB

Flanagan, Sir James Bernard, Kt., CBE

Fletcher, Sir Henry Egerton Aubrey-, Bt. (1782)

Fletcher, Sir James Muir Cameron, Kt.

Fletcher, Sir Leslie, Kt., DSC

Fletcher, *Air Chief Marshal* Sir Peter Carteret, KCB, OBE, DFC, AFC

Floissac, *Hon.* Sir Vincent Frederick, Kt., CMG, OBE, QC

Floyd, Sir Giles Henry Charles, Bt. (1816)

Foley, *Lt.-Gen.* Sir John Paul, KCB, OBE, MC

Foley, Sir (Thomas John) Noel, Kt., CBE

Follett, *Prof.* Sir Brian Keith, Kt., FRS

Foot, Sir Geoffrey James, Kt.

Foots, Sir James William, Kt.

Forbes, *Hon.* Sir Alastair Granville, Kt.

Forbes, *Maj.* Sir Hamish Stewart, Bt., MBE, MC (1823)

Forbes of Craigievar, Sir John Alexander Cumnock, Bt. (s. 1630)

Forbes, *Vice-Adm.* Sir John Morrison, KCB

Forbes, *Hon.* Sir Thayne John, Kt.

†Forbes of Pitsligo, Sir William Daniel Stuart-, Bt. (s. 1626)

Ford, Sir Andrew Russell, Bt. (1929)

Ford, Sir David Robert, KBE, LVO, OBE

Ford, *Maj.* Sir Edward William Spencer, KCB, KCVO

Ford, *Air Marshal* Sir Geoffrey Harold, KBE, CB, FEng.

Ford, *Prof.* Sir Hugh, Kt., FRS, FEng.

Ford, Sir James Anson St Clair-, Bt. (1793)

Ford, Sir John Archibald, KCMG, MC

Ford, Sir Richard Brinsley, Kt., CBE

Ford, *Gen.* Sir Robert Cyril, GCB, CBE

Foreman, Sir Philip Frank, Kt., CBE, FEng.

Forman, Sir John Denis, Kt., OBE

Forrest, *Prof.* Sir (Andrew) Patrick (McEwen), Kt.

Forrest, *Rear-Adm.* Sir Ronald Stephen, KCVO

Forster, Sir Archibald William, Kt., FEng.

Forster, Sir Oliver Grantham, KCMG, LVO

Forte, Hon. Sir Rocco John Vincent, Kt.

Forwood, Sir Dudley Richard, Bt. (1895)

Foster, *Prof.* Sir Christopher David, Kt.

Foster, Sir John Gregory, Bt. (1930)

Foster, Sir Norman Robert, Kt.

Foster, Sir Robert Sidney, GCMG, KCVO

Foulis, Sir Ian Primrose Liston-, Bt. (s. 1634)

Foulkes, Sir Nigel Gordon, Kt.

Fountain, *Hon.* Sir Cyril Stanley Smith, Kt.

Fowden, Sir Leslie, Kt., FRS

Fowke, Sir David Frederick Gustavus, Bt. (1814)

Fowler, Sir (Edward) Michael Coulson, Kt.

Fowler, Rt. Hon. Sir (Peter) Norman, Kt., MP

Fox, Sir (Henry) Murray, GBE

Fox, Rt. Hon. Sir (John) Marcus, Kt., MBE, MP

Fox, Rt. Hon. Sir Michael John, Kt.

Fox, Sir Paul Leonard, Kt., CBE

France, Sir Arnold William, GCB

France, Sir Christopher Walter, GCB

France, Sir Joseph Nathaniel, KCMG, CBE

Francis, Sir Horace William Alexander, Kt., CBE, FEng.

Frank, Sir Douglas George Horace, Kt., QC

Frank, Sir (Frederick) Charles, Kt., OBE, FRS

Frank, Sir Robert Andrew, Bt. (1920)

Frankel, Sir Otto Herzberg, Kt., D.SC., FRS

Franklin, Sir Michael David Milroy, KCB, CMG

Franks, Sir Arthur Temple, KCMG

Fraser, Sir Angus McKay, KCB, TD

Fraser, Sir Charles Annand, KCVO

Fraser, Gen. Sir David William, GCB, OBE

Fraser, Air Marshal Revd Sir (Henry) Paterson, KBE, CB, AFC

Fraser, Sir Ian, Kt., DSO, OBE

Fraser, Sir Ian James, Kt., CBE, MC

Fraser, Sir (James) Campbell, Kt.

Fraser, Prof. Sir James David, Bt. (1943)

Fraser, Sir William Kerr, GCB

Frederick, Sir Charles Boscawen, Bt. (1723)

Freeland, Sir John Redvers, KCMG

Freeman, Sir James Robin, Bt. (1945)

Freeman, Sir Ralph, Kt., CVO, CBE, FEng.

Freer, Air Chief Marshal Sir Robert William George, GBE, KCB

Freeth, Hon. Sir Gordon, KBE

French, Hon. Sir Christopher James Saunders, Kt.

Frere, Vice-Adm. Sir Richard Tobias, KCB

Fretwell, Sir (Major) John (Emsley), GCMG

Freud, Sir Clement Raphael, Kt.

Froggatt, Sir Leslie Trevor, Kt.

Froggatt, Sir Peter, Kt.

Frossard, Sir Charles Keith, KBE

Frost, Sir David Paradine, Kt., OBE

Frost, Hon. Sir (Thomas) Sydney, Kt.

Fry, Sir Peter Derek, Kt., MP

Fry, Hon. Sir William Gordon, Kt.

Fryberg, Sir Abraham, Kt., MBE

Fuchs, Sir Vivian Ernest, Kt., ph.D.

Fuller, Hon. Sir John Bryan Munro, Kt.

Fuller, Sir John William Fleetwood, Bt. (1910)

Fung, Hon. Sir Kenneth Ping-Fan, Kt., CBE

Furness, Sir Stephen Roberts, Bt. (1913)

Gadsden, Sir Peter Drury Haggerston, GBE, FEng.

Gage, Hon. Sir William Marcus, Kt.

Gainsford, Sir Ian Derek, Kt., DDS

Gairy, Rt. Hon. Sir Eric Matthew, Kt.

Gaius, Rt. Revd Saimon, KBE

Gallwey, Sir Philip Frankland Payne-, Bt. (1812)

Gam, Rt. Revd Sir Getake, KBE

Gamble, Sir David Hugh Norman, Bt. (1897)

Garden, Air Marshal Sir Timothy, KCB

Gardiner, Sir George Arthur, Kt., MP

Gardner, Sir Douglas Bruce Bruce-, Bt. (1945)

Gardner, Sir Edward Lucas, Kt., QC

Garland, Hon. Sir Patrick Neville, Kt.

Garland, Hon. Sir Ransley Victor, KBE

Garlick, Sir John, KCB

Garner, Sir Anthony Stuart, Kt.

Garnier, Rear-Adm. Sir John, KCVO, CBE

Garrick, Sir Ronald, Kt., CBE, FEng.

Garrioch, Sir (William) Henry, Kt.

Garrod, Lt.-Gen. Sir (John) Martin Carruthers, KCB, OBE

Garthwaite, Sir (William) Mark (Charles), Bt. (1919)

Gaskell, Sir Richard Kennedy Harvey, Kt.

Gatehouse, Hon. Sir Robert Alexander, Kt.

Geddes, Sir (Anthony) Reay (Mackay), KBE

George, Sir Arthur Thomas, Kt.

George, Sir Richard William, Kt.

Gerken, Vice-Adm. Sir Robert William Frank, KCB, CBE

Gery, Sir Robert Lucian Wade-, KCMG, KCVO

Gethin, Sir Richard Joseph St Lawrence, Bt. (I. 1665)

Ghurburrun, Sir Rabindrah, Kt.

Gibb, Sir Francis Ross (Frank), Kt., CBE, FEng.

Gibbings, Sir Peter Walter, Kt.

Gibbon, Gen. Sir John Houghton, GCB, OBE

Gibbons, Sir (John) David, KBE

Gibbons, Sir William Edward Doran, Bt. (1752)

Gibbs, Hon. Sir Eustace Hubert Beilby, KCVO, CMG

Gibbs, Rt. Hon. Sir Harry Talbot, GCMG, KBE

Gibbs, Sir Roger Geoffrey, Kt.

Gibbs, Field Marshal Sir Roland Christopher, GCB, CBE, DSO, MC

†Gibson, Revd Sir Christopher Herbert, Bt. (1931)

Gibson, Revd Sir David, Bt. (1926)

Gibson, Vice-Adm. Sir Donald Cameron Ernest Forbes, KCB, DSC

Gibson, Rt. Hon. Sir Peter Leslie, Kt.

Gibson, Rt. Hon. Sir Ralph Brian, Kt.

Giddings, Air Marshal Sir (Kenneth Charles) Michael, KCB, OBE, DFC, AFC

Gielgud, Sir (Arthur) John, Kt., CH

Giffard, Sir (Charles) Sydney (Rycroft), KCMG

Gilbert, Air Chief Marshal Sir Joseph Alfred, KCB, CBE

Gilbert, Sir Martin John, Kt., CBE

†Gilbey, Sir Walter Gavin, Bt. (1893)

Giles, Rear-Adm. Sir Morgan Charles Morgan-, Kt., DSO, OBE, GM

Gill, Sir Anthony Keith, Kt., FEng.

Gillett, Sir Robin Danvers Penrose, Bt., GBE, RD (1959)

Gilmour, Col. Sir Allan Macdonald, KCVO, OBE, MC

Gilmour, Sir John Edward, Bt., DSO, TD (1897)

Gingell, Air Chief Marshal Sir John, GBE, KCB, KCVO

Girolami, Sir Paul, Kt.

Girvan, Hon. Sir (Frederick) Paul, Kt.

Gladstone, Sir (Erskine) William, Bt. (1846)

Glasspole, Sir Florizel Augustus, GCMG, GCVO

Glen, Sir Alexander Richard, KBE, DSC

Glenn, Sir (Joseph Robert) Archibald, Kt., OBE

Glidewell, Rt. Hon. Sir Iain Derek Laing, Kt.

Glock, Sir William Frederick, Kt., CBE

Glover, Gen. Sir James Malcolm, KCB, MBE

Glover, Sir Victor Joseph Patrick, Kt.

Glyn, Sir Alan, Kt., ERD

Glyn, Sir Anthony Geoffrey Leo Simon, Bt. (1927)

Glyn, Sir Richard Lindsay, Bt. (1759 and 1800)

Goad, Sir (Edward) Colin (Viner), KCMG

Godber, Sir George Edward, GCB, DM

Goff, Sir Robert (William) Davis-, Bt. (1905)

Gold, Sir Arthur Abraham, Kt., CBE

Gold, Sir Joseph, Kt.

Goldberg, Prof. Sir Abraham, Kt., MD, D.SC., FRCP

Goldberg, Prof. Sir David Paul Brandes, Kt.

Goldman, Sir Samuel, KCB

Goldsmith, Sir James Michael, Kt.

Gombrich, Prof. Sir Ernst Hans Josef, Kt., OM, CBE, ph.D., FBA, FSA

Gooch, Sir (Richard) John Sherlock, Bt. (1746)

Gooch, Sir Trevor Sherlock (Sir Peter), Bt. (1866)

Goodall, Sir (Arthur) David Saunders, GCMG

Goodenough, Sir Richard Edmund, Bt. (1943)

Goodhart, Sir Philip Carter, Kt.

Goodhart, Sir Robert Anthony Gordon, Bt. (1911)

Goodhart, Sir William Howard, Kt., QC
Goodhew, Sir Victor Henry, Kt.
Goodison, Sir Alan Clowes, KCMG
Goodison, Sir Nicholas Proctor, Kt.
Goodman, Sir Patrick Ledger, Kt., CBE
Goodson, Sir Mark Weston Lassam, Bt. (1922)
Goodwin, Sir Matthew Dean, Kt., CBE
Goold, Sir George Leonard, Bt. (1801)
Gordon, Sir Alexander John, Kt., CBE
Gordon, Sir Andrew Cosmo Lewis Duff-, Bt. (1813)
Gordon, Sir Charles Addison Somerville Snowden, KCB
Gordon, Sir Keith Lyndell, Kt., CMG
Gordon, Sir (Lionel) Eldred (Peter) Smith-, Bt. (1838)
Gordon, Sir Robert James, Bt. (s. 1706)
Gordon, Sir Sidney Samuel, Kt., CBE
Gordon Lennox, Lord Nicholas Charles, KCMG, KCVO
†Gore, Sir Nigel Hugh St George, Bt. (I. 1622)
Gorham, Sir Richard Masters, Kt., CBE, DFC
Goring, Sir William Burton Nigel, Bt. (1627)
Gorst, Sir John Michael, Kt., MP
Gorton, Rt. Hon. Sir John Grey, GCMG, CH
Goschen, Sir Edward Christian, Bt., DSO (1916)
Gosling, Sir (Frederick) Donald, Kt.
Goswell, Sir Brian Lawrence, Kt.
Goulden, Sir (Peter) John, KCMG
Goulding, Sir (Ernest) Irvine, Kt.
Goulding, Sir (William) Lingard Walter, Bt. (1904)
Gourlay, Gen. Sir (Basil) Ian (Spencer), KCB, OBE, MC, RM
Gourlay, Sir Simon Alexander, Kt.
Govan, Sir Lawrence Herbert, Kt.
Gow, Gen. Sir (James) Michael, GCB
Gowans, Sir James Learmonth, Kt., CBE, FRCP, FRS
Graaff, Sir de Villiers, Bt., MBE (1911)
Grabham, Sir Anthony Henry, Kt.
Graham, Sir Alexander Michael, GBE
Graham, Sir Charles Spencer Richard, Bt. (1783)
Graham, Sir James Bellingham, Bt. (1662)
Graham, Sir James Thompson, Kt., CMG
Graham, Sir John Alexander Noble, Bt., GCMG (1906)
Graham, Sir John Moodie, Bt. (1964)
Graham, Sir Norman William, Kt., CB
Graham, Sir Peter, KCB, QC
Graham, Sir Peter Alfred, Kt., OBE
Graham, Lt.-Gen. Sir Peter Walter, KCB, CBE
†Graham, Sir Ralph Stuart, Bt. (1629)

Graham, Hon. Sir Samuel Horatio, Kt., CMG, OBE
Grandy, Marshal of the Royal Air Force Sir John, GCB, GCVO, KBE, DSO
Grant, Sir Archibald, Bt. (s. 1705)
Grant, Sir Clifford, Kt.
Grant, Sir (John) Anthony, Kt., MP
Grant, Sir (Matthew) Alistair, Kt.
Grant, Sir Patrick Alexander Benedict, Bt. (s. 1688)
Gray, Sir John Archibald Browne, Kt., SC.D., FRS
Gray, Vice-Adm. Sir John Michael Dudgeon, KBE, CB
Gray, Sir John Walton David, KBE, CMG
Gray, Lt.-Gen. Sir Michael Stuart, KCB, OBE
Gray, Sir Robert McDowall (Robin), Kt.
Gray, Sir William Hume, Bt. (1917)
Gray, Sir William Stevenson, Kt.
Graydon, Air Chief Marshal Sir Michael James, GCB, CBE
Grayson, Sir Jeremy Brian Vincent Harrington, Bt. (1922)
Green, Sir Allan David, KCB, QC
Green, Hon. Sir Guy Stephen Montague, KBE
Green, Sir Kenneth, Kt.
Green, Sir Owen Whitley, Kt.
†Green, Sir Stephen Lycett, Bt., TD (1886)
Greenaway, Sir John Michael Burdick, Bt. (1933)
Greenborough, Sir John, KBE
Greenbury, Sir Richard, Kt.
Greene, Sir (John) Brian Massy-, Kt.
Greengross, Sir Alan David, Kt.
Greening, Rear-Adm. Sir Paul Woollven, GCVO
Greenwell, Sir Edward Bernard, Bt. (1906)
Gregson, Sir Peter Lewis, GCB
Greig, Sir (Henry Louis) Carron, KCVO, CBE
Grenside, Sir John Peter, Kt., CBE
Grey, Sir Anthony Dysart, Bt. (1814)
Grierson, Sir Michael John Bewes, Bt. (s. 1685)
Grierson, Sir Ronald Hugh, Kt.
Griffin, Adm. Sir Anthony Templer Frederick Griffith, GCB
Griffin, Maj. Sir (Arthur) John (Stewart), KCVO
Griffin, Sir (Charles) David, Kt., CBE
Griffiths, Sir Eldon Wylie, Kt.
Griffiths, Sir John Norton-, Bt. (1922)
Grimwade, Sir Andrew Sheppard, Kt., CBE
Grindrod, Most Revd John Basil Rowland, KBE
Grinstead, Sir Stanley Gordon, Kt.
Grose, Vice-Adm. Sir Alan, KBE
Grotrian, Sir Philip Christian Brent, Bt. (1934)
Grove, Sir Charles Gerald, Bt. (1874)
Grove, Sir Edmund Frank, KCVO
Grugeon, Sir John Drury, Kt.

Grylls, Sir (William) Michael (John), Kt., MP
Guinness, Sir Alec, Kt., CH, CBE
Guinness, Sir Howard Christian Sheldon, Kt., VRD
Guinness, Sir Kenelm Ernest Lee, Bt. (1867)
Guise, Sir John Grant, Bt. (1783)
Gujadhur, Sir Radhamohun, Kt., CMG
Gull, Sir Rupert William Cameron, Bt. (1872)
Gumbs, Sir Emile Rudolph, Kt.
Gunn, Prof. Sir John Currie, Kt., CBE
Gunn, Sir Robert Norman, Kt.
Gunn, Sir William Archer, KBE, CMG
†Gunning, Sir Charles Theodore, Bt. (1778)
Gunston, Sir John Wellesley, Bt. (1938)
Gurdon, Prof. Sir John Bertrand, Kt., D.phil., FRS
Guthrie, Gen. Sir Charles Ronald Llewelyn, GCB, LVO, OBE
Guthrie, Sir Malcolm Connop, Bt. (1936)
Guy, Gen. Sir Roland Kelvin, GCB, CBE, DSO
Habakkuk, Sir John Hrothgar, Kt., FBA
Hackett, Gen. Sir John Winthrop, GCB, CBE, DSO, MC
Hadfield, Sir Ronald, Kt., QPM
Hadlee, Sir Richard John, Kt., MBE
Hadley, Sir Leonard Albert, Kt.
Hague, Prof. Sir Douglas Chalmers, Kt., CBE
Halberg, Sir Murray Gordon, Kt., MBE
Hale, Prof. Sir John Rigby, Kt.
Hall, Sir Arnold Alexander, Kt., FRS, FEng.
Hall, Sir Basil Brodribb, KCB, MC, TD
Hall, Air Marshal Sir Donald Percy, KCB, CBE, AFC
Hall, Sir Douglas Basil, Bt., KCMG (s. 1687)
Hall, Sir Ernest, Kt., OBE
Hall, Sir (Frederick) John (Frank), Bt. (1923)
Hall, Sir John, Kt.
Hall, Sir John Bernard, Bt. (1919)
Hall, Sir Peter Edward, KBE, CMG
Hall, Sir Peter Reginald Frederick, Kt., CBE
Hall, Sir Robert de Zouche, KCMG
Hall, Brig. Sir William Henry, KBE, DSO, ED
Halliday, Vice-Adm. Sir Roy William, KBE, DSC
Hallinan, Sir (Adrian) Lincoln, Kt.
Halpern, Sir Ralph Mark, Kt.
Halsey, Revd Sir John Walter Brooke, Bt. (1920)
Halstead, Sir Ronald, Kt., CBE
Ham, Sir David Kenneth Rowe-, GBE
Hambling, Sir (Herbert) Hugh, Bt. (1924)
Hamburger, Sir Sidney Cyril, Kt., CBE

Hamer, *Hon.* Sir Rupert James, KCMG, ED

Hamill, Sir Patrick, Kt., QPM

Hamilton, *Rt. Hon.* Sir Archibald Gavin, Kt., MP

Hamilton, Sir Edward Sydney, Bt. (1776 and 1819)

Hamilton, Sir James Arnot, KCB, MBE, FEng.

Hamilton, Sir Malcolm William Bruce Stirling-, Bt. (s. 1673)

Hamilton, Sir Michael Aubrey, Kt.

Hamilton, Sir (Robert Charles) Richard Caradoc, Bt. (s. 1646)

Hammett, *Hon.* Sir Clifford James, Kt.

Hammick, Sir Stephen George, Bt. (1834)

Hampel, Sir Ronald Claus, Kt.

Hampshire, Sir Stuart Newton, Kt., FBA

Hancock, Sir David John Stowell, KCB

Hancock, *Air Marshal* Sir Valston Eldridge, KBE, CB, DFC

Hand, *Most Revd* Geoffrey David, KBE

Handley, Sir David John Davenport-, Kt., OBE

Hanham, Sir Michael William, Bt., DFC (1667)

Hanley, Sir Michael Bowen, KCB

Hanmer, Sir John Wyndham Edward, Bt. (1774)

Hann, Sir James, Kt., CBE

Hannam, Sir John Gordon, Kt., MP

Hannay, Sir David Hugh Alexander, GCMG

Hanson, Sir Anthony Leslie Oswald, Bt. (1887)

†Hanson, Sir Charles Rupert Patrick, Bt. (1918)

Hanson, Sir John Gilbert, KCMG, CBE

Hardcastle, Sir Alan John, Kt.

Harders, Sir Clarence Waldemar, Kt., OBE

Hardie, Sir Charles Edgar Mathewes, Kt., CBE

Hardie, Sir Douglas Fleming, Kt., CBE

Harding, Sir Christopher George Francis, Kt.

Harding, Sir George William, KCMG, CVO

Harding, *Marshal of the Royal Air Force* Sir Peter Robin, GCB

Harding, Sir Roy Pollard, Kt., CBE

Hardman, Sir Henry, KCB

Hardy, Sir David William, Kt.

Hardy, Sir James Gilbert, Kt., OBE

Hardy, Sir Rupert John, Bt. (1876)

Hare, Sir Philip Leigh, Bt. (1818)

Harford, Sir (John) Timothy, Bt. (1934)

Hargroves, *Brig.* Sir Robert Louis, Kt., CBE

Harington, *Gen.* Sir Charles Henry Pepys, GCB, CBE, DSO, MC

Harington, Sir Nicholas John, Bt. (1611)

Harland, *Air Marshal* Sir Reginald Edward Wynyard, KBE, CB

Harley, *Lt.-Gen.* Sir Alexander George Hamilton, KBE, CB

Harman, *Gen.* Sir Jack Wentworth, GCB, OBE, MC

Harman, *Hon.* Sir Jeremiah LeRoy, Kt.

Harmsworth, Sir Hildebrand Harold, Bt. (1922)

Harpham, Sir William, KBE, CMG

Harris, *Prof.* Sir Alan James, Kt., CBE, FEng.

Harris, Sir Anthony Kyrle Travers, Bt. (1953)

Harris, *Prof.* Sir Henry, Kt., FRCP, FRCPath., FRS

Harris, *Lt.-Gen.* Sir Ian Cecil, KBE, CB, DSO

Harris, Sir Jack Wolfred Ashford, Bt. (1932)

Harris, *Air Marshal* Sir John Hulme, KCB, CBE

Harris, Sir William Gordon, KBE, CB, FEng.

Harrison, *Prof.* Sir Donald Frederick Norris, Kt., FRCS

Harrison, Sir Ernest Thomas, Kt., OBE

Harrison, Sir Francis Alexander Lyle, Kt., MBE, QC

Harrison, *Surgeon Vice-Adm.* Sir John Albert Bews, KBE

Harrison, *Hon.* Sir (John) Richard, Kt., ED

Harrison, *Hon.* Sir Michael Guy Vicat, Kt.

Harrison, Sir Michael James Harwood, Bt. (1961)

Harrison, *Prof.* Sir Richard John, Kt., FRS

Harrison, Sir (Robert) Colin, Bt. (1922)

Harrison, Sir Terence, Kt., FEng.

Harrop, Sir Peter John, KCB

Hart, Sir Graham Allan, KCB

Hartley, *Air Marshal* Sir Christopher Harold, KCB, CBE, DFC, AFC

Hartley, Sir Frank, Kt., CBE, Ph.D.

†Hartopp, *Lt. Cdr* Sir Kenneth Alston Cradock-, Bt., MBE, DSC (1796)

Hartwell, Sir (Francis) Anthony Charles Peter, Bt. (1805)

Harvey, Sir Charles Richard Musgrave, Bt. (1933)

Haselhurst, Sir Alan Gordon Barraclough, Kt., MP

Haskard, Sir Cosmo Dugal Patrick Thomas, KCMG, MBE

Haslam, *Hon.* Sir Alec Leslie, Kt.

Haslam, *Rear-Adm.* Sir David William, KBE, CB

Hassan, Sir Joshua Abraham, GBE, KCMG, LVO, QC

Hassett, *Gen.* Sir Francis George, KBE, CB, DSO, LVO

Hastings, Sir Stephen Lewis Edmonstone, Kt., MC

Hatty, *Hon.* Sir Cyril James, Kt.

Haughton, Sir James, Kt., CBE, QPM

Havelock, Sir Wilfrid Bowen, Kt.

Hawkins, Sir Arthur Ernest, Kt.

†Hawkins, Sir Howard Caesar, Bt. (1778)

Hawkins, Sir Paul Lancelot, Kt., TD

Hawley, Sir Donald Frederick, KCMG, MBE

†Hawley, Sir Henry Nicholas, Bt. (1795)

Haworth, Sir Philip, Bt. (1911)

Hawthorne, *Prof.* Sir William Rede, Kt., SC.D., FRS, FEng.

Hay, Sir David Osborne, Kt., CBE, DSO

Hay, Sir David Russell, Kt., CBE, FRCP, MD

Hay, Sir Hamish Grenfell, Kt.

Hay, Sir James Brian Dalrymple-, Bt. (1798)

†Hay, Sir John Erroll Audley, Bt. (s. 1663)

†Hay, Sir Ronald Frederick Hamilton, Bt. (s. 1703)

Haydon, Sir Walter Robert, KCMG

Hayes, Sir Brian David, GCB

Hayes, Sir Claude James, KCMG

Hayes, *Vice-Adm.* Sir John Osier Chattock, KCB, OBE

Hayr, *Air Marshal* Sir Kenneth William, KCB, KBE, AFC

Hayward, Sir Anthony William Byrd, Kt.

Hayward, Sir Jack Arnold, Kt., OBE

Haywood, Sir Harold, KCVO, OBE

Head, Sir Francis David Somerville, Bt. (1838)

Healey, Sir Charles Edward Chadwyck-, Bt. (1919)

Heap, Sir Desmond, Kt.

Heap, Sir Peter William, KCMG

Heath, *Rt. Hon.* Sir Edward Richard George, KG, MBE, MP

Heath, Sir Mark Evelyn, KCVO, CMG

Heath, *Air Marshal* Sir Maurice Lionel, KBE, CB, CVO

Heathcote, *Brig.* Sir Gilbert Simon, Bt., CBE (1733)

Heathcote, Sir Michael Perryman, Bt. (1733)

Heatley, Sir Peter, Kt., CBE

Heaton, Sir Yvo Robert Henniker-, Bt. (1912)

Heiser, Sir Terence Michael, GCB

Hellaby, Sir (Frederick Reed) Alan, Kt.

Henderson, Sir Denys Hartley, Kt.

Henderson, Sir (John) Nicholas, GCMG, KCVO

Henderson, Sir William MacGregor, Kt., D.SC.

Henley, Sir Douglas Owen, KCB

Henley, *Rear-Adm.* Sir Joseph Charles Cameron, KCVO, CB

Hennessy, Sir James Patrick Ivan, KBE, CMG

†Henniker, Sir Adrian Chandos, Bt. (1813)

Henry, Sir Denis Aynsley, Kt., OBE, QC

Henry, *Rt. Hon.* Sir Denis Robert Maurice, Kt.

Henry, *Hon.* Sir Geoffrey Arama, KBE
Henry, Sir James Holmes, Bt., CMG, MC, TD, QC (1923)
Henry, *Hon.* Sir Trevor Ernest, Kt.
Hepburn, Sir John Alastair Trant Kidd Buchan-, Bt. (1815)
Herbecq, Sir John Edward, KCB
Herbert, *Adm.* Sir Peter Geoffrey Marshall, KCB, OBE
Hermon, Sir John Charles, Kt., OBE, QPM
Heron, Sir Conrad Frederick, KCB, OBE
Heron, Sir Michael Gilbert, Kt.
Hervey, Sir Roger Blaise Ramsay, KCVO, CMG
Heseltine, *Rt. Hon.* Sir William Frederick Payne, GCB, GCVO
Hetherington, Sir Arthur Ford, Kt., DSC, FEng.
Hetherington, Sir Thomas Chalmers, KCB, CBE, TD, QC
Hewetson, Sir Christopher Raynor, Kt., TD
Hewett, Sir Peter John Smithson, Bt., MM (1813)
Hewitt, Sir (Cyrus) Lenox (Simson), Kt., OBE
Hewitt, Sir Nicholas Charles Joseph, Bt. (1921)
Heygate, Sir Richard John Gage, Bt. (1831)
Heyman, Sir Horace William, Kt.
Heywood, Sir Peter, Bt. (1838)
Hezlet, *Vice-Adm.* Sir Arthur Richard, KBE, CB, DSO, DSC
Hibbert, Sir Jack, KCB
Hibbert, Sir Reginald Alfred, GCMG
Hickey, Sir Justin, Kt.
Hickman, Sir (Richard) Glenn, Bt. (1903)
Hicks, Sir Robert, Kt., MP
Hidden, *Hon.* Sir Anthony Brian, Kt.
Hielscher, Sir Leo Arthur, Kt.
Higgins, Sir Christopher Thomas, Kt.
Higgins, *Hon.* Sir Malachy Joseph, Kt.
Higgins, *Rt. Hon.* Sir Terence Langley, KBE, MP
Higginson, Sir Gordon Robert, Kt., ph.D., FEng.
Highgate, Sir James Brown, Kt., CBE
Hildyard, Sir David Henry Thoroton, KCMG, DFC
Hill, Sir Alexander Rodger Erskine-, Bt. (1945)
Hill, Sir Arthur Alfred, Kt., CBE
Hill, Sir Brian John, Kt.
Hill, Sir James Frederick, Bt. (1917)
Hill, Sir John McGregor, Kt., ph.D., FEng.
Hill, Sir John Maxwell, Kt., CBE, DFC
†Hill, Sir John Rowley, Bt. (I. 1779)
Hill, *Vice-Adm.* Sir Robert Charles Finch, KBE, FEng.
Hill, Sir (Stanley) James (Allen), Kt., MP
Hillary, Sir Edmund, KG, KBE
Hillhouse, Sir (Robert) Russell, KCB

Hills, Sir Graham John, Kt.
Hine, *Air Chief Marshal* Sir Patrick Bardon, GCB, GBE
Hines, Sir Colin Joseph, Kt., OBE
Hinsley, *Prof.* Sir Francis Harry, Kt., OBE, FBA
Hirsch, *Prof.* Sir Peter Bernhard, Kt., ph.D., FRS
Hirst, *Rt. Hon.* Sir David Cozens-Hardy, Kt.
Hirst, Sir Michael William, Kt.
Hoare, Sir Peter Richard David, Bt. (1786)
Hoare, Sir Timothy Edward Charles, Bt., OBE (I. 1784)
Hobart, Sir John Vere, Bt. (1914)
Hobday, Sir Gordon Ivan, Kt.
Hobhouse, Sir Charles John Spinney, Bt. (1812)
Hobhouse, *Rt. Hon.* Sir John Stewart, Kt.
Hockaday, Sir Arthur Patrick, KCB, CMG
Hockley, *Gen.* Sir Anthony Heritage Farrar-, GBE, KCB, DSO, MC
†Hodge, Sir Andrew Rowland, Bt. (1921)
Hodge, Sir Julian Stephen Alfred, Kt.
Hodges, *Air Chief Marshal* Sir Lewis MacDonald, KCB, CBE, DSO, DFC
Hodgkin, *Prof.* Sir Alan Lloyd, OM, KBE, FRS, SC.D.
Hodgkin, Sir Gordon Howard Eliot, Kt., CBE
Hodgkinson, *Air Chief Marshal* Sir (William) Derek, KCB, CBE, DFC, AFC
Hodgson, Sir Maurice Arthur Eric, Kt., FEng.
Hodgson, *Hon.* Sir (Walter) Derek (Thornley), Kt.
Hodson, Sir Michael Robin Adderley, Bt. (I. 1789)
Hoffenberg, *Prof.* Sir Raymond, KBE
Hogg, Sir Christopher Anthony, Kt.
Hogg, Sir Edward William Lindsay-, Bt. (1905)
Hogg, *Vice-Adm.* Sir Ian Leslie Trower, KCB, DSC
Hogg, Sir John Nicholson, Kt., TD
†Hogg, Sir Michael David, Bt. (1846)
Holcroft, Sir Peter George Culcheth, Bt. (1921)
Holden, Sir David Charles Beresford, KBE, CB, ERD
Holden, Sir Edward, Bt. (1893)
Holden, Sir John David, Bt. (1919)
Holden, Sir John Henry, Bt. (1898)
Holder, *Air Marshal* Sir Paul Davie, KBE, CB, DSO, DFC, ph.D.
Holderness, Sir Richard William, Bt. (1920)
Holdgate, Sir Martin Wyatt, Kt., CB, ph.D.
Holdsworth, Sir (George) Trevor, Kt.
Holland, *Hon.* Sir Alan Douglas, Kt.
Holland, *Hon.* Sir Christopher John, Kt.

Holland, Sir Clifton Vaughan, Kt.
Holland, Sir Geoffrey, KCB
Holland, Sir Guy (Hope), Bt. (1917)
Holland, Sir Kenneth Lawrence, Kt., CBE, QFSM
Holland, Sir Philip Welsby, Kt.
Holliday, *Prof.* Sir Frederick George Thomas, Kt., CBE, FRSE
Hollings, *Hon.* Sir (Alfred) Kenneth, Kt., MC
Hollis, *Hon.* Sir Anthony Barnard, Kt.
Hollom, Sir Jasper Quintus, KBE
Holloway, *Hon.* Sir Barry Blyth, KBE
Holm, Sir Carl Henry, Kt., OBE
Holman, *Hon.* Sir (Edward) James, Kt.
Holmes, *Prof.* Sir Frank Wakefield, Kt.
Holmes, Sir Maurice Andrew, Kt.
Holmes, Sir Peter Fenwick, Kt., MC
Holroyd, *Air Marshal* Sir Frank Martyn, KBE, CB, FEng.
Holt, *Prof.* Sir James Clarke, Kt.
Holt, Sir Michael, Kt., CBE
Home, Sir William Dundas, Bt. (s. 1671)
Honeycombe, *Prof.* Sir Robert William Kerr, Kt., FRS, FEng.
Honywood, Sir Filmer Courtenay William, Bt. (1660)
Hood, Sir Harold Joseph, Bt., TD (1922)
Hookway, Sir Harry Thurston, Kt.
Hoole, Sir Arthur Hugh, Kt.
Hooper, *Hon.* Sir Anthony, Kt.
Hope, Sir (Charles) Peter, KCMG, TD
Hope, Sir Colin Frederick Newton, Kt.
Hope, *Rt. Revd and Rt. Hon.* David Michael, KCVO
Hope, Sir John Carl Alexander, Bt. (s. 1628)
Hopkin, Sir David Armand, Kt.
Hopkin, Sir (William Aylsham) Bryan, Kt., CBE
Hopkins, Sir Anthony Philip, Kt., CBE
Hopkins, Sir Michael John, Kt., CBE, RA, RIBA
Hopwood, *Prof.* Sir David Alan, Kt., FRS
Hordern, *Rt. Hon.* Sir Peter Maudslay, Kt., MP
Horlick, *Vice-Adm.* Sir Edwin John, KBE, FEng.
Horlick, Sir James Cunliffe William, Bt. (1914)
Horlock, *Prof.* Sir John Harold, Kt., FRS, FEng.
Hornby, Sir Derek Peter, Kt.
Hornby, Sir Simon Michael, Kt.
Horne, Sir Alan Gray Antony, Bt. (1929)
Horsfall, Sir John Musgrave, Bt., MC, TD (1909)
Horsley, *Air Marshal* Sir (Beresford) Peter (Torrington), KCB, CBE, LVO, AFC
†Hort, Sir Andrew Edwin Fenton, Bt. (1767)
Hosker, Sir Gerald Albery, KCB, QC

Hoskyns, Sir Benedict Leigh, Bt.
(1676)
Hoskyns, Sir John Austin
Hungerford Leigh, Kt.
Hotung, Sir Joseph Edward, Kt.
Houghton, Sir John Theodore, Kt.,
CBE, FRS
†Houldsworth, Sir Richard Thomas
Reginald, Bt. (1887)
Hounsfield, Sir Godfrey Newbold,
Kt., CBE
House, Lt.-Gen. Sir David George,
GCB, KCVO, CBE, MC
Houssemayne du Boulay, Sir Roger
William, KCVO, CMG
Howard, Sir (Hamilton) Edward de
Coucey, Bt., GBE (1955)
Howard, Prof. Sir Michael Eliot, Kt.,
CBE, MC
Howard, Maj.-Gen. Lord Michael
Fitzalan-, GCVO, CB, CBE, MC
Howard, Sir Walter Stewart, Kt., MBE
Howell, Sir Ralph Frederic, Kt., MP
Howells, Sir Eric Waldo Benjamin,
Kt., CBE
Howlett, Gen. Sir Geoffrey Hugh
Whitby, KBE, MC
Hoyle, Prof. Sir Fred, Kt., FRS
Hoyos, Hon. Sir Fabriciano
Alexander, Kt.
Huddie, Sir David Patrick, Kt., FENG.
Hudson, Sir Havelock Henry
Trevor, Kt.
Hudson, Lt.-Gen. Sir Peter, KCB, CBE
Huggins, Hon. Sir Alan Armstrong,
Kt.
Hughes, Sir David Collingwood, Bt.
(1773)
Hughes, Prof. Sir Edward Stuart
Reginald, Kt., CBE
Hughes, Sir Jack William, Kt.
Hughes, Air Marshal Sir (Sidney
Weetman) Rochford, KCB, CBE, AFC
Hughes, Sir Trevor Denby Lloyd-,
Kt.
Hughes, Sir Trevor Poulton, KCB
Hugo, Lt.-Col. Sir John Mandeville,
KCVO, OBE
Hull, Prof. Sir David, Kt.
†Hulse, Sir Edward Jeremy
Westrow, Bt. (1739)
Hume, Sir Alan Blyth, Kt., CB
Humphreys, Sir Olliver William, Kt.,
CBE
Humphreys, Sir (Raymond Evelyn)
Myles, Kt.
Hunn, Sir Jack Kent, Kt., CMG
Hunt, Sir David Wathen Stather,
KCMG, OBE
Hunt, Sir John Leonard, Kt., MP
Hunt, Adm. Sir Nicholas John
Streynsham, GCB, LVO
Hunt, Sir Peter John, Kt., FRICS
Hunt, Sir Rex Masterman, Kt., CMG
Hunt, Sir Robert Frederick, Kt., CBE,
FENG.
Hunter, Hon. Sir Alexander Albert,
KBE
Hunter, Sir Alistair John, KCMG
Hunter, Sir Ian Bruce Hope, Kt., MBE

Hunter, Prof. Sir Laurence Colvin,
Kt., CBE, FRSE
Hurn, Sir (Francis) Roger, Kt.
Hurrell, Sir Anthony Gerald, KCVO,
CMG
Husbands, Sir Clifford Straugh,
GCMG
Hutchinson, Hon. Sir Ross, Kt., DFC
Hutchison, Lt.-Cdr. Sir (George) Ian
Clark, Kt., RN
Hutchison, Rt. Hon. Sir Michael, Kt.
Hutchison, Sir Peter, Bt., CBE (1939)
Hutchison, Sir Peter Craft, Bt. (1956)
Hutton, Rt. Hon. Sir (James) Brian
Edward, Kt.
Huxley, Prof. Sir Andrew Fielding,
Kt., OM, FRS
Huxtable, Gen. Sir Charles Richard,
KCB, CBE
Hyatali, Hon. Sir Isaac Emanuel, Kt.
Hyslop, Sir Robert John (Robin)
Maxwell-, Kt.
Ibbs, Sir (John) Robin, KBE
Imbert, Sir Peter Michael, Kt., QPM
Imray, Sir Colin Henry, KBE, CMG
Inge, Field Marshal Sir Peter
Anthony, GCB
Ingham, Sir Bernard, Kt.
Ingilby, Sir Thomas Colvin William,
Bt. (1866)
Inglis, Sir Brian Scott, Kt.
Inglis of Glencorse, Sir Roderick
John, Bt. (s. 1703)
Ingram, Sir James Herbert Charles,
Bt. (1893)
Ingram, Sir John Henderson, Kt., CBE
Inkin, Sir Geoffrey David, Kt., OBE
†Innes, Sir David Charles Kenneth
Gordon, Bt. (NS 1686)
Innes of Edingight, Sir Malcolm
Rognvald, KCVO
Innes, Sir Peter Alexander Berowald,
Bt. (s. 1628)
Inniss, Hon. Sir Clifford de Lisle, Kt.
Irvine, Sir Donald Hamilton, Kt.,
CBE, MD, FRCGP
Irvine, Dr Sir Robin Orlando
Hamilton, Kt.
Irving, Prof. Sir Miles Horsfall, Kt.,
MD, FRCS, FRCSE
Isaacs, Sir Jeremy Israel, Kt.
Isham, Sir Ian Vere Gyles, Bt. (1627)
Jack, Hon. Sir Alieu Sulayman, Kt.
Jack, Sir David, Kt., CBE, FRS, FRSE
Jack, Sir David Emmanuel, GCMG,
MBE
Jackson, Air Chief Marshal Sir
Brendan James, GCB
Jackson, Sir (John) Edward, KCMG
Jackson, Sir Michael Roland, Bt.
(1902)
Jackson, Sir Nicholas Fane St
George, Bt. (1913)
Jackson, Sir Robert, Bt. (1815)
Jackson, Gen. Sir William Godfrey
Fothergill, GBE, KCB, MC
Jackson, Sir William Thomas, Bt.
(1869)
Jacob, Sir Isaac Hai, Kt., QC

Jacob, Hon. Sir Robert Raphael
Hayim (Robin), Kt.
Jacobi, Sir Derek George, Kt., CBE
Jacobi, Dr Sir James Edward, Kt., OBE
Jacobs, Sir David Anthony, Kt.
Jacobs, Hon. Sir Kenneth Sydney, KBE
Jacobs, Sir Piers, KBE
Jacobs, Sir Wilfred Ebenezer, GCMG,
GCVO, OBE, QC
Jacomb, Sir Martin Wakefield, Kt.
Jaffray, Sir William Otho, Bt. (1892)
James, Sir Cynlais Morgan, KCMG
James, Sir Gerard Bowes Kingston,
Bt. (1823)
James, Sir Robert Vidal Rhodes, Kt.
James, Sir Stanislaus Anthony, GCMG,
OBE
Jamieson, Air Marshal Sir David
Ewan, KBE, CB
Jansen, Sir Ross Malcolm, KBE
Jardine, Sir Andrew Colin Douglas,
Bt. (1916)
Jardine, Maj. Sir (Andrew) Rupert
(John) Buchanan-, Bt., MC (1885)
Jardine of Applegirth, Sir Alexander
Maule, Bt. (s. 1672)
Jarratt, Sir Alexander Anthony, Kt.,
CB
Jawara, Hon. Sir Dawda Kairaba, Kt.
Jay, Sir Antony Rupert, Kt., CVO
Jeewoolall, Sir Ramesh, Kt.
Jefferson, Sir George Rowland, Kt.,
CBE, FENG.
Jefferson, Sir Mervyn Stewart
Dunnington-, Bt. (1958)
Jeffreys, Prof. Sir Alec John, Kt., FRS
Jeffries, Hon. Sir John Francis, Kt.
Jehangir, Sir Hirji, Bt. (1908)
Jejeebhoy, Sir Rustom, Bt. (1857)
Jenkins, Sir Brian Garton, GBE
Jenkins, Sir Elgar Spencer, Kt., OBE
Jenkins, Sir Michael Romilly Heald,
KCMG
Jenkinson, Sir John Banks, Bt. (1661)
†Jenks, Sir Maurice Arthur Brian, Bt.
(1932)
Jennings, Prof. Sir Robert Yewdall,
Kt., QC
Jephcott, Sir (John) Anthony, Bt.
(1962)
Jessel, Sir Charles John, Bt. (1883)
Jewkes, Sir Gordon Wesley, KCMG
Joel, Hon. Sir Asher Alexander, KBE
John, Sir Rupert Godfrey, Kt.
Johns, Air Chief Marshal Sir Richard
Edward, KBE, CBE, LVO
Johnson, Rt. Hon. Sir David Powell
Croom-, Kt., DSC, VRD
Johnson, Gen. Sir Garry Dene, KCB,
OBE, MC
Johnson, Sir John Rodney, KCMG
†Johnson, Sir Patrick Eliot, Bt. (1818)
Johnson, Sir Peter Colpoys Paley, Bt.
(1755)
Johnson, Hon. Sir Robert Lionel, Kt.
Johnson, Sir Ronald Ernest Charles,
Kt., CB
Johnson, Sir Vassel Godfrey, Kt., CBE
Johnston, Sir (David) Russell, Kt., MP

Johnston, Sir John Baines, GCMG, KCVO

Johnston, Lt.-Col. Sir John Frederick Dame, GCVO, MC

Johnston, Lt.-Gen. Sir Maurice Robert, KCB, OBE

Johnston, Sir Thomas Alexander, Bt. (s. 1626)

Johnston, Sir William Robert Patrick Knox- (Sir Robin), Kt., CBE, RD

Johnstone, Sir (George) Richard Douglas, Bt. (s. 1700)

Johnstone, Sir (John) Raymond, Kt., CBE

Jolliffe, Sir Anthony Stuart, GBE

Jones, Gen. Sir (Charles) Edward Webb, KCB, CBE

Jones, Sir Christopher Lawrence-, Bt. (1831)

Jones, Sir David Akers-, KBE, CMG

Jones, Air Marshal Sir Edward Gordon, KCB, CBE, DSO, DFC

Jones, Sir (Edward) Martin Furnival, Kt., CBE

Jones, Sir Ewart Ray Herbert, Kt., D.SC., Ph.D., FRS

Jones, Sir Francis Avery, Kt., CBE, FRCP

Jones, Sir Gordon Pearce, Kt.

Jones, Sir Harry Ernest, Kt., CBE

Jones, Sir (John) Derek Alun-, Kt.

Jones, Sir John Henry Harvey-, Kt., MBE

Jones, Sir John Lewis, KCB, CMG

Jones, Sir John Prichard-, Bt. (1910)

Jones, Sir Keith Stephen, Kt.

Jones, Hon. Sir Kenneth George Illtyd, Kt.

Jones, Sir (Owen) Trevor, Kt.

Jones, Sir (Peter) Hugh (Jefferd) Lloyd-, Kt.

Jones, Sir Richard Anthony Lloyd, KCB

Jones, Sir Robert Edward, Kt.

Jones, Sir Simon Warley Frederick Benton, Bt. (1919)

Jones, Sir (Thomas) Philip, Kt., CB

Jones, Sir (William) Emrys, Kt.

Jones, Hon. Sir William Lloyd Mars-, Kt., MBE

Jones, Sir Wynn Normington Hugh-, Kt., LVO

†Joseph, Hon. Sir James Samuel, Bt. (1943)

Jowitt, Hon. Sir Edwin Frank, Kt.

Joyce, Lt.-Gen. Sir Robert John Hayman-, KCB, CBE

Judge, Rt. Hon. Sir Igor, Kt.

Judge, Sir Paul Rupert, Kt.

Jugnauth, Rt. Hon. Sir Anerood, KCMG, QC

Jungius, Vice-Adm. Sir James George, KBE

Junor, Sir John Donald Brown, Kt.

Jupp, Hon. Sir Kenneth Graham, Kt., MC

Kaberry, Hon. Sir Christopher Donald, Bt. (1960)

Kalms, Sir (Harold) Stanley, Kt.

Kalo, Sir Kwamala, Kt., MBE

Kan Yuet-Keung, Sir, GBE

Kapi, Hon. Sir Mari, Kt., CBE

Kaputin, Sir John Rumet, KBE, CMG

Katsina, The Emir of, KBE, CMG

Katz, Sir Bernard, Kt., FRS

Kausimae, Sir David Nanau, KBE

Kavali, Sir Thomas, Kt., OBE

Kawharu, Prof. Sir Ian Hugh, Kt.

Kay, Prof. Sir Andrew Watt, Kt.

Kay, Hon. Sir John William, Kt.

Kay, Hon. Sir Maurice Ralph, Kt.

Kaye, Sir David Alexander Gordon, Bt. (1923)

Kaye, Sir Emmanuel, Kt., CBE

Kaye, Sir John Phillip Lister Lister-, Bt. (1812)

Keane, Sir Richard Michael, Bt. (1801)

Keatinge, Sir Edgar Mayne, Kt., CBE

Keeble, Sir (Herbert Ben) Curtis, GCMG

Keene, Hon. Sir David Wolfe, Kt.

Keith, Prof. Sir James, KBE

Kellett, Sir Stanley Charles, Bt. (1801)

Kelly, Sir David Robert Corbett, Kt., CBE

Kelly, Rt. Hon. Sir (John William) Basil, Kt.

Kelly, Sir William Theodore, Kt., OBE

Kemball, Air Marshal Sir (Richard) John, KCB, CBE

Kemp, Sir (Edward) Peter, KCB

Kendrew, Sir John Cowdery, Kt., CBE, SC.D., FRS

Kenilorea, Rt. Hon. Sir Peter, KBE

Kennard, Lt.-Col. Sir George Arnold Ford, Bt. (1891)

Kennaway, Sir John Lawrence, Bt. (1791)

Kennedy, Sir Clyde David Allen, Kt.

Kennedy, Sir Francis, KCMG, CBE

Kennedy, Hon. Sir Ian Alexander, Kt.

Kennedy, Sir Ludovic Henry Coverley, Kt.

†Kennedy, Sir Michael Edward, Bt., (1836)

Kennedy, Rt. Hon. Sir Paul Joseph Morrow, Kt.

Kennedy, Air Chief Marshal Sir Thomas Lawrie, GCB, AFC

Kennedy-Good, Sir John, KBE

Kenny, Sir Anthony John Patrick, Kt., D.phil., D.Litt., FBA

Kenny, Gen. Sir Brian Leslie Graham, GCB, CBE

Kent, Sir Harold Simcox, GCB, QC

Kenyon, Sir George Henry, Kt.

Kermode, Sir (John) Frank, Kt., FBA

Kermode, Sir Ronald Graham Quale, KBE

Kerr, Hon. Sir Brian Francis, Kt.

Kerr, Adm. Sir John Beverley, GCB

Kerr, Sir John Olav, KCMG

Kerr, Rt. Hon. Sir Michael Robert Emanuel, Kt.

Kerruish, Sir (Henry) Charles, Kt., OBE

Kerry, Sir Michael James, KCB, QC

Kershaw, Sir (John) Anthony, Kt., MC

Keswick, Sir John Chippendale Lindley, Kt.

Kidd, Sir Robert Hill, KBE, CB

Kikau, Ratu Sir Jone Latianara, KBE

Killen, Hon. Denis James, KCMG

Killick, Sir John Edward, GCMG

Kimber, Sir Charles Dixon, Bt. (1904)

Kinahan, Sir Robert George Caldwell, Kt., ERD

King, Sir Albert, Kt., OBE

King, Gen. Sir Frank Douglas, GCB, MBE

King, Sir John Christopher, Bt. (1888)

King, Vice-Adm. Sir Norman Ross Dutton, KBE

King, Sir Richard Brian Meredith, KCB, MC

King, Sir Wayne Alexander, Bt. (1815)

Kingman, Prof. Sir John Frank Charles, Kt., FRS

Kingsland, Sir Richard, Kt., CBE, DFC

Kingsley, Sir Patrick Graham Toler, KCVO

Kinloch, Sir David, Bt. (s. 1686)

Kinloch, Sir David Oliphant, Bt. (1873)

Kipalan, Sir Albert, Kt.

Kirby, Hon. Sir Richard Clarence, Kt.

Kirkham, Sir Graham, Kt.

Kirkpatrick, Sir Ivone Elliott, Bt. (s. 1685)

Kirkwood, Hon. Sir Andrew Tristram Hammett, Kt.

Kirwan, Sir (Archibald) Laurence Patrick, KCMG, TD

Kitcatt, Sir Peter Julian, Kt., CB

Kitson, Gen. Sir Frank Edward, GBE, KCB, MC

Kitson, Sir Timothy Peter Geoffrey, Kt.

Kleinwort, Sir Richard Drake, Bt. (1909)

Klug, Sir Aaron, Kt., OM

Kneller, Sir Alister Arthur, Kt.

Knight, Sir Allan Walton, Kt., CMG

Knight, Sir Arthur William, Kt.

Knight, Sir Harold Murray, KBE, DSC

Knight, Air Chief Marshal Sir Michael William Patrick, KCB, AFC

Knill, Sir John Kenelm Stuart, Bt. (1893)

Knill, Prof. Sir John Lawrence, Kt., FEng.

Knott, Sir John Laurence, Kt., CBE

Knowles, Sir Charles Francis, Bt. (1765)

Knowles, Sir Durward Randolph, Kt., OBE

Knowles, Sir Leonard Joseph, Kt., CBE

Knowles, Sir Richard Marchant, Kt.

Knox, Sir Bryce Muir, KCVO, MC, TD

Knox, Sir David Laidlaw, Kt., MP

Knox, Hon. Sir John Leonard, Kt.

Knox, Hon. Sir William Edward, Kt.

Koraea, Sir Thomas, Kt.

Kornberg, *Prof.* Sir Hans Leo, Kt., D.SC., SC.D., Ph.D., FRS
Korowi, Sir Wiwa, GCMG
Kroto, *Prof.* Sir Harold Walter, Kt., FRS
Krusin, Sir Stanley Marks, Kt., CB
Kulukundis, Sir Elias George (Eddie), Kt., OBE
Kurongku, *Most. Revd* Peter, KBE
Labouchere, Sir George Peter, GBE, KCMG
Lacon, Sir Edmund Vere, Bt. (1818)
Lacy, Sir Hugh Maurice Pierce, Bt. (1921)
Lacy, Sir John Trend, Kt., CBE
Laddie, *Hon.* Sir Hugh Ian Lang, Kt.
Laidlaw, Sir Christophor Charles Fraser, Kt.
Laing, Sir (John) Maurice, Kt.
Laing, Sir (William) Kirby, Kt., FEng.
Laird, Sir Gavin Harry, Kt., CBE
Lake, Sir (Atwell) Graham, Bt. (1711)
Laker, Sir Frederick Alfred, Kt.
Lakin, Sir Michael, Bt. (1909)
Laking, Sir George Robert, KCMG
Lamb, Sir Albert (Larry), Kt.
Lamb, Sir Albert Thomas, KBE, CMG, DFC
Lambert, Sir Anthony Edward, KCMG
Lambert, Sir John Henry, KCVO, CMG
†Lambert, Sir Peter John Biddulph, Bt. (1711)
Laming, Sir (William) Herbert, Kt., CBE
Lampl, Sir Frank William, Kt.
Landale, Sir David William Neil, KCVO
Landau, Sir Dennis Marcus, Kt.
Lane, Sir David William Stennis Stuart, Kt.
Lang, *Lt.-Gen.* Sir Derek Boileau, KCB, DSO, MC
Langham, Sir James Michael, Bt. (1660)
Langley, *Hon.* Sir Gordon Julian Hugh, Kt.
Langley, *Maj.-Gen.* Sir Henry Desmond Allen, KCVO, MBE
Langrishe, Sir Hercules Ralph Hume, Bt. (I. 1777)
Lankester, Sir Timothy Patrick, KCB
Lapun, *Hon.* Sir Paul, Kt.
Larcom, Sir (Charles) Christopher Royde, Bt. (1868)
Large, Sir Andrew McLeod Brooks, Kt.
Large, Sir Peter, Kt., CBE
Larmour, Sir Edward Noel, KCMG
Lasdun, Sir Denys Louis, Kt., CH, CBE, FRIBA
Latey, *Rt. Hon.* Sir John Brinsmead, Kt., MBE
Latham, *Hon.* Sir David Nicholas Ramsey, Kt.
Latham, Sir Michael Anthony, Kt.
Latham, Sir Richard Thomas Paul, Bt. (1919)
Latimer, Sir (Courtenay) Robert, Kt., CBE
Latimer, Sir Graham Stanley, KBE

Lauder, Sir Piers Robert Dick-, Bt. (s. 1690)
Laughton, Sir Anthony Seymour, Kt.
Laurantus, Sir Nicholas, Kt., MBE
Laurence, Sir Peter Harold, KCMG, MC
Laurie, Sir Robert Bayley Emilius, Bt. (1834)
Lauti, *Rt. Hon.* Sir Toaripi, GCMG
Lavan, *Hon.* Sir John Martin, Kt.
Law, *Adm.* Sir Horace Rochfort, GCB, OBE, DSC
Lawes, Sir (John) Michael Bennet, Bt. (1882)
Lawler, Sir Peter James, Kt., OBE
Lawrence, Sir David Roland Walter, Bt. (1906)
Lawrence, Sir Guy Kempton, Kt., DSO, OBE, DFC
Lawrence, Sir Ivan John, Kt., QC, MP
Lawrence, Sir John Patrick Grosvenor, Kt., CBE
Lawrence, Sir John Waldemar, Bt., OBE (1858)
Lawrence, Sir William Fettiplace, Bt. (1867)
Laws, *Hon.* Sir John Grant McKenzie, Kt.
Lawson, Sir Christopher Donald, Kt.
Lawson, *Col.* Sir John Charles Arthur Digby, Bt., DSO, MC (1900)
Lawson, Sir John Philip Howard-, Bt. (1841)
Lawson, *Gen.* Sir Richard George, KCB, DSO, OBE
Lawton, *Prof.* Sir Frank Ewart, Kt.
Lawton, *Rt. Hon.* Sir Frederick Horace, Kt.
Layard, *Adm.* Sir Michael Henry Gordon, KCB, CBE
Layfield, Sir Frank Henry Burland Willoughby, Kt., QC
Lea, *Vice-Adm.* Sir John Stuart Crosbie, KBE
Lea, Sir Thomas William, Bt. (1892)
Leach, *Admiral of the Fleet* Sir Henry Conyers, GCB
Leahy, Sir Daniel Joseph, Kt.
Leahy, Sir John Henry Gladstone, KCMG
Learmont, *Gen.* Sir John Hartley, KCB, CBE
Leask, *Lt.-Gen.* Sir Henry Lowther Ewart Clark, KCB, DSO, OBE
Leather, Sir Edwin Hartley Cameron, KCMG, KCVO
Leaver, Sir Christopher, GBE
Le Bailly, *Vice-Adm.* Sir Louis Edward Stewart Holland, KBE, CB
Le Cheminant, *Air Chief Marshal* Sir Peter de Lacey, GBE, KCB, DFC
Lechmere, Sir Berwick Hungerford, Bt. (1818)
Ledwidge, Sir (William) Bernard (John), KCMG
Lee, Sir Arthur James, KBE, MC
Lee, *Air Chief Marshal* Sir David John Pryer, GBE, CB
Lee, *Brig.* Sir Leonard Henry, Kt., CBE
Lee, Sir Quo-wei, Kt., CBE

Leeds, Sir Christopher Anthony, Bt. (1812)
Lees, Sir David Bryan, Kt.
Lees, Sir Thomas Edward, Bt. (1897)
Lees, Sir Thomas Harcourt Ivor, Bt. (1804)
Lees, Sir (William) Antony Clare, Bt. (1937)
Leese, Sir John Henry Vernon, Bt. (1908)
Le Fanu, *Maj.* Sir (George) Victor (Sheridan), KCVO
le Fleming, Sir Quintin John, Bt. (1705)
Legard, Sir Charles Thomas, Bt. (1660)
Legg, Sir Thomas Stuart, KCB, QC
Leggatt, *Rt. Hon.* Sir Andrew Peter, Kt.
Leggatt, Sir Hugh Frank John, Kt.
Leggett, Sir Clarence Arthur Campbell, Kt., MBE
Leigh, Sir Geoffrey Norman, Kt.
Leigh, Sir Richard Henry, Bt. (1918)
Leighton, Sir Michael John Bryan, Bt. (1693)
Leitch, Sir George, KCB, OBE
Leith, Sir Andrew George Forbes-, Bt. (1923)
Le Marchant, Sir Francis Arthur, Bt. (1841)
Lemon, Sir (Richard) Dawnay, Kt., CBE
Leng, *Gen.* Sir Peter John Hall, KCB, MBE, MC
Lennard, *Revd* Sir Hugh Dacre Barrett-, Bt. (1801)
Leon, Sir John Ronald, Bt. (1911)
Leonard, *Rt. Revd and Rt. Hon.* Graham Douglas, KCVO
Leonard, *Hon.* Sir (Hamilton) John, Kt.
Lepping, Sir George Geria Dennis, GCMG, MBE
Le Quesne, Sir (Charles) Martin, KCMG
Le Quesne, Sir (John) Godfray, Kt., QC
Leslie, Sir Colin Alan Bettridge, Kt.
Leslie, Sir John Norman Ide, Bt. (1876)
†Leslie, Sir (Percy) Theodore, Bt. (s. 1625)
Leslie, Sir Peter Evelyn, Kt.
Lester, Sir James Theodore, Kt., MP
Lethbridge, Sir Thomas Periam Hector Noel, Bt. (1804)
Leupena, Sir Tupua, GCMG, MBE
Levene, Sir Peter Keith, KBE
Lever, Sir (Tresham) Christopher Arthur Lindsay, Bt. (1911)
Levey, Sir Michael Vincent, Kt., LVO
Levine, Sir Montague Bernard, Kt.
Levinge, Sir Richard George Robin, Bt. (I. 1704)
Lewando, Sir Jan Alfred, Kt., CBE
Lewinton, Sir Christopher, Kt.
Lewis, Sir David Courtenay Mansel, KCVO
Lewis, Sir Kenneth, Kt.

Lewthwaite, *Brig.* Sir Rainald Gilfrid, Bt., CVO, OBE, MC (1927)

Ley, Sir Ian Francis, Bt. (1905)

Leyland, Sir Philip Vyvyan Naylor-, Bt. (1895)

Lickiss, Sir Michael Gillam, Kt.

Lickley, Sir Robert Lang, Kt., CBE, FEng.

Lidderdale, Sir David William Shuckburgh, KCB

Liggins, *Prof.* Sir Graham Collingwood, Kt., CBE, FRS

Lighthill, Sir (Michael) James, Kt., FRS

Lightman, *Hon.* Sir Gavin Anthony, Kt.

Lighton, Sir Thomas Hamilton, Bt. (I. 1791)

Lim, Sir Han-Hoe, Kt., CBE

Linacre, Sir (John) Gordon (Seymour), Kt., CBE, AFC, DFM

Lindop, Sir Norman, Kt.

Lindsay, Sir James Harvey Kincaid Stewart, Kt.

Lindsay, *Hon.* Sir John Edmund Frederic, Kt.

Lindsay, Sir Ronald Alexander, Bt., (1962)

Lipworth, Sir (Maurice) Sydney, Kt.

Lithgow, Sir William James, Bt. (1925)

Little, *Most Revd* Thomas Francis, KBE

Littler, Sir (James) Geoffrey, KCB

Livesay, *Adm.* Sir Michael Howard, KCB

Llewellyn, Sir Henry Morton, Bt., CBE (1922)

Llewelyn, Sir John Michael Dillwyn-Venables-, Bt. (1890)

Lloyd, Sir Ian Stewart, Kt.

Lloyd, Sir (John) Peter (Daniel), Kt.

Lloyd, Sir Nicholas Markley, Kt.

Lloyd, *Rt. Hon.* Sir Peter Robert Cable, Kt., MP

Lloyd, Sir Richard Ernest Butler, Bt. (1960)

Loader, Sir Leslie Thomas, Kt., CBE

Loane, *Most Revd* Marcus Lawrence, KBE

Lobo, Sir Rogerio Hyndman, Kt., CBE

Lock, *Cdr.* Sir (John) Duncan, Kt.

Lockhart, Sir Simon John Edward Francis Sinclair-, Bt. (s. 1636)

Loder, Sir Giles Rolls, Bt. (1887)

Lodge, Sir Thomas, Kt.

Lofthouse, Sir Geoffrey, Kt., MP

Logan, Sir Donald Arthur, KCMG

Logan, Sir Raymond Douglas, Kt.

Lokoloko, Sir Tore, GCMG, GCVO, OBE

Lombe, *Hon.* Sir Edward Christopher Evans-, Kt.

Longden, Sir Gilbert James Morley, Kt., MBE

Longmore, *Hon.* Sir Andrew Centlivres, Kt.

Loram, *Vice-Adm.* Sir David Anning, KCB, CVO

Lorimer, Sir (Thomas) Desmond, Kt.

Los, *Hon.* Sir Kubulan, Kt., CBE

Lovell, Sir (Alfred Charles) Bernard, Kt., OBE, FRS

Lovelock, Sir Douglas Arthur, KCB

Loveridge, Sir John Warren, Kt.

Lovill, Sir John Roger, Kt., CBE

Low, Sir Alan Roberts, Kt.

Low, Sir James Richard Morrison-, Bt. (1908)

Lowe, *Air Chief Marshal* Sir Douglas Charles, GCB, DFC, AFC

Lowe, Sir Thomas William Gordon, Bt. (1918)

Lowry, Sir John Patrick, Kt., CBE

Lowson, Sir Ian Patrick, Bt. (1951)

Lowther, *Maj.* Sir Charles Douglas, Bt. (1824)

Loyd, Sir Francis Alfred, KCMG, OBE

Loyd, Sir Julian St John, KCVO

Lu, Sir Tseng Chi, Kt.

Lucas, Sir Cyril Edward, Kt., CMG, FRS

Lucas, Sir Thomas Edward, Bt. (1887)

Luce, *Rt Hon.* Sir Richard Napier, Kt.

Luckhoo, Sir Lionel Alfred, KCMG, CBE, QC

Lucy, Sir Edmund John William Hugh Cameron-Ramsay-Fairfax, Bt. (1836)

Luddington, Sir Donald Collin Cumyn, KBE, CMG, CVO

Lumsden, Sir David James, Kt.

Lus, *Hon.* Sir Pita, Kt., OBE

Lush, *Hon.* Sir George Hermann, Kt.

Lushington, Sir John Richard Castleman, Bt. (1791)

Luttrell, *Col.* Sir Geoffrey Walter Fownes, KCVO, MC

Lyell, *Rt. Hon.* Sir Nicholas Walter, Kt., QC, MP

Lygo, *Adm.* Sir Raymond Derek, KCB

Lyle, Sir Gavin Archibald, Bt. (1929)

Lyons, Sir Edward Houghton, Kt.

Lyons, Sir James Reginald, Kt.

Lyons, Sir John, Kt.

McAdam, Sir Ian William James, Kt., OBE

Macadam, Sir Peter, Kt.

McAlpine, Sir William Hepburn, Bt. (1918)

†Macara, Sir Hugh Kenneth, Bt. (1911)

Macartney, Sir John Barrington, Bt. (I. 1799)

McAvoy, Sir (Francis) Joseph, Kt., CBE

McCaffrey, Sir Thomas Daniel, Kt.

McCall, Sir (Charles) Patrick Home, Kt., MBE, TD

McCallum, Sir Donald Murdo, Kt., CBE, FEng.

McCamley, Sir Graham Edward, Kt., MBE

McCarthy, *Rt. Hon.* Sir Thaddeus Pearcey, KBE

McClellan, *Col.* Sir Herbert Gerard Thomas, Kt., CBE, TD

McClintock, Sir Eric Paul, Kt.

McColl, Sir Colin Hugh Verel, KCMG

McCollum, *Hon.* Sir William, Kt.

McConnell, Sir Robert Shean, Bt. (1900)

McCorkell, *Col.* Sir Michael William, KCVO, OBE, TD

McCowan, *Rt. Hon.* Sir Anthony James Denys, Kt.

McCowan, Sir Hew Cargill, Bt. (1934)

McCrea, *Prof.* Sir William Hunter, Kt., FRS

McCrindle, Sir Robert Arthur, Kt.

McCullough, *Hon.* Sir (Iain) Charles (Robert), Kt.

McCusker, Sir James Alexander, Kt.

MacDermott, *Rt. Hon.* Sir John Clarke, Kt.

McDermott, Sir (Lawrence) Emmet, KBE

MacDonald, *Gen.* Sir Arthur Leslie, KBE, CB

McDonald, Sir Duncan, Kt., CBE, FEng.

Macdonald of Sleat, Sir Ian Godfrey Bosville, Bt. (s. 1625)

Macdonald, Sir Kenneth Carmichael, KCB

Macdonald, *Vice-Adm.* Sir Roderick Douglas, KBE

McDonald, Sir Tom, Kt., OBE

McDonald, *Hon.* Sir William John Farquhar, Kt.

MacDougall, Sir (George) Donald (Alastair), Kt., CBE, FBA

McDowell, Sir Eric Wallalce, Kt., CBE

McDowell, Sir Henry McLorinan, KBE

Mace, *Lt.-Gen.* Sir John Airth, KBE, CB

McEwen, Sir John Roderick Hugh, Bt. (1953)

McFarland, Sir John Talbot, Bt. (1914)

Macfarlane, Sir (David) Neil, Kt.

Macfarlane, Sir George Gray, Kt., CB, FEng.

McFarlane, Sir Ian, Kt.

McGeoch, *Vice-Adm.* Sir Ian Lachlan Mackay, KCB, DSO, DSC

McGrath, Sir Brian Henry, KCVO

Macgregor, Sir Edwin Robert, Bt. (1828)

MacGregor of MacGregor, Sir Gregor, Bt. (1795)

McGregor, Sir Ian Alexander, Kt., CBE, FRS

MacGregor, Sir Ian Kinloch, Kt.

McGrigor, *Capt.* Sir Charles Edward, Bt. (1831)

McIntosh, *Vice-Adm.* Sir Ian Stewart, KBE, CB, DSO, DSC

McIntosh, Sir Malcolm Kenneth, Kt., ph.D.

McIntosh, Sir Ronald Robert Duncan, KCB

McIntyre, Sir Donald Conroy, Kt., CBE

McIntyre, Sir Meredith Alister, Kt.

MacKay, *Prof.* Sir Donald Iain, Kt., FRSE

Mackay, Sir (George Patrick) Gordon, Kt., CBE

McKay, Sir John Andrew, Kt., CBE
Mackechnie, Sir Alistair John, Kt.
McKee, *Maj.* Sir (William) Cecil, Kt., ERD
McKellen, Sir Ian Murray, Kt., CBE
McKenzie, Sir Alexander, KBE
Mackenzie, Sir Alexander Alwyne Henry Charles Brinton Muir-, Bt. (1805)
Mackenzie, *Vice-Adm.* Sir Hugh Stirling, KCB, DSO, DSC
†Mackenzie, Sir (James William) Guy, Bt. (1890)
Mackenzie, *Gen.* Sir Jeremy John George, KCB, OBE
†Mackenzie, Sir Peter Douglas, Bt. (s. 1673)
†Mackenzie, Sir Roderick McQuhae, Bt. (s. 1703)
McKenzie, Sir Roy Allan, KBE
Mackeson, Sir Rupert Henry, Bt. (1954)
MacKinlay, Sir Bruce, Kt., CBE
McKinnon, Sir James, Kt.
McKinnon, *Hon.* Sir Stuart Neil, Kt.
Mackintosh, Sir Cameron Anthony, Kt.
Macklin, Sir Bruce Roy, Kt., OBE
Mackworth, *Cdr.* Sir David Arthur Geoffrey, Bt. (1776)
McLaren, Sir Robin John Taylor, KCMG
MacLaurin, Sir Ian Charter, Kt.
Maclean, Sir Donald Og Grant, Kt.
†Maclean of Dunconnell, Sir Charles Edward, Bt. (1957)
McLean, Sir Francis Charles, Kt., CBE
MacLean, *Vice-Adm.* Sir Hector Charles Donald, KBE, CB, DSC
Maclean, Sir Lachlan Hector Charles, Bt. (NS 1631)
Maclean, Sir Robert Alexander, KBE
McLennan, Sir Ian Munro, KCMG, KBE
McLeod, Sir Charles Henry, Bt. (1925)
McLeod, Sir Ian George, Kt.
MacLeod, Sir (John) Maxwell Norman, Bt. (1924)
Macleod, Sir (Nathaniel William) Hamish, KBE
McLintock, Sir Michael William, Bt. (1934)
Maclure, Sir John Robert Spencer, Bt. (1898)
McMahon, Sir Brian Patrick, Bt. (1817)
McMahon, Sir Christopher William, Kt.
Macmillan, Sir (Alexander McGregor) Graham, Kt.
MacMillan, *Lt.-Gen.* Sir John Richard Alexander, KCB, CBE
McMullin, *Rt. Hon.* Sir Duncan Wallace, Kt.
Macnaghten, Sir Patrick Alexander, Bt. (1836)
McNamara, *Air Chief Marshal* Sir Neville Patrick, KBE

Macnaughton, *Prof.* Sir Malcolm Campbell, Kt.
McNee, Sir David Blackstock, Kt., QPM
McNeice, Sir (Thomas) Percy (Fergus), Kt., CMG, OBE
MacPhail, Sir Bruce Dugald, Kt.
Macpherson, Sir Ronald Thomas Steward (Tommy), CBE, MC, TD
Macpherson of Cluny, *Hon.* Sir William Alan, Kt., TD
McQuarrie, Sir Albert, Kt.
MacRae, Sir (Alastair) Christopher (Donald Summerhayes), KCMG
Macrae, *Col.* Sir Robert Andrew Scarth, KCVO, MBE
Macready, Sir Nevil John Wilfrid, Bt. (1923)
Mactaggart, Sir John Auld, Bt. (1938)
Macwhinnie, Sir Gordon Menzies, Kt., CBE
McWilliam, Sir Michael Douglas, KCMG
McWilliams, Sir Francis, GBE, FEng.
Madden, *Adm.* Sir Charles Edward, Bt., GCB (1919)
Maddocks, Sir Kenneth Phipson, KCMG, KCVO
Maddox, Sir John Royden, Kt.
Madel, Sir (William) David, Kt., MP
Madigan, Sir Russel Tullie, Kt., OBE
Magnus, Sir Laurence Henry Philip, Bt. (1917)
Maguire, *Air Marshal* Sir Harold John, KCB, DSO, OBE
Mahon, Sir (John) Denis, Kt., CBE
Mahon, Sir William Walter, Bt. (1819)
Maiden, Sir Colin James, Kt., D.phil.
Main, Sir Peter Tester, Kt., ERD
Maini, Sir Amar Nath, Kt., CBE
Maino, Sir Charles, KBE
†Maitland, Sir Charles Alexander, Bt. (1818)
Maitland, Sir Donald James Dundas, GCMG, OBE
Makins, Sir Paul Vivian, Bt. (1903)
Malcolm, Sir James William Thomas Alexander, Bt. (s. 1665)
Malet, Sir Harry Douglas St Lo, Bt. (1791)
Mallaby, Sir Christopher Leslie George, GCMG, GCVO
†Mallinson, Sir William James, Bt. (1935)
Malone, *Hon.* Sir Denis Eustace Gilbert, Kt.
Mamo, Sir Anthony Joseph, Kt., OBE
Mance, *Hon.* Sir Jonathan Hugh, Kt.
Manchester, Sir William Maxwell, KBE
Mander, Sir Charles Marcus, Bt. (1911)
Manduell, Sir John, Kt., CBE
Mann, *Rt. Hon.* Sir Michael, Kt.
Mann, *Rt. Revd* Michael Ashley, KCVO
Mann, Sir Rupert Edward, Bt. (1905)
Mansel, Sir Philip, Bt. (1622)
Mansfield, *Vice-Adm.* Sir (Edward) Gerard (Napier), KBE, CVO

Mansfield, *Prof.* Sir Peter, Kt., FRS
Mansfield, Sir Philip (Robert Aked), KCMG
Mantell, *Hon.* Sir Charles Barrie Knight, Kt.
Manton, Sir Edwin Alfred Grenville, Kt.
Manuella, Sir Tulaga, GCMG, MBE
Manzie, Sir (Andrew) Gordon, KCB
Mara, *Rt. Hon. Ratu* Sir Kamisese Kapaiwai Tuimacilai, GCMG, KBE
Margetson, Sir John William Denys, KCMG
Marjoribanks, Sir James Alexander Milne, KCMG
Mark, Sir Robert, GBE
Markham, Sir Charles John, Bt. (1911)
Marking, Sir Henry Ernest, KCVO, CBE, MC
Marling, Sir Charles William Somerset, Bt. (1882)
Marr, Sir Leslie Lynn, Bt. (1919)
Marriner, Sir Neville, Kt., CBE
Marriott, Sir Hugh Cavendish Smith-, Bt. (1774)
Marriott, Sir John Brook, KCVO
Marsden, Sir Nigel John Denton, Bt. (1924)
Marshall, Sir Arthur Gregory George, Kt., OBE
Marshall, Sir Colin Marsh, Kt.
Marshall, Sir Denis Alfred, Kt.
Marshall, *Prof.* Sir (Oshley) Roy, Kt., CBE
Marshall, Sir Peter Harold Reginald, KCMG
Marshall, Sir Robert Braithwaite, KCB, MBE
Marshall, Sir (Robert) Michael, Kt., MP
Martell, *Vice-Adm.* Sir Hugh Colenso, KBE, CB
Martin, Sir George Henry, Kt., CBE
Martin, *Vice-Adm.* Sir John Edward Ludgate, KCB, DSC
Martin, *Prof.* Sir (John) Leslie, Kt., ph.D.
Martin, *Prof.* Sir Laurence Woodward, Kt.
Martin, Sir (Robert) Bruce, Kt., QC
Marychurch, Sir Peter Harvey, KCMG
Masefield, Sir Peter Gordon, Kt.
Masire, Sir Ketumile, GCMG
Mason, *Hon.* Sir Anthony Frank, KBE
Mason, Sir (Basil) John, Kt., CB, D.SC., FRS
Mason, *Prof.* Sir David Kean, Kt., CBE
Mason, Sir Frederick Cecil, KCVO, CMG
Mason, Sir Gordon Charles, Kt., OBE
Mason, Sir John Charles Moir, KCMG
Mason, Sir John Peter, Kt., CBE
Mason, *Prof.* Sir Ronald, KCB, FRS
Matane, Sir Paulias Nguna, Kt., CMG, OBE
Mather, Sir (David) Carol (Macdonell), Kt., MC
Mather, Sir William Loris, Kt., CVO, OBE, MC, TD

Mathers, Sir Robert William, Kt.

Matheson, Sir (James Adam) Louis, KBE, CMG, FEng.

Matheson of Matheson, Sir Fergus John, Bt. (1882)

Matthews, Sir Peter Alec, Kt.

Matthews, Sir Peter Jack, Kt., CVO, OBE, QPM

Matthews, Sir Stanley, Kt., CBE

Maud, The Hon. Sir Humphrey John Hamilton, KCMG

†Maxwell, Sir Michael Eustace George, Bt. (s. 1681)

Maxwell, Sir Nigel Mellor Heron-, Bt. (s. 1683)

May, Sir Anthony Tristram Kenneth, Kt.

May, Rt. Hon. Sir John Douglas, Kt.

May, Sir Kenneth Spencer, Kt., CBE

May, Prof. Sir Robert McCredie, Kt., FRS

Mayhew, Rt. Hon. Sir Patrick Barnabas Burke, Kt., QC, MP

Maynard, Hon. Sir Clement Travelyan, Kt.

Maynard, Air Chief Marshal Sir Nigel Martin, KCB, CBE, DFC, AFC

Medlycott, Sir Mervyn Tregonwell, Bt. (1808)

Megarry, Rt. Hon. Sir Robert Edgar, Kt., FBA

Megaw, Rt. Hon. Sir John, Kt., CBE, TD

Meinertzhagen, Sir Peter, Kt., CMG

Melhuish, Sir Michael Ramsay, KBE, CMG

Mellon, Sir James, KCMG

Melville, Sir Harry Work, KCB, Ph.D., D.SC., FRS

Melville, Sir Leslie Galfreid, KBE

Melville, Sir Ronald Henry, KCB

Mensforth, Sir Eric, Kt., CBE, F.Eng.

Menter, Sir James Woodham, Kt., Ph.D., SC.D., FRS

Menteth, Sir James Wallace Stuart-, Bt. (1838)

Menzies, Sir Peter Thomson, Kt.

Meyer, Sir Anthony John Charles, Bt. (1910)

Meyjes, Sir Richard Anthony, Kt.

Meyrick, Sir David John Charlton, Bt. (1880)

Meyrick, Sir George Christopher Cadafael Tapps-Gervis-, Bt. (1791)

Miakwe, Hon. Sir Akepa, KBE

Michael, Sir Peter Colin, Kt., CBE

Middleton, Sir George Humphrey, KCMG

Middleton, Sir Lawrence Monck, Bt. (1662)

Middleton, Sir Peter Edward, GCB

Miers, Sir (Henry) David Alastair Capel, KBE, CMG

Milbank, Sir Anthony Frederick, Bt. (1882)

Milburn, Sir Anthony Rupert, Bt. (1905)

Miles, Sir Peter Tremayne, KCVO

Miles, Sir William Napier Maurice, Bt. (1859)

Millais, Sir Geoffrey Richard Everett, Bt. (1885)

Millar, Sir Oliver Nicholas, GCVO, FBA

Millar, Sir Ronald Graeme, Kt.

Millard, Sir Guy Elwin, KCMG, CVO

Miller, Sir Donald John, Kt., FRSE, FEng.

Miller, Sir Hilary Duppa (Hal), Kt.

Miller, Sir (Ian) Douglas, Kt.

Miller, Sir John Holmes, Bt. (1705)

Miller, Lt.-Col. Sir John Mansel, GCVO, DSO, MC

Miller, Sir (Oswald) Bernard, Kt.

Miller, Sir Peter North, Kt.

Miller, Sir Ronald Andrew Baird, Kt., CBE

Miller of Glenlee, Sir Stephen William Macdonald, Bt. (1788)

Millett, Rt. Hon. Sir Peter Julian, Kt.

Millichip, Sir Frederick Albert (Bert), Kt.

Milling, Air Marshal Sir Denis Crowley-, KCB, CBE, DSO, DFC

Mills, Vice-Adm. Sir Charles Piercy, KCB, CBE, DSC

Mills, Sir Frank, KCVO, CMG

Mills, Sir John Lewis Ernest Watts, Kt., CBE

Mills, Sir Peter Frederick Leighton, Bt. (1921)

Milman, Lt.-Col. Sir Derek, Bt. (1800)

Milne, Sir John Drummond, Kt.

†Milner, Sir Timothy William Lycett, Bt. (1717)

Milnes Coates, Sir Anthony Robert, Bt. (1911)

Mitchell, Air Cdre Sir (Arthur) Dennis, KBE, CVO, DFC, AFC

Mitchell, Sir David Bower, Kt., MP

Mitchell, Sir Derek Jack, KCB, CVO

Mitchell, Prof. Sir (Edgar) William John, Kt., CBE, FRS

Mitchell, Rt. Hon. Sir James FitzAllen, KCMG

Mitchell, Hon. Sir Stephen George, Kt.

Moate, Sir Roger Denis, Kt., MP

Mobbs, Sir (Gerald) Nigel, Kt.

Moberly, Sir John Campbell, KBE, CMG

Moberly, Sir Patrick Hamilton, KCMG

Moffat, Sir Brian Scott, Kt., OBE

Moffat, Lt.-Gen. Sir (William) Cameron, KBE

Mogg, Gen. Sir (Herbert) John, GCB, CBE, DSO

Moir, Sir Ernest Ian Royds, Bt. (1916)

Moller, Hon. Sir Lester Francis, Kt.

†Molony, Sir Thomas Desmond, Bt. (1925)

Molyneaux, Rt. Hon. Sir James Henry, KBE, MP

Monck, Sir Nicholas Jeremy, KCB

Monro, Sir Hector Seymour Peter, Kt., MP

Montgomery, Sir (Basil Henry) David, Bt. (1801)

Montgomery, Sir (William) Fergus, Kt., MP

Mookerjee, Sir Birendra Nath, Kt.

Moollan, Sir Abdool Hamid Adam, Kt.

Moollan, Hon. Sir Cassam (Ismael), Kt.

Moon, Sir Peter Wilfred Giles Graham-, Bt. (1855)

†Moon, Sir Roger, Bt. (1887)

Moore, Most Revd Desmond Charles, KBE

Moore, Sir Francis Thomas, Kt.

Moore, Sir Henry Roderick, Kt., CBE

Moore, Hon. Sir John Cochrane, Kt.

Moore, Maj.-Gen. Sir (John) Jeremy, KCB, OBE, MC

Moore, Sir John Michael, KCVO, CB, DSC

Moore, Prof. Sir Norman Winfrid, Bt. (1919)

Moore, Sir Patrick William Eisdell, Kt., OBE

Moore, Sir William Roger Clotworthy, Bt., TD (1932)

Morauta, Sir Mekere, Kt.

Mordaunt, Sir Richard Nigel Charles, Bt. (1611)

Moreton, Sir John Oscar, KCMG, KCVO, MC

Morgan, Vice-Adm. Sir Charles Christopher, KBE

Morgan, Maj.-Gen. Sir David John Hughes-, Bt., CB, CBE (1925)

Morgan, Sir John Albert Leigh, KCMG

Morison, Hon. Sir Thomas Richard Atkin, Kt.

Morland, Hon. Sir Michael, Kt.

Morland, Sir Robert Kenelm, Kt.

Morpeth, Sir Douglas Spottiswoode, Kt., TD

Morris, Air Marshal Sir Arnold Alec, KBE, CB, FEng.

Morris, Sir (James) Richard (Samuel), Kt., CBE, FEng.

Morris, Sir Keith Elliot Hedley, KBE, CMG

Morris, Prof. Sir Peter John, Kt., FRS

Morris, Sir Robert Byng, Bt. (1806)

Morris, Sir Trefor Alfred, Kt., CBE, QPM

Morris, Very Revd Sir William James, KCVO, Ph.D.

Morrison, Hon. Sir Charles Andrew, Kt.

Morrison, Sir Howard Leslie, Kt., OBE

Morritt, Hon. Sir (Robert) Andrew, Kt., CVO

Morrow, Sir Ian Thomas, Kt.

Morse, Sir Christopher Jeremy, KCMG

Morton, Adm. Sir Anthony Storrs, GBE, KCB

Morton, Sir (Robert) Alastair (Newton), Kt.

Moseley, Sir George Walker, KCB

Moser, Prof. Sir Claus Adolf, KCB, CBE, FBA

†Moss, Sir David John Edwards-, Bt. (1868)
Mostyn, *Gen.* Sir (Joseph) David Frederick, KCB, CBE
†Mostyn, Sir William Basil John, Bt. (1670)
Mott, Sir John Harmer, Bt. (1930)
†Mount, Sir (William Robert) Ferdinand, Bt. (1921)
Mountain, Sir Denis Mortimer, Bt. (1922)
Mowbray, Sir John, Kt.
Mowbray, Sir John Robert, Bt. (1880)
Muir, Sir Laurence Macdonald, Kt.
†Muir, Sir Richard James Kay, Bt. (1892)
Muirhead, Sir David Francis, KCMG, CVO
Mulcahy, Sir Geoffrey John, Kt.
Mullens, *Lt.-Gen.* Sir Anthony Richard Guy, KCB, OBE
Mummery, *Hon.* Sir John Frank, Kt.
Munn, Sir James, Kt., OBE
Munro, Sir Alan Gordon, KCMG
Munro, Sir Alasdair Thomas Ian, Bt. (1825)
Munro, Sir Ian Talbot, Bt. (s. 1634)
Munro, Sir Sydney Douglas Gun-, GCMG, MBE
Muria, *Hon.* Sir Gilbert John Baptist, Kt.
Murley, Sir Reginald Sydney, KBE, TD, FRCS
Murphy, Sir Leslie Frederick, Kt.
Murray, *Rt. Hon.* Sir Donald Bruce, Kt.
Murray, Sir Donald Frederick, KCVO, CMG
Murray, Sir James, KCMG
Murray, Sir John Antony Jerningham, Kt., CBE
Murray, *Prof.* Sir Kenneth, Kt., FRCPath., FRS, FRSE
Murray, Sir Nigel Andrew Digby, Bt. (s. 1628)
Murray, Sir Patrick Ian Keith, Bt. (s. 1673)
†Murray, Sir Rowland William Patrick, Bt. (s. 1630)
Mursell, Sir Peter, Kt., MBE
Musgrave, Sir Christopher Patrick Charles, Bt. (1611)
Musgrave, Sir Richard James, Bt. (I. 1782)
Musson, *Gen.* Sir Geoffrey Randolph Dixon, GCB, CBE, DSO
Myers, Sir Kenneth Ben, Kt., MBE
Myers, Sir Philip Alan, Kt., OBE, QPM
Myers, *Prof.* Sir Rupert Horace, KBE
Mynors, Sir Richard Baskerville, Bt. (1964)
Nabarro, Sir John David Nunes, Kt., MD, FRCP
Naipaul, Sir Vidiadhar Surajprasad, Kt.
Nairn, Sir Michael, Bt. (1904)
Nairn, Sir Robert Arnold Spencer-, Bt. (1933)

Nairne, *Rt. Hon.* Sir Patrick Dalmahoy, GCB, MC
Naish, Sir (Charles) David, Kt.
Nall, Sir Michael Joseph, Bt., RN (1954)
Namaliu, *Rt. Hon.* Sir Rabbie Langanai, Kt., CMG
†Napier, Sir Charles Joseph, Bt. (1867)
Napier, Sir John Archibald Lennox, Bt. (s. 1627)
Napier, Sir Oliver John, Kt.
Nasmith, *Prof.* Sir James Duncan Dunbar-, Kt., CBE, RIBA, FRSE
Neal, Sir Eric James, Kt., CVO
Neal, Sir Leonard Francis, Kt., CBE
Neale, Sir Gerrard Anthony, Kt.
Neave, Sir Paul Arundell, Bt. (1795)
Nedd, *Hon.* Sir Robert Archibald, Kt.
Neill, *Rt. Hon.* Sir Brian Thomas, Kt.
Neill, Sir Francis Patrick, Kt., QC
Neill, *Rt. Hon.* Sir Ivan, Kt., PC (NI)
Neill, Sir (James) Hugh, KCVO, CBE, TD
†Nelson, Sir Jamie Charles Vernon Hope, Bt. (1912)
Nelson, *Hon.* Sir Robert Franklyn, Kt.
Nelson, *Air Marshal* Sir (Sidney) Richard (Carlyle), KCB, OBE, MD
Nepean, *Lt.-Col.* Sir Evan Yorke, Bt. (1802)
Neubert, Sir Michael John, Kt., MP
Nevile, *Capt.* Sir Henry Nicholas, KCVO
Neville, Sir Roger Albert Gartside, Kt., VRD
New, *Maj.-Gen.* Sir Laurence Anthony Wallis, Kt., CB, CBE
Newall, Sir Paul Henry, Kt., TD
Newington, Sir Michael John, KCMG
Newman, Sir Francis Hugh Cecil, Bt. (1912)
Newman, Sir Geoffrey Robert, Bt. (1836)
Newman, *Hon.* Sir George Michael, Kt.
Newman, Sir Jack, Kt., CBE
Newman, Sir Kenneth Leslie, GBE, QPM
Newman, *Vice-Adm.* Sir Roy Thomas, KCB
Newman, *Col.* Sir Stuart Richard, Kt., CBE, TD
Newns, Sir (Alfred) Foley (Francis Polden), KCMG, CVO
Newsam, Sir Peter Anthony, Kt.
Newton, Sir (Charles) Wilfred, Kt., CBE
Newton, Sir (Harry) Michael (Rex), Bt. (1900)
Newton, Sir Kenneth Garnar, Bt., OBE, TD (1924)
Newton, Sir (Leslie) Gordon, Kt.
Ngata, Sir Henare Kohere, KBE
Nichol, Sir Duncan Kirkbride, Kt., CBE
Nicholas, Sir David, Kt., CBE
Nicholas, Sir Herbert Richard, Kt., OBE

Nicholas, Sir John William, KCVO, CMG
Nicholls, *Air Marshal* Sir John Moreton, KCB, CBE, DFC, AFC
Nicholson, Sir Bryan Hubert, Kt.
†Nicholson, Sir Charles Christian, Bt. (1912)
Nicholson, *Hon.* Sir David Eric, Kt.
Nicholson, *Rt. Hon.* Sir Michael, Kt.
Nicholson, Sir Paul Douglas, Kt.
Nicholson, Sir Robin Buchanan, Kt., Ph.D., FRS, FEng.
Nicoll, Sir William, KCMG
Nield, Sir Basil Edward, Kt., CBE, QC
Nightingale, Sir Charles Manners Gamaliel, Bt. (1628)
Nightingale, Sir John Cyprian, Kt., CBE, BEM, QPM
Nimmo, *Hon.* Sir John Angus, Kt., CBE
Nixon, Sir Edwin Ronald, Kt., CBE
Nixon, *Revd* Sir Kenneth Michael John Basil, Bt. (1906)
Noble, Sir David Brunel, Bt. (1902)
Noble, Sir Iain Andrew, Bt., OBE (1923)
Noble, Sir (Thomas Alexander) Fraser, Kt., MBE
Nombri, Sir Joseph Karl, Kt., ISO, BEM
Norman, Sir Arthur Gordon, KBE, DFC
Norman, Sir Mark Annesley, Bt. (1915)
Norman, Sir Robert Henry, Kt., OBE
Norman, Sir Robert Wentworth, Kt.
Norman, Sir Ronald, Kt., OBE
Normanton, Sir Tom, Kt., TD
Norris, *Air Chief Marshal* Sir Christopher Neil Foxley-, GCB, DSO, OBE
Norris, Sir Eric George, KCMG
North, Sir Thomas Lindsay, Kt.
North, Sir (William) Jonathan (Frederick), Bt. (1920)
Norton, *Vice-Adm. Hon.* Sir Nicholas John Hill-, KCB
Norwood, Sir Walter Neville, Kt.
Nossal, Sir Gustav Joseph Victor, Kt., CBE
Nott, *Rt. Hon.* Sir John William Frederic, KCB
Nourse, *Rt. Hon.* Sir Martin Charles, Kt.
Nugent, Sir John Edwin Lavallin, Bt. (I. 1795)
Nugent, *Maj.* Sir Peter Walter James, Bt. (1831)
Nugent, Sir Robin George Colborne, Bt. (1806)
Nursaw, Sir James, KCB, QC
Nuttall, Sir Nicholas Keith Lillington, Bt. (1922)
Nutting, *Rt. Hon.* Sir (Harold) Anthony, Bt. (1903)
Oakeley, Sir John Digby Atholl, Bt. (1790)
Oakes, Sir Christopher, Bt. (1939)
Oakshott, *Hon.* Sir Anthony Hendrie, Bt. (1959)
Oates, Sir Thomas, Kt., CMG, OBE

Obolensky, *Prof.* Sir Dimitri, Kt.
O'Brien, Sir Frederick William Fitzgerald, Kt.
O'Brien, Sir Richard, Kt., DSO, MC
O'Brien, Sir Timothy John, Bt. (1849)
O'Brien, *Adm.* Sir William Donough, KCB, DSC
O'Connell, Sir Maurice James Donagh MacCarthy, Bt. (1869)
O'Connor, *Rt. Hon.* Sir Patrick McCarthy, Kt.
O'Dea, Sir Patrick Jerad, KCVO
Odell, Sir Stanley John, Kt.
Ogden, Sir (Edward) Michael, Kt., QC
Ogilvie, Sir Alec Drummond, Kt.
Ogilvy, Hon. Sir Angus James Bruce, KCVO
Ogilvy, Sir Francis Gilbert Arthur, Bt. (s. 1626)
Ognall, *Hon.* Sir Harry Henry, Kt.
Ohlson, Sir Brian Eric Christopher, Bt. (1920)
Okeover, *Capt.* Sir Peter Ralph Leopold Walker-, Bt. (1886)
Olewale, *Hon.* Sir Niwia Ebia, Kt.
Oliphant, Sir Mark (Marcus Laurence Elwin), KBE, FRS
O'Loghlen, Sir Colman Michael, Bt. (1838)
Olver, Sir Stephen John Linley, KBE, CMG
O'Neil, *Hon.* Sir Desmond Henry, Kt.
Ongley, *Hon.* Sir Joseph Augustine, Kt.
Onslow, *Rt. Hon.* Sir Cranley Gordon Douglas, KCMG, MP
Onslow, Sir John Roger Wilmot, Bt. (1797)
Oppenheim, Sir Alexander, Kt., OBE, D.SC., FRSE
Oppenheim, Sir Duncan Morris, Kt.
Oppenheimer, Sir Michael Bernard Grenville, Bt. (1921)
Orde, Sir John Alexander Campbell-, Bt. (1790)
O'Regan, *Hon.* Sir John Barry, Kt.
O'Regan, *Dr* Sir Stephen Gerard (Tipene), Kt.
Orlebar, Sir Michael Keith Orlebar Simpson-, KCMG
Ormond, Sir John Davies Wilder, Kt., BEM
Orr, Sir David Alexander, Kt., MC
Osborn, Sir John Holbrook, Kt.
Osborn, Sir Richard Henry Danvers, Bt. (1662)
Osborne, Sir Peter George, Bt. (I. 1629)
Osifelo, Sir Frederick Aubarua, Kt., MBE
Osman, Sir (Abdool) Raman Mahomed, GCMG, CBE
Osmond, Sir Douglas, Kt., CBE
Osmond, Sir (Stanley) Paul, Kt., CB
Oswald, *Admiral of the Fleet* Sir (John) Julian Robertson, GCB
Otton, Sir Geoffrey John, KCB
Otton, *Rt. Hon.* Sir Philip Howard, Kt.

Oulton, Sir Antony Derek Maxwell, GCB, QC
Outram, Sir Alan James, Bt. (1858)
Overall, Sir John Wallace, Kt., CBE, MC
Owen, Sir Geoffrey, Kt.
Owen, Sir Hugh Bernard Pilkington, Bt. (1813)
Owen, Sir Hugo Dudley Cunliffe-, Bt. (1920)
Owen, *Hon.* Sir John Arthur Dalziel, Kt.
Owo, The Olowo of, Kt.
Oxburgh, *Prof.* Sir Ernest Ronald, KBE, ph.D., FRS
Oxford, Sir Kenneth Gordon, Kt., CBE, QPM
Packard, *Lt.-Gen.* Sir (Charles) Douglas, KBE, CB, DSO
Page, Sir (Arthur) John, Kt.
Page, Sir Frederick William, Kt., CBE, FEng.
Page, Sir John Joseph Joffre, Kt., OBE
Paget, Sir Julian Tolver, Bt., CVO (1871)
Paget, Sir Richard Herbert, Bt. (1886)
Pain, *Lt.-Gen.* Sir (Horace) Rollo (Squarey), KCB, MC
Pain, *Hon.* Sir Peter Richard, Kt.
Paine, Sir Christopher Hammon, Kt., FRCP, FRCR
Palin, *Air Chief Marshal* Sir Roger Hewlett, KCB, OBE
Palliser, *Rt. Hon.* Sir (Arthur) Michael, GCMG
Palmar, Sir Derek James, Kt.
Palmer, Sir (Charles) Mark, Bt. (1886)
Palmer, *Gen.* Sir (Charles) Patrick (Ralph), KBE
Palmer, Sir Geoffrey Christopher John, Bt. (1660)
Palmer, *Rt. Hon.* Sir Geoffrey Winston Russell, KCMG
Palmer, Sir John Chance, Kt.
Palmer, Sir John Edward Somerset, Bt. (1791)
Palmer, *Maj.-Gen.* Sir (Joseph) Michael, KCVO
Palmer, Sir Reginald Oswald, GCMG, MBE
Pantlin, Sir Dick Hurst, Kt., CBE
Paolozzi, Sir Eduardo Luigi, Kt., CBE, RA
Parbo, Sir Arvi Hillar, Kt.
Parish, Sir David Elmer Woodbine, Kt., CBE
Park, *Hon.* Sir Hugh Eames, Kt.
Parker, Sir (Arthur) Douglas Dodds-, Kt.
Parker, Sir Eric Wilson, Kt.
Parker, *Hon.* Sir Jonathan Frederic, Kt.
Parker, Sir Peter, KBE, LVO
Parker, Sir Richard (William) Hyde, Bt. (1681)
Parker, *Rt. Hon.* Sir Roger Jocelyn, Kt.

Parker, *Vice-Adm.* Sir (Wilfred) John, KBE, CB, DSC
Parker, Sir William Peter Brian, Bt. (1844)
Parkes, Sir Edward Walter, Kt., FEng.
Parkinson, Sir Nicholas Fancourt, Kt.
Parsons, Sir (John) Michael, Kt.
Parsons, Sir Richard Edmund (Clement Fownes), KCMG
Partridge, Sir Michael John Anthony, KCB
Pascoe, *Gen.* Sir Robert Alan, KCB, MBE
Pasley, Sir John Malcolm Sabine, Bt. (1794)
Paterson, Sir Dennis Craig, Kt.
Paterson, Sir John Valentine Jardine, Kt.
Patnick, Sir (Cyril) Irvine, Kt., OBE, MP
Paton, Sir (Thomas) Angus (Lyall), Kt., CMG, FRS, FEng.
Pattie, *Rt. Hon.* Sir Geoffrey Edwin, Kt., MP
Pattinson, Sir (William) Derek, Kt.
Pattullo, Sir (David) Bruce, Kt., CBE
Paul, Sir John Warburton, GCMG, OBE, MC
Paul, *Air Marshal* Sir Ronald Ian Stuart-, KBE
Payne, Sir Norman John, Kt., CBE, FEng.
Peach, Sir Leonard Harry, Kt.
Peacock, *Prof.* Sir Alan Turner, Kt., DSC
Pearce, Sir Austin William, Kt., CBE, ph.D., FEng.
Pearce, Sir (Daniel Norton) Idris, Kt., CBE, TD
Pearce, Sir Eric Herbert, Kt., OBE
Pearse, Sir Brian Gerald, Kt.
Pearson, Sir Francis Nicholas Fraser, Bt. (1964)
Pearson, *Gen.* Sir Thomas Cecil Hook, KCB, CBE, DSO
Peart, *Prof.* Sir William Stanley, Kt., MD, FRS
Pease, Sir (Alfred) Vincent, Bt. (1882)
Pease, Sir Richard Thorn, Bt. (1920)
Peat, Sir Gerrard Charles, KCVO
Peat, Sir Henry, KCVO, DFC
Peck, Sir Edward Heywood, GCMG
Peckham, *Prof.* Sir Michael John, Kt., FRCP, FRCPGlas., FRCR, FRCPath.
Pedder, *Air Marshal* Sir Ian Maurice, KCB, OBE, DFC
†Peek, Sir William Grenville, Bt. (1874)
Peek, *Vice-Adm.* Sir Richard Innes, KBE, CB, DSC
Peel, Sir John Harold, KCVO
Peel, Sir (William) John, Kt.
Peirse, Sir Henry Grant de la Poer Beresford-, Bt. (1814)
Peirse, *Air Vice-Marshal* Sir Richard Charles Fairfax, KCVO, CB
Pelgen, Sir Harry Friedrich, Kt., MBE
Pelly, Sir Richard John, Bt. (1840)

Pemberton, Sir Francis Wingate William, Kt., CBE

Penrose, *Prof.* Sir Roger, Kt., FRS

Percival, *Rt. Hon.* Sir (Walter) Ian, Kt., QC

Pereira, Sir (Herbert) Charles, Kt., D.SC., FRS

Perring, Sir Ralph Edgar, Bt. (1963)

Perris, Sir David (Arthur), Kt., MBE

Perry, Sir David Howard, KCB

Perry, Sir (David) Norman, Kt., MBE

Perry, Sir Michael Sydney, Kt., CBE

Pestell, Sir John Richard, KCVO

Peterkin, Sir Neville, Kt.

Peters, *Prof.* Sir David Keith, Kt., FRCP

Petersen, Sir Jeffrey Charles, KCMG

Petersen, Sir Johannes Bjelke-, KCMG

Peterson, Sir Christopher Matthew, Kt., CBE, TD

Petit, Sir Dinshaw Manockjee, Bt. (1890)

Peto, Sir Henry George Morton, Bt. (1855)

Peto, Sir Michael Henry Basil, Bt. (1927)

Petrie, Sir Peter Charles, Bt., CMG (1918)

Pettigrew, Sir Russell Hilton, Kt.

Pettit, Sir Daniel Eric Arthur, Kt.

Philips, *Prof.* Sir Cyril Henry, Kt.

Phillips, Sir Fred Albert, Kt., CVO

Phillips, Sir Henry Ellis Isidore, Kt., CMG, MBE

Phillips, Sir Horace, KCMG

Phillips, *Hon.* Sir Nicholas Addison, Kt.

Phillips, Sir Peter John, Kt., OBE

Phillips, Sir Robin Francis, Bt. (1912)

Pickering, Sir Edward Davies, Kt.

†Pickthorn, Sir James Francis Mann, Bt. (1959)

Pidgeon, Sir John Allan Stewart, Kt.

†Piers, Sir James Desmond, Bt. (i. 1661)

Pigot, Sir George Hugh, Bt. (1764)

Pigott, Sir Berkeley Henry Sebastian, Bt. (1808)

Pike, Sir Michael Edmund, KCVO, CMG

Pike, Sir Philip Ernest Housden, Kt., QC

Pilditch, Sir Richard Edward, Bt. (1929)

Pile, Sir Frederick Devereux, Bt., MC (1900)

Pile, Sir William Dennis, GCB, MBE

Pilkington, Sir Antony Richard, Kt.

Pilkington, Sir Thomas Henry Milborne-Swinnerton-, Bt. (s. 1635)

Pill, *Rt. Hon.* Sir Malcolm Thomas, Kt.

Pillar, *Adm.* Sir William Thomas, GBE, KCB

Pindling, *Rt. Hon.* Sir Lynden Oscar, KCMG

Pinker, Sir George Douglas, KCVO

Pinsent, Sir Christopher Roy, Bt. (1938)

Pippard, *Prof.* Sir (Alfred) Brian, Kt., FRS

Pirie, *Gp Capt* Sir Gordon Hamish, Kt., CVO, CBE

Pitakaka, Sir Moses Puibangara, GCMG

Pitblado, Sir David Bruce, KCB, CVO

Pitcher, Sir Desmond Henry, Kt.

Pitman, Sir Brian Ivor, Kt.

Pitoi, Sir Sere, Kt., CBE

Pitt, Sir Harry Raymond, Kt., PH.D., FRS

Pitts, Sir Cyril Alfred, Kt.

Plastow, Sir David Arnold Stuart, Kt.

†Platt, Sir (Frank) Lindsey, Bt. (1958)

Platt, Sir Harold Grant, Kt.

Platt, *Prof.* Hon. Sir Peter, Bt. (1959)

Playfair, Sir Edward Wilder, KCB

Pliatzky, Sir Leo, KCB

Plowman, *Hon.* Sir John Robin, Kt., CBE

Plumb, *Prof.* Sir John Harold, Kt.

Pohai, Sir Timothy, Kt., MBE

Pole, Sir (John) Richard (Walter Reginald) Carew, Bt. (1628)

Pole, Sir Peter Van Notten, Bt. (1791)

Pollen, Sir John Michael Hungerford, Bt. (1795)

Pollock, Sir George Frederick, Bt. (1866)

Pollock, Sir Giles Hampden Montagu-, Bt. (1872)

Pollock, *Admiral of the Fleet* Sir Michael Patrick, GCB, LVO, DSC

Ponsonby, Sir Ashley Charles Gibbs, Bt., KCVO, MC (1956)

Pontin, Sir Frederick William, Kt.

Poole, *Hon.* Sir David Anthony, Kt.

Poore, Sir Herbert Edward, Bt. (1795)

Pope, *Vice-Adm.* Sir (John) Ernle, KCB

Pope, Sir Joseph Albert, Kt., D.SC., PH.D.

Popplewell, *Hon.* Sir Oliver Bury, Kt.

†Porritt, Sir Jonathon Espie, Bt. (1963)

Portal, Sir Jonathan Francis, Bt. (1901)

Porter, Sir John Simon Horsbrugh-, Bt. (1902)

Porter, Sir Leslie, Kt.

Porter, *Air Marshal* Sir (Melvin) Kenneth (Drowley), KCB, CBE

Porter, *Rt. Hon.* Sir Robert Wilson, Kt., PC (NI), QC

Posnett, Sir Richard Neil, KBE, CMG

Potter, *Rt. Hon.* Sir Mark Howard, Kt.

Potter, *Maj.-Gen.* Sir (Wilfrid) John, KBE, CB

Potts, *Hon.* Sir Francis Humphrey, Kt.

Pound, Sir John David, Bt. (1905)

Pountain, Sir Eric John, Kt.

Powell, Sir (Arnold Joseph) Philip, Kt., CH, OBE, RA, FRIBA

Powell, Sir Charles David, KCMG

Powell, Sir Nicholas Folliott Douglas, Bt. (1897)

Powell, Sir Raymond, Kt., MP

Powell, Sir Richard Royle, GCB, KBE, CMG

Power, Sir Alastair John Cecil, Bt. (1924)

Prance, *Prof.* Sir Ghillean Tolmie, Kt., FRS

Prendergast, Sir (Walter) Kieran, KCVO, CMG

Prentice, *Hon.* Sir William Thomas, Kt., MBE

Prescott, Sir Mark, Bt. (1938)

Preston, Sir Ronald Douglas Hildebrand, Bt. (1815)

Prevost, Sir Christopher Gerald, Bt. (1805)

Price, Sir Charles Keith Napier Rugge-, Bt. (1804)

Price, Sir David Ernest Campbell, Kt.

Price, Sir Francis Caradoc Rose, Bt. (1815)

Price, Sir Frank Leslie, Kt.

Price, Sir (James) Robert, KBE

Price, Sir Leslie Victor, Kt., OBE

Price, Sir Norman Charles, KCB

Price, Sir Robert John Green-, Bt. (1874)

Prickett, *Air Chief Marshal* Sir Thomas Other, KCB, DSO, DFC

Prideaux, Sir Humphrey Povah Treverbian, Kt., OBE

†Primrose, Sir John Ure, Bt. (1903)

Pringle, *Air Marshal* Sir Charles Norman Seton, KBE, FEng.

Pringle, *Hon.* Sir John Kenneth, Kt.

Pringle, *Lt.-Gen.* Sir Steuart (Robert), Bt., KCB, RM (s. 1683)

Pritchard, Sir Neil, KCMG

Pritchett, Sir Victor Sawdon, Kt., CH, CBE

Proby, Sir Peter, Bt. (1952)

Prosser, Sir Ian Maurice Gray, Kt.

Proud, Sir John Seymour, Kt.

Pryke, Sir David Dudley, Bt. (1926)

Pugh, Sir Idwal Vaughan, KCB

Pugsley, *Prof.* Sir Alfred Grenvile, Kt., OBE, D.SC., FRS, FEng.

Pullen, Sir William Reginald James, KCVO

Pullinger, Sir (Francis) Alan, Kt., CBE

Pumphrey, Sir (John) Laurence, KCMG

Purchas, *Rt. Hon.* Sir Francis Brooks, Kt.

Purves, Sir William, Kt., CBE, DSO

Purvis, *Vice-Adm.* Sir Neville, KCB

Puttnam, Sir David Terrance, Kt., CBE

Quicke, Sir John Godolphin, Kt., CBE

Quigley, Sir (William) George (Henry), Kt., CB, PH.D.

Quilliam, *Hon.* Sir (James) Peter, Kt.

Quilter, Sir Anthony Raymond Leopold Cuthbert, Bt. (1897)

Quinlan, Sir Michael Edward, GCB

Quinton, Sir James Grand, Kt.

Radcliffe, Sir Sebastian Everard, Bt. (1813)

Radzinowicz, *Prof.* Sir Leon, Kt., LLD

Rae, *Hon.* Sir Wallace Alexander Ramsay, Kt.
Raeburn, Sir Michael Edward Norman, Bt. (1923)
Raeburn, *Maj.-Gen.* Sir (William) Digby (Manifold), KCVO, CB, DSO, MBE
Raffray, Sir Piat Joseph Raymond Andre, Kt.
Raikes, *Vice-Adm.* Sir Iwan Geoffrey, KCB, CBE, DSC
Raison, *Rt. Hon.* Sir Timothy Hugh Francis, Kt.
Ralli, Sir Godfrey Victor, Bt., TD (1912)
Ramdanee, Sir Mookteswar Baboolall Kailash, Kt.
Ramphal, Sir Shridath Surendranath, GCMG
Ramphul, Sir Baalkhristna, Kt.
Ramphul, Sir Indurduth, Kt.
Ramsay, Sir Alexander William Burnett, Bt. (1806)
Ramsay, Sir Allan John (Hepple), KBE, CMG
Ramsbotham, *Gen.* Sir David John, GCB, CBE
Ramsbotham, *Hon.* Sir Peter Edward, GCMG, GCVO
Ramsden, Sir John Charles Josslyn, Bt. (1689)
Ramsey, Sir Alfred Ernest, Kt.
Randle, *Prof.* Sir Philip John, Kt.
Ranger, Sir Douglas, Kt., FRCS
Rank, Sir Benjamin Keith, Kt., CMG
Rankin, Sir Alick Michael, Kt., CBE
Rankin, Sir Ian Niall, Bt. (1898)
Rasch, *Maj.* Sir Richard Guy Carne, Bt. (1903)
Rashleigh, Sir Richard Harry, Bt. (1831)
Ratford, Sir David John Edward, KCMG, CVO
Rattee, *Hon.* Sir Donald Keith, Kt.
Rattle, Sir Simon Dennis, Kt., CBE
Rault, Sir Louis Joseph Maurice, Kt.
Rawlins, *Surgeon Vice-Adm.* Sir John Stuart Pepys, KBE
Rawlinson, Sir Anthony Henry John, Bt. (1891)
Read, *Air Marshal* Sir Charles Frederick, KBE, CB, DFC, AFC
Read, *Gen.* Sir (John) Antony (Jervis), GCB, CBE, DSO, MC
Read, Sir John Emms, Kt.
†Reade, Sir Kenneth Ray, Bt. (1661)
Reay, *Lt.-Gen.* Sir (Hubert) Alan John, KBE
Redgrave, *Maj.-Gen.* Sir Roy Michael Frederick, KBE, MC
Redmayne, Sir Nicholas, Bt. (1964)
Redmond, Sir James, Kt., FEng.
Redwood, Sir Peter Boverton, Bt. (1911)
Reece, Sir Charles Hugh, Kt.
Reece, Sir James Gordon, Kt.
Reed, *Hon.* Sir Nigel Vernon, Kt., CBE
Rees, Sir (Charles William) Stanley, Kt., TD

Rees, Sir David Allan, Kt., PH.D., D.SC., FRS
Rees, *Prof.* Sir Martin John, Kt., FRS
Reeve, Sir Anthony, KCMG, KCVO
Reeves, *Most Revd* Paul Alfred, GCMG, GCVO
Reffell, *Adm.* Sir Derek Roy, KCB
Refshauge, *Maj-Gen.* Sir William Dudley, Kt., CBE
Reid, Sir Alexander James, Bt. (1897)
Reid, Sir (Harold) Martin (Smith), KBE, CMG
Reid, Sir Hugh, Bt. (1922)
Reid, Sir Norman Robert, Kt.
Reid, Sir Robert Paul, Kt.
Reid, Sir William Kennedy, KCB
Reiher, Sir Frederick Bernard Carl, KBE, CMG
Reilly, Sir (D'Arcy) Patrick, GCMG, OBE
Reilly, *Lt.-Gen.* Sir Jeremy Calcott, KCB, DSO
Renals, Sir Stanley, Bt. (1895)
Rennie, Sir John Shaw, GCMG, OBE
Renouf, Sir Clement William Bailey, Kt.
Renouf, Sir Francis Henry, Kt.
Renshaw, Sir (Charles) Maurice Bine, Bt. (1903)
Renwick, Sir Richard Eustace, Bt. (1921)
Renwick, Sir Robin William, KCMG
Reporter, Sir Shapoor Ardeshirji, KBE
Reynolds, Sir David James, Bt. (1923)
Reynolds, Sir Peter William John, Kt., CBE
Rhodes, Sir Basil Edward, Kt., CBE, TD
Rhodes, Sir John Christopher Douglas, Bt. (1919)
Rhodes, Sir Peregrine Alexander, KCMG
Rice, *Maj.-Gen.* Sir Desmond Hind Garrett, KCVO, CBE
Rice, Sir Timothy Miles Bindon, Kt.
Richard, Sir Cliff, Kt., OBE
Richards, Sir (Francis) Brooks, KCMG, D.SC.
Richards, *Lt.-Gen.* Sir John Charles Chisholm, KCB, KCVO, RM
Richards, Sir Rex Edward, Kt., D.SC., FRS
Richardson, Sir Anthony Lewis, Bt. (1924)
Richardson, *Rt. Hon.* Sir Ivor Lloyd Morgan, Kt.
Richardson, Sir (John) Eric, Kt., CBE
Richardson, Sir Michael John de Rougemont, Kt.
Richardson, *Lt.-Gen.* Sir Robert Francis, KCB, CVO, CBE
Richardson, Sir Simon Alaisdair Stewart-, Bt. (s. 1630)
Riches, Sir Derek Martin Hurry, KCMG
Riches, *Gen.* Sir Ian Hurry, KCB, DSO
Richmond, Sir Alan James, Kt.
Richmond, *Rt. Hon.* Sir Clifford Parris, KBE

Richmond, Sir John Frederick, Bt. (1929)
Richmond, *Prof.* Sir Mark Henry, Kt., FRS
Rickett, Sir Denis Hubert Fletcher, KCMG, CB
Ricketts, Sir Robert Cornwallis Gerald St Leger, Bt. (1828)
Riddell, Sir John Charles Buchanan, Bt., CVO (s. 1628)
Ridley, Sir Adam (Nicholas), Kt.
Ridsdale, Sir Julian Errington, Kt., CBE
Rigby, *Lt.-Col.* Sir (Hugh) John (Macbeth), Bt. (1929)
Riley, Sir Ralph, Kt., FRS
Rimer, *Hon.* Sir Colin Percy Farquharson, Kt.
Ring, Sir Lindsay Roberts, GBE
Ringadoo, *Hon.* Sir Veerasamy, GCMG
Ripley, Sir Hugh, Bt. (1880)
Risk, Sir Thomas Neilson, Kt.
Rix, *Hon.* Sir Bernard Anthony, Kt.
Rix, Sir John, Kt., MBE, FEng.
Roberts, Sir Bryan Clieve, KCMG, QC
Roberts, *Hon.* Sir Denys Tudor Emil, KBE, QC
Roberts, Sir Derek Harry, Kt., CBE, FRS, FEng.
Roberts, Sir (Edward Fergus) Sidney, Kt., CBE
Roberts, Sir Frank Kenyon, GCMG, GCVO
Roberts, *Brig.* Sir Geoffrey Paul Hardy-, KCVO, CB, CBE
Roberts, Sir Gilbert Howland Rookehurst, Bt. (1809)
Roberts, Sir Gordon James, Kt., CBE
Roberts, *Rt. Hon.* Sir (Ieuan) Wyn Pritchard, Kt., MP
Roberts, Sir Samuel, Bt. (1919)
Roberts, Sir Stephen James Leake, Kt.
Roberts, Sir William James Denby, Bt. (1909)
Robertson, Sir John Fraser, KCMG, CBE
Robertson, Sir Lewis, Kt., CBE, FRSE
Robertson, *Prof.* Sir Rutherford Ness, Kt., CMG
Robins, Sir Ralph Harry, Kt., FEng.
Robinson, Sir Albert Edward Phineas, Kt.
†Robinson, Sir Christopher Philipse, Bt. (1854)
Robinson, Sir John James Michael Laud, Bt. (1660)
†Robinson, Sir Dominick Christopher Lynch-, Bt. (1920)
Robinson, Sir Wilfred Henry Frederick, Bt. (1908)
Robotham, *Hon.* Sir Lascelles Lister, Kt.
Robson, *Prof.* Sir James Gordon, Kt., CBE
Robson, Sir John Adam, KCMG
Roch, *Rt. Hon.* Sir Ian Ormond, Kt.
Roche, Sir David O'Grady, Bt. (1838)
Rodgers, Sir (John Fairlie) Tobias, Bt. (1964)

Rodrigues, Sir Alberto Maria, Kt., CBE, ED

Roe, *Air Chief Marshal* Sir Rex David, GCB, AFC

Rogers, Sir Frank Jarvis, Kt.

Rogers, *Air Chief Marshal* Sir John Robson, KCB, CBE

Rogers, Sir Richard George, Kt., RA

Roll, *Revd* Sir James William Cecil, Bt. (1921)

Rooke, Sir Denis Eric, Kt., CBE, FRS, FEng.

Ropner, Sir John Bruce Woollacott, Bt. (1952)

Ropner, Sir Robert Douglas, Bt. (1904)

Roscoe, Sir Robert Bell, KBE

Rose, *Rt. Hon.* Sir Christopher Dudley Roger, Kt.

Rose, Sir Clive Martin, GCMG

Rose, Sir David Lancaster, Bt. (1874)

Rose, *Gen.* Sir (Hugh) Michael, KCB, CBE, DSO, QGM

Rose, Sir Julian Day, Bt. (1872 and 1909)

Rosier, *Air Chief Marshal* Sir Frederick Ernest, GCB, CBE, DSO

Ross, Sir (James) Keith, Bt., RD, FRCS (1960)

Ross, *Lt.-Gen.* Sir Robert Jeremy, KCB, OBE

Rosser, Sir Melvyn Wynne, Kt.

Rossi, Sir Hugh Alexis Louis, Kt.

Roth, *Prof.* Sir Martin, Kt., MD, FRCP

Rothnie, Sir Alan Keir, KCVO, CMG

Rothschild, Sir Evelyn Robert Adrian de, Kt.

Rougier, *Hon.* Sir Richard George, Kt.

Rous, *Lt.-Gen.* Hon. Sir William Edward, KCB, OBE

Rowe, Sir Jeremy, Kt., CBE

Rowell, Sir John Joseph, Kt., CBE

Rowland, *Air Marshal* Sir James Anthony, KBE, DFC, AFC

Rowlands, *Air Marshal* Sir John Samuel, GC, KBE

Rowley, Sir Charles Robert, Bt. (1836)

Rowley, Sir Joshua Francis, Bt. (1786)

Roxburgh, *Vice-Adm.* Sir John Charles Young, KCB, CBE, DSO, DSC

Royden, Sir Christopher John, Bt. (1905)

Rudd, Sir (Anthony) Nigel (Russell), Kt.

Rumbold, Sir Henry John Sebastian, Bt. (1779)

Rumbold, Sir Jack Seddon, Kt.

Runchorelal, Sir (Udayan) Chinubhai Madhowlal, Bt. (1913)

Runciman, *Hon.* Sir James Cochran Stevenson (Sir Steven Runciman), Kt., CH Rusby, *Vice-Adm.* Sir Cameron, KCB, LVO

Russell, Sir Charles Ian, Bt. (1916)

Russell, *Hon.* Sir David Sturrock West-, Kt.

Russell, Sir George, Kt., CBE

Russell, Sir George Michael, Bt. (1812)

Russell, *Prof.* Sir Peter Edward Lionel, Kt., D.Litt., FBA

Russell, Sir (Robert) Mark, KCMG

Russell, Sir Spencer Thomas, Kt.

Russell, *Rt. Hon.* Sir (Thomas) Patrick, Kt.

Rutter, Sir Frank William Eden, KBE

Rutter, *Prof.* Sir Michael Llewellyn, Kt., CBE, MD, FRS

Ryan, Sir Derek Gerald, Bt. (1919)

Rycroft, Sir Richard Newton, Bt. (1784)

Ryrie, Sir William Sinclair, KCB

Sabola, *Hon.* Sir Joaquim Claudino Gonsalves-, Kt.

Sachs, *Hon.* Sir Michael Alexander Geddes, Kt.

Sainsbury, Sir Robert James, Kt.

Sainsbury, *Rt. Hon.* Sir Timothy Alan Davan, Kt., MP

St Aubyn, Sir (John) Arscott Molesworth-, Bt. (1689)

St George, Sir George Bligh, Bt. (I. 1766)

St Johnston, Sir Kerry, Kt.

Sainty, Sir John Christopher, KCB

Sakzewski, Sir Albert, Kt.

Salt, Sir Patrick MacDonnell, Bt. (1869)

Salt, Sir (Thomas) Michael John, Bt. (1899)

Sampson, Sir Colin, Kt., CBE, QPM

Samuel, Sir Jon Michael Glen, Bt. (1898)

Samuelson, Sir (Bernard) Michael (Francis), Bt. (1884)

Samuelson, Sir Sydney Wylie, Kt., CBE

Sandberg, Sir Michael Graham Ruddock, Kt., CBE

Sanders, Sir John Reynolds Mayhew-, Kt.

Sanders, Sir Robert Tait, KBE, CMG

Sanderson, Sir Frank Linton, Bt. (1920)

Sarei, Sir Alexis Holyweek, Kt., CBE

Sarell, Sir Roderick Francis Gisbert, KCMG, KCVO

Sargant, Sir (Henry) Edmund, Kt.

Saunders, *Hon.* Sir John Anthony Holt, Kt., CBE, DSO, MC

Saunders, Sir Peter, Kt.

Sauzier, Sir (André) Guy, Kt., CBE, ED

Savage, Sir Ernest Walter, Kt.

Savile, Sir James Wilson Vincent, Kt., OBE

Saville, *Rt. Hon.* Sir Mark Oliver, Kt.

Say, *Rt. Revd* Richard David, KCVO

Schiemann, *Rt. Hon.* Sir Konrad Hermann Theodor, Kt.

Schneider, *Rt. Hon.* Sir Lancelot Raymond Adams-, KCMG

Scholey, Sir David Gerald, Kt., CBE

Scholey, Sir Robert, Kt., CBE, FEng.

Scholtens, Sir James Henry, KCVO

Schubert, Sir Sydney, Kt.

Schuster, Sir (Felix) James Moncrieff, Bt., OBE (1906)

Scipio, Sir Hudson Rupert, Kt.

Scoon, Sir Paul, GCMG, GCVO, OBE

Scopes, Sir Leonard Arthur, KCVO, CMG, OBE

Scott, Sir Anthony Percy, Bt. (1913)

Scott, Sir (Charles) Peter, KBE, CMG

Scott, Sir David Aubrey, GCMG

Scott, Sir Dominic James Maxwell-, Bt. (1642)

Scott, Sir Ian Dixon, KCMG, KCVO, CIE

Scott, Sir James Jervoise, Bt. (1962)

Scott, Sir Kenneth Bertram Adam, KCVO, CMG

Scott, Sir Michael, KCVO, CMG

Scott, *Rt. Hon.* Sir Nicholas Paul, KBE, MP

Scott, Sir Oliver Christopher Anderson, Bt. (1909)

Scott, *Prof.* Sir Philip John, KBE

Scott, *Rt. Hon.* Sir Richard Rashleigh Folliott, Kt.

Scott, Sir Robert David Hillyer, Kt.

Scott, Sir Walter John, Bt. (1907)

Scott, *Rear-Adm.* Sir (William) David (Stewart), KBE, CB

Scowen, Sir Eric Frank, Kt., MD, D.SC., LLD, FRCP, FRCS

Scrivenor, Sir Thomas Vaisey, Kt., CMG

Seale, Sir John Henry, Bt. (1838)

Seaman, Sir Keith Douglas, KCVO, OBE

Sebastian, Sir Cuthbert Montraville, GCMG, OBE

†Sebright, Sir Peter Giles Vivian, Bt. (1626)

Seccombe, Sir (William) Vernon Stephen, Kt.

Secombe, Sir Harry Donald, Kt., CBE

Seconde, Sir Reginald Louis, KCMG, CVO

Sedley, *Hon.* Sir Stephen John, Kt.

Seely, Sir Nigel Edward, Bt. (1896)

Seeto, Sir Ling James, Kt., MBE

Seeyave, Sir Rene Sow Choung, Kt., CBE

Seligman, Sir Peter Wendel, Kt., CBE

Sergeant, Sir Patrick, Kt.

Series, Sir (Joseph Michel) Emile, Kt., CBE

Serpell, Sir David Radford, KCB, CMG, OBE

Seton, Sir Iain Bruce, Bt. (s. 1663)

†Seton, Sir James Christall, Bt. (s. 1683)

Severne, *Air Vice-Marshal* Sir John de Milt, KCVO, OBE, AFC

Seymour, *Cdr.* Sir Michael Culme-, Bt., RN (1809)

Shakerley, Sir Geoffrey Adam, Bt. (1838)

†Shakespeare, Sir Thomas William, Bt. (1942)

Shapland, Sir William Arthur, Kt.

Sharp, Sir Adrian, Bt. (1922)

Sharp, Sir George, Kt., OBE

Sharp, Sir Kenneth Johnston, Kt., TD

Sharp, Sir Leslie, Kt., QPM

Sharp, Sir Milton Reginald, Bt. (1920)

Sharp, Sir Richard Lyall, KCVO, CB
Sharpe, *Hon.* Sir John Henry, Kt., CBE
Sharples, Sir James, Kt., QPM
Shattock, Sir Gordon, Kt.
Shaw, Sir Brian Piers, Kt.
Shaw, Sir (Charles) Barry, Kt., CB, QC
Shaw, Sir (George) Neville Bowan-, Kt.
Shaw, *Prof.* Sir John Calman, Kt., CBE, FRSE
Shaw, Sir (John) Giles (Dunkerley), Kt., MP
Shaw, Sir John Michael Robert Best-, Bt. (1665)
Shaw, Sir Neil McGowan, Kt.
Shaw, Sir Robert, Bt. (1821)
Shaw, Sir Roy, Kt.
Shaw, Sir Run Run, Kt., CBE
Sheehy, Sir Patrick, Kt.
Sheen, *Hon.* Sir Barry Cross, Kt.
Sheffield, Sir Reginald Adrian Berkeley, Bt. (1755)
Shehadie, Sir Nicholas Michael, Kt., OBE
Sheil, *Hon.* Sir John, Kt.
Sheldon, *Hon.* Sir (John) Gervase (Kensington), Kt.
Shelley, Sir John Richard, Bt. (1611)
Shelton, Sir William Jeremy Masefield, Kt.
Shepheard, Sir Peter Faulkner, Kt., CBE
Shepherd, Sir Colin Ryley, Kt., MP
Shepperd, Sir Alfred Joseph, Kt.
Sherlock, Sir Philip Manderson, KBE
Sherman, Sir Alfred, Kt.
Sherman, Sir Louis, Kt., OBE
Shersby, Sir (Julian) Michael, Kt., MP
Shields, Sir Neil Stanley, Kt., MC
Shields, *Prof.* Sir Robert, Kt., MD
Shiffner, Sir Henry David, Bt. (1818)
Shillington, Sir (Robert Edward) Graham, Kt., CBE
Shinwell, Sir Maurice Adrian, Kt.
Shock, Sir Maurice, Kt.
Short, *Brig.* Sir Noel Edward Vivian, Kt., MBE, MC
Shuckburgh, Sir Rupert Charles Gerald, Bt. (1660)
Siaguru, Sir Anthony Michael, KBE
Siddall, Sir Norman, Kt., CBE, FEng.
Sidey, *Air Marshal* Sir Ernest Shaw, KBE, CB, MD
Sie, Sir Banja Tejan-, GCMG
Simeon, Sir John Edmund Barrington, Bt. (1815)
Simmons, *Air Marshal* Sir Michael George, KCB, AFC
Simmons, Sir Stanley Clifford, Kt., FRCS, FRCOG
Simon, Sir David Alec Gwyn, Kt., CBE
Simonet, Sir Louis Marcel Pierre, Kt., CBE
Simpson, *Hon.* Sir Alfred Henry, Kt.
Simpson, Sir William James, Kt.
Sims, Sir Roger Edward, Kt., MP
Sinclair, Sir Clive Marles, Kt.
Sinclair, Sir George Evelyn, Kt., CMG, OBE

Sinclair, Sir Ian McTaggart, KCMG, QC
Sinclair, *Air Vice-Marshal* Sir Laurence Frank, GC, KCB, CBE, DSO
Sinclair, Sir Patrick Robert Richard, Bt. (s. 1704)
Sinclair, Sir Ronald Ormiston, KBE
Singer, *Prof.* Sir Hans Wolfgang, Kt.
Singer, *Hon.* Sir Jan Peter, Kt.
Singh, *Hon.* Sir Vijay Raghubir, Kt.
Singhania, Sir Padampat, Kt.
Sitwell, Sir (Sacheverell) Reresby, Bt. (1808)
Skeet, Sir Trevor Herbert Harry, Kt., MP
Skeggs, Sir Clifford George, Kt.
Skehel, Sir John James, Kt., FRS
Skingsley, *Air Chief Marshal* Sir Anthony Gerald, GBE, KCB
Skinner, Sir (Thomas) Keith (Hewitt), Bt. (1912)
Skipwith, Sir Patrick Alexander d'Estoteville, Bt. (1622)
Skyrme, Sir (William) Thomas (Charles), KCVO, CB, CBE, TD
Slack, Sir William Willatt, KCVO, FRCS
Slade, Sir Benjamin Julian Alfred, Bt. (1831)
Slade, *Rt. Hon.* Sir Christopher John, Kt.
Slaney, *Prof.* Sir Geoffrey, KBE
Slater, *Adm.* Sir John (Jock) Cunningham Kirkwood, GCB, LVO
Sleight, Sir Richard, Bt. (1920)
Sloan, Sir Andrew Kirkpatrick, Kt., QPM
Sloman, Sir Albert Edward, Kt., CBE
Smallwood, *Air Chief Marshal* Sir Denis Graham, GBE, KCB, DSO, DFC
Smart, *Prof.* Sir George Algernon, Kt., MD, FRCP
Smart, Sir Jack, Kt., CBE
Smedley, *Hon.* Sir (Frank) Brian, Kt.
Smedley, Sir Harold, KCMG, MBE
Smiley, *Lt.-Col.* Sir John Philip, Bt. (1903)
Smith, Sir Alan, Kt., CBE, DFC
Smith, Sir Alexander Mair, Kt., Ph.D.
Smith, Sir Andrew Colin Hugh-, Kt.
Smith, *Lt.-Gen.* Sir Anthony Arthur Denison-, KBE
Smith, Sir Charles Bracewell-, Bt. (1947)
Smith, Sir Christopher Sydney Winwood, Bt. (1809)
Smith, *Prof.* Sir Colin Stansfield, Kt., CBE
Smith, Sir Cyril, Kt., MBE
Smith, *Prof.* Sir David Cecil, Kt., FRS
Smith, *Air Chief Marshal* Sir David Harcourt-, GBE, KCB, DFC
Smith, Sir David Iser, KCVO
Smith, Sir Douglas Boucher, KCB
Smith, Sir Dudley (Gordon), Kt., MP
Smith, *Maj.-Gen.* Sir (Francis) Brian Wyldbore-, Kt., CB, DSO, OBE
Smith, *Prof.* Sir Francis Graham-, Kt., FRS
Smith, Sir Geoffrey Johnson, Kt., MP

Smith, Sir John Alfred, Kt., QPM
Smith, *Prof.* Sir John Cyril, Kt., CBE, QC, FBA
Smith, Sir John Hamilton-Spencer-, Bt. (1804)
Smith, Sir John Jonah Walker-, Bt. (1960)
Smith, Sir John Kenneth Newson-, Bt. (1944)
Smith, Sir John Lindsay Eric., Kt., CH, CBE
†Smith, Sir John Rathbone Vassar-, Bt. (1917)
Smith, Sir Joseph William Grenville, Kt., MD, FRCP
Smith, Sir Leslie Edward George, Kt.
Smith, Sir Michael John Llewellyn, KCVO, CMG
Smith, *Rt. Hon.* Sir Murray Stuart-, Kt.
Smith, Sir Raymond Horace, KBE
Smith, Sir Robert Courtney, Kt., CBE
Smith, Sir Robert Hill, Bt. (1945)
Smith, *Prof.* Sir Roland, Kt.
Smith, *Air Marshal* Sir Roy David Austen-, KBE, CB, CVO, DFC
Smith, *Lt.-Gen.* Sir Rupert Anthony, KCB, DSO, OBE, QGM
Smith, Sir (Thomas) Gilbert, Bt. (1897)
Smith, *Prof.* Sir Trevor Arthur, Kt.
Smith, *Adm.* Sir Victor Alfred Trumper, KBE, CB, DSC
Smith, Sir (William) Antony (John) Reardon-, Bt. (1920)
Smith, Sir (William) Richard Prince-, Bt. (1911)
Smithers, Sir Peter Henry Berry Otway, Kt., VRD, D.Phil.
Smyth, Sir Thomas Weyland Bowyer-, Bt. (1661)
Smyth, Sir Timothy John, Bt. (1955)
Soakimori, Sir Frederick Pa-Nukuanca, KBE, CPM
Soame, Sir Charles John Buckworth-Herne-, Bt. (1697)
Sobers, Sir Garfield St Auburn, Kt.
Solomon, Sir David Arnold, Kt., MBE
Solomon, Sir Harry, Kt.
Solti, Sir Georg, KBE
Somare, *Rt. Hon.* Sir Michael Thomas, GCMG, CH
Somers, *Rt. Hon.* Sir Edward Jonathan, Kt.
Somerset, Sir Henry Beaufort, Kt., CBE
Somerville, *Brig.* Sir John Nicholas, Kt., CBE
Somerville, Sir Quentin Charles Somerville Agnew-, Bt. (1957)
Sopwith, Sir Charles Ronald, Kt.
Soutar, *Air Marshal* Sir Charles John Williamson, KBE
South, Sir Arthur, Kt.
Southby, Sir John Richard Bilbe, Bt. (1937)
Southern, Sir Richard William, Kt., FBA
Southern, Sir Robert, Kt., CBE
Southey, Sir Robert John, Kt., CMG

Southgate, Sir Colin Grieve, Kt.

Southgate, Sir William David, Kt.

Southward, Sir Leonard Bingley, Kt., OBE

Southward, Sir Ralph, KCVO, FRCP

Southwood, *Prof.* Sir (Thomas) Richard (Edmund), Kt., FRS

Southworth, Sir Frederick, Kt., QC

Souyave, *Hon.* Sir (Louis) Georges, Kt.

Sowrey, *Air Marshal* Sir Frederick Beresford, KCB, CBE, AFC

Sparkes, Sir Robert Lyndley, Kt.

Sparrow, Sir John, Kt.

Spearman, Sir Alexander Young Richard Mainwaring, Bt. (1840)

Spedding, *Prof.* Sir Colin Raymond William, Kt., CBE

Spedding, Sir David Rolland, KCMG, CVO, OBE

Speed, Sir (Herbert) Keith, Kt., RD, MP

Speed, Sir Robert William Arney, Kt., CB, QC

Speelman, Sir Cornelis Jacob, Bt. (1686)

Speight, *Hon.* Sir Graham Davies, Kt.

Speir, Sir Rupert Malise, Kt.

Spencer, Sir Derek Harold, Kt., QC, MP

Spicer, Sir James Wilton, Kt., MP

Spicer, Sir Nicholas Adrian Albert, Bt., MB (1906)

Spicer, Sir William Michael Hardy, Kt., MP

Spiers, Sir Donald Maurice, Kt., CB, TD

Spooner, Sir James Douglas, Kt.

Spotswood, *Marshal of the Royal Air Force* Sir Denis Frank, GCB, CBE, DSO, DFC

Spratt, *Col.* Sir Greville Douglas, GBE, TD

Spring, Sir Dryden Thomas, Kt.

Spry, *Hon.* Sir John Farley, Kt.

Stabb, *Hon.* Sir William Walter, Kt., QC

Stainton, Sir (John) Ross, Kt., CBE

Stakis, Sir Reo Argiros, Kt.

Stamer, Sir (Lovelace) Anthony, Bt. (1809)

Stanbridge, *Air Vice-Marshal* Sir Brian Gerald Tivy, KCVO, CBE, AFC

Stanier, Sir Beville Douglas, Bt. (1917)

Stanier, *Field Marshal* Sir John Wilfred, GCB, MBE

Stanley, *Rt. Hon.* Sir John Paul, Kt., MP

†Staples, Sir Thomas, Bt. (I. 1628)

Stark, Sir Andrew Alexander Steel, KCMG, CVO

Starke, *Hon.* Sir John Erskine, Kt.

Starkey, Sir John Philip, Bt. (1935)

Starrit, Sir James, KCVO

Statham, Sir Norman, KCMG, CVO

Staughton, *Rt. Hon.* Sir Christopher Stephen Thomas Jonathan Thayer, Kt.

Staveley, Sir John Malfroy, KBE, MC

Staveley, *Admiral of the Fleet* Sir William Doveton Minet, GCB

Stear, *Air Chief Marshal* Sir Michael James Douglas, KCB, CBE

Steel, Sir David Edward Charles, Kt., DSO, MC, TD

Steel, *Rt. Hon.* Sir David Martin Scott, KBE, MP

Steel, *Maj.* Sir (Fiennes) Michael Strang, Bt. (1938)

Steele, Sir (Philip John) Rupert, Kt.

Steere, Sir Ernest Henry Lee-, KBE

Stenhouse, Sir Nicol, Kt.

Stening, *Col.* Sir George Grafton Lees, Kt., ED

Stephen, *Rt. Hon.* Sir Ninian Martin, KG, GCMG, GCVO, KBE

Stephenson, Sir Henry Upton, Bt. (1936)

Stephenson, *Rt. Hon.* Sir John Frederick Eustace, Kt.

Sternberg, Sir Sigmund, Kt.

Stevens, Sir Jocelyn Edward Greville, Kt., CVO

Stevens, Sir Laurence Houghton, Kt., CBE

Stevenson, *Vice-Adm.* Sir (Hugh) David, KBE

Stevenson, Sir Simpson, Kt.

Stewart, Sir Alan, KBE

Stewart, Sir Alan d'Arcy, Bt. (I. 1623)

Stewart, Sir David James Henderson-, Bt. (1957)

Stewart, Sir David John Christopher, Bt. (1803)

Stewart, Sir Edward Jackson, Kt.

Stewart, *Prof.* Sir Frederick Henry, Kt., PH.D., FRS, FRSE

Stewart, Sir Houston Mark Shaw-, Bt., MC, TD (S. 1667)

Stewart, Sir James Douglas, Kt.

Stewart, Sir James Moray, KCB

Stewart, Sir (John) Simon (Watson), Bt. (1920)

Stewart, Sir Robertson Huntly, Kt., CBE

Stewart, Sir Robin Alastair, Bt. (1960)

Stewart, Sir Ronald Compton, Bt. (1937)

Stewart, Prof. Sir William Duncan Paterson, Kt., FRS, FRSE

Stibbon, *Gen.* Sir John James, KCB, OBE

Stirling, Sir Alexander John Dickson, KBE, CMG

Stirling, Sir Angus Duncan Aeneas, Kt.

Stockdale, Sir Arthur Noel, Kt.

Stockdale, Sir Thomas Minshull, Bt. (1960)

Stocker, *Rt. Hon.* Sir John Dexter, Kt., MC, TD

Stoddart, *Wg Cdr.* Sir Kenneth Maxwell, KCVO, AE

Stoker, *Prof.* Sir Michael George Parke, Kt., CBE, FRCP, FRS, FRSE

Stokes, Sir John Heydon Romaine, Kt.

Stone, Sir Alexander, Kt., OBE

Stones, Sir William Frederick, Kt., OBE

Stonhouse, Sir Philip Allan, Bt. (1628)

Stonor, *Air Marshal* Sir Thomas Henry, KCB

Storey, *Hon.* Sir Richard, Bt., CBE (1960)

Stormonth Darling, Sir James Carlisle, Kt., CBE, MC, TD

Stott, Sir Adrian George Ellingham, Bt. (1920)

Stow, Sir Christopher Philipson-, Bt., DFC (1907)

Stow, Sir John Montague, GCMG, KCVO

Stowe, Sir Kenneth Ronald, GCB, CVO

Stracey, Sir John Simon, Bt. (1818)

Strachan, Sir Curtis Victor, Kt., CVO

Strachey, Sir Charles, Bt. (1801)

Straker, Sir Michael Ian Bowstead, Kt., CBE

Strawson, *Prof.* Sir Peter Frederick, Kt., FBA

Street, *Hon.* Sir Laurence Whistler, KCMG

Streeton, Sir Terence George, KBE, CMG

Stringer, Sir Donald Edgar, Kt., CBE

Strong, Sir Roy Colin, Kt., PH.D., FSA

Stronge, Sir James Anselan Maxwell, Bt. (1803)

Stroud, *Prof.* Sir (Charles) Eric, Kt., FRCP

Strutt, Sir Nigel Edward, Kt., TD

Stuart, Sir James Keith, Kt.

Stuart, Sir Kenneth Lamonte, Kt.

†Stuart, Sir Phillip Luttrell, Bt. (1660)

Stubblefield, Sir (Cyril) James, Kt., D.SC., FRS

Stubbs, Sir James Wilfrid, KCVO, TD

Stubbs, Sir William Hamilton, Kt., PH.D.

Stuceley, *Lt.* Sir Hugh George Coplestone Bampfylde, Bt. (1859)

Studd, Sir Edward Fairfax, Bt. (1929)

Studd, Sir Peter Malden, GBE, KCVO

Studholme, Sir Henry William, Bt. (1956)

Stuttaford, Sir William Royden, Kt., CBE

Style, *Lt.-Cdr.* Sir Godfrey William, Kt., CBE, DSC, RN

†Style, Sir William Frederick, Bt. (1627)

Suffield, Sir (Henry John) Lester, Kt.

Sugden, Sir Arthur, Kt.

Sullivan, Sir Desmond John, Kt.

Sullivan, Sir Richard Arthur, Bt. (1804)

Summerfield, *Hon.* Sir John Crampton, Kt., CBE

Sutherland, Sir John Brewer, Bt. (1921)

Sutherland, Sir Maurice, Kt.

Sutherland, *Prof.* Sir Stewart Ross, Kt., FBA

Sutherland, Sir William George MacKenzie, Kt.

Suttie, Sir (George) Philip Grant-,
Bt. (s. 1702)
Sutton, Sir Frederick Walter, Kt., OBE
Sutton, *Air Marshal* Sir John
Matthias Dobson, KCB
Sutton, Sir Richard Lexington, Bt.
(1772)
Swaffield, Sir James Chesebrough,
Kt., CBE, RD
Swaine, Sir John Joseph, Kt., CBE
Swallow, Sir William, Kt.
Swan, Sir Conrad Marshall John
Fisher, KCVO, ph.D.
Swan, Sir John William David, KBE
Swann, Sir Michael Christopher, Bt.,
TD (1906)
Swanwick, Sir Graham Russell, Kt.,
MBE
Swartz, *Hon.* Sir Reginald William
Colin, KBE, ED
Sweetnam, Sir (David) Rodney,
KCVO, CBE, FRCS
Swinburn, *Lt.-Gen.* Sir Richard Hull,
KCB
Swinson, Sir John Henry Alan, Kt.,
OBE
Swinton, *Maj.-Gen.* Sir John, KCVO,
OBE
Swire, Sir Adrian Christopher, Kt.
Swire, Sir John Anthony, Kt., CBE
Swynnerton, Sir Roger John Massy,
Kt., CMG, OBE, MC
Sykes, Sir Francis John Badcock, Bt.
(1781)
Sykes, Sir John Charles Anthony le
Gallais, Bt. (1921)
Sykes, *Prof.* Sir (Malcolm) Keith, Kt.
Sykes, Sir Richard, Kt.
Sykes, Sir Tatton Christopher Mark,
Bt. (1783)
Symington, *Prof.* Sir Thomas, Kt.,
MD, FRSE
Symons, *Vice-Adm.* Sir Patrick
Jeremy, KBE
Synge, Sir Robert Carson, Bt. (1801)
Tait, *Adm.* Sir (Allan) Gordon, KCB,
DSC
Tait, Sir James Sharp, Kt., D.SC., LLD.,
ph.D.
Tait, Sir Peter, KBE
Talbot, *Vice-Adm.* Sir (Arthur
Allison) FitzRoy, KBE, CB, DSO
Talbot, *Hon.* Sir Hilary Gwynne, Kt.
Talboys, *Rt. Hon.* Sir Brian Edward,
CH, KCB
Tancred, Sir Henry Lawson-, Bt.
(1662)
Tangaroa, *Hon.* Sir Tangoroa, Kt.,
MBE
Tange, Sir Arthur Harold, Kt., CBE
Tapsell, Sir Peter Hannay Bailey,
Kt., MP
Tate, Sir (Henry) Saxon, Bt. (1898)
Tavaiqia, *Ratu* Sir Josaia, KBE
Tavare, Sir John, Kt., CBE
Taylor, *Lt.-Gen.* Sir Allan Macnab,
KBE, MC
Taylor, Sir (Arthur) Godfrey, Kt.
Taylor, Sir Cyril Julian Hebden, Kt.

Taylor, Sir Edward Macmillan
(Teddy), Kt., MP
Taylor, Sir John Lang, KCMG
Taylor, Sir Nicholas Richard Stuart,
Bt. (1917)
Taylor, *Prof.* Sir William, Kt., CBE
Teagle, *Vice-Adm.* Sir Somerford
Francis, KBE
Tebbit, Sir Donald Claude, GCMG
Te Heuheu, Sir Hepi Hoani, KBE
Telford, Sir Robert, Kt., CBE, FEng.
Temple, Sir Ernest Sanderson, Kt.,
MBE, QC
Temple, Sir Rawden John Afamado,
Kt., CBE, QC
Temple, *Maj.* Sir Richard Anthony
Purbeck, Bt., MC (1876)
Templeton, Sir John Marks, Kt.
Tenison, Sir Richard Hanbury-,
KCVO
Tennant, *Capt.* Sir Iain Mark, KT
Tennant, Sir Anthony John, Kt.
Tennant, Sir Peter Frank Dalrymple,
Kt., CMG, OBE
Teo, Sir Fiatau Penitala, GCMG,
GCVO, ISO, MBE
Terry, Sir Michael Edward Stanley
Imbert-, Bt. (1917)
Terry, *Air Chief Marshal* Sir Peter
David George, GCB, AFC
Tetley, Sir Herbert, KBE, CB
Tett, Sir Hugh Charles, Kt.
Thatcher, Sir Denis, Bt., MBE, TD
(1990)
Thesiger, Sir Wilfred Patrick, KBE,
DSO
Thomas, Sir Derek Morison David,
KCMG
Thomas, Sir Frederick William, Kt.
Thomas, Sir (Godfrey) Michael
(David), Bt. (1694)
Thomas, Sir Jeremy Cashel, KCMG
Thomas, Sir (John) Alan, Kt.
Thomas, Sir John Maldwyn, Kt.
Thomas, *Prof.* Sir John Meurig, Kt.,
FRS
Thomas, Sir Keith Vivian, Kt.
Thomas, Sir Robert Evan, Kt.
Thomas, *Hon.* Sir Roger John
Laugharne, Kt.
Thomas, *Hon.* Sir Swinton Barclay,
Kt.
Thomas, Sir William James Cooper,
Bt., TD (1919)
Thomas, Sir (William) Michael
(Marsh), Bt. (1918)
Thomas, *Adm.* Sir (William) Richard
Scott, KCB, KCVO, OBE
Thompson, Sir Christopher Peile,
Bt. (1890)
Thompson, Sir Clive Malcolm, Kt.
Thompson, Sir Donald, Kt., MP
Thompson, Sir Gilbert Williamson,
Kt., OBE
Thompson, *Surgeon Vice-Adm.* Sir
Godfrey James Milton-, KBE
Thompson, *Vice-Adm.* Sir Hugh
Leslie Owen, KBE, FEng.
Thompson, Sir (Humphrey) Simon
Meysey-, Bt. (1874)

Thompson, *Prof.* Sir Michael
Warwick, Kt., D.SC
Thompson, Sir Paul Anthony, Bt.
(1963)
Thompson, Sir Peter Anthony, Kt.
Thompson, Sir Richard Hilton
Marler, Bt. (1963)
Thompson, Sir (Thomas) Lionel
Tennyson, Bt. (1806)
Thomson, Sir Adam, Kt., CBE
Thomson, Sir (Frederick Douglas)
David, Bt. (1929)
Thomson, Sir John, KBE, TD
Thomson, Sir John Adam, GCMG
Thomson, Sir John (Ian) Sutherland,
KBE, CMG
Thomson, Sir Mark Wilfrid Home,
Bt. (1925)
Thomson, Sir Thomas James, Kt.,
CBE, FRCP
Thorn, Sir John Samuel, Kt., OBE
Thorne, *Maj.-Gen.* Sir David
Calthrop, KBE, CVO
Thorne, Sir Neil Gordon, Kt., OBE,
TD
Thorne, Sir Peter Francis, KCVO, CBE
Thornton, Sir (George) Malcolm,
Kt., MP
Thornton, *Lt.-Gen.* Sir Leonard
Whitmore, KCB, CBE
Thornton, Sir Peter Eustace, KCB
Thorold, Sir Anthony Henry, Bt.,
OBE, DSC (1642)
Thorpe, *Hon.* Sir Mathew Alexander,
Kt.
Thouron, Sir John Rupert Hunt, KBE
Thwaites, Sir Bryan, Kt., ph.D.
Thwin, Sir U, Kt.
Tibbits, *Capt.* Sir David Stanley, Kt.,
DSC
Tickell, Sir Crispin Charles
Cervantes, GCMG, KCVO
Tidbury, Sir Charles Henderson, Kt.
Tikaram, Sir Moti, KBE
Tims, Sir Michael David, KCVO
Tindle, Sir Ray Stanley, Kt., CBE
Tippet, *Vice-Adm.* Sir Anthony
Sanders, KCB
Tippett, Sir Michael Kemp, Kt., OM,
CH, CBE
†Tipping, Sir David Gwynne Evans-,
Bt. (1913)
Tirvengadum, Sir Harry Krishnan,
Kt.
Titman, Sir John Edward Powis,
KCVO
Tod, *Air Marshal* Sir John Hunter
Hunter-, KBE, CB
Tod, *Vice-Adm.* Sir Jonathan James
Richard, KCB, CBE
Todd, *Prof.* Sir David, Kt., CBE
Todd, Sir Ian Pelham, KBE, FRCS
Todd, *Hon.* Sir (Reginald Stephen)
Garfield, Kt.
Tollemache, Sir Lyonel Humphry
John, Bt. (1793)
Tololo, Sir Alkan, KBE
Tomkins, Sir Alfred George, Kt., CBE
Tomkins, Sir Edward Emile, GCMG,
CVO

Tomkys, Sir (William) Roger, KCMG

Tomlinson, *Prof.* Sir Bernard Evans, Kt., CBE

Tooley, Sir John, Kt.

Tooth, Sir (Hugh) John Lucas-, Bt. (1920)

ToRobert, Sir Henry Thomas, KBE

Tory, Sir Geofroy William, KCMG

Touche, Sir Anthony George, Bt. (1920)

Touche, Sir Rodney Gordon, Bt. (1962)

Toulson, *Hon.* Sir Roger Grenfell, Kt.

Tovey, Sir Brian John Maynard, KCMG

ToVue, Sir Ronald, Kt., OBE

Towneley, Sir Simon Peter Edmund Cosmo William, KCVO

Townsend, *Rear-Adm.* Sir Leslie William, KCVO, CBE

Townsing, Sir Kenneth Joseph, Kt., CMG

Traill, Sir Alan Towers, GBE

Trant, *Gen.* Sir Richard Brooking, KCB

Travers, Sir Thomas à'Beckett, Kt.

Treacher, *Adm.* Sir John Devereux, KCB

Trehane, Sir (Walter) Richard, Kt.

Trelawny, Sir John Barry Salusbury-, Bt. (1628)

Trench, Sir Peter Edward, Kt., CBE, TD

Trescowthick, Sir Donald Henry, KBE

Trevelyan, Sir Geoffrey Washington, Bt. (1874)

Trevelyan, Sir Norman Irving, Bt. (1662)

Trewby, *Vice-Adm.* Sir (George Francis) Allan, KCB, FEng.

Trezise, Sir Kenneth Bruce, Kt., OBE

Trippier, Sir David Austin, Kt., RD

Tritton, Sir Anthony John Ernest, Bt. (1905)

†Trollope, Sir Anthony Simon, Bt. (1642)

Trotter, Sir Ronald Ramsay, Kt.

Troubridge, Sir Thomas Richard, Bt. (1799)

Troup, *Vice-Adm.* Sir (John) Anthony (Rose), KCB, DSC

Trowbridge, *Rear-Adm.* Sir Richard John, KCVO

Truscott, Sir George James Irving, Bt. (1909)

Tuck, Sir Bruce Adolph Reginald, Bt. (1910)

Tucker, *Hon.* Sir Richard Howard, Kt.

Tuckey, *Hon.* Sir Simon Lane, Kt.

Tuita, Sir Mariano Kelesimalefo, Kt., OBE

Tuite, Sir Christopher Hugh, Bt., ph.D. (1622)

Tuivaga, Sir Timoci Uluiburotu, Kt.

Tuke, Sir Anthony Favill, Kt.

Tumim, *His Hon.* Sir Stephen, Kt.

Tupper, Sir Charles Hibbert, Bt. (1888)

Turbott, Sir Ian Graham, Kt., CMG, CVO

Turing, Sir John Dermot, Bt. (s. 1638)

Turnberg, *Prof.* Sir Leslie Arnold, Kt., MD, FRCP

Turnbull, Sir Richard Gordon, GCMG

Turner, Sir Colin William Carstairs, Kt., CBE, DFC

Turner, *Hon.* Sir Michael John, Kt.

Turnquest, Sir Orville Alton, GCMG, QC

Tuti, *Revd* Dudley, KBE

Tuzo, *Gen.* Sir Harry Craufurd, GCB, OBE, MC

Tweedie, *Prof.* Sir David Philip, Kt.

Tyree, Sir (Alfred) William, Kt., OBE

Tyrwhitt, Sir Reginald Thomas Newman, Bt. (1919)

Udoma, *Hon.* Sir (Egbert) Udo, Kt.

Unsworth, *Hon.* Sir Edgar Ignatius Godfrey, Kt., CMG

Unwin, Sir (James) Brian, KCB

Ure, Sir John Burns, KCMG, LVO

Urquhart, Sir Brian Edward, KCMG, MBE

Urwick, Sir Alan Bedford, KCVO, CMG

Usher, Sir Leonard Gray, KBE

Usher, Sir (William) John Tevenar, Bt. (1899)

Ustinov, Sir Peter Alexander, Kt., CBE

Utting, Sir William Benjamin, Kt., CB

Vai, Sir Mea, Kt., CBE, ISO

Vallance, Sir Iain David Thomas, Kt.

Vallat, Sir Francis Aimé, GBE, KCMG, QC

Vallings, *Vice-Adm.* Sir George Montague Francis, KCB

Vanderfelt, Sir Robin Victor, KBE

van der Post, Sir Laurens Jan, Kt., CBE

Vane, Sir John Robert, Kt., D.phil., D.SC, FRS

Vanneck, *Air Cdre* Hon. Sir Peter Beckford Rutgers, GBE, CB, AFC

van Straubenzee, Sir William Radcliffe, Kt., MBE

Vasquez, Sir Alfred Joseph, Kt., CBE, QC

Vaughan, Sir Gerard Folliott, Kt., MP, FRCP

Vavasour, *Cdr.* Sir Geoffrey William, Bt., DSC, RN (1828)

Veale, Sir Alan John Ralph, Kt., FEng.

Verco, Sir Walter John George, KCVO

†Verney, Sir John Sebastian, Bt. (1946)

Verney, *Hon.* Sir Lawrence John, Kt., TD

Verney, Sir Ralph Bruce, Bt., KBE (1818)

Vernon, Sir James, Kt., CBE

Vernon, Sir Nigel John Douglas, Bt. (1914)

Vernon, Sir (William) Michael, Kt.

Vesey, Sir (Nathaniel) Henry (Peniston), Kt., CBE

Vestey, Sir (John) Derek, Bt. (1921)

Vial, Sir Kenneth Harold, Kt., CBE

Vick, Sir (Francis) Arthur, Kt., OBE, ph.D.

Vickers, *Lt.-Gen.* Sir Richard Maurice Hilton, KCB, LVO, OBE

Victoria, Sir (Joseph Aloysius) Donatus, Kt., CBE

Vincent, *Field Marshal* Sir Richard Frederick, GBE, KCB, DSO

Vincent, Sir William Percy Maxwell, Bt. (1936)

Vinelott, *Hon.* Sir John Evelyn, Kt.

Vines, Sir William Joshua, Kt., CMG

†Vyvyan, Sir Ralph Ferrers Alexander, Bt. (1645)

Waddell, Sir Alexander Nicol Anton, KCMG, DSC

Waddell, Sir James Henderson, Kt., CB

Wade, *Prof.* Sir Henry William Rawson, Kt., QC, FBA

Wade, *Air Chief Marshal* Sir Ruthven Lowry, KCB, DFC

Waite, *Rt. Hon.* Sir John Douglas, Kt.

Wake, Sir Hereward, Bt., MC (1621)

Wakefield, Sir (Edward) Humphry (Tyrell), Bt. (1962)

Wakefield, Sir Norman Edward, Kt.

Wakefield, Sir Peter George Arthur, KBE, CMG

Wakeford, *Air Marshal* Sir Richard Gordon, KCB, OBE, LVO, AFC

Wakeley, Sir John Cecil Nicholson, Bt., FRCS (1952)

†Wakeman, Sir Edward Offley Bertram, Bt. (1828)

Walford, Sir Christopher Rupert, Kt.

Walker, *Revd* Alan Edgar, Kt., OBE

Walker, *Gen.* Sir Antony Kenneth Frederick, KCB

Walker, Sir Baldwin Patrick, Bt. (1856)

Walker, Sir (Charles) Michael, GCMG

Walker, Sir Colin John Shedlock, Kt., OBE

Walker, Sir David Alan, Kt.

Walker, Sir Gervas George, Kt.

Walker, *Rt. Hon.* Sir Harold, Kt., MP

Walker, Sir Harold Berners, KCMG

Walker, *Maj.* Sir Hugh Ronald, Bt. (1906)

Walker, Sir James Graham, Kt., MBE

Walker, Sir James Heron, Bt. (1868)

Walker, *Air Marshal* Sir John Robert, KCB, CBE, AFC

Walker, *Lt.-Gen.* Sir Michael John Dawson, KCB, CBE

Walker, Sir Michael Leolin Forestier-, Bt. (1835)

Walker, Sir Patrick Jeremy, KCB

Walker, *Hon.* Sir Robert, Kt.

Walker, Sir Rodney Myerscough, Kt.

Walker, *Gen.* Sir Walter Colyear, KCB, CBE, DSO

Wall, Sir (John) Stephen, KCMG, LVO

Wall, *Hon.* Sir Nicholas Peter Rathbone, Kt.

Wall, Sir Patrick Henry Bligh, Kt., MC, VRD

Wall, Sir Robert William, Kt., OBE

Wallace, Sir Ian James, Kt., CBE

Waller, *Hon.* Sir (George) Mark, Kt.
Waller, *Rt. Hon.* Sir George Stanley,
Kt., OBE
Waller, Sir Robert William, Bt.
(I. 1780)
Walley, Sir John, KBE, CB
Wallis, Sir Peter Gordon, KCVO
Wallis, Sir Timothy William, Kt.
Walmsley, *Vice-Adm.* Sir Robert, KCB
Walsh, Sir Alan, Kt., D.SC., FRS
Walsh, *Prof.* Sir John Patrick, KBE
†Walsham, Sir Timothy John, Bt.
(1831)
Walter, Sir Harold Edward, Kt.
Walters, *Prof.* Sir Alan Arthur, Kt.
Walters, Sir Dennis Murray, Kt., MBE
Walters, Sir Frederick Donald, Kt.
Walters, Sir Peter Ingram, Kt.
Walters, Sir Roger Talbot, KBE, FRIBA
Walton, Sir John Robert, Kt.
Wan, Sir Wamp, Kt., MBE
Wanstall, *Hon.* Sir Charles Gray, Kt.
Ward, *Rt. Hon.* Sir Alan Hylton, Kt.
Ward, Sir Joseph James Laffey, Bt.
(1911)
Ward, *Maj.-Gen.* Sir Philip John
Newling, KCVO, CBE
Ward, Sir Timothy James, Kt.
Wardale, Sir Geoffrey Charles, KCB
Wardlaw, Sir Henry (John), Bt.
(s. 1631)
Wardle, Sir Thomas Edward Jewell,
Kt.
Waring, Sir (Alfred) Holburt, Bt.
(1935)
Warmington, Sir Marshall Denham
Malcolm, Bt. (1908)
Warner, Sir (Edward Courtenay)
Henry, Bt. (1910)
Warner, Sir Edward Redston, KCMG,
OBE
Warner, *Prof.* Sir Frederick Edward,
Kt., FRS, FEng.
Warner, Sir Gerald Chierici, KCMG
Warner, *Hon.* Sir Jean-Pierre Frank
Eugene, Kt.
†Warren, Sir Michael Blackley, Bt.
(1784)
Warren, Sir (Frederick) Miles, KBE
Warren, Sir Kenneth Robin, Kt.
Wass, Sir Douglas William Gretton,
GCB
Waterhouse, *Hon.* Sir Ronald Gough,
Kt.
Waterlow, Sir Christopher Rupert,
Bt. (1873)
Waterlow, Sir (James) Gerard, Bt.
(1930)
Waters, *Gen.* Sir (Charles) John, GCB,
CBE
Waters, Sir Thomas Neil Morris, Kt.
Wates, Sir Christopher Stephen, Kt.
Watkins, *Rt. Hon.* Sir Tasker, VC, GBE
Watson, Sir Bruce Dunstan, Kt.
Watson, Sir Duncan Amos, Kt., CBE
Watson, Sir (James) Andrew, Bt.
(1866)
Watson, Sir John Forbes Inglefield-,
Bt. (1895)

Watson, Sir Michael Milne-, Bt., CBE
(1937)
Watson, Sir (Noel) Duncan, KCMG
Watson, *Vice-Adm.* Sir Philip
Alexander, KBE, LVO
Watt, *Surgeon Vice-Adm.* Sir James,
KBE, FRCS
Watt, Sir James Harvie-, Bt. (1945)
Watts, Sir Arthur Desmond, KCMG
Watts, *Lt.-Gen.* Sir John Peter Barry
Condliffe, KBE, CB, MC
Wauchope, Sir Roger (Hamilton)
Don-, Bt. (s. 1667)
Way, Sir Richard George Kitchener,
KCB, CBE
Weatherall, *Prof.* Sir David John, Kt.,
FRS
Weatherall, *Vice-Adm.* Sir James
Lamb, KBE
Weatherstone, Sir Dennis, KBE
Weaver, Sir Tobias Rushton, Kt., CB
Webb, Sir Thomas Langley, Kt.
Webber, Sir Andrew Lloyd, Kt.
Webster, *Very Revd* Alan Brunskill,
KCVO
Webster, *Vice-Adm.* Sir John
Morrison, KCB
Webster, *Hon.* Sir Peter Edlin, Kt.
Wedderburn, Sir Andrew John
Alexander Ogilvy-, Bt. (1803)
Wedgwood, Sir (Hugo) Martin, Bt.
(1942)
Weekes, Sir Everton DeCourcey,
KCMG, OBE
Weinberg, Sir Mark Aubrey, Kt.
Weir, Sir Michael Scott, KCMG
Weir, Sir Roderick Bignell, Kt.
Welby, Sir (Richard) Bruno Gregory,
Bt. (1801)
Welch, Sir John Reader, Bt. (1957)
Weldon, Sir Anthony William, Bt.
(I. 1723)
Wellings, Sir Jack Alfred, Kt., CBE
†Wells, Sir Christopher Charles, Bt.
(1944)
Wells, Sir John Julius, Kt.
Westbrook, Sir Neil Gowanloch, Kt.,
CBE
Westerman, Sir (Wilfred) Alan, Kt.,
CBE
Weston, Sir Michael Charles Swift,
KCMG, CVO
Weston, Sir (Philip) John, KCMG
Whalen, Sir Geoffrey Henry, Kt., CBE
Wheeler, Sir Frederick Henry, Kt.,
CBE
Wheeler, Sir Harry Anthony, Kt.,
OBE
Wheeler, *Air Chief Marshal* Sir
(Henry) Neil (George), GCB, CBE,
DSO, DFC, AFC
Wheeler, *Rt. Hon.* Sir John Daniel,
Kt., MP
Wheeler, Sir John Hieron, Bt. (1920)
Wheeler, *Hon.* Sir Kenneth Henry,
Kt.
Wheeler, *Lt.-Gen.* Sir Roger Neil,
KCB, CBE
Whelcr, Sir Edward Woodford, Bt.
(1660)

Whent, Sir Gerald Arthur, Kt., CBE
Whishaw, Sir Charles Percival Law,
Kt.
Whitaker, *Maj.* Sir James Herbert
Ingham, Bt., OBE (1936)
White, Sir Christopher Robert
Meadows, Bt. (1937)
White, *Hon.* Sir Christopher Stuart
Stuart-, Kt.
White, Sir David Harry, Kt.
White, Sir George Stanley James, Bt.
(1904)
White, *Wg Cdr.* Sir Henry Arthur
Dalrymple-, Bt., DFC (1926)
White, *Adm.* Sir Hugo Moresby, GCB,
CBE
White, *Hon.* Sir John Charles, Kt.,
MBE
White, Sir John Woolmer, Bt. (1922)
White, Sir Lynton Stuart, Kt., MBE,
TD
White, *Adm.* Sir Peter, GBE
White, Sir Thomas Astley
Woollaston, Bt. (1802)
Whitehead, Sir John Stainton, GCMG,
CVO
Whitehead, Sir Rowland John
Rathbone, Bt. (1889)
Whiteley, Sir Hugo Baldwin
Huntington-, Bt. (1918)
Whiteley, *Gen.* Sir Peter John
Frederick, GCB, OBE, RM
Whitfield, Sir William, Kt., CBE
Whitford, *Hon.* Sir John Norman
Keates, Kt.
Whitley, *Air Marshal* Sir John René,
KBE, CB, DSO, AFC
Whitmore, Sir Clive Anthony, GCB,
CVO
Whitmore, Sir John Henry Douglas,
Bt. (1954)
Whittome, Sir (Leslie) Alan, Kt.
Wickerson, Sir John Michael, Kt.
Wicks, Sir James Albert, Kt.
Wicks, Sir Nigel Leonard, KCB, CVO,
CBE
†Wigan, Sir Michael Iain, Bt. (1898)
Wiggin, Sir Alfred William (Jerry),
Kt., TD, MP
†Wiggin, Sir Charles Rupert John,
Bt. (1892)
Wigram, *Revd Canon* Sir Clifford
Woolmore, Bt. (1805)
Wilbraham, Sir Richard Baker, Bt.
(1776)
Wilford, Sir (Kenneth) Michael,
GCMG
Wilkes, *Gen.* Sir Michael John, KCB,
CBE
Wilkins, Sir Graham John, Kt.
Wilkinson, Sir (David) Graham
(Brook) Bt. (1941)
Wilkinson, *Prof.* Sir Denys Haigh,
Kt., FRS
Wilkinson, *Prof.* Sir Geoffrey, Kt.,
FRS
Wilkinson, Sir Peter Allix, KCMG,
DSO, OBE
Wilkinson, Sir Philip William, Kt.
Willatt, Sir (Robert) Hugh, Kt.

Willcocks, Sir David Valentine, Kt., CBE, MC
Williams, Sir Alastair Edgcumbe James Dudley-, Bt. (1964)
Williams, Sir Alwyn, Kt., ph.D., FRS
Williams, Sir Arthur Dennis Pitt, Kt.
Williams, Sir (Arthur) Gareth Ludovic Emrys Rhys, Bt. (1918)
Williams, *Prof.* Sir Bruce Rodda, KBE
Williams, *Adm.* Sir David, GCB
Williams, *Prof.* Sir David Glyndwr Tudor, Kt.
Williams, Sir David Innes, Kt.
Williams, *Hon.* Sir Denys Ambrose, KCMG
Williams, Sir Donald Mark, Bt. (1866)
Williams, *Prof.* Sir (Edward) Dillwyn, Kt., FRCP
Williams, *Hon.* Sir Edward Stratten, KCMG, KBE
Williams, *Prof.* Sir Glanmor, Kt., CBE, FBA
Williams, Sir Henry Sydney, Kt., OBE
Williams, Sir John Robert, KCMG
Williams, Sir (Lawrence) Hugh, Bt. (1798)
Williams, Sir Leonard, KBE, CB
Williams, Sir Osmond, Bt., MC (1909)
Williams, *Prof.* Sir Robert Evan Owen, Kt., MD, FRCP
Williams, Sir (Robert) Philip Nathaniel, Bt. (1915)
Williams, Sir Robin Philip, Bt. (1953)
Williams, Sir (William) Maxwell (Harries), Kt.
Williamson, *Marshal of the Royal Air Force* Sir Keith Alec, GCB, AFC
Williamson, Sir (Nicholas Frederick) Hedworth, Bt. (1642)
Willink, Sir Charles William, Bt. (1957)
Willis, *Hon.* Sir Eric Archibald, KBE, CMG
Willis, *Vice-Adm.* Sir (Guido) James, KBE
Willis, *Air Chief Marshal* Sir John Frederick, KCB, CBE
Willison, *Lt.-Gen.* Sir David John, KCB, OBE, MC
Willison, Sir John Alexander, Kt., OBE
Wills, Sir David Seton, Bt. (1904)
Wills, Sir (Hugh) David Hamilton, Kt., CBE, TD
Wills, Sir John Vernon, Bt., TD (1923)
Wilmot, Sir Henry Robert, Bt. (1759)
†Wilmot, Sir Michael John Assheton Eardley-, Bt. (1821)
Wilsey, *Gen.* Sir John Finlay Willasey, GCB, CBE
Wilson, *Lt.-Gen.* Sir (Alexander) James, KBE, MC
Wilson, Sir Anthony, Kt.
Wilson, *Vice-Adm.* Sir Barry Nigel, KCB
Wilson, *Lt.-Col.* Sir Blair Aubyn Stewart-, KCVO
Wilson, Sir Charles Haynes, Kt.

Wilson, Sir David, Bt. (1920)
Wilson, Sir David Mackenzie, Kt.
Wilson, Sir Geoffrey Masterman, KCB, CMG
Wilson, Sir James William Douglas, Bt. (1906)
Wilson, Sir John Foster, Kt., CBE
Wilson, *Brig.* Sir Mathew John Anthony, Bt., OBE, MC (1874)
Wilson, *Hon.* Sir Nicholas Allan Roy, Kt.
Wilson, Sir Patrick Michael Ernest David McNair-, Kt., MP
Wilson, Sir Reginald Holmes, Kt.
Wilson, Sir Robert, Kt., CBE
Wilson, Sir Robert Donald, KBE
Wilson, *Rt. Revd* Roger Plumpton, KCVO, DD
Wilson, Sir Roland, KBE
Wilson, *Air Chief Marshal* Sir (Ronald) Andrew (Fellowes), KCB, AFC
Wilson, *Hon.* Sir Ronald Darling, KBE, CMG
Wilton, Sir (Arthur) John, KCMG, KCVO, MC
Wiltshire, Sir Frederick Munro, Kt., CBE
Wingate, *Capt.* Sir Miles Buckley, KCVO
Winnington, Sir Francis Salwey William, Bt. (1755)
Winskill, *Air Cdre* Sir Archibald Little, KCVO, CBE, DFC
Winterbottom, Sir Walter, Kt., CBE
Wiseman, Sir John William, Bt. (1628)
Wolfendale, *Prof.* Sir Arnold Whittaker, Kt., FRS
Wolfson, Sir Brian Gordon, Kt.
Wolseley, Sir Charles Garnet Richard Mark, Bt. (1628)
†Wolseley, Sir James Douglas, Bt. (I. 1745)
Wolstenholme, Sir Gordon Ethelbert Ward, Kt., OBE
Wombwell, Sir George Philip Frederick, Bt. (1778)
Womersley, Sir Peter John Walter, Bt. (1945)
Woo, Sir Leo Joseph, Kt.
Wood, Sir Alan Marshall Muir, Kt., FRS, FEng.
Wood, Sir Andrew Marley, KCMG
Wood, Sir Anthony John Page, Bt. (1837)
Wood, Sir David Basil Hill-, Bt. (1921)
Wood, Sir Frederick Ambrose Stuart, Kt.
Wood, Sir Ian Clark, Kt., CBE
Wood, *Prof.* Sir John Crossley, Kt., CBE
Wood, *Hon.* Sir John Kember, Kt., MC
Wood, Sir Martin Francis, Kt., OBE
Wood, Sir Russell Dillon, KCVO, VRD
Wood, Sir William Alan, KCVO, CB
Woodard, *Rear Adm.* Sir Robert Nathaniel, KCVO
Woodcock, Sir John, Kt., CBE, QPM

Woodfield, Sir Philip John, KCB, CBE
Woodhead, *Vice-Adm.* Sir (Anthony) Peter, KCB
Woodhouse, *Rt. Hon.* Sir (Arthur) Owen, KBE, DSC
Wooding, Sir Norman Samuel, Kt., CBE
Woodroffe, *Most Revd* George Cuthbert Manning, KBE
Woodroofe, Sir Ernest George, Kt., ph.D.
Woodruff, *Prof.* Sir Michael Francis Addison, Kt., D.SC., FRS, FRCS
Woods, Sir Colin Philip Joseph, KCVO, CBE
Woods, *Rt. Revd* Robert Wilmer, KCMG, KCVO
Woodward, *Hon.* Sir (Albert) Edward, Kt., OBE
Woodward, *Adm.* Sir John Forster, GBE, KCB
Woolf, Sir John, Kt.
Woollaston, Sir (Mountford) Tosswill, Kt.
Wordie, Sir John Stewart, Kt., CBE, VRD
Worsley, *Gen.* Sir Richard Edward, GCB, OBE
Worsley, Sir (William) Marcus (John), Bt. (1838)
Worsthorne, Sir Peregrine Gerard, Kt.
Wraight, Sir John Richard, KBE, CMG
Wratten, *Air Chief Marshal* Sir William John, KBE, CB, AFC
Wraxall, Sir Charles Frederick Lascelles, Bt. (1813)
Wrey, Sir George Richard Bourchier, Bt. (1628)
Wrigglesworth, Sir Ian William, Kt.
Wright, Sir Allan Frederick, KBE
Wright, Sir David John, KCMG, LVO
Wright, Sir Denis Arthur Hepworth, GCMG
Wright, Sir Edward Maitland, Kt., D.phil., LLD, D.SC., FRSE
Wright, *Hon.* Sir (John) Michael, Kt.
Wright, Sir (John) Oliver, GCMG, GCVO, DSC
Wright, Sir Paul Hervé Giraud, KCMG, OBE
Wright, Sir Peter Robert, Kt., CBE
Wright, Sir Richard Michael Cory-, Bt. (1903)
Wrightson, Sir Charles Mark Garmondsway, Bt. (1900)
Wrigley, *Prof.* Sir Edward Anthony (Sir Tony), Kt., ph.D., FBA
Wynn, Sir David Watkin Williams-, Bt. (1688)
Yacoub, *Prof.* Sir Magdi Habib, Kt., FRCS
Yang, *Hon.* Sir Ti Liang, Kt.
Yapp, Sir Stanley Graham, Kt.
Yardley, Sir David Charles Miller, Kt., LLD
Yarranton, Sir Peter George, Kt.
Yarrow, Sir Eric Grant, Bt., MBE (1916)
Yellowlees, Sir Henry, KCB

Yocklunn, Sir John (Soong Chung), KCVO

Yoo Foo, Sir (François) Henri, Kt.

Youens, Sir Peter William, Kt., CMG, OBE

Young, Sir Brian Walter Mark, Kt.

Young, Sir Colville Norbert, GCMG, MBE

Young, *Lt.-Gen.* Sir David Tod, KBE, CB, DFC

Young, *Rt. Hon.* Sir George Samuel Knatchbull, Bt., MP (1813)

Young, *Hon.* Sir Harold William, KCMG

Young, Sir John Kenyon Roe, Bt. (1821)

Young, *Hon.* Sir John McIntosh, KCMG

Young, Sir Leslie Clarence, Kt., CBE

Young, Sir Norman Smith, Kt.

Young, Sir Richard Dilworth, Kt.

Young, Sir Robert Christopher Mackworth-, GCVO

Young, Sir Roger William, Kt.

Young, Sir Stephen Stewart Templeton, Bt. (1945)

Young, Sir William Neil, Bt. (1769)

Younger, *Maj.-Gen.* Sir John William, Bt., CBE (1911)

Zeeman, *Prof.* Sir (Erik) Christopher, Kt., FRS

Zeidler, Sir David Ronald, Kt., CBE

Zissman, Sir Bernard Philip, Kt.

Zoleveke, Sir Gideon Pitabose, KBE

Zunz, Sir Gerhard Jacob (Jack), Kt., FEng.

Zurenuoc, Sir Zibang, KBE

The Military Knights of Windsor

The Military Knights of Windsor take part in all ceremonies of the Noble Order of the Garter and attend Sunday morning service in St George's Chapel, Windsor Castle, as representatives of the Knights of the Garter. The Knights receive a small stipend in addition to their army pensions and quarters in Windsor Castle.

The Knights of Windsor were originally founded in 1348 after the wars in France to assist English knights, who, having been prisoners in the hands of the French, had become impoverished by the payments of heavy ransoms. When Edward III founded the Order of the Garter later the same year, he incorporated the Knights of Windsor and the College of St George into its foundation and raised the number of Knights to 26 to correspond with the number of the Knights of the Garter. Known later as the Alms Knights or Poor Knights of Windsor, their establishment was reduced under the will of King Henry VIII to 13 and Statutes were drawn up by Queen Elizabeth I.

In 1833 King William IV changed their designation to The Military Knights and granted them their present uniform which consists of a scarlet tail-coat with white cross sword-belt, crimson sash and cocked hat with plume. The badges are the Shield of St George and the Star of the Order of the Garter.

Governor, Maj.-Gen. Peter Downward, CB, DSO, DFC

Military Knights, Brig. A. L. Atkinson, OBE; Brig. J. F. Lindner, OBE, MC; Maj. W. L. Thompson, MVO, MBE, DCM; Maj. L. W. Dickerson; Maj. J. C. Cowley, OBE, DCM; Maj. G. R. Mitchell, MBE, BEM; Lt.-Col. R. L. C. Tamplin; Maj. P. H. Bolton, MBE; Brig. T. W. Hackworth, OBE; Maj. R. J. Moore; Lt.-Col. R. R. Giles

Supernumerary, Brig. A. C. Tyler, CBE, MC

Dames Grand Cross and Dames Commanders

Style, 'Dame' before forename and surname, followed by appropriate post-nominal initials. Where such an award is made to a lady already in enjoyment of a higher title, the appropriate initials follow her name
Husband, Untitled
For forms of address, *see* page 136

Dame Grand Cross and Dame Commander are the higher classes for women of the Order of the Bath, the Order of St Michael and St George, the Royal Victorian Order, and the

Order of the British Empire. Dames Grand Cross rank after the wives of Baronets and before the wives of Knights Grand Cross. Dames Commanders rank after the wives of Knights Grand Cross and before the wives of Knights Commanders

Honorary Dames Commanders may be conferred on women who are citizens of countries of which The Queen is not head of state

---

LIST OF DAMES   *Revised to 31 August 1996*

Women peers in their own right and life peers are not included in this list. Female members of the royal family are not included in this list; details of the orders they hold are given on pages 117–8
If a dame has a double barrelled or hyphenated surname, she is listed under the final element of the name

Abaijah, Dame Josephine, DBE
Abel Smith, Lady, DCVO
Abergavenny, The Marchioness of, DCVO
Airlie, The Countess of, DCVO
Albemarle, The Countess of, DBE
Anderson, *Brig.* Hon. Dame Mary Mackenzie (Mrs Pihl), DBE
Anelay, Dame Joyce Anne, DBE
Anglesey, The Marchioness of, DBE
Anson, Lady (Elizabeth Audrey), DBE
Anstee, Dame Margaret Joan, DCMG
Arden, *Hon.* Dame Mary Howarth (Mrs Mance), DBE
Baker, Dame Janet Abbott (Mrs Shelley), CH, DBE
Ballin, Dame Reubina Ann, DBE
Barnes, Dame (Alice) Josephine (Mary Taylor), DBE, FRCP, FRCS
Barrow, Dame Jocelyn Anita (Mrs Downer), DBE
Barstow, Dame Josephine Clare (Mrs Anderson), DBE
Basset, Lady Elizabeth, DCVO
Bean, Dame Majorie Louise, DBE
Beaurepaire, Dame Beryl Edith, DBE
Bergquist, *Prof.* Dame Patricia Rose, DBE
Berry, Dame Alice Miriam, DBE
Blaize, Dame Venetia Ursula, DBE
Blaxland, Dame Helen Frances, DBE
Booth, *Hon.* Dame Margaret Myfanwy Wood, DBE
Bottomley, Dame Bessie Ellen, DBE
Bowman, Dame (Mary) Elaine Kellett-, DBE, MP
Boyd, Dame Vivienne Myra, DBE
Bracewell, *Hon.* Dame Joyanne Winifred (Mrs Copeland), DBE
Brain, Dame Margaret Anne (Mrs Wheeler), DBE
Brazill, Dame Josephine (Sister Mary Philippa), DBE

Bridges, Dame Mary Patricia, DBE
Brown, Dame Beryl Paston, DBE
Brown, Dame Gillian Gerda, DCVO, CMG
Browne, Lady Moyra Blanche Madeleine, DBE
Bryans, Dame Anne Margaret, DBE
Bryce, Dame Isabel Graham, DBE
Buttfield, Dame Nancy Eileen, DBE
Byford, Dame Hazel, DBE
Bynoe, Dame Hilda Louisa, DBE
Caldicott, Dame Fiona, DBE, FRCP, FRCPsych.
Cartland, Dame Barbara Hamilton, DBE
Cartwright, Dame Mary Lucy, DBE, SC.D., D.Phil., FRS
Cartwright, Dame Silvia Rose, DBE
Casey, Dame Stella Katherine, DBE
Cayford, Dame Florence Evelyn, DBE
Charles, Dame (Mary) Eugenia, DBE
Chesterton, Dame Elizabeth Ursula, DBE
Clark, *Prof.* Dame (Margaret) June, DBE, ph.D.
Clay, Dame Marie Mildred, DBE
Clayton, Dame Barbara Evelyn (Mrs Klyne), DBE
Cleland, Dame Rachel, DBE
Coll, Dame Elizabeth Anne Loosemore Esteve-, DBE
Cookson, Dame Catherine Ann, DBE
Corsar, The Hon. Dame Mary Drummond, DBE
Coulshed, Dame (Mary) Frances, DBE, TD
Crowe, Dame Sylvia, DBE
Daws, Dame Joyce Margaretta, DBE
Dell, Dame Miriam Patricia, DBE
Dench, Dame Judith Olivia (Mrs Williams), DBE
de Valois, Dame Ninette, OM, CH, DBE
Digby, Lady, DBE
Donaldson, Dame (Dorothy) Mary (Lady Donaldson of Lymington), GBE
Doyle, *Air Comdt.* Dame Jean Lena Annette Conan (Lady Bromet), DBE
Drake, *Brig.* Dame Jean Elizabeth Rivett-, DBE
Drew, Dame Jane Beverley (Mrs Fry), DBE, FRIBA

Dugdale, Kathryn, Lady, DCVO
Dumont, Dame Ivy Leona, DCMG
Ebsworth, *Hon.* Dame Ann Marian, DBE
Emerton, Dame Audrey Caroline, DBE
Engel, Dame Pauline Frances (Sister Pauline Engel), DBE
Evison, Dame Helen June Patricia, DBE
Fenner, Dame Peggy Edith, DBE, MP
Fitton, Dame Doris Alice (Mrs Mason), DBE
Fookes, Dame Janet Evelyn, DBE, MP
Fraser, Dame Dorothy Rita, DBE
Friend, Dame Phyllis Muriel, DBE
Fritchie, Dame Irene Tordoff (Dame Rennie Fritchie), DBE
Frost, Dame Phyllis Irene, DBE
Fry, Dame Margaret Louise, DBE
Gallagher, Dame Monica Josephine, DBE
Gardiner, Dame Helen Louisa, DBE, MVO
Gibbs, Dame Molly Peel, DBE
Giles, *Air Comdt.* Dame Pauline (Mrs Parsons), DBE, RRC
Golding, Dame (Cecilie) Monica, DBE
Goodman, Dame Barbara, DBE
Gordon, Dame Minita Elmira, GCMG, GCVO
Gow, Dame Jane Elizabeth (Mrs Whiteley), DBE
Grafton, The Duchess of, GCVO
Green, Dame Mary Georgina, DBE
Grey, Dame Beryl Elizabeth (Mrs Svenson), DBE
Grimthorpe, The Lady, DCVO
Guilfoyle, Dame Margaret Georgina Constance, DBE
Guthardt, *Revd Dr* Dame Phyllis Myra, DBE
Haig, Dame Mary Alison Glen-, DBE
Hale, *Hon.* Dame Brenda Marjorie (Mrs Farrand), DBE
Hammond, Dame Joan Hood, DBE
Harper, Dame Elizabeth Margaret Way, DBE
Harris, Dame (Muriel) Diana Reader-, DBE
Heilbron, *Hon.* Dame Rose, DBE

Henderson, Dame Louise Etiennette Sidonie, DBE
Henrison, Dame Anne Elizabeth Rosina, DBE
Herbison, Dame Jean Marjory, DBE, CMG
Hercus, *Hon.* Dame (Margaret) Ann, DCMG
Hetet, Dame Rangimarie, DBE
Higgins, *Prof.* Dame Rosalyn, DBE, QC
Hill, Dame Elizabeth Mary, DBE
Hill, *Air Cdre* Dame Felicity Barbara, DBE
Hiller, Dame Wendy (Mrs Gow), DBE
Hird, Dame Thora (Mrs Scott), DBE
Hogg, *Hon.* Dame Mary Claire (Mrs Koops), DBE
Howard, Dame (Rosemary) Christian, DBE
Hunter, Dame Pamela, DBE
Hurley, *Prof.* Dame Rosalinde (Mrs Gortvai), DBE
Hussey, Lady Susan Katharine, DCVO
Isaacs, Dame Albertha Madeline, DBE
James, Dame Naomi Christine (Mrs Haythorne), DBE
Jenkins, Dame (Mary) Jennifer (Lady Jenkins of Hillhead), DBE
Jessel, Dame Penelope, DBE
Jones, Dame Gwyneth (Mrs Haberfeld-Jones), DBE
Jones, Dame (Lilian) Pauline Neville-, DCMG
Kekedo, Dame Mary, DBE, BEM
Kekedo, Dame Rosalina Violet, DBE
Kelleher, Dame Joan, DBE
Kettlewell, *Comdt.* Dame Marion Mildred, DBE
Kilroy, Dame Alix Hester Marie (Lady Meynell), DBE
Kirby, Dame Georgina Kamiria, DBE
Kirk, Dame (Lucy) Ruth, DBE
Knight, Dame (Joan Christabel) Jill, DBE, MP
Kramer, *Prof.* Dame Leonie Judith, DBE
Lamb, Dame Dawn Ruth, DBE
Lewis, Dame Edna Leofrida (Lady Lewis), DBE
Lister, Dame Unity Viola, DBE
Litchfield, Dame Ruby Beatrice, DBE
Lott, Dame Felicity Ann Emwhyla (Mrs Woolf), DBE
Lowrey, *Air Comdt.* Dame Alice, DBE, RRC
Lympany, Dame Moura, DBE
Lynn, Dame Vera (Mrs Lewis), DBE
Mackinnon, Dame (Una) Patricia, DBE
Macknight, Dame Ella Annie Noble, DBE, MD
McLaren, Dame Anne Laura, DBE, FRCOG, FRS
Macmillan of Ovenden, Katharine, Viscountess, DBE
Major, Dame Malvina Lorraine (Mrs Fleming), DBE
Mann, Dame Ida Caroline, DBE, D.SC., FRCS
Markova, Dame Alicia, DBE
Martin, Rosamund Mary Holland-, Lady, DBE

Masters, Dame Sheila Valerie (Mrs Noakes), DBE
Metge, *Dr* Dame (Alice) Joan, DBE
Miller, Dame Mabel Flora Hobart, DBE
Miller, Dame Mary Elizabeth Hedley-, DCVO, CB
Mitchell, Dame Mona, DCVO
Mitchell, *Hon.* Dame Roma Flinders, DBE
Mitchell, Dame Wendy, DBE
Morrison, *Hon.* Dame Mary Anne, DCVO
Mueller, Dame Anne Elisabeth, DCB
Muldoon, Thea Dale, Lady, DBE, QSO
Mumford, Lady Mary Katharine, DCVO
Munro, Dame Alison, DBE
Murdoch, Dame Elisabeth Joy, DBE
Murdoch, Dame (Jean) Iris (Mrs Bayley), DBE
Murray, Dame (Alice) Rosemary, DBE, D.phil.
Ollerenshaw, Dame Kathleen Mary, DBE, D.phil.
Oxenbury, Dame Shirley Anne, DBE
Park, Dame Merle Florence (Mrs Bloch), DBE
Paterson, Dame Betty Fraser Ross, DBE
Peake, *Air Cdre* Dame Felicity Hyde, DBE, AE
Penhaligon, Dame Annette (Mrs Egerton), DBE
Plowden, The Lady, DBE
Poole, Dame Avril Anne Barker, DBE
Porter, Dame Shirley (Lady Porter), DBE
Prendergast, Dame Simone Ruth, DBE
Prentice, Dame Winifred Eva, DBE
Preston, Dame Frances Olivia Campbell-, DCVO
Price, Dame Margaret Berenice, DBE
Purves, Dame Daphne Helen, DBE
Pyke, Lady, DBE
Quinn, Dame Sheila Margaret Imelda, DBE
Railton, Dame Ruth (Mrs King), DBE
Rankin, Lady Jean Margaret Florence, DCVO
Raven, Dame Kathleen Annie (Mrs Ingram), DBE
Restieaux, *Dr* Dame Norma Jean, DBE
Riddelsdell, Dame Mildred, DCB, CBE
Ridley, Dame (Mildred) Betty, DBE
Ridsdale, Dame Victoire Evelyn Patricia (Lady Ridsdale), DBE
Rigg, Dame Diana, DBE
Rimington, Dame Stella, DCB
Robertson, *Comdt.* Dame Nancy Margaret, DBE
Roe, Dame Raigh Edith, DBE
Rue, Dame (Elsie) Rosemary, DBE
Rumbold, *Rt. Hon.* Dame Angela Claire Rosemary, DBE, MP
Salas, Dame Margaret Laurence, DBE
Salmond, *Prof.* Dame Mary Anne, DBE
Saunders, Dame Cicely Mary Strode, OM, DBE, FRCP
Schwarzkopf, Dame Elisabeth Friederike Marie Olga Legge-, DBE

Scott, Dame Catherine Campbell, DBE
Scott, Dame Jean Mary Monica Maxwell-, DCVO
Scott, Dame Margaret, (Dame Catherine Margaret Mary Denton), DBE
Shenfield, Dame Barbara Estelle, DBE
Sherlock, *Prof.* Dame Sheila Patricia Violet, DBE, MD, FRCP
Sibley, Dame Antoinette (Mrs Corbett), DBE
Sloss, *Rt. Hon.* Dame (Ann) Elizabeth (Oldfield) Butler-, DBE
Smieton, Dame Mary Guillan, DBE
Smith, *Hon.* Dame Janet Hilary (Mrs Mathieson), DBE
Smith, Dame Margaret Natalie (Maggie) (Mrs Cross), DBE
Smith, Dame Margot, DBE
Snagge, Dame Nancy Marion, DBE
Soames, Mary, Lady, DBE
Spark, Dame Muriel Sarah, DBE
Steel, *Hon.* Dame (Anne) Heather (Mrs Beattie), DBE
Stephens, *Air Comdt.* Dame Anne, DBE
Stewart, Dame Muriel Acadia, DBE
Sutherland, Dame Joan (Mrs Bonynge), OM, DBE
Szaszy, Dame Miraka Petricevich, DBE
Taylor, Dame Jean Elizabeth, DCVO
Te Atairangikaahu, Te Arikinui, Dame, DBE
Te Kanawa, Dame Kiri Janette (Mrs Park), DBE
Thorneycroft, Carla, Lady, CBE
Tilney, Dame Guinevere (Lady Tilney), DBE
Tinson, Dame Sue, DBE
Tizard, Dame Catherine Anne, GCMG, GCVO, DBE
Tokiel, Dame Rosa, DBE
Tyrwhitt, *Brig.* Dame Mary Joan Caroline, DBE, TD
Uatioa, Dame Mere, DBE
Uvarov, Dame Olga, DBE
Varley, Dame Joan Fleetwood, DBE
Wagner, Dame Gillian Mary Millicent (Lady Wagner), DBE
Wall, (Alice) Anne, (Mrs Michael Wall), DCVO
Wallace, Dame (Georgina Catriona Pamela) Augusta, DBE
Warburton, Dame Anne Marion, DCVO, CMG
Warwick, Dame Margaret Elizabeth Harvey Turner-, DBE, FRCP, FRCPEd.
Waterhouse, Dame Rachel Elizabeth, DBE, Ph.D.
Wedgwood, Dame (Cicely) Veronica, OM, DBE
Weir, Dame Gillian Constance (Mrs Phelps), DBE
Weston, Dame Margaret Kate, DBE
Williamson, Dame (Elsie) Marjorie, DBE, Ph.D.
Winstone, Dame Dorothy Gertrude, DBE, CMG

Decorations and Medals

ROYAL FLEET RESERVE LONG SERVICE AND GOOD
  CONDUCT MEDAL
ROYAL NAVAL WIRELESS AUXILIARY RESERVE LONG
  SERVICE AND GOOD CONDUCT MEDAL
AIR EFFICIENCY AWARD (AE), 1942
ULSTER DEFENCE REGIMENT MEDAL
THE QUEEN'S MEDAL. For champion shots in the RN, RM,
  RNZN, Army, RAF
CADET FORCES MEDAL, 1950
COASTGUARD AUXILIARY SERVICE LONG SERVICE
  MEDAL (formerly Coast Life Saving Corps Long
  Service Medal)
SPECIAL CONSTABULARY LONG SERVICE MEDAL
ROYAL OBSERVER CORPS MEDAL
CIVIL DEFENCE LONG SERVICE MEDAL
AMBULANCE SERVICE (EMERGENCY DUTIES) LONG
  SERVICE AND GOOD CONDUCT MEDAL
RHODESIA MEDAL
ROYAL ULSTER CONSTABULARY SERVICE MEDAL
SERVICE MEDAL OF THE ORDER OF ST JOHN
BADGE OF THE ORDER OF THE LEAGUE OF MERCY
VOLUNTARY MEDICAL SERVICE MEDAL, 1932
WOMEN'S VOLUNTARY SERVICE MEDAL
COLONIAL SPECIAL CONSTABULARY MEDAL

Foreign Orders, Decorations and Medals (in order of date)

THE VICTORIA CROSS (1856)
FOR CONSPICUOUS BRAVERY

VC

Ribbon, Crimson, for all Services (until 1918 it was blue for
the Royal Navy)

Instituted on 29 January 1856, the Victoria Cross was
awarded retrospectively to 1854, the first being held by Lt.
C. D. Lucas, RN, for bravery in the Baltic Sea on 21 June
1854 (gazetted 24 February 1857). The first 62 Crosses
were presented by Queen Victoria in Hyde Park, London,
on 26 June 1857.
  The Victoria Cross is worn before all other decorations,
on the left breast, and consists of a cross-pattée of bronze,
one and a half inches in diameter, with the Royal Crown
surmounted by a lion in the centre, and beneath there is
the inscription *For Valour*. Holders of the VC receive a tax-
free annuity of £1,300, irrespective of need or other
conditions. In 1911, the right to receive the Cross was
extended to Indian soldiers, and in 1920 to Matrons,
Sisters and Nurses, and the staff of the Nursing Services
and other services pertaining to hospitals and nursing, and
to civilians of either sex regularly or temporarily under
the orders, direction or supervision of the Naval, Military,
or Air Forces of the Crown.

SURVIVING RECIPIENTS OF THE VICTORIA CROSS
as at 31 August 1996

Agansing Rai, *Havildar*, MM (Gurkha Rifles)
  1944 *World War*
Ali Haidar, *Jemadar* (Frontier Force Rifles)
  1945 *World War*
Annand, *Capt.* R. W. (Durham Light Infantry)
  1940 *World War*

Bhan Bhagta Gurung, *Capt.* (2nd Gurkha Rifles)
  1945 *World War*
Bhandari Ram, *Capt.* (Baluch R.)
  1944 *World War*
Chapman, *Sgt.* E. T., BEM (Monmouthshire R.)
  1945 *World War*
Cruickshank, *Flt. Lt.* J. A. (RAFVR)
  1944 *World War*
Cutler, Sir Roden, AK, KCMG, KCVO, CBE (Australia)
  1941 *World War*
Fraser, *Lt.-Cdr.* I. E., DSC (RNR)
  1945 *World War*
Gaje Ghale, *Subedar* (Gurkha Rifles)
  1943 *World War*
Ganju Lama, *Jemadar*, MM (Gurkha Rifles)
  1944 *World War*
Gardner, *Capt.* P. J., MC (RTR)
  1941 *World War*
Gian Singh, *Jemadar* (Punjab R.)
  1945 *World War*
Gould, *Lt.* T. W. (RN)
  1942 *World War*
Hinton, *Sgt.* J. D. (NZMF)
  1941 *World War*
Jamieson, *Maj.* D. A., CVO (R. Norfolk R.)
  1944 *World War*
Kenna, *Pte.* E. (Australian M. F.)
  1945 *World War*
Kenneally, *C-Q-M-S* J. P. (Irish Guards)
  1943 *World War*
Lachiman Gurung, *Rifleman* (Gurkha Rifles)
  1945 *World War*
Merritt, *Lt.-Col.* C. C. I., CD (S. Saskatchewan R.)
  1942 *World War*
Norton, *Capt.* G. R., MM (SAMF)
  1944 *World War*
Payne, *WO* K. (Australian Army)
  1969 *Vietnam*
Porteous, *Col.* P. A. (RA)
  1942 *World War*
Rambahadur Limbu, *Lt.*, MVO (Gurkha Rifles)
  1965 *Sarawak*
Reid, *Flt. Lt.* W. (RAFVR)
  1943 *World War*
Smith, *Sgt.* E. A., CD (Seaforth Highlanders of Canada)
  1944 *World War*
Smythe, *Capt.* Q. G. M. (SAMF)
  1942 *World War*
Speakman-Pitt, *Sgt.* W. (Black Watch)
  1951 *Korea*
Tulbahadur Pun, *WO I* (Gurkha Rifles)
  1944 *World War*
Umrao Singh, *Sub-Major* (IA)
  1944 *World War*
Watkins, *Maj. Rt. Hon.* Sir Tasker, GBE (Welch R.)
  1944 *World War*
Wilson, *Lt.-Col.* E. C. T. (E. Surrey R.)
  1940 *World War*

210   Decorations and Medals

THE GEORGE CROSS (1940)
FOR GALLANTRY

GC

Ribbon, Dark blue, threaded through a bar adorned with laurel leaves

Instituted 24 September 1940 (with amendments, 3 November 1942).

The George Cross is worn before all other decorations (except the VC) on the left breast (when worn by a woman it may be worn on the left shoulder from a ribbon of the same width and colour fashioned into a bow). It consists of a plain silver cross with four equal limbs, the cross having in the centre a circular medallion bearing a design showing St George and the Dragon. The inscription *For Gallantry* appears round the medallion and in the angle of each limb of the cross is the Royal cypher 'G VI' forming a circle concentric with the medallion. The reverse is plain and bears the name of the recipient and the date of the award. The cross is suspended by a ring from a bar adorned with laurel leaves on dark blue ribbon one and a half inches wide.

The cross is intended primarily for civilians; awards to the fighting services are confined to cases for which purely military honours are not normally granted. It is awarded only for acts of the greatest heroism or of the most conspicuous courage in circumstances of extreme danger. From 1 April 1965, holders of the Cross have received a tax-free annuity of £1,300.

The royal warrant which ordained that the grant of the Empire Gallantry Medal should cease authorized holders of that medal to return it to the Central Chancery of the Orders of Knighthood and to receive in exchange the George Cross. A similar provision applied to posthumous awards of the Empire Gallantry Medal made after the outbreak of war in 1939. In October 1971 all surviving holders of the Albert Medal and the Edward Medal exchanged those decorations for the George Cross.

SURVIVING RECIPIENTS OF THE GEORGE CROSS
as at 31 August 1996

If the recipient originally received the Empire Gallantry Medal (EGM), the Albert Medal (AM) or the Edward Medal (EM), this is indicated by the initials in parenthesis.

Archer, *Col.* B. S. T., GC, OBE, ERD, 1941
Atkinson, T., GC (EGM), 1939
Baker, J. T., GC (EM), 1929
Bamford, J., GC, 1952
Beaton, J., GC, CVO, 1974
Biggs, *Maj.* K. A., GC, 1946
Bridge, *Cdr.* J., GC, GM, 1944
Butson, *Col.* A. R. C., GC, CD, MD (AM), 1948
Bywater, R. A. S., GC, GM, 1944
Errington, H., GC, 1941
Fairfax, F. W., GC, 1953
Farrow, K., GC (AM), 1948
Flintoff, H. H., GC (EM), 1944
Gledhill, A. J., GC, 1967
Gregson, J. S., GC (AM), 1943
Hawkins, E., GC (AM), 1943
Hodge, *Capt.* A. M., GC, VRD (EGM), 1940
Johnson, *WO1 (SSM)* B., GC, 1990

Kinne, D. G., GC, 1954
Lowe, A. R., GC (AM), 1949
Lynch, J., GC, BEM (AM), 1948
Malta, GC, 1942
Manwaring, T. G., GC (EM), 1949
Moore, R. V., GC, 1940
Moss, B., GC, 1940
Naughton, F., GC (EGM), 1937
Pearson, Miss J. D. M., GC (EGM), 1940
Pratt, M. K., GC, 1978
Purves, Mrs M., GC (AM), 1949
Raweng, Awang anak, GC, 1951
Riley, G., GC (AM), 1944
Rowlands, *Air Marshal* Sir John, GC, KBE, 1943
Sinclair, *Air Vice-Marshal* Sir Laurence, GC, KCB, CBE, DSO, 1941
Stevens, H. W., GC, 1958
Stronach, *Capt.* G. P., GC, 1943
Styles, *Lt.-Col.* S. G., GC, 1972
Taylor, *Lt.-Cdr.* W. H., GC, MBE, 1941
Walker, C., GC, 1972
Walker, C. H., GC (AM), 1942
Walton, E. W. K., GC (AM), 1948
Wilcox, C., GC (EM), 1949
Wiltshire, S. N., GC (EGM), 1930
Yates, P. W., GC (EM), 1932

Chiefs of Clans and Names in Scotland

Only chiefs of whole Names or Clans are included, except certain special instances (marked *) who, though not chiefs of a whole name, were or are for some reason (e.g. the Macdonald forfeiture) independent. Under decision (*Campbell-Gray*, 1950) that a bearer of a 'double or triple-barrelled' surname cannot be held chief of a part of such, several others cannot be included in the list at present.

THE ROYAL HOUSE: HM The Queen

AGNEW: Sir Crispin Agnew of Lochnaw, Bt., QC, 6 Palmerston Road, Edinburgh EH9 1TN

ANSTRUTHER: Sir Ralph Anstruther of that Ilk, Bt., GCVO, MC, Balcaskie, Pittenweem, Fife KY10 2RD

ARBUTHNOTT: The Viscount of Arbuthnott, CBE, DSC, Arbuthnott House, Laurencekirk, Kincardineshire AB30 1PA

BARCLAY: Peter C. Barclay of Towie Barclay and of that Ilk, 28A Gordon Place, London W8 4JE

BORTHWICK: The Lord Borthwick, TD, Crookston, Heriot, Midlothian EH38 5YS

BOYD: The Lord Kilmarnock, 194 Regent's Park Road, London NW1 8XP

BOYLE: The Earl of Glasgow, Kelburn, Fairlie, Ayrshire KA29 OBE

BRODIE: Ninian Brodie of Brodie, Brodie Castle, Forres, Morayshire IV36 OTE

BRUCE: The Earl of Elgin and Kincardine, KT, Broomhall, Dunfermline, Fife KY11 3DU

BUCHAN: David S. Buchan of Auchmacoy, Auchmacoy House, Ellon, Aberdeenshire

BURNETT: J. C. A. Burnett of Leys, Crathes Castle, Banchory, Kincardineshire

CAMERON: Sir Donald Cameron of Lochiel, KT, CVO, TD, Achnacarry, Spean Bridge, Inverness-shire

CAMPBELL: The Duke of Argyll, Inveraray, Argyll PA32 8XF

CARMICHAEL. Richard J. Carmichael of Carmichael, Carmichael, Thankerton, Biggar, Lanarkshire

CARNEGIE: The Duke of Fife, Elsick House, Stonehaven, Kincardineshire AB3 2NT

CATHCART: Maj.-Gen. The Earl Cathcart, CB, DSO, MC, Moor Hatches, West Amesbury, Salisbury SP4 7BH

CHARTERIS: The Earl of Wemyss and March, KT, Gosford House, Longniddry, East Lothian EH32 OPX

CLAN CHATTAN: M. K. Mackintosh of Clan Chattan, Maxwell Park, Gwelo, Zimbabwe

CHISHOLM: Alastair Chisholm of Chisholm (*The Chisholm*), Silver Willows, Beck Row, Bury St Edmunds

COCHRANE: The Earl of Dundonald, Lochnell Castle, Ledaig, Argyllshire

COLQUHOUN: Sir Ivar Colquhoun of Luss, Bt., Camstraddan, Luss, Dunbartonshire G83 8NX

CRANSTOUN: David A. S. Cranstoun of that Ilk, Corehouse, Lanark

CRICHTON: vacant

DARROCH: Capt. Duncan Darroch of Gourock, The Red House, Branksome Park Road, Camberley, Surrey

DAVIDSON: Duncan Davidson of Davidston, Durham Drive, Havelock North, New Zealand

DEWAR: Kenneth Dewar of that Ilk and Vogrie, The Dower House, Grayshott, Nr. Hindhead, Surrey

DRUMMOND: The Earl of Perth, PC, Stobhall, Perth PH2 6DR

DUNBAR: Sir James Dunbar of Mochrum, Bt., Bld 848 C.2, 66877 Flugplatz, Ramstein, Germany

DUNDAS: David D. Dundas of Dundas, 8 Derna Road, Kenwyn 7700, South Africa

DURIE: Raymond V. D. Durie of Durie, Court House, Pewsey, Wilts

ELIOTT: Mrs Margaret Eliott of Redheugh, Redheugh, Newcastleton, Roxburghshire

ERSKINE: The Earl of Mar and Kellie, Erskine House, Kirk Wynd, Clackmannan FK10 4JF

FARQUHARSON: Capt. A. Farquharson of Invercauld, MC, Invercauld, Braemar, Aberdeenshire AB35 5TT

FERGUSSON: Sir Charles Fergusson of Kilkerran, Bt., Kilkerran, Maybole, Ayrshire

FORBES: The Lord Forbes, KBE, Balforbes, Alford, Aberdeenshire AB33 8DR

FORSYTH: Alistair Forsyth of that Ilk, Ethie Castle, by Arbroath, Angus DD11 5SP

FRASER: The Lady Saltoun, Cairnbulg Castle, Fraserburgh, Aberdeenshire AB43 5TN

*FRASER (OF LOVAT): The Lord Lovat, Beaufort Lodge, Beauly, Inverness-shire IV4 7AZ

GAYRE: R. Gayre of Gayre and Nigg, Minard Castle, Minard, Inveray, Argyll PA32 8YB

GORDON: The Marquess of Huntly, Aboyne Castle, Aberdeenshire AB34 5JP

GRAHAM: The Duke of Montrose, Buchanan Auld House, Drymen, Stirlingshire

GRANT: The Lord Strathspey, The House of Lords, London SW1A OPW

GRIERSON: Sir Michael Grierson of Lag, Bt., 40C Palace Road, London SW2 3NJ

HAIG: The Earl Haig, OBE, Bemersyde, Melrose, Roxburghshire TD6 9DP

HALDANE: Martin Haldane of Gleneagles, Gleneagles, Auchterarder, Perthshire

HANNAY: Ramsey Hannay of Kirkdale and of that Ilk, Cardoness House, Gatehouse-of-Fleet, Kirkcudbrightshire

HAY: The Earl of Erroll, Woodbury Hall, Sandy, Beds

HENDERSON: John Henderson of Fordell, 7 Owen Street, Toowoomba, Queensland, Australia

HUNTER: Pauline Hunter of Hunterston, Plovers Ridge, Lon Cecrist, Treaddur Bay, Holyhead, Gwynedd

IRVINE OF DRUM: David C. Irvine of Drum, 20 Enville Road, Bowden, Altrincham, Cheshire WA14 2PQ

JARDINE: Sir Alexander Jardine of Applegirth, Bt., Ash House, Thwaites, Millom, Cumbria LA18 5HY

JOHNSTONE: The Earl of Annandale and Hartfell, Raehills, Lockerbie, Dumfriesshire

KEITH: The Earl of Kintore, The Stables, Keith Hall, Inverurie, Aberdeenshire AB51 OLD

KENNEDY: The Marquess of Ailsa, Cassillis House, Maybole, Ayrshire

KERR: The Marquess of Lothian, KCVO, Ferniehurst Castle, Jedburgh, Roxburghshire TN8 6NX

KINCAID: Mrs Heather V. Kincaid of Kincaid, 4 Watling Street, Leintwardine, Craven Arms, Shropshire

LAMONT: Peter N. Lamont of that Ilk, St Patrick's College, Manly, NSW 2095, Australia

LEASK: Madam Leask of Leask, 1 Vincent Road, Sheringham, Norfolk

LENNOX: Edward J. H. Lennox of that Ilk, Pools Farm, Downton on the Rock, Ludlow, Shropshire

LESLIE: The Earl of Rothes, Tanglewood, West Tytherley, Salisbury, Wilts SP5 1LX

LINDSAY: The Earl of Crawford and Balcarres, PC, Balcarres, Colinsburgh, Fife

LOCKHART: Angus H. Lockhart of the Lee, Newholme, Dunsyre, Lanark

LUMSDEN: Gillem Lumsden of that Ilk and Blanerne, Kinderslegh, Bois Avenue, Chesham Bois, Amersham

MACALESTER: William St J. S. McAlester of Loup and Kennox, 2 Avon Road East, Christchurch, Dorset

McBAIN: J. H. McBain of McBain, 7025, North Finger Rock Place, Tucson, Arizona, USA

MALCOLM (MACCALLUM): Robin N. L. Malcolm of Poltalloch, Duntrune Castle, Lochgilphead, Argyll

MACDONALD: The Lord Macdonald (*The Macdonald of Macdonald*), Kinloch Lodge, Sleat, Isle of Skye

*MACDONALD OF CLANRANALD: Ranald A. Macdonald of Clanranald, Grooms Bell, The Haining, Selkirk TD7 5LR

*MACDONALD OF SLEAT (CLAN HUSTEAIN): Sir Ian Bosville Macdonald of Sleat, Bt., Thorpe Hall, Rudston, Driffield, N. Humberside YO25 0JE

*MACDONELL OF GLENGARRY: Air Cdre Aeneas R. MacDonell of Glengarry, CB, DFC, Elonbank, Castle Street, Fortrose, Ross-shire IV10 8TH

MACDOUGALL: vacant

MACDOWALL: Fergus D. H. Macdowall of Garthland, 16 Tower Road, Nepean, Ontario, Canada

MACGREGOR: Sir Gregor MacGregor of MacGregor, Bt., Bannatyne, Newtyle, Blairgowrie, Perthshire PH12 8TR

MACINTYRE: James W. MacIntyre of Glenoe, 15301 Pine Orchard Drive, Apartment 3H, Silver Spring, Maryland, USA

MACKAY: The Lord Reay, House of Lords, London SW1

MACKENZIE: The Earl of Cromartie, Castle Leod, Strathpeffer, Ross-shire IV14 9AA

MACKINNON: Madam Anne Mackinnon of Mackinnon, 16 Purleigh Road, Bridgwater, Somerset

MACKINTOSH: *The Mackintosh of Mackintosh*, Moy Hall, Inverness IV13 7YQ

MACLACHLAN: Madam Marjorie MacLachlan of MacLachlan, Castle Lachlan, Argyll

MACLAREN: Donald MacLaren of MacLaren and Achleskine, Achleskine, Kirkton, Balquidder, Lochearnhead

MACLEAN: The Hon. Sir Lachlan Maclean of Duart, Bt., Arngask House, Glenfarg, Perthshire PH2 9QA

MACLENNAN: vacant

MACLEOD: John MacLeod of MacLeod, Dunvegan Castle, Isle of Skye

MACMILLAN: George MacMillan of MacMillan, Finlaystone, Langbank, Renfrewshire

MACNAB: J. C. Macnab of Macnab (*The Macnab*), Leuchars Castle Farmhouse, Leuchars, Fife KY16 0EY

MACNAGHTEN: Sir Patrick Macnaghten of Macnaghten and Dundarave, Bt., Dundarave, Bushmills, Co. Antrim

MACNEACAIL: Iain Macneacail of Macneacail and Scorrybreac, 12 Fox Street, Ballina, NSW, Australia

MACNEIL OF BARRA: Ian R. Macneil of Barra (*The Macneil of Barra*), Kisimul Castle, Barra

MACPHERSON: The Hon. Sir William Macpherson of Cluny, TD, Newtown Castle, Blairgowrie, Perthshire

MACTHOMAS: Andrew P. C. MacThomas of Finegand, c/o The Clan MacThomas Society, 19 Warriston Avenue, Edinburgh

MAITLAND: The Earl of Lauderdale, 12 St Vincent Street, Edinburgh

MAKGILL: The Viscount of Oxfuird, Hill House, St Mary Bourne, Andover, Hants SP11 6BG

MAR: The Countess of Mar, St Michael's Farm, Great Witley, Worcs WR6 6JB

MARJORIBANKS: Andrew Marjoribanks of that Ilk

MATHESON: Maj. Sir Fergus Matheson of Matheson, Bt., Old Rectory, Hedenham, Bungay, Suffolk NR35 2LD

MENZIES: David R. Menzies of Menzies, 20 Nardina Crescent, Dalkeith, Western Australia

MOFFAT: Madam Moffat of that Ilk, St Jasual, Bullocks Farm Lane, Wheeler End Common, High Wycombe

MONCREIFFE: vacant

MONTGOMERIE: The Earl of Eglinton and Winton, The Dutch House, West Green, Hartley Wintney, Hants

MORRISON: Dr Iain M. Morrison of Ruchdi, Magnolia Cottage, The Street, Walberton, Sussex

MUNRO: Hector W. Munro of Foulis, TD, Foulis Castle, Evanton, Ross-shire IV16 9UX

MURRAY: The Duke of Atholl, Blair Castle, Blair Atholl, Perthshire

NESBITT (or NISBET): Robert Nesbitt of that Ilk, Upper Roundhurst Farm, Roundhurst, Haslemere, Surrey

NICOLSON: The Lord Carnock, 90 Whitehall Court, London SW1A 2EL

OGILVY: The Earl of Airlie, KT, GCVO, PC, Cortachy Castle, Kirriemuir, Angus

RAMSAY: The Earl of Dalhousie, KT, GCVO, GBE, MC, Brechin Castle, Brechin, Angus DD7 6SH

RATTRAY: James S. Rattray of Rattray, Craighall, Rattray, Perthshire

ROBERTSON: Alexander G. H. Robertson of Struan (*Struan-Robertson*), The Breach Farm, Goudhurst Road, Cranbrook, Kent

ROLLO: The Lord Rollo, Pitcairns, Dunning, Perthshire

ROSE: Miss Elizabeth Rose of Kilravock, Kilravock Castle, Croy, Inverness

ROSS: David C. Ross of that Ilk, The Old Schoolhouse, Fettercairn, Kincardineshire

RUTHVEN: The Earl of Gowrie, PC, Castlemartin, Kilcullen, Co. Kildare, Republic of Ireland

SCOTT: The Duke of Buccleuch and Queensberry, KT, VRD, Bowhill, Selkirk

SCRYMGEOUR: The Earl of Dundee, Birkhill, Cupar, Fife

SEMPILL: The Lord Sempill, East Lodge, Druminnor, Rhynie, Aberdeenshire AB5 4LT

SHAW: John Shaw of Tordarroch, Newhall, Balblair, By Conon Bridge, Ross-shire

SINCLAIR: The Earl of Caithness, Churchill, Chipping Norton, Oxford OX7 5UX

SKENE: Danus Skene of Skene, Nether Pitleur, Strathmiglo, Fife

STIRLING: Fraser J. Stirling of Cader, 17 Park Row, Farnham, Surrey

STRANGE: Maj. Timothy Strange of Balcaskie, Little Holme, Porton Road, Amesbury, Wilts

SUTHERLAND: The Countess of Sutherland, House of Tongue, Brora, Sutherland

SWINTON: John Swinton of that Ilk, 123 Superior Avenue SW, Calgary, Alberta, Canada

TROTTER: Alexander Trotter of Mortonhall, Charterhall, Duns, Berwickshire

URQUHART: Kenneth T. Urquhart of Urquhart, 507 Jefferson Park Avenue, Jefferson, New Orleans, Louisiana 70121, USA

WALLACE: Ian F. Wallace of that Ilk, 5 Lennox Street, Edinburgh EH4 1QB

WEDDERBURN OF THAT ILK: The Master of Dundee, Birkhill, Cupar, Fife

WEMYSS: David Wemyss of that Ilk, Invermay, Forteviot, Perthshire

The Privy Council

The Sovereign in Council, or Privy Council, was the chief source of executive power until the system of Cabinet government developed in the 18th century. Now the Privy Council's main functions are to advise the Sovereign and to exercise its own statutory responsibilities independent of the Sovereign in Council (*see also* page 216).

Membership of the Privy Council is automatic upon appointment to certain government and judicial positions in the United Kingdom, e.g. Cabinet ministers must be Privy Counsellors and are sworn in on first assuming office. Membership is also accorded by The Queen to eminent people in the UK and independent countries of the Commonwealth of which Her Majesty is Queen, on the recommendation of the British Prime Minister. Membership of the Council is retained for life, except for very occasional removals.

The administrative functions of the Privy Council are carried out by the Privy Council Office (*see* page 334) under the direction of the Lord President of the Council, who is always a member of the Cabinet.

Lord President of the Council, The Rt. Hon. Antony Newton, OBE, MP
Clerk of the Council, N. H. Nicholls, CBE

MEMBERS *as at 31 August 1996*

HRH The Duke of Edinburgh, 1951
HRH The Prince of Wales, 1977

Aberdare, Lord, 1974
Ackner, Lord, 1980
Airlie, Earl of, 1984
Aitken, Jonathan, 1994
Aldington, Lord, 1954
Aldous, Sir William, 1995
Alebua, Ezekiel, 1988
Alison, Michael, 1981
Alport, Lord, 1960
Amery of Lustleigh, Lord, 1960
Ampthill, Lord, 1995
Ancram, Michael, 1996
Anthony, Douglas, 1971
Archer of Sandwell, Lord, 1977
Arnold, Sir John, 1979
Arthur, Hon. Owen, 1995
Ashdown, Paddy, 1989
Ashley of Stoke, Lord, 1979
Atkins, Robert, 1995
Auld, Sir Robin, 1995
Baker, Kenneth, 1984
Balcombe, Sir John, 1985
Barber, Lord, 1963

Barnett, Lord, 1975
Barwick, Sir Garfield, 1964
Beckett, Margaret, 1993
Beith, Alan, 1992
Beldam, Sir Roy, 1989
Belstead, Lord, 1983
Benn, Anthony, 1964
Bennett, Sir Frederic, 1985
Bevins, John, 1959
Biffen, John, 1979
Bingham of Cornhill, Lord, 1986
Birch, William, 1992
Bird, Vere, 1982
Bisson, Sir Gordon, 1987
Blair, Anthony, 1994
Blaker, Lord, 1983
Blatch, Baroness, 1993
Bolger, James, 1991
Booth, Albert, 1976
Boothroyd, Betty, 1992
Boscawen, Hon. Robert, 1992
Bottomley, Virginia, 1992
Boyd-Carpenter, Lord, 1954
Boyson, Sir Rhodes, 1987
Braine, Lord, 1985
Brandon of Oakbrook, Lord, 1978
Brathwaite, Sir Nicholas, 1991
Bridge of Harwich, Lord, 1975
Brightman, Lord, 1979
Brittan, Sir Leon, 1981
Brooke, Sir Henry, 1996
Brooke, Peter, 1988
Brown, Gordon, 1996
Brown, Sir Simon, 1992
Brown, Sir Stephen, 1983
Browne, Sir Patrick, 1974
Browne-Wilkinson, Lord, 1983
Buckley, Sir Denys, 1970
Butler, Sir Adam, 1984
Butler-Sloss, Dame Elizabeth, 1988
Caithness, Earl of, 1990
Callaghan of Cardiff, Lord, 1964
Cameron of Lochbroom, Lord, 1984
Campbell of Croy, Lord, 1970
Canterbury, The Archbishop of, 1991
Carlisle of Bucklow, Lord, 1979
Carr of Hadley, Lord, 1963
Carrington, Lord, 1959
Carswell, Sir Robert, 1993
Casey, Sir Maurice, 1986
Castle of Blackburn, Baroness, 1964
Cato, Robert, 1981
Chalfont, Lord, 1964
Chalker of Wallasey, Baroness, 1987
Chan, Sir Julius, 1981
Channon, Paul, 1980
Charteris of Amisfield, Lord, 1972
Chataway, Sir Christopher, 1970
Clark, Alan, 1991
Clark, Helen, 1990
Clark of Kempston, Lord, 1990
Clarke, Kenneth, 1984
Cledwyn of Penrhos, Lord, 1966
Cockfield, Lord, 1982

Cocks of Hartcliffe, Lord, 1976
Coggan, Lord, 1961
Colman, Fraser, 1986
Colnbrook, Lord, 1973
Compton, John, 1983
Concannon, John, 1978
Cook, Robin, 1996
Cooke of Thorndon, Lord, 1977
Cooper, Sir Frank, 1983
Cope, Sir John, 1988
Corfield, Sir Frederick, 1970
Cowen, Sir Zelman, 1981
Cradock, Sir Percy, 1993
Cranborne, Viscount, 1994
Crawford and Balcarres, Earl of, 1972
Crickhowell, Lord, 1979
Croom-Johnson, Sir David, 1984
Cumming-Bruce, Sir Roualeyn, 1977
Cunningham, Jack, 1993
Curry, David, 1996
Davies, Denzil, 1978
Davison, Sir Ronald, 1978
Dean of Harptree, Lord, 1991
Deedes, Lord, 1962
Dell, Edmund, 1970
Denham, Lord, 1981
Denning, Lord, 1948
Devonshire, Duke of, 1964
Dewar, Donald, 1996
Diamond, Lord, 1965
Dillon, Sir Brian, 1982
Dixon, Donald, 1996
Donaldson of Lymington, Lord, 1979
Dorrell, Stephen, 1994
Douglas, Sir William, 1977
Douglas-Hamilton, Lord James, 1996
du Cann, Sir Edward, 1964
Duff, Sir Antony, 1980
Dunn, Sir Robin, 1980
Eccles, Viscount, 1951
Eden of Winton, Lord, 1972
Eggar, Timothy, 1995
Eichelbaum, Sir Thomas, 1989
Emery, Sir Peter, 1993
Emslie, Lord, 1972
Erroll of Hale, Lord, 1960
Esquivel, Manuel, 1986
Evans, Sir Anthony, 1992
Eveleigh, Sir Edward, 1977
Farquharson, Sir Donald, 1989
Fellowes, Sir Robert, 1990
Ferrers, Earl, 1982
Floissac, Sir Vincent, 1992
Foot, Michael, 1974
Forsyth, Michael, 1995
Foster, Derek, 1993
Fowler, Sir Norman, 1979
Fox, Sir Marcus, 1995
Fox, Sir Michael, 1981
Fraser, Malcolm, 1976
Fraser of Carmyllie, Lord, 1989
Freeman, John, 1966
Freeman, Roger, 1993

Freeson, Reginald, 1976
Gairy, Sir Eric, 1977
Garel-Jones, Tristan, 1992
Gault, Thomas, 1992
Georges, Telford, 1986
Gibbs, Sir Harry, 1972
Gibson, Sir Peter, 1993
Gibson, Sir Ralph, 1985
Gibson-Watt, Lord, 1974
Gilbert, John, 1978
Gilmour of Craigmillar, Lord, 1973
Glenamara, Lord, 1964
Glidewell, Sir Iain, 1985
Goff of Chieveley, Lord, 1982
Goodlad, Alastair, 1992
Gorton, Sir John, 1968
Gowrie, Earl of, 1984
Gray of Contin, Lord, 1982
Griffiths, Lord, 1980
Gummer, John, 1985
Habgood, Rt Revd Lord, 1983
Hague, William, 1995
Hailsham of St Marylebone, Lord, 1956
Hamilton, Sir Archie, 1991
Hanley, Jeremy, 1994
Hardie Boys, Sir Michael, 1989
Harrison, Walter, 1977
Harvington, Lord, 1971
Hattersley, Roy, 1975
Hayhoe, Lord, 1985
Healey, Lord, 1964
Heath, Sir Edward, 1955
Heathcoat-Amory, David, 1996
Henry, Sir Denis, 1993
Herbison, Margaret, 1964
Heseltine, Michael, 1979
Heseltine, Sir William, 1986
Hesketh, Lord, 1991
Higgins, Sir Terence, 1979
Hirst, Sir David, 1992
Hobhouse, Sir John, 1993
Hoffmann, Lord, 1992
Hogg, Hon. Douglas, 1992
Holderness, Lord, 1959
Hope of Craighead, Lord, 1989
Hordern, Sir Peter, 1993
Howard, Michael, 1990
Howe of Aberavon, Lord, 1972
Howell, David, 1979
Howell, Lord, 1976
Hughes, Lord, 1970
Hunt, David, 1990
Hunt, Jonathan, 1989
Hurd, Douglas, 1982
Hutchison, Sir Michael, 1995
Hutton, Sir Brian, 1988
Ingraham, Hubert, 1993
Jauncey of Tullichettle, Lord, 1988
Jellicoe, Earl, 1963
Jenkin of Roding, Lord, 1973
Jenkins of Hillhead, Lord, 1964
Jones, Aubrey, 1955
Jopling, Michael, 1979
Judge, Sir Igor, 1996
Jugnauth, Sir Anerood, 1987
Kaufman, Gerald, 1978
Keith of Kinkel, Lord, 1976
Kelly, Sir Basil, 1984
Kenilorea, Sir Peter, 1979

Kennedy, Sir Paul, 1992
Kerr, Sir Michael, 1981
King, Thomas, 1979
Kingsdown, Lord, 1987
Kingsland, Lord, 1994
Kinnock, Neil, 1983
Knight, Gregory, 1995
Lamont, Norman, 1986
Lane, Lord, 1975
Lang, Ian, 1990
Lange, David, 1984
Lansdowne, Marquess of, 1964
Latasi, Kamuta, 1996
Latey, Sir John, 1986
Lauti, Sir Toaripi, 1979
Lawson of Blaby, Lord, 1981
Lawton, Sir Frederick, 1972
Leggatt, Sir Andrew, 1990
Leonard, Rt. Revd Graham, 1981
Lilley, Peter, 1990
Listowel, Earl of, 1946
Llewelyn-Davies of Hastoe, Baroness, 1975
Lloyd of Berwick, Lord, 1984
Lloyd, Sir Peter, 1994
London, The Bishop of, 1995
Longford, Earl of, 1948
Louisy, Allan, 1981
Lowry, Lord, 1974
Luce, Sir Richard, 1986
Lyell, Sir Nicholas, 1990
Mabon, Dickson, 1977
McCarthy, Sir Thaddeus, 1968
McCowan, Sir Anthony, 1989
MacDermott, Sir John, 1987
MacGregor, John, 1985
MacIntyre, Duncan, 1980
McKay, Ian, 1992
Mackay of Ardbrecknish, Lord, 1996
Mackay of Clashfern, Lord, 1979
Mackay of Drumadoon, Lord, 1996
McKinnon, Donald, 1992
Maclean, David, 1995
McMullin, Sir Duncan, 1980
Major, John, 1987
Manley, Michael, 1989
Mann, Sir Michael, 1988
Mara, Ratu Sir Kamisese, 1973
Marsh, Lord, 1966
Mason of Barnsley, Lord, 1968
Maude, Hon. Francis, 1992
Mawhinney, Brian, 1994
May, Sir John, 1982
Mayhew, Sir Patrick, 1986
Megarry, Sir Robert, 1978
Megaw, Sir John, 1969
Mellish, Lord, 1967
Mellor, David, 1990
Merlyn-Rees, Lord, 1974
Millan, Bruce, 1975
Millett, Sir Peter, 1994
Mitchell, Sir James, 1985
Molyneaux, Sir James, 1983
Monro, Sir Hector, 1995
Moore of Lower Marsh, Lord, 1986
Moore, Michael, 1990
Moore of Wolvercote, Lord, 1977
Morris, Alfred, 1979
Morris, Charles, 1978
Morris, John, 1970

Morris, Michael, 1994
Morritt, Sir Robert, 1994
Moyle, Roland, 1978
Murray, Hon. Lord, 1974
Murray, Sir Donald, 1989
Murray of Epping Forest, Lord, 1976
Murton of Lindisfarne, Lord, 1976
Mustill, Lord, 1985
Nairne, Sir Patrick, 1982
Namaliu, Sir Rabbie, 1989
Needham, Richard, 1994
Neill, Sir Brian, 1985
Newton, Antony, 1988
Nicholls of Birkenhead, Lord, 1995
Nicholson, Sir Michael, 1995
Nolan, Lord, 1991
Nott, Sir John, 1979
Nourse, Sir Martin, 1985
Nutting, Sir Anthony, 1954
Oakes, Gordon, 1979
O'Connor, Sir Patrick, 1980
O'Donnell, Turlough, 1979
O'Flynn, Francis, 1987
Oliver of Aylmerton, Lord, 1980
Onslow, Sir Cranley, 1988
Oppenheim-Barnes, Baroness, 1979
Orme, Stanley, 1974
Otton, Sir Philip, 1995
Owen, Lord, 1976
Paeniu, Bikenibeu, 1991
Palliser, Sir Michael, 1983
Palmer, Sir Geoffrey, 1986
Parker, Sir Roger, 1983
Parkinson, Lord, 1981
Patten, Christopher, 1989
Patten, John, 1990
Patterson, Percival, 1993
Pattie, Sir Geoffrey, 1987
Percival, Sir Ian, 1983
Perth, Earl of, 1957
Peyton of Yeovil, Lord, 1970
Phillips, Sir Nicholas, 1995
Pill, Sir Malcolm, 1995
Pindling, Sir Lynden, 1976
Portillo, Michael, 1992
Potter, Sir Mark, 1996
Powell, Enoch, 1960
Prentice, Lord, 1966
Prescott, John, 1994
Price, George, 1982
Prior, Lord, 1970
Puapua, Tomasi, 1982
Purchas, Sir Francis, 1982
Pym, Lord, 1970
Raison, Sir Timothy, 1982
Ramsden, James, 1963
Rawlinson of Ewell, Lord, 1964
Redwood, John, 1993
Rees, Lord, 1983
Renton, Lord, 1962
Renton, Timothy, 1989
Richard, Lord, 1993
Richardson, Sir Ivor, 1978
Richardson of Duntisbourne, Lord, 1976
Richmond, Sir Clifford, 1973
Rifkind, Malcolm, 1986
Rippon of Hexham, Lord, 1962
Robens of Woldingham, Lord, 1951
Roberts, Sir Wyn, 1991

Roch, Sir John, 1993
Rodger of Earlsferry, Lord, 1992
Rodgers of Quarry Bank, Lord, 1975
Rose, Sir Christopher, 1992
Roskill, Lord, 1971
Ross, *Hon.* Lord, 1985
Rumbold, Dame Angela, 1991
Runcie, Lord, 1980
Russell, Sir Patrick, 1987
Ryder, Richard, 1990
Sainsbury, Sir Timothy, 1992
St John of Fawsley, Lord, 1979
Sandiford, Erskine, 1989
Saville, Sir Mark, 1994
Scarman, Lord, 1973
Schiemann, Sir Konrad, 1995
Scott, Sir Nicholas, 1989
Scott, Sir Richard, 1991
Seaga, Edward, 1981
Seear, Baroness, 1985
Shawcross, Lord, 1946
Shearer, Hugh, 1969
Sheldon, Robert, 1977
Shephard, Gillian, 1992
Shepherd, Lord, 1965
Shore, Peter, 1967
Simmonds, Kennedy, 1984
Simon of Glaisdale, Lord, 1961
Sinclair, Ian, 1977
Slade, Sir Christopher, 1982
Slynn of Hadley, Lord, 1992

Smith, Sir Geoffrey Johnson, 1996
Somare, Sir Michael, 1977
Somers, Sir Edward, 1981
Stanley, Sir John, 1984
Staughton, Sir Christopher, 1988
Steel, Sir David, 1977
Stephen, Sir Ninian, 1979
Stephenson, Sir John, 1971
Stewartby, Lord, 1989
Steyn, Lord, 1992
Stocker, Sir John, 1986
Stodart of Leaston, Lord, 1974
Stott, Lord, 1964
Strathclyde, Lord, 1995
Stuart-Smith, Sir Murray, 1988
Talboys, Sir Brian, 1977
Taylor of Gosforth, Lord, 1988
Tebbit, Lord, 1981
Templeman, Lord, 1978
Thatcher, Baroness, 1970
Thomas of Gwydir, Lord, 1964
Thomas, Sir Swinton, 1994
Thomson, David, 1981
Thomson of Monifieth, Lord, 1966
Thorpe, Jeremy, 1967
Thorpe, Sir Matthew, 1995
Tizard, Robert, 1986
Tonypandy, Viscount, 1968
Trefgarne, Lord, 1989
Trumpington, Baroness, 1992
Ullswater, Viscount, 1994

Varley, Lord, 1974
Waddington, Lord, 1987
Waite, Sir John, 1993
Wakeham, Lord, 1983
Waldegrave, William, 1990
Walker, Sir Harold, 1979
Walker of Worcester, Lord, 1970
Waller, Sir George, 1976
Ward, Sir Alan, 1995
Watkins, Sir Tasker, 1980
Weatherill, Lord, 1980
Wheeler, Sir John, 1993
Whitelaw, Viscount, 1967
Wilberforce, Lord, 1964
Williams, Alan, 1977
Williams of Crosby, Baroness, 1974
Wilson of Langside, Lord, 1967
Windlesham, Lord, 1973
Wingti, Paias, 1987
Withers, Reginald, 1977
Woodhouse, Sir Owen, 1974
Woolf, Lord, 1986
Wylie, *Hon.* Lord, 1970
York, The Archbishop of, 1991
Young, Baroness, 1981
Young, Sir George, 1993
Young of Graffham, Lord, 1984
Younger of Prestwick, Lord, 1979
Zacca, Edward, 1992

The Privy Council of Northern Ireland

The Privy Council of Northern Ireland had responsibilities in Northern Ireland similar to those of the Privy Council in Great Britain until the Northern Ireland Act 1974 instituted direct rule and a UK Cabinet minister became responsible for the functions previously exercised by the Northern Ireland government.

Membership of the Privy Council of Northern Ireland is retained for life. The postnominal initials PC (NI)

are used to differentiate its members from those of the Privy Council.

MEMBERS *as at 31 August 1996*

Bailie, Robin, 1971
Bleakley, David, 1971
Bradford, Roy, 1969
Craig, William, 1963
Dobson, John, 1969
Kelly, Sir Basil, 1969

Kirk, Herbert, 1962
Long, William, 1966
Lowry, The Lord, 1971
McConnell, The Lord, 1964
McIvor, Basil, 1971
Morgan, William, 1961
Moyola, The Lord, 1966
Neill, Sir Ivan, 1950
Porter, Sir Robert, 1969
Simpson, Robert, 1969
Taylor, John, MP, 1970
West, Henry, 1960

Parliament

The United Kingdom constitution is not contained in any single document but has evolved in the course of time, formed partly by statute, partly by common law and partly by convention. A constitutional monarchy, the United Kingdom is governed by Ministers of the Crown in the name of the Sovereign, who is head both of the state and of the government.

The organs of government are the legislature (Parliament), the executive and the judiciary. The executive consists of HM Government (Cabinet and other Ministers) (*see* pages 275–6), government departments (*see* pages 277–356), local authorities (*see* Local Government), and public corporations operating nationalized industries or social or cultural services (*see* pages 277–356). The judiciary (*see* Law Courts and Offices) pronounces on the law, both written and unwritten, interprets statutes and is responsible for the enforcement of the law; the judiciary is independent of both the legislature and the executive.

THE MONARCHY

The Sovereign personifies the state and is, in law, an integral part of the legislature, head of the executive, head of the judiciary, the commander-in-chief of all armed forces of the Crown and the 'Supreme Governor' of the Church of England. The seat of the monarchy is in the United Kingdom. In the Channel Islands and the Isle of Man, which are Crown dependencies, the Sovereign is represented by a Lieutenant-Governor. In the member states of the Commonwealth of which the Sovereign is head of state, her representative is a Governor-General; in United Kingdom dependencies the Sovereign is usually represented by a Governor, who is responsible to the British Government.

Although the powers of the monarchy are now very limited, restricted mainly to the advisory and ceremonial, there are important acts of government which require the participation of the Sovereign. These include summoning, proroguing and dissolving Parliament, giving royal assent to bills passed by Parliament, appointing important office-holders, e.g. government ministers, judges, bishops and governors, conferring peerages, knighthoods and other honours, and granting pardon to a person wrongly convicted of a crime. An important function is appointing a Prime Minister, by convention the leader of the political party which enjoys, or can secure, a majority of votes in the House of Commons. In international affairs the Sovereign as head of state has the power to declare war and make peace, to recognize foreign states and governments, to conclude treaties and to annex or cede territory. However, as the Sovereign entrusts executive power to Ministers of the Crown and acts on the advice of her Ministers, which she cannot ignore, in practice royal prerogative powers are exercised by Ministers, who are responsible to Parliament.

Ministerial responsibility does not diminish the Sovereign's importance to the smooth working of government. She holds meetings of the Privy Council, gives audiences to her Ministers and other officials at home and overseas, receives accounts of Cabinet decisions, reads dispatches and signs state papers; she must be informed and consulted on every aspect of national life; and she must show complete impartiality.

COUNSELLORS OF STATE

In the event of the Sovereign's absence abroad, it is necessary to appoint Counsellors of State under letters patent to carry out the chief functions of the Monarch, including the holding of Privy Councils and giving royal assent to acts passed by Parliament. The normal procedure is to appoint as Counsellors three or four members of the royal family among those remaining in the United Kingdom.

In the event of the Sovereign on accession being under the age of eighteen years, or at any time unavailable or incapacitated by infirmity of mind or body for the performance of the royal functions, provision is made for a regency.

THE PRIVY COUNCIL

The Sovereign in Council, or Privy Council, was the chief source of executive power until the system of Cabinet government developed. Now its main function is to advise the Sovereign to approve Orders in Council and to advise on the issue of royal proclamations. The Council's own statutory responsibilities (independent of the powers of the Sovereign in Council) include powers of supervision over the registering bodies for the medical and allied professions. A full Council is summoned only on the death of the Sovereign or when the Sovereign announces his or her intention to marry. (For full list of Counsellors, *see* pages 213–5)

There are a number of advisory Privy Council committees, whose meetings the Sovereign does not attend. Some are prerogative committees, such as those dealing with legislative matters submitted by the legislatures of the Channel Islands and the Isle of Man or with applications for charters of incorporation; and some are provided for by statute, e.g. those for the universities of Oxford and Cambridge and the Scottish universities.

The Judicial Committee of the Privy Council is the final court of appeal from courts of the United Kingdom dependencies, courts of independent Commonwealth countries which have retained the right of appeal, courts of the Channel Islands and the Isle of Man, some professional and disciplinary committees, and church sources. The Committee is composed of Privy Counsellors who hold, or have held, high judicial office, although usually only three or five hear each case.

Administrative work is carried out by the Privy Council Office under the direction of the Lord President of the Council, a Cabinet Minister.

PARLIAMENT

Parliament is the supreme law-making authority and can legislate for the United Kingdom as a whole or for any parts of it separately (the Channel Islands and the Isle of Man are Crown dependencies and not part of the United Kingdom).

The main functions of Parliament are to pass laws, to provide (by voting taxation) the means of carrying on the work of government and to scrutinize government policy and administration, particularly proposals for expenditure. International treaties and agreements are by custom presented to Parliament before ratification.

Parliament emerged during the late 13th and early 14th centuries. The officers of the King's household and the King's judges were the nucleus of early Parliaments, joined by such ecclesiastical and lay magnates as the King might summon to form a prototype 'House of Lords', and occasionally by the knights of the shires, burgesses and proctors of the lower clergy. By the end of Edward III's reign a 'House of Commons' was beginning to appear; the first known Speaker was elected in 1377.

Parliamentary procedure is based on custom and precedent, partly formulated in the Standing Orders of both Houses (*see* Standing Orders, page 222), and each House has the right to control its own internal proceedings and to commit for contempt. The system of debate in the two Houses is similar; when a motion has been moved, the Speaker proposes the question as the subject of a debate. Members speak from wherever they have been sitting. Questions are decided by a vote on a simple majority. Draft legislation is introduced, in either House, as a bill. Bills can be introduced by a Government Minister or a private Member, but in practice the majority of bills which become law are introduced by the Government. To become law, a bill must be passed by each House (for parliamentary stages, *see* Bill, page 220) and then sent to the Sovereign for the royal assent, after which it becomes an Act of Parliament.

Proceedings of both Houses are public, except on extremely rare occasions. The minutes (called Votes and Proceedings in the Commons, and Minutes of Proceedings in the Lords) and the speeches (The Official Report of Parliamentary Debates, *Hansard*) are published daily. Proceedings are also recorded for transmission on radio and television and stored in the Parliamentary Recording Unit before transfer to the National Sound Archive. Television cameras have been allowed into the House of Lords since January 1985 and into the House of Commons since November 1989; committee meetings may also be televised.

By the Parliament Act of 1911, the maximum duration of a Parliament is five years (if not previously dissolved), the term being reckoned from the date given on the writs for the new Parliament. The maximum life has been prolonged by legislation in such rare circumstances as the two world wars (31 January 1911 to 25 November 1918; 26 November 1935 to 15 June 1945). Dissolution and writs for a general election are ordered by the Sovereign on the advice of the Prime Minister. The life of a Parliament is divided into sessions, usually of one year in length, beginning and ending most often in October or November.

THE HOUSE OF LORDS
London SWIA OPW
Tel 0171-219 3000

The House of Lords consists of the Lords Spiritual and Temporal. The Lords Spiritual are the Archbishops of Canterbury and York, the Bishops of London, Durham and Winchester, and the 21 senior diocesan bishops of the Church of England. The Lords Temporal consist of all hereditary peers of England, Scotland, Great Britain and the United Kingdom who have not disclaimed their peerages, life peers created under the Life Peerages Act 1958, and those Lords of Appeal in Ordinary created life peers under the Appellate Jurisdiction Act 1876, as amended (law lords). Disclaimants of a hereditary peerage lose their right to sit in the House of Lords but gain the right to vote at parliamentary elections and to offer themselves for election to the House of Commons (*see also* page 137). Those peers disqualified from sitting in the House include:

- aliens, i.e. any peer who is not a British citizen, a Commonwealth citizen (under the British Nationality Act 1981) or a citizen of the Republic of Ireland
- peers under the age of 21
- undischarged bankrupts or, in Scotland, those whose estate is sequestered
- peers convicted of treason

Peers who do not wish to attend sittings of the House of Lords may apply for leave of absence for the duration of a Parliament.

Until the beginning of this century the House of Lords had considerable power, being able to veto any bill submitted to it by the House of Commons, but those powers were greatly reduced by the Parliament Acts of 1911 and 1949 (*see* page 221).

Combined with its legislative role, the House of Lords has judicial powers as the ultimate Court of Appeal for courts in Great Britain and Northern Ireland, except for criminal cases in Scotland. These powers are exercised by the Lord Chancellor and the law lords.

Members of the House of Lords are unpaid. However, they are entitled to reimbursement of travelling expenses on parliamentary business within the UK and certain other expenses incurred for the purpose of attendance at sittings of the House, within a maximum for each day of £74.00 for overnight subsistence, £33.00 for day subsistence and incidental travel, and £32.00 for secretarial costs, postage and certain additional expenses.

COMPOSITION *as at 17 July 1996*
Archbishops and Bishops, 26
Peers by succession, 756 (16 women)
Hereditary Peers of first creation (including the Prince of Wales), 11
Life Peers under the Appellate Jurisdiction Act 1876, 24
Life Peers under the Life Peerages Act 1958, 378 (65 women)
Total 1,195
Of whom:
Peers without Writs of Summons, 84 (3 minors)
Peers on leave of absence from the House, 67

STATE OF PARTIES *as at 17 July 1996*
About half of the members of the House of Lords take the whip of one of the political parties. The other members sit on the cross-benches as independents or have no party affiliation.

Conservative, 468
Labour, 110
Liberal Democrats, 56
Cross-bench, 298
Other (including Bishops), 260 (of whom 151 are ineligible to attend)

OFFICERS

The House is presided over by the Lord Chancellor, who is *ex officio* Speaker of the House. A panel of deputy Speakers is appointed by Royal Commission. The first deputy Speaker is the Chairman of Committees, appointed at the beginning of each session, a salaried officer of the House who takes the chair in committee of the whole House and in some select committees. He is assisted by a panel of deputy chairmen, headed by the salaried Principal Deputy

Chairman of Committees, who is also chairman of the European Communities Committee of the House.

The permanent officers include the Clerk of the Parliaments, who is in charge of the administrative staff collectively known as the Parliament Office; the Gentleman Usher of the Black Rod, who is also Serjeant-at-Arms in attendance upon the Lord Chancellor and is responsible for security and for accommodation and services in the House of Lords; and the Yeoman Usher, who is Deputy Serjeant-at-Arms and assists Black Rod in his duties.

Speaker (£18,607), The Lord Mackay of Clashfern, PC
   Private Secretary, P. Kennedy
Chairman of Committees (£51,652), The Lord Boston of
   Faversham, QC
Principal Deputy Chairman of Committees (£47,673), The Lord
   Tordoff
Clerk of the Parliaments (£103,425), Sir Michael Wheeler-
   Booth, KCB
Clerk Assistant and Principal Finance Officer (£67,500 –
   £98,000), J. M. Davies
Reading Clerk and Clerk of Public Bills (£57,000 –£84,500),
   P. D. G. Hayter, LVO
Counsel to Chairman of Committees (£57,000 –£84,500),
   D. Rippengal, CB, QC; Sir James Nursaw, KCB, QC; Dr C. S.
   Kerse
Principal Clerks (£51,103 –£84,500), J. A. Vallance White
   (*Judicial Office and Fourth Clerk at the Table*); M. G.
   Pownall (*Clerk of the Journals*); B. P. Keith (*Private Bills*);
   D. R. Beamish (*Committees*); R. H. Walters, D.Phil.
Chief Clerks (£41,978 –£61,493), Dr F. P. Tudor; T. V.
   Mohan; E. C. Ollard
Senior Clerks (£29,107 –£44,101), Mrs M. E. Ollard (*seconded
   as Secretary to the Leader of the House and Chief Whip*); A.
   Makower; E. J. J. Wells; S. P. Burton; J. L. Goddard; Mrs
   M. B. Bloor; T. E. Radice
Clerks (£15,172 –£26,365), D. J. Batt; Dr C. Andrew Mylne;
   Miss L. J. Mouland; J. A. Vaughan
Clerk of the Records (£41,978 –£61,493), D. J. Johnson, FSA
Deputy Clerk of the Records (£32,962 –£53,481), S. K. Ellison
Establishment Officer, R. H. Walters, D.Phil.
Deputy Establishment Officer (£29,107 –£44,101), G.
   Embleton
Accountant (£29,107 –£53,481), C. Preece
Assistant Accountant (£22,410 –£28,932), Miss J. M.
   Lansdown
Computer Executive (£29,107 –£44,101), Ms S. C. White
Internal Auditor (£29,107 –£44,101), C. H. Rogers
Staff Adviser (£29,107 –£44,101), D. A. W. Dunn, ISO
Judicial Taxing Clerk (£22,410 –£28,932), C. G. Osborne
Librarian (£41,978 –£61,493), D. L. Jones
Deputy Librarian (£32,962 –£53,481), P. G. Davis, PH.D.
Senior Library Clerk (£29,107 –£44,101), Miss I. L. Victory,
   PH.D.
Examiners of Petitions for Private Bills, B. P. Keith; R. J.
   Willoughby
Gentleman Usher of the Black Rod and Serjeant-at-Arms
   (£57,000 –£84,500), Gen. Sir Edward Jones, KCB, CBE
Yeoman Usher of the Black Rod and Deputy Serjeant-at-Arms
   (£29,107 –£44,101), Air Vice-Marshal D. R. Hawkins,
   CB, MBE
Administration Officer (£29,107 –£44,101), Brig. A. J. M.
   Clark
Staff Superintendent, Maj. A. M. Charlesworth
Shorthand Writer (fees), Mrs P. J. Woolgar
Editor, Official Report (*Hansard*), (£39,566 –£57,910), Mrs
   M. E. Villiers
Deputy Editor, Official Report (£29,843 –£48,311), G. R.
   Goodbarne

THE HOUSE OF COMMONS
London SW1A 0AA
Tel 0171-219 3000

The members of the House of Commons are elected by universal adult suffrage. For electoral purposes, the United Kingdom is divided into constituencies, each of which returns one member to the House of Commons, the member being the candidate who obtains the largest number of votes cast in the constituency. To ensure equitable representation the four Boundary Commissions keep constituency boundaries under review and recommend any redistribution of seats which may seem necessary because of population movements, etc. The number of seats was raised to 640 in 1945, then reduced to 625 in 1948, and subsequently rose to 630 in 1955, 635 in 1970, 650 in 1983 and 651 in 1992. Of the present 651 seats, there are 524 for England, 38 for Wales, 72 for Scotland and 17 for Northern Ireland.

At the next general election the number of constituencies will increase to 659; 529 seats in England, 40 seats in Wales, 72 seats in Scotland, and 18 seats in Northern Ireland.

ELECTIONS

Elections are by secret ballot, each elector casting one vote; voting is not compulsory. When a seat becomes vacant between general elections, a by-election is held.

British subjects and citizens of the Irish Republic can stand for election as Members of Parliament (MPs) provided they are 21 or over and not subject to disqualification. Those disqualified from sitting in the House include:

– undischarged bankrupts
– people sentenced to more than one year's imprisonment
– clergy of the Church of England, Church of Scotland,
   Church of Ireland and Roman Catholic Church
– members of the House of Lords
– holders of certain offices listed in the House of Commons
   Disqualification Act 1975, e.g. members of the judiciary,
   Civil Service, regular armed forces, police forces, some
   local government officers and some members of public
   corporations and government commissions

For entitlement to vote in parliamentary elections, *see* Legal Notes section.

A candidate does not require any party backing but his or her nomination for election must be supported by the signatures of ten people registered in the constituency. A candidate must also deposit with the returning officer £500, which is forfeit if the candidate does not receive more than 5 per cent of the votes cast. All election expenses at a general election, except the candidate's personal expenses, are subject to a statutory limit of £4,330, plus 3.7 pence for each elector in a borough constituency or 4.9 pence for each elector in a county constituency.

See pages 226–32 for an alphabetical list of MPs, pages 237–67 for the results of the last General Election, and pages 234–5 for the results of recent by-elections.

STATE OF PARTIES *as at 13 July 1996*
Conservative, 324 (17 women)
Elected as Conservative but has resigned the whip, 1
Labour, 272 (38 women)
Liberal Democrats, 25 (4 women)
Plaid Cymru, 4
Scottish Nationalist, 4 (2 women)
Democratic Unionist, 3
Social Democratic and Labour, 4
Ulster Unionist, 9
United Kingdom Unionist, 1

The Speaker and three Deputy Speakers, 4 (2 women)
Total, 651 (63 women)

BUSINESS

The week's business of the House is outlined each Thursday by the Leader of the House, after consultation between the Chief Government Whip and the Chief Opposition Whip. A quarter to a third of the time will be taken up by the Government's legislative programme, and the rest by other business, e.g. question time. As a rule, bills likely to raise political controversy are introduced in the Commons before going on to the Lords, and the Commons claims exclusive control in respect of national taxation and expenditure. Bills such as the Finance Bill, which imposes taxation, and the Consolidated Fund Bills, which authorize expenditure, must begin in the Commons. A bill of which the financial provisions are subsidiary may begin in the Lords; and the Commons may waive its rights in regard to Lords' amendments affecting finance.

The Commons has a public register of MPs' financial and certain other interests; this is published annually as a House of Commons paper. Members must also disclose any relevant financial interest or benefit in a matter before the House when taking part in a debate, in certain other proceedings of the House, or in consultations with other MPs, with Ministers or civil servants.

MEMBERS' PAY AND ALLOWANCES

Since 1911 members of the House of Commons have received salary payments; facilities for free travel were introduced in 1924. Members are entitled to claim income tax relief on expenses incurred in the course of their parliamentary duties. Salary rates since 1911 are as follows:

1911	£400 p.a.	1981 June	£13,950 p.a.
1931	360	1982 June	14,510
1934	380	1983 June	15,308
1935	400	1984 Jan	16,106
1937	600	1985 Jan	16,904
1946	1,000	1986 Jan	17,702
1954	1,250	1987 Jan	18,500
1957	1,750	1988 Jan	22,548
1964	3,250	1989 Jan	24,107
1972 Jan	4,500	1990 Jan	26,701
1975 June	5,750	1991 Jan	28,970
1976 June	6,062	1992 Jan	30,854
1977 July	6,270	1994 Jan	31,687
1978 June	6,897	1995 Jan	33,189
1979 June	9,450	1996 Jan	34,085
1980 June	11,750	1996 July	43,000

In 1969 MPs were granted an allowance for secretarial and research expenses. In 1987 this became known as the Office Costs Allowance. From April 1996 the allowance is £43,098 a year.

Since 1972 MPs can claim reimbursement for the additional cost of staying overnight away from their main residence while on parliamentary business. From April 1996 this has been £11,976 a year and since 1984 has been non-taxable.

From 1980 provision was made enabling each MP in receipt of Office Costs Allowance to contribute sums to an approved pension scheme for the provision of a pension, or other benefits, for or in respect of persons whose salary is met by him/her from the Office Costs Allowance.

MEMBERS' PENSIONS

Pension arrangements for MPs were first introduced in 1964. The arrangements currently provide a pension of one-fiftieth of salary for each year of pensionable service with a maximum of two-thirds of salary at age 65. Pension is

payable normally at age 65, for men and women, or on later retirement. Pensions may be paid earlier, e.g. on ill-health retirement. The widow/widower of a former MP receives a pension of five-eighths of the late MP's pension. Pensions are index-linked. Members currently contribute 6 per cent of salary to the pension fund; there is an Exchequer contribution, currently slightly more than the amount contributed by MPs.

The House of Commons Members' Fund provides for annual or lump sum grants to ex-MPs, their widows or widowers, and children whose incomes are below certain limits. Alternatively, payments of £2,116 a year to ex-MPs with at least ten years' service and who left the House of Commons before October 1964, and £1,323 a year to their widows or widowers are made as of right. Members contribute £24 a year and the Exchequer £215,000 a year to the fund.

OFFICERS AND OFFICIALS

The House of Commons is presided over by the Speaker, who has considerable powers to maintain order in the House. A deputy, the Chairman of Ways and Means, and two Deputy Chairmen may preside over sittings of the House of Commons; they are elected by the House, and, like the Speaker, neither speak nor vote other than in their official capacity.

The staff of the House are employed by a Commission chaired by the Speaker. The heads of the six House of Commons departments are permanent officers of the House, not MPs. The Clerk of the House is the principal adviser to the Speaker on the privileges and procedures of the House, the conduct of the business of the House, and committees. The Serjeant-at-Arms is responsible for security, ceremonial, and for accommodation in the Commons part of the Palace of Westminster.

Speaker (£69,651), The Rt. Hon. Betty Boothroyd, MP (West Bromwich West)
Chairman of Ways and Means (£56,785), The Rt. Hon. Michael Morris, MP (Northampton South)
First Deputy Chairman of Ways and Means (£53,015), Sir Geoffrey Lofthouse, MP (Pontefract and Castleford)
Second Deputy Chairman of Ways and Means (£53,015), Dame Janet Fookes, DBE, MP (Plymouth Drake)

OFFICES OF THE SPEAKER AND CHAIRMAN OF WAYS AND MEANS

Speaker's Secretary (£42,180–£61,595), N. Bevan, CB
Chaplain to the Speaker, The Revd Canon D. Gray, TD
Secretary to the Chairman of Ways and Means, (£28,954–£43,802), Ms L. M. Gardner

DEPARTMENT OF THE CLERK OF THE HOUSE

Clerk of the House of Commons (£101,827), D. W. Limon, CB
Clerk Assistant (£67,500–£83,450), W. R. McKay, CB
Clerk of Committees (£67,500–£83,450), C. B. Winnifrith
Principal Clerks (£55,000–£67,650)
  Public Bills, R. B. Sands
  Table Office, G. Cubie
  Journals, A. J. Hastings
  Private Bills, R. J. Willoughby
  Select Committees, D. G. Millar
  Domestic Committees, M. R. Jack, PH.D.
  Overseas Office, R. W. G. Wilson
  Standing Committees, W. A. Proctor
  Second Clerk, Select Committees, Ms H. E. Irwin
  Financial Committees, Mrs J. Sharpe

Deputy Principal Clerks (£42,180–£61,595), S. A. L. Panton;
Ms A. Milner-Barry; F. A. Cranmer; R. J. Rogers; C. R. M.
Ward, ph.d.; D. W. N. Doig; D. L. Natzler; E. P. Silk; A. R.
Kennon; L. C. Laurence Smyth; S. J. Patrick;
D. J. Gerhold; C. J. Poyser; D. F. Harrison; S. J. Priestley;
A. H. Doherty; P. A. Evans; R. I. S. Phillips; R. G. James,
ph.d.; Ms P. A. Helme; D. R. Lloyd; B. M. Hutton; J. S.
Benger, d.phil.; Ms E. C. Samson; N. P. Walker; M. D.
Hamlyn
Senior Clerks (£28,954–£43,802), Mrs E. J. Flood; P. C.
Seaward, d.phil.; C. G. Lee; C. D. Stanton; A. Y. A. Azad;
C. A. Shaw; Ms L. M. Gardner; K. J. Brown; F. J. Reid; M.
Hennessy; G. R. Devine; Mrs E. A. J. Attridge (*acting*);
A. M. Kidner (*acting*); Ms J. Eldred (*acting*)
Clerks of Domestic Committees (£28,954–£43,802), P. G.
Moon; M. Clark
Examiners of Petitions for Private Bills, R. J. Willoughby; B. P.
Keith
Registrar of Members' Interests, R. J. Willoughby
Taxing Officer, R. J. Willoughby

Vote Office
Deliverer of the Vote (£42,180–£61,595), H. C. Foster
Deputy Deliverers of the Vote (£28,954–£43,802), J. F. Collins
(*Distribution*); F. W. Hallett (*Production*)

Speaker's Counsel
Speaker's Counsel (£55,000–£67,650), J. S. Mason, cb
Speaker's Counsel (European legislation) (£55,000–£67,650),
T. J. G. Pratt, cb
Speaker's Assistant Counsel (£42,180–£61,595), A. Akbar; J.
R. Mallinson

Department of the Serjeant-at-Arms
Serjeant-at-Arms (£55,000–£67,650), P. N. W. Jennings
Deputy Serjeant-at-Arms (£42,180–£61,595), M. J. A.
Cummins
Assistant Serjeant-at-Arms (£32,791–£53,108), P. A. J.
Wright
Deputy Assistant Serjeant-at-Arms (£28,954–£43,802), J. M.
Robertson; M. C. D. Harvey

Parliamentary Works Directorate
Director of Works (£55,060–£61,595), H. P. Webber
Deputy Director of Works (£32,791–£53,108), L. Brantingham

Communications Directorate
Director of Communications (£42,180–£61,595), C. G. Gilbert

Department of the Library
Librarian (£55,000–£67,650), Miss J. B. Tanfield
Deputy Librarian (£51,135–£61,595), Miss P. J. Baines
Service Directors (£42,180–£61,595), S. Z. Young; K. G.
Cuninghame; Mrs J. M. Wainwright
Heads of Section (£32,791–£53,108), C. C. Pond, ph.d.;
Mrs C. B. Andrews; R. C. Clements; Mrs J. M. Lourie;
R. J. Ware, d.phil.; C. R. Barclay; Mrs J. M. Fiddick; Mrs
C. M. Gillie; R. J. Twigger; Mrs G. L. Allen
Senior Library Clerks (£28,954–£43,802), Ms F. Poole; T. N.
Edmonds; R. J. Cracknell; Miss O. M. Gay; Miss E. M.
McInnes; Dr D. J. Gore; B. K. Winetrobe; Miss M. Baber;
Ms A. Walker; Mrs H. V. Holden; Mrs P. L. Carling; Miss
J. Seaton; A. J. L. Crompton; Miss P. J. Strickland; Miss
V. A. Miller; Ms H. M. Jeffs; M. P. Hillyard; Ms J. Roll;
Ms W. T. Wilson; S. A. Wise; E. H. Wood; P. Bowers; T. E.
Dodd; A. C. Seely; Ms J. K. Dyson; K. N. H. Parry (*acting*)

Department of Finance and Administration
Director of Finance and Administration (£55,000–£67,650),
J. Rodda
Accountant (£51,135–£61,595), A. R. Marskell

Deputy Accountant (£32,791–£53,108), M. Fletcher
Head of Establishments Office (£51,135–£61,595), B. A.
Wilson
Deputy Head of Establishments Office (£32,791–£53,108), J. A.
Robb
Head of Finance Office (£42,180–£61,595), M. J. Barram
Staff Inspector (£32,791–£53,108), R. C. Collins

Department of the Official Report
Editor (£51,135–£61,595), I. D. Church
Deputy Editor (£42,180–£61,595), P. Walker
Principal Assistant Editors (£32,791–£53,108), J. Gourley;
W. G. Garland; Miss H. Hales; Miss L. Sutherland
Assistant Editors (£32,791–£49,325), Miss V. Grainger; Miss
V. A. A. Clarke; S. M. Hutchinson; Miss C. Fogarty; Miss
V. A. Widgery; Ms K. Stewart; P. R. Hadlow

Refreshment Department
Director of Catering Services (£42,180–£61,595), Mrs S. J.
Harrison
Financial Controller (£28,954–£43,802), Mrs J. A. Rissen
Operations Manager (£28,954–£43,802), N. M. Hutson

PARLIAMENTARY INFORMATION

The following is a short glossary of aspects of the work of
Parliament. Unless otherwise stated, references are to
House of Commons procedures.

BILL – Proposed legislation is termed a bill. The stages of
a public bill (for private bills, *see* page 221) in the House of
Commons are as follows:
First Reading: There is no debate at this stage, which merely
constitutes an order to have the bill printed
Second Reading: The debate on the principles of the bill
Committee Stage: The detailed examination of a bill, clause
by clause. In most cases this takes place in a standing
committee, or the whole House may act as a committee. A
special standing committee may take evidence before
embarking on detailed scrutiny of the bill. Very rarely, a
bill may be examined by a select committee (*see* page 222)
Report Stage: Detailed review of a bill as amended in
committee
Third Reading: Final debate on a bill
Public bills go through the same stages in the House of
Lords, except that in almost all cases the committee stage is
taken in committee of the whole House.
A bill may start in either House, and has to pass through
both Houses to become law. Both Houses have to agree the
same text of a bill, so that the amendments made by the
second House are then considered in the originating
House, and if not agreed, sent back or themselves amended,
until agreement is reached.

CHILTERN HUNDREDS – A legal fiction, a nominal office
of profit under the Crown, the acceptance of which requires
an MP to vacate his seat. The Manor of Northstead is
similar. These are the only means by which an MP may
resign.

CLOSURE AND GUILLOTINE – To prevent deliberate
waste of time of either House, a motion may be made that
the question be now put. In the House of Commons, if the
Speaker decides that the rights of a minority are not being
prejudiced and 100 members support the closure motion in
a division, if carried, the original motion is put to the House
without further debate.
The guillotine represents a more rigorous and systematic application of the closure. Under this system, a bill

proceeds in accordance with a rigid timetable and discussion is limited to the time allotted to each group of clauses. The closure is hardly ever used in the Lords, and there is no procedure for a guillotine. The completion of business in the Lords is ensured by agreement from all sides of the House.

CONSOLIDATED FUND BILL – A bill to authorize issue of money to maintain Government services. The bill is dealt with without debate.

DISSOLUTION – Parliament comes to an end either by dissolution by the Sovereign, on the advice of the Prime Minister, or on the expiration of the term of five years for which the House of Commons was elected. Dissolution is normally effected by a royal proclamation.

EARLY DAY MOTION – A motion put on the notice paper by an MP without in general the real prospect of its being debated. Such motions are expressions of back-bench opinion.

EMERGENCY DEBATE – In the Commons a method of obtaining prompt discussion of a matter of urgency is by moving the adjournment under Standing Order No. 20 for the purpose of discussing a specific and important matter that should have urgent consideration. A member may ask leave to make this motion by giving written notice to the Speaker, usually before 12 noon, and if the Speaker considers the matter of sufficient importance and the House agrees, it is discussed usually at 7 p.m. on the following day.

FATHER OF THE HOUSE – The Member whose continuous service in the House of Commons is the longest. The present Father of the House is the Rt. Hon. Sir Edward Heath, KG, MBE, MP, elected first in 1950.

HANSARD – The official report of debates in both Houses (and in standing committees) published by HMSO, normally on the day after the sitting concerned.

HOURS OF MEETING – The House of Commons meets on Monday, Tuesday and Thursday at 2.30 p.m., on Wednesday at 10 a.m. and on Friday at 9.30 a.m.; there are ten Fridays without sittings in each session. The House of Lords normally meets at 2.30 p.m. Monday to Wednesday and at 3 p.m. on Thursday. In the latter part of the session, the House of Lords sometimes sits on Fridays at 11 a.m.

HYBRIDITY – A public bill which is considered to affect specific private or local interests, as distinct from all such interests of a single category, is called a hybrid bill and is subject to a special form of scrutiny to enable people affected to object. In the House of Lords, affirmative instruments may also be treated as hybrid.

LEADER OF THE OPPOSITION – In 1937 the office of Leader of the Opposition was recognized and a salary was assigned to the post. Since July 1996 the salary has been £83,332 (including parliamentary salary of £43,000). The present Leader of the Opposition is the Rt. Hon. Tony Blair, MP.

THE LORD CHANCELLOR – The Lord High Chancellor of Great Britain is (*ex officio*) the Speaker of the House of Lords. Unlike the Speaker of the House of Commons, he is a member of the Government, takes part in debates and votes in divisions. He has none of the powers to maintain order that the Speaker in the Commons has, these powers being exercised in the Lords by the House as a whole. The Lord Chancellor sits in the Lords on one of the Woolsacks, couches covered with red cloth and stuffed with wool. If he wishes to address the House in any way except formally as Speaker, he leaves the Woolsack.

NAMING – When a member has been named by the Speaker for a breach of order, i.e. contrary to the practice of the House, called by surname and not addressed as the 'Hon. Member for … (her/his constituency)', the Leader of the House moves that the offender 'be suspended from the service of the House' for (in the case of a first offence) a period of five sitting days. Should the member offend again, the period of suspension is increased.

OPPOSITION DAY – A day on which the topic for debate is chosen by the Opposition. There are twenty such days in a normal session. On seventeen days, subjects are chosen by the Leader of the Opposition; on the remaining three days by the leader of the next largest opposition party.

PARLIAMENT ACTS 1911 AND 1949 – Under these Acts, bills may become law without the consent of the Lords. Since at least the 18th century the Commons has had the privilege of having bills concerned with supply (i.e. taxation and money matters) passed without amendment by the Lords, though until 1911 the Lords retained the right to reject such bills outright.

By the Parliament Act 1911, a bill which has been endorsed by the Speaker of the House of Commons as a money bill, and has been passed by the Commons and sent up to the Lords at least one month before the end of a session, can become law without the consent of the Lords if it is not passed by them without amendment within a month.

Under the Parliament Acts 1911 and 1949, if the Lords reject any other public bill (except one to prolong the life of a Parliament) which has been passed by the Commons in two successive sessions, then that bill shall (unless the Commons direct to the contrary) become law without the consent of the Lords. The Lords have power, therefore, to delay a public bill for thirteen months from its first second reading in the House of Commons.

PRIME MINISTER'S QUESTIONS – The Prime Minister answers questions from 3.15 to 3.30 p.m. on Tuesdays and Thursdays. Nowadays the 'open question' predominates. Members tend to ask the Prime Minister what are his or her official engagements for the day; a supplementary question on virtually any topic can then be put.

PRIVATE BILL – A bill promoted by a body or an individual to give powers additional to, or in conflict with, the general law, and to which a special procedure applies to enable people affected to object.

PRIVATE MEMBERS' BILL – A public bill promoted by a Member who is not a member of the Government.

PRIVATE NOTICE QUESTION – A question adjudged of urgent importance on submission to the Speaker (in the Lords, the Leader of the House), answered at the end of oral questions, usually at 3.30 p.m.

PRIVILEGE – The following are covered by the privilege of Parliament:
(i) freedom from interference in going to, attending at, and going from, Parliament
(ii) freedom of speech in parliamentary proceedings
(iii) the printing and publishing of anything relating to the proceedings of the two Houses is subject to privilege
(iv) each House is the guardian of its dignity and may punish any insult to the House as a whole

PROROGATION – The bringing to an end, by the Sovereign on the advice of the Government, of a session of Parliament. Public bills which have not completed all their stages lapse on prorogation.

QUEEN'S SPEECH – The speech delivered by The Queen at the State Opening of Parliament, in which the Government's programme for the session is set forth. The speech is drafted by civil servants and approved by the Cabinet.

QUESTION TIME – Oral questions are answered by Ministers in the Commons from 2.30 to 3.30 p.m. every day except Friday. They are also taken at the start of the Lords sittings, with a daily limit of four oral questions.

ROYAL ASSENT – The royal assent is signified by letters patent to such bills and measures as have passed both Houses of Parliament (or bills which have been passed under the Parliament Acts 1911 and 1949). The Sovereign has not given royal assent in person since 1854. On occasion, for instance in the prorogation of Parliament, royal assent may be pronounced to the two Houses by Lords Commissioners. More usually royal assent is notified to each House sitting separately in accordance with the Royal Assent Act 1967. The old French formulae for royal assent are then endorsed on the acts by the Clerk of the Parliaments.

The power to withhold assent resides with the Sovereign but has not been exercised in the United Kingdom since 1707, in the reign of Queen Anne.

SCOTTISH GRAND COMMITTEE – Established in its present form in 1957, the committee consists of all 72 MPs representing Scottish constituencies, with a quorum of ten. The functions of the committee are to consider the principle of all public bills relating exclusively to Scotland (constituting in effect the bill's second reading); to consider the Scottish estimates on not less than six days a session; and to consider matters relating exclusively to Scotland on not more than six days a session. From the beginning of the 1994–5 session, the committee's powers were enhanced to allow oral questions, short debates, ministerial statements, and consideration of appropriate statutory instruments. The committee can meet on appointed days at specified places in Scotland.

The Scottish Affairs select committee is empowered to examine the expenditure, administration and policy of the Scottish Office, and the expenditure and administration of the Lord Advocate's Office.

SELECT COMMITTEES – Consisting usually of ten to 15 members of all parties, select committees are a means used by both Houses in order to investigate certain matters.

Most select committees in the House of Commons are now tied to departments; each committee investigates subjects within a government department's remit. There are other House of Commons select committees dealing with public accounts (i.e. the spending by the Government of money voted by Parliament) and European legislation, and also domestic committees dealing, for example, with privilege and procedure. Major select committees usually take evidence in public; their evidence and reports are published by HMSO.

The principal select committee in the House of Lords is that on the European Communities, which has, at present, six sub-committees dealing with all areas of Community policy. The House of Lords also has a select committee on science and technology, which appoints sub-committees to deal with specific subjects. In addition, ad hoc select committees have been set up from time to time to investigate specific subjects, e.g. overseas trade, murder and life imprisonment. There are also some joint committees of the two Houses, e.g. the Joint Committee on Statutory Instruments.

The following are the more important select committees:

DEPARTMENTAL COMMITTEES

Agriculture – Chair, Sir Jerry Wiggin, MP; Clerk, Mr Walker
Defence – Chair, Michael Colvin, MP; Clerks, Mr Kennon; Mr Shaw
Education and Employment – Chair, Sir Malcolm Thornton, MP; Clerk, Mr Hamlyn
Environment – Chair, Andrew Bennett, MP; Clerks, Mr Priestley; Ms Payne
Foreign Affairs – Chair, Rt. Hon. David Howell, MP; Clerks, Dr Ward; Mrs Davies
Health – Chair, Marion Roe, MP; Clerks, Dr James; Mr Healey
Home Affairs – Chair, Sir Ivan Lawrence, MP; Clerks, Mr Poyser; Mr Fox
National Heritage – Chair, Rt. Hon. Gerald Kaufman, MP; Clerk, Mr Patrick
Northern Ireland – Chair, Clive Soley, MP, Clerk, Mr Phillips
Science and Technology – Chair, Sir Giles Shaw, MP; Clerk, Ms Samson
Scottish Affairs – Chair, William McKelvey, MP; Clerk, Mr Doherty; Mr McGlashan
Social Security – Chair, Frank Field, MP; Clerk, Mr Laurence Smyth
Trade and Industry – Chair, Martin O'Neill, MP; Clerks, Mr Gerhold; Mrs Mulley
Transport – Chair, Rt. Hon. Paul Channon, MP; Clerks, Ms Long; Mr Stanton
Treasury – Chair, Sir Thomas Arnold, MP; Clerk, Mrs Sharpe
Welsh Affairs – Chair, Gareth Wardell, MP; Clerk, Ms Helme

NON-DEPARTMENTAL COMMITTEES

Deregulation – Chair, Barry Field, MP; Clerks, Mr Rogers; Mrs Flood
European Legislation – Chair, James Hood, MP; Clerks, Mr Rogers; Mr Lloyd
Parliamentary Commissioner – Chair, James Pawsey, MP; Clerk, Mr Azad
Procedure – Chair, Rt. Hon. Sir Peter Emery, MP; Clerks, Mr Natzler; Mr Rhys
Public Accounts – Chair, Rt. Hon. Robert Sheldon, MP; Clerk, Mr Brown
Public Service – Chair, Giles Radice, MP; Clerk, Dr Seaward
Standards and Privileges – Chair, Rt. Hon. Antony Newton, MP; Clerks, Mr Hastings; Mr Reid

THE SPEAKER – The Speaker of the House of Commons is the spokesman and president of the Chamber. He or she is elected by the House at the beginning of each Parliament or when the previous Speaker retires or dies. The Speaker neither speaks in debates nor votes in divisions except when the voting is equal.

STANDING ORDERS – Rules which have from time to time been agreed by each House of Parliament to regulate the conduct of its business. These orders may be amended or repealed, and are from time to time suspended or dispensed with.

STATE OPENING – This marks the start of each new session of Parliament. Parliament is normally opened, in the presence of both Houses, by The Queen in person, who makes the speech from the throne which outlines the Government's policies for the coming session (*see* Queen's Speech). In the absence of The Queen, Parliament is opened by Royal Commission, and the Queen's Speech is read by one of the Lords Commissioners specially appointed by letters patent for the occasion.

STRANGERS – Anyone who is not a Member or Officer of the House is a stranger. Visitors are generally admitted to debates of both Houses but may be excluded if the House so decides; in practice this happens only in time of war.

However, the cry of 'I spy strangers' causes the public gallery to be cleared, and occurs often.

VACANT SEATS – When a vacancy occurs in the House of Commons during a session of Parliament, the writ for the by-election is moved by a Whip of the party to which the member whose seat has been vacated belonged. If the House is in recess, the Speaker can issue a warrant for a writ, should two members certify to him that a seat is vacant.

WELSH GRAND COMMITTEE – First appointed in the 1959-60 session, the committee consists of all 38 MPs representing Welsh constituencies plus five other members nominated by the selection committee. The functions of the committee are to consider the principle of all public bills referred to it (constituting in effect the second reading of such a bill); and to consider matters relating exclusively to Wales.

The Welsh Affairs select committee is empowered to examine the expenditure, administration and policy of the Welsh Office.

WHIPS – In order to secure the attendance of Members of a particular party in Parliament on all occasions, and particularly on the occasion of an important vote, Whips (originally known as 'Whippers-in') are appointed. The written appeal or circular letter issued by them is also known as a 'whip', its urgency being denoted by the number of times it is underlined. Failure to respond to a three-line whip, headed 'Most important', is tantamount in the Commons to secession (at any rate temporarily) from the party. Whips are officially recognized by Parliament and are provided with office accommodation in both Houses. In both Houses, Government and some Opposition Whips receive salaries from public funds.

PUBLIC INFORMATION SERVICES
HOUSE OF COMMONS – Public Information Office, House of Commons, London SW1A 0AA. Tel: 0171-219 4272
HOUSE OF LORDS – The Journal and Information Office, House of Lords, London SW1A 0PW. Tel: 0171–219 3107

GOVERNMENT OFFICE

The Government is the body of Ministers responsible for the administration of national affairs, determining policy and introducing into Parliament any legislation necessary to give effect to government policy. The majority of Ministers are members of the House of Commons but members of the House of Lords or of neither House may also hold ministerial responsibility. The Lord Chancellor is always a member of the House of Lords. The Prime Minister is, by current convention, always a member of the House of Commons.

THE PRIME MINISTER
The office of Prime Minister, which had been in existence for nearly 200 years, was officially recognized in 1905 and its holder was granted a place in the table of precedence. The Prime Minister, by tradition also First Lord of the Treasury and Minister for the Civil Service, is appointed by the Sovereign and is usually the leader of the party which enjoys, or can secure, a majority in the House of Commons. Other Ministers are appointed by the Sovereign on the recommendation of the Prime Minister, who also allocates functions amongst Ministers and has the power to obtain their resignation or dismissal individually.

The Prime Minister informs the Sovereign of state and political matters, advises on the dissolution of Parliament, and makes recommendations for important Crown appointments, the award of honours, etc.

As the chairman of Cabinet meetings and leader of a political party, the Prime Minister is responsible for translating party policy into government activity. As leader of the Government, the Prime Minister is responsible to Parliament and to the electorate for the policies and their implementation.

The Prime Minister also represents the nation in international affairs, e.g. summit conferences.

THE CABINET
The Cabinet developed during the 18th century as an inner committee of the Privy Council, which was the chief source of executive power until that time. The Cabinet is composed of about twenty Ministers chosen by the Prime Minister, usually the heads of government departments (generally known as Secretaries of State unless they have a special title, e.g. Chancellor of the Exchequer), the leaders of the two Houses of Parliament, and the holders of various traditional offices.

The Cabinet's functions are the final determination of policy, control of government and co-ordination of government departments. The exercise of its functions is dependent upon enjoying majority support in the House of Commons. Cabinet meetings are held in private, taking place once or twice a week during parliamentary sittings and less often during a recess. Proceedings are confidential, the members being bound by their oath as Privy Counsellors not to disclose information about the proceedings.

The convention of collective responsibility means that the Cabinet acts unanimously even when Cabinet Ministers do not all agree on a subject. The policies of departmental Ministers must be consistent with the policies of the Government as a whole, and once the Government's policy has been decided, each Minister is expected to support it or resign.

The convention of ministerial responsibility holds a Minister, as the political head of his or her department, accountable to Parliament for the department's work. Departmental Ministers usually decide all matters within their responsibility, although on matters of political importance they normally consult their colleagues collectively. A decision by a departmental Minister is binding on the Government as a whole.

POLITICAL PARTIES

Before the reign of William and Mary the principal officers of state were chosen by and were responsible to the Sovereign alone and not to Parliament or the nation at large. Such officers acted sometimes in concert with one another but more often independently, and the fall of one did not, of necessity, involve that of others, although all were liable to be dismissed at any moment.

In 1693 the Earl of Sunderland recommended to William III the advisability of selecting a ministry from the political party which enjoyed a majority in the House of Commons and the first united ministry was drawn in 1696 from the Whigs, to which party the King owed his throne. This group became known as the Junto and was regarded with suspicion as a novelty in the political life of the nation, being a small section meeting in secret apart from the main body of Ministers. It may be regarded as the forerunner of the Cabinet and in course of time it led to the establishment of the principle of joint responsibility of Ministers, so that internal disagreement caused a change of personnel or resignation of the whole body of Ministers.

The accession of George I, who was unfamiliar with the English language, led to a disinclination on the part of the Sovereign to preside at meetings of his Ministers and caused the appearance of a Prime Minister, a position first acquired by Robert Walpole in 1721 and retained without interruption for 20 years and 326 days.

DEVELOPMENT OF PARTIES

In 1828 the Whigs became known as Liberals, a name originally given to it by its opponents to imply laxity of principles, but gradually accepted by the party to indicate its claim to be pioneers and champions of political reform and progressive legislation. In 1861 a Liberal Registration Association was founded and Liberal Associations became widespread. In 1877 a National Liberal Federation was formed, with headquarters in London. The Liberal Party was in power for long periods during the second half of the 19th century and for several years during the first quarter of the 20th century, but after a split in the party the numbers elected were small from 1931. In 1988, a majority of the Liberals agreed on a merger with the Social Democratic Party under the title Social and Liberal Democrats; since 1989 they have been known as the Liberal Democrats. A minority continue separately as the Liberal Party.

Soon after the change from Whig to Liberal the Tory Party became known as Conservative, a name believed to have been invented by John Wilson Croker in 1830 and to have been generally adopted about the time of the passing of the Reform Act of 1832 to indicate that the preservation of national institutions was the leading principle of the party. After the Home Rule crisis of 1886 the dissentient Liberals entered into a compact with the Conservatives, under which the latter undertook not to contest their seats, but a separate Liberal Unionist organization was maintained until 1912, when it was united with the Conservatives.

Labour candidates for Parliament made their first appearance at the general election of 1892, when there were 27 standing as Labour or Liberal-Labour. In 1900 the Labour Representation Committee was set up in order to establish a distinct Labour group in Parliament, with its own whips, its own policy, and a readiness to co-operate with any party which might be engaged in promoting legislation in the direct interest of labour. In 1906 the LRC became known as the Labour Party.

The Council for Social Democracy was announced by four former Labour Cabinet Ministers in January 1981 and on 26 March 1981 the Social Democratic Party was launched. Later that year the SDP and the Liberal Party formed an electoral alliance. In 1988 a majority of the SDP agreed on a merger with the Liberal Party (see above) but a minority continued as a separate party under the SDP title. In 1990 it was decided to wind up the party organization and its three sitting MPs were known as independent social democrats. None were returned at the 1992 general election.

Plaid Cymru was founded in 1926 to provide an independent political voice for Wales and to campaign for self-government in Wales.

The Scottish National Party was founded in 1934 to campaign for independence for Scotland.

The Social Democratic and Labour Party was founded in 1970, emerging from the civil rights movement of the 1960s, with the aim of promoting reform, reconciliation and partnership across the sectarian divide in Northern Ireland and of opposing violence from any quarter.

The Ulster Democratic Unionist Party was founded in 1971 to resist moves by the Official Unionist Party which were considered a threat to the Union. Its aims are to maintain Northern Ireland as an integral part of the United Kingdom; and to express unionist opinion and defend the interests of Ulster unionism.

The Ulster Unionist Council first met formally in 1905. Its objectives are to maintain Northern Ireland as an integral part of the United Kingdom; to express unionist opinion and defend the interests of Ulster unionism; and to promote the aims of the Ulster Unionist Party.

GOVERNMENT AND OPPOSITION

The government of the day is formed by the party which wins the largest number of seats in the House of Commons at a general election, or which has the support of a majority of members in the House of Commons. By tradition, the leader of the majority party is asked by the Sovereign to form a government, while the largest minority party becomes the official Opposition with its own leader and 'Shadow' Cabinet. Leaders of the Government and Opposition sit on the front benches of the Commons with their supporters (the back-benchers) sitting behind them.

FINANCIAL SUPPORT

Financial support to Opposition parties was introduced in 1975 and is commonly known as Short Money, after Edward Short, the Leader of the House at that time, who introduced the scheme. For 1996–7 financial assistance is:

Labour	£1,530,190.51
Liberal Democrats	316,480.54
Plaid Cymru	22,040.36
SNP	36,782.68
SDLP	23,134.12
Democratic Unionists	15,954.37
Ulster Unionists	46,357.18

PARTIES

The parties included here are those with MPs sitting in the House of Commons in the present Parliament. Addresses of other political parties may be found in the Societies and Institutions section.

CONSERVATIVE AND UNIONIST PARTY

Central Office, 32 Smith Square, London SW1P 3HH
Tel 0171-222 9000
Chairman, The Rt. Hon. Brian Mawhinney, MP
Deputy Chairman, Hon. Michael Trend, MP
Senior Treasurer, The Lord Hambro

SCOTTISH CONSERVATIVE AND UNIONIST CENTRAL OFFICE

Suite 1/1, 14 Links Place, Leith, Edinburgh EH6 7EZ
Tel 0131-555 2900
Chairman, Sir Michael Hirst
Deputy Chairman, Miss A. Goldie
Hon. Treasurer, W. Y. Hughes, CBE
Director of the Party in Scotland, R. Pratt, CBE

LABOUR PARTY

John Smith House, 150 Walworth Road, London SE17 1JT
Tel 0171-701 1234
Parliamentary Party Leader, The Rt. Hon. Tony Blair, MP
Deputy Party Leader, The Rt. Hon. John Prescott, MP
Leader in the Lords, The Lord Richard, PC, QC
Chair, Ms D. Jeuda
Vice-Chair, Ms C. Short, MP
Treasurer, T. Burlison
General Secretary, T. Sawyer

Shadow Cabinet as at end July 1996
Leader of the Opposition, The Rt. Hon. Tony Blair, MP
Deputy Leader, The Rt. Hon. John Prescott, MP
Defence, David Clark, MP
Disabled People's Rights, Tom Clarke, MP
Education and Employment, David Blunkett, MP
Environment and London, Frank Dobson, MP
Environment Protection, Michael Meacher, MP
Food, Agriculture and Rural Affairs, Gavin Strang, MP
Foreign and Commonwealth Affairs, The Rt. Hon. Robin Cook, MP
Health, Chris Smith, MP
Home Affairs, Jack Straw, MP
Leader of the House, Ann Taylor, MP
Northern Ireland, Marjorie Mowlam, MP
Overseas Development, Claire Short, MP
Scotland, George Robertson, MP
Social Security, Harriet Harman, MP
Trade and Industry, The Rt. Hon. Margaret Beckett, MP
Transport, Andrew Smith, MP
Treasury and Economic Affairs, The Rt. Hon. Gordon Brown, MP
Wales, Ron Davies, MP

National Heritage, The Rt. Hon. Jack Cunningham, MP
Chancellor of the Duchy of Lancaster, The Rt. Hon. Derek Foster, MP
Chief Secretary to the Treasury, Alistair Darling, MP

LABOUR CHIEF WHIPS
House of Lords, The Lord Graham of Edmonton
House of Commons, The Rt. Hon. Donald Dewar, MP

LIBERAL DEMOCRATS
4 Cowley Street, London SW1P 3NB
Tel 0171-222 7999
President, Robert Maclennan, MP
Hon. Treasurer, T. Razzall, CBE
General Secretary, G. Elson
Parliamentary Party Leader, The Rt. Hon. Paddy Ashdown, MP
Leader in the Lords, The Rt. Hon. the Lord Jenkins of Hillhead

LIBERAL DEMOCRAT SPOKESMEN *as at end May 1996*
Deputy Leader and Home Affairs, Alan Beith, MP
Agriculture and Rural Affairs, Paul Tyler, MP
Central/East Europe, Sir Russell Johnston, MP
Community Care, Archy Kirkwood, MP
Education, Employment and Training, Don Foster, MP
Energy, Fisheries, Jim Wallace, MP
Environment, Matthew Taylor, MP
EU Affairs, Charles Kennedy, MP
Foreign Affairs, Defence and Sport, Menzies Campbell, MP
Health and Welfare, Urban Policy, Simon Hughes, MP
Home Affairs, and Justice, Alex Carlile, QC, MP
Housing, Family and Women's Issues, Diana Maddock, MP
Local Government, David Rendel, MP
National Heritage, Constitution, Arts, Robert Maclennan, MP
Northern Ireland, The Lord Holme of Cheltenham
Overseas Development, Emma Nicholson, MP
Science and Technology, Nigel Jones, MP
Scottish Affairs, Ray Michie, MP
Social Security and Disability, Liz Lynne, MP
Trade and Industry, Nick Harvey, MP
Transport, David Chidgey, MP
Treasury, Malcolm Bruce, MP

LIBERAL DEMOCRAT WHIPS
House of Lords, The Lord Harris of Greenwich
House of Commons, Archy Kirkwood, MP (*Chief Whip*); Simon Hughes, MP (*Deputy Whip*)

WELSH LIBERAL DEMOCRATS
57 St Mary Street, Cardiff CF1 1FE
Tel 01222-382210
Party President, M. Thomas, OBE, QC
Party Leader, Alex Carlile, QC, MP
Chairman, P. Black
Treasurer, N. Howells
Secretary, J. Burree
Party Manager, Ms J. Lewis, MBE

SCOTTISH LIBERAL DEMOCRATS
4 Clifton Terrace, Edinburgh EH12 5DR
Tel 0131-337 2314
Party President, R. Thomson
Party Leader, Jim Wallace, MP
Convenor, Ms M. MacLaren
Hon. Treasurer, D. R. Sullivan
Chief Executive, A. Myles

PLAID CYMRU
51 Cathedral Road, Cardiff CF1 9HD
Tel 01222-231944
Party President, Dafydd Wigley, MP
Chairman, J. Evans
Treasurer, S. Morgan
Chief Executive/General Secretary, K. Davies

SCOTTISH NATIONAL PARTY
6 North Charlotte Street, Edinburgh EH2 4JH
Tel 0131-226 3661
Parliamentary Party Leader, Margaret Ewing, MP
Chief Whip, Andrew Welsh, MP
National Convener, Alex Salmond, MP
Senior Vice-Convener, Dr A. Macartney, MEP
National Treasurer, K. MacAskill
National Secretary, A. Morgan

NORTHERN IRELAND

SOCIAL DEMOCRATIC AND LABOUR PARTY
Cranmore House, 611 Lisburn Road, Belfast BT9 7GT
Tel 01232-668100
Parliamentary Party Leader, John Hume, MP, MEP
Deputy Leader, Seamus Mallon, MP
Chief Whip, Eddie McGrady, MP
Chairman, I. Stephenson
Hon. Treasurer, P. O'Hagan
Party Administrator, Mrs G. Cosgrove

ULSTER DEMOCRATIC UNIONIST PARTY
91 Dundela Avenue, Belfast BT4 3BU
Tel 01232-471155
Parliamentary Party Leader, Ian Paisley, MP, MEP
Deputy Leader, Peter Robinson, MP
Chairman, W. J. McClure
Hon. Treasurer, G. Campbell
General Secretary, N. Dodds

ULSTER UNIONIST PARTY
3 Glengall Street, Belfast BT12 5AE
Tel 01232-324601
Party Leader, David Trimble, MP
Chief Whip, Revd Martin Smyth, MP
Ulster Unionist Council
President, J. Cunningham
Chairman, D. Rogan
Hon. Treasurer, J. Allen, OBE
Party Secretary, J. Wilson

MEMBERS OF PARLIAMENT AS AT 31 JULY 1996

For abbreviations, *see* page 237
* Denotes membership of the last Parliament
†Elected at a by-election since the 1992 general election

*Abbott, Ms Diane J. (*b.* 1953) *Lab., Hackney North and Stoke Newington,* maj. 10,727

*Adams, Mrs Irene (*b.* 1948) *Lab., Paisley North,* maj. 9,329

Ainger, Nicholas R. (*b.* 1949) *Lab., Pembroke,* maj. 755

Ainsworth, Peter M. (*b.* 1956) *C., Surrey East,* maj. 17,656

Ainsworth, Robert W. (*b.* 1952) *Lab., Coventry North East,* maj. 11,676

*Aitken, Jonathan W. P. (*b.* 1942) *C., Thanet South,* maj. 11,513

*Alexander, Richard T. (*b.* 1934) *C., Newark,* maj. 8,229

*Alison, Rt. Hon. Michael J. H. (*b.* 1926) *C., Selby,* maj. 9,508

*Allason, Rupert W. S. (*b.* 1951) *C., Torbay,* maj. 5,787

*Allen, Graham W. (*b.* 1953) *Lab., Nottingham North,* maj. 10,743

*Alton, David P. (*b.* 1951) *LD, Liverpool, Mossley Hill,* maj. 2,606

*Amess, David A. A. (*b.* 1952) *C., Basildon,* maj. 1,480

Ancram, Rt. Hon. Michael A. F. J. K. (Earl of Ancram) (*b.* 1945) *C., Devizes,* maj. 19,712

*Anderson, Donald (*b.* 1939) *Lab., Swansea East,* maj. 23,482

Anderson, Mrs Janet (*b.* 1949) *Lab., Rossendale and Darwen,* maj. 120

*Arbuthnot, James N. (*b.* 1952) *C., Wanstead and Woodford,* maj. 16,885

*Armstrong, Miss Hilary J. (*b.* 1945) *Lab., Durham North West,* maj. 13,987

*Arnold, Jacques A. (*b.* 1947) *C., Gravesham,* maj. 5,493

*Arnold, Sir Thomas (*b.* 1947) *C., Hazel Grove,* maj. 929

*Ashby, David G. (*b.* 1940) *C., Leicestershire North West,* maj. 979

*Ashdown, Rt. Hon. J. J. D. (Paddy) (*b.* 1941) *LD, Yeovil,* maj. 8,833

*Ashton, Joseph W. (*b.* 1933) *Lab., Bassetlaw,* maj. 9,997

*Aspinwall, Jack H. (*b.* 1933) *C., Wansdyke,* maj. 13,341

*Atkins, Rt. Hon. Robert J. (*b.* 1946) *C., South Ribble,* maj. 5,973

*Atkinson, David A. (*b.* 1940) *C., Bournemouth East,* maj. 14,823

Atkinson, Peter (*b.* 1943) *C., Hexham,* maj. 13,438

Austin-Walker, John E. (*b.* 1944) *Lab., Woolwich,* maj. 2,225

*Baker, Rt. Hon. Kenneth W., CH (*b.* 1934) *C., Mole Valley,* maj. 15,950

*Baker, Nicholas B. (*b.* 1938) *C., Dorset North,* maj. 10,080

*Baldry, Antony B. (*b.* 1950) *C., Banbury,* maj. 16,720

Banks, Matthew (*b.* 1961) *C., Southport,* maj. 3,063

*Banks, Robert G., MBE (*b.* 1937) *C., Harrogate,* maj. 12,589

*Banks, Tony L. (*b.* 1943) *Lab., Newham North West,* maj. 9,171

*Barnes, Harold (*b.* 1936) *Lab., Derbyshire North East,* maj. 6,270

*Barron, Kevin J. (*b.* 1946) *Lab., Rother Valley,* maj. 17,222

Bates, Michael W. (*b.* 1961) *C., Langbaurgh,* maj. 1,564

†Batiste, Spencer L. (*b.* 1945) *C., Elmet,* maj. 3,261

*Battle, John D. (*b.* 1951) *Lab., Leeds West,* maj. 13,828

Bayley, Hugh (*b.* 1952) *Lab., York,* maj. 6,342

*Beckett, Rt. Hon. Margaret M. (*b.* 1953) *Lab., Derby South,* maj. 6,936

*Beggs, Roy (*b.* 1936) *UUP, Antrim East,* maj. 7,422

*Beith, Rt. Hon. Alan J. (*b.* 1943) *LD, Berwick-upon-Tweed,* maj. 5,043

*Bell, Stuart (*b.* 1938) *Lab., Middlesbrough,* maj. 15,784

*Bellingham, Henry C. (*b.* 1955) *C., Norfolk North West,* maj. 11,564

*Bendall, Vivian W. H. (*b.* 1938) *C., Ilford North,* maj. 9,071

*Benn, Rt. Hon. Anthony N. W. (*b.* 1925) *Lab., Chesterfield,* maj. 6,414

*Bennett, Andrew F. (*b.* 1939) *Lab., Denton and Reddish,* maj. 12,084

*Benton, Joseph E. (*b.* 1933) *Lab., Bootle,* maj. 29,442

Beresford, Sir Paul (*b.* 1946) *C., Croydon Central,* maj. 9,650

*Bermingham, Gerald E. (*b.* 1940) *Lab., St Helens South,* maj. 18,209

Berry, Roger L., D.Phil (*b.* 1948) *Lab., Kingswood,* maj. 2,370

Betts, Clive J. C. (*b.* 1950) *Lab., Sheffield, Attercliffe,* maj. 15,480

*Biffen, Rt. Hon. John W. (*b.* 1930) *C., Shropshire North,* maj. 16,211

*Blair, Rt. Hon. Anthony C. L. (*b.* 1953) *Lab., Sedgefield,* maj. 14,859

*Blunkett, David (*b.* 1947) *Lab., Sheffield, Brightside,* maj. 22,681

*Boateng, Paul Y. (*b.* 1951) *Lab., Brent South,* maj. 9,705

*Body, Sir Richard (*b.* 1927) *C., Holland with Boston,* maj. 13,831

*Bonsor, Sir Nicholas, Bt. (*b.* 1942) *C., Upminster,* maj. 13,821

Booth, Hartley, PH.D. (*b.* 1946) *C., Finchley,* maj. 6,388

*Boothroyd, Rt. Hon. Betty (*b.* 1929) *The Speaker, West Bromwich West,* maj. 7,830

*Boswell, Timothy E. (*b.* 1942) *C., Daventry,* maj. 20,274

*Bottomley, Peter J. (*b.* 1944) *C., Eltham,* maj. 1,666

*Bottomley, Rt. Hon. Virginia H. B. M. (*b.* 1948) *C., Surrey South West,* maj. 14,975

*Bowden, Sir Andrew, MBE (*b.* 1930) *C., Brighton, Kemptown,* maj. 3,056

*Bowis, John C., OBE (*b.* 1945) *C., Battersea,* maj. 4,840

*Boyes, Roland (*b.* 1937) *Lab., Houghton and Washington,* maj. 20,808

*Boyson, Rt. Hon. Sir Rhodes (*b.* 1925) *C., Brent North,* maj. 10,131

*Bradley, Keith J. C. (*b.* 1950) *Lab., Manchester, Withington,* maj. 9,735

Brandreth, Gyles D. (*b.* 1948) *C., City of Chester,* maj. 1,101

*Bray, Jeremy W., PH.D. (*b.* 1930) *Lab., Motherwell South,* maj. 14,013

*Brazier, Julian W. H. (*b.* 1953) *C., Canterbury,* maj. 10,805

*Bright, Sir Graham (*b.* 1942) *C., Luton South,* maj. 799

*Brooke, Rt. Hon. Peter L., CH (*b.* 1934) *C., City of London and Westminster South,* maj. 13,369

*Brown, Rt. Hon. J. Gordon, PH.D. (*b.* 1951) *Lab., Dunfermline East,* maj. 17,444

*Brown, Michael R. (*b.* 1951) *C., Brigg and Cleethorpes,* maj. 9,269

*Brown, Nicholas H. (*b.* 1950) *Lab., Newcastle upon Tyne East,* maj. 13,877

Browning, Mrs Angela F. (*b.* 1946) *C., Tiverton,* maj. 11,089

*Bruce, Ian C. (*b.* 1947) *C., Dorset South,* maj. 13,508

*Bruce, Malcolm G. (*b.* 1944) *LD, Gordon,* maj. 274

*Budgen, Nicholas W. (*b.* 1937) *C., Wolverhampton South West,* maj. 4,966

Burden, Richard (*b.* 1954) *Lab., Birmingham, Northfield,* maj. 630

*Burns, Simon H. M. (*b.* 1952) *C., Chelmsford,* maj. 18,260

*Burt, Alistair J. H. (*b.* 1955) *C., Bury North,* maj. 4,764

*Butcher, John P. (*b.* 1946) *C., Coventry South West,* maj. 1,436

Butler, Peter (*b.* 1951) *C., Milton Keynes North East,* maj. 14,176

*Butterfill, John V. (*b.* 1941) *C., Bournemouth West,* maj. 12,703

Byers, Stephen J. (*b.* 1953) *Lab., Wallsend,* maj. 19,470

Caborn, Richard G. (*b.* 1943) *Lab., Sheffield Central,* maj. 17,294

Callaghan, James (*b.* 1927) *Lab., Heywood and Middleton,* maj. 8,074

Campbell, Mrs Anne (*b.* 1940) *Lab., Cambridge,* maj. 580

Campbell, Ronald (*b.* 1943) *Lab., Blyth Valley,* maj. 8,044

Campbell, W. Menzies, CBE, QC (*b.* 1941) *LD, Fife North East,* maj. 3,308

◀Campbell-Savours, Dale N. (*b.* 1943) *Lab., Workington,* maj. 10,449

Canavan, Dennis A. (*b.* 1942) *Lab., Falkirk West,* maj. 9,812

Cann, James (*b.* 1946) *Lab., Ipswich,* maj. 265

Carlile, Alexander C., QC (*b.* 1948) *LD, Montgomery,* maj. 5,209

Carlisle, John R. (*b.* 1942) *C., Luton North,* maj. 13,094

Carlisle, Sir Kenneth (*b.* 1941) *C., Lincoln,* maj. 2,049

Carrington, Matthew H. M. (*b.* 1947) *C., Fulham,* maj. 6,579

Carttiss, Michael R. H. (*b.* 1938) *C., Great Yarmouth,* maj. 5,309

Cash, William N. P. (*b.* 1940) *C., Stafford,* maj. 10,900

◀Channon, Rt. Hon. H. Paul G. (*b.* 1935) *C., Southend West,* maj. 11,902

Chapman, Sir Sydney (*b.* 1935) *C., Chipping Barnet,* maj. 13,951

Chidgey, David W. G. (*b.* 1942) *LD, Eastleigh,* maj. 9,239

Chisholm, Malcolm (*b.* 1949) *Lab., Edinburgh, Leith,* maj. 4,985

Church, Ms Judith A. (*b.* 1953), *Lab., Dagenham,* maj. 13,344

Churchill, Winston S. (*b.* 1940) *C., Davyhulme,* maj. 4,426

Clapham, Michael (*b.* 1943) *Lab., Barnsley West and Penistone,* maj. 14,504

Clappison, W. James (*b.* 1956) *C., Hertsmere,* maj. 18,735

Clark, David G., PH.D. (*b.* 1939) *Lab., South Shields,* maj. 13,477

Clark, Dr Michael (*b.* 1935) *C., Rochford,* maj. 26,036

Clarke, Eric L. (*b.* 1933) *Lab., Midlothian,* maj. 10,334

Clarke, Rt. Hon. Kenneth H., QC (*b.* 1940) *C., Rushcliffe,* maj. 19,766

Clarke, Thomas, CBE (*b.* 1941) *Lab., Monklands West,* maj. 17,065

Clelland, David G. (*b.* 1943) *Lab., Tyne Bridge,* maj. 15,210

Clifton-Brown, Geoffrey R. (*b.* 1953) *C., Cirencester and Tewkesbury,* maj. 16,058

Clwyd, Ms Ann (*b.* 1937) *Lab., Cynon Valley,* maj. 21,364

Coe, Sebastian N., OBE (*b.* 1956) *C., Falmouth and Camborne,* maj. 3,267

Coffey, Ms M. Ann (*b.* 1946) *Lab., Stockport,* maj. 1,422

Cohen, Harry (*b.* 1949) *Lab., Leyton,* maj. 11,484

Colvin, Michael K. B. (*b.* 1932) *C., Romsey and Waterside,* maj. 15,304

Congdon, David L. (*b.* 1949) *C., Croydon North East,* maj. 7,473

Connarty, Michael (*b.* 1949) *Lab., Falkirk East,* maj. 7,969

Conway, Derek L. (*b.* 1953) *C., Shrewsbury and Atcham,* maj. 10,965

Cook, Francis (*b.* 1935) *Lab., Stockton North,* maj. 10,474

Cook, Rt. Hon. R. F. (Robin) (*b.* 1946) *Lab., Livingston,* maj. 8,105

Coombs, Anthony M. V. (*b.* 1952) *C., Wyre Forest,* maj. 10,341

Coombs, Simon C. (*b.* 1947) *C., Swindon,* maj. 2,826

Cope, Rt. Hon. Sir John (*b.* 1937) *C., Northavon,* maj. 11,861

Corbett, Robin (*b.* 1933) *Lab., Birmingham, Erdington,* maj. 4,735

Corbyn, Jeremy B. (*b.* 1949) *Lab., Islington North,* maj. 12,784

Cormack, Sir Patrick (*b.* 1939) *C., Staffordshire South,* maj. 22,633

Corston, Ms Jean (*b.* 1942) *Lab., Bristol East,* maj. 2,692

Couchman, James R. (*b.* 1942) *C., Gillingham,* maj. 16,638

*Cousins, James M. (*b.* 1944) *Lab., Newcastle upon Tyne Central,* maj. 5,288

*Cox, Thomas M. (*b.* 1930) *Lab., Tooting,* maj. 4,107

*Cran, James D. (*b.* 1944) *C., Beverley,* maj. 16,517

*Critchley, Sir Julian (*b.* 1930) *C., Aldershot,* maj. 19,188

*Cummings, John S. (*b.* 1943) *Lab., Easington,* maj. 26,390

*Cunliffe, Lawrence F. (*b.* 1929) *Lab., Leigh,* maj. 18,827

Cunningham, James (*b.* 1941) *Lab., Coventry South East,* maj. 1,311

*Cunningham, Rt. Hon. Dr John A. (Jack) (*b.* 1939) *Lab., Copeland,* maj. 2,439

†Cunningham, Ms Roseanna (*b.* 1951), *SNP, Perth and Kinross,* maj. 7,311

*Currie, Mrs Edwina (*b.* 1946) *C., Derbyshire South,* maj. 4,658

*Curry, Rt. Hon. David M. (*b.* 1944) *C., Skipton and Ripon,* maj. 19,330

Dafis, Cynog G. (*b.* 1938) *PC, Ceredigion and Pembroke North,* maj. 3,193

*Dalyell, Tam (Sir Thomas Dalyell of the Binns, Bt.) (*b.* 1932) *Lab., Linlithgow,* maj. 7,026

*Darling, Alistair M. (*b.* 1953) *Lab., Edinburgh Central,* maj. 2,126

Davidson, Ian (*b.* 1950) *Lab., Glasgow, Govan,* maj. 4,125

Davies, Bryan (*b.* 1939) *Lab., Oldham Central and Royton,* maj. 8,606

†Davies, Christopher (Chris) (*b.* 1954), *LD, Littleborough and Saddleworth,* maj. 1,993

*Davies, Rt. Hon. D. J. Denzil (*b.* 1938) *Lab., Llanelli,* maj. 19,270

*Davies, J. Quentin (*b.* 1944) *C., Stamford and Spalding,* maj. 22,869

*Davies, Ronald (*b.* 1946) *Lab., Caerphilly,* maj. 22,672

*Davis, David M. (*b.* 1948) *C., Boothferry,* maj. 17,535

*Davis, Terence A. G. (*b.* 1938) *Lab., Birmingham, Hodge Hill,* maj. 7,068

*Day, Stephen R. (*b.* 1948) *C., Cheadle,* maj. 15,778

Denham, John V. (*b.* 1953) *Lab., Southampton, Itchen,* maj. 551

Deva, Niranjan J. A. (*b.* 1948) *C., Brentford and Isleworth,* maj. 2,086

*Devlin, Timothy R. (*b.* 1959) *C., Stockton South,* maj. 3,369

*Dewar, Rt. Hon. Donald C. (*b.* 1937) *Lab., Glasgow, Garscadden,* maj. 13,340

*Dicks, Terence P. (*b.* 1937) *C., Hayes and Harlington,* maj. 53

*Dixon, Rt. Hon. Donald (*b.* 1929) *Lab., Jarrow,* maj. 17,907

*Dobson, Frank G. (*b.* 1940) *Lab., Holborn and St Pancras,* maj. 10,824

Donohoe, Brian H. (*b.* 1948) *Lab., Cunninghame South,* maj. 10,680

*Dorrell, Rt. Hon. Stephen J. (*b.* 1952) *C., Loughborough,* maj. 10,883

*Douglas-Hamilton, Rt. Hon. Lord James (*b.* 1942) *C., Edinburgh West,* maj. 879

*Dover, Densmore (*b.* 1938) *C., Chorley,* maj. 4,246

Dowd, James P. (*b.* 1951) *Lab., Lewisham West,* maj. 1,809

Duncan, Alan J. C. (*b.* 1957) *C., Rutland and Melton,* maj. 25,535

Duncan-Smith, G. Iain (*b.* 1954) *C., Chingford,* maj. 14,938

*Dunn, Robert J. (*b.* 1946) *C., Dartford,* maj. 10,314

*Dunnachie, James F. (*b.* 1930) *Lab., Glasgow, Pollok,* maj. 7,883

*Dunwoody, Hon. Mrs Gwyneth P. (*b.* 1930) *Lab., Crewe and Nantwich,* maj. 2,695

*Durant, Sir Anthony (*b.* 1928) *C., Reading West,* maj. 13,298

*Dykes, Hugh J. (*b.* 1939) *C., Harrow East,* maj. 11,098

Eagle, Ms Angela (*b.* 1961) *Lab., Wallasey,* maj. 3,809

*Eastham, Kenneth (*b.* 1927) *Lab., Manchester, Blackley,* maj. 12,389

*Eggar, Rt. Hon. Timothy J. C. (*b.* 1951) *C., Enfield North,* maj. 9,430

Elletson, Harold D. H. (*b.* 1960) *C., Blackpool North,* maj. 3,040

*Emery, Rt. Hon. Sir Peter (b. 1926) C., Honiton, maj. 16,511
*Enright, Rt. Hon. Derek A. (b. 1935) Lab., Hemsworth, maj. 22,075
Etherington, William (b. 1941) Lab., Sunderland North, maj. 17,004
*Evans, David J. (b. 1935) C., Welwyn Hatfield, maj. 8,465
*Evans, John (b. 1930) Lab., St Helens North, maj. 16,244
Evans, Jonathan P. (b. 1950) C., Brecon and Radnor, maj. 130
Evans, Nigel M. (b. 1957) C., Ribble Valley, maj. 6,542
Evans, Roger (b. 1947) C., Monmouth, maj. 3,204
*Evennett, David A. (b. 1939) C., Erith and Crayford, maj. 2,339
*Ewing, Mrs Margaret A. (b. 1945) SNP, Moray, maj. 2,844
Faber, David J. C. (b. 1961) C., Westbury, maj. 12,606
Fabricant, Michael L. D. (b. 1950) C., Staffordshire Mid, maj. 6,236
*Fatchett, Derek J. (b. 1945) Lab., Leeds Central, maj. 15,020
*Faulds, Andrew M. W. (b. 1923) Lab., Warley East, maj. 7,794
*Fenner, Dame Peggy, DBE (b. 1922) C., Medway, maj. 8,786
*Field, Barry J. A., TD (b. 1946) C., Isle of Wight, maj. 1,827
*Field, Frank (b. 1942) Lab., Birkenhead, maj. 17,613
*Fishburn, J. Dudley (b. 1946) C., Kensington, maj. 3,548
*Fisher, Mark (b. 1944) Lab., Stoke-on-Trent Central, maj. 13,420
*Flynn, Paul P. (b. 1935) Lab., Newport West, maj. 7,779
*Fookes, Dame Janet, DBE (b. 1936) C., Plymouth, Drake, maj. 2,013
*Forman, F. Nigel (b. 1943) C., Carshalton and Wallington, maj. 9,943
*Forsyth, Rt. Hon. Michael B. (b. 1954) C., Stirling, maj. 703
*Forsythe, Clifford (b. 1929) UUP, Antrim South, maj. 24,559
*Forth, Eric (b. 1944) C., Worcestershire Mid, maj. 9,870
*Foster, Rt. Hon. Derek (b. 1937) Lab., Bishop Auckland, maj. 10,087
Foster, Donald M. E. (b. 1937) LD, Bath, maj. 3,768
*Foulkes, George (b. 1942) Lab., Carrick, Cumnock and Doon Valley, maj. 16,626
*Fowler, Rt. Hon. Sir Norman (b. 1938) C., Sutton Coldfield, maj. 26,036
Fox, Dr Liam (b. 1961) C., Woodspring, maj. 17,509
*Fox, Rt. Hon. Sir Marcus, MBE (b. 1927) C., Shipley, maj. 12,382
*Fraser, John D. (b. 1934) Lab., Norwood, maj. 7,216
*Freeman, Rt. Hon. Roger N. (b. 1942) C., Kettering, maj. 11,154
*French, Douglas C. (b. 1944) C., Gloucester, maj. 6,058
*Fry, Sir Peter (b. 1931) C., Wellingborough, maj. 11,816
*Fyfe, Mrs Maria (b. 1938) Lab., Glasgow, Maryhill, maj. 13,419
*Galbraith, Samuel L. (b. 1945) Lab., Strathkelvin and Bearsden, maj. 3,162
*Gale, Roger J. (b. 1943) C., Thanet North, maj. 18,210
Gallie, Philip (b. 1939) C., Ayr, maj. 85
*Galloway, George (b. 1954) Lab., Glasgow, Hillhead, maj. 4,826
Gapes, Michael J. (b. 1952) Lab., Ilford South, maj. 402
*Gardiner, Sir George (b. 1935) C., Reigate, maj. 17,664
*Garel-Jones, Rt. Hon. (W. A. T.) Tristan (b. 1941) C., Watford, maj. 9,590
Garnier, Edward (b. 1952) C., Harborough, maj. 13,543
*Garrett, John L. (b. 1931) Lab., Norwich South, maj. 6,181
*George, Bruce T. (b. 1942) Lab., Walsall South, maj. 3,178
Gerrard, Neil F. (b. 1942) Lab., Walthamstow, maj. 3,022
*Gilbert, Rt. Hon. Dr John W. (b. 1927) Lab., Dudley East, maj. 9,200
*Gill, Christopher J. F., RD (b. 1936) C., Ludlow, maj. 14,152
Gillan, Ms Cheryl E. K. (b. 1952) C., Chesham and Amersham, maj. 22,220
*Godman, Norman A., PH.D. (b. 1938) Lab., Greenock and Port Glasgow, maj. 14,979

Godsiff, Roger D. (b. 1946) Lab., Birmingham, Small Heath, maj. 13,989
*Golding, Mrs Llinos (b. 1933) Lab., Newcastle under Lyme, maj. 9,839
*Goodlad, Rt. Hon. Alastair R. (b. 1943) C., Eddisbury, maj. 12,697
*Goodson-Wickes, Dr Charles (b. 1945) C., Wimbledon, maj. 14,761
*Gordon, Mrs Mildred (b. 1923) Lab., Bow and Poplar, maj. 8,404
*Gorman, Mrs Teresa E. (b. 1931) C., Billericay, maj. 22,494
*Gorst, Sir John (b. 1928) C., Hendon North, maj. 7,122
*Graham, Thomas (b. 1944) Lab., Renfrew West and Inverclyde, maj. 1,744
*Grant, Sir Anthony (b. 1925) C., Cambridgeshire South West, maj. 19,637
*Grant, Bernard A. M. (b. 1944) Lab., Tottenham, maj. 11,968
*Greenway, Harry (b. 1934) C., Ealing North, maj. 5,966
*Greenway, John R. (b. 1946) C., Ryedale, maj. 18,439
*Griffiths, Nigel (b. 1955) Lab., Edinburgh South, maj. 4,176
*Griffiths, Peter H. S. (b. 1928) C., Portsmouth North, maj. 13,881
*Griffiths, Winston J. (b. 1943) Lab., Bridgend, maj. 7,326
*Grocott, Bruce J. (b. 1940) Lab., The Wrekin, maj. 6,648
*Grylls, Sir Michael (b. 1934) C., Surrey North West, maj. 28,394
*Gummer, Rt. Hon. John S. (b. 1939) C., Suffolk Coastal, maj. 19,285
Gunnell, W. John (b. 1933) Lab., Leeds South and Morley, maj. 7,372
*Hague, Rt. Hon. William J. (b. 1961) C., Richmond (Yorks) maj. 23,504
*Hain, Peter G. (b. 1950) Lab., Neath, maj. 23,975
Hall, Michael T. (b. 1952) Lab., Warrington South, maj. 191
*Hamilton, Rt. Hon. Sir Archibald (b. 1941) C., Epsom and Ewell, maj. 20,021
*Hamilton, M. Neil (b. 1949) C., Tatton, maj. 15,860
*Hampson, Dr Keith (b. 1943) C., Leeds North West, maj. 7,671
*Hanley, Rt. Hon. Jeremy J. (b. 1945) C., Richmond and Barnes, maj. 3,869
*Hannam, Sir John (b. 1929) C., Exeter, maj. 4,045
Hanson, David G. (b. 1957) Lab., Delyn, maj. 2,039
*Hardy, Peter (b. 1931) Lab., Wentworth, maj. 22,449
*Hargreaves, Andrew R. (b. 1955) C., Birmingham, Hall Green, maj. 3,665
*Harman, Ms Harriet (b. 1950) Lab., Peckham, maj. 12,005
*Harris, David A. (b. 1937) C., St Ives, maj. 1,645
Harvey, Nicholas B. (b. 1961) LD, Devon North, maj. 794
*Haselhurst, Sir Alan (b. 1937) C., Saffron Walden, maj. 17,424
*Hattersley, Rt. Hon. Roy S. G. (b. 1932) Lab., Birmingham, Sparkbrook, maj. 13,572
Hawkins, Nicholas J. (b. 1957) C., Blackpool South, maj. 1,667
Hawksley, P. Warren (b. 1943) C., Halesowen and Stourbridge, maj. 9,582
*Hayes, Jeremy J. J. (b. 1953) C., Harlow, maj. 2,940
Heald, Oliver (b. 1954) C., Hertfordshire North, maj. 16,531
*Heath, Rt. Hon. Sir Edward, KG, MBE (b. 1916) C., Old Bexley and Sidcup, maj. 15,699
*Heathcoat-Amory, Rt. Hon. David P. (b. 1949) C., Wells, maj. 6,649
*Henderson, Douglas J. (b. 1949) Lab., Newcastle upon Tyne North, maj. 8,946
Hendron, Dr Joseph G. (b. 1932) SDLP, Belfast West, maj. 589
Hendry, Charles (b. 1959) C., High Peak, maj. 4,819
Heppell, John B. (b. 1948) Lab., Nottingham East, maj. 7,680
*Heseltine, Rt. Hon. Michael R. D. (b. 1933) C., Henley, maj. 18,392
*Hicks, Sir Robert (b. 1938) C., Cornwall South East, maj. 7,704

Higgins, Rt. Hon. Sir Terence, KBE (b. 1928) C., Worthing, maj. 16,533

Hill, Sir James (b. 1926) C., Southampton, Test, maj. 585

Hill, T. Keith (b. 1943) Lab., Streatham, maj. 2,317

Hinchliffe, David M. (b. 1948) Lab., Wakefield, maj. 6,590

Hodge, Ms Margaret E. (b. 1944) Lab., Barking, maj. 11,414

Hoey, Ms Catharine (Kate) L. (b. 1946) Lab., Vauxhall, maj. 10,488

Hogg, Rt. Hon. Douglas M., QC (b. 1945) C., Grantham, maj. 19,588

Hogg, Norman (b. 1938) Lab., Cumbernauld and Kilsyth, maj. 9,215

Home Robertson, John D. (b. 1948) Lab., East Lothian, maj. 10,036

Hood, James (b. 1948) Lab., Clydesdale, maj. 10,187

Hoon, Geoffrey W. (b. 1953) Lab., Ashfield, maj. 12,987

Horam, John R. (b. 1939) C., Orpington, maj. 12,935

Hordern, Rt. Hon. Sir Peter (b. 1929) C., Horsham, maj. 25,072

Howard, Rt. Hon. Michael, QC (b. 1941) C., Folkestone and Hythe, maj. 8,910

Howarth, Alan T., CBE (b. 1944) Lab., Stratford-upon-Avon, maj. 22,892

Howarth, George E. (b. 1949) Lab., Knowsley North, maj. 22,403

Howell, Rt. Hon. David A. R. (b. 1936) C., Guildford, maj. 13,404

Howell, Sir Ralph (b. 1923) C., Norfolk North, maj. 12,545

Howells, Kim S., ph.d. (b. 1946) Lab., Pontypridd, maj. 19,797

Hoyle, E. Douglas H. (b. 1930) Lab., Warrington North, maj. 12,622

Hughes, Kevin M. (b. 1952) Lab., Doncaster North, maj. 19,813

Hughes, Robert (b. 1932) Lab., Aberdeen North, maj. 9,237

Hughes, Robert G. (b. 1951) C., Harrow West, maj. 17,897

Hughes, Royston J. (b. 1925) Lab., Newport East, maj. 9,899

Hughes, Simon H. W. (b. 1951) LD, Southwark and Bermondsey, maj. 9,845

Hume, John, MEP (b. 1937) SDLP, Foyle, maj. 13,005

Hunt, Rt. Hon. David J. F., MBE (b. 1942) C., Wirral West, maj. 11,064

Hunt, Sir John (b. 1929) C., Ravensbourne, maj. 19,714

Hunter, Andrew R. F. (b. 1943) C., Basingstoke, maj. 21,198

Hurd, Rt. Hon. Douglas R., CH, CBE (b. 1930) C., Witney, maj. 22,568

Hutton, John M. P. (b. 1955) Lab., Barrow and Furness, maj. 3,578

Illsley, Eric E. (b. 1955) Lab., Barnsley Central, maj. 19,361

Ingram, Adam P. (b. 1947) Lab., East Kilbride, maj. 11,992

Jack, J. Michael (b. 1946) C., Fylde, maj. 20,991

Jackson, Ms Glenda, CBE (b. 1936) Lab., Hampstead and Highgate, maj. 1,440

Jackson, Mrs Helen (b. 1939) Lab., Sheffield, Hillsborough, maj. 7,068

Jackson, Robert V. (b. 1946) C., Wantage, maj. 16,473

Jamieson, David C. (b. 1947) Lab., Plymouth, Devonport, maj. 7,412

Janner, Hon. Greville E., QC (b. 1928) Lab., Leicester West, maj. 3,978

Jenkin, Hon. Bernard (b. 1959) C., Colchester North, maj. 16,492

Jenkins, Brian D. (b. 1942) Lab., Staffordshire South East, maj. 13,762

Jessel, Toby F. H. (b. 1934) C., Twickenham, maj. 5,711

Johnson Smith, Rt. Hon. Sir Geoffrey (b. 1924) C., Wealden, maj. 20,931

Johnston, Sir Russell (b. 1932) LD, Inverness, Nairn and Lochaber, maj. 458

Jones, Gwilym H. (b. 1947) C., Cardiff North, maj. 2,969

Jones, Ieuan W. (b. 1949) PC, Ynys Môn, maj. 1,106

Jones, Jon O. (b. 1954) Lab., Cardiff Central, maj. 3,465

Jones, Ms Lynne M., ph.d. (b. 1951) Lab., Birmingham, Selly Oak, maj. 2,060

*Jones, Martyn D. (b. 1947) Lab., Clwyd South West, maj. 4,941

Jones, Nigel D. (b. 1948) LD, Cheltenham, maj. 1,668

*Jones, Robert B. (b. 1950) C., Hertfordshire West, maj. 13,940

*Jones, S. Barry (b. 1938) Lab., Alyn and Deeside, maj. 7,851

*Jopling, Rt. Hon. T. Michael (b. 1930) C., Westmorland and Lonsdale, maj. 16,436

Jowell, Ms Tessa (b. 1947) Lab., Dulwich, maj. 2,056

*Kaufman, Rt. Hon. Gerald B. (b. 1930) Lab., Manchester, Gorton, maj. 16,279

Keen, Alan (b. 1937) Lab., Feltham and Heston, maj. 1,995

*Kellett-Bowman, Dame Elaine, DBE (b. 1924) C., Lancaster, maj. 2,953

*Kennedy, Charles P. (b. 1959) LD, Ross, Cromarty and Skye, maj. 7,630

Kennedy, Mrs Jane (b. 1958) Lab., Liverpool, Broadgreen, maj. 7,027

*Key, S. Robert (b. 1945) C., Salisbury, maj. 8,973

Khabra, Piara C. (b. 1924) Lab., Ealing, Southall, maj. 6,866

*Kilfoyle, Peter (b. 1946) Lab., Liverpool, Walton, maj. 28,299

*King, Rt. Hon. Thomas J., CH (b. 1933) C., Bridgwater, maj. 9,716

*Kirkhope, Timothy J. R. (b. 1945) C., Leeds North East, maj. 4,244

*Kirkwood, Archibald J. (b. 1946) LD, Roxburgh and Berwickshire, maj. 4,257

*Knapman, Roger M. (b. 1944) C., Stroud, maj. 13,405

Knight, Mrs Angela A. (b. 1950) C., Erewash, maj. 5,703

*Knight, Rt. Hon. Gregory (b. 1949) C., Derby North, maj. 4,453

*Knight, Dame Jill, DBE (b. 1923) C., Birmingham, Edgbaston, maj. 4,307

*Knox, Sir David (b. 1933) C., Staffordshire Moorlands, maj. 7,410

Kynoch, George A. B. (b. 1946) C., Kincardine and Deeside, maj. 4,495

Lait, Ms Jacqui (b. 1947) C., Hastings and Rye, maj. 6,634

*Lamont, Rt. Hon. Norman S. H. (b. 1942) C., Kingston upon Thames, maj. 10,153

*Lang, Rt. Hon. Ian B. (b. 1940) C., Galloway and Upper Nithsdale, maj. 2,468

*Lawrence, Sir Ivan, QC (b. 1936) C., Burton, maj. 5,996

Legg, Barry (b. 1949) C., Milton Keynes South West, maj. 4,687

*Leigh, Edward J. E. (b. 1950) C., Gainsborough and Horncastle, maj. 16,245

*Lennox-Boyd, Hon. Sir Mark (b. 1943) C., Morecambe and Lunesdale, maj. 11,509

*Lester, Sir James (b. 1932) C., Broxtowe, maj. 9,891

*Lestor, Miss Joan (b. 1931) Lab., Eccles, maj. 13,226

*Lewis, Terence (b. 1935) Lab., Worsley, maj. 10,012

†Liddell, Mrs Helen (b. 1950) Lab., Monklands East, maj. 1,640

Lidington, David R., ph.d. (b. 1956) C., Aylesbury, maj. 18,860

*Lilley, Rt. Hon. Peter B. (b. 1943) C., St Albans, maj. 16,404

*Litherland, Robert K. (b. 1930) Lab., Manchester Central, maj. 18,037

*Livingstone, Ken (b. 1945) Lab., Brent East, maj. 5,971

*Lloyd, Anthony J. (b. 1950) Lab., Stretford, maj. 11,137

*Lloyd, Rt. Hon. Sir Peter (b. 1937) C., Fareham, maj. 24,141

Llwyd, Elfyn (b. 1951) PC, Meirionnydd Nant Conwy, maj. 4,613

*Lofthouse, Sir Geoffrey (b. 1925) Lab., Pontefract and Castleford, maj. 23,495

*Lord, Michael N. (b. 1938) C., Suffolk Central, maj. 16,031

*Loyden, Edward (b. 1923) Lab., Liverpool, Garston, maj. 12,279

Luff, Peter J. (b. 1955) C., Worcester, maj. 6,152

*Lyell, Rt. Hon. Sir Nicholas, QC (b. 1938) C., Bedfordshire Mid, maj. 25,138

Sproat, Iain M. (*b.* 1938) *C., Harwich,* maj. 17,159
Squire, Ms Rachel (*b.* 1954) *Lab., Dunfermline West,* maj.
    7,484
*Squire, Robin C. (*b.* 1944) *C., Hornchurch,* maj. 9,165
*Stanley, Rt. Hon. Sir John (*b.* 1942) *C., Tonbridge and
    Malling,* maj. 21,558
*Steel, Rt. Hon. Sir David, KBE (*b.* 1938) *LD, Tweeddale,
    Ettrick and Lauderdale,* maj. 2,520
*Steen, Anthony D. (*b.* 1939) *C., South Hams,* maj. 13,711
*Steinberg, Gerald N. (*b.* 1945) *Lab., City of Durham,* maj.
    15,058
Stephen, B. Michael L. (*b.* 1942) *C., Shoreham,* maj. 14,286
*Stern, Michael C. (*b.* 1942) *C., Bristol North West,* maj. 45
Stevenson, George W. (*b.* 1938) *Lab., Stoke-on-Trent South,*
    maj. 6,909
*Stewart, J. Allan (*b.* 1942) *C., Eastwood,* maj. 11,688
*Stott, Roger, CBE (*b.* 1943) *Lab., Wigan,* maj. 21,842
*Strang, Gavin S., PH.D. (*b.* 1943) *Lab., Edinburgh East,* maj.
    7,211
*Straw, J. W. (Jack) (*b.* 1946) *Lab., Blackburn,* maj. 6,027
Streeter, Gary (*b.* 1955) *C., Plymouth, Sutton,* maj. 11,950
*Sumberg, David A. G. (*b.* 1941) *C., Bury South,* maj. 788
†Sutcliffe, Gerard (*b.* 1953) *Lab., Bradford South,* maj. 9,664
Sweeney, Walter E. (*b.* 1949) *C., Vale of Glamorgan,* maj. 19
Sykes, John D. (*b.* 1956) *C., Scarborough,* maj. 11,734
*Tapsell, Sir Peter (*b.* 1930) *C., Lindsey East,* maj. 11,846
*Taylor, Sir Edward (Teddy) (*b.* 1937) *C., Southend East,* maj.
    13,111
*Taylor, Ian C., MBE (*b.* 1945) *C., Esher,* maj. 20,371
*Taylor, Rt. Hon. John D. (*b.* 1937) *UUP, Strangford,* maj.
    8,911
*Taylor, John M. (*b.* 1941) *C., Solihull,* maj. 25,146
*Taylor, Matthew O. J. (*b.* 1963) *LD, Truro,* maj. 7,570
*Taylor, Mrs W. Ann (*b.* 1947) *Lab., Dewsbury,* maj. 634
*Temple-Morris, Peter (*b.* 1938) *C., Leominster,* maj. 16,680
Thomason, K. Roy, OBE (*b.* 1944) *C., Bromsgrove,* maj. 13,702
*Thompson, Sir Donald (*b.* 1931) *C., Calder Valley,* maj. 4,878
*Thompson, H. Patrick (*b.* 1935) *C., Norwich North,* maj. 266
*Thompson, John (*b.* 1928) *Lab., Wansbeck,* maj. 18,174
*Thornton, Sir Malcolm (*b.* 1939) *C., Crosby,* maj. 14,806
*Thurnham, Peter G. (*b.* 1938) *Ind. C., Bolton North East,* maj.
    185
†Timms, Stephen C. (*b.* 1955) *Lab., Newham North East,* maj.
    11,818
Tipping, S. Paddy (*b.* 1949) *Lab., Sherwood,* maj. 2,910
†Touhig, J. Donnelly (Don) (*b.* 1959) *Lab., Islwyn,* maj.
    13,097
Townend, John E. (*b.* 1934) *C., Bridlington,* maj. 16,358
*Townsend, Cyril D. (*b.* 1937) *C., Bexleyheath,* maj. 14,086
*Tracey, Richard P. (*b.* 1943) *C., Surbiton,* maj. 9,639
*Tredinnick, David A. S. (*b.* 1950) *C., Bosworth,* maj. 19,094
Trend, Hon. Michael St J. (*b.* 1952) *C., Windsor and
    Maidenhead,* maj. 12,928
†Trickett, Jon H. (*b.* 1950) *Lab., Hemsworth,* maj. 13,875
*Trimble, W. David (*b.* 1944) *UUP, Upper Bann,* maj. 16,163
*Trotter, Neville G. (*b.* 1932) *C., Tynemouth,* maj. 597
*Turner, Dennis (*b.* 1942) *Lab., Wolverhampton South East,*
    maj. 10,240
*Twinn, Dr Ian D. (*b.* 1950) *C., Edmonton,* maj. 593
Tyler, Paul A., CBE (*b.* 1941) *LD, Cornwall North,* maj. 1,921
*Vaughan, Sir Gerard (*b.* 1923) *C., Reading East,* maj. 14,555
*Vaz, N. Keith A. S. (*b.* 1956) *Lab., Leicester East,* maj. 11,316
*Viggers, Peter J. (*b.* 1938) *C., Gosport,* maj. 16,318
*Waldegrave, Rt. Hon. William A. (*b.* 1946) *C., Bristol West,*
    maj. 6,071
*Walden, George G. H., CMG (*b.* 1939) *C., Buckingham,* maj.
    19,791
*Walker, A. Cecil (*b.* 1924) *UUP, Belfast North,* maj. 9,625
*Walker, Rt. Hon. Sir Harold (*b.* 1927) *Lab., Doncaster
    Central,* maj. 10,682

*Walker, William C. (*b.* 1929) *C., Tayside North,* maj. 3,995
*Wallace, James R. (*b.* 1954) *LD, Orkney and Shetland,* maj.
    5,033
*Waller, Gary P. A. (*b.* 1945) *C., Keighley,* maj. 3,596
*Walley, Ms Joan L. (*b.* 1949) *Lab., Stoke-on-Trent North,* maj.
    14,777
*Ward, John D., CBE (*b.* 1925) *C., Poole,* maj. 12,831
*Wardell, Gareth L. (*b.* 1944) *Lab., Gower,* maj. 7,018
*Wardle, Charles F. (*b.* 1939) *C., Bexhill and Battle,* maj.
    16,307
*Wareing, Robert N. (*b.* 1930) *Lab., Liverpool, West Derby,* maj.
    20,425
Waterson, Nigel C. (*b.* 1950) *C., Eastbourne,* maj. 5,481
*Watson, Michael G. (*b.* 1949) *Lab., Glasgow Central,* maj.
    11,019
*Watts, John A. (*b.* 1947) *C., Slough,* maj. 514
*Wells, Bowen (*b.* 1935) *C., Hertford and Stortford,* maj. 20,210
*Welsh, Andrew P. (*b.* 1944) *SNP, Angus East,* maj. 954
*Wheeler, Rt. Hon. Sir John (*b.* 1940) *C., Westminster North,*
    maj. 3,733
*Whitney, Raymond W., OBE (*b.* 1930) *C., Wycombe,* maj.
    17,076
Whittingdale, John F. L., OBE (*b.* 1959) *C., Colchester South and
    Maldon,* maj. 21,821
Wicks, Malcolm H. (*b.* 1947) *Lab., Croydon North West,* maj.
    1,526
*Widdecombe, Miss Ann N. (*b.* 1947) *C., Maidstone,* maj.
    16,286
*Wiggin, Sir Jerry, TD (*b.* 1937) *C., Weston-super-Mare,* maj.
    5,342
*Wigley, Dafydd (*b.* 1943) *PC, Caernarfon,* maj. 14,476
*Wilkinson, John A. D. (*b.* 1940) *C., Ruislip-Northwood,* maj.
    19,791
Willetts, David L. (*b.* 1956) *C., Havant,* maj. 17,584
*Williams, Rt. Hon. Alan J. (*b.* 1930) *Lab., Swansea West,* maj.
    9,478
*Williams, Dr Alan W. (*b.* 1945) *Lab., Carmarthen,* maj. 2,922
*Wilshire, David (*b.* 1943) *C., Spelthorne,* maj. 19,843
*Wilson, Brian D. H. (*b.* 1948) *Lab., Cunninghame North,* maj.
    2,939
*Winnick, David J. (*b.* 1933) *Lab., Walsall North,* maj. 3,824
*Winterton, Mrs J. Ann (*b.* 1941) *C., Congleton,* maj. 11,120
*Winterton, Nicholas R. (*b.* 1938) *C., Macclesfield,* maj.
    22,767
*Wise, Mrs Audrey (*b.* 1935) *Lab., Preston,* maj. 12,175
*Wolfson, G. Mark (*b.* 1934) *C., Sevenoaks,* maj. 19,154
*Wood, Timothy J. R. (*b.* 1940) *C., Stevenage,* maj. 4,888
*Worthington, Anthony (*b.* 1941) *Lab., Clydebank and
    Milngavie,* maj. 12,430
*Wray, James (*b.* 1938) *Lab., Glasgow, Provan,* maj. 10,703
Wright, Anthony W., D.PHIL. (*b.* 1948) *Lab., Cannock and
    Burntwood,* maj. 1,506
*Yeo, Timothy S. K. (*b.* 1945) *C., Suffolk South,* maj. 17,289
*Young, David W. (*b.* 1930) *Lab., Bolton South East,* maj.
    12,691
*Young, Rt. Hon. Sir George, Bt. (*b.* 1941) *C., Ealing, Acton,*
    maj. 7,007

RETIRING MPs

The following MPs have announced that they will not be standing at the next general election:

Michael Alison, C., Selby
David Alton, LD, Liverpool Mossley Hill
Kenneth Baker, C., Mole Valley
Robert Banks, C., Harrogate and Knaresborough
John Biffen, C., Shropshire North
Jeremy Bray, Lab., Motherwell South
John Butcher, C., Coventry South West
Alex Carlile, LD, Montgomery
Sir Kenneth Carlisle, C., Lincoln
Paul Channon, C., Southend West
Sir Julian Critchley, C., Aldershot
Edwina Currie, C., Derbyshire South
Terry Dicks, C., Hayes and Harlington
Sir Anthony Durant, C., Reading West
Tim Eggar, C., Enfield North
Andrew Faulds, Lab., Warley East
Dudley Fishburn, C., Kensington
Sir Anthony Grant, C., Cambridgeshire South West
Sir Michael Grylls, C., Surrey North West
Sir John Hannam, C., Exeter
Peter Hardy, Lab., Wentworth
Roy Hattersley, Lab., Birmingham Sparkbrook
Sir Robert Hicks, C., Cornwall South East
Sir Peter Hordern, C., Horsham
David Howell, C., Guildford
Sir John Hunt, C., Ravensbourne
Douglas Hurd, C., Witney
Greville Janner, Lab., Leicester West
Sir Russell Johnston, LD, Inverness, Nairn and Lochaber
Dame Jill Knight, C., Birmingham Edgbaston
Sir Patrick McNair-Wilson, C., New Forest
Sir Patrick Mayhew, C., Tunbridge Wells
Sir David Mitchell, C., Hampshire North West
Sir Hector Monro, C., Dumfries
Sir Fergus Montgomery, C., Altrincham and Sale
Alf Morris, Lab., Manchester Wythenshawe
Steven Norris, C., Epping Forest
Sir Cranley Onslow, C., Woking
Stan Orme, Lab., Salford East
Bob Parry, Lab., Liverpool Riverside
Terry Patchett, Lab., Barnsley
John Patten, C., Oxford West and Abingdon
Sir Geoffrey Pattie, C., Chertsey and Walton
Tim Renton, C., Sussex Mid
Sir Wyn Roberts, C., Conwy
Richard Ryder, C., Mid Norfolk
Sir Giles Shaw, C., Pudsey
Peter Shore, Lab., Bethnal Green and Stepney
Sir Keith Speed, C., Ashford
Sir James Spicer, C., Dorset West
Sir David Steel, LD, Tweeddale, Ettrick and Lauderdale
Patrick Thompson, C., Norwich North
Peter Thurnham, Ind. C., Bolton North East
Neville Trotter, C., Tynemouth
George Walden, C., Buckingham
John Ward, C., Poole
Sir Jerry Wiggin, C., Weston-super-Mare
Mark Wolfson, C., Sevenoaks

The following MPs have been deselected by their constituency parties:
David Ashby, C., Leicestershire North West
David Young, Lab., Bolton South East

MEMBERS WITH SMALL MAJORITIES

The following MPs were returned in April 1992 with majorities of fewer than 1,000 votes

*Denotes membership of last Parliament

	Maj.
Walter Sweeney, C., Vale of Glamorgan	19
*Michael Stern, C., Bristol North West	45
*Terry Dicks, C., Hayes and Harlington	53
Phil Gallie, C., Ayr	85
Janet Anderson, Lab., Rossendale and Darwen	120
Jonathan Evans, C., Brecon and Radnor	130
Estelle Morris, Lab., Birmingham Yardley	162
*Peter Thurnham, C., Bolton North East	185
Mike Hall, Lab., Warrington South	191
*David Martin, C., Portsmouth South	242
Jamie Cann, Lab., Ipswich	265
*Patrick Thompson, C., Norwich North	266
*Malcolm Bruce, LD, Gordon	274
*William Powell, C., Corby	342
Mike Gapes, Lab., Ilford South	402
*Sir Russell Johnston, LD, Inverness, Nairn and Lochaber	458
*Alice Mahon, Lab., Halifax	478
*John Watts, C., Slough	514
John Denham, Lab., Southampton Itchen	551
Anne Campbell, Lab., Cambridge	580
*James Hill, C., Southampton Test	585
Dr Joe Hendron, SDLP, Belfast West	589
*Dr Ian Twinn, C., Edmonton	593
Neville Trotter, C., Tynemouth	597
Richard Burden, Lab., Birmingham Northfield	630
*Ann Taylor, Lab., Dewsbury	634
*Michael Forsyth, C., Stirling	703
*Phillip Oppenheim, C., Amber Valley	712
Nick Ainger, Lab., Pembroke	755
*David Sumberg, C., Bury South	788
Nick Harvey, LD, Devon North	794
*Graham Bright, C., Luton South	799
*David Shaw, C., Dover	833
*Lord James Douglas-Hamilton, C., Edinburgh West	879
*Sir Tom Arnold, C., Hazel Grove	929
*Andrew Welsh, SNP, Angus East	954
*David Ashby, C., Leicestershire North West	979
*Sir Wyn Roberts, C., Conwy	995

BY-ELECTIONS SINCE THE 1992 GENERAL ELECTION

NEWBURY
(6 May 1993)
*E.*81,081　*T.*71.25%

D. Rendel, *LD*	37,590
J. Davidson, *C.*	15,535
S. Billcliffe, *Lab.*	1,151
A. Sked, *Anti-Maastricht Anti Fed.*	601
A. Bannon, *C. Candidate*	561
S. Martin, *Commoners Party Movement*	435
'Lord' D. Sutch, *Loony*	432
J. Wallis, *Green*	341
R. Marlar, *Referendum*	338
J. Browne, *C. Rebel*	267
Ms L. St Clair, *Corrective*	170
W. Board, *Maastricht Referendum for Britain*	84
M. Grenville, *NLP*	60
J. Day, *People and Pensioners*	49
C. Palmer, *21st Century*	40
M. Grbin, *Defence of Children's Humanity Bosnia*	33
A. Page, *SDP*	33
Ms A. Murphy, *Comm. GB*	32
M. Stone, *Give Royal Billions to Schools*	21
LD majority	22,055

CHRISTCHURCH
(29 July 1993)
*E.*71,868　*T.*74.2%

Mrs D. Maddock, *LD*	33,164
R. Hayward, *C.*	16,737
N. Lickley, *Lab.*	1,453
A. Sked, *Anti-Maastricht Anti Fed.*	878
'Lord' D. Sutch, *Loony Rock-Roll*	404
A. Bannon, *C. Candidate*	357
P. Newman, *Sack Graham Taylor*	80
Ms T. B. Jackson, *Buy Daily Sport*	67
P. Hollyman, *Save NHS*	60
J. Crockard, *Highlander IV Wednesday Promotion Night*	48
M. Griffiths, *NLP*	45
M. Belcher, *Ian for King*	23
K. Fitzhugh, *Alfred Chicken*	18
J. Walley, *Rainbow Alliance Coalition*	16
LD majority	16,427

ROTHERHAM
(5 May 1994)
*E.*60,937　*T.*44.14%

D. MacShane, *Lab.*	14,912
D. Wildgoose, *LD*	7,958
N. Gibb, *C.*	2,649
'Lord' D. Sutch, *Loony*	1,114
K. Laycock, *NLP*	173
Lab. majority	6,954

BARKING
(9 June 1994)
*E.*50,454　*T.*38.6%

Ms M. Hodge, *Lab.*	13,704
G. White, *LD*	2,290
Ms T. May, *C.*	1,976
G. Needs, *NF*	551
G. Batten, *UK Ind.*	406
Ms H. Butensky, *NLP*	90
Lab. majority	11,414

BRADFORD SOUTH
(9 June 1994)
*E.*69,914　*T.*44.0%

G. Sutcliffe, *Lab.*	17,014
Ms H. Wright, *LD*	7,350
R. Farley, *C.*	5,475
'Lord' D. Sutch, *Loony*	727
K. Laycock, *NLP*	187
Lab. majority	9,664

DAGENHAM
(9 June 1994)
*E.*59,645　*T.*37.2%

Ms J. Church, *Lab.*	15,474
J. Fairrie, *C.*	2,130
P. Dunphy, *LD*	1,804
J. Tyndall, *BNP*	1,511
P. Compobassi, *UK Ind.*	457
M. Leighton, *NLP*	116
Lab. majority	13,344

EASTLEIGH
(9 June 1994)
*E.*91,736　*T.*58.9%

D. Chidgey, *LD*	24,473
Ms M. Birks, *Lab.*	15,234
S. Reid, *C.*	13,675
N. Farage, *UK Ind.*	952
'Lord' D. Sutch, *Loony*	783
P. Warburton, *NLP*	145
LD majority	9,239

NEWHAM NORTH EAST
(9 June 1994)
*E.*59,555　*T.*34.5%

S. Timms, *Lab.*	14,668
P. Hammond, *C.*	2,850
A. Kellaway, *LD*	821
A. Scholefield, *UK Ind.*	509
J. Homeless, *House Homeless People*	342
R. Archer, *NLP*	228
Ms V. Garman, *Buy the Daily Sport*	155
Lab. majority	11,818

MONKLANDS EAST
(30 June 1994)
*E.*48,391　*T.*70.17%

Mrs H. Liddell, *Lab.*	16,960
Ms K. Ullrich, *SNP*	15,320
S. Gallagher, *LD*	878
Ms S. Bell, *C.*	799
A. Bremner, *Network Against Criminal Justice Bill*	69
D. Paterson, *NLP*	58
Lab. majority	1,640

DUDLEY WEST
(15 December 1994)
*E.*87,633　*T.*46.95%

I. Pearson, *Lab.*	28,400
G. Postles, *C.*	7,706
M. Hadley, *LD*	3,154
M. S. Hyde, *Lib.*	548
M. R. Floyd, *UK Ind.*	590
A. Carmichael, *NF*	561
M. H. Nattrass, *New Britain*	146
Ms M. Nicholson, *FOREST*	77
J. D. Oldbury, *NLP*	70
C. R. Palmer, *21st Century*	55
Lab. majority	20,694

ISLWYN
(16 February 1995)
*E.*50,737　*T.*45.6%

D. Touhig, *Lab.*	16,030
J. Davies, *PC*	2,933
J. Bushell, *LD*	2,448
R. Buckland, *C.*	913
'Lord' D. Sutch, *Loony*	506
H. Hughes, *UK Ind.*	289
T. Rees, *NLP*	47
Lab. majority	13,097

PERTH AND KINROSS
(25 May 1995)
*E.*65,410　*T.*62.0%

Ms R. Cunningham, *SNP*	16,931
D. Alexander, *Lab.*	9,620
J. Godfrey, *C.*	8,990
Ms V. Linklater, *LD*	4,952
'Lord' D. Sutch, *Loony*	586
V. Linacre, *UK Ind.*	504
R. Harper, *Green*	223
M. Halford, *Scots Conservatory*	88
G. Black, *NLP*	54
SNP majority	7,311

DOWN NORTH
(15 June 1995)
*E.*68,662　*T.*38.7%

R. McCartney, *UK Unionist*	10,124
A. McFarland, *UUP*	7,232
Sir Oliver Napier, *All.*	6,970
A. Chambers, *Ind. Unionist*	2,170
S. Sexton, *C.*	583
M. Brooks, *Free Para Lee Clegg Now*	108
C. Carter, *Ulster's Ind. Voice*	101
J. Anderson, *NLP*	100
UK Unionist majority	2,892

LITTLEBOROUGH AND SADDLEWORTH (27 July 1995) £65,576 T.63.6%		HEMSWORTH (1 February 1996) £55,679 T.39.5%		STAFFORDSHIRE SOUTH EAST (11 April 1996) £70,199 T.60.3%	
C. Davies, *LD*	16,231	J. Trickett, *Lab.*	15,817	B. Jenkins, *Lab.*	26,155
P. Woolas, *Lab.*	14,238	N. Hazell, *C.*	1,942	J. James, *C.*	12,393
J. Hudson, *C.*	9,934	D. Ridgway, *LD*	1,516	Ms J. Davey, *LD*	2.042
'Lord' D. Sutch, *Loony*	782	Ms B. Nixon, *Soc. Lab.*	1,193	A. Smith, *UK Independence*	1,272
J. Whittaker, *UK Ind.*	549	'Lord' D. Sutch, *Loony*	652	'Lord' D. Sutch, *Loony*	506
P. Douglas, *C. Party*	193	P. Davies, *UK Ind.*	455	Ms S. Edwards, *National*	
Mr Blobby, *House Party*	105	Ms P. Alexander, *Green*	157	*Democrats*	358
A. Pitts, *Soc.*	46	M. Thomas, *Mark Thomas*		S. Mountford, *Lib.*	332
L. D. McLaren, *Old Lab.*	33	*Friday Nights Channel 4*	122	L.Taylor, *Churchill C.*	123
C. R. Palmer, *21st Century*	25	M. Cooper, *National*		News Bunny, *Official Bunny*	
LD majority	1,993	*Democrat*	111	*News Party*	85
		Ms D. Leighton, *NLP*	28	N. Samuelson, *Daily*	
		Lab. majority	13,875	*Loonylugs Earring-up the*	
				World	80
				D. Lucas, *NLP*	53
				F. Sandy, *Action Against*	
				Crime Life Means Life	53
				A. Wood, *Restoration of Death*	
				Penalty	45
				Lab. majority	13,762

Prime Ministers since 1782

Over the centuries there has been some variation in the determination of the dates of appointment of Prime Ministers. Where possible, the date given is that on which a new Prime Minister kissed the Sovereign's hands and accepted the commission to form a ministry. However, until the middle of the 19th century the dating of a commission or transfer of seals could be the date of taking office. Where the composition of the Government changed, e.g. became a coalition, but the Prime Minister remained the same, the date of the change of government is given.

The Marquess of Rockingham, *Whig*, 27 March 1782
The Earl of Shelburne, *Whig*, 4 July 1782
The Duke of Portland, *Coalition*, 2 April 1783
William Pitt, *Tory*, 19 December 1783
Henry Addington, *Tory*, 17 March 1801
William Pitt, *Tory*, 10 May 1804
The Lord Grenville, *Whig*, 11 February 1806
The Duke of Portland, *Tory*, 31 March 1807
Spencer Perceval, *Tory*, 4 October 1809
The Earl of Liverpool, *Tory*, 8 June 1812
George Canning, *Tory*, 10 April 1827
Viscount Goderich, *Tory*, 31 August 1827
The Duke of Wellington, *Tory*, 22 January 1828
The Earl Grey, *Whig*, 22 November 1830
The Viscount Melbourne, *Whig*, 16 July 1834
The Duke of Wellington, *Tory*, 17 November 1834
Sir Robert Peel, *Tory*, 10 December 1834
The Viscount Melbourne, *Whig*, 18 April 1835
Sir Robert Peel, *Tory*, 30 August 1841
Lord John Russell (subsequently the Earl Russell), *Whig*, 30 June 1846
The Earl of Derby, *Tory*, 23 February 1852
The Earl of Aberdeen, *Peelite*, 19 December 1852
The Viscount Palmerston, *Liberal*, 6 February 1855
The Earl of Derby, *Conservative*, 20 February 1858
The Viscount Palmerston, *Liberal*, 12 June 1859
The Earl Russell, *Liberal*, 29 October 1865

The Earl of Derby, *Conservative*, 28 June 1866
Benjamin Disraeli, *Conservative*, 27 February 1868
William Gladstone, *Liberal*, 3 December 1868
Benjamin Disraeli, *Conservative*, 20 February 1874
William Gladstone, *Liberal*, 23 April 1880
The Marquess of Salisbury, *Conservative*, 23 June 1885
William Gladstone, *Liberal*, 1 February 1886
The Marquess of Salisbury, *Conservative*, 25 July 1886
William Gladstone, *Liberal*, 15 August 1892
The Earl of Rosebery, *Liberal*, 5 March 1894
The Marquess of Salisbury, *Conservative*, 25 June 1895
Arthur Balfour, *Conservative*, 12 July 1902
Sir Henry Campbell-Bannerman, *Liberal*, 5 December 1905
Herbert Asquith, *Liberal*, 7 April 1908
Herbert Asquith, *Coalition*, 25 May 1915
David Lloyd-George, *Coalition*, 7 December 1916
Andrew Bonar Law, *Conservative*, 23 October 1922
Stanley Baldwin, *Conservative*, 22 May 1923
Ramsay MacDonald, *Labour*, 22 January 1924
Stanley Baldwin, *Conservative*, 4 November 1924
Ramsay MacDonald, *Labour*, 5 June 1929
Ramsay MacDonald, *Coalition*, 24 August 1931
Stanley Baldwin, *Coalition*, 7 June 1935
Neville Chamberlain, *Coalition*, 28 May 1937
Winston Churchill, *Coalition*, 10 May 1940
Winston Churchill, *Conservative*, 23 May 1945
Clement Attlee, *Labour*, 26 July 1945
Sir Winston Churchill, *Conservative*, 26 October 1951
Sir Anthony Eden, *Conservative*, 6 April 1955
Harold Macmillan, *Conservative*, 10 January 1957
Sir Alec Douglas-Home, *Conservative*, 19 October 1963
Harold Wilson, *Labour*, 16 October 1964
Edward Heath, *Conservative*, 19 June 1970
Harold Wilson, *Labour*, 4 March 1974
James Callaghan, *Labour*, 5 April 1976
Margaret Thatcher, *Conservative*, 4 May 1979
John Major, *Conservative*, 28 November 1990

General Election statistics

PRINCIPAL PARTIES IN PARLIAMENT since 1970

	1970	1974 Feb.	1974 Oct.	1979	1983	1987	1992
Conservative	330*	296	276	339	397	375	336
Labour	287	301	319	268	209	229	270
Liberal/LD	6	14	13	11	17	17	20
Social Democrat	—	1	—	—	6	5	—
Independent	5†	1	1	2	—	—	—
Plaid Cymru	—	2	3	2	2	3	4
Scottish Nationalist	1	7	11	2	2	3	3
Democratic Unionist	—	—	—	3	3	3	3
SDLP	—	1	1	1	1	3	4
Sinn Fein	—	—	—	—	1	1	—
Ulster Popular Unionist	—	—	—	—	1	1	1
Ulster Unionist‡	*	11	10	6	10	9	9
The Speaker	1	1	1	1	1	1	1
Total	630	635	635	635	650	650	651

* Including 8 Ulster Unionists
† Comprising: Independent Labour 1, Independent Unity 1, Protestant Unity 1, Republican Labour 1, Unity 1
‡ Comprises:
1974 (February) United Ulster Unionist Council 11
1974 (October) United Ulster Unionist 10
1979 Ulster Unionist 5, United Ulster Unionist 1
1983 Official Unionist 10

PARLIAMENTS since 1970

		Duration		
Assembled	Dissolved	yr	m.	d.
29 June 1970	8 February 1974	3	7	10
6 March 1974	20 September 1974	0	6	14
22 October 1974	7 April 1979	4	5	16
9 May 1979	13 May 1983	4	0	4
15 June 1983	18 May 1987	3	11	3
17 June 1987	16 March 1992	4	8	28
27 April 1992				

MAJORITIES IN THE COMMONS since 1970

Year	Party	Maj.
1970	Conservative	31
1974 Feb.	No majority	
1974 Oct.	Labour	5
1979	Conservative	43
1983	Conservative	144
1987	Conservative	102
1992	Conservative	21

VOTES CAST 1987 and 1992*

GENERAL ELECTION 1987

Conservative	13,760,525
Labour	10,029,944
Liberal/SDP Alliance	7,341,152
Scottish Nationalist	416,873
Plaid Cymru	123,589
†Green	89,753
Others	37,576

GENERAL ELECTION 1992

Conservative	14,048,283
Labour	11,559,735
Liberal Democrats	5,999,384
Scottish Nationalist	629,552
Plaid Cymru	154,439
Others	436,207

*Excluding Northern Ireland seats
†Excluding Ecology candidate in Northern Ireland

SIZE OF ELECTORATE 1992

	No. of electors	Average no. of electors per seat
England and Wales	38,648,000	68,800
Scotland	3,929,000	54,600
Northern Ireland	1,141,000	67,100
Total	43,719,000	67,200

PARLIAMENTARY CONSTITUENCIES as at 9 April 1992

The results of voting in each parliamentary division at the general election of 9 April 1992 are given below. The majority in the 1987 general election, and any by-elections between 1987 and 1992, is given below the 1992 result.

Symbols

E.   Total number of electors in the constituency at the 1992 general election

T.   Turnout of electors at the 1992 general election

*   Member of the last Parliament

Abbreviations

All.	Alliance Party (NI)
C.	Conservative
DUP	Democratic Unionist Party
Green	Green Party
Ind.	Independent
Lab.	Labour
L./All.	Liberal Alliance
LD	Liberal Democrat
Lib.	Liberal
PC	Plaid Cymru
SD	Social Democrat
SDLP	Social Democratic and Labour Party
SDP	Social Democrat Party
SF	Sinn Fein
SNP	Scottish National Party
UPUP	Ulster Popular Unionist Party
UUP	Ulster Unionist Party
ADS	After Dinner Speaker
AFE	Anti-Federal Europe
Alt.	Alternative
Anti Fed.	Anti Federalist League
Anti H.	Anti-Heseltine Independent
APAKBI	Anti-Paddy Ashdown Keep Britain Independent

AS	Anglo Saxon
Bastion	Bastion Party
BNP	British National Party
Brewer	Jolly Small Brewers Party
Brit. Ind.	British Independence Party
CD	Christian Democrat
Century	21st Century Party
Choice	People's Choice
CL	Communist League
Comm. GB	Communist Party of Great Britain
CRA	Chauvinist Raving Alliance
CSP	Common Sense Party
C. Thatch.	Conservative Thatcherite
DLC	Democrat Liberal Conservative
DOS	Doctor of Stockwell
EFRA	Epping Forest Residents Association
ERIP	Equal Representation in Parliament
EUVJJ	End Unemployment Vote Justice for the Jobless
FDP	Fancy Dress Party
Fellowship	Fellowship Party
FP	Feudal Party
FTA	Fair Trials Abroad
FTM	Forward to Mars Party
Fun	Funstermentalist
Gremloids	Gremloids
Hardcore	The Altern-8-ive (Hardcore) Party
Homeland	Independent British Homeland Defence
Hove C.	Official Conservative Hove Party
IFM	Irish Freedom Movement
ILP	Independent Labour Party
Ind. U.	Independent Unionist
Int. Comm.	International Communist Party
Islamic	Islamic Party
ISS	Illegal Sunday Shopping
JBR	Justice from British Rail

Loony	Official Monster Raving Loony Party
Loony G.	Loony Green
LP	Lodestar Party
LTU	Labour and Trade Union
MBI	Morecambe Bay Independent
NA	Noise Abatement
Nat.	Nationalist
NF	National Front
NLP	Natural Law Party
Pensioners	Pensioners' Party
PP	People's Party
PPP	Peoples' Peace Party
PR	Proportional Representation
Prog. Soc.	Independent Progressive Socialist
Prot. Ref.	Protestant Reformation
QFL	Quality for Life Party
RAVA	Rainbow Ark Voters Association
RCC	Revolutionary Christian Communist
Real Bean	Real Bean
Rev. Comm.	Revolutionary Communist
Rizz	Rizz Party – Rainbow
Scallywagg	Scallywagg
SML	Scottish Militant Labour
SOADDA	Struck Off and Die Doctor's Alliance
Soc.	Socialist
Soc. Lab.	Socialist Labour
True Lab.	True Labour
UTCHAP	Up The Creek Have A Party
WAR	Workers Against Racism
Wessex	Save Wessex
Whiplash	Whiplash Corrective
WP	Workers' Party
WRP	Workers' Revolutionary Party
WUWC	Wake Up Wokingham Campaign
YSOR	Young Socialist – Occupy Ravenscraig

ENGLAND

ALDERSHOT (Hants)
E.81,754   T.78.71%

J. Critchley, C.	36,974
A. Collett, LD	17,786
J. Anthony Smith, Lab.	8,552
D. Robinson, Lib.	1,038
C. majority	19,188

(June 1987, C. maj. 17,784)

ALDRIDGE-BROWNHILLS (W. Midlands)
E.63,404   T.82.55%

R. Shepherd, C.	28,431
N. Fawcett, Lab.	17,407
S. Reynolds, LD	6,503
C. majority	11,024

(June 1987, C. maj. 12,396)

ALTRINCHAM AND SALE (Greater Manchester)
E.65,897   T.80.66%

Sir F. Montgomery, C.	29,066
Ms M. Atherton, Lab.	12,275
J. Mulholland, LD	11,601
J. Renwick, NLP	212

C. majority	16,791

(June 1987, C. maj. 14,228)

AMBER VALLEY (Derbys)
E.70,155   T.84.69%

*Hon. P. Oppenheim, C.	27,418
J. Cooper, Lab.	26,706
G. Brocklebank, LD	5,294
C. majority	712

(June 1987, C. maj. 9,500)

ARUNDEL (W. Sussex)
E.79,241   T.77.06%

*Sir M. Marshall, C.	35,405
Dr J. Walsh, LD	15,542
R. Nash, Lab.	8,321
Mrs D. Renson, Lib.	1,103
R. Corbin, Green	693
C. majority	19,863

(June 1987, C. maj. 18,880)

ASHFIELD (Notts)
E.75,075   T.77.70%

G. Hoon, Lab.	32,018
L. Robertson, C.	19,031

J. Turton, LD	7,291
Lab. majority	12,987

(June 1987, Lab. maj. 4,400)

ASHFORD (Kent)
E.71,767   T.79.20%

*K. Speed, C.	31,031
Ms C. Headley, LD	13,672
Ms D. Cameron, Lab.	11,365
Dr A. Porter, Green	773
C. majority	17,359

(June 1987, C. maj. 15,488)

ASHTON-UNDER-LYNE (Greater Manchester)
E.58,701   T.73.87%

*Rt. Hon. R. Sheldon, Lab.	24,550
J. Pinniger, C.	13,615
C. Turner, LD	4,005
C. Hall, Lib.	907
J. Brannigan, NLP	289
Lab. majority	10,935

(June 1987, Lab. maj. 9,286)

Aylesbury (Bucks)
E.79,208   T.80.29%
D. Lidington, *C.*	36,500
Ms S. Bowles, *LD*	17,640
R. Priest, *Lab.*	8,517
N. Foster, *Green*	702
B. D'Arcy, *NLP*	239
C. majority	18,860
(June 1987, C. maj. 16,558)

Banbury (Oxon)
E.71,840   T.81.51%
*A. Baldry, *C.*	32,215
Ms A. Billingham, *Lab.*	15,495
G. Fisher, *LD*	10,602
Dr R. Ticiiati, *NLP*	250
C. majority	16,720
(June 1987, C. maj. 17,330)

Barking (Greater London)
E.50,454   T.69.99%
*Ms J. Richardson, *Lab.*	18,224
J. Kennedy, *C.*	11,956
S. Churchman, *LD*	5,133
Lab. majority	6,268
(June 1987, Lab. maj. 3,409)
See also page 234

Barnsley Central (S. Yorks)
E.55,373   T.70.53%
*E. Illsley, *Lab.*	27,048
D. Senior, *C.*	7,687
S. Cowton, *LD*	4,321
Lab. majority	19,361
(June 1987, Lab. maj. 19,051)

Barnsley East (S. Yorks)
E.54,051   T.72.73%
*T. Patchett, *Lab.*	30,346
J. Procter, *C.*	5,569
Ms S. Anginotti, *LD*	3,399
Lab. majority	24,777
(June 1987, Lab. maj. 23,511)

Barnsley West and Penistone (S. Yorks)
E.63,374   T.75.75%
M. Clapham, *Lab.*	27,965
G. Sawyer, *C.*	13,461
I. Nicolson, *LD*	5,610
D. Jones, *Green*	970
Lab. majority	14,504
(June 1987, Lab. maj. 14,191)

Barrow and Furness (Cumbria)
E.67,764   T.82.11%
J. Hutton, *Lab.*	26,568
*C. Franks, *C.*	22,990
C. Crane, *LD*	6,089
Lab. majority	3,578
(June 1987, C. maj. 3,928)

Basildon (Essex)
E.67,585   T.79.61%
*D. Amess, *C.*	24,159
J. Potter, *Lab.*	22,679
G. Williams, *LD*	6,967
C. majority	1,480
(June 1987, C. maj. 2,649)

Basingstoke (Hants)
E.82,952   T.82.79%
*A. Hunter, *C.*	37,521
D. Bull, *Lab.*	16,323

C. Curtis, *LD*	14,119
Ms V. Oldaker, *Green*	714
C. majority	21,198
(June 1987, C. maj. 17,893)

Bassetlaw (Notts)
E.58,583   T.92.97%
*J. Ashton, *Lab.*	29,061
Mrs C. Spelman, *C.*	19,064
M. Reynolds, *LD*	6,340
Lab. majority	9,997
(June 1987, Lab. maj. 5,613)

Bath (Avon)
E.63,689   T.82.54%
D. Foster, *LD*	25,718
*Rt. Hon. C. Patten, *C.*	21,950
Ms P. Richards, *Lab.*	4,102
D. McCanlis, *Green*	433
Ms M. Barker, *Lib.*	172
Dr A. Sked, *Anti Fed.*	117
J. Rumming, *Ind.*	79
LD majority	3,768
(June 1987, C. maj. 1,412)

Batley and Spen (W. Yorks)
E.76,417   T.79.63%
*Mrs E. Peacock, *C.*	27,629
Mrs E. Durkin, *Lab.*	26,221
G. Beever, *LD*	6,380
C. Lord, *Green*	628
C. majority	1,408
(June 1987, C. maj. 1,362)

Battersea (Greater London)
E.68,218   T.76.63%
*J. Bowis, *C.*	26,390
A. Dubs, *Lab.*	21,550
R. O'Brien, *LD*	3,659
I. Wingrove, *Green*	584
W. Stevens, *NLP*	98
C. majority	4,840
(June 1987, C. maj. 857)

Beaconsfield (Bucks)
E.64,268   T.82.27%
*T. Smith, *C.*	33,817
Ms A. Purse, *LD*	10,220
G. Smith, *Lab.*	7,163
W. Foulds, *Ind. C.*	1,317
A. Foss, *NLP*	196
Ms J. Martin, *ERIP*	166
C. majority	23,597
(June 1987, C. maj. 21,339)

Beckenham (Greater London)
E.59,440   T.77.86%
P. Merchant, *C.*	26,323
K. Ritchie, *Lab.*	11,038
Ms M. Williams, *LD*	8,038
G. Williams, *Lib.*	643
P. Shaw, *NLP*	243
C. majority	15,285
(June 1987, C. maj. 13,464)

Bedfordshire Mid
E.81,864   T.84.45%
*Rt. Hon. Sir N. Lyell, *C.*	40,230
R. Clayton, *Lab.*	15,092
N. Hills, *LD*	11,957
P. Cottier, *Lib.*	1,582
M. Lorys, *NLP*	279

C. majority	25,138
(June 1987, C. maj. 22,851)

Bedfordshire North
E.73,789   T.80.03%
*Sir T. Skeet, *C.*	29,920
P. Hall, *Lab.*	18,302
M. Smithson, *LD*	10,014
Ms L. Smith, *Green*	643
B. Bench, *NLP*	178
C. majority	11,618
(June 1987, C. maj. 16,505)

Bedfordshire South West
E.79,662   T.82.39%
*W. D. Madel, *C.*	37,498
B. Elliott, *Lab.*	16,225
M. Freeman, *LD*	10,988
P. Rollings, *Green*	689
D. Gilmour, *NLP*	239
C. majority	21,273
(June 1987, C. maj. 22,305)

Berkshire East
E.90,365   T.81.41%
*A. Mackay, *C.*	43,898
Ms L. Murray, *LD*	15,218
K. Dibble, *Lab.*	14,458
C. majority	28,680
(June 1987, C. maj. 22,626)

Berwick-upon-Tweed (Northumberland)
E.54,919   T.79.12%
*A. Beith, *LD*	19,283
Dr A. Henfrey, *C.*	14,240
Dr G. Adam, *Lab.*	9,933
LD majority	5,043
(June 1987, L./All. maj. 13,945)

Bethnal Green and Stepney (Greater London)
E.55,675   T.65.45%
*Rt. Hon. P. Shore, *Lab.*	20,350
J. Shaw, *LD*	8,120
Miss J. Emmerson, *C.*	6,507
R. Edmonds, *BNP*	1,310
S. Kelsey, *Comm. GB*	156
Lab. majority	12,230
(June 1987, Lab. maj. 5,284)

Beverley (Humberside)
E.81,198   T.79.69%
*J. Cran, *C.*	34,503
A. Collinge, *LD*	17,986
C. Challen, *Lab.*	12,026
D. Hetherington, *NLP*	199
C. majority	16,517
(June 1987, C. maj. 12,595)

Bexhill and Battle (E. Sussex)
E.65,850   T.78.99%
*C. Wardle, *C.*	31,330
Ms S. Prochak, *LD*	15,023
F. Taylor, *Lab.*	4,883
J. Prus, *Green*	594
Mrs M. Smith, *CSP*	190
C. majority	16,307
(June 1987, C. maj. 20,519)

Bexleyheath (Greater London)
E.57,684   T.82.17%
*C. Townsend, *C.*	25,606
J. Browning, *Lab.*	11,520

Ms W. Chaplin, *LD* 10,107
R. Cundy, *Ind.* 170
C. majority 14,086
(June 1987, C. maj. 11,687)

BILLERICAY (Essex)
*E.*80,388 *T.*82.34%
*Mrs T. Gorman, *C.* 37,406
F. Bellard, *LD* 14,912
Ms A. Miller, *Lab.* 13,880
C. majority 22,494
(June 1987, C. maj. 18,016)

BIRKENHEAD (Merseyside)
*E.*62,682 *T.*72.96%
*F. Field, *Lab.* 29,098
R. Hughes, *C.* 11,485
P. Williams, *LD* 4,417
Ms T. Fox, *Green* 543
Ms B. Griffiths, *NLP* 190
Lab. majority 17,613
(June 1987, Lab. maj. 15,372)

BIRMINGHAM EDGBASTON
(W. Midlands)
*E.*53,041 *T.*71.29%
*Dame J. Knight, *C.* 18,529
J. Wilton, *Lab.* 14,222
I. Robertson-Steel, *LD* 4,419
P. Simpson, *Green* 643
C. majority 4,307
(June 1987, C. maj. 8,581)

BIRMINGHAM ERDINGTON
(W. Midlands)
*E.*52,398 *T.*70.15%
*R. Corbett, *Lab.* 18,549
S. Hope, *C.* 13,814
Dr J. Campbell, *LD* 4,398
Lab. majority 4,735
(June 1987, Lab. maj. 2,467)

BIRMINGHAM HALL GREEN
(W. Midlands)
*E.*60,091 *T.*78.17%
*A. Hargreaves, *C.* 21,649
Ms J. Slowey, *Lab.* 17,984
D. McGrath, *LD* 7,342
C. majority 3,665
(June 1987, C. maj. 7,621)

BIRMINGHAM HODGE HILL
(W. Midlands)
*E.*57,651 *T.*70.82%
*T. Davis, *Lab.* 21,895
Miss E. Gibson, *C.* 14,827
S. Hagan, *LD* 3,740
E. Whicker, *NF* 370
Lab. majority 7,068
(June 1987, Lab. maj. 4,789)

BIRMINGHAM LADYWOOD
(W. Midlands)
*E.*56,970 *T.*65.92%
*Ms C. Short, *Lab.* 24,887
Mrs B. Ashford, *C.* 9,604
B. Worth, *LD* 3,068
Lab. majority 15,283
(June 1987, Lab. maj. 10,028)

BIRMINGHAM NORTHFIELD
(W. Midlands)
*E.*70,533 *T.*76.08%
R. Burden, *Lab.* 24,433
*R. King, *C.* 23,803
D. Cropp, *LD* 5,431
Lab. majority 630
(June 1987, C. maj. 3,135)

BIRMINGHAM PERRY BARR
(W. Midlands)
*E.*72,161 *T.*71.62%
*J. Rooker, *Lab.* 27,507
G. Green, *C.* 18,917
T. Philpott, *LD* 5,261
Lab. majority 8,590
(June 1987, Lab. maj. 6,933)

BIRMINGHAM SELLY OAK
(W. Midlands)
*E.*72,150 *T.*76.61%
Ms L. Jones, *Lab.* 25,430
*A. Beaumont-Dark, *C.* 23,370
D. Osborne, *LD* 5,679
P. Slatter, *Green* 535
C. Barwood, *NLP* 178
K. Malik, *Rev Comm* 84
Lab. majority 2,060
(June 1987, C. maj. 2,584)

BIRMINGHAM SMALL HEATH
(W. Midlands)
*E.*55,213 *T.*62.95%
R. Godsiff, *Lab.* 22,675
A. Qayyum Chaudhary, *C.* 8,686
H. Thomas, *LD* 2,575
Ms H. Clawley, *Green* 824
Lab. majority 13,989
(June 1987, Lab. maj. 15,521)

BIRMINGHAM SPARKBROOK
(W. Midlands)
*E.*51,677 *T.*66.80%
*Rt. Hon. R. Hattersley, *Lab.* 22,116
M. Khamisa, *C.* 8,544
D. Parry, *LD* 3,028
C. Alldrick, *Green* 833
Lab. majority 13,572
(June 1987, Lab. maj. 11,859)

BIRMINGHAM YARDLEY
(W. Midlands)
*E.*54,749 *T.*77.98%
Ms E. Morris, *Lab.* 14,884
*A. D. G. Bevan, *C.* 14,722
J. Hemming, *LD* 12,899
Miss P. Read, *NF* 192
Lab. majority 162
(June 1987, C. maj. 2,522)

BISHOP AUCKLAND (Durham)
*E.*72,572 *T.*76.52%
*D. Foster, *Lab.* 27,763
D. Williamson, *C.* 17,676
W. Wade, *LD* 10,099
Lab. majority 10,087
(June 1987, Lab. maj. 7,035)

BLABY (Leics)
*E.*81,790 *T.*83.39%
A. Robathan, *C.* 39,498
Ms E. Ranson, *Lab.* 14,151
Ms M. Lewin, *LD* 13,780

J. Peacock, *BNP* 521
Ms S. Lincoln, *NLP* 260
C. majority 25,347
(June 1987, C. maj. 22,176)

BLACKBURN (Lancs)
*E.*73,251 *T.*75.05%
*J. Straw, *Lab.* 26,633
R. Coates, *C.* 20,606
D. Mann, *LD* 6,332
R. Field, *Green* 878
Mrs M. Carmichael-Grimshaw, *LP* 334
W. Ayliffe, *NLP* 195
Lab. majority 6,027
(June 1987, Lab. maj. 5,497)

BLACKPOOL NORTH (Lancs)
*E.*58,087 *T.*77.55%
H. Elletson, *C.* 21,501
E. Kirton, *Lab.* 18,461
A. Lahiff, *LD* 4,786
Sir G. Francis, *Loony* 178
H. Walker, *NLP* 125
C. majority 3,040
(June 1987, C. maj. 7,321)

BLACKPOOL SOUTH (Lancs)
*E.*56,801 *T.*77.35%
N. Hawkins, *C.* 19,880
G. Marsden, *Lab.* 18,213
R. Wynne, *LD* 5,675
D. Henning, *NLP* 173
C. majority 1,667
(June 1987, C. maj. 6,744)

BLAYDON (Tyne & Wear)
*E.*66,044 *T.*77.69%
*J. McWilliam, *Lab.* 27,028
P. Pescod, *C.* 13,685
P. Nunn, *LD* 10,602
Lab. majority 13,343
(June 1987, Lab. maj. 12,488)

BLYTH VALLEY (Northumberland)
*E.*60,913 *T.*80.77%
*R. Campbell, *Lab.* 24,542
P. Tracey, *LD* 16,498
M. Revell, *C.* 7,691
S. Tyley, *Green* 470
Lab. majority 8,044
(June 1987, Lab. maj. 853)

BOLSOVER (Derbys)
*E.*66,693 *T.*78.94%
*D. Skinner, *Lab.* 33,973
T. James, *C.* 13,313
Ms S. Barber, *LD* 5,363
Lab. majority 20,660
(June 1987, Lab. maj. 14,120)

BOLTON NORTH EAST (Greater Manchester)
*E.*58,659 *T.*82.26%
*P. Thurnham, *C.* 21,644
D. Crausby, *Lab.* 21,459
B. Dunning, *LD* 4,971
P. Tong, *NLP* 181
C. majority 185
(June 1987, C. maj. 813)

BOLTON SOUTH EAST (Greater
Manchester)
E.65,600   T.75.53%
*D. Young, *Lab.*   26,906
N. Wood-Dow, *C.*   14,215
D. Lee, *LD*   5,243
W. Hardman, *Ind. Lab.*   2,894
L. Walch, *NLP*   290
Lab. majority   12,691
(June 1987, Lab. maj. 11,381)

BOLTON WEST (Greater
Manchester)
E.71,344   T.83.53%
*Hon. T. Sackville, *C.*   26,452
C. Morris, *Lab.*   25,373
Ms B. Ronson, *LD*   7,529
Ms J. Phillips, *NLP*   240
C. majority   1,079
(June 1987, C. maj. 4,593)

BOOTHFERRY (Humberside)
E.80,747   T.79.73%
*D. Davis, *C.*   35,266
Ms L. Coubrough, *Lab.*   17,731
J. Goss, *LD*   11,388
C. majority   17,535
(June 1987, C. maj. 18,970)

BOOTLE (Merseyside)
E.69,308   T.72.46%
*J. Benton, *Lab.*   37,464
C. Varley, *C.*   8,022
J. Cunningham, *LD*   3,301
Ms M. Hall, *Lib.*   1,174
T. Haynes, *NLP*   264
Lab. majority   29,442
(June 1987, Lab. maj. 24,477)
(May 1990, Lab. maj. 23,517)
(November 1990, Lab. maj. 19,465)

BOSWORTH (Leics)
E.80,234   T.84.13%
*D. Tredinnick, *C.*   36,618
D. Everitt, *Lab.*   17,524
G. Drozdz, *LD*   12,643
B. Fewster, *Green*   716
C. majority   19,094
(June 1987, C. maj. 17,016)

BOURNEMOUTH EAST (Dorset)
E.75,089   T.72.82%
*D. Atkinson, *C.*   30,820
N. Russell, *LD*   15,997
P. Brushett, *Lab.*   7,541
Ms S. Holmes, *NLP*   329
C. majority   14,823
(June 1987, C. maj. 14,683)

BOURNEMOUTH WEST (Dorset)
E.74,738   T.75.72%
*J. Butterfill, *C.*   29,820
Ms J. Dover, *LD*   17,178
B. Grower, *Lab.*   9,423
A. Springham, *NLP*   232
C. majority   12,642
(June 1987, C. maj. 12,651)

BOW AND POPLAR (Greater London)
E.56,685   T.65.84%
*Mrs M. Gordon, *Lab.*   18,487
P. Hughes, *LD*   10,083
S. Pearce, *C.*   6,876

J. Tyndall, *BNP*   1,107
S. Petter, *Green*   612
W. Hite, *NLP*   158
Lab. majority   8,404
(June 1987, Lab. maj. 4,631)

BRADFORD NORTH (W. Yorks)
E.66,719   T.73.38%
*T. Rooney, *Lab.*   23,420
M. Riaz, *C.*   15,756
D. Ward, *LD*   9,133
W. Beckett, *Loony*   350
M. Nasr, *Islamic*   304
Lab. majority   7,664
(June 1987, Lab. maj. 1,663)
(November 1990, Lab. maj. 9,514)

BRADFORD SOUTH (W. Yorks)
E.69,914   T.75.61%
*G. R. Cryer, *Lab.*   25,185
A. Popat, *C.*   20,283
B. Boulton, *LD*   7,243
M. Naseem, *Islamic*   156
Lab. majority   4,902
(June 1987, Lab. maj. 309)
See also page 234

BRADFORD WEST (W. Yorks)
E.70,016   T.69.90%
*M. Madden, *Lab.*   26,046
Dr A. Ashworth, *C.*   16,544
Dr. A. Griffiths, *LD*   5,150
P. Braham, *Green*   735
D. Pidcock, *Islamic*   471
Lab. majority   9,502
(June 1987, Lab. maj. 7,551)

BRAINTREE (Essex)
E.78,880   T.83.41%
*Rt. Hon. A. Newton, *C.*   34,415
I. Willmore, *Lab.*   16,921
Ms D. Wallis, *LD*   13,603
J. Abbott, *Green*   855
C. majority   17,494
(June 1987, C. maj. 16,857)

BRENT EAST (Greater London)
E.53,319   T.68.82%
*K. Livingstone, *Lab.*   19,387
D. Green, *C.*   13,416
M. Cummins, *LD*   3,249
Ms T. Dean, *Green*   548
Ms A. Murphy, *Comm. GB*   96
Lab. majority   5,971
(June 1987, Lab. maj. 1,653)

BRENT NORTH (Greater London)
E.58,917   T.70.57%
*Rt. Hon. Sir R. Boyson, *C.*   23,445
J. Moher, *Lab.*   13,314
P. Lorber, *LD*   4,149
T. Vipul, *Ind.*   356
T. Davids, *NLP*   318
C. majority   10,131
(June 1987, C. maj. 15,720)

BRENT SOUTH (Greater London)
E.56,034   T.64.10%
*P. Boateng, *Lab.*   20,662
R. Blackman, *C.*   10,957
M. Harskin, *LD*   3,658
D. Johnson, *Green*   479
C. Jani, *NLP*   166

Lab. majority   9,705
(June 1987, Lab. maj. 7,931)

BRENTFORD AND ISLEWORTH
(Greater London)
E.70,880   T.76.22%
N. Deva, *C.*   24,752
Ms A. Keen, *Lab.*   22,666
Ms J. Salmon, *LD*   5,683
J. Bradley, *Green*   927
C. majority   2,086
(June 1987, C. maj. 7,953)

BRENTWOOD AND ONGAR (Greater
London)
E.65,830   T.84.70%
E. Pickles, *C.*   32,145
Ms E. Bottomley, *LD*   17,000
F. Keohane, *Lab.*   6,080
Ms C. Bartley, *Green*   535
C. majority   15,145
(June 1987, C. maj. 18,921)

BRIDGWATER (Somerset)
E.71,567   T.79.51%
*Rt. Hon. T. King, *C.*   26,610
W. Revans, *Lab.*   16,894
P. James, *Lab.*   12,365
G. Dummett, *Green*   746
A. Body, *Ind.*   183
Ms G. Sanson, *NLP*   112
C. majority   9,716
(June 1987, C. maj. 11,195)

BRIDLINGTON (Humberside)
E.84,829   T.77.93%
*J. Townend, *C.*   33,604
J. Leeman, *LD*   17,246
S. Hatfield, *Lab.*   15,263
C. majority   16,358
(June 1987, C. maj. 17,321)

BRIGG AND CLEETHORPES
(Humberside)
E.82,377   T.77.98%
*M. Brown, *C.*   31,673
I. Cawsey, *Lab.*   22,404
Ms M. Cockbill, *LD*   9,374
N. Jacques, *Green*   790
C. majority   9,269
(June 1987, C. maj. 12,250)

BRIGHTON KEMPTOWN (E. Sussex)
E.57,646   T.76.14%
*A. Bowden, *C.*   21,129
Ms G. Haynes, *Lab.*   18,073
P. Scott, *LD*   4,461
Ms E. Overall, *NLP*   230
C. majority   3,056
(June 1987, C. maj. 9,260)

BRIGHTON PAVILION (E. Sussex)
E.57,616   T.76.81%
D. Spencer, *C.*   20,630
D. Lepper, *Lab.*   16,955
T. Pearce, *LD*   5,606
I. Brodie, *Green*   963
Ms E. Turner, *NLP*   103
C. majority   3,675
(June 1987, C. maj. 9,142)

BRISTOL EAST (Avon)
£62,577   T.80.40%
Ms J. Corston, *Lab.* 22,418
J. Sayeed, *C.* 19,726
J. Kiely, *LD* 7,903
J. Anderson, *NF* 270
Lab. majority 2,692
(June 1987, C. maj. 4,123)

BRISTOL NORTH WEST (Avon)
£72,726   T.82.35%
M. Stern, *C.* 25,354
D. Naysmith, *Lab.* 25,309
J. Taylor, *LD* 8,498
H. Long, *SD* 729
C. majority 45
(June 1987, C. maj. 6,952)

BRISTOL SOUTH (Avon)
£64,309   T.78.04%
Ms D. Primarolo, *Lab.* 25,164
J. Bercow, *C.* 16,245
P. Crossley, *LD* 7,892
J. Boxall, *Green* 756
N. Phillips, *NLP* 136
Lab. majority 8,919
(June 1987, Lab. maj. 1,404)

BRISTOL WEST (Avon)
£70,579   T.74.37%
Rt. Hon. W. Waldegrave, *C.* 22,169
C. Boney, *LD* 16,098
H. Bashforth, *Lab.* 12,992
A. Sawday, *Green* 906
D. Cross, *NLP* 104
B. Brent, *Rev. Comm.* 92
P. Hammond, *SOADDA* 87
T. Hedges, *Anti Fed.* 42
C. majority 6,071
(June 1987, C. maj. 7,703)

BROMSGROVE (H & W)
£71,111   T.82.49%
K. R. Thomason, *C.* 31,709
Ms C. Mole, *Lab.* 18,007
Ms A. Cassin, *LD* 8,090
J. Churchman, *Green* 856
C. majority 13,702
(June 1987, C. maj. 16,685)

BROXBOURNE (Herts)
£72,116   T.79.95%
Mrs M. Roe, *C.* 36,094
M. Hudson, *Lab.* 12,124
Mrs J. Davies, *LD* 9,244
G. Woolhouse, *NLP* 198
C. majority 23,970
(June 1987, C. maj. 22,995)

BROXTOWE (Notts)
£73,123   T.83.40%
J. Lester, *C.* 31,096
J. Walker, *Lab.* 21,205
J. Ross, *LD* 8,395
D. Lukehurst, *NLP* 293
C. majority 9,891
(June 1987, C. maj. 16,651)

BUCKINGHAM
£56,063   T.84.21%
G. Walden, *C.* 29,496
T. Jones, *LD* 9,705
K. White, *Lab.* 7,662

L. Sheaff, *NLP* 353
C. majority 19,791
(June 1987, C. maj. 18,526)

BURNLEY (Lancs)
£68,952   T.74.38%
*P. Pike, *Lab.* 27,184
Mrs B. Binge, *C.* 15,693
G. Birtwistle, *LD* 8,414
Lab. majority 11,491
(June 1987, Lab. maj. 7,557)

BURTON (Staffs)
£75,292   T.82.43%
*I. Lawrence, *C.* 30,845
Ms P. Muddyman, *Lab.* 24,849
R. Renold, *LD* 6,375
C. majority 5,996
(June 1987, C. maj. 9,830)

BURY NORTH (Greater Manchester)
£69,529   T.84.77%
*A. Burt, *C.* 29,266
J. Dobbin, *Lab.* 24,502
C. McGrath, *LD* 5,010
M. Sullivan, *NLP* 163
C. majority 4,764
(June 1987, C. maj. 6,929)

BURY SOUTH (Greater Manchester)
£65,793   T.82.10%
*D. Sumberg, *C.* 24,873
Ms H. Blears, *Lab.* 24,085
A. Cruden, *LD* 4,832
Mrs N. Sullivan, *NLP* 228
C. majority 788
(June 1987, C. maj. 2,679)

BURY ST EDMUNDS (Suffolk)
£79,967   T.78.38%
R. Spring, *C.* 33,554
T. Sheppard, *Lab.* 14,767
J. Williams, *LD* 13,814
Ms J. Lillis, *NLP* 550
C. majority 18,787
(June 1987, C. maj. 21,458)

CALDER VALLEY (W. Yorks)
£74,417   T.82.09%
*Sir D. Thompson, *C.* 27,753
D. Chaytor, *Lab.* 22,875
S. Pearson, *LD* 9,842
Ms V. Smith, *Green* 622
C. majority 4,878
(June 1987, C. maj. 6,045)

CAMBRIDGE
£69,022   T.73.18%
Mrs A. Campbell, *Lab.* 20,039
M. Bishop, *C.* 19,459
D. Howarth, *LD* 10,037
T. Cooper, *Green* 720
D. Brettell-Winnington, *Loony* 175
R. Chalmers, *NLP* 83
Lab. majority 580
(June 1987, C. maj. 5,060)

CAMBRIDGESHIRE NORTH EAST
£79,935   T.79.38%
*M. Moss, *C.* 34,288
M. Leeke, *LD* 19,195
R. Harris, *Lab.* 8,746
C. Ash, *Lib.* 998
Mrs M. Chalmers, *NLP* 227

C. majority 15,093
(June 1987, C. maj. 1,428)

CAMBRIDGESHIRE SOUTH EAST
£78,600   T.80.57%
*J. Paice, *C.* 36,693
R. Wotherspoon, *LD* 12,883
M. Jones, *Lab.* 12,688
J. Marsh, *Green* 836
Ms B. Langridge, *NLP* 231
C. majority 23,810
(June 1987, C. maj. 17,502)

CAMBRIDGESHIRE SOUTH WEST
£84,418   T.81.10%
*Sir A. Grant, *C.* 38,902
Ms S. Sutton, *LD* 19,265
K. Price, *Lab.* 9,378
Ms L. Whitebread, *Green* 699
F. Chalmers, *NLP* 225
C. majority 19,637
(June 1987, C. maj. 18,251)

CANNOCK AND BURNTWOOD
(Staffs)
£72,600   T.84.21%
A. Wright, *Lab.* 28,139
*G. Howarth, *C.* 26,633
P. Treasaden, *LD* 5,899
M. Hartshorne, *Loony* 469
Lab. majority 1,506
(June 1987, C. maj. 2,689)

CANTERBURY (Kent)
£75,181   T.78.12%
*J. Brazier, *C.* 29,827
M. Vye, *LD* 19,022
M. Whitemore, *Lab.* 8,936
Ms W. Arnall, *Green* 747
Ms S. Curphey, *NLP* 203
C. majority 10,805
(June 1987, C. maj. 14,891)

CARLISLE (Cumbria)
£55,140   T.79.39%
*E. Martlew, *Lab.* 20,479
C. Condie, *C.* 17,371
R. Aldersey, *LD* 5,740
Ms N. Robinson, *NLP* 190
Lab. majority 3,108
(June 1987, Lab. maj. 916)

CARSHALTON AND WALLINGTON
(Surrey)
£65,179   T.80.94%
*F. N. Forman, *C.* 26,243
T. Brake, *LD* 16,300
Ms M. Moran, *Lab.* 9,333
R. Steel, *Green* 614
D. Bamford, *Loony G.* 266
C. majority 9,943
(June 1987, C. maj. 14,409)

CASTLE POINT (Essex)
£66,229   T.80.50%
Dr R. Spink, *C.* 29,629
D. Flack, *Lab.* 12,799
A. Petchey, *LD* 10,208
Ms I. Willis, *Green* 683
C. majority 16,830
(June 1987, C. maj. 19,248)

CHEADLE (Greater Manchester)
E.66,131   T.84.43%

*S. Day, C.	32,504
Ms P. Calton, LD	16,726
Ms S. Broadhurst, Lab.	6,442
Ms P. Whittle, NLP	168
C. majority	15,778

(June 1987, C. maj. 10,631)

CHELMSFORD (Essex)
E.83,441   T.84.61%

*S. Burns, C.	39,043
H. Nicholson, LD	20,783
Dr R. Chad, Lab.	10,010
Ms E. Burgess, Green	769
C. majority	18,260

(June 1987, C. maj. 7,761)

CHELSEA (Greater London)
E.42,371   T.63.31%

*Rt. Hon. N. Scott, C.	17,471
Ms R. Horton, Lab.	4,682
Ms S. Broidy, LD	4,101
Ms N. Kortvelyessy, Green	485
D. Armstrong, Anti Fed.	88
C. majority	12,789

(June 1987, C. maj. 13,319)

CHELTENHAM (Glos)
E.79,808   T.80.32%

N. Jones, LD	30,351
J. Taylor, C.	28,683
Ms P. Tatlow, Lab.	4,077
M. Rendall, AFE	665
H. Brighouse, NLP	169
M. Bruce-Smith, Ind.	162
LD majority	1,668

(June 1987, C. maj. 4,896)

CHERTSEY AND WALTON (Surrey)
E.70,465   T.80.52%

*Rt. Hon. Sir G. Pattie, C.	34,163
A. Kremer, LD	11,344
Ms I. Hamilton, Lab.	10,791
Ms S. Bennell, NLP	444
C. majority	22,819

(June 1987, C. maj. 17,469)

CHESHAM AND AMERSHAM (Bucks)
E.69,895   T.81.93%

Ms C. Gillan, C.	36,273
A. Ketteringham, LD	14,053
Ms C. Atherton, Lab.	5,931
Ms C. Strickland, Green	753
T. Griffith-Jones, NLP	255
C. majority	22,220

(June 1987, C. maj. 19,440)

CHESTER, CITY OF
E.63,370   T.83.84%

G. Brandreth, C.	23,411
D. Robinson, Lab.	22,310
G. Smith, LD	6,867
T. Barker, Green	448
S. Cross, NLP	98
C. majority	1,101

(June 1987, C. maj. 4,855)

CHESTERFIELD (Derbys)
E.71,783   T.77.98%

*A. Benn, Lab.	26,461
A. Rogers, LD	20,047
P. Lewis, C.	9,473

Lab. majority	6,414

(June 1987, Lab. maj. 8,577)

CHICHESTER (W. Sussex)
E.82,124   T.77.77%

*R. A. Nelson, C.	37,906
P. Gardiner, LD	17,019
Ms D. Andrewes, Lab.	7,192
E. Paine, Green	876
Ms J. Weights, Lib.	643
Ms J. Jackson, NLP	238
C. majority	20,887

(June 1987, C. maj. 20,177)

CHINGFORD (Greater London)
E.55,401   T.78.41%

G. I. Duncan-Smith, C.	25,730
P. Dawe, Lab.	10,792
S. Banks, LD	5,705
D. Green, Lib.	602
J. Baguley, Green	575
Revd C. John, Ind.	41
C. majority	14,938

(June 1987, C. maj. 17,955)

CHIPPING BARNET (Greater London)
E.57,153   T.78.57%

*S. Chapman, C.	25,589
A. Williams, Lab.	11,638
D. Smith, LD	7,247
Ms D. Derksen, NLP	222
C. Johnson, Fun.	213
C. majority	13,951

(June 1987, C. maj. 14,871)

CHISLEHURST (Greater London)
E.53,782   T.78.89%

*R. Sims, C.	24,761
I. Wingfield, Lab.	9,485
W. Hawthorne, LD	6,683
I. Richmond, Lib.	849
Dr F. Speed, Green	652
C. majority	15,276

(June 1987, C. maj. 14,507)

CHORLEY (Lancs)
E.78,531   T.82.81%

*D. Dover, C.	30,715
R. McManus, Lab.	26,469
Ms J. Ross-Mills, LD	7,452
P. Leadbetter, NLP	402
C. majority	4,246

(June 1987, C. maj. 8,057)

CHRISTCHURCH (Dorset)
E.71,438   T.80.70%

*R. Adley, C.	36,627
Revd D. Bussey, LD	13,612
A. Lloyd, Lab.	6,997
J. Barratt, NLP	243
A. Wareham, CRA	175
C. majority	23,015

(June 1987, C. maj. 22,374)
See also page 234

CIRENCESTER AND TEWKESBURY (Glos)
E.88,299   T.82.05%

G. Clifton-Brown, C.	40,258
E. Weston, LD	24,200
T. Page, Lab.	7,262
R. Clayton, NLP	449

P. Trice-Rolph, Ind.	287
C. majority	16,058

(June 1987, C. maj. 12,662)

CITY OF LONDON AND WESTMINSTER SOUTH
E.55,021   T.63.08%

*Rt. Hon. P. Brooke, C.	20,938
C. Smith, Lab.	7,569
Ms J. Smithard, LD	5,392
G. Herbert, Green	458
P. Stockton, Loony	147
A. Farrell, IFM	107
R. Johnson, NLP	101
C. majority	13,369

(June 1987, C. maj. 12,034)

COLCHESTER NORTH (Essex)
E.86,479   T.79.11%

Hon. B. Jenkin, C.	35,213
Dr J. Raven, LD	18,721
D. Lee, Lab.	13,870
M. Tariq Shabbeer, Green	372
M. Mears, NLP	238
C. majority	16,492

(June 1987, C. maj. 13,623)

COLCHESTER SOUTH AND MALDON (Essex)
E.86,410   T.79.22%

J. Whittingdale, C.	37,548
I. Thorn, LD	15,727
C. Pearson, Lab.	14,158
M. Patterson, Green	1,028
C. majority	21,821

(June 1987, C. maj. 15,483)

COLNE VALLEY (W. Yorks)
E.72,043   T.81.97%

*G. Riddick, C.	24,804
J. Harman, Lab.	17,579
N. Priestley, LD	15,953
R. Stewart, Green	443
Mrs M. Staniforth, Loony	160
J. Hasty, Ind.	73
J. Tattersall, NLP	44
C. majority	7,225

(June 1987, C. maj. 1,677)

CONGLETON (Cheshire)
E.70,477   T.84.47%

*Mrs J. A. Winterton, C.	29,163
I. Brodie-Browne, LD	18,043
M. Finnegan, Lab.	11,927
P. Brown, NLP	399
C. majority	11,120

(June 1987, C. maj. 7,969)

COPELAND (Cumbria)
E.54,911   T.83.54%

*Dr J. Cunningham, Lab.	22,328
P. Davies, C.	19,889
R. Putnam, LD	3,508
J. Sinton, NLP	148
Lab. majority	2,439

(June 1987, Lab. maj. 1,894)

CORBY (Northants)
E.68,333   T.82.88%

*W. Powell, C.	25,203
A. Feather, Lab.	24,861
M. Roffe, LD	5,792
Ms J. Wood, Lib.	784

C. majority   342
(June 1987, C. maj. 1,805)

CORNWALL NORTH
E.76,844   T.81.51%
P. Tyler, LD   29,696
*Sir G. Neale, C.   27,775
F. Jordan, Lab.   4,103
P. Andrews, Lib.   678
G. Rowe, Ind.   276
Mrs H. Treadwell, NLP   112
LD majority   1,921
(June 1987, C. maj. 5,682)

CORNWALL SOUTH EAST
E.73,027   T.82.14%
*R. Hicks, C.   30,565
R. Teverson, LD   22,861
Mrs L. Gilroy, Lab.   5,536
Miss M. Cook, Lib.   644
A. Quick, Anti Fed.   227
Miss R. Allen, NLP   155
C. majority   7,704
(June 1987, C. maj. 6,607)

COVENTRY NORTH EAST
(W. Midlands)
E.64,787   T.73.20%
R. Ainsworth, Lab.   24,896
K. Perrin, C.   13,220
V. McKee, LD   5,306
*J. Hughes, Ind. Lab.   4,008
Lab. majority   11,676
(June 1987, Lab. maj. 11,867)

COVENTRY NORTH WEST
(W. Midlands)
E.50,670   T.77.63%
*G. Robinson, Lab.   20,349
Mrs A. Hill, C.   13,917
Ms A. Simpson, LD   5,070
Lab. majority   6,432
(June 1987, Lab. maj. 5,663)

COVENTRY SOUTH EAST
(W. Midlands)
E.48,796   T.74.87%
J. Cunningham, Lab.   11,902
Mrs M. Hyams, C.   10,591
*D. Nellist, Ind. Lab.   10,551
A. Armstrong, LD   3,318
N. Tompkinson, NF   173
Lab. majority   1,311
(June 1987, Lab. maj. 6,653)

COVENTRY SOUTH WEST
(W. Midlands)
E.63,474   T.80.14%
*J. Butcher, C.   23,225
R. Slater, Lab.   21,789
G. Sewards, LD   4,666
R. Wheway, Lib.   989
D. Morris, NLP   204
C. majority   1,436
(June 1987, C. maj. 3,210)

CRAWLEY (W. Sussex)
E.78,277   T.79.16%
*Hon. A. N. Soames, C.   30,204
Ms L. Moffatt, Lab.   22,439
G. Seekings, LD   8,558
M. Wilson, Green   766

C. majority   7,765
(June 1987, C. maj. 12,138)

CREWE AND NANTWICH (Cheshire)
E.74,993   T.81.87%
*Hon. Mrs G. Dunwoody, Lab.
65
B. Silvester, C.   25,370
G. Griffiths, LD   7,315
Ms N. Wilkinson, Green   651
Lab. majority   2,695
(June 1987, Lab. maj. 1,092)

CROSBY (Merseyside)
E.82,537   T.82.45%
*M. Thornton, C.   32,267
Ms M. Eagle, Lab.   17,461
Ms F. Clucas, LD   16,562
J. Marks, Lib.   1,052
S. Brady, Green   559
N. Paterson, NLP   152
C. majority   14,806
(June 1987, C. maj. 6,853)

CROYDON CENTRAL (Greater
London)
E.55,798   T.71.73%
Sir P. Beresford, C.   22,168
G. Davies, Lab.   12,518
Ms D. Richardson, LD   5,342
C. majority   9,650
(June 1987, C. maj. 12,617)

CROYDON NORTH EAST (Greater
London)
E.64,405   T.72.01%
D. Congdon, C.   23,835
Ms M. Walker, Lab.   16,362
J. Fraser, LD   6,186
C. majority   7,473
(June 1987, C. maj. 12,519)

CROYDON NORTH WEST (Greater
London)
E.57,241   T.70.76%
M. Wicks, Lab.   19,152
*H. Malins, C.   17,626
Ms L. Hawkins, LD   3,728
Lab. majority   1,526
(June 1987, C. maj. 3,988)

CROYDON SOUTH (Greater London)
E.64,768   T.77.57%
R. Ottaway, C.   31,993
P. Billenness, LD   11,568
Miss H. Salmon, Lab.   6,444
M. Samuel, Choice   239
C. majority   20,425
(June 1987, C. maj. 19,063)

DAGENHAM (Greater London)
E.59,645   T.70.65%
*B. Gould, Lab.   22,027
D. Rossiter, C.   15,294
C. Marquand, LD   4,824
Lab. majority   6,733
(June 1987, Lab. maj. 2,469)
See also page 234

DARLINGTON (Durham)
E.66,094   T.83.60%
A. Milburn, Lab.   26,556
*M. Fallon, C.   23,758
P. Bergg, LD   4,586

Dr D. Clarke, BNP   355
Lab. majority   2,798
(June 1987, C. maj. 2,661)

DARTFORD (Kent)
E.72,366   T.83.14%
*B. Dunn, C.   31,194
Dr H. Stoate, Lab.   20,880
Dr P. Bryden, LD   7,584
A. Munro, FDP   262
Ms A. Holland, NLP   247
C. majority   10,314
(June 1987, C. maj. 14,929)

DAVENTRY (Northants)
E.71,824   T.82.75%
*T. Boswell, C.   34,734
Ms L. Koumi, Lab.   14,460
A. Rounthwaite, LD   9,820
R. France, NLP   422
C. majority   20,274
(June 1987, C. maj. 19,690)

DAVYHULME (Greater Manchester)
E.61,679   T.81.82%
*W. Churchill, C.   24,216
B. Brotherton, Lab.   19,790
Ms J. Pearcey, LD   5,797
T. Brotheridge, NLP   665
C. majority   4,426
(June 1987, C. maj. 8,199)

DENTON AND REDDISH (Greater
Manchester)
E.68,463   T.76.77%
*A. Bennett, Lab.   29,021
J. Horswell, C.   16,937
Dr F. Ridley, LD   4,953
M. Powell, Lib.   1,296
J. Fuller, NLP   354
Lab. majority   12,084
(June 1987, Lab. maj. 8,250)

DERBY NORTH
E.73,176   T.80.65%
*G. Knight, C.   28,574
R. Laxton, Lab.   24,121
R. Charlesworth, LD   5,638
E. Wall, Green   383
P. Hart, NF   245
N. Onley, NLP   58
C. majority   4,453
(June 1987, C. maj. 6,280)

DERBY SOUTH
E.66,328   T.75.52%
*Mrs M. Beckett, Lab.   25,917
N. Brown, C.   18,981
S. Hartropp, LD   5,198
Lab. majority   6,936
(June 1987, Lab. maj. 1,516)

DERBYSHIRE NORTH EAST
E.70,707   T.83.61%
*H. Barnes, Lab.   28,860
J. Hayes, C.   22,590
D. Stone, LD   7,675
Lab. majority   6,270
(June 1987, Lab. maj. 3,720)

DERBYSHIRE SOUTH
E.82,342   T.85.49%
*Mrs E. Currie, C.   34,266
M. Todd, Lab.   29,608

Ms D. Brass, *LD*   6,236
T. Mercer, *NLP*   291
C. majority   4,658
(June 1987, C. maj. 10,311)

DERBYSHIRE WEST
*E.*71,201   *T.*84.99%
*P. McLoughlin, *C.*   32,879
R. Fearn, *LD*   14,110
S. Clamp, *Lab.*   13,528
C. majority   18,769
(June 1987, C. maj. 10,527)

DEVIZES (Wilts)
*E.*89,745   *T.*81.67%
M. Ancram, *C.*   39,090
Ms J. Mactaggart, *LD*   19,378
Ms R. Berry, *Lab.*   13,060
S. Coles, *Lib.*   962
D. Ripley, *Green*   808
C. majority   19,712
(June 1987, C. maj. 17,830)

DEVON NORTH
*E.*68,998   *T.*84.36%
N. Harvey, *LD*   27,414
*A. Speller, *C.*   26,620
P. Donner, *Lab.*   3,410
Ms C. Simmons, *Green*   658
G. Treadwell, *NLP*   107
LD majority   794
(June 1987, C. maj. 4,469)

DEVON WEST AND TORRIDGE
*E.*76,933   *T.*81.46%
*Miss E. Nicholson, *C.*   29,627
D. McBride, *LD*   26,013
D. Brenton, *Lab.*   5,997
Dr F. Williamson, *Green*   898
D. Collins, *NLP*   141
C. majority   3,614
(June 1987, C. maj. 6,468)

DEWSBURY (W. Yorks)
*E.*72,839   *T.*80.18%
*Mrs W. A. Taylor, *Lab.*   25,596
J. Whitfield, *C.*   24,962
R. Meadowcroft, *LD*   6,570
Lady J. Birdwood, *BNP*   660
N. Denby, *Green*   471
Mrs J. Marsden, *NLP*   146
Lab. majority   634
(June 1987, Lab. maj. 445)

DONCASTER CENTRAL (S. Yorks)
*E.*68,890   *T.*74.24%
*Rt. Hon. H. Walker, *Lab.*   27,795
W. Glossop, *C.*   17,113
C. Hampson, *LD*   6,057
M. Driver, *WRP*   184
Lab. majority   10,682
(June 1987, Lab. maj. 8,196)

DONCASTER NORTH (S. Yorks)
*E.*74,732   *T.*73.92%
K. Hughes, *Lab.*   34,135
R. Light, *C.*   14,322
S. Whiting, *LD*   6,787
Lab. majority   19,813
(June 1987, Lab. maj. 19,938)

DON VALLEY (S. Yorks)
*E.*76,327   *T.*76.25%
*M. Redmond, *Lab.*   32,008

N. Paget-Brown, *C.*   18,474
M. Jevons, *LD*   6,920
S. Platt, *Green*   803
Lab. majority   13,534
(June 1987, Lab. maj. 11,467)

DORSET NORTH
*E.*76,718   *T.*81.79%
*N. Baker, *C.*   34,234
Ms L. Siegle, *LD*   24,154
J. Fitzmaurice, *Lab.*   4,360
C. majority   10,080
(June 1987, C. maj. 11,907)

DORSET SOUTH
*E.*75,788   *T.*76.91%
*I. Bruce, *C.*   29,319
B. Ellis, *LD*   15,811
Dr A. Chedzoy, *Lab.*   12,298
Mrs J. Nager, *Ind.*   673
M. Griffiths, *NLP*   191
C. majority   13,508
(June 1987, C. maj. 15,067)

DORSET WEST
*E.*67,256   *T.*81.18%
*Sir J. Spicer, *C.*   27,766
R. Legg, *LD*   19,756
J. Mann, *Lab.*   7,082
C. majority   8,010
(June 1987, C. maj. 12,364)

DOVER (Kent)
*E.*68,962   *T.*83.50%
*D. Shaw, *C.*   25,395
G. Prosser, *Lab.*   24,562
M. Sole, *LD*   6,212
A. Sullivan, *Green*   637
P. Sherred, *Ind.*   407
B. Philp, *Ind. C.*   250
C. Percy, *NLP*   127
C. majority   833
(June 1987, C. maj. 6,541)

DUDLEY EAST (W. Midlands)
*E.*75,355   *T.*74.96%
*Dr J. Gilbert, *Lab.*   29,806
J. Holland, *C.*   20,606
I. Jenkins, *LD*   5,400
G. Cartwright, *NF*   675
Lab. majority   9,200
(June 1987, Lab. maj. 3,473)

DUDLEY WEST (W. Midlands)
*E.*86,632   *T.*82.08%
*J. Blackburn, *C.*   34,729
K. Lomax, *Lab.*   28,940
G. Lewis, *LD*   7,446
C. majority   5,789
(June 1987, C. maj. 10,244)
See also page 234

DULWICH (Greater London)
*E.*55,141   *T.*67.91%
Ms T. Jowell, *Lab.*   17,714
*G. Bowden, *C.*   15,658
Dr A. Goldie, *LD*   4,078
Lab. majority   2,056
(June 1987, C. maj. 180)

DURHAM, CITY OF
*E.*68,165   *T.*74.61%
*G. Steinberg, *Lab.*   27,095
M. Woodroofe, *C.*   12,037

N. Martin, *LD*   10,915
Ms S. J. Banks, *Green*   812
Lab. majority   15,058
(June 1987, Lab. maj. 6,125)

DURHAM NORTH
*E.*73,694   *T.*76.08%
*G. Radice, *Lab.*   33,567
Ms E. Sibley, *C.*   13,930
P. Appleby, *LD*   8,572
Lab. majority   19,637
(June 1987, Lab. maj. 18,433)

DURHAM NORTH WEST
*E.*61,139   *T.*75.58%
*Miss H. Armstrong, *Lab.*   26,734
Mrs T. May, *C.*   12,747
T. Farron, *LD*   6,728
Lab. majority   13,987
(June 1987, Lab. maj. 10,162)

EALING ACTON (Greater London)
*E.*58,687   *T.*76.03%
*Sir G. Young, *C.*   22,579
Ms Y. Johnson, *Lab.*   15,572
L. Rowe, *LD*   5,487
Ms A. Seibe, *Green*   554
T. Pitt-Aikens, *Ind. C.*   432
C. majority   7,007
(June 1987, C. maj. 12,233)

EALING NORTH (Greater London)
*E.*63,528   *T.*78.84%
*H. Greenway, *C.*   24,898
M. Stears, *Lab.*   18,932
P. Hankinson, *LD*   5,247
D. Earl, *Green*   554
C. Hill, *NF*   277
R. Davis, *CD*   180
C. majority   5,966
(June 1987, C. maj. 15,153)

EALING SOUTHALL (Greater
London)
*E.*65,574   *T.*75.49%
P. Khabra, *Lab.*   23,476
P. Treleaven, *C.*   16,610
*S. Bidwell, *True Lab.*   4,665
Ms P. Nandhra, *LD*   3,790
N. Goodwin, *Green*   964
Lab. majority   6,866
(June 1987, Lab. maj. 7,977)

EASINGTON (Durham)
*E.*65,061   *T.*72.46%
*J. Cummings, *Lab.*   34,269
W. Perry, *C.*   7,879
P. Freitag, *LD*   5,001
Lab. majority   26,390
(June 1987, Lab. maj. 24,639)

EASTBOURNE (E. Sussex)
*E.*76,103   *T.*80.97%
N. Waterson, *C.*   31,792
*D. Bellotti, *LD*   26,311
I. Gibbons, *Lab.*   2,834
D. Aherne, *Green*   391
Ms T. Williamson, *Lib.*   296
C. majority   5,481
(June 1987, C. maj 16,923)
(October 1990, LD maj. 4,550)

EASTLEIGH (Hants)
£91,736   T.82.91%
S. Milligan, *C.*   38,998
D. Chidgey, *LD*   21,296
Ms J. Sugrue, *Lab.*   15,768
C. majority   17,702
(June 1987, C. maj. 13,355)
See also page 234

ECCLES (Greater Manchester)
£64,910   T.74.12%
*Miss J. Lestor, *Lab.*   27,357
G. Ling, *C.*   14,131
G. Reid, *LD*   5,835
R. Duriez, *Green*   521
Miss J. Garner, *NLP*   270
Lab. majority   13,226
(June 1987, Lab. maj. 9,699)

EDDISBURY (Cheshire)
£75,089   T.82.55%
*A. Goodlad, *C.*   31,625
Ms N. Edwards, *Lab.*   18,928
D. Lyon, *LD*   10,543
A. Basden, *Green*   783
N. Pollard, *NLP*   107
C. majority   12,697
(June 1987, C. maj. 15,835)

EDMONTON (Greater London)
£63,052   T.75.66%
*Dr I. Twinn, *C.*   22,076
A. Love, *Lab.*   21,483
E. Jones, *LD*   3,940
Ms E. Solley, *NLP*   207
C. majority   593
(June 1987, C. maj. 7,286)

ELLESMERE PORT AND NESTON
(Cheshire)
£71,572   T.84.12%
A. Miller, *Lab.*   27,782
A. Pearce, *C.*   25,793
Ms E. Jewkes, *LD*   5,944
Dr M. Money, *Green*   589
Dr A. Rae, *NLP*   105
Lab. majority   1,989
(June 1987, C. maj. 1,853)

ELMET (W. Yorks)
£70,558   T.82.53%
*S. Batiste, *C.*   27,677
C. Burgon, *Lab.*   24,416
Mrs A. Beck, *LD*   6,144
C. majority   3,261
(June 1987, C. maj. 5,356)

ELTHAM (Greater London)
£51,989   T.78.72%
*P. Bottomley, *C.*   18,813
C. Efford, *Lab.*   17,147
C. McGinty, *LD*   4,804
A. Graham, *Ind. C.*   165
C. majority   1,666
(June 1987, C. maj. 6,460)

ENFIELD NORTH (Greater London)
£67,421   T.77.91%
*T. Eggar, *C.*   27,789
M. Upham, *Lab.*   18,359
Ms S. Tustin, *LD*   5,817
J. Markham, *NLP*   565

C. majority   9,430
(June 1987, C. maj. 14,015)

ENFIELD SOUTHGATE (Greater
London)
£64,311   T.76.28%
*M. Portillo, *C.*   28,422
Ms K. Livney, *Lab.*   12,859
K. Keane, *LD*   7,080
Ms M. Hollands, *Green*   696
C. majority   15,563
(June 1987, C. maj. 18,345)

EPPING FOREST (Essex)
£67,585   T.80.55%
*S. Norris, *C.*   32,407
S. Murray, *Lab.*   12,219
Mrs B. Austen, *LD*   9,265
A. O'Brien, *EFRA*   552
C. majority   20,188
(June 1987, C. maj. 21,513)
(December 1988, C. maj. 4,504)

EPSOM AND EWELL (Surrey)
£68,138   T.80.14%
*Rt. Hon. A. Hamilton, *C.*   32,861
M. Emerson, *LD*   12,840
R. Warren, *Lab.*   8,577
G. Hatchard, *NLP*   334
C. majority   20,021
(June 1987, C. maj. 20,761)

EREWASH (Derbys)
£75,627   T.83.78%
Mrs A. Knight, *C.*   29,907
S. Stafford, *Lab.*   24,204
P. Tuck, *LD*   8,606
L. Johnson, *BNP*   645
C. majority   5,703
(June 1987, C. maj. 9,754)

ERITH AND CRAYFORD (Kent)
£59,213   T.79.66%
*D. Evennett, *C.*   21,926
N. Beard, *Lab.*   19,587
Ms F. Jamieson, *LD*   5,657
C. majority   2,339
(June 1987, C. maj. 6,994)

ESHER (Surrey)
£58,840   T.80.80%
*I. Taylor, *C.*   31,115
J. Richling, *LD*   10,744
Ms J. Reay, *Lab.*   5,685
C. majority   20,371
(June 1987, C. maj. 19,068)

EXETER (Devon)
£76,723   T.82.21%
*Sir J. Hannam, *C.*   26,543
J. Lloyd, *Lab.*   22,498
G. Oakes, *LD*   12,059
Ms A. Micklem, *Lib.*   1,119
T. Brenan, *Green*   764
M. Turnbull, *NLP*   98
C. majority   4,045
(June 1987, C. maj. 7,656)

FALMOUTH AND CAMBORNE
(Cornwall)
£70,702   T.81.10%
S. Coe, *C.*   21,150
Ms T. Jones, *LD*   17,883
J. Cosgrove, *Lab.*   16,732

P. Holmes, *Lib.*   730
K. Saunders, *Green*   466
F. Zapp, *Loony*   327
A. Pringle, *NLP*   56
C. majority   3,267
(June 1987, C. maj. 5,039)

FAREHAM (Hants)
£81,124   T.81.85%
*P. Lloyd, *C.*   40,482
J. Thompson, *LD*   16,341
Ms E. Weston, *Lab.*   8,766
M. Brimecome, *Green*   818
C. majority   24,141
(June 1987, C. maj. 18,795)

FAVERSHAM (Kent)
£81,977   T.79.71%
*R. Moate, *C.*   32,755
Ms H. Brinton, *Lab.*   16,404
R. Truelove, *LD*   15,896
R. Bradshaw, *NLP*   294
C. majority   16,351
(June 1987, C. maj. 13,978)

FELTHAM AND HESTON (Greater
London)
£81,221   T.73.90%
A. Keen, *Lab.*   27,660
*P. Ground, *C.*   25,665
M. Hoban, *LD*   6,700
Lab. majority   1,995
(June 1987, C. maj. 5,430)

FINCHLEY (Greater London)
£52,907   T.77.64%
H. Booth, *C.*   21,039
Ms A. Marjoram, *Lab.*   14,651
Ms H. Leighter, *LD*   4,568
A. Gunstock, *Green*   564
Ms S. Johnson, *Loony*   130
J. Macrae, *NLP*   129
C. majority   6,388
(June 1987, C. maj. 8,913)

FOLKESTONE AND HYTHE (Kent)
£65,856   T.79.61%
*Rt. Hon. M. Howard, *C.*   27,437
Mrs L. Cufley, *LD*   18,527
P. Doherty, *Lab.*   6,347
A. Hobbs, *NLP*   123
C. majority   8,910
(June 1987, C. maj. 9,126)

FULHAM (Greater London)
£52,740   T.76.16%
*M. Carrington, *C.*   21,438
N. Moore, *Lab.*   14,859
P. Crystal, *LD*   3,339
Ms E. Streeter, *Green*   443
J. Darby, *NLP*   91
C. majority   6,579
(June 1987, C. maj. 6,322)

FYLDE (Lancs)
£63,573   T.78.50%
*M. Jack, *C.*   30,639
N. Cryer, *LD*   9,648
Ms C. Hughes, *Lab.*   9,382
P. Leadbetter, *NLP*   239
C. majority   20,991
(June 1987, C. maj. 17,772)

GAINSBOROUGH AND HORNCASTLE (Lincs)
E.72,038   T.80.87%

*E. Leigh, C.	31,444
N. Taylor, LD	15,199
Ms F. Jones, Lab.	11,619
C. majority	16,245

(June 1987, C. maj. 9,723)

GATESHEAD EAST (Tyne & Wear)
E.64,355   T.73.63%

*Miss J. Quin, Lab.	30,100
M. Callanan, C.	11,570
R. Beadle, LD	5,720
Lab. majority	18,530

(June 1987, Lab. maj. 17,228)

GEDLING (Notts)
E.68,953   T.82.34%

*A. J. B. Mitchell, C.	30,191
V. Coaker, Lab.	19,554
D. George, LD	6,863
Ms A. Miszeweka, NLP	168
C. majority	10,637

(June 1987, C. maj. 16,539)

GILLINGHAM (Kent)
E.71,851   T.80.32%

*J. Couchman, C.	30,201
P. Clark, Lab.	13,563
M. Wallbank, LD	13,509
C. MacKinlay, Ind.	248
D. Jolicoeur, NLP	190
C. majority	16,638

(June 1987, C. maj. 12,549)

GLANFORD AND SCUNTHORPE (Humberside)
E.73,479   T.78.91%

*E. Morley, Lab.	30,623
Dr A. Saywood, C.	22,211
W. Paxton, LD	4,172
C. Nottingham, SD	982
Lab. majority	8,412

(June 1987, Lab. maj. 512)

GLOUCESTER
E.80,578   T.80.24%

*D. French, C.	29,870
K. Stephens, Lab.	23,812
J. Sewell, LD	10,978
C. majority	6,058

(June 1987, C. maj. 12,035)

GLOUCESTERSHIRE WEST
E.80,007   T.83.89%

*P. Marland, C.	29,232
Ms D. Organ, Lab.	24,274
L. Boait, LD	13,366
A. Reeve, Brit. Ind.	172
C. Palmer, Century	75
C. majority	4,958

(June 1987, C. maj. 11,679)

GOSPORT (Hants)
E.69,638   T.76.79%

*P. Viggers, C.	31,094
M. Russell, LD	14,776
Ms M. Angus, Lab.	7,275
P. Ettie, Pensioners	332
C. majority	16,318

(June 1987, C. maj. 13,723)

GRANTHAM (Lincs)
E.83,463   T.79.29%

*Hon. D. Hogg, C.	37,194
S. Taggart, Lab.	17,606
J. Heppell, LD	9,882
J. Hiley, Lib.	1,500
C. majority	19,588

(June 1987, C. maj. 21,303)

GRAVESHAM (Kent)
E.70,740   T.83.48%

*J. Arnold, C.	29,322
G. Green, Lab.	23,829
D. Deedman, LD	5,269
A. Bunstone, Ind.	273
R. Khilkoff-Boulding, ILP	187
B. Buxton, Soc.	174
C. majority	5,493

(June 1987, C. maj. 8,792)

GREAT GRIMSBY (Humberside)
E.67,427   T.75.28%

*A. V. Mitchell, Lab.	25,895
P. Jackson, C.	18,391
Ms P. Frankish, LD	6,475
Lab. majority	7,504

(June 1987, Lab. maj. 8,784)

GREAT YARMOUTH (Norfolk)
E.68,263   T.77.94%

*M. Carttiss, C.	25,505
Ms B. Baughan, Lab.	20,196
M. Scott, LD	7,225
Ms P. Larkin, NLP	284
C. majority	5,309

(June 1987, C. maj. 10,083)

GREENWICH (Greater London)
E.47,789   T.74.63%

W. R. N. Raynsford, Lab.	14,630
*Mrs R. Barnes, SD	13,273
Mrs A. McNair, C.	6,960
R. McCracken, Green	483
R. Mallone, Fellowship	147
M. Hardee, UTCHAP	103
J. Small, NLP	70
Lab. majority	1,357

(June 1987, SDP/All. maj. 2,141)

GUILDFORD (Surrey)
E.77,265   T.78.48%

*Rt. Hon. D. Howell, C.	33,516
Mrs M. Sharp, LD	20,112
H. Mann, Lab.	6,781
A. Law, NLP	234
C. majority	13,404

(June 1987, C. maj. 12,607)

HACKNEY NORTH AND STOKE NEWINGTON (Greater London)
E.54,655   T.63.53%

*Ms D. Abbott, Lab.	20,083
C. Manson, C.	9,356
K. Fitchett, LD	3,996
Ms H. Hunt, Green	1,111
J. Windsor, NLP	178
Lab. majority	10,727

(June 1987, Lab. maj. 7,678)

HACKNEY SOUTH AND SHOREDITCH (Greater London)
E.57,935   T.63.82%

*B. Sedgemore, Lab.	19,730
A. Turner, C.	10,714
G. Wintle, LD	5,533
L. Lucas, Green	772
Ms G. Norman, NLP	226
Lab. majority	9,016

(June 1987, Lab. maj. 7,522)

HALESOWEN AND STOURBRIDGE (W. Midlands)
E.77,644   T.82.28%

P. W. Hawksley, C.	32,312
A. Hankon, Lab.	22,730
V. Sharma, LD	7,941
T. Weller, Green	908
C. majority	9,582

(June 1987, C. maj. 13,808)

HALIFAX (W. Yorks)
E.73,401   T.78.69%

*Ms A. Mahon, Lab.	25,115
T. Martin, C.	24,637
I. Howell, LD	7,364
R. Pearson, Nat.	649
Lab. majority	478

(June 1987, Lab. maj. 1,212)

HALTON (Cheshire)
E.74,906   T.78.34%

*Rt. Hon. G. Oakes, Lab.	35,025
G. Mercer, C.	16,821
D. Reaper, LD	6,104
S. Herley, Loony	398
N. Collins, NLP	338
Lab. majority	18,204

(June 1987, Lab. maj. 14,578)

HAMMERSMITH (Greater London)
E.47,229   T.71.90%

*C. Soley, Lab.	17,329
A. Hennessy, C.	12,575
J. Bates, LD	3,380
R. Crosskey, Green	546
K. Turner, NLP	89
Ms H. Szamuely, Anti Fed.	41
Lab. majority	4,754

(June 1987, Lab. maj. 2,415)

HAMPSHIRE EAST
E.92,139   T.80.35%

*M. Mates, C.	47,541
Ms S. Baring, LD	18,376
J. Phillips, Lab.	6,840
I. Foster, Green	1,113
S. Hale, RCC	165
C. majority	29,165

(June 1987, C. maj. 23,786)

HAMPSHIRE NORTH WEST
E.73,101   T.80.75%

*Sir D. Mitchell, C.	34,310
M. Simpson, LD	16,462
M. Stockwell, Lab.	7,433
Ms D. Ashley, Green	825
C. majority	17,848

(June 1987, C. maj. 13,437)

HAMPSTEAD AND HIGHGATE
(Greater London)
*E.*58,203   *T.*73.04%
Ms G. Jackson, *Lab.*   19,193
O. Letwin, *C.*   17,753
D. Wrede, *LD*   4,765
S. Games, *Green*   594
Dr R. Prosser, *NLP*   86
Ms A. Hall, *RAVA*   44
C. Scallywag Wilson, *Scallywag*   44
Captain Rizz, *Rizz*   33
Lab. majority   1,440
(June 1987, C. maj. 2,221)

HARBOROUGH (Leics)
*E.*76,514   *T.*82.11%
E. Garnier, *C.*   34,280
M. Cox, *LD*   20,737
Ms C. Mackay, *Lab.*   7,483
A. Irwin, *NLP*   328
C. majority   13,543
(June 1987, C. maj. 18,810)

HARLOW (Essex)
*E.*68,615   *T.*82.56%
J. Hayes, *C.*   26,608
W. Rammell, *Lab.*   23,668
Ms L. Spenceley, *LD*   6,375
C. majority   2,940
(June 1987, C. maj. 5,877)

HARROGATE (N. Yorks)
*E.*76,250   *T.*77.98%
R. Banks, *C.*   32,023
T. Hurren, *LD*   19,434
A. Wright, *Lab.*   7,230
A. Warneken, *Green*   780
C. majority   12,589
(June 1987, C. maj. 11,902)

HARROW EAST (Greater London)
*E.*74,733   *T.*77.83%
H. Dykes, *C.*   30,752
A. McNulty, *Lab.*   19,654
Ms V. Chamberlain, *LD*   6,360
P. Burrows, *Lib.*   1,142
Mrs S. Hamza, *NLP*   212
J. Lester, *Anti Fed.*   49
C. majority   11,098
(June 1987, C. maj. 18,273)

HARROW WEST (Greater London)
*E.*69,616   *T.*78.69%
R. G. Hughes, *C.*   30,240
C. Moraes, *Lab.*   12,343
C. Noyce, *LD*   11,050
G. Aitman, *Lib.*   845
Mrs J. Argyle, *NLP*   306
C. majority   17,897
(June 1987, C. maj. 15,444)

HARTLEPOOL (Cleveland)
*E.*67,968   *T.*76.07%
P. Mandelson, *Lab.*   26,816
G. Robb, *C.*   18,034
I. Cameron, *LD*   6,860
Lab. majority   8,782
(June 1987, Lab. maj. 7,289)

HARWICH (Essex)
*E.*80,260   *T.*77.70%
I. Sproat, *C.*   32,369
Mrs P. Bevan, *LD*   15,210

R. Knight, *Lab.*   14,511
Mrs E. McGrath, *NLP*   279
C. majority   17,159
(June 1987, C. maj. 12,082)

HASTINGS AND RYE (E. Sussex)
*E.*71,838   *T.*74.86%
Ms J. Lait, *C.*   25,573
M. Palmer, *LD*   18,939
R. Stevens, *Lab.*   8,458
Ms S. Phillips, *Green*   640
T. Howell, *Loony*   168
C. majority   6,634
(June 1987, C. maj. 7,347)

HAVANT (Hants)
*E.*74,217   *T.*79.01%
D. Willetts, *C.*   32,233
S. van Hagen, *LD*   14,649
G. Morris, *Lab.*   10,968
T. Mitchell, *Green*   793
C. majority   17,584
(June 1987, C. maj. 16,510)

HAYES AND HARLINGTON (Greater
London)
*E.*54,449   *T.*79.70%
T. Dicks, *C.*   19,489
J. McDonnell, *Lab.*   19,436
T. Little, *LD*   4,472
C. majority   53
(June 1987, C. maj. 5,965)

HAZEL GROVE (Greater
Manchester)
*E.*64,302   *T.*84.94%
Sir T. Arnold, *C.*   24,479
A. Stunell, *LD*   23,550
C. McAllister, *Lab.*   6,390
M. Penn, *NLP*   204
C. majority   929
(June 1987, C. maj. 1,840)

HEMSWORTH (W. Yorks)
*E.*55,679   *T.*75.91%
D. Enright, *Lab.*   29,942
G. Harrison, *C.*   7,867
Ms V. Megson, *LD*   4,459
Lab. majority   22,075
(June 1987, Lab. maj. 20,700)
(November 1991, Lab. maj. 11,087)
See also page 235

HENDON NORTH (Greater London)
*E.*51,513   *T.*75.08%
J. Gorst, *C.*   20,569
D. Hill, *Lab.*   13,447
P. Kemp, *LD*   4,136
Ms P. Duncan, *Green*   430
Ms P. Orr, *NLP*   95
C. majority   7,122
(June 1987, C. maj. 10,932)

HENDON SOUTH (Greater London)
*E.*48,401   *T.*72.38%
J. Marshall, *C.*   20,593
Ms L. Lloyd, *Lab.*   8,546
J. Cohen, *LD*   5,609
J. Leslie, *NLP*   289
C. majority   12,047
(June 1987, C. maj. 11,124)

HENLEY (Oxon)
*E.*64,702   *T.*79.84%
Rt. Hon. M. Heseltine, *C.*   30,835
D. Turner, *LD*   12,443
I. Russell-Swinnerton, *Lab.*   7,676
A. Plane, *Anti H.*   431
Ms S. Banerji, *NLP*   274
C. majority   18,392
(June 1987, C. maj. 17,082)

HEREFORD
*E.*69,676   *T.*81.29%
C. Shepherd, *C.*   26,727
G. Jones, *LD*   23,314
Ms J. Kelly, *Lab.*   6,005
C. Mattingly, *Green*   596
C. majority   3,413
(June 1987, C. maj. 1,413)

HERTFORD AND STORTFORD
*E.*76,654   *T.*81.05%
B. Wells, *C.*   35,716
C. White, *LD*   15,506
A. Bovaird, *Lab.*   10,125
J. Goth, *Green*   780
C. majority   20,210
(June 1987, C. maj. 17,140)

HERTFORDSHIRE NORTH
*E.*80,066   *T.*84.44%
O. Heald, *C.*   33,679
R. Liddle, *LD*   17,148
Ms S. Bissett Johnson, *Lab.*   16,449
B. Irving, *NLP*   339
C. majority   16,531
(June 1987, C. maj. 11,442)

HERTFORDSHIRE SOUTH WEST
*E.*70,836   *T.*83.76%
R. Page, *C.*   33,825
Ms A. Shaw, *LD*   13,718
A. Gale, *Lab.*   11,512
C. Adamson, *NLP*   281
C. majority   20,107
(June 1987, C. maj. 15,784)

HERTFORDSHIRE WEST
*E.*78,573   *T.*82.36%
R. Jones, *C.*   33,340
Mrs E. McNally, *Lab.*   19,400
M. Trevett, *LD*   10,464
J. Hannaway, *Green*   674
J. McAuley, *NF*   665
G. Harvey, *NLP*   175
C. majority   13,940
(June 1987, C. maj. 14,924)

HERTSMERE (Herts)
*E.*69,951   *T.*80.89%
W. J. Clappison, *C.*   32,133
Dr D. Souter, *Lab.*   13,398
Mrs Z. Gifford, *LD*   10,681
Ms D. Harding, *NLP*   373
C. majority   18,735
(June 1987, C. maj. 18,106)

HEXHAM (Northumberland)
*E.*57,812   *T.*82.37%
P. Atkinson, *C.*   24,967
I. Swithenbank, *Lab.*   11,529
J. Wallace, *LD*   10,344
J. Hartshorne, *Green*   781

C. majority   13,438
(June 1987, C. maj. 8,066)

HEYWOOD AND MIDDLETON
(Greater Manchester)
E.57,176   T.74.92%
*J. Callaghan, Lab.   22,380
E. Ollerenshaw, C.   14,306
Dr M. Taylor, LD   5,262
P. Burke, Lib.   757
Ms A. Scott, NLP   134
Lab. majority   8,074
(June 1987, Lab. maj. 6,848)

HIGH PEAK (Derbys)
E.70,793   T.84.62%
C. Hendry, C.   27,538
T. Levitt, Lab.   22,719
S. Molloy, LD   8,861
R. Floyd, Green   794
C. majority   4,819
(June 1987, C. maj. 9,516)

HOLBORN AND ST PANCRAS
(Greater London)
E.64,480   T.62.99%
*F. Dobson, Lab.   22,243
A. McHallam, C.   11,419
Ms J. Horne-Roberts, LD   5,476
P. Wolf-Light, Green   959
M. Hersey, NLP   212
R. Headicar, Soc.   175
N. Lewis, WAR   133
Lab. majority   10,824
(June 1987, Lab. maj. 8,853)

HOLLAND WITH BOSTON (Lincs)
E.67,900   T.77.93%
*Sir R. Body, C.   29,159
J. Hough, Lab.   15,328
N. Ley, LD   8,434
C. majority   13,831
(June 1987, C. maj. 17,595)

HONITON (Devon)
E.79,223   T.80.74%
*Sir P. Emery, C.   33,533
Ms J. Sharratt, LD   17,022
R. Davison, Lab.   8,142
D. Owen, Ind. C.   2,175
S. Hughes, Loony G.   1,442
G. Halliwell, Lib.   1,005
A. Tootill, Green   650
C. majority   16,511
(June 1987, C. maj. 16,562)

HORNCHURCH (Greater London)
E.60,522   T.79.78%
*R. Squire, C.   25,817
Ms L. Cooper, Lab.   16,652
B. Oddy, LD   5,366
T. Matthews, SD   453
C. majority   9,165
(June 1987, C. maj. 10,694)

HORNSEY AND WOOD GREEN
(Greater London)
E.73,491   T.75.85%
Mrs B. Roche, Lab.   27,020
A. Boff, C.   21,843
P. Dunphy, LD   5,547
Ms L. Crosbie, Green   1,051
P. Davies, NLP   197

W. Massey, Rev. Comm.   89
Lab. majority   5,177
(June 1987, C. maj. 1,779)

HORSHAM (W. Sussex)
E.84,158   T.81.27%
*Sir P. Hordern, C.   42,210
Ms J. Stainton, LD   17,138
S. Uwins, Lab.   6,745
Ms J. Elliott, Lib.   1,281
T. King, Green   692
J. Duggan, PPP   332
C. majority   25,072
(June 1987, C. maj. 23,907)

HOUGHTON AND WASHINGTON
(Tyne & Wear)
E.79,325   T.70.60%
*R. Boyes, Lab.   34,733
A. Tyrie, C.   13,925
O. Dumpleton, LD   7,346
Lab. majority   20,808
(June 1987, Lab. maj. 20,193)

HOVE (E. Sussex)
E.67,450   T.74.26%
*Hon. T. Sainsbury, C.   24,525
D. Turner, Lab.   12,257
A. Jones, LD   9,709
N. Furness, Hove C.   2,658
G. Sinclair, Green   814
J. Morilly, NLP   126
C. majority   12,268
(June 1987, C. maj. 18,218)

HUDDERSFIELD (W. Yorks)
E.67,604   T.72.32%
*B. Sheerman, Lab.   23,832
Ms J. Kenyon, C.   16,574
Ms A. Denham, LD   7,777
N. Harvey, Green   576
M. Cran, NLP   135
Lab. majority   7,258
(June 1987, Lab. maj. 7,278)

HULL EAST
E.69,036   T.69.29%
*J. Prescott, Lab.   30,092
J. Fareham, C.   11,373
J. Wastling, LD   6,050
C. Kinzell, NLP   323
Lab. majority   18,719
(June 1987, Lab. maj. 14,689)

HULL NORTH
E.71,363   T.66.71%
*J. K. McNamara, Lab.   26,619
B. Coleman, C.   11,235
A. Meadowcroft, LD   9,504
G. Richardson, NLP   253
Lab. majority   15,384
(June 1987, Lab. maj. 12,169)

HULL WEST
E.56,111   T.65.70%
*S. Randall, Lab.   21,139
D. Stewart, C.   10,554
R. Tress, LD   4,867
B. Franklin, NLP   308
Lab. majority   10,585
(June 1987, Lab. maj. 8,130)

HUNTINGDON (Cambs)
E.92,913   T.79.16%
*Rt. Hon. J. Major, C.   48,662
H. Seckleman, Lab.   12,432
A. Duff, LD   9,386
P. Wiggin, Lib.   1,045
Miss D. Birkhead, Green   846
Lord D. Sutch, Loony   728
M. Flanagan, C. Thatch.   231
Lord Buckethead, Gremloids   107
C. Cockell, FTM   91
D. Shepheard, NLP   26
C. majority   36,230
(June 1987, C. maj. 27,044)

HYNDBURN (Lancs)
E.58,539   T.83.97%
G. Pope, Lab.   23,042
*K. Hargreaves, C.   21,082
Ms Y. Stars, LD   4,886
S. Whittle, NLP   150
Lab. majority   1,960
(June 1987, C. maj. 2,220)

ILFORD NORTH (Greater London)
E.58,670   T.77.98%
*V. Bendall, C.   24,698
Ms L. Hilton, Lab.   15,627
R. Scott, LD   5,430
C. majority   9,071
(June 1987, C. maj. 12,090)

ILFORD SOUTH (Greater London)
E.55,741   T.76.83%
M. Gapes, Lab.   19,418
*N. Thorne, C.   19,016
G. Hogarth, LD   4,126
N. Bramachari, NLP   269
Lab. majority   402
(June 1987, C. maj. 4,572)

IPSWICH (Suffolk)
E.67,261   T.80.32%
J. Cann, Lab.   23,680
*M. Irvine, C.   23,415
J. White, LD   6,159
Ms J. Scott, Green   591
E. Kaplan, NLP   181
Lab. majority   265
(June 1987, C. maj. 874)

ISLE OF WIGHT
E.99,838   T.79.76%
*B. Field, C.   38,163
Dr P. Brand, LD   36,336
K. Pearson, Lab.   4,784
C. Daly, NLP   350
C. majority   1,827
(June 1987, C. maj. 6,442)

ISLINGTON NORTH (Greater
London)
E.56,270   T.67.26%
*J. Corbyn, Lab.   21,742
Mrs L. Champagnie, C.   8,958
Ms S. Ludford, LD   5,732
C. Ashby, Green   1,420
Lab. majority   12,784
(June 1987, Lab. maj. 9,657)

ISLINGTON SOUTH AND FINSBURY
(Greater London)
*E.*55,541   *T.*72.52%
C. Smith, *Lab.*	20,586
M. Jones, *C.*	9,934
C. Pryce, *LD*	9,387
Ms R. Hersey, *JBR*	149
Ms M. Avino, *Loony*	142
M. Spinks, *NLP*	83
Lab. majority	10,652

(June 1987, Lab. maj. 805)

JARROW (Tyne & Wear)
*E.*62,611   *T.*74.44%
D. Dixon, *Lab.*	28,956
T. Ward, *C.*	11,049
K. Orrell, *LD*	6,608
Lab. majority	17,907

(June 1987, Lab. maj. 18,795)

KEIGHLEY (W. Yorks)
*E.*66,358   *T.*82.58%
G. Waller, *C.*	25,983
T. Flanagan, *Lab.*	22,387
I. Simpson, *LD*	5,793
M. Crowson, *Green*	642
C. majority	3,596

(June 1987, C. maj. 5,606)

KENSINGTON (Greater London)
*E.*42,129   *T.*73.29%
J. D. Fishburn, *C.*	15,540
Ms A. Holmes, *Lab.*	11,992
C. Shirley, *LD*	2,770
Ms A. Burlingham-Johnson, *Green*	415
A. Hardy, *NLP*	90
Ms A. Bulloch, *Anti Fed.*	71
C. majority	3,548

(June 1987, C. maj. 4,447)
(July 1988, C. maj. 815)

KENT MID
*E.*74,459   *T.*79.66%
*A. Rowe, *C.*	33,633
T. Robson, *Lab.*	13,984
G. Colley, *LD*	11,476
G. Valente, *NLP*	224
C. majority	19,649

(June 1987, C. maj. 14,768)

KETTERING (Northants)
*E.*67,853   *T.*82.58%
*R. Freeman, *C.*	29,115
P. Hope, *Lab.*	17,961
R. Denton-White, *LD*	8,962
C. majority	11,154

(June 1987, C. maj. 11,327)

KINGSTON UPON THAMES (Greater London)
*E.*51,077   *T.*78.41%
*Rt. Hon. N. Lamont, *C.*	20,675
D. Osbourne, *LD*	10,522
R. Markless, *Lab.*	7,748
A. Amer, *Lib.*	771
D. Beaupre, *Loony*	212
G. Woollcoombe, *NLP*	81
A. Scholefield, *Anti Fed.*	42
C. majority	10,153

(June 1987, C. maj. 11,186)

KINGSWOOD (Avon)
*E.*71,727   *T.*83.85%
R. Berry, *Lab.*	26,774
*R. Hayward, *C.*	24,404
Ms J. Pinkerton, *LD*	8,960
Lab. majority	2,370

(June 1987, C. maj. 4,393)

KNOWSLEY NORTH (Merseyside)
*E.*48,761   *T.*72.81%
*G. Howarth, *Lab.*	27,517
S. Mabey, *C.*	5,114
J. Murray, *LD*	1,515
Mrs K. Lappin, *Lib.*	1,180
V. Ruben, *NLP*	179
Lab. majority	22,403

(June 1987, Lab. maj. 21,098)

KNOWSLEY SOUTH (Merseyside)
*E.*62,260   *T.*74.77%
*E. O'Hara, *Lab.*	31,933
L. Byrom, *C.*	9,922
I. Smith, *LD*	4,480
M. Raiano, *NLP*	217
Lab. majority	22,011

(June 1987, Lab. maj. 20,846)
(September 1990, Lab. maj. 11,367)

LANCASHIRE WEST
*E.*77,462   *T.*82.55%
C. Pickthall, *Lab.*	30,128
*K. Hind, *C.*	28,051
P. Reilly, *LD*	4,884
P. Pawley, *Green*	546
B. Morris, *NLP*	336
Lab. majority	2,077

(June 1987, C. maj. 1,353)

LANCASTER (Lancs)
*E.*58,714   *T.*78.78%
*Dame E. Kellett-Bowman, *C.*	21,084
Ms R. Henig, *Lab.*	18,131
J. Humberstone, *LD*	6,524
Ms G. Dowding, *Green*	433
R. Barcis, *NLP*	83
C. majority	2,953

(June 1987, C. maj. 6,453)

LANGBAURGH (Cleveland)
*E.*79,566   *T.*83.05%
M. Bates, *C.*	30,018
*A. Kumar, *Lab.*	28,454
P. Allen, *LD*	7,615
C. majority	1,564

(June 1987, C. maj. 2,088)
(November 1991, C. maj. 1,975)

LEEDS CENTRAL (W. Yorks)
*E.*62,058   *T.*61.29%
*D. Fatchett, *Lab.*	23,673
Mrs T. Holdroyd, *C.*	8,653
D. Pratt, *LD*	5,713
Lab. majority	15,020

(June 1987, Lab. maj. 11,505)

LEEDS EAST (W. Yorks)
*E.*61,695   *T.*70.02%
G. Mudie, *Lab.*	24,929
N. Carmichael, *C.*	12,232
P. Wrigley, *LD*	6,040
Lab. majority	12,697

(June 1987, Lab. maj. 9,526)

LEEDS NORTH EAST (W. Yorks)
*E.*64,372   *T.*76.89%
*T. Kirkhope, *C.*	22,462
F. Hamilton, *Lab.*	18,218
C. Walmsley, *LD*	8,274
J. Noble, *Green*	546
C. majority	4,244

(June 1987, C. maj. 8,419)

LEEDS NORTH WEST (W. Yorks)
*E.*69,406   *T.*72.84%
*Dr K. Hampson, *C.*	21,750
Ms B. Pearce, *LD*	14,079
Ms S. Egan, *Lab.*	13,782
D. Webb, *Green*	519
N. Nowosielski, *Lib.*	427
C. majority	7,671

(June 1987, C. maj. 5,201)

LEEDS SOUTH AND MORLEY
(W. Yorks)
*E.*63,107   *T.*72.58%
W. J. Gunnell, *Lab.*	23,896
R. Booth, *C.*	16,524
Ms J. Walmsley, *LD*	5,062
R. Thurston, *NLP*	327
Lab. majority	7,372

(June 1987, Lab. maj. 6,711)

LEEDS WEST (W. Yorks)
*E.*67,084   *T.*71.14%
*J. Battle, *Lab.*	26,310
P. Bartlett, *C.*	12,482
G. Howard, *LD*	4,252
M. Meadowcroft, *Lib.*	3,980
Ms A. Mander, *Green*	569
R. Tenny, *NF*	132
Lab. majority	13,828

(June 1987, Lab. maj. 4,692)

LEICESTER EAST
*E.*63,434   *T.*78.40%
*N. K. A. S. Vaz, *Lab.*	28,123
J. Stevens, *C.*	16,807
Ms S. Mitchell, *LD*	4,043
M. Frankland, *Green*	453
D. Taylor, *Homeland*	308
Lab. majority	11,316

(June 1987, Lab. maj. 1,924)

LEICESTER SOUTH
*E.*71,120   *T.*75.09%
*J. Marshall, *Lab.*	27,934
Dr M. Dutt, *C.*	18,494
Ms A. Crumbie, *LD*	6,271
J. McWhirter, *Green*	554
Ms P. Saunders, *NLP*	154
Lab. majority	9,440

(June 1987, Lab. maj. 1,877)

LEICESTER WEST
*E.*65,510   *T.*73.66%
*Hon. G. Janner, *Lab.*	22,574
J. Guthrie, *C.*	18,596
G. Walker, *LD*	6,402
Ms C. Wintram, *Green*	517
Ms J. Rosta, *NLP*	171
Lab. majority	3,978

(June 1987, Lab. maj. 1,201)

LEICESTERSHIRE NORTH WEST
E.72,414   T.86.11%

*D. Ashby, *C.*	28,379
D. Taylor, *Lab.*	27,400
J. Beckett, *LD*	6,353
J. Fawcett, *NLP*	229
C. majority	979
(June 1987, C. maj. 7,828)	

LEIGH (Greater Manchester)
E.70,064   T.75.02%

*L. Cunliffe, *Lab.*	32,225
J. Egerton, *C.*	13,398
R. Bleakley, *LD*	6,621
A. Tayler, *NLP*	320
Lab. majority	18,827
(June 1987, Lab. maj. 16,606)	

LEOMINSTER (H & W)
E.70,873   T.81.69%

*P. Temple-Morris, *C.*	32,783
D. Short, *LD*	16,103
C. Chappell, *Lab.*	6,874
Ms F. Norman, *Green*	1,503
Capt. E. Carlise, *Anti Fed.*	640
C. majority	16,680
(June 1987, C. maj. 14,075)	

LEWES (E. Sussex)
E.73,918   T.81.81%

*J. R. Rathbone, *C.*	33,042
N. Baker, *LD*	20,867
Ms A. Chapman, *Lab.*	5,758
A. Beaumont, *Green*	719
N. Clinch, *NLP*	87
C. majority	12,175
(June 1987, C. maj. 13,620)	

LEWISHAM DEPTFORD (Greater
London)
E.57,014   T.65.05%

*Mrs J. Ruddock, *Lab.*	22,574
Miss T. O'Neill, *C.*	10,336
Ms J. Brightwell, *LD*	4,181
Lab. majority	12,238
(June 1987, Lab. maj. 6,771)	

LEWISHAM EAST (Greater London)
E.57,674   T.74.78%

Mrs B. Prentice, *Lab.*	19,576
*Hon. C. Moynihan, *C.*	18,481
J. Hawkins, *LD*	4,877
Ms G. Mansour, *NLP*	196
Lab. majority	1,095
(June 1987, C. maj. 4,814)	

LEWISHAM WEST (Greater London)
E.59,317   T.73.11%

J. Dowd, *Lab.*	20,378
*J. Maples, *C.*	18,569
Ms E. Neale, *LD*	4,295
P. Coulam, *Anti Fed.*	125
Lab. majority	1,809
(June 1987, C. maj. 3,772)	

LEYTON (Greater London)
E.57,271   T.67.38%

*H. Cohen, *Lab.*	20,334
Miss C. Smith, *C.*	8,850
J. Fryer, *LD*	8,180
L. de Pinna, *Lib.*	561
K. Pervez, *Green*	412
R. Archer, *NLP*	256

Lab. majority	11,484
(June 1987, Lab. maj. 4,641)	

LINCOLN
E.78,905   T.79.15%

*K. Carlisle, *C.*	28,792
N. Butler, *Lab.*	26,743
D. Harding-Price, *LD*	6,316
Ms S. Wiggin, *Lib.*	603
C. majority	2,049
(June 1987, C. maj. 7,483)	

LINDSEY EAST (Lincs)
E.80,026   T.78.07%

*Sir P. Tapsell, *C.*	31,916
J. Dodsworth, *LD*	20,070
D. Shepherd, *Lab.*	9,477
Ms R. Robinson, *Green*	1,018
C. majority	11,846
(June 1987, C. maj. 8,616)	

LITTLEBOROUGH AND
SADDLEWORTH (Greater
Manchester)
E.65,576   T.81.61%

*G. Dickens, *C.*	23,682
C. Davies, *LD*	19,188
A. Brett, *Lab.*	10,649
C. majority	4,494
(June 1987, C. maj. 6,202)	
See also page 235	

LIVERPOOL BROADGREEN
E.60,080   T.69.59%

Mrs J. Kennedy, *Lab.*	18,062
Ms R. Cooper, *LD*	11,035
*T. Fields, *Soc. Lab.*	5,952
Mrs H. Roche, *C.*	5,405
S. Radford, *Lib.*	1,211
Mrs A. Brennan, *NLP*	149
Lab. majority	7,027
(June 1987, Lab. maj. 6,047)	

LIVERPOOL GARSTON
E.57,538   T.70.60%

*E. Loyden, *Lab.*	23,212
J. Backhouse, *C.*	10,933
W. Roberts, *LD*	5,398
A. Conrad, *Lib.*	894
P. Chandler, *NLP*	187
Lab. majority	12,279
(June 1987, Lab. maj. 13,777)	

LIVERPOOL MOSSLEY HILL
E.60,409   T.68.52%

*D. Alton, *LD*	19,809
N. Bann, *Lab.*	17,203
S. Syder, *C.*	4,269
B. Rigby, *NLP*	114
LD majority	2,606
(June 1987, L./All. maj. 2,226)	

LIVERPOOL RIVERSIDE
E.49,595   T.54.57%

*R. Parry, *Lab.*	20,550
Dr A. Zsigmond, *C.*	3,113
M. Akbar Ali, *LD*	2,498
L. Brown, *Green*	738
J. Collins, *NLP*	169
Lab. majority	17,437
(June 1987, Lab. maj. 20,689)	

LIVERPOOL WALTON
E.70,102   T.67.40%

*P. Kilfoyle, *Lab.*	34,214
B. Greenwood, *C.*	5,915
J. Lang, *LD*	5,672
T. Newall, *Lib.*	963
D. Carson, *Prot. Ref.*	393
Ms D. Raiano, *NLP*	98
Lab. majority	28,299
(June 1987, Lab. maj. 23,253)	
(July 1991, Lab. maj. 6,860)	

LIVERPOOL WEST DERBY
E.56,718   T.69.84%

*R. Wareing, *Lab.*	27,014
S. Fitzsimmons, *C.*	6,589
Ms G. Bundred, *LD*	4,838
D. Curtis, *Lib.*	1,021
C. Higgins, *NLP*	154
Lab. majority	20,425
(June 1987, Lab. maj. 20,496)	

LOUGHBOROUGH (Leics)
E.75,450   T.78.52%

*S. Dorrell, *C.*	30,064
A. Reed, *Lab.*	19,181
A. Stott, *LD*	8,953
I. Sinclair, *Green*	817
P. Reynolds, *NLP*	233
C. majority	10,883
(June 1987, C. maj. 17,648)	

LUDLOW (Salop)
E.68,935   T.80.87%

*C. Gill, *C.*	28,719
D. Phillips, *LD*	14,567
Ms B. Mason, *Lab.*	11,709
N. Appleton-Fox, *Green*	758
C. majority	14,152
(June 1987, C. maj. 11,699)	

LUTON NORTH (Beds)
E.76,857   T.81.91%

*J. Carlisle, *C.*	33,777
A. McWalter, *Lab.*	20,683
Ms J. Jackson, *LD*	7,570
R. Jones, *Green*	633
K. Buscombe, *NLP*	292
C. majority	13,094
(June 1987, C. maj. 15,573)	

LUTON SOUTH (Beds)
E.73,016   T.79.10%

*G. Bright, *C.*	25,900
W. McKenzie, *Lab.*	25,101
D. Rogers, *LD*	6,020
Ms L. Bliss, *Green*	550
D. Cooke, *NLP*	191
C. majority	799
(June 1987, C. maj. 5,115)	

MACCLESFIELD (Cheshire)
E.76,548   T.82.29%

*N. Winterton, *C.*	36,447
Mrs M. Longworth, *Lab.*	13,680
Dr P. Beatty, *LD*	12,600
Mrs C. Penn, *NLP*	268
C. majority	22,767
(June 1987, C. maj. 19,092)	

MAIDSTONE (Kent)
E.72,834　T.80.08%
*Miss A. Widdecombe, C.　31,611
Ms P. Yates, LD　15,325
Ms A. Logan, Lab.　10,517
Ms P. Kemp, Green　707
F. Ingram, NLP　172
C. majority　16,286
(June 1987, C. maj. 10,364)

MAKERFIELD (Greater Manchester)
E.71,425　T.76.09%
*I. McCartney, Lab.　32,832
Mrs D. Dickson, C.　14,714
S. Jeffers, LD　5,097
Ms S. Cairns, Lib.　1,309
C. Davies, NLP　397
Lab. majority　18,118
(June 1987, Lab. maj. 15,558)

MANCHESTER BLACKLEY
E.55,234　T.69.31%
*K. Eastham, Lab.　23,031
W. Hobhouse, C.　10,642
S. Wheale, LD　4,324
M. Kennedy, NLP　288
Lab. majority　12,389
(June 1987, Lab. maj. 10,122)

MANCHESTER CENTRAL
E.56,446　T.56.90%
*R. Litherland, Lab.　23,336
P. Davies, C.　5,299
M. Clayton, LD　3,151
A. Buchanan, CL　167
Ms V. Mitchell, NLP　167
Lab. majority　18,037
(June 1987, Lab. maj. 19,867)

MANCHESTER GORTON
E.62,410　T.60.84%
*Rt. Hon. G. Kaufman, Lab.　23,671
J. Bullock, C.　7,392
P. Harris, LD　5,327
T. Henderson, Lib.　767
M. Daw, Green　595
Ms P. Lawrence, Rev. Comm.　108
P. Mitchell, NLP　84
Ms C. Smith, Int. Comm.　30
Lab. majority　16,279
(June 1987, Lab. maj. 14,065)

MANCHESTER WITHINGTON
E.63,838　T.71.27%
*K. Bradley, Lab.　23,962
E. Farthing, C.　14,227
G. Hennell, LD　6,457
B. Candeland, Green　725
C. Menhinick, NLP　128
Lab. majority　9,735
(June 1987, Lab. maj. 3,391)

MANCHESTER WYTHENSHAWE
E.53,548　T.69.68%
*Rt. Hon. A. Morris, Lab.　22,591
K. McKenna, C.　10,595
S. Fenn, LD　3,633
G. Otten, Green　362
Ms E. Martin, NLP　133
Lab. majority　11,996
(June 1987, Lab. maj. 11,855)

MANSFIELD (Notts)
E.66,964　T.82.23%
*J. A. Meale, Lab.　29,932
G. Mond, C.　18,208
S. Thompstone, LD　6,925
Lab. majority　11,724
(June 1987, Lab. maj. 56)

MEDWAY (Kent)
E.61,736　T.80.22%
*Dame P. Fenner, C.　25,924
R. Marshall-Andrews, Lab.　17,138
C. Trice, LD　4,751
M. Austin, Lib.　1,480
P. Kember, NLP　234
C. majority　8,786
(June 1987, C. maj. 9,929)

MERIDEN (W. Midlands)
E.76,994　T.78.85%
*I. Mills, C.　33,462
N. Stephens, Lab.　18,763
Ms J. Morris, LD　8,489
C. majority　14,699
(June 1987, C. maj. 16,820)

MIDDLESBROUGH (Cleveland)
E.58,844　T.69.85%
*S. Bell, Lab.　26,343
P. Rayner, C.　10,559
Ms R. Jordan, LD　4,201
Lab. majority　15,784
(June 1987, Lab. maj. 14,958)

MILTON KEYNES NORTH EAST
(Bucks)
E.62,748　T.80.95%
P. Butler, C.　26,212
Ms M. Cosin, Lab.　12,036
P. Gaskell, LD　11,693
A. Francis, Green　529
Mrs M. Kavanagh-Dowsett, Ind. C.
　249
M. Simson, NLP　79
C. majority　14,176
(New constituency)

MILTON KEYNES SOUTH WEST
(Bucks)
E.66,422　T.77
B. Legg, C.　23,840
K. Wilson, Lab.　19,153
C. Pym, LD　7,429
Dr C. Field, Green　525
H. Kelly, NLP　202
C. majority　4,687
(New constituency)

MITCHAM AND MORDEN (Greater
London)
E.63,723　T.80.32%
*Rt. Hon. A. Rumbold, C.　23,789
Ms S. McDonagh, Lab.　22,055
J. Field, LD　4,687
T. Walsh, Green　655
C. majority　1,734
(June 1987, C. maj. 6,183)

MOLE VALLEY (Surrey)
E.66,949　T.81.97%
*Rt. Hon. K. Baker, C.　32,549
M. Watson, LD　16,599
Dr T. Walsh, Lab.　5,291

Ms J. Thomas, NLP　442
C. majority　15,950
(June 1987, C. maj. 16,076)

MORECAMBE AND LUNESDALE
(Lancs)
E.56,426　T.78.35%
*Hon. M. Lennox-Boyd, C.　22,507
Ms J. Yates, Lab.　10,998
A. Saville, LD　9,584
M. Turner, MBI　916
R. Marriott, NLP　205
C. majority　11,509
(June 1987, C. maj. 11,785)

NEWARK (Notts)
E.68,801　T.82.17%
*R. Alexander, C.　28,494
D. Barton, Lab.　20,265
P. Harris, LD　7,342
Ms P. Wood, Green　435
C. majority　8,229
(June 1987, C. maj. 13,543)

NEWBURY (Berks)
E.80,252　T.82.75%
Mrs J. Chaplin, C.　37,135
D. Rendel, LD　24,778
R. Hall, Lab.　3,962
J. Wallis, Green　539
C. majority　12,357
(June 1987, C. maj. 16,658)
See also page 234

NEWCASTLE UNDER LYME (Staffs)
E.66,595　T.80.34%
*Mrs L. Golding, Lab.　25,652
A. Brierley, C.　15,813
A. Thomas, LD　11,727
R. Lines, NLP　314
Lab. majority　9,839
(June 1987, Lab. maj. 5,132)

NEWCASTLE UPON TYNE CENTRAL
E.59,973　T.71.32%
*J. Cousins, Lab.　21,123
M. Summersby, C.　15,835
L. Opik, LD　5,816
Lab. majority　5,288
(June 1987, Lab. maj. 2,483)

NEWCASTLE UPON TYNE EAST
E.57,165　T.70.73%
*N. Brown, Lab.　24,342
J. Lucas, C.　10,465
A. Thompson, LD　4,883
G. Edwards, Green　744
Lab. majority　13,877
(June 1987, Lab. maj. 12,500)

NEWCASTLE UPON TYNE NORTH
E.66,187　T.76.80%
*D. Henderson, Lab.　25,121
I. Gordon, C.　16,175
P. Maughan, LD　9,542
Lab. majority　8,946
(June 1987, Lab. maj. 5,243)

NEW FOREST (Hants)
E.75,413　T.80.76%
*Sir P. McNair-Wilson, C.　37,986
Ms J. Vernon-Jackson, LD　17,581
M. Shutler, Lab.　4,989
Ms F. Carter, NLP　350

C. *majority* 20,405
(June 1987, C. maj. 21,732)

NEWHAM NORTH EAST (Greater London)
E.59,555　T.60.34%
*R. Leighton, *Lab.* 20,952
J. Galbraith, *C.* 10,966
J. Aves, *LD* 4,020
Lab. majority 9,986
(June 1987, Lab. maj. 8,236)
See also page 234

NEWHAM NORTH WEST (Greater London)
E.46,471　T.56.02%
*T. Banks, *Lab.* 15,911
M. Prisk, *C.* 6,740
A. Sawdon, *LD* 2,445
Ms A. Standford, *Green* 587
T. Jug, *Loony G.* 252
D. O'Sullivan, *Int. Comm.* 100
Lab. majority 9,171
(June 1987, Lab. maj. 8,496)

NEWHAM SOUTH (Greater London)
E.51,143　T.60.19%
*N. Spearing, *Lab.* 14,358
Ms J. Foster, *C.* 11,856
A. Kellaway, *LD* 4,572
Lab. majority 2,502
(June 1987, Lab. maj. 2,766)

NORFOLK MID
E.80,336　T.81.64%
*Rt. Hon. R. Ryder, *C.* 35,620
M. Castle, *Lab.* 16,672
J. Gleed, *LD* 13,072
Ms C. Waite, *NLP* 226
C. majority 18,948
(June 1987, C. maj. 18,008)

NORFOLK NORTH
E.73,780　T.80.84%
*R. Howell, *C.* 28,810
N. Lamb, *LD* 16,265
M. Cullingham, *Lab.* 13,850
Ms A. Zelter, *Green* 559
Ms S. Jackson, *NLP* 167
C. majority 12,545
(June 1987, C. maj. 15,310)

NORFOLK NORTH WEST
E.77,438　T.80.67%
*H. Bellingham, *C.* 32,554
Dr G. Turner, *Lab.* 20,990
A. Waterman, *LD* 8,599
S. Pink, *NLP* 330
C. majority 11,564
(June 1987, C. maj. 10,825)

NORFOLK SOUTH
E.81,647　T.83.99%
*Rt. Hon. J. MacGregor, *C.* 36,081
C. Brocklebank-Fowler, *LD* 18,516
C. Needle, *Lab.* 12,422
Ms S. Ross-Wagenknecht, *Green* 702
N. Clark, *NLP* 320
R. Peacock, *Ind.* 304
R. Watkins, *Ind. C.* 232
C. majority 17,565
(June 1987, C. maj. 12,418)

NORFOLK SOUTH WEST
E.77,652　T.79.30%
*Mrs G. Shephard, *C.* 33,637
Ms M. Page, *Lab.* 16,706
J. Marsh, *LD* 11,237
C. majority 16,931
(June 1987, C. maj. 20,436)

NORMANTON (W. Yorks)
E.65,562　T.76.35%
*W. O'Brien, *Lab.* 25,936
R. Sturdy, *C.* 16,986
M. Galdas, *LD* 7,137
Lab. majority 8,950
(June 1987, Lab. maj. 7,287)

NORTHAMPTON NORTH
E.69,139　T.78.52%
*A. Marlow, *C.* 24,865
Ms J. Thomas, *Lab.* 20,957
R. Church, *LD* 8,236
B. Spivack, *NLP* 232
C. majority 3,908
(June 1987, C. maj. 9,256)

NORTHAMPTON SOUTH
E.83,477　T.79.90%
*M. Morris, *C.* 36,882
J. Dickie, *Lab.* 19,909
G. Mabbutt, *LD* 9,912
C. majority 16,973
(June 1987, C. maj. 17,803)

NORTHAVON (Avon)
E.83,496　T.84.16%
*Rt. Hon. Sir J. Cope, *C.* 35,338
Ms H. Larkins, *LD* 23,477
Ms J. Norris, *Lab.* 10,290
Ms J. Greene, *Green* 789
P. Marx, *Lib.* 380
C. majority 11,861
(June 1987, C. maj. 14,270)

NORWICH NORTH (Norfolk)
E.63,308　T.81.82%
*H. P. Thompson, *C.* 22,419
I. Gibson, *Lab.* 22,153
D. Harrison, *LD* 6,706
L. Betts, *Green* 433
R. Arnold, *NLP* 93
C. majority 266
(June 1987, C. maj. 7,776)

NORWICH SOUTH (Norfolk)
E.63,603　T.80.60%
*J. Garrett, *Lab.* 24,965
D. Baxter, *C.* 18,784
C. Thomas, *LD* 6,609
A. Holmes, *Green* 803
B. Parsons, *NLP* 104
Lab. majority 6,181
(June 1987, Lab. maj. 336)

NORWOOD (Greater London)
E.52,496　T.65.87%
*J. Fraser, *Lab.* 18,391
J. Samways, *C.* 11,175
Ms S. Lawman, *LD* 4,087
S. Collins, *Green* 790
M. Leighton, *NLP* 138
Lab. majority 7,216
(June 1987, Lab. maj. 4,723)

NOTTINGHAM EAST
E.67,939　T.70.08%
J. Heppell, *Lab.* 25,026
*M. Knowles, *C.* 17,346
T. Ball, *LD* 3,695
A. Jones, *Green* 667
C. Roylance, *Lib.* 598
J. Ashforth, *NLP* 283
Lab. majority 7,680
(June 1987, C. maj. 456)

NOTTINGHAM NORTH
E.69,494　T.74.98%
*G. Allen, *Lab.* 29,052
I. Bridge, *C.* 18,309
A. Skelton, *LD* 4,477
A. Cadman, *NLP* 274
Lab. majority 10,743
(June 1987, Lab. maj. 1,665)

NOTTINGHAM SOUTH
E.72,796　T.74.22%
A. Simpson, *Lab.* 25,771
*M. Brandon-Bravo, *C.* 22,590
G. D. Long, *LD* 5,408
Ms J. Christou, *NLP* 263
Lab. majority 3,181
(June 1987, C. maj. 2,234)

NUNEATON (Warwicks)
E.70,906　T.83.70%
W. Olner, *Lab.* 27,157
*L. Stevens, *C.* 25,526
Ms R. Merritt, *LD* 6,671
Lab. majority 1,631
(June 1987, C. maj. 5,655)

OLD BEXLEY AND SIDCUP (Greater London)
E.49,449　T.81.94%
*Rt. Hon. E. Heath, *C.* 24,450
Ms D. Brierly, *Lab.* 8,751
D. Nicolle, *LD* 6,438
B. Rose, *Alt. C.* 733
R. Stephens, *NLP* 148
C. majority 15,699
(June 1987, C. maj. 16,274)

OLDHAM CENTRAL AND ROYTON (Greater Manchester)
E.61,333　T.74.20%
B. Davies, *Lab.* 23,246
Mrs T. Morris, *C.* 14,640
Ms A. Dunn, *LD* 7,224
I. Dalling, *NLP* 403
Lab. majority 8,606
(June 1987, Lab. maj. 6,279)

OLDHAM WEST (Greater Manchester)
E.54,063　T.75.65%
*M. Meacher, *Lab.* 21,580
J. Gillen, *C.* 13,247
J. Smith, *LD* 5,525
Ms S. Dalling, *NLP* 551
Lab. majority 8,333
(June 1987, Lab. maj. 5,967)

ORPINGTON (Greater London)
E.57,318　T.83.67%
J. Horam, *C.* 27,421
C. Maines, *LD* 14,486
S. Cowan, *Lab.* 5,512

R. Almond, *Lib.* 539
C. majority 12,935
(June 1987, C. maj. 12,732)

OXFORD EAST
£63,075   T.74.59%
*A. Smith, *Lab.* 23,702
Dr M. Mayall, *C.* 16,164
M. Horwood, *LD* 6,105
Mrs C. Lucas, *Green* 933
Miss A. Wilson, *NLP* 101
K. Thompson, *Rev. Comm.* 48
Lab. majority 7,538
(June 1987, Lab. maj. 1,288)

OXFORD WEST AND ABINGDON
£72,328   T.76.68%
*Rt. Hon. J. Patten, *C.* 25,163
Sir W. Goodhart, *LD* 21,624
B. Kent, *Lab.* 7,652
M. Woodin, *Green* 660
R. Jenking, *Lib.* 194
Miss S. Nelson, *Anti Fed.* 98
G. Wells, *NLP* 75
C. majority 3,539
(June 1987, C. maj. 4,878)

PECKHAM (Greater London)
£58,269   T.53.87%
*Ms H. Harman, *Lab.* 19,391
C. Frazer, *C.* 7,386
Mrs R. Colley, *LD* 4,331
G. Dacres, *WRP* 146
V. Emmanuel, *Whiplash* 140
Lab. majority 12,005
(June 1987, Lab. maj. 9,489)

PENDLE (Lancs)
£64,063   T.82.91%
G. Prentice, *Lab.* 23,497
*J. Lee, *C.* 21,384
A. Davies, *LD* 7,976
Mrs V. Thorne, *Anti Fed.* 263
Lab. majority 2,113
(June 1987, C. maj. 2,639)

PENRITH AND THE BORDER
(Cumbria)
£73,769   T.79.67%
*D. Maclean, *C.* 33,808
G. Walker, *LD* 15,359
J. Metcalfe, *Lab.* 8,871
R. Gibson, *Green* 610
I. Docker, *NLP* 129
C. majority 18,449
(June 1987, C. maj. 17,366)

PETERBOROUGH (Cambs)
£87,638   T.75.12%
*B. Mawhinney, *C.* 31,827
Ms J. Owens, *Lab.* 26,451
Ms A. Taylor, *LD* 5,208
E. Murat, *Lib.* 1,557
R. Heaton, *BNP* 311
P. Beasley, *PP* 271
C. Brettell, *NLP* 215
C. majority 5,376
(June 1987, C. maj. 9,784)

PLYMOUTH DEVONPORT (Devon)
£65,799   T.77.83%
D. Jamieson, *Lab.* 24,953
K. Simpson, *C.* 17,541

M. Mactaggart, *LD* 6,315
H. Luscombe, *SD* 2,152
F. Lyons, *NLP* 255
Lab. majority 7,412
(June 1987, SDP/All. maj. 6,470)

PLYMOUTH DRAKE (Devon)
£51,667   T.75.56%
*Dame J. Fookes, *C.* 17,075
P. Telford, *Lab.* 15,062
Ms V. Cox, *LD* 5,893
D. Stanbury, *SD* 476
Ms A. Harrison, *Green* 441
T. Pringle, *NLP* 95
C. majority 2,013
(June 1987, C. maj. 3,125)

PLYMOUTH SUTTON (Devon)
£67,430   T.81.17%
G. Streeter, *C.* 27,070
A. Pawley, *Lab.* 15,120
J. Brett-Freeman, *LD* 12,291
J. Bowler, *NLP* 256
C. majority 11,950
(June 1987, C. maj. 4,013)

PONTEFRACT AND CASTLEFORD
(W. Yorks)
£64,648   T.74.25%
*G. Lofthouse, *Lab.* 33,546
A. Rockall, *C.* 10,051
D. Ryan, *LD* 4,410
Lab. majority 23,495
(June 1987, Lab. maj. 21,626)

POOLE (Dorset)
£79,221   T.79.39%
*J. Ward, *C.* 33,445
B. Clements, *LD* 20,614
H. White, *Lab.* 6,912
M. Steen, *Ind. C.* 1,620
A. Bailey, *NLP* 303
C. majority 12,831
(June 1987, C. maj. 14,808)

PORTSMOUTH NORTH (Hants)
£79,592   T.77.05%
*P. Griffiths, *C.* 32,240
A. Burnett, *Lab.* 18,359
A. Bentley, *LD* 10,101
Ms H. Palmer, *Green* 628
C. majority 13,881
(June 1987, C. maj. 18,401)

PORTSMOUTH SOUTH (Hants)
£77,645   T.69.09%
*D. Martin, *C.* 22,798
M. Hancock, *LD* 22,556
S. Rapson, *Lab.* 7,857
A. Zivkovic, *Green* 349
W. Trend, *NLP* 91
C. majority 242
(June 1987, C. maj. 205)

PRESTON (Lancs)
£64,158   T.71.74%
*Mrs A. Wise, *Lab.* 24,983
S. O'Toole, *C.* 12,808
W. Chadwick, *LD* 7,897
Ms J. Ayliffe, *NLP* 341
Lab. majority 12,175
(June 1987, Lab. maj. 10,645)

PUDSEY (W. Yorks)
£70,847   T.80.14%
*Sir G. Shaw, *C.* 25,067
A. Giles, *Lab.* 16,095
D. Shutt, *LD* 15,153
Ms J. Wynne, *Green* 466
C. majority 8,972
(June 1987, C. maj. 6,436)

PUTNEY (Greater London)
£61,914   T.77.91%
*Rt. Hon. D. Mellor, *C.* 25,188
Ms J. Chegwidden, *Lab.* 17,662
J. Martyn, *LD* 4,636
K. Hagenbach, *Green* 618
P. Levy, *NLP* 139
C. majority 7,526
(June 1987, C. maj. 6,907)

RAVENSBOURNE (Greater London)
£57,259   T.81.24%
*Sir J. Hunt, *C.* 29,506
P. Booth, *LD* 9,792
E. Dyer, *Lab.* 6,182
I. Mouland, *Green* 617
P. White, *Lib.* 318
J. Shepheard, *NLP* 105
C. majority 19,714
(June 1987, C. maj. 16,919)

READING EAST (Berks)
£72,151   T.75.02%
*Sir G. Vaughan, *C.* 29,148
Ms G. Parker, *Lab.* 14,593
D. Thair, *LD* 9,528
Ms A. McCubbin, *Green* 861
C. majority 14,555
(June 1987, C. maj. 16,217)

READING WEST (Berks)
£67,937   T.77.98%
*Sir A. Durant, *C.* 28,048
P. Ruhemann, *Lab.* 14,750
K. Lock, *LD* 9,572
P. Unsworth, *Green* 613
C. majority 13,298
(June 1987, C. maj. 16,753)

REDCAR (Cleveland)
£62,494   T.77.73%
*Dr M. Mowlam, *Lab.* 27,184
R. Goodwill, *C.* 15,607
C. Abbott, *LD* 5,789
Lab. majority 11,577
(June 1987, Lab. maj. 7,735)

REIGATE (Surrey)
£71,853   T.78.54%
*Sir G. Gardiner, *C.* 32,220
B. Newsome, *LD* 14,556
Ms H. Young, *Lab.* 9,150
M. Dilcliff, *SD* 513
C. majority 17,664
(June 1987, C. maj. 18,173)

RIBBLE VALLEY (Lancs)
£64,996   T.85.73%
N. Evans, *C.* 29,178
*M. Carr, *LD* 22,636
R. Pickup, *Lab.* 3,649
D. Beesley, *Loony G.* 152
Ms N. Holmes, *NLP* 112

Parliament

254

C. majority 6,542
(June 1987, C. maj. 19,528)
(March 1991, LD maj. 4,641)

RICHMOND AND BARNES (Greater London)
*E.*53,081   *T.*85.01%
*J. Hanley, *C.* 22,894
Dr J. Tonge, *LD* 19,025
D. Touhig, *Lab.* 2,632
Ms J. Maciejowska, *Green* 376
C. Cunningham, *NLP* 89
R. Meacock, *QFL* 62
Ms A. Ellis-Jones, *Anti Fed.* 47
C. majority 3,869
(June 1987, C. maj. 1,766)

RICHMOND (N. Yorks)
*E.*82,879   *T.*78.41%
*W. Hague, *C.* 40,202
G. Irwin, *LD* 16,698
R. Cranston, *Lab.* 7,523
M. Barr, *Ind.* 570
C. majority 23,504
(June 1987, C. maj. 19,576)
(Feb 1989, C. maj. 2,634)

ROCHDALE (Greater Manchester)
*E.*69,522   *T.*76.47%
Ms E. Lynne, *LD* 22,776
D. Williams, *Lab.* 20,937
D. Goldie-Scott, *C.* 8,626
K. Henderson, *BNP* 620
V. Lucker, *NLP* 211
LD majority 1,839
(June 1987, L./All. maj. 2,779)

ROCHFORD (Essex)
*E.*76,869   *T.*82.99%
*Dr M. Clark, *C.* 38,967
N. Harris, *LD* 12,931
D. Quinn, *Lab.* 10,537
Ms L. Farmer, *Lib.* 1,362
C. majority 26,036
(June 1987, C. maj. 19,694)

ROMFORD (Greater London)
*E.*54,001   *T.*78%
*Sir M. Neubert, *C.* 23,834
Ms E. Gordon, *Lab.* 12,414
Ms P. Atherton, *LD* 5,329
F. Gibson, *Green* 546
C. majority 11,420
(June 1987, C. maj. 13,471)

ROMSEY AND WATERSIDE (Hants)
*E.*82,628   *T.*83.15%
*M. Colvin, *C.* 37,375
G. Dawson, *LD* 22,071
Mrs A. Mawle, *Lab.* 8,688
J. Spottiswood, *Green* 577
C. majority 15,304
(June 1987, C. maj. 15,272)

ROSSENDALE AND DARWEN (Lancs)
*E.*76,909   *T.*83.06%
Mrs J. Anderson, *Lab.* 28,028
*D. Trippier, *C.* 27,908
K. Connor, *LD* 7,226
J. Gaffney, *Green* 596
P. Gorrod, *NLP* 125
Lab. majority 120
(June 1987, C. maj. 4,982)

ROTHERHAM (S. Yorks)
*E.*60,937   *T.*71.68%
J. Boyce, *Lab.* 27,933
S. Yorke, *C.* 10,372
D. Wildgoose, *LD* 5,375
Lab. majority 17,561
(June 1987, Lab. maj. 16,012)
See also page 234

ROTHER VALLEY (S. Yorks)
*E.*68,303   *T.*74.98%
*K. Barron, *Lab.* 30,977
T. Horton, *C.* 13,755
K. Smith, *LD* 6,483
Lab. majority 17,222
(June 1987, Lab. maj. 15,790)

RUGBY AND KENILWORTH (Warwicks)
*E.*77,766   *T.*83.72%
*J. Pawsey, *C.* 34,110
J. Airey, *Lab.* 20,863
J. Roodhouse, *LD* 9,934
S. Withers, *NLP* 202
C. majority 13,247
(June 1987, C. maj. 16,264)

RUISLIP-NORTHWOOD (Greater London)
*E.*54,151   *T.*81.91%
*J. Wilkinson, *C.* 28,097
Ms R. Brooks, *Lab.* 8,306
H. Davies, *LD* 7,739
M. Sheehan, *NLP* 214
C. majority 19,791
(June 1987, C. maj. 16,971)

RUSHCLIFFE (Notts)
*E.*76,253   *T.*83.04%
*Rt. Hon. K. Clarke, *C.* 34,448
A. Chewings, *Lab.* 14,682
Dr A. Wood, *LD* 12,660
S. Anthony, *Green* 775
M. Maelor-Jones, *Ind. C.* 611
D. Richards, *NLP* 150
C. majority 19,766
(June 1987, C. maj. 20,839)

RUTLAND AND MELTON (Leics)
*E.*80,976   *T.*80.82%
A. Duncan, *C.* 38,603
Ms J. Taylor, *Lab.* 13,068
R. Lustig, *LD* 12,682
J. Berreen, *Green* 861
R. Grey, *NLP* 237
C. majority 25,535
(June 1987, C. maj. 23,022)

RYEDALE (N. Yorks)
*E.*87,048   *T.*81.73%
*J. Greenway, *C.* 39,888
Mrs E. Shields, *LD* 21,449
J. Healey, *Lab.* 9,812
C. majority 18,439
(June 1987, C. maj. 9,740)

SAFFRON WALDEN (Essex)
*E.*74,878   *T.*83.21%
*A. Haselhurst, *C.* 35,272
M. Hayes, *LD* 17,848
J. Kotz, *Lab.* 8,933
M. Miller, *NLP* 260

C. majority 17,424
(June 1987, C. maj. 16,602)

ST ALBANS (Herts)
*E.*74,188   *T.*83.47%
*Rt. Hon. P. Lilley, *C.* 32,709
Ms M. Howes, *LD* 16,305
K. Pollard, *Lab.* 12,016
C. Simmons, *Green* 734
D. Lucas, *NLP* 161
C. majority 16,404
(June 1987, C. maj. 10,881)

ST HELENS NORTH (Merseyside)
*E.*71,261   *T.*77.35%
*J. Evans, *Lab.* 31,930
B. Anderson, *C.* 15,686
J. Beirne, *LD* 7,224
Ms A. Lynch, *NLP* 287
Lab. majority 16,244
(June 1987, Lab. maj. 14,260)

ST HELENS SOUTH (Merseyside)
*E.*67,507   *T.*73.77%
*G. Bermingham, *Lab.* 30,391
Mrs P. Buzzard, *C.* 12,182
B. Spencer, *LD* 6,933
Dr H. Jump, *NLP* 295
Lab. majority 18,209
(June 1987, Lab. maj. 13,801)

ST IVES (Cornwall)
*E.*71,152   *T.*80.29%
*D. Harris, *C.* 24,528
A. George, *LD* 22,883
S. Warran, *Lab.* 9,144
Dr G. Stephens, *Lib.* 577
C. majority 1,645
(June 1987, C. maj. 7,555)

SALFORD EAST (Greater Manchester)
*E.*52,616   *T.*64.36%
*Rt. Hon. S. Orme, *Lab.* 20,327
D. Berens, *C.* 9,092
N. Owen, *LD* 3,836
M. Stanley, *Green* 463
C. Craig, *NLP* 150
Lab. majority 11,235
(June 1987, Lab. maj. 12,056)

SALISBURY (Wilts)
*E.*75,916   *T.*79.89%
*S. R. Key, *C.* 31,546
P. Sample, *LD* 22,573
S. Fear, *Lab.* 5,483
Dr S. Elcock, *Green* 609
S. Fletcher, *Ind.* 233
T. Abbott, *Wessex* 117
Ms A. Martell, *NLP* 93
C. majority 8,973
(June 1987, C. maj. 11,443)

SCARBOROUGH (N. Yorks)
*E.*76,364   *T.*77.18%
J. Sykes, *C.* 29,334
D. Billing, *Lab.* 17,600
B. Davenport, *LD* 11,133
Dr D. Richardson, *Green* 876
C. majority 11,734
(June 1987, C. maj. 13,626)

SEDGEFIELD (Durham)
E.61,024   *T*.77.06%
A. Blair, Lab.	28,453
N. Jopling, *C.*	13,594
G. Huntington, *LD*	4,982
Lab. majority	14,859
(June 1987, Lab. maj. 13,058)	

SELBY (N. Yorks)
E.77,178   *T*.80.16%
*Rt. Hon. M. Alison, C.	31,067
J. Grogan, *Lab.*	21,559
E. Batty, *LD*	9,244
C. majority	9,508
(June 1987, C. maj. 13,779)	

SEVENOAKS (Kent)
E.71,050   *T*.81.35%
*G. M. Wolfson, C.	33,245
R. Walshe, *LD*	14,091
Ms J. Evans, *Lab.*	9,470
Ms M. Lawrence, *Green*	786
P. Wakeling, *NLP*	210
C. majority	19,154
(June 1987, C. maj. 17,345)	

SHEFFIELD ATTERCLIFFE (S. Yorks)
E.69,177   *T*.71.81%
C. Betts, *Lab.*	28,563
G. Millward, *C.*	13,083
Ms H. Woolley, *LD*	7,283
G. Ferguson, *Green*	751
Lab. majority	15,480
(June 1987, Lab. maj. 17,191)	

SHEFFIELD BRIGHTSIDE (S. Yorks)
E.63,810   *T*.66.26%
*D. Blunkett, Lab.	29,771
T. Loughton, *C.*	7,090
R. Franklin, *LD*	5,273
D. Hyland, *Int. Comm.*	150
Lab. majority	22,681
(June 1987, Lab. maj. 24,191)	

SHEFFIELD CENTRAL (S. Yorks)
E.59,059   *T*.56.12%
*R. Caborn, Lab.	22,764
V. Davies, *C.*	5,470
A. Sangar, *LD*	3,856
G. Wroe, *Green*	750
M. Clarke, *EUVJJ*	212
Ms J. O'Brien, *CL*	92
Lab. majority	17,294
(June 1987, Lab. maj. 19,342)	

SHEFFIELD HALLAM (S. Yorks)
E.76,584   *T*.70.83%
*C. I. Patnick, C.	24,693
Dr P. Gold, *LD*	17,952
Ms V. Hardstaff, *Lab.*	10,930
M. Baker, *Green*	473
R. Hurford, *NLP*	101
Ms T. Clifford, *Rev. Comm.*	99
C. majority	6,741
(June 1987, C. maj. 7,637)	

SHEFFIELD HEELEY (S. Yorks)
E.70,953   *T*.70.89%
*W. Michie, Lab.	28,005
D. Beck, *C.*	13,051
P. Moore, *LD*	9,247
Lab. majority	14,954
(June 1987, Lab. maj. 14,440)	

SHEFFIELD HILLSBOROUGH
(S. Yorks)
E.77,343   *T*.77.19%
Mrs H. Jackson, *Lab.*	27,568
D. Chadwick, *LD*	20,500
S. Cordle, *C.*	11,640
Lab. majority	7,068
(June 1987, Lab. maj. 3,286)	

SHERWOOD (Notts)
E.73,354   *T*.85.48%
S. P. Tipping, *Lab.*	29,788
*A. Stewart, C.	26,878
J. Howard, *LD*	6,039
Lab. majority	2,910
(June 1987, C. maj. 4,495)	

SHIPLEY (W. Yorks)
E.68,816   *T*.82.12%
*Sir M. Fox, C.	28,463
Ms A. Lockwood, *Lab.*	16,081
J. Cole, *LD*	11,288
C. Harris, *Green*	680
C. majority	12,382
(June 1987, C. maj. 12,630)	

SHOREHAM (W. Sussex)
E.71,252   *T*.81.17%
B. M. L. Stephen, *C.*	32,670
M. King, *LD*	18,384
P. Godwin, *Lab.*	6,123
W. Weights, *Lib.*	459
J. Dreben, *NLP*	200
C. majority	14,286
(June 1987, C. maj. 17,070)	

SHREWSBURY AND ATCHAM (Salop)
E.70,620   *T*.82.45%
*D. Conway, C.	26,681
K. Hemsley, *LD*	15,716
Ms E. Owen, *Lab.*	15,157
G. Hardy, *Green*	677
C. majority	10,965
(June 1987, C. maj. 9,064)	

SHROPSHIRE NORTH
E.82,675   *T*.77.68%
*Rt. Hon. J. Biffen, C.	32,443
J. Stevens, *LD*	16,232
R. Hawkins, *Lab.*	15,550
C. majority	16,211
(June 1987, C. maj. 14,415)	

SKIPTON AND RIPON (N. Yorks)
E.75,628   *T*.81.34%
*D. Curry, C.	35,937
R. Hall, *LD*	16,607
Ms K. Allott, *Lab.*	8,978
C. majority	19,330
(June 1987, C. maj. 17,174)	

SLOUGH (Berks)
E.73,889   *T*.78.24%
*J. Watts, C.	25,793
E. Lopez, *Lab.*	25,279
P. Mapp, *LD*	4,041
J. Clark, *Lib.*	1,426
D. Alford, *Ind. Lab.*	699
A. Carmichael, *NF*	290
M. Creese, *NLP*	153
Ms E. Smith, *ERIP*	134
C. majority	514
(June 1987, C. maj. 4,090)	

SOLIHULL (W. Midlands)
E.77,303   *T*.81.61%
*J. Taylor, C.	38,385
M. Southcombe, *LD*	13,239
Ms N. Kutapan, *Lab.*	10,544
C. Hards, *Green*	925
C. majority	25,146
(June 1987, C. maj. 21,786)	

SOMERTON AND FROME (Somerset)
E.71,354   *T*.82.75%
M. Robinson, *C.*	28,052
D. Heath, *LD*	23,711
R. Ashford, *Lab.*	6,154
Ms L. Graham, *Green*	742
Ms J. Pollock, *Lib.*	388
C. majority	4,341
(June 1987, C. maj. 9,538)	

SOUTHAMPTON ITCHEN (Hants)
E.72,104   *T*.76.93%
J. Denham, *Lab.*	24,402
*C. Chope, C.	23,851
J. Hodgson, *LD*	7,221
Lab. majority	551
(June 1987, C. maj. 6,716)	

SOUTHAMPTON TEST (Hants)
E.72,932   *T*.77.40%
*S. J. A. Hill, C.	24,504
A. Whitehead, *Lab.*	23,919
Ms D. Maddock, *LD*	7,391
J. Michaelis, *Green*	535
D. Plummer, *NLP*	101
C. majority	585
(June 1987, C. maj. 6,954)	

SOUTHEND EAST (Essex)
E.56,708   *T*.73.80%
*Sir E. Taylor, C.	24,591
G. Bramley, *Lab.*	11,480
Ms J. Horne, *LD*	5,107
B. Lynch, *Lib.*	673
C. majority	13,111
(June 1987, C. maj. 13,847)	

SOUTHEND WEST (Essex)
E.64,198   *T*.77.80%
*Rt. Hon. P. Channon, C.	27,319
Ms N. Stimson, *LD*	15,417
G. Viney, *Lab.*	6,139
A. Farmer, *Lib.*	495
C. Keene, *Green*	451
P. Warburton, *NLP*	127
C. majority	11,902
(June 1987, C. maj. 8,400)	

SOUTH HAMS (Devon)
E.83,061   *T*.81.09%
*A. Steen, C.	35,951
V. Evans, *LD*	22,240
Ms E. Cohen, *Lab.*	8,091
C. Titmuss, *Green*	846
Mrs L. Summerville, *NLP*	227
C. majority	13,711
(June 1987, C. maj. 13,146)	

SOUTHPORT (Merseyside)
E.71,443   *T*.77.60%
M. Banks, *C.*	26,081
*R. Fearn, LD	23,018
J. King, *Lab.*	5,637
J. Walker, *Green*	545

G. Clements, NLP 159
C. majority 3,063
(June 1987, L./All. maj. 1,849)

SOUTH RIBBLE (Lancs)
E.78,173 T.82.99%
*R. Atkins, C. 30,828
Dr G. Smith, Lab. 24,855
S. Jones, LD 8,928
Dr R. Decter, NLP 269
C. majority 5,973
(June 1987, C. maj. 8,430)

SOUTH SHIELDS (Tyne & Wear)
E.59,392 T.70.07%
*D. Clark, Lab. 24,876
J. Howard, C. 11,399
A. Preece, LD 5,344
Lab. majority 13,477
(June 1987, Lab. maj. 13,851)

SOUTHWARK AND BERMONDSEY
(Greater London)
E.60,251 T.62.62%
*S. Hughes, LD 21,459
R. Balfe, Lab. 11,614
A. Raca, C. 3,794
S. Tyler, BNP 530
T. Blackham, NF 168
Dr G. Barnett, NLP 113
J. Grogan, CL 56
LD majority 9,845
June 1987, L./All. maj. 2,779

SPELTHORNE (Surrey)
E.69,343 T.80.36%
*D. Wilshire, C. 32,627
Ms A. Leedham, Lab. 12,784
R. Roberts, LD 9,202
Ms J. Wassell, Green 580
D. Rea, Loony 338
D. Ellis, NLP 195
C. majority 19,843
(June 1987, C. maj. 20,050)

STAFFORD
E.74,663 T.82.91%
*W. Cash, C. 30,876
D. Kidney, Lab. 19,976
Mrs J. Calder, LD 10,702
C. Peat, Hardcore 178
P. Lines, NLP 176
C. majority 10,900
(June 1987, C. maj. 13,707)

STAFFORDSHIRE MID
E.73,414 T.85.66%
M. Fabricant, C. 31,227
*Mrs S. Heal, Lab. 24,991
B. Stamp, LD 6,432
Ms D. Grice, NLP 239
C. majority 6,236
(June 1987, C. maj. 14,654)
(March 1990, Lab. maj. 9,449)

STAFFORDSHIRE MOORLANDS
E.75,036 T.83.66%
*D. Knox, C. 29,240
J. Siddelley, Lab. 21,830
Ms C. Jebb, LD 9,326
M. Howson, Anti Fed. 2,121
P. Davies, NLP 261

C. majority 7,410
(June 1987, C. maj. 14,427)

STAFFORDSHIRE SOUTH
E.82,758 T.81.54%
*P. Cormack, C. 40,266
B. Wylie, Lab. 17,633
I. Sadler, LD 9,584
C. majority 22,633
(June 1987, C. maj. 25,268)

STAFFORDSHIRE SOUTH EAST
E.70,199 T.82.05%
*D. Lightbown, C. 29,180
B. Jenkins, Lab. 21,988
Dr G. Penlington, LD 5,540
Miss J. Taylor, SD 895
C. majority 7,192
(June 1987, C. maj. 10,885)
See also page 235

STALYBRIDGE AND HYDE (Greater
Manchester)
E.68,189 T.73.46%
*T. Pendry, Lab. 26,207
S. Mort, C. 17,376
I. Kirk, LD 4,740
R. Powell, Lib. 1,199
D. Poyzer, Loony 337
E. Blomfield, NLP 238
Lab. majority 8,831
(June 1987, Lab. maj. 5,663)

STAMFORD AND SPALDING (Lincs)
E.75,153 T.81.16%
*J. Q. Davies, C. 35,965
C. Burke, Lab. 13,096
B. Lee, LD 11,939
C. majority 22,869
(June 1987, C. maj. 14,007)

STEVENAGE (Herts)
E.70,233 T.83.03%
*T. Wood, C. 26,652
Ms J. Church, Lab. 21,764
A. Reilly, LD 9,668
A. Calcraft, NLP 233
C. majority 4,888
(June 1987, C. maj. 5,340)

STOCKPORT (Greater Manchester)
E.58,095 T.82.27%
Ms M. A. Coffey, Lab. 21,096
*A. Favell, C. 19,674
Ms A. Corris, LD 6,539
Ms J. Filmore, Green 436
D. Saunders, NLP 50
Lab. majority 1,422
(June 1987, C. maj. 2,853)

STOCKTON NORTH (Cleveland)
E.69,451 T.76.83%
*F. Cook, Lab. 27,918
S. Brocklebank-Fowler, C. 17,444
Ms S. Fletcher, LD 7,454
K. McGarvey, Ind. Lab. 550
Lab. majority 10,474
(June 1987, Lab. maj. 8,801)

STOCKTON SOUTH (Cleveland)
E.75,959 T.82.77%
*T. Devlin, C. 28,418
J. Scott, Lab. 25,049
Ms K. Kirkham, LD 9,410

C. majority 3,369
(June 1987, C. maj. 774)

STOKE-ON-TRENT CENTRAL
(Staffs)
E.65,527 T.68.12%
*M. Fisher, Lab. 25,897
N. Gibb, C. 12,477
M. Dent, LD 6,073
N. Pullen, NLP 196
Lab. majority 13,420
(June 1987, Lab. maj. 9,770)

STOKE-ON-TRENT NORTH (Staffs)
E.73,141 T.73.42%
*Ms J. Walley, Lab. 30,464
L. Harris, C. 15,687
J. Redfern, LD 7,167
A. Morrison, NLP 387
Lab. majority 14,777
(June 1987, Lab. maj. 8,513)

STOKE-ON-TRENT SOUTH (Staffs)
E.71,316 T.74.33%
G. Stevenson, Lab. 26,380
R. Ibbs, C. 19,471
F. Jones, LD 6,870
Mrs E. Lines, NLP 291
Lab. majority 6,909
(June 1987, Lab. maj. 5,053)

STRATFORD-UPON-AVON
(Warwicks)
E.82,824 T.82.07%
*A. Howarth, C. 40,251
N. Fogg, LD 17,359
Ms S. Brookes, Lab. 8,932
R. Roughan, Green 729
A. Saunders, Ind. C. 573
M. Twite, NLP 130
C. majority 22,892
(June 1987, C. maj. 21,165)

STREATHAM (Greater London)
E.56,825 T.69.03%
K. Hill, Lab. 18,925
*Sir W. Shelton, C. 16,608
J. Pindar, LD 3,858
R. Baker, Green 443
A. Hankin, Islamic 154
Mrs C. Payne, ADS 145
J. Parsons, NLP 97
Lab. majority 2,317
(June 1987, C. maj. 2,407)

STRETFORD (Greater Manchester)
E.54,467 T.68.76%
*A. Lloyd, Lab. 22,300
C. Rae, C. 11,163
F. Beswick, LD 3,722
A. Boyton, NLP 268
Lab. majority 11,137
(June 1987, Lab. maj. 9,402)

STROUD (Glos)
E.82,553 T.84.49%
*R. Knapman, C. 32,201
D. Drew, Lab. 18,796
M. Robinson, LD 16,751
Ms S. Atkinson, Green 2,005
C. majority 13,405
(June 1987, C. maj. 12,375)

SUFFOLK CENTRAL
E.82,735   T.80.26%

*M. Lord, C.	32,917
Ms L. Henniker-Major, LD	16,886
J. Harris, Lab.	15,615
J. Matthissen, Green	800
Ms J. Wilmot, NLP	190
C. majority	16,031
(June 1987, C. maj. 16,290)	

SUFFOLK COASTAL
E.79,333   T.81.62%

*Rt. Hon. J. Gummer, C.	34,680
P. Monk, LD	15,395
T. Hodgson, Lab.	13,508
A. Slade, Green	943
Ms F. Kaplan, NLP	232
C. majority	19,285
(June 1987, C. maj. 15,280)	

SUFFOLK SOUTH
E.84,833   T.81.73%

*T. Yeo, C.	34,793
Ms K. Pollard, LD	17,504
S. Hesford, Lab.	16,623
T. Aisbitt, NLP	420
C. majority	17,289
(June 1987, C. maj. 16,243)	

SUNDERLAND NORTH (Tyne & Wear)
E.72,874   T.68.86%

W. Etherington, Lab.	30,481
Miss J. Barnes, C.	13,477
V. Halom, LD	5,389
Ms W. Lundgren, Lib.	841
Lab. majority	17,004
(June 1987, Lab. maj. 14,672)	

SUNDERLAND SOUTH (Tyne & Wear)
E.72,607   T.69.87%

*C. Mullin, Lab.	29,399
G. Howe, C.	14,898
J. Lennox, LD	5,844
T. Scouler, Green	596
Lab. majority	14,501
(June 1987, Lab. maj. 12,613)	

SURBITON (Greater London)
E.42,421   T.82.44%

*R. Tracey, C.	19,033
Ms B. Janke, LD	9,394
R. Hutchinson, Lab.	6,384
W. Parker, NLP	161
C. majority	9,639
(June 1987, C. maj. 9,741)	

SURREY EAST
E.57,878   T.82.53%

P. Ainsworth, C.	29,767
R. Tomlin, LD	12,111
Mrs G. Roles, Lab.	5,075
I. Kilpatrick, Green	819
C. majority	17,656
(June 1987, C. maj. 18,126)	

SURREY NORTH WEST
E.83,648   T.78.27%

*Sir M. Grylls, C.	41,772
Mrs C. Clark, LD	13,378
M. Hayhurst, Lab.	8,886
Ms Y. Hockey, Green	1,441

C. majority	28,394
(June 1987, C. maj. 23,575)	

SURREY SOUTH WEST
E.72,288   T.82.77%

*Mrs V. Bottomley, C.	35,008
N. Sherlock, LD	20,033
P. Kelly, Lab.	3,840
N. Bedrock, Green	710
K. Campbell, NLP	147
D. Newman, AS	98
C. majority	14,975
(June 1987, C. maj. 14,343)	

SUSSEX MID
E.80,827   T.82.85%

*Rt. Hon. T. Renton, C.	39,524
Ms M. Collins, LD	18,996
Ms L. Gregory, Lab.	6,951
H. Stevens, Green	772
P. Berry, Loony	392
P. Hodkin, PR	246
Dr A. Hankey, NLP	89
C. majority	20,528
(June 1987, C. maj. 18,292)	

SUTTON AND CHEAM (Greater London)
E.60,949   T.82.39%

Lady O. Maitland, C.	27,710
P. Burstow, LD	16,954
G. Martin, Lab.	4,980
J. Duffy, Green	444
Ms A. Hatchard, NLP	133
C. majority	10,756
(June 1987, C. maj. 15,718)	

SUTTON COLDFIELD (W. Midlands)
E.71,410   T.79.51%

*Rt. Hon. Sir N. Fowler, C.	37,001
J. Whorwood, LD	10,965
Ms J. Bott-Obi, Lab.	8,490
H. Meads, NLP	324
C. majority	26,036
(June 1987, C. maj. 21,183)	

SWINDON (Wilts)
E.90,067   T.81.46%

*S. Coombs, C.	31,749
J. D'Avila, Lab.	28,923
S. Cordon, LD	11,737
W. Hughes, Green	647
R. Gillard, Loony G.	236
V. Farrar, Ind.	78
C. majority	2,826
(June 1987, C. maj. 4,857)	

TATTON (Cheshire)
E.71,085   T.80.83%

*M. N. Hamilton, C.	31,658
J. Kelly, Lab.	15,798
Ms C. Hancox, LD	9,597
M. Gibson, FP	410
C. majority	15,860
(June 1987, C. maj. 17,094)	

TAUNTON (Somerset)
E.78,036   T.82.32%

*D. Nicholson, C.	29,576
Ms J. Ballard, LD	26,240
Ms J. Hole, Lab.	8,151
P. Leavey, NLP	279

C. majority	3,336
(June 1987, C. maj. 10,380)	

TEIGNBRIDGE (Devon)
E.74,892   T.83.43%

*P. Nicholls, C.	31,272
R. Younger-Ross, LD	22,416
R. Kennedy, Lab.	8,128
A. Hope, Loony	437
N. Hayes, NLP	234
C. majority	8,856
(June 1987, C. maj. 10,425)	

THANET NORTH (Kent)
E.70,978   T.76.02%

*R. Gale, C.	30,867
A. Bretman, Lab.	12,657
Ms J. Phillips, LD	9,563
Ms H. Dawe, Green	873
C. majority	18,210
(June 1987, C. maj. 17,480)	

THANET SOUTH (Kent)
E.62,441   T.78.17%

*J. Aitken, C.	25,253
M. James, Lab.	13,740
W. Pitt, LD	8,948
Ms S. Peckham, Green	871
C. majority	11,513
(June 1987, C. maj. 13,683)	

THURROCK (Essex)
E.69,171   T.78.15%

A. MacKinlay, Lab.	24,791
*T. Janman, C.	23,619
A. Banton, LD	5,145
C. Rogers, Pensioners	391
P. Compobassi, Anti Fed.	117
Lab. majority	1,172
(June 1987, C. maj. 690)	

TIVERTON (Devon)
E.71,024   T.82.98%

Mrs A. Browning, C.	30,376
D. Cox, LD	19,287
Ms S. Gibb, Lab.	5,950
D. Morrish, Lib.	2,225
P. Foggitt, Green	1,007
B. Rhodes, NLP	96
C. majority	11,089
(June 1987, C. maj. 9,212)	

TONBRIDGE AND MALLING (Kent)
E.77,292   T.82.66%

*Rt. Hon. Sir J. Stanley, C.	36,542
P. Roberts, LD	14,984
Ms M. O'Neill, Lab.	11,533
J. Tidy, Green	612
Mrs J. Hovarth, NLP	221
C. majority	21,558
(June 1987, C. maj. 16,429)	

TOOTING (Greater London)
E.68,306   T.74.79%

*T. Cox, Lab.	24,601
M. Winters, C.	20,494
B. Bunce, LD	3,776
Ms C. Martin, Lib.	1,340
P. Owens, Green	694
F. Anklesalria, NLP	119
M. Whitelaw, CD	64
Lab. majority	4,107
(June 1987, Lab. maj. 1,441)	

TORBAY (Devon)
E.71,171   *T*.80.63%

*R. Allason, C.	28,624
A. Sanders, LD	22,837
P. Truscott, Lab.	5,503
R. Jones, NF	268
Ms A. Thomas, NLP	157
C. majority	5,787
(June 1987, C. maj. 8,820)	

TOTTENHAM (Greater London)
E.68,319   *T*.65.60%

*B. Grant, Lab.	25,309
A. Charalambous, C.	13,341
A. L'Estrange, LD	5,120
P. Budge, Green	903
Ms M. Obomanu, NLP	150
Lab. majority	11,968
(June 1987, Lab. maj. 4,141)	

TRURO (Cornwall)
E.75,101   *T*.82.35%

*M. Taylor, LD	31,230
N. St Aubyn, C.	23,660
J. Geach, Lab.	6,078
L. Keating, Green	569
C. Tankard, Lib.	208
Ms M. Hartley, NLP	108
LD majority	7,570
(June 1987, L./All. maj. 4,753)	

TUNBRIDGE WELLS (Kent)
E.76,808   *T*.78.11%

*Rt. Hon. Sir P. Mayhew, C.	34,162
A. Clayton, LD	17,030
E. Goodman, Lab.	8,300
E. Fenna, NLP	267
R. Edey, ISS	236
C. majority	17,132
(June 1987, C. maj. 16,122)	

TWICKENHAM (Greater London)
E.63,072   *T*.84.27%

*T. Jessel, C.	26,804
Dr V. Cable, LD	21,093
M. Gold, Lab.	4,919
G. Gill, NLP	152
D. Griffith, DLC	103
A. Miners, Lib.	85
C. majority	5,711
(June 1987, C. maj. 7,127)	

TYNE BRIDGE (Tyne & Wear)
E.53,079   *T*.62.64%

*D. Clelland, Lab.	22,328
C. Liddell-Grainger, C.	7,118
J. Burt, LD	3,804
Lab. majority	15,210
(June 1987, Lab. maj. 15,573)	

TYNEMOUTH (Tyne & Wear)
E.74,955   *T*.80.39%

*N. Trotter, C.	27,731
P. Cosgrove, Lab.	27,134
P. Selby, LD	4,855
A. Buchanan-Smith, Green	543
C. majority	597
(June 1987, C. maj. 2,583)	

UPMINSTER (Greater London)
E.64,138   *T*.80.46%

*Sir N. Bonsor, C.	28,791
T. Ward, Lab.	14,970

T. Hurlstone, LD	7,848
C. majority	13,821
(June 1987, C. maj. 16,857)	

UXBRIDGE (Greater London)
E.61,744   *T*.78.87%

*J. M. Shersby, C.	27,487
R. Evans, Lab.	14,308
S. Carey, LD	5,900
I. Flindall, Green	538
M. O'Rourke, BNP	350
A. Deans, NLP	120
C. majority	13,179
(June 1987, C. maj. 15,970)	

VAUXHALL (Greater London)
E.62,473   *T*.62.35%

*Ms C. Hoey, Lab.	21,328
B. Gentry, C.	10,840
M. Tuffrey, LD	5,678
Ms P. Shepherd, Green	803
A. Khan, DOS	156
Ms S. Hill, Rev. Comm.	152
Lab. majority	10,488
(June 1987, Lab. maj. 9,019)	
(June 1989, Lab. maj. 9,766)	

WAKEFIELD (W. Yorks)
E.69,794   *T*.76.27%

*D. Hinchliffe, Lab.	26,964
D. Fanthorpe, C.	20,374
T. Wright, LD	5,900
Lab. majority	6,590
(June 1987, Lab. maj. 2,789)	

WALLASEY (Merseyside)
E.65,676   *T*.82.50%

Ms A. Eagle, Lab.	26,531
*Rt. Hon. L. Chalker, C.	22,722
N. Thomas, LD	4,177
Ms S. Davis, Green	650
G. Gay, NLP	105
Lab. majority	3,809
(June 1987, C. maj. 279)	

WALLSEND (Tyne & Wear)
E.77,941   *T*.74.12%

S. Byers, Lab.	33,439
Miss M. Gibbon, C.	13,969
M. Huscroft, LD	10,369
Lab. majority	19,470
(June 1987, Lab. maj. 19,384)	

WALSALL NORTH (W. Midlands)
E.69,604   *T*.74.98%

*D. Winnick, Lab.	24,387
R. Syms, C.	20,563
A. Powis, LD	6,629
K. Reynolds, NF	614
Lab. majority	3,824
(June 1987, Lab. maj. 1,790)	

WALSALL SOUTH (W. Midlands)
E.65,642   *T*.76.26%

*B. George, Lab.	24,133
L. Jones, C.	20,955
G. Williams, LD	4,132
R. Clarke, Green	673
J. Oldbury, NLP	167
Lab. majority	3,178
(June 1987, Lab. maj. 1,116)	

WALTHAMSTOW (Greater London)
E.49,140   *T*.72.35%

N. Gerrard, Lab.	16,251
*H. Summerson, C.	13,229
P. Leighton, LD	5,142
Ms J. Lambert, Green	594
V. Wilkinson, Lib.	241
A. Planton, NLP	94
Lab. majority	3,022
(June 1987, C. maj. 1,512)	

WANSBECK (Northumberland)
E.63,457   *T*.79.29%

*J. Thompson, Lab.	30,046
G. Sanderson, C.	11,872
B. Priestley, LD	7,691
N. Best, Green	710
Lab. majority	18,174
(June 1987, Lab. maj. 16,789)	

WANSDYKE (Avon)
E.77,156   *T*.84.33%

*J. Aspinwall, C.	31,389
D. Norris, Lab.	18,048
Ms D. Darby, LD	14,834
F. Hayden, Green	800
C. majority	13,341
(June 1987, C. maj. 16,144)	

WANSTEAD AND WOODFORD
(Greater London)
E.55,821   *T*.78.28%

*J. Arbuthnot, C.	26,204
Ms L. Brown, Lab.	9,319
G. Staight, LD	7,362
F. Roads, Green	637
A. Brickell, NLP	178
C. majority	16,885
(June 1987, C. maj. 16,412)	

WANTAGE (Oxon)
E.68,328   *T*.82.68%

*R. Jackson, C.	30,575
R. Morgan, LD	14,102
V. Woodell, Lab.	10,955
R. Ely, Green	867
C. majority	16,473
(June 1987, C. maj. 12,156)	

WARLEY EAST (W. Midlands)
E.51,717   *T*.71.72%

*A. Faulds, Lab.	19,891
G. Marshall, C.	12,097
A. Harrod, LD	4,547
A. Groucott, NLP	561
Lab. majority	7,794
(June 1987, Lab. maj. 5,585)	

WARLEY WEST (W. Midlands)
E.57,164   *T*.73.90%

J. Spellar, Lab.	21,386
Mrs S. Whitehouse, C.	15,914
Ms E. Todd, LD	4,945
Lab. majority	5,472
(June 1987, Lab. maj. 5,393)	

WARRINGTON NORTH (Cheshire)
E.78,548   *T*.77.38%

*E. D. H. Hoyle, Lab.	33,019
C. Daniels, C.	20,397
I. Greenhalgh, LD	6,965
B. Davies, NLP	400

Lab. majority	12,622
(June 1987, Lab. maj. 8,013)	

WARRINGTON SOUTH (Cheshire)
E.77,694   T.82.04%

M. Hall, *Lab.*	27,819
C. Butler, *C.*	27,628
P. Walker, *LD*	7,978
S. Benson, *NLP*	321
Lab. majority	191
(June 1987, C. maj. 3,609)	

WARWICK AND LEAMINGTON
E.71,259   T.81.54%

Sir D. Smith, *C.*	28,093
M. Taylor, *Lab.*	19,158
Ms S. Boad, *LD*	9,645
Ms J. Alty, *Green*	803
R. Newby, *Ind.*	251
J. Brewster, *NLP*	156
C. majority	8,935
(June 1987, C. maj. 13,982)	

WARWICKSHIRE NORTH
E.71,473   T.83.82%

M. O'Brien, *Lab.*	27,599
Hon. F. Maude, *C.*	26,145
N. Mitchell, *LD*	6,167
Lab. majority	1,454
(June 1987, C. maj. 2,829)	

WATFORD (Herts)
E.72,291   T.82.34%

W. A. T. T. Garel-Jones, *C.*	29,072
M. Jackson, *Lab.*	19,482
M. Oaten, *LD*	10,231
J. Hywel-Davies, *Green*	566
L. Davis, *NLP*	176
C. majority	9,590
(June 1987, C. maj. 11,736)	

WAVENEY (Suffolk)
E.84,181   T.81.81%

D. Porter, *C.*	33,174
E. Leverett, *Lab.*	26,472
A. Rogers, *LD*	8,925
D. Hook, *NLP*	302
C. majority	6,702
(June 1987, C. maj. 11,783)	

WEALDEN (E. Sussex)
E.74,665   T.80.83%

Sir G. Johnson Smith, *C.*	37,263
M. Skinner, *LD*	16,332
S. Billcliffe, *Lab.*	5,579
I. Guy-Moore, *Green*	1,002
Dr R. Graham, *NLP*	182
C. majority	20,931
(June 1987, C. maj. 20,110)	

WELLINGBOROUGH (Northants)
E.73,875   T.81.89%

P. Fry, *C.*	32,302
P. Sawford, *Lab.*	20,486
Ms J. Trevor, *LD*	7,714
C. majority	11,816
(June 1987, C. maj. 14,070)	

WELLS (Somerset)
E.69,833   T.82.71%

D. Heathcoat-Amory, *C.*	28,620
H. Temperley, *LD*	21,971
J. Pilgrim, *Lab.*	6,126
M. Fenner, *Green*	1,042

C. majority	6,649
(June 1987, C. maj. 8,541)	

WELWYN HATFIELD (Herts)
E.72,146   T.84.39%

*D. Evans, *C.*	29,447
R. Little, *Lab.*	20,982
R. Parker, *LD*	10,196
Ms E. Lucas, *NLP*	264
C. majority	8,465
(June 1987, C. maj. 10,903)	

WENTWORTH (S. Yorks)
E.64,914   T.74.03%

*P. Hardy, *Lab.*	32,939
M. Brennan, *C.*	10,490
Ms C. Roderick, *LD*	4,629
Lab. majority	22,449
(June 1987, Lab. maj. 20,092)	

**WEST BROMWICH EAST
(W. Midlands)**
E.56,940   T.75.25%

*P. Snape, *Lab.*	19,913
C. Blunt, *C.*	17,100
M. Smith, *LD*	5,360
J. Lord, *NF*	477
Lab. majority	2,813
(June 1987, Lab. maj. 983)	

**WEST BROMWICH WEST
(W. Midlands)**
E.57,655   T.70.41%

*Miss B. Boothroyd, *Lab.*	22,251
D. Swayne, *C.*	14,421
Miss S. Broadbent, *LD*	3,925
Lab. majority	7,830
(June 1987, Lab. maj. 5,253)	

WESTBURY (Wilts)
E.87,356   T.82.99%

D. Faber, *C.*	36,568
Ms V. Rayner, *LD*	23,962
W. Stallard, *Lab.*	9,642
P. Macdonald, *Lib.*	1,440
P. French, *Green*	888
C. majority	12,606
(June 1987, C. maj. 10,097)	

**WESTMINSTER NORTH (Greater
London)**
E.58,847   T.75.75%

*Sir J. Wheeler, *C.*	21,828
Ms J. Edwards, *Lab.*	18,095
J. Wigoder, *LD*	3,341
Ms A. Burke, *Green*	1,017
J. Hinde, *NLP*	159
M. Kelly, *Anti Fed.*	137
C. majority	3,733
(June 1987, C. maj. 3,310)	

**WESTMORLAND AND LONSDALE
(Cumbria)**
E.71,865   T.77.76%

*Rt. Hon. M. Jopling, *C.*	31,798
S. Collins, *LD*	15,362
D. Abbott, *Lab.*	8,436
R. Johnstone, *NLP*	287
C. majority	16,436
(June 1987, C. maj. 14,920)	

WESTON-SUPER-MARE (Avon)
E.78,839   T.79.75%

*A. W. Wiggin, *C.*	30,022
B. Cotter, *LD*	24,680
D. Murray, *Lab.*	6,913
Dr R. Lawson, *Green*	1,262
C. majority	5,342
(June 1987, C. maj. 7,998)	

WIGAN (Greater Manchester)
E.72,739   T.76.16%

*R. Stott, *Lab.*	34,910
E. Hess, *C.*	13,068
G. Davies, *LD*	6,111
K. White, *Lib.*	1,116
Ms A. Taylor, *NLP*	197
Lab. majority	21,842
(June 1987, Lab. maj. 20,462)	

WILTSHIRE NORTH
E.85,851   T.81.71%

*R. Needham, *C.*	39,028
Ms C. Napier, *LD*	22,640
Ms C. Reid, *Lab.*	6,945
Ms L. Howitt, *Green*	850
G. Hawkins, *Lib.*	622
S. Martiensson, *Bastion*	66
C. majority	16,388
(June 1987, C. maj. 10,939)	

WIMBLEDON (Greater London)
E.61,917   T.80.23%

*Dr C. Goodson-Wickes, *C.*	26,331
K. Abrams, *Lab.*	11,570
Ms A. Willott, *LD*	10,569
V. Flood, *Green*	860
H. Godfrey, *NLP*	181
G. Hadley, *Ind.*	170
C. majority	14,761
(June 1987, C. maj. 11,301)	

WINCHESTER (Hants)
E.79,218   T.83.46%

P. G. Malone, *C.*	33,113
A. Barron, *LD*	24,992
P. Jenks, *Lab.*	4,917
*J. Browne, *Ind. C.*	3,095
C. majority	8,121
(June 1987, C. maj. 7,479)	

**WINDSOR AND MAIDENHEAD
(Berks)**
E.77,327   T.81.68%

Hon. M. Trend, *C.*	35,075
J. Hyde, *LD*	22,147
Ms C. Attlee, *Lab.*	4,975
R. Williams, *Green*	510
D. Askwith, *Loony*	236
Miss E. Bigg, *Ind.*	110
M. Grenville, *NLP*	108
C. majority	12,928
(June 1987, C. maj. 17,836)	

WIRRAL SOUTH (Merseyside)
E.61,116   T.82.37%

*G. B. Porter, *C.*	25,590
Ms H. Southworth, *Lab.*	17,407
E. Cunniffe, *LD*	6,581
N. Birchenough, *Green*	584
G. Griffiths, *NLP*	182
C. majority	8,183
(June 1987, C. maj. 10,963)	

WIRRAL WEST (Merseyside)
E.62,453   T.81.57%

*Rt. Hon. D. Hunt, *C.*	26,852
Ms H. Stephenson, *Lab.*	15,788
J. Thornton, *LD*	7,420
Ms G. Bowler, *Green*	700
N. Broome, *NLP*	188
C. majority	11,064
(June 1987, C. maj. 12,723)	

WITNEY (Oxon)
E.78,521   T.81.89%

*Rt. Hon. D. Hurd, *C.*	36,256
J. Plaskitt, *Lab.*	13,688
I. Blair, *LD*	13,393
Ms C. Beckford, *Green*	716
Ms S. Catling, *NLP*	134
Miss M. Brown, *FTA*	119
C. majority	22,568
(June 1987, C. maj. 18,464)	

WOKING (Surrey)
E.80,842   T.79.20%

*Rt. Hon. C. Onslow, *C.*	37,744
Mrs D. Buckrell, *LD*	17,902
J. Dalgleish, *Lab.*	8,080
Mrs T. Macintyre, *NLP*	302
C. majority	19,842
(June 1987, C. maj. 16,544)	

WOKINGHAM (Berks)
E.85,914   T.82.41%

*J. Redwood, *C.*	43,497
P. Simon, *LD*	17,788
N. Bland, *Lab.*	8,846
P. Owen, *Loony*	531
P. Harriss, *WUWC*	148
C. majority	25,709
(June 1987, C. maj. 20,387)	

WOLVERHAMPTON NORTH EAST
(W. Midlands)
E.62,695   T.78%

K. Purchase, *Lab.*	24,106
*Mrs M. Hicks, *C.*	20,167
M. Gwinnett, *LD*	3,546
K. Bullman, *Lib.*	1,087
Lab. majority	3,939
(June 1987, C. maj. 204)	

WOLVERHAMPTON SOUTH EAST
(W. Midlands)
E.56,158   T.72.86%

*D. Turner, *Lab.*	23,215
P. Bradbourn, *C.*	12,975
R. Whitehouse, *LD*	3,881
Ms C. Twelvetrees, *Lib.*	850
Lab. majority	10,240
(June 1987, Lab. maj. 6,398)	

WOLVERHAMPTON SOUTH WEST
(W. Midlands)
E.67,288   T.78.28%

*N. Budgen, *C.*	25,969
S. Murphy, *Lab.*	21,003
M. Wiggin, *LD*	4,470
C. Hallmark, *Lib.*	1,237
C. majority	4,966
(June 1987, C. maj. 10,318)	

WOODSPRING (Avon)
E.77,534   T.83.21%

Dr L. Fox, *C.*	35,175
Ms N. Kirsen, *LD*	17,666
R. Stone, *Lab.*	9,942
N. Brown, *Lib.*	836
Ms R. Knifton, *Green*	801
B. Lee, *NLP*	100
C. majority	17,509
(June 1987, C. maj. 17,852)	

WOOLWICH (Greater London)
E.55,977   T.70.91%

J. Austin-Walker, *Lab.*	17,551
*J. Cartwright, *SD*	15,326
K. Walmsley, *C.*	6,598
Ms S. Hayward, *NLP*	220
Lab. majority	2,225
(June 1987, SDP/All. maj. 1,937)	

WORCESTER
E.74,211   T.80.99%

P. Luff, *C.*	27,883
R. Berry, *Lab.*	21,731
J. Caiger, *LD*	9,561
M. Foster, *Green*	592
M. Soden, *Brewer*	343
C. majority	6,152
(June 1987, C. maj. 10,453)	

WORCESTERSHIRE MID
E.84,269   T.81.07%

*E. Forth, *C.*	33,964
Ms J. Smith, *Lab.*	24,094
D. Barwick, *LD*	9,745
P. Davis, *NLP*	520
C. majority	9,870
(June 1987, C. maj. 14,911)	

WORCESTERSHIRE SOUTH
E.80,423   T.79.99%

*W. M. H. Spicer, *C.*	34,792
P. Chandler, *LD*	18,641
N. Knowles, *Lab.*	9,727
G. Woodford, *Green*	1,178
C. majority	16,151
(June 1987, C. maj. 13,645)	

WORKINGTON (Cumbria)
E.57,597   T.81.52%

*D. Campbell-Savours, *Lab.*	26,719
S. Sexton, *C.*	16,270
Ms C. Neale, *LD*	3,028
D. Langstaff, *Loony*	755
Ms N. Escott, *NLP*	183
Lab. majority	10,449
(June 1987, Lab. maj. 7,019)	

WORSLEY (Greater Manchester)
E.72,244   T.77.74%

*T. Lewis, *Lab.*	29,418
N. Cameron, *C.*	19,406
R. Boyd, *LD*	6,490
P. Connolly, *Green*	677
G. Phillips, *NLP*	176
Lab. majority	10,012
(June 1987, Lab. maj. 7,337)	

WORTHING (W. Sussex)
E.77,540   T.77.41%

*Rt. Hon. T. Higgins, *C.*	34,198
Mrs S. Bucknall, *LD*	17,665
J. Deen, *Lab.*	6,679

Mrs P. Beever, *Green*	806
N. Goble, *Lib.*	679
C. majority	16,533
(June 1987, C. maj. 18,501)	

THE WREKIN (Salop)
E.90,892   T.77.14%

*B. Grocott, *Lab.*	33,865
Mrs E. Holt, *C.*	27,217
A. West, *LD*	8,032
R. Saunders, *Green*	1,008
Lab. majority	6,648
(June 1987, Lab. maj. 1,456)	

WYCOMBE (Bucks)
E.72,564   T.78.01%

*R. Whitney, *C.*	30,081
T. Andrews, *LD*	13,005
J. Huddart, *Lab.*	12,222
J. Laker, *Green*	686
A. Page, *SD*	449
T. Anton, *NLP*	168
C. majority	17,076
(June 1987, C. maj. 13,819)	

WYRE (Lancs)
E.67,778   T.79.54%

*K. Mans, *C.*	29,449
D. Borrow, *Lab.*	17,785
J. Ault, *LD*	6,420
R. Perry, *NLP*	260
C. majority	11,664
(June 1987, C. maj. 14,661)	

WYRE FOREST (H & W)
E.73,550   T.82.36%

*A. Coombs, *C.*	28,983
R. Maden, *Lab.*	18,642
M. Jones, *LD*	12,958
C. majority	10,341
(June 1987, C. maj. 7,224)	

YEOVIL (Somerset)
E.73,057   T.81.98%

*Rt. Hon. J. J. D. Ashdown, *LD*	
58	
J. Davidson, *C.*	22,125
Ms V. Nelson, *Lab.*	5,765
J. Risbridger, *Green*	639
D. Sutch, *Loony*	338
R. Simmerson, *APAKBI*	70
LD majority	8,833
(June 1987, L./All. maj. 5,700)	

YORK (N. Yorks)
E.79,242   T.80.97%

H. Bayley, *Lab.*	31,525
*C. Gregory, *C.*	25,183
Ms K. Anderson, *LD*	6,811
S. Kenwright, *Green*	594
Ms P. Orr, *NLP*	54
Lab. majority	6,342
(June 1987, C. maj. 147)	

WALES

ABERAVON (W. Glamorgan)
E.51,650   T.77.57%
*Rt. Hon. J. Morris, Lab.   26,877
H. Williams, C.   5,567
Mrs M. Harris, LD   4,999
D. Saunders, PC   1,919
Capt. Beany, Real Bean   707
Lab. majority   21,310
(June 1987, Lab. maj. 20,609)

ALYN AND DEESIDE (Clwyd)
E.60,477   T.80.08%
*S. B. Jones, Lab.   25,206
J. Riley, C.   17,355
R. Britton, LD   4,687
J. Rogers, PC   551
V. Button, Green   433
J. Cooksey, Ind.   200
Lab. majority   7,851
(June 1987, Lab. maj. 6,383)

BLAENAU GWENT
E.55,638   T.78.13%
L. Smith, Lab.   34,333
D. Melding, C.   4,266
A. Burns, LD   2,774
A. Davies, PC   2,099
Lab. majority   30,067
(June 1987, Lab. maj. 27,861)

BRECON AND RADNOR (Powys)
E.51,509   T.85.94%
J. P. Evans, C.   15,977
*R. Livsey, LD   15,847
C. Mann, Lab.   11,634
Ms S. Meredudd, PC   418
H. Richards, Green   393
C. majority   130
(June 1987, L./All. maj. 56)

BRIDGEND (Mid Glamorgan)
E.58,531   T.80.44%
*W. Griffiths, Lab.   24,143
D. Unwin, C.   16,817
D. Mills, LD   4,827
A. Lloyd Jones, PC   1,301
Lab. majority   7,326
(June 1987, Lab. maj. 4,380)

CAERNARFON (Gwynedd)
E.46,468   T.78.15%
*D. Wigley, PC   21,439
P. Fowler, C.   6,963
Ms S. Mainwaring, Lab.   5,641
R. Arwel Williams, LD   2,101
G. Evans, NLP   173
PC majority   14,476
(June 1987, PC maj. 12,812)

CAERPHILLY (Mid Glamorgan)
E.64,529   T.77.20%
*R. Davies, Lab.   31,713
H. Philpott, C.   9,041
L. Whittle, PC   4,821
S. Wilson, LD   4,247
Lab. majority   22,672
(June 1987, Lab. maj. 19,167)

CARDIFF CENTRAL (S. Glamorgan)
E.57,716   T.74.35%
J. O. Jones, Lab.   18,014
*I. Grist, C.   14,549

Ms J. Randerson, LD   9,170
H. Marshall, PC   748
C. von Ruhland, Green   330
B. Francis, NLP   105
Lab. majority   3,465
(June 1987, C. maj. 1,986)

CARDIFF NORTH (S. Glamorgan)
E.56,721   T.84.15%
*G. H. Jones, C.   21,547
Ms J. Morgan, Lab.   18,578
Ms E. Warlow, LD   6,487
Ms E. Bush, PC   916
J. Morse, BNP   121
D. Palmer, NLP   86
C. majority   2,969
(June 1987, C. maj. 8,234)

CARDIFF SOUTH AND PENARTH
(S. Glamorgan)
E.61,484   T.77.25%
*A. Michael, Lab.   26,383
T. Hunter Jarvie, C.   15,958
P. Verma, LD   3,707
Ms B. Anglezarke, PC   776
L. Davey, Green   676
Lab. majority   10,425
(June 1987, Lab. maj. 4,574)

CARDIFF WEST (S. Glamorgan)
E.58,898   T.77.56%
*H. R. Morgan, Lab.   24,306
M. Prior, C.   15,015
Ms J. Gasson, LD   5,002
Ms P. Bestic, PC   1,177
A. Harding, NLP   184
Lab. majority   9,291
(June 1987, Lab. maj. 4,045)

CARMARTHEN (Dyfed)
E.68,887 T. 82.70%
*Dr A. W. Williams, Lab.   20,879
R. Thomas, PC   17,957
S. Cavenagh, C.   12,782
Mrs J. Hughes, LD   5,533
Lab. majority   2,922
(June 1987, Lab. maj. 4,317)

CEREDIGION AND PEMBROKE
NORTH (Dyfed)
E.66,180   T.77.36%
C. Dafis, PC   16,020
*G. Howells, LD   12,827
J. Williams, C.   12,718
J. Davies, Lab.   9,637
PC majority   3,193
(June 1987, L./All. maj. 4,700)

CLWYD NORTH WEST
E.67,351   T.78.64%
R. Richards, C.   24,488
C. Ruane, Lab.   18,438
R. Ingham, LD   7,999
T. Neil, PC   1,888
Ms M. Swift, NLP   158
C. majority   6,050
(June 1987, C. maj. 11,781)

CLWYD SOUTH WEST
E.60,607   T.81.52%
*M. Jones, Lab.   21,490
G. Owen, C.   16,549

G. Williams, LD   6,027
E. Lloyd Jones, PC   4,835
N. Worth, Green   351
Mrs J. Leadbetter, NLP   155
Lab. majority   4,941
(June 1987, Lab. maj. 1,028)

CONWY (Gwynedd)
E.53,576   T.78.85%
*Rt. Hon. Sir W. Roberts, C.   14,250
Revd R. Roberts, LD   13,255
Ms E. Williams, Lab.   10,883
R. Davies, PC   3,108
O. Wainwright, Ind. C.   637
Ms D. Hughes, NLP   114
C. majority   995
(June 1987, C. maj. 3,024)

CYNON VALLEY (Mid Glamorgan)
E.49,695   T.76.46%
*Ms A. Clwyd, Lab.   26,254
A. Smith, C.   4,890
T. Benney, PC   4,186
M. Verma, LD   2,667
Lab. majority   21,364
(June 1987, Lab. maj. 21,571)

DELYN (Clwyd)
E.66,591   T.83.40%
D. Hanson, Lab.   24,979
M. Whitby, C.   22,940
R. Dodd, LD   6,208
A. Drake, PC   1,414
Lab. majority   2,039
(June 1987, C. maj. 1,224)

GOWER (W. Glamorgan)
E.57,231   T.81.84%
*G. Wardell, Lab.   23,455
A. Donnelly, C.   16,437
C. Davies, LD   4,655
A. Price, PC   1,658
B. Kingzett, Green   448
G. Egan, Loony G.   114
M. Beresford, NLP   74
Lab. majority   7,018
(June 1987, Lab. maj. 5,764)

ISLWYN (Gwent)
E.51,079   T.81.48%
*Rt. Hon. N. Kinnock, Lab.   30,908
P. Bone, C.   6,180
M. Symonds, LD   2,352
Ms H. Jones, PC   1,636
Lord Sutch, Loony   547
Lab. majority   24,728
(June 1987, Lab. maj. 22,947)
See also page 234

LLANELLI (Dyfed)
E.65,058   T.77.80%
*Rt. Hon. D. Davies, Lab.   27,802
G. Down, C.   8,532
M. Phillips, PC   7,878
K. Evans, LD   6,404
Lab. majority   19,270
(June 1987, Lab. maj. 20,935)

MEIRIONNYDD NANT CONWY
(Gwynedd)
*E.*32,413   *T.*81.47%

E. Llwyd, *PC*	11,608
G. Lewis, *C.*	6,995
R. Williams, *Lab.*	4,978
Mrs R. Parry, *LD*	2,358
W. Pritchard, *Green*	471
PC majority	4,613
(June 1987, PC maj. 3,026)	

MERTHYR TYDFIL AND RHYMNEY
(Mid Glamorgan)
*E.*58,430   *T.*75.84%

*E. Rowlands, *Lab.*	31,710
R. Rowland, *LD*	4,997
M. Hughes, *C.*	4,904
A. Cox, *PC*	2,704
Lab. majority	26,713
(June 1987, Lab. maj. 28,207)	

MONMOUTH (Gwent)
*E.*59,147   *T.*86.06%

R. Evans, *C.*	24,059
*H. Edwards, *Lab.*	20,855
Mrs F. David, *LD*	5,562
M. Witherden, *Green/PC*	431
C. majority	3,204
(June 1987, C. maj. 9,350)	
(May 1991, Lab. maj. 2,406)	

MONTGOMERY (Powys)
*E.*41,386   *T.*79.87%

*A. Carlile, *LD*	16,031
Mrs J. France-Hayhurst, *C.*	10,822
S. Wood, *Lab.*	4,115
H. Parsons, *PC*	1,581
P. Adams, *Green*	508
LD majority	5,209
(June 1987, L./All. maj. 2,558)	

NEATH (W. Glamorgan)
*E.*56,392   *T.*80.58%

*P. Hain, *Lab.*	30,903
D. Adams, *C.*	6,928
Dr D. Evans, *PC*	5,145
M. Phillips, *LD*	2,467
Lab. majority	23,975
(June 1987, Lab. maj. 20,578)	
(April 1991, Lab. maj. 9,830)	

NEWPORT EAST (Gwent)
*E.*51,603   *T.*81.21%

*R. J. Hughes, *Lab.*	23,050
Mrs A. Emmett, *C.*	13,151
W. Oliver, *LD*	4,991
S. Ainley, *Green/PC*	716
Lab. majority	9,899
(June 1987, Lab. maj. 7,064)	

NEWPORT WEST (Gwent)
*E.*54,871   *T.*82.82%

*P. Flynn, *Lab.*	24,139
A. Taylor, *C.*	16,360
A. Toye, *LD*	4,296
P. Keelan, *PC*	653
Lab. majority	7,779
(June 1987, Lab. maj. 2,708)	

OGMORE (Mid Glamorgan)
*E.*52,195   *T.*80.62%

*R. Powell, *Lab.*	30,186
D. Edwards, *C.*	6,359
J. Warman, *LD*	2,868
Ms L. McAllister, *PC*	2,667
Lab. majority	23,827
(June 1987, Lab. maj. 22,292)	

PEMBROKE (Dyfed)
*E.*73,187   *T.*82.86%

N. Ainger, *Lab.*	26,253
*N. Bennett, *C.*	25,498
P. Berry, *LD*	6,625
C. Bryant, *PC*	1,627
R. Coghill, *Green*	484
M. Stoddart, *Anti Fed.*	158
Lab. majority	755
(June 1987, C. maj. 5,700)	

PONTYPRIDD (Mid Glamorgan)
*E.*61,685   *T.*79.25%

*K. Howells, *Lab.*	29,722
Dr P. Donnelly, *C.*	9,925
Dr D. Bowen, *PC*	4,448
S. Belzak, *LD*	4,180
Ms E. Jackson, *Green*	615
Lab. majority	19,797
(June 1987, Lab. maj. 17,277)	
(Feb. 1989, Lab. maj. 10,794)	

RHONDDA (Mid Glamorgan)
*E.*59,955   *T.*76.61%

*A. Rogers, *Lab.*	34,243
G. Davies, *PC*	5,427
J. Richards, *C.*	3,588
P. Nicholls-Jones, *LD*	2,431
M. Fisher, *Comm. GB*	245
Lab. majority	28,816
(June 1987, Lab. maj. 30,596)	

SWANSEA EAST (W. Glamorgan)
*E.*59,196   *T.*75.56%

*D. Anderson, *Lab.*	31,179
H. Davies, *C.*	7,697
R. Barton, *LD*	4,248
Ms E. Bonner-Evans, *PC*	1,607
Lab. majority	23,482
(June 1987, Lab. maj. 19,338)	

SWANSEA WEST (W. Glamorgan)
*E.*59,785   *T.*73.34%

*Rt. Hon. A. Williams, *Lab.*	23,238
R. Perry, *C.*	13,760
M. Shrewsbury, *LD*	4,620
Dr D. Lloyd, *PC*	1,668
B. Oubridge, *Green*	564
Lab. majority	9,478
(June 1987, Lab. maj. 7,062)	

TORFAEN (Gwent)
*E.*61,104   *T.*77.47%

*P. Murphy, *Lab.*	30,352
M. Watkins, *C.*	9,598
M. Hewson, *LD*	6,178
Dr J. Cox, *Green/PC*	1,210
Lab. majority	20,754
(June 1987, Lab. maj. 17,550)	

VALE OF GLAMORGAN
(S. Glamorgan)
*E.*66,672   *T.*81.93%

W. Sweeney, *C.*	24,220
*J. Smith, *Lab.*	24,201
K. Davies, *LD*	5,045
D. Haswell, *PC*	1,160
C. majority	19
(June 1987, C. maj 6,251)	
(May 1989, Lab. maj. 6,028)	

WREXHAM (Clwyd)
*E.*63,720   *T.*80.71%

*J. Marek, *Lab.*	24,830
O. Paterson, *C.*	18,114
A. Thomas, *LD*	7,074
G. Wheatley, *PC*	1,415
Lab. majority	6,716
(June 1987, Lab. maj. 4,152)	

YNYS MÔN (Gwynedd)
*E.*53,412   *T.*80.62%

*I. W. Jones, *PC*	15,984
G. Price Rowlands, *C.*	14,878
Dr R. Jones, *Lab.*	10,126
Ms P. Badger, *LD*	1,891
Mrs S. Parry, *NLP*	182
PC majority	1,106
(June 1987, PC maj. 4,298)	

SCOTLAND

ABERDEEN NORTH (Grampian)
*E.*60,217   *T.*66.52%

*R. Hughes, *Lab.*	18,845
J. McGugan, *SNP*	9,608
P. Cook, *C.*	6,836
Dr M. Ford, *LD*	4,772
Lab. majority	9,237
(June 1987, Lab. maj. 16,278)	

ABERDEEN SOUTH (Grampian)
*E.*58,881   *T.*69.78%

R. Robertson, *C.*	15,808
*F. Doran, *Lab.*	14,291
J. Davidson, *SNP*	6,223
Ms I. Keith, *LD*	4,767
C. majority	1,517
(June 1987, Lab. maj. 1,198)	

ANGUS EAST (Tayside)
*E.*63,170   *T.*75.03%

*A. Welsh, *SNP*	19,006
Dr R. Harris, *C.*	18,052
G. Taylor, *Lab.*	5,994
C. McLeod, *LD*	3,897
D. McCabe, *Green*	449
SNP majority	954
(June 1987, SNP maj. 1,544)	

ARGYLL AND BUTE (Strathclyde)
E.47,894   T.76.19%
*Mrs J. R. Michie, *LD*   12,739
J. Corrie, *C.*   10,117
Prof. N. MacCormick, *SNP*   8,689
D. Browne, *Lab.*   4,946
LD majority   2,622
(June 1987, L./All. maj. 1,394)

AYR (Strathclyde)
E.65,481   T.83.08%
P. Gallie, *C.*   22,172
A. Osborne, *Lab.*   22,087
Mrs B. Mullin, *SNP*   5,949
J. Boss, *LD*   4,067
R. Scott, *NLP*   132
C. majority   85
(June 1987, C. maj. 182)

BANFF AND BUCHAN (Grampian)
E.64,873   T.71.20%
*A. Salmond, *SNP*   21,954
S. Manson, *C.*   17,846
B. Balcombe, *Lab.*   3,803
Mrs R. Kemp, *LD*   2,588
SNP majority   4,108
(June 1987, SNP maj. 2,441)

CAITHNESS AND SUTHERLAND
(Highland)
E.30,905   T.71.93%
*R. Maclennan, *LD*   10,032
G. Bruce, *C.*   4,667
K. MacGregor, *SNP*   4,049
M. Coyne, *Lab.*   3,483
LD majority   5,365
(June 1987, SDP/All. maj. 8,494)

CARRICK, CUMNOCK AND DOON
VALLEY (Strathclyde)
E.55,330   T.76.94%
*G. Foulkes, *Lab.*   25,142
J. Boswell, *C.*   8,516
C. Douglas, *SNP*   6,910
Ms M. Paris, *LD*   2,005
Lab. majority   16,626
(June 1987, Lab. maj. 16,802)

CLACKMANNAN (Central)
E.48,963   T.78.34%
*M. O'Neill, *Lab.*   18,829
A. Brophy, *SNP*   10,326
J. Mackie, *C.*   6,638
Ms A. Watters, *LD*   2,567
Lab. majority   8,503
(June 1987, Lab. maj. 12,401)

CLYDEBANK AND MILNGAVIE
(Strathclyde)
E.47,337   T.77.79%
*A. Worthington, *Lab.*   19,637
G. Hughes, *SNP*   7,207
W. Harvey, *C.*   6,654
A. Tough, *LD*   3,216
Ms J. Barrie, *NLP*   112
Lab. majority   12,430
(June 1987, Lab. maj. 16,304)

CLYDESDALE (Strathclyde)
E.61,878   T.77.62%
*J. Hood, *Lab.*   21,418
Ms C. Goodwin, *C.*   11,231
I. Gray, *SNP*   11,084

Ms E. Buchanan, *LD*   3,957
S. Cartwright, *BNP*   342
Lab. majority   10,187
(June 1987, Lab. maj. 10,502)

CUMBERNAULD AND KILSYTH
(Strathclyde)
E.46,489   T.79.06%
*N. Hogg, *Lab.*   19,855
T. Johnston, *SNP*   10,640
I. Mitchell, *C.*   4,143
Ms J. Haddow, *LD*   2,118
Lab. majority   9,215
(June 1987, Lab. maj. 14,403)

CUNNINGHAME NORTH
(Strathclyde)
E.54,803   T.78.21%
*B. Wilson, *Lab.*   17,564
Ms E. Clarkson, *C.*   14,625
D. Crossan, *SNP*   7,813
D. Herbison, *LD*   2,864
Lab. majority   2,939
(June 1987, Lab. maj. 4,422)

CUNNINGHAME SOUTH
(Strathclyde)
E.49,010   T.75.88%
B. Donohoe, *Lab.*   19,687
R. Bell, *SNP*   9,007
S. Leslie, *C.*   6,070
B. Ashley, *LD*   2,299
W. Jackson, *NLP*   128
Lab. majority   10,680
(June 1987, Lab. maj. 16,633)

DUMBARTON (Strathclyde)
E.57,222   T.77.11%
*J. McFall, *Lab.*   19,255
T. Begg, *C.*   13,126
W. McKechnie, *SNP*   8,127
J. Morrison, *LD*   3,425
Ms D. Krass, *NLP*   192
Lab. majority   6,129
(June 1987, Lab. maj. 5,222)

DUMFRIES (D & G)
E.61,145   T.79.97%
*Sir H. Monro, *C.*   21,089
P. Rennie, *Lab.*   14,674
A. Morgan, *SNP*   6,971
N. Wallace, *LD*   5,749
G. McLeod, *Ind. Green*   312
T. Barlow, *NLP*   107
C. majority   6,415
(June 1987, C. maj. 7,493)

DUNDEE EAST (Tayside)
E.58,959   T.72.10%
*J. McAllion, *Lab.*   18,761
D. Coutts, *SNP*   14,197
S. Blackwood, *C.*   7,549
I. Yuill, *LD*   1,725
Ms S. Baird, *Green*   205
R. Baxter, *NLP*   77
Lab. majority   4,564
(June 1987, Lab. maj. 1,015)

DUNDEE WEST (Tayside)
E.59,953   T.69.82%
*E. Ross, *Lab.*   20,498
K. Brown, *SNP*   9,894
A. Spearman, *C.*   7,746

Ms E. Dick, *LD*   3,132
Ms E. Hood, *Green*   432
D. Arnold, *NLP*   159
Lab. majority   10,604
(June 1987, Lab. maj. 16,526)

DUNFERMLINE EAST (Fife)
E.50,179   T.75.62%
*J. G. Brown, *Lab.*   23,692
M. Tennant, *C.*   6,248
J. Lloyd, *SNP*   5,746
Ms T. Little, *LD*   2,262
Lab. majority   17,444
(June 1987, Lab. maj. 19,589)

DUNFERMLINE WEST (Fife)
E.50,948   T.76.44%
Ms R. Squire, *Lab.*   16,374
M. Scott-Hayward, *C.*   8,890
J. Smith, *SNP*   7,563
Ms E. Harris, *LD*   6,122
Lab. majority   7,484
(June 1987, Lab. maj. 9,402)

EAST KILBRIDE (Strathclyde)
E.64,080   T.80.01%
*A. Ingram, *Lab.*   24,055
Ms K. McAlorum, *SNP*   12,063
G. Lind, *C.*   9,781
Ms S. Grieve, *LD*   5,377
Lab. majority   11,992
(June 1987, Lab. maj. 12,624)

EAST LOTHIAN
E.66,699   T.82.37%
*J. Home Robertson, *Lab.*   25,537
J. Hepburne Scott, *C.*   15,501
G. Thomson, *SNP*   7,776
T. McKay, *LD*   6,126
Lab. majority   10,036
(June 1987, Lab. maj. 10,105)

EASTWOOD (Strathclyde)
E.63,685   T.80.97%
*J. A. Stewart, *C.*   24,124
P. Grant-Hutchison, *Lab.*   12,436
Miss M. Craig, *LD*   8,493
P. Scott, *SNP*   6,372
Dr L. Fergusson, *NLP*   146
C. majority   11,688
(June 1987, C. maj. 6,014)

EDINBURGH CENTRAL (Lothian)
E.56,527   T.69.26%
*A. Darling, *Lab.*   15,189
P. Martin, *C.*   13,063
Ms L. Devine, *SNP*   5,539
A. Myles, *LD*   4,500
R. Harper, *Green*   630
D. Wilson, *Lib.*   235
Lab. majority   2,126
(June 1987, Lab. maj. 2,262)

EDINBURGH EAST (Lothian)
E.45,687   T.73.89%
*G. Strang, *Lab.*   15,446
K. Ward, *C.*   8,235
D. McKinney, *SNP*   6,225
D. Scobie, *LD*   3,432
G. Farmer, *Green*   424
Lab. majority   7,211
(June 1987, Lab. maj. 9,295)

EDINBURGH LEITH (Lothian)
*E.*56,520　*T.*71.30%

M. Chisholm, *Lab.*		13,790
Ms F. Hyslop, *SNP*		8,805
M. Bin Ashiq Rizvi, *C.*		8,496
Mrs H. Campbell, *LD*		4,975
*R. Brown, *Ind. Lab.*		4,142
A. Swan, *NLP*		96
Lab. majority		4,985

(June 1987, Lab. maj. 11,327)

EDINBURGH PENTLANDS (Lothian)
*E.*55,567　*T.*80.18%

*Rt. Hon. M. Rifkind, *C.*		18,128
M. Lazarowicz, *Lab.*		13,838
Ms K. Caskie, *SNP*		6,882
K. Smith, *LD*		5,597
D. Rae, *NLP*		111
C. majority		4,290

(June 1987, C. maj. 3,745)

EDINBURGH SOUTH (Lothian)
*E.*61,355　*T.*72.67%

*N. Griffiths, *Lab.*		18,485
S. Stevenson, *C.*		14,309
B. McCreadie, *LD*		5,961
R. Knox, *SNP*		5,727
G. Manclark, *NLP*		108
Lab. majority		4,176

(June 1987, Lab. maj. 1,859)

EDINBURGH WEST (Lothian)
*E.*58,998　*T.*82.67%

*Lord J. Douglas-Hamilton, *C.*		18,071
D. Gorrie, *LD*		17,192
Ms I. Kitson, *Lab.*		8,759
G. Sutherland, *SNP*		4,117
A. Fleming, *Lib.*		272
Ms L. Hendry, *Green*		234
D. Bruce, *BNP*		133
C. majority		879

(June 1987, C. maj. 1,234)

FALKIRK EAST (Central)
*E.*51,918　*T.*76.91%

M. Connarty, *Lab.*		18,423
R. Halliday, *SNP*		10,454
K. Harding, *C.*		8,279
Miss D. Storr, *LD*		2,775
Lab. majority		7,969

(June 1987, Lab. maj. 14,023)

FALKIRK WEST (Central)
*E.*50,126　*T.*76.77%

*D. Canavan, *Lab.*		19,162
W. Houston, *SNP*		9,350
M. Macdonald, *C.*		7,558
M. Reilly, *LD*		2,414
Lab. majority		9,812

(June 1987, Lab. maj. 13,552)

FIFE CENTRAL
*E.*56,152　*T.*74.33%

*H. McLeish, *Lab.*		21,036
Mrs T. Marwick, *SNP*		10,458
Ms C. Cender, *C.*		7,353
C. Harrow, *LD*		2,892
Lab. majority		10,578

(June 1987, Lab. maj. 15,709)

FIFE NORTH EAST
*E.*53,747　*T.*77.84%

*W. M. Campbell, *LD*		19,430
Mrs M. Scanlon, *C.*		16,122
D. Roche, *SNP*		3,589
Miss L. Clark, *Lab.*		2,319
T. Flynn, *Green*		294
D. Senior, *Lib.*		85
LD majority		3,308

(June 1987, L./All. maj. 1,447)

GALLOWAY AND UPPER NITHSDALE
(D & G)
*E.*54,474　*T.*81.66%

*Rt. Hon. I. Lang, *C.*		18,681
M. Brown, *SNP*		16,213
J. Dowson, *Lab.*		5,766
J. McKerchar, *LD*		3,826
C. majority		2,468

(June 1987, C. maj. 3,673)

GLASGOW CATHCART (Strathclyde)
*E.*44,689　*T.*75.38%

*J. Maxton, *Lab.*		16,265
J. Young, *C.*		8,264
W. Steven, *SNP*		6,107
G. Dick, *LD*		2,614
Ms K. Allan, *Green*		441
Lab. majority		8,001

(June 1987, Lab. maj. 11,203)

GLASGOW CENTRAL (Strathclyde)
*E.*48,107　*T.*63.05%

*M. Watson, *Lab.*		17,341
B. O'Hara, *SNP*		6,322
E. Stewart, *C.*		4,208
Dr A. Rennie, *LD*		1,921
Ms I. Brandt, *Green*		435
T. Burn, *Comm. GB*		106
Lab. majority		11,019

(June 1987, Lab. maj. 17,253)
(June 1989, Lab. maj. 6,462)

GLASGOW GARSCADDEN
(Strathclyde)
*E.*41,289　*T.*71.13%

*D. Dewar, *Lab.*		18,920
R. Douglas, *SNP*		5,580
J. Scott, *C.*		3,385
C. Brodie, *LD*		1,425
W. Orr, *NLP*		61
Lab. majority		13,340

(June 1987, Lab. maj. 18,977)

GLASGOW GOVAN (Strathclyde)
*E.*45,822　*T.*76.03%

I. Davidson, *Lab.*		17,051
*J. Sillars, *SNP*		12,926
J. Donnelly, *C.*		3,458
R. Stewart, *LD*		1,227
D. Spaven, *Green*		181
Lab. majority		4,125

(June 1987, Lab. maj. 19,509)
(Nov. 1988, SNP maj. 3,554)

GLASGOW HILLHEAD (Strathclyde)
*E.*57,223　*T.*68.80%

*G. Galloway, *Lab.*		15,148
C. Mason, *LD*		10,322
Ms A. Bates, *C.*		6,728
Miss S. White, *SNP*		6,484
Ms L. Collie, *Green*		558
Ms H. Gold, *Rev. Comm.*		73

D. Patterson, *NLP*		60
Lab. majority		4,826

(June 1987, Lab. maj. 3,251)

GLASGOW MARYHILL (Strathclyde)
*E.*48,426　*T.*65.16%

*Mrs M. Fyfe, *Lab.*		19,452
C. Williamson, *SNP*		6,033
J. Godfrey, *C.*		3,248
J. Alexander, *LD*		2,215
P. O'Brien, *Green*		530
M. Henderson, *NLP*		78
Lab. majority		13,419

(June 1987, Lab. maj. 19,364)

GLASGOW POLLOK (Strathclyde)
*E.*46,139　*T.*70.74%

*J. Dunnachie, *Lab.*		14,170
T. Sheridan, *SML*		6,287
R. Gray, *C.*		5,147
G. Leslie, *SNP*		5,107
D. Jago, *LD*		1,932
Lab. majority		7,883

(June 1987, Lab. maj. 17,983)

GLASGOW PROVAN (Strathclyde)
*E.*36,560　*T.*65.31%

*J. Wray, *Lab.*		15,885
Ms A. MacRae, *SNP*		5,182
A. Rosindell, *C.*		1,865
C. Bell, *LD*		948
Lab. majority		10,703

(June 1987, Lab. maj. 18,372)

GLASGOW RUTHERGLEN
(Strathclyde)
*E.*52,709　*T.*75.23%

*T. McAvoy, *Lab.*		21,962
B. Cooklin, *C.*		6,692
J. Higgins, *SNP*		6,470
D. Baillie, *LD*		4,470
Ms B. Slaughter, *Int. Comm.*		62
Lab. majority		15,270

(June 1987, Lab. maj. 13,995)

GLASGOW SHETTLESTON
(Strathclyde)
*E.*51,910　*T.*68.91%

*D. Marshall, *Lab.*		21,665
Ms N. Sturgeon, *SNP*		6,831
N. Mortimer, *C.*		5,396
Ms J. Orskov, *LD*		1,881
Lab. majority		14,834

(June 1987, Lab. maj. 18,981)

GLASGOW SPRINGBURN
(Strathclyde)
*E.*45,842　*T.*65.65%

*M. Martin, *Lab.*		20,369
S. Miller, *SNP*		5,863
A. Barnett, *C.*		2,625
R. Ackland, *LD*		1,242
Lab. majority		14,506

(June 1987, Lab. maj. 22,063)

GORDON (Grampian)
*E.*80,103　*T.*73.86%

*M. Bruce, *LD*		22,158
J. Porter, *C.*		21,884
B. Adam, *SNP*		8,445
P. Morrell, *Lab.*		6,682
LD majority		274

(June 1987, L./All. maj. 9,519)

GREENOCK AND PORT GLASGOW
(Strathclyde)
E.52,053   T.73.72%
*N. Godman, *Lab.*   22,258
I. Black, *SNP*   7,279
Dr J. McCullough, *C.*   4,479
C. Lambert, *LD*   4,359
Lab. majority   14,979
(June 1987, Lab. maj. 20,055)

HAMILTON (Strathclyde)
E.61,531   T.76.15%
*G. Robertson, *Lab.*   25,849
W. Morrison, *SNP*   9,246
Ms M. Mitchell, *C.*   8,250
J. Oswald, *LD*   3,515
Lab. majority   16,603
(June 1987, Lab. maj. 21,662)

INVERNESS NAIRN AND LOCHABER
(Highland)
E.69,468   T.73.27%
*Sir R. Johnston, *LD*   13,258
D. Stewart, *Lab.*   12,800
F. Ewing, *SNP*   12,562
J. Scott, *C.*   11,517
J. Martin, *Green*   766
LD majority   458
(June 1987, L./All maj. 5,431)

KILMARNOCK AND LOUDOUN
(Strathclyde)
E.62,002   T.79.99%
*W. McKelvey, *Lab.*   22,210
A. Neil, *SNP*   15,231
R. Wilkinson, *C.*   9,438
Mrs K. Philbrick, *LD*   2,722
Lab. majority   6,979
(June 1987, Lab. maj. 14,127)

KINCARDINE AND DEESIDE
(Grampian)
E.66,617   T.78.74%
G. Kynoch, *C.*   22,924
*N. Stephen, *LD*   18,429
Dr A. Macartney, *SNP*   5,927
M. Savidge, *Lab.*   4,795
S. Campbell, *Green*   381
C. majority   4,495
(June 1987, C. maj. 2,063)
(Nov. 1991, LD maj. 7,824)

KIRKCALDY (Fife)
E.51,762   T.75.06%
*Dr L. Moonie, *Lab.*   17,887
S. Hosie, *SNP*   8,761
S. Wosley, *C.*   8,476
Ms S. Leslie, *LD*   3,729
Lab. majority   9,126
(June 1987, Lab. maj. 11,570)

LINLITHGOW (Lothian)
E.61,082   T.78.66%
*T. Dalyell, *Lab.*   21,603
K. MacAskill, *SNP*   14,577
Ms E. Forbes, *C.*   8,424
M. Falchikov, *LD*   3,446
Lab. majority   7,026
(June 1987, Lab. maj. 10,373)

LIVINGSTON (Lothian)
E.61,092   T.74.62%
*R. Cook, *Lab.*   20,245
P. Johnston, *SNP*   12,140
H. Gordon, *C.*   8,824
F. Mackintosh, *LD*   3,911
A. Ross-Smith, *Green*   469
Lab. majority   8,105
(June 1987, Lab. maj. 11,105)

MIDLOTHIAN
E.60,255   T.77.87%
E. Clarke, *Lab.*   20,588
A. Lumsden, *SNP*   10,254
J. Stoddart, *C.*   9,443
P. Sewell, *LD*   6,164
I. Morrice, *Green*   476
Lab. majority   10,334
(June 1987, Lab. maj. 12,253)

MONKLANDS EAST (Strathclyde)
E.48,391   T.75.07%
*Rt. Hon. J. Smith, *Lab.*   22,266
J. Wright, *SNP*   6,554
S. Walters, *C.*   5,830
P. Ross, *LD*   1,679
Lab. majority   15,712
(June 1987, Lab. maj. 16,389)
See also page 234

MONKLANDS WEST (Strathclyde)
E.49,269   T.77.45%
*T. Clarke, *Lab.*   23,384
K. Bovey, *SNP*   6,319
A. Lownie, *C.*   6,074
Ms S. Hamilton, *LD*   2,382
Lab. majority   17,065
(June 1987, Lab. maj. 18,333)

MORAY (Grampian)
E.63,255   T.72.46%
*Mrs M. Ewing, *SNP*   20,299
Ms R. Hossack, *C.*   17,455
C. Smith, *Lab.*   5,448
B. Sheridan, *LD*   2,634
SNP majority   2,844
(June 1987, SNP maj. 3,685)

MOTHERWELL NORTH
(Strathclyde)
E.57,290   T.76.71%
*Dr J. Reid, *Lab.*   27,852
D. Clark, *SNP*   8,942
R. Hargrave, *C.*   5,011
Miss H. Smith, *LD*   2,145
Lab. majority   18,910
(June 1987, Lab. maj. 23,595)

MOTHERWELL SOUTH
(Strathclyde)
E.50,042   T.76.17%
*J. Bray, *Lab.*   21,771
Mrs K. Ullrich, *SNP*   7,758
G. McIntosh, *C.*   6,097
A. Mackie, *LD*   2,349
D. Lettice, *YSOR*   146
Lab. majority   14,013
(June 1987, Lab. maj. 16,930)

ORKNEY AND SHETLAND
E.31,472   T.65.53%
*J. Wallace, *LD*   9,575
Dr P. McCormick, *C.*   4,542

J. Aberdein, *Lab.*   4,093
Mrs F. McKie, *SNP*   2,301
Ms C. Wharton, *NLP*   115
LD majority   5,033
(June 1987, L./All. maj. 3,922)

PAISLEY NORTH (Strathclyde)
E.46,403   T.73.39%
*Mrs I. Adams, *Lab.*   17,269
R. Mullin, *SNP*   7,940
D. Sharpe, *C.*   5,576
Miss E. McCartin, *LD*   2,779
D. Mellor, *Green*   412
N. Brennan, *NLP*   81
Lab. majority   9,329
(June 1987, Lab. maj. 14,442)
(Nov. 1990, Lab. maj. 3,770)

PAISLEY SOUTH (Strathclyde)
E.47,889   T.75.01%
*G. McMaster, *Lab.*   18,202
I. Lawson, *SNP*   8,653
Ms S. Laidlaw, *C.*   5,703
A. Reid, *LD*   3,271
S. Porter, *NLP*   93
Lab. majority   9,549
(June 1987, Lab. maj. 15,785)
(Nov. 1990, Lab. maj. 5,030)

PERTH AND KINROSS (Tayside)
E.65,410   T.76.86%
*Sir N. Fairbairn, *C.*   20,195
Ms R. Cunningham, *SNP*   18,101
M. Rolfe, *Lab.*   6,267
M. Black, *LD*   5,714
C. majority   2,094
(June 1987, C. maj. 5,676)
See also page 234

RENFREW WEST AND INVERCLYDE
(Strathclyde)
E.58,122   T.80.32%
*T. Graham, *Lab.*   17,085
Ms A. Goldie, *C.*   15,341
C. Campbell, *SNP*   9,444
S. Nimmo, *LD*   4,668
D. Maltman, *NLP*   149
Lab. majority   1,744
(June 1987, Lab. maj. 4,063)

ROSS, CROMARTY AND SKYE
(Highland)
E.55,524   T.73.90%
*C. Kennedy, *LD*   17,066
J. Gray, *C.*   9,436
R. Gibson, *SNP*   7,618
J. MacDonald, *Lab.*   6,275
D. Jardine, *Green*   642
LD majority   7,630
(June 1987, SDP/All. maj. 11,319)

ROXBURGH AND BERWICKSHIRE
(Borders)
E.43,485   T.77.71%
*A. Kirkwood, *LD*   15,852
S. Finlay-Maxwell, *C.*   11,595
M. Douglas, *SNP*   3,437
S. Lambert, *Lab.*   2,909
LD majority   4,257
(June 1987, L./All maj. 4,008)

STIRLING (Central)
E.58,266 T.82.29%
*M. Forsyth, C.   19,174
Ms K. Phillips, Lab.   18,471
G. Fisher, SNP   6,558
W. Robertson, LD   3,337
W. Thomson, Green   342
R. Sharp, Loony   68
C. majority   703
(June 1987, C. maj. 548)

STRATHKELVIN AND BEARSDEN
(Strathclyde)
E.61,116 T.82.33%
*S. Galbraith, Lab.   21,267
M. Hirst, C.   18,105
T. Chalmers, SNP   6,275

Ms B. Waterfield, LD   4,585
D. Whitley, NLP   90
Lab. majority   3,162
(June 1987, Lab. maj. 2,452)

TAYSIDE NORTH
E.55,969 T.77.64%
*W. Walker, C.   20,283
J. Swinney, SNP   16,288
S. Horner, LD   3,791
S. Maclennan, Lab.   3,094
C. majority   3,995
(June 1987, C. maj. 5,016)

TWEEDDALE, ETTRICK AND
LAUDERDALE (Borders)
E.39,493 T.78.04%
*Rt. Hon. Sir D. Steel, LD   12,296

L. Beat, C.   9,776
Mrs C. Creech, SNP   5,244
A. Dunton, Lab.   3,328
J. Hein, Lib.   177
LD majority   2,520
(June 1987, L./All. maj. 5,942)

WESTERN ISLES
E.22,784 T.70.35%
*C. MacDonald, Lab.   7,664
Ms F. MacFarlane, SNP   5,961
R. Heany, C.   1,362
N. Mitchison, LD   552
A. Price, Ind.   491
Lab. majority   1,703
(June 1987, Lab. maj. 2,340)

NORTHERN IRELAND

ANTRIM EAST
E.62,839 T.62.46%
*R. Beggs, UUP   16,966
N. Dodds, DUP   9,544
S. Neeson, All.   9,132
Miss M. Boal, C.   3,359
Ms A. Palmer, NLP   250
UUP majority   7,422
(June 1987, UUP maj. 15,360)

ANTRIM NORTH
E.69,124 T.65.82%
*Revd I. Paisley, DUP   23,152
J. Gaston, UUP   8,216
S. Farren, SDLP   6,512
G. Williams, All.   3,442
R. Sowler, C.   2,263
J. McGarry, SF   1,916
DUP majority   14,936
(June 1987, DUP maj. 23,234)

ANTRIM SOUTH
E.68,013 T.62.10%
*C. Forsythe, UUP   29,956
D. McClelland, SDLP   5,397
J. Blair, All.   5,224
H. Cushinan, SF   1,220
D. Martin, Loony G.   442
UUP majority   24,559
(June 1987, UUP maj. 19,587)

BELFAST EAST
E.52,833 T.67.74%
*P. Robinson, DUP   18,437
Dr J. Alderdice, All.   10,650
D. Greene, C.   3,314
Ms D. Dunlop, Ind. U.   2,256
J. O'Donnell, SF   679
J. Bell, WP   327
G. Redden, NLP   128
DUP majority   7,787
(June 1987, DUP maj. 9,798)

BELFAST NORTH
E.55,062 T.65.22%
*A. C. Walker, UUP   17,240
A. Maginness, SDLP   7,615
P. McManus, SF   4,693
T. Campbell, All.   2,246
Ms M. Redpath, C.   2,107

S. Lynch, NA   1,386
Ms M. Smith, WP   419
D. O'Leary, NLP   208
UUP majority   9,625
(June 1987, UUP maj. 8,560)

BELFAST SOUTH
E.52,032 T.64.54%
*Revd W. M. Smyth, UUP   16,336
Dr A. McDonnell, SDLP   6,266
J. Montgomery, All.   5,054
L. Fee, C.   3,356
S. Hayes, SF   1,123
P. Hadden, LTU   875
P. Lynn, WP   362
Ms T. Mullan, NLP   212
UUP majority   10,070
(June 1987, UUP maj. 11,954)

BELFAST WEST
E.54,609 T.73.19%
Dr J. Hendron, SDLP   17,415
*G. Adams, SF   16,826
F. Cobain, UUP   4,766
J. Lowry, WP   750
M. Kennedy, NLP   213
SDLP majority   589
(June 1987, SF maj. 2,221)

DOWN NORTH
E.68,662 T.65.47%
*J. Kilfedder, UPUP   19,305
Dr L. Kennedy, C.   14,371
Ms A. Morrow, All.   6,611
D. Vitty, DUP   4,414
A. Wilmot, NLP   255
UPUP majority   4,934
(June 1987, UPUP maj. 3,953)
See also page 234

DOWN SOUTH
E.76,093 T.80.92%
*E. McGrady, SDLP   31,523
D. Nelson, UUP   25,181
S. Fitzpatrick, SF   1,843
M. Healey, All.   1,542
Mrs S. McKenzie-Hill, C.   1,488
SDLP majority   6,342
(June 1987, SDLP maj. 731)

FERMANAGH AND SOUTH TYRONE
E.70,192 T.78.53%
*K. Maginnis, UUP   26,923
T. Gallagher, SDLP   12,810
F. Molloy, SF   12,604
D. Kettyles, Prog. Soc.   1,094
E. Bullick, All.   950
G. Cullen, NA   747
UUP majority   14,113
(June 1987, UUP maj. 12,823)

FOYLE
E.74,585 T.69.57%
*J. Hume, SDLP   26,710
G. Campbell, DUP   13,705
M. McGuinness, SF   9,149
Ms L. McIlroy, All.   1,390
G. McKenzie, WP   514
J. Burns, NLP   422
SDLP majority   13,005
(June 1987, SDLP maj. 9,860)

LAGAN VALLEY
E.72,645 T.67.39%
*Rt. Hon. J. H. Molyneaux, UUP
                                  29,772
S. Close, All.   6,207
H. Lewsley, SDLP   4,626
T. Coleridge, C.   4,423
P. Rice, SF   3,346
Ms A.-M. Lowry, WP   582
UUP majority   23,565
(June 1987, UUP maj. 23,373)

LONDONDERRY EAST
E.75,559 T.69.79%
*W. Ross, UUP   30,370
A. Doherty, SDLP   11,843
Ms P. Davey-Kennedy, SF   5,320
P. McGowan, All.   3,613
A. Elder, C.   1,589
UUP majority   18,527
(June 1987, UUP maj. 20,157)

NEWRY AND ARMAGH
E.67,508 T.77.87%
*S. Mallon, SDLP   26,073
J. Speers, UUP   18,982
B. Curran, SF   6,547
Mrs E. Bell, All.   972

SDLP majority	7,091
(June 1987, SDLP maj. 5,325)	

STRANGFORD
E.68,870   T.65.02%

*Rt. Hon. J. Taylor, UUP	19,517
S. Wilson, DUP	10,606
K. McCarthy, All.	7,585
S. Eyre, C.	6,782
D. Shaw, NLP	295
UUP majority	8,911
(June 1987, UUP maj. 20,646)	

ULSTER MID
E.69,071   T.79.28%

*Revd Dr R. T. W. McCrea, DUP	23,181
D. Haughey, SDLP	16,994
B. McElduff, SF	10,248
J. McLoughlin, Ind.	1,996
Ms A. Gormley, All.	1,506
H. Hutchinson, LTU	389
T. Owens, WP	285
J. Anderson, NLP	164
DUP majority	6,187
(June 1987, DUP maj. 9,360)	

UPPER BANN
E.67,446   T.67.43%

*W. D. Trimble, UUP	26,824
Mrs B. Rodgers, SDLP	10,661
B. Curran, SF	2,777
Dr W. Ramsey, All.	2,541
Mrs C. Jones, C.	1,556
T. French, WP	1,120
UUP majority	16,163
(June 1987, OUP maj. 17,361)	
(May 1990, OUP maj. 13,849)	

COMMONWEALTH PARLIAMENTARY ASSOCIATION (1911)

The Commonwealth Parliamentary Association consists of 135 branches in the national, state, provincial or territorial parliaments in the countries of the Commonwealth. Conferences and general assemblies are held every year in different countries of the Commonwealth.
President (1995–6), Y. B. Tan Sri Dato' Zahir Haji Ismail, MP, Speaker of the House of Representatives, Malaysia
Vice-President, (1995–6), Hon. Sir Ramesh Jeewoolall, MP, Speaker of the National Assembly, Mauritius
Chairman of the Executive Committee (1993–), Colin Shepherd, MP (United Kingdom)
Secretary-General, A. R. Donahoe, QC, Suite 700, Westminster House, 7 Millbank, London SWIP 3JA

UNITED KINGDOM BRANCH

Hon. Presidents, The Lord Chancellor; Madam Speaker
Chairman of Branch, The Rt. Hon. John Major, MP

Chairman of Executive Committee, Sir Ivan Lawrence, QC, MP
Secretary, P. Cobb, OBE, Westminster Hall, Houses of Parliament, London, SWIA OAA

THE INTER-PARLIAMENTARY UNION (1889)

To facilitate personal contact between members of all Parliaments in the promotion of representative institutions, peace and international co-operation.
Secretary-General, P. Cornillon, Place du Petit-Saconnex. BP 99, 1211 Geneva 19, Switzerland

BRITISH GROUP
Palace of Westminster, London SWIA OAA

Hon. Presidents, The Lord Chancellor; Madam Speaker
President, The Rt. Hon. John Major, MP
Chairman, Dame Jill Knight, DBE, MP
Secretary, D. Ramsay

European Parliament

European Parliament elections take place at five-yearly intervals. In mainland Britain MEPs are elected in all constituencies on a first-past-the-post basis; in Northern Ireland three MEPs are elected by proportional representation. From 1979 to 1994 the number of seats held by the UK in the European Parliament was 81. At the June 1994 election the number of seats increased to 87 (England 71, Wales 5, Scotland 8, Northern Ireland 3).

Since 1994, nationals of member states of the European Union have the right to vote in elections to the European Parliament in the UK. British subjects and citizens of the Irish Republic can stand in the UK for election to the European Parliament provided they are 21 or over and not subject to disqualification.

MEPs receive a salary from the parliaments or governments of their respective member states, set at the level of the national parliamentary salary and subject to national taxation rules (for salary of British MPs, see page 219).

UK MEMBERS AS AT END JULY 1996

*Denotes membership of the last European Parliament

*Adam, Gordon J., PH.D. (b. 1934), Lab., Northumbria, maj. 66,158

*Balfe, Richard A. (b. 1944), Lab., London South Inner, maj. 59,220

*Barton, Roger (b. 1945), Lab., Sheffield, maj. 50,288

Billingham, Mrs Angela T. (b. 1939), Lab., Northamptonshire and Blaby, maj. 26,085

*Bowe, David R. (b. 1955), Lab., Cleveland and Richmond, maj. 57,568

*Cassidy, Bryan M. D. (b. 1934), C., Dorset and Devon East, maj. 2,264

Chichester, Giles B. (b. 1946), C., Devon and Plymouth East, maj. 700

*Coates, Kenneth S. (b. 1930), Lab., Nottinghamshire North and Chesterfield, maj. 76,260

*Collins, Kenneth D. (b. 1939), Lab., Strathclyde East, maj. 52,340

Corrie, John A. (b. 1935), C., Worcestershire and Warwickshire South, maj. 1,204

*Crampton, Peter D. (b. 1932), Lab., Humberside, maj. 40,618

*Crawley, Mrs Christine M. (b. 1950), Lab., Birmingham East, maj. 55,120

Cunningham, Thomas A. (Tony) (b. 1952), Lab., Cumbria and Lancashire North, maj. 22,988

*David, Wayne (b. 1957), Lab., South Wales Central, maj. 86,082

*Donnelly, Alan J. (b. 1957), Lab., Tyne and Wear, maj. 88,380

Donnelly, Brendan P. (b. 1950), C., Sussex South and Crawley, maj. 1,746

*Elles, James E. M. (b. 1949), C., Buckinghamshire and Oxfordshire East, maj. 30,665

*Elliott, Michael N. (b. 1932), Lab., London West, maj. 42,275

Evans, Robert J. E. (b. 1956), Lab., London North West, maj. 17,442

*Ewing, Mrs Winifred M. (b. 1929), SNP, Highlands and Islands, maj. 54,916

*Falconer, Alexander (b. 1940), Lab., Scotland Mid and Fife, maj. 31,413

*Ford, J. Glyn (b. 1950), Lab., Greater Manchester East, maj. 55,986

*Green, Mrs Pauline (b. 1948), Lab., London North, maj. 48,348

Hallam, David J. A. (b. 1948), Lab., Herefordshire and Shropshire, maj. 1,850

Hardstaff, Mrs Veronica M. (b. 1941), Lab., Lincolnshire and Humberside South, maj. 13,745

*Harrison, Lyndon H. A. (b. 1947), Lab., Cheshire West and Wirral, maj. 47,176

Hendrick, Mark P. (b. 1958), Lab., Lancashire Central, maj. 12,191

*Hindley, Michael J. (b. 1947), Lab., Lancashire South, maj. 41,404

Howitt, Richard (b. 1961), Lab., Essex South, maj. 21,367

*Hughes, Stephen S. (b. 1952), Lab., Durham, maj. 111,638

*Hume, John, MP (b. 1937), SDLP, Northern Ireland, polled 161,992 votes

*Jackson, Mrs Caroline F., D.PHIL. (b. 1946), C., Wiltshire North and Bath, maj. 8,787

*Kellett-Bowman, Edward T. (b. 1931), C., Itchen, Test and Avon, maj. 6,903

Kerr, Hugh (b. 1944), Lab., Essex West and Hertfordshire East, maj. 3,067

Kinnock, Mrs Glenys E. (b. 1944), Lab., South Wales East, maj. 120,247

*Lomas, Alfred (b. 1928), Lab., London North East, maj. 57,085

Macartney, W. J. Allan, PH.D. (b. 1941), SNP, Scotland North East, maj. 31,227

McCarthy, Ms Arlene (b. 1960), Lab., Peak District, maj. 49,307

*McGowan, Michael (b. 1940), Lab., Leeds, maj. 53,082

*McIntosh, Ms Anne C. B. (b. 1954), C., Essex North and Suffolk South, maj. 3,633

*McMahon, Hugh R. (b. 1938), Lab., Strathclyde West, maj. 25,023

*McMillan-Scott, Edward H. C. (b. 1949), C., Yorkshire North, maj. 7,072

McNally, Mrs Eryl M. (b. 1942), Lab., Bedfordshire and Milton Keynes, maj. 33,209

*Martin, David W. (b. 1954), Lab., Lothians, maj 37,207

Mather, Graham C. S. (b. 1954), C., Hampshire North and Oxford, maj. 9,194

*Megahy, Thomas (b. 1929), Lab., Yorkshire South West, maj. 59,562

Miller, Bill (b. 1954), Lab., Glasgow, maj. 43,158

*Moorhouse, C. James O. (b. 1924), C., London South and Surrey East, maj. 8,739

Morgan, Ms Eluned (b. 1967), Lab., Wales Mid and West, maj. 29,234

*Morris, Revd David R. (b. 1930), Lab., South Wales West, maj. 84,970

Murphy, Simon F., PH.D. (b. 1962), Lab., Midlands West, maj. 54,823

Needle, Clive (b. 1956), Lab., Norfolk, maj. 26,287

*Newens, A. Stanley (b. 1930), Lab., London Central, maj. 25,059

*Newman, Edward (b. 1953), Lab., Greater Manchester Central, maj. 42,445

*Nicholson, James F. (b. 1945), UUUP, Northern Ireland, polled 133,459 votes

*Oddy, Ms Christine M. (b. 1955), Lab., Coventry and Warwickshire North, maj. 43,901

*Paisley, Revd Ian R. K., MP (b. 1926), DUP, Northern Ireland, polled 163,246 votes

Perry, Roy J. (b. 1943), C., Wight and Hampshire South, maj. 5,101

*Plumb, The Lord (b. 1925), C., Cotswolds, maj. 4,268
*Pollack, Ms Anita J. (b. 1946), Lab., London South West, maj. 30,975
Provan, James L. C. (b. 1936), C., South Downs West, maj. 21,067
*Read, Ms I. M. (Mel) (b. 1939), Lab., Nottingham and Leicestershire North West, maj. 39,668
*Seal, Barry H., ph.d. (b. 1937), Lab., Yorkshire West, maj. 48,197
*Simpson, Brian (b. 1953), Lab., Cheshire East, maj. 39,279
Skinner, Peter W. (b. 1959), Lab., Kent West, maj. 16,777
*Smith, Alexander (b. 1943), Lab., Scotland South, maj. 45,155
*Spencer, Thomas N. B. (b. 1948), C., Surrey, maj. 27,018
Spiers, Shaun M. (b. 1962), Lab., London South East, maj. 8,022
*Stevens, John C. C. (b. 1955), C., Thames Valley, maj. 758
*Stewart, Kenneth A. (b. 1925), Lab., Merseyside West, maj. 51,811 (see Stop-press)
*Stewart-Clark, Sir John, Bt. (b. 1929), C., Sussex East and Kent South, maj. 6,212
Sturdy, Robert W. (b. 1944), C., Cambridgeshire, maj. 3,942
Tappin, Michael (b. 1946), Lab., Staffordshire West and Congleton, maj. 40,277

Teverson, Robin (b. 1952), LD, Cornwall and Plymouth West, maj. 29,498
Thomas, David E. (b. 1955), Lab., Suffolk and Norfolk South West, maj. 12,535
*Titley, Gary (b. 1950), Lab., Greater Manchester West, maj. 58,635
*Tomlinson, John E. (b. 1939), Lab., Birmingham West, maj. 39,350
*Tongue, Ms Carole (b. 1955), Lab., London East, maj. 57,389
Truscott, Peter, ph.d. (b. 1959), Lab., Hertfordshire, maj. 10,304
Waddington, Mrs Susan A. (b. 1944), Lab., Leicester, maj. 20,284
Watson, Graham R. (b. 1956), LD, Somerset and Devon North, maj. 22,509
Watts, Mark F. (b. 1964), Lab., Kent East, maj. 635
*West, Norman, (b. 1935), Lab., Yorkshire South, maj. 88,309
*White, Ian (b. 1947), Lab., Bristol, maj. 29,955
Whitehead, Phillip (b. 1937), Lab., Staffordshire East and Derby, maj. 72,196
*Wilson, A. Joseph (b. 1937), Lab., Wales North, maj. 15,242
*Wynn, Terence (b. 1946), Lab., Merseyside East and Wigan, maj. 74,087

UK CONSTITUENCIES AS AT 9 JUNE 1994

Abbreviations	
Anti Fed.	UK Independence Anti-Federal
Anti Fed. C.	Official Anti-Federalist Conservative
Beanus	Eurobean from Planet Beanus
C. Non Fed.	Conservative Non-Federal Party
Capital P.	Restoration of Capital Punishment
Comm.	Communist
Comm. YBG	Communist Y Blaid Gomiwyddol
Const. NI	Constitutional Independence for N. Ireland
Corr.	Corrective Party
CPP	Christian People's Party
ICP	International Communist Party
ICP4	International Communist Party (4th International)
Ind. AES	Independent Anti-European Superstate
Ind. Out	Independent Out of Europe Party
Judo	European People's Party Judo Christian Alliance
Loony C	Raving Loony Commonsense
Loony CP	Monster Raving Loony Christian Party
Loony X	Monster Raving Loony Project X Party
MCCARTHY	Make Criminals Concerned About Our Response To Hostility and Yobbishness
MK	Mebyon Kernow
NCSA	Network Against Child Support Agency
Neeps	North East Ethnic Party, The Neeps
Rainbow	Rainbow Connection – Oui-Say-Non-Party
Sportsman	Sportsman Anti-Common Market Bureaucracy
UUUP	United Ulster Unionist Party

For other abbreviations, see page 237

ENGLAND

BEDFORDSHIRE AND MILTON KEYNES
E. 525,524   T. 38.74%

E. McNally, Lab.	94,837
Mrs E. Currie, C.	61,628
Ms M. Howes, LD	27,994
A. Sked, UK Independence	7,485
A. Francis, Green	6,804
A. Howes, New Britain	3,878
L. Sheaff, NLP	939
Lab. majority	33,209

(Boundary change since June 1989)

BIRMINGHAM EAST
E. 520,782   T. 29.77%

*Mrs C. Crawley, Lab.	90,291
A. Turner, C.	35,171
Ms C. Cane, LD	19,455
P. Simpson, Green	6,268
R. Cook, Soc.	1,969
M. Brierley, NLP	1,885
Lab. majority	55,120

(June 1989, Lab. maj. 46,948)

BIRMINGHAM WEST
E. 509,948   T. 28.49%

*J. Tomlinson, Lab.	77,957
D. Harman, C.	38,607
N. McGeorge, LD	14,603
Dr B. Juby, Anti Fed.	5,237
M. Abbott, Green	4,367
A. Carmichael, NF	3,727
H. Meads, NLP	789
Lab. majority	39,350

(June 1989, Lab. maj. 30,860)

BRISTOL
E. 503,218   T. 40.91%

*I. White, Lab.	90,790
The Earl of Stockton, C.	60,835
J. Barnard, LD	40,394

J. Boxall, Green	7,163
T. Whittingham, UK Independence	5,798
T. Dyball, NLP	876
Lab. majority	29,955

(Boundary change since June 1989)

BUCKINGHAMSHIRE AND OXFORDSHIRE EAST
E. 487,692   T. 37.31%

*J. Elles, C.	77,037
D. Enright, Lab.	46,372
Ms S. Bowles, LD	42,836
L. Roach, Green	8,433
Ms A. Micklem, Lib.	5,111
Dr G. Clements, NLP	2,156
C. majority	30,665

(Boundary change since June 1989)

CAMBRIDGESHIRE
E. 495,383   T. 35.91%

R. Sturdy, C.	66,921
Ms M. Johnson, Lab.	62,979
A. Duff, LD	36,114
Ms M. Wright, Green	5,756
P. Wiggin, Lib.	4,051
F. Chalmers, NLP	2,077
C. majority	3,942

(Boundary change since June 1989)

CHESHIRE EAST
E. 502,726   T. 32.46%

*B. Simpson, Lab.	87,586
P. Slater, C.	48,307
P. Harris, LD	20,552
D. Wild, Green	3,671
P. Dixon, Loony CP	1,600
P. Leadbetter, NLP	1,488
Lab. majority	39,279

(Boundary change since June 1989)

CHESHIRE WEST AND WIRRAL
E. 538,571   *T.* 36.78%

*L. Harrison, *Lab.*		106,160
D. Senior, *C.*		58,984
I. Mottershaw, *LD*		20,746
D. Carson, *British Home Rule*		6,167
M. Money, *Green*		5,096
A. Wilmot, *NLP*		929
Lab. majority		47,176

(Boundary change since June 1989)

CLEVELAND AND RICHMOND
E. 499,580   *T.* 35.26%

*D. Bowe, *Lab.*		103,355
R. Goodwill, *C.*		45,787
B. Moore, *LD*		21,574
G. Parr, *Green*		4,375
R. Scott, *NLP*		1,068
Lab. majority		57,568

(Boundary change since June 1989)

CORNWALL AND PLYMOUTH WEST
E. 484,697   *T.* 44.92%

R. Teverson, *LD*		91,113
*C. Beazley, *C.*		61,615
Mrs D. Kirk, *Lab.*		42,907
Mrs P. Garnier, *UK Independence*		
		6,466
P. Holmes, *Lib.*		6,414
Ms K. Westbrook, *Green*		4,372
Dr L. Jenkin, *MK*		3,315
F. Lyons, *NLP*		921
M. Fitzgerald, *Subsidiarity*		606
LD majority		29,498

(Boundary change since June 1989)

COTSWOLDS
E. 497,588   *T.* 39.27%

*The Lord Plumb, *C.*		67,484
Ms T. Kingham, *Lab.*		63,216
J. Thomson, *LD*		44,269
M. Rendell, *New Britain*		11,044
D. McCanlis, *Green*		8,254
H. Brighouse, *NLP*		1,151
C. majority		4,268

(Boundary change since June 1989)

COVENTRY AND WARWICKSHIRE NORTH
E. 523,448   *T.* 32.54%

*Ms C. Oddy, *Lab.*		89,500
Ms J. Crabb, *C.*		45,599
G. Sewards, *LD*		17,453
R. Meacham, *Free Trade*		9,432
P. Baptie, *Green*		4,360
R. Wheway, *Lib.*		2,885
R. France, *NLP*		1,098
Lab. majority		43,901

(Boundary change since June 1989)

CUMBRIA AND LANCASHIRE NORTH
E. 498,557   *T.* 40.78%

A. Cunningham, *Lab.*		97,599
*The Lord Inglewood, *C.*		74,611
R. Putnam, *LD*		24,233
R. Frost, *Green*		5,344
I. Docker, *NLP*		1,500
Lab. majority		22,988

(Boundary change since June 1989)

DEVON AND PLYMOUTH EAST
E. 524,320   *T.* 45.07%

G. Chichester, *C.*		74,953
A. Sanders, *LD*		74,253
Ms L. Gilroy, *Lab.*		47,596
D. Morrish, *Lib.*		14,621
P. Edwards, *Green*		11,172
R. Huggett, *Literal Democrat*		10,203
J. Everard, *Ind.*		2,629
A. Pringle, *NLP*		908
C. majority		700

(Boundary change since June 1989)

DORSET AND DEVON EAST
E. 531,842   *T.* 41.21%

*B. Cassidy, *C.*		81,551
P. Goldenberg, *LD*		79,287
A. Gardner, *Lab.*		34,856
M. Floyd, *UK Independence*		10,548
Mrs K. Bradbury, *Green*		8,642
I. Mortimer, *C. Non-Fed.*		3,229
M. Griffiths, *NLP*		1,048
C. majority		2,264

(Boundary change since June 1989)

DURHAM
E. 532,051   *T.* 35.62%

*S. Hughes, *Lab.*		136,671
P. Bradbourn, *C.*		25,033
Dr N. Martin, *LD*		20,935
S. Hope, *Green*		5,670
C. Adamson, *NLP*		1,198
Lab. majority		111,638

(June 1989, Lab. maj. 86,848)

ESSEX NORTH AND SUFFOLK SOUTH
E. 497,098   *T.* 41.33%

*Ms A. McIntosh, *C.*		68,311
C. Pearson, *Lab.*		64,678
S. Mole, *LD*		52,536
S. de Chair, *Ind. AES*		12,409
J. Abbott, *Green*		6,641
N. Pullen, *NLP*		884
C. majority		3,633

(Boundary change since June 1989)

ESSEX SOUTH
E. 487,221   *T.* 33.08%

R. Howitt, *Lab.*		71,883
L. Stanbrook, *C.*		50,516
G. Williams, *LD*		26,132
B. Lynch, *Lib.*		6,780
G. Rumens, *Green*		4,691
M. Heath, *NLP*		1,177
Lab. majority		21,367

(Boundary change since June 1989)

ESSEX WEST AND HERTFORDSHIRE EAST
E. 504,095   *T.* 36.39%

H. Kerr, *Lab.*		66,379
*Ms P. Rawlings, *C.*		63,312
Ms G. James, *LD*		35,695
B. Smalley, *Britain*		10,277
Ms F. Mawson, *Green*		5,632
P. Carter, *Sportsman*		1,127
L. Davis, *NLP*		1,026
Lab. majority		3,067

(Boundary change since June 1989)

GREATER MANCHESTER CENTRAL
E. 481,779   *T.* 29.11%

*E. Newman, *Lab.*		74,935
Mrs S. Mason, *C.*		32,490
J. Begg, *LD*		22,988
B. Candeland, *Green*		4,952
P. Burke, *Lib.*		3,862
P. Stanley, *NLP*		1,017
Lab. majority		42,445

(Boundary change since June 1989)

GREATER MANCHESTER EAST
E. 501,125   *T.* 27.17%

*G. Ford, *Lab.*		82,289
J. Pinniger, *C.*		26,303
A. Riley, *LD*		20,545
T. Clarke, *Green*		5,823
W. Stevens, *NLP*		1,183
Lab. majority		55,986

(Boundary change since June 1989)

GREATER MANCHESTER WEST
E. 512,618   *T.* 29.70%

*G. Titley, *Lab.*		94,129
D. Newns, *C.*		35,494
F. Harasiwka, *LD*		13,650
R. Jackson, *Green*		3,950
G. Harrison, *MCCARTHY*		3,693
T. Brotheridge, *NLP*		1,316
Lab. majority		58,635

(Boundary change since June 1989)

HAMPSHIRE NORTH AND OXFORD
E. 525,982   *T.* 38.31%

G. Mather, *C.*		72,209
Ms J. Hawkins, *LD*		63,015
J. Tanner, *Lab.*		48,525
D. Wilkinson, *UK Independence*		8,377
Dr M. Woodin, *Green*		7,310
H. Godfrey, *NLP*		1,027
R. Boston, *Boston Tea Party*		1,018
C. majority		9,194

(Boundary change since June 1989)

HEREFORDSHIRE AND SHROPSHIRE
E. 536,470   *T.* 38.69%

D. Hallam, *Lab.*		76,120
*Sir C. Prout, *C.*		74,270
J. Gallagher, *LD*		44,130
Ms F. Norman, *Green*		11,578
T. Mercer, *NLP*		1,480
Lab. majority		1,850

(Boundary change since June 1989)

HERTFORDSHIRE
E. 522,338   *T.* 40.11%

Dr P. Truscott, *Lab.*		81,821
P. Jenkinson, *C.*		71,517
D. Griffiths, *LD*		38,995
Ms L. Howitt, *Green*		7,741
M. Biggs, *New Britain*		6,555
J. McAuley, *NF*		1,755
D. Lucas, *NLP*		734
J. Laine, *Century*		369
Lab. majority		10,304

(Boundary change since June 1989)

HUMBERSIDE
E. 519,013   *T.* 32.38%

*P. Crampton, *Lab.*		87,296
D. Stewart, *C.*		46,678
Ms D. Wallis, *LD*		28,818
Ms S. Mummery, *Green*		4,170

Ms A. Miszewska, *NLP* 1,100
Lab. majority 40,618
(Boundary change since June 1989)

ITCHEN, TEST AND AVON
E. 550,406 *T.* 41.83%
*E. Kellett-Bowman, *C.* 81,456
A. Barron, *LD* 74,553
E. Read, *Lab.* 52,416
N. Farage, *UK Independence* 12,423
Ms F. Hulbert, *Green* 7,998
A. Miller-Smith, *NLP* 1,368
C. majority 6,903
(Boundary change since June 1989)

KENT EAST
E. 499,662 *T.* 40.34%
M. Watts, *Lab.* 69,641
*C. Jackson, *C.* 69,006
J. Macdonald, *LD* 44,549
C. Bullen, *UK Independence* 9,414
S. Dawe, *Green* 7,196
C. Beckley, *NLP* 1,746
Lab. majority 635
(Boundary change since June 1989)

KENT WEST
E. 505,658 *T.* 37.33%
P. Skinner, *Lab.* 77,346
*B. Patterson, *C.* 60,569
J. Daly, *LD* 33,869
C. Mackinlay, *UK Independence* 9,750
Ms P. Kemp, *Green* 5,651
J. Bowler, *NLP* 1,598
Lab. majority 16,777
(Boundary change since June 1989)

LANCASHIRE CENTRAL
E. 505,224 *T.* 33.23%
M. Hendrick, *Lab.* 73,420
*M. Welsh, *C.* 61,229
Ms J. Ross-Mills, *LD* 20,578
D. Hill, *Home Rule* 6,751
C. Maile, *Green* 4,169
Ms J. Ayliffe, *NLP* 1,727
Lab. majority 12,191
(Boundary change since June 1989)

LANCASHIRE SOUTH
E. 514,840 *T.* 33.14%
*M. Hindley, *Lab.* 92,598
R. Topham, *C.* 51,194
J. Ault, *LD* 17,008
J. Gaffney, *Green* 4,774
Mrs E. Rokas, *Ind.* 3,439
J. Renwick, *NLP* 1,605
Lab. majority 41,404
(Boundary change since June 1989)

LEEDS
E. 521,989 *T.* 30.03%
*M. McGowan, *Lab.* 89,160
N. Carmichael, *C.* 36,078
Ms J. Harvey, *LD* 17,575
M. Meadowcroft, *Lib.* 6,617
Ms C. Nash, *Green* 6,283
Ms S. Hayward, *NLP* 1,018
Lab. majority 53,082
(June 1989, Lab. maj. 42,518)

LEICESTER
E. 515,343 *T.* 37.63%
Ms S. Waddington, *Lab.* 87,048
A. Marshall, *C.* 66,764
M. Jones, *LD* 28,890
G. Forse, *Green* 8,941
Ms P. Saunders, *NLP* 2,283
Lab. majority 20,284
(Boundary change since June 1989)

LINCOLNSHIRE AND HUMBERSIDE
SOUTH
E. 539,981 *T.* 36.34%
Mrs V. Hardstaff, *Lab.* 83,172
*W. Newton Dunn, *C.* 69,427
K. Melton, *LD* 27,241
Ms R. Robinson, *Green* 8,563
E. Wheeler, *Lib.* 3,434
I. Selby, *NCSA* 2,973
H. Kelly, *NLP* 1,429
Lab. majority 13,745
(Boundary change since June 1989)

LONDON CENTRAL
E. 494,610 *T.* 32.57%
*S. Newens, *Lab.* 75,711
A. Elliott, *C.* 50,652
Ms S. Ludford, *LD* 20,176
Ms N. Kortvelyessy, *Green* 7,043
H. Le Fanu, *UK Independence* 4,157
C. Slapper, *Soc.* 1,593
Ms S. Hamza, *NLP* 1,215
G. Weiss, *Rainbow* 547
Lab. majority 25,059
(June 1989, Lab. maj. 11,542)

LONDON EAST
E. 511,523 *T.* 33.38%
*Ms C. Tongue, *Lab.* 98,759
Ms V. Taylor, *C.* 41,370
K. Montgomery, *LD* 15,566
G. Batten, *UK Independence* 5,974
J. Baguley, *Green* 4,337
O. Tillett, *Third Way Independence* 3,484
N. Kahn, *NLP* 1,272
Lab. majority 57,389
(June 1989, Lab. maj. 27,385)

LONDON NORTH
E. 541,269 *T.* 34.00%
*Mrs P. Green, *Lab.* 102,059
M. Keegan, *C.* 53,711
I. Mann, *LD* 15,739
Ms H. Jago, *Green* 5,666
I. Booth, *UK Independence* 5,099
G. Sabrizi, *Judo* 880
J. Hinde, *NLP* 856
Lab. majority 48,348
(June 1989, Lab. maj. 5,837)

LONDON NORTH EAST
E. 486,016 *T.* 26.60%
*A. Lomas, *Lab.* 80,256
S. Gordon, *C.* 23,171
K. Appiah, *LD* 10,242
Ms J. Lambert, *Green* 8,386
E. Murat, *NLP* 2,573
P. Compobassi, *UK Independence* 2,015
R. Archer, *NLP* 1,111
M. Fischer, *Comm. GB* 869
A. Hyland, *ICP4* 679

Lab. majority 57,085
(June 1989, Lab. maj. 47,767)

LONDON NORTH WEST
E. 481,272 *T.* 35.13%
R. Evans, *Lab.* 80,192
*The Lord Bethell, *C.* 62,750
Ms H. Leighter, *LD* 18,998
D. Johnson, *Green* 4,743
Ms A. Murphy, *Comm. GB* 858
Ms T. Sullivan, *NLP* 807
C. Palmer, *Century* 740
Lab. majority 17,442
(June 1989, C. maj. 7,400)

LONDON SOUTH AND SURREY EAST
E. 486,358 *T.* 34.38%
*J. Moorhouse, *C.* 64,813
Ms G. Rolles, *Lab.* 56,074
M. Reinisch, *LD* 32,059
J. Cornford, *Green* 7,046
J. Major, *Loony X* 3,339
A. Reeve, *Capital P.* 2,983
P. Levy, *NLP* 887
C. majority 8,739
(Boundary change since June 1989)

LONDON SOUTH EAST
E. 493,178 *T.* 35.38%
S. Spiers, *Lab.* 71,505
*P. Price, *C.* 63,483
J. Fryer, *LD* 25,271
I. Mouland, *Green* 6,399
R. Almond, *Lib.* 3,881
K. Lowne, *NF* 2,926
J. Small, *NLP* 1,025
Lab. majority 8,022
(Boundary change since June 1989)

LONDON SOUTH INNER
E. 510,609 *T.* 27.30%
*R. Balfe, *Lab.* 85,079
A. Boff, *C.* 25,859
A. Graves, *LD* 20,708
S. Collins, *Green* 6,570
M. Leighton, *NLP* 1,179
Lab. majority 59,220
(Boundary change since June 1989)

LONDON SOUTH WEST
E. 479,246 *T.* 34.35%
*Ms A. Pollack, *Lab.* 81,850
Prof. P. Treleaven, *C.* 50,875
G. Blanchard, *LD* 18,697
T. Walsh, *Green* 5,460
A. Scholefield, *UK Independence* 4,912
C. Hopewell, *Capital P.* 1,840
M. Simson, *NLP* 625
J. Quanjer, *Spirit of Europe* 377
Lab. majority 30,975
(Boundary change since June 1989)

LONDON WEST
E. 505,791 *T.* 36.02%
*M. Elliott, *Lab.* 94,562
R. Guy, *C.* 52,287
W. Mallinson, *LD* 21,561
J. Bradley, *Green* 6,134
G. Roberts, *UK Independence* 4,583
W. Binding, *NF* 1,963
R. Johnson, *NLP* 1,105
Lab. majority 42,275
(June 1989, Lab. maj. 14,808)

MERSEYSIDE EAST AND WIGAN
E. 518,196　T. 24.66%

*T. Wynn, *Lab.*	91,986
C. Manson, *C.*	17,899
Ms F. Clucas, *LD*	8,874
J. Melia, *Lib.*	4,765
L. Brown, *Green*	3,280
G. Hutchard, *NLP*	1,009
Lab. majority	74,087

(June 1989, Lab. maj. 76,867)

MERSEYSIDE WEST
E. 515,909　T. 26.18%

*K. Stewart, *Lab.*	78,819
C. Varley, *C.*	27,008
D. Bamber, *LD*	19,097
S. Radford, *Lib.*	4,714
Ms L. Lever, *Green*	4,573
J. Collins, *NLP*	852
Lab. majority	51,811

(June 1989, Lab. maj. 49,817)

MIDLANDS WEST
E. 533,742　T. 31.28%

S. Murphy, *Lab.*	99,242
M. Simpson, *C.*	44,419
G. Baldauf-Good, *LD*	12,195
M. Hyde, *Lib.*	5,050
C. Mattingly, *Green*	4,390
J. Oldbury, *NLP*	1,641
Lab. majority	54,823

(June 1989, Lab. maj. 42,364)

NORFOLK
E. 513,553　T. 44.25%

C. Needle, *Lab.*	102,711
*P. Howell, *C.*	76,424
P. Burall, *LD*	39,107
A. Holmes, *Green*	7,938
B. Parsons, *NLP*	1,075
Lab. majority	26,287

(Boundary change since June 1989)

NORTHAMPTONSHIRE AND BLABY
E. 524,916　T. 39.37%

Mrs A. Billingham, *Lab.*	95,317
*A. Simpson, *C.*	69,232
K. Scudder, *LD*	27,616
Ms A. Bryant, *Green*	9,121
I. Whitaker, *Ind.*	4,397
B. Spivack, *NLP*	972
Lab. majority	26,085

(Boundary change since June 1989)

NORTHUMBRIA
E. 516,680　T. 33.65%

*G. Adam, *Lab.*	103,087
J. Flack, *C.*	36,929
L. Opik, *LD*	20,195
D. Lott, *UK Independence*	7,210
J. Hartshorne, *Green*	5,714
L. Walch, *NLP*	740
Lab. majority	66,158

(June 1989, Lab. maj. 60,040)

NOTTINGHAM AND LEICESTERSHIRE NORTH WEST
E. 507,915　T. 37.68%

*Ms M. Read, *Lab.*	95,344
M. Brandon-Bravo, *C.*	55,676
A. Wood, *LD*	23,836
Ms S. Blount, *Green*	7,035
J. Downes, *UK Independence*	5,849

P. Walton, *Ind. Out*	2,710
Mrs J. Christou, *NLP*	927
Lab. majority	39,668

(Boundary change since June 1989)

NOTTINGHAMSHIRE NORTH AND CHESTERFIELD
E. 490,330　T. 36.95%

*K. Coates, *Lab.*	114,353
D. Hazell, *C.*	38,093
Ms S. Pearce, *LD*	21,936
G. Jones, *Green*	5,159
Ms S. Lincoln, *NLP*	1,632
Lab. majority	76,260

(Boundary change since June 1989)

PEAK DISTRICT
E. 511,357　T. 39.02%

Ms A. McCarthy, *Lab.*	105,853
R. Fletcher, *C.*	56,546
Ms S. Barber, *LD*	29,979
M. Shipley, *Green*	5,598
D. Collins, *NLP*	1,533
Lab. majority	49,307

(Boundary change since June 1989)

SHEFFIELD
E. 476,530　T. 27.50%

*R. Barton, *Lab.*	76,397
Ms S. Anginotti, *LD*	26,109
Ms K. Twitchen, *C.*	22,374
B. New, *Green*	4,742
M. England, *Comm.*	834
R. Hurford, *NLP*	577
Lab. majority	50,288

(Boundary change since June 1989)

SOMERSET AND DEVON NORTH
E. 517,349　T. 47.09%

G. Watson, *LD*	106,187
*Mrs M. Daly, *C.*	83,678
J. Pilgrim, *Lab.*	34,540
D. Taylor, *Green*	10,870
G. Livings, *New Britain*	7,165
M. Lucas, *NLP*	1,200
LD majority	22,509

(Boundary change since June 1989)

SOUTH DOWNS WEST
E. 486,793　T. 39.45%

J. Provan, *C.*	83,813
Dr J. Walsh, *LD*	62,746
Ms L. Armstrong, *Lab.*	32,344
E. Paine, *Green*	7,703
W. Weights, *Lib.*	3,630
P. Kember, *NLP*	1,794
C. majority	21,067

(Boundary change since June 1989)

STAFFORDSHIRE EAST AND DERBY
E. 519,553　T. 35.46%

P. Whitehead, *Lab.*	102,393
Ms J. Evans, *C.*	50,197
Ms D. Brass, *LD*	17,469
I. Crompton, *UK Independence*	6,993
R. Clarke, *Green*	4,272
R. Jones, *NF*	2,098
Ms D. Grice, *NLP*	793
Lab. majority	72,196

(Boundary change since June 1989)

STAFFORDSHIRE WEST AND CONGLETON
E. 502,395　T. 31.60%

M. Tappin, *Lab.*	84,337
A. Brown, *C.*	44,060
J. Stevens, *LD*	24,430
D. Hoppe, *Green*	4,533
D. Lines, *NLP*	1,403
Lab. majority	40,277

(Boundary change since June 1989)

SUFFOLK AND NORFOLK SOUTH WEST
E. 477,668　T. 38.38%

D. Thomas, *Lab.*	74,304
*A. Turner, *C.*	61,769
R. Atkins, *LD*	37,975
A. Slade, *Green*	7,760
E. Kaplan, *NLP*	1,530
Lab. majority	12,535

(Boundary change since June 1989)

SURREY
E. 514,130　T. 37.51%

*T. Spencer, *C.*	83,405
Mrs S. Thomas, *LD*	56,387
Ms F. Wolf, *Lab.*	30,894
Mrs S. Porter, *UK Independence*	7,717
H. Charlton, *Green*	7,198
J. Walker, *Ind. Britain in Europe*	4,627
Mrs J. Thomas, *NLP*	2,638
C. majority	27,018

(Boundary change since June 1989)

SUSSEX EAST AND KENT SOUTH
E. 513,550　T. 41.90%

*Sir J. Stewart-Clark, *C.*	83,141
D. Bellotti, *LD*	76,929
N. Palmer, *Lab.*	35,273
A. Burgess, *UK Independence*	9,058
Ms R. Addison, *Green*	7,439
Ms T. Williamson, *Lib.*	2,558
P. Cragg, *NLP*	765
C. majority	6,212

(Boundary change since June 1989)

SUSSEX SOUTH AND CRAWLEY
E. 492,413　T. 37.64%

B. Donnelly, *C.*	62,860
Ms J. Edmond Smith, *Lab.*	61,114
J. Williams, *LD*	41,410
Ms P. Beever, *Green*	9,348
D. Horner, *Ind. Euro-Sceptic*	7,106
N. Furness, *Anti-Fed. C.*	2,618
A. Hankey, *NLP*	901
C. majority	1,746

(Boundary change since June 1989)

THAMES VALLEY
E. 543,685　T. 34.80%

*J. Stevens, *C.*	70,485
J. Howarth, *Lab.*	69,727
N. Bathurst, *LD*	33,187
P. Unsworth, *Green*	6,120
J. Clark, *Lib.*	5,381
P. Owen, *Loony C*	2,859
M. Grenville, *NLP*	1,453
C. majority	758

(June 1989, C. maj. 26,491)

TYNE AND WEAR
E. 516,436   T. 28.02%

A. Donnelly, *Lab.*	107,604
I. Liddell-Grainger, *C.*	19,224
P. Maughan, *LD*	8,706
G. Edwards, *Green*	4,375
Ms W. Lundgren, *Lib.*	4,164
A. Fisken, *NLP*	650
Lab. majority	88,380

(June 1989, Lab. maj. 95,780)

WIGHT AND HAMPSHIRE SOUTH
E. 488,398   T. 37.16%

R. Perry, *C.*	63,306
M. Hancock, *LD*	58,205
Ms S. Fry, *Lab.*	40,442
J. Browne, *Ind.*	12,140
P. Fuller, *Green*	6,697
W. Treend, *NLP*	722
C. majority	5,101

(Boundary change since June 1989)

WILTSHIRE NORTH AND BATH
E. 496,591   T. 41.46%

*Mrs C. Jackson, *C.*	71,872
Ms J. Matthew, *LD*	63,085
Ms J. Norris, *Lab.*	50,489
P. Cullen, *Lib.*	6,760
M. Davidson, *Green*	5,974
T. Hedges, *UK Independence*	5,842
D. Cooke, *NLP*	1,148
Dr J. Day, *CPP*	725
C. majority	8,787

(Boundary change since June 1989)

WORCESTERSHIRE AND
WARWICKSHIRE SOUTH
E. 551,162   T. 37.98%

J. Corrie, *C.*	73,573
Ms G. Gschaider, *Lab.*	72,369
P. Larner, *LD*	44,168
Ms J. Alty, *Green*	9,273
C. Hards, *National Independence*	8,447
J. Brewster, *NLP*	1,510
C. majority	1,204

(Boundary change since June 1989)

YORKSHIRE NORTH
E. 475,686   T. 38.70%

*E. McMillan-Scott, *C.*	70,036
B. Regan, *Lab.*	62,964
M. Pitts, *LD*	43,171
Dr R. Richardson, *Green*	7,036
S. Withers, *NLP*	891
C. majority	7,072

(Boundary change since June 1989)

YORKSHIRE SOUTH
E. 523,401   T. 28.64%

*N. West, *Lab.*	109,004
J. Howard, *C.*	20,695
Ms C. Roderick, *LD*	11,798
P. Davies, *UK Independence*	3,948
J. Waters, *Green*	3,775
N. Broome, *NLP*	681
Lab. majority	88,309

(June 1989, Lab. maj. 91,784)

YORKSHIRE SOUTH WEST
E. 547,469   T. 29.03%

*T. Megahy, *Lab.*	94,025
Mrs C. Adamson, *C.*	34,463
D. Ridgway, *LD*	21,595

A. Cooper, *Green*	7,163
G. Mead, *NLP*	1,674
Lab. majority	59,562

(Boundary change since June 1989)

YORKSHIRE WEST
E. 490,078   T. 34.61%

*B. Seal, *Lab.*	90,652
R. Booth, *C.*	42,455
C. Bidwell, *LD*	20,452
R. Pearson, *New Britain*	8,027
C. Harris, *Green*	7,154
D. Whitley, *NLP*	894
Lab. majority	48,197

(Boundary change since June 1989)

WALES

SOUTH WALES CENTRAL
E. 477,182   T. 39.40%

*W. David, *Lab.*	115,396
Ms L. Verity, *C.*	29,314
G. Llywelyn, *PC*	18,857
J. Dixon, *LD*	18,471
C. von Ruhland, *Green*	4,002
R. Griffiths, *Comm. YBG*	1,073
G. Duguay, *NLP*	889
Lab. majority	86,082

(Boundary change since June 1989)

SOUTH WALES EAST
E. 454,794   T. 43.07%

Mrs G. Kinnock, *Lab.*	144,907
Mrs R. Blomfield-Smith, *C.*	24,660
C. Woolgrove, *LD*	9,963
C. Mann, *PC*	9,550
R. Coghill, *Green*	4,509
Ms S. Williams, *Welsh Soc.*	1,270
Dr R. Brussatis, *NLP*	1,027
Lab. majority	120,247

(Boundary change since June 1989)

SOUTH WALES WEST
E. 395,131   T. 39.92%

*Revd D. Morris, *Lab.*	104,263
R. Buckland, *C.*	19,293
J. Bushell, *LD*	15,499
Ms C. Adams, *PC*	12,364
Ms J. Evans, *Green*	4,114
Ms H. Evans, *NLP*	1,112
Capt. Beany, *Beanus*	1,106
Lab. majority	84,970

(Boundary change since June 1989)

WALES MID AND WEST
E. 401,529   T. 48.00%

Ms E. Morgan, *Lab.*	78,092
M. Phillips, *PC*	48,858
P. Bone, *C.*	31,606
Ms J. Hughes, *LD*	23,719
D. Rowlands, *UK Independence*	5,536
Dr C. Busby, *Green*	3,938
T. Griffith-Jones, *NLP*	988
Lab. majority	29,234

(Boundary change since June 1989)

WALES NORTH
E. 475,829   T. 45.34%

*J. Wilson, *Lab.*	88,091
D. Wigley, *PC*	72,849
G. Mon Hughes, *C.*	33,450

Ms R. Parry, *LD*	14,828
P. Adams, *Green*	2,850
D. Hughes, *NLP*	2,065
M. Cooksey, *Ind.*	1,623
Lab. majority	15,242

(Boundary change since June 1989)

SCOTLAND

GLASGOW
E. 463,364   T. 34.46%

W. Miller, *Lab.*	83,953
T. Chalmers, *SNP*	40,795
T. Sheridan, *SML*	12,113
R. Wilkinson, *C.*	10,888
J. Money, *LD*	7,291
P. O'Brien, *Green*	2,252
J. Fleming, *Soc.*	1,125
M. Wilkinson, *NLP*	868
C. Marsden, *ICP*	381
Lab. majority	43,158

(June 1989, Lab. maj. 59,232)

HIGHLANDS AND ISLANDS
E. 328,104   T. 39.09%

*Mrs W. Ewing, *SNP*	74,872
M. Macmillan, *Lab.*	19,956
M. Tennant, *C.*	15,767
H. Morrison, *LD*	12,919
Dr E. Scott, *Green*	3,140
M. Carr, *UK Independence*	1,096
Ms M. Gilmour, *NLP*	522
SNP majority	54,916

(June 1989, SNP maj. 44,695)

LOTHIANS
E. 520,943   T. 38.69%

*D. Martin, *Lab.*	90,531
K. Brown, *SNP*	53,324
Dr P. McNally, *C.*	33,526
Ms H. Campbell, *LD*	17,883
R. Harper, *Green*	5,149
J. McGregor, *Soc.*	637
M. Siebert, *NLP*	500
Lab. majority	37,207

(June 1989, Lab. maj. 38,826)

SCOTLAND MID AND FIFE
E. 546,060   T. 38.25%

*A. Falconer, *Lab.*	95,667
R. Douglas, *SNP*	64,254
P. Page, *C.*	28,192
Ms H. Lyall, *LD*	17,192
M. Johnston, *Green*	3,015
T. Pringle, *NLP*	532
Lab. majority	31,413

(June 1989, Lab. maj. 52,157)

SCOTLAND NORTH EAST
E. 575,748   T. 37.72%

A. Macartney, *SNP*	92,892
*H. McCubbin, *Lab.*	61,665
Dr R. Harris, *C.*	40,372
S. Horner, *LD*	18,008
K. Farnsworth, *Green*	2,569
Ms M. Ward, *Comm. GB*	689
L. Mair, *Neeps*	584
D. Paterson, *NLP*	371
SNP majority	31,227

(June 1989, Lab. maj. 2,613)

SCOTLAND SOUTH		STRATHCLYDE EAST		NORTHERN IRELAND	
E. 500,643 T. 40.14%		E. 492,618 T. 37.26%		Northern Ireland forms a three-member seat with a single transferable vote system	
*A. Smith, *Lab.*	90,750	*K. Collins, *Lab.*	106,476		
A. Hutton, *C.*	45,595	I. Hamilton, *SNP*	54,136		
Mrs C. Creech, *SNP*	45,032	B. Cooklin, *C.*	13,915	E. 1,150,304 T. 48.67%	
D. Millar, *LD*	13,363	R. Stewart, *LD*	6,383	*Revd I. Paisley, *DUP*	163,246
J. Hein, *Lib.*	3,249	A. Whitelaw, *Green*	1,874	*J. Hume, *SDLP*	161,992
Ms L. Hendry, *Green*	2,429	D. Gilmour, *NLP*	787	*J. Nicholson, *UUUP*	133,459
G. Gay, *NLP*	539	*Lab. majority*	52,340	Mrs M. Clark-Glass, *All.*	23,157
Lab. majority	45,155	(June 1989, Lab. maj. 60,317)		T. Hartley, *SF*	21,273
(June 1989, Lab. maj. 15,693)				Ms D. McGuinness, *SF*	17,195
		STRATHCLYDE WEST		F. Molloy, *SF*	16,747
		E. 489,129 T. 40.05%		Revd H. Ross, *Ulster Independence*	
		*H. McMahon, *Lab.*	86,957		7,858
		C. Campbell, *SNP*	61,934	Miss M. Boal, *C.*	5,583
		J. Godfrey, *C.*	28,414	J. Lowry, *WP*	2,543
		D. Herbison, *LD*	14,772	N. Cusack, *Ind. Lab.*	2,464
		Ms K. Allan, *Green*	2,886	J. Anderson, *NLP*	1,418
		Ms S. Gilmour, *NLP*	918	Mrs J. Campion, *Peace Coalition*	1,088
		Lab. majority	25,023	D. Kerr, *Independence for Ulster*	571
		(June 1989, Lab. maj. 39,591)		Ms S. Thompson, *NLP*	454
				M. Kennedy, *NLP*	419
				R. Mooney, *Const. NI*	400

Speakers of the Commons since 1708

The date of appointment given is the day on which the Speaker was first elected by the House of Commons. The appointment requires royal approbation before it is confirmed and this is usually given within a few days. The present Speaker is the 155th.

PARLIAMENT OF GREAT BRITAIN

Sir Richard Onslow (*Lord Onslow*), 16 November 1708
William Bromley, 25 November 1710
Sir Thomas Hanmer, 16 February 1714
Spencer Compton (*Earl of Wilmington*), 17 March 1715
Arthur Onslow, 23 January 1728
Sir John Cust, 3 November 1761
Sir Fletcher Norton (*Lord Grantley*), 22 January 1770
Charles Cornwall, 31 October 1780
Hon. William Grenville (*Lord Grenville*), 5 January 1789
Henry Addington (*Viscount Sidmouth*), 8 June 1789

PARLIAMENT OF THE UNITED KINGDOM

Sir John Mitford (*Lord Redesdale*), 11 February 1801

Charles Abbot (*Lord Colchester*), 10 February 1802
Charles Manners-Sutton (*Viscount Canterbury*), 2 June 1817
James Abercromby (*Lord Dunfermline*), 19 February 1835
Charles Shaw-Lefevre (*Viscount Eversley*), 27 May 1839
J. Evelyn Denison (*Viscount Ossington*), 30 April 1857
Sir Henry Brand (*Viscount Hampden*), 9 February 1872
Arthur Wellesley Peel (*Viscount Peel*), 26 February 1884
William Gully (*Viscount Selby*), 10 April 1895
James Lowther (*Viscount Ullswater*), 8 June 1905
John Whitley, 27 April 1921
Hon. Edward Fitzroy, 20 June 1928
Douglas Clifton-Brown (*Viscount Ruffside*), 9 March 1943
William Morrison (*Viscount Dunrossil*), 31 October 1951
Sir Harry Hylton-Foster, 20 October 1959
Horace King (*Lord Maybray-King*), 26 October 1965
Selwyn Lloyd (*Lord Selwyn-Lloyd*), 12 January 1971
George Thomas (*Viscount Tonypandy*), 2 February 1976
Bernard Weatherill (*Lord Weatherill*), 15 June 1983
Betty Boothroyd, 27 April 1992

The Government

Prime Minister, First Lord of the Treasury and Minister for the Civil Service
The Rt. Hon. John Major, MP, since November 1990
First Secretary of State and Deputy Prime Minister
The Rt. Hon. Michael Heseltine, MP, since July 1995
Lord High Chancellor
The Lord Mackay of Clashfern, PC, since October 1987
Chancellor of the Exchequer
The Rt. Hon. Kenneth Clarke, QC, MP, since May 1993
Secretary of State for the Home Department
The Rt. Hon. Michael Howard, QC, MP, since May 1993
Secretary of State for Foreign and Commonwealth Affairs
The Rt. Hon. Malcolm Rifkind, QC, MP, since July 1995
Lord President of the Council and Leader of the House of Commons
The Rt. Hon. Antony Newton, OBE, MP, since April 1992
Secretary of State for the Environment
The Rt. Hon. John Gummer, MP, since May 1993
Secretary of State for Social Security
The Rt. Hon. Peter Lilley, MP, since April 1992
Chief Secretary to the Treasury
The Rt. Hon. William Waldegrave, MP, since July 1995
Secretary of State for Trade and Industry and President of the Board of Trade
The Rt. Hon. Ian Lang, MP, since July 1995
Secretary of State for Northern Ireland
The Rt. Hon. Sir Patrick Mayhew, QC, MP, since April 1992
Secretary of State for National Heritage
The Rt. Hon. Virginia Bottomley, MP, since July 1995
Secretary of State for Education and Employment
The Rt. Hon. Gillian Shephard, MP, since July 1994 (Education)/July 1995 (Employment)
Secretary of State for Defence
The Rt. Hon. Michael Portillo, MP, since July 1995
Minister without Portfolio (Party chairman)
The Rt. Hon. Brian Mawhinney, MP, since July 1995
Secretary of State for Health
The Rt. Hon. Stephen Dorrell, MP, since July 1995
Lord Privy Seal and Leader of the House of Lords
Viscount Cranborne, PC, since July 1994
Secretary of State for Transport
The Rt. Hon. Sir George Young, Bt., MP, since July 1995
Minister of Agriculture, Fisheries and Food
The Rt. Hon. Douglas Hogg, QC, MP, since July 1995
Secretary of State for Scotland
The Rt. Hon. Michael Forsyth, MP, since July 1995
Chancellor of the Duchy of Lancaster and Minister for Public Service
The Rt. Hon. Roger Freeman, MP, since July 1995
Secretary of State for Wales
The Rt. Hon. William Hague, MP, since July 1995

LAW OFFICERS

Attorney-General
The Rt. Hon. Sir Nicholas Lyell, QC, MP, since April 1992
Lord Advocate
The Lord Mackay of Drumadoon, PC, QC, since May 1995
Solicitor-General
Sir Derek Spencer, QC, MP, since April 1992
Solicitor-General for Scotland
Paul Cullen, QC

MINISTERS OF STATE

Agriculture, Fisheries and Food
Anthony Baldry, MP
Office of Public Service
David Willetts, MP (*Paymaster-General*)
Defence
The Hon. Nicholas Soames, MP (*Armed Forces*)
James Arbuthnot, MP (*Defence Procurement*)
Education and Employment
Eric Forth, MP
The Lord Henley
Environment
The Rt. Hon. David Curry, MP (*Minister for Local Government*)
The Earl Ferrars, PC (*Minister for Environment and Countryside*)
Robert Jones, MP (*Minister for Construction, Planning and Energy Efficiency*)
Foreign and Commonwealth Affairs
The Baroness Chalker of Wallasey, PC (*Minister for Overseas Development*)
David Davis, MP (*Minister for Europe*)
The Rt. Hon. Jeremy Hanley, MP
Sir Nicholas Bonsor, MP
Health
Gerald Malone, MP
Home Office
The Rt. Hon. David Maclean, MP
The Baroness Blatch, PC
Ann Widdecombe, MP
National Heritage
Iain Sproat, MP (*Minister for Sport*)
Northern Ireland Office
The Rt. Hon. Sir John Wheeler, MP
The Rt. Hon. Michael Ancram, MP
Scottish Office
The Rt. Hon. Lord James Douglas-Hamilton, MP (*Home Affairs and Health*)
Social Security
The Lord Mackay of Ardbrecknish, PC
Alistair Burt, MP (*Social Security and Disabled People*)
Trade and Industry
The Lord Fraser of Carmyllie, PC, QC
Anthony Nelson, MP (*Minister for Trade*)
Gregory Knight, MP (*Minister of Industry and Energy*)
Transport
John Watts, MP
Treasury
Michael Jack, MP (*Financial Secretary*)
Angela Knight, MP (*Economic Secretary*)

UNDER-SECRETARIES OF STATE

Agriculture, Fisheries and Food
Angela Browning, MP
Timothy Boswell, MP
Defence
The Earl Howe
Education and Employment
Robin Squire, MP
James Paice, MP
Cheryl Gillan, MP
Environment
Sir Paul Beresford, MP
James Clappison, MP
Foreign Office
Liam Fox, MP
Health
The Baroness Cumberlege, CBE
John Horam, MP
Simon Burns, MP
Home Office
Timothy Kirkhope, MP
The Hon. Thomas Sackville, MP
Lord Chancellor's Department
Gary Streeter, MP
National Heritage
The Lord Inglewood
Northern Ireland
The Baroness Denton of Wakefield, CBE
Malcolm Moss, MP
Scottish Office
George Kynoch, MP (*Industry and Local Government*)
Raymond Robertson, MP (*Education, Housing and Fisheries*)
The Earl of Lindsay (*Agriculture, Forestry and the Environment*)
Social Security
Roger Evans, MP
Oliver Heald, MP
Andrew Mitchell, MP
Trade and Industry
Ian Taylor, MBE, MP (*Science and Technology*)
Richard Page, MP (*Small Business, Industry and Energy*)
John Taylor, MP (*Competition and Consumer Affairs*)
Transport
The Viscount Goschen
John Bowis, OBE, MP
Treasury
Phillip Oppenheim, MP (*Exchequer Secretary*)
The Lords Commissioners, *see* Government whips
Welsh Office
Gwilym Jones, MP
Jonathan Evans, MP

GOVERNMENT WHIPS

HOUSE OF LORDS

Captain of the Honourable Corps of Gentlemen-at-Arms (Chief Whip)
The Lord Strathclyde, PC
Captain of The Queen's Bodyguard of the Yeoman of the Guard (Deputy Chief Whip)
The Lord Chesham
Lords-in-Waiting
The Viscount Long; The Lord Lucas of Crudwell; The Earl of Courtown

Baronesses-in-Waiting
The Baroness Trumpington, PC; The Baroness Miller of Hendon

HOUSE OF COMMONS

Parliamentary Secretary to the Treasury (Chief Whip)
The Rt. Hon. Alastair Goodlad, MP
Treasurer of HM Household (Deputy Chief Whip)
Andrew Mackay, MP
Comptroller of HM Household
Timothy Wood, MP
Vice-Chamberlain of HM Household
Derek Conway, MP
Lords Commissioners
Bowen Wells, MP; Michael Bates, MP; Patrick McLoughlin, MP; Roger Knapman, MP; Richard Ottaway, MP
Assistant Whips
Gyles Brandeth, MP; Sebastian Coe, MP; Anthony Coombs, MP; Jacqui Lait, MP; Peter Ainsworth, MP

Government Departments and Public Offices

This section covers central government departments, executive agencies, regulatory bodies, other statutory independent organizations, and bodies which are government-financed or whose head is appointed by a government minister.

THE CIVIL SERVICE

Changes are currently being introduced into the civil service with the aim of reducing its functions to a central core and privatizing or contracting out the rest of its work. Many semi-autonomous executive agencies have already been established under the 'Next Steps' programme. Executive agencies operate within a framework set by the responsible minister which specifies policies, objectives and available resources. They are usually headed by a chief executive, who is responsible for the day-to-day operations of the agency and who is accountable to the minister for the use of resources and for the performance of the agency. Nearly 52 per cent of civil servants now work in executive agencies. Customs and Excise and the Inland Revenue, which employ a further 15 per cent of civil servants, also operate on 'Next Steps' lines. In April 1996 there were 494,300 permanent civil servants.

Most of the Home Civil Service's senior grades were formerly absorbed into an Open pay and grading structure. The Senior Civil Service came into being on 1 April 1996 and comprises civil servants formerly at Grade 5 level and above and all agency chief executives. All government departments and executive agencies are now responsible for their own pay and grading systems for civil servants outside the Senior Civil Service. In practice the grades of the former Open structure ar still currently being used in many organizations. The Open structure represented the following:

Grade Title
1   Permanent Secretary
1A   Second Permanent Secretary
2   Deputy Secretary
3   Under-Secretary
4   Chief Scientific Officer B, Professional and Technology Directing A
5   Assistant Secretary, Deputy Chief Scientific Officer, Professional and Technology Directing B
6   Senior Principal, Senior Principal Scientific Officer, Professional and Technology Superintending Grade
7   Principal, Principal Scientific Officer, Principal Professional and Technology Officer

SALARIES

MINISTERIAL SALARIES 1996–7

Ministers who are Members of the House of Commons receive a parliamentary salary (£43,000) in addition to their ministerial salary. The salaries in the right-hand column will come into effect on the day after the general election.

	From July 1996	After general election
Prime Minister	£58,557	£100,000
Secretary of State (Commons)	£43,991	£60,000
Secretary of State (Lords)	£58,876	£77,963
Minister of State (Commons)	£31,125	£31,125
Minister of State (Lords)	£51,838	£51,838
Parliamentary Under-Secretary (Commons)	£23,623	£23,623
Parliamentary Under-Secretary (Lords)	£43,632	£43,632

CIVIL SERVICE SALARIES 1996–7

Senior Civil Service (SCS)

Secretary of the Cabinet and Head of the Home Civil Service	£90,000–£154,500
Permanent Secretary to the Treasury	£90,000–£154,500
Head of the Diplomatic Service	£90,000–£154,500
Permanent Secretary	£90,000–£154,500
Band 9	£80,000–£113,300
Band 8	£73,200–£106,900
Band 7	£67,000–£100,900
Band 6	£61,200–£95,300
Band 5	£55,900–£90,000
Band 4	£51,000–£85,000
Band 3	£46,200–£75,600
Band 2	£41,900–£67,200
Band 1	£38,000–£59,700

Staff are placed in pay bands according to their level of responsibility and taking account of other factors such as experience and marketability. Movement within and between bands is based on performance. A recruitment and retention allowance of up to £3,000 may be paid at each department's discretion in addition to the salary ranges shown for bands 1 to 9.

Other Civil Servants

Following the delegation of responsibility for pay and grading to government departments and agencies from 1 April 1996, it is now not possible to show the pay rates for staff outside the Senior Civil Service. Individual departments and agencies have introduced or will be introducing their own pay systems.

ADJUDICATOR'S OFFICE
Haymarket House, 28 Haymarket, London SW1Y 4SP
Tel 0171-930 2292

The Adjudicator's Office opened in 1993 and investigates complaints made about the way the Inland Revenue, Customs and Excise or the Contributions Agency have handled an individual's affairs.
The Adjudicator, Ms E. Filkin
Head of Office, D. I. Richardson

ADVISORY, CONCILIATION AND ARBITRATION SERVICE
Brandon House, 180 Borough High Street, London
SE1 1LW
Tel 0171-210 3613

The Advisory, Conciliation and Arbitration Service (ACAS) is an independent organization set up under the Employment Protection Act 1975 (the provisions now being found in the Trade Union and Labour Relations (Consolidation) Act 1992). ACAS is directed by a Council consisting of a full-time chairman and part-time employer, trade union and independent members, all appointed by the Secretary of State for Trade and Industry. The functions of the Service are to promote the improvement of industrial relations in general, to provide facilities for conciliation, mediation and arbitration as means of avoiding and resolving industrial disputes, and to provide advisory and information services on industrial relations matters to employers, employees and their representatives.

ACAS also has regional offices in Birmingham, Bristol, Cardiff, Fleet, Glasgow, Leeds, Liverpool, London, Manchester, Newcastle upon Tyne and Nottingham.

Chairman, J. Hougham, CBE
Chief Conciliation Officer (G4), D. Evans

MINISTRY OF AGRICULTURE, FISHERIES AND FOOD
Whitehall Place, London SW1A 2HH
Tel 0171-238 6000; *enquiries* 0645-335577

The Ministry of Agriculture, Fisheries and Food is responsible for administering government policies on agriculture, horticulture and fisheries in England and policies relating to the safety and quality of food in the UK as a whole. In association with the Agriculture Departments of the Scottish, Welsh and Northern Ireland Offices and with the Intervention Board (*see* page 315), the Ministry is responsible for the negotiation and administration of the EU common agricultural and fisheries policies, for matters relating to the single European market, and for international agricultural and food trade policy. It commissions research to assist in the formulation and assessment of policy.

The Ministry administers policies on the control and eradication of animal, plant and fish diseases, and on assistance to capital investment in farm and horticultural businesses; it also has responsibilities relating to the protection and enhancement of the countryside and the marine environment as well as to flood defence and other rural issues.

The Ministry is responsible for ensuring public health standards in the manufacture, preparation and distribution of basic foods, and for planning to safeguard essential food supplies in times of emergency. It is responsible for government relations with the UK food and drink manufacturing industries and the food and drink importing, distributive and catering trades.

The Food Safety Directorate is responsible for many aspects of food safety and quality. These include pesticide safety approval, biotechnology, meat hygiene, animal health and welfare, and related public health issues.

Minister, The Rt. Hon. Douglas Hogg, QC, MP
  Principal Private Secretary (G7), W. F. G. Strang
  Private Secretary, M. H. Nisbet
  Parliamentary Private Secretary, G. Clifton-Brown, MP

Minister of State, Tony Baldry, QC, MP (*Farming and Fisheries*)
  Private Secretary, Miss R. J. Gower
Parliamentary Private Secretary, N. Evans, MP
Parliamentary Secretary, Timothy Boswell, MP (*Countryside*)
  Private Secretary, P. Green
Parliamentary Secretary, Angela Browning, MP (*Food*)
  Private Secretary, Mrs E. C. Ratcliffe
Parliamentary Clerk, Miss A. Evans
Permanent Secretary (G1), R. J. Packer
  Private Secretary, R. Campbell

ESTABLISHMENT DEPARTMENT
Director of Establishments (G3), J. W. Hepburn

†ESTABLISHMENTS (GENERAL) AND OFFICE SERVICES DIVISION
Head of Division (G6), Dr J. A. Bailey

WELFARE BRANCH
Whitehall Place (West Block), London SW1A 2HH
Tel 0171-238 6000
Chief Welfare Officer (SEO), D. J. Jones

†PERSONNEL MANAGEMENT AND DEVELOPMENT DIVISION
Head of Division (G5), T. J. Osmond

DEPARTMENTAL HEALTH AND SAFETY UNIT
Government Buildings, Hook Rise South, Tolworth, Surbiton, Surrey KT6 7NF
Tel 0181-330 4411
Head of Unit (G7), C. R. Bradburn

†TRAINING AND DEVELOPMENT BRANCH
Principal (G7), J. M. Cowley

BUILDING AND ESTATE MANAGEMENT
Eastbury House, 30–34 Albert Embankment,
London SE1 7TL
Tel 0171-238 6000
Head of Division (G5), J. A. S. Nickson

INFORMATION TECHNOLOGY DIRECTORATE
Government Buildings, Epsom Road, Guildford, Surrey
GU1 2LD
Tel 01483-68121
Director (G5), A. G. Matthews
Head of Strategies (G6), R. J. Long
Head of Applications (G6), D. D. Brown
Head of Infrastructure (G6), S. V. Soper

INFORMATION DIVISION
Whitehall Place (West Block), London SW1A 2HH
Tel 0171-238 6000
Chief Information Officer (G5), G. Blakeway
Chief Press Officer (G7), M. Smith
Chief Publicity Officer (G7), N. Wagstaffe
Principal Librarian (G7), P. McShane

FINANCE DEPARTMENT
19–29 Woburn Place, London WC1H 0LU
Tel 0171-270 8080
Principal Finance Officer (G3), P. Elliott

FINANCIAL POLICY DIVISION
Head of Division (G5), P. P. Nash

FINANCIAL MANAGEMENT DIVISION
Head of Division (G5), J. M. Lowi

†At Nobel/Ergon House, 17 Smith Square, London SW1P 3JR. Tel: 0171-238 6000

PROCUREMENT AND CONTRACTS DIVISION
Director of Audit (G5), D. V. Fisher

CAP SCHEMES MANAGEMENT
Head of Division (G5), Miss V. A. Smith

MARKET TESTING AND PROCUREMENT ADVICE
Director (G5), D. B. Rabey

RESOURCE MANAGEMENT STRATEGY UNIT
Head of Division (G5), Mrs J. Flint

LEGAL DEPARTMENT
55 Whitehall, London SWIA 2EY
Tel 0171-238 6000
Legal Adviser and Solicitor (G2), R. Woolman
Principal Assistant Solicitors (G3), D. J. Pearson; Ms C. A. Crisham

LEGAL DIVISIONS
Assistant Solicitor, Division A1 (G5), Dr M. R. Parke
Assistant Solicitor, Division A2 (G5), P. Kent
Assistant Solicitor, Division A3 (G5), T. J. Middleton
Assistant Solicitor, Division A4 (G5), P. D. Davis
Assistant Solicitor, Division B1 (G5), Mrs C. A. Davis
Assistant Solicitor, Division B2 (G4), Ms S. B. Spence
Assistant Solicitor, Division B3 (G5), A. I. Corbett
Assistant Solicitor, Division B4 (G5), Mrs F. C. Nash

INVESTIGATION UNIT
Chief Investigation Officer, Miss J. Panting

AGRICULTURAL COMMODITIES, TRADE AND FOOD PRODUCTION
Deputy Secretary (G2), Ms V. K. Timms

EUROPEAN UNION AND LIVESTOCK GROUP
Under-Secretary (G3), D. P. Hunter

DIVISIONS
Head, European Union I (G5), A. J. Lebrecht
Head, European Union II (G6), L. G. Mitchell
Head, Beef and Sheep (G5), J. R. Cowan
Head, Milk, Pigs, Eggs and Poultry (G5), B. J. Harding
Head, Livestock Quota Unit (G6), Ms L. Cornish

ARABLE CROPS AND HORTICULTURE
Under-Secretary (G3), D. H. Griffiths

DIVISIONS
Head, Cereals and Set-Aside (G4), G. M. Trevelyan
Head, Sugar, Tobacco, Oilseeds and Protein (G5), Mrs A. M. Blackburn
†*Head, Horticulture and Potatoes (G5)*, R. A. Saunderson

PLANT VARIETY RIGHTS OFFICE AND SEEDS DIVISION
White House Lane, Huntingdon Road, Cambridge
CB3 OLF
Tel 01223-277151
Head of Office (G5), D. A. Boreham

FOOD, DRINK AND MARKETING POLICY
Under-Secretary (G3), N. Thornton

DIVISIONS
Head, Food and Drinks Industry (G5), R. E. Melville
Head, International Relations and Export Promotion (G5), D. V. Orchard
Head, Trade Policy and Tropical Foods (G5), Miss S. E. Brown
†*Head, Market Task Force (G5)*, H. B. Brown

REGIONAL SERVICES AND DEFENCE GROUP
Under-Secretary (G3), R. A. Saunderson
Head, Deregulation, Agricultural Training and Resources (G5), A. R. Burne
Head, Plant Health and Plant Health and Seeds Inspectorate (G5), A. J. Perrins
Head, Flood and Coastal Protection (G5), Dr. J. Park

REGIONAL ORGANIZATION
Head, Regional Support Unit (G7), D. Putley

Regional Service Centres

ANGLIA REGION, Block B, Government Buildings, Brooklands Avenue, Cambridge CB2 2DR. Tel: 01223-462727. *Regional Director (G5)*, Miss C. J. Rabagliati
EAST MIDLANDS REGION, Government Buildings, Block 7, Chalfont Drive, Nottingham NG8 3SN. Tel: 0115-929 1191. *Regional Director (G6)*, G. Norbury
NORTH-EAST REGION, Government Buildings, Crosby Road, Northallerton, N. Yorks DL6 1AD. Tel: 01609-773751. *Regional Director (G6)*, P. Watson
NORTHERN REGION, Eden Bridge House, Lowther Street, Carlisle, Cumbria CA3 8DX. Tel: 01228-23400. *Regional Director (G5)*, J. P. Bradbury
NORTH MERCIA REGION, Berkeley Towers, Nantwich Road, Crewe, Cheshire CW2 6PT. Tel: 01270-69211. *Regional Director (G6)*, R. Bettley-Smith
SOUTH-EAST REGION, Block A, Government Buildings, Coley Park, Reading, Berks RGI 6DT. Tel: 01734-581222. *Regional Director (G6)*, Mrs V. Silvester
SOUTH MERCIA REGION, Block C, Government Buildings, Whittington Road, Worcester WR5 2LQ. Tel: 01905-763355. *Regional Director (G6)*, B. Davies
SOUTH-WEST REGION, Government Buildings, Alphington Road, Exeter EX2 8NQ. Tel: 01392-77951. *Regional Director (G6)*, M. R. W. Highman
WESSEX REGION, Block 3, Government Buildings, Burghill Road, Westbury-on-Trym, Bristol BSIO 6NJ. Tel: 01272-591000. *Regional Director (G6)*, Mrs A. J. L. Ould

FOOD SAFETY AND ENVIRONMENT GROUP
Deputy Secretary (G2), R. J. D. Carden

ENVIRONMENT GROUP
Under-Secretary (G3), D. J. Coates
Head, Conservation and Woodlands Policy (G5), Ms J. Allfrey
Head, Conservation Management Division (G5), P. M. Boyling
Head, Land Use and Rural Economy (G5), R. C. McIvor
Head, Land Use Planning Unit (G5), D. G. Sisson
Head, Environmental Protection (G5), D. E. Jones

†FOOD SAFETY AND SCIENCE GROUP
Under-Secretary (G3), G. Podger

DIVISIONS
Head, Food Hygiene (G5), Ms S. Nason
Head, Additives and Novel Foods (G5), Dr J. R. Bell
Head, Food Labelling and Standards (G5), G. Meekings
Head, Food Contaminants (G5), Dr R. Burt
Head, Consumers and Nutrition (G5), Miss E. J. Wordley
Head, Radiological Safety (G5), Dr M. G. Segal

†CHIEF SCIENTIST'S GROUP
Chief Scientist (G3), Dr D. W. F. Shannon

DIVISIONS
Head, Agriculture and Food Technology (G5), Dr J. C. Sherlock

Head, Food and Veterinary Science Division (*G5*),
Dr K. J. MacOwan
Head, Environment, Fisheries and International Science (*G5*),
Dr M. Parker
Head, Research Policy Co-ordination (*G5*), J. C. Suich

ANIMAL HEALTH AND VETERINARY GROUP
Government Buildings, Hook Rise South, Tolworth,
Surbiton, Surrey KT6 7NF
Tel 0181-330 4411
Under-Secretary (*G3*), B. H. B. Dickinson
Chief Veterinary Officer (*G3*), K. C. Meldrum, CB

DIVISIONS
Head, Animal Health (Disease Control) (*G5*), T. E. D. Eddy
Head, Animal Health (International Trade) (*G5*), R. A. Bell
Head, Meat Hygiene (*G5*), C. J. Lawson
Head, Services (*G6*), R. Gurd
Head, Animal Welfare (*G5*), C. J. Ryder

STATE VETERINARY SERVICE
Government Buildings, Hook Rise South, Tolworth,
Surbiton, Surrey KT15 3NB
Tel 0181-330 4411
Director of Veterinary Field Services (*G3*), I. Crawford

LASSWADE VETERINARY LABORATORY
East of Scotland College of Agriculture, The Bush Estate,
Penicuik, Midlothian EH26 0SA
Tel 0131-445 5371
Head of Laboratory (*G6*), Miss G. Mackenzie

†FISHERIES DEPARTMENT
Fisheries Secretary (*G3*), S. Wentworth

DIVISIONS
Head, Fisheries I (*G5*), A. Kuyk
Head, Fisheries II (*G5*), C. I. Llewellyn
Head, Fisheries III (*G5*), J. E. Robbs
Head, Fisheries IV (*G6*), B. S. Edwards
Chief Inspector, Sea Fisheries Inspectorate (*G6*), S. G. Elson

FISHERIES RESEARCH
Pakefield Road, Lowestoft, Suffolk NR33 0HT
Tel 01502-562244
Director of Fisheries Research and Development for Great Britain
(*G4*), P. W. Greig-Smith
Deputy Directors of Fisheries Research (*G5*), J. W. Horwood;
J. E. Portmann

FISHERIES LABORATORY
Pakefield Road, Lowestoft, Suffolk NR33 0HT
Tel 01502-562244

FISHERIES LABORATORY
Remembrance Avenue, Burnham-on-Crouch, Essex
CMO 8HA
Tel 01621-782658

FISHERIES EXPERIMENT STATION
Benarth Road, Conwy LL32 8UB
Tel 01492-593883

FISH DISEASES LABORATORY
33–33A Albany Road, Granby Industrial Estate,
Weymouth, Dorset DT4 9TU
Tel 01305-772137
Officer-in-Charge (*Principal Scientific Officer*) (*G6*), B. J. Hill,
PH.D.

ECONOMICS AND STATISTICS
Under-Secretary (*G3*), Dr J. M. Slater

DIVISIONS
Senior Economic Adviser, Economics and Statistics (Farm Business) (*G5*), J. P. Muriel
Senior Economic Adviser, Economics (International and Food) (*G5*), vacant
Senior Economic Adviser, Economics (Resource Use) (*G5*), R. W. Irving

STATISTICS DIVISION
Foss House, 1–2 Peasholme Green, King's Pool, York
YO1 2PX
Tel 01904-455328
Chief Statistician (Commodities and Food) (*G4*), Dr P. J. Lund
Chief Statistician (Census and Surveys) (*G5*), P. F. Helm

EXECUTIVE AGENCIES
ADAS (AGRICULTURAL DEVELOPMENT AND ADVISORY SERVICE)
ADAS Headquarters, Oxford Spires Business Park, The
Boulevard, Kidlington, Oxon OX5 1NZ
Tel 01865-842742
ADAS provides a range of consultancy services to the land-based industries. It is a joint executive agency of MAFF and the Welsh Office and carries out research, performs certain statutory functions and provides advice on policy for both departments. The Government has announced its intention of privatizing the commercial parts of ADAS.
Chief Executive, P. Needham
Director of Operations and Director for Wales, W. I. C. Davies
Research Director, Dr A. D. Hughes
Marketing Director, D. J. Hall
Finance Director, Dr C. Herring
Personnel Director, C. Ouseley

CENTRAL SCIENCE LABORATORY
The Innovation Centre, York Science Park, University
Road, Heslington, York YO1 5DG
Tel 01904-435120
The Central Science Laboratory was enlarged in 1994 by merging with the Food Science Laboratory, Norwich and the Torry Research Station, Aberdeen. The agency provides MAFF with technical support and policy advice on the protection and quality of the food supply and on related environmental issues.
Chief Executive (*G3*), Prof. P. I. Stanley
Research Director (*G5*), Prof. A. R. Hardy
Head of Food Science Laboratory (*G5*), Dr J. Gilbert, Norwich
Research Park, Colney Lane, Norwich NR4 7UQ. Tel:
01603-259350
Director, Torry Research Station (*G5*), Dr L. Cox, PO Box 31,
135 Abbey Road, Aberdeen AB9 8DG. Tel: 01224-877071

INTERVENTION BOARD
— *see* page 315

MEAT HYGIENE SERVICE
Foss House, 1–2 Peasholme Green, King's Pool, York
YO1 2PX
Tel 01904-455500
The Agency was launched in April 1995 and is responsible for the fresh meat hygiene enforcement arrangements formerly carried out by local authorities.
Chief Executive (*G4*), J. McNeill

---

†At Nobel/Ergon House, 17 Smith Square, London SW1P 3JR. Tel: 0171-238 6000

PESTICIDES SAFETY DIRECTORATE
Mallard House, King's Pool, 3 Peasholme Green, York
YOI 2PX
Tel 01904-640500

The Pesticides Safety Directorate is responsible for the evaluation and approval of pesticides and the development of policies relating to them, in order to protect consumers, users and the environment.
Chief Executive (*G4*), G. K. Bruce
Director (*Policy*) (*G5*), J. A. Bainton
Director (*Approvals*) (*G5*), Dr A. D. Martin

VETERINARY LABORATORIES AGENCY
Woodham Lane, New Haw, Addlestone, Surrey KT15 3NB
Tel 01932-341111

The Veterinary Laboratories Agency provides scientific and technical expertise in animal and public health.
Director and Chief Executive (*G3*), Dr T. W. A. Little
Director of Research (*G4*), Dr J. A. Morris
Director of Operations (*G5*), J. W. Harkness
Director of Veterinary Investigation Centres (*G5*),
   W. A. Edwards

VETERINARY MEDICINES DIRECTORATE
Woodham Lane, New Haw, Addlestone, Surrey KT15 3NB
Tel 01932-336911

The Veterinary Medicines Directorate is responsible for all aspects of licensing and control of animal medicines, including the protection of the consumer from hazardous or unacceptable residues.
Chief Executive and Director of Veterinary Medicines (*G4*),
   Dr J. M. Rutter
Director (*Policy*) (*G5*), R. Anderson
Director (*Licensing*) (*G5*), Dr K. N. Woodward
Secretary and Head of Business Unit (*G6*), J. FitzGerald
Licensing Manager, Pharmaceuticals and Feed Additives (*G6*),
   J. P. O'Brien
*Licensing Manager, Immunologicals and Suspected Adverse
   Reactions* (*SARS*) (*G6*), vacant

COLLEGE OF ARMS OR HERALDS
COLLEGE
Queen Victoria Street, London EC4V 4BT
Tel 0171-248 2762

The Sovereign's Officers of Arms (Kings, Heralds and Pursuivants of Arms) were first incorporated by Richard III. The powers vested by the Crown in the Earl Marshal (the Duke of Norfolk) with regard to state ceremonial are largely exercised through the College. The College is also the official repository of the arms and pedigrees of English, Northern Irish and Commonwealth (except Canadian) families and their descendants, and its records include official copies of the records of Ulster King of Arms, the originals of which remain in Dublin. The 13 officers of the College specialize in genealogical and heraldic work for their respective clients.

Arms have been and still are granted by letters patent from the Kings of Arms. A right to arms can only be established by the registration in the official records of the College of Arms of a pedigree showing direct male line descent from an ancestor already appearing therein as being entitled to arms, or by making application through the College of Arms for a grant of arms. Grants are made to corporations as well as to individuals.

The College of Arms is open Monday–Friday 10–4.
Earl Marshal, His Grace the Duke of Norfolk, KG, GCVO,
   CB, CBE, MC

KINGS OF ARMS
Garter, P. L. Gwynn-Jones, LVO
Clarenceux, J. P. B. Brooke-Little, CVO, FSA
Norroy and Ulster (*and Registrar*), D. H. B. Chesshyre, LVO,
   FSA

HERALDS
Windsor, T. D. Mathew
Somerset, T. Woodcock, LVO, FSA
Richmond (*and Earl Marshal's Secretary*), P. L. Dickinson
York, H. E. Paston-Bedingfeld
Chester, T. H. S. Duke
Lancaster, vacant

PURSUIVANTS
Bluemantle, R. J. B. Noel
Portcullis, W. G. Hunt, TD
Rouge Croix, D. V. White
Rouge Dragon, vacant

COURT OF THE LORD LYON
HM New Register House, Edinburgh EH1 3YT
Tel 0131-556 7255

The Court of the Lord Lyon is the Scottish Court of Chivalry (including the genealogical jurisdiction of the *Ri-Sennachie* of Scotland's Celtic Kings). The Lord Lyon King of Arms has jurisdiction, subject to appeal to the Court of Session and the House of Lords, in questions of heraldry and the right to bear arms. The Court also administers the Scottish Public Register of All Arms and Bearings and the Public Register of All Genealogies. Pedigrees are established by decrees of Lyon Court and by letters patent. As Royal Commissioner in Armory, the Lord Lyon grants patents of arms (which constitute the grantee and heirs noble in the Noblesse of Scotland) to 'virtuous and well-deserving' Scotsmen and to petitioners (personal or corporate) in Her Majesty's overseas realms of Scottish connection, and issues birthbrieves.
Lord Lyon King of Arms, Sir Malcolm Innes of Edingight,
   KCVO, WS

HERALDS
Albany, J. A. Spens, RD, WS
Rothesay, Sir Crispin Agnew of Lochnaw, Bt., QC
Ross, C. J. Burnett, FSA scot

PURSUIVANTS
Kintyre, J. C. G. George, FSA scot
Unicorn, Alastair Campbell of Airds, FSA scot
Carrick, Mrs C. G. W. Roads, MVO, FSA scot

Lyon Clerk and Keeper of Records, Mrs C. G. W. Roads, MVO,
   FSA scot
Procurator-Fiscal, D. F. Murby, WS
Herald Painter, Mrs J. Phillips
Macer, A. M. Clark

ARTS COUNCILS

The Arts Council of Great Britain was established as an independent body in 1946 to be the principal channel for the Government's support of the arts. In 1994 the Scottish and Welsh Arts Councils became autonomous and the Arts Council of Great Britain became the Arts Council of England.

The Arts Councils are responsible for the distribution of one-fifth of the proceeds of the National Lottery allocated to 'good causes'. They had made awards to the value of £402.760 million by the end of April 1996.

ARTS COUNCIL OF ENGLAND
14 Great Peter Street, London SW1P 3NQ
Tel 0171-333 0100

The Arts Council of England funds the major arts organizations in England and the ten Regional Arts Boards. It is funded by the Department of National Heritage and works closely with the Scottish Arts Council and the Arts Council of Wales.

The Council also provides advice, information and help to artists and arts organizations. Its objectives are to develop and improve the understanding and practice of the arts and to increase their accessibility to the public.

The Council distributes an annual grant from the Department of National Heritage; the grant for 1996-7 is £186.133 million.

Chairman, The Lord Gowrie, PC
Vice-Chairman, Sir Richard Rogers, RA
Members, R. Cork; Prof. R. Cowell; Prof. B. Cox, CBE;
C. Denton; Prof. C. Frayling; Ms M. Guillebaud;
Sir Ernest Hall, OBE; Dr D. Harrison, CBE;
G. Henderson; Ms T. Holt, CBE; Prof. A. Motion;
S. Phillips; Ms U. Prashar, CBE; C. Priestley, CB; R. Reed;
D. Reid; Ms S. Robinson; Ms P. Skene; R. Southgate;
two vacancies
Secretary-General, Ms M. Allen

REGIONAL ARTS BOARDS

EASTERN ARTS BOARD, Cherry Hinton Hall, Cherry Hinton Road, Cambridge CB1 4DW. Tel: 01223-215355.
Chair, Dr D. Harrison
EAST MIDLANDS ARTS BOARD, Mountfields House, Forest Road, Loughborough, Leics LE11 3HU. Tel: 01509-218292. *Chair*, Prof. R. Cowell
LONDON ARTS BOARD, Elme House, 133 Long Acre, London WC2E 9AF. Tel: 0171-240 1313. *Chair*, C. Priestley
NORTHERN ARTS BOARD, 9-10 Osborne Terrace, Newcastle upon Tyne NE2 1NZ. Tel: 0191-281 6334.
Chair, Mrs S. Robinson
NORTH-WEST ARTS BOARD, Manchester House, 22 Bridge Street, Manchester M3 3AB. Tel: 0161-834 9131.
Chair, Prof. B. Cox
SOUTH-EAST ARTS BOARD, 10 Mount Ephraim, Tunbridge Wells, Kent TN4 8AS. Tel: 01892-515210.
Chair, R. Reed
SOUTHERN ARTS BOARD, 13 St Clement Street, Winchester SO23 9DQ. Tel: 01962-855099. *Chair*, D. Reid
SOUTH-WEST ARTS BOARD, Bradninch Place, Gandy Street, Exeter EX4 3LS. Tel: 01392-218188. *Chair*, Ms M. Guillebaud
WEST MIDLANDS ARTS BOARD, 82 Granville Street, Birmingham B1 2LH. Tel: 0121-631 3121. *Chair*, R. Southgate
YORKSHIRE AND HUMBERSIDE ARTS BOARD, 21 Bond Street, Dewsbury, W. Yorks WF13 1AX. Tel: 01924-455555. *Chair*, Sir Ernest Hall

SCOTTISH ARTS COUNCIL
12 Manor Place, Edinburgh EH3 7DD
Tel 0131-226 6051

The Scottish Arts Council funds arts organizations in Scotland and is funded directly by the Scottish Office. The grant for 1996-7 is £24.47 million.
Chairman, M. Linklater
Vice-Chairman, Ms F. Walker

Members, Dr Sheila Brock; D. Connell; J. Denholm;
K. Geddes; G. Hallewell; P. Hamilton; R. Love;
Dr Rita McAllister; Dr I. McGowan; Ms M. MacLean;
Ms J. Richardson; Prof. E. Spiller; Ms L. Thomson
Director, Ms S. Reid
Lottery Director, D. Bonnar

ARTS COUNCIL OF WALES
Museum Place, Cardiff CF1 3NX
Tel 01222-394 711

The Arts Council of Wales funds arts organizations in Wales and is funded directly by the Welsh Office. The grant for 1996-7 is £14 million.
Chairman, Sir Richard Lloyd Jones, KCB
Members, Ms J. Davidson; M. Edwards; F. Evans; K. Evans;
Ms K. Gass; P. Griffiths; G. S. Jones; R. G. Jones;
M. Pepper; D. Richards; A. Roberts; E. Thomas; Prof. G. Thomas; Ms M. Vincentelli
Chief Executive, E. Jenkins

ARTS COUNCIL OF NORTHERN IRELAND
185 Stranmillis Road, Belfast BT9 5DU
Tel 01232-381591

The Arts Council of Northern Ireland disburses government funds in support of the arts in Northern Ireland. It is funded by the Department of Education for Northern Ireland, and the grant for 1996-7 is £6.85 million.
Chairman, D. Deeny, QC
Vice-Chairman, Sir Charles Brett
Members, J. Aiken; S. Burnside; F. Cobain; P. Donnelly;
Ms R. Duffy; Dr Tess Hurson; Ms K. Ingram;
Prof. Edna Longley; W. O'Connell; R. Pierce;
Ms C. Poulter; Ms I. Sandford; Prof. R. Welch
Chief Executive, B. Ferran

ART GALLERIES, ETC

ROYAL FINE ART COMMISSION
7 St James's Square, London SW1Y 4JU
Tel 0171-839 6537

Established in 1924, the Commission is an autonomous authority on the aesthetic implications of any project or development, primarily but not exclusively architectural, which affects the visual environment.
Chairman, The Lord St John of Fawsley, PC, FRSL
Commissioners, Miss S. Andreae; Prof. R. D. Carter, CBE;
E. Cullinan, CBE, RA; Sir Philip Dowson, CBE, PRA;
D. H. Fraser, RA; E. Hollinghurst; Sir Michael Hopkins, CBE, RA; S. A. Lipton; Prof. Margaret MacKeith, PH.D.;
H. T. Moggridge, OBE; Mrs J. Nutting; T. Osborne, FRICS; I. Ritchie; Prof. J. R. Steer, FSA; Miss W. Taylor, CBE; Q. Terry, FRIBA; Dr G. Worsley
Secretary, F. Golding

ROYAL FINE ART COMMISSION FOR SCOTLAND
9 Atholl Crescent, Edinburgh EH3 8HA
Tel 0131-229 1109

The Commission was established in 1927 and advises ministers and local authorities on the visual impact and quality of design of construction projects. It is an independent body and gives its opinions impartially.
Chairman, The Lord Cameron of Lochbroom, PC, FRSE
Commissioners, Prof. G. Benson; W. A. Cadell; Mrs K. Dalyell; A. S. Matheson, FRIBA; R. G. Maund; D. Page; Miss B. Rae; Prof. T. Ridley, FRSE; M. Turnbull; Prof. R. Webster; R. Wedgwood
Secretary, C. Prosser

NATIONAL GALLERY
Trafalgar Square, London WC2N 5DN
Tel 0171-839 3321

The National Gallery, which houses a permanent collection of western painting since the 13th century, was founded in 1824, following a parliamentary grant of £60,000 for the purchase and exhibition of the Angerstein collection of pictures. The present site was first occupied in 1838; a substantial extension to the north of the building with a public entrance in Orange Street was opened in 1975, and the Sainsbury wing was opened in 1991. Total government grant-in-aid for 1996–7 is £18.724 million.

BOARD OF TRUSTEES
Chairman, P. Hughes, CBE
Trustees, P. Troughton; Sir Derek Oulton, GCB, QC;
  E. Uglow; Sir Keith Thomas, FBA; The Hon. Simon
  Sainsbury; Lady Bingham; Sir Mark Richmond, SC.D.,
  FRS; A. Bennett; Lady Monck; Mrs P. Ridley; Sir Ewen
  Fergusson, GCMG, GCVO; R. Gavron, CBE; C. Le Brun;
  The Hon. R. G. H. Seitz

OFFICERS
Director, R. N. MacGregor
Chief Curator, Dr C. P. H. Brown
Senior Curators, Dr N. Penny; Dr S. Foister; Dr D. Gordon;
  J. Leighton
Chief Restorer, M. H. Wyld
Head of Exhibitions, M. J. Wilson
Scientific Adviser, Dr A. Roy
Director of Administration, J. MacAuslan
Head of Press and Public Relations, Miss J. Liddiard

NATIONAL PORTRAIT GALLERY
St Martin's Place, London WC2H 0HE
Tel 0171-306 0055

A grant was made in 1856 to form a gallery of the portraits of the most eminent persons in British history. The present building was opened in 1896 and an extension in 1933. There are four outstations displaying portraits in appropriate settings: Montacute House, Gawthorpe Hall, Beningbrough Hall and Bodelwyddan Castle. Total government grant-in-aid for 1996–7 is £4.914 million.

BOARD OF TRUSTEES
Chairman, H. Keswick
Trustees, The Lord President of the Council (*ex officio*);
  The President of the Royal Academy of Arts (*ex officio*);
  J. Roberts, CBE, D.phil.; The Lord Morris of Castle
  Morris, D.phil.; Prof. N. Lynton; Sir Eduardo Paolozzi;
  J. Tusa; Sir Antony Acland, GCMG, GCVO; Mrs
  J. E. Benson, LVO, OBE; Mrs W. Tumim, OBE; Sir David
  Scholey, CBE; Mrs C. Tomalin; Baroness Willoughby de
  Eresby; M. Hastings; Prof. The Earl Russell, FBA
Director (G3), C. Saumarez-Smith, ph.D.

TATE GALLERY
Millbank, London SW1P 4RG
Tel 0171-887 8000

The Tate Gallery comprises the national collections of British painting and 20th-century painting and sculpture. The Gallery was opened in 1897, the cost of erection (£80,000) being defrayed by Sir Henry Tate, who also contributed the nucleus of the present collection. The Turner wing was opened in 1910, galleries to contain the collection of modern foreign painting in 1926, and a new sculpture hall in 1937. In 1979 a further extension was built, and the Clore Gallery, for the Turner collection, was opened in 1987. The Tate Gallery Liverpool opened in 1988 and the Tate Gallery St Ives in 1993. Total government grant-in-aid for 1996–7 is £18.775 million.

BOARD OF TRUSTEES
Chairman, D. Stevenson, CBE
Trustees, Prof. Dawn Ades; The Lord Attenborough, CBE;
  The Hon. Mrs J. de Botton; Sir Richard Carew Pole;
  M. Craig-Martin; P. Doig; B. Gascoigne, FRSL;
  D. Gordon; Mrs P. Ridley; D. Verey; W. Woodrow

OFFICERS
Director (G3), N. Serota
Director of Public and Regional Services (G5), S. Nairne
Keeper of the British Collection (G5), A. Wilton
Keeper of the Modern Collection (G5), R. Morphet
Curator, Tate Gallery Liverpool (G6), L. Biggs
Curator, Tate Gallery St Ives (G6), M. Tooby

WALLACE COLLECTION
Hertford House, Manchester Square, London W1M 6BN
Tel 0171-935 0687

The Wallace Collection was bequeathed to the nation by the widow of Sir Richard Wallace, Bt. in 1897, and Hertford House was subsequently acquired by the Government. Total government grant-in-aid for 1996–7 is £1.9 million.
Director, Miss R. J. Savill
Head of Administration, A. W. Houldershaw

NATIONAL GALLERIES OF SCOTLAND
The Mound, Edinburgh EH2 2EL
Tel 0131-556 8921

The National Galleries of Scotland comprise the National Gallery of Scotland, the Scottish National Portrait Gallery and the Scottish National Gallery of Modern Art. There are also outstations at Paxton House, Berwickshire, and Duff House, Banffshire. Total government grant-in-aid for 1996–7 is £8.268 million.

TRUSTEES
Chairman of the Trustees, A. M. Grossart, CBE
Trustees, Mrs L. W. Gibbs; Lord Macfarlane of Bearsden;
  Dr T. Johnston; Prof. A. A. Tait; E. Hagman;
  Prof. E. Fernie; M. Shea; The Countess of Airlie, CVO;
  Mrs A. McCurley; Prof. J. R. Harper, CBE; Prof.
  Christina Lodder

OFFICERS
Director (G4), T. Clifford
Keeper of Conservation (G6), J. P. Dick, OBE
Head of Press and Information (G7), Mrs A. M. Wagener
Keeper of Education (G7), M. Cassin
Registrar (G7), Miss A. Buddle
Secretary (G6), Ms S. Edwards
Buildings (G7), R. Galbraith
Keeper, National Gallery of Scotland (G6), M. Clarke
Keeper, Scottish National Portrait Gallery (G6), D. Thomson,
  ph.D.
  Curator of Photography, Miss S. F. Stevenson
Keeper, Scottish National Gallery of Modern Art (G6),
  R. Calvocoressi

ASSEMBLY OMBUDSMAN FOR NORTHERN IRELAND AND NORTHERN IRELAND COMMISSIONER FOR COMPLAINTS
Progressive House, 33 Wellington Place, Belfast BT1 6HN
Tel 01232-233821

The Ombudsman is appointed under legislation with powers to investigate complaints by people claiming to have sustained injustice in consequence of maladministration arising from action taken by a Northern Ireland government department, or any other public body within his remit. Staff are presently seconded from the Northern Ireland Civil Service.

Commissioner, G. Burns, MBE
Deputy Commissioner, G. R. Dawson
Directors, C. O'Hare; R. Doherty

UK ATOMIC ENERGY AUTHORITY

Harwell, Didcot, Oxon OX11 0RA
Tel 01235-820220

The UKAEA was established by the Atomic Energy Authority Act 1954 and took over responsibility for the research and development of the civil nuclear power programme. The Authority increasingly evolved its operations, selling its products and services to the nuclear and non-nuclear sectors under the marketing title of AEA Technology while also continuing with the development of nuclear research and development.

The commercial arm, AEA Technology PLC, is now a science engineering services business which is legally separate from UKAEA and is due to be privatized by the end of 1996. UKAEA itself is responsible for the safe management and decommissioning of its radioactive plant and facilities used for the development of the UK's nuclear power programme. It is also responsible for maximizing the income from its still-operating active facilities, buildings and land on its six sites. UKAEA also undertakes special nuclear tasks for the Government, including the UK's contribution to the international fusion programme.

Chairman, UKAEA, Adm. Sir Kenneth Eaton
Chairman, AEA Technology PLC, Sir Anthony Cleaver
Chief Executive, UKAEA, Dr D. Pooley, CBE
Chief Executive, AEA Technology PLC, Dr P. Watson

AUDIT COMMISSIONS

AUDIT COMMISSION FOR LOCAL AUTHORITIES AND THE NATIONAL HEALTH SERVICE IN ENGLAND AND WALES

1 Vincent Square, London SW1P 2PN
Tel 0171-828 1212

The Audit Commission was set up in 1983 with responsibility for the external audit of local authorities. This remit was extended from 1990 to include the audit of the National Health Service bodies in England and Wales. The Commission appoints the auditors, who may be from the District Audit Service or from a private firm of accountants. The Commission is also responsible for promoting value for money in the services provided by local authorities and health bodies.

The Commission has 15–17 members appointed by the Secretary of State for the Environment in consultation with the Secretaries of State for Wales and for Health. Though appointed by the Secretary of State, the Commissioners are responsible to Parliament.

Chairman, R. Brooke
Deputy Chairman, C. Thompson
Controller of Audit, A. Foster
Chief Executive of District Audit Service, D. Prince

ACCOUNTS COMMISSION FOR SCOTLAND

18 George Street, Edinburgh EH2 2QU
Tel 0131-477 1234

The Commission was set up in 1975. It is responsible for securing the audit of the accounts of Scottish local authorities and certain joint boards and joint committees. On 1 April 1995 it assumed responsibility for securing the audit of National Health Service bodies in Scotland. Amongst its duties the Commission is required to deal with reports made by the Controller of Audit on items of account contrary to law; on incorrect accounting; and on losses due to misconduct, negligence and failure to carry out statutory duties. Since 1988 the Commission has had responsibility for value-for-money audits of authorities.

Members are appointed by the Secretary of State for Scotland.

Chairman, Prof. J. P. Percy
Controller of Audit, R. W. Black
Secretary, W. F. Magee

THE BANK OF ENGLAND

Threadneedle Street, London EC2R 8AH
Tel 0171-601 4444

The Bank of England was incorporated in 1694 under royal charter. It is the banker of the Government, on whose behalf it executes monetary policy and manages the note issue and the national debt. It is also responsible for promoting the efficiency and competitiveness of financial services. As the central reserve bank of the country, the Bank keeps the accounts of British banks, who maintain with it a proportion of their cash resources, and of most overseas central banks. The Bank is divided into two divisions, Monetary Stability and Financial Stability. (*See also* pages 604–5).

Governor, E. A. J. George
Deputy Governor, H. J. Davies
Directors, Sir David Cooksey; M. D. K. W. Foot; Sir John Hall; Mrs F. A. Heaton; P. H. Kent; Sir John Keswick; M. A. King; Sir David Lees; Ms S. V. Masters; Sir Christopher Morse, KCMG; J. Neill, CBE, PH.D.; I. Plenderleith; Sir David Scholey, CBE, FRSA; N. I. Simms; D. A. G. Simon; Sir Colin Southgate
Advisers to the Governor, Sir Peter Petrie; L. Berkowitz; I. G. Watt
Chief Cashier and Deputy Director, Banking and Market Services, G. E. A. Kentfield
Chief Registrar, P. W. F. Ironmonger
General Manager, Printing Works, A. W. Jarvis
Secretary, J. R. E. Footman
The Auditor, M. J. W. Phillips

BOUNDARY COMMISSIONS

The Commissions are constituted under the Parliamentary Constituencies Act 1986. The Speaker of the House of Commons is ex-officio chairman of all four commissions in the UK. Each of the four commissions is required by law to keep the parliamentary constituencies in their part of the UK under review. The latest review was completed in April 1995; the final proposals have been approved by Parliament and take effect at the next general election. Each of the three commissions in Great Britain is required by law to keep the European parliamentary constituencies in their part of Great Britain under review.

ENGLAND
St Catherine's House, 10 Kingsway, London WC2B 6JP
Tel 0171-396 2105
Deputy Chairman, vacant
Joint Secretaries, R. McLeod; S. Limpkin

WALES
St Catherine's House, 10 Kingsway, London WC2B 6JP
Tel 0171-396 2105
Deputy Chairman, The Hon. Mr Justice Kay
Joint Secretaries, R. McLeod; S. Limpkin

SCOTLAND
St Andrew's House, Edinburgh EHI 3DG
Tel 0131-244 2196/2027
Deputy Chairman, The Hon. Lord Davidson
Secretary, D. K. C. Jeffrey

NORTHERN IRELAND
Room 1/77, Old Admiralty Building, Whitehall, London
SWIA 2AZ
Tel 0171-210 6569
Deputy Chairman, The Hon. Mr Justice Pringle
Secretary, Ms C. Marson

BRITISH BROADCASTING CORPORATION
Broadcasting House, Portland Place, London WIA IAA
Tel 0171-580 4468
Television Centre, Wood Lane, London WI2 7RJ
Tel 0181-743 8000

The BBC was incorporated under royal charter as successor to the British Broadcasting Company Ltd, whose licence expired in 1926. Its current charter came into force in 1981 and a new charter will come into force on 1 January 1997. The chairman, vice-chairman and other governors are appointed by The Queen-in-Council. The BBC is financed by revenue from receiving licences for the home services and by grant-in-aid from Parliament for the World Service (radio). In June 1996 the BBC announced a restructuring of the corporation into six divisions: Production, Broadcast, News, Worldwide, Resources, and Corporate Centre.
For services, *see* Broadcasting section.

BOARD OF GOVERNORS

Chairman (£63,670), Sir Christopher Bland
Vice-Chairman (£16,340), The Lord Cocks of Hartcliffe, PC
National Governors (*each* £16,340), Sir Kenneth Bloomfield, KCB (*N. Ireland*); Dr G. Jones (*Wales*); N. Drummond (*Scotland*)
Governors (*each* £8,170), W. B. Jordan, CBE; Lord Nicholas Gordon Lennox, KCMG, KCVO; Mrs M. Spurr, OBE; Mrs J. Cohen; Sir David Scholey, CBE; R. Eyre, CBE; A. White, CBE

BOARD OF MANAGEMENT

EXECUTIVE COMMITTEE
Director-General, J. Birt
Deputy Director-General and Chief Executive, BBC Worldwide, R. Phillis
Chief Executives, R. Neil (*BBC Production*); W. Wyatt (*BBC Broadcast*); T. Hall (*BBC News*); R. Lynch (*BBC Resources*)
Directors, Ms M. Salmon (*Personnel*); Ms P. Hodgson (*Policy and Planning*); R. Baker-Bates (*Finance and IT*); C. Browne (*Corporate Affairs*)

WIDER BOARD OF MANAGEMENT
Managing Director, World Service, S. Younger

Directors, A. Yentob (*Programmes*); M. Jackson (*Television*); M. Bannister (*Radio*); Ms J. Drabble (*Education*); M. Byford (*Regional Broadcasting*)

OTHER SENIOR STAFF
The Secretary, M. Stevenson
Head of Continuous News, Ms J. Abramsky
Controller, BBC1, M. Jackson
Controller, BBC2, M. Thompson
Controller, Radio 1, M. Bannister
Controller, Radio 2, J. Moir
Controller, Radio 3, N. Kenyon
Controller, Radio 4, J. Boyle
Controller, Radio 5 Live, vacant
Controller, BBC Scotland, J. McCormick
Controller, BBC Wales, G. Talfan Davies
Controller, BBC N. Ireland, P. Loughrey
Head of Broadcasting, BBC South, J. Shearer
Head of Broadcasting, BBC North, C. Adams
Head of Broadcasting, BBC Midlands and East, N. Chapman
Controller, Editorial Policy, R. Ayre
Legal Adviser, G. Roscoe

BRITISH COAL CORPORATION
Charles House, 5–11 Lower Regent Street, London
SWIY 4LR
Tel 0171-201 4141

The British Coal Corporation (formerly the National Coal Board) was constituted in 1946 and took over the mines on 1 January 1947. The Coal Industry Act 1994 established the statutory framework for the privatization of British Coal's mining operations. British Coal's ownership of coal reserves and responsibility for licensing other coal producers were transferred to the Coal Authority, a non-departmental public body (*see* page 291). The sale of regional coal companies, into which British Coal's operational mining assets had been transferred, was concluded in December 1994. The Act also charged British Coal with the disposal of its non-mining activities. This process is continuing, and the bulk of the assets are expected to have been disposed of by early 1997. The British Coal Corporation will be wound up when the process is completed.
Chairman, J. N. Clarke
Executive Member, P. L. Hutchinson (*Secretary/Legal Adviser*)
Non-Executive Members, A. P. Hichens; Sir Robert Davidson, FENG.; D. B. Vaughan

---

THE BRITISH COUNCIL
10 Spring Gardens, London SWIA 2BN
Tel 0171-930 8466
Medlock Street, Manchester MI5
Tel 0161-957 7000

The British Council was established in 1934, incorporated by royal charter in 1940 and granted a supplemental charter in 1993. It is an independent, non-political organization which promotes Britain abroad. It is the UK's international network for education, culture and development services. The Council is represented in 228 towns and cities in 109 countries and runs 185 libraries, 95 teaching centres and 29 resource centres around the world.
Total funding in 1995–6, including Foreign and Commonwealth Office grants and contracted money, was £423.5 million.

Chairman, Sir Martin Jacomb
Deputy Chairman, The Lord Chorley
Director-General, Sir John Hanson, KCMG, CBE

BRITISH FILM COMMISSION
70 Baker Street, London WIM IDJ
Tel 0171-224 5000

The British Film Commission was set up in 1991 and is funded by the Department of National Heritage. The Commission promotes the UK as an international production centre, encourages the use of locations, facilities, services and personnel, and provides, at no charge to the enquirer, comprehensive advice and information relating to the practical aspects of filming in the UK.
Commissioner, Sir Sydney Samuelson, CBE
Chief Executive, A. Patrick

BRITISH FILM INSTITUTE
21 Stephen Street, London WIP 2LN
Tel 0171-255 1444

The British Film Institute was established in 1933 under royal charter. Its aims are to encourage the development of the art of film and its use as a record of contemporary life in Great Britain, and to foster the study, appreciation and use of films for television. It includes the National Film and Television Archive, the National Film Theatre and the Museum of the Moving Image, and it supports a network of 38 regional film theatres. The BFI Library contains the world's largest collection of material relating to film and television. Total government funding for 1996–7 is £16.5 million.
Chairman, J. Thomas
Director, W. Stevenson

BRITISH PHARMACOPOEIA COMMISSION
Market Towers, 1 Nine Elms Lane, London SW8 5NQ
Tel 0171-273 0561

The British Pharmacopoeia Commission sets standards for medicinal products used in human and veterinary medicines and is responsible for publication of the British Pharmacopoeia (a publicly-available statement of the standard that a product must meet throughout its shelf-life), the British Pharmacopoeia (Veterinary) and the selection of British Approved Names. It also participates in the work of the European Pharmacopoeia on behalf of the UK. It has 13 members who are appointed by the Secretary of State for Health, the Minister for Agriculture, Fisheries and Food, the Secretaries of State for Scotland and Wales, and the relevant Northern Ireland departments.
Chairman, Prof. D. Ganderton, OBE
Vice-Chairman, Dr D. H. Calam
Secretary and Scientific Director, Dr R. C. Hutton

BRITISH RAILWAYS BOARD
Euston House, 24 Eversholt Street, PO Box 100, London NWI IDZ
Tel 0171-928 5151

The British Railways Board came into being in 1963 under the terms of the Transport Act 1962. Under the Railways Act 1993, the activities of the Board have been restructured and are gradually being transferred to the private sector. For details of privatization and railway operations, *see* Transport section.
Chairman and Chief Executive (£180,000), J. K. Welsby, CBE
Finance and Planning, J. J. Jerram, CBE
Personnel, A. P. Watkinson
Engineering, Services and Safety, A. D. Roche
Part-time executive member, C. J. Campbell, CBE
Part-time non-executive members, P. Allen, CBE; J. Butler; K. H. M. Dixon; Sir William Francis, CBE; Miss K. T. Kantor; W. Wilson
Secretary, P. Trewin

BRITISH STANDARDS INSTITUTION (BSI)
389 Chiswick High Road, London W4 4AL
Tel 0181-996 9000

The British Standards Institution is the recognized authority in the UK for the preparation and publication of national standards for industrial and consumer products. In consultation with the interests concerned, BSI prepares standards relating to nearly every sector of the nation's industry and trade. It also represents the UK at European and international standards meetings. About 90 per cent of its standards work is now internationally linked. British Standards are issued for voluntary adoption, though in a number of cases compliance with a British Standard is required by legislation. Industrial and consumer products certified as complying with the relevant British Standard may carry the Institution's certification trade mark, known as the 'Kitemark'.
Chairman, V. E. Thomas, OBE
Chief Executive, B. Davis

BRITISH TOURIST AUTHORITY
Thames Tower, Black's Road, London W6 9EL
Tel 0181-846 9000

Established under the Development of Tourism Act 1969, the British Tourist Authority has specific responsibility for promoting tourism to Great Britain from overseas. It also has a general responsibility for the promotion and development of tourism and tourist facilities within Great Britain as a whole, and for advising the Secretary of State for National Heritage on tourism matters.
Chairman (*part-time*), D. Quarmby
Chief Executive, A. Sell

BRITISH WATERWAYS
Willow Grange, Church Road, Watford, Herts WDI 3QA
Tel 01923-226422

British Waterways is the navigation authority for over 2,000 miles of canals and river navigations in England,

Scotland and Wales. Some 380 miles are maintained and are being developed as commercial waterways for use by freight-carrying vessels. Another 1,200 miles, the cruising waterways, are being developed for boating, fishing and other leisure activities. The remaining 500 miles, the remainder waterways, are maintained with due regard to safety, public health and the preservation of amenities.

Chairman (part-time), B. Henderson, CBE
Vice-Chairman (part-time), Sir Peter Hutchison, Bt.
Members (all part-time), J. Gordon; D. H. R. Yorke;
    M. Cairns; Sir Neil Cossons; Ms J. Elvey; Ms J. Lewis-
    Jones
Chief Executive, D. Fletcher
Director of Corporate Services, R. J. Duffy

BROADCASTING STANDARDS COUNCIL
7 The Sanctuary, London SW1P 3JS
Tel 0171-233 0544

The Council was set up in 1988 but received its statutory powers under the Broadcasting Act 1990. Its role is advisory, not regulatory. It monitors the portrayal of violence, sex and matters of taste and decency in all broadcast programmes and advertisements on television, radio, cable and satellite services. The Council publishes a code of practice, considers complaints and conducts research into audience attitudes. Members of the Council are appointed by the Secretary of State for National Heritage. The appointments are part-time.

The Broadcasting Act 1996 provides for the merger of the BSC with the Broadcasting Complaints Commission to form the Broadcasting Standards Commission from 1 April 1997.

Chair (£42,700), The Lady Howe of Aberavon
Deputy Chairman (£32,250), The Lord Dubs
Members (each £12,845), Ms R. Bevan; Dame Fiona
    Caldicott, DBE; R. Kernohan, OBE; the Very
    Revd J. Lang; M. Parris; Ms S. O'Sullivan
Director, S. Whittle

THE BROADS AUTHORITY
Thomas Harvey House, 18 Colegate, Norwich NR3 1BQ
Tel 01603-610734

The Broads Authority is a special statutory authority set up under the Norfolk and Suffolk Broads Act 1988, with powers and responsibilities similar to those of National Park Authorities. The functions of the Authority are to conserve and enhance the natural beauty of the Broads; to promote the enjoyment of the Broads by the public; and to protect the interests of navigation. The Authority comprises 35 members, appointed by the local authorities in the area covered, environmental conservation bodies, the Environment Agency, and the Great Yarmouth Port Authority.

Chairman, J. S. Peel, CBE, MC
Chief Executive, M. A. Clark

THE CABINET OFFICE

The Cabinet Office comprises the Secretariat, who support Ministers collectively in the conduct of Cabinet business; and the Office of Public Service (OPS) which is responsible for the competitiveness agenda, the progress and develop-

ment of deregulation, the Citizen's Charter initiative, the Next Steps programme, policy on open government, senior Civil Service and public appointments, market testing and efficiency in the Civil Service, and Civil Service recruitment.

The OPS supports the Prime Minister in his capacity as Minister for the Civil Service, with responsibility for day-to-day supervision delegated to the Chancellor of the Duchy of Lancaster.

Prime Minister and Minister for the Civil Service,
    The Rt. Hon. John Major, MP

PRIME MINISTER'S OFFICE
10 Downing Street, London SW1A 2AA
Tel 0171-270 3000

Principal Private Secretary (G3), A. Allan
Private Secretaries (G5), J. E. Holmes (*Overseas Affairs*);
    M. Wallace (*Economic Affairs*); M. Adams (*Parliamentary
    Affairs*); (G7), Ms R. Reynolds (*Home Affairs*)
Assistant Private Secretaries, K. Waldock; Miss
    J. L. Wilkinson
Diary Secretary, Ms A. Warburton
Political Secretary, H. James
Policy Unit, N. Blackwell; Mrs K. Ramsey; D. Morris;
    J. Rees; D. Soskin; S. Williams; Ms C. Fairbairn;
    S. Walker
Parliamentary Private Secretary, J. Ward, MP
Chief Press Secretary (G2), J. Haslam
Deputy Chief Press Secretary (G5), vacant
*Secretary for Appointments, and Ecclesiastical Secretary to the
    Lord Chancellor (G2)*, J. Holroyd, CB
Parliamentary Clerk, R. Stone
Secretary of the Cabinet and Head of Home Civil Service,
    Sir Robin Butler, GCB, CVO
Private Secretary, Ms J. A. Polley

SECRETARIAT
70 Whitehall, London SW1A 2AS
Tel 0171-270 3000

Economic and Domestic Secretariat, K. Mackenzie, CB;
    W. A. Jeffrey
Defence and Overseas Affairs Secretariat, C. R. Budd, CMG;
    A. J. D. Pawson
Joint Intelligence Organization, J. Alpass; W. R. Fittall
European Secretariat, B. Bender; A. T. Cahn
Telecommunications Secretariat, R. Hope

OFFICE OF PUBLIC SERVICE (OPS)
*Horse Guards Road, London SW1P 3AL
Tel 0171-270 1234
70 Whitehall, London SW1A 2AS
Tel 0171-270 3000

First Secretary of State and Deputy Prime Minister,
    The Rt. Hon. Michael Heseltine, MP
Principal Private Secretary, M. Gibson
Private Secretary, R. Huxter
Special Advisers, Eileen, Lady Strathnaver; Dr A. Kemp
Chancellor of the Duchy of Lancaster, The Rt. Hon. Roger
    Freeman, MP
Principal Private Secretary, Ms J. Lemprière
Private Secretary, Mrs H. R. M. Paxman
Paymaster-General, David Willetts, MP
Private Secretary, J. B. McLaren
Second Permanent Secretary, R. Mountfield, CB
Private Secretary, M. S. Langdale

___

*Unless otherwise stated, this is the address and telephone number for divisions of the OPS

Parliamentary Clerk, Miss D. Smailes
Press Secretary (G5), B. Sutlieff

CITIZEN'S CHARTER UNIT
Government Offices, Great George Street, London
SWIP 3AL
Tel 0171-270 1826

Director, Miss E. C. Turton, CB
Deputy Directors, Mrs G. Craig; Dr C. Sanger

CENTRAL IT UNIT
1st Floor, Hampton House, 20 Albert Embankment,
London SEI 7TJ
Tel 0171-238 2015

Head of Unit, G. H. B. Jordan

EFFICIENCY AND EFFECTIVENESS GROUP
70 Whitehall, London SWIA 2AS
Tel 0171-270 0273

Prime Minister's Adviser on Efficiency and Effectiveness,
Sir Peter Levene, KBE
Head of Unit (G3), J. R. C. Oughton
Head of Next Steps Project Team, M. J. Cowper

AGENCIES GROUP
Ashley House, Monck Street, London SWIP 2BQ
Tel 0171-270 1234
Ministers' Adviser on Agencies, C. M. Brendish
Head of Agencies Group A, J. P. Henry
Head of Agencies Group B, Mrs M. J. Bloom

CIVIL SERVICE EMPLOYER GROUP
Head of Group, H. H. Taylor
Training and Development White Paper, Mrs J. I. Britton
Development and Equal Opportunities Division, Dr R. Price
Fast Stream and European Staffing Division, Dr J. G. Fuller
International Public Service Unit, C. J. Parry
Personnel Management and Conditions of Service Division,
J. Strachan
Top Management Programme, Ms H. Dudley (*Course Director*)
Civil Service Pensions Division, D. G. Pain

OFFICE OF THE COMMISSIONER FOR PUBLIC
APPOINTMENTS (OCPA)
Horse Guards Road, London SWIP 3AL
Tel 0171-270 5792
The role of the Commissioner for Public Appointments
(CPA) is to monitor, regulate and approve departmental
appointment procedures for ministerial appointments to
executive non-departmental public bodies and NHS
bodies. The Commissioner is appointed by Order in
Council.
Commissioner, Sir Leonard Peach
Head of the Office, Miss E. M. Goodison

OFFICE OF THE CIVIL SERVICE COMMISSIONERS
(OCSC)
Horse Guards Road, London SWIP 3AL
Tel 0171-270 5081

First Commissioner, Sir Michael Bett, CBE
Commissioners (part-time), D. J. Burr; M. D. Geddes; Ms J.
A. Hunt; H. J. F. McLean, CBE; Sir Leonard Peach;
K. Singh
Secretary to the Commissioners and Head of the Office, Miss
E. M. Goodison

INFORMATION OFFICER MANAGEMENT UNIT
Ashley House, 2 Monck Street, London SWIP 2BQ
Tel 0171-270 1234
Director, T. J. Perks

COMPETITIVENESS DIVISION
Head of Division, Dr R. C. Dobbie, CB

DEREGULATION UNIT
Director, Miss L. J. Neville-Rolfe

SENIOR CIVIL SERVICE GROUP
Director, B. M. Fox
Head of Senior Staff and Interchange Division, D. Laughrin
Head of Senior Pay and Contracts Division, J. A. Barker

MACHINERY OF GOVERNMENT AND STANDARDS
GROUP
70 Whitehall, London SWIA 2AS
Tel 0171-270 1234

Head of Group, D. A. Wilkinson
Head of Security Division, J. K. Barron

CEREMONIAL BRANCH
53 Parliament Street, London SWIA 2NG
Tel 0171-210 5056
Honours Nomination Unit: Tel 0171-210 5071
Ceremonial Officer, A. J. Merifield, CB

ESTABLISHMENT OFFICER'S GROUP
Queen Anne's Chambers, 28 Broadway, London SWIH 9JS
Tel 0171-270 3000
Principal Establishment and Finance Officer, R. W. D. Venning
Deputy Establishment Officer, K. Bastin
Senior Finance Officer, K. Tolladay

HISTORICAL AND RECORDS SECTION
Hepburn House, Marsham Street, London SWIP 4HW
Tel 0171-217 6032
Head of Section, Miss P. M. Andrews, OBE

EXECUTIVE AGENCIES

THE BUYING AGENCY
Royal Liver Building, Pier Head, Liverpool L3 IPE
Tel 0151-227 4262
The Agency provides a professional purchasing service to
government departments and other public bodies.
Chief Executive (G5), S. P. Sage

CCTA (THE GOVERNMENT CENTRE FOR
INFORMATION SYSTEMS)
Hampton House, 20 Albert Embankment, London SEI 7TJ
Tel 0171-238 2250
Rosebery Court, St Andrew's Business Park, Norwich
NR7 OHS
Tel 01603-704807
CCTA offers a range of specialist services in the field of
information technology and telecommunications. It be-
came an executive agency in April 1996.
Chief Executive, R. Assirati

CENTRAL OFFICE OF INFORMATION
— *see* page 289

CIVIL SERVICE COLLEGE
Sunningdale Park, Ascot, Berks SL5 OQE
Tel 01344-634000
11 Belgrave Road, London SWIV IRB
Tel 0171-834 6644
The College provides training in management and pro-
fessional skills for the public and private sectors.
Chief Executive (G3), Dr S. H. F. Hickey
Business Executives (G5/G6), C. W. H. Aitken; M. N. Barnes;
Mrs M. B. Chapman; Ms E. Chennells; G. W. Llewellyn;
M. Timmis; Miss M. A. Wood; Dr A. Wyatt

HMSO
— *see* page 346

PROPERTY ADVISERS TO THE CIVIL ESTATE
St Christopher House, Southwark Street, London SEI OTE
Tel 0171-921 1000

The Agency co-ordinates government activity on the civil estate, and provides general property guidance and support to government departments without in-house facilities. It was established in April 1996.
Chief Executive, N. Borrett

SECURITY FACILITIES EXECUTIVE
St Christopher House, Southwark Street, London SEI OTE
Tel 0171-921 4813

The Agency provides a range of security support services, products and systems for central government, the wider public sector and other approved customers.
Chief Executive (G5), J. C. King

CENTRAL ADJUDICATION SERVICES
Quarry House, Quarry Hill, Leeds LS2 7UB
Tel 0113-232 4000
New Court, 48 Carey Street, London WC2A 2LS
Tel 0171-412 1504

The Chief Adjudication Officer and Chief Child Support Officer are independent statutory authorities under the Social Security Act 1975 (as amended) and the Child Support Act 1991. They are appointed by the Secretary of State for Social Security to give advice to adjudication officers and child support officers, to keep under review the operation of the systems of adjudication, and to report annually to the Secretary of State on adjudication standards.

Adjudication officers make decisions of first instance on all claims for social security cash benefits, and child support officers make decisions of first instance on applications for child maintenance made to the Child Support Agency. Officers of the Chief Adjudication Officer also enter written observations on all appeals made to the Social Security Commissioners, and officers of the Chief Child Support Officer make written observations on appeals to the Child Support Commissioners.
Chief Adjudication Officer and Chief Child Support Officer, E. W. Hazlewood

---

CENTRAL OFFICE OF INFORMATION
Hercules Road, London SEI 7DU
Tel 0171-928 2345

The Central Office of Information (COI) is an executive agency which offers consultancy, procurement and project management services to central government for publicity, and provides specialist services in certain areas. Though the majority of COI's work is for government departments in the UK, it also procures a range of publicity materials for overseas consumption. Administrative responsibility for the COI rests with the Minister of Public Service within the Cabinet Office.
Chief Executive and Head of the Government Information Service (G3), G. M. Devereau
  Senior Personal Secretary, Mrs J. Rodrigues

MANAGEMENT BOARD
Members, G. M. Devereau; K. Williamson; R. Windsor; R. Smith
Secretary, Miss K. Gilding

DIRECTORS
Director, Client Services and Marketing (G6), vacant

Director, Advertising (G6), P. Buchanan
Director, Research (G6), M. Rigg
Director, Direct Marketing (G6), C. Noble
Director, Events (G6), A. Chard
Director, Press and Pictures (G6), V. Rowlands
Director, Publications (G6), J. Murray
Director, Publishing and Translations (G6), D. Beynon
Director, Films and Radio (G6), I. Hamilton
Principal Finance Officer (G5), K. Williamson
Director, Regional Network (G6), R. Haslam

NETWORK OFFICES

EASTERN, Three Crowns House, 72–80 Hills Road, Cambridge CB2 ILL. *Network Director (G7)*, Mrs V. Burdon
MIDLANDS EAST, 1st Floor, Severns House, 20 Middle Pavement, Nottingham NGI 7DW. *Network Director (G7)*, P. Smith
MIDLANDS WEST, Five Ways House, Islington Row Middleway, Edgbaston, Birmingham B15 ISH. *Network Director (G6)*, B. Garner
NORTH-EAST, Wellbar House, Gallowgate, Newcastle upon Tyne NEI 4TB. *Network Director (G7)*, H. Cozens
NORTH-WEST, Sunley Tower, Piccadilly Plaza, Manchester MI 4BD. *Network Director (G7)*, Mrs E. Jones
SOUTH-EAST, Hercules Road, London SEI 7DU. *Network Director (G6)*, D. Smith
SOUTH-WEST, The Pithay, Bristol BSI 2NF. *Network Director (G7)*, P. Whitbread
YORKSHIRE AND HUMBERSIDE, City House, New Station Street, Leeds LSI 4JG. *Network Director (G7)*, vacant

---

CERTIFICATION OFFICE FOR TRADE UNIONS AND EMPLOYERS' ASSOCIATIONS
180 Borough High Street, London SEI ILW
Tel 0171-210 3734/5

The Certification Office is an independent statutory authority. The Certification Officer is appointed by the Secretary of State for Trade and Industry and is responsible for receiving and scrutinizing annual returns from trade unions and employers' associations; for investigating allegations of financial irregularities in the affairs of a trade union or employers' association; for dealing with complaints concerning trade union elections; for ensuring observance of statutory requirements governing political funds and trade union mergers; and for certifying the independence of trade unions.
Certification Officer, E. G. Whybrew
Assistant Certification Officer, G. S. Osborne

SCOTLAND
58 Frederick Street, Edinburgh EH2 ILN
Tel 0131-226 3224
Assistant Certification Officer for Scotland, J. L. J. Craig

CHARITY COMMISSION
St Alban's House, 57–60 Haymarket, London SWIY 4QX
Tel 0171-210 4556
2nd Floor, 20 King's Parade, Queen's Dock, Liverpool L3 4DQ
Tel 0151-703 1500
Woodfield House, Tangier, Taunton, Somerset TAI 4BL
Tel 01823-345000

The Charity Commission is established under the Charities Act 1993 with the general function of promoting the effective use of charitable resources in England and

Wales. The Commission gives information and advice to charity trustees to make the administration of their charity more effective; investigates misconduct and the abuse of charitable assets, and takes or recommends remedial action; and maintains a public register of charities. The Commission does not have at its disposal any funds with which to make grants to organizations or individuals.

At the end of 1995 the total number of registered charities was 181,467.

Chief Commissioner (G3), R. Fries
Commissioner (G3), R. M. C. Venables
Commissioners (part-time) (G4), J. Bonds; Mrs T. Baring; Ms J. Warburton
Heads of Legal Sections (G5), J. A. Dutton; G. S. Goodchild; K. M. Dibble; S. Slack
Executive Director (G4), Mrs E. A. Shaw
Head of Policy Division (G5), Ms J. Munday
Establishment Officer (G5), Ms C. Stewart
Information Systems Controller (G5), Ms G. Cruickshank

The offices responsible for charities in Scotland and Northern Ireland are:

SCOTLAND – Scottish Charities Office, Crown Office, 25 Chambers Street, Edinburgh EH1 1LA. Tel: 0131-226 2626

NORTHERN IRELAND – Department of Health and Social Services, Charities Branch, Annexe 3, Castle Buildings, Stormont Estate, Belfast BT4 3RA. Tel: 01232-522 780

CHIEF ADJUDICATION OFFICER AND CHIEF CHILD SUPPORT OFFICER
— *see* Central Adjudication Services

CHILD SUPPORT AGENCY
— *see* page 345

CHURCH COMMISSIONERS
1 Millbank, London SW1P 3JZ
Tel 0171-222 7010

The Church Commissioners were established in 1948 by the amalgamation of Queen Anne's Bounty (established 1704) and the Ecclesiastical Commissioners (established 1836).

The Commissioners are responsible for the management of most of the Church of England's assets, the income from which is predominantly used to pay, house and pension the clergy. The Commissioners own nearly 137,000 acres of agricultural land, a number of residential estates in central London, and commercial property in Great Britain and the USA. They also carry out administrative duties in connection with pastoral reorganization and redundant churches, and have been designated by the General Synod as the central stipends authority of the Church of England.

The Commissioners are: the Archbishops of Canterbury and of York; the 41 diocesan bishops; five deans or provosts, ten other clergy and ten lay persons appointed by the General Synod; four lay persons nominated by The Queen; four persons nominated by the Archbishop of Canterbury; the Lord Chancellor; the Lord President of the Council; the First Lord of the Treasury; the Chancellor of the Exchequer; the Secretary of State for the Home Department; the Speaker of the House of Commons; the Lord Chief Justice; the Master of the Rolls; the Attorney-General; the Solicitor-General; the Lord Mayor and two Aldermen of the City of London; the Lord Mayor of York;

and one representative from each of the Universities of Oxford and Cambridge.

INCOME AND EXPENDITURE
for year ended 31 December 1995

	£ million
Total income	154.2
Net income	137.2
Investments	74.4
Property	63.5
Interest from loans, etc.	16.3
Total expenditure	143.0
Clergy stipends	41.7
Clergy and widows' pensions	76.9
Clergy houses	0.3
Episcopal and cathedral housing	2.3
Financial provision for resigning clergy	3.3
Commissioners' administration of central church functions	5.3
Episcopal administration and payments to Chapters	10.1
Church buildings	0.9
Administration costs of other bodies	2.2
Deficit for year	(5.6)

CHURCH ESTATES COMMISSIONERS
First, Sir Michael Colman, Bt.
Second, The Rt. Hon. Michael Alison, MP
Third, Mrs M. H. Laird

OFFICERS
Secretary, P. Locke
Deputy Secretary (Policy and Planning), R. S. Hopgood
Deputy Secretary (Finance and Investment), C. W. Daws
Assistant Secretaries:
    The Accountant, G. C. Baines
    Management Accountant, B. J. Hardy
    Chief Surveyor, A. C. Brown
    Computer Manager, J. W. Ferguson
    Estates, P. H. P. Shaw, LVO
    Investments Manager, A. S. Hardy
    Pastoral, Houses and Redundant Churches, M. D. Elengorn
    Stipends and Allocations, M. G. S. Farrell
    Senior Architect, J. A. Taylor
Official Solicitor, J. P. Guy

CIVIL AVIATION AUTHORITY
CAA House, 45–59 Kingsway, London WC2B 6TE
Tel 0171-379 7311

The CAA is responsible for the economic regulation of UK airlines by licensing air routes and air travel organizers and by approving fares for journeys outside the European Union; for the safety regulation of UK civil aviation by the certification of airlines and aircraft and by licensing aerodromes, flight crew and aircraft engineers; and, through a subsidiary company, National Air Traffic Services Ltd, for the provision of air traffic control and telecommunications services.

The CAA also advises the Government on aviation issues, represents consumer interests, conducts economic and scientific research, produces statistical data and provides specialist services and other training, and consultancy services to clients world-wide.

Chairman (part-time), Sir Malcolm Field
Secretary, R. J. Britton

THE COAL AUTHORITY
200 Lichfield Lane, Mansfield, Notts NG18 4RG
Tel 01623-427162

The Coal Authority was established under the Coal Industry Act 1994 to manage certain functions previously undertaken by British Coal, including ownership of unworked coal. It is responsible for licensing coal mining operations and for providing information on coal reserves and past and future coal mining. It settles subsidence claims not falling on coal mining operators. It is also responsible for the management and disposal of property, and for dealing with surface hazards such as abandoned coal mine shafts.
Chairman, Sir David White
Chief Executive, N. Washington, OBE

COMMONWEALTH DEVELOPMENT CORPORATION
1 Bessborough Gardens, London SW1V 2JQ
Tel 0171-828 4488

The Commonwealth Development Corporation (CDC) assists overseas countries in the development of their economies. Its sponsoring department is the Overseas Development Administration. Its main activity is providing long-term finance, as loans and risk capital, for financially viable and developmentally sound business enterprises. CDC's area of operations includes British dependent territories and, with ministerial approval, Commonwealth or other developing countries. At present, CDC is authorized to operate in more than 60 countries and territories. Its investments at the end of 1995 were £1,487 million.
Chairman (part-time), The Earl Cairns, CBE
Deputy Chairman (part-time), Sir William Ryrie, KCB
Chief Executive, Dr R. Reynolds

COMMONWEALTH SECRETARIAT
— *see* Index

COMMONWEALTH WAR GRAVES COMMISSION
2 Marlow Road, Maidenhead, Berks SL6 7DX
Tel 01628-34221

The Commonwealth War Graves Commission (formerly Imperial War Graves Commission) was founded by royal charter in 1917. It is responsible for the commemoration of 1,695,190 members of the forces of the Commonwealth who fell in the two world wars. More than one million graves are maintained in 23,198 burial grounds throughout the world. Over three-quarters of a million men and women who have no known grave or who were cremated are commemorated by name on memorials built by the Commission.
The funds of the Commission are derived from the six participating governments, i.e. the UK, Australia, Canada, India, New Zealand and South Africa.
President, HRH The Duke of Kent, KG, GCMG, GCVO, ADC
Chairman, The Secretary of State for Defence in the UK
Vice-Chairman, Air Chief Marshal Sir Joseph Gilbert, KCB, CBE

Members, The Secretary of State for the Environment in the UK; The High Commissioners in London for Australia, Canada, India, New Zealand and South Africa; Dame Janet Fookes, DBE, MP; Sir Nigel Mobbs; The Viscount Ridley, KG, GCVO, TD; Prof. R. J. O'Neill, AO; Mrs L. Golding, MP; Sir Harold Walker, KCMG; Gen. Sir John Akehurst, KCB, CBE; Adm. Sir John Kerr, GCB
Director-General and Secretary to the Commission, D. Kennedy
Deputy Director-General, R. J. Dalley
Directors, P. Noakes (*Finance*); A. Coombe (*Works*); D. C. Parker (*Horticulture*); D. R. Parker (*Personnel*); J. P. D. Gee, OBE (*Information and Secretariat*)
Legal Adviser and Solicitor, G. C. Reddie

IMPERIAL WAR GRAVES ENDOWMENT FUND
Trustees, The Lord Remnant, CVO (*Chairman*); Air Chief Marshal Sir Joseph Gilbert, KCB, CBE; A. C. Barker
Secretary to the Trustees, P. Noakes

COUNTRYSIDE COMMISSION
John Dower House, Crescent Place, Cheltenham, Glos GL50 3RA
Tel 01242-521381

The Countryside Commission was set up in 1968 and is an independent agency which promotes the conservation and enhancement of landscape beauty in England. It encourages the provision and improvement of facilities in the countryside, and works to secure access for open air recreation. Since 1982 the Commission has been funded by an annual grant from the Department of the Environment. Members of the Commission are appointed by the Secretary of State for the Environment.
In April 1996 the Commission's Countryside Stewardship initiative was transferred to the Ministry of Agriculture, Fisheries and Food.
Chairman, R. Simmonds
Commissioners, D. Barker, MBE; the Rt Revd A. Chesters; the Lord Denham, KBE; Dr Susan Owens; Prof. A. Patmore, CBE; W. Rogers-Coltman, OBE; R. Swarbrick, CBE; Mrs R. Thomas; Mrs S. Ward; D. Woodhall, CBE
Chief Executive (G3), R. G. Wakeford
Directors (G5), R. Clarke (*Policy*); M. J. Kirby (*Operations*); M. Taylor (*Resources*)
National Heritage Adviser, P. Walshe
Head of Corporate Planning (G7), N. Holliday
Head of Land Use Branch (G7), Ms P. Jones
Head of Recreation and Access Branch (G7), T. Robinson
Head of Public Affairs (G7), R. Roberts
Head of Finance and Establishments (G7), V. Ellis
Head of National Parks and Planning Branch (G7), R. Lloyd
Head of Environmental Protection Branch (G7), J. Worth
Regional Officers (G7), K. Buchanan (*Newcastle*); Dr M. Carroll (*Cambridge*); Dr S. A. Bucknall (*Leeds*); E. Holdaway (*Bristol*); Dr Liz Newton (*Manchester*); D. E. Coleman (*London*); T. Allen (*Birmingham*)
Special Initiatives, Dr M. Rawson (*Community Forests*)

COUNTRYSIDE COUNCIL FOR WALES/ CYNGOR CEFN GWLAD CYMRU
Plas Penrhos, Fford Penrhos, Bangor LL57 2LQ
Tel 01248-385500

The Countryside Council for Wales is the Government's statutory adviser on wildlife, countryside and maritime conservation matters in Wales, and it is the executive

authority for the conservation of habitats and wildlife. It promotes the protection of the Welsh landscape and encourages opportunities for public access and enjoyment of the countryside. It provides grant aid to local authorities, voluntary organizations and individuals to pursue countryside management. It is funded by the Welsh Office and accountable to the Secretary of State for Wales, who appoints its members.
Chairman, E. M. W. Griffith, CBE
Chief Executive, P. E. Loveluck, CBE
Director, Policy and Science, Dr M. E. Smith
Director, Conservation, I. R. Bonner

COVENT GARDEN MARKET AUTHORITY
Covent House, New Covent Garden Market, London sw8 5NX
Tel 0171-720 2211

The Covent Garden Market Authority is constituted under the Covent Garden Market Acts 1961 to 1977, the members being appointed by the Minister of Agriculture, Fisheries and Food. The Authority owns and operates the 56-acre New Covent Garden Markets (fruit, vegetables, flowers) which have been trading since 1974.
Chairman (part-time), W. P. Bowman, CBE
General Manager, Dr P. M. Liggins
Secretary, C. Farey

CRIMINAL INJURIES COMPENSATION AUTHORITY AND BOARD
Morley House, 26–30 Holborn Viaduct, London ECIA 2JQ
Tel 0171-842 6800
Tay House, 300 Bath Street, Glasgow G2 4JR
Tel 0141-331 2726

All applications for compensation for personal injury arising from crimes of violence in England, Scotland and Wales are dealt with at the above locations. (Separate arrangements apply in Northern Ireland.) Applications received up to 31 March 1996 were assessed on the basis of common law damages under the 1990 compensation scheme by the Criminal Injuries Compensation Board (CICB), which also hears appeals. Applications received on or after 1 April 1996 are assessed under a tariff-based scheme, made under the Criminal Injuries Compensation Act 1995, by the Criminal Injuries Compensation Authority (CICA); there is a separate avenue of appeal to the Criminal Injuries Compensation Appeals Panel (CICAP).
The Board was founded in 1964 by the Home Secretary and Secretary of State for Scotland under the prerogative powers of the Crown. The Authority and the Panel are established by the tariff-based scheme made under the Criminal Injuries Compensation Act 1995.
Chairman of the Criminal Injuries Compensation Board (part-time) (£35,306), The Lord Carlisle of Bucklow, PC, QC
Chief Executive of the Board and of the Criminal Injuries Compensation Authority, P. G. Spurgeon
Head of Legal Services, Mrs A. M. Johnstone
Operations Manager, E. McKeown
Chairman of the Criminal Injuries Compensation Appeals Panel, M. Lewer, QC
Secretary to the Board, Miss V. Jenson

CROFTERS COMMISSION
4–6 Castle Wynd, Inverness IV2 3EQ
Tel 01463-663450

The Crofters Commission is a statutory body established in 1955. It advises the Secretary of State for Scotland on all matters relating to crofting. It controls the letting, subletting and, in certain cases, the assignation or enlargement of crofts; the removal of land from crofting tenure; and the regulation of common grazings. It also administers schemes of agricultural assistance to crofters.
Chairman, I. MacAskill
Secretary (G6), M. Grantham

CROWN AGENTS FOR OVERSEA GOVERNMENTS AND ADMINISTRATIONS
St Nicholas House, St Nicholas Road, Sutton, Surrey SMI IEL
Tel 0181-643 3311

Incorporated under the Crown Agents Act 1979, the Crown Agents are commercial, financial and professional agents for governments and public authorities in over 120 countries, and for international bodies and other organizations, primarily in the public sector. The Government has announced its intention to transfer the Crown Agents to an independent foundation and the necessary legislation was passed in 1995.
Chairman, D. H. Probert, CBE
Managing Director, P. F. Berry

CROWN ESTATE
16 Carlton House Terrace, London SWIY 5AH
Tel 0171-210 4377

The land revenues of the Crown in England and Wales have been collected on the public account since 1760, when George III surrendered them to Parliament and received a fixed annual payment or Civil List. At the time of the surrender the gross revenues amounted to about £89,000 and the net return to about £11,000.
The land revenues in Ireland have been carried to the Consolidated Fund since 1820; from 1923, as regards the Republic of Ireland, they have been collected and administered by the Irish Government.
The land revenues in Scotland were transferred to the predecessors of the Crown Estate Commissioners in 1833.
In the year ended 31 March 1996, the gross income from the Crown Estate totalled £143 million. The sum of £94.6 million was paid to the Exchequer in 1995–6 as surplus revenue.
First Commissioner and Chairman (part-time), Sir Denys Henderson
Second Commissioner and Chief Executive, C. K. Howes, CB
Commissioners (part-time), R. B. Caws, CBE, FRICS; J. N. C. James, CBE; I. Grant; J. H. M. Norris, CBE; The Lord De Ramsey
Commissioner and Deputy Chief Executive, D. E. G. Griffiths
Deputy Chief Executive, D. E. Murray
Legal Adviser, M. L. Davies
Crown Estate Surveyor, C. F. Hynes
Urban Estates Managers, M. W. Dillon; A. Bickmore; R. Wyatt
Agricultural Estates Manager, R. J. Mulholland

Marine Estates Manager, F. G. Parrish
Information Systems Manager, D. Kingston-Smith
Valuation and Investment Analysis Manager, P. Shearmur
Internal Audit Manager, J. E. Ford
Finance Manager, J. G. Lelliott
Corporate Services Manager, M. E. Beckwith
Personnel Manager, R. J. Blake
Public Relations and Press Officer, Mrs G. Coates

SCOTLAND
10 Charlotte Square, Edinburgh EH2 4BR
Tel 0131-226 7241

Crown Estate Receiver for Scotland, M. J. Gravestock

WINDSOR ESTATE
The Great Park, Windsor, Berks SL4 2HT
Tel 01753-860222

Deputy Ranger and Surveyor, M. J. O'Lone

CROWN PROSECUTION SERVICE
— *see* pages 366–7

BOARD OF CUSTOMS AND EXCISE
*New King's Beam House, 22 Upper Ground, London
SE1 9PJ
Tel 0171-620 1313

Commissioners of Customs were first appointed in 1671 and housed by the King in London. The Excise Department was formerly under the Inland Revenue Department and was amalgamated with the Customs Department in 1909.

HM Customs and Excise is responsible for collecting and administering customs and excise duties and VAT, and advises the Chancellor of the Exchequer on any matters connected with them. The Department is also responsible for preventing and detecting the evasion of revenue laws and for enforcing a range of prohibitions and restrictions on the importation of certain classes of goods. In addition, the Department undertakes certain agency work on behalf of other departments, including the compilation of UK overseas trade statistics from customs import and export documents.

THE BOARD
Chairman (G1), Mrs V. P. M. Strachan, CB
  Private Secretaries, Ms C. Davis; A. Jones
Deputy Chairman, A. W. Russell, CB
Commissioners (G3), D. F. O. Battle; A. C. Sawyer; Mrs
  E. A. Woods; M. J. Eland; D. R. Howard; A. Paynter;
  M. Brown; R. McAfee
Head of Board's Secretariat, J. Bone

PUBLIC RELATIONS OFFICE
Tel 0171-865 5665

Head of Public Relations, Ms L. J. Sinclair

INFORMATION SYSTEMS DIRECTORATE
Alexander House, Victoria Avenue, Southend-on-Sea
SS99 1AU
Tel 01702-348944

Director, A. Paynter

CUSTOMS POLICY DIRECTORATE
Director, M. Eland

*Unless otherwise stated, this is the address and telephone number of directorates of the Board

EXCISE AND CENTRAL POLICY DIRECTORATE
Director, D. Howard

VAT POLICY DIRECTORATE
Director, M. Brown

PERSONNEL AND FINANCE DIRECTORATE
Director, D. Battle

CENTRAL OPERATIONS DIRECTORATE
Director, R. McAfee

Tariff and Statistical Office
Alexander House, Victoria Avenue, Southend-on-Sea
SS99 1AU
Tel 01702-348944

Controller, A. Cowley

Accounting Services Division
Alexander House, Victoria Avenue, Southend-on-Sea
SS99 1AU
Tel 01702-348944

Accountant and Comptroller-General, D. Robinson

COMPLIANCE DIRECTORATE
Director, Mrs E. A. Woods

PREVENTION DIRECTORATE
Director, A. Sawyer

National Investigation Service
Custom House, Lower Thames Street, London EC3R 6EE
Tel 0171-283 5353

Chief Investigation Officer, R. Kellaway

SOLICITOR'S OFFICE
Solicitor, D. Pickup
Deputy Solicitor, G. Fotherby

COLLECTORS OF HM CUSTOMS AND EXCISE (*G5*)
Anglia, R. C. Shepherd
Central England, A. Bowen
Eastern England, M. D. Patten
London Airports, M. Peach
London Central, J. Maclean
Northern England, H. Peden
Northern Ireland, T. W. Logan
North-west England, A. Allen
Scotland, C. Arnott
South-east England, W. I. Stuttle
South London and Thames, J. Priestly
Southern England, C. J. Packman
Thames Valley, J. Barnard
Wales, the West and Borders, H. Burnard

OFFICE OF THE DATA PROTECTION REGISTRAR
Wycliffe House, Water Lane, Wilmslow, Cheshire
SK9 5AF
Tel 01625-545700

The Office of the Data Protection Registrar was created by the Data Protection Act 1984. It is the Registrar's duty to compile and maintain the Register of data users and computer bureaux and to provide facilities for members of the public to examine the Register; to promote observance of data protection principles; to consider complaints made by data subjects; to disseminate information about the Act; to encourage the production of codes of practice by trade associations and other bodies; to guide data users in complying with data protection principles; to co-operate

with other parties to the Council of Europe Convention and act as UK authority for the purposes of Article 13 of the Convention; and to report annually to Parliament on the performance of her functions.
Registrar, Mrs E. France

DEER COMMISSION FOR SCOTLAND
Knowsley, 82 Fairfield Road, Inverness IV3 5LH
Tel 01463-231751

The Deer Commission for Scotland has the general functions of furthering the conservation and control of deer in Scotland. It has the statutory duty, with powers, to prevent damage to agriculture, forestry and the habitat by deer. The Commission also has the power to advise in the interest of conservation any owner of land on questions relating to the carrying of stocks of deer on that land, and to carry out research into matters of scientific importance relating to deer. It is funded by the Scottish Office.
Chairman (part-time), P. Gordon-Duff-Pennington, OBE
Chief Executive and Secretary, A. Rinning
Technical Director, R. W. Youngson

MINISTRY OF DEFENCE
— *see* pages 381–4

DESIGN COUNCIL
1 Oxendon Street, London SW1Y 4EE
Tel 0171-208 2121

The Design Council is incorporated by royal charter and is a registered charity. It aims to inspire the best use of design by the UK in order to improve prosperity and well-being. It works with government, industry and academia to generate information and practical tools for uptake in industry and education which demonstrate the contribution, value and effectiveness of design. Its sponsoring department is the Department of Trade and Industry.
Chairman, J. Sorrell, CBE
Chief Executive, A. Summers

THE DUCHY OF CORNWALL
10 Buckingham Gate, London SW1E 6LA
Tel 0171-834 7346

The Duchy of Cornwall was created by Edward III in 1337 for the support of his eldest son Edward, later known as the Black Prince. It is the oldest of the English duchies. The precursor of the duchy was the earldom of Cornwall, granted to Richard, younger brother of Henry III on his marriage four years after he had been granted the title of earl in 1227. The duchy is acquired by inheritance by the sovereign's eldest son either at birth or on the accession of his parent to the throne, whichever is the later. The primary purpose of the estate remains to provide an income for the Prince of Wales. The estate is mainly agricultural, consisting of 129,000 acres in 24 counties mainly in the south-west of England. The duchy also has some residential property, a number of shops and offices, and a Stock Exchange portfolio. Prince Charles is the 24th Duke of Cornwall.

THE PRINCE'S COUNCIL
Chairman, HRH The Prince of Wales, KG, KT, GCB

Lord Warden of the Stannaries, The Earl Peel
Receiver-General, The Earl Cairns, CBE
Attorney-General to the Prince of Wales, J. M. Sullivan, QC
Secretary and Keeper of the Records, J. N. C. James, CBE
Other members, Earl of Shelburne; Cdr. R. J. Aylard, CVO, RN; J. E. Pugsley; A. M. J. Galsworthy; C. Howes, CB; W. N. Hood, CBE; W. R. A. Ross

OTHER OFFICERS
Auditors, I. Brindle; H. Hughes
Sheriff (1996–7), Mrs J. Trench Morison

THE DUCHY OF LANCASTER
Lancaster Place, Strand, London WC2E 7ED
Tel 0171-836 8277

The estates and jurisdiction known as the Duchy of Lancaster have belonged to the reigning monarch since 1399 when John of Gaunt's son came to the throne as Henry IV. As the Lancaster Inheritance it goes back as far as 1265 when Henry III granted his youngest son Edmund lands and possessions following the Baron's war. In 1267 Henry gave Edmund the County, Honor and Castle of Lancaster and created him the first Earl of Lancaster. In 1351 Edward III created Lancaster a County Palatine.

The Chancellor of the Duchy of Lancaster is responsible for the administration of the Duchy, the appointment of justices of the peace in Lancashire, Greater Manchester and Merseyside and ecclesiastical patronage in the Duchy gift. The Chancellor is also a member of the Cabinet.
Chancellor of the Duchy of Lancaster, The Rt. Hon. Roger Freeman, MP
Attorney-General, T. A. W. Lloyd, QC
Receiver-General, M. C. G. Peat, CVO
Clerk of the Council, M. K. Ridley, CVO
Chief Clerk, Col. F. N. J. Davies

DEPARTMENT FOR EDUCATION AND EMPLOYMENT
Sanctuary Buildings, Great Smith Street, London SW1P 3BT
Tel 0171-925 5000
Caxton House, Tothill Street, London SW1H 9NF
Tel 0171-273 3000
Moorfoot, Sheffield S1 4PQ
Tel 0114-275 3275
Mowden Hall, Staindrop Road, Darlington DL3 9BG
Tel 01325-460155

The Department for Education and Employment was formed in July 1995, bringing together the functions of the former Department of Education with the training and labour market functions of the former Employment Department Group. It includes an executive agency, the Employment Service. The new Department aims to support economic growth and improve the nation's competitiveness and quality of life by raising standards of educational achievement and skill and by promoting an efficient and flexible labour market.
Secretary of State for Education and Employment, The Rt. Hon. Gillian Shephard, MP
Principal Private Secretary, A. T. Evans
Special Advisers, Dr. E. Cottrell; N. Heslop
Ministers of State, Eric Forth, MP; The Lord Henley
Private Secretaries, Ms C. Maye; Ms P. Clarke

Parliamentary Under-Secretaries of State, Robin Squire, MP;
James Paice, MP; Cheryl Gillan, MP
  Private Secretaries, D. McGrath; J. Kittmer;
  Ms S. Battarbee
Permanent Secretary, M. Bichard
  Private Secretary, Ms J. Ruff

EMPLOYMENT AND LIFETIME LEARNING DIRECTORATE

Director-General, N. Stuart
Heads of Divisions, M. Nicholas (*Employer Training Policy*);
  Ms F. Everiss (*Individual Commitment*)

EMPLOYMENT AND ADULT TRAINING
Director, P. Makeham
Heads of Divisions, I. Berry (*Employment Policy and
  Programmes*); A. Cranston (*Employment and Benefits*);
  E. Galvin (*Training Programmes*)

JSA PROJECT
Director, I. Stewart
JSA Project Manager, M. Allen

EQUAL OPPORTUNITIES, TECHNOLOGY AND OVERSEAS
LABOUR
Director, B. Niven
Heads of Divisions, Mrs J. Anderson, Ms S. Weber (*Sex and
  Race Equality*); Miss D. Fordham (*Disability Policy*);
  R. Ritzema (*Education and Training Technology*);
  N. Atkinson (*Overseas Labour Service*)

FINANCE DIRECTORATE

Director, L. Lewis
Heads of Divisions, D. Sandeman (*Expenditure*); Mrs I. Wilde
  (*Finance Policy*); D. Russell (*Programme Performance and
  Evaluation*); K. Beeton (*Efficiency*); P. Connor (*Accounting
  and Systems*); N. Thirtle (*Internal Audit*); P. Slade (*Private
  Finance Initiative*).

FURTHER AND HIGHER EDUCATION AND YOUTH TRAINING DIRECTORATE

Director-General, R. Dawe
Head of Division, M. Waring (*Education Business Links*)

FURTHER EDUCATION AND YOUTH TRAINING
Director, D. Forrester
Heads of Divisions, S. Kershaw (*16–19 Policy*); Mrs L.
  Ammon (*Choice and Careers*); J. Stanyer (*Further Education
  Support Unit*); Miss J. Benham (*Further Education*);
  R. Wye (*Training for Young People*)

HIGHER EDUCATION
Director, T. Clark
Heads of Divisions, Miss K. Fleay (*Higher Education Funding*);
  Miss C. Macready (*Higher Education Quality*); J. Moore
  (*Student Support*); T. Fellowes (*Higher Education and
  Employment*)

QUALIFICATIONS
Director, M. Richardson
Heads of Divisions, Miss C. Bienkowska (*School and College
  Based Qualifications*); J. West (*Qualifications for Work*);
  C. Barnham (*Qualifications Framework and GNVQ*)

INFORMATION DIRECTORATE

Director, J. Coe
Heads of Divisions, M. Paterson (*Media Relations*); J. Ross
  (*Publicity*)

LEGAL ADVISER'S OFFICE

Legal Adviser, R. Ricks
Heads of Divisions, F. Clarke; S. Harker; C. House; Ms R.
  Jeffreys; A. Preston

OPERATIONS DIRECTORATE

Director, J. Hedger
Heads of Divisions, P. Houten (*TECs and Careers Service
  Policy*); P. Lauener (*Resources and Budget Management*);
  Mrs P. Jones (*Financial Control, Operations*); P. Thomas
  (*Quality and Performance Improvement*); H. Sharp
  (*Government Office Policy and Management*); J. Fuller
  (*Sector Skills Partnership*)

PERSONNEL AND SUPPORT SERVICES DIRECTORATE

Director, D. Normington
Heads of Divisions, Ms C. Tyler (*Senior Staff Appointments
  and Development*); R. Hinchcliffe (*Information Systems*); Ms
  C. Johnson (*Personnel*); K. Jordan (*Procurement and
  Contracting*); J. Gordon (*Training and Development*);
  L. Webb (*Estates and Office Services*); T. Jeffery (*Human
  Resource Policy*)

SCHOOLS DIRECTORATE

Director-General, P. Owen
Head of Division, M. Richardson (*Curriculum and Assessment*)

SCHOOL PLACES, BUILDINGS AND GOVERNANCE
GROUP
Director, P. Shaw
Heads of Divisions, S. Marston (*Grant-Maintained Schools
  Policy*); A. Shaw (*Supply of School Places*); Ms A. Jackson
  (*Specialist Schools and School Governance*); J. Whitaker
  (*Schools Capital*); M. Hipkins (*Under-Fives*); C. Wells
  (*Nursery Vouchers Implementation*)

SCHOOL FUNDING, EFFECTIVENESS AND TEACHERS
GROUP
Director, N. Saunders
Heads of Divisions, A. Clarke (*School Recurrent Funding*);
  J. Street (*LEA Finance*); A. Wye (*School Teachers' Pay and
  Pensions*); Ms S. Scales (*Teacher Supply, Training and
  Qualifications*); M. Stark (*School Effectiveness*)

PUPILS, PARENTS AND YOUTH GROUP
Director, R. Smith
Heads of Divisions, A. Sargent (*Parental Choice*); R. Green
  (*Special Educational Needs Policy*); P. Thorpe (*Discipline
  and Attendance*); G. Holley (*Youth Service and Preparation
  for Adulthood*); M. Phipps (*Pupil Welfare*)

STRATEGY, INTERNATIONAL AND ANALYTICAL SERVICES DIRECTORATE

Director-General, G. Reid
Heads of Divisions, J. Dewsbury (*Briefing*); R. Harrison
  (*Strategy and Board Secretariat*)

ANALYTICAL SERVICES
Director, D. Allnutt
Heads of Divisions, J. Gardner (*Qualifications*); J. Elliott
  (*Youth and Further Education*); M. Chaplin (*Skills and
  Training Analysis*); D. Thompson (*Higher Education*); Ms
  J. Walton (*Schools, Teachers and General*); B. Butcher
  (*TECs and Lifetime Learning*); B. Wells (*Labour Market
  Analysis*); R. Bartholomew (*Social Analysis and Research*);
  Ms A. Brown (*School Resources and Modelling*)

INTERNATIONAL
Director, C. Tucker, CB

Heads of Divisions, Miss E. Hodkinson (*EC Education and Training*); Ms W. Harris (*European Union*); Ms E. Trewartha (*European Social Fund*); D. Brown (*International Relations*)
Assistant Director, Exports, Assistance and European Schools, R. Morgan

EXECUTIVE AGENCY

THE EMPLOYMENT SERVICE
St Vincent House, 30 Orange Street, London WC2H 7HT
Tel 0171-839 5600

The Employment Service is responsible for providing services and administering programmes to help unemployed people get back to work as quickly as possible and to make payments to those entitled to benefit.
Chief Executive (G3+), M. E. G. Fogden, CB
Senior Director of Operations (G3), D. Grover
Director of Finance and Resources (G3), D. Horne
Director of Policy and Process Design (G3), R. Phillips
Director of Human Resources (G4), K. White
Regional Directors (G4), R. Foster (*London and South-east*); (*G5*), Mrs A. Le Sage (*East Midlands*); P. Robson (*Northern*); J. Roberts (*North-west*); K. Pascoe (*South-west*); Miss R Thew (*West Midlands*); R. Lasko (*Yorkshire and Humberside*)
Director for Scotland (G5), A. R. Brown
Director for Wales (G5), Mrs S. Keyse

OFFICE OF ELECTRICITY REGULATION
Hagley House, Hagley Road, Birmingham B16 8QG
Tel 0121-456 2100
SCOTLAND: Regent Court, 70 West Regent Street, Glasgow G2 2QZ
Tel 0141-331 2678

The Office of Electricity Regulation (OFFER) is the regulatory body for the electricity supply industry in England, Scotland and Wales. Its functions are to promote competition in the generation and supply of electricity; to ensure that all reasonable demands for electricity are satisfied; to protect customers' interests in relation to prices, security of supply and quality of services; and to promote the efficient use of electricity. Headed by the Director-General of Electricity Supply, OFFER was set up under the Electricity Act 1989 but is independent of ministerial control.
Director-General of Electricity Supply, Prof. S. C. Littlechild
Deputy Director-General, C. P. Carter
Deputy Director-General for Scotland, G. L. Sims
Directors of Regulation and Business Affairs, T. M. Davis; J. Saunders
Director of Supply Competition, A. J. Boorman
Director of Consumer Affairs, Dr D. P. Hauser
Technical Director, Dr B. Wharmby
Director of Public Affairs, Miss J. D. Luke
Director of Administration, H. P. Jones
Legal Adviser, D. R. B. Bevan
Chief Examiner, J. D. Cooper

OFFICE OF ELECTRICITY REGULATION NORTHERN IRELAND
Brookmount Buildings, 42 Fountain Street, Belfast BT1 5EE
Tel 01232-311575

OFFER NI is the regulatory body for the electricity supply industry in Northern Ireland.

Director-General of Electricity Supply for Northern Ireland, D. McIldoon
Deputy Director-General, C. H. Coulthard

ENGLISH HERITAGE
— *see* Historic Buildings and Monuments Commission for England

ENGLISH NATURE
Northminster House, Peterborough PE1 1UA
Tel 01733-340345

English Nature (the Nature Conservancy Council for England) was established in 1991 and is responsible for advising the Secretary of State for the Environment on nature conservation in England. It promotes, directly and through others, the conservation of England's wildlife and natural features. It selects, establishes and manages National Nature Reserves and identifies and notifies Sites of Special Scientific Interest. It provides advice and information about nature conservation, and supports and conducts research relevant to these functions. Through the Joint Nature Conservation Committee (*see* page 329), it works with its sister organizations in Scotland and Wales on UK and international nature conservation issues.
Chairman, The Earl of Cranbrook
Chief Executive, Dr D. R. Langslow
Directors, Dr K. L. Duff; E. T. Idle; Miss C. E. M. Wood; Ms S. Collins

ENGLISH PARTNERSHIPS
16–18 Old Queen Street, London SW1H 9HP
Tel 0171-976 7070

English Partnerships, in statute the Urban Regeneration Agency, came into full operation in April 1994. Its primary aim is to secure the reclamation and reuse of vacant and derelict land throughout England for employment, green space, housing or any other use that will help to regenerate the area. It works in partnership with the public, private and voluntary sectors. Its sponsoring department is the Department of the Environment.
Chairman, The Lord Walker of Worcester, MBE, PC
Deputy Chairman, Sir Idris Pearce, CBE
Chief Executive, D. Taylor

DEPARTMENT OF THE ENVIRONMENT
Eland House, Bressenden Place, London SW1E 5DU
Tel 0171-890 3000
Ashdown House, 123 Victoria Street, London SW1E 6DE
Tel 0171-890 3000

The Department of the Environment is responsible for planning and land use; local government; housing and construction; inner city areas; new towns; environmental protection; conservation areas and countryside affairs; health and safety at work and energy efficiency.
Secretary of State for the Environment, The Rt. Hon. John Gummer, MP
Private Secretary, A. Davis
Special Advisers, T. Burke; K. Adams; L. O'Connor; G. Barwell
Parliamentary Private Secretary, D. French, MP

Minister for Local Government, The Rt. Hon. David Curry, MP
Private Secretary, B. Hackland
Minister for Planning, Construction and Energy Efficiency, Robert Jones, MP
Private Secretary, Mrs T. Vokes
Parliamentary Private Secretary to Mr Curry and Mr Jones, M. Banks, MP
Minister for Environment and Countryside, The Earl Ferrers, PC
Private Secretary, C. T. Wood
Parliamentary Under-Secretaries of State, Sir Paul Beresford, MP; James Clappison, MP
Private Secretaries, D. Gleave; J. Humphreys
Lord-in-Waiting, The Lord Lucas
Private Secretary, Miss A. Hemming
Parliamentary Clerk, T. Teehan
Permanent Secretary (G1), A. Turnbull, CB, CVO
Private Secretary, Mrs P. Allars

ORGANIZATION AND ESTABLISHMENTS
Principal Establishments Officer (G3), R. S. Dudding
Principal Finance Officer (G3), W. F. S. Rickett

PERSONNEL
Grade 5, K. G. Arnold; L. B. Hicks; Mrs M. Winckler
Chief Welfare Officer (G7), Miss E. T. Haines

FINANCE CENTRAL
Heads of Divisions (G5), M. J. Bailey; A. C. Allberry; P. D. Walton; M. R. Haselip; I. C. McBrayne
Grade 6, M. J. Burt; A. Brooks

ADMINISTRATION RESOURCES
Grade 5, J. J. O'Callaghan; Mrs H. Parker-Brown

DIRECTORATE OF COMMUNICATION
Director (G4), S. Dugdale
Grade 5, K. Kerslake

GOVERNMENT OFFICES CENTRAL UNIT
Under-Secretary (G3), A. G. Watson
Grade 5, T. Abraham; B. Hopson

HOUSING CONSTRUCTION, PLANNING AND COUNTRYSIDE GROUP
Deputy Secretary (G2), Mrs M. McDonald

SECRETARIAT
Grade 7, P. G. Tobia

HOUSING POLICY AND PRIVATE SECTOR
Under-Secretary (G3), Dr C. P. Evans
Grade 5, J. E. Roberts; Mrs H. Chipping; C. L. L. Braun

HOUSING AND URBAN MONITORING AND ANALYSIS
Under-Secretary (G3), Dr C. P. Evans
Grade 5, J. E. Turner; Mrs J. Littlewood; M. Hughes; S. Aldridge

HOUSING, SOCIAL POLICY AND RESOURCES
Under-Secretary (G3), Mrs D. S. Phillips
Grade 5, A. Wells; C. H. Bowden; R. S. Horsman; L. G. Packer

CONSTRUCTION SPONSORSHIP
Director (G3), P. Ward
Grade 5, J. P. Channing; J. N. Lithgow; Dr R. P. Thorogood
Grade 6, R. Wood

WILDLIFE AND COUNTRYSIDE DIRECTORATE
Under-Secretary (G3), J. P. Plowman
Grade 5, R. M. Pritchard; R. W. Bunce; R. Hepworth

PROPERTY AND BUILDINGS
Director (G4), D. O. McCreadie
Grade 5, J. M. Leigh-Pollitt; P. F. Everall
Grade 6, W. J. Marsh

PLANNING DIRECTORATE
Under-Secretary (G3), J. F. Ballard
Heads of Divisions (G5), D. N. Donaldson; R. Jones; W. E. Chapman; M. R. Ash; J. Zetter; R. C. Mabey; A. M. Oliver

CHIEF ECONOMIST DIRECTORATE
Chief Economist (G3), C. Riley
Economist (G6), R. Davies

LOCAL DEVELOPMENT GROUP
Deputy Secretary (G2), C. J. S. Brearley, CB

SECRETARIAT
HEO, E. A. Carter

LOCAL GOVERNMENT FINANCE POLICY DIRECTORATE
Director, Local Government Finance Policy (G3), N. Kinghan
Heads of Divisions (G5), Miss L. F. Bell; R. J. Gibson; M. J. C. Faulkner; Mrs P. Peneck; Dr C. Myerscough

LOCAL GOVERNMENT DIRECTORATE
Director (G3), Mrs L. A. Heath
Heads of Divisions (G5), M. H. Coulshed; P. Rowsell; J. R. Footit

REGENERATION DIRECTORATE
Director (G3), M. B. Gahagan
Heads of Divisions (G5), J. Jacobs; G. Lanfer; D. Liston-Jones; (G6), I. Nicol

PRIVATE FINANCE UNIT
Head of Unit (G5), J. McCarthy

LEGAL
Solicitor and Legal Adviser (G2), Mrs M. A. Morgan, CB
Deputy Solicitors (G3), A. D. Roberts; Ms S. D. Unerman; P. J. Szell
Assistant Solicitors (G5), J. L. Comber; I. D. Day; Mrs S. Headley; Mrs P. J. Conlon; Mrs G. Hedley-Dent; D. W. Jordan; Miss D. C. S. Phillips; Ms A. Brett-Holt; D. J. Noble

OFFICE OF THE CHIEF SCIENTIST
Chief Scientist (G3), Dr D. J. Fisk
Head of Division (G5), Dr A. J. Apling

ENVIRONMENT PROTECTION
Senior Director (G2), Miss D. A. Nichols

ENVIRONMENT AND INTERNATIONAL DIRECTORATE
Under-Secretary (G3), Dr D. J. Fisk
Heads of Divisions (G5), R. Mills; C. Whaley; Dr P. Hinchcliffe; Dr S. Brown; P. F. Unwin

ENVIRONMENT PROTECTION STATEGY AND WASTES DIRECTORATE
Under-Secretary (G3), P. J. Britton
Heads of Divisions (G5), Mrs L. A. C. Simcock; Mrs H. C. Hillier; B. Glicksman; J. Stevens; R. Wilson; J. Adams

WATER AND LAND DIRECTORATE
Director (G3), N. W. Summerton
Heads of Divisions (G5), A. J. C. Simcock; Dr N. R. Williams; P. Bristow

Drinking Water Inspectorate
Grade 5, M. J. Rouse

ENVIRONMENTAL AND ENERGY MANAGEMENT
DIRECTORATE
Under-Secretary (G3), J. Hobson
Heads of Divisions (G5), A. K. Galloway; Mrs G. Hackman;
H. Cleary
Grade 6, Dr A. Vincent

REGIONAL OFFICES
— *see* pages 302–3

EXECUTIVE AGENCIES
BUILDING RESEARCH ESTABLISHMENT
Garston, Watford, Herts WD2 7JR
Tel 01923-894040

The BRE carries out research and provides advice on the design, construction and performance of buildings, and supports government departments in their related responsibilities. The BRE is due to be privatized by February 1997.
Chief Executive (G3), R. G. Courtney
Deputy Chief Executive and Group Director (G4),
N. O. Milbank
Directors of Groups (G5), Dr V. H. C. Crisp; Dr A. B. Birtles;
R. Driscoll; M. Shaw
Director and Privatization Co-ordinator (G4), Dr W. D.
Woolley
Finance Director (G5), J. Horan
Personnel Director (G6), Mrs A. Elkeles

ORDNANCE SURVEY
— *see* page 331

PLANNING INSPECTORATE
Tollgate House, Houlton Street, Bristol BS2 9DJ
Tel 0117-987 8927

The Inspectorate is responsible for casework involving planning, housing, roads, environmental and related legislation. It is a joint executive agency of the Department of the Environment and the Welsh Office.
Chief Executive and Chief Planning Inspector (G3), C. Shepley
Deputy Chief Planning Inspector (G4), J. Greenfield
Assistant Chief Planning Inspectors (G5), R. E. Wilson; Mrs
S. Bruton; J. T. Graham; D. E. John
Director of Planning Appeals (G5), Ms S. Carter
Director of Finance and Management Services (G5), M. Brasher

QUEEN ELIZABETH II CONFERENCE CENTRE
Broad Sanctuary, London SW1P 3EE
Tel 0171-798 4010

The Centre provides conference and banqueting facilities for both private sector and government use.
Chief Executive (G5), M. C. Buck

THE ENVIRONMENT AGENCY
Hampton House, 20 Albert Embankment, London SE1 7TJ
Tel 0171-820 5012
Rio House, Waterside Drive, Aztec West, Almondsbury,
Bristol BS12 4UD
Tel 01454-624400

The Environment Agency came into being on 1 April 1996 under the Environment Act 1995. It brings together the work formerly undertaken by the National Rivers Authority, HM Inspectorate of Pollution, the waste regulation authorities and some technical units of the Department of the Environment. The Agency is responsible for pollution prevention and control in England and Wales, and for the management and use of water resources, including flood defences, fisheries and navigation. It has head offices in London and Bristol and eight regional offices which are mainly concerned with operational activities.

THE BOARD
Chairman, The Lord de Ramsey
Members, P. Burnham; Prof. R. Edwards; I. Farookhi;
E. Gallagher; Sir Richard George; N. Haigh, OBE;
C. Hampson, CBE; J. Harman; Mrs K. Morgan; J. Norris;
D. Osborn; Dr A. Powell; T. Rodgers; Mrs J. Wykes

THE EXECUTIVE
Chief Executive, E. Gallagher
Director of Finance, N. Reader
Director of Personnel, G. Duncan
Director of Pollution Prevention and Control, D. Slater
Director of Water Management, G. Mance
Director of Operations, A. Robertson
Director of Public Affairs, M. Wilson
Director of Legal Services, R. Navarro
Chief Scientist, J. Pentreath

ROYAL COMMISSION ON
ENVIRONMENTAL POLLUTION
Church House, Great Smith Street, London SW1P 3BZ
Tel 0171-276 2080

The Commission was set up in 1970 to advise on matters, both national and international, concerning the pollution of the environment; on the adequacy of research in this field; and the future possibilities of danger to the environment.
Chairman, Sir John Houghton, CBE, FRS
Members, Sir Geoffrey Allen, FRS; Revd Prof. M. C. Banner;
Prof. G.S. Boulton, FRS, FRSE; Prof. C. E. D. Chilvers;
Prof. R. Clift, OBE, FENG.; Dr P. Doyle, CBE, FRSE;
J. Flemming; Sir Martin Holdgate, CB; Prof. R. Macrory;
Prof. M. G. Marmot, PH.D.; Prof. J. G. Morris, CBE, FRS;
Dr Penelope A. Rowlatt; The Earl of Selborne, KBE, FRS
Secretary, D. R. Lewis

EQUAL OPPORTUNITIES COMMISSION
Overseas House, Quay Street, Manchester M3 3HN
Tel 0161-833 9244

Press Office, 36 Broadway, London SW1H 0XH. Tel: 0171-222 1110
Other Offices, Stock Exchange House, 7 Nelson Mandela Place, Glasgow G2 1QW. Tel: 0141-248 5833; Caerwys House, Windsor Place, Cardiff. Tel: 01222-343552

The Commission was set up by Parliament in 1975 as a result of the passing of the Sex Discrimination Act. It works towards the elimination of discrimination on the grounds of sex or marital status and to promote equality of opportunity between men and women generally. It is responsible to the Department for Education and Employment.
Chairwoman (£45,320), Ms K. Bahl
Deputy Chairwomen, Lady (Diana) Brittan, CBE; Mrs E.
Hodder
Members, Ms A. Gibson; Ms C. Wells, OBE; P. Smith;
Ms M. Berg; R. K.Fleeman; R. Grayson; Dr J. Stringer;
Ms E. Symons; Prof. T. Rees; Ms G. James
Chief Executive, P. Naish

EQUAL OPPORTUNITIES COMMISSION FOR NORTHERN IRELAND
Chamber of Commerce House, 22 Great Victoria Street, Belfast BT2 7BA
Tel 01232-242752
Chair and Chief Executive, Mrs J. Smyth

EXCHEQUER AND AUDIT DEPARTMENT
— *see* National Audit Office

ECGD (EXPORT CREDITS GUARANTEE DEPARTMENT)
PO Box 2200, 2 Exchange Tower, Harbour Exchange Square, London E14 9GS
Tel 0171-512 7000

ECGD (Export Credits Guarantee Department), the official export credit insurer, is a separate government department responsible to the President of the Board of Trade and functions under the Export and Investment Guarantees Act 1991. This enables ECGD to facilitate UK exports by making available export credit insurance to British firms engaged in selling overseas and to guarantee repayment to banks in Britain providing finance for export credit for goods sold on credit terms of two years or more. The Act also empowers ECGD to insure British private investment overseas against political risks such as war, expropriation and restrictions on remittances.
Chief Executive, W. B. Willott, CB
Group Directors (G3), V. P. Lunn-Rockliffe (*Asset Management*); J. R. Weiss (*Underwriting*); T. M. Jaffray (*Resource Management*)

DIVISIONS
Head, Finance (G5), J. C. W. Croall
Head, Central Services (G5), P. J. Callaghan
Head, Underwriting Divisions (G5), M. Lemmon (*Division 1*); M. D. Pentecost (*Division 3*); Mrs M. E. Maddox (*Division 4*); S. R. Dodgson (*Division 5*); C. J. Leeds (*Division 6*)
Head, Office of the General Counsel (G5), R. G. Elden
Head, International Debt (G5), A. Steele
Head, Claims (G5), R. F. Lethbridge
Head, Treasury Management (G5), J. S. Snowdon
Head, Risk Management (G5), P. J. Radford
Head, Chief Executive's Division (G5), R. Gotts
Head, IT Services (G6), E. J. Walsby
Head, Internal Audit (G6), G. Cassell
Head, Operational Research (G6), Ms R. Kaufman

EXPORT GUARANTEES ADVISORY COUNCIL
Chairman, R. T. Fox, CBE
Other Members, B. P. Dewe Mathews, CBE, TD; T. M. Evans, CBE; Sir Frank Lampl; G. W. Lynch; J. W. Melbourn, CBE; D. B. Newlands; Sir Derek Thomas, KCMG; The Viscount Weir

OFFICE OF FAIR TRADING
Field House, Bream's Buildings, London EC4A 1PR
Tel 0171-242 2858

The Office of Fair Trading is a non-ministerial government department headed by the Director-General of Fair Trading. It keeps commercial activities in the UK under review and seeks to protect consumers against unfair trading practices. The Director-General's consumer protection duties under the Fair Trading Act 1973, together with his responsibilities under the Consumer Credit Act 1974, the Estate Agents Act 1979, the Control of Misleading Advertisements Regulations 1988, and the Unfair Terms in Consumer Contracts Regulations 1994, are administered by the Office's Consumer Affairs Division. The Competition Policy Division is concerned with monopolies and mergers (under the Fair Trading Act 1973), and the Director-General's other responsibilities for competition matters, including those under the Restrictive Trade Practices Act 1976, the Resale Prices Act 1976, the Competition Act 1980, the Financial Services Act 1986 and the Broadcasting Act 1990. The Office is the UK competent authority on the application of the European Commission's competition rules, and also liaises with the Commission on consumer protection initiatives.
Director-General, J. Bridgeman
Deputy Director-General, J. W. Preston, CB

CONSUMER AFFAIRS DIVISION
Director (G3), G. Horton
Assistant Directors (G5), P. Casey; R. Watson; M. Graham

COMPETITION POLICY DIVISION
Director (G3), Dr M. Howe, CB
Assistant Directors (G5), A. J. White; H. L. Emden; E. L. Whitehorn; S. Wood; M. Parr

LEGAL DIVISION
Director (G3), Miss P. Edwards
Assistant Directors (G5), M. A. Khan; P. T. Rostron
Establishment and Finance Officer (G5), Miss C. Banks
Chief Information Officer (G6), D. Hill

FOREIGN AND COMMONWEALTH OFFICE
Downing Street, London SW1A 2AL
Tel 0171-270 3000

The Foreign and Commonwealth Office provides, mainly through diplomatic missions, the means of communication between the British Government and other governments and international governmental organizations for the discussion and negotiation of all matters falling within the field of international relations. It is responsible for alerting the British Government to the implications of developments overseas; for protecting British interests overseas; for protecting British citizens abroad; for explaining British policies to, and cultivating friendly relations with, governments overseas; and for the discharge of British responsibilities to the dependent territories.

Secretary of State, The Rt. Hon. Malcolm Rifkind, QC, MP
Principal Private Secretary, W. G. Ehrman
Private Secretaries, D. J. Chilcott; S. J. Sharpe
Special Advisers, C. Blunt; G. Carter
Minister of State (Minister for Overseas Development), The Baroness Chalker of Wallasey, PC
Private Secretary, R. Calvert
Parliamentary Private Secretary, A. Hargreaves, MP
Ministers of State, David Davis, MP (*Minister for Europe*); The Rt. Hon. Jeremy Hanley, MP; Sir Nicholas Bonsor, Bt., MP
Private Secretaries, M. Tatham; J. Slater; T. Barrow
Parliamentary Under-Secretary of State, Dr Liam Fox, MP
Parliamentary Relations Unit, E. Jenkinson (*Head*); A. Mehmet, MVO (*Deputy Head and Parliamentary Clerk*)
Permanent Under-Secretary of State and Head of the Diplomatic Service, Sir John Coles, KCMG
Private Secretary, J. King

Deputy Under-Secretaries, J. R. Young, CMG (*Chief Clerk*); P. Lever, CMG (*Economic Director*); J. Q. Greenstock, CMG (*Political Director*); A. Galsworthy; A. Burns, CMG; J. Rollo
Legal Adviser, Sir Franklin Berman, KCMG, QC
Deputy Political Director and UK Perm. Rep. on the Council of WEU, E. Jones Parry
Director of Information Systems, R. Dibble
Principal Finance Officer and Chief Inspector, K. R. Tebbit
Assistant Under-Secretaries, S. J. L. Wright; J. R. de Fonblanque; D. J. M. Dain; C. Battiscombe, CMG; W. Marsden, CMG; P. J. Torry; F. F. Mingay, CMG; R. H. Smith; F. N. Richards, CVO, CMG; R. Dales; G. Fry; A. Hunt, CMG; J. A. Shepherd, CMG
HM Vice-Marshal of the Diplomatic Corps, P. S. Astley, LVO

HEADS OF DEPARTMENTS (DS4)

*Aid Policy Department, S. Chakrabarti
Aviation and Maritime Department, R. A. Kealy
British Diplomatic Spouses Association, Mrs C. Young
Central European Department, H. Pearce
Commonwealth Co-ordination Department, D. A. Broad
Commonwealth Foreign and Security Policy Unit, Ms A. Pringle
Conference Unit, M. Dalton
Consular Division, S. F. Howarth
Cultural Relations Department, A. D. Sprake
Counter Terrorism Policy Department, T. Fean
Eastern Adriatic Unit, N. K. Darroch
Eastern Department, R. D. Wilkinson
*Economic Advisers Department, J. Rollo
*Economic Relations Department, N. Westcott
Engineering Services, I. Whitehead
Environment, Science and Energy Department, D. E. Lyscom
Equatorial Africa Department, Ms A. Grant
European Community Department (External), R. Stagg
European Community Department (Internal), A. J. Cary
Far Eastern and Pacific Department, D. Coates
Financial Compliance Unit, M. Mayhew
Fundamental Expenditure Review Unit, R. Brinkley
Home Estate Department, D. C. Brown, CMG
Hong Kong Department, S. L. Cowper Coles
Honours Unit, R. M. Sands
Human Rights Policy Unit, R. P. Nash
Information Department, P. J. Dun
Information Systems Department, P. McDermott
Internal Audit, R. Elias
Joint Assistance Unit (Central Europe), S. Laing
Joint Assistance Unit (Eastern Europe), M. McCulloch
†*Joint Export Promotion Directorate,* A. Hunt
Latin America Department, H. Hogger
Library and Records Department, S. I. Soutar
*Management Consultancy and Inspection Department, S. R. H. Pease
Medical and Welfare Unit, Miss D. M. Symes, OBE
Middle East Department, N. W. Browne
Migration and Visa Department, M. E. Frost
National Audit Office, R. Burwood
Near East and North Africa Department, P. W. Ford
News Department, N. E. Sheinwald
Non-Proliferation Department, B. Cleghorn
North America Department, P. J. Priestley
OSCE and Council of Europe, C. A. Munro
Overseas Estate Department, M. H. R. Bertram, CBE
Overseas Inspectorate, K. R. Tebbit (*Chief Inspector and Principal Finance Officer*)

Overseas Police Adviser, L. Grundy (*Senior Police Adviser*)
Permanent Under-Secretary's Department, P. January
Personnel Management Department, P. R. Sizeland
Personnel Policy Unit, Ms P. Major
Personnel Services Department, G. G. Wetherell
Policy Planning Staff, Miss A. M. Leslie
PROSPER, C. J. Edgerton, OBE
Protocol Department, R. S. Gorham (*First Assistant Marshal of the Diplomatic Corps*)
Purchasing Directorate, M. Gower
Republic of Ireland Department, D. A. Lamont
Research and Analysis Department, S. Jack
Resource and Finance Department, J. W. Thorp
Royal Matters Unit, B. Money
Security Department, T. Duggin
Security Policy Department, R. H. Gozney
Services, Planning and Resources Department, Mrs J. Link, LVO
South Asian Department, C. Elmes
South Atlantic and Antarctic Department, A. J. Longrigg
South-East Asian Department, N. J. Cox
Southern Africa Department, B. H. Dinwiddy
Southern European Department, H. B. Warren-Gash
Support Services Department, M. Carr
Training Department, I. W. Mackley
United Nations Department, Miss M. G. D. Evans, CMG
Western European Department, A. Layden
West Indian and Atlantic Department, C. Drace-Francis
Whitley Council, W. Evans

EXECUTIVE AGENCY

WILTON PARK CONFERENCE CENTRE
Wiston House, Steyning, W. Sussex BN44 3DZ
Tel 01903-815020

The Centre organizes international affairs conferences and is hired out to government departments and commercial users.
Chief Executive, R. Langhorne

THE SECRET INTELLIGENCE SERVICE (MI6)
Vauxhall Cross, PO Box 1300, London SE1 1BD

The Secret Intelligence Service produces secret intelligence in support of the Government's security, defence, foreign and economic policies. It was placed on a statutory footing by the Intelligence Services Act 1994. The Act also established an Intelligence Services Tribunal, which hears complaints made against the Service.
Director-General, Sir David Spedding, KCMG, CVO, OBE

GOVERNMENT COMMUNICATIONS HEADQUARTERS (GCHQ)
Priors Road, Cheltenham, Glos GL52 5AJ
Tel 01242-221491

GCHQ produces signal intelligence in support of the Government's security, defence, foreign and economic policies. It also provides advice and assistance to government departments and the armed forces on the security of their communications and information technology systems. It was placed on a statutory footing by the Intelligence Services Act 1994. The Act also established an Intelligence Services Tribunal, which hears complaints made against GCHQ.
Director, D. B. Omand

---

*Joint Foreign and Commonwealth Office/Overseas Development Administration department

†Joint Foreign and Commonwealth Office/Department of Trade and Industry directorate

CORPS OF QUEEN'S MESSENGERS
Support Services Department, Foreign and
Commonwealth Office, London SW1A 2AH
Tel 0171-270 2779

Superintendent of the Corps of Queen's Messengers,
Maj. I. G. M. Bamber
Queen's Messengers, Maj. J. E. A. Andre;
Cdr. D. H. Barraclough; Maj. A. N. D. Bols;
Lt.-Cdr. K. E. Brown; Lt.-Col. W. P. A. Bush;
Lt.-Col. M. B. de S. Clayton; Capt. G. Courtauld;
Maj. P. C. H. Dening-Smitherman;
Sqn. Ldr. J. S. Frizzell; Capt. N. C. E. Gardner;
Cdr. P. G. Gregson; Maj. D. A. Griffiths;
Wg Cdr. J. O. Jewiss; Lt.-Col. J. M. C. Kimmins;
Lt.-Col. R. C. Letchworth; Maj. D. R. Nevile;
Maj. K. J. Rowbottom; Maj. M. R. Senior;
Cdr. K. M. C. Simmons, AFC; Maj. P. M. O. Springfield;
Maj. J. S. Steele; Col. D. W. F. Taylor

FOREIGN COMPENSATION COMMISSION
Room 013, 4 Central Buildings, Matthew Parker Street,
London SW1H 9NL
Tel 0171-210 0400/5

The Commission was set up by the Foreign Compensation Act 1950 primarily to distribute, under Orders in
Council, funds received from other governments in
accordance with agreements to pay compensation for
expropriated British property and other losses sustained
by British nationals.
The Commission also has the duty of registering claims
for British-owned property in contemplation of agreements with other countries, and it has done so in seven
instances since 1950.
Chairman, A. W. E. Wheeler, CBE
Secretary, A. N. Grant

FORESTRY COMMISSION
231 Corstorphine Road, Edinburgh EH12 7AT
Tel 0131-334 0303

The Forestry Commission is the government department
responsible for forestry policy in Great Britain. It reports
directly to forestry ministers (i.e. the Secretary of State for
Scotland, who takes the lead role, the Minister of Agriculture, Fisheries and Food and the Secretary of State for
Wales), to whom it is responsible for advice on forestry
policy and for the implementation of that policy. There is a
statutorily-appointed Chairman and Board of Commissioners (four executive and seven non-executive) with
prescribed duties and powers.
The Commission's principal objectives are to protect
Britain's forests and woodlands; expand Britain's forest
area; enhance the economic value of the forest resources;
conserve and improve the biodiversity, landscape and
cultural heritage of forests and woodlands; develop opportunities for woodland recreation; and increase public
understanding of and community participation in forestry.
Forest Enterprise, a trading body operating as an executive
agency of the Commission, manages its forestry estate on a
multi-use basis.
Chairman (part-time) (£36,965), Sir Peter Hutchison, Bt.,
CBE
Director-General and Deputy Chairman (G2), D. J. Bills
Commissioner, Administration and Finance (G3), D. S. Grundy

Head of the Forestry Authority (G3), D. L. Foot
Secretary to the Commissioners (G5), T. J. D. Rollinson

FOREST ENTERPRISE, 231 Corstorphine Road, Edinburgh
EH12 7AT. Tel: 0131-334 0303. *Chief Executive (acting),*
G. M. Cowie

REGISTRY OF FRIENDLY SOCIETIES
15 Great Marlborough Street, London W1V 2LL
Tel 0171-437 9992

The Registry of Friendly Societies is a government
department serving three statutory bodies, the Building
Societies Commission, the Friendly Societies Commission, and the Central Office of the Registry of Friendly
Societies (together with the Assistant Registrar of Friendly
Societies for Scotland).
The Building Societies Commission was established by
the Building Societies Act 1986. The Commission is
responsible for the supervision of building societies and
administers the system of regulation. It also advises the
Treasury and other government departments on matters
relating to building societies.
The Friendly Societies Commission was established by
the Friendly Societies Act 1992. Its responsibilities for the
supervision of friendly societies parallel those of the
Building Societies Commission for building societies.
The Central Office of the Registry of Friendly Societies
provides a public registry for mutual organizations registered under the Building Societies Act 1986, Friendly
Societies Acts 1974 and 1992, and the Industrial and
Provident Societies Act 1965. It is responsible for the
supervision of friendly societies and credit unions, and
advises the Government on issues affecting those societies.

BUILDING SOCIETIES COMMISSION
Chairman, G. E. Fitchew
Deputy Chairman, M. Owen
Commissioners, J. M. Palmer; *T. F. Mathews, CBE;
*F. E. Worsley; *F. G. Sunderland; *N. Fox Bassett; *Sir
James Birrell
* part-time

FRIENDLY SOCIETIES COMMISSION
Chairman, D. W. Lee
Commissioners, F. da Rocha; *A. Wilson; *J. A. Geddes;
*P. E. Couse; *Dr J. Dine
* part-time

CENTRAL OFFICE
Chief Registrar, G. E. Fitchew
Assistant Registrars, A. J. Perrett; Ms S. Eden; D. A. W.
Stevens

THE REGISTRY
First Commissioner and Chief Registrar (G2), G. E. Fitchew

BUILDING SOCIETIES COMMISSION STAFF
Grade 3, M. Owen
Grade 4, J. M. Palmer
Grade 5, D. A. W. Stevens; W. Champion; M. Coombs;
E. Engstrom
Grade 6, N. F. Digance

FRIENDLY SOCIETIES COMMISSION STAFF
Grade 4, D. W. Lee
Grade 6, F. da Rocha

CENTRAL SERVICES STAFF
Legal Adviser (G4), A. J. Perrett
Establishment and Finance Officer (G5), J. Stevens

Legal Staff (G5), C. Gregory; *(G6)*, P. G. Ashcroft;
C. Stallard

REGISTRY OF FRIENDLY SOCIETIES, SCOTLAND
58 Frederick Street, Edinburgh EH2 1NB
Tel 0131-226 3224
Assistant Registrar (G5), J. L. J. Craig, WS

GAMING BOARD FOR GREAT BRITAIN
Berkshire House, 168–173 High Holborn, London
WC1V 7AA
Tel 0171-306 6200

The Board was established in 1968 and is responsible to the
Home Secretary. It is the regulatory body for casinos, bingo
clubs, gaming machines and the larger society and all local
authority lotteries in Great Britain. Its functions are to
ensure that those involved in organizing gaming and
lotteries are fit and proper to do so and to keep gaming free
from criminal infiltration; to ensure that gaming and
lotteries are run fairly and in accordance with the law; and
to advise the Home Secretary on developments in gaming
and lotteries so that the law can respond to change.
Chairman (part-time) (£33,995), Lady Littler
Secretary, T. Kavanagh

OFFICE OF GAS SUPPLY
Stockley House, 130 Wilton Road, London SW1V 1LQ
Tel 0171-828 0898

The Office of Gas Supply (Ofgas) is a regulatory body set
up under the Gas Act 1986. It is headed by the Director-
General of Gas Supply, who is independent of ministerial
control.
    The principal functions of Ofgas are to control British
Gas prices and levels of service; to protect the interests of
the gas consumer; and to facilitate the development of
competition in the gas market. Other functions are to grant
licences to gas suppliers and to investigate complaints.
Director-General, Ms C. Spottiswoode
Chief Economic Adviser, Dr Eileen Marshall
Legal Adviser, D. R. M. Long
Director, Public Affairs, C. Webb
Director, Consumer Affairs and Licensing, J. Golay
Director, Administration, R. Field

OFFICE OF GAS REGULATION NORTHERN IRELAND
Brookmount Buildings, 42 Fountain Street, Belfast BT1 5EE
Tel 01232-311575

OFGAS NI is the regulatory body for the gas industry in
Northern Ireland.
Director-General of Gas for Northern Ireland, D. McIldoon

GOVERNMENT ACTUARY'S DEPARTMENT
22 Kingsway, London WC2B 6LE
Tel 0171-211 2600

The Government Actuary provides a consulting service to
government departments, the public sector, and overseas
governments. The actuaries advise on social security
schemes and superannuation arrangements in the public

sector at home and abroad, on population and other
statistical studies, and on government supervision of
insurance companies and friendly societies.
Government Actuary, C. D. Daykin, CB
Directing Actuaries, D. G. Ballantine; D. H. Loades, CB; A. G.
Young
Chief Actuaries, E. I. Battersby; Ms W. M. Beaver; A. J.
Chamberlain; T. W. Hewitson; A. I. Johnston; D. Lewis;
J. C. A. Rathbone

GOVERNMENT HOSPITALITY FUND
8 Cleveland Row, London SW1A 1DH
Tel 0171-210 3000

The Government Hospitality Fund was instituted in 1908
for the purpose of organizing official hospitality on a
regular basis with a view to the promotion of international
goodwill. It is responsible to the Foreign and Commonwealth Office.
Minister in Charge, Sir Nicholas Bonsor, Bt., MP
Secretary, Col. T. Earl

GOVERNMENT OFFICES FOR THE REGIONS

The Government Offices for the Regions were established
in April 1994. They combine the former regional offices of
the Departments of the Environment, Trade and Industry,
Education and Employment, and Transport. The regional
directors are accountable to the Secretaries of State of all
four Departments. The offices' role is to promote a
coherent approach to competitiveness, sustainable economic development and regeneration using public and
private resources.
Central Unit, Room C10/19A, 2 Marsham Street, London
SW1P 3EB
Tel 0171-276 4629
Head of Central Unit (G3), G. Watson
Resources, Planning and Administration (G5), T. Abraham
Personnel Policy (G5), B. Hopson

EASTERN
Secretariat: Enterprise House, Vision Park, Histon,
Cambridge CB4 4DZ
Tel 01223-202065

Regional Director (G3), J. Turner
Directors (G5), C. Dunabin (*Housing, Environment and
Regeneration*); T. Bird (*Planning, Transport and Europe*);
M. Oldham (*Trade and Industry*); Mrs C. Hunter
(*Employment and Training*)

EAST MIDLANDS
Secretariat: The Belgrave Centre, Stanley Place, Talbot
Street, Nottingham NG1 5GG
Tel 0115-971 9971

Regional Director (G3), M. Lanyon
Directors (G4), D. Morrison (*Environment and Transport*);
(*G5*), M. Briggs (*Trade and Industry*); A. Davies
(*Employment and Training*)

LONDON
Secretariat: 10th Floor, Riverwalk House, 157–161
Millbank, London SW1P 4RR
Tel 0171-217 3456

Regional Director (G2), R. Young

Directors (*G3*), J. A. Owen (*Regeneration*); M. Lambirth (*Planning and Transport*); B. Glickman (*Skills Enterprise and Education*); (*G5*), Mrs J. Bridges (*Planning*); G. Emes (*Transport Assessment*); Mrs L. Meek (*Strategy and Co-ordination Unit*); (*G6*), A. Weeden (*Transport*)

MERSEYSIDE
Secretariat: Room 403, Graeme House, Derby Square, Liverpool L2 7SU
Tel 0151-224 6300

Regional Director (*G3*), J. Stoker
Directors (*G5*), I. Urqhart (*Skills and Enterprise*); S. Dunmore (*Regeneration, Transport and Planning*); Ms P. Jackson (*Competitiveness and Europe*)

NORTH-EAST
Secretariat: Room 404, Stangate House, 2 Groat Market, Newcastle upon Tyne NE1 1YN
Tel 0191-201 3300

Regional Director (*G3*), Ms P. Denham
Directors (*G5*), J. Darlington (*Planning, Environment and Transport*); Miss D. Caudle (*Regeneration and Housing*); A. Dell (*Competitiveness, Industry and Europe*); S. Geary (*Education Skills and Business Development*); (*G6*), Mrs D. Pearce (*Strategy and Resources*)

NORTH-WEST
Secretariat: 20th Floor, Sunley Tower, Piccadilly Plaza, Manchester M1 4BE
Tel 0161-952 4000

Regional Director (*G3*), Miss M. Neville-Rolfe
Directors, (*G5*), B. Isherwood (*Regeneration*); D. Higham (*Competitiveness*); P. Styche (*Infrastructure and Planning*); P. Keen (*Skills and Enterprise*); (*G6*), D. Duff (*TEC Operations and Finance*); D. Stewart (*Europe*)

SOUTH-EAST
Secretariat: 2nd Floor, Bridge House, 1 Walnut Tree Close, Guildford, Surrey GU1 4GA
Tel 01483-882481

Regional Director (*G3*), Mrs G. Ashmore
Directors (*G5*), G. B. Wilson (*Hants/IOW*); N. Wilson (*Berks/Oxon/Bucks*); J. Vaughan (*Kent*); E. Beston (*Surrey/E. and W. Sussex*); Mrs E. A. Baker (*Regional Strategy Team*)

SOUTH-WEST
Secretariat: 4th Floor, The Pithay, Bristol BS1 2PB
Tel 0117-900 1708

Regional Director (*G3*), B. H. Leonard
Directors (*G5*), S. McQuillin (*Devon and Cornwall*); M. Quinn (*Environment and Transport*); T. Shearer (*Education, Trade and Industry*); (*G6*), D. Way (*Strategy and Resources*)

WEST MIDLANDS
Secretariat: 6th Floor, 77 Paradise Circus, Queensway, Birmingham B1 2DT
Tel 0121-212 5000

Regional Director (*G3*), D. Ritchie
Directors (*G4*), Dr H. M. Sutton (*Trade, Industrial Development and Europe*); (*G5*), Mrs P. Holland (*Housing and Regeneration*); P. Langley (*Planning, Transport and Environment*); H. Tollyfield (*Education, Skills and Enterprise*); Mrs L. Eastwood (*Resource Management*)

YORKSHIRE AND HUMBERSIDE
Secretariat: PO Box 213, City House, New Station Street, Leeds LS1 4US
Tel 0113-280 0600

Regional Director (*G3*), J. Walker
Directors (*G4*), Ms S. Seymour (*Strategy and Europe*); (*G5*), I. Crowther (*Environment, Planning and Transport*); I. Kerry (*Regeneration*); G. Dyche (*Business, Enterprise and Skills*); (*G6*), N. Best (*Personnel and Resources*)

DEPARTMENT OF HEALTH
Richmond House, 79 Whitehall, London SW1A 2NS
Tel 0171-210 3000

The Department of Health is responsible for the provision of the National Health Service in England and for social care, including oversight of personal social services run by local authorities in England for children, the elderly, the infirm, the handicapped and other persons in need. It is responsible for health promotion and has functions relating to public and environmental health, food safety and nutrition. The Department is also responsible for the ambulance and emergency first aid services, under the Civil Defence Act 1948. The Department represents the UK at the European Union and other international organizations including the World Health Organization. It also supports UK-based healthcare and pharmaceutical industries.

Secretary of State for Health, The Rt. Hon. Stephen Dorrell, MP
  Principal Private Secretary, Ms C. Moriarty
  Private Secretaries, J. Holden; S. Gallagher
  Special Advisers, T. Hockley; T. Rycroft
  Parliamentary Private Secretary, D. Faber, MP
Minister of State, Gerald Malone, MP
  Private Secretary, Ms K. Fraser
  Parliamentary Private Secretary, N. Waterson, MP
Parliamentary Under-Secretaries of State, The Baroness Cumberlege, CBE; John Horam, MP; Simon Burns, MP
  Private Secretaries, Ms E. Woodeson;
  Mrs M. Weatherseed; A. Lapsley
Parliamentary Clerk, G. Wakeman
Permanent Secretary (*G1*), Sir Graham Hart, KCB
  Private Secretary, Dr M. Gray
Chief Medical Officer (*G1A*), Dr Sir Kenneth Calman, KCB
Chief Executive, NHS Executive (*G1A*), A. Langlands
Deputy Chief Medical Officer (*G2*), Dr J. S. Metters, CB

NATIONAL HEALTH SERVICE POLICY BOARD
Chairman, The Secretary of State for Health
Members, Gerald Malone, MP (*Minister of State*); The Baroness Cumberlege, CBE; J. Horam, MP; J. Bowis, OBE, MP (*Parliamentary Under-Secretaries*); Dr Sir Kenneth Calman, KCB (*Chief Medical Officer*); A. Langlands (*Chief Executive, NHS Executive*); Sir Graham Hart, KCB (*Permanent Secretary*); Mrs Y. Moores; B. Baker; Dr Sir Stuart Burgess, CBE; K. Ackroyd; Miss J. Trotter, OBE; J. Greetham, CBE; I. Mills; W. Wells; Prof. A. Breckenridge

PUBLIC HEALTH POLICY GROUP

HEALTH ASPECTS OF ENVIRONMENT AND FOOD DIVISION
Under-Secretary (*G3*), Dr E. Rubery
Head of Branches, Dr R. Skinner; Dr E. Smales; Mrs M. Fry; C. P. Kendall

SOCIAL CARE GROUP
Chief Social Services Inspector, Sir Herbert Laming, CBE
Head of Social Care Policy, T. R. H. Luce, CB
Deputy Chief Inspectors, D. Gilroy; Ms A. Nottage
Assistant Secretaries (*G5*), R. M. Orton; N. F. Duncan; D. P. Walden; Mrs E. Hunter-Johnston; R. Tyrrell

Assistant Chief Inspectors (HQ), J. Kennedy; F. Tolan; Mrs
W. Rose
Assistant Chief Inspectors (Regions), S. Allard; J. Cypher;
B. Riddell; A. Jones; D. G. Lambert; Mrs P. K. Hall;
C. P. Brearley; J. Fraser; Mrs L. Hoare; Ms J. Owen

HEALTH PROMOTION DIVISION
Under-Secretary (G3), G. J. F. Podger
Principal Medical Officer (G4), Dr D. McInnes
Assistant Secretaries (G5), J. F. Sharpe, CBE; Miss A. Mithani;
Ms L. Lockyer; K. J. Guinness

NURSING GROUP
Chief Nursing Officer/Director of Nursing (G3), Mrs
Y. Moores
Assistant Chief Nursing Officers (G4), Mrs P. Cantrill; Mrs G.
Stevens; *(G5)*, Dr G. Chapman; C. Butler

NHS EXECUTIVE
Quarry House, Quarry Hill, Leeds LS2 7UE
Tel 0113-254 5000

Chief Executive, A. Langlands
Director of Human and Corporate Resources, K. Jarrold
Director of Finance and Corporate Information, C. Reeves
Medical Director, Dr G. Winyard
Chief Nursing Officer, Mrs Y. Moores
Director of Research and Development, Prof. J. D. Swales
Director of Planning and Performance Management,
A. D. M. Liddell

PERSONNEL DIRECTORATE
Director of Human and Corporate Resources (G2), K. Jarrold

PERSONNEL DIVISION
Deputy Director (G3), M. Deegan
Under-Secretary (G3), R. M. Drury
Assistant Secretaries (G5), B. A. J. Bennett; Miss G. Newton;
Miss A. Simkins; Mrs E. Alkalifa

RESEARCH AND DEVELOPMENT DIVISION
Director of Research and Development, Prof. J. D. Swales
Deputy Director of Research Management (G4), Dr C.
Henshall
Assistant Secretaries (G5), Mrs J. Griffin; Dr P. Greenaway;
J. Ennis; Dr D. Gardiner
Senior Medical Officers (G5), Dr J. Toy; Dr S. Bannerjee; Dr
C. Law
Senior Principal Research Officers (G6), Ms A. Kauder;
Dr C. Davies
Nursing Officer (G6), Dr E. Meerabeau

HEALTH CARE DIRECTORATE
Deputy Chief Medical Officer (G2), Dr G. Winyard

PUBLIC HEALTH DIVISION
Grade 4, Dr T. Mann
Assistant Secretary (G5), P. Spellman
Senior Medical Officers (G5), Dr M. Charny; Dr I. Bowns;
Dr A. Lakhani; Dr J. Carpenter; Dr A. Burnett

MEDICAL EDUCATION, TRAINING AND STAFFING
DIVISION
Senior Principal Medical Officer (G3), J. R. W. Hangartner
Senior Medical Officers (G5), Dr R. Cairncross; Dr
C. Marvin; Dr S. Horsley
Assistant Secretaries (G5), S. D. Catling; T. Ashe;
R. Naysmith

PRIMARY CARE AND DENTAL SERVICES
Deputy Secretary (G2), A. D. M. Liddell

PRIMARY CARE DIVISION 2
Grade 4, J. A. Thompson
Senior Dental Officers, C. Audrey; K. A. Eaton; I. Cooper

DENTAL SERVICES BRANCH
Grade 4, J. A. Thompson
Head of Pharmaceutical and Optical Services (G5), G. Denham

OFFICE OF THE CHIEF DENTAL OFFICER
Chief Dental Officer, R. B. Mouatt
Dental Officer, A. J. Hawkes

OFFICE OF THE CHIEF PHARMACIST
Chief Pharmaceutical Officer (G4), B. H. Hartley

FINANCE AND PERFORMANCE DIRECTORATE
Director (G2), C. L. Reeves

FINANCE BRANCH
Under-Secretary (Health) (G3), A. B. Barton
Assistant Secretaries (G5), J. M. Brownlee; A. McNeil; R. J.
Tredgett; J. Stopes-Roe

FINANCE AND PERFORMANCE DIRECTORATE A
Deputy Director (G3), P. Garland
Heads of Branches (G5), H. Gwynn; A. Angilley; M. Sturges;
G. Hetherington; B. Derry; S. Bell

FINANCE AND PERFORMANCE DIVISION B
Deputy Director (G3), R. Douglas
Heads of Branches (G5), J. Tomlinson; S. Saunders;
M. Harris; D. J. Havelock

REGIONAL OFFICES
ANGLIA AND OXFORD, 6–12 Capital Drive, Linford
Wood, Milton Keynes MK14 6QP. *Chairman*, Sir Stuart
Burgess, CBE, PH.D., FRSC; *Regional Director*, Ms
B. Stocking
NORTHERN AND YORKSHIRE, John Snow House, Durham
University Science Park, Durham DH1 3YE. *Chairman*,
J. Greetham, CBE; *Regional Director*, Prof. L. Donaldson
NORTH THAMES, 40 Eastbourne Terrace, London W2 3QR.
Chairman, I. Mills; *Regional Director*, R. Kerr
NORTH WEST, 930–932 Birchwood Boulevard,
Millennium Park, Birchwood, Warrington WA3 7QN.
Chairman, Prof. A. Breckenridge; *Regional Director*,
R. Tinston
SOUTH AND WEST, Westward House, Lime Kiln Close,
Stoke Gifford, Bristol BS12 6SR. *Chairman*, Miss J.
Trotter, OBE; *Regional Director*, A. Laurance
SOUTH THAMES, 40 Eastbourne Terrace, London W2 3QR.
Chairman, W. Wells; *Regional Director*, C. Spry
TRENT, Fulwood House, Old Fulwood Road, Sheffield
S10 3TH. *Chairman*, K. Ackroyd, CBE; *Regional Director*,
N. McKay
WEST MIDLANDS, Arthur Thompson House, 146 Hagley
Road, Birmingham B16 9PA. *Chairman*, B. W. Baker;
Regional Director, B. Edwards, CBE

COMMISSIONING BOARD FOR HIGH SECURITY
PSYCHIATRIC SERVICES
NHS Executive North Thames Regional Office, 40
Eastbourne Terrace, London W2 3QR
Tel 0171-725 5662
Chairman, Mrs A.-M. Nelson
Director, R. Rowden

DEPARTMENTAL RESOURCES AND SERVICES GROUP
Deputy Secretary (G2), J. Pilling, CB

STATISTICS DIVISION
Director of Statistics (G3), Mrs R. J. Butler
Chief Statisticians (G5), R. K. Willmer; G. J. O. Phillpotts

DEPARTMENTAL MANAGEMENT
Principal Establishment Officer (G3), D. J. Clark
Assistant Secretaries (G5), Miss A. Stephenson; P. Allen;
J. E. Knight; Ms P. A. Stewart

INFORMATION SERVICES DIVISION
Head of Division (G4), Dr A. A. Holt
Heads of Branches (G5), J. Bilsby; Mrs L. Wishart; (*G6*),
Miss S. Blackburn; C. Horsey; Mrs R. Chinn; M.
Rainsford; (*G7*), Mrs J. Dainty

ECONOMICS AND OPERATIONAL RESEARCH DIVISION
(HEALTH)
Chief Economic Adviser (G3), C. H. Smee
Senior Economic Advisers (G5), Dr S. Harding; J. W. Hurst

INFORMATION DIVISION
Director of Information, Miss R. Christopherson
Deputy Directors, C. P. Wilson (*news*); Mrs A. Rea (*publicity*)

SOLICITOR'S OFFICE
Solicitor (G2), P. K. J. Thompson
Principal Assistant Solicitor (G3), Mrs G. S. Kerrigan

ADVISORY COMMITTEES

ADVISORY COMMITTEE ON THE MICROBIOLOGICAL
SAFETY OF FOOD, Room 601A, Skipton House, 80
London Road, London SE1 6LW. Tel: 0171-972 5049.
Chairman, Prof. D. Georgala
CLINICAL STANDARDS ADVISORY GROUP, Wellington
House, 133–155 Waterloo Road, London SE1 8UG. Tel:
0171-972 4926. *Chairman*, Prof. M. Harris
COMMITTEE ON THE SAFETY OF MEDICINES, Market
Towers, 1 Nine Elms Lane, London SW8 5NQ. Tel:
0171-273 0451. *Chairman*, Prof. M. D. Rawlins
MEDICINES COMMISSION, Market Towers, 1 Nine Elms
Lane, London SW8 5NQ. Tel: 0171-273 0365. *Chairman*,
Prof. D. Lawson, CBE, MD, FRCPED., FRCP(Glas.)

EXECUTIVE AGENCIES

MEDICINES CONTROL AGENCY
Market Towers, 1 Nine Elms Lane, London SW8 5NQ
Tel 0171-273 0000
The Agency controls medicines through licensing,
monitoring and inspection, and enforces safety standards.
Chief Executive, Dr K. H. Jones

MEDICAL DEVICES AGENCY
Hannibal House, Elephant and Castle, London SE1 6TE
Tel 0171-972 2000
The Agency safeguards the performance, quality and
safety of medical devices.
Director (G4), A. Kent

NHS ESTATES
1 Trevelyan Square, Boar Lane, Leeds LS1 6AE
Tel 0113-254 7000
The agency provides advice and support in the area of
healthcare estate functions to the NHS and the healthcare
industry.
Chief Executive (G3), J. C. Locke

NHS PENSIONS
Hesketh House, 200–220 Broadway, Fleetwood, Lancs
FY7 8LG
Tel 01253-774774
The agency administers the NHS occupational pension
scheme.
Chief Executive (G5), A. F. Cowan

SPECIAL HEALTH AUTHORITIES

ASHWORTH HOSPITAL, Parkbourn, Maghull, Merseyside
L31 1HW. Tel: 0151-473 0303. *Chief Nursing Officer*, Mrs J.
Miles
BROADMOOR HOSPITAL, Crowthorne, Berks RG45 7EG.
Tel: 01344-773111. *Chief Executive*, A. Franey
CENTRE FOR APPLIED MICROBIOLOGY AND RESEARCH,
Porton Down, Salisbury, Wilts SP4 0JG. Tel: 01980-
612100. *Director*, vacant
HEALTH EDUCATION AUTHORITY, Hamilton House,
Mabledon Place, London WC1H 9TX. Tel: 0171-383
3833. *Chairman*, A. Close; *Chief Executive*, S. Fortescue
NATIONAL BLOOD AUTHORITY, Oak House, Reeds
Crescent, Watford, Herts WD1 1QH. Tel: 01923-212121.
Chairman, Sir Colin Walker, OBE; *Chief Executive*, J. Adey
NHS LITIGATION AUTHORITY, 22–23 Blayds Yard,
Leeds LS1 4AD. Tel: 0113-244 6077. *Chairman*, Sir Bruce
Martin, QC
NHS SUPPLIES AUTHORITY, Apex Plaza, Forbury Road,
Reading, Berks RG1 1AX. Tel: 01734-595085. *Chairman*,
N. Ward; *National Director of Supplies*, T. Hunt, CBE
RAMPTON HOSPITAL, Retford, Notts DN22 0PD. Tel:
01777-248321. *Manager*, Mrs S. Foley

HEALTH AND SAFETY COMMISSION
Rose Court, 2 Southwark Bridge, London SE1 9HS
Tel 0171-717 6000

The Health and Safety Commission was created under the
Health and Safety at Work etc. Act 1974, with duties to
reform health and safety law, to propose new regulations,
and generally to promote the protection of people at work
and of the public from hazards arising from industrial and
commercial activity, including major industrial accidents
and the transportation of hazardous materials.

The Commission members are appointed by the
Secretary of State for the Environment, although the
Commission assists a number of Secretaries of State
concerned with aspects of its functions. It is made up of
representatives of employers, trades unions and local
authorities, and has a full-time chairman.

The Commission can appoint agents, and it works in
conjunction with local authorities who enforce the Act in
such premises as offices and warehouses.
Chairman, F. J. Davies, CBE
Members, R. Symons, CBE; E. Carrick; C. Chope, OBE; Dr
G. M. Schofield; A. Grant; Ms A. Scully, OBE; Ms C.
Atwell; Ms A. Gibson; Dr M. McKiernan
Secretary, T. A. Gates

HEALTH AND SAFETY EXECUTIVE
Rose Court, 2 Southwark Bridge, London SE1 9HS
Tel 0171-717 6000

The Health and Safety Executive is the Health and Safety
Commission's major instrument. Through its inspectorates it enforces health and safety law in the majority of

industrial premises, to protect people at work and the public. The Executive advises the Commission in its major task of laying down safety standards through regulations and practical guidance for many industrial processes, liaising as necessary with government departments and other institutions. The Executive is also the licensing authority for nuclear installations and the reporting officer on the severity of nuclear incidents in Britain. In carrying out its functions the Executive acts independently of the Government, guided only by the Commission as to general health and safety policy.

Director-General (G2), Miss J. H. Bacon, CB (*at G1A*)
Deputy Director-General (G2), D. C. T. Eves, CB (*HM Chief Inspector of Factories*)
Director, Field Operations Division (G3), Dr A. Ellis
Director, Nuclear Safety (G3), Dr S. A. Harbison
Director, Science and Technology (G3), Dr J. McQuaid
Director, Safety and Major Hazards Policy (G3), M. E. Addison
Director, Health Division (G3), Dr P. J. Graham
Director, Resources and Planning (G3), R. Hillier
Director, Offshore Safety (G3), R. S. Allison, CB

HIGHLANDS AND ISLANDS ENTERPRISE
Bridge House, 20 Bridge Street, Inverness IV1 1QR
Tel 01463-234171

Highlands and Islands Enterprise (HIE) was set up under the Enterprise and New Towns (Scotland) Act 1991. Its role is to design, direct and deliver enterprise development, training, environmental and social projects and services. HIE is made up of a strategic core body and ten Local Enterprise Companies (LECs) to which many of its individual functions are delegated. The LECs design and develop initiatives at local level covering a wide range of economic and community development, training and environmental improvements.
Chairman, F. Morrison, CBE
Chief Executive, I. A. Robertson, CBE

HISTORIC BUILDINGS AND MONUMENTS COMMISSION FOR ENGLAND (ENGLISH HERITAGE)
23 Savile Row, London W1X 1AB
Tel 0171-973 3000

Under the National Heritage Act 1983, the duties of the Commission are to secure the preservation of ancient monuments and historic buildings; to promote the preservation and enhancement of conservation areas; and to promote the public's enjoyment of, and advance their knowledge of, ancient monuments and historic buildings and their preservation. The Commission has advisory committees on historic buildings and areas, ancient monuments, cathedrals and churches, parks and gardens, and London. It is funded by the Department of National Heritage.
Chairman, Sir Jocelyn Stevens, CVO
Commissioners, HRH The Duke of Gloucester; The Lord Cavendish of Furness; Ms B. Cherry; Sir David Wilson; Mrs C. Lycett-Green; J. Seymour; G. Wilson; A. Fane; Lady Gass; Prof. E. Fernie, CBE; R. MacCormac; Ms K. McLeod; R. Morris, FSA
Chief Executive (acting), Ms J. Sharman

HISTORIC BUILDINGS COUNCIL FOR WALES
Brunel House, 2 Fitzalan Road, Cardiff CF2 1UY
Tel 01222-500200

The Council's function is to advise the Secretary of State for Wales on the built heritage through Cadw: Welsh Historic Monuments (*see* page 356), which is an executive agency within the Welsh Office.
Chairman, T. Lloyd, FSA
Members, W. Lindsay Evans; R. Haslam; Dr P. Morgan; Mrs S. Furse; Dr S. Unwin; Dr E. Wiliam
Secretary, R. W. Hughes

HISTORIC BUILDINGS COUNCIL FOR SCOTLAND
Longmore House, Salisbury Place, Edinburgh EH9 1SH
Tel 0131-668 8787

The Historic Buildings Council for Scotland is the advisory body to the Secretary of State for Scotland on matters related to buildings of special architectural or historical interest and in particular to proposals for awards by him of grants for the repair of buildings of outstanding architectural or historical interest or lying within outstanding conservation areas.
Chairman, Sir Raymond Johnstone, CBE
Members, R. Cairns; Sir Ilay Campbell, Bt.; M. Ellington; Dr J. Frew; Lady Jane Grosvenor; J. Hunter Blair; I. Hutchison, OBE; K. Martin; Miss G. Nayler; Revd C. Robertson; Mrs F. Walker
Secretary, Ms S. Adams

ROYAL COMMISSION ON THE HISTORICAL MONUMENTS OF ENGLAND
National Monuments Record Centre, Kemble Drive, Swindon SN2 2GZ
Tel 01793-414700
London Search Room: 55 Blandford Street, London W1H 3AF.
Tel: 0171-208 8200

The Royal Commission on the Historical Monuments of England was established in 1908. It is the national body of architectural and archaeological survey and record and manages England's public archive of heritage information, the National Monuments Record. It is funded by the Department of National Heritage.
Chairman, The Lord Faringdon
Commissioners, Prof. R. Bradley, FSA; D. J. Keene, PH.D.; Prof. G. I. Meirion-Jones, PH.D., FSA; Prof. A. C. Thomas, CBE, D.Litt., FSA; R. D. H. Gem, PH.D., FSA; T. R. M. Longman; R. A. Yorke; Miss A. Riches, FSA; Dr M. Airs, FSA; Prof. M. Fulford, PH.D., FSA; Dr M. Palmer, FSA; Miss A. Arrowsmith
Secretary, T. G. Hassall, FSA

ROYAL COMMISSION ON THE ANCIENT AND HISTORICAL MONUMENTS OF WALES

Crown Building, Plas Crug, Aberystwyth SY23 INJ
Tel 01970-621233

The Royal Commission was established in 1908 to make an inventory of the ancient and historical monuments of Wales and Monmouthshire. It is currently empowered by a royal warrant of 1992 to survey, record, publish and maintain a database of ancient and historical and maritime sites and structures, and landscapes in Wales. The Commission is funded by the Welsh Office and is also responsible for the National Monuments Record of Wales, which is open daily for public reference, for the supply of archaeological information to the Ordnance Survey, for the co-ordination of archaeological aerial photography in Wales, and for sponsorship of the regional Sites and Monuments Records.

Chairman, Prof. J. B. Smith
Commissioners, Prof. R. W. Brunskill, OBE, PH.D., FSA (*Vice-Chairman*); Prof. R. A. Griffiths, PH.D., D.Litt.; D. Gruffyd Jones; R. M. Haslam, FSA; Prof. G. B. D. Jones, D.Phil., FSA; Mrs A. Nicol; S. B. Smith; Prof. G. J. Wainwright, MBE, PH.D., FSA; E. Wiliam, PH.D., FSA
Secretary, P. R. White, FSA

ROYAL COMMISSION ON THE ANCIENT AND HISTORICAL MONUMENTS OF SCOTLAND

John Sinclair House, 16 Bernard Terrace, Edinburgh EH8 9NX
Tel 0131-662 1446

The Royal Commission was established in 1908 and is appointed to provide for the survey and recording of ancient and historical monuments connected with the culture, civilization and conditions of life of the people in Scotland from the earliest times. It is funded by the Scottish Office. The Commission compiles and maintains the National Monuments Record of Scotland as the national record of the archaeological and historical environment. The National Monuments Record is open for reference Monday–Thursday 9.30–4.30, Friday 9.30–4.

Chairman, Sir William Fraser, GCB, FRSE
Commissioners, Prof. J. M. Coles, PH.D., FBA; Prof. J. D. Dunbar-Nasmith, CBE, FRIBA; Prof. Rosemary Cramp, CBE, FSA; Prof. T. C. Smout, CBE, FRSE, FBA; The Hon. Lord Cullen; Dr Deborah Howard, FSA; Prof. R. A. Paxton, FRSE; Dr Barbara Crawford, FSA, FSA SCOT.; Miss A. Riches
Secretary, R. J. Mercer, FSA, FRSE

ANCIENT MONUMENTS BOARD FOR WALES

Brunel House, 2 Fitzalan Road, Cardiff CF2 IUY
Tel 01222-500200

The Ancient Monuments Board for Wales advises the Secretary of State for Wales on his statutory functions in respect of ancient monuments.

Chairman, Prof. R. R. Davies, CBE, D.Phil., FBA

Members, R. G. Keen; Mrs F. M. Lynch Llewellyn, FSA; Prof. W. H. Manning, PH.D., FSA; Prof. J. B. Smith; Prof. W. E. Davies, PH.D., FBA; M. J. Garner
Secretary, S. Morris

ANCIENT MONUMENTS BOARD FOR SCOTLAND

Longmore House, Salisbury Place, Edinburgh EH9 ISH
Tel 0131-668 8764

The Ancient Monuments Board for Scotland advises the Secretary of State for Scotland on the exercise of his functions, under the Ancient Monuments and Archaeological Areas Act 1979, of providing protection for monuments of national importance. Protection may be provided by including a monument in a statutory list of protected monuments, by acquisition, or by guardianship in which the Secretary of State assumes responsibility for maintenance.

Chairman, Prof. M. Lynch, PH.D., FRSE
Members, A. Wright; Mrs E. V. W. Proudfoot, FSA, FSA SCOT.; Mrs K. Dalyell, FSA SCOT.; J. H. A. Gerrard, FRSA, FSA SCOT.; P. Clarke; L. J. Masters, FSA; Dr Anna Ritchie, FSA, FSA SCOT.; R. D. Kernohan, OBE; Dr Janet Morgan, FSA SCOT.; Prof. C. D. Morris, FSA, FSA SCOT.; R. J. Mercer, FRSE, FSA, FSA SCOT.; W. D. H. Sellar, FSA SCOT.; B. Mackie; Miss L. M. Thoms, FSA SCOT.
Secretary, R. A. J. Dalziel
Assessor, D. J. Breeze, PH.D., FRSE, FSA SCOT.

HOME-GROWN CEREALS AUTHORITY

Hamlyn House, Highgate Hill, London N19 5PR
Tel 0171-263 3391

Set up under the Cereals Marketing Act 1965, the Authority consists of seven members representing UK cereal growers, seven representing dealers in, or processors of, grain and two independent members. The Authority's functions are to improve the production and marketing of UK-grown cereals and oilseeds through a research and development programme, to provide a market information service, to promote UK cereals in export markets and to support work at Food from Britain. The Authority also undertakes agency work for the Intervention Board in connection with the application in the UK of the Common Agricultural Policy for cereals.

Chairman, G. B. Nelson, CBE
Chief Executive, A. J. Williams

HOME OFFICE

50 Queen Anne's Gate, London SW1H 9AT
Tel 0171-273 4000

The Home Office deals with those internal affairs in England and Wales which have not been assigned to other government departments. The Home Secretary is particularly concerned with the administration of justice; criminal law; the treatment of offenders, including probation and the prison service; the police; immigration and nationality; passport policy matters; community relations; certain public safety matters; and fire and civil emergencies services. The Home Secretary personally is the link between The Queen and the public, and exercises certain powers on her behalf, including that of the Royal Pardon.

Other subjects dealt with include electoral arrangements; addresses and petitions to The Queen; ceremonial and formal business connected with honours; requests for extradition of criminals; scrutiny of local authority bye-laws; granting of licences for scientific procedures involving animals; cremations, burials and exhumations; firearms; dangerous drugs and poisons; general policy on laws relating to shops, liquor licensing, gaming and lotteries, and marriage; theatre and cinema licensing; and race relations policy.

The Home Secretary is also the link between the UK government and the governments of the Channel Islands and the Isle of Man.

Secretary of State for the Home Department, The Rt. Hon. Michael Howard, QC, MP
Principal Private Secretary (*SCS*), K. D. Sutton
Private Secretaries, Mrs M. K. Bramwell; C. Harnett; D. Redhouse
Special Adviser, P. Rock
Parliamentary Private Secretary, D. Lidington, MP
Ministers of State, The Rt. Hon. David Maclean, MP; Ann Widdecombe, MP; The Baroness Blatch, CBE, PC
Private Secretaries, Miss S. Gooch; A. E. Jones; J. Sedgwick
Special Adviser, Miss R. Whetstone
Parliamentary Private Secretary to Baroness Blatch and Mr Maclean, D. Evennett, MP
Parliamentary Under-Secretary of State, Timothy Kirkhope, MP
Private Secretary, G. Park
Parliamentary Under-Secretary of State, The Hon. Tom Sackville, MP
Private Secretary, Miss C. McCombie
Parliamentary Clerk, Mrs R. Robinson
Permanent Under-Secretary of State (*G1*), R. T. J. Wilson, CB
Private Secretary, Ms J. L. Hutcheon
Chief Medical Officer (*at Department of Health*), Dr Sir Kenneth Calman, KCB

CENTRAL SECRETARIAT

Head of Secretariat (*acting*) (*SCS*), Mrs M. Wooldridge

COMMUNICATION DIRECTORATE

Director, Communication (*SCS*), M. Granatt
Deputy Head of Communication (*Head of News*) (*SCS*), B. Butler
Head of Publicity and Corporate Services (*G6*), C. Skinner
Assistant Director, Co-ordination (*G7*), A. Underwood
Chief Press Officer (*G7*), B. McBride
Head of Information and Library Services (*G7*), P. Griffiths

CONSTITUTIONAL AND COMMUNITY POLICY DIRECTORATE

Director (*SCS*), Miss C. Sinclair
Heads of Units (*SCS*), Mrs G. Catto; R. Evans; M. Gillespie; S. B. Hickson

ANIMALS (SCIENTIFIC PROCEDURES) INSPECTORATE
Chief Inspector (*SCS*), Dr R. Watt
Superintendent Inspector (*SCS*), Dr J. Anderson
Inspectors (*G6*), Dr R. Curtis; Dr V. Navaratnam; D. Rutty; Dr R. South; Dr C. Wilkins

GAMING BOARD FOR GREAT BRITAIN
— *see* page 302

CORPORATE RESOURCES DIRECTORATE

Grenadier House, 99–105 Horseferry House, London SW1P 2DD
Tel 0171-273 4000
Clive House, Petty France, London SW1H 9HD
Tel 0171-273 4000
Director (*SCS*), Miss P. Drew
Heads of Units (*SCS*), Dr M. Allnutt; B. Caffarey; A. R. Edwards; S. Wharton
Senior Principals (*G6*), T. Cobley; J. Daly; D. Houghton; J. G. Jones; R. Jones; T. Lewis; D. Meakin

CRIMINAL POLICY DIRECTORATE

Director (*SCS*), J. Halliday, CB
Deputy Director (*SCS*), J. Lyon
Heads of Units (*SCS*), M. Boyle; R. Childs; I. Chisholm; Mrs F. Clarkson; E. Grant; A. Harding; P. Honour; Ms H. Jackson; N. Varney
Senior Principals (*G6*), Ms A. Fletcher; H. Marriage; A. Macfarlane

CENTRAL DRUGS PREVENTION UNIT
Horseferry House, Dean Ryle Street, London SW1P 2AW
Tel 0171-273 4000
Head of Unit (*G6*), A. Norbury

HOME OFFICE CRIME PREVENTION COLLEGE
The Hawkhills, Easingwold, York YO6 3EG
Tel 01347-825060
Director, J. Acton

HM INSPECTORATE OF PROBATION
Chief Inspector (*SCS*), G. W. Smith, CBE
Assistant Chief Inspector (*G6*), G. Childs

CRIMINAL INJURIES COMPENSATION AUTHORITY
— *see* page 292

FIRE AND EMERGENCY PLANNING DIRECTORATE

Horseferry House, Dean Ryle Street, London SW1P 2AW
Tel 0171-273 4000
50 Queen Anne's Gate, London SW1H 9AT
Tel 0171-273 4000
Director (*SCS*), Mrs S. Street
Heads of Units (*SCS*), E. Guy; Mrs V. Harris; Miss S. Paul; Dr D. Peace
Civil Emergencies Adviser, D. Bawtree, CB

HM FIRE SERVICE INSPECTORATE
HM Chief Inspector, B. T. A. Collins, OBE
HM Territorial Inspectors, D. McCallum, OBE; P. Morphew, QFSM; N. Musselwhite, CBE; G. P. Reid, QFSM; A. Rule, QFSM
Lay Inspector, P. Cummings
HM Inspectors, W. Ambalino; D. Berry; G. P. Bowles; S. D. Christian; M. T. Franklin; D. Kent; E. G. Pearn, QFSM; K. Phillips; R. M. Simpson, OBE; A. C. Wells, QFSM; D. Wright
Principal (*G7*), K. O'Sullivan

EMERGENCY PLANNING COLLEGE
The Hawkhills, Easingwold, Yorks YO6 3EG
Tel 01347-821406
Senior Principal (*G6*), A. R. Blackley
College Secretary (*G7*), A. Richmond

IMMIGRATION AND NATIONALITY DIRECTORATE, AND EU AND INTERNATIONAL UNIT

Lunar House, 40 Wellesley Road, Croydon, Surrey CR9 2BY
Tel 0181-686 0688
Apollo House, 36 Wellesley Road, Croydon, Surrey CR9 3RR
Tel 0181-686 0333
50 Queen Anne's Gate, London SW1H 9AT
Tel 0171-273 4000
India Buildings, 3rd Floor, Water Street, Liverpool L2 0QN
Tel 0151-227 3939

Director-General (SCS), T. Walker
Deputy Directors-General (SCS), A. R. Rawsthorne (*Policy*); T. Flesher (*Operations*)
Heads of Directorates (SCS), J. Acton; Miss V. M. Dews; E. B. Nicholls; Mrs E. C. L. Pallett; J. Potts; A. Walmsley; R. M. Whalley; R. G. Yates
Senior Principals (G6), P. Dawson; B. Downie; C. Saunders; G. Stadlen

IMMIGRATION SERVICE

Director (Ports) (SCS), T. Farrage
Deputy Directors (G6), G. Boiling, MBE; V. Hogg
Director (Enforcement) (SCS), D. Cooke
Deputy Director (G6), D. McDonough

EU AND INTERNATIONAL UNIT

Head of Unit (SCS), P. Edwards

LEGAL ADVISER'S BRANCH

Legal Adviser (SCS), D. E. J. Nissen
Deputy Legal Advisers (SCS), Mrs S. A. Evans; D. Seymour
Assistant Legal Advisers (SCS), R. J. Clayton; J. R. O'Meara; C. M. L. Osborne; S. A. Parker

ORGANIZED AND INTERNATIONAL CRIME DIRECTORATE

Director (SCS), J. Warne
Heads of Units (SCS), J. Duke-Evans; P. Wrench
Senior Principal (G6), J. Nicholson

NATIONAL CRIMINAL INTELLIGENCE SERVICE
— see page 376

INQUIRY INTO LEGISLATION AGAINST TERRORISM
Reviewer, The Lord Lloyd
SCS, A. Cory

PLANNING AND FINANCE DIRECTORATE

50 Queen Anne's Gate, London SW1H 9AT
Tel 0171-273 4000
Horseferry House, Dean Ryle Street, London SW1P 2AW
Tel 0171-273 4000

Director (SCS), S. Norris, CB
Heads of Units (SCS), R. Eagle; L. Haugh
Senior Principals (G6), P. Davies; B. Elliott; I. Gaskell; A. K. Holman; R. McBurney; Ms E. Sparrow

POLICE POLICY DIRECTORATE

Director (SCS), S. Boys Smith
Heads of Units (SCS), N. Benger; R. Fulton; Miss D. Loudon; C. Pelham; N. Sanderson
Senior Principals (G6), N. Burham; R. Ginman; Dr G. Laycock

NATIONAL DIRECTORATE OF POLICE TRAINING
National Director of Police Training, P. Ryan, QPM

Central Administration Unit
Senior Principal (G6), P. Curwen

POLICE STAFF COLLEGE
Bramshill House, Bramshill, Hook, Hants RG27 0JW
Tel 0125-126 2931
Head of Higher Training, Mrs S. Davies, QPM

POLICE INFORMATION TECHNOLOGY ORGANIZATION
Horseferry House, Dean Ryle Street, London SW1P 2AW
Tel 0171-273 4000

Chief Executive (SCS), Miss J. MacNaughton
Senior Managers (SCS), B. Buck; M. Goulding
Senior Principals (G6), M. Hart; J. Hamer; D. Rowe; Dr G. Turnbull

HENDON DATA CENTRE
Aerodrome Road, Colindale, London NW9 5LN
Tel 0181-200 2424

Head of Unit (G6), J. Ladley

POLICE SCIENTIFIC DEVELOPMENT BRANCH
Woodcock Hill, Sandridge, St Albans, Herts AL4 9HQ
Tel 01727-865051
Director (SCS), B. R. Coleman, OBE
Research Director (G6), Dr P. Young

Langhurst House, Langhurstwood Road, Nr Horsham, W. Sussex RH12 4WX
Tel 01403-255451
Head of Unit Langhurst (G6), Dr G. Thomas

HM INSPECTORATE OF CONSTABULARY

HM Chief Inspector of Constabulary (SCS), D. J. O'Dowd, CBE, QPM
HM Inspectors (SCS), D. Crompton, CBE, QPM; G. J. Dear, QPM; C. Smith, CBE, CVO, QPM; P. J. Winship, QPM; J. Stevens, QPM
Lay Inspectors, P. T. G. Hobbs; Dr A. Williams
Senior Principal (G6), L. Davidoff

METROPOLITAN POLICE COMMITTEE AND SECRETARIAT
Clive House, Petty France, London SW1H 9HD
Tel 0171-273 4000

Head of Secretariat (SCS), Mrs C. Crawford

RESEARCH AND STATISTICS DIRECTORATE

Director (SCS), C. Nuttall
Heads of Units (SCS), C. Lewis; D. Moxon; P. Wood
Senior Principals (G6), G. Barclay; Dr B. Butcher; Dr S. Field; P. Jordan; Mrs C. Lehman; Mrs P. Mayhew; R. Taylor; Ms J. Vennard; Mrs M. Wilkinson

PRISON SERVICE MONITORING UNIT

Head of Unit (SCS), R. Weatherill

HM INSPECTORATE OF PRISONS

HM Chief Inspector (SCS), Gen. Sir David Ramsbotham, GCB, CBE
HM Deputy Chief Inspector (SCS), C. Allen
HM Inspectors (Governor 1), R. Jacques; T. Wood

PRISONS OMBUDSMAN

— see page 334

PAROLE BOARD FOR ENGLAND AND WALES

— see pages 332–3

THE SECURITY SERVICE (MI5)

Thames House, PO Box 3255, London SWIP IAE

The Security Service was placed on a statutory footing by the Security Service Act 1989 and is headed by a director-general who is directly accountable to the Home Secretary. The function of the Service is the protection of national security, in particular against threats from espionage, terrorism and sabotage, from the activities of agents of foreign powers, and from actions intended to overthrow or undermine parliamentary democracy by political, industrial or violent means. It is also the Service's function to safeguard the economic well-being of the UK against threats posed by the actions or intentions of persons outside the British Islands. Under the Security Service Act 1996 the Service's role has been extended to support the police and customs in the prevention and detection of serious crime. Under the Intelligence Services Act 1994, the Intelligence and Security Committee of Parliamentarians was established to oversee the work of all three intelligence services. The Security Service Tribunal and Commissioner (*see* page 344) investigate complaints about the Service from the public.

Director-General, S. Lander

HM PRISON SERVICE

Cleland House, Page Street, London SWIP 4LN
Tel 0171-217 6000

An executive agency of the Home Office.

SALARIES 1996–7

Governor 1	£46,467–£48,025
Governor 2	£41,959–£43,206
Governor 3	£36,236–£36,566
Governor 4	£29,817–£31,974
Governor 5	£26,320–£28,639

THE PRISONS BOARD

Director-General (SCS), R. R. Tilt
Director of Personnel (SCS), D. Scott
Director of Finance (SCS), B. Landers
Director of Security and Programmes (SCS), A. J. Pearson
Directors of Operations (SCS), A. Papps (*North*); A. Walker (*South*); P. Wheatley (*Dispersals*)
Director of Services (SCS), H. Taylor
Director of Health Care (SCS), Dr M. Longfield
Non-Executive Members, F. W. Bentley; Sir Duncan Nichol, CBE

PRISON SERVICE HEADQUARTERS

Heads of Groups (SCS), R. Smith (*Custody*); W. J. Abbott (*Security*); I. Boon (*Pay and Industrial Relations*); K. Heal (*Programmes Policy*); Miss S. Paul (*Health Care Policy*); Mrs E. J. Grimsey (*Personnel Planning*); T. Wilson (*Contracts and Competitions*); J. Le Vay (*Planning*); P. Sleightholme (*Systems Strategy*); (*G6*), Mrs H. Bayne (*Lifer*); Mrs A. Nelson (*Prison Service Communications*); K. Lockyer (*Secretariat*)
Strategic Development Adviser (SMO), Dr L. Joyce
Heads of Services (Gov. 1), C. Davidson (*Training*); (*Gov. 3*), Mrs U. McCullom-Gordon (*Staff Care and Welfare*); (*SCS*), R. Haines (*Construction*); Miss L. Gill (*Prisoner Services*); (*G6*), vacant (*Office Services*); Mrs Y. Wilmott (*Nursing*); Dr C. McDougall (*Personnel*); J. Gunderson (*Prisoner Escorts and Custody*); S. Jenner (*Internal Audit*); J. Powls (*IT Services*); A. Pay (*Accounting*); (*G7*), T. Kelly (*Personnel Finance*); (*PMO*), Dr D. Howells (*Healthcare Professional Development*)
Chaplain-General and Archdeacon of the Prison Service, Ven. D. Fleming
Chief Education Adviser (G6), I. G. Benson
Chief Physical Education Adviser (G6), M. W. Denton

PRISON ENTERPRISE AND ACTIVITY SERVICES

Block A, Whitgift Centre, Wellesley Road, Croydon, Surrey CR9 3LY
Tel 0181-686 8710
Director (SCS), P. R. A. Fulton

SUPPLY AND TRANSPORT SERVICES

Crown House, 52 Elizabeth Street, Corby, Northants
Tel 01536-202101
Director (SCS), D. J. C. Kent

AREA MANAGERS

Directorate of Operations (North)
East Midlands (SCS), J. Blakey
Mercia (SCS), D. Curtis
Mersey and Manchester (SCS), R. Halward
North-East (SCS), R. Mitchell
North-West (SCS), D. I. Lockwood
Yorkshire (SCS), T. Bone

Directorate of Operations (South)
Central (SCS), J. Dring
Kent (SCS), T. Murtagh, OBE
London North and East Anglia (SCS), A. de Frisching
London South (SCS), P. J. Kitteridge
South Coast (SCS), J. Perriss
Wales and the West (SCS), J. May

PRISONS

ACKLINGTON, Morpeth, Northumberland NE65 9XF. *Governor,* I. Woods
ALBANY, Newport, Isle of Wight PO30 5RS. *Governor,* S. O'Neill
ALDINGTON, Ashford, Kent TN25 7BQ. *Governor,* D. A. Bratton
ASHWELL, Oakham, Leics LE15 7LS. *Governor,* C. Bushell
*ASKHAM GRANGE, Askham Richard, York YO2 3PT. *Governor,* H. E. Crew
BEDFORD, St Loyes Street, Bedford MK40 IHG. *Governor,* E. Willets
BELMARSH, Western Way, Thamesmead, London SE28 OEB. *Governor,* W. S. Duff
BIRMINGHAM, Winson Green Road, Birmingham B18 4AS. *Governor,* G. Gregory-Smith
BLAKENHURST (private prison), Hewell Lane, Redditch, Worcs B97 6QS. *Monitor,* P. J. Hanglin
BLANTYRE HOUSE, Goudhurst, Cranbrook, Kent TN17 2NH. *Governor,* B. Pollett
BLUNDESTON, Lowestoft, Suffolk NR32 5BG. *Governor,* S. Robinson
BRISTOL, Cambridge Road, Bristol BS7 8PS. *Governor,* R. D. Dixon
BRIXTON, PO Box 369, Jebb Avenue, London SW2 5XF. *Governor,* Dr A. Coyle
BROCKHILL, Redditch, Worcs B97 6RD. *Governor,* K. Naisbitt
BUCKLEY HALL (private prison), Buckley Road, Rochdale, Lancs OL12 9DP. *Monitor,* Miss V. Bird
BULLINGDON, Padrick Haugh Road, Arncott, Bicester, Oxon OX6 0PZ. *Governor,* Mrs S. E. Payne
*BULLWOOD HALL, High Road, Hockley, Essex SS5 4TE. *Governor,* Mrs E. Butler
CAMP HILL, Newport, Isle of Wight PO30 5PB. *Governor,* S. Moore
CANTERBURY, Longport, Canterbury, Kent CT1 IPJ. *Governor,* G. Davies
CARDIFF, Knox Road, Cardiff CF2 IUG. *Governor,* N. D. Clifford
CHANNINGS WOOD, Denbury, Newton Abbott, Devon TQ12 6DW. *Governor,* J. K. Petherick
CHELMSFORD, Springfield Road, Chelmsford, Essex CM2 6LQ. *Governor,* vacant

COLDINGLEY, Bisley, Woking, Surrey GU24 9EX. *Governor*,
J. Smith
*COOKHAM WOOD, Cookham Wood, Rochester, Kent
ME1 3LU. *Governor*, I. Smout
DARTMOOR, Princetown, Yelverton, Devon PL20 6RR.
Governor, J. Lawrence
DONCASTER (private prison), Off North Bridge,
Marshgate, Doncaster DN5 8UX. *Director*, K. Rogers
DORCHESTER, North Square, Dorchester, Dorset DT1 1JD.
Governor, R. Walker
DOWNVIEW, Sutton Lane, Sutton, Surrey SM2 5PD.
Governor, D. M. Lancaster
*DRAKE HALL, Eccleshall, Staffs ST21 6LQ. *Governor*,
G. Hughes
*DURHAM, Old Elvet, Durham DH1 3HU. *Governor*,
R. Mitchell
*EAST SUTTON PARK, Sutton Valence, Maidstone, Kent
ME17 3DF. *Governor*, Mrs C. J. Galbally
*ELMLEY, Church Road, Eastchurch, Sheerness, Kent
ME12 4DZ. *Governor*, A. Smith
ERLESTOKE HOUSE, Devizes, Wilts SN10 5TU. *Governor*,
vacant
EVERTHORPE, Brough, North Humberside HU15 1RB.
Governor, R. Smith
EXETER, New North Road, Exeter, Devon EX4 4EX.
Governor, T. C. H. Newth
FEATHERSTONE, New Road, Featherstone,
Wolverhampton WV10 7PU. *Governor*, C. Scott
FORD, Arundel, W. Sussex BN18 0BX. *Governor*,
D. A. Godfrey
FRANKLAND, Frankland, Brasside, Durham, DH1 5YD.
Governor, P. J. Leonard
FULL SUTTON, Full Sutton, York YO4 1PS. *Governor*,
J. W. Staples
GARTH, Ulnes Walton Lane, Leyland, Preston, Lancs
PR5 3NE. *Governor*, W. Rose-Quirie
GARTREE, Leicester Road, Market Harborough, Leics
LE16 7RP. *Governor*, R. J. Perry
GLOUCESTER, Barrack Square, Gloucester GL1 2JN.
Governor, R. Dempsey
GRENDON, Grendon Underwood, Aylesbury, Bucks
HP18 0TL. *Governor*, T. C. Newell
HASLAR, Dolphin Way, Gosport, Hants PO12 2AW.
Governor, I. Truffet
HAVERIGG, Haverigg Camp, Millom, Cumbria LA18 4NA.
Governor, B. Wilson
HEWELL GRANGE, Redditch, Worcs B97 6QQ. *Governor*,
D. W. Bamber
HIGHDOWN, Sutton Lane, Sutton, Surrey SM2 5PJ.
Governor, S. Pryor
HIGHPOINT, Stradishall, Newmarket, Suffolk CB8 9YG.
Governor, C. D. Sherwood
HINDLEY, Gibson Street, Bickershaw, Hindley, Wigan,
Lancs WN2 5TH. *Governor*, L. Lavender
HOLLESLEY BAY COLONY, Hollesley, Woodbridge,
Suffolk IP12 3JS. *Governor*, M. F. Clarke
*HOLLOWAY, Parkhurst Road, London N7 0NU. *Governor*,
M. Sheldrick
HOLME HOUSE, Holme House Road, Stockton-on-Tees,
Cleveland TS18 2QU. *Governor*, D. Roberts
HULL, Hedon Road, Hull, N. Humberside HU9 5LS.
Governor, M. Newell
KINGSTON, Milton Road, Portsmouth PO3 6AS. *Governor*,
J. R. Dovell
KIRKHAM, Preston, Lancs PR4 2RA. *Governor*, A. F. Jennings
KIRKLEVINGTON GRANGE, Yarm, Cleveland TS15 9PA.
Governor, Mrs P. Midgley
LANCASTER, The Castle, Lancaster LA1 1YL. *Governor*,
D. G. McNaughton

LATCHMERE HOUSE, Church Road, Ham Common,
Richmond, Surrey TW10 5HH. *Governor*, E. Butt
LEEDS, Armley, Leeds LS12 2TJ. *Governor*, A. J. Fitzpatrick
LEICESTER, Welford Road, Leicester LE2 7AJ. *Governor*,
M. Egan
LEWES, Brighton Road, Lewes, E. Sussex BN7 1EA.
Governor, J. F. Dixon
LEYHILL, Wotton-under-Edge, Glos GL12 8HL. *Governor*,
D. T. Williams
LINCOLN, Greetwell Road, Lincoln LN2 4BD. *Governor*,
D. Shaw
LINDHOLME, Bawtry Road, Hatfield, Woodhouse,
Doncaster DN7 6EE. *Governor*, M. Shann
LITTLEHEY, Perry, Huntingdon, Cambs PE18 0SR. *Governor*,
M. L. Knight
LIVERPOOL, 68 Hornby Road, Liverpool L9 3DF. *Governor*,
B. Duncan
LONG LARTIN, South Littleton, Evesham, Worcs
WR11 5TZ. *Governor*, J. Mullen
MAIDSTONE, County Road, Maidstone ME14 1UZ. *Governor*,
H. Bagshaw
MANCHESTER, Southall Street, Manchester M60 9AH.
Governor, P. Earnshaw
MOORLAND, Hatfield Woodhouse, Doncaster DN7 6BW.
Governor, C. R. Griffiths
MORTON HALL, Swinderby, Lincoln LN6 9PS. *Governor*,
S. G. Wagstaffe
THE MOUNT, Molyneaux Avenue, Bovingdon, Hemel
Hempstead HP3 0NZ. *Governor*, Mrs M. Donnelly
*NEW HALL, Dial Wood, Flockton, Wakefield, W. Yorks
WF4 4AX. *Governor*, D. England
NORTH SEA CAMP, Freiston, Boston, Lincs PE22 0QX.
Governor, M. A. Lewis
NORWICH, Mousehold, Norwich NR1 4LU. *Governor*,
N. Wall
NOTTINGHAM, Perry Road, Sherwood, Nottingham
NG5 3AG. *Governor*, P. J. Bennett
OXFORD, New Road, Oxford OX1 1LZ. *Governor*, Mrs S. E.
Payne
PARKHURST, Newport, Isle of Wight PO30 5NX. *Governor*,
D. M. Morrison
PENTONVILLE, Caledonian Road, London N7 8TT.
Governor, K. Brewer
PRESTON, 2 Ribbleton Lane, Preston, Lancs OR1 5AB.
Governor, R. J. Crouch
RANBY, Ranby, Retford, Notts DN22 8EU. *Governor*,
T. J. Williams
*RISLEY, Warrington Road, Risley, Warrington WA3 6BP.
Governor, vacant
ROCHESTER, Rochester, Kent ME1 3QS. *Governor*,
R. A. Chapman
RUDGATE, Wetherby, W. Yorks LS23 7AZ. *Governor*,
H. Jones
SEND, Ripley Road, Send, Woking, Surrey GU23 7LJ.
Governor, S. Guy-Gibbons
SHEPTON MALLET, Cornhill, Shepton Mallet, Somerset
BA4 5LU. *Governor*, P. O'Sullivan
SHREWSBURY, The Dana, Shrewsbury, Salop SY1 2HR.
Governor, K. Beaumont
STAFFORD, 54 Gaol Road, Stafford ST16 3AW. *Governor*,
R. Feeney
STANDFORD HILL, Church Road, Eastchurch, Sheerness,
Kent ME12 4AA. *Governor*, D. M. Twiner
STOCKEN, Stocken Hall Road, Stretton, Nr Oakham,
Leics LE15 7RD. *Governor*, D. Hall
STOKE HEATH, Market Drayton, Shropshire TF9 2JL.
Governor, J. Aldridge

---

*Women's establishments/establishments with units for women

*Styal, Wilmslow, Cheshire SK9 4HR. *Governor,*
M. Goodwin
Sudbury, Sudbury, Derbys DE6 5HW. *Governor,* P. E. Salter
Swaleside, Eastchurch, Isle of Sheppey, Kent ME12 4AX.
Governor, R. Tasker
Swansea, Oystermouth Road, Swansea SA1 2SR. *Governor,*
J. Heyes
Usk, 29 Maryport Street, Usk, Gwent NP5 1XP. *Governor,*
N. J. Evans
The Verne, Portland, Dorset DT5 1EQ. *Governor,*
T. M. Turner
Wakefield, Love Lane, Wakefield WF2 9AG. *Governor,*
R. Doughty
Wandsworth, PO Box 757, Heathfield Road, London
SW18 3HS. *Governor,* C. G. Clark, OBE
Wayland, Wayland, Griston, Thetford, Norfolk IP25 6RL.
Governor, M. Spurr
Wealstun, Wetherby, W. Yorks LS23 7AY. *Governor,*
G. Barnard
Wellingborough, Millers Park, Doddington Road,
Wellingborough, Northants NN8 2NH. *Governor,*
J. Whetton
Whatton, Whatton, Notts NG13 9FQ. *Governor,*
B. McCourt
Whitemoor, Longhill Road, March, Cambs PE15 0PR.
Governor, R. B. Clarke
Winchester, Romsey Road, Winchester, Hants
SO22 5DF. *Governor,* M. K. Pascoe
Woodhill, Tattenhoe Street, Milton Keynes MK4 4DA.
Governor, Ms M. Gorman
Wormwood Scrubs, PO Box 757, Du Cane Road,
London W12 0AE. *Governor,* J. F. Perris
Wymott, Moss Lane, Ulnes Walton, Leyland, Preston,
Lancs PR5 3LW. *Governor,* G. Brunskill

YOUNG OFFENDER INSTITUTIONS

Aylesbury, Bierton Road, Aylesbury, Bucks HP20 1EH.
Governor, N. Pascoe
Brinsford, New Road, Featherstone, Wolverhampton
WV10 7PY. *Governor,* B. Payling
*Bullwood Hall, High Road, Hockley, Essex SS5 4TE.
Governor, Mrs E. Butler
Castington, Morpeth, Northumberland NE65 9XF.
Governor, C. Harder
Deerbolt, Bowes Road, Barnard Castle, Co. Durham
DL12 9BG. *Governor,* P. Atkinson
Dover, The Citadel, Western Heights, Dover, Kent
CT17 9DR. *Governor,* B. W. Sutton
*Drake Hall, Eccleshall, Staffs ST21 6LQ. *Governor,*
G. Hughes
*East Sutton Park, Sutton Valence, Maidstone, Kent
ME17 3DF. *Governor,* Mrs C. J. Galbally
Eastwood Park, Falfield, Wotton-under-Edge, Glos
GL12 8DB. *Governor,* P. Winkley
Feltham, Bedfont Road, Feltham, Middx TW13 4ND.
Governor, I. Ward
Glen Parva, Tigers Road, Wigston, Leics LE8 2TN.
Governor, C. Williams
Guys Marsh, Shaftesbury, Dorset SP7 0AH. *Governor,*
R. Gaines
Hatfield, Hatfield, Doncaster DN7 6EL. *Governor,*
H. Jones
Hollesley Bay Colony, Hollesley, Woodbridge,
Suffolk IP12 3JS. *Governor,* M. F. Clarke
Huntercombe, Huntercombe Place, Nuffield, Henley-
on-Thames RG9 5SB. *Governor,* D. Strong
Lancaster Farms, Stone Row Head, off Quernmore
Road, Lancaster LA1 3QZ. *Governor,* D. J. Waplington

*Women's establishments/establishments with units for women

*New Hall, Dial Wood, Flockton, Wakefield WF4 4AX.
Governor, D. England
Northallerton, East Road, Northallerton, N. Yorks
DL6 1NW. *Governor,* D. P. G. Appleton
Onley, Willoughby, Rugby, Warks CV23 8AP. *Governor,*
J. N. Brooke
Portland, Easton, Portland, Dorset DT5 1DL. *Governor,*
D. Brisco
Prescoed, 29 Maryport Street, Usk NP4 0TD. *Governor,*
N. J. Evans
Stoke Heath, Market Drayton, Salop TF9 2JL. *Governor,*
J. Aldridge
*Styal, Wilmslow, Cheshire, SK9 4HR. *Governor,*
M. Goodwin
Swinfen Hall, Lichfield, Staffs WS14 9QS. *Governor,* J. P.
Francis
Thorn Cross, Arley Road, Appleton Thorn,
Warrington WA4 4RL. *Governor,* I. Windebank
Werrington, Stoke-on-Trent ST9 0DX. *Governor,*
B. Stanhope
Wetherby, York Road, Wetherby, W. Yorks LS22 5ED.
Governor, P. J. Atkinson

REMAND CENTRES

Brinsford, New Road, Featherstone, Wolverhampton
WV10 7PY. *Governor,* B. Payling
Cardiff, Knox Road, Cardiff CF2 1UG. *Governor,*
N. D. Clifford
Exeter, New North Road, Exeter, Devon EX4 4EX.
Governor, T. C. H. Newth
Feltham, Bedfont Road, Feltham, Middx TW13 4ND.
Governor, I. Ward
Glen Parva, Tigers Road, Wigston, Leics LE8 2TN.
Governor, C. Williams
Lancaster Farms, Stone Rowe Head, Off Quernmore
Road, Lancaster LA1 3QZ. *Governor,* D. J. Waplington
Low Newton, Brasside, Durham DH1 5SD. *Governor,*
vacant
Norwich, Mousehold, Norwich, Norfolk NR1 4LU.
Governor, N. Wall
Reading, Forbury Road, Reading, Berks RG1 3HY.
Governor, W. Payne
The Wolds (private remand prison), Everthorpe,
Brough, N. Humberside HU15 2JZ. *Director,* J. McDonnell

FIRE SERVICE COLLEGE
Moreton-in-Marsh, Glos GL56 0RH
Tel 01608-650831

An executive agency of the Home Office.
Chief Executive, N. K. Finlayson
Commandant, T. Glossop, QFSM
Dean, Dr R. Willis-Lee
Director of Development and Services (G7), Dr T. Jeans

FORENSIC SCIENCE SERVICE HEADQUARTERS
Metropolitan Police Forensic Science Laboratory, 109
Lambeth Road, London SE1 7LP
Tel 0171-230 1212
Priory House, Gooch Street North, Birmingham B5 6QQ
Tel 0121-607 6800

An executive agency of the Home Office.
Director-General (SCS), Dr J. Thompson
Director of Business Development (SCS), T. Howitt
Director of Finance (SCS), R. Anthony
Chief Scientist (G6), Dr. B. Bramley
Corporate Service Manager (G6), Dr W. D. Wilson
Director of Operations and Head of Personnel (G6),
M. Loveland
Director of Service (G6), Dr D. Werrett

UK PASSPORT AGENCY
Clive House, Petty France, London SW1H 9HD
Tel 0171-799 2728
An executive agency of the Home Office.
Chief Executive (SCS), D. Gatenby
Deputy Chief Executive and Director of Operations (G6),
T. Lonsdale
Director of Resources (G6), K. J. Sheehan
Director of Systems (G6), R. G. Le Marechal

HORSERACE TOTALISATOR BOARD
74 Upper Richmond Road, London SW15 2SU
Tel 0181-874 6411

The Horserace Totalisator Board was established by the
Betting, Gaming and Lotteries Act 1963, as successor to the
Racecourse Betting Control Board. Its function is to
operate totalisators on approved racecourses in Great
Britain, and it also provides on- and off-course cash and
credit offices. Under the Horserace Totalisator and Betting
Levy Board Act 1972, it is further empowered to offer bets
at starting price (or other bets at fixed odds) on any sporting
event. The chairman and members of the Board are
appointed by the Home Secretary.
Chairman (£95,000), The Lord Wyatt of Weeford (*until
April 1997*)
Chief Executive, B. McDonnell

HOUSING CORPORATION
149 Tottenham Court Road, London W1P 0BN
Tel 0171-393 2000

Established by Parliament in 1964, the Housing Corporation registers, promotes, funds and supervises housing
associations. The Corporation's duties were extended
under the provisions of the Housing Act 1988 to cover the
payment of capital and revenue grants to housing associations, advice for tenants interested in Tenants' Choice,
and the approval and revocation of potential new landlords
under this policy. The Corporation is funded by the
Department of the Environment.
There are over 2,200 registered associations in England
providing more than 600,000 homes for people in need of
housing. Housing associations are non-profit making
bodies run by voluntary committees.
Chairman, Sir Brian Pearse
Chief Executive, A. Mayer

HUMAN FERTILIZATION AND
EMBRYOLOGY AUTHORITY
Paxton House, 30 Artillery Lane, London E1 7LS
Tel 0171-377 5077

The Authority was established under the Human Fertilization and Embryology Act 1990. Its function is to license
persons carrying out any of the following activities: the
creation or use of embryos outside the body in the
provision of infertility treatment services; the use of
donated gametes in infertility treatment; the storage of
gametes or embryos; and research on human embryos. The
Authority also keeps under review information about
embryos and, when requested to do so, gives advice to the
Secretary of State for Health.
Chairman, Mrs R. Deech

Deputy Chairman, Lady (Diana) Brittan
Members, Prof. R. J. Berry; Mrs J. Denton; Ms E. Forgan;
D. Greggains; Mrs J. Harbison; Prof. S. Hillier; The
Most Revd R. Holloway; Prof. M. Johnson; R. Jones;
Miss P. Keith; Dr B. Lieberman; Mrs A. Mays; Dr
A. McLaren; Dr J. Naish; Prof. A. Nichol; Prof.
A. Templeton; Prof. Revd A. Thiselton; Ms
J. Tugendhat; J. Williams
Chief Executive, Mrs S. McCarthy

INDEPENDENT COMMISSION FOR POLICE
COMPLAINTS FOR NORTHERN IRELAND
Chamber of Commerce House, 22 Great Victoria Street,
Belfast BT2 7LP
Tel 01232-244821

The Independent Commission for Police Complaints was
established under the Police (Northern Ireland) Order
1987. It has powers to supervise the investigation of certain
categories of serious complaints, can direct that disciplinary charges be brought, and has oversight of the
informal resolution procedure for less serious complaints.
Chairman, J. Grew
Chief Executive, B. McClelland

INDEPENDENT REVIEW SERVICE FOR
THE SOCIAL FUND
4th Floor, Centre City Podium, 5 Hill Street,
Birmingham B5 4UB
Tel 0121-606 2100

The Social Fund Commissioner is appointed by the
Secretary of State for Social Security. The Commissioner
appoints Social Fund Inspectors, who provide an independent review of decisions made by Social Fund Officers in
the Benefits Agency of the Department of Social Security.
Social Fund Commissioner, J. Scampion

INDEPENDENT TELEVISION COMMISSION
33 Foley Street, London W1P 7LB
Tel 0171-255 3000

The Independent Television Commission replaced the
Independent Broadcasting Authority in 1991. The Com-
mission is responsible for licensing and regulating all
commercially funded television services broadcast from
the UK. Members are appointed by the Secretary of State
for National Heritage.
Chairman (£63,670), Sir George Russell, CBE
Deputy Chairman, Earl of Dalkeith
Members, R. Goddard; Mrs E. Wynne Jones; Dr J. Beynon,
FENG.; Ms J. Goffe; Dr Maria Moloney; J. Ranelagh; Dr
M. Shea
Chief Executive, P. Rogers
Secretary, M. Redley

INDUSTRIAL INJURIES ADVISORY COUNCIL
6th Floor, The Adelphi, 1–11 John Adam Street, London
WC2N 6HT
Tel 0171-962 8066

The Industrial Injuries Advisory Council is a statutory body under the Social Security Act 1975 which considers and advises the Secretary of State for Social Security on regulations and other questions relating to industrial injuries benefits or their administration.
Chairman, Prof. A. J. Newman Taylor, OBE, FRCP
Secretary, R. Wakely

BOARD OF INLAND REVENUE
Somerset House, London WC2R 1LB
Tel 0171-438 6420

The Board of Inland Revenue was constituted under the Inland Revenue Board Act 1849, by the consolidation of the Board of Excise and the Board of Stamps and Taxes. In 1909 the administration of excise duties was transferred to the Board of Customs. The Board of Inland Revenue administers and collects direct taxes – income tax, corporation tax, capital gains tax, inheritance tax, stamp duty, and petroleum revenue tax – and advises the Chancellor of the Exchequer on policy questions involving them.
The Department is organized into a series of accountable management units. The day-to-day operations in assessing and collecting tax and in providing internal support services are carried out by Executive Offices. The Department's Valuation Office is an executive agency responsible for providing valuation services for rating, council tax, Inland Revenue and other public sector purposes. In 1995–6 the Inland Revenue collected £97,000 million in tax.

THE BOARD
Chairman (*G1*), Sir Anthony Battishill, KCB
  Private Secretary, Miss S. Woollard
Deputy Chairmen (*G2*), S. C. T. Matheson, CB; C. W. Corlett, CB
Director-General (*G2*), G. H. Bush

DIVISIONS
Director, Personnel Division (*G3*), J. Gant
Director, Business and Management Services Division (*G3*), J. Yard
Director, Change Management Division and Self-Assessment Programme, D. A. Smith
Principal Finance Officer (*G3*), R. R. Martin
Director, Policy Co-ordination Unit, P. Lewis
Director, Business Operations Division (*G3*), M. A. Johns
Director, Quality Development Division (*G3*), K. V. Deacon
Director, Company Tax Division and Financial Institutions Division (*G3*), M. F. Cayley
Director, International Division (*G3*), I. Spence
Director, Business Profits Division (*G3*), E. J. Gribbon
Director, Personal Tax Division (*G3*), E. McGivern
Director, Capital and Valuation Division, and Savings and Investment Division (*G3*), B. A. Mace

EXECUTIVE OFFICES
ACCOUNTS OFFICE (CUMBERNAULD), Cumbernauld, Glasgow G70 5TR. *Controller*, A. Geddes, OBE

ACCOUNTS OFFICE (SHIPLEY), Shipley, Bradford, W. Yorks BD98 8AA. *Controller*, P. Clark, OBE

CAPITAL TAXES OFFICE
Ferrers House, PO Box 38, Castle Meadow Road, Nottingham NG2 1BB
Controller, B. D. Kent

CAPITAL TAXES OFFICE (SCOTLAND)
Mulberry House, 16 Picardy Place, Edinburgh EH1 3NB
Registrar, I. Fraser

CORPORATE COMMUNICATIONS OFFICE
North-West Wing, Bush House, Aldwych, London WC2B 4PP
Controller, R. N. Hooper

ENFORCEMENT OFFICE
Durrington Bridge House, Barrington Road, Worthing, W. Sussex BN12 4SE
Controller, Mrs S. F. Walsh

FINANCIAL ACCOUNTING OFFICE
South Block, Barrington Road, Worthing, W. Sussex BN12 4XH
Controller, J. D. Easey

FINANCIAL INTERMEDIARIES AND CLAIMS OFFICE
St John's House, Merton Road, Bootle L26 9BB
Controller, D. A. Hartnett

INTERNAL AUDIT OFFICE
North-West Wing, Bush House, Aldwych, London WC2B 4PP
Controller, N. R. Buckley

LARGE GROUP OFFICE
New Court, Carey Street, London WC2A 2JE
Controller, R. A. J. Jones

OIL TAXATION OFFICE
Melbourne House, Aldwych, London WC2B 4LL
Controller, R. C. Mountain

PENSION SCHEMES OFFICE
Yorke House, PO Box 62, Castle Meadow Road, Nottingham NG2 1BG
Controller, S. J. McManus

SOLICITOR'S OFFICE
East Wing, Somerset House, London WC2R 1LB
Solicitor (*G2*), B. E. Cleave, CB

SOLICITOR'S OFFICE (SCOTLAND)
80 Lauriston Place, Edinburgh EH3 9SL
Solicitor, I. K. Laing

SPECIAL COMPLIANCE OFFICE
Angel Court, 199 Borough High Street, London SE1 1HZ
Controller, F. J. Brannigan

STAMP OFFICE
South-West Wing, Bush House, Strand, London WC2B 4QN
Controller, K. S. Hodgson

STATISTICS AND ECONOMICS OFFICE
West Wing, Somerset House, Strand, London WC2R 1LB
Director, R. Ward

TRAINING OFFICE
Lawres Hall, Riseholme Park, Lincoln LN2 2BJ
Controller, T. Kuczys

REGIONAL EXECUTIVE OFFICES
INLAND REVENUE EAST, Midgate House, Peterborough PE1 1TD. *Controller*, M. J. Hodgson

INLAND REVENUE LONDON, New Court, Carey Street, London WC2A 2JE. *Controller,* J. F. Carling
INLAND REVENUE NORTH, 100 Russell Street, Middlesbrough, Cleveland TS1 2RZ. *Controller,* R. I. Ford
INLAND REVENUE NORTH-WEST, The Triad, Stanley Road, Bootle, Merseyside L20 3PD. *Controller,* I. S. Gerrie
INLAND REVENUE SOUTH-EAST, Dukes Court, Dukes Street, Woking GU21 5XR. *Controller,* D. L. S. Bean
INLAND REVENUE SOUTH-WEST, Longbrook House, New North Road, Exeter EX4 4QU. *Controller,* Mrs M. E. Williams
INLAND REVENUE SOUTH YORKSHIRE, Concept House, 5 Young Street, Sheffield S1 4LF. *Controller,* A. C. Sleeman
INLAND REVENUE WALES AND MIDLANDS, 1st Floor, Phase 11 Building, Ty Glas Avenue, Llanishen, Cardiff CF4 5TS. *Controller,* M. W. Kirk
INLAND REVENUE SCOTLAND, 80 Lauriston Place, Edinburgh EH3 9SL. *Controller,* O. J. Clarke
INLAND REVENUE NORTHERN IRELAND, Dorchester House, 52–58 Great Victoria Street, Belfast BT2 7QE. *Controller,* R. S. T. Ewing

VALUATION OFFICE AGENCY
New Court, 48 Carey Street, London WC2A 2JE
Tel 0171-324 1183/1057
Meldrum House, 15 Drumsheugh Gardens, Edinburgh EH3 7UN
Tel 0131-225 4938

Chief Executive, Ms V. Lowe
Chief Valuer, Scotland, A. MacLaren

ADJUDICATOR'S OFFICE
— *see* page 277

INTERCEPTION COMMISSIONER
c/o The Home Office, 50 Queen Anne's Gate, London SW1H 9AT

The Commissioner is appointed by the Prime Minister. He keeps under review the issue by the Home Secretary, the Foreign Secretary, and the Secretaries of State for Scotland and for Northern Ireland, of warrants under the Interception of Communications Act 1985 and safeguards made in respect of intercepted material obtained through the use of such warrants. He is also required to give all such assistance as the Interception of Communications Tribunal may require to enable it to carry out its functions, and to submit an annual report to the Prime Minister with respect to the carrying out of his functions.
Commissioner, The Lord Nolan, PC

INTERCEPTION OF COMMUNICATIONS TRIBUNAL
PO Box 44, London SE1 0TX
Tel 0171-273 4096

Under the Interception of Communications Act 1985, the Tribunal is required to investigate applications from any person who believes that communications sent to or by them have been intercepted in the course of their transmission by post or by means of a public telecommunications system. The Tribunal comprises senior members of the legal profession, who are appointed by The Queen.
President, The Hon. Mr Justice Macpherson of Cluny
Vice-President, Sir David Calcutt, QC
Members, P. Scott, QC; W. Carmichael; R. Seabrook, QC

INTERVENTION BOARD
PO Box 69, Reading RG1 3YD
Tel 0118-958 3626

The Intervention Board was established as a government department in 1972 and became operational in 1973; it became an executive agency in 1990. The Board is responsible for the implementation of European Union regulations covering the market support arrangements of the Common Agricultural Policy. Members are appointed by and are responsible to the Minister of Agriculture, Fisheries and Food and the Secretaries of State for Scotland, Wales and Northern Ireland.
Chairman, A. Marshall
Chief Executive (G3), G. Trevelyan

HEADS OF DIVISIONS
External Trade Division (G5), G. N. Dixon
Internal Market Division (G5), H. MacKinnon
Corporate Services Division (G5), J. W. M. Peffers
Finance Division (G5), G. R. R. Jenkins
Legal Division (G5), J. F. McCleary
Chief Accountant (G6), R. Bryant
Procurement and Supply (G6), P. J. Offer
Information Systems (G7), T. G. Lamberstock
Internal Market Operations (G6), J. A. Sutton

LAND AUTHORITY FOR WALES
The Custom House, Customhouse Street, Cardiff CF1 5AP
Tel 01222-223444

The Authority, established under the Local Government Planning and Land Act 1980, is responsible for identifying and acquiring land suitable for development in Wales and making it available for development by others.
Chairman (part-time) (£33,305), Sir Geoffrey Inkin, OBE
Chief Executive, B. Ryan, FRICS

LAND REGISTRIES

HM LAND REGISTRY
Lincoln's Inn Fields, London WC2A 3PH
Tel 0171-917 8888

The registration of title to land was first introduced in England and Wales by the Land Registry Act 1862; HM Land Registry operates today under the Land Registration Acts 1925 to 1988. The object of registering title to land is to create and maintain a register of land-owners whose title is guaranteed by the state and so to simplify the transfer, mortgage and other dealings with real property. Registration on sale is now compulsory throughout England and Wales. The register has been open to inspection by the public since 1990.

HM Land Registry is an executive agency administered under the Lord Chancellor by the Chief Land Registrar. The work is decentralized to a number of regional offices. The Chief Land Registrar is also responsible for the Land Charges Department and the Agricultural Credits Department.

HEADQUARTERS OFFICE
Chief Land Registrar and Chief Executive, Dr S. J. Hill
Solicitor to Land Registry, C. J. West
Director of Corporate Services, E. G. Beardsall
Senior Land Registrar, Mrs J. G. Totty
Director of Operations, G. N. French

Director of Information Technology, P. J. Smith
Director of Management Services, P. R. Laker
Land Registrar, M. L. Wood
Deputy Establishment Officer, J. Hodder
Controller of Operations Development, A. W. Howarth

COMPUTER SERVICES DIVISION
Burrington Way, Plymouth PL5 3LP
Tel 01752-779831
Head of Services Division, P. A. Maycock
Head of Development Division, R. J. Smith

LAND CHARGES AND AGRICULTURAL CREDITS
DEPARTMENT
Burrington Way, Plymouth PL5 3LP
Tel 01752-635600
Superintendent of Land Charges (G7), J. Hughes

DISTRICT LAND REGISTRIES
BIRKENHEAD – Old Market House, Hamilton Street,
  Birkenhead L41 5FL. Tel: 0151-473 1110. *District Land
  Registrar*, M. G. Garwood
COVENTRY – Leigh Court, Torrington Avenue, Coventry
  CV4 9XZ. Tel: 01203-860860. *District Land Registrar*,
  S. P. Kelway
CROYDON – Sunley House, Bedford Park, Croydon
  CR9 3LE. Tel: 0181-781 9100. *District Land Registrar*,
  D. M. J. Moss
DURHAM – Southfield House, Southfield Way, Durham
  DH1 5TR. Tel: 0191-301 3500. *District Land Registrar*,
  C. W. Martin
GLOUCESTER – Twyver House, Bruton Way, Gloucester
  GL1 1DQ. Tel: 01452-511111. *District Land Registrar*,
  W. W. Budden
HARROW – Lyon House, Lyon Road, Harrow, Middx
  HA1 2EU. Tel: 0181-427 8811. *District Land Registrar*,
  J. V. Timothy
KINGSTON UPON HULL – Earle House, Portland Street,
  Hull HU2 8JN. Tel: 01482-223244. *District Land Registrar*,
  S. R. Coveney
LEICESTER – Thames Tower, 99 Burleys Way, Leicester
  LE1 3UB. Tel: 0116-265 4000. *District Land Registrar*, Mrs
  J. A. Goodfellow
LYTHAM – Birkenhead House, Lytham St Annes, Lancs
  FY8 5AB. Tel: 01253-849849. *District Land Registrar*,
  J. G. Cooper
NOTTINGHAM – Chalfont Drive, Nottingham NG8 3RN.
  Tel: 0115-935 1166. *District Land Registrar*,
  P. J. Timothy
PETERBOROUGH – Touthill Close, City Road,
  Peterborough PE1 1XN. Tel: 01733-288288. *District Land
  Registrar*, L. M. Pope
PLYMOUTH – Plumer House, Tailyour Road, Crownhill,
  Plymouth PL6 5HY. Tel: 01752-636000. *District Land
  Registrar*, A. J. Pain
PORTSMOUTH – St Andrews Court, St Michael's Road,
  Portsmouth PO1 2JH. Tel: 01705-768888. *District Land
  Registrar*, S. R. Sehrawat
STEVENAGE – Brickdale House, Swingate, Stevenage,
  Herts SG1 1XG. Tel: 01438-788888. *District Land Registrar*,
  C. Tate
SWANSEA – Tybryn Glas, High Street, Swansea SA1 1PW.
  Tel: 01792-458877. *District Land Registrar*,
  G. A. Hughes.
TELFORD – Parkside Court, Hall Park Way, Telford TF3
  4LR. Tel: 01952-290355. *District Land Registrar*,
  M. A. Roche
TUNBRIDGE WELLS – Curtis House, Hawkenbury,
  Tunbridge Wells, Kent TN2 5AQ. Tel: 01892-510015.
  District Land Registrar, G. R. Tooke

WEYMOUTH – 1 Cumberland Drive, Weymouth, Dorset
  DT4 9TT. Tel: 01305-776161. *District Land Registrar*, Mrs
  P. M. Reeson
YORK – James House, James Street, York YO1 3YZ. Tel:
  01904-450000. *District Land Registrar*, Mrs R. F. Lovel

REGISTERS OF SCOTLAND (EXECUTIVE
AGENCY)
Meadowbank House, 153 London Road, Edinburgh
EH8 7AU
Tel 0131-659 6111

The Registers of Scotland is an executive agency of the
Scottish Office. The Registers consist of: General Register
of Sasines and Land Register of Scotland; Register of
Deeds in the Books of Council and Session; Register of
Protests; Register of Judgments; Register of Service of
Heirs; Register of the Great Seal; Register of the Quarter
Seal; Register of the Prince's Seal; Register of Crown
Grants; Register of Sheriffs' Commissions; Register of the
Cachet Seal; Register of Inhibitions and Adjudications;
Register of Entails; Register of Hornings.

The General Register of Sasines and the Land Register
of Scotland form the chief security in Scotland of the rights
of land and other heritable (or real) property.
Chief Executive and Keeper of the Registers of Scotland (G4),
  A. W. Ramage
Deputy Chief Executive (G5), J. K. Mason
Deputy Keeper (G5), A. G. Rennie
Senior Directors (G6), B. J. Corr; A. M. Falconer
Directors (G7), R. Glen (*Human resources*); Miss
  M. M. D. Archer (*Land Register*); D. McCallum (*Land
  Register*); L. J. Mitchell (*Sasines*); A. M. Gardiner (*Land
  Register*); I. M. Nicol (*Finance*); Ms A. Rooney
  (*Communications*); T. Wilson (*Commercial*)

LAW COMMISSION
Conquest House, 37–38 John Street, London WC1N 2BQ
Tel 0171-453 1220

The Law Commission was set up in 1965, under the Law
Commissions Act 1965, to make proposals to the Government for the examination of the law in England and Wales
and for its revision where it is unsuited for modern
requirements, obscure, or otherwise unsatisfactory. It
recommends to the Lord Chancellor programmes for the
examination of different branches of the law and suggests
whether the examination should be carried out by the
Commission itself or by some other body. The Commission is also responsible for the preparation of Consolidation
and Statute Law (Repeals) Bills.
Chairman, The Hon. Mrs Justice Arden
Commissioners, C. Harpum; A. S. Burrows; Miss D. Faber;
  S. Silber, QC
Secretary, M. W. Sayers

SCOTTISH LAW COMMISSION
140 Causewayside, Edinburgh EH9 1PR
Tel 0131-668 2131

The Commission keeps the law in Scotland under review
and makes proposals for its development and reform. It is
responsible to the Scottish Courts Administration (*see* page
368).
Chairman, The Hon. Lord Davidson

Commissioners (*full-time*), Dr E. M. Clive; N. R. Whitty; (*part-time*) Prof. K. G. C. Reid; W. Nimmo Smith, QC
Secretary, J. G. S. MacLean

LAW OFFICERS' DEPARTMENTS
Legal Secretariat to the Law Officers, Attorney-General's Chambers, 9 Buckingham Gate, London SW1E 6JP
Tel 0171-828 7155
Attorney-General's Chambers, Royal Courts of Justice, Belfast BT1 3JY
Tel 01232-235111

The Law Officers of the Crown for England and Wales are the Attorney-General and the Solicitor-General. The Attorney-General, assisted by the Solicitor-General, is the chief legal adviser to the Government and is also ultimately responsible for all Crown litigation. He has overall responsibility for the work of the Law Officers' Departments (the Treasury Solicitor's Department, the Crown Prosecution Service, the Serious Fraud Office and the Legal Secretariat to the Law Officers). He has a specific statutory duty to superintend the discharge of their duties by the Director of Public Prosecutions (who heads the Crown Prosecution Service) and the Director of the Serious Fraud Office. The Director of Public Prosecutions for Northern Ireland is also responsible to the Attorney-General for the performance of his functions. The Attorney-General has additional responsibilities in relation to aspects of the civil and criminal law.
Attorney-General (*£46,745), The Rt. Hon. Sir Nicholas Lyell, QC, MP
 Private Secretary, S. M. Whatton
Solicitor-General (*£38,329), Sir Derek Spencer, QC, MP
 Private Secretary, S. M. Whatton
 Parliamentary Private Secretary, E. Garnier, QC, MP
Legal Secretary (*G2*), Miss J. L. Wheldon, CB
Deputy Legal Secretary (*G3*), S. J. Wooler
* In addition to a parliamentary salary of £43,000

LEGAL AID BOARD
85 Gray's Inn Road, London WC1X 8AA
Tel 0171-813 1000

The Legal Aid Board has the general function of ensuring that advice, assistance and representation are available in accordance with the Legal Aid Act 1988. In 1989 it took over from the Law Society responsibility for administering legal aid. The Board is a non-departmental government body whose members are appointed by the Lord Chancellor.
Chairman, Sir Tim Chessells
Deputy Chairman, H. Hodge
Members, S. Orchard (*Chief Executive*); J. Crosby; Ms J. Dunkley; C. George; B. Harvey; Ms K. Markus; Ms D. Payne; Ms P. Pearce; G. Pulman, QC; D. Sinker; K. Winberg

SCOTTISH LEGAL AID BOARD
44 Drumsheugh Gardens, Edinburgh EH3 7SW
Tel 0131-226 7061

The Scottish Legal Aid Board was set up under the Legal Aid (Scotland) Act 1986. It is responsible for ensuring that advice, assistance and representation are available in

accordance with the Act. The Board is a non-departmental government body whose members are appointed by the Secretary of State for Scotland.
Chairman, Ms C. A. M. Davis
Members, Mrs K. Blair; Mrs P. M. M. Bowman; Mrs S. Campbell; Mrs J. Couper; Prof. P. H. Grinyer; Sheriff A. Jessop; N. Kuenssberg; R. J. Livingstone; C. N. McEachran, QC; Ms Y. Osman; R. Scott; A. F. Wylie, QC
Chief Executive, R. Scott

OFFICE OF THE LEGAL SERVICES OMBUDSMAN
22 Oxford Court, Oxford Street, Manchester M2 3WQ
Tel 0161-236 9532

The Legal Services Ombudsman is appointed by the Lord Chancellor under the Courts and Legal Services Act 1990 to oversee the handling of complaints against solicitors, barristers and licensed conveyancers by their professional bodies. A complainant must first complain to the relevant professional body before raising the matter with the Ombudsman. The Ombudsman is independent of the legal profession and his services are free of charge.
Legal Services Ombudsman, M. Barnes
Secretary, S. Murray

OFFICE OF THE SCOTTISH LEGAL SERVICES OMBUDSMAN
2 Greenside Lane, Edinburgh EH1 3AH
Tel 0131-556 5574
Scottish Legal Services Ombudsman, G. S. Watson

LIBRARIES

LIBRARY AND INFORMATION COMMISSION
2 Sheraton Street, London W1V 4BH
Tel 0171-411 0056

The Commission is an independent body set up by the Secretary of State for National Heritage in 1995 to advise the Government and others on library and information matters, notably in the areas of research strategy and international links. It also aims to promote co-operation and co-ordination between different types of information services.
Chairman, M. Evans
Commissioners, D. Adams; E. Arram; Sir Charles Chadwyck-Healey; Dr G. Chambers; Prof. M. Collier; Prof. Judith Elkin; Dr B. Lang; D. Law; Dr R. McKee; Rabbi Julia Neuberger; Sir Peter Swinnerton-Dyer; Dr Sandra Ward; M. Wood
Executive Secretary, vacant

THE BRITISH LIBRARY
96 Euston Road, London NW1 2DB
Tel 0171-412 7000

The British Library was established in 1973. It is the UK's national library and occupies the central position in the library and information network. The Library aims to serve scholarship, research, industry, commerce and all other major users of information. Its services are based on collections which include over 18 million volumes, 1 million discs, and 55,000 hours of tape recordings, at 18 buildings in London and one complex in West Yorkshire. The British Library's new purpose-built accommodation at St Pancras, London NW1 is scheduled to open to the public in a phased programme starting in late 1997. Government grant-in-aid to the British Library in 1996–7 is £85.1 million; the British Library St Pancras Project receives £21.5 million. The Library's sponsoring department is the Department of National Heritage.

Access to the Humanities and Social Sciences reading rooms is limited to holders of a British Library Reader's Pass; information about eligibility is available from the Reader Admissions Office. The reading rooms of the Science Reference and Information Service are open to the general public without charge or formality.

Opening hours of services vary; most services are closed for one week each year. Specific information should be checked by telephone.

BRITISH LIBRARY BOARD
96 Euston Road, London NW1 2DB
Tel 0171-412 7262

Chairman, Dr J. Ashworth
Chief Executive and Deputy Chairman (G2), Dr B. Lang
Deputy Chief Executive (G4), D. Russon
Director-General, Collections and Services (G4), D. Bradbury
Part-time Members, T. J. Rix; D. Peake; The Hon.
  E. Adeane, cvo; Sir Matthew Farrer, gcvo; Mrs
  P. M. Lively, OBE; Prof. M. Anderson, FBA, FRSE;
  A. Bloom; B. Naylor; J. Ritblat

BRITISH LIBRARY, BOSTON SPA
Boston Spa, Wetherby, W. Yorks LS23 7BQ
Tel 01937-546000

DOCUMENT SUPPLY CENTRE, *Director (acting)* (G5), M. Smith
NATIONAL BIBLIOGRAPHIC SERVICE. Tel: 01937-546585.
  Director (G6), R. Smith
London Unit, 2 Sheraton Street, London WIV 4BH. Tel:
  0171-412 7077
ACQUISITIONS PROCESSING AND CATALOGUING, *Director*
  (G5), S. Ede
COMPUTING AND TELECOMMUNICATIONS. Tel: 01937-
  546879. *Director (G5),* J. R. Mahoney

BRITISH LIBRARY, LONDON
Great Russell Street, London WC1B 3DG
Tel 0171-412 7000

St Pancras Project Director (G4), D. Lyman
Director of Project Services St Pancras Planning (G6), Dr
  R. Coman

ADMINISTRATION, 2 Sheraton Street, London WIV 4BH.
  Tel: 0171-412 7132. *Director (G5),* D. Gesua
PRESS AND PUBLIC RELATIONS, 96 Euston Road, London
  NW1 2DB. Tel: 0171-412 7111. *Head (G7),* M. Jackson
PUBLIC SERVICES. Tel: 0171-412 7626. *Director (G5),* Ms
  J. Carr
Exhibitions and Education Service. Tel: 0171-412 7595
Reader Admissions. Tel: 0171-412 7677
HUMANITIES AND SOCIAL SCIENCES. Tel: 0171-412 7676.
  Director (G5), A. Phillips
West European Collections, Slavonic and East European
  Collections, English Language Collections. Tel: 0171-412
  7676
Social Policy Information Service. Tel: 0171-412 7536
Information Sciences Service (BLISS), Ridgmount Street,
  London WCIE 7AE. Tel: 0171-412 7688
Newspaper Library, Colindale Avenue, London NW9 5HE.
  Tel: 0171-412 7353
National Sound Archive, 29 Exhibition Road, London SW7
  2AS. Tel: 0171-412 7440

COLLECTIONS AND PRESERVATION. Tel: 0171-412 7676.
  Director (G5), Dr M. Foot
Preservation Service (National Preservation Office). Tel: 0171-
  412 7612

SPECIAL COLLECTIONS. Tel: 0171-412 7513. *Director*
  (G5), Dr A. Prochaska
Oriental and India Office Collections, 197 Blackfriars Road,
  London SEI 8NG. Tel: 0171-412 7873
Western Manuscripts. Tel: 0171-412 7513
Map Library. Tel: 0171-412 7700
Music Library. Tel: 0171-412 7528
Philatelic Collections. Tel: 0171-412 7729

SCIENCE REFERENCE AND INFORMATION SERVICE,
  25 Southampton Buildings, London WC2A 1AW. Tel:
  0171-412 7494; 9 Kean Street, London WC2B 4AT. Tel:
  0171-412 7288. *Director (G5),* A. Gomersall

RESEARCH AND INNOVATION CENTRE, 2 Sheraton
  Street, London WIV 4BH. Tel: 0171-412 7055. *Director*
  (G6), N. Macartney

NATIONAL LIBRARY OF SCOTLAND
George IV Bridge, Edinburgh EH1 1EW
Tel 0131-226 4531

The Library, which was founded as the Advocates' Library in 1682, became the National Library of Scotland in 1925. It is funded by the Scottish Office. It contains about six million books and pamphlets, 18,000 current periodicals, 230 newspaper titles and 100,000 manuscripts. It has an unrivalled Scottish collection.

The Reading Room is for reference and research which cannot conveniently be pursued elsewhere. Admission is by ticket issued to an approved applicant. Opening hours: Reading Room, weekdays, 9.30–8.30 (Wednesday, 10–8.30); Saturday 9.30–1. Map Library, weekdays, 9.30–5 (Wednesday, 10–5); Saturday 9.30–1. Exhibition, weekdays, 10–5; Saturday 10–5; Sunday 2–5. Scottish Science Library, weekdays, 9.30–5 (Wednesday, 10–8.30).
Chairman of the Trustees, The Earl of Crawford and
  Balcarres, PC
Librarian and Secretary to the Trustees (G4), I. D. McGowan
Secretary of the Library (G6), M. C. Graham
Keeper of Printed Books (G6), Ms A. Matheson, PH.D.
Keeper of Manuscripts (G6), I. C. Cunningham
Director of Public Services (G6), A. M. Marchbank, PH.D.
Director of Electronic Information (G6), B. Gallivan

NATIONAL LIBRARY OF WALES/
LLYFRGELL GENEDLAETHOL CYMRU
Aberystwyth SY23 3BU
Tel 01970-623816

The National Library of Wales was founded by Royal Charter in 1907, and is maintained by annual grant from the Welsh Office. It contains about four million printed books, 40,000 manuscripts, four million deeds and documents, numerous maps, prints and drawings, and a sound and moving image collection. It specializes in manuscripts and books relating to Wales and the Celtic peoples. It is the repository for pre-1858 Welsh probate records, manorial records and tithe documents, and certain legal records. Readers' room open weekdays, 9.30–6 (Saturday 9.30–5); closed first week of October. Admission by Reader's Ticket.
President, Prof. Emeritus J. Gwynn Williams
Librarian (G4), Dr J. L. Madden
Heads of Departments (G6), M. W. Mainwaring
  (Administration and Technical Services); G. Jenkins
  (Manuscripts and Records); Dr W. R. M. Griffiths *(Printed
  Books);* Dr D. H. Owen *(Pictures and Maps)*

LIGHTHOUSE AUTHORITIES

CORPORATION OF TRINITY HOUSE
Trinity House, Tower Hill, London EC3N 4DH
Tel 0171-480 6601

Trinity House, the first general lighthouse and pilotage authority in the kingdom, was granted its first charter by Henry VIII in 1514. The Corporation is the general lighthouse authority for England, Wales and the Channel Islands and maintains 67 lighthouses (of which 11 are manned), 14 major floating aids to navigation (e.g. light vessels) and more than 400 buoys. It also has certain statutory jurisdiction over aids to navigation maintained by local harbour authorities and is responsible for dealing with wrecks dangerous to navigation, except those occurring within port limits or wrecks of HM ships.

The Trinity House Lighthouse Service is maintained out of the General Lighthouse Fund which is provided from light dues levied on ships calling at ports of the UK and the Republic of Ireland. The Corporation is also a deep-sea pilotage authority and a charitable organization.

The affairs of the Corporation are controlled by a board of Elder Brethren and the Secretary. A separate board, which comprises Elder Brethren, senior staff and outside representatives, currently controls the Lighthouse Service. The Elder Brethren also act as nautical assessors in marine cases in the Admiralty Division of the High Court of Justice.

ELDER BRETHREN
Master, HRH The Duke of Edinburgh, KG, KT
Deputy Master, Rear-Adm. P. B. Rowe, CBE, LVO
Elder Brethren, Capt. D. J. Orr; Capt. N. M. Turner, RD; Capt. Sir Malcolm Edge, KCVO; HRH The Prince of Wales, KT; HRH The Duke of York, CVO, ADC; Capt. R. N. Mayo, CBE; Capt. Sir David Tibbits, DSC, RN; Capt. D. A. G. Dickens; Capt. J. E. Bury; Capt. J. A. N. Bezant, DSC, RD, RNR (retd.); Capt. D. J. Cloke; Capt. Sir Miles Wingate, KCVO; The Rt. Hon. Sir Edward Heath, KG, MBE, MP; Capt. I. R. C. Saunders; Capt. P. F. Mason, CBE; Capt. T. Woodfield, OBE; Sir Eric Drake, CBE; The Lord Simon of Glaisdale, PC; Admiral of the Fleet the Lord Lewin, KG, GCB, LVO, DSC; Capt. D. T. Smith, RN; Cdr. Sir Robin Gillett, BT., GBE, RD, RNR; The Lord Cuckney; The Lord Carrington, KG, GCMG, CH, MC, PC; Sir Brian Shaw; The Lord Mackay of Clashfern, PC; Sir Adrian Swire; Capt. P. H. King; The Lord Sterling of Plaistow, CBE, RNR; Cdr. M. J. Rivett-Carnac, RN; Capt. C. M. C. Stewart; Adm. Sir Jock Slater, GCB, LVO

OFFICERS
Secretary, R. F. Dobb
Director of Finance, K. W. Clark
Director of Engineering, M. G. B. Wannell
Director of Administration, D. I. Brewer
General Manager Operations, Capt. J. M. Barnes
Human Resources and Communications Manager,
 N. J. Cutmore
Operations Administration Manager, S. J. W. Dunning
Legal and Insurance Manager, J. D. Price
Navigation Manager, Mrs K. Hossain
Deputy Director of Engineering, P. N. Hyde
Senior Inspector of Shipping, J. R. Dunnett
Media and Communication Officer, H. L. Cooper

COMMISSIONERS OF NORTHERN LIGHTHOUSES
84 George Street, Edinburgh EH2 3DA
Tel 0131-226 7051

The Commissioners of Northern Lighthouses are the general lighthouse authority for Scotland and the Isle of Man. The present board owes its origin to an Act of Parliament passed in 1786. At present the Commissioners operate under the Merchant Shipping Act 1894 and are 19 in number.

The Commissioners control 8 major manned lighthouses, 76 major automatic lighthouses, 112 minor lights and many lighted and unlighted buoys. They have a fleet of two motor vessels.

COMMISSIONERS
The Lord Advocate; the Solicitor-General for Scotland; the Lord Provosts of Edinburgh, Glasgow and Aberdeen; the Provost of Inverness; the Convener of Argyll and Bute Council; the Sheriffs-Principal of North Strathclyde, Tayside, Central and Fife, Grampian, Highlands and Islands, South Strathclyde, Dumfries and Galloway, Lothians and Borders, and Glasgow and Strathkelvin; A. J. Struthers; W. F. Hay, CBE; Capt. D. M. Cowell; Adm. Sir Michael Livesay, KCB; The Lord Maclay

OFFICERS
Chief Executive, Capt. J. B. Taylor, RN
Director of Finance, D. Gorman
Director of Engineering, W. Paterson
Director of Operations and Navigational Requirements,
 P. J. Christmas

LOCAL COMMISSIONERS

COMMISSION FOR LOCAL ADMINISTRATION IN ENGLAND
21 Queen Anne's Gate, London SW1H 9BU
Tel 0171-915 3210

Local Commissioners (local government ombudsmen) are responsible for investigating complaints from members of the public against local authorities (but not town and parish councils); police authorities; the Commission for New Towns (housing functions); urban development corporations (town and country planning functions) and certain other authorities. The Commissioners are appointed by the Crown on the recommendation of the Secretary of State for the Environment.

Certain types of action are excluded from investigation, including personnel matters and commercial transactions unless they relate to the purchase or sale of land. Complaints can be sent direct to the Local Government Ombudsman or through a councillor, although the Local Government Ombudsman will not consider a complaint unless the council has had an opportunity to investigate and reply to a complainant.

A free booklet *Complaint about the council? How to complain to the Local Government Ombudsman* is available from the Commission's office.

Chairman of the Commission and Local Commissioner
 (£95,051), E. B. C. Osmotherly, CB
Vice-Chairman and Local Commissioner (£77,875), Mrs
 P. A. Thomas
Local Commissioner (£76,875), J. R. White
Member (*ex officio*), The Parliamentary Commissioner for Administration
Secretary (£48,135), G. D. Adams

COMMISSION FOR LOCAL ADMINISTRATION IN WALES
Derwen House, Court Road, Bridgend CF31 1BN
Tel 01656-661325

The Local Commissioner for Wales has similar powers to the Local Commissioners in England. The Commissioner is appointed by the Crown on the recommendation of the Secretary of State for Wales. A free leaflet *Your Local Ombudsman in Wales* is available from the Commission's office.
Local Commissioner, E. R. Moseley
Secretary, D. Bowen
Member (ex officio), The Parliamentary Commissioner for Administration

COMMISSIONER FOR LOCAL ADMINISTRATION IN SCOTLAND
23 Walker Street, Edinburgh EH3 7HX
Tel 0131-225 5300

The Local Commissioner for Scotland has similar powers to the Local Commissioners in England, and is appointed by the Crown on the recommendation of the Secretary of State for Scotland.
Local Commissioner, F. C. Marks, OBE
Deputy and Secretary, Ms J. H. Renton

LONDON REGIONAL TRANSPORT
55 Broadway, London SW1H 0BD
Tel 0171-222 5600

Subject to the financial objectives and principles approved by the Secretary of State for Transport, London Regional Transport has a general duty to provide or secure the provision of public transport services for Greater London.
Chairman (£154,500), P. Ford
Member, and Managing Director of London Transport Board (£68,967), C. Hodson, CBE
Member for Finance (£92,784), A. J. Sheppeck
Member, and Managing Director of London Underground Ltd (£108,635), D. Tunnicliffe

LORD ADVOCATE'S DEPARTMENT
2 Carlton Gardens, London SW1Y 5AA
Tel 0171-210 1010

The Law Officers for Scotland are the Lord Advocate and the Solicitor-General for Scotland. The Lord Advocate's Department is responsible for drafting Scottish legislation, for providing legal advice to other departments on Scottish questions and for assistance to the Law Officers for Scotland in certain of their legal duties.
Lord Advocate (£57,241), The Lord Mackay of Drumadoon, PC, QC
Private Secretary, A. G. Maxwell
Solicitor-General for Scotland (£48,985), Paul Cullen, QC
Private Secretary, A. G. Maxwell
Legal Secretary and First Scottish Parliamentary Counsel (G2), J. C. McCluskie, QC
Assistant Legal Secretaries and Scottish Parliamentary Counsel (G3), G. M. Clark; G. Kowalski; P. J. Layden, TD; C. A. M. Wilson
Assistant Legal Secretary and Depute Scottish Parliamentary Counsel (G5), J. D. Harkness

LORD CHANCELLOR'S DEPARTMENT
Selborne House, 54–60 Victoria Street, London SW1E 6QB
Tel 0171-210 8500

The Lord Chancellor is the principal legal adviser of the Crown, Speaker of the House of Lords, President of the House of Lords as an Appellate Court, of the Court of Appeal, and of the Chancery Division of the High Court of Justice, and acting President of the Judicial Committee of the Privy Council. The Lord Chancellor appoints Justices of the Peace (except in Lancashire) and advises the Crown on the appointment of most members of the higher judiciary. He is responsible for promoting general reforms in the civil law, for the procedure of the civil courts and for legal aid schemes. He is a member of the Cabinet. He also has ministerial responsibility for magistrates' courts, which are administered locally. Administration of the Supreme Court and county courts in England and Wales was taken over by the Court Service, an executive agency of the department, in April 1995.

The Lord Chancellor is also responsible for ensuring that letters patent and other formal documents are passed in the proper form under the Great Seal of the Realm, of which he is the custodian. The work in connection with this is carried out under his direction in the Office of the Clerk of the Crown in Chancery.
Lord Chancellor (£132,178), The Lord Mackay of Clashfern, PC
Private Secretary, P. Kennedy
Parliamentary Private Secretary, P. Luff, MP
Parliamentary Secretary, Gary Streeter, MP
Private Secretary, A. Clegg
Permanent Secretary (G1), Sir Thomas Legg, KCB, QC
Private Secretary, Ms M. Cale

CROWN OFFICE
House of Lords, London SW1A 0PW
Clerk of the Crown in Chancery (G1), Sir Thomas Legg, KCB, QC
Deputy Clerk of the Crown in Chancery (G2), M. Huebner, CB
Clerk of the Chamber, C. I. P. Denyer

JUDICIAL APPOINTMENTS GROUP
Tel 0171-210 8926
Head of Group (G3), R. E. K. Holmes
Grade 5, D. E. Staff (*Policy and Conditions of Service*); Mrs M. Pigott (*Circuit Bench*); Miss J. Killick (*Circuit Bench*); E. Adams (*District Bench and Tribunals*); R. Venne (*Magistrates' Appointments*)

Judicial Studies Board
14 Little St James's Street, London SW1A 1DP
Tel 0171-925 0185
Grade 5, P. G. Taylor

POLICY GROUP
Tel 0171-210 8719
Head of Group (G2), I. M. Burns, CB
Heads of Divisions (G5), S. Smith (*Legal Aid*); Ms J. Rowe (*Criminal Policy*); D. Gladwell (*Civil Justice*); R. Sams (*Law Reform and Tribunals*); W. Arnold (*Family Policy*); P. G. Harris (*Legal Aid Reform*); A. J. Finlay (*Woolf Inquiry*)
Head of Secretariat and Agency Monitoring Unit (G7), Ms A. Jones

LEGAL ADVISER'S GROUP
Tel 0171-210 0711
Legal Adviser (G3), R. H. H. White

Grade 4, M. H. Collon (*Legal Advice and Litigation*)
Grade 5, J. Watherston (*International*); M. Kron (*Rules of Court and Regulations*)

CORPORATE SERVICES GROUP
Tel 0171-210 5503

Director of Corporate Services and Principal Establishment and Finance Officer (G3), Mrs N. A. Oppenheimer
Grade 5, Ms H. Tuffs (*Personnel Management*); A. Cogbill (*Finance*); A. Maultby (*Planning and Communications*)
Grade 6, K. Cregeen (*Accommodation and Magistrates' Courts Building*); A. Rummins (*Internal Audit*); K. Garrett (*Statutory Publications Office*)

MAGISTRATES' COURTS GROUP
Tel 0171-210 8809

Head of Group (G3), L. C. Oates
Grade 5, M. E. Ormerod
Grade 6, P. Duffin

ECCLESIASTICAL PATRONAGE
10 Downing Street, London SW1A 2AA
Tel 0171-930 4433

Secretary for Ecclesiastical Patronage, J. H. Holroyd, CB
Assistant Secretary for Ecclesiastical Patronage, N. C. Wheeler

MAGISTRATES' COURTS' SERVICE INSPECTORATE
Southside, 105 Victoria Street, London SW1E 6QJ
Tel 0171-210 1655

Chief Inspector (G5), Mrs R. L. Melling
Senior Inspectors (G6), Ms J. Eeles; D. Gear; C. Monson; Ms S. Steel

LORD CHANCELLOR'S ADVISORY COMMITTEE ON STATUTE LAW
6 Spring Gardens, London SW1A 2BP
Tel 0171-389 3244

The Advisory Committee advises the Lord Chancellor on all matters relating to the revision, modernization and publication of the statute book.
Chairman, The Lord Chancellor
Deputy Chairman, Sir Thomas Legg, KCB, QC
Members, Sir Michael Wheeler-Booth, KCB; Sir Clifford Boulton, KCB; The Hon. Mr Justice Brooke; The Hon. Lord Davidson; C. Jenkins, CB, QC; J. C. McCluskie, QC; G. Hosker, CB, QC; R. Brodie, CB; R. H. H White; J. Gibson; Dr P. Freeman; (*ex officio*) First Legislative Counsel, Northern Ireland
Secretary, C. Carey

EXECUTIVE AGENCIES

THE COURT SERVICE
Southside, 105 Victoria Street, London SW1E 6QT
Tel 0171-210 1775

The Court Service provides administrative support to the Supreme Court of England and Wales, county courts and a number of tribunals.
Chief Executive (G2), M. Huebner
Grade 5, P. Handcock (*operational support*)

Finance and Administration Group
Director (G3), C. W. V. Everett
Grade 5, K. Pogson (*resources*); Miss B. Kenny (*personnel and training*); P. Jacobs (*project manager, LOCCS*); A. Shaw (*accommodation, procurement, libraries and records*); P. White (*information technology (ISD)*)

Royal Courts of Justice
Strand, London WC2A 2LL
Tel 0171-936 6000
Administrator, G. E. Calvett

For Supreme Court departments and offices and circuit administrators, *see* Law Courts and Offices section

HM LAND REGISTRY
— *see* pages 315–16

PUBLIC RECORD OFFICE
— *see* pages 336–7

PUBLIC TRUST OFFICE
— *see* page 335

LORD GREAT CHAMBERLAIN'S OFFICE
House of Lords, London SW1A 0PW
Tel 0171-219 3100

The Lord Great Chamberlain is a Great Officer of State, the office being hereditary since the grant of Henry I to the family of De Vere, Earls of Oxford. The Lord Great Chamberlain is responsible for the Royal Apartments of the Palace of Westminster, i.e. The Queen's Robing Room, the Royal Gallery and, in conjunction with the Lord Chancellor and Madam Speaker, Westminster Hall. The Lord Great Chamberlain has particular responsibility for the internal administrative arrangements within the House of Lords for State Openings of Parliament.
Lord Great Chamberlain, The Marquess of Cholmondeley
Secretary to the Lord Great Chamberlain, Gen. Sir Edward Jones, KCB, CBE
Clerks to the Lord Great Chamberlain, Mrs S. E. Douglas; Miss R. M. Wilkinson

---

LORD PRIVY SEAL'S OFFICE
Privy Council Office, 68 Whitehall, London SW1A 2AT
Tel 0171-270 3000

The Lord Privy Seal is a member of the Cabinet and Leader of the House of Lords. He has no departmental portfolio, but is a member of a number of domestic and economic Cabinet committees. He is responsible to the Prime Minister for the organization of government business in the House and has a responsibility to the House itself to advise it on procedural matters and other difficulties which arise.
Lord Privy Seal, and Leader of the House of Lords, Viscount Cranborne, PC
Principal Private Secretary, Mrs J. Hope
Private Secretary (House of Lords), Mrs M. Ollard
Special Adviser, Ms S. McEwen
Parliamentary Private Secretary, J. Sykes, MP

LOTTERY, OFFICE OF THE NATIONAL
— *see* page 328

OFFICE OF MANPOWER ECONOMICS
Oxford House, 76 Oxford Street, London W1N 9FD
Tel 0171-467 7244

The Office of Manpower Economics was set up in 1971. It is an independent non-statutory organization which is responsible for servicing independent review bodies which advise on the pay of various public service groups (*see* Review Bodies, page 337), the Pharmacists Review Panel and the Police Negotiating Board. The Office is also responsible for servicing *ad hoc* bodies of inquiry and for

undertaking research into pay and associated matters as requested by the Government.
OME Director, M. J. Horsman
Director, Statistics and Office Services, G. S. Charles
Director, Armed Forces Secretariat, A. Hughes
Director, Health Secretariat, and OME Deputy Director, Miss S. M. Haird
Director, Teachers' and Police Secretariats, P. J. H. Edwards
Director, Senior Salaries Secretariat, Mrs C. Haworth
Press Liaison Officer, M. C. Cahill

MENTAL HEALTH ACT COMMISSION
Maid Marian House, 56 Hounds Gate, Nottingham
NG1 6BG
Tel 0115-950 4040

The Mental Health Act Commission was established in 1983. Its functions are to keep under review the operation of the Mental Health Act 1983; to visit and meet patients detained under the Act; to investigate complaints falling within the Commission's remit; to operate the consent to treatment safeguards in the Mental Health Act; to publish a biennial report on its activities; to monitor the implementation of the Code of Practice; and to advise ministers. Commissioners are appointed by the Secretary of State for Health.
Chairman, The Viscountess Runciman of Doxford, OBE
Vice-Chairman, N. Pleming
Chief Executive (G6), W. Bingley

MILLENNIUM COMMISSION
2 Little Smith Street, London SW1P 3DH
Tel 0171-340 2001

The Millennium Commission was established in February 1994 and is funded by the Department of National Heritage. It is an independent body which distributes 20 per cent of the money allocated to 'good causes' from National Lottery proceeds to projects to mark the millennium. The Commission had made awards totalling £494 million by April 1996.
Chairman, The Rt. Hon. Virginia Bottomley, MP
Members, Prof. Heather Couper, FRAS; Earl of Dalkeith; The Lord Glentoran, CBE; Sir John Hall; The Rt. Hon. M. Heseltine, MP; S. Jenkins; M. Montague, CBE; Miss P. Scotland, QC
Chief Executive, Miss J. A. Page, CBE

MONOPOLIES AND MERGERS COMMISSION
New Court, 48 Carey Street, London WC2A 2JT
Tel 0171-324 1407

The Commission was established in 1949 as the Monopolies and Restrictive Practices Commission and became the Monopolies and Mergers Commission under the Fair Trading Act 1973. Its role is to investigate and report on matters which are referred to it by the Secretary of State for Trade and Industry or the Director-General of Fair Trading or, in the case of privatized industries, by the appropriate regulator. Its decisions are determined by the criteria set out in the legislation covering the different types of reference. The main types of reference which can be made are: monopolies; mergers; newspaper mergers;

general, involving general practices in an industry; restrictive labour practices; competition, involving anti-competitive practices of individual firms; public sector audits; privatized industries; and Channel 3 (ITV) networking arrangements between holders of regional Channel 3 licences. References may be made under the Fair Trading Act 1973, the Competition Act 1980, the Broadcasting Act or other relevant statutes.

The Commission consists of about 35 members, including a full-time chairman and three part-time deputy chairmen, all appointed by the Secretary of State for Trade and Industry. Each inquiry is conducted on behalf of the Commission by a group of four to six members who are appointed by the chairman.
Chairman (£97,440), G. D. W. Odgers
Deputy Chairmen (£40–£60,000), D. Morris, PH.D.; P. H. Dean, CBE; D. G. Goyder, CBE
Members (£13,765/*£9,175 each), Prof. J. Beatson; Prof. M. Cave; R. H. F. Croft, CB; *R. Davies; Prof. S. Eilon; *J. Evans; *N. H. Finney, OBE; *Sir Archibald Forster; *Sir Ronald Halstead, CBE; D. B. Hammond; *Ms P. A. Hodgson; D. J. Jenkins, MBE; H. H. Liesner, CB; R. Lyons; P. Mackay; *N. F. Matthews; Prof. J. S. Metcalfe, CBE; *Mrs K. Mortimer; *R. Munson; Prof. D. Newbery; Dr Gill Owen; *Prof. J. F. Pickering; *L. Priestley; R. Prosser; Prof. Judith Rees; Dr Ann Robinson; *J. K. Roe; *Dr Lynda Rouse; *G. H. Stacy, CBE; Mrs C. Tritton, QC; Prof. G. Whittington
Secretary, Miss P. Boys
* Reserve members

MUSEUMS

MUSEUMS AND GALLERIES COMMISSION
16 Queen Anne's Gate, London SW1H 9AA
Tel 0171-233 4200

Established in 1931 as the Standing Commission on Museums and Galleries, the Commission was renamed and took up new functions in 1981. Its sponsor department is the Department of National Heritage. The Commission advises the Government, including the Department of Education for Northern Ireland, the Scottish Education Department and the Welsh Office, on museum affairs. Commissioners are appointed by the Prime Minister.

The Commission's executive functions include providing the services of the Museums Security Adviser; allocating grants to the seven Area Museum Councils in England; funding and monitoring the work of the Museum Documentation Association; and administering grant schemes for non-national museums. The Commission administers the arrangements for government indemnities and the acceptance of works of art in lieu of inheritance tax, and its Conservation Unit advises on conservation and environmental standards. A registration scheme for museums in the UK is operated by the Commission.
Chairman, J. Joll
Members, The Marchioness of Anglesey, DBE; J. Baer; Prof. P. Bateson, FRS; The Baroness Brigstocke; Prof. R. Buchanan; The Viscountess Cobham; R. Foster; L. Grossman; Adm. Sir John Kerr, GCB; J. Last, CBE; Prof. D. Michie; The Lord Rees, PC, QC; R. H. Smith; A. Warhurst, CBE; Mrs C. Wilson
Director and Secretary, T. Mason

THE BRITISH MUSEUM
Great Russell Street, London WC1B 3DG
Tel 0171-636 1555

The British Museum houses the national collection of antiquities, coins and paper money, medals, and prints and drawings. The ethnographical collections are displayed at the Museum of Mankind. The British Museum may be said to date from 1753, when Parliament approved the holding of a public lottery to raise funds for the purchase of the collections of Sir Hans Sloane and the Harleian manuscripts, and for their proper housing and maintenance. The building (Montagu House) was opened in 1759. The present buildings were erected between 1823 and the present day, and the original collection has increased to its present dimensions by gifts and purchases. Total government grant-in-aid for 1996–7 is £33.196 million.

BOARD OF TRUSTEES
Appointed by the Sovereign, HRH The Duke of Gloucester, GCVO
Appointed by the Prime Minister, N. Barber; Prof. Gillian Beer, FBA; Sir John Boyd; J. Browne, FENG.; Sir Matthew Farrer, GCVO; Sir Peter Harrop, KCB; Sir Michael Hopkins, CBE, RA, RIBA; Sir Joseph Hotung; S. Keswick; Hon. Mrs M. Marten, OBE; Sir John Morgan, KCMG; The Rt. Hon. Sir Timothy Raison; Prof. G. H. Treitel, DCL, FBA, QC
Nominated by the Learned Societies, Prof. Jean Thomas, CBE (*Royal Society*); A. Jones, RA (*Royal Academy*); Sir Claus Moser, KCB, CBE, FBA (*British Academy*); The Lord Renfrew of Kaimsthorn, FBA, FSA (*Society of Antiquaries*)
Appointed by the Trustees of the British Museum, G. C. Greene, CBE (*Chairman*); Sir David Attenborough, CH, CVO, CBE, FRS; Prof. Rosemary Cramp, CBE, FSA; The Lord Egremont; Dr Jennifer Montagu, FBA

OFFICERS
Director (*G2*), Dr R. G. W. Anderson, FRSC, FSA
Deputy Director (*G4*), Miss J. M. Rankine
Secretary (*G6*), Mrs C. Nihoul Parker
Head of Public Services (*G6*), G. A. L. House
Head of Press and Public Relations (*SIO*), A. E. Hamilton
Head of Design (*G6*), Miss M. Hall, OBE
Head of Education (*G7*), J. F. Reeve
Head of Administration (*G5*), C. E. I. Jones
Head of Building Development and Planning (*G5*), K. T. Stannard
Head of Building Management (*G6*), T. R. A. Giles
Head of Finance (*G7*), Miss S. E. Davies
Head of Personnel and Office Services (*G7*), Miss B. A. Hughes

KEEPERS
Keeper of Prints and Drawings (*G5*), A. V. Griffiths
Keeper of Coins and Medals (*G5*), Dr A. M. Burnett
Keeper of Egyptian Antiquities (*G5*), W. V. Davies
Keeper of Western Asiatic Antiquities (*G5*), Dr J. E. Curtis
Keeper of Greek and Roman Antiquities (*G5*), Dr D. J. R. Williams
Keeper of Medieval and Later Antiquities (*G5*), N. M. Stratford
Keeper of Prehistoric and Romano-British Antiquities (*G5*), Dr T. M. Potter
Keeper of Japanese Antiquities (*G5*), L. R. H. Smith
Keeper of Oriental Antiquities (*G5*), R. J. Knox
Keeper of Ethnography (*G5*), B. J. Mack
Keeper of Scientific Research (*G5*), Dr S. G. E. Bowman
Keeper of Conservation (*G5*), W. A. Oddy

NATURAL HISTORY MUSEUM
Cromwell Road, London SW7 5BD
Tel 0171-938 9123

The Natural History Museum originates from the natural history departments of the British Museum, which grew extensively during the 19th century and in 1860 the natural history collection was moved from Bloomsbury to a new location. Part of the site of the 1862 International Exhibition in South Kensington was acquired for the new museum, and the Museum opened to the public in 1881. In 1963 the Natural History Museum became completely independent with its own body of trustees. The Walter Rothschild Zoological Museum, Tring, bequeathed by the second Lord Rothschild, has formed part of the Museum since 1938. The Geological Museum merged with the Natural History Museum in 1985. Total government grant-in-aid for 1996–7 is £27.445 million.

BOARD OF TRUSTEES
Appointed by the Prime Minister: Sir Robert May, FRS (*Chairman*); The Baroness Blackstone, PH.D.; Mrs J. M. d'Abo; Sir Denys Henderson; Sir Crispin Tickell, GCMG, KCVO; Dame Anne McLaren, DBE, FRS; Prof. Sir Ronald Oxburgh, FRS; Sir Richard Sykes
Nominated by the Royal Society, Prof. J. L. Harper, CBE, FRS
Appointed by the Trustees of the Natural History Museum, Prof. Sir Brian Follett, FRS; Prof. K. O'Nions, FRS; The Lord Palumbo

SENIOR STAFF
Director, N. R. Chalmers, PH.D.
Director of Science, Prof. P. Henderson, D.phil.
Science Policy Co-ordinator, Ms N. Donlon
Secretary and Head of Corporate Services, C. J. E. Legg
Head of Development and Marketing, Mrs T. Burman
Keeper of Zoology, C. R. Curds, D.SC
Director, Tring Zoological Museum, I. R. Bishop, OBE
Keeper of Entomology, Dr R. P. Lane
Keeper of Botany, S. Blackmore, PH.D.
Keeper of Palaeontology, L. R. M. Cocks, D.SC
Keeper of Mineralogy, Dr A. Fleet
Head of Finance, J. Card
Head of Personnel, Mrs P. H. I. Orchard
Head of Library and Information Services, vacant
Head of Education and Exhibitions (*G5*), Dr G. Clarke
Head of Visitor Services, Mrs W. B. Gullick
Head of Estates, G. Pellow

THE SCIENCE MUSEUM
South Kensington, London SW7 2DD
Tel 0171-938 8000

The Science Museum, part of the National Museum of Science and Industry, houses the national collections of science, technology, industry and medicine. The Museum began as the science collection of the South Kensington Museum and first opened in 1857. In 1883 it acquired the collections of the Patent Museum and in 1909 the science collections were transferred to the new Science Museum, leaving the art collections with the Victoria and Albert Museum.

Some of the Museum's commercial aircraft, agricultural machinery, and road and rail transport collections are at Wroughton, Wilts. The Museum is also responsible for the National Railway Museum, York; the National Museum of Photography, Film and Television, Bradford; and the Concorde Exhibition at the Fleet Air Arm Museum, Yeovilton.

Total government grant-in-aid for 1996–7 is £20.63 million.

BOARD OF TRUSTEES
Chairman, Dr P. Williams, CBE
Members, HRH The Duke of Kent, KG, GCMG, GCVO, ADC;
Dr Mary Archer; The Viscount Downe; G. Dyke;
Miss M. S. Goldring, OBE; Dr Anne Grocock; Mrs
A. Higham, OBE; Mrs J. Kennedy, OBE; Dr Bridget
Ogilvie; Sir David Puttnam; Sir Michael Quinlan, GCB;
L. de Rothschild, CBE; Sir Christopher Wates

OFFICERS
Director, Sir Neil Cossons, OBE, FSA
Assistant Director and Head of Resource Management
Division, J. J. Defries
Head of Personnel and Training, C. Gosling
Head of Finance, Ms A. Caine
Assistant Director and Head of Collections Division, Dr T.
Wright
Head of Physical Sciences and Engineering Group,
Dr D. A. Robinson
Head of Life and Communications Technologies Group,
Dr R. F. Bud
Head of Collections Management Group, Dr S. Keene
Assistant Director and Head of Public Affairs Division,
C. M. Pemberton
Assistant Director and Head of Science Communication Division,
Prof. J. R. Durant
Head of Education and Programmes, Dr R. Jackson
Head of Exhibitions, Dr G. Farmelo
Assistant Director and Head of Project Development Division,
Mrs G. M. Thomas
Head of Design, T. Molloy
Head of National Railway Museum, A. Scott
Head of National Museum of Photography, Film and Television,
Ms A. Nevill

VICTORIA AND ALBERT MUSEUM
South Kensington, London SW7 2RL
Tel 0171-938 8500

The national museum of all branches of fine and applied art
and design, the Victoria and Albert Museum descends
directly from the Museum of Manufactures, which opened
in Marlborough House in 1852 after the Great Exhibition
of 1851. The Museum was moved in 1857 to become part of
the South Kensington Museum. It was renamed the
Victoria and Albert Museum in 1899. It also houses the
National Art Library and Print Room.

The branch museum at Bethnal Green, which houses
the Museum of Childhood, was opened in 1872 and the
building is the most important surviving example of the
type of glass and iron construction used by Paxton for the
Great Exhibition. The Museum is also responsible for the
Wellington Museum (Apsley House), and the Theatre
Museum. Total government grant-in-aid for 1996–7 is
£30.6 million.

BOARD OF TRUSTEES
Chairman, The Lord Armstrong of Ilminster, GCB, CVO
Deputy Chairman, Sir Michael Butler, GCMG
Members, The Lord Barnett, PC; Miss N. Campbell; Sir
Clifford Chetwood; The Viscountess Cobham;
E. Dawe; R. Fitch, CBE; Prof. C. Frayling, PH.D.;
R. Gorlin; Pamela, Lady Harlech; Sir Terence Heiser,
GCB; A. Irby III; Sir Nevil Macready, Bt., CBE;
Miss A. Plowden; Prof. M. Podro, PH.D., FBA; M. Saatchi;
J. Scott, FSA; A. Snow; Prof. J. Steer, FSA; A. Wheatley
Secretary to the Board of Trustees (G7), P. A. Wilson

OFFICERS
Director (G3), A. C. N. Borg, CBE, PH.D.
Assistant Directors (G5), T. Stevens (*Collections*); J. W. Close
(*Administration*)

Head of Buildings and Estate (G5), J. G. Charlesworth
Head of Collections (G5), Mrs G. F. Miles
Head of Conservation Department (G5), Dr J. Ashley-Smith
Head of Finance and Central Services (G5), Miss R. M. Sykes
Development Director, D. Charlton
Head of Education (G6), D. Anderson
Curator, Ceramics Collection (G6), Dr O. Watson
Curator, Far Eastern Collection (G6), Miss R. Kerr
Curator, Furniture and Woodwork Collection (G6), C. Wilk
Curator, Indian and South-East Asian Collection (G6),
Dr D. Swallow
Curator, Metalwork Collection (G6), Mrs P. Glanville
Head of Personnel (G6), Mrs G. Henchley
Curator, Prints, Drawings and Paintings Collection (G6),
Miss S. B. Lambert
Head of Public Affairs (G5), R. Cole-Hamilton
Head of Research (G5), P. Greenhalgh
Curator, Sculpture Collection (G6), P. E. D. Williamson
Curator, Textiles and Dress Collection (G6), Mrs V. D. Mendes
Managing Director, V. and A. Enterprises Ltd, M. Cass
Curator and Chief Librarian, National Art Library (G5),
J. F. van den Wateren
Head of Bethnal Green Museum of Childhood (G6), A. P. Burton
Head of Theatre Museum (G6), Ms M. Benton
Curator of Wellington Museum (*Apsley House*), J. R. S. Voak

MUSEUM OF LONDON
London Wall, London EC2Y 5HN
Tel 0171-600 3699

The Museum of London illustrates the history of London
from prehistoric times to the present day. It opened in 1976
and is based on the amalgamation of the former Guildhall
Museum and London Museum. The Museum is controlled by a Board of Governors, appointed (nine each) by
the Government and the Corporation of London. The
Museum is funded jointly by the Department of National
Heritage and the Corporation of London, each contributing £4.313 million in 1996–7.
Chairman of Board of Governors, P. Revell-Smith, CBE
Director, M. G. Hebditch, CBE, FSA

COMMONWEALTH INSTITUTE
Kensington High Street, London W8 6NQ
Tel 0171-603 4535

The Commonwealth Institute is the UK centre responsible
for promoting the Commonwealth in Britain through
exhibitions, educational programmes, publications, resources and information. The Institute houses an Education Centre, a Commonwealth Resource Centre and
Literature Library, and a Conference and Events Centre.
Its galleries are currently closed for refurbishment and will
reopen with new exhibitions in spring 1997.

The Institute is an independent statutory body, partially
funded by the British government with contributions from
other Commonwealth governments. It is controlled by a
Board of Governors which includes the High Commis-
sioners of all Commonwealth countries represented in
London. Total government grant-in-aid for 1996–7 is
£1 million.
Director-General, S. Cox
Administrative and Commercial Director, P. Kennedy
Projects Director, Dr J. Stevenson

IMPERIAL WAR MUSEUM
Lambeth Road, London SE1 6HZ
Tel 0171-416 5000

The Museum, founded in 1917, illustrates and records all
aspects of the two world wars and other military operations

involving Britain and the Commonwealth since 1914. It was opened in its present home, formerly Bethlem Hospital or Bedlam, in 1936. The Museum also administers HMS *Belfast* in the Pool of London, Duxford Airfield near Cambridge and the Cabinet War Rooms in Westminster.

Total government grant-in-aid for 1996–7 is £10.678 million.

Director-General, R. W. K. Crawford
Secretary, J. J. Chadwick
Assistant Directors, D. A. Needham (*Administration*); Miss K. J. Carmichael (*Collections*); G. Marsh (*Planning and Development*)
Head of Personnel Services, Miss L. Court
Head of Finance, Mrs P. A. Whitfield
Head of Information Systems, J. C. Barrett
Head of Support Systems, G. P. McCartney
Director of Duxford Airfield, E. O. Inman
Director of HMS Belfast, E. J. Wenzel

Keepers
Department of Museum Services, C. Dowling, D.Phil.
Department of Documents, R. W. A. Suddaby
Department of Exhibits and Firearms, D. J. Penn
Department of Printed Books, G. M. Bayliss, ph.d.
Department of Art, Miss A. H. Weight
Department of Film, R. B. N. Smither
Department of Photographs, Miss K. J. Carmichael
Department of Sound Records, Mrs M. A. Brooks
Department of Marketing and Trading, Miss A. Godwin
Curator of the Cabinet War Rooms, P. Reed

NATIONAL MARITIME MUSEUM
Greenwich, London SE10 9NF
Tel 0181-858 4422

Established by Act of Parliament in 1934, the National Maritime Museum illustrates the maritime history of Great Britain in the widest sense, underlining the importance of the sea and its influence on the nation's power, wealth, culture, technology and institutions. The Museum is in three groups of buildings in Greenwich Park – the main building, the Queen's House (built by Inigo Jones, 1616–35) and the Old Royal Observatory (including Wren's Flamsteed House). Total government grant-in-aid for 1996–7 is £10.5 million.
Director, R. L. Ormond

NATIONAL ARMY MUSEUM
Royal Hospital Road, London SW3 4HT
Tel 0171-730 0717

The National Army Museum covers the history of five centuries of the British Army. It was established by royal charter in 1960. Total government grant-in-aid for 1996–7 is £3.293 million.
Director, I. G. Robertson
Assistant Directors, D. K. Smurthwaite; A. J. Guy;
  Maj. P. R. Bateman

ROYAL AIR FORCE MUSEUM
Grahame Park Way, London NW9 5LL
Tel 0181-205 2266

Situated on the former airfield at RAF Hendon, the Museum illustrates the development of aviation from before the Wright brothers to the present-day RAF. Total government grant-in-aid for 1996–7 is £3.14 million.
Director, Dr M. A. Fopp
Deputy Director, J. D. Freeborn
Keepers, P. Elliott; D. F. Lawrence

NATIONAL MUSEUMS AND GALLERIES ON MERSEYSIDE
William Brown Street, Liverpool L3 8EN
Tel 0151-207 0001

The Board of Trustees of the National Museums and Galleries on Merseyside was established in 1986 to take over responsibility for the museums and galleries previously administered by Merseyside County Council. The Board is responsible for the Liverpool Museum, the Merseyside Maritime Museum (incorporating HM Customs and Excise National Museum), the Museum of Liverpool Life, the Lady Lever Art Gallery, the Walker Art Gallery and Sudley House, and a centre for museum conservation which opened in autumn 1996. Total government grant-in-aid for 1996–7 is £13.1 million.
Chairman of the Board of Trustees, D. McDonnell
Director, R. Foster
Head of Central Services, P. Sudbury, ph.d.
Keeper of Art Galleries, J. Treuherz
Keeper of Conservation, A. Durham
Keeper, Liverpool Museum, E. Greenwood
Keeper, Merseyside Maritime Museum and Museum of Liverpool Life, M. Stammers

NATIONAL MUSEUMS AND GALLERIES OF WALES/AMGUEDDFEYDD AC ORIELAU CENEDLAETHOL CYMRU
Cathays Park, Cardiff CF1 3NP
Tel 01222-397951

The National Museums and Galleries of Wales comprise the National Museum and Gallery, the Museum of Welsh Life, the Roman Legionary Museum, Turner House Art Gallery, the Welsh Slate Museum, the Segontium Roman Museum, the Museum of the Welsh Woollen Industry and the Welsh Industrial and Maritime Museum. Total funding from the Welsh Office for 1996–7 is £11.552 million.
President, C. R. T. Edwards
Vice-President, M. C. T. Pritchard, CBE

Officers
Director, C. Ford, CBE
Assistant Directors, T. Arnold (*Resource Management*);
  C. Thomas (*Public Services*); A. Southall (*Museums Development*); I. Fell (*Education and Interpretation*); Dr E. Williams (*Collections and Research*)
Keeper of Geology, M. G. Bassett, ph.d.
Keeper of Botany, B. A. Thomas, ph.d.
Keeper of Zoology, P. M. Morgan
Keeper of Archaeology (*acting*), R. Brewer
Curator, Museum of Welsh Life, vacant
Keepers, E. Scourfield, ph.d.; J. Williams-Davies
Officer in Charge, Roman Legionary Museum, P. Guest, ph.d.
Keeper in Charge, Turner House Art Gallery, D. Alston
Keeper in Charge, Welsh Slate Museum, D. Roberts, ph.d.
Officer in Charge, Segontium Roman Museum, R. J. Brewer
Officer in Charge, Museum of the Welsh Woollen Industry, E. Scourfield, ph.d.
Keeper, Welsh Industrial and Maritime Museum, E. S. Owen-Jones, ph.d.

NATIONAL MUSEUMS OF SCOTLAND
Chambers Street, Edinburgh EH1 1JF
Tel 0131-225 7534

The National Museums of Scotland comprise the Royal Museum of Scotland, the Scottish United Services Museum, the Scottish Agricultural Museum, the Museum of Flight, the Biggar Gasworks Museum and Shambellie House Museum of Costume. Total funding from the Scottish Office for 1996–7 is £19.685 million.

BOARD OF TRUSTEES
Chairman, R. Smith, FSA SCOT.
Members, Prof. L. Bown, OBE; R. D. Cramond, CBE, FSA SCOT.;
Countess of Dalkeith; Prof. T. Devine; Dr Lesley
Glasser, FRSE; S. G. Gordon, CBE; Sir Alistair Grant;
Prof. P. H. Jones; A. Massie; Dr Anna Ritchie; The
Countess of Rosebery; Sir John Thomson; Dr Veronica
Van Heyingen

OFFICERS
Director (G3), M. Jones, FSA, FSA SCOT., FRSA
Depute Director (Resources) and Project Director, Museum of
Scotland (G5), I. Hooper, FSA SCOT.
Depute Director (Collections) and Keeper of History and Applied
Art (G5), Miss D. Idiens, FRSA, FSA SCOT.
Keeper of Archaeology, D. V. Clarke, PH.D., FSA, FSA SCOT.
Keeper of Geology (G5), vacant
Keeper of Natural History (G5), M. Shaw, D.Phil.
Keeper of Science, Technology and Working Life (G5),
D. J. Bryden, PH.D., FSA
Head of Public Affairs (G6), Ms M. Bryden
Head of Museum Services (G6), S. R. Elson, FSA SCOT.
Head of Administration (G6), A. G. Young
Campaign Director, Museum of Scotland, S. Brock, PH.D., FRSA
Keeper, Scottish United Services Museum, S. C. Wood
Curator, Scottish Agricultural Museum, G. Sprott
Curator, Museum of Flight, Sqn. Ldr. R. Major
Curator, Biggar Gasworks Museum, J. Crompton
Keeper, Shambellie House Museum of Costume, Miss N. Tarrant

NATIONAL AUDIT OFFICE
157–197 Buckingham Palace Road, London SW1W 9SP
Tel 0171–798 7000
Audit House, 23–24 Park Place, Cardiff CF1 3BA
Tel 01222-378661
22 Melville Street, Edinburgh EH3 7NS
Tel 0131-244 2736

The National Audit Office came into existence under the National Audit Act 1983 to replace and continue the work of the former Exchequer and Audit Department. The Act reinforced the Office's total financial and operational independence from the Government and brought its head, the Comptroller and Auditor-General, into a closer relationship with Parliament as an officer of the House of Commons.
The National Audit Office provides independent information, advice and assurance to Parliament and the public about all aspects of the financial operations of government departments and many other bodies receiving public funds. It does this by examining and certifying the accounts of these organizations and by regularly publishing reports to Parliament on the results of its value for money investigations of the economy, efficiency and effectiveness with which public resources have been used. The National Audit Office is also the auditor by agreement of the accounts of certain international and other organizations. In addition, the Office authorizes the issue of public funds to government departments.
Comptroller and Auditor-General, Sir John Bourn, KCB
Private Secretary, F. Grogan
Deputy Comptroller and Auditor-General, R. N. Le Marechal, CB
Assistant Auditors-General, T. Burr; J. A. Higgins; L. H. Hughes, CB; J. Marshall; M. C. Pfleger; Miss C. Mawhood

Directors, C. K. Beauchamp; B. Hogg; J. Parsons; J. M. Pearce; A. G. Roberts; R. A. Skeen; A. Fiander; M. Daynes; R. J. Eales; J. Colman; B. Payne; N. Sloan; D. Woodward; Ms W. Kenway-Smith; R. Frith; J. Cavanagh; R. Maggs; M. Sinclair; J. Robertson; M. Whitehouse

NATIONAL CONSUMER COUNCIL
20 Grosvenor Gardens, London SW1W 0DH
Tel 0171-730 3469

The National Consumer Council was set up by the Government in 1975 to give an independent voice to consumers in the UK. Its job is to advocate the consumer interest to decision-makers in national and local government, industry and regulatory bodies, business and the professions. It does this through a combination of research and campaigning. It is funded by a grant-in-aid from the Department of Trade and Industry.
Chairman, D. Hatch, CBE
Vice-Chairman, Mrs A. Scully, OBE
Director, R. Evans

NATIONAL DEBT OFFICE
— see National Investment and Loans Office

DEPARTMENT OF NATIONAL HERITAGE
2–4 Cockspur Street, London SW1Y 5DH
Tel 0171-211 6000

The Department of National Heritage was established in 1992 and is responsible for government policy relating to the arts, broadcasting, the press, museums and galleries, libraries, sport and recreation, heritage and tourism. It funds the Arts Councils and other arts bodies, including the National Heritage Memorial Fund. It also funds the Museums and Galleries Commission, the national museums and galleries in England, the British Library, the Sports Council, the British Tourist Authority and the English Tourist Board, and the British Film Institute. It is responsible for the issue of export licences on works of art, antiques and collector's items; the Government Art Collection; the built heritage, including the Royal Parks and Historic Royal Palaces executive agencies; and statistical services including the International Passenger Survey and broadcasting statistics. The Department is also responsible for policy and implementation of the National Lottery. On 1 May 1996 the Department assumed responsibility from the Home Office for the voluntary sector and charities.
Secretary of State for National Heritage, The Rt. Hon. Virginia Bottomley, MP
Private Secretary, D. Fawcett
Special Adviser, A. Pepper
Parliamentary Private Secretary, N. Hawkins, MP
Minister of State, Iain Sproat, MP
Private Secretary, Ms D. Wells
Parliamentary Private Secretary, A. Robathan, MP
Parliamentary Under-Secretary, The Lord Inglewood
Lady-in-Waiting, The Baroness Trumpington
Parliamentary Clerk, C. Hutson
Permanent Secretary (G1), G. H. Phillips, CB
Private Secretary, Ms C. Pillmen

LIBRARIES, GALLERIES AND MUSEUMS GROUP
Head of Group (G3), Miss S. Booth, CBE
Head of Libraries and Information Services Division (G5), D. Wilson
Head of Museums and Galleries Division (G5), P. Gregory

Director, Government Art Collection (G6), Dr Wendy Baron, OBE
Head of Cultural Property Unit (G7), M. Helston

ARTS, SPORTS AND LOTTERY GROUP
Head of Group (G3), A. Ramsay
Head of Arts Division (G5), Ms M. Leech
Head of National Lottery Division (G5), S. MacDonald
Head of Sport and Recreation Division (G5), S. Broadley

BROADCASTING AND MEDIA GROUP
Head of Group (G3), P. Wright
Head of Broadcasting Policy Division (G5), N. Kroll
Head of Media Division (G5), Dr K. Gray

HERITAGE AND TOURISM GROUP
Head of Group (G3), D. Chesterton
Head of Heritage Division (G5), A. Corner
Head of Tourism Division (G5), Ms J. Evans

VOLUNTARY AND COMMUNITY DIVISION
Head of Division (G5), H. Webber

RESOURCES AND SERVICES GROUP
Director (G4), N. Pittman
Director of Finance and Corporate Planning (G5), Ms A.
  Stewart
Director of Implementation and Review (G5), R. MacLachlan
Director of Personnel (G5), G. Jones

INFORMATION
Head of Information (G5), A. Marre

EXECUTIVE AGENCIES

HISTORIC ROYAL PALACES
Hampton Court Palace, East Molesey, Surrey KT8 9AU
Tel 0181-781 9750

The Historic Royal Palaces agency manages the Tower of
London, Hampton Court Palace, Kensington Palace State
Apartments and the Royal Ceremonial Dress Collection,
Kew Palace with Queen Charlotte's Cottage, and the
Banqueting House, Whitehall.
Chief Executive, D. C. Beeton
Director of Finance and Resources, A. Cornwell
Surveyor of the Fabric, S. Bond
Director of Public Affairs, P. D. Hammond
Curator, Historic Royal Palaces, Dr S. J. Thurley
Commercial Director, C. MacDonald
Director, Hampton Court Palace, R. Evans, FRICS
Resident Governor, HM Tower of London, Maj.-Gen.
  M. G. Field
Administrator, Kensington Palace, N. J. Arch

ROYAL PARKS AGENCY
The Old Police House, Hyde Park, London W2 2UH
Tel 0171-298 2000

The agency is responsible for maintaining and developing
the royal parks.
Chief Executive (G5), D. Welch

NATIONAL HERITAGE MEMORIAL FUND
20 King Street, London SW1Y 6QY
Tel 0171-930 0963

The National Heritage Memorial Fund is an independent
body established in 1980 as a memorial to those who have
died for the UK. The Fund is empowered by the National
Heritage Act 1980 to give financial assistance towards the
cost of acquiring, maintaining or preserving land, buildings, works of art and other objects of outstanding interest
which are also of importance to the national heritage. The
Fund is administered by 13 trustees who are appointed by
the Prime Minister.

The National Lottery Act 1993 designated the Fund as
distributor of the heritage share of proceeds from the
National Lottery (one fifth of the proceeds to the 'good
causes'). In effect, this positioned the Fund as an umbrella
organization operating two funds: the Heritage Memorial
Fund and the Heritage Lottery Fund. The Heritage
Memorial Fund receives an annual grant from the Depart-
ment of National Heritage (£8 million in 1996–7). The
Heritage Lottery Fund had made awards to the value of
£256.6 million by July 1996.
Chairman, The Lord Rothschild
Trustees, Dr E. Anderson; Sir Richard Carew Pole, Bt.;
  W. L. Evans; Sir Nicholas Goodison; Sir Martin
  Holdgate; Mrs C. Hubbard; Sir Martin Jacomb;
  J. Keegan; The Lord Macfarlane of Bearsden;
  Prof. P. J. Newbould; Mrs J. Nutting; Mrs C. Porteous;
  Dame Sue Tinson, DBE
Director, Ms A. Case

NATIONAL INSURANCE JOINT AUTHORITY
The Adelphi, 1–11 John Adam Street, London WC2N 6HT
Tel 0171-962 8523

The Authority's function is to co-ordinate the operation of
social security legislation in Great Britain and Northern
Ireland, including the necessary financial adjustments
between the two National Insurance Funds.
Members, The Secretary of State for Social Security; the
  Head of the Department of Health and Social Services
  for Northern Ireland.
Secretary, M. Driver

NATIONAL INVESTMENT AND LOANS OFFICE
1 King Charles Street, London SW1A 2AP
Tel 0171-270 3861

The National Investment and Loans Office was set up in
1980 by the merger of the National Debt Office and the
Public Works Loan Board. The Office provides staff and
services for the National Debt Commissioners and the
Public Works Loan Commissioners. The National Debt
Office is responsible for the investment and management
of statutory funds relating to the surplus monies of certain
government bodies; the management of some residual
operations relating to the national debt; and the facilitation
of raising funds by central government following Article
104 of the Maastricht Treaty, in pursuance of section 211 of
the Finance Act 1993. The function of the Public Works
Loan Board is to make loans for capital purposes from
central government funds to local authorities and to collect
repayments.
Director, I. H. Peattie
Establishment Officer, A. G. Ladd

NATIONAL DEBT OFFICE
Comptroller-General, I. H. Peattie

PUBLIC WORKS LOAN BOARD
Chairman, Sir Robin Dent, KCVO
Deputy Chairman, A. D. Loehnis, CMG

Other Commissioners, Miss V. J. Di Palma, OBE;
R. A. Chapman; A. Morton; G. G. Williams;
L. B. Woodhall; Ms S. V. Masters; Mrs R. V. Hale;
R. Burton; J. A. Parkes; J. Andrews
Secretary, I. H. Peattie
Assistant Secretary, Miss L. M. Ashcroft

OFFICE OF THE NATIONAL LOTTERY
2 Monck Street, London SW1P 2BQ
Tel 0345-125596

The Office of the National Lottery (OFLOT) was
established as a non-ministerial government department
under the National Lottery Act 1993. It regulates the
National Lottery operations and licenses games promoted
as part of the Lottery.

About 28 per cent of national lottery proceeds is
currently allocated equally to five 'good causes': the arts,
charities, heritage, sport and the Millennium Fund. More
than £1,400 million had been allocated to the good causes
by 31 March 1996.
Director-General (G2), P. Davis
Deputy Director-General (G5), Ms D. Kahn
Head of Compliance Regulation (G5), K. Dunn

NATIONAL LOTTERY CHARITIES BOARD
St Vincent House, 30 Orange Street, London WC2H 7HH
Tel 0171-747 5300

The Board is the independent body set up under the
National Lottery Act 1993 to distribute funds from the
Lottery to support charitable, benevolent and philan-
thropic organizations (one-fifth of the 28 per cent allocated
to 'good causes'). There are 22 Board members including
the chairman. Members are appointed by the Secretary of
State for National Heritage. The Board's main aim is to
help meet the needs of those at greatest disadvantage in
society and to improve the quality of life in the community
through themed grants programmes in the UK and an
international grants programme for UK-based charities
working abroad. The Board is also piloting a small grants
scheme in Wales. By June 1996 the Board had awarded
4,689 grants totalling £319 million.
Chairman, The Hon. D. Sieff
Chief Executive, T. Hornsby
Members, Mrs T. Baring; A. Bhatia; G. Bowie; Mrs
J. Churchman; I. Clarke; Ms S. Clarke; Ms P. de Lima;
A. Higgins; T. Jones; Ms A. Jordan; Ms J. Kaufmann;
W. Kirkpatrick; Ms A. McGinley; Ms M. McWilliams;
W. G. Morrison; A. Phillips; Ms L. Quinn; Sir Adam
Ridley; J. Simpson, OBE; N. Stewart; Prof. Sir Eric
Stroud, FRCP; C. Woodcock

NATIONAL PHYSICAL LABORATORY
Queen's Road, Teddington, Middx TW11 0LW
Tel 0181-977 3222

The Laboratory is government-owned but contractor-
operated. It develops and disseminates national measurement standards.
Managing Director, Dr J. Rae

NATIONAL RADIOLOGICAL PROTECTION BOARD
Chilton, Didcot, Oxon OX11 0RQ
Tel 01235-831600

The National Radiological Protection Board is an independent statutory body created by the Radiological
Protection Act 1970. It is the national point of authoritative
reference on radiological protection for both ionizing and
non-ionizing radiations, and has issued recommendations
on limiting human exposure to electromagnetic fields and
radiation from a range of sources, including X-rays, the Sun
and power generators. Its sponsoring department is the
Department of Health.
Chairman, Prof. Sir Keith Peters
Director, Prof. R. H. Clarke

DEPARTMENT FOR NATIONAL SAVINGS
Charles House, 375 Kensington High Street, London
W14 8SD
Tel 0171-605 9300

The Department for National Savings was established as a
government department in 1969. It became an executive
agency of the Treasury in July 1996. The Department is
responsible for the administration of a wide range of
schemes for personal savers.
Chief Executive, P. Bareau
Deputy Director (G3), K. Chivers
Director, Operations (G5), D. H. Monaghan
Director, Information Systems (G5), A. S. McGill
Director, Personnel (G5), D. S. Speedie
Director, Finance (G5), M. A. Nicholls
Director, Marketing (G5), Miss A. Nash
Director, Policy and Product Development (G5),
P. N. S. Hickman-Robertson

For details of schemes, *see* National Savings section

OFFICE FOR NATIONAL STATISTICS
Great George Street, London SW1P 3AQ
Tel 0171-270 3000

The Office for National Statistics was created in April 1996
by the merger of the Central Statistical Office and the
Office of Population, Censuses and Surveys. It is an
executive agency of the Treasury and is responsible for
the full range of functions previously carried out by those
offices. This includes responsibility for preparing and
interpreting key economic statistics for government
policy; collecting and publishing business statistics; publishing annual and monthly statistical digests; providing
researchers, analysts and other customers with a statistical
service; administration of the marriage laws and local
registration of births, marriages and deaths in England and
Wales; provision of population estimates and projections
and statistics on health and other demographic matters in
England and Wales; population censuses in England and
Wales; surveys for government departments and public
bodies; and promoting these functions within the UK, the
European Union and internationally to provide a statistical
service to meet European Union and international requirements.

The office for National Statistics is also responsible for
establishing and maintaining a central database of key

economic and social statistics produced to common classifications, definitions and standards.

Chief Executive, Prof. T. Holt
Directors (*G3*), J. Calder; J. Fox; J. Kidgell; L. Mayhew; M. Pepper; D. Roberts
Principal Establishment Officer (*G5*), E. Williams
Principal Finance Officer (*G5*), B. Smith
Head of Information (*G6*), I. Scott
Parliamentary Clerk, L. Land

JOINT NATURE CONSERVATION COMMITTEE
Monkstone House, City Road, Peterborough PEI IJY
Tel 01733-62626

The Committee was established under the Environmental Protection Act 1990. It advises the Government and others on UK and international nature conservation issues and disseminates knowledge on these subjects. It establishes common standards for the monitoring of nature conservation and research, and analyses the resulting information. It commissions research relevant to these roles, and provides guidance to English Nature, Scottish Natural Heritage, the Countryside Council for Wales and the Department of the Environment for Northern Ireland.

Chairman, The Earl of Selborne, KBE, FRS
Chief Officer, Dr A. E. Brown
Director, Dr M. A. Vincent

NOLAN COMMITTEE
— *see* page 346

NORTHERN IRELAND AUDIT OFFICE
106 University Street, Belfast BT7 IEU
Tel 01232-251000

The primary aim of the Northern Ireland Audit Office is to provide independent assurance, information and advice to Parliament on the proper accounting for Northern Ireland departmental and certain other public expenditure, revenue, assets and liabilities; on regularity and propriety; and on the economy, efficiency and effectiveness of the use of resources.

Comptroller and Auditor-General for Northern Ireland,
   J. M. Dowdall

NORTHERN IRELAND OFFICE
Whitehall, London SWIA 2AZ
Tel 0171-210 3000
Stormont Castle, Belfast BT4 3ST
Tel 01232-520700

The Northern Ireland Office was established in 1972, when the Northern Ireland (Temporary Provisions) Act transferred the legislative and executive powers of the Northern Ireland Parliament and Government to the UK Parliament and a Secretary of State.

The Northern Ireland Office is responsible primarily for security issues, law and order and prisons, and for matters relating to the political and constitutional future of the province. It also deals with international issues as they affect Northern Ireland, including the Anglo-Irish Agreement. The Northern Ireland departments are responsible

for the administration of social, industrial and economic policies.

The names of most civil servants are not listed for security reasons.

Secretary of State for Northern Ireland, The Rt. Hon. Sir Patrick Mayhew, QC, MP
   Special Adviser, D. Campbell-Bannerman
   Parliamentary Private Secretary, J. Cran, MP
Ministers of State, The Rt. Hon. Michael Ancram, MP; The Rt. Hon. Sir John Wheeler, MP
   Parliamentary Private Secretary to Michael Ancram, H. Elletson, MP
Parliamentary Under-Secretaries of State, The Baroness Denton of Wakefield, CBE; Malcolm Moss, MP
Permanent Under-Secretary of State (*G1*), Sir John Chilcot, KCB
Second Permanent Under-Secretary of State, Head of the Northern Ireland Civil Service, Sir David Fell, KCB

LONDON
Deputy Secretary (Political Director)
Under-Secretaries (*G3*), (Associate Political Director); (Security and International; Constitutional and Political; Economic and Social); (Establishment and Finance)
SCS, (Information Services)

BELFAST
Deputy Secretary (Political Director)
Under-Secretaries (Associate Political Director); (Security); (Criminal Justice); (Political); (Establishment and Finance)

EXECUTIVE AGENCIES
COMPENSATION AGENCY, Royston House, Upper Queen Street, Belfast BTI 6FD. Tel: 01232-2499444
PRISON SERVICE AGENCY, Dundonald House, Upper Newtownards Road, Belfast B4 3SU. Tel: 01232-520700

DEPARTMENT OF AGRICULTURE FOR NORTHERN IRELAND
Dundonald House, Upper Newtownards Road, Belfast BT4 3SB
Tel 01232-520100

Parliamentary Under-Secretary of State, The Baroness Denton of Wakefield, CBE
Permanent Secretary (*G2*)
Under-Secretaries (*G3*), (Central Services and Rural Development); (Food and Farm Policy); (Agri-Environment Policy, Forestry and Fisheries); (Veterinary); (Science); (Agri-Food Development)

EXECUTIVE AGENCY
INTERVENTION BOARD
— *see* page 315

DEPARTMENT OF ECONOMIC DEVELOPMENT NORTHERN IRELAND
Netherleigh, Massey Avenue, Belfast BT4 2JP
Tel 01232-529900

Parliamentary Under-Secretary of State, The Baroness Denton of Wakefield, CBE
Permanent Secretary (*G2*)
Under-Secretaries (*G3*), (Resources Group); (Regulatory Services Group)
INDUSTRIAL DEVELOPMENT BOARD, IDB House, 64 Chichester Street, Belfast BTI 4JX. Tel: 01232-233233

EXECUTIVE AGENCIES

INDUSTRIAL RESEARCH AND TECHNOLOGY UNIT, Netherleigh, Massey Avenue, Belfast BT4 2JP. Tel: 01232-529900

TRAINING AND EMPLOYMENT AGENCY (NORTHERN IRELAND), Clarendon House, 39–49 Adelaide Street, Belfast BT2 8FD. Tel: 01232-541541

DEPARTMENT OF EDUCATION FOR NORTHERN IRELAND
Rathgael House, Balloo Road, Bangor, Co. Down BT19 7PR
Tel 01247-279279

Minister of State, The Rt. Hon. Michael Ancram, MP
Permanent Secretary (G2)
Under-Secretaries (G3), (Schools); (Finance and Corporate Services); (Education and Training Inspectorate)

DEPARTMENT OF THE ENVIRONMENT FOR NORTHERN IRELAND
Clarence Court, 10–18 Adelaide Street, Belfast BT2 8GB
Tel 01232-540540

Parliamentary Under-Secretary of State, Malcolm Moss, MP
Permanent Secretary (G2)
Under-Secretaries (G3), (Personnel, Finance, Housing and Local Government); (Rural and Urban Affairs); (Roads, Water and Transport); (Planning, Works and Environment)

EXECUTIVE AGENCIES

CONSTRUCTION SERVICE, Churchill House, Victoria Square, Belfast BT1 4QW. Tel: 01232-250284

DRIVER AND VEHICLE LICENSING AGENCY (NORTHERN IRELAND), County Hall, Castlerock Road, Coleraine, Co. Londonderry BT51 3HS. Tel: 01265-41200

DRIVER AND VEHICLE TESTING AGENCY (NORTHERN IRELAND), Balmoral Road, Belfast BT12 6QL. Tel: 01232-681831

ENVIRONMENT AND HERITAGE SERVICE, Commonwealth House, Castle Street, Belfast BT1 1GU. Tel: 01232-251477

LAND REGISTERS OF NORTHERN IRELAND, Lincoln Building, 27–45 Great Victoria Street, Belfast BT2 7SL. Tel: 01232-251515

ORDNANCE SURVEY OF NORTHERN IRELAND, Colby House, Stranmillis Court, Belfast BT9 5BJ. Tel: 01232-255755

PLANNING SERVICE, Clarence Court, 10–18 Adelaide Street, Belfast BT2 8GB. Tel: 01232-540540

PUBLIC RECORD OFFICE (NORTHERN IRELAND) – *see* page 337

RATE COLLECTION AGENCY (NORTHERN IRELAND), Oxford House, 49–55 Chichester Street, Belfast BT1 4HH. Tel: 01232-252252

ROADS SERVICE, Clarence Court, 10–18 Adelaide Street, Belfast BT2 8GB. Tel: 01232-540540

WATER SERVICE, Northland House, 3 Frederick Street, Belfast BT1 2NR. Tel: 01232-244711

ADVISORY BODIES

HISTORIC BUILDINGS COUNCIL FOR NORTHERN IRELAND, c/o Environment and Heritage Service, Historic Monuments and Buildings, Commonwealth House, Castle Street, Belfast BT1 1GU. Tel: 01232-251477

COUNCIL FOR NATURE CONSERVATION AND THE COUNTRYSIDE, c/o Environment and Heritage Service, Commonwealth House, Castle Street, Belfast BT1 1GU. Tel: 01232-251477

DEPARTMENT OF FINANCE AND PERSONNEL
Rosepark, Belfast BT4 3SW
Tel 01232-520400

Minister of State, The Rt. Hon. Sir John Wheeler, MP
Permanent Secretary (G2)
Under-Secretaries (G3), (Supply Group); (Resources Control and Professional Services Group); (Central Personnel Group); (Government Purchasing Service)

NORTHERN IRELAND CIVIL SERVICE (NICS)
Stormont Castle, Belfast BT4 3TT
Tel 01232-520700

Head of Civil Service (G1A), Sir David Fell, KCB
Under-Secretaries (G3), (Central Secretariat); (Legal Services); (Office of the Legislative Council)

GENERAL REGISTER OFFICE (NORTHERN IRELAND)
Oxford House, 49–65 Chichester Street, Belfast BT1 4HL
Tel 01232-252000

Registrar-General (G6)

EXECUTIVE AGENCY

VALUATION AND LANDS AGENCY, Queen's Court, 56–66 Upper Queen Street, Belfast BT4 6FD. Tel: 01232-439303

DEPARTMENT OF HEALTH AND SOCIAL SERVICES NORTHERN IRELAND
Dundonald House, Upper Newtownards Road, Belfast BT4 3SF
Tel 01232-520500

Parliamentary Under-Secretary of State, Malcolm Moss, MP
Permanent Secretary (G2)
Chief Medical Officer (G2A)
Under-Secretaries (G3), (Health and Social Services Group); (Health and Social Policy); (Medical and Allied Services); (Central Management and Social Security Policy Group)

EXECUTIVE AGENCIES

NORTHERN IRELAND CHILD SUPPORT AGENCY, Great Northern Tower, 17 Great Victoria Street, Belfast BT2 7AD. Tel: 01232-339000

NORTHERN IRELAND HEALTH AND SOCIAL SERVICES ESTATES AGENCY, Stoney Road, Dundonald, Belfast BT16 0US. Tel: 01232-520025

NORTHERN IRELAND SOCIAL SECURITY AGENCY, Castle Buildings, Stormont, Belfast BT4 3SJ. Tel: 01232-520520

OCCUPATIONAL PENSIONS BOARD
PO Box 2EE, Newcastle upon Tyne NE99 2EE
Tel 0191-225 6414

The Occupational Pensions Board (OPB) is an independent statutory body set up under the Social Security Act 1973 to administer the contracting-out of occupational pensions from the State Earnings Related Pension Scheme (SERPS), and to advise the Secretary of State. Its functions have been extended by subsequent legislation and it is now also responsible for administering equal access, preservation, and modification requirements and appropriate personal pension schemes. Following the Social Security Act 1990, the OPB was appointed as Registrar of Occupational and Personal Pension Schemes and granted powers to make grants to approved bodies in the field. The OPB now funds the operation of the Occupational Pensions Advisory Service (OPAS).

The OPB is to be dissolved on 5 April 1997 under the Pension Act 1995. It will be replaced by the Occupational Pensions Regulatory Authority (OPRA).

Chairman, P. D. Carr, CBE
Deputy Chairman, Miss C. H. Dawes, OBE
Secretary to the Board and General Manager of Executive Office (*G6*), M. McLean
Chief Executive, OPRA, Ms C. Johnston

OMBUDSMEN

— *see* Local Commissioners *and* Parliamentary Commissioner. For non-statutory Ombudsmen, *see* Index

ORDNANCE SURVEY

Romsey Road, Maybush, Southampton SO16 4GU
Tel 01703-792000

Ordnance Survey is the national mapping agency for Britain. It became an executive agency in 1990 and reports to the Secretary of State for the Environment.

Ordnance Survey maintains a large-scale database (which replaces the large-scale plans previously available) from which site-centred plans can be plotted at a variety of scales. It also produces a wide range of small-scale maps, co-publishes several series of atlases and guidebooks, and is becoming increasingly involved in the supply of mapping as data.

Director-General and Chief Executive, Prof. D. Rhind

OVERSEAS DEVELOPMENT ADMINISTRATION

94 Victoria Street, London SW1E 5JL
Tel 0171-917 7000
Abercrombie House, Eaglesham Road, East Kilbride, Glasgow G75 8EA
Tel 01355-844000

The Overseas Development Administration of the Foreign and Commonwealth Office deals with British development assistance to overseas countries. This includes both capital aid on concessional terms and technical assistance (mainly in the form of specialist staff abroad and training facilities in the UK), whether provided directly to developing countries or through the various multilateral aid organizations, including the United Nations and its specialized agencies.

Minister for Overseas Development, The Baroness Chalker of Wallasey, PC
Private Secretary (*G7*), R. Calvert
Parliamentary Private Secretary, A. Hargreaves, MP
Permanent Secretary (*SCS*), J. M. M. Vereker
Private Secretary, B. Mellor

PROGRAMMES

Director-General (*SCS*), B. R. Ireton
Head of Emergency Aid Department (*SCS*), P. A. Bearpark

AFRICA
Director (*SCS*), P. D. M. Freeman
Heads of Departments (*SCS*), Mrs B. M. Kelly, CBE (*Africa, Greater Horn and Co-ordination*); S. Ray (*West and North Africa*); M. A. Wickstead (*British Development Division in East Africa*); A. G. Coverdale (*British Development Division in Central Africa*); J. H. S. Chard (*British Development Division in South Africa*)

ASIA
Director (*SCS*), J. V. Kerby
Heads of Departments (*SCS*), A. D. Davis (*East Asia and Pacific*); Ms S. E. Unsworth (*British Development Co-operation Office*); Ms M. H. Vowles (*Western Asia*); A. K. C. Wood (*South-East Asia Development Division*); K. L. Sparkhall (*Aid Management Office*)

EASTERN EUROPE AND WESTERN HEMISPHERE
Director (*SCS*), J. A. L. Faint
Heads of Departments (*SCS*), M. C. McCulloch (*Joint Assistance Department* (*Eastern*)); J. S. Laing (*Joint Assistance Department* (*Central Europe*)); B. P. Thomson (*British Development Division in the Caribbean*); (*G6*), D. R. Curran (*Latin America, Caribbean and Atlantic*); (*G7*), J. D. Moye (*EBRD Unit*)

ECONOMICS AND GOVERNANCE
Director, and Chief Economic Adviser (*SCS*), J. B. W. Wilmshurst
Chief Statistician (*SCS*), A. B. Williams
Head of Asia, Latin America and Oceans Economics (*G6*), P. J. Ackroyd
Head of African Economics Department (*SCS*), M. G. Foster
Head of International Economics Department (*SCS*), P. D. Grant
Senior Small-Scale Enterprise Adviser (*G6*), D. L. Wright
Senior Economic Advisers (*G6*), Ms R. L. Turner; P. L. Owen; P. J. Dearden; P. J. Landymore; E. Hawthorn; F. C. Clift; J. L. Hoy
Head of Government Institutions Advisory Department (*SCS*), R. J. Wilson
Senior Government and Institutions Advisers (*G6*), Dr G. W. Glentworth; D. W. Baker; Mrs A. Newsum; S. Sharples; J. G. Clarke
Senior Police Adviser (*G6*), L. H. Grundy

HUMAN RESOURCE DEVELOPMENT
Director, and Chief Health and Population Adviser (*SCS*), Dr D. N. Nabarro
Senior Health and Population Advisers (*G6*), Dr P. J. Key; J. N. Lambert; Ms J. M. Isard; S. Tyson; R. N. Grose; Ms C. M. Sergeant
Chief Social Development Adviser (*G6*), Dr R. Eyben
Senior Social Development Advisers (*G6*), Ms P. M. Holden; Dr A. M. Coles
Chief Education Adviser (*SCS*), Ms M. A. Harrison
Senior Education Advisers (*G6*), Dr C. Treffgarne; M. E. Seath; M. D. Francis; R. T. Allsop; Dr D. B. Pennycuick; S. E. Packer; Dr K. M. Lillis; Dr G. R. H. Jones
Senior Technical Education Adviser (*G6*), C. Lewis

PRODUCTIVE CAPACITY AND ENVIRONMENT
Director, and Chief Natural Resources Adviser (*SCS*), A. J. Bennett
Head of Environment Policy Department (*SCS*), D. P. Turner
Head of Natural Resources Policy and Advisory Department, and Deputy Chief Natural Resources Adviser (*SCS*), J. M. Scott
Head of Natural Resources Research Department (*SCS*), Dr I. H. Haines
Senior Natural Resources Advisers (*G6*), Ms F. Proctor; R. C. Fox; M. J. Wilson; A. J. Tainsh; J. R. F. Hansell; Dr B. E. Grimwood; J. A. Harvey; A. Hall
Natural Resources Systems Programme Manager (*G6*), J. C. Barrett
Senior Environment and Research Adviser (*G6*), Ms L. C. Brown
Senior Fisheries Advisers (*G6*), R. W. Beales; Dr J. Tarbit
Senior Forestry Advisers (*G6*), J. M. Hudson; I. A. Napier
Senior Animal Health Advisers (*G6*), G. G. Freeland; Ms L. M. Bell
Chief Engineering Adviser (*SCS*), J. W. Hodges

Senior Engineering Advisers (G6), B. Dolton; C. I. Ellis; P. J.
Davies; D. F. Gillett; P. W. D. H. Roberts; M. F.
Sergeant; R. J. Cadwallader; C. J. Hunt
Senior Water Resources Adviser (G6), A. Wray
Senior Architectural and Physical Planning Adviser (G6), M. W.
Parkes
Senior Electrical and Mechanical Adviser (G6), R. P. Jones
Senior Renewable Energy and Research Adviser (G6),
A. Gilchrist
Industrial Training Adviser (G7), D. G. Marr

RESOURCES

Director-General (SCS), R. G. Manning
Heads of Departments (SCS), J. R. Drummond (*Personnel*);
D. S. Fish (*Procurement, Appointments and NGO*); P. Aylett
(*Information*); G. M. Stegmann (*Aid Policy and Resources*);
B. W. Hammond (*Information Systems*); R. A. Elias
(*Internal Audit Unit*); C. P. Raleigh (*Evaluation*); (*G6*),
R. Plumb (*Overseas Pensions*); K. D. Grimshaw (*Sponsored
Organizations Unit*)
Assistant Establishment Officer (G6), J. A. Anning

INTERNATIONAL DEVELOPMENT AFFAIRS
Director (SCS), N. B. Hudson, CB
Heads of Departments (SCS), D. J. Batt (*European Union*); J. C.
Machin (*United Nations and Commonwealth*); M. E. Cund
(*International Financial Institutions*)

OFFICE OF THE PARLIAMENTARY COMMISSIONER FOR ADMINISTRATION AND HEALTH SERVICE COMMISSIONER
Church House, Great Smith Street, London SWIP 3BW
Tel 0171-276 2130 (*Parliamentary Commissioner*); 0171-217
4051 (*Health Service Commissioner*)

The Parliamentary Commissioner for Administration (the
Parliamentary Ombudsman) is independent of Government and is an officer of Parliament. He is responsible for
investigating complaints referred to him by MPs from
members of the public who claim to have sustained
injustice in consequence of maladministration by or on
behalf of government departments and certain non-
departmental public bodies. Certain types of action by
government departments or bodies are excluded from
investigation. The Parliamentary Commissioner is also
responsible for investigating complaints, referred by MPs,
alleging that access to official information has been
wrongly refused under the Code of Practice on Access to
Government Information 1994.

The Health Service Commissioners (the Health Service
Ombudsmen) for England, for Scotland and for Wales are
responsible for investigating complaints against National
Health Service authorities and trusts that are not dealt with
by those authorities to the satisfaction of the complainant.
Complaints can be referred direct by the member of the
public who claims to have sustained injustice or hardship in
consequence of the failure in a service provided by a
relevant body, failure of that body to provide a service or in
consequence of any other action by that body. (The
Ombudsmens' jurisdiction now covers complaints about
family doctors, dentists, pharmacists and opticians, and
complaints about actions resulting from clinical judgment.)
The Health Service Ombudsmen are also responsible for
investigating complaints that information has been wrongly refused under the Code of Practice on Openness in the
National Health Service 1995. The three offices are
presently held by the Parliamentary Commissioner.
*Parliamentary Commissioner and Health Service Commissioner
(G1)*, Sir William Reid, KCB (*until end 1996*)

Deputy Parliamentary Commissioners (G3), J. E. Avery;
J. Tate
Deputy Health Service Commissioners (G3), C. H. Wilson;
Miss M. I. Nisbet
Directors, Parliamentary Commissioner (G5), Mrs
A. H. P. Bates; D. J. Coffey; Mrs S. P. Maunsell;
J. L. Railton; A. Watson
Directors, Health Service Commissioners (G5), Miss
H. Bainbridge; D. P. Flaherty; N. J. Jordan;
R. H. Keynes; D. R. G. Pinchin; P. Pugh
Finance and Establishment Officer (G6), T. G. Hull

PARLIAMENTARY COMMISSIONER FOR STANDARDS
House of Commons, London SWIA OAA
Tel 0171-219 0320

Following recommendations of the Committee on Standards in Public Life (the Nolan Committee) the House of
Commons agreed to the appointment of an independent
Parliamentary Commissioner for Standards. The Commissioner was appointed with effect from November 1995
and has responsibility for maintaining and monitoring the
operation of the Register of Members' Interests; advising
Members of Parliament and the new select committee on
standards and privileges on the interpretation of the rules
on disclosure and advocacy and on other questions of
propriety; and receiving and, if he thinks fit, investigating
complaints about the conduct of MPs.
Parliamentary Commissioner for Standards, Sir Gordon
Downey, KCB

PARLIAMENTARY COUNSEL
36 Whitehall, London SWIA 2AY
Tel 0171-210 6633

Parliamentary Counsel draft all government bills (i.e.
primary legislation) except those relating exclusively to
Scotland, the latter being drafted by the Lord Advocate's
Department. They also advise on all aspects of parlia-
mentary procedure in connection with such bills and draft
government amendments to them as well as any motions
(including financial resolutions) necessary to secure their
introduction into, and passage through, Parliament.
First Counsel (SCS), J. C. Jenkins, CB, QC
Counsel (SCS), D. W. Saunders, CB; E. G. Caldwell, CB;
E. G. Bowman, CB; G. B. Sellers, CB; E. R. Sutherland, CB;
P. F. A. Knowles, CB; S. C. Laws, CB; R. S. Parker; Miss
C. E. Johnston; P. J. Davies

PAROLE BOARD FOR ENGLAND AND WALES
Abell House, John Islip Street, London SWIP 4LH
Tel 0171-217 5314

The Board was constituted under the Criminal Justice Act
1967 and continued under the Criminal Justice Act 1991.
Its duty is to advise the Home Secretary with respect to
matters referred to it by him which are connected with the
early release or recall of prisoners. Its functions include
giving directions concerning the release on licence of
prisoners serving discretionary life sentences and of certain
prisoners serving long-term determinate sentences; and
making recommendations to the Home Secretary concerning the early release on licence of other prisoners, the
conditions of parole and licences and the variation and

cancellation of such conditions, and the recall of long-term and life prisoners while on licence.
Chairman, The Lord Belstead, PC
Vice-Chairman, The Hon. Mr Justice Alliott
Chief Executive, M. S. Todd

PAROLE BOARD FOR SCOTLAND
Calton House, 5 Redheughs Rigg, Edinburgh EH12 9HW
Tel 0131-244 8755

The Board directs and advises the Secretary of State for Scotland on the release of prisoners on licence, and related matters.
Chairman, I. McNee
Vice-Chairman, Sheriff G. Shiach
Secretary, H. P. Boyle

PATENT OFFICE
Cardiff Road, Newport NP9 1RH
Tel 0645-500505

The Patent Office is an executive agency of the Department of Trade and Industry. The duties of the Patent Office are to administer the Patent Acts, the Registered Designs Act and the Trade Marks Act, and to deal with questions relating to the Copyright, Designs and Patents Act 1988. The Search and Advisory Service carries out commercial searches through patent information. In 1994–5 the Office granted 9,530 patents and registered 7,806 designs and 28,828 trade and service marks.
Comptroller-General (G3), P. R. S. Hartnack
Assistant Comptroller, Intellectual Property Policy Directorate (Supt. Examiner), G. Jenkins
Assistant Comptroller, Patents and Designs (G4), R. J. Marchant
Assistant Registrar, Trade Marks (G4), Miss A. Brimelow
Head of Administration and Resources (G5), C. Octon
Head of ADP Unit (G6), G. Bennett

PAYMASTER
The Office of HM Paymaster-General
Sutherland House, Russell Way, Crawley, W. Sussex
RH10 1UH
Tel 01293-560999
Alencon Link, Basingstoke, Hants RG21 7JB
Tel 01256-846488

PAYMASTER, the Office of HM Paymaster-General, was formed by the consolidation in 1835 of various separate pay departments. Its function is that of paying agent for government departments other than the revenue departments. Most of its payments are made through banks, to whose accounts the necessary transfers are made at the Bank of England. The calculation and payment of over 1.5 million public service pensions is an important feature of its work. The Office became an executive agency of the Treasury in 1993 but is to be privatized in 1997.
Paymaster-General, David Willetts, MP
Assistant Paymaster-General/Chief Executive (G5), K. Sullens

OFFICE OF THE PENSIONS OMBUDSMAN
11 Belgrave Road, London SW1V 1RB
Tel 0171-834 9144

The Pensions Ombudsman is appointed by the Secretary of State for Social Security under the Pension Schemes Act 1993 to deal with complaints against, and disputes with, occupational and personal pension schemes. He is completely independent.
Pensions Ombudsman, Dr J. T. Farrand

POLICE COMPLAINTS AUTHORITY
10 Great George Street, London SW1P 3AE
Tel 0171-273 6450

The Police Complaints Authority was established under the Police and Criminal Evidence Act 1984 to provide an independent system for dealing with serious complaints by members of the public against police officers in England and Wales. It is funded by the Home Office. The authority has powers to supervise the investigation of certain categories of serious complaints and certain statutory functions in relation to the disciplinary aspects of complaints. It does not deal with police operational matters; these are usually dealt with by the Chief Constable of the relevant force.
Chairman (acting), P. Moorhouse
Deputy Chairman (Investigations), J. Cartwright
Deputy Chairman (Discipline), P. W. Moorhouse
Members, Mrs L. Cawsey; N. Dholakia, OBE; J. Elliott; Miss L. Haye; A. Kelly; Mrs M. Meacher; Mrs C. Mitchell; E. Wignall; A. Williams

INDEPENDENT COMMISSION FOR POLICE COMPLAINTS FOR NORTHERN IRELAND
— see page 313

POLITICAL HONOURS SCRUTINY COMMITTEE
Cabinet Office, 53 Parliament Street, London SW1A 2NG
Tel 0171-210 5058

The function of the Political Honours Scrutiny Committee (a committee of Privy Councillors) was set out in an Order of Council in 1991 and amended by Orders in Council in 1992 and 1994. The Prime Minister submits certain particulars to the Committee about persons proposed to be recommended for honour for their political services. The Committee, after such enquiry as they think fit, report to the Prime Minister whether, so far as they believe, the persons whose names are submitted to them are fit and proper persons to be recommended.
Chairman, The Lord Pym, MC, PC
Members, The Lord Cledwyn of Penrhos, CH, PC; The Lord Thomson of Monifieth, KT, PC
Secretary, A. J. Merifield, CB

PORT OF LONDON AUTHORITY
Devon House, 58–60 St Katharine's Way, London E1 9LB
Tel 0171-265 2656

The Port of London Authority is a public trust constituted under the Port of London Act 1908 and subsequent

legislation. It is the governing body for the Port of London, covering the tidal portion of the River Thames from Teddington to the seaward limit. The Board comprises a chairman and up to seven but not less than four non-executive members appointed by the Secretary of State for Transport, and up to four but not less than one executive members appointed by the Board.
Chairman, Sir Brian Shaw
Vice-Chairman, J. H. Kelly, CBE
Chief Executive, D. Jeffery
Secretary, G. E. Ennals

THE POST OFFICE
148 Old Street, London EC1V 9HQ
Tel 0171-490 2888

Crown services for the carriage of government dispatches were set up in about 1516. The conveyance of public correspondence began in 1635 and the mail service was made a parliamentary responsibility with the setting up of a Post Office in 1657. Telegraphs came under Post Office control in 1870 and the Post Office Telephone Service began in 1880. The National Girobank service of the Post Office began in 1968. The Post Office ceased to be a government department in 1969 when responsibility for the running of the postal, telecommunications, giro and remittance services was transferred to a public authority called the Post Office. The 1981 British Telecommunications Act separated the functions of the Post Office, making it solely responsible for postal services and Girobank. Girobank was privatized in 1990.

The chairman, chief executive and members of the Post Office Board are appointed by the Secretary of State for Trade and Industry but responsibility for the running of the Post Office as a whole rests with the Board in its corporate capacity.

FINANCIAL RESULTS £m	1994–5	1995–6
Post Office Group		
Turnover	5,878	6,210
Profit before tax	472	422
Royal Mail		
Turnover	4,540	4,804
Profit before tax	430	354
Parcelforce		
Turnover	481	471
Profit (loss) before tax	(30)	1
Post Office Counters		
Turnover	1,118	1,195
Profit before tax	30	35

POST OFFICE BOARD
Chairman, Sir Michael Heron
Chief Executive, J. Roberts, CBE
Members, R. Close (*Managing Director, Finance*); J. Cope (*Managing Director, Strategy and Personnel*)
Secretary, R. Osmond
For postal services, *see* pages 510–12

PRIME MINISTER'S OFFICE
— *see* page 287

PRISONS OMBUDSMAN FOR ENGLAND AND WALES
St Vincent House, 30 Orange Street, London WC2H 7HH
Tel 0171-389 1527

The post of Prisons Ombudsman was instituted in 1994. The Ombudsman is appointed by the Home Secretary and is an independent point of appeal for prisoners' grievances about their lives in prison, including disciplinary issues. The Ombudsman cannot investigate grievances relating to issues which are the subject of litigation or criminal proceedings, decisions taken by ministers, or actions of bodies outside the prison service.
Prisons Ombudsman, Sir Peter Woodhead, KCB

For Scotland, *see* Scottish Prisons Complaints Commission

PRIVY COUNCIL OFFICE
Whitehall, London SW1A 2AT
Tel 0171-270 3000

The Office is responsible for the arrangements leading to the making of all royal proclamations and Orders in Council; for certain formalities connected with ministerial changes; for considering applications for the granting (or amendment) of royal charters; for the scrutiny and approval of by-laws and statutes of chartered bodies; and for the appointment of High Sheriffs and many Crown and Privy Council appointments to governing bodies.
Lord President of the Council (and Leader of the House of Commons), The Rt. Hon. Antony Newton, OBE, MP
Private Secretary, P. Cohen
Special Adviser, P. Moman
Parliamentary Private Secretary, J. Couchman, MP
Clerk of the Council (G3), N. H. Nicholls, CBE
Deputy Clerk of the Council (G5), Miss K. P. Makin, OBE
Senior Clerk, Miss M. A. McCullagh

PROCURATOR FISCAL SERVICE
— *see* pages 369–70

PUBLIC HEALTH LABORATORY SERVICE
61 Colindale Avenue, London NW9 5DF
Tel 0181-200 1295

The Public Health Laboratory Service comprises nine groups of laboratories, the Central Public Health Laboratory and the Communicable Disease Surveillance Centre. The PHLS provides diagnostic microbiological services to hospitals, and has reference facilities that are available nationally. It collates information on the incidence of infection, and when necessary it institutes special inquiries into outbreaks and the epidemiology of infectious disease. It also undertakes bacteriological surveillance of the quality of food and water for local authorities and others.
Chairman, Dr M. P. W. Godfrey, CBE, FRCP
Deputy Chairman, A. Graham-Dixon, QC
Director, Dr Diana Walford, FRCP, FRCPath.
Deputy Directors, Prof. B. I. Duerden, MD, FRCPath.
(*Programmes*); K. M. Saunders (*Corporate Planning and Resources*)
Board Secretary, K. M. Saunders

CENTRAL PUBLIC HEALTH LABORATORY
Colindale Avenue, London NW9 5HT
Director, Prof. S. P. Borriello

COMMUNICABLE DISEASES SURVEILLANCE CENTRE
Colindale Avenue, NW9 5EQ
Director, Dr C. L. R. Bartlett

OTHER SPECIAL LABORATORIES AND UNITS
ANAEROBE REFERENCE UNIT, Public Health Laboratory,
Cardiff. *Director,* Prof. B. I. Duerden, MD, FRCPath.
CRYPTOSPROIDIUM REFERENCE UNIT, Public Health
Laboratory, Rhyl. *Director,* D. N. Looker
GONOCOCCUS REFERENCE UNIT, Public Health
Laboratory, Bristol. *Director,* A. E. Jephcott, MD
LEPTOSPIRA REFERENCE LABORATORY, Public Health
Laboratory, Hereford. *Director,* Dr T. J. Coleman
MALARIA REFERENCE LABORATORY, London School of
Hygiene and Tropical Medicine, London WC1. *Directors,*
Prof. D. J. Bradley, DM; D. C. Warhurst, PH.D., FRCPath.
MENINGOCOCCAL REFERENCE LABORATORY, Public
Health Laboratory, Manchester. *Director,* Dr
B. A. Oppenheim
MYCOBACTERIUM REFERENCE UNIT, Public Health
Laboratory, Dulwich, London. *Director,*
Dr F. Drobniewski
MYCOLOGY REFERENCE LABORATORY, Public Health
Laboratory, Bristol. *Director,* Dr D. Warnock; Public
Health Laboratory, Leeds. *Director,* Prof. E. G. V. Evans
PARASITOLOGY REFERENCE LABORATORY, Hospital for
Tropical Diseases, London. *Director,* Dr P. L. Chiodini
TOXOPLASMA REFERENCE LABORATORIES, Public Health
Laboratory, Swansea. *Director,* D. H. M. Joynson; Public
Health Laboratory, Tooting, London. *Director,* Prof.
A. R. M. Coates

PHLS GROUPS OF LABORATORIES AND GROUP
DIRECTORS
East, Dr Philippa M. B. White
Midlands, Dr R. E. Warren
North, Dr N. F. Lightfoot
North-West, Dr P. Morgan-Capner
South Thames, Prof. R. Y. Cartwright
South-West, Dr K. A. V. Cartwright
Trent, Dr P. J. Wilkinson
Wessex, Dr S. A. Rousseau
Wales, Dr A. J. Howard

REGISTRAR OF PUBLIC LENDING RIGHT
Bayheath House, Prince Regent Street,
Stockton-on-Tees TS18 1DF
Tel 01642-604699

Under the Public Lending Right system, in operation since
1983, payment is made from public funds to authors whose
books are lent out from public libraries. Payment is made
once a year and the amount each author receives is
proportionate to the number of times (established from a
sample) that each registered book has been lent out during
the previous year. The Registrar of PLR, who is appointed
by the Secretary of State for National Heritage, compiles
the register of authors and books. Only living authors
resident in the UK or Germany are eligible to apply. (The
term 'author' covers writers, illustrators, translators, and
some editors/compilers.)

A payment of two pence was made in 1995–6 for each
estimated loan of a registered book, up to a top limit of
£6,000 for the books of any one registered author; the
money for loans above this level is used to augment the
remaining PLR payments. In February 1996, the sum of

£4.330 million was made available for distribution to
20,127 registered authors and assignees as the annual
payment of PLR.

The PLR Advisory Committee advises the Secretary of
State for National Heritage and the Registrar of Public
Lending Right. Its members are appointed by the Secretary
of State.
Chairman of Advisory Committee, P. S. Ziegler, CVO
Registrar, Dr J. G. Parker

PUBLIC RECORD OFFICE
— *see* page 336

PUBLIC TRUST OFFICE
Stewart House, 24 Kingsway, London WC2B 6JX
Tel 0171-269 7000

COURT FUNDS OFFICE, 22 Kingsway, London WC2B 6LE
Tel 0171-936 6000

The Public Trust Office became an executive agency of
the Lord Chancellor's Department in 1994. The chief
executive of the agency holds the statutory titles of Public
Trustee and Accountant-General of the Supreme Court.

The Public Trustee is a trust corporation created to
undertake the business of executorship and trusteeship; she
can act as executor or administrator of the estate of a
deceased person, or as trustee of a will or settlement. The
Public Trustee is also responsible for the performance of
all the administrative, but not the judicial, tasks required of
the Court of Protection under Part VII of the Mental
Health Act 1983, relating to the management and administration of the property and affairs of persons suffering
from mental disorder. The Public Trustee also acts as
Receiver when so directed by the Court, usually where
there is no other person willing or able so to act.

The Accountant-General of the Supreme Court,
through the Court Funds Office, is responsible for the
investment and accounting of funds in court for persons
under a disability, monies in court subject to litigation and
statutory deposits.
Chief Executive (Public Trustee and Accountant-General), Ms
J. C. Lomas
Assistant Public Trustee, Mrs S. Hutcheson
Investment Manager, H. Stevenson
Chief Property Adviser, A. Nightingale

MENTAL HEALTH SECTOR
Head, Mrs H. M. Bratton
Receivership Activity, D. Adams
Protection Activity, P. L. Hales

TRUSTS AND FUNDS SECTOR
Head, F. J. Eddy
Court Funds Activity, R. Anns
Trust Activity, M. Munt

ESTABLISHMENTS AND FINANCE SECTOR
Head, E. A. Bloomfield
Finance, M. Guntrip
Planning, Mrs N. M. Hunt

PUBLIC WORKS LOAN BOARD
— *see* National Investment and Loans Office

COMMISSION FOR RACIAL EQUALITY
Elliot House, 10–12 Allington Street, London SW1E 5EH
Tel 0171-828 7022

The Commission was established in 1977, under the Race Relations Act 1976, to work towards the elimination of discrimination and promote equality of opportunity and good relations between different racial groups. It is funded by the Home Office.
Chairman, H. Ouseley
Deputy Chairs, Mrs Z. Manzoor; H. Harris
Members, R. Purkiss; Dr D. Neil; Ms M. Cunningham; Dr R. Chandran; Dr Z. Khan; M. Hastings; M. Jogee; Dr J. Singh; Ms J. Mellor
Executive Director, D. Sharma

THE RADIO AUTHORITY
Holbrook House, 14 Great Queen Street, London WC2B 5DG
Tel 0171-430 2724

The Radio Authority was established in 1991 under the Broadcasting Act 1990. It is the regulator and licensing authority for all independent radio services. Members of the Authority are appointed by the Secretary of State for National Heritage; senior executive staff are appointed by the Authority.
Chairman, Sir Peter Gibbings
Deputy Chairman, M. Moriarty, CB
Members, Ms J. Francis; M. Reupke; Lady Sheil; A. Reid; Mrs H. Tennant
Chief Executive, A. Stoller
Deputy Chief Executive, D. Vick
Secretary to the Authority, J. Norrington

OFFICE OF THE RAIL REGULATOR
1 Waterhouse Square, 138–142 Holborn, London EC1N 2ST
Tel 0171-282 2000

The Office of the Rail Regulator was set up under the Railways Act 1993. It is headed by the Rail Regulator, who is independent of ministerial control. The Regulator's main functions are the licensing of operators of railway assets; the approval of agreements for access by those operators to track, stations and light maintenance depots; the enforcement of domestic competition law; and consumer protection. The Regulator also sponsors a network of rail users' consultative committees, which represent the interests of passengers.
Rail Regulator, J. A. Swift, QC
Director, Personnel, Finance and Administration, P. D. Murphy
Director, Economic Regulation Group, C. W. Bolt
Director, Railway Network Group, C. J. F. Brown
Director, Passenger Services Group, J. A. Rhodes
Chief Legal Adviser, M. R. Brocklehurst

RECORD OFFICES

ADVISORY COUNCIL ON PUBLIC RECORDS
Secretariat: Public Record Office, Ruskin Avenue, Kew, Richmond, Surrey TW9 4DU
Tel 0181-876 3444

Council members are appointed by the Lord Chancellor, under the Public Records Act 1958, to advise him on matters concerning public records in general and, in particular, on those aspects of the work of the Public Record Office which affect members of the public who make use of it. The Council meets quarterly and produces an annual report which is published alongside the Report of the Keeper of Public Records as a House of Commons sessional paper.
Chairman, The Master of the Rolls
Secretary, T. R. Padfield

THE PUBLIC RECORD OFFICE
Ruskin Avenue, Kew, Richmond, Surrey TW9 4DU
Tel 0181-876 3444

The Public Record Office, originally established in 1838 under the Master of the Rolls, was placed under the direction of the Lord Chancellor in 1958. It became an executive agency in 1992. The Lord Chancellor appoints a Keeper of Public Records, whose duties are to co-ordinate and supervise the selection of records of government departments and the law courts for permanent preservation, to safeguard the records and to make them available to the public. There is a separate record office for Scotland (*see* page 337).

The Office holds records of central government dating from the Domesday Book (1086) to the present. Under the Public Records Act 1967 they are normally open to inspection when 30 years old, and are then available, without charge, in the reading rooms, Monday–Friday, 9.30–5.
Keeper of Public Records (G3), Mrs S. Tyacke
Director, Public Services Division (G5), Dr E. Hallam Smith
Director, Archival Services Division (G5), Dr N. G. Cox
Director, Corporate Services Division (G5), Dr D. Simpson

HOUSE OF LORDS RECORD OFFICE
House of Lords, London SW1A 0PW
Tel 0171-219 3074

Since 1497, the records of Parliament have been kept within the Palace of Westminster. They are in the custody of the Clerk of the Parliaments. In 1946 a record department was established to supervise their preservation and their availability to the public. The search room of the office is open to the public Monday–Friday, 9.30–5 (Tuesday to 8, by appointment).

Some three million documents are preserved, including Acts of Parliament from 1497, journals of the House of Lords from 1510, minutes and committee proceedings from 1610, and papers laid before Parliament from 1531. Amongst the records are the Petition of Right, the Death Warrant of Charles I, the Declaration of Breda, and the Bill of Rights. The House of Lords Record Office also has charge of the journals of the House of Commons (from 1547), and other surviving records of the Commons (from 1572), including documents relating to private bill legislation from 1818. Among other documents are the records of the Lord Great Chamberlain, the political papers of certain members of the two Houses, and documents relating to

Parliament acquired on behalf of the nation. A permanent exhibition was established in the Royal Gallery in 1979.
Clerk of the Records (£40,807–£59,754), D. J. Johnson, FSA
Deputy Clerk of the Records (£32,054–£51,975), S. K. Ellison
Assistant Clerk of the Records (£18,611–£32,731), D. L. Prior

ROYAL COMMISSION ON HISTORICAL MANUSCRIPTS
Quality House, Quality Court, Chancery Lane, London WC2A 1HP
Tel 0171-242 1198

The Commission was set up by royal warrant in 1869 to enquire and report on collections of papers of value for the study of history which were in private hands. In 1959 a new warrant enlarged these terms of reference to include all historical records, wherever situated, outside the Public Records and gave it added responsibilities as a central co-ordinating body to promote, assist and advise on their proper preservation and storage. The Commission, which is responsible to the Department of National Heritage, has published over 200 volumes of reports.

It also maintains the National Register of Archives (NRA), which contains over 39,000 unpublished lists and catalogues of manuscript collections describing the holdings of local record offices, national and university libraries, specialist repositories and others in the UK and overseas. The NRA can be searched using computerized indices which are available in the Commission's search room.

The Commission also administers the Manorial and Tithe Documents Rules on behalf of the Master of the Rolls.
Chairman, The Rt. Hon. Sir Thomas Bingham
Commissioners, The Lord Blake, FBA; Prof. S. F. C. Milsom, FBA; P. T. Cormack, FSA, MP; D. G. Vaisey, FSA; The Lord Egremont and Leconfield; Sir Matthew Farrer, GCVO; Miss B. Harvey, FBA, FSA; Sir John Sainty, KCB, FSA; Prof. R. H. Campbell, OBE, PH.D.; Very Revd H. E. C. Stapleton, FSA; Sir Keith Thomas, PBA; Mrs C. M. Short; The Earl of Scarbrough; Mrs A. Dundas-Bekker; G. E. Aylmer, D.Phil, FBA; Mrs S. J. Davies, PH.D.
Secretary, C. J. Kitching, PH.D., FSA

SCOTTISH RECORDS ADVISORY COUNCIL
HM General Register House, Edinburgh EH1 3YY
Tel 0131-556 6585

The Council was established under the Public Records (Scotland) Act 1937. Its members are appointed by the Secretary of State for Scotland and it may submit proposals or make representations to the Secretary of State, the Lord Justice General or the Lord President of the Court of Session on questions relating to the public records of Scotland.
Chairman, Prof. M. Anne Crowther
Secretary, D. M. Abbott

SCOTTISH RECORD OFFICE
HM General Register House, Edinburgh EH1 3YY
Tel 0131-535 1314

The history of the national archives of Scotland can be traced back to the 13th century. The Scottish Record Office keeps the administrative records of pre-Union Scotland, the registers of central and local courts of law, the public registers of property rights and legal documents, and many collections of local and church records and private archives. Certain groups of records, mainly the modern records of government departments in Scotland, the Scottish railway records, the plans collection, and

private archives of an industrial or commercial nature, are preserved in the branch repository at the West Register House in Charlotte Square. The search rooms in both buildings are open Monday–Friday, 9–4.45. A permanent exhibition at the West Register House and changing exhibitions at the General Register House are open to the public on weekdays, 10–4. The National Register of Archives (Scotland), which is a branch of the Scottish Record Office, is based in the West Register House.

The Scottish Record Office became an executive agency of the Scottish Office in 1993.
Keeper of the Records of Scotland, P. M. Cadell
Deputy Keeper, Dr P. D. Anderson

PUBLIC RECORD OFFICE (NORTHERN IRELAND)
66 Balmoral Avenue, Belfast BT9 6NY
Tel 01232-251318

The Public Record Office (Northern Ireland) is responsible for identifying and preserving Northern Ireland's archival heritage and making it available to the public. It is an executive agency of the Department of the Environment for Northern Ireland. The search room is open on weekdays, 9.15–4.15 (Thursday, 9.15–8.45).
Chief Executive (G5), Dr A. P. Malcomson

CORPORATION OF LONDON RECORDS OFFICE
Guildhall, London EC2P 2EJ
Tel 0171-332 1251

The Corporation of London Records Office contains the municipal archives of the City of London which are regarded as the most complete collection of ancient municipal records in existence. The collection includes charters of William the Conqueror, Henry II, and later kings and queens to 1957; ancient custumals: Liber Horn, Dunthorne, Custumarum, Ordinacionum, Memorandorum and Albus, Liber de Antiquis Legibus, and collections of Statutes; continuous series of judicial rolls and books from 1252 and Council minutes from 1275; records of the Old Bailey and Guildhall Sessions from 1603; financial records from the 16th century; the records of London Bridge from the 12th century; and numerous subsidiary series and miscellanea of historical interest. Readers' Room open Monday–Friday, 9.30–4.45.
Keeper of the City Records, The City Secretary
City Archivist, J. R. Sewell
Deputy City Archivist, Mrs J. M. Bankes

RESEARCH COUNCILS
— *see* pages 701–6

REVIEW BODIES

The secretariat for these bodies is provided by the Office of Manpower Economics (*see* page 321)

ARMED FORCES PAY

The Review Body on Armed Forces Pay was appointed in 1971 to advise the Prime Minister on the pay and allowances of members of naval, military and air forces of the Crown and of any women's service administered by the Defence Council.
Chairman, G. M. Hourston

Members, C. M. Bolton; Mrs K. Coleman, OBE; J. C. L. Cox, CBE; J. Crosby; Sir Gavin Laird; G. Neely; Air Chief Marshal Sir Roger Palin, KCB, OBE; Mrs D. Venables

DOCTORS' AND DENTISTS' REMUNERATION

The Review Body on Doctors' and Dentists' Remuneration was set up in 1971 to advise the Prime Minister on the remuneration of doctors and dentists taking any part in the National Health Service.
Chairman, C. B. Gough
Members, Mrs B. Brewer; Mrs C. Hui; M. Innes; R. Jackson; C. King, CBE; Dr E. Nelson; D. Penton

NURSING STAFF, MIDWIVES, HEALTH VISITORS AND PROFESSIONS ALLIED TO MEDICINE

The Review Body for nursing staff, midwives, health visitors and professions allied to medicine was set up in 1983 to advise the Prime Minister on the remuneration of nursing staff, midwives and health visitors employed in the National Health Service; and also of physiotherapists, radiographers, remedial gymnasts, occupational therapists, orthoptists, chiropodists, dietitians and related grades employed in the National Health Service.
Chairman, B. Rigby
Members, Mrs A. Dean; Mrs S. Gleig; L. Haddon; Ms R. Lea; Miss A. Mackie, OBE; K. Miles; Prof. Gillian Raab

SCHOOL TEACHERS

The School Teachers' Review Body (STRB) is a statutory body, set up under the School Teachers' Pay and Conditions Act 1991. It is required to examine and report on such matters relating to the statutory conditions of employment of school teachers in England and Wales as may be referred to it by the Secretary of State for Education and Employment. The STRB's reports are submitted to the Prime Minister and the Secretary of State and the latter is required to publish them.
Chairman, A. R. Vineall
Members, Mrs B. Amey; Mrs J. Cuthbertson; P. Gedling; M. Harding; Miss J. Langdon

SENIOR SALARIES

A Top Salaries Review Body was set up in 1971 to advise the Prime Minister on the remuneration of the higher judiciary and other judicial appointments, senior civil servants, and senior officers of the armed forces. In 1993 its name was changed to the Senior Salaries Review Body, and its remit was officially extended to cover the pay, pensions and allowances of MPs, ministers and others whose pay is determined by a Ministerial and Other Salaries Order, and the allowances of peers.
Chairman, Sir Michael Perry, CBE
Members, M. Beloff, QC; Mrs R. Day; G. M. Hourston; Sir Sydney Lipworth, QC; Miss P. Mann; Mrs Y. Newbold; M. Sheldon; Sir Anthony Wilson

ROYAL BOTANIC GARDEN EDINBURGH
Inverleith Row, Edinburgh EH3 5LR
Tel 0131-552 7171

The Royal Botanic Garden Edinburgh (RBGE) originated as the Physic Garden, established in 1670 beside the Palace of Holyroodhouse. Since 1986, RBGE has been adminis-

tered by a Board of Trustees established under the National Heritage (Scotland) Act 1985. It receives an annual grant from the Scottish Office.

RBG Edinburgh is an international centre for scientific research on plant diversity, maintaining collections of living plants and reference resources, including a herbarium of some two million specimens of preserved plants. Other statutory functions of RBGE include the provision of education and information on botany and horticulture, and the provision of public access to the living plant collections.

The Garden moved to its present site at Inverleith, Edinburgh in 1821. There are also three specialist gardens: Younger Botanic Garden Benmore, near Dunoon, Argyllshire; Logan Botanic Garden, near Stranraer, Wigtownshire; and Dawyck Botanic Garden, near Stobo, Peeblesshire. Public opening hours: RBGE, daily (except Christmas Day and New Year's Day) November–February 10–4; March–April and September–October 10–6; May–August 10–8; specialist gardens, 15 March–October 10–6. Admission free to RBGE; small admission charge to specialist gardens.
Chairman of the Board of Trustees, Prof. M. Wilkins, FRSE
Regius Keeper, Prof. D. S. Ingram, SC.D, FRSE
Deputy Keeper, Dr D. J. Mann

ROYAL BOTANIC GARDENS KEW
Richmond, Surrey TW9 3AB
Tel 0181-940 1171
Wakehurst Place, Ardingly, nr Haywards Heath,
W. Sussex RH17 6TN
Tel 01444-892701

The Royal Botanic Gardens (RBG) Kew were originally laid out as a private garden for Kew House for George III's mother, HRH Princess Augusta, in 1759. They were much enlarged in the 19th century, notably by the inclusion of the grounds of the former Richmond Lodge. In 1965 the garden at Wakehurst Place was acquired; it is owned by the National Trust and managed by RBG Kew. Under the National Heritage Act 1983 a Board of Trustees was set up to administer the Gardens which in 1984 became an independent body supported by a grant-in-aid from the Ministry of Agriculture, Fisheries and Food.

The functions of RBG Kew are to carry out research into plant sciences, to disseminate knowledge about plants and to provide the public with the opportunity to gain knowledge and enjoyment from the Gardens' collections. There are extensive national reference collections of living and preserved plants and a comprehensive library and archive. The main emphasis is on plant conservation and biodiversity.

Open daily (except Christmas Day and New Year's Day) from 9.30 a.m. The closing hour varies from 4 p.m. in midwinter to 6 p.m. on weekdays and 7.30 p.m. on Sundays and Bank Holidays in mid-summer. Admission (1996, £4.50. Concessionary schemes available. Glasshouses, 9.30–4.30 (winter); 9.30–5.30 (summer). No dogs except guide-dogs for the blind.

BOARD OF TRUSTEES
Chairman, R. A. E. Herbert, CBE

Members, R. P. Bauman; The Viscount Blakenham; Sir Jeffery Bowman; C. D. Brickell, CBE; Prof. W. G. Chaloner, FRS; Prof. H. Dickinson; Miss A. Ford; S. de Grey; Lady Lennox-Boyd; The Lady Renfrew of Kaimsthorn, PH.D.; The Earl of Selbourne, KBE, FRS (*Queen's Trustee*)
Director, Prof. Sir Ghillean Prance, FRS

ROYAL COMMISSION FOR THE EXHIBITION OF 1851
Sherfield Building, Imperial College of Science, Technology and Medicine, London SW7 2AZ
Tel 0171-594 8790

The Royal Commission was incorporated by supplemental charter as a permanent Commission after winding up the affairs of the Great Exhibition of 1851. Its object is to promote scientific and artistic education by means of funds derived from its Kensington estate, purchased with the surplus left over from the Great Exhibition.
President, HRH The Duke of Edinburgh, KG, KT, PC
Chairman, Board of Management, Sir Denis Rooke, CBE, FRS, FEng.
Secretary to Commissioners, J. P. W. Middleton, CB

THE ROYAL MINT
Llantrisant, Pontyclun, Mid Glamorgan CF72 8YT
Tel 01443-222111

The prime responsibility of the Royal Mint is the provision of United Kingdom coinage, but it actively competes in world markets for a share of the available circulating coin business and, based on the last ten years, two-thirds of the 15,000 tonnes of coins produced annually is exported to more than 100 countries. The Mint also manufactures special proof and uncirculated quality coins in gold, silver and other metals; military and civil decorations and medals; commemorative and prize medals; and royal and official seals.
    The Royal Mint became an executive agency of the Treasury in 1990.
Master of the Mint, The Chancellor of the Exchequer (*ex officio*)
Deputy Master and Comptroller, R. de L. Holmes

ROYAL NATIONAL THEATRE BOARD
South Bank, London, SE1 9PX
Tel 0171-928 2033

The chairman and members of the Board of the Royal National Theatre are appointed by the Secretary of State for National Heritage.
Chairman, Sir Christopher Hogg
Members, The Hon. P. Benson; The Hon. Lady Cazalet; M. Codron, CBE; Lady Greenbury; Ms S. Hall; Ms K. Jones; S. Lipton; D. Nandy; M. Oliver; The Rt. Hon. Sir Michael Palliser, GCMG; T. Stoppard, CBE; P. Wiegand; S. Yassukovich, CBE
Company Secretary and Head of Finance, A. Blackstock
Board and Committee Secretary, M. McGregor

RURAL DEVELOPMENT COMMISSION
141 Castle Street, Salisbury, Wilts. SP1 3TP
Tel 01722-336255

The Rural Development Commission is the government agency for economic and social development in rural England. The Commission gives advice to the Government and undertakes activities aimed at stimulating job creation and the provision of essential services in the countryside. Its sponsoring department is the Department of the Environment.
Chairman, The Lord Shuttleworth
Deputy Chairman, R. Thompson
Chief Executive, R. Butt

SCOTTISH COURTS ADMINISTRATION
— *see* page 368

SCOTTISH ENTERPRISE
120 Bothwell Street, Glasgow G2 7JP
Tel 0141-248 2700

In 1991 Scottish Enterprise took over the economic development and environmental improvement functions of the Scottish Development Agency and the training functions of the Training Agency in lowland Scotland. It is funded by the Scottish Office and its remit is to further the development of Scotland's economy, to enhance the skills of the Scottish workforce, to promote Scotland's international competitiveness and to improve the environment. Many of its functions are contracted out to a network of local enterprise companies. Through Locate in Scotland (*see* page 342), Scottish Enterprise is also concerned with attracting firms to Scotland.
Chairman, Sir Donald MacKay
Chief Executive, C. Beveridge, CBE

SCOTTISH ENVIRONMENT PROTECTION AGENCY
Erskine Court, The Castle Business Park, Stirling FK9 4TR
Tel 01786-457700

The Scottish Environment Protection Agency came into being on 1 April 1996 under the Environment Act 1995. It brings together the work formerly undertaken by HM Industrial Pollution Inspectorate, the river purification authorities, and district and islands councils in respect of waste regulation and some air pollution controls. It has regional offices in East Kilbride, Riccarton and Dingwall, and 17 local offices throughout Scotland. It receives funding from the Scottish Office.

THE BOARD
Chairman, Prof. W. Turmeau, CBE
Members, B. Baird; A. Buchan; B. Fitzgerald; G. Gordon, OBE; D. Hughes Hallett, FRICS; Prof. C. Johnston; C. McChord; C. McLatchie; Ms A. Magee; Ms J. Shaw

THE EXECUTIVE
Chief Executive, A. Paton
Director of Corporate Services, Dr G. King
Director of Environmental Strategy, Ms P. Henton
Director, North Region, Prof. D. Mackay
Director, East Region, W. Halcrow
Director, West Region, J. Beveridge

SCOTTISH HOMES
Thistle House, 91 Haymarket Terrace, Edinburgh
EH12 5HE
Tel 0131-313 0044

Scottish Homes, the national housing agency for Scotland, aims to improve the quality and variety of housing available in Scotland by working in partnership with the public and private sectors. The agency is a major funder of new and improved housing provided by housing associations and private developers. It is currently transferring its own 34,000 rented houses to alternative landlords. It is also involved in housing research and in piloting innovative housing solutions. Board members are appointed by the Secretary of State for Scotland.
Chairman, J. Ward, CBE
Chief Executive, P. McKinlay

SCOTTISH NATURAL HERITAGE
12 Hope Terrace, Edinburgh EH9 2AS
Tel 0131-447 4784

Scottish Natural Heritage came into existence in 1992 under the Natural Heritage (Scotland) Act 1991. It provides advice on nature conservation to all those whose activities affect wildlife, landforms and features of geological interest in Scotland, and seeks to develop and improve facilities for the enjoyment of the Scottish countryside. It is funded by the Scottish Office.
Chairman, M. Magnusson, KBE
Chief Executive, R. Crofts
Chief Scientific Adviser, M. B. Usher
Director of Policy, J. Thomson
Director of Resources, L. Montgomery

SCOTTISH OFFICE

The Secretary of State for Scotland is responsible in Scotland for a wide range of statutory functions which in England and Wales are the responsibility of a number of departmental ministers. He also works closely with ministers in charge of Great Britain departments on topics of special significance to Scotland within their fields of responsibility. His statutory functions are administered by five main departments collectively known as the Scottish Office. The departments are: the Scottish Office Agriculture, Environment and Fisheries Department; the Scottish Office Development Department; the Scottish Office Education and Industry Department; the Scottish Office Department of Health; and the Scottish Office Home Department.

In addition there are a number of other Scottish departments for which the Secretary of State has some degree of responsibility; these include the Scottish Courts Administration, the General Register Office, the Scottish Record Office and the Department of the Registers of Scotland. The Secretary of State also bears ministerial responsibility for the activities in Scotland of several statutory bodies, such as the Forestry Commission, whose functions extend throughout Great Britain.

Dover House, Whitehall, London, SW1A 2AU
Tel 0171-270 3000

Secretary of State for Scotland, The Rt. Hon. Michael Forsyth, MP
Private Secretary (G5), C. M. A. Lugton
Special Advisers, G. Warner; Mrs J. Low
Parliamentary Private Secretary, B. Jenkin, MP
Minister of State, The Rt. Hon. Lord James Douglas-Hamilton, MP (*Home Affairs and Health*)
Private Secretary, A. T. F. Johnston
Parliamentary Private Secretary, N. Deva, MP
Parliamentary Under-Secretaries of State, Raymond Robertson, MP (*Education, Housing and Fisheries*); George Kynoch, MP (*Industry and Local Government*); The Earl of Lindsay (*Agriculture, Forestry and the Environment*)
Private Secretaries, S. Farrell; D. McLaren; J. M. Pryce
Parliamentary Clerk, Mrs L. J. Stirling
Permanent Under-Secretary of State (G1), Sir Russell Hillhouse, KCB
Private Secretary, Miss L. M. Harper

LIAISON DIVISION
Assistant Secretary (G5), E. W. Ferguson

MANAGEMENT GROUP SUPPORT STAFF
Principal (G7), M. Grant

St Andrew's House, Edinburgh EH1 3DG
Tel 0131-556 8400

PERSONNEL GROUP
16 Waterloo Place, Edinburgh EH1 3DN
Tel 0131-556 8400
Principal Establishment Officer (G3), C. C. MacDonald
Assistant Secretary (G5), G. D. Calder

FINANCE DIVISION
Victoria Quay, Edinburgh EH6 6QQ
Tel 0131-556 8400
Principal Finance Officer (G3), J. S. G. Graham
Assistant Secretaries (G5), Dr P. S. Collings; D. Crawley; D. G. N. Reid; W. T. Tait
Head of Accountancy Services Unit (G6), I. M. Smith
Assistant Director of Finance Strategy (G6), I. A. McLeod

SOLICITOR'S OFFICE
For the Scottish departments and certain UK services, including HM Treasury, in Scotland
Solicitor (G2), R. Brodie, CB
Deputy Solicitor (G3), R. M. Henderson
Divisional Solicitors (G4), J. L. Jamieson; (G5), R. Bland (*seconded to Scottish Law Commission*); G. C. Duke; I. H. Harvie; H. F. Macdiarmid; J. G. S. Maclean; N. Raven; Mrs L. A. Wallace

SCOTTISH OFFICE INFORMATION DIRECTORATE
For the Scottish departments and certain UK services
Director (G5), Ms E. S. B. Drummond
Deputy Director (G6), W. A. McNeill

SCOTTISH OFFICE AGRICULTURE, ENVIRONMENT AND FISHERIES DEPARTMENT
Pentland House, 47 Robb's Loan, Edinburgh EH14 1TY
Tel 0131-556 8400
Secretary (G2), A. M. Russell
Under-Secretaries (G3), T. A. Cameron (*Agriculture*); S. F. Hampson (*Environment*)
Fisheries Secretary (G3), I. W. Gordon
Assistant Secretaries (G5), D. A. Brew; D. R. Dickson; J. Duffy; M. B. Foulis; R. A. Grant; C. K. McIntosh; A. J. Matheson; A. J. Rushworth; I. M. Whitelaw
Chief Agricultural Officer (G4), W. A. Macgregor
Deputy Chief Agricultural Officer (G5), J. I. Woodrow

Assistant Chief Agricultural Officers (G6), J. A. Hardie;
A. Robb; A. J. Robertson
Chief Agricultural Economist (G6), J. R. Wildgoose, D.phil.
Chief Food and Dairy Officer (G7), S. D. Rooke
Principal Surveyor (G6), I. W. Anderson, FRICS
Scientific Adviser (G5), T. W. Hegarty, Ph.D.
Senior Principal Scientific Officers (G6), Mrs L. A. D. Turl;
Dr Rosi Waterhouse

FISHERIES RESEARCH SERVICES
Marine Laboratory, PO Box 101, Victoria Road, Torry,
Aberdeen AB9 8DB
Tel 01224-876544

Director of Fisheries Research for Scotland (G4),
Prof. A. D. Hawkins, Ph.D., FRSE
Deputy Director (G5), J. Davies

Freshwater Fisheries Laboratory
Faskally, Pitlochry, Perthshire PH6 5LB
Tel 01796-472060

Senior Principal Scientific Officers (G6), Dr R. M. Cook; Dr
J. M. Davies; Dr A. E. Ellis; Dr A. L. S. Munro;
R. G. J. Shelton; Dr P. A. Stewart; Dr C. S. Wardle
Inspector of Salmon and Freshwater Fisheries for Scotland (G7),
D. A. Dunkley

ENVIRONMENTAL AFFAIRS GROUP
Under-Secretary (G3), S. F. Hampson
Assistant Secretaries (G5), J. W. L. Lonie; T. D. MacDonald;
J. A. Rennie
Chief Water Engineer, D. MacDonald
Ecological Adviser (G6), Dr J. Miles

DIRECTORATE OF ADMINISTRATIVE SERVICES
Victoria Quay, Edinburgh EH6 6QQ
Tel 0131-556 8400

Director of Administrative Services (G3), R. S. B. Gordon
Director of Efficiency Unit (G5), Ms I. M. Low
Chief Estates Officer (G6), J. A. Andrew

Saughton House, Broomhouse Drive, Edinburgh EH11 3DX
Head of Information Technology (G5), A. M. Brown
Head of IT Services (G6), I. W. Goodwin
Director of Telecommunications (G6), K. Henderson, OBE

James Craig Walk, Edinburgh EH1 3BA
Head of Purchasing and Supplies (G5), D. Ramsay

EXECUTIVE AGENCIES

INTERVENTION BOARD
— see page 315

SCOTTISH AGRICULTURAL SCIENCE AGENCY
East Craig, Edinburgh EH12 8NJ
The Agency provides scientific information and advice on
agricultural and horticultural crops and the environment,
and has various statutory and regulatory functions.
Director (G5), Dr R. K. M. Hay
Deputy Director (G6), S. R. Cooper
Senior Principal Scientific Officers (G6), A. D. Ruthven;
W. J. Rennie

SCOTTISH FISHERIES PROTECTION AGENCY
Pentland House, 47 Robb's Loan, Edinburgh EH14 1TY
Tel 0131-556 8400
The Agency enforces fisheries law and regulations in
Scottish waters and ports.
Chief Executive (G5), Capt. P. Du Vivier, RN
Director of Corporate Strategy and Resources (G6), J. B. Roddin
Director of Operational Enforcement (G6), R. J. Walker
Marine Superintendent, Capt. R. M. Mill-Irving

SCOTTISH OFFICE DEVELOPMENT
DEPARTMENT
Victoria Quay, Edinburgh EH6 6QQ
Tel 0131-556 8400

Secretary (G2), H. H. Mills, CB
Under-Secretaries (G3), D. J. Belfall; J. W. Elvidge
Assistant Secretaries (G5), M. T. Affolter; J. A. Ewing;
D. Hart; D. Henderson; J. D. Gallacher; W. Howat;
K. W. McKay; J. R. McQueen; D. A. Middleton; R. Tait;
G. M. D. Thomson
Senior Economic Adviser (G5), C. L. Wood

PROFESSIONAL STAFF
*Director of Construction and Building Control Group and Chief
Architect (G3)*, J. E. Gibbons, Ph.D., FSA SCOT.
*Deputy Director of Construction and Building Control Group and
Deputy Chief Architect (G5)*, G. Gray
*Deputy Director of Construction and Building Control Group and
Chief Quantity Surveyor (G5)*, A. J. Wyllie
Chief Planner (G4), A. Mackenzie
Chief Statistician (G5), Dr J. Cuthbert

INQUIRY REPORTERS
Robert Stevenson House, 2 Greenside Lane, Edinburgh
EH1 3AG
Tel 0131-244 5680
Chief Reporter (G3), Miss G. Pain
Deputy Chief Reporter (G5), R. M. Hickman

NATIONAL ROADS DIRECTORATE
Victoria Quay, Edinburgh EH6 6QQ
Tel 0131-556 8400

Director of Roads (G3), J. Innes
Deputy Chief Engineers (G5), J. A. Howison (*Roads*),
N. B. MacKenzie (*Bridges*)

EXECUTIVE AGENCY

HISTORIC SCOTLAND
Longmore House, Salisbury Place, Edinburgh EH9 1SH
Tel 0131-668 8600
The agency's role is to protect Scotland's historic monu-
ments, buildings and lands, and to promote public under-
standing and enjoyment of them.
Chief Executive (G3), G. N. Munro
Directors (G5), F. J. Lawrie; I. Maxwell; B. Naylor; (*G6*),
S. Rosie
Chief Inspector of Ancient Monuments, Dr D. J. Breeze
Chief Inspector, Building Division, J. R. Hume

SCOTTISH OFFICE EDUCATION AND
INDUSTRY DEPARTMENT
Victoria Quay, Edinburgh EH6 6QQ
Tel 0131-556 8400

Secretary (G2), G. R. Wilson, CB
Under-Secretaries (G3), J. S. B. Martin; E. J. Weeple
Assistant Secretaries (G5), A. W. Fraser; I. G. F. Gray;
R. Irvine; R. D. Jackson; G. McHugh; Miss M. Maclean;
A. K. MacLeod; Mrs R. Menlowe; Mrs V. Macniven
Chief Statistician (G5), C. R. Macleans

HM INSPECTORS OF SCHOOLS
Senior Chief Inspector (G3), D. A. Osler
Depute Senior Chief Inspector (G4), G. H. C. Donaldson
Chief Inspectors (G5), J. Boyes; J. T. Donaldson; Miss
K. M. Fairweather; D. E. Kelso; J. J. McDonald;
A. S. McGlynn; M. Roebuck; H. M. Stalker;
R. M. S. Tuck
There are 79 Grade 6 Inspectors

INDUSTRIAL EXPANSION
Meridian Court, 5 Cadogan Street, Glasgow G2 6AT
Tel 0141-248 2855

Under-Secretary (G3), G. Robson
Industrial Adviser, D. Blair
Scientific Adviser, Prof. D. J. Tedford
Assistant Secretaries (G5), M. T. S. Batho; W. Malone; Ms J. Morgan; Dr J. Rigg

LOCATE IN SCOTLAND
120 Bothwell Street, Glasgow G2 7JP
Tel 0141-248 2700

Director (G4), M. Togneri

SCOTTISH TRADE INTERNATIONAL
120 Bothwell Street, Glasgow G2 7JP
Tel 0141-248 2700

Director, D. Taylor

EXECUTIVE AGENCIES

STUDENT AWARDS AGENCY FOR SCOTLAND
Gyleview House, 3 Redheughs Rigg, Edinburgh EH12 9HH
Tel 0131-244 5867

Chief Executive, K. MacRae

SCOTTISH OFFICE PENSIONS AGENCY
St Margaret's House, 151 London Road, Edinburgh
EH8 7TG
Tel 0131-556 8400

The Agency is responsible for the pension arrangements of some 300,000 people, mainly NHS and teaching services employees and pensioners.
Chief Executive, N. MacLeod
Directors (G7), G. Mowat (*Policy*); A. M. Small (*Operations*); M. J. McDermott (*Resources and Customer Services*)

SCOTTISH OFFICE DEPARTMENT OF HEALTH
St Andrew's House, Edinburgh EH1 3DG
Tel 0131-556 8400

NATIONAL HEALTH SERVICE IN SCOTLAND
MANAGEMENT EXECUTIVE
Chief Executive (G3), G. R. Scaife
Director of Purchasing (G4), Dr K. J. Woods
Director of Primary Care (G5), Mrs A. Robson
Director of Finance (G5), S. Featherstone
Director of Human Resources (G5), M. Sibbald
Director of Nursing, Miss A. Jarvie
Medical Director (G3), Dr A. B. Young, FRCPE
Director of Trusts (G4), P. Wilson
Director of Information Services, NHS, C. B. Knox
Director of Estates, H. R. McCallum
Chief Pharmacist (G5), W. Scott
Chief Scientist, Prof. I. A. D. Bouchier, CBE, FRCP
Chief Dental Officer, J. R. Wild

PUBLIC HEALTH POLICY UNIT
Head of Unit and Chief Medical Officer (G2), Dr R. E. Kendell, CBE
Deputy Chief Medical Officer (G3), Dr A. B. Young, FRCPE
Under-Secretary (G3), Mrs N. Munro
Assistant Secretary (G5), J. T. Brown
Principal Medical Officers, Dr J. V. Basson; Dr Rosalind Skinner; Dr Elizabeth Sowler
Senior Medical Officers, Dr Angela Anderson; P. W. Brooks; Dr J. Cumming; Dr D. J. Ewing; Dr A. Findlay; Dr D. Jolliffe; Dr A. Keel; Dr Patricia Madden; Dr R. Simmons

NATIONAL HEALTH SERVICE, SCOTLAND

HEALTH BOARDS
ARGYLL AND CLYDE, Ross House, Hawkhead Road, Paisley PA2 7BN. *Chairman*, M. D. Jones; *General Manager*, I. C. Smith
AYRSHIRE AND ARRAN, PO Box 13, Seafield House, Doonfoot Road, Ayr KA7 4DW. *Chairman*, J. W. G. Donaldson, CBE; *General Manager*, J. M. Eckford, OBE
BORDERS, Huntlyburn, Melrose, Roxburghshire TD6 9DB. *Chairman*, D. A. C. Kilshaw; *General Manager*, D. A. Peters, OBE
DUMFRIES AND GALLOWAY, Nithbank, Dumfries DG1 2SD. *Chairman*, Mrs J. D. Tulloch; *General Manager*, D. Banks
FIFE, Springfield House, Cupar KY7 5PR. *Chairman*, R. Baker, OBE; *General Manager*, Miss P. Frost
FORTH VALLEY, 33 Spittal Street, Stirling FK8 1DX. *Chairman (acting)*, E. Bell-Scott; *General Manager*, D. Hird
GRAMPIAN, Summerfield House, 2 Eday Road, Aberdeen AB9 1RE. *Chairman*, C. MacLeod, CBE; *General Manager*, F. E. L. Hartnett, OBE
GREATER GLASGOW, 112 Ingram Street, Glasgow G1 1ET. *Chairman*, Sir Robert Calderwood; *General Manager (acting)*, T. A. Divers
HIGHLAND, Reay House, 17 Old Edinburgh Road, Inverness IV2 3HG. *Chairman*, J. D. M. Robertson, CBE; *General Manager*, Dr G. V. Stone
LANARKSHIRE, 14 Beckford Street, Hamilton, Lanarkshire ML3 0TA. *Chairman*, I. Livingstone, OBE; *General Manager*, Prof. F. Clark, CBE
LOTHIAN, 148 The Pleasance, Edinburgh EH8 9RS. *Chairman*, Dr J. W. Baynham, CBE; *General Manager*, J. Lusby
ORKNEY, Balfour Hospital, New Scapa Road, Kirkwall, Orkney KW15 1BQ. *Chairman*, J. Leslie; *General Manager*, E. Jackson
SHETLAND, Brevik House, South Road, Lerwick ZW1 0RB. *Chairman*, Mrs F. Grains, OBE; *General Manager*, B. J. Atherton
TAYSIDE, PO Box 75, Vernonholme, Riverside Drive, Dundee DD1 9NL. *Chairman*, J. C. MacFarlane, CBE; *General Manager*, Miss L. Barrie
WESTERN ISLES, 37 South Beach Street, Stornoway, Isle of Lewis PA87 2BN. *Chairman*, A. Matheson; *General Manager*, R. Mullan

HEALTH EDUCATION BOARD FOR SCOTLAND
Woodburn House, Canaan Lane, Edinburgh EH10 4SG
Tel 0131-447 8044

Chairman, D. Campbell
General Manager, Dr A. Tannahill

STATE HOSPITAL
Carstairs Junction, Lanark ML11 8RP
Tel 01555-840293

Chairman, P. Hamilton-Grierson
General Manager, R. Manson

COMMON SERVICES AGENCY
Trinity Park House, South Trinity Road, Edinburgh
EH5 3SE
Tel 0131-552 6255

Chairman, G. Scaife
General Manager (acting), Dr F. Gibb

SCOTTISH OFFICE HOME DEPARTMENT
St Andrew's House, Edinburgh EH1 3DG
Tel 0131-556 8400

Secretary (G2), J. Hamill

Under-Secretaries (G3), N. G. Campbell; D. J. Essery; Mrs G. M. Stewart
Assistant Secretaries (G5), C. Baxter; Mrs M. H. Brannan; Mrs M. B. Gunn; R. S. T. MacEwen; D. Macniven, TD
Chief Research Officer, Dr C. P. A. Levein
Senior Principal Research Officer (G6), Dr Jacqueline Tombs

SOCIAL WORK SERVICES GROUP
James Craig Walk, Edinburgh EH1 3BA
Tel 0131-556 8400
Under-Secretary (G3), N. G. Campbell
Assistant Secretaries (G5), G. A. Anderson; Ms L. J. Clare; J. W. Sinclair
Chief Inspector of Social Work Services, A. Skinner
Assistant Chief Inspectors, Ms M. L. Hunt; F. A. O'Leary; Mrs A. Ottley; D. Pia; I. C. Robertson; A. Sabine

OTHER APPOINTMENTS
HM Chief Inspector of Constabulary, J. Boyd, CBE, QPM
HM Chief Inspector of Prisons, C. Fairweather, OBE
Commandant, Scottish Police College, H. I. Watson, QPM
HM Chief Inspector of Fire Service, N. Morrison
Commandant, Scottish Fire Service Training School, D. Grant, QFSM

MENTAL WELFARE COMMISSION FOR SCOTLAND
25 Drumsheugh Gardens, Edinburgh EH3 7NS
Tel 0131-225 7034

Chairman, Hon. Lady Cosgrove
Commissioners, Mrs N. Bennie; P. H. Brodie; Mrs F. Cotter; Mrs M. Jeffcoat; Dr M. Livingston; Dr D. McCall-Smith; Dr M. McCreadie; D. J. Macdonald; Ms L. M. Noble; I. Ross; Dr E. M. Thomas; W. Gent; Ms M. Whoriskey; A. Robb

COUNSEL TO THE SECRETARY OF STATE FOR SCOTLAND UNDER THE PRIVATE LEGISLATION PROCEDURE (SCOTLAND) ACT 1936
50 Frederick Street, Edinburgh EH2 1EN
Tel 0131-226 6499

Senior Counsel, G. S. Douglas, QC
Junior Counsel, N. M. P. Morrison

EXECUTIVE AGENCIES

REGISTERS OF SCOTLAND
— see page 316

SCOTTISH COURT SERVICE
— see page 368

SCOTTISH PRISON SERVICE
Calton House, 5 Redheughs Rigg, Edinburgh EH12 9HW
Tel 0131-556 8400
Chief Executive of Scottish Prison Service (G3), E. W. Frizzell
Director of Custody (G4), P. Withers
Director, Human Resources (G5), F. Coyle
Director, Finance and Information Systems (G5), W. Pretswell
Director, Strategy and Corporate Affairs (G5), D. A. Stewart
Deputy Director, Regime Services and Supplies (G6), vacant
Deputy Director, Estates and Buildings (G6), B. Paterson
Area Director, South and West (G5), J. Pearce
Area Director, North and East (G5), P. Russell
Governor, Scottish Prison Service College, J. Matthews

PRISONS
ABERDEEN, Craiginches, Aberdeen AB9 2HN. Governor, J. Bywalec

BARLINNIE, Barlinnie, Glasgow G33 2QX. Governor, R. L. Houchain
CASTLE HUNTLY YOUNG OFFENDERS INSTITUTION, Castle Huntly, Longforgan, nr Dundee DD2 5HL. Governor, K. Rennie
CORNTON VALE, Cornton Road, Stirling FK9 5NY. Governor, vacant
DUMFRIES YOUNG OFFENDERS INSTITUTION, Terregles Street, Dumfries DG2 9AX. Governor, G. Taylor
DUNGAVEL, Dungavel House, Strathaven, Lanarkshire ML10 6RF. Governor, Ms M. Wood
EDINBURGH, 33 Stenhouse Road, Edinburgh EH1 3LN. Governor, J. Durno
FRIARTON, Friarton, Perth PH2 8DW. Governor, E. A. Gordon
GLENOCHIL PRISON AND YOUNG OFFENDERS INSTITUTION, King O'Muir Road, Tullibody, Clackmannanshire FK10 3AD. Governor, L. McBain
GREENOCK, Gateside, Greenock PA16 9AH. Governor, R. MacCowan
LONGRIGGEND REMAND INSTITUTION, Longriggend, nr Airdrie, Lanarkshire ML6 7TL. Governor, A. MacDonald
LOW MOSS, Low Moss, Bishopbriggs, Glasgow G64 2QB. Governor, W. Middleton
NORANSIDE, Noranside, Fern, by Forfar, Angus DD8 3QY. Governor, E. Brownsmith
PENNINGHAME, Penninghame, Newton Stewart DG8 6RG. Governor, H. Ross
PERTH, 3 Edinburgh Road, Perth PH2 8AT. Governor, M. Duffy
PETERHEAD, Salthouse Head, Peterhead, Aberdeenshire AB4 6YY. Governor, W. Rattray
POLMONT YOUNG OFFENDERS INSTITUTION, Brightons, Falkirk, Stirlingshire FK2 0AB. Governor, D. Gunn
PORTERFIELD, Porterfield, Inverness IV2 3HH. Governor, W. M. Weir
SHOTTS, Shotts ML7 4LF. Governor, W. McKinlay
SHOTTS UNIT, Shotts ML7 4LF. Governor, A. McVicar
SHOTTS NATIONAL INDUCTION UNIT, Shotts ML7 4LE. Governor, Ms S. Brookes

SCOTTISH RECORD OFFICE
— see page 337

GENERAL REGISTER OFFICE
New Register House, Edinburgh EH1 3YT
Tel 0131-334 0380

The General Register Office for Scotland is an associated department of the Scottish Office. It is the office of the Registrar-General for Scotland, who has responsibility for civil registration and the taking of censuses in Scotland and has in his custody the following records: the statutory registers of births, deaths, still births, adoptions, marriages and divorces; the old parish registers (recording births, deaths and marriages, etc., before civil registration began in 1855); and records of censuses of the population in Scotland. Hours of public access: Monday–Friday 9–4.30.
Registrar-General, J. Meldrum
Deputy Registrar-General, B. V. Philp
Senior Principal (G6), D. A. Orr
Principals (G7), D. B. L. Brownlee; R. C. Lawson; F. D. Garvie
Statisticians (G7), J. Arrundale; G. W. L. Jackson; F. G. Thomas

SCOTTISH PRISONS COMPLAINTS COMMISSION

Government Buildings, Broomhouse Drive, Edinburgh EHII 3XD
Tel 0131-244 8423

The Commission was established in 1994. It is an independent body to which prisoners in Scottish prisons can make application in relation to any matter where they have failed to obtain satisfaction from the Prison Service's internal grievance procedures. Clinical judgments made by medical officers, matters which are the subject of legal proceedings and matters relating to sentence, conviction and parole decision-making are excluded from the Commission's jurisdiction. The Commissioner is appointed by the Secretary of State for Scotland.
Commissioner, Dr J. McManus

SEA FISH INDUSTRY AUTHORITY

18 Logie Mill, Logie Green Road, Edinburgh EH7 4HG
Tel 0131-558 3331

Established under the Fisheries Act 1981, the Authority is required to promote the efficiency of the sea fish industry. It carries out research relating to the industry and gives advice on related matters. It provides training, promotes the marketing, consumption and export of sea fish and sea fish products, and may provide financial assistance for the improvement of fishing vessels in respect of essential safety equipment. It is responsible to the Ministry of Agriculture, Fisheries and Food.
Chairman, E. Davey
Chief Executive, P. D. Chaplin

THE SECURITY SERVICE COMMISSIONER

c/o PO Box 18, London SEI OTZ

The Commissioner is appointed by the Prime Minister. He keeps under review the issue of warrants by the Home Secretary under the Intelligence Services Act 1994, and is required to help the Security Service Tribunal by investigating complaints which allege interference with property and by offering all such assistance in discharging its functions as it may require. He is also required to submit an annual report on the discharge of his functions to the Prime Minister.
Commissioner, The Rt. Hon. Lord Justice Stuart-Smith

SECURITY SERVICE TRIBUNAL

PO Box 18, London SEI OTZ
Tel 0171-273 4095

The Security Service Act 1989 established a tribunal of three to five senior members of the legal profession, independent of the Government and appointed by The Queen, to investigate complaints from any person about anything which they believe the Security Service has done to them or to their property.
President, The Rt. Hon. Lord Justice Simon Brown
Vice-President, Sheriff J. McInnes, QC
Member, Sir Richard Gaskell

SERIOUS FRAUD OFFICE

Elm House, 10–16 Elm Street, London WCIX OBJ
Tel 0171-239 7272

The Serious Fraud Office is an autonomous department under the superintendence of the Attorney-General. Its remit is to investigate and prosecute serious and complex fraud. (Other fraud cases are currently handled by the fraud investigation unit of the Crown Prosecution Service.) The scope of its powers covers England, Wales and Northern Ireland. The staff includes lawyers, accountants and other support staff; investigating teams work closely with the police.
Director, G. Staple, CB

DEPARTMENT OF SOCIAL SECURITY

Richmond House, 79 Whitehall, London SWIA 2NS
Tel 0171-238 0800

The Department of Social Security is responsible for the payment of benefits and the collection of contributions under the National Insurance and Industrial Injuries schemes, and for the payment of child benefit, one-parent benefit, Income Support and Family Credit. It administers the Social Fund, and is responsible for assessing the means of applicants for legal aid. It is also responsible for the payment of war pensions and the operation of the child maintenance system.
Secretary of State for Social Security, The Rt. Hon. Peter Lilley, MP
  Private Secretary, S. Czerniawski
  Special Adviser, P. Barnes
  Parliamentary Private Secretary, P. Merchant, MP
Minister of State, Alistair Burt, MP (*Social Security and Disabled People*)
  Private Secretary, G. Tempest-Hay
Minister of State, The Lord Mackay of Ardbrecknish, PC
  Private Secretary, Ms C. Payne
Parliamentary Under-Secretaries of State, Roger Evans, MP; Andrew Mitchell, MP; Oliver Heald, MP
  Private Secretaries, M. Baldock; J. Vincent; C. Lewis
  Parliamentary Private Secretary, D. Congdon, MP
Permanent Secretary (*G1*), Mrs A. E. Bowtell, CB
  Private Secretary, B. Hearn

CORPORATE MANAGEMENT GROUP
Director (*G2*), J. Tross

PERSONNEL AND HQ SUPPORT SERVICES DIRECTORATE
Director, S. Hewitt
Section Heads (*G5*), T. Perl; (*G7*), R. Yeats; B. Glew; J. Elliott

*ANALYTICAL SERVICES DIVISION
Director (*G3*), D. Stanton
Chief Statisticians (*G5*), N. Dyson; M. McDowall
Senior Economic Advisers (*G5*), J. Ball; G. Harris
Deputy Chief Scientific Officer (*G5*), D. Barnbrook
Chief Research Officer (*G5*), Ms S. Duncan

FINANCE DIVISION
Grade 3, S. Lord

---

*At the Adelphi, 1–11 John Adam Street, London WC2N 6HT. Tel: 0171-962 8000

SOCIAL SECURITY POLICY GROUP
Head of Policy Group (G2), C. Kelly
Policy Directors (G3), R. Allen; M. Whippman; Miss
M. Peirson, CB; D. Brereton
Policy Managers (G5), Mrs A. Lingwood; D. Jackson; Ms
S. Graham; B. O'Gorman; Miss J. Moore; M. Street;
J. Groombridge; Mrs C. Rookes; B. Calderwood; Miss
J. Leibling; D. Allsop; C. Evans; J. Hughes; P. Cleasby;
G. Bowen; Ms K. Limm; P. Morgan; Mrs L. Richards;
Ms J. Shersby; (G6), B. Layton; I. Williams

INFORMATION DIRECTORATE
Head of Information (G5), S. Reardon
Deputy Head of Information (G6), T. Grace
Principal Information Officer (G7), J. Bretherton
Chief Publicity Officer (G7), Ms H. Midlane

SOLICITOR'S OFFICE
Solicitor (G2), P. K. J. Thompson

SOLICITOR'S DIVISION A
New Court, 48 Carey Street, London WC2A 2LS
Tel 0171-412 1465

Principal Assistant Solicitor (G3), J. A. Catlin
Assistant Solicitors (G5), R. Powell; J. M. Swainson; Mrs
G. Massiah; K. K. Baublys; Mrs F. A. Logan;
S. M. Cooper

SOLICITOR'S DIVISION B
New Court, 48 Carey Street, London WC2A 2LS
Tel 0171-412 1404

Solicitor (G2), P. K. J. Thompson
Assistant Solicitors (G5), R. G. S. Aitken; W. H. Connell; Ms
S. Edwards

SOLICITOR'S DIVISION C
New Court, 48 Carey Street, London WC2A 2LS
Tel 0171-412 1341

Principal Assistant Solicitor (G3), Mrs G. S. Kerrigan
Assistant Solicitors (G5), P. Milledge; R. J. Dormer; Miss
M. E. Trefgarne; Mrs S. Walker; Miss G. E. Parker

MAXWELL PENSIONS UNIT
7 St James's Square, London SW1Y 4JU
Tel 0171-839 3599

Director (G5), R. P. Cleasby

EXECUTIVE AGENCIES

BENEFITS AGENCY
Quarry House, Quarry Hill, Leeds LS2 7UA
Tel 0113-232 4000

The Agency administers claims for and payments of social
security benefits.
Chief Executive, P. Mathison
Private Secretary, Ms E. Clayton
Directors, D. Riggs (*Finance*); P. Murphy (*Personnel and
Communications*); Ms U. Brennan (*Change Management*);
A. Cleveland (*Project Director*); G. McCorkell (*Project
Director*); J. Lutton (*North*); T. Edge (*South*)

Benefits Agency Medical Services
Principal Medical Officers, Dr M. Aylward; Dr P. Dewis; Dr
C. Hudson; Dr P. Doughty

CHILD SUPPORT AGENCY
Quay House, The Waterfront, Brierley Hill, W. Midlands
DY1 1XZ
Tel 01384-488488

The Agency was set up in April 1993. It is responsible for
the administration of the Child Support Act and for the

assessment, collection and enforcement of maintenance
payments for all new cases.
Chief Executive, Miss A. Chant
Directors, S. Heminsley; C. Francis; M. Davison; C. Peters;
M. Isaacs

CONTRIBUTIONS AGENCY
DSS Longbenton, Benton Park Road, Newcastle upon
Tyne NE98 1YX
Tel 0191-213 5000

The Agency collects and records National Insurance
contributions, maintains individual records, and provides
an advisory service on National Insurance matters.
Chief Executive (G3), Mrs F. Boardman
Deputy Chief Executive (G5), G. Bertram
Management Board, K. Wilson; T. Lord; D. Slater; K. Elliott
Non-Executive Members, J. Wilson; B. Glassberg

INFORMATION TECHNOLOGY SERVICES AGENCY
4th Floor, Verulam Point, Station Way, St Albans, Herts
AL1 5HE
Tel 01727-815838

The Agency maintains and oversees policies on infor-
mation technology strategy, procurement, technical stan-
dards and security.
Chief Executive, I. Magee
Directors, J. Thomas; N. Haighton; G. Hextall; J. Brewood;
G. Kemp; P. Sharkey; C. Brown; T. Edkins
Non-Executive Director, T. Drury

WAR PENSIONS AGENCY
Norcross, Blackpool, Lancs FY5 3WP
Tel 01253-858858

The Agency administers the payment of war disablement
and war widows' pensions and provides welfare services
and support to war disablement pensioners, war widows
and their dependants and carers. It became an executive
agency in 1994.
Chief Executive, K. Caldwell

Central Advisory Committee on War Pensions
Room 1138, The Adelphi, 1–11 John Adam Street,
London WC2N 6HT
Tel 0171-962 8028
Secretary, S. Adams

ADVISORY BODIES

NATIONAL DISABILITY COUNCIL, 6th Floor, The
Adelphi, 1–11 John Adam Street, London WC2N 6HT.
Tel: 0171-712 2099. *Chairman*, D. Grayson; *Secretary*,
Ms K. Archer
SOCIAL SECURITY ADVISORY COMMITTEE, New Court,
Carey Street, London WC2A 2LS. Tel 0171-412 1507.
Chairman, Sir Thomas Boyd-Carpenter, KBE; *Secretary*,
L. C. Smith

SPORTS COUNCIL
16 Upper Woburn Place, London WC1H 0QP
Tel 0171-388 1277

The Sports Council is an independent body established in
1972 by royal charter. It promotes the development of sport
and fosters the provision of facilities for sport and recreation in Great Britain. Government funding for 1996–7 is
£47 million.
The Council is also responsible, with the other Sports
Councils, for administering the Lottery Sports Fund,

which distributes the funds allocated to sport from the proceeds of the National Lottery. The Council had made awards to the value of £248 million by July 1996.

In the autumn of 1996 the Council will be replaced by a United Kingdom Sports Council and an English Sports Council.

Chairman, Sir Rodney Walker

Chief Executive, D. Casey

For Sports Councils for Scotland, Wales and N. Ireland, *see* page 707.

OFFICE FOR STANDARDS IN EDUCATION (OFSTED)
Alexandra House, 33 Kingsway, London WC2B 6SE
Tel 0171-421 6800

A non-ministerial government department established in 1992 to keep the Secretary of State and the public informed about the standards and management of schools in England, and to establish and monitor an independent inspection system for maintained schools in England. *See also* page 432.

HM Chief Inspector, C. Woodhead
Director of Administration, Mrs H. Douglas
Directors of Inspection, A. J. Rose, CBE; M. J. Tomlinson

TEAM MANAGERS
Planning and Resource, Miss J. Phillips
Personnel Management, C. Payne
Contracts, C. Bramley
Communications, Media and Public Relations, J. Lawson
Information Systems, M. Childs
Administrative Support and Estates Management, K. Francis
Competition and Compliance, Ms E. Slater
Training and Assessment of Independent Inspectors, Miss E. Pagliacci
Inspection Quality, Monitoring and Development, P. Matthews
LEA Reviews, Reorganization Proposals and Independent Schools, D. Singleton
School Improvement, Ms E. Passmore
Additional Inspector Project, Ms S. O'Sullivan
Nursery and Primary, K. Lloyd
Secondary, C. Gould
Post-Compulsory, D. West
Special Educational Needs, C. Marshall
Research, Analysis and International, Ms C. Agambar
Teacher Education and Training, D. Taylor
Nursery Education Scheme, D. Bradley
Specialist Advisers, J. Stannard; N. Bufton; B. Ponchaud; A. Dobson; M. Ive; G. Goldstein; J. Hamer; P. Smith; Ms J. Mills; G. Clay; P. Jones; I. Wragg
There are about 200 HM Inspectors

COMMITTEE ON STANDARDS IN PUBLIC LIFE
Horse Guards Road, London SW1P 3AL
Tel 0171-270 5875

The Committee on Standards in Public Life (the Nolan Committee) was set up in October 1994. It is a standing body whose chairman and members are appointed by the Prime Minister. Its remit is to examine concerns about standards of conduct of all holders of public office, including arrangements relating to financial and commercial activities, and to make recommendations as to any

changes in current arrangements which might be required to ensure the highest standards of propriety in public life. The committee does not investigate individual allegations of misconduct.
Chairman, The Lord Nolan, PC
Members, Sir Clifford Boulton, GCB; Sir Martin Jacomb; Prof. A. King; The Rt. Hon. T. King, CH, MP; The Rt. Hon. P. Shore, MP; The Lord Thomson of Monifieth, PC; Sir William Utting, CB; Dame Anne Warburton, DCVO, CMG; Ms D. Warwick
Secretary (SCS), A. Riddell

HMSO (HER MAJESTY'S STATIONERY OFFICE)
St Crispins, Duke Street, Norwich NR3 1PD
Tel 01603-622211

HMSO (Her Majesty's Stationery Office) was established in 1786. It provides printing, binding and business supplies to government departments and publicly funded organizations. It was an executive agency accountable to the Chancellor of the Duchy of Lancaster (the Minister of Public Service) within the Cabinet Office but was privatized in September 1996. HMSO is also the Government's publisher, and has bookshops for the sale of government publications in seven cities as well as appointed agents in other UK cities and throughout the world. HMSO obtains most of its supplies and printing from commercial sources, but about 20 per cent of its printing requirement, such as Hansard and Bills and Acts of Parliament, is produced in its own printing works.
Controller and Chief Executive (acting), M. D. Lynn
Board Directors, C. J. Penn; C. N. Southgate; P. J. Macdonald, CBE

DIRECTORS
Client Publishing, A. Cole
Parliamentary and Statutory Publishing, E. Hendry
Book Sales and Service, B. Minett
Office Supplies, V. G. Bell
Business Systems, D. C. Kerry
Copiers, P. Barnard
Print, A. A. Smith (*Norwich*); G. Aldus (*London*); M. McNeill (*Manchester and Logistics*); C. Mills (*Security*)
Furniture, G. A. H. Turner
HMSO Wales, A. McCabe
HMSO Scotland, G. Heaford
HMSO N. Ireland, S. Barker
BIRMINGHAM – *Bookshop*, 68–69 Bull Street, Birmingham B4 6AB
BRISTOL, Distribution Park, Hawkley Drive, Woodlands Lane, Bradley Stoke, Bristol BS12 0BF. *Bookshop*, 33 Wine Street, Bristol BS1 2BH
LONDON – *Publications Centre*, 51 Nine Elms Lane, London SW8 5DR. *Bookshop*, 49 High Holborn, London WC1V 6HB
MANCHESTER, Broadway, Chadderton, Oldham, Lancs OL9 9QH. *Bookshop*, 9–21 Princess Street, Manchester M60 8AS
SCOTLAND, South Gyle Crescent, Edinburgh EH12 9EB. *Bookshop*, 71 Lothian Road, Edinburgh EH3 9AZ
WALES – *Bookshop*, The Friary, Cardiff CF1 4AA
NORTHERN IRELAND, IDB House, Chichester Street, Belfast BT1 4PS. *Bookshop*, 16 Arthur Street, Belfast BT1 4GD

OFFICE OF TELECOMMUNICATIONS
50 Ludgate Hill, London EC4M 7JJ
Tel 0171-634 8700

The Office of Telecommunications (Oftel) is a non-ministerial government department which is responsible for supervising telecommunications activities in the UK. Its principal functions are to ensure that holders of telecommunications licences comply with their licence conditions; to maintain and promote effective competition in telecommunications; and to promote the interests of purchasers and other users of telecommunication services and apparatus in respect of prices, quality and variety.

The Director-General has powers to deal with anti-competitive practices and monopoly situations. He also has a duty to consider all reasonable complaints and representations about telecommunication apparatus and services.

Director-General, D. G. Cruickshank
Deputy Director-General, Mrs A. Walker
Director of Network Competition, Mrs A. Taylor
Director of Consumer Affairs, Ms C. Farnish
Director of Licensing, Ms S. Chambers
Director of Licence Enforcement and Fair Trading, C. J. C. Wright
Technical Director, P. Walker
Economic Director, A. Bell
Legal Director, D. H. M. Ingham
Director of Information, D. Redding
Director of Service Competition and International Affairs, Ms C. Varley

TOURIST BOARDS
(For British Tourist Authority, *see* page 286)

The English Tourist Board, the Scottish Tourist Board, the Wales Tourist Board and the Northern Ireland Tourist Board are responsible for developing and marketing the tourist industry in their respective countries. The Boards' main objectives are to promote holidays and to encourage the provision and improvement of tourist amenities.

ENGLISH TOURIST BOARD, Thames Tower, Black's Road, London w6 9EL. Tel: 0181-846 9000. *Chief Executive,* T. Bartlett
SCOTTISH TOURIST BOARD, 23 Ravelston Terrace, Edinburgh EH4 3EU. Tel: 0131-332 2433. *Chief Executive,* D. D. Reid
WALES TOURIST BOARD, Brunel House, 2 Fitzalan Road, Cardiff CF2 1UY. Tel: 01222-499909. *Chief Executive,* J. French
NORTHERN IRELAND TOURIST BOARD, St Anne's Court, 59 North Street, Belfast BT1 1NB. Tel: 01232-231221. *Chief Executive,* I. Henderson

DEPARTMENT OF TRADE AND INDUSTRY
1 Victoria Street, London SW1H 0ET
Tel 0171-215 5000

Business Link: Tel 0800-500200
Business in Europe: Tel 0117-944 4888
Innovation Enquiry Line: Tel 0171-215 1217

The Department is responsible for international trade policy, including the promotion of UK trade interests in the European Union, GATT, OECD, UNCTAD and other international organizations; the promotion of UK exports and assistance to exporters; policy in relation to industry and commerce, including industrial relations policy; policy towards small firms; regional industrial assistance; legislation and policy in relation to the Post Office; competition policy and consumer protection; the development of national policies in relation to all forms of energy and the development of new sources of energy, including international aspects of energy policy; policy on science and technology research and development; space policy; standards, quality and design; company legislation; and the regulation of insurance industries.

President of the Board of Trade and Secretary of State for Trade and Industry, The Rt. Hon. Ian Lang, MP
Principal Private Secretary, J. Alty
Private Secretaries, R. Jenkinson; A. Phillipson
Parliamentary Private Secretary, S. Coombe, MP
Minister for Industry and Energy, The Rt. Hon. Gregory Knight, MP
Private Secretary, M. Hilton
Parliamentary Private Secretary, R. Spring, MP
Minister for Trade, Anthony Nelson, MP
Private Secretary, U. Marthaler
Minister of State, The Rt. Hon. The Lord Fraser of Carmyllie, QC
Private Secretary, C. Pook
Parliamentary Under-Secretary of State for Science and Technology, Ian Taylor, MBE, MP
Private Secretary, Ms H. Stanley
Parliamentary Under-Secretary of State for Small Business, Industry and Energy, Richard Page, MP
Private Secretary, I. McKenzie
Parliamentary Under-Secretary of State for Competition and Consumer Affairs, John Taylor, MP
Private Secretary, P. Hadley
British Overseas Trade Board Chairman, M. Laing, CBE
Private Secretary, Ms S. Brown
Parliamentary Clerk, T. Williams
Permanent Secretary, M. Scholar, CB
Private Secretary, C. Hannant
Second Permanent Secretary, Chief Scientific Adviser and Head of Office of Science and Technology, Sir Robert May, FRS
Private Secretary, R. Clay
Directors-General, Sir John Cadogan, CBE, FRS (*Director-General of the Research Councils*); C. W. Roberts, CB (*Trade Policy and Export Promotion*); D. Durie, CMG (*Regional and Small- and Medium-Sized Enterprises*); B. Hilton, CB (*Corporate and Consumer Affairs*); A. Hammond, CB (*The Solicitor*); C. Henderson, CB (*Energy*); A. C. Hutton (*Resources and Services*); A. Macdonald, CB (*Industry*)

DIVISIONAL ORGANIZATION

‡AEROSPACE AND DEFENCE INDUSTRIES DIRECTORATE
Director of Aerospace and Defence Industries, R. Foster
Directors, M. Coolican; S. I. Charik

BRITISH NATIONAL SPACE CENTRE
Bridge Place, 88–89 Eccleston Square, London SW1V 1PT
Director-General, D. R. Davis
Deputy Director-General, D. Leadbeater
Directors, H. Evans; Dr P. Murdin; Dr D. Lumley

BUSINESS LINK DIRECTORATE
Director of Business Link, V. Brown
Directors, J. Reid; P. Bentley; P. Waller

CENTRAL POLICY UNIT
Director, Dr C. Bell

‡At 151 Buckingham Palace Road, London SW1W 9SS

‡CHEMICALS AND BIOTECHNOLOGY DIRECTORATE
Director of Chemicals and Biotechnology, M. Baker
Directors, Ms G. Alliston; Dr E. A. M. Baker

COAL DIRECTORATE
Director, A. Berry

‡COMMUNICATIONS AND INFORMATION INDUSTRIES
DIRECTORATE
Director of Communications and Information Industries,
W. MacIntyre
Directors, J. Neilson; N. McMillan; D. Hendon;
N. Worman; D. Hopkins; S. Pride

COMPANY LAW DIRECTORATE
Director of Company Law, Mrs S. Brown
Directors, N. D. Peace; D. E. Love

CONSUMER AFFAIRS AND COMPETITION POLICY
DIRECTORATE
Director of Consumer Affairs and Competiton Policy, P. Salvidge
Directors, A. Cooper; M. Higson; P. Masson; Miss D. Gane;
Dr A. Eggington; G. Boon

ECONOMICS AND STATISTICS DIRECTORATE
Chief Economic Adviser, D. R. Coates
Directors, Dr D. S. Higham; S. Penneck; M. S. Bradley

ELECTRICITY DIRECTORATE
Director of Electricity, J. Green

ENERGY POLICY AND ANALYSIS UNIT
Director of Energy Policy and Analysis, M. Keay
Directors, E. Evans; G. C. White

ENERGY TECHNOLOGIES DIRECTORATE
Director, G. Bevan

‡ENGINEERING, AUTOMOTIVE AND METALS
DIRECTORATE
Director of Engineering, Automotive and Metals, M. O'Shea
Directors, H. Brown; J. Grewe; R. Poole; A. Vinall; A. Wilks

ENGINEERING INSPECTORATE
Director of Engineering Inspectorate, Dr P. Fenwick

‡ENVIRONMENT DIRECTORATE
Director of Environment, Dr C. Hicks

‡ESTATES AND FACILITIES MANAGEMENT
DIRECTORATE
Director, M. Coolican

EUROPEAN COHESION DIRECTORATE
Director, D. Miner

EUROPE DIRECTORATE
Kingsgate House, 66–74 Victoria Street, London
SW1E 6SW
Director, B. Stow

EXPORT CONTROL AND NON-PROLIFERATION
DIRECTORATE
Kingsgate House, 66–74 Victoria Street, London
SW1E 6SW
Director of Export Control and Non-Proliferation,
R. J. Meadway
Directors, A. J. Mantle, P. H. Agrell

EXPORT PROMOTION DIRECTORATE
Kingsgate House, 66–74 Victoria Street, London
SW1E 6SW
Directors, M. Mowlam (*The Americas*); M. Cohen (*Asia
Pacific*); K. Levinson (*Central and Eastern Europe*); S. Lyle
Smythe (*Business in Europe*); N. Armour (*Middle East,
Near East and North Africa*); N. McInnes (*Sub-Saharan
Africa and South Asia*)

EXPORT SERVICES DIRECTORATE
Kingsgate House, 66–74 Victoria Street, London
SW1E 6SW
Director, A. Reynolds

FINANCE AND RESOURCE MANAGEMENT DIRECTORATE
Director of Finance and Resource Management, M. Roberts
Directors, Dr S. Sklaroff; K. Hills; N. Nandra; J. P. Clayton

IMPORT POLICY DIRECTORATE
Kingsgate House, 66–74 Victoria Street, London
SW1E 6SW
Director, S. Bowen

INDUSTRIAL RELATIONS DIRECTORATE
Director of Industrial Relations, Ms H. Leiser
Directors, K. Masson; R. Niblett; A. Wright; Mrs
Z. Hornstein; P. Parker

‡INDUSTRY ECONOMICS AND STATISTICS
DIRECTORATE
Director, Dr N. Owen

INFORMATION DIRECTORATE
Director of Information, Ms J. M. Caines
Director of News, M. Ricketts
Director of Publicity, Miss P. R. A. Freedman

‡INFORMATION MANAGEMENT AND TECHNOLOGY
DIRECTORATE
Director, R. Wheeler

‡INNOVATION UNIT
Director, Dr A. Keddie

INSURANCE DIRECTORATE
Director of Insurance, J. Spencer
Directors, R. Allen; R. Hobbs; K. Long; J. Whitlock

INTERNAL AUDIT
Bridge Place, 88–89 Eccleston Square, London SW1V 1PT
Director of Internal Audit, A. C. Elkington

INTERNATIONAL ECONOMICS DIRECTORATE
Kingsgate House, 66–74 Victoria Street, London
SW1E 6SW
Director, C. Moir

INVEST IN BRITAIN BUREAU
Chief Executive, A. Fraser

INVESTIGATIONS AND ENFORCEMENT DIRECTORATE
10 Victoria Street, London SW1H 0NN
Director of Investigations and Enforcement, J. Phillips
Directors, G. Horne; J. Sibley; R. Burns; T. Dunstan;
S. Clements

JOINT EXPORT PROMOTION DIRECTORATE
(FCO/DTI)
Kingsgate House, 66–74 Victoria Street, London
SW1E 6SW
Director-General of Export Promotion, F. R. Mingay, CMG
Directors, D. Saunders; (*DS4*), M. Dougal

LEGAL RESOURCE MANAGEMENT AND BUSINESS LAW
UNIT
10 Victoria Street, London SW1H 0NN
The Solicitor and Director-General, A. Hammond, CB
Director, J. Burnett

LEGAL SERVICES DIRECTORATE A
10 Victoria Street, London SW1H 0NN
Director of Legal A, J. Stanley

---

‡At 151 Buckingham Palace Road, London SW1W 9SS

Legal Directors, I. Mathers; J. Roberts; Miss N. O'Flynn;
S. Hyett; Miss G. Richmond

LEGAL SERVICES DIRECTORATE B
10 Victoria Street, London SW1H 0NN
Director of Legal B, P. Bovey
Legal Directors, R. Baker; Ms R. Jeffreys; T. Susman;
B. Welch; A. Woods

LEGAL SERVICES DIRECTORATE C
10 Victoria Street, London SW1H 0NN
Director of Legal C, Miss K. Morton
Legal Directors, S. Milligan; R. Perkins; R. Green;
M. Bucknill; C. Raikes

MANAGEMENT BEST PRACTICE
Director of Management Best Practice, Dr K. Poulter
Directors, Dr I. Harrison; J. Sutton

NEW ISSUES AND DEVELOPING COUNTRIES
Kingsgate House, 66–74 Victoria Street, London
SW1E 6SW
Director, C. Bridge

NUCLEAR INDUSTRIES DIRECTORATE
Director of Nuclear Industries, N. Hirst
Directors, Mrs H. Haddon; S. D. Spivey; Dr M. Draper;
J. Rhodes

NUCLEAR POWER PRIVATIZATION TEAM
Director, C. Wilcock

**OFFICE OF SCIENCE AND TECHNOLOGY: SCIENCE AND
ENGINEERING BASE DIRECTORATE**
Albany House, 84–86 Petty France, London SW1H 9ST
Director, Science and Engineering Base, A. Quigley
Directors, A. Carter; K. Root

**OFFICE OF SCIENCE AND TECHNOLOGY:
TRANSDEPARTMENTAL SCIENCE AND TECHNOLOGY
DIRECTORATE**
Albany House, 84–86 Petty France, London SW1H 9ST
Director, Transdepartmental Science and Technology, Ms H.
Williams
Directors, R. Wright; C. De Grouchy

OIL AND GAS DIRECTORATE
Director of Oil and Gas, M. J. Michell
Directors, J. R. V. Brook; S. Price; A. Wilson
Director of Oil and Gas Royalties Office, A. Cran

Oil and Gas Office (Aberdeen)
Atholl House, 86–88 Guild Street, Aberdeen AB9 1DR
Tel 01224-213557
Director, A. S. Wilson

OIL AND GAS PROJECTS AND SUPPLIES OFFICE
Tay House, 300 Bath Street, Glasgow G2 4DX
Tel 0141-228 3646
Kingsgate House, 66–74 Victoria Street, London
SW1H 6SW
Tel 0171-215 5000
Chief Executive, Oil Supplies Office, M. Stanley
Directors, P. Dunn; K. Forrest; B. Gallagher; K. Mayo

‡**POST OFFICE RETAILING AND TEXTILES
DIRECTORATE**
Director of Post Office Retailing and Textiles, I. M. Jones
Director, C. Jackson

PROJECTS EXPORT PROMOTION DIRECTORATE
Director of Projects Export Promotion, D. J. Hall
Directors, A. G. Atkinson; D. Marsh

REGIONAL ASSISTANCE DIRECTORATE
Director, D. Miner

REGIONAL POLICY DIRECTORATE
Director, D. Smith

SENIOR STAFF MANAGEMENT
Director, R. Rogers

**SMALL- AND MEDIUM-SIZED ENTERPRISES (SME)
POLICY DIRECTORATE**
St Mary's House, Level 2, c/o Moorfoot, Sheffield S1 4PQ
Director, R. Anderson

**SMALL- AND MEDIUM-SIZED ENTERPRISES (SME)
TECHNOLOGY DIRECTORATE**
Director, R. Allpress

STAFF PAY AND CONDITIONS
Director of Personnel, vacant
Director, C. Johnston

STAFF PERSONNEL OPERATIONS
Director, I. Cameron

‡**TECHNOLOGY AND STANDARDS DIRECTORATE**
Director of Technology and Standards, Dr D. Evans
Directors, R. T. King; I. C. Downing; J. M. Barber;
G. C. Riggs

TRADE POLICY DIRECTORATE
Kingsgate House, 66–74 Victoria Street, London
SW1E 6SW
Director, J. Hunt

BRITISH OVERSEAS TRADE BOARD
Kingsgate House, 66–74 Victoria Street, London SW1E
6SW
Tel 0171-215 5000

President, The President of the Board of Trade
Chairman, M. Laing, CBE
Vice-Chairman, HRH The Duke of Kent, KG, GCMG, GCVO
Members, Dr D. Baldwin, CBE; A. Buxton; I. L. Dale, OBE;
A. Turner; P. Goodwin, CBE; D. Lanigan, CBE;
R. Mingay, CMG; R. Burman, CBE; The Rt. Hon. Sir
Michael Palliser, GCMG; Sir Brian Pearse;
C. W. Roberts, CB; B. D. Taylor, CBE; B. Willott;
A. Burns, CMG; D. Peake; A. Hunt, CMG
Secretary, Dr D. Walker

REGIONAL OFFICES
— see pages 302–3

EXECUTIVE AGENCIES

COMPANIES HOUSE
Companies House, Crown Way, Cardiff CF4 3UZ
Tel 01222-388588
London Search Room, 55–71 City Road, London EC1Y 1BB
Tel 0171-253 9393
37 Castle Terrace, Edinburgh EH1 2EB
Tel 0131-535 5800

Companies House incorporates companies, registers company documents and provides company information.
Registrar of Companies for England and Wales, J.Holden
Registrar for Scotland, J. Henderson

THE INSOLVENCY SERVICE
PO Box 203, 21 Bloomsbury Street, London WC1B 3QW
Tel 0171-637 1110

The Service administers and investigates the affairs of bankrupts and companies in compulsory liquidation; deals with the disqualification of directors in all corporate

failures; regulates insolvency practitioners and their professional bodies; provides banking and investment services for bankruptcy and liquidation estates; and advises ministers on insolvency policy issues.
Inspector-General and Chief Executive, P. R. Joyce
Deputy Inspectors-General, D. J. Flynn; M. C. A. Osborne

NATIONAL WEIGHTS AND MEASURES LABORATORY
Stanton Avenue, Teddington, Middx TW11 0JZ
Tel 0181-943 7272
The Laboratory administers weights and measures legislation, carries out type examination, calibration and testing, and runs courses on metrological topics.
Chief Executive (G5), Dr S. Bennett

PATENT OFFICE
— *see* page 333

RADIOCOMMUNICATIONS AGENCY
New King's Beam House, 22 Upper Ground, London
SE1 9SA
Tel 0171-211 0211
The Agency is responsible for most civil radio matters other than telecommunications broadcasting policy and the radio equipment market.
Chief Executive (G3), J. Norton

DEPARTMENT OF TRANSPORT
Great Minster House, 76 Marsham Street, London
SW1P 4DR
Tel 0171-271 5000

The Department of Transport is responsible for land, sea and air transport, including sponsorship of the rail and bus industries; airports; domestic and international civil aviation; shipping and the ports industry; navigational lights, pilotage, HM Coastguard and marine pollution; motorways and other trunk roads; oversight of road transport including vehicle standards, registration and licensing, driver testing and licensing, bus and road freight licensing, regulation of taxis and private hire cars and road safety; and oversight of local authorities' transport planning, including payment of Transport Supplementary Grant.
Secretary of State for Transport, The Rt. Hon. Sir George Young, Bt., MP
  Private Secretary, Miss B. Hill
  Parliamentary Private Secretary, Dr C. Goodson-Wickes, MP
Minister of State, John Watts, MP (*Railways, Roads and Local Transport*)
  Private Secretary, S. M. Ghagan
  Parliamentary Private Secretary, T. Dicks, MP
Parliamentary Under-Secretaries, The Viscount Goschen (*Aviation and Shipping*); John Bowis, OBE, MP (*Transport in London and Road Safety*)
  Private Secretaries, S. Heard; L. Sambrook
Parliamentary Clerk, Miss P. Gaunt
Permanent Under-Secretary of State, Sir Patrick Brown, KCB
  Private Secretary, Miss V. H. Dickinson

INFORMATION
Head of Information, D. McMillan

RESOURCES
Director of Resources, D. J. Rowlands, CB

PERSONNEL
Director of Personnel and Change Management, R. Bird
SCS, R. D. Bayly; G. Kemp

Grade 6, B. Meakins
Grade 7, J. Gibson
Chief Welfare Officer (G7), Miss E. T. Haines

FINANCE
SCS, B. Wadsworth
Accounting Adviser, A. R. Allum
Heads of Divisions, R. Bennett; M. Reece; P. A. Sanders

EXECUTIVE AGENCIES DIRECTORATE
SCS, A. C. Melville

INTERNAL AUDIT
Ashdown House, Sedlescombe Road North, Hastings, E. Sussex TN37 7GA
Tel 01424-458306
Head of Branch, M. J. Reece

CENTRAL SERVICES
Ashdown House, Sedlescombe Road North, Hastings, E. Sussex TN37 7GA
Tel 01424-458306
Director, M. R. Newey
Heads of Divisions, I. R. Heawood (*Management Support Services*); G. L. Jones (*Departmental Procurement Unit*)
Grade 6, I. Harris (*Accommodation and Office Services*); P. Waller (*IT Management Unit*)

STATISTICAL SERVICES
Romney House, 43 Marsham Street, London SW1P 3PY
Tel 0171-276 8513
SCS, Miss B. J. Wood; Dr R. L. Butchart; P. J. Capell; R. P. Donachie

CHIEF SCIENTIST
Chief Scientist, Dr D. H. Metz

TRANSPORT SECURITY
Portland House, Stag Place, London SW1E 5BH
Tel 0171-460 3016
Director and Co-ordinator, R. D. Lord
SCS, Mrs A. M. Moss

MOBILITY UNIT
Head of Unit, Miss E. A. Frye

RAILWAYS
Director of Railways, N. L. J. Montagu, CB

RAILWAY INFRASTRUCTURE
Director of Railways (General), R. J. Griffins
Heads of Divisions, Dr J. H. Denning (*Railways 1A*); Miss P. M. Williams (*International Railways*); M. Fuhr (*Rail Link Bill*); P. Cox (*Railways Economics*); A. P. Moss (*Channel Tunnel*)

RAILWAY PRIVATIZATION
Director of Railway Privatization, Mrs J. M. Williams
Heads of Divisions, P. H. McCarthy; R. Linnard; R. S. Peal; D. Priestley

CHANNEL TUNNEL SAFETY AUTHORITY
SCS, E. A. Ryder, CB

ROADS, LOCAL TRANSPORT AND TRANSPORT POLICY
Director of Roads and Local Transport, P. Wood

NATIONAL ROADS POLICY DIRECTORATE
Director of National Roads Policy, H. Wenban-Smith
Heads of Divisions, T. Worsley (*Highways Economic and Traffic Appraisal*); Dr C. M. Woodman (*Highways Policy and Programmes*); Mrs C. M. Dixon (*Tolling and Private Finance*)

URBAN AND LOCAL TRANSPORT
Director of Urban and Local Transport, R. A. Allan
Heads of Divisions, A. B. Murray (*Buses and London Transport*); E. C. Neve (*Taxis and London Projects*); M. R. Pitwood (*Local Transport Policy*); M. A. Walsh (*Economics, Local Transport and General*); A. S. D. Whybrow (*Traffic Policy*); M. F. Talbot (*Driver Information and Traffic Management*)

ROAD AND VEHICLE SAFETY
Director of Road and Vehicle Safety, Miss S. J. Lambert
Heads of Divisions, I. R. Jordan (*Vehicle Standards and Engineering*); Dr R. M. Kimber (*Road Safety*); J. L. Gansler (*Licensing and Roadworthiness Policy*); J. R. Fells (*Road Haulage*); (*G6*), J. Winder (*Traffic Area Network Unit*)

TRANSPORT POLICY UNIT
Head of Unit, D. R. Instone

DEPARTMENTAL MEDICAL ADVISER
SCS, Dr P. A. M. Diamond, OBE

AVIATION GROUP
Director of General Civil Aviation, A. J. Goldman, CB
SCS, Ms A. Munro (*Airport Policy*); Ms M. J. Clare (*CAA and Safety Policy*); M. C. Mann (*Economics Aviation Maritime International*); Ms E. A. Duthie (*Noise and Pollution*)

INTERNATIONAL AVIATION NEGOTIATIONS
Director of International Aviation Negotiations, A. T. Baker
SCS, N. J. Starling; Dr P. H. Martin

AIR ACCIDENTS INVESTIGATION BRANCH
Royal Aerospace Establishment, Farnborough, Hants
GU14 6TD
Tel 01252-510300
Chief Inspector of Air Accidents, K. P. R. Smart, CBE
Deputy Chief Inspector of Air Accidents, R. C. McKinlay

SHIPPING DIRECTORATE
Director of Shipping, R. E. Clarke
Heads of Divisions, J. F. Wall; R. T. Bishop; G. D. Rowe

MARINE ACCIDENTS INVESTIGATION BRANCH
5–7 Brunswick Place, Southampton SO1 2AN
Tel 01703-232424
Chief Inspector of Marine Accidents, Capt. P. B. Marriott

REGIONAL OFFICES
— *see* pages 302–3

EXECUTIVE AGENCIES

COASTGUARD AGENCY
Spring Place, 105 Commercial Road, Southampton
SO15 1EG
Tel 01703-329100
The Agency's role is to minimize loss of life among seafarers and coastal users, and to minimize pollution from ships to sea and coastline.
Chief Executive, C. J. Harris
Chief Coastguard, J. Astbury

DRIVER AND VEHICLE LICENSING AGENCY
Longview Road, Morriston, Swansea SA6 7JL
Tel 01792-772151
The Agency issues driving licences, registers and licenses vehicles, and collects excise duty.
Chief Executive, Dr S. J. Ford
Heads of Divisions, R. J. Verge; T. J. Horton; J. C. Betts

DRIVING STANDARDS AGENCY
Stanley House, Talbot Street, Nottingham NG1 5GU
Tel 0115-947 4222
The Agency's role is to carry out driving tests and approve driving instructors.
Chief Executive, B. L. Herdan

HIGHWAYS AGENCY
St Christopher House, Southwark Street, London SE1 0TE
Tel 0171-928 3666
The Agency is responsible for the management and maintenance of the motorway and trunk road network and for road construction and improvement.
Chief Executive, L. J. Haynes

Finance Directorate
Director, J. Seddon
Heads of Divisions, P. A. Houston (*Finance and Procurement*); J. Bradley (*Lands, Claims and Graphics*); D. Kershaw (*Computing*)

Private Finance Directorate
Director, P. G. Collis

Human Resources Directorate
Director, K. A. Wyatt

Engineering and Environmental Policy Directorate
Director, T. A. Rochester
Deputy Director, J. A. Kerman
Head of Divisions, Mrs V. A. Bodnar (*Agency Environmental Policy*); N. S. Organ (*Road Engineering and Environmental*); A. J. Pickett (*Bridges Engineering*)

Road Programme Directorate
Director, J. W. Fellows
Deputy Director, D. York
Heads of Divisions, D. A. Holland (*Technical Services*); K. McKenzie (*Administrative Services*); D. E. Oddy (*Motorways Operations*); R. R. Bineham (*Northern Operations*); D. Ward (*Southern Operations*); J. P. Boud (*Construction Operations*); D. E. Oddy (*Administrative Operations*)

Network Management and Maintenance Directorate
Director, B. J. Billington
Deputy Director, P. E. Nutt
Heads of Divisions, R. Eastman (*Network Policy Division*); M. G. Quinn (*Network Control Division*); K. A. Lasbury (*Northern Network Management*); W. S. C. Wadrup (*Midland Network Management*); A. D. Rowland (*Southern Network Management*); R. T. Thorndike (*London Network Management*)

MARINE SAFETY AGENCY
Spring Place, 105 Commercial Road, Southampton
SO15 1EG
Tel 01703-329100
The Agency's role is to develop, promote and enforce high standards of marine safety and to minimize the risk of pollution of the marine environment from ships.
Chief Executive, R. M. Bradley
Directors, W. A. Graham (*Ship Construction and Navigation*); A. Cubbin (*Marine Safety Operations and Seafarers Standards*); (*G6*), R. Padgett (*Finance, Personnel and Corporate Services*)

VEHICLE CERTIFICATION AGENCY
1 Eastgate Office Centre, Eastgate Road, Bristol BS5 6XX
Tel 0117-951 5151
The Agency tests and certificates vehicles to UK and international standards.
Chief Executive, D. W. Harvey

VEHICLE INSPECTORATE
Berkeley House, Croydon Street, Bristol BS5 0DA
Tel 0117-954 3274

The Agency carries out annual testing and inspection of heavy goods and other vehicles and administers the MOT testing scheme.
Chief Executive, R. J. Oliver
Deputy Chief Executive, J. A. T. David

TRAFFIC DIRECTOR FOR LONDON
College House, Great Peter Street, London SW1P 3LN
Tel 0171-222 4545

The Traffic Director for London is a non-departmental public body which is independent from the Department of Transport but responsible to the Secretary of State for Transport and to Parliament. Its role is to co-ordinate the introduction of the Priority (Red) Route Network in London and monitor its operation.
Traffic Director for London, D. Turner

TRAFFIC AREA OFFICES

LICENSING AUTHORITIES AND TRAFFIC COMMISSIONERS
EASTERN (Nottingham and Cambridge), Brig. C. M. Boyd
NORTH-EASTERN (Newcastle upon Tyne and Leeds), K. R. Waterworth
NORTH-WESTERN (Manchester), K. R. Waterworth
SCOTTISH (Edinburgh), Brig. M. W. Betts
SOUTH-EASTERN AND METROPOLITAN (Eastbourne), Brig. M. H. Turner
SOUTH WALES (Cardiff), J. Mervyn
WESTERN (Bristol), J. Mervyn
WEST MIDLANDS (Birmingham), J. Mervyn

THE TREASURY
Parliament Street, London SW1P 3AG
Tel 0171-270 3000

The Office of the Lord High Treasurer has been continuously in commission for well over 200 years. The Lord High Commissioners of HM Treasury are the First Lord of the Treasury (who is also the Prime Minister), the Chancellor of the Exchequer and five junior Lords (who are government whips in the House of Commons). This Board of Commissioners is assisted at present by the Chief Secretary, a Parliamentary Secretary who is also the government Chief Whip, a Financial Secretary, an Economic Secretary, the Paymaster-General, and the Permanent Secretary.

The Prime Minister is not primarily concerned in the day-to-day aspects of Treasury business; the management of the Treasury devolves upon the Chancellor of the Exchequer and the other Treasury ministers.

The Chief Secretary is responsible for the planning and control of public expenditure; public sector pay, excluding the Civil Service; value for money in the public services (including the 'Next Steps' programme); and export credit.

The Financial Secretary has responsibility for parliamentary financial business; the legislative programme; oversight of the Inland Revenue; Inland Revenue taxes (excluding stamp duties); and privatization, competition and deregulation policy.

The Economic Secretary has responsibility for monetary policy; the financial system (including financial institutions); international finance issues and institutions; Economic and Monetary Union; stamp duties; wider

share-ownership; Treasury interest in small firms' policy; procurement policy; economic briefing; the Valuation Office Agency; the Royal Mint; the Department for National Savings; the Registry of Friendly Societies; the National Investment and Loans Office; the Office for National Statistics; and the Government Actuary's Department.

The Exchequer Secretary to the Treasury is responsible for general oversight of Customs and Excise; Customs and Excise duties and taxes; assisting the Chief Secretary on public expenditure planning and control; Treasury interest in women's issues; charities; the environment (including energy efficiency); the EC budget; general accounting issues; PAYMASTER (*see* page 333) and ministerial correspondence.

All Treasury ministers are concerned in tax matters.
Prime Minister and First Lord of the Treasury, The Rt. Hon. John Major, MP
Chancellor of the Exchequer, The Rt. Hon. Kenneth Clarke, QC, MP
  Principal Private Secretary, N. I. MacPherson
  Private Secretary, A. Gibbs
  Special Adviser, A. Teasdale
Chief Secretary to the Treasury, The Rt. Hon. William Waldegrave, MP
  Private Secretary, P. Raynes
  Special Adviser, P. Gardner
Financial Secretary to the Treasury, Michael Jack, MP
  Private Secretary, D. Finch
  Parliamentary Private Secretary, M. Fabricant, MP
Economic Secretary, Angela Knight, MP
  Private Secretary, Ms S. Tebbutt
Exchequer Secretary to the Treasury, The Rt. Hon. Phillip Oppenheim, MP
  Private Secretary, Ms P. Murray
  Special Adviser to the Treasury Ministers, E. Troup
Parliamentary Secretary to the Treasury and Government Chief Whip (*£36,613), The Rt. Hon. Alastair Goodlad, MP
  Private Secretary, M. Maclean
  Special Adviser, Miss S. C. Hole, OBE
Treasurer of HM Household and Deputy Chief Whip (*£31,125), Andrew Mackay, MP
Comptroller of HM Household (*£20,029), Timothy Wood, MP
Vice-Chamberlain of HM Household (*20,029), Derek Conway, MP
Lord Commissioners of the Treasury (*£20,029), M. Bates, MP; B. Wells, MP; P. McLoughlin, MP; R. Knapman, MP; R. Ottaway, MP
Assistant Whips (*£20,029), G. Brandreth, MP; S. Coe, MP; A. Coombs, MP; Mrs J. Lait, MP; P. Ainsworth, MP
Parliamentary Clerk, D. S. Martin
Panel of Independent Forecasters to the Treasury, G. Davies; T. Congdon; Prof. P. Minford, CBE; Ms K. Barker; Ms B. Rosewell; M. Weale
Permanent Secretary to the Treasury (G1), Sir Terence Burns, GCB
  Private Secretary, C. Guest
Head of Government Accountancy Service and Chief Accountancy Adviser to the Treasury, A. Likierman

DIRECTORATES

Leader, Ministerial Support Team, N. Macpherson
Leader, Communications Team, Ms J. Rutter
Leader, Strategy Team, N. Holgate

---

*In addition to a parliamentary salary of £43,000

MACROECONOMIC POLICY AND PROSPECTS
Director, Prof. A. Budd
Deputy Directors, J. Grice; A. O'Donnell, CB (*until end 1996*)
Team Leaders, M. Bradbury; J. S. Cunliffe; C. M. Kelly;
A. Kilpatrick; S. W. Matthews; S. Pickford; D. Savage

INTERNATIONAL FINANCE
Director, Sir Nigel Wicks, KCB, CVO, CBE
Deputy Directors, P. McIntyre; D. L. C. Peretz, CB
Team Leaders, S. Brooks; R. Fellgett; N. J. Ilett;
Ms S. Owen; D. Roe

BUDGET AND PUBLIC FINANCES
Director, P. R. C. Gray
Deputy Directors, S. W. Boys-Smith; †E. J. W. Gieve; C. J.
Mowl
Team Leaders, B. Byers; D. Deaton; Ms R. Kosmin;
N. M. Hansford; S. N. Matthews; M. Parkinson;
A. W. Ritchie; P. Short; S. N. Wood; P. Wynn Owen

SPENDING
Director, R. P. Culpin, CB, CVO
Deputy Directors, †N. Glass; Miss G. M. Noble;
Ms A. Perkins; P. N. Sedgwick
Team Leaders, P. Brook; S. Chakrabarti; D. Griffiths;
J. Halligan; A. Hudson; M. Neale; T. J. Sutton;
I. V. W. Taylor; Ms R. Thompson; Ms S. Walker

FINANCIAL MANAGEMENT, REPORTING AND AUDIT
Director (Chief Accountancy Adviser), A. Likierman
Deputy Director, †J. E. Mortimer
Team Leaders, K. Bradley; C. Butler; Mrs R. M. Dunn;
P. Holden; N. Holgate; Ms A. M. Jones

FINANCE, REGULATION AND INDUSTRY
Director, S. Robson
Deputy Directors, A. Whiting; M. L. Williams
Team Leaders, H. J. Bush; J. Colling; Mrs P. C. Diggle;
C. Farthing; J. J. Heywood; J. May; C. R. Pickering;
A. Sharples; Ms J. Simpson; P. Wanless

PERSONNEL AND SUPPORT
Director, Ms M. O'Mara
Team Leaders, I. Cooper; S. Judge; D. Rayson

EXECUTIVE AGENCIES

DEPARTMENT FOR NATIONAL SAVINGS
— *see* page 328

PAYMASTER
— *see* page 333

ROYAL MINT
— *see* page 339

OFFICE FOR NATIONAL STATISTICS
— *see* page 328

THE TREASURY SOLICITOR
DEPARTMENT OF HM PROCURATOR-GENERAL AND
TREASURY SOLICITOR
Queen Anne's Chambers, 28 Broadway, London
SWIH 9JS
Tel 0171-210 3000

The Treasury Solicitor's Department provides legal services for many government departments. Those without
their own lawyers are provided with legal advice, and both
they and other departments are provided with litigation
services. The Treasury Solicitor is also the Queen's

†Combined Deputy Director and Head of Team

Proctor, and is responsible for collecting Bona Vacantia
on behalf of the Crown. The Department became an
executive agency in April 1996.
HM Procurator-General and Treasury Solicitor (SCS), M. L.
Saunders, CB, QC
Deputy Treasury Solicitor (SCS), D. A. Hogg

CENTRAL ADVISORY DIVISION
SCS, Mrs I. G. Letwin

LITIGATION DIVISION
SCS, D. Brummell; F. L. Croft; Mrs D. Babar;
A. D. Lawton; A. Leithead; P. R. Messer; Mrs
J. B. C. Oliver; D. Palmer; R. J. Phillips; A. J. Sandal;
P. F. O. Whitehurst
Grade 6, Miss P. J. Carroll

QUEEN'S PROCTOR DIVISION
Queen's Proctor (SCS), M. L. Saunders, CB, QC
Assistant Queen's Proctor (SCS), Mrs D. Babar

RESOURCES AND SERVICES DIVISION
Principal Establishment and Finance Officer and Security Officer
(SCS), A. J. E. Hollis
Deputy Establishment Officer (G7), Ms H. Donnelly
Finance Officer (G7), C. A. Woolley
Information Systems Manager (G7), G. N. Younger
Business Support Manager (G7), J. Hoadly

BONA VACANTIA DIVISION
SCS, R. A. D. Jackson

EUROPEAN DIVISION
SCS, J. E. G. Vaux; J. E. Collins; D. Macrae

NATIONAL HERITAGE DIVISION
SCS, P. C. Jenkins

OFFICE OF PUBLIC SERVICE DIVISION
SCS, M. C. L. Carpenter

MINISTRY OF DEFENCE ADVISORY DIVISION
Metropole Building, Northumberland Avenue, London
WC2N 5BL
Tel 0171-218 4691
SCS, A. M. C. Inglese; Mrs P. A. Dayer; C. P. J.
Muttukumaru

DEPARTMENT FOR EDUCATION AND EMPLOYMENT
ADVISORY DIVISION
Caxton House, Tothill Street, London SW1H 9NF
Tel 0171-273 3000
SCS, R. N. Ricks; C. House; Miss R. Jeffreys;
N. A. D. Lambert; F. D. W. Clarke; A. D. Preston;
S. T. Harker

DEPARTMENT OF TRANSPORT ADVISORY DIVISION
Great Minster House, 76 Marsham Street, London
SW1P 4DR
Tel 0171-271 5000
SCS, M. C. P. Thomas; D. J. Aries; P. D. Coopman;
C. W. M. Ingram; A. G. Jones; R. Lines; N. C. Thomas

HM TREASURY ADVISORY DIVISION
Treasury Chambers, Parliament Street, London SW1P 3AG
Tel 0171-270 3000
SCS, M. A. Blythe; M. J. Hemming; Mrs V. Collett; Miss
J. V. Stokes; J. R. J. Braggins

GOVERNMENT PROPERTY LAWYERS
Riverside Chambers, Castle Street, Taunton, Somerset
TA1 4AP
Tel 01823-345200
An executive agency of the Treasury Solicitor's Depart-
ment.
Chief Executive (G3), P. Horner

Group Directors (G5), M. Benmayor; I. P. Parker;
M. F. Rawlins; A. M. Scarfe
Director of Lands Advisory (G5), R. C. Paddock

COUNCIL ON TRIBUNALS
7th Floor, 22 Kingsway, London WC2B 6LE
Tel 0171-936 7045

The Council on Tribunals is an independent statutory body. It keeps under review the constitution and working of the various tribunals which have been placed under its general supervision, and considers and reports on administrative procedures relating to statutory inquiries. It is consulted by government departments on proposals for legislation affecting tribunals and inquiries, and on proposals where the need for an appeals procedure may arise. It also offers advice on draft primary legislation. Some 70 tribunals are currently under the Council's supervision.
The Scottish Committee of the Council generally considers Scottish tribunals and matters relating only to Scotland.
Members of the Council are appointed by the Lord Chancellor and the Lord Advocate. The Scottish Committee is composed partly of members of the Council designated by the Lord Advocate and partly of others appointed by him. The Parliamentary Commissioner for Administration is *ex officio* a member of both the Council and the Scottish Committee.
Chairman, The Lord Archer of Sandwell, PC, QC
Members, The Parliamentary Commissioner for
    Administration; Mrs A. Anderson; T. N. Biggart, CBE, WS
    (*Chairman of the Scottish Committee*); Mrs S. Friend, MBE;
    C. Heaps; Prof. M. J. Hill; R. H. Jones, CVO; Dr
    C. A. Kaplan; I. D. Penman, CB; Prof. M. Partington;
    S. M. D. Brown; S. R. Davie, CB
Secretary, J. D. Saunders

SCOTTISH COMMITTEE OF THE COUNCIL ON
TRIBUNALS
44 Palmerston Place, Edinburgh EH12 5BJ
Tel 0131-220 1236

Chairman, T. N. Biggart, CBE, WS
Members, The Parliamentary Commissioner for
    Administration; Mrs H. Sheerin, OBE; Ms M. Burns;
    Mrs A. Middleton; I. D. Penman, CB; Mrs P. Y. Berry,
    MBE
Secretary, Mrs E. M. MacRae

TRIBUNALS
— *see* pages 372–5

UNRELATED LIVE TRANSPLANT REGULATORY AUTHORITY
Department of Health, Room 520, Eileen House,
80–94 Newington Causeway, London SE1 6EF
Tel 0171-972 2739

The Unrelated Live Transplant Regulatory Authority (ULTRA) is a statutory body established in 1990. In every case where the transplant of an organ within the definition of the Human Organ Transplants Act 1989 is proposed between a living donor and a recipient who are not genetically related, the proposal must be referred to ULTRA. Applications must be made by registered medical practitioners.

The Authority comprises a chairman and ten members appointed by the Secretary of State for Health. The secretariat is provided by Department of Health officials.
Chairman, Prof. M. Bobrow, CBE
Members, Revd Prof. G. R. Dunstan, CBE; Dr J. F. Douglas;
    Dr P. A. Dyer; Mrs D. Eccles; A. Hooker;
    S. G. Macpherson; Prof. N. P. Mallick;
    Prof. J. R. Salaman; Miss S. M. Taber; J. Wellbeloved
Administrative Secretary, J. R. Walden
Medical Secretary, Dr P. Doyle

WALES YOUTH AGENCY
Leslie Court, Lon-y-Llyn, Caerphilly CF83 1BQ
Tel 01222-880088

The Wales Youth Agency is a non-departmental public body funded by the Welsh Office. Its functions include the encouragement and development of the partnership between statutory and voluntary agencies relating to young people; the promotion of staff development and training; and the extension of marketing and information services in the relevant fields. The board of directors is appointed by the Secretary of State for Wales; directors do not receive a salary.
Chairman of the Board of Directors, G. Davies
Vice-Chairman of the Board of Directors, Dr H. Williamson
Executive Director, B. Williams

OFFICE OF WATER SERVICES
Centre City Tower, 7 Hill Street, Birmingham B5 4UA
Tel 0121-625 1300

The Office of Water Services (Ofwat) was set up under the Water Act 1989 and is the independent economic regulator of the water and sewerage companies in England and Wales. Ofwat's main duties are to ensure that the companies can finance and carry out the functions specified in the Water Industry Act 1991 and to protect the interests of water customers. Ofwat is a non-ministerial government department headed by the Director-General of Water Services. The Director-General has established ten regional customer service committees which are concerned solely with the interests of water customers. They are fully independent of the water industry with their own statutory identity and duty to investigate customer complaints and represent the interest of water customers. Representation of customer interests at national level is the responsibility of the Ofwat National Customer Council (ONCC), whose membership comprises the ten regional chairmen and the Director-General.
The Director-General is independent of ministerial control and directly accountable to Parliament.
Director-General of Water Services, I. C. R. Byatt

WELSH DEVELOPMENT AGENCY
Principality House, The Friary, Cardiff CF1 4AE
Tel 0345-775577/66

The Agency was established under the Welsh Development Agency Act 1975. Its remit is to help further the regeneration of the economy and improve the environment in Wales. The Agency's main activities include site assembly, provision of premises, encouraging investment by the private sector in property development, grant-

aiding land reclamation, stimulating quality urban and rural development, promoting Wales as a location for inward investment, helping to boost the growth, profitability and competitiveness of indigenous Welsh companies, and providing investment capital for industry. Its sponsoring department is the Welsh Office.
Chairman, D. Rowe-Beddoe
Deputy Chairman, R. Lewis
Chief Executive, B. Hartop

WELSH OFFICE

The Welsh Office has responsibility in Wales for ministerial functions relating to health and personal social services; education, except for terms and conditions of service and student awards; training; the Welsh language, arts and culture; the implementation of the Citizen's Charter in Wales; local government; housing; water and sewerage; environmental protection; sport; agriculture and fisheries; forestry; land use, including town and country planning and countryside and nature conservation; new towns; non-departmental public bodies and appointments in Wales; ancient monuments and historic buildings and the Welsh Arts Council; roads; tourism; financial assistance to industry; the Strategic Development Scheme in Wales and the Programme for the Valleys; the operation of the European Regional Development Fund in Wales and other European Community matters; civil emergencies; and all financial aspects of these matters, including Welsh rate support grant.

Gwydyr House, Whitehall, London SW1A 2ER
Tel 0171-270 3000

Secretary of State for Wales, The Rt. Hon. William Hague, MP
  Private Secretary, Dr J. Milligan
Parliamentary Under-Secretaries, Gwilym Jones, MP;
  Jonathan Evans, MP
  Private Secretaries, V. R. Watkin; W. S. Gear
  Special Adviser, B. Towns
Parliamentary Clerk, A. Green
Permanent Secretary (*G1*), Mrs R. Lomax
  Private Secretary, Ms J. M. Brown

Cathays Park, Cardiff CF1 3NQ
Tel 01222-825111

LEGAL GROUP
Legal Adviser (*G3*), D. G. Lambert
Deputy Legal Adviser (*G5*), J. H. Turnbull

INFORMATION DIVISION
Director of News (*G7*), R. Lehnert
Principal Publicity Officer (*G7*), W. J. Edwards

ESTABLISHMENT GROUP
Principal Establishment Officer (*G3*), C. D. Stevens
Heads of Divisions (*G5*), R. M. Abel; G. A. Thomas;
  Ms H. Angus
Chief Statistician (*G5*), W. R. L. Alldritt
Head of Health Statistics and Analysis Unit (*G6*), P. J. Fullerton
Head of Training and Education Intelligence Unit (*G6*), Mrs C. Fullerton

FINANCE GROUP
Principal Finance Officer (*G3*), R. A. Wallace
Heads of Divisions (*G5*), D. T. Richards; L. A. Pavelin
Senior Economic Adviser (*G5*), M. G. Phelps

Grade 6, M. G. Horlock
Head of Internal Audit (*G6*), D. Howarth

AGRICULTURE, ECONOMIC DEVELOPMENT, AND INDUSTRY AND TRAINING
Deputy Secretary (*G2*), J. F. Craig, CB

AGRICULTURE DEPARTMENT
Head of Department (*G3*), L. K. Walford
Heads of Divisions (*G5*), D. R. Thomas; Mrs A. M. Jackson
Divisional Executive Officers (*G7*), W. K. Griffiths
  (*Carmarthen*); E. Hughes (*Caernarfon*); J. C. Alexander
  (*Llandrindod Wells*)

ECONOMIC DEVELOPMENT GROUP
Head of Group (*G3*), M. J. Cochlin
Heads of Divisions (*G5*), B. J. Mitchell; A. D. Lansdown;
  M. L. Evans

INDUSTRY AND TRAINING DEPARTMENT
Director (*G3*), D. W. Jones
Industrial Director (*G4*), J. Cameron
Heads of Divisions (*G5*), G. T. Evans; H. Brodie;
  N. E. Thomas; (*G6*), Dr R. J. Loveland

EDUCATION, HOUSING, HEALTH AND SOCIAL SERVICES, TRANSPORT, LOCAL GOVERNMENT, PLANNING AND ENVIRONMENT
Deputy Secretary (*G2*), J. W. Lloyd, CB

EDUCATION DEPARTMENT
Head of Department (*G3*), S. H. Martin
Heads of Divisions (*G5*)°, W. G. Davies; H. Evans;
  R. J. Davies; Dr H. F. Rawlings

OFFICE OF HM CHIEF INSPECTOR FOR SCHOOLS IN WALES
Chief Inspector (*G4*)°, R. L. James
Staff Inspectors (*G5*)°, S. J. Adams; J. R. N. Evans;
  T. E. Parry; G. Thomas; P. Thomas
There are 45 Grade 6 Inspectors.
Head of Administration (*G7*), J. Roberts

LOCAL GOVERNMENT GROUP
Head of Group (*G3*), J. D. Shortridge
Heads of Divisions (*G5*), A. C. Wood; M. J. Clancy;
  Mrs B. J. M. Wilson; Mrs E. A. Taylor
Chief Inspector, Social Services Inspectorate (*Wales*) (*G5*),
  D. G. Evans
Deputy Chief Inspectors, J. F. Mooney; R. C. Woodward
Social Services Inspectors (*G7*), D, Barker; D. A. Brushett;
  G. H. Davies; Miss R. E. Evans; I. Forster;
  Mrs J. Jenkins; C. D. Vyvyan; Mrs P. White

HEALTH DEPARTMENT
Director (*G3*), P. R. Gregory
Heads of Divisions (*G5*), D. H. Jones; D. A. Pritchard; M. D. Chown; B. Wilcox; R. C. Williams; A. G. Thornton

HEALTH PROFESSIONAL GROUP
Chief Medical Officer (*G3*), Dr D. J. Hine
Principal Medical Officers (*G4*), Dr B. Fuge; Dr J. K. Richmond
Senior Medical Officers (*G5*), Dr J. Ludlow; Dr H. N. Williams; Dr P. Salter; Dr P. Lyne
Medical Adviser (*part-time*), Dr J. Andrew
Chief Dental Officer (*G5*), D. M. Heap
Senior Dental Officer (*G5*), P. Langmaid
Chief Scientific Adviser (*G5*), Dr J. A. V. Pritchard
Deputy Scientific Adviser (*G6*), Dr E. O. Crawley
Chief Pharmaceutical Adviser (*G5*), Miss C. W. Howells

°Based at Ty Glas Road, Llanishen, Cardiff CF4 5LE. Tel: 01222-761456

Chief Environmental Health Adviser (G5), R. Alexander
Deputy Environmental Health Adviser (G6), D. Worthington

NURSING DIVISION
Chief Nursing Officer, Miss M. Bull
Deputy Chief Nursing Officer, Mrs B. Melvin
Nursing Officers, Mrs S. M. Drayton; P. Johnson; Mrs
J. Sait; M. F. Tonkin

TRANSPORT, PLANNING AND ENVIRONMENT GROUP
Head of Group (G3), G. C. G. Craig
Director of Highways (G4), K. J. Thomas°
Deputy Director of Highways (G5), J. G. Evans*
Head of Division (G5), D. I. Westlake°
Chief Planning Adviser (G5), W. P. Roderick
Superintending Engineers (G6), J. R. Rees*; B. H. Hawker,
OBE*
Chief Estates Adviser (G6), G. K. Hoad
Senior Principal (G6), P. R. Marsden
Scientific Adviser (G6), Dr H. Prosser
Principal Planning Officers (G7), L. Owen; J. V. Spear
Principal Research Officers (G7), A. S. Dredge;
Ms L. J. Roberts
Principal Estates Officer (G7), R. W. Wilson
*Principal Professional and Technology Officers, Highways
Directorate° (G7)*, M. J. Gilbert*; I. A. Grindulis;
A. P. Howcroft; A. L. Perry; R. H. Powell; S. C. Shouler;
J. Collins; K. J. Alexander; R. H. Hooper*; R. K. Cone;
J. Dawkins; T. Dorken; R. Shaw; M. J. A. Parker;
V. S. Pownall*

LOCAL GOVERNMENT REORGANIZATION GROUP
Head of Group (G3), J. D. Shortridge

HEALTH AUTHORITIES

BRO TAF, Churchill House, Churchill Way, Cardiff CF1
4TW. *Chair*, Mrs K. Thomas; *Chief Executive*, Mrs G.
Todd
DYFED POWYS, St David's Hospital, Carmarthen SA31 3HB.
Chair, Mrs V. Bourne; *Chief Executive*, Mrs P. Stansbie
GWENT, Mamhilad House, Mamhilad, Pontypool NP4
0YP. *Chair*, Hon. Mrs L. Price; *Chief Executive*, J. Hallett
MORGANNWG, The Oldway Centre, 36 Orchard Street,
Swansea SA1 5AQ. *Chair*, H. Thomas; *Chief Executive*,
Mrs J. Williams
NORTH WALES, Preswylfa, Hendy Road, Mold CH7 1PZ.
Chair, Dr A. Kenrick; *Chief Executive*, B. Jones

EXECUTIVE AGENCIES

AGRICULTURAL DEVELOPMENT AND ADVISORY
SERVICE (ADAS)
— *see* page 280

CADW: WELSH HISTORIC MONUMENTS
Brunel House, Fitzalan Road, Cardiff CF2 1UY
Tel 01222-500200
Cadw supports the preservation, conservation, apprecia-
tion and enjoyment of the built heritage in Wales.
Chief Executive, T. Cassidy
Director of Policy and Administration, R. W. Hughes
Conservation Architect (G6), J. D. Hogg
*Principal Inspector of Ancient Monuments and Historic
Buildings*, J. R. Avent

Based at:
°Ty Glas Road, Llanishen, Cardiff CF4 5LE. Tel: 01222-761456
*Government Buildings, Dinerth Road, Rhos-on-Sea, Colwyn Bay
LL28 4UL. Tel: 01492-44261

Inspectors of Ancient Monuments and Historic Buildings,
J. K. Knight; A. D. McLees; Dr S. E. Rees; R. C. Turner;
M. J. Yates

INTERVENTION BOARD
— *see* page 315

PLANNING INSPECTORATE
Cathays Park, Cardiff CF1 3NQ
Tel 01222-823892
A joint executive agency of the Department of the
Environment and the Welsh Office (*see* page 298).
Chief Executive and Chief Inspector of Planning (G3),
C. Shepley
Assistant Chief Planning Inspector (G5), Mrs S. Bruton

WOMEN'S NATIONAL COMMISSION
Level 4, Caxton House, Tothill Street, London SW1H 9NF
Tel 0171-273 5486

The Women's National Commission is an independent
advisory committee to the Government. Its remit is to
ensure that the informed opinions of women are given their
due weight in the deliberations of the Government. The
Commission's 50 members are all women who are elected
or appointed by national organizations with a large and
active membership of women. The organizations include
the women's sections of the major political parties, trade
unions and religious groups, professional women's organizations and other bodies broadly representative of women.
The Commission's sponsoring department is the Department for Education and Employment.
Government Co-Chairman, Mrs A. Browning, MP
Elected Co-Chairman, Mrs E. Bavidge
Joint Secretaries, Ms J. Bailey; Ms W. Brown

CIVIL SERVICE STAFF

BY PRINCIPAL DEPARTMENTS *As at 1 April 1995*

		Of whom
	Total	in agencies
Agriculture, Fisheries and Food	10,567	4,164
Cabinet Office	2,405	887
Customs and Excise	24,132	—
Defence	116,139	32,403
Education	2,507	391
Employment Department Group	49,553	39,852
Environment	7,054	2,541
Foreign Office	5,978	30
Health	4,496	1,058
Home Office	50,889	41,323
Inland Revenue	59,093	4,531
Lord Chancellor's Department	11,605	10,383
Scottish Departments	13,158	7,571
Social Security	89,248	86,455
Trade and Industry	10,247	5,103
Transport	12,792	10,491
Treasury	1,127	—
Welsh Office	2,224	227
Other departments	43,679	19,238
TOTAL	516,893	266,648

Law Courts and Offices

THE JUDICIAL COMMITTEE OF THE PRIVY COUNCIL

The Judicial Committee of the Privy Council is primarily the final court of appeal for the United Kingdom dependent territories and those independent Commonwealth countries which have retained the avenue of appeal upon achieving independence (Antigua and Barbuda, The Bahamas, Barbados, Belize, Brunei, Dominica, The Gambia, Jamaica, Kiribati, Mauritius, New Zealand, St Christopher and Nevis, St Lucia, St Vincent and the Grenadines, Trinidad and Tobago, and Tuvalu). The Committee also hears appeals from the Channel Islands and the Isle of Man and the disciplinary and health committees of the medical and allied professions. It has a limited jurisdiction to hear appeals under the Pastoral Measure 1983. In 1995 the Judicial Committee heard 69 appeals and 69 petitions for special leave to appeal.

The members of the Judicial Committee include the Lord Chancellor, the Lords of Appeal in Ordinary (*see* page 358), other Privy Councillors who hold or have held high judicial office and certain judges from the Commonwealth.

PRIVY COUNCIL OFFICE (JUDICIAL COMMITTEE), Downing Street, London SW1A 2AJ. Tel: 0171-270 0483. *Registrar of the Privy Council*, D. H. O. Owen; *Chief Clerk*, F. G. Hart

The Judicature of England and Wales

The legal system of England and Wales is separate from those of Scotland and Northern Ireland and differs from them in law, judicial procedure and court structure, although there is a common distinction between civil law (disputes between individuals) and criminal law (acts harmful to the community).

The supreme judicial authority for England and Wales is the House of Lords, which is the ultimate Court of Appeal from all courts in Great Britain and Northern Ireland (except criminal courts in Scotland) for all cases except those concerning the interpretation and application of European Community law, including preliminary rulings requested by British courts and tribunals, which are decided by the European Court of Justice (*see* page 773). As a Court of Appeal the House of Lords consists of the Lord Chancellor and the Lords of Appeal in Ordinary (law lords).

The Supreme Court of Judicature comprises the Court of Appeal, the High Court of Justice and the Crown Court. The High Court of Justice is the superior civil court and is divided into three divisions. The Chancery Division is concerned mainly with equity, bankruptcy and contentious probate business. The Queen's Bench Division deals with commercial and maritime law, serious personal injury and medical negligence cases, cases involving a breach of contract and professional negligence actions. The Family Division deals with matters relating to family law. Sittings are held at the Royal Courts of Justice in London or at 126 District Registries outside the capital. High Court judges sit alone to hear cases at first instance. Appeals from lower courts are heard by two or three judges, or by single judges of the appropriate division. The Restrictive Practices Court, set up under the Restrictive Trade Practices Act 1956, and the Official Referees' Courts, which deal almost exclusively with cases concerning the construction industry, are also part of the High Court. Appeals from the High Court are heard in the Court of Appeal (Civil Division), presided over by the Master of the Rolls, and may go on to the House of Lords.

In criminal matters the decision to prosecute in the majority of cases rests with the Crown Prosecution Service, the independent prosecuting body in England and Wales (*see* page 366–7). At the head of the service is the Director of Public Prosecutions, who discharges her duties under the superintendence of the Attorney-General. Certain categories of offence continue to require the Attorney-General's consent for prosecution.

The Crown Court sits in about 90 centres, divided into six circuits, and is presided over by High Court judges, full-time circuit judges, and part-time recorders and assistant recorders, sitting with a jury in all trials which are contested. There were 332 assistant recorders at 30 June 1996. The Crown Court deals with trials of the more serious criminal offences, the sentencing of offenders committed for sentence by magistrates' courts (when the magistrates consider their own power of sentence inadequate), and appeals from magistrates' courts. Magistrates usually sit with a circuit judge or recorder to deal with appeals and committals for sentence. Appeals from the Crown Court, either against sentence or conviction, are made to the Court of Appeal (Criminal Division), presided over by the Lord Chief Justice. A further appeal from the Court of Appeal to the House of Lords can be brought if a point of law of general public importance is considered to be involved.

Minor criminal offences (summary offences) are dealt with in magistrates' courts, which usually consist of three unpaid lay magistrates (justices of the peace) sitting without a jury, who are advised on points of law and procedure by a legally-qualified clerk to the justices. There were 30,326 justices of the peace at 1 January 1996. In busier courts a full-time, salaried and legally-qualified stipendiary magistrate presides alone. Cases involving people under 18 are heard in youth courts, specially constituted magistrates' courts which sit apart from other courts. Preliminary proceedings in a serious case to decide whether there is evidence to justify committal for trial in the Crown Court are also dealt with in the magistrates' courts. Appeals from magistrates' courts against sentence or conviction are made to the Crown Court. Appeals upon a point of law are made to the High Court, and may go on to the House of Lords.

Most minor civil cases are dealt with by the county courts, of which there are about 270 (details may be found in the local telephone directory). Cases are heard by circuit judges or district judges. There were 331 district judges at 31 May 1996. For cases involving small claims there are special simplified procedures. Where there are financial limits on county court jurisdiction, claims which exceed those limits may be tried in the county courts with the consent of the parties, or in certain circumstances on transfer from the High Court. Outside London, bankruptcy proceedings can be heard in designated county courts. Magistrates' courts can deal with certain classes of civil case and committees of magistrates license public houses, clubs and betting shops. For the implementation of the Children Act 1989, a new structure of hearing centres was set up in 1991 for family proceedings cases, involving magistrates' courts (family proceedings courts), divorce county courts, family hearing centres and care centres. Appeals in family matters heard in the family proceedings courts go to the Family Division of the High Court; affiliation appeals and appeals from decisions of the licensing committees of magistrates go to the Crown Court. Appeals from county courts are heard in the Court of Appeal (Civil Division), and may go on to the House of Lords.

On 26 July 1996 the Master of the Rolls (Lord Woolf) published proposals for a radical reform of the civil justice system in England and Wales aimed at making procedures simpler, quicker and cheaper.

Coroners' courts investigate violent and unnatural deaths or sudden deaths where the cause is unknown. Cases may be brought before a local coroner (a senior lawyer or doctor) by doctors, the police, various public authorities or members of the public. Where a death is sudden and the cause is unknown, the coroner may order a post-mortem examination to determine the cause of death rather than hold an inquest in court.

Judicial appointments are made by The Queen; the most senior appointments are made on the advice of the Prime Minister and other appointments on the advice of the Lord Chancellor.

Under the provisions of the Criminal Appeal Act 1995, a Commission is being set up to direct and supervise investigations into possible miscarriages of justice and to refer cases to the courts on the grounds of conviction and sentence; these functions were formerly the responsibility of the Home Secretary. The Commission will be based in Birmingham and is expected to start work by the end of 1996.

THE HOUSE OF LORDS
AS FINAL COURT OF APPEAL

The Lord High Chancellor
The Rt. Hon. the Lord Mackay of Clashfern, *born* 1927, *apptd* 1987

LORDS OF APPEAL IN ORDINARY (each £122,231)
Style, The Rt. Hon. Lord —

Rt. Hon. Lord Goff of Chieveley, *born* 1926, *apptd* 1986
Rt. Hon. Lord Browne-Wilkinson, *born* 1930, *apptd* 1991
Rt. Hon. Lord Mustill, *born* 1931, *apptd* 1992
Rt. Hon. Lord Slynn of Hadley, *born* 1930, *apptd* 1992
Rt. Hon. Lord Lloyd of Berwick, *born* 1929, *apptd* 1993
Rt. Hon. Lord Nolan, *born* 1928, *apptd* 1994
Rt. Hon. Lord Nicholls of Birkenhead, *born* 1933, *apptd* 1994
Rt. Hon. Lord Steyn, *born* 1932, *apptd* 1995
Rt. Hon. Lord Hoffman, *born* 1934, *apptd* 1995
Rt. Hon. Lord Hope of Craighead, *born* 1938, *apptd* 1996
Rt. Hon. Lord Clyde, *born* 1932, *apptd* 1996

Registrar, The Clerk of the Parliaments (*see* page 218)

SUPREME COURT OF JUDICATURE

COURT OF APPEAL

The Master of the Rolls (£122,231), The Rt. Hon. Lord Woolf, *born* 1933, *apptd* 1996
Secretary, Miss V. Seymour
Clerk, D. G. Grimmett

LORDS JUSTICES OF APPEAL (each £117,190)
Style, The Rt. Hon. Lord/Lady Justice [surname]

Rt. Hon. Sir Martin Nourse, *born* 1932, *apptd* 1985
Rt. Hon. Dame Elizabeth Butler-Sloss, DBE, *born* 1933, *apptd* 1988
Rt. Hon. Sir Murray Stuart-Smith, *born* 1927, *apptd* 1988
Rt. Hon. Sir Christopher Staughton, *born* 1933, *apptd* 1988
Rt. Hon. Sir Anthony McCowan, *born* 1928, *apptd* 1989
Rt. Hon. Sir Roy Beldam, *born* 1925, *apptd* 1989
Rt. Hon. Sir Andrew Leggatt, *born* 1930, *apptd* 1990
Rt. Hon. Sir Paul Kennedy, *born* 1935, *apptd* 1992
Rt. Hon. Sir David Hirst, *born* 1925, *apptd* 1992
Rt. Hon. Sir Simon Brown, *born* 1937, *apptd* 1992
Rt. Hon. Sir Anthony Evans, *born* 1934, *apptd* 1992
Rt. Hon. Sir Christopher Rose, *born* 1937, *apptd* 1992
Rt. Hon. Sir John Waite, *born* 1932, *apptd* 1993
Rt. Hon. Sir John Roch, *born* 1934, *apptd* 1993
Rt. Hon. Sir Peter Gibson, *born* 1934, *apptd* 1993
Rt. Hon. Sir John Hobhouse, *born* 1932, *apptd* 1993
Rt. Hon. Sir Denis Henry, *born* 1931, *apptd* 1993
Rt. Hon. Sir Mark Saville, *born* 1936, *apptd* 1994
Rt. Hon. Sir Peter Millett, *born* 1932, *apptd* 1994
Rt. Hon. Sir Swinton Thomas, *born* 1931, *apptd* 1994
Rt. Hon. Sir Andrew Morritt, CVO, *born* 1938, *apptd* 1994
Rt. Hon. Sir Philip Otton, *born* 1933, *apptd* 1995
Rt. Hon. Sir Robin Auld, *born* 1937, *apptd* 1995
Rt. Hon. Sir Malcolm Pill, *born* 1938, *apptd* 1995
Rt. Hon. Sir William Aldous, *born* 1936, *apptd* 1995
Rt. Hon. Sir Alan Ward, *born* 1938, *apptd* 1995
Rt. Hon. Sir Michael Hutchison, *born* 1933, *apptd* 1995
Rt. Hon. Sir Konrad Schiemann, *born* 1937, *apptd* 1995
Rt. Hon. Sir Nicholas Phillips, *born* 1938, *apptd* 1995
Rt. Hon. Sir Mathew Thorpe, *born* 1938, *apptd* 1995
Rt. Hon. Sir Mark Potter, *born* 1937, *apptd* 1996
Rt. Hon. Sir Henry Brooke, *born* 1936, *apptd* 1996
Rt. Hon. Sir Igor Judge, *born* 1941, *apptd* 1996
Rt. Hon. Sir Mark Waller, *born* 1940, *apptd* 1996
Rt. Hon. Sir John Mummery, *born* 1938, *apptd* 1996

Ex officio Judges, The Lord High Chancellor; the Lord Chief Justice of England; the Master of the Rolls; the President of the Family Division; and the Vice-Chancellor

COURT OF APPEAL (CRIMINAL DIVISION)
Judges, The Lord Chief Justice of England; the Master of the Rolls; Lords Justices of Appeal; and Judges of the High Court of Justice

COURTS-MARTIAL APPEAL COURT
Judges, The Lord Chief Justice of England; the Master of the Rolls; Lords Justices of Appeal; and Judges of the High Court of Justice

HIGH COURT OF JUSTICE
CHANCERY DIVISION

President, The Lord High Chancellor
The Vice-Chancellor (£117,190), The Rt. Hon. Sir Richard Scott, *born* 1934, *apptd* 1994
Clerk, W. Northfield, BEM

JUDGES (each £104,431)
Style, The Hon. Mr/Mrs Justice [surname]

Hon. Sir Jeremiah Harman, *born* 1930, *apptd* 1982
Hon. Sir John Knox, *born* 1925, *apptd* 1985
Hon. Sir Donald Rattee, *born* 1937, *apptd* 1989
Hon. Sir Francis Ferris, TD, *born* 1932, *apptd* 1990
Hon. Sir John Chadwick, ED, *born* 1941, *apptd* 1991
Hon. Sir Jonathan Parker, *born* 1937, *apptd* 1991
Hon. Sir John Lindsay, *born* 1935, *apptd* 1992
Hon. Dame Mary Arden, DBE, *born* 1947, *apptd* 1993
Hon. Sir Edward Evans-Lombe, *born* 1937, *apptd* 1993
Hon. Sir Robin Jacob, *born* 1941, *apptd* 1993
Hon. Sir William Blackburne, *born* 1944, *apptd* 1993
Hon. Sir Gavin Lightman, *born* 1939, *apptd* 1994
Hon. Sir Robert Walker, *born* 1938, *apptd* 1994
Hon. Sir Robert Carnwath, *born* 1945, *apptd* 1994
Hon. Sir Colin Rimer, *born* 1944, *apptd* 1994
Hon. Sir Hugh Laddie, *born* 1946, *apptd* 1995

HIGH COURT OF JUSTICE IN BANKRUPTCY
Judges, The Vice-Chancellor and judges of the Chancery
    Division of the High Court

COMPANIES COURT
Judges, The Vice Chancellor and judges of the Chancery
    Division of the High Court

PATENT COURT (APPELLATE SECTION)
Judge, The Hon. Mr Justice Jacob

QUEEN'S BENCH DIVISION

The Lord Chief Justice of England (£132,178) The Rt. Hon.
    the Lord Bingham of Cornhill, *born* 1933, *apptd* 1996
Private Secretary, E. Adams
Clerk, J. Bond

JUDGES (each £104,431)
Style, The Hon. Mr/Mrs Justice [surname]

Hon. Sir Christopher French, *born* 1925, *apptd* 1979
Hon. Sir Charles McCullough, *born* 1931, *apptd* 1981
Hon. Sir Oliver Popplewell, *born* 1927, *apptd* 1983
Hon. Sir Richard Tucker, *born* 1930, *apptd* 1985
Hon. Sir Patrick Garland, *born* 1929, *apptd* 1985
Hon. Sir Michael Turner, *born* 1931, *apptd* 1985
Hon. Sir John Alliott, *born* 1932, *apptd* 1986
Hon. Sir Harry Ognall, *born* 1934, *apptd* 1986
Hon. Sir John Owen, *born* 1925, *apptd* 1986
Hon. Sir Humphrey Potts, *born* 1931, *apptd* 1986
Hon. Sir Richard Rougier, *born* 1932, *apptd* 1986
Hon. Sir Ian Kennedy, *born* 1930, *apptd* 1986
Hon. Sir Stuart McKinnon, *born* 1938, *apptd* 1988
Hon. Sir Scott Baker, *born* 1937, *apptd* 1988
Hon. Sir Edwin Jowitt, *born* 1929, *apptd* 1988
Hon. Sir Douglas Brown, *born* 1931, *apptd* 1996
Hon. Sir Michael Morland, *born* 1929, *apptd* 1989
Hon. Sir Roger Buckley, *born* 1939, *apptd* 1989
Hon. Sir Anthony Hidden, *born* 1936, *apptd* 1989
Hon. Sir Michael Wright, *born* 1932, *apptd* 1990
Hon. Sir Charles Mantell, *born* 1937, *apptd* 1990
Hon. Sir John Blofeld, *born* 1932, *apptd* 1990
Hon. Sir Peter Cresswell, *born* 1944, *apptd* 1991
Hon. Sir Anthony May, *born* 1940, *apptd* 1991
Hon. Sir John Laws, *born* 1945, *apptd* 1992
Hon. Dame Ann Ebsworth, DBE, *born* 1937, *apptd* 1992
Hon. Sir Simon Tuckey, *born* 1941, *apptd* 1992
Hon. Sir David Latham, *born* 1942, *apptd* 1992
Hon. Sir Christopher Holland, *born* 1937, *apptd* 1992
Hon. Sir John Kay, *born* 1943, *apptd* 1992
Hon. Sir Richard Curtis, *born* 1933, *apptd* 1992

Hon. Sir Stephen Sedley, *born* 1939, *apptd* 1992
Hon. Dame Janet Smith, DBE, *born* 1940, *apptd* 1992
Hon. Sir Anthony Colman, *born* 1938, *apptd* 1992
Hon. Sir Anthony Clarke, *born* 1943, *apptd* 1993
Hon. Sir John Dyson, *born* 1943, *apptd* 1993
Hon. Sir Thayne Forbes, *born* 1938, *apptd* 1993
Hon. Sir Michael Sachs, *born* 1932, *apptd* 1993
Hon. Sir Stephen Mitchell, *born* 1941, *apptd* 1993
Hon. Sir Rodger Bell, *born* 1939, *apptd* 1993
Hon. Sir Michael Harrison, *born* 1939, *apptd* 1993
Hon. Sir Bernard Rix, *born* 1944, *apptd* 1993
Hon. Dame Heather Steel, DBE, *born* 1940, *apptd* 1993
Hon. Sir William Gage, *born* 1938, *apptd* 1993
Hon. Sir Jonathan Mance, *born* 1943, *apptd* 1993
Hon. Sir Andrew Longmore, *born* 1944, *apptd* 1993
Hon. Sir Thomas Morison, *born* 1939, *apptd* 1993
Hon. Sir Richard Buxton, *born* 1938, *apptd* 1993
Hon. Sir David Keene, *born* 1941, *apptd* 1994
Hon. Sir Andrew Collins, *born* 1942, *apptd* 1994
Hon. Sir Maurice Kay, *born* 1942, *apptd* 1995
Hon. Sir Brian Smedley, *born* 1934, *apptd* 1995
Hon. Sir Anthony Hooper, *born* 1937, *apptd* 1995
Hon. Sir Alexander Butterfield, *born* 1942, *apptd* 1995
Hon. Sir George Newman, *born* 1941, *apptd* 1995
Hon. Sir David Poole, *born* 1938, *apptd* 1995
Hon. Sir Martin Moore-Bick, *born* 1946, *apptd* 1995
Hon. Sir Gordon Langley, *born* 1943, *apptd* 1995
Hon. Sir Roger Thomas, *born* 1947, *apptd* 1996
Hon. Sir Robert Nelson, *born* 1942, *apptd* 1996
Hon. Sir Roger Toulson, *born* 1946, *apptd* 1996
Hon. Sir Michael Astill, *born* 1938, *apptd* 1996
Hon. Sir Alan Moses, *born* 1945, *apptd* 1996

FAMILY DIVISION

President (£117,190) Rt. Hon. Sir Stephen Brown, *born*
    1929, *apptd* 1988
Secretary, Mrs S. Leung
Clerk, Mrs S. Bell

JUDGES (each £104,431)
Style, The Hon. Mr/Mrs Justice [surname]

Hon. Sir Anthony Hollis, *born* 1927, *apptd* 1982
Hon. Sir Edward Cazalet, *born* 1936, *apptd* 1988
Hon. Sir Robert Johnson, *born* 1933, *apptd* 1989
Hon. Dame Joyanne Bracewell, DBE, *born* 1934, *apptd* 1990
Hon. Sir Michael Connell, *born* 1939, *apptd* 1991
Hon. Sir Peter Singer, *born* 1944, *apptd* 1993
Hon. Sir Nicholas Wilson, *born* 1945, *apptd* 1993
Hon. Sir Nicholas Wall, *born* 1945, *apptd* 1993
Hon. Sir Andrew Kirkwood, *born* 1944, *apptd* 1993
Hon. Sir Christopher Stuart-White, *born* 1933, *apptd* 1993
Hon. Dame Brenda Hale, DBE, *born* 1945, *apptd* 1994
Hon. Sir Hugh Bennett, *born* 1943, *apptd* 1995
Hon. Sir Edward Holman, *born* 1947, *apptd* 1995
Hon. Dame Mary Hogg, *born* 1947, *apptd* 1995
Hon. Sir Christopher Sumner, *born* 1939, *apptd* 1996

RESTRICTIVE PRACTICES COURT
Room 410, Thomas More Building, Royal Courts of
Justice, Strand, London WC2A 2LL
Tel 0171-936 6727

President, The Hon. Mr Justice Buckley
Judges, The Hon. Mr Justice Ferris; The Hon. Mr Justice
    Buxton
Lay Members, B. M. Currie; Sir Lewis Robertson, CBE;
    R. Garrick, CBE; S. J. Ahearne; J. A. Graham; Mrs D. H.
    Hatfield; S. McDowall; J. A. Scott; B. D. Colgate;
    J. A. C. King
Clerk of the Court, M. Buckley

OFFICIAL REFEREES' COURTS
St Dunstan's House, 133–137 Fetter Lane, London
EC4A 1HD
Tel 0171-936 7427

JUDGES (each £89,123)
His Hon. Judge Lewis, QC (*Senior Official Referee*)
His Hon. Judge Bowsher, QC
His Hon. Judge Loyd, QC
His Hon. Judge Hicks, QC
His Hon. Judge Havery, QC
His Hon. Judge Lloyd, QC
His Hon. Judge Newman, QC
His Hon. Judge Thornton, QC
His Hon. Judge Wilcox

Chief Clerk, Miss B. Joy

LORD CHANCELLOR'S DEPARTMENT
— *see* Government Departments and Public Offices

SUPREME COURT DEPARTMENTS AND OFFICES
Royal Courts of Justice, London WC2A 2LL
Tel 0171-936 6000

DIRECTOR'S OFFICE
Director, G. E. Calvert
Deputy Director, J. Selch
Group Manager, Family Proceedings and Probate Service, R. P.
  Knight
Finance and Court Business Officer, K. T. Fairweather

ADMIRALTY AND COMMERCIAL REGISTRY AND MARSHAL'S OFFICE
Registrar (£62,621), P. Miller
Marshal and Chief Clerk (G7), A. Ferrigno

BANKRUPTCY DEPARTMENT
Chief Registrar (£76,716), G. L. Pimm
Bankruptcy Registrars (£62,621), W. S. James;
  J. A. Simmonds; D. G. Scott; P. J. S. Rawson
Chief Clerk (SEO), M. Brown

CENTRAL OFFICE OF THE SUPREME COURT
Senior Master of the Supreme Court (*QBD*), *and Queen's
  Remembrancer* (£76,716), M. McKenzie, QC
Masters of the Supreme Court (*QBD*) (£62,621),
  P. B. Creightmore; D. L. Prebble; G. H. Hodgson;
  J. Trench; M. Tennant; P. Miller; N. O. G. Murray;
  I. H. Foster; G. H. Rose; P. G. A. Eyre
Chief Clerk (G7), P. Emery

CHANCERY DIVISION
Chief Clerk (G7), P. Emery

CHANCERY CHAMBERS
Chief Master of the Supreme Court (£76,716), J. M. Dyson
Masters of the Supreme Court (£62,621), G. A. Barratt; J. I.
  Winegarten; J. A. Moncaster, R. A. Bowman
Chief Clerk (SEO), G. Robinson
Conveyancing Counsel of the Supreme Court, W. D. Ainger;
  H. M. Harrod; A. C. Taussig

COMPANIES COURT
Registrar (£62,621), M. Buckley
Chief Clerk (SEO), M. Brown

COURT OF APPEAL CIVIL DIVISION
Registrar (£76,716), J. D. R. Adams
Chief Clerk (SEO), Miss H. M. Goddard

COURT OF APPEAL CRIMINAL DIVISION
Registrar (£76,716), M. McKenzie, QC
Deputy Registrar (G5), Mrs L. G. Knapman
Chief Clerk (G7), M. Bishop

COURTS-MARTIAL APPEALS OFFICE
Registrar (£76,716), M. McKenzie, QC
Chief Clerk (G7), M. Bishop

CROWN OFFICE OF THE SUPREME COURT
Master of the Crown Office, and Queen's Coroner and Attorney
  (£76,716), M. McKenzie, QC
Head of Crown Office (G5), Mrs L. Knapman
Chief Clerk (G7), M. Bishop

EXAMINERS OF THE COURT
Empowered to take examination of witnesses in all
Divisions of the High Court
R. G. Wood; Mrs G. M. Kenne; R. M. Planterose; Miss
  V. E. I. Selvaratnam

RESTRICTIVE PRACTICES COURT
Clerk of the Court, M. Buckley
Chief Clerk (SEO), M. Brown

SUPREME COURT TAXING OFFICE
Chief Master (£76,716), P. T. Hurst
Masters of the Supreme Court (£62,621), M. Ellis; T. H.
  Seager Berry; C. C. Wright; P. A. Rogers; G. N. Pollard;
  J. E. O'Hare
Court Manager, Mrs H. Oakey
Chief Taxing Officer (G7), T. J. Ryan

COURT OF PROTECTION
Stewart House, 24 Kingsway, London WC2B 6HD
Tel 0171-269 7000
Master (£76,716), D. A. Lush

ELECTION PETITIONS OFFICE
Room E218, Royal Courts of Justice, Strand, London
WC2A 2LL
Tel 0171-936 6131

The office accepts petitions and deals with all matters
relating to the questioning of parliamentary, European
Parliament and local government elections, and with
applications for relief under the Representation of the
People legislation.
Prescribed Officer, R. L. Turner
Chief Clerk, Miss J. L. Waine

OFFICE OF THE LORD CHANCELLOR'S VISITORS
Stewart House, 24 Kingsway, London WC2B 6HD
Tel 0171-269 7317

Legal Visitor, A. R. Tyrrell
Medical Visitors, K. Khan; W. B. Sprey; E. Mateu;
  S. E. Malapatra; A. Bailey; A. Kaeser

OFFICIAL RECEIVERS' DEPARTMENT
21 Bloomsbury Street, London WC1B 3SS
Tel 0171-323 3090

Senior Official Receiver, M. C. A. Osborne
Official Receivers, M. J. Pugh; L. T. Cramp; J. Norris

OFFICIAL SOLICITOR'S DEPARTMENT
81 Chancery Lane, London WC2B 6HD
Tel 0171-911 7105

Official Solicitor to the Supreme Court, P. M. Harris

Deputy Official Solicitor, H. J. Baker
Chief Clerk (G7), R. Lancaster

PRINCIPAL REGISTRY (FAMILY DIVISION)
Somerset House, London WC2R 1LP
Tel 0171-936 6000

Senior District Judge (£76,716), G. B. N. A. Angel
District Judges (£62,621), R. B. Rowe; B. P. F. Kenworthy-
Browne; Mrs K. T. Moorhouse; M. J. Segal; R. Conn;
Miss I. M. Plumstead; G. J. Maple; Miss I I. C. Bradley;
K. J. White; A. R. S. Bassett-Cross; N. A. Grove;
M. C. Berry; Miss S. M. Bowman; C. Million; P. Waller;
Miss P. Cushing; R. Harper; G. C. Brasse
Group Manager, Family Proceedings and Probate Service (G6),
R. P. Knight

District Probate Registrars
Birmingham and Stoke-on-Trent, C. Marsh
Brighton and Maidstone, M. N. Emery
Bristol, Exeter and Bodmin, R. H. P. Joyce
Ipswich, Norwich and Peterborough, D. N. Mee
Leeds, Lincoln and Sheffield, A. P. Dawson
Liverpool, Lancaster and Chester, B. J. Thomas
Llandaff, Bangor, Carmarthen and Gloucester, R. F. Yeldam
Manchester and Nottingham, M. A. Moran
Newcastle, Carlisle, York and Middlesbrough, P. Sanderson
Oxford, R. R. Da Costa
Winchester, A. K. Biggs

OFFICE OF THE JUDGE ADVOCATE OF
THE FLEET
The Law Courts, Barker Road, Maidstone ME16 8EQ
Tel 01622-754966

Judge Advocate of the Fleet (£76,716), His Hon. Judge
Sessions

OFFICE OF THE JUDGE ADVOCATE-
GENERAL OF THE FORCES
(*Joint Service for the Army and the Royal Air Force*)
22 Kingsway, London WC2B 6LE
Tel 0171-305 7910

Judge Advocate-General (£89,123), His Hon. Judge J. W.
Rant, CB, QC
Vice-Judge Advocate-General (£76,716), E. G. Moelwyn-
Hughes
Assistant Judge Advocates-General (£49,400–£57,000), D. M.
Berkson; M. A. Hunter; J. P. Camp; Miss S. E. Woollam;
R. C. C. Seymour; I. H. Pearson; R. G. Chapple; J. F. T.
Bayliss

HIGH COURT AND CROWN COURT
CENTRES

First-tier centres deal with both civil and criminal cases
and are served by High Court and circuit judges. Second-
tier centres deal with criminal cases only and are served
by High Court and circuit judges. Third-tier centres deal
with criminal cases only and are served only by circuit
judges.
   A management structure review of the Court Service is
currently in progress and is likely to result in changes in
the groups within circuits, which would take effect by 1
April 1997.

MIDLAND AND OXFORD CIRCUIT
First-tier – Birmingham, Lincoln, Nottingham, Oxford,
Stafford, Warwick
Second-tier – Leicester, Northampton, Shrewsbury,
Worcester
Third-tier – Coventry, Derby, Grimsby, Hereford,
Peterborough, Stoke-on-Trent, Wolverhampton
Circuit Administrator, R. Stoate, The Priory Courts, 6th
Floor, 33 Bull Street, Birmingham B4 6DW. Tel: 0121-
681 3000
Courts Administrators: Birmingham Group, P. Barton;
Nottingham Group, Mrs E. A. Folman; *Stafford Group*, A. F.
Parker

NORTH-EASTERN CIRCUIT
First-tier – Leeds, Newcastle upon Tyne, Sheffield,
Teesside
Second-tier – Bradford, York
Third-tier – Doncaster, Durham, Kingston-upon-Hull
Circuit Administrator, P. J. Farmer, 17th Floor, West Riding
House, Albion Street, Leeds LS1 5AA. Tel: 0113-251
1200
Courts Administrators: Leeds Group, P. Delany, OBE; *Newcastle
upon Tyne Group*, K. Budgen; *Sheffield Group*, G. Bingham

NORTHERN CIRCUIT
First-tier – Carlisle, Liverpool, Manchester, Preston
Third-tier – Barrow-in-Furness, Bolton, Burnley,
Lancaster
Circuit Administrator, R. A. Vincent, 15 Quay Street,
Manchester M60 9FD. Tel: 0161-833 1005
Courts Administrators: Manchester Group, Mrs A. Prior;
Liverpool Group, D. A. Beaumont; *Preston Group*,
Mrs C. A. Mayer

SOUTH-EASTERN CIRCUIT
First-tier – Chelmsford, Lewes, Norwich
Second-tier – Ipswich, London (Central Criminal Court),
Luton, Maidstone, Reading, St Albans
Third-tier – Aylesbury, Basildon, Brighton, Bury St
Edmunds, Cambridge, Canterbury, Chichester,
Guildford, King's Lynn, London (Croydon, Harrow,
Inner London Sessions House, Isleworth, Kingston
upon Thames, Knightsbridge, Middlesex Guildhall,
Snaresbrook, Southwark, Wood Green, Woolwich),
Southend
Circuit Administrator, J. Brindley, New Cavendish House,
18 Maltravers Street, London WC2R 3EU. Tel: 0171-936
7235
Deputy Circuit Administrator, P. Stockton
Courts Administrators: Chelmsford Group, M. Littlewood;
Maidstone Group, Mrs H. Hartwell; *Kingston Group*,
J. L. Powell; *London Group* (Civil), D. Marsh; *London
Group* (Crime), G. F. Addicott

The High Court in Greater London sits at the Royal
Courts of Justice.

WALES AND CHESTER CIRCUIT
First-tier – Caernarfon, Cardiff, Chester, Mold, Swansea
Second-tier – Carmarthen, Merthyr Tydfil, Newport,
Welshpool
Third-tier – Dolgellau, Haverfordwest, Knutsford,
Warrington
Circuit Administrator, V. Grove, Churchill House,
Churchill Way, Cardiff CF1 4HH. Tel: 01222-396925

Courts Administrators: Cardiff Group, A. M. Eshelby; *Chester Group*, T. D. Beckett

WESTERN CIRCUIT

First-tier – Bristol, Exeter, Truro, Winchester
Second-tier – Dorchester, Gloucester, Plymouth, Weymouth
Third-tier – Barnstaple, Bournemouth, Newport (IOW), Portsmouth, Salisbury, Southampton, Swindon, Taunton
Circuit Administrator, R. J. Clark, Bridge House, Clifton Down, Bristol BS8 4BN. Tel: 0117-974 3763
Courts Administrators: Bristol Group, A. C. Butler; *Exeter Group*, J. Ardern; *Winchester Group*, D. Ryan

CIRCUIT JUDGES

Senior Circuit Judges, each £89,123
Circuit Judges, each £76,716
Style, His/Her Hon. Judge [surname]
Senior Presiding Judge, The Rt. Hon. Lord Justice Auld

MIDLAND AND OXFORD CIRCUIT

Presiding Judges, Hon. Mr Justice Jowitt; Hon. Mr Justice Latham

W. A. L. Allardice; F. A. Allen; Miss C. Alton;
B. J. Appleby, QC; D. P. Bennett; R. S. A. Benson;
I. J. Black, QC; J. G. Boggis, QC; R. W. A. Bray;
D. W. Brunning; J. J. Cavell; F. A. Chapman;
P. N. R. Clark; R. R. B. Cole; T. G. E. Corrie; P. F. Crane;
*P. J. Crawford, QC (*Recorder of Birmingham*);
I. T. R. Davidson, QC; P. N. de Mille; T. M. Dillon, QC;
C. H. Durman; B. A. Farrer, QC; Miss E. N. Fisher;
J. E. Fletcher; A. C. Geddes; R. J. H. Gibbs, QC; V. E. Hall;
J. Hall; D. R. D. Hamilton; S. T. Hammond;
G. C. W. Harris, QC; M. K. Harrison-Hall; M. J. Heath;
C. R. Hodson; J. R. Hopkin; R. H. Hutchinson;
R. P. V. Jenkins; A. W. P. King; M. K. Lee, QC;
D. L. McCarthy; A. W. McCreath; D. D. McEvoy, QC;
M. H. Mander; K. Matthewman, QC; W. D. Matthews;
R. G. May; H. R. Mayor, QC; N. J. Mitchell; P. R. Morrell;
J. I. Morris; A. J. H. Morrison; M. D. Mott; A. J. D. Nicholl;
R. T. N. Orme; R. C. C. O'Rorke; J. F. F. Orrell;
D. S. Perrett, QC; C. J. Pitchers; R. F. D. Pollard;
F. M. Potter; D. P. Pugsley; J. R. Pyke; R. J. Rubery;
J. A. O. Shand; J. R. S. Smyth; D. P. Stanley; P. J. Stretton;
G. C. Styler; H. C. Tayler, QC; A. B. Taylor; M. B. Ward;
D. J. R. Wilcox; H. Wilson; J. W. Wilson;
K. S. W. Wilson Mellor, QC; C. G. Young

NORTH-EASTERN CIRCUIT

Presiding Judges, Hon. Mr Justice Hooper; Hon. Mrs Justice Smith

J. R. S. Adams; J. Altman; T. G. F. Atkinson; T. W. Barber;
J. E. Barry; G. N. Barr Young; R. Bartfield;
D. R. Bentley, QC; P. H. Bowers; A. N. J. Briggs;
D. M. A. Bryant; J. W. M. Bullimore; B. Bush; M. C. Carr;
M. L. Cartlidge; P. J. Charlesworth; P. J. Cockroft;
G. J. K. Coles, QC; J. Crabtree; M. T. Cracknell;
W. H. R. Crawford, QC; Mrs J. Davies; I. J. Dobkin;
E. J. Faulks; P. J. Fox, QC; A. N. Fricker, QC; M. S. Garner;
A. R. Goldsack, QC; R. A. Grant; S. P. Grenfell;
G. F. R. Harkins; P. M. L. Hoffman; R. Hunt;
A. E. Hutchinson, QC; N. H. Jones, QC; G. H. Kamil;
T. D. Kent-Jones, TD; G. M. Lightfoot; R. P. Lowden;
A. G. McCallum; A. C. Macdonald; M. K. Mettyear;
R. J. Moore; A. L. Myerson, QC; D. A. Orde;
Miss H. E. Paling; P. E. Robertshaw; R. M. Scott;
A. Simpson; L. Spittle; J. Stephenson; *R. A. R. Stroyan, QC

(*Recorder of Newcastle upon Tyne*); Mrs L. Sutcliffe;
J. A. Swanson; M. J. Taylor; R. C. Taylor; J. D. G. Walford;
M. Walker; P. H. C. Walker; *B. Walsh, QC;
J. S. Wolstenholme; D. R. Wood

NORTHERN CIRCUIT

Presiding Judge, Hon. Mr Justice Forbes

M. P. Allweis; H. H. Andrew, QC; J. F. Appleton; A. W. Bell;
R. C. W. Bennett; Miss I. Bernstein; M. S. Blackburn;
R. Brown; J. K. Burke, QC; I. B. Campbell; F. B. Carter, QC;
B. I. Caulfield; D. Clark; D. C. Clarke, QC; G. M. Clifton;
I. W. Crompton; *R. E. Davies, QC (*Recorder of Manchester*);
M. Dean, QC; Miss A. E. Downey; B. R. Duckworth;
S. B. Duncan; Miss D. B. Eaglestone; T. K. Earnshaw;
G. A. Ensor; D. M. Evans, QC; S. J. D. Fawcus; P. S. Fish;
J. R. B. Geake; D. S. Gee; W. George; J. A. D. Gilliland, QC;
R. G. Hamilton; J. A. Hammond; F. D. Hart, QC;
M. Hedley; T. B. Hegarty, QC; T. D. T. Hodson;
F. R. B. Holloway; R. C. Holman; N. J. G. Howarth;
G. W. Humphries; C. E. F. James; P. M. Kershaw, QC
(*Commercial Circuit Judge*); H. L. Lachs; P. M. Lakin;
J. M. Lever, QC; R. J. D. Livesey, QC; R. Lockett; D. Lynch;
D. I. Mackay; J. B. Macmillan; D. G. Maddison;
B. C. Maddocks; C. J. Mahon; J. A. Morgan; W. P. Morris;
T. J. Mort; F. D. Owen, TD; R. E. I. Pickering; J. C. Phipps;
D. A. Pirie; A. J. Proctor; J. H. Roberts; Miss G. D. Ruaux;
H. S. Singer; E. Slinger; W. P. Smith; Miss E. M. Steel;
C. B. Tetlow; J. P. Townend; I. J. C. Trigger;
P. W. G. Urquhart; W. R. Wickham (*Recorder of Liverpool*);
K. H. P. Wilkinson; B. Woodward

SOUTH-EASTERN CIRCUIT

Presiding Judges, Hon. Mr Justice Gage; Hon. Mr Justice Wright

M. F. Addison; F. J. Aglionby; A. R. L. Ansell;
S. A. Anwyl, QC; J. A. Baker; J. B. Baker, QC;
M. F. Baker, QC; M. J. D. Baker; A. F. Balston;
G. S. Barham; C. J. A. Barnett, QC; W. E. Barnett, QC;
K. Bassingthwaighte; G. A. Bathurst Norman;
P. J. L. Beaumont, QC; N. E. Beddard; M. G. Binning;
G. J. Binns; J. E. Bishop; B. M. B. Black; H. O. Blacksell,
QC; J. G. Boal, QC; A. V. Bradbury; P. N. Brandt;
L. J. Bromley, QC; A. E. Brookes; R. G. Brown;
J. M. Bull; G. N. Butler, QC; *N. M. Butter, QC;
H. J. Byrt, QC; C. V. Callman; J. Q. Campbell;
B. E. Capstick, QC; M. J. Carroll; B. E. F. Catlin;
B. L. Charles, QC; P. C. L. Clark; P. C. Clegg; S. H. Colgan;
P. H. Collins; C. C. Colston, QC; S. S. Coltart; Viscount
Colville of Culross, QC; J. S. Colyer, QC; C. D. Compston;
T. A. C. Coningsby, QC; J. G. Conner; R. D. Connor;
M. J. Cook; R. A. Cooke; G. H. Coombe; M. R. Coombe;
A. Cooray; P. E. Copley; Dr E. Cotran; P. R. Cowell;
R. C. Cox; J. F. Crocker; D. L. Croft, QC; H. M. Crush;
D. M. Cryan; P. Curl; G. L. Davies; I. H. Davies, TD;
W. L. M. Davies, QC; W. N. Denison, QC (*Common Serjeant*);
J. E. Devaux; M. N. Devonshire, TD; A. L. E. Diamond, QC;
P. H. Downes; W. H. Dunn, QC; A. H. Durrant;
C. M. Edwards; Q. T. Edwards, QC; D. F. Elfer; QC;
D. R. Ellis; C. Elwen; F. P. L. Evans; S. J. Evans;
J. D. Farnworth; P. Fingret; J. J. Finney; P. Ford;
J. J. Fordham; G. C. F. Forrester; Ms D. A. Freedman;
R. Gee; L. Gerber; C. A. H. Gibson;
Miss A. F. Goddard, QC; S. A. Goldstein; P. W. Goldstone;
M. B. Goodman; C. G. M. Gordon; J. B. Gosschalk;
J. H. Gower, QC; M. Graham; B. S. Green, QC;
P. B. Greenwood; D. J. Griffiths; G. D. Grigson;
R. B. Groves, TD, VRD; N. T. Hague, QC;
A. B. R. Hallgarten, QC; Miss G. Hallon; P. J. Halnan;
J. Hamilton; C. R. H. Hardy; B. Hargrove, OBE, QC;

M. F. Harris; R. G. Hawkins, QC; R. J. Haworth;
R. M. Hayward; A. H. Head; A. N. Hitching; D. Holden;
A. C. W. Hordern, QC; K. A. D. Hornby; R. W. Howe;
M. Hucker; Sir David Hughes-Morgan, Bt., CB, CBE;
J. G. Hull, QC; M. J. Hyam; D. A. Inman; A. B. Issard-
Davies; Dr P. J. E. Jackson; C. P. James; T. J. C. Joseph;
S. S. Katkhuda; M. Kennedy, QC; A. M. Kenny; T. R. King;
L. G. Krikler; L. H. C. Lait; P. St J. H. Langan, QC;
Capt. J. B. R. Langdon, RN; G. F. B. Laughland, QC;
R. Laurie; T. Lawrence; D. M. Levy, QC; S. H. Lloyd;
F. R. Lockhart; D. B. D. Lowe; Capt. S. Lyons;
K. M. McHale; K. A. Machin, QC; K. C. Macrae; T. Maher;
B. A. Marder, QC; F. J. M. Marr-Johnson; L. A. Marshall;
D. N. N. Martineau; N. A. Medawar, QC; D. B. Meier;
D. J. Mellor; G. D. Mercer; D. Q. Miller; F. I. Mitchell;
H. M. Morgan; D. Morton Jack; R. T. Moss; Miss
M. J. S. Mowat; J. I. Murchie; T. M. E. Nash;
Mrs N. F. Negus; M. H. D. Neligan; Mrs M. F. Norrie;
Brig. A. P. Norris, OBE; P. W. O'Brien; M. A. Oppenheimer;
D. A. Paiba; D. J. Parry; Mrs N. Pearce; Prof. D. S. Pearl;
Miss V. A. Pearlman; B. P. Pearson; J. R. Peppitt, QC;
F. H. L. Petre; N. A. J. Philpot; D. C. Pitman; J. R. Platt;
P. B. Pollock; T. G. Pontius; W. D. C. Poulton;
H. C. Pownall, QC; S. Pratt; R. J. C. V. Prendergast;
E. E. Previté, QC; B. H. Pryor, QC; J. E. Pullinger;
D. W. Radford; J. W. Rant, QC; E. V. P. Reece;
M. P. Reynolds; G. K. Rice; M. S. Rich, QC; N. P. Riddell;
G. Rivlin, QC; S. D. Robbins; D. A. H. Rodwell, QC;
J. W. Rogers, QC; G. H. Rooke, TD, QC; P. C. R. Rountree;
J. H. Rucker; T. R. G. Ryland; R. B. Sanders;
A. R. G. Scott-Gall; J. S. Sennitt; J. L. Sessions;
J. D. Sheerin; D. R. A. Sich; A. G. Simmons; K. T. Simpson;
P. R. Simpson; M. Singh, QC; J. K. E. Slack, TD;
S. P. Sleeman; P. M. J. Slot; C. M. Smith, QC; S. A. R. Smith;
R. J. Southan; S. B. Spence; W. F. C. Thomas;
A. G. Y. Thorpe; A. H. Tibber; C. H. Tilling; J. T. Turner;
C. J. M. Tyrer; Mrs A. P. Uziell-Hamilton; J. E. van der
Werff; Sir Lawrence Verney, TD (*Recorder of London*);
A. O. R. Vick, QC; T. L. Viljoen; Miss M. S. Viner, CBE, QC;
R. Wakefield; R. Walker; S. P. Waller; D. B. Watling, QC;
V. B. Watts; *F. J. White; S. R. Wilkinson; R. J. Winstanley;
E. G. Wrintmore; K. H. Zucker, QC

WALES AND CHESTER CIRCUIT

Presiding Judges, Hon. Mr Justice Curtis; Hon. Mr
Justice Kay

K. E. Barnett; M. R. Burr; S. P. Clarke; T. R. Crowther, QC;
J. T. Curran; Miss J. M. P. Daley; G. H. M. Daniel;
Sir Robin David, QC; D. T. A. Davies; J. B. S. Diehl, QC;
D. E. H. Edwards; G. O. Edwards, QC; Lord Elystan-
Morgan; D. R. Evans, QC; T. M. Evans, QC; J. W. Gaskell;
*M. Gibbon, QC; D. R. Halbert; D. J. Hale; D. M. Hughes;
G. J. Jones; H. D. H. Jones; G. E. Kilfoil; T. E. I. Lewis-
Bowen; C. G. Masterman; D. G. Morgan; D. G. Morris;
D. C. Morton; T. H. Moseley, QC; P. J. Price, QC;
E. J. Prosser, QC; H. E. P. Roberts, QC; S. M. Stephens, QC;
H. V. Williams, QC

WESTERN CIRCUIT

Presiding Judges, Hon. Mr Justice Butterfield; Hon. Mr
Justice Tuckey

P. T. S. Batterbury; J. F. Beashel; Miss J. A. M. Bonvin;
C. L. Boothman; M. J. L. Brodrick; J. M. J. Burford, QC;
R. D. H. Bursell, QC; J. R. Chalkley; M. G. Cotterill;
G. W. A. Cottle; S. C. Darwall Smith; Mrs S. P. Darwall
Smith; Mrs L. H. Davies; *M. Dyer; J. D. Foley;
D. L. Griffiths; J. D. Griggs; Mrs C. M. A. Hagen;
P. J. C. R. Hooton; G. B. Hutton; R. E. Jack, QC;
A. G. H. Jones; T. N. Mackean; Miss S. M. D. McKinney;

I. S. McKintosh; I. G. McLean; J. G. McNaught;
T. J. Milligan; J. Neligan; E. G. Neville; S. K. O'Malley;
S. K. Overend; R. Price; R. C. Pryor, QC; J. N. P. Rudd;
A. Rutherford; Miss A. O. H. Sander; D. H. D. Selwood;
R. M. Shawcross; D. A. Smith, QC; W. E. M. Taylor;
P. M. Thomas; A. A. R. Thompson, QC;
H. J. M. Tucker, QC; D. M. Webster, QC; J. H. Weeks, QC;
J. R. Whitley; J. S. Wiggs; J. A. J. Wigmore; J. C. Willis;
J. H. Wroath

RECORDERS (each £366 per day)

F. A. Abbott; R. D. I. Adam; J. D. R. Adams; P. C. Ader;
R. J. P. Aikens, QC; J. F. Akast; D. J. Ake; R. Akenhead, QC;
I. D. G. Alexander, QC; C. D. Allan, QC; C. J. Alldis;
J. H. Allen, QC; D. M. Altaras; A. J. Anderson, QC;
W. P. Andreae-Jones, QC; P. J. Andrews, QC;
R. A. Anelay, QC; M. G. Anthony; Miss L. E. Appleby, QC;
J. F. A. Archer, QC; Lord Archer of Sandwell, PC, QC;
A. J. Arlidge, QC; E. K. Armitage, QC; P. J. B. Armstrong;
G. K. Arran; R. Ashton; J. M. Aspinall, QC; E. G. Aspley;
N. J. Atkinson, QC; D. S. Aubrey; M. G. Austin-Smith, QC;
M. J. S. Axtell; W. S. Aylen, QC; P. D. Babb;
J. F. Badenoch, QC; Miss P. H. Badley; A. B. Baillie;
N. R. J. Baker, QC; S. W. Baker; C. G. Ball, QC; P. R. Barclay;
A. Barker, QC; B. J. Barker, QC; D. Barker, QC;
G. E. Barling, QC; D. N. Barnard; D. M. W. Barnes, QC;
H. J. Barnes; T. P. Barnes, QC; A. J. Barnett;
R. A. Barratt, QC; R. Bartfield; D. A. Bartlett;
G. R. Bartlett, QC; J. C. T. Barton, QC; D. C. Bate, QC;
S. D. Batten, QC; P. D. Batty, QC; J. J. Baughan, QC;
R. A. Bayliss; D. M. Bean; J. Beatson; C. H. Beaumont;
R. V. M. E. Behar; C. O. J. Behrens; R. W. Belben;
P. Bennett, QC; P. C. Benson; R. A. Benson, QC;
H. L. Bentham, QC; D. M. Berkson; C. R. Berry;
M. Bethel, QC; J. P. V. Bevan; J. C. Beveridge, QC;
Mrs C. V. Bevington; N. Bidder; I. G. Bing;
P. V. Birkett, QC; M. I. Birnbaum; W. J. Birtles;
P. W. Birts, QC; B. G. D. Blair, QC; J. A. Blair-Gould;
A. N. H. Blake; P. E. Bleasdale; C. Bloom, QC;
D. J. Blunt, QC; O. S. P. Blunt, QC; D. R. L. Bodey, QC;
R. H. Bond; G. T. K. Boney, QC; J. J. Boothby;
D. J. Boulton; S. N. Bourne-Arton, QC; S. C. Boyd, QC;
J. J. Boyle; D. L. Bradshaw; W. T. S. Braithwaite, QC;
N. D. Bratza, QC; G. B. Breen; D. J. Brennan, QC;
M. L. Brent, QC; G. J. B. G. Brice, QC; J. N. W. Bridges-
Adams; A. J. Brigden; P. J. Briggs; D. R. Bright;
R. P. Brittain; R. A. Britton; J. Bromley-Davenport;
S. C. Brown, QC; D. J. M. Browne, QC; J. N. Browne;
A. J. N. Brunner, QC; R. V. Bryan; A. Bueno, QC;
P. E. Bullock; J. P. Burgess; J. P. Burke, QC;
H. W. Burnett, QC; R. H. Burns; S. J. Burnton, QC;
G. Burrell, QC; M. J. Burton, QC; K. Bush; A. J. Butcher, QC;
Miss J. Butler; C. W. Byers; M. D. Byrne;
Mrs B. A. Calvert, QC; D. Calvert-Smith;
R. Camden Pratt, QC; Miss S. M. C. Cameron, QC;
A. N. Campbell, QC; J. M. Caplan, QC; G. M. C. Carey, QC;
A. C. Carlile, MP; The Lord Carlisle of
Bucklow, PC, QC; H. B. H. Carlisle, QC; J. J. Carter-
Manning, QC; R. Carus, QC; Mrs J. R. Case; P. D. Cattan;
Miss M. T. Catterson; J. A. Chadwin, QC;
N. M. Chambers, QC; Miss D. C. Champion;
V. R. Chapman; J. M. Cherry, QC; J. R. Cherryman, QC;
C. F. Chruszcz, QC; C. H. Clark, QC; C. S. C. S. Clarke, QC;
P. W. Clarke; P. R. J. Clarkson, QC; T. Clayson;
A. S. L. Cleary; W. Clegg, QC; T. A. Clover; M. F. Coates;
Miss S. Coates; W. P. Coates; D. J. Cocks, QC;
J. J. Coffey, QC; T. A. Coghlan, QC; W. J. Coker, QC;
J. R. Cole; A. J. S. Coleman; N. J. Coleman;
P. J. D. Coleridge, QC; N. B. C. Coles, QC;

A. R. Collender, QC; P. N. Collier, QC; J. M. Collins;
I. Collis; Ms M. Colton; Mrs J. R. Comyns; G. D. Conlin;
C. S. Cook; K. B. Coonan, QC; A. E. M. Cooper;
Miss B. P. Cooper, QC; P. J. Cooper, QC;
Miss S. M. Corkhill; C. J. Cornwall; P. J. Cosgrove, QC;
Miss D. R. Cotton, QC; J. S. Coward, QC;
Mrs L. M. Cox, QC; P. Crampin, QC; N. Crichton;
D. I. Crigman, QC; M. L. S. Cripps; C. A. Critchlow;
D. R. Crome; Mrs J. Crowley; J. D. Crowley, QC;
W. R. H. Crowther, QC; T. S. Culver;
Miss E. A. M. Curnow, QC; P. D. Curran;
J. W. O. Curtis, QC; M. J. Curwen; K. C. Cutler;
A. J. G. Dalziel; Mrs P. M. T. Dangor; P. M. Darlow;
A. M. Darroch; G. W. Davey; C. P. M. Davidson;
A. R. M. Davies; J. T. L. Davies; R. L. Davies, QC;
W. E. Davis; A. W. Dawson; D. H. Day, QC; J. J. Deave;
J. B. Deby, QC; P. G. Dedman; Mrs P. A. Deeley;
C. F. Dehn, QC; P. A. de la Piquerie; M. A. de Navarro, QC;
R. L. Denyer, QC; S. C. Desch, QC; H. A. D. de Silva;
P. N. Digney; C. E. Dines; A. D. Dinkin, QC; D. R. Dobbin;
P. Dodgson; R. A. M. Doggett; Ms B. Dohmann, QC;
D. T. Donaldson, QC; A. M. Donne, QC; A. F. S. Donovan;
A. K. Dooley; J. Dowse; S. M. Duffield; P. R. Dunkels, QC;
J. D. Durham Hall, QC; R. T. Dutton; J. M. Dyson;
D. Eady, QC; H. W. P. Eccles, QC; C. N. Edelman, QC;
A. H. Edwards; Miss S. M. Edwards, QC; G. Elias, QC;
E. A. Elliott; R. C. Elly; J. A. Elvidge; R. M. Englehart, QC;
T. M. English; D. A. Evans, QC; D. H. Evans, QC;
F. W. H. Evans; G. W. R. Evans, QC; M. Evans, QC;
M. J. Evans; M. A. Everall, QC; Sir Graham Eyre, QC;
T. M. Faber; W. D. Fairclough; R. B. Farley, QC;
P. M. Farmer, QC; D. J. Farrer, QC; P. E. Feinberg, QC;
R. Fernyhough, QC; M. C. Field; J. E. Finestein;
J. E. P. Finnigan; D. T. Fish; D. P. Fisher, QC;
G. D. Flather, CBE, QC; P. E. J. Focke, QC;
R. A. Fordham, QC; A. J. Forrest; M. D. P. Fortune;
D. R. Foskett, QC; J. R. Foster, QC; Miss R. M. Foster;
J. H. Fryer-Spedding, OBE; M. Furness; M. Gale, QC;
C. J. E. Gardner, QC; C. R. Garside, QC; R. C. Gaskell;
S. A. G. L. Gault; A. H. Gee, QC; I. W. Geering, QC;
D. S. Geey; D. C. Gerrey; J. S. Gibbons, QC;
A. J. Gilbart, QC; F. H. S. Gilbert, QC; N. J. Gilchrist;
K. Gillance; N. B. D. Gilmour, QC; L. Giovene;
A. T. Glass, QC; H. B. Globe, QC; Miss E. Gloster, QC;
H. K. Goddard, QC; H. A. Godfrey, QC;
Ms L. S. Godfrey, QC; J. J. Goldberg, QC;
J. B. Goldring, QC; P. H. Goldsmith, QC;
L. C. Goldstone, QC; I. F. Goldsworthy, QC;
A. J. J. Gompertz, QC; A. A. Gordon; J. R. W. Goss;
T. J. C. Goudie, QC; A. A. Goymer; G. Gozem;
A. S. Grabiner, QC; C. A. St J. Gray; G. Gray, QC;
H. Green, QC; Miss J. E. G. Greenberg, QC;
A. E. Greenwood; J. C. Greenwood; J. G. Grenfell, QC;
R. D. Grey, QC; R. H. Griffith-Jones; J. P. G. Griffiths, QC;
M. G. Grills; M. S. E. Grime, QC; P. Grobel;
P. H. Gross, QC; M. A. W. Grundy; S. J. Gullick;
A. S. Hacking, QC; M. F. Haigh; J. W. Haines; N. J. Hall;
S. J. Hall; J. P. N. Hallam; D. T. Hallchurch;
Miss H. C. Hallett, QC; G. M. Hamilton, TD, QC;
I. M. Hamilton; Miss S. Hamilton, QC; P. L. Hamlin;
J. Hampton; J. L. Hand, QC; Miss R. S. A. Hare, QC;
R. D. Harman, QC; G. T. Harrap; P. J. Harrington, QC;
D. M. Harris, QC; D. Harrison; R. M. Harrison, QC;
H. M. Harrod; J. M. Harrow; C. P. Hart-Leverton, QC;
B. Harvey; C. S. Harvey, MBE, TD; J. G. Harvey;
M. L. T. Harvey, QC; D. W. Hatton, QC;
T. S. A. Hawkesworth, QC; W. G. Hawkesworth;
J. M. Haworth; R. W. P. Hay; Prof. D. J. Hayton;
Miss J. E. Hayward; R. Hayward-Smith, QC;
A. T. Hedworth, QC; G. E. Heggs; R. A. Henderson, QC;

R. H. Q. Henriques, QC; M. J. Henshell;
P. J. M. Heppel, QC; R. C. Herman; M. S. Heslop QC;
T. Hewitt; B. J. Higgs, QC; E. M. Hill, QC; J. W. Hillyer;
A. J. H. Hilton, QC; Ms E. J. Hindley, QC; W. T. J. Hirst;
J. D. Hitchen; S. A. Hockman, QC; A. J. C. Hoggett, QC;
D. A. Hollis, VRD, QC; C. J. Holmes; J. F. Holt; R. M. Hone;
A. T. Hoolahan, QC; A. D. Hope; S. Hopkins;
M. A. P. Hopmeier; M. Horowitz, QC; Miss R. Horwood-Smart; C. P. Hotten, QC; B. F. Houlder, QC;
M. N. Howard, QC; C. I. Howells; M. J. Hubbard, QC;
A. P. G. Hughes, QC; Mrs H. M. Hughes; Miss
J. C. A. Hughes, QC; P. T. Hughes, QC; R. P. Hughes;
T. M. Hughes, QC; J. Hugill, QC; L. D. Hull;
W. G. B. Hungerford; D. P. Hunt; D. R. N. Hunt, QC;
P. J. Hunt, QC; I. G. A. A. Hunter, QC; M. Hussain, QC;
J. G. K. Hyland; B. A. Hytner, QC; R. A. G. Inglis;
P. R. Isaacs; S. Jack; D. G. A. Jackson; M. R. Jackson;
R. M. Jackson, QC; I. E. Jacob; P. J. Jacobs;
N. F. B. Jarman, QC; J. M. Jarvis, QC; J. R. Jarvis;
A. H. Jeffreys; D. A. Jeffreys, QC; J. Jeffs, QC;
J. D. Jenkins, QC; D. B. Johnson, QC; D. A. F. Jones;
D. L. Jones; N. G. Jones; R. A. Jones, QC; S. E. Jones, QC;
T. G. Jones; W. H. Joss; H. M. Joy; P. S. L. Joyce, QC;
R. W. S. Juckes; M. D. L. Kalisher, QC; M. L. Kallipetis, QC;
I. G. F. Karsten, QC; R. G. Kaye, QC; C. B. Kealy;
M. L. Keane; K. R. Keen, QC; B. R. Keith, QC; C. L. Kelly;
C. J. B. Kemp; D. Kennett Brown; D. M. Kerr;
L. D. Kershen, QC; M. I. Khan; G. M. Khayat, QC;
R. I. Kidwell, QC; T. R. A. King, QC; W. M. Kingston, QC;
R. C. Klevan, QC; B. J. Knight, QC; M. S. Knott;
Miss P. E. Knowles; C. Knox; Miss J. C. M. Korner, QC;
S. E. Kramer, QC; Miss L. J. Kushner, QC; P. E. Kyte, QC;
L. P. Laity; C. A. Lamb; N. R. W. Lambert; D. A. Landau;
D. G. Lane, QC; T. J. Langdale, QC; B. F. J. Langstaff, QC;
D. H. Latham; R. B. Latham, QC; S. W. Lawler, QC;
Sir Ivan Lawrence, QC, MP; M. H. Lawson, QC;
G. S. Lawson-Rogers, QC; P. L. O. Leaver, QC;
D. Lederman, QC; B. W. T. Leech; I. Leeming, QC;
C. H. de V. Leigh, QC; Sir Godfrey Le Quesne, QC;
H. B. G. Lett; B. L. Lever; B. H. Leveson, QC; S. Levine;
A. E. Levy, QC; M. E. Lewer, QC; A. K. Lewis, QC;
B. W. Lewis; M. ap G. Lewis, QC; R. S. Lewis;
C. C. D. Lindsay, QC; S. J. Linehan, QC; J. S. Lipton;
B. J. E. Livesey, QC; C. G. Llewellyn-Jones, QC;
C. J. Lockhart-Mummery, QC; A. J. C. Lodge, QC;
T. Longbotham; D. C. Lovell-Pank, QC; G. W. Lowe;
N. H. Lowe; J. A. M. Lowen; G. W. Lowther; F. D. L. Loy;
Mrs C. M. Ludlow; E. Lyons, QC; R. G. B. McCombe, QC;
A. G. McDowall; A. G. MacDuff, QC; K. M. P. Macgill;
C. I. McGonigal; R. J. McGregor-Johnson;
R. D. Machell, QC; J. V. Machin; B. M. McIntyre;
C. C. Mackay, QC; D. L. Mackie; R. G. McKinnon;
W. N. McKinnon; N. A. McKittrick; I. A. B. McLaren, QC;
I. McLeod; N. R. B. Macleod, QC; N. J. C. McLusky;
A. G. Mainds; A. H. R. Maitland; A. R. Malcolm;
H. J. Malins; M. E. Mann, QC; The Hon. G. R. J. Mansfield;
A. C. B. Markham-David; R. L. Marks; A. S. Marron, QC;
P. Marsh; R. G. Marshall-Andrews, QC; G. C. Marson;
H. R. A. Martineau; C. P. Mather; D. Matheson, QC;
P. R. Matthews; Mrs P. Matthews, QC;
P. B. Mauleverer, QC; R. B. Mawrey, QC; J. F. M. Maxwell;
R. Maxwell, QC; Mrs P. R. May; M. Meggeson;
N. F. Merriman, QC; C. S. J. Metcalf; J. T. Milford, QC;
K. S. H. Miller; R. A. Miller; S. M. Miller, QC;
J. B. M. Milmo, QC; D. C. Milne, QC; Miss C. M. Miskin;
Miss A. E. Mitchell; A. P. Mitchell; C. R. Mitchell;
D. C. Mitchell; J. R. Mitchell; J. E. Mitting, QC; F. R. Moat;
E. G. Moelwyn-Hughes; C. R. D. Moger, QC;
D. R. P. Mole, QC; H. J. Montlake; M. G. C. Moorhouse;
D. W. Morgan; G. E. Moriarty, QC; A. P. Morris, QC; The

Rt. Hon. J. Morris, QC, MP; C. Morris-Coole;
C. J. Moss, QC; P. C. Mott, QC; R. W. Moxon-Browne, QC;
J. H. Muir; F. J. Muller, QC; G. S. Murdoch, QC;
I. P. Murphy, QC; M. J. A. Murphy, QC; N. O. G. Murray;
N. J. Mylne, QC; H. G. Narayan; D. E. Neuberger, QC;
R. E. Newbold; A. R. H. Newman, QC; G. Nice, QC;
C. A. A. Nicholls, QC; C. V. Nicholls, QC; A. S. T. E. Nicol;
A. E. R. Noble; B. Nolan, QC; M. C. Norman; J. M. Norris;
P. H. Norris; J. G. Nutting, QC; D. P. O'Brien, QC;
E. M. Ogden, QC; Mrs F. M. Oldham, QC; S. Oliver-
Jones, QC; R. W. Onions; C. P. L. Openshaw, QC;
M. N. O'Sullivan; D. B. W. Ouseley, QC; R. M. Owen, QC;
T. W. Owen; N. D. Padfield, QC; S. R. Page;
D. C. J. Paget, QC; A. O. Palmer, QC; A. W. Palmer, QC;
D. P. Pannick, QC; A. D. W. Pardoe, QC; S. A. B. Parish;
G. C. Parkins, QC; G. E. Parkinson; M. P. Parroy, QC;
D. J. Parry; E. O. Parry; M. A. Parry Evans;
N. S. K. Pascoe, QC; A. Patience, QC; J. G. Paulusz;
W. E. Pawlak; R. J. Pearse Wheatley; J. V. Pegden;
D. H. Perry-Davey, QC; J. Perry, QC; M. Pert, QC;
B. J. Phelvin; J. A. Phillips; W. B. Phillips;
M. A. Pickering, QC; T. O. Pillay; C. J. Pitchford, QC;
The Hon. B. M. D. Pitt; Miss E. F. Platt, QC; R. Platts;
J. R. Playford, QC; A. G. S. Pollock, QC; A. R. Porten, QC;
L. R. Portnoy; Mrs R. M. Poulet, QC; T. W. Preston, QC;
D. Price; G. A. L. Price, QC; J. A. Price, QC; J. C. Price;
N. P. L. Price, QC; H. W. Prosser; A. C. Pugh, QC;
G. V. Pugh, QC; G. F. Pulman, QC; C. P. B. Purchas, QC;
R. M. Purchas, QC; N. R. Purnell, QC; P. O. Purnell, QC;
Q. C. W. Querelle; D. A. Radcliffe; Mrs N. P. Radford, QC;
Ms A. J. Rafferty, QC; T. W. H. Raggatt, QC; A. Rankin, QC;
A. D. Rawley, QC; P. R. Raynor, QC; L. F. Read, QC;
J. H. Reddihough; A. R. F. Redgrave, QC; J. Reeder, QC;
P. Rees; C. E. Reese, QC; J. R. Reid, QC; P. C. Reid;
P. C. Rhodes; R. E. Rhodes, QC; D. G. Rice; D. W. Richards;
S. P. Richards; H. A. Richardson; S. V. Riordan, QC;
G. Risius; Miss J. H. Ritchie, QC; M. W. Roach;
A. J. Roberts, QC; J. M. Roberts; J. M. G. Roberts, QC;
A. J. Robertson; V. Robinson, QC; D. E. H. Robson, QC;
G. W. Roddick, QC; Miss D. J. Rodgers;
J. M. T. Rogers, QC; P. F. G. Rook, QC; W. M. Rose;
J. G. Ross; J. G. Ross Martyn; P. C. Rouch; J. J. Rowe, QC;
R. J. Royce, QC; M. W. Rudland; A. A. Rumbelow, QC;
N. J. Rumfitt, QC; R. J. Rundell; R. R. Russell;
G. C. Ryan, QC; J. R. T. Rylance; C. R. A. Sallon, QC;
C. N. Salmon; D. A. Salter; J. E. A. Samuels, QC;
A. T. Sander; G. R. Sankey, QC; N. L. Sarony;
J. H. B. Saunders, QC; M. P. Sayers, QC; R. J. Scholes, QC;
Miss P. Scriven, QC; R. J. Seabrook, QC; C. Seagroatt, QC;
M. R. Selfe; W. P. L. Sellick; O. M. Sells, QC; D. Serota, QC;
R. W. Seymour, QC; A. J. Seys-Llewellyn; A. R. F. Sharp;
P. P. Shears; S. J. Sher, QC; Miss J. Shipley;
J. M. Shorrock, QC; S. R. Silber, QC; P. F. Singer, QC;
J. C. N. Slater, QC; A. C. Smith; A. C. Smith, QC;
D. H. Smith, QC; R. D. H. Smith, QC; R. S. Smith, QC;
Ms Z. P. Smith; C. J. Smyth; S. M. Solley, QC; R. F. Solman;
E. Somerset Jones, QC; R. C. Southwell, QC;
R. C. E. Southwell; M. H. Spence, QC; J. Spencer, QC;
M. G. Spencer, QC; S. M. Spencer, QC;
R. V. Spencer Bernard; D. P. Spens, QC; R. W. Spon-Smith;
D. W. Steel, QC; D. Steer, QC; M. T. Steiger, QC;
D. H. Stembridge, QC; Mrs L. J. Stern, QC;
A. W. Stevenson, TD; J. S. H. Stewart, QC;
R. M. Stewart, QC; W. R. Stewart Smith; A. C. Steynor;
G. J. C. Still; D. A. Stockdale, QC; D. M. A. Stokes, QC;
M. G. T. Stokes, QC; E. D. R. Stone, QC; J. B. Storey, QC;
P. L. Storr; T. M. F. Stow, QC; D. M. A. Strachan, QC;
M. Stuart-Moore, QC; F. R. C. Such; A. B. Suckling, QC;
J. M. Sullivan, QC; Ms L. E. Sullivan, QC; D. M. Sumner;
J. P. C. Sumption, QC; M. A. Supperstone, QC; P. J. Susman;

R. P. Sutton, QC; C. J. Sutton-Mattocks;
Miss C. J. Swift, QC; D. R. Swift; L. Swift, QC;
M. R. Swift, QC; Miss H. H. Swindells, QC;
C. J. M. Symons, QC; J. P. Tabor, QC; J. A. Tackaberry, QC;
R. K. K. Talbot; R. B. Tansey, QC; G. F. Tattersall, QC;
E. Taylor; J. J. Teare; R. H. Tedd, QC; A. D. Temple, QC;
V. B. A. Temple, QC; M. H. Tennant;
D. M. Thomas, OBE, QC; D. O. Thomas, QC; P. A. Thomas;
R. L. Thomas, QC; R. M. Thomas; R. U. Thomas, QC;
P. J. Thompson; D. K. Ticehurst, QC; A. C. Tickle;
J. Tiley; M. B. Tillett, QC; J. W. Tinnion;
R. N. Titheridge, QC; S. M. Tomlinson, QC;
R. S. W. Tonking; J. K. Toulmin, CMG, QC;
J. B. S. Townend, QC; C. M. Treacy, QC; H. B. Trethowan;
A. D. H. Trollope, QC; M. G. Tugendhat, QC;
H. W. Turcan; D. A. Turner, QC; P. A. Twigg, QC;
A. R. Tyrrell, QC; N. E. Underhill, QC; J. G. G. Ungley;
N. P. Valios, QC; N. C. van der Bijl; A. R. Vandermeer, QC;
D. A. J. Vaughan, QC; M. J. D. Vere-Hodge, QC;
J. P. Wadsworth, QC; S. P. Waine; J. J. Wait; Miss
A. P. Wakefield; R. M. Wakerley, QC; W. H. Waldron, QC;
Mrs E. A. Walker; R. A. Walker, QC; R. J. Walker, QC;
T. E. Walker, QC; Sir Jonah Walker-Smith, Bt.;
T. M. Walsh; C. T. Walton; J. J. Wardlow; J. C. Warner;
J. Warren, QC; N. J. Warren; D. E. B. Waters; Sir James
Watson, Bt.; B. J. Waylen; A. R. Webb; R. S. Webb, QC;
A. S. Webster, QC; M. Weisman; P. Weitzman, QC;
C. S. Welchman; C. P. C. Whelon; G. Whitburn, QC;
C. H. Whitby, QC; G. B. N. White; W. J. M. White;
D. R. B. Whitehouse, QC; R. P. Whitehurst;
P. G. Whiteman, QC; P. J. M. Whiteman, TD;
A. Whitfield, QC; D. G. Widdicombe, QC; C. T. Wide, QC;
R. Wigglesworth; A. D. F. Wilcken; A. F. Wilkie, QC;
N. V. M. Wilkinson; Miss E. Willers;
G. H. G. Williams, QC; The Lord Williams of Mostyn, QC;
Miss J. A. Williams; J. G. Williams, QC; J. L. Williams, QC;
M. J. Williams; W. L. Williams, QC;
Miss H. E. Williamson, QC; S. W. Williamson, QC;
A. J. D. Wilson, QC; A. M. Wilson, QC; C. Wilson-
Smith, QC; G. W. Wingate-Saul, QC; M. E. Wolff;
H. Wolton, QC; D. A. Wood, QC; N. A. Wood; W. R. Wood;
L. G. Woodley, QC; Miss S. Woodley; J. T. Woods;
W. C. Woodward, QC; N. G. Wootton; T. H. Workman;
Miss A. M. Worrall, QC; D. Worsley; P. F. Worsley, QC;
J. J. Wright; M. P. Yelton; D. E. M. Young, QC

STIPENDIARY MAGISTRATES

PROVINCIAL (each £62,621)

Cheshire, P. K. Dodd, OBE, *apptd* 1991
Devon, P. H. Wassall, *apptd* 1994
East and West Sussex, P. C. Tain, *apptd* 1992
Essex, K. A. Gray, *apptd* 1995
Greater Manchester, W. D. Fairclough, *apptd* 1982;
   Miss J. E. Hayward, *apptd* 1991; A. Berg, *apptd* 1994;
   C. R. Darnton, *apptd* 1994
Hampshire, T. G. Cowling, *apptd* 1989
Humberside, N. H. White, *apptd* 1985
Lancashire/Merseyside, J. Finestein, *apptd* 1992
Leicestershire, D. M. Meredith, *apptd* 1995
Merseyside, D. R. G. Tapp, *apptd* 1992; P. S. Ward, *apptd*
   1994; P. J. Firth, *apptd* 1994
Middlesex, N. A. McKittrick, *apptd* 1989; S. N. Day, *apptd*
   1991
Mid Glamorgan, Miss P. J. Watkins, *apptd* 1995
Norfolk, N. P. Heley, *apptd* 1994
North-East London, G. E. Cawdron, *apptd* 1993

Nottinghamshire, P. F. Nuttall, *apptd* 1991; M. L. R. Harris, *apptd* 1991
Shropshire, P. H. R. Browning, *apptd* 1994
South Glamorgan, G. R. Watkins, *apptd* 1993
South Yorkshire, J. A. Browne, *apptd* 1992; W. D. Thomas, *apptd* 1989; M. A. Rosenberg, *apptd* 1993; P. H. F. Jones, *apptd* 1995; Mrs S. E. Driver, *apptd* 1995
Staffordshire, P. G. G. Richards, *apptd* 1991
West Midlands, W. M. Probert, *apptd* 1983; B. Morgan, *apptd* 1989; I. Gillespie, *apptd* 1991; M. F. James, *apptd* 1991; C. M. McColl, *apptd* 1994
West Yorkshire, F. D. L. Loy, *apptd* 1972; Mrs P. A. Hewitt, *apptd* 1990; G. A. K. Hodgson, *apptd* 1993

Metropolitan

Chief Metropolitan Stipendiary Magistrate and Chairman of Magistrates' Courts Committee for Inner London Area (£76,716), P. G. N. Badge, *apptd* 1992 (*Bow Street*)

Magistrates (each £62,621)

Bow Street, The Chief Magistrate; R. D. Bartle, *apptd* 1972; H. N. Evans, *apptd* 1990; P. A. M. Clark, *apptd* 1996
Camberwell Green, C. P. M. Davidson, *apptd* 1984; H. Gott, *apptd* 1992; Miss E. Roscoe, *apptd* 1994; R. House, *apptd* 1995; Miss C. S. R. Tubbs, *apptd* 1996
Clerkenwell, M. L. R. Romer, *apptd* 1972; C. J. Bourke, *apptd* 1972; B. Loosley, *apptd* 1989
Family Proceedings and Youth Courts, London NW1, G. Wicks, *apptd* 1987; N. Crichton, *apptd* 1987
Greenwich and Woolwich, D. A. Cooper, *apptd* 1991; P. S. Wallis, *apptd* 1993; H. Riddle, *apptd* 1995
Highbury Corner, Miss D. Quick, *apptd* 1986; A. T. Evans, *apptd* 1990; D. Simpson, *apptd* 1993
Horseferry Road, G. Parkinson, *apptd* 1982; A. R. Davies, *apptd* 1985; G. Breen, *apptd* 1986; Mrs K. R. Keating, *apptd* 1987
Marlborough Street, T. H. Workman, *apptd* 1986; Miss D. Wickham, *apptd* 1989
Marylebone, D. Kennett-Brown, *apptd* 1982; K. Maitland-Davies, *apptd* 1984; A. C. Baldwin, *apptd* 1990; C. Pratt, *apptd* 1990
Old Street, M. A. Johnstone, *apptd* 1980; Mrs L. Morgan, *apptd* 1995
South-Western, S. G. Clixby, *apptd* 1981; C. D. Voelcker, *apptd* 1982; A. Ormerod, *apptd* 1988
Thames, I. Bing, *apptd* 1989; W. A. Kennedy, *apptd* 1991; M. J. Read, *apptd* 1993; S. Dawson, *apptd* 1994
Tower Bridge, Mrs J. R. Comyns, *apptd* 1982; R. D. Philips, *apptd* 1989; M. Kelly, *apptd* 1992
Wells Street, Miss A. M. Jennings, *apptd* 1972; Ms G. Babington-Browne, *apptd* 1991
West London, T. English, *apptd* 1986; D. Thomas, *apptd* 1990
Unattached Magistrates, C. S. F. Black, *apptd* 1993; I. M. Baker, *apptd* 1990; Mrs E. Rees, *apptd* 1994; S. Somjee, *apptd* 1995; J. B. Coleman, *apptd* 1995; Miss D. Lachhar, *apptd* 1996

Magistrates' Courts Committee for the Inner London Area
65 Romney Street, London SW1P 3RD
Tel 0171-799 3332

Justices' Chief Executive and Clerk to the Committee (*£80,000), Miss C. Glenn
Justices' Clerk (*Training*) (£*48,971), Miss A. F. Damazer

* 1995–6 figure

CROWN PROSECUTION SERVICE
50 Ludgate Hill, London EC4M 7EX
Tel 0171-273 8000

The Crown Prosecution Service (CPS) is responsible for the independent review and conduct of criminal proceedings instituted by police forces in England and Wales, with the exception of cases conducted by the Serious Fraud Office (*see* page 344) and certain minor offences.

The Director of Public Prosecutions is the head of the Service and discharges her statutory functions under the superintendence of the Attorney-General.

The Service comprises a headquarters office and 14 Areas covering England and Wales. Each of the CPS Areas is supervised by a Chief Crown Prosecutor.

For salary information, *see* page 277

Director of Public Prosecutions (*G1*), Mrs B. Mills, QC
Director of Corporate Services (*G3*), D. Nooney
Director of Casework Evaluation (*G3*), C. Newell
Director of Casework Services (*G3*), G. Duff

CPS AREAS

CPS Anglia, Queen's House, 58 Victoria Street, St Albans AL1 3HZ. Tel: 01727-818100. *Chief Crown Prosecutor* (*G4*), R. J. Chronnell
CPS Central Casework, 50 Ludgate Hill, London EC4M 7EX. Tel: 0171-273 8000. *Chief Crown Prosecutor* (*G4*), D. Kyle
CPS East Midlands, 2 King Edward Court, King Edward Street, Nottingham NG1 1EL. Tel: 0115-948 0480. *Chief Crown Prosecutor* (*G4*), B. T. McArdle
CPS Humber, Greenfield House, Scotland Street, Sheffield S3 7DQ. Tel: 0114-291 2164. *Chief Crown Prosecutor* (*G4*), D. Adams, CBE
CPS London, Portland House, Stag Place, London SW1E 5BH. Tel: 0171-915 5700. *Chief Crown Prosecutor* (*G3*), G. D. Etherington
CPS Mersey/Lancashire, 7th Floor (South), Royal Liver Building, Pier Head, Liverpool L3 1HN. Tel: 0151-236 7575. *Chief Crown Prosecutor* (*G4*), G. Brown
CPS Midlands, 14th Floor, Colmore Gate, 2 Colmore Row, Birmingham B3 2QA. Tel: 0121-629 7202. *Chief Crown Prosecutor* (*G4*), D. Blundell
CPS North, Wellbar House, Gallowgate, Newcastle upon Tyne NE1 4TX. Tel: 0191-261 1858. *Chief Crown Prosecutor* (*G4*), M. Graham
CPS North-West, PO Box 377, 8th Floor, Sunlight House, Quay Street, Manchester M60 3LU. Tel: 0161-837 7402. *Chief Crown Prosecutor* (*G4*), A. R. Taylor
CPS Severn/Thames, Artillery House, Heritage Way, Droitwich, Worcester WR9 8YB. Tel: 01905-793763. *Chief Crown Prosecutor* (*G4*), N. Franklin
CPS South-East, 1 Onslow Street, Guildford, Surrey GU1 4YA. Tel: 01483-882600. *Chief Crown Prosecutor* (*G4*), C. Nicholls
CPS South-West, 8 Kew Court, Pynes Hill, Rydon Lane, Exeter EX2 5SS. Tel: 01392-445422. *Chief Crown Prosecutor* (*G4*), P. Boeuf
CPS Wales, Tudor House, 16 Cathedral Road, Cardiff CF1 9LJ. Tel: 01222-783000. *Chief Crown Prosecutor* (*G4*), R. A. Prickett
CPS Yorkshire, 6th Floor, Ryedale Building, 60 Piccadilly, York YO1 1NS. Tel: 01904-610726. *Chief Crown Prosecutor* (*G4*), D. V. Dickenson

The Scottish Judicature

Scotland has a legal system separate from and differing greatly from the English legal system in enacted law, judicial procedure and the structure of courts.

In Scotland the system of public prosecution is headed by the Lord Advocate and is independent of the police, who have no say in the decision to prosecute. The Lord Advocate, discharging his functions through the Crown Office in Edinburgh, is responsible for prosecutions in the High Court, sheriff courts and district courts. Prosecutions in the High Court are prepared by the Crown Office and conducted in court by one of the law officers, by an advocate-depute, or by a solicitor advocate. In the inferior courts the decision to prosecute is made and prosecution is preferred by procurators fiscal, who are lawyers and full-time civil servants subject to the directions of the Crown Office. A permanent legally-qualified civil servant known as the Crown Agent is responsible for the running of the Crown Office and the organization of the Procurator Fiscal Service, of which he is the head.

Scotland is divided into six sheriffdoms, each with a full-time Sheriff Principal. The sheriffdoms are further divided into sheriff court districts, each of which has a legally-qualified, resident sheriff or sheriffs, who are the judges of the court.

In criminal cases sheriffs principal and sheriffs have the same powers; sitting with a jury of 15 members, they may try more serious cases on indictment, or, sitting alone, may try lesser cases under summary procedure. Minor summary offences are dealt with in district courts which are administered by the district and the islands local government authorities and presided over by lay justices of the peace (of whom there are about 4,200) and, in Glasgow only, by stipendiary magistrates. Juvenile offenders (children under 16) may be brought before an informal children's hearing comprising three local lay people. The superior criminal court is the High Court of Justiciary which is both a trial and an appeal court. Cases on indictment are tried by a High Court judge, sitting with a jury of 15, in Edinburgh and on circuit in other towns. Appeals from the lower courts against conviction or sentence are heard also by the High Court, which sits as an appeal court only in Edinburgh. There is no further appeal to the House of Lords in criminal cases.

In civil cases the jurisdiction of the sheriff court extends to most kinds of action. Appeal against decisions of the sheriff may be made to the Sheriff Principal and thence to the Court of Session, or direct to the Court of Session, which sits only in Edinburgh. The Court of Session is divided into the Inner and the Outer House. The Outer House is a court of first instance in which cases are heard by judges sitting singly, sometimes with a jury of 12. The Inner House, itself subdivided into two divisions of equal status, is mainly an appeal court. Appeals may be made to the Inner House from the Outer House as well as from the sheriff court. An appeal may be made from the Inner House to the House of Lords.

The judges of the Court of Session are the same as those of the High Court of Justiciary, the Lord President of the Court of Session also holding the office of Lord Justice General in the High Court. Senators of the College of Justice are Lords Commissioners of Justiciary as well as judges of the Court of Session. On appointment, a Senator takes a judicial title, which is retained for life. Although styled 'The Hon./Rt. Hon. Lord —', the Senator is not a peer.

The office of coroner does not exist in Scotland. The local procurator fiscal inquires privately into sudden or suspicious deaths and may report findings to the Crown Agent. In some cases a fatal accident inquiry may be held before the sheriff.

COURT OF SESSION AND HIGH COURT OF JUSTICIARY

The Lord President and Lord Justice General (£122,231)
The Rt. Hon. the Lord Rodger of Earlsferry, *born* 1944, *apptd* 1996
Secretary, Mrs M. Small

INNER HOUSE
Lords of Session (each £117,190)

FIRST DIVISION
The Lord President
Hon. Lord Sutherland (Ranald Sutherland), *born* 1932, *apptd* 1985
Hon. Lord Cullen (William Cullen), *born* 1935, *apptd* 1986

SECOND DIVISION
Lord Justice Clerk (£121,190), The Rt. Hon. Lord Ross (Donald Ross), *born* 1927, *apptd* 1985
Rt. Hon. The Lord McCluskey, *born* 1929, *apptd* 1984
Hon. Lord Morison (Alastair Morison), *born* 1931, *apptd* 1985
Hon. Lord Weir (Bruce Weir), *born* 1931, *apptd* 1985

OUTER HOUSE
Lords of Session (each £104,431)

Hon. Lord Prosser (William Prosser), *born* 1934, *apptd* 1986
Hon. Lord Kirkwood (Ian Kirkwood), *born* 1932, *apptd* 1987
Hon. Lord Coulsfield (John Cameron), *born* 1934, *apptd* 1987
Hon. Lord Milligan (James Milligan), *born* 1934, *apptd* 1988
Hon. Lord Caplan (Philip Caplan), *born* 1929, *apptd* 1989
Rt. Hon. The Lord Cameron of Lochbroom, *born* 1931, *apptd* 1989
Hon. Lord Marnoch (Michael Bruce), *born* 1938, *apptd* 1990
Hon. Lord MacLean (Ranald MacLean), *born* 1938, *apptd* 1990
Hon. Lord Penrose (George Penrose), *born* 1938, *apptd* 1990
Hon. Lord Osborne (Kenneth Osborne), *born* 1937, *apptd* 1990
Hon. Lord Abernethy (Alistair Cameron), *born* 1938, *apptd* 1992
Hon. Lord Johnston (Alan Johnston), *born* 1942, *apptd* 1994
Hon. Lord Gill (Brian Gill), *born* 1942, *apptd* 1994
Hon. Lord Hamilton (Arthur Hamilton), *born* 1942, *apptd* 1995
Hon. Lord Dawson (Thomas Dawson), *born* 1948, *apptd* 1995
Hon. Lord Macfadyen (Donald Macfadyen), *born* 1945, *apptd* 1995
Hon. Lady Cosgrove (Hazel Aronson), *born* 1946, *apptd* 1996

COURT OF SESSION AND HIGH COURT OF JUSTICIARY

Parliament House, Parliament Square, Edinburgh EHI IRQ
Tel 0131-225 2595

Principal Clerk of Session and Justiciary (£36,739–£54,815),
H. S. Foley
Deputy Principal Clerk of Justiciary and Administration
(£24,724–£38,290), T. Fyffe
Deputy Principal Clerk of Session and Principal Extractor
(£24,724–£38,290), G. McKeand
Deputy Principal Clerk (Keeper of the Rolls)
(£24,724–£38,290), T. M. Thomson
Depute Clerks of Session and Justiciary (£19,215–£25,289),
N. J. Dowie; I. Smith; T. Higgins; T. B. Cruickshank;
Q. Oliver; F. Shannly; A. S. Moffat; D. J. Shand; G. Ellis;
D. G. Lynn; R. Cockburn; W. Dunn; A. Finlayson;
C. Armstrong; S. Hindes; P. Crow; R. McMillan;
G. Prentice; S. Walker; R. Jenkins; J. O. McLean; M.
Weir

SCOTTISH COURTS ADMINISTRATION

Hayweight House, 23 Lauriston Street, Edinburgh EH3 9DQ
Tel 0131-229 9200

The Scottish Courts Administration is responsible to the Secretary of State for Scotland for the performance of the Scottish Court Service and central administration pertaining to the judiciary in the Supreme and Sheriff Courts; and to the Lord Advocate for certain aspects of court procedures, jurisdiction and legislation, law reform and other matters.
Director (G2), J. Hamill
Deputy Director (*Legal Policy*) (*Assistant Solicitor*) (G5),
P. M. Beaton
Deputy Director (*Resources and Liaison*) (G6), D. Stewart

SCOTTISH COURT SERVICE
Hayweight House, 23 Lauriston Street, Edinburgh EH3 9DQ
Tel 0131-229 9200

The Scottish Court Service became an executive agency within the Scottish Courts Administration in 1995. It is responsible to the Secretary of State for Scotland for the provision of staff, court houses and associated services for the Supreme and Sheriff Courts.
Chief Executive, M. Ewart

SHERIFF COURT OF CHANCERY

27 Chambers Street, Edinburgh EHI ILB
Tel 0131-225 2525

The Court deals with service of heirs and completion of title in relation to heritable property.
Sheriff of Chancery, C. G. B. Nicholson, QC

HM COMMISSARY OFFICE

27 Chambers Street, Edinburgh EHI ILB
Tel 0131-225 2525

The Office is responsible for issuing confirmation, a legal document entitling a person to execute a deceased person's will, and other related matters.
Commissary Clerk, J. L. Anderson

SCOTTISH LAND COURT

1 Grosvenor Crescent, Edinburgh EHI2 5ER
Tel 0131-225 3595

The court deals with disputes relating to agricultural and crofting land in Scotland.

Chairman (£89,123), The Hon. Lord Philip (Alexander Philip), QC
Members, D. D. McDiarmid; D. M. Macdonald; J. Kinloch (*part-time*)
Principal Clerk, K. H. R. Graham, WS

SHERIFFDOMS

SALARIES

Sheriff Principal	£89,123
Sheriff	£76,716
Regional Sheriff Clerk	£28,975–£56,295
Sheriff Clerk	£11,208–£39,324

*Floating Sheriff

GRAMPIAN, HIGHLANDS AND ISLANDS

Sheriff Principal, D. J. Risk
Regional Sheriff Clerk, J. Robertson

SHERIFFS AND SHERIFF CLERKS
Aberdeen and Stonehaven, D. W. Bogie; G. C. Warner;
D. Kelbie; L. A. S. Jessop; A. Pollock; *Sheriff Clerks*,
Mrs E. Laing (*Aberdeen*); I. Smith (*Stonehaven*)
Peterhead and Banff, K. A. McLernan; *Sheriff Clerk*,
A. Hempseed (*Peterhead*); *Sheriff Clerk Depute*, Mrs
F. L. MacPherson (*Banff*)
Elgin, N. McPartlin; *Sheriff Clerk*, M. McBey
Inverness, Lochmaddy, Portree, Stornoway, Dingwall, Tain, Wick and Dornoch, W. J. Fulton; D. Booker-Milburn;
J. O. A. Fraser; I. A. Cameron; *Sheriff Clerks*, J. Robertson
(*Inverness*); W. Cochrane (*Dingwall*); *Sheriff Clerks Depute*,
Miss M. Campbell (*Lochmaddy and Portree*); Mrs
M. Macdonald (*Stornoway*); L. MacLachlan (*Tain*); Mrs
J. McEwan (*Wick*); Miss R. MacSween (*Dornoch*)
Kirkwall and Lerwick, C. S. Mackenzie; *Sheriff Clerks Depute*,
R. Cantwell (*Kirkwall*); A. C. Norris (*Lerwick*)
Fort William, C. G. McKay (also *Oban*); *Sheriff Clerk Depute*,
D. Hood

TAYSIDE, CENTRAL AND FIFE

Sheriff Principal, J. J. Maguire, QC
Regional Sheriff Clerk, J. S. Doig

SHERIFFS AND SHERIFF CLERKS
Arbroath and Forfar, K. A. Veal; *C. N. R. Stein; *Sheriff Clerks*,
M. Herbertson (*Arbroath*); S. Munro (*Forfar*)
Dundee, R. A. Davidson; A. L. Stewart, QC; *J. N. Young;
C. Smith (also *Cupar*); *Sheriff Clerk*, J. S. Doig
Perth, J. F. Wheatley; J. C. McInnes, QC; *Sheriff Clerk*,
W. Jones
Falkirk, A. V. Sheehan; A. J. Murphy; *Sheriff Clerk*,
D. Forrester
Stirling, The Hon. R. E. G. Younger; *Mrs A. M. Cowan;
Sheriff Clerk, J. Clark
Alloa, W. M. Reid; *Sheriff Clerk*, G. McKeand
Cupar, C. Smith (also *Dundee*); *Sheriff Clerk*, R. Hughes
Dunfermline, J. S. Forbes; C. W. Palmer; *Sheriff Clerk*,
W. McCulloch
Kirkcaldy, W. J. Christie; Mrs L. G. Patrick; *Sheriff Clerk*,
I. Hay

LOTHIAN AND BORDERS

Sheriff Principal, C. G. B. Nicholson, QC
Regional Sheriff Clerk, J. Anderson

SHERIFFS AND SHERIFF CLERKS
Edinburgh, vacant (also *Peebles*); R. G. Craik, QC;
G. I. W. Shiach; Miss I. A. Poole; R. J. D. Scott;
A. M. Bell; J. M. S. Horsburgh, QC; G. W. S. Presslie (also
Haddington); J. A. Farrell; *A. Lothian; *F. J. Keane;
I. D. Macphail, QC; C. N. Stoddart; A. B. Wilkinson, QC;
Mrs D. J. B. Robertson; N. M. P. Morrison, QC; *Sheriff
Clerk*, J. Anderson
Peebles, vacant (also *Edinburgh*); *Sheriff Clerk Depute*,
R. McArthur
Linlithgow, H. R. MacLean; G. R. Fleming; *Sheriff Clerk*,
R. Sinclair
Haddington, G. W. S. Presslie (also *Edinburgh*); *Sheriff Clerk*,
J. O'Donnell
Jedburgh and Duns, J. V. Paterson; *Sheriff Clerk*,
J. W. Williamson
Selkirk, J. V. Paterson; *Sheriff Clerk Depute*, L. McFarlane

NORTH STRATHCLYDE
Sheriff Principal, R. C. Hay, CBE
Regional Sheriff Clerk, A. A. Brown

SHERIFFS AND SHERIFF CLERKS
Oban, C. G. McKay (also *Fort William*); *Sheriff Clerk Depute*,
G. Whitelaw
Dumbarton, J. T. Fitzsimons; T. Scott; S. W. H. Fraser;
Sheriff Clerk, P. Corcoran
Paisley, R. G. Smith; J. Spy; C. K. Higgins; N. Douglas;
*D. J. Pender; *W. Dunlop (also *Campbeltown*); *Sheriff
Clerk*, A. A. Brown
Greenock, J. Herald (also *Rothesay*); Sir Stephen Young;
Sheriff Clerk, J. Tannahill
Kilmarnock, T. M. Croan; D. B. Smith; T. F. Russell; *Sheriff
Clerk*, N. R. Weir
Dunoon, A. W. Noble; *Sheriff Clerk Depute*, Mrs C. Carson
Campbeltown, *W. Dunlop (also *Paisley*); *Sheriff Clerk Depute*,
P. G. Hay
Rothesay, J. Herald (also *Greenock*); *Sheriff Clerk Depute*, Mrs
S. Gracie

GLASGOW AND STRATHKELVIN
Sheriff Principal, N. D. MacLeod, QC
Regional Sheriff Clerk, I. Scott

SHERIFFS AND SHERIFF CLERKS
Glasgow, A. C. Horsfall, QC (*seconded to Scottish Lands
Tribunal*); B. Kearney; G. H. Gordon, CBE, PH.D., QC;
B. A. Lockhart; I. G. Pirie; Mrs A. L. A. Duncan;
G. J. Evans; E. H. Galt; A. C. Henry; J. K. Mitchell;
A. G. Johnston; J. P. Murphy; M. Sischy; Miss
S. A. O. Raeburn, QC; D. Convery; J. McGowan;
B. A. Kerr, QC; Mrs C. M. A. F. Gimblett;
I. A. S. Peebles, QC; C. W. McFarlane, QC; K. M. Maciver;
Sheriff Clerk, I. Scott

SOUTH STRATHCLYDE, DUMFRIES AND GALLOWAY
Sheriff Principal, G. L. Cox, QC
Regional Sheriff Clerk, M. Bonar

SHERIFFS AND SHERIFF CLERKS
Hamilton, L. Cameron; A. C. MacPherson; W. F. Lunny;
D. C. Russell; V. J. Canavan (also *Airdrie*); W. E. Gibson;
H. Stirling; J. H. Stewart; *Sheriff Clerk*, P. Feeney
Lanark, J. D. Allan; *H. S. Neilson; *Sheriff Clerk*, J. Lynn
Ayr, N. Gow, QC; R. G. McEwan, QC; *C. B. Miller; *Sheriff
Clerk*, G. W. Waddell

Stranraer and Kirkcudbright, J. R. Smith (also *Dumfries*);
Sheriff Clerks, W. McIntosh (*Stranraer*); B. Lindsay
(*Kirkcudbright*)
Dumfries, K. G. Barr; M. J. Fletcher; J. R. Smith (also
Stranraer and Kirkcudbright); *Sheriff Clerk*, P. McGonigle
Airdrie, V. J. Canavan (also *Hamilton*); R. H. Dickson;
I. C. Simpson; *Sheriff Clerk*, M. Bonar

STIPENDIARY MAGISTRATES

GLASGOW
R. Hamilton, *apptd* 1984; J. B. C. Nisbet, *apptd* 1984;
R. B. Christie, *apptd* 1985; Mrs J. A. M. MacLean, *apptd*
1990

PROCURATOR FISCAL SERVICE

CROWN OFFICE
25 Chambers Street, Edinburgh EH1 1LA
Tel 0131-226 2626
Crown Agent (*£65,990–£79,396), J. D. Lowe, CB
Deputy Crown Agent (*£45,278–£54,815), N. McFadyen

PROCURATORS FISCAL

*SALARIES

Regional Procurator Fiscal–grade 3	£52,704–£62,817
Regional Procurator Fiscal–grade 4	£45,278–£54,815
Procurator Fiscal–upper level	£36,739–£54,815
Procurator Fiscal–lower level	£26,418–£45,078

*1994–5 figures; grades and salaries were under review at the time
of going to press

GRAMPIAN, HIGHLANDS AND ISLANDS REGION
Regional Procurator Fiscal, A. D. Vannett (*Aberdeen*)
Procurators Fiscal, E. K. Barbour (*Stonehaven*);
A. J. M. Colley (*Banff*); Mrs D. Wilson (*Peterhead*);
J. F. MacKay (*Elgin*); A. N. MacDonald (*Wick*);
J. Bamber (*Portree, Lochmaddy*); F. Redman (*Stornoway*);
G. K. Buchanan (*Inverness*); D. K. Adam (*Kirkwall,
Lerwick*); Mrs A. Neizer (*Fort William*); D. R. Hingston
(*Dingwall, Dornoch, Tain*)

TAYSIDE, CENTRAL AND FIFE REGION
Regional Procurator Fiscal, B. K. Heywood (*Dundee*)
Procurators Fiscal, I. C. Walker (*Forfar*); I. A. McLeod
(*Perth*); J. J. Miller (*Falkirk*); C. Ritchie (*Stirling*);
I. D. Douglas (*Alloa*); E. B. Russell (*Cupar*);
R. T. Hamilton (*Dunfermline*); Miss E. C. Munro
(*Kirkcaldy*)

LOTHIAN AND BORDERS REGION
Regional Procurator Fiscal, R. F. Lees (*Edinburgh*)
Procurators Fiscal, D. McNeill (*Peebles*); Miss L. M. Ruxton
(*Linlithgow*); A. J. P. Reith (*Haddington*); A. R. G. Fraser
(*Duns, Jedburgh*); D. McNeill (*Selkirk*)

NORTH STRATHCLYDE REGION
Regional Procurator Fiscal, J. D. Friel (*Paisley*)
Procurators Fiscal, I. Henderson (*Campbeltown*);
C. C. Donnelly (*Dumbarton*); W. S. Carnegie (*Greenock,
Rothesay*); D. L. Webster (*Dunoon*); J. G. MacGlennan
(*Kilmarnock*); B. R. Maguire (*Oban*)

GLASGOW AND STRATHKELVIN REGION
Regional Procurator Fiscal, A. C. Normand (*Glasgow*)

SOUTH STRATHCLYDE, DUMFRIES AND GALLOWAY
REGION
Regional Procurator Fiscal, F. R. Crowe (*Hamilton*)
Procurators Fiscal, S. R. Houston (*Lanark*); D. A. Brown
(*Ayr*); F. Walkingshaw (*Stranraer*); D. J. Howdle
(*Dumfries, Stranraer, Kirkcudbright*); D. Spiers (*Airdrie*)

Northern Ireland Judicature

In Northern Ireland the legal system and the structure of
courts closely resemble those of England and Wales; there
are, however, often differences in enacted law.

The Supreme Court of Judicature of Northern Ireland
comprises the Court of Appeal, the High Court of Justice
and the Crown Court. The practice and procedure of
these courts is similar to that in England. The superior
civil court is the High Court of Justice, from which an
appeal lies to the Northern Ireland Court of Appeal; the
House of Lords is the final civil appeal court.

The Crown Court, served by High Court and county
court judges, deals with criminal trials on indictment.
Cases are heard before a judge and, except those involving
offences specified under emergency legislation, a jury.
Appeals from the Crown Court against conviction or
sentence are heard by the Northern Ireland Court of
Appeal; the House of Lords is the final court of appeal.

The decision to prosecute in cases tried on indictment
and in summary cases of a serious nature rests in Northern
Ireland with the Director of Public Prosecutions, who is
responsible to the Attorney-General. Minor summary
offences are prosecuted by the police.

Minor criminal offences are dealt with in magistrates'
courts by a legally qualified resident magistrate and,
where an offender is under 17, by juvenile courts each
consisting of a resident magistrate and two lay members
specially qualified to deal with juveniles (at least one of
whom must be a woman). In June 1996 there were 942
justices of the peace in Northern Ireland. Appeals from
magistrates' courts are heard by the county court, or by
the Court of Appeal on a point of law or an issue as to
jurisdiction.

Magistrates' courts in Northern Ireland can deal with
certain classes of civil case but most minor civil cases are
dealt with in county courts. Judgments of all civil courts
are enforceable through a centralized procedure administered by the Enforcement of Judgments Office.

SUPREME COURT OF JUDICATURE
The Royal Courts of Justice, Belfast BT1 3JF
Tel 01232-235111

Lord Chief Justice of Northern Ireland (£122,231)
    The Rt. Hon. Sir Brian Hutton, *born* 1931, *apptd* 1988
Principal Secretary, G. W. Johnston

LORDS JUSTICES OF APPEAL (each £117,190)
Style, The Rt. Hon. Lord Justice [surname]
Rt. Hon. Sir John MacDermott, *born* 1927, *apptd* 1987
Rt. Hon. Sir Robert Carswell, *born* 1934, *apptd* 1993
Rt. Hon. Sir Michael Nicholson, *born* 1933, *apptd* 1995

PUISNE JUDGES (each £104,431)
Style, The Hon. Mr Justice [surname]
Hon. Sir William McCollum, *born* 1933, *apptd* 1987
Hon. Sir Anthony Campbell, *born* 1936, *apptd* 1988
Hon. Sir John Sheil, *born* 1938, *apptd* 1989
Hon. Sir Brian Kerr, *born* 1948, *apptd* 1993
Hon. Sir John Pringle, *born* 1929, *apptd* 1993
Hon. Sir Malachy Higgins, *born* 1944, *apptd* 1993
Hon. Sir Paul Girvan, *born* 1948, *apptd* 1995

MASTERS OF THE SUPREME COURT (each £62,621)
Master, Queen's Bench and Appeals and Clerk of the Crown,
    J. W. Wilson, QC
Master, High Court, Mrs D. M. Kennedy
Master, Office of Care and Protection, F. B. Hall
Master, Chancery Office, R. A. Ellison
Master, Bankruptcy and Companies Office, J. B. C. Glass
Master, Probate and Matrimonial Office, R. T. Millar
Master, Taxing Office, J. C. Napier

OFFICIAL SOLICITOR
Official Solicitor to the Supreme Court of Northern Ireland,
    C. W. G. Redpath

COUNTY COURTS

JUDGES (each £89,123)
Style, His Hon. Judge [surname]
Judge Curran, QC; Judge McKee, QC; Judge Gibson, QC;
Judge Hart, QC; Judge Petrie, QC; Judge Smyth, QC; Judge
Markey, QC; Judge McKay, QC; Judge Chambers, QC
(*Chief Social Security and Child Support Commissioner*); Judge
Martin, QC; Judge Brady, QC

RECORDERS (each £89,123)
Belfast, Judge Russell, QC
Londonderry, Judge Burgess

MAGISTRATES' COURTS

RESIDENT MAGISTRATES (each £62,621)
There are 17 resident magistrates in Northern Ireland.

CROWN SOLICITOR'S OFFICE
PO Box 410, Royal Courts of Justice, Belfast BT1 3JY
Tel 01232-542555

Crown Solicitor, N. P. Roberts

DEPARTMENT OF THE DIRECTOR OF
PUBLIC PROSECUTIONS
Royal Courts of Justice, Belfast BT1 3NX
Tel 01232-542444

Director of Public Prosecutions, A. Fraser, CB, QC
Deputy Director of Public Prosecutions, D. Magill

NORTHERN IRELAND COURT SERVICE
Windsor House, Bedford Street, Belfast BT2 7LT
Tel 01232-328594

Director (G3)

Ecclesiastical Courts

Original jurisdiction is exercised by the consistory court of each diocese in England, presided over by the Chancellor of that diocese. Appellate jurisdiction is exercised by the provincial courts detailed below, by the Court for Ecclesiastical Causes Reserved, and by commissions of review (the membership of these being newly constituted for each case).

COURT OF ARCHES (PROVINCE OF CANTERBURY)
Registry, 16 Beaumont Street, Oxford OX1 2LZ
Tel 01865-241974

Dean of the Arches, The Rt. Worshipful Sir John Owen

COURT OF THE VICAR-GENERAL OF THE PROVINCE OF CANTERBURY
Registry, 16 Beaumont Street, Oxford OX1 2LZ
Tel 01865-241974

Vicar-General, The Rt. Worshipful Miss S. Cameron, QC

CHANCERY COURT OF YORK
Registry, 1 Peckitt Street, York YO1 1SG
Tel 01904-623487

Auditor, The Rt. Worshipful Sir John Owen

THE VICAR-GENERAL OF THE PROVINCE OF YORK
Registry, 1 Peckitt Street, York YO1 1SG
Tel 01904-623487

Vicar-General, His Honour the Worshipful Judge
T. A. C. Coningsby, QC

COURT OF FACULTIES
Registry, 1 The Sanctuary, London SW1P 3JT
Tel 0171-222 5381

Office for the issue of special and common marriage licences, appointment of notaries public, etc. Office hours, Monday–Friday, 10–4.

Master of the Faculties, The Rt. Worshipful Sir John Owen

The Probation Service

ENGLAND AND WALES

The Probation Service is employed in each area (55 in total) by an independent committee of justices and it provides a professional social work agency in the courts, with responsibility for a wide range of duties which include:

(a) a pre-sentence report service for the criminal courts
(b) provision of a range of non-custodial measures involving the supervision of offenders in the community
(c) supervisory aftercare for offenders released from custody, together with social work in penal establishments and help for the families of those serving sentences
(d) an enquiry, conciliation and supervision service in the divorce and domestic courts
(e) support for and promotion of preventive and containment measures in the community designed to reduce the level of crime and domestic breakdown

It is a direct grant service funded 80 per cent from the Home Office and 20 per cent from the relevant local authority.

Its national representative bodies are:
THE CENTRAL PROBATION COUNCIL, 38 Belgrave Square, London SW1X 8NT. Tel: 0171-245 9364. *Director*, I. Miles

THE ASSOCIATION OF CHIEF OFFICERS OF PROBATION, 20–30 Lawefield Lane, Wakefield WF2 8SP. Tel: 01924-361156. *General Secretary*, Ms M. Honeyball

THE NATIONAL ASSOCIATION OF PROBATION OFFICERS, 3 Chivalry Road, London SW11 1HT. Tel: 0171-223 4887. *General Secretary*, Ms J. McKnight

SCOTLAND

The probation service in Scotland is a statutory duty of local authorities under section 27 of the Social Work (Scotland) Act 1968. Social workers supervise and provide advice, guidance and assistance to those persons living in their area who are subject to a court's supervision order. This is done by social workers as part of their normal duties and not by a separate probation staff.

NORTHERN IRELAND

The Probation Board for Northern Ireland provides a probation service throughout Northern Ireland. Its function and range of duties is similar to that of the Probation Service in England and Wales (*see* above), except that in Northern Ireland work in divorce and domestic courts is the responsibility of the social services and not the Probation Board. The Probation Board is a statutory body whose 14 members are appointed by the Secretary of State for Northern Ireland and it receives its funding from the Northern Ireland Office.

Tribunals

AGRICULTURAL LAND TRIBUNALS
c/o Land Use and Rural Economy Division, Ministry of
Agriculture, Fisheries and Food, Nobel House, 17 Smith
Square, London SWIP 3JR
Tel 0171-238 6991

Agricultural Land Tribunals were set up under the
Agriculture Act 1947 and settle disputes and other issues
between agricultural landlords and tenants. They also
settle drainage disputes between neighbours.

There are seven tribunals covering England and one
covering Wales. For each tribunal the Lord Chancellor
appoints a chairman and one or more deputies, who must
be barristers or solicitors of at least seven years standing.
The Lord Chancellor also appoints lay members to three
statutory panels of members: the 'landowners' panel, the
'farmers' panel and the 'drainage' panel.

Each of the eight tribunals is an independent statutory
body with jurisdiction only within its own area. A separate
tribunal is constituted for each case, and consists of a chairman (who may be the chairman or one of the deputy chairmen) and two lay members nominated by the chairman.
Chairmen (England) (£233 a day), W. D. Greenwood;
K. J. Fisher; P. A. de la Piquerie; C. H. Beaumont;
M. K. Lee; G. L. Newsom; His Hon. Judge Robert Taylor
Chairman (Wales) (£233 a day), W. J. Owen

COMMONS COMMISSIONERS
4th Floor, 35 Old Queen Street, London SWIH 9JA
Tel 0171-222 0038

The Commons Commissioners are responsible for de-
ciding disputes arising under the Commons Registration
Act 1965 and the Common Land (Rectification of
Registers) Act 1989. They also enquire into the ownership
of unclaimed common land. Commissioners are appointed
by the Lord Chancellor.
Chief Commons Commissioner (part-time) (£40,358),
D. M. Burton
Commissioner, I. L. R. Romer
Clerk, Miss F. A. A. Buchan

COPYRIGHT TRIBUNAL
25 Southampton Buildings, London WC2A IAY
Tel 0171- 438 4776

The Copyright Tribunal is the successor to the Performing
Right Tribunal which was established by the Copyright
Act 1956 to resolve various classes of copyright dispute,
principally in the field of collective licensing. Its juris-
diction was extended by the Copyright, Designs and
Patents Act 1988 and the Broadcasting Act 1990.

The chairman and two deputy chairmen are appointed
by the Lord Chancellor. Up to eight ordinary members are
appointed by the Secretary of State for Trade and Industry.
Chairman (£316 a day), J. M. Bowers
Secretary, Miss J. E. M. Durdin

DATA PROTECTION TRIBUNAL
c/o The Home Office, Queen Anne's Gate, London
SWIH 9AT
Tel 0171-273 3386

The Data Protection Tribunal was established under the
Data Protection Act 1984 to determine appeals against
decisions of the Data Protection Registrar (*see* page 293).
The chairman and two deputy chairmen are appointed by
the Lord Chancellor and must be legally qualified. Lay
members are appointed by the Home Secretary to represent the interests of data users or data subjects.

A tribunal consists of a legally-qualified chairman sitting
with equal numbers of the lay members appointed to
represent the interests of data users and data subjects.
Chairman (£359 a day), J. A. C. Spokes, QC
Secretary, D. Anderson

EMPLOYMENT APPEAL TRIBUNAL
Central Office, Audit House, 58 Victoria Embankment,
London EC4Y ODS
Tel 0171-273 1041
Divisional Office, 52 Melville Street, Edinburgh EH3 7HF
Tel 0131-225 3963

The Employment Appeal Tribunal was established as a
superior court of record under the provisions of the
Employment Protection Act 1975, hearing appeals on a
question of law arising from any decision of an industrial
tribunal.

A tribunal consists of a legally-qualified chairman and
two lay members, one from each side of industry. They are
appointed by The Queen on the recommendation of the
Lord Chancellor and the Secretary of State for Trade and
Industry.
President, The Hon. Mr Justice Morison
Scottish Chairman, The Hon. Lord Johnston
Registrar, Miss V. J. Selio

IMMIGRATION APPELLATE AUTHORITIES
Thanet House, 231 Strand, London WC2R IDA
Tel 0171-353 8060

The Immigration Appeal Adjudicators hear appeals from
immigration decisions concerning the need for, and refusal
of, leave to enter or remain in the UK, refusals to grant
asylum, decisions to make deportation orders and directions to remove persons subject to immigration control
from the UK. The Immigration Appeal Tribunal hears
appeals direct from decisions to make deportation orders in
matters concerning conduct contrary to the public good
and refusals to grant asylum. Its principal jurisdiction is,
however, the hearing of appeals from adjudicators by the
party (Home Office or individual) who is aggrieved by the
decision. Appeals are subject to leave being granted by the
tribunal.

An adjudicator sits alone. The tribunal sits in divisions of
three, normally a legally qualified member and two lay

members. Members of the tribunal and adjudicators are appointed by the Lord Chancellor.

IMMIGRATION APPEAL TRIBUNAL
President (£80,176), G. W. Farmer
Vice-Presidents, Prof. D. C. Jackson; Mrs J. Chatwani

IMMIGRATION APPEAL ADJUDICATORS
Chief Adjudicator, His Hon. Judge Pearl
Deputy Chief Adjudicator, vacant

INDEPENDENT TRIBUNAL SERVICE
City Gate House, 39–45 Finsbury Square, London
EC2A 1PX
Tel 0171-814 6500

The service is the judicial authority which exercises judicial and administrative control over the independent social security and child support appeal tribunals, medical and disability appeal tribunals, and vaccine damage tribunals.
President, His Hon. Judge Bassingthwaighte
Chief Executive, S. Williams

INDUSTRIAL TRIBUNALS

CENTRAL OFFICE (ENGLAND AND WALES)
19–29 Woburn Place, London WC1H 0LU
Tel 0171-273 8659

Industrial Tribunals for England and Wales sit in 11 regions. The tribunals deal with matters of employment law, redundancy, dismissal, contract disputes, sexual, racial and disability discrimination, and related areas of dispute which may arise in the workplace. A central registration unit records all applications and maintains a public register at Southgate Street, Bury St Edmunds, Suffolk IP33 2AQ. The tribunals are funded by the Department of Trade and Industry. In April 1997 the tribunals will be renamed the Employment Tribunal Service.

Chairmen, who may be full-time or part-time, are legally qualified. They are appointed by the Lord Chancellor. Tribunal members are nominated by specified employer and employee groups and appointed by the Secretary of State for Trade and Industry.
President, His Hon. Judge Lawrence

CENTRAL OFFICE (SCOTLAND)
Eagle Building, 215 Bothwell Street, Glasgow G2 7TS
Tel 0141-204 0730

Tribunals in Scotland have the same remit as those in England and Wales. Chairmen are appointed by the Lord President of the Court of Session and lay members by the Secretary of State for Trade and Industry.
President (£89,123), Mrs D. Littlejohn

INDUSTRIAL TRIBUNALS AND THE FAIR EMPLOYMENT TRIBUNAL (NORTHERN IRELAND)
Long Bridge House, 20–24 Waring Street, Belfast BT1 2EB
Tel 01232-327666

The industrial tribunal system in Northern Ireland was set up in 1965 and is similar to the system operating in the rest of the UK. The main legislation in Northern Ireland giving jurisdiction to industrial tribunals to hear complaints relating to employment matters corresponds to legislation enacted in Great Britain, except that there is no equivalent legislation to the Race Relations Act.

Since 1990 there has been a separate Fair Employment Tribunal in Northern Ireland. The Fair Employment Tribunal hears and determines individual cases of alleged religious or political discrimination in employment. Employers can also appeal to the Fair Employment Tribunal if they consider the directions of the Fair Employment Commission to be unreasonable, inappropriate or unnecessary, and the Fair Employment Commission can make application to the Tribunal for the enforcement of undertakings or directions with which an employer has not complied.

The president, vice-president and part-time chairmen of the Fair Employment Tribunal are appointed by the Lord Chancellor. The full-time chairman and the part-time chairmen of the industrial tribunals and the panel members to both the industrial tribunals and the Fair Employment Tribunal are appointed by the Department of Economic Development Northern Ireland.
President of the Industrial Tribunals and the Fair Employment Tribunal (£89,123), J. Maguire, CBE
Vice-President of the Industrial Tribunals and the Fair Employment Tribunal, Mrs M. P. Price
Secretary, J. Murphy

LANDS TRIBUNAL
48–49 Chancery Lane, London WC2A 1JR
Tel 0171-936 7200

The Lands Tribunal is an independent judicial body constituted by the Lands Tribunal Act 1949 for the purpose of determining a wide range of questions relating to the valuation of land, rating appeals from valuation tribunals and the discharge or modification of restrictive covenants. The Act also empowers the tribunal to accept the function of arbitration under references by consent. The tribunal consists of a president and a number of other members, who are appointed by the Lord Chancellor.
President, His Hon. Judge Marder, QC
Members (£76,716), Dr T. Hoyes, FRICS; M. St J. Hopper, FRICS; P. H. Clarke, FRICS
Member (part-time), His Hon. Judge Rich, QC
Members (part-time) (£349 a day), J. C. Hill, TD; A. P. Musto, FRICS
Registrar, C. A. McMullan

LANDS TRIBUNAL FOR SCOTLAND
1 Grosvenor Crescent, Edinburgh EH12 5ER
Tel 0131-225 7996

The Lands Tribunal for Scotland was constituted by the Lands Tribunal Act 1949. Its remit is the same as the tribunal for England and Wales but also covers questions relating to tenants' rights. The president is appointed by the Lord President of the Court of Session.
President, The Hon. Lord Philip, QC
Members (£76,716), Sheriff A. C. Horsfall, QC; A. R. MacLeary; J. Devine
Member (part-time) (£349 a day), R. A. Edwards, CBE, WS
Clerk, N. Tainsh

MENTAL HEALTH REVIEW TRIBUNALS

The Mental Health Review Tribunals are independent judicial bodies established under the Mental Health Act 1959 and which now operate under the Mental Health Act 1983. They are responsible for reviewing the cases of patients compulsorily detained under the Act's provisions. They have the power to discharge the patient, to recommend leave of absence, delayed discharge, transfer to another hospital or that a guardianship order be made, and to reclassify both restricted and unrestricted patients. There are eight tribunals in England, each headed by a regional chairman who is appointed by the Lord Chancellor's Department on a part-time basis. Each tribunal is made up of at least three members, and must include a lawyer, who acts as president (£239 a day), a medical member (£226 a day) and a lay member (£97 a day).

The Mental Health Review Tribunals' secretariat is based in five regional offices:

LIVERPOOL, 3rd Floor, Cressington House, 249 St Mary's Road, Garston, Liverpool L19 0NF. Tel: 0151-494 0095. *Clerk,* Mrs B. Foot

LONDON (NORTH), Spur 3, Block 1, Government Buildings, Honeypot Lane, Stanmore, Middx HA7 1AY. Tel: 0171-972 3734. *Clerk,* P. Barnett

LONDON (SOUTH), Block 3, Crown Offices, Kingston Bypass Road, Surbiton, Surrey KT6 5QN. Tel: 0181-268 4520. *Clerk,* C. Lilly

NOTTINGHAM, Spur A, Block 5, Government Buildings, Chalfont Drive, Western Boulevard, Nottingham NG8 3RZ. Tel: 0115-929 4222. *Clerk,* M. Chapman

WALES, 4th Floor, Crown Buildings, Cathays Park, Cardiff CF1 3NQ. Tel: 01222-825328. *Clerk,* Mrs C. Thomas

NATIONAL HEALTH SERVICE TRIBUNAL

The NHS Tribunal was set up under the National Health Service Act 1977. It inquires into representations that the continued inclusion of a family practitioner (doctor, dentist, pharmacist or optician) on a Family Practitioner Committee's list would be prejudicial to the efficiency of the services concerned. The tribunal sits when required, about eight times a year, and usually in London. The chairman is appointed by the Lord Chancellor and members are appointed by the Secretary of State for Health.

Chairman (£295 a day), A. Whitfield, QC
Deputy Chairmen, Miss E. Platt, QC; Dr R. N. Ough
Clerk, I. D. Keith, East Hookers, Twineham, nr Haywards Heath, W. Sussex RH17 5NN. Tel: 01444-881345

NATIONAL HEALTH SERVICE TRIBUNAL (SCOTLAND)
Erskine House, 68 Queen Street, Edinburgh EH2 4NN
Tel 0131-226 6541

The tribunal was set up under the National Health Service (Scotland) Act 1978, and exists to consider representations that the continued inclusion of a registered doctor, dentist, optometrist or pharmacist on a health board's list would be prejudicial to the continuing efficiency of the service in question.

The tribunal meets when required and is composed of a chairman, one lay member, and one practitioner member drawn from a representative professional panel. The chairman is appointed by the Lord President of the Court of Session, and the lay member and the members of the professional panel are appointed by the Secretary of State for Scotland.

Chairman (£295 a day), W. C. Galbraith, QC
Lay member, J. D. M. Robertson
Clerk to the Tribunal, D. G. Brash, WS

PENSIONS APPEAL TRIBUNALS

CENTRAL OFFICE (ENGLAND AND WALES)
48–49 Chancery Lane, London WC2A 1JR
Tel 0171-936 7034

The Pensions Appeal Tribunals are responsible for hearing appeals from ex-servicemen or women and widows who have had their claims for a war pension rejected by the Secretary of State for Social Security. The Entitlement Appeal Tribunals hear appeals in cases where the Secretary of State has refused to grant a war pension. The Assessment Appeal Tribunals hear appeals against the Secretary of State's assessment of the degree of disablement caused by an accepted condition.

The tribunal members are appointed by the Lord Chancellor.

President (£62,621), J. R. T. Holt
Secretary, W. Thomas

PENSIONS APPEAL TRIBUNALS FOR SCOTLAND
20 Walker Street, Edinburgh EH3 7HS
Tel 0131-220 1404
President (£282 a day), C. N. McEachran, QC

OFFICE OF THE SOCIAL SECURITY AND CHILD SUPPORT COMMISSIONERS
Harp House, 83–86 Farringdon Street, London EC4A 4DH
Tel 0171-353 5145
23 Melville Street, Edinburgh EH3 7PW
Tel 0131-225 2201

The Social Security Commissioners are the final statutory authority to decide appeals relating to entitlement to social security benefits. The Child Support Commissioners are the final statutory authority to decide appeals relating to child support. Appeals may be made in relation to both matters only on a point of law. The Commissioners' jurisdiction covers England, Wales and Scotland. There are 17 commissioners; they are all qualified lawyers.

Chief Social Security Commissioner and Chief Child Support Commissioner, His Hon. Judge Machin, QC
Secretary, S. Hill (*London*); E. Barschtschyk (*Edinburgh*)

OFFICE OF THE SOCIAL SECURITY AND CHILD SUPPORT COMMISSIONERS FOR NORTHERN IRELAND
Lancashire House, 5 Linenhall Street, Belfast BT2 8AA
Tel 01232-332344

The role of Northern Ireland Social Security and Child Support Commissioners is similar to that of the Commissioners in Great Britain. There are two commissioners for Northern Ireland.

Chief Commissioner, His Hon. Judge Chambers, QC
Registrar of Appeals, W. D. Pollock

THE SOLICITORS' DISCIPLINARY TRIBUNAL
227–228 Strand, London WC2A IBA
Tel 0171-242 0219

The Solicitors' Disciplinary Tribunal was constituted under the provisions of the Solicitors Act 1974. It is an independent statutory body whose members are appointed by the Master of the Rolls. The tribunal considers applications made to it alleging either professional misconduct and/or a breach of the statutory rules by which solicitors are bound against an individually named solicitor, former solicitor, or registered foreign lawyer. The tribunal's jurisdiction extends to solicitor's clerks, in respect of whom they may make an order restricting that clerk's employment by solicitors. The president and solicitor members do not receive remuneration.
President, G. B. Marsh
Clerk, Mrs S. C. Elson

SPECIAL COMMISSIONERS OF INCOME TAX
15–19 Bedford Avenue, London WC1B 3AS
Tel 0171-631 4242

The Special Commissioners are an independent body appointed by the Lord Chancellor to hear complex appeals against decisions of the Board of Inland Revenue and its officials. In addition to the Presiding Special Commissioner there are two full-time and 12 deputy special commissioners; all are legally qualified.
Presiding Special Commissioner, His Hon. Stephen Oliver, QC
Special Commissioners (£62,621), T. H. K. Everett;
    D. A. Shirley
Clerk, R. P. Lester

TRAFFIC COMMISSIONERS
c/o Scottish Traffic Area, Argyle House, 3 Lady Lawson Street, Edinburgh EH3 9SE
Tel 0131-529 8500

The Traffic Commissioners are responsible for the licensing of operators of heavy goods and public service vehicles. They also have responsibility for appeals relating to the licensing of operators and for disciplinary cases involving the conduct of drivers of these vehicles. There are seven Commissioners in the eight traffic areas covering Great Britain. Each Traffic Commissioner constitutes a tribunal for the purposes of the Tribunals and Inquiries Act 1971. For Traffic Area Offices and Commissioners, *see* page 352.
Senior Traffic Commissioner (£54,029), M. Betts

TRANSPORT TRIBUNAL
48–49 Chancery Lane, London WC2A IJR
Tel 0171-936 7493

The Transport Tribunal was set up in 1947 and hears appeals against decisions made by Traffic Commissioners at public inquiries. The tribunal consists of a legally-qualified president, two legal members who may sit as chairmen, and five lay members. The president and legal members are appointed by the Lord Chancellor and the lay members are appointed by the Secretary of State for Transport.
President (part-time), His Hon. Judge Main, QC
Legal members (£257 a day), His Hon. Judge Brodrick (*part-time*); R. Owen, QC
Lay members (£206 a day), T. W. Hall; J. W. Whitworth; G. Simms; Miss E. B. Haran; P. Rogers
Secretary, W. Thomas

VALUATION TRIBUNALS
c/o Warwickshire Valuation Tribunal, 2nd Floor, Walton House, 11 Parade, Leamington Spa, Warks CV32 4DG
Tel 01926-421875

The Valuation Tribunals hear appeals concerning the council tax, non-domestic rating and land drainage rates in England and Wales. They also have residual jurisdiction to hear appeals concerning the community charge, the pre-1990 rating list, disabled rating and mixed hereditaments. There are 56 tribunals in England, and eight in Wales. Each tribunal is a separate independent body; those in England are funded by the Department of the Environment and those in Wales by the Welsh Office. A separate tribunal is constituted for each hearing, and normally consists of a chairman and two other members. Members are appointed by the local authority/authorities, and serve on a voluntary basis. A National Committee of Valuation Tribunals considers all matters affecting valuations tribunals in England, and the President of the Council of Wales Valuation Tribunals performs the same function in Wales.
President, National Committee of Valuation Tribunals, A. H. W. Kennard
Secretary, National Committee of Valuation Tribunals, B. P. Massen
National President, Council of Wales Valuation Tribunal, P. J. Law

VAT AND DUTIES TRIBUNALS
15–19 Bedford Avenue, London WC1B 3AS
Tel 0171-631 4242

VAT and Duties Tribunals are administered by the Lord Chancellor's Department in England and Wales, and by the Secretary of State in Scotland. They are independent, and decide disputes between taxpayers and the Commissioners of Customs and Excise. In England and Wales, the president and chairmen are appointed by the Lord Chancellor and members are appointed by the Treasury. Chairmen in Scotland are appointed by the Lord President of the Court of Session.
President, His Hon. Stephen Oliver, QC
Vice-President, England and Wales (£66,621), A. W. Simpson
Vice-President, Scotland (£66,621), R. A. Bennett, CBE, QC
Vice-President, Northern Ireland (£66,621), D. C. Morgan, QC
Registrar, R. P. Lester

TRIBUNAL CENTRES
EDINBURGH, 44 Palmerston Place, Edinburgh EH12 5BJ. Tel: 0131-226 3551
LONDON (including Belfast), 15–19 Bedford Avenue, London WC1B 3AS. Tel: 0171-631 4242
MANCHESTER, Warwickgate House, Warwick Road, Old Trafford, Manchester M16 0GP. Tel: 0161-872 6471

The Police Service

There are 52 police forces in the United Kingdom, each responsible for policing in its area. Most forces' area is conterminous with one or more local authority areas. Policing in London is carried out by the Metropolitan Police and the City of London Police; in Northern Ireland by the Royal Ulster Constabulary; and by the Isle of Man, States of Jersey, and Guernsey forces in their respective islands and bailiwicks. National services include the National Criminal Intelligence Service and the National Missing Persons Bureau (see below).

Each police force is maintained by a police authority. The authorities of English and Welsh forces comprise local councillors, magistrates and independent members. In Scotland, there are eight joint police boards made up of local councillors. In London the authority for the Metropolitan Police is the Home Secretary, advised by the Metropolitan Police Committee; for the City of London Police the authority is a committee of the Corporation of London and includes councillors and magistrates. In Northern Ireland the Secretary of State appoints the police authority.

Police authorities are financed by central and local government grants and a precept on the council tax. Subject to the approval of the Home Secretary and to regulations, they appoint the chief constable. In England and Wales they are responsible for publishing annual policing plans and annual reports, setting local objectives and a budget, and levying the precept. The police authorities in Scotland are responsible for setting a budget, providing the resources necessary to police the area adequately, appointing officers of the rank of Assistant Chief Constable and above, and determining the number of officers and civilian staff in the force. The structure and responsibilities of the police authority in Northern Ireland are under review.

The Home Secretary and the Secretaries of State for Scotland and Northern Ireland are responsible for the organization, administration and operation of the police service. They make regulations covering matters such as police ranks, discipline, hours of duty, and pay and allowances. All police forces are subject to inspection by HM Inspectors of Constabulary, who report to the respective Secretary of State.

COMPLAINTS

The investigation and resolution of a serious complaint against a police officer in England and Wales is subject to the scrutiny of the Police Complaints Authority. An officer who is disciplined by his chief constable, whether as a result of a complaint or not, may appeal to the Home Secretary. In Scotland, chief constables are obliged to investigate a complaint against one of their officers; if there is a suggestion of criminal activity, the complaint is investigated by an independent public prosecutor. In Northern Ireland complaints are investigated by the Independent Commission for Police Complaints.

BASIC RATES OF PAY from 1 September 1996*

Chief Constable	
No fixed term	£59,742–£85,431
Fixed term appointment	£62,730–£89,598
Assistant Chief Constable-designate	80% of their Chief Constable's pay
Assistant Chief Constable	
No fixed term	£50,769–£58,278
Fixed term appointment	£53,310–£61,191
Superintendent	£38,724–£46,362
Chief Inspector	£32,937–£35,589*
Inspector	£29,466–£32,067*
Sergeant	£22,785–£26,574*
Constable	£14,916–£23,607*
Metropolitan Police	
Metropolitan Commissioner	£90,148
Deputy Commissioner	£83,712–£94,593
Assistant Commissioner	£75,699–£83,343
Commander	£50,769–£61,191

The rank of Chief Superintendent was abolished in April 1995. Existing appointments continue and receive the higher ranges of the pay scale for Superintendents

*These pay scales apply from 1 September 1996. Other pay scales apply from 1 September 1995; pay negotiations still in progress at time of going to press

THE SPECIAL CONSTABULARY

Each police force has its own special constabulary, made up of volunteers who work in their spare time. Special Constables have full police powers within their force and adjoining force areas, and assist regular officers with routine policing duties.

NATIONAL CRIMINAL INTELLIGENCE SERVICE

The function of the National Criminal Intelligence Service (NCIS) is to gather, collate and disseminate information and intelligence on serious crime of a regional national and international nature. It is independent of any other police organization.

Headquarters: Spring Gardens, 2 Citadel Place, London SEII 5EF. Tel: 0171-238 8000

Strength, 570

Director-General, A. H. Pacey, CBE, QPM

Deputy Director-General (Director (Intelligence)), J. P. Hamilton, QPM

Director, International Division, P. J. Byrne, MBE

Director, UK Division, P. L. Clay

Director, Resources Division, R. Creedon

NATIONAL MISSING PERSONS BUREAU

The Police National Missing Persons Bureau (PNMPB) acts as a central clearing house of information, receiving reports about vulnerable missing persons that are still outstanding after 28 days and details of unidentified persons or remains within 48 hours of being found from all forces in England and Wales. Reports are also received from Scottish police forces, the RUC, and foreign police forces via Interpol.

Headquarters: New Scotland Yard, Broadway, London SWIH 0BG. Tel: 0171-230 1212

Director, C. J. Coombes

FORENSIC SCIENCE SERVICE

A new national Forensic Science Service was created in April 1996 by the merger of the Forensic Science Service and the Metropolitan Police Forensic Science Laboratory. It provides support and advice for the investigation of scenes of crime, scientific analysis of material, and inter-

pretation of scientific results. Services are concentrated at sites in London, Birmingham, Chorley and Wetherby.
Headquarters: Priory House, Gooch Street North, Birmingham B5 6QQ. Tel: 0121-666 6606
Chief Executive, Dr J. Thompson

POLICE AUTHORITIES

Strength: actual strength of force as at mid 1996
Chair: chairman/convener of the police authority/police committee/joint police board

ENGLAND

AVON AND SOMERSET CONSTABULARY, *HQ,* PO Box 37, Valley Road, Portishead, Bristol BS20 8QJ. Tel: 01275-818181. *Strength,* 2,978; *Chief Constable,* D. J. Shattock, CBE, QPM; *Chair,* I. Hoddell

BEDFORDSHIRE POLICE, *HQ,* Woburn Road, Kempston, Bedford MK43 9AX. Tel: 01234-841212. *Strength,* 1,130; *Chief Constable,* M. O'Byrne, QPM; *Chair,* A. P. Hendry, CBE

CAMBRIDGESHIRE CONSTABULARY, *HQ,* Hinchingbrooke Park, Huntingdon, Cambs PE18 8NP. Tel: 01480-456111. *Strength,* 1,270; *Chief Constable,* D. G. Gunn, QPM; *Chair,* J. Reynolds

CHESHIRE CONSTABULARY, *HQ,* Nuns Road, Chester CH1 2PP. Tel: 01244-350000. *Strength,* 2,003; *Chief Constable,* J. M. Jones, QPM; *Chair,* R. Tilling

CLEVELAND CONSTABULARY, *HQ,* PO Box 70, Ladgate Lane, Middlesbrough TS8 9EH. Tel: 01642-326326. *Strength,* 1,428; *Chief Constable,* B. D. D. Shaw, QPM; *Chair,* A. Gwenlan

CUMBRIA CONSTABULARY, *HQ,* Carleton Hall, Penrith, Cumbria CA10 2AU. Tel: 01768-891999. *Strength,* 1,118; *Chief Constable,* A. G. Elliott, QPM; *Chair,* R. Watson

DERBYSHIRE CONSTABULARY, *HQ,* Butterley Hall, Ripley, Derbyshire DE5 3RS. Tel: 01773-570100. *Strength,* 1,765; *Chief Constable,* J. F. Newing, QPM; *Chair,* K. Wilkinson

DEVON AND CORNWALL CONSTABULARY, *HQ,* Middlemoor, Exeter EX2 7HQ. Tel: 0990-777444. *Strength,* 2,944; *Chief Constable,* J. S. Evans, QPM; *Chair,* B. Homer, OBE

DORSET POLICE FORCE, *HQ,* Winfrith, Dorchester, Dorset DT2 8DZ. Tel: 01929-462727. *Strength,* 1,269; *Chief Constable,* D. W. Aldous, QPM; *Chair,* Sir Stephen Hammick, Bt.

DURHAM CONSTABULARY, *HQ,* Aykley Heads, Durham DH1 5TT. Tel: 0191-386 4929. *Strength,* 1,404; *Chief Constable,* F. W. Taylor, QPM; *Chair,* J. Knox

ESSEX POLICE, *HQ,* PO Box 2, Springfield, Chelmsford CM2 6DA. Tel: 01245-491491. *Strength,* 2,915; *Chief Constable,* J. H. Burrow, CBE; *Chair,* E. Peel

GLOUCESTERSHIRE CONSTABULARY, *HQ,* Holland House, Lansdown Road, Cheltenham, Glos GL51 6QH. Tel: 01242-521321. *Strength,* 1,160; *Chief Constable,* A. J. P. Butler, QPM; *Chair,* R. Somers, PH.D.

GREATER MANCHESTER POLICE, *HQ,* PO Box 22 (S. West PDO), Chester House, Boyer Street, Manchester M16 0RE. Tel: 0161-872 5050. *Strength,* 7,186; *Chief Constable,* D. Wilmot, QPM; *Chair,* S. Murphy

HAMPSHIRE CONSTABULARY, *HQ,* West Hill, Winchester, Hants SO22 5DB. Tel: 01962-868133. *Strength,* 3,351; *Chief Constable,* J. C. Hoddinott, CBE, QPM; *Chair,* M. J. Clark

HERTFORDSHIRE CONSTABULARY, *HQ,* Stanborough Road, Welwyn Garden City, Herts AL8 6XF. Tel: 01707-354200. *Strength,* 1,716; *Chief Constable,* P. Sharpe, QPM; *Chair,* R. Gordon

HUMBERSIDE POLICE, *HQ,* Queens Gardens, Kingston upon Hull HU1 3DJ. Tel: 01482-326111. *Strength,* 2,036; *Chief Constable,* D. A. Leonard, QPM; *Chair,* I. A. Cawsey

KENT CONSTABULARY, *HQ,* Sutton Road, Maidstone, Kent ME15 9BZ. Tel: 01622-690690. *Strength,* 3,156; *Chief Constable,* J. D. Phillips, QPM; *Chair,* Sir John Grugeon

LANCASHIRE CONSTABULARY, *HQ,* PO Box 77, Hutton, Preston, Lancs PR4 5SB. Tel: 01772-614444. *Strength,* 3,202; *Chief Constable,* Mrs P. A. Clare, QPM; *Chair,* Mrs R. B. Henig

LEICESTERSHIRE CONSTABULARY, *HQ,* PO Box 999, Leicester LE99 1AZ. Tel: 0116-253 0066. *Strength,* 1,919; *Chief Constable,* K. Povey, QPM; *Chair,* R. A. Wann

LINCOLNSHIRE POLICE, *HQ,* PO Box 999, Lincoln LN5 7PH. Tel: 01522-532222. *Strength,* 1,176; *Chief Constable,* J. P. Bensley, QPM; *Chair,* R. Staples

MERSEYSIDE POLICE, *HQ,* PO Box 59, Canning Place, Liverpool L69 1JD. Tel: 0151-709 6010. *Strength,* 4,446; *Chief Constable,* Sir James Sharples, QPM; *Chair,* Ms C. Gustafason

NORFOLK CONSTABULARY, *HQ,* Martineau Lane, Norwich NR1 2DJ. Tel: 01603-768769. *Strength,* 1,392; *Chief Constable,* K. R. Williams, QPM; *Chair,* B. J. Landale

NORTHAMPTONSHIRE POLICE, *HQ,* Wootton Hall, Northampton NN4 0JQ. Tel: 01604-700700. *Strength,* 1,200; *Chief Constable,* new appointment awaited; *Chair,* Dr M. Dickie

NORTHUMBRIA POLICE, *HQ,* Ponteland, Newcastle upon Tyne NE20 0BL. Tel: 01661-872555. *Strength,* 3,736; *Chief Constable,* J. A. Stevens, QPM; *Chair,* G. Gill

NORTH YORKSHIRE POLICE, *HQ,* Newby Wiske Hall, Newby Wiske, Northallerton, N. Yorks DL7 9HA. Tel: 01609-783131. *Strength,* 1,331; *Chief Constable,* D. M. Burke, QPM; *Chair,* Mrs A. F. Harris

NOTTINGHAMSHIRE CONSTABULARY, *HQ,* Sherwood Lodge, Arnold, Nottingham NG5 8PP. Tel: 0115-967 0999. *Strength,* 2,367; *Chief Constable,* C. F. Bailey, QPM; *Chair,* C. P. Winterton

SOUTH YORKSHIRE POLICE, *HQ,* Snig Hill, Sheffield S3 8LY. Tel: 0114-276 8522. *Strength,* 4,825; *Chief Constable,* R. Wells, QPM; *Chair,* C. Swindells

STAFFORDSHIRE POLICE, *HQ,* Cannock Road, Stafford ST17 0QG. Tel: 01785-257717. *Strength,* 2,215; *Chief Constable,* J. W. Giffard; *Chair,* J. T. Meir

SUFFOLK CONSTABULARY, *HQ,* Martlesham Heath, Ipswich IP5 7QS. Tel: 01473-613500. *Strength,* 1,127; *Chief Constable,* A. T. Coe, QPM; *Chair,* M. N. Smith

SURREY POLICE, *HQ,* Mount Browne, Sandy Lane, Guildford, Surrey GU3 1HG. Tel: 01483-571212. *Strength,* 1,676; *Chief Constable,* D. J. Williams, QPM; *Chair,* A. C. Tisdall

SUSSEX POLICE, *HQ,* Malling House, Church Lane, Lewes, E. Sussex BN7 2DZ. Tel: 01273-475432. *Strength,* 3,099; *Chief Constable,* P. Whitehouse, QPM; *Chair,* Dr J. M. M. Walsh, RD

THAMES VALLEY POLICE, *HQ,* Oxford Road, Kidlington, Oxon OX5 2NX. Tel: 01865-846000. *Strength,* 3,724; *Chief Constable,* C. Pollard, QPM; *Chair,* Mrs D. J. Priestley

WARWICKSHIRE CONSTABULARY, *HQ,* PO Box 4, Leek Wootton, Warwick CV35 7QB. Tel: 01926-415000. *Strength,* 977; *Chief Constable,* P. D. Joslin, QPM; *Chair,* F. Pithie

WEST MERCIA CONSTABULARY, *HQ,* PO Box 55, Hindlip Hall, Hindlip, Worcester WR3 8SP. Tel: 01905-723000. *Strength,* 2,061; *Chief Constable,* D. C. Blakey, QPM; *Chair,* G. Raxster

WEST MIDLANDS POLICE, *HQ,* PO Box 52, Lloyd House, Colmore Circus, Queensway, Birmingham B4 6NQ. Tel: 0121-626 5000. *Strength,* 7,280; *Chief Constable,* E. Crew, QPM; *Chair,* R. Jones

WEST YORKSHIRE POLICE, *HQ,* PO Box 9, Laburnum
Road, Wakefield, W. Yorks WF1 3QP. Tel: 01924-375222.
Strength, 5,118; *Chief Constable,* K. Hellawell, QPM; *Chair,*
T. Brennan
WILTSHIRE CONSTABULARY, *HQ,* London Road, Devizes,
Wilts SN10 2DN. Tel: 01380-722341. *Strength,* 1,120; *Chief
Constable,* W. R. Girven, QPM; *Chair,* H. A. Woolnough

WALES

DYFED–POWYS POLICE, *HQ,* PO Box 99, Llangunnor,
Carmarthen, Dyfed SA31 2PF. Tel: 01267-222020.
Strength, 1,002; *Chief Constable,* R. White, CBE, QPM; *Chair,*
W. J. W. Evans
GWENT CONSTABULARY, *HQ,* Croesyceiliog, Cwmbran
NP44 2XJ. Tel: 01633-838111. *Strength,* 1,210; *Chief
Constable,* new appointment awaited; *Chair,* D. Turnbull
NORTH WALES POLICE, *HQ,* Glan-y-don, Colwyn Bay,
Clwyd LL29 8AW. Tel: 01492-517171. *Strength,* 1,381;
Chief Constable, M. J. Argent, QPM; *Chair,* G. Bartley
SOUTH WALES CONSTABULARY, *HQ,* Cowbridge Road,
Bridgend CF31 3SU. Tel: 01656-655555. *Strength,* 2,994;
Chief Constable, A. T. Burden, QPM; *Chair,* B. P. Murray

SCOTLAND

CENTRAL SCOTLAND POLICE, *HQ,* Randolphfield, Stirling
FK8 2HD. Tel: 01786-456000. *Strength,* 657; *Chief Constable,*
W. J. M. Wilson, QPM; *Convener,* Mrs J. Burness
DUMFRIES AND GALLOWAY CONSTABULARY, *HQ,*
Cornwall Mount, Dumfries DG1 1PZ. Tel: 01387-252112.
Strength, 383; *Chief Constable,* W. Rae; *Chair,* K. Cameron
FIFE CONSTABULARY, *HQ,* Detroit Road, Glenrothes, Fife
KY6 2RJ. Tel: 01592-418888. *Strength,* 797; *Chief Constable,*
J. P. Hamilton, QPM; *Chair,* A. Keddie
GRAMPIAN POLICE, *HQ,* Queen Street, Aberdeen AB10 1ZA.
Tel: 01224-639111. *Strength,* 1,166; *Chief Constable,*
I. T. Oliver, QPM, Ph.D.; *Chair,* Prof. J. Thomaneck
LOTHIAN AND BORDERS POLICE, *HQ,* Fettes Avenue,
Edinburgh EH4 1RB. Tel: 0131-311 3131. *Strength,* 2,519;
Chief Constable, R. Cameron, QPM; *Chair,* E. Drummond
NORTHERN CONSTABULARY, *HQ,* Perth Road, Inverness
IV2 3SY. Tel: 01463-715555. *Strength,* 643; *Chief Constable,*
W. A. Robertson, QPM; *Chair,* N. Graham
STRATHCLYDE POLICE, *HQ,* 173 Pitt Street, Glasgow
G2 4JS. Tel: 0141-532 2000. *Strength,* 7,216; *Chief
Constable,* J. Orr, OBE; *Chair,* W. Timoney
TAYSIDE POLICE, *HQ,* PO Box 59, West Bell Street,
Dundee DD1 9JU. Tel: 01382-223200. *Strength,* 1,090;
Chief Constable, W. A. Spence, QPM; *Chair,* A. Shand

NORTHERN IRELAND

ROYAL ULSTER CONSTABULARY, *HQ,* Brooklyn, Knock
Road, Belfast BT5 6LE. Tel: 01232-650222. *Strength,* 8,429;
Chief Constable, R. Flanagan; *Chair,* P. Armstrong

ISLANDS

ISLAND POLICE FORCE, *HQ,* Hospital Lane, St Peter Port,
Guernsey GY1 2QN. Tel: 01481-725111. *Strength,* 146;
Chief Officer (acting), Supt. G. W. Denning; *President, States
Committee for Home Affairs,* M. Torode
STATES OF JERSEY POLICE, *HQ,* Rouge Bouillon, PO Box
789, St Helier, Jersey JE2 3ZA. Tel: 01534-612612.
Strength, 243; *Chief Officer,* R. H. Le Breton; *Chair,*
M. Wavell
ISLE OF MAN CONSTABULARY, *HQ,* Glencrutchery Road,
Douglas, Isle of Man IM2 4RG. Tel: 01624-631212.
Strength, 213; *Chief Constable,* R. E. N. Oake; *Chairman,*
Police Committee, Hon. R. K. Corkill

METROPOLITAN POLICE SERVICE
New Scotland Yard, Broadway, London SW1H 0BG
Tel 0171-230 1212

Establishment, 27,994
Commissioner, Sir Paul Condon, QPM
Deputy Commissioner, B. Hayes, CBE, QPM
Receiver, P. Fletcher

OPERATIONAL AREAS
Assistant Commissioners, A. J. Speed, QPM (*Central*);
    B. H. Skitt, BEM, QPM (*North-West*); A. Dunn, QPM (*North-
    East*); W. I. R. Johnston, QPM (*South-East*); P. Manning,
    QPM (*South-West*)
Deputy Assistant Commissioners, D. Flanders, QPM;
    M. J. Sullivan, OBE, QPM
Commanders, D. M. T. Kendrick, QPM; J. F. Purnell, GM, QPM;
    T. D. Laidlaw, QPM; C. R. Pearman; A. L. Rowe, QPM;
    M. Briggs; M. R. Campbell; W. I. Griffiths, BEM; S. C.
    Pilkington; D. A. Ray, QPM; R. Gaspar; D. Gilbertson;
    Mrs J. Stichbury; J. Townsend

SPECIALIST OPERATIONS DEPARTMENT
Assistant Commissioner, D. C. Veness, QPM
Deputy Assistant Commissioners, J. A. Howley, QPM;
    A. G. Fry, QPM
Commanders, R. C. Marsh, QPM; B. G. Moss, QPM;
    J. G. D. Grieve; R. A. C. Ramm

COMPLAINTS INVESTIGATION BUREAU
Commander, I. G. Quinn

INSPECTORATE
Commander, B. J. Luckhurst

OTHER DEPARTMENTS
Director, Strategic Co-ordination, Mrs B. Reeves
Director, Personnel, Mrs H. Maslen
Director, Consultancy and Information Services, Mrs
    S. Merchant
Director, Public Affairs, Mrs S. Cullum
Solicitor, D. Hamilton
Director, Technology, N. Boothman
Director, Property Services, T. G. Lawrence

CITY OF LONDON POLICE
26 Old Jewry, London EC2R 8DJ
Tel 0171-601 2222

Strength (January 1996), 937
The City of London Police is responsible for policing the
City of London. Though small, the area includes one of the
most important financial centres in the world and the force
has particular expertise in areas such as fraud investigation
as well as the areas required of any police force.
    The force has a wholly elected police authority, the
police committee of the Corporation of London, which
appoints the Commissioner.
Commissioner (£91,764), W. Taylor, QPM
Assistant Commissioner (£71,577), P. Nove
Commander (£61,191), J. Davison
Chairman of Police Committee, Maj.-Gen. P. Maclellan, CB,
    CVO, MBE

BRITISH TRANSPORT POLICE
15 Tavistock Place, London WC1H 9SJ
Tel 0171-388 7541

Strength (March 1996), 2,165
British Transport Police is the national police force for the railways in England, Wales and Scotland, including the London Underground system and the Docklands Light Railway. The Chief Constable reports to the British Transport Police Committee. The members of the Committee are appointed by the British Railways Board, Railtrack and London Underground Ltd.
Chief Constable, D. O'Brien, OBE, QPM
Deputy Chief Constable, A. Parker, QPM

MINISTRY OF DEFENCE POLICE
MDP Wethersfield, Braintree, Essex CM7 4AZ
Tel 01371-854000

Strength (April 1996), 4,019
The Ministry of Defence Police is an agency of the Ministry of Defence. It is a national civilian police force whose officers are appointed by the Secretary of State for Defence. It is responsible for the policing of all military land, stations and establishments in the United Kingdom. The agency also has certain responsibilities for the civilian Ministry of Defence Guard Service.
Chief Constable, W. E. E. Boreham, OBE
Deputy Chief Constable, A. V. Comben
Head of Secretariat, J. A. Smallwood

ROYAL PARKS CONSTABULARY
The Old Police House, Hyde Park, London W2 2UH
Tel 0171-298 2000

Strength (May 1996), 177
The Royal Parks Constabulary is maintained by the Royal Parks Agency, an executive agency of the Department of National Heritage, and is responsible for the policing of eight royal parks in and around London. These comprise an area in excess of 6,300 acres. Officers of the force are appointed under the Parks Regulations Act 1872 as amended.
Chief Officer, W. Ross
Deputy Chief Officer, A. McLean

UK ATOMIC ENERGY AUTHORITY CONSTABULARY
Building E6, Culham Laboratory, Abingdon,
Oxon OX14 3DB
Tel 01235-463760

Strength (July 1996), 479
The Constabulary is responsible for policing UK Atomic Energy Authority and British Nuclear Fuels PLC establishments and for escorting nuclear material between establishments. The Chief Constable is responsible, through the Atomic Energy Authority Police Committee, to the President of the Board of Trade.
Chief Constable, A. J. Pointer, QPM
Assistant Chief Constable, W. H. Pryke

STAFF ASSOCIATIONS

ASSOCIATION OF CHIEF POLICE OFFICERS OF ENGLAND, WALES AND NORTHERN IRELAND, Room 311, Wellington House, 67–73 Buckingham Gate, London SW1E 6BE. Tel: 0171-230 7184. Represents Chief Constables, Deputy and Assistant Chief Constables in England, Wales and Northern Ireland, and officers of the rank of Commander and above in the Metropolitan and City of London Police. *General Secretary*, Miss M. C. E. Barton
THE POLICE SUPERINTENDENTS' ASSOCIATION OF ENGLAND AND WALES, 67A Reading Road, Pangbourne, Reading RG8 7JD. Tel: 01189-844005. Represents officers of the rank of Superintendent. *Secretary*, Chief Supt. D. A. Clark
THE POLICE FEDERATION OF ENGLAND AND WALES, 15–17 Langley Road, Surbiton, Surrey KT6 6LP. Tel: 0181-399 2224. Represents officers up to and including the rank of Chief Inspector. *General Secretary*, L. Williams
ASSOCIATION OF CHIEF POLICE OFFICERS IN SCOTLAND, Police Headquarters, Fettes Avenue, Edinburgh EH4 1RB. Tel: 0131-311 3051. Represents the Chief Constables, Deputy and Assistant Chief Constables of the Scottish police forces. *Hon. Secretary*, H. R. Cameron, QPM
THE ASSOCIATION OF SCOTTISH POLICE SUPERINTENDENTS, Secretariat, 173 Pitt Street, Glasgow G2 4JS. Tel: 0141-221 5796. Represents officers of the rank of Superintendent. *Hon. Secretary*, Chief Supt. A. Forrest
THE SCOTTISH POLICE FEDERATION, 5 Woodside Place, Glasgow G3 7QF. Tel: 0141-332 5234. Represents officers up to and including the rank of Chief Inspector. *General Secretary*, D. J. Keil, QPM
THE SUPERINTENDENTS' ASSOCIATION OF NORTHERN IRELAND, MSU RUC Station, Musgrave Street, Belfast BT1 3HX. Tel: 01232-700507. Represents Superintendents and Chief Superintendents in the RUC. *Hon. Secretary*, Supt. W. T. Brown
THE POLICE FEDERATION FOR NORTHERN IRELAND, Royal Ulster Constabulary, Garnerville, Garnerville Road, Belfast BT4 2NX. Tel: 01232-760831. Represents officers up to and including the rank of Chief Inspector. *Secretary*, D. A. McClurg

Crime Statistics

ENGLAND AND WALES

CRIMINAL JUSTICE STATISTICS 1994

Number of arrests	1,753,000,000
Notifiable offences recorded	5,036,000
Notifiable offences cleared up	1,320,000
Clear-up rate	26%
*Number of offenders cautioned	308,000
Defendants proceeded against at magistrates' courts	1,947,000
Defendants found guilty at magistrates' courts	1,340,000
Defendants tried at Crown Courts	86,000
Defendants found guilty at Crown Courts	68,000
Defendants sentenced at Crown Courts after summary conviction	3,000
Total offenders found guilty at both courts	1,408,000
*Total offenders found guilty or cautioned	1,716,000

*Excludes motoring offences

AVERAGE LENGTH OF SENTENCE 1994 *in months*

	Males aged 21 and over	Females aged 21 and over
Magistrates' courts	3.1	2.5–2.6
Crown court	21.6	18.6

OFFENDERS SENTENCED BY TYPE OF SENTENCE OR ORDER 1994

Absolute discharge	25,900
Conditional discharge	108,900
Fine	1,055,200
Probation order	50,500
Supervision order	9,200
Community service order	49,500
Attendance sentence order	7,300
Combination order	12,400
Young offender institution	16,800
Imprisonment:	
Suspended	3,200
Unsuspended	52,400
Otherwise dealt with	19,100
All sentences or orders: total	1,407,100
Of which:	
Immediate custody	69,200
Community sentences	128,900

Source: HMSO – *Criminal Statistics England and Wales 1994*

SCOTLAND

CRIMINAL JUSTICE STATISTICS 1994

Total crimes and offences recorded	990,981
Number of persons proceeded against	178,292
Persons with charge proved	158,119

PERSONS WITH CHARGE PROVED *by main penalty* 1994

Absolute discharge	430
Remit to children's hearing	122
Admonition or caution	15,967
Compensation order	1,659
Fine	112,428
Probation	6,011
Community service order	5,430
Insanity, hospital or guardianship order	118
Detention of child	28
Young offender institution	4,426
Prison	11,500
All penalties: total	158,119

Source: Scottish Office – *Annual Abstract of Statistics 1995*

POLICE STRENGTHS 1996

	Male	Female	Total
ENGLAND AND WALES			
Total officers	108,615	18,262	126,877
Ethnic minority officers	1,793	484	2,277
Special constables	12,803	6,925	19,728
Civilians	20,821	32,112	52,933
SCOTLAND			
Officers	12,627	1,885	14,512
Special constables	1,523	454	1,977
Civilians	1,539	2,518	4,057
NORTHERN IRELAND			
Officers	7,536	893	8,429
Special constables	977	545	1,522
Civilians	732	2,032	2,764

Sources: Home Office; Scottish Office; RUC

Defence

The armed forces of the United Kingdom comprise the Royal Navy, the Army and the Royal Air Force. The Queen is commander-in-chief of all the armed forces. The Ministry of Defence, headed by a Secretary of State, provides the support structure for the armed forces. Within the Ministry of Defence, the Defence Council has overall responsibility for running the armed forces. The Chief of Staff of each service reports through the Chief of the Defence Staff to the Secretary of State on matters relating to the running of his service. The Chief of Staff also chairs the executive committee of the appropriate service board, which manages the service in accordance with centrally-determined objectives and budgets. The military-civilian Central Staffs, headed by the Vice-Chief of the Defence Staff and the Second Permanent Under-Secretary of State, are responsible for policy, operational requirements, commitments, financial management, resource planning and civilian personnel management. The Procurement Executive is responsible for purchasing equipment. The Defence Intelligence Staff and the Defence Scientific Staff also form part of the Ministry of Defence.

As a result of the 1994 'Front Line First' defence costs study, the Ministry of Defence has been restructured and a permanent Joint Headquarters for the conduct of joint operations was set up at Northwood in April 1996. The Joint Headquarters connects the policy and strategic functions of the MoD Head Office with the conduct of operations and strengthens the policy/executive division.

ARMED FORCES STRENGTHS *as at 1 April 1996*

All Services	222,417
Men	206,660
Women	15,757
Royal Naval Services	48,307
Men	44,676
Women	3,631
Army	109,387
Men	102,858
Women	6,529
Royal Air Force	64,723
Men	59,126
Women	5,597

DEPLOYMENT; *as at April 1996*

Outside Great Britain, army units were stationed in the south Atlantic, Belize, Brunei, Cyprus, the Falkland Islands, Germany, Gibraltar, the Gulf, Hong Kong (the Brigade of Gurkhas), Northern Ireland and Turkey. Royal Air Force units were stationed in the central Atlantic, the eastern Atlantic and North Sea, the Channel, Cyprus, the Falkland Islands, Germany, Gibraltar, the Gulf, Hong Kong, Italy, Northern Ireland, Turkey and the former Yugoslavia.

Members of the British armed forces were also deployed with the United Nations Force in Cyprus (UNFICYP), the United Nations Iraq-Kuwait Observer Mission (UNIKOM), the Implementation Force in the former Yugoslavia (IFOR) and as military observers with the United Nations Mission in Georgia/Organization for Security and Co-operation in Europe (UNOMIG/OSCE).

DEFENCE CUTS

*DEFENCE CASH PROVISION IN REAL TERMS

	£ million
1994–5 outturn	22,562
1995–6 estimated outturn	20,653
1996–7 plans	20,293
1997–8 plans	20,258

*At 1994–5 prices, based on GDP assumptions in the 1996–7 Financial Statement and Budget Report

SERVICE PERSONNEL

	Royal Navy	Army	RAF
1990 strength	63,200	152,800	89,700
1991 target for 1995	55,000	116,000	75,000
July 1994 target for 2000	49,100	117,800	62,500
May 1995 plans for 1996	48,000	117,000	66,500
May 1996 plans for 1 April 1997	46,000	111,000	57,000

MoD CIVILIAN PERSONNEL

1990–1 level	170,642
February 1994 level	144,010
April 1994 target for 1996	128,700
1 April 1996 level	127,700
July 1994 target for 2000	121,600
May 1996 target for 2002	115,800

MINISTRY OF DEFENCE

Main Building, Whitehall, London SW1A 2HB
Tel 0171-218 6645

For ministerial and civil service salaries, *see* page 277
For Services salaries, *see* pages 390–2

Secretary of State for Defence, The Rt. Hon. Michael Portillo, MP
  Private Secretary, Ms M. Aldred
  Special Adviser, Ms A. Broom
  Parliamentary Private Secretary, D. Ames, MP
Minister of State for the Armed Forces, The Hon. Nicholas Soames, MP
  Private Secretary, D. King
Minister of State for Defence Procurement, The Rt. Hon. James Arbuthnot, MP
  Private Secretary, J. Wright
Parliamentary Private Secretary to Mr Soames and Mr Arbuthnot, N. Hawkins, MP
Parliamentary Under-Secretary of State, The Earl Howe
  Private Secretary, G. Dean
Permanent Under-Secretary of State (G1), R. C. Mottram
  Private Secretary, D. Stephens
Chief of the Defence Staff, Field Marshal Sir Peter Inge, GCB (*until early 1997*)

THE DEFENCE COUNCIL

The Defence Council is responsible for running the Armed Forces. It is chaired by the Secretary of State for Defence and consists of: the Ministers of State; the Parliamentary Under-Secretary of State; the Permanent Under-Secretary of State; the Chief of the Defence Staff; the Chief of the

Naval Staff; the Chief of the General Staff; the Chief of the Air Staff; the Vice-Chief of the Defence Staff; the Chief Scientific Adviser; the Chief of Defence Procurement; and the Second Permanent Under-Secretary of State.

CHIEFS OF STAFF

CHIEF OF THE NAVAL STAFF

Chief of the Naval Staff and First Sea Lord, Adm. Sir Jock Slater, GCB, LVO, ADC
Asst Chief of the Naval Staff, Rear-Adm. J. J. Blackham

CHIEF OF THE GENERAL STAFF

Chief of the General Staff, Gen. Sir Charles Guthrie, GCB, LVO, OBE, ADC *(Gen.)*
Asst Chief of the General Staff, Maj.-Gen. M. A. Willcocks
Director-General, Development and Doctrine, Lt.-Gen. M. D. Jackson, CBE

CHIEF OF THE AIR STAFF

Chief of the Air Staff, Air Chief Marshal Sir Michael Graydon, GCB, CBE, ADC
Asst Chief of the Air Staff, Air Vice-Marshal T. I. Jenner, CB
British-American Community Relations, Air Marshal Sir John Kemball (retd)
Chief Executive, National Air Traffic Services (G2), D. J. McLauchlan

CENTRAL STAFFS

Vice-Chief of the Defence Staff, Air Chief Marshal Sir John Willis, KCB, CBE
Second Permanent Under-Secretary of State (G1A), Sir Moray Stewart, KCB
Defence Services Secretary, Air Vice-Marshal P. J. Harding, CB, CBE, AFC
Deputy CDS (Commitments), Lt.-Gen. Sir Alexander Harley, KBE, CB
Asst Under-Secretary (Home and Overseas) (G3), B. R. Hawtin
Asst CDS (Operations), Air Vice-Marshal A. J. Harrison
Asst CDS (Logistics), Maj.-Gen. G. A. Ewer
Deputy CDS (Systems), Vice-Adm. J. H. Dunt
Asst CDS, Operational Requirements (Sea Systems), Rear-Adm. R. T. R. Phillips
Asst CDS, Operational Requirements (Land Systems), Maj.-Gen. E. F. G. Burton, OBE
Asst CDS, Operational Requirements (Air Systems), Air Vice-Marshal C. C. C. Coville, CB
Director-General, Information and Communications Services, Maj.-Gen. W. J. P. Robins, OBE
Deputy CDS (Programmes and Personnel), Air Marshal P. T. Squire, DFC, AFC
Asst CDS (Programmes), Rear-Admiral N. R. Essenhigh
Surgeon-General, Surgeon Vice-Adm. A. L. Revell, QHS
Chief Executive, Defence Dental Agency, Air Vice-Marshal J. Mackey, QHDS
Director, Defence Nursing Services, Air Cdre V. M. Hand
Director-General, Defence Medical Training, Maj.-Gen. C. G. Callow
Deputy Under-Secretary (Policy) (G2), R. P. Hatfield, CBE
Asst Under-Secretary (Policy) (G3), G. W. Hopkinson
Asst CDS (Policy), Air Vice-Marshal J. C. French

DEFENCE INFORMATION STAFF

Press Secretary and Chief of Information (G4), Ms G. Samuel
Deputy Press Secretary and Director of Information (Policy and Procurement) (G5), I. Lee
Director, Public Relations (Navy), Capt. C. Beagley, RN
Director, Public Relations (Army), Brig. P. C. C. Trousdell
Director, Public Relations (RAF), Air Cdre G. L. McRobbie

MANAGEMENT AND FINANCE

Deputy Under-Secretaries (G2), J. F. Howe, CB, OBE *(Civilian Management);* R. T. Jackling, CB, CBE *(Resources, Finance and Programmes)*
Defence Housing Executive (G3), C. J. I. James
Asst Under-Secretaries (G3), D. C. R. Heyhoe *(General Finance);* I. D. Fauset *(Civilian Personnel Management);* B. A. E. Taylor *(Civilian Policy Management);* C. V. Balmer *(Financial Management);* Miss A. Walker *(Service Personnel);* vacant *(Director-General of Management and Organization);* D. J. Seammen *(Programmes);* D. Fisher *(Systems);* A. Inglese *(Legal Adviser)*
Defence Estate Organization (G4), J. Mustow *(Works);* A. Boardman *(Land)*
Chief Statistical Adviser and Chief Executive of Defence Analytical Services Agency, P. Altobell
Chief Executive, Defence Bills Agency, T. R. Thurgate

DEFENCE INTELLIGENCE STAFF

Chief of Defence Intelligence
Director-General, Intelligence (Assessments)
Director-General, Scientific and Technical Intelligence
Director-General, Management and Support of Intelligence
Director-General, Intelligence Geographic Resources
Director, Defence Intelligence (Secretariat) (G5)

DEFENCE SCIENTIFIC STAFF

Chief Scientific Adviser (G1A), Prof. Sir David Davies, KBE
Chief Scientist (G2), P. D. Ewins, CB
Nuclear Weapon Safety Adviser (G2), Dr A. Ferguson
Deputy Chief Scientists (G3), P. M. Sutcliffe *(Research and Technology);* M. Earwicker *(Scrutiny and Analysis)*
Asst Chief Scientific Adviser (Nuclear) (G4), P. W. Roper
Chief Executive, Defence Evaluation and Research Agency (G2), J. A. R. Chisholm

SECOND SEA LORD/COMMANDER-IN-CHIEF NAVAL HOME COMMAND

Second Sea Lord and C.-in-C. Naval Home Command, Adm. Sir Michael Boyce, KCB, OBE
Director-General, Naval Personnel (Strategy and Plans) and Chief of Staff to Second Sea Lord, Rear-Adm. R. B. Lees
Asst Under-Secretary (Naval Personnel) (G3), J. M. Moss, CB
Flag Officer Training and Recruiting, Rear-Adm. J. H. S. McAnally, LVO
Naval Secretary and Director-General, Naval Manning, Rear-Adm. F. M. Malbon
Director-General, Naval Medical Services, Surgeon Rear-Adm. A. Craig, QHP
Director-General, Naval Chaplaincy Services, Ven. M. W. Bucks, QHC

NAVAL SUPPORT COMMAND

Chief of Fleet Support, Vice-Adm. Sir Toby Frere, KCB
Asst Under-Secretary (Fleet Support) (G3), D. J. Gould
Director-General, Fleet Support (Ships) (G3), R. V. Babbington
Director-General, Naval Bases and Supply (N), Rear-Adm. J. A. Trewby
Director-General, Naval Bases and Supply and Chief Inspector of Explosives (G4), D. J. Stevens
Director-General, Fleet Support (Operations and Plans), Rear-Adm. P. Spencer
Director-General, Aircraft (Navy), Rear-Adm. D. J. Wood
Flag Officer Scotland, N. England and N. Ireland, Rear-Adm. J. G. Tolhurst, CB

Hydrographer of the Royal Navy and Chief Executive,
Hydrographic Office, Rear-Adm. J. P. Clarke, CB, LVO, MBE

COMMANDER-IN-CHIEF FLEET

C.-in-C. Fleet, Adm. Sir Peter Abbott, KCB
Deputy Commander Fleet and Chief of Staff, Vice-Adm. Sir
  Jonathan Tod, KCB, CBE
Chief of Staff (Operations) and Flag Officer Submarines, Rear-
  Adm. J. F. Perowne
Flag Officer Surface Flotilla, Vice-Adm. J. R. Brigstocke
Flag Officer Sea Training, Rear-Adm. P. M. Franklyn
Flag Officer Naval Aviation, Rear-Adm. T. W. Loughran
Commandant-General, Royal Marines, Maj.-Gen. D. A. S.
  Pennefather, CB, OBE

QUARTERMASTER-GENERAL'S DEPARTMENT

Quartermaster-General, Lt.-Gen. S. Cowan, CBE
Chief of Staff, Maj.-Gen. K. O'Donoghue, CBE
Asst Under-Secretary (Quartermaster) (G3), N. H. R. Evans
Director-General, Logistic Support (Army), Maj.-Gen.
  M. S. White, CBE
Director-General, Equipment (Army), Maj.-Gen.
  P. J. G. Corp, CB
Chief Executive, Logistics Information Systems Agency, Brig.
  A. W. Pollard
Chief Executive, Defence Postal and Courier Service, Brig.
  T. M. Brown, OBE
Chief Executive, Defence Transport and Movements Executive,
  Brig. M. G. R. Hodson, CBE
Chief Executive, Defence Clothing and Textiles Agency, Brig.
  M. J. Roycroft

ADJUTANT-GENERAL'S DEPARTMENT

Adjutant-General, Gen. Sir Michael Rose, KCB, CBE, DSO,
  QGM
Chief of Staff to the Adjutant-General, Maj.-Gen. R. A. Oliver,
  OBE
Director-General, Army Manning and Recruiting, Maj.-Gen.
  D. L. Burden, CB, CBE
Chaplain-General, Revd Dr V. Dobbins
Director, Army Legal Services, Maj.-Gen. A. P. V. Rogers, OBE
Head, Command Secretariat (G4), W. A. Perry
Military Secretary, Maj.-Gen. M. I. E. Scott, CBE, DSO
Director-General, Army Medical Services, Maj.-Gen. W. R.
  Short
Director-General, Individual Training, and Chief Executive,
  Army Individual Training Organization, Maj.-Gen. C. L.
  Elliott, MBE
Commandant, Royal Military Academy, Sandhurst, Maj.-Gen.
  J. F. Deverell, OBE
Commandant, Royal Military College of Science, Maj.-Gen.
  D. J. M. Jenkins, CBE

COMMANDER-IN-CHIEF LAND COMMAND

Commander-in-Chief, Land Command, Gen. Sir Roger
  Wheeler, KCB, CBE
Deputy Commander-in-Chief, Land Command, and Inspector-
  General, Territorial Army, Lt.-Gen. H. W. R. Pike, DSO,
  MBE
Chief of Staff, HQ Land Command, Maj.-Gen. C. G. C.
  Vyvyan, CBE
Deputy Chief of Staff, HQ Land Command, Maj.-Gen. R. A.
  Cordy-Simpson
Command Secretariat (G3), J. S. Pitt-Brooke

HQ STRIKE COMMAND

Air Officer Commanding-in-Chief, Air Chief Marshal Sir
  William Wratten, KBE, CB, AFC
Chief of Staff and Deputy Commander-in-Chief, Air Marshal
  G. A. Robertson, CBE
Senior Air Staff Officer, Air Vice-Marshal D. A. Hurrell
Air Officer Administration, Air Vice-Marshal T. B.
  Sherrington, OBE
Air Officer Commanding, No. 1 Group, Air Vice-Marshal
  J. R. Day
Air Officer Engineering and Supply, Air Vice-Marshal
  D. J. Saunders, CBE
Air Officer Commanding, No. 11/18 Group, Air Vice-Marshal
  C. R. Spink
Head, Command Secretariat (G5), J. P. Thatcher

HQ LOGISTIC COMMAND

Air Officer Commanding-in-Chief and Air Member for Logistics,
  Air Chief Marshal Sir John Allison, KCB, CBE
Chief of Staff, Land Command, Air Vice-Marshal C. G.
  Terry, CB, OBE
Air Officer Communications Information Systems and Air Officer
  Commanding Signals Units, Air Vice-Marshal B. C.
  McCandless
Director-General, Support Management (RAF), Air Vice-
  Marshal P. D. Markey
Command Secretary (G3), H. Griffiths
Chief Executive, RAF Maintenance Group Agency, Air Vice-
  Marshal R. H. Kyle, MBE

HQ PERSONNEL AND TRAINING COMMAND

Air Member for Personnel and Air Officer Commanding-in-
  Chief, Air Marshal Sir David Cousins, KCB, AFC
Chief of Staff and Director-General, Strategic Policy and Plans,
  Air Vice-Marshal M. D. Smart
Air Officer Training, Air Vice-Marshal J. A. G. May, CB, CBE
Air Secretary, Air Vice-Marshal R. P. O'Brien, OBE
Commandant, RAF Staff College, Bracknell, Air Vice-Marshal
  M. Van der Veen
Commandant, RAF Staff College, Cranwell, Air Vice-Marshal
  A. J. Stables
Director-General, Medical Services (RAF), Air Vice-Marshal
  J. A. Baird, QHP
Director, Legal Services (RAF), Air Vice-Marshal
  G. W. Carleton
Chaplain-in-Chief (RAF), Ven. P. R. Turner, QHC

PROCUREMENT EXECUTIVE

EXECUTIVE

Chief of Defence Procurement, Vice-Adm. Sir Robert
  Walmsley, KCB
Director-General, Land Systems and Master-General of the
  Ordnance, Lt.-Gen. Sir Robert Hayman-Joyce, KCB, CBE
Deputy Chief of Defence Procurement (Operations), Air Marshal
  Sir Roger Austin, KCB, AFC
Deputy Chief of Defence Procurement (Support) (G3),
  M. J. V. Bell

BUSINESS UNITS

Director-General (Business Strategy) (G3), J. A. Gulvin, CB
Director-General (Finance) (G3), B. Miller
President of the Ordnance Board, Air Vice-Marshal P. J.
  O'Reilly
Director-General, Commercial Directorate (G3), A. T. Phipps
Principal Director, Pricing and Quality Services (G4), N. J.
  Bennett

Director-General, Submarines (G3), C. V. Betts
Director-General, Surface Ships and Acting Controller of the Navy, Rear-Adm. F. P. Scourse, MBE
Director-General, Surface Weapons (Naval) (G4), A. M. Stagg
Chief, Strategic Systems Executive, Rear-Adm. P. A. M. Thomas
Director-General (Nuclear) (G4), Dr D. R. Glue
Director, Nuclear Projects (G4), R. A. Russell
Director-General, Command Information Systems (G3), J. D. Maines
Director-General, Air Systems 1, Air Vice-Marshal P. C. Norriss, CB, AFC
Director-General, Air Systems 2 (G3), G. E. Roe
Director-General, Weapons and Electronic Systems (G3), G. N. Beaven
Head of Defence Export Services (G2), C. B. G. Masefield
Military Deputy to Head of DES, Rear-Adm. J. F. T. G. Salt (retd)
Director-General, Marketing (G3), D. J. Bowen
Asst Under-Secretary (Export Policy and Finance) (G4), Dr A. M. Fox
Director-General, Saudi Armed Forces Project, Air Marshal I. D. Macfadyen, CB, OBE
Principal Directors of Contracts (G4), P. A. Gerard (*Navy*); A. V. Carey (*Ordnance*); S. L. Porter (*Air*)

DEFENCE AGENCIES

ARMY BASE REPAIR ORGANIZATION, Monxton Road, Andover, Hants SP11 8HT. Tel: 01264-383295. *Chief Executive*, J. R. Drew, CBE
ARMY BASE STORAGE AND DISTRIBUTION AGENCY, Monxton Road, Andover, Hants SP11 8HT. Tel: 01264-383334. *Chief Executive*, Brig. K. J. W. Goad, ADC
ARMY INDIVIDUAL TRAINING ORGANIZATION, Trenchard Lines, Upavon, Pewsey, Wilts SN9 6BE. Tel: 01980-615024. *Chief Executive*, Maj.-Gen. C. L. Elliott, MBE
ARMY TECHNICAL SUPPORT AGENCY, Room 23/11, Portway, Monxton Road, Andover, Hants SP11 8HT. Tel: 01264-383161. *Chief Executive*, J. R. Prince
DEFENCE ANALYTICAL SERVICES AGENCY, Northumberland House, Northumberland Avenue, London WC2N 5BP. Tel: 0171-218 0729. *Chief Executive*, P. Altobell
DEFENCE ANIMAL CENTRE, Welby Lane, Melton Mowbray, Leics LE13 0SL. Tel: 01664-410694. *Chief Executive*, Col. A. H. Roache
DEFENCE BILLS AGENCY, Room 410, Mersey House, Drury Lane, Liverpool L2 7PX. Tel: 0151-242 2234. *Chief Executive*, T. R. Thurgate
DEFENCE CLOTHING AND TEXTILES AGENCY, Monxton Road, Andover, Hants SP11 8HT. Tel: 01264-382216. *Chief Executive*, Brig. M. J. Roycroft
DEFENCE DENTAL AGENCY, Room 102, Lacon House, Theobalds Road, London WC1X 8RY. Tel: 0171-305 5733. *Chief Executive*, Air Vice-Marshal J. Mackey, QHDS
DEFENCE EVALUATION AND RESEARCH AGENCY, Farnborough, Hants GU14 6TD. Tel: 01252-392000. *Chief Executive*, J. A. R. Chisholm
DEFENCE MEDICAL SUPPLIES AGENCY, Defence Medical Equipment Depot, Drummond Barracks, Ludgershall, Andover, Hants SP11 9RU. Tel: 01264-798606. *Chief Executive*, B. Nimick
DEFENCE POSTAL AND COURIER SERVICE, Inglis Barracks, Mill Hill, London NW7 1PX. Tel: 0181-818 6300. *Director and Chief Executive*, Brig. T. M. Brown, OBE
DEFENCE SECONDARY CARE AGENCY, Room 1216, Empress State Building, Lillie Road, London SW6 1TR. Tel: 0171-305 6190. *Chief Executive*, R. Smith

DEFENCE TRANSPORT AND MOVEMENTS EXECUTIVE, Monxton Road, Andover, Hants SP11 8HT. Tel: 01264-382139. *Chief Executive*, Brig. M. G. R. Hodson, CBE
DISPOSAL SALES AGENCY, 7th Floor, 6 Hercules Road, London SED J. Tel: 0171-261 8853. *Chief Executive*, M. Westgate
HYDROGRAPHIC OFFICE, ADMIRALTY WAY, Taunton, Somerset TAI 2DN. Tel: 01823-337900. *Chief Executive, and Hydrographer of the Royal Navy*, Rear-Adm. J. P. Clarke, CB, LVO, MBE
JOINT AIR RECONNAISSANCE INTELLIGENCE CENTRE, RAF Brampton, Huntingdon, Cambs PE18 8QL. Tel: 01480-52151. *Chief Executive*, Gp Capt N. J. Pearson
LOGISTIC INFORMATION SYSTEMS AGENCY, Monxton Road, Andover, Hants SP11 8HT. Tel: 01264-382815. *Chief Executive*, Brig. A. W. Pollard
METEOROLOGICAL OFFICE, London Road, Bracknell, Berks RG12 2SZ. Tel: 01344-420242. *Chief Executive*, Prof. J. C. R. Hunt, FRS
MILITARY SURVEY, Elmwood Avenue, Feltham, Middx TW13 7AH. Tel: 0181-818 2193. *Chief Executive*, Brig. P. R. Wildman, OBE
MINSTRY OF DEFENCE POLICE, Wethersfield, Braintree, Essex CM7 4AZ. Tel: 01371-854000. *Chief Executive*, Chief Constable W. E. E. Boreham, OBE
NAVAL AIRCRAFT REPAIR ORGANIZATION, Royal Naval Yard, Fleetlands, Gosport, Hants PO13 0AW. Tel: 01705-544910. *Chief Executive*, Capt. W. S. Graham, RN
NAVAL RECRUITING AND TRAINING AGENCY, Victory Building, HM Naval Base, Portsmouth, Hants PO1 3LS. Tel: 01705-727602. *Chief Executive*, Rear-Adm. J. H. S. McAnally, LVO
PAY AND PERSONNEL AGENCY, Warminster Road, Bath BA1 5AA. Tel: 01225-828105. *Chief Executive*, M. A. Rowe
RAF MAINTENANCE GROUP AGENCY, RAF Brampton, Huntingdon, Cambs PE18 8QL. Tel: 01480-52151 ext. 6300. *Chief Executive*, Air Vice-Marshal R. H. Kyle, MBE
RAF SIGNALS ENGINEERING ESTABLISHMENT, RAF Henlow, Beds SG16 6DN. Tel: 01462-851515 ext. 7625. *Chief Executive*, Air Cdre P. C. Ayee
RAF TRAINING GROUP AGENCY, RAF Innsworth, Gloucester GL3 1EZ. Tel: 01452-712612 ext. 5302. *Chief Executive*, Air Vice-Marshal J. A. G. May, CB, CBE
SERVICE CHILDREN'S EDUCATION, BFPO 140. Tel: 00-49 2161 473296. *Chief Executive*, I. S. Mitchelson

The Royal Navy

LORD HIGH ADMIRAL OF THE UNITED KINGDOM
HM The Queen

ADMIRALS OF THE FLEET

HRH The Prince Philip, Duke of Edinburgh, KG, KT, OM, GBE, AC, QSO, PC, *apptd* 1953
The Lord Hill-Norton, GCB, *apptd* 1971
Sir Michael Pollock, GCB, LVO, DSC, *apptd* 1974
Sir Edward Ashmore, GCB, DSC, *apptd* 1977
The Lord Lewin, KG, GCB, LVO, DSC, *apptd* 1979
Sir Henry Leach, GCB, *apptd* 1982
Sir William Staveley, GCB, *apptd* 1989
Sir Julian Oswald, GCB, *apptd* 1993
Sir Benjamin Bathurst, GCB, *apptd* 1995

ADMIRALS

Slater, Sir Jock, GCB, LVO, ADC (*Chief of the Naval Staff and First Sea Lord*)
White, Sir Hugo, GCB, CBE (*Governor and C.-in-C. Gibraltar*)

Boyce, Sir Michael, KCB, OBE, ADC (*C.-in-C. Naval Home Command and Second Sea Lord*)
Abbott, Sir Peter, KCB (*C.-in-C. Fleet*)

VICE-ADMIRALS

Frere, Sir Toby, KCB (*Chief of Fleet Support*)
Moore, M. A. C., LVO (*Chief of Staff to Commander, Allied Naval Forces Southern Europe*)
Walmsley, Sir Robert, KCB (*Chief of Defence Procurement*)
Revell, A. I., QHS (*Surgeon-General*)
Tod, Sir Jonathan, KCB, CBE (*Deputy Comd. Fleet and Chief of Staff*)
Gretton, M. P. (*Supreme Allied Commander Atlantic's Representative in Europe*)
Dunt, J. H. (*Deputy CDS (Systems)*)
Brigstocke, J. R. (*Flag Officer Surface Flotilla*)
Garnett, I. D. G. (*Military Assistant, Supreme Allied Commander Atlantic*)

REAR-ADMIRALS

Wilkinson, N. J., CB (*Commandant, Joint Services Defence College*)
Tolhurst, J. G., CB (*Flag Officer Scotland, N. England and N. Ireland*)
Blackham, J. J. (*Asst Chief of Naval Staff*)
Essenhigh, N. R. (*Asst CDS (Programmes)*)
Craig, A., QHP (*Director-General, Naval Medical Services*)
Haddacks, P. K. (*Asst CDS (Policy and Requirements) to Supreme Allied Commander Europe*)
West, A. W. J., DSC (*Commander, UK Task Group*)
Trewby, J. A. (*Director-General Naval Bases and Supply*)
Clarke, J. P., CB, LVO, MBE (*Hydrographer of the Navy and Chief Executive, Hydrographic Office Defence Support Agency*)
Blackburn, D. A. J. (*Head of British Defence Staff Washington*)
Scourse, F. P., MBE (*Director-General, Surface Ships and Acting Controller of the Navy*)
Franklyn, P. M. (*Flag Officer Sea Training*)
Perowne, J. F. (*Chief of Staff (Operations), Flag Officer Submarines, COMSUBEASTLANT and COMSUBNORTHWEST*)
Wood, D. J. (*Director-General, Aircraft (Navy)*)
Lees, R. B. (*Director-General, Naval Personnel (Strategy and Plans) and Chief of Staff to Second Sea Lord*)
Spencer, P. (*Director-General, Fleet Support (Operations and Plans)*)
Loughran, T. W. (*Flag Officer Naval Aviation*)
Thomas, P. A. M. (*Chief, Strategic Systems Executive*)
Malbon, F. M. (*Naval Secretary and Director-General, Naval Manning*)
Armstrong, J. H. A. J. (*Senior Naval Member, Royal College of Defence Studies*)
McAnally, J. H. S., LVO (*Flag Officer Training and Recruiting*)
Phillips, R. T. R. (*Asst CDS Operational Requirements (Sea Systems)*)
Ross, A. B. (*Asst Director Operations Divn International Military Staff*)

HM FLEET AS AT 1 APRIL 1996

SUBMARINES

TRIDENT
Operational: Vanguard, Victorious*

POLARIS
Operational: Repulse

FLEET
Operational: Sceptre, Spartan, Splendid, Talent, Trafalgar, Trenchant, Triumph
Refitting/standby: Sovereign, Superb, Tireless, Torbay, Turbulent

ANTI-SUBMARINE WARFARE (ASW) CARRIERS
Operational: Illustrious, Invincible
Refitting/standby: Ark Royal

ASSAULT SHIPS
Operational: Fearless
Refitting/standby: Intrepid

DESTROYERS

TYPE 42
Operational: Birmingham, Edinburgh, Exeter, Glasgow, Gloucester, Liverpool, Manchester, Nottingham, Southampton, York
Refitting/standby: Cardiff, Newcastle

FRIGATES

TYPE 23
Operational: Argyll, Iron Duke, Lancaster, Marlborough, Monmouth, Montrose, Northumberland, Richmond*, Somerset*, Westminster
Refitting/standby: Norfolk

TYPE 22
Operational: Battleaxe, Beaver, Boxer, Brave, Brazen, Brilliant, Campbeltown, Chatham, Cornwall, Cumberland, London, Sheffield
Refitting/standby: Coventry

OFFSHORE PATROL

CASTLE CLASS
Operational: Dumbarton Castle, Leeds Castle

ISLAND CLASS
Operational: Alderney, Anglesey, Guernsey, Lindisfarne, Orkney, Shetland

MINEHUNTERS

HUNT CLASS
Operational: Atherstone, Berkeley, Bicester, Brecon, Chiddingfold, Cottesmore, Dulverton, Hurworth, Ledbury, Middleton, Quorn
Refitting/standby: Brocklesby, Cattistock

SANDOWN CLASS
Operational: Bridport, Cromer, Inverness, Sandown, Walney

PATROL CRAFT

PEACOCK CLASS
Operational: Peacock, Plover, Starling

RIVER CLASS
Operational: Arun, Blackwater, Itchen, Orwell, Spey

COASTAL TRAINING CRAFT †
Operational: Archer, Biter, Blazer, Charger, Dasher, Example, Exploit, Explorer, Express, Loyal Chancellor, Loyal Watcher, Puncher, Pursuer, Smiter

---

*   Engaged in trials or training
†   Operated by the University Royal Naval Units

GIBRALTAR SEARCH AND RESCUE CRAFT
Operational: Ranger, Trumpeter

ROYAL YACHT

Operational: Britannia

ICE PATROL SHIP

Operational: Endurance

SURVEY SHIPS

Operational: Bulldog, Gleaner, Hecla, Herald
Refitting/standby: Beagle, Roebuck

SOLD/DECOMMISSIONED 1995–6

Renown

OTHER PARTS OF THE NAVAL SERVICE

ROYAL MARINES

The Royal Marines were formed in 1664 and are part of the
Naval Service. Their primary purpose is to conduct
amphibious and land warfare. The principal operational
units are 3 Commando Brigade Royal Marines, an
amphibious all-arms brigade trained to operate in arduous
environments, which is a core element of the UK's Joint
Rapid Reaction Force; Comacchio Group Royal Marines,
which is responsible for the security of nuclear weapon
facilities; and Special Boat Service Royal Marines, the
maritime special forces. The Royal Marines also provide
detachments for warships and land-based naval parties as
required. The Royal Marines Band Service provides
military musical support for the Naval Service. The
headquarters of the Royal Marines is at Portsmouth, along
with the Royal Marines School of Music, and principal
bases are at Plymouth, Arbroath, Poole, Taunton and
Chivenor. The Corps of Royal Marines is about 6,500
strong.
Commandant-General, Royal Marines, Maj.-Gen. D. A. S.
Pennefather, CB, OBE

ROYAL MARINES RESERVE (RMR)

The Royal Marines Reserve is a commando-trained
volunteer force with the principal role, when mobilized,
of supporting the Royal Marines. There are RMR centres
in London, Glasgow, Bristol, Liverpool and Newcastle.
The current strength of the RMR is about 1,000.
Director, RMR, Col. J. Q. Davis

ROYAL FLEET AUXILIARY (RFA)

The Royal Fleet Auxiliary supplies ships of the fleet with
fuel, food, water, spares and ammunition while at sea. Its
ships are manned by merchant seamen. In April 1996 there
were 21 ships in the RFA.

FLEET AIR ARM

The Fleet Air Arm was established in 1937 and operates
aircraft (including helicopters) for the Royal Navy. In April
1996 there were 218 aircraft in the Fleet Air Arm.

ROYAL NAVAL RESERVE (RNR)

The Royal Naval Reserve is a totally integrated part of the
Royal Navy. It comprises about 3,500 men and women
nationwide who volunteer to train in their spare time for a

variety of sea and shore tasks which they would carry out in
time of crisis or war.
Director, Naval Reserves, Capt N. R. Hodgson, RN

QUEEN ALEXANDRA'S ROYAL NAVAL
NURSING SERVICE

The first nursing sisters were appointed to naval hospitals
in 1884 and the Queen Alexandra's Royal Naval Nursing
Service (QARNNS) gained its current title in 1902.
Nursing ratings were introduced in 1960 and men were
integrated into the Service in 1982; both men and women
serve as officers and ratings. Female medical assistants
were introduced in 1987. Qualified staff and learners are
mainly based at the UK Royal Naval Hospitals, and
continue their responsibility for the health and fitness of
naval personnel. The strength is about 600.
Patron, HRH Princess Alexandra, the Hon. Lady Ogilvy
Matron-in-Chief, Capt. C. M. Taylor

The Army

THE QUEEN

FIELD MARSHALS

HRH The Prince Philip, Duke of Edinburgh, KG, KT, OM,
    GBE, AC, QSO, PC, *apptd* 1953
Sir James Cassels, GCB, KBE, DSO, *apptd* 1968
The Lord Carver, GCB, CBE, DSO, MC, *apptd* 1973
Sir Roland Gibbs, GCB, CBE, DSO, MC, *apptd* 1979
The Lord Bramall, KG, GCB, OBE, MC, *apptd* 1982
Sir John Stanier, GCB, MBE, *apptd* 1985
Sir Nigel Bagnall, GCB, CVO, MC, *apptd* 1988
The Lord Vincent of Coleshill, GBE, KCB, DSO, Col. Cmdt.
    RA, *apptd* 1991
Sir John Chapple, GCB, CBE, *apptd* 1992
HRH The Duke of Kent, KG, GCMG, GCVO, ADC, *apptd* 1993
Sir Peter Inge, GCB, Col. Green Howards, Col. Cmdt.
    APTC (*Chief of the Defence Staff, until early* 1997), *apptd*
    1994

GENERALS

Guthrie, Sir Charles, GCB, LVO, OBE, ADC (*Gen.*), (*Chief of the
    General Staff*)
Mackenzie, Sir Jeremy, KCB, OBE, Col. Cmdt. AG Corps,
    Col. The Highlanders (*D. SACEUR*)
Rose, Sir Michael, KCB, CBE, DSO, QGM, ADC (*Adjutant-
    General*)
Wheeler, Sir Roger, KCB, CBE, Col. Cmdt. Int. Corps, Col.
    RIR (*C.-in-C., Land*)

LIEUTENANT-GENERALS

Foley, Sir John, KCB, OBE, MC, Col. Cmdt. The Light
    Division
Walker, Sir Michael, KCB, CBE, Col. Cmdt. The Queen's
    Division, Col. Cmdt. AAC (*Commandant NATO Rapid
    Reaction Corps*)
Harley, Sir Alexander, KBE, CB, Col. Cmdt. RRA (*Deputy
    CDS (Commitments)*)
Smith, Sir Rupert, KCB, DSO, OBE, QGM, Col. Cmdt.
    Parachute Regiment, Col. Cmdt. Corps of REME (*GOC
    Northern Ireland*)
Cowan, S., CBE, Col. QGS (*Quartermaster-General*)
Hayman-Joyce, Sir Robert, KCB, CBE, Col. Cmdt. RAC
    (*Director-General, Land Systems and Master-General of the
    Ordnance*)

Pike, H. W. R., DSO, MBE, Col. Cmdt. SASC (*Deputy C.-in-C., Land, and Inspector-General, Territorial Army*)
Grant, S. C., CB, Col. QLR (*Commandant, Royal College of Defence Studies*)
Jackson, M. D., CBE (*Director-General, Development and Doctrine*)
Wallace, C. B. Q., OBE, Col. Cmdt. 2 RGJ (*Comd. Permanent Joint HQ*)

MAJOR-GENERALS

Courage, W. J., CB, MBE (*Director-General, TA*)
Burton, E. F. G., OBE (*Asst CDS, Operational Requirements (Land Systems)*)
Freer, I. L., CB, CBE, Col. Staffords
Dutton, B. H., CBE, Col. Cmdt. POW Division (*Comd. British Forces Hong Kong*)
Robins, W. J. P., OBE (*Director-General, Information and Communications Services*)
Kennedy, A. I. G., CB, CBE (*Senior Army Member, Royal College of Defence Studies*)
Mackay-Dick, I. C., MBE (*GOC London District*)
Scott, M. I. E., CBE, DSO (*Military Secretary*)
Burden, D. L., CB, CBE, Col. Cmdt. Royal Logistics Corps (*Director-General, Army Manning and Recruiting*)
Cordingley, P. A. J., DSO (*GOC 2 Divn*)
Willcocks, M. A. (*Asst Chief of the General Staff*)
Cordy-Simpson, R. A. (*Deputy Chief of Staff, HQ Land Command*)
Deverell, J. F., OBE (*Commandant RMAS*)
Pigott, A. D., CBE, Col. Cmdt. The Queen's Gurkha Engineers (*Comdt. Staff College*)
Hall, J. M. F. C., OBE, Col. Cmdt. The Scottish Division, Col. Cmdt. RAVC (*GOC Scotland*)
McAfee, R. W. M., CBE, Col. Cmdt. RTR (*Comd. Multinational Divn Central (Airmobile*)
Richards, N. W. F., OBE (*GOC HQ 4 Divn*)
Vyvyan, C. G. C., Col. Cmdt. 1 RGJ (*Chief of Staff, HQ Land*)
White, M. S., CBE (*Director-General, Logistic Support (Army)*)
Jenkins, D. J. M., CBE (*Commandant RMCS*)
Rogers, A. P. V., OBE (*Director, Army Legal Services*)
Granville-Chapman, T. J., CBE (*Commandant Joint Services Command and Staff College*)
Drewienkiewicz, K. J. (*Director of Support LANDCENT*)
Oliver, R. A., OBE (*Chief of Staff, Adjutant-General's Dept.*)
Sulivan, T. J., CBE (*Chief of Staff HQ ACE Rapid Reaction Corps*)
Corp, P. J. G., CB, Col. Cmdt. REME (*Director-General, Equipment (Army)*)
Pack, S. J. (*Comd. British Forces Gibraltar*)
Pennefather, D. A. S., CB, OBE (*Commandant-General, Royal Marines*)
Elliott, C. L., MBE (*Chief Executive, Army Individual Training Organization*)
Drewry, C. F., CBE (*GOC UK Support Command (Germany)*)
Ewer, G. A. (*Asst CDS (Logistics)*)
Short, W. R., QHP (*Director-General, Army Medical Services*)
Callow, C. G., CBE (*Director-General, Defence Medical Training*)
O'Donoghue, K., CBE (*Chief of Staff, HQ Quartermaster-General*)
Kiszely, J. P., MC (*GOC 1 (UK) Armd Division*)
Searby, R. V. (*GOC 5 Divn*)

CONSTITUTION OF THE ARMY

The regular forces include the following arms, branches and corps. They are listed in accordance with the order of

precedence within the British Army. Soldiers' record offices are shown at the end of each group; all the record offices are due to move to Kentigern House, Glasgow, by July 1997. Records of officers are maintained at the Ministry of Defence.

THE ARMS

HOUSEHOLD CAVALRY – The Household Cavalry Regiment (The Life Guards and The Blues and Royals). *Records*, Queen's Park, Chester
ROYAL ARMOURED CORPS – Cavalry Regiments: 1st The Queen's Dragoon Guards; The Royal Scots Dragoon Guards (Carabiniers and Greys); The Royal Dragoon Guards; The Queen's Royal Hussars (The Queen's Own and Royal Irish); 9th/12th Royal Lancers (Prince of Wales's); The King's Royal Hussars; The Light Dragoons; The Queen's Royal Lancers; Royal Tank Regiment, comprising two regular regiments. *Records*, Queen's Park, Chester
ARTILLERY – Royal Regiment of Artillery. *Records*, Imphal Barracks, Fulford Road, York
ENGINEERS – Corps of Royal Engineers. *Records*, Kentigern House, Brown Street, Glasgow
SIGNALS – Royal Corps of Signals. *Records*, Kentigern House, Brown Street, Glasgow

THE INFANTRY

The Foot Guards and regiments of Infantry of the Line are grouped in divisions as follows:
GUARDS DIVISION – Grenadier, Coldstream, Scots, Irish and Welsh Guards. *Divisional Office*, HQ Infantry, Imber Road, Warminster, Wilts. *Training Centre*, Infantry Training Centre, Vimy Barracks, Catterick, N. Yorks. *Records*, Imphal Barracks, Fulford Road, York
SCOTTISH DIVISION – The Royal Scots (The Royal Regiment); The Royal Highland Fusiliers (Princess Margaret's Own Glasgow and Ayrshire Regiment); The King's Own Scottish Borderers; The Black Watch (Royal Highland Regiment); The Highlanders (Seaforth, Gordons and Camerons); The Argyll and Sutherland Highlanders (Princess Louise's). *Divisional Office*, HQ Infantry, Imber Road, Warminster, Wilts. *Training Centre*, Infantry Training Centre, Vimy Barracks, Catterick, N. Yorks. *Records*, Imphal Barracks, Fulford Road, York.
QUEEN'S DIVISION – The Princess of Wales's Royal Regiment (Queen's and Royal Hampshire's); The Royal Regiment of Fusiliers; The Royal Anglian Regiment. *Divisional Office*, HQ Infantry, Imber Road, Warminster, Wilts. *Training Centre*, Infantry Training Centre, Vimy Barracks, Catterick, N. Yorks. *Records*, Higher Barracks, Exeter
KING'S DIVISION – The King's Own Royal Border Regiment; The King's Regiment; The Prince of Wales's Own Regiment of Yorkshire; The Green Howards (Alexandra, Princess of Wales's Own Yorkshire Regiment); The Queen's Lancashire Regiment; The Duke of Wellington's Regiment (West Riding). *Divisional Office*, HQ Infantry, Imber Road, Warminster, Wilts. *Training Centre*, Infantry Training Centre, Vimy Barracks, Catterick, N. Yorks. *Records*, Imphal Barracks, Fulford Road, York
THE ROYAL IRISH REGIMENT (one general service and six home service battalions) – 27th (Inniskilling), 83rd, 87th and the Ulster Defence Regiment. *Regimental HQ and Training Centre*, St Patrick's Barracks, BFPO 808. *Records*, Imphal Barracks, Fulford Road, York

PRINCE OF WALES's DIVISION – The Devonshire and Dorset Regiment; The Cheshire Regiment; The Royal Welch Fusiliers; The Royal Regiment of Wales (24th/41st Foot); The Royal Gloucestershire, Berkshire and Wiltshire Regiment; The Worcestershire and Sherwood Foresters Regiment (29th/45th Foot); The Staffordshire Regiment (The Prince of Wales's). *Divisional Office,* HQ Infantry, Imber Road, Warminster, Wilts. *Training Centre,* Infantry Training Centre, Vimy Barracks, Catterick, N. Yorks. *Records,* Imphal Barracks, Fulford, York

LIGHT DIVISION – The Light Infantry; The Royal Green Jackets. *Divisional Office,* HQ Infantry, Imber Road, Warminster, Wilts. *Training Centre,* Infantry Training Centre, Vimy Barracks, Catterick, N. Yorks. *Records,* Higher Barracks, Exeter

BRIGADE OF GURKHAS – The Royal Gurkha Rifles; The Queen's Gurkha Engineers; Queen's Gurkha Signals; The Queen's Own Gurkha Transport Regiment. *Regimental HQ, Training Centre* and *Records,* Queen Elizabeth Barracks, Church Crookham, Fleet, Aldershot, Hants

THE PARACHUTE REGIMENT (three regular battalions) – *Regimental HQ,* Browning Barracks, Aldershot, Hants. *Training Centre,* Infantry Training Centre, Vimy Barracks, Catterick, N. Yorks. *Records,* Higher Barracks, Exeter

SPECIAL AIR SERVICE REGIMENT – *Regimental HQ and Training Centre,* Stirling Lines, Hereford. *Records,* Higher Barracks, Exeter

ARMY AIR CORPS – *Regimental HQ* and *Training Centre,* Middle Wallop, Stockbridge, Hants. *Records,* Higher Barracks, Exeter

SERVICES/ARMS*

Royal Army Chaplains' Department – *Regimental HQ* and *Training Centre,* Netheravon House, Netheravon, Wilts SP4 9NF

The Royal Logistic Corps – *Regimental HQ,* Blackdown Barracks, Deepcut, Camberley, Surrey. *Training Centre,* Princess Royal Barracks, Deepcut, Camberley, Surrey. *Records,* Kentigern House, Brown Street, Glasgow; South Wigston, Leicester; Higher Barracks, Exeter

Royal Army Medical Corps – *Regimental HQ* and *Training Centre,* Keogh Barracks, Ashvale, Aldershot, Hants. *Records,* Queen's Park, Chester

Corps of Royal Electrical and Mechanical Engineers – *Regimental HQ* and *Training Centre,* Hazebrouck Barracks, Isaac Newton Road, Arborfield, Reading, Berks. *Records,* Glen Parva Barracks, Saffron Road, Wigston, Leicester

Adjutant-General's Corps – *Corps HQ* and *Training Centre,* Worthy Down, Winchester, Hants. *Records,* Queen's Park, Chester

Royal Army Veterinary Corps – *Corps HQ,* Gallowey Road, Aldershot, Hants. *Regimental HQ* and *Training Centre,* Welby Lane Camp, Elmhurst Avenue, Melton Mowbray, Leics. *Records,* Higher Barracks, Exeter

Small Arms School Corps – *Corps HQ* and *Training Centre,* School of Infantry, Imber Road, Warminster, Wilts. *Records,* Higher Barracks, Exeter

Royal Army Dental Corps – *Regimental HQ,* Evelyn Woods Road, Aldershot, Hants. *Training Centre,* Keogh Barracks, Ashvale, Aldershot, Hants. *Records,* Queen's Park, Chester

*Intelligence Corps – *Corps HQ* and *Training Centre,* Templer Barracks, Ashford, Kent. *Records,* Higher Barracks, Exeter

Army Physical Training Corps – *Regimental HQ* and *Training Centre,* Queen's Avenue, Aldershot, Hants. *Records,* Higher Barracks, Exeter

General Service Corps – *Records,* Imphal Barracks, Fulford Road, York

Queen Alexander's Royal Army Nursing Corps – *Regimental HQ* and *Training Centre,* Keogh Barracks, Ashvale, Aldershot, Hants. *Records,* Queen's Park, Chester

Corps of Army Music – *Corps HQ* and *Training Centre,* Army School of Music, Netherhall, Kneller Road, Twickenham, Middx. *Records,* Higher Barracks, Exeter

ARMY EQUIPMENT HOLDINGS

The Army is equipped (as at November 1995) with 662 tanks, 3,470 armoured combat vehicles or ACV lookalikes, 511 artillery pieces, 48 landing craft and 236 helicopters.

THE TERRITORIAL ARMY (TA)

The Territorial Army is designed to be a General Reserve to the Army. It exists to reinforce the regular Army as and when required, with individuals, sub-units or units either in the UK or overseas, and to provide the framework and basis for regeneration and reconstitution in times of national emergency. The TA also provides an essential link between the military and civilian communities. Its structure has recently been reviewed. Its peacetime establishment is 59,000.

Inspector-General, Lt.-Gen. H. W. R. Pike, DSO, MBE

QUEEN ALEXANDRA'S ROYAL ARMY NURSING CORPS

The Queen Alexandra's Royal Army Nursing Corps (QARANC) was founded in 1902 as Queen Alexandra's Imperial Military Nursing Service (QAIMNS) and gained its present title in 1949. The QARANC has trained nurses for the register since 1950 and has many other nursing employments. Since 1992 men have been eligible to join the QARANC. The Corps provides service in military hospitals in the UK (including Northern Ireland), Germany, Hong Kong, Cyprus, Falkland Islands, Belize and wherever they may be needed world-wide.

Colonel-in-Chief, HRH The Princess Margaret, Countess of Snowdon, GCVO, CI

Matron-in-Chief (Army) and Director, Army Nursing Services, Col. J. Arigho

The Royal Air Force

THE QUEEN

MARSHALS OF THE ROYAL AIR FORCE

HRH The Prince Philip, Duke of Edinburgh, KG, KT, OM, GBE, AC, QSO, PC, *apptd* 1953

Sir John Grandy, GCB, GCVO, KBE, DSO, *apptd* 1971

Sir Denis Spotswood, GCB, CBE, DSO, DFC, *apptd* 1974

Sir Michael Beetham, GCB, CBE, DFC, AFC, *apptd* 1982

Sir Keith Williamson, GCB, AFC, *apptd* 1985

The Lord Craig of Radley, GCB, OBE, *apptd* 1988

AIR CHIEF MARSHALS

Graydon, Sir Michael, GCB, CBE, ADC (*Chief of the Air Staff*)

Stear, Sir Michael, KCB, CBE (*Deputy C.-in-C. Allied Forces Central Europe*)

Johns, Sir Richard, KCB, CBE, LVO (*C.-in-C. Allied Forces North-Western Europe*)
Wratten, Sir William, KBE, CB, AFC, ADC (*AOC.-in-C. Strike Command and Comd. Allied Air Forces North-Western Europe*)
Willis, Sir John, KCB, CBE (*Vice-Chief of the Defence Staff*)
Allison, Sir John, KCB, CBE (*Air Officer Commanding-in-Chief and Air Member for Logistics*)

AIR MARSHALS

Austin, Sir Roger, KCB, AFC (*Deputy Chief of Defence Procurement (Operations)*)
Macfadyen, I. D., CB, OBE (*Director-General, Saudi Armed Forces Project*)
Cheshire, Sir John, KBE, CB (*UK Military Representative to NATO Military Committee, Brussels*)
Cousins, Sir David, KCB, AFC (*Air Member for Personnel and Air Officer Commanding-in-Chief*)
Squire, P. T., DFC, AFC (*Deputy CDS (Programmes and Personnel)*)
Robertson, G. A., CBE (*Chief of Staff and Deputy C.-in-C. Strike Command*)
Bagnall, A. J. C., CB, OBE (*Deputy C.-in-C. Allied Air Forces Central Europe*)

AIR VICE-MARSHALS

Harding, P. J., CB, CBE, AFC (*Defence Services Secretary*)
Baird, J. A., QHP (*Director-General, Medical Services (RAF)*)
Saunders, D. J., CBE (*Air Officer Engineering and Supply*)
Chapple, R., QHP (*Principal Medical Officer, RAF Support Command*)
Norriss, P. C., CB, AFC (*Director-General, Air Systems 1*)
Kyle, R. H., MBE (*Chief Executive, RAF Maintenance Group Agency*)
Mackey, J., QHDS (*Chief Executive, Defence Dental Agency*)
Sherrington, T. B., OBE (*Air Officer Admin., Strike Command*)
Carleton, G. W. (*Director, Legal Services (RAF)*)
Coville, C. C. C., CB (*Asst CDS Operational Requirements (Air Systems)*)
O'Brien, R. P., OBE (*Air Secretary*)
May, J. A. G., CB, CBE (*Air Officer Training*)
Terry, C. G., CB, OBE (*Chief of Staff, Logistic Command, and Chief Engineer (RAF)*)
Feesey, J. D. L. (*Director-General, Policy and Plans*)
Goddard, P. J., AFC (*Senior Directing Staff (Air), Royal College of Defence Studies*)
Goodall, R. H., CBE, AFC (*Chief of Staff, Permanent Joint HQ*)
Jenner, T. I., CB (*Asst Chief of the Air Staff*)
Day, J. R. (*AOC No. 1 Group*)
Harrison, A. J. (*Asst CDS (Operations)*)
Millar, P. (*Comd. British Forces Cyprus*)
Stables, A. J. (*Commandant RAF Staff College, Cranwell*)
Hull, D. H., QHS (*Dean of Air Force Music*)
Hurrell, D. A. (*Senior Air Staff Officer*)
Markey, P. D. (*Director-General, Support Management (RAF)*)
McCandless, B. C. (*Air Officer Communications Information Systems and Air Officer Commanding Signals Units*)
French, J. C. (*Asst CDS (Policy)*)
Van der Veen, M. (*Cmdt., RAF Staff College Bracknell*)
Smart, M. D. (*Chief of Staff, Personnel and Training Command, and Director-General, Strategic Policy and Plans*)
O'Reilly, P. J. (*President of the Ordnance Board*)
Spink, C. R. (*AOC No. 11/18 Group*)
Elder, R. D.
Jackson, M. R.
Thompson, J. H.

CONSTITUTION OF THE ROYAL AIR FORCE

The RAF consists of three commands: Strike Command, Personnel and Training Command and Logistics Command. Strike Command is responsible for all the RAF's front-line forces. Its roles include strike/attack, air defence, reconnaissance, maritime patrol, strategic air transport, air-to-air refuelling, search and rescue, and aero-medical facilities. Personnel and Training Command is responsible for personnel administration and training in the RAF. Logistics Command is responsible for all logistics, engineering and materiel support.

RAF EQUIPMENT *as at 1 July 1996*

Aircraft – 249 Tornado, 70 Harrier, 54 Jaguar, 9 Canberra, 29 Nimrod, 26 VC10, 9 Tristar, 55 Hercules, 11 BAe, 7 Sentry, 4 Andover, 100 Hawk, 116 Bulldog, 10 Domenie, 2 Islander, 10 Jetstream, 73 Tucano
Helicopters – 37 Puma, 50 Wessex, 19 Sea King, 34 Chinook, 21 Gazelle
Rapier missiles

ROYAL AUXILIARY AIR FORCE (RAUXAF)

Formed in 1924, the Auxiliary Air Force received the prefix 'Royal' in 1947 in recognition of its war record. The RAUXAF supports the RAF in maritime air operations, air and ground defence of airfields, air movements and aero-medical evacuation. The RAUXAF and the RAFVR are due to be merged in 1997.
Air Commodore-in-Chief, HM The Queen
Director of Personnel Management (Airmen) and Controller of Reserve Forces (RAF), Air Cdre M. L. Jackson, OBE

ROYAL AIR FORCE VOLUNTEER RESERVE (RAFVR)

The Royal Air Force Volunteer Reserve was created in 1936 to train the increased number of aircrew who were seen as necessary for the forthcoming conflict. The RAFVR was reconstituted in 1947 following war service. It provides specialist personnel who fill specific wartime intelligence support, photo interpretation and public relations appointments. A small number of RAFVR aircrew augment regular crews on Nimrod (Maritime Reconnaissance) aircraft in wartime. The RAFVR and the RAUXAF are due to be merged in 1997.
Director of Personnel Management (Airmen) and Controller of Reserve Forces (RAF), Air Cdre M. L. Jackson, OBE

PRINCESS MARY'S ROYAL AIR FORCE NURSING SERVICE

The Princess Mary's Royal Air Force Nursing Service (PMRAFNS) offers commissions to Registered General Nurses (RGN) with a minimum of two years experience after obtaining RGN and normally with a second qualification. RGNs with no additional experience or qualification are recruited as non-commissioned officers in the grade of Staff Nurse.
Air Chief Commandant, HRH Princess Alexandra, the Hon. Lady Ogilvy, GCVO
Matron-in-Chief, Gp Capt R. H. Williams

SERVICE SALARIES

The following rates of pay apply from 1 December 1996. The increasing integration of women in the armed services is reflected in equal pay for equal work and the X factor addition is now the same for men and women (12 per cent).

Annual salaries are derived from daily rates in whole pence and rounded to the nearest £.

The pay rates shown are for Army personnel. The rates apply also to personnel of equivalent rank and pay band in the other services.

OFFICERS' SALARIES

MAIN SCALE

Rank	Daily	Annual	Rank	Daily	Annual
Second Lieutenant	£38.53	£14,063	Special List Lieutenant-Colonel	£113.72	£41,508
Lieutenant			Lieutenant-Colonel		
On appointment	50.93	18,589	On appointment with less than 19 years service	115.84	42,282
After 1 year in the rank	52.27	19,079	After 2 years in the rank or with 19 years service	118.89	43,395
After 2 years in the rank	53.61	19,568	After 4 years in the rank or with 21 years service	121.94	44,508
After 3 years in the rank	54.95	20,057	After 6 years in the rank or with 23 years service	124.99	45,621
After 4 years in the rank	56.29	20,546	After 8 years in the rank or with 25 years service	128.04	46,735
Captain			Colonel		
On appointment	64.90	23,689	On appointment	134.65	49,147
After 1 year in the rank	66.65	24,327	After 2 years in the rank	138.19	50,439
After 2 years in the rank	68.40	24,966	After 4 years in the rank	141.73	51,731
After 3 years in the rank	70.15	25,605	After 6 years in the rank	145.27	53,024
After 4 years in the rank	71.90	26,244	After 8 years in the rank	148.81	54,316
After 5 years in the rank	73.65	26,882	Brigadier	165.09	60,258
After 6 years in the rank	75.40	27,521	Major-General	181.62	66,291
Major			Lieutenant-General	205.58	75,000
On appointment	82.34	30,054	General	277.35	101,233
After 1 year in the rank	84.38	30,799	Field Marshal	344.80	125,852
After 2 years in the rank	86.42	31,543			
After 3 years in the rank	88.46	32,288			
After 4 years in the rank	90.50	33,033			
After 5 years in the rank	92.54	33,777			
After 6 years in the rank	94.58	34,522			
After 7 years in the rank	96.62	35,266			
After 8 years in the rank	98.66	36,011			

SALARIES OF OFFICERS COMMISSIONED FROM THE RANKS (LIEUTENANTS AND CAPTAINS ONLY)

YEARS OF COMMISSIONED SERVICE	YEARS OF NON-COMMISSIONED SERVICE FROM AGE 18					
	Less than 12 years		12 years but less than 15 years		15 years or more	
	Daily	Annual	Daily	Annual	Daily	Annual
On commissioning	£71.67	£26,160	£75.36	£27,506	£79.05	£28,853
After 1 year service	73.52	26,835	77.21	28,182	80.26	29,295
After 2 years service	75.36	27,506	79.05	28,853	81.45	29,729
After 3 years service	77.21	28,182	80.26	29,295	82.64	30,164
After 4 years service	79.05	28,853	81.45	29,729	83.83	30,598
After 5 years service	80.26	29,295	82.64	30,164	85.02	31,032
After 6 years service	81.45	29,729	83.83	30,598	86.21	31,467
After 8 years service	82.64	30,164	85.02	31,032	87.40	31,901
After 10 years service	83.83	30,598	86.21	31,467	87.40	31,901
After 12 years service	85.02	31,032	87.40	31,901	87.40	31,901
After 14 years service	86.21	31,467	87.40	31,901	87.40	31,901
After 16 years service	87.40	31,901	87.40	31,901	87.40	31,901

SOLDIERS' SALARIES

The pay structure below officer level is divided into pay bands. Jobs at each rank are allocated to bands according to their score in the job evaluation system. Length of service is from age 18.

Scale A: committed to serve/have completed less than 6 years
Scale B: committed to serve/have completed 6 years but less than 9 years
Scale C: committed to serve/have completed more than 9 years

Daily rates of pay effective from 1 December 1996 are:

Rank	Scale A		
	Band 1	Band 2	Band 3
Private			
Class 4	£24.14	£ —	£ —
Class 3	27.04	31.39	36.22
Class 2	30.23	34.62	39.45
Class 1	32.88	37.26	42.08
Lance-Corporal			
Class 3	32.88	37.26	42.08
Class 2	35.12	39.51	44.73
Class 1	37.78	42.17	47.39
Corporal			
Class 2	40.41	44.78	50.00
Class 1	43.38	47.74	52.96

	Band 4	Band 5	Band 6	Band 7
Sergeant	£47.80	£52.56	£57.75	£ —
Staff Sergeant	50.55	55.29	60.51	66.78
Warrant Officer				
Class 2	54.05	58.81	65.21	71.62
Class 1	57.64	62.38	68.88	75.27

Scale B			
	Band 1	Band 2	Band 3
Private			
Class 4	£24.44	£ —	£ —
Class 3	27.34	31.69	36.52
Class 2	30.53	34.92	39.75
Class 1	33.18	37.56	42.38

Rank	Scale B (contd)		
	Band 1	Band 2	Band 3
Lance-Corporal			
Class 3	33.18	37.56	42.38
Class 2	35.42	39.81	45.03
Class 1	38.08	42.47	47.69
Corporal			
Class 2	40.71	45.08	50.30
Class 1	43.68	48.04	53.26

	Band 4	Band 5	Band 6	Band 7
Sergeant	£48.10	£52.86	£58.05	£ —
Staff Sergeant	50.85	55.59	60.81	66.08
Warrant Officer				
Class 2	54.35	59.11	65.51	71.92
Class 1	57.94	62.68	69.18	75.57

Scale C			
	Band 1	Band 2	Band 3
Private			
Class 4	£24.89	£ —	£ —
Class 3	27.79	32.14	36.97
Class 2	30.98	35.37	40.20
Class 1	33.63	38.01	42.83
Lance-Corporal			
Class 3	33.63	38.01	42.83
Class 2	35.87	40.26	45.48
Class 1	38.53	42.92	48.14
Corporal			
Class 2	41.16	45.53	50.75
Class 1	44.13	48.49	53.71

	Band 4	Band 5	Band 6	Band 7
Sergeant	£48.55	£53.31	£58.50	£ —
Staff Sergeant	51.30	56.04	61.26	67.53
Warrant Officer				
Class 2	54.80	59.56	65.96	72.37
Class 1	58.39	63.13	69.63	76.02

RELATIVE RANK – ARMED FORCES

	Royal Navy		*Army*		*Royal Air Force*
1	Admiral of the Fleet	1	Field Marshal	1	Marshal of the RAF
2	Admiral (Adm.)	2	General (Gen.)	2	Air Chief Marshal
3	Vice-Admiral (Vice-Adm.)	3	Lieutenant-General (Lt.-Gen.)	3	Air Marshal
4	Rear-Admiral (Rear-Adm.)	4	Major-General (Maj.-Gen.)	4	Air Vice-Marshal
5	Commodore (1st & 2nd class) (Cdre)	5	Brigadier (Brig.)	5	Air Commodore (Air Cdre)
6	Captain (Capt.)	6	Colonel (Col.)	6	Group Captain (Gp Capt)
7	Commander (Cdr.)	7	Lieutenant-Colonel (Lt.-Col.)	7	Wing Commander (Wg Cdr.)
8	Lieutenant-Commander (Lt.-Cdr.)	8	Major (Maj.)	8	Squadron Leader (Sqn. Ldr.)
9	Lieutenant (Lt.)	9	Captain (Capt.)	9	Flight Lieutenant (Flt. Lt.)
10	Sub-Lieutenant (Sub-Lt.)	10	Lieutenant (Lt.)	10	Flying Officer (FO)
11	Acting Sub-Lieutenant (Acting Sub-Lt.)	11	Second Lieutenant (2nd Lt.)	11	Pilot Officer (PO)

SERVICE RETIRED PAY ON COMPULSORY RETIREMENT

Those who leave the services having served at least five years, but not long enough to qualify for the appropriate immediate pension, now qualify for a preserved pension and terminal grant, both of which are payable at age 60. The tax-free resettlement grants shown below are payable on release to those who qualify for a preserved pension and who have completed nine years service from age 21 (officers) or 12 years from age 18 (other ranks).

The annual rates for army personnel are given. The rates apply also to personnel of equivalent rank in the other services, including the nursing services.

OFFICERS

Applicable to officers who give full pay service on the active list on or after 30 November 1996

No. of years reckonable service over age 21	Capt. and below	Major	Lt.-Col.	Colonel	Brigadier	Major-General	Lieutenant-General	General
16	£ 7,843	£ 9,414	£12,368	£ —	£ —	£ —	£ —	£ —
17	8,208	9,861	12,940	—	—	—	—	—
18	8,573	10,309	13,512	15,705	—	—	—	—
19	8,937	10,756	14,084	16,370	—	—	—	—
20	9,302	11,203	14,656	17,035	—	—	—	—
21	9,667	11,650	15,229	17,699	—	—	—	—
22	10,032	12,098	15,801	18,364	21,190	—	—	—
23	10,397	12,545	16,373	19,029	21,860	—	—	—
24	10,762	12,992	16,945	19,694	22,529	24,785	—	—
25	11,126	13,440	17,517	20,359	23,199	25,552	—	—
26	11,491	13,887	18,089	21,024	23,869	26,258	—	—
27	11,856	14,334	18,661	21,689	24,538	26,995	30,542	—
28	12,221	14,781	19,233	22,354	25,208	27,731	31,375	—
29	12,586	15,229	19,805	23,019	25,877	28,468	32,209	—
30	12,951	15,676	20,378	23,683	26,547	29,205	33,042	44,598
31	13,315	16,123	20,950	24,348	27,216	29,941	33,875	45,723
32	13,680	16,570	21,522	25,013	27,886	30,678	34,708	46,848
33	14,045	17,018	22,094	25,678	28,555	31,414	35,542	47,972
34	14,410	17,465	22,666	26,343	29,225	32,151	36,375	49,097

Field Marshal – active list retired pay at the rate of £61,037 a year

WARRANT OFFICERS, NCOS AND PRIVATES

Applicable to soldiers who give full pay service on or after 30 November 1996

No. of years reckonable service	Below Corporal	Corporal	Sergeant	Staff Sergeant	Warrant Officer Class II	Warrant Officer Class I
22	£4,551	£5,798	£6,433	£ 7,323	£ 7,570	£ 8,368
23	4,710	6,000	6,658	7,579	7,838	8,669
24	4,869	6,203	6,882	7,834	8,106	8,970
25	5,028	6,405	7,107	8,090	8,375	9,270
26	5,186	6,608	7,331	8,346	8,643	9,571
27	5,345	6,810	7,556	8,601	8,911	9,872
28	5,504	7,012	7,781	8,857	9,179	10,173
29	5,663	7,215	8,005	9,113	9,447	10,474
30	5,822	7,417	8,230	9,368	9,716	10,774
31	5,981	7,620	8,454	9,624	9,984	11,075
32	6,140	7,822	8,679	9,880	10,252	11,376
33	6,299	8,024	8,904	10,135	10,520	11,677
34	6,457	8,227	9,128	10,391	10,788	11,978
35	6,616	8,429	9,353	10,647	11,057	12,278
36	6,775	8,632	9,577	10,902	11,325	12,579
37	6,934	8,834	9,802	11,158	11,593	12,880

RESETTLEMENT GRANTS

Terminal grants are in each case three times the rate of retired pay or pension. There are special rates of retired pay for certain other ranks not shown above. Lower rates are payable in cases of voluntary retirement.

A gratuity of £2,665 is payable for officers with short service commissions for each year completed. Resettlement grants are: officers £9,174; non-commissioned ranks £6,041.

Archbishops of Canterbury since 1414

Henry Chichele (1362–1443), translated 1414
John Stafford (?–1452), translated 1443
John Kemp (c.1380–1454), translated 1452
Thomas Bourchier (c.1410–86), translated 1454
John Morton (c.1420–1500), translated 1486
Henry Deane (?–1503), translated 1501
William Warham (1450–1532), translated 1503
Thomas Cranmer (1489–1556), translated 1533
Reginald Pole (1500–58), translated 1556
Matthew Parker (1504–75), translated 1559
Edmund Grindal (c.1519–83), translated 1576
John Whitgift (c.1530–1604), translated 1583
Richard Bancroft (1544–1610), translated 1604
George Abbot (1562–1633), translated 1611
William Laud (1573–1645), translated 1633
William Juxon (1582–1663), translated 1660
Gilbert Sheldon (1598–1677), translated 1663
William Sancroft (1617–93), translated 1678
John Tillotson (1630–94), translated 1691
Thomas Tenison (1636–1715), translated 1695
William Wake (1657–1737), translated 1716

John Potter (c.1674–1747), translated 1737
Thomas Herring (1693–1757), translated 1747
Matthew Hutton (1693–1758), translated 1757
Thomas Secker (1693–1768), translated 1758
Hon. Frederick Cornwallis (1713–83), translated 1768
John Moore (1730–1805), translated 1783
Charles Manners-Sutton (1755–1828), translated 1805
William Howley (1766–1848), translated 1828
John Bird Sumner (1780–1862), translated 1848
Charles Longley (1794–1868), translated 1862
Archibald Campbell Tait (1811–82), translated 1868
Edward White Benson (1829–1896), translated 1883
Frederick Temple (1821–1902), translated 1896
Randall Davidson (1848–1930), translated 1903
Cosmo Lang (1864–1945), translated 1928
William Temple (1881–1944), translated 1942
Geoffrey Fisher (1887–1972), translated 1945
Michael Ramsey (1904–88), translated 1961
Donald Coggan (1909–), translated 1974
Robert Runcie (1921–), translated 1980
George Carey (1935–), translated 1991

Archbishops of York since 1606

Tobias Matthew (1546–1628), translated 1606
George Montaigne (1569–1628), translated 1628
Samuel Harsnett (1561–1631), translated 1629
Richard Neile (1562–1640), translated 1632
John Williams (1582–1650), translated 1641
Accepted Frewen (1588–1664), translated 1660
Richard Sterne (1596–1683), translated 1664
John Dolben (1625–86), translated 1683
Thomas Lamplugh (1615–91), translated 1688
John Sharp (1645–1714), translated 1691
William Dawes (1671–1724), translated 1714
Launcelot Blackburn (1658–1743), translated 1724
Thomas Herring (1693–1757), translated 1743
Matthew Hutton (1693–1758), translated 1747
John Gilbert (1693–1761), translated 1757
Robert Hay Drummond (1711–76), translated 1761

William Markham (1719–1807), translated 1777
Edward Vernon Harcourt (1757–1847), translated 1808
Thomas Musgrave (1788–1860), translated 1847
Charles Longley (1794–1868), translated 1860
William Thomson (1819–90), translated 1862
William Connor Magee (1821–91), translated 1891
William Maclagan (1826–1910), translated 1891
Cosmo Lang (1864–1945), translated 1909
William Temple (1881–1944), translated 1929
Cyril Garbett (1875–1955), translated 1942
Michael Ramsey (1904–88), translated 1956
Donald Coggan (1909–), translated 1961
Stuart Blanch (1918–94), translated 1975
John Habgood (1927–), translated 1983
David Hope (1940–), translated 1995

Popes since 1800

The family name is in italics

Pius VII, *Chiaramonti*, elected 1800
Leo XII, *della Genga*, elected 1823
Pius VIII, *Castiglioni*, elected 1829
Gregory XVI, *Cappellari*, elected 1831
Pius IX, *Mastai-Ferretti*, elected 1846
Leo XIII, *Pecci*, elected 1878
Pius X, *Sarto*, elected 1903
Benedict XV, *della Chiesa*, elected 1914

Pius XI, *Ratti*, elected 1922
Pius XII, *Pacelli*, elected 1939
John XXIII, *Roncalli*, elected 1958
Paul VI, *Montini*, elected 1963
John Paul I, *Luciani*, elected 1978
John Paul II, *Wojtyla*, elected 1978

Adrian IV is the only Englishman to be elected pope. He was born Nicholas Breakspear at Langley, near St Albans, and was elected Pope in 1154 on the death of Anastasius IV. He died in 1159.

The Christian Churches

The Church of England

The Church of England is the established (i.e. state) church in England and the mother church of the Anglican Communion. A Church of England already existed when Pope Gregory sent Augustine to evangelise the English in AD 596. During the Middle Ages conflicts between Church and State culminated in the Act of Supremacy in 1534. This repudiated papal supremacy and declared Henry VIII to be the supreme head of the Church in England. Since 1559 the English monarch has been termed the Supreme Governor of the Church of England. The Thirty-Nine Articles, a set of doctrinal statements which, together with the Book of Common Prayer of 1662 and the Ordinal, define the position of the Church of England, were adopted in their final form in 1571 and include the emphasis on personal faith and the authority of the scriptures common to the Protestant Reformation throughout Europe.

The Church of England is divided into the two provinces of Canterbury and York, each under an archbishop. The two provinces are subdivided into 44 dioceses. Decisions on matters concerning the Church of England are made by the General Synod, established in 1970. It also discusses and expresses opinion on any other matter of religious or public interest. The General Synod has 574 members in total, divided between three houses: the House of Bishops, the House of Clergy and the House of Laity. It is presided over jointly by the Archbishops of Canterbury and York and normally meets twice a year. The Synod has the power, delegated by Parliament, to frame statute law (known as a Measure) on any matter concerning the Church of England. A Measure must be laid before both Houses of Parliament, who may accept or reject it but cannot amend it. Once accepted the Measure is submitted for royal assent and then has the full force of law. The Synod appoints a number of committees, boards and councils which deal with, or advise on, a wide range of matters. In addition to the General Synod, there are synods of clergy and laity at diocesan level.

A report of a commission headed by the Bishop of Durham recommending changes to the national structures of the Church of England was accepted by the General Synod in November 1995; a draft Measure will be brought before the Synod in November 1996 and the changes, which include the creation of an Archbishops' Council, are likely to be implemented in 1998.

In 1994 the Church of England had an electoral roll membership of 1.5 million, of whom about 1.1 million regularly attended Sunday services. There are (1995 figures) two archbishops, 106 diocesan, suffragan and (stipendiary) assistant bishops, 9,333 other male and 820 female full-time stipendiary clergy, and over 16,000 churches and places of worship. (The Diocese in Europe is not included in these figures.)

THE ORDINATION OF WOMEN

On 11 November 1992, the General Synod of the Church of England voted to permit the ordination of women as priests by majorities of 75 per cent in the House of Bishops, 70.4 per cent in the House of Clergy, and 67.3 per cent in the House of Laity. After receiving parliamentary approval and royal assent, the canon was promulged in the General Synod in February 1994 and the first 32 women priests were ordained on 12 March 1994 by the Bishop of Bristol.

The Priests (Ordination of Women) Measure 1993 contains provisions safeguarding the position of bishops and parishes who are opposed to the priestly ministry of women. In November 1993 the General Synod agreed to the appointment of up to three 'provincial visitors' to work with those who are unable to accept the ministry of bishops ordaining women priests. The provincial visitors, who are suffragan bishops in the newly created sees of Ebbsfleet (Province of Canterbury), Beverley (Province of York) and Richborough (Province of Canterbury), are allowed to carry out confirmations and ordinations in parishes opposed to women priests, as long as they have the permission of the diocesan bishop. Clergy who feel compelled to leave the ministry are entitled to financial assistance.

PORVOO COMMON STATEMENT

The Porvoo Common Statement was drawn up by the British and Irish Anglican churches and the Nordic and Baltic Lutheran churches and was approved by the General Synod of the Church of England in July 1995. In the House of Bishops the motion was approved by 34 votes to 0, in the House of Clergy by 176 votes to 8, and in the House of Laity by 169 votes to 15.

Churches that agree the statement regard baptized members of each other's churches as members of their own, and allow free interchange of episcopally ordained ministers within the rules of each church.

GENERAL SYNOD OF THE CHURCH OF ENGLAND, Church House, Dean's Yard, London SW1P 3NZ. Tel: 0171-222 9011. *Secretary-General*, P. Mawer

HOUSE OF BISHOPS: *Chairman*, The Archbishop of Canterbury; *Vice-Chairman*, The Archbishop of York

HOUSE OF CLERGY: *Joint Chairmen*, Revd Dr J. Sentamu; Canon J. Stanley

HOUSE OF LAITY: *Chairman*, Dr Christina Baxter; *Vice-Chairman*, Dr P. Giddings

STIPENDS 1996–7

Archbishop of Canterbury	£47,070
Archbishop of York	£41,420
Bishop of London	£38,440
Other diocesan bishops	£25,520
Suffragan bishops	£20,980
Deans and provosts	£20,980
Residentiary canons	£17,160
Incumbents and clergy of similar status	£13,450*

*national average

STIPENDIARY CLERGY *as at 31 December 1995*

	Male	Female
Bath and Wells	234	20
Birmingham	192	25
Blackburn	261	5
Bradford	123	8
Bristol	143	19
Canterbury	179	15
Carlisle	159	13
Chelmsford	406	31

	Male	Female
Chester	284	14
Chichester	348	8
Coventry	153	17
Derby	184	10
Durham	229	28
Ely	154	20
Exeter	279	9
Gloucester	168	14
Guildford	187	23
Hereford	121	12
Leicester	162	14
Lichfield	348	37
Lincoln	204	28
Liverpool	256	32
London	514	45
Manchester	304	22
Newcastle	160	9
Norwich	203	16
Oxford	404	46
Peterborough	147	9
Portsmouth	116	9
Ripon	147	24
Rochester	226	19
St Albans	270	29
St Edmundsbury and Ipswich	175	15
Salisbury	234	14
Sheffield	195	18
Sodor and Man	22	0
Southwark	350	49
Southwell	187	23
Truro	125	3
Wakefield	184	17
Winchester	250	12
Worcester	153	16
York	300	23
TOTAL	9,440	820

Province of Canterbury

CANTERBURY

103RD ARCHBISHOP AND PRIMATE OF ALL ENGLAND
Most Revd and Rt. Hon. George L. Carey, PH.D., *cons.* 1987, *trans.* 1991, *apptd* 1991; Lambeth Palace, London SE1 7JU. *Signs* George Cantuar:

BISHOPS SUFFRAGAN
Dover, Rt. Revd J. Richard A. Llewellin, *cons.* 1985, *apptd* 1992; Upway, St Martin's Hill, Canterbury, CT1 1PR
Maidstone, Rt. Revd Gavin H. Reid, *cons.* 1992, *apptd* 1992; Bishop's House, Pett Lane, Charing, Ashford TN27 0DL
Ebbsfleet, Rt. Revd John Richards, *cons.* 1994, *apptd* 1994 (provincial episcopal visitor); The Rectory, Church Leigh, Stoke-on-Trent, Staffs ST10 4PT
Richborough, Rt. Revd Edwin Barnes, *cons.* 1995, *apptd* 1995 (provincial episcopal visitor); St Stephen's House, Marston Street, Oxford OX4 1JX

DEAN
Very Revd John Arthur Simpson, *apptd* 1986

CANONS RESIDENTIARY
P. Brett, *apptd* 1983; R. H. C. Symon, *apptd* 1994; Dr M. Chandler, *apptd* 1995; Ven. J. Pritchard, *apptd* 1996

Organist, D. Flood, FRCO, *apptd* 1988

ARCHDEACONS
Canterbury, Ven. J. Pritchard, *apptd* 1996
Maidstone, Ven. P. Evans, *apptd* 1989

Vicar-General of Province and Diocese, Chancellor S. Cameron, QC
Commissary-General, His Hon. Judge Richard Walker
Joint Registrars of the Province, F. E. Robson, OBE; B. J. T. Hanson, CBE
Diocesan Registrar and Legal Adviser, R. H. B. Sturt
Diocesan Secretary, D. Kemp, Diocesan House, Lady Wootton's Green, Canterbury CT1 1NQ. Tel: 01227-459401

LONDON

132ND BISHOP
Rt. Revd Richard C. Chartres; The Old Deanery, Dean's Court, London EC4V 5AA. *Signs* Richard Londin:

AREA BISHOPS
Edmonton, Rt. Revd Brian J. Masters, *cons.* 1982, *apptd* 1984; 1 Regent's Park Terrace, London NW1 7EE
Kensington, Rt. Revd Michael Colclough, *cons.* 1996, *apptd* 1996; 19 Campden Hill Square, London W8 7JY
Stepney, Rt. Revd Dr John M. Sentamu, *cons.* 1996, *apptd* 1996; 63 Coborn Road, London E3 2DB
Willesden, Rt. Revd Graham G. Dow, *cons.* 1992, *apptd* 1992; 173 Willesden Lane, London NW6 7YN

BISHOP SUFFRAGAN
Fulham, Rt. Revd John Broadhurst, *cons.* 1996, *apptd* 1996; c/o The Old Deanery, Dean's Court, London EC4V 5AA

DEAN OF ST PAUL'S
Very Revd John H. Moses, PH.D., *apptd* 1996

CANONS RESIDENTIARY
Ven. G. Cassidy, *apptd* 1987; R. J. Halliburton, *apptd* 1990; M. J. Saward, *apptd* 1991
Registrar and Receiver of St Paul's, Brig. R. W. Acworth, CBE
Organist, J. Scott, FRCO, *apptd* 1990

ARCHDEACONS
Charing Cross, Ven. W. Jacob, *apptd* 1996
Hackney, Ven. C. Young, *apptd* 1992
Hampstead, Ven. P. Wheatley, *apptd* 1995
London, Ven. G. Cassidy, *apptd* 1987
Middlesex, Ven. M. Colmer, *apptd* 1996
Northolt, Ven. P. Broadbent, *apptd* 1995

Chancellor, Miss S. Cameron, QC, *apptd* 1992
Registrar and Legal Secretary, D. W. Faull, OBE
Diocesan Secretary, C. J. A. Smith, 36 Causton Street, London SW1P 4AU. Tel: 0171-932 1100

WINCHESTER

96TH BISHOP
Rt. Revd Michael C. Scott-Joynt, *cons.* 1987, *trans.* 1995, *apptd* 1995; Wolvesey, Winchester SO23 9ND. *Signs* Michael Winton:

BISHOPS SUFFRAGAN
Basingstoke, Rt. Revd D. Geoffrey Rowell, *cons.* 1994, *apptd* 1994; Little Acorns, Boynes Wood Road, Medstead GU34 5EA
Southampton, vacant; Ham House, The Crescent, Romsey SO51 7NG

DEAN
Very Revd Michael Till, *apptd* 1996

Dean of Jersey (*A Peculiar*), Very Revd John Seaford, *apptd* 1993
Dean of Guernsey (*A Peculiar*), Very Revd Marc Trickey, *apptd* 1995

CANONS RESIDENTIARY
A. K. Walker, *apptd* 1987; Ven. A. F. Knight, *apptd* 1991; P. B. Morgan, *apptd* 1994
Organist, D. Hill, FRCO, *apptd* 1988

ARCHDEACONS
Basingstoke, Ven. A. F. Knight, *apptd* 1990
Winchester, Ven. A. G. Clarkson, *apptd* 1984

Chancellor, C. Clark, *apptd* 1993
Registrar and Legal Secretary, P. M. White
Diocesan Secretary, R. Anderton, Church House, 9 The Close, Winchester, Hants SO23 9LS. Tel: 01962-844644

BATH AND WELLS

76TH BISHOP
Rt. Revd James L. Thompson, *cons.* 1978, *apptd* 1991; The Palace, Wells BA5 2PD. *Signs* James Bath & Wells

BISHOP SUFFRAGAN
Taunton, Rt. Revd J. H. Richard Lewis, *cons.* 1992, *apptd* 1992; Sherford Farm House, Sherford, Taunton TA1 3RF

DEAN
Very Revd Richard Lewis, *apptd* 1990

CANONS RESIDENTIARY
P. de N. Lucas, *apptd* 1988; G. O. Farran, *apptd* 1985; R. Acworth, *apptd* 1993; P. G. Walker, *apptd* 1994
Organist, M. Archer, *apptd* 1996

ARCHDEACONS
Bath, Ven. R. J. S. Evens, *apptd* 1996
Taunton, Ven. R. M. C. Frith, *apptd* 1992
Wells, Ven. R. Acworth, *apptd* 1993

Chancellor, T. Briden, *apptd* 1993
Registrar and Legal Secretary, T. Berry
Diocesan Secretary, N. Denison, The Old Deanery, Wells, Somerset BA5 2UG. Tel: 01749-670777

BIRMINGHAM

7TH BISHOP
Rt. Revd Mark Santer, *cons.* 1981, *apptd* 1987; Bishop's Croft, Harborne, Birmingham B17 0BG. *Signs* Mark Birmingham

BISHOP SUFFRAGAN
Aston, Rt. Revd John Austin, *cons.* 1992, *apptd* 1992; Strensham House, 8 Strensham Hill, Moseley, Birmingham B13 8AG

PROVOST
Very Revd Peter A. Berry, *apptd* 1986

CANONS RESIDENTIARY
Ven. C. J. G. Barton, *apptd* 1990; Revd D. Lee, *apptd* 1996
Organist, M. Huxley, FRCO, *apptd* 1986

ARCHDEACONS
Aston, Ven. C. J. G. Barton, *apptd* 1990
Birmingham, Ven. J. F. Duncan, *apptd* 1985

Chancellor, His Honour Judge Aglionby, *apptd* 1970
Registrar and Legal Secretary, H. Carslake
Diocesan Secretary, J. Drennan, 175 Harborne Park Road, Harborne, Birmingham B17 0BH. Tel: 0121-427 5141

BRISTOL

54TH BISHOP
Rt. Revd Barry Rogerson, *cons.* 1979, *apptd* 1985; Bishop's House, Clifton Hill, Bristol BS8 1BW. *Signs* Barry Bristol

BISHOP SUFFRAGAN
Swindon, Rt. Revd Michael Doe, *cons.* 1994, *apptd* 1994; Mark House, Field Rise, Old Town, Swindon SN1 4HP

DEAN
vacant

CANONS RESIDENTIARY
A. L. J. Redfern, *apptd* 1987; J. L. Simpson, *apptd* 1989; P. F. Johnson, *apptd* 1990
Organist, C. Brayne, *apptd* 1990

ARCHDEACONS
Bristol, Ven. D. J. Banfield, *apptd* 1990
Swindon, Ven. M. Middleton, *apptd* 1992

Chancellor, Sir David Calcutt, QC, *apptd* 1971
Registrar and Legal Secretary, D. Ratcliffe
Diocesan Secretary, Mrs L. Farrall, Diocesan Church House, 23 Great George Street, Bristol, Avon BS1 5QZ. Tel: 0117-921 4411

CHELMSFORD

8TH BISHOP
Rt. Revd John F. Perry, *cons.* 1989, *apptd* 1996; Bishopscourt, Margaretting, Ingatestone CM4 0HD. *Signs* John Chelmsford

BISHOPS SUFFRAGAN
Barking, Rt. Revd Roger F. Sainsbury, *cons.* 1991, *apptd* 1991; 110 Capel Road, Forest Gate, London E7 0JS
Bradwell, Rt. Revd Laurence Green, *cons.* 1993, *apptd* 1993; The Vicarage, Orsett Road, Horndon-on-the-Hill, Stanford-le-Hope, Essex SS17 8NS
Colchester, Rt. Revd Edward Holland, *cons.* 1986, *apptd* 1995; 1 Fitzwalter Road, Lexden, Colchester CO3 3SS

PROVOST
vacant

CANONS RESIDENTIARY
T. Thompson, *apptd* 1988; B. P. Thompson, *apptd* 1988; D. Knight, *apptd* 1991
Organist, Dr G. Elliott, PH.D., FRCO, *apptd* 1981

ARCHDEACONS
Colchester, Ven. E. C. F. Stroud, *apptd* 1983
Harlow, Ven. P. F. Taylor, *apptd* 1996
Southend, Ven. D. Jennings, *apptd* 1992
West Ham, Ven. M. J. Fox, *apptd* 1996

Chancellor, Miss S. M. Cameron, QC, *apptd* 1970
Registrar and Legal Secretary, B. Hood
Diocesan Secretary, D. Phillips, 53 New Street, Chelmsford, Essex CM1 1AT. Tel: 01245-266731

CHICHESTER

102ND BISHOP
Rt. Revd Eric W. Kemp, DD, *cons.* 1974, *apptd* 1974; The Palace, Chichester PO19 1PY. *Signs* Eric Cicestr:

BISHOPS SUFFRAGAN
Horsham, Rt. Revd Lindsay G. Urwin, *cons.* 1993, *apptd* 1993; Bishop's House, 21 Guildford Road, Horsham, W. Sussex RH12 1LU
Lewes, vacant; Beacon House, Berwick, Polegate BN26 6ST

DEAN
Very Revd John D. Treadgold, LVO, *apptd* 1989

CANONS RESIDENTIARY
R. T. Greenacre, *apptd* 1975; F. J. Hawkins, *apptd* 1981
Organist, A. J. Thurlow, FRCO, *apptd* 1980

ARCHDEACONS
Chichester, Ven. M. Brotherton, *apptd* 1991
Horsham, Ven. W. C. L. Filby, *apptd* 1983
Lewes and Hastings, Ven. H. Glaisyer, *apptd* 1991

Chancellor, His Honour Judge Q. T. Edwards, QC, *apptd* 1978
Registrar and Legal Secretary, C. L. Hodgetts
Diocesan Secretary, J. Prichard, Diocesan Church House, 211 New Church Road, Hove, E. Sussex BN3 4ED. Tel: 01273-421021

COVENTRY

7TH BISHOP
Rt. Revd Simon Barrington-Ward, *cons.* 1985, *apptd* 1985; The Bishop's House, 23 Davenport Road, Coventry CV5 6PW. *Signs* Simon Coventry

BISHOP SUFFRAGAN
Warwick, Rt. Revd Anthony M. Priddis, *cons.* 1996, *apptd* 1996; 139 Kenilworth Road, Coventry CV4 7AF

PROVOST
Very Revd John F. Petty, *apptd* 1987

CANONS RESIDENTIARY
P. Oestreicher, *apptd* 1986; V. Faull, *apptd* 1994; J. C. Burch, *apptd* 1995
Organist, A. P. Leddington Wright, *apptd* 1984

ARCHDEACONS
Coventry, Ven. H. I. L. Russell, *apptd* 1989
Warwick, Ven. M. J. J. Paget-Wilkes, *apptd* 1990

Chancellor, Sir William Gage, *apptd* 1980
Registrar and Legal Secretary, D. J. Dumbleton
Diocesan Secretary, Mrs I. Chapman, Church House, Palmerston Road, Coventry CV5 6FJ. Tel: 01203-674328

DERBY

6TH BISHOP
Rt. Revd Jonathan S. Bailey, *cons.* 1992, *apptd* 1995; Derby Church House, Full Street, Derby DE1 3DR. *Signs* Jonathan Derby

BISHOP SUFFRAGAN
Repton, Rt. Revd F. Henry A. Richmond, *cons.* 1986, *apptd* 1986; Repton House, Lea, Matlock DE4 5JP

PROVOST
Very Revd Benjamin H. Lewers, *apptd* 1981

CANONS RESIDENTIARY
G. A. Chesterman, *apptd* 1989; Ven. I. Gatford, *apptd* 1992; G. O. Marshall, *apptd* 1992; R. M. Parsons, *apptd* 1993
Organist, P. Gould, *apptd* 1982

ARCHDEACONS
Chesterfield, Ven. D. C. Garnett, *apptd* 1996
Derby, Ven. I. Gatford, *apptd* 1992

Chancellor, J. W. M. Bullimore, *apptd* 1981
Registrar and Legal Secretary, J. S. Battie
Diocesan Secretary, R. J. Carey, Derby Church House, Full Street, Derby DE1 3DR. Tel: 01332-382233

ELY

67TH BISHOP
Rt. Revd Stephen W. Sykes, *cons.* 1990, *apptd* 1990; The Bishop's House, Ely, Cambs CB7 4DW. *Signs* Stephen Ely

BISHOP SUFFRAGAN
Huntingdon, vacant; 14 Lynn Road, Ely, Cambs CB6 1DA

DEAN
Very Revd Michael Higgins, *apptd* 1991

CANONS RESIDENTIARY
D. J. Green, *apptd* 1980; J. Inge, *apptd* 1996
Organist, P. Trepte, FRCO, *apptd* 1991

ARCHDEACONS
Ely, Ven. J. Watson, *apptd* 1993
Huntingdon, vacant
Wisbech, Ven. J. Rone, *apptd* 1995

Chancellor, W. Gage, QC
Joint Registrars, W. H. Godfrey; P. F. B. Beesley (*Legal Secretary*)
Diocesan Secretary, Dr M. Lavis, Bishop Woodford House, Barton Road, Ely, Cambs CB7 4DX. Tel: 01353-663579

EXETER

69TH BISHOP
Rt. Revd G. Hewlett Thompson, *cons.* 1974, *apptd* 1985; The Palace, Exeter EX1 1HY. *Signs* Hewlett Exon:

BISHOPS SUFFRAGAN
Crediton, Rt. Revd Richard S. Hawkins, *cons.* 1988, *apptd* 1996; 10 The Close, Exeter EX1 1EZ
Plymouth, Rt. Revd John H. Garton, *cons.* 1996, *apptd* 1996; 31 Riverside Walk, Tamerton Foliot, Plymouth PL5 4AQ

DEAN
Very Revd Keith B. Jones, *apptd* 1996

CANONS RESIDENTIARY
A. C. Mawson, *apptd* 1979; K. C. Parry, *apptd* 1991
Organist, L. A. Nethsingha, FRCO, *apptd* 1973

ARCHDEACONS
Barnstaple, Ven. T. Lloyd, *apptd* 1989
Exeter, Ven. A. F. Tremlett, *apptd* 1994
Plymouth, Ven. R. G. Ellis, *apptd* 1982
Totnes, Preb. R. T. Gilpin, *apptd* 1996

Chancellor, Sir David Calcutt, QC, *apptd* 1971
Registrar and Legal Secretary, R. K. Wheeler

Diocesan Secretary, Revd R. Huddleson, Diocesan House, Palace Gate, Exeter, Devon EX1 1HX. Tel: 01392-72686

GIBRALTAR IN EUROPE

BISHOP
Rt. Revd John Hind, *cons.* 1991, *apptd* 1993; 14 Tufton Street, London SW1P 3QZ. *Signs* John Gibraltar

BISHOP SUFFRAGAN
In Europe Rt. Revd Henry Scriven, *cons.* 1995, *apptd* 1994; 14 Tufton Street, London SW1P 3QZ

Vicar-General, Canon W. G. Reid
Dean, Cathedral Church of the Holy Trinity, Gibraltar, Very Revd B. W. Horlock, OBE
Chancellor, Pro-Cathedral of St Paul, Valletta, Malta, Canon A. Woods
Chancellor, Pro-Cathedral of the Holy Trinity, Brussels, Belgium, Canon N. Walker

ARCHDEACONS
Aegean, Ven. S. J. B. Peake
North-West Europe, Ven. G. G. Allen
France, Ven. M. Draper
Gibraltar, Ven. K. Robinson
Italy, Rt. Revd E. Devenport
Scandinavia and Germany, Ven. D. Ratcliff
Switzerland, Ven. P. J. Hawker, OBE

Chancellor, Sir David Calcutt, QC
Registrar and Legal Secretary, J. G. Underwood
Diocesan Secretary, Canon W. G. Reid, 14 Tufton Street, London SW1P 3QZ. Tel: 0171-976 8001

GLOUCESTER

39TH BISHOP
Rt. Revd David Bentley, *cons.* 1986, *apptd* 1993; Bishopscourt, Gloucester GL1 2BQ. *Signs* David Gloucestr

BISHOP SUFFRAGAN
Tewkesbury, Rt. Revd John S. Went, *cons.* 1995, *apptd* 1995; Green Acre, Hempsted, Gloucester GL2 6LG

DEAN
Very Revd Nicholas A. S. Bury, *apptd* 1996

CANONS RESIDENTIARY
R. D. M. Grey, *apptd* 1982; N. Chatfield, *apptd* 1992; N. Heavisides, *apptd* 1993; C. H. Morgan, *apptd* 1996

Organist, D. Briggs, FRCO, *apptd* 1994

ARCHDEACONS
Cheltenham, Ven. J. A. Lewis, *apptd* 1988
Gloucester, Ven. C. J. H. Wagstaff, *apptd* 1982

Chancellor and Vicar-General, Ms D. J. Rogers, *apptd* 1990
Registrar and Legal Secretary, C. G. Peak
Diocesan Secretary, M. Williams, Church House, College Green, Gloucester GL1 2LY. Tel: 01452-410022

GUILDFORD

8TH BISHOP
Rt. Revd John W. Gladwin, *cons.* 1994, *apptd* 1994; Willow Grange, Woking Road, Guildford GU4 7QS. *Signs* John Guildford

BISHOP SUFFRAGAN
Dorking, Rt. Revd Ian Brackley, *cons.* 1996, *apptd* 1995; 13 Pilgrims Way, Guildford GU4 8AD

DEAN
Very Revd Alexander G. Wedderspoon, *apptd* 1987

CANONS RESIDENTIARY
R. D. Fenwick, *apptd* 1990; J. Schofield, *apptd* 1995; Revd Dr Maureen Palmer
Organist, A. Millington, FRCO, *apptd* 1982

ARCHDEACONS
Dorking, Ven. M. Wilson, *apptd* 1995
Surrey, Ven. R. Reiss, *apptd* 1995

Chancellor, His Hon. Judge Goodman
Registrar and Legal Secretary, P. F. B. Beesley
Diocesan Secretary, Mrs K. Ingate, Diocesan House, Quarry Street, Guildford GU1 3XG. Tel: 01483-571826

HEREFORD

103RD BISHOP
Rt. Revd John Oliver, *cons.* 1990, *apptd* 1990; The Palace, Hereford HR4 9BN. *Signs* John Hereford

BISHOP SUFFRAGAN
Ludlow, Rt. Revd Dr John Saxbee, *cons.* 1994, *apptd* 1994; Bishop's House, Halford, Craven Arms, Shropshire SY7 9BT

DEAN
Very Revd Robert A. Willis, *apptd* 1992

CANONS RESIDENTIARY
P. Iles, *apptd* 1983; J. Tiller, *apptd* 1984; J. Butterworth, *apptd* 1994
Organist, Dr R. Massey, FRCO, *apptd* 1974

ARCHDEACONS
Hereford, Ven. L. G. Moss, *apptd* 1992
Ludlow, Rt. Revd J. C. Saxbee, *apptd* 1992

Chancellor, J. M. Henty
Joint Registrars and Legal Secretaries, V. T. Jordan; P. F. B. Beesley
Diocesan Secretary, Miss S. Green, The Palace, Hereford HR4 9BL. Tel: 01432-353863

LEICESTER

5TH BISHOP
Rt. Revd Thomas F. Butler, PH.D., LL D, *cons.* 1985, *apptd* 1991; Bishop's Lodge, 10 Springfield Road, Leicester LE2 3BD. *Signs* Thomas Leicester

STIPENDIARY ASSISTANT BISHOP
Rt. Revd William Down, *cons.* 1990, *apptd* 1995

PROVOST
Very Revd Derek Hole, *apptd* 1992

CANONS RESIDENTIARY
M. T. H. Banks, *apptd* 1988; M. Wilson, *apptd* 1988
Organist, J. T. Gregory, *apptd* 1994

ARCHDEACONS
Leicester, Ven. M. Edson, *apptd* 1994
Loughborough, Ven. I. Stanes, *apptd* 1992

Chancellor, N. Seed, *apptd* 1989
Registrars and Legal Secretaries, P. C. E. Morris; R. H. Bloor

Diocesan Secretary, J. Cryer, Church House, 3–5 St Martin's East, Leicester LEI 5FX. Tel: 0116-262 7445

LICHFIELD

97TH BISHOP
Rt. Revd Keith N. Sutton, *cons.* 1978, *apptd* 1984; Bishop's House, The Close, Lichfield WS13 7LG. *Signs* Keith Lichfield

BISHOPS SUFFRAGAN
Shrewsbury, Rt. Revd David M. Hallatt, *cons.* 1994, *apptd* 1994; 68 London Road, Shrewsbury SY2 6PG
Stafford, Rt. Revd Christopher J. Hill, *cons.* 1996, *apptd* 1996; Ash Garth, Broughton Crescent, Barlaston, Staffs ST12 9DD
Wolverhampton, Rt. Revd Michael G. Bourke, *cons.* 1993, *apptd* 1993; 61 Richmond Road, Wolverhampton WV3 9JH

DEAN
Very Revd Tom Wright, *apptd* 1993

CANONS RESIDENTIARY
Ven. R. B. Ninis, *apptd* 1974; A. N. Barnard, *apptd* 1977; J. Howe, *apptd* 1988; C. W. Taylor, *apptd* 1995

Organist, A. Lumsden, *apptd* 1992

ARCHDEACONS
Lichfield, Ven. R. B. Ninis, *apptd* 1974
Salop, Ven. G. Frost, *apptd* 1987
Stoke-on-Trent, Ven. D. Ede, *apptd* 1989

Chancellor, His Honour Judge Shand
Registrar and Legal Secretary, J. P. Thorneycroft
Diocesan Secretary, D. R. Taylor, St Mary's House, The Close, Lichfield, Staffs WS13 7LD. Tel: 01543-414551

LINCOLN

70TH BISHOP
Rt. Revd Robert M. Hardy, *cons.* 1980, *apptd* 1987; Bishop's House, Eastgate, Lincoln LN2 1QQ. *Signs* Robert Lincoln

BISHOPS SUFFRAGAN
Grantham, Rt. Revd William Ind, *cons.* 1987, *apptd* 1987; Fairacre, Barrowby High Road, Grantham NG31 8NP
Grimsby, Rt. Revd David Tustin, *cons.* 1979, *apptd* 1979; Bishop's House, Church Lane, Irby-upon-Humber, Grimsby DN37 7JR

DEAN
Very Revd Brandon D. Jackson, *apptd* 1989

CANONS RESIDENTIARY
B. R. Davis, *apptd* 1977; A. J. Stokes, *apptd* 1992; V. White, *apptd* 1994

Organist, C. S. Walsh, FRCO, *apptd* 1988

ARCHDEACONS
Lincoln, Ven. A. Hawes, *apptd* 1995
Lindsey, vacant
Stow, Ven. R. J. Wells, *apptd* 1989

Chancellor, His Honour Judge Goodman, *apptd* 1971
Registrar and Legal Secretary, D. M. Wellman
Diocesan Secretary, P. Hamlyn Williams, The Old Palace, Lincoln LN2 1PU. Tel: 01522-529241

NORWICH

70TH BISHOP
Rt. Revd Peter J. Nott, *cons.* 1977, *apptd* 1985; Bishop's House, Norwich NR3 1SB. *Signs* Peter Norvic:

BISHOPS SUFFRAGAN
Lynn, Rt. Revd David Conner, *cons.* 1994, *apptd* 1994; The Old Vicarage, Castle Acre, King's Lynn PE32 2AA
Thetford, Rt. Revd Hugo F. de Waal, *cons.* 1992, *apptd* 1992; Rectory Meadow, Bramerton, Norwich NR14 7DW

DEAN
Very Revd Stephen Platten, *apptd* 1995

CANONS RESIDENTIARY
M. F. Perham, *apptd* 1992; Ven. C. J. Offer, *apptd* 1994; R. J. Hanmer, *apptd* 1994

Organist, D. Dunnett, *apptd* 1996

ARCHDEACONS
Lynn, Ven. A. C. Foottit, *apptd* 1987
Norfolk, Ven. A. M. Handley, *apptd* 1993
Norwich, Ven. C. J. Offer, *apptd* 1994

Chancellor, His Honour J. H. Ellison, VRD, *apptd* 1955
Registrar and Legal Secretary, J. W. F. Herring
Diocesan Secretary, D. Adeney, Diocesan House, 109 Dereham Road, Easton, Norwich, Norfolk NR9 5ES. Tel: 01603-880853

OXFORD

41ST BISHOP
Rt. Revd Richard D. Harries, *cons.* 1987, *apptd* 1987; Diocesan Church House, North Hinksey, Oxford OX2 0NB. *Signs* Richard Oxon:

AREA BISHOPS
Buckingham, Rt. Revd Colin J. Bennetts, *cons.* 1994, *apptd* 1994; Sheridan, Grimms Hill, Great Missenden HP16 9BD
Dorchester, Rt. Revd Anthony J. Russell, *cons.* 1988, *apptd* 1988; Holmby House, Sibford Ferris, Banbury, Oxon OX15 5RG
Reading, vacant; Greenbanks, Old Bath Road, Sonning, Reading RG4 0SY

DEAN OF CHRIST CHURCH
Very Revd John H. Drury, *apptd* 1991

CANONS RESIDENTIARY
Ven. F. V. Weston, *apptd* 1982; O. M. T. O'Donovan, D.Phil., *apptd* 1982; J. M. Pierce, *apptd* 1987; J. S. K. Ward, *apptd* 1991; R. Jeffery, *apptd* 1996; Prof. J. Webster, *apptd* 1996
Organist, S. Darlington, FRCO, *apptd* 1985

ARCHDEACONS
Berkshire, Ven. M. A. Hill, *apptd* 1992
Buckingham, Ven. J. A. Morrison, *apptd* 1989
Oxford, Ven. F. V. Weston, *apptd* 1982

Chancellor, P. T. S. Boydell, QC, *apptd* 1958
Registrar and Legal Secretary, Dr F. E. Robson
Secretary to the Diocesan Board of Finance, T. Landsbert, Diocesan Church House, North Hinksey, Oxford OX2 0NB. Tel: 01865-244566

PETERBOROUGH

37TH BISHOP
Rt. Revd Ian P. M. Cundy, *cons.* 1992, *apptd* 1996; The Palace, Peterborough PEI IYA. *Signs* Ian Petriburg:

BISHOP SUFFRAGAN
Brixworth, Rt. Revd Paul E. Barber, *cons.* 1989, *apptd* 1989; 4 The Avenue, Dallington, Northampton NNI 4RZ

DEAN
Very Revd Michael Bunker, *apptd* 1992

CANONS RESIDENTIARY
T. R. Christie, *apptd* 1980; J. Higham, *apptd* 1983; T. Willmott, *apptd* 1989
Organist, C. S. Gower, FRCO, *apptd* 1977

ARCHDEACONS
Northampton, Ven. M. R. Chapman, *apptd* 1991
Oakham, Ven. B. Fernyhough, *apptd* 1977

Chancellor, T. A. C. Coningsby, QC, *apptd* 1989
Registrar and Legal Secretary, R. Hemingray
Diocesan Secretary, K. H. Hope-Jones, The Palace, Peterborough, Cambs PEI IYB. Tel: 01733-64448

PORTSMOUTH

8TH BISHOP
Rt. Revd Dr Kenneth W. Stevenson, *cons.* 1995, *apptd* 1995; Bishopswood, 23 The Avenue, Fareham, Hants PO14 INT. *Signs* Kenneth Portsmouth

PROVOST
Very Revd Michael Yorke, *apptd* 1994

CANONS RESIDENTIARY
C. J. Bradley, *apptd* 1990; D. T. Isaac, *apptd* 1990; Jane Hedges, *apptd* 1993
Organist, D. Price, *apptd* 1996

ARCHDEACONS
Isle of Wight, Ven. K. M. L. H. Banting, *apptd* 1996
Portsmouth, Ven. G. P. Knowles, *apptd* 1993

Chancellor, His Honour Judge Aglionby, *apptd* 1978
Registrar and Legal Secretary, Miss H. A. G. Tyler
Diocesan Secretary, M. F. Jordan, Cathedral House, St Thomas's Street, Portsmouth, Hants PO1 2HA. Tel: 01705-825731

ROCHESTER

106TH BISHOP
Rt. Revd Dr Michael Nazir-Ali, *cons.* 1984, *apptd* 1994; Bishopscourt, Rochester MEI ITS. *Signs* Michael Roffen:

BISHOP SUFFRAGAN
Tonbridge, Rt. Revd Brian A. Smith, *cons.* 1993, *apptd* 1993; Bishop's Lodge, St Botolph's Road, Sevenoaks TNI3 3AG

DEAN
Very Revd Edward F. Shotter, *apptd* 1990

CANONS RESIDENTIARY
E. R. Turner, *apptd* 1981; R. J. R. Lea, *apptd* 1988; J. Armson, *apptd* 1989; N. Warren, *apptd* 1989
Organist, R. Sayer, FRCO, *apptd* 1995

ARCHDEACONS
Bromley, Ven. G. Norman, *apptd* 1994
Rochester, Ven. N. L. Warren, *apptd* 1989
Tonbridge, Ven. Judith Rose

Chancellor, His Honour Judge M. B. Goodman, *apptd* 1971
Registrar, O. R. Woodfield
Legal Secretary, D. W. Faull, OBE
Diocesan Secretary, P. Law, St Nicholas Church, Boley Hill, Rochester MEI ISL. Tel: 01634-830333

ST ALBANS

9TH BISHOP
Rt. Revd Christopher W. Herbert, *cons.* 1995, *apptd* 1995; Abbey Gate House, St Albans AL3 4HD. *Signs* Christopher St Albans

BISHOPS SUFFRAGAN
Bedford, Rt. Revd John H. Richardson, *cons.* 1994, *apptd* 1994; 168 Kimbolton Road, Bedford MK41 8DN
Hertford, Rt. Revd Robin J. N. Smith, *cons.* 1990, *apptd* 1990; Hertford House, Abbey Mill Lane, St Albans AL3 4HE

DEAN
Very Revd Christopher Lewis, *apptd* 1993

CANONS RESIDENTIARY
C. Garner, *apptd* 1984; G. R. S. Ritson, *apptd* 1987; M. Sansom, *apptd* 1988; C. R. J. Foster, *apptd* 1994
Organist, Dr B. Rose, *apptd* 1988

ARCHDEACONS
Bedford, Ven. M. L. Lesiter, *apptd* 1993
St Albans, Ven. P. B. Davies, *apptd* 1987

Chancellor, His Honour Judge Bursell, QC, *apptd* 1992
Registrar and Legal Secretary, D. N. Cheetham
Diocesan Secretary, L. Nicholls, Holywell Lodge, 41 Holywell Hill, St Albans ALI IHE. Tel: 01727-854532

ST EDMUNDSBURY AND IPSWICH

BISHOP
vacant; Bishop's House, 4 Park Road, Ipswich IPI 3ST. *Signs* – St Edmundsbury and Ipswich

BISHOP SUFFRAGAN
Dunwich, Rt. Revd Timothy J. Stevens, *cons.* 1995, *apptd* 1995; The Old Vicarage, Stowupland, Stowmarket IP14 4BQ

PROVOST
Very Revd J. Atwell, *apptd* 1995

CANONS RESIDENTIARY
A. M. Shaw, *apptd* 1989; M. E. Mingins, *apptd* 1993
Organist, M. Cousins, *apptd* 1993

ARCHDEACONS
Ipswich, Ven. T. A. Gibson, *apptd* 1987
Sudbury, Ven. J. Cox, *apptd* 1995
Suffolk, Ven. G. Arrand, *apptd* 1994

Chancellor, His Honour Sir John Blofeld, QC, *apptd* 1974
Registrar and Legal Secretary, Revd J. D. Mitson
Diocesan Secretary, I. Dodd, 13–15 Tower Street, Ipswich IPI 3BG. Tel: 01473-211028

SALISBURY

77TH BISHOP
Rt. Revd David S. Stancliffe, *cons.* 1993, *apptd* 1993; South Canonry, The Close, Salisbury SP1 2ER. *Signs* David Sarum

BISHOPS SUFFRAGAN
Ramsbury, Rt. Revd Peter St G. Vaughan, *cons.* 1989, *apptd* 1989; Bishop's House, Urchfont, Devizes, Wilts SN10 4QH
Sherborne, Rt. Revd John D. G. Kirkham, *cons.* 1976, *apptd* 1976; Little Bailie, Sturminster Marshall, Wimborne BH21 4AD

DEAN
Very Revd Derek Watson, *apptd* 1996

CANONS RESIDENTIARY
D. J. C. Davies, *apptd* 1985; D. M. K. Durston, *apptd* 1992; June Osborne, *apptd* 1995
Organist, R. G. Seal, FRCO, *apptd* 1968

ARCHDEACONS
Dorset, Ven. G. E. Walton, *apptd* 1982
Sarum, Ven. B. J. Hopkinson, *apptd* 1986
Sherborne, Ven. P. C. Wheatley, *apptd* 1991
Wilts, Ven. B. J. Smith, *apptd* 1980

Chancellor, His Honour J. H. Ellison, VRD, *apptd* 1955
Registrar and Legal Secretary, F. M. Broadbent
Diocesan Secretary, Revd Karen Curnock, Church House, Crane Street, Salisbury SP1 2QB. Tel: 01722-411922

SOUTHWARK

8TH BISHOP
Rt. Revd Robert K. Williamson, *cons.* 1984, *trans.* 1991, *apptd* 1991; Bishop's House, 38 Tooting Bec Gardens, London SW16 1QZ. *Signs* Robert Southwark

AREA BISHOPS
Croydon, Rt. Revd Dr Wilfred D. Wood, DD, *cons.* 1985, *apptd* 1985; St Matthew's House, George Street, Croydon CR0 1PE
Kingston upon Thames, Rt Revd Martin Wharton, *cons.* 1992, *apptd* 1992; *Kingston Episcopal Area Office*, Whitelands College, West Hill, London SW15 3SN
Woolwich, Rt. Revd Colin O. Buchanan, *cons.* 1985, *apptd* 1996; c/o Trinity House, 4 Chapel Court, Borough High Street, London SE1 1HW

PROVOST
Very Revd Colin B. Slee, *apptd* 1994

CANONS RESIDENTIARY
Dr M. Kitchen, *apptd* 1988; D. Painter, *apptd* 1991; Helen Cunliffe, *apptd* 1995
Organist, P. Wright, FRCO, *apptd* 1989

ARCHDEACONS
Croydon, Ven. V. A. Davies, *apptd* 1994
Lambeth, Ven. C. R. B. Bird, *apptd* 1988
Lewisham, Ven. D. J. Atkinson, *apptd* 1996
Reigate, Ven. M. Baddeley, *apptd* 1996
Southwark, Ven. D. L. Bartles-Smith, *apptd* 1985
Wandsworth, Ven. D. Gerrard, *apptd* 1989

Chancellor, vacant
Registrar and Legal Secretary, P. Morris

Diocesan Secretary, M. Cawte, Trinity House, 4 Chapel Court, Borough High Street, London SE1 1HW. Tel: 0171-403 8686

TRURO

13TH BISHOP
Rt. Revd Michael T. Ball, *cons.* 1980, *apptd* 1990; Lis Escop, Truro TR3 6QQ. *Signs* Michael Truro

BISHOP SUFFRAGAN
St Germans, Rt. Revd Graham R. James, *cons.* 1993, *apptd* 1993; 32 Falmouth Road, Truro TR1 2HX

DEAN
Very Revd David J. Shearlock, *apptd* 1982

CANONS RESIDENTIARY
P. R. Gay, *apptd* 1994; K. P. Mellor, *apptd* 1994; P. D. Goodridge, *apptd* 1996
Organist, A. Nethsingha, FRCO, *apptd* 1994

ARCHDEACONS
Cornwall, Ven. J. T. McCabe, *apptd* 1996
Bodmin, Ven. R. D. C. Whiteman, *apptd* 1989

Chancellor, P. T. S. Boydell, QC, *apptd* 1957
Registrar and Legal Secretary, M. J. Follett
Diocesan Secretary, C. B. Gorton, Diocesan House, Kenwyn, Truro TR1 3DU. Tel: 01872-74351

WORCESTER

BISHOP
vacant; The Bishop's House, Hartlebury Castle, Kidderminster DY11 7XX. *Signs* – Worcester

BISHOP SUFFRAGAN
Dudley, Rt. Revd Dr Rupert Hoare, *cons.* 1993, *apptd* 1993; The Bishop's House, Brooklands, Halesowen Road, Cradley Heath B64 7JF

DEAN
vacant

CANONS RESIDENTIARY
Ven. F. Bentley, *apptd* 1984; D. G. Thomas, *apptd* 1987; I. M. MacKenzie, *apptd* 1989
Organist, A. Lucas, *apptd* 1996

ARCHDEACONS
Dudley, Ven. J. Gathercole, *apptd* 1987
Worcester, Ven. F. Bentley, *apptd* 1984

Chancellor, P. T. S. Boydell, QC, *apptd* 1959
Registrar and Legal Secretary, M. Huskinson
Diocesan Secretary, J. Stanbury, The Old Palace, Deansway, Worcester WR1 2JE. Tel: 01905-20537

ROYAL PECULIARS

WESTMINSTER
The Collegiate Church of St Peter
Dean, vacant
Sub Dean and Archdeacon, A. E. Harvey, *apptd* 1987
Canons of Westminster, A. E. Harvey, *apptd* 1982; D. C. Gray, *apptd* 1987; C. D. Semper, *apptd* 1987; D. H. Hutt, *apptd* 1995

Chapter Clerk and Receiver-General, Rear-Adm. K. A. Snow,
CB, *apptd* 1987
Organist, M. Neary, FRCO, *apptd* 1988
Registrar, S. J. Holmes, MVO, 20 Dean's Yard, London
SWIP 3PA
Legal Secretary, C. L. Hodgetts

WINDSOR

The Queen's Free Chapel of St George within Her Castle of Windsor
Dean, Very Revd Patrick R. Mitchell, FSA, *apptd* 1989
Canons Residentiary, J. A. White, *apptd* 1982; D. M. Stanesby,
ph.D., *apptd* 1985; M. A. Moxon, *apptd* 1990; L. F. P.
Gunner, *apptd* 1996
Chapter Clerk, Lt.-Col. N. J. Newman, *apptd* 1990, Chapter
Office, The Cloisters, Windsor Castle, Windsor, Berks
SL4 INJ
Organist, J. Rees-Williams, FRCO, *apptd* 1991

Province of York

YORK

96TH ARCHBISHOP AND PRIMATE OF ENGLAND
Most Revd and Rt. Hon. David M. Hope, KCVO, D.Phil., LL D,
cons. 1985, *trans.* 1995, *apptd* 1995; Bishopthorpe, York
YO2 1QE. *Signs* David Ebor:

BISHOPS SUFFRAGAN
Hull, Rt. Revd James S. Jones, *cons.* 1994, *apptd* 1994; Hullen
House, Woodfield Lane, Hessle, Hull HU13 OES
Selby, Rt. Revd Humphrey V. Taylor, *cons.* 1991, *apptd* 1991;
10 Precentor's Court, York YO1 2ES
Whitby, Rt. Revd Gordon Bates, *cons.* 1983, *apptd* 1983;
60 West Green, Stokesley, Middlesbrough TS9 5BD
Beverley, Rt. Revd John Gaisford, *cons.* 1994, *apptd* 1994
(provincial episcopal visitor); 3 North Lane, Roundhay,
Leeds LS8 2QJ

DEAN
Very Revd Raymond Furnell, *apptd* 1994

CANONS RESIDENTIARY
J. Toy, ph.D., *apptd* 1983; R. Metcalfe, *apptd* 1988;
P. J. Ferguson, *apptd* 1995; E. R. Norman, ph.D., DD, *apptd* 1995
Organist, P. Moore, FRCO, *apptd* 1983

ARCHDEACONS
Cleveland, Ven. C. J. Hawthorn, *apptd* 1991
East Riding, Ven. H. F. Buckingham, *apptd* 1988
York, Ven. G. B. Austin, *apptd* 1988

Official Principal and Auditor of the Chancery Court,
J. A. D. Owen, QC
Chancellor of the Diocese, His Honour Judge Coningsby, QC,
apptd 1977
Vicar-General of the Province and Official Principal of the
Consistory Court, His Honour Judge Coningsby, QC
Registrar and Legal Secretary, L. P. M. Lennox
Diocesan Secretary, K. W. Dodgson, Church House,
Ogleforth, York YO1 2JE. Tel: 01904-611696

DURHAM

92ND BISHOP
Rt. Revd A. Michael A. Turnbull, *cons.* 1988, *apptd* 1994;
Auckland Castle, Bishop Auckland DL14 7NR. *Signs*
Michael Dunelm:

BISHOP SUFFRAGAN
Jarrow, Rt. Revd Alan Smithson, *cons.* 1990, *apptd* 1990; The
Old Vicarage, Hallgarth, Pittington, Durham DH6 1AB

DEAN
Very Revd John R. Arnold, *apptd* 1989

CANONS RESIDENTIARY
M. C. Perry, *apptd* 1970; R. L. Coppin, *apptd* 1974; Ven. J. D.
Hodgson, *apptd* 1983; D. W. Brown, *apptd* 1990; G. S. Pedley,
apptd 1993
Organist, J. B. Lancelot, FRCO, *apptd* 1985

ARCHDEACONS
Auckland, Ven. G. G. Gibson, *apptd* 1993
Durham, Ven. J. D. Hodgson, *apptd* 1993

Chancellor, His Honour Judge Bursell, QC, *apptd* 1989
Registrar and Legal Secretary, D. M. Robertson
Diocesan Secretary, W. Hurworth, Auckland Castle, Bishop
Auckland, Co. Durham DL14 7QJ. Tel: 01388-604515

BLACKBURN

7TH BISHOP
Rt. Revd Alan D. Chesters, *cons.* 1989, *apptd* 1989; Bishop's
House, Ribchester Road, Blackburn BB1 9EF. *Signs* Alan
Blackburn

BISHOPS SUFFRAGAN
Burnley, Rt. Revd Martyn W. Jarrett, *cons.* 1994, *apptd* 1994;
Dean House, 449 Padiham Road, Burnley BB12 6TE
Lancaster, Rt. Revd John Nicholls, *cons.* 1990, *apptd* 1990;
Wheatfields, 7 Dallas Road, Lancaster LA1 1TN

PROVOST
Very Revd David Frayne, *apptd* 1992

CANONS RESIDENTIARY
K. J. Parfitt, *apptd* 1994; J. R. Hall, *apptd* 1994; D. M. Galilee,
apptd 1995; A. D. Hindley, *apptd* 1996
Organist, G. Stewart, *apptd* 1995

ARCHDEACONS
Blackburn, Ven. F. J. Marsh, *apptd* 1996
Lancaster, Ven. K. H. Gibbons, *apptd* 1981

Chancellor, J. W. M. Bullimore, *apptd* 1990
Registrar and Legal Secretary, T. A. Hoyle
Diocesan Secretary, Revd M. J. Wedgeworth, Diocesan
Office, Cathedral Close, Blackburn BB1 5AA. Tel: 01254-
54421

BRADFORD

8TH BISHOP
Rt. Revd David J. Smith, *cons.* 1987, *apptd* 1992;
Bishopscroft, Ashwell Road, Heaton, Bradford BD9 4AU.
Signs David Bradford

Provost
Very Revd John S. Richardson, *apptd* 1990

Canons Residentiary
C. G. Lewis, *apptd* 1993; G. Smith, *apptd* 1996
Organist, A. Horsey, frco, *apptd* 1986

Archdeacons
Bradford, Ven. D. H. Shreeve, *apptd* 1984
Craven, Ven. M. L. Grundy, *apptd* 1994

Chancellor, D. M. Savill, qc, *apptd* 1976
Registrar and Legal Secretary, J. G. H. Mackrell
Diocesan Secretary, M. Halliday, Cathedral Hall, Stott Hill,
Bradford bd1 4et. Tel: 01274-725958

CARLISLE

65th Bishop
Rt. Revd Ian Harland, *cons.* 1985, *apptd* 1989; Rose Castle,
Dalston, Carlisle ca5 7bz. *Signs* Ian Carliol:

Bishop Suffragan
Penrith, Rt. Revd Richard Garrard, *cons.* 1994, *apptd* 1994;
Holm Croft, Castle Road, Kendal, Cumbria la9 7au

Dean
Very Revd Henry E. C. Stapleton, *apptd* 1988

Canons Residentiary
R. A. Chapman, *apptd* 1978; Ven. D. C. Turnbull, *apptd* 1993;
D. W. V. Weston, *apptd* 1994; C. Hill, *apptd* 1996
Organist, J. Suter, frco, *apptd* 1991

Archdeacons
Carlisle, Ven. D. C. Turnbull, *apptd* 1993
West Cumberland, vacant
Westmorland and Furness, Ven. D. T. I. Jenkins, *apptd* 1995

Chancellor, His Honour Judge Aglionby, *apptd* 1991
Registrar and Legal Secretary, Mrs S. Holmes
Diocesan Secretary, Canon C. Hill, Church House, West
Walls, Carlisle ca3 8ue. Tel: 01228-22573

CHESTER

40th Bishop
Rt. Revd Peter R. Forster, ph.d., *cons.* 1996, *apptd* 1996;
Bishop's House, Chester chi 2jd. *Signs* Peter Cestr:

Bishops Suffragan
Birkenhead, Rt. Revd Michael L. Langrish, *cons.* 1993, *apptd*
1993; 67 Bidston Road, Oxton, Birkenhead l43 6tr
Stockport, Rt. Revd Geoffrey M. Turner, *cons.* 1994, *apptd*
1994; Bishop's Lodge, Back Lane, Dunham Town,
Altrincham, Cheshire wa14 4sg

Dean
Very Revd Dr Stephen S. Smalley, *apptd* 1986

Canons Residentiary
R. M. Rees, *apptd* 1990; O. A. Conway, *apptd* 1991; Dr
T. J. Dennis, *apptd* 1994; J. W. S. Newcome, *apptd* 1994
Organist, R. Fisher, frco, *apptd* 1968

Archdeacons
Chester, Ven. C. Hewetson, *apptd* 1994
Macclesfield, Ven. R. J. Gillings, *apptd* 1994

Chancellor, H. H. Lomas, *apptd* 1977
Registrar and Legal Secretary, A. K. McAllester
Diocesan Secretary, P. J. Mills, Diocesan House, Raymond
Street, Chester chi 4pn. Tel: 01244-379222

LIVERPOOL

6th Bishop
Rt. Revd David S. Sheppard, *cons.* 1969, *apptd* 1975; Bishop's
Lodge, Woolton Park, Liverpool l25 6dt. *Signs* David
Liverpool

Bishop Suffragan
Warrington, Rt. Revd John Packer, *cons.* 1996, *apptd* 1996;
c/o Martinsfield, Elm Avenue, Great Crosby, Liverpool
l23 2sx

Dean
Very Revd Rhys D. C. Walters, obe, *apptd* 1983

Canons Residentiary
D. J. Hutton, *apptd* 1983; M. C. Boyling, *apptd* 1994; N. T.
Vincent, *apptd* 1995
Organist, Prof. I. Tracey, *apptd* 1980

Archdeacons
Liverpool, Ven. R. L. Metcalf, *apptd* 1994
Warrington, Ven. C. D. S. Woodhouse, *apptd* 1981

Chancellor, R. G. Hamilton
Registrar and Legal Secretary, R. H. Arden
Diocesan Secretary, K. Cawdron, Church House, 1 Hanover
Street, Liverpool l1 3dw. Tel: 0151-709 9722

MANCHESTER

10th Bishop
Rt. Revd Christopher J. Mayfield, *cons.* 1985, *apptd* 1993;
Bishopscourt, Bury New Road, Manchester m7 4le.
Signs Christopher Manchester

Bishops Suffragan
Bolton, Rt. Revd David Bonser, *cons.* 1991, *apptd* 1991;
4 Sandfield Drive, Lostock, Bolton bl6 4du
Hulme, Rt. Revd Colin J. F. Scott, *cons.* 1984, *apptd* 1984;
1 Raynham Avenue, Didsbury, Manchester m20 0bw
Middleton, Rt. Revd Stephen Venner, *cons.* 1994, *apptd* 1994;
The Hollies, Manchester Road, Rochdale ol11 3qy

Dean
Very Revd Kenneth Riley, *apptd* 1993

Canons Residentiary
Ven. R. B. Harris, *apptd* 1980; J. R. Atherton, ph.d., *apptd* 1984;
A. E. Radcliffe, *apptd* 1991; P. Denby, *apptd* 1995
Organist, C. Stokes, *apptd* 1992

Archdeacons
Bolton, Ven. L. M. Davies, *apptd* 1992
Manchester, Ven. R. B. Harris, *apptd* 1980
Rochdale, Ven. J. M. M. Dalby, *apptd* 1991

Chancellor, G. C. H. Spafford, *apptd* 1976
Registrar and Legal Secretary, M. Darlington
Diocesan Secretary, Mrs J. Park, Diocesan Church House,
90 Deansgate, Manchester m3 2gh. Tel: 0161-833 9521

NEWCASTLE

10th Bishop
Rt. Revd Andrew A. K. Graham, *cons.* 1977, *apptd* 1981;
Bishop's House, 29 Moor Road South, Gosforth,
Newcastle upon Tyne ne3 1pa. *Signs* A. Newcastle

STIPENDIARY ASSISTANT BISHOP
Rt. Revd Kenneth Gill, *cons.* 1972, *apptd* 1980

PROVOST
Very Revd Nicholas G. Coulton, *apptd* 1990

CANONS RESIDENTIARY
R. Langley, *apptd* 1985; P. R. Strange, *apptd* 1986;
I. F. Bennett, *apptd* 1988; Ven. P. Elliott, *apptd* 1993

Organist, T. G. Hone, FRCO, *apptd* 1987

ARCHDEACONS
Lindisfarne, Ven. M. E. Bowering, *apptd* 1987
Northumberland, Ven. P. Elliott, *apptd* 1993

Chancellor, His Honour A. J. Blackett-Ord, CVO, *apptd* 1971
Registrar and Legal Secretary, Mrs B. J. Lowdon
Diocesan Secretary, J. M. Craster, Church House, Grainger
Park Road, Newcastle upon Tyne NE4 8SX. Tel: 0191-
226 0622

RIPON

11TH BISHOP
Rt. Revd David N. de L. Young, *cons.* 1977, *apptd* 1977;
Bishop Mount, Ripon HG4 5DP. *Signs* David Ripon

BISHOP SUFFRAGAN
Knaresborough, Rt. Revd Malcolm J. Menin, *cons.* 1986, *apptd*
1986; 16 Shaftesbury Avenue, Roundhay, Leeds LS8 1DT

DEAN
Very Revd John Methuen, *apptd* 1995

CANONS RESIDENTIARY
P. J. Marshall, *apptd* 1985; M. R. Glanville-Smith, *apptd* 1990;
Revd K. Punshon, *apptd* 1996

Organist, K. Beaumont, FRCO, *apptd* 1994

ARCHDEACONS
Leeds, Ven. J. M. Oliver, *apptd* 1992
Richmond, Ven. K. Good, *apptd* 1993

Chancellor, His Honour Judge Grenfell, *apptd* 1992
Registrar and Legal Secretary, J. R. Balmforth
Diocesan Secretary, G. M. Royal, Diocesan Office, St Mary's
Street, Leeds LS9 7DP. Tel: 0113-248 7487

SHEFFIELD

5TH BISHOP
Rt. Revd David R. Lunn, *cons.* 1980, *apptd* 1980;
Bishopscroft, Snaithing Lane, Sheffield S10 3LG. *Signs*
David Sheffield

BISHOP SUFFRAGAN
Doncaster, Rt. Revd. Michael F. Gear, *cons.* 1993, *apptd* 1993;
Bishops Lodge, Hooton Roberts, Rotherham S65 4PF

PROVOST
Very Revd Michael Sadgrove, *apptd* 1995

CANONS RESIDENTIARY
T. M. Page, *apptd* 1982; Ven. S. R. Lowe, *apptd* 1988;
C. M. Smith, *apptd* 1991; Jane E. M. Sinclair, *apptd* 1993

Organist, S. Lole, *apptd* 1994

ARCHDEACONS
Doncaster, Ven. B. L. Holdridge, *apptd* 1994
Sheffield, Ven. S. R. Lowe, *apptd* 1988

Chancellor, Prof. J. D. McClean, *apptd* 1992

Registrar and Legal Secretary, C. P. Rothwell
Diocesan Secretary, C. A. Beck, FCIS, Diocesan Church
House, 95–99 Effingham Street, Rotherham S65 1BL. Tel:
0114-283 7547

SODOR AND MAN

79TH BISHOP
Rt. Revd Noel D. Jones, CB, *cons.* 1989, *apptd* 1989; The
Bishop's House, Quarterbridge Road, Douglas, Isle of
Man IM2 3RF. *Signs* Noel Sodor and Man

CANONS
B. H. Kelly, *apptd* 1980; J. Sheen, *apptd* 1991; F. H. Bird, *apptd*
1993; D. Whitworth, *apptd* 1996

ARCHDEACON
Isle of Man, Ven. B. H. Partington, *apptd* 1996

Vicar-General and Chancellor, Ms C. Faulds
Registrar and Legal Secretary, C. J. Callow
Diocesan Secretary, The Hon. C. Murphy, c/o Cooil
Voorath, The Cronk, Ballaugh, Isle of Man IM7 5AX. Tel:
01624-897880

SOUTHWELL

9TH BISHOP
Rt. Revd Patrick B. Harris, *cons.* 1973, *apptd* 1988; Bishop's
Manor, Southwell NG25 0JR. *Signs* Patrick Southwell

BISHOP SUFFRAGAN
Sherwood, Rt. Revd Alan W. Morgan, *cons.* 1989, *apptd* 1989;
Sherwood House, High Oakham Road, Mansfield
NG18 5AJ

PROVOST
Very Revd David Leaning, *apptd* 1991

CANONS RESIDENTIARY
D. P. Keene, *apptd* 1981; I. G. Collins, *apptd* 1985;
M. R. Austin, *apptd* 1988

Organist, P. Hale, *apptd* 1989

ARCHDEACONS
Newark, Ven. D. C. Hawtin, *apptd* 1992
Nottingham, Ven. G. Ogilvie, *apptd* 1996

Chancellor, J. Shand, *apptd* 1981
Registrar and Legal Secretary, C. C. Hodson
Diocesan Secretary, B. Noake, Dunham House, Westgate,
Southwell, Notts NG25 0JL. Tel: 01636-814331

WAKEFIELD

11TH BISHOP
Rt. Revd Nigel S. McCulloch, *cons.* 1986, *apptd* 1992;
Bishop's Lodge, Woodthorpe Lane, Wakefield WF2 6JL.
Signs Nigel Wakefield

BISHOP SUFFRAGAN
Pontefract, Rt. Revd John Finney, *cons.* 1993, *apptd* 1993;
Pontefract House, 181A Manygates Lane, Wakefield
WF2 7DR

PROVOST
Very Revd John E. Allen, *apptd* 1982

CANONS RESIDENTIARY
R. D. Baxter, *apptd* 1986; I. C. Knox, *apptd* 1989; G. Nairn-Briggs, *apptd* 1992
Organist, J. Bielby, FRCO, *apptd* 1972

ARCHDEACONS
Halifax, Ven. R. Inwood, *apptd* 1995
Pontefract, Ven. J. Flack, *apptd* 1992

Chancellor, P. Collier, QC, *apptd* 1992
Registrar and Legal Secretary, L. Box
Diocesan Secretary, J. Clark, Church House, 1 South Parade, Wakefield WF1 1LP. Tel: 01924-371802

The Anglican Communion

The Anglican Communion consists of 37 independent provincial or national Christian churches throughout the world, many of which are in Commonwealth countries and originated from missionary activity by the Church of England. There is no single world authority linking the Communion, but all recognize the leadership of the Archbishop of Canterbury and have strong ecclesiastical and historical links with the Church of England. Every ten years all the bishops in the Communion meet at the Lambeth Conference, convened by the Archbishop of Canterbury. The Conference has no policy-making authority but is an important forum for the discussion of issues of common concern. The Anglican Consultative Council was set up in 1968 to function between conferences and the meeting of the Primates every two years.

There are about 70 million Anglicans and 800 archbishops and bishops world-wide.

THE CHURCH IN WALES

The Anglican Church was the established church in Wales from the 16th century until 1920, when the estrangement of the majority of Welsh people from Anglicanism resulted in disestablishment. Since then the Church in Wales has been an autonomous province consisting of six sees, with one of the diocesan bishops being elected Archbishop of Wales by an electoral college comprising elected lay and clerical members.

The legislative body of the Church in Wales is the Governing Body, which has 356 members in total, divided between the three orders of bishops, clergy and laity. It is presided over by the Archbishop of Wales and meets twice annually. Its decisions are binding upon all members of the Church. There are about 100,000 members of the Church in Wales, with six bishops, about 700 stipendiary clergy and 1,142 parishes.

THE GOVERNING BODY OF THE CHURCH IN WALES, 39 Cathedral Road, Cardiff CF1 9XF. Tel: 01222–231638. *Secretary-General,* J. W. D. McIntyre

10TH ARCHBISHOP OF WALES, Most Revd Alwyn R. Jones (Bishop of St Asaph), *elected* 1991

THE RT. REVD BISHOPS
Bangor (79*th*), Rt. Revd Dr Barry C. Morgan, *b.* 1947, *cons.* 1993, *elected* 1992; Tŷ'r Esgob, Bangor LL57 2SS. *Signs* Barry Bangor. *Stipendiary clergy,* 69
Llandaff (101*st*), Rt. Revd Roy T. Davies, *b.* 1934, *cons.* 1985, *elected* 1985; Llys Esgob, The Cathedral Green, Llandaff, Cardiff CF5 2YE. *Signs* Roy Landav. *Stipendiary clergy,* 158

Monmouth (8*th*), Rt. Revd Rowan D. Williams, *b* 1950, *cons.* 1992, *elected* 1992; Bishopstow, Stow Hill, Newport NP9 4EA. *Signs* Rowan Monmouth. *Stipendiary clergy,* 120
St Asaph (74*th*), Most Revd Alwyn R. Jones, *b.* 1934, *cons.* 1982, *elected* 1982; Esgobty, St Asaph, Clwyd LL17 0TW. *Signs* Alwyn Cambrensis. *Stipendiary clergy,* 112
St David's (126*th*), Rt. Revd D. Huw Jones, *b.* 1934, *cons.* 1993, *elected* 1995; Llys Esgob, Abergwili, Carmarthen SA31 2JG. *Signs* Huw St Davids. *Stipendiary clergy,* 132
Swansea and Brecon (7*th*), Rt. Revd Dewi M. Bridges, *b.* 1933, *cons.* 1988, *elected* 1988; Ely Tower, Brecon, Powys LD3 9DE. *Signs* Dewi Swansea & Brecon. *Stipendiary clergy,* 100

The stipend of a diocesan bishop of the Church in Wales is £24,901 a year from 1996

THE SCOTTISH EPISCOPAL CHURCH

The Scottish Episcopal Church was founded after the Act of Settlement (1690) established the presbyterian nature of the Church of Scotland. The Scottish Episcopal Church is in full communion with the Church of England but is autonomous. The governing authority is the General Synod, an elected body of 180 members which meets once a year. The diocesan bishop who convenes and presides at meetings of the General Synod is called the Primus and is elected by his fellow bishops.

There are 54,382 members of the Scottish Episcopal Church, of whom 33,795 are communicants. There are seven bishops, 210 stipendiary clergy, and 320 churches and places of worship.

THE GENERAL SYNOD OF THE SCOTTISH EPISCOPAL CHURCH, 21 Grosvenor Crescent, Edinburgh EH12 5EE. Tel: 0131-225 6357. *Secretary-General,* J. F. Stuart

PRIMUS OF THE SCOTTISH EPISCOPAL CHURCH, Most Revd Richard F. Holloway (Bishop of Edinburgh), *elected* 1992

THE RT. REVD BISHOPS
Aberdeen and Orkney, A. Bruce Cameron, *b.* 1941, *cons.* 1992, *apptd* 1992. *Clergy,* 19
Argyll and the Isles, Douglas M. Cameron, *b.* 1935, *cons.* 1993, *apptd* 1992. *Clergy,* 9
Brechin, Robert T. Halliday, *b.* 1932, *cons.* 1990, *apptd* 1990. *Clergy,* 19
Edinburgh, Richard F. Holloway, *b.* 1933, *cons.* 1986, *apptd* 1986. *Clergy,* 53
Glasgow and Galloway, John M. Taylor, *b.* 1932, *cons.* 1991, *apptd* 1991. *Clergy,* 48
Moray, Ross and Caithness, Gregor Macgregor, *b.* 1933, *cons.* 1994, *apptd* 1994. *Clergy,* 13
St Andrews, Dunkeld and Dunblane, Michael H. G. Henley, *b.* 1938, *cons.* 1995, *apptd* 1995. *Clergy,* 30

The minimum stipend of a diocesan bishop of the Scottish Episcopal Church was £19,278 in 1996

THE CHURCH OF IRELAND

The Anglican Church was the established church in Ireland from the 16th century but never secured the allegiance of a majority of the Irish and was disestablished in 1871. The Church in Ireland is divided into the provinces of Armagh and Dublin, each under an archbishop. The provinces are subdivided into 12 dioceses.

The legislative body is the General Synod, which has 660 members in total, divided between the House of Bishops and the House of Representatives. The Archbishop of Armagh is elected by the House of Bishops; other episcopal elections are made by an electoral college.

There are about 375,000 members of the Church of Ireland, with two archbishops, ten bishops, about 600 clergy and about 1,000 churches and places of worship.

CENTRAL OFFICE, Church of Ireland House, Church Avenue, Rathmines, Dublin 6. Tel: 00-353-1-4978422. *Chief Officer and Secretary of the Representative Church Body,* R. H. Sherwood; *Assistant Secretary of the General Synod,* D. G. Meredith

PROVINCE OF ARMAGH

ARCHBISHOP OF ARMAGH AND PRIMATE OF ALL IRELAND, Most Revd Robert H. A. Eames, PH.D., *b.* 1937, *cons.* 1975, *trans.* 1986. *Clergy,* 50

THE RT. REVD BISHOPS
Clogher, Brian D. A. Hannon, *b.* 1936, *cons.* 1986, *apptd* 1986. *Clergy,* 34
Connor, James E. Moore, *b.* 1933, *cons.* 1995, *apptd.* 1995. *Clergy,* 104
Derry and Raphoe, James Mehaffey, PH.D., *b.* 1931, *cons.* 1980, *apptd* 1980. *Clergy,* 55
Down and Dromore, Gordon McMullan, PH.D., TH.D., *b.* 1934, *cons.* 1980, *trans.* 1986. *Clergy,* 107
Kilmore, Elphin and Ardagh, Michael H. G. Mayes, *b.* 1941, *cons.* 1993, *apptd* 1993. *Clergy,* 28
Tuam, Killala and Achonry, John R. W. Neill, *b.* 1945, *cons.* 1986, *apptd* 1986. *Clergy,* 12

PROVINCE OF DUBLIN

ARCHBISHOP OF DUBLIN, BISHOP OF GLENDALOUGH, AND PRIMATE OF IRELAND, Most Revd Walton N. F. Empey, *b.* 1934, *cons.* 1981, *trans.* 1985, 1996. *Clergy,* 88

THE RT. REVD BISHOPS
Cashel and Ossory, Noel V. Willoughby, *b.* 1926, *cons.* 1980, *apptd* 1980. *Clergy,* 34
Cork, Cloyne and Ross, Robert A. Warke, *b.* 1930, *cons.* 1988, *apptd* 1988. *Clergy,* 29
Limerick and Killaloe, Edward F. Darling, *b.* 1933, *cons.* 1985, *apptd* 1985. *Clergy,* 24
Meath and Kildare, Most Revd Robert L. Clarke, *b.* 1949, *cons.* 1996, *trans.* 1996. *Clergy,* 23

Anglican Communion Overseas

ANGLICAN CHURCH OF AOTEAROA, NEW ZEALAND AND POLYNESIA

PRIMATE AND ARCHBISHOP OF AOTEAROA, NEW ZEALAND AND POLYNESIA, The Most Revd Brian N. Davis (Bishop of Wellington), *cons.* 1980, *apptd* 1986

THE RT. REVD BISHOPS
Aotearoa, Whakahuhui Vercoe, *cons.* 1981, *apptd* 1981
Auckland, John Paterson, *cons.* 1995, *apptd* 1995
Christchurch, David Coles, *cons.* 1990, *apptd* 1990
Dunedin, Penelope Jamieson, *cons.* 1990, *apptd* 1990
Nelson, Derek Eaton, *cons.* 1990, *apptd* 1990
Polynesia, Jabez Bryce, *cons.* 1975, *apptd* 1975
Waiapu, Murray Mills, *cons.* 1991, *apptd* 1991

Waikato, David Moxon, *cons.* 1993, *apptd* 1993
Wellington, see above

ANGLICAN CHURCH OF AUSTRALIA

PRIMATE OF AUSTRALIA, The Most Revd Keith Rayner (Archbishop of Melbourne), *cons.* 1969, *apptd* 1991

PROVINCE OF NEW SOUTH WALES

METROPOLITAN
Archbishop of Sydney, The Most Revd R. Harry Goodhew, *cons.* 1982, *apptd* 1993

THE RT. REVD BISHOPS
Armidale, Peter Chiswell, *cons.* 1976, *apptd* 1976
Bathurst, Bruce W. Wilson, *cons.* 1984, *apptd* 1989
Canberra and Goulburn, George V. Browning, *cons.* 1985, *apptd* 1993
Grafton, Bruce A. Schultz, *cons.* 1983, *apptd* 1985
Newcastle, Roger A. Herft, *cons.* 1986, *apptd* 1993
Riverina, Bruce Q. Clark, *cons.* 1993, *apptd* 1993

PROVINCE OF QUEENSLAND

METROPOLITAN
Archbishop of Brisbane, The Most Revd Peter Hollingworth, *cons.* 1985, *apptd* 1990

THE RT. REVD BISHOPS
North Queensland, Clyde M. Wood, *cons.* 1983, *apptd* 1996
Northern Territory, Richard F. Appleby, *cons.* 1992, *apptd* 1992
Rockhampton, Ronald F. Stone, *cons.* 1992, *apptd* 1996

PROVINCE OF SOUTH AUSTRALIA

METROPOLITAN
Archbishop of Adelaide, The Most Revd Ian G. C. George, *cons.* 1989, *apptd* 1991

THE RT. REVD BISHOPS
The Murray, Graham H. Walden, *cons.* 1981, *apptd* 1989
Willochra, W. David H. McCall, *cons.* 1987, *apptd* 1987

PROVINCE OF VICTORIA

METROPOLITAN
Archbishop of Melbourne, The Most Revd Keith Rayner, *cons.* 1969, *apptd* 1990 (*see* above)

THE RT. REVD BISHOPS
Ballarat, R. David Silk, *cons.* 1994, *apptd* 1994
Bindigo, R. David Bowden, *cons.* 1995, *apptd* 1995
Gippsland, Arthur L. V. Jones, *cons.* 1994, *apptd* 1994
Wangaratta, Paul Richardson, *cons.* 1987, *apptd* 1995

PROVINCE OF WESTERN AUSTRALIA

METROPOLITAN
Archbishop of Perth, The Most Revd Peter F. Carnley, PH.D., *cons.* 1981, *apptd* 1981

THE RT. REVD BISHOPS
Bunbury, Hamish J. U. Jamieson, *cons.* 1974, *apptd* 1984
North-West Australia, Anthony Nicholls, *cons.* 1992, *apptd* 1992

EXTRA-PROVINCIAL DIOCESE

Bishop of Tasmania, Rt. Revd Phillip K. Newell, AO, *cons.* 1982, *apptd* 1982

EPISCOPAL ANGLICAN CHURCH OF BRAZIL
Igreja Episcopal Anglicana Do Brasil

PRIMATE, The Most Revd Glauco Soares de Lima (Bishop of São Paulo), *cons.* 1989, *apptd* 1994

THE RT. REVD BISHOPS
Brasilia, Almir dos Santos, *cons.* 1989, *apptd* 1989
Central Brazil, Sydney A. Ruiz, *cons.* 1985, *apptd* 1985
Northern Brazil, Clovis E. Rodrigues, *cons.* 1985, *apptd* 1986
Pelotas, Luiz O. P. Prado, *cons.* 1987, *apptd* 1989
São Paulo, see above, *apptd* 1989
Southern Brazil, Claudio V. S. Gastal, *cons.* 1984, *apptd* 1984
South-Western Brazil, Jubal P. Neves, *cons.* 1993, *apptd* 1993

CHURCH OF THE PROVINCE OF BURUNDI

ARCHBISHOP OF PROVINCE, The Most Revd Samuel Sindamuka (Bishop of Matana), *cons.* 1975, *apptd* 1989

THE RT. REVD BISHOPS
Bujumbura, Pie Ntukamazina, *cons.* 1990, *apptd* 1990
Buye, Samuel Ndayisenga, *apptd* 1979
Gitega, Jean Nduwayo, *apptd* 1985
Matana, see above

ANGLICAN CHURCH OF CANADA

ARCHBISHOP AND PRIMATE, The Most Revd Michael G. Peers, *cons.* 1977, *elected* 1986

PROVINCE OF BRITISH COLUMBIA
METROPOLITAN
Archbishop of Kootenay, The Most Revd David Crawley, *cons.* 1990, *elected* 1994

THE RT. REVD BISHOPS
British Columbia, Barry Jenks, *cons.* 1992, *elected* 1992
Caledonia, John Hannen, *cons.* 1981, *elected* 1981
Cariboo, James Cruickshank, *cons.* 1992, *elected* 1992
Kootenay, see above, *elected* 1990
New Westminster, Michael Ingham, *cons.* 1994, *elected* 1993
Yukon, Terrence O. Buckle, *cons.* 1993, *elected* 1995

PROVINCE OF CANADA
METROPOLITAN
Archbishop of Western Newfoundland, The Most Revd Stewart S. Payne, *cons.* 1978, *elected* 1990

THE RT. REVD BISHOPS
Central Newfoundland, Edward Marsh, *cons.* 1990, *elected* 1990
Eastern Newfoundland and Labrador, Donald Harvey, *cons.* 1993, *elected* 1992
Fredericton, George Lemon, *cons.* 1989, *elected* 1989
Montreal, Andrew Hutchison, *cons.* 1990, *elected* 1990
Nova Scotia, Arthur Peters, *cons.* 1982, *elected* 1982
Quebec, Bruce Stavert, *cons.* 1991, *elected* 1991
Western Newfoundland, see above

PROVINCE OF ONTARIO
METROPOLITAN
Archbishop of Huron, The Most Revd Percival O'Driscoll, *cons.* 1987, *elected* 1993

THE RT. REVD BISHOPS
Algoma, Ronald Ferris, *cons.* 1981, *elected* 1995
Huron, see above
Moosonee, Caleb Lawrence, *cons.* 1980, *elected* 1980
Niagara, Walter Asbil, *cons.* 1990, *elected* 1990
Ontario, Peter Mason, *cons.* 1992, *elected* 1992
Ottawa, John Baycroft, *cons.* 1985, *elected* 1993
Toronto, Terence Finlay, *cons.* 1986, *elected* 1990

PROVINCE OF RUPERT'S LAND
METROPOLITAN
Archbishop of Calgary, The Most Revd Barry Curtis, *cons.* 1983, *elected* 1994

THE RT. REVD BISHOPS
Arctic, J. Christopher Williams, *cons.* 1987, *elected* 1991
Athabasca, John Clarke, *cons.* 1992, *elected* 1992
Brandon, Malcolm Harding, *cons.* 1992, *elected* 1992
Calgary, see above, *elected* 1983
Edmonton, Kenneth Genge, *cons.* 1988, *elected* 1988
Keewatin, vacant
Qu' Appelle, Eric Bays, *cons.* 1986, *elected* 1986
Rupert's Land, Patrick Lee, *cons.* 1994, *elected* 1994
Saskatchewan, Anthony Burton, *cons.* 1993, *elected* 1993
Saskatoon, Thomas Morgan, *cons.* 1985, *elected* 1993

CHURCH OF THE PROVINCE OF CENTRAL AFRICA

ARCHBISHOP OF PROVINCE, The Most Revd Walter P. K. Makhulu (Bishop of Botswana), *cons.* 1979, *apptd* 1980

THE RT. REVD BISHOPS
Botswana, see above
Central Zambia, Titus Zhenje
Eastern Zambia, John R. Osmers
Harare, Jonathan Siyachitema, *cons.* 1981
Lake Malawi, Peter Nyanja, *cons.* 1978, *apptd* 1978
The Lundi, vacant
Lusaka, Stephen Mumba, *cons.* 1981, *apptd* 1981
Manicaland, Elijah Masuko, *cons.* 1981, *apptd* 1981
Matabeleland, Theophilus Naledi, *cons.* 1987, *apptd* 1987
Northern Malawi, Jackson C. Biggers
Northern Zambia, Bernard Malango, *cons.* 1988, *apptd* 1988
Southern Malawi, Nathaniel Aipa, *cons.* 1987, *apptd* 1987

CHURCH OF THE PROVINCE OF THE INDIAN OCEAN

ARCHBISHOP OF PROVINCE, The Most Revd Remi Rabenirina (Bishop of Atananarivo), *cons.* 1984, *apptd* 1995

THE RT. REVD BISHOPS
Antananarivo, see above, *apptd* 1984
Antsiranana, Keith Benzies, OBE, *cons.* 1982, *apptd* 1982
Mahajanga, vacant
Mauritius, Rex Donat, *cons.* 1984, *apptd* 1984
Seychelles, French Chang-Him, *cons.* 1979, *apptd* 1979
Toamasina, Donald Smith, *cons.* 1990, *apptd* 1990

HOLY CATHOLIC CHURCH IN JAPAN
Nippon Sei Ko Kai

PRIMATE, The Most Revd James T. Yashiro (Bishop of Kita Kanto), *cons.* 1985, *apptd* 1994

THE RT. REVD BISHOPS
Chubu, Samuel W. Hoyo, *cons.* 1987, *apptd* 1987
Hokkaido, Augustine H. Amagi, *cons.* 1987, *apptd* 1987
Kita Kanto, see above, *apptd* 1985
Kobe, John J. Furumoto, *cons.* 1992, *apptd* 1992
Kyoto, Barnabas M. Muto, *cons.* 1995, *apptd* 1995
Kyushu, Joseph N. Iida, *cons.* 1982, *apptd* 1982
Okinawa, Paul S. Nakamura, *cons.* 1972, *apptd* 1972
Osaka, Augustine K. Takano, *cons.* 1995, *apptd* 1995
Tohoku, John T. Sato, *cons.* 1996, *apptd* 1996
Tokyo, John M. Takeda, *cons.* 1988, *apptd* 1988
Yokohama, Raphael S. Kajiwara, *cons.* 1984, *apptd* 1984

EPISCOPAL CHURCH IN JERUSALEM AND THE MIDDLE EAST

PRESIDENT-BISHOP, Rt. Revd Samir Kafity, *apptd* 1986

THE RT. REVD BISHOPS
Jerusalem, Samir Kafity, *cons.* 1984, *apptd* 1986
Iran, Iraj Mottahedeh, *cons.* 1990, *apptd* 1990
Egypt, Ghais A. Malik, *cons.* 1984, *apptd* 1984
Cyprus and the Gulf, Clive Handford, *cons.* 1990, *apptd* 1996

CHURCH OF THE PROVINCE OF KENYA

ARCHBISHOP OF PROVINCE (*acting*), Rt Revd David Gitari (Bishop of Kirinyaga), *cons.* 1975, *apptd* 1994

THE RT. REVD BISHOPS
Butere, Horace Etemesi, *cons.* 1993, *apptd* 1993
Eldoret, Stephen Kewasis, *cons.* 1992, *apptd* 1992
Embu, Moses Njue, *cons.* 1990, *apptd* 1990
Kajiado, vacant
Katakwa, Eliud Okiring, *cons.* 1991, *apptd* 1991
Kirinyaga, see above, *apptd* 1975
Kitui, Benjamin Nzimbi, *cons.* 1985, *apptd* 1995
Machakos, vacant
Maseno North, vacant
Maseno South, Francis Mwayi-Abiero, *cons.* 1994, *apptd* 1994
Maseno West, Joseph Wasonga, *cons.* 1991, *apptd* 1991
Mombasa, Julius Kalu, *cons.* 1994, *apptd* 1994
Mount Kenya Central, Julius G. Gachuche, *cons.* 1993, *apptd* 1993
Mount Kenya South, vacant
Mount Kenya West, Alfred Chipman, *cons.* 1993, *apptd* 1993
Mumias, William Wesa
Nairobi, vacant
Nakuru, Stephen M. Njihia, *cons.* 1990, *apptd* 1990
Nambale, Josiah M. Were, *cons.* 1993, *apptd* 1993
Southern Nyanza, Haggai Nyang', *cons.* 1990, *apptd* 1993
Taita/Taveta, Samson M. Mwaluda, *cons.* 1993, *apptd* 1993

CHURCH OF THE PROVINCE OF KOREA

ARCHBISHOP OF PROVINCE, The Most Revd Bundo C. H. Kim (Bishop of Pusan), *cons.* 1988, *apptd* 1995

THE RT. REVD BISHOPS
Daejon, Paul Hwan Yoon, *cons.* 1987, *apptd* 1988
Pusan, see above
Seoul, Matthew C. B. Chung, *cons.* 1995, *apptd* 1995

CHURCH OF THE PROVINCE OF MELANESIA

ARCHBISHOP OF PROVINCE, The Most Revd Ellison L. Pogo (Bishop of Central Melanesia), *cons.* 1981, *apptd* 1994

THE RT. REVD BISHOPS
Banks and Torres, Walter Ling, *cons.* 1996, *apptd* 1996
Central Melanesia, see above
Hanuato'o, James Mason, *cons.* 1991, *apptd* 1991
Malaita, Terry M. Brown, *cons.* 1996, *apptd* 1996
Temotu, Lazarus Munamua, *cons.* 1987, *apptd* 1987
Vanuatu, Michael Tavoa, *cons.* 1990, *apptd* 1990
Ysabel, Walter Siba, *cons.* 1990, *apptd* 1994

EPISCOPAL CHURCH OF MEXICO

ARCHBISHOP OF PROVINCE, The Most Revd José G. Saucedo (Bishop of Cuernavaca), *cons.* 1958, *elected* 1995

THE RT. REVD BISHOPS
Cuernavaca, see above, *apptd* 1989
Mexico, Sergio Carrauza-Gomez, *cons.* 1989, *apptd* 1989
Northern Mexico, German Martinez-Marquez, *cons.* 1987, *apptd* 1987
South-East Mexico, Claro Huerta-Rames, *cons.* 1980, *apptd* 1989
Western Mexico, Samuel Espinoza-Venegas, *cons.* 1981, *apptd* 1983

CHURCH OF THE PROVINCE OF MYANMAR

ARCHBISHOP OF PROVINCE, The Most Revd Andrew Mya Han (Bishop of Yangon), *cons.* 1988, *apptd* 1988

THE RT. REVD BISHOPS
Hpa'an, Daniel Hoi Kyin, *cons.* 1992, *apptd* 1992
Mandalay, Andrew Hla Aung, *cons.* 1988, *apptd* 1988
Myitkyina, John Shan Lum, *cons.* 1994, *apptd* 1994
Sittwe, Barnabas Theaung Hawi, *cons.* 1978, *apptd* 1980
Toungoo, John Wilme, *cons.* 1994, *apptd* 1994
Yangon (Rangoon), see above

CHURCH OF THE PROVINCE OF NIGERIA

ARCHBISHOP OF PROVINCE, The Most Revd Joseph Adetiloye (Bishop of Lagos), *apptd* 1991

THE RT. REVD BISHOPS
Aba, A. O. Iwuagwu, *apptd* 1985
Abuja, Peter Akinola, *apptd* 1989
Akoko, J. O. K. Olowokure, *apptd* 1986
Akure, Emmanuel B. Gbonigi, *apptd* 1983
Asaba, Roland N. C. Nwosu, *apptd* 1977
Awka, Maxwell S. C. Anikwenwa, *apptd* 1987
Bauchi, Emmanuel O. Chukwuma, *apptd* 1990
Benin, Peter Onekpe

Calabar, W. G. Ekprikpo
Egba-Abeokuta, Matthew O. Owadayo
Egbado, Timothy I. O. Bolaji
Ekiti, C. A. Akinbola, *apptd* 1986
Enugu, Gideon N. Otubelu, *apptd* 1969
Ibadan, Gideon I. Olajide, *apptd* 1988
Ife, Gabriel B. Oloniyo
Ijebu, Abraham O. Olowoyo, *apptd* 1990
Ijebu Remo, E. O. I. Ogundana, *apptd* 1984
Ikale-Ilaje, J. Akin Omoyajowo
Ilesha, E. A. Ademowo, *apptd* 1989
Jos, B. A. Kwashi
Kaduna, Titus Ogbonyomi, *apptd* 1975
Kafanchan, William Diya, *apptd* 1990
Kano, B. O. Omosebi, *apptd* 1990
Katsina, J. S. Kwasu, *apptd* 1990
Kwara, Jeremiah O. A. Fabuluje
Lagos, see above, *apptd* 1985
Lokoja, George Bako
Maiduguri, E. K. Mani, *apptd* 1990
Makurdi, Nathan Nyom
Mbaise, Cyril Chukwka Anyanwu
Minna, Nathaniel Yisa, *apptd* 1990
The Niger, Jonathan A. Onyemelukwe, *apptd* 1975
Niger Delta, Samuel O. Elenwo, *apptd* 1981
Nsukka, Jonah Ilonuba
Oke-Osun, Abraham O. Awoson
Okigwe North, Alfred Nwaizuzu
Okigwe South, Bennett Okoro
Orlu, Samuel C. N. Ebo, *apptd* 1984
Ondo, Samuel O. Aderin, *apptd* 1981
Osun, Seth O. Fagbemi, *apptd* 1987
Owerri, Benjamin C. Nwankiti, *apptd* 1968
Owo, Peter A. Adebiyi
Sabongida Ora, Albert A. Agbaje
Sokoto, J. A. Idowu-Fearon, *apptd* 1990
Ukwa, Uju Obinya
Umuahia, Ngochukwe U. Ezuoke
Uyo, Ebenezar E. Nglass
Warri, Nathaniel Enuku
Yola, Chris O. Efobi, *apptd* 1990

ANGLICAN CHURCH OF PAPUA NEW GUINEA

ARCHBISHOP OF PROVINCE, The Most Revd James Ayong (Bishop of Aipo Rongo), *cons.* 1995, *elected* 1996

THE RT. REVD BISHOPS
Aipo Rongo, see above, *elected* 1995
Dogura, Tevita Talanoa, *cons.* 1992, *elected* 1992
New Guinea Islands, Michael Hough, *cons.* 1996, *elected* 1996
Popondota, Reuben Tariambari, *cons.* 1995, *elected* 1994
Port Moresby, Isaac Gadebo, *cons.* 1983, *elected* 1983

EPISCOPAL CHURCH IN THE PHILIPPINES

PRIME BISHOP, The Most Revd Narciso V. Ticobay, *cons.* 1986, *apptd* 1993

THE RT. REVD BISHOPS
Central Philippines, Manuel C. Lumpias, *cons.* 1977, *apptd* 1978
North Central Philippines, Joel A. Pachao, *cons.* 1993, *apptd* 1993
Northern Luzon, Ignacio C. Soliba, *cons.* 1990, *apptd* 1990
Northern Philippines, Robert L. Longid, *cons.* 1983, *apptd* 1986

Southern Philippines, James B. Manguramas, *cons.* 1993, *apptd* 1993

CHURCH OF THE PROVINCE OF RWANDA

ARCHBISHOP OF PROVINCE, The Most Revd Augustin Nshamihigo (Bishop of Shyira), *apptd* 1992 (currently in exile)

THE RT. REVD BISHOPS
Butare, Venuste Mutiganda
Byumba, Onesphore Rwaje
Cyangugu, Daniel Nduhura (currently in exile)
Kibungo, Augustin Mvunabandi (currently in exile)
Kigali, Jonathan Ruhumuliza
Kigeme, Norman Kayumba
Shyira, see above, *apptd* 1984
Shyogwe, Samuel Musubyimana (currently in exile)

CHURCH OF THE PROVINCE OF SOUTHERN AFRICA

Metropolitan
Archbishop of Cape Town, The Most Revd Winston H. N. Ndungane, *cons.* 1991, *trans.* 1996

THE RT. REVD BISHOPS
Bloemfontein, Thomas Stanage, *cons.* 1978, *trans.* 1982
Christ the King, Peter Lee, *cons.* 1990, *elected* 1990
George, Derek Damant, *cons.* 1985, *elected* 1985
Grahamstown, David Russell, *cons.* 1986, *trans.* 1987
Johannesburg, Duncan Buchanan, *cons.* 1986, *elected* 1986
Kimberley and Kuruman, vacant
Klerksdorp, David Nkwe, *cons.* 1990, *elected* 1990
Lebombo, Dinis Sengulane, *cons.* 1976, *elected* 1976
Lesotho, Philip Mokuku, *cons.* 1978, *elected* 1978
Namibia, James Kauluma, *cons.* 1978, *elected* 1981
Natal, Michael Nuttall, *cons.* 1975, *trans.* 1982
Niassa, Paulino Manhique, *cons.* 1986, *elected* 1986
Port Elizabeth, Eric Pike, *cons.* 1989, *trans.* 1993
Pretoria, Richard Kraft, *cons.* 1982, *elected* 1982
St Helena, John Ruston, *cons.* 1985, *trans.* 1991
St John's, Jacob Dlamini, *cons.* 1980, *elected* 1985
St Mark the Evangelist, Rollo Le Feuvre, *cons.* 1987, *elected* 1987
South-Eastern Transvaal, David Beetge, *cons.* 1990, *elected* 1990
Swaziland, Lawrence Zulu, *cons.* 1975, *trans.* 1993
Umzimvubu, Geoffrey Davies, *cons.* 1987, *elected* 1991
Zululand, Peter Harker, *cons.* 1993, *elected* 1993

Order of Ethiopia, Sigqibo Dwane, *cons.* 1983, *apptd* 1983

ANGLICAN CHURCH OF THE SOUTHERN CONE OF AMERICA

PRESIDING BISHOP, Rt. Revd Maurice Sinclair (Bishop of Northern Argentina), *cons.* 1990

THE RT. REVD BISHOPS
Argentina, David Leake, *cons.* 1969, *apptd* 1990
Bolivia, Gregory Venables, *cons.* 1993
Chile, Colin Bazley, *cons.* 1969, *apptd* 1977
Northern Argentina, see above, *apptd* 1990
Paraguay, John Ellison, *cons.* 1988, *apptd* 1988

Peru and Bolivia, vacant
Uruguay, Harold Godfrey, *cons.* 1986, *apptd* 1986

PROVINCE OF THE EPISCOPAL CHURCH OF THE SUDAN

ARCHBISHOP OF PROVINCE, The Most Revd Benjamin
W. Yugusuk (Bishop of Juba)

THE RT. REVD BISHOPS
Bor, Nathaniel Garang
Cueibet, Ruben M. Makoi
El Obeil, Kurkeil M. Khamis
Juba, see above
Kaduguli, Peter El Birish
Kajo-keji, Manaseh B. Dawidi
Khartoum, Bulus Idris Tia
Lainya, Eliaba L. Menasona
Lui, Ephraim Natana
Malakal, Kedekia Mabior
Maridi, Joseph Marona
Mundri, Dr Eluzai G. Munda
Port Sudan, vacant
Rajaf, Michael S. Lugor
Renk, Daniel Deng
Rokon, Francis Loyo
Rumbek, Gabriel R. Jur
Torit, Wilson A. Ogwok
Wau, Henery Riak
Yambio, Daniel Zindo, *cons.* 1984, *apptd* 1984
Yei, Seme L. Solomone
Yirol, Benjamin Mangar

CHURCH OF THE PROVINCE OF TANZANIA

ARCHBISHOP OF PROVINCE, The Most Revd John
A. Ramadhani (Bishop of Zanzibar and Tanga), *cons.*
1980, *apptd* 1984

THE RT. REVD BISHOPS
Central Tanganyika, Godfrey Mhogolo, *cons.* 1989, *apptd*
1989
Dar es Salaam, Basil Sambano, *cons.* 1992, *apptd* 1992
Kagera, Edwin Nyamubi, *cons.* 1993, *apptd* 1993
Mara, vacant
Masasi, Christopher Sadiki, *cons.* 1992, *apptd* 1992
Morogoro, Dudley Mageni, *cons.* 1987, *apptd* 1987
Mount Kilimanjaro, Simon Makundi, *cons.* 1991, *apptd* 1991
Mpwapwa, Simon Chiwanga, *cons.* 1991, *apptd* 1991
Rift Valley, Alpha Mohamed, *cons.* 1982, *apptd* 1991
Ruaha, Donald Mtetemela, *cons.* 1982, *apptd* 1990
Ruvuma, Stanford Shauri, *cons.* 1989, *apptd* 1989
South-West Tanganyika, Charles Mwaigoga, *cons.* 1983, *apptd*
1983
Tabora, Francis Ntiruka, *cons.* 1989, *apptd* 1989
Victoria Nyanza, John Changae, *cons.* 1993, *apptd* 1993
Western Tanganyika, Gerard Mpango, *cons.* 1983, *apptd* 1983
Zanzibar and Tanga, see above

CHURCH OF THE PROVINCE OF UGANDA

ARCHBISHOP OF PROVINCE, The Most Revd Livingstone
Mpalanyi-Nkoyoyo (Bishop of Kampala)

THE RT. REVD BISHOPS
Bukedi, Nicodemus Okille, *apptd* 1984
Bunyoro-Kitara, Wilson N. Turumanya
Busoga, Cyprian Bamwoze, *apptd* 1972
Central Buganda, George Sinabulya
East Ankole, Elisha Kyamugambi, *cons.* 1992, *apptd* 1992
Kampala, see above
Karamoja, Peter Lomongin, *apptd* 1987
Kigezi, William Rukirande
Kinkizi, John Ntegyereize
Kitgum, Macleord B. Ochola II
Lango, Melchizedek Otim, *apptd* 1976
Luwero, Mesusera Bugimbi, *cons.* 1990, *apptd* 1990
Madi and West Nile, Enoch Drati
Mbale, Israel Koboyi, *cons.* 1992, *apptd* 1992
Mityana, Wilson Mutebi, *apptd* 1977
Muhabura, Ernest M. Shalita, *cons.* 1990, *apptd* 1990
Mukono, Michael Ssenyimba
Namirembe, Samuel B. Ssekkadde
Nebbi, Henry L. Orombi, *cons.* 1993, *apptd* 1993
North Kigezi, John Kahijwa
North Mbale, Peter Mudonyi, *cons.* 1992, *apptd* 1992
Northern Uganda, Gideon Oboma
Ruwenzori, Eustace Kamanyire, *apptd* 1981
Soroti, Geresom Ilukor, *apptd* 1976
South Ruwenzori, Zebidee Masereka
West Ankole, Yorumu Bamunoba, *apptd* 1977
West Buganda, Christopher Senyonjo, *apptd* 1974

EPISCOPAL CHURCH IN THE USA

PRESIDING BISHOP AND PRIMATE, Most Revd Edmond
Lee Browning, DD, *cons.* 1968, *apptd* 1986

RT. REVD BISHOPS
Province I
Connecticut, Clarence Coleridge, *cons.* 1981, *apptd* 1994
Maine, vacant
Massachusetts, M. Thomas Shaw, *cons.* 1994, *apptd* 1995
New Hampshire, Douglas E. Theuner, *cons.* 1986, *apptd* 1986
Rhode Island, Geralyn Wolfe, *cons.* 1996, *apptd* 1996
Vermont, Mary A. Mcleod, *cons.* 1993, *apptd* 1993
Western Massachusetts, vacant

Province II
Albany, David S. Ball, *cons.* 1984, *apptd* 1984
Central New York, David B. Joslin, *cons.* 1991, *apptd* 1992
Europe, Convocation of American Churches in, Jeffery
Rowthorn, *cons.* 1987
Haiti, Zaché Duracin, *cons.* 1993, *apptd* 1994
Long Island, Orris Walker, *cons.* 1988, *apptd* 1991
New Jersey, Joe M. Doss, *cons.* 1993, *apptd* 1993
New York, Richard Grein, *cons.* 1981, *apptd* 1989
Newark, John S. Spong, *cons.* 1976, *apptd* 1979
Rochester, William G. Burrill, *cons.* 1984, *apptd* 1984
Virgin Islands, Telésforo Isaac (*Bishop-in-charge*), *cons.* 1972
Western New York, David C. Bowman, *cons.* 1986, *apptd* 1987

Province III
Bethlehem, Paul Marshall, *cons.* 1996, *apptd* 1996
Central Pennsylvania, Michael W. Creighton, *cons.* 1995
Delaware, C. Cabell Tennis, *cons.* 1986, *apptd* 1986
Easton, Martin G. Townsend, *cons.* 1992, *apptd* 1993
Maryland, Robert Ihloff, *cons.* 1995

---

*missionary diocese

North-Western Pennsylvania, Robert D. Rowley jun., *cons.* 1989, *apptd* 1991
Pennsylvania, Allen L. Bartlett, *cons.* 1986, *apptd* 1987
Pittsburgh, Alden M. Hathaway, *cons.* 1981, *apptd* 1983
Southern Virginia, Frank Vest, *cons.* 1985, *apptd* 1991
South-Western Virginia, A. Heath Light, *cons.* 1979, *apptd* 1979
Virginia, Peter J. Lee, *cons.* 1984, *apptd* 1985
Washington, Ronald Haines, *cons.* 1986, *apptd* 1990
West Virginia, John H. Smith, *cons.* 1989, *apptd* 1989

Province IV

Alabama, Robert O. Miller, *cons.* 1988, *apptd* 1988
Atlanta, Frank K. Allan, *cons.* 1988, *apptd* 1989
Central Florida, John Howe, *cons.* 1989, *apptd* 1990
Central Gulf Coast, Charles F. Duvall, *cons.* 1981, *apptd* 1981
East Carolina, Sidney Saunders, *cons.* 1979, *apptd* 1983
East Tennessee, Robert G. Tharp, *cons.* 1991, *apptd* 1992
Florida, Stephen Jecko, *cons.* 1994, *apptd* 1994
Georgia, Henry Louttit, *cons.* 1994, *apptd* 1994
Kentucky, Ted Gulick, *cons.* 1964
Lexington, Don A. Wimberley, *cons.* 1984, *apptd* 1985
Louisiana, James B. Brown, *cons.* 1976, *apptd* 1976
Mississippi, Alfred C. Marble jun., *cons.* 1991, *apptd* 1993
North Carolina, Robert Johnson, *cons.* 1994, *apptd* 1994
South Carolina, Edward Salmon jun., *cons.* 1990, *apptd* 1990
South-East Florida, Calvin O. Schofield jun., *cons.* 1979, *apptd* 1980
South-West Florida, Rogers Harris, *cons.* 1989, *apptd* 1989
Tennessee, Bertram N. Herlong, *cons.* 1993, *apptd* 1993
Upper South Carolina, Dorsey F. Henderson, *cons.* 1995
West Tennessee, James Coleman, *cons.* 1993
Western North Carolina, Robert Johnson, *cons* 1989, *apptd* 1990

Province V

Chicago, Frank T. Griswold III, *cons.* 1985, *apptd* 1987
Eastern Michigan, Edwin M. Leidel jun., *cons.* 1996, *apptd* 1996
Eau Claire, William C. Wantland, *cons.* 1980, *apptd* 1980
Fond Du Lac, Russell Jacobus, *cons.* 1994, *apptd* 1994
Indianapolis, Edward W. Jones, *cons.* 1977, *apptd* 1977
Michigan, R. Stewart Wood, *cons.* 1990, *apptd* 1990
Milwaukee, Roger J. White, *cons.* 1984, *apptd* 1985
Missouri, Hays Rockwell, *cons.* 1991, *apptd* 1991
Northern Indiana, Francis C. Gray, *cons.* 1986, *apptd* 1987
Northern Michigan, Thomas K. Ray, *cons.* 1982, *apptd* 1982
Ohio, J. Clark Grew, *cons.* 1994, *apptd* 1994
Quincy, Keith L. Ackerman, *cons.* 1994, *apptd* 1994
Southern Ohio, Herbert Thompson jun., *cons.* 1988, *apptd* 1992
Springfield, Peter H. Beckwith, *cons.* 1991
Western Michigan, Edward L. Lee jun., *cons.* 1989, *apptd* 1989

Province VI

Colorado, William Winterrowd, *cons.* 1991, *apptd* 1991
Iowa, C. Christopher Epting, *cons.* 1988, *apptd* 1988
Minnesota, James Jelinek, *cons.* 1993, *apptd* 1993
Montana, Charles I. Jones, *cons.* 1986, *apptd* 1986
Nebraska, James E. Krotz, *cons.* 1989, *apptd* 1989
North Dakota, Andrew H. Fairfield, *cons.* 1990, *apptd* 1990
South Dakota, Creighton Robertson, *cons.* 1994, *apptd* 1994
Wyoming, Bob G. Jones, *cons.* 1977, *apptd* 1977

Province VII

Arkansas, Larry Maze, *cons.* 1994, *apptd* 1994
Dallas, James Stanton, *cons.* 1993, *apptd* 1993
Fort Worth, Jack Iker, *cons.* 1993, *apptd* 1994
Kansas, William E. Smalley, *cons.* 1989, *apptd* 1989
North-West Texas, Sam B. Hulsey, *cons.* 1980, *apptd* 1980

Oklahoma, Robert M. Moodey, *cons.* 1988, *apptd* 1989
Rio Grande, Terence Kelshaw, *cons.* 1989, *apptd* 1989
Texas, Claude Payne, *cons.* 1994
West Missouri, John C. Buchanan, *cons.* 1989, *apptd* 1989
West Texas, James E. Folts, *cons.* 1996, *apptd* 1996
Western Kansas, Vernon Strickland, *cons.* 1995
Western Louisiana, Robert Hargrove, *cons.* 1989, *apptd* 1990

Province VIII

Alaska, vacant
Arizona, Robert R. Shahan, *cons.* 1992, *apptd* 1993
California, William E. Swing, *cons.* 1979, *apptd* 1980
El Camino Real, Richard L. Skimpfky, *cons.* 1990, *apptd* 1990
Eastern Oregon, Rustin R. Kimsey, *cons.* 1980, *apptd* 1980
Hawaii, Richard Chang, *cons.* 1997, *apptd* 1996
Idaho, John Thornton, *cons.* 1990, *apptd* 1990
Los Angeles, Frederick L. Borsch, *cons.* 1988, *apptd* 1988
Navajoland Area Mission, Steven T. Plummer, *cons.* 1989, *apptd* 1989
Nevada, Stewart C. Zabriskie, *cons.* 1986, *apptd* 1986
Northern California, Jerry A. Lamb, *cons.* 1991, *apptd* 1992
Olympia, Vincent W. Warner, *cons.* 1989, *apptd* 1990
Oregon, Robert L. Ladehoff, *cons.* 1985, *apptd* 1986
San Diego, Gethin B. Hughes, *cons.* 1992, *apptd* 1992
San Joaquin, John-David Schofield, *cons.* 1988, *apptd* 1989
Spokane, Frank Terry, *cons.* 1990, *apptd* 1991
Taiwan, John C. T. Chien, *cons.* 1988, *apptd* 1988
Utah, George E. Bates, *cons.* 1986, *apptd* 1986

Province IX

Central Ecuador, Neptali L. Moreno, *cons.* 1990, *apptd* 1990
Colombia, Bernardo Merino-Botero, *cons.* 1979, *apptd* 1979
Dominican Republic, Julio C. Holguin, *apptd* 1991
Guatemala, Armando Guerra, *cons.* 1982, *apptd* 1982
Honduras, Leopold Frade, *cons.* 1984, *apptd* 1984
Nicaragua, Sturdie W. Downs, *cons.* 1985, *apptd* 1985
Panama, Clarence W. Hayes, *cons.* 1995
El Salvador, Martin Barahona, *cons.* 1992, *apptd* 1992

Extra-Provincial

Costa Rica, Cornelius J. Wilson, *cons.* 1978, *apptd* 1978
Puerto Rico, David Alvarez, *cons.* 1987, *apptd* 1987
Venezuela, Orlando Guerrero, *cons.* 1995

CHURCH OF THE PROVINCE OF WEST AFRICA

ARCHBISHOP OF PROVINCE, The Most Revd Robert Okine (Bishop of Koforidua), *cons.* 1981, *apptd* 1993

THE RT. REVD BISHOPS
Accra, Francis W. B. Thompson, *cons.* 1983, *apptd* 1983
Bo, Samuel S. Gbonda, *cons.* 1994, *apptd* 1994
Cape Coast, Kobina Quashie, *apptd* 1992
Freetown, vacant
Gambia, Solomon T. Johnson, *cons.* 1990, *apptd* 1990
Guinea, vacant
Koforidua, see above, *apptd* 1981
Kumasi, Edmund Yeboah, *cons.* 1985, *apptd* 1985
Liberia, vacant
Sekondi, Theophilus Annobil, *cons.* 1981, *apptd* 1981
Sunyani / Tamale, Joseph Dadson, *cons.* 1981, *apptd* 1981

The Anglican Church of Cameroon is a missionary area of the Province

CHURCH IN THE PROVINCE OF THE WEST INDIES

ARCHBISHOP OF PROVINCE, The Most Revd Orland Lindsay (Bishop of North-Eastern Caribbean and Aruba), *cons.* 1970, *apptd* 1986

THE RT. REVD BISHOPS
Barbados, Rufus Broome
Belize, Sylvestre D. Romero-Palma
Guyana, Randolph George, *cons.* 1976, *apptd* 1980
Jamaica, Neville de Souza, *cons.* 1973, *apptd* 1979
Nassau and the Bahamas, Michael Eldon, CMG, *cons.* 1971, *apptd* 1972
North-Eastern Caribbean and Aruba, see above
Trinidad and Tobago, Rawle Douglin
Windward Islands, Sehon Goodridge

CHURCH OF THE PROVINCE OF ZAÏRE

ARCHBISHOP OF PROVINCE, The Most Revd Byankya Njojo (Bishop of Boga-Zaïre), *cons.* 1980, *apptd* 1992

THE RT. REVD BISHOPS
Boga-Zaïre, see above, *apptd* 1980
Bukavu, Balafuga Dirokpa, *cons.* 1982, *apptd* 1982
Kisangani, Sylvestre Tibafa, *cons.* 1980, *apptd* 1980
Maniema, vacant
Nord-Kivu, Methusela Munzenda, *cons.* 1992, *apptd* 1992
Shaba, Emmanuel Kolini, *cons.* 1980, *apptd* 1980

OTHER CHURCHES AND EXTRA-PROVINCIAL DIOCESES

ANGLICAN CHURCH OF BERMUDA, The Rt. Revd Ewen Ratteray, *apptd* 1996
EPISCOPAL CHURCH OF CUBA, The Rt. Revd Jorge Perera Hurtado, *apptd* 1995
HONG KONG AND MACAO, The Rt. Revd Peter Kwong
KUCHING, The Rt. Revd Datuk John Leong Chee Yun
LUSITANIAN CHURCH (*Portuguese Episcopal Church*), The Rt. Revd Fernando da Luz Soares, *apptd* 1971
SPANISH REFORMED EPISCOPAL CHURCH, The Rt. Revd Carlos Lozano Lopez, *apptd* 1995

The Church of Scotland

The Church of Scotland is the established (i.e. state) church of Scotland. The Church is Reformed and evangelical in doctrine, and presbyterian in constitution. In 1560 the jurisdiction of the Roman Catholic Church in Scotland was abolished and the first assembly of the Church of Scotland ratified the Confession of Faith, drawn up by a committee including John Knox. In 1592 Parliament passed an Act guaranteeing the liberties of the Church and its presbyterian government. James VI (James I of England) and later Stuart monarchs attempted to restore episcopacy, but a presbyterian church was finally restored in 1690 and secured by the Act of Settlement (1690) and the Act of Union (1707). The Free Church of Scotland was formed in 1843 in a dispute over patronage and state interference; in 1900 most of its ministers joined with the United Presbyterian Church (formed in 1847) to form the United Free Church of Scotland. In 1929 most of this body rejoined the Church of Scotland to form the united Church of Scotland.

The Church of Scotland is presbyterian in its organization, i.e. based on a hierarchy of councils of ministers and elders and, since 1990, of members of a diaconate. At local level the kirk session consists of the parish minister and ruling elders. At district level the presbyteries, of which there are 47, consist of all the ministers in the district, one ruling elder from each congregation, and those members of the diaconate who qualify for membership. The General Assembly is the supreme authority, and is presided over by a Moderator chosen annually by the Assembly. The Sovereign, if not present in person, is represented by a Lord High Commissioner who is appointed each year by the Crown.

The Church of Scotland has about 700,000 members, 1,200 ministers and 1,600 churches. There are about 100 ministers and other personnel working overseas.

Lord High Commissioner (1996), HRH The Princess Royal KG, GCVO
Moderator of the General Assembly (1996), The Rt. Revd J. H. McIndoe
Principal Clerk, The Very Revd J. L. Weatherhead, DD
Depute Clerk, Revd F. A. J. MacDonald
Procurator, A. Dunlop, QC
Law Agent and Solicitor of the Church, Mrs J. S. Wilson
Parliamentary Agent, I. McCulloch (*London*)
General Treasurer, D. F. Ross
CHURCH OFFICE, 121 George Street, Edinburgh EH2 4YN. Tel: 0131-225 5722

PRESBYTERIES AND CLERKS
Edinburgh, Revd W. P. Graham
West Lothian, Revd D. Shaw
Lothian, J. D. McCulloch
Melrose and Peebles, Revd J. H. Brown
Duns, Revd A. C. D. Cartwright
Jedburgh, Revd A. D. Reid
Annandale and Eskdale, Revd C. B. Haston
Dumfries and Kirkcudbright, Revd G. M. A. Savage
Wigtown and Stranraer, Revd D. Dutton
Ayr, Revd J. Crichton
Irvine and Kilmarnock, Revd C. G. F. Brockie
Ardrossan, Revd D. Broster
Lanark, Revd I. D. Cunningham
Paisley, Revd J. P. Cubie
Greenock, Revd D. Mill
Glasgow, Revd A. Cunningham
Hamilton, Revd J. H. Wilson
Dumbarton, Revd D. P. Munro
South Argyll, Revd R. H. McNidder
Dunoon, Revd R. Samuel
Lorn and Mull, Revd W. Hogg
Falkirk, Revd D. E. McClements
Stirling, Revd B. W. Dunsmore
Dunfermline, Revd W. E. Farquhar
Kirkcaldy, Revd B. L. Tomlinson
St Andrews, Revd J. W. Patterson
Dunkeld and Meigle, Revd A. F. Chisholm
Perth, Revd D. Main
Dundee, Revd J. A. Roy
Angus, Revd R. J. Ramsay
Aberdeen, Revd A. Douglas
Kincardine and Deeside, Revd J. W. S. Brown
Gordon, Revd I. U. Thomson
Buchan, Revd R. Neilson
Moray, Revd D. J. Ferguson

Abernethy, Revd J. A. I. MacEwan
Inverness, Revd A. S. Younger
Lochaber, Revd A. Ramsay
Ross, Revd R. M. MacKinnon
Sutherland, Revd J. L. Goskirk
Caithness, Revd M. G. Mappin
Lochcarron/Skye, Revd A. I. Macarthur
Uist, Revd A. P. J. Varwell
Lewis, Revd T. S. Sinclair
Orkney (Finstown), Revd T. Hunt
Shetland (Lerwick), Revd N. R. Whyte
England (London), Revd W. A. Cairns
Europe (Portugal), Revd J. W. McLeod

The minimum stipend of a minister in the Church of Scotland in 1996 was £15,348

The Roman Catholic Church

The Roman Catholic Church is one world-wide Christian Church acknowledging as its head the Bishop of Rome, known as the Pope (Father). The Pope is held to be the successor of St Peter and thus invested with the power which was entrusted to St Peter by Jesus Christ. A direct line of succession is therefore claimed from the earliest Christian communities. Papal authority over the doctrine and jurisdiction of the Church in western Europe developed early and was unrivalled after the split with the Eastern Orthodox Church until the Protestant Reformation in the 16th century. With the fall of the Roman Empire the Pope also became an important political leader. His temporal power is now limited to the 107 acres of the Vatican City State.

The Pope exercises spiritual authority over the Church with the advice and assistance of the Sacred College of Cardinals, the supreme council of the Church. He is also advised about the concerns of the Church locally by his ambassadors, who liaise with the Bishops' Conference in each country.

In addition to advising the Pope, those members of the Sacred College of Cardinals who are under the age of 80 also elect a successor following the death of a Pope. The assembly of the Cardinals at the Vatican for the election of a new Pope is known as the Conclave in which, in complete seclusion, the Cardinals elect by a secret ballot; a two-thirds majority is necessary before the vote can be accepted as final. When a Cardinal receives the necessary votes, the Dean of the Sacred College formally asks him if he will accept election and the name by which he wishes to be known. On his acceptance of the office the Conclave is dissolved and the First Cardinal Deacon announces the election to the assembled crowd in St Peter's Square. On the first Sunday or Holyday following the election, the new Pope assumes the pontificate at High Mass in St Peter's Square. A new pontificate is dated from the assumption of the pontificate.

The number of cardinals was fixed at 70 by Pope Sixtus V in 1586, but has been steadily increased since the pontificate of John XXIII and now stands at 160 (as at end June 1996).

The Roman Catholic Church universally and the Vatican City State are run by the Curia, which is made up of the Secretariat of State, the Sacred Council for the Public Affairs of the Church, and various congregations, secretariats and tribunals assisted by commissions and offices. The congregations are permanent commissions for conducting the affairs of the Church and are made up of cardinals, one of whom occupies the office of prefect. Below the Secretariat of State and the congregations are the secretariats and tribunals, all of which are headed by cardinals. (The Curial cardinals are analogous to ministers in charge of government departments.)

The Vatican State has its own diplomatic service, with representatives known as nuncios. Papal nuncios with full diplomatic recognition are given precedence over all other ambassadors to the country to which they are appointed; where precedence is not recognised the Papal representative is known as a pro-nuncio. Where the representation is only to the local churches and not to the government of a country, the Papal representative is known as an apostolic delegate. The Roman Catholic Church has an estimated 890.9 million adherents world-wide.

SOVEREIGN PONTIFF

His Holiness Pope John Paul II (Karol Wojtyla), *born* Wadowice, Poland, 18 May 1920; *ordained priest* 1946; *appointed Archbishop* of Krakow 1964; *created Cardinal* 1967; *assumed pontificate* 16 October 1978

SECRETARIAT OF STATE

Secretary of State, HE Cardinal Angelo Sodano
First Section (General Affairs), Mgr G. Re (Archbishop of Vescovio)
Second Section (Relations with other states), Mgr J. L. Tauran (Archbishop of Telepte)

BISHOPS' CONFERENCE

The Roman Catholic Church in England and Wales is governed by the Bishops' Conference, membership of which includes the Diocesan Bishops, the Apostolic Exarch of the Ukrainians, the Bishop of the Forces and the Auxiliary Bishops. The Conference is headed by the President (Cardinal Basil Hume, Archbishop of Westminster) and Vice-President. There are five departments, each with an episcopal chairman: the Department for Christian Life and Worship (the Archbishop of Southwark), the Department for Mission and Unity (the Bishop of Arundel and Brighton), the Department for Catholic Education and Formation (the Bishop of Leeds), the Department for Christian Responsibility and Citizenship (the Bishop of Plymouth), and the Department for International Affairs.

The Bishops' Standing Committee, made up of all the Archbishops and the chairman of each of the above departments, has general responsibility for continuity and policy between the plenary sessions of the Conference. It prepares the Conference agenda and implements its decisions. It is serviced by a General Secretariat. There are also agencies and consultative bodies affiliated to the Conference.

The Bishops' Conference of Scotland has as its president Archbishop Winning of Glasgow and is the permanently constituted assembly of the Bishops of Scotland. To promote its work, the Conference establishes various agencies which have an advisory function in relation to the Conference. The more important of these agencies are called Commissions and each one has a Bishop President who, with the other members of the Commissions, are appointed by the Conference.

The Irish Episcopal Conference has as its acting president Archbishop Connell of Dublin. Its membership comprises all the Archbishops and Bishops of Ireland and it appoints various Commissions to assist it in its work. There are three types of Commissions: (a) those made up of lay and clerical members chosen for their skills and experience, and staffed by full-time expert secretariats; (b) Commissions whose members are selected from existing institutions and whose services are supplied on a part-time basis; and (c) Commissions of Bishops only.

The Roman Catholic Church in Britain and Ireland has an estimated 8,992,000 members, 11 archbishops, 67 bishops, 11,260 priests, and 8,588 churches and chapels open to the public.

Bishops' Conferences secretariats:

ENGLAND AND WALES, 39 Eccleston Square, London SWIV IPD. Tel: 0171-630 8220. *General Secretary*, The Rt. Revd Philip Carroll

SCOTLAND, Candida Casa, 8 Corsehill Road, Ayr, Scotland KA7 2ST. Tel: 01292-256750. *General Secretary*, The Rt. Revd Maurice Taylor, Bishop of Galloway

IRELAND, Iona, 65 Newry Road, Dundalk, Co. Louth. *Executive Secretary*, Revd Hugh G. Connelly

GREAT BRITAIN

APOSTOLIC NUNCIO TO THE UNITED KINGDOM OF GREAT BRITAIN AND NORTHERN IRELAND
The Most Revd Luigi Barbarito, 54 Parkside, London SWI9 5NE. Tel: 0181-946 1410

ENGLAND AND WALES

THE MOST REVD ARCHBISHOPS
Westminster, HE Cardinal Basil Hume, *cons.* 1976
  Auxiliaries, Victor Guazzelli, *cons.* 1970; Vincent Nichols, *cons.* 1992; James J. O'Brien, *cons.* 1977; Patrick O'Donoghue, *cons.* 1993
  Clergy, 789
  Archbishop's Residence, Archbishop's House, Ambrosden Avenue, London SWIP IQJ. Tel: 0171-834 4717
Birmingham, Maurice Couve de Murville, *cons.* 1982, *apptd* 1982
  Auxiliaries, Terence Brain, *cons.* 1991; Philip Pargeter, *cons.* 1989
  Clergy, 524
  Diocesan Curia, Cathedral House, St Chad's Queensway, Birmingham B4 6EX. Tel: 0121-236 5535
Cardiff, John A. Ward, *cons.* 1981, *apptd* 1983
  Clergy, 146
  Diocesan Curia, Archbishop's House, 41–43 Cathedral Road, Cardiff CFI 9HD. Tel: 01222-220411
Liverpool, Patrick Kelly, *cons.* 1984, *apptd* 1996
  Auxiliaries, John Rawsthorne, *cons.* 1981; Vincent Malone, *cons.* 1989
  Clergy, 602
  Diocesan Curia, 152 Brownlow Hill, Liverpool L3 5RQ. Tel: 0151-709 4801
Southwark, Michael Bowen, *cons.* 1970, *apptd* 1977
  Auxiliaries, Charles Henderson, *cons.* 1972; Howard Tripp, *cons.* 1980; John Jukes, *cons.* 1980
  Clergy, 504
  Diocesan Curia, Archbishop's House, 150 St George's Road, London SEI 6HX. Tel: 0171-928 5592

THE RT. REVD BISHOPS
Arundel and Brighton, Cormac Murphy-O'Connor, *cons.* 1977. *Clergy*, 286. *Diocesan Curia*, Bishop's House, The Upper Drive, Hove, E. Sussex BN3 6NE. Tel: 01273-506387
Brentwood, Thomas McMahon, *cons.* 1980, *apptd* 1980. *Clergy*, 167. *Bishop's Office*, Cathedral House, Ingrave Road, Brentwood, Essex CMI5 8AT. Tel: 01277-232266
Clifton, Mervyn Alexander, *cons.* 1972, *apptd* 1975. *Clergy*, 235. *Diocesan Curia*, Egerton Road, Bishopston, Bristol BS7 8HU. Tel: 0117-924 1378

East Anglia, Peter Smith, *cons.* 1995, *apptd* 1995. *Clergy*, 133. *Diocesan Curia*, The White House, 21 Upgate, Poringland, Norwich NR14 7SH. Tel: 01508-492202
Hallam, Gerald Moverley, *cons.* 1968, *apptd* 1980 (has retired, but continuing until successor appointed). *Clergy*, 98. *Bishop's Residence*, 'Quarters', Carsick Hill Way, Sheffield SIO 3LT. Tel: 0114-230 9101
Hexham and Newcastle, Michael Ambrose Griffiths, *cons.* 1992. *Clergy*, 281. *Diocesan Curia*, Bishop's House, East Denton Hall, 800 West Road, Newcastle upon Tyne NE5 2BJ. Tel: 0191-228 0003
Lancaster, John Brewer, *cons.* 1971, *apptd* 1985. *Clergy*, 255. *Bishop's Residence*, Bishop's House, Cannon Hill, Lancaster LAI 5NG. Tel: 01524-32231
Leeds, David Konstant, *cons.* 1977, *apptd* 1985. *Clergy*, 235. *Diocesan Curia*, 7 St Marks Avenue, Leeds LS2 9BN. Tel: 0113-244 4788
Menevia (Wales), Daniel Mullins, *cons.* 1970, *apptd* 1987. *Clergy*, 63. *Diocesan Curia*, 115 Walter Road, Swansea SAI 5RE. Tel: 01792-644017
Middlesbrough, John Crowley, *cons.* 1986, *apptd* 1992. *Clergy*, 182. *Diocesan Curia*, 50A The Avenue, Linthorpe, Middlesbrough, Cleveland TS5 6QT. Tel: 01642-850505
Auxiliary, Thomas O'Brien, *cons.* 1981
Northampton, Patrick Leo McCartie, *cons.* 1977, *apptd* 1990. *Clergy*, 163. *Diocesan Curia*, Bishop's House, Marriott Street, Northampton NN2 6AW. Tel: 01604-715635
Nottingham, James McGuinness, *cons.* 1972, *apptd* 1975. *Clergy*, 204. *Diocesan Curia*, Willson House, Derby Road, Nottingham NGI 5AW. Tel: 0115-953 9800
Plymouth, Christopher Budd, *cons.* 1986. *Clergy*, 156. *Diocesan Curia*, Vescourt, Hartley Road, Plymouth PL3 5LR. Tel: 01752-772950
Portsmouth, F. Crispian Hollis, *cons.* 1987, *apptd* 1989. *Clergy*, 264. *Bishop's Residence*, Bishop's House, Edinburgh Road, Portsmouth, Hants POI 3HG. Tel: 01705-820894
Salford, vacant. *Clergy*, 391. *Diocesan Curia*, Cathedral House, 250 Chapel Street, Salford M3 5LL. Tel: 0161-834 9052
Shrewsbury, Brian Noble, *cons.* 1995, *apptd* 1995. *Clergy*, 202. *Diocesan Curia*, 2 Park Road South, Birkenhead, Merseyside L43 4UX. Tel: 0151-652 9855
Wrexham (Wales), Edwin Regan, *apptd* 1994. *Clergy*, 91. *Diocesan Curia*, Bishop's House, Sontley Road, Wrexham, Clwyd LLI3 7EW. Tel: 01978-262726

SCOTLAND

THE MOST REVD ARCHBISHOPS
St Andrews and Edinburgh, Keith Patrick O'Brian, *cons.* 1985
  Auxiliary, Kevin Rafferty, *cons.* 1990
  Clergy, 201
  Diocesan Curia, 106 Whitehouse Loan, Edinburgh EH9 IBD. Tel: 0131-452 8244
Glasgow, HE Cardinal Thomas Winning, *cons.* 1971, *apptd* 1974
  Clergy, 303
  Diocesan Curia, 196 Clyde Street, Glasgow GI 4JY. Tel: 0141-226 5898

THE RT. REVD BISHOPS
Aberdeen, Mario Conti, *cons.* 1977. *Clergy*, 58. *Bishop's Residence*, 156 King's Gate, Aberdeen AB2 6BR. Tel: 01224-319154
Argyll and the Isles, Roderick Wright, *cons.* 1990. *Clergy*, 32. *Diocesan Curia*, St Mary's, Belford Road, Fort William, Inverness-shire PH33 6BT. Tel: 01397-706046
Dunkeld, Vincent Logan, *cons.* 1981. *Clergy*, 55. *Diocesan Curia*, 26 Roseangle, Dundee DDI 4LR. Tel: 01382-25453
Galloway, Maurice Taylor, *cons.* 1981. *Clergy*, 66. *Diocesan Curia*, 8 Corsehill Road, Ayr KA7 2ST. Tel: 01292-266750

Motherwell, Joseph Devine, *cons.* 1977, *apptd* 1983. *Clergy,* 180. *Diocesan Curia,* Coursington Road, Motherwell MLI IPW. Tel: 01698-269114
Paisley, John A. Mone, *cons.* 1984, *apptd* 1988. *Clergy,* 95. *Diocesan Curia,* Cathedral House, 8 East Buchanan Street, Paisley, Renfrewshire PAI IHS. Tel: 0141-889 3601

IRELAND

There is one hierarchy for the whole of Ireland. Several of the dioceses have territory partly in the Republic of Ireland and partly in Northern Ireland.

APOSTOLIC NUNCIO TO IRELAND
The Most Revd Emanuele Gerada (titular Archbishop of Nomenta), 183 Navan Road, Dublin 7. Tel: 00 353 1-380577

THE MOST REVD ARCHBISHOPS
Armagh, HE Cardinal Cahal B. Daly, *cons.* 1990
Coadjutor, Sean Brady
Auxiliary, Gerard Clifford, *cons.* 1991
Clergy, 183
Diocesan Curia, Ara Coeli, Armagh BT61 7QY. Tel: 01861-522045
Cashel, Dermot Clifford, *cons.* 1986
Clergy, 136
Archbishop's Residence, Archbishop's House, Thurles, Co. Tipperary. Tel: 00 353 504-21512
Dublin, Desmond Connell, *cons.* 1988, *apptd* 1988
Auxiliaries, Donal Murray, *cons.* 1982; Dermot O'Mahony, *cons.* 1975; James Moriarty, *cons.* 1992; Eamonn Walsh, *cons.* 1990; Desmond Williams, *cons.* 1985; Fiachra O'Ceallaigh, *cons* 1994; James Kavanagh, *cons.* 1996
Clergy, 994
Archbishop's Residence, Archbishop's House, Drumcondra, Dublin 9. Tel: 00 353 1-8373732
Tuam, Michael Neary, *cons.* 1992
Clergy, 180
Archbishop's Residence, Archbishop's House, Tuam, Co. Galway. Tel: 00 353 93-24166

THE MOST REVD BISHOPS
Achonry, Thomas Flynn, *cons.* 1975. *Clergy,* 62. *Bishop's Residence,* Bishop's House, Ballaghadaderreen, Co. Roscommon. Tel: 00 353 907-60021
Ardagh and Clonmacnois, Colm O'Reilly, *cons.* 1983. *Clergy,* 100. *Diocesan Office,* Bishop's House, St Michael's, Longford, Co. Longford. Tel: 00 353 43-46432
Clogher, Joseph Duffy, *cons.* 1979. *Clergy,* 108. *Bishop's Residence,* Bishop's House, Monaghan. Tel: 00 353 47 81019
Clonfert, Joseph Kirby, *cons.* 1988. *Clergy,* 71. *Bishop's Residence,* St Brendan's, Coorheen, Loughrea, Co. Galway. Tel: 00 353 91-41560
Cloyne, John Magee, *cons.* 1987. *Clergy,* 158. *Diocesan Centre,* Cobh, Co. Cork. Tel: 00 353 21-811430
Cork and Ross, Michael Murphy, *cons.* 1976. *Clergy,* 338. *Diocesan Office,* Bishop's House, Redemption Road, Cork. Tel: 00 353 21-301717
Auxiliary, John Buckley, *cons.* 1984
Derry, Seamus Hegarty, *cons.* 1984, *apptd* 1994. *Clergy,* 157. *Bishop's Residence,* Bishop's House, St Eugene's Cathedral, Derry BT48 9AP. Tel: 01504-262302
Auxiliary, Francis Lagan, *cons.* 1988

Down and Connor, Patrick J. Walsh, *cons.* 1991. *Clergy,* 248. *Bishop's Residence,* Lisbreen, 73 Somerton Road, Belfast, Co. Antrim DTI5 4DE. Tel: 01232-776185
Auxiliaries, Anthony Farquhar, *cons.* 1983; William Philbin, *cons.* 1991; Michael Dallat, *cons.* 1994
Dromore, Francis Brooks, *cons.* 1976. *Clergy,* 78. *Bishop's Residence,* Bishop's House, Violet Hill, Newry, Co. Down BT35 6PN. Tel: 01693-62444
Elphin, Christopher Jones, *cons.* 1994. *Clergy,* 101. *Bishop's Residence,* St Mary's, Sligo. Tel: 00 353 71-62670
Ferns, Brendon Comiskey, *cons.* 1980. *Clergy,* 161. *Bishop's Office,* Bishop's House, Summerhill, Wexford. Tel: 00 353 53-22177
Galway and Kilmacduagh, James McLoughlin, *cons.* 1993. *Clergy,* 90. *Diocesan Office,* The Cathedral, Galway. Tel: 00 353 91-63566
Kerry, William Murphy, *cons.* 1995. *Clergy,* 149. *Bishop's Residence,* Bishop's House, Killarney, Co. Kerry. Tel: 00 353 64-31168
Kildare and Leighlin, Laurence Ryan, *cons.* 1984. *Clergy,* 136. *Bishop's Residence,* Bishop's House, Carlow. Tel: 00 353 503-31102
Killala, Thomas Finnegan, *cons.* 1970. *Clergy,* 62. *Bishop's Residence,* Bishop's House, Ballina, Co. Mayo. Tel: 00 353 96-21518
Killaloe, William Walsh, *cons.* 1994. *Clergy,* 149. *Bishop's Residence,* Westbourne, Ennis, Co. Clare. Tel: 00 353 65-28638
Kilmore, Francis McKiernan, *cons.* 1972. *Clergy,* 115. *Bishop's Residence,* Bishop's House, Cullies, Co. Cavan. Tel: 00 353 49-31496
Limerick, Donal Murray, *cons.* 1996. *Clergy,* 152. *Diocesan Offices,* 66 O'Connell Street, Limerick. Tel: 00 353 61-315856
Meath, Michael Smith, *cons.* 1984, *apptd* 1990. *Clergy,* 141. *Bishop's Residence,* Bishop's House, Dublin Road, Mullingar, Co. Westmeath. Tel: 00 353 44-48841
Ossory, Laurence Forristal, *cons.* 1980. *Clergy,* 111. *Bishop's Residence,* Sion House, Kilkenny. Tel: 00 353 56-62448
Raphoe, Philip Boyce, *cons.* 1994. *Clergy,* 96. *Bishop's Residence,* Ard Adhamhnáin, Letterkenny, Co. Donegal. Tel: 00 353 74-21208
Waterford and Lismore, William Lee, *cons.* 1993. *Clergy,* 130. *Bishop's Residence,* Woodleigh, Summerville Avenue, Waterford. Tel: 00 353 51-71432

RESIDENTIAL ARCHBISHOPRICS THROUGHOUT THE WORLD

ALBANIA
Durrës-Tirana, Brok K. Mirdita
Shkodër, Frano Illia

ALGERIA
Algiers, Henri Teissier

ANGOLA
Huambo, Francisco Viti
Luanda, HE Cardinal Alexandre do Nascimento
Lubango, Manuel Franklin da Costa
Coadjutor, Zacarias Kamwenho

ARGENTINA
Bahia Blanca, Romulo Garcia
Buenos Aires, HE Cardinal Antonio Quarracino
Córdoba, HE Cardinal Raúl Francisco Primatesta
Corrientes, Domingo S. Castagna
La Plata, Carlos Galán
Mendoza, Jose M. Arancibia

Paraná, Estanislao Esteban Karlic
Resistencia, Carmelo J. Giaquinta
Rosario, Eduardo Vicente Miras
Salta, Moises J. Blanchoud
San Juan de Cuyo, Italo Severino Di Stefano
Santa Fe, Edgardo Gabriel Storni
Tucumán, Arsenio R. Casado

AUSTRALIA
Adelaide, Leonard Anthony Faulkner
Brisbane, John A. Bathersby
Canberra, Francis P. Carroll
Hobart, Joseph E. D'Arcy
Melbourne, Thomas Francis Little
Perth, Barry J. Hickey
Sydney, HE Cardinal Edward B. Clancy

AUSTRIA
Salzburg, Georg Eder
Vienna, Christoph Schoenborn

BANGLADESH
Dhaka, Michael Rozario

BELARUS
Minsk-Mohilev Archdiocese, HE Cardinal Kazimierz Swiatek

BELGIUM
Malines-Bruxelles, HE Cardinal Godfried Danneels

BENIN
Cotonou, Isidore de Souzá

BOLIVIA
Cochabamba, Rene Fernandez Apaza
La Paz, Luis Sainz Hinojosa
Santa Cruz de la Sierra, Julio T. Sandoval
Sucre, Jesus G. Pérez Rodriguez

BOSNIA HERCEGOVINA
Vrhbosna, Sarajevo, HE Cardinal Vinko Puljić

BRAZIL
Aparacida, HE Cardinal Aloisio Lorscheider
Aracaju, Luciano José Cabral Duarte
Bélem do Pará, Vicente Joaquim Zico
Belo Horizonte, Serafim Fernandes de Araújo
Botucatu, Antonio M. Mucciolo
Brasilia, HE Cardinal Jose Freire Falcao
Campinas, Gilberto Pereira Lopes
Campo Grande, Vitorio Pavanello
Cascavel, Lucio I. Baumgaertner
Cuiaba, Bonifacio Piccinini
Curitiba, Pedro Antonio Fedalto
Diamantina, Geraldo Majelo Reis
Florianópolis, Eusebio Oscar Scheid
Fortaleza, vacant
Goiania, Antonio Ribeiro de Oliveira
Juiz de Fora, Clovis Frainer
Londrina, Albano Bortoletto Cavallin
Maceió, Edvaldo G. Amaral
Manaus, Luiz S. Vieira
Mariana, Luciano Mendes de Almeida
Maringá, Jaime Luis Coelho
Natal, Heitor de Araujo Sales
Niteroi, Carlos A. Navarro
Olinda and Recife, José Cardoso Sobrinho
Palmas, Alberto T. Corrèa
Paraiba, Marcello Pinto Carvalheira
Porto Alegre, Altamiro Rossato
Porto Velho, José Martins da Silva
Pouso Alegre, vacant
Ribeirão Preto, Arnaldo Ribeiro
São Luis do Maranhão, Paulo Eduardo de Andrade Ponte

São Paulo, HE Cardinal Paulo Evaristo Arns
São Salvador da Bahia, HE Cardinal Lucas Moreira Neves
São Sebastião do Rio de Janeiro, HE Cardinal Eugenio de Araújo Sales
Sorocaba, José Lambert
Teresina, Miguel F. Camara Filho
Uberaba, Aloisio R. Oppermann
Vitória, Silvestre L. Scandian

BURKINA
Ouagadougou, Jean-Marie Untaani Compaore

BURUNDI
Gitega, Joachim Ruhuna

CAMEROON
Bamenda, Paul Verdzekov
Douala, HE Cardinal Christian W. Tumi
Garoua, Antoine Ntalou
Yaoundé, Jean Zoa

CANADA
Edmonton, Joseph N. MacNeil
Gatineau-Hull, Roger Ebacher
Grouard-McLennon, Henri Légaré
Halifax, Austin-Emile Burke
Keewatin-Le Pas, Peter Alfred Sutton
Kingston, Francis John Spence
Moncton, vacant
Montreal, HE Cardinal Jean-Claude Turcotte
Ottawa, Marcel A. Gervais
Quebec, Maurice Couture
Regina, Peter Mallon
Rimouski, Bertrand Blanchet
St Boniface, Antoine Hacault
St Johns, Newfoundland, James H. MacDonald
Sherbrooke, Jean Marie Fortier
    Coadjutor, Andre Gaumond
Toronto, Aloysius Matthew Ambrosic
Vancouver, Adam J. Exner
Winnipeg, Leonard J. Wall; (Ukrainian rite), Michael Bzdel

CAUCASIA
Caucasia Apostolic Administrator, Jean-Paul Gobel

CENTRAL AFRICAN REPUBLIC
Bangui, Joachim N'Dayen

CHAD
Ndjamena, Charles Vandame

CHILE
Antofagasta, Patricio Infante Alfonso
Concepción, Antonio M. Casamitjana
La Serena, Francisco J. Cox Huneeus
Puerto Montt, Savino B. Cazzaro Bertollo
Santiago de Chile, HE Cardinal Carlos Oviedo Cavada

CHINA
Anking, Huai-Ning, vacant
Canton, vacant
Changsha, vacant
Chungking, vacant
Foochow, Min-Hou, vacant
Hangchow, vacant
Hankow, vacant
Kaifeng, vacant
Kunming, vacant
Kweyang, vacant
Lanchow, vacant
Mukden, vacant
Nanchang, vacant
Nanking, vacant
Nanning, vacant

Peking (Beijing), vacant
Sian, vacant
Suiyüan, Francis Wang Hsueh-Ming
Taiyuan, vacant
Tsinan, vacant

COLOMBIA
Barranquilla, Felix Maria Torres Parra
Bogotá, Pedro Rubiano Sáenz
Bucaramanga, Dario Castrillon Hoyos
Cali, Isaias Duarte Cancino
Cartagena, Carlos José Ruiseco Vieira
Ibague, Juan S. Jaramillo
Manizales, José de Jesús Pimiento Rodriguez
Medellin, Hector Rueda Hernández
Nueva Pamplona, Victor M. Lopez Forero
Popayán, Alberto G. Jaramillo
Santa Fe de Antioquia, Ignacio Gomez Afistizabal
Tunja, Augusto Trujillo Arango

CONGO
Brazzaville, Barthélémy Batantu

COSTA RICA
San José, Román Arrieta Villalobos

CÔTE D'IVOIRE
Abidjan, Bernard Agre
Bouake, Vital Komenan Yao
Gagnoa, Noel Kokora-Tekry
Korhogo, Auguste Nobou

CROATIA
Rijeka-Senj, Anton Tamarut
Split-Makarska, Ante Juric
Zadar, Marijan Oblak
Zagreb, HE Cardinal Franjo Kuharić

CUBA
San Cristóbal de la Habana, HE Cardinal Jaime Lucas Ortega
    y Alamino
Santiago de Cuba, Pedro Meurice Estiu

CYPRUS
Cyprus (Maronite seat at Nicosia), Boutros Gemayel

CZECH REPUBLIC
Olomouc, Jan Graubner
Prague, HE Cardinal Miloslav Vlk

DOMINICAN REPUBLIC
Santiago de los Caballeros, Juan A. F. Santana
Santo Domingo, HE Cardinal Nicolás de Jesús López
    Rodriguez

ECUADOR
Cuenca, Alberto Luna Tobar
Guayaquil, Ignacio Larrea Holguin
Quito, Antonio J. González Zumárraga

EQUATORIAL GUINEA
Malabo, Idlefonso Obama Obono

ETHIOPIA
Addis Ababa, HE Cardinal Paul Tzadua

FRANCE
Aix, Louis-Marie Bille
Albi, Roger Meindre
Auch, vacant
Avignon, Raymond Bouchex
Besançon, Lucien Daloz
Bordeaux, HE Cardinal Pierre Eyt
Bourges, Pierre Plateau
Cambrai, Jacques Delaporte
Chambéry, Claude Feidt

Lyon, Jean Balland
Marseilles, Bernard Panafieu
Paris, HE Cardinal J. M. Lustiger
Reims, Gerard Defois
Rennes, Jacques Jullien
Rouen, Joseph Duval
Sens, vacant
Strasbourg, Charles Amarin Brand
Toulouse, André Collini
Tours, Joan Honoré

FRENCH POLYNESIA
Papeete, Michel Coppenrath

GABON
Libreville, André Fernand Anguilé

GERMANY
Bamberg, Karl Braun
Berlin, HE Cardinal George M. Sterzinsky
Cologne, HE Cardinal Joachim Meisner
Freiburg im Breisgau, Oskar Saier
Munich and Freising, HE Cardinal Friedrich Wetter
Paderborn, Johannes Joachim Degenhardt

GHANA
Accra, Dominic K. Andoh
Cape Coast, Peter Kodwo A. Turkson
Tamale, Gregory E. Kpiebaya

GREECE
Athens, Nicholaos Foscolos
Corfu, Antonio Varthalitis
Naxos, Nicolaos Printesis
Rhodes, vacant (Apostolic Administrator, Nicholaos
    Foscolos)

GUATEMALA
Guatemala, Prospero Penados del Barrio

GUINEA
Conakry, Robert Sarah

HAITI
Cap-Haitien, François Gayot
Port au Prince, François-Wolff Ligondé

HONDURAS
Tegucigalpa, Oscar A. Maradiaga

HONG KONG
Hong Kong, HE Cardinal J. B. Wu Cheng Chung

HUNGARY
Eger, Istvan Seregely
Esztergom, HE Cardinal Laslo Paskai
Kalocsa, Laszlo Danko

INDIA
Agra, Cecil de Sa
Bangalore, Alphonsus Mathias
Bhopal, Paschal Topno
Bombay, HE Cardinal I. Pimenta
Calcutta, Henry Sebastian D'Souza
Changanacherry, Joseph Powathil
Cuttack-Bhubaneswar, Raphael Cheenath
Delhi, Alan de Lastic
Ernakulam, HE Cardinal Anthony Padiyara
Goa and Daman, Raul Nicolau Gonsalves
Hyderabad, Saminini Arulappa
Madras and Mylapore, James M. Arul Das
Madurai, Marianus Arokiasamy
Nagpur, Leobard D'Souza
Pondicherry and Cuddalore, Michael Augustine
Ranchi, Telesphore P. Toppo
Shillong-Gauhati, Tarcisius Resto Phanrang

Trivandrum (Syrian Melekite rite), Cyril Baselios
   Malancharuvil
Verapoly, Cornelius Elanjikal

INDONESIA
Ende, Donatus Djagom
Jakarta, vacant
Kupang, Gregorius Manteiro
Medan, Alfred Gonti Pius Datubara
Merauke, Jacobus Duivenvoorde
Pontianak, Hieronymus Herculanus Bumbun
Semarang, HE Cardinal Julius R. Darmaatmadja
Ujung Pandang, Johannes Liku Ada'

IRAN
Ahváz, Hanna Zora
Tehran, Youhannan Semaan Issayi
Urmyā, Thomas Meram

IRAQ
Arbil, Hanna Markho
Baghdad (Latin rite), Paul Dahdah; (Syrian rite), Athanase
   M. S. Matoka; (Armenian rite), Paul Coussa; (Chaldean
   rite), Raphaël Bidawid
Basra, vacant
Kirkuk, André Sana
Mosul (Chaldean rite), Georges Garmo; (Syrian rite),
   Cyrille E. Benni

ISRAEL (*see also* Patriarchs, page 421)
Akka (Greek Melekite Catholic rite), Maximos Salloum

ITALY
Acerenza, Michele Scandiffio
Amalfi, Beniamino De Palma
Ancona, Franco Festorazzi
Bari, Mariano Magrassi
Benevento, Serafino Sprovieri
Bologna, HE Cardinal Giacomo Biffi
Brindisi, Settimio Todisco
Cagliari, Otterino Pietro Alberti
Camerino, Piergiòrgìo Nesti
Campobasso-Boiano, Ettore Di Filippo
Capua, Luigi Diligenza
Catania, Luigi Bommarito
Catanzaro, Antonio Cantisani
Chieti, Edoardo Menichelli
Conza, Mario Milano
Cosenza, Dino Trabalzini
Crotone-Santa Severina, Giuseppe Agostino
Fermo, Cleto Bellucci
Ferrara, Carlo Caffarra
Florence, HE Cardinal Silvano Piovanelli
Foggia, Giuseppe Casale
Gaeta, Vincenzo Farano
Genoa, Dionigi Tettamanzi
Gorizia and Gradisca, Antonio Vitale Bommarco
Lanciano, Enzio D'Antonio
L'Aquila, Mario Peressin
Lecce, Cosmo F. Ruppi
Lucca, Bruno Tommasi
Manfredonia, Vincenzo D'Addario
Matera, Antonio Ciliberti
Messina, Ignazio Cannavó
Milan, HE Cardinal Carlo Maria Martini
Modena, Santo B. Quadri
Monreale, Salvatore Cassisa
Naples, HE Cardinal Michele Giordano
Oristano, Pier Luigi Tiddia
Otranto, Francesco Cacucci
Palermo, Salvatore De Giorgi
Perugia, Giuseppe Chiaretti

Pescara-Penne, Francesco Cuccarese
Pisa, Alessandro Plotti
Potenza, Ennio Appignanesi
Ravenna, Luigi Amaducci
Reggio Calabria, Vittorio L. Mondello
Rossano-Cariati, Andrea Cassone
Salerno, Gerardo Pierro
Sassari, Salvatore Isgrò
Siena, Gaetano Bonicelli
Siracusa, Giuseppe Costanzo
Sorrento, Felice Cece
Spoleto, Riccardo Fontana
Taranto, Luigi Papa
Trani and Barletta, Carmelo Cassati
Trento, Giovanni Sartori
Turin, HE Cardinal Giovanni Saldarini
Udine, Alfredo Battisti
Urbino, Donato U. Bianchi
Vercelli, Enrico Masseroni

JAMAICA
Kingston, Edgerton R. Clarke

JAPAN
Nagasaki, Francis Xavier Shimamoto
Osaka, Paul Hisao Yasuda
Tokyo, HE Cardinal Peter Seiichi Shirayanagi

JORDAN
Petra and Filadelfia (Greek Melekite Catholic rite), George
   El-Murr

KAZAKHSTAN
Karaganda Apostolic Administration (Latin rite), Apostolic
   Administrator, Mgr Jan Lenga (titular Bishop of Arba)

KENYA
Kisumu, Zacchaeus Okoth
Mombasa, John Njenga
Nairobi, HE Cardinal Maurice Otunga
Nyeri, Nicodemus Kirima

KOREA
Kwang Ju, Victorinus Kong-Hi Youn
Seoul, HE Cardinal Stephen Sou Hwan Kim
Tae Gu, Paul Moun-Hi Ri

LATVIA
Riga, Jānis Pujats

LEBANON
Antelias (Maronite rite), Joseph Mohsen Bechara
Baalbek, Eliopoli (Greek Melekite Catholic rite), Salim
   Bustros
Baniyas (Greek Melekite Catholic rite), Antoine Hayek
Beirut (Greek Melekite Catholic rite), Habib Bacha;
   (Maronite rite), Khalil Abinader; (Armenian rite), Jean
   P. Kasparian
Saida (Greek Melekite Catholic rite), Georges Kwaiter
Tripoli (Maronite rite), Gabriel Toubia; (Greek Melekite
   Catholic rite), George Riashi
Tyre (Greek Melekite Catholic rite), Jean A. Haddad;
   (Maronite rite), Maroun Sader
Zahle and Furzol (Greek Melekite Catholic rite), Andre
   Haddad

LESOTHO
Maseru, Bernard Mohlalisi

LIBERIA
Monrovia, Michael Kpakala Francis

LITHUANIA
Kaunas, Sigitas Tamkevicius
Vilnius, Audris J. Bačkis

LUXEMBOURG
Luxembourg, Fernand Franck

MADAGASCAR
Antananarive, HE Cardinal Armand G. Razafindratandra
Antsiranana, Albert Joseph Tsiahoana
Fianarantsoa, Philibert Randriambololona

MALAWI
Blantyre, James Chiona

MALAYSIA
Kuala Lumpur, Anthony S. Fernandez
Kuching, Peter Chung Hoan Ting

MALI
Bamako, Luc Auguste Sangaré

MALTA
Malta, Joseph Mercieca

MARTINIQUE
Fort de France, Maurice Marie-Sainte

MEXICO
Acapulco, Rafael Bello Ruiz
Antequera, Hector G. Martìnez
Chihuahua, José Fernández Arteaga
Durango, José M. Perez
Guadalajara, HE Cardinal Juan Sandoval Iniguez
Hermosillo, Carlos Quintero Arce
Jalapa, Sergio Obeso Rivera
Mexico City, Norberto R. Carrera
Monterrey, HE Cardinal Adolfo Suarez Rivera
Morelia, Alberto S. Inda
Puebla de los Angeles, Rosendo Huesca Pacheco
San Luis Potosi, Arturo A. Szymanski Ramirez
Tlalnepantla, Manuel P. Gil Gonzalez
Yucatán, Emilio C. B. Belaunzaran

MONACO
Monaco, Joseph-Marie Sardou

MOROCCO
Rabat, Hubert Michon
Tangier, Antonio J. Peteiro Freire

MOZAMBIQUE
Beira, Jaime P. Goncalves
Maputo, HE Cardinal Alexandre José Maria dos Santos
Nampula, Manuel Vieira Pinto

MYANMAR (BURMA)
Mandalay, Alphonse U. Than Aung
Yangon (Rangoon), Gabriel Thohey Mahn Gaby

NAMIBIA
Windhoek, Bonifatius Haushiku

NETHERLANDS
Utrecht, HE Cardinal Adrianus J. Simonis

NEW ZEALAND
Wellington, HE Cardinal Thomas Stafford Williams

NICARAGUA
Managua, HE Cardinal Miguel Obando Bravo

NIGERIA
Jos, Gabriel G. Ganaka
Kaduna, Peter Yariyok Jatau
Lagos, Anthony Okogie
Onitsha, Albert K. Obiefuna

OCEANIA
Agaña, Anthony Sablan Apuron
Honiara, Adrian Thomas Smith
Nouméa, Michel-Marie-Bernard Calvet

Papeete, Michel-Gaspard Copenrath
Samoa, Apia and Tokelau, HE Cardinal Pio Taofino'u
Suva, Petero Mataca

PAKISTAN
Karachi, Simeon Pereira

PANAMA
Panama, Jose Dimas C. Delgado

PAPUA NEW GUINEA
Madang, Benedict To Varpin
Mount Hagen, Michael Meier
Port Moresby, Peter Kurongku
Rabaul, Karl Hesse

PARAGUAY
Asuncion, Felipe Santiago B. Avalos

PERU
Arequipa, Luis Sanchez-Moreno Lira
Ayacucho o Huamanga, Juan L. C. Thorne
Cuzco, Alcides Mendoza Castro
Huancayo, Jose P. Rios Reynoso
Lima, HE Cardinal Augusto Vargas Alzamora
Piura, Oscar Rolando Cantuarias Pastor
Trujillo, Manuel Prado Pérez-Rosas

PHILIPPINES
Caceres, Leonardo Legazpi
Cagayan de Oro, Jesus B. Tuquib
Capiz, Onesimo C. Gordoncillo
Cebu, HE Cardinal Ricardo Vidal
Cotabato, Philip Francis Smith
Davao, Antonio Mabutas
Jaro, Alberto J. Piamonte
Lingayen-Dagupan, Oscar V. Cruz
Lipa, Gaudencio B. Rosales
Manila, HE Cardinal Jaime L. Sin
Nueva Segovia, Orlando Quevedo
Ozamiz, Jesus Dosado
Palo, Pedro R. Dean
San Fernando, Paciano Aniceto
Tuguegarao, Diosdado A. Talamayan
Zamboanga, Carmelo D. F. Morelos

POLAND
Bialystok, Stanislaw Szymecki
Czestochowa, Stanislaw Nowak
Gdańsk, Tadeusz Goclowski
Gniezno, Henryk Muszyński
Katowice, Damian Zimoń
Kraków, HE Cardinal Franciszek Macharski
Lodz, Wladyslaw Ziolek
Lublin, Boleslaw Pylak
Poznań, Jerzy Stroba
Przemyśl of the Latins, Jozef Michalik
Szczecin-Kamień, Marian Przykucki
Warmia, Edmund Piszcz
Warsaw, HE Cardinal Józef Glemp
Wroclaw, HE Cardinal Henryk Roman Gulbinowicz

PORTUGAL
Braga, Eurico Dias Nogueira
Evora, Maurilio Jorge Quintal de Gouveia

PUERTO RICO
San Juan, HE Cardinal Luis Aponte Martinez

ROMANIA
Alba Julia (Latin rite), Gyorgy-Miklos Jakubinyi
Bucareşti, Ioan Robu
Fagaras and Alba Julia (Romanian Byzantine rite), Lucian Muresan

RUSSIA
Moscow Apostolic Administration (covering European Russia),
Apostolic Administrator, Archbishop Tadeusz
Kondrusiewicz
Novosibirsk Apostolic Administration (covering Siberia),
Apostolic Administrator, Mgr Joseph Werth, SJ (titular
Bishop of Bulna)

RWANDA
Kigali, Thaddée Ntihinyurwa

ST LUCIA
Castries, Kelvin E. Felix, OBE

EL SALVADOR
San Salvador, Fernando S. Lacalle

SENEGAL
Dakar, HE Cardinal Hyacinthe Thiandoum

SIERRA LEONE
Freetown and Bo, Joseph Ganda

SINGAPORE
Singapore, Gregory Yong Sooi Ngean

SLOVAK REPUBLIC
Trnava, Jan Sokol

SLOVENIA
Ljubljana, Alojzij Šuštar

SOUTH AFRICA
Bloemfontein, Peter John Butelezi
Cape Town, Lawrence Patrick Henry
Durban, Wilfrid Fox Napier
Pretoria, George Francis Daniel

SPAIN
Barcelona, HE Cardinal Ricardo Maria Carles Gordó
Burgos, Santiago Martinez Acebes
Granada, José Méndez Asensio
Madrid, Antonio M. Rouco Varela
Oviedo, Gabino Diaz Merchán
Pamplona, Fernando S. Aquilar
Santiago de Compostela, vacant
Sevilla, Carlos Amigo Vallejo
Tarragona, Ramon Torrella Cascante
Toledo, Francisco A. Martinez
Valencia, Agustin Garcia-Gasco Vicente
Valladolid, José Delicado Baeza
Zaragoza, Eliaz Yanez Alvarez

SRI LANKA
Colombo, Nicholas Marcus Fernando

SUDAN
Juba, Paulino Lukudu Loro
Khartoum, Gabriel Zubeir Wako

SYRIA
Alep, Beroea, Halab (Greek Melekite Catholic rite), Jean-
Clement Jeanbart; (Syrian rite), Raboula A. Beylouni;
(Maronite rite), Pierre Callaos; (Armenian rite), Boutros
Marayati
Baniyas (Greek Melekite Catholic rite), Antoine Hayek
Bosra, Bostra, Boulos Nassif Borkhoche
Damascus (Greek Melekite Catholic rite), S. B. Maximos
V. Hakim; (Syrian rite), Eustache J. Mounayer;
(Maronite rite), Hamid A. Mourany
Hassaké-Nisibi, Georges Habib Hafouri
Homs, Emesa (Greek Melekite Catholic rite), Abraham
Nehmé; (Syrian Catholic rite), Basile Daoud
Laodicea (Greek Melekite Catholic rite), Fares Maakaroun

TAIWAN
Taipei, Joseph Ti-Kang

TANZANIA
Dar es Salaam, Polycarp Pengo
Mwanza, Antony Mayala
Songea, Norbert W. Mtega
Tabora, Mario E. A. Mgulunde

THAILAND
Bangkok, HE Cardinal Michael Michai Kitbunchu
Tharé and Nonseng, Lawrence Khai Saen-Phon-On

TOGO
Lomé, Philippe F. K. Kpodzro

TRINIDAD
Port of Spain, Gordon Anthony Pantin

TURKEY
Diarbekir, Paul Karatas
Istanbul (*Constantinople*), Jean Tcholakian
Izmir, Giuseppe G. Bernardini

UGANDA
Kampala, HE Cardinal Emmanuel Wamala

UKRAINE
Lvov (Latin rite), Marian Jaworski (Archbishop of Lvov of
the Latins); (Ukrainian rite), HE Cardinal Myroslav
I. Lubachivsky (Major Archbishop of Lvov of the
Ukrainians)

URUGUAY
Montevideo, José Gottardi Cristelli

USA
Anchorage, Francis Thomas Hurley
Atlanta, John F. Donoghue
Baltimore, HE Cardinal William Henry Keeler
Boston, HE Cardinal Bernard F. Law
Chicago, HE Cardinal Joseph L. Bernardin
Cincinnati, Daniel E. Pilarczyk
Denver, James Francis Stafford
Detroit, HE Cardinal Adam J. Maida
Dubuque, Jerome G. Hanus
Hartford, Daniel A. Cronin
Indianapolis, Daniel Mark Buechlein
Kansas City, James P. Keleher
Los Angeles, HE Cardinal Roger M. Mahony
Louisville, Thomas C. Kelly
Miami, John C. Favalora
Milwaukee, Rembert G. Weakland
Mobile, Oscar H. Lipscomb
Newark, Theodore E. McCarrick
New Orleans, Francis B. Schulte
New York, HE Cardinal John J. O'Connor
Oklahoma City, Eusebius Joseph Beltran
Omaha, Elden Curtiss
Philadelphia, HE Cardinal Anthony J. Bevilacqua;
(Ukrainian rite), Stephen Sulyk
Pittsburgh (Byzantine rite), Judson M. Procyk
Portland (*Oregon*), vacant
St Louis (*Missouri*), Justin F. Rigali
St Paul and Minneapolis, Harry J. Flynn
San Antonio, Patrick F. Flores
San Francisco, William J. Levada
Santa Fe, Michael Sheehan
Seattle, Thomas J. Murphy
Washington, HE Cardinal James A. Hickey

VENEZUELA
Barquisimeto, Julio Manuel Chirivella Varela
Calabozo, Helimenas de J. R. Paredes
Caracas, Ignacio A. V. Garcia
Ciudad Bolívar, Medardo Luzardo Romero
Cumana, Alfredo J. R. Figueroa

Maracaibo, Ramon O. Perez Morales
Mérida, Baltazar P. Cardozo
Valencia, Jorge Liberato Urosa Savino

VIETNAM
Hanoi, HE Cardinal Paul Joseph Pham Dinh Tung
Hue, *Apostolic Administrator*, Etienne N. N. Thê
Thanh-Phô Hôchiminh, *Apostolic Administrator*, Mgr Nicolas Huynh Van Nghi

YUGOSLAV FEDERAL REPUBLIC
Bar, Petar Perkolić
Belgrade, Franc Perko

ZAÏRE
Bukavu, Christophe Munzihirwa Mwene Ngabo
Kananga, Bakole wa Ilunga
Kinshasa, HE Cardinal Frederick Etsou-Nzabi-Bamungwabi
Kisangani, Laurent Monsengwo Pasinya
Lubumbashi, Kabanga Songasonga
Mbandaka-Bikoro, Joseph Kumuondala Mbimba

ZAMBIA
Kasama, James Spaita
Lusaka, Adrian Mungandu

ZIMBABWE
Harare, Patrick Chakaipa

PATRIARCHS IN COMMUNION WITH THE ROMAN CATHOLIC CHURCH

Alexandria, HB Stephanos II Ghattas (Patriarch for Catholic Copts); HB Parthenios III (Greek Orthodox Patriarch of Alexandria and All Africa)
Antioch, HB Ignace Antoine II Hayek (Patriarch for Syrian rite Catholics); HB Maximos V. Hakim (Patriarch for Greek Melekite rite Catholics); HE Cardinal Nasrallah Pierre Sfeir (Patriarch for Maronite rite Catholics)
Jerusalem, HB Michel Sabbah (Patriarch for Latin rite Catholics); HB Maximos V. Hakim (Patriarch for Greek Melekite rite Catholics)
Babilonia of the Chaldeans, HB Raphael I Bidawid
Cilicia of the Armenians, HB Jean Pierre XVIII Kasparian (Patriarch for Armenian rite Catholics)
Oriental India, Archbishop Raul Nicolau Gonsalves
Lisbon, HE Cardinal Antonio Ribeiro
Venice, HE Cardinal Marco Ce

Other Churches in the UK

AFRICAN AND AFRO-CARIBBEAN CHURCHES

There are more than 160 Christian churches or groups of African or Afro-Caribbean origin in the UK. These include the Apostolic Faith Church, the Cherubim and Seraphim Church, the New Testament Church Assembly, the New Testament Church of God, the Wesleyan Holiness Church and the Aladura Churches.

The Afro-West Indian United Council of Churches and the Council of African and Afro-Caribbean Churches UK (which was initiated as the Council of African and Allied Churches in 1979 to give one voice to the various Christian churches of African origin in the UK) are the media through which the member churches can work jointly to provide services they cannot easily provide individually.

There are about 70,000 adherents of African and Afro-Caribbean churches in the UK, and about 1,000 congregations. The Afro-West Indian United Council of Churches has about 30,000 individual members, 135 ministers and 65 places of worship. The Council of African and Afro-Caribbean Churches UK has about 17,000 members, 250 ministers and 75 congregations.

AFRO-WEST INDIAN UNITED COUNCIL OF CHURCHES, c/o New Testament Church of God, Arcadian Gardens, High Road, London N22 5AA. Tel: 0181-888 9427. *Chairman*, Revd E. Brown
COUNCIL OF AFRICAN AND AFRO-CARIBBEAN CHURCHES UK, 31 Norton House, Sidney Road, London SW9 0UJ. Tel: 0171-274 5589. *Chairman*, His Grace The Most Revd Father Olu A. Abiola

ASSOCIATED PRESBYTERIAN CHURCHES OF SCOTLAND

The Associated Presbyterian Churches came into being in 1989 as a result of a division within the Free Presbyterian Church of Scotland. Following two controversial disciplinary cases, the culmination of deepening differences within the Church, a presbytery was formed calling itself the Associated Presbyterian Churches (APC). The Associated Presbyterian Churches has about 1,000 members, 15 ministers and 20 churches.
Clerk of the Scottish Presbytery, Revd Dr M. MacInnes, Drumalin, 16 Drummond Road, Inverness IV2 4NB. Tel: 01463-223983

THE BAPTIST CHURCH

Baptists trace their origins to John Smyth, who in 1609 in Amsterdam reinstituted the baptism of conscious believers as the basis of the fellowship of a gathered church. Members of Smyth's church established the first Baptist church in England in 1612. They came to be known as 'General' Baptists and their theology was Arminian, whereas a later group of Calvinists who adopted the baptism of believers came to be known as 'Particular' Baptists. The two sections of the Baptists were united into one body, the Baptist Union of Great Britain and Ireland, in 1891. In 1988 the title was changed to the Baptist Union of Great Britain.

Baptists emphasize the complete autonomy of the local church, although individual churches are linked in various kinds of associations. There are international bodies (such as the Baptist World Alliance) and national bodies, but some Baptist churches belong to neither. However, in Great Britain the majority of churches and associations belong to the Baptist Union of Great Britain. There are also Baptist Unions in Wales, Scotland and Ireland which are much smaller than the Baptist Union of Great Britain, and there is some overlap of membership.

There are over 38 million Baptist church members world-wide; in the Baptist Union of Great Britain there are 157,000 members, 1,864 pastors and 2,130 churches. In the Baptist Union of Scotland there are 14,328 members, 140 pastors and 171 churches. In the Baptist Union of Wales there are 24,178 members, 118 pastors and 537 churches. In the Baptist Union of Ireland there are 8,454 members, 83 pastors and 109 churches.
President of the Baptist Union of Great Britain (1996–7), Revd John C. James

General Secretary, Revd D. R. Coffey, Baptist House, PO Box 44, 129 Broadway, Didcot, Oxon OX11 8RT. Tel: 01235-512077

THE CHURCH OF CHRIST, SCIENTIST

The Church of Christ, Scientist was founded by Mary Baker Eddy in the USA in 1879 to 'reinstate primitive Christianity and its lost element of healing'. Christian Science teaches the need for spiritual regeneration and salvation from sin, but is best known for its reliance on prayer alone in the healing of sickness. Adherents believe that such healing is a law, or Science, and is in direct line with that practised by Jesus Christ (revered, not as God, but as the Son of God) and by the early Christian Church.

The denomination consists of The First Church of Christ, Scientist, in Boston, Massachusetts, USA (the Mother Church) and its branch churches in over 60 countries world-wide. Branch churches are democratically governed by their members, while a five-member Board of Directors, based in Boston, is authorized to transact the business of the Mother Church. The Bible and Mary Baker Eddy's book, *Science and Health with Key to the Scriptures*, are used at services; there are no clergy. Those engaged in full-time healing are called practitioners, of whom there are 3,500 world-wide.

No membership figures are available, since Mary Baker Eddy felt that numbers are no measure of spiritual vitality and ruled that such statistics should not be published. There are over 2,400 branch churches world-wide, including nearly 200 in the UK.

CHRISTIAN SCIENCE COMMITTEE ON PUBLICATION, 2 Elysium Gate, 126 New Kings Road, London SW6 4LZ. Tel: 0171-371 0600. *District Manager for Great Britain and Ireland*, A. Grayson

THE CHURCH OF JESUS CHRIST OF LATTER-DAY SAINTS

The Church (often referred to as 'the Mormons') was founded in New York State, USA, in 1830, and came to Britain in 1837. The oldest continuous branch in the world is to be found in Preston, Lancs. Mormons are Christians who claim to belong to the 'Restored Church' of Jesus Christ. They believe that true Christianity died when the last original apostle died, but that it was given back to the world by God and Christ through Joseph Smith, the Church's founder and first president. They accept and use the Bible as scripture, but believe in continuing revelation from God and use additional scriptures, including *The Book of Mormon: Another Testament of Jesus Christ*. The importance of the family is central to the Church's beliefs and practices. Church members set aside Monday evenings as Family Home Evenings when Christian family values are taught. Polygamy was formally discontinued in 1890.

The Church has no paid ministry; local congregations are headed by a leader chosen from amongst their number. The world governing body, based in Utah, USA, is the three-man First Presidency, assisted by the Quorum of the Twelve Apostles.

There are about 9 million members world-wide, with about 170,000 adherents in Britain in over 350 congregations.

President of the Europe North Area (including Britain), Elder C. O. Samuelson, jun.

BRITISH HEADQUARTERS, Church Offices, 751 Warwick Road, Solihull, W. Midlands B91 3DQ. Tel: 0121-711 2244

THE CONGREGATIONAL FEDERATION

The Congregational Federation was founded by members of Congregational churches in England and Wales who did not join the United Reformed Church (q.v.) in 1972. There are also churches in Scotland and Australia affiliated to the Federation. The Federation exists to encourage congregations of believers to worship in free assembly, but it has no authority over them and emphasizes their right to independence and self-government.

The Federation has 11,923 members, 71 recognized ministers and 313 churches in England, Wales and Scotland.

President of the Federation (1996-7), F. Wroe
General Secretary, G. M. Adams, The Congregational Centre, 4 Castle Gate, Nottingham NG1 7AS. Tel: 0115-941 3801

THE FREE CHURCH OF ENGLAND

The Free Church of England is a union of two bodies in the Anglican tradition, the Free Church of England, founded in 1844 as a protest against the Oxford Movement in the established Church, and the Reformed Episcopal Church, founded in America in 1873 but which also had congregations in England. As both Churches sought to maintain the historic faith, tradition and practice of the Anglican Church since the Reformation, they decided to unite as one body in England in 1927. The historic episcopate was conferred on the English Church in 1876 through the line of the American bishops, who had pioneered an open table Communion policy towards members of other denominations.

The Free Church of England has 1,550 members, 38 ministers and 26 churches in England. It also has three house churches and three ministers in New Zealand, and one church and one minister in St Petersburg, Russia.

General Secretary, Revd W. J. Lawler, 45 Broughton Road, Wallasey, Merseyside L44 4DT. Tel: 0151-638 2564

THE FREE CHURCH OF SCOTLAND

The Free Church of Scotland was formed in 1843 when over 400 ministers withdrew from the Church of Scotland as a result of interference in the internal affairs of the church by the civil authorities. In 1900, all but 26 ministers joined with others to form the United Free Church (most of which rejoined the Church of Scotland in 1929). In 1904 the remaining 26 ministers were recognized by the House of Lords as continuing the Free Church of Scotland.

The Church maintains strict adherence to the Westminster Confession of Faith (1648) and accepts the Bible as the sole rule of faith and conduct. Its General Assembly meets annually. It also has links with Reformed Churches overseas. The Free Church of Scotland has 6,000 members, 110 ministers and 140 churches.

General Treasurer, I. D. Gill, The Mound, Edinburgh EH1 2LS. Tel: 0131-226 5286

THE FREE PRESBYTERIAN CHURCH OF SCOTLAND

The Free Presbyterian Church of Scotland was formed in 1893 by two ministers of the Free Church of Scotland who refused to accept a Declaratory Act passed by the Free Church General Assembly in 1892. The Free Presbyterian Church of Scotland is Calvinistic in doctrine and emphasizes observance of the Sabbath. It adheres strictly to the Westminster Confession of Faith of 1648.

The Church has about 3,000 members in Scotland and about 7,000 in overseas congregations. It has 26 ministers and 50 churches.

Moderator, Revd J. R. Tallach, Free Presbyterian Manse, Raasay, by Kyle IV40 8PB. Tel: 01478-660216

Clerk of Synod, Revd J. MacLeod, 16 Matheson Road, Stornoway, Isle of Lewis HSI 2LA. Tel: 01851-702755

THE INDEPENDENT METHODIST CHURCHES

The Independent Methodist Churches seceded from the Wesleyan Methodist Church in 1805 and remained independent when the Methodist Church in Great Britain was formed in 1932. They are mainly concentrated in the industrial areas of the north of England.

The churches are Methodist in doctrine but their organization is congregational. All the churches are members of the Independent Methodist Connexion of Churches. The controlling body of the Connexion is the Annual Meeting, to which churches send delegates. The Connexional President is elected annually. Between annual meetings the affairs of the Connexion are handled by departmental committees. Ministers are appointed by the churches and trained through the Connexion. The ministry is open to both men and women and is unpaid.

There are 3,400 members, 106 ministers and 101 churches in Great Britain.

Connexional President (1996–7), H. G. Gleave
General Secretary, J. M. Day, The Old Police House, Croxton, Stafford ST21 6PE. Tel: 0163-062 0671

JEHOVAH'S WITNESSES

The movement now known as Jehovah's Witnesses grew from a Bible study group formed by Charles Taze Russell in 1872 in Pennsylvania, USA. In 1896 it adopted the name of the Watch Tower Bible and Tract Society, and in 1931 its members became known as Jehovah's Witnesses. Jehovah's (God's) Witnesses believe in the Bible as the word of God, and consider it to be inspired and historically accurate. They take the scriptures literally, except where there are obvious indications that they are figurative or symbolic, and reject the doctrine of the Trinity. Witnesses believe that the earth will remain for ever and that all those approved of by Jehovah will have eternal life on a cleansed and beautified earth; only 144,000 will go to heaven to rule with Christ. They believe that the second coming of Christ and his thousand-year reign on earth have been imminent since 1914, and that Armageddon (a final battle in which evil will be defeated) will precede Christ's rule of peace. They refuse to take part in military service, and do not accept stimulants or blood transfusions. They publish a magazine, *The Watchtower.*

The 12-member world governing body is based in New York, USA. Witnesses world-wide are divided into branches, countries or areas, districts, circuits and congregations. There are overseers at each level, and two assemblies are held annually for each circuit. There is no paid ministry, but each congregation has elders assigned to look after various duties and every Witness is assigned homes to visit in their congregation.

There are over 5 million Jehovah's Witnesses worldwide, with 130,000 Witnesses in the UK organized into over 1,400 congregations.

BRITISH ISLES HEADQUARTERS, Watch Tower House, The Ridgeway, London NW7 IRN. Tel: 0181-906 2211

THE LUTHERAN CHURCH

Lutheranism is based on the teachings of Martin Luther, the German leader of the Protestant Reformation. The authority of the scriptures is held to be supreme over Church tradition and creeds, and the key doctrine is that of justification by faith alone.

Lutheranism is one of the largest Protestant denominations and it is particularly strong in northern Europe and the USA. Some Lutheran churches are episcopal, while others have a synodal form of organization; unity is based on doctrine rather than structure. Most Lutheran churches are members of the Lutheran World Federation, based in Geneva.

Lutheran services in Great Britain are held in many languages to serve members of different nationalities. English-language congregations are members either of the Lutheran Church in Great Britain–United Synod, or of the Evangelical Lutheran Church of England. The United Synod and most of the various national congregations are members of the Lutheran Council of Great Britain.

There are over 70 million Lutherans world-wide; in Great Britain there are 27,000 members, 45 ministers and 100 churches.

Chairman of the Lutheran Council of Great Britain, Very Revd R. J. Patkai, 8 Collingham Gardens, London SW5 OHW. Tel: 0171-373 1141

THE METHODIST CHURCH

The Methodist movement started in England in 1729 when the Revd John Wesley, an Anglican priest, and his brother Charles met with others in Oxford and resolved to conduct their lives and study by 'rule and method'. In 1739 the Wesleys began evangelistic preaching and the first Methodist chapel was founded in Bristol in the same year. In 1744 the first annual conference was held, at which the Articles of Religion were drawn up. Doctrinal emphases included repentance, faith, the assurance of salvation, social concern and the priesthood of all believers. After John Wesley's death in 1791 the Methodists withdrew from the established Church to form the Methodist Church. Methodists gradually drifted into many groups, but in 1932 the Wesleyan Methodist Church, the United Methodist Church and the Primitive Methodist Church united to form the Methodist Church in Great Britain as it now exists.

The governing body and supreme authority of the Methodist Church is the Conference, but there are also 33 district synods, consisting of all the ministers and selected lay people in each district, and circuit meetings of the ministers and lay people of each circuit.

There are over 60 million Methodists world-wide; in Great Britain (1995 figures) there are 380,269 members, 3,660 ministers, 12,611 lay preachers and 6,678 churches.
President of the Conference in Great Britain (1996–7), Revd N. T. Collinson
Vice-President of the Conference (1996–7), Ms J. S. Pickard
Secretary of the Conference, Revd B. E. Beck, Methodist Church, Conference Office, 25 Marylebone Road, London NW1 5JR. Tel: 0171-486 5502

THE METHODIST CHURCH IN IRELAND

The Methodist Church in Ireland is closely linked to British Methodism but is autonomous. It has 17,964 members, 199 ministers, 289 lay preachers and 233 churches.
President of the Conference in Ireland (1996–7), Revd K. Best, 11 Clearwater, Clooney Road, Londonderry BT47 1BE. Tel: 01504-42644
Secretary of the Conference in Ireland, Revd E. T. I. Mawhinney, 1 Fountainville Avenue, Belfast BT9 6AN. Tel: 01232-324554

THE ORTHODOX CHURCH

The Orthodox Church (or Eastern Orthodox Church) is a communion of self-governing Christian churches recognizing the honorary primacy of the Oecumenical Patriarch of Constantinople.

In the first millennium of the Christian era the faith was slowly formulated. Between AD 325 and 787 there were seven Oecumenical Councils at which bishops from the entire Christian world assembled to resolve various doctrinal disputes which had arisen. The estrangement between East and West began after Constantine moved the centre of the Roman Empire from Rome to Constantinople, and it gained momentum after the temporal administration was divided. Linguistic and cultural differences between Greek East and Latin West served to encourage separate ecclesiastical developments which became pronounced in the tenth and early 11th centuries.

The administration of the church was divided between five ancient patriarchates: Rome and all the West, Constantinople (the imperial city – the 'New Rome'), Jerusalem and all Palestine, Antioch and all the East, and Alexandria and all Africa. Of these, only Rome was in the Latin West and after the Great Schism in 1054, Rome developed a structure of authority centralized on one source, the Papacy, while the Orthodox East maintained the style of localized administration.

To the older patriarchates were later added the Patriarchates of Russia, Georgia, Serbia, Bulgaria and Romania. The Orthodox Church also includes autocephalous (self-governing) national churches in Greece, Cyprus, Poland, Albania, Czechoslovakia and Sinai, and autonomous national churches in Finland and Japan. The Estonian and Latvian Orthodox Churches are in practice part of the Moscow Patriarchate. The Belorussians and Ukrainians have recently been given greater autonomy by Moscow, but some Ukrainians have broken away to establish an independent Ukrainian Patriarchate. In Macedonia the local hierarchy has declared itself independent of the Serbian Patriarchate. The Russian dioceses in the diaspora fall into four groups: those under the direct control of the Moscow Patriarchate; the Russian Orthodox Church Outside Russia, sometimes known as the Synod in Exile; the Russian Archdiocese centred at the cathedral in rue Daru, Paris, which is part of the Patriarchate in Constantinople;

and the Orthodox Church in America, which was granted autocephalous status in 1970.

The position of Orthodox Christians is that the faith was fully defined during the period of the Oecumenical Councils. In doctrine it is strongly trinitarian, and stresses the mystery and importance of the sacraments. It is episcopal in government. The structure of the Orthodox Christian year differs from that of western Churches (*see* page 82).

Orthodox Christians throughout the world are estimated to number about 150 million.

PATRIARCHS
Archbishop of Constantinople, New Rome and Oecumenical Patriarch, Bartholomew, *elected* 1991
Pope and Patriarch of Alexandria and All Africa, Parthenios III, *elected* 1987
Patriarch of Antioch and All the East, Ignatios IV, *elected* 1979
Patriarch of Jerusalem and All Palestine, Diodoros, *elected* 1981
Patriarch of Moscow and All Russia, Alexei II, *elected* 1990
Archbishop of Tbilisi and Mtskheta, Catholicos-Patriarch of All Georgia, Ilia II, *elected* 1977
Archbishop of Pec, Metropolitan of Belgrade and Karlovci, Patriarch of Serbia, Paul, *elected* 1990
Archbishop of Bucharest and Patriarch of Romania, Teoctist, *elected* 1986
Metropolitan of Sofia and Patriarch of Bulgaria, Maxim, *elected* 1971
Patriarch of Kiev and All Ukraine, Philaret, *elected* 1995 (not recognized by any other Patriarchate)

ORTHODOX CHURCHES IN THE UK

THE PATRIARCHATE OF ANTIOCH

Until 1995 the Patriarchate of Antioch was represented in Britain by one Arabic language parish with one priest. A group of ex-Anglicans (the 'Pilgrimage to Orthodoxy') was received into the Patriarchate of Antioch in 1995. There are now eight parishes served by eight priests. In Britain the Patriarchate is represented by the Revd Fr Samir Gholam, 1A Redhill Street, London NW1 4BG. Tel: 0171-383 0403

THE GREEK ORTHODOX CHURCH (PATRIARCHATE OF CONSTANTINOPLE)

The presence of Greek Orthodox Christians in Britain dates back to 1677 when Archbishop Joseph Geogirenes of Samos fled from Turkish persecution and came to London, where a church was built for him in Soho. The present Greek cathedral in Moscow Road, Bayswater, was opened for public worship in 1879 and the Diocese of Thyateira and Great Britain was established in 1922. There are now 114 parishes and other communities (including monasteries) in Great Britain, served by five bishops and 91 churches.

In Great Britain the Patriarchate of Constantinople is represented by Archbishop Gregorios of Thyateira and Great Britain, 5 Craven Hill, London W2 3EN. Tel: 0171-723 4787.

THE RUSSIAN ORTHODOX CHURCH (PATRIARCHATE OF MOSCOW) AND THE RUSSIAN ORTHODOX CHURCH OUTSIDE RUSSIA

The earliest records of Russian Orthodox Church activities in Britain date from the visit to England of Tsar Peter I at the beginning of the 18th century. Clergy were sent from Russia to serve the chapel established to minister to the staff of the Imperial Russian Embassy in London.

After 1917 the Church of Russia was persecuted. The Patriarch of Moscow, St Tikhon the New Martyr, anathematized both the atheistic persecutors of the Church and all who collaborated with them. Because of the civil war normal administrative contact with Russian Orthodox Christians outside the country was impossible, and he therefore authorized the establishment of a higher church administration, i.e. a synod in exile, by Russian bishops who were then outside Russia. This is the origin of the Russian Orthodox Church Outside Russia. The attitude of the Church of Russia to the former Soviet regime was always a source of contention between the two hierarchies; tensions are now lessening but remain unresolved.

In Britain the Patriarchate of Moscow is represented by Metropolitan Anthony of Sourozh, 67 Ennismore Gardens, London SW7 1NH. Tel: 0171-584 0096. He is assisted by one archbishop, one vicar bishop and 13 priests. There are 27 parishes and smaller communities.

The Russian Orthodox Church Outside Russia is represented by Archbishop Mark of Richmond and Great Britain (also Archbishop of Berlin and Germany), 14 St Dunstan's Road, London W6 8RB. Tel: 0181-748 4232. There are eight communities, including two monasteries, served by four priests.

THE SERBIAN ORTHODOX CHURCH (PATRIARCHATE OF SERBIA)

There was a small congregation of Orthodox Christian Serbs in London before the Second World War, but most Serbian parishes in Britain have been established since 1945. There is no resident bishop as the parishes are part of the Serbian Orthodox Diocese of Western Europe, which has its centre in Germany. There are 33 parishes and smaller communities in Britain served by 13 priests.

In Britain the Patriarchate of Serbia is represented by the Episcopal Vicar, the Very Revd Milun Kostic, 89 Lancaster Road, London W11 1QQ. Tel: 0171-727 8367.

OTHER NATIONALITIES

Most of the Ukrainian parishes in Britain have now joined the Patriarchate of Constantinople, leaving just one Ukrainian parish in Britain under the care of the Patriarch of Kiev. The Latvian, Polish and some Belorussian parishes are also under the care of the Patriarchate of Constantinople. The Patriarchate of Romania has one parish served by two priests. The Patriarchate of Bulgaria has one parish served by one priest. The Belorussian Autocephalous Orthodox Church has five parishes served by two priests.

ORTHODOX CHURCH PUBLIC RELATIONS OFFICE, St George Orthodox Information Service, 64 Prebend Gardens, London W6 0XU. Tel: 0181-741 9624. *Secretary,* A. Bond

PENTECOSTAL CHURCHES

Pentecostalism is inspired by the descent of the Holy Spirit upon the apostles at Pentecost. The movement began in Los Angeles, USA, in 1906 and is characterized by baptism with the Holy Spirit, divine healing, speaking in tongues (glossolalia), and a literal interpretation of the scriptures. The Pentecostal movement in Britain dates from 1907. Initially, groups of Pentecostalists were led by laymen and did not organize formally. However, in 1915 the Elim Foursquare Gospel Alliance (more usually called the Elim Pentecostal Church) was founded in Ireland by George Jeffreys and in 1924 about 70 independent assemblies formed a fellowship, the Assemblies of God in Great Britain and Ireland. The Apostolic Church grew out of the 1904−5 revivals in South Wales and was established in 1916, and the New Testament Church of God was

established in England in 1953. In recent years many aspects of Pentecostalism have been adopted by the growing charismatic movement within the Roman Catholic, Protestant and Eastern Orthodox churches.

There are about 22 million Pentecostalists world-wide, with about 130,000 adult adherents in Great Britain and Ireland.

THE APOSTOLIC CHURCH, International Administration Offices, PO Box 389, 24−27 St Helens Road, Swansea SA1 1ZH. Tel: 01792-473992. *President,* Pastor P. Cawthorne; *Administrator,* Pastor M. Davies. The Apostolic Church has about 130 churches, 5,500 adherents and 83 ministers

THE ASSEMBLIES OF GOD IN GREAT BRITAIN AND IRELAND, General Offices, 106−114 Talbot Street, Nottingham NG1 5GH. Tel: 0115-947 4525. *General Superintendent,* W. Shenton; *General Administrator,* B. D. Varnam. The Assemblies of God has 645 churches, about 75,000 adherents (including children) and 678 accredited ministers

THE ELIM PENTECOSTAL CHURCH, PO Box 38, Cheltenham, Glos GL50 3HN. Tel: 01242-519904. *General Superintendent,* Pastor I. W. Lewis; *Administrator,* Pastor B. Hunter. The Elim Pentecostal Church has about 470 churches, 50,000 adherents and 475 accredited ministers

THE NEW TESTAMENT CHURCH OF GOD, Main House, Overstone Park, Overstone, Northampton NN6 0AD. Tel: 01604-645944. *National Overseer,* Revd Dr R. O. Brown. The New Testament Church of God has 110 organized congregations, 7,500 baptized members, about 20,000 adherents and 242 accredited ministers

THE PRESBYTERIAN CHURCH IN IRELAND

The Presbyterian Church in Ireland is Calvinistic in doctrine and presbyterian in constitution. Presbyterianism was established in Ireland as a result of the Ulster plantation in the early 17th century, when English and Scottish Protestants settled in the north of Ireland.

There are 21 presbyteries and five regional synods under the chief court known as the General Assembly. The General Assembly meets annually and is presided over by a Moderator who is elected for one year. The ongoing work of the Church is undertaken by 18 boards under which there are a number of specialist committees.

There are about 304,000 Presbyterians in Ireland, mainly in the north, in 562 congregations and with 400 ministers.

Moderator (1996−7), Rt. Revd Dr D. H. Allen
Clerk of Assembly and General Secretary, Revd S. Hutchinson, Church House, Belfast BT1 6DW. Tel: 01232-322284

THE PRESBYTERIAN CHURCH OF WALES

The Presbyterian Church of Wales or Calvinistic Methodist Church of Wales is Calvinistic in doctrine and presbyterian in constitution. It was formed in 1811 when Welsh Calvinists severed the relationship with the established church by ordaining their own ministers. It secured its own confession of faith in 1823 and a Constitutional Deed in 1826, and since 1864 the General Assembly has met annually, presided over by a Moderator elected for a year. The doctrine and constitutional structure of the Presbyterian Church of Wales was confirmed by Act of Parliament in 1931−2.

The Church has 51,720 members, 136 ministers and 939 churches.
Moderator (1996–7), Revd A. Wynne Edwards
General Secretary, Revd D. H. Owen, 53 Richmond Road, Cardiff CF2 3UP. Tel: 01222-494913

THE RELIGIOUS SOCIETY OF FRIENDS (QUAKERS)

Quakerism is a movement, not a church, which was founded in the 17th century by George Fox and others in an attempt to revive what they saw as 'primitive Christianity'. The movement was based originally in the Midlands, Yorkshire and north-west England, but there are now Quakers in 36 countries around the world. The colony of Pennsylvania, founded by William Penn, was originally Quaker.

Emphasis is placed on the experience of God in daily life rather than on sacraments or religious occasions. There is no church calendar. Worship is largely silent and there are no appointed ministers; the responsibility for conducting a meeting is shared equally among those present. Social reform and religious tolerance have always been important to Quakers, together with a commitment to non-violence in resolving disputes.

There are 213,800 Quakers world-wide, with over 19,000 in Great Britain and Ireland. There are about 490 meeting houses in Great Britain.
CENTRAL OFFICES: (GREAT BRITAIN) Friends House, Euston Road, London NW1 2BJ. Tel: 0171-387 3601; (IRELAND) Swanbrook House, Morehampton Road, Dublin 4. Tel: 00 353 1-683684

THE SALVATION ARMY

The Salvation Army was founded by a Methodist minister, William Booth, in the east end of London in 1865, and has since become established in 101 countries world-wide. It was first known as the Christian Mission, and took its present name in 1878 when it adopted a quasi-military command structure intended to inspire and regulate its endeavours and to reflect its view that the Church was engaged in spiritual warfare. Salvationists emphasize evangelism, social work and the relief of poverty.

The world leader, known as the General, is elected by a High Council composed of the Chief of the Staff and senior ranking officers known as commissioners.

There are 1,341,841 members, 17,276 active officers (full-time ordained ministers) and 14,558 worship centres and outposts world-wide. In Great Britain and Ireland there are 66,183 members, 1,763 active officers and 993 worship centres.
General, P. A. Rader
UK Territorial Commander, Commissioner D. Pender
TERRITORIAL HEADQUARTERS, PO Box 249, 101 Queen Victoria Street, London EC4P 4EP. Tel: 0171-236 5222

THE SEVENTH-DAY ADVENTIST CHURCH

The Seventh-day Adventist Church was founded in 1863 in the USA. Its members look forward to the second coming of Christ and observe the Sabbath (the seventh day) as a day of rest, worship and ministry. The Church bases its faith and practice wholly on the Bible and has developed 27 fundamental beliefs.

The World Church is divided into 12 divisions, each made up of unions of churches. The Seventh-day Adventist Church in the British Isles is known as the British Union of Seventh-day Adventists and is a member of the Trans-European Division. In the British Isles the administrative organization of the church is arranged in three tiers: the local churches; the regional conferences for south England, north England, Wales, Scotland and Ireland; and the national 'union' conference.

There are about 9 million Adventists and 38,816 churches in 208 countries world-wide. In the UK and Ireland there are 18,734 members, 162 ministers and 247 churches.
President of the British Union Conference, Pastor C. R. Perry
BRITISH ISLES HEADQUARTERS, Stanborough Park, Watford WD2 6JP. Tel: 01923-672251

UNDEB YR ANNIBYNWYR CYMRAEG
The Union of Welsh Independents

The Union of Welsh Independents was formed in 1872 and is a voluntary association of Welsh Congregational Churches and personal members. It is entirely Welsh-speaking. Congregationalism in Wales dates back to 1639 when the first Welsh Congregational Church was opened in Gwent. Member Churches are Calvinistic in doctrine and congregationalist in organization. Each church has complete independence in the government and administration of its affairs.

The Union has 42,442 members, 150 ministers and 555 member churches.
President of the Union (1996–7), Revd F. M. Jones
General Secretary, Revd D. Morris Jones, Tŷ John Penry, 11 Heol Sant Helen, Swansea SA1 4AL. Tel: 01792-652542

UNITARIAN AND FREE CHRISTIAN CHURCHES

Unitarianism has its historical roots in the Judaeo-Christian tradition but questions the deity of Christ and the doctrine of the trinity. It allows the individual to embrace insights from all the world's faiths and philosophies, as there is no formal creed. It is accepted that beliefs may evolve in the light of personal experience.

Unitarian communities first became established in Poland and Transylvania in the 16th century. The first avowedly Unitarian place of worship in the British Isles opened in London in 1774. The General Assembly of Unitarian and Free Christian Churches came into existence in 1928 as the result of the amalgamation of two earlier organizations.

There are about 10,000 Unitarians in Great Britain and Ireland, and 150 Unitarian ministers. About 250 self-governing congregations and fellowship groups, including a small number overseas, are members of the General Assembly.
GENERAL ASSEMBLY OF UNITARIAN AND FREE CHRISTIAN CHURCHES, Essex Hall, 1–6 Essex Street, Strand, London WC2R 3HY. Tel: 0171-240 2384. *General Secretary*, J. J. Teagle

THE UNITED REFORMED CHURCH

The United Reformed Church was formed by the union of most of the Congregational churches in England and Wales with the Presbyterian Church of England in 1972.

Congregationalism dates from the mid 16th century. It is Calvinistic in doctrine, and its followers form independent self-governing congregations bound under God by covenant, a principle laid down in the writings of Robert Browne (1550–1633). From the late 16th century the movement was driven underground by persecution, but the cause was defended at the Westminster Assembly in 1643 and the Savoy Declaration of 1658 laid down its principles. Congregational churches formed county associations for mutual support and in 1832 these associations merged to form the Congregational Union of England and Wales.

The Presbyterian Church in England also dates from the mid 16th century, and was Calvinistic and evangelical in its doctrine. It was governed by a hierarchy of courts.

In the 1960s there was close co-operation locally and nationally between Congregational and Presbyterian Churches. This led to union negotiations and a Scheme of Union, supported by Act of Parliament in 1972. In 1981 a further unification took place, with the Reformed Association of Churches of Christ becoming part of the URC. In its basis the United Reformed Church reflects local church initiative and responsibility with a conciliar pattern of oversight. The General Assembly is the central body, and is made up of equal numbers of ministers and lay members.

The United Reformed Church is divided into 12 Provinces, each with a Provincial Moderator who chairs the Synod, and 75 Districts. There are 102,582 members, 774 full-time stipendiary ministers, 219 non-stipendiary ministers and 1,768 local churches.

General Secretary, Revd A. G. Burnham, 86 Tavistock Place, London WC1H 9RT. Tel: 0171-916 2020

THE WESLEYAN REFORM UNION

The Wesleyan Reform Union was founded by Methodists who left or were expelled from Wesleyan Methodism in 1849 following a period of internal conflict. Its doctrine is conservative evangelical and its organization is congregational, each church having complete independence in the government and administration of its affairs. The main concentration of churches is in Yorkshire.

The Union has 2,516 members, 20 ministers, 143 lay preachers and 122 churches.

President (1996–7), S. Bown
General Secretary, Revd E. W. Downing, Wesleyan Reform Church House, 123 Queen Street, Sheffield S1 2DU. Tel: 0114-272 1938

Non-Christian Faiths

BUDDHISM

Buddhism originated in northern India, in the teachings of Siddharta Gautama, who was born near Kapilavastu about 560 BC. After a long spiritual quest he experienced enlightenment beneath a tree at the place now known as Bodhgaya, and began missionary work.

Fundamental to Buddhism is the concept that there is no such thing as a permanent soul or self; when someone dies, consciousness is the only one of the elements of which they were composed which is lost. All the other elements regroup in a new body and carry with them the consequences of the conduct of the earlier life (known as the law of *karma*). This cycle of death and rebirth is broken only when the state of *nirvana* has been reached. Buddhism steers a middle path between belief in personal immortality and belief in death as the final end.

The Four Noble Truths of Buddhism (*dukkha*, suffering; *tanha*, a thirst or desire for continued existence which causes dukkha; *nirvana*, the final liberation from desire and ignorance; and *ariya*, the path to nirvana) are all held to be universal and to sum up the *dhamma* or true nature of life. Necessary qualities to promote spiritual development are *sila* (morality), *samadhi* (meditation) and *panna* (wisdom).

There are two main schools of Buddhism: *Theravada* Buddhism, the earliest extant school, which is more traditional, and *Mahayana* Buddhism, which began to develop about 100 years after the Buddha's death and is more liberal; it teaches that all people may attain Buddahood. Important schools which have developed within Mahayana Buddhism are *Zen* Buddhism, *Nichiren* Buddhism and Pure Land Buddhism or *Amidism*. There are also distinctive Tibetan forms of Buddhism. Buddhism began to establish itself in the West at the beginning of the 20th century.

The scripture of Theravada Buddhism is the *Pali Canon*, which dates from the first century BC. Mahayana Buddhism uses a Sanskrit version of the Pali Canon but also has many other works of scripture.

There is no set time for Buddhist worship, which may take place in a temple or in the home. Worship centres around *paritta* (chanting), acts of devotion centring on the image of the Buddha, and, where possible, offerings to a relic of the Buddha. Buddhist festivals vary according to local traditions and within Theravada and Mahayana Buddhism. For religious purposes Buddhists use solar and lunar calendars, the New Year being celebrated in April. Other festivals mark events in the life of the Buddha.

There is no supreme governing authority in Buddhism. In the United Kingdom communities representing all schools of Buddhism have developed and operate independently. The Buddhist Society was established in 1924; it runs courses and lectures, and publishes books about Buddhism. It represents no one school of Buddhism.

There are estimated to be at least 300 million Buddhists world-wide, and about 275 organizations and groups, an estimated 25,000 adherents and 15 temples or monasteries in the United Kingdom.

THE BUDDHIST SOCIETY, 58 Eccleston Square, London SWIV IPH. Tel: 0171-834 5858. *General Secretary*, R. C. Maddox

HINDUISM

Hinduism has no historical founder but is known to have been highly developed in India by about 1200 BC. Its adherents originally called themselves Aryans; Muslim invaders first called the Aryans 'Hindus' (derived from the word 'Sindhu', the name of the river Indus) in the eighth century.

Hinduism's evolution has been complex and it embraces many different religious beliefs, mythologies and practices. Most Hindus hold that *satya* (truthfulness), *ahimsa* (non-violence), honesty, physical labour and tolerance of other faiths are essential for good living. They believe in one supreme spirit (*Brahman*), and in the transmigration of *atman* (the soul). Most Hindus accept the doctrine of *karma* (consequences of actions), the concept of *samsara* (successive lives) and the possibility of all atmans achieving *moksha* (liberation from samsara) through *jnana* (knowledge), *yoga* (meditation), *karma* (work or action) and *bhakti* (devotion).

Most Hindus offer worship to *murtis* (images or statues) representing different aspects of Brahman, and follow their *dharma* (religious and social duty) according to the traditions of their *varna* (social class), *ashrama* (stage in life), *jati* (caste) and *kula* (family).

Hinduism's sacred texts are divided into *shruti* ('heard' or divinely inspired), including the *Vedas*, or *smriti* ('remembered' tradition), including the *Ramayana*, the *Mahabharata*, the *Puranas* (ancient myths), and the sacred law books. Most Hindus recognize the authority of the *Vedas*, the oldest holy books, and accept the philosophical teachings of the *Upanishads*, the *Vedanta Sutras* and the *Bhagavad-Gita*.

Brahman is formless, limitless and all-pervading, and is represented in worship by murtis which may be male or female and in the form of a human, animal or bird. Brahma, Vishnu and Shiva are the most important gods worshipped by Hindus; their respective consorts are Saraswati, Lakshmi and Durga or Parvati, also known as Shakti. There are held to have been ten *avatars* (incarnations) of Vishnu, of whom the most important are Rama and Krishna. Other popular gods are Ganesha, Hanuman and Subrahmanyam. All gods are seen as aspects of the supreme God, not as competing deities.

Orthodox Hindus revere all gods and goddesses equally, but there are many sects, including the Hare-Krishna movement (ISKCon), the Arya Samaj, the Swami Narayan Hindu mission and the Satya Sai-Baba movement. Worship in the sects is concentrated on one deity to the exclusion of others. In some sects a human *guru* (spiritual teacher), usually the head of the organization, is revered more than the deity, while in other sects the guru is seen as the source of spiritual guidance.

Hinduism does not have a centrally-trained and ordained priesthood. The pronouncements of the *shankaracharyas* (heads of monasteries) of Shringeri, Puri, Dwarka and Badrinath are heeded by the orthodox but may be ignored by the various sects.

The commonest form of worship is a *puja*, in which offerings of red and yellow powders, rice grains, water, flowers, food, fruit, incense and light are made to the image of a deity. Puja may be done either in a home shrine or a *mandir* (temple). Many British Hindus celebrate life-cycle rituals with Sanskrit mantras for naming a baby, the sacred thread (an initiation ceremony), marriage and cremation. For details of the Hindu calendar, main festivals etc, see pages 84–5.

The largest communities of Hindus in Britain are in Leicester, London, Birmingham and Bradford, and developed as a result of immigration from India, east Africa and Sri Lanka. Many Hindus now are British by birth, with English as their first language; the main ethnic languages are Gujarati, Hindi, Punjabi, Tamil, Bengali and Marathi.

There are an estimated 800 million Hindus world-wide; there are about 360,000 adherents and over 150 temples in the UK.

ARYA PRATINIDHI SABHA (UK) AND ARYA SAMAJ
LONDON, 69A Argyle Road, London W13 0LY. Tel: 0181-991 1732. *Director*, Prof. S. N. Bharadwaj
BHARATIYA VIDYA BHAVAN, Old Church Building, 4A Castletown Road, London W14 9HQ. Tel: 0171-381 3086. *Executive Director*, Dr M. Nandakumara
INTERNATIONAL SOCIETY FOR KRISHNA CONSCIOUSNESS (ISKCon), Bhaktivedanta Manor, Letchmore Heath, nr Watford, Herts WD2 8EP. Tel: 01923-857244. *Governing Body Commissioner*, H. H. Sivarama Swami
NATIONAL COUNCIL OF HINDU TEMPLES (UK), c/o Shree Sanatan Mandir, Weymouth Street, off Catherine Street, Leicester LE4 6FP. Tel: 0116-266 1402. *Secretary*, V. Aery
SWAMINARAYAN HINDU MISSION, 105-119 Brentfield Road, London NW10 8JB. Tel: 0181-965 2651. *Head of Mission*, Admaswarup Swami
VISHWA HINDU PARISHAD (UK), 48 Wharfedale Gardens, Thornton Heath, Surrey CR7 6LB. Tel: 0181-684 9716. *General Secretary*, K. Ruparelia

ISLAM

Islam (which means 'peace arising from submission to the will of Allah' in Arabic) is a monotheistic religion which originated in Arabia through the Prophet Muhammad, who was born in Mecca (Makkah) in AD 570. Islam spread to Egypt, North Africa, Spain and the borders of China in the century following the prophet's death, and is now the predominant religion in Indonesia, the Near and Middle East, North and parts of West Africa, Pakistan, Bangladesh, Malaysia and some of the republics of the former Soviet Union. There are also large Muslim communities in many other countries.

For Muslims (adherents of Islam), God (*Allah*) is one and holds absolute power. His commands were revealed to mankind through the prophets, who include Abraham, Moses and Jesus, but his message was gradually corrupted until revealed finally and in perfect form to Muhammad through the angel *Jibril* (Gabriel) over a period of 23 years. This last, incorruptible message has been recorded in the *Qur'an* (Koran), which contains 114 divisions called *surahs*, each made up of *ayahs*, and is held to be the essence of all previous scriptures. The *Ahadith* are the records of the Prophet Muhammad's deeds and sayings (the *Sunnah*) as recounted by his immediate followers. A culture and a system of law and theology gradually developed to form a distinctive Islamic civilization. Islam makes no distinction between sacred and worldly affairs and provides rules for every aspect of human life. The *Shari'ah* is the sacred law of Islam based upon prescriptions derived from the Qur'an and the Sunnah of the Prophet.

The 'five pillars of Islam' are *shahadah* (a declaration of faith in the oneness and supremacy of Allah and the messengership of Muhammad); *salat* (formal prayer, to be

performed five times a day facing the *Ka'bah* (sacred house) in the holy city of Mecca); *zakat* (welfare due); *saum* (fasting during the month of Ramadan); and *hajj* (pilgrimage to Mecca); some Muslims would add *jihad* (striving for the cause of good and resistance to evil).

Two main groups developed among Muslims. *Sunni* Muslims accept the legitimacy of Muhammad's first four *caliphs* (successors as head of the Muslim community) and of the authority of the Muslim community as a whole. About 90 per cent of Muslims are *Sunni* Muslims. *Shi'ites* recognize only Muhammad's son-in-law Ali as his rightful successor and the *Imams* (descendants of Ali, not to be confused with *imams* (prayer leaders or religious teachers)) as the principal legitimate religious authority. The largest group within *Shi'ism* is *Twelver Shi'ism*, which has been the official school of law and theology in Iran since the 16th century; other subsects include the *Ismailis* and the *Druze*, the latter being an offshoot of the Ismailis and differing considerably from the main body of Muslims.

There is no organized priesthood, but learned men such as *ulama*, *imams* and *ayatollahs* are accorded great respect. The *Sufis* are the mystics of Islam. Mosques are centres for worship and teaching and also for social and welfare activities. For details of the Muslim calendar and festivals, *see* page 86.

Islam was first known in western Europe in the eighth century AD when 800 years of Muslim rule began in Spain. Later, Islam spread to eastern Europe. More recently, Muslims came to Europe from Africa, the Middle East and Asia in the late 19th century. Both the Sunni and Shi'ah traditions are represented in Britain, but the majority of Muslims in Britain adhere to Sunni Islam.

The largest communities are in London, Liverpool, Manchester, Birmingham, Bradford, Cardiff, Edinburgh and Glasgow. There is no central organization, but the Islamic Cultural Centre, which is the London Central Mosque, and the Imams and Mosques Council are influential bodies; there are many other Muslim organizations in Britain.

There are about 1,000 million Muslims world-wide, with more than one million adherents and about 900 mosques in Britain.

IMAMS AND MOSQUES COUNCIL, 20–22 Creffield Road, London W5 3RP. Tel: 0181-992 6636. *Director of the Council and Principal of the Muslim College*, Dr M. A. Z. Badawi
ISLAMIC CULTURAL CENTRE, 146 Park Road, London NW8 7RG. Tel: 0171-724 3363. *Director (acting)*, H. Al-Majed
MUSLIM WORLD LEAGUE, 46 Goodge Street, London W1P 1FJ. Tel: 0171-636 7568. *Director*, B. A. Alim
UNION OF MUSLIM ORGANIZATIONS OF THE UK AND EIRE, 109 Campden Hill Road, London W8 7TL. Tel: 0171-229 0538. *Geneal Secretary*, Dr S. A. Pasha

JUDAISM

Judaism is the oldest monotheistic faith. The primary authority of Judaism is the Hebrew Bible or *Tanakh*, which records how the descendants of Abraham were led by Moses out of their slavery in Egypt to Mount Sinai where God's law (*Torah*) was revealed to them as the chosen people. The *Talmud*, which consists of commentaries on the *Mishnah* (the first text of rabbinical Judaism), is also held to be authoritative, and may be divided into two main categories: the *halakah* (dealing with legal and ritual matters) and the *Aggadah* (dealing with theological and ethical matters not directly concerned with the regulation of conduct). The *Midrash* comprises rabbinic writings containing biblical interpretations in the spirit of the *Aggadah*. The *halakah* has become a source of division; Orthodox Jews regard Jewish law as derived from God and therefore unalterable; Reform and Liberal Jews seek to interpret it in the light of contemporary considerations; and Conservative Jews aim to maintain most of the traditional rituals but to allow changes in accordance with that tradition. Reconstructionist Judaism, a 20th-century movement, regards Judaism as a culture rather than a theological system and therefore accepts all forms of Jewish practice.

The family is the basic unit of Jewish ritual, with the synagogue playing an important role as the centre for public worship and religious study. A synagogue is led by a group of laymen who are elected to office. The Rabbi is primarily a teacher and spiritual guide. The Sabbath is the central religious observance. For details of the Jewish calendar, fasts and festivals, *see* page 85. Most British Jews are descendants of either the *Ashkenazim* of central and eastern Europe or the *Sephardim* of Spain and Portugal.

The Chief Rabbi of the United Hebrew Congregations of the Commonwealth is appointed by a Chief Rabbinate Conference, and is the rabbinical authority of the Orthodox sector of the Ashkenazi Jewish community. His authority is not recognized by the Reform Synagogues of Great Britain (the largest progressive group), the Union of Liberal and Progressive Synagogues, the Union of Orthodox Hebrew Congregations, the Federation of Synagogues, the Sephardi community, or the Assembly of Masorti Synagogues. He is, however, generally recognized both outside the Jewish community and within it as the public religious representative of the totality of British Jewry.

The *Beth Din* (Court of Judgment) is the rabbinic court. The *Dayanim* (Assessors) adjudicate in disputes or on matters of Jewish law and tradition; they also oversee dietary law administration. The Chief Rabbi is President of the *Beth Din* of the United Synagogue.

The Board of Deputies of British Jews was established in 1760 and is the representative body of British Jewry. The basis of representation is mainly synagogal, but communal organizations are also represented. It watches over the interests of British Jewry and seeks to counter anti-Jewish discrimination.

There are over 12.5 million Jews world-wide; in Great Britain and Ireland there are an estimated 300,000 adherents and about 350 synagogues. Of these, 185 congregations and about 150 rabbis and ministers are under the jurisdiction of the Chief Rabbi; 99 orthodox congregations have a more independent status; and 72 congregations do not recognize the authority of the Chief Rabbi.

CHIEF RABBINATE, 735 High Road, London N12 0US. Tel: 0181-343 6301. *Chief Rabbi*, Dr Jonathan Sacks; *Executive Director*, J. Kestenbaum

BETH DIN (COURT OF THE CHIEF RABBI), 735 High Road, London N12 0US. Tel: 0181-343 6280. *Registrar*, J. Phillips; *Dayanim*, Rabbi C. Ehrentreu; Rabbi I. Binstock; Rabbi C. D. Kaplin; Rabbi M. Gelley

BOARD OF DEPUTIES OF BRITISH JEWS, Commonwealth House, 1–19 New Oxford Street, London WC1A 1NF. Tel: 0171-543 5400. *President*, E. Tabachnik, QC; *Chief Executive*, N. A. Nagler

ASSEMBLY OF MASORTI SYNAGOGUES, 766 Finchley Road, London NW11 7TH. Tel: 0181-201 8772. *Development Director*, H. Freedman

FEDERATION OF SYNAGOGUES, 65 Watford Way, London NW4 3AQ. Tel: 0181-202 2263. *Administrator*, G. Kushner

REFORM SYNAGOGUES OF GREAT BRITAIN, The Sternberg Centre for Judaism, Manor House, 80 East

End Road, London N3 2SY. Tel: 0181-349 4731. *Chief Executive*, Rabbi T. Bayfield

SPANISH AND PORTUGUESE JEWS' CONGREGATION, 2 Ashworth Road, London W9 1JY. Tel: 0171-289 2573. *Chief Executive*, Mrs J. Velleman

UNION OF LIBERAL AND PROGRESSIVE SYNAGOGUES, The Montagu Centre, 21 Maple Street, London W1P 6DS. Tel: 0171-580 1663. *Director*, Mrs R. Rosenberg

UNION OF ORTHODOX HEBREW CONGREGATIONS, 140 Stamford Hill, London N16 6QT. Tel: 0181-802 6226. *Executive Director*, Rabbi A. Klein

UNITED SYNAGOGUE HEAD OFFICE, 735 High Road, London N12 0US. Tel: 0181-343 8989. *Chief Executive*, J. M. Lew

---

SIKHISM

The Sikh religion dates from the birth of Guru Nanak in the Punjab in 1469. 'Guru' means teacher but in Sikh tradition has come to represent the divine presence of God giving inner spiritual guidance. Nanak's role as the human vessel of the divine guru was passed on to nine successors, the last of whom (Guru Gobind Singh) died in 1708. The immortal guru is now held to reside in the sacred scripture, *Guru Granth Sahib*, and so to be present in all Sikh gatherings.

Guru Nanak taught that there is one God and that different religions are like different roads leading to the same destination. He condemned religious conflict, ritualism and caste prejudices. The fifth Guru, Guru Arjan largely compiled the Sikh Holy Book, a collection of hymns (*gurbani*) known as the *Adi Granth*. It includes the writings of the first five Gurus and the ninth Guru, and selected writings of Hindu and Muslim saints whose views are in accord with the Gurus' teachings. Guru Arjan also built the Golden Temple at Amritsar, the centre of Sikhism. The tenth Guru, Guru Gobind Singh, passed on the guruship to the sacred scripture, Guru Granth Sahib. He also founded the *Khalsa*, an order intended to fight against tyranny and injustice. Male initiates to the order added 'Singh' to their given names and women added 'Kaur'. Guru Gobind Singh also made five symbols obligatory: *kaccha* (a special undergarment), *kara* (a steel bangle), *kirpan* (a small sword), *kesh* (long unshorn hair, and consequently the wearing of a turban), and *kangha* (a comb). These practices are still compulsory for those Sikhs who are initiated into the *Khalsa* (the *Amritdharis*). Those who do not seek initiation are known as *Sahajdharis*.

There are no professional priests in Sikhism; anyone with a reasonable proficiency in the Punjabi language can conduct a service. Worship can be offered individually or communally, and in a private house or a *gurdwara* (temple). Sikhs are forbidden to eat meat prepared by ritual slaughter; they are also asked to abstain from smoking, alcohol and other intoxicants. For details of the Sikh calendar and main celebrations, *see* page 86.

There are about 20 million Sikhs world-wide and about 400,000 adherents and more than 250 gurdwaras in Great Britain. The largest communities are in London, Bradford, Leeds, Huddersfield, Birmingham, Nottingham, Coventry and Wolverhampton. Every gurdwara manages its own affairs and there is no central body in the UK. The Sikh Missionary Society provides an information service.

SIKH CULTURAL SOCIETY OF GREAT BRITAIN, 88 Mollison Way, Edgware, Middx HA8 5QW. Tel: 0181-952 1215. *General Secretary*, A. S. Chhatwal

SIKH MISSIONARY SOCIETY UK, 10 Featherstone Road, Southall, Middx UB2 5AA. Tel: 0181-574 1902. *Hon. Secretary*, T. S. Manget

Education

For addresses of national education departments, *see* Government Departments and Public Offices. For other addresses, *see* Education Directory

Responsibility for education in the United Kingdom is largely decentralized. Overall responsibility for all aspects of education in England lies with the Secretary of State for Education and Employment; in Wales with the Secretary of State for Wales; in Scotland with the Secretary of State for Scotland acting through the Scottish Office Education and Industry Department; and in Northern Ireland with the Secretary of State for Northern Ireland.

The main concerns of the education departments (the Department for Education and Employment (DFEE), the Welsh Office, the Scottish Office Education and Industry Department (SOEID), and the Department of Education for Northern Ireland (DENI)) are the formulation of national policies for education and the maintenance of consistency in educational standards. They are responsible for the broad allocation of resources for education, for the rate and distribution of educational building and for the supply, training and superannuation of teachers.

EXPENDITURE

In the UK in 1993–4, provisional expenditure on education was (£ million):

Schools	19,676.2
Further and higher education	8,965.3
Other education and related expenditure	3,336.5

Most of this expenditure is incurred by local authorities, which make their own expenditure decisions according to their local situations and needs. Expenditure on education by central government departments, in real terms, was (£ million):

	1995–6 estimated outturn	1996–7 planned
DFEE	10,753	10,766
Welsh Office	520.6	529.4
SOEID	1,281	1,326
DENI	1,323	1,370

The bulk of direct expenditure by the DFEE, the Welsh Office and SOEID is directed towards supporting higher education in universities and colleges through the Higher Education Funding Councils (HEFCs) and further education and sixth form colleges through the Further Education Funding Councils (FEFCs) in England and Wales and directly from central government in Scotland. In addition, the DFEE funds grant-maintained schools (through the Funding Agency for Schools), the City Technology Colleges (CTCs) and the City College for the Technology of the Arts, and pays grants to Technology Colleges.

The Welsh Office also funds grants for higher and further education, grant-maintained schools, educational services and research, and supports bilingual education and the Welsh language.

In Scotland the main elements of central government expenditure, in addition to those outlined above, are grant-aided special schools, self-governing schools, student awards and bursaries, curriculum development, special educational needs and community education.

The Department of Education for Northern Ireland directly funds higher education, teacher education, teacher salaries and superannuation, student awards, further education, grant-maintained integrated schools, and voluntary grammar schools.

Current net expenditure on education by local education authorities in England, Wales, and Scotland, and education and library boards in Northern Ireland is (£ million):

	1995–6 estimated outturn	1996–7 planned
England	19,990	18,000
Wales	1,235.5	1,241.5
Scotland	2,515.5	2,503.1
Northern Ireland	953	936

LOCAL EDUCATION ADMINISTRATION

The education service at present is a national service in which the provision of most school education is locally administered; its administration is still largely decentralized.

In England and Wales the education service is administered by local education authorities (LEAs), which carry the day-to-day responsibility for providing most state primary and secondary education in their areas, although the planning and supply of school places is to be shared with the Funding Agency for Schools as the number of grant-maintained schools grows. They also share with the FEFCs the duty to provide adult education to meet the needs of their areas.

The LEAs own and maintain schools and colleges, build new ones and provide equipment. Most of the public money spent on education is disbursed by the local authorities. LEAs are financed largely from the council tax and aggregate external finance (AEF) from the Department of the Environment in England and the Welsh Office in Wales.

The powers of local education authorities as regards the control of schools have been modified in recent years and schools can choose to opt out of local authority control. These grant-maintained (GM) schools are funded by the Funding Agency for Schools in England. Those in Wales are funded by the Welsh Office at present but the Schools Funding Council for Wales will take over when the number of grant-maintained schools is sufficient to warrant the change. Primary schools can apply for grant-maintained status as a group as well as individually. An Education Association can be set up to take over the management of failing schools where both the LEA and the governing body have not brought about improvements identified as necessary by inspection.

The duty of providing education locally in Scotland rests with the education authorities. They are responsible for the construction of buildings, the employment of teachers and other staff, and the provision of equipment and materials. Devolved School Management (DSM) was introduced for all primary and secondary schools by April 1996, although the deadline has been extended to April 1998 in primary schools with headteachers who teach full-time and to April 1997 in all special schools.

The powers of local authorities over educational institutions under their control have been reduced also in Scotland. Education authorities are required to establish school boards consisting of parents and teachers as well as co-opted members, responsible among other things for the appointment of staff. Schools can choose to withdraw from local authority control and become self-governing; the institution of Technology Academies directly funded by central government has been provided for; at least half the members of further education college councils must be drawn from employers, and substantial functions have been delegated to these new councils.

Education is administered locally in Northern Ireland by five education and library boards, whose costs are met in full by DENI. A review of educational administration has taken place and as a result the boards are to be reduced in number from five to three. All grant-aided schools include elected parents and teachers on their boards of governors. Provision has been made for schools wishing to provide integrated education to have grant-maintained integrated status from the outset. All schools and colleges of further education have full responsibility for their own budgets, including staffing costs. The Council for Catholic Maintained Schools forms an upper tier of management for Catholic schools and provides advice on matters relating to management and administration.

THE INSPECTORATE

The Office for Standards in Education (OFSTED) is a non-ministerial government department in England headed by HM Chief Inspector of Schools (HMCI). OFSTED's remit is regularly to inspect all maintained schools and report on and thereby improve standards of achievement. All state schools are inspected by teams of independent inspectors on contract to OFSTED, including educationalists and lay people and headed by registered inspectors. There are also additional inspectors (AIs), who are mostly headteachers and deputy heads on secondment to OFSTED for the inspection of primary schools. HM Inspectors (HMI) within OFSTED report on good practice in schools and other educational issues based on inspection evidence. From 1997 for secondary and from 1998 for primary, schools will be inspected once every six years or more frequently if there is cause. A summary of the inspection report must be sent to parents of each pupil by the school, followed by a copy of the governors' action plan thereon. OFSTED's counterpart in Wales is the Office of HM Chief Inspector of Schools in Wales (OHMCI Wales), where inspection of maintained schools is carried out on a five-year cycle. The inspection of further and higher education in England and Wales is the responsibility of inspectors appointed to the respective funding councils.

HM Inspectorate in Scotland carries out the inspection of schools and further education institutions in Scotland, using teams which include lay people, and in addition requires schools to produce a document setting out their educational targets for two years ahead and a report on progress over the previous two years. The inspection of higher education is the responsibility of inspectors appointed to the Higher Education Funding Council for Scotland.

Inspection is carried out in Northern Ireland by the Department of Education's Education and Training Inspectorate, using teams which include lay people. The Inspectorate also performs an advisory function to the Secretary of State for Northern Ireland. From September 1992 a five-year cycle of inspection was introduced.

There were, in 1996–7, 200 HMIs who act as special advisers to OFSTED, 1,500 registered inspectors, 6,400 team inspectors in England, 40 HMIs and about 888 registered inspectors and team members in Wales, 93 HMIs in Scotland and 60 members of the Inspectorate in Northern Ireland.

SCHOOLS AND PUPILS

Schooling is compulsory in Great Britain for all children between five and 16 years and between four and 16 years in Northern Ireland. Some provision is made for children under five and many pupils remain at school after the minimum leaving age. No fees are charged in any publicly maintained school in England, Wales and Scotland. In Northern Ireland, fees are paid by pupils in preparatory departments of grammar schools, but pupils admitted to the secondary departments of grammar schools do not pay fees.

In the UK, parents have a right to express a preference for a particular school and have a right to appeal if dissatisfied. The policy, known as more open enrolment, requires schools to admit children up to the limit of their capacity if there is a demand for places, and to publish their criteria for selection if they are over-subscribed, in which case parents have a right of appeal.

The 'Parents' Charter', available free from education departments, is a booklet which tells parents about the education system. Schools are now required to make available information about themselves, their public examination results, truancy rates, and destination of leavers. Corporal punishment is no longer legal in publicly maintained schools in the UK.

FALL AND RISE IN NUMBERS

In primary education, and increasingly in secondary education, pupil numbers in the UK declined through the 1980s. In nursery and primary schools pupil numbers reached their lowest figure of 4.6 million in 1986. They stood at 5.1 million in 1995 and are expected to increase gradually year by year until by 2000 they reach about 5.6 million. In secondary schools pupil numbers peaked at 4.6 million in 1981. They stood at 3.65 million in 1995 and are projected to rise to about 4.1 million in 2005.

ENGLAND AND WALES

There are two main categories of school in England and Wales: publicly maintained schools, which charge no fees; and independent schools, which charge fees (see pages 435–6). Publicly maintained schools are maintained by local education authorities except for grant-maintained schools and City Technology Colleges.

The number of schools by category in 1995 was:

Maintained schools	24,116
County	15,876
Voluntary	7,175
controlled	2,991
aided	4,134
special agreement*	50
Grant-maintained	1,032
Wales	17
CTCs and CCTAs	16
Independent schools	2,325
TOTAL	26,441

* There are no special agreement schools in Wales

County schools are owned by LEAs and wholly funded by them. They are non-denominational and provide primary and secondary education. Voluntary schools also provide primary and secondary education. Although the buildings are in many cases provided by the voluntary bodies (mainly religious denominations), they are financially maintained by an LEA. In controlled schools the LEA bears all costs. In aided schools the building is usually provided by the voluntary body. The managers or governors are responsible for repairs to the school building and for improvements and alterations to it, though the DFEE may reimburse part of approved capital expenditure, while the LEA pays for internal maintenance and other running costs. Special agreement schools are those where the LEA may, by special agreement, pay between one-half and three-quarters of the cost of building a new, or extending an existing, voluntary school, almost always a secondary school

Under the Local Management of Schools (LMS) initiative, LEAs are required to delegate at least 85 per cent of school budgets, including staffing costs, directly to schools. LEAs continue to retain responsibility for various services, including transport and school meals.

Governing bodies – All publicly maintained schools have a governing body, usually made up of a number of parent representatives, governors appointed by the LEA if the school is LEA maintained, the headteacher (unless he or she chooses otherwise), and serving teachers. Schools can appoint up to four sponsor governors from business who will be expected to provide financial and managerial assistance. Governors are responsible for the overall policies of schools and their academic aims and objectives; they also control matters of school discipline and the appointment and dismissal of staff. Governing bodies select inspectors for their schools, are responsible for action as a result of inspection reports and are required to make those reports and their action plans thereon available to parents.

Technology Colleges and Language Colleges – The Specialist Schools programme is open to all state secondary schools wishing to specialize in the teaching of technology, mathematics and science (Technology Colleges) and modern foreign languages (Language Colleges). In addition to the normal funding arrangements, the colleges receive business sponsorship (up to four sponsor governors may sit on governing bodies) and complementary capital grants up to £100,000 from central government, together with extra annual funding of £100 a pupil to assist the delivery of an enhanced curriculum. By September 1996, there were 151 technology colleges and 30 language colleges. In Wales the Technology Schools Initiative provides grants to enhance technology teaching to those schools successful in attracting funding through open competition.

Grant-maintained (GM) schools – All secondary and primary schools, whether maintained or independent, are eligible to apply for grant-maintained status, subject to a ballot of parents. GM schools are maintained directly by the Secretary of State and the Welsh Office, not the LEA, and are wholly run by their own governing body. They also have the freedom to borrow commercially to fund capital projects. The Funding Agency for Schools pays grants to GM schools in England. The Schools Funding Council for Wales will be instituted when the number of GM schools justifies the change in funding arrangements. As of September 1996 about 60 per cent of grant-maintained schools were secondary schools.

City Technology Colleges (CTCs) and *City Colleges for the Technology of the Arts (CCTAs)* are state-aided but independent of LEAs. Their aim is to widen the choice of secondary education in disadvantaged urban areas and to teach a broad curriculum with an emphasis on science, technology, business understanding and arts technologies. Capital costs are shared by government and sponsors from industry and commerce, and running costs are covered by a per capita grant from the DFEE in line with comparable costs in an LEA maintained school. The first city technology college opened in 1988 in Solihull. The first CCTA, known as Britschool, opened in Croydon in 1991.

SCOTLAND

The number of schools by category in 1995 was:

Publicly maintained schools:
Education authority	3,843
Grant-aided	10
Self-governing	3
Independent schools	116
TOTAL	3,972

Education authority schools (known as public schools) are financed jointly by the authorities and central government. Grant-aided schools are conducted by voluntary managers who receive grants direct from the SOEID. Independent schools receive no direct grant and charge fees, but are subject to inspection and registration. An additional category is that of self-governing schools opting to be managed entirely by a board of management consisting of the headteacher, parent and staff representatives and co-opted members. The change of status requires a ballot of parents and the publication of proposals by the board, and the achievement of self-government is subject to a final decision by the Secretary of State. These schools remain in the public sector and are funded by direct government grant set to match the resources the school would have received under education authority management. Three have so far been established.

Education authorities are required to establish school boards to participate in the administration and management of schools. These boards consist of elected parents and staff members as well as co-opted members.

Technology Academies (TAs) – The Self-Governing Schools etc. (Scotland) Act 1989 provides for setting up technology academies in areas of urban deprivation. These secondary schools are intended to be so placed as to draw on a wide catchment, and to offer a broad curriculum with an emphasis on science and technology. They are to be founded and managed in partnership with industrial sponsors, with central government meeting the running costs by grant-aid thereafter. None has yet been set up.

NORTHERN IRELAND

The number of schools by category in 1995 was:

Grant-aided schools:
Controlled	683
Voluntary maintained	555
Voluntary grammar	53
Integrated schools	32
Independent schools	20
TOTAL	1,343

Controlled schools are controlled by the education and library boards with all costs paid from public funds. Voluntary maintained schools, mainly under Roman Catholic management, receive grants towards capital costs and running costs in whole or in part. Voluntary grammar schools may be under Roman Catholic or non-denominational management and receive grants from the DENI. All grant-aided schools include elected parents and teachers on their boards of governors, whose responsibilities also include financial management under the Local Management of Schools (LMS) initiative. About 85 per cent of the potential funds available to schools are now delegated to them. Voluntary maintained and voluntary grammar schools can apply for designation as a new category of voluntary school, which is eligible for a 100 per cent as opposed to 85 per cent grant. Such schools are managed by a board of governors on which no single interest group has a majority of nominees.

The majority of children in Northern Ireland are educated in schools which in practice are segregated on religious lines. Integrated schools exist to educate Protestant and Roman Catholic children together. There are two types: grant-maintained integrated schools which are funded by DENI; and controlled integrated schools funded by the education and library boards. Procedures are in place for balloting parents in existing segregated schools to determine whether they want instead to have integrated schools. By September 1996, 32 integrated schools had been established, 11 of them secondary.

THE STATE SYSTEM

NURSERY EDUCATION – Nursery education is for children from two to five years and is not compulsory. It takes place in nursery schools or nursery classes in primary schools. The number of children receiving nursery education in the UK in 1994-5 was:

In maintained nursery schools	85,100
In primary schools	976,100
In non-maintained nursery schools	63,900
TOTAL	1,125,100
% of total three- and four-year-old population	57%

Many children also attend pre-school playgroups organized by parents and voluntary bodies such as the Pre-School Learning Alliance. In order to increase participation in nursery education, every parent of a four-year-old is to be given a voucher worth £1,100 exchangeable for up to three terms of pre-school education. The scheme was piloted in 1996 and will be fully operational in England and Wales by April 1997 and in Northern Ireland by September 1997. In Scotland the pilot began in August 1996, prior to the introduction of the scheme in August 1997.

PRIMARY EDUCATION – Primary education begins at five years in Great Britain and four years in Northern Ireland, and is almost always co-educational. In England, Wales and Northern Ireland the transfer to secondary school is generally made at 11 years. In Scotland, the primary school course lasts for seven years and pupils transfer to secondary courses at about the age of 12.

Primary schools consist mainly of infants' schools for children aged five to seven, junior schools for those aged seven to 11, and combined junior and infant schools for both age groups. First schools in some parts of England cater for ages five to ten as the first stage of a three-tier system: first, middle and secondary. Many primary schools provide nursery classes for children under five (*see* above).

Primary schools (UK) 1994-5

No. of primary schools	23,938
No. of pupils	5,250,600
Pupils under five years	976,100

Pupil-teacher ratios in maintained primary schools were:

	1992–3	1993–4
England	22.2	22.5
Wales	22.1	22.3
Scotland	19.3	19.5
Northern Ireland	22.3	21.7
UK	21.9	21.5

The average size of classes 'as taught' was 25.8 in 1994 but fell to 25.5 in 1995.

MIDDLE SCHOOLS – Middle schools (which take children from first schools), mostly in England, cover varying age ranges between eight and 14 and usually lead on to comprehensive upper schools.

SECONDARY EDUCATION – Secondary schools are for children aged 11 to 16 and for those who choose to stay on to 18. At 16, many students prefer to move on to tertiary or sixth form colleges (*see* page 439). Most secondary schools in England, Wales and Scotland are co-educational. The largest secondary schools have over 1,500 pupils but only 27 per cent of the schools take over 1,000 pupils.

Secondary schools 1995

	England and Wales	Scotland	N. Ireland
No. of pupils	3,128,401	314,904	150,036
% over 16 years	9.9%	11.3%	13.6%
Average class size	21	19.4	n/
Pupil-teacher ratio	16.1	12.9	15.

In England and Wales the main types of secondary schools are: comprehensive schools (86.2 per cent of pupils in England, 100 in Wales), whose admission arrangements are without reference to ability or aptitude; middle deemed secondary schools for children aged variously between eight and 14 years who then move on to senior comprehensive schools at 12, 13 or 14 (5.5 per cent of pupils in England); secondary modern schools (3.1 per cent of pupils in England) providing a general education with a practical bias; secondary grammar schools (4.0 per cent of pupils in England) with selective intake providing an academic course from 11 to 16–18 years; and technical schools (0.1 per cent in England), providing an integrated academic and technical education.

In Scotland all pupils in education authority secondary schools attend schools with a comprehensive intake. Most of these schools provide a full range of courses appropriate to all levels of ability from first to sixth year.

In most areas of Northern Ireland there is a selective system of secondary education with pupils transferring either to grammar schools (40 per cent of pupils in 1995) or secondary schools (59.7 per cent of pupils in 1995) at 11–1. years of age. Parents can choose the school they would like their children to attend and all those who apply must be admitted if they meet the criteria. If a school is oversubscribed beyond its statutory admissions number, selection is on the basis of published criteria, which, for most grammar schools, place emphasis on performance in the transfer procedure tests which are set and administered by the Northern Ireland Council for the Curriculum, Examinations and Assessment. When parents consider that a school has not applied its criteria fairly they have access to independent appeals tribunals. Grammar schools provide an academic type of secondary education with A-levels at the end of the seventh year, while secondary non-grammar schools follow a curriculum suited to a wider range of aptitudes and abilities.

SPECIAL EDUCATION – Special education is provided for children with special educational needs, usually because they have a disability which either prevents or hinders them from making use of educational facilities of a kind generally provided for children of their age in schools within the area of the local authority concerned. Wherever possible, such children are educated in ordinary schools, taking the parents' wishes into account, and schools are required to publish their policy for pupils with special educational needs. LEAs in England and Wales are required to identify and secure provision for the needs of children with learning difficulties, to involve the parents in any decision and draw up a formal statement of the child's special educational needs and how they intend to meet them, all within statutory time limits. Parents have a right to appeal to a Special Educational Needs (SEN) Tribunal if they disagree with the statement. A code of practice similar to that in England and Wales is to be introduced in

Northern Ireland. A SEN Tribunal will operate there from September 1997.

Maintained special schools are run by education authorities which pay all the costs of maintenance, but under the terms of Local Management of Schools (LMS), those able and wishing to manage their own budgets may choose to do so. These schools are also able to apply to become grant-maintained. Non-maintained special schools are run by voluntary bodies; they may receive some grant from central government for capital expenditure and for equipment but their current expenditure is met primarily from the fees charged to education authorities for pupils placed in the schools. Some independent schools provide education wholly or mainly for children with special educational needs and are required to meet similar standards to those for maintained and non-maintained special schools. It is intended that pupils with special education needs should have access to as much of the national curriculum as possible, but there is provision for them to be exempt from it or for it to be modified to suit their capabilities. The number of full-time pupils with special needs in January 1995 was:

Special schools: total	112,300
England	95,300
Wales	3,300
Scotland	9,100
N. Ireland	4,600
Hospital schools: total	200
Public sector primary and secondary	
schools: total	134,300
England	112,800
Wales	10,900
Scotland	5,700
N. Ireland	3,200

In Scotland, school placing is a matter of agreement between education authorities and parents. Parents have the right to say which school they want their child to attend, and a right of appeal where their wishes are not being met. Whenever possible, children with special needs are integrated into ordinary schools. However, for those who require a different environment or specialized facilities, there are special schools, both grant-aided by central government and independent, and special classes within ordinary schools. Education authorities are required to respond to reasonable requests for independent special schools and to send children with special needs to schools outside Scotland if appropriate provision is not available within the country.

ALTERNATIVE PROVISION

There is no legal obligation on parents in the UK to educate their children at school provided that the local education authority is satisfied that the child is receiving full-time education suited to its age, abilities and aptitudes. The education authority need not be informed that a child is being educated at home unless the child is already registered at a state school. In this case the parents must arrange for the child's name to be removed from the school's register (by writing to the headteacher) before education at home can begin. Failure to do so leaves the parents liable to prosecution for condoning non-attendance.

In most cases an initial visit is made by an education adviser or education welfare officer, and sometimes subsequent inspections are made, but practice varies according to the individual education authority. There is no requirement for parents educating their children at home to be in possession of a teaching qualification.

Information and support on all aspects of home education can be obtained from Education Otherwise (see page 449).

INDEPENDENT SCHOOLS

Independent schools receive no grants from public funds, but they can apply to the Secretaries of State for grant-maintained status within the public sector. They charge fees, and are owned and managed under special trusts, with profits being used for the benefit of the schools concerned. There is a wide variety of provision, from kindergartens to large day and boarding schools, and from experimental schools to traditional institutions. A number of independent schools have been instituted by religious and ethnic minorities.

All independent schools in the UK are open to inspection by approved inspectors (see page 432) and must register with the appropriate government education department. The education departments lay down certain minimum standards and can make schools remedy any unacceptable features of their building or instruction and exclude any unsuitable teacher or proprietor. Most independent schools offer a similar range of courses to state schools and enter pupils for the same public examinations. Introduction of the national curriculum and the associated education targets and assessment procedures is not obligatory in the independent sector.

The term public schools is often applied to those independent schools in membership of the Headmasters' and Headmistresses' Conference, the Governing Bodies Association or the Governing Bodies of Girls' Schools Association. Most public schools are single-sex but there are some mixed schools and an increasing number of schools have mixed sixth forms.

Preparatory schools are so-called because they prepare pupils for the common entrance examination to senior independent schools. Most cater for pupils from about seven to 13 years. The common entrance examination is set by the Common Entrance Examination Board, but marked by the independent school to which the pupil intends to go. It is taken at 13 by boys, and from 11 to 13 by girls. The number of schools and pupils in 1994–5 was:

	No. of schools	No. of pupils	Pupil-teacher ratio
England	2,259	556,572	10.3
Wales	62	10,297	10.1
Scotland	116	32,600	10.2
N. Ireland	21	941	10.8

Most independent schools in Scotland follow the English examination system, i.e. GCSE followed by A-levels, although some take the Scottish Education Certificate at Standard grade followed by Highers or Advanced Highers.

ASSISTED PLACES SCHEME

The Assisted Places Scheme enables children to attend independent secondary schools which their parents could not otherwise afford. The scheme provides help with tuition fees and other expenses, except boarding costs, on a sliding scale depending on the family's income. The proportion of pupils receiving full fee remission is about 46 per cent. In the 1996–7 academic year, 35,830 places were offered at the 372 participating schools in England and Wales. The 55 participating schools in Scotland admitted about 3,000 pupils on the scheme in 1995–6, which, unlike that in England and Wales, is cash-limited.

The proportion of pupils receiving full fee remission was about 47 per cent.

The scheme is administered and funded in England by the DFEE, in Wales by the Welsh Office, and in Scotland by the SOEID. The scheme does not operate in Northern Ireland as the independent sector admits non-fee-paying pupils. There is, however, a similar scheme known as the Talented Children's Scheme to help pupils gifted in music and dance.

Further information can be obtained from the Independent Schools Information Service (*see* page 449).

THE CURRICULUM

ENGLAND AND WALES

The national curriculum was introduced in primary and secondary schools between autumn 1989 and autumn 1996, for the period of compulsory schooling from five to 16. It is mandatory in all maintained schools. As originally proposed, it was widely criticized for being too prescriptive and time-consuming. Following revision in 1994 its requirements were substantially reduced; the revisions were implemented in August 1995 for key stages 1 to 3 and from August 1996 for key stage 4.

The statutory subjects at key stages 1 and 2 (5–11 year olds) are:

Core subjects	*Foundation subjects*
English	Design and technology
Welsh, for Welsh-speaking schools in Wales	Information technology
Mathematics	History
Science	Geography
	Welsh, in Wales
	Art
	Music
	PE

At key stage 3 (11- to 14-year olds) all pupils must study a modern foreign language. At key stage 4 (14- to 16-year olds) pupils are required to take GCSEs in the core subjects and at least a GCSE short course in a modern foreign language and design and technology (optional subjects in Wales); they must also continue to study, although they are not required to take examinations in, information technology and PE. Other foundation subjects are optional. Religious education must be taught across all key stages, following a locally agreed syllabus; parents have the right to remove their children if they wish.

National tests and tasks in English and mathematics at key stage 1, with the addition of science at key stages 2 and 3, are in place. Teachers make their own assessments of their pupils' progress to set alongside the test results. At key stage 4 the GCSE and vocational equivalents will be the main form of assessment.

For several years the DFEE and the Welsh Office have published tables showing pupils' performance in A-level, AS-level, GCSE and GNVQ examinations school by school. Similar tables showing the results of the 1996 tests and teacher assessments for 11-year-olds will be published for the first time in 1997. Approximately 700,000 pupils in each of the age groups take the tests each year in England and Wales.

In Wales in 1994–5 the Welsh language was in use as the main or secondary medium of instruction or taught as a second language in 98.4 per cent of primary schools. In secondary schools Welsh was taught as a first or second language in 96.6 per cent of schools. It constitutes a core subject of the national curriculum in schools in which Welsh is taught as a first language and a foundation subject in the others, although there is provision for exemptions to

be made; by September 1999 all pupils will be taught Welsh throughout the period of compulsory schooling. A two-year review of assessment arrangements for the national curriculum is taking place.

In England the School Curriculum and Assessment Authority (SCAA), an independent government agency funded by the DFEE, is responsible for advising the Secretary of State on the school curriculum and school tests and examinations. In Wales its functions are performed by the Curriculum and Assessment Authority for Wales (ACAC), funded by the Welsh Office.

SCOTLAND

The content and management of the curriculum in Scotland are not prescribed by statute but are the responsibility of education authorities and individual headteachers. Advice and guidance is provided by the SOEID and the Scottish Consultative Council on the Curriculum. SOEID has produced guidelines on the structure and balance of the curriculum for the 5–14 age group as well as for each of the curriculum areas. There are also guidelines on assessment across the whole curriculum, on reporting to parents, and on standardized national tests for English language and mathematics at five levels for this age group. A major programme to extend modern language teaching to primary schools is in progress. The curriculum for 14- to 16-year-olds includes study within each of eight modes: language and communication, mathematical studies, science, technology, social studies, creative activities, physical education, and religious and moral education. There is a recommended percentage of class time to be devoted to each area over the two years. Provision is made for teaching in Gaelic in Gaelic-speaking areas.

For 16- to 18-year-olds, there is available a modular system of vocational courses, certificated by the Scottish Vocational Education Council, in addition to academic courses and a new unified framework of courses and awards is to be introduced in 1998–9.

The Scottish Consultative Council on the Curriculum has responsibility for development and advisory work on the curriculum in Scottish schools.

NORTHERN IRELAND

A curriculum common to all grant-aided schools exists. Pupils are required to study religious education and, depending on which key stage they have reached, certain subjects from six broad areas of study: English, mathematics, science and technology; the environment and society; creative and expressive studies and, in key stages 3 and 4, language studies. The statutory curriculum requirements at key stages 1 to 3 have been revised and new programmes of study were introduced in September 1996. Six cross-curricular educational themes, which include information technology and education for mutual understanding, are woven through the main subjects of the curriculum. Irish is a foundation subject in schools that use it as a medium of instruction.

The assessment of pupils for all compulsory subjects, broadly in line with practice in England and Wales, will take place at the ages of eight, 11, 14 and 16. Statutory assessment will be introduced in 1996–7. The GCSE will be used to assess 16-year-olds.

The Northern Ireland Council for the Curriculum, Examinations and Assessment (NICCEA) monitors and advises the department and teachers on all matters relating to the curriculum, assessment arrangements and examinations in grant-aided schools in Northern Ireland. It conducts GCSE, A- and AS-level examinations, pupil assessment at key stages and administers the transfer procedure tests.

RECORDS OF ACHIEVEMENT

The National Record of Achievement (NRA) is being reviewed and will be relaunched in September 1997. It sets down the range of a school-leaver's achievements and activities both inside and outside the classroom, including those not tested by examination. It is issued to all those leaving school in England, Wales and Northern Ireland and its use is to be extended within further and higher education, training and employment. It is not compulsory in Scotland but is available to all education authorities for issue to school leavers. Parents in England and Wales must receive a written yearly progress report on all aspects of their child's achievements. There is a similar commitment for Northern Ireland. In Scotland the school report card gives parents information on their child's progress.

THE PUBLIC EXAMINATION SYSTEM

ENGLAND, WALES AND NORTHERN IRELAND

Until the end of 1987, secondary school pupils at the end of compulsory schooling around the age of 16, and others, took the General Certificate of Education (GCE) Ordinary-level or the Certificate of Secondary Education (CSE). From 1988 these were replaced by a single system of examinations, the General Certificate of Secondary Education (GCSE), which is usually taken after five years of secondary education. The GCSE is the main method of assessing the performance of pupils at age 16 in all national curriculum subjects required to be assessed at the end of compulsory schooling. The structure of the exam is being adapted in accordance with national curriculum requirements; new subject criteria were published in 1995 to govern GCSE syllabuses introduced in 1996 for first examination in 1998. From September 1996 GCSE short course qualifications in a wide range of subjects were introduced. As a rule the syllabus will take half the time of a GCSE course.

The GCSE differs from its predecessors in that there are syllabuses based on national criteria covering course objectives, content and assessment methods; differentiated assessment (i.e. different papers or questions for different ranges of ability); and grade-related criteria (i.e. grades awarded on absolute rather than relative performance). The GCSE certificates are awarded on a seven-point scale, A to G. From 1994 there has been an additional 'starred' A grade (A*), to recognize the achievement of the highest attainers at GCSE. Grades A to C are the equivalent of the corresponding O-level grades A to C or CSE grade 1. Grades D, E, F and G record achievement at least as high as that represented by CSE grades 2 to 5. All GCSE syllabuses, assessments and grading procedures are monitored by the School Curriculum and Assessment Authority (see page 436) to ensure that they conform to the national criteria

In the UK in 1993–4, 84 per cent of all 15-year-olds achieved one or more higher grade GCSE, SCE Standard grade, or equivalent results, 1.4 per cent fewer than in 1992-.

In Wales the Certificate of Education is intended for 16-year-olds for whom no suitable examination exists. In 1995, 7,107 candidates took the examination, of whom 92.8 per cent obtained pass or better.

From 1991, many maintained schools have offered BTEC Firsts (see page 439) and an increasing number offer BTEC Nationals. National Vocational Qualifications in the form of General NVQs have been available to students in schools from 1992 (see page 440). The Part 1 GNVQ has been piloted from 1995. It is a two-year course available at foundation and intermediate levels, broadly equivalent to two GCSEs.

The General Diploma was introduced in 1995 for 16- to 18-year-olds achieving GCSE at grades A* to C in English, mathematics and science, plus two other GCSEs at the same grades or their vocational equivalent.

Advanced (A-level) examinations are taken by those who choose to continue their education after GCSE. A-level courses last two years and have traditionally provided the foundation for entry to higher education. A-levels are marked on a seven-point scale, from A to E, N (narrow failure) and U (unclassified), which latter grade will not be certificated.

Advanced Supplementary level (AS-level) examinations were introduced in 1987 as an alternative to, and to complement, A-level examinations. AS-levels are for full-time A-level students but are also open to other students. An AS-level syllabus covers not less than half the amount of ground covered by the corresponding A-level syllabus and, where possible, is related to it. An AS-level course lasts two years and requires not less than half the teaching time of the corresponding A-level course, and two AS-levels are equivalent to one A-level. AS-level passes are graded A to E, with grade standards related to the A-level grades.

In the UK in 1993–4, 190,000 school pupils (47 per cent boys, 53 per cent girls) achieved one or more passes at A-level or SCE H-grade, an increase of 1.6 per cent on the previous year. Of those in Great Britain who entered for at least one A-level, or at least two SCE H-grades, 44 per cent studied sciences (58 per cent boys, 42 per cent girls) and 56 per cent studied arts/social studies (41 per cent of boys, 59 per cent of girls).

Most examining boards allow the option of an additional paper of greater difficulty to be taken by A-level candidates to obtain what is known as a Special-level or Scholarship-level qualification. S-level papers are available in most of the traditional academic subjects and are marked on a three-point scale.

The City & Guilds Foundation Programmes at pre-16 and Diploma of Vocational Education at post-16 replaced the Certificate of Pre-Vocational Education (CPVE) at post-16 in schools and colleges from 1992. It is intended for a wide ability range, including pupils who might not go on to A-levels but would like to continue their education on completion of compulsory secondary schooling.

The Diploma of Vocational Education provides recognition of achievement at two levels: foundation and intermediate; the latter broadly corresponding to the GNVQ (see page 440) at intermediate and advanced levels. The intermediate level is being phased out in favour of the corresponding GNVQs. Within guidelines schools and colleges design their own courses, which stress activity-based learning, core skills which include application of number, communication and information technology, and work experience. The Diploma of Vocational Education is mainly for those who want to find out what aptitudes they may have and to prepare themselves for work, but who are not yet committed to a particular occupation. According to level, it can be taken alongside other courses such as GCSEs, A- or AS-levels. At foundation level it can provide a context for the introduction of GNVQ units into the key stage 4 curriculum.

SCOTLAND

Scotland has its own system of public examinations. At the end of the fourth year of secondary education, at about the age of 16, pupils take the Standard grade (which has replaced the Ordinary grade) of the Scottish Certificate of Education. Standard grade courses and examinations have been designed to suit every level of ability, with assessment against nationally determined standards of performance.

For most courses there are three separate examination papers at the end of the two-year Standard grade course. They are set at Credit (leading to awards at grade 1 or 2), General (leading to awards at grade 3 or 4) and Foundation (leading to awards at grade 5 or 6) levels. Grade 7 is available to those who, although they have completed the course, have shown no significant level of attainment. Normally pupils will take examinations covering two pairs of grades, either grades 1–4 or grades 3–6. Most candidates take seven or eight Standard grade examinations.

The Higher grade of the Scottish Certificate of Education is normally taken one year after Standard grade, at the age of 17 or thereabouts. It is common for pupils to be presented for four or more Higher grades at a single diet of the examination.

The Certificate of Sixth Year Studies (CSYS) is designed to give direction and purpose to sixth-year work by encouraging pupils who have completed their main subjects at Higher grade to study a maximum of three of these subjects in depth. Pupils may also use the sixth year to gain improved or additional Higher grades or Standard grades. A major programme of reform, 'Higher Still', is afoot which will draw all upper secondary qualifications into a single framework by 1998–9. There will be five levels of attainment, the first three corresponding to Standard grade levels, plus Higher and Advanced Higher (which will replace CSYS). Students will study individual units (of 40 or 80 hours) which will be internally assessed, and may combine these into courses (with external assessment) or group awards.

The examining body for the Scottish Certificate of Education and the Certificate of Sixth Year Studies is the Scottish Examination Board (SEB).

National Certificates provide an alternative to, and complement Highers and CSYS. They are awarded to pupils normally over the age of 16 who have successfully completed a programme of vocational courses based on modular study units, and the assessment system is based on national criteria. National Certificates are awarded by the Scottish Vocational Education Council (SCOTVEC) (*see also* page 440).

The Scottish Qualifications Authority (SQA) will take over the existing functions of SEB and SCOTVEC and will administer the new 'Higher Still' qualifications from April 1997.

THE INTERNATIONAL BACCALAUREATE

The International Baccalaureate is an internationally recognized two-year pre-university course and examination designed to facilitate the mobility of students and to promote international understanding. Candidates must offer one subject from each of six subject groups, at least three at higher level and the remainder at subsidiary level. Single subjects can be offered, for which a certificate is received. There are 34 schools and colleges in the UK which offer the International Baccalaureate diploma.

TEACHERS

ENGLAND AND WALES

Teachers are appointed by local education authorities, school governing bodies, or school managers. Those in publicly maintained schools must be approved as qualified by the Secretary of State. To become a qualified teacher it is necessary to have successfully completed a course of initial teacher training, usually either a Bachelor of Education (B.Ed.) degree or the Postgraduate Certificate of Education (PGCE) at an accredited institution, but a one-year course is being considered which will qualify certain non-graduates to teach at nursery and infant level.

With certain exceptions the profession at present has an all graduate entry. Teachers in further education are not required to have qualified teacher status, though roughly half have a teaching qualification and most have industrial, commercial or professional experience. The new National Qualification for Headship (NQH) is to be piloted until July 1997 and will be introduced in September of that year.

Teacher training was formerly largely integrated with the rest of higher education, with training places concentrated in universities and institutes or colleges of education, but it has now become largely school-based, with student teachers on secondary PGCE courses spending two-thirds of their training in the classroom. Changes have also been made to primary phase teacher training to make it more school-based and to give schools a role in course design and delivery. Individual schools or consortia of schools and CTCs can bid for funds from the DFEE to carry out their own teacher training, including recruitment of students, subject to approval of their proposed training programme by the Teacher Training Agency (TTA) and monitoring and evaluation by the Office for Standards in Education (OFSTED). Funds are given to schools to meet the costs of designing and delivering the courses, and students receive flat-rate bursaries.

The Teacher Training Agency began operations in September 1994. The TTA accredits institutions in England providing initial teacher training for school teachers which meet both criteria published by the Secretary of State and appropriate quality standards. The TTA funds all types of teacher training in England whether run by universities, colleges or schools, and some educational research. It has responsibility for the Licensed Teacher Scheme, which is designed to attract into the teaching profession entrants over 24 years of age without formal teaching qualifications but with relevant training and experience; licensees undertake a two-year training programme devised by the school which appoints them.

The Higher Funding Council for Wales exercises similar functions in respect of Wales. The TTA also acts as a central source of information and advice for both England and Wales about entry to teaching, and has responsibilities relating to the continuing professional development of teachers.

The Specialist Teacher Assistant (STA) scheme was introduced in September 1994 to provide trained support to qualified teachers in the teaching of reading, writing and arithmetic to young pupils.

SCOTLAND

All teachers in maintained schools must be registered with the General Teaching Council for Scotland. They are registered provisionally for a two-year probationary period which can be extended if necessary. Only graduates are accepted as entrants to the profession; primary school teachers undertake either a four-year vocational degree course or a one-year postgraduate course, while teachers of academic subjects in secondary school undertake the latter. As a result of a review of initial teacher training instituted in 1992 a greater proportion of training is now classroom based. The colleges of education provide both in-service and pre-service training for teachers and are funded by the Scottish Higher Education Funding Council.

NORTHERN IRELAND

Teacher training in Northern Ireland is provided by the two universities and two colleges of education. The colleges are concerned with teacher education mainly for the primary school sector. They also provide B.Ed. courses for intending secondary school teachers of religious education, commercial studies, and craft, design and

:chnology. With these exceptions, the training of teachers
▸r secondary schools is provided in the education depart-
▴ents of the universities. A professional qualification is not
▴andatory to teach in secondary schools. A review of
▸imary and secondary teacher training has taken place as a
:sult of which from 1996−7 all student teachers will spend
▴ore time in the classroom. The current probationary year
to be replaced by a two-year induction period by 1996−7.

CCREDITATION OF TRAINING INSTITUTIONS

dvice to central government on the accreditation, content
▴d quality of initial teacher training courses is given in
ngland by the TTA, in Wales by the HEFCW and in
▾orthern Ireland by validating bodies. These bodies
so monitor and disseminate good practice, assisted in
▾orthern Ireland by the Teacher Education Committee.
   In Scotland all training courses in colleges of education
▴ust be approved by the SOEID and a validating body.

▾EWLY-TRAINED TEACHERS

▴f teachers who in 1994 had successfully completed initial
aining courses in the UK, 17,400 had completed a
ostgraduate course and 10,000 a course for non-graduates.
   Because of a shortage of teachers in certain secondary
▴bjects, from 1996-7 providers of initial teacher training
▴ll be able to apply for funds from the TTA to provide
nhanced courses, and scholarships and bursaries to attract
ainee teachers onto one- or two-year full-time courses in
▾iority subjects. The subjects are: science; mathematics;
▴odern languages (including Welsh in Wales); design and
▸chnology; information technology, and religious edu-
▴tion.

▸RVING TEACHERS 1993-4 *(full-time and full-time equiva-
▴nt)*

▴ublic sector schools	452,000
Primary	212,000
Secondary	223,000
Special	17,000
▸E and HE establishments	145,380
▾niversities	32,000
▸OTAL	629,380

▴LARIES

▴ualified teachers in England, Wales and Northern
▸eland, other than heads and deputy heads, are paid on an
▸-point scale. Entry points and placement depend on
▴alifications, experience, responsibilities, excellence, and
▸cruitment and retention factors as calculated by the
▸levant body, i.e. the governing body or the LEA. There is
statutory superannuation scheme in maintained schools.
   Teachers in Scotland are paid on a ten-point scale. The
▴try point depends on type of qualification, and additional
▴lowances are payable under certain circumstances.

▴laries from 1 April 1996

	England, Wales and N. Ireland	Scotland
▴ead	£25,371–£55,566	£26,376–£48,858
▸eputy head	£24,564–£40,407	£26,376–£36,558
▸eacher	£12,462–£33,375	£12,510–£20,796

URTHER EDUCATION

"he Education Reform Act 1988 defines further education
▸ all provision outside schools to people aged over 16 of
▴ucation up to and including A-level and its equivalent.
"he Further Education Funding Councils for England and

Wales, the Scottish Office Education and Industry Department and the Education and Library Boards in Northern
Ireland have a duty to secure provision of adequate
facilities for further education in their areas.

ENGLAND AND WALES

Further education and sixth form colleges are funded
directly by central government through the Further
Education Funding Council for England (FEFCE) and
the Further Education Funding Council for Wales
(FEFCW). These councils are also responsible for the
assessment of quality, in which the Councils' inspectorates
play a key role. The colleges are controlled by autonomous
further education corporations, which include substantial
representation from industry and commerce, and which
own their own assets and employ their own staff. Their
funding is determined in part by the number of students
enrolled.
   In England and Wales further education courses are
taught at a variety of institutions. These include universities which were formerly polytechnics, colleges of higher
education, colleges of further education (some of which
also offer higher education courses), and tertiary colleges
and sixth form colleges, which concentrate on the provision of normal sixth form school courses as well as a range
of vocational courses. A number of institutions specific to a
particular form of training, e.g. the Royal College of Music,
are also involved.
   Teaching staff in further education establishments are
not necessarily required to have teaching qualifications
although many do so, but they are subject to regular
appraisal of teaching performance.
   Further education tends to be broadly vocational in
purpose and employers are often involved in designing
courses. It ranges from lower-level technical and commercial courses through courses for those aiming at higher-
level posts in industry, commerce and administration, to
professional courses. Facilities for GCSE courses, the
Diploma of Vocational Education, AS-levels and A-level
courses are also provided (*see* pages 437–8). These courses
can form the foundation for progress to higher education
qualifications.
   The main courses and examinations in the vocational
field, all of which link in with the National Vocational
Qualification (NVQ) framework (*see* below), are offered by
the following bodies, but there are also many others:
   The Business and Technology Education Council
(BTEC) and London Examinations have merged to form
the Edexcel Foundation. Edexcel courses and qualifications will continue to be known by their original names.
They provide programmes of study across a wide range of
subject areas. The main qualifications are the BTEC First
Certificate and the BTEC First Diploma; the BTEC
National Certificate and the BTEC National Diploma;
the BTEC Higher National Diploma; BTEC NVQs; and
BTEC foundation, intermediate and advanced GNVQs in
some vocational areas. BTEC First and National diplomas
will be phased out gradually as GNVQs are introduced.
   City & Guilds specializes in developing qualifications
and assessments for work-related, general education and
leisure qualifications. It awards nationally recognized
certificates in over 500 subjects, many of which are NVQs,
SVQs and GNVQs. Its progressive structure of awards
spans seven levels, from foundation to the highest level of
professional competence.
   RSA Examinations Board schemes cover a wide range of
vocational qualifications, including accounting, business
administration, customer service, management, language
schemes, information technology and teaching qualifications. A wide range of NVQs and GNVQs are offered

and a policy operates of credit accumulation, so that candidates can take a single unit or complete qualifications.

There are 589 further education establishments and sixth form colleges in England and Wales and 4,390 adult education centres. In 1994–5 there were 702,200 full-time and sandwich-course students and 1,369,384 part-time students on further education courses.

SCOTLAND

Further education comprises non-advanced courses up to SCE Highers grade, GCE A-level and SCOTVEC vocational courses. Further education colleges are currently funded by central government but a further education funding council is proposed at a later stage. Courses are taught mainly at colleges of further education, including technical colleges, and in some schools.

Further education colleges are incorporated bodies, with boards of management which run them and employ staff. The boards include the principal and staff and student representatives among their ten to 16 members, and at least half the members must have experience of commerce, industry or the practice of a profession.

The Scottish Vocational Education Council (SCOTVEC) awards qualifications for most occupations. It awards at non-advanced level the National Certificate which is available in over 3,000 individual modules and covers the whole range of non-advanced further education provision in Scotland. Students may study for the National Certificate on a full-time, part-time, open learning or work-based learning basis. National Certificate modules can be taken in further education colleges, secondary schools and other centres, normally from the age of 16 onwards. SCOTVEC also offers modular advanced-level HNC/HND qualifications and a few post-graduate or post-experience qualifications which are available in further education colleges and higher education institutions. SCOTVEC accredits and awards Scottish Vocational Qualifications (SVQs) which are analogous with the system of NVQs which operates in the rest of the UK. SVQs are essentially work-based but are also available in further education colleges and other centres.

The Record of Education and Training (RET) has been introduced to provide a single certificate recording SCOTVEC achievements; an updated version is provided as and when necessary. SCOTVEC also administers the National Record of Achievement in Scotland on behalf of the Scottish Office.

In 1993–4 there were 40,654 full-time and sandwich-course students and 80,051 part-time students on non-advanced vocational courses of further education in the 43 further education colleges and five colleges of education.

NORTHERN IRELAND

The Education and Library Boards currently plan the further education provision to be made by colleges under their management subject to approval by the Department of Education for Northern Ireland. From August 1997 all colleges will become free-standing corporate bodies and the planning will transfer to DENI, which will also fund the colleges directly.

Financial powers and responsibilities are delegated to the boards of governors of the colleges. The boards must include at least 50 per cent membership from the professions, local business or industry, or other fields of employment relevant to the activities of the college.

On reaching school-leaving age, pupils may attend colleges of further education to pursue the same type of vocational courses as are provided in colleges in England and Wales, administered by the same examining bodies.

In 1995–6 Northern Ireland had 17 institutions of further education, and there were 21,096 full-time students and 51,885 part-time students on non-advanced vocational courses of further education.

COURSE INFORMATION

Applications for further education courses are generally made directly to the colleges concerned. Information on further education courses in the UK and addresses of colleges can be found in the *Directory of Further Education* published annually by the Careers Research and Advisory Centre.

NATIONAL VOCATIONAL QUALIFICATIONS

The National Council for Vocational Qualifications (NCVQ) was set up by the Government in 1986 to achieve a coherent national framework for vocational qualifications in England, Wales and Northern Ireland. The Council does not award qualifications but accredits National Vocational Qualifications (NVQs), General National Vocational Qualifications (GNVQs) and core skills. Candidates are assessed through awarding bodies who bestow the qualifications where candidates reach the required standards. SCOTVEC (*see* above) performs similar functions in Scotland, but its role includes the awarding of qualifications.

From September 1992 General National Vocational Qualifications (GNVQs) were introduced into colleges and schools as a vocational alternative to academic qualifications. They cover broad categories in the NVQ framework and are aimed at those wishing to familiarize themselves with a range of opportunities. Advanced GNVQ or the vocational A-level is designed to be equivalent to two A-levels; intermediate is equivalent to four or five good GCSEs. Foundation GNVQs became available in September 1994.

HIGHER EDUCATION

The term higher education is used to describe education above A-level, Advanced Higher grade and their equivalent, which is provided in universities and colleges of higher education and in some further education colleges.

The Further and Higher Education Act 1992 and parallel legislation in Scotland removed the distinction between higher education provided by the universities which were funded by the Universities Funding Council (UFC), and that provided in England and Wales by the former polytechnics and colleges of higher education funded by the Polytechnics and Colleges Funding Council (PCFC), and in Scotland by the former central institutions and other institutions funded by central government. All are now funded by the Higher Education Funding Councils for England, Wales and Scotland. Other provisions brought the non-university sector in line with the universities, allowing all polytechnics, and other higher education institutions which satisfy the necessary criteria to award their own taught course and research degrees and to adopt the title of university. All the polytechnics and all colleges have since adopted the title of university. The change of name does not affect the legal constitution of the institutions.

The number of students in higher eduction in the UK in 1994-5 was:

	Universities	Other	Total
Full-time, sandwich	814,000	206,000	1,420,000
% female	48%	51%	
Part-time	525,000	162,000	687,000
% female	24%	49%	
Overseas	114,400	9,700	124,100
TOTAL	1,453,400	377,700	1,831,100

The proportion of 16- to 20-year-olds entering full-time higher education in Great Britain rose from 12.2 per cent in 1985–6 to 25.6 per cent in 1994–5. The number of mature entrants (those aged 21 and over when starting an undergraduate course and 25 and over when starting a postgraduate course) to higher education in Great Britain in 1995 (excluding those at the Open University) was 459,000. The number of full-time and part-time students on science courses in 1994–5 was 365,600, of whom 21.5 per cent were female.

UNIVERSITIES AND COLLEGES

The universities are self-governing institutions established by royal charter or Act of Parliament. They have academic freedom and are responsible for their own academic appointments, curricula and student admissions and award their own degrees.

Responsibility for universities in England rests with the Secretary of State for Education and Employment, and in their territories with the Secretaries of State for Scotland, Wales and Northern Ireland. Advice to the Government on matters relating to the universities is provided by the Higher Education Funding Councils for England, Wales and Scotland, and by the Northern Ireland Higher Education Council. The HEFCs receive a block grant from central government which they allocate to the universities and colleges. The grant is allocated directly by central government in Northern Ireland.

There are now 88 universities in the UK, where only 47 existed prior to the Further and Higher Education Acts 1992. Of the 88, 71 are in England (including one federal university), two (one a federal institution) in Wales, 13 in Scotland and two in Northern Ireland.

The pre-1992 universities each have their own system of internal government but broad similarities exist. Most are run by two main bodies: the senate, which deals primarily with academic issues and consists of members elected from within the university; and the council, which is the supreme body and is responsible for all appointments and promotions, and bidding for and allocation of financial resources. At least half the members of the council are drawn from outside the university. Joint committees of senate and council are becoming increasingly common.

Those universities which were formerly polytechnics (38) or other higher education institutions (3) and the colleges of higher education (47) are run by higher education corporations (HECs), which are controlled by boards of governors whose members were initially appointed by the Secretaries of State but which will subsequently make their own appointments. At least half the members of each board must be drawn from industry, business, commerce and the professions.

In 1994-5 full-time student enrolments in England and Wales were:

	Universities	Other
England		
Undergraduates	660,200	146,800
% overseas	10%	4%
Postgraduates	95,800	9,600
% overseas	34%	14.5%
Wales		
Undergraduates	39,500	16,600
% overseas	11.4%	6%
Postgraduates	5,900	700
% overseas	30.5%	0%

Higher education courses funded by the respective HEFCs are also taught in some further education colleges in England and Wales. In England in 1994-5 there were over 36,000 students (8 per cent of total higher education student numbers) on such courses and 564 (0.72 per cent of higher education student numbers) in Wales.

The non-residential Open University provides courses nationally leading to degrees. Teaching is through a combination of television and radio programmes, correspondence, tutorials, short residential courses and local audio-visual centres. No qualifications are needed for entry. The Open University offers a modular programme of undergraduate courses by credit accumulation and post-experience and postgraduate courses, including a programme of higher degrees which comprises B.Phil., M.Phil. and Ph.D. through research, and MA, MBA and M.Sc. through taught courses. The Open University throughout the UK is funded by the Higher Education Funding Council for England. Its recurrent grant for 1994-5 was £110.8 million. In 1996, about 97,000 undergraduates were registered at the Open University, of whom about 50 per cent were women. Estimated cost (1996) of a six-credit degree was around £3,200 including course fees of £1,800.

The independent University of Buckingham provides a two-year course leading to a bachelor's degree and its tuition fees were £9,460 for 1996. It receives no capital or recurrent income from the Government but its students are eligible for mandatory awards from local education authorities. Its academic year consists of four terms of ten weeks each.

ACADEMIC STAFF

Each university and college appoints its own academic staff on its own conditions. However, there is a common salary structure and, except for Oxford and Cambridge, a common career structure in those universities formerly funded by the UFC and a common salary structure for the former PCFC sector. The Universities and Colleges Employers Association (UCEA) acts as a pay agency for universities and colleges.

Teaching staff in higher education require no formal teaching qualification, but teacher trainers are required to spend a certain amount of time in schools to ensure that they have sufficient recent practical experience.

In 1994–5, there were 70,439 full-time and part-time teaching and research staff in institutions of higher education in the UK.

Salary scales for staff in the former UFC sector differ from those in the former polytechnics and colleges; it is hoped eventually to amalgamate them. The 1995–6 salary scales for non-clinical academic staff in universities formerly funded by the UFC are:

Professor from	£31,999
Senior lecturer	£27,747–£31,357
Lecturer grade B	£20,677–£26,430
Lecturer grade A	£15,154–£19,848

The salaries of clinical academic staff are kept broadly comparable to those of doctors and dentists in the National Health Service.

Salary scales for lecturers in the former polytechnics, now universities, and colleges of higher education in England, Wales and Northern Ireland are (September 1995):

Head of Department	from £26,304
Principal lecturer	£25,474–£32,030
Senior lecturer	£20,381–£26,931
Lecturer	£13,100–£21,838

The salary scales for staff in Scotland are (April 1995):

Head of department/professor	from £32,058
Senior lecturer	£24,044–£31,081
Lecturer	£14,607–£26,216

FINANCE

Although universities and colleges are expected to look to a wider range of funding sources than before, and to generate additional revenue in collaboration with industry, they are still largely financed, directly or indirectly, from government resources.

In 1994–5 the total income of institutions of higher education in the UK was £10 million (£9.4 million in 1993–4). Grants from the funding councils amounted to £4.4 million (£3.5 million in 1993–4), forming 43.6 per cent of total income (37 per cent in 1993-4). Income from research grants and contracts was £1.4 million, an increase of 0.1 per cent on the previous year.

In the academic year 1994–5 the HEFCs' recurrent grant to institutions outside their sector and to LEAs for the provision of higher education courses was £79.4 million.

COURSES

In the UK all universities, including the Open University, and some colleges award their own degrees and other qualifications and can act as awarding and validating bodies for neighbouring colleges which are not yet accredited. The Higher Education Quality Council (HEQC), funded by institutional contributions, advises the Secretaries of State on applications for degree-awarding powers.

Higher education courses last full-time for at least four weeks or, if part-time, involve more than 60 hours of instruction. Facilities exist for full-time and part-time study, day release, sandwich or block release. Credit accumulation and transfer (CATS) is a system of study which is becoming widely available. It allows a student to achieve a final qualification by accumulating credits for courses of study successfully achieved, or even professional experience, over a period. Credit transfer information and values are carried on an electronic database called ECCTIS 2000, which is available in most careers offices and many schools and colleges.

Higher education courses include: first degree and postgraduate (including research); Diploma in Higher Education (Dip.HE); Higher National Diploma (HND) and Higher National Certificate (HNC); and preparation for professional examinations. The in-service training of teachers is also included, but from September 1994 has been funded in England by the TTA (see page 438), not the HEFC.

The Diploma of Higher Education (Dip.HE) is a two-year diploma usually intended to serve as a stepping-stone to a degree course or other further study. The Dip.HE is awarded by the institution itself if it is accredited; by an accredited institution of its choice if not. The BTEC Higher National Certificate (HNC) is awarded after two years part-time study. The BTEC Higher National Diploma (HND) is awarded after two years full-time, or three years sandwich-course or part-time study.

With the exception of certain Scottish universities where master is sometimes used for a first degree in arts subjects, undergraduate courses lead to the title of Bachelor, Bachelor of Arts (BA) and Bachelor of Science (B.Sc.) being the most common. For a higher degree the titles are: Master of Arts (MA), Master of Science (M.Sc.) (usually taught courses) and the research degrees of Master of Philosophy (M.Phil.) and Doctor of Philosophy (Ph.D. or, at a few universities, D.Phil.).

Most undergraduate courses at British universities and colleges of higher education run for three years, except in Scotland and at the University of Keele where they may take four years. Professional courses in subjects such as medicine, dentistry and veterinary science take longer. Details of courses on offer and of predicted entry requirements for the following year's intake are provided in *University and College Entrance: Official Guide*, published annually by the Universities and Colleges Admissions Service (UCAS), which includes degree, Dip.HE and HND courses at all universities (excluding the Open University) and most colleges of HE (for address, see page 451).

Postgraduate studies vary in length. Taught courses which lead to certificates, diplomas or master's degrees usually take one year full-time or two years part-time. Research degrees take from two to three years full-time and much longer if completed on a part-time basis. Details of taught courses and research degree opportunities can be found in *Graduate Studies*, published annually for the Careers Research and Advisory Centre (CRAC) by Hobsons Publishing plc (for address, see page 451).

Post-experience short courses are forming an increasing part of higher education provision, reflecting the need to update professional and technical training. Most of these courses fund themselves.

ADMISSIONS

The target number of students entering higher education has been set at 30 per cent of the 18- to 19-year-old age group. Apart from quotas for medical, dental and veterinary students, there are no limits set for other subjects and the individual university or college decides which students to accept. The formal entry requirements to most degree courses are two A-levels at grade E or above (or equivalent), and to HND courses one A-level (or equivalent). In practice, most offers of places require qualifications in excess of this, higher requirements usually reflecting the popularity of a course. These requirements do not, however, exclude applications from students with a variety of non-GCSE qualifications or unquantified experience and skills.

For admission to a degree, Dip.HE or HND, potential students apply through a central clearing house. All universities and most colleges providing higher education courses in the UK are members of the Universities and Colleges Admission Service (UCAS). Applicants are supplied with an application form and a *UCAS Handbook*, available from schools, colleges and careers offices or direct from UCAS, and may apply to a maximum of eight institutions/courses on the UCAS form. The only exception among universities is the Open University, which conducts its own admissions.

Applications for undergraduate teacher training courses are made through UCAS. Details of initial teacher training courses in Scotland can be obtained from colleges of education and those universities offering such courses, and from the Committee of Scottish Higher Education Principals (COSHEP).

For admission as a postgraduate student, universities and colleges normally require a good first degree in a subject related to the proposed course of study or research, but other experience and qualifications will be considered on merit. Most applications are made to individual institutions but there are two clearing houses of relevance. Postgraduate teacher training courses in England and Wales utilize the Graduate Teacher Training Registry (*see* page 451). Applications to postgraduate teacher training courses in Scotland are made through the Teacher Education Admissions Clearing House (TEACH) (*see* page 451). Applications for PGCE courses at institutions in Northern Ireland are made to the Department of Education for Northern Ireland. For social work the Social Work Admissions System operates (*see* page 451).

SCOTLAND

The Scottish Higher Education Funding Council (SHEFC) funds 21 institutions of higher education, including 13 universities. The universities are broadly managed as described above and each institution of higher education is managed by an independent governing body which includes representatives of industrial, commercial, professional and educational interests. Most of the courses outside the universities have a vocational orientation and a substantial number are sandwich courses.

Full-time higher education student enrolments in 1994–5 were:

	Universities	Other
Undergraduates	91,100	36,200
% overseas	8.2%	2.2%
Postgraduates	12,300	1,900
% overseas	48.2%	10.5%

There were 29,098 students on higher education courses in further education colleges, 21 per cent of total higher education students.

NORTHERN IRELAND

In Northern Ireland advanced courses are provided by 17 institutions of further education and by the two universities. As well as offering first and postgraduate degrees, the University of Ulster offers courses leading to the BTEC Higher National Diploma and professional qualifications. Applications to undertake courses of higher education other than degree courses are made to the institutions direct. Full-time higher education student enrolments in 1994–5 were:

	Universities	Other
Undergraduates	21,000	3,600
% overseas	16.6%	9%
Postgraduates	2,700	600
% overseas	7.4%	0%

There were 6,832 students enrolled on advanced courses of higher education in the institutions of further education, 25 per cent of higher education student numbers.

FEES

The tuition fees for students with mandatory awards (*see* below) are paid by the grant-awarding body. Students from member states of the European Union pay fees at home student rates. Since 1980–1 students from outside the EU have paid fees that are meant to cover the cost of their education, but financial help is available under a number of schemes. Information about these schemes is available from British Council offices world-wide.

Universities and colleges are free to set their own charges for students from non-EU countries. Undergraduate fees for the academic year 1996–7 for home and EU students are £750 for arts courses (band 1), £1,600 for laboratory or workshop based courses, mainly science (band 2), and £2,800 for clinical courses (band 3).

For postgraduate students, the maximum tuition fee that will be reimbursed through the awards system is £2,490 in 1996–7.

GRANTS FOR STUDENTS

Students in the UK who plan to take a full-time or sandwich course of further study after leaving school may be eligible for a grant. A parental contribution is deductible on a sliding scale dependent on income. For married students this may be deducted from their spouse's income instead. However, parental contribution is not deducted from the grant to students over 25 years of age who have been self-supporting for at least three years. The main rates of mandatory grant have been frozen since 1991–2 as it is envisaged that students will increasingly support themselves by loans. Tuition fees are paid in full for all students in receipt of a grant, regardless of parental income, and they are usually paid direct to the university or college by the education authority.

Grants are paid by local education authorities in England, Wales and Northern Ireland, of which 100 per cent of the cost is reimbursed by central government, and by the SOEID in Scotland through the Students Award Agency. Applications are made to the authority in the area in which the student normally lives. Applications should not, however, be made earlier than the January preceding the start of the course.

TYPES OF GRANT

Grants are of two kinds: mandatory and discretionary. Mandatory grants are those which awarding authorities must pay to students who are attending designated courses and who can satisfy certain other conditions. Such a grant is awarded normally to enable the student to attend only one designated course and there is no general entitlement to an award for any particular number of years. Discretionary grants are those for which each awarding authority has discretion to decide its own policy.

Designated courses are those full-time or sandwich courses leading to: a degree; the Diploma of Higher Education; the BTEC Higher National Diploma; initial teacher-training courses, including those for the postgraduate certificate of education and the art teachers' certificate or diploma; a university certificate or diploma course lasting at least three years; other qualifications which are specifically designated as being comparable to first degree courses; and the SCOTVEC Higher National Diploma. The local education authority should be consulted for advice about eligibility for a grant.

A means-tested maintenance grant, usually paid once a term, covers periods of attendance during term as well as the Christmas and Easter vacations, but not the summer vacation. The basic grant rates for 1996–7 are:

Living in	Grant	Grant to Scottish students
College/lodgings in London area	2,105	2,035
College/lodgings outside London area	1,710	1,645
Parental home	1,400	1,260

Additional allowances are available if, for example, the course requires a period of study abroad.

LEA and SOEID expenditure on student fees and maintenance in 1994–5 was £2,926.8 million; 923,465 mandatory awards were made.

STUDENT LOANS

The Education (Student Loans) Act 1990 legislated for interest-free but indexed top-up loans of up to £2,035 in 1996–7 to be made available to eligible students in the UK. The Government expects that at least £766.7 million will be taken up in loans in 1996–7.

Students apply direct to the Student Loans Company Ltd (see page 451), which will require a certificate of eligibility from their place of study. Loans are available to students on designated courses within the scope of mandatory awards and the same residency conditions apply. Repayment is normally over five to seven years, although it can be deferred if income is at or below 85 per cent of national average earnings (about £14,500 a year). From the 1997-8 academic year private financial institutions will receive subsidies to allow them to offer loans on the same terms as the Student Loans Company.

ACCESS FUNDS

Access funds are allocated by education departments to the appropriate funding councils in England, Wales and Scotland and administered by further and higher education institutions. In Northern Ireland they are allocated by central government to the institutions direct. They are available to students whose access to higher education might otherwise be inhibited by financial considerations or where real financial difficulties are faced. For the academic year 1996–7, provision in the UK will be £28.9 million.

POSTGRADUATE AWARDS

Unlike funding for undergraduates, which is mandatory for most degree and equivalent level courses, grants for postgraduate study are usually discretionary. Grants are also often dependent on the class of first degree, especially for research degrees.

An increasing number of scholarships are available from research charities, endowments, and particular industries or companies. For residents in England and Wales, several schemes of postgraduate bursaries or studentships are funded by the DFEE, the government research councils, the Ministry of Agriculture, Fisheries and Food, and the British Academy, which awards grants for study in the humanities.

In Scotland postgraduate funding is provided by the SOEID, the Scottish Office Agriculture and Fisheries Department, and the research councils as in England and Wales.

Awards in Northern Ireland are made by the DENI, the Department of Agriculture for Northern Ireland, and the Medical Research Council.

In the UK in 1993–4, 21,400 awards were made. The national rates in 1996–7 are:

Living in	12-month scholarship	30-week bursary
College/lodgings in London area	5,845	3,460
College/lodgings outside London area	4,645	2,735
Parental home	3,420	2,065

ADULT AND CONTINUING EDUCATION

The term adult education covers a broad spectrum of educational activities ranging from non-vocational courses of general interest, through the acquiring of special vocational skills needed in industry or commerce, to study for a degree at the Open University.

The responsibility for securing adult and continuing education in England and Wales is statutory and shared between the Further Education Funding Councils, which are responsible for and fund those courses which take place in their sector and lead to academic and vocational qualifications, prepare students to undertake further or higher education courses, or confer basic skills; the Higher Education Funding Councils, which fund advanced courses of continuing education; and LEAs, which are responsible for those courses which do not fall within the remit of the funding councils. Funding in Northern Ireland is through the education and library boards and in Scotland by the Scottish Office Education and Industry Department.

PROVIDERS

Courses specifically for adults are provided by many bodies. They include, in the statutory sector: local education authorities in England and Wales; in Scotland the education authorities and the SOEID; education and library boards in Northern Ireland; further education colleges; higher education colleges; universities, especially the Open University and Birkbeck College of the University of London; residential colleges; the BBC, independent television and local radio stations. There are also a number of voluntary bodies.

The LEAs in England and Wales operate through 'area' adult education centres (4,390 in 1995), institutes or colleges, and the adult studies departments of colleges of further education. The SOEID funds adult education, including that provided by the universities and the Workers' Educational Association, at vocational further education colleges (47 in 1995) and evening centres (162 in 1995). In addition, SOEID provides grants to a number of voluntary organizations. Provision in the statutory sector in Northern Ireland is the responsibility of the universities and the education and library boards, which operate 17 further education colleges and a number of community schools.

The involvement of universities in adult education and continuing education has diversified considerably and is supported by a variety of administrative structures ranging from dedicated departments to a devolved approach. Birkbeck College in the University of London caters solely for part-time students. Those institutions and colleges formerly in the PCFC sector in England and Wales, because of their range of courses and flexible patterns of student attendance, provide opportunities in the field of adult and continuing education. The Forum for the Advancement of Continuing Education (FACE) promotes collaboration between institutions of higher education active in this area. The Open University, in partnership with the BBC, provides distance teaching leading to first degrees, and also offers post-experience and higher degree courses (see page 459).

Of the voluntary bodies, the biggest is the Workers' Educational Association (WEA) which operates throughout the UK, reaching about 150,000 adult students annually. The FEFC for England, the SOEID, and LEAs make grants towards provision.

The National Institute of Adult Continuing Education (England and Wales) (NIACE) provides information and advice to organizations and providers on all aspects of adult continuing education. NIACE conducts research, project and development work, and is funded by the DFEE, LEAs and other funding bodies. The Welsh committee, NIACE Cymru, receives financial support from the Welsh Office, support in kind from the Welsh Joint Education Committee, and advises government, voluntary bodies and education providers on adult continuing education and training matters in Wales. In Scotland advice on adult and community education, and promotion thereof, is provided by the Scottish Community Education Council. The Northern Ireland Council for Adult Education has an advisory role. Its membership includes representatives of the education and library boards and of most organizations involved in the field, together with an assessor appointed by DENI.

Membership of the Universities Association for Continuing Education is open to any university or university college in the UK. It promotes university continuing education, facilitates the interchange of information, and supports research and development work in continuing education.

COURSES

Although lengths vary, most courses are part-time. Long-term residential colleges in England and Wales are grant-aided by the FEFCs and provide full-time courses lasting one or two years. Some colleges and centres offer short-term residential courses, lasting from a few days to a few weeks, in a wide range of subjects. Local education authorities directly sponsor many of the colleges, while others are sponsored by universities or voluntary organizations. A directory of learning holidays, *Time to Learn*, is published by NIACE.

GRANTS

Although full-time courses at degree level attract mandatory awards, for courses below that level all students over the age of 19 must pay a fee. However, discretionary grants may be available. Adult education bursaries for students at the long-term residential colleges of adult education are the responsibility of the colleges themselves. The awards are administered for the colleges by the Awards Officer of the Residential Colleges Committee for students resident in England and are funded by the FEFC for England in English colleges; for colleges in Wales they are funded and administered by the FEFC for Wales; and for colleges in Scotland and Northern Ireland they are funded by central government and administered by the education authorities. A booklet, *Adult Education Bursaries,* can be obtained from the Awards Officer, Adult Education Bursaries, c/o Ruskin College (*see* page 461).

NUMBERS

There are no comprehensive statistics covering all aspects of adult education. However, enrolments on evening courses in the UK numbered 1,480,000 in 1994–5 (65.8 per cent women). This number included 722,000 students at adult education centres.

Education Directory

LOCAL EDUCATION AUTHORITIES

ENGLAND

COUNTY COUNCILS

BEDFORDSHIRE, County Hall, Cauldwell Street, Bedford MK42 9AP. Tel: 01234-363222. *Director*, D. G. Wadsworth

BERKSHIRE, PO Box 902, Shire Hall, Shinfield Park, Reading RG2 9XE. Tel: 0118-923 3652. *Chief Education Officer*, S. R. Goodchild

BUCKINGHAMSHIRE, County Hall, Aylesbury HP20 1UA. Tel: 01296-382641. *Director*, D. McGahey

CAMBRIDGESHIRE, Castle Court, Shire Hall, Cambridge CB3 0AP. Tel: 01223-317990. *Director*, A. Baxter

CHESHIRE, County Hall, Chester CH1 1SQ. Tel: 01244-602306. *Director*, D. Cracknell

CORNWALL, County Hall, Truro TR1 3AY. Tel: 01872-322000. *Secretary for Education*, J. Harris

CUMBRIA, 5 Portland Square, Carlisle CA1 1PU. Tel: 01228-606060. *Director*, J. Nellist

DERBYSHIRE, County Hall, Matlock DE4 3AG. Tel: 01629-580000. *Chief Education Officer*, Ms V. Hannon

DEVON, County Hall, Topsham Road, Exeter EX2 4QG. Tel: 01392-382039. *Chief Education Officer*, S. W. Jenkin

DORSET, County Hall, Colliton Park, Dorchester DT1 1XJ. Tel: 01305-224166. *Director*, R. H. Ely

DURHAM, County Hall, Durham DH1 5UJ. Tel: 0191-386 4411. *Director*, K. Mitchell

EAST SUSSEX, PO Box 4, County Hall, St Anne's Crescent, Lewes BN7 1SG. Tel: 01273-481000. *Director*, D. Mallen

ESSEX, PO Box 47, A Block, County Hall, Victoria Road South, Chelmsford CM1 1LD. Tel: 01245-492211. *Director*, P. A. Lincoln

GLOUCESTERSHIRE, Shire Hall, Gloucester GL1 2TP. Tel: 01452-425302. *Chief Education Officer*, K. D. Anderson, CBE

HAMPSHIRE, The Castle, Winchester SO23 8UG. Tel: 01962-841841. *Director*, P. J. Coles

HEREFORD AND WORCESTER, County Hall, Spetchley Road, Worcester WR5 2NP. Tel: 01905-766347. *County Education Officer*, D. A. J. Stanley

HERTFORDSHIRE, County Hall, Hertford SG13 8DF. Tel: 01992-555701. *Director*, M. Instone

ISLE OF WIGHT, County Hall, Newport PO30 1UD. Tel: 01983-823400. *Director*, A. Kaye

KENT, Springfield, Maidstone ME14 2LJ. Tel: 01622-671411. *Director*, R. Pryke

LANCASHIRE, PO Box 61, County Hall, Preston PR1 8RJ. Tel: 01772-254868. *Chief Education Officer*, C. J. Trinick

LEICESTERSHIRE, County Hall, Glenfield, Leicester LE3 8RF. Tel: 0116-265 6300. *Director*, Mrs J. A. M. Strong

LINCOLNSHIRE, County Offices, Newland, Lincoln LN1 1YQ. Tel: 01522-552222. *Director*, N. J. Riches

NORFOLK, County Hall, Martineau Lane, Norwich NR1 2DH. Tel: 01603-222222. *Director*, M. H. Edwards

NORTHAMPTONSHIRE, PO Box 149, County Hall, Northampton NN1 1AU. Tel: 01604-236252. *Director*, J. R. Atkinson

NORTHUMBERLAND, County Hall, Morpeth NE61 2EF. Tel: 01670-533000. *Director*, C. C. Tipple

NORTH YORKSHIRE, County Hall, Northallerton DL7 8AD. Tel: 01609-780780. *Director*, Miss C. Welbourn

NOTTINGHAMSHIRE, County Hall, West Bridgford, Nottingham NG2 7QP. Tel: 0115-982 3823. *Director*, R. Valentine

OXFORDSHIRE, Macclesfield House, New Road, Oxford OX1 1NA. Tel: 01865-815449. *Director*, G. Badman

SHROPSHIRE, The Shirehall, Abbey Foregate, Shrewsbury SY2 6ND. Tel: 01743-254302. *Director*, Ms C. Adams

SOMERSET, County Hall, Taunton TA1 4DY. Tel: 01823-333451. *Chief Education Officer*, N. Henwood

STAFFORDSHIRE, Wedgwood Building, Tipping Street, Stafford ST16 2DH. Tel: 01785-223121. *Chief Education Officer*, P. J. Hunter, PH.D.

SUFFOLK, St Andrew House, County Hall, Ipswich IP4 1LJ. Tel: 01473-264627. *County Education Officer*, D. J. Peachey

SURREY, County Hall, Penrhyn Road, Kingston upon Thames KT1 2DN. Tel: 0181-541 9501. *County Education Officer*, Dr P. Gray

WARWICKSHIRE, PO Box 24, 22 Northgate Street, Warwick CV34 4SR. Tel: 01926-410410. *Director*, E. Wood

WEST SUSSEX, County Hall, West Street, Chichester PO19 1RF. Tel: 01243-777100. *Director*, R. D. C. Bunker

WILTSHIRE, County Hall, Trowbridge BA14 8JH. Tel: 01225-713000. *Chief Education Officer*, Dr L. Davies

UNITARY COUNCILS

BARNSLEY, Berneslai Close, Barnsley S70 2HS. Tel: 01226-770770. *Director*, D. Dalton

BATH AND NORTH-EAST SOMERSET, Northgate House, Upper Borough Walls, Bath BA1 2JD. Tel: 01225-460628. *Director*, R. Jones

BIRMINGHAM, Council House, Margaret Street, Birmingham B3 3BU. Tel: 0121-235 2550. *Chief Education Officer*, T. Brighouse

BOLTON, Paderborn House, Civic Centre, Bolton BL1 1JW. Tel: 01204-522311. *Director*, Mrs M. Blenkinsop

BRADFORD, Flockton House, Flockton Road, Bradford BD4 7RY. Tel: 01274-751840. *Director*, Ms D. Cavanagh

BRISTOL, Council House, College Green, Bristol BS1 5TR. Tel: 0117-922 2000. *Director*, R. Riddell

BURY, Athenaeum House, Market Street, Bury BL9 0BN. Tel: 0161-253 5652. *Chief Education Officer (acting)*, G. Talbot

CALDERDALE, Northgate House, Northgate, Halifax HX1 1UN. Tel: 01422-357257. *Director*, I. Jennings

COVENTRY, Council House, Earl Street, Coventry CV1 5RR. Tel: 01203-833333. *Chief Education Officer*, Ms. C. Goodwin

DONCASTER, PO Box 266, The Council House, College Road, Doncaster DN1 3AD. Tel: 01302-734444. *Director*, A. M. Taylor

DUDLEY, Westox House, 1 Trinity Road, Dudley DY1 1JB. Tel: 01384-452200. *Chief Education Officer*, R. Colligan

EAST RIDING OF YORKSHIRE, County Hall, Beverley HU17 9BA. Tel: 01482-887700. *Director*, J. Ginnever

GATESHEAD, Civic Centre, Regent Street, Gateshead NE8 1HH. Tel: 0191-477 1011. *Director*, J. D. Arbon

HARTLEPOOL, Civic Centre, Victoria Road, Hartlepool TS24 8AY. Tel: 01429-266522. *Director*, J. J. Fitt

KINGSTON UPON HULL, Essex House, Alfred Gelder Street, Kingston upon Hull HU1 1YD. Tel: 01482-610610. *Director*, Ms J. E. Taylor

KIRKLEES, Oldgate House, 2 Oldgate, Huddersfield HD1 6QW. Tel: 01484-422133. *Chief Education Officer*, R. Vincent

KNOWSLEY, Huyton Hey Road, Huyton, Merseyside L36 5YH. Tel: 0151-443 3232. *Director of Education*, P. Wylie

LEEDS, Merrion House, Leeds LS2 8DT. Tel: 0113-247 5575. *Chief Education Officer*, J. Rawlinson

LIVERPOOL, 14 Sir Thomas Street, Liverpool L1 6BJ. Tel: 0151-227 3911. *Director*, M. F. Cogley

MANCHESTER, Cumberland House, Crown Square, Manchester M60 3BB. Tel: 0161-234 7125. *Chief Education Officer*, R. Jobson

MIDDLESBROUGH, Civic Centre, Middlesbrough TS1 2QQ. Tel: 01642-262001. *Director*, M. Shorney

NEWCASTLE UPON TYNE, Civic Centre, Newcastle upon Tyne NE1 8PU. Tel: 0191-232 8520. *Education Officer*, D. Bell

NORTH EAST LINCOLNSHIRE, Eleanor Street, Grimsby DN31 1HU. Tel: 01472-323025. *Head of Education*, G. Hill

NORTH LINCOLNSHIRE, Pittwood House, Ashby Road, Scunthorpe DN16 1AB. Tel: 01724-296296. *Director*, T. Thomas

NORTH SOMERSET, Town Hall, Weston-Super-Mare BS23 1UJ. Tel: 01934-888888. *Director*, Ms J. Wreford

NORTH TYNESIDE, Stephenson House, Stephenson Street, North Shields NE30 1QA. Tel: 0191-200 5151. *Director*, L. Walton

OLDHAM, Town Hall, Middleton Road, Chadderton, Oldham OL9 6PP. Tel: 0161-911 4203. *Director*, Mrs H. Holmes

REDCAR AND CLEVELAND, Council Offices, Kirkleatham Street, Redcar TS10 1RT. Tel: 01642-444000. *Chief Education Officer*, K. Bruton

ROCHDALE, PO Box 70, Municipal Offices, Smith Street, Rochdale OL16 1YD. Tel: 01706-47474. *Director*, B. Atkinson

ROTHERHAM, Norfolk House, Walker Place, Rotherham S60 1QT. Tel: 01709-822500. *Education Officer*, H. C. Bower

ST HELENS, Rivington Centre, Rivington Road, St Helens WA10 4ND. Tel: 01744-456000. *Director*, B. M. Mainwaring

SALFORD, Chapel Street, Salford M3 5LT. Tel: 0161-832 9751. *Chief Education Officer*, D. Johnston

SANDWELL, PO Box 41, Shaftesbury House, 402 High Street, West Bromwich B70 9LT. Tel: 0121-525 7366. *Director*, S. Gallacher

SEFTON, Town Hall, Oriel Road, Bootle, Merseyside L20 7AE. Tel: 0151-922 4040. *Education Officer*, J. A. Marsden

SHEFFIELD, Leopold Street, Sheffield S1 1RJ. Tel: 0114-272 6341. *Director*, vacant

SOLIHULL, PO Box 20, Council House, Solihull B91 3QU. Tel: 0121-704 6000. *Director*, D. Nixon

SOUTH GLOUCESTERSHIRE, Bowling Hill, Chipping Sodbury BS17 6JX. Tel: 01454-863253. *Director*, Ms T. Gillespie

SOUTH TYNESIDE, Town Hall and Civic Offices, Westoe Road, South Shields NE32 2RL. Tel: 0191-427 1717. *Director*, I. L. Reid

STOCKPORT, Stopford House, Piccadilly, Stockport SK1 3XE. Tel: 0161-474 3808. *Director*, M. K. J. Hunt

STOCKTON-ON-TEES, Municipal Buildings, Church Road, Stockton-on-Tees TS18 1XE. Tel: 01642-670067. *Head of Education*, S. Bradford

SUNDERLAND, PO Box 101, Civic Centre, Burdon Road, Sunderland SR2 7DN. Tel: 0191-553 1000. *Director*, J. Williams

TAMESIDE, Council Offices, Wellington Road, Ashton-under-Lyne OL6 6DL. Tel: 0161-342 8355. *Director*, A. M. Webster

TRAFFORD, PO Box 19, Sale Town Hall, Tatton Road, Sale M33 1YR. Tel: 0161-912 1212. *Director*, A. Lee

WAKEFIELD, County Hall, Bond Street, Wakefield WF1 2QL. Tel: 01924-306090. *Education Officer*, J. McLeod

WALSALL, Civic Centre, Darwall Street, Walsall WS1 1DQ. Tel: 01922-650000. *Director*, T. Howard

WIGAN, Gateway House, Standishgate, Wigan WN1 1AE. Tel: 01942-244991. *Education Officer*, R. Clark

WIRRAL, Hamilton Building, Conway Street, Birkenhead L41 4FD. Tel: 0151-666 2121. *Director*, D. Rigby

WOLVERHAMPTON, Civic Centre, St Peter's Square, Wolverhampton WV1 1RR. Tel: 01902-27811. *Director*, R. Lockwood

YORK, 10-12 George Hudson Street, York YO1 1ZG. Tel: 01904-615191. *Director*, M. Peters

LONDON

*Inner London borough

BARKING AND DAGENHAM, Town Hall, Barking, Essex IG11 7LU. Tel: 0181-592 4500. *Education Officer*, A. Larbalestier

BARNET, Old Town Hall, Friern Barnet Lane, London N11 3DL. Tel: 0181-359 2000. *Director*, M. Daubney

BEXLEY, Hill View, Hill View Drive, Welling, Kent DA16 3RY. Tel: 0181-303 7777. *Director*, P. McGee

BRENT, Chesterfield House, 9 Park Lane, Wembley, Middx HA9 7RW. Tel: 0181-937 3020. *Chief Education Officer (acting)*, P. Doherty

BROMLEY, Civic Centre, Stockwell Close, Bromley BR1 3UH. Tel: 0181-464 3333. *Director*, vacant

*CAMDEN, Crowndale Centre, 218-220 Eversholt Street, London NW1 1BD. Tel: 0171-911 1525. *Education Officer*, R. Litchfield

*CITY OF LONDON, Education Department, Corporation of London, PO Box 270, Guildhall, London EC2P 2EJ. Tel: 0171-332 1750. *City Education Officer*, D. Smith

*CITY OF WESTMINSTER, PO Box 240, City Hall, 64 Victoria Street, London SW1E 6QP. Tel: 0171-798 2771. *Director*, Mrs D. McGrath

CROYDON, Taberner House, Park Lane, Croydon CR9 1TP. Tel: 0181-686 4433. *Director*, P. Benians

EALING, Perceval House, 14-16 Uxbridge Road, London W5 2HL. Tel: 0181-758 5484. *Director*, vacant

ENFIELD, PO Box 56, Civic Centre, Silver Street, Enfield EN1 3XQ. Tel: 0181-967 9423. *Director*, Ms L. Graham

*GREENWICH, Riverside House, Woolwich High Street, London, SE18 6DN. Tel: 0181-854 8888. *Director*, J. Kramer

*HACKNEY, Edith Cavell Building, Enfield Road, London N1 5AZ. Tel: 0171-214 8400. *Director (acting)*, S. Roberts

*HAMMERSMITH AND FULHAM, Cambridge House, Cambridge Grove, London W6 4LE. Tel: 0181-576 5477. *Director*, Ms C. Whatford

HARINGEY, 48 Station Road, Wood Green, London N22 4TY. Tel: 0181-975 9700. *Director*, Miss J. Tonge

HARROW, PO Box 22, Civic Centre, Harrow HA1 2UW. Tel: 0181-424 1304. *Director*, Mrs C. Gilbert

HAVERING, Broxhill Centre, Broxhill Road, Harold Hill, Romford RM4 1XN. Tel: 01708-772222. *Director*, C. Hardy

HILLINGDON, Civic Centre, High Street, Uxbridge, Middx UB8 1UW. Tel: 01895-250111. *Director*, Mrs G. Andrews

448   Education

HOUNSLOW, Civic Centre, Lampton Road, Hounslow, Middx TW3 4DN. Tel: 0181-862 5301. *Director,* J. D. Trickett
*ISLINGTON, Laycock Street, London N1 1TH. Tel: 0171-457 5753. *Education Officer,* Dr H. Nicole
*KENSINGTON AND CHELSEA, Town Hall, Hornton Street, London W8 7NX. Tel: 0171-937 5464. *Director,* R. Wood
KINGSTON UPON THAMES, Guildhall, High Street, Kingston upon Thames KT1 1EU. Tel: 0181-547 5220. *Director,* J. Braithwaite
*LAMBETH, Blue Star House, 234–244 Stockwell Road, London SW9 9SP. Tel: 0171-926 2248. *Director,* Ms H. DuQuesnay, CBE
*LEWISHAM, Laurence House, 1 Catford Road, London SE6 4SW. Tel: 0181-695 6000. *Director,* Ms A. Efunshile
MERTON, Civic Centre, London Road, Morden, Surrey SM4 5DX. Tel: 0181-554 3251. *Director,* Ms J. Cairns
NEWHAM, Broadway House, 322 High Street, London E15 1AJ. Tel: 0181-555 5552. *Director,* I. Harrison
REDBRIDGE, Lynton House, 255–259 High Road, Ilford IG1 1NN. Tel: 0181-478 3020. *Director,* D. E. Capper
RICHMOND UPON THAMES, Regal House, London Road, Twickenham TW1 3QS. Tel: 0181-891 7500. *Director,* G. Alexander
*SOUTHWARK, 1 Bradenham Close, London SE17 2BA. Tel: 0171-525 5000. *Director,* G. Mott
SUTTON, The Grove, Carshalton, Surrey SM5 3AL. Tel: 0181-770 6568. *Director,* Dr I. Birnbaum
*TOWER HAMLETS, Mulberry Place, 5 Clove Crescent, London E14 2BG. Tel: 0171-364 5000. *Education Officer,* Mrs A. Sofer
WALTHAM FOREST, Municipal Offices, High Road, Leyton, London E10 5QJ. Tel: 0181-527 5544. *Chief Education Officer,* A. Lockhart
*WANDSWORTH, Town Hall, Wandsworth High Street, London SW18 2PU. Tel: 0181-871 6000. *Director,* P. Robinson

WALES

ANGLESEY, Glanhwfa Road, Llangefni LL77 7EY. Tel: 01248-752900. *Director,* R. P. Jones
BLAENAU GWENT, Civic Centre, Ebbw Vale NP3 6XB. Tel: 01495-355434. *Director,* B. Mawby
BRIDGEND, Sunnyside Offices, Bridgend CF31 4AR. Tel: 01656-766211. *Director,* D. Matthews
CAERNARFONSHIRE AND MERIONETHSHIRE, Swyddfa'r Cyngor, Caernarfon LL55 1SH. Tel: 01286-679012. *Director,* D. Whittall
CAERPHILLY, Caerphilly Road, Ystrad Mynach, Hengoed CF82 7EP. Tel: 01443-816016. *Director,* N. Harries
CARDIFF, County Hall, Atlantic Wharf, Cardiff CF1 5UW. Tel: 01222-872000. *Director,* T. Davies
CARMARTHENSHIRE, Pibwrlwyd, Carmarthen SA31 2NH. Tel: 01267-234567. *Director,* K. P. Davies
CEREDIGION, Swyddfa'r Sir, Aberystwyth SY23 2DE. Tel: 01970-633600. *Director,* R. Williams
CONWY, Government Buildings, Dinerth Road, Colwyn Bay LL28 5AX. Tel: 01492-544261. *Director,* R. E. Williams
DENBIGHSHIRE, Phase IV, Shire Hall, Mold CH7 6GR. Tel: 01824-706700. *Director,* E. Lewis
FLINTSHIRE, County Hall, Mold CH7 6ND. Tel: 01352-704010. *Director,* K. McDonogh
MERTHYR TYDFIL, Civic Centre, Castle Street, Merthyr Tydfil CF47 8AN. Tel: 01685-724614. *Director,* D. Jones
MONMOUTHSHIRE, County Hall, Cwmbran NP44 2XH. Tel: 01633-838838. *Director,* D. Young

NEATH AND PORT TALBOT, Civic Centre, Port Talbot SA13 1PJ. Tel: 01639-763333. *Director,* V. Thomas
NEWPORT, Civic Centre, Newport NP9 4UR. Tel: 01633-232000. *Director,* G. Bingham
PEMBROKESHIRE, Cambria House, Haverfordwest SA61 1TP. Tel: 01437-764551. *Director,* G. Davies
POWYS, County Hall, Llandrindod Wells LD1 5LG. Tel: 01597-826433. *Director,* M. Barker
RHONDDA, CYNON, TAFF, Grawen Street, Porth CF39 0BU. Tel: 01433-687666. *Director,* K. Ryley
SWANSEA, Room 1.1.10, County Hall, Oystermouth Road, Swansea SA1 3SN. Tel: 01792-636351. *Director,* M. Brunt
TORFAEN, County Hall, Cwmbran NP44 2WH. Tel: 01633-832403. *Director,* M. de Val
VALE OF GLAMORGAN, Civic Offices, Holton Road, Barry CF63 4RU. Tel: 01466-709100. *Director,* A. Davies
WREXHAM, Roxburgh House, Hill Street, Wrexham LL11 1SN. Tel: 01978-297400. *Director,* T. Garner

SCOTLAND

ABERDEEN CITY, Summerhill Education Centre, Stronsay Drive, Aberdeen AB15 6JA. Tel: 01224-208626. *Director,* J. Stodter
ABERDEENSHIRE, Woodhill House, Westburn Road, Aberdeen AB16 5GB. Tel: 01224-665420. *Director,* M. White
ANGUS, County Buildings, Market Street, Forfar DD8 3LG. Tel: 01307-461460. *Director,* J. Anderson
ARGYLL AND BUTE, Argyll House, Alexandra Parade, Dunoon PA23 8HI. Tel: 01369-704000. *Director,* A. C. Morton
CITY OF EDINBURGH, Council Headquarters, George IV Bridge, Edinburgh EH1 1UQ. Tel: 0131-200 2000. *Director,* Ms E. Reid
CLACKMANNANSHIRE, Lime Tree House, Alloa FK10 1EX. Tel: 01259-452435. *Director,* K. Bloomer
DUMFRIES AND GALLOWAY, Education Headquarters, 30 Edinburgh Road, Dumfries DG1 1JQ. Tel: 01387-260000. *Director,* K. MacLeod
DUNDEE CITY, Floor 8, Tayside House, 28 Crichton Street, Dundee DD1 3RJ. Tel: 01382-223281. *Director,* Ms A. Wilson
EAST AYRSHIRE, Council Headquarters, London Road, Kilmarnock KA3 7BU. Tel: 01563-576017. *Director,* J. Mulgrew
EAST DUMBARTONSHIRE, Bocleirla House, 100 Milngavie Road, Bearsden, Glasgow G61 2TQ. Tel: 0141-942 9000. *Director,* I. Mills
EAST LOTHIAN, Council Buildings, Haddington EH41 3HA. Tel: 01620-827827. *Director,* A. Blackie
EAST RENFREWSHIRE, Council Offices, Eastwood Park, Rouken Glen Road, Giffnock, Glasgow G46 6UG. Tel: 0141-621 3430. *Director,* Ms E. J. Currie
FALKIRK, McLaren House, Marchmont Avenue, Polmont, Falkirk FK2 0NZ. Tel: 01324-506600. *Director,* G. Young
FIFE, Rothesay House, North Street, Glenrothes KY7 5PN. Tel: 01592-413656. *Director,* A. Mackay
GLASGOW CITY, Education Offices, 129 Bath Street, Glasgow G2 2SY. Tel: 0141-287 6898. *Director,* K. Corsar
HIGHLAND, Glenurquhart Road, Inverness IV3 5NX. Tel: 01463-702801. *Director,* A. C. Gilchrist
INVERCLYDE, 105 Dalrymple Street, Greenock PA15 1HT. Tel: 01475-724400. *Director,* B. McLeary
MIDLOTHIAN, Education Division, Greenhall Centre, Gowkshill, Gorebridge EH23 4PE. Tel: 01875-823699. *Director,* D. MacKay
MORAY, Academy Street, Elgin IV30 1LL. Tel. 01343-541144. *Director,* K. Gavin

NORTH AYRSHIRE, Cunninghame House, Irvine KA12 8EE. Tel: 01294-324100. *Director,* J. Travers

NORTH LANARKSHIRE, Municipal Buildings, Kildonan Street, Coatbridge ML5 3LF. Tel: 01236-812222. *Director,* M. O'Neil

ORKNEY ISLANDS, Council Offices, School Place, Kirkwall, Orkney KW15 1WY. Tel: 01856-873535. *Director,* J. J. Anderson

PERTH AND KINROSS, 6–8 South Methven Street, Perth PH1 5PF. Tel: 01783-476200. *Director,* R. McKay

RENFREWSHIRE, South Building, Cotton Street, Paisley PA1 1BU. Tel: 0141-842 5601. *Director,* Mrs S. Rae

SCOTTISH BORDERS, Council Headquarters, Newtown St Boswells, Melrose TD6 0SA. Tel: 01835-824000. *Director,* J. Christie

SHETLAND ISLANDS, Schlumberger, Gremista Industrial Estate, Lerwick ZE1 0PX. Tel: 01595-744300. *Director,* J. Halcrow

SOUTH AYRSHIRE, County Buildings, Wellington Square, Ayr KA7 1DR. Tel: 01292-612000. *Director,* M. McCabe

SOUTH LANARKSHIRE, Council Offices, Almada Street, Hamilton ML3 0AA. Tel: 01698-454444. *Director,* Ms M. Allan

STIRLING, Council Headquarters, Viewforth, Stirling FK8 2ET. Tel: 01786-442680. *Director,* G. Jeyes

WEST DUMBARTONSHIRE, Garshake Road, Dumbarton G82 3PU. Tel: 01389-737000. *Director,* I. McMurdo

WEST LOTHIAN, Lindsay House, South Bridge Street, Bathgate EH48 1TS. Tel: 01506-776000. *Director,* R. Stewart

WESTERN ISLES ISLANDS, Council Offices, Sandwick Road, Stornoway HS1 2BW. Tel: 01851-703773. *Director,* N. Galbraith

NORTHERN IRELAND

EDUCATION AND LIBRARY BOARDS

BELFAST, 40 Academy Street, Belfast BT1 2NQ. Tel: 01232-564000. *Chief Executive,* T. G. J. Moag

NORTH EASTERN, County Hall, 182 Galgorm Road, Ballymena, Co. Antrim BT42 1HN. Tel: 01266-653333. *Chief Executive,* G. Topping

SOUTH EASTERN, 18 Windsor Avenue, Belfast BT9 6EF. Tel: 01232-381188. *Chief Executive,* T. Nolan, OBE

SOUTHERN, 3 Charlemont Place, The Mall, Armagh BT61 9AX. Tel: 01861-512200. *Chief Executive,* J. G. Kelly

WESTERN, 1 Hospital Road, Omagh, Co. Tyrone BT79 0AW. Tel: 01662-240240. *Chief Executive,* J. Martin

ISLANDS

GUERNSEY, Grange Road, St Peter Port GY1 1RQ. Tel: 01481-710821. *Director,* D. T. Neale

JERSEY, PO Box 142, JE4 8QJ. Tel: 01534-509500. *Director,* B. Grady

ISLE OF MAN, Department of Education, Murray House, 5–11 Mount Havelock, Douglas IM1 2SG. Tel: 01624-685685. *Director,* G. A. Baker

ISLES OF SCILLY, Town Hall, St Mary's TR21 0LW. Tel: 01720-422537. *Secretary for Education,* P. S. Hygate

ADVISORY BODIES

SCHOOLS

EDUCATION OTHERWISE, PO Box 7420, London N9 9SG. *Helpline,* tel: 0891-518303

INTERNATIONAL BACCALAUREATE, Peterson House, Fortran Road, St Mellons, Cardiff CF3 0LT. Tel: 01222-774000. *Director of Examinations,* C. Carthew

NATIONAL ADVISORY COUNCIL FOR EDUCATION TRAINING AND TARGETS, 7th Floor, 222 Grays Inn Road, London WC1X 8HL. Tel: 0171-211 4529. *Chairman,* P. Davis; *Director,* P. Chorley

NATIONAL COUNCIL FOR EDUCATIONAL TECHNOLOGY, Milburn Hill Road, Science Park, Coventry CV4 7JJ. Tel: 01203-416994. *Chief Executive,* Mrs M. Bell

SPECIAL EDUCATIONAL NEEDS TRIBUNAL, 71 Victoria Street, London SW1H 0HW. Tel: 0171-925 6925. *President,* T. Aldridge; *Secretary,* Ms J. Saraga

INDEPENDENT SCHOOLS

GOVERNING BODIES ASSOCIATION, The Coach House, Pickforde Lane, Ticehurst, E. Sussex TN5 7BJ. Tel: 01580-200855. *Secretary,* D. G. Banwell

GOVERNING BODIES OF GIRLS' SCHOOLS ASSOCIATION, The Coach House, Pickforde Lane, Ticehurst, E. Sussex TN5 7BJ. Tel: 01580-200855. *Secretary,* D. G. Banwell

INDEPENDENT SCHOOLS EXAMINATIONS BOARD, Jordan House, Christchurch Road, New Milton, Hants BH25 6QJ. Tel: 01425-621111. *Administrator,* Mrs J. Williams

INDEPENDENT SCHOOLS INFORMATION SERVICE, 56 Buckingham Gate, London SW1E 6AG. Tel: 0171-630 8793. *National Director,* D. J. Woodhead

THE ISJC ASSISTED PLACES COMMITTEE, 26 Queen Anne's Gate, London SW1H 9AN. Tel: 0171-222 9595. *Secretary,* P. F. V. Waters

FURTHER EDUCATION

FURTHER EDUCATION DEVELOPMENT AGENCY, Dumbarton House, 68 Oxford Street, London W1N 0DA. Tel: 0171-436 0020. *Chief Executive,* S. Crowne

NATIONAL COUNCIL FOR VOCATIONAL QUALIFICATIONS, 222 Euston Road, London NW1 2BZ. Tel: 0171-387 9898. *Chief Executive,* J. Hillier

Regional Advisory Councils

ASSOCIATION OF COLLEGES IN THE EASTERN REGION, Merlin Place, Milton Road, Cambridge CB4 4DP. Tel: 01223–424022. *Chief Executive,* J. Graystone

CENTRA (EDUCATION AND TRAINING SERVICES) LTD, Duxbury Park, Duxbury Hall Road, Chorley, Lancs PR7 4AT. Tel: 01257-241428. *Chief Executive,* N. Bailey

EMFEC (EAST MIDLAND FURTHER EDUCATION COUNCIL), Robins Wood House, Robins Wood Road, Aspley, Nottingham NG8 3NH. Tel: 0115-929 3291. *Chief Executive,* R. Ainscough

NCFE (NORTHERN COUNCIL FOR FURTHER EDUCATION), 5 Grosvenor Villas, Grosvenor Road, Newcastle upon Tyne NE2 2RU. Tel: 0191-281 3242. *Chief Executive,* J. F. Pearce

SOUTHERN REGIONAL COUNCIL FOR FURTHER EDUCATION AND TRAINING, The Mezzanine Suite, PO Box 2055, Civic Centre, Reading RG1 7ET. Tel: 01734-390592. *Chief Executive,* B. J. Knowles

SOUTH WEST ASSOCIATION FOR FURTHER EDUCATION AND TRAINING, Bishops Hull House, Bishops Hull, Taunton, Somerset TA1 5RA. Tel: 01823-335491. *Chief Executive,* S. Fisher

WELSH JOINT EDUCATION COMMITTEE, 245 Western Avenue, Cardiff CF5 2YX. Tel: 01222-265000. *Secretary,* C. Heycock

Yorkshire and Humberside Association for Further and Higher Education, 13 Wellington Road East, Dewsbury, W. Yorks WF13 1XG. Tel: 01924-450900. *Chief Executive*, Prof. N. Woodhead

HIGHER EDUCATION

Association of Commonwealth Universities, John Foster House, 36 Gordon Square, London WC1H 0PF. Tel: 0171–387 8572. *Secretary-General*, Prof. M. G. Gibbons

Committee of Vice-Chancellors and Principals of the Universities of the United Kingdom, 29 Tavistock Square, London WC1H 9EZ. Tel: 0171-387 9231. *Chairman*, Prof. G. Roberts, FRS; *Chief Executive* Ms D. Warwick

Higher Education Quality Council, 344–354 Gray's Inn Road, London WC1X 8BP. Tel: 0171-837 2223. *Company Secretary*, G. L. Middleton

Northern Ireland Higher Education Council, Rathgael House, Balloo Road, Bangor BT19 7PR. Tel: 01247–279333. *Chairman*, Sir Kenneth Bloomfield, KCB; *Secretary*, J. Coote

---

CURRICULUM COUNCILS

Awdurdod Cwricwlwm acAsesu Cymru/ Curriculum and Assessment Authority for Wales, Castle Buildings, Womanby Street, Cardiff CF1 9SX. Tel: 01222-344946. *Chief Executive*, J. V. Williams

Northern Ireland Council for the Curriculum, Examinations and Assessment, 29 Clarendon Road, Belfast BT1 3BG. Tel: 01232-261200. *Chief Executive*, Mrs C. Coxhead

School Curriculum and Assessment Authority, Newcombe House, 45 Notting Hill Gate, London W11 3JB. Tel: 0171–229 1234. *Chairman*, Sir Ron Dearing, CB; *Chief Executive*, N. Tate, PH.D.

Scottish Consultative Council on the Curriculum, Gardyne Road, Broughty Ferry, Dundee DD5 1NY. Tel: 01382-455053. *Chief Executive*, C. E. Harrison

---

EXAMINING BODIES

GCSE

London Examinations and Assessment Council, Stewart House, 32 Russell Square, London WC1B 5DN. Tel: 0171-331 4000. *Chief Executive*, Ms C. Townsend, PH.D.

Midland Examining Group, 1 Hills Road, Cambridge CB1 2EU. Tel: 01223-553311. *Chief Executive*, R. R. McLone, PH.D. (Part of UCLES)

Northern Examinations and Assessment Board, Devas Street, Manchester M15 6EX. Tel: 0161-953 1180. *Chief Executive*, Mrs K. Tattersall

Northern Ireland Council for the Curriculum, Examinations and Assessment, Beechill House, 42 Beechill Road, Belfast BT8 4RS. Tel: 01232-704666. *Chief Executive*, Mrs C. Coxhead

SEG (Southern Examining Group), Stag Hill House, Guildford, Surrey GU2 5XJ. Tel: 01483-506506. *Secretary-General*, J. A. Day

Welsh Joint Education Committee, 245 Western Avenue, Cardiff CF5 2YX. Tel: 01222-265000. *Chief Executive*, C. Heycock

A-LEVEL

Associated Examining Board, Stag Hill House, Guildford, Surrey GU2 5XJ. Tel: 01483-506506. *Secretary-General*, J. A. Day

London Examinations and Assessment Council, Stewart House, 32 Russell Square, London WC1B 5DN. Tel: 0171-331 4000. *Chief Executive*, Ms C. Townsend, PH.D.

Northern Examinations and Assessment Board, Devas Street, Manchester M15 6EX. Tel: 0161-953 1180. *Chief Executive*, Mrs K. Tattersall

Northern Ireland Council for the Curriculum, Examinations and Assessment, Beechill House, 42 Beechill Road, Belfast BT8 4RS. Tel: 01232-704666. *Chief Executive*, Mrs C. Coxhead

Oxford and Cambridge Examinations and Assessment Council (OCEAC), Syndicate Buildings, 1 Hills Road, Cambridge CB1 2EU. Tel: 01223-553311; Ewert House, Ewert Place, Oxford OX2 7BZ. Tel: 01865-54291 (OCEAC is part of UCLES)

Oxford and Cambridge Schools Examination Board, *see* OCEAC

University of Cambridge Local Examinations Syndicate (UCLES), *see* OCEAC

University of Oxford Delegacy of Local Examinations, *see* OCEAC

Welsh Joint Education Committee, 245 Western Avenue, Cardiff CF5 2YX. Tel: 01222-265000. *Chief Executive*, C. Heycock

SCOTLAND

Scottish Examination Board, Ironmills Road, Dalkeith, Midlothian EH22 1LE. Tel: 0131-663 6601. *Chief Executive*, H. A. Long, PH.D.

Scottish Qualifications Authority, Hanover House, 24 Douglas Street, Glasgow G2 7NQ. Tel: 0141-248 7900

Scottish Vocational Education Council (SCOTVEC), Hanover House, 24 Douglas Street, Glasgow G2 7NQ. Tel: 0141-248 7900. *Chief Executive*, T. J. McCool, CBE

FURTHER EDUCATION

City & Guilds, 1 Giltspur Street, London EC1A 9DD. Tel: 0171-294 2468. *Director-General*, N. Carey, PH.D.

The Edexcel Foundation (BTEC and London Examinations and Assessment Council), Stewart House, 32 Russell Square, London WC1B 5DN. Tel: 0171-331 4000. *Chief Executive*, Ms C. Townsend, PH.D.

RSA Examinations Board, Westwood Way, Coventry CV4 8HS. Tel: 01203-470033. *Chief Executive*, M. F. Cross

---

FUNDING COUNCILS

SCHOOLS

Funding Agency for Schools, Albion Wharf, 25 Skeldergate, York YO1 2XL. Tel: 01904-661661. *Chairman*, Sir Christopher Benson; *Chief Executive*, M. Collier

FURTHER EDUCATION

Further Education Funding Council for England, Cheylesmore House, Quinton Road, Coventry CV1 2WT. Tel: 01203-863000. *Chief Executive*, Prof. D. Melville

FURTHER EDUCATION FUNDING COUNCIL FOR WALES, Lambourne House, Cardiff Business Park, Llanishen, Cardiff CF4 5GL. Tel: 01222-761861. *Chief Executive*, Prof. J. A. Andrews

SCOTTISH FURTHER EDUCATION FUNDING UNIT, Scottish Office Education and Industry Department, First Floor West, Victoria Quay, Edinburgh EH6 6QQ. Tel: 0131-244 0278. *Director*, R. D. Jackson

HIGHER EDUCATION

HIGHER EDUCATION FUNDING COUNCIL FOR ENGLAND, Northavon House, Coldharbour Lane, Bristol BS16 1QD. Tel: 0117-931 7317. *Chief Executive*, Prof. B. Fender

HIGHER EDUCATION FUNDING COUNCIL FOR WALES, Lambourne House, Cardiff Business Park, Llanishen, Cardiff CF4 5GL. Tel: 01222-761861. *Chief Executive*, Prof. J. A. Andrews

SCOTTISH HIGHER EDUCATION FUNDING COUNCIL, Donaldson House, 97 Haymarket Terrace, Edinburgh EH12 5HD. Tel: 0131-313 6500. *Chief Executive*, Prof. J. Sizer, CBE

STUDENT LOANS COMPANY LTD, 100 Bothwell Street, Glasgow G2 7JD. Tel: 0141-306 2000. *Chief Executive*, C. Ward

TEACHER TRAINING AGENCY, Portland House, Stag Place, London SW1E 5TT. Tel: 0171-925 3700. *Chairman*, G. Parker, CBE; *Chief Executive*, Ms A. Millett

---

ADMISSIONS AND COURSE INFORMATION

CAREERS RESEARCH AND ADVISORY CENTRE (CRAC), Sheraton House, Castle Park, Cambridge CB3 0AX. Tel: 01223-460277. *Director*, D. McGregor. *Publishers*, Hobsons Publishing PLC, Bateman Street, Cambridge CB2 1LZ

COMMITTEE OF SCOTTISH HIGHER EDUCATION PRINCIPALS (COSHEP), St Andrew House, 141 West Nile Street, Glasgow G1 2RN. Tel: 0141-353 1880. *Secretary*, Dr R. L. Crawford

GRADUATE TEACHER TRAINING REGISTRY, Fulton House, Jessop Avenue, Cheltenham, Glos GL50 3SH. Tel: 01242-225868. *Registrar*, Mrs M. Griffiths

SOCIAL WORK ADMISSIONS SYSTEM, Fulton House, Jessop Avenue, Cheltenham, Glos GL50 3SH. Tel: 01242-225977. *Admissions Officer*, Mrs M. Griffiths

TEACHER EDUCATION ADMISSIONS CLEARING HOUSE (TEACH) (Scottish postgraduate only), PO Box 165, Holyrood Road, Edinburgh EH8 8AT. *Registrar*, Miss R. C. Williamson

UNIVERSITIES AND COLLEGES ADMISSIONS SERVICE, Fulton House, Jessop Avenue, Cheltenham, Glos GL50 3SH. Tel: 01242-222444. *Chief Executive*, M. A. Higgins, PH.D.

UNIVERSITIES

THE UNIVERSITY OF ABERDEEN (1495)
Regent Walk, Aberdeen AB9 1FX
Tel 01224-272014
Full-time students (1995–6), 10,843
Chancellor, Sir Kenneth Alexander, FRSE (1987)
Vice-Chancellor, Prof. C. D. Rice
Registrar, Dr P. J. Murray

Secretary, N. R. D. Begg
Rector, I. Hamilton, QC (1993–6)

THE UNIVERSITY OF ABERTAY DUNDEE
(1994)
Bell Street, Dundee DD1 1HG
Tel: 01382-308000
Full-time students (1995–6), 4,000
Chancellor, The Earl of Airlie, KT, GCVO, PC
Vice-Chancellor, Prof. B. King
Registrar, Prof. J. McGoldrick
Secretary, D. Hogarth

ANGLIA POLYTECHNIC UNIVERSITY (1992)
Bishop Hall Lane, Chelmsford, Essex CM1 1SQ
Tel 01245-493131
Full-time students (1995–6), 10,545
Chancellor, The Lord Prior, PC (1992)
Vice-Chancellor, M. Malone-Lee, CB
Head of Student Administration, D. Davies
Secretary, S. G. Bennett

ASTON UNIVERSITY (1966)
Aston Triangle, Birmingham B4 7ET
Tel 0121-359 3611
Full-time students (1995–6), 4,500
Chancellor, Sir Adrian Cadbury (1979)
Vice-Chancellor, Prof. M. Wright
Registrar and Secretary, R. D. A. Packhan

THE UNIVERSITY OF BATH (1966)
Claverton Down, Bath BA2 7AY
Tel 01225-826826
Full-time students (1995–6), 5,610
Chancellor, Sir Denys Henderson (1993)
Vice-Chancellor, Prof. V. D. Vandelinde
Registrar, J. A. Bursey

THE UNIVERSITY OF BIRMINGHAM (1900)
Edgbaston, Birmingham B15 2TT
Tel 0121-414 3344
Full-time students (1995–6), 17,000
Chancellor, Sir Alexander Jarratt, CB (1983)
Vice-Chancellor, Prof. M. Irvine, PH.D.
Registrar and Secretary, D. R. Holmes

BOURNEMOUTH UNIVERSITY (1992)
Poole House, Talbot Campus, Fern Barrow,
Dorset BH12 5BB
Tel 01202-524111
Full-time students (1994–5), 8,200
Chancellor, The Baroness Cox (1992)
Vice-Chancellor, Prof. G. Slater
Registrar, N. Richardson
Secretary, R. Allen

THE UNIVERSITY OF BRADFORD (1966)
Bradford BD7 1DP
Tel 01274-733466
Full-time students (1995–6), 6,769
Chancellor, Sir Trevor Holdsworth (1992)
Vice-Chancellor, Prof. D. J. Johns, PH.D., D.SC. (1989)
Registrar and Secretary, N. J. Andrew

THE UNIVERSITY OF BRIGHTON (1992)
Mithras House, Lewes Road, Brighton BN2 4AT
Tel 01273-600900
Full-time students (1995–6), 10,800
Chairman of the Board, M. J. Aldrich

Director, Prof. D. J. Watson
Deputy Director, D. E. House

THE UNIVERSITY OF BRISTOL (1909)
Senate House, Tyndall Avenue, Bristol BS8 1TH
Tel 0117-928 9000
Full-time students (1995–6), 10,833
Chancellor, Sir Jeremy Morse, KCMG (1989)
Vice-Chancellor, Sir John Kingman, FRS
Registrar, J. H. M. Parry
Secretary, Ms K. McKenzie, D.phil.

BRUNEL UNIVERSITY (1966)
Uxbridge, Middx UB8 3PH
Tel 01895-274000
Full-time students (1995–6), 12,441
Chancellor, The Earl of Halsbury, FRS (1966)
Vice-Chancellor, Prof. M. J. H. Sterling
Secretary-General and Registrar, D. Neave

THE UNIVERSITY OF BUCKINGHAM (1983)
(Founded 1976 as University College at Buckingham)
Buckingham MK18 1EG
Tel 01280-814080
Full-time students (1995–6), 976
Chancellor, The Baroness Thatcher, KG, OM, PC, FRS (1992)
Vice-Chancellor, Prof. R. H. Taylor (from Jan. 1997)
Director of Administration, J. Elder

THE UNIVERSITY OF CAMBRIDGE
University Offices, The Old Schools, Cambridge CB2 1TN
Tel 01223-337733
Undergraduates in residence (1995–6), 11,115

UNIVERSITY OFFICERS, ETC.

Chancellor, HRH The Duke of Edinburgh, KG, KT, OM, GBE, PC (1977)
Vice-Chancellor, Prof. A. N. Broers, ph.D., FRS (1996)
High Steward, The Lord Runcie, PC, DD (1991)
Deputy High Steward, The Lord Richardson of Duntisbourne, PC, MBE, TD (1983)
Commissary, The Lord Oliver of Aylmerton, PC (*Trinity Hall*) (1989)
Proctors, D. J. H. Garling, SC.D. (*St John's*); O. Rackham, ph.D. (*Corpus Christi*) (1996)
Orator, A. J. Bowen (*Jesus*) (1993)
Registrary, S. G. Fleet, ph.D. (*Downing*) (1983)
Deputy Registrary, N. J. B. A. Branson, ph.D. (*Darwin*) (1993)
Librarian, P. K. Fox (*Selwyn*) (1994)
Treasurer, Ms J. Womack (*Trinity*) (1993)
Secretary-General of the Faculties, D. A. Livesey, ph.D. (*Emmanuel*) (1992)
Director of the Fitzwilliam Museum, D. D. Robinson (*Clare*) (1995)

COLLEGES AND HALLS, ETC.
with dates of foundation

CHRIST'S (1505), *Master,* A. J. Munro, ph.D. (1995)
CHURCHILL (1960), *Master,* Sir John Boyd, KCMG (1996)
CLARE (1326), *Master,* Prof. B. A. Hepple, LL D (1993)
CLARE HALL (1966), *President,* Prof. G. P. K. Beer, Litt.D., FBA (1994)
CORPUS CHRISTI (1352), *Master,* Prof. Sir Tony Wrigley, ph.D. (1994)
DARWIN (1964), *Master,* Prof. G. E. R. Lloyd, ph.D., FBA (1989)
DOWNING (1800), *Master,* Prof. D. A. King, FRS (1995)
EMMANUEL (1584), *Master,* Prof. J. E. Ffowcs-Williams, SC.D. (1996)

FITZWILLIAM (1966), *Master,* Prof. A. W. Cuthbert, ph.D., FRS (1991)
GIRTON (1869), *Mistress,* Mrs J. J. d'A. Campbell, CMG (1992)
GONVILLE AND CAIUS (1348), *Master,* N. MacKendrick (1996)
HOMERTON (1824) (for B.Ed. students), *Principal,* Mrs K. B. Pretty, ph.D. (1991)
HUGHES HALL (1885) (for post-graduate students), *President,* J. T. Dingle, D.sc. (1993)
JESUS (1496), *Master,* Prof. the Lord Renfrew of Kaimsthorn, SC.D. (1986)
KING'S (1441), *Provost,* Prof. P. P. G. Bateson, SC.D., FRS (1987)
*LUCY CAVENDISH COLLEGE (1965) (for women research students and mature and affiliated undergraduates), *President,* The Baroness Perry of Southwark (1994)
MAGDALENE (1542), *Master,* Prof. Sir John Gurdon, D.phil., FRS (1995)
*NEW HALL (1954), *President,* Mrs A. Lonsdale (1996)
*NEWNHAM (1871), *Principal,* Ms O. S. O'Neill, CBE (1992)
PEMBROKE (1347), *Master,* Sir Roger Tomkys, KCMG (1992)
PETERHOUSE (1284), *Master,* Prof. Sir John Meurig Thomas, FRS (1993)
QUEENS' (1448), *President,* Lord Eatwell (from Jan. 1997)
ROBINSON (1977), *Warden,* Prof. the Lord Lewis of Newnham, SC.D., FRS (1977)
ST CATHARINE'S (1473), *Master,* Prof. Sir Terence English (1993)
ST EDMUND'S (1896), *Master,* Prof. R. B. Heap, SC.D. (1996)
ST JOHN'S (1511), *Master,* Prof. P. Goddard, ph.D., FRS (1994)
SELWYN (1882), *Master,* D. Harrison, CBE, SC.D., F.eng. (1993)
SIDNEY SUSSEX (1596), *Master,* Prof. G. Horn, SC.D., FRS (1992)
TRINITY (1546), *Master,* Sir Michael Atiyah, ph.D., FRS, FRSE (1990)
TRINITY HALL (1350), *Master,* Sir John Lyons, ph.D. (1984)
WOLFSON (1965), *President,* G. Johnson ph.D. (1994)
*College for women only

THE UNIVERSITY OF CENTRAL ENGLAND IN BIRMINGHAM (1992)
Perry Barr, Birmingham B42 2SU
Tel 0121-331 5000
Full-time students (1995–6), 11,000
Chancellor, The Lord Mayor of Birmingham
Vice-Chancellor, Dr P. C. Knight, CBE
Secretary and Registrar, Ms M. Penlington

THE UNIVERSITY OF CENTRAL LANCASHIRE (1992)
Preston PR1 2HE
Tel 01772-201201
Full-time students (1995–6), 13,856
Chancellor, Sir Francis Kennedy, KCMG, CBE
Vice-Chancellor, B. G. Booth
Academic Registrar, L. Munro
Secretary, Ms P. M. Ackroyd

THE CITY UNIVERSITY (1966)
Northampton Square, London EC1V 0HB
Tel 0171-477 8000
Full-time students (1995–6), 6,837
Chancellor, The Rt. Hon. the Lord Mayor of London

Vice-Chancellor, Prof. R. N. Franklin, CBE, D.Phil., D.SC.
Academic Registrar, A. H. Seville, PH.D.
Secretary, M. M. O'Hara

COVENTRY UNIVERSITY (1992)
Priory Street, Coventry CV1 5FB
Tel 01203-631313
Full-time students (1995–6), 13,035
Chancellor, The Lord Plumb, MEP
Vice-Chancellor, M. Goldstein, Ph.D., D.SC.
Academic Registrar, J. Gledhill, PH.D.
Secretary, Ms L. Arlidge

CRANFIELD UNIVERSITY (1969)
(Founded as Cranfield Institute of Technology)
Cranfield, Beds MK43 0AL
Tel 01234-750111
Full-time students (1995–6), 2,355
Chancellor, The Lord Kings Norton, PH.D., FENg. (1969)
Vice-Chancellor, Prof. F. R. Hartley, D.SC.
Secretary and Registrar, J. K. Pettifer

DE MONTFORT UNIVERSITY (1992)
The Gateway, Leicester LE1 9BH
Tel 0116-255 1551
Full-time students (1995–6), 26,000
Chancellor, Sir Clive Whitmore, GCB, CVO
Vice-Chancellor, Prof. K. Barker, CBE
Academic Registrar, V. E. Critchlow

THE UNIVERSITY OF DERBY (1993)
(formerly Derbyshire College of Higher Education)
Kedleston Road, Derby DE22 1GB
Tel 01332-622222
Full-time students (1995–6), 9,500
Chancellor, Sir Christopher Ball
Vice-Chancellor, Prof. R. Waterhouse
Registrar, Mrs J. Fry
Secretary, R. Gillis

THE UNIVERSITY OF DUNDEE (1967)
Dundee DD1 4HN
Tel 01382-223181
Full-time students (1995–6), 8,170
Chancellor, Sir James Black, FRCP, FRS (1992)
Vice-Chancellor, Dr I. J. Graham-Bryce
Academic Secretary, Dr I. Francis
Secretary, R. Seaton
Rector, S. Fry (1995–8)

THE UNIVERSITY OF DURHAM
(Founded 1832; re-organized 1908, 1937 and 1963)
Old Shire Hall, Durham DH1 3HP
Tel 0191-374 2000
Full-time students (1995–6), 8,804
Chancellor, Sir Peter Ustinov, CBE, FRSL
Vice-Chancellor, Prof. E. A. V. Ebsworth, CBE, PH.D., SC.D.,
 FRSE
Registrar and Secretary, J. C. F. Hayward

COLLEGES
COLLINGWOOD, *Principal*, Prof. G. H. Blake, PH.D.
GRADUATE SOCIETY, *Principal*, M. Richardson, PH.D.
GREY, *Master*, V. E. Watts
HATFIELD, *Master*, Prof. T. P. Burt, PH.D.
ST AIDAN'S, *Principal*, R. J. Williams
ST CHAD'S, *Principal*, Revd D. W. H. Arnold, PH.D.
ST CUTHBERT'S SOCIETY, *Principal*, S. G. C. Stoker
ST HILD AND ST BEDE, *Principal*, J. V. Armitage, PH.D.
ST JOHN'S, *Principal*, D. V. Day

ST MARY'S, *Principal*, Miss J. M. Kenworthy
TREVELYAN, *Principal*, Prof. M. Todd
UNIVERSITY (DURHAM), *Master*, E. C. Salthouse, PH.D.
UNIVERSITY (STOCKTON), *Principal*, J. C. F. Hayward
USHAW, *President*, Rt. Revd Mgr R. Atherton, OBE
VAN MILDERT, *Principal*, Ms J. Turner, PH.D.

THE UNIVERSITY OF EAST ANGLIA (1963)
Norwich NR4 7TJ
Tel 01603 456161
Full-time students (1995–6), 7,500
Chancellor, Sir Geoffrey Allen, FEng, FRS (1994)
Vice-Chancellor, Dame Elizabeth Esteve-Coll, DBE
Registrar and Secretary, M. G. E. Paulson-Ellis, OBE

THE UNIVERSITY OF EAST LONDON (1992)
Longbridge Road, Dagenham, Essex RM8 2AS
Tel 0181-590 7000
Full-time students (1995–6), 10,080
Chancellor, vacant
Vice-Chancellor, Prof. F. Gould
Secretary and Registrar, A. Ingle

THE UNIVERSITY OF EDINBURGH (1583)
7–11 Nicolson Street, Edinburgh EH8 9BE
Tel 0131-650 1000
Full-time students (1995–6), 15,358
Chancellor, HRH The Prince Philip, Duke of Edinburgh,
 KG, KT, OM, GBE, PC, FRS (1952)
Vice-Chancellor, Prof. Sir Stewart Sutherland, FBA, FRSE
Secretary, M. J. B. Lowe, PH.D.
Rector, Dr. M. Macleod (1994–7)

THE UNIVERSITY OF ESSEX (1964)
Wivenhoe Park, Colchester CO4 3SQ
Tel 01206-873333
Full-time students (1995–6), 5,645
Chancellor, The Rt. Hon. Sir Patrick Nairne, GCB, MC, LL D
 (1983)
Vice-Chancellor, I. Crewe
Registrar and Secretary, A. F. Woodburn

THE UNIVERSITY OF EXETER (1955)
Northcote House, The Queen's Drive, Exeter EX4 4QJ
Tel 01392-263263
Full-time students (1995–6), 8,000
Chancellor, Sir Rex Richards, D.SC., FRS (1981)
Vice-Chancellor, Sir Geoffrey Holland, KCB
Academic Registrar and Secretary, I. H. C. Powell

GLAMORGAN UNIVERSITY (1992)
Treforest, Pontypridd CF37 1DL
Tel 01443-480480
Full-time students (1995–6), 11,598
Chancellor, The Lord Rees, PC, QC
Vice-Chancellor, Prof. A. L. Webb
Academic Registrar, J. O'Shea
Secretary, J. L. Bracegirdle

THE UNIVERSITY OF GLASGOW (1451)
Glasgow G12 8QQ
Tel 0141-339 8855
Full-time students (1995–6), 15,302
Chancellor, Sir William Kerr Fraser
Vice-Chancellor, Prof. G. Davies, PH.D., FEng.
Secretary, D. Mackie
Rector, R. Wilson (1996–9)

GLASGOW CALEDONIAN UNIVERSITY
(1993)
Cowcaddens Road, Glasgow G4 OBA
Tel 0141-331 3000
Full-time students (1995–6), 9,700
Chancellor, The Lord Nickson, KBE
Vice-Chancellor, Prof. J. S. Mason, ph.D.
Secretary, B. M. Murphy

THE UNIVERSITY OF GREENWICH (1992)
Bexley Road, Eltham, London SE9 2PQ
Tel 0181-331 8000
Full-time students (1995–6), 15,130
Chancellor, The Baroness Young
Vice-Chancellor, Dr D. E. Fussey
Academic Registrar, A. I. Mayfield
Secretary, J. M. Charles

HERIOT-WATT UNIVERSITY (1966)
Riccarton, Edinburgh EH14 4AS
Tel 0131-449 5111
Full-time students (1995–6), 9,219
Chancellor, The Lord Mackay of Clashfern, PC, QC, FRSE
  (1979)
Vice-Chancellor, Prof. A. G. J. MacFarlane, CBE, ph.D., FRS,
  FRSE, FEng. (1989)
Secretary, P. L. Wilson

THE UNIVERSITY OF HERTFORDSHIRE
(1992)
College Lane, Hatfield, Herts AL10 9AB
Tel 01707-284000
Full-time students (1995–6), 13,504
Chancellor, Sir Ian MacLaurin
Vice-Chancellor, Prof. N. K. Buxton
Registrar and Secretary, P. G. Jeffreys

THE UNIVERSITY OF HUDDERSFIELD
(1992)
Queensgate, Huddersfield HD1 3DH
Tel 01484-422288
Full-time students (1995–6), 10,524
Chancellor, vacant
Vice-Chancellor, Prof. J. R. Tarrant, ph.D.
Academic Registrar, M. E. Bond
Secretary, G. W. Downs

THE UNIVERSITY OF HULL (1954)
Cottingham Road, Hull HU6 7RX
Tel 01482-346311
Full-time students (1995–6), 12,200
Chancellor, The Lord Armstrong of Ilminster, GCB, CVO
Vice-Chancellor, Prof. D. Dilks, FRSL
Registrar and Secretary, D. J. Lock

KEELE UNIVERSITY (1962)
Keele, Newcastle under Lyme, Staffs ST5 5BG
Tel 01782-621111
Full-time students (1995–6), 5,700
Chancellor, Sir Claus Moser, KCB, CBE, FBA (1986)
Vice-Chancellor, Prof. J. V. Finch
Registrar, D. Cohen, ph.D.
Director of Academic Affairs, Dr E. F. Slade

THE UNIVERSITY OF KENT AT
CANTERBURY (1965)
Canterbury CT2 7NZ
Tel 01227-764000
Full-time students (1995–6), 8,441
Chancellor, Sir Crispin Tickell, GCMG, KCVO

Vice-Chancellor, Prof. R. Sibson, ph.D.
Secretary and Registrar, T. Mead, ph.D.

KINGSTON UNIVERSITY (1992)
Penrhyn Road, Kingston upon Thames,
Surrey KT1 2EE
Tel 0181-547 2000
Full-time students (1995–6), 13,678
Chancellor, Sir Frank Lampl
Vice-Chancellor, R. C. Smith, CBE, ph.D.
Secretary, R. Abdulla

THE UNIVERSITY OF LANCASTER (1964)
Bailrigg, Lancaster LA1 4YW
Tel 01524-65201
Full-time students (1995–6), 9,926
Chancellor, HRH Princess Alexandra, the Hon. Lady
  Ogilvy, GCVO (1964)
Vice-Chancellor, Prof. W. Ritchie, OBE
Secretary, S. A. C. Lamley

THE UNIVERSITY OF LEEDS (1904)
Leeds LS2 9JT
Tel 0113-243 1751
Full-time students (1995–6), 19,419
Chancellor, HRH The Duchess of Kent, GCVO (1966)
Vice-Chancellor, Prof. A. G. Wilson
Secretary and Registrar, D. Robinson, ph.D.

LEEDS METROPOLITAN UNIVERSITY (1992)
Calverley Street, Leeds LS1 3HE
Tel 0113-283 2600
Full-time students (1995–6), 10,825
Chairman of the Board of Governors, L. Silver
Vice-Chancellor, Prof. L. Wagner
Head of Registry Services, M. Christie
Secretary, M. Wilkinson

THE UNIVERSITY OF LEICESTER (1957)
University Road, Leicester LE1 7RH
Tel 0116-252 2522
Full-time students (1995–6), 8,516
Chancellor, Sir Michael Atiyah, OM, ph.D., D.SC. (1995)
Vice-Chancellor, K. J. R. Edwards, ph.D.
Registrar and Secretary, K. J. Julian

THE UNIVERSITY OF LINCOLNSHIRE AND
HUMBERSIDE
(University of Humberside founded 1992; re-organized
1996)
Humberside Campus: Cottingham Road, Hull HU6 7RT
Tel 01482-440550
Lincoln Campus: Lincoln LN2 4YF
Tel 01522-882000
Full-time students (1995–6), 11,410
Chancellor, Dr J. H. Hooper, CBE
Vice-Chancellor, Prof. R. P. King
Registrar, F. S. Marks
Secretary, Ms M. Harries-Jenkins

THE UNIVERSITY OF LIVERPOOL (1903)
Senate House, Abercromby Square, Liverpool L69 3BX
Tel 0151-794 2010
Full-time students (1995–6), 12,993
Chancellor, The Lord Owen, CH, PC
Vice-Chancellor, Prof. P. N. Love, CBE
Registrar and Secretary, M. D. Carr

LIVERPOOL JOHN MOORES UNIVERSITY (1992)
Rodney House, 70 Mount Pleasant, Liverpool L3 5UX
Tel 0151-231 2121
Full-time students (1995–6), 14,825
Chancellor, J. Moores, CBE
Vice-Chancellor, Prof. P. Toyne
Registrar and Secretary, Ms A. Wild

THE UNIVERSITY OF LONDON (1836)
Senate House, Malet Street, London WCIE 7HU
Tel 0171-636 8000
Internal students (1995–6), 79,230, External students, 22,116
Visitor, HM The Queen in Council
Chancellor, HRH The Princess Royal, KG, GCVO, FRS (1981)
Vice-Chancellor, Prof. A. Rutherford, CBE
Chairman of the Council, The Lord Woolf, PC
Chairman of Convocation, Prof. Sir William Taylor, CBE

COLLEGES OF THE UNIVERSITY
BIRKBECK COLLEGE, Malet Street, London
WCIE 7HX. *Master*, The Baroness Blackstone, PH.D.
CHARING CROSS AND WESTMINSTER MEDICAL SCHOOL,
The Reynolds Building, St Dunstan's Road, London
W6 8RP. *Dean*, Prof. R. M. Greenhalgh, FRCS
GOLDSMITHS COLLEGE, Lewisham Way, New Cross,
London SE14 6NW. *Warden*, Prof. K. J. Gregory, PH.D.
HEYTHROP COLLEGE, Kensington Square, London
W8 5HQ. *Principal*, C. J. Moss, D.phil.
IMPERIAL COLLEGE OF SCIENCE, TECHNOLOGY AND
MEDICINE (includes St Mary's Hospital Medical
School), South Kensington, London SW7 2AZ. *Rector*,
Prof. Sir Ronald Oxburgh, KBE, FRS
INSTITUTE OF CANCER RESEARCH, Royal Cancer
Hospital, Chester Beatty Laboratories, 17A Onslow
Gardens, London SW7 3AL. *Chief Executive*, Prof.
P. B. Garland, PH.D., FRSE
INSTITUTE OF EDUCATION, 20 Bedford Way, London
WCIH OAL. *Director*, Prof. P. Mortimore
KING'S COLLEGE LONDON (includes King's College
School of Medicine and Dentistry), Strand, London
WC2R 2LS. *Principal*, Prof. A. Lucas, PH.D.
Associated Institute:
Institute of Psychiatry, De Crespigny Park, Denmark Hill,
London SE5 8AF. *Dean*, Prof. S. Checkley
LONDON BUSINESS SCHOOL, Sussex Place, Regent's Park,
London NWI 4SA. *Principal*, Prof. G. S. Bain, D.phil.
THE LONDON HOSPITAL MEDICAL COLLEGE, Turner
Street, London EI 2AD. *Dean*, Prof. Sir Colin Berry,
FRCPath.
LONDON SCHOOL OF ECONOMICS AND POLITICAL
SCIENCE, Houghton Street, London WC2A 2AE. *Director*,
J. M. Ashworth, PH.D., D.SC.
LONDON SCHOOL OF HYGIENE AND TROPICAL
MEDICINE, Keppel Street, London WCIE 7HT. *Dean*,
Prof. H. Spencer
QUEEN MARY AND WESTFIELD COLLEGE (incorporating
St Bartholomew's and the Royal London School of
Medicine and Dentistry), Mile End Road, London
EI 4NS. *Principal*, Prof. G. Zellick, PH.D.
ROYAL FREE HOSPITAL SCHOOL OF MEDICINE, Rowland
Hill Street, London NW3 2PF. *Dean*, Prof. A. J.
Zuckerman, MD, FRCP
ROYAL HOLLOWAY, Egham Hill, Egham, Surrey TW20
OEX. *Principal*, Prof. N. Gowar, M.phil.
ROYAL POSTGRADUATE MEDICAL SCHOOL,
Hammersmith Hospital, Du Cane Road, London
WI2 7HT. *Dean*, Prof. Sir Colin Dollery, FRCP

ROYAL VETERINARY COLLEGE, Royal College Street,
London NWI OTU. *Principal and Dean*, Prof. L. E. Lanyon,
PH.D.
ST BARTHOLOMEW'S AND THE ROYAL LONDON SCHOOL
OF MEDICINE AND DENTISTRY, *see* Queen Mary and
Westfield College
ST GEORGE'S HOSPITAL MEDICAL SCHOOL, Cranmer
Terrace, London SW17 ORE. *Dean*, Prof. R. Boyd
SCHOOL OF ORIENTAL AND AFRICAN STUDIES,
Thornhaugh Street, Russell Square, London
WCIH OXG. *Director*, Sir Tim Lankester, KCB
SCHOOL OF PHARMACY, 29–39 Brunswick Square,
London WCIN IAX. *Dean*, Prof. A. T. Florence, PH.D.,
FRSE
SCHOOL OF SLAVONIC AND EAST EUROPEAN STUDIES,
Senate House, Malet Street, London WCIE 7HU. *Director*,
Prof. M. A. Branch, PH.D.
UNITED MEDICAL AND DENTAL SCHOOLS OF GUY'S AND
ST THOMAS' HOSPITALS, Guy's, London Bridge,
London SEI 9RT; St Thomas', Lambeth Palace Road,
London SEI 7EH. *Principal*, Prof. C. Chantler, FRCP
UNIVERSITY COLLEGE LONDON (including UCL
Medical School), Gower Street, London
WCIE 6BT. *Provost*, Sir Derek Roberts, CBE, FRS
WYE COLLEGE, Wye, Near Ashford, Kent
TN25 5AH. *Principal*, Prof. J. H. D. Prescott, PH.D.

SCHOOL OF ADVANCED STUDY
Senate House, Malet Street, London WCIE 7HU. *Dean*, Prof.
T. C. Daintith
Comprises:
INSTITUTE OF ADVANCED LEGAL STUDIES, Charles
Clore House, 17 Russell Square, London
WCIB 5DR. *Director*, Prof. B. A. K. Rider
INSTITUTE OF CLASSICAL STUDIES, 31–34 Gordon
Square, London WCIH OPY. *Director*, Prof.
R. R. K. Sorabji, FBA
INSTITUTE OF COMMONWEALTH STUDIES, 27–28 Russell
Square, London WCIB 5DS. *Director*, Prof. J. Manor
INSTITUTE OF GERMANIC STUDIES, 29 Russell Square,
London WCIB 5DP. *Hon. Director*, E. M. Batley
INSTITUTE OF HISTORICAL RESEARCH, Senate House,
Malet Street, London WCIE 7HU. *Director*, Prof.
P. K. O'Brien, D.phil.
INSTITUTE OF LATIN AMERICAN STUDIES, 31 Tavistock
Square, London WCIH 9HA. *Director*, Prof. V. G. Bulmer-
Thomas, D.phil.
INSTITUTE OF ROMANCE STUDIES, Senate House, Malet
Street, London WCIE 7HU. *Hon. Director*, Prof. A. Lavers,
PH.D.
INSTITUTE OF UNITED STATES STUDIES, Senate House,
Malet Street, London WCIE 7HU. *Director*, Prof.
G. L. McDowell, PH.D.
WARBURG INSTITUTE, Woburn Square, London
WCIH OAB. *Director*, Prof. C. N. J. Mann, PH.D.

INSTITUTES AND ASSOCIATE INSTITUTIONS
BRITISH INSTITUTE IN PARIS, 9–11 rue de Constantine,
75340 Paris, Cedex 07, France. *Director*, Prof.
C. L. Campos, PH.D. *London office*: Senate House, Malet
Street, London WCIE 7HU
CENTRE FOR DEFENCE STUDIES, King's College London,
Strand, London WC2R 2LS. *Director*, Prof. L. Freedman
CENTRE FOR ENGLISH STUDIES, Senate House, Malet
Street, London WCIE 7HU. *Director*, Dr W. L. Chernaik
COURTAULD INSTITUTE OF ART, North Block, Somerset
House, Strand, London WC2R ORN. *Director*, Prof. E. C.
Fernie
INSTITUTE OF ZOOLOGY, Royal Zoological Society,
Regent's Park, London NWI 4RY. *Director*, Prof. M.
Gosling.

JEWS' COLLEGE, 44A Albert Road, London NW4 2SJ.
Principal, Rabbi Dr D. Sinclair
ROYAL ACADEMY OF MUSIC, Marylebone Road, London
NWI 5HT. *Principal,* Prof. C. Price
ROYAL COLLEGE OF MUSIC, Prince Consort Road,
London SW7 2BS. *Director,* Ms J. Ritterman, PH.D.
TRINITY COLLEGE OF MUSIC, 11–13 Mandeville Place,
London WIM 6AQ. *Principal,* G. Henderson
UNIVERSITY MARINE BIOLOGICAL STATION MILLPORT,
Isle of Cumbrae, Scotland KA28 OEG. *Director,* Prof.
J. Davenport, PH.D., D.SC., FRSE

LONDON GUILDHALL UNIVERSITY (1993)
133 Whitechapel High Street, London EI 7QA
Tel 0171-320 1000
Full-time students (1995–6), 13,000
Patron, HRH The Prince Philip, Duke of Edinburgh, KG,
    KT, OM, GBE, PC, FRS
Provost, Prof. R. Floud, D.phil.
Academic Registrar, Ms J. Grinstead
Secretary, N. Maude

LOUGHBOROUGH UNIVERSITY OF
TECHNOLOGY (1966)
Loughborough, Leics LEII 3TU
Tel 01509-263171
Full-time students (1994–5), 9,963
Chancellor, Sir Denis Rooke, CBE, FRS, FEng (1989)
Vice-Chancellor, Prof. D.Wallace, PH.D., FRS, FRSE
Registrar, D. E. Fletcher, PH.D.
Academic Secretary, N. A. McHard

THE UNIVERSITY OF LUTON (1993)
(formerly Luton College of Higher Education)
Park Square, Luton LUI 3JU
Tel 01582-34111
Full-time students (1995–6), 9,000
Chancellor, Sir David Plastow
Vice-Chancellor, Dr A. Wood
Head of Admissions, S. Kendall

THE UNIVERSITY OF MANCHESTER
(Founded 1851; re-organized 1880 and 1903)
Oxford Road, Manchester MI3 9PL
Tel: 0161-275 2000
Full-time students (1995–6), 16,569
Chancellor, The Lord Flowers, FRS
Vice-Chancellor, Prof. M. B. Harris, CBE, PH.D.
Registrar and Secretary, E. Newcomb
Academic Secretary, D. A. Richardson

UNIVERSITY OF MANCHESTER
INSTITUTE OF SCIENCE AND
TECHNOLOGY (1824)
PO Box 88, Manchester M60 IQD
Tel 0161-236 3311
Full-time students (1995–6), 6,000
Chancellor, Prof. Sir Roland Smith, PH.D. (1995)
Vice-Chancellor, Prof. R. F. Boucher, FEng.
Registrar and Secretary, P. C. C. Stephenson

MANCHESTER METROPOLITAN
UNIVERSITY (1992)
All Saints, Manchester MI5 6BH
Tel 0161-247 2000
Full-time students (1995–6), 22,000
Chancellor, The Duke of Westminster, OBE, TD
Vice-Chancellor, Sir Kenneth Green
Academic Registrar, J. Karczewski-Slowikowski
Secretary, T. A. Hendley

MIDDLESEX UNIVERSITY (1992)
White Hart Lane, London NI7 8HR
Tel 0181-362 5000
Full-time students (1994–5), 16,084
Chancellor, The Baroness Platt of Writtle
Vice-Chancellor, vacant
Registrar and Secretary, G. Jones

NAPIER UNIVERSITY (1992)
219 Colinton Road, Edinburgh EHI4 IDJ
Tel 0131-444 2266
Full-time students (1995–6), 7,753
Chancellor, The Lord Younger of Prestwick, KCVO, TD, PC,
    FRSE
Vice-Chancellor, Prof. J. Mavor
Secretary and Registrar, I. J. Miller

THE UNIVERSITY OF NEWCASTLE UPON
TYNE
(Founded 1852; re-organized 1908, 1937 and 1963)
6 Kensington Terrace, Newcastle upon Tyne NEI 7RU
Tel 0191-222 6000
Full-time students (1995–6), 12,703
Chancellor, The Viscount Ridley, KG, GCVO, TD (1989)
Vice-Chancellor, J. R. G. Wright
Registrar, D. E. T. Nicholson

THE UNIVERSITY OF NORTH LONDON
(1992)
166–220 Holloway Road, London N7 8DB
Tel 0171-607 2789
Full-time students (1995–6), 10,710
Vice-Chancellor, B. Roper
Academic Registrar, Dr M. Storey
Secretary, J. McParland

THE UNIVERSITY OF NORTHUMBRIA AT
NEWCASTLE (1992)
Ellison Place, Newcastle upon Tyne NEI 8ST
Tel 0191-232 6002
Full-time students (1995–6), 16,656
Chancellor, The Lord Glenamara, CH, PC (1984)
Vice-Chancellor, Prof. G. Smith
Registrar, Mrs C. Penna
Secretary, R. A. Bott

THE UNIVERSITY OF NOTTINGHAM (1948)
University Park, Nottingham NG7 2RD
Tel 0115-951 5151
Full-time students (1995–6), 13,425
Chancellor, Sir Ron Dearing, CB, FEng. (1993)
Vice-Chancellor, Prof. Sir Colin Campbell
Registrar, D. J. Allen

NOTTINGHAM TRENT UNIVERSITY (1992)
Burton Street, Nottingham NGI 4BU
Tel 0115-941 8418
Full-time students (1995–6), 18,213
Vice-Chancellor, Prof. R. Cowell, PH.D.
Academic Registrar, D. W. Samson
Secretary, S. Smith

THE UNIVERSITY OF OXFORD
University Offices, Wellington Square, Oxford OXI 2JD
Tel 01865-270001
Students in residence (1995–6), 15,300

UNIVERSITY OFFICERS, ETC.

Chancellor, The Lord Jenkins of Hillhead, OM, PC (*Balliol*),
    elected 1987

High Steward, The Lord Goff of Chieveley, PC (*Lincoln* and *New College*), *elected* 1990
Vice-Chancellor, Dr P. M. North, CBE, QC, FBA (*Jesus*), *elected* 1993
Proctors, Dr J. R. T. Garfitt (*Magdalen*); Dr J. C. N. Horder (*Worcester*), *elected* 1996
Assessor, Dr N. G. Bowles (*St Anne's*), *elected* 1996
Public Orator, J. Griffin (*Balliol*), *elected* 1992
Bodley's Librarian, D. G. Vaisey (*Exeter*), *elected* 1986
Keeper of Archives, D. G. Vaisey (*Exeter*), *elected* 1995
Director of the Ashmolean Museum, Prof. C. J. White, CVO (*Worcester*), *elected* 1985
Registrar of the University, A. J. Dorey, D.phil. (*Linacre*), *elected* 1979
Surveyor to the University, P. M. R. Hill, *elected* 1993
Secretary of Faculties, A. P. Weale (*Worcester*), *elected* 1984
Secretary of the Chest, J. R. Clements, *elected* 1995
Deputy Registrar (Administration), P. W. Jones (*Green*), *elected* 1991

OXFORD COLLEGES AND HALLS
with dates of foundation

ALL SOULS (1438), *Warden*, Prof. J. Davis (1994)
BALLIOL (1263), *Master*, C. R. Lucas, D.phil. (1994)
BRASENOSE (1509), *Principal*, The Lord Windlesham, CVO, PC (1989)
CHRIST CHURCH (1546), *Dean*, Very Revd J. H. Drury (1991)
CORPUS CHRISTI (1517), *President*, Prof. Sir Keith Thomas, FBA (1986)
EXETER (1314), *Rector*, Prof. M. Butler (1994)
GREEN (1979), *Warden*, Sir Crispin Tickell, GCMG, KCVO (1990)
HERTFORD (1874), *Principal*, Sir Walter Bodmer, FRS (1996)
JESUS (1571), *Principal*, Dr P. M. North, CBE, FBA (1984)
KEBLE (1868), *Warden*, A. Cameron, FBA, FSA (1994)
KELLOG (1990), *President*, G. P. Thomas, PH.D. (1990)
LADY MARGARET HALL (1878), *Principal*, Sir Brian Fall, KCMG (1995)
LINACRE (1962), *Principal*, Dr P. A. Slack (1996)
LINCOLN (1427), *Rector*, E. K. Anderson, FRSE (1994)
MAGDALEN (1458), *President*, A. D. Smith, CBE (1988)
MANSFIELD (1886), *Principal*, D. I. Marquand (1996)
MERTON (1264), *Warden*, Dr. J Rawson, FBA (1994)
NEW COLLEGE (1379), *Warden*, Prof. A. J. Ryan (1996)
NUFFIELD (1937), *Warden*, Prof. A. Atkinson, FBA (1994)
ORIEL (1326), *Provost*, E. W. Nicholson, DD, FBA (1990)
PEMBROKE (1624), *Master*, Prof. R. Stevens, DCL (1993)
QUEEN'S (1340), *Provost*, G. Marshall (1993)
ST ANNE'S (1952) (originally Society of Oxford Home-Students (1879)), *Principal*, Mrs R. L. Deech (1991)
ST ANTONY'S (1950), *Warden*, The Lord Dahrendorf, KBE, PH.D., FBA (1987)
ST CATHERINE'S (1962), *Master*, The Lord Plant of Highfield (1994)
ST CROSS (1965), *Master*, R. C. Repp, D.phil. (1987)
ST EDMUND HALL (*c.*1278), *Principal*, His Hon. Stephen Tumin (1996)
*ST HILDA'S (1893), *Principal*, Miss E. Llewellyn-Smith, CB (1990)
ST HUGH'S (1886), *Principal*, D. Wood, QC (1991)
ST JOHN'S (1555), *President*, W. Hayes, D.phil. (1987)
ST PETER'S (1929), *Master*, J. P. Barron, D.phil. (1991)
SOMERVILLE (1879), *Principal*, Dr F. Caldicott (1996)
TEMPLETON (1965), *President*, Dr M. van Clemm (1996)

TRINITY (1554), *President*, The Hon. Michael J. Beloff, QC (1996)
UNIVERSITY (1249), *Master*, W. J. Albery, D.phil., FRS (1989)
WADHAM (1612), *Warden*, J. S. Flemming (1993)
WOLFSON (1966), *President*, Sir David Smith, D.phil. (1994)
WORCESTER (1714), *Provost*, R. G. Smethurst (1991)

BLACKFRIARS (1921), *Regent*, Revd B. E. A. Davies (1994)
CAMPION HALL (1896), *Master*, Revd J. A. Munitiz (1989)
GREYFRIARS (1910), *Warden*, Revd M. W. Sheehan, D.phil. (1990)
MANCHESTER (1786), *Principal*, Revd R. Waller, PH.D. (1990)
REGENT'S PARK (1810), *Principal*, Revd P. S. Fiddes, D.phil. (1989)
ST BENET'S HALL (1897), *Master*, Revd H. Wansbrough, OSB (1991)

OXFORD BROOKES UNIVERSITY (1993)
Headington, Oxford OX3 0BP
Tel 01865-741111
Full-time students (1995–6), 8,000
Chancellor, Ms H. Kennedy, QC
Vice-Chancellor, Dr C. Booth
Deputy Vice-Chancellor, Corporate Services, B. Summers
Academic Secretary, Ms L. Winders

THE UNIVERSITY OF PAISLEY (1992)
(formerly Paisley College of Technology)
High Street, Paisley PA1 2BE
Tel 0141-848 3000
Full-time students (1993–4), 6,162
Chancellor, Sir Robert Easton, CBE
Vice-Chancellor, Prof. R. W. Shaw
Registrar, D. Rigg
Secretary, J. Fraser

THE UNIVERSITY OF PLYMOUTH (1992)
Drake Circus, Plymouth PL4 8AA
Tel 01752-600600
Full-time students (1995–6), 18,305
Vice-Chancellor, Prof. J. Bull
Registrar, Dr C. J. Sparrow

THE UNIVERSITY OF PORTSMOUTH (1992)
University House, Winston Churchill Avenue, Portsmouth PO1 2UP
Tel 01705-876543
Full-time students (1995–6), 14,612
Chancellor, The Lord Palumbo
Vice-Chancellor (acting), Dr M. Bateman
Academic Registrar, A. Rees
Secretary, R. Moore

THE QUEEN'S UNIVERSITY OF BELFAST (1908)
Belfast BT7 1NN
Tel 01232-245133
Full-time students (1994–5), 11,000
Chancellor, Sir David Orr
Vice-Chancellor, Sir Gordon Beveridge, PH.D., FRSE
Academic Secretary, Dr G. Baird
Administrative Secretary, D. Wilson

THE UNIVERSITY OF READING (1926)
Whiteknights, PO Box 217, Reading RG6 2AH
Tel 0118-987 5123
Full-time students (1995–6), 11,000

* College for women only

Chancellor, The Lord Carrington, KG, GCMG, CH, MC, PC (1992)
Vice-Chancellor, Prof. R. Williams
Registrar, D. C. R. Frampton

THE ROBERT GORDON UNIVERSITY (1992)
Schoolhill, Aberdeen AB10 1FR
Tel 01224-262210
Full-time students (1995–6), 6,500
Chancellor, Sir Bob Reid (1993)
Vice-Chancellor, Dr D. A. Kennedy
Secretary, D. Caldwell

THE UNIVERSITY OF ST ANDREWS (1411)
College Gate, St Andrews KY16 9AJ
Tel 01334-476161
Full-time students (1995–6), 5,930
Chancellor, Sir Kenneth Dover, D.Litt., FRSE, FBA (1981)
Vice-Chancellor, Prof. S. Arnott, CBE, SC.D., FRS, FRSE
Secretary of Court, D. J. Corner
Rector, D. Findlay, QC (1994–7)

THE UNIVERSITY OF SALFORD (1967)
Salford M5 4WT
Tel 0161-745 5000
Full-time students (1995–6), 13,000
Chancellor, Sir Walter Bodmer, PH.D., FRS
Vice-Chancellor, Prof. T. M. Husband, PH.D., FEng.
Registrar, M. D. Winton, PH.D.

THE UNIVERSITY OF SHEFFIELD (1905)
8 Palmerston Road, Sheffield S10 2TE
Tel 0114-276 8555
Full-time students (1995–6), 18,400
Chancellor, The Lord Dainton, PH.D., SC.D., FRS (1979)
Vice-Chancellor, Prof. G. G. Roberts, PH.D., D.SC., FRS
Registrar and Secretary, J. S. Padley, PH.D.

SHEFFIELD HALLAM UNIVERSITY (1992)
Pond Street, Sheffield S1 1WB
Tel 0114-272 0911
Full-time students (1995–6), 20,000
Chancellor, Sir Bryan Nicholson
Vice-Chancellor, J. Stoddart, CBE
Registrar, Ms J. Tory
Secretary, Ms S. Neocosmos

THE UNIVERSITY OF SOUTHAMPTON (1952)
Highfield, Southampton SO17 1BJ
Tel 01703-595000
Full-time students (1995–6), 12,500
Chancellor, The Earl of Selbourne, KBE, FRS
Vice-Chancellor, Prof. H. Newby, CBE, PH.D.
Secretary and Registrar, J. F. D. Lauwerys
Academic Registrar, R. Knight

SOUTH BANK UNIVERSITY (1992)
103 Borough Road, London SE1 0AA
Tel 0171-898 8989
Full-time students (1994–5), 15,000
Chancellor, C. McLaren
Vice-Chancellor, Prof. G. Bernbaum
Registrar, R. Phillips
Secretary, Mrs L. Gander

STAFFORDSHIRE UNIVERSITY (1992)
College Road, Stoke-on-Trent ST4 2DE
Tel 01782-294000
Full-time students (1995–6), 13,223

Chancellor, The Lord Ashley of Stoke, CH, PC
Vice-Chancellor, Prof. C. E. King, PH.D.
Academic Registrar, Miss F. Francis
Secretary, K. Sproston

THE UNIVERSITY OF STIRLING (1967)
Stirling FK9 4LA
Tel 01786-467055
Full-time students (1995–6), 5,300
Chancellor, The Lord Balfour of Burleigh, FRSE (1988)
Vice-Chancellor, Prof. A. Miller, PH.D., FRSE
Academic Registrar, D. Wood
Secretary, K. J. Clarke

THE UNIVERSITY OF STRATHCLYDE (1964)
McCance Building, John Anderson Campus, Glasgow G1 1XQ
Tel 0141-552 4400
Full-time students (1995–6), 14,100
Chancellor, The Lord Tombs, LL D, D.SC., FEng. (1990)
Vice-Chancellor, Prof. J. P. Arbuthnott, SC.D., FRSE
Secretary, P. W. A. West

THE UNIVERSITY OF SUNDERLAND (1992)
Langham Tower, Ryhope Road, Sunderland SR2 7EE
Tel 0191-515 2000
Full-time students (1994–5), 12,588
Vice-Chancellor, Ms A. Wright, PH.D.
Academic Registrar, S. Porteous
Secretary, J. D. Pacey

THE UNIVERSITY OF SURREY (1966)
Guildford, Surrey GU2 5XH
Tel 01483-300800
Full-time students (1995–6), 7,500
Chancellor, HRH The Duke of Kent, KG, GCMG, GCVO (1977)
Vice-Chancellor, Prof. R. J. Dowling, PH.D., FEng.
Secretary and Registrar, H. W. B. Davies

THE UNIVERSITY OF SUSSEX (1961)
Falmer, Brighton BN1 9RH
Tel 01273-606755
Full-time students (1995–6), 8,731
Chancellor, The Duke of Richmond and Gordon (1985)
Vice-Chancellor, Prof. G. Conway, PH.D.
Registrar and Secretary, B. Gooch

THE UNIVERSITY OF TEESSIDE (1992)
Middlesbrough TS1 3BA
Tel 01642-218121
Full-time students (1994–5), 9,700
Chancellor, Sir Leon Brittan
Vice-Chancellor, Prof. D. Fraser
University Secretary, J. M. McClintock

THAMES VALLEY UNIVERSITY (1992)
St Mary's Road, Ealing, London W5 5RF
Tel 0181-579 5000
Full-time students (1995–6), 11,500
Chancellor, P. Hamlyn, CBE
Vice-Chancellor, M. Fitzgerald, PH.D.
Head of Registry, P. Head
Secretary, Ms M. Joyce

THE UNIVERSITY OF ULSTER (1984)
(Amalgamation of New University of Ulster and Ulster Polytechnic)
Cromore Road, Coleraine BT52 1SA
Tel 01265-44141
Full-time students (1995–6), 13,548

Chancellor, Rabbi J. Neuberger
Vice-Chancellor, Prof. Sir Trevor Smith
Academic Registrar, K. Miller, ph.d.

THE UNIVERSITY OF WALES (1893)
King Edward VII Avenue, Cathays Park, Cardiff CF1 3NS
Tel 01222-382656
Full-time students (1995–6), 45,000
Chancellor, HRH The Prince of Wales, KG, KT, GCB, PC (1976)
Senior Vice-Chancellor, Prof. K. Robbins, D.Litt., D.Phil., FRSE
Secretary-General, J. D. Pritchard

COLLEGES AND INSTITUTIONS
UNIVERSITY COLLEGE OF NORTH WALES, Bangor LL57 2DG. Tel: 01248-351151. *Vice-Chancellor*, Prof. H. R. Evans, ph.d., FEng. (1995)
UNIVERSITY COLLEGE OF WALES, ABERYSTWYTH, Old College, King Street, Aberystwyth SY23 2AX. Tel: 01970-623111. *Vice-Chancellor*, Prof. D. Llwyd Morgan, D.Phil. (1995)
UNIVERSITY OF WALES, CARDIFF, PO Box 920, Cardiff CF1 3XP. Tel: 01222-874000. *Vice-Chancellor*, Prof. E. B. Smith, ph.d., D.Sc. (1993)
UNIVERSITY OF WALES COLLEGE, NEWPORT, College Crescent, Caerleon NP6 1YG. Tel: 01633-432020. *Principal*, Prof. K. J. Overshott, ph.d.
UNIVERSITY OF WALES COLLEGE OF MEDICINE, Heath Park, Cardiff CF4 4XN. Tel: 01222-747747. *Vice-Chancellor*, Prof. I. R. Cameron, FRCP (1994)
UNIVERSITY OF WALES INSTITUTE, CARDIFF, Llandaff Centre, Western Avenue, Cardiff CF5 2SG. Tel: 01222-551111. *Principal*, J. D. Winslow
UNIVERSITY OF WALES, LAMPETER, Lampeter SA48 7ED. Tel: 01570-422351. *Principal*, Prof. K. Robbins, D.Litt., D.Phil., FRSE (1992)
UNIVERSITY OF WALES, SWANSEA, Singleton Park, Swansea SA2 8PP. Tel: 01792-205678. *Vice-Chancellor*, Prof. R. H. Williams, ph.d., FRS (1994)

THE UNIVERSITY OF WARWICK (1965)
Coventry CV4 7AL
Tel 01203-523523
Full-time students (1995–6), 13,300
Chancellor, Sir Shridath Surendranath Ramphal, GCMG, QC (1989)
Vice-Chancellor, Prof. Sir Brian Follett, FRS, D.Sc.
Registrar, M. L. Shattock, OBE

THE UNIVERSITY OF WESTMINSTER (1992)
309 Regent Street, London W1R 8AL
Tel 0171-911 5000
Full-time students (1995–6), 9,000
Rector, Dr G. M. Copland
Deputy-Rector, A. Dart
Registrar, Ms J. Hopkinson

THE UNIVERSITY OF THE WEST OF ENGLAND, BRISTOL (BRISTOL UWE) (1992)
Coldharbour Lane, Bristol BS16 1QY
Tel 0117-965 6261
Full-time students (1995–6), 13,622
Chancellor, Dame Elizabeth Butler-Sloss, DBE
Vice-Chancellor, A. C. Morris
Academic Registrar, Ms M. J. Carter
Secretary, W. Evans

THE UNIVERSITY OF WOLVERHAMPTON (1992)
Wulfruna Street, Wolverhampton WV1 1SB
Tel 01902-321000
Full-time students (1995–6), 17,296
Chancellor, The Earl of Shrewsbury and Talbot
Vice-Chancellor, Prof. M. J. Harrison

THE UNIVERSITY OF YORK (1963)
Heslington, York YO1 5DD
Tel 01904-430000
Full-time students (1995–6), 5,600
Chancellor, Dame Janet Baker, CH, DBE
Vice-Chancellor, Prof. R. U. Cooke, ph.d.
Registrar, D. J. Foster

THE OPEN UNIVERSITY (1969)
Walton Hall, Milton Keynes MK7 6AA
Tel 01908-274066
Students and clients (1996), c.200,000
Tuition by correspondence linked with special radio and television programmes, video and audio cassettes, computing, residential schools and a locally-based tutorial and counselling service. The University awards degrees of BA, B.Sc., B.Phil., MA, MBA, MBA (Technology), M.Eng., M.Sc., M.Phil., Ph.D., D.Ed., D.Sc. and D.Litt. There are faculties and schools of arts; education; health and social welfare; management; mathematics and computing; modern languages; science; social sciences; technology; and a wide range of qualification courses and study packs.
Chancellor, The Rt. Hon. Betty Boothroyd, MP
Vice-Chancellor, Sir John Daniel
Secretary, D. J. Clinch

THE ROYAL COLLEGE OF ART (1837)
Kensington Gore, London SW7 2EU
Tel 0171-584 5020
Under royal charter (1967) the Royal College of Art grants the degrees of Doctor, Doctor of Philosophy, Master of Philosophy and Master of Arts.
Students (1995–6), 770 (all postgraduate)
Provost, The Earl of Snowdon, GCVO
Rector and Vice-Provost, Prof. C. Frayling
Registrar, A. Selby

COLLEGES

It is not possible to name here all the colleges offering courses of higher or further education. The list does not include colleges forming part of a polytechnic or a university. The English colleges that follow are confined to those in the Higher Education Funding Council for England sector; there are many more colleges in England providing higher education courses, some with HEFCFE funding.

The list of colleges in Wales, Scotland and Northern Ireland includes institutions providing at least one full-time course leading to a first degree granted by an accredited validating body.

ENGLAND

BATH COLLEGE OF HIGHER EDUCATION, Newton Park, Newton St Loe, Bath BA2 9BN. Tel: 01225-873701. *Director*, F. Morgan
BISHOP GROSSETESTE COLLEGE, Lincoln LN1 3DY. Tel: 01522-527347. *Principal*, Ms E. Baker

BOLTON INSTITUTE OF HIGHER EDUCATION, Deane Road, Bolton BL3 5AB. Tel: 01204-528851. *Principal,* R. Oxtoby, PH.D.

BRETTON HALL, West Bretton, Wakefield, W. Yorks WF4 4LG. Tel: 01924-830261. *Principal,* Prof. G. H. Bell

BUCKINGHAMSHIRE COLLEGE, Queen Alexandra Road, High Wycombe, Bucks HP11 2JZ. Tel: 01494-522141. *Director,* Prof. P. B. Mogford

CANTERBURY CHRIST CHURCH COLLEGE, North Holmes Road, Canterbury, Kent CT1 1QU. Tel: 01227-767700. *Principal,* M. H. A. Berry, TD

THE CENTRAL SCHOOL OF SPEECH AND DRAMA, Embassy Theatre, Eton Avenue, London NW3 3HY. Tel: 0171-722 8183. *Principal,* Prof. R. S. Fowler, FRSA

CHELTENHAM AND GLOUCESTER COLLEGE OF HIGHER EDUCATION, PO Box 220, The Park, Cheltenham, Glos GL50 2QF. Tel: 01242-532700. *Director,* Miss J. O. Trotter, OBE

CHICHESTER INSTITUTE OF HIGHER EDUCATION, College Lane, Chichester, West Sussex PO19 4PE. Tel: 01243-816000. *Director,* P. E. D. Robinson

COLLEGE OF ST MARK AND ST JOHN, Derriford Road, Plymouth PL6 8BH. Tel: 01752-777188. *Principal,* Dr W. J. Rea

DARTINGTON COLLEGE OF ARTS, Totnes, Devon TQ9 6EJ. Tel: 01803-862224. *Principal,* Prof. K. Thompson

EDGE HILL UNIVERSITY COLLEGE, St Helens Road, Ormskirk, Lancs L39 4QP. Tel: 01695-575171. *Director,* Dr. J. Cater

FALMOUTH COLLEGE OF ARTS, Woodlane, Falmouth, Cornwall TR11 4RA. Tel: 01326-211077. *Principal,* Prof. A. G. Livingston

HARPER ADAMS AGRICULTURAL COLLEGE, Newport, Shropshire TF10 8NB. Tel: 01952-820280. *Principal,* G. R. McConnell

HOMERTON COLLEGE, Cambridge CB2 2PH. Tel: 01223-507111. *Principal,* Mrs K. Pretty, PH.D.

INSTITUTE OF ADVANCED NURSING EDUCATION, Royal College of Nursing, 20 Cavendish Square, London W1M 0AB. Tel: 0171-409 3333. *Director,* Prof. A. Kitson

KENT INSTITUTE OF ART AND DESIGN, Oakwood Park, Maidstone ME16 8AG (*also* New Dover Road, Canterbury CT1 3AN; and Fort Pitt, Rochester ME1 1DZ). Tel: 01622-691471/757286. *Director,* Prof. V. Grylls

KING ALFRED'S COLLEGE OF HIGHER EDUCATION, Winchester SO22 4NR. Tel: 01962-841515. *Principal,* Prof. J. P. Dickinson

LIVERPOOL HOPE UNIVERSITY COLLEGE, Hope Park, Liverpool L16 9JD. Tel: 0151-737 3477. *Rector,* Prof. S. Lee

THE LONDON INSTITUTE, 65 Davies Street, London W1Y 2DA. Tel: 0171-514 6000. *Rector,* Sir William Stubbs Comprising:
Camberwell College of Arts, Peckham Road, London SE5 8UF
Central St Martins College of Art and Design, Southampton Row, London WC1B 4AP
Chelsea College of Art and Design, Manresa Road, London SW3 6LS
London College of Fashion, 20 John Prince's Street, London W1M 0BJ
London College of Printing and Distributive Trades, Elephant and Castle, London SE1 6SB

LOUGHBOROUGH COLLEGE OF ART AND DESIGN, Epinal Way, Loughborough, Leics LE11 3GE. Tel: 01509-261515. *Principal,* T. Kavanagh

LSU COLLEGE OF HIGHER EDUCATION, The Avenue, Southampton SO17 1BG. Tel: 01703-228761. *Principal,* Dr A. C. Chitnis

NENE COLLEGE, Park Campus, Boughton Green Road, Northampton NN2 7AL. Tel: 01604-735500. *Director,* S. M. Gaskell, PH.D.

NEWMAN COLLEGE, Genners Lane, Bartley Green, Birmingham B32 3NT. Tel: 0121-476 1181. *Principal,* Prof. B. Ray

ROEHAMPTON INSTITUTE LONDON, Senate House, Roehampton Lane, London SW15 5PU. Comprises Digby Stuart College, Froebel Institute College, Southlands College and Whitelands College. Tel: 0181-392 3000. *Rector,* Prof. S. C. Holt, PH.D.

ROSE BRUFORD COLLEGE, Lamorbey Park, Sidcup, Kent DA15 9DF. Tel: 0181-300 3024. *Principal,* R. Ely

ROYAL NORTHERN COLLEGE OF MUSIC, 124 Oxford Road, Manchester M13 9RD. Tel: 0161-273 6283. *Principal,* Prof. E. Gregson

SOUTHAMPTON INSTITUTE, East Park Terrace, Southampton SO14 0YN. Tel: 01703-319000. *Director,* Prof. D. G. Leyland

SURREY INSTITUTE OF ART AND DESIGN, Falkner Road, The Hart, Farnham, Surrey GU9 7DS. Tel: 01252-722441. *Director,* N. J. Taylor

TRINITY AND ALL SAINTS' COLLEGE, Brownberrie Lane, Horsforth, Leeds LS18 5HD. Tel: 0113-283 7100. *Principal,* Dr G. L. Turnbull

UNIVERSITY COLLEGE CHESTER, Cheyney Road, Chester CH1 4BJ. Tel: 01244-375444. *Principal,* Canon E. V. Binks

UNIVERSITY COLLEGE OF RIPON AND YORK ST JOHN, Lord Mayor's Walk, York YO3 7EX. Tel: 01904-656771. *Principal,* Prof. R. A. Butlin

UNIVERSITY COLLEGE OF S. MARTIN, Lancaster LA1 3JD. Tel: 01524-63446. *Principal,* D. Edynbry, PH.D.

UNIVERSITY COLLEGE SCARBOROUGH, Filey Road, Scarborough YO11 3AZ. Tel: 01723-362392. *Principal,* R. A. Withers, PH.D.

WESTHILL COLLEGE, Weoley Park Road, Selly Oak, Birmingham B29 6LL. Tel: 0121-472 7245. *Principal,* Dr J. G. Priestley

WESTMINSTER COLLEGE, Oxford OX2 9AT. Tel: 01865-247644. *Principal,* Revd Dr R. Ralph

WINCHESTER SCHOOL OF ART, Park Avenue, Winchester, Hants SO23 8DL. Tel: 01962-842500. *Head of School,* Prof. K. Crouan

WORCESTER COLLEGE OF HIGHER EDUCATION, Henwick Grove, Worcester WR2 6AJ. Tel: 01905-855000. *Principal,* Ms D. Urwin

WALES

THE NORTH-EAST WALES INSTITUTE OF HIGHER EDUCATION, Plas Coch, Mold Road, Wrexham LL11 2AW. Tel: 01978-290666. *Principal,* Prof. J. O. Williams, PH.D., D.SC.

SWANSEA INSTITUTE OF HIGHER EDUCATION, Townhill Road, Swansea SA2 0UT. Tel: 01792-481000. *Principal,* G. Stockdale, PH.D.

TRINITY COLLEGE, Carmarthen SA31 3EP. Tel: 01267-237971. *Principal,* D. C. Jones-Davies, OBE

WELSH COLLEGE OF MUSIC AND DRAMA, Castle Grounds, Cathays Park, Cardiff CF1 3ER. Tel: 01222-342854. *Principal,* E. Fivet

SCOTLAND

BELL COLLEGE OF TECHNOLOGY, Almada Street, Hamilton ML3 0JB. Tel: 01698-283100. *Principal,* J. Reid

DUMFRIES AND GALLOWAY COLLEGE, Heathhall, Dumfries DG1 3QZ. Tel: 01387-261261. *Principal,* J. W. M. Neil

FIFE COLLEGE OF FURTHER AND HIGHER EDUCATION,
St Brycedale Avenue, Kirkcaldy, Fife KY1 1EX. Tel:
01592-268591. *Principal,* D. A. Huckle
GLASGOW SCHOOL OF ART, 167 Renfrew Street, Glasgow
G3 6RQ. Tel: 0141-353 4500. *Director,* Prof. D. Cameron
NORTHERN COLLEGE OF EDUCATION, Hilton Place,
Aberdeen AB24 4FA. Tel: 01224-283500; Gardyne Road,
Dundee DD5 1NY. Tel: 01382-464000. *Principal,*
D. A. Adams
QUEEN MARGARET COLLEGE, Clerwood Terrace,
Edinburgh EH12 8TS. Tel: 0131-317 3000; Duke Street,
Edinburgh EH6 8HF. Tel: 0131-317 3355. *Principal,* Dr J.
Stringer
ROYAL SCOTTISH ACADEMY OF MUSIC AND DRAMA, 100
Renfrew Street, Glasgow G2 3DB. Tel: 0141-332 4101.
Principal, Dr P. Ledger, CBE, FRSE
SAC (SCOTTISH AGRICULTURAL COLLEGE), Central
Office, West Mains Road, Edinburgh EH9 3JG. Tel:
0131-535 4000. Campuses at Aberdeen, Auchincruive,
Ayr, and Edinburgh. *Principal,* Prof. P. C. Thomas
ST ANDREW'S COLLEGE OF EDUCATION, Duntocher
Road, Bearsden, Glasgow G61 4QA. Tel: 0141-943 1424.
Principal, Prof. B. J. McGettrick, OBE

NORTHERN IRELAND

EAST DOWN INSTITUTE OF FURTHER AND HIGHER
EDUCATION, Market Street, Downpatrick, Co. Down
BT30 6ND. Tel: 01396-615815. *Principal,* T. L. Place
ST MARY'S COLLEGE, 191 Falls Road, Belfast BT12 6FE.
Tel: 01232-327678. *Principal,* Revd M. O'Callaghan
STRANMILLIS COLLEGE, Stranmillis Road, Belfast
BT9 5DY. Tel: 01232-381271. *Principal,* Dr J. R. McMinn

ADULT AND CONTINUING EDUCATION

FORUM FOR THE ADVANCEMENT OF CONTINUING
EDUCATION (FACE), Department of Continuing
Education, University of Plymouth, Plymouth PL4 8AA.
Tel: 01752-232374. *Chair,* C. Bell
NATIONAL INSTITUTE OF ADULT CONTINUING
EDUCATION, 21 De Montfort Street, Leicester LE1 7GE.
Tel: 0116-255 1451. *Director,* A. Tuckett
NIACE CYMRU, 245 Western Avenue, Cardiff CF5 2YX.
Tel: 01222-265001. *Associate Director,* Ms A. Poole
NORTHERN IRELAND COUNCIL FOR ADULT EDUCATION,
c/o Western Education and Library Board, 1 Hospital
Road, Omagh, Co. Tyrone BT79 0AW. Tel: 01662-
240240. *Chairman,* J. Martin; *Education Officer,* Ms
T. Devine
THE RESIDENTIAL COLLEGES COMMITTEE, c/o Ruskin
College, Oxford OX1 2HE. Tel: 01865-556360. *Awards
Officer,* Mrs F. A. Bagchi
SCOTTISH COMMUNITY EDUCATION COUNCIL,
Rosebery House, 9 Haymarket Terrace, Edinburgh
EH12 5EZ. Tel: 0131-313 2488. *Chief Executive,*
C. McConnell
THE UNIVERSITIES ASSOCIATION FOR CONTINUING
EDUCATION, Department of Adult Continuing
Education, University of Leeds, Leeds LS2 9JT. Tel:
0113-233 3184. *Secretary,* Prof. R. Taylor
THE WORKERS' EDUCATIONAL ASSOCIATION, Temple
House, 17 Victoria Park Square, London E2 9PB. Tel:
0181-983 1515. *General Secretary,* R. Lochrie

LONG-TERM RESIDENTIAL COLLEGES FOR ADULT EDUCATION

COLEG HARLECH, Harlech, Gwynedd LL46 2PU. Tel:
01766-780363. *Warden,* J. W. England
CO-OPERATIVE COLLEGE, Stanford Hall, Loughborough,
Leics LE12 5QR. Tel: 01509-852333. *Chief Executive,*
R. Wildgusp
FIRCROFT COLLEGE, 1018 Bristol Road, Selly Oak,
Birmingham B29 6LH. Tel: 0121-472 0116. *Principal,*
K. Jackson
HILLCROFT COLLEGE, South Bank, Surbiton, Surrey
KT6 6DF. Tel: 0181-399 2688. For women only.
Principal, Ms J. Ireton
NEWBATTLE ABBEY COLLEGE, Dalkeith, Midlothian
EH22 3LL. Tel: 0131-663 1921. *Principal,* W. M. Conboy
NORTHERN COLLEGE, Wentworth Castle, Stainborough,
Barnsley, S. Yorks S75 3ET. Tel: 01226-776000. *Principal,*
Prof. R. H. Fryer
PLATER COLLEGE, Pullens Lane, Oxford OX3 0DT. Tel:
01865-741676. *Principal,* M. Blades
RUSKIN COLLEGE, Walton Street, Oxford OX1 2HE. Tel:
01865-54331. *Principal,* S. Yeo, D.Phil.

PROFESSIONAL EDUCATION
Excluding postgraduate study

The organizations listed below are those which, by
providing specialist training or conducting examinations,
control entry into a profession, or organizations responsible for maintaining a register of those with professional
qualifications in their sector.
  Many professions now have a largely graduate entry,
and possession of a first degree can exempt entrants from
certain of the professional examinations. Enquiries about
obtaining professional qualifications should be made to the
relevant professional organization(s). Details of higher
education providers of first degrees may be found in
University and College Entrance: Official Guide (available from
UCAS, *see* page 451).

ACCOUNTANCY

The main bodies granting membership on examination
after a period of practical work are:
INSTITUTE OF CHARTERED ACCOUNTANTS IN ENGLAND
AND WALES, Chartered Accountants' Hall, PO Box 433,
Moorgate Place, London EC2P 2BJ. Tel: 0171-920 8100.
Secretary and Chief Executive, A. J. Colquhoun
INSTITUTE OF CHARTERED ACCOUNTANTS OF
SCOTLAND, 27 Queen Street, Edinburgh EH2 1LA. Tel:
0131-225 5673. *Chief Executive,* P. W. Johnston
CHARTERED ASSOCIATION OF CERTIFIED
ACCOUNTANTS, 29 Lincoln's Inn Fields, London
WC2A 3EE. Tel: 0171-242 6855. *Chief Executive,* Mrs
A. L. Rose
CHARTERED INSTITUTE OF MANAGEMENT
ACCOUNTANTS, 63 Portland Place, London W1N 4AB.
Tel: 0171-637 2311. *Secretary,* J. S. Chester, OBE
CHARTERED INSTITUTE OF PUBLIC FINANCE AND
ACCOUNTANCY, 3 Robert Street, London WC2N 6BH.
Tel: 0171-543 5600. *Director,* N. P. Hepworth, OBE

ACTUARIAL SCIENCE

Two professional organizations grant qualifications after
examination:

INSTITUTE OF ACTUARIES, Staple Inn Hall, High Holborn, London WC1V 7QJ. Tel: 0171-242 0106. *Secretary-General*, A. G. Tait. Enquiries to Actuarial Education Service, Napier House, 4 Worcester Street, Oxford OX1 2AW. Tel: 01865-794144
FACULTY OF ACTUARIES IN SCOTLAND, 40–44 Thistle Street, Edinburgh EH2 1EN. Tel: 0131-220 4555. *Secretary*, W. W. Mair

ARCHITECTURE

The Education and Professional Development Committee of the Royal Institute of British Architects sets standards and guides the whole system of architectural education throughout the UK. The RIBA recognizes courses at 38 schools of architecture in the UK for exemption from their own examinations.
THE ROYAL INSTITUTE OF BRITISH ARCHITECTS, 66 Portland Place, London W1N 4AD. Tel: 0171-580 5533. *President*, O. Luder; *Director-General*, A. Reid, PH.D.

Schools of architecture outside the universities include:
THE ARCHITECTURAL ASSOCIATION, 34–36 Bedford Square, London WC1B 3ES. *Secretary*, E. A. Le Maistre
PRINCE OF WALES'S INSTITUTE OF ARCHITECTURE, 14–15 Gloucester Gate, London NW1 4HG. Tel: 0171-916 7380. *Director*, Dr R. John

BANKING

Professional organizations granting qualifications after examination are:
CHARTERED INSTITUTE OF BANKERS, 90 Bishopsgate, London EC2N 4AS. Tel: 0171-444 7111. *Chief Executive*, G. Shreeve
CHARTERED INSTITUTE OF BANKERS IN SCOTLAND, 19 Rutland Square, Edinburgh EH1 2DE. Tel: 0131-229 9869. *Chief Executive*, Dr C. W. Munn

BIOLOGY, CHEMISTRY, PHYSICS

Professional qualifications are awarded by:
INSTITUTE OF BIOLOGY, 20–22 Queensberry Place, London SW7 2DZ. Tel: 0171-581 8333. *President*, Prof. R. B. Heap; *General Secretary*, Dr R. H. Priestley
INSTITUTE OF PHYSICS, 76–78 Portland Place, London W1N 4AA. Tel: 0171-470 4800. *Chief Executive*, Dr A. D. W. Jones
ROYAL SOCIETY OF CHEMISTRY, Burlington House, Piccadilly, London W1V 0BN. Tel: 0171-437 8656. *President*, E. Able; *Secretary-General*, T. D. Inch, PH.D.

BUILDING

Examinations are conducted by:
CHARTERED INSTITUTE OF BUILDING, Englemere, King's Ride, Ascot, Berks SL5 8TB. Tel: 01344-23355. *Chief Executive*, K. Banbury
INSTITUTE OF BUILDING CONTROL, 21 High Street, Ewell, Epsom, Surrey KT17 1SB. Tel: 0181-393 6860. *Chief Executive*, Ms R. Raywood
INSTITUTE OF CLERKS OF WORKS OF GREAT BRITAIN, 41 The Mall, London W5 3TJ. Tel: 0181-579 2917/8. *Secretary*, A. P. Macnamara

BUSINESS, MANAGEMENT AND ADMINISTRATION

Professional bodies conducting training and/or examinations in business, administration, management or commerce include:

AMETS (ASSOCIATION FOR MANAGEMENT EDUCATION AND TRAINING IN SCOTLAND), c/o University of Stirling, Stirling FK9 4LA. Tel: 01786-450906. *Vice-Chairman*, M. Makower
THE ASSOCIATION OF MBAs, 15 Duncan Terrace, London N1 8BZ. Tel: 0171-837 3375. Publishes a directory giving details of MBA courses provided at UK institutions. *Director*, R. McCormick
CAM FOUNDATION (COMMUNICATIONS, ADVERTISING AND MARKETING EDUCATION FOUNDATION), Abford House, 15 Wilton Road, London SW1V 1NJ. Tel: 0171-828 7506. *General Secretary*, J. Knight
CHARTERED INSTITUTE OF HOUSING, Octavia House, Westwood Business Park, Westwood Way, Coventry CV4 8JP. Tel: 01203-694433. *Chief Executive*, Ms C. Laird
CHARTERED INSTITUTE OF MARKETING, Moor Hall, Cookham, Maidenhead, Berks SL6 9QH. Tel: 01628-427500. *Director-General*, S. Cuthbert
CHARTERED INSTITUTE OF PURCHASING AND SUPPLY, Easton House, Easton on the Hill, Stamford, Lincs PE9 3NZ. Tel: 01780-56777. *Director-General*, P. Thomson
CHARTERED INSTITUTE OF TRANSPORT, 80 Portland Place, London W1N 4DP. Tel: 0171-636 9952. *Director*, Mrs S. Gross
FACULTY OF SECRETARIES AND ADMINISTRATORS, Brightstowe, Catteshall Lane, Godalming, Surrey GU7 1LJ. Tel: 01483-454213. *Secretary*, Mrs D. M. Rummery
HENLEY MANAGEMENT COLLEGE, Greenlands, Henley-on-Thames, Oxon RG9 3AU. Tel: 01491-571454. *Principal*, Prof. R. Wild, PH.D., D.SC.
INSTITUTE OF ADMINISTRATIVE MANAGEMENT, 40 Chatsworth Parade, Petts Wood, Orpington, Kent BR5 1RW. Tel: 01689-875555. *Chief Executive*, Prof. G. Robinson
INSTITUTE OF CHARTERED SECRETARIES AND ADMINISTRATORS, 16 Park Crescent, London W1N 4AH. Tel: 0171-580 4741. *Chief Executive*, M. J. Ainsworth
INSTITUTE OF CHARTERED SHIPBROKERS, 3 St Helen's Place, London EC3A 6EJ. Tel: 0171-628 5559. *Director*, Mrs B. Fletcher
INSTITUTE OF EXPORT, Export House, 64 Clifton Street, London EC2A 4HB. Tel: 0171-247 9812. *Director-General*, I. J. Campbell
INSTITUTE OF HEALTH SERVICES MANAGEMENT, 39 Chalton Street, London NW1 1JD. Tel: 0171-388 2626. *Director*, Ms K. Caines
INSTITUTE OF MANAGEMENT, Management House, Cottingham Road, Corby, Northants NN17 1TT. Tel: 01536-204222. *Director-General*, R. Young
INSTITUTE OF PERSONNEL AND DEVELOPMENT, IPD House, Camp Road, London SW19 4UX. Tel: 0181-971 9000. *Director-General*, G. Armstrong
INSTITUTE OF PRACTITIONERS IN ADVERTISING, 44 Belgrave Square, London SW1X 8QS. Tel: 0171-235 7020. *Secretary*, J. Raad
LONDON CHAMBER OF COMMERCE AND INDUSTRY EXAMINATIONS BOARD, Marlowe House, Station Road, Sidcup, Kent DA15 7BJ. Tel: 0181-302 0261. *Chief Executive*, W. J. Swords

DANCE

IMPERIAL SOCIETY OF TEACHERS OF DANCING, Imperial House, 22–26 Paul Street, London EC2A 4QE. Tel: 0171-377 1577. *Chief Executive*, M. J. Browne
ROYAL ACADEMY OF DANCING, 36 Battersea Square, London SW11 3RA. Tel: 0171-223 0091. *Chief Executive*, D. Watchman; *Artistic Director*, Miss L. Wallis

ROYAL BALLET SCHOOL, 155 Talgarth Road, London WI4 9DE. Tel: 0181-748 6335. Also at White Lodge, Richmond Park, Surrey TWIO 5HR. Tel: 0181-876 5547. *Director,* Dame Merle Park, DBE

DEFENCE

ROYAL COLLEGE OF DEFENCE STUDIES, Seaford House, 37 Belgrave Square, London SWIX 8NS. Tel: 0171-915 4800. Prepares selected senior officers and officials for responsibilities in the direction and management of defence and security. *Commandant,* Lt.-Gen. S. C. Grant, CB

ROYAL NAVAL COLLEGES

BRITANNIA ROYAL NAVAL COLLEGE, Dartmouth, Devon TQ6 OHJ. Tel: 01803-832141. Provides general and academic officer training. *Captain,* Capt. A. P. Masterton-Smith
ROYAL NAVAL COLLEGE, Greenwich, London SEIO 9NN. Tel: 0181-858 2154. *Admiral President,* Rear-Adm. J. B. Blackham; *Dean of the College,* Prof. G. Till, PH.D.

MILITARY COLLEGES

DIRECTORATE OF EDUCATIONAL AND TRAINING SERVICES, Director-General Adjutant General's Corp, Worthy Down, Winchester, Hants SO21 2RG. Tel: 01962-887665. *Director,* Brig. A. D. Thompson
ROYAL MILITARY ACADEMY SANDHURST, Camberley, Surrey GUI5 4PQ. Tel: 01276-63344. *Commandant,* Maj.-Gen. J. F. Deverell, OBE
ROYAL MILITARY COLLEGE OF SCIENCE, Shrivenham, Swindon, Wilts SN6 8LA. Tel: 01793-785435. Students from UK and overseas study from degree to postgraduate levels in management, science and technology. The College is a faculty of Cranfield University. *Commandant,* Maj.-Gen. D. J. M. Jenkins, CBE; *Principal,* Prof. P. Hutchinson
STAFF COLLEGE, Camberley, Surrey GUI5 4NP. Tel: 01276-412632. *Commandant,* Maj.-Gen. A. D. Piggott, CBE

ROYAL AIR FORCE COLLEGES

ROYAL AIR FORCE COLLEGE, Cranwell, Sleaford, Lincs. NG34 8HB. Selects all officer and aircrew entrants to the RAF and provides initial training for all officer entrants to the RAF. Also provides specialist training for junior officers of some ground branches and supervision of elementary flying training, general service training for University Air Squadrons, and supervision of the Air Cadet Organization. *Air Officer Commanding and Commandant,* Air Vice-Marshal A. J. Stables, CBE
ROYAL AIR FORCE STAFF COLLEGE, Bracknell, Berks RGI2 9DD. Prepares selected senior officers for high-grade command and staff appointments. Two-thirds of the students are RAF officers; the others are officers from the other UK Services and overseas air forces. *Air Officer Commanding and Commandant,* Air Vice-Marshal M. van der Veen
ROYAL AIR FORCE TRAINING, DEVELOPMENT AND SUPPORT UNIT, RAF Halton, Aylesbury, Bucks HP22 5PG. Tel: 01296-623535. *Commanding Officer,* Gp Capt K. L. Sherit

DENTISTRY

To be entitled to be registered in the Dentists Register, a person must hold the degree or diploma in dental surgery of a university in the UK or the diploma of any of the licensing authorities (the Royal Colleges of Surgeons of England and of Edinburgh, and the Royal College of Physicians and Surgeons of Glasgow). Nationals of an EU member state holding an appropriate European diploma, and holders of certain overseas diplomas, may also be registered. The Dentists Register is maintained by:
THE GENERAL DENTAL COUNCIL, 37 Wimpole Street, London WIM 8DQ. Tel: 0171-486 2171. *Chief Executive,* Mrs R. M. J. Hepplewhite

DIETETICS

See also FOOD AND NUTRITION SCIENCE

The professional association is the British Dietetic Association. Full membership is open to dietitians holding a recognized qualification, who may also become State Registered Dietitians through the Council for Professions Supplementary to Medicine (*see* Medicine)
THE BRITISH DIETETIC ASSOCIATION, 7th Floor, Elizabeth House, 22 Suffolk Street, Queensway, Birmingham BI ILS. Tel: 0121-643 5483. *Administrator,* J. Grigg

DRAMA

The national validating body for courses providing training in drama for the professional theatre is the National Council for Drama Training. It currently has accredited courses at the following: Academy of Live and Recorded Arts; Arts Educational Schools; Birmingham School of Speech Training and Dramatic Art; Bristol Old Vic Theatre School; Central School of Speech and Drama; Drama Centre, London; Drama Studio, London; Guildford School of Acting; Guildhall School of Music and Drama, London; London Academy of Music and Dramatic Art; Manchester Metropolitan University School of Theatre; Mountview Theatre School; Oxford School of Drama, Woodstock; Queen Margaret College, Edinburgh; Rose Bruford College, Sidcup; Royal Academy of Dramatic Art, London; Royal Scottish Academy of Music and Drama; Webber Douglas Academy of Dramatic Art; Welsh College of Music and Drama.
The accreditation of a course in a school does not necessarily imply that other courses of different type or duration in the same school are also accredited.
THE NATIONAL COUNCIL FOR DRAMA TRAINING, 5 Tavistock Place, London WCIH 9SN. *Executive Secretary,* Ms A. Bailey

ENGINEERING

The Engineering Council supervises the engineering profession through the 39 nominated engineering institutions who are represented on its Board for Engineers' Regulation. Working with and through the institutions, the Council sets the standards for the registration of individuals, and also the accreditation for academic courses in universities and colleges and the practical training in industry.
THE ENGINEERING COUNCIL, 10 Maltravers Street, London WC2R 3ER. Tel: 0171-240 7891. *Director-General,* M. Heath

The principal qualifying bodies are:
BRITISH COMPUTER SOCIETY, 1 Sanford Street, Swindon SNI IHJ. Tel: 01793-417417. *Chief Executive,* Ms J. Scott
CHARTERED INSTITUTION OF BUILDING SERVICES ENGINEERS, 222 Balham High Road, London SWI2 9BS. Tel: 0181-675 5211. *Secretary,* A. V. Ramsay
INSTITUTION OF CHEMICAL ENGINEERS, Davis Building, 165–189 Railway Terrace, Rugby, Warks CV2I 3HQ. Tel: 01788-578214. *Chief Executive,* Dr T. J. Evans

INSTITUTION OF CIVIL ENGINEERS, 1 Great George Street, London SW1P 3AA. Tel: 0171-222 7722. *Director-General*, R. S. Dobson, OBE, FEng.

INSTITUTION OF ELECTRICAL ENGINEERS, Savoy Place, London WC2R 0BL. Tel: 0171-240 1871. *Secretary*, Dr J. C. Williams, FEng.

INSTITUTE OF ENERGY, 18 Devonshire Street, London W1N 2AU. Tel: 0171-580 7124. *Secretary*, J. E. H. Leach

INSTITUTION OF GAS ENGINEERS, 21 Portland Place, London W1N 3AF. Tel: 0171-636 6603. *Secretary*, Mrs S. M. Raine

INSTITUTE OF MARINE ENGINEERS, The Memorial Building, 76 Mark Lane, London EC3R 7JN. Tel: 0171-481 8493. *Secretary*, J. E. Sloggett, OBE

INSTITUTE OF MATERIALS, 1 Carlton House Terrace, London SW1Y 5DB. Tel: 0171-839 4071. *Secretary*, Dr J. A. Catterall

INSTITUTE OF MEASUREMENT AND CONTROL, 87 Gower Street, London WC1E 6AA. Tel: 0171-387 4949. *Secretary*, M. J. Yates

INSTITUTION OF MECHANICAL ENGINEERS, 1 Birdcage Walk, London SW1H 9JJ. Tel: 0171-222 7899. *Director-General*, Dr R. Pike

INSTITUTION OF MINING AND METALLURGY, 44 Portland Place, London W1N 4BR. Tel: 0171-580 3802. *Secretary*, M. J. Jones

INSTITUTION OF MINING ENGINEERS, Danum House, 6A South Parade, Doncaster DN1 2DY. Tel: 01302-320486. *Secretary*, Dr G. J. M. Woodrow

INSTITUTE OF PHYSICS, 76–78 Portland Place, London W1N 4AA. Tel: 0171-470 4800. *Chief Executive*, Dr A. Jones

INSTITUTION OF STRUCTURAL ENGINEERS, 11 Upper Belgrave Street, London SW1X 8BH. Tel: 0171-235 4535. *Chief Executive*, Dr J. W. Dougill

ROYAL AERONAUTICAL SOCIETY, 4 Hamilton Place, London W1V 0BQ. Tel: 0171-499 3515. *Director*, R. J. Kennett

ROYAL INSTITUTION OF NAVAL ARCHITECTS, 10 Upper Belgrave Street, London SW1X 8BQ. Tel: 0171-235 4622. *Secretary*, J. Rosewarn

FILM AND TELEVISION

Training for graduates intending to make a career in film and television production is provided by the National Film and Television School, which provides courses in production, direction, animation, camera work and other specialisms. Short post-experience courses to enable professionals to update or expand their skills are also provided.

NATIONAL FILM AND TELEVISION SCHOOL, Station Road, Beaconsfield, Bucks HP9 1LJ. Tel: 01494-671234. *Director*, H. Camre

FOOD AND NUTRITION SCIENCE
See also DIETETICS

Scientific and professional bodies include:

INSTITUTE OF FOOD SCIENCE & TECHNOLOGY, 5 Cambridge Court, 210 Shepherd's Bush Road, London W6 7NJ. Tel: 0171-603 6316. *Chief Executive*, Ms H. G. Wild

NUTRITION SOCIETY, 10 Cambridge Court, 210 Shepherds Bush Road, London W6 7NJ. Tel: 0171-602 0228. *Hon. Secretary*, Prof. J. Mathers

FORESTRY AND TIMBER STUDIES

Professional organizations include:

COMMONWEALTH FORESTRY ASSOCIATION, c/o Oxford Forestry Institute, South Parks Road, Oxford OX1 3RB. Tel: 01865-275072. *Chairman*, P. J. Wood

INSTITUTE OF CHARTERED FORESTERS, 7A St Colme Street, Edinburgh EH3 6AA. Tel: 0131-225 2705. *Secretary*, Mrs M. W. Dick

ROYAL FORESTRY SOCIETY OF ENGLAND, WALES AND NORTHERN IRELAND, 102 High Street, Tring, Herts HP23 4AF. Tel: 01442-822028. *Director*, J. E. Jackson, ph.D.

ROYAL SCOTTISH FORESTRY SOCIETY, The Stables, Dalkeith Country Park, Dalkeith, Midlothian EH22 2NA. Tel: 0131-660 9480. *Director*, M. Osborne

FUEL AND ENERGY SCIENCE

The principal professional bodies are:

INSTITUTE OF ENERGY, 18 Devonshire Street, London W1N 2AU. Tel: 0171-580 7124. *Secretary*, J. Leach

INSTITUTION OF GAS ENGINEERS, 21 Portland Place, London W1N 3AF. Tel: 0171-636 6603. *Secretary*, Mrs S. M. Raine

INSTITUTE OF PETROLEUM, 61 New Cavendish Street, London W1M 8AR. Tel: 0171-467 7100. *Director-General*, I. Ward

HOTELKEEPING, CATERING AND INSTITUTIONAL MANAGEMENT
See also DIETETICS, and FOOD AND NUTRITION SCIENCE

The qualifying professional body in these areas is:

HOTEL AND CATERING INTERNATIONAL MANAGEMENT ASSOCIATION, 191 Trinity Road, London SW17 7HN. Tel: 0181-672 4251. *Chief Executive*, D. Wood

INDUSTRIAL AND VOCATIONAL TRAINING

There are 120 industry training organizations, employer-led independent organizations whose role includes setting the standards of National and Scottish Vocational Qualifications.

NATIONAL COUNCIL OF INDUSTRY TRAINING ORGANIZATIONS, 10 Meadowcourt, Amos Road, Sheffield S9 1BX. Tel: 0114-261 9926. *Chair*, Ms L. Millington; *Administrator*, Miss J. Maisari

INSURANCE

Organizations conducting examinations and awarding diplomas are:

ASSOCIATION OF AVERAGE ADJUSTERS, 200 Aldersgate Street, London EC1A 4JJ. Tel: 0171-956 0099. *Hon. Secretary*, D. W. Taylor

CHARTERED INSTITUTE OF LOSS ADJUSTERS, Manfield House, 1 Southampton Street, London WC2R 0LR. Tel: 0171-240 1496. *Director*, A. F. Clack

CHARTERED INSURANCE INSTITUTE, 20 Aldermanbury, London EC2V 7HY. Tel: 0171-606 3835. *Director-General*, Prof. D. E. Bland

JOURNALISM

Courses for trainee newspaper journalists are available at 20 centres. One-year full-time courses are available for selected students and 18-week courses for graduates. Particulars of all these courses are available from the National Council for the Training of Journalists. Short courses for mid-career development can be arranged, as can various distance learning courses. The NCTJ also offers Assessor, Internal Verifier (IV) and Accreditation of Prior Achievement (APA) training, and NVQs.

For periodical journalists, there are eight centres running courses approved by the Periodicals Training Council.

THE NATIONAL COUNCIL FOR TRAINING OF JOURNALISTS, Latton Bush Centre, Southern Way, Harlow, Essex CM18 7BL. Tel: 01279-430009. *Chief Executive,* R. Selwood

THE PERIODICALS TRAINING COUNCIL, Queen's House, 55–56 Lincoln's Inn Field, London WC2A 3LJ. Tel: 0171-404 4168. *Executive Director,* Ms J. Butcher

LAW

THE BAR

Admission to the Bar of England and Wales is controlled by the Inns of Court, admission to the Bar of Northern Ireland by the Honorable Society of the Inn of Court of Northern Ireland and admission as an Advocate of the Scottish Bar is controlled by the Faculty of Advocates. The governing body of the barristers' branch of the legal profession in England and Wales is the General Council of the Bar. The governing body in Northern Ireland is the Honorable Society of the Inn of Court of Northern Ireland, and the Faculty of Advocates is the governing body of the Scottish Bar. The education and examination of students training for the Bar of England and Wales is regulated by the General Council of the Bar. The Inns of Court School of Law is currently the sole provider of the Bar's vocational course but from September 1997 there will be other institutions validated to provide the course. Those who intend to practise at the Bar of England and Wales must pass the Bar's vocational course.

THE GENERAL COUNCIL OF THE BAR, 3 Bedford Row, London WC1R 4DB. Tel: 0171-242 0082. *Chairman,* D. Peury-Davey, QC; *Chief Executive,* N. Morison

FACULTY OF ADVOCATES, Advocates Library, Parliament House, Edinburgh EH1 1RF. Tel: 0131-226 5071. *Dean,* A. R. Hardie, QC; *Clerk,* I. G. Armstrong

THE HONORABLE SOCIETY OF THE INN OF COURT OF NORTHERN IRELAND, Royal Courts of Justice, Belfast BT1 3JF. Tel: 01232-235111. *Treasurer* (1996), F. C. Elliott, QC; *Under-Treasurer,* J. A. L. McLean, QC

The Inns of Court

THE INNER TEMPLE, London EC4Y 7HL. Tel: 0171-797 8250. *Treasurer,* The Rt. Hon. Lord Justice Staughton; *Sub-Treasurer,* Brig. P. A. Little, CBE

THE MIDDLE TEMPLE, London EC4Y 9AT. Tel: 0171-427 4800. *Treasurer,* The Lord Nicholls, QC; *Deputy Treasurer,* Sir David Calcutt, QC

GRAY'S INN, 8 South Square, London WC1R 5EU. Tel: 0171-405 8164. *Treasurer,* His Hon. Judge Lewis, QC; *Under-Treasurer,* D. Machin

LINCOLN'S INN, London WC2A 3TL. Tel: 0171-405 1393. *Treasurer,* Sir Maurice Drake, DFC; *Under-Treasurer,* Capt. P. M. Carver, RN

INNS OF COURT SCHOOL OF LAW, 39 Eagle Street, London WC1R 4AJ. Tel: 0171-404 5787. *Chairman,* The Hon. Mr Justice Hooper; *Dean,* Mrs M. A. Phillips

SOLICITORS

Qualifications for solicitor are obtainable only from one of the Law Societies, which control the education and examination of trainee solicitors and the admission of solicitors.

LAW SOCIETY OF ENGLAND AND WALES, 113 Chancery Lane, London WC2A 1PL. Tel: 0171-242 1222. *President* (1996–7), J. A. Girling; *Vice-President* (1996–7), P. Sycamore; *Secretary-General,* Ms J. M. Betts

THE COLLEGE OF LAW provides courses for the Common Professional Examination and Legal Practice Course at Braboeuf Manor, St Catherines, Guildford, Surrey GU3 1HA; 14 Store Street, London WC1E 7DE; Christleton Hall, Chester CH3 7AB; Bishopthorpe Road, York YO2 1QA

OFFICE FOR THE SUPERVISION OF SOLICITORS, Victoria Court, 8 Dormer Place, Leamington Spa, Warks CV32 5AE. Tel: 01926-820082. The Office is an establishment of the Law Society set up to handle complaints about solicitors

LAW SOCIETY OF SCOTLAND, Law Society's Hall, 26 Drumsheugh Gardens, Edinburgh EH3 7YR. Tel: 0131-226 7411. *President* (1996–7), A. G. McCulloch; *Secretary,* K. W. Pritchard, OBE

LAW SOCIETY OF NORTHERN IRELAND, Law Society House, 98 Victoria Street, Belfast BT1 3JZ. Tel: 01232-231614. *Secretary,* M. C. Davey

LIBRARIANSHIP AND INFORMATION SCIENCE/MANAGEMENT

The Library Association accredits degree and postgraduate courses in library and information science which are offered by 18 universities in the UK. A full list of accredited degree and postgraduate courses is available from its Information Service. The Association also maintains a professional register of Chartered Members open to graduate ordinary members of the Association.

THE LIBRARY ASSOCIATION, 7 Ridgmount Street, London WC1E 7AE. Tel: 0171-636 7543. *Chief Executive,* R. Shimmon

MATERIALS STUDIES

The qualifying body is:

INSTITUTE OF MATERIALS, 1 Carlton House Terrace, London SW1Y 5DB. Tel: 0171-839 4071. *Secretary,* Dr J. A. Catterall

MEDICINE

EXAMINING BODY FOR DIPLOMAS

UNITED EXAMINING BOARD, Apothecaries Hall, Black Friars Lane, London EC4V 6EJ. Tel: 0171-236 1180. *Chairman,* P. Edmond, CBE; *Registrar,* A. M. Wallington-Smith

COLLEGES/SOCIETIES HOLDING POSTGRADUATE MEMBERSHIP AND DIPLOMA EXAMINATIONS

ROYAL COLLEGE OF ANAESTHETISTS, 48–49 Russell Square, London WC1B 4JY. Tel: 0171-813 1900. *President,* Prof. C. Prys-Roberts; *Chief Executive,* Sir Geoffrey de Deney, KCVO

ROYAL COLLEGE OF GENERAL PRACTITIONERS, 14 Princes Gate, London SW7 1PU. Tel: 0171-581 3232. *Hon. President,* Dr L. Newman, OBE; *Hon. Secretary,* Dr W. Reith

ROYAL COLLEGE OF OBSTETRICIANS AND GYNAECOLOGISTS, 27 Sussex Place, London NW1 4RG. Tel: 0171-262 5425. *President,* Dr N. Patel; *Secretary,* P. A. Barnett

ROYAL COLLEGE OF PATHOLOGISTS, 2 Carlton House Terrace, London SW1Y 5AF. Tel: 0171-930 5861. *President,* Prof. A. J. Bellingham, FRCP, FRCPath.; *Secretary,* K. Lockyer

ROYAL COLLEGE OF PHYSICIANS, 11 St Andrews Place, London NW1 4LE. Tel: 0171-935 1174. *President,* Prof. Sir Leslie Turnberg; *Secretary,* D. B. Lloyd

ROYAL COLLEGE OF PHYSICIANS AND SURGEONS OF GLASGOW, 232–242 St Vincent Street, Glasgow G2 5RJ. Tel: 0141-221 6072. *President*, Prof. N. McKay; *Hon. Secretary*, Dr S. Slater

ROYAL COLLEGE OF PHYSICIANS OF EDINBURGH, 9 Queen Street, Edinburgh EH2 1JQ. Tel: 0131-225 7324. *President*, Dr J. D. Cash; *Secretary*, Dr J. Thomas

ROYAL COLLEGE OF PSYCHIATRISTS, 17 Belgrave Square, London SW1X 8PG. Tel: 0171-235 2351. *President*, Dr R. Kendell; *Secretary*, Mrs V. Cameron

ROYAL COLLEGE OF RADIOLOGISTS, 38 Portland Place, London W1N 4QJ. Tel: 0171-636 4432. *President*, Dr M. J. Brindle; *Secretary*, A. J. Cowles

ROYAL COLLEGE OF SURGEONS OF EDINBURGH, Nicolson Street, Edinburgh EH8 9DW. Tel: 0131-527 1600. *President*, Prof. Sir Robert Shields; *Secretary*, Ms A. Campbell

ROYAL COLLEGE OF SURGEONS OF ENGLAND, 35–43 Lincoln's Inn Fields, London WC2A 3PN. Tel: 0171-405 3474. *President*, Sir Rodney Sweetnam, KCVO, CBE; *Secretary*, R. H. E. Duffett

SOCIETY OF APOTHECARIES OF LONDON, 14 Black Friars Lane, London EC4V 6EJ. Tel: 0171-236 1189. *Clerk*, R. J. Stringer

PROFESSIONS SUPPLEMENTARY TO MEDICINE

The standard of professional education in biomedical sciences, chiropody, dietetics, occupational therapy, orthoptics, physiotherapy and radiography is the responsibility of seven professional boards, which also publish an annual register of qualified practitioners. The work of the boards is co-ordinated by the Council for Professions Supplementary to Medicine.

THE COUNCIL FOR PROFESSIONS SUPPLEMENTARY TO MEDICINE, Park House, 184 Kennington Park Road, London SE11 4BU. Tel: 0171-582 0866. *Registrar*, M. D. Hall

BIOMEDICAL SCIENCES

Qualifications from higher or further education establishments and training in medical laboratories are required for progress to the professional examinations and qualifications of the Institute of Biomedical Science.

INSTITUTE OF BIOMEDICAL SCIENCE, 12 Coldbath Square, London EC1R 5HL. Tel: 0171-636 8192. *Chief Executive*, A. Potter

CHIROPODY

Professional recognition is granted by the Society of Chiropodists and Podiatrists to students who are awarded B.Sc. degrees in Podiatry or Podiatric Medicine after attending a course of full-time training for three or four years at one of the 14 recognized schools in the UK (11 in England and Wales, two in Scotland and one in Northern Ireland). Qualifications granted and degrees recognized by the Society are approved by the Chiropodists Board for the purpose of State Registration, which is a condition of employment within the National Health Service.

THE SOCIETY OF CHIROPODISTS AND PODIATRISTS, 53 Welbeck Street, London W1M 7HE. Tel: 0171-486 3381. *General Secretary*, J. G. C. Trouncer

See also DIETETICS

OCCUPATIONAL THERAPY

Professional qualifications are awarded by the College of Occupational Therapists upon completion of one of the 29 training courses approved by the College. The courses are normally degree-level courses based in higher education institutions.

COLLEGE OF OCCUPATIONAL THERAPISTS, 6–8 Marshalsea Road, London SE1 1HL. Tel: 0171-357 6480. *Secretary*, J. Thompson

See also OPHTHALMIC AND DISPENSING OPTICS

ORTHOPTICS

Orthoptists undertake the diagnosis and treatment of all types of squint and other anomalies of binocular vision, working in close collaboration with ophthalmologists. The training and maintenance of professional standards are the responsibility of the Orthoptists Board of the Council for the Professions Supplementary to Medicine. The professional body is the British Orthoptic Society. Training is at degree level.

THE BRITISH ORTHOPTIC SOCIETY, Tavistock House North, Tavistock Square, London WC1H 9HX. *Hon. Secretary*, Mrs A. Charnock

OSTEOPATHY

Osteopathy is accorded statutory regulation by the Osteopaths Act 1993. There are currently four bodies that accredit courses leading to a qualification in Osteopathy but these are due to be replaced by a General Osteopathic Council when it opens a new register, expected to be in 1997. Osteopathy is becoming an all-graduate profession. Courses vary in length from three to five years, granting various qualifications from diploma to honours degree. Shorter courses are available for qualified doctors. Details of accrediting institutions and courses can be obtained from the Osteopathic Information Service.

OSTEOPATHIC INFORMATION SERVICE, PO Box 2074, Reading, Berks RG1 4YR. Tel: 01734-512051. *Public Relations Manager*, B. Daniels

PHYSIOTHERAPY

Full-time three- or four-year degree courses are available at 31 recognized schools in the UK. Information about courses leading to eligibility for Membership of the Chartered Society of Physiotherapy and to State Registration is available from the Chartered Society of Physiotherapy.

THE CHARTERED SOCIETY OF PHYSIOTHERAPY, 14 Bedford Row, London WC1R 4ED. Tel: 0171-306 6666. *Secretary*, vacant

RADIOGRAPHY AND RADIOTHERAPY

In order to practise both diagnostic and therapeutic radiography in the UK, it is necessary to have successfully completed a course of education and training recognized by the Privy Council. Such courses are offered by universities throughout the UK and lead to the award of a degree in radiography. Further information is available from the college.

THE COLLEGE OF RADIOGRAPHERS, 2 Carriage Row, 183 Eversholt Street, London NW1 1BU. Tel: 0171-391 4500. *Chief Executive*, S. Evans

COMPLEMENTARY MEDICINE

Professional courses are validated by:

INSTITUTE FOR COMPLEMENTARY MEDICINE, PO Box 194, London SE16 1QZ. Tel: 0171-237 5165. *Director*, A. Baird

MERCHANT NAVY TRAINING SCHOOLS

OFFICERS

WARSASH MARITIME CENTRE, Southampton Institute, Newtown Road, Warsash, Southampton SO31 9ZL. Tel: 01489-576161. *Dean*, Capt. G. B. Angas

SEAFARERS

INDEFATIGABLE SCHOOL, Plas Llanfair, Llanfairpwll, Anglesey LL61 6NT. Tel: 01248 714338. *Headmaster*, Capt. P. White

NATIONAL SEA TRAINING CENTRE, North West Kent College, Dering Way, Gravesend, Kent DA12 2JJ. Tel: 01474-363656. *Head of Faculty*, R. MacDonald

MUSIC

ASSOCIATED BOARD OF THE ROYAL SCHOOLS OF MUSIC, 14 Bedford Square, London WC1B 3JG. Tel: 0171-636 5400. The Board conducts graded music examinations in over 80 countries and provides other services to music education through its professional development department and publishing company. *Chief Executive*, R. Morris

GUILDHALL SCHOOL OF MUSIC AND DRAMA, Silk Street, London EC2Y 8DT. Tel: 0171-628 2571. *Principal*, I. Horsbrugh

LONDON COLLEGE OF MUSIC, Thames Valley University, St Mary's Road, London W5 5RF. Tel: 0181-231 2304. *Director*, A. Creamer

ROYAL ACADEMY OF MUSIC, Marylebone Road, London NW1 5HT. Tel: 0171-873 7373. *Principal*, Prof. C. Price

ROYAL COLLEGE OF MUSIC, Prince Consort Road, London SW7 2BS. Tel: 0171-589 3643. *Director*, Ms J. Ritterman, PH.D.

ROYAL COLLEGE OF ORGANISTS, 7 St Andrew Street, London EC4A 3LQ. Tel: 0171-936 3606. *Chief Executive*, Dr M. Nicholas

ROYAL NORTHERN COLLEGE OF MUSIC, 124 Oxford Road, Manchester M13 9RD. Tel: 0161-273 6283. *Principal*, Prof. E. Gregson

ROYAL SCOTTISH ACADEMY OF MUSIC AND DRAMA, 100 Renfrew Street, Glasgow G2 3DB. Tel: 0141-332 4101. *Principal*, Dr P. Ledger, CBE, FRSE

TRINITY COLLEGE OF MUSIC, 11–13 Mandeville Place, London W1M 6AQ. Tel: 0171-935 5773. *Principal*, G. Henderson

NURSING

All nurses must be registered with the UK Central Council for Nursing, Midwifery and Health Visiting. Courses leading to registration as a nurse are at least three years in length. There are also some programmes which are combined with degrees. Students study in colleges of nursing or in institutions of higher education. Courses offer a combination of theoretical and practical experience in a variety of settings. Different courses lead to different types of registration, including: Registered General Nurse (RGN) or Registered Nurse (RN), Registered Mental Nurse (RMN), Registered Mental Handicap Nurse (RMHN), Registered Sick Children Nurse (RSCN), Registered Midwife (RM) and Registered Health Visitor (RHV). The various national boards, listed below, are responsible for validating courses in nursing.

The Royal College of Nurses is the professional union representing nurses and provides higher education through its Institute.

UK CENTRAL COUNCIL FOR NURSING, MIDWIFERY AND HEALTH VISITING, 23 Portland Place, London W1N 4JT. Tel: 0171-637 7181. *Chief Executive and Registrar*, Ms S. Norman

ENGLISH NATIONAL BOARD FOR NURSING, MIDWIFERY AND HEALTH VISITING, Victory House, 170 Tottenham Court Road, London W1P 0HA. Tel: 0171-388 3131. *Chief Executive*, A. P. Smith

NATIONAL BOARD FOR NURSING, MIDWIFERY AND HEALTH VISITING FOR NORTHERN IRELAND, Centre House, 79 Chichester Street, Belfast BT1 4JE. Tel: 01232-238152. *Chief Executive*, Dr O. D'A. Slevin

NATIONAL BOARD FOR NURSING, MIDWIFERY AND HEALTH VISITING FOR SCOTLAND, 22 Queen Street, Edinburgh EH2 1NT. Tel: 0131-226 7371. *Chief Executive*, Mrs L. Mitchell

WELSH NATIONAL BOARD FOR NURSING, MIDWIFERY AND HEALTH VISITING, Floor 13, Pearl Assurance House, Greyfriars Road, Cardiff CF1 3AG. Tel: 01222-395535. *Chief Executive*, Mrs A. Ravey

THE ROYAL COLLEGE OF NURSING OF THE UNITED KINGDOM, 20 Cavendish Square, London W1M 0AB. Tel: 0171-409 3333. *General Secretary*, Miss C. Hancock; *Principal of the RCN Institute*, Prof. A. Kitson

OPHTHALMIC AND DISPENSING OPTICS

Professional bodies are:

THE ASSOCIATION OF BRITISH DISPENSING OPTICIANS, 6 Hurlingham Business Park, Sulivan Road, London SW6 3DU. Tel: 0171-736 0088. Grants qualifications as a dispensing optician. *Registrar*, D. G. Baker

THE COLLEGE OF OPTOMETRISTS, 10 Knaresborough Place, London SW5 0TG. Tel: 0171-373 7765. Grants qualifications as an optometrist. *General Secretary*, P. D. Leigh

PHARMACY

Information may be obtained from the Secretary and Registrar of the Royal Pharmaceutical Society of Great Britain.

ROYAL PHARMACEUTICAL SOCIETY OF GREAT BRITAIN, 1 Lambeth High Street, London SE1 7JN. Tel: 0171-735 9141. *Secretary and Registrar*, J. Ferguson, OBE

PHOTOGRAPHY

The professional body is:

BRITISH INSTITUTE OF PROFESSIONAL PHOTOGRAPHY, Fox Talbot House, Amwell End, Ware, Herts SG12 9HN. Tel: 01920-464011. *Chief Executive*, A. Mair

PRINTING

Details of training courses in printing can be obtained from the Institute of Printing and the British Printing Industries Federation. In addition to these examining and organizing bodies, examinations are held by various independent regional examining boards in further education.

BRITISH PRINTING INDUSTRIES FEDERATION, 11 Bedford Row, London WC1R 4DX. Tel: 0171-242 6904. *Director-General*, T. P. E. Machin

INSTITUTE OF PRINTING, 8A Lonsdale Gardens, Tunbridge Wells, Kent TN1 1NU. Tel: 01892-538118. *Secretary-General*, D. Freeland

SOCIAL WORK

The Central Council for Education and Training in Social Work promotes education and training for social work and social care in the UK. It approves education and training

programmes, including those leading to its qualifying award, the Diploma in Social Work.
THE CENTRAL COUNCIL FOR EDUCATION AND TRAINING IN SOCIAL WORK, Derbyshire House, St Chad's Street, London WC1H 8AD. Tel: 0171-278 2455. *Chairman*, J. Greenwood; *Director*, T. Hall

SPEECH AND LANGUAGE THERAPY

The Royal College of Speech and Language Therapists provides details of courses leading to qualification as a speech and language therapist. Other professionals may become Associates of the College. A directory of registered members is published annually.
THE ROYAL COLLEGE OF SPEECH AND LANGUAGE THERAPISTS, 7 Bath Place, Rivington Street, London EC2A 3DR. Tel: 0171-613 3855. *Director*, Mrs P. Evans

SURVEYING

The qualifying professional bodies include:
ARCHITECTS AND SURVEYORS INSTITUTE, St Mary House, 15 St Mary Street, Chippenham, Wilts SN15 3WD. Tel: 01249-444505. *Chief Executive*, C. G. A. Nash, OBE
ASSOCIATION OF BUILDING ENGINEERS, Jubilee House, Billing Brook Road, Weston Favell, Northampton NN3 8NW. Tel: 01604-404121. *Chief Executive*, B. D. Hughes
INCORPORATED SOCIETY OF VALUERS AND AUCTIONEERS (1968), 3 Cadogan Gate, London SW1X 0AS. Tel: 0171-235 2282. *Chief Executive*, H. Whitty
INSTITUTE OF REVENUES, RATING AND VALUATION, 41 Doughty Street, London WC1N 2LF. Tel: 0171-831 3505. *Director*, C. Farrington
ROYAL INSTITUTION OF CHARTERED SURVEYORS (incorporating The Institute of Quantity Surveyors), 12 Great George Street, London SW1P 3AD. Tel: 0171-222 7000. *Chief Executive*, Ms C. Makin

TEACHING

Teachers in publicly maintained schools must be approved as qualified by the Secretary of State in England and the General Teaching Council in Scotland, usually after a course at an accredited institution. Non-graduates usually qualify by way of a three- or four-year course leading to a Bachelor of Education (B.Ed.) honours degree, or a first degree course (BA, B.Sc.) taken concurrently with a certificate of education. Graduates take a one-year post-graduate certificate of education (PGCE). Teacher training courses may now also be developed and delivered by schools in England, subject to approval of their proposed training programme by the Teacher Training Agency and monitoring and evaluation by OFSTED (*see also* pages 438–9).

Details of courses in England and Wales are contained in the *Handbook of Degree and Advanced Courses* published annually by the National Association of Teachers in Further and Higher Education. Details of courses in Scotland can be obtained from colleges of education, universities, from COSHEP, and from TEACH (*see* page 451). Details of courses in Northern Ireland can be obtained from the Department of Education for Northern Ireland. Applications for teacher training courses in Northern Ireland are made to the institutions direct. For applications, *see* pages 442–3.

TEXTILES

THE TEXTILE INSTITUTE, International Headquarters, 10 Blackfriars Street, Manchester M3 5DR. Tel: 0161-834 8457. *Chief Executive (acting)*, Dr J. McPhee

THEOLOGICAL COLLEGES

The number of students training for the ministry in the academic year 1995–6 is shown in parenthesis. Those marked * show figures for 1994–5.

ANGLICAN

COLLEGE OF THE RESURRECTION, Mirfield, W. Yorks WF14 0BW. Tel: 01924-490441. (20). *Principal*, Revd Dr D. J. Lane
CRANMER HALL, St John's College, Durham DH1 3RJ. Tel: 0191-374 3579. (59). *Principal*, D. V. Day
OAK HILL COLLEGE, Chase Side, London N14 4PS. Tel: 0181-449 0467. (45). *Principal*, Revd Dr D. Peterson
RIDLEY HALL, Cambridge CB3 9HG. Tel: 01223-353040. (50). *Principal*, Revd G. A. Cray
RIPON COLLEGE, Cuddesdon, Oxford OX44 9EX. Tel: 01865-874404. (75). *Principal (acting)*, Revd Dr B. Castle
ST JOHN's COLLEGE, Chilwell Lane, Bramcote, Nottingham NG9 3DS. Tel: 0115-925 1114. (75). *Principal*, Revd Dr J. Goldingay
ST MICHAEL's THEOLOGICAL COLLEGE, Llandaff, Cardiff CF5 2YJ. Tel: 01222-563379/116. (30). *Principal*, Revd Canon J. H. L. Rowlands
ST STEPHEN's HOUSE, 16 Marston Street, Oxford OX4 1JX. Tel: 01865-247874. (50). *Principal*, Revd J. Sheehy
THEOLOGICAL INSTITUTE OF THE SCOTTISH EPISCOPAL CHURCH, 21 Inverleith Terrace, Edinburgh EH3 5NS. Tel: 0131-343 2038. (27). *Principal*, Revd R. A. Nixon
TRINITY COLLEGE, Stoke Hill, Bristol BS9 1JP. Tel: 0117-968 2803. (120). *Principal*, Revd Canon D. Gillett
WESTCOTT HOUSE, Jesus Lane, Cambridge CB5 8BP. Tel: 01223-350074. (57). *Principal*, Revd M. G. V. Roberts
WYCLIFFE HALL, 54 Banbury Road, Oxford OX2 6PW. Tel: 01865-274200. (67). *Principal*, Revd Dr A. McGrath

BAPTIST

BRISTOL BAPTIST COLLEGE, Woodland Road, Bristol BS8 1UN. Tel: 0117-926 0248. (25). *Principal*, Revd Dr B. Haymes
NORTHERN BAPTIST COLLEGE, Luther King House, Brighton Grove, Rusholme, Manchester M14 5JP. Tel: 0161-224 2214. (21). *Principal*, Revd Dr R. L. Kidd
NORTH WALES BAPTIST COLLEGE, Ffordd Ffriddoedd, Bangor LL57 2EH. Tel: 01248-362608. (2). *Warden*, Revd Dr D. D. Morgan
REGENT's PARK COLLEGE, Oxford OX1 2LB. Tel: 01865-288120. (24). *Principal*, Revd Dr P. S. Fiddes
THE SCOTTISH BAPTIST COLLEGE, 12 Aytoun Road, Glasgow G41 5RN. Tel: 0141-424 0747. (13). *Principal*, Revd K. B. E. Roxburgh
SOUTH WALES BAPTIST COLLEGE, 54 Richmond Road, Cardiff CF2 3UR. Tel: 01222-496060. (24). *Principal*, Revd D. H. Matthews
SPURGEON's COLLEGE, South Norwood Hill, London SE25 6DJ. Tel: 0181-653 0850. (80). *Principal*, Revd M. Quicke

CHURCH OF SCOTLAND

CHRIST's COLLEGE, 25 High Street, Old Aberdeen AB2 3EE. Tel: 01224-272138. (30). *Master*, Revd Prof. A. Main, TD, Ph.D.
NEW COLLEGE, Mound Place, Edinburgh EH1 2LU. Tel: 0131-650 8900. (33). *Principal*, Revd Dr R. Page

TRINITY COLLEGE, 4 The Square, University of
Glasgow, Glasgow G12 8QQ. Tel: 0141-339 8855. (70).
Principal, Revd Prof. G. M. Newlands

CONGREGATIONAL

COLLEGE OF THE WELSH INDEPENDENTS, 38 Pier Street,
Aberystwyth. *Principal,* Revd Dr E. S. John
SCOTTISH CONGREGATIONAL COLLEGE, St Colm's, 20
Inverleith Terrace, Edinburgh EH3 5NS. Tel: 0131-315
3595. (1). *Principal,* Revd Dr J. W. S. Clark

ECUMENICAL

QUEEN'S COLLEGE, Somerset Road, Edgbaston,
Birmingham B15 2QH. Tel: 0121-454 1527. (70).
Principal, Revd P. Fisher

METHODIST

EDGHILL THEOLOGICAL COLLEGE, 9 Lennoxvale, Belfast
BT9 5BY. Tel: 01232-665870. (19). *Principal,* Revd D. D.
Cooke, PH.D.
HARTLEY VICTORIA COLLEGE, Northern Federation for
Training in Ministry, Luther King House, Brighton
Grove, Manchester M14 5JP. Tel: 0161-224 2215. (22).
Principal, Revd G. Slater
WESLEY COLLEGE, College Park Drive, Henbury Road,
Bristol BS10 7QD. Tel: 0117-959 1200. (63). *Principal,*
Revd Dr N. Richardson
WESLEY HOUSE, Jesus Lane,Cambridge CB5 8BJ. Tel:
01223-350609. (30). *Principal,* Revd Dr I. H. Jones
WESLEY STUDY CENTRE, 55 The Avenue, Durham
DH1 4EB. Tel: 0191-386 1833. (24). *Director,* Revd
P. Luscombe, PH.D.

NON-DENOMINATIONAL

ST MARY'S COLLEGE, The University, St Andrews, Fife
KY16 9JU. Tel: 01334-462851. (180). *Principal,* Dr
R. A. Piper

PRESBYTERIAN

UNION THEOLOGICAL COLLEGE, Belfast BT7 1JT. Tel:
01232-325374. (*41). *Principal,* Revd Prof. T. S. Reid

PRESBYTERIAN CHURCH OF WALES

UNITED THEOLOGICAL COLLEGE, Aberystwyth SY23 2LT.
Tel: 01970-624574. (20). *Principal,* Revd Prof. E. N.
Roberts

ROMAN CATHOLIC

ALLEN HALL, 28 Beaufort Street, London SW3 5AA. Tel:
0171-351 1296. (*35). *Principal,* Revd K. Barltrop, STL
CAMPION HOUSE COLLEGE, 112 Thornbury Road,
Isleworth, Middx TW7 4NN. Tel: 0181-560 1924. (23).
Principal, Revd C. C. Dykehoff, SJ
OSCOTT COLLEGE, Chester Road, Sutton Coldfield,
W. Midlands B73 5AA. Tel: 0121-354 7117. (50). *Rector,*
Rt. Revd P. McKinney, STL
ST JOHN'S SEMINARY, Wonersh, Guildford, Surrey
GU5 0QX. Tel: 01483-892217. (70). *Rector,* Fr
K. Haggerty, STL
SCOTUS COLLEGE, 2 Chesters Road, Bearsden, Glasgow
G61 4AG. Tel: 0141-942 8384. (50). *Rector,* Rt Revd M. J.
Conway
USHAW COLLEGE, Durham DH7 9RH. Tel: 0191-373 1366.
(64). *President,* Revd J. O'Keefe

UNITARIAN

UNITARIAN COLLEGE, Northern Federation for Training
in Ministry, Luther King House, Brighton Grove,
Rusholme, Manchester M14 5JP. Tel: 0161-224 2849. (5).
Principal, Revd L. Smith, PH.D.

UNITED REFORMED

BALA-BANGOR INDEPENDENT COLLEGE, Bangor
LL57 2EH. (*15). *Principal,* R. T. Jones, D.phil., DD
MANSFIELD COLLEGE, Mansfield Road, Oxford OX1 3TF.
Tel: 01865-270999. (25). *Principal,* Prof. D. Marquand
NORTHERN COLLEGE, Northern Federation for Training
in Ministry, Luther King House, Brighton Grove,
Rusholme, Manchester M14 5JP. Tel: 0161-224 4381.
(24). *Principal,* Revd Dr D. R. Peel
WESTMINSTER COLLEGE, Madingley Road, Cambridge
CB3 0AA. Tel: 01223-353997. (28). *Principal,* Revd D. G.
Cornick, PH.D.

JEWISH

JEWS' COLLEGE, Albert Road, London NW4 2SJ. Tel: 0181-
203 6427. (10). *Principal,* Rabbi Dr D. Sinclair
LEO BAECK COLLEGE, Sternberg Centre for Judaism, 80
East End Road, London N3 2SY. Tel: 0181-349 4525.
(17). *Principal,* Rabbi Prof. J. Magonet

TOWN AND COUNTRY PLANNING

Degree and diploma courses in town planning are accred-
ited by the Royal Town Planning Institute.
THE ROYAL TOWN PLANNING INSTITUTE, 26 Portland
Place, London W1N 4BE. Tel: 0171-636 9107. *Secretary-
General,* R. Upton

TRANSPORT

Qualifying examinations in transport management and
logistics leading to chartered professional status are
conducted by the Chartered Institute of Transport.
THE CHARTERED INSTITUTE OF TRANSPORT, 80
Portland Place, London W1N 4DP. Tel: 0171-636 9952.
Director, Mrs S. Gross

Independent Schools

The following pages list those independent schools whose
Head is a member of the Headmasters' and Headmistress'
Conference, the Society of Headmasters and
Headmistresses of Independent Schools or the Girls'
Schools Association

THE HEADMASTERS' AND HEADMISTRESS' CONFERENCE

Chairman (1997), M. B. Mavor (Rugby School)
Secretary, V. S. Anthony, 130 Regent Road, Leicester
LEI 7PG. Tel: 0116-285 4810
Membership Secretary, D. E. Prince, 1 Russell House, Bepton
Road, Midhurst, W. Sussex GU29 9NB. Tel: 01730-
815635. The annual meeting is, as a rule, held at the end
of September or early in October

* Woodard Corporation School, 1 The Sanctuary, London
  SW1P 3JT. Tel: 0171-222 5381
† Girls in VI form
‡ Co-educational
° 1995 figures

Name of School	Foun-ded	No. of pupils	Annual fees £ Boarding	Day	Head (with date of appointment)
ENGLAND AND WALES			Boarding	Day	
Abbotsholme School, Staffs	1889	240‡	11,850	7,920	D. J. Farrant (1984)
Abingdon School, Oxon	1256	780	10,332	5,571	M. St J. Parker (1975)
Ackworth School, W. Yorks	1779	375‡	9,705	5,529	M. J. Dickinson (1995)
Aldenham School, Herts	1597	377†	11,919	8,175	S. R. Borthwick (1994)
Alleyn's School, London SE22	1619	925‡	—	5,895	Dr C. H. R. Niven (1992)
Ampleforth College (*RC*), Yorks	1802	540	12,555	6,480	Revd G. F. L. Chamberlain, OSB (1993)
*Ardingly College, W. Sussex	1858	450‡	12,225	9,465	J. W. Flecker (1980)
Arnold School, Blackpool	1896	823‡	—	3,900	W. T. Gillen (1993)
Ashville College, Harrogate	1877	574‡	9,237	4,938	M. H. Crosby (1987)
Bablake School, Coventry	1560	876‡	—	3,975	Dr S. Nuttall (1991)
Bancroft's School, Essex	1727	749‡	—	6,051	Dr P. R. Scott (1996)
Barnard Castle School, Co. Durham	1883	516‡	8,940	5,292	F. S. McNamara (1980)
Batley Grammar School, W. Yorks	1612	547‡	—	3,882	W. M. Duggan (1995)
Bedales School, Hants	1893	400‡	13,647	10,236	Mrs A. A. Willcocks (1995)
Bedford Modern School	1566	930	9,179	4,839	S. Smith (1996)
Bedford School	1552	708	11,670	7,350	Dr I. P. Evans (1990)
Berkhamsted School, Herts	1541	500†	11,664	9,821	Dr P. Chadwick (1996)
Birkenhead School, Merseyside	1860	690	—	3,897	S. J. Haggett (1988)
°Bishop's Stortford College, Herts	1868	337†	10,320	7,440	J. Trotman (1996)
*Bloxham School, Oxon	1860	356‡	12,655	9,915	D. K. Exham (1991)
Blundell's School, Devon	1604	420‡	12,135	7,410	J. Leigh (1992)
Bolton School	1524	850	—	4,626	A. W. Wright (1983)
Bootham School, York	1823	346‡	10,161	6,594	I. M. Small (1988)
Bradfield College, Berks	1850	620†	12,825	9,621	P. B. Smith (1985)
Bradford Grammar School	1662	920†	—	4,428	S. R. Davidson (1996)
Brentwood School, Essex	1557	1,048‡	10,620	6,075	J. A. B. Kelsall (1993)
Brighton College, E. Sussex	1845	488‡	12,450	8,190	J. D. Leach (1987)
Bristol Grammar School	1532	1,040‡	—	4,089	C. E. Martin (1986)
Bromsgrove School, Worcs	1553	640‡	10,605	6,750	T. M. Taylor (1986)
Bryanston School, Dorset	1928	630‡	13,230	8,820	T. D. Wheare (1983)
Bury Grammar School, Lancs	1634	700	—	3,876	K. Richards (1990)
Canford School, Dorset	1923	540‡	13,000	9,750	J. D. Lever (1992)
Caterham School, Surrey	1811	750‡	11,730	6,090	R. A. E. Davey (1995)
Charterhouse, Surrey	1611	720‡	13,341	11,022	Revd J. S. Witheridge (1996)
Cheadle Hulme School, Cheshire	1855	980‡	—	4,296	D. J. Wilkinson (1990)
Cheltenham College, Glos	1841	580†	12,690	9,585	P. D. V. Wilkes (1990)
Chetham's School of Music, Manchester	1653	258‡	15,975	12,366	Revd Canon P. F. Hullah (1992)
Chigwell School, Essex	1629	370†	9,993	6,573	D. F. Gibbs (1996)
Christ College, Brecon	1541	340‡	9,972	7,728	D. P. Jones (1996)
Christ's Hospital, W. Sussex	1553	820‡	varies	—	Dr P. C. D. Southern (1996)
Churcher's College, Hants	1722	575‡	9,810	5,250	G. W. Buttle (1988)

Name of School	Foun-ded	No. of pupils	Annual fees £		Head (with date of appointment)
			Boarding	Day	
City of London Freemen's School, Surrey	1854	530‡	9,988	6,291	D. C. Haywood (1987)
City of London, London EC4	1442	870	—	6,120	R. Dancey (1995)
Clifton College, Bristol	1862	630‡	12,500	8,900	H. Monro (1991)
Colfe's School, London SE12	1652	720†	—	5,730	Dr D. Richardson (1990)
Colston's Collegiate School, Bristol	1710	450‡	10,590	5,745	D. G. Crawford (1995)
Cranleigh School, Surrey	1863	490‡	12,990	9,615	T. A. A. Hart (1984)
Culford School, Suffolk	1881	400‡	10,920	7,107	J. S. Richardson (1992)
Dame Allan's School, Newcastle upon Tyne	1705	418†	—	3,570	D. W. Welsh (*Principal*) (1996)
Dauntsey's School, Wilts	1543	640‡	11,070	6,816	C. R. Evans (1985)
Dean Close School, Cheltenham	1884	445‡	12,840	8,955	C. J. Bacon (1979)
Denstone College, Staffs	1873	300‡	11,328	8,052	D. Derbyshire (from January 1997)
Douai School (*RC*), Berks	1903	205‡	10,545	6,780	Dr E. Power, OSB (1993)
Dover College, Kent	1871	250‡	11,820	6,450	M. P. G. Wright (1991)
Downside School (*RC*), Somerset	1607	301	11,685	6,180	Revd Dom. A. Sutch (*Master*) (1995)
Dulwich College, London SE21	1619	1,390	12,636	6,318	G. G. Able (*Master*) (from January 1997)
Durham School	1414	299†	11,748	7,644	M. A. Lang (1982)
Eastbourne College, E Sussex	1867	477‡	12,084	8,936	C. M. P. Bush (1993)
Ellesmere College, Shropshire	1884	300‡	11,100	7,350	B. J. Wignall (1996)
Eltham College, London SE9	1842	590†	12,081	5,724	D. M. Green (1990)
Emanuel School, London SE11	1594	760‡	—	4,950	T. Jones-Parry (1994)
Epsom College, Surrey	1855	652‡	12,204	9,066	A. H. Beadles (1993)
Eton College, Berks	1440	1,270	13,410	—	J. E. Lewis (1994)
Exeter School	1633	700†	8,475	4,470	N. W. Gamble (1992)
Felsted School, Essex	1564	350‡	12,978	10,239	S. C. Roberts (1993)
Forest School, London E17	1834	825‡	9,087	5,790	A. G. Boggis (*Warden*) (1992)
Framlingham College, Suffolk	1864	450‡	10,170	6,528	Mrs. G. M. Randall (1994)
Frensham Heights, Surrey	1925	295‡	11,985	7,770	P. de Voil (1993)
Giggleswick School, N. Yorks	1512	320‡	12,120	8,040	A. P. Millard (1993)
The Grange School, Cheshire	1978	575‡	—	3,675	E. S. Marshall (1977)
Gresham's School, Norfolk	1555	520‡	12,435	8,700	J. H. Arkell (1991)
Haberdashers' Aske's School, Herts	1690	1,100	—	6,021	J. W. R. Goulding (1996)
Haileybury, Herts	1862	586†	13,338	9,672	S. A. Westley (*Master*) (1996)
Hampton School, Middx	1557	945	—	5,280	B. R. Martin (from April 1997)
Harrow School, Middx	1571	785	13,830	—	N. R. Bomford (1991)
Hereford Cathedral School	1384	622‡	8,235	4,755	Dr H. C. Tomlinson (1987)
Highgate School, London N6	1565	615	—	7,515	R. P. Kennedy (1989)
Hulme Grammar School, Oldham	1611	684	—	3,726	T. J. Turvey (1995)
Hurstpierpoint College, W. Sussex	1849	350‡	11,940	9,330	S. Meek (1995)
Hymers College, Hull	1889	743‡	—	3,735	J. C. Morris (1990)
Ipswich School, Suffolk	1390	595†	9,111	5,331	I. G. Galbraith (1993)
John Lyon School, Middx	1876	520	—	5,790	Revd T. J. Wright (1986)
Kelly College, Devon	1877	300‡	11,670	7,335	M. Turner (1995)
Kent College, Canterbury	1885	500‡	10,770	6,048	E. B. Halse (1995)
Kimbolton School, Cambs	1600	560‡	9,450	5,520	R. V. Peel (1987)
King Edward VI School, Southampton	1553	950‡	—	5,016	P. B. Hamilton (1996)
King Edward VII School, Lytham	1908	495	—	3,875	P. J. Wilde (1993)
King Edward's School, Bath	1552	665†	—	4,548	P. J. Winter (1993)
King Edward's School, Birmingham	1552	890	—	4,725	H. R. Wright (*Chief Master*) (1991)
King Edward's School, Witley, Surrey	1553	421‡	9,450	6,540	R. J. Fox (1988)
King Henry VIII School, Coventry	1545	810‡	—	3,975	T. J. Vardon (1994)
King's College, Taunton	1880	450‡	12,030	7,920	R. S. Funnell (1988)
King's College School, London SW19	1829	720	—	6,840	R. M. Reeve (1980)
King's School, Bruton, Somerset	1519	334†	11,355	8,055	R. I. Smyth (1993)
King's School, Canterbury	600	740‡	13,440	9,285	Revd K. H. Wilkinson (1996)
King's School, Chester	1541	510	—	4,230	A. R. D. Wickson (1981)
King's School, Ely, Cambs	970	400‡	12,030	8,055	R. H. Youdale (1992)
King's School, Gloucester	1541	350‡	10,650	6,300	P. Lacey (1992)
King's School, Macclesfield	1502	1,120‡	—	4,350	A. G. Silcock (1987)
King's School, Rochester, Kent	604	320‡	12,375	7,110	Dr I. R. Walker (1986)
King's School, Tynemouth	1860	670‡	—	3,924	Dr D. Younger (1993)

Name of School	Foun-ded	No. of pupils	Annual fees £		Head (with date of appointment)
			Boarding	Day	
King's School, Worcester	1541	802‡	9,099	5,250	Dr J. M. Moore (1983)
Kingston Grammar School, Surrey	1561	600‡	—	5,715	C. D. Baxter (1991)
Kingswood School, Bath	1748	450‡	11,829	7,350	G. M. Best (1987)
*Lancing College, W. Sussex	1848	515†	12,630	9,495	C. J. Saunders (1993)
Latymer Upper School, London w6	1624	955†	—	6,180	C. Diggory (1991)
Leeds Grammar School	1552	917	—	4,845	B. W. Collins (1986)
Leicester Grammar School	1981	606‡	—	4,320	J. B. Sugden (1989)
Leighton Park School, Reading	1890	370‡	11,754	8,820	J. Dunston (1996)
The Leys School, Cambridge	1875	420‡	12,300	8,790	Revd J. C. A. Barrett (1990)
Liverpool College	1840	620‡	—	4,290	B. R. Martin (Principal) (1992)
Llandovery College, Carmarthenshire	1848	235‡	9,987	6,516	Dr C. E. Evans (Warden) (1988)
Lord Wandsworth College, Hants	1912	475‡	9,972	7,752	G. de W. Waller (1993)
Loughborough Grammar School	1495	940	8,586	4,662	D. N. Ireland (1984)
Magdalen College School, Oxford	1480	516	—	5,094	P. M. Tinniswood (Master) (1991)
Malvern College, Worcs	1865	648‡	12,750	9,270	H. C. K. Carson (from January 1997)
Manchester Grammar School	1515	1,411	—	4,344	G. M. Stephen, ph.d (High Master) (1994)
Marlborough College, Wilts	1843	800‡	13,425	9,465	E. J. H. Gould (Master) (1993)
Merchant Taylors' School, Liverpool	1620	730	—	3,933	S. J. R. Dawkins (1985)
Merchant Taylors' School, Middx	1561	750	11,520	6,920	J. R. Gabitass (1991)
Millfield, Street, Somerset	1935	1,220‡	13,785	8,820	C. S. Martin (1990)
Mill Hill School, London nw7	1807	530†	12,045	7,815	W. R. Winfield (1996)
Monkton Combe School, Bath	1868	326‡	12,195	8,400	M. J. Cuthbertson (1990)
Monmouth School, Gwent	1614	570	8,664	5,202	T. H. P. Haynes (1995)
Mount St Mary's College (RC), Sheffield	1842	290‡	9,420	6,150	P. B. Fisher (1991)
Newcastle under Lyme School	1874	1,150‡	—	3,755	Dr R. M. Reynolds (Principal) (1990)
Norwich School	1250	630†	—	4,800	C. D. Brown (1984)
Nottingham High School	1513	826	—	4,923	C. S. Parker (1995)
Oakham School, Rutland	1584	1,000‡	12,240	6,840	A. R. M. Little (1996)
The Oratory School (RC), Berks	1859	380	12,300	8,595	S. W. Barrow (1992)
Oundle School, Northants	1556	835‡	13,380	—	D. B. McMurray (1984)
Pangbourne College, Berks	1917	329‡	11,880	8,310	A. B. E. Hudson (1988)
Perse School, Cambridge	1615	525†	—	4,839	N. P. V. Richardson (1994)
Plymouth College	1877	587‡	9,580	4,995	A. J. Morsley (1992)
Pocklington School, York	1514	620‡	8,904	5,109	J. N. D. Gray (1992)
Portsmouth Grammar School	1732	820‡	—	4,755	A. C. V. Evans (1983)
Prior Park College (RC), Bath	1830	500‡	10,758	5,949	R. G. G. Mercer, d.phil (1996)
Queen Elizabeth GS, Wakefield	1591	751	—	4,368	R. P. Mardling (1985)
Queen Elizabeth's GS, Blackburn	1567	950†	—	4,140	Dr D. S. Hempsall (1995)
Queen Elizabeth's Hospital, Bristol	1590	500	7,431	4,131	Dr R. Gliddon (1986)
Queen's College, Taunton	1843	480‡	9,693	6,354	C. T. Bradnock (1991)
Radley College, Oxon	1847	614	12,900	—	R. M. Morgan (Warden) (1991)
Ratcliffe College (RC), Leicester	1844	490‡	9,459	6,309	T. A. Kilbride (1996)
Reading Blue Coat School	1646	550†	10,050	5,514	Revd A. C. E. Sanders (1974)
Reed's School, Surrey	1813	350†	10,767	8,142	D. E. Prince (1983)
Reigate Grammar School, Surrey	1675	820‡	—	5,160	P. V. Dixon (1996)
Rendcomb College, Glos	1920	241‡	10,800	8,550	J. Tolputt (1987)
Repton School, Derby	1557	560‡	12,120	9,120	G. E. Jones (1987)
RNIB New College, Worcester	1987	122‡	22,636	15,090	Mrs H. Williams (Principal) (1995)
Rossall School, Lancs	1844	400‡	11,628	4,368	R. D. W. Rhodes (1988)
Royal Grammar School, Guildford	1552	840	—	5,980	T. M. S. Young (1992)
Royal Grammar School, Newcastle upon Tyne	1545	935	—	3,885	J. F. X. Miller (1994)
Royal Grammar School, Worcester	1291	773	—	4,590	W. A. Jones (1993)
Rugby School, Warwicks	1567	740‡	13,290	10,440	M. B. Mavor, cvo (1990)
Rydal Penrhos School, Conwy	1880	380‡	10,242	7,389	N. W. Thorne (1991)
Ryde School (with Upper Chine), Isle of Wight	1921	460‡	8,870	4,350	M. D. Featherstone (1990)
St. Albans School, Herts	1570	654†	—	5,865	A. R. Grant (1993)
St Ambrose College, Cheshire	1946	700	—	3,624	G. E. Hester (1991)
St. Bede's College (RC), Manchester	1876	1,000‡	—	3,990	J. Byrne (1983)
St Bees School, Cumbria	1583	285‡	11,016	7,578	P. A. Chamberlain (1988)

Name of School	Foun-ded	No. of pupils	Annual fees £		Head (with date of appointment)
			Boarding	Day	
St Benedict's School (RC), London w5	1902	591†	—	5,220	Dr A. J. Dachs (1987)
St Dunstan's College, London se6	1888	643‡	—	5,745	J. D. Moore (1993)
St Edmund's College (RC), Herts	1568	450‡	10,320	6,480	D. J. J. McEwen (1984)
St Edmund's School, Canterbury	1749	300‡	12,570	8,220	A. N. Ridley (1994)
St Edward's College (RC), Liverpool	1853	750‡		3,798	J. E. Waszek (1992)
St Edward's School, Oxford	1863	560†	12,855	9,465	D. Christie (Warden) (1988)
St George's College (RC), Surrey	1869	530†	—	6,795	J. A. Peake (1995)
St John's School, Surrey	1851	400†	11,100	7,650	C. H. Tongue (1993)
St Lawrence College in Thanet, Kent	1879	370‡	11,835	7,905	M. Slater (1996)
St Mary's College (RC), Merseyside	1919	630‡	—	3,894	W. Hammond (1991)
St Paul's School, London sw13	1509	780	12,765	8,490	R. S. Baldock (High Master) (1992)
St Peter's School, York	627	479‡	10,419	6,066	A. F. Trotman (1995)
Sedbergh School, Cumbria	1525	315	12,150	8,505	C. H. Hirst (1995)
Sevenoaks School, Kent	1418	939‡	12,087	7,362	T. R. Cookson (1996)
Sherborne School, Dorset	1550	600	13,125	10,005	P. H. Lapping (1988)
Shrewsbury School	1552	690	12,990	9,150	F. E. Maidment (1988)
Silcoates School, W. Yorks	1820	422‡	—	5,562	A. P. Spillane (1991)
Solihull School, W. Midlands	1560	810†	—	4,530	P. S. J. Derham (1996)
Stamford School, Lincs	1532	570	8,600	4,300	G. J. Timm (1978)
Stockport Grammar School	1487	985‡	—	4,086	I. Mellor (1996)
Stonyhurst College (RC), Lancs	1593	400†	12,045	7,500	A. J. F. Aylward (1996)
Stowe School, Bucks	1923	550†	4,263	2,935	J. G. L. Nichols (1988)
Sutton Valence School, Kent	1576	380‡	11,700	7,485	N. A. Sampson (1994)
Taunton School	1847	483‡	11,355	7,260	B. B. Sutton (1987)
Tettenhall College, Wolverhampton	1863	220‡	9,147	5,640	Dr P. C. Bodkin (1994)
Tonbridge School, Kent	1553	680	13,620	9,612	J. M. Hammond (1990)
Trent College, Nottingham	1868	700‡	10,899	6,690	J. S. Lee (1988)
Trinity School, Surrey	1596	850	—	5,622	B. J. Lenon (1995)
Truro School	1879	810‡	8,958	4,812	G. A. G. Dodd (1993)
University College School, London nw3	1830	700	—	7,200	K. J. Durham (1996)
Uppingham School, Leics	1584	630†	13,320	7,995	Dr S. C. Winkley (1991)
Warwick School	914	806	10,419	4,854	Dr P. J. Cheshire (1988)
Wellingborough School, Northants	1595	510‡	9,780	5,595	F. R. Ullmann (1993)
Wellington College, Berks	1856	795†	12,750	9,300	C. J. Driver (Master) (1989)
Wellington School, Somerset	1837	547‡	8,394	4,596	A. J. Rogers (1990)
Wells Cathedral School, Somerset	1180	598‡	9,651	5,667	J. S. Baxter (1986)
West Buckland School, Devon	1858	455‡	9,450	5,130	M. Downward (1979)
Westminster School, London sw1	1560	675†	13,530	10,125	D. M. Summerscale (1986)
Whitgift School, Surrey	1596	1,105	—	5,826	C. A. Barnett, d.phil (1991)
William Hulme's GS, Manchester	1887	761‡	—	4,449	P. D. Briggs (1987)
Winchester College, Hants	1382	680	13,944	10,458	J. P. Sabben-Clare (1985)
Wisbech Grammar School, Cambs	1379	640‡	—	4,890	R. S. Repper (1988)
Wolverhampton Grammar School	1512	770‡	—	5,100	B. Trafford (1990)
Woodbridge School, Suffolk	1662	540‡	9,279	5,646	S. H. Cole (1994)
Woodhouse Grove School, Bradford	1812	560‡	9,450	5,565	D. Humphreys (1996)
Worksop College, Notts	1895	350‡	11,325	7,800	R. A. Collard (1994)
Worth School (RC), W. Sussex	1959	315	11,952	8,109	Fr C. Jamison (1994)
Wrekin College, Shropshire	1880	270‡	11,910	6,540	P. M. Johnson (1991)
Wycliffe College, Glos	1882	364‡	12,750	9,000	D. C. M. Prichard (1994)
Yarm School, N. Yorks	1978	520†	—	4,750	R. N. Tate (1978)

SCOTLAND

Name of School	Foun-ded	No. of pupils	Annual fees £		Head (with date of appointment)
Daniel Stewart's and Melville College, Edinburgh	1832	780	8,640	4,320	P. J. F. Tobin (Principal) (1989)
Dollar Academy, Clackmannanshire	1818	767‡	9,612	4,338	J. S. Roberston (Rector) (1994)
The Edinburgh Academy	1824	580†	11,265	5,283	J. V. Light (Rector) (1995)
Fettes College, Edinburgh	1870	495‡	12,810	8,655	M. T. Thyne, frse (1988)
George Heriot's School, Edinburgh	1659	980‡	—	3,936	K. P. Pearson (1983)
George Watson's College, Edinburgh	1741	1,278‡	8,646	4,299	F. E. Gerstenberg (Principal) (1985)
Glasgow Academy	1845	585‡	—	4,485	D. Comins (Rector) (1994)
Glenalmond College, Perth	1841	325‡	12,480	8,325	I. G. Templeton (Warden) (1992)
Gordonstoun School, Moray	1934	420‡	12,480	8,055	M. C. S.-R. Pyper (1990)

Name of School	Foun-ded	No. of pupils	Annual fees £		Head (with date of appointment)
			Boarding	Day	
High School of Dundee	1239	750‡	—	4,170	R. Nimmo, OBE (Rector) (1977)
High School of Glasgow	1124	635‡	—	4,518	R. G. Easton (1983)
Hutcheson's Grammar School, Glasgow	1641	1,213‡	—	3,986	D. R. Ward (Rector) (1987)
Kelvinside Academy, Glasgow	1878	425	—	4,720	J. H. Duff (Rector) (1980)
Loretto School, Midlothian	1827	317‡	12,195	8,130	K. J. Budge (1995)
Merchiston Castle School, Edinburgh	1833	330	11,985	7,965	D. M. Spawforth (1980)
Morrison's Academy, Crieff	1860	449‡	11,121	3,828	G. H. Edwards (Rector) (1996)
Robert Gordon's College, Aberdeen	1729	958‡	—	4,185	B. R. W. Lockhart (1996)
St Aloysius' College, Glasgow	1859	820‡	—	3,300	Revd A. Porter, SJ (1995)
Strathallan School, Perth	1913	495‡	11,775	8,211	A. W. McPhail (1993)

NORTHERN IRELAND

Name of School	Foun-ded	No. of pupils	Annual fees £		Head (with date of appointment)
°Bangor Grammar School, Co. Down	1856	920	—	400	T. W. Patton (1979)
Belfast Royal Academy	1785	1,364‡	—	80	W. M. Sillery (1980)
Campbell College, Belfast	1894	705	5,556	1,041	Dr R. J. I. Pollock (1987)
Coleraine Academical Institution	1856	850	6,600	2,910	R. S. Forsythe (1984)
Methodist College, Belfast	1868	1,853‡	5,792	230	T. W. Mulryne (Principal) (1988)
Portora Royal School, Enniskillen	1618	100	—	42	R. L. Bennett (1983)
Royal Belfast Academical Institution	1810	1,050	—	420	R. M. Ridley (Principal) (1990)

CHANNEL ISLANDS AND ISLE OF MAN

Name of School	Foun-ded	No. of pupils	Annual fees £		Head (with date of appointment)
Elizabeth College, Guernsey	1563	555†	6,660	2,610	J. H. F. Doulton (1988)
King William's College, Isle of Man	1668	320‡	11,580	8,250	P. K. Fulton-Peebles (Principal) (1996)
Victoria College, Jersey	1852	620	—	1,776	J. Hydes (1992)

EUROPE

Name of School	Foun-ded	No. of pupils	Annual fees £		Head (with date of appointment)
Aiglon College, Switzerland	1949	280‡	Fr.45,340	Fr.31,170	R. McDonald (1994)
British School in the Netherlands	1935	490‡	—	Gld.20,490	M. J. Cooper (Principal) (1990)
British School of Brussels	1970	502‡	—	Fr.648,000	Ms J. M. Bray (Principal) (1992)
British School of Paris	1954	320‡	Fr.105,000	Fr.75,000	M. Honour (Principal) (1991)
°The English School, Nicosia, Cyprus	1900	834‡	—	C£1,700	A. M. Hudspeth (1988)
The International School of Geneva	1924	1,000‡	Fr.42,720	Fr.19,040	G. Walker, OBE (Director-General) (1991)
The International School of Paris	1964	220‡	—	Fr.82,000	N. M. Prentki (1988)
King's College, Madrid		n/a‡	—	n/a	Dr G. Percy
St Columba's College, Dublin	1843	265‡	Ir£6,135	Ir£3,540	T. E. Macey (Warden) (1988)
St Edward's College, Malta	1929	600†	—	LM.765	G. Briscoe (1989)
St George's English School, Rome	1958	350‡	—	L.19.4m	B. Gardner (1994)
°Sir James Henderson British School, Milan	1969	170‡	—	L.15m	C. T. G. Leech (Principal) (1986)

OTHER OVERSEAS MEMBERS

AFRICA

DIOCESAN COLLEGE, Rondebosch, SA. Head, C. N. Watson
FALCON COLLEGE, PO Esigodini, Zimbabwe. Head, P. N. Todd
HILTON COLLEGE, Kwazulu-Natal, SA. Head, M. J. Nicholson
MICHAELHOUSE, Balgowan, SA. Head, J. H. Pluke
PETERHOUSE, Marondera, Zimbabwe. Head, M. A. Bawden
ST GEORGE'S COLLEGE, Harare, Zimbabwe. Head, K. F. Brennan
ST JOHN'S COLLEGE, Johannesburg, SA. Head, R. J. D. Clarence
ST STITHIAN'S COLLEGE, Randburg, SA. Head, D. B. Wylde

AUSTRALIA

ANGLICAN CHURCH GRAMMAR SCHOOL, Brisbane, Queensland. Head, C. V. Ellis
BRIGHTON GRAMMAR SCHOOL, Brighton, Victoria. Head, R. L. Rofe
BRISBANE BOYS' COLLEGE, Toowong, Queensland. Head, G. M. Cujes
CAMBERWELL GRAMMAR SCHOOL, Balwyn, Victoria. Head, C. F. Black
CANBERRA GRAMMAR SCHOOL, Redhill, ACT. Head, T. C. Murray
CAULFIELD GRAMMAR SCHOOL, Elsternwick, Victoria. Head, S. H. Newton
CHRIST CHURCH GRAMMAR SCHOOL, Claremont, W. Australia. Head, J. J. S. Madin
CRANBROOK SCHOOL, Sydney, NSW. Head, Dr B. N. Carter
THE GEELONG COLLEGE, Geelong, Victoria. Head, Ms P. Turner

GEELONG GRAMMAR SCHOOL, Corio, Victoria. *Head,*
L. Hannah
GUILDFORD GRAMMAR SCHOOL, Guildford, W. Australia.
Head, J. M. Moody
HAILEYBURY COLLEGE, Keysborough, Victoria. *Head,*
A. H. M. Aikman
THE HALE SCHOOL, Wembley Downs, W. Australia. *Head,*
R. J. Inverarity
THE ILLAWARRA GRAMMAR SCHOOL, Wollongong, NSW.
Head, Revd P. J. R. Smart
THE KING'S SCHOOL, Parramatta, NSW. *Head,*
J. A. Wickham
KINROSS WOLAROI SCHOOL, Orange, NSW. *Head,*
A. E. S. Anderson
KNOX GRAMMAR SCHOOL, Wahroonga, NSW. *Head,*
Dr I. Paterson
MELBOURNE GRAMMAR SCHOOL, South Yarra, Victoria.
Head, A. P. Sheahan
MENTONE GRAMMAR SCHOOL, Mentone, Victoria. *Head,*
N. Clark
NEWINGTON COLLEGE, Stanmore, NSW. *Head,*
M. E. Smee
ST PETER'S COLLEGE, St Peter's, S. Australia. *Head,*
R. L. Burchnall
SCOTCH COLLEGE, Adelaide, S. Australia. *Head,* K. Webb
SCOTCH COLLEGE, Melbourne, Victoria. *Head,*
Dr F. G. Donaldson
SCOTCH COLLEGE, Claremont, W. Australia. *Head,*
W. R. Dickinson
THE SCOTS COLLEGE, Sydney, NSW. *Head,* Dr R. L. Iles
THE SCOTS SCHOOL, Bathurst, NSW. *Head,* R. D. Fraser
THE SOUTHPORT SCHOOL, Southport, Queensland. *Head,*
B. A. Cook
SYDNEY CHURCH OF ENGLAND GRAMMAR SCHOOL,
Sydney, NSW. *Head,* R. A. I. Grant
SYDNEY GRAMMAR SCHOOL, Darlinghurst, NSW. *Head,*
Dr R. D. Townsend
WESLEY COLLEGE, Melbourne, Victoria. *Head,*
D. G. McArthur
WESTBOURNE AND WILLIAMSTOWN GRAMMAR
SCHOOLS, Hoppers Crossing, Victoria. *Head,* G. G. Ryan

CANADA

BRENTWOOD COLLEGE SCHOOL, Mill Bay, BC. *Head,*
W. T. Ross
GLENLYON-NORFOLK SCHOOL, Victoria, BC. *Head,*
D. Brooks
HILLFIELD-STRATHALLAN COLLEGE, Hamilton, Ontario.
Head, W. S. Boyer
PICKERING COLLEGE, Newmarket, Ontario. *Head,* vacant
ST ANDREW'S COLLEGE, Aurora, Ontario. *Head,*
R. P. Bedard
TRINITY COLLEGE SCHOOL, Port Hope, Ontario. *Head,*
R. C. N. Wright
UPPER CANADA COLLEGE, Toronto, Ontario. *Head,*
J. D. Blakey

HONG KONG

ISLAND SCHOOL, Borrett Road. *Head,* D. J. James
KING GEORGE V SCHOOL, Kowloon. *Head,* M. J. Behennah

INDIA

BISHOP COTTON SCHOOL, Shimla. *Head,* K. Mustafi
THE CATHEDRAL AND JOHN CONNON SCHOOL, Bombay.
Head, D. E. W. Shaw
THE LAWRENCE SCHOOL, Sanawar. *Head,* Dr H. S. Dhillon
THE SCINDIA SCHOOL, Gwalior. *Head,* A. N. Dar

MALAYSIA

KOLEJ TUANKU JA'AFAR, Negeri Sembilan. *Head,*
S. Morris

NEW ZEALAND

CHRIST'S COLLEGE, Christchurch. *Head,* Dr M. J. Rosser
KING'S COLLEGE, Auckland. *Head,* J. S. Taylor
ST ANDREW'S COLLEGE, Christchurch. *Head,* B. Maister
THE COLLEGIATE SCHOOL, Wanganui. *Head,*
T. S. McKinley
WAITAKI BOYS' HIGH SCHOOL, Oamaru. *Head,*
B. R. Gollop

PAKISTAN

AITCHISON COLLEGE, Lahore. *Head,* S. Khan

SOUTH AMERICA

ACADEMIA BRITANICA CUSCATLECA, Santa Tecla, El
Salvador. *Head,* R. Braund
THE BRITISH SCHOOLS, Montevideo, Uruguay. *Head,*
C. D. T. Smith
MARKHAM COLLEGE, Lima, Peru. *Head,* W. J. Baker
ST ANDREW'S SCOTS SCHOOL, Buenos Aires, Argentina.
Head, A. G. F. Fisher
ST GEORGE'S COLLEGE, Buenos Aires, Argentina. *Head,*
N. P. O. Green
ST PAULS' SCHOOL, São Paulo, Brazil. *Head,*
M. T. M. C. McCann

USA

ST MARK'S COLLEGE, Southborough, Massachusetts.
Head, A. J. de V. Hill

ADDITIONAL MEMBERS

The headteachers of some maintained schools are by
invitation Additional Members of the HMC. They include
the following:

BISHOP WORDSWORTH'S SCHOOL, Salisbury. *Head,*
C. D. Barnett
DURHAM JOHNSTON COMPREHENSIVE SCHOOL, Durham.
Head, J. Dunford
EGGBUCKLAND COMMUNITY COLLEGE, Plymouth. *Head,*
H. E. Green
HAYWARDS HEATH SIXTH FORM COLLEGE, W. Sussex.
Head, B. W. Derbyshire
HINCHINGBROOKE SCHOOL, Huntington, Cambs. *Head,*
P. J. Downes
THE JUDD SCHOOL, Tonbridge, Kent. *Head,* K. A. Starling
LISKEARD SCHOOL AND COMMUNITY COLLEGE, Liskeard,
Cornwall. *Head,* A. D. Wood
THE LONDON ORATORY SCHOOL, London SW6. *Head,*
J. C. McIntosh
PRESCOT COLLEGE, Prescot, Merseyside. *Head,*
P. A. Barlow
PRINCE HENRY'S GRAMMAR SCHOOL, Otley, W Yorks.
Head, M. Franklin
PRINCE WILLIAM SCHOOL, Oundle, Cambs. *Head,*
C. J. Lowe
THE ROYAL GRAMMAR SCHOOL, Lancaster. *Head,*
P. J. Mawby
ST ANSELM'S COLLEGE, Birkenhead, Merseyside. *Head,*
C. J. Cleugh
ST JOHN'S SCHOOL, Marlborough, Wilts. *Head,* J. T. Price

SOCIETY OF HEADMASTERS AND HEADMISTRESSES OF INDEPENDENT SCHOOLS

The Society was founded in 1961 and, in general, represents smaller boarding schools.

Secretary, I. D. Cleland, Celedston, Rhosesmore Road, Halkyn, Holywell CH8 8DL. Tel: 01352-781102

Headmasters of the following schools are members of both HMC and SHMIS; details of these schools appear in the HMC list: Abbotsholme School, Bedales School, Churcher's College, City of London Freemen's School, Colston's Collegiate School, King's School, Gloucester, King's School, Tynemouth, Lord Wandsworth College, Pang-bourne College, Reading Blue Coat School, Reed's School, Rendcomb College, Ryde School, St George's College, Silcoates School, Tettenhall College, Wisbech Grammar School, Woodbridge School, Yarm School

* Woodard Corporation School
† Girls in VI form
‡ Co-educational
° 1995 figures
§ Entry into SHMIS subject to confirmation

Name of School	Foun-ded	No. of pupils	Annual fees £		Head (with date of appointment)
			Boarding	Day	
Abbey Gate College, Saighton, Chester	1977	300‡	—	4,221	E. W. Mitchell (1991)
Austin Friars School (*RC*), Carlisle	1951	304‡	7,956	4,734	M. G. Taylor (1994)
Bearwood College, Berks	1827	220‡	10,500	5,850	Dr R. J. Belcher (1993)
Bedstone College, Shropshire	1948	200‡	10,500	6,006	M. S. Symonds (1991)
°Bembridge School, Isle of Wight	1919	200‡	9,270	4,620	J. High (1986)
Bentham School, N. Yorks	1726	220‡	9,450	4,710	T. Halliwell (1995)
Bethany School, Kent	1866	275‡	9,819	6,282	W. M. Harvey (1988)
Birkdale School, Sheffield	1904	500†	—	4,599	Revd M. D. A. Hepworth (1983)
Box Hill School, Surrey	1959	260‡	10,530	6,300	Dr R. A. S. Atwood (1987)
Carmel College (*Jewish*), Oxon	1948	143‡	13,000	7,500	P. D. Skelker (1984)
Claremont Fan Court School, Surrey	1932	306‡	9,435	5,970	Mrs. P. B. Farrar (*Principal*) (1994)
Claysmore School, Dorset	1896	290‡	11,640	8,145	D. J. Beeby (1986)
Cokethorpe School, Oxon	1957	225‡	12,420	8,010	P. J. S. Cantwell (1995)
Duke of York's Royal Military School, Dover	1803	500‡	795	—	Col. G. H. Wilson (1992)
Elmhurst Ballet School, Surrey	1903	72‡	9,570	7,020	J. McNamara (*Principal*) (1995)
Embley Park School, Romsey, Hants	1946	250‡	9,945	6,060	D. F. Chapman (1987)
Ewell Castle School, Surrey	1926	320†	—	4,635	R. A. Fewtrell (1983)
Friends' School, Essex	1702	230‡	10,614	6,369	Ms J. Laing (1996)
°Fulneck School (Boys), W. Yorks	1753	425‡	8,655	4,620	Mrs B. A. Heppell (1994)
*Grenville College, Devon	1954	300‡	10,551	5,175	Dr M. C. V. Cane (1992)
Halliford School, Middx	1956	281†	—	4,680	J. R. Crook (1984)
Hipperholme Grammar School, Halifax	1648	322‡	—	3,750	C. C. Robinson (1988)
Keil School, Dumbarton	1915	220‡	9,300	5,100	J. A. Cummings (1993)
Kingham Hill School, Oxon	1886	210‡	9,945	5,970	M. H. Payne (*Warden*) (1990)
Kirkham Grammar School, Lancs	1549	545‡	7,500	3,870	B. Stacey (1991)
Langley School, Norfolk	1910	247‡	10,500	5,460	S. J. W. McArthur (1989)
Lord Mayor Treloar College, Hants	1908	114‡	40,452	30,339	N. Clark (1989)
Milton Abbey School, Dorset	1954	83	12,090	8,070	W. J. Hughes-D'Aeth (1995)
Oswestry School, Shropshire	1407	245‡	9,591	5,556	P. K. Smith (1995)
The Purcell School (music), Middx	1962	144‡	17,343	11,283	K. J. Bain (1983)
Rannoch School, Perth	1959	230‡	10,764	5,655	M. Barratt (1982)
Rishworth School, W. Yorks	1724	400‡	9,900	4,818	M. J. Elford (1992)
°Rougemont School, Torfaen	1919	170‡	—	4,602	I. Brown (1995)
Royal Hospital School, Ipswich	1712	650‡	7,875	4,050	N. K. D. Ward (1995)
Royal Russell School, Surrey	1853	450‡	10,035	5,550	Dr J. R. Jennings (1996)
°Royal School, Dungannon, N. Ireland	1614	700‡	5,726	85	P. D. Hewitt (1984)
Royal Wolverhampton School	1850	310‡	10,545	5,385	Mrs B. A. Evans (1995)
Ruthin School, Denbighshire	1574	171‡	10,350	6,510	J. S. Rowlands (1993)
St Bede's School, E. Sussex	1979	450‡	11,925	7,200	R. A. Perrin (1978)
St Christopher School, Letchworth	1915	330‡	11,454	6,489	C. Reid (1980)
St David's College, Conwy	1965	210	10,178	6,619	W. Seymour (1991)
Scarborough College, N. Yorks	1898	360‡	9,843	5,337	T. L. Kirkup (1996)
Seaford College, W. Sussex	1884	290‡	10,250	6,450	R. C. Hannaford (1990)
Shebbear College, Devon	1841	240‡	9,816	5,268	R. J. Buley (1983)
Shiplake College, Oxon	1959	295	11,730	7,890	N. V. Bevan (1988)
Sibford School, Oxon	1842	250‡	10,035	5,310	Ms S. Freestone (from January 1997)
Sidcot School, North Somerset	1808	405‡	9,930	5,925	C. J. Greenfield (1986)

Name of School	Foun-ded	No. of pupils	Annual fees £		Head (with date of appointment)
			Boarding	Day	
Stafford Grammar School, Staffs	1982	300‡	—	4,080	M. S. James (1992)
Stanbridge Earls School, Hants	1952	180‡	12,120	3,690	H. Moxon (1984)
Sunderland High School	1887	246‡	—	3,915	Ms C. Rendle-Short (1993)
Warminster School, Wilts	1707	290‡	9,690	5,610	T. D. Holgate (1990)
Yehudi Menuhin School (music), Surrey	1963	50‡	varies	varies	N. Chisholm (1988)

GIRLS' SCHOOLS ASSOCIATION

THE GIRLS' SCHOOLS ASSOCIATION, 130 Regent Road, Leicester LEI 7PG. Tel: 0116-254 1619
President (from Jan. 1997), Mrs J. Lang
Secretary, Ms S. Cooper

CSC Church Schools Company, Church Schools House, Chapel Street, Titchmarsh, Kettering, Northants NNI4 3DA. Tel: 01832-735105
§ Girls Public Day School Trust, 26 Queen Anne's Gate, London SWIH 9AN. Tel: 0171-222 9595
* Woodard Corporation School
† Boys in VI form
‡ Co-educational
° 1995 figures

Name of School	Foun-ded	No. of pupils	Annual fees £		Head (with date of appointment)
			Boarding	Day	
ENGLAND AND WALES					
Abbey School, Reading	1887	710	—	4,350	Miss B. C. L. Sheldon (1991)
Abbot's Hill, Herts	1912	160	10,710	6,330	Mrs K. Lewis (from January 1997)
Adcote School for Girls, Shropshire	1907	94	9,540	5,295	Mrs S. B. Cecchet (1979)
Alice Ottley School, Worcester	1883	573	—	5,052	Miss C. Sibbit (1986)
Amberfield School, Ipswich	1952	170	—	3,990	Mrs L. A. Lewis (1992)
Ashford School, Kent	1910	366	11,319	6,513	Mrs P. Metham (1992)
Atherley School, Southampton (CSC)	1926	246	—	4,482	Mrs C. Madina (1994)
Badminton School, Bristol	1858	300	11,850	6,600	C. J. T. Gould (1981)
Bath High School	1875	450	—	4,140	Miss M. A. Winfield (1985)
Bedford High School	1882	740	9,453	4,995	Mrs B. E. Stanley (1995)
Bedgebury School, Kent	1860	224	11,301	6,996	Mrs L. J. Griffin (1995)
Beechwood Sacred Heart (RC), Kent	1915	160	11,190	6,675	T. S. Hodkinson (1993)
Belvedere School, Liverpool	1880	482	—	4,140	Mrs C. H. Evans (1992)
Benenden School, Kent	1923	430	13,260	—	Mrs G. duCharme (1985)
Berkhamsted School, Herts	1888	400†	10,113	5,973	Dr P. Chadwick (1996)
Birkenhead High School	1901	682	—	4,140	Mrs K. R. Irving (1986)
Blackheath High School, London SE3	1880	358	—	4,920	Miss R. K. Musgrave (1989)
Bolton School, Lancs	1877	804	—	4,626	Miss E. J. Panton (1994)
Bradford Girls' Grammar School	1875	650	—	4,200	Mrs L. J. Warrington (1987)
Brighton and Hove High School	1876	506	—	4,140	Miss R. A. Woodbridge (1989)
Brigidine School, Windsor	1948	210	—	4,680	Mrs M. B. Cairns (1986)
Bromley High School, Kent	1883	543	—	4,920	Mrs E. J. Hancock (1989)
Bruton School, Somerset	1900	501	7,761	4,011	Mrs J. M. Wade (1987)
Burgess Hill School, W. Sussex	1906	360	9,675	5,730	Mrs R. F. Lewis (1992)
Bury Grammar School, Lancs	1884	800	—	3,876	Miss J. M. Lawley (1987)
Casterton School, Carnforth, Lancs	1823	350	9,618	6,030	A. F. Thomas (1990)
Central Newcastle High School	1895	612	—	4,140	Mrs A. M. Chapman (1985)
Channing School, London N6	1885	322	—	5,880	Mrs I. R. Raphael (1984)
Cheltenham Ladies' College, Glos	1853	844	12,900	8,190	Mrs A. V. Tuck (Principal) (1996)
City of London School for Girls, London EC2	1894	548	—	5,427	Mrs Y. A. Burne, PH.D. (1995)
Clifton High School, Bristol	1877	412	8,535	4,470	Mrs Y. G. Graham (1996)
Cobham Hall, Kent	1962	180	13,500	8,250	Mrs R. J. McCarthy (1989)
Colston's Girls' School, Bristol	1891	490	—	3,840	Mrs J. P. Franklin (1989)
Combe Bank School, Kent	1868	210	—	6,030	Miss N. Spurr (1993)
Commonweal Lodge School, Surrey	1916	100	—	4,680	Mrs S. Law (1995)
Cranford House School, Oxon	1931	80	—	4,920	Mrs A. B. Gray (1992)
Croft House School, Dorset	1941	100	10,215	7,215	M. P. Hawkins (1993)

Name of School	Foun-ded	No. of pupils	Annual fees £		Head (with date of appointment)
			Boarding	Day	
Croham Hurst School, Surrey	1899	320	—	4,890	Miss S. C. Budgen (1994)
§Croydon High School, Surrey	1874	714	—	4,920	Mrs P. E. Davies (1990)
°Dame Allan's Girls' School, Newcastle upon Tyne	1705	388†	—	3,570	T. A. Willcocks (Principal) (1988)
Derby High School	1892	320	—	4,500	G. H. Goddard, ph.d. (1983)
Downe House, Berks	1907	640	12,915	9,360	Mrs A. G Watkin (acting) (1996)
Dunottar School, Surrey	1926	290	—	4,875	Ms M. Skinner (from January 1997)
Durham High School for Girls	1884	273	—	4,593	Miss M. L. Walters (1992)
°Edgbaston Church of England College	1886	350	—	4,275	Mrs A. Varley-Tipton (1992)
Edgbaston High School for Girls	1876	495	—	4,425	Mrs S. J. Horsman (1987)
Edgehill College, Devon	1884	350‡	10,050	5,490	Mrs E. M. Burton (1987)
Elmslie Girls' School, Lancs	1918	170	—	4,425	Miss E. M. Smithies (1978)
Farlington School, W. Sussex	1896	250	9,870	6,090	Mrs P. M. Mawer (1992)
Farnborough Hill, Hants	1889	530	—	4,782	Miss R. McGeoch (1996)
Farringtons and Stratford House, Kent	1911	260	10,278	5,205	Mrs B. J. Stock (1987)
Francis Holland School, London nw1	1878	366	—	5,640	Mrs P. H. Parsonson (1988)
Francis Holland School, London sw1	1881	190	—	6,330	Mrs J. A. Anderson (1982)
Gateways School, Leeds	1941	180	—	3,750	Mrs J. E. Stephen (1994)
°Godolphin School, Wilts	1726	387	10,779	6,456	Miss J. Horsburgh (1996)
Godolphin and Latymer School, London w6	1905	716	—	6,285	Miss M. Rudland (1986)
Greenacre School, Surrey	1933	218	—	5,250	Mrs P. M. Wood (1990)
Guildford High School (CSC)	1888	519	—	5,385	Mrs S. H. Singer (1991)
Haberdashers' Aske's School for Girls, Herts	1873	825	—	4,410	Mrs P. Penney (1991)
Haberdashers' Monmouth School	1891	646	8,592	4,521	Mrs. D. L. Newman (1992)
Harrogate Ladies' College	1893	300	9,495	6,324	Dr M. J. Hustler (1996)
Headington School, Oxford	1915	541	9,600	4,830	Mrs H. A. Fender (1996)
Heathfield School, Ascot, Berks	1900	210	13,125	—	Mrs J. M. Benammar (1992)
§Heathfield School, Pinner, Middx	1900	293	—	4,920	Mrs J. Merritt (1988)
Hethersett Old Hall School, Norwich	1928	215	9,225	4,650	Mrs V. M. Redington (1983)
Highclare School, W. Midlands	1932	173†	—	4,380	Mrs C. A. Hanson (1974)
Hollygirt School, Nottingham	1877	220	—	3,795	Mrs M. R. Banks (1985)
Holy Child School, Birmingham	1933	148	—	4,725	Mrs J. M. C. Hill (1993)
Holy Trinity College, Bromley	1886	270	—	4,347	Mrs D. A. Bradshaw (1994)
Holy Trinity School, Kidderminster	1903	200	—	3,885	Mrs S. M. Bell (1990)
Howell's School, Denbigh	1859	206	10,485	6,840	Mrs M. Steel (1991)
§Howell's School, Llandaff, Cardiff	1860	552	—	4,140	Mrs C. J. Fitz (1991)
Hull High School (CSC)	1890	146	—	4,125	Mrs M. A. Benson (1994)
Hulme Grammar School, Oldham	1895	530	—	3,726	Miss M. S. Smolenski (1992)
Ilford Ursuline High School, Essex	1903	350	—	4,575	Miss J. Reddington (1990)
§Ipswich High School	1878	463	—	4,140	Miss V. C. MacCuish (1993)
James Allen's Girls' School, London se22	1741	740	—	6,150	Mrs M. Gibbs (1994)
Kent College	1885	240	11,700	6,960	Miss B. J. Crompton (1990)
King Edward VI High School for Girls, Birmingham	1883	550	—	4,500	Ms S. H. Evans (1996)
King's HS for Girls, Warwick	1879	560	—	4,350	Mrs J. M. Anderson (1987)
Kingsley School, Warks	1884	600	—	4,485	Mrs M. A. Webster (1988)
Lady Eleanor Holles School, Middx	1711	692	—	5,520	Miss E. M. Candy (1981)
La Retraite School, Wilts	1953	120	—	4,845	Mrs R. A. Simmons (1994)
Lavant House Rosemead School, W. Sussex	1919	134	10,425	5,850	Mrs S. E. Watkins (1996)
Leeds Girls' High School	1876	600	—	4,617	Miss P. A. Randall (1977)
Leicester High School	1906	300	—	4,500	Mrs P. A. Watson (1992)
Lincoln Minster School	1905	200‡	8,000	4,500	Mrs M. Bradley (1996)
Loughborough High School	1850	529	—	4,194	Miss J. E. L. Harvatt (1978)
Luckley-Oakfield School, Berks	1895	240	8,349	5,175	R. C. Blake (1984)
Malvern Girls' College, Worcs	1893	160	12,285	8,190	Revd P. D. Newton (acting) (1996)
Manchester High School	1874	700‡	—	4,185	Miss E. M. Diggory (1994)
Manor House School, Little Bookham, Surrey	1927	140	8,190	5,640	Mrs L. Mendes (1989)
Maynard School, Exeter	1877	484	—	4,440	Miss F. Murdin (1980)
Merchant Taylors' School, Liverpool	1888	660	—	3,933	Mrs J. I. Mills (1994)
Moira House School, E. Sussex	1875	215	11,340	7,320	A. R. Underwood (1975)
More House School, London sw1	1953	200	—	5,700	Miss M. Connell (1991)
Moreton Hall, Shropshire	1913	280	11,700	8,100	J. Forster (1992)

Name of School	Foun-ded	No. of pupils	Annual fees £		Head (with date of appointment)
			Boarding	Day	
Mount School, York	1831	251	10,170	6,255	Miss B. J. Windle (1986)
Newcastle upon Tyne Church HS	1885	365	—	3,960	Mrs L. G. Smith (1996)
New Hall School, Chelmsford, Essex	1642	410	10,830	6,930	Sr Anne-Marie (1996)
Northampton High School	1878	587	—	4,275	Mrs L. A. Mayne (1988)
North Foreland Lodge, Hants	1909	150	11,550	7,050	Miss S. Cameron (1996)
North London Collegiate School	1850	745	—	5,124	Mrs J. L. Clanchy (1986)
Northwood College, Middx	1878	418	—	5,172	Mrs J. A. Mayou (1991)
Norwich High School	1875	645	—	4,140	Mrs V. C. Bidwell (1985)
Nottingham High School	1875	820	—	4,140	Mrs A. C. Rees (1996)
Notting Hill and Ealing High School	1873	564	—	4,920	Mrs S. M. Whitfield (1991)
Ockbrook School, Derby	1799	470	7,392	3,978	Miss D. P. Bolland (1995)
Old Palace School, Surrey	1887	599	—	4,293	Miss K. L. Hilton (1974)
Oxford High School	1875	551	—	4,140	Miss F. Lusk (from January 1997)
Palmers Green High School, London N21	1905	140	—	4,650	Mrs S. Grant (1989)
Parsons Mead, Surrey	1897	250	9,270	5,280	Miss E. B. Plant (1990)
Perse School for Girls, Cambridge	1881	540	—	4,935	Miss H. S. Smith (1989)
Peterborough High School	1939	170	8,838	4,401	Mrs A. J. V. Storey (1977)
Pipers Corner School, Bucks	1930	300	9,702	5,808	Mrs V. M. Staltensfield (1996)
Polam Hall School, Co. Durham	1848	320	9,159	4,479	Mrs H. C. Hamilton (1986)
Portsmouth High School	1882	511	—	4,140	Mrs J. M. Dawtrey (1984)
Princess Helena College, Herts	1820	150	10,410	7,245	J. Jarvis (1995)
Prior's Field, Surrey	1902	230	10,287	6,867	Mrs J. M. McCallum (1987)
Putney High School, London SW15	1893	573	—	4,920	Mrs E. Merchant (1991)
Queen Anne's School, Berks	1698	175	11,820	7,740	Mrs D. Forbes (1993)
Queen Ethelburga's College, York	1912	200	11,397	7,497	Mrs G. L. Richardson (Principal) (1993)
Queen Margaret's School, York	1901	360	10,626	6,732	Dr G. A. H. Chapman (1992)
Queen Mary School, Lytham, Lancs	1930	460	—	3,870	Miss M. C. Ritchie (1981)
Queen's College, London W1	1848	368	—	6,105	Lady Goodhart (1991)
Queen's Gate School, London SW7	1891	240	—	5,325	Mrs A. M. Holyoak (Principal) (1988)
Queen's School, Chester	1878	468	—	4,545	Miss D. M. Skilbeck (1989)
Queenswood, Herts	1894	400	11,958	7,374	Ms C. Farr (Principal) (1996)
Redland High School for Girls, Bristol	1882	352	—	4,200	Mrs C. Lear (1989)
Red Maids' School, Bristol	1634	503	7,776	3,888	Miss S. Hampton (1987)
Rickmansworth Masonic School, Herts	1788	540	8,811	5,361	Mrs I. M. Andrews (1992)
Roedean School, Brighton	1885	400	13,635	7,740	Mrs A. R. Longley (1984)
The Royal School, Bath	1864	210	11,001	5,886	Mrs E. McKendrick (1994)
The Royal School, Surrey	1840	320	10,017	6,363	C. Brooks (1985)
Rydal Penrhos School (Girls), Colwyn Bay	1880	216	9,720	6,660	C. M. J. Allen (1993)
Rye St Antony School (RC), Oxford	1930	350	8,880	5,280	Miss A. M. Jones (1990)
St Albans High School, Herts	1889	532	—	5,040	Mrs C. Y. Daly (1994)
St Andrew's School, Bedford	1897	140	—	3,912	Mrs J. M. Mark (1995)
St Anne's School, Cumbria	1863	250	9,540	6,330	R. D. Hunter (1996)
St Antony's-Leweston School (RC), Dorset	1891	290	10,935	7,140	Miss B. A. King (1996)
St Catherine's School, Surrey	1885	471	9,630	5,880	Mrs C. M. Oulton (1994)
St David's School, Middx	1716	230	9,585	5,394	Mrs J. G. Osborne (1985)
St Dunstan's Abbey School, Devon	1850	180	8,652	4,860	R. A. Bye (1990)
St Elphin's School, Derbys	1844	160	10,197	5,940	Mrs V. E. Fisher (1994)
St Felix School, Suffolk	1897	195	11,100	7,200	Mrs S. R. Campion (1991)
St Francis' College (RC), Herts	1933	196	9,810	5,025	Miss M. Hegarty (1993)
St Gabriel's School, Berks	1929	158	—	5,034	D. Cobb (1990)
St George's School, Ascot, Berks	1923	290	12,150	7,350	Mrs A. M. Griggs (1989)
School of S. Helen and S. Katharine, Oxon	1903	522	—	4,704	Mrs C. L. Hall (1993)
St Helen's School, Middx	1899	609	9,576	5,082	Mrs D. M. Jefkins (1995)
S. Hilary's School, Cheshire	1880	120	—	4,230	Ms G. M. Case (1995)
St James's and the Abbey, Worcs	1896	177	11,565	7,308	Miss E. M. Mullenger (1986)
St Joseph's Convent School (RC), Berks	1909	378	—	4,065	Mrs V. Brookes (1990)
St Leonards-Mayfield School, E. Sussex	1850	525	10,740	7,160	Sr J. Sinclair (1980)
St Margaret's School, Bushey, Herts	1749	335	9,210	5,625	Miss M. de Villiers (1992)
St Margaret's School, Exeter	1904	350	7,104	4,323	Mrs M. D'Albertanson (1993)
St Martin's School, Solihull	1941	212	—	4,590	Mrs S. J. Williams (1988)
School of S. Mary and S. Anne, Abbots Bromley, Staffs	1874	227	11,205	7,485	A. J. Grigg (1989)

Name of School	Foun-ded	No. of pupils	Annual fees £		Head (with date of appointment)
			Boarding	Day	
St Mary's Convent School, Worcester	1934	220	—	3,780	Miss G. Morrissey (1995)
St Mary's Hall, Brighton	1836	263	9,315	6,180	Mrs P. J. James (1991)
St Mary's School (RC), Ascot, Berks	1885	338	12,246	7,705	Sr M. F. Orchard (1982)
°St Mary's School, Calne, Wilts	1872	307	11,550	6,825	Mrs C. Shaw (1996)
St Mary's School, Cambridge	1898	555	7,410	4,140	Ms M. Conway (1989)
St Mary's School, Colchester	1908	210	—	3,960	Mrs G. M. G. Mouser (1981)
°St Mary's School, Gerrards Cross	1872	190	—	4,995	Mrs F. Balcombe (1995)
St Mary's School (RC), Shaftesbury	1945	310	9,990	6,420	Sr M. Campion Livesey (1985)
St Mary's School, Wantage, Oxon	1873	220	11,550	7,698	Mrs S. Bodinham (1994)
St Maur's Senior School, Weybridge	1898	390	—	4,530	Mrs M. E. Dodds (1991)
St Paul's Girls' School, London w6	1904	620	—	6,627	Miss J. Gough (High Mistress) (1992)
St Swithun's School, Winchester	1884	455	11,580	6,990	Ms H. Harvey, ph.D. (1995)
St Teresa's School, Dorking	1928	330	10,785	5,325	L. Allan (1987)
Selwyn School, Glos		130	8,430	4,800	Miss L. M. Brown (1994)
§Sheffield High School	1878	545	—	4,140	Mrs M. A. Houston (1989)
Sherborne School for Girls, Dorset	1899	430	12,240	8,550	Miss J. M. Taylor (1985)
§Shrewsbury High School	1885	406	—	4,140	Miss S. Gardner (1990)
Sir William Perkins's School, Surrey	1725	590	—	4,170	Miss S. Ross (1994)
§South Hampstead High School, London NW3	1876	630	—	4,920	Mrs J. G. Scott (1993)
Stamford High School, Lincs	1876	713	8,616	4,308	Miss G. K. Bland (1978)
Stonar School, Wilts	1921	402	9,915	5,490	Mrs S. Hopkinson (1985)
Stover School, Devon	1932	188	8,580	4,559	P. E. Bujak (1994)
§Streatham Hill and Clapham High School, London SW2	1887	419	—	4,920	Miss G. M. Ellis (1979)
Surbiton High School, Surrey (CSC)	1884	597	—	5,130	Miss M. G. Perry (1993)
§Sutton High School, Surrey	1884	494	—	4,920	Mrs A. J. Coutts (1995)
§Sydenham High School, London SE26	1887	458	—	4,920	Mrs G. Baker (1988)
Talbot Heath, Dorset	1886	418	9,150	5,250	Mrs C. Dipple (1991)
Teesside High School, Stockton-on-Tees	1970	400	—	3,936	Miss J. F. Hamilton (1995)
Tormead School, Surrey	1905	502	—	5,370	Mrs H. E. M. Alleyne (1992)
Truro High School	1880	350	8,364	4,551	J. Graham-Brown (1992)
Tudor Hall School, Oxon	1850	262	10,545	6,570	Miss N. Godfrey (1984)
Ursuline College, Kent	1904	360‡	10,600	5,400	Sr A. Montgomery (1995)
Wakefield Girls' High School	1878	741	—	4,368	Mrs P. A. Langham (1987)
Walthamstow Hall, Kent	1838	315	12,360	6,660	Mrs J. S. Lang (1984)
Wentworth College, Dorset	1871	241	9,330	5,850	Miss S. D. Coe (1990)
Westfield School, Newcastle upon Tyne	1962	220	—	4,392	Mrs M. Farndale (1990)
West Heath, Kent	1867	110	12,030	8,070	Mrs A. Williamson (Principal) (1994)
Westholme School, Lancs	1923	625	—	3,690	Mrs L. Croston (Principal) (1988)
Westonbirt School, Glos	1928	220	11,340	7,380	Mrs G. Hylson-Smith (1986)
§Wimbledon High School, London SW19	1880	569	—	4,920	Dr J. L. Clough (1995)
Wispers School, Surrey	1946	120	9,507	6,117	L. H. Beltran (1980)
Withington Girls' School, Manchester	1890	525	—	3,930	Mrs M. Kenyon (1986)
Woldingham School, Surrey	1842	530	12,009	7,263	P. Dineen, ph.D. (1985)
°Wychwood School, Oxford	1897	160	6,885	4,350	Mrs M. L. Duffill (1981)
Wycombe Abbey School, Bucks	1896	500	12,780	9,585	Mrs J. M. Goodland (1989)
Wykeham House School, Fareham, Hants	1913	300	—	4,059	Mrs R. M. Kamaryc (1995)

SCOTLAND

Kilgraston School, Perthshire	1930	180	10,335	5,955	Mrs J. L. Austin (1993)
Laurel Park School, Glasgow	1903	550	—	3,969	Mrs E. Surber (1996)
Mary Erskine School, Edinburgh	1694	652	8,640	4,320	P. F. J. Tobin (Principal) (1989)
St Denis and Cranley School, Edinburgh	1858	130	9,975	5,085	Mrs S. Duncanson (1996)
St George's School, Edinburgh	1888	568	9,075	4,575	J. McClure, D.phil. (1994)
St Leonards School, St Andrews	1877	280	12,366	6,540	Mrs M. James (1988)
St Margaret's School, Aberdeen	1846	219	—	3,924	Miss L. M. Ogilvie (1989)
St Margaret's School, Edinburgh	1890	363	8,685	4,305	Miss A. Mitchell (1994)

CHANNEL ISLANDS

The Ladies' College, Guernsey	1872	359	—	2,250	Miss M. E. Macdonald (Principal) (1992)

Social Welfare

National Health Service
and Local Authority Personal Social Services

The National Health Service came into being on 5 July 1948 as a result of the National Health Service Act 1946, covering England and Wales, and separate legislation for Scotland and Northern Ireland. The Acts placed a duty on the relevant Secretaries of State to promote the establishment of a comprehensive health service designed to secure improvement in the mental and physical health of the people and the prevention, diagnosis and treatment of illness. The National Health Service is administered in England by the Secretary of State for Health, and in Wales, Scotland and Northern Ireland by the Secretaries of State for Wales, Scotland and Northern Ireland.

The National Health Service covers a comprehensive range of hospital, specialist, family practitioner (medical, dental, ophthalmic and pharmaceutical), artificial limb and appliance, ambulance, and community health services. Everyone normally resident in the UK is entitled to use any of these services without charge, except where charges are specifically provided for by statute, e.g. prescriptions.

In addition, the Secretary of State for Health is responsible under the Local Authority Social Services Act 1970 for the provision by local authorities of social services for the elderly, the disabled, those with mental disorders and for families and children.

The NHS is financed mainly from taxation and the cost met from moneys voted by Parliament. The estimated level of expenditure in 1996–7 is £42,600 million.

STRUCTURE
The National Health Service and Community Care Act 1990 reformed management and patient care. The Act provided for more streamlined Regional and District Health Authorities and Family Health Services Authorities, and for the establishment of NHS Trusts, which operate as self-governing health care providers. One result of the Act is that health care is provided through NHS contracts, where one body (the purchaser) is responsible for obtaining the appropriate health care for its population from another body (the provider). From 1 April 1993, the Community Care Reforms introduced changes in the way care is administered for the elderly, the mentally ill, the physically handicapped and people with learning disabilities.

On 31 March 1996 the eight Regional Health Authorities (RHAs) in England were replaced by eight NHS Executive regional offices which have taken on the functions of the RHAs. They are responsible for regional planning, the allocation of resources to Health Authorities (HAs) and general practitioner fundholders, and the promotion of national policies and priorities, and are directly accountable to the Secretary of State for Health.

From April 1996, 100 new Health Authorities (HAs) replaced the District Health Authorities and Family Health Service Authorities and have taken on the combined duties and responsibilities of both. They are responsible for developing strategies, in liaison with general practitioners, the public, local authorities and other public bodies, to improve health and secure a comprehensive range of health and health-care services for their local populations within national guidelines. HAs'

resources are allocated by the NHS Executive headquarters, to which they are also accountable for their performance.

HEALTH SERVICES

FAMILY DOCTOR SERVICE
In England and Wales the Family Doctor Service (or General Medical Services) was managed by 98 Family Health Services Authorities (FHSAs) which also organized the general dental, pharmaceutical and ophthalmic services for their areas. These functions are now the responsibility of the Health Authorities (HAs). In England the chairman is appointed by the Secretary of State and the non-executive members by the regional offices of the NHS Executive. In Wales the chairman and non-executive members are appointed by the Secretary of State.

Any doctor may take part in the Family Doctor Service (provided the area in which he/she wishes to practise has not already an adequate number of doctors) and about 28,000 general practitioners in England and Wales do so. They may at the same time have private fee-paying patients. Family doctors are paid for their NHS work in accordance with a scheme of remuneration which includes a basic practice allowance, capitation fees, reimbursement of certain practice expenses and payments for out-of-hours work.

The National Health Service and Community Care Act 1990 enables general practitioner practices to apply for fundholding status. This makes the practice responsible for its own NHS budget for a specified range of goods and services. Since 1 April 1996 there have been two types of general practitioner fundholding: Standard fundholders, for practices with at least 5,000 patients, who purchase a full range of in- and out-patient services; and Community fundholders, for smaller practices of at least 3,000 patients, who purchase only community nursing services and diagnostic tests. There are currently 3,000 fundholding units, comprising 3,735 practices. Fundholding practices are monitored by the HAs on behalf of the NHS Executive regional offices.

Everyone aged 16 or over can choose their doctor (parents or guardians choose for children under 16) and the doctor is also free to accept a person or not as he or she chooses. A person may change their doctor if they wish, by going to the surgery of a general practitioner of their choice who is willing to accept them, and either handing in their medical card to register or filling in a form. When people are away from home they can still use the Family Doctor Service if they ask to be treated as temporary residents, and in an emergency, if a person's own doctor is not available, any doctor in the service will give treatment and advice.

Patients are treated either in the doctor's surgery or, when necessary, at home. Doctors may prescribe for their patients all drugs and medicines which are medically necessary for their treatment and also a certain number of surgical appliances (the more elaborate being provided through hospitals).

DENTAL SERVICE
Dentists, like doctors, may take part in the NHS and also have private patients. About 16,000 of the dentists available

for general practice in England provide NHS general dental services. They are responsible to the HAs in whose areas they provide services.

Patients are free to go to any dentist who is taking part in the NHS and willing to accept them. Dentists are paid a capitation fee and payment for certain treatments for patients registered with them who are under 18 years of age. They receive payment for items of treatment for individual adult patients and, in addition, a continuing care payment for those registered with them.

Patients are asked to pay 80 per cent of the cost of NHS dental treatment. The maximum charge for a course of treatment is £325. There is no charge for arrest of bleeding, repairs to dentures, home visits by the dentist or re-opening a surgery in an emergency (in these two cases, payment will be for treatment given in the normal way). The following are exempt from dental charges/have charges remitted:

(i)   young people under 18
(ii)   full-time students under 19
(iii)   women who were pregnant when accepted for treatment
(iv)   women who have had a child in the previous 12 months
(v)   people or the partners of people who receive income support, family credit, disability working allowance or income-based jobseeker's allowance

Leaflet HC11 available from post offices and local social security offices explains how other people on a low income can, depending on their financial circumstances, get free treatment or help with charges.

PHARMACEUTICAL SERVICE

Patients may obtain medicines, appliances and oral contraceptives prescribed under the NHS from any pharmacy whose owner has entered into arrangements with the HA to provide this service. Almost all pharmacy owners have done so and display notices that they dispense under the NHS; the number of these pharmacies in England and Wales in March 1996 was about 10,500. There are also some appliance suppliers who only provide special appliances. In rural areas where access to a pharmacy may be difficult, patients may be able to obtain medicines, etc., from their doctor.

Except for contraceptives (for which there is no charge), a charge of £5.50 is payable for each item supplied unless the patient is exempt and the declaration on the back of the prescription form is completed. Exemptions cover:

(i)   children under 16
(ii)   full-time students under 19
(iii)   men and women aged 60 and over
(iv)   pregnant women
(v)   women who have had a baby within the last 12 months
(vi)   people suffering from certain medical conditions
(vii)   people who receive income support or family credit and their dependants
(viii) people who receive disability working allowance and their partners
(ix)   people who receive income-based jobseeker's allowance, and their partners
(x)   people who hold an AG2 certificate issued by the Health Benefits Division, and their dependants
(xi)   war pensioners (for their accepted disablements)

Prepayment certificates (£28.50 valid for four months, £78.40 valid for a year) may be purchased by those patients not entitled to exemption who require frequent pre-scriptions. Further information about the exemption and prepayment arrangements is given in leaflet HC11.

GENERAL OPHTHALMIC SERVICES

General Ophthalmic Services, which are administered by HAs, form part of the ophthalmic services available under the NHS. The NHS sight test is available free to:

(i)   children under 16
(ii)   full-time students under the age of 19
(iii)   people in receipt of income support, income-based jobseeker's allowance or family credit, and their partners
(iv)   people in receipt of disability working allowance and their partners
(v)   people prescribed complex lenses
(vi)   the registered blind and partially sighted
(vii)   diagnosed diabetic and glaucoma patients
(viii) close relatives aged 40 or over of diagnosed glaucoma patients

Those on a low income may qualify for help with the cost.

Certain groups are automatically entitled to help with the purchase of glasses under an NHS voucher scheme:

(i)   children under 16
(ii)   full-time students under 19
(iii)   people in receipt of income support, income-based jobseeker's allowance or family credit, and their partners
(iv)   people in receipt of disability working allowance and their partners
(v)   people wearing certain complex lenses
(vi)   people whose spectacles are lost or damaged as a result of their disability, injury or illness

The value of the voucher depends on the lenses required. Vouchers may be used to help pay for the glasses or contact lenses of the patient's choice. People with a low income may claim help on form AG1. Glasses or contact lenses should not be purchased until the result of a claim is known as no refunds can be given. Booklet G11 gives further details.

Diagnosis and specialist treatment of eye conditions is available through the Hospital Eye Service as well as the provision of glasses of a special type.

Testing of sight may be carried out by any ophthalmic medical practitioner or ophthalmic optician. The optician must give the prescription, and a voucher if eligible, to the patient who can take this to any supplier of glasses of his/her choice to have dispensed. However, only registered opticians can supply glasses to children and to people registered as blind or partially sighted.

PRIMARY HEALTH CARE SERVICES

Primary health care services include the general medical, dental, ophthalmic and pharmaceutical services. They also include community services run by HAs, health centres and clinics, family planning outside the hospital service, and preventive activities in the community including vaccination, immunization and fluoridation.

The district nursing and health visiting services include community psychiatric nursing for mentally ill people living outside hospital, and school nursing for the health surveillance of schoolchildren of all ages. Ante- and post-natal care and chiropody are also an integral part of the primary health care service.

COMMUNITY CHILD HEALTH SERVICES

Pre-school services at GP surgeries or child health clinics provide regular surveillance of children's physical, mental and emotional health and development, and advice to parents on their children's health and welfare.

The School Health Service provides for the medical and dental examination of schoolchildren, and advises the local education authority, the school, the parents and the pupil of any health factors which may require special consideration during the pupil's school life. GPs are increasingly undertaking child health surveillance to improve the preventive health care of children.

HOSPITALS AND OTHER SERVICES

The Secretary of State for Health has a duty to provide, to such extent as he/she considers necessary to meet all reasonable requirements, hospital and other accommodation; medical, dental, nursing and ambulance services; other facilities for the care of expectant and nursing mothers and young children; facilities for the prevention of illness and the care and after-care of persons suffering from illness; and such other services as are required for the diagnosis and treatment of illness. Rehabilitation services (occupational therapy, physiotherapy and speech therapy) may also be provided for those who need it and surgical and medical appliances are supplied in appropriate cases. NHS services and equipment should be free of charge unless current legislation on prescriptions states otherwise.

Specialists and consultants who work in the NHS can engage in private practice, including the treatment of their private patients in NHS hospitals. Any private work a consultant does is additional to NHS duties.

Trusts

The National Health Service and Community Care Act 1990 enables hospitals and other providers of health care to become independent of health authority control as self-governing NHS Trusts run by boards of directors. The Trusts derive their income principally from contracts to provide health services to health authorities and fund-holding general practitioners. As at April 1995 there were 433 trusts, representing the majority of hospitals in England.

Charges

In a number of hospitals, accommodation is available for the treatment of private in-patients who undertake to pay the full costs of hospital accommodation and services and (usually) separate medical fees to a specialist as well. The amount of the medical fees is a matter for agreement between doctor and patient. Hospital charges for private in-patients are set locally at a commercial rate.

Certain hospitals have accommodation in single rooms or small wards which, if not required for patients who need privacy for medical reasons, may be made available to patients who desire it as an amenity for a small charge. These patients are still NHS patients and are treated as such.

There is no charge for drugs supplied to NHS hospital in-patients but out-patients pay £5.50 an item unless they are exempt.

With certain exceptions, hospital out-patients have to pay fixed charges for dentures, contact lenses and certain appliances. Glasses may be obtained either from the hospital or an optician and the charge will be related to the type of lens prescribed and the choice of frame.

PERSONAL SOCIAL SERVICES

Local authorities are responsible for personal social services within their area. Each authority has a Director of Social Services and a Social Services Committee responsible for the social services functions placed upon them by the Local Authority Social Services Act 1970.

FINANCE

ENGLAND

COST OF NATIONAL HEALTH AND PERSONAL SOCIAL SERVICES 1994

	£ million
All services	38,466
Central government services: total	31,275
Central administration	227
Health Authorities, current	22,656
Health Authorities, capital	618
Family Health Services Authorities:	
Administration and related services	78
General medical	1,840
Pharmaceutical	3,051
General dental	1,223
General ophthalmic	192
Other	1,391
Personal social services	7,191

Source: HMSO – *Health and Personal Social Services Statistics for England 1995*

WALES

GROSS CENTRAL GOVERNMENT SUPPORT FOR HEALTH AND PERSONAL SOCIAL SERVICES 1993–4*

	£ thousand
Total	2,095,990
District Health Authorities	1,308,658
NHS Trusts	47,743
General medical	110,195
Pharmaceutical	224,038
General dental	67,963
General ophthalmic	13,532
Welfare foods	13,470
Other	310,391

* Excludes local authority expenditure on personal social services funded through general grants
Source: Welsh Office – *Digest of Welsh Statistics 1995*

SCOTLAND

NET COSTS OF THE NATIONAL HEALTH SERVICE 1994–5

	£ thousand
Total cost	4,335,737
Central administration	8,966
Total NHS cost	4,326,771
NHS contributions	423,293
Net costs to Exchequer	3,903,478
Health Board administration	93,844
Hospital and community health services	3,087,729
Family practitioner services	855,141
Centre health services	198,478
State hospital	19,824
Training	27,165
Research	10,062
Disabled services	2,230
Welfare foods	13,910
Miscellaneous health services	18,388

Source: Scottish Office – *Annual Abstract of Statistics 1995*

EMPLOYEES

HEALTH AND PERSONAL SOCIAL SERVICES
WORKFORCE (*Great Britain*)

Health Service staff and practitioners: total	979,081
Dental Practice Board staff	722
Statutory authorities staff	4,380
Family Health Services practitioners: total	60,965
Of whom:	
General medical practitioners	34,421
General dental practitioners	18,630
Ophthalmic medical practitioners	735
Ophthalmic opticians	7,179
Directly employed staff: total	913,014
Of whom:	
Medical staff	56,736
Dental staff	2,947
Nursing and midwifery staff	429,160
Professionals allied to medical staff	48,338
Scientific and professional staff	17,043
Professional and technical staff	43,458
Administrative and clerical staff	182,390
Works and maintenance staff	19,249
Ambulance staff	21,379
Ancillary staff	91,064
Others	1,250
*Personal social services staff	237,752
Total	1,216,833

*England only
Source: HMSO – *Annual Abstract of Statistics 1996*

NUMBER OF BEDS AND PATIENT ACTIVITY

ENGLAND AND WALES 1993

	England	Wales
In-patients:		
Average daily available beds	219,000	17,500
Average daily occupation of beds	n/a	13,500
Persons waiting for admission at 31 March	995,000	61,000
Day-case admissions	2,106,000	201,400
Ordinary admissions	7,988,000	n/a
Out-patient attendances:		
New patients	9,685,000	1,254,100*
Total attendances	38,233,000	3,494,800
Accident and emergency:		
New patients	11,365,000	n/a
Total attendances	13,289,000	n/a
Family Health Services:		
Number of patients per doctor	1,902	1,739
Prescriptions dispensed	413,300,000	34,300,000
NHS sight tests conducted	5,935,000	397,000
Pairs of glasses dispensed/ vouchers paid for	3,485,000	254,000
Number of adult courses of dental treatment	24,848,000	1,399,000

n/a not available
* 1992 figure

SCOTLAND 1993

In-patients:	
Average available staffed beds	46,700
Average occupied beds	38,100
Out-patient attendances:	
New patients	2,457,000
Total attendances	6,086,000
Primary Care Services:	
Average number of patients per principal doctor	1,542
Prescriptions dispensed	48,180,000
NHS sight tests conducted	568,000
Pairs of glasses supplied	440,000
Number of courses of dental treatment completed	2,647,000

Source: HMSO – *Annual Abstract of Statistics 1996*

National Insurance and Related Cash Benefits

The state insurance and assistance schemes, comprising schemes of national insurance and industrial injuries insurance, national assistance, and non-contributory old age pensions came into force from 5 July 1948. The Ministry of Social Security Act 1966 replaced national assistance and non-contributory old age pensions with a scheme of non-contributory benefits. These and subsequent measures relating to social security provision in Great Britain were consolidated by the Social Security Act 1975; the Social Security (Consequential Provisions) Act 1975; and the Industrial Injuries and Diseases (Old Cases) Act 1975. Corresponding measures were passed for Northern Ireland. The Social Security Pensions Act 1975 introduced a new state pensions scheme in 1978, and the graduated pension scheme 1961 to 1975 has been wound up, existing rights being preserved. Under the Pensions Act 1995 the age of retirement is to be 65 for both men and women, this being phased in between 2010 and 6 April 2020. The Pensioners' Payments and Social Security Act 1979 provided for a £10 Christmas bonus for pensioners in 1979 and for the payment of a bonus in succeeding years at levels then to be determined. The Child Benefit Act 1975 replaced family allowances (introduced 1946) with child benefit and one parent benefit. Some of this legislation has been superseded by the provisions of the Social Security Acts 1968 to 1992.

NATIONAL INSURANCE SCHEME

The National Insurance (NI) scheme operates under the Social Security Contributions and Benefits Act 1992 and the Social Security Administration Act 1992, and orders and regulations made thereunder. The scheme is financed by contributions payable by earners, employers and others (such as non-employed persons paying voluntary contributions). It provides the funds required for paying the benefits payable under the Social Security Acts out of the National Insurance Fund and not out of other public money, and for the making of payments towards the cost of the National Health Service. In 1991 the Redundancy Fund was absorbed into the National Insurance Fund. The yearly Treasury supplement to the National Insurance Fund was abolished in 1989. A Treasury grant was introduced from 1993.

CONTRIBUTIONS

National Insurance contributions are of four classes:

CLASS 1 CONTRIBUTIONS

These are earnings-related, based on a percentage of the employee's earnings.

Primary Class 1 contributions are payable by employed earners and office-holders over age 16 with gross earnings at or above the lower earnings limit of £61.00 per week. Employees earning less than the lower earnings limit do not pay any contributions. For those with gross earnings at or above this level, contributions are payable on all earnings up to an upper limit of £455.00 per week. 'Gross earnings' include overtime pay, commission, bonus, etc., without deduction of any superannuation contributions. Contributions are paid at 2 per cent of earnings up to the lower earnings limit, plus contributions at a higher percentage on earnings between the lower earning limit and the employees' upper earnings limit. Employees contributing at the reduced rate continue to pay at that rate on earnings up to and including the employees' upper earnings limit.

Secondary Class 1 contributions are payable by employers of employed earners, and by the appropriate authorities in the case of office-holders. In 1985 the upper earnings limit for employers' contributions was abolished and secondary contributions are payable on all the employee's earnings if they reach or exceed £61.00 per week.

Women who marry for the first time no longer have a right to elect not to pay the full contribution rate. Married women and widows who before 12 May 1977 elected not to pay contributions at the full rate retain the right to pay a reduced rate over the same earnings range, which includes a contribution to the National Health Service. They lose this right if, after 5 April 1978, there are two consecutive tax years in which they receive no earnings on which primary Class 1 contributions are payable and in which they have not been at any time self-employed earners. No primary contributions are due on earnings paid for a period on or after the employee's pension age, even when retirement is deferred.

Primary contributions are deducted from earnings by the employer and are paid, together with the employer's contributions, to the Inland Revenue along with income tax collected under the PAYE system.

For the period 6 April 1996 to 5 April 1997 the earnings brackets determining Class 1 contributions are:

Earnings bracket	Weekly earnings
1	£61.00–109.99
2	110.00–154.99
3	155.00–209.99
4	210.00–455.00
5	over 455.00

CLASS 2 CONTRIBUTIONS

These are flat-rate, paid weekly by self-employed earners over age 16. Those with earnings below £3,430 a year for the tax year 1996–7 can apply for exemption from liability to pay Class 2 contributions. People who while self-employed are exempted from liability to pay contributions on the grounds of small earnings may pay either Class 2 or Class 3 contributions voluntarily. Self-employed earners (whether or not they pay Class 2 contributions) may also be liable to pay Class 4 contributions based on profits or gains within certain limits. There are special rules for those who are concurrently employed and self-employed.

Married women and widows can no longer choose not to pay Class 2 contributions. Those who elected not to pay Class 2 contributions before 12 May 1977 retain the right until there is a period of two consecutive tax years after 5 April 1978 in which they were not at any time either self-employed earners or had earnings on which primary Class 1 contributions were payable.

CLASS 3 CONTRIBUTIONS

These are voluntary flat-rate contributions payable by persons over age 16 who would otherwise be unable to qualify for retirement pension and certain other benefits because they have an insufficient record of Class 1 or Class 2 contributions. Married women and widows who on or before 11 May 1977 elected not to pay Class 1 (full rate) or Class 2 contributions cannot pay Class 3 contributions while they retain this right.

CLASS 4 CONTRIBUTIONS

These are payable by self-employed earners, whether or not they pay Class 2 contributions, on annual profits or gains from a trade, profession or vocation chargeable to income tax under Schedule D, where these fall between £6,860 and £23,660 a year. The maximum Class 4 contribution, payable on profits or gains of £23,660 or more, is £1,008.

Class 4 contributions are generally assessed and collected by the Inland Revenue along with Schedule D income tax. Self-employed persons under 16 or who at the beginning of a tax year are over pension age even where retirement is deferred, are not liable to pay Class 4 contributions. There are special rules for people who have more than one job or who pay Class 1 contributions on earnings which are chargeable to income tax under Schedule D.

Regulations state the cases in which earners may be exempted from liability to pay contributions, and the conditions upon which contributions are credited to persons who are exempted. Leaflet NI 208 is obtainable from local social security offices.

CONTRIBUTION RATES
FROM 6 APRIL 1996 TO 5 APRIL 1997

CLASS 1 CONTRIBUTIONS – EMPLOYEE'S RATES
Not Contracted Out

Earnings bracket	Percentage of reckonable income			
	On first £61.00		On earnings from £61.00–£455.00	
	standard	reduced	standard	reduced
1	2	3.85	10	3.85
2	2	3.85	10	3.85
3	2	3.85	10	3.85
4	2	3.85	10	3.85
5	*2	*3.85	*10	*3.85

CLASS 1 CONTRIBUTIONS – EMPLOYEE'S RATES
Contracted Out (*see also* page 487)

Earnings bracket	On first £61.00		On earnings from £61.00–£455.00	
	standard	reduced	standard	reduced
1	2	3.85	8.2	3.85
2	2	3.85	8.2	3.85
3, 4	2	3.85	8.2	3.85
5	*2	*3.85	*8.2	*3.85

*To a maximum of £455.00 per week

CLASS 1 CONTRIBUTIONS – EMPLOYER'S RATES

Earnings bracket	On first £61.00	On earnings from £61.00– £455.00	On any earnings over £455.00
1	3.0	0.0	0
2	5.0	2.0	0
3	7.0	4.0	0
4	10.2	7.2	0
5	10.2	7.2	10.2

CLASS 2 CONTRIBUTIONS, £6.05 weekly flat rate

CLASS 3 CONTRIBUTIONS, £5.95

CLASS 4 CONTRIBUTIONS, 8% of profits or gains

The Social Security (Contributions) Act 1991 added a new class of contributions: 1A, payable in respect of car fuel

by persons liable to pay secondary Class 1 contributions. It was effective from the 1991–2 tax year.

THE STATE EARNINGS RELATED PENSION SCHEME (SERPS)

The Social Security Pensions Act 1975 which came into force in 1978 aimed to reduce reliance upon means-tested benefit in old age, in widowhood and in chronic ill-health by providing better pensions; to ensure that occupational pension schemes which are contracted out of part of the state scheme fulfil the conditions of a good scheme; that pensions are adequately protected against inflation; and that in both the state and occupational schemes men and women are treated equally. Modifications to the schemes have been made since 1978 and further changes come into effect in April 1997 (*see* below).

Under the state earnings-related pension scheme, retirement, invalidity and widow's pensions for employees are related to the earnings on which NI contributions have been paid. For employees of either sex with a complete insurance record, the scheme provides a category A retirement pension in two parts, a basic and an additional pension. The basic pension corresponds to the old personal flat-rate national insurance pension. The additional pension is 1.25 per cent of average earnings between the lower weekly earnings limit for Class 1 contribution liability and the upper earnings limit for each year of such earnings under the scheme, and will thus build up to 25 per cent in twenty years. Retirement, widow's and invalidity pensions under the new scheme started to be paid in 1979. Since 1979 the basic retirement pension has been augmented for employed earners by the additional pension related to earnings, but it will be 20 years before these additional pensions become payable at the full rate.

The additional pension will be calculated in a different way for individuals who reach pension age after 6 April 1999. The changes are to be phased in over ten years. From 2010 a lifetime's earnings will be included in the calculation and for years from 1988–9 onwards the accrual rate on these surplus earnings will be 20 per cent. The accrual rate on surplus earnings for the years from 1978–9 to 1987–8 will remain at 25 per cent.

Actual earnings are to be revalued in terms of the earnings level current in the last complete tax year before pension age (or death or incapacity). Both components of pensions in payment will be uprated annually in line with the movement of prices. Graduated retirement pensions in payment, and rights to such pensions earned by people who are still working, will be brought into the annual review of benefits.

Self-employed persons pay contributions towards the basic pension. Employees with earnings below the lower limit and people not in employment may contribute voluntarily for basic pension. Although no primary Class 1 contributions or Class 2 or Class 4 contributions are payable by persons who work beyond pension age (65 for men, 60 for women), the employer's liability for secondary Class 1 contributions continues if earnings are at or above the lower earnings limit. Class 4 contributions are still payable up to the end of the tax year during which pension age is reached.

Widows will get the whole of any additional pensions earned by their husbands with their widowed mother's allowances or widow's pensions; and can add to the retirement pensions earned by their own contributions any additional pensions earned by their husbands up to the maximum payable on one person's contributions. Men whose wives die when they are both over pension age can add together their own and their wives' pension rights in the same way.

The scheme permits years of home responsibilities to reduce the number of qualifying years (since 1978) needed by women for retirement pension. The range of short-term social security benefits and industrial injury benefits under the Social Security Act 1975 continues with only minor changes.

CONTRACTED-OUT AND PERSONAL PENSION SCHEMES

Members of occupational pension schemes which meet the standards laid down in the Pension Schemes Act 1993 can be contracted-out of the state earnings-related pension scheme (SERPS).

Until 1988 occupational pension schemes could contract out only if they promised a pension that was related to earnings (a contracted-out salary-related scheme). They must provide a pension that is not less than the guaranteed minimum pension (GMP), which is broadly equivalent to the state earnings-related pension. Since 6 April 1988 occupational pension schemes which promise a minimum level of contributions (a contracted-out money purchase scheme) have also been able to contract out. They provide a pension based on how much has been paid in and invested and how much these investments have grown.

Since 1988 employees have been able to start their own personal pension instead of staying in SERPS. This choice is open to all employees even if their employer has a pension scheme. A personal pension, like a contracted-out money purchase scheme, provides a pension based on the fund built up in the scheme over the years plus the results of the way they have been invested.

The decision on whether or not an occupational pension scheme may become contracted-out lies with the Occupational Pension Board, an independent statutory body which has a general responsibility for supervising contracting-out. They also consider and approve personal pension schemes which can be used instead of state additional pension.

The state earnings-related pension payable to a member of a contracted-out salary-related scheme, or his widow, will be reduced by the amount of GMP payable (which in the case of a widow must be at least half of the late husband's GMP entitlement). Members of contracted-out money purchase schemes and personal pension schemes, or their widows, have no GMP entitlement as such. But the state earnings-related pension payable will be reduced by an amount equivalent to a GMP (or widow's GMP).

Since 1988 contracted-out salary-related schemes must also provide a widower's GMP which must be at least half of the late wife's GMP entitlement built up from 6 April 1988. (A scheme need not provide entitlement to a GMP for widowers of earners dying before April 1989.) Contracted-out money purchase schemes and personal pension schemes must provide half-rate widower's benefit.

In contracted-out occupational pension schemes, both the employee and the employer pay the lower (rebated) rate of National Insurance contributions on earnings between the lower and upper earnings limits in recognition that full SERPS will not be paid. The amount of the rebate is determined by the Secretary of State after receiving advice from the Government Actuary and is normally reviewed every five years (see also page 486).

An employee who chooses a personal pension in place of SERPS or their employer's pension scheme must pay NI contributions at the full ordinary rate (the employer's share must also be paid at the same rate). The DSS pays the difference between the lower contracted-out rate and the full ordinary rate directly into the personal pension scheme.

The Pensions Act 1995 introduces a number of changes to the present system of contracting-out. From April 1997, the links between SERPS and contracting-out will be broken, and thereafter people will no longer accrue entitlement to SERPS for periods of contracted-out service, but will still be entitled to pension rights earned before April 1997. Contracted-out salary-related schemes will no longer have to provide a GMP. Instead, they will have to satisfy a new scheme-based test as one of the requirements for the issue of a contracting-out certificate. GMPs accrued before April 1997 will still form part of the occupational pension and will be subject to the rules currently in force. All occupational pension schemes will be required to provide inflation-proofing of up to 5 per cent on the whole pension accrued after April 1997. There will also be age-related National Insurance contribution rebates, from April 1997, for people who leave SERPS and join a contracted-out money purchase or personal pension scheme. The rebate will be lower for younger people and higher for older people. This should mean that most people will be able to stay in their contracted-out money purchase or personal pension scheme until they retire.

The Occupational Pensions Board will be abolished from April 1997, and the Contributions Agency, an executive agency of the Department of Social Security, will process elections to contract-out.

NATIONAL INSURANCE FUND

The National Insurance Fund receives all social security contributions (less only the National Health Service) and it bears the cost of all contributory benefits provided by the Social Security Acts and the cost of administration.

Approximate receipts and payments of the National Insurance Fund for the year ended 31 March 1995, were:

Receipts	£'000
Balance, 1 April 1994	4,548,652
Contributions under the Social Security Acts (net of SSP/SMP)	37,863,479
Treasury Grant	6,280,000
Compensation from Consolidated Fund for SSP/SMP recoveries	541,000
Income from investments	363,950
Other receipts	82,003
	49,679,084

Payments	£'000	£'000
Unemployment benefit	1,299,483	
Sickness benefit	341,840	
Invalidity benefit	7,705,134	
Maternity allowance	27,000	
Widow's benefit	1,022,000	
Guardian's allowance and child's special allowance	1,000	
Retirement pension	28,744,810	
Pensioners' lump sum payments	123,305	39,264,572
Personal pensions		1,956,618
Transfers to Northern Ireland		145,000
Administration		1,279,888
Other payments		8,879
Redundancy payments		196,528
Balance, 31 March 1995		6,827,599
		49,679,084

BENEFITS

The benefits payable under the Social Security Acts are as follows:

CONTRIBUTORY BENEFITS
Incapacity benefit
Maternity allowance
Widow's benefit, comprising widow's payment, widowed
    mother's allowance and widow's pension
Retirement pensions, categories A and B

NON-CONTRIBUTORY BENEFITS
Child benefit
One parent benefit
Guardian's allowance
Invalid care allowance
Mobility allowance
Severe disablement allowance
Attendance allowance
Disability living allowance
Disability working allowance
Retirement pensions, categories C and D
Income support
Family credit
Social fund

BENEFITS FOR INDUSTRIAL INJURIES, DISABLEMENT
AND DEATH

OTHER
Statutory sick pay
Statutory maternity pay
Jobseeker's allowance

Leaflets relating to the various benefits and payments are obtainable from local social security offices.

CONTRIBUTORY BENEFITS

Entitlement to contributory benefits depends on contribution conditions being satisfied either by the claimant or by some other person (depending on the kind of benefit). The class or classes of contribution which for this purpose are relevant to each benefit are:

Jobseeker's allowance (contribution-based)	Class 1
Incapacity benefit	Class 1 or 2
Maternity allowance	Class 1 or 2
Widow's benefits	Class 1, 2 or 3
Retirement pensions categories A and B	Class 1, 2 or 3

The system of contribution conditions relates to yearly levels of earnings on which contributions have been paid. The contribution conditions for different benefits are set out in leaflets available at local social security offices.

JOBSEEKER'S ALLOWANCE

Jobseeker's allowance replaced unemployment benefit and income support for unemployed people under pension age from 7 October 1996. There are two routes of entitlement: a contribution-based route, paid as a personal rate to individuals for up to six months, and an income-based route, based on savings and income and payable for a claimant and their dependants for as long as they satisfy the rules. Rates of jobseeker's allowance corrrespond to income support rates.

A person wishing to claim jobseeker's allowance must be unemployed, capable of work and available for any work which they can reasonably be expected to do, usually for at least 40 hours a week. They must actively seek work. They must agree and sign a 'Jobseeker's Agreement', which will set out each claimant's plans to find work.

A person will be disqualified from jobseeker's allowance if they have left a job voluntarily or through misconduct, if they refuse to take up an offer of employment or if they fail to attend a training scheme or employment programme. Hardship payments may not be available except where a person may be vulnerable, e.g. if sick or pregnant, or for those with children or caring responsibilities.

INCAPACITY BENEFIT

Incapacity benefit replaced state sickness benefit and invalidity benefit on 13 April 1995. Short-term incapacity benefit consists of a lower rate payable for the first 28 weeks of sickness, and a higher rate payable after 28 weeks. Long-term benefit is payable after 52 weeks and is not payable after pension age. The terminally ill and those entitled to the highest rate care component of disability living allowance are able to get the long-term rate after 28 weeks rather than 52 weeks. Incapacity benefit is taxable after 28 weeks of incapacity. Former sickness and invalidity benefit claimants were transferred to incapacity benefit on equivalent rates and special transitional arrangements apply.

Two rates of age addition are paid with long-term benefit based on the claimant's age when incapacity started. The higher rate is payable where incapacity for work commenced before the age of 35; and the lower rate where incapacity commenced before the age of 45. Increases for dependents are also payable with short and long-term incapacity benefit.

A new medical test of incapacity, the 'all work test', was introduced for incapacity benefit as well as other benefits paid on the basis of incapacity for work. The medical test normally applies after 28 weeks of incapacity for work and assesses ability to perform a range of work-related activities rather than the ability to perform a specific job. The new test applies to most former sickness and invalidity benefit claimants.

MATERNITY BENEFIT

Statutory maternity pay (SMP) is administered by employers (*see* page 493). The state maternity allowance scheme covers women who are self-employed or otherwise do not qualify for SMP. The Maternity (Compulsory Leave) Regulations 1994 apply to both schemes and effectively prohibit women from working for two weeks after the date of childbirth.

A woman may qualify for maternity allowance (MA) if she has been working and paying contributions at the full rate for at least 26 weeks in the 66-week period which ends one week before the week the baby is due. She also has an element of choice in deciding when to stop work and receive MA, which is not payable for any period she works. Women employed at the 15th week before the baby is due will receive £54.55 per week for up to 18 weeks, and self-employed and unemployed women will receive £47.35 for up to 18 weeks.

WIDOW'S BENEFITS

Only the late husband's contributions of any class count for widow's benefit in any of its three forms:

Widow's payment – may be received by a woman who at her husband's death is under 60, or whose husband was not entitled to a Category A retirement pension when he died

Widowed mother's allowance – payable to a widow if she is entitled or treated as entitled to child benefit, or if she is expecting her husband's baby

Widow's pension – a widow may receive this pension if aged 45 or over at the time of her husband's death (40 or over if widowed before 11 April 1988) or when her widowed mother's allowance ends. If aged 55 or over (50 or over if widowed before 11 April 1988) she will receive the full widow's pension rate

Widow's benefit of any form ceases upon remarriage or during a period in which she lives with a man as his wife.

RETIREMENT PENSION: CATEGORIES A AND B

A Category A pension is payable for life to men or women on their own contributions if they are over pension age (65 for a man and 60 for a woman).

Where a person defers making a claim at 65 (60 for a woman) or later opts to be treated as if he/she had not made a claim, and does not draw a Category A pension, the weekly rate of pension is increased when he or she finally makes a claim or reaches the age of 70 (65 for a woman), in respect of weeks when pension is forgone during the five years after reaching minimum pension age. Details of the increase in the rate of pension due to deferred retirement are given in leaflet NP46, available at social security offices. If a married man defers his own Category A pension, his wife has to defer receiving her Category B pension based on his contribution record. During this time she earns increments to the Category B pension, provided she does not claim retirement pension or graduated retirement benefit in her own right; increments are payable to her (and not her husband) when they both claim their pensions.

A Category B pension is normally payable for life to a woman on her husband's contributions when he has claimed, or is over 70, and has qualified for his own Category A pension, and she has reached 60. It is also payable on widowhood after 60 whether or not the late husband had retired and qualified for his own pension. The pension is payable at the rate of the increase for a wife while the husband is alive, and at the single person's rate on widowhood after 60. Where a woman is widowed before she reaches 60, a Category B pension is paid to her on reaching 60 at the same rate as her widow's pension if she claims. If a woman qualifies for a pension of each category she receives whichever pension is the larger.

The earnings rule, which stated that anyone who had qualified for a pension would have it reduced if he or she earned more than a certain amount, was abolished in 1989. Where an adult dependant is living with the claimant, an adult dependants increase (£36.60) will only be payable if the dependant's earnings do not exceed the rate of jobseeker's allowance for a single person (*see* below). For the purpose of the dependency rule only, earnings will include payments by way of occupational or personal pension. The earnings of a separated spouse affect the increase of retirement pension if they exceed £36.60 a week.

Income support is payable to men between 65 and 70 and women between 60 and 65 who have not claimed their retirement pension and who would have been entitled to a retirement pension if they had claimed at pension age. This applies in the case of incapacity benefit if incapacity for work is the result of an industrial accident or prescribed disease. These rates of benefit for people over pension age are shown in leaflet NI 196. A retirement pension will be increased by the amount of any invalidity allowance the pensioner was getting within the period of eight weeks and one day before reaching minimum pension age but this will be offset against any additional pension or GMP. An age addition of 25p per week is payable if a retirement pensioner is aged 80 or over.

GRADUATED RETIREMENT BENEFIT

Graduated NI contributions were first payable from 1961 and were calculated as a percentage of earnings between certain bands. They were discontinued in 1975. Any graduated pension which an employed person over 18 and under 70 (65 for a woman) had earned by paying graduated contributions will be paid when the contributor claims retirement pension or at 70 (65 for a woman), in addition to any retirement pension for which he or she qualifies.

Graduated retirement benefit is at the rate of 7.90p a week (April 1996) for each 'unit' of graduated contributions paid by the employee (half a unit or more counts as a whole unit). A unit of contributions is £7.50 for men and £9.00 for women of graduated contributions paid.

A wife can get a graduated pension in return for her own graduated contributions, but not for her husband's. A widow, or a widower whose wife died after 5 April 1979 when they were both over pensionable age, gets a graduated addition to his/her retirement pension equal to half of any graduated additions earned by his/her late spouse, plus any additions earned by his/her own graduated contributions. If a person defers making a claim beyond 65 (60 for a woman), entitlement may be increased by one seventh of a penny per £1 of its weekly rate for each complete week of deferred retirement, as long as the retirement is deferred for a minimum of seven weeks.

WEEKLY RATES OF BENEFIT
from April 1996

Jobseeker's allowance (contribution-based)

Person under 18	£28.85
Person aged 18–24	37.90
Person over 25	47.90
Couple	75.20

Short-term incapacity benefit

Person under pension age – lower rate	46.15
*Person under pension age – higher rate	54.55
Increase for adult dependant	28.55
*Person over pension age	58.65
Increase for adult dependant	33.15

Long-term incapacity benefit

Person (under or over pension age)	61.15
Increase for adult dependant	36.60
Age addition – lower rate	6.45
Age addition – higher rate	12.90

Invalidity allowance: maximum amount payable

Higher rate	12.90
Middle rate	8.10
Lower rate	4.05

Maternity allowance

Employed	54.55
Self-employed or unemployed	47.35

Widow's benefits

Widow's payment (lump sum)	1,000.00
*Widowed mother's allowance	61.15
*Widow's pension	61.15

Retirement pension: categories A and B

Single person	61.15
Increase for wife/other adult dependant	36.60

*These benefits attract an increase for each dependent child (in addition to child benefit) of £9.90 for the first or only child and £11.15 for each subsequent child

NON-CONTRIBUTORY BENEFITS

CHILD BENEFIT

Child benefit is payable for virtually all children aged under 16, and for those aged 16 to 18 who are studying full-time up to and including A-level or equivalent standard. It is also payable for a short period if the child has left school recently and is registered for work or youth training at a careers office.

ONE-PARENT BENEFIT

This benefit may be paid to a person in receipt of child benefit who is responsible for bringing up one or more children on his/her own. It is a flat rate non-means tested, non-contributory benefit payable for the eldest child.

GUARDIAN'S ALLOWANCE

Where the parents of a child are dead, the person who has the child in his/her family may claim a guardian's allowance in addition to child benefit. The allowance, in exceptional circumstances, is payable on the death of only one parent.

INVALID CARE ALLOWANCE

Invalid care allowance is payable to persons of working age who are not gainfully employed because they are regularly and substantially engaged in caring for a severely disabled person who is receiving attendance allowance, the middle or highest rate of disability living allowance care component or constant attendance allowance, paid at not less than the normal maximum rate, under the industrial injuries or war pensions schemes.

SEVERE DISABLEMENT ALLOWANCE

Persons who have been incapable of work for a continuous period of at least 28 weeks but who do not qualify for contributory incapacity benefit may be entitled to severe disablement allowance. People who first become incapable of work after their 20th birthday must also be at least 80 per cent disabled or have been disabled for a continuous period of at least 28 weeks.

ATTENDANCE ALLOWANCE

This is payable to disabled people over 65 who need a lot of care or supervision because of physical or mental disability for a period of at least six months. People not expected to live for six months because of an illness do not have to wait six months. The allowance has two rates: the lower rate is for day or night care, and the higher rate is for day and night care.

DISABILITY LIVING ALLOWANCE

This is payable to disabled people under 65 who have personal care and mobility needs because of an illness or disability for a period of at least three months and are likely to have those needs for a further six months or more. People not expected to live for six months because of an illness do not have to wait three months. The allowance has two components: the care component, which has three rates, and the mobility component, which has two rates. The rates depend on the care and mobility needs of the claimant. The mobility component is payable only to those aged five or over.

DISABILITY WORKING ALLOWANCE

This is a tax-free, income-related benefit for people who are working 16 hours a week or more but have an illness or disability which puts them at a disadvantage in getting a job. To qualify a person must be aged 16 or over and must, at the date of the claim, have one of the 'qualifying benefits',

such as disability living allowance. The amount payable depends on the size of the family and weekly income. The allowance is not payable if any savings exceed £16,000.

RETIREMENT PENSION: CATEGORIES C AND D

A Category C pension is provided, subject to a residence test, for persons who were over pensionable age on 5 July 1948, and for women whose husbands are so entitled if they are over pension age, with increases for adult and child dependants. A Category D pension is provided for others when they reach 80 if they are not already getting a retirement pension of any category or if they are getting that pension at less than these rates. An age addition of 25p per week is payable if persons entitled to retirement pension are aged 80 or over.

WEEKLY RATES OF BENEFIT
from April 1996

Child benefit (first child)	£10.80
Each subsequent child	8.80
One-parent benefit	
First or only child of certain lone parents	6.30
Guardian's allowance (eldest child)	9.85
Each subsequent child	11.05
* *Severe disablement allowance*	
†Basic rate	35.55
Under 40	12.40
40–49	7.80
50–59	3.90
Increase for wife/other adult dependant	21.15
* *Invalid care allowance*	36.60
Increase for wife/other adult dependant	21.90
Attendance allowance	
Higher rate	46.70
Lower rate	31.20
Disability living allowance	
Care component	
Higher rate	46.70
Middle rate	31.20
Lower rate	12.40
Mobility component	
Higher rate	32.65
Lower rate	12.40
Disability working allowance	
Single person	48.25
Couple or single parent	75.60
Child aged under 11	11.75
aged 11–15	19.45
aged 16–17	24.15
aged 18	33.80
Disabled child allowance	20.40
Thirty hours allowance	10.30
‡Applicable amount (income threshold)	
Single person	54.75
Couple or single parent	73.00
*Retirement pension: categories *C and D*	
Single person	36.60
Increase for wife/other adult dependant (not payable with Category D pension)	21.90

*These benefits attract an increase for each dependent child (in addition to child benefit) of £9.90 for the first or only child and £11.15 for each subsequent child

†The age addition applies to the age when incapacity began

‡70 pence is deducted from the maximum DWA payable (this is obtained by adding up the appropriate allowance for each person in the family) for every £ coming in each week over the appropriate applicable amount. Where weekly income is below the applicable amount, maximum DWA is payable

INCOME SUPPORT

Income support is a benefit for those aged 18 and over (although certain vulnerable 16- and 17-year-olds may be eligible) whose income falls below set levels. Others who may be eligible include people who are over 60, bringing up children alone, unable to work through sickness or disability, or caring for a disabled person. Except in special cases income support is not available to those who work for more than 24 hours per week or who have a partner who works for more than 16 hours per week. Income support for unemployed people was replaced by jobseeker's allowance from 7 October 1996.

Income support is not payable if the claimant, or claimant and partner, have capital or savings in excess of £8,000. For capital or savings in excess of £3,000 a deduction of £1 is made for every £250, or part of £250, held.

Sums payable depend on fixed allowances laid down by law for people in different circumstances. If both partners are entitled to income support, either may claim it for the couple. People receiving income support may be able to receive housing benefit, help with mortgage or home loan interest and help with health care. They may also be eligible for help with exceptional expenses from the Social Fund. Leaflet IS20 gives a detailed explanation of income support.

Special rates may apply to some people living in residential care or nursing homes. Details are available from local social security offices.

INCOME SUPPORT PREMIUMS

Income support premiums are additional weekly payments for those with special needs. People qualifying for more than one premium will normally only receive the highest single premium for which they qualify. However, family premium, disabled child's premium, severe disability premium and carer premium are payable in addition to other premiums.

People with children qualify for a family premium if they have at least one child; a disabled child's premium if they have a child who receives disability living allowance or is registered blind; or a lone parent premium if they are bringing up one or more children alone. If someone receives invalid care allowance, they qualify for the carer premium.

Long-term sick or disabled people qualify for a disability premium if they or their partner are receiving certain benefits because they are disabled or cannot work; are registered blind; or if the claimant, but not their partner, is incapable of work or receiving statutory sick pay for at least 364 days (not broken by any period longer than 56 days), or 196 days if terminally ill. If someone is living alone and they are in receipt of attendance allowance, or disability living allowance at the middle or higher rate, without anyone receiving invalid care allowance for looking after them, they may qualify for a severe disability premium in addition to a disability premium.

People qualify for a pensioner premium if they or their partner are aged between 60 and 74, an enhanced pensioner premium if they or their partner are aged between 75 and 79, and a higher pensioner premium if they or their partner are aged 80 or over. A higher pensioner premium is also payable to people aged between 60 and 79 who receive attendance allowance, disability living allowance, long-term incapacity benefit or severe disablement allowance, or who are registered blind.

WEEKLY RATES OF BENEFIT
from April 1996

Income support

Single people	
aged 16–17	£28.85
aged 16–17 (certain circumstances)	37.90
aged 18–24	37.90
aged 25 and over	47.90
aged 18 and over and a single parent	47.90

Couples*	
both under 18	57.20
one or both aged 18 or over	75.20

For each child in a family	
under 11	16.45
aged 11–15	24.10
†aged 16–17	28.85
†aged 18 and over	37.90

Premiums	
Family premium	10.55
Disabled child's premium	20.40
Carer's premium	13.00
Lone parent premium	5.20
Disability premium	
Single	20.40
Couple	29.15
Severe disability premium	
Single	36.40
Couple (one person qualified)	36.40
Couple (both qualified)	72.80
Pensioner premium	
Single	19.15
Couple	28.90
Higher pensioner premium	
Single	25.90
Couple	37.05
Enhanced pensioner premium	
Single	21.30
Couple	31.90

*Where one or both partners are aged under 18, their personal allowance will depend on their situation
†If in full-time education up to A-level or equivalent standard

FAMILY CREDIT

Family credit is a tax-free benefit for working families with children. To qualify, a family must include at least one child under 16 (under 19 if in full-time education up to A-level or equivalent standard) and the claimant, or partner if there is one, must be working for at least 16 hours per week. It does not matter which partner is working and they may be employed or self-employed. The right to family credit does not depend on NI contributions and the same rates of benefit are paid to one- and two-parent families. Family credit is not payable if the claimant, or claimant and partner, have capital or savings in excess of £8,000. The rate of benefit is affected if capital or savings in excess of £3,000 are held. The rate of benefit payable depends upon the claimant's (and partner's) net income (excluding child benefit, one-parent benefit and the first £15.00 of any maintenance in payment), number of children and children's ages, and the number of hours worked. Family credit is paid for 26 weeks and the amount payable will usually remain the same throughout this period, regardless of change of circumstances. In certain cases where there are formal childcare arrangements for children under 11, costs of up to £60 per week will be taken into account. Up to £10.30 a week extra is paid to parents working 30 hours or more a week. Payment is made weekly via post offices or every four weeks directly into a bank or building society account. Family credit is claimed by post. A claim pack FC1 which includes a claim form can be obtained at a post office or social security office or call the Family Credit Helpline on 01253-500050. In two-parent families the woman should claim.

WEEKLY RATES OF BENEFIT
from week commencing 9 April 1996
The maximum amount will be payable where net income is no more than £73.00 a week. Where net income exceeds that amount, the maximum credit is reduced by 70 per cent of the excess and the result is the family credit payable. The maximum rate consists of:

Adult credit (for one or two parents)	£46.45
plus for each child	
aged under 11	11.75
aged 11–15	19.45
aged 16–17	24.15
aged 18	33.80

CLAIMS AND QUESTIONS

With a few exceptions, claims and questions relating to social security benefits are decided by statutory authorities who act independently of the Department of Social Security and Department for Education and Employment.

The first of the statutory authorities, the Adjudication Officer, determines entitlement to benefit. A client who is dissatisfied with that decision has the right of appeal to an independent social security appeal tribunal. There is a further right of appeal to a Social Security Commissioner against the tribunal's decision but leave to appeal must first be obtained. Appeals to the Commissioner must be on a point of law. Provision is also made for the determination of certain questions by the Secretary of State for Social Security.

Disablement questions are decided by adjudicating medical authorities or medical appeal tribunals. Appeal to the Commissioner against a tribunal's decision is with leave and on a point of law only.

Leaflet NI246, which is available from social security offices, explains how to appeal, and leaflet NI260 is a guide to reviews and appeals.

THE SOCIAL FUND

The Social Fund helps people with expenses which are difficult to meet from regular income. Regulated maternity, funeral and cold weather payments are decided by Adjudication Officers and are not cash-limited. Discretionary community care grants, and budgeting and crisis loans are decided by Social Fund Officers and come out of a yearly budget which is allocated to each district (1996–7, grants £97 million; loans £321.5 million; £1 million set aside as a contingency reserve).

REGULATED PAYMENTS
Maternity Payments
A payment of up to £100 for each baby expected, born or adopted. It is payable to people on income support, disability working allowance and family credit and is non-repayable.

Funeral Payments
Payable for specified funeral director's charges, plus the necessary cost of all burial or cremation expenses reasonably incurred by people receiving income support, disability working allowance, family credit, council tax benefit or housing benefit. It is recoverable from the estate of the deceased.

Cold Weather Payments
£8.50 for any consecutive seven days when the average temperature is 0°C or below in their area. These are paid to people on income support who are pensioners, disabled or parents with a child under the age of five. They are non-repayable.

DISCRETIONARY PAYMENTS
Community Care Grants
They are intended to help people on income support to move into the community or avoid institutional or residential care; ease exceptional pressures on families; care for a prisoner on release on temporary licence; and/or meet certain essential travelling expenses. They are non-repayable.

Budgeting Loans
These are interest-free loans to people who have been receiving income support for at least six months, for intermittent expenses that may be difficult to budget for.

Crisis Loans
These are interest-free loans to anyone, whether receiving benefit or not, who is without resources in an emergency, where there is no other means of preventing serious risk or damage to their health or safety.

Loans are normally repaid over a period of up to 78 weeks at 15, 10 or 5 per cent of income support (less housing costs), depending on other commitments.

SAVINGS
Savings over £500 (£1,000 for people aged 60 or over) are taken into account for maternity and funeral payments, community care grants and budgeting loans. All savings are taken into account for crisis loans. Savings are not taken into account for cold weather payments.

APPEALS AND REVIEWS
For regulated payments there is a right of appeal (except in the case of cold weather payments, which do not carry the right of appeal although a question may be raised by a claimant if they believe they should have received a payment) to an independent Social Security Appeal Tribunal and thereafter to a Social Security Commissioner. For discretionary payments there is a review system where persons can ask for a review at the local office with a further right of review to an independent Social Fund Inspector.

INDUSTRIAL INJURIES, DISABLEMENT AND DEATH BENEFITS

The industrial injuries scheme, administered under the Social Security Contributions and Benefits Act 1992, provides a range of benefits designed to compensate for disablement resulting from an industrial accident (i.e. an accident arising out of and in the course of an employed earner's employment) or from a prescribed disease due to the nature of a person's employment. Rates of benefit are increased annually.

BENEFITS

Disablement benefit is normally payable 15 weeks (90 days) after the date of accident or onset of disease if the employed earner suffers from loss of physical or mental faculty such that the resulting disablement is assessed at not less than 14 per cent. The amount of disablement benefit payable varies according to the degree of disablement (in the form of a percentage) assessed by an adjudicating medical authority or medical appeal tribunal.

Disablement assessed at less than 14 per cent does not normally attract basic benefit except for certain chest diseases. A weekly pension is payable where the assessment of disablement is between 14 and 100 per cent (assessments of 14 to 19 per cent are payable at the 20 per cent rate). Payment can be made for a limited period or for life. The basic rates are applicable to adults and to juveniles entitled to an increase for a child or adult dependant; other juveniles receive lower rates.

Basic rates of pension are not related to the pensioner's loss of earning power, and are payable whether he/she is in work or not. There is provision for increases of pension if the pensioner requires constant attendance or if his/her disablement is exceptionally severe. A pensioner may draw statutory sick pay or incapacity benefit as appropriate, in addition to disablement pension, during spells of incapacity for work.

Regulations impose certain obligations on claimants and beneficiaries and on employers, including, in the case of claimants for disablement benefit, that of submitting themselves for medical examination.

SUPPLEMENTARY ALLOWANCES

Special schemes under the Industrial Injuries and Diseases (Old Cases) Act 1975 provide supplementary allowances to those entitled to receive weekly payments of workmen's compensation for loss of earnings due to injury at work, or disease contracted during employment before 5 July 1948 when the industrial injuries scheme was introduced. Other schemes under the Act provide allowances to those who contracted slowly-developing diseases during employment before July 1948 where neither workmen's compensation nor industrial injuries benefits are payable. A lump sum death benefit of up to £300 may also be payable to a dependant of such a person. Leaflet NI196 provides details relating to these allowances.

WEEKLY RATES OF BENEFIT
from April 1996
Disablement benefit/pension
Degree of disablement

100 per cent	£99.00
90	89.10
80	79.20
70	69.30
60	59.40
50	49.50
40	39.60
30	29.70
20	19.80
‡Unemployability supplement	61.15
Addition for adult dependant (subject to earnings rule)	36.60

Reduced earnings allowance (maximum)	£39.60
Constant attendance allowance (normal maximum rate)	39.70
Exceptionally severe disablement allowance	39.70

*There is a weekly benefit for those under 18 with no dependants which is set at a lower rate
†This benefit attracts an increase for each dependent child (in addition to child benefit) of £9.90 for the first child and £11.15 for each subsequent child

CLAIMS AND QUESTIONS

Provision is made for the determination of certain questions by the Secretary of State for Social Security, and of 'disablement questions' by a medical board (or a single doctor) or, on appeal, by a medical appeal tribunal. An appeal on a point of law against a medical appeal tribunal decision is determined by the Social Security Commissioner.

Claims for benefit and certain questions arising in connection with a claim for or award of benefit (e.g. whether the accident arose out of and in the course of the employment) are determined by an adjudication officer appointed by the Secretary of State, or a social security appeal tribunal, or in certain circumstances, on further appeal, by the Commissioners.

OTHER BENEFITS

STATUTORY SICK PAY

Employers usually pay statutory sick pay (SSP) to their employees for up to 28 weeks of sickness in any period of incapacity for work. SSP is paid at £54.55 a week and is subject to PAYE tax and NI deductions. Employees who cannot get SSP may be able to claim incapacity benefit. Employers can recover some SSP costs under the percentage threshold scheme where a large part of the workforce is off sick at the same time. Where SSP payments exceed 13 per cent of the employer's total NI liability for any tax month the employer can recover excess SSP paid above the 13 per cent threshold. Leaflet NI 244 is obtainable from local Social Security offices.

STATUTORY MATERNITY PAY

In general, employers pay statutory maternity pay to pregnant women who have been employed by them full or part-time for at least 26 weeks before the end of the 'qualifying week', which is 15 weeks before the week the baby is due, and whose earnings are on average at least at the lower earnings limit for the payment of NI contributions. All women who meet these conditions receive payment of 90 per cent of their average earnings for six weeks, followed by a maximum of 12 weeks at £54.55. Women have some choice in deciding when to begin maternity leave but SMP is not payable for any week in which work is done. Employers are reimbursed for 92 per cent of the SMP they pay (105.5 per cent for those whose annual NI liability is £20,000 or less).

War Pensions

The War Pensions Agency, an executive agency of the Department of Social Security (DSS), awards war pensions under The Naval, Military and Air Forces, Etc. (Disablement and Death) Service Pensions Order 1983 to members of the armed forces in respect of the periods 4 August 1914 to 30 September 1921 and subsequent to 3 September 1939 (including present members of the armed forces). War pensions for the period 1 October 1921 to 2 September 1939 were dealt with by the Ministry of Defence until July 1996 when the DSS became responsible for the provision of war pensions for this period. There is also a scheme for civilians and civil defence workers in respect of the 1939–45 war, and other schemes for groups such as merchant seamen and Polish armed forces who served under British command.

PENSIONS

War disablement pension is awarded for the disabling effects of any injury, wound or disease which is attributable to, or has been aggravated by, conditions of service in the armed forces. It cannot be paid until the serviceman or woman has left the armed forces.

Disablement is assessed by comparison of the disabled person's health with that of a normal, healthy person of the same age and sex, without taking into account the disabled person's earning capacity or occupation, and is expressed on a percentage scale up to 100 per cent. Disablement of 20 per cent and above, for which a pension is awarded, is assessed in steps of 10 per cent. Maximum assessment does not necessarily imply total incapacity. For assessment of less than 20 per cent a lump sum is usually payable. No award is made where disablement in respect of noise-induced sensorineural hearing loss is assessed at less than 20 per cent.

The dependency allowance in respect of a wife or child was abolished in 1992 and an equivalent amount incorporated into the basic war disablement pension.

War widow's pension is awarded where death occurs as a result of service or where a war disablement pensioner was receiving constant attendance allowance at the time of his death, or would have been receiving it if he were not in hospital, in which case his widow has automatic entitlement to a war widow's pension, regardless of the cause of death. Additional allowances are payable for dependent children, in addition to child benefit. From July 1995 a war widow's pension, which is withdrawn on remarriage, can be restored on subsequent widowhood or divorce.

A lower weekly rate is payable to war widows of men below the rank of Lieutenant-Colonel who are under the age of 40, without children and capable of maintaining themselves. This is increased to the standard rate at age 40.

Rank additions to both disablement gratuities and widow's pensions may be paid where the rank held was above that of private (or equivalent).

SUPPLEMENTARY ALLOWANCES

A number of supplementary allowances may be awarded to a war pensioner which are intended to meet various needs, such as mobility, unemployability, constant nursing care, which may result from disablement or death and take account of its particular effect on the pensioner or spouse.

The principal supplementary allowances are:

Unemployability supplement – paid to a war pensioner whose pensioned disablement is so serious as to make him unemployable. An invalidity allowance may also be payable if the incapacity for work began more than five years before normal retirement age.

Allowance for lowered standard of occupation – awarded to a partially disabled pensioner whose pensioned disablement permanently prevents him from following his regular occupation. The allowance, together with the basic war disablement pension, must not exceed pension at the 100 per cent rate.

Constant attendance allowance – awarded if the pensioner is receiving a pension at the 80 per cent rate or more and needs care and attendance because of the disability. It is paid at one of four rates depending on how much care is needed.

Widow's child's allowance – paid in addition to child benefit.

Other supplementary allowances include exceptionally severe disablement allowance, severe disablement occupational allowance, treatment allowance, mobility supplement, comforts allowance, clothing allowance, age allowance and widow's age allowance. There is a rent allowance available on a war widow's pension.

Decisions on supplementary allowances are made on a discretionary basis and there is no provision for a statutory right of appeal against them. However, war pensioners may discuss any aspect of their pension position with their local war pensions committee, which may be able to arrange help or make representations to the DSS.

WAR PENSIONERS ABROAD

The DSS is responsible for the payment of war pensions, and, where necessary, meeting the cost of treatment for accepted disablement, to pensioners who reside overseas. They receive the same pension rates and annual upratings as war pensioners in this country.

SOCIAL SECURITY BENEFITS

Most social security benefits are paid in addition to the basic war disablement pension or war widow's pension. Any retirement pension for which a war widow qualifies on her own contributions, and any graduated retirement benefit or additional earnings-related pension inherited from her husband, can be paid in addition to her war widow's pension.

A war pensioner or war widow who claims income support, family credit or disability working allowance has the first £10 of pension disregarded. A similar provision operates for housing benefit and council tax benefit; but the local authority may, at its discretion, disregard any or all of the balance.

CLAIMS AND QUESTIONS

Where a claim in respect of death or disablement is made no later than seven years after the termination of service, the claimant does not have to prove that the disablement or death on which the claim is based is related to service and receives the benefit of any reasonable doubt. Where a claim in respect of death or disablement is made more than seven years after the termination of service the claimant has to show that disablement or death is related to service. However, the claim succeeds if reliable evidence is produced which raises a reasonable doubt whether or not disablement or death is related to service. There is no time limit for making a claim for war pension.

Independent pensions appeal tribunals hear appeals against the decisions of the DSS on entitlement and assessment of disablement in respect of the 1939–45 war and subsequent service cases. There are no time limits within which an entitlement appeal must be made but there are time limits within which an assessment appeal should be made. However, there are now no rights of appeal in the 1914–21 war disablement cases, the great majority of which were given final assessment in the 1920s with a 12 months' right of appeal at the time. An appeal by a 1914 war widow must be made within twelve months of the date on which the rejection of the claim is notified.

WAR PENSIONERS WELFARE SERVICE

The DSS operates a war pensioners welfare service to advise and assist war pensioners and their widows on any matters affecting their welfare. Welfare officers are attached to war pensioners' welfare offices located in the major towns, and the service is available to any war pensioner or war widow who needs it.

The current rates of all war pensions and allowances are listed in WPA leaflet 9, *Rates of War Pensions and Allowances*, obtainable from war pensioners welfare offices, HMSO, Broadway, Chadderton, Oldham OL9 9QH, or by phoning the War Pension Helpline on 01253-858858.

WEEKLY RATES OF PENSIONS AND ALLOWANCES
from week commencing 8 April 1996

War disablement pension
Degree of disablement:

100 per cent	£105.00
90 per cent	94.50
80 per cent	84.00
70 per cent	73.50
60 per cent	63.00
50 per cent	52.50
40 per cent	42.00
30 per cent	31.50
20 per cent	21.00

Unemployability supplement

Personal allowance	64.90
Increase for wife/other adult dependant	36.50
Increase for first child	9.90
Increase for other children	11.15

Allowance for lowered standard of occupation

(maximum)	39.60

Widow's pension
(widow of Private or equivalent rank)

Standard rate	79.35
Increase for first child	14.10
Increase for other children	15.35
Childless widow under 40	18.35

Widow's age allowance

aged 65–69	9.05
aged 70–79	17.40
aged 80 and over	25.90

The Water Industry

ENGLAND AND WALES

In England and Wales the Secretaries of State for the Environment and for Wales have overall responsibility for water policy and set the environmental and health and safety standards for the water industry. The Director-General of Water Services, as the independent economic regulator, is responsible for ensuring that the private water companies are able to fulfil their statutory obligation to provide water supply and sewerage services, and for protecting the interests of consumers.

The Minister of Agriculture, Fisheries and Food and the Secretary of State for Wales are responsible for policy relating to land drainage, flood protection, sea defences and the protection and development of fisheries.

The Environment Agency is responsible for water quality and the control of pollution, the management of water resources and nature conservation. The Drinking Water Inspectorate and local authorities are responsible for the quality of drinking water.

THE WATER COMPANIES

Until 1989 nine regional water authorities in England and the Welsh Water Authority in Wales were responsible for water supply and the development of water resources, sewerage and sewage disposal, pollution control, fresh-water fisheries, flood protection, water recreation, and environmental conservation. The Water Act 1989 provided for the creation of a privatized water industry under public regulation, and the functions of the regional water authorities were taken over by ten holding companies and the regulatory bodies.

Of the 99 per cent of the population of England and Wales who are connected to a public water supply, 75 per cent are supplied by the water companies (through their principal operating subsidiaries, the water service companies). The remaining 25 per cent are supplied by statutory water companies which were already in the private sector. Most of these have public limited company (PLC) status and many are now French-owned. They are represented by the Water Companies Association. The ten water service companies are also responsible for sewerage and sewage disposal in England and Wales. The Water Services Association is the trade association for all the water service companies except Wessex Water Services.

Water Service Companies

ANGLIAN WATER SERVICES LTD, Anglian House, Ambury Road, Huntingdon, Cambs PE18 6NZ

DWR CYMRU (WELSH WATER), Cambrian Way, Brecon, Powys LD3 7HP

NORTHUMBRIAN WATER LTD, Abbey Road, Pity Me, Durham DH1 5FJ

NORTH WEST WATER LTD, Dawson House, Liverpool Road, Great Sankey, Warrington WA5 3LW

SEVERN TRENT WATER LTD, 2297 Coventry Road, Sheldon, Birmingham B26 3PU

SOUTHERN WATER SERVICES LTD, Southern House, Yeoman Road, Worthing, W. Sussex BN13 3NX

SOUTH WEST WATER SERVICES LTD, Peninsula House, Rydon Lane, Exeter EX2 7HR

THAMES WATER UTILITIES LTD, Nugent House, Vastern Road, Reading RG1 8DB

WESSEX WATER SERVICES LTD, Wessex House, Passage Street, Bristol BS2 0JQ

YORKSHIRE WATER SERVICES LTD, West Riding House, 67 Albion Street, Leeds LS1 5AA

WATER COMPANIES ASSOCIATION, 1 Queen Anne's Gate, London SW1H 9BT. Tel: 0171-222 0644. *Chief Executive*, Ms P. Taylor

WATER SERVICES ASSOCIATION, 1 Queen Anne's Gate, London SW1H 9BT. Tel: 0171-957 4567. *Chief Executive*, Miss J. Langdon

REGULATORY BODIES

The Office of Water Services (Ofwat) (*see* page 354) was set up under the Water Act 1989 and is the independent economic regulator of the water and sewerage companies in England and Wales. Ofwat's main duty is to ensure that the companies can finance and carry out their statutory functions and to protect the interests of water customers. Ofwat is a non-ministerial government department headed by the Director-General of Water Services, who is appointed by the Secretaries of State for the Environment and for Wales.

An independent national body, the National Rivers Authority, took over the regulatory and river management functions of the regional water authorities. It had statutory duties and powers in relation to water resources, pollution control, flood defence, fisheries, recreation, conservation and navigation in England and Wales. On 1 April 1996 the statutory duties, powers and functions of the National Rivers Authority were transferred to the new Environment Agency (*see* page 298).

The Drinking Water Inspectorate (*see* page 297) is responsible for assessing the quality of the drinking water supplied by the water companies, inspecting the companies themselves and investigating any accidents affecting drinking water quality. The Chief Inspector presents an annual report to the Secretaries of State for the Environment and for Wales.

METHODS OF CHARGING

In England and Wales, most householders still pay for domestic water supply and sewerage services through charges based on the assessed value of their property under the old domestic rating system. Industrial and most commercial users are charged according to consumption, which is recorded by meter.

The Water Industry Act 1991 gives the water companies until 2000 to decide on and introduce a suitable method of charging. The main options under consideration are a flat-rate licence fee, property banding, and metering. The Government believes metering to be the best basis for payment. However, extension of the use of meters to all households will take considerable time to achieve. The Government has therefore decided to allow water companies to continue to use the old domestic rating system as a basis for their unmeasured charges after 2000.

SCOTLAND

Overall responsibility for national water policy in Scotland rests with the Secretary of State for Scotland. Most aspects of water policy are administered through the Scottish Office Agriculture, Environment and Fisheries Department.

Water supply and sewerage services were formerly local authority responsibilities and the Central Scotland Water Development Board had the function of developing new sources of water supply for the purpose of providing water in bulk to water authorities whose limits of supply were within the board's area. The Local Government etc. Scotland) Act 1994 provided for three new public water authorities, covering the north, east and west of Scotland respectively, to be established to take over the provision of water and sewerage services from 1 April 1996. From that date the Central Scotland Water Development Board was abolished. The new authorities are accountable to Parliament through the Secretary of State for Scotland. The Act also provided for a Scottish Water and Sewerage Customers Council to be established to represent consumer interests. It will monitor the performance of the authorities; approve charges schemes; investigate complaints; and keep the Secretary of State advised on standards of service and customer relations.

The new Scottish Environment Protection Agency (SEPA) (*see* page 339) is responsible for promoting the cleanliness of Scotland's rivers, lochs and coastal waters. SEPA is also responsible for controlling pollution.

EAST OF SCOTLAND WATER AUTHORITY, Pentland Gait, 597 Calder Road, Edinburgh EH11 4HJ. Tel: 0131-453 7500. *Chief Executive*, R. Rennet
NORTH OF SCOTLAND WATER AUTHORITY, Caledonia House, 63 Academy Street, Inverness IV1 1LU. Tel: 01463-245400. *Chief Executive*, A. Findlay
SCOTTISH WATER AND SEWERAGE CUSTOMERS COUNCIL, Suite 4, Ochil House, Springkerse Business Park, Stirling FK7 7XE. Tel: 01786-430200. *Director*, Dr V. Nash
WEST OF SCOTLAND WATER AUTHORITY, 419 Balmore Road, Glasgow G22 6NU. Tel: 0141-355 3555. *Chief Executive*, E. Chambers

METHODS OF CHARGING

The water authorities set charges for domestic and non-domestic water and sewerage provision through charges schemes which have to be approved by the Scottish Water and Sewerage Customers Council. The authorities must publish a summary of their charges schemes.

NORTHERN IRELAND

In Northern Ireland ministerial responsibility for water services lies with the Secretary of State for Northern Ireland. The Water Service, which is an executive agency of the Department of the Environment for Northern Ireland, is responsible for policy and co-ordination with regard to supply, distribution and cleanliness of water, and the provision and maintenance of sewerage services.

The Water Service (*see* page 330) is divided into four regions, the Eastern, Northern, Western and Southern Divisions. These are based in Belfast, Ballymena, Londonderry and Craigavon respectively.

On major issues the Department of the Environment for Northern Ireland seeks the views of the Northern Ireland Water Council, a body appointed to advise the Department on the exercise of its water and sewerage functions. The Council includes representatives from agriculture, angling, industry, commerce, tourism, trade unions and local government.

METHODS OF CHARGING

Usually householders do not pay separately for water and sewerage services; the costs of these services are allowed for in the Northern Ireland regional rate. Water consumed by industry, commerce and agriculture in excess of 100 cubic metres (22,000 gallons) per half year is charged through meters. Traders operating from industrially rated premises are required to pay for the treatment and disposal of the trade effluent which they discharge into the public sewerage system.

Energy

THE COAL INDUSTRY

Coal has been mined in Britain for centuries and the availability of coal was crucial to the industrial revolution of the 18th and 19th centuries. Mines were in private ownership until 1947 when they were nationalized and came under the management of the National Coal Board (later the British Coal Corporation). In addition to producing coal at its own deep-mine and opencast sites, British Coal was responsible for licensing private operators.

PRIVATIZATION

Under the Coal Industry Act 1994, a new body, the Coal Authority (see page 291), was established to take over ownership of coal reserves and to issue licences to private mining companies as part of the privatization of British Coal. The Coal Authority also deals with the physical legacy of mining, e.g. subsidence damage claims, and is responsible for holding and making available all existing records.

The Government offered the mines for sale in five businesses based in the separate regions of Scotland, Wales and the North-East and two based on the central areas of the Midlands and Yorkshire. All five businesses were sold, the three businesses in England being sold to a single purchaser as one company. Coal production in the UK is now undertaken entirely in the private sector.

SUPPLY AND DEMAND

The main domestic customer for coal is the electricity supply industry, but the latter's demand for coal has declined as it turns increasingly to alternative fuels. National Power has announced that it expects to close ten of its 18 coal-fired power stations by 2000.

Supply 1994	million tonnes
Production of deep-mined coal	31.1
Production of opencast coal	16.6
Recovered slurry, fines, etc.	0.3
Imports	15.0
Change in colliery stocks	−4.2
Change in stocks at opencast sites	−0.5
Total supply	67.7

Home consumption 1994	
Electricity supply industry	62.4
Coke ovens	8.6
Low temperature carbonization plants	0.5
Manufactured fuel plants	0.7
Railways	—
Collieries	—
Industry	4.9
Domestic	3.9
Public services	0.5
Miscellaneous	0.2
Total home consumption	81.7
Overseas shipments and bunkers	1.0
Total consumption and shipments	82.7
*Change in distributed stocks	−14.6
†Balance	0.4

*Stock change excludes industrial and domestic stocks
†This is the balance between supply and consumption, shipments and changes in known distributed stocks
Source: HMSO – Annual Abstract of Statistics 1996

THE GAS INDUSTRY

The gas industry in the United Kingdom was nationalized in 1949 under the Gas Act 1948, and operated as the Gas Council. The Gas Act 1972 replaced the Gas Council with the British Gas Corporation and led to greater centralization of the industry. The British Gas Corporation was privatized in 1986 as British Gas PLC and is currently the main supplier of gas in Great Britain. The Office of Gas Supply (see page 302) is the regulatory body for the gas industry.

In 1993 the Monopolies and Mergers Commission found that British Gas's integrated business in Great Britain as a gas trader and the owner of the gas transportation system could be expected to operate against the public interest, and it recommended that the company divest itself of its gas trading activities in Great Britain. The President of the Board of Trade subsequently announced that competition would be introduced into the domestic gas supply market, and that British Gas should separate fully its supply and transportation operations; it would not, however, be required to divest itself of its supply business. Competition is now being introduced into the domestic gas market. The first tranche took place in April 1996 when a pilot project involving 500,000 customers in Cornwall, Devon and Wales was implemented. The second tranche will commence in April 1997, when competition will be extended to cover two million customers in the south of England. In April 1998 competition will be extended to cover all customers in Great Britain.

FUEL INPUT AND GAS OUTPUT: GAS SALES 1994

Fuel input to gas industry	GWh
Petroleum (million tonnes)	—
*Petroleum gases	52
Natural gas	—
Coke oven gas	—
Total to gas works	—
Natural gas for direct supply	729,374
Total fuel input	729,426

Gas output and sales	
Gas output:	
Town gas	30
Natural gas supplied direct	729,374
Gross total available	729,404
Own use	−2,743
†Statistical difference	−20,444
Total sales	706,217

*Butane, propane, ethane and refinery tail gases
†Supply greater than recorded demand (−). Includes losses in distribution
Source: HMSO – Annual Abstract of Statistics 1996

NATURAL GAS CONSUMPTION 1995p

	GWh
Domestic	326,010
Electricity generators	145,455
Iron and steel industry	20,581
Other industries	152,896
Other	109,585
Total	754,527

p provisional
Source: Department of Trade and Industry

BRITISH GAS

The principal business of British Gas PLC is the purchase, transmission and sale of natural gas to domestic, industrial and commercial customers in Great Britain. It is increasingly seeking to exploit overseas markets. British Gas has hydrocarbon exploration and production operations offshore and onshore, both in Great Britain and overseas, and it has an interest in gas-related activities world-wide.

British Gas is divided into three parts: the UK Gas Business, Exploration and Production, and International Downstream. In 1994 it restructured its UK operations to separate its gas supply business from its gas transportation business. Its regional structure was abolished and has been replaced by four business units: TransCo, which provides transportation and storage services to shippers; British Gas Trading, which sells gas to domestic, industrial and commercial customers; Retail, which markets gas and other appliances through a national chain of shops; and Service, which handles the servicing and installation of gas central heating and other equipment. British Gas has announced plans to demerge; final proposals will be tabled in 1997.

BRITISH GAS PLC, The Adelphi, 1–11 John Adam Street, London WC2N 6HT. Tel: 0171-321 2880. *Chairman and Chief Executive*, R. V. Giordano

BRITISH GAS FINANCE
£ million

	1994	1995
Turnover		
TransCo	3,103	3,126
Trading	8,238	7,604
Exploration and production	1,161	1,268
Other activities	480	821
†Overseas gas supply	669	—
Less: intra-group sales	(3,953)	(4,218)
Total	9,698	8,601
Operating costs include:		
Raw materials and consumables	3,397	2,955
Employee costs	1,691	1,492
Exceptional costs	195	394
Current cost depreciation	1,365	1,275
Total	8,711	8,018
Current cost profit on ordinary activities	1,020	590
Gearing adjustment	67	92
Net interest payable	(184)	(92)
Current cost profit before tax	918	607
Current cost profit after tax	414	136
Minority shareholders' interest	(4)	(6)
Current cost profit attributable to British Gas shareholders	410	130
Dividends	(631)	(637)
Transfer from reserves	(221)	(507)

* 1994 restated on an estimated basis
† Discontinued June 1994

SUPPLY AND TRANSMISSION

British Gas obtains natural gas from fields on mainland Britain, in coastal waters and in the North Sea. It also imports gas from other countries. In 1994 total production of gas by British Gas from UK continental shelf fields was 350 billion cubic feet; in 1995 total production was 429 billion cubic feet.

The mainland national transmission system is operated by British Gas, with other gas suppliers entering contracts to use the system. British Gas operates six reception terminals. The length of mains in use in 1995 was 269,600

km: 251,700 km of distribution mains and 17,900 km of transmission mains.

THE ELECTRICITY INDUSTRY

Under the Electricity Act 1989 twelve regional public electricity supply companies were formed from the twelve area electricity boards in England and Wales; the companies were floated on the stock market in 1990. Four companies were formed from the Central Electricity Generating Board: three generating companies (National Power PLC, Nuclear Electric PLC and PowerGen PLC) and the National Grid Company PLC. National Power PLC and PowerGen PLC were floated on the stock market in 1991, the Government retaining a 40 per cent holding in both companies. In 1995 a second flotation took place when the Government sold its remaining 40 per cent holding in the two companies. Shares in the National Grid Company PLC were demerged from the regional electricity companies and floated on the stock market in December 1995.

In Scotland, three new companies were formed: Scottish Power PLC, Scottish Hydro-Electric PLC and Scottish Nuclear Ltd. Flotation of Scottish Power PLC and Scottish Hydro-Electric PLC on the stock market took place in 1991.

Two new companies, British Energy PLC and Magnox Electric PLC, were formed from the combined assets of Scottish Nuclear Ltd and Nuclear Electric PLC in April 1996. British Energy PLC is due to be floated on the stock market in the summer of 1996; Magnox Electric is to remain in public ownership.

In Northern Ireland, Northern Ireland Electricity PLC was set up in 1993 under a 1991 Order in Council. It has been floated on the stock market.

A trade and representational organization, the Electricity Association, was created by the newly formed electricity companies; its principal subsidiaries were Electricity Association Services Ltd (for representational and professional services) and Electricity Association Technology Ltd (for distribution and utilization research, development and technology transfer). Electricity Association Technology Ltd (now renamed EA Technology Ltd) left the Electricity Association group of companies in 1993.

The Offices of Electricity Regulation (*see* page 296) are the regulatory bodies for the industry.

Competition is to be introduced into the domestic electricity market on 1 April 1998.

ELECTRICITY ASSOCIATION SERVICES LTD, 30 Millbank, London SW1P 4RD. Tel: 0171-963 5700. *Chief Executive*, P. E. G. Daubeney

EA TECHNOLOGY LTD, Capenhurst, Chester CHI 6ES. Tel: 0151-339 4181. *Managing Director*, Dr S. F. Exell

SUPPLY COMPANIES

BRITISH ENERGY PLC, 10 Lochside Place, Edinburgh EH12 9DF. Tel: 0131-527 2000. *Chief Executive*, Dr R. Hawley
MAGNOX ELECTRIC PLC, Berkeley Centre, Berkeley, Glos GL13 9PB. Tel: 01453-810451. *Chief Executive*, R. Hall
THE NATIONAL GRID COMPANY PLC, National Grid House, Kirby Corner Road, Coventry CV4 8JY. Tel: 01203-537777. *Chief Executive*, D. Jones
NATIONAL POWER PLC, Windmill Hill Business Park, Whitehill Way, Swindon, Wilts SN5 9NX. Tel: 01793-877777. *Chief Executive*, K. Henry
POWERGEN PLC, 53 New Broad Street, London EC2M 1JJ. Tel: 0171-638 5742. *Chief Executive*, E. Wallis

500   Energy

REGIONAL ELECTRICITY COMPANIES

EASTERN ELECTRICITY PLC, PO Box 40, Wherstead, Ipswich IP2 9AQ
EAST MIDLANDS ELECTRICITY PLC, PO Box 444, Wollaton, Nottingham NG8 1EZ
LONDON ELECTRICITY PLC, Templar House, 81–87 High Holborn, London WC1V 6NU
MANWEB PLC, Sealand Road, Chester CH1 4LR
MIDLANDS ELECTRICITY PLC, Mucklow Hill, Halesowen, W. Midlands B62 8BP
NORTHERN ELECTRIC PLC, Carliol House, Newcastle upon Tyne NE99 1SE
NORWEB PLC, Talbot Road, Manchester M16 0MQ
SEEBOARD PLC, Forest Gate, Brighton Road, Crawley, W. Sussex RH11 9BH
SOUTHERN ELECTRIC PLC, Littlewick Green, Maidenhead, Berks SL6 3QB
SWALEC PLC, St Mellons, Cardiff CF3 9XW
SOUTH WESTERN ELECTRICITY PLC, 800 Park Avenue, Aztec West, Almondsbury, Avon BS12 4SE
YORKSHIRE ELECTRICITY GROUP PLC, Scarcroft, Leeds LS14 3HS

SCOTTISH COMPANIES

SCOTTISH HYDRO-ELECTRIC PLC, 16 Rothesay Terrace, Edinburgh EH3 7SE. Tel: 0131-225 1361. *Chief Executive*, R. Young
SCOTTISH POWER PLC, 1 Atlantic Quay, Glasgow G2 8SP. Tel: 0141-248 8200. *Chief Executive*, I. Robinson

NORTHERN IRELAND

NORTHERN IRELAND ELECTRICITY PLC, PO Box 2, Danesfort, 120 Malone Road, Belfast BT9 5HT. Tel: 01232-661100. *Chief Executive*, Dr P. Haren

GENERATION, SUPPLY AND CONSUMPTION
gigawatt-hours

	1993	1994
Electricity generated		
Major power producers: total	300,514	302,807
Conventional steam stations	187,786	175,362
Nuclear stations	84,433	83,944
Gas turbines and oil engines	359	244
Combined cycle gas turbine stations	22,811	36,971
Hydro-electric stations:		
Natural flow	3,522	4,317
Pumped storage	1,437	1,463
Renewables other than hydro	165	506
Electricity used on works: total	19,287	17,504
Major generating companies	17,391	15,921
Other generators	1,896	1,583
Electricity supplied (gross)		
Major power producers: total	283,123	286,886
Conventional steam stations	178,312	167,289
Nuclear stations	76,839	76,412
Gas turbines and oil engines	324	233
Combined cycle gas turbine stations	22,611	36,815
Hydro-electric stations:		
Natural flow	3,513	4,265
Pumped storage	1,388	1,417
Renewables other than hydro	136	455
Electricity used in pumping		
Major power producers	1,948	2,051

Electricity supplied (net): total	301,845	305,828
Major power producers	281,175	284,835
Other generators	20,670	20,993
Net imports	16,721	16,887
Electricity available	318,561	322,715
Losses in transmission, etc	22,815	26,520
Electricity consumption: total	295,746	296,195
Fuel industries	9,615	7,669
Final users: total	286,130	288,527
Industrial sector	96,842	97,855
Domestic sector	100,456	100,644
Other sectors	88,833	90,028

Source: HMSO – *Annual Abstract of Statistics 1996*

Transport

Source: HMSO – Annual Abstract of Statistics 1996

GOODS TRANSPORT 1994

TOTAL TONNE KILOMETRES (*millions*)	220,800
Road	143,700
Rail (British Rail only)	13,300
Water: coastwise oil products*	28,700
Water: other*	23,500
Pipelines (except gases)	11,600
TOTAL (*million tonnes*)	2,051
Road	1,689
Rail (British Rail only)	97
Water: coastwise oil products*	43
Water: other*	97
Pipelines (except gases)	125

'Coastwise' includes all sea traffic within the UK, Isle of Man and Channel Islands. 'Other' means other coastwise plus inland waterway traffic and one-port traffic

Source: HMSO – Annual Abstract of Statistics 1996

PASSENGER TRANSPORT 1994p
Million passenger kilometres (estimated)

TOTAL	689,000
Air	5,000
Rail*	35,000
Road: Public service vehicles	43,000
Cars, vans and taxis	596,000
Motorcycles	4,000
Pedal cycles	5,000

* provisional
†including London Regional Transport and Passenger Transport Executive railway systems

Source: HMSO – Annual Abstract of Statistics 1996

AIR PASSENGERS 1995*

ALL UK AIRPORTS: TOTAL	131,100,157
LONDON AREA AIRPORTS: TOTAL	83,330,537
Battersea Heliport	4,022
Gatwick	22,550,131
Heathrow	54,469,173
London City	553,989
Luton	1,829,205
Southend	4,210
Stansted	3,919,827
OTHER UK AIRPORTS: TOTAL	47,769,600
Aberdeen	2,255,557
Barra	7,665
Barrow-in-Furness	344
Belfast City	1,283,500
Belfast International	2,374,506
Benbecula	38,942
Biggin Hill	5,259
Birmingham	5,328,469
Blackpool	75,961
Bournemouth	103,388
Bristol	1,468,123
Cambridge	33,004
Cardiff	1,068,582
Carlisle	1,514
Coventry	3,523
Dundee	16,397
East Midlands	1,891,215
Edinburgh	3,384,432
Exeter	191,101
Glasgow	5,528,771
Gloucestershire	2,763
Hawarden	46
Humberside	289,348
Inverness	285,221
Islay	20,400
Isle of Man	561,235
Isles of Scilly–St Mary's	119,110
–Tresco	24,094
Kent International	2,621
Kirkwall	104,994
Leeds/Bradford	931,697
Lerwick (Tingwall)	4,411
Liverpool	505,786
Londonderry	64,897
Lydd	258
Manchester	14,750,949
Newcastle	2,527,503
Norwich	258,470
Penzance Heliport	90,462
Plymouth	106,182
Prestwick	330,691
Scatsta	14,623
Shoreham	2,398
Southampton	519,841
Stornoway	95,733
Sumburgh	505,407
Teesside	462,127
Tiree	5,602
Unst	74,505
Wick	47,973
CHANNEL IS. AIRPORTS: TOTAL	2,569,589
Alderney	85,472
Guernsey	833,464
Jersey	1,650,653

*Total terminal, transit, scheduled and charter passengers

Source: Civil Aviation Authority

AERODROMES/AIRPORTS

The following aerodromes in the UK, the Isle of Man and the Channel Islands are either state owned or licensed for use by civil aircraft. A number of unlicensed aerodromes not included in this list are also available for private use by special permission. Aerodromes designated as Customs airports are printed in small capitals. Customs facilities are available at certain other aerodromes by special arrangement.

BAA   Owned by BAA PLC
H   Licensed for helicopters
HIAL   Operated by Highland and Islands Airports Ltd
L   Owned by municipal authority
M   Military aerodromes – civil availability by prior permission
P   Private ownership
S   Government owned and operated

ENGLAND AND WALES
Aberporth, Dyfed   M
Andrewsfield, Essex
Barrow (Walney Island), Cumbria
Bembridge, IOW
Benson, Oxon   M
Beverley/Linley Hill, N. Humberside
BIGGIN HILL, Kent   P
BIRMINGHAM   P
Blackbushe, Hants
BLACKPOOL, Lancs   P
Bodmin, Cornwall
Boscombe Down, Wilts   M
Bourn, Cambridge
BOURNEMOUTH, Dorset   P
BRISTOL   P
Brize Norton, Oxford   M
Brough, N. Humberside
Caernarfon, Gwynedd
CAMBRIDGE   P
CARDIFF   P
Carlisle, Cumbria   L
Chichester (Goodwood), Sussex
Chivenor, Devon   M
Church Fenton, N. Yorks   M
Clacton, Essex
Compton Abbas, Dorset
Cosford, Wolverhampton   M
COVENTRY, W. Midlands   L
Cranfield, Beds
Cranwell, Lincs   M
Crowfield, Suffolk
Culdrose, Cornwall   M
Denham, Bucks
Derby
Dishforth, N. Yorks   M
Dunkeswell, Devon
Dunsfold, Surrey   L
Duxford, Cambs   L
Eaglescott, Devon
Earls Colne, Halstead

EAST MIDLANDS, Derbys   P
Elstree, Herts
EXETER, Devon
Fairoaks, Surrey
Farnborough, Hants   S
Fenland, Lincs
Filton, Bristol
Finningley, S. Yorks   M
Fowlmere, Cambs
Full Sutton, N. Yorks
Gloucestershire (Staverton)   P
Great Yarmouth (North Denes), Norfolk   H
Halfpenny Green, Staffs
Halton, Bucks   M
Haverfordwest, Dyfed   L
Hawarden, Clwyd
Hucknall, Notts
HUMBERSIDE   P
Ipswich, Suffolk
Isle of Wight/Sandown
Land's End (St Just), Cornwall
Lashenden, Headcorn, Kent
LEEDS/BRADFORD   P
Lee-on-Solent, Hants   M
Leicester
Linton-on-Ouse, Yorks   M
Little Gransden, Beds
LIVERPOOL   P
Llanbedr, Gwynedd   M
LONDON/CITY
LONDON/GATWICK   BAA
LONDON/HEATHROW   BAA
LONDON/LUTON   P
LONDON/STANSTED   BAA
London/Westland Heliport   H
LYDD, Kent
Lyneham, Wilts   M
MANCHESTER   P
Manchester (Barton)
MANSTON/KENT INTERNATIONAL   M
Mona, Gwynedd   M
Netherthorpe, S. Yorks
NEWCASTLE UPON TYNE   P
Newton, Notts   M
Northampton (Sywell)
Northolt, Middx   M
NORWICH, Norfolk   L
Nottingham
Old Sarum, Wilts
Oxford (Kidlington)
Penzance, Cornwall   H
Perranporth, Cornwall
Peterborough (Conington)
Peterborough (Sibson)
PLYMOUTH (ROBOROUGH), Devon
Portland Naval, Dorset   MH
Redhill, Surrey
Retford/Gamston, Notts
Rochester, Kent
St Mawgan, Cornwall   M
Sandtoft, Humberside
Scilly Isles (St Mary's)   L
Seething, Norfolk
Shawbury, Shropshire   M
Sherburn-in-Elmet, N. Yorks
Shipdham, Norfolk
Shobdon, Herefordshire
SHOREHAM, W. Sussex   P
Silverstone, Northants

Sleap, Shropshire
SOUTHAMPTON   P
SOUTHEND, Essex   P
Stapleford, Essex
Sturgate, Lincs
Swansea   L
TEESSIDE   P
Thruxton, Hants
Tresco, Isles of Scilly   H
Turweston, Northants
Valley, Gwynedd   M
Warton, Lancs
Wattisham, Suffolk   M
Wellesbourne Mountford, Warwick
Welshpool, Powys
Weston, Avon   H
White Waltham, Berks
Wickenby, Lincs
Woodford, Gtr Manchester
Woodvale, Merseyside   M
Wycombe Air Park (Booker), Bucks
Yeovil, Somerset
Yeovilton, Somerset   M

SCOTLAND
ABERDEEN (DYCE)   BAA
Barra, Hebrides
Benbecula, Hebrides   HIAL
Campbeltown   HIAL
Cumbernauld, Strathclyde
Dundee   L
Eday, Orkneys   L
EDINBURGH   BAA
Fair Isle, Shetlands
Fife   L
Flotta, Orkneys
GLASGOW   BAA
Inverness (Dalcross)   HIAL
Islay (Port Ellen), Hebrides   HIAL
Kirkwall, Orkneys   HIAL
Lerwick (Tingwall), Shetlands   L
Leuchars, Fife   M
North Ronaldsay, Orkneys   L
Papa Westray, Orkneys   L
Perth (Scone)
PRESTWICK, Ayrshire   BAA
Sanday, Orkneys   L
Scatsta, Shetlands
Stornoway, Hebrides   HIAL
Stronsay, Orkneys   L
SUMBURGH, Shetlands   HIAL
Tiree, Hebrides   HIAL
Unst, Shetlands   L
West Freugh, Dumfries   S
Westray, Orkneys   L
Whalsay, Shetlands
Wick, Caithness   HIAL

NORTHERN IRELAND
BELFAST (ALDERGROVE)
Belfast (City)
Enniskillen (St Angelo), Co. Fermanagh   L
Londonderry (Eglinton)   L
Newtownards, Co. Down

ISLANDS
ALDERNEY, CI   S
GUERNSEY, CI   S
ISLE OF MAN   S
JERSEY, CI   S

RAILWAYS

Britain pioneered railways and a railway network was developed across Britain by private companies in the course of the 19th century. In 1948 the main railway companies were nationalized and were run by a public authority, the British Transport Commission. The Commission was replaced by the British Railways Board in 1963. On 1 April 1994 the British Railways Board ceased to be responsible for the provision of rail services in Britain but continues as operator (under the operating name British Rail) of all train services until they are sold or franchised to the private sector.

Prior to privatization, management of the railways had been organized into the business sectors of InterCity, Network SouthEast, Regional Railways, Trainload Freight and Railfreight Distribution. These businesses have ceased to exist corporately but the names will continue to be used for trading purposes in the short term. European Passenger Services Ltd was set up to manage international passenger rail services through the Channel Tunnel and ownership was transferred to the Government in May 1994.

PRIVATIZATION

Since 1 April 1994, ownership of track and land has been vested in a new company, Railtrack, which was floated on the Stock Exchange in May 1996. Railtrack manages the track and charges for access to it and is responsible for signalling and timetabling. It does not operate train services. It owns the freehold of stations, but station management is being privatized under management contract or lease arrangements. Initially, Railtrack's infrastructure support functions were provided by 20 British Rail service companies; these companies have now been sold into the private sector. Railtrack will invest in infrastructure principally using finance raised by track charges, and will take investment decisions in consultation with rail operators.

Passenger services have been divided into 25 train-operating units, which are gradually being franchised to private sector operators. The private sector will eventually also be able to run completely new services with a right of open access to the track. The Government will continue to subsidize loss-making but socially necessary rail services. The franchising director is responsible for awarding franchises by competitive tendering, monitoring the performance of the franchisees, and allocating and administering government subsidy payments.

British Rail's passenger rolling stock has been divided between three subsidiary companies which will lease rolling stock to franchisees. The three companies were transferred to government ownership in July 1995 and were sold to the private sector in February 1996. The bulk freight haulage companies and Rail Express Systems, which carries Royal Mail traffic, have been sold to English, Welsh and Scottish Railways. The European business of Railfreight Distribution will be privatized when the Channel Tunnel freight services have been developed. The domestic and deep-sea container business (Freightliner) was sold in May 1996. British Rail's technical support and specialist function businesses are also being sold.

The independent Rail Regulator is responsible for the licensing of new railway operators, approving access agreements, promoting the use and development of the network, and protecting the interests of rail users.

BRITISH RAILWAYS BOARD, see page 286

RAILTRACK, 40 Bernard Street, London WCIN IBY. Tel: 0171-344 7100. *Chairman*, R. Horton. *Chief Executive*, J. Edmonds, CBE

OFFICE OF PASSENGER RAIL FRANCHISING (OPRAF), Golding's House, 2 Hay's Lane, London SEI 2HB. Tel: 0171-940 4200. *Franchising Director*, J. O'Brien

OFFICE OF THE RAIL REGULATOR (ORR), 1 Waterhouse Square, Holborn Bars, 138–142 Holborn, London ECIN 2SU. Tel: 0171-282 2000. *Rail Regulator*, J. Swift

RAIL OPERATIONS

At 31 March 1996, Railtrack had about 20,000 miles of standard gauge lines and sidings in use, representing over 10,000 miles of route of which about 3,000 miles were electrified. Standard rail on main line has a weight of 110 lb per yard.

Loaded train miles run in passenger service totalled 231.3 million. Passenger journeys made during the year totalled 718.7 million, including 325.6 million made by holders of season tickets. The average distance of each passenger journey on ordinary fare was 34.1 miles; and on season ticket, 14.5 miles. Passenger stations in use in 1996 numbered 2,514. Train miles run in freight service totalled 24.5 million.

On 31 March 1996 British Rail employed 63,982 staff (94,344 at 31 March 1995). Including subsidiaries, the group total at 31 March 1996 was 64,259 (100,264 at 31 March 1995).

FINANCIAL RESULTS

Railtrack

In 1994–5 Railtrack showed an operating profit of £305 million and a pre-tax profit of £189 million.

	£ million
Income	
Passenger	1,955
Freight	191
Property rental	82
Other	47
Total	2,275
Costs	
Production and management	501
Infrastructure maintenance	696
Asset maintenance plan charge	483
Joint industry costs	197
Depreciation	93
Total	1,970

British Rail

British Rail's profit and loss account for 1995–6 showed a profit of £58 million after interest and extraordinary items, compared with a profit of £362 million in 1994–5. The railway operating surplus was £13.7 million (including a write-off of £500 million against Channel Tunnel freight services) compared with a surplus of £571 million for the previous year.

	£ million
*Income	
Passenger	4,394
Freight and Parcels	444
Railfreight Distribution	47
Others	164
Infrastructure services	1,019
Group Services	317
Total	6,385

Operating expenditure

Staff costs	1,919
Railtrack access charges	2,155
Rolling stock leasing	487
Materials, supplies and services	1,162
Depreciation	102
Amortization of deferred grant	(27)
Own work capitalized	(1)
Total	5,797
Operating profit	588
Profit on disposals	176
Restructuring costs	(51)
Exceptional items	(575)
Profit before interest	138
Interest	(80)
Group profit	58

*Income includes government grants totalling £2,010 million

ACCIDENTS ON RAILWAYS

	1993–4	1994–5
Train accidents: total	977	907
Persons killed: total	6	12
Passengers	0	3
Railway staff	0	5
Others	6	4
Persons injured: total	246	296
Passengers	134	190
Railway staff	95	83
Others	17	23
Other accidents through movement of		
railway vehicles		
Persons killed	26	27
Persons injured	2,373	2,417
Other accidents on railway premises		
Persons killed	9	3
Persons injured	8,244	7,933
Trespassers and suicides		
Persons killed	253	254
Persons injured	97	85

THE CHANNEL TUNNEL

The earliest recorded scheme for a submarine transport connection between Britain and France was in 1802. Tunnelling has begun simultaneously on both sides of the Channel three times: in 1881, in the early 1970s, and on 1 December 1987, when construction workers began to bore the first of the three tunnels which form the current project. They 'holed through' the first tunnel (the service tunnel) on 1 December 1990 and tunnelling was completed in June 1991. The tunnel was officially inaugurated by The Queen and President Mitterrand of France on 6 May 1994.

In January 1986 the concession for construction and operation of the tunnel and its services was awarded to a paired Anglo-French private-sector company, CTG-FM, wholly owned by Eurotunnel. Eurotunnel's costs from establishment in 1986 to the first commercial service in 1994 were about £8,700 million. The funds available to Eurotunnel amount to £10,535 million, raised through equity and loans. Eurotunnel expect to achieve cash-flow break-even in 1998. On 14 September 1995 Eurotunnel suspended interest payments on its 'junior' debt (i.e. all money raised before a rights issue in 1994) in line with its credit agreement. This gives Eurotunnel up to March 1997 to discuss a restructuring of its finances with interested parties.

Passenger services (Eurostar) run from Waterloo station in London to Paris and Brussels. Connecting services from Edinburgh and Manchester via London began in 1995 and through services from these cities, not stopping in London, are scheduled to begin in September 1996. Vehicle shuttle services (Le Shuttle) operate between Folkestone and Calais.

The submarine link comprises three tunnels. There are two rail tunnels, each carrying trains in one direction, which measure 24.93 ft (7.6 m) in diameter. Between them lies a smaller service tunnel, measuring 15.75 ft (4.8 m) in diameter. The service tunnel is linked to the rail tunnels by 130 cross-passages for maintenance and safety purposes. The tunnels are 31 miles (50 km) long, 24 miles (38 km) of which is under the sea-bed at an average depth of 132 ft (40 m). The rail terminals are situated at Folkestone and Calais, and the tunnels go underground at Shakespeare Cliff, Dover, and Sangatte, west of Calais.

RAIL LINKS

The route for the British Channel Tunnel rail link was confirmed by the Government in 1994. The rail link will run from Folkestone to a proposed new terminal at St Pancras station, London, but at present services run into a terminal at Waterloo station, London.

Construction of the rail link will be financed by the private sector with a substantial government contribution. A private sector consortium, London and Continental Railways Ltd, will be responsible for the design, construction and ownership of the rail link, and has taken over Union Railways and European Passenger Services Ltd, who will operate international services from London through the Channel tunnel. Construction is expected to be completed in 2003.

Infrastructure developments in France have been completed and high-speed trains run from Calais to Paris, linking the Channel tunnel with the high-speed European network.

ROADS

HIGHWAY AUTHORITIES

The powers and responsibilities of highway authorities in England and Wales are set out in the Highways Acts 1980; for Scotland there is separate legislation.

Responsibility for trunk road motorways and other trunk roads in Great Britain rests in England with the Secretary of State for Transport, in Scotland with the Secretary of State for Scotland, and in Wales with the Secretary of State for Wales. The costs of construction, improvement and maintenance are paid for by central government. The highway authority for non-trunk roads in England, Wales and Scotland is, in general, the unitary authority, county council or London borough council in whose area the roads lie. In Northern Ireland the Department of the Environment for Northern Ireland is the statutory road authority responsible for public roads and their maintenance and construction; the Roads Service executive agency (*see* page 330) carries out these functions on behalf of the Department.

FINANCE

The Government contributes towards capital expenditure through Transport Supplementary Grant (TSG) in England and Transport Grant (TG) in Wales. Grant rates are determined by the respective Secretaries of State; at present, grant is paid at 50 per cent of expenditure accepted for grant in England and Wales.

In England TSG is paid towards capital spending on highways and the regulation of traffic; current expenditure is funded by revenue support grant (i.e. central government grants to local authorities for non-specific services). TSG is also paid towards capital spending on bridge assessment and strengthening; towards structural maintenance on the primary route network; and towards all principal 'A' roads. In Wales TG is paid towards capital expenditure only; current expenditure is funded by revenue support grant.

For the financial year 1996–7 local authorities in England will receive £236 million in TSG. Total estimated expenditure on building and maintaining motorways and trunk roads in England in 1995–6 was £1,785 million; estimated outturn for 1996–7 is £1,569 million.

For the financial year 1996–7 local authorities in Wales will receive up to £39 million in TG. Total expenditure on roads in Wales in 1994–5 was £298.4 million.

The Scottish Office receives a block vote from Parliament and the Secretary of State for Scotland determines how much is allocated towards roads. Total expenditure on building and maintaining trunk roads in Scotland was estimated at £234 million in 1995–6.

In Northern Ireland expenditure on roads in 1995–6 was estimated at £150 million, and estimated expenditure for 1996–7 is £153 million.

PRIVATE FINANCE

The Government is seeking to encourage greater involvement by the private sector in the design, finance, construction and operation of roads. A research programme is under way to assess the technology necessary for the introduction of electronic motorway tolls.

ROAD BUILDING PROGRAMME

In 1995 the Government conducted a review of its programme of improving the motorway and trunk road network, resulting in the withdrawal in November 1995 of 77 schemes deemed to be unnecessary or environmentally

unacceptable and the suspension of preparation work on 104 other schemes. In winter 1995, 35 schemes were under construction, 37 schemes were being taken forward as Design, Build, Finance and Operate (DBFO), i.e. privately-financed, schemes and a further 112 were being progressed under conventional funding arrangements.

ROAD LENGTHS (in miles) as at April 1995

	Total roads	Trunk roads (including motorways)	Motorways*
England	174,207	6,448	1,678
Wales	21,001	1,057	78
Scotland	32,698	1,950	179
N. Ireland	15,018	1,460†	69
UK	242,925	10,916	2,004

*There were in addition 27.3 miles of local authority motorway in England and 16.7 miles in Scotland
†'A' roads; there are no designated trunk roads in N. Ireland

MOTORWAYS

England and Wales:

M1	London to Yorkshire
M2	London to Faversham
M3	London to Southampton
M4	London to South Wales
M5	Birmingham to Exeter
M6	Catthorpe to Carlisle
M10	St Albans spur
M11	London to Cambridge
M18	Rotherham to Goole
M20	London to Folkestone
M23	London to Gatwick
M25	London orbital
M26	M20 to M25 spur
M27	Southampton bypass
M32	M4 to Bristol spur
M40	London to Birmingham
M41	London to West Cross
M42	South-west of Birmingham to Measham
M45	Dunchurch spur
M50	Ross spur
M53	Chester to Birkenhead
M54	M6 to Telford
M55	Preston to Blackpool
M56	Manchester to Chester
M57	Liverpool outer ring
M58	Liverpool to Wigan
M61	Manchester to Preston
M62	Liverpool to Hull
M63	Manchester southern ring road
M65	Calder Valley
M66	Manchester eastern ring road to Rochdale
M67	Manchester Hyde to Denton
M69	Coventry to Leicester
M180	South Humberside

Scotland:

M8	Edinburgh-Newhouse, Baillieston-West Ferry Interchange
M9	Edinburgh to Stirling
M73	Maryville to Mollisburn
M74	Glasgow-Paddy's Ridde Bridge, Cleughbrae-Gretna
M77	Ayr Road Route
M80	Stirling to Haggs/Glasgow (M8) to Stepps
M90	Inverkeithing to Perth
M876	Dennyloanhead (M80) to Kincardine Bridge

Northern Ireland:

M1	Belfast to Dungannon
M2	Belfast to Antrim
M3	Belfast Cross Harbour Bridge
M5	M2 to Greencastle
M12	M1 to Craigavon
M22	Antrim to Randalstown

ROAD USE

ESTIMATED TRAFFIC ON ALL ROADS (GREAT BRITAIN) 1995

Million vehicle kilometres

All motor vehicles	430,900
Cars and taxis	353,200
Two-wheeled motor vehicles	4,100
Buses and coaches	4,700
Light vans	39,100
Other goods vehicles	29,800
Total goods vehicles	68,900
Pedal cycles	4,500

Source: Department of Transport

BUSES AND COACHES (GREAT BRITAIN) 1994–5

Number of vehicles (31 March 1995)	75,300
Vehicle kilometres (millions)	4,106
Local bus passenger journeys (millions)	4,420
Passenger receipts (£ million)	3,335

ROAD GOODS TRANSPORT (GREAT BRITAIN) 1995
Analysis by mode of working and by gross weight of vehicle

Estimated tonne kilometres (thousand million)	143.7
Own account	37.2
Public haulage	106.5
By gross weight of vehicle (billion tonne kilometres)	
Not over 25 tonnes	24.7
Over 25 tonnes	119.0
Estimated tonnes carried (millions)	1,609.0
Own account	622.0
Public haulage	987.0
By gross weight of vehicle (million tonnes)	
Not over 25 tonnes	467.0
Over 25 tonnes	1,142.0

Source: Department of Transport

ROAD ACCIDENTS 1995

Road accidents	230,376
Vehicles involved:	
Pedal cycles	25,462
Motor vehicles	388,603
Total casualties	310,506
Pedestrians	47,029
Vehicle users	263,477
Killed*	3,621
Pedestrians	1,038
Pedal cycles	213
All two-wheeled motor vehicles	445
Cars and taxis	1,749
Others	176

*Died within 30 days of accident

	Killed	Injured
1965	7,952	389,986
1970	7,499	355,869
1975	6,366	318,584
1980	6,010	323,000
1985	5,165	312,359
1990	5,217	335,924
1993	3,814	302,206
1994	3,650	311,539
1995	3,621	306,885

DRIVING LICENCES

It is necessary to hold a valid full licence in order to drive on public roads in the UK. Learner drivers obtain a provisional driving licence before starting to learn to drive and must then pass a test to obtain a full driving licence. There are separate tests for driving motor cycles, cars, passenger-carrying vehicles (PCVs) and large goods vehicles (LGVs). Drivers must hold full car entitlement before they can apply for PCV or LGV entitlements. In 1996, 36.4 million people in the UK held a valid driving licence (full or provisional). The minimum age for driving motor cars, light goods vehicles up to 3.5 tonnes and motor cycles is 17 (moped, 16).

The Driver and Vehicle Licensing Agency is responsible for issuing driving licences, registering and licensing vehicles, and collecting excise duty in Great Britain. In Northern Ireland the Driver and Vehicle Licensing Agency (Northern Ireland) has similar responsibilities.

DRIVING LICENCE FEES *since October 1994*

First provisional licence	£21.00
Changing a provisional to a full licence after passing a driving test	free
Renewal of licence	£6.00
Renewal of licence including PCV or LGV entitlements	£21
Medical renewal	free
Medical renewal (over 70)	£6.00
Duplicate Licence	£6.00
Exchange Licence	£6.00
Removing endorsements	£6.00
New licence after a period of disqualification	£12.00
New licence after disqualification for some drinking and driving offences	£20

DRIVING TESTS

The Driving Standards Agency is responsible for carrying out driving tests and approving driving instructors in Great Britain. In Northern Ireland the Driver and Vehicle Testing Agency (Northern Ireland) is responsible for testing drivers and vehicles.

About 1.6 million car driving tests were conducted in Great Britain in 1995–6 of which 45.7 per cent resulted in a pass. In addition over 80,000 lorry and bus tests were undertaken, of which 48 per cent were successful. Over 108,000 motorcycle tests were undertaken, of which 70.1 per cent were successful.

*DRIVING TEST FEES (weekday rate/evening and Saturday rate)

For cars	£28.50/£38.50
†For motor cycles	£36/£47.50
For lorries, buses	£62/£80
For invalid carriages	free

*Since 1 July 1996 most candidates for car and motor cycle tests have also been required to take a written driving theory test, for which there is a separate fee of £15. Theory tests for lorry and bus drivers will be introduced on 1 January 1997
†Almost all motor cyclists are required to have completed Compulsory Basic Training, organized by DSA-approved training bodies. Prices vary. The exemption from CBT for full car licence holders will end on 1 January 1997

An extended driving test was introduced in 1992 for those convicted of dangerous driving. The fee is £57/£77.50 (car) or £72/£92 (motorcycle).

MOTOR VEHICLES

Vehicles must be licensed before they can be driven on public roads. They must also be approved as roadworthy by the Vehicle Certification Agency. The Vehicle Inspectorate carries out annual testing and inspection of goods vehicles, buses and coaches.

The number of vehicles with current licences in 1995 was:

	Britain	N. Ireland
Private and light goods	23,000,000	523,000
Motor cycles, scooters, mopeds	603,000	9,000
Public transport vehicles	82,000	2,000
Heavy goods vehicles	410,000	16,000
Agricultural tractors	317,000	2,000
Others	45,000	11,000
Total	25,679,000	612,000

These totals include 1,094,000 vehicles exempt from licensing.

VEHICLE LICENCES

Since 1974 registration and first licensing of vehicles has been through local offices (known as Vehicle Registration Offices) of the Department of Transport's Driver and Vehicle Licensing Centre in Swansea. The records of existing vehicles are held at Swansea. Local facilities for relicensing are available as follows:

(i) with a licence reminder (form V11) in person at any post office which deals with vehicle licensing, or post it to the post office shown on the form

(ii) with a vehicle licence renewal (form V10). Applicants may normally apply in person at any licensing post office. They will need to take their vehicle registration document; if this is not available the applicant must complete form V62 which is held at post offices. Postal applications can be made to the post offices shown on form V100, available at any post office. This form also provides guidance on registering and licensing vehicles.

Details of the present duties chargeable on motor vehicles are available at post offices and Vehicle Registration Offices. The Vehicle Excise and Registration Act 1994 provides *inter alia* that any vehicle kept on a public road but not used on roads is chargeable to excise duty as if it were in use. All non-commercial vehicles over 25 years old are exempt from vehicle excise duty.

VEHICLE EXCISE DUTY RATES *since 1 July 1995*

	12 months £	6 months £
Motor Cars		
Light vans, cars, taxis, etc.	140.00	77.00
Motor Cycles		
With or without sidecar, not over 150 cc	15.00	—
With or without sidecar, 150–250 cc	35.00	—
Electric motorcycles (including tricycles)	15.00	—
Others	55.00	30.25
Tricycles (not over 450 kg)		
Not over 150 cc	15.00	—
Others	55.00	30.25
Buses		
Seating 9–16 persons	150.00	82.50
Seating 17–35 persons	200.00	110.00
Seating 36–60 persons	300.00	165.00
Seating over 60 persons	450.00	247.50

MoT TESTING

Cars, motor cycles, motor caravans, light goods and dual-purpose vehicles more than three years old must be covered by a current MoT test certificate. The certificate must be renewed annually. Copies of the legislation governing MoT testing can be obtained from any bookshop which stocks HMSO publications. The legislation comprises the Road Traffic Act 1988 (Sections 45 and 46), the Motor Vehicles (Test) Regulations 1981, and subsequent amendments. The MoT testing scheme is administered by the Vehicle Inspectorate.

A fee is payable to MoT testing stations, which must be authorized to carry out tests. The maximum fees, which are prescribed by regulations, are:

For cars and light vans	£28.66
For solo motor cycles	£11.90
For motor cycle combinations	£20.00
For three-wheeled vehicles	£23.40
For non-public service vehicle buses	£35.12
For light goods vehicles	£28.66
For goods vehicles	£30.68

SHIPPING

PRINCIPAL MERCHANT FLEETS 1995

Flag	No	Gross tonnage
Panama	5,777	71,921,698
Liberia	1,666	59,800,742
Greece	1,863	29,434,695
Cyprus	1,674	24,652,547
Bahamas	1,176	23,602,812
Japan	9,438	19,913,211
Norway (NIS)	700	18,902,880
Malta	1,164	17,678,303
China	2,948	16,943,220
Russia	5,160	15,202,349
Singapore	1,344	13,610,818
*United States of America	5,292	12,760,810
Hong Kong	399	8,794,766
Philippines	1,524	8,743,769
India	916	7,126,850
Korea (South)	2,246	6,972,148
Italy	1,397	6,699,484
Turkey	1,075	6,267,629
Saint Vincent	1,029	6,164,878
Taiwan	683	6,104,294
Germany	1,146	5,626,178
Denmark (DIS)	450	5,119,877
Brazil	551	5,076,695
Ukraine	1,142	4,613,003
United Kingdom	1,454	4,412,683
Netherlands	1,059	3,409,241
Malaysia	685	3,282,878
Marshall Islands	95	3,098,574
Bermuda	86	3,047,535
Sweden	621	2,955,425
Iran	424	2,902,431
Australia	627	2,853,061
Indonesia	2,196	2,770,513
Norway	1,515	2,648,030
Romania	421	2,536,421
Canada	886	2,401,047
Poland	516	2,358,043
Isle of Man	146	2,300,402
French Antarctic Territory	77	2,266,040
Kuwait	213	2,057,044
WORLD TOTAL	82,890	490,662,091

NIS   Norwegian International Ship Register – offshore registry
*Excluding ships of United States Reserve Fleet
DIS   Danish International Register of Shipping – offshore registry
Source: Lloyd's Register of Shipping

MERCHANT SHIPS COMPLETED 1995

Country of Build	No.	Gross tonnage
Japan	592	9,262,882
Korea (South)	158	6,264,282
Germany	91	1,120,991
Denmark	25	1,003,032
*China	64	783,688
Poland	39	523,650
Taiwan	16	488,083
Italy	19	395,360
Finland	8	316,606
France	13	253,991
Spain	41	250,743
Romania	18	229,321
Netherlands	76	205,181
*Ukraine	16	184,637
Croatia	7	178,626
Brazil	7	172,245
Norway	35	146,785
United Kingdom	22	125,775
Singapore	51	98,933
Bulgaria	7	91,598
*Russia	19	82,846
India	13	40,840
Turkey	12	30,506
Slovakia	13	29,856
Sweden	2	28,916
Other countries	169	157,528

For Registration in

Panama	256	7,186,380
Liberia	71	3,804,849
Hong Kong	39	1,260,039
Philippines	31	819,842
Japan	296	796,653
Germany	61	742,393
China	49	679,636
Greece	20	641,015
Cyprus	33	537,732
Marshall Islands	9	481,513
Singapore	95	469,173
Malaysia	27	436,376
Denmark (DIS)	12	412,601
Bahamas	16	369,536
Taiwan	14	357,355
Norway (NIS)	15	351,101
Italy	16	310,739
United Kingdom	20	307,695
India	17	266,996
Norway	15	194,948
Malta	13	187,482
Netherlands	45	178,159
Antigua and Barbuda	29	169,684
French Antarctic Territory	6	155,132
Isle of Man	4	147,144
Other countries	324	1,202,728
WORLD TOTAL	1,533	22,466,901

*Information incomplete
DIS   Danish International Register of Shipping – offshore registry
NIS   Norwegian International Ship Register – offshore registry
Source: Lloyd's Register of Shipping

BRITISH-REGISTERED* TRADING VESSELS
of 500 Gross Tons and Over *as at end 1994*

Type of vessel	No.	Gross tonnage
Tankers[1]	113	2,481,000
Bulk carriers[2]	14	294,000
Specialized carriers[3]	13	110,000
Container (fully cellular)	34	1,236,000
Ro-Ro[4]	84	874,000
Other general cargo	93	212,000
Passenger[5]	9	281,000
Total	360	5,488,000

* Registered in the UK and British Crown dependencies
1 Includes oil, gas, chemical and other specialized tankers
2 Includes combination bulk carriers: ore/oil and ore bulk/oil carriers
3 Includes livestock, car and chemical carriers
4 Roll-on, roll-off passenger and cargo vessels
5 Cruise liner and other passenger vessels
Source: HMSO – *Annual Abstract of Statistics 1996*

SEAPORT TRAFFIC OF GREAT BRITAIN 1994
By Mode of Appearance

	Million gross tonnes
FOREIGN TRAFFIC: *Imports*	184.9
Bulk fuel traffic	71.2
Other bulk traffic	46.2
Container and roll-on traffic	49.6
Semi-bulk traffic	16.6
Conventional traffic	1.4
FOREIGN TRAFFIC: *Exports*	178.6
Bulk fuel traffic	112.1
Other bulk traffic	21.3
Container and roll-on traffic	38.8
Semi-bulk traffic	5.3
Conventional traffic	1.1
DOMESTIC TRAFFIC*	154.6
Bulk fuel traffic	105.1
Other bulk traffic	33.9
Container and roll-on traffic	10.5
Semi-bulk traffic	0.4
Conventional traffic	0.5
Non-oil traffic with UK offshore installations	4.1
TOTAL FOREIGN AND DOMESTIC TRAFFIC	518.1

* Domestic traffic refers to traffic through the ports of Great Britain only, to all parts of the UK, Isle of Man and the Channel Islands. Traffic to and from offshore installations, landing of sea-dredged aggregates and material shipped for dumping at sea included

Source: HMSO – *Annual Abstract of Statistics 1996*

SEABORNE TRADE OF THE UK 1994p
Exports (Including Re-exports) Plus Imports by Sea

	Million tonnes	% carried by UK-registered vessels*
By weight		
All cargo	352.9	12
Dry bulk cargo	84.9	9
Other dry cargo	110.8	15
Tanker cargo	157.2	12
	£ million	
By value		
All cargo	2,178,800	25
Dry bulk cargo	74,800	9
Other dry cargo	1,970,800	28
Tanker cargo	133,200	12

p provisional
* Relates to trade with countries outside the EU
Source: HMSO – *Annual Abstract of Statistics 1996*

PASSENGER MOVEMENT BY SEA 1994

Arrivals plus departures at UK seaports by place of embarkation or landing*

All passenger movements	37,038,000
Irish Republic	3,478,000
Belgium	2,878,000
France†	27,224,000
Netherlands	1,987,000
Other EU countries	896,000
Other European and Mediterranean countries‡	305,000
USA	31,100
Rest of the world	3,100
Pleasure cruises beginning and/or ending at UK seaports	236,000

* Passengers are included at both departure and arrival if their journeys begin and end at a UK seaport
† Includes hovercraft passengers
‡ Includes North Africa and Middle East Mediterranean countries

Source: HMSO – *Annual Abstract of Statistics 1996*

Communications

Postal Services

Responsibility for running postal services rests in the UK with a public authority, the Post Office (*see* page 334). The Secretary of State for Trade and Industry has powers to suspend the monopoly of the Post Office in certain areas and to issue licences to other bodies to provide an alternative service. Non-Post Office bodies are permitted to transfer mail between document exchanges and to deliver letters, provided that a minimum fee of £1 per letter is charged. Charitable organizations are allowed to carry and deliver Christmas and New Year cards.

INLAND POSTAL SERVICES AND REGULATIONS

INLAND LETTER POST RATES*

Not over	1st class†	2nd class†
60 g	26p	20p
100 g	39p	31p
150 g	49p	38p
200 g	60p	45p
250 g	70p	55p
300 g	80p	64p
350 g	92p	73p
400 g	£1.04	83p
450 g	£1.17	93p
500 g	£1.30	£1.05
600 g	£1.60	£1.25
700 g	£2.00	£1.45
750 g	£2.15	£1.55 (not
800 g	£2.30	admissible
900 g	£2.55	over 750 g)
1,000 g	£2.50	
Each extra 250 g or part thereof	70p	

UK PARCEL RATES

Not over		Not over	
1 kg	£2.70	8 kg	£6.10
2 kg	£3.30	10 kg	£7.10
4 kg	£4.70	30 kg	£8.40
6 kg	£5.25		

*Postcards travel at the same rates as letter post
†There is a two-tier postal delivery system in the UK with first class letters normally being delivered the following day and second class post within three days

OVERSEAS POSTAL SERVICES AND REGULATIONS

OVERSEAS SURFACE MAIL RATES

Letters

Not over		Not over	
20 g	31p	450 g	£2.88
60 g	52p	500 g	£3.18
100 g	75p	750 g	£4.70
150 g	£1.06	1,000 g	£6.21
200 g	£1.36	1,250 g	£7.71
250 g	£1.66	1,500 g	£9.21
300 g	£1.97	1,750 g	£10.71
350 g	£2.27	2,000 g	£12.21
400 g	£2.57		

AIRMAIL LETTER RATES

Europe: Letters

Not over		Not over	
20 g	26p	260 g	£1.82
20 g non EC	31p	280 g	£1.95
40 g	44p	300 g	£2.07
60 g	56p	320 g	£2.20
80 g	69p	340 g	£2.32
100 g	82p	360 g	£2.45
120 g	94p	380 g	£2.57
140 g	£1.07	400 g	£2.70
160 g	£1.19	420 g	£2.82
180 g	£1.32	440 g	£2.95
200 g	£1.44	460 g	£3.08
220 g	£1.57	480 g	£3.20
240 g	£1.69	*500 g	£3.33

* Max. 2 kg

Outside Europe: Letters

	Not over 10 g	Not over 20 g	Over 20 g
Zone 1	43p	63p	varies
Zone 2	43p	63p	varies

For airmail letter zones outside Europe, *see* pages 515–6

STAMPS

Postage stamps are sold in values of 1p, 2p, 4p, 5p, 6p, 10p, 19p, 20p, 25p, 26p, 29p, 30p, 31p, 35p, 36p, 37p, 38p, 39p, 41p, 43p, 50p, 63p, £1, £1.50, £2.00, £5.00, and £10.00. Books or rolls of first and second class stamps are also available. Stamps are sold at Post Offices and some other outlets, including stationers and newsagents.

PREPAID STATIONERY

Aerogrammes to all destinations are 36p. Forces Aerogrammes are free to certain destinations.

Prepaid envelopes:
Standard services (DL size)

	1st class	2nd class
single	31p	25p
packet of 10	£2.85	£2.25

Guaranteed services	Special Delivery	Registered	Registered Plus
C4, 500g	£4.00	£4.30	£4.90
C5, 250g	3.30	3.60	4.20

Printed postage stamps cut from envelopes, postcards, newspaper wrappers, etc., may be used as stamps in payment of postage, provided that they are not imperfect or defaced.

POSTAL ORDERS

Postal orders (British pattern) are issued and paid at nearly all post offices in the UK and in many other countries.

Postal orders are printed with a counterfoil for denominations of 50p and £1, followed by £1 steps to £10, £15 and £20. Postage stamps may be affixed in the space provided to increase the value of the postal order by up to 49p. Charges (in addition to the value of the postal order): Up to £1, 25p; £2–£4, 42p; £5–£7, 58p; £8–£10, 66p; £15, 80p; £20, 85p.

The name of the payee must be inserted on the postal order. If not presented within six months of the last day of the month of issue, orders must be sent to the local customer services manager of Post Office Counters Ltd (listed in the telephone directory) to ascertain whether the order may still be paid. If the counterfoil has been retained postal orders not more than four years out of date may be paid when presented with the counterfoil at a post office.

RESTRICTIONS

Articles which may not be sent in the post include offensive or dangerous articles, packets likely to impede Post Office sorters, and certain kinds of advertisement.

Under Department of Trade and Industry regulations the exportation of some goods by post is prohibited except under Department of Trade licence. Enquiries should be addressed to the Export Data Branch, Overseas Trade Divisions, Department of Trade and Industry, 1 Victoria Street, London SW1H OET. Tel: 0171-215 5000.

SPECIAL DELIVERY SERVICES

DATAPOST

A guaranteed service for the delivery of documents and packages: (i) Datapost Sameday offers same working day collection and delivery in many areas; (ii) Datapost 10 (for delivery before 10 a.m.) and Datapost 12 (for delivery before noon) offer next working day delivery nationwide and are available only to certain destinations. Items may be collected or handed in at post offices. There are also Datapost links with a number of overseas countries. Parcelforce 24 (next working day delivery) and 48 (delivery in two working days) offer a similar guaranteed service.

ROYAL MAIL SPECIAL DELIVERY

A guaranteed next-day delivery service by 12.30 p.m. to most UK destinations for first class letters and packets. The fee of £2.70 plus first class postage is refunded if next working day delivery is not achieved, provided that items are posted before latest recommended posting times.

SWIFTAIR

Express delivery of airmail letters and packets up to 2 kg anywhere in the world. Items normally arrive at least one day in advance of normal air mail. Charge (in addition to postage), £2.70.

OTHER SERVICES

ADVICE OF DELIVERY

Written confirmation of delivery from the post office at the stated destination. Charge: 33p (inland); 40p (international); plus postage.

CASH ON DELIVERY (INLAND AND INTERNATIONAL)

Inland: an amount up to £500 can, under certain conditions, be collected and remitted to the sender of a parcel containing an invoice. Invoice values of over £100 are only collectable at Post Office premises. Charge per parcel

(exclusive of postage and registration): customers under contract, £1.70; other customers, £2.00; COD enquiry, £1.70.

Overseas: this service is only available with Parcelforce International Standard or Economy service. The following fee is added to postage charges, based on the value of the item to be delivered:

Value	Fee
Up to £200	£5.20
£200–£400	£9.05
£400–£600	£15.00
£600–£1,000	£19.15
£1,000–£1,500	£23.30

CERTIFICATE OF POSTING

Issued free on request at time of posting.

COMPENSATION (INLAND AND INTERNATIONAL)

Inland: compensation up to a maximum of £26 may be paid where it can be shown that a letter was damaged or lost in the post due to the fault of the Post Office, its employees or agents. The Post Office does not accept responsibility for loss or damage arising from faulty packing. Charges: Parcelforce – compensation up to £20 per parcel for loss or damage if a certificate of posting has been obtained. Compensation Fee Certificate of Posting – 70p, up to £150 compensation; £1.25, up to £500 compensation.

International: if a certificate of posting is produced, compensation up to a maximum of £26 may be given for loss or damage in the UK to uninsured parcels to or from most overseas countries. No compensation will be paid for any loss or damage due to the action of the Queen's Enemies.

INTERNATIONAL REPLY COUPONS

Coupons used to prepay replies to letters, exchangeable abroad for stamps representing the minimum surface mail letter rate from the country concerned to the UK. Charge: 60p each.

NEWSPAPER POST

Copies of newspapers registered at the Post Office may be posted only by the publisher or their agents in open-ended wrappers or unsealed envelopes approved by the Post Office, or tied with string removable without cutting. Wrappers and envelopes must be prominently marked 'newspaper post' in the top left-hand corner. The only additional writing or printing permitted is 'with compliments', the name and address of sender, request for return if undeliverable, and a page reference. Items receive first class letter service.

POSTE RESTANTE

Poste Restante is solely for travellers and is for three months in any one town. A packet may be addressed to any post office, except town sub-offices, and should state 'Poste Restante' or 'to be called for' in the address. Redirection from a Poste Restante is undertaken for up to three months. Letters for an expected ship at a port are kept for two months, otherwise letters are kept for two weeks, or one month if from abroad. At the end of this period mail is treated as undeliverable or is returned.

RECORDED DELIVERY (INLAND)

Provides a record of posting and delivery of letters and ensures a signature on delivery. This service is recommended for items of little or no monetary value. Charge: 60p plus postage.

REDIRECTION

By agent of addressee: mail other than parcels, business reply and freepost items may be reposted free not later than the day after delivery (not counting Sundays and public holidays) if unopened and if original addressee's name is unobscured. Parcels may be redirected free within the same time limits only if the original and substituted address are in the same local parcel delivery area (or the London postal area). Registred packets must be taken to a post office and are re-registered free up to the day after delivery.

By the Post Office: a printed form obtainable from the Post Office must be signed by the person to whom the letters are to be addressed. A fee is payable for each different surname on the application form. Charges: up to 1 calendar month, £6.00 (abroad, £12.00); up to 3 calendar months, £13.00 (£26.00); up to 12 calendar months, £30.00 (£60.00).

REGISTERED MAIL (INLAND AND INTERNATIONAL)

Inland: all packets must be handed to the post office and a certificate of posting obtained. Charges (plus postage): up to £500 compensation, £3.00; Registered Plus for compensation between £500 and £1,500, £3.30; up to £2,200 compensation, £3.60. Consequential Loss Insurance provides cover up to £10,000:

Compensation up to	Standard fee in addition to registered fee and postage
£1,000	45p
£2,500	60p
£5,000	85p
£7,500	£1.10
£10,000	£1.35

Compensation in respect of currency or other forms of monetary worth is given only if money is sent by registered letter post. Compensation cannot be paid in the case of any packet containing prohibited articles (*see* Restrictions). Compensation is only paid for well-packed fragile articles and not for exceptionally fragile or perishable articles.

International: packets containing valuable papers, documents or articles can be insured as letters, or as parcels if the country of destination does not accept dutiable goods in the letter post. For HM ships abroad and members of the Army and RAF overseas using BFPO numbers, parcels only are insurable up to £140 at a fee of £1.20. Charges (plus airmail postage): compensation up to £500, £3.00; up to £1,000, £4.00.

SMALL PACKETS POST (INTERNATIONAL)

Permits the transmission of goods up to 2 kg to all countries, in the same mails as printed papers (NB: to Myanmar (Burma) and Papua New Guinea there is a limit of 500 g). Packets can be sealed and can contain personal correspondence relating to the contents. Registration is allowed as insurance as long as the item is packed in a way complying with any insurance regulations. A customs declaration is required and the packet must be marked with 'small packet' and a return address. Instructions for the disposal of undelivered packets must be given at the time of posting. An undeliverable packet will be returned to the sender at his/her expense.

Surface Mail: World-wide

Not over		Not over	
100 g	50p	450 g	£1.67
150 g	67p	500 g	£1.84
200 g	84p	750 g	£2.68
250 g	£1.00	1,000 g	£3.51
300 g	£1.17	1,500 g	£5.21
350 g	£1.34	2,000 g	£6.91
400 g	£1.51		

SPECIAL DELIVERY
See above

UNDELIVERED AND UNPAID MAIL

Undelivered mail is returned to the sender provided the return address is indicated either on the outside of the envelope or inside. If the sender's address is not available items not containing property are destroyed. If the packet contains something of value it is retained for up to three months. Undeliverable second class mail containing newspapers, magazines or commercial advertising is destroyed.

All unpaid or underpaid letters are treated as second class mail. The recipient is charged the amount of underpayment plus 15p per item. Parcels over 750 g are charged at first class rates plus 15p.

Public Telecommunications Services

Under the British Telecommunications Act 1981 British Telecom (now BT) was created to provide a national public telecommunications service. The Telecommunications Act 1984 removed BT's monopoly on running the public telecommunications system and BT was privatized in 1984.

The Telecommunications Act 1984 also established the Office of Telecommunications (Oftel) as the independent regulatory body for the telecommunications industry (*see also* Government Departments and Public Offices).

PUBLIC TELECOMMUNICATIONS OPERATORS

Until 1991 the three licensed fixed-link public telecommunications operators (PTOs) in the UK were BT, Mercury Communications Ltd, and Kingston Communications (Hull) PLC. In March 1991 the Government announced that it was opening up the existing duopoly of the two major fixed-link operators and would be en-couraging applications for telecommunications licences. Since then the Department of Trade and Industry has received over 200 applications for new licences. Around 25 PTO licences have been granted.

BT's obligations under its operating licence continue to include the provision of a universal telecommunications service; a service in rural areas; and essential services, such as public call boxes and emergency services.

Mercury Communications is licensed to provide national and international public telecommunications services for residential and business customers. These services utilize the digital network created by Mercury. Mercury can also provide the following services: public and private telephone services; national and international switched voice and data services; electronic messaging (private circuits and networks (national and international), integrated voice and data); data network services; customer equipment; and mobile communications services.

In June 1996 the Government announced that it was liberalizing international facilities licensing in the UK. The end of the BT/Mercury duopoly means that other operators are now able to apply for licences to own and operate their own international telecommunications networks.

PRIVATE TELEPHONE SERVICES

There are over 260 private telephone companies which offer information on a variety of subjects such as the weather, stock market analysis, horoscopes, etc., on the BT network. Other services are available on the Mercury and Racal Vodaphone networks.

The lines and equipment are provided by BT under condition that services adhere to the codes of practice of the Independent Committee for the Supervision of Standards of Telephone Information Services. All services are charged at 48p per minute (peak and standard rate) or 36p per minute (cheap rate).

MOBILE TELEPHONE SYSTEMS

Cellular telephone network systems allow calls to be made to and from mobile telephones. The four companies licensed by the Department of Trade and Industry to provide competing cellular telephone systems are Cellnet, jointly owned by BT and Securicor; One-2-One, jointly owned by Cable and Wireless and US West; Orange, owned by Hutchison Telecom UK Ltd; and Racal Vodafone Ltd, owned by the Racal Electronics Group.

INLAND TELEPHONES

An individual customer can install an extension telephone socket or apparatus in their own home without the need to buy the items from any of the licensed public telecommunications operators. However, it is necessary to possess a special style of master-socket which must be supplied by the public network operator. Although an individual need not buy or rent an apparatus from a PTO, a telephone bought from a retail outlet must be of an approved standard compatible with the public network (indicated by a green disc on the label).

BT EXCHANGE LINE RENTALS (*including VAT*)

	Per quarter
Residential, exclusive	£25.69
Light user scheme	£25.69
Business, exclusive	£41.13

BT TELEPHONE APPARATUS RENTAL

Residential	from £4.47
Business	from £4.70
Private payphone	from £35.00

EXCHANGE LINE CONNECTION AND TAKE-OVER CHARGES (*including VAT*)

BT

New line	£116.33
Removing customer	£0.00
Take-over of existing lines:	
Simultaneous (same day)	£0.00
Non-simultaneous	£9.99

Mercury

Initial and annual administration charge	£23.00

RATES

BT and Mercury local and dialled national calls are charged by the second. Calls made from payphones are charged in 10p units. There is a 5p minimum charge on all BT calls and a 3p minimum charge on Mercury calls. All charges are subject to VAT, except those from payphones which are VAT inclusive. VAT charges on ordinary lines are calculated as a percentage of the total quarterly (BT)/monthly (Mercury) bill.

The charge per second depends on the time of day and the distance of the call:

BT	Mercury	
Daytime	Standard	Monday to Friday 8 a.m. to 6 p.m.
Cheap	Economy	Monday to Friday 6 p.m. to 8 a.m.*
Weekend	Weekend	Midnight Friday to midnight Sunday

*also Christmas Day, Boxing Day and New Year's Day

Local rate
Regional rate – up to 35 miles (56 km)
National rate – over 35 miles (56 km) (including Channel Islands and Isle of Man)
'm' rate – dialled calls to mobile phones

DIALLED CALL TIME pence per minute charges (*including VAT*)

	BT	Mercury
Local		
Daytime	4.00	*
Cheap	1.70	*
Weekend	1.00	*
Regional rate		
Daytime/Standard	8.30	7.52
Cheap/Economy	4.00	2.82
Weekend	3.30	2.82
National rate		
Daytime/Standard	8.80	7.52
Cheap/Economy	4.65	2.82
Weekend	3.30	2.82
'm' rate		
Daytime/Standard	41.05	32.90†
Cheap/Economy	28.32	23.03†
Weekend	12.05	23.03†

*Mercury advises customers to use BT or cable for local calls

†Calls to One-2-One and Orange mobile phones are charged at the following pence per minute rates:

Standard	12.69
Economy/Weekend	7.99

OPERATOR-CONNECTED CALLS

Operator-connected calls from ordinary lines are generally subject to a three-minute minimum charge (and thereafter by the minute) which varies with distance and time of day. Operator-connected calls from payphones are charged in three-minute periods at the payphone tariff. For calls that have to be placed through the operator because a dialled call has failed, the charge is equivalent to the dialled rate, subject normally to the three-minute minimum.

Higher charges apply to other operator-connected calls, including special services calls and those to mobile phones, the Irish Republic and the Channel Islands.

PHONECARDS

BT phonecards to the value of £2, £5, £10 and £20 are available from post offices and other outlets for use in specially designated public telephone boxes. Each phonecard unit is equivalent to a 10p coin in a payphone. Special public payphones at major railway stations and airports also accept commercial credit cards.

INTERNATIONAL TELEPHONES

All UK customers have access to International Direct Dialling (IDD) and can dial direct to numbers on most exchanges in over 200 countries world-wide. Details about how to make calls are given in dialling code information and in the International Telephone Guide.

For countries without IDD, calls have to be made through the International Operator. All operator-connected calls are subject to a three-minute minimum charge. Thereafter the call is charged by the minute.

Countries which can be called on IDD fall into one of 13 international charge bands depending on location. Charges in each band also vary according to the time of day; cheap rate dialled calls are available to all countries at certain times, but there is no reduced rate for operator-connected calls. Details of current international telephone charges can be obtained from the International Operator.

For International Dialling Codes, *see* pages 515–6

OTHER TELECOMMUNICATIONS SERVICES

TELEX SERVICE

There are now 208 countries that can be reached by the BT telex service from the UK, over 200 of them by direct dialling. For most customers, direct dialled calls to international destinations are charged by the second. Calls via the BT operator are charged in one-minute steps with a three-minute minimum, plus a surcharge of £1.30 a call. Operator-connected calls are charged at between 39p and £1.60 a minute depending upon the country called.

Calls made via BT's Telex Plus store and forward facility attract normal telex charges and a handling charge of 13p for inland delivered messages and 30p for international delivered messages.

TELEMESSAGE

Telemessages can be sent by telephone or telex within the UK for 'hard copy' delivery the next working day, including Saturdays. To achieve this, a telemessage must be telephoned/telexed before 10 p.m. Monday to Saturday (7 p.m. Sundays and Bank Holidays). Dial 100 (190 in London, Birmingham and Glasgow) and ask for the Telemessage Service or see the telex directory for codes.

A telemessage costs £5 for the first 50 words and £2.75 for each subsequent group of 50 words – the name and address are free. A sender's copy costs 85p. A selection of cards is available for special occasions at 80p per card. All prices are subject to VAT.

INTERNATIONAL TELEMESSAGE

Telemessage is also available to the USA. For next working day delivery a telemessage must be filed by 10 p.m. UK time Monday to Saturday (7 p.m. Sundays and Bank Holidays). US addresses must include the ZIP code. Charges are £7.25 for the first 50 words and £3.60 for each subsequent group of 50 words. The name and address are free but all charges are subject to VAT.

BT SERVICES

OPERATOR SERVICES – 100
    For difficulties
    For the following call services: alarm calls (booking charge £2.70); advice of duration and charge (charge £1.80); charge card calls (charge £1.50); freephone calls; international personal calls (charge £2.15–£4.30); transferred charge calls (charge £1.80); subscriber controlled transfer (All charges exclude VAT)
INTERNATIONAL OPERATOR – 155
DIRECTORY ENQUIRIES – 192 (25p charge per call)
INTERNATIONAL DIRECTORY ENQUIRIES – 153
EMERGENCY SERVICES – 999
    Services include fire service; police service; ambulance service; coastguard; lifeboat; cave rescue; mountain rescue
FAULTS – 151
TELEMESSAGE – 100 (190 in London, Birmingham and Glasgow)
INTERNATIONAL TELEMESSAGE – 100 (190 in London, Birmingham and Glasgow). The service is only available to the USA
INTERNATIONAL TELEGRAMS – 100 (190 in London, Birmingham and Glasgow). The service is available world-wide
MARITIME SERVICES – 100
    Includes Ship's Telegram Service and Ship's Telephone Service
BT INMARSAT SATELLITE SERVICE – 155
ALL OTHER CALL ENQUIRIES – 191

Airmail and IDD Codes

AIRMAIL ZONES (AZ)
The table includes airmail letter zones for countries outside Europe, and destinations to which European and European Union airmail letter rates apply (*see also* page 510).
(*Source: Post Office*)

1 airmail zone 1
2 airmail zone 2
e Europe
eu European Union

INTERNATIONAL DIRECT DIALLING (IDD)
International dialling codes are composed of four elements which are dialled in sequence:

(i) the international code
(ii) the country code (*see* below)
(iii) the area code
(iv) the customer's telephone number

Calls to some countries must be made via the international operator. (*Source: BT*)

† Calls must be made via the international operator
p A pause in dialling is necessary whilst waiting for a second tone
* Varies in some areas

Country	AZ	IDD from UK	IDD to UK
Afghanistan	1	00 93	†
Albania	e	00 355	†
Algeria	1	00 213	00*p*44
Andorra	eu	00 376	00 44
Angola	1	00 244	†
Anguilla	1	00 1 809	001 44
Antigua and Barbuda	1	00 1 268	011 44
Argentina	1	00 54	00 44
Armenia	e	00 374	810 44
Aruba	1	00 297	†
Ascension Island	1	00 247	01 44
Australia	2	00 61	00 11 44
Austria	eu	00 43	00 44
Azerbaijan	e	00 994	810 44
Azores	eu	00 351	00 44
Bahamas	1	00 1 809	011 44
Bahrain	1	00 973	0 44
Bangladesh	1	00 880	00 44
Barbados	1	00 1 246	011 44
Belarus	e	00 375	810 44
Belgium	eu	00 32	00 44
Belize	1	00 501	†
Benin	1	00 229	00*p*44
Bermuda	1	00 1 441	1 44
Bhutan	1	00 975	00 44
Bolivia	1	00 591	00 44
Bosnia-Hercegovina	e	00 387	99 44
Botswana	1	00 267	00 44
Brazil	1	00 55	00 44
British Virgin Islands	1	00 1 809 49	011 44
Brunei	1	00 673	00 44
Bulgaria	e	00 359	00 44
Burkina Faso	1	00 226	00 44
Burundi	1	00 257	90 44
Cambodia	1	00 855	†
Cameroon	1	00 237	00 44
Canada	1	00 1	011 44

Country	AZ	IDD from UK	IDD to UK
Canary Islands	eu	00 34	07*p*44
Cape Verde	1	00 238	00 44
Cayman Islands	1	00 1 345	0 44
Central African Republic	1	00 236	00*p*44
Chad	1	00 235	†
Chile	1	00 56	00 44
China	?	00 86	00 44
Colombia	1	00 57	90 44
Comoros	1	00 269	†
Congo	1	00 242	00 44
Cook Islands	2	00 682	00 44
Costa Rica	1	00 506	00 44
Côte d'Ivoire	1	00 225	00 44
Croatia	e	00 385	99 44
Cuba	1	00 53	†
Cyprus	e	00 357	00 44
Czech Republic	e	00 42	00 44
Denmark	eu	00 45	009 44
Djibouti	1	00 253	00 44
Dominica	1	00 1 809	011 44
Dominican Republic	1	00 1 809	†
Ecuador	1	00 593	00 44
Egypt	1	00 20	00 44
Equatorial Guinea	1	00 240	19 44
Eritrea	1	00 291	†
Estonia	e	00 372	810 44
Ethiopia	1	00 251	00 44
Falkland Islands	1	00 500	01 44
Faroe Islands	e	00 298	009 44
Fiji	2	00 679	05 44
Finland	eu	00 358	00 44
France	eu	00 33	00 44
French Guiana	1	00 594	†
French Polynesia	2	00 689	00 44
Gabon	1	00 241	00 44
The Gambia	1	00 220	00 44
Georgia	e	00 7	810 44
Germany	eu	00 49	00 44
Ghana	1	00 233	00 44
Gibraltar	eu	00 350	00 44
Greece	eu	00 30	00 44
Greenland	e	00 299	009 44
Grenada	1	00 1 809	011 44
Guadeloupe	1	00 590	00 44
Guam	2	00 671	00 44
Guatemala	1	00 502	00 44
Guinea	1	00 224	†
Guinea-Bissau	1	00 245	†
Guyana	1	00 592	011 44
Haiti	1	00 509	†
Honduras	1	00 504	00 44
Hong Kong	1	00 852	001 44
Hungary	e	00 36	00 44
Iceland	e	00 354	00 44
India	1	00 91	00 44
Indonesia	1	00 62	00 44
Iran	1	00 98	00 44
Iraq	1	00 964	00 44
Ireland, Republic of	eu	00 353	00 44
Israel	1	00 972	00 44
Italy	eu	00 39	00 44
Jamaica	1	00 1 809	†
Japan	2	00 81	001 44
Jordan	1	00 962	00 44*
Kazakhstan	e	00 7	810 44
Kenya	1	00 254	00 44
Kiribati	2	00 686	09 44

Country	AZ	IDD from UK	IDD to UK
Korea, North	2	00 850	010 44
Korea, South	2	00 82	001 44
Kuwait	1	00 965	00 44
Kyrgystan	e	00 7	810 44
Laos	1	00 856	†
Latvia	e	00 371	810 44
Lebanon	1	00 961	00 44
Lesotho	1	00 266	00 44
Liberia	1	00 231	00 44
Libya	1	00 218	00 44
Liechtenstein	e	00 41 75	00 44
Lithuania	e	00 370	810 44
Luxembourg	eu	00 352	00 44
Macao	1	00 853	00 44
Macedonia	e	00 389	99 44
Madagascar	1	00 261	16p44
Madeira	eu	00 351 91	00 44*
Malawi	1	00 265	101 44
Malaysia	1	00 60	00 44
Maldives	1	00 960	00 44
Mali	1	00 223	00 44
Malta	e	00 356	00 44
Mariana Islands, Northern	2	00 670	010 44
Marshall Islands	2	00 692	012 44
Martinique	1	00 596	19p44
Mauritania	1	00 222	00 44
Mauritius	1	00 230	00 44
Mayotte	1	00 269	19p44
Mexico	1	00 52	98 44
Micronesia, Federated States of	2	00 691	†
Moldova	e	00 373	810 44
Monaco	eu	00 377 93	19p44
Mongolia	2	00 976	†
Montenegro	e	00 381	99 44
Montserrat	1	00 1 664	†
Morocco	1	00 212	00p44
Mozambique	1	00 258	00 44
Myanmar	1	00 95	0 44
Namibia	1	00 264	09 44
Nauru	2	00 674	00 44
Nepal	1	00 977	00 44
Netherlands	eu	00 31	00 44
Netherlands Antilles	1	00 599	00 44
New Caledonia	2	00 687	00 44
New Zealand	2	00 64	00 44
Nicaragua	1	00 505	00 44
Niger	1	00 227	00 44
Nigeria	1	00 234	009 44
Niue	2	00 683	†
Norfolk Island	2	00 672	00 44
Norway	e	00 47	095 44
Oman	1	00 968	00 44
Pakistan	1	00 92	00 44
Palau	2	00 680	†
Panama	1	00 507	00 44
Papua New Guinea	2	00 675	05 44
Paraguay	1	00 595	002 44 / 003 44
Peru	1	00 51	00 44
Philippines	2	00 63	00 44
Poland	e	00 48	0p044
Portugal	eu	00 351	00 44
Puerto Rico	1	00 1 787	135 44
Qatar	1	00 974	044
Réunion	1	00 262	19p44
Romania	e	00 40	00 44

Country	AZ	IDD from UK	IDD to UK
Russia	e	00 7	810 44
Rwanda	1	00 250	00 44
St Helena	1	00 290	01 44
St Kitts and Nevis	1	00 1 809	†
St Lucia	1	00 1 758	0 44
St Pierre and Miquelon	1	00 508	19p44
St Vincent and the Grenadines	1	00 1 809	00 44
El Salvador	1	00 503	00 44
Samoa, American	1	00 684	1 44
San Marino	eu	00 378	00 44
São Tomé and Príncipe	1	00 239	00 44
Saudi Arabia	1	00 966	00 44
Senegal	1	00 221	00p44
Serbia	e	00 381	99 44
Seychelles	1	00 248	0 44
Sierra Leone	1	00 232	00 44
Singapore	1	00 65	005 44
Slovak Republic	e	00 42	00 44
Slovenia	e	00 386	99 44
Solomon Islands	1	00 677	00 44
Somalia	1	00 252	†
South Africa	1	00 27	09 44
Spain	eu	00 34	07p44
Sri Lanka	1	00 94	00 44
Sudan	1	00 249	†
Suriname	1	00 597	00 44
Swaziland	1	00 268	00 44
Sweden	eu	00 46	009 44p
Switzerland	e	00 41	00 44
Syria	2	00 963	00 44
Taiwan	1	00 886	002 44
Tajikistan	e	00 7	810 44
Tanzania	1	00 255	00 44
Thailand	1	00 66	001 44
Tibet	2	00 86	00 44
Togo	1	00 228	00 44
Tonga	2	00 676	00 44
Trinidad and Tobago	1	00 1 809	01 44
Tristan da Cunha	1	†	†
Tunisia	2	00 216	00 44
Turkey	e	00 90	00 44
Turkmenistan	e	00 993	810 44
Turks and Caicos Islands	1	00 1 809	0 44
Tuvalu	1	00 688	00 44
Uganda	1	00 256	00 44
Ukraine	e	00 380	810 44
United Arab Emirates	1	00 971	00 44
Uruguay	2	00 598	00 44
USA	1	00 1	011 44
Alaska		00 1 907	011 44
Hawaii		00 1 808	011 44
Uzbekistan	e	00 7	810 44
Vanuatu	1	00 678	00 44
Vatican City State	eu	00 39 66982	00 44
Venezuela	1	00 58	00 44
Vietnam	1	00 84	00 44
Virgin Islands (US)	2	00 1 809	011 44
Western Samoa	1	00 685	†
Yemen	1	00 967	00 44
Yugoslav Fed. Rep.	e	00 381	99 44
Zaïre	1	00 243	00 44
Zambia	1	00 260	00 44
Zimbabwe	1	00 263	00 44

Development Corporations

NEW TOWNS

COMMISSION FOR THE NEW TOWNS
Glen House, Stag Place, London SW1E 5AJ
Tel 0171-828 7722

The Commission was established under the New Towns Act 1959. Its remit is to hold, manage and turn to account the property of development corporations transferred to the Commission; and to dispose of property so transferred and any other property held by it, as soon as it considers it expedient to do so. In carrying out its remit the Commission must have due regard to the convenience and welfare of persons residing, working or carrying on business there and, until disposal, the maintenance and enhancement of the value of the land held and return obtained from it.

The Commission has such responsibilities in Basildon, Bracknell, Central Lancashire, Corby, Crawley, Harlow, Hatfield, Hemel Hempstead, Milton Keynes, Northampton, Peterborough, Redditch, Skelmersdale, Stevenage, Telford, Warrington and Runcorn, Washington, and Welwyn Garden City. The Commission has minimal responsibilities (principally financial and litigation) in Aycliffe and Peterlee, and Cwmbran following the wind-up of their development corporations in 1988.

In May 1996 the Government proposed that the Commission should take on responsibility for any assets and liabilities remaining when urban development corporations and housing action trusts are wound up. Legislation relating to the extension of the Commission's role was before Parliament at the time of going to press.
Chairman, Dr J. R. G. Bradfield, CBE
Members, R. B. Caws, CBE; F. C. Graves, OBE; Sir Brian Jenkins, GBE; M. H. Mallinson; Lady Marsh; J. Trustram Eve
Chief Executive, N. J. Walker

REGIONAL OFFICES
NORTH (Central Lancashire, Skelmersdale, Warrington and Runcorn, Washington, Aycliffe and Peterlee), New Town House, Buttermarket Street, Warrington WA1 2LF. Tel: 01925-651144. *Director*, C. Mackrell
CENTRAL (Milton Keynes, Corby, Northampton), Saxon Court, 502 Avebury Boulevard, Central Milton Keynes MK9 3HS. Tel: 01908-692692. *Director*, J. Napleton
WEST MIDLANDS (Redditch, Telford), Jordan House West, Hall Court, Hall Park Way, Telford TF3 4NN. Tel: 01952-293131. *Director*, C. Mackrell
SOUTH (Basildon, Bracknell, Crawley, Harlow, Hatfield, Hemel Hempstead, Peterborough, Stevenage, Welwyn Garden City), Glen House, Stag Place, London SW1E 5AJ. Tel: 0171-828 7722. *Director*, G. D. Johnston

DEVELOPMENT CORPORATIONS
WALES
DEVELOPMENT BOARD FOR RURAL WALES (1977), Ladywell House, Newtown, Powys SY16 1JB. Tel: 01686-626965. *Chairman*, D. Rowe-Beddoe; *Chief Executive*, J. Taylor

SCOTLAND
CUMBERNAULD (1956), Cumbernauld House, Cumbernauld G67 3JH. *Chairman*, D. W. Mitchell, CBE. *General Manager*, D. R. Lind. Area, 7,788 acres. Population, 52,200. To be wound up December 1996
EAST KILBRIDE (1947), wound up 31 December 1995
GLENROTHES (1948), wound up 31 December 1995
IRVINE (1966), Perceton House, Irvine, Ayrshire KA11 2AL. *Chairman*, CBE. *Managing Director*, J. Murdoch. Area, 16,000 acres. Population, 56,300. To be wound up March 1997
LIVINGSTON (1962), 1 Bell Square, Brucefield Industrial Park, Livingston, West Lothian EH54 9BY. *Chairman*, R. S. Watt, CBE. *Chief Executive*, J. A. Pollock. Area, 6,868 acres. Population, 44,000. To be wound up December 1996

URBAN DEVELOPMENT CORPORATIONS

Urban development corporations were established under the Local Government, Planning and Land Act 1980. Their remit is to bring land and buildings in selected areas back into effective use by developing infrastructure, housing, employment and the environment. The corporations encourage business, especially from overseas, to invest in the area and can provide grants to assist commercial and industrial development.

ENGLAND
BIRMINGHAM HEARTLANDS (1992), Waterlinks House, Richard Street, Birmingham, B7 4AA. Tel: 0121-333 3060. *Chairman*, Sir Reginald Eyre; *Chief Executive*, J. Beeston. Area, 1,000 hectares. To be wound up March 1998
BLACK COUNTRY (1987), Black Country House, Rounds Green Road, Oldbury B69 2RD. Tel: 0121-511 2000. *Chairman*, G. Carter, CBE; *Chief Executive*, D. Morgan. Area, 2,600 hectares. To be wound up March 1998
BRISTOL, wound up 31 December 1995
CENTRAL MANCHESTER, wound up 31 March 1996
LEEDS, wound up 31 March 1995
LONDON DOCKLANDS (1981), Thames Quay, 191 Marsh Wall, London E14 9TJ. Tel: 0171-512 3000. *Chairman*, M. Pickard; *Chief Executive*, E. Sorensen. Area, 2,226 hectares. To be wound up March 1998
MERSEYSIDE (1981), Royal Liver Buildings, Pier Head, Liverpool L3 1JH. Tel: 0151-236 6090. *Chairman*, Sir Desmond Pitcher; *Chief Executive*, C. Farrow. Area, 960 hectares. To be wound up March 1998
PLYMOUTH (1993), Royal William Yard, Plymouth PL1 3RP. Tel: 01752-256132. *Chairman*, Lord Chilver, FRS; *Chief Executive*, G. Tinbrell. Area, 67 hectares. To be wound up March 1998
SHEFFIELD (1988), Don Valley House, Saville Street East, Sheffield S4 7UQ. Tel: 0114-272 0100. *Chairman*, H. Sykes; *Chief Executive*, G. Kendall. Area, 800 hectares. To be wound up March 1997
TEESSIDE (1987), Dunedin House, Riverside Quay, Stockton-on-Tees TS17 6BJ. Tel: 01642-677123. *Chairman*, Sir Ronald Norman, OBE; *Chief Executive*, D. Hall. Area, 4,600 hectares. To be wound up March 1998

518   Development Corporations

TRAFFORD PARK (1987), Waterside, Trafford Wharf Road, Trafford Park, Manchester M17 1EX. Tel: 0161-848 8000. *Chairman*, W. Morgan; *Chief Executive*, M. Shields. Area, 1,270 hectares. To be wound up March 1998

TYNE AND WEAR (1987), Scotswood House, Newcastle Business Park, Newcastle upon Tyne NE4 7YL. Tel: 0191-226 1234. *Chairman*, Sir Paul Nicholson; *Chief Executive*, A. Balls, CB. Area, 2,400 hectares. To be wound up March 1998

WALES

CARDIFF BAY (1987), Baltic House, Mount Stuart Square, Cardiff CF1 6DH. Tel: 01222-823958. *Chairman*, Sir Geoffrey Inkin, OBE; *Chief Executive*, M. Boyce. Area, 1,094 hectares

NORTHERN IRELAND

LAGANSIDE (1989), Clarendon Building, 15 Clarendon Road, Belfast BT1 3BG. Tel: 01232-328507. *Chairman*, The Duke of Abercorn; *Chief Executive*, G. Mackey. Area, 122 hectares

HM Coastguard

Founded in 1822, originally to guard the coasts against smuggling, HM Coastguard's role today is the very different one of guarding and saving life at sea. The Service is responsible for co-ordinating all civil maritime search and rescue operations around the 10,500 mile coastline of Great Britain and Northern Ireland and 1,000 miles into the Atlantic. In addition, it co-operates with search and rescue organizations of neighbouring countries in western Europe and around the Atlantic seaboard. The Service maintains a 24-hour radar watch on the Dover Strait, providing a Channel navigation information service for all shipping in one of the busiest sea lanes in the world. It also liaises very closely with the off-shore oil and gas industry and with merchant shipping companies.

Since 1978 HM Coastguard has been organized into six regions, each with a Regional Controller. Each region is subdivided into districts under District Controllers, operating from Maritime Rescue Co-ordination Centres or Sub-Centres. In all there are 21 of these centres. They are on 24-hour watch and are fitted with a comprehensive range of communications equipment. They are supported by some 357 smaller stations staffed by part-time Auxiliary Coastguards under the direction of Regulars, each of which keeps its parent centre fully informed of day-to-day casualty risk, particularly on the more remote danger spots around the coast.

Between 1 January and 31 December 1995, the 450 Regular and 3,500 Auxiliary Coastguards co-ordinated 12,220 incidents requiring search and rescue facilities,

resulting in assistance being given to 19,384 persons. All distress telephone and radio calls are centralized on the 21 centres, which are on the alert for people or vessels in distress, shipping hazards and pollution incidents. Using telecommunications equipment, including satellite, they can alert and co-ordinate the most appropriate rescue facilities; RNLI lifeboats, Royal Navy, RAF or Coastguard helicopters, fixed-wing aircraft, vessels in the vicinity, or Coastguard shore and cliff rescue teams.

For those who regularly sail in local waters or make longer passages, the Coastguard Yacht and Boat Safety Scheme provides a valuable free service. Its aim is to give the Coastguard a record of the details of craft, their equipment and normal operating areas. Yacht and Boat Safety Scheme cards are available from all Coastguard stations, harbourmasters' offices, and most yacht clubs and marinas as well as Coastguard Headquarters.

Members of the public who see an accident or a potentially dangerous incident on or around the coast should dial 999 and ask for the Coastguard.

On 1 April 1994 HM Coastguard and the Marine Pollution Control Unit together formed the Coastguard Agency, an executive agency of the Department of Transport.

Coastguard Headquarters and Office of the Chief Coastguard, Spring Place, 105 Commercial Road, Southampton SO15 1EG. Tel: 01703-329100

Local Government

The Local Government Acts of 1972, 1985 and 1992, the Local Government (Wales) Act 1994, the Local Government (Scotland) Act 1973 and the London Government Act 1963 are the main Acts which have brought about the present structure of local government in Great Britain. This structure has been in effect in England and Wales since 1974, with alterations in 1986, 1995 and 1996; and in Scotland since 1975.

The structure in England is based on two tiers of local authorities (county councils and district councils) in the non-metropolitan areas; and a single tier of metropolitan and London borough councils in the six metropolitan areas of England and in London respectively.

Following recent reviews of the structure of local government in England by the Local Government Commission, 46 unitary (all-purpose) authorities have been or are being created to cover certain areas in the non-metropolitan counties. The remaining county areas will continue to have two tiers of local authorities. The county and district councils in the Isle of Wight were replaced by a single unitary authority on 1 April 1995; the former counties of Avon, Cleveland and Humberside were abolished on 1 April 1996 and replaced by unitary authorities; York became a unitary authority at the same date. Changes in other areas will take effect in April 1997 and April 1998.

Legislation passed in 1994 abolishes the two-tier structure in Wales and Scotland with effect from 1 April 1996 and replaces it with a single tier of unitary authorities.

Local authorities are empowered or required by various Acts of Parliament to carry out functions in their areas. The legislation concerned comprises public general Acts and 'local' Acts which local authorities have promoted as private bills.

ELECTIONS

Local elections are normally held on the first Thursday in May. Generally, all British subjects or citizens of the Republic of Ireland of 18 years or over who are resident on the qualifying date in the area for which the election is being held, are entitled to vote at local government elections. A register of electors is prepared and published annually by local electoral registration officers.

A returning officer has the overall responsibility for an election. Voting takes place at polling stations, arranged by the local authority and under the supervision of a presiding officer specially appointed for the purpose. Candidates, who are subject to various statutory qualifications and disqualifications designed to ensure that they are suitable persons to hold office, must be nominated by electors for the electoral area concerned.

In England, the Local Government Commission is responsible for carrying out periodic reviews of electoral arrangements and making proposals to the Secretary of State for changes found necessary. In Wales and Scotland these matters are the responsibility of the Local Boundary Commission for Wales and the Local Boundary Commission for Scotland respectively.

LOCAL GOVERNMENT COMMISSION FOR ENGLAND, Dolphyn Court, 10–11 Great Turnstile, Lincoln's Inn Fields, London WCIV 7JU. Tel: 0171-430 8400

INTERNAL ORGANIZATION

The council as a whole is the final decision-making body within any authority. Councils are free to a great extent to make their own internal organizational arrangements.

Normally, questions of policy are settled by the full council, while the administration of the various services is the responsibility of committees of councillors. Day-to-day decisions are delegated to the council's officers, who act within the policies laid down by the councillors.

FINANCE

Local government in England, Wales and Scotland is financed from four sources: the council tax, non-domestic rates, government grants, and income from fees and charges for services. (For arrangements in Northern Ireland, *see* page 522.)

COUNCIL TAX

Under the Local Government Finance Act 1992, from 1 April 1993 the council tax replaced the community charge (which had been introduced in April 1989 in Scotland and April 1990 in England and Wales in place of domestic rates).

The council tax is a local tax levied by each local council. Liability for the council tax bill usually falls on the owner-occupier or tenant of a dwelling which is their sole or main residence. Council tax bills may be reduced because of the personal circumstances of people resident in a property, and there are discounts in the case of dwellings occupied by fewer than two adults.

In England, each county council, each district council and, from 1 April 1996, each police authority sets its own council tax rate. The district councils collect the combined council tax, and the county councils and police authorities claim their share from the district councils' collection funds. In Wales, each county and county borough council and each police authority sets its own council tax rate. The county and county borough councils collect the combined council tax and the police authorities claim their share from the collection funds. In Scotland each island council and unitary authority sets its own rate of council tax.

The tax relates to the value of the dwelling. Each dwelling is placed in one of eight valuation bands, ranging from A to H, based on the property's estimated market value as at 1 April 1991.

The valuation bands and ranges of values in England, Wales and Scotland are:

England

A	Up to £40,000	E	£88,001–£120,000
B	£40,001–£52,000	F	£120,001–£160,000
C	£52,001–£68,000	G	£160,001–£320,000
D	£68,001–£88,000	H	Over £320,000

Wales

A	Up to £30,000	E	£66,001–£90,000
B	£30,001–£39,000	F	£90,001–£120,000
C	£39,001–£51,000	G	£120,001–£240,000
D	£51,001–£66,000	H	Over £240,000

Scotland

A	Up to £27,000	E	£58,001–£80,000
B	£27,001–£35,000	F	£80,001–£106,000
C	£35,001–£45,000	G	£106,001–£212,000
D	£45,001–£58,000	H	Over £212,000

The council tax within a local area varies between the different bands according to proportions laid down by law. The charge attributable to each band as a proportion of the Band D charge set by the council is approximately:

A	67%	E	122%
B	78%	F	144%
C	89%	G	167%
D	100%	H	200%

The band D rate is given in the tables on pages 540–45 (England), 552 (London), 555 (Wales), and 560 (Scotland). There may be variations from the given figure within each district council area because of different parish or community precepts being levied.

NON-DOMESTIC RATES

Non-domestic (business) rates are collected by billing authorities; these are the district councils in those areas of England with two tiers of local government and unitary authorities in other parts of England, the county and county borough councils in Wales (since April 1996), and the councils and islands councils in Scotland. In respect of England and Wales, the Local Government Finance Act 1988 provides for liability for rates to be assessed on the basis of a poundage (multiplier) tax on the rateable value of property (hereditaments). Separate multipliers are set by the appropriate Secretaries of State in England, Wales and Scotland, and rates are collected by the billing authority for the area where a property is located. Rate income collected by billing authorities is paid into a national non-domestic rating (NNDR) pool and redistributed to individual authorities on the basis of the adult population figure as prescribed by the appropriate Secretary of State. The rates pools are maintained separately in England, Wales and Scotland. For the years 1995–6 to 2000–1 actual payment of rates in certain cases are subject to transitional arrangements, to phase in the larger increases and reductions in rates resulting from the effects of the 1995 revaluation.

Rates are levied in Scotland in accordance with the Local Government (Scotland) Act 1975. For 1995–6, the Secretary of State for Scotland prescribed a single non-domestic rates poundage to apply throughout the country at the same level as the uniform business rate (UBR) in England. Rate income is pooled and redistributed to local authorities on a per capita basis. For the year 1995–6 payment of rates was subject to transitional arrangements to phase in the effect of the 1995 revaluation.

Rateable values for the rating lists came into force on 1 April 1995. They are derived from the rental value of property as at 1 April 1993 and determined on certain statutory assumptions by valuation officers of the Valuation Office Agency in England and Wales, and by Regional Assessors in Scotland. New property which is added to the list, and significant changes to existing property, necessitate amendments to the rateable value on the same basis. Rating lists (valuation rolls in Scotland) remain in force until the next general revaluation. Such revaluations take place every five years, the next being in 2000.

Certain types of property are exempt from rates, e.g. agricultural land and buildings, and places of public religious worship. Charities and other non-profit-making organizations may receive full or partial relief. Empty property is liable to pay rates at 50 per cent, except for certain specified classes which are exempt entirely.

GOVERNMENT GRANTS

In addition to specific grants in support of revenue expenditure on particular services, central government pays revenue support grant to local authorities. This grant is paid to each local authority so that if each authority spends at a level sufficient to provide a standard level of service, all authorities in the same class can set broadly the same council tax.

COMPLAINTS

Commissioners for Local Administration in England, Wales and Scotland (*see* pages 319–20) are responsible for investigating complaints from members of the public who claim to have suffered injustice as a consequence of maladministration in local government or in certain local bodies.

The Northern Ireland Commissioner for Complaints fulfils a similar function in Northern Ireland, investigating complaints about local authorities and certain public bodies.

THE QUEEN'S REPRESENTATIVES

The Lord Lieutenant of a county is the permanent local representative of the Crown in that county. The appointment of Lord Lieutenants is now regulated by the Reserve Forces Act 1980. They are appointed by the Sovereign on the recommendation of the Prime Minister. The retirement age is 75. The office of Lord Lieutenant dates from 1557, and its holder was originally responsible for the maintenance of order and for local defence in the county. The duties of the post include attending on royalty during official visits to the county, performing certain duties in connection with armed forces of the Crown (and in particular the reserve forces), and making presentations of honours and awards on behalf of the Crown. In England, Wales and Northern Ireland, the Lord Lieutenant usually also holds the office of *Custos Rotulorum*. As such, he or she acts as head of the county's commission of the peace (which recommends the appointment of magistrates).

The office of Sheriff (from the Old English shire-reeve of a county was created in the tenth century. The Sheriff was the special nominee of the Sovereign, and the office reached the peak of its influence under the Norman kings. The Provisions of Oxford (1258) laid down a yearly tenure of office. Since the mid-16th century the office has been purely civil, with military duties taken over by the Lord Lieutenant of the county. The Sheriff (commonly known as 'High Sheriff') attends on royalty during official visits to the county, acts as the returning officer during parliamentary elections in county constituencies, attends the opening ceremony when a High Court judge goes on circuit, executes High Court writs, and appoints under-sheriffs to act as deputies. The appointments and duties of the High Sheriffs in England and Wales are laid down by the Sheriffs Act 1887.

The serving High Sheriff submits a list of names of possible future sheriffs to a tribunal which chooses three names to put to the Sovereign. The tribunal nominates the High Sheriff annually on 12 November and the Sovereign pricks the name of the Sheriff to succeed in the following year. The term of office runs from 25 March to the following 24 March (the civil and legal year before 1752). No person may be chosen twice in three years if there is any other suitable person in the county.

CIVIC DIGNITIES

District councils in England may petition for a royal charter granting borough or 'city' status to the district. County councils in Wales may petition for a royal charter granting county borough or 'city' status to the council.

In England and Wales the chairman of a borough or county borough council may be called a mayor, and the chairman of a city council a Lord Mayor. Parish councils in England and Wales may call themselves 'town councils', in which case their chairman is the town mayor.

In Scotland the chairman of a district council may be known as a convenor; a provost is the equivalent of a mayor. The chairmen of the councils for the cities of Aberdeen, Dundee, Edinburgh and Glasgow are Lord Provosts.

ENGLAND

(For London, *see* below)

There are currently 36 non-metropolitan counties; all (apart from the Isle of Wight) are divided into non-metropolitan districts. In addition, there are 13 unitary authorities created in April 1996, and a further 36 unitary authorities will come into being in April 1997 and April 1998. At present there are 286 non-metropolitan districts; by 1998 there will be 282. The populations of most of the new unitary authorities are in the range of 100,000 to 300,000. The non-metropolitan districts have populations broadly in the range of 60,000 to 100,000; some, however, have larger populations, because of the need to avoid dividing large towns, and some in mainly rural areas have smaller populations.

Six metropolitan counties cover the main conurbations outside Greater London: Tyne and Wear, West Midlands, Merseyside, Greater Manchester, West Yorkshire and South Yorkshire. They are divided into 36 metropolitan districts, most of which have a population of over 200,000.

There are about 10,000 parishes, in 219 of the non-metropolitan and 18 of the metropolitan districts.

ELECTIONS

For districts, non-metropolitan counties and for about 8,000 parishes, there are elected councils, consisting of directly elected councillors. The councillors elect annually one of their number as chairman.

Generally, councillors serve four years and there are no elections of district and parish councillors in county election years. In metropolitan districts, one-third of the councillors for each ward are elected each year except in the year when county elections take place elsewhere. Non-metropolitan districts can choose whether to have elections by thirds or whole council elections. In the former case, one-third of the council, as nearly as may be, is elected in each year of metropolitan district elections. If whole council elections are chosen, these are held in the year midway between county elections.

FUNCTIONS

In non-metropolitan areas, functions are divided between the districts and counties, those requiring the larger area or population for their efficient performance going to the county. The metropolitan district councils, with the larger population in their areas, already had wider functions than non-metropolitan councils, and following abolition of the metropolitan county councils were given most of their functions also. A few functions continue to be exercised over the larger area by joint bodies, made up of councillors from each district.

The allocation of functions is as follows:

County councils: education; strategic planning; traffic, transport and highways; fire service; consumer protection; refuse disposal; smallholdings; social services; libraries

Non-metropolitan district councils: local planning; housing; highways (maintenance of certain urban roads and off-street car parks); building regulations; environmental health; refuse collection; cemeteries and crematoria

Non-metropolitan unitary councils: their functions are all those listed above, except that the fire service is exercised by a joint body

Concurrently by county and district councils: recreation (parks, playing fields, swimming pools); museums; encouragement of the arts, tourism and industry

The Police and Magistrates Court Act 1994 set up police authorities in England and Wales separate from the local authorities.

PARISH COUNCILS

Parishes with 200 or more electors must generally have parish councils, which means that over three-quarters of the parishes have councils. A parish council comprises at least five members, the number being fixed by the district council. Elections are held every four years, at the time of the election of the district councillor for the ward including the parish. All parishes have parish meetings, comprising the electors of the parish. Where there is no council, the meeting must be held at least twice a year.

Parish council functions include: allotments; encouragement of arts and crafts; community halls, recreational facilities (e.g. open spaces, swimming pools), cemeteries and crematoria; and many minor functions. They must also be given an opportunity to comment on planning applications. They may, like county and district councils, spend limited sums for the general benefit of the parish. They levy a precept on the district councils for their funds.

FINANCE

Aggregate external finance for 1996–7 was originally determined at £35,652 million. Of this, specific and special grants were estimated at £4,892 million. £18,024 million was in respect of revenue support grant and £12,736 million was support from the national non-domestic pool. Total standard spending by local authorities considered for grant purposes was £44,927 million.

The average council taxes, expressed in terms of Band C, two-adult properties for 1996–7, were: inner London boroughs and the City of London £633; outer London boroughs £606; metropolitan districts £725; shire areas £632. The average for England was £647.

National non-domestic rate (or uniform business rate) for 1996–7 is 44.9p. The provisional amount estimated to be raised from central, local and Crown lists is £12.5 billion. Total rateable value held on draft local authority lists at 31 December 1995 was £29.7 billion. The amount to be redistributed to authorities from the pool in 1996–7 is £12.7 billion.

Under the Local Government and Housing Act 1989, local authorities have four main ways of paying for capital expenditure: borrowing and other forms of extended credit; capital grants from central government towards some types of capital expenditure; 'usable' capital receipts from the sale of land, houses and other assets; and revenue.

The amount of capital expenditure which a local authority can finance by borrowing (or other forms of credit) is effectively limited by the credit approvals issued to it by central government. Most credit approvals can be used for any local authority service; these are known as basic credit approvals. Others are for particular projects or services; these are known as supplementary credit approvals.

Generally, the 'usable' part of a local authority's capital receipts consists of 25 per cent of receipts from the sale of council houses and 50 per cent of most other receipts. The balance has to be set aside as provision for repaying debt and meeting other credit liabilities.

EXPENDITURE

Local authority budgeted net revenue expenditure for 1996–7 was (1996–7 cash prices):

Service	£m
Education	19,062
Personal social services	7,903
Police	6,296
Highway maintenance	1,730
Fire	1,285
Civil defence and other Home Office services	542
Magistrates courts	306
Public transport and parking	646
Housing benefit administration	5,406
Non-housing revenue account housing	354
Libraries, museums and art galleries	755
Swimming pools and recreation	497
Local environmental services	5,247
Other services	365
Net current expenditure	50,394
Capital charges	2,307
Capital charged to revenue	800
Other non-current expenditure	3,645
Interest receipts	−699
Gross revenue expenditure	56,447
Specific and special grants outside AEF	−9,032
Other income	−73
Revenue expenditure	47,342
Specific and special grants inside AEF	−1,549
Net revenue expenditure	45,793
AEF = aggregate external finance	

LONDON

Since the abolition of the Greater London Council in 1986, the Greater London area has not had a single local government body. The area is divided into 32 borough councils, which have a status similar to the metropolitan district councils in the rest of England, and the Corporation of the City of London.

LONDON BOROUGH COUNCILS

The London boroughs have whole council elections every four years, in the year immediately following the county council election year. The next elections will be held in 1998.

The borough councils have responsibility for the following functions: building regulations; cemeteries and crematoria; consumer protection; education; youth employment; environmental health; electoral registration; food; drugs; housing; leisure services; libraries; local planning; local roads; museums; parking; recreation (parks, playing fields, swimming pools); refuse collection and street cleansing; social services; town planning; and traffic management.

THE CORPORATION OF LONDON
(*see also* pages 547–9)

The Corporation of London is the local authority for the City of London. Its legal definition is 'The Mayor and

Commonalty and Citizens of the City of London'. It is governed by the Court of Common Council, which consists of the Lord Mayor, 24 other aldermen, and 130 common councilmen. The Lord Mayor and two sheriffs are nominated annually by the City guilds (the livery companies) and elected by the Court of Aldermen. Aldermen and councilmen are elected by businesses in the 25 wards into which the City is divided; councilmen must stand for re-election annually. The Council is a legislative assembly, and there are no political parties.

The Corporation has the same functions as the London borough councils. In addition, it runs the City of London Police; is the health authority for the Port of London; has health control of animal imports throughout Greater London, including at Heathrow airport; owns and manages public open spaces throughout Greater London; runs the Central Criminal Court; and runs Billingsgate, Smithfield and Spitalfields markets.

THE CITY GUILDS (LIVERY COMPANIES)

The livery companies of the City of London grew out of early medieval religious fraternities and began to emerge as trade and craft guilds, retaining their religious aspect, in the 12th century. From the early 14th century, only members of the trade and craft guilds could call themselves citizens of the City of London. The guilds began to be called livery companies, because of the distinctive livery worn by the most prosperous guild members on ceremonial occasions, in the late 15th century.

By the early 19th century the power of the companies within their trades had begun to wane, but those wearing the livery of a company continued to play an important role in the government of the City of London. Liverymen still have the right to nominate the Lord Mayor and sheriffs, and most members of the Court of Common Council are liverymen (*see also* page 549).

GREATER LONDON SERVICES

After the abolition of the Greater London Council (GLC) in 1986, the London boroughs took over most of its functions. Successor bodies have also been set up for certain functions.

The London Residuary Body (LRB) was set up in 1986 to deal with residual matters of the GLC which could not easily be transferred elsewhere and in 1990 became responsible for residual matters relating to the Inner London Education Authority. The LRB completed its work and was wound up in 1995, having transferred most residual Greater London matters to the London Borough of Bromley and inner London matters to the Royal Borough of Kensington and Chelsea.

WALES

The Local Government (Wales) Act 1994 abolished the two-tier structure of eight county and 37 district councils which had existed since 1974, and replaced it, from 1 April 1996, with 22 unitary authorities. The new authorities were elected in May 1995. Each unitary authority has inherited all the functions of the previous county and district councils, except fire services (which are provided by three combined fire authorities, composed of representatives of the unitary authorities) and National Parks (which are the responsibility of three independent National Park authorities).

The Police and Magistrates Courts Act 1994 set up four police authorities with effect from 1 April 1995: Dyfed-Powys, Gwent, North Wales, and South Wales.

COMMUNITY COUNCILS

In Wales parishes have been replaced by communities. Unlike England, where many areas are not in any parish, communities have been established for the whole of Wales, approximately 865 communities in all. Community meetings may be convened as and when desired.

Community councils exist in 734 communities and further councils may be established at the request of a community meeting. Community councils have broadly the same range of powers as English parish councils. Community councillors are elected en bloc at the same time as a unitary authority election and for a term of four years.

FINANCE

Aggregate external finance for 1996–7 is £2,517.9 million. This comprises revenue support grant of £1,821.1 million, specific grants of £237.8 million, and support from the national non-domestic rate pool of £459.0 million. Total standard spending by local authorities considered for grant purposes is £2,867.6 million.

The average council tax levied in Wales for 1996–7 is £462, comprising unitary authorities £416 and police authorities £46.

National non-domestic rates (or uniform business rate) in Wales for 1996–7 is 40.5p. The amount estimated to be raised is £459 million. Total rateable value held on local authority lists at 31 December 1995 was £1,324 million.

SCOTLAND

The Local Government etc. (Scotland) Act abolished the two-tier structure of nine regional and 53 district councils which had existed since 1975 and replaced it, from 1 April 1996, with 29 unitary authorities on the mainland; the three islands councils remain. The new authorities were elected in April 1995. Each unitary authority has inherited all the functions of the regional and district councils, except water and sewerage (which are provided by three public bodies whose members will be appointed by the Secretary of State for Scotland) and reporters panels (which have become a national agency).

ELECTIONS

The unitary authorities consist of directly elected councillors. Elections take place every three years; the next elections are in 1999. In 1996 the register showed 3,971,203 electors in Scotland.

FUNCTIONS

The functions of the councils and islands councils are: education; social work; strategic planning; the provision of infrastructure such as roads; consumer protection; flood prevention; coast protection; valuation and rating; the police and fire services; civil defence; electoral registration; public transport; registration of births, deaths and marriages; housing; leisure and recreation; development control and building control; environmental health; licensing; allotments; public conveniences; the administration of district courts.

COMMUNITY COUNCILS

Unlike the parish councils and community councils in England and Wales, Scottish community councils are not local authorities. Their purpose as defined in statute is to ascertain and express the views of the communities which they represent, and to take in the interests of their communities such action as appears to be expedient or practicable. Over 1,000 community councils have been established under schemes drawn up by district and islands councils in Scotland.

Since April 1996 community councils have had an enhanced role, becoming statutory consultees on local planning issues and on the decentralization schemes which the new councils have to draw up for delivery of services.

FINANCE

Figures for 1995–6 show total receipts from non-domestic rates of £1,244.4 million and £759.6 million from the council tax. The unified business rate for 1995–6 was 43p and the average Band D council tax payable was £624. The average Band D council water charge payable was £84.

NORTHERN IRELAND

For the purpose of local government Northern Ireland has a system of 26 single-tier district councils.

ELECTIONS

There are 582 members of the councils, elected for periods of four years at a time on the principle of proportional representation.

FUNCTIONS

The district councils have three main roles. These are:

Executive: responsibility for a wide range of local services including building regulations; community services; consumer protection; cultural facilities; environmental health; miscellaneous licensing and registration provisions, including dog control; litter prevention; recreational and social facilities; refuse collection and disposal; street cleansing; and tourist development

Representative: nominating representatives to sit as members of the various statutory bodies responsible for the administration of regional services such as drainage, education, fire, health and personal social services, housing, and libraries

Consultative: acting as the medium through which the views of local people are expressed on the operation in their area of other regional services, notably conservation (including water supply and sewerage services), planning, and roads, provided by those departments of central government which have an obligation, statutory or otherwise, to consult the district councils about proposals affecting their areas

FINANCE

Local government in Northern Ireland is funded by a system of rates (a local property tax calculated by using the rateable value of a property multiplied by an amount per pound of rateable value). Rates are collected by the Department of the Environment for Northern Ireland and consist of a regional rate made by the Department of Finance and Personnel and a district rate made by individual district councils.

In 1995–6 approximately £430 million was raised in rates in Northern Ireland and the total rateable value was £237.3 million. The average domestic poundage levied was 167.27p and the average non-domestic rate poundage was 241.27p.

Political Composition of Local Councils

AS AT END MAY 1996

Abbreviations:

C.	Conservative
Com.	Communist
Dem.	Democrat
Green	Green
Ind.	Independent
Lab.	Labour
Lib.	Liberal
LD	Liberal Democrat
MK	Mebyon Kernow
NP	Non-political/Non-party
PC	Plaid Cymru
RA	Ratepayers'/Residents' Associations
SD	Social Democrat
SNP	Scottish National Party

ENGLAND

COUNTY COUNCILS

*Unitary council

Bedfordshire	Lab. 31, C. 27, LD 14, Ind. 1
Berkshire	LD 34, Lab. 25, C. 14, Ind. 2, Lib. 1
Buckinghamshire	C. 37, LD 16, Lab. 13, Ind. 4, Ind. C. 1
Cambridgeshire	C. 33, Lab. 21, LD 21, Ind. 1, Lib. 1
Cheshire	Lab. 34, C. 22, LD 14
Cornwall	LD 40, Ind. 25, Lab. 7, C. 6, MK 1
Cumbria	Lab. 39, C. 28, Ind. 2, LD 14
Derbyshire	Lab. 51, C. 21, LD 8, Ind. 1, vacant 3
Devon	LD 39, Lab. 21, C. 17, Ind. 4, Lib. 3, Ind. C. 1
Dorset	LD 39, C. 27, Lab. 6, Ind. 5
Durham	Lab. 56, C. 6, LD 6, Ind. 4
East Sussex	LD 30, C. 22, Lab. 18
Essex	Lab. 35, LD 32, C. 30, Ind. 1
Gloucestershire	LD 30, Lab. 19, Ind. C. 12
Hampshire	LD 48, C. 28, Lab. 23, Ind. 3
Hereford and Worcester	C. 25, Lab. 24, LD 20, Ind. 6, vacant 1
Hertfordshire	Lab. 31, C. 24, LD 19, Ind. 2, vacant 1
*Isle of Wight	LD 34, C. 5, Ind. 5, Lab 3, others 1
Kent	C. 41, Lab. 31, LD 27
Lancashire	Lab. 53, C. 34, LD 11, vacant 1
Leicestershire	Lab. 37, C. 30, LD 17, Ind. C. 1
Lincolnshire	C. 31, Lab. 24, LD 16, Ind. 5
Norfolk	C. 33, Lab. 32, LD 17, Ind. 2
Northamptonshire	Lab. 35, C. 26, LD 5, Ind. 2
Northumberland	Lab. 39, C. 13, LD 13, Ind. 1
North Yorkshire	LD 29, C. 26, Lab. 11, Ind. 7, vacant 1
Nottinghamshire	Lab. 58, C. 24, LD 6
Oxfordshire	Lab. 24, C. 23, LD 20, Green 2, Ind. C. 1

Shropshire	C. 24, Lab. 24, LD 15, Ind. 2, Ind. Lab. 1
Somerset	LD 40, C. 13, Lab. 3, Ind. 1
Staffordshire	Lab. 52, C. 20, LD 5, Ind. 2, RA 2, vacant 1
Suffolk	Lab. 32, C. 25, LD 19, Ind. 4
Surrey	C. 33, LD 28, Lab. 10, RA 3, Ind. 2
Warwickshire	Lab. 30, C. 19, LD 10, Ind. 3
West Sussex	LD 34, C. 26, Lab. 9, vacamt 1
Wiltshire	LD 34, C. 17, Lab. 17

UNITARY COUNCILS

Barnsley	Lab. 63, Ind. 2, C. 1
Bath and North-East Somerset	LD 27, Lab. 21, C. 16, vacant 1
Birmingham	Lab. 87, LD 17, C. 13
Bolton	Lab. 48, C. 6, LD 6
Bradford	Lab. 71, C. 13, LD 6
Bristol	Lab. 52, C. 6, LD 10
Bury	Lab. 41, C. 4, LD 3
Calderdale	Lab. 29, C. 7, LD 7, Ind. 1
Coventry	Lab. 50, C. 4
Doncaster	Lab. 58, C. 3, LD 2
Dudley	Lab. 60, C. 8, LD 4
East Riding of Yorkshire	Lab. 23, C. 19, LD 18, Ind. 7
Gateshead	Lab. 51, LD 14, Lib. 1
Hartlepool	Lab. 40, LD 4, C. 2, Ind. C. 1
Kingston upon Hull	Lab. 59, LD 1
Kirklees	Lab. 45, LD 18, C. 6, Green 1, Ind. 1, vacant 1
Knowsley	Lab. 65, LD 1
Leeds	Lab. 82, LD 9, C. 8
Liverpool	Lab. 51, LD 42, Ind. Lab. 3, Lib. 2, C. 1
Manchester	Lab. 84, LD 15
Middlesbrough	Lab. 45, LD 4, C. 2, Ind. 1, Ind. Lab. 1
Newcastle upon Tyne	Lab. 65, LD 13
North East Lincolnshire	Lab. 32, LD 7, C. 2, Ind. 1
North Lincolnshire	Lab. 35, C. 7
North Somerset	LD 30, C. 17, Lab. 6, Ind. 4, Green 1, Lib. 1
North Tyneside	Lab. 45, C. 8, LD 6, Ind. 1
Oldham	Lab. 36, LD 24
Redcar and Cleveland	Lab. 49, LD 7, Ind. 2, C. 1
Rochdale	Lab. 36, LD 17, C. 6, vacant 1
Rotherham	Lab. 65, C. 1
St Helens	Lab. 44, LD 9, C. 1
Salford	Lab. 57, LD 3
Sandwell	Lab. 60, LD 9, C. 2, Ind. Lab. 1
Sefton	Lab. 32, LD 24, C. 13
Sheffield	Lab. 55, LD 31, C. 1
Solihull	C. 16, Lab. 16, LD 12, Ind. 6, vacant 1
South Gloucestershire	Lab. 31, LD 30, C. 8, Ind. Lab. 1
South Tyneside	Lab. 52, LD 6, others 2
Stockport	LD 31, Lab. 27, Ind. 3, C. 2
Stockton-on-Tees	Lab. 44, C. 7, LD 4
Sunderland	Lab. 67, C. 4, LD 3, Ind. 1
Tameside	Lab. 54, LD 1, others 2
Trafford	Lab. 35, C. 23, LD 5
Wakefield	Lab. 61, C. 2
Walsall	Lab. 25, C. 13, LD 5, Ind. C. 1, Ind. 1, others 15
Wigan	Lab. 69, LD 2, Ind. 1
Wirral	Lab. 41, C. 16, LD 9
Wolverhampton	Lab. 46, C. 12, LD 2
York	Lab. 30, LD 17, C. 3, Ind. 2, vacant 1

NON-METROPOLITAN DISTRICT
COUNCILS

*Denotes councils where one-third of councillors retire
each year except in the year of county council elections

*Adur	LD 29, Lab. 6, C. 2, Ind. 2
Allerdale	Lab. 37, C. 7, Ind. 7, LD 4
Alnwick	LD 11, Lab. 7, Ind. 3, C. 2, others 6
Amber Valley	Lab. 39, C. 4
Arun	C. 29, LD 14, Lab. 10, Ind. 3
Ashfield	Lab. 33
Ashford	C. 19, LD 14, Lab. 11, Ind. C. 1, Ind. 1, others 3
Aylesbury Vale	LD 33, C. 12, Ind. 6, Lab. 5, others 2
Babergh	Ind. 12, Lab. 12, C. 9, LD 7, others 2
*Barrow-in-Furness	Lab. 29, C. 4, others 5
*Basildon	Lab. 24, LD 17, C. 1
*Basingstoke and Deane	C. 23, LD 17, Lab. 14, Ind. 3
*Bassetlaw	Lab. 35, C. 6, LD 3, Ind. 2, others 4
*Bedford	Lab. 22, LD 14, C. 10, Ind. 7
Berwick upon Tweed	LD 12, Ind. 10, C. 2, Lab. 2, Ind. Lib. 1, others 1
Blaby	Lab. 16, C. 11, LD 9, Ind. 2, Ind. C. 1
*Blackburn	Lab. 45, C. 12, LD 3
Blackpool	Lab. 38, LD 3, C. 2, vacant 1
Blyth Valley	Lab. 39, LD 7, Ind. Lab. 1
Bolsover	Lab. 35, Ind. 1, RA 1
Boston	Lab. 10, Ind. 7, LD 7, C. 5, others 5
Bournemouth	LD 28, C. 19, Ind. 4, Lab. 6
Bracknell Forest	Lab. 22, C. 12, LD 6
Braintree	Lab. 37, C. 10, Ind. 7, LD 6
Breckland	Lab. 24, C. 18, Ind. 8, LD 2, Green 1
*Brentwood	Lib. 25, C. 12, Lab. 2
Bridgnorth	Ind. 9, Lab. 6, Ind. C. 5, LD 4, C. 3, Ind. Lab. 1, NP 1, others 4
*Brighton	Lab. 29, C. 16, Ind. C. 3
Broadland	Lab. 20, C. 12, LD 12, Ind. 5
Bromsgrove	Lab. 24, C. 12, LD 1, others 2
*Broxbourne	C. 25, Lab. 15, LD 2
Broxtowe	Lab. 36, C. 7, LD 5, Ind. 1
*Burnley	Lab. 38, LD 8, C. 1, Ind. 1
*Cambridge	Lab. 23, LD 18, C. 1
*Cannock Chase	Lab. 40, LD 2
Canterbury	LD 24, Lab. 15, C. 10
Caradon	Ind. 18, LD 18, Lab. 2, RA 2, C. 1
*Carlisle	Lab. 33, C. 14, LD 3, Ind. 1
Carrick	LD 19, Ind. 8, Lab. 8, C. 7, MK 1, others 2
Castle Morpeth	Lab. 12, Ind. 10, C. 6, LD 6
Castle Point	Lab. 34, C. 5
Charnwood	Lab. 30, C. 15, LD 5, Ind. 2
Chelmsford	LD 32, C. 13, Lab. 7, Ind. 4
*Cheltenham	LD 34, C. 3, Ind. 3, Lab. 1
*Cherwell	Lab. 28, C. 16, LD 8
*Chester	Lab. 27, LD 18, C. 13, Ind. 2
Chesterfield	Lab. 37, LD 10
Chester-le-Street	Lab. 30, C. 1, Ind. 1, LD 1
Chichester	LD 25, C. 21, Ind. 4, Lab. 1
Chiltern	LD 24, C. 22, RA 2, Ind. 1, Lab. 1
*Chorley	Lab. 35, LD 7, C. 5, Ind. 1

Christchurch	LD 11, C. 8, Ind. 6
*Colchester	LD 33, Lab. 15, C. 11, RA 1
*Congleton	LD 28, Lab. 11, C. 5, Ind. LD 1
Copeland	Lab. 37, C. 12, Ind. 2
Corby	Lab. 24, LD 2, C. 1
Cotswold	Ind. 16, LD 9, Ind. C. 5, Lab. 4, C. 3, others 8
*Craven	LD 18, C. 6, Lab. 6, Ind. 4
*Crawley	Lab. 28, C. 2, LD 2
*Crewe and Nantwich	Lab. 38, C. 15, LD 3, Ind. 1
Dacorum	Lab. 33, C. 19, LD 4, Ind. 2
Darlington	Lab. 36, C. 13, LD 2, Ind. 1
Dartford	Lab. 35, C. 10, RA 1, Ind. Lab. 1
*Daventry	C. 15, Lab. 15, Ind. 3, LD 2
*Derby	Lab. 39, C. 3, LD 2
Derbyshire Dales	LD 16, Ind. C. 15, Lab. 8
Derwentside	Lab. 50, Ind. 5
Dover	Lab. 39, C. 13, LD 4
Durham	Lab. 38, LD 7, Ind. 4
Easington	Lab. 44, Lib. 3, Ind. 2, Ind. Lab. 2
*Eastbourne	LD 21, C. 8, vacant 1
East Cambridgeshire	Ind. 14, LD 13, NP 6, Lab. 3, Ind. C. 1
East Devon	C. 31, LD 19, Ind. 10
East Dorset	LD 23, C. 12, Ind. 1
East Hampshire	LD 26, C. 12, Ind. 4
East Hertfordshire	C. 23, LD 16, Lab. 8, Ind. 2, RA 1
*Eastleigh	LD 31, C. 7, Lab. 6
East Lindsey	NP 34, Lab. 14, LD 7, Green 3, others 2
East Northamptonshire	Lab. 25, C. 9, LD 2
East Staffordshire	Lab. 36, C. 4, Ind. C. 3, LD 3
Eden	Ind. 31, LD 4, Lab. 2
*Ellesmere Port and Neston	Lab. 36, C. 5
*Elmbridge	C. 21, RA 21, LD 9, Lab. 8, Ind. 1
*Epping Forest	Lab. 18, LD 16, C. 13, RA 9, Ind. 3
Epsom and Ewell	RA 33, Lab. 3, LD 3
Erewash	Lab. 39, C. 10, Ind. 2, LD 1
*Exeter	Lab. 24, LD 7, Lib. 3, C. 2
*Fareham	LD 21, C. 8, Lab. 8, others 5
Fenland	Lab. 19, C. 14, Ind. 4, LD 2, vacant 1
Forest Heath	C. 10, LD 6, Ind. 5, Lab. 4
Forest of Dean	Lab. 28, Ind. 8, LD 5, NP 5, C. 1, others 1, vacant 1
Fylde	C. 17, Ind. 12, Lab. 6, LD 4, others 10
Gedling	Lab. 29, C. 20, LD 7, Ind. 1
*Gillingham	LD 29, Lab. 10, C. 2, Ind. 1
*Gloucester	Lab. 25, LD 8, C. 2
*Gosport	LD 18, Lab. 7, C. 5
Gravesham	Lab. 33, C. 10, Ind. 1
*Great Yarmouth	Lab. 38, C. 9, LD 1
Guildford	LD 23, C. 13, Lab. 6, Ind. 3
*Halton	Lab. 46, LD 7
Hambleton	C. 25, Ind. 15, Lab. 4, LD 3
Harborough	LD 16, C. 11, Lab. 8, Ind. 2
*Harlow	Lab. 39, LD 3
*Harrogate	LD 44, C. 10, Lab. 4, Ind. 1
*Hart	LD 15, C. 12, Lab. 8
*Hastings	LD 17, Lab. 15
*Havant	LD 20, Lab. 11, C. 8, Ind. 3
*Hereford	LD 22, Lab. 5
*Hertsmere	Lab. 22, C. 8, LD 8, Ind. 1
High Peak	Lab. 30, C. 5, LD 5, Ind. 4

Hinckley and Bosworth	*LD* 16, *Lab.* 13, *C.* 5	*Penwith	*LD* 11, *Lab.* 9, *Ind.* 8, *C.* 4,
Horsham	*LD* 22, *C.* 18, *Ind.* 3		*MK* 2
Hove	*Lab.* 16, *C.* 11, *LD* 3	*Peterborough	*Lab.* 29, *C.* 13, *Lib.* 3, *LD* 2,
*Huntingdonshire	*C.* 33, *LD* 13, *Lab.* 5, *Ind.* 2		*Ind.* 1
*Hyndburn	*Lab.* 44, *C.* 3	Plymouth	*Lab.* 55, *C.* 5
*Ipswich	*Lab.* 41, *C.* 6, *LD* 1	Poole	*LD* 23, *C.* 13, *Lab.* 3
Kennet	*Ind.* 14, *Lab.* 9, *C.* 9, *LD* 8	*Portsmouth	*Lab.* 21, *LD* 12, *C.* 6
Kerrier	*Lab.* 15, *LD* 13, *Ind.* 12, *others* 4	*Preston	*Lab.* 32, *C.* 13, *SD* 12
Kettering	*Lab.* 32, *C.* 6, *Ind.* 3, *LD* 3,	*Purbeck	*LD* 11, *Ind.* 5, *C.* 3, *Lab.* 3
	vacant 1	*Reading	*Lab.* 35, *LD* 6, *C.* 4
Kings Lynn and West		*Redditch	*Lab.* 25, *C.* 3, *LD* 1
Norfolk	*Lab.* 37, *Ind. C.* 16, *LD* 6, *Ind.* 1	*Reigate and Banstead	*C.* 15, *Lab.* 14, *LD* 14, *RA* 4,
Lancaster	*Lab.* 33, *C.* 11, *Ind.* 9, *LD* 5,		*Ind.* 2
	Ind. C. 1, *others* 1	Restormel	*LD* 30, *NP* 9, *Lab.* 4, *C.* 1
Leicester	*Lab.* 40, *LD* 8, *C.* 7, *vacant* 1	Ribble Valley	*LD* 19, *C.* 18, *Ind. C.* 1, *Lab.* 1
*Leominster	*Ind.* 16, *LD* 7, *Lab.* 6, *C.* 3,	Richmondshire	*Ind.* 22, *LD* 9, *C.* 2, *SD* 1
	Ind. C. 3, *Green* 1	Rochester-upon-Medway	*Lab.* 44, *LD* 5, *C.* 1
Lewes	*LD* 28, *C.* 16, *Lab.* 2, *Ind.* 1,	*Rochford	*LD* 23, *Lab.* 11, *RA* 3, *C.* 2
	RA 1	*Rossendale	*Lab.* 31, *C.* 5
Lichfield	*Lab.* 33, *C.* 19, *LD* 2, *Ind.* 1,	Rother	*LD* 21, *C.* 14, *Ind.* 5, *Lab.* 5
	Ind. Lab. 1	*Rugby	*Lab.* 22, *C.* 11, *LD* 5, *others* 10
*Lincoln	*Lab.* 33	*Runnymede	*C.* 21, *Lab.* 14, *Ind.* 6, *LD* 1
Luton	*Lab.* 36, *LD* 9, *C.* 3	Rushcliffe	*C.* 26, *Lab.* 17, *LD* 10, *Ind.* 1
*Macclesfield	*C.* 33, *Lab.* 12, *LD* 11, *RA* 3,	*Rushmoor	*LD* 18, *Lab.* 14, *C.* 13
	vacant 1	Rutland	*Ind.* 11, *LD* 5, *C.* 2, *Lab.* 2
*Maidstone	*LD* 22, *Lab.* 18, *C.* 10, *Ind.* 5	Ryedale	*Ind.* 9, *LD* 9, *C.* 4, *Lab.* 1
Maldon	*C.* 16, *Lab.* 7, *Ind.* 6, *LD* 1	*St Albans	*LD* 39, *Lab.* 11, *C.* 6, *vacant* 1
Malvern Hills	*LD* 18, *Ind.* 11, *NP* 7, *C.* 6,	St Edmundsbury	*Lab.* 22, *C.* 15, *LD* 5, *Ind.* 2
	Green 3, *Lab.* 3, *Ind. C.* 2,	Salisbury	*LD* 30, *Lab.* 11, *C.* 9, *Ind.* 8
	vacant 1	Scarborough	*Lab.* 24, *C.* 13, *Ind.* 8, *LD* 4
Mansfield	*Lab.* 45, *C.* 1	Sedgefield	*Lab.* 47, *Ind.* 2
Melton	*LD* 9, *C.* 8, *Lab.* 5, *Ind.* 4	Sedgemoor	*C.* 21, *Lab.* 13, *LD* 12, *Ind.* 3
Mendip	*LD* 21, *Lab.* 9, *C.* 8, *Ind.* 3, *RA* 2	Selby	*Lab.* 26, *C.* 9, *Ind.* 5, *LD* 1
Mid Bedfordshire	*C.* 22, *Lab.* 20, *Ind.* 6, *LD* 5	Sevenoaks	*C.* 20, *C.* 17, *Lab.* 11, *Ind.* 5
Mid Devon	*LD* 21, *Ind.* 17, *Lab.* 1, *Lib.* 1	Shepway	*LD* 20, *C.* 19, *Lab.* 14, *Ind.* 3
Mid Suffolk	*Lab.* 17, *LD* 11, *C.* 6, *Ind.* 5,	*Shrewsbury and Atcham	*Lab.* 22, *LD* 13, *C.* 8, *Ind.* 5
	others 1	*Slough	*Lab.* 36, *Lib.* 3, *Ind.* 1
*Mid Sussex	*LD* 28, *C* 18, *Ind.* 4, *Lab.* 4	*Southampton	*Lab.* 29, *LD* 13, *C.* 3
Milton Keynes	*Lab.* 30, *LD* 18, *C.* 2, *Ind.* 1	*South Bedfordshire	*Lab.* 24, *LD* 15, *C.* 11, *Ind.* 3
*Mole Valley	*LD* 18, *C.* 11, *Ind.* 9, *Lab.* 2,	South Bucks	*C.* 19, *Ind.* 17, *LD* 4
	vacant 1	*South Cambridgeshire	*Ind.* 21, *C.* 13, *LD* 11, *Lab.* 10
Newark and Sherwood	*Lab.* 37, *C.* 10, *LD* 5, *Ind.* 2	South Derbyshire	*Lab.* 27, *C.* 6, *others* 1
Newbury	*LD* 37, *C.* 6, *Ind.* 2	*Southend-on-Sea	*LD* 18, *Lab.* 11, *C.* 10
*Newcastle-under-Lyme	*Lab.* 42, *LD* 10, *C.* 4	South Hams	*C.* 16 , *Ind.* 16 , *LD* 10, *Lab.* 2
New Forest	*LD* 32, *C.* 23, *Ind.* 3	*South Herefordshire	*Ind.* 23, *LD* 13, *others* 2,
Northampton	*Lab.* 34, *LD* 8, *C.* 1		*vacant* 1
North Cornwall	*Ind.* 25, *LD* 12, *C.* 1	South Holland	*Ind.* 17, *Lab.* 10, *C.* 7, *others* 4
North Devon	*LD* 31, *Ind.* 11, *C.* 1, *others* 1	South Kesteven	*Lab.* 18, *C.* 13, *Ind.* 11, *LD* 7,
North Dorset	*LD* 19, *Ind.* 12, *C.* 1, *Lab.* 1,		*Ind. Lab.* 3, *Lib.* 2, *others* 3
North East Derbyshire	*Lab.* 42, *C.* 4, *LD* 3, *Ind. Lab.* 2,	*South Lakeland	*LD* 25, *Ind.* 11, *C.* 10, *Lab.* 6
	Ind. 1, *vacant* 1	South Norfolk	*LD* 30, *C.* 12, *Lab.* 3, *Ind.* 2
*North Hertfordshire	*Lab.* 26, *C.* 16, *LD* 7, *Ind.* 1	South Northamptonshire	*C.* 15, *Lab.* 10, *Ind.* 8, *LD* 7
North Kesteven	*Lab.* 15, *LD* 8, *Ind.* 6, *C.* 4,	South Oxfordshire	*LD* 21, *Lab.* 13, *C.* 9, *Ind.* 5,
	others 6		*others* 2
North Norfolk	*Lab.* 19, *Ind.* 12, *LD* 12, *C.* 3	South Ribble	*Lab.* 29, *C.* 16, *LD* 9
North Shropshire	*Ind.* 7, *Lab.* 6, *C.* 2, *LD* 1,	South Shropshire	*NP* 9, *LD* 8, *Ind.* 7, *Green* 2,
	others 24		*Lab.* 1, *others* 13
North Warwickshire	*Lab.* 29, *C.* 4, *Ind.* 1	South Somerset	*LD* 45, *C.* 8, *Ind.* 6, *Lab.* 1
North West		South Staffordshire	*C.* 26, *Lab.* 15, *Lib.* 4, *RA* 3,
Leicestershire	*Lab.* 35, *C.* 3, *Ind. C.* 2		*Ind. C.* 1, *Ind.* 1
North Wiltshire	*LD* 30, *C.* 12, *Lab.* 6, *Ind.* 4	Spelthorne	*C.* 21, *Lab.* 16, *LD* 3
*Norwich	*Lab.* 37, *LD* 11	Stafford	*Lab.* 33, *C.* 16, *LD* 10, *Ind.* 1
Nottingham	*Lab.* 51, *LD* 2, *C.* 1, *Green* 1	*Staffordshire Moorlands	*Lab.* 27, *C.* 11, *LD* 7, *Ind.* 3,
*Nuneaton and Bedworth	*Lab.* 42, *C.* 3		*others* 8
*Oadby and Wigston	*LD* 25, *C.* 1	*Stevenage	*Lab.* 38, *LD* 1
Oswestry	*Lab.* 10, *C.* 5, *LD* 5, *others* 9	*Stoke-on-Trent	*Lab.* 60
*Oxford	*Lab.* 39, *LD* 9, *Green* 3	*Stratford-upon-Avon	*LD* 24, *C.* 17, *Ind.* 9, *Lab.* 5
*Pendle	*LD* 29, *Lab.* 19, *C.* 3	*Stroud	*Lab.* 27, *LD* 11, *C.* 7, *Ind.* 5,
			Green 4, *vacant* 1

Suffolk Coastal	*C.* 19, *LD* 16, *Lab.* 15, *Ind.* 5
Surrey Heath	*C.* 24, *LD* 8, *Lab.* 4
*Swale	*LD* 23, *Lab.* 19, *C.* 6, *Ind.* 1,
*Tamworth	*Lab.* 27, *Ind.* 3
*Tandridge	*LD* 19, *C.* 16, *Lab.* 7
Taunton Deane	*LD* 29, *C.* 14, *Lab.* 7, *Ind.* 3
Teesdale	*Lab.* 12, *Ind.* 11, *NP* 6, *C.* 2
Teignbridge	*LD* 25, *Ind.* 21, *Lab.* 7, *C.* 5
Tendring	*Lab.* 37, *Ind.* 9, *C.* 8, *LD* 6
Test Valley	*C.* 22, *LD* 22
Tewkesbury	*Ind.* 22, *LD* 8, *Lab.* 5, *others* 1
*Thamesdown	*Lab.* 41, *LD* 9, *C.* 3, *Ind.* 1
Thanet	*Lab.* 44, *LD* 4, *C.* 4, *Ind.* 2
*Three Rivers	*LD* 23, *C.* 17, *Lab.* 8
*Thurrock	*Lab.* 37, *C.* 2
*Tonbridge and Malling	*C.* 23, *LD* 21, *Lab.* 11
*Torbay	*LD* 25, *C.* 5, *Lab.* 5, *Ind. LD* 1
Torridge	*LD* 13, *Ind.* 9, *NP* 6, *Lab.* 5,
	C. 2, *Green* 1
*Tunbridge Wells	*LD* 27, *C.* 14, *Lab.* 6, *Ind.* 1
Tynedale	*Lab.* 19, *LD* 13, *C.* 11, *Ind.* 4
Uttlesford	*LD* 19, *C.* 12, *Ind.* 7, *Lab.* 4
Vale of White Horse	*LD* 34, *C.* 11, *Lab.* 5, *Ind.* 1
Vale Royal	*Lab.* 42, *C.* 15, *LD* 3
Wansbeck	*Lab.* 46
Warrington	*Lab.* 48, *LD* 11, *C.* 1
Warwick	*Lab.* 17, *C.* 13, *LD* 11, *Ind.* 4
*Watford	*Lab.* 21, *LD* 9, *C.* 6
*Waveney	*Lab.* 44, *C.* 2, *LD* 2
Waverley	*LD* 37, *C.* 17, *Lab.* 2, *Ind.* 1
Wealden	*C.* 29, *LD* 24, *Ind.* 5
Wear Valley	*Lab.* 35, *Ind.* 3, *LD* 2
Wellingborough	*Lab.* 16, *C.* 15, *Ind.* 3
*Welwyn Hatfield	*Lab.* 32, *C.* 15
West Devon	*LD* 15, *Ind.* 14, *Lab.* 1
West Dorset	*C.* 18, *Ind.* 17, *LD* 14, *Lab.* 5,
	SD 1
*West Lancashire	*Lab.* 35, *C.* 20
*West Lindsey	*LD* 19, *Ind.* 10, *Lab.* 3, *C.* 2,
	others 3
*West Oxfordshire	*Ind.* 15, *LD* 14, *Lab.* 11, *C.* 9
West Somerset	*C.* 11, *Ind.* 10, *Lab.* 8, *LD* 3
West Wiltshire	*LD* 28, *C.* 8, *Lab.* 4, *Ind.* 3
*Weymouth and Portland	*Lab.* 15, *LD* 14, *RA* 4, *Ind.* 2
*Winchester	*LD* 36, *C.* 9, *Lab.* 6, *Ind.* 4
Windsor and Maidenhead	*LD* 32, *C.* 17, *Ind.* 7, *Lab.* 2
*Woking	*LD* 18, *C.* 10, *Lab.* 7
*Wokingham	*LD* 29, *C.* 24, *Ind.* 1
*Worcester	*Lab.* 23, *C.* 9, *LD* 3, *Ind.* 1
*Worthing	*LD* 25, *C.* 11
Wrekin	*Lab.* 38, *C.* 3, *Ind. Lab.* 2, *LD* 2,
	Ind. 1
Wychavon	*C.* 18, *LD* 15, *Lab.* 9, *Ind.* 5,
	vacant 2
Wycombe	*C.* 24, *LD* 19, *Lab.* 15, *Ind.* 2
Wyre	*Lab.* 30, *C.* 18, *LD* 4, *RA* 2,
	Ind. C. 1, *vacant* 1
*Wyre Forest	*Lab.* 26, *LD* 8, *C.* 3, *Lab.* 3,
	Ind. 2

GREATER LONDON BOROUGHS

Barking and Dagenham	*Lab.* 47, *RA* 3, *LD* 1
Barnet	*C.* 29, *Lab.* 25, *LD* 6
Bexley	*C.* 24, *Lab.* 24, *LD* 14
Brent	*C.* 33, *Lab.* 28, *LD* 5
Bromley	*C.* 32, *LD* 21, *Lab.* 7
Camden	*Lab.* 48, *C.* 7, *LD* 4
City of Westminster	*C.* 45, *Lab.* 15
Croydon	*Lab.* 40, *C.* 30

Ealing	*Lab.* 49, *C.* 19, *LD* 3
Enfield	*Lab.* 41, *C.* 24, *Ind. C.* 1
Greenwich	*Lab.* 46, *C.* 8, *SD* 4, *LD* 3,
	Ind. Lab. 1
Hackney	*Lab.* 33, *C* 13, *LD* 2, *vacant* 2
Hammersmith and	
Fulham	*Lab.* 33, *C.* 13, *LD* 2, *vacant* 2
Haringey	*Lab.* 57, *C.* 2
Harrow	*LD* 29, *C.* 16, *Lab.* 14, *Ind.* 1,
	others 3
Havering	*Lab.* 28, *RA* 17, *C.* 12, *LD* 2,
	others 4
Hillingdon	*Lab.* 41, *C.* 25, *others* 3
Hounslow	*Lab.* 50, *C.* 6, *LD* 4
Islington	*Lab.* 37, *LD* 13, *C.* 1, *Ind.* 1
Kensington and Chelsea	*C.* 39, *Lab.* 15
Kingston upon Thames	*LD* 27, *C.* 17, *Lab.* 6
Lambeth	*LD* 25, *Lab.* 24, *C.* 14, *Ind.* 1
Lewisham	*Lab.* 63, *LD* 2, *C.* 1, *others* 1
Merton	*Lab.* 39, *C.* 10, *Ind.* 5, *LD* 3
Newham	*Lab.* 60
Redbridge	*Lab.* 28, *C.* 24, *Lib.* 9, *vacant* 1
Richmond upon Thames	*LD* 43, *C.* 7, *Lab.* 2
Southwark	*Lab.* 35, *LD* 24, *C.* 3, *Ind. Lib.* 1,
	others 1
Sutton	*LD* 47, *Lab.* 5, *C.* 4
Tower Hamlets	*Lab.* 43, *LD* 7
Waltham Forest	*Lab.* 26, *C.* 16, *LD* 14,
	Ind. Lab. 1
Wandsworth	*C.* 45, *Lab.* 16

WALES SINCE 1 APRIL 1996

Anglesey	*Ind.* 26, *PC* 7, *Lab.* 6, *C.* 1
Blaenau Gwent	*Lab.* 33, *Ind.* 5, *C.* 1, *Ind. Lab.* 1,
	Lib. 1, *PC* 1
Bridgend	*Lab.* 45, *Ind.* 2, *Ind. Lab.* 1
Caernarfonshire and	*PC* 45, *Ind.* 20, *Lab.* 11, *LD* 4,
Merionethshire	*others* 2
Caerphilly	*Lab.* 56, *PC* 9, *Ind.* 3
Cardiff	*Lab.* 56, *LD* 9, *C.* 1, *PC* 1
Carmarthenshire	*Lab.* 37, *Ind.* 29, *PC* 8, *LD* 3,
	Ind. Lab. 2, *others* 1, *vacant* 1
Ceredigion	*Ind.* 24, *LD* 11, *PC* 8, *Lab.* 1
Conwy	*LD* 18, *Ind.* 10, *C.* 9, *PC* 4
Denbighshire	*Lab.* 20, *Ind.* 19, *PC* 7, *LD* 3
Flintshire	*Lab.* 45, *LD* 6, *C.* 3, *others* 18
Merthyr Tydfil	*Lab.* 30, *Ind.* 3
Monmouthshire	*Lab.* 26, *C.* 11, *Ind.* 4, *LD* 1
Neath and Port Talbot	*Lab.* 50, *PC* 3, *RA* 3, *Ind.* 2,
	LD 2, *SD* 1, *others* 2,
	vacant 1
Newport	*Lab.* 46, *C.* 1
Pembrokeshire	*Ind.* 39, *Lab.* 14, *LD* 3, *PC* 3,
	others 1
Powys	*Ind.* 61, *Lab.* 9, *LD* 9, *C.* 3, *PC* 1
Rhondda, Cynon, Taff	*Lab.* 58, *PC* 12, *Ind.* 3, *vacant* 1
Swansea	*Lab.* 56, *Ind.* 9, *LD* 7, *C.* 1
Torfaen	*Lab.* 41, *C.* 1, *Ind.* 1, *LD* 1
Vale of Glamorgan	*Lab.* 36, *C.* 5, *PC* 5, *Ind. C.* 1
Wrexham	*Lab.* 33, *Ind. C.* 7 , *Ind. Lab.* 2,
	NP 1, *others* 8

SCOTLAND since 1 April 1996

Aberdeen City	Lab. 30, LD 10, C. 9, SNP 1
Aberdeenshire	LD 15, SNP 15, Ind. 13, C. 4
Angus	SNP 21, C. 2, LD 2, Ind. 1
Argyll and Bute	Ind. 21, SNP 4, C. 3, LD 3, Lab. 2
City of Edinburgh	Lab. 34, C. 14, LD 10
Clackmannanshire	Lab. 8, SNP 3, C. 1
Dumfries and Galloway	Ind. 28, Lab. 20, LD 10, SNP 9, C. 2, others 1
Dundee City	Lab. 28, C. 4, SNP 3, Ind. Lab. 1
East Ayrshire	Lab. 22, SNP 8
East Dumbartonshire	Lab. 15, LD 9, C. 2
East Lothian	Lab. 15, C. 3
East Renfrewshire	C. 9, Lab. 8, LD 2, RA 1
Falkirk	Lab. 23, SNP 8, Ind. 3, C. 2
Fife	Lab. 54, LD 25, SNP 9, Ind. 2, others 2
Glasgow City	Lab. 77, C. 3, LD 1, SNP 1, others 1

Highland	Ind. 48, SNP 9, Lab. 7, LD 6, C. 1, vacant 1
Inverclyde	Lab. 14, LD 5, C. 1
Midlothian	Lab. 13, SNP 2
Moray	SNP 13, Lab. 3, Ind. 2
North Ayrshire	Lab. 27, C. 1, Ind. 1, SNP 1
North Lanarkshire	Lab. 60, SNP 7, Ind. 2
Orkney Islands	Ind. 28
Perth and Kinross	SNP 18, Lab. 6, LD 5, C. 2, Ind. 1
Renfrewshire	Lab. 20, SNP 13, LD 3, C. 2, others 2
Scottish Borders	Ind. 22, LD 17, SNP 8, NP 6, C. 3, Lab. 2,
Shetland Islands	NP 11, Ind. 8, LD 2, Lab. 1, Ind. Lab. 1, others 3
South Ayrshire	Lab. 21, C. 4
South Lanarkshire	Lab. 54, SNP 8, C. 2, LD 2, others 8
Stirling	Lab. 13, C. 7, SNP 2
West Dumbartonshire	Lab. 14, SNP 7, Ind. 1
Western Isles	Ind. 25, Lab. 5
West Lothian	Lab. 15, SNP 11, C. 1

Patron Saints

ST GEORGE
Patron Saint of England

St George is believed to have been born in Cappadocia, of Christian parents, in the latter part of the third century and to have served with distinction as a soldier under the Emperor Diocletian, including a visit to England on a military mission. When the persecution of Christians was ordered, St George sought a personal interview to remonstrate with the Emperor and after a profession of faith resigned his military commission. Arrest and torture followed and he was martyred at Nicomedia on 23 April 303, a day ordered to be kept in remembrance as a national festival by the Council of Oxford in 1222, although it was not until the reign of Edward III that he was made patron saint of England.

St George's connection with a dragon seems to date from the close of the sixth century and to be due to the transfer of his remains from Nicomedia to Lydda, close to the scene of the legendary exploit of Perseus in rescuing Andromeda and slaying the sea monster, credit for which became attached to the Christian martyr.

ST DAVID
Patron Saint of Wales

St David is believed to have been born towards the beginning and to have died towards the end of the sixth century. St David was an eloquent preacher, who founded the monastery at Menevia, now St David's. He became the patron of Wales, but there is no record of any papal canonization before 1181. His annual festival is observed on 1 March.

ST ANDREW
Patron Saint of Scotland

St Andrew, one of the apostles and brother of Simon Peter, was born at Bethsaida on the Sea of Galilee and lived at Capernaum. He preached the Gospel in Asia Minor and in Scythia along the shores of the Black Sea and became the patron saint of Russia. It is believed that he suffered crucifixion at Patras in Achaea, on a *crux decussata* (now known as St Andrew's Cross) and that his relics were removed from Patras to Constantinople and thence to St Andrews, probably in the eighth century, since which time he has been the patron saint of Scotland. The festival of St Andrew is held on 30 November.

ST PATRICK
Patron Saint of Ireland

St Patrick was born, probably in England, about 389 and was carried off to Ireland as a slave about 16 years later, escaping to Gaul at the age of 22. He was ordained deacon at Auxerre and having been consecrated Bishop in 432 was dispatched to Wicklow to reorganize the Christian communities in Ireland. He founded the see of Armagh and introduced Latin into Ireland as the language of the Church. He died c.461 and his festival is celebrated on 17 March.

England

The Kingdom of England lies between 55° 46′ and 49° 57′ 30″ N. latitude (from a few miles north of the mouth of the Tweed to the Lizard), and between 1° 46′ E. and 5° 43′ W. (from Lowestoft to Land's End). England is bounded on the north by the Cheviot Hills; on the south by the English Channel, on the east by the Straits of Dover (Pas de Calais) and the North Sea; and on the west by the Atlantic Ocean, Wales and the Irish Sea. It has a total area of 50,351 sq. miles (130,410 sq. km): land 50,058 sq. miles (129,652 sq. km); inland water 293 sq. miles (758 sq. km).

POPULATION

The population at the 1991 census was 46,382,050 (males 22,469,707; females 23,912,343). The average density of the population in 1991 was 3.6 persons per hectare.

FLAG

The flag of England is the cross of St George, a red cross on a white field (cross gules in a field argent). The cross of St George, the patron saint of England, has been used since the 13th century.

RELIEF

There is a marked division between the upland and lowland areas of England. In the extreme north the Cheviot Hills (highest point, The Cheviot, 2,674 ft) form a natural boundary with Scotland. Running south from the Cheviots, though divided from them by the Tyne Gap, is the Pennine range (highest point, Cross Fell, 2,930 ft), the main orological feature of the country. The Pennines culminate in the Peak District of Derbyshire (Kinder Scout, 2,088 ft). West of the Pennines are the Cumbrian mountains, which include Scafell Pike (3,210 ft), the highest peak in England, and to the east are the Yorkshire Moors, their highest point being Urra Moor (1,490 ft).

In the west, the foothills of the Welsh mountains extend into the bordering English counties of Shropshire (the Wrekin, 1,334 ft; Long Mynd, 1,694 ft) and Hereford and Worcester (the Malvern Hills – Worcestershire Beacon, 1,394 ft). Extensive areas of high land and moorland are also to be found in the south-western peninsula formed by Somerset, Devon and Cornwall: principally Exmoor (Dunkery Beacon, 1,704 ft), Dartmoor (High Willhays, 2,038 ft) and Bodmin Moor (Brown Willy, 1,377 ft). Ranges of low, undulating hills run across the south of the country, including the Cotswolds in the Midlands and south-west, the Chilterns to the north of London, and the North (Kent) and South (Sussex) Downs of the south-east coastal areas.

The lowlands of England lie in the Vale of York, East Anglia and the area around the Wash. The lowest-lying are the Cambridgeshire Fens in the valleys of the Great Ouse and the River Nene, which are below sea-level in places. Since the 17th century extensive drainage has brought much of the Fens under cultivation. The North Sea coast between the Thames and the Humber, low-lying and formed of sand and shingle for the most part, is subject to erosion and defences against further incursion have been built along many stretches.

HYDROGRAPHY

The Severn is the longest river in Great Britain, rising in the north-eastern slopes of Plynlimon (Wales) and entering England in Shropshire with a total length of 220 miles (354 km) from its source to its outflow into the Bristol Channel, where it receives on the east the Bristol Avon, and on the west the Wye, its other tributaries being the

Vyrnwy, Tern, Stour, Teme and Upper (or Warwickshire) Avon. The Severn is tidal below Gloucester, and a high bore or tidal wave sometimes reverses the flow as high as Tewkesbury (13½ miles above Gloucester). The scenery of the greater part of the river is very picturesque and beautiful, and the Severn is a noted salmon river, some of its tributaries being famous for trout. Navigation is assisted by the Gloucester and Berkeley Ship Canal (16¾ miles), which admits vessels of 350 tons to Gloucester. The Severn Tunnel was begun in 1873 and completed in 1886 at a cost of £2 million and after many difficulties from flooding. It is 4 miles 628 yards in length (of which 2¼ miles are under the river). The Severn road bridge between Haysgate, Gwent, and Almondsbury, Glos, with a centre span of 3,240 ft, was opened in 1966.

The longest river wholly in England is the Thames, with a total length of 215 miles (346 km) from its source in the Cotswold hills to the Nore, and is navigable by ocean-going ships to London Bridge. The Thames is tidal to Teddington (69 miles from its mouth) and forms county boundaries almost throughout its course; on its banks are situated London, Windsor Castle, the oldest royal residence still in regular use, Eton College and Oxford, the oldest university in the kingdom.

Of the remaining English rivers, those flowing into the North Sea are the Tyne, Wear, Tees, Ouse and Trent from the Pennine Range, the Great Ouse (160 miles), which rises in Northamptonshire, and the Orwell and Stour from the hills of East Anglia. Flowing into the English Channel are the Sussex Ouse from the Weald, the Itchen from the Hampshire Hills, and the Axe, Teign, Dart, Tamar and Exe from the Devonian hills. Flowing into the Irish Sea are the Mersey, Ribble and Eden from the western slopes of the Pennines and the Derwent from the Cumbrian mountains.

The English Lakes, noteworthy for their picturesque scenery and poetic associations, lie in Cumbria, the largest being Windermere (10 miles long), Ullswater and Derwent Water.

ISLANDS

The Isle of Wight is separated from Hampshire by the Solent. The capital, Newport, stands at the head of the estuary of the Medina, Cowes (at the mouth) being the chief port. Other centres are Ryde, Sandown, Shanklin, Ventnor, Freshwater, Yarmouth, Totland Bay, Seaview and Bembridge.

Lundy (the name means Puffin Island), 11 miles north-west of Hartland Point, Devon, is about two miles long and about half a mile wide on average, with a total area of about 1,116 acres, and a population of about 20. It became the property of the National Trust in 1969 and is now principally a bird sanctuary.

The Isles of Scilly consist of about 140 islands and skerries (total area, 6 sq. miles/10 sq. km) situated 28 miles south-west of Land's End. Only five are inhabited: St Mary's, St Agnes, Bryher, Tresco and St Martin's. The population is 1,978. The entire group has been designated a Conservation Area, a Heritage Coast, and an Area of Outstanding Natural Beauty, and has been given National Nature Reserve status by the Nature Conservancy Council because of its unique flora and fauna. Tourism and the winter/spring flower trade for the home market form the basis of the economy of the Isles. The island group is a recognized rural development area.

EARLY HISTORY

Archaeological evidence suggests that England has been inhabited since at least the Palaeolithic period, though the extent of the various Palaeolithic cultures was dependent upon the degree of glaciation. The succeeding Neolithic and Bronze Age cultures have left abundant remains throughout the country, the best-known of these being the henges and stone circles of Stonehenge (ten miles north of Salisbury, Wilts) and Avebury (Wilts), both of which are believed to have been of religious significance. In the latter part of the Bronze Age the Goidels, a people of Celtic race, and in the Iron Age other Celtic races of Brythons and Belgae, invaded the country and brought with them Celtic civilization and dialects, place names in England bearing witness to the spread of the invasion over the whole kingdom.

THE ROMAN CONQUEST

The Roman conquest of Gaul (57–50 BC) brought Britain into close contact with Roman civilization, but although Julius Caesar raided the south of Britain in 55 BC and 54 BC, conquest was not undertaken until nearly 100 years later. In AD 43 the Emperor Claudius dispatched Aulus Plautius, with a well-equipped force of 40,000, and himself followed with reinforcements in the same year. Success was delayed by the resistance of Caratacus (Caractacus), the British leader from AD 48–51, who was finally captured and sent to Rome, and by a great revolt in AD 61 led by Boudicca (Boadicea), Queen of the Iceni; but the south of Britain was secured by AD 70, and Wales and the area north to the Tyne by about AD 80.

In AD 122, the Emperor Hadrian visited Britain and built a continuous rampart, since known as Hadrian's Wall, from Wallsend to Bowness (Tyne to Solway). The work was entrusted by the Emperor Hadrian to Aulus Platorius Nepos, legate of Britain from AD 122 to 126, and it was intended to form the northern frontier of the Roman Empire.

The Romans administered Britain as a province under a Governor, with a well-defined system of local government, each Roman municipality ruling itself and its surrounding territory, while London was the centre of the road system and the seat of the financial officials of the Province of Britain. Colchester, Lincoln, York, Gloucester and St Albans stand on the sites of five Roman municipalities, and Wroxeter, Caerleon, Chester, Lincoln and York were at various times the sites of legionary fortresses. Well-preserved Roman towns have been uncovered at or near Silchester (*Calleva Atrebatum*), ten miles south of Reading, Wroxeter (*Viroconium Cornoviorum*), near Shrewsbury, and St Albans (*Verulamium*) in Hertfordshire.

Four main groups of roads radiated from London, and a fifth (the Fosse) ran obliquely from Lincoln through Leicester, Cirencester and Bath to Exeter. Of the four groups radiating from London, one ran south-east to Canterbury and the coast of Kent, a second to Silchester and thence to parts of western Britain and south Wales, a third (later known as Watling Street) ran through Verulamium to Chester, with various branches, and the fourth reached Colchester, Lincoln, York and the eastern counties.

In the fourth century Britain was subject to raids along the east coast by Saxon pirates, which led to the establishment of a system of coast defence from the Wash to Southampton Water, with forts at Brancaster, Burgh Castle (Yarmouth), Walton (Felixstowe), Bradwell, Reculver, Richborough, Dover, Lympne, Pevensey and Porchester (Portsmouth). The Irish (Scoti) and Picts in the north were also becoming more aggressive; from about AD 350

incursions became more frequent and more formidable. As the Roman Empire came under attack increasingly towards the end of the fourth century, many troops were removed from Britain for service in other parts of the empire. The island was eventually cut off from Rome by the Teutonic conquest of Gaul, and with the withdrawal of the last Roman garrison early in the fifth century, the Romano-British were left to themselves.

SAXON SETTLEMENT

According to legend, the British King Vortigern called in the Saxons to defend him against the Picts, the Saxon chieftains being Hengist and Horsa, who landed at Ebbsfleet, Kent, and established themselves in the Isle of Thanet; but the events during the one and a half centuries between the final break with Rome and the re-establishment of Christianity are unclear. However, it would appear that in the course of this period the raids turned into large-scale settlement by invaders traditionally known as Angles (England north of the Wash and East Anglia), Saxons (Essex and southern England) and Jutes (Kent and the Weald), which pushed the Romano-British into the mountainous areas of the north and west, Celtic culture outside Wales and Cornwall surviving only in topographical names. Various kingdoms were established at this time which attempted to claim overlordship of the whole country, hegemony finally being achieved by Wessex (capital, Winchester) in the ninth century. This century also saw the beginning of raids by the Vikings (Danes), which were resisted by Alfred the Great (871–899), who fixed a limit to the advance of Danish settlement by the Treaty of Wedmore (878), giving them the area north and east of Watling Street, on condition that they adopt Christianity.

In the tenth century the kings of Wessex recovered the whole of England from the Danes, but subsequent rulers were unable to resist a second wave of invaders. England paid tribute (*Danegeld*) for many years, and was invaded in 1013 by the Danes and ruled by Danish kings from 1016 until 1042, when Edward the Confessor was recalled from exile in Normandy. On Edward's death in 1066 Harold Godwinson (brother-in-law of Edward and son of Earl Godwin of Wessex) was chosen King of England. After defeating (at Stamford Bridge, Yorkshire, 25 September) an invading army under Harald Hadraada, King of Norway (aided by the outlawed Earl Tostig of Northumbria, Harold's brother), Harold was himself defeated at the Battle of Hastings on 14 October 1066, and the Norman conquest secured the throne of England for Duke William of Normandy, a cousin of Edward the Confessor.

CHRISTIANITY

Christianity reached the Roman province of Britain from Gaul in the third century (or possibly earlier); Alban, traditionally Britain's first martyr, was put to death as a Christian during the persecution of Diocletian (22 June 303), at his native town Verulamium; and the Bishops of Londinium, Eboracum (York), and Lindum (Lincoln) attended the Council of Arles in 314. However, the Anglo-Saxon invasions submerged the Christian religion in England until the sixth century when conversion was undertaken in the north from 563 by Celtic missionaries from Ireland led by St Columba, and in the south by a mission sent from Rome in 597 which was led by St Augustine, who became the first archbishop of Canterbury. England appears to have been converted again by the end of the seventh century and followed, after the Council of Whitby in 663, the practices of the Roman Church, which brought the kingdom into the mainstream of European thought and culture.

PRINCIPAL CITIES

BIRMINGHAM

Birmingham (West Midlands) is Britain's second city. It is a focal point in national communications networks with a rapidly expanding International Airport. The generally accepted derivation of 'Birmingham' is the *ham* (dwelling-place) of the *ing* (family) of *Beorma*, presumed to have been Saxon. During the Industrial Revolution the town grew into a major manufacturing centre. In 1889 Birmingham was granted city status.

Despite the decline in manufacturing, Birmingham is still a major hardware trade and motor component industry centre. As well as the National Exhibition Centre and the Aston Science Park, recent developments include the International Convention Centre and the National Indoor Arena.

The principal buildings are the Town Hall (1834–50); the Council House (1879); Victoria Law Courts (1891); Birmingham University (1906–9); the 13th-century Church of St Martin-in-the-Bull-Ring (rebuilt 1873); the Cathedral (formerly St Philip's Church) (1711) and the Roman Catholic Cathedral of St Chad (1839–41).

BRADFORD

Bradford (West Yorkshire) lies on the southern edge of the Yorkshire Dales National Park, including within its boundaries the village of Haworth, home of the Brontë sisters, and Ilkley Moor.

Originally a Saxon township, Bradford received a market charter in 1251 but developed only slowly until the industrialization of the textile industry brought rapid growth during the 19th century; it was granted its city charter in 1897. The prosperity of that period is reflected in much of the city's architecture, particularly the public buildings: City Hall (1873), Wool Exchange (1867), St George's Hall (Concert Hall, 1853), Cartwright Hall (Art Gallery, 1904) and the Technical College (1882). Other chief buildings are the Cathedral (15th century) and Bolling Hall (14th century).

Textiles still play an important part in the city's economy but industry is now more broadly based, including engineering, micro-electronics, printing and chemicals. The city has a strong financial services sector, and a growing tourism industry.

BRISTOL

Bristol was a Royal Borough before the Norman Conquest. The earliest form of the name is *Bricgstow*. In 1373 it received from Edward III a charter granting it county status.

The chief buildings include the 12th-century Cathedral (with later additions), with Norman chapter house and gateway, the 14th-century Church of St Mary Redcliffe, Wesley's Chapel, Broadmead, the Merchant Venturers' Almshouses, the Council House (1956), Guildhall, Exchange (erected from the designs of John Wood in 1743), Cabot Tower, the University and Clifton College. The Roman Catholic Cathedral at Clifton was opened in 1973.

The Clifton Suspension Bridge, with a span of 702 feet over the Avon, was projected by Brunel in 1836 but was not completed until 1864. Brunel's SS *Great Britain*, the first ocean-going propeller-driven ship, is now being restored in the City Docks from where she was launched in 1843.

The docks themselves have been extensively restored and redeveloped.

CAMBRIDGE

Cambridge, a settlement far older than its ancient University, lies on the River Cam or Granta. The city is a county town and regional headquarters. Its industries include electronics, high technology research and development, and biotechnology. Among its open spaces are Jesus Green, Sheep's Green, Coe Fen, Parker's Piece, Christ's Pieces, the University Botanic Garden, and the Backs, or lawns and gardens through which the Cam winds behind the principal line of college buildings. East of the Cam, King's Parade, upon which stand Great St Mary's Church, Gibbs' Senate House and King's College Chapel with Wilkins' screen, joins Trumpington Street to form one of the most beautiful throughfares in Europe.

University and college buildings provide the outstanding features of Cambridge architecture but several churches (especially St Benet's, the oldest building in the city, and St Sepulchre's, the Round Church) are also notable. The Guildhall (1939) stands on a site of which at least part has held municipal buildings since 1224.

CANTERBURY

Canterbury, the Metropolitan City of the Anglican Communion, has a history going back to prehistoric times. It was the Roman *Durovernum Cantiacorum* and the Saxon *Cant-wara-byrig* (stronghold of the men of Kent). Here in 597 St Augustine began the conversion of the English to Christianity, when Ethelbert, King of Kent, was baptized. Of the Benedictine St Augustine's Abbey, burial place of the Jutish Kings of Kent (whose capital Canterbury was), only ruins remain. St Martin's Church, on the eastern outskirts of the city, is stated by Bede to have been the place of worship of Queen Bertha, the Christian wife of King Ethelbert, before the advent of St Augustine.

In 1170 the rivalry of Church and State culminated in the murder in Canterbury Cathedral, by Henry II's knights, of Archbishop Thomas Becket, whose shrine became a great centre of pilgrimage, as described by Chaucer in his *Canterbury Tales*. After the Reformation pilgrimages ceased, but the prosperity of the city was strengthened by an influx of Huguenot refugees, who introduced weaving. The poet and playwright Christopher Marlowe was born and reared in Canterbury, and there are also literary associations with Defoe, Dickens, Joseph Conrad and Somerset Maugham.

The Cathedral, with architecture ranging from the 11th to the 15th centuries, is world famous. Modern pilgrims are attracted particularly to the Martyrdom, the Black Prince's Tomb, the Warriors' Chapel and the many examples of medieval stained glass.

The medieval city walls are built on Roman foundations and the 14th-century West Gate is one of the finest buildings of its kind in the country.

The 1,000 seat Marlowe Theatre is a centre for the Canterbury Arts Festival each autumn.

CARLISLE

Carlisle is situated at the confluence of the River Eden and River Caldew, 309 miles north-west of London and about ten miles from the Scottish border. It was granted a charter in 1158.

The city stands at the western end of Hadrian's Wall and dates from the original Roman settlement of *Luguvalium*. Granted to Scotland in the tenth century, Carlisle is not included in the Domesday Book. William Rufus reclaimed the area in 1092 and the castle and city walls were built to guard Carlisle and the western border; the citadel is a Tudor addition to protect the south of the city. Border disputes were common until the problem of the Debateable Lands was settled in 1552. During the Civil War the city remained Royalist; in 1745 Carlisle was besieged for the last time by the Young Pretender.

The Cathedral, originally a 12th-century Augustinian priory, was enlarged in the 13th and 14th centuries after the diocese was created in 1133. To the south is a restored Tithe Barn and nearby the 18th-century church of St Cuthbert, the third to stand on a site dating from the seventh century.

Carlisle is the major shopping, commercial and agricultural centre for the area, and industries include the manufacture of metal goods, biscuits and textiles. However, the largest employer is the services sector, notably in central and local government, retailing and transport. The city has an important communications position at the centre of a network of major roads, as an important stage on the main west coast rail services, and with its own airport at Crosby-on-Eden.

CHESTER

Chester is situated on the River Dee, and was granted borough and city status in 1974. Its recorded history dates from the first century when the Romans founded the fortress of *Deva*. The city's name is derived from the Latin *castra* (a camp or encampment). During the Middle Ages, Chester was the principal port of north-west England but declined with the silting of the Dee estuary and competition from Liverpool. The city was also an important military centre, notably during Edward I's Welsh campaigns and the Elizabethan Irish campaigns. During the Civil War, Chester supported the King and was besieged from 1643 to 1646. Chester's first charter was granted *c.*1175 and the city was incorporated in 1506. The office of Sheriff is the earliest created in the country (*c.*1120s), and in 1992 the Mayor was granted the title of Lord Mayor. He/she also enjoys the title 'Admiral of the Dee'.

The city's architectural features include the city walls (an almost complete two-mile circuit), the unique 13th-century Rows (covered galleries above the street-level shops), the Victorian Gothic Town Hall (1869), the Castle (rebuilt 1788 and 1822) and numerous half-timbered buildings. The Cathedral was a Benedictine abbey until the Dissolution. Remaining monastic buildings include the chapter house, refectory and cloisters and there is a modern free-standing bell tower. The Norman church of St John the Baptist was a cathedral church in the early Middle Ages.

Chester is a thriving retail, business and tourist centre.

COVENTRY

Coventry (West Midlands) is an important industrial centre, producing vehicles, machine tools, agricultural machinery, man-made fibres, aerospace components and telecommunications equipment. New investment has come from financial services, power transmission, professional services and education.

The city owes its beginning to Leofric, Earl of Mercia, and his wife Godiva who, in 1043, founded a Benedictine monastery. The guildhall of St Mary dates from the 14th century, three of the city's churches date from the 14th and 15th centuries, and 16th-century almshouses may still be seen. Coventry's first cathedral was destroyed at the Reformation, its second in the 1940 blitz (the walls and spire remain) and the new cathedral designed by Sir Basil Spence, consecrated in 1962, now draws innumerable visitors.

Coventry is the home of the University of Warwick and its Science Park, Coventry University, the Westwood Business Park, the Cable and Wireless College, and the Museum of British Road Transport.

DERBY

Derby stands on the banks of the River Derwent, and its name dates back to 880 when the Danes settled in the locality and changed the original Saxon name of *Northworthy* to *Deoraby*.

Derby has a wide range of industries: its products include aero engines, pipework, specialized mechanical engineering equipment, textiles, chemicals, plastics and the Royal Crown Derby porcelain. The city is an established railway centre, the site of British Rail's Technical Centre with its research laboratories.

Buildings of interest include St Peter's Church and the Old Abbey Building (14th century), the Cathedral (1525), St Mary's Roman Catholic Church (1839) and the Industrial Museum, formerly the Old Silk Mill (1721). The traditional city centre is complemented by the Eagle Centre and 'out-of-centre' retail developments. In addition to the Derby Playhouse, the Assembly Rooms are a multi-purpose venue.

The first charter granting a Mayor and Aldermen was that of Charles I in 1637. Previous charters date back to 1154. It was granted city status in 1977.

DURHAM

The city of Durham is a district in the county of Durham and a major tourist attraction because of its prominent Norman Cathedral and Castle set high on a wooded peninsula overlooking the River Wear. The Cathedral was founded as a shrine for the body of St Cuthbert in 995. The present building dates from 1093 and among its many treasures is the tomb of the Venerable Bede (673–735). Durham's Prince Bishops had unique powers up to 1836, being lay rulers as well as religious leaders. As a palatinate Durham could have its own army, nobility, coinage and courts. The Castle was the main seat of the Prince Bishops for nearly 800 years; it is now used as a college by the University. The University, founded on the initiative of Bishop William Van Mildert, is England's third oldest.

Among other buildings of interest is the Guildhall in the Market Place which dates originally from the 14th century. Much work has been carried out to conserve this area, forming part of the city's major contribution to the Council of Europe's Urban Renaissance Campaign. Annual events include Durham's Regatta in June (claimed to be the oldest rowing event in Britain) and the Annual Gala (formerly Durham Miners' Gala) in July.

The economy of Durham has undergone a significant change with the replacement of mining as the dominant industry by 'white collar' employment. Although still a predominantly rural area, the industrial and commercial sector is growing and a wide range of manufacturing and service industries are based on industrial estates in and around the city.

EXETER

Exeter lies on the River Exe ten miles from the sea. It was granted a charter by Henry II. The Romans founded *Isca Dumnoniorum* in the first century AD, and in the third century a stone wall (much of which remains) was built, providing protection against Saxon, and then Danish invasions. After the Conquest, the city led resistance to William in the west until reduced by siege. The Normans built the ringwork castle of Rougemont, the gatehouse and one tower of which remain, although the rest was pulled down in 1784. The first bridge across the Exe was built in the early 13th century. The city's main port was situated downstream at Topsham until the construction in the 1560s of the first true canal in England, the redevelopment of which in 1700 brought seaborne trade direct to the city. Exeter was the Royalist headquarters in the west during the Civil War.

The diocese of Exeter was established by Edward the Confessor in 1050, although a minster existed near the Cathedral site from the late seventh century. A new cathedral was built in the 12th century but the present building was begun c.1275, although incorporating the Norman towers, and completed about a century later. The Guildhall dates from the 12th century and there are many other medieval buildings in the city, as well as architecture in the Georgian and Regency styles, and the Custom House (1680). Damage suffered by bombing in 1942 led to the redevelopment of the city centre.

Exeter's prosperity from medieval times was based on trade in wool and woollen cloth (commemorated by Tuckers Hall), which remained at its height until the late 18th century when export trade was hit by the French wars. Subsequently Exeter has developed as an administrative and commercial centre, notably in the distributive trades, light manufacturing industries and tourism.

KINGSTON UPON HULL

Hull (officially Kingston upon Hull) lies at the junction of the River Hull with the Humber, 22 miles from the North Sea. It is one of the major seaports of the United Kingdom. It has docks covering a water area of 172 acres, equipped to handle cargoes by unit-load techniques, and is a departure point for car ferry services to continental Europe. There is a variety of industry and service industries, as well as increasing tourism and conference business.

The city, restored after heavy air raid damage during the Second World War, has good office and administrative buildings, its municipal centre being the Guildhall, its educational centres the University of Hull and Humberside University and its religious centre the Parish Church of the Holy Trinity. The old town area is being renovated and includes a marina and shopping complex. Just west of the city is the Humber Bridge, the world's longest single-span suspension bridge.

Kingston upon Hull was so named by Edward I. City status was accorded in 1897 and the office of Mayor raised to the dignity of Lord Mayor in 1914.

LEEDS

Leeds (West Yorkshire), situated in the lower Aire Valley, is a junction for road, rail, canal and air services and an important manufacturing and commercial centre. Seventy-three per cent of employment is in services, notably the distributive trades, public administration, medical services and business services. The main manufacturing industries are mechanical engineering, printing and publishing, metal goods and furniture.

The principal buildings are the Civic Hall (1933), the Town Hall (1858), the Municipal Buildings and Art Gallery (1884) with the Henry Moore Gallery (1982), the Corn Exchange (1863) and the University. The Parish Church (St Peter's) was rebuilt in 1841; the 17th-century St John's Church has a fine interior with a famous English Renaissance screen; the last remaining 18th-century church in the city is Holy Trinity in Boar Lane (1727). Kirkstall Abbey (about three miles from the centre of the city), founded by Henry de Lacy in 1152, is one of the most

complete examples of Cistercian houses now remaining. Temple Newsam, birthplace of Lord Darnley, was acquired by the Council in 1922. The present house was largely rebuilt by Sir Arthur Ingram in about 1620. Adel Church, about five miles from the centre of the city, is a fine Norman structure. The new Royal Armouries Museum houses the collection of antique arms and armour formerly held at the Tower of London.

Leeds was first incorporated by Charles I in 1626. The earliest forms of the name are Loidis or Ledes, the origins of which are obscure.

LEICESTER

Leicester is situated geographically in the centre of England. It dates back to pre-Roman times and was one of the five Danish Burghs. In 1589 Queen Elizabeth I granted a charter to the city and the ancient title was confirmed by letters patent in 1919.

The principal industries are hosiery, knitwear, footwear manufacturing and engineering. The growth of Leicester as a hosiery centre increased rapidly from the introduction there of the first stocking frame in 1670 and today it has some of the largest hosiery factories in the world.

The principal buildings are the Town Hall, the New Walk Centre, the University of Leicester, De Montfort University, De Montfort Hall, one of the finest concert halls in the provinces seating over 2,750 people, and the Granby Halls, an indoor sports facility. The ancient churches of St Martin (now Leicester Cathedral), St Nicholas, St Margaret, All Saints, St Mary de Castro, and buildings such as the Guildhall, the 14th-century Newarke Gate, the Castle and the Jewry Wall Roman site still exist. The Haymarket Theatre was opened in 1973 and The Shires shopping centre in 1992.

LINCOLN

Situated 40 miles inland on the River Witham, Lincoln derives its name from a contraction of *Lindum Colonia*, the settlement founded in AD 48 by the Romans to command the crossing of Ermine Street and Fosse Way. Sections of the third-century Roman city wall can be seen, including an extant gateway (Newport Arch), and excavations have discovered traces of a sewerage system unique in Britain. The Romans also drained the surrounding fenland and created a canal system, laying the foundations of Lincoln's agricultural prosperity and also of the city's importance in the medieval wool trade as a port and Staple town.

As one of the Five Boroughs of the Danelaw, Lincoln was an important trading centre in the ninth and tenth centuries and medieval prosperity from the wool trade lasted until the 14th century, enabling local merchants to build parish churches (of which three survive), and attracting in the 12th century a Jewish community (Jew's House and Court, Aaron's House). However, the removal of the Staple to Boston in 1369 heralded a decline from which the city only recovered fully in the 19th century when improved fen drainage made Lincoln agriculturally important and improved canal and rail links led to industrial development, mainly in the manufacture of machinery, components and engineering products.

The castle was built shortly after the Conquest and is unusual in having two mounds; on one motte stands a Keep (Lucy's Tower) added in the 12th century. It currently houses one of the four surviving copies of the Magna Carta. The Cathedral was begun c.1073 when the first Norman bishop moved the see of Lindsey to Lincoln, but was mostly destroyed by fire and earthquake in the 12th century. Rebuilding was begun by St Hugh and completed over a century later. Other notable architectural features are the 12th-century High Bridge, the oldest in Britain still to carry buildings, and the Guildhall situated above the 15th–16th-century Stonebow gateway.

LIVERPOOL

Liverpool (Merseyside) on the right bank of the River Mersey, three miles from the Irish Sea, is the United Kingdom's foremost port for the Atlantic trade. Tunnels link Liverpool with Birkenhead and Wallasey.

There are 2,100 acres of dockland on both sides of the river and the Gladstone and Royal Seaforth Docks can accommodate the largest vessels afloat. Annual tonnage of cargo handled is approximately 27.8 million tonnes. The main imports are crude oil, grain, ores, edible oils, timber, containers and break-bulk cargo. Liverpool Free Port, Britain's largest, was opened in 1984.

Liverpool was created a free borough in 1207 and a city in 1880. From the early 18th century it expanded rapidly with the growth of industrialization and the Atlantic trade. Surviving buildings from this date include the Bluecoat Chambers (1717, formerly the Bluecoat School), the Town Hall (1754, rebuilt to the original design 1795), and buildings in Rodney Street, Canning Street and the suburbs. Notable from the 19th and 20th centuries are the Anglican Cathedral, built from the designs of Sir Giles Gilbert Scott (the foundation stone was laid in 1904, and the building was completed only in 1980), the Catholic Metropolitan Cathedral (designed by Sir Frederick Gibberd, consecrated 1967) and St George's Hall (1838–54), regarded as one of the finest modern examples of classical architecture. The refurbished Albert Dock (designed by Jesse Hartley) contains the Merseyside Maritime Museum and Tate Gallery, Liverpool.

In 1852 an Act was obtained for establishing a public library, museum and art gallery; as a result Liverpool had one of the first public libraries in the country. The Brown, Picton and Hornby Libraries now form one of the country's major libraries. The Victoria Building of Liverpool University, the Royal Liver, Cunard and Mersey Docks & Harbour Company buildings at the Pier Head, the Municipal Buildings and the Philharmonic Hall are other examples of the city's fine buildings.

MANCHESTER

Manchester (the *Mamucium* of the Romans, who occupied it in AD 79) is a commercial and industrial centre with a population engaged in the engineering, chemical, clothing, food processing and textile industries, and in education. Banking, insurance and a growing leisure industry are among the prime commercial activities. The city is connected with the sea by the Manchester Ship Canal, opened in 1894, 35½ miles long, and accommodating ships up to 15,000 tons. Manchester Airport handles 15 million passengers yearly.

The principal buildings are the Town Hall, erected in 1877 from the designs of Alfred Waterhouse, together with a large extension of 1938; the Royal Exchange (1869, enlarged 1921); the Central Library (1934); Heaton Hall; the 17th-century Chetham Library; the Rylands Library (1900), which includes the Althorp collection; the University precinct; the 15th-century Cathedral (formerly the parish church); G-MEX exhibition centre and the Free Trade Hall. Recent developments include the Manchester Arena, the largest indoor arena in Europe. Manchester is the home of the Hallé Orchestra, the Royal Northern College of Music, the Royal Exchange Theatre and seven public art galleries. Metrolink, the new light rail system, opened in 1992.

The town received its first charter of incorporation in 1838 and was created a city in 1853. The title of City was retained under local government reorganization.

NEWCASTLE UPON TYNE

Newcastle upon Tyne (Tyne and Wear), on the north bank of the River Tyne, is eight miles from the North Sea. A cathedral and university city, it is the administrative, commercial and cultural centre for north-east England and the principal port. It is an important manufacturing centre with a wide variety of industries.

The principal buildings include the Castle Keep (12th century), Black Gate (13th century), Blackfriars (13th century), West Walls (13th century), St Nicholas's Cathedral (15th century, fine lantern tower), St Andrew's Church (12th–14th century), St John's (14th–15th century), All Saints (1786 by Stephenson), St Mary's Roman Catholic Cathedral (1844), Trinity House (17th century), Sandhill (16th-century houses), Guildhall (Georgian), Grey Street (1834–9), Central Station (1846–50), Laing Art Gallery (1904), University of Newcastle Physics Building (1962) and Medical Building (1985), Civic Centre (1963), Central Library (1969) and Eldon Square Shopping Development (1976). Open spaces include the Town Moor (927 acres) and Jesmond Dene. Nine bridges span the Tyne at Newcastle.

The city derives its name from the 'new castle' (1080) erected as a defence against the Scots. In 1400 it was made a county, and in 1882 a city.

NORWICH

Norwich (Norfolk) grew from an early Anglo-Saxon settlement near the confluence of the Rivers Yare and Wensum, and now serves as provincial capital for the predominantly agricultural region of East Anglia. The name is thought to relate to the most northerly of a group of Anglo-Saxon villages or *wics*. The city's first known charter was granted in 1158 by Henry II.

Norwich serves its surrounding area as a market town and commercial centre, banking and insurance being prominent among the city's businesses. From the 14th century until the Industrial Revolution, Norwich was the regional centre of the woollen industry, but now the biggest single industry is financial services and principal trades are engineering, printing, shoemaking, double glazing, and the production of chemicals, clothing and food processing. Norwich is accessible to seagoing vessels by means of the River Yare, entered at Great Yarmouth, 20 miles to the east.

Among many historic buildings are the Cathedral (completed in the 12th century and surmounted by a 15th-century spire 315 feet in height), the keep of the Norman castle (now a museum and art gallery), the 15th-century flint-walled Guildhall (now a tourist information centre), some thirty medieval parish churches, St Andrew's and Blackfriars' Halls, the Tudor houses preserved in Elm Hill and the Georgian Assembly House. The University of East Anglia is located on a site at Earlham on the city's western boundary.

NOTTINGHAM

Nottingham stands on the River Trent and is connected by canal with the Atlantic Ocean and the North Sea. *Snotinga-ham* or *Notingeham*, literally the homestead of the people of Snot, is the Anglo-Saxon name for the Celtic settlement of *Tigguocobauc*, or the house of caves. In 878, Nottingham became one of the Five Boroughs of the Danelaw. William the Conqueror ordered the construction of Nottingham

Castle, while the town itself developed rapidly under Norman rule. Its laws and rights were later formally recognized by Henry II's charter in 1155. The Castle became a favoured residence of King John. In 1642 King Charles I raised his personal standard at Nottingham Castle at the start of the Civil War.

Nottingham is a major sporting centre, home to Nottingham Forest FC, Notts County FC (the world's oldest Football league side), Nottingham Racecourse and the National Watersports Centre. The principal industries include textiles, pharmaceuticals, food manufacturing, engineering and telecommunications. There are two universities within the city boundaries.

Architecturally, Nottingham has a wealth of notable buildings, particularly those designed in the Victorian era by T. C. Hine and Watson Fothergill. The City Council owns the Castle, of Norman origin but restored in 1878, Wollaton Hall (1580–8), Newstead Abbey (home of Lord Byron), the Guildhall (1888) and Council House (1929). St Mary's, St Peter's and St Nicholas's Churches are of interest, as is the Roman Catholic Cathedral (Pugin, 1842–4).

Nottingham was granted city status in 1897.

OXFORD

Oxford is a university city, an important industrial centre, and a market town. Industry played a minor part in Oxford until the motor industry was established in 1912.

It is for its architecture that Oxford is of most interest to the visitor, its oldest specimens being the reputedly Saxon tower of St Michael's church, the remains of the Norman castle and city walls, and the Norman church at Iffley. It is chiefly famous, however, for its Gothic buildings, such as the Divinity Schools, the Old Library at Merton College, William of Wykeham's New College, Magdalen College and Christ Church and many other college buildings. Later centuries are represented by the Laudian quadrangle at St John's College, the Renaissance Sheldonian Theatre by Wren, Trinity College Chapel, and All Saints Church; Hawksmoor's mock-Gothic at All Souls College, and the 18th-century Queen's College. In addition to individual buildings, High Street and Radcliffe Square, just off it, both form architectural compositions of great beauty. Most of the Colleges have gardens, those of Magdalen, New College, St John's and Worcester being the largest.

PLYMOUTH

Plymouth is situated on the borders of Devon and Cornwall at the confluence of the Rivers Tamar and Plym. The city has a long maritime history; it was the home port of Sir Francis Drake and the starting point for his circumnavigation of the world, as well as the last port of call for the *Mayflower* when the Pilgrim Fathers sailed for the New World in 1620. Today Plymouth is host to many international yacht races. The Barbican harbour area has many Elizabethan buildings and on Plymouth Hoe stands Smeaton's lighthouse, the third to be built on the Eddystone Rocks 13 miles offshore.

The city centre was rebuilt following extensive war damage, and comprises a large shopping centre, municipal offices, law courts and public buildings. The main employment is provided at the naval base, though many industrial firms and service industries have become established in the post-war period and the city is a growing tourism centre. In 1982 the Theatre Royal was opened. In conjunction with the Cornwall County Council, the Tamar Bridge was constructed linking the city by road with Cornwall.

PORTSMOUTH

Portsmouth occupies Portsea Island, Hampshire, with boundaries extending to the mainland. It is a centre of industry and commerce, including many high technology and manufacturing industries. It is the British headquarters of several major international companies. The Royal Navy base still has a substantial work-force, although this has decreased in recent years. The commercial port and continental ferry port is owned and run by the City Council, and carries passengers and vehicles to France and northern Spain.

A major port since the 16th century, Portsmouth is also a thriving seaside resort catering for thousands of visitors annually. Among many historic attractions are Lord Nelson's flagship, HMS *Victory*, the Tudor warship *Mary Rose*, Britain's first 'ironclad' warship, HMS *Warrior*, the D-Day Museum, Charles Dickens' birthplace at 393 Old Commercial Road, the Royal Naval and Royal Marine museums, Southsea Castle (built by Henry VIII), the Round Tower and Point Battery, which for hundreds of years have guarded the entrance to Portsmouth Harbour, Fort Nelson on Portsdown Hill and the Sealife Centre.

ST ALBANS

The origins of St Albans, situated on the River Ver, stem from the Roman town of *Verulamium*. Named after the first Christian martyr in Britain, who was executed here, St Albans has developed around the Norman Abbey and Cathedral Church (consecrated 1115), built partly of materials from the old Roman city. The museums house Iron Age and Roman artefacts and the Roman Theatre, unique in Britain, has a stage as opposed to an amphitheatre. Archaeological excavations in the city centre have revealed evidence of pre-Roman, Saxon and medieval occupation.

The town's significance grew to the extent that it was a signatory and venue for the drafting of the Magna Carta. It was also the scene of riots during the Peasants' Revolt, the French King John was imprisoned there after the Battle of Poitiers, and heavy fighting took place there during the Wars of the Roses.

Previously controlled by the Abbot, the town achieved a charter in 1553 and city status in 1877. The street market, first established in 1553, is still an important feature of the city, as are many hotels and inns which survive from the days when St Albans was an important coach stop. Tourist attractions include historic churches and houses, and a 15th-century clock tower.

The city now contains a wide range of firms, with special emphasis on micro-technology and electronics, particularly in the medical field. In addition, it is the home of the Royal National Rose Society, and of Rothamsted Park, the agricultural research centre.

SHEFFIELD

Sheffield (South Yorkshire), the centre of the special steel and cutlery trades, is situated at the junction of the Sheaf, Porter, Rivelin and Loxley valleys with the River Don. Though its cutlery, silverware and plate have long been famous, Sheffield has other and now more important industries: special and alloy steels, engineering, tool-making and medical equipment. Sheffield has two universities and is an important research centre.

The parish church of St Peter and St Paul, founded in the 12th century, became the Cathedral Church of the Diocese of Sheffield in 1914. The Roman Catholic Cathedral Church of St Marie (founded 1847) was created Cathedral for the new diocese of Hallam in 1980. Parts of the present building date from c.1435. The principal buildings are the Town Hall (1897), the Cutlers' Hall (1832), City Hall (1932), Graves Art Gallery (1934), Mappin Art Gallery, the Crucible Theatre and the restored 19th-century Lyceum theatre, which dates from 1897 and was reopened in 1990. Three major sports venues were opened in 1990 to 1991.

Sheffield was created a city in 1893 and in 1974 retained its city status.

Master Cutler of the Company of Cutlers in Hallamshire 1995–6,
    D. R. Stone

SOUTHAMPTON

Southampton is the leading British deep-sea port on the Channel and is situated on one of the finest natural harbours in the world. The first charter was granted by Henry II and Southampton was created a county of itself in 1447. In 1964 it was granted city status.

There were Roman and Saxon settlements on the site of the city, which has been an important port since the time of the Conquest due to its natural deep-water harbour. The oldest church is St Michael's (1070) which has an unusually tall spire built in the 18th century as a landmark for navigators of Southampton Water. Other buildings and monuments within the city walls are the Tudor House Museum, God's House Tower, the Bargate museum, the Tudor Merchants Hall, the Weigh-house, West Gate, King John's House, Long House, Wool House, the ruins of Holy Rood Church, St Julien's Church and the Mayflower Memorial. The medieval town walls, built for artillery, are among the most complete in Europe. Public open spaces total over 1,000 acres and comprise 9 per cent of the city's area. The Common covers an area of 328 acres in the central district of the city and is mostly natural parkland. Two recent additions to work in marine technology in Southampton are Europe's leading oceanographic research centre (part of the University) and the marine science and technology business park.

STOKE-ON-TRENT

Stoke-on-Trent (Staffordshire), standing on the River Trent and familiarly known as The Potteries, is the main centre of employment for the population of North Staffordshire. The city is the largest clayware producer in the world (china, earthenware, sanitary goods, refractories, bricks and tiles) and also has a wide range of other manufacturing industry, including steel, chemicals, engineering and tyres. Extensive reconstruction has been carried out in recent years.

The city was formed by the federation of the separate municipal authorities of Tunstall, Burslem, Hanley, Stoke, Fenton, and Longton in 1910 and received its city status in 1925.

WINCHESTER

Winchester, the ancient capital of England, is situated on the River Itchen. The city is rich in architecture of all types but the Cathedral takes pride of place. The longest Gothic cathedral in the world, it was built in 1079–93 and exhibits examples of Norman, Early English and Perpendicular styles. Winchester College, founded in 1382, is one of the most famous public schools, the original building (1393) remaining largely unaltered. St Cross Hospital, another great medieval foundation, lies one mile south of the city. The almshouses were founded in 1136 by Bishop Henry de Blois, and Cardinal Henry Beaufort added a new almshouse of 'Noble Poverty' in 1446. The chapel and dwell-

ings are of great architectural interest, and visitors may still receive the 'Wayfarer's Dole' of bread and ale.

Excavations have done much to clarify the origins and development of Winchester. Part of the forum and several of the streets of the Roman town have been discovered; excavations in the Cathedral Close have uncovered the entire site of the Anglo-Saxon cathedral (known as the Old Minster) and parts of the New Minster which was built by Alfred's son Edward the Elder and is the burial place of the Alfredian dynasty. The original burial place of St Swithun, before his remains were translated to a site in the present cathedral, was also uncovered.

Excavations in other parts of the city have thrown much light on Norman Winchester, notably on the site of the Royal Castle (adjacent to which the new Law Courts have been built) and in the grounds of Wolvesey Castle, where the great house built by Bishops Giffard and Henry de Blois in the 12th century has been uncovered. The Great Hall, built by Henry III between 1222 and 1236 survives and houses the Arthurian Round Table.

YORK

The city of York is an archiepiscopal seat. Its recorded history dates from AD 71, when the Roman Ninth Legion established a base under Petilius Cerealis which later became the fortress of *Eburacum*. In Anglo-Saxon times the city was the royal and ecclesiastical centre of Northumbria, and after capture by a Viking army in AD 866 it became the capital of the Viking kingdom of Jorvik. By the 14th century the city had become a great mercantile centre, mainly because of its control of the wool trade, and was used as the chief base against the Scots. Under the Tudors its fortunes declined, though Henry VIII made it the headquarters of the Council of the North. Excavations on many sites, including Coppergate, have greatly expanded knowledge of Roman, Viking and medieval urban life.

With its development as a railway centre in the 19th century the commercial life of York expanded. The principal industries are the manufacture of chocolate, scientific instruments and sugar. It is the location of several government departments.

The city is rich in examples of architecture of all periods. The earliest church was built in AD 627 and, in the 12th to 15th centuries, the present Minster was built in a succession of styles. Other examples within the city are the medieval city walls and gateways, churches and guildhalls. Domestic architecture includes the Georgian mansions of The Mount, Micklegate and Bootham.

English Counties and Shires

LORD LIEUTENANTS AND HIGH SHERIFFS

County/Shire	Lord Lieutenant	High Sheriff, 1996–7
Bedfordshire	S. C. Whitbread	J. J. M. Glasse
Berkshire	P. L. Wroughton	C. Spence
Bristol	J. Tidmarsh, MBE	G. Ferguson
Buckinghamshire	Sir Nigel Mobbs (from Jan. 1997)	R. E. Morris-Adams
Cambridgeshire	J. G. P. Crowden	N. H. M. Chancellor
Cheshire	W. Bromley Davenport	Sir Anthony Pilkington
Cornwall	Lady Holborow	Mrs D. Morrison
Cumbria	J. A. Cropper	H. C. F. Bowring
Derbyshire	J. K. Bather	Brig. C. E. Wilkinson, CBE, TD
Devon	The Earl of Morley	Mrs Y. M. V. Tremlett
Dorset	The Lord Digby	W. J. Weld
Durham	D. J. Grant, CBE	J. A. Marr
East Riding of Yorkshire	R. Marriott, TD	T. Martin
East Sussex	Adm. Sir Lindsay Bryson, KCB, FEng.	J. Fooks
Essex	The Lord Braybrooke	P. T. Thistlethwayte
Gloucestershire	H. W. G. Elwes	J. G. Peel
Greater London	Field Marshal the Lord Bramall, KG, GCB, OBE, MC	Sir Cyril Taylor
Greater Manchester	Col. J. B. Timmins, OBE, TD	Mrs M. F. MacKinnon Firth, OBE
Hampshire	Mrs F. M. Fagan	M. Radcliffe
Hereford and Worcester	Sir Thomas Dunne, KCVO	Mrs R. S. Clive
Hertfordshire	S. A. Bowes Lyon	R. Dimsdale
Isle of Wight	*C. D. J. Bland	Mrs J. A. Griffin
Kent	The Lord Kingsdown, KG, PC	P. Smallwood
Lancashire	Sir Simon Towneley, KCVO	T. R. H. Kimber
Leicestershire	T. G. M. Brooks	G. N. Corah
Lincolnshire	Mrs B. K. Cracroft-Eley	J. Milligan-Manby
Merseyside	A. W. Waterworth	Mrs J. A. Grundy
Norfolk	Sir Timothy Colman, KG	I. D. R. MacNicol, FRICS
Northamptonshire	J. L. Lowther, CBE	M. F. Collcutt
Northumberland	The Viscount Ridley, KG, GCVO, TD	J. F. C. Festing
North Yorkshire	Sir Marcus Worsley, Bt.	J. L. C. Pratt
Nottinghamshire	Sir Andrew Buchanan, Bt.	T. Parr
Oxfordshire	H. L. J. Brunner	M. Cochrane
Shropshire	A. E. H. Heber-Percy	T. W. E. Corbett
Somerset	Sir John Vernon Wills, Bt., TD	C. Thomas-Everard, FRICS
South Yorkshire	The Earl of Scarbrough	W. G. A. Warde-Norbury
Staffordshire	J. A. Hawley, TD	S. E. Mitchell
Suffolk	The Lord Belstead, PC	J. Kerr, MBE
Surrey	R. E. Thornton, OBE	A. Sanders
Tyne and Wear	Sir Ralph Carr-Ellison, TD	Dr M. L. Fisher
Warwickshire	The Viscount Daventry	Maj. J. W. Oakes
West Midlands	R. R. Taylor, OBE	J. D. Saville
West Sussex	Maj.-Gen. Sir Philip Ward, KCVO, CBE	J. Knight
West Yorkshire	J. Lyles	J. S. Behrens
Wiltshire	Lt.-Gen. Sir Maurice Johnston, KCB, OBE	A. W. M. Christie-Miller

* Lord Lieutenant and Governor

COUNTY COUNCILS: Area, Population, Finance

Council	Administrative headquarters	Area (hectares)	Population 1994	Total demand upon collection fund 1996–7
Bedfordshire	County Hall, Bedford	123,468	543,100	£89,379,000
Berkshire	Shire Hall, Shinfield Park, Reading	125,901	769,200	137,660,000
Buckinghamshire	County Hall, Aylesbury	188,279	658,400	118,700,000
Cambridgeshire	Shire Hall, Cambridge	340,181	686,900	107,400,000
Cheshire	County Hall, Chester	233,325	975,600	178,581,418
Cornwall	County Hall, Truro	356,442†	479,600†	76,054,000
Cumbria	The Courts, Carlisle	682,451	490,200	86,787,000
Derbyshire	County Offices, Matlock	263,098	954,100	152,900,000
Devon	County Hall, Exeter	671,096	1,053,400	164,585,000
Dorset	County Hall, Dorchester	265,433	673,000	117,656,209
Durham	County Hall, Durham	243,369	607,800	81,899,510
East Sussex	Pelham House, St Andrew's Lane, Lewes	179,530	726,500	129,431,000
Essex	County Hall, Chelmsford	367,167	1,569,900	259,656,000
Gloucestershire	Shire Hall, Gloucester	264,270	549,500	88,913,412
Hampshire	The Castle, Winchester	378,022	1,605,700	255,214,000
Hereford and Worcester	County Hall, Worcester	392,650	699,900	109,882,000
Hertfordshire	County Hall, Hertford	163,601	1,005,400	179,025,000
§Isle of Wight	County Hall, Newport, IOW	38,063	124,600	27,783,500
Kent	County Hall, Maidstone	373,063	1,546,300	25,500,000
Lancashire	County Hall, Preston	306,957	1,424,000	237,191,000
Leicestershire	County Hall, Glenfield, Leicester	255,297	916,900	133,221,000
Lincolnshire	County Offices, Newland, Lincoln	591,791	605,600	91,135,000
Norfolk	County Hall, Norwich	537,482	768,500	118,458,000
Northamptonshire	County Hall, Northampton	236,721	594,800	90,465,384
Northumberland	County Hall, Morpeth	503,165	307,700	51,222,531
North Yorkshire	County Hall, Northallerton	803,741	726,100	91,048,594
Nottinghamshire	County Hall, Nottingham	216,090	1,030,900	172,615,513
Oxfordshire	County Hall, Oxford	260,798	590,200	109,594,000
Shropshire	The Shirehall, Shrewsbury	349,013	416,500	63,709,000
Somerset	County Hall, Taunton	345,233	477,900	82,000,000
Staffordshire	County Buildings, Stafford	271,616	1,054,400	145,145,432
Suffolk	County Hall, Ipswich	379,664	649,500	101,722,000
Surrey	County Hall, Kingston upon Thames	167,924	1,041,200	211,700,000
Warwickshire	Shire Hall, Warwick	198,052	496,300	90,714,000
West Sussex	County Hall, Chichester	198,935	722,100	134,600,000
Wiltshire	County Hall, Trowbridge	347,883	586,300	95,323,000

Source for population figures: OPCS Monitor PP1 96/1, 29 February 1996
† Including Isles of Scilly
§ Unitary authority since April 1995

COUNTY COUNCILS: Officers and Chairman

Council	Chief Executive	County Treasurer	Chairman of County Council
Bedfordshire	D. Cleggett	*B. Phelps	B. K. W. Gibbons
Berkshire	°G. B. Scotford, OBE	†I. Thompson	M. L. Tomkinson
Buckinghamshire	I. Crookall	**J. Beckerlegg	K. I. Ross
Cambridgeshire	A. G. Lister	*D. Earle	J. L. Gluza
Cheshire	M. E. Pitt	‡‡J. E. H. Whiteoak	W. E. Leathwood
Cornwall	J. Mills	F. Twyning	A. R. J. Horn
Cumbria	J. E. Burnet	§R. F. Mather	C. L. Tuley, MBE
Derbyshire	J. S. Raine	P. Swaby	H. Lowe
Devon	P. Jenkinson	J. Glasby	E. J. Kingston
Dorset	P. K. Harvey	A. P. Peel	Mrs P. A. Hymers
Durham	K. W. Smith	J. Kirkby	J. Walker
East Sussex	††Mrs C. Miller	J. Davies	D. Norcross
Essex	K. W. S. Ashurst	K. D. Neale	W. Archibald
Gloucestershire	M. Honey	**J. R. Cockroft	F. R. Thompson
Hampshire	P. C. B. Robertson	J. E. Scotford, CBE	N. A. Best, CBE
Hereford and Worcester	J. W. Turnbull	P. Middleborough	J. W. Wardle, MBE
Hertfordshire	B. Ogley	*C. Sweeney	Mrs I. Tarry, CBE
Isle of Wight	‡F. Hetherington	J. Pulsford	Mrs M. O'Neill Stolworthy
Kent	P. R. Sabin	*P. Martin	P. Morgan
Lancashire	G. A. Johnson	B. G. Aldred	D. Yates
Leicestershire	J. B. Sinnott	R. Hale	J. M. Roberts
Lincolnshire	J. Barrow	P. Brittain	Mrs E. Davies
Norfolk	T. J. Byles	R. D. Summers	R. D. Phelan
Northamptonshire	J. V. Picking	*R. Paver	J. J. Gardner
Northumberland	°°K. Morris	*K. Morris	T. Wallace
North Yorkshire	J. A. Ransford	J. S. Moore	T. K. Hull
Nottinghamshire	P. Housden	R. Latham	B. Grocock
Oxfordshire	J. Harwood	C. Gray	D. Buckle
Shropshire	A. J. Barnish	N. T. Pursey	G. Raxster
Somerset	B. M. Tanner	C. N. Bilsland	R. B. Clark
Staffordshire	B. A. Price	R. G. Tettenborn, OBE	W. F. Austin
Suffolk	P. F. Bye	P. B. Atkinson	K. J. Doran
Surrey	P. Coen	‡‡P. Derrick	Baroness Thomas of Walliswood, OBE
Warwickshire	I. G. Caulfield	S. R. Freer	B. Kirton
West Sussex	D. P. Rigg	Mrs H. Kilpatrick	C. Robinson
Wiltshire	Dr K. Robinson	D. Chalker	Mrs J. M. Wood

* Director of Finance
° County Manager
† County Finance Officer
** Director of Corporate Services
°° Managing Director
†† Head of Paid Service
‡‡ Director of Resources
§ Director of Corporate Finance
‡ Clerk to the Council

540   Local Government

Unitary Councils

SMALL CAPITALS denote CITY status
§ Denotes Metropolitan council

Council	Population 1994	Band D charge 1996*	Chief Executive	Mayor (a) Lord Mayor (b) Chairman 1996–7
§Barnsley	226,500	£554.08	J. Edwards	C. Rowe
Bath and North-East Somerset	†158,692	675.00	T. du Sautoy	Ms M. Feeny
§BIRMINGHAM	1,008,400	681.02	M. Lyons	(a) Ms M. Arnott-Job
§Bolton	265,200	732.90	B. Collinge	E. Johnson
§BRADFORD	481,700	646.94	R. Penn	(a) G. Mitchell
BRISTOL	†374,300	871.46	Ms L. de Groot	Ms J. McLaren
§Bury	182,200	651.71	D. J. Burton	T. Holt
§Calderdale	193,600	740.80	M. Ellison	Ms D. Neal
§COVENTRY	302,500	808.68	I. Roxburgh	(a) S. Hodson
§Doncaster	292,500	592.52	J. D. Hale	Mrs D. M. Layton
§Dudley	312,200	637.29	A. V. Astling	W. P. Cody
East Riding of Yorkshire	†310,000	729.87	D. Stephenson	(b) P. Rounding
§Gateshead	202,400	778.50	L. N. Elton	W. Maddison
Hartlepool	†90,409	836.69	B. J. Dinsdale	H. J. Bishop
KINGSTON UPON HULL	†265,000	655.29	I. Crookham	(a) J. S. Mulgrove, MBE
§Kirklees	386,900	759.00	R. V. Hughes	Ms A. Harrison
§Knowsley	154,000	774.04	D. Henshaw	J. Gallagher
§LEEDS	724,400	635.29	‡P. Smith	(a) M. J. Bedford
§LIVERPOOL	474,000	1006.46	P. Bounds	(a) F. Doran
§MANCHESTER	431,100	838.36	A. Sandford	(a) D. Shaw
Middlesbrough	†146,000	639.45	D. W. Ashton	R. Regan
§NEWCASTLE UPON TYNE	283,600	770.82	G. N. Cook	(a) L. A. Russell
North East Lincolnshire	†164,000	735.48	R. Bennett	(b) L. T. Taylor
North Lincolnshire	†153,000	886.82	Dr M. Garnett	Ms J. Metcalfe
North Somerset	†177,000	615.93	P. May	(b) D. Walker
§North Tyneside	194,100	743.17	Executive Directorate	R. W. Schofield
§Oldham	220,400	768.00	C. Smith	(a) A. Griffiths
Redcar and Cleveland	†144,000	858.00	A. W. Kilburn	(b) Ms F. Christie
§Rochdale	207,100	726.68	J. F. D. Pierce	S. Emmott
§Rotherham	256,300	676.89	J. Bell	J. P. Wardle
§St Helens	181,000	777.87	Mrs C. Hudson	A. Worth
§SALFORD	230,700	813.75	J. C. Willis	J. Gaffney
§Sandwell	293,700	679.23	N. Summers	R. S. Badham
§Sefton	292,400	749.82	G. J. Haywood	T. J. Francis
§SHEFFIELD	530,100	725.17	Mrs P. J. Gordon	(a) P. Price
§Solihull	202,000	616.73	Dr N. H. Perry	L. W. P. Kyles
South Gloucestershire	†220,000	640.00	**M. Robinson	(b) L. Bishop
§South Tyneside	156,700	708.66	‡‡P. J. Haigh	W. E. Brady
§Stockport	291,400	803.48	J. Schultz	Ms A. Graham
Stockton-on-Tees	†176,600	746.03	G. Garlick	R. Gibson
§SUNDERLAND	297,200	652.24	Dr C. W. Sinclair	(a) I. Galbraith
§Tameside	221,800	756.00	M. J. Greenwood	M. P. Ballagher
§Trafford	218,100	591.66	W. Allan Lewis	L. T. Murkin
§WAKEFIELD	317,300	580.53	R. Mather	(a) K. Bolland
§Walsall	263,900	718.49	D. C. Winchurch	R. Worrall
§Wigan	310,000	699.60	S. M. Jones	A. B. Coyle, OBE
§Wirral	333,100	773.70	A. White	Mrs N. M. Lea
§Wolverhampton	245,100	725.04	D. Anderson	G. F. Howells
YORK	†104,100	574.24	D. Clark	(a) K. King

Source of 1994 population figures: OPCS Monitor PP1 96/1, 29 February 1996
† 1996 figures given for new unitary authorities
* For explanation of council tax, see pages 519–20
‡ The Chief Officer
** Head of Paid Service
‡‡ Director of Corporate Services

Non-Metropolitan Councils

SMALL CAPITALS denote CITY status
§ Denotes Borough status
Source of population figures: OPCS Monitor PP1 96/1, 29 February 1996
For explanation of council tax, see pages 519–20

Council	Population 1994	Band D charge 1996	Chief Executive	Chairman 1996–7 (a) Mayor (b) Lord Mayor
Adur, West Sussex	57,900	£654.00	F. M. G. Staden	D. Hancock
§Allerdale, Cumbria	96,100	699.39	C. J. Hart	(a) Mrs J. Tweddle
Alnwick, Northumberland	30,600	680.00	L. St Ruth	J. Hinson
§Amber Valley, Derbyshire	114,500	679.14	P. M. Carney	(a) E. J. Chapman
Arun, West Sussex	134,300	628.03	I. Sumnall	Mrs J. Goad
Ashfield, Nottinghamshire	109,900	690.72	†N. Bernasconi	Mrs G. Thierry
§Ashford, Kent	94,800	585.35	D. Lambert	(a) S. J. G. Koowaree
Aylesbury Vale, Bucks	152,000	570.00	B. Hurley	Mrs A. Davies
Babergh, Suffolk	78,800	598.44	D. C. Bishop	Mrs J. Law
§Barrow-in-Furness, Cumbria	72,100	733.33	T. O. Campbell	(a) S. Derbyshire
Basildon, Essex	162,100	651.96	J. Robb	Ms A. Bruce
§Basingstoke and Deane, Hants	147,200	569.64	Ms K. Sporle	(a) L. T. Garland
Bassetlaw, Notts	105,500	716.93	M. S. Havenhand	B. Macaulay
§Bedford	137,000	635.51	L. W. Gould	(a) A. Bagchi
§Berwick-upon-Tweed, Northumberland	26,500	683.46	E. O. Cawthorn	(a) J. D. Lockie
Blaby, Leics	85,300	528.52	‡E. Hemsley	J. T. Roper
§Blackburn, Lancs	140,100	781.31	G. L. Davies	(a) Ms M. Leaver
§Blackpool, Lancs	154,000	665.93	G. E. Essex-Crosby	(a) L. Kersh
§Blyth Valley, Northumberland	80,600	663.50	D. Crawford	(a) R. Allan
Bolsover, Derbyshire	70,800	721.25	J. R. Fotherby	C. R. Moseby
§Boston, Lincs	54,200	628.92	I. Ward	(a) C. A. Tebbs
§Bournemouth, Dorset	160,100	579.96	D. Newell	(a) Mrs J. Moore
§Bracknell Forest, Berks	104,600	551.08	A. J. Targett	(a) T. Wheaton
Braintree, Essex	123,600	588.33	Ms A. Ralph	E. Bishop
Breckland, Norfolk	112,200	577.00	R. Garnett	A. Stasiak
Brentwood, Essex	71,800	583.38	C. P. Sivell	(a) C. Myers
Bridgnorth, Shropshire	50,400	611.30	Mrs T. M. Elliott	R. Lane
§Brighton, East Sussex	154,900	579.94	G. Jones	(a) I. Duncan
Broadland, Norfolk	110,100	574.72	J. H. Bryant	D. Dewgrade
Bromsgrove, Hereford and Worcs	94,000	566.41	R. P. Bradshaw	R. Clayton
§Broxbourne, Herts	82,400	558.73	M. J. Walker	(a) Mrs J. E. E. Ball
§Broxtowe, Notts	112,200	716.29	M. Brown	(a) J. White
§Burnley, Lancs	90,500	747.19	R. Ellis	(a) P. A. White
CAMBRIDGE	113,000	629.65	R. Hammond	(a) J. Durrant
Cannock Chase, Staffs	90,800	633.45	M. G. Kemp	T. F. Smith
CANTERBURY, Kent	133,900	607.95	Dr C. Gay	(b) C. Wake
Caradon, Cornwall	78,900	611.00	J. Neal	E. G. Lewis
CARLISLE, Cumbria	103,300	727.97	R. S. Brackley	(a) C. Johnston
Carrick, Cornwall	84,400	628.98	P. M. Kidwell-Talbot	P. C. Tregunna
§Castle Morpeth, Northumberland	50,200	680.05	P. Wilson	(a) Mrs K. Morris
§Castle Point, Essex	85,900	636.84	B. Rollinson	(a) D. Williams
§Charnwood, Leics	153,100	616.89	S. M. Peatfield	(a) K. Brailsford
§Chelmsford, Essex	155,800	597.28	M. Easteal	(a) F. Mountain
§Cheltenham, Glos	106,800	596.52	C. Nye	(a) Mrs P. Thomas
Cherwell, Oxon	127,500	621.00	G. J. Handley	R. E. Groves, MBE
CHESTER, Cheshire	120,600	666.00	P. F. Durham	(b) Ms L. Price
§Chesterfield, Derbyshire	101,100	676.08	D. R. Shaw	(a) G. Waddours
Chester-le-Street, Co. Durham	54,200	623.34	J. A. Greensmith	D. Meek
Chichester, West Sussex	103,100	584.45	C. E. Evans	A. J. French
Chiltern, Bucks	91,400	613.35	A. Goodrum	Miss P. A. Appleby, MBE
§Chorley, Lancs	96,900	687.35	J. W. Davies	(a) M. Coombes
§Christchurch, Dorset	42,700	568.67	M. A. Turvey	(a) E. W. Wood
§Colchester, Essex	149,600	607.61	J. Cobley	(a) W. Sanford

†Managing Director
‡Finance and General Manager

Council	Population 1994	Band D charge 1996	Chief Executive	Chairman 1996–7 (a) Mayor (b) Lord Mayor
§Congleton, Cheshire	85,500	£656.22	†P. Cooper	(a) Mrs K. A. Thomas
§Copeland, Cumbria	71,000	681.85	Dr J. Stanforth	(a) Ms J. Pickering
Corby, Northants	52,800	616.30	T. Simmons	(a) J. Cowling
Cotswold, Glos	80,800	585.00	N. Howells	Mrs S. M. H. Herdman
Craven, North Yorkshire	51,100	581.00	Ms G. Taylor, PH.D	R. Walker
§Crawley, W. Sussex	90,000	614.79	M. D. Sander	(a) J. G. Smith
§Crewe and Nantwich, Cheshire	111,400	674.68	A. Wenham	(a) L. Cooper
§Dacorum, Herts	134,200	569.85	K. Hunt	(a) M. Young
§Darlington, Co. Durham	100,600	659.71	B. Keel	(a) G. Plummer
§Dartford, Kent	83,400	597.67	C. R. Shepherd	(a) H. Phillips
Daventry, Northants	64,100	744.69	R. J. Symons, RD	J. S. H. Russell
DERBY	230,500	664.79	R. H. Cowlishaw	(a) A. Mullarkey
Derbyshire Dales	68,600	656.92	D. Wheatcroft	C. P. Brindley
Derwentside, Co. Durham	87,000	706.16	N. F. Johnson	H. S. Guildford
Dover, Kent	106,900	598.68	J. P. Moir, TD	P. T. Wilson
DURHAM	89,100	642.39	C. G. Firmin	(a) J. S. Anderson
Easington, Co. Durham	98,000	744.00	*P. Innes	D. Myers
§Eastbourne, East Sussex	88,200	639.07	S. E. Conway	(a) R. G. Kirtley
East Cambridgeshire	63,300	447.03	R. C. Carr	H. J. L. Fitch
East Devon	122,800	572.09	F. J. Vallender	B. Willoughby
East Dorset	80,700	586.40	A. Breakwell	N. P. Evans
East Hampshire	108,200	593.73	B. P. Roynon	H. Cunliffe
East Hertfordshire	121,600	550.97	R. J. Bailey	J. O. Ranger
§Eastleigh, Hants	110,800	589.57	C. Tapp	(a) D. Horne
East Lindsey, Lincs	121,400	611.69	P. Haigh	Lt.-Gen. J. L. M. Dymoke, MBE
East Northamptonshire	70,000	606.47	R. K. Heath	Dr P. Wix
East Staffordshire	99,000	601.98	F. W. Saunders	(a) Mrs J. Dean
Eden, Cumbria	47,300	704.42	I. W. Bruce	J. B. Thornborrow
§Ellesmere Port and Neston, Cheshire	81,400	689.86	S. Ewbank	(a) Ms J. Walker
§Elmbridge, Surrey	119,700	616.95	D. W. L. Jenkins	(a) H. Ashton
Epping Forest, Essex	118,900	597.67	J. Burgess	R. Barnes
§Epsom and Ewell, Surrey	69,000	582.16	D. J. Smith	(a) Mrs H. Dodd
§Erewash, Derbyshire	107,100	664.74	G. A. Pook	(a) P. A. Jeffery
EXETER, Devon	104,500	562.37	W. H. Bassett	(a) I. Mitchell
§Fareham, Hants	101,800	526.98	A. A. Davies	(a) D. J. Murray
Fenland, Cambs	78,500	499.00	N. R. Topliss	B. E. A. Diggle
Forest Heath, Suffolk	64,000	566.07	S. W. Catchpole	Mrs S. D. Crickmere
Forest of Dean, Glos	75,400	619.89	‡R. A. Willis	B. W. Hobman
§Fylde, Lancs	74,000	692.12	J. R. Wilkinson	(a) A. W. Jealous
§Gedling, Notts	111,700	705.54	D. Kennedy	(a) R. B. Marshall
§Gillingham, Kent	96,200	583.80	J. A. McBride	(a) Mrs D. Smith
GLOUCESTER	104,700	572.93	G. Garbutt	(a) T. Haines
§Gosport, Hants	74,700	609.52	M. Crocker	(a) K. H. Brown
§Gravesham, Kent	92,900	558.63	E. V. J. Seager	(a) A. Cunningham, MBE
§Great Yarmouth, Norfolk	88,700	577.94	R. Packham	P. W. Dye
§Guildford, Surrey	126,200	586.11	D. T. Watts	(a) J. D. Woodhatch
§Halton, Cheshire	123,700	646.05	M. Cuff	(a) F. Nyland
Hambleton, North Yorkshire	82,900	497.52	P. C. O'Brien (acting)	D. J. Dennis
Harborough, Leics	70,900	619.32	M. C. Wilson	B. Summers
Harlow, Essex	73,100	704.55	*D. Byrne	Ms D. Pennick
§Harrogate, North Yorkshire	148,400	626.30	P. M. Walsh	(a) P. Broadbank
Hart, Hants	83,300	588.41	G. R. Jelbart	H. Eastwood
§Hastings, East Sussex	82,600	643.35	R. A. Carrier	(a) G. White
§Havant, Hants	119,400	613.78	R. Smith	(a) Mrs V. Steel
HEREFORD	50,500	577.68	C. E. S. Willis	(a) L. M. H. Andrews
§Hertsmere, Hertfordshire	94,200	582.44	P. H. Copland	(a) J. Nolan
§High Peak, Derbyshire	87,300	696.53	R. P. H. Brady	(a) D. Lomax
§Hinckley and Bosworth, Leics	97,700	586.85	°I. G. Davis	(a) D. J. Wood
Horsham, West Sussex	114,300	587.34	M. J. Pearson	A. Chisholm
§Hove, East Sussex	91,300	604.28	J. P. Teasdale	(a) L. E. Hamilton

† Managing Director
* General Manager
‡ Head of Paid Service
° Head of Technical Services

Council	Population 1994	Band D charge 1996	Chief Executive	Chairman 1996-7 (a) Mayor (b) Lord Mayor
Huntingdonshire, Cambs	149,900	£537.91	D. Monks	J. G. Rignall
§Hyndburn, Lancs	79,600	751.49	M. Chambers	(a) M. M. Yousaf
§Ipswich, Suffolk	114,100	671.13	J. D. Herir	(a) P. Smart
Kennet, Wilts	73,800	578.60	P. L. Owens	D. Parker
Kerrier, Cornwall	88,900	613.87	G. G. Cox	T. J. Bray
§Kettering, Northants	79,200	626.49	P. Walker	(a) B. Morgan
§King's Lynn and West Norfolk	131,000	587.47	A. E. Pask	(a) A. M. Evans
LANCASTER, Lancs	135,000	689.64	J. Burrows	(a) Mrs J. Horner
LEICESTER	293,400	686.41	R. Green	(b) C. S. Batty
Leominster, Hereford and Worcs	40,900	558.96	†Mrs M. Holborow	M. J. Kimbery
Lewes, East Sussex	88,400	633.13	J. N. Crawford	J. E. Lewry
Lichfield, Staffs	93,600	533.40	J. T. Thompson	W. J. Wilson
LINCOLN	84,600	625.17	A. Sparke	(a) A. Morgan
§Luton, Beds	180,800	650.64	Mrs K. Jones	(a) M. D. Hand
§Macclesfield, Cheshire	151,500	669.95	B. W. Longden	(a) H. R. Harrison
§Maidstone, Kent	138,500	627.95	J. D. Makepeace	(a) M. Robertson
Maldon, Essex	53,500	581.46	E. A. P. Plumridge	R. G. Boyce
Malvern Hills, Hereford and Worcs	90,700	595.50	M. J. Jones	J. Tretheway
Mansfield, Notts	102,100	692.93	R. P. Goad	M. Hall
§Melton, Leics	46,600	616.25	P. M. Murphy	(a) R. Hyslop
Mendip, Somerset	98,000	639.45	G. Jeffs	C. F. Lockey
Mid Bedfordshire	114,900	616.58	C. A. Tucker	D. Harrowell
Mid Devon	66,400	585.37	M. I. R. Bull	D. J. Allen
Mid Suffolk	79,100	608.17	G. Chilton	M. Shave
Mid Sussex	125,100	604.00	W. J. H. Hatton	Ms A. Jones
§Milton Keynes, Bucks	188,400	657.13	H. Miller	(a) D. L. Lewis
Mole Valley, Surrey	79,000	567.22	H. Kerswell	Mrs J. Marsh
Newark and Sherwood, Notts	104,100	766.34	†R. G. Dix	B. L. D'Arcy
Newbury, Berks	141,600	595.94	P. E. McMahon	J. I. Morgan
§Newcastle under Lyme, Staffs	123,100	589.06	J. Dunn	(a) G. O'Kane Cairns
New Forest, Hants	166,400	609.00	†I. B. Mackintosh	Miss S. A. Cooke
§Northampton	187,600	670.05	R. J. B. Morris	(a) J. S. Bains
North Cornwall	76,900	616.73	D. Brown	A. Hirst
North Devon	86,200	567.15	D. T. Cunliffe	Mrs F. E. Webber
North Dorset	55,300	575.92	Ms E. Peters	M. F. Lane
North East Derbyshire	99,200	704.60	‡Mrs C. A. Gilbey	Ms M. Simpson
North Hertfordshire	114,300	585.42	J. S. Philp	Mrs A. E. Carss
North Kesteven, Lincs	82,000	600.71	S. Lamb	G. W. Chambers
North Norfolk	94,300	588.13	B. A. Barrell	A. L. Dennis
North Shropshire	54,400	636.72	D. Pearce	A. Boughey
§North Warwickshire	61,400	665.00	J. Hutchinson	(a) Mrs A. Forwood
North West Leicestershire	83,100	619.79	M. J. Diaper	W. J. Wildgoose
North Wiltshire	118,900	622.21	R. Marshall	A. S. R. Jackson
NORWICH, Norfolk	127,800	641.38	J. R. Packer	(b) R. Quinn
NOTTINGHAM	282,400	769.23	E. F. Cantle	(a) B. Parker
§Nuneaton and Bedworth, Warwickshire	119,100	705.79	‡‡J. Walton	(a) J. Glass
§Oadby and Wigston, Leics	53,100	627.06	Mrs R. E. Hyde	(a) J. Kaufman
§Oswestry, Shropshire	34,300	621.14	D. A. Towers	(a) Mrs A. H. Bickerton
OXFORD	132,800	688.40	R. S. Block	(b) Ms B. Keen
§Pendle, Lancs	85,700	751.49	S. Barnes	(a) F. Clifford
Penwith, Cornwall	59,600	613.60	‡F. H. Murton	P. Badrock
PETERBOROUGH, Cambs	158,700	588.10	W. E. Samuel	(a) M. A. Choudhary
PLYMOUTH, Devon	255,800	649.78	Mrs A. Stone	(b) Mrs S. Y. Bellamy
§Poole, Dorset	138,100	587.70	J. W. Brooks	(a) B. A. Greenwood
PORTSMOUTH, Hants	189,300	572.13	N. Gurney	(b) M. Hancock
§Preston, Lancs	133,100	748.48	J. Carr	(a) R. Marshall
Purbeck, Dorset	44,500	500.00	P. B. Croft	D. A. Budd
§Reading, Berks	138,500	696.26	D. Bligh	(a) R. J. Day
§Redditch, Hereford and Worcs	78,400	619.60	**Ms S. Manzie	(a) R. T. Vickers
§Reigate and Banstead, Surrey	118,300	591.21	M. Bacon	(a) J. A. Chiles

† Managing Director
‡ Head of Paid Service
‡‡ Borough Manager
** Borough Director

Council	Population 1994	Band D charge 1996	Chief Executive	Chairman 1996–7 (a) Mayor (b) Lord Mayor
§Restormel, Cornwall	89,000	£600.15	Mrs P. Crowson	(a) Mrs S. Blaylock
§Ribble Valley, Lancs	51,800	697.33	O. Hopkins	(a) Ms E. Lowe
Richmondshire, N. Yorkshire	45,100	579.07	H. Tabiner	R. Alderson
ROCHESTER UPON MEDWAY, Kent	145,500	512.82	R. I. Gregory	(a) H. Housby
Rochford, Essex	75,800	604.00	R. Lovell	P. Beckers
§Rossendale, Lancs	65,600	761.69	J. S. Hartley	(a) L. Forshaw
Rother, East Sussex	86,000	619.20	D. F. Powell	M. J. Jones
§Rugby, Warwickshire	86,600	676.06	Miss D. M. Colley	(a) S. G. Humphries
§Runnymede, Surrey	75,100	528.15	T. N. Williams	(a) Mrs M. H. Taylor
§Rushcliffe, Notts	103,000	681.04	J. Saxton	(a) A. H. Cooper
§Rushmoor, Hants	85,800	580.79	R. Upton	(a) M. Banner
Rutland, Leics	33,600	631.70	F. Allen Dobson	B. Montgomery
Ryedale, North Yorkshire	93,900	618.01	M. Walker	A. C. Farnaby
ST ALBANS, Herts	128,700	587.58	E. A. Hackford	(a) Revd R. Donald
§St Edmundsbury, Suffolk	92,800	597.13	G. R. Toft	(a) W. Cownley
Salisbury, Wilts	110,000	598.54	D. R. J. Rawlinson	I. West
§Scarborough, N. Yorkshire	108,700	578.97	J. M. Trebble	(a) J. E. Agar
Sedgefield, Co. Durham	91,400	728.07	A. J. Roberts	K. Noble
Sedgemoor, Somerset	101,400	605.24	A. G. Lovell	G. A. Buchanan
Selby, North Yorkshire	92,000	559.68	M. Connor	J. A. Heppenstal
Sevenoaks, Kent	109,900	618.74	B. C. Cova, MBE	D. Coates
Shepway, Kent	96,500	631.67	R. J. Thompson	K. D. Hudson
§Shrewsbury and Atcham	94,600	610.55	D. Bradbury	(a) K. Brennand
§Slough, Berks	104,900	534.28	Mrs C. Coppell	(a) Mrs M. Atkinson
SOUTHAMPTON, Hants	211,700	592.48	J. Cairns	(a) Ms D. Altwood
South Bedfordshire	110,400	670.72	T. D. Rix	E. Snoxell
South Buckinghamshire	63,900	560.00	C. R. Furness	Mrs P. Burry
South Cambridgeshire	123,600	517.02	J. S. Ballantyne	Mrs S. Saunders
South Derbyshire	75,100	667.96	D. J. Dugdale	Mrs J. Mead
§Southend-on-Sea, Essex	169,900	581.73	°D. Moulson	(a) H. P. Gibeon
South Hams, Devon	79,100	585.89	M. S. Carpenter	Mrs J. I. Roskruge
South Herefordshire	54,100	580.73	A. Hughes	Mrs R. F. Lincoln
South Holland, Lincs	70,400	636.77	C. J. Simpkins	J. R. Pearl
South Kesteven, Lincs	115,200	605.38	K. R. Cann	K. Joynson
South Lakeland, Cumbria	100,300	700.96	A. F. Winstanley	M. C. Bentley
South Norfolk	104,500	562.59	A. G. T. Kellett	Viscountess Knollys
South Northamptonshire	73,000	655.33	K. Whitehead	P. Henson
South Oxfordshire	121,800	514.45	R. Watson	Mrs S. M. Cooper
§South Ribble, Lancs	103,600	688.56	P. Halsall	(a) Mrs B. R. Greenland
South Shropshire	39,300	601.82	G. C. Biggs, MBE	R. D. Phillips
South Somerset	148,300	640.52	M. Usher	Mrs Gail Coleshill
South Staffordshire	104,400	529.24	L. Barnfield	J. L. Evans
§Spelthorne, Surrey	91,400	591.78	M. B. Taylor	(a) G. G. Blampied
§Stafford	122,500	577.86	J. K. M. Krawiec	(a) J. T. Holland
Staffordshire Moorlands	95,100	594.16	B. J. Preedy	G. S. Eyre
§Stevenage, Herts	75,900	626.05	H. L. Miller	(a) B. G. Dunnell
STOKE-ON-TRENT, Staffs	245,200	644.64	B. Smith	(b) J. P. Birkin
Stratford-on-Avon, Warwicks	109,500	632.62	I. B. Prosser	S. B. Ribbans
Stroud, Glos	106,300	647.68	R. M. Ollin	Mrs M. E. A. Nolder
Suffolk Coastal	113,200	608.38	T. K. Griffin	R. Burgon
§Surrey Heath	81,900	587.52	N. M. Pughe	(a) C. Gimblett
§Swale, Kent	117,200	558.87	J. C. Edwards	(a) E. Madgwick
§Tamworth, Staffs	71,800	571.52	C. Moore	(a) R. R. Dermid
Tandridge, Surrey	76,700	601.00	P. J. D. Thomas	R. B. Clements
§Taunton Deane, Somerset	98,200	596.17	†Mrs S. Douglas	(a) J. G. Dunkley, OBE
Teesdale, Co. Durham	24,200	644.93	C. M. Anderson	O. Hedley
Teignbridge, Devon	114,100	573.48	B. T. Jones	R. Astbury
Tendring, Essex	130,900	596.80	D. Mitchell-Gears	B. Mixter
§Test Valley, Hants	105,300	573.61	A. Jones	(a) B. I. Palmer
§Tewkesbury, Glos	75,400	503.59	H. Davis	(a) H. Chamberlayne
§Thamesdown, Wilts	173,500	619.73	‡R. Clegg	(a) M. K. Caton
Thanet, Kent	125,300	434.00	D. Ralls, CBE, DFC	Mrs M. Davies

° Town Clerk
‡ General Manager
‡ Head of Paid Service

Council	Population 1994	Band D charge 1996	Chief Executive	Chairman 1996–7 (a) Mayor (b) Lord Mayor
Three Rivers, Herts	83,100	£606.60	A. Robertson	Ms N. Spellman
§Thurrock, Essex	131,400	605.34	K. Barnes	(a) S. Josling
§Tonbridge and Malling, Kent	102,800	591.09	T. Thompson	(a) Ms J. Cresswell
§Torbay, Devon	123,000	567.86	A. J. Hodgkiss (acting)	(a) Mrs C. Milward
Torridge, Devon	54,700	546.26	R. K. Brasington	W. J. Brook
§Tunbridge Wells, Kent	102,700	580.34	R. J. Stone	(a) R. Baker
Tynedale, Northumberland	57,700	659.85	A. Baty	Mrs M. J. Howard
Uttlesford, Essex	67,500	591.81	K. Ivory	E. C. Abrahams
Vale of White Horse, Oxon	113,200	612.63	D. J. Heavens	R. T. Johnston
§Vale Royal, Cheshire	114,700	670.00	W. R. T. Woods	(a) E. G. Redford
Wansbeck, Northumberland	62,200	690.90	A. G. White	J. A. Graham
§Warrington, Cheshire	186,700	680.12	M. I. M. Sanders	(a) Mrs M. Roblin
Warwick	119,800	654.21	Ms J. Barrett	Mrs J. Evans
§Watford, Herts	76,200	666.47	Ms C. Hassan	(a) P. Harrison
Waveney, Suffolk	107,600	590.41	M. Berridge	T. Carter
§Waverley, Surrey	114,800	575.30	Miss C. L. Pointer	(a) Mrs G. Beel
Wealden, East Sussex	134,900	613.14	D. R. Holness	Mrs V. Chidson
Wear Valley, Co. Durham	63,300	714.09	°Mrs C. Hughes	S. Dent
§Wellingborough, Northants	68,100	499.50	J. E. Thewlass	(a) S. Dholakia
Welwyn Hatfield, Herts	94,700	610.69	D. Riddle	A. Appleby
§West Devon	46,700	603.18	J. S. Ligo	(a) J. Darch
West Dorset	88,600	561.53	R. C. Rennison	T. Frost
West Lancashire	110,200	717.32	B. A. Knight	R. A. Pendleton
West Lindsey, Lincs	77,700	623.67	R. W. Nelsey	J. Turner
West Oxfordshire	95,000	557.41	N. J. B. Robson	E. J. Cooper
West Somerset	32,000	636.19	C. Rockall	S. Pugsley
West Wiltshire	110,000	585.33	R. S. While	T. Chivers
§Weymouth and Portland, Dorset	62,900	582.49	M. N. Ashby	(a) B. Ellis
WINCHESTER, Hants	101,800	599.83	D. H. Cowan	(a) B. V. Blunt
§Windsor and Maidenhead, Berks	137,800	590.94	D. Lunn	(a) Mrs A. Sheldon
§Woking, Surrey	89,000	575.30	P. Russell	(a) J. G. B. Coombe
Wokingham, Berks	141,700	623.75	Mrs G. C. Norton	Ms D. Carpenter
WORCESTER	89,500	582.15	††D. Wareing	(a) L. Thomas
§Worthing, West Sussex	97,400	610.11	M. J. Ball	(a) P. Green
Wrekin, Shropshire	143,400	660.00	D. G. Hutchison	S. Bradley
Wychavon, Hereford and Worcs	104,600	578.80	W. S. Nott	R. Mason
Wycombe, Bucks	162,600	603.52	R. J. Cummins	(a) Mrs E. M. Barratt
§Wyre, Lancs	103,900	694.29	M. Brown	(a) R. V. Allen
Wyre Forest, Hereford and Worcs	97,200	601.00	W. S. Baldwin	N. Knowles

° Executive Director
†† Principal Director

Roman Names of English Towns and Cities

Bath	Aquae Sulis
Canterbury	Durovernum Cantiacorum
Carlisle	Luguvalium
Chelmsford	Caesaromagus
Chester	Deva
Chichester	Noviomagus Regnensium
Cirencester	Corinium Dobunnorum
Colchester	Camulodunum
Doncaster	Danum
Dorchester	Durnovaria
Dover	Dubris
Exeter	Isca Dumnoniorum
Gloucester	Glevum

Leicester	Ratae Corieltauvorum
Lincoln	Lindum
London	Londinium
Manchester	Mamucium
Newcastle upon Tyne	Pons Aelius
Pevensey	Anderetium
Rochester	Durobrivae
St Albans	Verulamium
Salisbury (Old Sarum)	Sorviodunum
Silchester	Calleva Atrebatum
Winchester	Venta Belgarum
Wroxeter	Viroconium Cornoviorum
York	Eburacum

LOCAL GOVERNMENT CHANGES IN ENGLAND

CHANGES FROM 1 APRIL 1997
UA Unitary Authority

Present county (no. of DCs at present)

Bedfordshire (4)	UA in Luton; rest remain two-tier
Buckinghamshire (5)	UA in Milton Keynes; rest remain two-tier
Derbyshire (9)	UA in Derby; rest remain two-tier
Dorset (8)	UAs in Bournemouth, Poole; rest remain two-tier
Durham (8)	UA in Darlington; rest remain two-tier
East Sussex	UA in Brighton and Hove; rest remain two-tier
Hampshire (13)	UAs in Portsmouth, Southampton; rest remain two-tier
Leicestershire (9)	UAs in Leicester, Rutland; rest remain two-tier
Staffordshire (9)	UA in Stoke-on-Trent; rest remain two-tier
Wiltshire (5)	UA in Thamesdown; rest remain two-tier

CHANGES PROPOSED FROM 1 APRIL 1998
Present county (no. of DC's at present)

Berkshire (6)	UAs in Bracknell Forest, Newbury, Reading, Slough, Windsor and Maidenhead, Wokingham
Cambridgeshire (6)	UA in Peterborough; rest remain two-tier
Cheshire (8)	UAs in Halton, Warrington; rest remain two-tier
Devon (10)	UAs in Plymouth, Torbay; rest remain two-tier
Essex (14)	UAs in Southend, Thurrock; rest remain two-tier
Hereford and Worcester (9)	UA in Herefordshire (pre-1974 boundary); Worcestershire retains two tiers
Kent (14)	UA in Rochester and Gillingham; rest remain two-tier
Lancashire (14)	UAs in Blackburn, Blackpool; rest remain two-tier
Nottinghamshire (8)	UA in Nottingham; rest remain two-tier
Shropshire (6)	UA in The Wrekin; rest remain two-tier

No changes are proposed in the following:
Cornwall; Cumbria; Gloucestershire; Hertfordshire; Lincolnshire; Norfolk; Northamptonshire; Northumberland; Oxfordshire; Somerset; Suffolk; Surrey; Warwickshire; West Sussex

The Cinque Ports

As their name implies, the Cinque Ports were originally five in number: Hastings, New Romney, Hythe, Dover and Sandwich. They were formed during the 11th century to defend the Channel coast and, after the Norman Conquest, were recognized as a Confederation by a charter of 1278. The 'antient towns' of Winchelsea and Rye were added at some time after the Conquest. The other members of the Confederation, known as Limbs, are Lydd, Faversham, Folkestone, Deal, Tenterden, Margate and Ramsgate.

Until 1855 the duty of the Cinque Ports was to provide ships and men for the defence of the state in return for considerable privileges, such as tax exemptions and the framing of by-laws. Of these privileges only jurisdiction in Admiralty remains.

The Barons of the Cinque Ports have the ancient privilege of attending the Coronation ceremony and are allotted special places in Westminster Abbey.

Lord Warden of the Cinque Ports, HM Queen Elizabeth the Queen Mother
Judge, Court of Admiralty, G. Darling, RD, QC
Registrar, I. G. Gill, LVO, 3 Waterloo Crescent, Dover, Kent CT16 1LA. Tel: 01304-225225

LORD WARDENS OF THE CINQUE PORTS *since* 1904

The Marquess Curzon	1904
The Prince of Wales	1905
The Earl Brassey	1908
The Earl Beauchamp	1913
The Marquess of Reading	1934
The Marquess of Willingdon	1936
Winston Churchill	1941
Sir Robert Menzies	1965
HM Queen Elizabeth the Queen Mother	1978

London

THE CORPORATION OF LONDON
(see also page 522)

The City of London is the historic centre at the heart of London known as 'the square mile' around which the vast metropolis has grown over the centuries. The City's residential population is 5,500. The civic government is carried on by the Corporation of London through the Court of Common Council.

The City is the financial and business centre of London and includes the head offices of the principal banks, insurance companies and mercantile houses, in addition to buildings ranging from the historic interest of the Roman Wall and the 15th-century Guildhall, to the massive splendour of St Paul's Cathedral and the architectural beauty of Wren's spires.

The City of London was described by Tacitus in AD 62 as 'a busy emporium for trade and traders'. Under the Romans it became an important administration centre and hub of the road system. Little is known of London in Saxon times, when it formed part of the kingdom of the East Saxons. In 886 Alfred recovered London from the Danes and reconstituted it a burgh under his son-in-law. In 1066 the citizens submitted to William the Conqueror who in 1067 granted them a charter, which is still preserved, establishing them in the rights and privileges they had hitherto enjoyed.

THE MAYORALTY

The Mayoralty was probably established about 1189, the first Mayor being Henry Fitz Ailwyn who filled the office for 23 years and was succeeded by Fitz Alan (1212–14). A new charter was granted by King John in 1215, directing the Mayor to be chosen annually, which has ever since been done, though in early times the same individual often held the office more than once. A familiar instance is that of 'Whittington, thrice Lord Mayor of London' (in reality four times, 1397, 1398, 1406, 1419); and many modern cases have occurred. The earliest instance of the phrase 'Lord Mayor' in English is in 1414. It was used more generally in the latter part of the 15th century and became invariable from 1535 onwards. At Michaelmas the liverymen in Common Hall choose two Aldermen who have served the office of Sheriff for presentation to the Court of Aldermen, and one is chosen to be Lord Mayor for the following mayoral year.

LORD MAYOR'S DAY

The Lord Mayor of London was previously elected on the feast of St Simon and St Jude (28 October), and from the time of Edward I, at least, was presented to the King or to the Barons of the Exchequer on the following day, unless that day was a Sunday. The day of election was altered to 16 October in 1346, and after some further changes was fixed for Michaelmas Day in 1546, but the ceremonies of admittance and swearing-in of the Lord Mayor continued to take place on 28 and 29 October respectively until 1751. In 1752, at the reform of the calendar, the Lord Mayor was continued in office until 8 November, the 'New Style' equivalent of 28 October. The Lord Mayor is now presented to the Lord Chief Justice at the Royal Courts of Justice on the second Saturday in November to make the final declaration of office, having been sworn in at Guildhall on the preceding day. The procession to the Royal Courts of Justice is popularly known as the Lord Mayor's Show.

REPRESENTATIVES

Aldermen are mentioned in the 11th century and their office is of Saxon origin. They were elected annually between 1377 and 1394, when an Act of Parliament of Richard II directed them to be chosen for life.

The Common Council, elected annually on the first Friday in December, was, at an early date, substituted for a popular assembly called the Folkmote. At first only two representatives were sent from each ward, but the number has since been greatly increased.

OFFICERS

Sheriffs were Saxon officers; their predecessors were the wic-reeves and portreeves of London and Middlesex. At first they were officers of the Crown, and were named by the Barons of the Exchequer; but Henry I (in 1132) gave the citizens permission to choose their own Sheriffs, and the annual election of Sheriffs became fully operative under King John's charter of 1199. The citizens lost this privilege, as far as the election of the Sheriff of Middlesex was concerned, by the Local Government Act 1888; but the liverymen continue to choose two Sheriffs of the City of London, who are appointed on Midsummer Day and take office at Michaelmas.

The office of Chamberlain is an ancient one, the first contemporary record of which is 1237. The Town Clerk (or Common Clerk) is mentioned in 1274.

ACTIVITIES

The work of the Corporation is assigned to a number of committees which present reports to the Court of Common Council. These Committees are: City Lands and Bridge House Estates, Policy and Resources, Finance, Planning and Transportation, Central Markets, Billingsgate and Leadenhall Markets, Spitalfields Market, Police, Port and City of London Health and Social Services, Libraries, Art Galleries and Records, Boards of Governors of Schools, Music and Drama (Guildhall School of Music and Drama), Establishment, Housing, Gresham (City side), Hampstead Heath Management, Epping Forest and Open Spaces, West Ham Park, Privileges, Barbican Residential and Barbican Centre (Barbican Arts and Conference Centre).

The City's estate, in the possession of which the Corporation of London differs from other municipalities, is managed by the City Lands and Bridge House Estates Committee, the chairmanship of which carries with it the title of Chief Commoner.

The Honourable the Irish Society, which manages the Corporation's estates in Ulster, consists of a Governor and five other Aldermen, the Recorder, and 19 Common Councilmen, of whom one is elected Deputy Governor.

THE LORD MAYOR 1995–6*
The Rt. Hon. the Lord Mayor, Sir Leonard Chalstrey
  Secretary, Air Vice-Marshal M. Dicken, CB

THE SHERIFFS 1996–7
Sir Peter Levene, KBE (Alderman, Portsoken) and K. E. Ayers; elected, 26 June 1995; assumed office, 28 September 1995

---

* The Lord Mayor for 1996–7 was elected on Michaelmas Day. See Stop-press

OFFICERS, ETC
Town Clerk and Chamberlain, B. P. Harty
Chief Commoner (1996), P. J. Willoughby
Clerk, The Honourable the Irish Society, S. Waley, The Irish
Chamber, St Dunstan's House, 2–4 Carey Lane, London
EC2V 8AA

THE ALDERMEN

Name and Ward	CC	Ald.	Shff.	Lord Mayor
Sir Peter Gadsden, GBE,				
Farringdon Wt.	1969	1971	1970	1979
Sir Christopher Leaver, GBE,				
Dowgate	1973	1974	1979	1981
Sir Alan Traill, GBE,				
Langbourn	1970	1975	1982	1984
Sir David Rowe-Ham, GBE,				
Bridge	—	1976	1984	1986
Sir Christopher Collett, GBE,				
Broad Street	1973	1979	1985	1988
Sir Hugh Bidwell, GBE,				
Billingsgate	—	1979	1986	1989
Sir Alexander Graham, GBE,				
Queenhithe	1978	1979	1986	1990
Sir Brian Jenkins, GBE,				
Cordwainer	—	1980	1987	1991
Sir Paul Newall, TD, Walbrook	1980	1981	1989	1993
Sir Christopher Walford,				
Farringdon Wn.	—	1982	1990	1994
Sir Leonard Chalstrey, Vintry	1981	1984	1993	1995

All the above have passed the Civic Chair

Roger Cork, Tower	1978 1983	1992
Richard Nichols, Candlewick	1983 1984	1994
Sir Peter Levene, KBE,		
Portsoken	1983 1984	
Clive Martin, OBE, TD, Aldgate	— 1985	
Bryan Toye, Lime Street	— 1983	
Peter Bull, Cheap	1968 1984	
David Howard, Cornhill	1972 1986	
James Oliver, Bishopsgate	1980 1987	
Gavyn Arthur, Cripplegate	1988 1991	
Robert Finch, Coleman Street	— 1992	
Richard Agutter, Castle		
Baynard	— 1995	
Michael Savory, Bread Street	1980 1996	
David Brewer, Bassishaw	1992 1996	
Nicholas Anstee, Aldersgate	1987 1996	

THE COMMON COUNCIL

Deputy: Each Common Councilman so described serves as
deputy to the Alderman of her/his ward

Absalom, J. D. (1994)	Farringdon Wt.
Angell, E. H. (1991)	Cripplegate Wt.
Archibald, Deputy W. W. (1986)	Cornhill
Bailey, J. (1993)	Cripplegate Wt.
Ballard, K. A., MC (1969)	Castle Baynard
Balls, H. D. (1970)	Castle Baynard
Barker, Deputy J. A. (1981)	Cripplegate Wt.
Barnes-Yallowley, H. M. F. (1986)	Coleman Street
Beale, Deputy M. J. (1979)	Lime Street
Bird, J. L. (1977)	Bridge
Biroum-Smith, P. L. (1988)	Dowgate
Block, S. A. A. (1983)	Cheap
Bowman, J. C. R. (1995)	Aldgate
Bradshaw, D. J. (1991)	Cripplegate Wn.
Bramwell, F. M. (1983)	Langbourn
Brewster, J. W., OBE (1994)	Bassishaw

Brighton, R. L. (1984)	Portsoken
Brooks, W. I. B. (1988)	Billingsgate
Brown, Deputy D. T. (1971)	Walbrook
Caspi, D. (1994)	Bridge
Cassidy, Deputy M. J. (1989)	Coleman Street
Catt, B. F. (1982)	Farringdon Wn.
Chadwick, R. A. H. (1994)	Tower
Challis, G. H., CBE (1978)	Langbourn
Cohen, Mrs C. M. (1986)	Lime Street
Cole, Lt.-Col. Sir Colin, KCB, KCVO, TD	
(1964)	Castle Baynard
Collinson, Miss A. H. (1991)	Farringdon Wt.
Cotgrove, D. (1991)	Lime Street
Coven, Deputy Mrs E. O., CBE (1972)	Dowgate
Currie, Miss S. E. M. (1985)	Cripplegate Wt.
Daily-Hunt, R. B. (1989)	Cripplegate Wt.
Darwin, G. E. (1995)	Farringdon Wt.
Davis, C. B. (1991)	Bread Street
Delderfield, D. W. (1995)	Farringdon Wt.
Dove, W. H., MBE (1993)	Bishopsgate
Dunitz, A. A. (1984)	Portsoken
Edwards, Deputy R. D. K. (1978)	Bassishaw
Eskenzi, A. N. (1970)	Farringdon Wn.
Evans, Deputy Mrs J. (1975)	Farringdon Wt.
Eve, R. A. (1980)	Cheap
Everett, K. M. (1984)	Candlewick
Farthing, R. B. C. (1981)	Aldgate
Fell, J. A. (1982)	Queenhithe
FitzGerald, Deputy R. C. A. (1981)	Bread Street
Forbes, G. B. (1993)	Bishopsgate
Fraser, S. J. (1993)	Coleman Street
Fraser, W. B. (1981)	Vintry
Galloway, A. D. (1981)	Broad Street
Gillon, G. M. F. (1995)	Cordwainer
Ginsburg, S. (1990)	Bishopsgate
Gowman, Miss A. (1991)	Dowgate
Graves, A. C. (1985)	Bishopsgate
Green, C. (1994)	Aldersgate
Hall, B. R. H. (1995)	Farringdon Wn.
Halliday, Mrs P. (1992)	Walbrook
Hardwick, Dr P. B. (1987)	Aldgate
Harries, R. E. (1995)	Cripplegate Wt.
Harris, B. N. (1996)	Broad Street
Hart, Deputy M. G. (1970)	Bridge
Haynes, J. E. H. (1986)	Cornhill
Henderson, Deputy J. S., OBE (1975)	Langbourn
Henderson-Begg, M. (1977)	Coleman Street
Hilliard, N. R. M. (1994)	Farringdon Wt.
Holland, Deputy J., CBE (1972)	Aldgate
Holliday, Mrs E. H. L. (1987)	Vintry
Horlock, Deputy H. W. S. (1969)	Farringdon Wn.
Hughesdon, J. S. (1991)	Broad Street
Jackson, L. St J. T. (1978)	Bread Street
Keep, Mrs B. (1987)	Cripplegate Wn.
Kellett, Mrs M. W. F. (1986)	Tower
Kemp, D. L. (1984)	Coleman Street
Knowles, S. K. (1984)	Candlewick
Lawrence, G. A. (1994)	Farringdon Wt.
Lawson, G. C. H. (1971)	Portsoken
Littlestone, N. (1993)	Aldersgate
MacLellan, A. P. W. (1989)	Walbrook
McNeil, I. D. (1977)	Lime Street
Malins, J. H., QC (1981)	Farringdon Wt.
Martin, R. C. (1986)	Queenhithe
Martinelli, P. J. (1994)	Bassishaw
Mayhew, Miss J. (1986)	Queenhithe
Mitchell, Deputy C. R. (1971)	Castle Baynard
Mizen, Deputy D. H. (1979)	Broad Street
Mobsby, Deputy D. J. L. (1985)	Billingsgate

Morgan, *Deputy* B. L., CBE (1963)   *Bishopsgate*
Moss, A. D. (1989)   *Tower*
Nash, *Deputy* Mrs J. C. (1983)   *Aldersgate*
Neary, J. E. (1982)   *Aldgate*
Newman, Mrs P. B. (1989)   *Aldersgate*
Northall-Laurie, P. D. (1975)   *Walbrook*
Owen, Mrs J. (1975)   *Langbourn*
Owen-Ward, J. R. (1983)   *Bridge*
Parmley, A. C. (1992)   *Vintry*
Pembroke, *Deputy* Mrs A. M. F. (1978)   *Cheap*
Platts-Mills, J. F. F., *QC*   *Farringdon Wt.*
Ponsonby of Shulbrede, *Deputy* Lady
  (1981)   *Farringdon Wt.*
Pulman, *Deputy* G. A. G. (1983)   *Tower*
Punter, C. (1993)   *Cripplegate Wn.*
Reed, *Deputy* J. L., MBE (1967)   *Farringdon Wn.*
Revell-Smith, *Deputy* P. A., CBE (1959)   *Vintry*
Rigby, P. P., CBE (1972)   *Farringdon Wn.*
Robinson, Mrs D. C. (1989)   *Bishopsgate*
Roney, *Deputy* E. P. T., CBE (1974)   *Bishopsgate*
Samuel, *Deputy* Mrs I., MBE (1971)   *Portsoken*
Sargant, K. A. (1991)   *Cornhill*
Saunders, *Deputy* R. (1975)   *Candlewick*
Scriven, R. G. (1984)   *Candlewick*
Sellon, S. A., OBE, TD (1990)   *Cordwainer*
Shalit, D. M. (1972)   *Farringdon Wn.*
Sharp, *Deputy* Mrs I. M. (1974)   *Queenhithe*
Sherlock, M. R. C. (1992)   *Dowgate*
Simpson, A. S. J. (1987)   *Aldersgate*
Smith, Miss A. M. (1995)   *Farringdon Wt.*
Snyder, *Deputy* M. J. (1986)   *Cordwainer*
Spanner, J. H., TD (1984)   *Broad Street*
Stevenson, F. P. (1994)   *Cripplegate Wn.*
Stone, H. V. (1993)   *Billingsgate*
Taylor, J. A. F., TD (1991)   *Bread Street*
Trotter, J. (1993)   *Billingsgate*
Walsh, S. (1990)   *Farringdon Wt.*
Warner, D. W. (1994)   *Cripplegate Wn.*
White, Dr J. W. (1986)   *Cornhill*
Willoughby, P. J. (1985)   *Bishopsgate*
Wilmot, R. T. D. (1973)   *Cordwainer*
Wilson, A. B., CBE (1984)   *Cheap*
Wixley, G. R. A., CBE, TD (1964)   *Coleman Street*
Woodward, *Deputy* C. D., CBE (1971)   *Cripplegate Wn.*
Wooldridge, F. D. (1988)   *Farringdon Wn.*

The City Guilds
(Livery Companies)

The constitution of the livery companies has been unchanged for centuries. There are three ranks of membership: freemen, liverymen and assistants. A person can become a freeman by patrimony (through a parent having been a freeman); by servitude (through having served an apprenticeship to a freeman); or by redemption (by purchase).

Election to the livery is the prerogative of the company, who can elect any of its freemen as liverymen. Assistants are usually elected from the livery and form a Court of Assistants which is the governing body of the company. The Master (in some companies called the Prime Warden) is elected annually from the assistants.

As at June 1996, 23,750 liverymen of the guilds were entitled to vote at elections at Common Hall.

The order of precedence, omitting extinct companies, is given in parenthesis after the name of each company in the list below. In certain companies the election of Master or Prime Warden for the year does not take place till the autumn. In such cases the Master or Prime Warden for 1995–6 is given.

THE TWELVE GREAT COMPANIES
In order of civic precedence

MERCERS (*1*). *Hall*, Ironmonger Lane, London EC2V 8HE. *Livery*, 226. *Clerk*, G. M. M. Wakeford, OBE. *Master*, J. Hedges
GROCERS (*2*). *Hall*, Princes Street, London EC2R 8AD. *Livery*, 312. *Clerk*, C. G. Mattingley, CBE. *Master*, C. D. Stewart-Smith, CBE
DRAPERS (*3*). *Hall*, Throgmorton Avenue, London EC2N 2DQ. *Livery*, 243. *Clerk*, A. L. Lang, MBE. *Master*, Vice-Adm. Sir Geoffrey Dalton, KCB
FISHMONGERS (*4*). *Hall*, London Bridge, London EC4R 9EL. *Livery*, 366. *Clerk*, K. S. Waters. *Prime Warden*, M. Drummond, OBE
GOLDSMITHS (*5*). *Hall*, Foster Lane, London EC2V 6BN. *Livery*, 275. *Clerk*, R. D. Buchanan-Dunlop, CBE. *Prime Warden*, S. L. Devlin, CMG
MERCHANT TAYLORS (*6/7*). *Hall*, 30 Threadneedle Street, London EC2R 8AY. *Livery* 312. *Clerk*, D. A. Peck. *Master*, P. H. Ryan, CBE
SKINNERS (*6/7*). *Hall*, 8 Dowgate Hill, London EC4R 2SP. *Livery*, 370. *Clerk*, Capt. D. Hart-Dyke, CBE, LVO, RN. *Master*, A. Crawshaw
HABERDASHERS (*8*). *Hall*, Staining Lane, London EC2V 7DD. *Livery*, 320. *Clerk*, Capt. R. J. Fisher, RN. *Master*, D. G. C. Inglefield
SALTERS (*9*). *Hall*, 4 Fore Street, London EC2Y 5DE. *Livery*, 165. *Clerk*, Col. M. P. Barneby. *Master*, A. Dawson Paul
IRONMONGERS (*10*). *Hall*, Shaftesbury Place, Barbican, London EC2Y 8AA. *Livery*, 224. *Clerk*, J. A. Oliver. *Master*, R. H. Hunting
VINTNERS (*11*). *Hall*, Upper Thames Street, London EC4V 3BJ. *Livery*, 308. *Clerk*, Brig. G. Read, CBE. *Master*, T. J. Hood
CLOTHWORKERS (*12*). *Hall*, Dunster Court, Mincing Lane, London EC3R 7AH. *Livery*, 200. *Clerk*, M. G. T. Harris. *Master*, R. L. L. Davis

OTHER CITY GUILDS
In alphabetical order

ACTUARIES (*91*). *Livery*, 190. *Clerk*, P. D. Esslemont, 16A Cadogan Square, London SW1X 0JU. *Master*, M. H. Field, CBE

AIR PILOTS AND AIR NAVIGATORS, GUILD OF (*81*). *Livery*, 415. *Grand Master*, HRH The Prince Philip, Duke of Edinburgh, KG, KT. *Clerk*, Gp Capt. W. M. Watkins, Cobham House, 291 Gray's Inn Road, London WC1X 8QF. *Master*, Dr I. C. Perry

APOTHECARIES, SOCIETY OF (*58*). *Hall*, 14 Black Friars Lane, London EC4V 6EJ. *Livery*, 1,286. *Clerk*, Lt.-Col. R. J. Stringer. *Master*, Dr F. B. Gibberd

ARBITRATORS (*93*). *Livery*, 234. *Clerk*, Lt.-Col. I. R. P. Green, 2 Bolts Hill, Castle Camps, Cambs CB1 6TL. *Master*, C. J. Evans

ARMOURERS AND BRASIERS (*22*). *Hall*, 81 Coleman Street, London EC2R 5BJ. *Livery*, 125. *Clerk*, Cdr. T. J. K. Sloane, OBE. *Master*, M. J. Paton

BAKERS (*19*). *Hall*, Harp Lane, London EC3R 6DP. *Livery*, 389. *Clerk (acting)*, J. W. Tompkins. *Master*, J. Moon

BARBERS (*17*). *Hall*, Monkwell Square, Wood Street, London EC2Y 5BL. *Livery*, 235. *Clerk*, Brig. A. F. Eastburn. *Master*, R. R. C. Bloomfield, CBE

BASKETMAKERS (*52*). *Livery*, 341. *Clerk*, Maj. G. J. Flint-Shipman, TD, 48 Seymour Walk, London SW10 9NF. *Prime Warden*, J. Heffernan

BLACKSMITHS (*40*). *Livery*, 239. *Clerk*, R. C. Jorden, 27 Cheyne Walk, Grange Park, London N21 1DB. *Prime Warden*, R. Lyons

BOWYERS (*38*). *Livery*, 105. *Clerk*, J. R. Owen-Ward, 261 Green Lanes, London N13 4XE. *Master*, P. J. Begent

BREWERS (*14*). *Hall*, Aldermanbury Square, London EC2V 7HR. *Livery*, 115. *Clerk*, C. W. Dallmeyer. *Master*, M. R. M. Foster

BRODERERS (*48*). *Livery*, 158. *Clerk*, P. J. C. Crouch, 11 Bridge Road, East Molesey, Surrey KT8 9EU. *Master*, B. E. Toye

BUILDERS MERCHANTS (*88*). *Livery*, 183. *Clerk*, Miss S. M. Robinson, TD, 14 Charterhouse Square, London EC1M 6AX. *Master*, D. Bedford

BUTCHERS (*24*). *Hall*, 87 Bartholomew Close, London EC1A 7EB. *Livery*, 650. *Clerk*, J. C. M. Chapman. *Master*, Mrs S. Reid

CARMEN (*77*). *Livery*, 430. *Clerk*, Cdr. R. M. H. Bawtree, OBE, 35–37 Ludgate Hill, London EC4M 7JN. *Master*, J. M. B. Gotch

CARPENTERS (*26*). *Hall*, 1 Throgmorton Avenue, London EC2N 2JJ. *Livery*, 150. *Clerk*, Maj.-Gen. P. T. Stevenson, OBE. *Master*, D. Hornsby

CHARTERED ACCOUNTANTS (*86*). *Livery*, 345. *Clerk*, C. Bygrave, The Rustlings, Valley Close, Studham, Dunstable, Beds LU6 2QN. *Master*, W. S. C. Richards

CHARTERED ARCHITECTS (*98*). *Livery*, 150. *Clerk*, J. Griffiths, 28 Palace Road, East Molesey, Surrey KT8 9DL. *Master*, Mrs S. Reid

CHARTERED SECRETARIES AND ADMINISTRATORS (*87*). *Livery*, 225. *Hon. Clerk*, W. C. Hammond, MBE, St Dunstan's House, Carey Lane, London EC2V 8AA. *Master*, G. S. Finn

CHARTERED SURVEYORS (*85*). *Livery*, 350. *Clerk*, Mrs A. L. Jackson, 16 St Mary-at-Hill, London EC3R 8EE. *Master*, D. H. Pepper

CLOCKMAKERS (*61*). *Livery*, 220. *Clerk*, Gp Capt P. H. Gibson, MBE, Room 66–67 Albert Buildings, 49 Queen Victoria Street, London EC4N 4SE. *Master*, Air Vice-Marshal P. H. Latham, CB, AFC

COACHMAKERS AND COACH-HARNESS MAKERS (*72*). *Livery*, 420. *Clerk*, Maj. W. H. Wharfe, 149 Banstead Road, Ewell, Epsom, Surrey KT17 3HL. *Master*, J. Smillie

CONSTRUCTORS (*99*). *Livery*, 119. *Clerk*, L. L. Brace, 181 Fentiman Road, London SW8 1JY. *Master*, P. A. Everett

COOKS (*35*). *Livery*, 75. *Clerk*, M. C. Thatcher, 35 Great Peter Street, London SW1P 3LR. *Master*, Revd J. K. L. Powell

COOPERS (*36*). *Hall*, 13 Devonshire Square, London EC2M 4TH. *Livery*, 260. *Clerk*, J. A. Newton. *Master*, J. B. Holden

CORDWAINERS (*27*). *Livery* 152. *Clerk*, Lt.-Col. J. R. Blundell, RM, Eldon Chambers, 30 Fleet Street, London EC4Y 1AA. *Master*, T. C. Weber-Brown

CURRIERS (*29*). *Livery*, 96. *Clerk*, Gp Capt F. J. Hamilton, Kestrel Cottage, East Knoyle, Salisbury SP3 6AD. *Master*, R. G. Blaber

CUTLERS (*18*). *Hall*, Warwick Lane, London EC4M 7BR. *Livery*, 115. *Clerk*, K. S. G. Hinde, TD. *Master*, J. A. L. Evans, CBE

DISTILLERS (*69*). *Livery*, 260. *Clerk*, C. V. Hughes, 71 Lincoln's Inn Fields, London WC2A 3JF. *Master*, A. W. C. Edwards

DYERS (*13*). *Hall*, 10 Dowgate Hill, London EC4R 2ST. *Livery*, 121. *Clerk*, J. R. Chambers. *Prime Warden*, R. S. Brooks

ENGINEERS (*94*). *Livery*, 281. *Clerk*, Cdr. B. D. Gibson, Kiln Bank, Bodle Street Green, Hailsham, E. Sussex BN27 4UA. *Master*, Prof. Sir Frederick Crawford, FENG.

ENVIRONMENTAL CLEANERS (*97*). *Livery*, 185. *Clerk*, S. J. Holt, Whitethorns, Rannoch Road, Crowborough, E. Sussex TN6 1RA. *Master*, A. W. E. Ellison

FAN MAKERS (*76*). *Livery*, 205. *Clerk*, Lt.-Col. I. R. P. Green, 2 Bolts Hill, Castle Camps, Cambs CB1 6TL. *Master*, A. S. Collins, TD

FARMERS (*80*). *Hall*, 3 Cloth Street, London EC1A 7LD. *Livery*, 300. *Clerk*, Miss M. L. Winter. *Master*, W. M. Cornish

FARRIERS (*55*). *Livery*, 360. *Clerk*, H. W. H. Ellis, 37 The Uplands, Loughton, Essex IG10 1NQ. *Master*, T. L. Baker

FELTMAKERS (*63*). *Livery*, 170. *Clerk*, Lt.-Col. C. J. Holroyd, Providence Cottage, Chute Cadley, Andover, Hants SP11 9EB. *Master*, Capt. P. Cobb, OBE, RN

FLETCHERS (*39*). *Hall*, 3 Cloth Street, London EC1A 7LD. *Livery*, 110. *Clerk*, J. R. Owen-Ward. *Master*, L. S. Johnson

FOUNDERS (*33*). *Hall*, 1 Cloth Fair, London EC1A 7HT. *Livery*, 175. *Clerk*, A. J. Gillett. *Master*, R. G. Lightfoot

FRAMEWORK KNITTERS (*64*). *Livery*, 210. *Clerk*, H. W. H. Ellis, Whitegarth Chambers, 37 The Uplands, Loughton, Essex IG10 1NQ. *Master*, T. M. Fraser

FRUITERERS (*45*). *Livery*, 270. *Clerk*, Lt.-Col. L. G. French, Chapelstones, 84 High Street, Codford St Mary, Warminster, Wilts BA12 0ND. *Master*, M. J. Tanguy

FUELLERS (*95*). *Livery*, 65. *Clerk*, S. J. Lee, Fords, 134 Ockford Road, Godalming, Surrey GU7 1RG. *Master*, Brig. C. E. Wilkinson

FURNITURE MAKERS (*83*). *Livery*, 257. *Clerk*, Mrs J. A. Wright, 9 Little Trinity Lane, London EC4V 2AD. *Master*, H. P. Joscelyne

GARDENERS (*66*). *Livery*, 248. *Clerk*, Col. N. G. S. Gray, 25 Luke Street, London EC2A 4AR. *Master*, I. B. Flanagan

GIRDLERS (*23*). *Hall*, Basinghall Avenue, London EC2V 5DD. *Livery*, 80. *Clerk*, Lt.-Col. R. Sullivan. *Master*, Sir Gordon Pirie, CVO, CBE

GLASS-SELLERS (*71*). *Livery*, 165. *Hon. Clerk*, B. J. Rawles, 175 Aragon Avenue, Thames Ditton, Surrey KT7 0PY. *Master*, J. G. Thorpe

GLAZIERS AND PAINTERS OF GLASS (*53*). *Hall*, 9 Montague Close, London SE1 9DD. *Livery*, 270. *Clerk*, P. R. Batchelor. *Master*, M. C. Tosh

GLOVERS (*62*). *Livery*, 280. *Clerk*, Mrs M. Hood, 71 Ifield Road, London SW10 9AU. *Master*, A. S. Fishman

GOLD AND SILVER WYRE DRAWERS (74). *Livery,* 325. *Clerk,*
J. R. Williams, 50 Cheyne Avenue, London E18 2DR.
Master, N. S. Nichols

GUNMAKERS (73). *Livery,* 280. *Clerk,* J. M. Riches, The
Proof House, 48–50 Commercial Road, London E1 1LP.
Master, R. W. Whittaker

HORNERS (54). *Livery,* 260. *Clerk,* S. J. Holt, Whitethorns,
Rannoch Road, Crowborough, E. Sussex TN6 1RA. *Master,*
D. J. Rogers

INFORMATION TECHNOLOGISTS (100). *Livery,* 255. *Clerk,*
Mrs G. Davies, 30 Aylesbury Street, London EC1R OER.
Master, K. Arnold, OBE

INNHOLDERS (32). *Hall,* College Street, London EC4R 2RH.
Livery, 130. *Clerk,* J. R. Edwardes Jones. *Master,* A. House

INSURERS (92). *Hall,* 20 Aldermanbury, London EC2V 7HY.
Livery, 373. *Clerk,* V. D. Webb. *Master,* B. V. Day

JOINERS AND CEILERS (41). *Livery,* 130. *Clerk,* Mrs A. L.
Jackson, 75 Meadway Drive, Horsell, Woking, Surrey
GU21 4TF. *Master,* S. K. Riddick

LAUNDERERS (89). *Hall,* 9 Montague Close, London
SE1 9DD. *Livery,* 230. *Clerk,* vacant. *Master,* D. R. Browne

LEATHERSELLERS (15). *Hall,* 15 St Helen's Place, London
EC3A 6DQ. *Livery,* 150. *Clerk,* Capt. J. G. F. Cooke, OBE, RN.
Master, D. W. Dove

LIGHTMONGERS (96). *Livery,* 132. *Clerk,* D. B. Wheatley, 53
Leithcote Gardens, London SW16 2UX. *Master,* D. J.
Collins

LORINERS (57). *Livery,* 350. *Clerk,* J. R. Williams, 50 Cheyne
Avenue, London E18 2DR. *Master,* A. Bischoff

MAKERS OF PLAYING CARDS (75). *Livery,* 149. *Clerk,* M. J.
Smyth, 6 The Priory, Godstone, Surrey RH9 8NL. *Master,*
M. H. Goodall

MARKETORS (90). *Livery,* 243. *Clerk,* Mrs G. Dutty, 14
Charterhouse Square, London EC1M 6AX. *Master,*
D. Thomas

MASONS (30). *Livery,* 125. *Clerk,* T. F. Ackland, 261 Green
Lanes, London N13 4XE. *Master,* B. Woodman

MASTER MARINERS, HONOURABLE COMPANY OF (78).
HQS *Wellington,* Temple Stairs, Victoria Embankment,
London WC2R 2PN. *Livery,* 250. *Clerk,* J. A. V. Maddock.
Admiral, HRH The Duke of Edinburgh, KG, KT. *Master,*
Capt. G. T. Davies

MUSICIANS (50). *Livery,* 320. *Clerk,* S. F. N. Waley, St
Dunstan's House, 2–4 Carey Lane, London EC2V 8AA.
Master, A. M. Burnett-Brown

NEEDLEMAKERS (65). *Livery,* 240. *Clerk,* M. G. Cook, 5
Staple Inn, London WC1V 7QH. *Master,* B. G. Amery

PAINTER-STAINERS (28). *Hall,* 9 Little Trinity Lane,
London EC4V 2AD. *Livery,* 308. *Clerk,* Col. W. J. Chesshyre.
Master, G. F. Jacobs

PATTENMAKERS (70). *Livery,* 179. *Clerk,* C. L. K. Ledger, 17
Orchard Close, The Rutts, Bushey Heath, Herts WD2
1LW. *Master,* J. A. V. Townsend

PAVIORS (56). *Livery,* 250. *Clerk,* R. F. Coe, 154 Dukes
Avenue, New Malden, Surrey KT3 4HR. *Master,* J. Luff

PEWTERERS (16). *Hall,* Oat Lane, London EC2V 7DE. *Livery,*
113. *Clerk,* Cdr. A. Steiner, OBE. *Master,* J. P. Hull

PLAISTERERS (46). *Hall,* 1 London Wall, London EC4Y 5JU.
Livery, 208. *Clerk,* R. Vickers. *Master,* B. Lincoln

PLUMBERS (31). *Livery,* 349. *Clerk,* Lt.-Col. R. J. A. Paterson-
Fox, 49 Queen Victoria Street, London EC4N 4SA.
Master, C. D. Smith

POULTERS (34). *Livery,* 173. *Clerk,* A. W. Scott, 23 Orchard
Drive, Chorleywood, Herts WD3 5QN. *Master,* M. B.
Savory

SADDLERS (25). *Hall,* 40 Gutter Lane, London EC2V 6BR.
Livery, 70. *Clerk,* Gp Capt W. S. Brereton Martin, CBE.
Master, W. Price

SCIENTIFIC INSTRUMENT MAKERS (84). *Hall,* 9 Montague
Close, London SE1 9DD. *Livery,* 232. *Clerk,* F. G. Everard.
Master, W. Lyons

SCRIVENERS (44). *Livery,* 215. *Clerk,* P. C. Stevens, HQS
Wellington, Temple Stairs, Victoria Embankment,
London WC2R 2PN. *Master,* H. J. W. Harman

SHIPWRIGHTS (59). *Livery,* 420. *Clerk,* Capt. R. F. Channon,
RN, Ironmongers' Hall, Barbican, London EC2Y 8AA.
Permanent Master, HRH The Duke of Edinburgh, KG, KT.
Prime Warden, J. G. M. Hart

SOLICITORS (79). *Livery,* 265. *Clerk,* Miss S. M. Robinson,
TD, 14 Charterhouse Square, London EC1M 6AX. *Master,*
W. King

SPECTACLE MAKERS (60). *Livery,* 370. *Clerk,* C. J. Eldridge,
Apothecaries' Hall, Black Friars Lane, London EC4V 6EL.
Master, C. Stone

STATIONERS AND NEWSPAPER MAKERS (47). *Hall,* Ave
Maria Lane, London EC4M 7DD. *Livery,* 439. *Clerk,* Brig.
D. G. Sharp. *Master,* R. Fullick

TALLOW CHANDLERS (21). *Hall,* 4 Dowgate Hill, London
EC4R 2SH. *Livery,* 180. *Clerk,* Brig. W. K. L. Prosser, CBE, MC.
Master, C. A. Holborow, OBE, TD, MD, FRCS

TIN PLATE WORKERS alias Wire Workers (67). *Livery,* 174.
Clerk, S. J. Holt, Whitethorns, Rannoch Road,
Crowborough, E. Sussex TN6 1RA. *Master,* Dr
R. S. A. White

TOBACCO PIPE MAKERS AND TOBACCO BLENDERS (82).
Livery, 161. *Clerk,* N. J. Hallings-Pott, Hackhurst Farm,
Lower Dicker, Hailsham, E. Sussex BN27 4BP. *Master,*
R. L. H. Merton

TURNERS (51). *Livery,* 180. *Clerk,* Maj.-Gen. D. Shaw, CB,
CBE, c/o Apothecaries' Hall, Black Friars Lane, London
EC4V 6EL. *Master,* J. N. Ciclitira

TYLERS AND BRICKLAYERS (37). *Livery,* 130. *Clerk,*
J. Griffiths, 28 Palace Road, East Molesey, Surrey
KT8 9DL. *Master,* B. G. Holliday, MC.

UPHOLDERS (49). *Livery,* 200. *Clerk,* G. J. K. Darby,
Kirstone, Beckenham Place Park, Beckenham, Kent BR3
2BN. *Master,* D. S. Austin

WAX CHANDLERS (20). *Hall,* Gresham Street, London EC2V
7AD. *Livery,* 88. *Clerk,* Cdr J. Stevens. *Master,* D. La Riece

WEAVERS (42). *Livery,* 125. *Clerk,* Mrs F. Newcombe,
Saddlers' House, Gutter Lane, London EC2V 6BR. *Upper
Bailiff,* S. A. A. Block

WHEELWRIGHTS (68). *Livery,* 250. *Clerk,* M. G. Cook, 9
Staple Inn, London WC1V 7QH. *Master,* B. P. Boreham

WOOLMEN (43). *Livery,* 135. *Clerk,* F. Allen, Hollands,
Hedsor Road, Bourne End, Bucks SL8 5EC. *Master,*
M. D. Abrahams, CBE

FIREFIGHTERS (*No livery*), Freemen, 110. *Clerk,* T. Morris, 20
Aldermanbury, London EC2V 7GF. *Master,* K. Barnes

PARISH CLERKS (*No livery*). *Members,* 90. *Clerk,* Lt.-Col.
B. J. N. Coombes, 1 Dean Trench Street, London SW1P
3HB. *Master,* Revd G. L. Blacktop

WATER CONSERVATORS (*No livery*). *Freemen,* 162. *Clerk,*
H. B. Berridge, MBE, 20 Aldermanbury, London EC2V 7GF.
Master, E. W. Flaxman.

WATERMEN AND LIGHTERMEN (*No livery*). *Craft Owning
Freemen,* 300. *Hall,* 18 St Mary-at-Hill, London EC3R 8EE.
Clerk, R. G. Crouch. *Master,* Capt. Sir Malcolm Edge,
KCVO

WORLD TRADERS (*No livery*). *Freemen,* 83. *Clerk,*
J. T. Norman, 13 Pinewood Road, Branksome Park,
Poole, Dorset BH13 6JP. *Master,* J. Davis, CBE

LONDON BOROUGH COUNCILS

Council	Municipal offices	Population 1994	Band D charge 1996	Chief Executive (*Managing Director)	Mayor (a) Lord Mayor 1996–7
Barking and Dagenham	°Dagenham, RM10 7BN	155,000	£576.00	W. C. Smith	J. Thomas
Barnet	†The Burroughs, Hendon, NW4 4BG	308,200	636.85	M. M. Caller	Ms P. Coleman
Bexley	‡Bexleyheath, Kent DA6 7LB	220,400	583.92	C. Duffield	R. Brierly
Brent	†Forty Lane, Wembley, HA9 9EZ	244,500	455.50	G. Benham	Ms L. Patel
Bromley	°Bromley, BR1 3UH	293,000	540.00	M. Blanch	P. Woods
§Camden	†Judd Street, WC1H 9JE	182,500	778.60	S. Bundred	Ms G. Lazenby
§CITY OF WESTMINSTER	City Hall, Victoria Street, SW1E 6QP	190,100	295.00	*W. C. Roots	(a) R. Davis
Croydon	Taberner House, Park Lane, Croydon CR9 3JS	326,800	593.00	D. Wechsler	P. Spalding
Ealing	†Uxbridge Road, W5 2HL	289,800	532.00	Ms G. Guy	M. Patil
Enfield	°Enfield, EN1 3XA	259,800	616.88	D. Plank	P. Cunneen
§Greenwich	†Wellington Street, SE18 6PW	212,200	763.29	C. Roberts	Ms J. Gillman
§Hackney	†Mare Street, E8 1EA	192,500	855.13	A. Elliston	Ms L. Hibberd
§Hammersmith and Fulham	†King Street, W6 9JU	156,600	725.00	*N. Newton	I. Coleman
Haringey	°Wood Green, N22 4LE	212,300	780.00	G. Singh	R. Blanchard
Harrow	°Harrow, HA1 2UH	210,300	579.69	A. G. Redmond	A. Hamlin
Havering	†Romford, RM1 3BD	231,700	595.00	H. W. Tinworth	I. Cameron
Hillingdon	°Uxbridge, UB8 1UW	243,000	593.32	C. Rippingale	Ms J. Blundell
Hounslow	°Lampton Road, Hounslow, TW3 4DN	202,700	661.68	R. Kerslake	Ms M. Brister
§Islington	†Upper Street, N1 2UD	175,200	853.39	Ms L. Fullick	Ms S. Marks
§Kensington and Chelsea (RB)	†Hornton Street, W8 7NX	151,500	503.94	R. A. Taylor	J. Corbet-Singleton
Kingston upon Thames (RB)	Guildhall, Kingston upon Thames KT1 1EU	138,500	569.48	B. Quoroll	I. Reid
§Lambeth	†Brixton Hill, SW2 1RW	260,700	665.00	Ms H. Rabbatts	A. Bays
§Lewisham	†Catford, SE6 4RU	242,400	629.45	B. Quirk	Ms F. Hayee
Merton	°London Road, Morden, SM4 5DX	177,200	644.67	Ms S. Charteris	S. Flegg
Newham	†East Ham, E6 2RP	226,800	594.00	Ms W. Thomson	Ms S. Ahmad
Redbridge	†Ilford, IG1 1DD	225,100	581.00	M. J. Frater	R. Hoskins
Richmond upon Thames	°York Street, Twickenham, TW1 3AA	172,000	683.00	R. L. Harbord	M. Rolands
§Southwark	†Peckham Road, SE5 8UB	228,800	730.91	W. Coomber	Ms J. Khachik
Sutton	‡St Nicholas Way, Sutton, SM1 1EA	173,400	579.06	Mrs P. Hughes	S. Theed
§Tower Hamlets	107 Commercial Street, E1 6BG	170,500	645.91	Ms S. Pierce	A. Jacob
Waltham Forest	†Forest Road, Walthamstow, E17 4JF	221,800	737.83	A. Tobias	R. J. Wheatley
§Wandsworth	†Wandsworth, SW18 2PU	266,600	431.26	G. K. Jones	Miss D. Whittingham

§   Inner London Borough
RB Royal Borough
°   Civic Centre
†   Town Hall
‡   Civic Offices
Source of population statistics: OPCS Monitor PP1 95/1, 17 August 1995
For explanation of council tax, *see* pages 519–20

Wales

The Principality of Wales (Cymru) occupies the extreme west of the central southern portion of the island of Great Britain, with a total area of 8,015 sq. miles (20,758 sq. km): land 7,965 sq. miles (20,628 sq. km); inland water 50 sq. miles (130 sq. km). It is bounded on the north by the Irish Sea, on the south by the Bristol Channel, on the east by the English counties of Cheshire, Shropshire, Hereford and Worcester, and Gloucestershire, and on the west by St George's Channel.

Across the Menai Straits is the island of Ynys Môn (Anglesey) (276 sq. miles), communication with which is facilitated by the Menai Suspension Bridge (1,000 ft long) built by Telford in 1826, and by the tubular railway bridge (1,100 ft long) built by Stephenson in 1850. Holyhead harbour, on Holy Isle (north-west of Anglesey), provides accommodation for ferry services to Dublin (70 miles).

POPULATION

The population at the 1991 Census was 2,811,865 (males 1,356,886; females 1,454,979). The average density of population in 1991 was 1.36 persons per hectare.

RELIEF

Wales is a country of extensive tracts of high plateau and shorter stretches of mountain ranges deeply dissected by river valleys. Lower-lying ground is largely confined to the coastal belt and the lower parts of the valleys. The highest mountains are those of Snowdonia in the north-west (Snowdon, 3,559 ft), Berwyn (Aran Fawddwy, 2,971 ft), Cader Idris (Pen y Gadair, 2,928 ft), Dyfed (Plynlimon, 2,467 ft), and the Black Mountain, Brecon Beacons and Black Forest ranges in the south-east (Carmarthen Van, 2,630 ft, Pen y Fan, 2,906 ft, Waun Fâch, 2,660 ft).

HYDROGRAPHY

The principal river rising in Wales is the Severn (*see* page 529), which flows from the slopes of Plynlimon to the English border. The Wye (130 miles) also rises in the slopes of Plynlimon. The Usk (56 miles) flows into the Bristol Channel, through Gwent. The Dee (70 miles) rises in Bala Lake and flows through the Vale of Llangollen, where an aqueduct (built by Telford in 1805) carries the Pontcysyllte branch of the Shropshire Union Canal across the valley. The estuary of the Dee is the navigable portion, 14 miles in length and about five miles in breadth, and the tide rushes in with dangerous speed over the 'Sands of Dee'. The Towy (68 miles), Teifi (50 miles), Taff (40 miles), Dovey (30 miles), Taf (25 miles) and Conway (24 miles), the last named broad and navigable, are wholly Welsh rivers.

The largest natural lake is Bala (Llyn Tegid) in Gwynedd, nearly four miles long and about one mile wide. Lake Vyrnwy is an artificial reservoir, about the size of Bala, and forms the water supply of Liverpool; Birmingham is supplied from reservoirs in the Elan and Claerwen valleys.

WELSH LANGUAGE

According to the 1991 Census results, the percentage of persons of three years and over able to speak Welsh was:

Clwyd	18.2	Powys	20.2
Dyfed	43.7	S. Glamorgan	6.5
Gwent	2.4	W. Glamorgan	15.0
Gwynedd	61.0		
Mid Glamorgan	8.5	Wales	18.7

The 1991 figure represents a slight decline from 18.9 per cent in 1981 (1971, 20.8 per cent; 1961, 26 per cent).

FLAG

The flag of Wales, the Red Dragon (Y Ddraig Goch), is a red dragon on a field divided white over green (per fess argent and vert a dragon passant gules). The flag was augmented in 1953 by a royal badge on a shield encircled with a riband bearing the words *Ddraig Goch Ddyry Cychwyn* and imperially crowned, but this augmented flag is rarely used.

EARLY HISTORY

The earliest inhabitants of whom there is any record appear to have been subdued or exterminated by the Goidels (a people of Celtic race) in the Bronze Age. A further invasion of Celtic Brythons and Belgae followed in the ensuing Iron Age. The Roman conquest of southern Britain and Wales was for some time successfully opposed by Caratacus (Caractacus or Caradog), chieftain of the Catuvellauni and son of Cunobelinus (Cymbeline). South-east Wales was subjugated and the legionary fortress at Caerleon-on-Usk established by about AD 75–77; the conquest of Wales was completed by Agricola about AD 78. Communications were opened up by the construction of military roads from Chester to Caerleon-on-Usk and Caerwent, and from Chester to Conwy (and thence to Carmarthen and Neath). Christianity was introduced during the Roman occupation, in the fourth century.

ANGLO-SAXON ATTACKS

The Anglo-Saxon invaders of southern Britain drove the Celts into the mountain stronghold of Wales, and into Strathclyde (Cumberland and south-west Scotland) and Cornwall, giving them the name of *Waelisc* (Welsh), meaning 'foreign'. The West Saxons' victory of Deorham (AD 577) isolated Wales from Cornwall and the battle of Chester (AD 613) cut off communication with Strathclyde and northern Britain. In the eighth century the boundaries of the Welsh were further restricted by the annexations of Offa, King of Mercia, and counter-attacks were largely prevented by the construction of an artificial boundary from the Dee to the Wye (Offa's Dyke).

In the ninth century Rhodri Mawr (844–878) united the country and successfully resisted further incursions of the Saxons by land and raids of Norse and Danish pirates by sea, but at his death his three provinces of Gwynedd (north), Powys (mid) and Deheubarth (south) were divided among his three sons, Anarawd, Mervyn and Cadell. Cadell's son Hywel Dda ruled a large part of Wales and codified its laws but the provinces were not united again until the rule of Llewelyn ap Seisyllt (husband of the heiress of Gwynedd) from 1018 to 1023.

THE NORMAN CONQUEST

After the Norman conquest of England, William I created palatine counties along the Welsh frontier, and the Norman barons began to make encroachments into Welsh territory. The Welsh princes recovered many of their losses during the civil wars of Stephen's reign and in the early 13th century Owen Gruffydd, prince of Gwynedd, was the dominant figure in Wales. Under Llewelyn ap Iorwerth (1194–1240) the Welsh united in powerful resistance to English incursions and Llewelyn's privileges and *de facto* independence were recognized in Magna Carta. His grandson, Llewelyn ap Gruffydd, was the last native

prince; he was killed in 1282 during hostilities between the
Welsh and English, allowing Edward I of England to
establish his authority over the country. On 7 February
1301, Edward of Caernarvon, son of Edward I, was created
Prince of Wales, a title which has subsequently been borne
by the eldest son of the sovereign.

Strong Welsh national feeling continued, expressed in
the early 15th century in the rising led by Owain Glyndŵr,
but the situation was altered by the accession to the English
throne in 1485 of Henry VII of the Welsh House of Tudor.
Wales was politically assimilated to England under the Act
of Union of 1535, which extended English laws to the
Principality and gave it parliamentary representation for
the first time.

EISTEDDFOD

The Welsh are a distinct nation, with a language and
literature of their own, and the national bardic festival
(Eisteddfod), instituted by Prince Rhys ap Griffith in 1176,
is still held annually (for date, *see* page 12). These
Eisteddfodau (sessions) form part of the *Gorsedd* (assembly),
which is believed to date from the time of Prydian, a ruling
prince in an age many centuries before the Christian era.

PRINCIPAL CITIES

CARDIFF

Cardiff, at the mouth of the Rivers Taff, Rhymney and Ely,
is the capital city of Wales and a major administrative,
commercial and business centre. It has many industries,
including steel and cigars, and its flourishing port is within
the Cardiff Bay area, subject of a major redevelopment
until the year 2000.

The many fine buildings include the City Hall, the
National Museum of Wales, University Buildings, Law
Courts, Welsh Office, County Hall, Police Headquarters,
the Temple of Peace and Health, Llandaff Cathedral, the
Welsh National Folk Museum at St Fagans, Cardiff Castle,
the New Theatre, the Sherman Theatre and the Welsh
College of Music and Drama. More recent buildings
include St David's Hall, Cardiff International Arena and
World Trade Centre, and the Welsh National Ice Rink.
The Millenium Stadium is to be completed for the 1999
rugby World Cup.

SWANSEA

Swansea (*Abertawe*) is a city and a seaport. The Gower
peninsula was brought within the city boundary under
local government reform in 1974. The trade of the port
includes coal, steel products, containerized goods and the
import and export of petroleum products and petrochemicals.

The principal buildings are the Norman Castle (rebuilt
*c.*1330), the Royal Institution of South Wales, founded in
1835 (including Library), the University College at
Singleton, and the Guildhall, containing the Brangwyn
panels. More recent buildings include the Industrial and
Maritime Museum, the new Maritime Quarter and Marina
and the leisure centre.

Swansea was chartered by the Earl of Warwick,
*c.*1158–84, and further charters were granted by King
John, Henry III, Edward II, Edward III and James II,
Cromwell (two) and the Marcher Lord William de Breos.

LOCAL COUNCILS

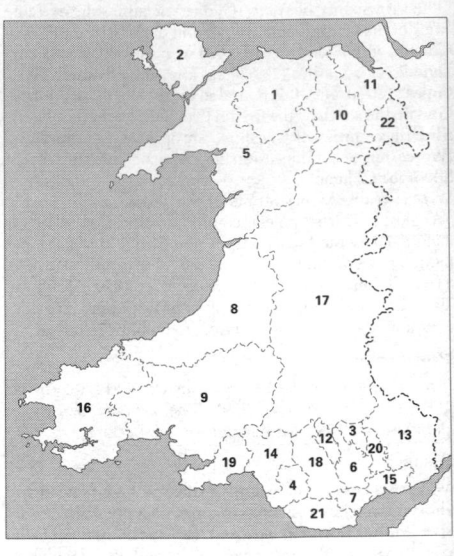

Key	County
1	Conwy
2	Anglesey
3	Blaenau Gwent
4	Bridgend
5	Caernarfonshire and Merionethshire
6	Caerphilly
7	Cardiff
8	Ceredigion
9	Carmarthenshire
10	Denbighshire
11	Flintshire
12	Merthyr Tydfil
13	Monmouthshire
14	Neath and Port Talbot
15	Newport
16	Pembrokeshire
17	Powys
18	Rhondda, Cynon, Taff
19	Swansea
20	Torfaen
21	The Vale of Glamorgan
22	Wrexham

LORD LIEUTENANTS AND HIGH SHERIFFS

County	Lord Lieutenant	High Sheriff, 1996–7
Clwyd	Sir William Gladstone, Bt.	R. H. W. Graham-Palmer
Dyfed	Sir David Mansel Lewis, KCVO	D. C. Jones-Davies, OBE
Gwent	Sir Richard Hanbury-Tenison, KCVO	I. F. Donald
Gwynedd	R. E. Meuric Rees, CBE	Maj. D. O. Carpenter
Mid Glamorgan	M. A. McLaggan	D. Clayton-Jones, TD
Powys	M. L. Bourdillon	W. A. D. Windham
South Glamorgan	Capt. N. Lloyd-Edwards	R. P. V. Rees, OBE
West Glamorgan	R. C. Hastie, CBE	R. Lewis

LOCAL COUNCILS

SMALL CAPITALS denote CITY status
§ Denotes Borough status

Council	Administrative headquarters	Population (latest estimate)	Band D charge 1996	Chief Executive	Chairman 1996–7 (a) Mayor (b) Lord Mayor
Anglesey	Llangefni	70,000	£416.81	L. Gibson	G. W. Roberts
§Blaenau Gwent	Ebbw Vale	73,300	430.00	R. Leadbetter, OBE	(a) M. B. Dally
§Bridgend	Bridgend	130,874	542.04	I. K. Lewis	(a) Mrs M. Butcher
Caernarfonshire and Merionethshire	Caernarfon	117,000	469.00	G. Jones	D. Orwig
§Caerphilly	Hengoed	170,000	462.69	M. Davies	(a) L. Lewis
CARDIFF	Cardiff	306,500	375.83	B. Davies	(b) J. Phillips
Carmarthenshire	Carmarthen	169,000	520.00	R. Morgan	D. T. Davies, OBE, MM
Ceredigion	Aberaeron	69,700	446.53	O. Watkin	G. Ellis
§Conwy	Conwy	110,700	401.26	C. D. Barker	W. Jones
Denbighshire	Ruthin	91,000	491.22	H. V. Thomas	R. Webb
Flintshire	Mold	144,000	500.48	P. McGreevy	Mrs I. Fellows, MBE
§Merthyr Tydfil	Merthyr Tydfil	60,000	495.46	R. V. Morris	(a) W. Smith
Monmouthshire	Cwmbran	81,000	409.06	J. Redfearn	V. G. Thomas
§Neath and Port Talbot	Port Talbot	140,000	561.76	K. Sawyers	(a) R. Jones
§Newport	Newport	130,000	389.00	R. D. Blair	(a) L. R. Turnball
Pembrokeshire	Haverfordwest	117,000	373.22	B. Parry-Jones	D. J. Thomas
Powys	Llandrindod Wells	123,600	433.86	N. Pringle	D. M. Jones
§Rhondda Cynon Taff	Tonypandy	232,581	493.00	G. R. Thomas	(a) R. Roberts
SWANSEA	Swansea	231,000	402.69	Ms V. Sugar	(b) D. Thomas
§Torfaen	Pontypool	90,700	438.35	Dr C. L. Grace	(a) S. P. Smith
§Vale of Glamorgan	Barry	119,200	424.92	D. Foster	N. Brown
§Wrexham	Wrexham	123,500	489.13	D. A. Griffin	(a) Mrs B. Greenaway

For explanation of council tax, see pages 519–20

Scotland

The Kingdom of Scotland occupies the northern portion of the main island of Great Britain and includes the Inner and Outer Hebrides, and the Orkney, Shetland, and many other islands. It lies between 60° 51′ 30″ and 54° 38′ N. latitude and between 1° 45′ 32″ and 6° 14′ W. longitude, with England to the south, the Atlantic Ocean on the north and west, and the North Sea on the east.

The greatest length of the mainland (Cape Wrath to the Mull of Galloway) is 274 miles, and the greatest breadth (Buchan Ness to Applecross) is 154 miles. The customary measurement of the island of Great Britain is from the site of John o' Groats house, near Duncansby Head, Caithness, to Land's End, Cornwall, a total distance of 603 miles in a straight line and approximately 900 miles by road.

The total area of Scotland is 30,420 sq. miles (78,789 sq. km); land 29,767 sq. miles (77,097 sq. km), inland water 653 sq. miles (1,692 sq. km).

POPULATION

The population at the 1991 Census was 4,998,567 (males 2,391,961; females 2,606,606). The average density of the population in 1991 was 0.65 persons per hectare.

RELIEF

There are three natural orographic divisions of Scotland. The southern uplands have their highest points in Merrick (2,766 ft), Rhinns of Kells (2,669 ft), and Cairnsmuir of Carsphairn (2,614 ft), in the west; and the Tweedsmuir Hills in the east (Hartfell 2,651 ft, Dollar Law 2,682 ft, Broad Law 2,756 ft).

The central lowlands, formed by the valleys of the Clyde, Forth and Tay, divide the southern uplands from the northern Highlands, which extend almost from the extreme north of the mainland to the central lowlands, and are divided into a northern and a southern system by the Great Glen.

The Grampian Mountains, which entirely cover the southern Highland area, include in the west Ben Nevis (4,406 ft), the highest point in the British Isles, and in the east the Cairngorm Mountains (Cairn Gorm 4,084 ft, Braeriach 4,248 ft, Ben Macdui 4,296 ft). The north-western Highland area contains the mountains of Wester and Easter Ross (Carn Eige 3,880 ft, Sgurr na Lapaich 3,775 ft).

Created, like the central lowlands, by a major geological fault, the Great Glen (60 miles long) runs between Inverness and Fort William, and contains Loch Ness, Loch Oich and Loch Lochy. These are linked to each other and to the north-east and south-west coasts of Scotland by the Caledonian Canal, providing a navigable passage between the Moray Firth and the Inner Hebrides.

HYDROGRAPHY

The western coast is fragmented by peninsulas and islands, and indented by fjords (sea-lochs), the longest of which is Loch Fyne (42 miles long) in Argyll. Although the east coast tends to be less fractured and lower, there are several great drowned inlets (firths), e.g. Firth of Forth, Firth of Tay, Moray Firth, as well as the Firth of Clyde in the west.

The lochs are the principal hydrographic feature. The largest in Scotland and in Britain is Loch Lomond (27 sq. miles), in the Grampian valleys; the longest and deepest is Loch Ness (24 miles long and 800 feet deep), in the Great Glen; and Loch Shin (20 miles long) and Loch Maree in the Highlands.

The longest river is the Tay (117 miles), noted for its salmon. It flows into the North Sea, with Dundee on the estuary, which is spanned by the Tay Bridge (10,289 ft) opened in 1887 and the Tay Road Bridge (7,365 ft) opened in 1966. Other noted salmon rivers are the Dee (90 miles) which flows into the North Sea at Aberdeen, and the Spey (110 miles), the swiftest flowing river in the British Isles, which flows into Moray Firth. The Tweed, which gave its name to the woollen cloth produced along its banks, marks in the lower stretches of its 96-mile course the border between Scotland and England.

The most important river commercially is the Clyde (106 miles), formed by the junction of the Daer and Portrail water, which flows through the city of Glasgow to the Firth of Clyde. During its course it passes over the picturesque Falls of Clyde, Bonnington Linn (30 ft), Corra Linn (84 ft), Dundaff Linn (10 ft) and Stonebyres Linn (80 ft), above and below Lanark. The Forth (66 miles), upon which stands Edinburgh, the capital, is spanned by the Forth (Railway) Bridge (1890), which is 5,330 feet long, and the Forth (Road) Bridge (1964), which has a total length of 6,156 feet (over water) and a single span of 3,000 feet.

The highest waterfall in Scotland, and the British Isles, is Eas a'Chùal Aluinn with a total height of 658 feet (200 m), which falls from Glas Bheinn in Sutherland. The Falls of Glomach, on a head-stream of the Elchaig in Wester Ross, have a drop of 370 feet.

GAELIC LANGUAGE

According to the 1991 Census, 1.4 per cent of the population of Scotland, mainly in the Highlands and western coastal regions, were able to speak the Scottish form of Gaelic.

FLAG

The flag of Scotland is known as the Saltire. It is a white diagonal cross on a blue field (saltire argent in a field azure) and represents St Andrew, the patron saint of Scotland.

THE SCOTTISH ISLANDS

The Hebrides did not become part of the Kingdom of Scotland until 1266, when they were ceded to Alexander III by Magnus of Norway. Orkney and Shetland fell to the Scottish Crown as a pledge for the unpaid dowry of Margaret of Denmark, wife of James III, in 1468, the Danish claims to suzerainty being relinquished in 1590 when James VI married Anne of Denmark.

ORKNEY

The Orkney Islands (total area 375½ sq. miles) lie about six miles north of the mainland, separated from it by the Pentland Firth. Of the 90 islands and islets (holms and skerries) in the group, about one-third are inhabited.

The total population at the 1991 Census was 19,612; the 1991 populations of the islands shown here include those of smaller islands forming part of the same civil parish.

Mainland, 15,128	Rousay, 291
Burray, 363	Sanday, 533
Eday, 166	Shapinsay, 322
Flotta and Fara, 126	South Ronaldsay, 943
Graemsay and Hoy, 477	Stronsay, 382
North Ronaldsay, 92	Westray, 704
Papa Westray, 85	

The islands are rich in Pictish and Scandinavian remains, the most notable being the Stone Age village of Skara Brae, the burial chamber of Maeshowe, the many brochs (Pictish towers) and St Magnus Cathedral. Scapa Flow, between the

Mainland and Hoy, was the war station of the British Grand Fleet from 1914 to 1919 and the scene of the scuttling of the surrendered German High Seas Fleet (21 June, 1919).

Most of the islands are low-lying and fertile, and farming (principally beef cattle) is the main industry. Flotta, to the south of Scapa Flow, is now the site of the oil terminal for the Piper, Claymore and Tartan fields in the North Sea.

The capital is Kirkwall (population 6,881) on Mainland.

SHETLAND

The Shetland Islands have a total area of 551 sq. miles and a population at the 1991 Census of 22,522. They lie about 50 miles north of the Orkneys, with Fair Isle about half-way between the two groups. Out Stack, off Muckle Flugga, one mile north of Unst, is the most northerly part of the British Isles (60° 51' 30" N. lat.).

There are over 100 islands, of which 16 are inhabited. Populations at the 1991 census were:

Mainland, 17,596	Muckle Roe, 115
Bressay, 352	Trondra, 117
East Burra, 72	Unst, 1,055
Fair Isle, 67	West Burra, 857
Fetlar, 90	Whalsay, 1,041
Housay, 85	Yell, 1,075

Shetland's many archaeological sites include Jarlshof, Mousa and Clickhimin, and its long connection with Scandinavia has resulted in a strong Norse influence on its place-names and dialect.

Industries include fishing, knitwear and farming. In addition to the fishing fleet there are fish processing factories, while the traditional handknitting of Fair Isle and Unst is supplemented now with machine-knitted garments. Farming is mainly crofting, with sheep being raised on the moorland and hills of the islands. Latterly the islands have become an important centre of the North Sea oil industry, with pipelines from the Brent and Ninian fields running to the terminal at Sullom Voe, the largest of its kind in Europe. Lerwick is the main centre for supply services for offshore oil exploration and development.

The capital is Lerwick (population 7,901) on Mainland.

THE HEBRIDES

Until the closing years of the 13th century the Hebrides included other Scottish islands in the Firth of Clyde, the peninsula of Kintyre (Argyllshire), the Isle of Man, and the (Irish) Isle of Rathlin. The origin of the name is stated to be the Greek *Eboudai*, latinized as *Hebudes* by Pliny, and corrupted to its present form. The Norwegian name *Sudreyjar* (Southern Islands) was latinized as *Sodorenses*, a name that survives in the Anglican bishopric of Sodor and Man.

There are over 500 islands and islets, of which about 100 are inhabited, though mountainous terrain and extensive peat bogs mean that only a fraction of the total area is under cultivation. Stone, Bronze and Iron Age settlement has left many remains, including those at Callanish on Lewis, and Norse colonization has influenced language, customs and place-names. Occupations include farming (mostly crofting and stock-raising), fishing and the manufacture of tweeds and other woollens. Tourism is also an important factor in the economy.

The Inner Hebrides lie off the west coast of Scotland and relatively close to the mainland. The largest and best-known is Skye (area 643 sq. miles; pop. 8,868; chief town, Portree), which contains the Cuillin Hills (Sgurr Alasdair 3,257 ft), the Red Hills (Beinn na Caillich 2,403 ft), Bla Bheinn (3,046 ft) and The Storr (2,358 ft). Skye is also

famous as the refuge of the Young Pretender in 1746. Other islands in the Highland Region include Raasay (pop. 163), Rum, Eigg and Muck.

Islands in the Strathclyde Region include Arran (pop. 4,474) containing Goat Fell (2,868 ft); Coll and Tiree (pop. 940); Colonsay and Oronsay (pop. 106); Islay (area 235 sq. miles; pop. 3,538); Jura (area 160 sq. miles; pop. 196) with a range of hills culminating in the Paps of Jura (Beinn-an-Oir, 2,576 ft, and Beinn Chaolais, 2,477 ft); and Mull (area 367 sq. miles; pop. 2,708; chief town Tobermory) containing Ben More (3,171 ft).

The Outer Hebrides, separated from the mainland by the Minch, now form the Western Isles Islands Council area (area 1,119 sq. miles; population at the 1991 Census 29,600). The main islands are Lewis with Harris (area 770 sq. miles, pop. 21,737), whose chief town, Stornoway, is the administrative headquarters; North Uist (pop. 1,404); South Uist (pop. 2,106); Baleshare (55); Benbecula (pop. 1,803) and Barra (pop. 1,244). Other inhabited islands include Bernera (262), Berneray (141), Eriskay (179), Grimsay (215), Scalpay (382) and Vatersay (72).

EARLY HISTORY

The Picts, believed to be of non-Aryan origin, seem to have inhabited the whole of northern Britain and to have spread over the north of Ireland. Remains are most frequent in Caithness and Sutherland and the Orkney Islands.

Celts arrived from Belgic Gaul during the latter part of the Bronze Age and in the early Iron Age and, except in the extreme north of the mainland and in the islands, the civilization and speech of the people were definitely Celtic at the time of the Roman invasion of Britain.

THE ROMAN INVASION

In AD 79–80 Julius Agricola extended the Roman conquests in Britain by advancing into Caledonia and building a line of fortifications across the isthmus between the Forth and Clyde, but after a victory at Mons Graupius he was recalled. Hadrian's Wall, mostly complete by AD 130, marked the frontier until about AD 143 when the frontier moved north to the Forth–Clyde isthmus and was secured by the Antonine Wall. From about AD 155 the Antonine Wall was damaged by frequent attacks and by the end of the second century the northern limit of Roman Britain had receded to Hadrian's Wall.

THE SCOTS

After the withdrawal or absorption of the Roman garrison of Britain there were many years of tribal warfare between the Picts and Scots (the Gaelic tribe then dominant in Ireland), the Brythonic Waelisc (Welsh) of Strathclyde (south-west Scotland and Cumberland), and the Anglo-Saxons of Lothian. The Waelisc were isolated from their kinsmen in Wales by the victory of the West Saxons at Chester (613), and towards the close of the ninth century the Scots under Kenneth Mac Alpin became the dominant power in Caledonia. In the reign of Malcolm I (943–954) Strathclyde was brought into subjection, the English lowland kingdom (Lothian) being conquered by Malcolm II (1005–1034).

From the late 11th century until the mid 16th century there were constant wars between Scotland and England, the outstanding figures in the struggle being William Wallace, who defeated the English at Stirling Bridge (1297) and Robert Bruce, who won the battle of Bannockburn (1314). James IV and many of his nobles fell at the disastrous battle of Flodden (1513).

THE JACOBITE REVOLTS

In 1603 James VI of Scotland succeeded Elizabeth I on the throne of England (his mother, Mary Queen of Scots, was the great-granddaughter of Henry VII), his successors reigning as sovereigns of Great Britain, although political union of the two countries did not occur until 1707. After the abdication (by flight) in 1688 of James VII and II, the crown devolved upon William III (grandson of Charles I) and Mary (elder daughter of James VII and II). In 1689 Graham of Claverhouse roused the Highlands on behalf of James VII and II, but died after a military success at Killiecrankie.

After the death of Anne (younger daughter of James VII and II), the throne devolved upon George I (great-grandson of James VI and I). In 1715, armed risings on behalf of James Stuart (the Old Pretender) led to the indecisive battle of Sheriffmuir, and the Jacobite movement died down until 1745, when Charles Stuart (the Young Pretender) defeated the Royalist troops at Prestonpans and advanced to Derby (1746). From Derby, the adherents of 'James VIII and III' (the title claimed for his father by Charles Stuart) fell back on the defensive, and the movement was finally crushed at Culloden (16 April 1746).

PRINCIPAL CITIES

ABERDEEN

Aberdeen, 130 miles north-east of Edinburgh, received its charter as a Royal Burgh in 1179. Scotland's third largest city, Aberdeen is the second largest Scottish fishing port and the main centre for offshore oil exploration and production. It is also an ancient university town and distinguished research centre. Other industries include engineering, food processing, textiles, paper manufacturing and chemicals.

Places of interest include King's College, St Machar's Cathedral, Brig o' Balgownie, Duthie Park and Winter Gardens, Hazlehead Park, the Kirk of St Nicholas, Mercat Cross, Marischal College and Marischal Museum, Provost Skene's House, Art Gallery, James Dun's House, Satrosphere Hands-On Discovery Centre, and Aberdeen Maritime Museum in Provost Ross's House.

DUNDEE

Dundee, a Royal Burgh, is situated on the north bank of the Tay estuary. The city's port and dock installations are important to the offshore oil industry and the airport also provides servicing facilities. Principal industries include textiles, computers and other electronic industries, lasers, printing, tyre manufacture, food processing, carpets, engineering, clothing manufacture and tourism.

The unique City Churches – three churches under one roof, together with the 15th-century St Mary's Tower – are the most prominent architectural feature. Dundee has two historic ships: the Dundee-built RRS *Discovery* which took Capt. Scott to the Antarctic lies alongside Discovery Quay, and the frigate *Unicorn*, the only British-built wooden warship still afloat, is moored in Victoria Dock. Places of interest include Mills Public Observatory, the Tay road and rail bridges, McManus Galleries, Barrack Street Museum, Claypotts Castle, Broughty Castle and Verdant Works (Textile Heritage Centre).

EDINBURGH

Edinburgh is the capital of and seat of government in Scotland. The city is built on a group of hills and contains in Princes Street one of the most beautiful thoroughfares in the world.

The principal buildings are the Castle, which includes St Margaret's Chapel, the oldest building in Edinburgh, and near it, the Scottish National War Memorial; the Palace of Holyroodhouse; Parliament House, the present seat of the judicature; three universities (Edinburgh, Heriot-Watt, Napier); St Giles' Cathedral (restored 1879–83); St Mary's (Scottish Episcopal) Cathedral (Sir Gilbert Scott); the General Register House (Robert Adam); the National and the Signet Libraries; the National Gallery; the Royal Scottish Academy; the National Portrait Gallery; and the Edinburgh International Conference Centre, opened in 1995.

GLASGOW

Glasgow, a Royal Burgh, is the principal commercial and industrial centre in Scotland. The city occupies the north and south banks of the Clyde, formerly one of the chief commercial estuaries in the world. The principal industries include engineering, electronics, finance, chemicals and printing. The city has also developed recently as a tourism and conference centre.

The chief buildings are the 13th-century Gothic Cathedral, the University (Sir Gilbert Scott), the City Chambers, the Royal Concert Hall, St Mungo Museum of Religious Life and Art, Pollok House, the School of Art (Mackintosh), Kelvingrove Art Galleries, the Gallery of Modern Art, the Burrell Collection museum and the Mitchell Library. The city is home to the Scottish National Orchestra, Scottish Opera and Scottish Ballet.

LORD LIEUTENANTS

Title	Name
Aberdeenshire	Capt. C. A. Farquharson
Angus	The Earl of Airlie, KT, GCVO, PC
Argyll and Bute	The Duke of Argyll
Ayrshire and Arran	Maj. R. Y. Henderson, TD
Banffshire	J. A. S. McPherson, CBE
Berwickshire	Maj.-Gen. Sir John Swinton, KCVO, OBE
Caithness	Maj. G. T. Dunnett, TD
Clackmannan	Lt.-Col. R. C. Stewart, CBE, TD
Dumfries	Capt. R. C. Cunningham-Jardine
Dumbartonshire	Brig. D. D. G. Hardie, TD
East Lothian	Sir Hew Hamilton-Dalrymple, Bt., KCVO
Fife	The Earl of Elgin and Kincardine KT
Inverness	The Lord Gray of Contin, PC
Kincardineshire	The Viscount of Arbuthnott, CBE, DSC, FRSE
Lanarkshire	H. B. Sneddon, CBE
Midlothian	Capt. G. W. Burnet, LVO
Moray	Air Vice-Marshal G. A. Chesworth, CB, OBE, DFC
Nairn	The Earl of Leven and Melville
Orkney	Brig. M. G. Dennison
Perth and Kinross	Sir David Montgomery, Bt.
Renfrewshire	The Lord Goold
Ross and Cromarty	Capt. R. W. K. Stirling of Fairburn TD

Roxburgh, Ettrick
and Lauderdale
Shetland
Stirling and Falkirk

Sutherland
The Stewartry of
Kirkcudbright

The Duke of Buccleugh and
Queensberry, KT, VRD
J. H. Scott
Lt.-Col. J. Stirling of Garden, CBE,
TD, FRICS
Maj.-Gen. D. Houston, CBE

Lt.-Gen. Sir Norman Arthur, KCB

Tweeddale
West Lothian
Western Isles
Wigtown

Capt. J. D. B. Younger
The Earl of Morton
The Viscount Dunrossil, CMG
Maj. E. S. Orr-Ewing

The Lord Provosts of the four city districts of Aberdeen,
Dundee, Edinburgh and Glasgow are Lord Lieutenants for
those districts *ex officio*

LOCAL COUNCILS

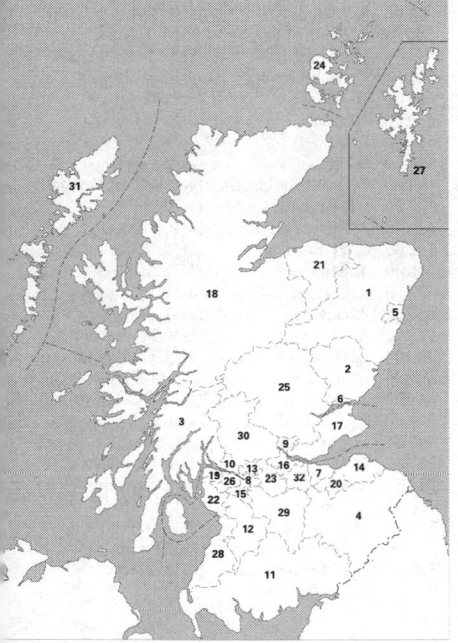

Key	Council
1	Aberdeenshire
2	Angus
3	Argyll and Bute
4	Scottish Borders
5	Aberdeen City
6	Dundee City
7	City of Edinburgh
8	Glasgow City
9	Clackmannanshire
10	West Dumbartonshire
11	Dumfries and Galloway
12	East Ayrshire
13	East Dumbartonshire
14	East Lothian
15	East Renfrewshire
16	Falkirk
17	Fife
18	Highland
19	Inverclyde
20	Midlothian
21	Moray
22	North Ayrshire
23	North Lanarkshire
24	Orkney Islands Council
25	Perth and Kinross
26	Renfrewshire
27	Shetland Islands Council
28	South Ayrshire
29	South Lanarkshire
30	Stirling
31	Western Isles Islands Council
32	West Lothian

LOCAL COUNCILS

Council	Administrative headquarters	Population (latest estimate)	Band D charge 1996	Chief Executive	Chairman (a) Convener (b) Provost (c) Lord Provost
Aberdeen City	Aberdeen	219,120	£909.51	D. Paterson	(c) Ms M. Farquhar
Aberdeenshire	Aberdeen	226,530	591.00	A. Campbell	(a) Dr C. S. Millar
Angus	Forfar	111,750	659.00	A. B. Watson	(b) Mrs F. M. Duncan
Argyll and Bute	Lochgilphead	90,000	652.00	J. McLellan	(a) J. Wilson
City of Edinburgh	Edinburgh	447,550	812.00	T. Aitchson	(c) E. Milligan
Clackmannanshire	Alloa	47,679	744.50	R. Allan	(b) R. Elder
Dundee City	Dundee	151,010	882.50	A. Stephen	(c) M. J. Rolfe
Dumfries and Galloway	Dumfries	147,900	833.33	I. F. Smith	(a) A. T. Baldwick
East Ayrshire	Kilmarnock	124,000	793.50	D. Montgomery	(b) R. Stirling
East Dumbartonshire	Glasgow	110,000	668.00	C. Mallon	(b) J. Dempsey
East Lothian	Haddington	86,800	670.00	J. Linsay	(a) P. O'Brien
East Renfrewshire	Glasgow	86,780	621.00	P. Daniels	O. Taylor
Falkirk	Falkirk	142,800	624.00	W. Weir	(b) A. Fowler
Fife	Glenrothes	351,600	694.00	Dr J. A. Markland	(a) J. W. MacDougall
Glasgow City	Glasgow	618,430	897.00	J. F. Anderson	(c) P. Lally
Highland	Inverness	207,500	620.00	A. McCourt	(a) P. J. Peacock
Inverclyde	Greenock	89,380	762.00	G. H. Bettison	(b) Ms C. Allen
Midlothian	Dalkeith	79,880	718.00	T. Muir	(b) D. Molloy
Moray	Elgin	87,150	607.50	A. Connell	(a) G. McDonald
North Ayrshire	Irvine	139,000	660.00	B. Devine	(a) G. Steven
North Lanarkshire	Motherwell	326,750	758.00	A. Cowe	(b) V. Matheison
Orkney Islands	Kirkwall	19,700	480.00	R. H. Gilbert	(a) H. Halcro-Johnston
Perth and Kinross	Perth	130,740	696.50	H. Robertson	(b) J. Culliven
Renfrewshire	Paisley	176,970	830.00	T. Scholes	(b) Ms N. Allison
Scottish Borders	Melrose	105,300	558.00	A. M. Croall	(a) A. L. Tulley
Shetland Islands	Lerwick	23,090	443.21	M. E. Green	(a) Canon L. S. Smith
South Ayrshire	Ayr	114,000	731.00	G. W. F. Thorley	(b) R. Campbell
South Lanarkshire	Hamilton	307,510	717.75	A. MacNish	(b) S. Casserly
Stirling	Stirling	81,630	730.50	K. Yates	(b) J. Paterson
West Dumbartonshire	Dumbarton	97,790	812.00	M. J. Watters	(b) P. O'Neill
West Lothian	Livingston	148,190	678.00	A. M. Linkston	(a) J. Thomas
West Isles Islands	Stornoway	29,393	550.00	B. W. Stewart	(a) D. Mackay

For explanation of council tax, *see* pages 519–20

Northern Ireland

Northern Ireland has a total area of 5,461 sq. miles (14,144 sq. km): land, 5,215 sq. miles (13,506 sq. km); inland water and tideways, 246 sq. miles (638 sq. km).

The population of Northern Ireland at the 1991 Census was 1,577,836 (males, 769,071; females, 808,765). The average density of population in 1991 was 1.11 persons per hectare.

In 1991 the number of persons in the various religious denominations (expressed as percentages of the total population) were: Roman Catholic, 38.4; Presbyterian, 21.4; Church of Ireland, 17.7; Methodist, 3.8; others 7.7; none, 3.7; not stated, 7.3.

PRINCIPAL CITIES

BELFAST

Belfast, the administrative centre of Northern Ireland, is situated at the mouth of the River Lagan at its entrance to Belfast Lough. The city grew, owing to its easy access by sea to Scottish coal and iron, to be a great industrial centre.

The principal buildings are of a relatively recent date and include the Parliament Buildings at Stormont, the City Hall, the Law Courts, the Public Library and the Museum and Art Gallery.

Belfast received its first charter of incorporation in 1613 and was created a city in 1888; the title of Lord Mayor was conferred in 1892.

LONDONDERRY

Londonderry (originally Derry) is situated on the River Foyle, and has important associations with the City of London. The Irish Society was created by the City of London in 1610, and under its royal charter of 1613 it fortified the city and was for long closely associated with its administration. Because of this connection the city was incorporated in 1613 under the new name of Londonderry.

The city is famous for the great siege of 1688–9, when for 105 days the town held out against the forces of James II until relieved by sea. The city walls are still intact and form a circuit of almost a mile around the old city.

Interesting buildings are the Protestant Cathedral of St Columb's (1633) and the Guildhall, reconstructed in 1912 and containing a number of beautiful stained glass windows, many of which were presented by the livery companies of London.

CONSTITUTION AND GOVERNMENT

As part of the United Kingdom, Northern Ireland is subject to the same fundamental constitutional provisions which apply to the rest of the United Kingdom. It had its own parliament and government from 1921 to 1972, but after increasing civil unrest the Northern Ireland (Temporary Provisions) Act 1972 transferred the legislative and executive powers of the Northern Ireland parliament and government to the UK Parliament and a Secretary of State. The Northern Ireland Constitution Act 1973 provided for devolution in Northern Ireland through an assembly and executive, and in January 1974 a power-sharing executive was formed by the Northern Ireland political parties. This arrangement collapsed in May 1974 and since then Northern Ireland has been governed by direct rule under the

provisions of the Northern Ireland Act 1974. This allows Parliament to approve all laws for Northern Ireland and places the Northern Ireland department under the direction and control of the Secretary of State for Northern Ireland.

Attempts have been made by successive governments to find a means of restoring a widely acceptable form of devolved government to Northern Ireland. A 78-member Assembly was elected by proportional representation in 1982. However, it was dissolved four years later after it failed to discharge its responsibilities of making proposals for the resumption of devolved government and of monitoring the work of the Northern Ireland departments.

In 1985 the governments of the United Kingdom and the Republic of Ireland signed the Anglo-Irish Agreement, establishing an intergovernmental conference in which the Irish government may put forward views and proposals on certain aspects of Northern Ireland affairs.

Discussions between the British and Irish governments and the main Northern Ireland parties began in 1991. It was agreed that any political settlement would need to address three key relationships: those within Northern Ireland; those within the island of Ireland (north/south); and those between the British and Irish governments (east/west). Although round table talks ended in 1992 the process continued from September 1993 as separate bilateral discussions with three of the Northern Ireland parties (the DUP declined to participate).

On 15 December 1993 the British and Irish governments published the Joint Declaration complementing the political talks, and making clear that any settlement would need to be founded on principles of democracy and consent. The declaration also stated that all democratically mandated parties could be involved in political talks as long as they permanently renounced paramilitary violence.

The provisional IRA and loyalist paramilitary groups announced cease-fires on 31 August and 13 October 1994 respectively. The Government initiated a series of separate exploratory meetings with Sinn Fein and loyalist representatives in December 1994. The purposes of these were: to explore the basis upon which Sinn Fein and the loyalist representatives would come to be admitted to an inclusive political talks process; to exchange views on how they would be able to play the same role as the current constitutional parties in the public life of Northern Ireland; and to examine the practical consequences of the ending of violence.

In February 1995 the Prime Minister launched *A Framework for Accountable Government in Northern Ireland* and, with the Irish Prime Minister, *A New Framework for Agreement*. These outlined what a comprehensive political settlement might look like. The ideas were intended to facilitate multilateral dialogue involving the Northern Ireland parties and the British government. To this end the Secretary of State for Northern Ireland (Sir Patrick Mayhew) initiated separate bilateral meetings with the leaders of the main parties. The Government had previously given an undertaking to submit the final outcome of political talks to the electorate of Northern Ireland for approval in a referendum.

In the autumn of 1995 the Prime Minister said that Sinn Fein would not be invited to all-party talks until the IRA had decommissioned its arms; the IRA ruled out any decommissioning of weapons in advance of a political settlement. In November 1995 the Prime Minister and the

Irish Prime Minister agreed to set up a three-member international body chaired by a former US senator, George Mitchell, to advise both governments on suitable methods of decommissioning arms. The international body reported in January 1996 that no weapons would be decommissioned before the start of all-party talks and that a compromise agreement was necessary under which weapons would be decommissioned during negotiations. The Prime Minister accepted the report and proposed that elections should be held to provide a pool of representatives to conduct all-party talks. On 9 February 1996 the IRA called off its cease-fire. On 30 May 1996 elections were held to a peace forum. On 10 June all-party talks opened at Stormont Castle; Sinn Fein delegates were turned away because the IRA had failed to reinstate its cease-fire. The peace forum met for the first time on 14 June 1996; it was boycotted by Sinn Fein members. On 29 June 1996 the all-party talks were suspended for six weeks after disagreements over the issue of decommissioning arms.

FLAG

The official national flag of Northern Ireland is now the Union Flag. The flag formerly in use (a white, six-pointed star in the centre of a red cross on a white field, enclosing a red hand and surmounted by a crown) has not been used since the imposition of direct rule.

ECONOMY

FINANCE

Taxation in Northern Ireland is largely imposed and collected by the United Kingdom government. After deducting the cost of collection and of Northern Ireland's contributions to the European Community the balance, known as the Attributed Share of Taxation, is paid over to the Northern Ireland Consolidated Fund. Northern Ireland's revenue is insufficient to meet its expenditure and is supplemented by a grant-in-aid.

	1995–6*	1996–7**
Public income	£6,579,018,105	£7,027,800,000
Public expenditure	6,510,447,437	7,027,800,000

* Outturn
** Estimate

PRODUCTION

The products of the engineering and allied industries, which employed 25,400 persons in 1993, were valued at £1,723 million. The textiles industry, employing about 11,200 persons, produced products valued at approximately £536 million. The food products, beverages and tobacco industry, employing about 22,700 persons, produced goods valued at £3,962 million.

In 1995 1,375 persons were employed in mining and quarrying operations in Northern Ireland and the minerals raised (22,119,008 tonnes) were valued at £55,982,254.

COMMUNICATIONS

The total tonnage handled by Northern Ireland ports in 1995 was 20 million. Regular ferry, freight and container services operate to ports in Great Britain and Europe from 18 ports, including Belfast, Coleraine, Larne, Londonderry and Warrenpoint.

The Northern Ireland Transport Holding Company is largely responsible for the supervision of the subsidiary companies, Ulsterbus and Citybus (which operate the public road passenger services) and Northern Ireland Railways. Road freight services are also provided by a large number of hauliers operating competitively under licence.

Belfast International Airport was privatized in July 1994. It has substantial passenger and freight handling facilities and provides scheduled and chartered services on domestic and international routes.

Scheduled services also operate from Belfast City Airport (BCA) to 21 UK destinations and from City of Derry Airport (Londonderry) to Glasgow, Manchester and to Belfast, providing links to many of the locations serviced by BCA.

Northern Ireland Counties

County	Area* (sq. miles)	Lord Lieutenant	High Sheriff, 1996
Antrim	1,093	The Lord O'Neill, TD	D. de Burgh Kinahan
‡Belfast City	25	Col. J. E. Wilson, OBE	S. Bride
Armagh	484	The Earl of Caledon	Dr M. Patton
Down	945	W. J. Hall	W. S. Brown
Fermanagh	647	The Earl of Erne	G. Burns
†Londonderry	798	Sir Michael McCorkell, KCVO, OBE, TD	T. C. Boyd
‡Londonderry City	3.4	J. T. Eaton, CBE, TD	D. Chatis
Tyrone	1,211	The Duke of Abercorn	J. R. H. Ellis

* Excluding inland waters and tideways
‡ Denotes County Borough
† Excluding the City of Londonderry

District Councils

SMALL CAPITALS denotes CITY status
§ Denotes Borough Council

Council	Population (30 June 1994)	Net Annual Value	Council Clerk	Chairman †Mayor 1996
§Antrim, Co. Antrim	46,039	£7,445,831	S. J. Magee	†F. R. H. Marks
§Ards, Co. Down	66,533	8,447,579	D. J. Fallows	†R. Gibson
				†R. Ferguson
ARMAGH, Co. Armagh	52,053	5,548,105	D. R. D. Mitchall	†J. A. Speers
§Ballymena, Co. Antrim	57,132	8,903,765	M. G. Rankin	†J. Currie
§Ballymoney, Co. Antrim	24,478	2,770,364	J. C. Alderdice	†J. A. Gaston
Banbridge, Co. Down	37,083	4,384,059	R. Gilmore	W. McCracken
Belfast, Co. Antrim and Co. Down	295,649	57,800,052	B. Hanna	S. I. G. Adamson (Lord Mayor)
§Carrickfergus, Co. Antrim	34,747	4,798,829	R. Boyd	†S. McCambey
§Castlereagh, Co. Down	63,206	8,734,158	J. White	†Mrs I. Robinson
§Coleraine, Co. Londonderry	53,866	8,193,577	W. E. Andrews	†Mrs P. E. A. Armitage
Cookstown, Co. Tyrone	31,096	3,345,957	M. McGuckin	S. A. Glasgow
§Craigavon, Co. Armagh	77,359	11,363,669	M. Graham (acting)	†M. Casey
Derry, Co. Londonderry	100,614	13,540,468	T. J. Keanie	†R. Dallas
Down, Co. Down	59,695	6,627,612	O. O'Connor	W. J. F. Biggerstaff
Dungannon, Co. Tyrone	45,847	5,159,683	W. J. Beattie	V. Currie N. R. D. Mulligan
Fermanagh, Co. Fermanagh	54,446	6,384,167	Mrs A. McGinley	S. Foster
§Larne, Co. Antrim	29,904	4,157,956	G. McKinley	†S. C. McAllister
§Limavady, Co. Londonderry	29,845	3,101,729	J. K. Stevenson	†M. Gault
§Lisburn, Co. Antrim and Co. Down	102,882	14,813,451	M. S. Fielding	†G. Morrison
Magherafelt, Co. Londonderry	36,643	3,859,691	J. A. McLaughlin	P. H. McErlain
Moyle, Co. Antrim	14,751	1,632,504	R. G. Lewis	A. G. Kane
Newry and Mourne, Co. Down and Co. Armagh	82,671	8,865,124	K. O'Neill	J. E. B. Hanna
§Newtownabbey, Co. Antrim	78,145	11,882,556	N. Dunn (acting)	†W. G. Snoddy
§North Down, Co. Down	72,914	10,437,089	A. McDowell	†Mrs R. L. Cree
Omagh, Co. Tyrone	45,915	5,014,191	J. P. McKinney	S. Shields
Strabane, Co. Tyrone	35,886	3,446,404	Dr V. R. Eakin	E. Turner

The Isle of Man

Ellan Vannin

The Isle of Man is an island situated in the Irish Sea, in latitude 54° 3'–54° 25' N. and longitude 4° 18'–4° 47' W., nearly equidistant from England, Scotland and Ireland. Although the early inhabitants were of Celtic origin, the Isle of Man was part of the Norwegian Kingdom of the Hebrides until 1266, when this was ceded to Scotland. Subsequently granted to the Stanleys (Earls of Derby) in the 15th century and later to the Dukes of Atholl, it was brought under the administration of the Crown in 1765. The island forms the bishopric of Sodor and Man.

The total land area is 221 sq. miles (572 sq. km). The report on the 1991 Census showed a resident population of 69,788 (males, 33,693; females, 36,095). The main language in use is English. There are no remaining native speakers of Manx Gaelic but 643 people are able to speak the language.
CAPITAL – ΨDouglas; population (1991), 22,214. ΨCastletown (3,152) is the ancient capital; the other towns are ΨPeel (3,829) and ΨRamsey (6,496)
FLAG – A red flag charged with three conjoined armoured legs in white and gold
TYNWALD DAY – 5 July.

GOVERNMENT

The Isle of Man is a self-governing Crown dependency, having its own parliamentary, legal and administrative system. The British Government is responsible for international relations and defence. Under the UK Act of Accession, Protocol 3, the island's relationship with the European Community is limited to trade alone and does not extend to financial aid. The Lieutenant-Governor is The Queen's personal representative in the island.

The legislature, Tynwald, is the oldest parliament in the world in continuous existence. It has two branches: the Legislative Council and the House of Keys. The Council consists of the President of Tynwald, the Bishop of Sodor and Man, the Attorney-General (who does not have a vote) and eight members elected by the House of Keys. The House of Keys has 24 members, elected by universal adult suffrage. The branches sit separately to consider legislation and sit together, as Tynwald Court, for most other parliamentary purposes.

The presiding officer in Tynwald Court is the President of Tynwald, elected by the members, who also presides over sittings of the Legislative Council. The presiding officer of the House of Keys is Mr Speaker, who is elected by members of the House.

The principal members of the Manx Government are the Chief Minister and nine departmental ministers, who comprise the Council of Ministers.

Lieutenant-Governor, His Excellency Sir Timothy Daunt, KCMG
ADC to the Lieutenant-Governor, M. M. Wood
President of Tynwald, The Hon. Sir Charles Kerruish, OBE
Speaker, House of Keys, The Hon. J. C. Cain
The First Deemster and Clerk of the Rolls, His Honour J. W. Corrin, CBE
Clerk of Tynwald, Secretary to the House of Keys and Counsel to the Speaker, Prof. T. St J. N. Bates
Clerk of Legislative Council and Clerk Assistant of Tynwald, T. A. Bawden
Attorney-General, J. M. Kerruish, QC
Chief Minister, The Hon. M. R. Walker, CBE
Chief Secretary, J. F. Kissack
Chief Financial Officer, J. A. Cashen

ECONOMY

Most of the income generated in the island is earned in the services sector with financial and business services being considerably larger than the traditional industry of tourism. Manufacturing industry is also a major generator of income whilst the island's other traditional industries of agriculture and fishing now play a smaller role in the economy.

Under the terms of Protocol 3, the island has free access to EU markets for its products.

The island's unemployment rate is approximately 4 per cent and price inflation is around 3 per cent per annum.

FINANCE

The budget for 1996–7 provided for net expenditure of £226 million. The principal sources of government revenue are taxes on income and expenditure. Income tax is payable at a rate of 15 per cent on the first £9,000 of taxable income for single resident individuals and 20 per cent on the balance, after personal allowances; these bands are doubled for married couples. The rate of income tax is 20 per cent on the whole taxable income of non-residents and companies. By agreement with the British Government, the island keeps most of its rates of indirect taxation (VAT and duties) the same as those in the United Kingdom, but this agreement may be terminated by either party. However, VAT on tourist accommodation is charged at 5 per cent. A reciprocal agreement on national insurance benefits and pensions exists between the Governments of the Isle of Man and the United Kingdom. Taxes are also charged on property (rates), but these are comparatively low.

The major government expenditure items are health, social security and education, which account for 60 per cent of the government budget. The island makes a voluntary annual contribution to the United Kingdom for defence and other external services.

Although the island has a limited relationship with the European Union, it neither contributes money to nor receives funds from the EU budget.

The Channel Islands

The Channel Islands, situated off the north-west coast of France (at distances of from ten to 30 miles), are the only portions of the Dukedom of Normandy still belonging to the Crown, to which they have been attached since the Conquest. They were the only British territory to come under German occupation during the Second World War, following invasion on 30 June to 1 July 1940. The islands were relieved by British forces on 9 May 1945, and 9 May (Liberation Day) is now observed as a bank and public holiday.

The islands consist of Jersey (28,717 acres/11,630 ha), Guernsey (15,654 acres/6,340 ha), and the dependencies of Guernsey: Alderney (1,962 acres/795 ha), Brechou (74/30), Great Sark (1,035/419), Little Sark (239/97), Herm 320/130), Jethou (44/18) and Lihou (38/15) – a total of 48,083 acres/19,474 ha, or 75 sq. miles/194 sq. km. In 1991 the population of Jersey was 84,082; and of Guernsey, 58,867; Alderney, 2,297 and Sark, 575. The official languages are English and French but French is being supplanted by English, which is the language in daily use. In country districts of Jersey and Guernsey and throughout Sark a Norman-French *patois* is also in use, though to a declining extent.

GOVERNMENT

The islands are Crown dependencies with their own legislative assemblies (the States in Jersey, Guernsey and Alderney, and the Court of Chief Pleas in Sark), and systems of local administration and of law, and their own courts. Acts passed by the States require the sanction of The Queen-in-Council. The British Government is responsible for defence and international relations. The Channel Islands have trading rights alone within the European Union; these rights do not include financial aid.

In both Bailiwicks the Lieutenant-Governor and Commander-in-Chief, who is appointed by the Crown, is the personal representative of The Queen and the channel of communication between the Crown (via the Privy Council) and the island's government.

The government of each Bailiwick is conducted by committees appointed by the States. Justice is administered by the Royal Courts of Jersey and Guernsey, each consisting of the Bailiff and 12 elected Jurats. The Bailiffs of Jersey and Guernsey, appointed by the Crown, are President of the States and of the Royal Courts of their respective islands.

Each Bailiwick constitutes a deanery under the jurisdiction of the Bishop of Winchester (*see* Index).

ECONOMY

A mild climate and good soil have led to the development of intensive systems of agriculture and horticulture, which form a significant part of the economy. Equally important are invisible earnings, principally from tourism and banking and finance, the low rate of income tax (20p in the £ in Jersey and Guernsey; no tax of any kind in Sark) and the absence of super-tax and death duties making the islands a popular tax-haven.

Principal exports are agricultural produce and flowers; imports are chiefly machinery, manufactured goods, food, fuel and chemicals. Trade with the UK is regarded as internal.

British currency is legal tender in the Channel Islands but each Bailiwick issues its own coins and notes (*see* page 603). They also issue their own postage stamps; UK stamps are not valid.

JERSEY

Lieutenant-Governor and Commander-in-Chief of Jersey, His Excellency Gen. Sir Michael Wilkes, KCB, CBE, *apptd* 1995
  Secretary and ADC, Col. A. J. C. Woodrow, OBE
Bailiff of Jersey, Sir Philip Bailhache, Kt.
Deputy Bailiff, F. C. Hamon
Attorney-General, M. C. St J. Burt, QC
Receiver-General, Gp Capt R. Green, OBE
Solicitor-General, Miss S. C. Nicolle, QC
Greffier of the States, G. H. C. Coppock
States Treasurer, G. M. Baird

FINANCE

Year to 31 Dec.	1994	1995
Revenue income	£393,418,443	£417,271,388
Revenue expenditure	356,827,170	376,752,850
Capital expenditure	74,762,593	67,886,094
Public debt	0	0

CHIEF TOWN – ΨSt Helier, on the south coast of Jersey
FLAG – A white field charged with a red saltire cross, and the arms of Jersey in the upper centre

GUERNSEY AND DEPENDENCIES

Lieutenant-Governor and Commander-in-Chief of the Bailiwick of Guernsey and its Dependencies, His Excellency Vice-Adm. Sir John Coward, KCB, DSO, *apptd* 1994
  Secretary and ADC, Capt. D. P. L. Hodgetts
Bailiff of Guernsey, Sir Graham Dorey
Deputy Bailiff, de V. G. Carey
HM Procureur and Receiver-General, A. C. K. Day, QC
HM Comptroller, G. R. Rowland, QC
States Supervisor, M. J. Brown

FINANCE

Year to 31 Dec.	1994	1995
Revenue	£164,719,000	£171,506,000
Expenditure	143,957,000	152,222,000

CHIEF TOWNS – ΨSt Peter Port, on the east coast of Guernsey; St Anne on Alderney
FLAG – White, bearing a red cross of St George, with a gold cross overall in the centre

ALDERNEY

President of the States, G. W. Baron
Clerk of the States, D. V. Jenkins
Clerk of the Court, A. Johnson

SARK

Seigneur of Sark, J. M. Beaumont
The Seneschal, L. P. de Carteret
The Greffier, J. P. Hamon

OTHER DEPENDENCIES

Brechou, Lihou and Jethou are leased by the Crown. Herm is leased by the States of Guernsey.

Conservation and Heritage

Countryside Conservation

NATIONAL PARKS

ENGLAND AND WALES

The ten National Parks of England and Wales were set up under the provisions of the National Parks and Access to the Countryside Act 1949 to conserve and protect scenic landscapes from inappropriate development and to provide access to the land for public enjoyment.

The Countryside Commission is the statutory body which has the power to designate National Parks in England, and the Countryside Council for Wales is responsible for National Parks in Wales. Designations in England are confirmed by the Secretary of State for the Environment, and those in Wales by the Secretary of State for Wales. The designation of a National Park does not affect the ownership of the land or remove the rights of the local community. Although the parks are administered through local government, the majority of the land is owned by private landowners (74 per cent) or by bodies such as the National Trust (7 per cent) and the Forestry Commission (7 per cent). The National Park Authorities own only 2.3 per cent of the land in the National Parks.

The Environment Act 1995 will replace the existing National Park committees and boards with free-standing National Park Authorities (NPAs) and will also widen the duties of the NPAs to include fostering the economic and social well-being of local communities within the National Parks. NPAs are the authorities responsible for park administration. They also influence land use and development, and deal with planning applications. The NPAs appoint the National Park Officer for the National Park they administer.

In Wales, the three National Parks have had free-standing NPAs since 1 April 1996. Two-thirds of the members are local authority representatives and one-third are appointed by the Secretary of State for Wales with advice from the Countryside Council for Wales.

In England, two free-standing NPAs already exist: the Peak Park Joint Planning Board and the Lake District Special Planning Board. These are autonomous authorities which are financially independent. These two Boards and the five other NPAs in England will be replaced on 1 April 1997 by free-standing NPAs. Membership will be split between local authority representatives and members appointed by the Secretary of State for the Environment, with the local authority representatives in a majority of one.

Central government provides 75 per cent of the funding for the parks through the National Park Supplementary Grant (the National Park Grant in Wales). The remaining 25 per cent is supplied by the local authorities concerned. Approved net expenditure for all National Parks in England and Wales in 1996–7 was £28,372,602.

The Countryside Commission has stated that other areas are regarded as being worthy of National Parks status. Two areas considered as having equivalent status are the Broads and the New Forest (see page 567).

The National Parks (with date designation confirmed) are:

BRECON BEACONS (1957), 1,351 sq. km/522 sq. miles – The park lies in Powys (66 per cent), Carmarthenshire, Rhondda, Cynon and Taff, Merthyr Tydfil, Blaenau Gwent and Monmouthshire. The park is centred on the Beacons, Pen y Fan, Corn Du and Cribyn, but also includes the valley of the Usk, the Black Mountains to the east and the Black Mountain to the west. There are information centres at Brecon, Craig-y-nos Country Park, Abergavenny and Llandovery, a study centre at Danywenallt and a day visitor centre near Libanus. *Information Office*, 7 Glamorgan Street, Brecon, Powys LD3 7DP. Tel: 01874-624437. *National Park Officer*, M. Fitton

DARTMOOR (1951 and 1994), 954 sq. km/368 sq. miles – The park lies wholly in Devon. It consists of moorland and rocky granite tors, and is rich in prehistoric remains. There are information centres at Newbridge, Tavistock, Bovey Tracey, Steps Bridge, Princetown and Postbridge. *Information Office*, Parke, Haytor Road, Bovey Tracey, Devon TQ13 9JQ. Tel: 01626-832093. *National Park Officer*, N. Atkinson

EXMOOR (1954), 693 sq. km/268 sq. miles – The park lies in Somerset (71 per cent) and Devon. Exmoor is a moorland plateau inhabited by wild ponies and red deer. There are many ancient remains and burial mounds. There are information centres at Lynmouth, County Gate, Dulverton and Combe Martin. *Information Office*, Exmoor House, Dulverton, Somerset TA22 9HL. Tel: 01398-23665. *National Park Officer*, K. Bungay

LAKE DISTRICT (1951), 2,292 sq. km/885 sq. miles – The park lies wholly in Cumbria. The Lake District includes England's highest mountains (Scafell Pike, Helvellyn and Skiddaw) but it is most famous for its glaciated lakes. There are information centres at Keswick, Waterhead, Hawkshead, Seatoller, Bowness, Grasmere, Coniston, Glenridding and Pooley Bridge, an information van at Gosforth and a park centre at Brockhole, Windermere. *Information Office*, Brockhole, Windermere, Cumbria LA23 1LJ. Tel: 01539-446601. *National Park Officer*, J. Toothill

NORTHUMBERLAND (1956), 1,049 sq. km/405 sq. miles – The park lies wholly in Northumberland. It is an area of hill country stretching from Hadrian's Wall to the Scottish Border. There are information centres at Ingram, Once Brewed, Rothbury, Housesteads, Harbottle and Kielder, and an information caravan at Cawfields. *Information Office*, Eastburn, South Park, Hexham, Northumberland NE46 1BS. Tel: 01434-605555. *National Park Officer*, G. Taylor

NORTH YORK MOORS (1952), 1,436 sq. km/554 sq. miles – The park lies in North Yorkshire (96 per cent) and Redcar and Cleveland. It consists of woodland and moorland, and includes the Hambleton Hills and the Cleveland Way. There are information centres at Danby, Pickering, Sutton Bank, Ravenscar, Helmsley and Hutton-le-Hole, and a day study centre at Danby.

Information Office, The Old Vicarage, Bondgate, Helmsley, York YO6 5BP. Tel: 01439-70657. *National Park Officer*, D. Arnold-Forster

PEAK DISTRICT (1951), 1,438 sq. km/555 sq. miles – The park lies in Derbyshire (64 per cent), Staffordshire, South Yorkshire, Cheshire, West Yorkshire and Greater Manchester. The Peak District includes the gritstone moors of the 'Dark Peak' and the limestone dales of the 'White Peak'. There are information centres at Bakewell, Edale, Fairholmes and Castleton, and information points at Torside (in the Longdendale Valley) and at Hartington (former station). *Information Office*, Aldern House, Baslow Road, Bakewell, Derbyshire DE45 1AE. Tel: 01629-814321. *National Park Officer*, C. Harrison

PEMBROKESHIRE COAST (1952 and 1995), 584 sq. km/225 sq. miles – The park lies wholly in Pembrokeshire. It includes cliffs, moorland and Skomer Island. There are information centres at Tenby, St David's, Pembroke, Newport, Kilgetty, Haverfordwest and Broad Haven. *Information Office*, Winch Lane, Haverfordwest, Pembrokeshire SA61 1PY. Tel: 01437-764636. *National Park Officer*, N. Wheeler

SNOWDONIA (1951), 2,142 sq. km/827 sq. miles – Snowdonia lies in Gwynedd and Conwy. It is an area of deep valleys and rugged mountains. There are information centres at Aberdovey, Bala, Betws y Coed, Blaenau Ffestiniog, Conwy, Harlech, Dolgellau and Llanberis. *Information Office*, Penrhyndeudraeth, Gwynedd LL48 6LF. Tel: 01766-770274. *National Park Officer*, I. Huws.

YORKSHIRE DALES (1954), 1,769 sq. km/683 sq. miles – The park lies in North Yorkshire (88 per cent) and Cumbria. The Yorkshire Dales are composed primarily of limestone overlaid in places by millstone grit. The three peaks of Ingleborough, Whernside and Pen-y-Ghent are within the park. There are information centres at Clapham, Grassington, Hawes, Aysgarth Falls, Malham and Sedbergh. *Information Office*, Yorebridge House, Bainbridge, Leyburn, N. Yorks DL8 3BP. Tel: 01969-50456. *National Park Officer*, R. Harvey

Two other areas considered to have equivalent status to national parks are the Broads and the New Forest. The Broads Authority, a special statutory authority, was established in 1989 to develop, conserve and manage the Norfolk and Suffolk Broads (*see also* Government Departments and Public Offices). The Government declared in 1992 its intention of giving the New Forest a status equivalent to that of a National Park by declaring it an 'area of national significance'.

THE BROADS (1989), 303 sq. km/117 sq. miles – The Broads are located between Norwich and Great Yarmouth on the flood plains of the five rivers flowing through the area to the sea. The area is one of fens, winding waterways, woodland and marsh. The 40 or so broads are man-made, and are connected to the rivers by dykes, providing over 200 km of navigable waterways. There are information centres at Beccles, Hoveton, North-west Tower (Yarmouth), Ranworth and Toad Hole.

Broads Authority, Thomas Harvey House, 18 Colegate, Norwich NR3 1BQ. Tel: 01603-610734. *Chief Executive*, A. Clark

THE NEW FOREST, 376 sq. km/145 sq. miles – The forest has been protected since 1079 when it was declared a royal hunting forest. The area consists of forest, ancient woodland and heathland. Much of the Forest is managed by the Forestry Commission, which provides several camp-sites. The main villages are Brockenhurst, Burley and Lyndhurst, which has a visitor centre.

The Forestry Commission, Office of the Deputy Surveyor of the New Forest and the New Forest Committee, The Queen's House, Lyndhurst, Hants SO43 7NH. Tel: 01703-284149

SCOTLAND AND NORTHERN IRELAND

The National Parks and Access to the Countryside Act 1949 dealt only with England and Wales and made no provision for Scotland or Northern Ireland. Although there are no national parks in these two countries, there is power to designate them in Northern Ireland under the Amenity Lands Act 1965 and the Nature Conservation and Amenity Lands Order (Northern Ireland) 1985. In 1989 the Scottish Office asked Scottish Natural Heritage to report on whether national parks should be designated in Scotland.

AREAS OF OUTSTANDING NATURAL BEAUTY

ENGLAND AND WALES

Under the National Parks and Access to the Countryside Act 1949, provision was made for the designation of Areas of Outstanding Natural Beauty (AONBs) by the Countryside Commission. The Countryside Act 1968 further defines the role of AONBs, suggesting that they should show due regard for the interests of other land users, such as agriculture and forestry groups. The Countryside Commission continues to be responsible for AONBs in England but since April 1991 the Countryside Council for Wales has been responsible for the Welsh AONBs. Designations in England are confirmed by the Secretary of State for the Environment and those in Wales by the Secretary of State for Wales.

Although less emphasis is placed upon the provision of open-air enjoyment for the public than in the national parks, AONBs are areas which are no less beautiful and require the same degree of protection to conserve and enhance the natural beauty of the countryside. This includes protecting flora and fauna, geological and other landscape features. In AONBs planning and management responsibilities are split between county and district councils. There are 19 which cross local authority boundaries. Finance for the AONBs is provided by grant-aid.

The 41 Areas of Outstanding Natural Beauty (with date designation confirmed) are:

ANGLESEY (1967), Anglesey, 215 sq. km/83 sq. miles

ARNSIDE AND SILVERDALE (1972), Cumbria/Lancashire, 75 sq. km/29 sq. miles

BLACKDOWN HILLS (1991), Devon/Somerset, 370 sq. km/143 sq. miles.

CANNOCK CHASE (1958), Staffordshire, 68 sq. km/26 sq. miles

CHICHESTER HARBOUR (1964), Hampshire/West Sussex, 74 sq. km/29 sq. miles

CHILTERNS (1965; extended 1990), Bedfordshire/ Hertfordshire/Buckinghamshire/Oxfordshire, 833 sq. km/322 sq. miles

CLWYDIAN RANGE (1985), Denbighshire/Flintshire, 156 sq. km/60 sq. miles

CORNWALL (1959; Camel estuary 1983), 958 sq. km/370 sq. miles

COTSWOLDS (1966; extended 1990), Gloucestershire/ Wiltshire/Warwickshire/Hereford and Worcester/ Somerset, 2,038 sq. km/787 sq. miles

CRANBORNE CHASE AND WEST WILTSHIRE DOWNS (1983), Dorset/Hampshire/Somerset/Wiltshire, 983 sq. km/379 sq. miles

DEDHAM VALE (1970; extended 1978, 1991), Essex/Suffolk, 90 sq. km/35 sq. miles

EAST DEVON (1963), 268 sq. km/103 sq. miles

NORTH DEVON (1960), 171 sq. km/66 sq. miles

SOUTH DEVON (1960), 337 sq. km/130 sq. miles

DORSET (1959), 1,129 sq. km/436 sq. miles

FOREST OF BOWLAND (1964), Lancashire/North Yorkshire, 802 sq. km/310 sq. miles

GOWER (1956), Swansea, 189 sq. km/73 sq. miles

EAST HAMPSHIRE (1962), 383 sq. km/148 sq. miles

SOUTH HAMPSHIRE COAST (1967), 77 sq. km/30 sq. miles

HIGH WEALD (1983), Kent/Surrey/East Sussex/West Sussex, 1,460 sq. km/564 sq. miles

HOWARDIAN HILLS (1987), North Yorkshire, 204 sq. km/79 sq. miles

KENT DOWNS (1968), 878 sq. km/339 sq. miles

LINCOLNSHIRE WOLDS (1973), 558 sq. km/215 sq. miles

LLEYN (1957), Gwynedd, 155 sq. km/60 sq. miles

MALVERN HILLS (1959), Hereford and Worcester/Gloucestershire, 105 sq. km/40 sq. miles

MENDIP HILLS (1972; extended 1989), Somerset, 198 sq. km/76 sq. miles

NIDDERDALE (1994), North Yorkshire, 603 sq. km/233 sq. miles

NORFOLK COAST (1968), 451 sq. km/174 sq. miles

NORTH PENNINES (1988), Cumbria/Durham/Northumberland, 1,983 sq. km/766 sq. miles

NORTHUMBERLAND COAST (1958), 135 sq. km/52 sq. miles

QUANTOCK HILLS (1957), Somerset, 99 sq. km/38 sq. miles

ISLES OF SCILLY (1976), 16 sq. km/6 sq. miles

SHROPSHIRE HILLS (1959), 804 sq. km/310 sq. miles

SOLWAY COAST (1964), Cumbria, 115 sq. km/44 sq. miles

SUFFOLK COAST AND HEATHS (1970), 403 sq. km/156 sq. miles

SURREY HILLS (1958), 419 sq. km/162 sq. miles

SUSSEX DOWNS (1966), 983 sq. km/379 sq. miles

TAMAR VALLEY (1995), Cornwall/Devon, 195 sq. km/115 sq. miles

NORTH WESSEX DOWNS (1972), Berkshire/Hampshire/Oxfordshire/Wiltshire, 1,730 sq. km/668 sq. miles

ISLE OF WIGHT (1963), 189 sq. km/73 sq. miles

WYE VALLEY (1971), Monmouthshire/Gloucestershire/Hereford and Worcester, 326 sq. km/126 sq. miles

NORTHERN IRELAND

The Department of the Environment for Northern Ireland, with advice from the Council for Nature Conservation and the Countryside, designates Areas of Outstanding Natural Beauty in Northern Ireland. At present there are nine and these cover a total area of approximately 284,948 hectares (704,121 acres).

ANTRIM COAST AND GLENS, Co. Antrim, 70,600 ha/174,452 acres

CAUSEWAY COAST, Co. Antrim, 4,200 ha/10,378 acres

LAGAN VALLEY, Co. Down, 2,072 ha/5,119 acres

LECALE COAST, Co. Down, 3,108 ha/7,679 acres

MOURNE, Co. Down, 57,012 ha/140,876 acres

NORTH DERRY, Co. Londonderry, 12,950 ha/31,999 acres

RING OF GULLION, Co. Armagh, 15,353 ha/37,938 acres

SPERRIN, Co. Tyrone/Co. Londonderry, 101,006 ha/249,585 acres

STRANGFORD LOUGH, Co. Down, 18,647 ha/46,077 acres

NATIONAL SCENIC AREAS

No Areas of Outstanding Natural Beauty are designated in Scotland. However, National Scenic Areas have a broadly equivalent status. Scottish Natural Heritage recognize areas of national scenic significance. At mid 1996 there were 40, covering a total area of 1,001,800 hectare (2,475,448 acres).

Development within National Scenic Areas is dealt with by the local planning authority, who are required to consul Scottish Natural Heritage concerning certain categories c development. Land management uses can also be modifie in the interest of scenic conservation. The Secretary o State for Scotland has limited powers of interventio should a planning authority and Scottish Natural Heritag disagree.

ASSYNT-COIGACH, Highland, 90,200 ha/222,884 acres

BEN NEVIS AND GLEN COE, Highland/Argyll and Bute/Perthshire and Kinross, 101,600 ha/251,053 acres

CAIRNGORM MOUNTAINS, Highland/Aberdeenshire/Moray, 67,200 ha/166,051 acres

CUILLIN HILLS, Highland, 21,900 ha/54,115 acres

DEESIDE AND LOCHNAGAR, Aberdeenshire/Angus, 40,000 ha/98,840 acres

DORNOCH FIRTH, Highland, 7,500 ha/18,532 acres

EAST STEWARTRY COAST, Dumfries and Galloway, 4,500 ha/11,119 acres

EILDON AND LEADERFOOT, Borders, 3,600 ha/8,896 acres

FLEET VALLEY, Dumfries and Galloway, 5,300 ha/13,096 acres

GLEN AFFRIC, Highland, 19,300 ha/47,690 acres

GLEN STRATHFARRAR, Highland, 3,800 ha/9,390 acres

HOY AND WEST MAINLAND, Orkney Islands, 14,800 ha/36,571 acres

JURA, Argyll and Bute, 21,800 ha/53,868 acres

KINTAIL, Highland, 15,500 ha/38,300 acres

KNAPDALE, Argyll and Bute, 19,800 ha/48,926 acres

KNOYDART, Highland, 39,500 ha/97,604 acres

KYLE OF TONGUE, Highland, 18,500 ha/45,713 acres

KYLES OF BUTE, Argyll and Bute, 4,400 ha/10,872 acres

LOCHNA KEAL, MULL, Argyll and Bute, 12,700 ha/31,382 acres

LOCH LOMOND, Argyll and Bute/Stirling/West Dumbartonshire, 27,400 ha/67,705 acres

LOCH RANNOCH AND GLEN LYON, Perthshire and Kinross/Stirling, 48,400 ha/119,596 acres

LOCH SHIEL, Highland, 13,400 ha/33,111 acres

LOCH TUMMEL, Perthshire and Kinross, 9,200 ha/22,733 acres

LYNN OF LORN, Argyll and Bute, 4,800 ha/11,861 acres

MORAR, MOIDART AND ARDNAMURCHAN, Highland, 13,500 ha/33,358 acres

NORTH-WEST SUTHERLAND, Highland, 20,500 ha/50,65 acres

NITH ESTUARY, Dumfries and Galloway, 9,300 ha/22,980 acres

NORTH ARRAN, North Ayrshire, 23,800 ha/58,810 acres

RIVER EARN, Perthshire and Kinross, 3,000 ha/7,413 acres

RIVER TAY, Perthshire and Kinross, 5,600 ha/13,838 acres

ST KILDA, Western Isles, 900 ha/2,224 acres

SCARBA, LUNGA AND THE GARVELLACHS, Argyll and Bute, 1,900 ha/4,695 acres

SHETLAND, Shetland Islands, 11,600 ha/28,664 acres

SMALL ISLES, Highland, 15,500 ha/38,300 acres

South Lewis, Harris and North Uist, Western Isles, 109,600 ha/270,822 acres
South Uist Machair, Western Isles, 6,100 ha/15,073 acres
The Trossachs, Stirling, 4,600 ha/11,367 acres
Trotternish, Highland, 5,000 ha/12,355 acres
Upper Tweeddale, Borders, 10,500 ha/25,945 acres
Wester Ross, Highland, 145,300 ha/359,036 acres

THE NATIONAL FOREST

The National Forest will be planted in about 200 square miles of Derbyshire, Leicestershire and Staffordshire. About 30 million trees, of mixed species but mainly broadleaved, will be planted over the next 20 years and beyond, and will eventually cover about one-third of the designated area. The project is funded by the Department of the Environment. It was developed in 1992–5 by the Countryside Commission and is now run by the National Forest Company. Competitive bids for woodland creation projects are submitted to the National Forest Company by anybody who wishes to undertake a project, and are considered under the National Forest tender scheme. Sixteen tenders were approved in the first round of the scheme in 1995. The second round of the scheme closed for bids on 31 March 1996; approval of these tenders will be given in autumn 1996. The third round opens for bids on 1 January 1997.
National Forest Company, Enterprise Glade, Bath Lane, Moira, Swadlincote, Derbys DE12 6BD. Tel: 01283-551211. *Chief Executive*, Ms S. Bell

Nature Conservation Areas

SITES OF SPECIAL SCIENTIFIC INTEREST

Site of Special Scientific Interest (SSSI) is a legal notification applied to land in England, Scotland or Wales which English Nature (EN), Scottish Natural Heritage (SNH), or the Countryside Council for Wales (CCW) identifies as being of special interest because of its flora, fauna, geological or physiographical features. In some cases, SSSI are managed as nature reserves.
EN, SNH and CCW must notify the designation of a SSSI to the local planning authority, every owner/occupier of the land, and the relevant Secretary of State. Forestry and agricultural departments and a number of other bodies are also informed of this notification.
Objections to the notification of a SSSI can be made and ultimately considered at a full meeting of the Council of EN or the Statutory Protection Committee of CCW. In Scotland an objection will be dealt with by the appropriate regional board or the main board of SNH, depending on the nature of the objection. Unresolved objections on scientific grounds must be referred to the Advisory Committee for SSSI.
The protection of these sites depends on the co-operation of individual landowners and occupiers. Owner/occupiers must consult EN, SNH or CCW and gain written consent before they can undertake certain listed activities on the site. Funds are available through management agreements and grants to assist owners and

occupiers in conserving sites' interests. As a last resort a site can be purchased.
The number and area of SSSIs in Britain as at 31 March 1996 was:

	no.	hectares	acres
England	3,874	920,696	2,274,119
Scotland	1,398	895,227	2,211,211
Wales	909	208,076	514,156

NORTHERN IRELAND
In Northern Ireland 93 Areas of Special Scientific Interest (ASSIs) have been established by the Department of the Environment for Northern Ireland. These cover a total area of 76,061.5 hectares (704,121 acres).

NATIONAL NATURE RESERVES

National Nature Reserves are defined in the National Parks and Access to the Countryside Act 1949 as land designated for the study and preservation of flora and fauna, or of geological or physiographical features.
English Nature (EN), Scottish Natural Heritage (SNH) or the Countryside Council for Wales (CCW) can designate as a National Nature Reserve land which is being managed as a nature reserve under an agreement with one of the statutory nature conservation agencies; land held and managed by EN, SNH or CCW; or land held and managed as a nature reserve by another approved body. EN, SNH or CCW can make by-laws to protect reserves from undesirable activities; these are subject to confirmation by the relevant Secretary of State.
The number and area of National Nature Reserves in Britain as at 31 March 1996 was:

	no.	hectares	acres
England	173	68,222	168,577
Scotland	70	113,238	279,698
Wales	55	17,719	43,784

NORTHERN IRELAND
National Nature Reserves are established and managed by the Department of the Environment for Northern Ireland, with advice from the Council for Nature Conservation and the Countryside. There are 45 National Nature Reserves covering 4,574 hectares (11,297 acres).

LOCAL NATURE RESERVES

Local Nature Reserves are defined in the National Parks and Access to the Countryside Act 1949 as land designated for the study and preservation of flora and fauna, or of geological or physiographical features. The Act gives local authorities in England, Scotland and Wales the power to acquire, declare and manage local nature reserves in consultation with English Nature, Scottish Natural Heritage and the Countryside Council for Wales. Conservation trusts can also own and manage non-statutory local nature reserves.
The number and area of designated Local Nature Reserves in Britain as at 31 March 1996 was:

	no.	hectares	acres
England	519	18,431	45,543
Scotland	23	7,456	18,416
Wales	31	5,006	12,370

An additional 33 km of linear trails are designated as Local Nature Reserves.

FOREST NATURE RESERVES

Forest Enterprise (an executive agency of the Forestry Commission) is responsible for the management of the Commission's forests. It has created 46 Forest Nature Reserves with the aim of protecting and conserving special forms of natural habitat, flora and fauna. There are about 300 SSSI on the estates, some of which are also Nature Reserves.

Forest Nature Reserves extend in size from under 50 hectares (124 acres) to over 500 hectares (1,236 acres). The largest include the Black Wood of Rannoch, by Loch Rannoch; Cannop Valley Oakwoods, Forest of Dean; Culbin Forest, near Forres; Glen Affric, near Fort Augustus; Kylerhea, Skye; Pembrey, Carmarthen Bay; Starr Forest, in Galloway Forest Park; and Wyre Forest, near Kidderminster.

NORTHERN IRELAND

There are 36 Forest Nature Reserves in Northern Ireland, covering 1,759 hectares (4,346 acres). They are designated and administered by the Forest Service, a division of the Department of Agriculture for Northern Ireland. There are also 15 National Nature Reserves on Forest Service-owned property.

MARINE NATURE RESERVES

The Wildlife and Countryside Act 1981 gives the Secretary of State for the Environment (and the Secretaries of State for Wales and for Scotland where appropriate) power to designate Marine Nature Reserves, and English Nature, Scottish Natural Heritage and the Countryside Council for Wales powers to select and manage these reserves.

Marine Nature Reserves provide protection for marine flora and fauna, and geological and physiographical features on land covered by tidal waters or parts of the sea in or adjacent to Great Britain. Reserves also provide opportunities for study and research.

The three statutory Marine Nature Reserves are:

LUNDY (1986), Bristol Channel
SKOMER (1990), Dyfed
STRANGFORD LOUGH (1995), Northern Ireland

Two other areas proposed for designation as reserves are: the Menai Strait, and Bardsey Island and part of the Lleyn peninsula, both in Wales.

A number of non-statutory marine reserves have been set up by conservation groups.

Wildlife Conservation

PROTECTED SPECIES

The Wildlife and Countryside Act 1981 gives legal protection to a wide range of wild animals and plants. Subject to parliamentary approval, the Secretary of State for the Environment may vary the animals and plants given legal protection. The most recent variation of Schedules 5 and 8 came into effect in October 1992.

ANIMALS, ETC.

Under Section 9 and Schedule 5 of the Act it is illegal without a licence to kill, injure, take, possess or sell any of the animals mentioned below (whether alive or dead) and to disturb its place of shelter and protection or to destroy that place.

‡Adder (*Vipera berus*)
§Allis shad (*alosa alosa*)
Anemone, Ivell's Sea (*Edwardsia ivelli*)
Anemone, Startlet Sea (*Nematosella vectensis*)
Apus (*Triops cancriformis*)
Bat, Horseshoe (*Rhinolophidae*, all species)
Bat, Typical (*Vespertilionidae*, all species)
Beetle (*Hypebaeus flavipes*)
Beetle, Lesser Silver Water (*Hydrochara caraboides*)
§Beetle, Mire Pill (*Curimopsis nigrita*)
Beetle, Rainbow Leaf (*Chrysolina cerealis*)
Beetle, Violet Click (*Limoniscus violaceus*)
Beetle, Water (*Graphoderus zonatus*)
Beetle, Water (*Paracymus aeneus*)
Burbot (*Lota lota*)
*Butterfly, Adonis Blue (*Lysandra bellargus*)
*Butterfly, Black Hairstreak (*Strymonidia pruni*)
*Butterfly, Brown Hairstreak (*Thecla betulae*)
*Butterfly, Chalkhill Blue (*Lysandra coridon*)
*Butterfly, Chequered Skipper (*Carterocephalus palaemon*)
*Butterfly, Duke of Burgundy Fritillary (*Hamearis lucina*)
*Butterfly, Glanville Fritillary (*Melitaea cinxia*)
Butterfly, Heath Fritillary (*Mellicta athalia* (or *Melitaea athalia*))
Butterfly, High Brown Fritillary (*Argynnis adippe*)
Butterfly, Large Blue (*Maculinea arion*)
*Butterfly, Large Copper (*Lycaena dispar*)
*Butterfly, Large Heath (*Coenonympha tullia*)
*Butterfly, Large Tortoiseshell (*Nymphalis polychloros*)
*Butterfly, Lulworth Skipper (*Thymelicus acteon*)
*Butterfly, Marsh Fritillary (*Eurodryas aurinia*)
*Butterfly, Mountain Ringlet (*Erebia epiphron*)
*Butterfly, Northern Brown Argus (*Aricia artaxerxes*)
*Butterfly, Pearl-bordered Fritillary (*Boloria euphrosyne*)
*Butterfly, Purple Emperor (*Apatura iris*)
*Butterfly, Silver Spotted Skipper (*Hesperia comma*)
*Butterfly, Silver-studded Blue (*Plebejus argus*)
*Butterfly, Small Blue (*Cupido minimus*)
Butterfly, Swallowtail (*Papilio machaon*)

*Butterfly, White Letter Hairstreak (*Stymonida w-album*)
*Butterfly, Wood White (*Leptidea sinapis*)
Cat, Wild (*Felis silvestris*)
Cicada, New Forest (*Cicadetta montana*)
**Crayfish, Atlantic Stream (*Austropotamobius pallipes*)
Cricket, Field (*Gryllus campestris*)
Cricket, Mole (*Gryllotalpa gryllotalpa*)
Dolphin (*Cetacea*)
Dormouse (*Muscardinus avellanarius*)
Dragonfly, Norfolk Aeshna (*Aeshna isosceles*)
*Frog, Common (*Rana temporaria*)
Grasshopper, Wart-biter (*Decticus verrucivorus*)
Hatchet Shell, Northern (*Thyasira gouldi*)
Lagoon Snail (*Paludinella littorina*)
Lagoon Snail, De Folin's (*Caecum armoricum*)
Lagoon Worm, Tentacled (*Alkmaria romijni*)
Leech, Medicinal (*Hirudo medicinalis*)
Lizard, Sand (*Lacerta agilis*)
‡Lizard, Viviparous (*Lacerta vivipara*)
Marten, Pine (*Martes martes*)
Moth, Barberry Carpet (*Pareulype berberata*)
Moth, Black-veined (*Siona lineata* (or *Idaea lineata*))
Moth, Essex Emerald (*Thetidia smaragdaria*)
Moth, New Forest Burnet (*Zygaena viciae*)
Moth, Reddish Buff (*Acosmetia caliginosa*)
Moth, Sussex Emerald (*Thalera fimbrialis*)
Moth, Viper's Bugloss (*Hadena irregularis*)
†Mussel, Freshwater Pearl (*Margaritifera margaritifera*)
Newt, Great Crested (or Warty) (*Triturus cristatus*)
*Newt, Palmate (*Triturus helveticus*)
*Newt, Smooth (*Triturus vulgaris*)
Otter, Common (*Lutra lutra*)
Porpoise (*Cetacea*)
Sandworm, Lagoon (*Armandia cirrhosa*)
††Sea Fan, Pink (*Eunicella verrucosa*)
Sea-Mat, Trembling (*Victorella pavida*)
Sea Slug, Lagoon (*Tenellia adspersa*)
Shrimp, Fairy (*Chirocephalus diaphanus*)
Shrimp, Lagoon Sand (*Gammarus insensibilis*)
‡Slow-worm (*Anguis fragilis*)
Snail, Glutinous (*Myxas glutinosa*)
Snail, Sandbowl (*Catinella arenaria*)
‡Snake, Grass (*Natrix natrix* (*Natrix helvetica*))
Snake, Smooth (*Coronella austriaca*)
Spider, Fen Raft (*Dolomedes plantarius*)
Spider, Ladybird (*Eresus niger*)
Squirrel, Red (*Sciurus vulgaris*)
Sturgeon (*Acipenser sturio*)
*Toad, Common (*Bufo bufo*)
Toad, Natterjack (*Bufo calamita*)
Turtle, Marine (*Dermochelyidae* and *Cheloniidae*, all species)
Vendace (*Coregonus albula*)
Walrus (*Odobenus rosmarus*)
Whale (*Cetacea*)
Whitefish (*Coregonus lavaretus*)

PLANTS

Under Section 13 and Schedule 8 of the Wildlife and Countryside Act 1981, it is illegal without a licence to pick, uproot, sell or destroy any of the plants mentioned below and, unless authorized, to uproot any wild plant.

Adder's tongue, Least (*Ophioglossum lusitanicum*)
Alison, Small (*Alyssum alyssoides*)
Blackwort (*Southbya nigrella*)
Broomrape, Bedstraw (*Orobanche caryophyllacea*)

---

* the offence relates to 'sale' only
** the offence relates to 'taking' and 'sale' only
† the offence relates to 'killing and injuring' only
‡ the offence relates to 'killing, injuring and sale'
§ the offence relates to 'killing, injuring and taking'
§§ the offence relates only to damaging, destroying or obstructing access to a shelter or protection
†† the offence relates to killing, injuring, taking, possession and sale

Broomrape, Oxtongue (*Orobanche loricata*)
Broomrape, Thistle (*Orobanche reticulata*)
Cabbage, Lundy (*Rhynchosinapis wrightii*)
Calamint, Wood (*Calamintha sylvatica*)
Caloplaca, Snow (*Caloplaca nivalis*)
Catapyrenium, Tree (*Catapyrenium psoromoides*)
Catchfly, Alpine (*Lychnis alpina*)
Catillaria, Laurer's (*Catellaria laureri*)
Centaury, Slender (*Centaurium tenuiflorum*)
Cinquefoil, Rock (*Potentilla rupestris*)
Cladonia, Upright Mountain (*Cladonia stricta*)
Clary, Meadow (*Salvia pratensis*)
Club-rush, Triangular (*Scirpus triquetrus*)
Colt's-foot, Purple (*Homogyne alpina*)
Cotoneaster, Wild (*Cotoneaster integerrimus*)
Cottongrass, Slender (*Eriophorum gracile*)
Cow-wheat, Field (*Melampyrum arvense*)
Crocus, Sand (*Romulea columnae*)
Crystalwort, Lizard (*Riccia bifurca*)
Cudweed, Broad-leaved (*Filago pyramidata*)
Cudweed, Jersey (*Gnaphalium luteoalbum*)
Cudweed, Red-tipped (*Filago lutescens*)
Diapensia (*Diapensia lapponica*)
Dock, Shore (*Rumex rupestris*)
Earwort, Marsh (*Jamesoniella undulifolia*)
Eryngo, Field (*Eryngium campestre*)
Fern, Dickie's bladder (*Cystopteris dickieana*)
Fern, Killarney (*Trichomanes speciosum*)
Flapwort, Norfolk (*Leiocolea rutheana*)
Fleabane, Alpine (*Erigeron borealis*)
Fleabane, Small (*Pulicaria vulgaris*)
Frostwort, Pointed (*Gymnomitrion apiculatum*)
Galingale, Brown (*Cyperus fuscus*)
Gentian, Alpine (*Gentiana nivalis*)
Gentian, Dune (*Gentianella uliginosa*)
Gentian, Early (*Gentianella anglica*)
Gentian, Fringed (*Gentianella ciliata*)
Gentian, Spring (*Gentiana verna*)
Germander, Cut-leaved (*Teucrium botrys*)
Germander, Water (*Teucrium scordium*)
Gladiolus, Wild (*Gladiolus illyricus*)
Goosefoot, Stinking (*Chenopodium vulvaria*)
Grass-poly (*Lythrum hyssopifolia*)
Grimmia, Blunt-leaved (*Grimmia unicolor*)
Gyalecta, Elm (*Gyalecta ulmi*)
Hare's-ear, Sickle-leaved (*Bupleurum falcatum*)
Hare's-ear, Small (*Bupleurum baldense*)
Hawk's-beard, Stinking (*Crepis foetida*)
Hawkweed, Northroe (*Hieracium northroense*)
Hawkweed, Shetland (*Hieracium zetlandicum*)
Hawkweed, Weak-leaved (*Hieracium attenuatifolium*)
Heath, Blue (*Phyllodoce caerulea*)
Helleborine, Red (*Cephalanthera rubra*)
Helleborine, Young's (*Epipactis youngiana*)
Horsetail, Branched (*Equisetum ramosissimum*)
Hound's-tongue, Green (*Cynoglossum germanicum*)
Knawel, Perennial (*Scleranthus perennis*)
Knotgrass, Sea (*Polygonum maritimum*)
Lady's-slipper (*Cypripedium calceolus*)
Lecanactis, Churchyard (*Lecanactis hemisphaerica*)
Lecanora, Tarn (*Lecanora achariana*)
Lecidea, Copper (*Lecidea inops*)
Leek, Round-headed (*Allium sphaerocephalon*)
Lettuce, Least (*Lactuca saligna*)
Lichen, Arctic Kidney (*Nephroma arcticum*)
Lichen, Ciliate Strap (*Heterodermia leucomelos*)
Lichen, Coralloid Rosette (*Heterodermia propagulifera*)
Lichen, Ear-lobed Dog (*Peltigera lepidophora*)
Lichen, Forked Hair (*Bryoria furcellata*)
Lichen, Golden Hair (*Teloschistes flavicans*)

Lichen, Orange Fruited Elm (*Caloplaca luteoalba*)
Lichen, River Jelly (*Collema dichotomum*)
Lichen, Scaly Breck (*Squamarina lentigera*)
Lichen, Stary Breck (*Buellia asterella*)
Lily, Snowdon (*Lloydia serotina*)
Liverwort (*Petallophyllum ralfsi*)
Liverwort, Lindenberg's Leafy (*Adelanthus lindenbergianus*)
Marsh-mallow, Rough (*Althaea hirsuta*)
Marshwort, Creeping (*Apium repens*)
Milk-parsley, Cambridge (*Selinum carvifolia*)
Moss (*Drepanocladius vernicosus*)
Moss, Alpine Copper (*Mielichoferia mielichoferi*)
Moss, Baltic Bog (*Sphagnum balticum*)
Moss, Blue Dew (*Saelania glaucescens*)
Moss, Blunt-leaved Bristle (*Orthotrichum obtusifolium*)
Moss, Bright Green Cave (*Cyclodictyon laetevirens*)
Moss, Cordate Beard (*Barbula cordata*)
Moss, Cornish Path (*Ditrichum cornubicum*)
Moss, Derbyshire Feather (*Thamnobryum angustifolium*)
Moss, Dune Thread (*Bryum mamillatum*)
Moss, Glaucous Beard (*Barbula glauca*)
Moss, Green Shield (*Buxbaumia viridis*)
Moss, Hair Silk (*Plagiothecium piliferum*)
Moss, Knothole (*Zygodon forsteri*)
Moss, Large Yellow Feather (*Scorpidium turgescens*)
Moss, Millimetre (*Micromitrium tenerum*)
Moss, Multifruited River (*Cryphaea lamyana*)
Moss, Nowell's Limestone (*Zygodon gracilis*)
Moss, Rigid Apple (*Bartramia stricta*)
Moss, Round-leaved Feather (*Rhyncostegium rotundifolium*)
Moss, Schleicher's Thread (*Bryum schleicheri*)
Moss, Triangular Pygmy (*Acaulon triquetrum*)
Moss, Vaucher's Feather (*Hypnum vaucheri*)
Mudwort, Welsh (*Limosella australis*)
Naiad, Holly-leaved (*Najas marina*)
Naiad, Slender (*Najas flexilis*)
Orache, Stalked (*Halimione pedunculata*)
Orchid, Early Spider (*Ophrys sphegodes*)
Orchid, Fen (*Liparis loeselii*)
Orchid, Ghost (*Epipogium aphyllum*)
Orchid, Lapland Marsh (*Dactylorhiza lapponica*)
Orchid, Late Spider (*Ophrys fuciflora*)
Orchid, Lizard (*Himantoglossum hircinum*)
Orchid, Military (*Orchis militaris*)
Orchid, Monkey (*Orchis simia*)
Pannaria, Caledonia (*Pannaria ignobilis*)
Parmelia, New Forest (*Parmelia minarum*)
Parmentaria, Oil Stain (*Parmentaria chilensis*)
Pear, Plymouth (*Pyrus cordata*)
Penny-cress, Perfoliate (*Thlaspi perfoliatum*)
Pennyroyal (*Mentha pulegium*)
Pertusaria, Alpine Moss (*Pertusaria bryontha*)
Physcia, Southern Grey (*Physcia tribacioides*)
Pigmyweed (*Crassula aquatica*)
Pine, Ground (*Ajuga chamaepitys*)
Pink, Cheddar (*Dianthus gratianopolitanus*)
Pink, Childling (*Petroraghia nanteuilii*)
Plantain, Floating Water (*Luronium natans*)
Pseudocyphellaria, Ragged (*Pseudocyphellaria lacerata*)
Psora, Rusty Alpine (*Psora rubiformis*)
Ragwort, Fen (*Senecio paludosus*)
Ramping-fumitory, Martin's (*Fumaria martinii*)
Rampion, Spiked (*Phyteuma spicatum*)
Restharrow, Small (*Ononis reclinata*)
Rock-cress, Alpine (*Arabis alpina*)
Rock-cress, Bristol (*Arabis stricta*)
Rustwort, Western (*Marsupella profunda*)
Sandwort, Norwegian (*Arenaria norvegica*)
Sandwort, Teesdale (*Minuartia stricta*)
Saxifrage, Drooping (*Saxifraga cernua*)

Saxifrage, Marsh (*Saxifrage hirulus*)
Saxifrage, Tufted (*Saxifraga cespitosa*)
Solenopsora, Serpentine (*Solenopsora liparina*)
Solomon's-seal, Whorled (*Polygonatum verticillatum*)
Sow-thistle, Alpine (*Cicerbita alpina*)
Spearwort, Adder's-tongue (*Ranunculus ophioglossifolius*)
Speedwell, Fingered (*Veronica triphyllos*)
Speedwell, Spiked (*Veronica spicata*)
Star-of-Bethlehem, Early (*Gagea bohemica*)
Starfruit (*Damasonium alisma*)
Stonewort, Bearded (*Chara canescens*)
Stonewort, Foxtail (*Lamprothamnium papulosum*)
Strapwort (*Corrigiola litoralis*)
Turpswort (*Geocalyx graveolens*)
Violet, Fen (*Viola persicifolia*)
Viper's-grass (*Scorzonera humilis*)
Water-plantain, Ribbon-leaved (*Alisma gramineum*)
Wood-sedge, Starved (*Carex depauperata*)
Woodsia, Alpine (*Woodsia alpina*)
Woodsia, Oblong (*Woodsia ilvensis*)
Wormwood, Field (*Artemisia campestris*)
Woundwort, Downy (*Stachys germanica*)
Woundwort, Limestone (*Stachys alpina*)
Yellow-rattle, Greater (*Rhinanthus serotinus*)

WILD BIRDS

The Wildlife and Countryside Act 1981 lays down a close season for wild birds (other than game birds) from 1 February to 31 August inclusive, each year. Exceptions to these dates are made for:

Capercaillie and (except Scotland) *Woodcock* – 1 February to 30 September
Snipe – 1 February to 11 August
Wild Duck and *Wild Goose* (below high water mark) – 21 February to 31 August

Birds which may be killed or taken outside the close season (except on Sundays and on Christmas Day in Scotland, and on Sundays in prescribed areas of England and Wales) are the above-named, plus coot, certain wild duck (gadwall, goldeneye, mallard, pintail, pochard, shoveler, teal, tufted duck, wigeon), certain wild geese (Canada, greylag, pink-footed, white-fronted (in England and Wales only)), moorhen, golden plover and woodcock.

Certain wild birds may be killed or taken subject to the conditions of a general licence at any time by authorized persons: crow, collared dove, gull (great and lesser black-backed or herring), jackdaw, jay, magpie, pigeon (feral or wood), rook, sparrow (house), and starling. Conditions usually apply where the birds pose a threat to agriculture, public health, air safety, other bird species, and to prevent the spread of disease.

All other British birds are fully protected by law throughout the year.

CLOSE SEASONS AND TIMES

GAME BIRDS

In each case the dates are inclusive:

Black game – 11 December to 19 August (31 August in Somerset, Devon and New Forest)
Grouse – 11 December to 11 August
Partridge – 2 February to 31 August
Pheasant – 2 February to 30 September
Ptarmigan – (Scotland only) 11 December to 11 August

*It is also unlawful in England and Wales to kill this game on a Sunday or Christmas Day

HUNTING AND GROUND GAME

There is no statutory close time for fox-hunting or rabbit-shooting, nor for hares. However, by an Act passed in 1892 the sale of hares or leverets in Great Britain is prohibited from 1 March to 31 July inclusive. The recognized date for the opening of the fox-hunting season is 1 November, and it continues till the following April.

DEER

The statutory close seasons for deer (all dates inclusive) are:

	England and Wales	Scotland
Fallow deer		
Male	1 May–31 July	1 May–31 July
Female	1 Mar.–31 Oct.	16 Feb.–20 Oct.
Red deer		
Male	1 May–31 July	21 Oct.–30 June
Female	1 Mar.–31 Oct.	16 Feb.–20 Oct.
Roe deer		
Male	1 Nov.–31 Mar.	21 Oct.–31 Mar.
Female	1 Mar.–31 Oct.	1 April–20 Oct.
Sika deer		
Male	1 May–31 July	21 Oct.–30 June
Female	1 Mar.–31 Oct.	16 Feb.–20 Oct.
Red/Sika hybrids		
Male	—	21 Oct.–30 June
Female	—	16 Feb.–20 Oct.

ANGLING

Game Fishing
Where local by-laws neither specify nor dispense with an annual close-season, the statutory close times for game fishing are: Trout, 1 October to end February; Salmon, 1 November to 31 January.

Coarse Fishing
Responsibility for the fisheries function of the National Rivers Authority, including licensing and regulation, passed to the Environment Agency on 1 April 1996. The statutory close season for coarse fish in England and Wales runs from 15 March to 15 June on all rivers, streams and drains. Close season arrangements for canals vary from region to region. The close season on all lakes, ponds and reservoirs is at the discretion of the fishery owner, except on the Norfolk Broads and certain Sites of Special Scientific Interest where the statutory close season still applies. It is necessary in all cases to check with the Environment Agency regional office concerning the area (details can be found in the local telephone directory).

Licences
Purchase of a national rod fishing licence is legally required of anglers wishing to fish with rod and line in all waters within the area of the Environment Agency.

	Salmon and sea trout	Non-migratory trout and coarse fish
Full	£55.00	£15.00
Concessionary	27.50	7.50
Eight-day	13.50	4.50
One-day	4.50	1.50

Concessionary licences are available for juniors (12–16 years), for senior citizens (65 years and over), and disabled who are in receipt of invalidity benefit or severe disability allowance. Those in receipt of a war pension which includes unemployability supplements are also eligible.

Historic Buildings and Monuments

LISTING

Under the Planning (Listed Buildings and Conservation Areas) Act 1990, the Secretary of State for National Heritage has a statutory duty to compile lists of buildings or groups of buildings in England which are of special architectural or historic interest. Under the Ancient Monuments and Archaeological Areas Act 1979 as amended by the National Heritage Act 1983, the Secretary of State is also responsible for compiling a schedule of ancient monuments. Decisions are taken on the advice of English Heritage (see page 306).

Listed buildings are classified into Grade I, Grade II* and Grade II. There are currently about 500,000 individual listed buildings in England, of which about 95 per cent are Grade II listed. Almost all pre-1700 buildings are listed, and most buildings of 1700 to 1840. English Heritage is carrying out thematic surveys of particular types of buildings with a view to making recommendations for listing, and members of the public may propose a building for consideration. The main purpose of listing is to ensure that care is taken in deciding the future of a building. No changes which affect the architectural or historic character of a listed building can be made without listed building consent (in addition to planning permission where relevant). Applications for listed building consent are normally dealt with by the local planning authority, although English Heritage is always consulted about proposals affecting Grade I and Grade II* properties. It is a criminal offence to demolish a listed building, or alter it in such a way as to affect its character, without consent.

There are currently about 16,000 scheduled monuments in England. English Heritage is carrying out a Monuments Protection Programme assessing archaeological sites with a view to making recommendations for scheduling, and members of the public may propose a monument for consideration. All monuments proposed for scheduling are considered to be of national importance. Where buildings are both scheduled and listed, ancient monuments legislation takes precedence. The main purpose of scheduling a monument is to preserve it for the future and to protect it from damage, destruction or any unnecessary interference. Once a monument has been scheduled, scheduled monument consent is required before any works are carried out which would damage or alter the monument in any way. The scope of the control is more extensive and more detailed than that applied to listed buildings, but certain minor works, as detailed in the Ancient Monuments Class Consents Order 1994, may be carried out without consent. It is a criminal offence to carry out unauthorized work to scheduled monuments.

Under the Planning (Listed Buildings and Conservation Areas) Act 1990 and the Ancient Monuments and Archaeological Areas Act 1979, the Secretary of State for Wales is responsible for listing buildings and scheduling monuments in Wales on the advice of Cadw (see page 356), the Historic Buildings Council for Wales (see page 306) and the Ancient Monuments Board for Wales (see page 307). The criteria for evaluating buildings are similar to those in England and the same listing system is used. There are about 18,000 listed buildings and about 2,800 scheduled monuments in Wales.

Under the Town and County Planning (Scotland) Act 1972 and the Ancient Monuments and Archaeological Areas Act 1979, the Secretary of State for Scotland is responsible for listing buildings and scheduling monuments in Scotland on the advice of Historic Scotland (see page 341), the Historic Buildings Council for Scotland (see

page 306) and the Ancient Monuments Board for Scotland (see page 307). The criteria for evaluating buildings are similar to those in England but an A, B, C grading system is used. There are about 42,000 listed buildings and about 6,000 scheduled monuments in Scotland.

Under the Planning (Northern Ireland) Order 1991 and the Historic Monuments and Archaeological Objects (Northern Ireland) Order 1995, the Department of the Environment for Northern Ireland (see page 330) is responsible for listing buildings and scheduling monuments in Northern Ireland on the advice of the Historic Buildings Council for Northern Ireland and the Historic Monuments Council for Northern Ireland. The criteria for evaluating buildings are similar to those in England but no official grading system is used. There are about 8,565 listed buildings and 1,120 scheduled monuments in Northern Ireland.

The Government proposes to reform the system for protecting the built heritage in Great Britain. In March 1995 public consultation was introduced on listing recommendations arising from English Heritage's thematic surveys of particular building types, and a Green Paper was published in May 1996.

OPENING TO THE PUBLIC

The following is a selection of the many historic buildings and monuments open to the public. The admission charges given are the standard charges for 1996–7; many properties have concessionary rates for children, etc. Opening hours vary. Many properties are closed in winter and some are also closed in the mornings. Most properties are closed on Christmas Eve, Christmas Day, Boxing Day and New Year's Day, and many are closed on Good Friday. During the winter season, most English Heritage monuments are closed on Mondays and Tuesdays and monuments in the care of Cadw are closed on Sunday mornings. Information about a specific property should be checked by telephone.

*Closed in winter (usually November–March)
†Closed in winter, and in mornings in summer

ENGLAND

EH English Heritage property
NT National Trust property

*A LA RONDE (NT), Exmouth, Devon. Tel: 01395-265514. Closed Sat. morning and Fri. Adm. £3.10. Unique 16-sided house built in 1796

*ALNWICK CASTLE, Northumberland. Tel: 01665-510777. Closed Fri. Adm. £4.70; grounds only £4.20. Seat of the Dukes of Northumberland since 1309; Italian Renaissance-style interior

ALTHORP, Northants. Tel: 01604-770107. Opening times and prices subject to change. House originally built in early 16th century. Fine art collection

†ANGLESEY ABBEY (NT), Cambs. Tel: 01223-811200. Closed Mon. (except Bank Holidays) and Tues. Gardens open daily July to Sept. Adm. £5.50 (£6.50 Sun. and Bank Holidays); gardens only, £3.20. House built c.1600; bought by Lord Fairhaven in early 20th century. Outstanding grounds with unique statuary

APSLEY HOUSE, London W1. Tel: 0171-499 5676. Closed Mon. Adm £3.00. Built by Robert Adam 1771-8, home of the Dukes of Wellington since 1817 and known as 'No. 1 London'. Collection of fine and decorative arts

ARUNDEL CASTLE, W. Sussex. Tel: 01903-883136.
Closed Sat. and Good Fri. Adm. charge. Castle dating
from the Norman Conquest. Seat of the Dukes of
Norfolk

AVEBURY (NT), Wilts. Adm. free. Remains of stone circles
constructed 4,000 years ago surrounding the later
village of Avebury. Also *Alexander Keiller Museum*. Tel:
01672-539250. Adm. £1.50

BANQUETING HOUSE, Whitehall, London SW1. Tel: 0171-
839 8919. Closed Sun. and Bank Holidays. Adm. £3.00.
Designed by Inigo Jones; ceiling paintings by Rubens,
Site of the execution of Charles I

BASILDON PARK (NT), Berks. Tel: 01734-843040. Closed
Mon. (except Bank Holidays) and Tues. Adm. £3.70;
grounds only, £1.50. Palladian house built in 1776;
unusual octagonal room

BATTLE ABBEY (EH), E. Sussex. Tel: 01424-773792. Adm.
£3.50. Remains of the abbey founded by William the
Conqueror on the site of the Battle of Hastings

BEAULIEU, Hants. Tel: 01590-612345. Adm. charge.
House and gardens, Beaulieu Abbey and exhibition of
monastic life, National Motor Museum (*see also* page
581)

BEESTON CASTLE (EH), Cheshire. Tel: 01829-260464.
Adm. £2.20. Thirteenth-century inner ward with
gatehouse and towers, and remains of large outer ward

BELTON HOUSE (NT), Grantham, Lincs. Tel: 01476-
566116. Closed Mon. (except Bank Holidays) and Tues.
Adm. £4.50. Fine 17th-century house in landscaped
park

BELVOIR CASTLE, nr Grantham, Lincs. Tel: 01476-
870262. Closed Mon. and Fri. except Bank Holidays.
Adm. £4.25. Seat of the Dukes of Rutland; 19th-century
Gothic-style castle

BERKELEY CASTLE, Glos. Tel: 01453-810332. Opening
times vary. Adm. £4.50. Completed 1153; site of the
murder of Edward II (1327). Elizabethan terraced
gardens

BLENHEIM PALACE, Woodstock, Oxon. Tel: 01993-
811325. Adm. charge. Seat of the Dukes of
Marlborough and Winston Churchill's birthplace;
designed by Vanbrugh

BLICKLING HALL (NT), Norfolk. Tel: 01263-733084.
Closed Mon. (except Bank Holidays) and Thurs. Adm.
£5.50 (£6.50 Sun. and Bank Holidays; garden only
tickets available. Jacobean house with state rooms,
Long Gallery, formal gardens, temple and 18th-
century orangery

BODIAM CASTLE (NT), E. Sussex. Tel: 01580-830436.
Closed Mon. in winter. Adm. £2.70. Well-preserved
medieval moated castle

BOLSOVER CASTLE (EH), Derbys. Tel: 01246-823349.
Closed Mon. and Tues. in winter. Adm. £2.60. Notable
for its 17th-century buildings

BOSCOBEL HOUSE (EH), Shropshire. Tel: 01902-850244.
Closed Mon. and Tues. in winter. Adm. £3.50. Timber-
framed 17th-century hunting lodge, refuge of fugitive
Charles II

BOUGHTON HOUSE, Northants. Tel: 01536-515731.
House open Aug. only; grounds May to Sept. except
Fri. State rooms by prior booking. Adm. £4.00; grounds
£1.50. A 17th-century house with French-style
additions

BOWOOD HOUSE, Wilts. Tel: 01249-812102. Adm. £4.80.
An 18th-century house in Capability Brown park, with
lake, temple and arboretum

BROADLANDS, Hants. Tel: 01794-516878. Open July-
Sept. Adm. £5.00. Palladian mansion in Capability
Brown parkland. Mountbatten exhibition

BRONTË PARSONAGE, Haworth, W. Yorks. Tel: 01535-
642323. Closed Jan.- Feb. Adm. £3.80. Home of the
Brontë sisters; museum and memorabilia

BUCKFAST ABBEY, Devon. Tel: 01364-642519. Adm. free.
Medieval monastery rebuilt 1907-1938

*BUCKINGHAM PALACE, London SW1. Tel: 0171-839 1377.
Open daily for eight weeks from early Aug. each year.
Adm. £8.50. Purchased by George III in 1762, it has
been the Sovereign's official London residence since
1837. Eighteen state rooms, including the Throne
Room; also the Picture Gallery

BUCKLAND ABBEY (NT), Devon. Tel: 01822-853607.
Closed Thurs. In winter open only weekend
afternoons. Adm. £4.20. A 13th-century Cistercian
monastery. Home of Sir Francis Drake

*BURGHLEY HOUSE, Stamford, Lincs. Tel: 01780-52451.
Adm. £5.50. Late Elizabethan house; vast state
apartments

†CALKE ABBEY (NT), Derbys. Tel: 01332-863822. Closed
Thurs. and Fri. Adm. £4.70, by timed ticket. Baroque
18th-century mansion

CARISBROOKE CASTLE (EH), Isle of Wight. Tel: 01983-
522107. Adm. £3.80. Norman castle; prison of Charles I
1647-8

CARLISLE CASTLE (EH), Cumbria. Tel: 01228-591922.
Adm. £2.50. Medieval castle, prison of Mary Queen of
Scots

*CARLYLE'S HOUSE (NT), Cheyne Row, London SW3. Tel:
0171-352 7087. Home of Thomas Carlyle

CASTLE ACRE PRIORY (EH), Norfolk. Tel: 01760-755394.
Closed Mon. and Tues. in winter. Adm. £2.50. Remains
include 12th-century church and prior's lodgings

*CASTLE DROGO (NT), Devon. Tel: 01647-433306. Castle
closed Fri. Adm. £4.80; grounds only, £2.20. Granite
castle designed by Lutyens

*CASTLE HOWARD, N. Yorks. Tel: 01653-684333. Adm.
£6.50; grounds only, £4.00. Designed by Vanbrugh
1699-1726; mausoleum designed by Hawksmoor

CASTLE RISING CASTLE (EH), Norfolk. Tel: 01553-
631330. Closed Mon. and Tues. in winter. Adm. £2.00.
A 12th-century keep in a massive earthwork with
gatehouse and bridge

†CHARTWELL (NT), Kent. Tel: 01732-866368. Closed Fri.
and Mon. (except Bank Holidays). Adm. £4.50; grounds
only, £2.00. Home of Sir Winston Churchill

*CHATSWORTH, Derbys. Tel: 01246-582204. Adm. £5.75.
Tudor mansion with later additions in magnificent
parkland

CHESTERS ROMAN FORT (EH), Northumberland. Tel:
01434-681379. Adm. £2.50. Fine example of a Roman
cavalry fort

*CHYSAUSTER ANCIENT VILLAGE (EH), Cornwall. Tel:
01326-212044. Adm. £1.50. Romano-Cornish village,
2nd and 3rd century AD, on a probably late Iron Age site

CLIFFORD'S TOWER (EH), York. Tel: 01904-646940. Adm.
£1.60. A 13th-century tower built on a mound

†CLIVEDEN (NT), Berks. Tel: 01628-605069. House open
Thurs. and Sun. only, gardens daily. Adm. £4.00, £1.00
extra for house. Former home of the Astors, now an
hotel set in garden and woodland

CORBRIDGE ROMAN SITE (EH), Northumberland. Tel:
01434-632349. Closed Mon. and Tues. in winter. Adm.
£2.50. Excavated central area of a Roman town and
successive military bases

CORFE CASTLE (NT), Dorset. Tel: 01929-481294. Nov.-
Jan. open weekend afternoons only. Adm. £3.00.
Ruined former royal castle dating from 11th century

†CROFT CASTLE (NT), Herefordshire. Tel: 01568-780246.
Closed Mon. (except Bank Holidays) and Tues.; April
and Oct. open weekends only. Adm. £3.20. Pre-
Conquest border castle with Georgian-Gothic interior

DEAL CASTLE (EH), Kent. Tel: 01304-372762. Closed
Mon. and Tues. in winter. Adm. £2.80. Largest and most
complete of the coastal defence forts built by Henry
VIII

DICKENS HOUSE, Doughty Street, London WC1. Tel: 0171-405 2127. Closed Sun. Adm. £3.50. House occupied by Dickens 1837-9; manuscripts, furniture and portraits

DR JOHNSON'S HOUSE, 17 Gough Square, London EC4. Tel: 0171-353 3745. Closed Sun. and Bank Holidays. Adm. £3.00. Home of Samuel Johnson

DOVE COTTAGE, Grasmere, Cumbria. Tel: 015394-35544. Closed Jan. and early Feb. Adm. £4.10. Wordsworth's home 1799-1808; museum and memorabilia

DOVER CASTLE (EH), Kent. Tel: 01304-201628. Adm. £6.00. Castle with Roman, Saxon and Norman features; wartime operations rooms

DUNSTANBURGH CASTLE (EH), Northumberland. Tel: 01665-576231. Closed Mon. and Tues. in winter. Adm. £1.50. A 14th-century castle on a cliff, with a substantial gatehouse-keep

FARLEIGH HUNGERFORD CASTLE (EH), Somerset. Tel: 01225-754026. Adm. £1.50. Late 14th-century castle with two courts and chapel with tomb of Sir Thomas Hungerford

*FARNHAM CASTLE KEEP (EH), Surrey. Tel: 01252-713393. Adm. £2.00. Large 12th-century shell-keep on motte

FOUNTAINS ABBEY (NT), nr Ripon, N. Yorks. Tel: 01765-608888. Closed Fri. Nov.-Jan. Adm. £4.00. Ruined Cistercian monastery; 18th-century landscaped gardens of Studley Royal estate

FRAMLINGHAM CASTLE (EH), Suffolk. Tel: 01728-724189. Adm. £2.50. Castle (c.1200) with high curtain walls enclosing an almshouse (1639)

FURNESS ABBEY (EH), Cumbria. Tel: 01229-823420. Adm. £2.30. Remains of church and conventual buildings founded in 1123

GLASTONBURY ABBEY, Somerset. Tel: 01458-832267. Adm. £2.50. Ruins of a 12th-century abbey rebuilt after fire. Site of an early Christian settlement

GOODRICH CASTLE (EH), Herefordshire. Tel: 01600-890538. Adm. £2.20. Remains of 13th- and 14th-century castle with 12th-century keep

GREENWICH, London SE10. *Royal Observatory.* Closed Sun. mornings. Adm. charge. Former Royal Observatory (founded 1675) where the time ball and zero meridian of longitude can be seen. *The Queen's House.* Tel: 0181-858 4422. Closed Sun. mornings. Adm. charge. Designed for Queen Anne, wife of James I, by Inigo Jones. *Painted Hall and Chapel* (Royal Naval College). Closed mornings. Visitors are admitted to Sunday service in the chapel at 11 a.m. except during college vacations

GRIMES GRAVES (EH), Norfolk. Tel: 01842-810656. Closed Mon. and Tues. in winter. Adm. £1.50. Neolithic flint mines. One shaft can be descended

*GUILDHALL, London EC2. Tel: 0171-332 1460. Closed Sat. Adm. free. Centre of civic government of the City. Built c.1440; facade built 1788-9

*HADDON HALL, Derbys. Tel: 01629-812855. Closed Sun. in July and Aug. except Bank Holiday weekend. Adm. £4.50. Well-preserved 12th-century manor house

HAILES ABBEY (EH), Glos. Tel: 01242-602398. Closed Mon. and Tues. in winter. Adm. £2.20. Ruins of a 13th-century Cistercian monastery

†HAM HOUSE (NT), Richmond, Surrey. Tel: 0181-940 1950. Closed Thurs. and Fri. Adm. £4.00. Garden open all year except Fri. Adm. free. Stuart house with fine interiors

HAMPTON COURT PALACE, East Molesey, Surrey. Tel: 0181-781 9500. Adm. £7.50. A 16th-century palace with additions by Wren. Gardens with maze; Tudor tennis court (summer only)

†HARDWICK HALL (NT), Derbys. Tel: 01246-850430. Closed Mon. (except Bank Holidays), Tues. and Fri.: grounds open daily, all year. Adm £5.50; grounds only £2.50. Built 1591-7 by Bess of Hardwick; notable furnishings

*HARDY'S COTTAGE (NT), Higher Bockhampton, Dorset. Tel: 01305-262366. Interior open only by appointment. Adm. £2.50. Garden open daily, adm. free. Birthplace of Thomas Hardy

*HAREWOOD HOUSE, W. Yorks. Tel: 0113-288 6331. Adm. charge. An 18th-century house designed by John Carr and Robert Adam; park by Capability Brown

†HATFIELD HOUSE, Herts. Tel: 01707-262823. Closed Mon. (except Bank Holidays). Adm. charge. Jacobean house built by Robert Cecil, and family home of the Cecils. Surviving wing of royal Palace of Hatfield (1497)

HELMSLEY CASTLE (EH), N. Yorks. Tel: 01439-770442. Closed Mon. and Tues. in winter. Adm. £2.00. A 12th-century keep and curtain wall with 16th-century buildings. Spectacular earthwork defences

†HEVER CASTLE, Kent. Tel: 01732-865224. Adm. charge. A 13th-century double-moated castle, childhood home of Anne Boleyn

*HOLKER HALL, Cumbria. Tel: 015395-58328. Closed Sat. Adm. charge. Former home of the Dukes of Devonshire; award-winning gardens

†HOLKHAM HALL, Norfolk. Tel: 01328-710227. Closed Fri. and Sat. Adm. £3.00. Fine Palladian mansion

HOUSESTEADS ROMAN FORT (EH), Northumberland. Tel: 01434-344363. Adm. £2.50. Excavated infantry fort on Hadrian's Wall with extra-mural civilian settlement

†HUGHENDEN MANOR (NT), High Wycombe. Tel: 01494-532580. Closed Mon. (except Bank Holidays) and Tues.; open weekends only in March. Adm. £3.60. Home of Disraeli; small formal garden

JANE AUSTEN'S HOUSE, Chawton, Hants. Tel: 01420-83262. Closed Mon.-Fri. in Jan. and Feb. Adm. £2.00. Jane Austen's home 1809-17

KEATS HOUSE, Keats Grove, London NW3. Tel: 0171-435 2062. Closed Sun. mornings in summer, mornings except Sat. in winter. Adm. free. Home of John Keats 1818-20

*KELMSCOTT MANOR, nr Lechlade, Glos. Tel: 01367-252486. Open Wed. and third Sat. in every month. Adm. £6.00. Summer home of William Morris, with products of Morris and Co.

KENILWORTH CASTLE (EH), Warks. Tel: 01926-852078. Adm. £2.50. Castle showing many styles of building from 1155 to 1649

*KENSINGTON PALACE, London W8. Tel: 0171-937 9561. Adm. £5.50. Built in 1605 and enlarged by Wren; bought by William and Mary in 1689. Birthplace of Queen Victoria

KENWOOD (EH), Hampstead Lane, London NW3. Tel: 0181-348 1286. Adm. free. Adam villa housing the Iveagh bequest of paintings and furniture. Open-air concerts in summer

*KEW PALACE, Surrey. Tel: 0181-332 5189. Adm. £1.00 (plus £4.50 adm. to Kew Gardens). Built in 1631 as the Dutch House; residence of George III.

†KINGSTON LACY HOUSE (NT), Dorset. Tel: 01202-883402. Closed Thurs. and Fri. Adm. £5.50; grounds only, £2.20. A 17th-century house with 19th-century alterations; important collection of paintings

†KNEBWORTH HOUSE, Herts. Tel: 01438-812661. Closed Mon. (except Bank Holidays), and Mon.-Fri. April, May and Sept. Adm. £4.50; grounds only, £3.50. Tudor manor house concealed by 19th-century Gothic decoration; Lutyens gardens

*KNOLE (NT), Kent. Tel: 01732-450608. Closed Mon. (except Bank Holidays), Tues. and Thurs. morning. Adm. £4.50; park free to pedestrians. House dating from 1456 set in parkland; fine art treasures

LAMBETH PALACE, London SE1. Tel: 0171-928 8282. Visits by written application. Official residence of the Archbishop of Canterbury. A 19th-century house with parts dating from the 12th century

*LANERCOST PRIORY (EH), Cumbria. Tel: 016977-3030. Adm. £1.00. The nave of the Augustinian priory church, c.1166, is still used; remains of other claustral buildings

*LANHYDROCK (NT), Cornwall. Tel: 01208-73320. Closed Mon. (except Bank Holidays). Garden open daily including in winter. Adm. £5.90; gardens only, £3.00. House dating from the 17th century; 45 rooms, including kitchen and nursery

LEEDS CASTLE, Kent. Tel: 01622-765400. Adm. £8.00; park only, £6.00. Castle dating from the 9th century, on two islands in a lake

*LEVENS HALL, Cumbria. Tel: 015395-60321. Closed Fri. and Sat. Adm. charge. Elizabethan house with unique topiary garden (1694). Steam engine collection

LINCOLN CASTLE. Tel: 01522-511068. Adm. £2.00. Built by William the Conqueror in 1068

LINDISFARNE PRIORY (EH), Northumberland. Tel: 01289-389200. Open all year, subject to tide times. Adm. £2.50. Bishopric of the Northumbrian kingdom destroyed by the Danes; re-established in the 11th century as a Benedictine priory, now ruined

†LITTLE MORETON HALL (NT), Cheshire. Tel: 01260-272018. Closed Mon. (except Bank Holidays) and Tues. Adm. £3.60. Timber-framed moated manor house with knot garden

LONGLEAT HOUSE, Warminster. Tel: 01985-844400. Open daily; safari park closed winter. Adm. charge. Elizabethan house in Italian Renaissance style

LULLINGSTONE ROMAN VILLA (EH), Kent. Tel: 01322-863467. Adm. £2.00. Large villa occupied for much of the Roman period; fine mosaics

†LUTON HOO, Beds. Tel: 01582-22955. Open Fri.-Sun. and Bank Holiday Mon. Adm. £5.50. Houses the Wernher collection of china, glass, pictures and other *objets d'art*

MANSION HOUSE, London EC4. Tel: 0171-626 2500. Group visits only, by prior arrangement. Adm. free. The official residence of the Lord Mayor of London

MARBLE HILL HOUSE (EH), Twickenham, Middx. Tel: 0181-892 5115. Closed Mon. and Tues. in winter. Adm. £2.50. English Palladian villa with Georgian paintings and furniture

*MICHELHAM PRIORY, E. Sussex. Tel: 01323-844224. Adm. £3.80. Tudor house built onto an Augustinian priory

MIDDLEHAM CASTLE (EH), N. Yorks. Tel: 01969-623899. Closed Mon. and Tues. in winter. Adm. £1.60. A 12th-century keep within later fortifications. Childhood home of Richard III

†MONTACUTE HOUSE (NT), Somerset. Tel: 01935-823289. Closed Tues; grounds open all year. Adm. £5.00; grounds only, £2.80. Elizabethan house with National Portrait Gallery portraits from period

MOUNT GRACE PRIORY (EH), N. Yorks. Tel: 01609-883494. Closed Mon. and Tues. in winter. Adm. £2.40. Carthusian monastery, with remains of monastic buildings

NETLEY ABBEY (EH), Hants. Tel: 01705-527667. Adm. free. Remains of Cistercian abbey, used as house in Tudor period

OLD SARUM (EH), Wilts. Tel: 01722-335398. Adm. £1.70. Earthworks enclosing remains of the castle and the 11th-century cathedral

ORFORD CASTLE (EH), Suffolk. Tel: 013944-50472. Adm. £2.00. Circular keep of c.1170 and remains of coastal defence castle built by Henry II

*OSBORNE HOUSE (EH), Isle of Wight. Tel: 01983-200022. Adm. £6.00. Queen Victoria's seaside residence

†OSTERLEY PARK HOUSE (NT), Isleworth, Middx. Tel: 0181-560 3918. Closed Mon. (except Bank Holidays) and Tues; grounds open all year. Adm. £3.70; grounds free. Elizabethan mansion set in parkland

PENDENNIS CASTLE (EH), Cornwall. Tel: 01326-316594. Adm. £2.50. Well-preserved coastal defence castle built by Henry VIII

†PENSHURST PLACE, Kent. Tel: 01892-870307. Adm. £5.50; grounds only, £4.00. House with medieval Baron's Hall and 14th-century gardens

†PETWORTH (NT), W. Sussex. Tel: 01798-342207. Closed Mon. (except Bank Holidays) and Fri. Adm. £4.20; grounds free. Late 17th-century house set in deer park

PEVENSEY CASTLE (EH), E. Sussex. Tel: 01323-762604. Closed Mon. and Tues. in winter. Adm. £2.00. Walls of a 4th-century Roman fort enclosing remains of an 11th-century castle

PEVERIL CASTLE (EH), Derbys. Tel: 01433-620613. Adm. £1.50. A 12th-century castle defended on two sides by precipitous rocks

†POLESDEN LACY (NT), Surrey. Tel: 01372-458203. Closed Mon. (except Bank Holidays) and Tues.; open weekends only in March. Grounds open daily all year. Adm. £6.00; grounds only £3.00. Regency villa remodelled in the Edwardian era. Fine paintings and furnishings

PORTCHESTER CASTLE (EH), Hants. Tel: 01705-378291. Adm. £2.50. Walls of a late Roman fort enclosing a Norman keep and an Augustinian priory church

*POWDERHAM CASTLE, Devon. Tel: 01626-890243. Closed Sat. Adm. £4.40. Medieval castle with 18th- and 19th-century alterations

†RABY CASTLE, Co. Durham. Tel: 01833-660202. Closed Sat. (except Bank Holiday weekends). Limited opening in May and June. Adm. £3.50; grounds only, £1.00. A 14th-century castle with walled gardens

*RAGLEY HALL, Warks. Tel: 01789-762090. Closed Mon. (except Bank Holidays) and Fri.; grounds open daily. Adm. £4.50. A 17th-century house with gardens, park and lake

RICHBOROUGH CASTLE (EH), Kent. Tel: 01304-612013. Adm. £2.00. Landing-site of the Claudian invasion in AD 43, with 3rd-century stone walls

RICHMOND CASTLE (EH), N. Yorks. Tel: 01748-822493. Adm. £1.80. A 12th-century keep with 11th-century curtain wall and domestic buildings

RIEVAULX ABBEY (EH), N. Yorks. Tel: 01439-798228. Adm. £2.50. Remains of a Cistercian abbey founded c.1131

ROCHESTER CASTLE (EH), Kent. Tel: 01634-402276. Adm. £2.50. An 11th-century castle partly on the Roman city wall, with a square keep of c.1130

†ROCKINGHAM CASTLE, Northants. Tel: 01536-770240. Open Sun. and Thurs. only (and Bank Holiday Mon. and Tues., and Tues. in Aug.). Adm. £3.80; gardens only, £2.40. Built by William the Conqueror

ROYAL PAVILION, Brighton. Tel: 01273-603005. Adm. charge. Palace of George IV, in Chinese style with Indian exterior and Regency gardens

†RUFFORD OLD HALL (NT), Lancs. Tel: 01704-821254. Closed Thurs. and Fri. Adm. £3.00; garden only, £1.60. A 16th-century hall with unique screen

ST AUGUSTINE'S ABBEY (EH), Canterbury, Kent. Tel: 01227-767345. Adm. £1.50. Remains of Benedictine monastery, with Norman church, on site of abbey founded AD 598 by St Augustine

ST MAWES CASTLE (EH), Cornwall. Tel: 01326-270526. Closed Mon. and Tues. in winter. Adm. £2.00. Coastal defence castle built by Henry VIII comprising central tower and three bastions

ST MICHAEL'S MOUNT (NT), Cornwall. Tel: 01736-710507. Closed Sat. and Sun. No regular ferry service in winter; castle open as tide, weather, etc., permit. Adm. £3.70. A 14th-century castle with later additions and alterations, off the coast at Marazion

*SANDRINGHAM, Norfolk. Tel: 01553-772675. Closed for three weeks in summer and when the Royal Family is in residence. Adm. £4.00; grounds only, £3.00. The Queen's private residence; a neo-Jacobean house built in 1870

SCARBOROUGH CASTLE (EH), N. Yorks. Tel: 01723-372451. Closed Mon. and Tues. in winter. Adm. £1.80. Remains of 12th-century keep and curtain walls

†SHERBORNE CASTLE, Dorset. Tel: 01935-813182. Open Thurs., Sat., Sun. and Bank Holiday Mon. Adm. charge. Early 12th-century castle owned by Sir Walter Raleigh

*SHUGBOROUGH (NT), Staffs. Tel: 01889-881388. Adm. house, servants' quarters and farm, £8.00; each site alone, £3.50. House set in 18th-century park with monuments, temples and pavilions in the Greek Revival style

SKIPTON CASTLE, N. Yorks. Tel: 01756-792442. Closed Sun. mornings. Adm. £3.40. D-shaped castle with six round towers and beautiful inner courtyard

†SMALLHYTHE PLACE (NT), Kent. Tel: 01580-762334. Closed Thurs.-Fri. (open Good Friday). Adm. £2.50. Half-timbered 16th-century house; home of Ellen Terry 1899-1928

†STANFORD HALL, Leics. Tel: 01788-860250. Open Sat.-Sun.; also Bank Holiday Mon. and Tues. Adm. £3.50; grounds only, £1.90. William and Mary house with Stuart portraits. Motorcycle museum

STONEHENGE (EH), Wilts. Tel: 01980-624715. Adm. £3.50. Prehistoric monument consisting of a series of concentric stone circles surrounded by a ditch and bank

STONELEIGH ABBEY, Warks. Tel: 01285-659771. Open by appointment only; closed weekends. Early 18th-century Georgian mansion on the site of a Cistercian abbey

†STONOR PARK, Oxon. Tel: 01491-638587. Opening days vary. Adm. £4.00. Medieval house with Georgian facade. Centre of Roman Catholicism after the Reformation

†STOURHEAD (NT), Wilts. Tel: 01985-844785. Closed Thurs.-Fri. Gardens open daily all year. Adm. £4.20; gardens, £4.20. English Palladian mansion with famous gardens

*STRATFIELD SAYE HOUSE, Hants. Tel: 01256-882882. Closed Fri. Adm. charge. House built 1630-40; home of the Dukes of Wellington since 1817

STRATFORD-UPON-AVON, Warks. *Shakespeare's Birthplace* with Shakespeare Centre; *Anne Hathaway's Cottage*, home of Shakespeare's wife; *Mary Arden's House*, home of Shakespeare's mother; *New Place*, where Shakespeare died; and *Hall's Croft*, home of Shakespeare's daughter. Tel: 01789-204016. Adm. charges. Also *Grammar School* attended by Shakespeare, *Holy Trinity Church*, where Shakespeare is buried, *Royal Shakespeare Theatre* (burnt down 1926, rebuilt 1932) and *Swan Theatre* (opened 1986)

*SUDELEY CASTLE, Glos. Tel: 01242-602308. Adm. £5.40; grounds only, £4.00. Castle built in 1442; restored in the 19th century

*SYON HOUSE, Brentford, Middx. Tel: 0181-560 0881. Opening times vary. Adm. £5.50; grounds only, £2.50. Built on the site of a former monastery; Adam interior

TILBURY FORT (EH), Essex. Tel: 01375-858489. Closed Mon. and Tues. in winter. Adm. £2.00. A 17th-century coastal fort

TINTAGEL CASTLE (EH), Cornwall. Tel: 01840-770328. Adm. £2.50. A 12th-century cliff-top castle and Dark Age settlement site

TOWER OF LONDON, London EC3. Tel: 0171-709 0765. Adm. charge. Royal palace and fortress begun by William the Conqueror in 1078. Houses the Crown Jewels

*TRERICE (NT), Cornwall. Tel: 01637-875404. Closed Tues. Adm. £3.80. Elizabethan manor house

TYNEMOUTH PRIORY AND CASTLE (EH), Tyne and Wear. Tel: 0191-257 1090. Closed Mon. and Tues. in winter. Adm. £1.50. Remains of a Benedictine priory, founded 1090, on Saxon monastic site. First World War gun battery open Sat., Sun. and Bank Holidays

†UPPARK (NT), W. Sussex. Tel: 01730-825415. Closed Fri. and Sat. Adm. £5.00 by timed ticket. Late 17th-century house, completely restored after fire. Fetherstonhaugh art collection

WALMER CASTLE (EH), Kent. Tel: 01304-364288. Closed Mon. and Tues. in winter; closed Jan.-Feb. and when the Lord Warden is in residence. Adm. £3.80. One of Henry VIII's coastal defence castles, now the residence of the Lord Warden of the Cinque Ports

WALTHAM ABBEY (EH), Essex. Adm. free. Ruined abbey including the nave of the abbey church, 'Harold's Bridge' and late 14th-century gatehouse. Traditionally the burial place of Harold II (1066)

WARKWORTH CASTLE (EH), Northumberland. Tel: 01665-711423. Adm. £2.00. A 15th-century keep amidst earlier ruins, with 14th-century hermitage (open Wed. and Sun. in summer only) upstream

WARWICK CASTLE. Tel: 01926-408000. Adm. £8.75. Medieval castle with Madam Tussaud's waxworks, in Capability Brown parkland

WHITBY ABBEY (EH), N. Yorks. Tel: 01947-603568. Adm. £1.60. Remains of Norman church on the site of a monastery founded in AD 657

*WILTON HOUSE, Wilts. Tel: 01722-743115. Adm. £6.00; grounds only, £3.50. A 17th-century house on the site of a Tudor house and Saxon abbey. Notable art collection

WINDSOR CASTLE, Berks. Tel: 01753-831118 for recorded information on opening times. Adm. £9.50, including the Castle precincts. Official residence of The Queen; oldest royal residence still in regular use. Includes state apartments and Queen Mary's Dolls' House. Restoration work in progress on fire-damaged state rooms (which may still be viewed). Also *St George's Chapel*

WOBURN ABBEY, Beds. Tel: 01525-290666. Closed Nov. and Dec.; also Mon.-Fri. in Jan. and Feb. Adm. £6.80. Built on the site of a Cistercian abbey; seat of the Dukes of Bedford. Important art collection; antiques centre

WROXETER ROMAN CITY (EH), Shropshire. Tel: 01743-761330. Closed Mon. and Tues. in winter. Adm. £2.50. Second-century public baths and part of the forum of the Roman town of Viroconium

WALES

c Property of Cadw: Welsh Historic Monuments
NT National Trust property

BEAUMARIS CASTLE (C), Anglesey. Tel: 01248-810361. Adm. £2.20. Fine concentrically-planned castle, still almost intact

CAERLEON ROMAN BATHS AND AMPHITHEATRE (C), nr Newport. Tel: 01633-422518. Closed Sun. morning in winter. Adm. £1.70, joint ticket with Legionary Museum £2.85. Rare example of a legionary bath-house and late 1st-century arena surrounded by bank for spectators

CAERNARFON CASTLE (C). Tel: 01286-677617. Adm. £3.80. Important Edwardian castle built, with the town wall, between 1283 and 1330

CAERPHILLY CASTLE (C). Tel: 01222-883143. Adm. £2.20. Concentrically-planned castle (c.1270) notable for its scale and use of water defences

CARDIFF CASTLE. Tel: 01222-878100. Adm. charge. Castle built on the site of a Roman fort; spectacular towers and rich interior

CASTELL COCH (C), nr Cardiff. Tel: 01222-810101. Adm. £2.20. Rebuilt 1875-90 on medieval foundations

CHEPSTOW CASTLE (C). Tel: 01291-624065. Adm. £3.00. Rectangular keep amid extensive fortifications

CONWY CASTLE (C). Tel: 01492-592358. Adm. £3.00. Built by Edward I, 1283-7

*CRICCIETH CASTLE (C). Tel: 01766-522227. Adm. £2.20. Native Welsh 13th-century castle, altered by Edward I

DENBIGH CASTLE (C). Tel: 01745-813979. Adm. free. Remains of the castle (begun 1282), including triple-towered gatehouse

HARLECH CASTLE (C). Tel: 01766-780552. Adm. £3.00. Well-preserved Edwardian castle, constructed 1283-90, on an outcrop above the former shore-line

PEMBROKE CASTLE. Tel: 01646-681510. Adm. £2.95. Castle founded in 1093, with a Great Tower 75 feet tall; birthplace of King Henry VII

‡PENRHYN CASTLE (NT), Bangor. Tel: 01248-353084. Closed Tues. Adm. £4.50; grounds only, £3.00. Neo-Norman castle built in the 19th century. Industrial railway museum

PORTMEIRION, Penrhyndeudraeth. Tel: 01766-770228. Adm. £3.20 (April-Oct.); reduced rate in winter. Village in Italianate style

‡POWIS CASTLE (NT), nr Welshpool. Tel: 01938-554336. Closed Mon. (except Bank Holidays) and Tues. (except July and Aug.). Adm. £6.00; garden only, £4.00. Medieval castle with interior in variety of styles, 17th-century gardens and Clive of India museum

RAGLAN CASTLE (C). Tel: 01291-690228. Adm. £2.20. Remains of 15th-century castle with moated hexagonal keep

ST DAVIDS BISHOP'S PALACE (C), St Davids. Tel: 01437-720517. Closed Sun. mornings in winter. Adm. £1.70. Remains of residence of Bishops of St Davids built 1328-47

TINTERN ABBEY (C), nr Chepstow. Tel: 01291-689251. Adm. £2.20. Remains of 13th-century church and conventual buildings of a Cistercian monastery

*TRETOWER COURT AND CASTLE (C), nr Crickhowell. Tel: 01874-730279. Adm. £2.20. Medieval house with remains of 12th-century castle nearby

SCOTLAND

HS Historic Scotland property
NTS National Trust for Scotland property

ANTONINE WALL (HS), between the Clyde and the Forth. Adm. free. Built about AD 142, consists of ditch, turf rampart and road, with forts every two miles

BALMORAL CASTLE, Aberdeenshire. Tel: 013397-42334. Open May-July. Closed Sun. Adm. £3.00. Mid 19th-century Baronial-style castle built for Victoria and Albert. The Queen's private residence

BLACK HOUSE, ARNOL (HS), Lewis, Western Isles. Tel: 01851-710395. Closed Sun.; also Fri. in winter. Adm. £1.50. Traditional Lewis thatched house

*BLAIR CASTLE, Blair Atholl. Tel: 01796-481207. Adm. £5.00. Mid 18th-century mansion with 13th-century tower; seat of the Dukes of Atholl

*BONAWE IRON FURNACE (HS), Argyll and Bute. Tel: 01866-822432. Closed Sun. mornings. Adm. £2.00. Charcoal-fuelled ironworks founded in 1753

†BOWHILL, Selkirk. Tel: 01750-22204. House open July only; grounds early May to late summer except Fri. Adm. £4.00; grounds only, £1.00. Seat of the Dukes of Buccleuch and Queensberry. Fine collection of paintings, including portrait miniatures

BROUGH OF BIRSAY (HS), Orkney. Adm. free. Remains of Norse church and village on the tidal island of Birsay

CAERLAVEROCK CASTLE (HS), nr Dumfries. Tel: 01387-770244. Closed Sun. mornings. Adm. £2.00. Fine early classical Renaissance building

CALLANISH STANDING STONES (HS), Lewis, Western Isles. Adm. free. Standing stones in a cross-shaped setting, dating from 3000 BC

CATHER TUNS (BROWN AND WHITE) (HS), Aberdeenshire. Adm. free. Two large Iron Age hill forts

*CAWDOR CASTLE, Inverness. Tel: 01667-404615. Adm. £4.70; grounds only, £2.50. A 14th-century keep with 15th- and 17th-century additions

CLAVA CAIRNS (HS), Highland. Adm. free. Late Neolithic or early Bronze Age cairns

*CRATHES CASTLE (NTS), nr Banchory. Tel: 01330-844525. Garden and grounds open all year. Adm. £4.10; garden and grounds only, £1.60; castle only, £1.60. A 16th-century baronial castle in woodland, fields and gardens

*CULZEAN CASTLE (NTS), S. Ayrshire. Tel: 01655-760274. Country park open all year. Adm. £5.50; country park only, £3.50; castle only, £3.50. An 18th-century Adam castle with oval staircase and circular saloon

*DRUMLANRIG CASTLE, nr Dumfries. Tel: 01848-331682. Closed Thurs. Adm. charge. Castle with baroque decorative features and notable art and furniture collections

DRYBURGH ABBEY (HS), Borders. Tel: 01835-822381. Closed Sun. mornings. Adm. £2.00. A 12th-century abbey containing tomb of Sir Walter Scott

*DUNVEGAN CASTLE, Skye. Tel: 01470-521206. Closed Sun. mornings. Adm. £4.00; gardens only, £2.50. A 13th-century castle with later additions; the home of the chiefs of the Clan MacLeod. Boat trips to seal colony

EDINBURGH CASTLE (HS). Tel: 0131-225 9846. Adm. £5.50; war memorial free. Includes the Scottish National War Memorial, Scottish United Services Museum and historic apartments

EDZELL CASTLE (HS), Aberdeenshire. Tel: 01356-648631. Closed Sun. mornings; also Thurs. afternoons and Fri. in winter. Adm. £2.00. Medieval tower house; unique walled garden

*EILEAN DONAN CASTLE, Wester Ross. Tel: 01599-555202. Adm. £2.50. A 13th-century castle with Jacobite relics

ELGIN CATHEDRAL (HS), Moray. Tel: 01343-547171. Closed Sun. mornings; also Thurs. afternoons and Fri. in winter. Adm. £1.50. A 13th-century cathedral with fine chapterhouse

*FLOORS CASTLE, Kelso. Tel: 01573-223333. In Oct. open Sun. and Wed. only. Adm. £3.80. Largest inhabited castle in Scotland; seat of the Dukes of Roxburghe
FORT GEORGE (HS), Highland. Tel: 01667-462777. Closed Sun. mornings. Adm. £2.50. An 18th-century fort
*GLAMIS CASTLE, Angus. Tel: 01307-840242. Adm. £4.70; grounds only, £2.20. Seat of the Lyon family (later Earls of Strathmore and Kinghorne) since 1372
GLASGOW CATHEDRAL (HS). Tel: 0141-552 6891. Closed Sun. mornings. Adm. free. Medieval cathedral with elaborately vaulted crypt
GLENELG BROCH (HS), Highland. Adm. free. Two broch towers with well-preserved structural features
*HOPETOUN HOUSE, nr Edinburgh. Tel: 0131-331 2451. Adm. £3.80; grounds only, £2.00. House designed by Sir William Bruce, enlarged by William Adam
HUNTLY CASTLE (HS). Tel: 01466-793191. Closed Sun. mornings; also Thurs. afternoons and Fri. in winter. Adm. £2.00. Ruin of a 16th- and 17th-century house
*INVERARAY CASTLE, Argyll. Tel: 01499-302203. Closed Fri. (except July-Aug.) and Sun. morning. Woods open all year. Adm. £4.00. Gothic-style 18th-century castle; seat of the Dukes of Argyll
IONA ABBEY, Inner Hebrides. Tel: 01681-700404. Adm. £2.00. Monastery founded by St Columba in AD 563
*JARLSHOF (HS), Shetland. Tel: 01950-460112. Closed Sun. mornings. Adm. £2.00. Remains from Stone Age
JEDBURGH ABBEY (HS), Borders. Tel: 01835-863925. Closed Sun. mornings. Adm. £2.50. Romanesque and early Gothic church founded about 1138
KELSO ABBEY (HS), Borders. Closed Sun. mornings. Adm. free. Remains of great abbey church founded 1128
LINLITHGOW PALACE (HS). Tel: 01506-842896. Closed Sun. mornings. Adm. £2.00. Ruin of royal palace in park setting. Birthplace of Mary, Queen of Scots
MAES HOWE CHAMBERED CAIRN (HS), Orkney. Tel: 01856-761606. Closed Sun. Mornings; also Thurs. mornings and Wed. in winter. Adm. £2.00. Neolithic tomb plundered by Vikings
*MEIGLE SCULPTURED STONE (HS), Angus. Tel: 011828-64612. Closed Sun. mornings. Adm. £1.20. Celtic Christian stones
MELROSE ABBEY (HS), Borders. Tel: 01896-822562. Closed Sun. mornings. Adm. £2.50. Ruin of Cistercian abbey founded c.1136
MOUSA BROCH (HS), Shetland. Adm. free. Finest surviving Iron Age broch tower
NETHER LARGIE CAIRNS (HS), Argyll and Bute. Adm. free. Bronze Age and Neolithic cairns
NEW ABBEY CORN MILL (HS), nr Dumfries. Tel: 01387-850260. Closed Sun. mornings; also Thurs. afternoons and Fri. in winter. Adm. £2.00. Water-powered mill
PALACE OF HOLYROODHOUSE, Edinburgh. Tel: 0131-556 7371. Closed when The Queen is in residence. Adm. £5.00. The Queen's official Scottish residence. Main part of the palace built 1671-9
RING OF BROGAR (HS), Orkney. Adm. free. Neolithic circle of upright stones with an enclosing ditch
RUTHWELL CROSS (HS), Dumfries and Galloway. Adm. free. Seventh-century Anglian cross
ST ANDREWS CASTLE AND CATHEDRAL (HS), Fife. Tel: 01334-477196 (castle); 01334-472563 (cathedral). Adm. £2.00 (castle); £1.50 (cathedral). Closed Sun. mornings. Ruins of 13th-century castle and remains of the largest cathedral in Scotland
*SCONE PALACE, Perth. Tel: 01738-552300. Adm. £4.70; grounds only, £2.35. House built 1802-13 on the site of a medieval palace
SKARA BRAE (HS), Orkney. Tel: 01856-841815. Closed Sun. mornings. Adm. £2.50. Stone-Age village
*SMAILHOLM TOWER (HS), Borders. Closed Sun. mornings. Adm. £1.50. Well-preserved tower-house

STIRLING CASTLE (HS). Tel: 01786-450000. Adm. £3.50. Great Hall and gatehouse of James IV, palace of James V, Chapel Royal remodelled by James VI
TANTALLON CASTLE (HS), E. Lothian. Tel: 01620-892727. Closed Sun. mornings; also Thurs. afternoons and Fri. in winter. Adm. £2.00. Fortification with earthwork defences and a 14th-century curtain wall with towers
*THREAVE CASTLE (HS), Dumfries and Galloway. Tel: 08314-168512. Closed Sun. mornings. Adm. £1.50, including ferry trip. Late 14th-century tower on an island; reached by boat, long walk to castle
URQUHART CASTLE (HS), Loch Ness. Tel: 01456-450551. Adm. £3.00. Closed Sun. morning in winter. Castle remains with well-preserved tower on shore of loch

NORTHERN IRELAND

DE Property in the care of the Northern Ireland Department of the Environment
NT National Trust property

CARRICKFERGUS CASTLE (DE), Co. Antrim. Tel: 01960-351273. Closed Sun. mornings. Adm. £2.70. Castle begun in 1180 and garrisoned until 1928
†CASTLE COOLE (NT), Enniskillen. Tel: 01365-322690. Closed Thurs. May-Aug. and Mon.-Fri. in April and Sept. Adm. house, £2.60; estate, £1.50 per car. An 18th-century mansion by James Wyatt in parkland
†CASTLE WARD (NT), Co. Down. Tel: 01396-881204. Closed Thurs. May-Aug. and Mon.-Fri. in April, Sept. and Oct; grounds open all year. Adm. house, £2.60; estate, £3.50 per car. An 18th-century house with Classical west and Gothic east fronts
*DEVENISH ISLAND (DE), Co. Fermanagh. Closed Sun. mornings and Mon. Adm. £2.25. Island monastery founded in the 6th century by St Molaise
DOWNHILL CASTLE (NT), Co. Londonderry. Tel: 01265-848728. Adm. free. Ruins of palatial house in landscaped estate including Mussenden Temple. Temple closed in winter and Mon.-Fri. (except Bank Holidays) in April-June and Sept.
DUNLUCE CASTLE (DE), Co. Antrim. Tel: 012657-31938. Closed Sun. morning (except July and Aug.) Adm. £1.50. Ruins of 16th-century stronghold of the MacDonnells
†FLORENCE COURT (NT), Co. Fermanagh. Tel: 01365-348249. Closed Tues., and Mon.-Fri. (except Bank Holidays) in April and Sept.; grounds open all year. Adm. £2.60; estate £1.50 per car. Mid 18th-century house with rococo plasterwork
*GREY ABBEY (DE), Co. Down. Tel: 01247-788585. Closed Sun. morning and Mon. Adm £1.00. Substantial remains of a Cistercian abbey founded in 1193
HILLSBOROUGH FORT (DE), Co. Down. Closed Sun. mornings and Mon. Adm. free. Built in 1650
†MOUNT STEWART (NT), Co. Down. Tel: 012477-88387. Closed Tues., and Mon.-Fri. in April and Oct. Adm. £3.00. An 18th-century house, childhood home of Lord Castlereagh
NENDRUM MONASTERY (DE), Mahee Island, Co. Down. Closed Sun. mornings and Mon., also Mon.-Fri. in winter. Adm 75p. Founded in the 5th century by St Machaoi
*TULLY CASTLE (DE), Co. Fermanagh. Closed Sun. mornings and Mon. Adm. £1.00. Fortified house and bawn built in 1613
*WHITE ISLAND (DE), Co. Fermanagh. Closed Sun. mornings and Mon. Adm. £2.25. Tenth-century monastery and 12th-century church. Access by ferry

Museums and Galleries

There are more than 2,000 museums and galleries in the United Kingdom. About 1,600 are registered with the Museums and Galleries Commission (*see* page 322), which indicates that they have an appropriate constitution, are soundly financed, have adequate collection management standards and public services, and have access to professional curatorial advice. Museums must achieve full or provisional registration status in order to be eligible for grants from the Museums and Galleries Commission and from Area Museums Councils. Over 700 of the registered museums are run by a local authority.

The national museums and galleries (i.e. the British Museum, the Imperial War Museum, the National Army Museum, the National Galleries of Scotland, the National Gallery, the National Maritime Museum, the National Museums and Galleries on Merseyside, the National Museum of Wales, the National Museums of Scotland, the National Portrait Gallery, the Natural History Museum, the RAF Museum, the Royal Armouries, the Science Museum, the Tate Gallery, the Ulster Folk and Transport Museum, the Ulster Museum, the Victoria and Albert Museum, and the Wallace Collection) receive direct government grant-in-aid. Local authority museums are funded by the local authority and may also receive grants from the Museums and Galleries Commission. Independent museums and galleries mainly rely on their own resources but are also eligible for grants from the Museums and Galleries Commission.

Ten Area Museum Councils in the United Kingdom, which are independent charities that receive an annual grant from the Museums and Galleries Commission, give advice and support to the museums in their area and may offer improvement grants. They also circulate exhibitions and assist with training and marketing.

OPENING TO THE PUBLIC

The following is a selection of the museums and art galleries in the United Kingdom. The admission charges given are the standard charges for 1996-7, where a charge is made; many museums have concessionary rates for children, etc. Opening hours vary. Most museums are closed on Christmas Eve, Christmas Day, Boxing Day and New Year's Day; many are closed on Good Friday, and some are closed on May Day Bank Holiday. Some smaller museums close at lunchtimes. Information about a specific museum or gallery should be checked by telephone.

* Local authority museum/gallery

ENGLAND

BARNARD CASTLE, Co. Durham – *The Bowes Museum*, Westwick Road. Tel: 01833 -690606. Closed Sun. mornings. Adm. £3.00. European art from the late medieval period to the 19th century; music and costume galleries; English period rooms from Elizabeth I to Victoria; local archaeology

BATH – *American Museum in Britain*, Claverton Manor. Tel: 01225-460503. Closed mornings and Mon. (except Bank Holidays); also closed in winter (except on application). Adm. £5.00 (including house); grounds and galleries only, £2.00. American decorative arts from the 17th to 19th centuries

Museum of Costume, Bennett Street. Tel: 01225-477752. Adm. £3.50. Fashion from the 16th century to the present day

Roman Baths Museum, Abbey Church Yard. Tel: 01225-477774. Adm. (including 18th-century Pump Room) £5.60. Museum adjoins the remains of a Roman baths and temple complex

Victoria Art Gallery, Bridge Street. Tel: 01225-477772. Closed Sun. and Bank Holidays. Adm. free. European Old Masters and British art since the 18th century

BEAMISH, Co. Durham – *Beamish, The North of England Open Air Museum*. Tel: 01207-231811. Closed Mon. and Fri. in winter. Adm. charge. Recreated northern town *c*.1900, with rebuilt and furnished local buildings, colliery village, farm, railway station, tramway, Pockerley Manor and horse-yard (set *c*.1800)

BEAULIEU, Hants – *National Motor Museum*. Tel: 01590 - 612345. Adm. charge. Displays of over 250 vehicles dating from 1895 to the present day

BEVERLEY, N. Humberside – *Museum of Army Transport*, Flemingate. Tel: 01482-860445. Adm. charge. Field workshop, amphibious assault landing, railway section and aircraft

BIRMINGHAM – *Aston Hall*, Albert Road. Tel: 0121-327 0062. Closed mornings and in winter. Adm. free. Jacobean house containing paintings, furniture and tapestries from 17th to 19th centuries

Birmingham Nature Centre, Edgbaston. Tel: 0121-472 7775. Closed Mon.-Sat. in winter. Adm. £1.50. Indoor and outdoor enclosures displaying British wildlife

City Museum and Art Gallery, Chamberlain Square. Tel: 0121-235 2834. Closed Sun. mornings. Adm. free (except Gas Hall). Includes notable collection of Pre-Raphaelites

Museum of Science and Industry, Newhall Street. Tel: 0121-235 1661. Closed Sun. mornings. Adm. free. Vehicles and industrial machinery from the Industrial Revolution to the present; interactive science centre and mechanical musical instrument collection

BRADFORD – *Cartwright Hall Art Gallery*, Lister Park. Tel: 01274-493313. Closed Mon. (except Bank Holidays). Adm. free. British 19th- and 20th-century fine art

Industrial Museum and Horses at Work, Moorside Road. Tel: 01274-631756. Closed Mon. (except Bank Holidays). Adm. charge. Engineering, textiles, transport and social history exhibits, including recreated back-to-back cottages, shire horses and horse tram-rides

National Museum of Photography, Film and Television, Pictureville. Tel: 01274-727488. Closed Mon. Adm. free. Photography, film and television equipment and materials, including the only IMAX cinema in the UK and the only public Cinerama theatre in the world

BRIGHTON – *Brighton Museum and Art Gallery*, Church Street. Tel: 01273-603005. Closed Sun. mornings and Wed. Adm. free. Includes fine art, design, fashion, archaeology, Brighton history

BRISTOL – *Arnolfini Gallery*, Narrow Quay. Tel: 0117-929 9191. Adm. free; charge for cinema and events. Contemporary visual arts, dance, theatre, film and music

Blaise Castle House Museum, Henbury. Tel: 0117-950 6789. Closed Mon. Adm. free. Agricultural and social history collections in an 18th-century mansion

Bristol Industrial Museum, Prince Street. Tel: 0117-925 1470. Closed Mon. Adm. charge. Industrial, maritime and transport collections

*City Museum and Art Gallery, Queen's Road. Tel: 0117-922 3571. Adm. charge. Includes fine and decorative art, oriental art, and Bristol ceramics and paintings
CAMBRIDGE – *Duxford Airfield, Duxford. Tel: 01223-835000. Adm. £5.95. Displays of military and civil aircraft, tanks, guns and naval exhibits
Fitzwilliam Museum, Trumpington Street. Tel: 01223-332900. Closed Mon. (except some Bank Holidays) and Sun. mornings. Adm. free. Antiquities, fine and applied arts, clocks, ceramics, manuscripts, furniture, sculpture, coins and medals, temporary exhibitions
CARLISLE – *Tullie House Museum and Art Gallery, Castle Street. Tel: 01228-34781. Closed Sun. mornings. Adm. charge to Border galleries only; ground floor, Old Tullie House and Jacobean galleries, adm. free. Prehistoric archaeology, Hadrian's Wall, Viking and medieval Cumbria, and the social history of Carlisle; also British 19th- and 20th-century art and English porcelain
CHESTER – *Grosvenor Museum, Grosvenor Street. Tel: 01244-321616. Closed Sun. mornings. Adm. free. Roman collections, natural history, art, Chester silver, local history and costume
CHICHESTER – *Weald and Downland Open Air Museum*, Singleton. Tel: 01243-811348. Closed Mon.,Tues., Thurs., Fri. in winter. Adm. £4.20. Rebuilt vernacular buildings from south-east England; includes medieval houses, agricultural and rural craft buildings and a working watermill
COLCHESTER – *Colchester Castle Museum, Castle Park. Tel: 01206-282939. Closed Sun. mornings. Adm. £3.00. Local archaeological antiquities and displays on Roman Colchester; tours of the Roman vaults, castle walls and chapel with medieval and prison displays
COVENTRY – *Herbert Art Gallery and Museum, Jordan Well. Tel: 01203-832381. Closed Sun. mornings. Local history, archaeology and industry, natural history, oriental ceramics, and fine and decorative art
Museum of British Road Transport, Hales Street. Tel: 01203-832425. Adm. £3.30. Hundreds of motor vehicles and bicycles
CRICH, nr Matlock, Derbys – National Tramway Museum. Tel: 01773-852565. Closed in winter. Open weekends and Bank Holidays, Mon.-Thurs. April-Sept., and some Fridays. Adm. £5.40. Open-air working museum with tram rides
DERBY – *Derby Museum and Art Gallery, The Strand. Tel: 01332-255586. Closed Sun. mornings and Bank Holiday mornings. Adm. free. Includes paintings by Joseph Wright of Derby and Derby porcelain
Industrial Museum, off Full Street. Tel: 01332-255308. Closed Sun. mornings and Bank Holiday mornings. Adm. free. Rolls-Royce aero engine collection and a railway engineering gallery
DORCHESTER – Dorset County Museum, High West Street. Tel: 01305-262735. Closed Sun. (except July and Aug.) Adm. £2.35. Includes a collection of Thomas Hardy's manuscripts, books, notebooks and drawings
EXETER – Exeter Maritime Museum, The Haven. Tel: 01392-58075. Adm. £4.25. Collection of working boats from around the world
*Royal Albert Memorial Museum, Queen Street. Tel: 01392-265858. Closed Sun. Adm. free. Natural history, archaeology, ethnography, and fine and decorative art including Exeter silver
GAYDON, Warwick – British Motor Industry Heritage Trust, Banbury Road. Tel: 019626-641188. Adm. charge. History of British motor industry from 1890 to present; classic vehicles; engineering gallery; Corgi and Lucas collections

GLOUCESTER, – National Waterways Museum, The Docks. Tel: 01452-318054. Adm. £4.50. History of Britain's canals and inland waterways
GOSPORT, Hants. – Royal Navy Submarine Museum, Haslar Jetty Road. Tel: 01705-529217. Adm. £3.50. Underwater warfare, including the submarine Alliance; historical and nuclear galleries; and first Royal Navy submarine
HALIFAX – Eureka! The Museum for Children, Discovery Road. Tel: 01426-983191. Adm. £4.75 (over age 12), £3.75 (ages 3-12), free (under age 3). Saver ticket £14.75. Museum designed for children up to age 12
HULL – *Ferens Art Gallery, Queen Victoria Square. Tel: 01482-613902. Closed Sun. mornings. Adm.: non-residents £1.00; residents free. European art, especially Dutch 17th-century paintings, British portraits from 17th to 20th centuries, and marine paintings
*Town Docks Museum, Queen Victoria Square. Tel: 01482-613902. Closed Sun. mornings. Adm.: non-residents £1.00; residents free. Whaling, fishing and navigation exhibits
HUNTINGDON – *Cromwell Museum, Grammar School Walk. Tel: 01480-425830. Closed Mon., and mornings (except Sat. and Sun.) in winter. Adm. free. Portraits and memorabilia relating to Oliver Cromwell
IPSWICH – *Christchurch Mansion and Wolsey Art Gallery, Christchurch Park. Tel: 01473-253246. Closed Sun. mornings and Mon. Adm. free. Tudor house with paintings by Gainsborough, Constable and other Suffolk artists; furniture and 18th-century ceramics. Art gallery for temporary exhibitions
LEEDS – *Abbey House Museum, Kirkstall. Tel: 0113-275 5821. Closed Sun. mornings and Mon. Adm. charge. Toys, games, dolls, and three full-sized period streets
*City Art Gallery, The Headrow. Tel: 0113-247 8248. Closed Sun. mornings. Adm. free. British and European paintings including English watercolours, modern sculpture, Henry Moore gallery, print room
*City Museum, Calverley Street. Tel: 0113-247 8275. Closed Sun. and Mon. Adm. free. Natural history, archaeology, ethnography and coin collections
*Royal Armouries Museum, Armouries Drive. Tel: 0113-220 1900. Adm. £6.95. Antique arms and armour formerly held by Tower of London; five galleries including tournament, war, oriental arms, etc., jousting and simulated fights
LEICESTER – *Jewry Wall Museum, St Nicholas Circle. Tel: 0116-247 3021. Closed Sun. mornings. Adm. free. Archaeology, Roman Jewry Wall and baths, and mosaics
*Leicestershire Museum and Art Gallery, New Walk. Tel: 0116-255 4100. Closed Sun. mornings. Adm. free. Natural history, geology, ancient Egypt gallery, European art and decorative arts
*Snibston Discovery Park, Coalville. Tel: 01530-510851. Adm. charge. Open-air science and industry museum on site of a coal mine; country park with nature trail
LINCOLN – *Museum of Lincolnshire Life, Burton Road. Tel: 01522-528448. Closed Sun. mornings in winter. Adm. charge. Social history and agricultural collection
*Usher Gallery, Lindum Road. Tel: 01522-527980. Closed Sun. mornings. Adm. £1.00. Watches, miniatures, porcelain, silver; collection of Peter de Wint works; Lincolnshire topography; Tennyson memorabilia
LIVERPOOL – Lady Lever Art Gallery, Wirral. Tel: 0151-645 3623. Closed Sun. mornings. Adm. free. Paintings, furniture and porcelain
Liverpool Museum, William Brown Street. Tel: 0151-207 0001. Closed Sun. mornings. Adm. free (except to the Planetarium). Includes Egyptian mummies, weapons and classical sculpture; planetarium, aquarium, vivarium and natural history centre

Merseyside Maritime Museum, Albert Dock. Tel: 0151-207 0001. Joint adm. charge with the Museum of Liverpool Life. Floating exhibits, working displays and craft demonstrations; incorporates *HM Customs and Excise National Museum*
Museum of Liverpool Life, Mann Island. Tel: 0151-207 0001. Joint adm. charge with the Merseyside Maritime Museum. The history of Liverpool
Sudley House, Mossley Hill Road. Tel: 0151-724 3245. Closed Sun. mornings. Adm. free. Late 18th- and 19th-century British paintings in former shipowner's home
Tate Gallery Liverpool, Albert Dock. Tel: 0151-709 3223. Closed Mon. (except Bank Holidays). Adm. free. Twentieth-century painting and sculpture
Walker Art Gallery, William Brown Street. Tel: 0151-207 0001. Closed Sun. mornings. Adm. free. Paintings from the 14th to 20th centuries
LONDON: GALLERIES – *Barbican Art Gallery*, Barbican Centre, EC2. Tel: 0171-382 7105. Temporary exhibitions
Courtauld Institute Galleries, Somerset House, Strand, WC2. Tel: 0171-873 2526. Closed Sun. mornings. Adm. £3.00. The University of London galleries
Dulwich Picture Gallery, College Road, SE21. Tel: 0181-693 5254. Closed Sun. mornings and Mon. Adm. £2.00 (free on Fri.). Built by Sir John Soane to house 17th- and 18th-century paintings
Hayward Gallery, South Bank Centre, SE1. Tel: 0171-928 3144. Adm. £5.00. Temporary exhibitions
National Gallery, Trafalgar Square, WC2. Tel: 0171-839 3321. Closed Sun. mornings. Adm. free. Western painting from the 13th to 20th centuries; early Renaissance collection in the Sainsbury wing
National Portrait Gallery, St Martin's Place, WC2. Tel: 0171-306 0055. Closed Sun. mornings and some Bank Holidays. Adm. free. Portraits of eminent people in British history
Percival David Foundation of Chinese Art, Gordon Square, WC1. Tel: 0171-387 3909. Closed weekends and Bank Holidays. Adm free. Chinese ceramics; charge for use of reference library
Photographers Gallery, Great Newport Street, WC2. Tel: 0171-831 1772. Closed Sun. Adm. free. Temporary exhibitions
The Queen's Gallery, Buckingham Palace, SW1. Tel: 0171-839 1377. Adm. £3.50. Art from the Royal Collection
Royal Academy of Arts, Piccadilly, W1. Tel: 0171-439 7438. Adm. charge. British art since 1750 and temporary exhibitions; annual Summer Exhibition
Serpentine Gallery, Kensington Gardens, W2. Tel: 0171-723 9072. Adm. free. Temporary exhibitions
Tate Gallery, Millbank, SW1. Tel: 0171-887 8000. Closed Sun. mornings. Adm. free (charge for special exhibitions). British painting and 20th-century painting and sculpture
Wallace Collection, Manchester Square, W1. Tel: 0171-935 0687. Closed Sun. mornings. Adm. free. Paintings and drawings, French 18th-century furniture, armour, porcelain and clocks
Whitechapel Art Gallery, Whitechapel High Street, E1. Tel: 0171-522 7878. Closed Mon. Adm. free to most exhibitions. Temporary exhibitions of modern art
LONDON: MUSEUMS – *Bank of England Museum*, Threadneedle Street, EC2. Tel: 0171-601 5545. Closed weekends and Bank Holidays. Adm. free. History of the Bank since 1694
Bethnal Green Museum of Childhood, Cambridge Heath Road, E2. Tel: 0181-980 3204. Closed Sun. mornings and Fri. Adm. free but donations invited. Toys, games and exhibits relating to the social history of childhood

British Museum, Great Russell Street, WC1. Tel: 0171-636 1555. Closed Sun. mornings. Adm. free. Antiquities, coins, medals, prints and drawings, European history galleries
Cabinet War Rooms, King Charles Street, SW1. Tel: 0171-930 6961. Adm. £4.20. Underground rooms used by Churchill and the Government during the Second World War
Commonwealth Institute, Kensington High Street, W8. Tel: 0171-603 4535. Closed for redevelopment until spring 1997. Exhibitions on Commonwealth nations, visual arts and crafts
Cutty Sark, Greenwich, SE10. Tel: 0181-858 3445. Adm. £3.25. Restored and rerigged tea clipper with exhibits on board. Sir Francis Chichester's round-the-world yacht, *Gipsy Moth IV*, can also be seen (separate adm. charge)
Design Museum, Shad Thames, SE1. Tel: 0171-378 6055. Adm. £4.75. The development of design and the mass-production of consumer objects
Geffrye Museum, Kingsland Road, E2. Tel: 0171-739 9893. Closed Mon.; also Sun. and Bank Holiday mornings. Adm. free. English urban domestic interiors from 1600-1950s; also paintings, furniture, decorative arts, walled herb garden and knot garden
HMS Belfast, Morgans Lane, Tooley Street, SE1. Tel: 0171-407 6434. Adm £4.40. Life on a warship, illustrated on World War II warship.
Horniman Museum and Gardens, London Road, SE23. Tel: 0181-699 1872. Closed Sun. mornings. Adm. free. Museum of ethnography, musical instruments, natural history and aquarium. Reference library (by appointment)
Imperial War Museum, Lambeth Road, SE1. Tel: 0171-416 5000. Reference departments closed Sat. (except by appointment) and Sun. Adm. £4.50 (free after 4.30 p.m. daily). All aspects of the two world wars and other military operations involving Britain and the Commonwealth since 1914
Jewish Museum, Albert Street, NW1. Tel: 0171-284 1997. Closed Fri., Sat., public and Jewish holidays. Adm. £3.00. Jewish life, history and religion
London Transport Museum, Covent Garden, WC2. Tel: 0171-379 6344. Adm. charge. Vehicles, photographs and graphic art relating to the history of transport in London
MCC Museum, Lord's, NW8. Tel: 0171-289 1611. Open match days (closed Sun. mornings); also conducted tours by appointment with Tours Manager. Adm. charge. Cricket museum
Museum of Garden History, Lambeth Palace Road SE1. Tel: 0171-401 8865. Open daily except Sat. Closed Dec.-Feb. Adm free. Exhibition of aspects of garden history and re-created 17th-century garden
Museum of London, London Wall, EC2. Tel: 0171-600 3699. Closed Sun. mornings and Mon. Adm. £3.50 (free after 4.30 p.m. daily). History of London from prehistoric times to present day
Museum of Mankind, Burlington Gardens, W1. Tel: 0171-437 2224. Closed Sun. mornings. Adm. free. The ethnographical collections of the British Museum
Museum of the Moving Image, South Bank, SE1. Tel: 0171-401 2636. Adm. £5.95. History of the moving image in cinema and television
National Army Museum, Royal Hospital Road, SW3. Tel: 0171-730 0717. Adm. free. History of the British soldier; the Indian Army room at the Royal Military Academy, Sandhurst, may be viewed by appointment
National Maritime Museum, Greenwich, SE10. Tel: 0181-858 4422. Reference library closed Sat. (except by appointment) and Sun. Comprises the main building,

the Old Royal Observatory and the Queen's House (*see page* 576). Adm. charge. Maritime history of Britain
Natural History Museum, Cromwell Road, sw7. Tel: 0171-938 9123. Adm. £5.50. Natural history collections
Royal Air Force Museum, Colindale, nw9. Tel: 0181-205 2266. Adm. £5.20. Aviation from before the Wright brothers to the present-day RAF; historic aircraft
Royal Mews, Buckingham Palace, sw1. Tel: 0171-839 1377. Open Tues.-Thurs. afternoons in summer, Wed. only in winter. Adm. £3.50. Carriages, coaches, stables and horses
Science Museum, Exhibition Road, sw7. Tel: 0171-938 8000. Adm. charge. Science, technology, industry and medicine collections
Shakespeare Globe Exhibition, Bankside, se1. Tel: 0171-928 6406. Adm. £4.00. Recreation of Elizabethan theatre using 16th-century techniques
Sherlock Holmes Museum, Baker Street, nw1. Tel: 0171-935 8866. Adm. £5.00. Recreated rooms of the fictional detective
Sir John Soane's Museum, Lincoln's Inn Fields, wc2. Tel: 0171-430 0175. Closed Sun. and Mon. Adm. free. Art and antiques, temporary exhibitions
Theatre Museum, Russell Street, wc2. Tel: 0171-836 7891. Closed Mon. Adm. £3.00. History of the performing arts
Tower Bridge Experience, se1. Tel: 0171-378 1928. Adm. £5.50. History of the bridge and display of Victorian steam machinery; panoramic views from walkways
Victoria and Albert Museum, Cromwell Road, sw7. Tel: 0171-938 8500. Closed Mon. mornings. Adm. £5.00. Includes National Art Library and Print Room (closed Sun. and Mon.) Adm. free but donations invited. Fine and applied art and design, including furniture, glass, textiles, dress collections
Wellington Museum, Apsley House, w1 (*see* page 574)
Wimbledon Lawn Tennis Museum, Church Road, sw19. Tel: 0181-946 6131. Closed Sun. mornings and Mon. Adm. £2.50. Tennis trophies, fashion and memorabilia
MANCHESTER – *City Art Galleries*, Mosley Street and Princess Street. Tel: 0161-236 5244. Closed Sun. mornings. Adm. free. Includes Old Masters, Turner, Gainsborough, Stubbs, the Pre-Raphaelites and 20th century art
Gallery of English Costume, Rusholme. Tel: 0161-224 5217. Closed Sun., Mon. Adm. free. Exhibits from the 16th to 20th centuries
Manchester Museum, Oxford Road. Tel: 0161-275 2634. Closed Sun. Adm. free. Archaeology, archery, botany, Egyptology, entomology, ethnography, geology, natural history, numismatics, oriental and zoology collections
Museum of Science and Industry, Castlefield. Tel: 0161-832 1830. Adm. £4.00. On site of world's oldest passenger railway station; galleries relating to space, energy, power, transport, aviation and social history; interactive science centre
Whitworth Art Gallery, Oxford Road. Tel: 0161-275 7450. Closed Sun. mornings. Adm. free. Watercolours, drawings, prints, textiles, wallpapers and 20th-century British art
NEWCASTLE UPON TYNE – *Laing Art Gallery*, Higham Place. Tel: 0191-232 7734. Closed Sun. mornings. Adm. free. British and European art, ceramics, glass, silver, textiles and costume; local arts and crafts
Newcastle Discovery Museum, West Blandford Square. Tel: 0191-232 6789. Closed Sun. Adm. free. Local history, fashion, power, and Tyneside's maritime history; hands-on science centre

NEWMARKET – *National Horseracing Museum*, High Street. Tel: 01638-667333. Closed Mon. (except Bank Holidays, July and Aug.), Sun. mornings and Jan.-March. Adm. £3.30. Paintings, trophies and exhibits relating to horseracing
NORWICH – *Castle Museum*. Tel: 01603-223624. Closed Sun. mornings. in winter. Adm. charge. Art (including Norwich school), archaeology, natural history, teapot collection; guided tours of battlements and dungeons
NOTTINGHAM – *Brewhouse Yard Museum*, Castle Boulevard. Tel: 0115-948 3504. Adm. free (except weekends and Bank Holidays). Daily life from the 17th to 20th centuries
Castle Museum. Tel: 0115-948 3504. Adm. free (except weekends and Bank Holidays). Paintings, ceramics, silver and glass; history of Nottingham
Industrial Museum, Wollaton Park. Tel: 0115-928 4602. Closed Sun. mornings, and Mon.-Wed. in winter. Adm. free (except weekends and Bank Holidays). Lacemaking machinery, steam engines and transport exhibits
Museum of Costume and Textiles, Castle Gate. Tel: 0115-948 3504. Adm. free. Costume displays from 1790 to the mid 20th-century in period rooms
Natural History Museum, Wollaton Park. Tel: 0115-928 1333. Closed Sun. mornings. Adm. free (except weekends and Bank Holidays) Local natural history and wildlife dioramas
OXFORD – *Ashmolean Museum*, Beaumont Street. Tel: 01865-278000. Closed Mon. (except Bank Holidays) and Sun. mornings. Adm. free. European and Oriental fine and applied arts, archaeology, Egyptology and numismatics
Museum of Modern Art, Pembroke Street. Tel: 01865-722733. Closed Mon. Adm. £2.50. Temporary exhibitions
Oxford University Museum, Parks Road. Tel: 01865-272950. Closed mornings (except for school parties by appointment) and Sun. Adm. free. Entomology, geology, mineralogy and zoology
PLYMOUTH – *City Museum and Art Gallery*, Drake Circus. Tel: 01752-264878. Closed Mon. (except Bank Holidays) and Sun. Adm. free. Local and natural history, ceramics, silver, Old Masters, temporary exhibitions
The Dome, The Hoe. Tel: 01752-603300. Adm. charge. Maritime history museum
PORTSMOUTH – *Charles Dickens Birthplace Museum*, Old Commercial Road. Tel: 01705-827261. Closed in winter. Adm. charge. Dickens memorabilia
D-Day Museum, Clarence Esplanade. Tel: 01705-827261. Adm. charge. Includes the Overlord Embroidery
Naval Heritage Area, HM Naval Base. Story of the Royal Navy using HMS *Victory* (tel: 01705-819604), HMS *Warrior* (tel: 01705-291379), and the *Mary Rose* (tel: 01705-750521). Separate adm. charge to each, combined tickets available
Royal Naval Museum, HM Naval Base. Tel: 01705-733060. Adm. charge. History of the Royal Navy
PRESTON – *Harris Museum and Art Gallery*, Market Square. Tel: 01772-258248. Closed Sun. and Bank Holidays. Adm. free. British art since the 18th century, ceramics, glass, costume and local history; also contemporary exhibitions
ST ALBANS – *Verulamium Museum*, St Michael's. Tel: 01727-819339. Closed Sun. mornings. Adm. £2.60. Iron Age and Roman Verulamium, including wall plasters, jewellery, mosaics and room reconstructions
ST IVES, Cornwall – *Tate Gallery St Ives*, Porthmeor Beach. Tel: 01736-796226. Closed Mon. Oct.-March. Adm. £3.00. Painting and sculpture by artists associated with St Ives

SHEFFIELD – *City Museum and Mappin Art Gallery*, Weston Park. Tel: 0114-276 8588. Closed Mon. Adm. free. Includes applied arts, natural history, archaeology and ethnography, 19th- and 20th-century art
Graves Art Gallery, Surrey Street. Tel: 0114-273 5858. Closed Sun. Adm. free. British art from the 16th to 20th centuries. Old Masters and non-European art
Kelham Island Industrial Museum, off Alma Street. Tel: 0114-272 2106. Closed Fri. and Sat. Adm. charge. Local industrial and social history
Shepherd Wheel, off Hangingwater Road. Tel: 0114-236 7731. Closed Mon. and Tues. Adm. free. Water-powered cutlery-grinding wheel and workshops
STOKE-ON-TRENT – *City Museum and Art Gallery*, Hanley. Tel: 01782-202173. Closed Sun. mornings. Adm. free. Pottery, china and porcelain collections
Etruria Industrial Museum, Etruria. Tel: 01782-287557. Closed Mon. and Tues. Adm. free. Britain's sole surviving steam-powered potter's mill
Gladstone Pottery Museum, Longton. Tel: 01782-319232. Adm. charge. A working Victorian pottery. Pottery factory tours are available by arrangement Mon.-Fri., except during factory holidays, at the following: *Royal Doulton*, Burslem; *Spode*, Stoke; *John Beswick*, Longton; *Wedgwood*, Barlaston; *W. Moorcroft*, Cobridge; *H & R Johnson Tiles*, Tunstall; *Moorland Pottery*, Burslem; *Peggy Davies Ceramics*, Stoke; *Staffordshire Enamels*, Longton; *St George's Fine Bone China*, Hanley
STYAL, Cheshire – *Quarry Bank Mill*. Tel: 01625-527468. Closed Mon. in winter. Adm. charge. Working mill illustrating history of cotton industry; costumed display at restored Apprentice House
TELFORD – *Ironbridge Gorge Museum*. Tel: 01952-433522. Smaller sites closed in winter. Adm. charge for each site; £8.95 for all sites (ticket valid until all sites have been visited). First iron bridge; early 20th-century working town; Museum of the River; Museum of Iron; Jackfield Tile Museum; Coalport China Museum
TRING, Herts – *Tring Zoological Museum*, Akeman Street. Tel: 01442-824181. Closed Sun. mornings. Adm. £2.20. Display of more than 4,000 animal species
WAKEFIELD – *Yorkshire Sculpture Park*, West Bretton. Tel: 01924-830302. Adm. free. Open-air sculpture gallery including works by Moore, Hepworth, Frink and others
WORCESTER – *City Museum and Art Gallery*, Foregate Street. Tel: 01905-25371. Closed Thurs. and Sun. Adm. free. Includes a military museum, 19th-century chemist's shop and changing art exhibitions
Museum of Worcester Porcelain and Royal Worcester Factory, Severn Street. Tel: 01905-23221. Closed Sun. Adm. £1.50. Worcester porcelain collection; factory tours on weekdays
WROUGHTON, nr Swindon, Wilts – *Science Museum*, Wroughton Airfield. Tel: 01793-814466. Open selected summer weekends only. Adm. charge. Air displays and some of the Science Museum's transport and agricultural collection
YEOVIL, Somerset – *Fleet Air Arm Museum*, Royal Naval Air Station, Yeovilton. Tel: 01935-840565. Adm. charge. History of naval aviation; historic aircraft, including Concorde 002
Montacute House, Montacute. Tel: 01935-823289. Closed mornings and Tues.; also closed in winter. Adm. £4.80. Elizabethan and Jacobean portraits from the National Portrait Gallery
YORK – *Beningbrough Hall*, Shipton-by-Beningbrough. Tel: 01904-470666. Closed Thurs. and Fri. (except Good Friday and July-Aug.); also closed in winter. Adm. £4.50. Portraits from the National Portrait Gallery

Castle Museum. Tel: 01904-653611. Adm. £4.20. Reconstructed streets; costume and military collections
City Art Gallery, Exhibition Square. Tel: 01904-623839. Closed Sun. mornings. Adm. free. European and British painting spanning seven centuries; modern pottery
Jorvik Viking Centre, Coppergate. Tel: 01904-643211. Adm. £4.95. Reconstruction of Viking York
National Railway Museum, Leeman Road. Tel: 01904-621261. Adm. £4.50. Includes locomotives, rolling stock and carriages
Yorkshire Museum, Museum Gardens. Tel: 01904-629745. Closed Sun. mornings in winter. Adm. £3.00. Yorkshire life from Roman to medieval times; geology gallery

WALES

BODELWYDDAN, Denbighshire – *Bodelwyddan Castle*. Tel: 01745-584060. Opening times vary. Adm. charge. Portraits from the National Portrait Gallery, furniture from the Victoria and Albert Museum and sculptures from the Royal Academy
CAERLEON – *Roman Legionary Museum*. Tel: 01633-423134. Closed Sun. mornings. Adm. charge. Material from the site of the Roman fortress of Isca and its suburbs
CARDIFF – *National Museum of Wales*, Cathays Park. Tel: 01222-397951. Closed Sun. mornings and Mon. (except Bank Holidays). Adm. charge. Includes natural sciences, archaeology and Impressionist paintings
Museum of Welsh Life, St Fagans. Tel: 01222-569441. Adm. charge. Open-air museum with re-erected buildings, agricultural equipment and costume
Welsh Industrial and Maritime Museum, Bute Street. Tel: 01222-481919. Closed Sun. mornings and Mon. (except Bank Holidays). Adm. charge. Power, railways, locomotives and shipping exhibitions; miniature railway
DRE-FACH FELINDRE, nr Llandysul – *Museum of the Welsh Woollen Industry*. Tel: 01559-370929. Closed Sun., and Sat. in winter. Adm. charge. Exhibitions, a working woollen mill and craft workshops
LLANBERIS, nr Caernarfon – *Welsh Slate Museum*. Tel: 01286-870630. Closed in winter (except by appointment). Adm. charge. Former slate quarry with original machinery and plant; slate crafts demonstrations
SWANSEA – *Glyn Vivian Art Gallery and Museum*, Alexandra Road. Tel: 01792-655006. Closed Mon. (except Bank Holidays). Adm. free. Paintings, ceramics, Swansea pottery and porcelain, clocks, glass and Welsh art
Swansea Maritime and Industrial Museum, Museum Square. Tel: 01792-650351. Closed Mon. (except Bank Holidays). Adm. free. Includes a working woollen mill and historic boats

SCOTLAND

ABERDEEN – *Aberdeen Art Gallery*, Schoolhill. Tel: 01224-646333. Closed Sun. mornings. Adm. free. Art from the 18th to 20th centuries
Aberdeen Maritime Museum, Shiprow. Tel: 01224-585788. Closed Sun. Adm. free. Maritime history, including shipbuilding and North Sea oil
EDINBURGH – *City Art Centre*, Market Street. Tel: 0131-529 3993. Closed Sun. Adm. free. Late 19th- and 20th-century art and temporary exhibitions

*Huntly House Museum, Canongate. Tel: 0131-529 4143.
Closed Sun. Adm. free. Local history, silver, glass and
Scottish pottery
*Museum of Childhood, High Street. Tel: 0131-529 4142.
Closed Sun. Adm. free. Toys, games, clothes and
exhibits relating to the social history of childhood
Museum of Flight, East Fortune Airfield, nr North
Berwick. Tel: 01620-880308. Closed in winter. Adm.
charge. Display of more than 30 aircraft
National Gallery of Scotland, The Mound. Tel: 0131-556
8921. Closed Sun. mornings. Adm. free. Paintings,
drawings and prints from the 16th to 20th centuries, and
the national collection of Scottish art
*The People's Story, Canongate. Tel: 0131-529 4057.
Closed Sun. Adm. free. Edinburgh life since the 18th
century
Royal Museum of Scotland, Chambers Street. Tel: 0131-
225 7534. Closed Sun. mornings. Adm. free. Scottish and
international collections from prehistoric times to the
present
Scottish Agricultural Museum, Ingliston. Tel: 0131-225
7534. Closed in winter and on Sun.; also on Sat. in May
and Sept. Adm. free. History of agriculture in Scotland
Scottish National Portrait Gallery, Queen Street. Tel:
0131-556 8921. Closed Sun. mornings. Adm. free.
Portraits of eminent people in Scottish history, and the
national collection of photography
Scottish National Gallery of Modern Art, Belford Road. Tel:
0131-556 8921. Closed Sun. mornings. Adm. free.
Twentieth-century painting, sculpture and graphic art
Scottish United Services Museum, Edinburgh Castle. Tel:
0131-225 7534. Closed Sun. mornings in winter. Adm.
free. History of the armed forces of Scotland
*The Writer's Museum, Lawnmarket. Tel: 0131-529 4901.
Closed Sun. Adm. free. Robert Louis Stevenson, Walter
Scott and Robert Burns exhibits
FORT WILLIAM – West Highland Museum, Cameron Square.
Tel: 01397-702169. Closed until May 1997. Includes
tartan collections and exhibits relating to 1745 uprising
GLASGOW – *Burrell Collection, Pollokshaws Road. Tel:
0141-649 7151. Adm. free. Nineteenth-century
paintings, textiles, furniture, ceramics, stained glass and
silver
*Gallery of Modern Art, Queen Street. Tel: 0141-229 1996.
Adm. free. Collection of contemporary Scottish and
world art
*Glasgow Art Gallery and Museum, Kelvingrove. Tel: 0141-
287 2000. Adm. free. Includes Old Masters, 19th-
century French paintings and armour collection
Hunterian Art Gallery, Hillhead Street. Tel: 0141-330
5431. Closed Sun. Adm. free. Rennie Mackintosh and
Whistler collections; also Old Masters and modern
prints
*McLellan Galleries, Sauchiehall Street. Tel: 0141-331
1854. Adm. charge. Temporary exhibitions
*Museum of Transport, Bunhouse Road. Tel: 0141-287
2000. Adm. free. Includes a reproduction of a 1938
Glasgow street, cars since the 1930s, trams and a
Glasgow subway station
*People's Palace Museum, Glasgow Green. Tel: 0141-554
0223. Adm. free. History of Glasgow since 1175
*Pollok House, Pollokshaws Road. Tel: 0141-649 7547.
Adm. free. Spanish paintings, furniture, silver and
ceramics
*St Mungo Museum of Religious Life and Art, Castle Street.
Tel: 0141-553 2557. Adm. free. Explores universal
themes through objects of all the main world religions

NORTHERN IRELAND

BELFAST – Ulster Museum, Botanic Gardens. Tel: 01232-
383000. Closed weekend mornings. Adm. free. Irish
antiquities, natural and local history, fine and applied
arts
HOLYWOOD, Co. Down – Ulster Folk and Transport Museum,
Cultra. Tel: 01232-428428. Closed Sun. mornings, also
Sat. mornings in winter. Adm. £3.30. Indoor galleries
and reconstructed buildings in the open air, Irish
National Railway and Titanic exhibitions
LONDONDERRY – The Tower Museum, Union Hall Place.
Tel: 01504-372411. Closed Sun. morning July-Aug.;
Sun. and Mon. (except Bank Holidays) Sep.-June. Adm.
£3.00. Tells the story of Ireland through the history of
Londonderry
OMAGH, Co. Tyrone – Ulster American Folk Park,
Castletown. Tel: 01662-243292. Closed weekends in
winter. Adm. £3.50. Open-air museum telling the story
of Ulster's emigrants to America; restored or recreated
dwellings and workshops; ship and dockside gallery

Sights of London

For historic buildings, museums and galleries in London, *see* pages 574–80 and 583–4

ALEXANDRA PALACE, Wood Green, London N22 4AY. Tel: 0181-365 2121. The Victorian Palace was severely damaged by fire in 1980 but was restored, and reopened in 1988. Alexandra Palace now provides modern facilities for exhibitions, conferences, banquets and leisure activities. There is an ice rink, open daily, and a boating lake.

BARBICAN CENTRE, Silk Street, London EC2Y 8DS. Tel: 0171-638 4141. Owned, funded and managed by the Corporation of London, the Barbican Centre opened in 1982 and houses the 1,166-seat Barbican Theatre, a 200-seat studio theatre (The Pit), and the 2,026-seat Barbican Hall. There are also three cinemas, two art galleries, a sculpture court, a lending library, trade exhibition and conference facilities, and shops.

BRIDGES. The bridges over the Thames (from east to west) are:

The Queen Elizabeth II Bridge, opened 1991, from Dartford to Thurrock

Tower Bridge, opened 1894 (*see also* page 584)

London Bridge, opened after rebuilding by Rennie, 1831; the new London Bridge opened 1973

Alexandra Bridge (railway bridge), built 1863–6

Southwark Bridge (Rennie), built 1814–19; rebuilt 1912–21

Blackfriars Railway Bridge, completed 1864

Blackfriars Bridge, built 1760–9; rebuilt 1860–9; widened 1907–10

Waterloo Bridge (Rennie), opened 1817; rebuilt 1937–42

Hungerford Railway Bridge (Brunel), suspension bridge built 1841–5; replaced by present railway and footbridge 1863

Westminster Bridge (width 84 ft), opened 1750; rebuilt 1854–62

Lambeth Bridge, built 1862; rebuilt 1929–32

Vauxhall Bridge, built 1811–16; rebuilt 1895–1906

Grosvenor Bridge (railway bridge), built 1859–60; rebuilt 1963–7

Chelsea Bridge, built 1851–8; replaced by suspension bridge 1934; widened 1937

Albert Bridge, opened 1873; restructured (Bazalgette) 1884; strengthened 1971–3

Battersea Bridge (Holland), opened 1772; rebuilt (Bazalgette) 1890

Battersea Railway Bridge, opened 1863

Wandsworth Bridge, opened 1873; rebuilt 1940

Putney Railway Bridge, opened 1889

Putney Bridge, built 1727–9; rebuilt (Bazalgette) 1882–6; starting point of Oxford and Cambridge Boat Race

Hammersmith Bridge, built 1824–7; rebuilt (Bazalgette) 1883–7

Barnes Railway Bridge (also pedestrian), built 1846–9; restructured 1893

Chiswick Bridge, opened 1933

Kew Railway Bridge, opened 1869

Kew Bridge, built 1758–9; rebuilt and renamed King Edward VII Bridge 1903

Richmond Lock; lock, weir and footbridge opened 1894

Twickenham Bridge, opened 1933

Richmond Railway Bridge, opened 1848; restructured 1906–8

Richmond Bridge, built 1774–7; widened 1937

Teddington Lock, footbridge opened 1889; marks the end of the tidal reach of the Thames

Kingston Bridge, built 1825–8; widened 1914

Hampton Court Bridge, built 1753; replaced by iron bridge 1865; present bridge built 1933

CEMETERIES. *Abney Park*, Stamford Hill, N16 (35 acres), tomb of General Booth, founder of the Salvation Army, and memorials to many Nonconformist divines. *Brompton*, Old Brompton Road, SW10 (40 acres), graves of Sir Henry Cole, Emmeline Pankhurst, John Wisden. *City of London Cemetery and Crematorium*, Aldersbrook Road, E12 (200 acres). *Golders Green Crematorium*, Hoop Lane, NW11 (12 acres), with Garden of Rest and memorials to many famous men and women. *Hampstead*, Fortune Green Road, NW6 (36 acres), graves of Kate Greenaway, Lord Lister, Marie Lloyd. *Highgate*, Swains Lane, N6 (38 acres), tombs of George Eliot, Faraday and Marx; guided tours only, west side, £3.00. *Kensal Green*, Harrow Road, W10 (70 acres), tombs of Thackeray, Trollope, Sydney Smith, Wilkie Collins, Tom Hood, George Cruikshank, Leigh Hunt, I. K. Brunel and Charles Kemble. Churchyard of the former *Marylebone Chapel*, Marylebone High Street, W1, Charles Wesley and his son Samuel Wesley buried; chapel demolished in 1949, now Garden of Rest. *Nunhead*, Linden Grove, SE15 (26 acres), closed in 1969, recently restored and opened for burials. *St Marylebone Cemetery and Crematorium*, East End Road, N2 (47 acres). *West Norwood Cemetery and Crematorium*, Norwood High Street, SE27 (42 acres), tombs of Sir Henry Bessemer, Mrs Beeton, Sir Henry Tate and Joseph Whitaker (*Whitaker's Almanack*).

CENOTAPH, Whitehall, London SW1. The word 'cenotaph' means 'empty tomb'. The monument, erected 'To the Glorious Dead', is a memorial to all ranks of the sea, land and air forces who gave their lives in the service of the Empire during the First World War. Designed by Sir Edwin Lutyens and erected as a temporary memorial in 1919, it was replaced by a permanent structure unveiled by George V on Armistice Day 1920. An additional inscription was made after the Second World War to commemorate those who gave their lives in that conflict.

CHARTERHOUSE, Sutton's Hospital, Charterhouse Square, London EC1M 6AN. Tel: 0171-253 9503. A Carthusian monastery from 1371 to 1537, purchased in 1611 by Thomas Sutton, who endowed it as a hospital for aged men 'of gentle birth' and a school for poor scholars (removed to Godalming in 1872). Open to visitors on Wednesdays at 2.15 (April–July). Admission £3.00. *Registrar and Clerk to the Governors*, Lt.-Col. I. Macdonald.

CHELSEA PHYSIC GARDEN, 66 Royal Hospital Road, London SW3 4HS. Tel: 0171-352 5646. A garden of general botanical research, maintaining a wide range of rare and unusual plants. The garden was established in 1673 by the Society of Apothecaries. Open Wednesday and Sunday p.m. during summer months. All enquiries to the Curator.

DOWNING STREET, London SW1. Number 10 Downing Street is the official town residence of the Prime Minister, No. 11 of the Chancellor of the Exchequer and No. 12 is the office of the Government Whips. The street was named after Sir George Downing, Bt., soldier and diplomatist, who was MP for Morpeth from 1660 to 1684.

Chequers, a Tudor mansion in the Chilterns near Princes Risborough, was presented by Lord and Lady Lee of Fareham in 1917 to serve, from 1921, as a country residence for the Prime Minister of the day.

GEORGE INN, Borough High Street, London SE1. The last galleried inn in London, built in 1677. Now run as an ordinary public house.

GREENWICH, London SE10. *The Royal Naval College* was until 1873 the Greenwich Hospital. It was built by Charles II, largely from designs by John Webb, and by Queen Anne and William III, from designs by Wren. It stands on the site of an ancient royal palace and of the more recent Palace of Placentia constructed by Humphrey, Duke of Gloucester (1391–1447), son of Henry IV. Henry VIII, Mary I and Elizabeth I were born in the royal palace (which reverted to the Crown in 1447) and Edward VI died there. *Greenwich Park* (196½ acres) was enclosed by Humphrey, Duke of Gloucester, and laid out by Charles II from the designs of Le Nôtre. On a hill in Greenwich Park is the former Royal Observatory (founded 1675). Its buildings are now managed by the National Maritime Museum (*see* pages 583–4) and the first observatory is named Flamsteed House, after John Flamsteed (1646–1719), the first Astronomer Royal. *The Cutty Sark*, the last of the famous tea clippers, has been preserved as a memorial to ships and men of a past era (*see* page 583). The yacht *Gipsy Moth IV* is preserved alongside the *Cutty Sark*.

HORSE GUARDS, Whitehall, London SW1. Archway and offices built about 1753. The mounting of the guard takes place at 11 a.m. (10 a.m. on Sundays) and the dismounted inspection at 4 p.m. Only those on the Lord Chamberlain's list may drive through the gates and archway into *Horse Guards' Parade* (230,000 sq. ft), where the Colour is 'trooped' on The Queen's official birthday.

THE HOUSES OF PARLIAMENT, Westminster, London SW1. The royal palace of Westminster, originally built by Edward the Confessor, was the normal meeting place of Parliament from about 1340. St Stephen's Chapel was used from about 1550 for the meetings of the House of Commons, which had previously been held in the Chapter House or Refectory of Westminster Abbey. The House of Lords met in an apartment of the royal palace.

The fire of 1834 destroyed much of the palace and the present Houses of Parliament were erected on the site from the designs of Sir Charles Barry and Augustus Welby Pugin between 1840 and 1867. The chamber of the House of Commons was destroyed by bombing in 1941 and a new Chamber designed by Sir Giles Gilbert Scott was used for the first time in 1950.

Westminster Hall was the only part of the old palace of Westminster to survive the fire of 1834. It was built by William Rufus (1097–9) and altered by Richard II (1394–9). The hammerbeam roof of carved oak dates from 1396–8. The Hall was the scene of the trial of Charles I.

The *Victoria Tower* of the House of Lords is about 330 ft high, and when Parliament is sitting the Union flag flies by day from its flagstaff. The *Clock Tower* of the House of Commons is about 320 ft high and contains 'Big Ben', the hour bell said to be named after Sir Benjamin Hall, First Commissioner of Works when the original bell was cast in 1856. This bell, which weighed 16 tons 11 cwt, was found to be cracked in 1857. The present bell (13½ tons) is a recasting of the original and was first brought into use in 1859. The dials of the clock are 23 ft in diameter, the hands being 9 ft and 14 ft long (including balance piece). A light is displayed from the Clock Tower at night when Parliament is sitting.

For security reasons tours of the Houses of Parliament are available only to those who have made advance arrangements through an MP or peer.

Admission to the Strangers' Gallery of the House of Lords is arranged by a peer or by queue via St Stephen's Entrance. Admission to the Strangers' Gallery of the House of Commons is by Members' order (Members' orders should be sought several weeks in advance), or by queue via St Stephen's Entrance. Queues are usually shorter after 6 p.m. Monday–Thursday and on Wednesday morning. Overseas visitors may write to the Public Information Office to obtain a permit to tour the Houses of Parliament, or obtain cards of introduction from their Embassy or High Commission to attend the public gallery.

INNS OF COURT. The *Inner* and *Middle Temple*, Fleet Street/Victoria Embankment, London EC4, have occupied since the early 14th century the site of the buildings of the Order of Knights Templars. *Inner Temple Hall* is open by appointment on application to the Treasurer's Office. *Middle Temple Hall* (1562–70) is open when not in use, Monday–Friday 10–11.30 and 3–4; closed on public holidays. In Middle Temple Gardens (not open to the public) Shakespeare (Henry VI, Part I) places the incident which led to the 'Wars of the Roses' (1455–85). *Temple Church*, London EC4, has a nave which forms one of five remaining round churches in England. Open Wednesday–Friday 10–4. Services: 8.30 and 11.15 a.m. except in August and September. *Master of the Temple*, Revd Canon J. Robinson.

Lincoln's Inn, Chancery Lane/Lincoln's Inn Fields, London WC2, occupies the site of the palace of a former Bishop of Chichester and of a Black Friars monastery. The hall and library buildings are of 1845, although the library is first mentioned in 1474; the old hall (late 15th century) and the chapel were rebuilt c.1619–23. Halls open by appointment, chapel and gardens, Monday–Friday 12–2.30. Chapel services Sunday 11.30 a.m. during law terms. *Lincoln's Inn Fields* (7 acres). The square was laid out by Inigo Jones.

Gray's Inn, Holborn/Gray's Inn Road, London WC1. Early 14th century; hall 1556–8. Chapel services 11.15 a.m. (during law dining terms only). Holy Communion first Sunday in every month except August–September. Gardens open Monday–Friday 12–2.30. Tel: 0171-405 8164.

No other 'Inns' are active, but there are remains of *Staple Inn*, a gabled front on Holborn (opposite Gray's Inn Road). *Clement's Inn* (near St Clement Danes Church), *Clifford's Inn*, Fleet Street, and *Thavies Inn*, Holborn Circus, are all rebuilt. *Serjeants' Inn*, Fleet Street, and another (demolished 1910) of the same name in Chancery Lane, were composed of Serjeants-at-Law, the last of whom died in 1922.

KEW GARDENS, Surrey – *see* index.

LLOYD'S, Lime Street, London EC3M 7HA. Society of private underwriters which evolved during the 18th century from Lloyds Coffee House. The present building was opened for business in May 1986, and houses the Lutine Bell. Underwriting is on four floors with a total area of 114,000 sq. feet. A visitors' gallery is open Monday–Friday for pre-booked groups.

LONDON PARKS, ETC.

Royal Parks

Bushy Park (1,099 acres), Surrey. Adjoining Hampton Court, contains avenue of horse-chestnuts enclosed in a fourfold avenue of limes planted by William III. 'Chestnut Sunday' (when the trees are in full bloom with their 'candles') is usually about 1 to 15 May

Green Park (49 acres), London W1. Between Piccadilly and St James's Park, with Constitution Hill leading to Hyde Park Corner

Greenwich Park (196½ acres), London SE10

Hampton Court Gardens (54 acres), Surrey
Hampton Court Green (17 acres), Surrey
Hampton Court Park (622 acres), Surrey
Hyde Park (341 acres), London w1/w2. From Park Lane to Kensington Gardens, containing the Serpentine. Fine gateway at Hyde Park Corner, with Apsley House, the Achilles Statue, Rotten Row and the Ladies' Mile. To the north-east is the Marble Arch, originally erected by George IV at the entrance to Buckingham Palace and re-erected in the present position in 1851
Kensington Gardens (275 acres), London w2/w8. From the western boundary of Hyde Park to Kensington Palace, containing the Albert Memorial and Peter Pan statue
Kew, Royal Botanic Gardens, see page 338
Regent's Park and Primrose Hill (464 acres), London nw1. From Marylebone Road to Primrose Hill surrounded by the Outer Circle and divided by the Broad Walk leading to the Zoological Gardens
Richmond Park (2,469 acres), Surrey
St James's Park (93 acres), London sw1. From Whitehall to Buckingham Palace. Ornamental lake of 12 acres. The original suspension bridge built in 1857 was replaced in 1957. The Mall leads from the Admiralty Arch to Buckingham Palace, Birdcage Walk from Storey's Gate to Buckingham Palace
Maintained by the Corporation of London
Ashtead Common (500 acres), Surrey
Burnham Beeches and Fleet Wood (540 acres), Bucks. Purchased by the Corporation for the benefit of the public in 1880, Fleet Wood (65 acres) being presented in 1921
Coulsdon Common (133 acres), Surrey
Epping Forest (6,000 acres), Essex. Purchased by the Corporation and opened to the public in 1882. The present forest is 12 miles long by 1 to 2 miles wide, about one-tenth of its original area
Farthing Downs (121 acres), Surrey
Hampstead Heath (789 acres), London nw3. Including Golders Hill (36 acres) and Parliament Hill (271 acres)
Highgate Wood (70 acres), London n6/n10
Kenley Common (138 acres), Surrey
Queen's Park (30 acres), London nw6
Riddlesdown (90 acres), Surrey
Spring Park (51 acres), Kent
West Ham Park (77 acres), London e15
West Wickham Common (25 acres), Kent
Woodredon and Warlies Park Estate (740 acres), Waltham Abbey
Also smaller open spaces within the City of London, including Finsbury Circus Gardens
LONDON PLANETARIUM, Marylebone Road, London nw1 5lr. Tel: 0171-935 6861. Open daily (except Christmas Day), star show and interactive exhibits 12.20–5.00. Admission charge.
MADAME TUSSAUD's, Marylebone Road, London nw1 5lr. Tel: 0171-935 6861. Waxwork exhibition. Open daily (except Christmas Day) 9–5.30. Admission charge.
MARKETS. The London markets are mostly administered by the Corporation of London. Billingsgate (fish), Thames Street site dating from 1875, a market site for over 1,000 years, moved to the Isle of Dogs in 1982. Borough, se1 (vegetables, fruit, flowers, etc.), established on present site 1756, privately owned and run. Covent Garden (vegetables, fruit, flowers, etc.), established in 1661 under a charter of Charles II, moved in 1973 to Nine Elms. Leadenhall, ec3 (meat, poultry, fish, etc.), built 1881, part recently demolished. London Fruit Exchange, Brushfield Street, built by Corporation of London 1928–9 as buildings for Spitalfields market; not connected with the market since it moved in 1991. Petticoat Lane, Middlesex Street, e1, a market has existed on the site for over 500 years, now a Sunday morning market selling almost anything. Portobello Road, w11, originally for herbs and horse-trading from 1870; became famous for antiques after the closure of the Caledonian Market in 1948; Saturdays. Smithfield, Central Meat, Fish, Fruit, Vegetable and Poultry Markets, built 1851–66, the site of St Bartholomew's Fair from 12th to 19th century, new hall built 1963, market refurbished 1993–4. Spitalfields, e1 (vegetables, fruit, etc.), established 1682, modernized 1928, moved to Leyton in 1991.
MARLBOROUGH HOUSE, Pall Mall, London sw1a 5hx. Built by Wren for the first Duke of Marlborough and completed in 1711, the house reverted to the Crown in 1835. In 1863 it became the London house of the Prince of Wales and was the London home of Queen Mary until her death in 1953. In 1959 Marlborough House was given by The Queen as a centre for Commonwealth government conferences and it was opened as such in 1962. The Queen's Chapel, Marlborough Gate, begun in 1623 from the designs of Inigo Jones for the Infanta Maria of Spain, and completed for Queen Henrietta Maria, is open to the public for services on Sundays at 8.30 a.m. and 11.15 a.m. between Easter Day and end July (see St James's Palace for winter services in The Chapel Royal).
LONDON MONUMENT (commonly called The Monument), Monument Street, London ec3. Built from designs of Wren, 1671–7, to commemorate the Great Fire of London, which broke out in Pudding Lane on 2 September 1666. The fluted Doric column is 120 ft high; the moulded cylinder above the balcony supporting a flaming vase of gilt bronze is an additional 42 ft; the column is based on a square plinth 40 ft high (with fine carvings on the west face) making a total height of 202 ft. Splendid views of London from gallery at top of column (311 steps).
MONUMENTS (sculptor's name in parenthesis). Albert Memorial (Durham), Kensington Gore; Royal Air Force (Blomfield), Victoria Embankment; Viscount Alanbrooke, Whitehall; Beaconsfield, Parliament Square; Beatty (Macmillan), Trafalgar Square; Belgian Gratitude (setting by Blomfield, statue by Rousseau), Victoria Embankment; Boadicea (or Boudicca), Queen of the Iceni (Thornycroft), Westminster Bridge; Brunel (Marochetti), Victoria Embankment; Burghers of Calais (Rodin), Victoria Tower Gardens, Westminster; Burns (Steel), Embankment Gardens; Canada Memorial (Granche), Green Park; Carlyle (Boehm), Chelsea Embankment; Cavalry (Jones), Hyde Park; Edith Cavell (Frampton), St Martin's Place; Cenotaph (Lutyens), Whitehall; Charles I (Le Sueur), Trafalgar Square; Charles II (Gibbons), South Court, Chelsea Hospital; Churchill (Roberts-Jones), Parliament Square; Cleopatra's Needle (68½ ft high, c.1500 BC, erected on the Thames Embankment in 1877–8; the sphinxes are Victorian); Clive (Tweed), King Charles Street; Captain Cook (Brock), The Mall; Crimean, Broad Sanctuary; Oliver Cromwell (Thornycroft), outside Westminster Hall; Cunningham (Belsky), Trafalgar Square; Gen. Charles de Gaulle, Carlton Gardens; Lord Dowding (Faith Winter), Strand; Duke of Cambridge (Jones), Whitehall; Duke of York (124 ft), Carlton House Terrace; Edward VII (Mackennal), Waterloo Place; Elizabeth I (1586, oldest outdoor statue in London; from Ludgate), Fleet Street; Eros (Shaftesbury Memorial) (Gilbert), Piccadilly Circus; Marechal Foch (Mallisard, copy of one in Cassel, France), Grosvenor Gardens; Charles James Fox (Westmacott), Bloomsbury Square; George III (Cotes Wyatt), Cockspur Street; George IV (Chantrey), riding without stirrups, Trafalgar Square;

George V (Reid Dick), Old Palace Yard; *George VI* (Macmillan), Carlton Gardens; *Gladstone* (Thornycroft), Strand; *Guards'* (Crimea) (Bell), Waterloo Place; (Great War) (Ledward, figures, Bradshaw, cenotaph), Horse Guards' Parade; *Haig* (Hardiman), Whitehall; *Sir Arthur (Bomber) Harris* (Faith Winter), Strand; *Irving* (Brock), north side of National Portrait Gallery; *James II* (Gibbons and/or pupils), Trafalgar Square; *Jellicoe* (Wheeler), Trafalgar Square; *Samuel Johnson* (Fitzgerald), opposite St Clement Danes; *Kitchener* (Tweed), Horse Guards' Parade; *Abraham Lincoln* (Saint-Gaudens, copy of one in Chicago), Parliament Square; *Milton* (Montford), St Giles, Cripplegate; *The Monument* (*see* above); *Mountbatten*, Foreign Office Green; *Nelson* (170 ft 2 in), Trafalgar Square, with Landseer's lions (cast from guns recovered from the wreck of the *Royal George*); *Florence Nightingale* (Walker), Waterloo Place; *Palmerston* (Woolner), Parliament Square; *Peel* (Noble), Parliament Square; *Pitt* (Chantrey), Hanover Square; *Portal* (Nemon), Embankment Gardens; *Prince Consort* (Bacon), Holborn Circus; *Queen Elizabeth Gate*, Hyde Park Corner; *Raleigh* (Macmillan), Whitehall; *Richard I (Coeur de Lion)* (Marochetti), Old Palace Yard; *Roberts* (Bates), Horse Guards' Parade; *Franklin D. Roosevelt* (Reid Dick), Grosvenor Square; *Royal Artillery* (South Africa) (Colton), The Mall; (Great War), Hyde Park Corner; *Captain Scott* (Lady Scott), Waterloo Place; *Shackleton* (Sarjeant Jagger), Kensington Gore; *Shakespeare* (Fontana, copy of one by Scheemakers in Westminster Abbey), Leicester Square; *Smuts* (Epstein), Parliament Square; *Sullivan* (Goscombe John), Victoria Embankment; *Trenchard* (Macmillan), Victoria Embankment; *Victoria Memorial*, in front of Buckingham Palace; *George Washington* (Houdon copy), Trafalgar Square; *Wellington* (Boehm), Hyde Park Corner; (Chantrey) riding without stirrups, outside Royal Exchange; *John Wesley* (Adams Acton), City Road; *William III* (Bacon), St James's Square; *Wolseley* (Goscombe John), Horse Guards' Parade.

PORT OF LONDON. The Port of London covers the tidal section of the River Thames from Teddington to the seaward limit (the outer Tongue buoy and the sunk light vessel), a distance of 150 km. The governing body is the Port of London Authority (PLA). Eighty-eight per cent of the total port traffic is handled at privately operated riverside terminals between Fulham and Canvey Island, the rest at the enclosed dock at Tilbury, 40 km below London Bridge. Passenger vessels and cruise liners can be handled at moorings at Greenwich, Tower Bridge and Tilbury.

ROMAN REMAINS. The city wall of Roman *Londinium* was largely rebuilt during the medieval period but sections may be seen near the White Tower in the Tower of London; at Tower Hill; at Coopers' Row; at All Hallows, London Wall, its vestry being built on the remains of a semi-circular Roman bastion; at St Alphage, London Wall, showing a succession of building repairs from the Roman until the late medieval period; and at St Giles, Cripplegate. Sections of the great forum and basilica, more than 165 metres square, have been encountered during excavations in the area of Leadenhall, Gracechurch Street and Lombard Street. Traces of Roman activity along the river include a massive riverside wall built in the late Roman period, and a succession of Roman timber quays along Lower and Upper Thames Street.

Other major buildings are the provincial governor's palace in Cannon Street; the amphitheatre at Guildhall; remains of a bath-building, preserved in Lower Thames Street; and the temple of Mithras in Walbrook.

ROYAL ALBERT HALL, Kensington Gore, London SW7 2SR. Tel: 0171-589 3203. The elliptical hall, one of the largest in the world, was completed in 1871, and since 1941 has been the venue each summer for the Promenade Concerts founded in 1895 by Sir Henry Wood. Other events include pop and classical music concerts, dance, opera, sporting events, conferences and banquets.

ROYAL HOSPITAL, CHELSEA, Royal Hospital Road, London SW3 4SR. Tel: 0171-730 0161. Founded by Charles II in 1682, and built by Wren; opened in 1692 for old and disabled soldiers. Open Monday–Saturday 10–12, daily 2–4. The extensive grounds include the former Ranelagh Gardens and are the venue for the Chelsea Flower Show each May. *Governor*, Gen. Sir Brian Kenny, GCB, CBE; *Lt.-Governor and Secretary*, Maj.-Gen. F. G. Sugden, CB, CBE.

ROYAL OPERA HOUSE, Covent Garden, London WC2E 9DD. Home of The Royal Ballet (1931) and The Royal Opera (1946). The Royal Opera House is the third theatre to be built on the site, opening 1858; the first was opened in 1732. The theatre is due to close for redevelopment from July 1997 to autumn 1999.

ST JAMES'S PALACE, Pall Mall, London SW1. Built by Henry VIII; the Gatehouse and Presence Chamber remain; later alterations were made by Wren and Kent. The Chapel Royal is open for services on Sundays at 8.30 a.m. and 11.15 a.m. between the beginning of October and Good Friday (*see* Marlborough House for summer services in The Queen's Chapel). Representatives of foreign powers are still accredited 'to the Court of St James's'. *Clarence House* (1825) in the palace precinct is the home of The Queen Mother.

ST PAUL'S CATHEDRAL, London EC4M 8AD. Built 1675–1710, cost £747,660. The cross on the dome is 365 ft above the ground level, the inner cupola 218 ft above the floor. 'Great Paul' in the south-west tower weighs nearly 17 tons. The organ by Father Smith (enlarged by Willis and rebuilt by Mander) is in a case carved by Grinling Gibbons, who also carved the choir stalls. Open for sightseeing Monday–Saturday 8.30–4.00. Admission to cathedral and crypt: £3.50, children £2.00; Galleries £2.50/£1.50. Services: Sundays, 8, 11 and 3.15. Weekdays, 7.30, 8, 12.30 and 5 (Saturday Mattins 8.30 a.m.).

SOMERSET HOUSE, Strand and Victoria Embankment, London WC2. The river façade (600 ft. long) was built in 1776–86 from the designs of Sir William Chambers; the eastern extension, which houses part of King's College, was built by Smirke in 1829. Somerset House was the property of Lord Protector Somerset, at whose attainder in 1552 the palace passed to the Crown, and it was a royal residence until 1692.

SOUTH BANK, London SE1. The arts complex on the south bank of the River Thames includes the South Bank Centre, owned and managed by the South Bank Board, which consists of the 2,903-seat *Royal Festival Hall* (opened in 1951 for the Festival of Britain), the adjacent 1,056-seat *Queen Elizabeth Hall*, the 368-seat *Purcell Room*, and the 77-seat Voice Box. Tel: 0171-960 4242.

The *National Film Theatre* (opened 1952), administered by the British Film Institute, has three auditoria showing almost 2,000 films a year. The London Film Festival is held here every November. Tel: 0171-928 3232.

The *Royal National Theatre* opened in 1976 and stages classical, modern, new and neglected plays in its three auditoria: the 1,160-seat Olivier theatre, the 890-seat Lyttelton theatre and the Cottesloe theatre which seats up to 400. Tel: 0171-928 2252.

SOUTHWARK CATHEDRAL, London SE1 9DA. Mainly 13th century, but the nave is largely rebuilt. The tomb of John Gower (1330–1408) is between the Bunyan and Chaucer memorial windows in the north aisle; Shakespeare's effigy backed by a view of Southwark and the Globe Theatre in the south aisle; the tomb of Bishop Andrewes (died 1626) is near the screen. The lady chapel was the scene of the consistory courts of the reign of Mary (Gardiner and Bonner) and is still used as a consistory court. John Harvard, after whom Harvard University is named, was baptized here in 1607, and the chapel by the north choir aisle is his memorial chapel. Open 8.30–6, admission free. Services: Sundays, 11, 3. Weekdays, 8, 12.45, 5.30 (sung on Tuesdays and Fridays), Saturdays, 9.

THAMES EMBANKMENTS. The *Victoria Embankment*, on the north side from Westminster to Blackfriars, was constructed by Sir Joseph Bazalgette (1819–91) for the Metropolitan Board of Works, 1864–70; the seats, of which the supports of some are a kneeling camel, laden with spicery, and of others a winged sphinx, were presented by the Grocers' Company and by W. H. Smith, MP, in 1874; the *Albert Embankment*, on the south side from Westminster Bridge to Vauxhall, 1866–9; the *Chelsea Embankment*, 1871–4. The total cost exceeded £2,000,000. Bazalgette also inaugurated the London main drainage system, 1858–65. A medallion (*Flumini vincula posuit*) has been placed on a pier of the Victoria Embankment to commemorate the engineer.

THAMES FLOOD BARRIER. Officially opened in May 1984, though first used in February 1983, the barrier consists of ten rising sector gates which span 570 yards from bank to bank of the Thames at Woolwich Reach. When not in use the gates lie horizontally, allowing shipping to navigate the river normally; when the barrier is closed, the gates turn through 90 degrees to stand vertically more than 50 feet above the river bed. The barrier took eight years to complete and can be raised within about 30 minutes.

THAMES TUNNELS. The *Rotherhithe Tunnel*, opened 1908, connects Commercial Road, London E14, with Lower Road, Rotherhithe; it is 1 mile 332 yards long, of which 525 yards are under the river. The first *Blackwall Tunnel* (northbound vehicles only), opened 1897, connects East India Dock Road, Poplar, with Blackwall Lane, East Greenwich. The height restriction on the northbound tunnel is 13ft 4in. A second tunnel (for southbound vehicles only) opened 1967. The lengths of the tunnels measured from East India Dock Road to the Gate House on the south side are 6,215 ft (old tunnel) and 6,152 ft. *Greenwich Tunnel* (pedestrians only), opened 1902, connects the Isle of Dogs, Poplar, with Greenwich; it is 406 yards long. The *Woolwich Tunnel* (pedestrians only), opened 1912, connects North and South Woolwich below the passenger and vehicular ferry from North Woolwich Station, London E16, to High Street, Woolwich, London SE18; it is 552 yards long.

WALTHAM CROSS, Herts. At Waltham Cross is one of the crosses (partly restored) erected by Edward I to mark a resting place of the corpse of Queen Eleanor on its way to Westminster Abbey. Ten crosses were erected, but only those at Geddington, Northampton and Waltham survive; 'Charing' Cross originally stood near the spot now occupied by the statue of Charles I at Whitehall.

WESTMINSTER ABBEY, London SW1. Built between 1050 and 1745; contains the chapel of Henry VII, chapter house and cloisters, Edward the Confessor's shrine, tombs of kings and queens and many other monuments, including the grave of 'The Unknown Warrior' and Poets' Corner. The Coronation Chair encloses the

Stone of Scone, removed from Scotland by Edward I in 1296. Open on weekdays 9.20–6. Admission to the Royal Chapels, Poets' Corner, Quire and Statesmen's Aisle £4.00, con. £2.00/£1.00. Last admission Monday–Friday 3.45 p.m., Saturday 4.45 p.m. Nave open on Sundays between services. Services: Sundays, 8, 10, 11.15, 3, 6.30 (generally preceded by an organ recital). Monday–Friday, 7.30, 8, 12.30, 5. Saturdays, 8, 9.20, 3.

WESTMINSTER CATHEDRAL, Ashley Place, London SW1P 1QW. Roman Catholic cathedral built 1895–1903 from the designs of J. F. Bentley. The campanile is 283 feet high. Cathedral open 6.50 a.m.–7 p.m. Masses: Sundays, 7, 8, 9, 10.30 (sung), 12, 5.30 and 7; Solemn Vespers and Benediction 3.30. Monday–Friday, 7, 8, 8.30, 9, 10.30, 12.30, 1.05 and 5.30 (sung). Morning Prayer 7.40, Vespers 5. Saturdays 8, 8.30, 9, 10.30 (sung), 12.30 and 6, Morning Prayer 7.40, Vespers 5.30. Holy days of obligation, Low Masses 7, 8, 8.30, 9, 10.30, 12.30, 1.05, 5.30 (sung) and 7.

ZOOLOGICAL GARDENS (London Zoo), Regent's Park, London NW1. Tel: 0171-722 3333. Opened in 1828. Open daily (except Christmas Day) 10–5.30 March–September, 10–4 in winter. Admission £7.50.

LONDON TOURISM BOARD AND CONVENTION BUREAU, 26 Grosvenor Gardens, London SW1W 0DU. Tourist information: 0171-730 3450

Hallmarks

Hallmarks are the symbols stamped on gold, silver or platinum articles to indicate that they have been tested at an official Assay Office and that they conform to one of the legal standards. With certain exceptions, all gold, silver or platinum articles are required by law to be hallmarked before they are offered for sale. Hallmarking was instituted in England in 1300 under a statute of Edward I.

MODERN HALLMARKS

Normally a complete modern hallmark consists of four symbols – the sponsor's mark, the assay office mark, the standard mark and the date letter. Additional marks have been authorized from time to time.

SPONSOR'S MARK

Instituted in England in 1363, the sponsor's mark was originally a device such as a bird or fleur-de-lis. Now it consists of the initial letters of the name or names of the manufacturer or firm. Where two or more sponsors have the same initials, there is a variation in the surrounding shield or style of letters.

STANDARD MARK

The standard mark indicates that the content of the precious metal in the alloy from which the article is made, is not less than the legal standard. The legal standard is the minimum content of precious metal by weight in parts per thousand, and the standards are:

Gold	916.6	(22 carat)
	750	(18 carat)
	585	(14 carat)
	375	(9 carat)
Silver	958.4	(Britannia)
	925	(sterling)
Platinum	950	

The metals are marked as follows, if they are manufactured in the United Kingdom:

GOLD – a crown followed by the millesimal figure for the standard, e.g. 916 for 22 carat (see table above)

SILVER – Britannia silver: a full-length figure of Britannia. Sterling silver: a lion passant (England) or a lion rampant (Scotland)

 Britannia Silver

 Sterling Silver (England)

 Sterling Silver (Scotland)

PLATINUM – an orb

ASSAY OFFICE MARK

This mark identifies the particular assay office at which the article was tested and marked. The British assay offices are:

LONDON, Goldsmiths' Hall, London EC2V 8AQ. Tel: 0171-606 8975

BIRMINGHAM, Newhall Street, Birmingham B3 1SB. Tel: 0121-236 6951

 Gold and platinum

 Silver

SHEFFIELD, 137 Portobello Street, Sheffield S1 4DS. Tel: 0114–275 5111

EDINBURGH, 39 Manor Place, Edinburgh EH3 7EB. Tel: 0131-226 1122

Assay offices formerly existed in other towns, e.g. Chester, Exeter, Glasgow, Newcastle, Norwich and York, each having its own distinguishing mark.

DATE LETTER

The date letter shows the year in which an article was assayed and hallmarked. Each alphabetical cycle has a distinctive style of lettering or shape of shield. The date letters were different at the various assay offices and the particular office must be established from the assay office mark before reference is made to tables of date letters.

The table on page 593 shows specimen shields and letters used by the London Assay Office on silver articles in each period from 1498. The same letters are found on gold articles but the surrounding shield may differ. Since 1 January 1975, each office has used the same style of date letter and shield for all articles.

OTHER MARKS

FOREIGN GOODS

Since 1842 foreign goods imported into Britain have been required to be hallmarked before sale. The marks consist of the importer's mark, a special assay office mark, the figure denoting fineness (fineness mark) and the annual date letter.

The following are the assay office marks for gold imported articles. For silver and platinum the symbols remain the same but the shields differ in shape.

 London

 Birmingham

 Sheffield

 Edinburgh

CONVENTION HALLMARKS

Special marks at authorized assay offices of the signatory countries of the International Convention (Austria, Denmark, Finland, Ireland, Norway, Portugal, Sweden, Switzerland and the UK) are legally recognized in the United Kingdom as approved hallmarks. These consist of a sponsor's mark, a common control mark, a fineness mark (arabic numerals showing the standard in parts per thousand), and an assay office mark. There is no date letter.

The fineness marks are:

Gold	750	(18 carat)
	585	(14 carat)
	375	(9 carat)
Silver	925	(sterling)
Platinum	950	

The common control marks are:

 Gold (18 carat)

 Silver

 *Platinum*

DUTY MARKS

In 1784 an additional mark of the reigning sovereign's head was introduced to signify that the excise duty had been paid. The mark became obsolete on the abolition of the duty in 1890.

COMMEMORATIVE MARKS

There are three other marks to commemorate special events: the silver jubilee of King George V and Queen Mary in 1935, the coronation of Queen Elizabeth II in 1953, and her silver jubilee in 1977.

LONDON (GOLDSMITHS' HALL) DATE LETTERS FROM 1498

		from	to
𝕰𝕷	Black letter, small	1498–9	1517–8
🅰	Lombardic	1518–9	1537–8
🅰	Roman and other capitals	1538–9	1557–8
🅰	Black letter, small	1558–9	1577–8
🅰	Roman letter, capitals	1578–9	1597–8
𝔸	Lombardic, external cusps	1598–9	1617–8
𝒆	Italic letter, small	1618–9	1637–8
🅱	Court hand	1638–9	1657–8

		from	to
𝖆	Black letter, capitals	1658–9	1677–8
𝖆	Black letter, small	1678–9	1696–7
ʆ	Court hand	1697	1715–6
𝐀	Roman letter, capitals	1716–7	1735–6
𝖺	Roman letter, small	1736–7	1738–9
𝖉	Roman letter, small	1739–40	1755–6
𝕬	Old English, capitals	1756–7	1775–6
𝖆	Roman letter, small	1776–7	1795–6
𝐀	Roman letter, capitals	1796–7	1815–6
𝖆	Roman letter, small	1816–7	1835–6
𝕬	Old English, capitals	1836–7	1855–6
𝖃	Old English, small	1856–7	1875–6
🅐	Roman letter, capitals [A to M *square* shield N to Z as shown]	1876–7	1895–6
𝖆	Roman letter, small	1896–7	1915–6
𝖆	Black letter, small	1916–7	1935–6
𝐀	Roman letter, capitals	1936–7	1955–6
𝑎	Italic letter, small	1956–7	1974
𝐴	Italic letter, capitals	1975	

Economic Statistics

GOVERNMENT RECEIPTS AND EXPENDITURE

GENERAL GOVERNMENT RECEIPTS £ billion

	Outturn 1994–5	Forecast 1995–6	Forecast 1996–7
Income tax	63.1	68.9	70.2
Corporation tax	19.4	24.7	26.6
Value added tax	41.8	44.0	47.9
Excise duties	27.0	28.3	30.8
Other taxes and royalties	40.3	43.8	46.3
Social security contributions	42.1	44.4	46.9
Other receipts	16.4	17.7	16.1
Total general government receipts	250.0	271.9	284.8

Source: HM Treasury – *Financial Statement and Budget Report 1996–7*

THE CONTROL TOTAL AND GENERAL GOVERNMENT EXPENDITURE
(*excluding privatization proceeds*) £ million

	Estimated outturn 1995–6	Plans/ projections 1996–7
Central government expenditure	181,100	184,000
Local authority expenditure	74,400	74,500
Financing requirements of nationalized industries	−70	−840
Reserve	—	2,500
Control total	255,500	260,200
Cyclical social security	14,000	13,900
Central government debt interest	20,500	22,300
Accounting adjustments	9,600	9,700
General government expenditure excluding privatization proceeds	299,600	306,100
GGE excluding privatization proceeds as a percentage of GDP	42%	40.5%

Source: HM Treasury – *Financial Statement and Budget Report 1996–7*

CONTROL TOTAL EXPENDITURE BY DEPARTMENT
£ million

	Estimated outturn 1995–6	New plans 1996–7
Defence	21,210	21,420
Foreign Office	1,470	1,090
Overseas Development	2,370	2,290
Agriculture, Fisheries and Food	2,930	3,020
Trade and Industry	3,670	2,910
ECGD	30	10
Transport	4,620	4,180
DoE – Housing	6,700	5,840
DoE – Urban and environment	2,370	2,400
DoE – Local government	30,320	31,320
Home Office	6,600	6,520
Legal departments	2,710	2,720
Education and Employment	14,190	14,040
National Heritage	1,020	960
Health	32,930	33,750
Long-term care	—	60
Social security	73,730	76,810
Scotland	14,470	14,550
Wales	6,720	6,800
Northern Ireland	7,820	8,010
Chancellor of the Exchequer's departments	3,300	3,200
Cabinet Office	1,120	960
European Communities	2,890	2,300
Local authority self-financed expenditure	12,300	12,500
Reserve	—	2,500
Control total	255,500	260,200

Source: HM Treasury – *Financial Statement and Budget Report 1996–7*

FINANCING REQUIREMENTS OF NATIONALIZED INDUSTRIES £ million

Department and industry	Estimated outturn 1995–6	Plans 1996–7
Trade and Industry	430	−290
British Coal	60	100
British Shipbuilders	0	−20
Nuclear Electric	370	40
Post Office	−210	−300
British Nuclear Fuels	210	−120
Transport	1,310	1,340
Railways*	340	400
Civil Aviation Authority	40	−10
London Transport	940	950
DoE – Environment	50	50
British Waterways Board	50	50
Scotland	−20	30
Caledonian MacBrayne Ltd	10	10
Scottish Nuclear	−40	20
Scottish Transport Group	0	0
Highlands and Islands Airports	10	10
Total	1,760	1,130

* Includes British Rail, Railtrack, Union Railways and European Passenger Services
Source: HM Treasury – *Financial Statement and Budget Report 1996–7*

LOCAL AUTHORITY EXPENDITURE   £ million

	Estimated outturn 1995–6	Plans 1996–7
CURRENT		
Aggregate External Finance		
England	34,770	35,650
Scotland	5,320	5,380
Wales	2,460	2,510
Total Aggregate External Finance	42,550	43,560
Other current grants	14,090	13,510
TOTAL CURRENT	56,640	57,070
CAPITAL		
Capital grants	1,900	1,760
Credit approvals	3,580	3,180
TOTAL CAPITAL SUPPORT	5,480	4,940
Total Central Government Support to Local Authorities	62,100	62,000
Local Authority Self-Financed Expenditure	12,300	12,500
TOTAL LOCAL AUTHORITY EXPENDITURE	74,400	74,500

Source: HM Treasury – Financial Statement and Budget Report 1996–7

PUBLIC SECTOR BORROWING REQUIREMENT

	Outturn 1994–5	Forecast 1995–6	Forecast 1996–7
PSBR (£ billion)	35.9	29.0	22.4
As % of GDP	5¼	4	3

Source: HM Treasury – Financial Statement and Budget Report 1996–7

GDP BY INDUSTRY 1994 BEFORE DEPRECIATION BUT AFTER STOCK APPRECIATION
£ million

Agriculture, hunting, forestry and fishing	11,548
Mining and quarrying, including gas and oil extraction	13,078
Manufacturing	171,272
Electricity, gas and water supply	15,458
Construction	31,035
Wholesale and retail trade; repairs; hotels and restaurants	83,472
Transport, storage and communication	49,039
Financial intermediation; real estate; renting and business activities	154,550
Public administration, national defence and compulsory social security	38,797
Education; health; social work	69,116
Other services, including sewerage and refuse disposal	22,044
TOTAL	609,409
less adjustment for financial services	29,828
Statistical discrepancy (income adjustment)	−441
GROSS DOMESTIC PRODUCT	579,140

Source: HMSO – Annual Abstract of Statistics 1996

BALANCE OF PAYMENTS 1994   *£ million*

CURRENT ACCOUNT

Visible trade	
Exports (fob)	134,611
Imports (fob)	145,349
Visible balance	−10,738
Invisibles	
Credits	123,046
Debits	114,136
Invisibles balance	8,910
of which:	
Services balance	3,790
Investment income	10,519
Transfers balance	−5,399
CURRENT BALANCE	−1,828

*TRANSACTIONS IN EXTERNAL ASSETS
AND LIABILITIES

Investment overseas by UK residents	
Direct	−16,412
Portfolio	18,552
Total UK investment overseas	2,140
Investment in the UK by overseas residents	
Direct	6,677
Portfolio	31,836
Total overseas investment in UK	38,513
Foreign currency lending abroad by UK banks	−49,967
Foreign currency borrowing abroad by UK banks	41,121
Net foreign currency transactions of UK banks	−8,846
Sterling lending abroad by UK banks	339
Sterling borrowing and deposit liabilities abroad of UK banks	6,214
Net sterling transactions of UK banks	6,553
Deposits with and lending to banks abroad by UK non-bank private sector	−10,686
Borrowing from banks abroad by:	
UK non-bank private sector	−1,867
Public corporations	−118
General government	−133
Official reserves (additions to −, drawings on +)	−1,045
Other external assets of:	
UK non-bank private sector and public corporations	20,475
General government	−619
Other external liabilities of:	
UK non-bank private sector and public corporations	−48,600
General government	674

NET TRANSACTIONS IN ASSETS AND LIABILITIES	−3,561
BALANCING ITEM	5,389

* Assets: increase −/decrease; +
Liabilities: increase +/decrease−
Source: HMSO – *Annual Abstract of Statistics 1996*

VISIBLE TRADE OF THE UK
ON A BALANCE OF PAYMENTS BASIS   *£ million*

	Exports	Imports	Visible balance
1985	77,991	81,336	−3,345
1986	72,627	82,186	−9,559
1987	79,153	90,735	−11,582
1988	80,346	101,826	−21,480
1989	92,154	116,837	−24,683
1990	101,718	120,527	−18,809
1991	103,413	113,697	−10,284
1992	107,343	120,447	−13,104
1993	121,414	134,623	−13,209
1994	134,611	145,349	−10,738

Source: HMSO – *Annual Abstract of Statistics 1996*

VALUE OF UK EXPORTS 1995
BY DESTINATION   *£ million*

European Community	88,647.4
Other western Europe	6,446.0
Eastern Europe	3,757.3
North America	20,506.8
Other America	2,530.5
Middle East and North Africa	7,533.5
Sub-Saharan Africa	3,663.8
Asia and Oceania	19,713.8
Low-value exports	553.8
Total non-EC exports	64,705.1
Total exports	153,352.5

Source: HM Customs and Excise

VALUE OF UK IMPORTS 1995
BY SOURCE   *£ million*

European Community	92,911.1
Other western Europe	10,701.8
Eastern Europe	3,374.1
North America	23,038.1
Other America	2,825.2
Middle East and North Africa	3,426.7
Sub-Saharan Africa	2,551.8
Asia and Oceania	28,827.9
Low-value imports	398.1
Total non-EC imports	75,143.9
Total imports	168,055.0

Source: HM Customs and Excise

EMPLOYMENT

LABOUR FORCE BY AGE 1994 (GREAT BRITAIN)

Age	
16–24	4,710,000
25–44	14,301,000
45–59	7,922,000
60–64	1,051,000
65 and over	437,000
Total	28,421,000

ECONOMIC STATUS OF PEOPLE OF WORKING AGE (GREAT BRITAIN)
AS AT SPRING 1995 *Percentages*

	Male	Female
Working full time	71	38
Working part time	5	28
Unemployed	9	5
Inactive	15	29
Total	100	100

Source: HMSO – *Social Trends 26*

AVERAGE GROSS WEEKLY EARNINGS OF FULL-TIME EMPLOYEES (GREAT BRITAIN)
AS AT APRIL 1995

	£
All adults	336.3
All men	374.6
Men, manual	291.3
Men, non-manual	443.3
All women	269.8
Women, manual	188.1
Women, non-manual	288.1

Source: HMSO – *Annual Abstract of Statistics 1996*

UNEMPLOYMENT BY STANDARD REGIONS
SEASONALLY ADJUSTED, AT 9 MAY 1996*

	Total	% of workforce
United Kingdom	2,167,600	7.7
England:		
North	138,900	10.0
Yorkshire and Humberside	194,600	8.3
East Midlands	137,100	7.2
East Anglia	61,500	5.8
South East	663,400	7.3
South West	152,500	6.4
West Midlands	194,200	7.8
North West	238,200	8.3
Wales	104,800	8.3
Scotland	196,900	8.1
Northern Ireland	85,600	11.1

Note: Percentages calculated using mid-1995 estimates of total employees in employment, unemployed, self-employed and HM Forces, and participants in work-related government training schemes
* provisional
Source: Office for National Statistics

UNEMPLOYMENT RATES BY AGE 1995 (UK)
Percentages

Age	Male	Female
16–19	19.6	14.8
20–29	14.0	9.2
30–39	8.3	6.5
40–49	7.1	5.0
50–64/59	9.2	4.2
65/60 and over	2.7	2.4
All ages	10.1	6.8

Source: HMSO – *Social Trends 26*

INDUSTRIAL STOPPAGES 1995 (UK)

Duration	
Not more than 5 days	176
6–10 days	14
11–20 days	6
21–30 days	5
31–50 days	1
More than 50 days	3
Total number of stoppages	205

TRADE UNION MEMBERSHIP (UK)

	1982	1992
Number of trade unions	408	268
Membership	11,593,000	9,048,000

Source: HMSO – *Annual Abstract of Statistics 1996*

598   Economic Statistics

HOUSEHOLDS AND THEIR EXPENDITURE 1994[1]

NUMBER OF HOUSEHOLDS
SUPPLYING DATA 6,853
Total number of persons 16,617
Total number of adults[2] 12,365

DISTRIBUTION BY TENURE
Rented unfurnished 27.9%
Rented furnished 3.9%
Rent-free 1.3%
Owner-occupied 67.4%

AVERAGE NUMBER OF PERSONS
PER HOUSEHOLD
All persons 2.425
Males 1.162
Females 1.263
Adults[2] 1.804
  Persons under 65 1.444
  Persons 65 and over 0.360
Children[2] 0.621
  Children under 2 0.073
  Children 2 and under 5 0.113
  Children 5 and under 18 0.435
Persons economically active 1.150
Persons not economically active 1.275
  Men 65 and over, women 60 and over 0.391
  Others 0.883

HOUSEHOLD EXPENDITURE ON COMMODITIES AND
SERVICES – WEEKLY AVERAGE

	£	As % of total
Housing[3]	46.42	16.4
Fuel, light and power	12.95	4.6
Food	30.43	17.8
Alcoholic drink	12.32	4.3
Tobacco	5.61	2.0
Clothing and footwear	17.13	6.0
Household goods	22.66	8.0
Household services	15.08	5.3
Personal goods and services	10.78	3.8
Motoring expenditure	36.17	12.8
Fares and other travel costs	6.64	2.3
Leisure goods	13.89	4.9
Leisure services	31.20	11.0
Miscellaneous	2.30	0.8
Total	283.58	100.0

[1]Information derived from the Family Expenditure Survey; relates to the UK
[2]Adults = all persons 18 and over and married persons under 18 Children = all unmarried persons under 18
[3]Excludes mortgage payments but includes imputed expenditure (i.e. the weekly equivalent of rateable value)
Source: HMSO – Annual Abstract of Statistics 1996

SOURCES OF HOUSEHOLD INCOME 1994*

AVERAGE WEEKLY INCOME BY SOURCE (£)
Wages and salaries 237.94
Self-employment 35.25
Investments 16.23
Annuities and pensions (other than social security benefits) 23.48
Social security benefits 49.86
Other sources 6.49
Total 359.25

SOURCES AS A PERCENTAGE OF TOTAL HOUSEHOLD INCOME (%)
Wages and salaries 64.4
Self-employment 9.5
Investments 4.4
Annuities and pensions (other than social security benefits) 6.4
Social security benefits 13.5
Other sources 1.8
Total 100.0

* Information derived from the Family Expenditure Survey; relates to the UK. Number of households supplying data, 6,853
Source: HMSO – Annual Abstract of Statistics 1996

AVAILABILITY OF CERTAIN DURABLE GOODS 1994*
PERCENTAGE OF HOUSEHOLDS

Car	69.0
One	45.0
Two	20.0
Three or more	4.0
Central heating, full or partial	84.3
Washing machine	89.0
Refrigerator or fridge/freezer	98.5
Freezer or fridge/freezer	85.7
Television	98.3†
Telephone	91.1
Home computer	19.1†
Video recorder	76.4

* Information derived from the Family Expenditure Survey; relates to the UK. Number of households supplying data, 6,853
† 1992 figure
Source: HMSO – Annual Abstract of Statistics 1996

Cost of Living and Inflation Rates

The first cost of living index to be calculated took July 1914 as 100 and was based on the pattern of expenditure of working-class families in 1914. The cost of living index was superseded in 1947 by the general index of retail prices (RPI), although the older term is still popularly applied to it.

GENERAL INDEX OF RETAIL PRICES

The general index of retail prices measures the changes month by month in the average level of prices of goods and services purchased by most households in the United Kingdom. The spending pattern on which the index is based is revised each year, mainly using information from the Family Expenditure Survey. The expenditure of certain higher income households and of households mainly dependent on state pensions is excluded.

The index is compiled using a selection of over 600 goods and services and the prices charged for these items are collected at regular intervals in about 180 locations throughout the country. For the index, the price changes are weighted in accordance with the pattern of consumption of the average family.

INFLATION RATE

The twelve-monthly percentage change in the 'all items' index of the RPI is usually referred to as the rate of inflation. The percentage change in prices between any two months/years can be obtained using the following formula:

$$\frac{\text{Later date RPI} - \text{Earlier date RPI}}{\text{Earlier date RPI}} \times 100$$

e.g. to find the rate of inflation for 1988, using the annual averages for 1987 and 1988:

$$\frac{106.9 - 101.9}{101.9} \times 100 = 4.9\%$$

PURCHASING POWER OF THE POUND

Changes in the internal purchasing power of the pound may be defined as the 'inverse' of changes in the level of prices; when prices go up, the amount which can be purchased with a given sum of money goes down. To find the purchasing power of the pound in one month or year, given that it was 100p in a previous month or year, the calculation would be:

$$100p \times \frac{\text{Earlier month/year RPI}}{\text{Later month/year RPI}}$$

Thus, if the purchasing power of the pound is taken to be 100p in 1975, the comparable purchasing power in 1995 would be:

$$100p \times \frac{34.2}{149.1} = 22.94p$$

For longer term comparisons, it has been the practice to use an index which has been constructed by linking together the RPI for the period 1962 to date; an index derived from the consumers expenditure deflator for the period from 1938 to 1962; and the prewar 'Cost of Living' index for the

period 1914 to 1938. This long-term index enables the internal purchasing power of the pound to be calculated for any year from 1914 onwards. It should be noted that these figures can only be approximate.

	Long-term index of consumer goods and services (Jan. 1987 = 100)	Comparable purchasing power of £1 in 1995	Rate of inflation (annual average)
1914	2.8	53.25	
1915	3.5	42.60	
1920	7.0	21.30	
1925	5.0	29.82	
1930	4.5	33.13	
1935	4.0	37.28	
1938	4.4	33.89	
There are no official figures for 1939–45			
1946	7.4	20.15	
1950	9.0	16.57	
1955	11.2	13.31	
1960	12.6	11.83	
1965	14.8	10.07	
1970	18.5	8.06	
1975	34.2	4.36	
1980	66.8	2.23	18.0
1981	74.8	1.99	11.9
1982	81.2	1.84	8.6
1983	84.9	1.76	4.6
1984	89.2	1.67	5.0
1985	94.6	1.58	6.1
1986	97.8	1.52	3.4
1987	101.9	1.46	4.2
1988	106.9	1.39	4.9
1989	115.2	1.29	7.8
1990	126.1	1.18	9.5
1991	133.5	1.12	5.9
1992	138.5	1.08	3.7
1993	140.7	1.06	1.6
1994	144.1	1.03	2.4
1995	149.1	1.00	3.5

Gaming and Lotteries

Gaming and lotteries in the UK are officially regulated and may only be run by licensed operators or in licensed premises. Responsibility for policy and the laws on gaming and lotteries rests with the Home Secretary. Supervision of gaming and lottery operations is mostly the responsibility of the Gaming Board of Great Britain, although the National Lottery (see below) is regulated by the Director-General of the National Lottery through the Office of the National Lottery.

Most betting is on horseracing and greyhound racing, and may take place at racecourses and greyhound tracks, or at off-course betting offices. The amount spent on on-course betting cannot be calculated precisely since no duty is payable on it and therefore no returns are made; however, it is estimated to be about 10 per cent of the figures for off-course betting.

Off-Course Betting (UK)

	£ million
1993–4	6,385
1994–5	6,562
1995–6	6,257p

p provisional
Source: Horserace Totalisator Board

Other forms of gaming and lotteries include the following (for National Lottery, see below):

Number of casinos operating	119
Drop	£2,461m
Bingo clubs licensed	972
Amount staked (£ million)	£811m
Gaming machines licensed	271,272*
Society lottery schemes registered	377
Local authority lottery schemes registered	25
Number of lotteries held under registered schemes	1,144
Total ticket sales (£ million)	£38.74m

* 1993–4 figure
Source: Annual Report of the Gaming Board of Great Britain 1994–5

THE NATIONAL LOTTERY

The National Lottery is run by a private company, Camelot. The Office of the National Lottery regulates the National Lottery operations and licenses games promoted as part of the Lottery.

The first National Lottery tickets draw was made on 19 November 1994 and scratchcards were introduced on 25 March 1995. Tickets and scratchcards cost £1. The average number of tickets sold each week in the first year of the Lottery was about 63,893,000, and the average number of scratchcards sold each week was about 32,813,000. An estimated two-thirds of the adult population buy lottery tickets each week and spend an average of £2.60. About 15–20 per cent of the adult population purchases scratch-cards; accurate data is difficult to obtain but it is estimated that most players buy about three scratchcards a week. From November 1994 to February 1996 more than £5,900 million was raised by the National Lottery.

Fifty per cent of the proceeds are used in prize money; the Government receives 12 per cent in tax; the retailer receives 5 per cent; Camelot receives 5 per cent; and the remaining 28 per cent is divided equally between the five 'good causes' (see below). If the jackpot prize is not won, it is 'rolled over' to the following week; the first multi-million jackpot prize of £17,880,000 was won by one individual on 10 December 1994 as the result of a roll-over. The highest individual win to date was £22,590,000 on 10 June 1995.

LOTTERY AWARDS

Seventy-seven per cent of awards made by the 11 disbursing bodies were for less than £100,000; 2.4 per cent were for more than £1 million. Most awards are conditional on partnership funding being obtained from other sources.

Awards Made to February 1996

Awards, Total - 5,121 to the total value of £1,225,957,787

Arts Awards, Total - 842 awards to the total value of £319,533,744

Arts Council of England - 466 awards to the total value of £280,876,872. Twelve awards were for more than £3 million, including £55 million to the Royal Opera House, Covent Garden, £41.1 million to the Lowry Centre and £30 million to Sadler's Wells Theatre

Arts Council of Wales - 159 awards to the total value of £10,263,012. Three awards were for more than £1 million, including £2 million to the Cardiff Old Library Trust

Scottish Arts Council - 142 awards to the total value of £22,986,792. Six awards were for more than £1 million, including £3 million to the Edinburgh Festival Society

Arts Council of Northern Ireland - 75 awards to the total value of £5,407,067. Three awards were for more than £300,000, including £3 million to Armagh City and District Council for a new theatre/arts centre

Millennium Commission - 310 awards to the total value of £443,448,385. Thirteen awards were for more than £10 million, including £50 million to the new Tate Gallery of Modern Art, £50 million to the Earth Centre, Conisbrough, £46 million to South Glamorgan County Council and the Welsh Rugby Union for the Millennium Stadium, £42.5 million to Sustrans National Cycle Network, £40 million to the Renaissance of Portsmouth Harbour and £21.5 million to the Millennium Seed Bank at the Royal Botanic Gardens, Kew

National Heritage Memorial Fund - 221 awards to the total value of £117,001,647. Seven awards were for more than £5 million, including £13.25 million to the Sir Winston Churchill Archive Trust, £10.277 million to the National Trust for Scotland for the Mar Lodge Estate, £8 million to the National Gallery for Seurat's The Channel of Gravelines and £7.65 million to the Lowry Centre

National Lottery Charities Board - 2,460 awards to the total value of £159,081,946. Twelve awards were for more than £500,000, including £682,000 to St Chad's Community Project, Tyne and Wear, £666,177 to Strathclyde Poverty Alliance, £647,725 to Wirral Mind and £600,000 to Barnado's

Sport Awards, Total - 1,288 awards to the total value of £186,892,065

THE SPORTS COUNCIL - 911 awards to the total value of
£152,066,880. Nine awards were for more than £3
million, including £5.756 to North Tyneside Council
for the regeneration of Smith Park, £4.895 million to
the London Borough of Hackney for the Clissold
Leisure Centre and £4.417 million to the Jubilee
Sailing Trust, Hants
SPORTS COUNCIL FOR WALES - 111 awards to the total
value of £9,763,218. Two awards were for more than
£500,000, including £1.418 million to Wrexham
Maelor Borough Council for its swimming baths
SCOTTISH SPORTS COUNCIL - 166 awards to the total
value of £18,474,658. Four awards were for more than
£700,000, including £1.5 million to Tayside Regional
Council for the Maryfield Regional Sports Complex
SPORTS COUNCIL FOR NORTHERN IRELAND - 100 awards
to the value of £6,587,309. Three awards were for more
than £400,000, including £500,000 to Lisburn
Racquets Club

REGIONAL BREAKDOWN OF AWARDS BY VALUE
To February 1996

	% of total UK population	*% of value of total awards made*
England	83.3	71.86
London		22.67
North-West		10.04
North-East		3.95
Yorks and Humberside		7.15
Eastern		5.50
East Midlands		2.25
West Midlands		4.52
South-West		4.34
South-East		9.65
Merseyside		1.28
England-wide		0.52
Scotland	8.9	10.10
Wales	5.0	10.33
N. Ireland	2.8	2.27
UK-wide projects		5.45

Sources: Department of National Heritage; Office of the National Lottery

Finance

British Currency

COIN

Gold Coins	Nickel-Brass Coins
*One hundred pounds	‡Two pounds £2
£100	One pound £1
*Fifty pounds £50	
*Twenty-five pounds £25	Cupro-Nickel Coins
*Ten pounds £10	Crown £5 (since 1990)
Five pounds £5	‡50 pence 50p
Two pounds £2	Crown 25p (pre-1990)
Sovereign £1	20 pence 20p
Half-Sovereign 50p	§10 pence 10p
	¶5 pence 5p
†Silver Coins	
(Maundy Money)	Bronze Coins
Fourpence 4p	2 pence 2p
Threepence 3p	1 penny 1p
Twopence 2p	Copper-plated Steel Coins
Penny 1p	2 penny 2p
	1 penny 1p

*Britannia gold bullion coins, introduced in October 1987
†Gifts of special money distributed by the Sovereign annually on Maundy Thursday to the number of aged poor men and women corresponding to the Sovereign's own age
‡A new £2 coin will be introduced on 1 November 1997 and a new 50p coin on 1 September 1997
§New 10 pence coin introduced on 30 September 1992
¶New 5 pence coin introduced on 27 June 1990

GOLD COIN

Gold ceased to circulate during the First World War. Since then controls on buying, selling and holding gold coin have been imposed at various times but subsequently have been revoked. Under the Exchange Control (Gold Coins Exemption) Order 1979 gold coins may now be imported and exported without restriction, except gold coins which are more than 50 years old and valued at a sum in excess of £8,000; these cannot be exported without specific authorization from the Department of Trade and Industry.

In 1982 the Government introduced VAT on sales of all gold coin.

SILVER COIN

Prior to 1920 silver coins were struck from sterling silver, an alloy of which 925 parts in 1,000 were silver. In 1920 the proportion of silver was reduced to 500 parts. From 1 January 1947 all 'silver' coins, except Maundy money, have been struck from cupro-nickel, an alloy of copper 75 parts and nickel 25 parts, except for the 20p, composed of copper 84 parts, nickel 16 parts. Maundy coins continue to be struck from sterling silver.

BRONZE COIN

Bronze, introduced in 1860 to replace copper, is an alloy of copper 97 parts, zinc 2.5 parts and tin 0.5 part. These proportions have been subject to slight variations in the past. Bronze was replaced by copper-plated steel in September 1992.

LEGAL TENDER

Gold, dated 1838 onwards, if not below least current weight, is legal tender to any amount. £5 (Crown since 1990), £2 and £1 coins are legal tender to any amount; 50p, 25p (Crown pre-1990) and 20p coins are legal tender up to £10; 10p and 5p coins are legal tender up to £5, and 2p and 1p coins are legal tender for amounts up to 20p.

Farthings ceased to be legal tender on 31 December 1960, the halfpenny on 1 August 1969, the halfcrown on 1 January 1970, the threepence and penny on 31 August 1971, the sixpence on 30 June 1980, the decimal halfpenny on 31 December 1984, the old 5p on 31 December 1990, and the old 10p on 30 June 1993.

The decimal system was introduced on 15 February 1971. Since 1982 the word 'new' in 'new pence' displayed on decimal coins has been dropped.

The Channel Islands and the Isle of Man issue their own coinage, which are legal tender only in the island of issue. For denominations, see page 603.

Metal		Standard weight (g)	Standard diameter (cm)
Penny	bronze	3.564	2.032
Penny	copper-plated steel	3.564	2.032
2 pence	bronze	7.128	2.591
2 pence	copper-plated steel	7.128	2.591
5p	cupro-nickel	3.25	1.80
10p	cupro-nickel	6.5	2.45
20p	cupro-nickel	5.0	2.14
25p Crown	cupro-nickel	28.276	3.861
50p	cupro-nickel	13.5	3.0
£1	nickel-brass	9.5	2.25
£2	nickel-brass	15.98	2.84
£5 Crown	cupro-nickel	28.28	3.861

The 'remedy' is the amount of variation from standard permitted in weight and fineness of coins when first issued from the Mint.

The Trial of the Pyx is the examination by a jury to ascertain that coins made by the Royal Mint, which have been set aside in the pyx (or box), are of the proper weight, diameter and composition required by law. The trial is held annually, presided over by the Queen's Remembrancer (the Senior Master of the Supreme Court), with a jury of freemen of the Company of Goldsmiths.

BANKNOTES

Bank of England notes are currently issued in denominations of £5, £10, £20 and £50 for the amount of the fiduciary note issue, and are legal tender in England and Wales. Banknotes which are no longer legal tender are payable when presented at the head office of the Bank of England in London.

The old white notes for £10, £20, £50, £100, £500 and £1,000, which were issued until April 1943, ceased to be legal tender in May 1945, and the old white £5 note in March 1946.

The white £5 note issued between October 1945 and September 1956, the £5 notes issued between 1957 and 1963, (bearing a portrait of Britannia) and the first series to bear a portrait of The Queen, issued between 1963 and 1971, ceased to be legal tender in March 1961, June 1967 and September 1973 respectively.

The series of £1 notes issued during the years 1928 to 1960 and the 10 shilling notes issued from 1928 to 1961 (those without the royal portrait) ceased to be legal tender in May and October 1962 respectively. The £1 note first issued in March 1960 (bearing on the back a representation of Britannia) and the £10 note first issued in February 1964 (bearing a lion on the back), both bearing a portrait of The Queen on the front, ceased to be legal tender in June 1979. The £5 note first issued in 1978 ceased to be legal tender on 11 March 1988. The 10 shilling note was replaced by the 50p coin in October 1969, and ceased to be legal tender on 21 November 1970.

The D series of banknotes was introduced in 1970 and ceased to be legal tender from 1991 onwards. The predominant identifying feature of each note was the portrayal on the back of a prominent figure from British history:

£1	Feb. 1978–March 1988	Sir Isaac Newton
£5	Nov. 1971–Nov. 1991	The Duke of Wellington
£10	Feb. 1975–May 1994	Florence Nightingale
£20	July 1970–March 1993	William Shakespeare
£50	March 1981–Sept. 1996	Sir Christopher Wren

The £1 coin was introduced on 21 April 1983 to replace the £1 note.

The E series of notes was introduced in June 1990, replacing the D series. The historical figures portrayed in this series are:

£5	June 1990–	George Stephenson
£10	April 1992–	Charles Dickens
£20	June 1991–	Michael Faraday
£50	April 1994–	Sir John Houblon

NOTE CIRCULATION

Note circulation is highest at the two peak spending periods of the year, around Christmas and during the summer holiday period. The total value of notes in circulation at 20 December 1995 was £21,270 million, compared to £20,060 million at 21 December 1994.

The value of notes in circulation at end February 1995 and 1996 was:

	1995	1996
£1*	£57m	£56m
£5	£1,072m	£1,067m
£10	£5,348m	£5,688m
£20	£7,723m	£8,579m
£50	£2,852m	£3,104m
Other notes†	£1,004m	£1,154m
Total	£18,056m	£19,648m

* No £1 notes have been issued since 1984
† Includes higher value notes used internally in the Bank of England, e.g. as cover for the note issues of banks of issue in Scotland and Northern Ireland in excess of their permitted issue

OTHER BANKNOTES

SCOTLAND – Banknotes are issued by three Scottish banks. The Royal Bank of Scotland issues notes for £1, £5, £10, £20 and £100. The Bank of Scotland and the Clydesdale Bank issue notes for £5, £10, £20, £50 and £100. Scottish notes are not legal tender in Scotland but they are an authorized currency and enjoy there a status comparable to that of the Bank of England note.

NORTHERN IRELAND – Banknotes are issued by four banks in Northern Ireland. The Bank of Ireland, the Northern Bank and the Ulster Bank issue notes for £5,

£10, £20, £50 and £100. The First Trust Bank issues notes for £10, £20, £50 and £100. Northern Ireland notes are not legal tender in Northern Ireland but they circulate widely and enjoy a status comparable to that of Bank of England notes.

CHANNEL ISLANDS – The States of Guernsey issues its own currency notes and coinage. The notes are for £1, £5, £10, £20 and £50, and the coins are for 1p, 2p, 5p, 10p, 20p, 50p, £1, £2 and £5. The States of Jersey issues its own currency notes and coinage. The notes are for £1, £5, £10, £20 and £50, and the coins are for 1p, 2p, 5p, 10p, 20p, 50p and £1. There are plans to issue a smaller 50p coin and a new £2 coin in late 1997.

THE ISLE OF MAN – The Isle of Man Government issues notes for £1, £5, £10, £20 and £50. Although these notes are only legal tender in the Isle of Man, they are accepted at face value in branches of the clearing banks in the UK. The Isle of Man issues coins for 1p, 2p, 5p, 10p, 20p, 50p, £1, £2 and £5.

Although none of the series of notes specified above is legal tender in the UK, they are generally accepted by the banks irrespective of their place of issue. At one time the banks made a commission charge for handling Scottish and Irish notes but this was abolished some years ago.

Banking

Deposit-taking institutions may be broadly divided into two sectors: the monetary sector, which is predominantly banks and is supervised by the Bank of England; and those institutions outside the monetary sector, of which the most important are the building societies and the National Savings Bank.

The main institutions within the British banking system are the Bank of England (the central bank), the retail banks, the merchant banks, the overseas banks, and the discount houses.

The Banking Act 1987 established a single category of authorized institutions eligible to carry out banking business. Under the 1987 Act, the Bank of England exercises a regulatory role over the banking system; it also ensures the efficient functioning of payment and settlement systems and efficient services. In its role as the central bank, the Bank of England acts as banker to the Government and as a note-issuing authority. It is responsible for executing monetary policy and therefore sets the base rates.

BANK BASE RATES 1995–6

13 December 1995	6.50%
18 January 1996	6.25%
8 March 1996	6.00%
6 June 1996	5.75%

RETAIL BANKS

The major retail banks (sometimes referred to as clearing banks) are Abbey National, Bank of Scotland, Barclays, Lloyds/TSB, Midland, National Westminster and the Royal Bank of Scotland Group.

Retail banks offer a wide variety of financial services to companies and individuals, including current and deposit accounts, loan facilities, automated teller (cashpoint) machines, cheque guarantee cards, credit cards and debit cards.

The Banking Ombudsman scheme provides independent and impartial arbitration in disputes between a bank and its customer (*see also* page 627).

Banking hours differ throughout Great Britain. Many banks now open longer hours and Saturday mornings, and hours vary from branch to branch. Current core opening hours are:
ENGLAND AND WALES: Monday–Friday 9.30–4.30
SCOTLAND: Monday–Friday, 9.30–4.00
NORTHERN IRELAND: Monday–Friday 9.30–4.30
(Wednesdays 10–4.30); Northern Bank, 10–3.30, Thursdays 9.30–5

PAYMENT CLEARINGS

The Association for Payment Clearing Services (APACS) is an umbrella organization for payment clearings in the UK. It operates three clearing companies:
– BACS Ltd is the UK's automated clearing house for bulk clearing of electronic debits and credits (e.g. direct debits and salary credits)
– the Cheque and Credit Clearing Company Ltd operates bulk clearing systems for inter-bank cheques and paper credit items in England and Wales
– CHAPS Clearing Company Ltd provides same-day clearing for high-value electronic funds transfers throughout the UK
Membership of APACS and the clearing companies is open to any appropriately regulated financial institution providing payment services and meeting the relevant membership criteria. As at June 1996, APACS had 21 members, comprising the major banks and building societies.

ASSOCIATION FOR PAYMENT CLEARING SERVICES (APACS), Mercury House, Triton Court, 14 Finsbury Square, London EC2A 1BR. Tel: 0171-711 6200. *Head of Public Affairs*, R. Tyson-Davies
BACS LTD, De Havilland Road, Edgware, Middx HA8 5QA. *Chief Executive*, G. Younger
CHEQUE AND CREDIT CLEARING COMPANY LTD, Mercury House, Triton Court, 14 Finsbury Square, London EC2A 1BR
CHAPS CLEARING COMPANY LTD, Mercury House, Triton Court, 14 Finsbury Square, London EC2A 1BR

AUTHORIZED INSTITUTIONS

Banking in the UK is regulated by the Banking Act 1987 as amended by the European Community's Second Banking Co-ordination Directive, which came into effect on 1 January 1993.

The Directive permits banks incorporated in one EU member state to carry on certain banking activities in another member state without the need for authorization by that state. Consequently, the Bank of England no longer authorizes banks incorporated in other EU states with branches in the UK so that they may accept deposits in the UK; the authorization of their home state supervisor is sufficient provided that certain notification requirements are met. However, UK-incorporated subsidiaries of banks incorporated in other EU states which wish to accept

MAJOR RETAIL BANKS: FINANCIAL RESULTS 1995

Bank Group	P/L before taxation £m	P/L after taxation £m	Total assets £m	Number of UK branches
Abbey National	1,098	682	103,132	675
Bank of Scotland	545	335	44,099.1	420
Barclays	2,083	1,407	168,826	2,033
Lloyds/TSB	1,650	1,071	148,047	3,100
Midland	998	637	93,627	1,740
NatWest Group	1,753	1,240	168,272	2,700
Royal Bank of Scotland Group PLC	602	400	51,044	724

deposits in the UK continue to need authorization by the Bank of England.

As at end February 1996, a total of 539 institutions were authorized to carry out business in the UK, 375 institutions authorized under the Banking Act 1987 and 164 institutions recognized under the Second Banking Co-ordination Directive as European authorized institutions (EAIs):

UK-incorporated	220
Incorporated outside the UK	319
Of which:	
Incorporated outside the EEA	155
EAIs with UK branches entitled to accept deposits in UK	103
Other EAIs	61

The following lists show the institutions authorized or entitled to accept deposits in the UK and covered by the UK's deposit protection scheme, as at 30 August 1996.

AUTHORIZED BY THE BANK OF ENGLAND

UK-INCORPORATED
(Including partnerships formed under the law of any part of the UK)
*In administration

ABC International Bank PLC
AMC Bank Ltd
ANZ Grindlays Bank PLC
AY Bank Ltd
Abbey National PLC
Abbey National Treasury Services PLC
Adam & Company PLC
Afghan National Credit & Finance Ltd
Airdrie Savings Bank
Alexanders Discount PLC
Alliance Trust (Finance) Ltd
Allied Bank Philippines (UK) PLC
Allied Trust Bank Ltd
Alpha Bank London Ltd
Anglo-Romanian Bank Ltd
Henry Ansbacher & Co. Ltd
Arbuthnot Latham & Co. Ltd
Assemblies of God Property Trust
Associates Capital Corporation Ltd
Avco Trust PLC

Banamex Investment Bank PLC
Bank Leumi (UK) PLC
Bank of America International Ltd
Bank of Cyprus (London) Ltd
Bank of Montreal Europe Ltd
Bank of Scotland
Bank of Scotland Treasury Services PLC
Bank of Tokyo-Mitsubishi (UK) Ltd
Bank of Wales PLC
Bankers Trust International PLC
Bankgesellschaft Berlin (UK) PLC
Banque Nationale de Paris PLC
The Baptist Union Corporation Ltd
Barclays Bank PLC
Barclays Bank Trust Company Ltd
Barclays de Zoete Wedd Ltd
Baring Brothers Ltd
Belmont Bank Ltd
Beneficial Bank PLC
*Bishopscourt (BB & Co.) Ltd
British Arab Commercial Bank Ltd
British Bank of the Middle East
British Linen Bank Ltd

British Railways Savings Company Ltd
Brown, Shipley & Co. Ltd

CIBC Wood Gundy Bank PLC
CLF Municipal Bank PLC
Cafcash Ltd
Cater Allen Ltd
Central Hispano Bank (UK) Ltd
Chartered Trust PLC
Charterhouse Bank Ltd
Chase Investment Bank Ltd
Cheltenham and Gloucester PLC
Chemical Investment Bank Ltd
Citibank International PLC
Clive Discount Company Ltd
Close Brothers Ltd
Clydesdale Bank PLC
Consolidated Credits Bank Ltd
The Co-operative Bank PLC
Coutts & Co.
Crédit Agricole Lazard Financial Products Bank
Credit Suisse Financial Products
Cyprus Credit Bank (UK) Ltd

Daiwa Europe Bank PLC
Dalbeattie Finance Co. Ltd
Dao Heng Bank (London) PLC
Davenham Trust PLC
Direct Line Financial Services Ltd
Dorset, Somerset & Wilts Investment Society Ltd
Dryfield Trust PLC
Dunbar Bank PLC
Duncan Lawrie Ltd

Eccles Savings and Loans Ltd
Exeter Bank Ltd

FIBI Bank (UK) PLC
Fairmount Capital Management Ltd
Financial & General Bank PLC
James Finlay Bank Ltd
First National Bank PLC
First National Commercial Bank PLC
First Personal Bank PLC
First Trust Bank (AIB Group Northern Ireland PLC)
Robert Fleming & Co. Ltd
Ford Credit Europe PLC
Forward Trust Ltd
Forward Trust Personal Finance Ltd
Frizzell Bank Ltd

Gartmore Money Management Ltd
Gerrard & National Ltd
Girobank PLC
Goldman Sachs International Bank
Granville Bank Ltd
Gresham Trust PLC
Guinness Mahon & Co. Ltd

HFC Bank PLC
HSBC Equator Bank PLC
HSBC Investment Bank PLC
Habibsons Bank Ltd
Hambros Bank Ltd
Hampshire Trust PLC
The Hardware Federation Finance Co. Ltd
Harrods Bank Ltd
Harton Securities Ltd
Havana International Bank Ltd
The Heritable and General Investment Bank Ltd
Hill Samuel Bank Ltd
C. Hoare & Co.

Julian Hodge Bank Ltd
Humberclyde Finance Group Ltd

3i PLC
3i Group PLC
IBJ International PLC
Iran Overseas Investment Bank Ltd
Italian International Bank PLC

Jordan International Bank PLC
Leopold Joseph & Sons Ltd

KDB Bank (UK) Ltd
KEXIM Bank (UK) Ltd
King & Shaxson Ltd
Kleinwort Benson Ltd
Kleinwort Benson Investment Management Ltd
Korea Long Term Credit Bank International Ltd

LTCB International Ltd
Lazard Brothers & Co. Ltd
Lloyds Bank PLC
Lloyds Bank (BLSA) Ltd
Lloyds Bowmaker Ltd
Lloyds Private Banking Ltd
Lombard & Ulster Ltd
Lombard Bank Ltd
Lombard North Central PLC
London Scottish Bank PLC
London Trust Bank PLC

MBNA International Bank Ltd
W. M. Mann & Co. (Investments) Ltd
Marks and Spencer Financial Services Ltd
Matheson Bank Ltd
Matlock Bank Ltd
Meghraj Bank Ltd
Mellon Europe Ltd
Merrill Lynch International Bank Ltd
Methodist Chapel Aid Association Ltd
Midland Bank PLC
Midland Bank Trust Company Ltd
Minories Finance Ltd
Minster Trust Ltd
Samuel Montagu & Co. Ltd
Morgan Grenfell & Co. Ltd
Moscow Narodny Bank Ltd
Mutual Trust and Savings Ltd

NIIB Group Ltd
NWS Bank PLC
National Bank of Egypt International Ltd
National Bank of Kuwait (International) PLC
National Mortgage Bank PLC
National Westminster Bank PLC
NationsBank Europe Ltd
Nikko Bank (UK) PLC
Noble Grossart Ltd
Nomura Bank International PLC
Northern Bank Ltd
Northern Bank Executor & Trustee Company Ltd

Paine Webber International Bank Ltd
Pointon York Ltd
Private Bank and Trust Company Ltd

R. Raphael & Sons PLC
Rathbone Bros & Co. Ltd
Rea Brothers Ltd
Reliance Bank Ltd
Riggs AP Bank Ltd
Riyad Bank Europe Ltd
N. M. Rothschild & Sons Ltd
Royal Bank of Canada Europe Ltd
Royal Bank of Scotland PLC

RoyScot Trust PLC
Ruffler Bank PLC

SBI European Bank PLC
Sabanci Bank PLC
Sanwa International PLC
Saudi American Bank (UK) Ltd
Saudi International Bank (Al-Bank Al-Saudi Al-Alami Ltd)
Schroder Leasing Ltd
J. Henry Schroder & Co. Ltd
Scotiabank (UK) Ltd
Scottish Amicable Money Managers Ltd
Scottish Widows Bank PLC
Seccombe Marshall & Campion PLC
Secure Trust Bank PLC
Singer & Friedlander Ltd
Smith & Williamson Securities
Southsea Mortgage & Investment Co. Ltd
Standard Bank London Ltd
Standard Chartered Bank
Sun Banking Corporation Ltd

TSB Bank PLC
TSB Bank Scotland PLC
Tokai Bank Europe PLC
Toronto Dominion Bank Europe Ltd
Turkish Bank (UK) Ltd

UCB Bank PLC
Ulster Bank Ltd
Union Discount Company Ltd
United Bank of Kuwait PLC
United Dominions Trust Ltd
United Trust Bank Ltd
Unity Trust Bank PLC

Wagon Finance Ltd
S. G. Warburg & Co. Ltd
Weatherbys & Co. Ltd
Wesleyan Savings Bank Ltd
Western Trust & Savings Ltd
West Merchant Bank Ltd
Whiteaway Laidlaw Bank Ltd
Wintrust Securities Ltd
Woodchester Credit Lyonnais PLC

Yamaichi Bank (UK) PLC
Yorkshire Bank PLC

INCORPORATED OUTSIDE THE EUROPEAN ECONOMIC AREA
(Including partnerships or other unincorporated associations formed under the law of any member state of the European Union other than the UK)

†Provisional liquidator appointed

ABSA Bank Ltd
Allied Bank of Pakistan Ltd
American Express Bank Ltd
Arab African International Bank
Arab Bank PLC
Arab Banking Corporation BSC
Arab National Bank
Asahi Bank Ltd
Ashikaga Bank Ltd
Australia & New Zealand Banking Group Ltd

BSI – Banca della Svizzera Italiana
Banca Serfin SA
Banco de la Nación Argentina
Banco do Brasil SA
Banco do Estado de São Paulo SA
Banco Inverlat SA

Banco Mercantil de São Paulo SA
Banco Nacional de Mexico SA
Banco Real SA
Bancomer SA
Bangkok Bank Public Company Ltd
Bank Julius Baer & Co. Ltd
Bank Bumiputra Malaysia Berhad
PT Bank Ekspor Impor Indonesia (Persero)
Bank Handlowy w Warszawie SA
Bank Hapoalim BM
Bank Mellat
Bank Melli Iran
PT Bank Negara Indonesia (Persero)
Bank of America NT & SA
Bank of Baroda
The Bank of N. T. Butterfield & Son Ltd
Bank of Ceylon
Bank of China
Bank of East Asia Ltd
Bank of Fukuoka Ltd
Bank of India
Bank of Montreal
Bank of New York
Bank of Nova Scotia
Bank of Tokyo Ltd
Bank of Tokyo-Mitsubishi Ltd
Bank of Yokohama Ltd
Bank Saderat Iran
Bank Sepah-Iran
Bank Tejarat
Bank von Ernst & Co. Ltd
Bankers Trust Company
Beirut Riyad Bank SAL

Canadian Imperial Bank of Commerce
Canara Bank
Capital One Bank
Chang Hwa Commercial Bank Ltd
Chase Manhattan Bank NA
Chemical Bank
Chiba Bank Ltd
Cho Hung Bank
Chuo Trust & Banking Co. Ltd
Citibank NA
Commercial Bank of Korea Ltd
Commonwealth Bank of Australia
CoreStates Bank NA
Crédit Suisse
Cyprus Popular Bank Ltd

Dai-Ichi Kangyo Bank Ltd
Daiwa Bank Ltd
Development Bank of Singapore Ltd
Discount Bank and Trust Company

Emirates Bank International PJSC

First Bank of Nigeria PLC
First Commercial Bank
First National Bank of Boston
First National Bank of Chicago
First Union National Bank
Fleet National Bank
Fuji Bank Ltd

Ghana Commercial Bank
Gulf International Bank BSC

Habib Bank AG Zurich
Habib Bank Ltd
Hanil Bank
Harris Trust and Savings Bank
Hiroshima Bank Ltd
Hokkaido Takushoku Bank Ltd

Hokuriku Bank Ltd
Hongkong and Shanghai Banking Corporation Ltd
The Industrial Bank of Japan Ltd
Joyo Bank Ltd
KorAm Bank
Korea Exchange Bank
Korea First Bank
The Long-Term Credit Bank of Japan Ltd
Macquarie Bank Ltd
Malayan Banking Berhad
Mashreq Bank PSC
Mellon Bank NA
Mitsubishi Trust and Banking Corporation
Mitsui Trust & Banking Co. Ltd
Morgan Guaranty Trust Company of New York
NBD Bank
Nacional Financiera SNC
National Australia Bank Ltd
National Bank of Abu Dhabi
National Bank of Canada
The National Bank of Dubai Public Joint Stock Company
National Bank of Pakistan
NationsBank NA
NationsBank of Texas NA
Nedcor Bank Ltd
Nippon Credit Bank Ltd
Norinchukin Bank
Northern Trust Company
Oversea-Chinese Banking Corporation Ltd
Overseas Trust Bank Ltd
Overseas Union Bank Ltd
People's Bank
Philippine National Bank
Qatar National Bank SAQ
†Rafidain Bank
Republic National Bank of New York
Riggs Bank NA
Riyad Bank
Royal Bank of Canada
Sakura Bank Ltd
Sanwa Bank Ltd
Saudi American Bank
Saudi British Bank
Seoulbank
Shanghai Commercial Bank Ltd
Shinhan Bank
Siam Commercial Bank Public Company Ltd
Sonali Bank
State Bank of India
State Street Bank and Trust Company
Sumitomo Bank Ltd
Sumitomo Trust & Banking Co. Ltd
Swiss Bank Corporation
Syndicate Bank
TC Ziraat Bankasi
Thai Farmers Bank Public Company Ltd
Tokai Bank Ltd
Toronto-Dominion Bank
Toyo Trust & Banking Company Ltd
Türkiye İş Bankası AŞ
Uco Bank
Union Bancaire Privée CBI-TDB
Union Bank of Nigeria PLC
Union Bank of Switzerland

United Bank Ltd
United Mizrahi Bank Ltd
United Overseas Bank Ltd

Westpac Banking Corporation

Yasuda Trust & Banking Co. Ltd

Zambia National Commercial Bank Ltd
Zivnostenská Banka AS

EUROPEAN AUTHORIZED INSTITUTIONS
ENTITLED TO ESTABLISH UK BRANCHES

The following are entitled to establish branches in the UK
for the purpose of accepting deposits in the UK. The
country of the home state supervisory authority is in
parenthesis.

ABN AMRO Bank NV (Netherlands)
AIB Capital Markets PLC (Republic of Ireland)
AIB Finance Ltd (Republic of Ireland)
Allied Irish Banks PLC (Republic of Ireland)
Alpha Credit Bank AE (Greece)
Anglo Irish Bank Corporation PLC (Republic of Ireland)

BfG Bank AG (Germany)
Banca Cassa di Risparmio di Torino SpA (Italy)
Banca Commerciale Italiana (Italy)
Banca di Roma SpA (Italy)
Banca March SA (Spain)
Banca Monte dei Paschi di Siena SpA (Italy)
Banca Nazionale dell'Agricoltura SpA (Italy)
Banca Nazionale del Lavoro SpA (Italy)
Banca Popolare di Milano (Italy)
Banca Popolare di Novara (Italy)
Banco Ambrosiano Veneto SpA (Italy)
Banco Bilbao-Vizcaya (Spain)
Banco Central Hispanoamericano SA (Spain)
Banco de Sabadell (Spain)
Banco di Napoli SpA (Italy)
Banco di Sicilia SpA (Italy)
Banco Español de Crédito SA (Spain)
Banco Espirito Santo e Comercial de Lisboa (Portugal)
Banco Exterior de España SA (Spain)
Banco Nacional Ultramarino SA (Portugal)
Banco Português do Atlântico (Portugal)
Banco Santander (Spain)
Banco Santander de Negocios SA (Spain)
Banco Totta & Açores SA (Portugal)
Bank Austria AG (Austria)
Bank Brussels Lambert (Belgium)
Bankgesellschaft Berlin AG (Germany)
The Bank of Ireland (Republic of Ireland)
Banque Arabe et Internationale d'Investissement (France)
Banque Banorabe (France)
Banque Française de l'Orient (France)
Banque Française du Commerce Extérieur (France)
Banque Indosuez (France)
Banque Internationale à Luxembourg SA (Luxembourg)
Banque Nationale de Paris (France)
Banque Paribas (France)
Bayerische Hypotheken-und Wechsel-Bank AG
    (Germany)
Bayerische Landesbank Girozentrale (Germany)
Bayerische Vereinsbank AG (Germany)
Belgolaise SA (Belgium)
Berliner Bank AG (Germany)
Berliner Handels-und Frankfurter Bank (Germany)
Byblos Bank Belgium SA (Belgium)

CARIPLO (Cassa di Risparmio delle Provincie Lombarde
    SpA) (Italy)

Caisse Nationale de Crédit Agricole (France)
Cariverona Banca SpA (Italy)
Christiania Bank og Kreditkasse (Norway)
Commerzbank AG (Germany)
Compagnie Financière de CIC et de l'Union Européenne
    (France)
Confederacion Española de Cajas de Ahorros (Spain)
Creditanstalt-Bankverein (Austria)
Crédit Commercial de France (France)
Crédit du Nord (France)
Crédit Lyonnais (France)
Credito Italiano (Italy)

De Nationale Investeringsbank NV (Netherlands)
Den Danske Bank Aktieselskab (Denmark)
Den norske Bank ASA (Norway)
Deutsche Bank AG (Germany)
Deutsche Genossenschaftsbank (Germany)
Dresdner Bank AG (Germany)

Equity Bank Ltd (Republic of Ireland)
Ergobank SA (Greece)

First National Building Society (Republic of Ireland)

Generale Bank (Belgium)
Generale Bank Nederland NV (Netherlands)
GiroCredit Bank Aktiengesellschaft der Sparkassen
    (Austria)

Hamburgische Landesbank Girozentrale (Germany)

ICC Bank PLC (Repulic of Ireland)
ICS Building Society (Republic of Ireland)
ING Bank NV (Netherlands)
Indosuez Carr Futures SNC (France)
Industrial Bank of Korea Europe SA (Luxembourg)
Ionian and Popular Bank of Greece SA (Greece)
Irish Nationwide Building Society (Republic of Ireland)
Irish Permanent PLC (Republic of Ireland)
Istituto Bancario San Paolo di Torino SpA (Italy)

Jyske Bank (Denmark)

Kas-Associatie NV (Netherlands)
Kredietbank NV (Belgium)

Landesbank Berlin Girozentrale (Germany)
Landesbank Hessen-Thüringen Girozentrale (Germany)

MeesPierson NV (Netherlands)
Merita Bank Ltd (Finland)

National Bank of Greece SA (Greece)
Norddeutsche Landesbank Girozentrale (Germany)

Postipankki Ltd (Finland)

Rabobank (Coöperatieve Centrale Raiffeisen-
    Boerenleenbank BA) (Netherlands)
Raiffeisen Zentralbank Osterreich AG (Austria)

Skandinaviska Enskilda Banken AB (publ) (Sweden)
Société Générale (France)
Südwestdeutsche Landesbank Girozentrale (Germany)
Svenska Handelsbanken AB (publ) (Sweden)
SwedBank (Sparbanken Sverige AB (publ)) (Sweden)

Triodosbank NV (Netherlands)

Ulster Bank Markets Ltd (Republic of Ireland)
Unibank AS (Denmark)

Westdeutsche Landesbank Girozentrale (Germany)

The National Debt

Net central government borrowing each year represents an addition to the National Debt. At the end of March 1995 the National Debt amounted to some £349,200 million of which about £18,500 million was in currencies other than sterling. Of the £330,700 million sterling debt, £235,000 million consisted of gilt-edged stock; of this, 31 per cent had a maturity of up to five years, 43 per cent a maturity of over five years and up to 15 years, and 26 per cent a maturity of over 15 years or undated. The remaining sterling debt was made up mainly of national savings (£48,900 million), certificates of tax deposits, Treasury bills, and Ways and Means advances (very short-term internal government borrowing).

Sizeable trust funds have been established over the past 50 years for the purpose of reducing the National Debt. The National Fund was established in 1927 with an original gift of £499,878. At 31 March 1996 it was valued at £115,238,395; it is administered by Baring Trust Co. Ltd. The Elsie Mackay Fund was established in 1929 with an original gift of £527,809 to run for 45–50 years. It was wound up in 1979, when it was valued at £4,902,864. The John Buchanan Fund was established in 1932 with gifts totalling £36,702 to run for 50 years. It was wound up in 1982, when it was valued at £204,138.

Slang Terms for Money
(Reproduced from *Whitaker's Almanack* 1891)

In addition to the ordinary terms there are others which, although puzzling to a foreigner, are tolerably well understood in this country. In Scotland, a man who flies 'kites' may not be worth a 'bodle', and in England not worth a 'mag' – coins which no ever saw. Such a man will toss you for a 'bob'. He, of course, would be shunned by the lady who lost a 'pony' on last year's Oaks, and by her husband who lost a 'monkey' on the Derby at Epsom a day or two previously. A gentleman who is worth a 'plum' (£100,000) need never be short of 'tin'; while the outcast who begs a few 'coppers' in order to procure a bed generally has no 'blunt'. The following words are commonly in use:

A Joey = 4d.
A Tanner = 6d.
A Bob = 1s.
Half a Bull = 2s. 6d.
A Bull = 5s.
A Quid = £1
A Pony = £25
A Monkey = £500
A Kite = An accommodation Bill
Browns = Copper or bronze
Tin = Money generally
Blunt = Silver, or money in general

Mutual Societies

FRIENDLY SOCIETIES IN BRITAIN

Friendly societies are voluntary mutual organizations, the main purposes of which are the provision of relief or maintenance during sickness, unemployment or retirement, and the provision of life assurance. Many of the older traditional societies complement their business activities by social activity and a general care for individual members in ways normally outside the scope of a purely commercial organization. There are three main categories of friendly societies: societies with separately registered branches, commonly called orders; centralized societies, which conduct business directly with members (having no separately registered branches); and collecting societies. Collecting societies conduct industrial assurance business and are subject to the requirements of the Industrial Assurance Acts in addition to the Friendly Societies Acts. Industrial assurance is life assurance for which the premiums are payable at intervals of less than two months and are received by means of collectors who make house-to-house visits for the purpose.

The Friendly Societies Act 1974 allows three other main classes of society to be registered: benevolent societies, working men's clubs and specially authorized societies. Benevolent societies are established for any charitable or benevolent purpose, to provide the same type of benefits as would be permissible for a friendly society, but in contrast the benefits must be for persons who are not members instead of, or in addition to, members. Working men's clubs provide social and recreational facilities for members. Specially authorized societies are registered for any purpose authorized by the Treasury as a purpose to which some or all of the provisions of the 1974 Act ought to be extended. Examples are societies for the promotion of science, literature and the fine arts, or to enable members to pursue an interest in sports and games.

The most recent legislation, the Friendly Societies Act 1992, created a new legislative framework for friendly societies, enabling them to provide a wider range of services to their members and allowing them to compete on more equal terms with other financial institutions. At the same time it provided for more flexible prudential supervision to safeguard members of societies.

The Act enables friendly societies to incorporate and establish subsidiaries to provide various financial and other services to their members and the public. By 31 March 1995, 23 societies had incorporated and ten of these had set up one or more subsidiaries. The activities which subsidiaries are able to conduct include those to establish and manage unit trust schemes and personal equity plans; to arrange for the provision of credit, whether as agents or providers; to carry on long-term or general insurance business; to provide insurance intermediary services; to provide fund management services for trustees of pension funds; to administer estates and execute trusts of wills; and to establish and manage sheltered housing, residential homes for the elderly, hospitals and nursing homes.

The Act established a new framework to oversee friendly societies, including a Friendly Societies Commission, whose principal functions are to regulate the activities of friendly societies, promote their financial stability and protect members' funds. All friendly societies carrying on insurance or non-insurance business require authorization by the Commission, which has a broad range of prudential powers. Friendly societies were also to be brought within the scope of the Policyholders Protection Act 1975, the statutory investor protection scheme covering insurance policyholders.

In April 1995 the Treasury, with the assistance of the Commission, issued a consultation document as required by the Deregulation and Contracting Out Act 1994. This sets out proposals to amend the Friendly Societies Act 1992 in ways which would ease the administrative burden for friendly societies without removing any necessary protection for their members. Following the end of the consultation period the Deregulation (Friendly Societies Act 1992) Order 1996 was made on 29 April 1996, to come into force on 1 August 1996. A working party established to explore other areas where administrative burdens on societies might be eliminated or reduced has made further deregulation proposals to be considered by the Friendly Societies Commission.

As part of the Deregulation Initiative the Government agreed to review the Industrial Assurance Acts and the Treasury published a consultation document seeking views on proposals either to repeal or amend the Acts. The Industrial Assurance Act 1923 was intended to curb abuses which were widespread at the time, specifically in relation to overselling; obtaining signatures to proposal forms without regard to full disclosure of medical history (which led to insurers refusing to pay on subsequent death on the ground of non-disclosure of material fact); various forms of misrepresentation on the canvass of new policies; and restrictive practices by the collectors. Comments received from interested bodies will be translated into practical measures to reduce regulation governing this type of business.

The principal statistics at the end of 1994 are given in the table below.

	No. of societies	No. of members 000s	Benefits paid £000s	Total funds £000s
Orders and branches	1,160*	299	8,775	186,358
Collecting societies	21	6,423†	278,934	4,626,720
Other centralized societies	316	2,718	454,960	3,845,844
Benevolent societies	73	320	9,323	39,262
Working men's clubs	2,303	2,001	n/a	227,960
Specially authorized societies				
Loans	5	13	n/a	151
Others	129	87	806	22,375

* 18 orders, 1,142 branches
† Includes 4.7 million policies rather than members in the case of eight collecting societies

INDUSTRIAL AND PROVIDENT SOCIETIES IN BRITAIN

The familiar 'Co-op' societies are amongst the wide variety which are registered under the Industrial and Provident Societies Act 1965. This consolidating Act, which is administered by the Chief Registrar of Friendly Societies, provides for the registration of societies and lays down the broad framework within which they must operate. Internal relations of societies are governed by their registered rules.

Registration under the Act confers upon a society corporate status by its registered name with perpetual succession and a common seal, and limited liability. A society qualifies for registration if it is carrying on an industry, business or trade, and it satisfies the Registrar either (a) that it is a bona fide co-operative society, or (b) that in view of the fact that its business is being, or is intended to be, conducted for the benefit of the community, there are special reasons why it should be registered under the Act rather than as a company under the Companies Act.

The Credit Unions Act 1979 added a new class of society registerable under the 1965 Act. It also made provision for the supervision of these savings and loan bodies. Unlike other classes, the role of the Registry is solely that of a registration authority, it is for credit unions the prudential supervisor, seeking to encourage the prudent safekeeping of investors' money.

During 1994 the number of registered societies of all classes decreased by 266 to 10,738 but the number of credit unions increased by 48 to 475. Assets of industrial and provident societies totalled £35,158 million, more than half of which is held in the 4,090 housing societies. The principal statistics at the end of 1994 are given in the table below.

	No. of socie-ties	No. of mem-bers 000s	Funds of members £000s	Total assets £000s
Retail	133	6,820	1,327,904	2,710,703
Wholesale and productive	159	48	609,604	1,362,734
Agricultural	1,012	305	217,416	727,282
Fishing	87	7	7,261	18,940
Clubs	3,703	2,536	323,495	537,519
General service	1,079	303	764,384	10,952,420
Housing	4,090	189	8,096,265	18,787,936
Credit unions	475	154	57,990	60,670
TOTAL	10,738	10,362	11,404,319	35,158,204

BUILDING SOCIETIES IN THE UK

The Building Societies Act 1986 gave building societies a completely new legal framework, the first since the initial comprehensive building society legislation in 1874. It made provision for a Building Societies Commission to promote the protection of shareholders and depositors, the financial stability of societies, and to administer the system of regulation of building societies provided under the Act. The chairman of the Commission is also Chief Registrar of Friendly Societies (see Index). Much of the Act is concerned with the powers of control of the Commission and provision in relation to the management of societies, accounts, audit and so on. But the greatest impact flowed from the new powers which societies could adopt, leading to an increased range of services which they might provide. There were also some significant changes in relation to members' rights.

In 1994 the Government announced a review of the Act and the outcome of the first stage of the review included measures designed to give societies opportunities to develop and introduce extra competition into matters where they had not previously been able to operate directly, e.g. owning an insurance company offering buildings contents and mortgage protection insurance policies. Following extensive consultations, the Government announced the outcome of the second stage of the review on 24 February 1995, outlining its intention to replace the current prescriptive legislative framework governing building societies' powers by a more permissive regime. In future, with a few exceptions, a society will be able to pursue any activities set out in its memorandum, subject to a statutory principal purpose requirement and to overall limits on the composition of assets and liabilities. Following the announcement, Commission and Treasury staff developed a new policy framework to carry forward this proposal, in consultation with the Building Societies Association.

In March 1996 the Government published a draft Building Societies Bill for consultation. The bill will introduce a widened definition of the principal purpose of a building society and a generally permissive regime allowing societies to pursue any of the activities set out in their memoranda. The new principal purpose, which defines what a building society is, will no longer be limited to lending for owner-occupation, but will allow societies to finance rented housing as well as, or even instead of, further involvement in the owner-occupied sector.

Outside the area of the principal purpose and the 'nature limits' which support it, societies will legally be free to develop their business according to normal commercial criteria, provided the activities they wish to undertake are covered by the society's memorandum and subject to the board's responsibilities under the 1986 Act to conduct the business prudently. As an exception from the generally permissive regime and in view of the importance to their members of their risk-averse reputation, societies will continue to be prohibited from engaging in speculative trading in securities, currencies or commodities.

To balance this liberalization of the statutory framework, the criteria of prudent management are to be enhanced. In addition, the Building Societies Commission will be required to publish a statement of principles explaining how it interprets the criteria of prudent management and how it would expect to exercise its statutory powers.

In parallel with these deregulatory measures, the Government announced a range of proposals to enhance the accountability of societies' boards to their members, in particular through improved information about members' rights and by making the procedures for electing directors more transparent. Some of the accountability measures have been included in the proposed bill; others will be put into effect voluntarily by societies.

During 1995 the number of authorized societies reduced to 80 as a result of the merger of the Halifax and the Leeds Permanent and of the take-over of the Cheltenham and Gloucester by Lloyds Bank, both of which took effect on 1 August 1995. During the first quarter of 1996 the City and Metropolitan and the Stroud and Swindon approved a merger and this took effect on 19 April. The take-over of the National and Provincial by Abbey National, to take effect on 5 August, and a further merger, between the Cumberland and West Cumbria, to take effect at the end of

September, will leave the number of authorized societies at 77.

In addition to National and Provincial, there are at present five other societies (Halifax, Woolwich, Alliance and Leicester, Northern Rock, and Bristol and West) which have announced plans to demutualize, either by conversion or take-over, which are likely to take effect (if approved by members) over the next two years. If all these societies carry through their plans, the total assets of the building society sector would, on present figures, be reduced by around 60 per cent. The remaining sector of some 70 societies would still account for a substantial minority of both the savings and mortgage markets, with group assets of £120 billion, 17 million investors and 2.75 million borrowers.

OMBUDSMAN SCHEME

Societies must belong to an ombudsman scheme for the investigation of complaints. Matters to be covered by the scheme include operation of share and deposit accounts, loans (but not the making of new loans), money transmission services, foreign exchange services, agency payments and receipts, and the provision of credit. Grounds for complaint include breach of the Act or contract, unfair treatment or maladministration, and where the complainant has suffered pecuniary loss or expense or inconvenience. A society must agree to be bound by decisions of the adjudicator unless it agrees to give notice to its members and the public of its reasons for not doing so. For address of the Building Societies Ombudsman scheme, see page 627.

BUILDING SOCIETIES 1994–5

	1994	1995
No. of societies – total	96	94
– authorized	82	80
No. of shareholders (000s)	38,150	38,998
No. of depositors (000s)	5,509	6,307
No. of borrowers (000s)	7,370	7,178
Share balances (£m)	201,812	200,853
Deposit balances (£m)	71,900	69,220
Mortgage balances (£m)	236,658	233,358
Total assets (£m)	301,011	299,921
Advances during year		
No. (000s)	1,093	1,047
Amount (£m)	36,792	39,200

MORTGAGE ARREARS AND REPOSSESSIONS

The economic recession resulted in a sharp rise in mortgage arrears and repossessions, with more than 75,000 properties repossessed in 1991. That total fell by 7,000 in 1992 as a result of a greater willingness by societies to enter into arrangements with borrowers. The number continued to decline in the following two years. In 1994 repossessions fell to less than 50,000 for the first time since 1990 but remained at much the same level in 1995. Details of loans outstanding and properties repossessed for recent years are shown below.

	1988	1989	1990	1991	1992	1993	1994	1995
No. of loans at end year (000s)	8,564	9,125	9,415	9,815	9,922	10,137	10,410	10,521
Properties repossessed in year								
Number	18,510	15,810	43,890	75,540	68,540	58,540	49,190	49,410
%	0.22	0.17	0.47	0.77	0.70	0.58	0.47	0.47

INTEREST RATES: MORTGAGE AND SHARE 1991–6

The interest rates prevailing on mortgage lending and share investment vary from society to society and in relation to the type or amount of loan or investment.

The interval between the payments or compounding of interest is crucial in determining the competitiveness of particular societies' accounts. In order to make a true comparison of interest rates, the annual percentage rate or APR, which should appear in all advertisements and leaflets, must be used.

	1991	1992	1993	1994	1995	1996 1st quarter
Average bank base rate	11.70	9.56	6.01	5.46	6.70	6.23
Building societies average mortgage rate	12.72	10.65	8.09	7.68	7.84	7.13
Building societies average share rate	10.88	8.45	5.78	5.36	5.62	4.79

SOCIETIES WITH TOTAL ASSETS EXCEEDING £1 MILLION AT END OF FINANCIAL YEAR 1995

Name of Society* and head office address	Share investors	Total assets £'000
Alliance and Leicester, 49 Park Lane, London WIY 4EQ	3,260,435	22,846,100
Barnsley, Regent Street, Barnsley, South Yorks S70 2EH	35,795	187,120
Bath Investment, 20 Charles Street, Bath BAI IHY	14,500	55,864
Beverley, 57 Market Place, Beverley, N. Humberside HUI7 8AA	6,693	42,082
Birmingham Midshires, PO Box 81, Pendeford Business Park, Wobaston Road, Wolverhampton, WV9 5HZ	748,415	6,724,700
Bradford and Bingley, Crossflatts, Bingley, West Yorks BD16 2UA	1,742,425	15,658,402
Bristol and West, Broad Quay, Bristol BS99 7AX	1,194,707	8,589,000
Britannia, Britannia House, Cheadle Road, Leek, Staffs ST13 5RG	1,218,720	14,916,000
Buckinghamshire, High Street, Chalfont St Giles, Bucks HP8 4QB	8,200	67,481
Cambridge, 32 St Andrew's Street, Cambridge CB2 3AR	47,000	367,892
Catholic, 7 Strutton Ground, London SWIP 2HY	3,703	27,312
Century, 21 Albany Street, Edinburgh EHI 3QW	2,047	12,376
Chelsea, Thirlestaine Hall, Thirlestaine Road, Cheltenham, Glos GL53 7AL	176,124	2,606,205
Chesham, 12 Market Square, Chesham, Bucks HP5 IER	16,621	104,462
Cheshire, Castle Street, Macclesfield, Cheshire SKII 6AH	232,098	1,509,056
Chorley and District, Key House, Foxhole Road, Chorley, Lancs PR7 INZ	10,222	67,330
City and Metropolitan, 219 High Street, Bromley, Kent BRI IPR	11,763	102,169
Clay Cross, Eyre Street, Clay Cross, Chesterfield S45 9NS	3,475	16,320
Coventry, PO Box 9, High Street, Coventry CVI 5QN	531,990	3,379,072
Cumberland, Cumberland House, Castle Street, Carlisle CA3 8RX	154,336	581,351
Darlington, Sentinel House, Lingfield Way, Darlington, Co. Durham DLI 4PR	46,389	300,582
Derbyshire, Duffield Hall, Duffield, Derby DE56 IAG	296,689	1,844,106
Dudley, Dudley House, Stone Street, Dudley DYI INP	21,684	85,535
Dunfermline, Caledonia House, Carnegie Avenue, Dunfermline, Fife KYII 5PJ	160,313	1,005,984
Earl Shilton, 22 The Hollow, Earl Shilton, Leicester LE9 7NB	11,203	57,967
Ecology, 18 Station Road, Cross Hills, Keighley, West Yorks BD20 7EH	4,255	18,362
Furness, 51–55 Duke Street, Barrow-in-Furness LAI4 IRT	61,149	351,561
Gainsborough, 9 Lord Street, Gainsborough, Lincs DN2I 2DD	6,443	30,261
Greenwich, 279–283 Greenwich High Road, London SEIO 8NL	22,429	174,790
Halifax, Trinity Road, Halifax, West Yorks HXI 2RG	11,600,000	98,654,500
Hanley Economic, Granville House, Festival Park, Hanley, Stoke-on-Trent, Staffs STI 5TB	27,546	174,951
Harpenden, 14 Station Road, Harpenden, Herts AL5 4SE	10,190	48,290
Hinckley and Rugby, Upper Bond Street, Hinckley, Leics LEIO IDG	48,042	301,098
Holmesdale, 43 Church Street, Reigate, Surrey RH2 OAE	6,572	68,708
Ilkeston Permanent, 24–26 South Street, Ilkeston, Derby DE7 5HQ	3,753	16,341
Ipswich, 44 Upper Brook Street, Ipswich IP4 IDP	35,405	190,580
Kent Reliance, Reliance House, Manor Road, Chatham, Kent ME4 6AF	42,705	253,674
Lambeth, 118–120 Westminster Bridge Road, London SEI 7XE	44,127	580,417
Leeds and Holbeck, 105 Albion Street, Leeds LSI 5AS	309,402	2,612,524
Leek United, 50 St Edward Street, Leek, Staffs ST13 5DH	53,844	356,110
Londonderry Provident, 31A Carlisle Road, Londonderry BT48 6JJ	1,087	8,347
Loughborough, 6 High Street, Loughborough, Leics LEII 2QB	14,152	108,572
Manchester, 18–20 Bridge Street, Manchester M3 3BU	12,534	111,325
Mansfield, Regent House, Regent Street, Mansfield, Notts NGI8 ISS	20,227	115,143
Market Harborough, Welland House, The Square, Market Harborough, Leics LEI6 7PD	35,845	224,486
Marsden, 6–20 Russell Street, Nelson, Lancs. BB9 7NJ	61,952	262,809
Melton Mowbray, 39 Nottingham Street, Melton Mowbray, Leics LEI3 INR	32,155	201,489
Mercantile, Mercantile House, The Silverlink Business Park, Wallsend, Tyne and Wear NE28 9NY	24,935	134,339
Monmouthshire, John Frost Square, Newport, Gwent NP9 IPX	29,722	190,629
National and Provincial, Provincial House, Bradford BDI INL	2,338,336	14,133,000
National Counties, National Counties House, Church Street, Epsom, Surrey KTI7 4NL	15,726	406,961
Nationwide, Nationwide House, Pipers Way, Swindon SN38 IQQ	6,191,252	37,617,130
Newbury, 17–20 Bartholomew Street, Newbury, Berks RGI4 5LY	31,740	239,096
Newcastle, Portland House, New Bridge Street, Newcastle upon Tyne NEI 8AL	170,522	1,405,511
Northern Rock, Northern Rock House, Gosforth, Newcastle upon Tyne NE3 4PL	1,113,670	11,559,072
Norwich and Peterborough, Peterborough Business Park, Lynchwood, Peterborough PE2 6WZ	196,978	1,561,239
Nottingham, 5–13 Upper Parliament Street, Nottingham NGI 2BX	143,535	958,296
Nottingham Imperial, Imperial House, 72 Bridgford Road, West Bridgford, Nottingham NG2 6AP	7,201	43,608
Penrith, 7 King Street, Penrith, Cumbria CAII 7AR	6,076	49,371
Portman, Portman House, Richmond Hill, Bournemouth, Dorset BH2 6EP	616,553	3,512,939
Principality, PO Box 89, Principality Buildings, Queen Street, Cardiff CFI IUA	237,563	1,413,199

Name of Society* and head office address	Share investors	Total assets £'000
Progressive, 33–37 Wellington Place, Belfast BT1 6HH	51,956	376,851
Saffron Walden, Herts and Essex, 1A Market Street, Saffron Walden, Essex CB10 1HX	45,249	247,834
Scarborough, Prospect House, 442/444 Scalby Road, Scarborough, North Yorks YO12 6EQ	103,837	503,743
Scottish, 23 Manor Place, Edinburgh EH3 7XE	19,522	113,542
Shepshed, Bull Ring, Shepshed, Loughborough, Leics LE12 9QD	7,022	35,299
Skipton, The Bailey, Skipton, North Yorks BD23 1DN	261,450	3,036,548
Stafford Railway, 4 Market Square, Stafford ST16 2JH	9,048	51,159
Staffordshire, Jubilee House, PO Box 66, 84 Salop Street, Wolverhampton WV3 0SA	203,154	1,005,384
Standard, 64 Church Way, North Shields, Tyne and Wear NE29 0AF	2,431	15,874
Stroud and Swindon, Rowcroft, Stroud, Glos GL5 3BG	114,728	713,427
Swansea, 11 Cradock Street, Swansea SA1 3EW	3,484	30,022
Teachers, Allenview House, Hanham Road, Wimborne, Dorset BH21 1AG	11,061	124,087
Tipton and Coseley, 70 Owen Street, Tipton, West Midlands DY4 8HG	21,045	109,468
Universal, Universal House, Kings Manor, Newcastle upon Tyne NE1 6PA	32,000	245,015
Vernon, 19 St Petersgate, Stockport, Cheshire SK1 1HF	30,033	128,420
West Bromwich, 374 High Street, West Bromwich, West Midlands B70 8LR	340,803	1,767,102
West Cumbria, Cumbria House, Murray Road, Workington CA14 2AD	6,690	35,775
Woolwich, Watling Street, Bexleyheath, Kent DA6 7RR	3,507,000	28,005,300
Yorkshire, Yorkshire House, Yorkshire Drive, Bradford BD5 8LJ	809,141	6,411,644

* 'Building Society' are the last words in every society's name

National Savings

Investment and Ordinary Accounts

On 31 May 1996, there were about 16,012,335 active accounts with the sum of approximately £1,414.5 million due to depositors in ordinary accounts and about 4,557,786 active accounts with the sum of approximately £8,857.9 million due to depositors in investment accounts.

Interest is earned at 2.75 per cent per year on each ordinary account for every complete calendar month in which the balance is £500 or more, provided the account is kept open for the whole of 1996 (31 December 1995 to 1 January 1997); and at 1.75 per cent per year for other months or for accounts opened or closed during 1996. The minimum deposit is £10; maximum balance £10,000 plus interest credited. On 31 May 1996 the average amount held in ordinary accounts was approximately £89.

The investment account pays a higher rate of interest depending on the account balance (the current rate can be found at any post office). The minimum deposit is £20; maximum balance £100,000 plus interest credited. On 31 May 1996 the average amount held in investment accounts was approximately £1,943.

Premium Bonds

Premium Bonds are a government security which were first introduced in 1956. Premium Bonds enable savers to enter a regular draw for tax-free prizes, while retaining the right to get their money back. A sum equivalent to interest on each bond is put into a prize fund and distributed by monthly prize draws. (The rate of interest is 4.75 per cent a year from 1 May 1996.) The prizes are drawn by ERNIE (electronic random number indicator equipment) and are free of all UK income tax and capital gains tax.

Bonds are in units of £1, with a minimum purchase of £100; above this, purchases must be in multiples of £10, up to a maximum holding limit of £20,000 per person. The scheme offers a facility to reinvest prize wins automatically. Upon completion of an automatic prize reinvestment mandate, holders receive new bonds which are immediately eligible for future prize draws. Bonds can only be held in the name of an individual and not by organizations.

Bonds become eligible for prizes once they have been held for one clear calendar month following the month of purchase. Each £1 unit can win only one prize per draw, but it will be awarded the highest for which it is drawn. Bonds remain eligible for prizes until they are repaid. When a holder dies, bonds remain eligible for prizes up to and including the twelfth monthly draw after the month in which the holder dies.

By April 1996 bonds to the value of £10,726 million had been sold. Of these £4,071 million had been cashed, leaving £6,665 million still invested. By the April 1996 prize draw, 52.4 million prizes totalling £3,131 million had been distributed since the first prize draw in June 1957.

Income Bonds

National Savings Income Bonds were introduced in 1982. They are suitable for those who want to receive regular monthly payments of interest while preserving the full cash value of their capital. The bonds are sold in multiples of £1,000. The minimum holding is £2,000 and the maximum £250,000 (sole or joint holding).

Interest is calculated on a day-to-day basis and paid monthly. Interest is taxable but is paid without deduction of tax at source. The bonds have a guaranteed life of ten years, but may be repaid at par before maturity on giving three months' notice. Repayment is also possible without

giving notice but incurs a penalty. If the sole or sole surviving holder dies, however, no fixed period of notice is required and there is no loss of interest for repayment made within the first year.

Net investment in National Savings Income Bonds was £10,398 million at the end of April 1996.

Pensioners Guaranteed Income Bonds

Pensioners Guaranteed Income Bonds were introduced in January 1994 and are designed for people aged 60 and over who wish to receive regular monthly payments with a rate of interest that is fixed for a five-year period whilst preserving the full cash value of their investment.

The minimum limit for each purchase is £500. The maximum holding is £50,000 (£100,000 for a joint holding); within those limits bonds can be bought for any amount in pounds and pence. The rate of interest is fixed and guaranteed for the first five years. Interest is taxable but is paid without deduction of tax at source.

Holders can apply for repayment (or part repayment of a bond subject to the minimum holding limits) by giving 60 days notice (if repayment is before the fifth anniversary date). No interest is earned during the notice period. If repayment is requested within two weeks of any fifth anniversary of purchase, there is no formal period of notice. Repayment is possible without giving notice but a penalty is incurred. On the death of a holder or sole surviving investor in a joint holding repayment will be made without notice. Interest will be paid in full up to the date of repayment.

Net investment in Pensioners Guaranteed Income Bonds was £4,449 million at the end of March 1996.

Children's Bonus Bonds

Children's Bonus Bonds were introduced in 1991. The latest issue, Issue H, was introduced in January 1996. They can be bought for any child under 16 and will go on growing in value until he or she is 21. The bonds are sold in multiples of £25. The minimum holding is £25. The maximum holding in Issue H is £1,000 per child. This is in addition to holdings of earlier issues of the bond (excluding interest and bonuses). Bonds for children under 16 must be held by a parent or guardian.

Children's Bonus Bonds (Issue H) earn 5 per cent a year over five years. A bonus (18.28 per cent) of the purchase price is added at the fifth anniversary. This is equal to 6.75 per cent a year compound. All returns are totally exempt from UK income tax. No interest is earned on bonds cashed in before the first anniversary of purchase. Bonuses are only payable if the bond is held until the next bonus date. Bonds over five years old continue to earn interest and bonuses until the holder is 21, when they should be cashed in. If bonds are not cashed in on the holder's 21st birthday, they earn no interest after that birthday.

FIRST Option Bonds

FIRST (Fixed Interest Rate Savings Tax-paid) Option Bonds were introduced in 1992. They offer guaranteed rates without the need for long-term commitment for personal savers over 16. They can be held indefinitely and will continue to grow in value at rates of interest fixed for 12 months at a time. Tax is deducted from the interest at source. The minimum purchase is £1,000 and the maximum holding is £250,000. Withdrawals can be made without penalty at any anniversary date and there is no formal notice period for repayment. No interest is earned on repayments before the first anniversary.

CAPITAL BONDS

National Savings Capital Bonds were introduced in 1989. The latest series, Series J, was introduced in January 1996. Capital Bonds offer capital growth over five years with guaranteed returns at fixed rates. The interest is taxable each year (for those who pay income tax) but is not deducted at source. The minimum purchase is £100. There is a maximum holding limit of £250,000 from Series B onwards.

Capital Bonds will be repaid in full with all interest gained at the end of five years. No interest is earned on bonds repaid in the first year. Reinvestment or extension terms may also be available.

GILTS ON THE NATIONAL SAVINGS STOCK REGISTER

Government stock or 'gilts' are Stock Exchange securities issued by the Government. They usually have a life of between five and 15 years and most pay a guaranteed fixed rate of interest twice a year throughout this period. When they reach the end of this period they are 'redeemed' (which means repaid) at their face value.

The National Savings Stock Register (NSSR) enables investors to buy and sell gilts by post. It is now possible to have most new issues of gilts registered on the NSSR. Interest on gilts held on the NSSR, although taxable, is paid in full without deduction of tax at source.

NATIONAL SAVINGS CERTIFICATES

RECENT ISSUES

The amount, including accrued interest, index-linked increase or bonus remaining to the credit of investors in National Savings Certificates on 30 April 1996 was approximately £20,030.4 million. In 1995–6, approximately £3,469.6 million was subscribed and £2,259.8 million (excluding interest, index-linked increase or bonus) was repaid. Interest, index-linked increase, bonus or other sum payable is free of UK income tax (including investment income surcharge) and capital gains tax.

From June 1982, savings certificates of the 7th to 36th Issues will be extended on general extension rates as they reach the end of their existing extension periods. The percentage interest rate is determined by the Treasury and any change in this general extension rate will be applicable from the first of the month following its announcement. Under the system, a certificate earns interest for each complete period of three months beyond the expiry of the previous extension terms. Within each three-month period, interest is calculated separately for each month at the rate applicable from the beginning of that month. The interest for each month is one-twelfth of the annual rate (i.e. it does not vary with the number of days in the month) and is capitalized annually on the anniversary of the date of purchase. The current rate of interest under the general extension rate is given in leaflets available at post offices.

FOURTH INDEX-LINKED ISSUE
1 August 1986–30 June 1990
Maximum holding: 200 units
Unit cost: £25
Interest per unit: the repayment value, subject to their being held for one year, is related to the movement of the UK General Index of Retail Prices. In addition, there is guaranteed extra interest of 3 per cent for the first year; 3.25 per cent for the second year; 3.5 per cent for the third year; 4.5 per cent for the fourth year, and 6 per cent for the fifth year. This interest is worth 4.04 per cent compound over a full five years. Certificates held beyond the fifth anniversary earn index-linking plus half a per cent interest on each following anniversary*

THIRTY-FOURTH ISSUE
22 July 1988–16 June 1990
Maximum holding: 40 units, plus facilities to hold up to a further 400 units
Unit cost: £25
Value after five years: £35.89
Interest per unit: after one year the repayment value increases by 6 per cent for ordinarily held 34th Issue. However, reinvestment certificates earn interest during the first year at a rate of 6 per cent a year for each three-month period. Thereafter, all 34th Issue earn 6.25 per cent after two years; 6.5 per cent after three years; 7 per cent after four years; and 7.5 per cent after five years*

THIRTY-FIFTH ISSUE
18 June 1990–14 March 1991
Maximum holding: 40 units, plus special facilities to hold up to a further 400 units
Unit cost: £25
Value after five years: £39.36
Interest per unit: after one year the repayment value increases by 6.5 per cent for ordinarily held 35th Issue. However, reinvestment certificates earn interest during the first year at a rate of 6.5 per cent a year. Thereafter, all 35th Issue earn 7 per cent after two years; 7.75 per cent after three years; 8.5 per cent after four years; and 9.5 per cent after five years

FIFTH INDEX-LINKED ISSUE
2 July 1990–12 November 1992
Maximum holding: 400 units, plus special facilities to hold up to a further 400 units
Unit cost: £25
Interest per unit: the repayment value, subject to their being held for one year, is related to the movement of the UK General Index of Retail Prices. In addition, there is guaranteed extra interest which is paid from the date of purchase for each full year the certificates are held. After the first year the return is the Retail Price Index (RPI) only. Certificates repaid before the first anniversary date earn RPI for each complete month held from the purchase date. For the second year, the RPI plus 0.5 per cent; for the third, the RPI plus 1 per cent; for the fourth, the RPI plus 2 per cent; and at the fifth anniversary, RPI plus 4.5 per cent. Certificates held beyond the fifth anniversary earn the index-linked return only

THIRTY-SIXTH ISSUE
2 April 1991–2 May 1992
Maximum holding: 400 units, plus special facilities to hold up to a further 400
Unit cost: £25
Value after five years: £37.59
Interest per unit: after one year the repayment value increases by 5.5 per cent for ordinarily held 36th Issue. However, reinvestment certificates earn interest during the first year at a rate of 5.5 per cent a year. Thereafter, all 36th Issue earn 6 per cent after two years; 6.75 per cent after three years; 7.5 per cent after four years; and 8.5 per cent after five years

THIRTY-SEVENTH ISSUE
13 May 1992–5 August 1992
Maximum holding: 300 units, plus special facilities to hold up to a further 400
Unit cost: £25
Value after five years: £36.74
Interest per unit: after one year the repayment value increases by 5.5 per cent for ordinarily held 37th Issue. However, reinvestment certificates earn interest during the first year at a rate of 5.5 per cent a year. After one year, £1.38 is added; during the second year 41 pence per completed three months; during the third year, 56 pence per completed three months; during the fourth year, 71 pence per completed three months; and during the fifth year, 91 pence per completed three months

THIRTY-EIGHTH ISSUE
24 August 1992–22 September 1992
Maximum holding: 200 units, plus special facilities to hold up to a further 400
Unit cost: £25
Value after five years: £35.89
Interest per unit: after one year the repayment value increases by 5.25 per cent for ordinarily held 38th Issue. However, reinvestment certificates earn interest during the first year at a rate of 5.25 per cent a year. After one year, £1.31 is added; during the second year 41 pence per completed three months; during the third year, 50 pence per completed three months; during the fourth year,

63 pence per completed three months; and during the fifth year, 86 pence per completed three months

THIRTY-NINTH ISSUE
5 October 1992–12 November 1992
Maximum holding: 50 units, plus special facilities to hold up to a further 100
Unit cost: £100
Value after five years: £138.63
Interest per unit: after one year the repayment value increases by 4.6 per cent for ordinarily held 39th Issue. However, reinvestment certificates earn interest during the first year at a rate of 4.6 per cent a year. After one year, £4.60 is added; during the second year, £1.37 per completed three months; during the third year, £1.86 per completed three months; during the fourth year, £2.32 per completed three months; and during the fifth year, £2.96 per completed three months

FORTIETH ISSUE
7 December 1992–16 December 1993
Maximum holding: 400 units, plus special facilities to hold up to a further 800
Unit cost: £100; reinvestment certificates £25
Value after five years: £132.25
Interest per unit: after one year the repayment value increases by 4 per cent for ordinarily held 40th Issue. However, reinvestment certificates earn interest during the first year at a rate of 4 per cent a year. On a £100 unit after one year, £4 is added; during the second year, £1.15 per completed three months; during the third year, £1.56 per completed three months; during the fourth year, £1.54 per completed three months; and during the fifth year, £2.42 per completed three months

SIXTH INDEX-LINKED ISSUE
7 December 1992–16 December 1993
Maximum holding: 400 units, plus special facilities to hold up to a further 800
Unit cost: £100; reinvestment certificates £25
Interest per unit: the repayment value, subject to their being held for one year, is related to the movement of the UK General Index of Retail Prices. In addition, there is a guaranteed extra interest of 1.5 per cent for the first year; 2 per cent for the second year; 2.75 per cent for the third year; 3.75 per cent for the fourth year; and 6.32 per cent for the fifth year. This is worth 3.25 per cent compound over the full five years. Reinvestment certificates repaid before the first anniversary date earn RPI plus extra interest of 1.5 per cent a year for each complete month

SEVENTH INDEX-LINKED ISSUE
17 December 1993–19 September 1994
Maximum holding: 400 units, plus special facilities to hold up to a further 800
Unit cost: £100; reinvestment certificates £25
Interest per unit: the repayment value, subject to their being held for one year, is related to the movement of the UK General Index of Retail Prices. In addition, there is a guaranteed extra interest of 1.25 per cent for the first year; 1.75 per cent for the second year; 2.5 per cent for the third year; 3.5 per cent for the fourth year and 6.07 per cent for the fifth year. This is worth 3 per cent compound over the full five years. Reinvestment certificates repaid before the first anniversary date will earn RPI plus extra interest of 1.25 per cent a year for each complete month

FORTY-FIRST ISSUE
17 December 1993–19 December 1994
Maximum holding: 400 units, plus special facilities to hold up to a further 800
Unit cost: £100; reinvestment certificates £25
Value after five years: £130.08
Interest per unit: after one year the repayment value increased by 3.65 per cent for ordinarily held 41st Issue. However, reinvestment certificates if encashed before the first anniversary earn interest at 3.65 per cent for each complete period of three months. On a £100 unit after one year, £3.65 is added; during the second year, £1.05 per completed three months; during the third year, £1.45 per completed three months; during the fourth year, £1.82 per completed three months; and during the fifth year, £2.28 per completed three months

FORTY-SECOND ISSUE
20 September 1994–25 January 1996
Maximum holding: £10,000, plus special facilities to hold up to a further £20,000

Unit cost: certificates may be purchased for any amount, subject to a minimum purchase at any time of £100; reinvestment certificates are available for any amount and are not subject to a minimum purchase requirement
Value after five years: £132.88
Interest: after one year the repayment value increases by 4 per cent for ordinarily held 42nd Issue. However, reinvestment certificates if encashed before the first anniversary earn interest at 4 per cent for each complete period of three months. On a £100 certificate after one year £4.00 is added; during the second year £1.19 per completed three months; during the third year, £1.49 per completed three months; during the fourth year, £1.93 per completed three months; and during the fifth year, £2.59 per completed three months

EIGHTH INDEX-LINKED ISSUE
20 September 1994–25 January 1996
Maximum holding: £10,000, plus special facilities to hold up to a further £20,000
Unit cost: certificates may be purchased for any amount, subject to a minimum purchase at any time of £100; reinvestment certificates are available for any amount and are not subject to a minimum purchase requirement
Interest: the repayment value, subject to their being held for one year, is related to the movement of the UK General Index of Retail Prices. In addition, there is a guaranteed extra interest of 1.25 per cent for the first year, 1.75 per cent for the second year, 2.5 per cent for the third year, 3.5 per cent for the fourth year and 6.07 per cent for the fifth year. This is worth 3 per cent compound over the full five years. Reinvestment certificates repaid before the first anniversary date will earn RPI plus extra interest of 1.25 per cent a year for each complete month

FORTY-THIRD ISSUE
26 January 1996–
Maximum holding: £10,000, plus special facilities to hold up to a further £20,000
Unit cost: certificates may be purchased for any amount, subject to a minimum purchase at any time of £100; reinvestment certificates are available for any amount and are not subject to a minimum purchase requirement
Value after five years: £129.77
Interest: after one year the repayment value increases by 3.75 per cent for ordinarily held 43rd Issue. However, reinvestment certificates if encashed before the first anniversary earn interest at 3.75 per cent a year for each complete period of three months. On a £100 unit after one year, £3.75 is added; during the second year, £1.07 per completed three months; during the third year, £1.35 per completed three months; during the fourth year, £1.74 per completed three months; and during the fifth year, £2.33 per completed three months

NINTH INDEX-LINKED ISSUE
26 January 1996–
Maximum holding: £10,000, plus special facilities to hold up to a further £20,000
Unit cost: certificates may be purchased for any amount, subject to a minimum purchase at any time of £100; reinvestment certificates are available for any amount and are not subject to a minimum purchase requirement
Interest: the repayment value, subject to their being held for one year, is related to the movement of the UK General Index of Retail Prices. In addition, there is a guaranteed extra interest of 1 per cent for the first year, 1.25 per cent for the second year, 2 per cent for the third year, 3 per cent for the fourth year and 5.31 per cent for the fifth year. This is worth 2.5 per cent per annum compound over the full five years. Reinvestment certificates repaid before the first anniversary date will earn RPI plus extra interest of 1 per cent a year for each complete month

*As announced by the Treasury

Insurance

The Insurance Companies Act 1982 empowers the Department of Trade and Industry to authorize corporate bodies to transact insurance in the United Kingdom provided they comply with the financial and other regulations detailed in the Act. At the end of 1995 there were 821 insurance companies with authorization from the DTI to transact one or more classes of insurance business. However, with the establishment of the single European insurance market on 1 July 1994 an insurer authorized in any of the European Union (EU) countries can now transact insurance in the UK without further formality; this creates a potential market of about 5,300 insurance companies.

Under the Financial Services Act 1986, the Securities and Investments Board (SIB) is empowered to make, monitor and enforce rules about the conduct of investment business. Insurance companies offering investment contracts like life insurance, pensions, unit trusts and annuities can either obtain authorization direct from SIB or from one of the self-regulating organizations (SROs). For life insurance the SRO is the Personal Investment Authority (PIA) (*see* page 626).

Disputes between policy holders and insurers may be referred to the Insurance Ombudsman or, if appropriate, the PIA Ombudsman or the Pensions Ombudsman (*see* page 627).

THE EUROPEAN UNION

On 1 July 1994 the single market for insurance in the European Union officially came into existence. In 1994 the total premium income of EU insurers amounted to ECU 430 billion, of which UK premiums comprised 21 per cent, second only to Germany's 23.5 per cent. Cross-border cover is now possible for anyone seeking insurance although the number of people or organizations taking advantage of this freedom remains small because of language difficulties or fear of having to deal with an unfamiliar legal system if problems occur.

Most insurers have, to date, opted for selling on an establishment basis (establishing a branch in the country concerned) rather than a services basis (selling from a base outside the country). The total number of companies operating in the EU fell in 1995, and some commentators believe a period of pan-European mergers and take-overs might be imminent.

The work towards total harmonization continues but will not be completed for some time to come.

ASSOCIATION OF BRITISH INSURERS

Ninety per cent of the world-wide business of insurance companies is transacted by the 450 members of the Association of British Insurers (ABI) (51 Gresham Street, London EC2V 7HQ), a trade association which represents both life and general insurers. On general insurance (motor, household, holiday, etc.), ABI acts as a regulatory organization for insurance intermediaries who do not qualify to be registered brokers.

INSURANCE BROKERS

The Insurance Brokers Registration Act 1977 empowers the Insurance Brokers Registration Council (IBRC) (15 St Helen's Place, London EC3A 6DS) as the statutory body responsible for the registration of insurance brokers. The Council is responsible for the registration and training of insurance brokers, conduct of business, and discipline, and it lays down rules relating to such matters as accounting practice, staff qualifications, advertising, etc.

It is possible to act as an insurance intermediary without being registered with the IBRC but unregistered intermediaries are forbidden to use the words 'Insurance Broker' as a title.

IBRC Registered Brokers 1995

Registered individuals	14,899
Limited companies registered	2,302
Sole traders and partnerships	1,126
(containing 1,940 partners and directors)	

BALANCE OF PAYMENTS

The insurance industry's contribution to the balance of payments was £3,925 million in 1994 (£4,814 million in 1993).

GENERAL INSURANCE

General insurance companies and their customers had a good year in 1995. Premiums fell in many classes of business, while insurance companies achieved good profits.

The world-wide general business trading result was a profit of 10.7 per cent of net premium income. This was slightly down on 1994 but the second best performance since 1988. Loss prevention measures played a major part in this good result but the increases in the cost of claims for subsidence and winter weather damage suggests that the days of premium reductions may be coming to an end.

In the UK, the motor sector reversed the trend of the last two years and recorded a small loss of £34 million. This is largely due to the intense competition among motor insurers which has forced net premium income down by 7 per cent to £5,948 million. Non-motor business was still in profit but this reduced from £950 million to £403 million.

Overseas general business again recorded a loss but this was down on 1994. US motor insurance losses were reduced from £50 million to £12 million but elsewhere the figure worsened slightly from £244 million to £274 million. Non-motor figures for the USA saw a reduction in the loss of £350 million in 1994 to £281 million. Elsewhere the losses were reduced from £181 million to £117 million.

BRITISH INSURANCE COMPANIES

The following insurance company figures refer to members and certain non-members of the ABI.

CLAIMS STATISTICS (£ million)

	1994	1995
Domestic claims		
Theft	634	566
Fire	191	209
Weather	282	267
Subsidence	125	326
Business interruption	—	—
Total	1,232	1,368
Commercial claims		
Theft	203	206
Fire	424	492
Weather	106	94
Subsidence	—	—
Business interruption	205	175
Total	938	967

WORLD-WIDE GENERAL BUSINESS TRADING RESULT

	1994 £m	1995 £m
Net written premiums	34,884	36,805
Underwriting profit (loss) for one year account business	359	(321)
Transfer to profit and loss account for other business		
Marine, Aviation, Transport	(281)	(93)
Other	(221)	(163)
Total underwriting result	(143)	(577)
Net investment income	4,089	4,513
Overall trading profit	3,946	3,936
Profit as % of premium income	11.3	10.7

LLOYD'S OF LONDON

Lloyd's of London is an incorporated society of private underwriters who provide an international market for almost all types of insurance. Lloyd's currently earns a gross premium income of around £8,000 million for underwriters each year. Much of this business comes from outside Great Britain and makes a valuable contribution to the balance of payments.

Today, a policy is underwritten at Lloyd's by private individuals with unlimited liability and the newly included corporate members admitted for the first time in 1992. Specialist underwriters accept insurance risks at Lloyd's on behalf of members (often referred to as 'names') grouped in syndicates. There are currently around 250 syndicates of varying sizes, some with over 2,000 names, each managed by an underwriting agent approved by the Council of Lloyd's.

Lloyd's membership is drawn from many sources. Industry, commerce and the professions are strongly represented, while many members work at Lloyd's either for brokerage firms or for underwriting agencies. Underwriting membership of Lloyd's is open to anyone provided they meet the stringent financial requirements of the Corporation of Lloyd's. Substantial financial assets have to be shown and a deposit lodged with the Corporation as security for underwriting liabilities. This deposit, which must be in the form of approved securities, is determined at 30 per cent of the member's annual premium income and showing nominal means.

Lloyd's is incorporated by an Act of Parliament (Lloyd's Acts 1871–1982) and is governed by a council of 18 members. Market management is handled by a Market Board of 19 members (comprising six working members of the Council, the chief executive officer, six further working members, three external members and three Corporation executives). Regulation is supervised by a Board of 16 members (comprising six nominated members of the Council, five external members of the Council, four working members and the Solicitor to the Corporation).

WORLD-WIDE GENERAL BUSINESS UNDERWRITING RESULT

	1994					1995				
	UK	Other EU	USA	Other	Total	UK	Other EU	USA	Other	Total
Motor										
Premiums: £m	6,371	1,480	1,633	1,551	11,035	5,948	1,871	1,637	1,627	11,083
Profit (loss): £m	297	(154)	(50)	(90)	4	(34)	(175)	(12)	(99)	(320)
% of premiums	4.7	(10.4)	(3.0)	(5.8)	0.0	0.6	(9.3)	(0.7)	(6.1)	(2.9)
Non-motor										
Premiums: £m	12,052	1,764	2,188	2,455	18,459	12,275	2,661	2,292	2,665	19,893
Profit (loss): £m	950	(120)	(350)	(61)	419	403	(72)	(281)	(45)	6
% of premiums	7.9	(6.8)	(16.0)	(2.5)	2.3	3.3	(2.7)	(12.2)	(1.7)	0.0

NET PREMIUM INCOME BY TERRITORY 1995

	UK £m	Other EU countries £m	USA £m	Other £m	Total £m
Motor	5,948	1,871	1,637	1,627	11,083
Non-motor	12,275	2,661	2,292	2,665	19,893
Marine, aviation and transport	1,416	262	269	277	2,223
Reinsurance	1,027	607	8	1,174	2,816
Other three-year business	560	10	5	216	791
Total general business	21,226	5,410	4,211	5,958	36,805
Ordinary long-term	42,968	4,653	2,798	3,901	54,320
Industrial long-term	1,217				1,217
Total long-term business	44,185	4,653	2,798	3,901	55,537

620   Insurance

The Corporation is a non-profit making body chiefly financed by its members' subscriptions. It provides the premises, administrative staff and services enabling Lloyd's underwriting syndicates to conduct their business. It does not, however, assume corporate liability for the risks accepted by its members, who remain responsible to the full extent of their personal means for their underwriting affairs.

Lloyd's syndicates have no direct contact with the public. All business is transacted through insurance brokers accredited by the Corporation of Lloyd's. In addition, non-Lloyd's brokers in the United Kingdom, when guaranteed by Lloyd's brokers, are able to deal directly with Lloyd's motor syndicates, a facility which has made the Lloyd's market more accessible to the insuring public.

Lloyd's also provides the most comprehensive shipping intelligence service in the world. The shipping and other information received from Lloyd's agents, shipowners, news agencies and other sources throughout the world is collated and distributed to the media as well as to the maritime and commercial sectors in general. *Lloyd's List* is London's oldest daily newspaper and contains news of general commercial interest as well as shipping information. *Lloyd's Shipping Index*, also published daily, lists some 25,000 ocean-going vessels in alphabetical order and gives the latest known report of each.

DEVELOPMENTS IN 1995

After losses totalling over £8,000 million for the late 1980s and early 1990s, Lloyd's latest results, which, because of Lloyd's three-year accounting period, were for the year 1993, showed a profit of £1,084 million (pure year result). Despite this, the Lloyd's insurance market, which has faced litigation, dissatisfaction and even the suggestion of closure, has some way to go before its troubles are over.

The market's problems stem from very bad trading results and allegations by the names that the market was incompetently and fraudulently run. This has led to two rescue plans. The first was in 1994 and offered names about £900 million in settlement of their litigation; it was rejected. The latest offer involves the setting-up of a reinsurance arrangement for the pre-1992 losses and a settlement of around £3.1 billion in return for an end to all litigation. Not all names are happy with this offer but it is believed the majority will accept it when it is formally put to the vote.

It is believed that by the end of 1996 Lloyd's will have satisfied sufficient numbers of names for the market to contemplate a more settled future.

LLOYD'S MEMBERSHIP

	1993	1994	1995
Total no. of underwriting members participating			
Individuals	19,537	17,526	14,744
Corporate	—	95	140

GROSS MARKET CAPACITY

	1993	1994	1995
Average market capacity per member			
Individual	£449,000	£534,000	£531,000
Corporate	—	16,947,000	16,856,000

LLOYD'S GLOBAL ACCOUNTS
as at 31 December 1995

	1992 and prior years of account £m	1992 total £m
Gross premiums written (net of brokerage)	9,130	8,492
Outward reinsurance premiums	2,799	2,575
Net premiums	6,331	5,917
Reinsurance to close premiums received from earlier years of account	3,897	3,551
Amounts retained to meet all known and unknown outstanding liabilities brought forward	8,413	9,992
Total premiums	18,641	19,460
Gross claims paid	11,284	8,802
Reinsurers' share	5,283	3,350
Net claims	6,001	5,452
Reinsurance premiums paid to close the year of account into Equitas	—	11,582
Other reinsurance premiums paid to close the year of account	3,573	1,474
Amounts retained to meet all known and unknown outstanding liabilities carried forward	9,891	238
Adjustment in respect of double count	(240)	—
Difference on exchange (Equitas)	—	44
Total claims	19,225	18,790
Underwriting result	(584)	670
Other profit (loss) on exchange	39	(12)
Syndicate operating expenses	(663)	(712)
Balance on technical account	(1,208)	(54)
Investment income	663	848
Investment expenses and charges	(10)	(13)
Investment gains less losses	(195)	110
Result before personal expenses	(750)	891
Personal expenses	(443)	(666)
Result after personal expenses	(1,193)	225

LLOYD'S RESULTS 1993

	Marine 1992 £m	1993 £m	Non-marine 1992 £m	1993 £m	Aviation 1992 £m	1993 £m	Motor 1992 £m	1993 £m
Net premiums	1,377	1,400	3,509	3,047	446	457	977	988
Pure year result	148	526	(201)	881	14	138	125	175

LIFE INSURANCE AND PENSIONS

The stagnant housing market throughout the year and the continuing publicity given to the Securities and Investment Board investigation into the quality of advice on opting out of company pension schemes had a serious effect on the sale of life and pension products at the beginning of 1995. The insurance companies have been attempting to discover the true position throughout the year but problems in obtaining information from occupational pension schemes are said to have caused considerable delays. More cynical commentators have attributed the delay to the insurance companies dragging their feet.

Towards the end of 1995, however, confidence was beginning to return and the overall figures for the year showed a small rise, with world-wide net premium income rising by 3 per cent to £55,537 million. Also, during 1995 the Goverment announced plans for the transfer of some welfare state provision to the private sector. These plans could see a rapid expansion in areas such as long-term health care and critical illness cover.

The year was quieter on the regulation side, although insurers remain convinced that the present regime is over-elaborate and over-prescriptive.

PREMIUM INCOME FOR WORLD-WIDE LONG-TERM INSURANCE BUSINESS

	1994 £m	1995 £m
Ordinary Branch		
Business written in UK		
Annual premiums		
Life	11,146	11,677
Annuities	62	53
Pensions	9,732	10,086
Single premiums		
Life	8,602	8,337
Annuities	593	380
Pensions	11,229	11,873
Other	461	562
Business written overseas		
Annual premiums	4,849	5,580
Single premiums	5,974	5,772
Industrial Business	1,291	1,217

PAYMENTS TO POLICYHOLDERS

	1994 £m	1995 £m
Ordinary Branch		
Payments to UK policyholders	28,880	31,259
Payments to overseas policyholders	7,079	8,390
Industrial Branch		
Payments to UK policyholders	2,169	2,194
Total	38,128	41,852

INVESTMENTS OF INSURANCE COMPANIES 1995

Investment of funds	Long-term business £m	General business £m
Index-linked British Government securities	8,951	827
British Government authority securities (excluding those above)	67,864	13,060
Other government, provincial and municipal stocks	37,357	14,188
Debentures, loan stocks, etc.	52,677	8,005
Ordinary stocks and shares	303,330	19,615
Mortgages	15,090	1,562
Real property and ground rents	38,396	4,256
Other invested assets	25,958	11,008
Net current assets	6,063	6,648
Total net assets	555,686	79,170
Gross income for year on investment holdings (gross of tax and interest paid)	29,300	4,878
Interest payable in year	458	365

INDIVIDUAL PENSIONS: NEW BUSINESS 1994–5

	Annual premium policies		Single premium policies	
	No. new policies	New premiums £m	No. new policies	New premiums £m
1994				
1st quarter	275,000	273	120,000	929
2nd quarter	275,000	275	117,000	933
3rd quarter	229,000	224	69,000	657
4th quarter	225,000	245	73,000	624
1995				
1st quarter	211,000	209	70,000	596
2nd quarter	234,000	251	96,000	695
3rd quarter	196,000	212	63,000	565
4th quarter	190,000	24	71,000	632

DIRECTORY OF INSURANCE COMPANIES

Classes of insurance undertaken		*Group membership*
G	General	(CU) Commercial Union
L	Life	(ES) Eagle Star
M	Marine	(GA) General Accident
Re	Reinsurance	(GRE) Guardian Royal Exchange
		(NU) Norwich Union
		(R) Royal
		(SA) Sun Alliance

Nature of business	*Name of company*	*Head Office address*
GLM Re	AGF	41 Botolph Lane, London EC3R 8DL
L	AIG Life (UK)	Alico House, 22 Addiscombe Road, Croydon CR9 5AZ
GM Re	Albion	9–13 Fenchurch Buildings, London EC3M 5HR
L	Alico	Alico House, 22 Addiscombe Road, Croydon CR9 5AZ
GLM	Alliance Assurance (SA)	1 Bartholomew Lane, London EC2N 2AB
L	Allied Dunbar	Allied Dunbar Centre, Swindon SN1 1EL
G	Ansvar	31 St Leonards Road, Eastbourne BN21 3UR
GM	Atlas (GRE)	Royal Exchange, London EC3V 3LS
L	Australian Mutual Provident	100 Temple Street, Bristol BS1 6EA
L	Axa Equity and Law	Amersham Road, High Wycombe HP13 5AL
G	Baptist	1 Merchant Street, London E3 4LY
L	Barclays Life	94 St Paul's Churchyard, London EC4M 8EH
GLM Re	Black Sea and Baltic	65 Fenchurch Street, London EC3M 4EV
M	Bradford (SA)	Bowling Mill, Dean Clough, Halifax HX3 5WA
L	Britannia Life	Britannia Court, 50 Bothwell Street, Glasgow G2 6HR
GL	Britannic	Moor Green, Moseley, Birmingham B13 8QF
M	British & Foreign Marine (R)	New Hall Place, Liverpool
Engineering	British Engine (R)	Longridge House, Manchester M60 4DT
GLM	British Equitable (GRE)	Royal Exchange, London EC3V 3LS
L	British Life Office	Reliance House, Mount Ephraim, Tunbridge Wells, Kent TN4 8BL
G	British Oak (GRE)	Royal Exchange, London EC3V 3LS
L	Caledonian (GRE)	Royal Exchange, London EC3V 3LS
GM	Cambrian (GRE)	Royal Exchange, London EC3V 3LS
L	Canada Life	Canada Life House, Potters Bar, Herts EN6 5BA
GM	Car & General (GRE)	Royal Exchange, London EC3V 3LS
L	Century Life	Century House, 5 Old Bailey, London EC4M 7BA
GL	Cigna	PO Box 42, Greenock, Renfrewshire PA15 1AB
L	Citibank Life	21–23 Perrymount Road, Haywards Heath, W. Sussex RH16 3TH
L	City of Glasgow Friendly	200 Bath Street, Glasgow G2 4HJ
L	Clerical, Medical Group	15 St James Square, London SW1Y 4LQ
L	Colonial Mutual	Colonial Mutual House, Chatham Maritime, Kent ME14 4YY
GLM Re	Commercial Union	St Helen's, 1 Undershaft, London EC3P 3DQ
L	Commercial Union Life	St Helen's, 1 Undershaft, London EC3P 3DQ
L	Confederation Life	Lytton Way, Stevenage, Herts SG1 2NN
G	Congregational and General	Currer House, Currer Street, Bradford BD1 5BA
GLM Re	Co-operative	Miller Street, Manchester M60 0AL
GLM Re	Cornhill	57 Ladymead, Guildford GU1 1DB
L	Crown Financial Management	Crown House, Crown Square, Woking GU21 1XW
GL	Direct Line Insurance	3 Edridge Road, Croydon CR9 1AG
GM	Dominion	52–54 Leadenhall Street, London EC3A 2AQ
GLM Re	Eagle Star	60 St Mary Axe, London EC3A 8JQ
GL Re	Ecclesiastical	Beaufort House, Brunswick Road, Gloucester GL1 1JZ
GL	Economic	Economic House, 25 London Road, Sittingbourne ME10 1PE
Animal Ins.	Equine and Livestock	PO Box 100, Ouseburn, York YO5 9SZ
L	Equitable Life	Walton Street, Aylesbury HP21 7QW
G	Federation General	PO Box 196, Redhill, Surrey RH1 1FG
L	Friends' Provident	United Kingdom House, Castle Street, Salisbury SP1 3SH
GM Re	Gan	Gan House, 12 Arthur Street, London EC4R 9BT
GM Re	General Accident	Pitheavlis, Perth, Scotland PH2 0NH
L	General Accident Life	2 Rougier Street, York YO1 1HR
GLM Re	GRE	Royal Exchange, London EC3V 3LS
G	Gresham Fire & Accident	11 Queen Victoria Street, London EC4N 4XP
GM	Guarantee Society (GA)	42–47 Minories, London EC3N 1BX
L	Guardian Assurance (GRE)	Royal Exchange, London EC3V 3LS

Nature of business	*Name of company*	*Head Office address*
GLM Re	Hibernian	Haddington Road, Dublin 4
L	Hill Samuel	NLA Tower, Addiscombe Road, Croydon CR9 6BP
GL	Ideal	Pitmaston, Moseley, Birmingham B13 8NG
L	Irish Life	Irish Life Centre, Victoria Street, St Albans AL1 5TS
GF	Iron Trades	Iron Trades House, 21–24 Grosvenor Place, London SW1X 7JA
GLM Re	Legal and General	Temple Court, 11 Queen Victoria Street, London EC4N 4TP
L	Liberty Life	Liberty House, Station Road, New Barnet EN5 1PA
GF	Licenses & General (GRE)	Royal Exchange, London EC3V 3LS
L	Lincoln National (UK) PLC	The Quays, 101–105 Oxford Road, Uxbridge, UB8 1LZ
GM	Liverpool Marine & General (SA)	1 Bartholomew Lane, London EC2N 2AB
L	Liverpool Victoria Friendly	Victoria House, Southampton Row, London WC1B 4DB
GM	Local Government Guarantee (GRE)	Royal Exchange, London EC3V 3LS
GM Re	Lombard General	Lombard House, 182 High Street, Tonbridge TN9 1BY
GM	London & Edinburgh	The Warren, Worthing, W. Sussex BN14 9QD
L	London & Manchester	Winslade Park, Exeter, Devon EX5 1DS
L	M & G Assurance	Three Quays, Tower Hill, London EC3R 6BQ
L	Manulife	St George's Way, Stevenage SG1 1HP
M	Marine (R)	34–36 Lime Street, London EC3M 7JE
M Re	Maritime (NU)	Surrey Street, Norwich NR1 3NS
L	Medical, Sickness, Annuity and Life	Pynes Hill House, Rydon Lane, Exeter EX2 5SP
Re	Mercantile & General	Moorfields House, Moorfields, London EC4R 9BJ
L	Merchant Investors (MI Group)	St Bartholomew's House, Lewins Mead, Bristol BS1 2NH
GF	Methodist	Brazennose House, Brazennose Street, Manchester M2 5AS
L	MGM Assurance	MGM House, Heene Road, Worthing BN11 2DY
G	Motor Union (GRE)	Royal Exchange, London EC3V 3LS
L	NPI	NPI House, Tunbridge Wells, Kent TN1 2UE
GL	Nalgo Insurance Association	137 Euston Road, London NW1 2AU
L	National Mutual Life	The Priory, Hitchin, Herts SG5 2DW
Engineering	National Vulcan Eng. Ins. Group (SA)	St Mary's Parsonage, Manchester M60 9AP
G	Navigators & General (ES)	113 Queens Road, Brighton BN1 3XN
GL Re	NFU Avon	Tiddington Road, Stratford-upon-Avon CV37 7BJ
G	NIG Skandia	Crown House, 145 City Road, London EC1V 1LP
L	NM Financial Management	Enterprise House, Isambard Brunel Road, Portsmouth PO1 2AW
GM	Norwich Union Fire	PO Box 6, Surrey Street, Norwich NR1 3NS
L	Norwich Union Life	PO Box 4, Surrey Street, Norwich NR1 3NG
GLM Re	Pearl	The Pearl Centre, Lynchwood, Peterborough PE2 6FY
GL Sickness	Permanent	Pynes Hill House, Pynes Hill, Rydon Lane, Exeter EX2 5SP
GLM	Phoenix (SA)	1 Bartholomew Lane, London EC2N 2AB
L	Property Growth	Phoenix House, Redcliff Hill, Bristol BS1 6SX
L	Provident Mutual Life	Six Hills Way, Stevenage, Herts SG1 2ST
F	Provincial	Stramongate, Kendal, Cumbria LA9 4BE
GLM Re	Prudential	142 Holborn Bars, London EC1N 2NH
GL	Refuge	Refuge House, Alderley Road, Wilmslow, Cheshire SK9 1PF
GM	Reliance Marine (GRE)	Royal Exchange, London EC3V 3LS
L	Reliance Mutual	Reliance House, Mount Ephraim, Tunbridge Wells, Kent TN4 8BL
G	Road Transport & General (GA)	Pitheavlis, Perth PH2 0NH
G	Royal Exchange	Royal Exchange, London EC3V 3LS
L	Royal Heritage Life	Royal Insurance House, Business Park, Peterborough PE2 6GG
G	Royal Insurance	New Hall Place, Liverpool L69 3EN
L	Royal Life	PO Box 30, New Hall Place, Liverpool L69 3HS
L	Royal Liver	Royal Liver Building, Pier Head, Liverpool L3 1HT
GL	Royal London	Royal London House, Middleborough, Colchester CO1 1RA
L	Royal National Pension Fund for Nurses	Burdett House, 15 Buckingham Street, Strand, London WC2N 6ED
F	Salvation Army	117–121 Judd Street, London WC1H 9NN
L	Save & Prosper	1 Finsbury Avenue, London EC2M 2QY
L	Scottish Amicable	150 St Vincent Street, Glasgow G2 5NQ
Engineering	Scottish Boiler (GA)	PO Box 131, 825 Wilmslow Road, Didsbury, Manchester M20 8GS
L	Scottish Equitable	28 St Andrew Square, Edinburgh EH2 1YE
L	Scottish Friendly	16 Blythswood Square, Glasgow G2 6HJ
M	Scottish General (GA)	PO Box 896, 103 Westerhill Road, Bishopbriggs, Glasgow G64 2QX
L	Scottish Legal Life	95 Bothwell Street, Glasgow G2 7HY
L	Scottish Life	19 St Andrew Square, Edinburgh EH2 1YE
L	Scottish Mutual	109 St Vincent Street, Glasgow G2 5HN

Nature of business	Name of company	Head Office address
L	Scottish Provident Institution	6 St Andrew Square, Edinburgh EH2 1YE
GLM	Scottish Union & National (NU)	Surrey Street, Norwich NR1 3NS
L	Scottish Widows'	15 Dalkeith Road, Edinburgh EH16 5BU
GM	Sea (SA)	1 Bartholomew Lane, London EC2N 2AB
L	Stalwart Assurance	Stalwart House, 142 South Street, Dorking RH4 2EV
L	Standard Life	3 George Street, Edinburgh EH2 2XZ
GM	State Assurance (GRE)	Royal Exchange, London EC3V 3LS
GLM	Sun Alliance (SA)	1 Bartholomew Lane, London EC2N 2AB
GM	Sun Insurance Office (SA)	1 Bartholomew Lane, London EC2N 2AB
L	Sun Life Assurance	107 Cheapside, London EC2N 6DU
L Re	Sun Life of Canada	Basing View, Basingstoke, Hants RG21 2DZ
L	Swiss Life	Swiss Life House, 24–26 South Park, Sevenoaks TN13 1BG
L	Swiss Pioneer Life	16 Crosby Road North, Waterloo, Liverpool L22 0NY
GL	Teacher's Assurance	Tringham House, Wessex Fields, Deansleigh Road, Bournemouth BH7 7DT
L	Tunstall & District	Station Chambers, Tunstall, Stoke-on-Trent ST6 6DU
G Re	UAP Provincial Insurance	Stramongate, Kendal, Cumbria LA9 4BE
M	Ulster Marine (GA)	Pitheavlis, Perth PH2 0NH
L	UIA Insurance Ltd	Kings Court, London Road, Stevenage SG1 2TP
GM	Union Insurance Society of Canton (GRE)	Royal Exchange, London EC3V 3LS
GL	United Friendly	42 Southwark Bridge Road, London SE1 9HE
GL Re	Wesleyan Assurance	Colmore Circus, Birmingham B4 6AR
L	Winterthur Life	Winterthur Way, Basingstoke RG21 6SZ
L	Windsor Life	Windsor House, Telford TF3 4NB
GM Re	Zurich	Zurich House, Stanhope Road, Portsmouth PO1 1DU
L	Zurich Life	Hippodrome House, 11 Guildhall Walk, Portsmouth PO1 2RL

The London Stock Exchange

The London Stock Exchange Ltd serves the needs of government, industry and investors by providing facilities for raising capital and a central market-place for securities trading. This market-place covers government stocks (called gilts), UK and overseas company shares (called equities and fixed interest stocks), and traditional options.

PRIMARY MARKETS

The Exchange serves the needs of industry by providing a mechanism where companies can raise capital for development and growth through the issue of securities. For a company entering the market for the first time there is a choice of possible Stock Exchange markets, depending upon the size, history and requirements of the company. The first is the listed market, which exists for well-established companies, which must comply with stringent criteria relating to all aspects of their operations. At present, companies coming to this market require a three-year trading record with a minimum of 25 per cent of the shares held in public hands. The Alternative Investment Market (AIM) began trading in June 1995. It enables small, young and growing companies to raise capital, widen their investor base and have their shares traded on a regulated market without the expense of a full Stock Exchange listing. The Unlisted Securities Market was established in 1980 with the smaller and newer company in mind but closed at the end of 1996.

Once admitted to the Exchange, all companies are obliged to keep their shareholders informed of their progress, making announcements of a price-sensitive nature through the Exchange's company announcements department.

At the end of 1995 there were 2,078 UK companies listed on the London Stock Exchange; their equity capital had a total market value of £900,000 million, an increase of 16 per cent on the 1994 figure of £775,000 million. Also, 525 foreign companies were listed, with a total equity market value of £2,357,000 million. The Alternative Investment Market attracted 121 companies in its first six months of operation, with a total equity market value of £2,300 million.

UK and Irish equity turnover in 1995 was £646,000 million, with an average 38,957 bargains and £2,600 million value a day. Foreign equity turnover averaged 13,886 bargains and £3,100 million value a day. In 1995 the most valuable country sectors in terms of market capitalization were Malaysia (£6,500 million), South Africa (£7,200 million), South Korea (£3,800 million), Taiwan (£2,000 million) and Thailand (£5,400 million).

BIG BANG

During 1986 the London Stock Exchange went through the greatest period of change in its 200-year history. In March 1986 it opened its doors for the first time to overseas and corporate membership of the Exchange, allowing banks, insurance companies and overseas securities houses to become members of the Exchange and to buy existing member firms. On 27 October 1986, three major reforms took place, changes which became known as 'Big Bang':

- abolition of scales of minimum commissions, allowing clients to negotiate freely with their brokers about the charge for their services
- abolition of the separation of member firms into brokers and jobbers: firms are now broker/dealers, able to act as agents on behalf of clients; to act as principals buying and

selling shares for their own account; and to become registered market makers, making continuous buying and selling prices in specific securities
- the introduction of the Stock Exchange automated quotations (SEAQ) system

Of all these changes, the implementation of SEAQ has had the most visible effect. Dealing in stocks and shares now takes place via the telephone in the firms' own dealing rooms, rather than face to face on the floor of the Exchange. The new systems also provide increased investor protection. All deals taking place via the Exchange's SEAQ system are recorded on a database which can be used to resolve disputes or to carry out investigations.

Members of the London Stock Exchange buy and sell shares on behalf of the public, as well as institutions such as pension funds or insurance companies. In return for transacting the deal, the broker will charge a commission, which is usually based upon the value of the transaction. The market makers, or wholesalers, in each security do not charge a commission for their services, but will quote the broker two prices, a price at which they will buy and a price at which they will sell. It is the middle of these two prices which is published in lists of Stock Exchange prices in newspapers.

REGULATORY BODIES

The London Stock Exchange Ltd and the Securities and Futures Authority are the two regulatory bodies. They were formed under the provisions of the Financial Services Act 1986, which requires investment businesses to be authorized and regulated by a self-regulating organization (SRO), of which the Securities and Futures Authority is one. The Act also requires business to be conducted through a recognized investment exchange (RIE). The London Stock Exchange is an RIE, regulating three main markets: UK equities, international equities and gilts.

THE GOVERNING BOARD

The London Stock Exchange has its headquarters in London, and representative offices around the UK. At present there are about 318 member firms.

The governing board is responsible for overall policy and the strategic direction of the Exchange. The board consists of representatives drawn from listed companies, investors and other major users, elected at the annual general meeting, and the Government Broker, the Chief Executive and up to five senior executives of the Stock Exchange.

LONDON STOCK EXCHANGE, Old Broad Street, London EC2N 1HP. Tel: 0171-797 1000
Chairman, J. Kemp-Welch
Chief Executive, G. Casey
Government Broker, I. Plenderleith (*Deputy Chairman*)
Other Board members, G. Allen, CBE; G. Allen; R. Barfield; J. Bond; D. Brydon, OBE; S. Cooke; Ms C. Dann; M. Kaneko; R. Kilsby; M. Marks; R. Metzler; M. Radcliffe; I. Salter; N. Sherlock; B. Solomons; G. Vardey; N. Verey; Ms F. Wicker-Miurin

Investment Business Regulation

The present supervisory framework of Britain's financial services industry was established under the Financial Services Act 1986 which came into force on 29 April 1988. Since that date, it has been a criminal offence to conduct investment business without authorization, unless specifically exempt from the authorization requirement.

The Securities and Investments Board (SIB) is the designated agency under the Financial Services Act 1986 for regulating the activities of investment businesses in the UK. Although not a statutory body, the SIB has statutory powers under the Act to recognize self-regulating organizations, professional bodies, investment exchanges and clearing houses, and directly to authorize firms to undertake investment business in the UK.

The SIB oversees the regulation of all investment business in the UK. It is not responsible for areas involving public issues, takeovers and mergers, and insider dealing investigation. Its area of authority overlaps with that of the Bank of England, the Department of Trade and Industry (for insurance companies) and the Building Societies Commission where their respective member bodies are carrying out investment business.

The regulatory sanctions of the SIB are as follows:
1 It may issue public or private reprimands
2 It may restrict business
3 It may suspend authorization
4 It may withdraw authorization
5 In certain cases it may take out a civil injunction
6 It may petition the courts for the winding up of companies
7 It may ban persons from the industry for life

CENTRAL REGISTER

The SIB maintains the Central Register of all firms who are authorized to carry on investment business. The entry for each firm gives its name, address and telephone number; an SIB reference number; its authorization status; its appropriate regulatory body; and whether it can handle client money.

INVESTORS COMPENSATION SCHEME

The Investors Compensation Scheme, run by a management company as part of the overall investor protection offered by the SIB, comes into play when authorized firms become insolvent owing money to private investors. It is funded by means of a levy on all member firms, according to their size and category. The maximum compensation that the scheme can pay to an investor is £48,000.

SECURITIES AND INVESTMENTS BOARD LTD, Gavrelle House, 2–14 Bunhill Row, London EC1Y 8RA. Tel: 0171-638 1240. *Chairman*, Sir Andrew Large; *Chief Executive*, A. Winckler
CENTRAL REGISTER CHECKLINE: 0171-929 3652

SELF-REGULATING ORGANIZATIONS

The SIB recognizes self-regulating organizations (SROs), which are responsible to the SIB for ensuring financial supervision in their respective sectors of investment business. Most members of the financial services industry obtain their authorization by being members of an SRO.

The following are recognized by the SIB as being able to provide proper regulation of the investment business carried out by their members, and the necessary standard of investor protection:

IMRO (Investment Management Regulatory Organization), 5th Floor, Lloyd's Chambers, Portsoken Street, London E1 8BT. Tel: 0171-390 5000
*†PIA (Personal Investment Authority), 1 Canada Square, Canary Wharf, London E14 5AZ. Tel: 0171-538 8860
SFA (Securities and Futures Authority Ltd), Cottons Centre, Cottons Lane, London SE1 2QB. Tel: 0171-378 9000
* PIA also regulates the activities of friendly societies
† PIA replaced FIMBRA and LAUTRO as the main SRO for the retail sector with effect from 18 July 1994

RECOGNIZED PROFESSIONAL BODIES

The SIB is empowered to recognize professional bodies (RPBs) who, as a result, can authorize their members for investment business. Such business must not form the whole or main part of the total business undertaken by the firm.

INSTITUTE OF CHARTERED ACCOUNTANTS IN ENGLAND AND WALES, Chartered Accountants Hall, PO Box 433, Moorgate Place, London EC2P 2BJ. Tel: 0171-920 8100
INSTITUTE OF CHARTERED ACCOUNTANTS OF SCOTLAND, 27 Queen Street, Edinburgh EH2 1LA. Tel: 0131-225 5673
THE ULSTER SOCIETY OF THE INSTITUTE OF CHARTERED ACCOUNTANTS IN IRELAND, 11 Donegall Square South, Belfast BT1 5JE. Tel: 01232-321600
CHARTERED ASSOCIATION OF CERTIFIED ACCOUNTANTS, 29 Lincoln's Inn Fields, London WC2A 3EE. Tel: 0171-242 6855
INSTITUTE OF ACTUARIES, Staple Inn Hall, High Holborn, London WC1V 7QJ. Tel: 0171-242 0106
INSURANCE BROKERS REGISTRATION COUNCIL, 15 St Helen's Place, London EC3A 6DS. Tel: 0171-588 4387
THE LAW SOCIETY, 113 Chancery Lane, London WC2A 1PL. Tel: 0171-242 1222
LAW SOCIETY OF SCOTLAND, Law Society's Hall, 26 Drumsheugh Gardens, Edinburgh EH3 7YR. Tel: 0131-226 7411
LAW SOCIETY OF NORTHERN IRELAND, Law Society House, 98 Victoria Street, Belfast BT1 3JZ. Tel: 01232-231614

RECOGNIZED INVESTMENT EXCHANGES

Investment exchanges are exempt from needing authorization from the SIB as an investment business. However, to be a recognized investment exchange (RIE), each must fulfil the following requirements: adequate financial resources; proper conduct of business rules; a proper market in its products; procedures for recording transactions; effective monitoring and enforcement of rules; proper arrangements for the clearing and performance of contracts.

INTERNATIONAL PETROLEUM EXCHANGE (IPE), International House, 1 St Katharine's Way, London E1 9UN. Tel: 0171-481 0643
LONDON STOCK EXCHANGE (LSE), Old Broad Street, London EC2N 1HP. Tel: 0171-797 1000
LONDON COMMODITY EXCHANGE LTD, 1 Commodity Quay, St Katharine Dock, London E1 9AX. Tel: 0171-481 2080
LONDON INTERNATIONAL FINANCIAL FUTURES AND OPTIONS EXCHANGE (LIFFE), Cannon Bridge, London EC4R 3XX. Tel: 0171-623 0444

London Metal Exchange Ltd (LME), 56 Leadenhall Street, London EC3A 2BJ. Tel: 0171-264 5555

The London Securities and Derivatives Exchange Ltd (OMLX), Milestone House, 107 Cannon Street, London EC4N 5AD. Tel: 0171-283 0678

Tradepoint Financial Networks plc, 35 King Street, London WC2E 8JD. Tel: 0171-240 8000

The following exchanges are recognized by the Treasury as offering adequate investor protection:

Belgium Futures and Options Exchange (BELFOX), Palais de la Bourse, rue Henri Maus Straat 2, 1000 Brussels, Belgium. Tel: 00-32-2-512 8040

Chicago Board of Trade (CBOT), European Office, 52–54 Gracechurch Street, London EC3V 0EH. Tel: 0171-929 0021

Chicago Mercantile Exchange (CME), Pinnacle House, 23–26 St Dunstan's Hill, London EC3R 8HL. Tel: 0171-623 2550

Delta Government Options Corporation, c/o Sullivan and Cromwell, 125 Broad Street, New York 10004-2498, USA. Tel: 00-1-212-558 4675

MATIF, 176 rue Montmatre, 75083 Paris, Cedex 02, France. Tel: 00 331-4028 8282

MEFF RF, Via Laietana, 58-08003 Barcelona, Spain. Tel: 00-34 3 412 1128

MEFF RV, Torre Picasso, Planta 26, 28820 Madrid, Spain. Tel: 00-34 1 585 0800

National Association of Securities Dealers Automated Quotations System (Nasdaq), 43 London Wall, London EC2M 5TB. Tel: 0171-374 6969

New York Mercantile Exchange (NYMEX), 35 Piccadilly, London W1V 9PB. Tel: 0171-734 1280

Paris Bourse, London Representative, 199 Bishopsgate, London EC2M 3TT. Tel: 0171-814 6624

SCMC–MONEP,London Representative, 199 Bishopsgate, London EC2M 3TT. Tel: 0171-814 6624

Stockholm Stock Exchange, Källargränd 2, PO Box 1256, S-111 82 Stockholm, Sweden. Tel: 00-46-8-613 8618

Sydney Futures Exchange Ltd, 30–32 Grosvenor Street, Sydney, NSW 2000, Australia. Tel: 00-612 256 0555

RECOGNIZED CLEARING HOUSES

A recognized clearing house (RCH) must satisfy the same kind of criteria to obtain recognition as the RIEs. There is one RCH which acts as a clearing house for some of the above RIEs:

London Clearing House Ltd (LCH), Roman Wall House, 1–2 Crutched Friars, London EC3N 2AN. Tel: 0171-265 2000

DESIGNATED INVESTMENT EXCHANGES

The SIB has drawn up a list of 51 overseas exchanges (known as DIEs) whose operations are set in a regulatory context which provides investor protection equivalent to that available from RIEs. Designation does not allow an overseas investment exchange to do business in the UK and, while showing that an exchange meets certain basic criteria, it carries no guarantee for the investor.

OMBUDSMAN SCHEMES

Independent ombudsman schemes have been set up for banks, building societies, insurance companies, financial institutions and independent financial advisers. They provide an independent and impartial method of resolving disputes that arise between a company and its customer. In most ombudsman schemes there is a council which appoints and supervises the Ombudsman. The Ombudsman Council is composed of people representing public and consumer interests and member companies. The schemes are funded in various ways: annual subscription from member companies, a levy on member companies according to the size of their assets, a charge for each complaint handled against a particular company, or a combination of these.

The Investment Ombudsman is responsible for resolving disputes that arise between a customer and a member company of IMRO. The Personal Investment Authority (PIA) Ombudsman is primarily responsible for resolving complaints against PIA members about personal investments.

The Pensions Ombudsman is appointed by the Secretary of State for Social Security under the Pension Schemes Act 1993, and is responsible to Parliament. He can resolve grievances between an individual and his/her pension scheme (but not National Insurance benefits). His decisions are binding on both parties. A statutory levy on pension schemes, based on the number of members therein, contributes to the funding of the scheme.

The Office of the Banking Ombudsman, 70 Gray's Inn Road, London WC1X 8NB. Tel: 0171-404 9944. *Banking Ombudsman*, D. Thomas

The Office of the Building Societies Ombudsman, Millbank Tower, Millbank, London SW1P 4XS. Tel: 0171-931 0044. *Building Societies Ombudsman*, B. Murphy

The Insurance Ombudsman Bureau, City Gate One, 135 Park Street, London SE1 9EA. Tel: 0171-928 4488. *Insurance Ombudsman*, W. Merricks

The Office of the Investment Ombudsman, 6 Frederick's Place, London EC2R 8BT. Tel: 0171-796 3065. *Investment Ombudsman*, P. Dean, CBE

The Pensions Ombudsman, 11 Belgrave Road, London SW1V 1RB. Tel: 0171-834 9144. *Pensions Ombudsman*, Dr J. T. Farrand

The PIA Ombudsman Bureau, 3rd Floor, Centre Point, 103 New Oxford Street, London WC1A 1QH. Tel: 0171-240 3838. *Principal Ombudsman*, S. Edell; *Ombudsman*, R. Prior

THE TAKEOVER PANEL

The Takeover Panel was set up in 1968 in response to concern about practices unfair to shareholders in take-over bids for public and certain private companies. Its principal objective is to ensure equality of treatment, and fair opportunity for all shareholders to consider on its merits an offer that would result in the change of control of a company. It is a non-statutory body that operates the City code on take-overs and mergers.

The chairman, deputy chairmen and three lay members of the panel are appointed by the Bank of England. The remainder are representatives of the banking, insurance, investment, pension fund and accountancy professional bodies, the CBI, IMRO and the Stock Exchange.

The Takeover Panel, PO Box 226, The Stock Exchange Building, London, EC2P 2JX. Tel: 0171-382 9026. *Chairman*, Sir David Calcutt, QC

Stamp Duties

Stamp duty is a tax on documents. There are a number of separate duties, under different heads of charge. The Finance Act 1990 included provisions abolishing all the stamp duty charges on transactions in shares from a date to be fixed by Treasury order (which has not yet been made). The Finance Act 1991 removed the stamp duty charges on documents relating to all other types of property except land and buildings, again from a date to be specified (no date yet specified). The Chancellor has indicated that these provisions are unlikely to be brought into force for two to three years. In the list of documents which follows, those which will be affected by the above provisions are indicated with an asterisk*.

TIME FOR STAMPING

A stampable instrument may, subject to exceptions, be stamped without penalty if presented for stamping within 30 days after its date of first execution. Where wholly executed abroad, the period begins to run from the date of arrival in the UK.

Instruments presented after the proper time (subject to special provisions in some cases and subject to the Commissioner's power to mitigate) are subject to a penalty equal to the unpaid duty (and interest thereon if duty exceeds £10) plus £10.

AGREEMENT FOR LEASE, see LEASES

AGREEMENT FOR SALE OF PROPERTY

Charged with *ad valorem* duty as if an actual conveyance on sale, with certain exceptions, e.g. agreements for the sale of land, stocks and shares, goods, wares or merchandise, or a ship (*see* S. 59 (1), Stamp Act 1891). If *ad valorem* duty is paid on an agreement in accordance with this provision, the subsequent conveyance or transfer is not chargeable with any *ad valorem* duty and the Commissioners will upon application either place a denoting stamp on such conveyance or transfer or will transfer the *ad valorem* duty thereto. Further, if such an agreement is rescinded, not performed, etc., the Commissioners will return the *ad valorem* duty paid.

ASSIGNMENT

By way of sale, *see* CONVEYANCE
By way of gift, *see* VOLUNTARY DISPOSITION

*BEARER INSTRUMENT

Inland bearer instrument, i.e. share warrant, stock certificate to bearer or any other instrument to bearer by which stock can be transferred, issued by a company or body formed or established in the UK, 1.5 per cent

Overseas bearer instrument, i.e. such an instrument issued in Great Britain by a company formed out of the UK, 1.5 per cent

BILL OF SALE, ABSOLUTE, *see* CONVEYANCE ON SALE

CONTRACT, *see* AGREEMENT

CONVEYANCE OR TRANSFER ON SALE
(In the case of a Voluntary Disposition, *see* below)

Conveyance or transfer on sale of any property (except stock or marketable securities), where the conveyance or transfer contains a certificate of value certifying that the transaction does not form part of a larger transaction or a series of transactions in respect of which the aggregate amount or value of the consideration exceeds £60,000, *nil*

Exceeds £60,000 (for every £100 or fraction of £100), £1

If the conveyance or transfer on sale does not contain the appropriate statement, duty at the full rate of £1 for every £100 or fraction of £100 will be payable whatever the amount of the consideration.

Conveyances to charities are exempt from duty under this head provided the instrument is stamped with a denoting stamp.

CONVEYANCE OR TRANSFER OF ANY OTHER KIND
Fixed duty, 50p

However, under the Stamp Duty (Exempt Instruments) Regulations 1987, instruments which would otherwise fall under this head are exempt from stamp duty provided that the document is duly certified. The certificate must contain a sufficient description of the category into which the instrument falls, and must be signed by the transferor, his solicitor or agent: 'I/We hereby certify that this instrument falls within category … in the Schedule to the Stamp Duty (Exempt Instruments) Regulations 1987.'

COVENANT, for original creation and sale of any annuity, *see* CONVEYANCE

DECLARATION OF TRUST
Not being a will or settlement, 50p

DEMISE, *see* LEASES

DUPLICATE OR COUNTERPART
Same duty as original, but not to exceed 50p

GIFT, *see* VOLUNTARY DISPOSITION

LEASES (INCLUDING AGREEMENTS FOR LEASES)

Lease or tack for any definite term less than a year of any furnished dwelling-house or apartments where the rent for such term exceeds £500, £1

Of any lands, tenements, etc., in consideration of any rent, according to the following:

Annual rent not exceeding	†Term not exceeding			Exceeding 100 yrs
	7 yrs	35 yrs	100 yrs	
£	£ p	£ p	£ p	£ p
5	nil	0.10	0.60	1.20
10	nil	0.20	1.20	2.40
15	nil	0.30	1.80	3.60
20	nil	0.40	2.40	4.80
25	nil	0.50	3.00	6.00
50	nil	1.00	6.00	12.00
75	nil	1.50	9.00	18.00
100	nil	2.00	12.00	24.00
150	nil	3.00	18.00	36.00
200	nil	4.00	24.00	48.00
250	nil	5.00	30.00	60.00
300	nil	6.00	36.00	72.00
350	nil	7.00	42.00	84.00
400	nil	8.00	48.00	96.00
450	nil	9.00	54.00	108.00
500	nil	10.00	60.00	120.00
Exceeding £500, *for every* £50 *or fraction thereof*	0.50	1.00	6.00	12.00

†If the term is indefinite the same duty is payable as if the term did not exceed seven years.

Where a consideration other than rent is payable, the same rule applies where the consideration does not exceed £60,000 as under conveyance or transfer on sale (except stock or marketable securities), provided that any rent payable does not exceed £600 a year and a certificate of value is included in the conveyance or transfer.

Where a lease is granted pursuant to a prior agreement for lease, the agreement itself is liable to duty. Credit for any duty paid on the agreement will be given against the duty payable on the lease and the Commissioners will place a denoting stamp on the lease. Where there is no prior agreement for lease, the lease must contain a certificate that it has not been made in pursuance of an agreement.

Leases to charities are exempt from duty under this head provided the instrument is stamped with a denoting stamp.

MORTGAGES, exempt

TRANSFER OF STOCK AND SHARES BY SALE, 0.5 per cent

UNIT TRUST INSTRUMENT

Unit Trust Instrument duty was abolished in the Finance Act 1988. Transfer of property to a unit trust or agreement to transfer units is generally subject to Conveyance on Sale duty.

By the Finance Act 1989, the transfer of units in certain authorized unit trusts is no longer subject to duty.

VOLUNTARY DISPOSITION, *inter vivos*

Fixed duty, 50p

However, under the Stamp Duty (Exempt Intruments) Regulations 1987, instruments which would otherwise fall under this head are exempt from stamp duty provided that the document is certified as falling within category L in the schedule to the Regulations. *See* Conveyance or Transfer of Any Other Kind, above.

Taxation

INCOME TAX

Income tax is charged annually on the income of individuals for a year of assessment commencing on 6 April and ending on the following 5 April. The rates of tax and the calculation of liability frequently differ, sometimes substantially, as between one year of assessment and another. The following information is confined to the year of assessment 1996–7, ending on 5 April 1997; it has only limited application to earlier years because the basis used for calculating liability to United Kingdom income tax and the steps which must be taken to discharge that liability have both been significantly affected by recent changes.

The first of these changes, introduced on 6 April 1990, was the independent taxation of husband and wife. The second change occurred on 6 April 1996 at the beginning of the 1996–7 year of assessment and introduces self-assessment.

Liability to income tax is determined by establishing the taxable income for a year of assessment. That income will be reduced by an individual's personal allowance and perhaps by some other allowances or reliefs. The first £3,900 of taxable income remaining is assessable to income tax at the lower rate of 20 per cent. Disregarding income from 'savings', the next £21,600 is taxed at the basic rate of 24 per cent. Should any excess over £25,500 (£3,900 plus £21,600) remain, this will be taxable at the higher rate of 40 per cent.

Company dividends, interest and other forms of 'savings income' do not incur liability at the basic rate of 24 per cent. Income of this nature is taxable at 20 per cent unless the individual's taxable income exceeds £25,500, when liability may arise at 40 per cent on the excess.

Certain allowances and reliefs are given at the rate of 15 or 20 per cent as a deduction from income tax payable. These adjustments can only be made once the full amount of tax otherwise due has been calculated.

The tables below show the income tax payable for 1996–7 by an individual on the amount of income specified, after deducting the personal allowance and providing relief for the married couple's allowance, where appropriate. Elderly persons over the age of 74 years may pay less tax, unless their income is substantial. Some taxpayers may be entitled to transitional allowance following the introduction of independent taxation, together with other reliefs which reduce the tax payable below the amount shown by the tables. These tables have been structured on the assumption that none of the income arises from savings. Should income of this nature be received, less tax may be due.

Trustees administering settled property are chargeable to income tax at the basic rate of 24 per cent. Where the trustees retain discretionary powers or income is accumulated, there will also be liability to the additional rate of 10 per cent. Companies residing in the UK are not liable to income tax but suffer corporation tax on income, profit and gains.

The charge to income tax arises on all taxable income accruing from sources in the UK. Individuals who are resident in this territory may also become liable on income arising overseas. An individual is resident in the UK if he or she normally resides here. Persons not normally residing in the UK may become resident if they visit this territory for periods which average three months or more throughout period of years, or are present for at least 183 days in particular year.

Income arising overseas will often incur liability to foreign taxation. If that income is also chargeable to UK income tax, excessive liability could arise. The UK has

SINGLE PERSONS AND MARRIED WOMEN					MARRIED MEN				
Income	Persons under 65		Persons 65 or over*		Income	Couples under 65		Couples 65 or over†	
£	Income tax £	Average rate %	Income tax £	Average rate %	£	Income tax £	Average rate %	Income tax £	Average rate %
4,000	47	1.2	—	—	4,000	—	—	—	—
5,000	247	4.9	18	0.4	5,000	—	—	—	—
6,000	447	7.5	218	3.6	6,000	179	3.0	—	—
7,000	647	9.2	418	6.0	7,000	379	5.4	—	—
8,000	860	10.8	618	7.7	8,000	592	7.4	151	1.9
9,000	1,100	12.2	826	9.2	9,000	832	9.2	358	4.0
10,000	1,340	13.4	1,066	10.7	10,000	1,072	10.7	598	6.0
12,000	1,820	15.2	1,546	12.9	12,000	1,552	12.9	1,078	9.0
14,000	2,300	16.4	2,026	14.5	14,000	2,032	14.6	1,558	11.1
16,000	2,780	17.4	2,602	16.3	16,000	2,512	15.7	2,134	13.3
18,000	3,260	18.1	3,260	18.1	18,000	2,992	16.6	2,831	15.7
20,000	3,740	18.7	3,740	18.7	20,000	3,472	17.4	3,461	17.3
25,000	4,940	19.8	4,940	19.8	25,000	4,672	18.7	4,672	18.7
30,000	6,258	20.9	6,258	20.9	30,000	5,990	20.0	5,990	20.0
40,000	10,258	25.6	10,258	25.6	40,000	9,990	25.0	9,990	25.0
50,000	14,258	28.5	14,258	28.5	50,000	13,990	28.0	13,990	28.0
60,000	18,258	30.4	18,258	30.4	60,000	17,990	30.0	17,990	30.0
100,000	34,258	34.3	34,258	34.3	100,000	33,990	34.0	33,990	34.0

* Persons aged 75 or over suffer less tax on income falling below £18,000 on this table

† Persons aged 75 or over suffer less tax on income falling below £18,000 on this table

concluded double taxation agreements with many overseas territories and these ensure that the same slice of income is not doubly taxed. In the absence of such an agreement, foreign tax suffered can usually be relieved under the domestic code when calculating liability to UK income tax.

INDEPENDENT TAXATION

Since the introduction of independent taxation on 6 April 1990, a husband and wife have been separately taxed, with each entitled to their own personal allowance. In most situations any unused personal allowance available to one spouse cannot be transferred to the other. A married man 'living with' his wife can obtain a married couple's allowance. In the absence of any claim, this allowance must be used by the husband but where any balance remains the surplus may be transferred to the wife. It is possible for a married woman to claim half the basic married couple's allowance as of right. In addition, the entire basic allowance may be claimed by the wife, if her husband so agrees.

Each spouse may obtain other allowances and reliefs where the required conditions are satisfied. Income must be accurately allocated between a husband and wife by reference to the individual beneficially entitled to that income. Where income arises from jointly-held assets, this must be apportioned equally between husband and wife. However, in those cases where the beneficial interests in jointly-held assets are not equal, a special declaration can be made to apportion income by reference to the actual interests in that income.

SELF-ASSESSMENT

A fundamental change in the structure of UK taxation was introduced on 6 April 1996 and applies for 1996–7 and future years. This change, known as self-assessment, does not affect the amount of income tax payable. However, it significantly amends the compliance requirements which many individuals must satisfy, and also changes the procedure for discharging liability to income tax.

The system which applied for 1995–6 and earlier years required the taxpayer to complete a tax return showing profits, gains and income chargeable to income tax and capital gains tax also. The Inland Revenue then raised the appropriate assessment, or assessments, showing the amount of tax due, unless that tax had already been discharged. If these assessments were correct, tax would fall due for payment on the appropriate date or dates.

The self-assessment system also requires the taxpayer to deliver a completed tax return. This must normally be submitted by 31 January following the end of the year of assessment to which the return relates. In addition to completing the return, the taxpayer must calculate the amount of income tax due. If a taxpayer does not wish to calculate the tax due, the return must be forwarded to the Inland Revenue not later than the previous 30 September; an Inland Revenue representative will then calculate the amount of tax, using the information disclosed by the return, and advise the taxpayer. This is the only advantage of providing a completed return not later than 30 September, as it remains the responsibility of the taxpayer to submit payments of income tax on time.

There may be three different payment dates when discharging income tax due for a year of assessment:
a) an interim payment due on 31 January in the year of assessment itself
b) a second interim payment due on the following 31 July
c) a balancing payment, or possibly a repayment, on the following 31 January

The two interim payments will be based on tax payable for the previous year of assessment but liability may be reduced where income has fallen or even avoided entirely where the amounts are small.

Although all individuals could be affected by self-assessment, its impact will largely be restricted to about nine million persons receiving tax returns and comprising self-employed individuals, those receiving income from the exploitation of land in the UK, and others with investment income liable to higher rate income tax. Individuals whose only income comprises earnings from an employment where the PAYE system applies are largely unaffected.

Failure to submit completed tax returns by 31 January or to discharge payments of income tax on time will incur a liability to interest, surcharges and penalties.

Self-assessment is not limited to income tax but extends also to capital gains tax. However, there is no requirement to make interim payments on account of capital gains tax as the entire amount due for disposals taking place in a year of assessment must be discharged on the following 31 January.

INCOME TAXABLE

Income tax is assessed and collected under several Schedules. Each Schedule determines the extent of liability and establishes the amount to be included in taxable income. In some instances the actual income arising in a year of assessment will be charged to income tax for that year.

A different basis of assessment may be used for income taxable under Cases I to V of Schedule D. For many years income was assessed under these Cases on a 'preceding year' basis. This involved measuring income for the year by reference to that arising in a previous year or period but there were special rules where a new source was acquired or an existing source discontinued. The 'preceding year' basis is being replaced by a 'current year' basis of assessment. This requires that business profits assessable under Case I or Case II of Schedule D will be those for the accounting period ending in the year of assessment, with special adjustments for the opening and closing years of a business. Other income assessable under Schedule D will be that which arises in the actual year of assessment.

The current year basis applies at the outset for new sources commenced on and after 6 April 1994. Sources existing before that date will become subject to the current year basis in 1997–8, although special rules will apply to achieve a smooth transition from the old basis to the new. These rules mean that a form of averaging will often be used to establish the profits or income for 1996–7.

Following the withdrawal of income tax liability for most commercial woodlands in the UK, Schedule B no longer applies. Schedule C has also been withdrawn as the result of recent developments. The contents of the remaining schedules are shown below.

Schedule A

Tax is charged under Schedule A on the annual profits or gains arising from any business carried on for the exploitation of land in the UK. Whilst the broad scope of this Schedule has remained unchanged for many years, substantial amendments were made to the calculation of profits and gains for 1995–6 and future years. The calculation of liability for a Schedule A business, as it is now described, adopts principles identical to those used when establishing the profits or gains of a trade, profession or vocation. Rents and other income from the exploitation of land will be included in the calculation, and outgoings incurred wholly and exclusively for the purposes of the Schedule A business may be deducted from income.

Schedule A does not extend to profits from farming, market gardening or woodlands, nor does it apply to mineral rents and royalties. Premiums arising on the grant of a lease for a period not exceeding 50 years in duration are treated as rents. However, the amount of the taxable premium may be reduced by 2 per cent for each complete year, after the first 12 months, of the leasing period. Income arising from the provision of certain furnished holiday accommodation attracts a number of tax advantages not otherwise available for most income chargeable under Schedule A.

Receipts not exceeding £3,250 annually and accruing to an individual from letting property furnished in his or her own home are not chargeable to income tax.

Schedule D

This Schedule is divided into six Cases:

Cases I and II – profits arising from trades, professions and vocations, including farming and market gardening. Capital expenditure incurred on assets used for business purposes will often produce an entitlement to capital allowances which reduce the profits chargeable. These profits may also be reduced by claims for loss relief and other matters.

Case III – interest on government stocks not taxed at source (e.g. war loan and British savings bonds), interest on National Savings Bank deposits and discounts. Interest up to £70 on ordinary National Savings Bank deposits is exempt from income tax. The exemption applies to both husband and wife separately. Interest on National Savings Bank special investment accounts is not exempt. Interest and other items of savings income received after 5 April 1996 incur no liability at the basic rate of 24 per cent.

Cases IV and V – interest from overseas securities, rents, dividends and all other income accruing outside the UK. Assessment is based on the full amount of income arising, whether remitted to the UK or retained overseas, but individuals who are either not domiciled in the UK or who are ordinarily resident overseas may be taxed on a remittance basis. Overseas pensions are taxable but the amount arising may be reduced by 10 per cent for assessment purposes. Dividends and interest on most overseas investments are chargeable only at the lower rate of 20 per cent and the higher rate of 40 per cent.

Case VI – sundry profits and annual receipts not assessed under any other Case or Schedule. These may include insurance commissions, post-cessation receipts and numerous other receipts specifically charged under Case VI.

Schedule E

All emoluments from an office or employment are assessable under this Schedule. There are three Cases:

Case I – applies to all emoluments of an individual resident and ordinarily resident in the UK.

Case II – of application where the individual is not resident or not ordinarily resident and extends to emoluments for duties undertaken in the UK.

Case III – applies in rare situations to other emoluments remitted to the UK.

Although earnings for duties performed overseas may be assessable under Case I where the employee is resident and ordinarily resident in the UK, a foreign earnings deduction of 100 per cent may be available, which reduces the overseas assessable earnings to nil. This deduction can be obtained where duties are performed overseas for a

continuous period reaching or exceeding 365 days and is confined to earnings from the overseas activity.

A 'receipts basis' applies for determining the year of assessment in which earnings must be taxed. Where emoluments are assessable under Case I or Case II, the date of receipt will comprise the earlier of the date of payment, or the date entitlement arises. In the case of company directors it is the earlier of these two dates, with the addition of the following three which establish the time of receipt: the date emoluments are credited in the company's books; where emoluments for a period are determined after the end of that period, the date of determination; where emoluments for a period are determined in that period, the last day of that period.

The emoluments assessable under Schedule E include all salaries, wages, director's fees and other money sums. In addition, there are a wide range of benefits which must be added to taxable emoluments. These include the provision of living accommodation on advantageous terms and advantages arising from the use of vouchers.

Further taxable benefits accrue to directors and also to employees receiving emoluments of £8,500 or more in the year of assessment. These benefits include the reimbursement of expenses, the availability of motor cars for private motoring, the provision of petrol or other fuel for private motoring, the use of vans, the provision of interest-free loans, and other benefits provided at the employer's expense. The cost of providing a limited range of child care facilities may be excluded.

In arriving at the amount to be assessed under Schedule E, all expenses incurred wholly, exclusively and necessarily in the performance of the duties may be deducted. This includes fees and subscriptions paid to certain professional bodies and learned societies. Fees paid to managers by entertainers, actors and others assessable under Schedule E may be deducted, up to a maximum of 17.5 per cent of earnings.

Compensation for loss of office and other sums received on the termination of an office or employment are assessable to tax. However, the first £30,000 may be excluded with only the balance remaining chargeable, unless the compensatory payment is linked with the retirement of the recipient.

Earnings received from an approved profit-related pay scheme are exempt from income tax.

Schedule F

This Schedule is concerned with company dividends and distributions. A UK resident company paying a dividend or making a distribution must account to the Inland Revenue for advance corporation tax. A shareholder residing in the UK obtains the dividend or distribution together with a tax credit equal to one-quarter of the sum received for 1996–7. The dividend or distribution is regarded as having suffered income tax, equal to the tax credit, at the lower rate of 20 per cent. Where the shareholder is not liable, or not fully liable, at that rate a repayment can be obtained. Dividends and distributions comprise income from savings and incur no liability to income tax at the basic rate of 24 per cent (*see* below).

Some payments made by an unquoted trading company to redeem or purchase its own shares are not treated as distributions.

Building society and bank interest

Many payments of interest by building societies and banks are received after the deduction of income tax at the lower rate of 20 per cent. However, investors not liable to income tax may arrange to receive interest gross, with no tax being deducted on payment. Others who suffer income tax be deduction can obtain a repayment in whole or in part if they are not fully liable at the lower rate. This income also comprises income from savings, which is taxable as outlined below.

INCOME FROM SAVINGS

Some forms of investment income attract reduced rates of income tax in 1996–7. These rates are limited to 'income from savings', an expression which includes:
(a) bank interest
(b) building society interest
(c) interest on government securities
(d) all other forms of interest
(e) the income element of purchased life annuities
(f) dividends from UK companies
This list is not exhaustive and may be extended to include dividends and other income of a similar nature arising outside the UK. Not all forms of investment income are included in the list; a notable exception is income from letting property.

A great deal of interest will be received after deduction of income tax at the lower rate of 20 per cent. Dividends have a tax credit attached which effectively represents tax at the rate of 20 per cent on the grossed-up equivalent. The significance of these rates is that income from savings will be taxed at 20 per cent where the income of the recipient is sufficiently substantial. There is no liability at the basic rate of 24 per cent but where taxable income exceeds £25,500, the excess is liable at the higher rate of 40 per cent. As tax will usually have been deducted at source at 20 per cent, higher rate liability arises at a further 20 per cent (40 per cent less 20 per cent). When calculating liability, income from savings is treated as the 'top slice' of the taxpayer's income.

INCOME NOT TAXABLE

This includes interest on National Savings certificates, most scholarship income, bounty payments to members of the armed services and annuities payable to the holders of certain awards. Dividend income arising from investments in personal equity plans and venture capital trusts may be exempt from tax. Income received under most maintenance agreements and court orders made after 30 June 1988 will not be liable to tax. Nor will payments made under many deeds of covenant be recognized for tax purposes, unless the recipient is a charity. Interest arising on a tax exempt special savings account (TESSA) opened with a building society or bank will be exempt from tax if the account is maintained throughout a five-year period.

SOCIAL SECURITY BENEFITS

Many social security benefits are not liable to income tax. These include income support, family credit, maternity allowance, child benefit, war widow's pension and disability living allowance, among others. The limited range of benefits which are taxable includes the retirement pension, widow's pension, widowed mother's allowance, and unemployment benefits. Short-term sick pay and maternity pay payable by an employer are also chargeable to tax. Incapacity benefit, introduced to replace invalidity benefit and sickness benefit, is chargeable to tax but no liability arises for the first 28 weeks of receiving benefit.

PAY AS YOU EARN

The Pay As You Earn (PAYE) system is not an independent form of taxation but is designed to collect income tax by deduction from most emoluments. When paying emoluments to employees, an employer is usually required to deduct income tax and account for that tax to the Inland Revenue. In many cases this deduction procedure will fully exhaust the individual's liability to income tax, unless there is other income. The date of 'receipt' used for assessment purposes (see above) also identifies the date of 'payment' when establishing liability for PAYE.

The PAYE system is also used to collect tax on certain payments made 'in kind'. This includes payment in the form of gold bullion, diamonds and marketable securities, among others.

ALLOWANCES

The allowances available to individuals for 1996–7 are:

Personal allowance

Each individual receives a basic personal allowance of £3,765. This is increased to £4,910 for individuals over the age of 64 on 5 April 1997, and further increased to £5,090 for those over the age of 74 on the same date. The increased allowance is available for those who died during the year of assessment but who would otherwise have achieved the appropriate age not later than 5 April 1997.

The amount of the increased personal allowance for older taxpayers will be reduced by one-half of total income in excess of £15,200. This reduction in the allowance will continue until it has been reduced to the basic personal allowance of £3,765.

Apart from limited transitional matters mentioned below, any unused part of the personal allowance of one spouse cannot be transferred to the other.

The personal allowance is given as a deduction in calculating taxable income and may therefore produce relief at the rate of 20, 24 or 40 per cent, as appropriate.

Married couple's allowance

A married man who was living with' his wife at any time in the year ending on 5 April 1997 is entitled to a married couple's allowance. The basic allowance is £1,790. This may be increased to £3,115 if either the husband or the wife is 65 years or over at any time in the year ending on 5 April 1997. A further increase to £3,155 can be obtained where either party to the marriage was 75 or over on 5 April 1997. Where an individual would otherwise have reached either age by 5 April 1997, but who died earlier in the year, the increased allowance is given.

The amount of the increased married couple's allowance may be reduced where the income of the husband (excluding the income of the wife) exceeds £15,200. The reduction will comprise:
(a) one-half of the husband's total income in excess of £15,200, less
(b) the amount of any reduction made when calculating the husband's increased personal allowance
This reduction in the married couple's allowance cannot reduce that allowance below the basic amount of £1,790.

If husband and wife were married during 1996–7 the married couple's allowance of £1,790, or any increased sum, must be reduced by one-twelfth for each complete month commencing on 6 April 1996 and preceding the date of marriage.

Unlike the personal allowance, the married couple's allowance does not reduce taxable income. Relief is granted by reducing the tax payable by 15 per cent of the allowance. Should the allowance exceed taxable income, no tax will be due.

In the absence of any further action the married couple's allowance will be given to the husband. If he is unable to utilize all or any part of that allowance due to an absence of income, the husband may transfer the unused portion to his wife. The decision whether or not to transfer remains at the discretion of the husband.

However, a wife may file an election to obtain one-half of the basic married couple's allowance as of right, leaving the husband with the balance of that allowance. Alternatively, the couple may jointly elect that the entire basic allowance should be allocated to the wife only. Except in the year of marriage, the election must be made before the commencement of the year of assessment to which it is to apply. Should either spouse be unable to utilize his or her share of the married couple's allowance the unused part may be transferred to the other spouse.

Additional personal allowance

An allowance of £1,790 is available to a single person who has a qualifying child resident with him or her in 1996–7. The allowance can also be obtained by a married man whose wife is totally incapacitated by physical or mental infirmity throughout the year.

A 'qualifying child' for 1996–7 must be born during the year, be under the age of 16 years at the commencement of the year, or be over the age of 16 at the commencement of the year and either receiving full-time instruction at a university, college, school or other educational establishment or undergoing training for a trade, profession or vocation throughout a minimum period of two years. It is also necessary that the child is the claimant's own, a stepchild of the claimant, an illegitimate child if the parents married after the child's birth, or an adopted child under the age of 18 at the time of adoption. Alternatively it must be shown that the child was either born during 1996–7 or under the age of 18 at the commencement of the year and maintained by the claimant at his or her own expense during the whole of the succeeding 12-month period.

Only one additional personal allowance of £1,790 can be obtained by an individual notwithstanding the number of children involved. Where an unmarried couple are living together as husband and wife, it is not possible for both to obtain the additional personal allowance. The allowance is given by reducing tax payable at the rate of 15 per cent of £1,790.

Widow's bereavement allowance

For the year of assessment in which a husband dies his surviving widow may obtain a widow's bereavement allowance, which is £1,790 for 1996–7. It is a requirement that the parties were 'living together' immediately before the husband's death. A similar allowance will be available in the year following death, unless the widow remarried in the year of death. No widow's bereavement allowance can be obtained for future years. Relief is granted by reducing tax payable at the rate of 15 per cent of £1,790.

Blind person's allowance

An allowance of £1,250 is available to an individual if at any time during the year ending on 5 April 1997, he or she was registered as blind on a register maintained by a local authority. If the individual is 'living with' a wife or husband, any unused part of the blind person's allowance can be transferred to the other spouse. The allowance reduces taxable income and may therefore give rise to relief at the taxpayer's highest rate of tax suffered.

Transitional allowances

There are three limited transitional allowances which are intended to ensure that the introduction of independent taxation on 6 April 1990 did not increase liability to income tax for subsequent years. These allowances comprise:
(a) an increased personal allowance available to a wife where the husband cannot fully use that allowance in 1996–7

(b) a special personal allowance available to a husband where his wife falls into a higher age group, namely over 64 or over 74
(c) a married couple's allowance available to a separated husband not 'living with' his wife if the separation occurred before 6 April 1990
Recent increases in tax allowances imply that heading (b) has become obsolete.

Life Assurance Relief

Life assurance deduction relief is limited to premiums paid on policies made before 14 March 1984. No relief is available for policies issued after this date. Where the terms of a policy made before 14 March 1984 are subsequently varied or extended to produce increased benefits, future premiums paid may no longer qualify for relief.

When paying premiums under a qualifying policy made before 14 March 1984, the payer will deduct and retain income tax at the rate of 12.5 per cent. The ability to retain deductions made in this manner is not affected by the payer's liability to income tax on taxable income. No restriction to the deduction procedure arises if aggregate premiums paid during a year of assessment do not exceed £1,500 (calculated before deducting tax). Should premiums exceed this amount, relief will be confined to £1,500 or one-sixth of total income, whichever is the greater. Where sums deducted exceed the maximum limit, the excess must be accounted for to the Inland Revenue.

Interest

In addition to personal and blind person's allowances, which reduce taxable income, and other allowances which reduce tax payable, further reliefs may be available to an individual. These include payments of interest.

In some instances, interest paid by a business proprietor may be included when calculating profits chargeable to income tax under Case I or Case II of Schedule D. In addition, relief for interest paid on a loan applied to acquire or develop land may be obtained by including the outlay in the calculation of income chargeable under Schedule A. However, many private individuals cannot obtain relief in this manner and must satisfy stringent requirements before relief will be forthcoming. In general terms it is a requirement that before interest can qualify for relief it must be paid for a qualifying purpose. Relief will not be available to the extent that interest exceeds a reasonable commercial rate and no relief is forthcoming for interest on an overdraft.

For 1996–7 relief will be available on the following payments:
(a) Interest on a loan to purchase, develop or improve an interest in land owned by the individual and used as the only or main residence of that individual. 'Land' includes large houseboats and also caravans used for residential purposes. No relief is available for interest on loans applied after 5 April 1988 for the development or improvement of land, unless the work involves the construction of a new building. Relief is available for interest paid on a loan applied to acquire a property which is the only or main residence of a dependent relative, a separated spouse or a divorced former spouse, but only where that person occupied the property before 6 April 1988. Relief may also be forthcoming for interest on a loan used to acquire some other property, perhaps to be used as the only or main residence on retirement, by an individual who is compelled to occupy property by reason of his or her work. If the loan, or aggregate of several loans, exceeds £30,000, relief is restricted to interest on that amount. Where two or more persons apply loans after 31 July

1988 to acquire interests in a single building, those persons cannot, collectively, obtain relief for interest on more than £30,000 in relation to that building. Relief is given by reducing tax payable at the rate of 15 per cent of the qualifying interest.

(b) Interest on a loan made to acquire an interest in a close company or in a partnership, or to advance money to such a person

(c) Interest on a loan to a member of a partnership to acquire machinery or plant for use in the partnership business

(d) Interest on a loan to an employed person to acquire machinery or plant for the purposes of his/her employment

(e) Interest on a loan made for the purpose of contributing capital to an industrial co-operative

(f) Interest on a loan applied for investment in an employee-controlled company

(g) Interest on a loan made to elderly persons for the purchase of an annuity where the loan is secured on land. If the loan exceeds £30,000, relief is limited to interest on this amount. This relief is restricted to income tax at the basic rate of 24 per cent

(h) Interest on a loan to personal representatives to provide funds for the payment of inheritance tax

Relief for many payments of mortgage interest is obtained through a special scheme known as MIRAS (mortgage interest relief at source). This applies to interest paid to a building society, bank, insurance company and certain other approved persons. When making payments of this nature in 1996–7 the payer will deduct and retain income tax at the rate of 15 per cent. This will provide the payer with full relief at that rate and no other relief will be necessary. Qualifying payments of interest outside the MIRAS scheme continue to produce relief by reducing tax payable at the rate of 15 per cent.

Other relief under headings (b) to (h) (but not (g)) are given by deducting interest from taxable income. This enables the taxpayer to obtain relief at his or her top rate suffered.

OTHER OUTGOINGS

Many employees pay contributions to an approved occupational pension scheme. The amount of their contributions may be deducted when calculating emoluments assessable under Schedule E. Relief should also be available for any additional voluntary contributions paid.

Self-employed individuals and those receiving earnings not covered by an occupational pension scheme may contribute under personal pension scheme arrangements. These individuals may also pay premiums under retirement annuity schemes if the arrangements were concluded before 1 July 1988. Contributions paid under both headings and which do not exceed upper limits may obtain income tax relief by deduction from taxable income.

Subject to a maximum of £100,000 in any one year, the cost of subscribing for shares in an unquoted trading company may qualify for relief under the Enterprise Investment Scheme. Many requirements must be satisfied before this relief can be obtained, but husband and wife may each take advantage of the £100,000 annual maximum. Relief is given by reducing tax payable at the rate of 20 per cent of the share subscription cost. Further relief, also to a maximum of £100,000 and given at the rate of 20 per cent, is available for a subscription of shares in a venture capital trust company.

CAPITAL GAINS TAX

An individual is chargeable to capital gains tax on chargeable gains which accrue to him or her during a year of assessment ending on 5 April. The application of the tax has been amended substantially in recent years and the following information is confined to the year of assessment 1996–7, ending on 5 April 1997.

Liability extends to individuals who are either resident or ordinarily resident for the year but special rules apply where a person permanently leaves the UK or comes to this territory for the purpose of acquiring residence. Non-residents are not liable to capital gains tax unless, exceptionally, they carry on a business in the UK through a branch or agency.

Trustees residing in the UK are chargeable to capital gains tax but chargeable gains accruing to companies are assessable to corporation tax.

Capital gains tax is chargeable on the total of chargeable gains which accrue to a person in a year of assessment, after subtracting allowable losses arising in the same year. Unused allowable losses brought forward from some earlier year may be offset against current chargeable gains but in the case of individuals this must not reduce the net chargeable gains for 1996–7 below £6,300. It is possible to utilize trading losses against chargeable gains where those losses have not been offset against income.

RATE OF TAX

Where the net chargeable gains accruing to an individual during 1996–7 do not exceed £6,300 there will be no liability to capital gains tax. If the net gains exceed £6,300 the excess is chargeable at the taxpayer's marginal rate of income tax. This is achieved by adding the excess net chargeable gains to the amount of income chargeable to income tax. The rate attributable to this top slice will disclose the rate of capital gains tax payable, which may be at 20 per cent, 24 per cent, 40 per cent or a combination of the three. Although income tax rates are used, capital gains remains a separate tax.

Capital gains tax for 1996–7 falls due for payment in full on 31 January 1998. If payment is delayed beyond this date, interest or surcharges may be imposed.

HUSBAND AND WIFE

Independent taxation requires that a husband and wife 'living together' are separately assessed to capital gains tax. Each spouse must independently calculate his or her gains and losses, with each entitled to the annual exemption of £6,300. No liability to capital gains tax arises from the transfer of assets between husband and wife 'living together'.

DISPOSAL OF ASSETS

Before liability to capital gains tax can arise a disposal, or deemed disposal, of an asset must take place. This occurs not only where assets are sold or exchanged but applies on the making of a gift. There is also a disposal of assets where any capital sum is derived from assets, for example, where compensation is received for loss or damage to an asset.

The date on which a disposal must be treated as having taken place will determine the year of assessment into which the chargeable gain or allowable loss falls. In those cases where a disposal is made under an unconditional contract, the time of disposal will be that when the contract was entered into and not the subsequent date of conveyance or transfer. A disposal under a conditional contract or option is treated as taking place when the contract becomes unconditional or the option is exercised. Disposals by way of gift are undertaken when the gift becomes effective.

VALUATION OF ASSETS

The amount actually received as consideration for the disposal of an asset will be the sum from which very limited outgoings must be deducted for the purpose of establishing the gain or loss. In some cases, however, the consideration passing will not accurately reflect the value of the asset and a different basis must be used. This applies, in particular, where an asset is transferred by way of gift or otherwise than by a bargain made at arm's length. Such transactions are deemed to take place for a consideration representing market value, which will determine both the disposal proceeds accruing to the transferor and the cost of acquisition to the transferee.

Market value represents the price which an asset might reasonably be expected to fetch on a sale in the open market. In the case of unquoted shares or securities, it is to be assumed that the hypothetical purchaser in the open market would have available all the information which a prudent prospective purchaser of shares or securities might reasonably require if he were proposing to purchase them from a willing vendor by private treaty and at arm's length. This is an important consideration as the amount of information deemed to be available to a hypothetical purchaser may materially affect the price 'reasonably' offered in an open market situation. The market value of unquoted shares or securities will usually be established following negotiations with the Shares Valuation Division of the Capital Taxes Office. The valuation of land and interests in land in the UK will be dealt with by the District Valuer.

Special rules apply to determine the market value of shares quoted on the Stock Exchange.

DEDUCTION FOR OUTGOINGS

Once the actual or notional disposal proceeds have been determined, it only remains to subtract eligible outgoings for the purpose of computing the gain or loss. There is the general rule that any outgoings deducted, or which are available to be deducted, when calculating income tax liability must be ignored. Subject to this, deductions will usually be limited to:

(a) the cost of acquiring the asset, together with incidental costs wholly and exclusively incurred in connection with the acquisition

(b) expenditure incurred wholly and exclusively on the asset in enhancing its value, being expenditure reflected in the state or nature of the asset at the time of the disposal, and any other expenditure wholly and exclusively incurred in establishing, preserving or defending title to, or a right over, the asset

(c) the incidental costs of making the disposal

Where the disposal concerns a leasehold interest having less than 50 years to run, any expenditure falling under (a) and (b) must be written off throughout the duration of the lease. This recognizes that a lease is a wasting asset which, at the termination of the leasing period, will retain no value.

ASSETS HELD ON 31 MARCH 1982

Where the disposal relates to assets held on 31 March 1982, the actual cost of acquisition will not usually enter into the calculation of gain. It is to be assumed that such assets were acquired on 31 March 1982 for a consideration representing market value on that date. The increase in value, if any, occurring before 31 March 1982 will not be assessable to capital gains tax.

INDEXATION ALLOWANCE

An indexation allowance may be available when calculating any gain on the disposal of an asset. This allowance is based on percentage increases in the retail prices index between the month of March 1982 or the month in which expenditure is incurred, if later, and the month of disposal. The increase is applied to the items of expenditure in (a) and (b) above to determine the amount of the indexation allowance. However, if the asset was acquired before 31 March 1982, the allowance will be based on market value at 31 March 1982.

Previously the indexation allowance could be subtracted from the gain, added to the loss or used to convert a gain into a loss. However, for disposals taking place after 29 November 1993 the indexation allowance may only be applied to reduce a gain. It cannot increase the amount of a loss, and where the allowance exceeds the amount of a gain it only remains necessary to reduce the gain to nil.

EXEMPTIONS

There is a general exemption from liability to capital gains tax where the net gains of an individual for 1996–7 do not exceed £6,300. This general exemption applies separately to a husband and to his wife where the parties are 'living together'.

The disposal of many assets will not give rise to chargeable gains or allowable losses and these assets include:

(a) private motor cars
(b) government securities
(c) loan stock and other securities (but not shares)
(d) options and contracts relating to securities within (b) and (c)
(e) National Savings Certificates, Premium Bonds, Defence Bonds and National Development Bonds
(f) currency of any description acquired for personal expenditure outside the UK
(g) decorations awarded for valour
(h) betting wins and pools, lottery or games prizes
(i) compensation or damages for any wrong or injury suffered by an individual in his/her person or in his/her profession or vocation
(j) life assurance and deferred annuity contracts where the person making the disposal is the original beneficial owner
(k) dwelling-houses and land enjoyed with the residence which is an individual's only or main residence
(l) tangible movable property, the consideration for the disposal of which does not exceed £6,000
(m) certain tangible movable property which is a wasting asset having a life not exceeding 50 years
(n) assets transferred to charities and other bodies
(o) works of art, historic buildings and similar assets
(p) assets used to provide maintenance funds for historic buildings
(q) assets transferred to trustees for the benefit of employees

DWELLING-HOUSES

Exemption from capital gains tax will usually be available for any gain which accrues to an individual from the disposal of, or of an interest in, a dwelling-house or part of a dwelling-house which has been his/her only or main residence. The exemption extends to land which has been occupied and enjoyed with the residence as its garden or grounds. Some restriction may be necessary where the land exceeds half a hectare.

The gain will not be chargeable to capital gains tax if the dwelling-house, or part, has been the individual's only or main residence throughout the period of ownership, or throughout the entire period except for all or any part of the last three years. A proportionate part of the gain will be exempt in other cases if the dwelling-house has been the individual's only or main residence for part only of the period of ownership. In the case of property acquired before 31 March 1982, the period of ownership is treated as commencing on this date.

Where part of the dwelling-house has been used exclusively for business purposes, that part of the gain attributable to business use will not be exempt. It will be comparatively unusual for any part to be used exclusively for such a purpose, except perhaps in the case of doctors' or dentists' surgeries.

In those cases where part of a qualifying dwelling-house has been used to provide rented residential accommodation this non-personal use may frequently be ignored when calculating exemption from capital gains tax, unless relatively substantial sums are involved.

Dwellings occupied by dependent relatives or separated or divorced former spouses, may also qualify for the exemption, but only where occupation commenced before 6 April 1988.

ROLL-OVER RELIEF – BUSINESS ASSETS

Persons carrying on business will often undertake the disposal of an asset and use the proceeds to finance the acquisition of a replacement asset. Where this situation arises a claim for roll-over relief may be available. The broad effect of such a claim is that all or part of the gain arising on the disposal of the old asset may be disregarded. The gain or part is then subtracted from the cost of acquiring the replacement asset. As this cost is reduced, any gain arising from the future disposal of the replacement asset will be correspondingly increased, unless of course a further roll-over situation then develops.

It remains a requirement that both the old and the replacement asset must be used for the purpose of the taxpayer's business. Relief will only be available if the acquisition of the replacement asset takes place within a period commencing twelve months before, and ending three years after, the disposal of the old asset, although the Inland Revenue retain a discretion to extend this period where the circumstances were such that it was impossible for the taxpayer to acquire the replacement asset before the expiration of the normal time limit.

Whilst many business assets qualify for roll-over relief there are exceptions.

ROLL-OVER RELIEF – SHARES

An additional form of roll-over relief was introduced for disposals taking place after 15 March 1993 and matched with the acquisition of shares in unquoted companies. The conditions governing this relief were subsequently relaxed on several occasions and from 29 November 1994, gains arising on the disposal of virtually any asset will enable an individual, and some trustees, to contemplate the availability of roll-over relief. It is a necessary requirement that the individual or trustee making the disposal acquires shares in a qualifying unquoted trading company. Most shareholdings in trading companies will qualify unless the company also undertakes non-trading activities. An unusual feature of roll-over relief on the reinvestment in shares is that, subject to upper limits, the individual or trustee can roll over any part of the chargeable gain arising on the disposal of assets. The ability to select the amount to be rolled over enables the claimant to leave undisturbed the remaining gain, which can be offset against available losses or perhaps used to absorb the annual exemption of £6,300.

DEFERRAL RELIEF

A novel form of roll-over relief was introduced for disposals taking place after 28 November 1994. Gains arising from such disposals may be matched, in whole or in part, with an investment in shares under the Enterprise Investment Scheme. To the extent that the investment qualifies for income tax relief, any part of the gain arising on disposal, not exceeding the investment qualifying for relief, may become the subject of a claim. Unlike the more usual form of roll-over relief, this claim does not eliminate or reduce the chargeable gain. It has the effect of deferring that gain until the time of some future event, which will usually be identified by the disposal of shares.

A similar form of deferral relief is available for gains arising on disposals taking place after 5 April 1995. It is a necessary requirement that the individual undertaking the disposal makes a qualifying investment in a venture capital trust company. To the extent of the gain arising, which must not exceed the amount of the investment qualifying for income tax relief, that gain is deferred until the time of a future event, which will normally comprise the disposal of shares in the venture capital trust.

HOLD-OVER RELIEF – GIFTS

The gift of an asset is treated as a disposal made for a consideration equal to market value, with a corresponding acquisition by the transferee at an identical value. In the case of gifts made by individuals and a limited range of trustees to a transferee resident in the UK, a form of hold-over relief may be available. Relief is limited to the transfer of certain assets, including the following:

(a) assets used for the purposes of a trade or similar activity carried on by the transferor or his/her personal company

(b) shares or securities of a trading company which is neither quoted on a stock exchange nor dealt in on the Unlisted Securities Market

(c) shares or securities of a trading company which is quoted or listed but which is the transferor's personal company

(d) many interests in agricultural property qualifying for agricultural property relief for inheritance tax purposes

(e) assets involved in transactions which are lifetime transfers for inheritance tax purposes, other than potentially exempt transfers

The effect of the claim is similar to that following a claim for roll-over relief on the disposal of business assets, but adjustments will be necessary where some consideration is given for the transfer, the asset has not been used for business purposes throughout the period of ownership, or not all assets of a company are used for business purposes.

RETIREMENT RELIEF

Retirement relief is available to an individual who disposes by way of sale or gift of the whole or part of a business. It does not necessarily follow that the isolated disposal of assets will represent the disposal of the whole or part of a business. The main condition for granting this relief is that throughout a period of at least one year the business has been owned either by the individual or by a trading company in which the individual retained a sufficient shareholding interest. The relief extends also to cases where an individual disposes by way of sale or gift of shares or securities of a company. It must be demonstrated that the company was a trading company, that the individual retained a sufficient shareholding interest, and that he/she was engaged as a full-time working officer or employee.

638   Taxation

An individual who has attained the age of 50 years at the time of a disposal taking place after 27 November 1995 may obtain retirement relief up to a maximum of £625,000. The amount of this relief must be reduced if the underlying conditions have not been satisfied throughout a ten-year period. With a single exception no retirement relief can be obtained if the disposal occurs before the individual's 50th birthday. This exception arises where an individual is compelled to retire early on the grounds of ill-health. The normal retirement relief may then be obtained. Any retirement relief must be subtracted from the net gains arising on disposal, leaving the balance remaining, if any, chargeable to capital gains tax in the normal manner.

DEATH

No capital gains tax is chargeable on the value of assets retained at the time of death. However, the personal representatives administering the deceased's estate are deemed to acquire those assets for a consideration representing market value on death. This ensures that any increase in value occurring before the date of death will not be chargeable to capital gains tax. If a legatee or other person acquires an asset under a will or intestacy no chargeable gain will accrue to the personal representatives, and the person taking the asset will also be treated as having acquired it at the time of death for its then market value.

INHERITANCE TAX

Liability to inheritance tax may arise on a limited range of lifetime gifts and other dispositions and also on the value of assets retained, or deemed to be retained, at the time of death. An individual's domicile at the time of any gift or on death is an important matter. Domicile will generally be determined by applying normal rules, although special considerations may be necessary where an individual was previously domiciled in the UK but subsequently acquired a domicile of choice overseas. Where a person was domiciled in the UK at the time of a disposition or on death the location of assets is immaterial and full liability to inheritance tax arises. Individuals domiciled outside the UK are, however, chargeable to inheritance tax only on transactions affecting assets located in the UK.

The assets of husband and wife are not merged for inheritance tax purposes. Each spouse is treated as a separate individual entitled to receive the benefit of his or her exemptions, reliefs and rates of tax. Where husband and wife retain similar assets, e.g. shares in the same family company, special 'related property' provisions may require the merger of those assets for valuation purposes only.

LIFETIME GIFTS AND DISPOSITIONS

Gifts and dispositions made during lifetime fall under four broad headings, namely:
(a) dispositions which are not transfers of value
(b) exempt transfers
(c) potentially exempt transfers
(d) chargeable transfers

Dispositions which are not transfers of value
Several lifetime transactions are not treated as transfers of value and may be entirely disregarded for inheritance tax purposes. These include transactions not intended to confer gratuitous benefit, the provision of family maintenance, the waiver of the right to receive remuneration or dividends, and the grant of agricultural tenancies for full consideration.

Exempt transfers
Certain transfers are treated as exempt transfers and incur no liability to inheritance tax. The main exempt transfers are listed below:

Transfers between spouses – Transfers between husband and wife are usually exempt. However, if the transferor is, but the transferee spouse is not, domiciled in the UK, transfers will be exempt only to the extent that the total does not exceed £55,000. Unlike the requirement used for income tax and capital gains tax purposes, it is immaterial whether husband and wife are living together.

Annual exemption – The first £3,000 of gifts and other dispositions made in a year ending on 5 April is exempt. If the exemption is not used, or not wholly used, in any year the balance may be carried forward to the following year only. The annual exemption will only be available for a potentially exempt transfer if that transfer subsequently becomes chargeable by reason of the donor's death.

Small gifts – Outright gifts of £250 or less to any person in one year ending 5 April are exempt.

Normal expenditure – A transfer made during lifetime and comprising normal expenditure is exempt. To obtain this exemption it must be shown that:
(a) the transfer was made as part of the normal expenditure of the transferor
(b) taking one year with another, the transfer was made out of income
(c) after allowing for all transfers of value forming part of normal expenditure the transferor was left with sufficient income to maintain his or her usual standard of living

Gifts in consideration of marriage – These are exempt if they satisfy certain requirements. The amount allowed will be governed by the relationship between the donor and a party to the marriage. The allowable amounts comprise:
(a) gifts by a parent, £5,000
(b) gifts by a grandparent, £2,500
(c) gifts by a party to the marriage, £2,500
(d) gifts by other persons, £1,000

Gifts to charities – These are exempt from liability.

Gifts to political parties – Gifts which satisfy certain requirements are generally exempt.

Gifts for national purposes – Gifts made to an extensive list of bodies are exempt from liability. These include, among others, the National Gallery, the British Museum, the National Trust, the National Art Collections Fund, the National Heritage Memorial Fund, the Historic Buildings and Monuments Commission for England (English Heritage), any local authority, any university or university college in the UK.

A number of other gifts made for the public benefit are also exempt.

Potentially exempt transfers
Lifetime gifts and dispositions which are neither to be ignored nor comprise exempt transfers incur possible liability to inheritance tax. However, relief is available for a range of potentially exempt transfers. These comprise gifts made by an individual to:
(a) a second individual
(b) trustees administering an accumulation and maintenance trust
(c) trustees administering a disabled person's trust
    The accumulation and maintenance trust mentioned in (b) must provide that on reaching a specified age, not exceeding 25 years, a beneficiary will become absolutely entitled to trust assets or obtain an interest in possession in the income from those assets.

Additions to the above list affect settled property administered by trustees where an individual, or individuals, retain an interest in possession. The transfer of assets to, the removal of assets from, or the rearrangement of interests in such property comprise potentially exempt transfers if the person transferring an interest and the person benefiting from the transfer are both individuals. No immediate liability to inheritance tax will arise on the making of a potentially exempt transfer. Should the donor survive for a period of seven years, immunity from liability will be confirmed. However, the donor's death within the seven-year *inter vivos* period produces liability if the amounts involved are sufficiently substantial (*see* below).

Chargeable transfers

Any remaining lifetime gifts or dispositions which are neither to be ignored nor represent exempt transfers or potentially exempt transfers, incur liability to inheritance tax. The range of such chargeable transfers is severely limited and is broadly confined to transfers made to or affecting discretionary trusts, transfers to non-individuals and transfers involving companies.

GIFTS WITH RESERVATION

A lifetime gift of assets made at any time after 17 March 1986 may incur additional liability to inheritance tax if the donor retains some interest in the subject matter of the gift. This may arise, for example, where a parent transfers a dwelling-house to a son or daughter and continues to occupy the property or to enjoy some benefit from that property. The retention of a benefit may be ignored where it is enjoyed in return for full consideration, perhaps a commercial rent, or where the benefit arises from changed circumstances which could not have been foreseen at the time of the original gift. The gift with reservation provisions will not usually apply to most exempt transfers.

There are three possibilities which may arise where the donor reserves or enjoys some benefit from the subject matter of a previous gift and subsequently dies, namely:

(a) if no benefit is enjoyed within a period of seven years before death there can be no further liability

(b) if the benefit ceased to be enjoyed within a period of seven years before the date of death, the original donor is deemed to have made a potentially exempt transfer representing the value of the asset at the time of cessation

(c) if the benefit is enjoyed at the time of death, the value of the asset must be included in the value of the deceased's estate on death

It must be emphasized that the existence of a benefit enjoyed at any time within a period of seven years before death will establish liability to tax on gifts with reservation, notwithstanding that the gift may have been made many years earlier, providing it was undertaken after 17 March 1986.

DEATH

Immediately before the time of death an individual is deemed to make a transfer of value. This transfer will comprise the value of assets forming part of the deceased's estate after subtracting most liabilities. Any exempt transfers may, however, be excluded. These include transfers for the benefit of a surviving spouse, a charity and a qualifying political party, together with bequests to approved bodies and for national purposes.

Death may also trigger three additional liabilities, namely:

(a) A potentially exempt transfer made within the period of seven years ending on death loses its potential status and becomes chargeable to inheritance tax

(b) The value of gifts made with reservation may incur liability if any benefit was enjoyed within a period of seven years preceding death

(c) Additional tax may become payable for chargeable lifetime transfers made within seven years before death

VALUATIONS

The valuation of assets is an important matter as this will establish the value transferred for lifetime dispositions and also the value of a person's estate at the time of death. The value of property will represent the price which might reasonably be expected from a sale in the open market. This price cannot be reduced on the grounds that, should the whole property be placed on the market simultaneously, values would be depressed.

In some cases it may be necessary to incorporate the value of 'related property'. This will include property comprised in the estate of the transferor's spouse and certain property previously transferred to charities. The purpose of the related property valuation rules is not to add the value of the property to the estate of the transferor. Related property must be merged to establish the aggregate value of the respective interests and this value is then apportioned, usually on a *pro rata* basis, to the separate interests.

The value of shares and securities quoted on the Stock Exchange will be determined by extracting figures from the daily list of official prices.

Where quoted shares and securities are sold or the quotation is suspended within a period of 12 months following the date of death, a claim may be made to substitute the proceeds or subsequent value for the value on death. This claim will only be beneficial if the gross proceeds realized are lower or the value has fallen below market value at the time of death. A similar claim may be available for interests in land sold within a period of four years following death.

RELIEF FOR ASSETS

Special relief is made available for certain assets, notably:

Woodlands

Where woodlands pass on death the value will usually be included in the deceased's estate. However, an election may be made in respect of land in the UK on which trees or underwood is growing to delete the value of those assets. Relief is confined to the value of trees or underwood and does not extend to the land on which they are growing. Liability to inheritance tax will arise if and when the trees or underwood are sold on a future occasion.

Agricultural property

Relief is available for the agricultural value of agricultural property. Such property must be occupied and used for agricultural purposes and relief is confined to the agricultural value only.

The value transferred, either on a lifetime gift or on death, must be determined. This value may then be reduced by a percentage. The percentage has changed from time to time but for events taking place after 9 March 1992 a 100 per cent deduction will be available if the transferor retained vacant possession or could have obtained that possession within a period of 12 months following the transfer. In other cases, notably including land let to tenants, a lower deduction of 50 per cent is usually available. However, this lower deduction may be increased to 100 per cent if the letting was made after 31 August 1995.

It remains a requirement that the agricultural property was either occupied by the transferor for the purposes of agriculture throughout a two-year period ending on the date of the transfer, or was owned by him/her throughout a period of seven years ending on that date and also occupied for agricultural purposes.

Business property

Where the value transferred is attributable to relevant business property, that value may be reduced by a percentage. The reduction in value applies to:
(a) property consisting of a business or an interest in a business
(b) shares or securities of an unquoted company which provided the transferor with more than 25 per cent of voting rights
(c) other unquoted shares or securities not falling within (b)
(d) shares or securities of a quoted company which provided the transferor with control
(e) any land, building, machinery or plant which, immediately before the transfer, was used wholly or mainly for the purposes of a business carried on by a company of which the transferor had control
(f) any land, building, machinery or plant which, immediately before the transfer, was used wholly or mainly for the purposes of a business carried on by a partnership of which the transferor was a partner
(g) any land, building, machinery or plant which, immediately before the transfer, was used wholly or mainly for the purposes of a business carried on by the transferor and was then settled property in which he or she retained an interest in possession

The percentage deductions have changed from time to time. For events occurring after 9 March 1992 a deduction of 100 per cent is available for assets falling within (a) and (b). The deductions for unquoted shares in (c) became 50 per cent but this was increased to 100 per cent for events taking place after 5 April 1996. A deduction of 50 per cent remains for assets within (d) to (g).

It is a general requirement that the property must have been retained for a period of two years before the transfer or death and restrictions may be necessary if the property has not been used wholly for business purposes. The same property cannot obtain both business property relief and the relief available for agricultural property.

CALCULATION OF TAX PAYABLE

The calculation of inheritance tax payable adopts the use of a cumulative total. Each chargeable lifetime transfer is added to the total with a final addition made on death. The top slice added to the total for the current event determines the rate at which inheritance tax must be paid. However, the cumulative total will only include transfers made within a period of seven years before the current event and those undertaken outside this period must be excluded.

Lifetime chargeable transfers

The value transferred by the limited range of lifetime chargeable transfers must be added to the seven-year cumulative total to calculate whether any inheritance tax is due. Should the nil rate band be exceeded, tax will be imposed on the excess at one-half of the rate shown below. However, if the donor dies within a period of seven years from the date of the chargeable lifetime transfer, additional tax may be due. This is calculated by applying tax at the full rate (in substitution for the one-half rate previously used). The amount of tax is then reduced to a percentage by

applying tapering relief. This percentage is governed by the number of years from the date of the lifetime gift to the date of death and is as follows:

Period of years before death	
Not more than 3	100%
More than 3 but not more than 4	80%
More than 4 but not more than 5	60%
More than 5 but not more than 6	40%
More than 6 but not more than 7	20%

Should this exercise produce liability greater than that previously paid at the one-half rate on the lifetime transfer, additional tax, representing the difference, must be discharged. Where the calculation shows an amount falling below tax paid on the lifetime transfer, no additional liability can arise nor will the shortfall become repayable.

Tapering relief will, of course, only be available if the calculation discloses a liability to inheritance tax. There can be no liability to the extent that the lifetime transfer falls within the nil rate band.

Potentially exempt transfers

Where a potentially exempt transfer loses immunity from liability due to the donor's death within the seven-year *inter vivos* period, the value transferred by that transfer enters into the cumulative total. Any liability to inheritance tax will be calculated by applying the full rate shown below, reduced to the percentage governed by tapering relief if the original transfer occurred more than three years before death. Liability can only arise to the extent, if any, that the nil rate band is exceeded.

Death

The final addition to the seven-year cumulative total will comprise the value of an estate on death. Inheritance tax will be calculated by applying the full rate shown below to the extent the nil rate band is exceeded. No tapering relief can be obtained.

RATES OF TAX

In earlier times there were several rates of inheritance tax which progressively increased as the value transferred grew in size. However, for events taking place after 5 April 1996, a nil rate applies to the first £200,000. Any excess is charged at the single positive rate of 40 per cent.

Only one-half of the 40 per cent rate (namely 20 per cent) will be applicable for chargeable lifetime transfers.

PAYMENT OF TAX

Inheritance tax usually falls due for payment six months after the end of the month in which the chargeable transaction takes place. Where a transfer other than that made on death occurs after 5 April and before the following 1 October, tax falls due on the following 30 April, although there are some exceptions to this general rule.

Inheritance tax attributable to the transfer of certain land, controlling shareholding interests, unquoted shares, businesses and interests in businesses, together with agricultural property, may usually be satisfied by instalments spread over ten years. Except in the case of non-agricultural land, where interest is charged on outstanding instalments, no liability to interest arises where tax is paid on the due date. In all cases, delay in the payment of tax may incur liability to interest.

SETTLED PROPERTY

Complex rules apply to establish inheritance tax liability on settled property. Where a person is beneficially entitled to an interest in possession, that person is effectively deemed to own the property in which the interest subsists

It follows that where the interest comes to an end during the beneficiary's lifetime and some other person becomes entitled to the property or interest, the beneficiary is treated as having made a transfer of value. However, this will usually comprise a potentially exempt transfer. In addition, no liability will arise where the property vests in the absolute ownership of the previous beneficiary. The death of a person entitled to an interest in possession will require the value of the underlying property to be added to the value of the deceased's estate.

In the case of other settled property where there is no interest in possession (e.g. discretionary trusts), liability to tax will arise on each ten-year anniversary of the trust. There will also be liability if property ceases to be held on discretionary trusts before the first ten-year anniversary date is reached or between anniversaries. The rate of tax suffered will be governed by several considerations, including previous dispositions made by the settlor of the trust, transactions concluded by the trustees, and the period throughout which property has been held in trust.

Accumulation and maintenance settlements which require assets to be distributed, or interests in income to be created, not later than a beneficiary's 25th birthday may be exempt from any liability to inheritance tax.

CORPORATION TAX

Profits, gains and income accruing to companies resident in the UK incur liability to corporation tax. Non-resident companies are immune from this tax unless they carry on a trade in the UK through a permanent establishment, branch or office. Companies residing outside the UK may be liable to income tax at the basic rate on other income arising in the UK, perhaps from letting property. The following comments are confined to companies resident in the UK and have little application to those residing overseas.

Liability to corporation tax is governed by the profits, gains or income for an accounting period. This is usually the period for which financial accounts are made up, and in the case of companies preparing accounts to the same accounting date annually will comprise successive periods of 12 months.

RATE OF TAX

The amount of profits or income for an accounting period must be determined on normal taxation principles. The special rules which apply to individuals where a source of income is acquired or discontinued are ignored and consideration is confined to the actual profits or income for an accounting period.

The rate of corporation tax is fixed for a financial year ending on 31 March. Where the accounting period of a company overlaps this date and there is a change in the rate of corporation tax, profits and income must be apportioned.

In recent years the full rate of corporation tax has been as follows:

Financial year
Ending 31 March 1990 ... 35%
31 March 1991 ... 34%
31 March 1992, 1993, 1994, 1995, 1996, 1997 ... 33%

SMALL COMPANIES RATE

Where the profits of a company do not exceed stated limits, corporation tax becomes payable at the small companies rate. It is the amount of profits and not the size of the company which governs the application of this rate.

In recent years the small companies rate has been as follows:

Financial year
Ending 31 March 1990, 1991,
1992, 1993, 1994, 1995, 1996 ... 25%
31 March 1997 ... 24%

The level of profits which a company may derive without losing the benefit of the small companies rate is frequently changed. For each year ending on 31 March 1995, 31 March 1996 and 31 March 1997 the limit is £300,000. Where profits exceed £300,000 but fall below £1,500,000 marginal small companies rate relief applies. The effect of marginal relief is that the average rate of corporation tax imposed on all profits steadily increases from the lower small companies rate to the full rate of 33 per cent, with tax being imposed on profits in the margin at approximately 35 per cent.

Different upper limits and marginal rates applied for earlier years. Where the accounting period of a company overlaps 31 March, profits must be apportioned to establish the appropriate rate for each part of those profits.

The lower limit of £300,000 and the upper limit of £1,500,000 apply to a period of 12 months and must be proportionately reduced for shorter periods. Some restriction in the small companies rate and the marginal rate may be necessary if there are two or more associated companies, namely companies under common control.

The small companies rate is not available for close investment-holding companies. These are mainly investment companies, other than those receiving most of their income from letting land and property.

CAPITAL GAINS

Chargeable gains arising to a company are calculated in a manner similar to that used for individuals. However, companies cannot obtain the annual exemption of £6,300. Nor are they assessed to capital gains tax. In place of this tax companies suffer liability to corporation tax on chargeable gains. Tax is suffered on the full chargeable gain, after subtracting relief for losses, if any.

DISTRIBUTIONS

Dividends and other qualifying distributions made by a UK resident company are not satisfied after deduction of income tax. However, when making a distribution a company is required to account to the Inland Revenue for advance corporation tax. The amount of this tax is based on the distribution and changes in the rate have been introduced in recent years as follows:

Distribution	Rate
Year ending 5 April 1993	one third
Year ending 5 April 1994	nine thirty-firsts
Year ending 5 April 1995	one quarter
Year ending 5 April 1996	one quarter
Year ending 5 April 1997	one quarter

Advance corporation tax accounted for in this manner in relation to distributions made in an accounting period may usually be set against a company's corporation tax liability for the same period. Some restrictions are imposed on the amount which can be offset but any surplus may be carried forward, or perhaps carried backwards, and set against corporation tax paid or due for other accounting periods.

A UK resident shareholder receiving a qualifying distribution also obtains a tax credit based on the distribution made. Over the same five-year period the tax credit will be calculated as follows:

Distribution	Rate
Year ending 5 April 1993	one third
Year ending 5 April 1994	one quarter
Year ending 5 April 1995	one quarter
Year ending 5 April 1996	one quarter
Year ending 5 April 1997	one quarter

The total income of the individual therefore comprises the aggregate of the distribution and the tax credit, with that credit representing income tax at the rate of 20 per cent on the total amount in the more recent years. If the individual is not liable or not fully liable to income tax at this rate, all or part of the tax credit can be refunded by the Inland Revenue. There is no liability on distributions at the basic rate but individuals with substantial income incur liability to income tax at the higher rate of 40 per cent on the aggregate of the distribution and the tax credit. With tax deemed to have been suffered at the lower rate of 20 per cent the additional liability will be limited to the excess over this rate, which is also 20 per cent.

INTEREST

On making many payments of interest after 5 April 1996 a company is required to deduct income tax at the lower rate of 20 per cent and account for the tax deducted to the Inland Revenue. The gross amount of interest paid will usually comprise a charge on income to be offset against profits on which corporation tax becomes payable.

GROUPS OF COMPANIES

Each company within a group is separately charged to corporation tax on profits, gains and income. However, where one group member realizes a loss, other than a capital loss, a claim may be made to offset the deficiency against profits of some other member of the same group.

Claims are also available to avoid the payment of advance corporation tax on distributions, or the deduction of income tax on the payment of interest, for transactions between members of a group of companies. The transfer of capital assets from one member of a group to a fellow member will incur no liability to tax on chargeable gains.

PAY AND FILE

A recently introduced 'pay and file' system now affects all companies. Under this system tax is payable nine months following the end of the accounting period involved, with accounts and returns being submitted three months later. Failure to satisfy corporation tax or to submit documents within these time limits will result in a liability to discharge interest and penalties.

Although the pay and file system retains some similarity with self-assessment, there are differences. These are likely to be removed shortly when full self-assessment is extended to companies.

VALUE ADDED TAX

Value added tax (VAT) is charged on the value of the supplies made by a registered trader and extends to both the supply of goods and the supply of services. It is administered by Customs and Excise.

Liability to account for VAT arises on the value of goods imported into the UK from sources outside the European Community. In contrast goods imported by a trader from a second trader in a member state of the European Community attract no VAT on importation. Instead there is an acquisition tax whereby a trader who acquires goods must include the acquisition in his normal VAT return and

account for the tax due. A UK trader who exports goods to a member state will not be required to account for VAT on the supply, if that trader observes the requirements laid down by regulations.

REGISTRATION

All traders, including professional men and women and companies, making taxable supplies of a value exceeding stated limits are required to register for VAT purposes. Taxable supplies represent the supply of goods and services potentially chargeable with VAT. The limits which govern mandatory registration are amended annually but from 29 November 1995 an unregistered trader must register:

(a) at any time, if there are reasonable grounds for believing that the value of taxable supplies in the next 30 days will exceed £47,000.

(b) at the end of any month if the value of taxable supplies in the 12 months then ending has exceeded £47,000.

Liability to register under (b) may be avoided if it can be shown that the value of supplies in the period of 12 months then beginning will not exceed £45,000. There may, however, be liability to register immediately where a business is taken over from another trader as a 'going concern'.

Where the limits governing mandatory registration have been exceeded, it is necessary for the trader to notify Customs and Excise. In the event of failure to provide prompt notification, the person concerned will be required to account for VAT from the proper registration date.

A trader whose taxable supplies do not reach the mandatory registration limits may apply for voluntary registration. This step may be thought advisable to recover input tax or to compete with other registered traders.

A registered trader may submit an application for deregistration if the value of taxable supplies subsequently falls. From 29 November 1995, an application for deregistration can be made if the value of taxable supplies for the year beginning on the application date is not expected to exceed £45,000.

INPUT TAX

A registered trader will both suffer tax (input tax) when obtaining goods or services for the purposes of his business and also become liable to account for tax (output tax) on the value of goods and services which he supplies. Relief can usually be obtained for input tax suffered, either by setting that tax against output tax due or by repayment. Most items of input tax can be relieved in this manner but there are exceptions, including the prohibition of relief for the cost of business entertaining. Where a registered trader makes both exempt supplies and also taxable supplies to his customers or clients, there may be some restriction in the amount of input tax which can be recovered.

OUTPUT TAX

When making a taxable supply of goods or services a registered trader must account for output tax, if any, on the value of the supply. Usually the price charged by the registered trader will be increased by adding VAT but failure to make the required addition will not remove liability to account for output tax.

The application of output tax, and also input tax, may be affected where a trader is using the special second-hand goods scheme.

EXEMPT SUPPLIES

No VAT is chargeable on the supply of goods or services which are treated as exempt supplies. These include the provision of burial and cremation facilities, insurance, finance and education. The granting of a lease to occupy land or the sale of land will usually comprise an exempt supply, but there are numerous exceptions. In particular, the sale of new non-domestic buildings or certain buildings used by charities cannot be treated as exempt supplies.

A taxable person may elect to tax rents and other supplies of buildings and agricultural land not used for residential or charitable purposes.

Exempt supplies do not enter into the calculation of taxable supplies which governs liability to mandatory registration. Such supplies made by a registered trader may, however, limit the amount of input tax which can be relieved. It is for this reason that the election may be useful.

RATES OF TAX

Two rates of VAT have applied since 1 April 1991, namely:
(a) a zero, or nil, rate
(b) a standard rate of 17.5 per cent
In addition, a special reduced rate of 8 per cent has applied to supplies of domestic fuel since March 1994. Although no tax is due on a zero-rated supply, this does comprise a taxable supply which must be included in the calculation which governs liability to register.

ZERO-RATING

A large number of supplies are zero-rated. The following list is not exhaustive but indicates the wide range of supplies which may be included under this heading:
(a) the supply of many items of food and drink for human consumption. This does not include ice creams, chocolates, sweets, potato crisps and alcoholic drinks. Nor does it extend to supplies made in the course of catering or to items supplied for consumption in a restaurant or café. Whilst the supply of cold items, e.g. sandwiches, for consumption away from the supplier's premises, is zero-rated, the supply of hot food, for example fish and chips, is not
(b) animal feeding stuffs
(c) sewerage and water, unless supplied for industrial purposes
(d) books, brochures, pamphlets, leaflets, newspapers, maps and charts
(e) talking books for the blind and handicapped, and wireless sets for the blind
(f) supplies of services, other than professional services, when constructing a new domestic building or a building to be used by a charity. The supply of materials for such a building is also zero-rated, together with the sale or the grant of a long lease for these buildings. Alterations to some protected buildings are also zero-rated
(g) the transportation of persons in a vehicle, ship or aircraft designed to carry not less than 12 persons
(h) supplies of drugs, medicines and other aids for the handicapped
(i) supplies of clothing and footwear for young persons
(j) exports

COLLECTION OF TAX

Registered traders submit VAT returns for accounting periods usually of three months duration but arrangements can be made to submit returns on a monthly basis. Very large traders must account for tax on a monthly basis but this does not affect the three-monthly return. The return will show both the output tax due for supplies made by the trader in the accounting period and also the input tax for which relief is claimed. If the output tax exceeds input tax the balance must be remitted with the VAT return. Where input tax suffered exceeds the output tax due the registered

trader may claim recovery of the excess from Customs and Excise.

This basis for collecting tax explains the structure of VAT. Where supplies are made between registered traders the supplier will account for an amount of tax which will usually be identical to the tax recovered by the person to whom the supply is made. However, where the supply is made to a person who is not a registered trader there can be no recovery of input tax and it is on this person that the final burden of VAT eventually falls.

In those cases where goods are acquired by a UK trader from a supplier within a member state of the European Community the trader must also account for the tax due on acquisition.

An optional scheme is available for registered traders having an annual turnover of taxable supplies not exceeding £300,000. Such traders may, if they wish, render returns annually. Nine interim payments of VAT will be paid on account, with a final balancing payment accompanying submission of the return. The number of interim payments may be reduced if turnover does not exceed £100,000.

BAD DEBTS

Many retailers operate special retail schemes for calculating the amount of VAT due. These schemes are, broadly, based on the volume of consideration received in an accounting period. Should a customer fail to pay for goods or services supplied, there will be no consideration on which VAT falls to be calculated.

To avoid the problem of bad debts incurred by traders not operating a special retail scheme, an optional system of cash accounting is available. This scheme, confined to traders with annual taxable supplies not exceeding £350,000, enables returns to be made on a cash basis, in substitution for the normal supply basis. Traders using such a scheme will not, of course, include bad debts in the calculation of cash receipts.

Where neither the cash accounting arrangements nor the special retail scheme applies, output tax falls due on the value of the supply and liability is not affected by failure to receive consideration. However, where a debt is more than six months old and is written off in the supplier's books, relief for bad debts will be forthcoming.

OTHER SPECIAL SCHEMES

In addition to the schemes for retailers, there are several special schemes applied to calculate the amount of VAT due and which also limit the ability to recover input tax. Before 1 January 1995 these schemes were confined to a limited range of goods, but on and after this date virtually all second-hand goods have been brought within special margin schemes.

FARMERS

Farmers may elect to apply a special flat rate scheme. This scheme is available to farmers who are not registered traders. Under the scheme a flat-rate addition of 4 per cent may be made on sales, with the amount of the addition being retained by the farmer. Registered traders to whom such a supply is made may treat the 4 per cent addition as recoverable input tax.

Duty and Tax-free Allowances

Travellers are entitled to the allowances in either of the columns below (but not both) for any category of goods (*see* Notes on Allowances). Passengers under 17 are not, however, entitled to tobacco and drinks allowances.

COLUMN 1	COLUMN 2
Goods obtained duty and tax-free in the European Union (e.g. in duty-free shops), or duty and tax-free on a ship or aircraft, or goods obtained outside the European Union	Suggested guidelines for goods obtained duty and tax paid in the European Union
Tobacco goods	*Tobacco goods*
200 cigarettes	800 cigarettes
or	*plus*
100 cigarillos	400 cigarillos
or	*plus*
50 cigars	200 cigars
or	*plus*
250 grammes of tobacco	1 kg of tobacco
Alcoholic drinks	*Alcoholic drinks*
2 litres of still table wine	90 litres of still table wine (not more than 60 litres should
plus	be sparkling wine)
1 litre over 22% vol. (e.g. spirits and strong	*plus*
liqueurs)	10 litres over 22% vol. (e.g. spirits and strong liqueurs)
or	*plus*
2 litres not over 22% vol. (e.g. low strength liqueurs,	20 litres not over 22% vol. (e.g. low strength liqueurs,
fortified wine or sparkling wine)	fortified wine)
or	*plus*
A further 2 litres of still table wine	110 litres of beer
Perfume	*Perfume*
50 grammes (60 cc or 2 fl oz)	No limit
Toilet water	*Toilet water*
250 cc (9 fl oz)	No limit
Other goods	*Other goods*
£75 worth	No limit

NB: A maximum of 50 litres of beer may be imported duty-free, subject to the limitations of the 'Other goods' monetary allowance.

Anyone visiting the United Kingdom for less than six months is also entitled to bring in, free of duty and tax, all personal effects (except tobacco goods, alcoholic drinks and perfume) which they intend to take with them when they leave.

NOTES ON ALLOWANCES

1 The countries of the European Union are Austria, Belgium, Denmark, Finland, France, Germany, Greece, the Irish Republic, Italy, Luxembourg, the Netherlands, Portugal, Spain (but not the Canary Islands), Sweden, and the United Kingdom (but not the Channel Islands)

2 The allowances apply only to goods carried and cleared by travellers at the time of their arrival

3 The allowances do not apply to goods brought in for sale or for other commercial purposes

4 Reduced allowances apply to certain persons crossing the Irish land boundary and to seamen and aircrew members

5 Whisky, gin, rum, brandy, vodka and most liqueurs normally exceed 22% vol. (38.8° proof) but advocaat, cassis, fraise, suze and aperitifs may be less. Fortified wines include port, sherry, vermouth and madeira. Sparkling wines include champagne, perelada, spumante and semi-sparkling wines. Still table wines include claret, Sauterne, Graves and Chianti. Burgundy, Chablis, hock and Moselle may be either sparkling or still, depending on manufacture

6 Goods obtained duty and tax-free or outside the European Union may not be mixed with goods of the same category obtained duty and tax paid in the European Union to obtain the higher allowance, e.g. the higher allowance for tobacco goods will not apply if any of the items in that category were obtained duty and tax-free or outside the European Union

7 Where there are alternative quantities within a category of goods they may be apportioned. For example, 100 cigarettes (half allowance) plus 50 cigarillos (half allowance)

8 One litre is approximately 1¾ pints or 35 fl oz

9 A cigarillo is a cigar with a maximum weight of 3 grammes

PROHIBITED AND RESTRICTED GOODS

Customs officers are able to provide full information. This is a list of more frequently met items:

Controlled drugs (such as opium, heroin, morphine, cocaine, cannabis, amphetamines, lysergide (LSD) and barbiturates)

Firearms (including gas pistols, electric shock batons and similar weapons), ammunition and explosives (including fireworks)

Offensive weapons (including certain types of knife, swordsticks, knuckle-dusters and other martial arts equipment)

Counterfeit currency and other counterfeit goods, such as fake watches and sports shirts; goods bearing a false indication of their place of manufacture or in breach of UK copyright

Obscene books, magazines, films, videotapes, laser discs, computer discs and other material, horror comics

Radio transmitters (walkie-talkies, Citizen's Band radios, cordless telephones, etc.) not approved for use in the UK

Meat and poultry, and most of their products, including ham, bacon, sausage, paté, eggs, milk and cream. (Exception: 1 kg per passenger of fully cooked meat or poultrymeat products in cans or other hermetically-sealed containers of glass or foil)

Plants, parts thereof and plant produce, including trees and shrubs, soil, potatoes and certain other vegetables, fruit, bulbs and seeds

Anglers' lead weights

Most animals and birds, whether alive or dead (e.g. stuffed), certain fish and fish eggs, whether live or dead, or bees

Certain articles derived from rare species including fur skins, ivory, reptile leather and goods made from them

NB: Cats, dogs and other mammals, including mice, rats, guinea-pigs and gerbils, must not be landed unless a British import licence (rabies) has previously been issued.

EXPORT CONTROL

The following are some of the goods subject to export control and should be declared to the customs officer. There are formalities to be completed in respect of these goods prior to arrival at the port of exportation and further information is available through any local office of Customs and Excise (address in the telephone directory).

Controlled drugs
Firearms and ammunition
Photographic material over 50 years old and valued at £6,000 or more
Portraits (including sculptures) of British historical personages which are over 50 years old and valued at £6,000 or more
Antiques, collectors' items, etc. (including paintings and other works of art) over 50 years old and valued at £39,600 or more
Certain archaeological material
Most live animals and birds, and items made from animals occurring wild in the UK

The Queen's Awards

The Queen's Award for Export Achievement and The Queen's Award for Technological Achievement were instituted by royal warrant in 1976. The two separate awards took the place of The Queen's Award to Industry, which had been instituted in 1965. In 1992 the scheme was extended with the launch of a third award, The Queen's Award for Environmental Achievement.

The export and technological awards are designed to recognize and encourage outstanding achievements in exporting goods or services from the United Kingdom and in advancing process or product technology. The purpose of the environmental award is to recognize and encourage product and process development which has major benefits for the environment and which is commercially successful.

The awards differ from a personal royal honour in that they are given to a unit as a whole, management and employees working as a team. They may be applied for by any organization within the United Kingdom, the Channel Islands or the Isle of Man producing goods or services which meet the criteria for the awards. Eligibility is not influenced in any way by the particular activities of the unit applying, its location, or size. Units or agencies of central and local government with industrial functions, as well as research associations, educational institutions and bodies of a similar character, are also eligible, provided that they can show they have contributed to industrial efficiency.

Each award is formally conferred by a grant of appointment and is symbolized by a representation of its emblem cast in stainless steel and encapsulated in a transparent acrylic block.

Awards are held for five years and holders are entitled to fly the appropriate award flag and to display the emblem on the packaging of goods produced in this country, on the goods themselves, on the unit's stationery, in advertising and on certain articles used by employees. Units may also display the emblem of any previous current awards during the five years.

Awards are announced on 21 April (the birthday of The Queen) and published formally in a special supplement to the London Gazette.

AWARDS OFFICE

All enquiries about the scheme and requests for application forms (completed forms must be returned by 31 October) should be made to: The Secretary, The Queen's Awards Office, Bridge Place, 88–89 Eccleston Square, London SW1V 1PT. Tel: 0171-222 2277.

EXPORT ACHIEVEMENT

The criterion upon which recommendations for an award for export achievement are based is a substantial and sustained increase in export earnings to a level which is outstanding for the products or services concerned and for the size of the applicant unit's operations. Account will be taken of any special market factors described in the application. Applicants for the award will be expected to explain the basis of the achievement (e.g. improved marketing organization or new initiative to cater for export markets) and this will be taken into consideration. Export earnings considered will include receipts by the applicant unit in this country from the export of goods produced in this country, and the provision of services to non-residents. Account will be taken of the overseas expenses incurred other than marketing expenses. Income from profits (after overseas tax) remitted to this country from the applicant unit's direct investments in its overseas branches, subsidiaries or associates in the same general line of business will be taken into account, but not receipts from profits on other overseas investments or by interest on overseas loans or credits.

In 1996, The Queen's Award for Export Achievement was conferred on the following concerns:

Anglo Beef Processors Ltd, Blisworth, Northants
Audience Systems Ltd, Westbury, Wilts
Autoflame Engineering Ltd, London SE6
Avesta Sheffield Ltd, Sheffield
Bartle Bogle Hegarty Ltd, London W1
Bass Beers Worldwide Ltd, Birmingham
Beamech Group Ltd, Manchester
Beck & Pollitzer Engineering Ltd, Dartford, Kent
Biotrace Ltd, Bridgend, Mid Glam
J. Blackledge & Son Ltd, Chorley, Lancs
Brett Martin Ltd, Newtownabbey, Co. Antrim
Bridge of Weir Leather Company Ltd, Bridge of Weir, Renfrewshire
British Chrome & Chemicals, Stockton-on-Tees, Cleveland
British Steel Special Sections (Skinningrove), Carlin How, Saltburn-by-the-Sea, Cleveland
Burberrys Ltd, Manufacturing and Export Division, London E9
Camlaw Ltd, Tamworth, Staffs
Chadwyck-Healey Ltd, Cambridge
The Chartered Association of Certified Accountants (ACCA), London WC2
Toby Churchill Ltd, Cambridge
Cincinnati Milacron (UK) Ltd, Machine Tool Division, Birmingham
Corsair Toiletries Ltd, St Albans, Herts
Dairy Produce Packers Ltd, Coleraine, Co. Londonderry
Designers Guild Ltd, London W11
Digi-Media Vision Ltd (trading as DMV), Eastleigh, Hants
Dunlop Hydraulic Hose Ltd, Gateshead
EBI Foods Ltd, Abingdon, Oxon
Edwards High Vacuum International, Crawley, W. Sussex
English Hop Products Ltd, Tonbridge, Kent
Epichem Ltd, Wirral, Merseyside
Eurostock Meat Marketing Ltd, Newry, Co. Down

Evans Medical Ltd, Leatherhead, Surrey
Fermec Holdings Ltd, Manchester
J. & S. Franklin Ltd, London WC2
GPT Public Networks Group, Coventry
Garigue, London SW5
Gates Power Transmission Ltd, Dumfries
Genesis Tilemates Ltd, Stokesley, N. Yorks
Glass Eels Ltd, Gloucester
Gossard, Leighton Buzzard, Beds
William Grant & Sons Ltd, Motherwell, Lanarkshire
Guinness Brewing Worldwide Ltd, London NW10
HSB Engineering Insurance Ltd, London EC3
Halcrow Holdings Ltd, London w6
Healey & Baker, London w1
International Diamalt Co Ltd, Newark, Notts
International Labmate Ltd, St Albans, Herts
IPTest Ltd, Guildford, Surrey
JCB Materials Handling Ltd, Rocester, Staffs
JCB Special Products Ltd, Stoke-on-Trent, Staffs
Laminar Medica Ltd, Tring, Herts
Lilly Industries Ltd, Basingstoke, Hants
Lombard Risk Systems Ltd, London EC4
Magneco Metrel (UK) Ltd, Shildon, Co. Durham
Maybridge Chemical Company Ltd, Tintagel, Cornwall
McCalls Special Products, Sheffield
McKechnie Vehicle Components, Extrusion Operation, Milton Keynes
Mechatherm International Ltd, Kingswinford, W. Midlands
Mivan Ltd, Antrim, Co. Antrim
Mobile Systems International PLC, London E14
Molypress Ltd, Calne, Wilts
Abraham Moon & Sons Ltd, Leeds
Morrisflex Ltd, Consumable Tools Division, Daventry, Northants
Morrison Bowmore Distillers Ltd, Glasgow
Motorola Ltd, European Cellular Infrastructure Division, Swindon
Motorola Ltd, Europe, Middle East and Africa Cellular Subscriber Division, Bathgate, West Lothian
Mott MacDonald Group Ltd, Croydon, Surrey
Mulberry Company (Design) Ltd, Home Division, Shepton Mallet, Somerset
New Holland (UK) Ltd, Basildon, Essex
Newbridge Networks Ltd, Newport, Gwent
Nikwax Ltd, Wadhurst, E. Sussex
Nortel Radio Infrastructure, GPS Unit, Paignton, Devon
Ocular Sciences Ltd, Southampton
Orb Electrical Steels Ltd, Newport, Gwent
Oxford Metrics Ltd, Oxford
Oxford University Press, Oxford
Pamarco Europe Ltd, Warrington, Cheshire
Paper Makers Export Ltd, Wellingborough, Northants
Paradise Datacom Ltd, Tiptree, Essex
Parkman Consultants Ltd, Sutton, Surrey
Percell Group Ltd, Newport, Gwent
Puretone Ltd, Rochester, Kent
Queensgate Instruments Ltd, Bracknell, Berks
Quick Controls Ltd, Manchester
RBR Armour Ltd, London SE1
Reilor Ltd, Preston, Lancs
Reynard Racing Cars Ltd, Bicester, Oxon
Robinson Special Packaging, Chesterfield, Derbys
Robobond Ltd (trading as Emafyl), London SE18
Segal Quince Wicksteed Ltd, Swavesey, Cambs
Sinclair International Ltd, Norwich
Smith's Environmental Products Ltd, Chelmsford, Essex
Speedibake Ltd, Northampton
Statestrong Ltd, Lytham, Lancs
Steel Wheels Ltd, Kidderminster, Worcs

Storehouse PLC, London NW1
Swiftpack Automation Ltd, Alcester, Warks
Syfer Technology Ltd, Norwich
Terex Equipment Ltd, Motherwell, Lanarkshire
Thermopol Ltd, Crawley, W. Sussex
TRAK Microwave Ltd, Dundee
Unipath Ltd, Consumer and Clinical Diagnostics, Bedford
Universal Bulk Handling Ltd, Burscough, Lancs
Van Leer Metallized Products Ltd, Caerphilly, Mid Glam
Visual Communications Group Ltd, London E14
Weetabix Ltd, Kettering, Northants
Willis Corroon Group PLC, Financial Risks and Specie Division, London EC3
Windsong International Ltd, Orpington, Kent

TECHNOLOGICAL ACHIEVEMENT

The criterion upon which recommendations for an award for technological achievement are based is a significant advance, leading to increased efficiency, in the application of technology to a production or development process in British industry or the production for sale of goods which incorporate new and advanced technological qualities. An award is only granted for production or development processes which have achieved commercial success.

In 1996 The Queen's Award for Technological Achievement was conferred on the following concerns:

Affinity Chromatography Ltd, Ballasalla, IOM – *innovating means of separating protein pharmaceuticals*
Amersham Healthcare, Little Chalfont, Bucks – *Metastron: a therapeutic option for treating metastatic bone pain*
Bede Scientific Instruments Ltd, Bowburn, Co. Durham – *direct drive x-ray diffractometer*
Chas A. Blatchford & Sons Ltd, Products Division, Basingstoke, Hants – *electro-mechanical computer controlled lower limb prostheses*
Digi-Media Vision Ltd (trading as DMV), Eastleigh, Hants – *professional digital video compression technology*
Glaxo Research and Development Ltd, Greenford, Middx – *Sumatriptan-Imigran: medicine for migraine and cluster headache*
Marks & Spencer PLC, London W1 – *'dry' discharge method for garment panel printing*
Oxford Magnet Technology Ltd, Witney, Oxon – *open C magnet system for magnetic resonance imaging scanner*
Philips Medical Systems (Radiotherapy), Crawley, W. Sussex – *multileaf collimator for radiotherapy treatment machine*
Rover Group Ltd, Electronics and Control Systems, Coventry – *microprocessor controlled engine management system*
Scimat Ltd, Swindon, Wilts – *membranes for the rechargeable battery industry*
Smith & Nephew PLC, Group Research Centre, York – *IV3000: materials innovation in infection control*
Ultra Electronics Ltd, Noise and Vibration Systems Division, Greenford, Middx – *system for reducing cabin noise in turboprop aircraft*
Institute of Biotechnology, University of Cambridge, Cambridge – *innovating means of separating protein pharmaceuticals*
Wace Screen, Wakefield, W. Yorks – *'dry' discharge method for garment panel printing*
Westwind Air Bearings Ltd, Poole, Dorset – *aerodynamic spindle for optical scanning*

ENVIRONMENTAL ACHIEVEMENT

The criterion upon which recommendations for an award for environmental achievement are based is a significant advance in the application by British industry of the development of products, technology or processes which offer major benefits in environmental terms compared to existing products, technology or processes. An award is only granted for products, technology or processes which have achieved commercial success.

In 1996 The Queen's Award for Environmental Achievement was conferred on the following concerns:

Brook Hansen, Huddersfield, W. Yorks – *energy efficient electric motors*

Hoover Ltd, Merthyr Tydfil, Mid Glam – *environmentally advanced washing machine range*

Hydro Chemicals Ltd (Hydrocare), Immingham, Lincs – *Nutriox process for elimination of odour and septicity in municipal sewer networks*

International Combustion Ltd, Derby – *EnviroNOx: low NOx burners for power stations*

Lucas Diesel Systems, Stonehouse, Glos – *electronic unit injector systems for diesel engines*

Ultra Hydraulics Ltd, Mobile Products Division, Cheltenham, Glos – *'Stealth' ultra quiet, high performance external gear pumps for off highway and mechanical handling vehicles*

Chemical Elements

Element	Symbol	Atomic Number	Element	Symbol	Atomic Number	Element	Symbol	Atomic Number
Actinium	Ac	89	Hafnium	Hf	72	Promethium	Pm	61
Aluminium	Al	13	Helium	He	2	Protactinium	Pa	91
Americium	Am	95	Holmium	Ho	67	Radium	Ra	88
Antimony	Sb	51	Hydrogen	H	1	Radon	Rn	86
Argon	Ar	18	Indium	In	49	Rhenium	Re	75
Arsenic	As	33	Iodine	I	53	Rhodium	Rh	45
Astatine	At	85	Iridium	Ir	77	Rubidium	Rb	37
Barium	Ba	56	Iron	Fe	26	Ruthenium	Ru	44
Berkelium	Bk	97	Krypton	Kr	36	Samarium	Sm	62
Beryllium	Be	4	Lanthanum	La	57	Scandium	Sc	21
Bismuth	Bi	83	Lawrencium	Lr	103	Selenium	Se	34
Boron	B	5	Lead	Pb	82	Silicon	Si	14
Bromine	Br	35	Lithium	Li	3	Silver	Ag	47
Cadmium	Cd	48	Lutetium	Lu	71	Sodium	Na	11
Caesium	Cs	55	Magnesium	Mg	12	Strontium	Sr	38
Calcium	Ca	20	Manganese	Mn	25	Sulphur	S	16
Californium	Cf	98	Mendelevium	Md	101	Tantalum	Ta	73
Carbon	C	6	Mercury	Hg	80	Technetium	Tc	43
Cerium	Ce	58	Molybdenum	Mo	42	Tellurium	Te	52
Chlorine	Cl	17	Neodymium	Nd	60	Terbium	Tb	65
Chromium	Cr	24	Neon	Ne	10	Thallium	Tl	81
Cobalt	Co	27	Neptunium	Np	93	Thorium	Th	90
Copper	Cu	29	Nickel	Ni	28	Thulium	Tm	69
Curium	Cm	96	Niobium	Nb	41	Tin	Sn	50
Dysprosium	Dy	66	Nitrogen	N	7	Titanium	Ti	22
Einsteinium	Es	99	Nobelium	No	102	Tungsten (Wolfram)	W	74
Erbium	Er	68	Osmium	Os	76	Uranium	U	92
Europium	Eu	63	Oxygen	O	8	Vanadium	V	23
Fermium	Fm	100	Palladium	Pd	46	Xenon	Xe	54
Fluorine	F	9	Phosphorus	P	15	Ytterbium	Yb	70
Francium	Fr	87	Platinum	Pt	78	Yttrium	Y	39
Gadolinium	Gd	64	Plutonium	Pu	94	Zinc	Zn	30
Gallium	Ga	31	Polonium	Po	84	Zirconium	Zr	40
Germanium	Ge	32	Potassium	K	19			
Gold	Au	79	Praseodymium	Pr	59			

Legal Notes

IMPORTANT

These notes outline certain aspects of the law as they might affect the average person. They are intended only as a broad guideline and are by no means definitive. The information is believed to be correct at the time of going to press but the law is constantly changing so expert advice should always be taken. In some cases, sources of further information are given in these notes.

It is always advisable to consult a solicitor without delay; timely advice will set your mind at rest but sitting on your rights can mean that you lose them. Anyone who does not have a solicitor already can contact the Citizens' Advice Bureau (addresses in the telephone directory or at any post office or town hall), the Law Society (113 Chancery Lane, London WC2A 1PL) or the Law Society of Scotland (26 Drumsheugh Gardens, Edinburgh EH3 7YR) for assistance in finding one.

The legal aid and legal aid and assistance schemes exist to make the help of a lawyer available to those who would not otherwise be able to afford one. Entitlement depends upon an individual's means (see pages 660) but a solicitor or Citizens' Advice Bureau will be able to advise about entitlement.

ADOPTION OF CHILDREN

In England and Wales the adoption of children is mainly governed by the Adoption Act 1976 and the Children Act 1989.

Anyone over 21, whether married, single, widowed or divorced, can legally adopt a child. Married couples must adopt 'jointly', unless one partner cannot be found, is incapable of making an application, or if a separation is likely to be permanent. Unmarried couples may not adopt 'jointly' although one partner in that couple may adopt. The only organizations allowed to arrange adoptions are the social services departments of local authorities or voluntary agencies such as Barnardo's which are registered as adoption agencies with the local authorities.

Once an adoption has been arranged, a court order is necessary to make it legal. These are obtained from the High Court (Family Division) or from a county or family proceedings court. The child's natural parents (or guardians) must consent to the adoption, unless the court dispenses with the consent, e.g. where the natural parent has neglected the child or is incapable of giving consent. Once adopted, the child has the same status as a child born to the adoptive parents and the natural parents cease to have any rights or responsibilities where the child is concerned. The adopted child will be treated as the natural child of the adoptive parents for the purposes of intestate succession, national insurance, family allowances, etc. The adopted child ceases to have any rights to the estates of his/her natural parents.

Registration and Certificates

All adoptions are registered in the Registers of Adopted Children kept by the Office of National Statistics for adoptions in England and Wales, and by the General Register Office for adoptions in Scotland. Certificates from the registers can be obtained in a similar way to birth certificates (see page 650).

Tracing Natural Parents or Children Who Have Been Adopted

Adult adopted people may apply to the Registrar-General for information to enable him/her to obtain a full birth certificate. Before being supplied with this information the adopted person will be informed that counselling services are available to him/her. There is also an Adoption Contact Register (created after the 1989 Act) in which details of adopted people and of parents who gave their children up to adoption may be recorded. The BAAF (see below) can provide addresses of organizations which offer advice, information and counselling to adopted people, adoptive parents and people who have had their children adopted.

Scotland

The relevant legislation is the Adoption (Scotland) Act 1978 (as amended by the Children Act 1995) and the provisions are similar to those described above. In Scotland, petitions for adoption are made to the Sheriff Court or the Court of Session.

Further information can be obtained from:
BRITISH AGENCIES FOR ADOPTION AND FOSTERING (BAAF), Skyline House, 200 Union Street, London SE1 0LY. Tel: 0171-593 2000

BIRTHS (REGISTRATION)

The birth of a child must be registered within 42 days of birth at the register office of the district in which the baby was born. In England and Wales it is possible to give the particulars to be registered at any other register office. Responsibility for registering the birth rests with the parents, except in the case of an illegitimate child, when the mother is responsible for registration. Responsibility rests firstly with the parents but if they fail, particulars may be given to the registrar by:
– a relative of either parent (in Scotland only)
– the occupier of the house in which the baby was born
– a person present at the birth
– the person having charge of the child
Failure to register the birth within 42 days without reasonable cause may leave the parents liable to a penalty.

If the parents were married at the time of the birth, either parent may register the birth and details about both parents will be entered on the register. If the parents were unmarried at the time of the birth, the father's details are entered only if both parents attend or if the parents have made a statutory declaration confirming the identity of the father. Copies of the forms necessary to make such a declaration are available at the register offices. A short birth certificate is issued free when the birth is registered.

Still Births

If a baby is stillborn, i.e. born dead after the 24th week of pregnancy, the birth must be registered. The doctor or midwife who attends the birth or afterwards examines the body of the child will issue a Medical Certificate of Stillbirth and this must be presented at the register office.

RE-REGISTRATION

In certain circumstances it may be necessary to re-register a birth, e.g. where the birth of an illegitimate child is legitimated by the subsequent marriage of the parents. It is also possible to re-register the birth of an illegitimate child so that the father's name is entered on the register; the mother must agree to re-registration in such cases.

BIRTH AT SEA

The master of a British ship must record any birth on board and send particulars to the Registrar-General of Shipping.

BIRTH ABROAD

Births of British subjects occurring abroad are registered with consular officers and certificates of birth are subsequently available from the Registrar-General. The registration of births among members of the armed forces that occur abroad or on military ships or aircraft is governed by the Registration of Births, Deaths and Marriages (Special Provisions) Act 1957.

SCOTLAND

In Scotland the birth of a child must be registered within 21 days at the register office of either the district in which the baby was born or the district in which the mother was resident at the time of the birth.

If the child is born, either in or out of Scotland, on a ship, aircraft or land vehicle that ends its journey at any place in Scotland, the child, in most cases, will be registered as if born in that place.

CERTIFICATES OF BIRTHS, DEATHS OR MARRIAGES

Certificates of births, deaths or marriages that have taken place in England and Wales since 1837 can be obtained from the Office of National Statistics (General Register Office). Applications can be made:
- by a personal visit to the General Register Office in London between 8.30 a.m. and 4.30 p.m., Monday to Friday
- by postal application to the General Register Office in Southport

Certificates are also available from the Superintendent Registrar for the district in which the event took place or, in the case of marriage certificates, from the minister of the church in which the marriage took place. Any register office can advise about the best way to obtain certificates.

There is no charge for the short birth certificate issued when a birth is registered. The fees for other certificates (from 1 April 1996) are:
Obtained from Registrar
Full certificate of birth, death or marriage, £2.50
Copy of an entry of birth, death or marriage, £2.50
Certificate of birth, death or marriage for certain statutory purposes, £2.00
Short certificate of birth, £2.00
Certificate of death issued to certain professional bodies, £2.50
Obtained from Superintendent Registrar
Full certificate of birth, death or marriage, £5.50
Copy of an entry of birth, death or marriage, £5.50
Certificate of birth, death or marriage for certain statutory purposes, £2.00

Short certificate of birth, £3.00
General Search (Superintendent Registrar)
General search in indexes not exceeding six successive hours, £17.00
Each verification exceeding the eight covered by the general search fee, £2.50

When a particular entry in the register is specified, there is no fee for a search in the indexes.

The Society of Genealogists has many records of baptisms, marriages and deaths prior to 1837.

SCOTLAND

Certificates of births, deaths or marriages that have taken place in Scotland since 1855 can be obtained from the General Register Office or from the appropriate local registrar. The General Register Office also keeps the Register of Divorces (including decrees of declaration of nullity of marriage), and holds parish registers dating from before 1855.

Fees for certificates (from 1 April 1996) are:
Certificates (full or abbreviated) of birth, death or marriage
Personal visit, £10
Postal application, £12
Extract marriage certificate
In the month following the ceremony, £7
More than one month after the ceremony, £10
Extract from the Register of Divorces
Personal visit, £10
Postal application, £12
Extract of entries in parish records prior to 1855
Search fee, £12

Further information can be obtained from:
THE GENERAL REGISTER OFFICE, Office for National Statistics, St Catherine's House, London WC2B 6JP. Tel: 0171-396 2828
POSTAL APPLICATION SECTION, Office for National Statistics, Smedley Hydro, Trafalgar Road, Birkdale, Southport, Merseyside PR8 2HH. Tel: 0151-471 4800
THE GENERAL REGISTER OFFICE, New Register House, Edinburgh EH1 3YT. Tel: 0131-334 0380
THE SOCIETY OF GENEALOGISTS, 14 Charterhouse Buildings, Goswell Road, London ECIM 7BA. Tel: 0171-251 8799

BRITISH CITIZENSHIP

The British Nationality Act 1981 which came into force on 1 January 1983 established three types of citizenship to replace the single form of Citizenship of the UK and Colonies created by the British Nationality Act 1948. The three forms of citizenship are: British Citizenship; British Dependent Territories Citizenship; and British Overseas Citizenship. Three residual categories were created: British Subjects; British Protected Persons; and British Nationals (Overseas).

BRITISH CITIZENSHIP

Almost everyone who was a citizen of the UK and colonies and had a right of abode in the UK prior to the 1981 Act became British citizens when the Act came into force. British citizens have the right to live permanently in the UK and are free to leave and re-enter the UK at any time.

A person born on or after 1 January 1983 in the UK (including, for this purpose, the Channel Islands and the Isle of Man) is entitled to British citizenship if he/she falls into one of the following categories:

- he/she has a parent who is a British citizen
- he/she has a parent who is settled in the UK
- he/she is a newborn infant found abandoned in the UK
- his/her parents subsequently settle in the UK
- he/she lives in the UK for the first ten years of his/her life and is not absent for more than 90 days in each of those years
- he/she is adopted in the UK and one of the adopters is a British Citizen

A person born outside the UK may acquire British citizenship if he/she falls into one of the following categories:

- he/she has a parent who is a British citizen otherwise than by descent, e.g. a parent who was born in the UK
- he/she has a parent who is a British citizen serving the Crown overseas
- the Home Secretary consents to his/her registration while he/she is a minor
- he/she is a British Dependent Territories citizen, a British Overseas citizen, a British subject or a British protected person and has been lawfully resident in the UK for five years
- he/she is a British Dependent Territories citizen who acquired that citizenship from a connection with Gibraltar
- he/she is adopted (*see* above) or naturalized (*see* below)

Where parents are married, the status of either may confer citizenship on their child. If a child is illegitimate, the status of the mother determines the child's citizenship.

Under the 1981 Act, Commonwealth citizens and citizens of the Republic of Ireland were entitled to registration as British citizens before 1 January 1988. In 1985 citizens of the Falkland Islands were granted British citizenship.

Renunciation of British citizenship must be registered with the Home Secretary and will be revoked if no new citizenship or nationality is acquired within six months. If the renunciation was required in order to retain or acquire another citizenship or nationality, the citizenship may be reacquired once.

BRITISH DEPENDENT TERRITORIES CITIZENSHIP

Under the 1981 Act, this type of citizenship was conferred on citizens of the UK and colonies by birth, naturalization or registration in British Dependent Territories. British Dependent Territories citizens may be entitled to registration as British citizens on completion of five years' legal residence in the UK.

On 1 July 1997 citizens of Hong Kong who do not qualify to register as British citizens under the British Nationality (Hong Kong) Act 1990 will lose their British Dependent Territories citizenship on the handover of sovereignty to China; they may, however, apply to register as British Nationals (Overseas).

Eligibility for British Dependent Territories citizenship is determined by similar rules to those for acquiring British citizenship, except that the connection is with the dependent territory rather than with the UK.

BRITISH OVERSEAS CITIZENSHIP

Under the 1981 Act, this type of citizenship was conferred on any UK and colonies citizens who did not qualify for British citizenship or citizenship of the British Dependent Territories. British Overseas citizenship may be acquired by the wife and minor children of a British Overseas citizen in certain circumstances. British Overseas citizens may be entitled to registration as British citizens on completion of five years' legal residence in the UK.

RESIDUAL CATEGORIES

British subjects, British protected persons and British Nationals (Overseas) may be entitled to registration as British citizens on completion of five years' legal residence in the UK.

Citizens of the Republic of Ireland who were also British subjects before 1 January 1949 can retain that status if they fulfill certain conditions.

EUROPEAN UNION CITIZENSHIP

British citizens (including Gibraltarians who are registered as such) are also EU citizens and are entitled to travel freely to other EU countries to work, study, reside and set up a business. EU citizens have the same rights with respect to the United Kingdom.

NATURALIZATION

Naturalization is granted at the discretion of the Home Secretary. The basic requirements are five years' residence (three years if the applicant is married to a British citizen), good character, adequate knowledge of the English, Welsh or Scottish Gaelic language, and an intention to reside permanently in the UK.

STATUS OF ALIENS

Aliens may not hold public office or vote in Britain and they may not own a British ship or aircraft. Citizens of the Republic of Ireland are not deemed to be aliens.

Further information can be obtained from the Home Office, Nationality Division, 3rd Floor, India Buildings, Water Street, Liverpool L2 0QN. Tel: 0151-236 4723

CONSUMER LAW

SALE OF GOODS

A sale of goods contract is the most common type of contract. It is governed by the Sale of Goods Act 1979 (as amended by the Sale and Supply of Goods Act 1994). The Act provides protection for buyers by implying terms into every sale of goods contract. These terms are:

- a condition that the seller will pass good title to the buyer (unless the seller agrees to transfer only such title as he has)
- where the seller sells goods by reference to a description, a condition that the goods will match that description and, where the sale is by sample and description, a condition that the bulk of the goods will correspond with such sample and description
- where goods are sold by a business seller, a condition that the goods will be of satisfactory quality if they meet the standard that a reasonable person would regard as satisfactory taking into account any description of the goods, the price, and all other relevant circumstances. The quality of the goods includes their state and condition, relevant aspects being whether they are suitable for their common purpose, their appearance and finish, freedom from minor defects and their safety and durability. This term will not be implied, however, if a buyer has examined the goods and should have noticed the defect or if the seller specifically drew the buyer's attention to the defect
- where goods are sold by a business seller, a condition that the goods are reasonably fit for any purpose made known to the seller by the buyer, unless the buyer does not rely on the seller's judgement, or it is not reasonable for him/her to do so

– where goods are sold by sample, conditions that the bulk of the sample will correspond with the sample in quality, that the buyer will have a reasonable opportunity of comparing the two and that the goods are free from any defect rendering them unsatisfactory which would not be obvious from the sample

Some of the above terms can be excluded from contracts by the seller. The seller's right to do this is, however, restricted by the Unfair Contract Terms Act 1977. The Act offers more protection to a buyer who 'deals as a consumer', that is where the sale is a business sale, the goods are of a type ordinarily bought for private use and the goods are bought by a buyer who is not a business buyer. In a sale by auction or competitive tender, a buyer never deals as consumer. Also, a seller can never exclude the implied term as to title mentioned above.

Hire-purchase Agreements

Terms similar to those implied in contracts of sales of goods are implied into contracts of hire-purchase, under the Supply of Goods (Implied Terms) Act 1973. The 1977 Act limits the exclusion of these implied terms as before.

Supply of Goods and Services

Under the Supply of Goods and Services Act 1982, similar terms are also implied in other types of contract under which ownership of goods passes, e.g. a contract for 'work and materials' such as supplying new parts while servicing a car, and contracts for the hire of goods. These types of contracts have additional implied terms:
– that the supplier will use reasonable care and skill
– that the supplier will carry out the service in a reasonable time (unless the time has been agreed)
– that the supplier will make a reasonable charge (unless the charge has already been agreed)
The 1977 Act limits the exclusion of these implied terms in a similar manner as before.

Unfair Terms

The Unfair Terms in Consumer Contracts Regulations 1994 apply to contracts between business sellers (or suppliers of goods and services) and consumers, where the terms have not been individually negotiated, i.e. where the terms were drafted in advance so that the consumer was unable to influence those terms. An unfair term is one which operates to the detriment of the consumer. An unfair term does not bind the consumer but the contract will continue to bind the parties if it is capable of existing without the unfair term. The regulations contain a non-exhaustive list of terms which are regarded as unfair. Whether a term is regarded as fair or not will depend on many factors, including the nature of the goods or services, the surrounding circumstances (such as the bargaining strength of both parties) and the other terms in the contract.

Trade Descriptions

It is a criminal offence under the Trade Descriptions Act 1968 for a business seller to apply a false trade description of goods or to supply or offer to supply any goods to which a false description has been applied. A 'trade description' includes descriptions of quality, size, composition, fitness for purpose and method, place and date of manufacture of the goods. It is also an offence to give a false indication of the price of goods. Prosecutions are brought by trading standards inspectors.

Fair Trading

The Fair Trading Act 1973 is designed to protect the consumer. It provides for the appointment of a Director-General of Fair Trading, one of whose duties is to review commercial activities in the UK relating to the supply of goods and services to consumers. An example of a practice which has been prohibited by a reference made under this Act is that of business sellers posing in advertisements as private sellers.

Consumer Protection

Under the Consumer Protection Act 1987, producers of goods are liable for any damage exceeding £275 caused by a defect in their product (subject to certain defences).

The Consumer Protection (Cancellation of Contracts Concluded Away from Business Premises) Regulations 1987 allow consumers a seven-day period in which to cancel contracts for the supply of goods and services, where the contracts were made during an unsolicited visit to the consumer's home or workplace. This only applies to contracts where the cost exceeds £35.

Consumer Credit

In matters relating to the provision of credit (or the supply of goods on hire or hire-purchase), consumers are also protected by the Consumer Credit Act 1974. Under this Act a licence, issued by the Director-General of Fair Trading, is required to conduct a consumer credit or consumer hire business or to deal in credit brokerage, debt adjusting, counselling or collecting. Any 'fit' person may apply to the Director-General of Fair Trading for a licence, which is normally renewable after ten years. A licence is not necessary if such types of business are only transacted occasionally, or if only exempt agreements are involved. The provisions of the Act only apply to 'regulated' agreements, i.e. those that are with individuals or partnerships, those that are not exempt (such as certain local authority and building society loans), and those where the total credit does not exceed £15,000. Provisions include:
– the terms of the regulated agreement can be altered by the creditor provided the agreement gives him/her the right to do so; in such cases the debtor must be given proper notice of this
– in order for a creditor to enforce a regulated agreement, the agreement must comply with certain formalities and must be properly executed. The debtor must also be given specified information by the creditor or his/her broker or agent during the negotiations which take place before the signing of the agreement. The agreement must state certain information such as the amount of credit, the annual percentage rate of interest and the amount and timing of repayments
– if an agreement is signed other than at the creditor's (or credit broker's or negotiator's) place of business and oral representations were made in the debtor's presence during discussions pre-agreement, the debtor has a right to cancel the agreement. Time for cancellation expires five clear days after the debtor receives a second copy of the agreement. The agreement must inform the debtor of his right to cancel and how to cancel
– if the debtor is in arrears (or otherwise in breach of the agreement), the creditor must serve a default notice before taking any action such as repossessing the goods
– if the agreement is a hire-purchase or conditional sale agreement, the creditor cannot repossess the goods without a court order if the debtor has paid one-third of the total price of the goods

– in agreements where the debtor is required to make grossly exorbitant payments or where the agreement grossly contravenes the ordinary principles of fair trading, the debtor may request that the court alter or set aside some of the terms of the agreement. The agreement can also be reopened during enforcement proceedings by the court itself

Where a credit reference agency has been used to check the debtor's financial standing, the creditor must give the agency's name to the debtor, who is entitled to see the agency's file on him. A fee of £1 is payable to the agency.

SCOTLAND

The legislation governing the sale and supply of goods applies to Scotland as follows:
– the Sale of Goods Act 1979 applies with some modifications and it has been amended by the Sale and Supply of Goods Act 1994
– the Supply of Goods (Implied Terms) Act 1973 applies
– the Supply of Goods and Services Act 1982 does not extend to Scotland but some of its provisions were introduced by the Sale and Supply of Goods Act 1994
– only Parts II and III of the Unfair Contract Terms Act 1977 apply
– the Trade Descriptions Act 1968 applies with minor modifications
– the Consumer Credit Act 1974 applies

PROCEEDINGS AGAINST THE CROWN

Until 1947, proceedings against the Crown were generally possible only by a procedure known as a petition of right, which put the litigant at a considerable disadvantage. The Crown Proceedings Act 1947 placed the Crown (not the Sovereign in his/her private capacity, but as the embodiment of the State) largely in the same position as a private individual. The Act did not, however, extinguish or limit the Crown's prerogative or statutory powers, and it granted immunity to HM ships and aircraft. It also left certain Crown privileges unaffected. The Act largely abolished the special procedures which previously applied to civil proceedings by and against the Crown. Civil proceedings may be instituted against the appropriate government department or against the Attorney-General.

In Scotland proceedings against the Crown founded on breach of contract could be taken before the 1947 Act and no special procedures applied. The Crown could, however, claim certain special pleas. The 1947 Act applies in part to Scotland and brings the practice of the two countries as closely together as the different legal systems permit. Civil proceedings may be instituted against the Lord Advocate representing the appropriate government department.

DEATHS

WHEN A DEATH OCCURS

If the death was expected, the doctor who attended the deceased during their final illness should be contacted. If the death was sudden or unexpected the police should also be contacted. For stillbirths, see pages 649–50.

If the cause of death is quite clear the doctor will provide:
– a medical certificate that shows the cause of death (this will be in a sealed envelope, addressed to the registrar)

– a formal notice that states that the doctor has signed the medical certificate and gives instructions on getting the death registered

If the death was known to be caused by a natural illness but the doctor wishes to know more about the cause of death, he/she may ask the relatives for permission to carry out a post-mortem examination. This should not delay the funeral.

In England and Wales a coroner is responsible for investigating deaths occurring in the following circumstances:
– when no doctor has treated the deceased during his or her last illness or when the doctor attending the patient did not see him or her within 14 days before death, or after death; or
– when the death occured during an operation or before recovery from the effect of an anaesthetic; or
– when the death was sudden and unexplained or attended by suspicious circumstances; or
– when the death might be due to an industrial injury or disease, or to accident, violence, neglect or abortion, or to any kind of poisoning; or
– the death occurred in prison or in police custody

The doctor will write on the formal notice that the death has been referred to the coroner; if the coroner ascertains that the death was due to natural causes, he/she will then issue a notification which gives the cause of death so that the death can be registered. If the cause of death is not due to a natural cause, the coroner is obliged to hold an inquest.

In Scotland the office of coroner does not exist. The local procurator fiscal inquires into sudden or suspicious deaths. A fatal accident inquiry will be held before the sheriff where the death has resulted from an accident during the course of the employment of the person who has died, or where the person who has died was in legal custody, or where the Lord Advocate deems it in the public interest that an inquiry be held.

REGISTERING A DEATH

In England and Wales the death must be registered by the registrar of births and deaths for the sub-district in which it occurred; details can be obtained from the telephone directory, from the doctor or local council, or at a post office or police station. In January 1996 the Government published proposals to allow information concerning a death to be given before any registrar of births and deaths in England and Wales. The registrar would pass the relevant details to the registrar for the district where the death occurred, who would then register the death. At the time of going to press the implementation of these proposals was imminent. In Scotland a death may be registered in any registration district in which the deceased was ordinarily resident immediately before his/her death.

In England and Wales the death must normally be registered within five days; in Scotland it must be registered within eight days. If the death has been referred to the coroner it cannot be registered until the registrar has received authority from the coroner to do so. Failure to register a death involves a penalty.

If the death occurred at a house, the death may be registered by:
– any relative of the deceased present at the death or residing in the sub-district where the death occurred
– any person present at the death
– the occupier or any inmate of the house if he/she knew of the occurrence of the death
– any person causing the disposal of the body

The person registering the death should take the medical certificate of the cause of death with them; it is also useful, though not essential, to take the deceased's

birth certificate or passport, medical card (if possible), pension documents and life assurance details. The registrar will issue a certificate for burial or cremation and a certificate of registration of death; both are free of charge. A death certificate is a certified copy of the entry in the death register; these can be provided on payment of a fee and may be required for the following purposes:
– probate or letters of administration
– bank and building society accounts
– insurance companies
– pension claims

If the death occurred abroad or on a foreign ship or aircraft, the death should be registered according to the local regulations of the relevant country and a death certificate should be obtained. The death should also be registered with the British Consul in that country so that a record is kept in England and Wales.

After 12 months of death or the finding of a dead body, no death can be registered without the consent of the Registrar-General.

BURIAL AND CREMATION

In most circumstances in England and Wales a certificate for burial or cremation must be obtained from the registrar before the burial or cremation can take place. If the death has been referred to the coroner this may delay the funeral. In Scotland a body may be buried (but not cremated) before the death is registered.

Most funerals are arranged by a funeral director. The funeral costs can normally be repaid out of the deceased's estate and will be given priority over any other claims. If the deceased has left a will it may contain directions concerning the funeral; however, these directions need not be followed by the executor.

The deceased's papers should also indicate whether a grave space had already been arranged. Most town churchyards and many suburban churchyards are no longer open for burial because they are full. Most cemeteries are non-denominational and may be owned by local authorities or private companies; fees vary.

If the body is to be cremated an application form, two cremation certificates (for which there is a charge) or a certificate for cremation if the death was referred to the coroner, and a certificate signed by the medical referee must be completed in addition to the certificate for burial or cremation (the form is not required if the coroner has issued a certificate for cremation). All the forms are available from the funeral director or crematorium. Most crematoria are run by local authorities; fees vary. Ashes may be scattered, buried in a churchyard or cemetery, or kept.

The registrar must be notified of the date, place and means of disposal of the body within 96 hours (England and Wales) or three days (Scotland).

If the death occurred abroad or on a foreign ship or aircraft, a local burial or cremation may be arranged. If the body is to be brought back to England or Wales, a death certificate from the relevant country or an authorization for the removal of the body from that country will be required. To arrange a funeral in England or Wales an authenticated translation of a foreign death certificate or a death certificate issued in Scotland or Northern Ireland which must show the cause of death, is needed, together with a certificate of no liability to register from the registrar in England and Wales in whose sub-district it is intended to bury or cremate the body. If it is intended to cremate the body a cremation order will be required from the Home Office or a certificate for cremation.

Further information can be obtained from:
THE GENERAL REGISTER OFFICE, Office for National Statistics, St Catherine's House, 10 Kingsway, London WC2B 6JP. Tel: 0171-242 0262
THE GENERAL REGISTER OFFICE, New Register House, Edinburgh EH1 3YT. Tel: 0131-334 0380

DIVORCE AND RELATED MATTERS

ENGLAND AND WALES

There are two types of matrimonial suit: those seeking the annulment of a marriage, and those seeking a judicial separation or divorce. To obtain an annulment, judicial separation or divorce in England and Wales, one or both of the parties must have their permanent home in England and Wales when the petition is started, or have been living in England and Wales for at least a year on the day the petition is started. All cases are commenced in divorce county courts or in the Divorce Registry in London. If a suit is defended it may be transferred to the High Court.

NULLITY OF MARRIAGE

A marriage is invalid from the beginning if:
– the parties were within the prohibited degrees of consanguinity, affinity or adoption (*see* page 662)
– the parties were not male and female
– either of the parties was already married (if the polygamous marriage was entered into outside England and Wales, it is invalid if either of the parties lived in England or Wales at the time of the marriage)
– either of the parties was under the age of 16
– the formalities of the marriage were defective, e.g. the marriage did not take place in an authorized building, and both parties knew of the defect

In the case of those aged 16 to 17, absence of parental consent does not invalidate the marriage.

A marriage may be voidable (i.e. a decree of nullity may be obtained but in the meantime the marriage remains valid) on the following grounds:
– either party was unable to consummate the marriage
– the respondent wilfully refused to consummate the marriage (insistence on the use of contraceptives does not constitute wilful refusal to consummate, but may constitute unreasonable behaviour for the purpose of divorce and may be allowed as a defence to a charge of desertion)
– either party did not validly consent to the marriage, in consequence of duress, mistake, unsoundness of mind, or otherwise
– either party was suffering from a mental disorder at the time of the marriage
– the respondent was suffering from a communicable venereal disease at the time of the marriage, and the petitioner did not know this
– the respondent was pregnant by another man at the time of the marriage, and the petitioner did not know this

In the last four circumstances, proceedings must generally be instituted within three years of the date of the marriage.

A decree of nullity only annuls the marriage from the date of the decree, and any children of the marriage are legitimate. Children of a void marriage are illegitimate unless the father lived in England and Wales at the time of the birth (or father's death, if earlier) and at the time of conception (or marriage, if later) both or either of the parents reasonably believed the marriage was valid.

When a marriage has been annulled, both parties are free to marry again.

SEPARATION

A couple may enter into an agreement to separate by consent but for the agreement to be valid it must be followed by an immediate separation; a solicitor should be contacted and will usually advise that a court order be obtained.

Judicial separation does not dissolve a marriage and it is not necessary to prove that the marriage has irretrievably broken down. Either party can petition for a judicial separation at any time; the grounds listed below as grounds for divorce are also grounds for judicial separation.

DIVORCE

Divorce dissolves the marriage and leaves both parties at liberty to marry again. Neither party can petition for divorce until at least one year after the date of the marriage. The fee for starting a divorce petition is £80. The sole ground for divorce is the irretrievable breakdown of the marriage; this must be proved on one or more of the following grounds:

– the respondent has committed adultery and the petitioner finds it intolerable to live with him/her; however the petitioner cannot rely on an act of adultery by the other party if they have lived together for more than six months after the discovery that adultery had been committed

– the respondent has behaved in such a way that the petitioner cannot reasonably be expected to continue living with him/her

– the respondent deserted the petitioner for two years immediately before the petition. Desertion may be defined as a voluntary withdrawal from cohabitation by the respondent without just cause and against the wishes of the petitioner; where one party is guilty of serious misconduct which forces the other party to leave, the party at fault is said to be guilty of constructive desertion

– the respondent and the petitioner have lived separately for two years immediately before the petition and the respondent consents to the decree

– the respondent and the petitioner have lived separately for five years immediately before the petition

A total period of less than six months during which the parties have resumed living together is disregarded in determining whether the prescribed period of separation or desertion has been continuous (but cannot be included as part of the period of separation).

The Matrimonial Causes Act 1973 requires the solicitor for the petitioner in certain cases to certify that the possibility of a reconciliation has been discussed with the petitioner.

THE DECREE NISI

A decree nisi does not dissolve or annul the marriage but must be obtained before a divorce or annulment can take place.

Where the suit is undefended, the evidence normally takes the form of a sworn written statement made by the petitioner which is considered by a district judge. If the judge is satisfied that the petitioner has proved the contents of the petition, he/she will set a date for the pronouncement of the decree nisi in open court; neither party need attend.

If the judge is not satisfied that the petitioner has proved the contents of the petition, or if the suit is defended, the petition will be heard in open court with the parties giving oral evidence.

THE DECREE ABSOLUTE

The decree nisi is usually made absolute after six weeks and on the application of the petitioner. The fee for applying for a decree absolute is £20. If the judge thinks it may be necessary to exercise any of his/her rights under the Children Act 1989, he/she can in exceptional circumstances delay the granting of the decree absolute. The decree absolute dissolves or annuls the marriage.

CHILDREN

Neither parent is now awarded 'custody' of any children of the marriage in England and Wales. The term 'parent with care' is used to describe the parent who lives with the child or children; the parent who does not normally live with the child or children is termed the 'absent parent'. The courts will deal with issues of contact and residence involving children; in all court cases concerning children, whether connected to a matrimonial suit or not, the welfare of the child is the paramount consideration.

MAINTENANCE, ETC.

Either party may be liable to pay maintenance to their former spouse. If there were any children of the marriage, both parents have a legal responsibility to support them financially if they can afford to do so. These so-called ancillary matters, including any property settlements, may be settled before the divorce goes through but currently can go on long after the marriage is dissolved.

The courts are responsible for assessing maintenance for the former spouse, taking into account each party's income and essential outgoings and other aspects of the case. The court also deals with any maintenance for a child which has been treated by the spouses as a 'child of the family', e.g. a stepchild, and any property settlements.

The Child Support Agency (CSA) was set up under the Child Support Act 1991 and is now responsible for assessing the maintenance that absent parents should pay for their natural or adopted children (whether or not a marriage has taken place). The CSA accepts applications only when all the people involved are habitually resident in the UK; the courts will continue to deal with cases where one of the people involved lives abroad. The CSA deals with all new cases, and is gradually taking on cases where the parent with care (or his/her new partner) was already receiving income support, family credit or disability working allowance before 5 April 1993. People with existing court orders or written maintenance agreements made before 5 April 1993 should continue to use the courts. Where it is already collecting child maintenance, the CSA has the power to offer a collection and enforcement service for certain other payments of maintenance.

A formula is used to work out how much child maintenance is payable. The formula ensures that after the payment of child maintenance the absent parent's income, and that of any second family he/she may now have, remains significantly above basic income support rates. Also, no absent parent will normally be assessed to pay more than 30 per cent of his/her net income in current child maintenance, or more than 33 per cent if he/she is also liable for any arrears. Absent parents are normally expected to pay at least a minimum amount of child maintenance (currently £4.80 a week).

A scheme is expected to be introduced by the end of 1997 which will allow for greater flexibility in the calculation of maintenance payments. The scheme will allow absent parents to have certain special expenses offset against their income before their maintenance liability is calculated, or to have a property and capital transfer ('clean break' settlement) taken into account; there will also be some additional grounds which may result in liability being increased.

Some cases involving unusual circumstances are treated as special cases and the assessment is modified. Where there is financial need (e.g. because of disability or continuing education), maintenance may be ordered for children even beyond the age of 18.

The level of maintenance is reviewed automatically every two years. Either parent can report a change of circumstances and request a review at any time. An independent complaints examiner for the CSA is to be appointed in early 1997.

If the absent parent does not pay the child maintenance, the CSA may make an order for payments to be deducted directly from his/her salary or wages; if all other methods fail, the CSA may take court action to enforce the payment.

COURT ORDERS

Magistrates' courts used for domestic proceedings are now called family proceedings courts. A spouse can apply to the family proceedings court for a court order on the ground that the other spouse:
- has failed to pay reasonable maintenance for the applicant
- has failed to make a proper contribution towards the reasonable maintenance of a 'child of the family'
- has deserted the applicant
- has behaved in such a way that the applicant cannot reasonably be expected to live with the respondent

If the case is proved, the court can order:
- periodical payments for the applicant and/or a 'child of the family'
- a lump sum payment (not exceeding £1,000) to the applicant and/or a 'child of the family'

In deciding what orders (if any) to make, the court must consider guidelines which are similar to those governing financial orders in divorce cases. There are also special provisions relating to consent orders and separation by agreement. An order may be enforceable even if the parties are living together, but in some cases it will cease to have effect if they continue to do so for six months.

DOMESTIC VIOLENCE

If one spouse has been subjected to violence at the hands of the other, it is now possible to obtain a court order very quickly to restrain further violence and if necessary to have the other spouse excluded from the home. Such orders may also relate to unmarried couples. A person disobeying such a court order is liable to be imprisoned for contempt of court.

IMPENDING LEGISLATION

A bill is currently before Parliament under the provisions of which irretrievable breakdown would be the sole ground for divorce; the partner initiating the divorce would be required to attend an information session about the nature of divorce and the options available; and divorce would be granted after one year, or 18 months if the couple have children, during which time the couple would have the chance to take part in mediation sessions to make arrangements concerning children, property and money. If the bill becomes law, these changes will not be effective until 1998 at the earliest.

SCOTLAND

Although there is separate legislation for Scotland covering nullity of marriage, judicial separation, divorce and ancillary matters, the provisions are in most respects the same as those for England and Wales. The following is confined to those points on which the law in Scotland differs.

A suit for judicial separation or divorce may be raised in the Court of Session; it may also be raised in the Sheriff Court if either party was resident in the sheriffdom for 40 days immediately before the date of the action or for 40 days ending not more than 40 days before the date of the action. The fee for starting a divorce petition is £70 in the Sheriff Court.

When adultery is cited as proof that the marriage has broken down irretrievably, it is not necessary in Scotland to prove also that it is intolerable for the petitioner to live with the respondent. In the case of desertion, irretrievable breakdown is not established if cohabitation is resumed for a period of more than three months after the two-year desertion period has expired.

The court is responsible for seeking to promote a reconciliation between the spouses. Where a divorce action has been raised, it may be postponed by the court to enable the parties to seek to effect a reconciliation if the court feels that there may be a reasonable prospect of such reconciliation. If the parties do cohabit during such postponement, no account is taken of the cohabitation if the action later proceeds.

In actions for divorce and separation, the court has the power to award custody of any children of the marriage. The welfare of the children is of paramount importance, and the fact that a spouse has caused the breakdown of the marriage does not in itself preclude him or her from being awarded custody.

A simplified procedure for 'do-it-yourself' divorce was introduced in 1983 for certain divorces. If the action is based on two or five years' separation and will not be opposed, and if there are no children under 16 and no financial claims, the applicant can write directly to the local sheriff court or to the Court of Session for the appropriate forms to enable him or her to proceed. The fee is £55, unless the applicant receives income support, family credit or legal advice and assistance, in which case there is no fee.

The decree absolute is known in Scotland as the extract decree. The fee for applying for an extract decree is £14.

Further information can be obtained from any divorce county court, solicitor or Citizens' Advice Bureau, the Lord Chancellor's Department or the Lord Advocate's Department (for entries, see Index), or the following:
THE PRINCIPAL REGISTRY, Somerset House, London WC2R ILP. Tel: 0171-936 6983
THE COURT OF SESSION, Divorce Section (SP), Parliament House, Edinburgh EH1 IRQ. Tel: 0131-225 2595
THE CHILD SUPPORT AGENCY, PO Box 55, Brierley Hill, W. Midlands DY5 IYL. Tel: 0345-133133

EMPLOYMENT LAW

PAY AND CONDITIONS

Under the Employment Protection (Consolidation) Act 1978 (as amended by the Trade Union Reform and Employment Rights Act 1993), employers must give each employee based in Great Britain and employed for more than one month a written statement containing the following information:
- names of employer and employee
- date when employment began
- remuneration and intervals at which it will be paid
- job title or description of job
- hours and place(s) of work

– holiday entitlement and holiday pay
– entitlement to sick leave and sick pay
– details of pension scheme(s)
– length of notice period that employer and employee need to give to terminate employment, or the end date for a fixed-term contract
– details of any collective agreement which affects the terms of employment
– details of disciplinary and grievance procedures
– if the employee is to work outside the UK for more than one month, the period of such work and the currency in which payment is made

This must be given to the employee within two months of the start of their employment.

SICK PAY

Employees absent from work through illness or injury are entitled to receive Statutory Sick Pay (SSP) from the employer for a maximum period of 28 weeks in any three-year period. This applies to all employees, both men and women, up to the age of 65.

DEDUCTIONS FROM PAY

Under the Wages Act 1986, employers may not make deductions from an employee's wages without the employee's prior written consent or unless authorized by statute (e.g. deductions for national insurance or tax).

PART-TIME EMPLOYEES

The Employment Protection (Part-time Employees) Regulations 1995 extend the rights of part-time workers and in most circumstances bring into line the treatment of part-time and full-time workers.

SUNDAY TRADING

The Sunday Trading Act 1994 gave new rights to shop workers. They have the right not to be dismissed, selected for redundancy or to suffer any detriment (such as the denial of overtime, promotion or training) if they refuse to work on Sundays. This does not apply to those who, under their contracts, are employed to work on Sundays.

TRADE UNION MEMBERSHIP

Under employment legislation, employees or potential employees may not be penalized because they are or are not a member of a trade union.

DISPUTES

Where it has not been possible to settle a dispute in the workplace, it may be possible for employees to make a complaint to an industrial tribunal. ACAS (the Advisory, Conciliation and Arbitration Service; for entry, *see* Index) offers advice and conciliation in employment disputes.

TERMINATION OF EMPLOYMENT

An employee may be dismissed without notice if guilty of gross misconduct but in other cases a period of notice must be given by the employer. The minimum periods of notice specified in the Employment Protection (Consolidation) Act 1978 are:
– at least one week if the employee has been continuously employed for one month or more but for less than two years
– at least two weeks if the employee has been continuously employed for two years or more. A week is added for every complete year of continuous employment up to 12 years
– at least 12 weeks for those who have been continuously employed for 12 years or more

– longer periods apply if these are specified in the contract of employment

If an employee is dismissed with less notice than he/she is entitled to, the employer is generally liable to pay wages for the period of proper notice (or for the period of the contract for those on fixed-term contracts). Generally, no notice needs to be given of the expiry of a fixed-term contract.

REDUNDANCY

An employee dismissed because of redundancy may be entitled to a lump sum. This applies if:
– the employee has at least two years' continuous service (qualified as for unfair dismissal, below)
– the employee is actually dismissed by the employer (even in cases of voluntary redundancy)
– dismissal is due to a reduction in the work force

An employee may not be entitled to a redundancy payment if offered a new job by the same employer. The amount of payment depends on the length of service, the salary and the age of the employee.

UNFAIR DISMISSAL

Complaints about unfair dismissal are dealt with by an industrial tribunal. Any employee, with two years' continuous service (although this requirement has been questioned in a recent court of appeal case) subject to exceptions, regardless of their hours of work, can make a complaint to the tribunal. At the tribunal the employer must prove that he/she acted reasonably in dismissing the employee and that the dismissal was due to one or more of the following reasons:
– the employee's capability for the job
– the employee's conduct
– redundancy
– a legal restriction preventing the continuation of the employee's contract
– some other substantial reason

If the employee is found to have been unfairly dismissed, the tribunal can order that he/she be reinstated or compensated.

DISCRIMINATION

Discrimination in employment on the grounds of sex, race or (subject to wide exceptions) disability is unlawful. The following legislation applies to those employed in Great Britain but not to employees in Northern Ireland or to those who work mainly abroad:
– The Equal Pay Act 1970 (as amended) entitles men and women to equality in matters related to their contracts of employment. Those doing like work for the same employer are entitled to the same pay and conditions regardless of their sex
– The Sex Discrimination Act 1975 (as amended by the Sex Discrimination Act 1986) makes it unlawful to discriminate on grounds of sex or marital status. This covers all aspects of employment, including advertising for recruits, terms offered, opportunities for promotion and training, and dismissal procedures
– The Race Relations Act 1976 gives individuals the right not to be discriminated against in employment matters on the grounds of race, colour, nationality, or ethnic or national origins. It applies to all aspects of employment
– The Disability Discrimination Act 1995 makes discrimination against a disabled person in all aspects of employment unlawful. Unlike sex and race discrimination, an employer may show that the treatment is justified and that the employer acted reasonably. Employers with 20 or fewer employees are exempt

The Equal Opportunities Commission and the Commission for Racial Equality (for entries, *see* Index) have the function of eliminating such discriminations in the workplace and can provide further information and assistance.

In Northern Ireland like provisions exist but are constituted in separate legislation. The Fair Employment (Northern Ireland) Act 1989 adds specific provisions aimed at preventing religious discrimination.

ILLEGITIMACY AND LEGITIMATION

The Children Act 1989 gives the mother parental responsibility for the child when she is not married to the father. The father can acquire parental responsibility either by agreement with her (in prescribed form) or by applying to the court. If an illegitimate child is to be adopted, the father's consent is required only where he has been awarded parental rights by the court.

Every child born to a married woman during marriage is presumed to be legitimate, unless the couple are separated under court order when the child is conceived, in which case the child is presumed not to be the husband's child. It is possible to challenge the presumption of legitimacy or illegitimacy through civil proceedings.

LEGITIMATION

Under the Legitimacy Act 1976, an illegitimate person automatically becomes legitimate when his/her parents marry. This applies even where one of the parents was married to a third person at the time of the birth. In such cases it is necessary to re-register the birth of the child. In Scotland, the relevant legislation is the Legitimation (Scotland) Act 1968 which came into operation on 8 June 1968, on which date thousands of existing illegitimate children were regarded as legitimate.

RIGHTS OF ILLEGITIMATE PEOPLE

For the purposes of most legislation, illegitimate and legitimate people have the same rights and responsibilities. In particular, under the Family Law Reform Acts 1969 and 1987, legitimate and illegitimate children have broadly the same rights on an intestacy. Furthermore, in any will made after 31 December 1969, it is assumed that any reference to children or relatives will include those who are illegitimate and those related through another person who is illegitimate. In Scotland, illegitimate and legitimate people are given equal status under the Law Reform (Parent and Child) Act 1986.

In Scotland, the father of an illegitimate child has a responsibility to provide for that child until he/she is 16. The mother of the child can take action in court if this is not done. The court will also decide on custody and access issues.

JURY SERVICE

A person charged with any but the most minor offences is entitled to be tried by jury, although jury trials are now unusual in civil cases. There are 12 members of a jury in England and Wales. In Scotland there are 12 members of a jury in a civil case in the Court of Session, seven in the Sheriff Court, and 15 in a criminal trial. Jurors are normally asked to serve for ten working days, although jurors selected for longer cases are expected to sit for the duration of the trial.

Every parliamentary or local elector between the ages of 18 and 70 who has lived in the UK (including, for this purpose, the Channel Islands and the Isle of Man) for any period of at least five years since reaching the age of 13 is qualified to serve on a jury unless he/she is ineligible or disqualified.

ENGLAND AND WALES

Those ineligible for jury service include:
– those who have at any time been judges, magistrates or senior court officials
– those who have within the previous ten years been concerned with the adminstration of justice (e.g. barristers, solicitors and their clerks, court officials, coroners, police officers, prison officers and probation officers)
– priests of any religion and vowed members of religious communities
– certain sufferers from mental illness

Those disqualified from jury service include:
– those who have at any time been sentenced by a court in the UK (including, for this purpose, the Channel Islands and the Isle of Man) to a term of imprisonment or custody of five years or more
– those who have within the previous ten years served any part of a sentence of imprisonment, youth custody or detention, been detained in a young offenders' institution, received a suspended sentence of imprisonment or order for detention, or received a community service order
– those who have within the previous five years been placed on probation

Those who may be excused as of right from jury service include:
– persons over the age of 65
– members and officers of the Houses of Parliament
– full-time serving members of the armed forces
– registered and practising members of the medical, dental, nursing, veterinary and pharmaceutical professions
– those who have served on a jury in the previous two years

The court has the discretion to excuse a juror from service, or defer the date of service, if the service would be a hardship to the juror. If a person serves on a jury knowing himself/herself to be ineligible or disqualified, he/she is liable to be fined up to £1,000 or £5,000 respectively. Jurors failing to attend without good cause are liable to be fined up to £1,000. The defendant can object to any juror if he/she can show that the juror is ineligible, disqualified, or biased against him/her.

A juror may claim travelling expenses, a subsistence allowance and an allowance for other financial loss (e.g. loss of earnings or benefits, fees paid to carers or child-minders) up to a stated limit.

It is an offence for a juror to discuss a case with anyone who is not a member of the jury, even after the trial is over. A jury's verdict must normally be unanimous, but if no verdict has been reached after two hours' consideration (or such longer period as the court deems to be reasonable) a majority verdict is acceptable if ten jurors agree to it.

It is an offence to intimidate, threaten or harm a juror.

SCOTLAND

Qualification criteria for jury service in Scotland are similar to those in England and Wales, except that the maximum age for a juror is 65, and those who have within the previous five years been concerned with the administration of justice are ineligible for service. Ministers of religion, persons in holy orders and those who have served on a jury in the previous five years are excusable as of right.

The maximum fine for a person serving on a jury knowing himself/herself to be ineligible is £1,000. The maximum fine for failing to attend without good cause is £400.

Further information can obtained from:
THE COURT SERVICE, Southside, 105 Victoria Street, London SWIE 6QT. Tel: 0171-210 1775
THE CLERK OF JUSTICIARY, High Court of Justiciary, Parliament House, Edinburgh EHI IRQ. Tel: 0131-225 2595

LANDLORD AND TENANT

When a property is rented to a tenant, the rights and responsibilities of the landlord and the tenant are determined largely by the tenancy agreement but also by statutory provisions. Some of the main provisions are outlined below but it is advisable to contact the Citizens' Advice Bureau or the local authority housing department for further information.

RESIDENTIAL LETTINGS

The provisions outlined here apply only where the tenant lives in a separate dwelling from the landlord and where the dwelling is the tenant's only or main home. It does not apply to licensees such as lodgers, guests or service occupiers.

The 1996 Housing Bill includes proposals which will radically change certain aspects of the legislation referred to below, in particular the grant of assured and assured shorthold tenancies under the Housing Act 1988. It is advisable to check whether the new legislation has come into force before relying on the provisions set out below.

ASSURED TENANCIES

Most new lettings will be assured tenancies and under the Housing Act 1988 the tenants are given certain rights. The tenant may stay as long as he/she wishes unless the landlord has grounds for repossession, e.g. if the tenant breaks the terms of the agreement. The rent payable is that agreed with the landlord unless the rent has been fixed by the rent assessment committee of the local authority. The tenant or the landlord may request that the committee set the rent in line with open market rents for that type of property. Any rent increases that are to take place should be written into the agreement but failing that, the landlord must give advance notice of the increase.

It is also common for new lettings to be assured shorthold tenancies. This is a type of assured tenancy and the same conditions and rights apply except that the tenancy lasts for a specified period of time. The tenancy must be for at least six months. At the end of the tenancy the landlord can agree to another tenancy or can repossess the property. The landlord must give the tenant a notice stating that the tenancy is an assured shorthold tenancy. These notices are available at law stationers.

REGULATED TENANCIES

Before the Housing Act 1988 came into force (15 January 1989) there were regulated tenancies; some are still in existence and are protected by the Rent Act 1977. Under this Act it is possible for the landlord or the tenant to apply to the local rent officer to have a 'fair' rent registered. The fair rent is then the maximum rent payable.

SECURE TENANCIES

Secure tenancies are generally given to tenants of local authorities, housing associations and certain other bodies. This gives the tenant lifelong tenure unless the terms of the agreement are broken by the tenant. In certain circumstances those with secure tenancies may have the right to buy their property. In practice this right is generally only available to council tenants.

AGRICULTURAL PROPERTY

Tenancies in agricultural properties are governed by the Agricultural Holdings Act 1986 and the Rent (Agricultural) Act 1976, which give similar protections to those described above, e.g. security of tenure, right to compensation for disturbance, etc. The Agricultural Holdings (Scotland) Act 1991 applies similar provisions to Scotland.

EVICTION

Under the Protection from Eviction Act 1977 (as amended by the Housing Act 1988), a landlord must give reasonable notice that he/she is to evict the tenant, and in most cases a possession order, granted in court, is necessary. Notice is generally to be at least four weeks and in prescribed statutory form (notices are available from law stationers). It is illegal for a landlord to evict a person by putting their belongings onto the street, by changing the locks and so on. It is also illegal for a landlord to harass a tenant in any way in order to persuade him/her to give up the tenancy.

LANDLORD RESPONSIBILITIES

Under the Landlord and Tenant Act 1985, where the term of the lease is less than seven years the landlord is responsible for maintaining the structure and exterior of the property and all installations for the supply of water, gas and electricity, for sanitation, and for heating and hot water.

LEASEHOLDERS

Legally leaseholders have bought a long lease rather than a property and in certain limited circumstances the landlord can end the tenancy. Under the Leasehold Reform Act 1967 (as amended by the Housing Acts 1969, 1974 and 1980), leaseholders of houses may have the right to buy the freehold or to take an extended lease for a term of 50 years. This applies to leases where the term of the lease is over 21 years and where the leaseholder has occupied the house as his/her main residence for the last three years, or for a total of three years over the last ten.

The Leasehold Reform, Housing and Urban Development Act came into force in 1993 and allows the leaseholders of flats in certain circumstances to buy the freehold of the building in which they live.

Responsibility for maintenance of the structure, exterior and interior of the building should be set out in the lease. Usually the upkeep of the interior of his/her part of the property is the responsibility of the leaseholder, and responsibility for the structure, exterior and common interior areas is shared between the freeholder and the leaseholder(s).

BUSINESS LETTINGS

The Landlord and Tenant Acts 1927 and 1954 (as amended) give security of tenure to the tenants of most business premises. The landlord can only evict the tenant on one of the grounds laid down in the 1954 Act, and in some cases where the landlord repossesses the property the tenant may be entitled to compensation.

SCOTLAND

In Scotland assured and short assured tenancies exist for lettings after 2 January 1989 and are similar to assured tenancies in England and Wales. The relevant legislation is the Housing (Scotland) Act 1988.

Most tenancies created before 2 January 1989 were regulated tenancies and the Rent (Scotland) Act 1984 still applies where these exist. The Act defines, among other things, the circumstances in which a landlord can increase the rent when improvements are made to the property. The provisions of the Rent Act do not apply to tenancies where the landlord is the Crown, a local authority, the development corporation of a new town or a housing corporation.

The Housing (Scotland) Act 1987 and its provisions relate to local authority responsibilities for housing, the right to buy, and local authority secured tenancies. The provisions are broadly similar to England and Wales.

In Scotland, business premises are not controlled by statute to the same extent as in England and Wales, although the Shops (Scotland) Act 1949 gives some security to tenants of shops. Tenants of shops can apply to the sheriff for a renewal of tenancy if threatened with eviction. This application may be dismissed if the landlord has offered to sell the property to the tenant at an agreed price. The Act extends to properties where the Crown or government departments are the landlords or the tenants.

Under the Leases Act 1449 the landlord's successors (either purchasers or creditors) are bound by the agreement made with any tenants so long as the following conditions are met:
- the lease, if for more than one year, must be in writing
- there must be a rent
- there must be a term of expiry
- the tenant must have entered into possession

Many leases contain references to term and quarter days. The statutory dates of these are listed on page 9.

LEGAL AID

Under the Legal Aid Act 1988 (as amended) and the Legal Aid (Scotland) Act 1986, people on low or moderate incomes may qualify for help with the costs of legal advice or representation. The scheme is administered in England and Wales by the Legal Aid Board and in Scotland by the Scottish Legal Aid Board (for entries, *see* Index). There are three types of legal aid: civil legal aid, legal advice and assistance, and criminal legal aid.

CIVIL LEGAL AID

Applications for legal aid are made through a solicitor; the Citizens' Advice Bureau will have addresses for local solicitors. Franchised solicitors are those approved by the Legal Aid Boards, which can provide details.

Civil legal aid is available for proceedings in the following:
- the House of Lords
- the High Court
- the Court of Appeal
- county courts
- lands tribunals
- the Employment Appeal Tribunal
- the Restrictive Practices Court
- the Commons Commissioners
- civil proceedings in magistrates' courts
- family proceedings courts

It is not available for the following:
- tribunals other than those mentioned above
- defamation proceedings
- obtaining the decree in undefended divorce and judicial separation
- court cases outside England and Wales

ELIGIBILITY

The Legal Aid Board will only grant a civil legal aid certificate where:
- the applicant qualifies financially, and
- the applicant has reasonable grounds for taking or defending the action, and
- it is reasonable to grant legal aid in the circumstances of the case. For example, civil legal aid will not be granted where it appears that the applicant will gain only trivial advantage from the proceedings

In order to qualify for civil legal aid, a person's disposable income must be £7,403 a year or less and their disposable capital must be £6,750 or less. (The financial limits are different for pensioners and in personal injury claims). Disposable income is the total income, less outgoings such as tax and national insurance contributions, rent, council tax, etc., with allowances made for dependants. The income of a spouse or cohabitee is taken into account unless they are living apart or have a contrary interest in the proceedings. Disposable capital includes savings, insurances, any personal possessions of substantial value, property owned (but not the property in which the person lives, the furniture and fittings in that property, or the equipment of the person's trade).

CONTRIBUTIONS

Some of those who qualify for legal aid will have to contribute towards their legal costs:
- if in receipt of income support, no contributions are due
- if annual disposable income is between £2,498 and £7,403, a contribution must be made from disposable income
- if disposable capital is over £3,000, all disposable capital in excess of £3,000 must be paid as a contribution

Contributions from disposable income are paid monthly for as long as the person has legal aid. The amount of the contribution depends on the amount of disposable income in excess of £2,498; the greater the excess income, the greater the contribution. Contributions from capital are payable immediately.

STATUTORY CHARGES

A statutory charge is made if a person receives money or property in a case for which they have received legal aid. This means that the amount paid by the Legal Aid Fund on their behalf is deducted from the amount that the person receives. This does not apply if the court has ordered that the costs be paid by the other party or if the payments are for maintenance. In family proceedings cases, the first £2,500 is exempt and the statutory charge is taken from anything in excess of that.

In urgent cases, e.g. domestic violence, legal aid may be granted without the means test. This will be carried out later and the person will have to reimburse the Legal Aid Fund for any aid that they received which exceeded their entitlement.

SCOTLAND

Civil legal aid is available for cases in the following:
- the House of Lords
- the Court of Session
- the Lands Valuation Appeal Court
- the Scottish Land Court

– sheriff courts
– the Lands Tribunal for Scotland
– the Employment Appeal Tribunals
– the Restrictive Practices Court
Eligibility for civil legal aid is assessed in a similar way to that in England and Wales, though the financial limits differ in some respects and are as follows:
– a person is eligible if disposable income is £8,158 or less and disposable capital is £6,750 or less
– if disposable income is between £2,498 and £8,158, contributions are payable
– if disposable capital exceeds £3,000, contributions are payable

LEGAL ADVICE AND ASSISTANCE

The legal aid and assistance scheme (commonly referred to as the green form scheme) covers the costs of getting advice and help from a solicitor, and, in some cases, representation in court under the 'assistance by way of representation' scheme (see below).
A person is eligible for legal advice and assistance if:
– they have a disposable income of £75 a week or less and disposable capital of £1,000 or less
– they are eligible for income support or family credit (unless they have disposable capital of more than £1,000)
There are no contributions under this scheme.
If a person is eligible, the Legal Aid Board will pay for up to two hours' work by a solicitor on behalf of the person (three hours where drafting a petition for divorce). The solicitor must seek the approval of the Legal Aid Board to claim for longer periods of time. The work the solicitor does may include giving advice, writing letters, making an application for civil/criminal legal aid, seeking the advice of a barrister, etc. The scheme does not cover any form of proceedings before a court or tribunal.
Any money or property recovered with the help of legal advice and assistance will be subject to a 'solicitor's charge', which is similar to a statutory charge in civil legal aid but with some differences.

ASSISTANCE BY WAY OF REPRESENTATION

This type of assistance is available for most cases in a family proceedings court and to patients before a mental health review tribunal. It covers the cost of preparing a case and of legal representation in the court.
Under this scheme the two-hour limit does not apply and the approval of the Legal Aid Board is needed in all cases. The income and capital limits are different to legal advice and assistance. In order to qualify, a person's disposable income must be £162 a week or less and their savings must not exceed £3,000. There is no means test for patients due before a mental health review tribunal. Contributions may have to be made and a solicitor's charge will apply to money or property recovered (as with legal advice and assistance).

DUTY SOLICITORS

The Legal Aid Act 1988 also provides free advice and assistance to anyone questioned by the police (whether under arrest or helping the police with their enquiries). No means test or contributions are required for this. The advice or assistance can be from the duty solicitor at the police station, from a person's own solicitor or from any local solicitor (a list is available at police stations).
Duty solicitors are usually available at the magistrates' court, in criminal cases, for advice and/or representation on first appearances. This assistance is not means-tested.
The Legal Aid Fund also covers the costs of a solicitor present in the buildings of family proceedings or county

courts who may be requested by the court to advise or represent someone in need of help.

SCOTLAND

Legal advice and assistance operates in a similar way in Scotland. A person is eligible:
– if disposable income does not exceed £162 a week. If disposable income is between £67 and £162 a week, contributions are payable
– if disposable capital does not exceed £1,000 (£1,335 if the person has one dependant, £1,535 if two dependants).
There are no contributions from capital

CRIMINAL LEGAL AID

It is up to the criminal court in which proceedings are to take place to grant criminal legal aid. The court will do this if it is desirable in the interests of justice (e.g. if there are important questions of law to be argued or the case is so serious that if found guilty the person may go to prison) and the person needs help to pay their legal costs.
Criminal legal aid covers the cost of preparing a case and legal representation (including the cost of a barrister) in criminal proceedings. It is also available for appeals against verdicts or sentences in magistrates' courts, the Crown Court or the Court of Appeal. It is not available for bringing a private prosecution in a criminal court.
If granted criminal legal aid, either the person may choose their own solicitor or the court will assign one. Contributions to the legal costs must be paid by anyone who has a disposable income of over £49 a week or disposable capital of over £3,000. These contributions are payable each month and will probably be returned to the person if they are acquitted. If the payments are not made, the legal aid order may be revoked.

SCOTLAND

The procedure for application for criminal legal aid depends on the circumstances of each case. In solemn cases (more serious cases, e.g. homicide) heard before a jury, it is for the court to decide whether to grant legal aid. In summary cases (less serious) the procedure depends on whether the person is in custody:
– anyone taken into custody has the right to free legal aid from the duty solicitor up to and including the first court appearance
– if the person is not in custody and wishes to plead guilty, they are not entitled to criminal legal aid but may be entitled to legal advice and assistance, including assistance by way of representation
– if the person is not in custody and wishes to plead not guilty, they can apply for criminal legal aid. This must be done within 14 days of the first court appearance at which they made the plea
The criteria used to assess whether or not criminal legal aid should be granted is similar to the criteria for England and Wales.

MARRIAGE

Any two persons may marry provided that:
– they are at least 16 years old on the day of the marriage (in England and Wales persons under the age of 18 must generally obtain the consent of their parents; if consent is refused an appeal may be made to the High Court, the county court or a court of summary jurisdiction)
– they are not related to one another in a way which would prevent their marrying (see below)

- they are unmarried (a person who has already been married must produce documentary evidence that the previous marriage has been ended by death, divorce or annulment)
- they are not of the same sex
- they are capable of understanding the nature of a marriage ceremony and of consenting to marriage
- the marriage would be regarded as valid in any foreign country of which either party is a citizen

DEGREES OF RELATIONSHIP

A marriage between persons within the prohibited degrees of consanguinity, affinity or adoption is void.

A man may not marry his mother, daughter, grandmother, granddaughter, sister, aunt, niece, great-grandmother, great-granddaughter, adoptive mother, former adoptive mother, adopted daughter or former adopted daughter. In some circumstances he may now be allowed to marry his former wife's daughter, former wife's granddaughter, father's former wife or grandfather's former wife.

A woman may not marry her father, son, grandfather, grandson, brother, uncle, nephew, great-grandfather, great-grandson, adoptive father, former adoptive father, adopted son or former adopted son. In some circumstances she may now be allowed to marry her former husband's son, former husband's grandson, mother's former husband or grandmother's former husband.

ENGLAND AND WALES

TYPES OF MARRIAGE CEREMONY

It is possible to marry by either religious or civil ceremony. A religious ceremony can take place at a church or chapel of the Church of England or the Church in Wales, or at any other place of worship which has been formally registered by the Registrar-General.

A civil ceremony can take place at a register office, a registered building or any other premises approved by the local authority.

An application for an approved premises licence must be made by the owners or trustees of the building concerned; it cannot be made by the prospective marriage couple. Approved premises must be regularly open to the public so that the marriage can be witnessed; the venue must be deemed to be a permanent and immovable structure. Open-air ceremonies are prohibited.

Non-Anglicans may be married under the Registrar-General's licence in unregistered premises where one of the parties is seriously ill, is not expected to recover, and cannot be moved to registered premises. Detained and housebound persons may be married at their place of residence.

MARRIAGE IN THE CHURCH OF ENGLAND OR THE CHURCH IN WALES

Marriage by banns

The marriage must take place in a parish in which one of the parties lives, or in a church in another parish if it is the usual place of worship of either or both of the parties. The banns must be called in the parish in which the marriage is to take place on three Sundays before the day of the ceremony; if either or both of the parties lives in a different parish the banns must also be called there. After three months the banns are no longer valid.

Marriage by common licence

The vicar who is to conduct the marriage will arrange for a common licence to be issued by the diocesan bishop; this dispenses with the necessity for banns. One of the parties must have lived in the parish for 15 days immediately before the issuing of the licence or must usually worship at the church. Affidavits are prepared from the personal instructions of one of the parties and the licence will be given to the applicant in person.

Marriage by special licence

A special licence is granted by the Archbishop of Canterbury in special circumstances for the marriage to take place at any place, with or without previous residence in the parish, or at any time. Application must be made to the Faculty Office of the Archbishop of Canterbury, 1 The Sanctuary, London SW1P 3JT. Tel: 0171-222 5381.

Marriage by certificate

The marriage can be conducted on the authority of the superintendent registrar's certificate, provided that the vicar's consent is obtained. One of the parties must live in the parish or must usually worship at the church.

MARRIAGE BY OTHER RELIGIOUS CEREMONY

One of the parties must normally live in the registration district where the marriage is to take place. In addition to giving notice to the superintendent registrar (*see* below), it may also be necessary to book a registrar to be present at the ceremony.

CIVIL MARRIAGE

A marriage may be conducted at any register office, registered building or approved premises in England and Wales. The superintendent registrar of the district should be contacted, and, if the marriage is to take place at approved premises, the necessary arrangements at the venue must also be made.

NOTICE OF MARRIAGE

Unless it is to take place by banns or under common or special licence in the Church of England or the Church in Wales, a notice of the marriage must be given in person to the superintendent registrar. Notice of marriage may be given in the following ways:
- by certificate. Both parties must have lived in a registration district in England or Wales for at least seven days immediately before giving notice at the local register office. If they live in different registration districts, notice must be given in both districts. The marriage can take place in any register office in England and Wales 21 days after notice has been given
- by licence (often known as 'special licence'). One of the parties must have lived in a registration district in England or Wales for at least 15 days before giving notice at the register office; the other party need only be a resident of, or be physically in, England and Wales on the day notice is given. The marriage can take place one clear day (other than a Sunday, Christmas Day or Good Friday) after notice has been given

A notice of marriage is valid for three months. It is not therefore possible to give formal notice of a marriage more than three months before it is to take place, but it should be possible to make an advance (provisional) booking 12 months before the ceremony. In this case it is still necessary to give formal notice three months before the marriage. When giving notice of the marriage it is necessary to produce official proof, if relevant, that any previous marriage has ended in divorce or death; it is also useful, but not necessary, to take birth certificates or passports as proof of identity.

SOLEMNIZATION OF THE MARRIAGE

On the day of the wedding there must be at least two other people present who are prepared to act as witnesses and sign the marriage register. A registrar of marriages must be present at a marriage in a register office or at approved premises, but an authorized person may act in the capacity of registrar in a registered building.

If the marriage takes place at approved premises, the room must be separate from any other activity on the premises at the time of the ceremony, and no food or drink can be sold or consumed in the room during the ceremony or for one hour beforehand.

The marriage must be solemnized between 8 a.m. and 6 p.m., with open doors. The parties must at some time during the ceremony make the following declaration: 'I declare that I know of no legal reason why I, A. B., may not be joined in marriage to C. D.' Alternatively, the couple may answer 'I am' to the question 'Are you, A. B., free lawfully to marry C. D.?'. Each party must also say to the other: 'I, A. B., take you, C. D., to be my wedded wife [or husband]'.

A civil marriage cannot contain any religious aspects, but it may be possible for non-religious music and/or poetry readings to be included. It may also be possible to embellish the marriage vows taken by the couple.

If both parties are Jews, they may be married in a synagogue which has a certified marriage secretary or in a private house. The wedding may take place at any time of day and must be registered by the secretary of the synagogue of which the man is a member. The presence of a registrar of marriages is not necessary.

If both parties are members of the Society of Friends (Quakers), they may be married in a Friends' meeting-house. The marriage must be registered by the registering officer of the Society appointed to act for the district in which the meeting-house is situated. The presence of a registrar of marriages is not necessary.

CIVIL FEES *from 1 April 1996*

Fee for entry in the marriage notice book, £19
Marriage certificate on day of marriage, £2.50
Total fees for preliminaries for marriage under Registrar-General's licence, £15

Marriage at a register office or registered building
By certificate, where both parties live in the same district, £44
By certificate, where the parties live in different districts, £63
By licence, £89
These amounts include the fee of £25 for the registrar's attendance on the day of the wedding.

Marriage on approved premises
By certificate, where both parties live in the same district, £19
By certificate, where the parties live in different districts, £38
By licence, £64
Additional fees must be paid for the attendance of the superintendent registrar or the registrar on the day of the wedding; these fees are set by the local authority. A further charge is likely to be made by the owners of the building for the use of the premises.

Marriage in a religious building
(other than in the Church of England or the Church in Wales)
By certificate, where both parties live in the same district, £19
By certificate, where the parties live in different districts, £38

By licence, £64
An additional fee of £35 must be paid for the registrar's attendance on the day of the wedding unless an authorized person appointed by the trustees of the building is to register the marriage. Additional fees may also be charged by the trustees of the building and by the person who performs the ceremony.

ECCLESIASTICAL FEES *from 1 January 1996*

(Church of England and Church in Wales*)
Marriage by banns
For publication of banns, £12
For certificate of banns issued at time of publication, £7
For marriage service, £114
Marriage by common licence
Fee for licence varies, but about £50
Marriage by special licence
Fee for licence, £95
Further fees may be payable for additional facilities at the marriage, e.g. the organist's fee.

*Some of the above fees may not apply to the Church in Wales

SCOTLAND

REGULAR MARRIAGES

A regular marriage is one which is celebrated by a minister of religion or authorized registrar or other celebrant. Proclamation of banns is not required in Scotland. Each of the parties must complete a marriage notice form and return it to the district registrar for the area in which they are to be married, irrespective of where they live, at least 15 days before the ceremony is due to take place.

A marriage schedule, which is prepared by the registrar, will be issued to one or both of the parties in person up to seven days before a religious marriage; for a civil marriage the schedule will be available at the ceremony. The schedule must be handed to the celebrant before the ceremony starts; it must be signed immediately after the wedding and the marriage must be registered within three days.

The authority to conduct a marriage is deemed to be vested in the person conducting the ceremony rather than the building in which it takes place; open-air ceremonies are therefore permissable in Scotland.

MARRIAGE BY HABIT AND REPUTE

If two people live together constantly as husband and wife and are generally held to be such by the neighbourhood and among their friends and relations, there may arise a presumption from which marriage can be inferred. Before such a marriage can be registered, however, a decree of declarator of marriage must be obtained from the Deputy Principal Clerk of the Court of Session.

CIVIL FEES *from 1 April 1996*

Fee for a statutory notice of intention to marry, £11 per person
Fee for solemnization of marriage in a register office, £40

Further information can be obtained from:
THE GENERAL REGISTER OFFICE, Office for National Statistics, Smedley Hydro, Trafalgar Road, Birkdale, Southport PR8 2HH. Tel: 01704-569824
THE GENERAL REGISTER OFFICE FOR SCOTLAND, New Register House, Edinburgh EH1 3YT. Tel: 0131-334 0380

TOWN AND COUNTRY PLANNING

The principal legislation governing the development of land and buildings in England and Wales is the Town and Country Planning Act 1990 (as amended by the Planning and Compensation Act 1991). The equivalent legislation in Scotland is the Town and Country Planning (Scotland) Act 1972. The uses of buildings are classified by the Town and Country Planning (Use Classes) Order 1987 (as amended) in England and Wales, and in Scotland by the Town and Country Planning (Use Classes) (Scotland) Order 1989. It is advisable in all cases to contact the planning department of the local authority to check whether planning or other permission is needed.

PLANNING PERMISSION

Planning permission is needed if the work involves:
– making a material change in use, such as dividing off part of the house so that it can be used as a separate home or dividing off part of the house for commercial use, e.g. for a workshop
– going against the terms of the original planning permission, e.g. there may be a restriction on fences in front gardens on an open-plan estate
– obstructing the view of road users
– new or wider access to a main road
– additions or extensions to flats or maisonettes, even if they were originally converted from a house
Planning permission is not needed to carry out internal alterations or work which does not affect the external appearance of the building.
    There are certain types of development for which the Secretary of State for the Environment has granted general permissions. These include:
– house extensions and additions (including conservatories, loft conversions, garages and dormer windows). Up to 10 per cent or up to 50 cubic metres (whichever is the greater) can be added to the original house for terraced houses. Up to 15 per cent or 70 cubic metres (whichever is the greater) to other kinds of houses. The maximum that can be added to any house is 115 cubic metres
– buildings such as garden sheds and greenhouses so long as they are no more than 3 metres high (or 4 metres if the roof is ridged), are no nearer to a highway than the house, and at least half the ground around the house remains uncovered by buildings
– adding a porch with a ground area of less than 3 square metres and that is less than 3 metres in height
– putting up fences, walls and gates of under 1 metre in height if next to a road and under 2 metres elsewhere
– laying patios, paths or driveways for domestic use

OTHER RESTRICTIONS

It may be necessary to obtain other types of permissions before carrying out any development. These permissions are separate from planning permission and apply regardless of whether or not planning permission is needed, e.g.:
– building regulations will probably apply if a new building is to be erected, if an existing one is to be altered or extended, or if the work involves building over a drain or sewer. The building control department of the local authority will advise on this
– any alterations to a listed building or the grounds of a listed building must be approved by the local authority
– local authority approval is necessary if a building (or, in some circumstances, gates, walls, fences or railings) in a

conservation area is to be demolished; each local authority keeps a register of all local buildings that are in conservation areas
– many trees are protected by tree preservation orders and must not be pruned or taken down without local authority consent
– bats and other species are protected and English Nature, the Countryside Council for Wales or Scottish Natural Heritage (for entries, see Index) must be notified before any work is carried out that will affect the habitat of protected species, e.g. timber treatment, renovation or extensions of lofts
– any development in areas designated as a National Park, an Area of Outstanding National Beauty, a National Scenic Area or in the Norfolk or Suffolk Broads is subject to greater restrictions. The local planning authority will advise or refer enquirers to the relevant authority

VOTERS' QUALIFICATIONS

Those entitled to vote at parliamentary, European Union (EU) and local government elections are those who are:
– resident in the constituency or ward on the qualifying date i.e. 10 October in the year before the electoral register (see below) comes into effect; in Northern Ireland the qualifying date is 15 September and voters must have been resident in Northern Ireland for the three months leading up to that date
– over 18 years old
– Commonwealth (which includes British) citizens or citizens of the Republic of Ireland
    British citizens resident abroad are entitled to vote, for 20 years after leaving Britain, as overseas electors in parliamentary and EU elections in the constituency in which they were last resident. Members of the armed forces, Crown servants and employees of the British Council who are overseas and their spouses are entitled to vote regardless of how long they have been abroad.
    European Union citizens resident in the UK may vote in EU and local government elections.
    The following people are not entitled to vote:
– peers, and peeresses in their own right, who are members of the House of Lords (except that they may vote in EU and local government elections)
– patients detained under mental health legislation
– voluntary mental patients (unless they make a prescribed declaration)
– those serving prison sentences
– those convicted within the previous five years of corrupt or illegal election practices

REGISTERING TO VOTE

Voters must be entered on an electoral register, which runs from 16 February in one year to 15 February in the following year. The registration officer for each constituency is responsible for preparing and publishing the register. A registration form is sent to all households in the autumn of each year and the householder is required to provide details of all occupants who are eligible to vote, including ones who will reach their 18th birthday in the year covered by the register. Those who fail to give the required information or who give false information are liable to be fined. A draft register is usually published at the end of November. Any person whose name has been omitted may ask to be registered and should contact the registration officer. Anyone on the register may object to the inclusion of another person's name, in which case he/she should notify the registration officer, who will investigate that person's eligibility. Supplementary electors lists are published throughout the duration of the register.

VOTING

Voting is not compulsory in the UK. Those who wish to vote must generally vote in person at the allotted polling station. Those who will be away at the time of the election, those who will not be able to attend in person due to physical incapacity or the nature of their occupation, and those who have changed address during the period for which the register is valid, may apply for a postal vote or nominate a proxy to vote for them. Overseas electors who wish to vote must do so by proxy.

Further information can be obtained from the local authority's electoral registration officer in England and Wales or the regional valuation assessor in Scotland (details in local telephone directories), or the Chief Electoral Officer in Northern Ireland (65–67 Chichester Street, Belfast BT1 4JD. Tel: 01232-245353).

WILLS AND INTESTACY

In a will a person leaves instructions as to the disposal of their property after they die. A will is also used to appoint executors, give directions as to the disposal of the body, appoint guardians for children and, for larger estates, can operate to reduce the level of inheritance tax. It is best to have a will drawn up by a solicitor but if a solicitor is not employed, the following points must be taken into account:
– if possible the will must not be prepared on behalf of another person by someone who is to benefit from it
– the language used must be clear and unambiguous and it is better to avoid the use of legal terms where the same thing can be expressed in plain language
– it is better to rewrite the whole document if a mistake is made. If necessary, alterations can be made by striking through the words with a pen, alongside which the witnesses and the person making the will must write their names or place their initials. No alteration of any kind should be made after the will has been executed
– if the person later wishes to change the will or part of it, it is better to write a new will revoking the old. The use of codicils (documents written as supplements or containing modifications to the will) should be left to a solicitor
– the will should be typed or printed, or if handwritten be legible and preferably in ink. Commercial will forms can be obtained from some stationers
   The form of a will varies to suit different cases; the following is an example of how a will might be written. The notes after this example explain the terms used and procedures that need to be followed in drawing up a will.

This is the last will and testament of me [*Thomas Smith*] of [*Heather Cottage, Prospero Road, Manchester* MI 4DK] which I make this [*seventeenth*] day of [*May 1997*] and I revoke all previous wills and testamentary dispositions.

1. I appoint as my executors and trustees [*Ann Green of _____ and Richard Brown of_____*]. In my will the expression 'my Trustees' means any executors and trustees for the time being of my will and of any trust arising under it.

2. I give all my property to [*such of my children as shall survive me by 28 days and if more than one in equal shares* or as the case may be].

or

2. I give to [*Pamela Henderson of_____*] the sum of [£_____] and to [*Michael Broadbent of_____*] the sum of [£_____] and to [*Ruth Walker of_____*] all of my [*books* or as the case may be]

and

3. I give everything not otherwise disposed of to [*Richard Black of_____*]

Signed by the testator in our joint presence and then by us in his.

Thomas Smith
[*Signature of the person making the will*]

Elizabeth Wall
[*Signature of witness*] of 67 Beatrice Lane, Manchester MI 4DK, journalist

William Jones
[*Signature of witness*] of 17 Paris Road, Manchester MI 4DK, tailor

TERMS TO AVOID USING

Keep the will as simple as possible. Try to avoid using the following terms, as they have specific legal meaning:
– real property
– personal property
– goods and chattels
– my money

SPECIFIC GIFTS AND LEGACIES

Gifts of specific items usually fail if the property is not owned by the person making the will on their death. It is better in all cases where such gifts are made, to leave some person or persons 'the residue of my property' even if it seems that all property has already been disposed of in the will.

LAPSED LEGATEES

If a person who has been left property in a will dies before the person who made the will, the gift cannot take effect and the property becomes part of the residuary estate.
   If the person who has been left the residuary estate dies before the person who made the will, their share will generally pass to the closest relatives of the person who made the will unless the will names a beneficiary such as a charity who will take as a 'long stop' if the gift of residue is unable to take effect for any reason.
   It is always better to draw up a new will if a beneficiary predeceases the person who made the will.

EXECUTORS

It is usual to appoint two executors, although one is sufficient. No more than four persons can deal with the estate of the person who has died. The name and address of each executor should be given in full (the addresses are not essential but including them adds clarity to the document).
   Executors must be 18 years of age or over. An executor may be a beneficiary of the will.

WITNESSES

Someone who is a beneficiary of a will, or the spouse of a beneficiary, ought not to act as a witness or else they will be unable to take their gift. Husband and wife can both act as witnesses provided neither benefits from the will. A blind person cannot witness a will.
   It is better that a person does not act as an executor and as a witness. The identity of the witnesses should be made as explicit as possible.

EXECUTION OF A WILL

The person making the will should sign his/her name at the foot of the document, in the presence of the two witnesses. The witnesses must then sign their names in the presence of each other and in the presence of the person making the will. If this procedure is not adhered to, the will may be considered invalid. There are certain exceptional circumstances where these rules are relaxed, e.g. where the person may be too ill to sign, and in these cases the attestation clause which normally reads 'signed by the testator in the presence of …' should be reworded as follows:

The will was read over to Thomas Smith in our presence when he stated that he understood it. It was then signed on his behalf by Thomas Brown in the presence of the testator and by his direction in our joint presence and then by us in his.

CAPACITY TO MAKE A WILL

Anyone aged 18 or over can make a will. However, if there is any suspicion that the person making the will is not, through reasons of infirmity or age, fully in command of his/her faculties, it is advisable to arrange for a medical practitioner to examine the person making the will at the time it is to be executed to verify their mental capacity and to record that opinion in writing, and to ask his/her doctor to act as a witness. If a person is not mentally able to make a will, the Court may do this for him/her under provisions contained in the Mental Health Act 1983.

REVOCATION

A will may be revoked in a number of ways:
– a later will revokes an earlier one if it says so or if it is completely inconsistent with it. Otherwise the earlier will is only revoked where it is inconsistent with the later one
– a will is also revoked if the physical document on which it is written is destroyed by the person whose will it is. There must be an intention to revoke the will. It is not sufficient to obliterate the will with a pen
– a will is revoked when the person marries, unless it is clear from the will that the person intended the will to stand after the marriage
– where a marriage is ended by a decree of divorce or annulled or declared void, gifts to the spouse and the appointment of the spouse as executor will take effect as if the former spouse had died on the date on which the marriage is dissolved or annulled unless the will makes it clear that this will not happen

PROBATE AND LETTERS OF ADMINISTRATION

Probate is granted to the executors named in a will and once granted, the executors are obliged to carry out the instructions of the will. Letters of administration are granted where no executor is named in a will or is willing or able to act or where there is no valid will; this gives a person, often the next of kin, similar powers and duties to those of an executor.

Applications for probate or for letters of administration can be made to the Principal Registry of the Family Division, to a district probate registry or to a probate sub-registry. Applicants will need the following documents: the original will (if any); a certificate of death; particulars of all property and assets left by the deceased; a list of debts and funeral expenses. Certain property, up to the value of £5,000, may be disposed of without a grant of probate or administration.

WHERE TO FIND A PROVED WILL

Since 1858 wills which have been proved, that is wills on which probate or letters of administration have been granted, must have been proved at the Principal Registry of the Family Division or at a district probate registry. The Lord Chancellor has power to direct where the original documents are kept but most are filed where they were proved and may be inspected there and a copy obtained. The Principal Registry also holds copies of all wills proved at district probate registries and these may be inspected at Somerset House. An index of all grants, both of probate and of letters of administration, is compiled by the Principal Registry and may be seen either at the Principal Registry or at a district probate registry.

It is also possible to discover when a grant of probate or letters of administration is issued by requesting a standing search. In response to a request and for a small fee, a district probate registry will supply the names and addresses of executors or administrators and the registry in which the grant was made, of any grant in the estate of a specified person made in the previous 12 months or following six months. This is useful for applicants under the Inheritance (Provision for Family and Dependants) Act 1975 (see Intestacy, page 667) and for creditors of the deceased.

SCOTLAND

In Scotland any person over 12 and of sound mind can make a will. The person making the will can only freely dispose of what is known as the 'dead's part' of the estate because:
– the spouse has the right to inherit one-third of the moveable estate if there are children or other descendants, and one-half of it if there are not
– children are entitled to one-third of the moveable estate if there is a surviving spouse, and one-half of it if there is not

The remaining portion is the dead's part, and legacies and bequests are payable from this. Debts are payable out of the whole estate before any division.

From August 1995, wills no longer needed to be 'holographed' and it is now only necessary to have one witness. The person making the will still needs to sign each page. It is better that the will is not witnessed by a beneficiary although the attestation would still be sound and the beneficiary would not have to relinquish the gift (as is the case in England and Wales).

Subsequent marriage does not revoke a will but the birth of a child who is not provided for may do so. A will may be revoked by a subsequent will, either expressly or by implication, but in so far as the two can be read together both have effect. If a subsequent will is revoked, the earlier will is revived.

Wills may be registered in the Books of the Sheriffdom in which the deceased lived or in the Books of Council and Session at the Registers of Scotland. The original will can be inspected and a copy obtained for small fee.

CONFIRMATION

Confirmation (probate) is obtained in the sheriff court of the sheriffdom in which the deceased was resident at the time of death. Executives are either 'nominate' (named by the deceased in the will) or 'dative' (appointed by the court in cases where no executor is named in a will or in cases of intestacy). Applicants for confirmation must first provide an inventory of the deceased's estate and a schedule of debts, with an affidavit. In estates under £17,000 gross, confirmation can be obtained under a simplified procedure at reduced fees. the local sheriff clerk's office can provide assistance.

Further information can be obtained from:
PRINCIPAL REGISTRY (FAMILY DIVISION), Somerset
House, London, WC2R 1LP. Tel: 0171-936 6000
REGISTERS OF SCOTLAND, Meadowbank House, 153
London Road, Edinburgh, EH8 7AU. Tel: 0131-659 6111

INTESTACY

Intestacy occurs when someone dies without leaving a will.
In such cases the person's estate (property, possessions,
other assets following the payment of debts) passes to
certain members of the family. The relevant legislation is
the Administration of Estates Act 1925, as amended by
various legislation including the Intestates Estates Act
1952, and the Law Reform (Succession) Act 1995 and
Orders made there under. Some of the provisions of this
legislation are described below. If a will has been written
that disposes of only part of a person's property, these rules
apply to the intestate part.

If the person (intestate) leaves a spouse and children
(legitimate, illegitimate and adopted children and other
descendants), the estate is divided as follows:
– the spouse takes the 'personal chattels' (household
  articles, including cars, but nothing used for business
  purposes), £125,000 (with interest payable at 6 per cent
  from the time of the death until payment) and a life
  interest in half of the rest of the estate (which can be
  capitalized by the spouse if he/she wishes)
– the rest of the estate goes to the children*
If the person leaves a spouse but no children:
– the spouse takes the personal chattels, £200,000 (interest
  payable as before) and full ownership of half of the rest of
  the estate
– the other half of the rest of the estate goes to the parents
  (equally, if both alive) or, if none, to the brothers and
  sisters of the whole blood*
– if there are no parents or brothers or sisters of the whole
  blood or their issue, the spouse takes the whole estate
If there is no surviving spouse, the estate is distributed
among those who survive the intestate as follows:
– to surviving children*, but if none to
– parents (equally, if both alive), but if none to
– brothers and sisters of the whole blood*, but if none to
– brothers and sisters of the half blood*, but if none to
– grandparents (equally, if more than one), but if none to
– aunts and uncles of the whole blood*, but if none to
– aunts and uncles of the half blood*, but if none to
– the Crown, Duchy of Lancaster or the Duke of Cornwall
  (bona vacantia)
* To inherit, a member of these groups must survive the
intestate and attain 18, or marry under that age. If they die
under 18 (unless married under that age), their share goes
to others, if any, in the same group. If any member of these
groups predeceases the intestate, their share is divided
equally among their children.

In England and Wales the provisions of the Inheritance
(Provision for Family and Dependants) Act 1975 may
allow other people to claim provision from the deceased's
assets. This Act also applies to cases where a will has been
made and allows a person to apply to the Court if they feel
that the will or rules of intestacy or both do not make
adequate provision for them. The Court can order
payment from the deceased's assets or the transfer of
property from them if the applicant's claim is accepted.
The application must be made within six months of the
grant of probate or letters of administration and the
following people can make an application:
– the spouse
– a former spouse who has not remarried
– a child of the deceased

– someone treated as a child of the deceased's family
– someone maintained by the deceased
– someone who has cohabited for two years before the
  death in the same household as the deceased or as the
  husband or wife of the deceased

SCOTLAND

Under the Succession (Scotland) Act 1964, no distinction is
made between 'moveable' and 'heritable' property in
intestacy cases.

A surviving spouse is entitled to 'prior rights'. This
means that the spouse has the right to inherit:
– the matrimonial home up to a value of £110,000, or one
  matrimonial home if there is more than one, or, in certain
  circumstances, the value of the matrimonial home
– the furnishings and contents of that home, up to the value
  of £20,000
– £30,000 if the deceased left children or other descendants, or £50,000 if not
These figures are increased from time to time by order of
the Secretary of State.

Once prior rights have been satisfied, what remains of
the estate is generally divided between the surviving
spouse and children (legitimate and illegitimate) according to 'legal' rights. Legal rights are:
Jus relicti(ae) – the right of a surviving spouse to one-half of
  the net moveable estate, after satisfaction of prior rights,
  if there are no surviving children; if there are surviving
  children, the spouse is entitled to one-third of the net
  moveable estate
Legitim – the right of surviving children to one-half of the
  net moveable estate if there is no surviving spouse; if
  there is a surviving spouse, the children are entitled to
  one-third of the net moveable estate after the satisfaction
  of prior rights
Where there is no surviving spouse or children, half of
the estate is taken by the parents and half by the brothers
and sisters. Failing that, the lines of succession, in general,
are:
– to descendants
– if no descendants, then to collaterals (i.e. brothers and
  sisters) and parents
– surviving spouse
– if no collaterals or parents or spouse, then to ascendants
  collaterals (i.e. aunts and uncles), and so on in an
  ascending scale
– if all lines of succession fail, then to the Crown
Relatives of the whole blood are preferred to relatives of
the half blood. The right of representation, i.e. the right of
the issue of a person who would have succeeded if he/she
had survived the intestate, also applies.

Intellectual Property

COPYRIGHT

Copyright protects all original literary, dramatic, musical and artistic works (including photographs, maps and plans), published editions of works, computer programs, sound recordings, films (including video), broadcasts (including satellite broadcasts) and cable programmes (including on-line information services). Under copyright the creators of these works can control the various ways in which their material may be exploited, the rights broadly covering copying, adapting, issuing copies to the public, performing in public, and broadcasting the material.

Copyright protection in the United Kingdom is automatic and there is no registration system. The Copyright, Designs and Patents Act 1988 determined the length of copyright protection for various types of works created after 1 August 1989. The term of copyright protection on works created before that date was governed by the legislation in place when they were created. However, an EC directive, effective from January 1996, amended previous legislation with regard to certain types of works, and now the term of copyright protection for literary, dramatic, musical and artistic works lasts until 70 years after the death of the author; for film it lasts for 70 years after the death of the last surviving author, i.e. director, author of the screenplay, scriptwriter or composer of the music. Sound recordings are protected for 50 years after their publication, and broadcasts and cable programmes for 50 years from the end of the year in which the first broadcast/transmission is made. Published editions remain under copyright protection for 25 years from the end of the year in which the edition was published.

The main international treaties protecting copyright are the Berne Convention for the Protection of Literary and Artistic Works, the Rome Convention for the Protection of Performers, Producers of Phonograms and Broadcasting Organizations, and the Universal Copyright Convention (UCC); the UK is a signatory to these conventions. Copyright material created by UK nationals or residents is protected in each country which is a member of the conventions by the national law of that country. A full list of participating countries may be obtained from the Patent Office.

LICENSING

Reproduction of copyright material without seeking permission in each instance may be permitted under licence. (For a list of licensing agencies, *see* page 669.) The International Federation of Reproduction Rights Organizations facilitates agreements between its member licensing agencies and on behalf of its members with organizations such as the World Intellectual Property Organization, UNESCO, the European Union and the Council of Europe.

LEGAL DEPOSIT

Publishers are legally obliged to send one copy of a new publication to each of the copyright deposit libraries within one month of publication. The aim of legal deposit is to keep a complete national archive of published works as a current reference and information source. The copyright deposit libraries are the British Library, the Bodleian Library in Oxford, Cambridge University Library, the National Library of Scotland, the National Library of Wales, and Trinity College Library in Dublin.

The British Library's Legal Deposit Office is split between two locations; books and other publications are deposited at Boston Spa, and newspapers and periodicals at the Newspaper Legal Deposit Office in London. All publications for the other four copyright libraries in the UK are dealt with by the Agent for Copyright Libraries.

PATENTS

A patent is a document issued by the Patent Office relating to an invention and giving the proprietor monopoly rights, effective within the United Kingdom (including the Isle of Man). In return the patentee pays a fee to cover the costs of processing the patent and publicly discloses details of the invention.

To qualify for a patent an invention must be new, must exhibit an inventive step, and must be capable of industrial application. The patent is valid for a maximum of 20 years from the date on which the application was filed, subject to payment of annual fees from the end of the fourth year.

The Patent Office, established in 1852, is responsible for ensuring that all stages of an application comply with the Patents Act 1977, and that the invention meets the criteria for a patent. Patent Office Examiners check that the invention is new and innovative by searching previously published documents on the Patent Office databank, which contains details of some two million British patents, together with published international and European applications. The contents of the databank and of the Science Reference Library, which developed from the library established at the Patent Office, are available to the public.

The World Intellectual Property Organization (WIPO), a United Nations body, is responsible for administering many of the international conventions on intellectual property. The Patent Co-operation Treaty allows inventors to file a single application for patent rights in some or all of the 85 contracting states. This application is searched by an International Searching Authority and published by the International Bureau of WIPO. It may also be the subject of an (optional) international preliminary examination. Applicants must then deal directly with the patent offices in the countries where they are seeking patent rights.

The European Patent Convention, linked to the Patent Co-operation Treaty, allows inventors to obtain patent rights in all 17 contracting states by filing a single European patent application which is processed by the European Patent Office (EPO). Once granted, the patent is subject to national laws in each signatory country. To comply with security requirements, an applicant resident in the UK must file a European patent application with the UK Patent Office unless the Patent Office gives permission for it to be filed directly with the EPO. The EPO office for international patent documentation acts as an information, collection and reference centre for patent offices around the world.

TRADE MARKS

Trade marks are a means of identification, whether a word or device or a combination of both, a logo, or the shape of goods or their packaging, which enable traders to make their goods or services readily distinguishable from those supplied by other traders. Registration prevents other traders using the same or a similar trade mark for similar products or services for which the mark is registered.

In the UK trade marks are registered at the Trade Marks Registry in the Patent Office. In order to qualify for registration a mark must be capable of distinguishing its proprietor's goods or services from those of other undertakings. It should be non-deceptive and not easily confused with a mark that has already been registered for the same or similar goods or services. The relevant current legislation is the Trade Marks Act 1994.

It is possible to obtain an international trade mark registration, effective in 46 countries, under the Madrid Agreement. UK companies cannot take advantage of this because the UK is not a party to this agreement. Following revision of UK trade marks law, however, the UK has ratified the protocol to the Madrid Agreement, and British companies can now obtain international trade mark registration through a single application to WIPO in those countries party to the protocol.

EC trade mark regulation is now in force and is administered by the Office for Harmonization in the Internal Market (trade marks and designs) in Alicante, Spain. The office registers EC trade marks, which are a unitary right valid throughout the European Union. The national registration of trade marks in member states is continuing in parallel with the EC trade mark.

DESIGN PROTECTION

Design protection covers the outward appearance of an article and takes two forms in the UK, registered design and design right, which are not mutually exclusive. Registered design protects the aesthetic appearance of an article, including shape, configuration, pattern or ornament, although artistic works such as sculptures are excluded, being generally protected by copyright. In order to qualify for protection, a design must be new and materially different from earlier UK published designs. The owner of the design must apply to the Designs Registry at the Patent Office. Initial registration lasts for five years and is extendible in five-yearly steps to a maximum of 25 years. The current legislation is the Registered Designs Act 1949 (as amended).

There is no international design registry currently available to UK applicants; in general, separate applications must be made in each country in which protection is sought. Proposals for an EC design regulation are being discussed. If adopted, these would result in a unitary design right valid throughout the European Union, obtainable via a single application.

Design right is an automatic right which applies to the shape or configuration of articles and does not require registration. Unlike registered design, two-dimensional designs do not qualify for protection but designs of semiconductor chips (topographies) are protected by design right. Designs must be original and non-commonplace. The term of design right is ten years from first marketing of the design and the right is effective only in the UK. The current legislation is Part 3 of the Copyright, Designs and Patents Act 1988.

INTELLECTUAL PROPERTY ORGANIZATIONS

AGENT FOR THE COPYRIGHT LIBRARIES, 100 Euston Street, London NW1 2HQ. Tel: 0171-380 0240. *Agent*, A. T. Smail
CHARTERED INSTITUTE OF PATENT AGENTS, Staple Inn Buildings, London WC1V 7PZ. Tel: 0171-405 9450
DESIGNS REGISTRY, The Patent Office, Cardiff Road, Newport NP9 1RH. Tel: 0645-500505
EUROPEAN PATENT OFFICE, *Headquarters*, Erhardstrasse 27, D-80331 Munich, Germany. Tel: Munich 23990
INTERNATIONAL FEDERATION OF REPRODUCTION RIGHTS ORGANIZATIONS (IFRRO), Goethestrasse 49, D-80336 Munich, Germany. Tel: Munich 514120
LEGAL DEPOSIT OFFICE, The British Library, Boston Spa, Wetherby, West Yorkshire LS23 7BY. Tel: 01937-546267
NEWSPAPER LEGAL DEPOSIT OFFICE, The British Library Newspaper Library, 120 Colindale Avenue, London NW9 5LF. Tel: 0171-412 7378
OFFICE FOR HARMONIZATION IN THE INTERNAL MARKET (TRADE MARKS AND DESIGNS) (CTMO), 20 Avenida de la Aguilera, 03007 Alicante, Spain
THE PATENT OFFICE, Cardiff Road, Newport NP9 1RH. Tel: 0645-500505
REGISTRY OF COPYRIGHT AT STATIONERS' HALL, The Registrar, Stationers' Hall, Ave Maria Lane, London EC4M 7DD. Tel: 0171-248 2934
SCIENCE REFERENCE LIBRARY, 25 Southampton Buildings, London WC2A 1AW. Tel: 0171-412 7494
TRADE MARKS REGISTRY, The Patent Office, Cardiff Road, Newport NP9 1RH. Tel: 0645-500505
WORLD INTELLECTUAL PROPERTY ORGANIZATION (WIPO), 34 chemin des Colombettes, 1211 Geneva 20, Switzerland. Tel: Geneva 730 9246

COPYRIGHT LICENSING/COLLECTING AGENCIES

AUTHORS' LICENSING AND COLLECTING SOCIETY, 74 New Oxford Street, London WC1A 1EF. Tel: 0171-255 2034
CHRISTIAN COPYRIGHT LICENSING, PO Box 1339, Eastbourne, E. Sussex BN21 4YF. Tel: 01323-417711
COPYRIGHT LICENSING AGENCY LTD, 90 Tottenham Court Road, London W1P 0LP. Tel: 0171-436 5931
DESIGN AND ARTISTS COPYRIGHT AGENCY, Parchment House, 13 Northburgh Street, London EC1V 0AH. Tel: 0171-336 8811
EDUCATIONAL RECORDING AGENCY, 74 New Oxford Street, London WC1A 1EF. Tel: 0171-436 4883
INTERNATIONAL FEDERATION OF THE PHONOGRAPHIC INDUSTRIES, 54 Regent Street, London W1R 5PJ. Tel: 0171-434 3521
MECHANICAL COPYRIGHT PROTECTION SOCIETY, Elgar House, 41 Streatham High Road, London SW16 1ER. Tel: 0181-664 4400
NEWSPAPER LICENSING AGENCY, 17 Lyons Crescent, Tonbridge, Kent TN9 1EX. Tel: 01732-360333
PERFORMING RIGHT SOCIETY, 29–33 Berners Street, London W1P 4AA. Tel: 0171-580 5544
PHONOGRAPHIC PERFORMANCE LTD, Ganton House, 14–22 Ganton Street, London W1V 1LB. Tel: 0171-437 0311
PUBLISHERS LICENSING SOCIETY, 90 Tottenham Court Road, London W1P 9HE. Tel: 0171-436 5931
VIDEO PERFORMANCE LTD, Ganton House, 14–22 Ganton Street, London W1V 1LB. Tel: 0171-437 0311

The Media

Broadcasting

The British Broadcasting Corporation (*see* page 285) is responsible for public service broadcasting in the UK. Its role is to provide high-quality programmes with wide-ranging appeal that educate, inform and entertain. Its constitution and finances are governed by royal charter and agreement. On 1 May 1996 a new royal charter came into force, establishing the framework for the BBC's activities until 2006.

The Independent Television Commission (*see* page 313) and the Radio Authority (*see* page 336) were set up under the terms of the Broadcasting Act 1990. The ITC is the regulator and licensing authority for all commercially-funded television services, including cable and satellite services. The Radio Authority is the regulator and licensing authority for all independent radio services.

There are rules on cross-media ownership to prevent undue concentration of ownership. These were amended by the Broadcasting Act 1996. Radio companies are now permitted to own one AM, one FM and one other (AM or FM) service; ownership of the third licence is subject to a public interest test. Local newspapers with a circulation under 20 per cent in an area are also allowed to own one AM, one FM and one other service, and may control a regional Channel 3 television service subject to a public interest test. Local newspapers with a circulation between 20 and 50 per cent in an area may own one AM and one FM service, subject to a public interest test, but may not control a regional Channel 3 service. Those with a circulation over 50 per cent may own one radio service in the area (provided that more than one independent local radio service serves the area) subject to a public interest test.

Ownership controls on the number of television or radio licences have been removed; holdings are now restricted to 15 per cent of the total television audience or 15 per cent of the total points available in the radio points scheme. Ownership controls on cable operators have also been removed. National newspapers with less than 20 per cent of national circulation may apply to control any broadcasting licences, subject to a public interest test. National newspapers with more than 20 per cent of national circulation may not have more than a 20 per cent interest in a licence to provide a Channel 3 service, Channel 5 or national and local analogue radio services.

COMPLAINTS

The Broadcasting Complaints Commission (BCC) was set up in 1981. It considers and adjudicates upon complaints of unfair treatment or unwarranted infringement of privacy in all broadcast programmes and advertisements on television, radio, cable and satellite services. The Broadcasting Standards Council (BSC) was set up under the Broadcasting Act 1990. It is an advisory body which monitors the portrayal of violence, sex and matters of taste and decency in all broadcast programmes and advertisements on television, radio, cable and satellite services. The BCC and BSC will be merged in April 1997 to form the Broadcasting Standards Commission.

BROADCASTING COMPLAINTS COMMISSION, 7 The Sanctuary, London SW1P 3JS. Tel: 0171-233 0544. *Chairman*, The Lord Pilkington of Oxenford; *Secretary*, H. Bauer

BROADCASTING STANDARDS COUNCIL, 7 The Sanctuary, London SW1P 3JS. Tel: 0171-233 0544. *Chair*, The Lady Howe of Aberavon; *Director*, C. Shaw, CBE

TELEVISION

All channels are broadcast in colour on 625 lines UHF from a network of transmitting stations which are owned and operated by the BBC and by National Transcommunications Ltd. Transmissions are available to more than 99 per cent of the population. In November 1995 the Secretary of State for National Heritage announced that the transmission facilities of the BBC would be privatized.

The total number of receiving television licences in the UK at end June 1996 was 21,150,868, of which 552,964 were for monochrome receivers and 20,597,904 for colour receivers. Annual television licence fees are: monochrome £30; colour £89.50.

No overall statistics are available for subscriptions to satellite television services; British Sky Broadcasting had 5,349,000 subscribers in the UK at March 1996, though about 33 per cent of these view through cable. At April 1996 the ITC recorded 1,422,868 homes connected to cable television.

DIGITAL TELEVISION

Digital television broadcasting is a new technique for improving the quality of the current reception of television programmes. It uses digital modulation to provide a consistently high quality of reception and digital compression to make more effective use of the frequency channels available than PAL, the analogue system currently used. A preliminary frequency plan for digital television broadcasting was submitted to the Government by the ITC in early 1996.

The Broadcasting Act 1996 provides for the licensing of 20 or more digital terrestrial television channels (on six frequency channels or 'multiplexes'). Existing national television broadcasters (the BBC, ITV, Channel 4 and the new Channel 5) will be offered guaranteed access to digital frequencies and all programmes broadcast on existing analogue channels will have to be broadcast on the equivalent digital service.

BBC TELEVISION
Television Centre, Wood Lane, London W12 7RJ
Tel 0181-743 8000

The BBC's experiments in television broadcasting started in 1929 and in 1936 the BBC began the world's first public service of high-definition television from Alexandra Palace. The BBC broadcasts two UK-wide television services, BBC 1 and BBC 2; outside England these services are designated BBC Scotland on 1, BBC Scotland on 2, BBC 1 Northern Ireland, BBC 2 Northern Ireland, BBC Wales on 1 and BBC Wales on 2.

BBC WORLDWIDE TELEVISION
Woodlands, 80 Wood Lane, London W12 OTT
Tel 0181-576 2000

BBC Worldwide Television is responsible for the BBC's commercial television activity. It was created in May 1994 by the merger of the television activity of BBC Enterprises and the channel businesses of BBC World Service Television. In 1995–6 BBC Worldwide Television licensed more than 15,000 hours of programming to over 80 countries. Its core service is a 24-hour news and information channel, BBC World, which is distributed in Europe, Asia, Africa, Australia and the Middle East. Output from the channel is also re-broadcast in New Zealand, Canada and a range of Asian and African countries. BBC Prime is a subscription entertainment channel available across Europe.

INDEPENDENT TELEVISION

The ITV franchises for the 15 regional companies and for breakfast television were allocated new ten-year licences from January 1993. A new independent national television channel was due to be established by autumn 1993, but the ITC decided not to award the licence to Channel Five Holdings Ltd, the only applicant. The ITC received a further four bids for the licence in May 1995. The winner was Channel 5 Broadcasting Ltd and the new channel will be launched in February 1997, provided the company has retuned video recorders and satellite receivers in 90 per cent of the homes affected by interference because of the frequency to be used by Channel 5.

ITV NETWORK CENTRE/ITV ASSOCIATION
200 Gray's Inn Road, London WC1X 8HF
Tel 0171-843 8000

The ITV Network Centre is wholly owned by the ITV companies and undertakes the commissioning and scheduling of those television programmes which are shown across the ITV network. Through its sister organization, the ITV Association, it also provides a range of services to the ITV companies where a common approach is required.

Network Director, M. Plantin
Director, ITV Association, B. Cox

INDEPENDENT TELEVISION NETWORK COMPANIES

ANGLIA TELEVISION (owned by MAI) (*eastern England*), Anglia House, Norwich NR1 3JG. Tel: 01603-615151
BORDER TELEVISION PLC (*the Borders*), Television Centre, Carlisle CA1 3NT. Tel: 01228-25101
CARLTON TELEVISION LTD (*London* (*weekdays*)), 101 St Martin's Lane, London WC2N 4AZ. Tel: 0171-240 4000
CENTRAL INDEPENDENT TELEVISION PLC (owned by Carlton Communications) (*the Midlands*), Central House, Broad Street, Birmingham B1 2JP. Tel: 0121-643 9898
CHANNEL TELEVISION LTD (*Channel Islands*), The Television Centre, St Helier, Jersey JE2 3ZD. Tel: 01534-68999
GRAMPIAN TELEVISION PLC (*northern Scotland*), Queen's Cross, Aberdeen AB9 2XJ. Tel: 01224-646464
GRANADA TELEVISION LTD (*north-west England*), Granada TV Centre, Quay Street, Manchester M60 9EA. Tel: 0161-832 7211
HTV GROUP (*Wales and western England*), HTV Wales, Television Centre, Culverhouse Cross, Cardiff CF5 6XJ. Tel: 01222-590590; HTV Ltd, Television Centre, Bath Road, Bristol BS4 3HG. Tel: 0117-977 8366
LONDON WEEKEND TELEVISION (owned by Granada Group) (*London* (*weekends*)), London Television Centre, Upper Ground, London SE1 9LT. Tel: 0171-620 1620
MERIDIAN BROADCASTING LTD (owned by MAI) (*south and south-east England*), Television Centre, Southampton SO9 5HZ. Tel: 01703-222555
SCOTTISH TELEVISION PLC (*central Scotland*), Cowcaddens, Glasgow G2 3PR. Tel: 0141-300 3000

TYNE TEES TELEVISION LTD (*north-east England*), The Television Centre, City Road, Newcastle upon Tyne NE1 2AL. Tel: 0191-261 0181
ULSTER TELEVISION PLC (*Northern Ireland*), Havelock House, Ormeau Road, Belfast BT7 1EB. Tel: 01232-328122
WESTCOUNTRY TELEVISION LTD (*south-west England*), Western Wood Way, Langage Science Park, Plymouth PL7 5BG. Tel: 01752-333333
YORKSHIRE TELEVISION LTD (*Yorkshire*), The Television Centre, Leeds LS3 1JS. Tel: 0113-243 8283

OTHER INDEPENDENT TELEVISION COMPANIES

CHANNEL FOUR TELEVISION CORPORATION, 124 Horseferry Road, London SW1P 2TX. Tel: 0171-396 4444. Provides a service to the UK except Wales, and is charged to cater for interests under-represented by the ITV network companies. Channel 4 sells its own advertising. The ITV companies are currently required to provide some financial support for Channel 4 if Channel 4's income falls below a certain point; they benefit financially if Channel 4's revenues are higher. The Government has announced plans to phase out this arrangement. In 1995 Channel 4 gave the ITV companies £57.2 million. In return ITV promotes Channel 4 programmes.
GMTV LTD (*breakfast television*), The London Television Centre, Upper Ground, London SE1 9TT. Tel: 0171-827 7000
INDEPENDENT TELEVISION NEWS LTD, 200 Gray's Inn Road, London WC1X 8XZ. Tel: 0171-833 3000
TELETEXT LTD, 101 Farm Lane, London SW6 1QJ. Tel: 0171-386 5000. Provides teletext services for the ITV companies and Channel 4
WELSH FOURTH CHANNEL AUTHORITY (Sianel Pedwar Cymru), Parc Ty Glas, Llanishen, Cardiff CF4 5DU. Tel: 01222-747444. S4C schedules Welsh language programmes and relays most Channel 4 programmes

DIRECT BROADCASTING BY SATELLITE TELEVISION

BRITISH SKY BROADCASTING LTD, Grant Way, Isleworth, Middx TW7 5QD. Tel: 0171-705 3000. Broadcasts ten channels which are wholly owned by Sky (Sky One, Sky News, Sky Sports, Sky Sports 2, Sky Sports Gold, Sky Movies, The Movie Channel, Sky Movies Gold, Sky Soap and Sky Travel). Sky also co-operates with four joint ventures and broadcasts 14 channels for third parties.

RADIO

UK domestic radio services are broadcast across three wavebands: FM (or VHF), medium wave (also referred to as AM) and long wave (used by BBC Radio 4). In the UK the FM waveband extends in frequency from 87.5 MHz to 108 MHz and the medium wave band extends from 531 kHz to 1602 kHz. Some radios are still calibrated in wavelengths rather than frequency. To convert frequency to wavelength, divide 300,000 by the frequency in kHz.

DIGITAL RADIO

Digital audio broadcasting (DAB) is a new technique for improving the robustness of high fidelity radio services, especially compared with current FM and AM radio transmissions. It was developed in a collaborative research project under the pan-European EUREKA initiative and has been adopted as a world standard for new digital radio systems. DAB allows more services to be broadcast to a higher technical quality in a given amount of radio spectrum, and provides the data facility for text or pictures associated with sound programmes. The frequencies allocated for terrestrial DAB in the UK are 217.5 to 230 MHz.

The Broadcasting Act 1996 provides for the licensing of up to 42 digital radio services (on seven frequency channels or 'multiplexes'). The BBC has been allocated a multiplex capable of broadcasting six to eight national stereo services; BBC DAB broadcasts began in the London area in September 1995. A national DAB multiplex has also been made available to the Radio Authority. Local and regional services would use the remaining five frequency channels currently allocated. Analogue services will eventually be withdrawn.

BBC RADIO
Broadcasting House, Portland Place, London WIA IAA
Tel 0171-580 4468

BBC Radio broadcasts five national services to the UK, Isle of Man and the Channel Islands. There is also a tier of national regional services in Wales, Scotland and Northern Ireland and 38 local radio stations in England and the Channel Islands. In Wales there are two regional services based on the Welsh and English languages respectively.

BBC NATIONAL SERVICES
RADIO 1 (Contemporary pop music, social action campaigns and comedy) – 24 hours a day. *Frequencies:* FM 97.6–99.8 MHz, coverage 99%

RADIO 2 (Popular music, entertainment, comedy and the arts) – 24 hours a day. *Frequencies:* FM 88–90.2 MHz, coverage 99%

RADIO 3 (Classical music, drama, documentaries, poetry, and schools programmes) – 24 hours a day. *Frequencies:* FM 90.2–92.4 MHz, coverage 99%

RADIO 4 (News, documentaries, drama, entertainment, and cricket on long wave in season) – 5.55 a.m.–1.00 a.m. daily, with BBC World Service overnight. *Frequencies:* FM in England 92.4–94.6 MHz, elsewhere 92.4–96.1 and 103.5–105 MHz, coverage 99%; LW 198 kHz/ 1515m, plus eight local fillers on MW

RADIO 5 LIVE (News and sport) – 24 hours a day. *Frequencies:* MW 693 kHz and 909 kHz, plus one local filler

BBC NATIONAL REGIONAL SERVICES
RADIO SCOTLAND *Frequencies:* MW 810 kHz plus two local fillers; FM 92.5–94.7 MHz, coverage 99%. Local programmes on FM as above: HIGHLANDS; NORTH-EAST (also MW 990 kHz); BORDERS; SOUTH-WEST (also MW 585 kHz); ORKNEY; SHETLAND. RADIO NAN GAIDHEAL (Gaelic service) (FM 103.5–105 MHz) available in Western Highlands and Islands, Moray Firth and central Scotland; also available on MW 990 kHz in Aberdeen

RADIO ULSTER *Frequencies:* MW 1341 kHz, plus two local fillers; FM 92.4–96.1 MHz, coverage 96%. Local programmes on RADIO FOYLE *Frequencies:* MW 792 kHz; FM 93.1 MHz

RADIO WALES *Frequencies:* MW 882 kHz plus two local fillers, coverage 96%

RADIO CYMRU (Welsh-language) *Frequencies:* FM 92.4–96.1 and 103.5–105 MHz, coverage 96%

BBC LOCAL RADIO STATIONS
There are 38 local stations serving England and the Channel Islands:

BRISTOL, PO Box 194, Bristol BS99 7QT. Tel: 0117-974 1111; 14–15 Paul Street, Taunton TA1 3PF. Tel: 01823-252437. *Frequencies:* MW 1548 kHz, 1323 kHz (*Somerset Sound*), 94.9/95.5/104.6 FM

CAMBRIDGESHIRE, Broadcasting House, 104 Hills Road, Cambridge CB2 1LD. Tel: 01223-259696. *Frequencies:* MW 1026/1449 kHz, 96/95.7 FM

CLEVELAND, PO Box 95 FM, Newport Road, Middlesbrough, Cleveland TS1 5DG. Tel: 01642-225211. *Frequencies:* 95.0/95.8 FM

CORNWALL, Phoenix Wharf, Truro, Cornwall TR1 1UA. Tel: 01872-75421. *Frequencies:* MW 630/657 kHz, 95.2/ 96.0/103.9 FM

CUMBRIA, Annetwell Street, Carlisle CA3 8BB. Tel: 01228-592444. *Frequencies:* MW 756/1458/837 kHz, 95.2/ 95.6/96.1/104.2 FM

DERBY, PO Box 269, Derby DE1 3HL. Tel: 01332-361111. *Frequencies:* MW 1116 kHz, 94.2/95.3/104.5 FM

DEVON, PO Box 5, Broadcasting House, Seymour Road, Plymouth PL1 1XT. Tel: 01752-260323. *Frequencies:* MW 801/990/1458/801 kHz, 103.4/96.0/95.8/94.8 FM

ESSEX, 198 New London Road, Chelmsford CM2 9AB. Tel: 01245-262393. *Frequencies:* MW 765/729/1530 kHz, 103.5/95.3 FM

GLOUCESTERSHIRE, London Road, Gloucester GL1 1SW. Tel: 01452-308585. *Frequencies:* 95.0/104.7/95.8 FM

GLR (GREATER LONDON RADIO), 35c Marylebone High Street, London WIA 4LG. Tel: 0171-224 2424. *Frequency:* 94.9 FM

GMR (GREATER MANCHESTER RADIO), PO Box 951, Oxford Road, Manchester M60 1SD. Tel: 0161-200 2000. *Frequency:* 95.1 FM

GUERNSEY, Commerce House, Les Banques, St Peter Port, Guernsey. Tel: 01481-728977. *Frequencies:* MW 1116 kHz, 93.2 FM

HEREFORD AND WORCESTER, Hylton Road, Worcester WR2 5WW. Tel: 01905-748485. *Frequencies:* MW 738/ 819 kHz, 104.6/104.0/94.7 FM

HUMBERSIDE, 9 Chapel Street, Hull HU1 3NU. Tel: 01482-323232. *Frequencies:* MW 1485 kHz, 95.9 FM

JERSEY, 18 Parade Road, St Helier, Jersey. Tel: 01534-870000. *Frequencies:* MW 1026 kHz, 88.8 FM

KENT, Sun Pier, Chatham, Kent ME4 4EZ. Tel: 01634-830505. *Frequencies:* MW 774/1602 kHz, 96.7/97.6/ 104.2 FM

LANCASHIRE, 26 Darwen Street, Blackburn BB2 2EA. Tel: 01254-262411. *Frequencies:* MW 855/1557 kHz, 95.5/ 104.5/103.9 FM

LEEDS, Broadcasting House, Woodhouse Lane, Leeds LS2 9PN. Tel: 0113-244 2131. *Frequencies:* MW 774 kHz, 92.4/95.3/103.9 FM

LEICESTER, Epic House, Charles Street, Leicester LE1 3SH. Tel: 0116-251 6688. *Frequencies:* MW 837 kHz, 104.9 FM

LINCOLNSHIRE, PO Box 219, Newport, Lincoln LN1 3XY. Tel: 01522-511411. *Frequencies:* MW 1368 kHz, 94.9 FM

MERSEYSIDE, 55 Paradise Street, Liverpool L1 3BP. Tel: 0151-708 5500. *Frequencies:* MW 1485 kHz, 95.8 FM

NEWCASTLE, Broadcasting Centre, Barrack Road, Newcastle upon Tyne NE99 1RN. Tel: 0191-232 4141. *Frequencies:* MW 1458 kHz, 95.4/104.4/96.0 FM

NORFOLK, Norfolk Tower, Surrey Street, Norwich NR1 3PA. Tel: 01603-617411. *Frequencies:* MW 855/873 kHz, 95.1/104.4 FM

NORTHAMPTON, Broadcasting House, Abington Street, Northampton NN1 2BE. Tel: 01604-239100. *Frequencies:* MW 1107 kHz, 104.2/106.3 FM

NOTTINGHAM, York House, Mansfield Road, Nottingham NG1 3JB. Tel: 0115-955 0500. *Frequencies:* MW 1584/1521 kHz, 103.8/95.5 FM

SHEFFIELD, Ashdell Grove, 60 Westbourne Road, Sheffield S10 2QU. Tel: 0114-268 6185. *Frequencies:* MW 1035 kHz, 94.7/104.1/88.6 FM

SHROPSHIRE, 2–4 Boscobel Drive, Shrewsbury SY1 3TT Tel: 01743-248484. *Frequencies:* MW 756/1584 kHz, 95.0/96.0 FM

SOLENT, Broadcasting House, Havelock Road, Southampton SO14 7PW. Tel: 01703-631311. *Frequencies:* MW 999/1359 kHz, 96.1/103.8 FM

SOUTHERN COUNTIES, Broadcasting Centre, Guildford GU2 5AP. Tel: 01483-306306. *Frequencies:* 95–95.3/ 104–104.8 FM

STOKE, Cheapside, Hanley, Stoke-on-Trent ST1 1JJ. Tel: 01782-208080. *Frequencies:* MW 1503 kHz, 94.6 FM

SUFFOLK, Broadcasting House, St Matthew's Street, Ipswich IP1 3EP. Tel: 01473-250000. *Frequencies:* 103.9/ 104.6 FM

THAMES VALLEY FM, 269 Banbury Road, Oxford OX2 7DW. Tel: 01865-311444. *Frequencies:* 95.2/104.1/104.4/ 95.4/94.6 FM

THREE COUNTIES RADIO, PO Box 3CR, Luton, Beds LU1 5XL. Tel: 01582-441000. *Frequencies:* MW 1161/630 kHz, 104.5/95.5/103.8 FM

WILTSHIRE SOUND, Broadcasting House, Prospect Place, Swindon SN1 3RW. Tel: 01793-513626. *Frequencies:* MW 1332/1368 kHz, 103.6/104.3/103.5/104.9 FM

WM (WEST MIDLANDS), Pebble Mill Road, Birmingham B5 7SD. Tel: 0121-414 8484; 25 Warwick Road, Coventry CV1 2WR. Tel: 01203-559911. *Frequencies:* MW 828/1458 kHz, 95.6 FM; 94.8/103.7 FM (Coventry and Warwickshire)

YORK, 20 Bootham Row, York YO3 7BR. Tel: 01904-641351. *Frequencies:* MW 666/1260 kHz, 103.7/104.3/95.5 FM

BBC WORLD SERVICE

Bush House, Strand, London WC2B 4PH
Tel 0171-240 3456

The BBC World Service broadcasts over 1,000 hours of programmes a week in 44 languages including English. Of the 135 transmitters in use, 40 are in the UK and 95 overseas. In addition the World Service supplies programmes to more than 1,000 radio stations and stations in over 90 countries.

The World Service is organized into six regions, each responsible for programmes in English as well as regional languages.

AFRICA AND THE MIDDLE EAST, Arabic, French, Hausa, Kinyarwanda/Kirundi, Portuguese, Somali and Swahili; English programmes including *Network Africa* and *Focus on Africa*.

ASIA PACIFIC, Burmese, Cantonese, Indonesian, Mandarin, Thai and Vietnamese; English programmes including *East Asia Today*.

EUROPE, Albanian, Bulgarian, Croatian, Czech, Finnish, German, Greek, Hungarian, Macedonian, Polish, Romanian, Serbian, Slovak and Slovene; English programmes including *Europe Today*.

FORMER SOVIET UNION AND SOUTH-WEST ASIA, Azeri, Kazakh, Kyrgyz, Pashto, Persian, Russian, Turkish, Ukrainian and Uzbek.

SOUTH ASIA, Bengali, Hindi, Nepali, Sinhala, Tamil and Urdu; English programmes including *South Asia Report*.

THE AMERICAS, Portuguese for Brazil, Spanish; English programmes including *Caribbean Report* and *Calling the Falklands*.

BBC ENGLISH teaches English world-wide through radio, television and a wide range of published courses

BBC INTERNATIONAL BROADCASTING AND AUDIENCE RESEARCH carries out audience research and sells printed publications and data

BBC MONITORING supplies news and information from the output of overseas radio and television stations and news agency sources

BBC MPM (Marshall Plan of the Mind) makes programmes about business, democracy and management for countries of the former Soviet Union

BBC RADIO INTERNATIONAL sells a wide range of BBC radio programmes on CD to broadcasters in over 100 countries

BBC WORLD SERVICE TRAINING runs journalism, management and skills training courses for overseas broadcasters

INDEPENDENT RADIO

The Radio Authority began advertising new licences for the development of commercial radio in January 1991. Since then it has awarded three national licences, 60 new local radio licences (including six regional licences) and one additional service licence (to use the spare capacity in an existing channel which is not used by the programme service). The Authority has also issued over 1,300 restricted service licences (for temporary low-powered radio services).

In February 1996 the Authority completed re-advertising the 125 licences that were originally awarded by the Authority's predecessor, the Independent Broadcasting Authority.

The Authority will continue to advertise about two licences a month in 1997.

COMMERCIAL RADIO COMPANIES ASSOCIATION, 77 Shaftesbury Avenue, London W1V 7AD. Tel: 0171-306 2603. *Director*, P. Brown

INDEPENDENT NATIONAL RADIO STATIONS

CLASSIC FM, Academic House, 24–28 Oval Road, London NW1 7DQ. Tel: 0171-284 3000. 24 hours a day. *Frequencies:* FM 99.9–101.9 MHz

TALK RADIO UK, PO Box 1089, London W1A 1PP. Tel: 0171-636 1089. 24 hours a day. *Frequencies:* MW 1053/ 1089 kHz

VIRGIN RADIO, 1 Golden Square, London W1R 4DJ. Tel: 0171-434 1215. 24 hours a day. *Frequencies:* MW 1215/ 1197/1233/1242/1260 kHz

INDEPENDENT REGIONAL LOCAL RADIO STATIONS

CENTURY RADIO (*North-east*), PO Box 100, Gateshead NE8 2YY. Tel: 0191-477 6666. *Frequencies:* 100.7/101.8/96.2/ 96.4 FM

GALAXY 101 (*Severn Estuary*), PO Box 1010, Bristol or Cardiff. Tel: 0117-924 0111. *Frequencies:* 101 FM; 97.2 FM (Bristol)

HEART FM (*West Midlands*), 1 The Square, 111 Broad Street, Birmingham B15 1AS. Tel: 0121-626 1007. *Frequency:* 100.7 FM

JAZZ FM 100.4 (*North-west*), The World Trade Centre, Exchange Quay, Manchester M5 3EJ. Tel: 0161-877 1004. *Frequency*, 100.4 FM

KISS 105, 2A Joseph's Well, Hanover Way, Park Lane, Leeds LS3 1AB. Tel: 0113-246 0105. *Frequencies (from Feb. 1997):* 105.1 FM (Leeds); 105.6 FM (Bradford and Sheffield); 105.8 FM (Hull)

SCOT FM (*Central Scotland*), 1 Albert Quay, Leith Docks, Edinburgh EH6 7DN. Tel: 0131-554 6677. *Frequencies:* 100.3/101.1 FM

INDEPENDENT LOCAL RADIO STATIONS

AMBER RADIO, St George's Plain, 47–49 Colegate, Norwich NR3 1DB. Tel: 01603-630621; Radio House, Alpha Business Park, White House Road, Ipswich IP1 5LT. Tel: 01473-461000. *Frequencies:* MW 1152 kHz (Norfolk); 1170/1251 kHz (Suffolk)

A1 FM, Radio House, 11 Woodland Road, Darlington DL3 7BJ. Tel: 01325-255552. *Frequency:* 103.2 FM

ASIAN SOUND RADIO, Globe House, Southall Street, Manchester M3 ILG. Tel: 0161-288 1000. *Frequencies:* MW 1377/963 kHz

THE BAY, PO Box 969, St George's Quay, Lancaster LA1 3LD. Tel: 01524-848747. *Frequencies:* 96.9/102.3/103.2 FM

THE BEACH, PO Box 103.4, Lowestoft, Suffolk NR32 2TL; PO Box 103.4, Great Yarmouth, Norfolk NR29 4UL. Tel: 07000-001035. *Frequency:* 103.4 FM

BEACON RADIO, 267 Tettenhall Road, Wolverhampton WV6 0DQ. Tel: 01902-838383. *Frequencies:* 97.2/103.1 FM

B97, 55 Goldington Road, Bedford MK40 3LS. Tel: 01234-272400. *Frequency:* 96.9 FM

THE BREEZE, Radio House, Clifftown Road, Southend-on-Sea, Essex SS1 1SX. Tel: 01702-333711. *Frequency:* MW 1359 kHz (Chelmsford); 1431 kHz (Southend)

BROADLAND 102, St George's Plain, 47–49 Colegate, Norwich NR3 1DB. Tel: 01603-630621. *Frequency:* 102.4 FM

BRUNEL CLASSIC GOLD, PO Box 2020, Watershed, Canon's Road, Bristol BS99 7SN. Tel: 0117-984 3200; PO Box 2020, Lime Kiln, Wootton Bassett, Wilts SN4 7EX. Tel: 01793-440301. *Frequencies:* MW 1260 kHz (Bristol); 1161 kHz (Swindon); 936 kHz (West Wilts)

CAPITAL FM AND GOLD, 29–30 Leicester Square, London WC2H 7LE. Tel: 0171-766 6000. *Frequencies:* MW 1548 kHz (*Gold*), 95.8 FM

CENTRAL FM, John Player Building, Stirling Enterprise Park, Stirling FK7 7YJ. Tel: 01786-451188. *Frequency:* 103.1 FM

CFM, PO Box 964, Carlisle, Cumbria CA1 3NG. Tel: 01228-818964. *Frequencies:* 96.4 FM; 102.5 FM (Penrith); 102.2 FM (Workington); 103.4 FM (Whitehaven)

CHANNEL 103 FM, 6 Tunnel Street, St Helier, Jersey JE2 4LU. Tel: 01543-888103. *Frequency:* 103.7 FM

CHANNEL TRAVEL RADIO, Eurotunnel UK Terminal, Main Control Building, PO Box 2000, Folkestone, Kent CT18 8XY. Tel: 01303-283873. *Frequency:* 107.6 FM

CHELTENHAM RADIO, Radio House, PO Box 99, Cheltenham, Glos GL53 7YX. Tel: 01242-261555. *Frequency:* MW 603 kHz

CHILTERN FM, Chiltern Road, Dunstable, Beds LU6 1HQ. Tel: 01582-666001. *Frequency:* 97.6 FM

CHOICE FM BIRMINGHAM, 95 Broad Street, Birmingham B15 1AU. Tel: 0121-616 1000. *Frequency:* 102.4 FM

CHOICE FM LONDON, 16–18 Trinity Gardens, London SW9 8DP. Tel: 0171-738 7969. *Frequency:* 96.9 FM

CITY FM, 8–10 Stanley Street, Liverpool L1 6AF. Tel: 0151-227 5100. *Frequency:* 96.7 FM

CLASSIC GOLD 774, Old Talbot House, Southgate Street, Gloucester GL1 2DQ. Tel: 01452-423791. *Frequency:* MW 774 kHz

CLASSIC GOLD 792/828, Chiltern Road, Dunstable, Beds LU6 1HQ. Tel: 01582-666001. *Frequency:* MW 792 kHz (Bedford); 828 kHz (Luton)

CLASSIC GOLD 828, 5 Southcote Road, Bournemouth, Dorset BH1 3LR. Tel: 01202-294881. *Frequency:* MW 828 kHz

CLASSIC GOLD 1332 AM, PO Box 2020, Queensgate Centre, Peterborough PE1 1LL. Tel: 01733-460460. *Frequency:* MW 1332 kHz

CLASSIC GOLD 1359, Hertford Place, Coventry CV1 3TT. Tel: 01203-868200. *Frequency:* MW 1359 kHz

CLASSIC GOLD 1431 AM, PO Box 210, Reading RG31 7RZ. Tel: 01189-254400. *Frequency:* MW 1431 kHz

CLASSIC GOLD 1557, The Broadcast Centre, 19–21 St Edmunds Road, Northampton NN1 5DY. Tel: 01604-792411. *Frequency:* MW 1557 kHz

CLYDE 1 AND 2, Clydebank Business Park, Clydebank, Glasgow G81 2RX. Tel: 0141-306 2200. *Frequencies:* MW 1152 kHz, 102.5 FM; 97.0 FM (Vale of Leven); 103.3 FM (Firth of Clyde)

COAST FM, The Studios, 41 Conwy Road, Colwyn Bay. Tel: 01492-534555. *Frequency:* 96.3 FM

COOL FM, PO Box 974, Belfast BT1 1RT. Tel: 01247-817181. *Frequency:* 97.4 FM

COUNTRY 1035 AM, Unit 7, Hurlingham Business Park, Sullivan Road, London SW6 3DU. Tel: 0171-384 1175. *Frequency:* 1035 kHz

COUNTY SOUND RADIO 1476 AM, Dolphin House, North Street, Guildford GU1 4AA. Tel: 01483-300964. *Frequency:* MW 1476 kHz

DELTA RADIO 97.1 FM, 65 Weyhill, Haslemere, Surrey GU27 1HN. Tel: 01428-651971. *Frequency:* 97.1 FM

DOWNTOWN RADIO, Newtownards, Co. Down BT23 4ES. Tel: 01247-815555. *Frequencies:* MW 1026 kHz (Belfast); 102.4 FM (Londonderry); 96.4 FM (Limavady); 96.6 FM (Enniskillen)

ELEVEN SEVENTY, PO Box 1170, High Wycombe, Bucks HP13 6YT. Tel: 01494-446611. *Frequency:* MW 1170 kHz

ESSEX FM, Radio House, Clifftown Road, Southend-on-Sea, Essex SS1 1SX. Tel: 01702-333711. *Frequencies:* 96.3 FM (Southend), 102.6 FM (Chelmsford)

FAME 1521, Broadfield House, Brighton Road, Crawley, W. Sussex RHII 9TT. Tel: 01293-519161. *Frequency:* MW 1521 kHz

FM 102 – THE BEAR, The Guard House Studios, Banbury Road, Stratford-upon-Avon, Warks CV37 7HX. Tel: 01789-262636. *Frequency:* 102.0 FM

FM 103 HORIZON, Broadcast Centre, Vincent Avenue, Crownhill, Milton Keynes, Bucks MK8 0AB. Tel: 01908-269111. *Frequency:* 103.3 FM

FORTH FM, Forth House, Forth Street, Edinburgh EH1 3LF. Tel: 0131-556 9255. *Frequencies:* 97.3/97.6 FM

FOX FM, Brush House, Pony Road, Oxford OX4 2XR. Tel: 01865-871000. *Frequencies:* 102.6/97.4 FM

GEM-AM, 29–31 Castle Gate, Nottingham NG1 7AP. Tel: 0115-952 7000. *Frequencies:* MW 999/945 kHz

GEMINI AM, Hawthorn House, Exeter Business Park, Exeter EX1 3QS. Tel: 01392-444444. *Frequencies:* MW 666/954 kHz

GEMINI FM, Hawthorn House, Exeter Business Park, Exeter EX1 3QS. Tel: 01392-444444. *Frequencies:* 97.0/96.4/103.0 FM

GNR (GREAT NORTH RADIO), Newcastle upon Tyne NE99 1BB. Tel: 0191-420 3040. *Frequencies:* MW 1152/1170 kHz

GOLD RADIO, Longmead, Shaftesbury, Dorset SP7 8QQ. Tel: 01747-855711. *Frequency:* 97.4 FM

GREAT YORKSHIRE GOLD, Radio House, 900 Herries Road, Sheffield S6 1RH. Tel: 0114-285 2121; Forster Square, Bradford BD1 5NE. Tel: 01274-731521. *Frequencies:* MW 1548/1305/990 kHz (S. Yorks, N. Midlands); 1278/1530 kHz (W. Yorks); 1161 kHz (Humberside)

GWR FM (Bristol and Bath), PO Box 2000, Watershed, Canon's Road, Bristol bs99 7sn. Tel: 0117-984 3200. *Frequencies:* 96.3/103.0 FM

GWR FM (Wiltshire), PO Box 2000, Swindon sn4 7ex. Tel: 01793-440300. *Frequencies:* 97.2 FM (Swindon); 102.2 FM (West Wilts)

Hallam FM, Radio House, 900 Herries Road, Sheffield s6 1rh. Tel: 0114-285 3333. *Frequencies:* 97.4 FM (Sheffield); 102.9/103.4 FM (Rotherham); 102.9 FM (Barnsley); 103.4 FM (Doncaster)

Heart 106.2, The Chrysalis Building, Bramley Road, London w10 6sp. Tel: 0171-468 1062. *Frequency:* 106.2 FM

Heartland FM, The Curling Rink, Lower Oakfield, Pitlochry, Perthshire ph16 5hq. Tel: 01796-474040. *Frequency:* 97.5 FM

Invicta FM and SuperGold, Radio House, John Wilson Business Park, Whitstable, Kent ct5 3qx. Tel: 01227-772004. *Frequencies:* MW 1242 kHz (West Kent), 603 kHz (East Kent); 103.1 FM (Maidstone and Medway), 102.8 FM (Canterbury), 95.9 FM (Thanet), 97.0 FM (Dover), 96.1 FM (Ashford)

Island FM, 12 Westerbrook, St Sampson, Guernsey gy2 4qq. Tel: 01481-42000. *Frequencies:* 93.7 FM (Alderney); 104.7 FM (Guernsey)

Isle of Wight Radio, Dodnor Park, Newport, Isle of Wight po30 5xe. Tel: 01983-822557. *Frequency:* MW 1242 kHz

Jazz FM 102.2, 26–27 Castlereagh Street, London w1h 6dj. Tel: 0171-706 4100. *Frequency:* 102.2 FM

KCBC 1584 AM, Unit 1, Centre 2000, Robinson Close, Telford Way Industrial Estate, Kettering, Northants nn16 8pu. Tel: 01536-412413. *Frequency:* MW 1584 kHz

Key 103, PO Box 103, Manchester m1 4aw. Tel: 0161-236 9913. *Frequency:* 103.0 FM

KFM, 1 East Street, Tonbridge, Kent tn9 1ar. Tel: 01732-369200. *Frequencies:* 96.2/101.6 FM

Kingston FM Ltd, The Teddington Studios, Teddington Lock, Teddington, Middx tw11 9nt. Tel: 0181-614 2400. (*From early 1997*)

Kiss 100 FM, Kiss House, 80 Holloway Road, London n7 8jg. Tel: 0171-700 6100. *Frequency:* 100.0 FM

Kiss 102, Kiss House, PO Box 102, Manchester m60 1gj. Tel: 0161-228 0102. *Frequency:* 102 FM

Kix 96, PO Box 962, Coventry cv1 4xx. Tel: 01203-525656. *Frequency:* 96.2 FM

KL.FM, PO Box 77, Blackfriars Street, King's Lynn, Norfolk pe30 1nn. Tel: 01553-772777. *Frequency:* 96.7 FM

Lantern FM, The Light House, 17 Market Place, Bideford, N. Devon ex39 2dr. Tel: 01237-424444. *Frequency:* 96.2 FM

LBC 1152, 200 Gray's Inn Road, London wc1x 8xz. Tel: 0171-973 1152. *Frequency:* MW 1152 kHz

Leicester Sound, Granville House, Granville Road, Leicester le1 7rw. Tel: 0116-256 1300. *Frequency:* 103.2 FM

Lincs FM, Witham Park, Waterside South, Lincoln ln5 7jn. Tel: 01522-549900. *Frequency:* 102.2 FM/96.7 FM (Grantham Relay)

London Greek Radio, Florentia Village, Vale Road, London n4 1td. Tel: 0181-800 8001. *Frequency:* 103.3 FM

London News 97.3 FM, 200 Gray's Inn Road, London wc1x 8xz. Tel: 0171-973 1152. *Frequency:* 97.3 FM

London Turkish Radio LTR, 185b High Road, Wood Green, London n22 6ba. Tel: 0181-881 0606. *Frequency:* MW 1584 kHz

Magic 828, PO Box 2000, 51 Burley Road, Leeds ls3 1lr. Tel: 0113-245 2299. *Frequency:* MW 828 kHz

Marcher Gold, The Studios, Mold Road, Gwersyllt, Nr Wrexham ll11 4af. Tel: 01978-752202. *Frequency:* MW 1260 kHz

Max AM, Forth House, Forth Street, Edinburgh eh1 3lf. Tel: 0131-556 9255. *Frequency:* MW 1548 kHz

Mellow 1557, Media Centre, 2 St Johns Wynd, Culver Square, Colchester co1 1wq. Tel: 01206-764466. *Frequency:* MW 1557 kHz

Melody FM, 180 Brompton Road, London sw3 1hf. Tel: 0171-581 1054. *Frequency:* 105.4 FM

Mercia FM, Hertford Place, Coventry cv1 3tt. Tel: 01203-868200. *Frequencies:* 97.0/102.9 FM

Mercury FM, Broadfield House, Brighton Road, Crawley, W. Sussex rh11 9tt. Tel: 01293-519161. *Frequency:* 102.7 FM

Metro FM, Newcastle upon Tyne ne99 1bb. Tel: 0191-420 0971. *Frequencies:* 97.1/103.0 /103.2/102.6 FM

MFM, The Studios, Mold Road, Gwersyllt, Nr Wrexham ll11 4af. Tel: 01978-752202. *Frequencies:* 103.4/97.1 FM

Minster FM, PO Box 123, Dunnington, York yo1 5zx. Tel: 01904-488888. *Frequency:* 104.7 FM

Mix 96, Friars Square Studios, Bourbon Street, Aylesbury, Bucks hp20 2pz. Tel: 01296-399396. *Frequency:* 96.2 FM

Moray Firth Radio, PO Box 271, Inverness iv3 6sf. Tel: 01463-224433. *Frequencies:* MW 1107 kHz, 97.4/96.6 FM

NECR (North-East Community Radio), Town House, Kintore, Inverurie, Aberdeenshire ab51 0us. Tel: 01467-632909. *Frequency:* 102.1 FM

Nevis Radio, Inverlochy, Fort William, Inverness-shire ph33 6lu. Tel: 01397-700007. *Frequency:* 96.6 FM

96.3 Aire FM, PO Box 2000, 51 Burley Road, PO Box 2000, Leeds ls3 ilr. Tel: 0113-245 2299. *Frequency:* 96.3 FM

96.3 QFM, 26 Lady Lane, Paisley pa1 2lg. Tel: 0141-887 9630. *Frequency:* 96.3 FM

96.4 FM BRMB, Radio House, Aston Road North, Birmingham b6 4bx. Tel: 0121-359 4481. *Frequency:* 96.4 FM

96.4 The Eagle, Dolphin House, North Street, Guildford, Surrey gu1 4aa. Tel: 01483-300964. *Frequency:* 96.4 FM

96.6 FM Classic Hits, 7 Hatfield Road, St Albans, Herts al1 3rs. Tel: 01727-831966. *Frequency:* 96.6 FM

96.7 BCR, Russell Court Building, Claremont Street, Lisburn Road, Belfast bt9 6jx. Tel: 01232-438500. *Frequency:* 96.7 FM

97.2 Stray FM, PO Box 972, Station Parade, Harrogate hg1 5yf. Tel: 01423-522972. *Frequency:* 97.2 FM

Northants Radio, The Broadcast Centre, 19–21 St Edmunds Road, Northampton nn1 5dy. Tel: 01604-792411. *Frequency:* 96.6 FM

NorthSound One and Two, 45 Kings Gate, Aberdeen ab15 4el. Tel: 01224-632234. *Frequencies:* MW 1035 kHz, 96.9/97.6/103 FM

Oban FM, McLeod Units, Lochavullin Estate, Oban, Argyll. Tel: 01631-570057. *Frequency:* 103.3 FM

Ocean FM, Radio House, Whittle Avenue, Segensworth West, Fareham, Hants po15 5sh. Tel: 01489-589911. *Frequencies:* 97.5/96.7 FM

102.7 Hereward FM, PO Box 225, Queensgate Centre, Peterborough pe1 1xj. Tel: 01733-460460. *Frequency:* 102.7 FM

1152 Xtra AM, Radio House, Aston Road North, Birmingham b6 4bx. Tel: 0121-359 4481. *Frequency:* MW 1152 kHz

1458 LITE AM, PO Box 1458, Quay West, Trafford Park, Manchester M17 1FL. Tel: 0161-872 1458. *Frequency:* MW 1458 kHz

ORCHARD FM, Haygrove House, Taunton TA3 7BT. Tel: 01823-338448. *Frequencies:* 102.6/97.1 FM

PICCADILLY 1152, PO Box 1152, Manchester M1 4AW. Tel: 0161-236 9913. *Frequency:* MW 1152 kHz

PIRATE FM 102, Carn Brea Studios, Wilson Way, Redruth, Cornwall TR15 3XX. Tel: 01209-314400; 12 Chapel Street, Devonport, Plymouth PL1 4DS. Tel: 01752-605301. *Frequencies:* 102.2 FM (East Cornwall and West Devon); 102.8 FM (West Cornwall and Isles of Scilly)

PLYMOUTH SOUND AM, Earl's Acre, Plymouth PL3 4HX. Tel: 01752-227272. *Frequency:* MW 1152 kHz

PLYMOUTH SOUND FM, Earl's Acre, Plymouth PL3 4HX. Tel: 01752-227272. *Frequencies:* 97.0/96.6 FM

POWERFM, Radio House, Whittle Avenue, Segensworth West, Fareham, Hants PO15 5SH. Tel: 01489-589911. *Frequency:* 103.2 FM

PREMIER RADIO, Glen House, Stag Place, London SW1E 5AG. Tel: 0171-233 6705. *Frequencies:* MW 1305/1332/1413 kHz

THE PULSE, Forster Square, Bradford BD1 5NE. Tel: 01274-731521. *Frequencies:* 97.5 FM (Bradford); 102.5 FM (Huddersfield and Halifax)

Q102.9, The Riverside Suite, The Old Waterside Railway Station, Duke Street, Waterside, Londonderry BT47 1DH. Tel: 01504-44449. *Frequency:* 102.9 FM

Q103 FM, Enterprise House, The Vision Park, Chivers Way, Histon, Cambridge CB4 4WW. Tel: 01223-235255. *Frequencies:* 103.0 FM (Cambridge); 97.4 FM (Newmarket)

RADIO BORDERS, Tweedside Park, Galashiels TD1 3TD. Tel: 01896-759444. *Frequencies:* 96.8/97.5/103.1/103.4 FM

RADIO CEREDIGION, Yr Hen Ysgol Gymraeg, Ffordd Alexandra, Aberystwyth SY23 1LF. Tel: 01970-627999. *Frequencies:* 103.3/96.6 FM

RADIO CITY 1548 AM, 8–10 Stanley Street, Liverpool L1 6AF. Tel: 0151-227 5100. *Frequency:* MW 1548 kHz

RADIO MALDWYN, The Studios, The Park, Newtown SY16 2NZ. Tel: 01686-623555. *Frequency:* MW 756 kHz

RADIO 1521, Carn Business Park, Craigavon, Co. Armagh BT63 5RH. Tel: 01762-330033. *Frequency:* MW 1521 kHz

RADIO TAY, 6 North Isla Street, Dundee DD3 7JQ. Tel: 01382-200800. *Frequencies:* MW 1161 kHz, 102.8 FM (Dundee); 1584 kHz, 96.4 FM (Perth)

RADIO WAVE, 965 Mowbray Drive, Blackpool, Lancs FY3 7JR. Tel: 01253-304965. *Frequency:* 96.5 FM

RADIO XL 1296 AM, KMS House, Bradford Street, Birmingham B12 0JD. Tel: 0121-753 5353. *Frequency:* MW 1296 kHz

RAM FM, The Market Place, Derby DE1 3AA. Tel: 01332-292945. *Frequency:* 102.8 FM

RED DRAGON FM, Radio House, West Canal Wharf, Cardiff CF1 5XJ. Tel: 01222-384041. *Frequencies:* 97.4 FM (Newport); 103.2 FM (Cardiff)

RED ROSE GOLD and RED ROSE ROCK FM, PO Box 999, St Paul's Square, Preston, Lancs PR1 1XS. Tel: 01772-556301. *Frequencies:* MW 999 kHz (*Gold*), 97.4 FM (*Rock FM*)

RTM RADIO, Harrow Manor Way, Thamesmead South, London SE2 9XH. Tel: 0181-311 3112. *Frequency:* 103.8 FM

SABRAS SOUND, Radio House, 63 Melton Road, Leicester LE4 6PN. Tel: 0116-261 0666. *Frequency:* MW 1260 kHz

SEVERN SOUND FM, Old Talbot House, Southgate Street, Gloucester GL1 2DQ. Tel: 01452-423791. *Frequencies:* 103.0/102.4 FM

SGR COLCHESTER, Abbeygate Two, 9 Whitewell Road, Colchester CO2 7DE. Tel: 01206-575859. *Frequency:* 96.1 FM

SGR-FM, PO Box 250, Bury St Edmunds, Suffolk IP33 1AD. Tel: 01284-701511; Radio House, Alpha Business Park, White House Road, Ipswich IP1 5LT. Tel: 01473-461000. *Frequencies:* 97.1 FM (Ipswich); 96.4 FM (Bury)

SIBC, Market Street, Lerwick, Shetland ZE1 0JN. Tel: 01595-695299. *Frequency:* 96.2 FM

SIGNAL CHESHIRE, Regent House, Heaton Lane, Stockport SK4 1BX. Tel: 0161-480 5445. *Frequencies:* 104.9/96.4 FM

SIGNAL ONE AND SIGNAL GOLD, Stoke Road, Stoke-on-Trent ST4 2SR. Tel: 01782-747047. *Frequencies:* MW 1170 kHz, 102.6/99.9 FM

SOUND WAVE, PO Box 964, Victoria Road, Gowerton, Swansea SA4 3AB. Tel: 01792-511964. *Frequency:* 96.4 FM

SOUTH COAST RADIO, Radio House, Whittle Avenue, Segensworth West, Fareham, Hants PO15 5SH. Tel: 01489-589911; Radio House, PO Box 2000, Brighton BN14 2SS. Tel: 01273-430111. *Frequencies:* MW 945/1170/1557/1323 kHz

SOUTHERN FM, Radio House, PO Box 2000, Brighton BN41 2SS. Tel: 01273-430111. *Frequencies:* 103.5 FM (Brighton); 96.9 FM (Newhaven); 102.4 FM (Eastbourne); 102.0 FM (Hastings)

SOUTH WEST SOUND, Campbell House, Bankend Road, Dumfries DG1 4TH. Tel: 01387-250999. *Frequency:* 97.0 FM

SPECTRUM INTERNATIONAL RADIO, 80 Silverthorne Road, London SW8 3XA. Tel: 0171-627 4433. *Frequency:* MW 558 kHz

SPIRE FM, City Hall Studios, Malthouse Lane, Salisbury, Wilts SP2 7QQ. Tel: 01722-416644. *Frequency:* 102.0 FM

SPIRIT FM, Dukes Court, Bognor Road, Chichester, W. Sussex PO19 2FX. Tel: 01243-773600. *Frequencies:* 96.6/102.3 FM

STAR FM, Tristar Broadcasting Ltd, The Observatory Shopping Centre, Slough, Berks SL1 1LH. Tel: 01753-551016. *Frequency:* 106.6 FM

SUN CITY 103.4, 39 Holmeside, Sunderland SR1 3HY. Tel: 0191-567 3333. *Frequency:* 103.4 FM

SUNRISE FM, Sunrise House, 30 Chapel Street, Little Germany, Bradford BD1 5DN. Tel: 01274-735043. *Frequency:* 103.2 FM

SUNRISE RADIO, Sunrise House, Sunrise Road, Southall, Middx UB2 4AU. Tel: 0181-574 6666. *Frequency:* MW 1458 kHz

SUNSHINE 855, Sunshine House, Waterside, Ludlow, Shropshire SY8 1GS. Tel: 01584-873795. *Frequency:* MW 855 kHz

SWANSEA SOUND, PO Box 1170, Victoria Road, Gowerton, Swansea SA4 3AB. Tel: 01792-511170. *Frequency:* MW 1170 kHz

TEN 17, Latton Bush Centre, Southern Way, Harlow, Essex CM18 7BU. Tel: 01279-432415. *Frequency:* 101.7 FM

TFM, Yale Crescent, Thornaby, Stockton-on-Tees, Cleveland TS17 6AA. Tel: 01642-615111. *Frequencies:* 96.6 FM

TOUCH RADIO, West Canal Wharf, Cardiff CF1 5XY. Tel: 01222-237878. *Frequencies:* MW 1359 kHz (Cardiff); 1305 kHz (Newport)

TOWNLAND RADIO 828 AM, 2c Park Avenue, Cookstown, Co. Tyrone BT80 8AH. Tel: 016487-64828. *Frequency:* MW 828 kHz

TRENT-FM, 29–31 Castle Gate, Nottingham NG1 7AP. Tel: 0115-952 7000. *Frequency:* 96.2/96.5 FM

2CR FM, 5 Southcote Road, Bournemouth BH1 3LR. Tel: 01202-294881. *Frequency:* 102.3 FM

2-TEN FM, PO Box 210, Reading RG31 7RZ. Tel: 01189-254400. *Frequencies:* 97.0/102.9 FM

VALLEY SOUND LTD, PO Box 1116, Ebbw Vale NP3 5YJ. Tel: c/o *Swansea Sound,* 01792-511170. *Frequency:* MW 1116 kHz

VIKING FM, Commercial Road, Hull HU1 2SG. Tel: 01482-325141. *Frequency:* 96.9 FM

VIRGIN RADIO LONDON, 1 Golden Square, London WIR 4DJ. Tel: 0171-434 1215. *Frequency:* 105.8 FM

VIVA! 963 AM, 26–27 Castlereagh Street, London W1H 6DJ. Tel: 0171-706 9963. *Frequency:* MW 963 kHz

WABC, 267 Tettenhall Road, Wolverhampton WV6 0DQ. Tel: 01902-838383. *Frequencies:* MW 990 kHz (Wolverhampton); 1017 kHz (Shrewsbury and Telford)

WESSEX FM, Radio House, Trinity Street, Dorchester, Dorset DT1 1DJ. Tel: 01305-250333. *Frequencies:* 97.2/96.0 FM

WEST SOUND AM, Radio House, 54A Holmston Road, Ayr KA7 3BE. Tel: 01292-283662. *Frequencies:* MW 1035 kHz, 96.7/97.5 FM

WEY VALLEY RADIO, Prospect Place, Mill Lane, Alton, Hants GU34 2SY. Tel: 01420-544444. *Frequencies:* 102/101.6 FM

WYVERN AM and FM, 5 Barbourne Terrace, Worcester WR1 3JZ. Tel: 01905-612212. *Frequencies:* MW 954 kHz, 97.6 FM (Hereford); 1530 kHz, 102.8 FM (Worcester); 96.7 FM (Kidderminster)

YORKSHIRE COAST RADIO, PO Box 962, Scarborough, N. Yorks YO12 5YX. Tel: 01723-500962. *Frequencies:* 96.2/103.1 FM

YORKSHIRE DALES RADIO LTD, Harefield Hall, Pateley Bridge, N. Yorks HG3 5UD. Tel: 01423-712223. (*From March 1997*)

SERVICES BROADCASTING

The British Forces Broadcasting Service (BFBS) and the Services Sound and Vision Corporation (SSVC) television, both part of the SSVC group of companies, provide HM Forces and their families with radio and television broadcasting. The broadcasting service covers Britain and Northern Ireland, Cyprus, Germany, Gibraltar, the Falkland Islands, Hong Kong, Belize, Bosnia and Brunei.

SSVC, Chalfont Grove, Gerrards Cross, Bucks SL9 8TN. Tel: 01494-874461. *Managing Director,* D. O. Crwys-Williams, CB

The Press

The newspaper and periodical press in the UK is large and diverse, catering for a wide variety of views and interests. There is no state control or censorship of the press, though it is subject to the laws on publication and the Press Complaints Commission (*see* below) was set up by the industry as a means of self-regulation.

The press is not state-subsidized and receives few tax concessions. The income of most newspapers and periodicals is derived largely from sales and from advertising; the press is the largest advertising medium in Britain.

SELF-REGULATION

When the report of the Committee on Privacy and Related Matters, chaired by David Calcutt, QC, was published in June 1990, the then Home Secretary (David Waddington) said that the Government would review the performance of a non-statutory Press Complaints Commission after 18 months of operation to determine whether statutory measures were required. The *Calcutt Review of Press Self-Regulation* was presented to Parliament by the then Secretary of State for National Heritage (Peter Brooke) in January 1993 (for summary, *see* Whitaker's Almanack 1994).

COMPLAINTS

The Press Complaints Commission was founded by the newspaper and magazine industry in January 1991 to replace the Press Council (established in 1953). It is a voluntary, non-statutory body set up to operate the press's self-regulation system, and funded by the industry through the Press Standards Board of Finance.

The Commission's objects are to consider, adjudicate, conciliate, and resolve complaints of unfair treatment by the press; and to ensure that the press maintains the highest professional standards with respect for generally recognized freedoms, including freedom of expression, the public's right to know, and the right of the press to operate free from improper pressure. The Commission judges newspaper and magazine conduct by a code of practice drafted by editors, agreed by the industry and ratified by the Commission.

Seven of the Commission's members are editors of national, regional and local newspapers and magazines, and nine, including the chairman, are drawn from other fields. One member has been appointed Privacy Commissioner with special powers to investigate complaints about invasion of privacy.

PRESS COMPLAINTS COMMISSION, 1 Salisbury Square, London EC4Y 8AE. Tel: 0171-353 1248. *Chairman,* Lord Wakeham, PC; *Director,* G. Black

---

NEWSPAPERS

Newspapers are usually financially independent of any political party, though most adopt a political stance in their editorial comments, usually reflecting proprietorial influence. Ownership of the national and regional daily newspapers is concentrated in the hands of large corporations whose interests cover publishing and communications. There are rules on cross-media ownership to prevent undue concentration of newspaper ownership. The Broad-casting Act 1996 amended the rules on cross-media ownership (*see* page 670).

There are about 15 daily and ten Sunday national papers, about 80 regional daily papers, and several hundred local papers that are published weekly or twice-weekly. Scotland, Wales and Northern Ireland all have at least one daily and one Sunday national paper.

Newspapers are usually published in either broadsheet or tabloid format. The 'quality' daily papers, i.e. those providing detailed coverage of a wide range of public matters, have a broadsheet format. The tabloid papers take a more popular approach and are more illustrated.

NATIONAL DAILY NEWSPAPERS

DAILY EXPRESS, Ludgate House, 245 Blackfriars Road, London SE1 9UX. Tel: 0171-928 8000
DAILY MAIL, Northcliffe House, 2 Derry Street, London W8 5TT. Tel: 0171-938 6000
DAILY MIRROR, 1 Canada Square, Canary Wharf, London E14 5AP. Tel: 0171-293 3000
DAILY SPORT, 19 Great Ancoats Street, Manchester M60 4BT. Tel: 0161-236 4466
DAILY STAR, Ludgate House, 245 Blackfriars Road, London SE1 9UX. Tel: 0171-928 8000
DAILY TELEGRAPH, 1 Canada Square, Canary Wharf, London E14 5DT. Tel: 0171-538 5000
THE EUROPEAN, 200 Gray's Inn Road, London WC1X 8NE. Tel: 0171-418 7777
FINANCIAL TIMES, 1 Southwark Bridge, London SE1 9HL. Tel: 0171-873 3000
THE GUARDIAN, 119 Farringdon Road, London EC1R 3ER. Tel: 0171-278 2332
THE HERALD, 195 Albion Street, Glasgow G1 1QP. Tel: 0141-552 6255
THE INDEPENDENT, 1 Canada Square, Canary Wharf, London E14 5DL. Tel: 0171-293 2000
MORNING STAR, 1–3 Ardleigh Road, London N1 4HS. Tel: 0171-254 0033
RACING POST, 112–120 Coombe Lane, London SW2 0BA. Tel: 0181-879 3377
THE SCOTSMAN, 20 North Bridge, Edinburgh EH1 1YT. Tel: 0131-225 2468
THE SPORTING LIFE, Orbit House, 1 New Fetter Lane, London EC4A 1AR. Tel: 0171-822 2119
THE SUN, 1 Virginia Street, London E1 9XN. Tel: 0171-782 4000
THE TIMES, 1 Pennington Street, London E1 9XN. Tel: 0171-782 5000

REGIONAL DAILY NEWSPAPERS

Aberdeen: PRESS AND JOURNAL, and EVENING EXPRESS, PO Box 43, Lang Stracht, Mastrick, AB9 8AF
Aylesford: KENT TODAY, Messenger House, New Hythe Lane, Larkfield, ME20 6SG
Barrow-in-Furness: NORTH-WEST EVENING MAIL, Newspaper House, Abbey Road, LA14 5QS
Basildon: EVENING ECHO, Newspaper House, Chester Hall Lane, SS14 3BL
Belfast: BELFAST TELEGRAPH, 124–144 Royal Avenue, BT1 1EB; IRISH NEWS AND BELFAST MORNING NEWS, 113–117 Donegall Street, BT1 2GE; NEWS LETTER, 46–56 Boucher Crescent, BT12 6QY
Birmingham: THE BIRMINGHAM POST, and BIRMINGHAM EVENING MAIL, 28 Colmore Circus, Queensway, B4 6AX

Blackburn: LANCASHIRE EVENING TELEGRAPH, Newspaper House, High Street, BB1 1HT
Blackpool: EVENING GAZETTE, PO Box 20, Preston New Road, FY4 4AU
Bolton: BOLTON EVENING NEWS, Churchgate, BL1 1DE
Bournemouth: EVENING ECHO, Richmond Hill, BH2 6HH
Bradford: TELEGRAPH AND ARGUS, Hall Ings, BD1 1JR
Brighton: EVENING ARGUS, Argus House, Crowhurst Road, Hollingbury, BN1 8AR
Bristol: BRISTOL EVENING POST, and WESTERN DAILY PRESS, Temple Way, BS99 7HD
Burton-on-Trent: BURTON MAIL, 65–68 High Street, DE14 1LE
Cambridge: CAMBRIDGE EVENING NEWS, 51 Newmarket Road, CB5 8EJ
Cardiff: SOUTH WALES ECHO, and WESTERN MAIL, Thomson House, Havelock Street, CF1 1WR
Carlisle: NEWS AND STAR, Newspaper House, Dalston Road, CA2 5UA
Chelmsford: ESSEX CHRONICLE, Westway, Essex CM1 3BE
Cheltenham: GLOUCESTERSHIRE ECHO, 1 Clarence Parade, GL50 3NZ
Colchester: EVENING GAZETTE, Oriel House, 43–44 North Hill, CO1 1TZ
Coventry: COVENTRY EVENING TELEGRAPH, Corporation Street, CV1 1FP
Darlington: NORTHERN ECHO, Priestgate, DL1 1NF
Derby: DERBY EVENING TELEGRAPH, Northcliffe House, Meadow Road, DE1 2DW
Dundee: COURIER AND ADVERTISER, and EVENING TELEGRAPH AND POST, 2 Albert Square, DD1 9QJ
Edinburgh: EDINBURGH EVENING NEWS, 20 North Bridge, EH1 1YT
Exeter: EXPRESS AND ECHO, Heron Road, Sowton, EX2 7NF
Glasgow: DAILY RECORD, 40 Anderston Quay, G3 8DA; EVENING TIMES, 195 Albion Street, G1 1QP; SCOTTISH DAILY EXPRESS, Park House, Park Circus Place, G3 6AF
Gloucester: THE GLOUCESTERSHIRE CITIZEN, St John's Lane, GL1 2AY
Greenock: GREENOCK TELEGRAPH, 2 Crawford Street, PA15 1LH
Grimsby: GRIMSBY EVENING TELEGRAPH, 80 Cleethorpe Road, DN31 3EH
Guernsey: GUERNSEY EVENING PRESS AND STAR, PO Box 57, Braye Road, Vale, GY1 3BW
Halifax: HALIFAX EVENING COURIER, PO Box 19, Courier Buildings, King Cross Street, HX1 2SF
Huddersfield: HUDDERSFIELD DAILY EXAMINER, PO Box A26, Queen Street South, HD1 2TD
Hull: HULL DAILY MAIL, Blundell's Corner, Beverley Road, HU3 1XS
Ipswich: EAST ANGLIAN DAILY TIMES, and EVENING STAR, 30 Lower Brook Street, IP4 1AN
Jersey: JERSEY EVENING POST, PO Box 582, Five Oaks, St Saviour, JE4 8XQ
Kettering: NORTHAMPTONSHIRE EVENING TELEGRAPH, Northfield Avenue, NN16 9TT
Leeds: YORKSHIRE EVENING POST, and YORKSHIRE POST, PO Box 168, Wellington Street, LS1 1RF
Leicester: LEICESTER MERCURY, St George Street, LE1 9FQ
Lincoln: LINCOLNSHIRE ECHO, Brayford Wharf East, LN5 7AT
Liverpool: DAILY POST, and LIVERPOOL ECHO, PO Box 48, Old Hall Street, L69 3EB
London: THE EVENING STANDARD, Northcliffe House, 2 Derry Street, W8 5TT
Manchester: MANCHESTER EVENING NEWS, 164 Deansgate, M60 2RR
Middlesbrough: EVENING GAZETTE, Gazette Buildings, Borough Road, TS1 3AZ

Mold: EVENING LEADER, Mold Business Park, Wrexham Road, CH7 1XY
Newcastle upon Tyne: EVENING CHRONICLE, and THE JOURNAL, Thomson House, Groat Market, NE1 1ED
Newport: SOUTH WALES ARGUS, Cardiff Road, Maesglas, NP9 1QW
Northampton: CHRONICLE AND ECHO, Upper Mounts, NN1 3HR
Norwich: EASTERN DAILY PRESS, and EVENING NEWS, Prospect House, Rouen Road, NR1 1RE
Nottingham: NOTTINGHAM EVENING POST, PO Box 99, Forman Street, NG1 4AB
Nuneaton: HEARTLAND EVENING NEWS, Newspaper House, 11–15 Newtown Road, CV11 4HR
Oldham: EVENING CHRONICLE, 172 Union Street, OL1 1EQ
Oxford: THE OXFORD MAIL, Newspaper House, Osney Mead, OX2 0EJ
Paisley: PAISLEY DAILY EXPRESS, 1 Woodside Terrace, Glasgow G3 7UY
Peterborough: PETERBOROUGH EVENING TELEGRAPH, New Priestgate House, 57 Priestgate, PE1 1JW
Plymouth: WESTERN MORNING NEWS, and EVENING HERALD, 17 Brest Road, Derriford Business Park, PL6 5AA
Portsmouth: THE NEWS, The News Centre, Hilsea, PO2 9SX
Preston: LANCASHIRE EVENING POST, Oliver's Place, Fulwood, PR2 9ZA
Reading: EVENING POST, 8 Tessa Road, RG1 8NS
Scarborough: SCARBOROUGH EVENING NEWS, 17–23 Aberdeen Walk, YO11 1BB
Scunthorpe: SCUNTHORPE EVENING TELEGRAPH, Telegraph House, Doncaster Road, DN15 7RE
Sheffield: THE STAR; THE DONCASTER STAR; ROTHERHAM STAR, York Street, S1 1PU
South Shields: SHIELDS GAZETTE, and SUNDERLAND ECHO, Chapter Row, NE33 1BL
Southampton: SOUTHERN DAILY ECHO, 45 Above Bar, SO14 7AA
Stoke-on-Trent: EVENING SENTINEL, Sentinel House, Etruria, ST1 5SS
Swansea: SOUTH WALES EVENING POST, Adelaide Street, SA1 1QT
Swindon: EVENING ADVERTISER, and THE BATH CHRONICLE, Newspaper House, 100 Victoria Road, SN1 3BE
Telford: SHROPSHIRE STAR, Ketley, TF1 4HU
Torquay: HERALD EXPRESS, Harmsworth House, Barton Hill Road, TQ2 8JN
Weymouth: DORSET EVENING ECHO, 57 St Thomas Street, DT4 8EU
Wigan: WIGAN EVENING POST, Martland Mill, Martland Mill Lane, WN5 0LX
Wolverhampton: EXPRESS AND STAR, 51–53 Queen Street, WV1 3BU
Worcester: WORCESTER EVENING NEWS, Hylton Road, WR2 5JX
York: YORKSHIRE EVENING PRESS, PO Box 29, 76–86 Walmgate, YO1 1YN

WEEKLY NEWSPAPERS

AL MAJALLA, Arab Press House, 184 High Holborn, London WC1V 7AP. Tel: 0171-831 8181
ASIAN TIMES, 3rd Floor, Tower House, 141–149 Fonthill Road, London N4 3HF. Tel: 0171-281 1191
CARIBBEAN TIMES, 3rd Floor, Tower House, 141–149 Fonthill Road, London N4 3HF. Tel: 0171-281 1191
THE GUARDIAN WEEKLY, 119 Farringdon Road, London EC1R 3ER. Tel: 0171-278 2332
INDEPENDENT ON SUNDAY, 1 Canada Square, Canary Wharf, London E14 5DL. Tel: 0171-293 2000

INDIA TIMES, Global House, 90 Ascot Gardens, Southall, Middx UB1 2SB. Tel: 0181-575 0151

THE MAIL ON SUNDAY, Northcliffe House, 2 Derry Street, London W8 5TS. Tel: 0171-938 6000

NEWS OF THE WORLD, 1 Virginia Street, London E1 9XN. Tel: 0171-782 4000

THE OBSERVER, 119 Farringdon Road, London EC1 RER. Tel: 0171-278 2332

THE PEOPLE, 1 Canada Square, Canary Wharf, London E14 5AP. Tel: 0171-293 3000

SCOTLAND ON SUNDAY, 20 North Bridge, Edinburgh EH1 1YT. Tel: 0131-225 2468

SUNDAY EXPRESS, Ludgate House, 245 Blackfriars Road, London SE1 9UX. Tel: 0171-928 8000

SUNDAY MAIL, 40 Anderston Quay, Glasgow G3 8DA. Tel: 0141-248 7000

SUNDAY MIRROR, 1 Canada Square, Canary Wharf, London E14 5AP. Tel: 0171-293 3000

SUNDAY POST, Courier Place, Dundee DD1 9QJ. Tel: 01382-223131

SUNDAY SPORT, 848B Melton Road, Thurmaston, Leicester LE4 8BJ. Tel: 0116-269 4892

THE SUNDAY TELEGRAPH, 1 Canada Square, Canary Wharf, London E14 5AR. Tel: 0171-538 5000

THE SUNDAY TIMES, 1 Pennington Street, London E1 9XW. Tel: 0171-782 5000

THE VOICE, 370 Coldharbour Lane, London SW9 8PL. Tel: 0171-737 7377

WALES ON SUNDAY, Thomson House, Havelock Street, Cardiff CF1 1WR. Tel: 01222-583583

WEEKLY NEWS, Courier Place, Dundee DD1 9QJ. Tel: 01382-223131

THE WEEKLY TELEGRAPH, 1 Canada Square, Canary Wharf, London E14 5DT. Tel: 0171-538 6298

RELIGIOUS PAPERS

Alt. = Alternate; *M.* = Monthly; *Q.* = Quarterly; *W.* = Weekly

BAPTIST TIMES, PO Box 54, 129 The Broadway, Didcot, Oxon OX11 8XB. *W.*

CATHOLIC HERALD, Herald House, Lamb's Passage, Bunhill Row, London EC1Y 8TQ. *W.*

CHALLENGE – THE GOOD NEWS PAPER, Revenue Buildings, Chapel Road, Worthing, W. Sussex BN11 1BQ. *M.*

CHRISTIAN HERALD, Herald House, 96 Dominion Road, Worthing, W. Sussex BN14 8JP. *W.*

THE CHURCH OF ENGLAND NEWSPAPER, 10 Little College Street, London SW1P 3SH. *W.*

CHURCH OF IRELAND GAZETTE, 36 Bachelor's Walk, Lisburn, Co. Antrim, BT28 1XN. *W.*

CHURCH TIMES, 33 Upper Street, London N1 6PN. *W.*

ENGLISH CHURCHMAN, 22 Lesley Avenue, Canterbury, Kent CT1 3LF. *Alt. W.*

THE FRIEND, Drayton House, 30 Gordon Street, London WC1H 0BQ. *W.*

THE INQUIRER, Essex Hall, 1–6 Essex Street, London WC2R 3HY. *Alt. M.*

JEWISH CHRONICLE, 25 Furnival Street, London EC4A 1JT. *W.*

JEWISH TELEGRAPH, Telegraph House, 11 Park Hill, Bury Old Road, Prestwich, Manchester M25 0HH. *W.*

LIFE AND WORK, Church of Scotland, 121 George Street, Edinburgh EH2 4YN. *M.*

METHODIST RECORDER, 122 Golden Lane, London EC1Y 0TL. *W.*

MIDDLE WAY, Buddhist Society, 58 Eccleston Square, London SW1V 1PH. *Q.*

ORTHODOX OUTLOOK, 42 Withen's Lane, Wallasey, Wirral, Merseyside L43 7NN. *Alt. M.*

PRESBYTERIAN HERALD, Church House, Fisherwick Place, Belfast BT1 6DW. *Ten times a year*

QUAKER MONTHLY, Friends House, Euston Road, London NW1 2BJ. *M.*

REFORM, United Reformed Church, 86 Tavistock Place, London WC1H 9RT. *Eleven times a year*

SIKH MESSENGER, 43 Dorset Road, London SW19 3EZ. *Q.*

THE TABLET, 1 King Street Cloisters, Clifton Walk, London W6 0QZ. *W.*

THE UNIVERSE, 1st Floor, St James Building, Oxford Street, Manchester M1 6FP. *W.*

THE WAR CRY, 101 Queen Victoria Street, London EC4P 4EP. *W.*

PERIODICALS

There are about 7,700 periodicals published in Britain. These are classified as consumer, i.e. general interest, or as trade, professional or academic.

CONSUMER PERIODICALS

Alt. = Alternate; *M.* = Monthly; *Q.* = Quarterly; *W.* = Weekly

AMATEUR PHOTOGRAPHER, King's Reach Tower, Stamford Street, London SE1 9LS. *W.*

ANGLING TIMES, Bretton Court, Bretton, Peterborough PE3 8DZ. *W.*

THE ANTIQUE COLLECTOR, 7 St John's Road, Harrow, Middx HA1 2EE. *Alt. M.*

APOLLO, 29 Chesham Place, London SW1X 8HB. *M.*

ARENA, 3rd Floor, Block A, Exmouth House, Pine Street, London EC1R 0JL. *Ten times a year*

THE ARTIST, Caxton House, 63–65 High Street, Tenterden, Kent TN30 6BD. *M.*

ASTRONOMY NOW, Douglas House, 32–34 Simpson Road, Bletchley, Milton Keynes, Bucks MK1 1BA. *M.*

ATHLETICS WEEKLY, Bretton Court, Bretton, Peterborough PE3 8DZ. *W.*

AUTOCAR AND MOTOR, 38–42 Hampton Road, Teddington, Middx TW11 0JE. *W.*

BBC GARDENER'S WORLD, Woodlands, 80 Wood Lane, London W12 0TT. *M.*

BBC GOOD FOOD, Woodlands, 80 Wood Lane, London W12 0TT. *M.*

BBC WILDLIFE MAGAZINE, Woodlands, 80 Wood Lane, London W12 0TT. *M.*

BELFAST GAZETTE (*Official*), 64 Chichester Street, Belfast BT1 4PS. *W.*

BELLA, 2nd Floor, Shirley House, 25–27 Camden Road, London NW1 9LL. *W.*

BEST, 10th Floor, Portland House, Stag Place, London SW1E 5AU. *W.*

BIRDS, RSPB, The Lodge, Sandy, Beds SG19 2DL. *Q.*

BIRD WATCHING, Bretton Court, Bretton, Peterborough PE3 8DZ. *M.*

BOXING NEWS, PO Box 300, London SW15 5QF. *W.*

BRIDES & SETTING UP HOME, Vogue House, Hanover Square, London WIR 0AD. *Alt. M.*

THE BURLINGTON MAGAZINE, 6 Bloomsbury Square, London WC1A 2LP. *M.*

CAMPING & CARAVANNING, Greenfields House, Westwood Way, Coventry CV4 8JH. *M.*

CAR, Abbots Court, 34 Farringdon Lane, London EC1R 3AU. *M.*

CAT WORLD, 10 Western Road, Shoreham-by-Sea, W. Sussex BN43 5WD. *M.*

CHAT, King's Reach Tower, Stamford Street, London SE1 9LS. *W.*

CLASSIC AND SPORTSCAR, 38–42 Hampton Road, Teddington, Middx TW11 0JE. *M.*

CLASSIC CD, Beauford Court, 30 Monmouth Street, Bath BA1 2BW. *M.*

CLOTHES SHOW MAGAZINE, 80 Wood Lane, London W12 0TT. *M.*

COARSE ANGLING, King's Reach Tower, Stamford Street, London SE1 9LS. *M.*

COIN NEWS, PO Box 20, Axminster, Devon EX13 7YT. *M.*

COMPANY, National Magazine House, 72 Broadwick Street, London W1V 2BP. *M.*

COMPETITORS JOURNAL, PO Box 300, London SW15 5QF. *Alt. W.*

COMPUTER SHOPPER, 19 Bolsover Street, London W1P 7HJ. *M.*

COMPUTER AND VIDEO GAMES, Priory Court, 30–32 Farringdon Road, London EC1R 3AU. *M.*

COSMOPOLITAN, National Magazine House, 72 Broadwick Street, London W1V 2BP. *M.*

COUNTRY HOMES AND INTERIORS, King's Reach Tower, Stamford Street, London SE1 9LS. *M.*

COUNTRY LIFE, King's Reach Tower, Stamford Street, London SE1 9LS. *W.*

COUNTRY LIVING MAGAZINE, National Magazine House, 72 Broadwick Street, London W1V 2BP. *M.*

THE COUNTRYMAN, Link House, Dingwall Avenue, Croydon, Surrey CR9 2TA. *Alt. M.*

CRICKETER INTERNATIONAL, Beech Hanger, Ashurst, Tunbridge Wells, Kent TN3 9ST. *M.*

CYCLING WEEKLY, King's Reach Tower, Stamford Street, London SE1 9LS. *W.*

THE DALESMAN, Stable Courtyard, Broughton Hall, Skipton, N. Yorks BD23 3AE. *M.*

DALTONS WEEKLY, CI Tower, St George's Square, New Malden, Surrey KT3 4JA. *W.*

DANCE AND DANCERS, 214 Panther House, 38 Mount Pleasant, London WC1X 0AP. *M.*

DANCING TIMES, Clerkenwell House, 45–47 Clerkenwell Green, London EC1R 0EB. *M.*

DOGS TODAY, Pankhurst Farm, Bagshot Road, West End, Woking, Surrey GU24 9QR. *M.*

DOG WORLD, 9 Tufton Street, Ashford, Kent TN23 1QN. *W.*

THE ECOLOGIST, Agriculture House, Bath Road, Sturminster Newton, Dorset DT10 1DU. *Alt. M.*

THE ECONOMIST, 25 St James's Street, London SW1A 1HG. *W.*

EDINBURGH GAZETTE (*Official*), PO Box 276, London SW8 5DT. *Alt. W.*

ELLE, Victory House, 14 Leicester Place, London WC2H 7BP. *M.*

EMPIRE, 42–48 Great Portland Street, London W1N 5AH. *M.*

ESQUIRE, National Magazine House, 72 Broadwick Street, London W1V 2BP. *M.*

ESSENTIALS, King's Reach Tower, Stamford Street, London SE1 9LS. *M.*

EVERYWOMAN, 9 St Albans Place, London N1 0NX. *M.*

EXCHANGE AND MART, Link House, 25 West Street, Poole, Dorset BH15 1LL. *W.*

THE FACE, 3rd Floor, Block A, Exmouth House, Pine Street, London EC1R 0JL. *M.*

FAMILY CIRCLE, King's Reach Tower, Stamford Street, London SE1 9LS. *M.*

FHM, Mappin House, 4 Winsley Street, London W1N 7AR. *M.*

THE FIELD, King's Reach Tower, Stamford Street, London SE1 9LS. *M.*

FILM REVIEW, 9 Blades Court, Deodar Road, London SW15 2NU. *M.*

FORE!, Bretton Court, Bretton, Peterborough PE3 8DZ. *M.*

GARDEN NEWS, Apex House, Oundle Road, Peterborough PE2 9NP. *W.*

GAY TIMES, Ground Floor, Worldwide House, 116–134 Bayham Street, London NW1 0BA. *M.*

GEOGRAPHICAL MAGAZINE, Unit 2, 7 Chalcot Road, Utopia Village, London NW1 8LX. *M.*

GIBBONS STAMP MONTHLY, 5 Parkside, Christchurch Road, Ringwood, Hants BH24 3SH. *M.*

GOLF WORLD, Bretton Court, Bretton, Peterborough PE3 8DZ. *M.*

GOOD HOLIDAY MAGAZINE, 91 High Street, Esher, Surrey KT10 9QD. *Q.*

GOOD HOUSEKEEPING, National Magazine House, 72 Broadwick Street, London W1V 2BP. *M.*

GQ, Vogue House, Hanover Square, London W1R 0AD. *M.*

GRAMOPHONE, 177–179 Kenton Road, Harrow, Middx HA3 0HA. *M.*

GRANTA, 2–3 Hanover Yard, Noel Road, London N1 8BE. *Q.*

GUIDING, 17–19 Buckingham Palace Road, London SW1W 0PT. *M.*

HANSARD, *see* Parliamentary Debates

HARPERS AND QUEEN, National Magazine House, 72 Broadwick Street, London W1V 2BP. *M.*

HELLO!, 69–71 Upper Ground, London SE1 9PQ. *W.*

HOMES AND GARDENS, King's Reach Tower, Stamford Street, London SE1 9LS. *M.*

HORSE AND HOUND, King's Reach Tower, Stamford Street, London SE1 9LS. *W.*

HOUSE AND GARDEN, Vogue House, Hanover Square, London W1R 0AD. *M.*

HOUSE BEAUTIFUL, National Magazine House, 72 Broadwick Street, London W1V 2BP. *Ten times a year*

i–D MAGAZINE, 44 Earlham Street, London WC2H 9LA. *M.*

IDEAL HOME, King's Reach Tower, Stamford Street, London SE1 9LS. *M.*

ILLUSTRATED LONDON NEWS, 20 Upper Ground, London SE1 9PF. *Twice a year*

IN BRITAIN, Haymarket House, 1 Oxendon Street, London SW1Y 4EE. *M.*

IRISH POST, Uxbridge House, 464 Uxbridge Road, Hayes, Middx UB4 0SP. *W.*

JAZZ JOURNAL INTERNATIONAL, 1–5 Clerkenwell Road, London EC1M 5PA. *M.*

JUST SEVENTEEN, Victory House, 14 Leicester Place, London WC2H 7BP. *W.*

LABOUR RESEARCH, 78 Blackfriars Road, London SE1 8HF. *M.*

THE LADY, 39–40 Bedford Street, London WC2E 9ER. *W.*

LAND AND LIBERTY, 177 Vauxhall Bridge Road, London SW1V 1EU. *Alt. W.*

LITERARY REVIEW, 51 Beak Street, London W1R 3LF. *M.*

LONDON GAZETTE (*Official*) Room 413, HMSO Publications Centre, 51 Nine Elms Lane, London SW8 5DR. *Five times a week*

LONDON REVIEW OF BOOKS, 28–30 Little Russell Street, London WC1A 2HN. *Alt. W.*

LONDON WEEKLY ADVERTISER, 137 George Lane, London E18 1AJ. *W.*

MAJESTY, 26–28 Hallam Street, London W1N 6NP. *M.*

MARIE CLAIRE, 2 Hatfields, London SE1 9PG. *M.*

MELODY MAKER (MM), King's Reach Tower, Stamford Street, London SE1 9LS. *W.*

METEOROLOGICAL MAGAZINE, HMSO, PO Box 276, London SW8 5DT. *M.*

MIZZ, King's Reach Tower, Stamford Street, London SE1 9LS. *Alt. W.*

MODEL BOATS, Nexus House, Boundary Way, Hemel Hempstead, Herts HP2 7ST. *M.*

MONEYWISE, Berkeley Square House, Berkeley Square, London WIX 6AB. *M.*

MORE!, Victory House, 14 Leicester Place, London WC2H 7BP. *Alt. W.*

MOTHER AND BABY, Victory House, 14 Leicester Place, London WC2H 7BP. *M.*

MOTOR CYCLE NEWS, 20–22 Station Road, Kettering, Northants NN15 7HH. *W.*

MOTORING NEWS, Standard House, Bonhill Street, London EC2A 4DA. *W.*

MOTOR SPORT, Standard House, Bonhill Street, London EC2A 4DA. *M.*

MY WEEKLY, 80 Kingsway East, Dundee DD4 8SL. *W.*

NATIONAL STUDENT EXTRA, PO Box 5, Glossop, Derbys SK13 8PT. *Alt. M.*

NATURE, Porters South, Crinan Street, London NI 9XW. *W.*

NEEDLECRAFT, Beauford Court, 30 Monmouth Street, Bath BAI 2BW. *Thirteen times a year*

NEW INTERNATIONALIST, 55 Rectory Road, Oxford OX4 IBW. *M.*

NEW MUSICAL EXPRESS (NME), King's Reach Tower, Stamford Street, London SE1 9LS. *W.*

NEW SCIENTIST, King's Reach Tower, Stamford Street, London SE1 9LS. *W.*

NEW STATESMAN AND SOCIETY, Foundation House, Perseverance Works, 38 Kingsland Road, London E2 8DQ. *W.*

NEWSWEEK, 18 Park Street, London WIY 4HH. *W.*

NEW WOMAN, Victory House, 14 Leicester Place, London WC2H 7BP. *M.*

19, King's Reach Tower, Stamford Street, London SE1 9LS. *M.*

OK!, Northern and Shell Tower, City Harbour, London EI4 9GL. *M.*

THE OLDIE, 26 Charlotte Street, London WIP IHJ. *Alt. W.*

OPERA, IA Mountgrove Road, London N5 2LU. *M.*

OPERA NOW, 241 Shaftesbury Avenue, London WC2H 8EH. *Alt. M.*

OPTIONS, King's Reach Tower, Stamford Street, London SE1 9LS. *M.*

OUR DOGS, 5 Oxford Road, Station Approach, Manchester M60 ISX. *W.*

PARENTS, Victory House, 14 Leicester Place, London WC2H 7BP. *M.*

PARLIAMENTARY DEBATES (COMMONS) (Hansard), HMSO, PO Box 276, London SW8 5DT. *Daily or weekly during parliamentary session*

PARLIAMENTARY DEBATES (LORDS) (Hansard), HMSO, PO Box 276, London SW8 5DT. *Daily or weekly during parliamentary session*

PC USER, Greater London House, Hampstead Road, London NWI 7QZ. *Alt. W.*

PEOPLE'S FRIEND, 80 Kingsway East, Dundee DD4 8SL. *W.*

POETRY REVIEW, 22 Betterton Street, London WC2H 9BU. *Q.*

PONY, Haslemere House, Lower Street, Haslemere, Surrey GU27 2PE. *M.*

PRACTICAL BOAT OWNER, Westover House, West Quay Road, Poole, Dorset BHI5 IJG. *M.*

PRACTICAL CARAVAN, 60 Waldegrave Road, Teddington, Middx TWII 8LG. *M.*

PRACTICAL GARDENING, Apex House, Oundle Road, Peterborough PE2 9NP. *M.*

THE PRACTICAL HOUSEHOLDER AND NEW DIY, Nexus House, Azalea Drive, Swanley, Kent BR8 8HY. *M.*

PRACTICAL PARENTING, King's Reach Tower, Stamford Street, London SE1 9LS. *M.*

PRACTICAL PHOTOGRAPHY, Apex House, Oundle Road, Peterborough PE2 9NP. *M.*

PRIMA, 9th Floor, Portland House, Stag Place, London SWIE 5AU. *M.*

PRIVATE EYE, 6 Carlisle Street, London WIV 5RG. *Alt. W.*

PROGRESS (*Braille type*), RNIB, Technical Consumer Services Division, Orton Southgate, Peterborough PE2 OXU. *M.*

THE PUZZLER, Glenthorne House, Hammersmith Grove, London W6 OLG. *M.*

Q, Mappin House, 4 Winsley Street, London WIN 7AR. *M.*

THE RACING CALENDAR, British Horseracing Board Publications, c/o Weatherbys International Services, Sanders Road, Wellingborough, Northants NN8 4BX. *W.*

RADIO TIMES, Woodlands, 80 Wood Lane, London WI2 OTT. *W.*

RAILWAY MAGAZINE, King's Reach Tower, Stamford Street, London SE1 9LS. *M.*

RAILWAY MODELLER, Peco Publications, Beer, Seaton, Devon EXI2 3NA. *M.*

READER'S DIGEST, Berkeley Square House, Berkeley Square, London WIX 6AB. *M.*

RIDING, Corner House, Foston, Grantham, Lincs NG32 2JU. *M.*

RUGBY LEAGUER, Martland Mill, Martland Mill Lane, Wigan, Lancs WN5 OLX. *W.*

RUGBY WORLD AND POST, Weirbank, Bray on Thames, Maidenhead, Berks SL6 2ED. *M.*

SCOTS MAGAZINE, 2 Albert Square, Dundee DDI 9QJ. *M.*

SCOTTISH FIELD, PO Box 1, Oban, Argyll PA34 5PY. *M.*

SCOUTING, Baden-Powell House, Queen's Gate, London SW7 5JS. *M.*

SEA ANGLER, Bretton Court, Bretton, Peterborough PE3 8DZ. *M.*

SHE, National Magazine House, 72 Broadwick Street, London WIV 2BP. *M.*

SHOOT, King's Reach Tower, Stamford Street, London SE1 9LS. *W.*

SHOOTING TIMES AND COUNTRY MAGAZINE, King's Reach Tower, Stamford Street, London SE1 9LS. *W.*

SKY MAGAZINE, 5th Floor, Mappin House, 4 Winsley Street, London WIN 7AR. *M.*

SLIMMING MAGAZINE, Victory House, 14 Leicester Place, London WC2H 7BP. *Ten times a year*

SMASH HITS, 5th Floor, Mappin House, 4 Winsley Street, London WIN 7AR. *Alt. W.*

THE SPECTATOR, 56 Doughty Street, London WCIN 2LL. *W.*

THE STRAD, 7 St John's Road, Harrow, Middx HAI 2EE. *M.*

TATLER, Vogue House, Hanover Square, London WIR OAD. *Ten times a year*

TENNIS WORLD, The Spendlove Centre, Enstone Road, Charlbury, Oxford OX7 3PQ. *M.*

THIS ENGLAND, Alma House, 73 Rodney Road, Cheltenham, Glos GL50 IYQ. *Q.*

TIME INTERNATIONAL, Brettenham House, Lancaster Place, London WC2E 7TL. *W.*

TIME OUT, Universal House, 251 Tottenham Court Road, London WIP OAB. *W.*

THE TIMES EDUCATIONAL SUPPLEMENT, Admiral House, 66–68 East Smithfield, London EI 9XY. *W.*

THE TIMES HIGHER EDUCATION SUPPLEMENT, Admiral House, 66–68 East Smithfield, London EI 9XY. *W.*

THE TIMES LITERARY SUPPLEMENT, Admiral House, 66–68 East Smithfield, London EI 9XY. *W.*

TRIBUNE, 308 Gray's Inn Road, London WCIX 8DY. *W.*

TROUT AND SALMON, Bretton Court, Bretton, Peterborough PE3 8DZ. *M.*

TV TIMES, King's Reach Tower, Stamford Street, London SE1 9LS. *W.*

VACHER'S PARLIAMENTARY COMPANION, 113 High Street, Berkhamsted, Herts HP4 2DJ. *Q.*

VANITY FAIR, Vogue House, Hanover Square, London WIR OAD. *M.*

Viz Magazine, The Boat House, Crabtree Lane, London sw6 6lu. *Alt. M.*

Vogue, Vogue House, Hanover Square, London wir oad. *M.*

Vox, King's Reach Tower, Stamford Street, London se1 9ls. *M.*

Weather, 104 Oxford Road, Reading rg1 7ll. *M.*

Welsh Nation, 51 Cathedral Road, Cardiff cf1 9hd. *Twice a year*

Which?, 2 Marylebone Road, London nw1 4dx. *M.*

Woman, King's Reach Tower, Stamford Street, London se1 9ls. *W.*

Woman and Home, King's Reach Tower, Stamford Street, London se1 9ls. *M.*

Woman's Journal, King's Reach Tower, Stamford Street, London se1 9ls. *M.*

Woman's Own, King's Reach Tower, Stamford Street, London se1 9ls. *W.*

Woman's Realm, King's Reach Tower, Stamford Street, London se1 9ls. *W.*

Woman's Weekly, King's Reach Tower, Stamford Street, London se1 9ls. *W.*

The World of Interiors, Vogue House, Hanover Square, London wir oad. *Eleven times a year*

Yachting Monthly, King's Reach Tower, Stamford Street, London se1 9ls. *M.*

TRADE, PROFESSIONAL AND ACADEMIC PERIODICALS

Alt. = Alternate; *M.* = Monthly; *Q.* = Quarterly; *W.* = Weekly

Accountancy, Institute of Chartered Accountants, 40 Bernard Street, London wc1n 1ld. *M.*

Accountancy Age, VNU House, 32–34 Broadwick Street, London w1a 2hg. *W.*

Accountants' Magazine, Institute of Chartered Accountants of Scotland, 27 Queen Street, Edinburgh eh2 1la. *Alt. M.*

The Actuary, Government Actuary's Department, 22 Kingsway, London wc2b 6le. *M.*

Agriculture and Equipment International, Yew Tree House, Horne, Horley, Surrey rh6 9jp. *Alt. M.*

Antiquaries Journal, Osney Mead, Oxford ox2 oel. *Annual*

Antique Dealer and Collectors' Guide, PO Box 805, London se10 8td. *M.*

Antiques Trade Gazette, 17 Whitcomb Street, London wc2h 7pl. *W.*

The Architects' Journal, 151 Rosebery Avenue, London ec1r 4qx. *W.*

The Architectural Review, 151 Rosebery Avenue, London ec1r 4qx. *M.*

Armed Forces Defence International, 21 Hawley Road, London nw1 8rp. *Q.*

The Author, Society of Authors, 84 Drayton Gardens, London sw10 9sb. *Q.*

Banking World (Chartered Institute of Bankers), Haymarket House, 1 Oxendon Street, London sw1y 4ee. *Alt. M.*

The Biochemist, The Biochemical Society, 59 Portland Place, London w1n 3aj. *Alt. M.*

Biologist, Institute of Biology, 20–22 Queensberry Place, London sw7 2dz. *Five times a year*

The Bookseller, 12 Dyott Street, London wc1a 1df. *W.*

Brain, Osney Mead, Oxford ox2 oel. *Alt. M.*

Brewing and Distilling International, Southbound House, 163 Burton Road, Burton-on-Trent, Staffs de14 3dp. *M.*

British Baker, Maclaren House, 19 Scarbrook Road, Croydon cr9 1qh. *W.*

British Dental Journal, BMA House, Tavistock Square, London w1h 9jr. *Alt. W.*

British Food Journal, 60–62 Toller Lane, Bradford, W. Yorks bd8 9by. *Eleven times a year*

British Jeweller, 67 Clerkenwell Road, London ec1r 5bh. *Eleven times a year*

British Journal for the Philosophy of Science, Osney Mead, Oxford ox1 oel. *Q.*

British Journal of Photography, 244–249 Temple Chambers, Temple Avenue, London ec4a odt. *W.*

British Journal of Psychiatry, Royal College of Psychiatrists, 17 Belgrave Square, London sw1x 8pg. *M.*

British Journal of Psychology, British Psychological Society, 13a Church Lane, London n2 8dx. *Q.*

The British Journal of Social Work, Osney Mead, Oxford ox2 oel. *Alt. M.*

British Medical Journal, British Medical Association, BMA House, Tavistock Square, London w1h 9jr. *W.*

British Printer, 151 Rosebery Avenue, London ec1r 4qx. *M.*

British Tax Review, South Quay Plaza, 183 Marsh Wall, London e14 9ft. *Alt. M.*

British Veterinary Journal, 24–28 Oval Road, London nw1 7dx. *Alt. M.*

Building, Builder House, 1 Millharbour, London e14 9ra. *W.*

Building Trade & Industry, 131–133 Duckmoor Road, Ashton Gate, Bristol bs3 2bh. *M.*

Business Connections, Node Court, Drivers End, Codicote, Hitchin, Herts sg4 8tr. *Q.*

Business Education Today, 128 Long Acre, London wc2e 9an. *Alt. W.*

Cabinet Maker, Miller Freeman House, Sovereign Way, Tonbridge, Kent tn9 1rw. *W.*

Campaign, 174 Hammersmith Road, London w6 7jp. *W.*

Carpet and Floorcoverings Review, Miller Freeman House, Sovereign Way, Tonbridge, Kent tn9 1rw. *Alt. W.*

Caterer and Hotelkeeper, Quadrant House, The Quadrant, Sutton, Surrey sm2 5as. *W.*

Chemist and Druggist, Miller Freeman House, Sovereign Way, Tonbridge, Kent tn9 1rw. *W.*

Chemistry and Industry, 14–15 Belgrave Square, London sw1x 8ps. *Alt. W.*

Chemistry in Britain, Royal Society of Chemistry, Burlington House, Piccadilly, London w1v obn. *M.*

Child Education, Villiers House, Clarendon Avenue, Leamington Spa, Warks cv32 5pr. *M.*

Classical Music, 241 Shaftesbury Avenue, London wc2h 8eh. *W.*

Classical Quarterly, Osney Mead, Oxford ox2 oel. *Twice a year*

Classical Review, Osney Mead, Oxford ox2 oel. *Twice a year*

Computer Weekly, Quadrant House, The Quadrant, Sutton, Surrey sm2 5as. *W.*

Computing, VNU House, 32–34 Broadwick Street, London w1a 2hg. *W.*

Construction News, 151 Rosebery Avenue, London ec1r 4qx. *W.*

Container Management, The Baltic Centre, Great West Road, Brentford, Middx tw8 9bu. *M.*

Contract Journal, Quadrant House, The Quadrant, Sutton, Surrey sm2 5as. *W.*

Control and Instrumentation, Miller Freeman House, 30 Calderwood Street, London se18 6qh. *M.*

Crafts Magazine, Crafts Council, 44a Pentonville Road, London n1 9by. *Alt. M.*

CRIMINOLOGIST, East Row, Little London, Chichester, W. Sussex PO19 1PG. *Q.*

DAIRY FARMER AND DAIRY BEEF PRODUCER, 2 Wharfedale Road, Ipswich IP1 4LG. *M.*

DAIRY INDUSTRIES INTERNATIONAL, Wilmington House, Church Hill, Wilmington, Dartford, Kent DA2 7EF. *M.*

THE DENTIST, Warman House, 20 Leas Road, Guildford, Surrey GU1 4QT. *M.*

DESIGN WEEK, St Giles House, 49–50 Poland Street, London W1V 4AX. *W.*

THE DIRECTOR, Institute of Directors, Mountbarrow House, 6–20 Elizabeth Street, London SW1W 9RB. *M.*

THE ECONOMIC JOURNAL, 108 Cowley Road, Oxford OX4 1JF. *Alt. M.*

EDUCATION, 128 Long Acre, London WC2E 9AN. *W.*

ELECTRICAL AND RADIO TRADING, Quadrant House, The Quadrant, Sutton, Surrey SM2 5AS. *W.*

ELECTRICAL REVIEW, Quadrant House, The Quadrant, Sutton, Surrey SM2 5AS. *Alt. W.*

ELECTRICAL TIMES, Quadrant House, The Quadrant, Sutton, Surrey SM2 5AS. *Eleven times a year*

ELECTRONIC ENGINEERING, Miller Freeman House, 30 Calderwood Street, London SE18 6QH. *M.*

ENERGY MANAGEMENT, 19 Scarbrook Road, Croydon, Surrey CR9 1QH. *Alt. M.*

THE ENGINEER, Miller Freeman House, 30 Calderwood Street, London SE18 6QH. *W.*

ENGINEERING, Chester Court, High Street, Knowle, Solihull, W. Midlands B93 0LL. *Eleven times a year*

THE ENGLISH HISTORICAL REVIEW, Longman House, Edinburgh Gate, Harlow, Essex CM20 2JE. *Five times a year*

ENGLISH TODAY, Cambridge University Press, The Edinburgh Building, Shaftesbury Road, Cambridge CB2 2RU. *Q.*

THE ENVIRONMENTALIST, 2–6 Boundary Row, London SE1 8HN. *Q.*

EQUITY JOURNAL, Guild House, Upper St Martin's Lane, London WC2H 9EG. *Q.*

ESTATES GAZETTE, 151 Wardour Street, London W1V 4BN. *W.*

FAIRPLAY INTERNATIONAL SHIPPING WEEKLY, 20 Ullswater Crescent, Ullswater Business Park, Coulsdon, Surrey CR5 2HR. *W.*

FARMERS WEEKLY, Quadrant House, The Quadrant, Sutton, Surrey SM2 5AS. *W.*

FASHION WEEKLY, 67 Clerkenwell Road, London EC1R 5BH. *W.*

FIRE, Queensway House, 2 Queensway, Redhill, Surrey RH1 1QS. *M.*

FIRE PREVENTION, Fire Protection Association, Melrose Avenue, Borehamwood, Herts WD6 2BJ. *Ten times a year*

FISH, Institute of Fisheries Management, 151 Cove Road, Farnborough, Hants GU1 4HQ. *Q.*

FISH TRADER, Queensway House, 2 Queensway, Redhill, Surrey RH1 1QS. *M.*

FLIGHT INTERNATIONAL, Quadrant House, The Quadrant, Sutton, Surrey SM2 5AS. *W.*

FOOD TRADE REVIEW, Station House, Hortons Way, Westerham, Kent TN16 1BZ. *M.*

FORESTRY AND BRITISH TIMBER, Miller Freeman House, Sovereign Way, Tonbridge, Kent TN9 1RW. *M.*

FOUNDRY TRADE JOURNAL, Queensway House, 2 Queensway, Redhill, Surrey RH1 1QS. *Alt. W.*

FROZEN AND CHILLED FOODS, Queensway House, 2 Queensway, Redhill, Surrey RH1 1QS. *M.*

FUEL, The Boulevard, Langford Lane, Kidlington, Oxford OX5 1GB. *M.*

GARDEN TRADE NEWS, Apex House, Oundle Road, Peterborough PE2 9NP. *Eight times a year*

GAS WORLD INTERNATIONAL, PO Box 105, 25–31 Ironmonger Row, London EC1 VPN. *Q.*

GEOGRAPHY, Geographical Association, 343 Fulwood Road, Sheffield S10 3BP. *Q.*

GEOLOGICAL MAGAZINE, Cambridge University Press, The Edinburgh Building, Shaftesbury Road, Cambridge CB2 2RU. *Alt. M.*

GLASS AND GLAZING PRODUCTS, Maclaren House, 19 Scarbrook Road, Croydon CR9 1QH. *M.*

GREECE AND ROME, Osney Mead, Oxford OX2 0EL. *Twice a year*

THE GROCER, Broadfield Park, Crawley, W. Sussex RH11 9RT. *W.*

GROWER, Nexus House, Azalea Drive, Swanley, Kent BR8 8HY. *W.*

HAIRDRESSERS' JOURNAL INTERNATIONAL, Quadrant House, The Quadrant, Sutton, Surrey SM2 5AS. *W.*

THE HEALTH SERVICE JOURNAL, Porters South, 4–6 Crinan Street, London N1 9SQ. *W.*

HEALTH VISITOR, BMA House, Tavistock Square, London WC1H 9JR. *M.*

HEATING, VENTILATING AND PLUMBING, PO Box 13, Hereford House, Bridle Path, Croydon, Surrey CR9 4NL. *M.*

HISTORY TODAY, 20 Old Compton Street, London W1V 5PE. *M.*

INDEPENDENT RETAILER, Alliance House, 14 Pierpoint Street, Worcester WR1 1TA. *M.*

INDUSTRIAL EXCHANGE AND MART, Link House, West Street, Poole, Dorset BH1 5LL. *W.*

INDUSTRIAL RELATIONS JOURNAL, 108 Cowley Road, Oxford OX4 1JF. *Alt. M.*

INTERNATIONAL AFFAIRS, Cambridge University Press, The Edinburgh Building, Shaftesbury Road, Cambridge CB2 2RU. *Q.*

JANE'S INFORMATION WEEKLY, Sentinel House, 163 Brighton Road, Coulsdon, Surrey CR5 2NH. *W.*

THE JOURNALIST, National Union of Journalists, Acorn House, 314 Gray's Inn Road, London WC1X 8DP. *Alt. M.*

JOURNAL OF ALTERNATIVE AND COMPLEMENTARY MEDICINE, 9 Rickett Street, London SW6 1RU. *M.*

JOURNAL OF THE BRITISH ASTRONOMICAL ASSOCIATION, Burlington House, Piccadilly, London W1V 9AG. *Alt. M.*

JOURNAL OF THE CHEMICAL SOCIETY, Thomas Graham House, Science Park, Milton Road, Cambridge CB4 4WF. *Irregular*

JUSTICE OF THE PEACE REPORTS, East Row, Little London, Chichester, W. Sussex PO19 1PG. *Alt. W.*

THE LANCET, 42 Bedford Square, London WC1B 3SL. *W.*

LAW QUARTERLY REVIEW, South Quay Plaza, 183 Marsh Wall, London E14 9FT. *Q.*

THE LAW REPORTS, 3 Stone Buildings, Lincoln's Inn, London WC2A 3XN. *M.*

LAW SOCIETY'S GAZETTE, 50 Chancery Lane, London WC2A 1SX. *W.*

LEATHER, Miller Freeman House, Sovereign Way, Tonbridge, Kent TN9 1RW. *M.*

LIBRARY ASSOCIATION RECORD, 7 Ridgmount Street, London WC1 EAE. *M.*

LLOYD'S LOADING LIST, Collwyn House, Sheepen Place, Colchester, Essex CO3 3LP. *W.*

LLOYD'S SHIPPING INDEX, Collwyn House, Sheepen Place, Colchester, Essex CO3 3LP. *W.*

LOCAL GOVERNMENT CHRONICLE, 33–39 Bowling Green Lane, London EC1 RDA. *W.*

MACHINERY AND PRODUCTION ENGINEERING, Franks Hall, Franks Lane, Horton Kirby, Dartford, Kent DA4 9LL. *Alt. M.*

MACHINERY MARKET, 6 Blyth Road, Bromley, Kent BR1 3RX. *W.*

MANAGEMENT ACCOUNTING, Chartered Institute of Management Accountants, 63 Portland Place, London WIN 4AB. *M.*

MANAGEMENT TODAY, 22 Lancaster Gate, London W2 3LY. *M.*

MANUFACTURING CHEMIST, Miller Freeman House, 30 Calderwood Street, London SE18 6QH. *M.*

MARKETING, 174 Hammersmith Road, London W6 7JP. *W.*

MARKETING WEEK, St Giles House, 49–50 Poland Street, London WIV 4AX. *W.*

MATERIALS RECYCLING WEEKLY, Maclaren House, 19 Scarbrook Road, Croydon, Surrey CR9 1QH. *W.*

MATERIALS WORLD, Institute of Materials, 1 Carlton House Terrace, London SW1 YDB. *M.*

MEAT TRADES' JOURNAL, Maclaren House, 19 Scarbrook Road, Croydon, Surrey CR9 1QH. *W.*

MEDIA WEEK, 33–39 Bowling Green Lane, London ECI RDA. *W.*

METALS INDUSTRY NEWS, Queensway House, 2 Queensway, Redhill, Surrey RHI 1QS. *Q.*

MIND, Osney Mead, Oxford OX2 OEL. *Q.*

MINING JOURNAL, 60 Worship Street, London EC2A 2HD. *W.*

MOTOR TRANSPORT, Quadrant House, The Quadrant, Sutton, Surrey SM2 5AS. *W.*

MUNICIPAL JOURNAL, 32 Vauxhall Bridge Road, London SW1 VSS. *W.*

MUNICIPAL REVIEW AND AMA NEWS, 35 Great Smith Street, London SW1 PBJ. *Ten times a year*

MUSEUMS JOURNAL, Museums Association, 42 Clerkenwell Close, London ECI RPA. *M.*

THE MUSICAL TIMES, 7 St John's Road, Harrow, Middx HAI 2EE. *M.*

MUSIC AND LETTERS, Osney Mead, Oxford OX2 OEL. *Q.*

MUSIC WEEK, 8th Floor, Ludgate House, 245 Blackfriars Road, London SE1 9UR. *W.*

NOTES AND QUERIES, Osney Mead, Oxford OX2 OEL. *Q.*

NUCLEAR ENGINEERING INTERNATIONAL, Quadrant House, The Quadrant, Sutton, Surrey SM2 5AS. *M.*

NURSING TIMES, Porters South, Crinan Street, London NI 9SQ. *W.*

OFF-LICENCE NEWS, Broadfield Park, Crawley, W. Sussex RHII 9RT. *W.*

OPTICIAN, Quadrant House, The Quadrant, Sutton, Surrey SM2 5AS. *W.*

OPTOMETRY TODAY, Association of Optometrists, 233–234 Blackfriars Road, London SE1 8NW. *Alt. W.*

PACKAGING WEEK, Miller Freeman House, Sovereign Way, Tonbridge, Kent TN9 IRW. *W.*

PC PLUS, Beauford Court, Kingsgate House, 536 Kings Road, London OTE. *M.*

PERSONAL COMPUTER WORLD, VNU House, 32–34 Broadwick Street, London WIA 2HG. *M.*

PERSONNEL MANAGEMENT, Institute of Personnel Management, 17 Britton Street, London ECIM 5NQ. *M.*

PHARMACEUTICAL JOURNAL, Royal Pharmaceutical Society of Great Britain, 1 Lambeth High Street, London SE1 7JN. *W.*

PHILOSOPHY, (Royal Institute of Philosophy), Cambridge University Press, The Edinburgh Building, Shaftesbury Road, Cambridge CB2 2RU. *Q.*

THE PHOTOGRAPHER, British Institute of Professional Photography, Fox Talbot House, Amwell End, Ware, Herts SG12 9HN. *M.*

PHYSICS WORLD, Techno House, Redcliffe Way, Bristol BSI 6NX. *M.*

PLUMBING AND HEATING NEWS, Peterson House, Northbank, Berryhill Industrial Estate, Droitwich, Worcs WR9 9BL. *M.*

POLICE REVIEW, South Quay Plaza 2, 183 Marsh Wall, London E14 9FS. *W.*

THE PRACTITIONER, Miller Freeman House, 30 Calderwood Street, London SE18 6QH. *M.*

PRINTING WORLD, Miller Freeman House, Sovereign Way, Tonbridge, Kent TN9 IRW. *W.*

PROBATION JOURNAL, National Association of Probation Officers, 3–4 Chivalry Road, London SW1 IHT. *Q.*

PROFESSIONAL CARE OF MOTHER AND CHILD, PO Box 100, Chichester, W. Sussex PO19 IXR. *Ten times a year*

THE PSYCHOLOGIST, The British Psychological Society, St Andrews House, 48 Princess Road East, Leicester LEI 7DR. *M.*

PULP AND PAPER (EUROPE), Miller Freeman House, Sovereign Way, Tonbridge, Kent TN9 IRW. *Ten times a year*

QUARRY MANAGEMENT, 7 Regent Street, Nottingham NGI 5BY. *M.*

RAILWAY GAZETTE INTERNATIONAL, Quadrant House, The Quadrant, Sutton, Surrey SM2 5AS. *M.*

RATING & VALUATION REPORTER, 4 Breams Buildings, London EC4 AAQ. *M.*

RETAIL NEWSAGENT, Robert Taylor House, 11 Angel Gate, City Road, London ECIV 2PT. *W.*

RETAIL WEEK, Maclaren House, PO Box 109, Croydon CR9 1QH. *W.*

THE REVIEW OF ENGLISH STUDIES, Osney Mead, Oxford OXI OEL. *Q.*

RUSI JOURNAL, Royal United Services Institute for Defence Studies, Whitehall, London SW1 AET. *Alt. M.*

SHIPPING WORLD & SHIPBUILDER, 4 Hubbard Road, Houndsmill, Basingstoke, Hants RG21 2UH. *M.*

SHOE & LEATHER NEWS, 67 Clerkenwell Road, London ECIR 5BH. *M.*

SMALLHOLDER, High Street, Stoke Ferry, King's Lynn, Norfolk PE3 3SF. *M.*

SOCIOLOGICAL REVIEW, 108 Cowley Road, Oxford OX4 IJF. *Q.*

SOLICITORS' JOURNAL, 21–27 Lamb's Conduit Street, London WCIN 3NJ. *W.*

SPORTS TRADER, Nexus House, Azalea Drive, Swanley, Kent BR8 8HY. *M.*

THE STAGE AND TELEVISION TODAY, Stage House, 47 Bermondsey Street, London SE1 3XT. *W.*

THE STRUCTURAL ENGINEER, 11 Upper Belgrave Street, London SWIX 8BH. *Alt. W.*

THE SURVEYOR, 32 Vauxhall Bridge Road, London SW1 VSS. *W.*

TAXATION PRACTITIONER, (Chartered Institute of Taxation), Tolley House, 2 Addiscombe Road, Croydon, Surrey CR9 5AF. *M.*

TAXI, Licensed Taxi Drivers' Association, Taxi House, 7–11 Woodfield Road, London W9 2BA. *Alt. W.*

THE TEACHER, National Union of Teachers, Hamilton House, Mabledon Place, London WCI HBD. *Eight times a year*

TEACHING HISTORY, 59A Kennington Park Road, London SEII 4JH. *Q.*

TELEVISION, Royal Television Society, Holborn Hall, 100 Gray's Inn Road, London WCI XAL. *Eight times a year*

TEXTILE HORIZONS, 8 De Montfort Street, Leicester LEI 7GA. *M.*

TEXTILE MONTH, 76 Kirkgate, Bradford, W. Yorks BDI ITB. *M.*

TOBACCO, Queensway House, 2 Queensway, Redhill, Surrey RHI 1QS. *Alt. M.*

TOWN AND COUNTRY PLANNING, Town and Country Planning Association, 17 Carlton House Terrace, London SWIY 5AS. *M.*

TOWN PLANNING REVIEW, Liverpool University Press,
Senate House, Liverpool L69 3BX. *Q.*
TOY TRADER, Turret House, 171–173 High Street,
Rickmansworth, Herts WD3 ISN. *M.*
TRADE MARKS JOURNAL, Patent Office, 25 Southampton
Buildings, London WC2A 1AY. *W.*
THE TRADER, Link House, West Street, Poole, Dorset
BH1 5LL. *M.*
TRAVEL TRADE GAZETTE (UK & IRELAND), Miller
Freeman House, 30 Calderwood Street, London SE18
6QH. *W.*
TTJ-TIMBER TRADES JOURNAL, Miller Freeman House,
Sovereign Way, Tonbridge, Kent TN9 1RW. *W.*
UK PRESS GAZETTE, 33–39 Bowling Green Lane, London
EC1R ODA. *W.*
WEEKLY LAW REPORTS, 3 Stone Buildings, Lincoln's Inn,
London WC2A 3XN. *W.*
WOODCARVING, Castle Place, 166 High Street, Lewes,
E. Sussex BN7 1XU. *Ten times a year*
WORLD'S FAIR, 2 Daltry Street, Oldham, Lancs OL1 4BB. *W.*

NEWS AGENCIES IN LONDON

News agencies provide general, business, sport and
television news to a variety of subscribers including the
press, other media, and industrial, commercial, financial
and business users.

THE ASSOCIATED PRESS LTD (AP), 12 Norwich Street,
London EC4A 4BP. Tel: 0171-353 1515
CENTRAL PRESS FEATURES LTD, 20 Spectrum House,
32–34 Gordon House Road, London NW5 1LP. Tel: 0171-
284 1433
EXTEL FINANCIAL LTD, Fitzroy House, 13–17 Epworth
Street, London EC2 ADL. Tel: 0171-825 8000
HAYTERS, 146–148 Clerkenwell Road, London EC1R 5DP.
Tel: 0171-837 7171
PARLIAMENTARY AND EEC NEWS SERVICE, 19 Douglas
Street, London SW1P 4PA. Tel: 0171-233 8283
THE PRESS ASSOCIATION, 292 Vauxhall Bridge Road,
London SW1V 1AE. Tel: 0171-963 7000
REUTERS LTD, 85 Fleet Street, London EC4P 4AJ. Tel:
0171-250 1122
TWO-TEN COMMUNICATIONS LTD, 210 Old Street,
London EC1 VUN. Tel: 0171-490 8111
UNITED PRESS INTERNATIONAL (UK) LTD,
2 Greenwich View, Millharbour, London E14 9NN. Tel:
0171-538 0932

Book Publishers

More than 15,000 firms, individuals and societies have published one or more books in recent years. The list which follows is a selective one comprising those firms whose names are most familiar to the general public. A fuller list, *Whitaker Directory of Publishers*, containing some 3,000 names and addresses is published annually in March by the publishers of *Whitaker's Almanack*.

ADDISON-WESLEY PUBLISHERS, Finchampstead Road, Wokingham, Berks RG11 2NZ. Tel: 01734-794000

ALLAN (IAN), Coombelands House, Coombelands Lane, Addlestone, Surrey KT15 1HY. Tel: 01932-855909

ALLEN (J. A.), 1 Lower Grosvenor Place, London SW1W 0EL. Tel: 0171-834 0090

ALLISON & BUSBY, 179 King's Cross Road, London WC1X 9BZ. Tel: 0171-833 1042

APPLE PRESS, 6 Blundell Street, London N7 9BH. Tel: 0171-700 8521/7

ARMADA BOOKS, 77 Fulham Palace Road, London W6 8JB. Tel: 0181-741 7070

ARMS & ARMOUR PRESS, 125 Strand, London WC2R 0BB. Tel: 0171-420 5555

ARNOLD, 338 Euston Road, London NW1 3BH. Tel: 0171-873 6000

ARROW BOOKS, 20 Vauxhall Bridge Road, London SW1V 2SA. Tel: 0171-973 9700

ATHLONE PRESS, 1 Park Drive, London NW11 7SG. Tel: 0181-458 0888

AURUM PRESS, 25 Bedford Avenue, London WC1B 3AT. Tel: 0171-637 3225

AUTOMOBILE ASSOCIATION, Norfolk House, Priestly Road, Basingstoke, Hants RG24 9NY. Tel: 01256-491524

BAILLIÈRE TINDALL, 24 Oval Road, London NW1 7DX. Tel: 0171-267 4466

BANTAM BOOKS, 61 Uxbridge Road, London W5 5SA. Tel: 0181-579 2652

BARRIE & JENKINS, 20 Vauxhall Bridge Road, London SW1V 2SA. Tel: 0171-973 9690

BARTHOLOMEW, 77 Fulham Palace Road, London W6 8JB. Tel: 0181-741 7070

BATSFORD (B. T.), 4 Fitzhardinge Street, London W1H 0AH. Tel: 0171-486 8484

BBC BOOKS, 80 Wood Lane, London W12 0TT. Tel: 0181-576 2570

BLACK (A. & C.), 35 Bedford Row, London WC1R 4JH. Tel: 0171-242 0946

BLACKIE CHILDREN'S BOOKS, 27 Wrights Lane, London W8 5TZ. Tel: 0171-416 3000

BLACKWELL PUBLISHERS, 108 Cowley Road, Oxford OX4 1JF. Tel: 01865-791100

BLANDFORD PRESS, 125 Strand, London WC2R 0BB. Tel: 0171-420 5555

BLOOMSBURY PUBLISHING, 2 Soho Square, London W1V 6HB. Tel: 0171-494 2111

BODLEY HEAD, 20 Vauxhall Bridge Road, London SW1V 2SA. Tel: 0171-973 9730

BOXTREE, 21 Broadwall, London SE1 9PL. Tel: 0171-928 9696

BOYARS (MARION), 24 Lacy Road, London SW15 1NL. Tel: 0181-788 9522

BRIMAX BOOKS, 4 Studlands Park Industrial Estate, Exning Road, Newmarket, Suffolk CB8 7AU. Tel: 01638-664611

BRITISH MUSEUM PRESS, 46 Bloomsbury Street, London WC1B 3QQ. Tel: 0171-323 1234

BUTTERWORTH & Co., 35 Chancery Lane, London WC2A 1ER. Tel: 0171-400 2500

CADOGAN BOOKS, London House, Parkgate Road, London SW11 4NQ. Tel: 0171-738 1961

CALDER PUBLICATIONS, 179 King's Cross Road, London WC1X 9BZ. Tel: 0171-833 1300

CAMBRIDGE UNIVERSITY PRESS, The Edinburgh Building, Cambridge CB2 2RU. Tel: 01223-312393

CANONGATE BOOKS, 14 High Street, Edinburgh EH1 1TE. Tel: 0131-557 5111

CAPE (JONATHAN), 20 Vauxhall Bridge Road, London SW1V 2SA. Tel: 0171-973 9730

CASSELL, 125 Strand, London WC2R 0BB. Tel: 0171-420 5555

CAVENDISH PUBLISHING, The Glass House, Wharton Street, London WC1X 9PX. Tel: 0171-278 8000

CENTURY PUBLISHING Co., *see* Random House UK

CHAMBERS, 24 Great Titchfield Street, London, W1P 7AD. Tel: 0171-631 0878

CHANCELLOR PRESS, 81 Fulham Road, London SW3 6RB. Tel: 0171-581 9393

CHAPMAN & HALL, 2 Boundary Row, London SE1 8HN. Tel: 0171-865 0066

CHAPMAN (GEOFFREY), 125 Strand, London WC2R 0BB. Tel: 0171-420 5555

CHAPMANS PUBLISHERS, 5 Upper St Martin's Lane, London WC2H 9EA. Tel: 0171-240 3444

CHATTO & WINDUS, 20 Vauxhall Bridge Road, London SW1V 2SA. Tel: 0171-973 9740

CHIVERS PRESS, Windsor Bridge Road, Bath BA2 3AX. Tel: 01225-335336

CHURCH HOUSE PUBLISHING, Church House, Great Smith Street, London SW1P 3NZ. Tel: 0171-222 9011

CHURCHILL LIVINGSTONE, 1–3 Baxter's Place, Leith Walk, Edinburgh EH1 3AF. Tel: 0131-556 2424

COLLINS (WILLIAM), *see* HarperCollins Publishers

CONSTABLE & Co., 3 The Lanchesters, 162 Fulham Palace Road, London W6 9ER. Tel: 0181-741 3663

CONSUMERS' ASSOCIATION, *see* Which? Books

CORGI BOOKS, 61 Uxbridge Road, London W5 5SA. Tel: 0181-579 2652

CROWOOD PRESS, The Stable Block, Crowood Lane, Ramsbury, Marlborough, Wilts SN8 2HR. Tel: 01672-520320

DARTON, LONGMAN & TODD, 1 Spencer Court, 140 Wandsworth High Street, London SW18 4JJ. Tel: 0181-875 0134

DAVID & CHARLES, Brunel House, Newton Abbot, Devon TQ12 4PU. Tel: 01626-61121

DEAN & SON, 81 Fulham Road, London SW3 6RB. Tel: 0171-581 9393

DENT (J. M.) & SONS, 5 Upper St Martin's Lane, London WC2H 9EA. Tel: 0171-240 3444

DEUTSCH (ANDRE), 106 Great Russell Street, London WC1B 3LJ. Tel: 0171-580 2746

DORLING KINDERSLEY, 9 Henrietta Street, London WC2E 8PS. Tel: 0171-836 5411

DOUBLEDAY, 61 Uxbridge Road, London W5 5SA. Tel: 0181-579 2652

DUCKWORTH & Co., 48 Hoxton Square, London N1 6PB. Tel: 0171-729 5986

EBURY PRESS, 20 Vauxhall Bridge Road, London SW1V 2SA. Tel: 0171-973 9690

ELEMENT BOOKS, The Old School House, The Courtyard, Bell Street, Shaftesbury, Dorset SP7 8BP. Tel: 01747-851448

ELLIOT RIGHT WAY BOOKS, Kingswood Building, Kingswood, Tadworth, Surrey KT20 6TD. Tel: 01737-832202

ELSEVIER SCIENCE, The Boulevard, Langford Lane, Kidlington, Oxon OX5 1GB. Tel: 01865-843000

ENCYCLOPAEDIA BRITANNICA INTERNATIONAL, Carew House, Station Approach, Wallington, Surrey SM6 0DA. Tel: 0181-669 4355

EPWORTH PRESS, c/o SCM Press, 9-17 St Albans Place, London N1 0NX. Tel: 0171-359 8033

EVANS BROS, 2A Portman Mansions, Chiltern Street, London W1M 1LE. Tel: 0171-935 7160

EVERYMAN, see Orion Publishing Group

EVERYMAN'S LIBRARY, 79 Berwick Street, London W1V 3PF. Tel: 0171-287 0035

FABER & FABER, 3 Queen Square, London WC1N 3AU. Tel: 0171-465 0045

FLAMINGO, see HarperCollins Publishers

FONTANA, 77 Fulham Palace Road, London W6 8JB. Tel: 0181-741 7070

FOULIS (G. T.), Sparkford, Yeovil, Somerset BA22 7JJ. Tel: 01963-440635

FOULSHAM (W.) & Co., Bennetts Close, Cippenham, Slough SL1 5AP. Tel: 01753-526769

FOURTH ESTATE, 6 Salem Road, London W2 4BU. Tel: 0171-727 8993

FRENCH (SAMUEL), 52 Fitzroy Street, London W1P 6JR. Tel: 0171-387 9373

GAIA BOOKS, 20 High Street, Stroud GL5 1AS. Tel: 01453-752985

GIBBONS (STANLEY), 5 Parkside, Christchurch Road, Ringwood, Hants BH24 3SH. Tel: 01425-472363

GINN & Co., Prebendal House, Parson's Fee, Aylesbury, Bucks HP20 2QZ. Tel: 01296-394442

GOLLANCZ (VICTOR), 125 Strand, London WC2R 0BB. Tel: 0171-420 5555

GOWER PUBLISHING Co., Croft Road, Aldershot, Hants GU11 3HR. Tel: 01252-331551

GRANTA BOOKS, 2 Hanover Yard, London N1 8BE. Tel: 0171-704 9776

GUINNESS PUBLISHING, 33 London Road, Enfield, Middx EN2 6DJ. Tel: 0181-367 4567

HALE (ROBERT), 45 Clerkenwell Green, London EC1R 0HT. Tel: 0171-251 2661

HAMILTON (HAMISH), 27 Wrights Lane, London W8 5TZ. Tel: 0171-416 3000

HAMLYN (PAUL), 81 Fulham Road, London SW3 6RB. Tel: 0171-581 9393

HARCOURT BRACE, 24 Oval Road, London NW1 7DX. Tel: 0171-267 4466

HARPERCOLLINS PUBLISHERS, 77 Fulham Palace Road, London W6 8JB. Tel: 0181-741 7070

HARRAP, 24 Great Titchfield Street, London W1P 7AD. Tel: 0171-631 0878

HAYNES (J. H.), Sparkford, Yeovil, Somerset BA22 7JJ. Tel: 01963-440635

HEADLINE BOOK PUBLISHING, see Hodder Headline

HEINEMANN (WILLIAM), 81 Fulham Road, London SW3 6RB. Tel: 0171-581 9393

HERBERT PRESS, 46 Northchurch Road, London N1 4EJ. Tel: 0171-254 4379

HIPPO BOOKS, 1-19 New Oxford Street, London WC1A 1NU. Tel: 0171-421 9000

HMSO, PO Box 276, London SW8 5DT. Tel: 0171-873 0011

HODDER & STOUGHTON, see Hodder Headline

HODDER HEADLINE, 338 Euston Road, London NW1 3BH. Tel: 0171-873 6000

HOGARTH PRESS, 20 Vauxhall Bridge Road, London SW1V 2SA. Tel: 0171-973 9740

HUTCHINSON, see Random House UK

JARROLD PUBLISHING, Whitefriars, Norwich NR3 1TR. Tel: 01603-763300

JORDAN PUBLISHING, 21 St Thomas Street, Bristol BS1 6JS. Tel: 0117-923 0600

JOSEPH (MICHAEL), 27 Wrights Lane, London W8 5TZ. Tel: 0171-416 3000

KEGAN PAUL INTERNATIONAL, PO Box 256, London WC1B 3SW. Tel: 0171-580 5511

KINGFISHER BOOKS, 24 Great Titchfield Street, London W1P 7AD. Tel: 0171-631 0878

KINGSWAY PUBLICATIONS, Lottbridge Drove, Eastbourne BN23 6NT. Tel: 01323-410930

KOGAN PAGE, 120 Pentonville Road, London N1 9JN. Tel: 0171-278 0433

LADYBIRD BOOKS, Beeches Road, Loughborough LE11 2NQ. Tel: 01509-268021

LAROUSSE, 24 Great Titchfield Street, London W1P 7AD. Tel: 0171-631 0878

LASCELLES (ROGER), 47 York Road, Brentford, Middx TW8 0QP. Tel: 0181-847 0935

LAWRENCE & WISHART, 99A Wallis Road, London E9 5LN. Tel: 0181-533 2506

LENNARD PUBLISHING, Windmill Cottage, Mackerye End, Harpenden, Herts AL5 5DR. Tel: 01582-715866

LETTS OF LONDON, 24 Nutford Place, London W1H 6DQ. Tel: 0171-724 7773

LINCOLN (FRANCES), 4 Torriano Mews, Torriano Avenue, London NW5 2RZ. Tel: 0171-284 4009

LION PUBLISHING, Sandy Lane West, Oxford OX4 5HG. Tel: 01865-747550

LITTLE, BROWN & Co., Brettenham House, Lancaster Place, London WC2E 7EN. Tel: 0171-911 8000

LONGMAN, Edinburgh Gate, Harlow, Essex CM20 2JE. Tel: 01279-426721

LUND HUMPHRIES, 1 Russell Gardens, London NW11 9NN. Tel: 0181-458 6314

LUTTERWORTH PRESS, PO Box 60, Cambridge CB1 2NT. Tel: 01223-350865

MACDONALD & EVANS, 128 Long Acre, London WC2E 9AN. Tel: 0171-379 7383

MACDONALD YOUNG BOOKS, 61 Western Road, Hove, E. Sussex BN3 1JD. Tel: 01273-722561

McGRAW-HILL, Shoppenhangers Road, Maidenhead, Berks SL6 2QL. Tel: 01628-23432

MACMILLAN PUBLISHERS, 25 Eccleston Place, London SW1W 9NF. Tel: 0171-881 8000

MACRAE (JULIA), 20 Vauxhall Bridge Road, London SW1V 2SA. Tel: 0171-973 9750

MAINSTREAM PUBLISHING Co. (EDINBURGH), 7 Albany Street, Edinburgh EH1 3UG. Tel: 0131-557 2959

MAMMOTH, 81 Fulham Road, London SW3 6RB. Tel: 0171-581 9393

MANDALA, see HarperCollins Publishers

MANDARIN, 81 Fulham Road, London SW3 6RB. Tel: 0171-581 9393

METHUEN LONDON, 81 Fulham Road, London SW3 6RB. Tel: 0171-581 9393

MILLS & BOON, 18 Paradise Road, Richmond, Surrey TW9 1SR. Tel: 0181-948 0444

MINERVA PRESS, 195 Knightsbridge, London SW7 1RE. Tel: 0171-225 3113

MITCHELL BEAZLEY, 81 Fulham Road, London SW3 6RB. Tel: 0171-581 9393

MOWBRAY, 125 Strand, London WC2R 0BB. Tel: 0171-420 5555

MURRAY (JOHN), 50 Albemarle Street, London W1X 4BD. Tel: 0171-493 4361

NATIONAL CHRISTIAN EDUCATION COUNCIL, 1020 Bristol Road, Selly Oak, Birmingham B29 6LB. Tel: 0121-472 4242

NELSON (THOMAS), Mayfield Road, Walton-on-Thames KT12 5PL. Tel: 01932-252211

NEW ENGLISH LIBRARY, see Hodder Headline

NEXUS SPECIAL INTEREST, Nexus House, Boundary Way, Hemel Hempstead, Herts HP2 7ST. Tel: 01442-66551

NISBET & Co., 78 Tilehouse Street, Hitchin, Herts SG5 2DY. Tel: 01462-438331

NOVELLO & CO., 8 Frith Street, London W1V 5TZ. Tel: 0171-434 0066

OCTOPUS BOOKS, 81 Fulham Road, London SW3 6RB Tel: 0171-581 9393

OLIVER & BOYD, Edinburgh Gate, Harlow, Essex CM20 2JE. Tel: 01279-426721

O'MARA (MICHAEL) BOOKS, 9 Lion Yard, Tremadoc Road, London SW4 7NQ. Tel: 0171-720 8643

ORCHARD BOOKS, 96 Leonard Street, London EC2A 4RH. Tel: 0171-739 2929

ORION PUBLISHING GROUP, 5 Upper St Martin's Lane, London WC2H 9EA. Tel: 0171-240 3444

OWEN (PETER), 73 Kenway Road, London SW5 0RE. Tel: 0171-373 5628

OXFORD UNIVERSITY PRESS, Walton Street, Oxford OX2 6DP. Tel: 01865-56767

PAN BOOKS, 25 Eccleston Place, London SW1W 9NF. Tel: 0171-881 8000

PAVILION BOOKS, 26 Upper Ground, London SE1 9PD. Tel: 0171-620 1666

PELHAM BOOKS, 27 Wrights Lane, London W8 5TZ. Tel: 0171-416 3000

PENGUIN BOOKS, 27 Wrights Lane, London W8 5TZ. Tel: 0171-416 3000

PERGAMON PRESS, The Boulevard, Langford Lane, Kidlington, Oxon OX5 1GB. Tel: 01865-843000

PHAIDON PRESS, Regent's Wharf, All Saints Street, London N1 9PA. Tel: 0171-843 1000

PHILIP (GEORGE), 81 Fulham Road, London SW3 6RB. Tel: 0171-581 9393

PIATKUS BOOKS, 5 Windmill Street, London W1P 1HF. Tel: 0171-631 0710

PICADOR, see Pan Books

PICCADILLY PRESS, 5 Castle Road, London NW1 8PR. Tel: 0171-267 4492

PINTER PUBLISHERS, 125 Strand, London WC2R 0BB. Tel: 0171-420 5555

PITKIN PICTORIALS, Healey House, Dene Road, Andover, Hants SP10 2AA. Tel: 01264-334303

PITMAN PUBLISHING, 128 Long Acre, London WC2E 9AN. Tel: 0171-379 7383

QUARTET BOOKS, 27 Goodge Street, London W1P 2LD. Tel: 0171-636 3992

QUILLER PRESS, 46 Lillie Road, London SW6 1TN. Tel: 0171-499 6529

RANDOM HOUSE UK, 20 Vauxhall Bridge Road, London SW1V 2SA. Tel: 0171-973 9000

READER'S DIGEST, 25 Berkeley Square, London W1X 6AB. Tel: 0171-629 8144

RELIGIOUS & MORAL EDUCATION PRESS, St Mary's Works, St Mary's Plain, Norwich NR3 3BH. Tel: 01603-615995

ROUGH GUIDES, 1 Mercer Street, London WC2H 9QJ. Tel: 0171-379 3329

ROUTLEDGE, 11 New Fetter Lane, London EC4P 4EE. Tel: 0171-583 9855

ST ANDREW PRESS, 121 George Street, Edinburgh EH2 4YN. Tel: 0131-225 5722

SCM PRESS, 9-17 St Albans Place, London N1 0NX. Tel: 0171-359 8033

SCRIPTURE UNION, 207-209 Queensway, Bletchley, Milton Keynes, MK2 2EB. Tel: 01908-856000

SECKER & WARBURG, 81 Fulham Road, London SW3 6RB. Tel: 0171-581 9393

SERPENT'S TAIL PUBLISHING, 4 Blackstock Mews, London N4 2BT. Tel: 0171-354 1949

SEVERN HOUSE, 9 Sutton High Street, Sutton SM1 1DF. Tel: 0181-770 3930

SHELDON PRESS, Holy Trinity Church, Marylebone Road, London NW1 4DU. Tel: 0171-387 5282

SIDGWICK & JACKSON, 25 Eccleston Place, London SW1W 9NF. Tel: 0171-881 8000

SIMON & SCHUSTER, Campus 400, Maylands Avenue, Hemel Hempstead, Herts HP2 7EZ. Tel: 01442-881900

SINCLAIR-STEVENSON, 81 Fulham Road, London SW3 6RB. Tel: 0171-581 9393

SOUVENIR PRESS, 43 Great Russell Street, London WC1B 3PA. Tel: 0171-580 9307

SPCK, Holy Trinity Church, Marylebone Road, London NW1 4DU. Tel: 0171-387 5282

SPON (E. & F. N.), 2 Boundary Row, London SE1 8HN. Tel: 0171-865 0066

STEPHENS (PATRICK), Sparkford, Yeovil BA22 7JJ. Tel: 01963-440635

SUTTON PUBLISHING, Phoenix Mill, Far Thrupp, Stroud, Glos GL5 2BU. Tel: 01453-731114

SWEET & MAXWELL, 100 Avenue Road, London NW3 3PS. Tel: 0171-393 7000

THAMES & HUDSON, 30 Bloomsbury Street, London WC1B 3QP. Tel: 0171-636 5488

THORNES (STANLEY) (PUBLISHERS), Ellenborough House, Wellington Street, Cheltenham, Glos GL50 1YD. Tel: 01242-228888

THORSONS, 77 Fulham Palace Road, London W6 8JB. Tel: 0181-741 7070

TIMES BOOKS, 77 Fulham Palace Road, London W6 8JB. Tel: 0181-741 7070

UNIVERSITY OF WALES PRESS, 6 Gwennyth Street, Cardiff CF2 4YD. Tel: 01222-231919

USBORNE PUBLISHING, Usborne House, 83-85 Saffron Hill, London EC1N 8RT. Tel: 0171-430 2800

VIKING, 27 Wrights Lane, London W8 5TZ. Tel: 0171-416 3000

VIRAGO PRESS, 20 Vauxhall Bridge Road, London SW1V 2SA. Tel: 0171-973 9750

VIRGIN PUBLISHING, 33-34 Grand Union Centre, 332 Ladbroke Grove, London W10 5AH. Tel: 0181-968 7554

WALKER BOOKS, 87 Vauxhall Walk, London SE11 5HJ. Tel: 0171-793 0909

WARD LOCK, 125 Strand, London WC2R 0BB. Tel: 0171-420 5555

WARD LOCK EDUCATIONAL CO., 1 Christopher Road, East Grinstead, W. Sussex RH19 3BT. Tel: 01342-318980

WARNE (FREDERICK), see Penguin Books

WATTS BOOKS, 96 Leonard Street, London EC2A 4RH. Tel: 0171-739 2929

WAYLAND (PUBLISHERS), 61 Western Road, Hove, E. Sussex BN3 1JD. Tel: 01273-722561

WEIDENFELD & NICOLSON, 5 Upper St Martin's Lane, London WC2H 9EA. Tel: 0171-240 3444

WHICH? BOOKS, Consumer's Association, 2 Marylebone Road, London NW1 4DF. Tel: 0171-830 6000

WHITAKER (J.), 12 Dyott Street, London WC1A 1DF. Tel: 0171-420 6000

WILEY (JOHN) & SONS, Baffins Lane, Chichester, W. Sussex PO19 1UD. Tel: 01243-779777

WISDEN (JOHN), 25 Down Road, Merrow, Guildford GU1 2PY. Tel: 01483-570358

Annual Reference Books

If the address of the editorial office of a publication differs from the address to which orders should be sent, the address given is usually the one for orders

AA HOTEL GUIDE, Invicta House, Sir Thomas Longley Road, Medway City Estate, Rochester, Kent ME2 4DU. (Oct.) £13.99

ADVERTISER'S ANNUAL, East Grinstead House, East Grinstead, W. Sussex RH19 1XA. 3 vol. £187.00

AEROSPACE EUROPE, Riverbank House, Angel Lane, Tonbridge, Kent TN9 1SE. £75.00

ALLIED DUNBAR INVESTMENT AND SAVINGS HANDBOOK, 12–14 Slaidburn Crescent, Southport, Merseyside PR9 9YF. £24.99

ALLIED DUNBAR TAX HANDBOOK, 12–14 Slaidburn Crescent, Southport, Merseyside PR9 9YF. £24.99

ANNUAL ABSTRACT OF STATISTICS, HMSO, PO Box 276, London SW8 5DT. (Feb.) £35.95

ANNUAL REGISTER: A RECORD OF WORLD EVENTS, 12–14 Slaidburn Crescent, Southport, Merseyside PR9 9YF. £99.00

ANTIQUE SHOPS OF BRITAIN, GUIDE TO THE, 5 Church Street, Woodbridge, Suffolk IP12 1DS. £14.95

ART SALES INDEX, 1 Thames Street, Weybridge, Surrey KT13 8JG. 2 vol. £105.00

ART WORLD DIRECTORY, 1 Stewarts Court, 220 Stewarts Road, London SW8 4UO. (Jan.) £9.95

ASSOCIATION OF CONSULTING ENGINEERS DIRECTORY OF MEMBERS FIRMS, Alliance House, 12 Caxton Street, London SW1H 0QL. £10.00

ASTRONOMICAL ALMANAC, HMSO, PO Box 276, London SW8 5DT. (Dec.) £21.00

ATHLETICS: ASSOCIATION OF TRACK AND FIELD STATISTICIANS YEAR BOOK, Waldenbury, North Common, North Chailey, Lewes, E. Sussex BN8 4DR. (May) £14.95

AUTOMOBILE YEAR, Waldenbury, North Common, North Chailey, Lewes, E. Sussex BN8 4DR. £29.95

BAILY'S HUNTING DIRECTORY, Chesterton Mill, French's Road, Cambridge CB4 3NP. (Nov.) £29.95

BANKER'S ALMANAC, East Grinstead House, East Grinstead, W. Sussex RH19 1XE. 3 vol. £320.00

BENEDICTINE AND CISTERCIAN MONASTIC YEAR BOOK, Ampleforth Abbey, York YO6 4EN. (Dec.) £2.25

BENN'S MEDIA, Riverbank House, Angel Lane, Tonbridge, Kent TN9 1SE. 3 vol. £330.00

BIRMINGHAM POST AND MAIL YEAR BOOK AND WHO'S WHO, 137 Newhall Street, Birmingham B3 1SF. (Sept.) £32.90

BPIF SERVICES AND LIST OF MEMBERS, 11 Bedford Row, London WC1R 4DX. £90.00

BRASSEY'S DEFENCE YEAR BOOK, PO Box 269, Abingdon, Oxon OX14 4YN. £36.00

BRITAIN: AN OFFICIAL HANDBOOK, HMSO, PO Box 276, London SW8 5DT. (Jan.) £27.50

BRITANNICA BOOK OF THE YEAR, Carew House, Station Approach, Wallington, Surrey SM6 0DA. (May) £76.00

BRITISH CLOTHING INDUSTRY YEAR BOOK, 11 The Swan Courtyard, Charles Edward Road, Yardley, Birmingham B26 1BU. £45.00

BRITISH EXPORTS, East Grinstead House, East Grinstead, W. Sussex RH19 1XA. £150.00

BRITISH MUSIC YEARBOOK, 241 Shaftesbury Avenue, London WC2H 8EH. £19.95

BRITISH PERFORMING ARTS YEAR BOOK, 241 Shaftesbury Avenue, London WC2H 8EH. (Jan.) £18.95

BRITISH PLASTICS AND RUBBER DIRECTORY, Catalyst House, 159 Clapham High Street, London SW4 7SS. £10.00

BROWN'S NAUTICAL ALMANAC DAILY TIDE TABLES, 4–10 Darnley Street, Glasgow G41 2SD. (Sept.) £34.50

BUILDING AND CONSTRUCTION INDEX, Riverbank House, Angel Lane, Tonbridge, Kent TN9 1SE. (Jan.) £62.00

BUILDING SOCIETIES YEAR BOOK, South Quay Plaza, 183 Marsh Wall, London E14 9FS. £65.00

BUSES YEARBOOK, 39 Milton Park, Abingdon, Oxon OX14 4TD. £11.99

BUTTERWORTHS LAW DIRECTORY AND LEGAL SERVICES DIRECTORY, Maypole House, Maypole Road, East Grinstead, W. Sussex RH19 1HH. (Feb.) 2 vol. £49.00

CATHOLIC DIRECTORY OF ENGLAND AND WALES, St James's Buildings, Oxford Street, Manchester M1 6FP. £23.50

CHARITIES DIGEST, 501–505 Kingsland Road, London E8 4AU. £16.95

CHEMICAL INDUSTRY EUROPE, Riverbank House, Angel Lane, Tonbridge, Kent TN9 1SE. £89.00

CHEMIST AND DRUGGIST DIRECTORY, Riverbank House Angel Lane, Tonbridge, Kent TN9 1SE. £102.00

CHRISTIES' REVIEW OF THE SEASON, 1 Stewart's Court, 220 Stewart's Road, London SW8 4UD. (Nov.) £30.00

CHURCH OF ENGLAND YEAR BOOK, St Mary's Works, St Mary's Plain, Norwich NR3 3BH. (Jan.) £20.00

CHURCH OF SCOTLAND YEAR BOOK, 121 George Street, Edinburgh EH2 4YN. (Sept.) £10.00

CITY OF LONDON DIRECTORY AND LIVERY COMPANIES GUIDE, Seatrade House, 42–48 North Station Road, Colchester, Essex CO1 1RB. £20.50, £18.50

CIVIL SERVICE YEAR BOOK, HMSO, PO Box 276, London SW8 5DT. (Feb.) £23.00

COMMONWEALTH UNIVERSITIES YEAR BOOK, 36 Gordon Square, London WC1H 0PF. (July) 2 vol. £130.00

COMMONWEALTH YEAR BOOK, 24 Willow Street, London EC2A 4BH. (May) £50.00

COMPUTER USERS' YEAR BOOK, Woodside, Hinksey Hill Oxford OX1 5BE. 3 vol. £250.00

CONCRETE YEAR BOOK, Thomas Telford House, 1 Heron Quay, London E14 4JD. £55.00

CURRENT LAW YEAR BOOK, Cheriton House, North Way Andover, Hants SP10 5BE. £115.00

DIPLOMATIC SERVICE LIST, HMSO, PO Box 276, London SW8 5DT. (April) £21.00

DIRECTORY OF DIRECTORS, Units 1A and 1B, Learoyd Road, Mountfield Road Industrial Estate, New Romney, Kent TN28 8XU. (Jan.) 2 vol. £204.00

DIRECTORY OF FURTHER EDUCATION, Bateman Street, Cambridge CB2 1LZ. (June) £56.95, £46.95

DIRECTORY OF HIGHER EDUCATION, Bateman Street, Cambridge CB2 1LZ. (June) £56.95, £46.95

DIRECTORY OF OFFICIAL ARCHITECTURE AND PLANNING, 12–14 Slaidburn Crescent, Southport, Merseyside PR9 9YF. £75.00

DIY TRADE BUYERS GUIDE, Riverbank House, Angel Lane, Tonbridge, Kent TN9 1SE. £69.00

DOD'S PARLIAMENTARY COMPANION, Hurst Green, Etchingham, E. Sussex TN19 7PX. £85.00

EDUCATION AUTHORITIES' DIRECTORY AND ANNUAL, Derby House, Bletchingley Road, Merstham, Surrey RH1 3DN. (Jan.) £65.00, £55.00

EDUCATION YEAR BOOK, 12–14 Slaidburn Crescent, Southport, Merseyside PR9 9YF. £85.00

ELECTRICAL AND ELECTRONIC TRADES DIRECTORY, Michael Faraday House, Six Hills Way, Stevenage, Herts SG1 2AY. (Feb.) £77.00

ELECTRICITY SUPPLY HANDBOOK, PO Box 935, Finchingfield, Braintree, Essex CM7 4LN. (Feb.) £40.00

EUROPA WORLD YEAR BOOK, 18 Bedford Square, London WC1B 3JN. 2 vol. £345.00

EUROPEAN FOOD TRADES DIRECTORY, 32 Vauxhall Bridge Road, London SW1V 2SS. 2 vol. £140.00

EUROPEAN GLASS DIRECTORY AND BUYER'S GUIDE, 2 Queensway, Redhill, Surrey RH1 1QS. £119.35

FLIGHT INTERNATIONAL DIRECTORY, PO Box 1315, Potters Bar, Herts EN6 1PU. 2 vol. £48.00, £60.00

FROZEN AND CHILLED FOODS YEAR BOOK, Queensway House, 2 Queensway, Redhill, Surrey RH1 1QS. £119.35

FURNITURE AND FURNISHINGS INDUSTRY, DIRECTORY OF THE, Riverbank House, Angel Lane, Tonbridge, Kent TN9 1SE. £98.00

GAS INDUSTRY DIRECTORY, Riverbank House, Angel Lane, Tonbridge, Kent TN9 1SE. (Oct.) £89.00

GIBBONS' STAMPS OF THE WORLD CATALOGUE, 5 Parkside, Christchurch Road, Ringwood, Hants BH24 3SH. (Oct.) 3 vol. £24.95, £24.95, £22.95

GOOD FOOD GUIDE, Bath Road, Harmondsworth, West Drayton, Middx UB7 0DA. £14.99

GOOD GUIDE TO BRITAIN, Church Road, Tiptree, Colchester CO5 0SR. (Nov.) £14.99

GOOD HOTEL GUIDE, Brunel Road, Houndmills, Basingstoke, Hants RG21 2XS. £14.99

GOVERNMENT AND MUNICIPAL BUYERS GUIDE, Riverbank House, Angel Lane, Tonbridge, Kent TN9 1SE. (Jan.) £82.00

GRADUATE STUDIES, Bateman Street, Cambridge CB2 1LZ. (July) £99.95

GUINNESS BOOK OF ANSWERS, 33 London Road, Enfield EN2 6DJ. £14.99

GUINNESS BOOK OF RECORDS, 33 London Road, Enfield EN2 6DJ. (Oct.) £15.99

HEALTH AND SOCIAL SERVICES YEARBOOK, 39 Chalton Street, London NW1 1JD. £115.00

HEALTH CARE BUYERS GUIDE, Riverbank House, Angel Lane, Tonbridge, Kent TN9 1SE. £78.00

HISTORIC HOUSES, CASTLES AND GARDENS, East Grinstead House, East Grinstead, W. Sussex RH19 1XA. (March) £7.99

HOLLIS UK PRESS AND PR ANNUAL, Harlequin House, 7 High Street, Teddington TW11 8EY. (Oct.) £97.50

HUTCHINS' PRICED SCHEDULES, PO Box 5, Rushden, Northants NN10 6XJ. £55.00

INDEPENDENT SCHOOLS YEAR BOOK, PO Box 19, Huntingdon, Cambs PE19 3SF. £24.00

INSURANCE DIRECTORY AND YEAR BOOK, Garrard House, 2–6 Homesdale Road, Bromley, Kent BR2 9WL. (Jan.) 4 vol. £405.00

INTERNATIONAL PAPER DIRECTORY, PHILLIPS', Riverbank House, Angel Lane, Tonbridge, Kent TN9 1SE. £120.00

INTERNATIONAL WHO'S WHO, 18 Bedford Square, London WC1R 4JH. (Sept.) £160.00

INTERNATIONAL YEARBOOK AND STATESMEN'S WHO'S WHO, East Grinstead House, East Grinstead, W. Sussex RH19 1XA. (April) £170.00

JANE'S ALL THE WORLD'S AIRCRAFT, Sentinel House, 163 Brighton Road, Coulsdon, Surrey CR5 2NH. (Oct.) £225.00

JANE'S ARMOUR AND ARTILLERY, Sentinel House, 163 Brighton Road, Coulsdon, Surrey CR5 2NH. (Nov.) £225.00

JANE'S FIGHTING SHIPS, Sentinel House, 163 Brighton Road, Coulsdon, Surrey CR5 2NH. £225.00

JANE'S HIGH SPEED MARINE TRANSPORTATION, Sentinel House, 163 Brighton Road, Coulsdon, Surrey CR5 2NH. £210.00

JANE'S INFANTRY WEAPONS, Sentinel House, 163 Brighton Road, Coulsdon, Surrey CR5 2NH. (Aug.) £195.00

JANE'S INTERMODAL TRANSPORTATION, Sentinel House, 163 Brighton Road, Coulsdon, Surrey CR5 2NH. (Nov.) £210.00

JANE'S NAVAL WEAPON SYSTEMS, Sentinel House, 163 Brighton Road, Coulsdon, Surrey CR5 2NH. £330.00

JANE'S WORLD RAILWAYS, Sentinel House, 163 Brighton Road, Coulsdon, Surrey CR5 2NH. £235.00

JEWISH YEAR BOOK, Star Road, Partridge Green, Horsham, W. Sussex RH13 8LD. (Feb.) £24.00

KELLY'S BUSINESS DIRECTORY, East Grinstead House, East Grinstead, W. Sussex RH19 1XA. £175.00

KEMPE'S ENGINEERS YEAR BOOK, Riverbank House, Angel Lane, Tonbridge, Kent TN9 1SE. £105.00

KIME'S INTERNATIONAL LAW DIRECTORY, 12–14 Slaidburn Crescent, Southport, Merseyside PR9 9YF. (Dec.) £75.00

LAXTON'S BUILDING PRICE BOOK, East Grinstead House, East Grinstead, W. Sussex RH19 1XA. 2 vol. £94.00

LIBRARY ASSOCIATION YEARBOOK, 7 Ridgmount Street, London WC1E 7AE. (June) £37.50

LLOYD'S LIST OF SHIPOWNERS, 71 Fenchurch Street, London EC3M 4BS. (Sept.) £115.00

LLOYD'S MARITIME DIRECTORY, Sheepen Place, Colchester CO3 3LP. (Jan.) £160.00

LLOYD'S NAUTICAL YEAR BOOK, Sheepen Place, Colchester CO3 3LP. (Sept.) £48.00

LLOYD'S REGISTER OF SHIPS, 71 Fenchurch Street, London EC3M 4BS. (July) 3 vol. £425.00

LYLE OFFICIAL ANTIQUES PRICE GUIDE, Glenmayne, Galashiels TD1 3NR. £17.95

MACMILLAN NAUTICAL ALMANACK, Brunel Road, Houndmills, Basingstoke, Hants RG21 2XS. £27.99

MAGISTRATES' COURT GUIDE, Halsbury House, 35 Chancery Lane, London WC2A 1EL. £23.95

MEDICAL DIRECTORY, 12–14 Slaidburn Crescent, Southport, Merseyside PR9 9YF. (June) 3 vol. £170.00

MEDICAL REGISTER, 44 Hallam Street, London W1N 6AE. (March) 3 vol. £90.00

MIDDLE EAST AND NORTH AFRICA, 18 Bedford Square, London WC1B 3JN. (Oct.) £185.00

MILLER'S ANTIQUES PRICE GUIDE, The Cellars, 5 High Street, Tenterden, Kent TN30 6BN. £21.99

MINING ANNUAL REVIEW, PO Box 10, Edenbridge, Kent TN8 5NE. £70.00

MINING INTERNATIONAL YEAR BOOK, 12–14 Slaidburn Crescent, Southport, Merseyside PR9 9YF. (June) £165.00

MOTOR INDUSTRY OF GREAT BRITAIN WORLD AUTOMOTIVE STATISTICS, Forbes House, Halkin Street, London SW1X 7DS. (Oct.) £75.00

MOTOR SHIP DIRECTORY, PO Box 935, Finchingfield, Braintree, Essex CM7 4LN. (Oct.) £75.00

MUNICIPAL YEARBOOK AND PUBLIC SERVICES DIRECTORY, 32 Vauxhall Bridge Road, London SW1V 2SS. (Dec.) 2 vol. £165.00

MUSEUMS AND GALLERIES IN GREAT BRITAIN AND IRELAND, East Grinstead House, East Grinstead, W. Sussex RH19 1XA. (Oct.) £7.50

NAUTICAL ALMANAC, HMSO, PO Box 276, London SW8 5DT. (Oct.) £19.50

PACKAGING INDUSTRY DIRECTORY, Riverbank House, Angel Lane, Tonbridge, Kent TN9 1SE. £87.00

PEARS CYCLOPEDIA, 27 Wright's Lane, London w8 5TZ. £15.99

PEOPLE OF TODAY, 73–77 Britannia Road, PO Box 357, London sw6 2JY. (April) £97.50

PHOTOGRAPHY YEAR BOOK, Fountain House, 2 Gladstone Road, Kingston upon Thames, Surrey KT1 3HD. £24.95

POLYMERS, PAINT AND COLOUR YEAR BOOK, Queensway House, 2 Queensway, Redhill, Surrey RH1 1QS. £106.30

PORTS OF THE WORLD, Sheepen Place, Colchester, Essex CO3 3LP. £170.00

PRINTING TRADES DIRECTORY, Riverbank House, Angel Lane, Tonbridge, Kent TN9 1SE. £102.00

PUBLIC AUTHORITIES DIRECTORY, Lansdowne Mews, 196 High Street, Tonbridge, Kent TN9 1EF. (Jan.) £89.00

PUBLIC SERVICES YEARBOOK, 12–14 Slaidburn Crescent, Southport, Merseyside PR9 9YF. (April) £25.00

PUBLISHING, DIRECTORY OF, Artillery House, Artillery Row, London SW1P 1RT. (Oct.) £55.00

RAC EUROPEAN HOTEL GUIDE, 39 Milton Park, Abingdon, Oxon OX14 4TD. £8.99

RAC HOTEL GUIDE, 39 Milton Park, Abingdon, Oxon OX14 4TD. £9.99

RAILWAY DIRECTORY, PO Box 935, Finchingfield, Braintree, Essex CM7 4LN. (Dec.) £80.00

REGIONAL TRENDS, HMSO, PO Box 276, London sw8 5DT. (July) £35.95

RETAIL DIRECTORY OF THE UNITED KINGDOM, 32 Vauxhall Bridge Road, London SW1V 2SS. £155.00

RIBA DIRECTORY OF PRACTICES, 39 Moreland Street, London EC1V 8BB. (Oct.) £57.75

ROTHMAN'S FOOTBALL YEAR BOOK, 39 Milton Park, Abingdon, Oxon OX14 4TD. (Aug.) £30.00, £17.99

ROTHMAN'S RUGBY LEAGUE YEAR BOOK, 39 Milton Park, Abingdon, Oxon OX14 4TD. (Sept.) £16.99

ROTHMAN'S RUGBY UNION YEAR BOOK, 39 Milton Park, Abingdon, Oxon OX14 4TD. (Sept.) £16.99

ROYAL AND ANCIENT GOLFER'S HANDBOOK, Brunel Road, Houndmills, Basingstoke, Hants RG21 2XS. (April) £45.00, £18.99

ROYAL SOCIETY YEAR BOOK, 6 Carlton House Terrace, London SW1Y 5AG. (Feb.) £17.75

RUFF'S GUIDE TO THE TURF AND SPORTING LIFE ANNUAL, Orbit House, 1 New Fetter Lane, London EC4A 1AR. (Jan.) £40.00

SALVATION ARMY YEAR BOOK, 117–121 Judd Street, London WC1H 9NN. (April) £5.50

SCOTTISH CURRENT LAW YEAR BOOK, 21 Alva Street, Edinburgh EH2 4PS. 2 vol. £98.00

SCOTTISH LAW DIRECTORY, 59 George Street, Edinburgh EH2 2LQ. £34.00

SEABY STANDARD CATALOGUE OF BRITISH COINS, PO Box 4, Braintree, Essex CM7 7QY. (Sept.) £12.99

SELL'S PRODUCTS AND SERVICES DIRECTORY, Riverbank House, Angel Lane, Tonbridge, Kent TN9 1SE. (June) £90.00

SHEET METAL INDUSTRIES YEAR BOOK, Queensway House, 2 Queensway, Redhill, Surrey RH1 1QS. £73.00

SHOWCASE INTERNATIONAL MUSIC BOOK, 12 Felix Avenue, London N8 9TL. £32.00

SOCIAL SERVICES YEAR BOOK, 12–14 Slaidburn Crescent, Southport, Merseyside PR9 9YF. (April) £97.00

SOCIAL TRENDS, HMSO, PO Box 276, London sw8 5DT. (Jan.) £35.95

SOLICITORS AND BARRISTERS, DIRECTORY OF, 50 Chancery Lane, London WC2A 1SX. £55.00

SPON'S ARCHITECTS' AND BUILDERS' PRICE BOOK, Cheriton House, North Way, Andover, Hants SP10 5BE. £69.50

SPON'S MECHANICAL AND ELECTRICAL SERVICES PRICE BOOK, Cheriton House, North Way, Andover, Hants SP10 5BE. £72.50

STATESMAN'S YEARBOOK, Brunel House, Houndmills, Basingstoke, Hants RG21 2XS. (Aug.) £49.00

STOCK EXCHANGE OFFICIAL YEAR BOOK, Brunel House, Houndmills, Basingstoke, Hants RG21 2XS. £225.00

STONE'S JUSTICES' MANUAL, PO Box 3000, Halsbury House, 35 Chancery Lane, London WC2A 1EL. 3 vol. (May) £220.00

STUDENT BOOK, Brunel Road, Houndmills, Basingstoke, Hants RG21 2XS. (March) £12.99

TANKER REGISTER, 12 Camomile Street, London EC3A 7BP. (April) £155.00

TIMBER TRADES ADDRESS BOOK, Riverbank House, Angel Lane, Tonbridge, Kent TN9 1SE. £66.00

TRAINING AND ENTERPRISE DIRECTORY, 120 Pentonville Road, London N1 9JN. £27.50

TRAVEL TRADE GAZETTE DIRECTORY, Riverbank House, Angel Lane, Tonbridge, Kent TN9 1SE. (April) £70.00

UK KOMPASS REGISTER, East Grinstead House, East Grinstead, W. Sussex RH19 1XD. 5 vol. £900.00

UNITED KINGDOM MINERALS YEARBOOK, British Geological Survey, Keyworth, Nottingham NG12 5GG. £30.00

UNITED REFORMED CHURCH YEAR BOOK, 86 Tavistock Place, London WC1H 9RT. (Sept.) £8.50

UNIT TRUST YEAR BOOK, Maple House, 149 Tottenham Court Road, London W1P 9LL. £250.00

UNIVERSITY AND COLLEGE ENTRANCE, 14 Cooper's Row, London EC3N 2BH. (June) £18.95

VETERINARY ANNUAL, PO Box 269, Abingdon, Oxon. OX14 4YN. £59.50

WATER SERVICES YEAR BOOK, Queensway House, 2 Queensway, Redhill, Surrey RH1 1QS. (Oct.) £75.00

WHITAKER DIRECTORY OF PUBLISHERS, 12 Dyott Street, London WC1A 1DF. (March) £15.00

WHITAKER'S ALMANACK, 12 Dyott Street, London WC1A 1DF. (Nov.) £55.00, £35.00

WHITAKER'S BOOKS IN PRINT, 12 Dyott Street, London WC1A 1DF. (Jan.) 5 vol. £295.00

WHITAKER'S CONCISE ALMANACK, 12 Dyott Street, London WC1A 1DF. (Nov.) £9.99

WHO OWNS WHOM?, Holmers Farm Way, High Wycombe, Bucks HP12 4UL. 2 vol. £338.00

WHO'S WHO, PO Box 19, Huntingdon, Cambs PE19 3SF. £95.00

WILLING'S PRESS GUIDE, Units 1A and 1B, Learoyd Road, Mountfield Road Industrial Estate, New Romney, Kent TN28 8XU. (Feb.) 2 vol. £162.00

WISDEN CRICKETERS' ALMANACK, Bath Road, Harmondsworth, West Drayton, Middx UB7 0DA. (April) £24.50

WORLD HOTEL DIRECTORY, 12–14 Slaidburn Crescent, Southport, Merseyside PR9 9YF. £125.00

WORLD INSURANCE, 12–14 Slaidburn Crescent, Southport, Merseyside PR9 9YF. £160.00

WORLD MINERAL STATISTICS, British Geological Survey, Keyworth, Notts NG12 5GG. (Sept.) 2 vol. £73.50

WORLD OF LEARNING, 18 Bedford Square, London WC1B 3JN. (Jan.) 2 vol. £220.00

WORLD SHIPPING DIRECTORY, PO Box 96, Coulsdon, Surrey CR5 2TE. £99.00

WRITERS' AND ARTISTS' YEAR BOOK, PO Box 19, Huntingdon, Cambs PE19 3SF. (Sept.) £10.99

Employers' and Trade Associations

At 31 December 1995 there were 114 employers' associations listed by the Certification Officer (*see* page 289). Most national employers' associations are members of the Confederation of British Industry (CBI). For ACAS, the Certification Office, the Commission for Racial Equality, the Equal Opportunities Commission, the Health and Safety Commission, the Industrial Tribunals and Review Bodies, *see* Index.

CONFEDERATION OF BRITISH INDUSTRY
Centre Point, 103 New Oxford Street, London WC1A 1DU
Tel 0171-379 7400

The Confederation of British Industry was founded in 1965 and is an independent non-party political body financed by industry and commerce. It exists primarily to ensure that the Government understands the intentions, needs and problems of British business. It is the recognized spokesman for the business viewpoint and is consulted as such by the Government.

The CBI represents, directly and indirectly, some 250,000 companies, large and small, from all sectors.

The governing body of the CBI is the 400-strong Council, which meets monthly in London under the chairmanship of the President. It is assisted by some 27 expert standing committees which advise on the main aspects of policy. There are 13 regional councils and offices covering the administrative regions of England, Wales, Scotland and Northern Ireland. There is also an office in Brussels.

President, Sir Colin Marshall
Director-General, J. Adair Turner
Secretary, M. W. Hunt

ASSOCIATIONS

ADVERTISING ASSOCIATION, Abford House, 15 Wilton Road, London SW1V 1NJ. Tel: 0171-828 2771. *Director-General,* A. Brown

AEROSPACE COMPANIES LTD, SOCIETY OF BRITISH, 60 Petty France, London SW1H 9EU. Tel: 0171-227 1000. *Director,* Sir Barry Duxbury, KCB, CBE

APPAREL AND TEXTILE CONFEDERATION LTD, BRITISH, 5 Portland Place, London WIN 3AA. Tel: 0171-636 7788. *Director-General,* J. R. Wilson

BAKERS, FEDERATION OF, 20 Bedford Square, London WC1B 3HF. Tel: 0171-580 4252. *Director,* A. Casdagli, CBE

BANKERS' ASSOCIATION, BRITISH, 105–108 Old Broad Street, London EC2N 1EX. Tel: 0171-216 8800. *Director-General,* T. P. Sweeney

BLC (BRITISH LEATHER CONFEDERATION) – THE LEATHER TECHNOLOGY CENTRE, Leather Trade House, Kings Park Road, Moulton Park, Northampton NN3 6JD. Tel: 01604-494131. *Chief Executive,* K. T. W. Alexander, PH.D.

BREWERS' AND LICENSED RETAILERS' ASSOCIATION, 42 Portman Square, London W1H 0BB. Tel: 0171-486 4831. *Director,* R. W. Simpson

BUILDING EMPLOYERS CONFEDERATION, 82 New Cavendish Street, London W1M 8AD. Tel: 0171-580 5588. *Director-General,* I. A. Deslandes

BUILDING MATERIAL PRODUCERS, NATIONAL COUNCIL OF, 26 Store Street, London WC1E 7BT. Tel: 0171-323 3770. *Director-General,* N. M. Chaldecott, OBE

CHAMBER OF SHIPPING LTD, Carthusian Court, 12 Carthusian Street, London EC1M 6EB. Tel: 0171-417 8400. *Director-General,* Adm. Sir Nicholas Hunt, GCB, LVO

CHEMICAL INDUSTRIES ASSOCIATION LTD, Kings Buildings, Smith Square, London SW1P 3JJ. Tel: 0171-834 3399. *Director-General,* Dr E. G. Finer

CLOTHING INDUSTRY ASSOCIATION LTD, BRITISH, 5 Portland Place, London WIN 3AA. Tel: 0171-636 7788. *Director,* J. R. Wilson

DAIRY INDUSTRY FEDERATION, 19 Cornwall Terrace, London NW1 4QP. Tel: 0171-486 7244. *Director-General,* J. P. Price

ELECTROTECHNICAL AND ALLIED MANUFACTURERS' ASSOCIATIONS, FEDERATION OF BRITISH (BEAMA), Westminster Tower, 3 Albert Embankment, London SE1 7SL. Tel: 0171-793 3000. *Director-General,* J. G. Gaddes

ENGINEERING EMPLOYERS' FEDERATION, Broadway House, Tothill Street, London SW1H 9NQ. Tel: 0171-222 7777. *Director-General,* G. R. Mackenzie, F.ENG.

FARMERS' UNION, NATIONAL (NFU), 164 Shaftesbury Avenue, London WC2H 8HL. Tel: 0171-331 7200. *Director-General,* R. MacDonald

FARMERS' UNION OF SCOTLAND, NATIONAL, Rural Centre-West Mains, Ingliston, Newbridge, Midlothian EH28 8LT. Tel: 0131-335 3111. *Chief Executive,* T. J. Brady

FARMERS' UNION, ULSTER, 475 Antrim Road, Belfast BT15 3DA. Tel: 01232-370222. *Director-General,* A. MacLaughlin

FINANCE AND LEASING ASSOCIATION, 18 Upper Grosvenor Street, London W1X 9PB. Tel: 0171-491 2783. *Director,* M. Hall

FOOD AND DRINK FEDERATION, 6 Catherine Street, London WC2B 5JJ. Tel: 0171-836 2460. *Director-General,* M. P. Mackenzie

FREIGHT TRANSPORT ASSOCIATION LTD, Hermes House, 157 St John's Road, Tunbridge Wells, Kent TN4 9UZ. Tel: 01892-526171. *Director-General,* D. C. Green

INSURERS, ASSOCIATION OF BRITISH, 51 Gresham Street, London EC2V 7HQ. Tel: 0171-600 3333. *Director-General,* M. Boléat

KNITTING INDUSTRIES' FEDERATION LTD, 53 Oxford Street, Leicester LE1 5XY. Tel: 0116-254 1608. *Director,* J. P. Harrison

LEATHER PRODUCERS' ASSOCIATION, Leather Trade House, Kings Park Road, Moulton Park, Northampton NN3 6JD. Tel: 01604-494131. *National Secretary,* J. Purvis

MANAGEMENT CONSULTANCIES ASSOCIATION, 11 West Halkin Street, London SW1X 8JL. Tel: 0171-235 3897. *Executive Director,* B. O'Rorke

MARINE INDUSTRIES FEDERATION, BRITISH, Meadlake Place, Thorpe Lea Road, Egham, Surrey TW20 8HE. Tel: 01784-473377. *Executive Chairman,* A. V. Beechey

MARKET TRADERS' FEDERATION, NATIONAL, Hampton House, Hawshaw Lane, Hoyland, Barnsley S74 0HA. Tel: 01226-749021. *General Secretary,* D. E. Feeny

MASTER BUILDERS, FEDERATION OF, Gordon Fisher House, 14–15 Great James Street, London WC1N 3DP. Tel: 0171-242 7583. *Director-General*, J. D. Maiden
MOTOR MANUFACTURERS AND TRADERS LTD, SOCIETY OF, Forbes House, Halkin Street, London SW1X 7DS. Tel: 0171-235 7000. *Chief Executive*, R. E. Thompson
NEWSPAPER PUBLISHERS ASSOCIATION LTD, 34 Southwark Bridge Road, London SE1 9EU. Tel: 0171-928 6928. *Director*, D. Pollock
NEWSPAPER SOCIETY, Bloomsbury House, 74–77 Great Russell Street, London WC1B 3DA. Tel: 0171-636 7014. *Director*, D. Nisbet-Smith, CBE
OFFICE SYSTEMS AND STATIONERY FEDERATION, BRITISH, 6 Wimpole Street, London W1M 8AS. Tel: 0171-637 7692. *Chief Executive*, new appointment awaited
PAPER FEDERATION OF GREAT BRITAIN LTD, Papermakers House, Rivenhall Road, Swindon SN5 7BD. Tel: 01793-886086. *Director-General*, W. J. Bartlett
PASSENGER TRANSPORT UK, CONFEDERATION OF, Imperial House, 15–19 Kingsway, London WC2B 6UN. Tel: 0171-240 3131. *Director-General*, Mrs V. Palmer, OBE
PLASTICS FEDERATION, BRITISH, 6 Bath Place, Rivington Street, London EC2A 3JE. Tel: 0171-457 5000. *Director-General*, D. R. Jones
PORTS ASSOCIATION, BRITISH, Africa House, 64–78 Kingsway, London WC2B 6AH. Tel: 0171-242 1200. *Director*, D. Whitehead
PRINTING INDUSTRIES FEDERATION, BRITISH, 11 Bedford Row, London WC1R 4DX. Tel: 0171-242 6904. *Director-General*, T. P. E. Machin
PRIVATE MARKET OPERATORS, ASSOCIATION OF, 4 Worrygoose Lane, Rotherham S60 4AD. Tel: 01709-700072. *Secretary*, D. J. Glasby
PROPERTY FEDERATION, BRITISH, 35 Catherine Place, London SW1E 6DY. Tel: 0171-828 0111. *Director-General*, W. A. McKee
PUBLISHERS ASSOCIATION, THE, 19 Bedford Square, London WC1B 3HJ. Tel: 0171-580 6321. *Chief Executive*, C. Bradley, CBE
RADIO COMPANIES ASSOCIATION, COMMERCIAL, 77 Shaftesbury Avenue, London W1V 7AD. Tel: 0171-306 2603. *Chief Executive*, P. Brown
RETAIL CONSORTIUM, BRITISH, Bedford House, 69–79 Fulham High Street, London SW6 3JW. Tel: 0171-371 5185. *Director-General*, J. N. W. May
RETAIL NEWSAGENTS, NATIONAL FEDERATION OF, Yeoman House, Sekforde Street, London EC1R 0HD. Tel: 0171-253 4225. *Chief Executive*, R. Clarke
ROAD FEDERATION, BRITISH, Pillar House, 194–202 Old Kent Road, London SE1 5TG. Tel: 0171-703 9769. *Director*, R. Diment
ROAD HAULAGE ASSOCIATION LTD, Roadway House, 35 Monument Hill, Weybridge, Surrey KT13 8RN. Tel: 01932-841515. *Director-General*, D. B. H. Colley, CB, CBE
RUBBER MANUFACTURERS' ASSOCIATION LTD, BRITISH, 90 Tottenham Court Road, London W1P 0BR. Tel: 0171-580 2794. *Director*, W. R. Pollock
SPORT AND ALLIED INDUSTRIES FEDERATION LTD, BRITISH, Federation House, National Agricultural Centre, Stoneleigh Park, Warks CV8 2RF. Tel: 01203-414999. *Chief Executive*, Dr J. Hooper
TIMBER GROWERS ASSOCIATION, 5 Dublin Street Lane South, Edinburgh EH1 3PX. Tel: 0131-538 7111. *Chief Executive*, P. H. Wilson
TIMBER MERCHANTS' ASSOCIATION, BRITISH, Stocking Lane, Hughenden Valley, High Wycombe, Bucks HP14 4JZ. Tel: 01494-563602. *Secretary*, G. Waugh
TIMBER TRADE FEDERATION, Clareville House, 26–27 Oxendon Street, London SW1Y 4EL. Tel: 0171-839 1891. *Director-General*, P. G. Harris

UK OFFSHORE OPERATORS ASSOCIATION LTD, 3 Hans Crescent, London SW1X 0LN. Tel: 0171-589 5255. *Director-General*, Dr H. W. D. Hughes, OBE
UK PETROLEUM INDUSTRY ASSOCIATION LTD, 9 Kingsway, London WC2B 6XF. Tel: 0171-240 0289. *Director-General*, Dr M. A. Frend

Trade Unions

At 31 December 1995 there were 256 trade unions listed by the Certification Officer (*see* page 289). In 1994 8,230,545 people were members of listed trade unions, compared with 8,665,944 in 1993. Nearly 80 per cent of trade union members belong to unions affiliated to the TUC (*see* below).

The Central Arbitration Committee arbitrates in industrial disputes between trade unions and employers, and determines disclosure of information complaints. The Commissioner for the Rights of Trade Union Members provides assistance to individuals taking action against their trade union when they have not been afforded their statutory rights or when specific union rules have been breached. The Commissioner for Protection Against Unlawful Industrial Action assists individuals who have been, or are likely to be, deprived of goods or services because of industrial action unlawfully organized by a trade union.

For ACAS, the Certification Office, the Commission for Racial Equality, the Equal Opportunities Commission, the Health and Safety Commission, the Industrial Tribunals and Review Bodies, *see* Index.

THE CENTRAL ARBITRATION COMMITTEE, Brandon House, 180 Borough High Street, London SE1 ILW. Tel: 0171-210 3737/8. *Chairman*, Prof. Sir John Wood, CBE; *Secretary*, S. Gouldstone
THE COMMISSIONER FOR THE RIGHTS OF TRADE UNION MEMBERS, 1st Floor, Bank Chambers, 2A Rylands Street, Warrington, Cheshire WA1 1EN. Tel: 01925-415771. *Commissioner*, G. Corless
THE COMMISSIONER FOR PROTECTION AGAINST UNLAWFUL INDUSTRIAL ACTION, 2nd Floor, Bank Chambers, 2A Rylands Street, Warrington, Cheshire WA1 1EN. Tel: 01925-414128. *Commissioner*, G. Corless

---

TUC-AFFILIATED TRADE UNIONS

TRADES UNION CONGRESS (TUC)
Congress House, 23–28 Great Russell Street, London WC1B 3LS
Tel 0171-636 4030

The Trades Union Congress, founded in 1868, is an independent association of trade unions. The TUC promotes the rights and welfare of those in work and helps the unemployed. It helps its member unions promote membership in new areas and industries, and campaigns for rights at work for all employees, including part-time and temporary workers, whether union members or not. TUC representatives sit on many public bodies at national and international level. It makes representatins to government, political parties, employers and international bodies such as the European Union.

The governing body of the TUC is the annual Congress. Between Congresses, business is conducted by a General Council, which meets five times a year, and an Executive Committee, which meets monthly. The full-time staff is headed by the General Secretary who is elected by Congress and is a permanent member of the General Council.

Affiliated unions (in 1995–6) totalled 73 with a total membership of about 6,800,000.

President (1996–7), A. Dubbins (GPMU)
General Secretary, J. Monks, *elected* 1993

SCOTTISH TRADES UNION CONGRESS
Middleton House, 16 Woodlands Terrace, Glasgow G3 6DF
Tel 0141-332 4946

The Congress was formed in 1897 and acts as a national centre for the trade union movement in Scotland. In 1996 it consisted of 47 unions with a membership of 670,632 and 28 directly affiliated Trades Councils.

The Annual Congress in April elects a 36-member General Council on the basis of eight industrial sections.
Chairperson, Ms M. Harrison
General Secretary, C. Christie

AFFILIATED UNIONS AS AT 1 SEPTEMBER 1996 (Number of members in parenthesis)

AMALGAMATED ENGINEERING AND ELECTRICAL UNION (AEEU) (750,000), Hayes Court, West Common Road, Bromley, Kent BR2 7AU. Tel: 0181-462 7755. *General Secretary*, K. Jackson
ASSOCIATED METALWORKERS UNION (AMU) (1,400), 92 Worsley Road North, Worsley, Manchester M28 5QW. Tel: 01204-793245. *General Secretary*, R. Marron
ASSOCIATED SOCIETY OF LOCOMOTIVE ENGINEERS AND FIREMEN (ASLEF) (15,741), 9 Arkwright Road, London NW3 6AB. Tel: 0171-431 0275. *General Secretary*, L. Adams
ASSOCIATION OF FIRST DIVISION CIVIL SERVANTS (11,000), 2 Caxton Street, London SW1H 0QH. Tel: 0171-222 6242. *General Secretary*, Ms E. Symons
ASSOCIATION OF MAGISTERIAL OFFICERS (5,050), 231 Vauxhall Bridge Road, London SW1V 1EG. Tel: 0171-630 5455. *General Secretary*, Ms R. Eagleson
ASSOCIATION OF UNIVERSITY TEACHERS (36,000), United House, 9 Pembridge Road, London W11 3JY. Tel: 0171-221 4370. *General Secretary*, D. Triesman
BAKERS, FOOD AND ALLIED WORKERS' UNION (29,676), Stanborough House, Great North Road, Stanborough, Welwyn Garden City, Herts AL8 7TA. Tel: 01707-260150. *General Secretary*, J. R. Marino
BANKING, INSURANCE AND FINANCE UNION (125,000), Sheffield House, 1B Amity Grove, London SW20 0LG. Tel: 0181-946 9151. *General Secretary*, E. Sweeney
BRITISH ACTORS' EQUITY ASSOCIATION (43,000), Guild House, Upper St Martin's Lane, London WC2H 9EG. Tel: 0171-379 6000. *General Secretary*, I. McGarry
BRITISH AIR LINE PILOTS ASSOCIATION (BALPA) (5,500), 81 New Road, Harlington, Hayes, Middx UB3 5BG. Tel: 0181-476 4000. *General Secretary*, C. Darke
BRITISH ASSOCIATION OF COLLIERY MANAGEMENT (4,200), 17 South Parade, Doncaster, S. Yorks DN1 2DN. Tel: 01302-349152. *General Secretary*, P. M. Carragher
BRITISH ORTHOPTIC SOCIETY (830), Tavistock House North, London WC1H 9HX. Tel: 0171-387 7992. *Executive Secretary*, Ms J. Brown
BROADCASTING, ENTERTAINMENT, CINEMATOGRAPH AND THEATRE UNION (BECTU) (30,000), 111 Wardour Street, London W1V 4AY. Tel: 0171-437 8506. *General Secretary*, R. Bolton
CARD SETTING MACHINE TENTERS' SOCIETY (88), 48 Scar End Lane, Staincliffe, Dewsbury, W. Yorks WF12 4NY. Tel: 01924-400206. *Secretary*, A. Moorhouse

CERAMIC AND ALLIED TRADES UNION (22,234), Hillcrest House, Garth Street, Hanley, Stoke-on-Trent STI 2AB. Tel: 01782-272755. *General Secretary*, G. Bagnall

THE CHARTERED SOCIETY OF PHYSIOTHERAPY (32,000), 14 Bedford Row, London WCIR 4ED. Tel: 0171-306 6666. *Secretary*, T. Simon

CIVIL AND PUBLIC SERVICES ASSOCIATION (122,500), 160 Falcon Road, London SWII 2LN. Tel: 0171-924 2727. *General Secretary*, B. Reamsbottom

COMMUNICATION MANAGERS' ASSOCIATION (15,100), CMA House, Ruscombe Road, Twyford, Reading RGI0 9JD. Tel: 01734-342300. *General Secretary*, T. L. Deegan

COMMUNITY AND DISTRICT NURSING ASSOCIATION (5,000), Thames Valley University, 8 University House, Ealing Green, London W5 5ED. Tel: 0181-231 2776. *General Secretary*, Ms A. Keen

COMMUNITY AND YOUTH WORKERS UNION (3,000), Unit 302, The Argent Centre, 60 Frederick Street, Birmingham BI 3HS. Tel: 0121-244 3344. *General Secretary*, D. Nicholls

COMMUNICATION WORKERS UNION (280,000), CWU House, Crescent Lane, London SW4 9RN. Tel: 0171-622 9977. *Joint General Secretaries*, A. I. Young, A. Johnson

THE EDUCATIONAL INSTITUTE OF SCOTLAND (49,633), 46 Moray Place, Edinburgh EH3 6BH. Tel: 0131-225 6244. *General Secretary*, R. A. Smith

ENGINEERING AND FASTENER TRADE UNION (268), 42 Galton Road, Warley, West Midlands B67 5JU. Tel: 0121-429 2594. *General Secretary*, J. Burdis

ENGINEERS' AND MANAGERS' ASSOCIATION (32,000), Flaxman House, Gogmore Lane, Chertsey, Surrey KTI6 9JS. Tel: 01932-577007. *General Secretary*, D. A. Cooper

THE FIRE BRIGADES UNION (50,442), Bradley House, 68 Coombe Road, Kingston upon Thames, Surrey KT2 7AE. Tel: 0181-541 1765. *General Secretary*, K. Cameron

GENERAL UNION OF ASSOCIATIONS OF LOOM OVERLOOKERS (430), 9 Wellington Street, St Johns, Blackburn, Lancs BBI 8AF. Tel: 01254-51760. *President*, D. J. Rishton

GMB (formerly General, Municipal, Boilermakers and Allied Trades Union) (790,000), 22–24 Worple Road, London SWI9 4DD. Tel: 0181-947 3131. *General Secretary*, J. Edmonds

GRAPHICAL, PAPER AND MEDIA UNION (200,000), 63–67 Bromham Road, Bedford MK40 2AG. Tel: 01234-351521. *General Secretary*, A. D. Dubbins

HOSPITAL CONSULTANTS AND SPECIALISTS ASSOCIATION (2,358), 1 Kingsclere Road, Overton, Basingstoke, Hants RG25 3JA. Tel: 01256-771777. *Chief Executive*, S. J. Charkham

INDEPENDENT UNION OF HALIFAX STAFF (19,652), Simmons House, 46 Old Bath Road, Charvil, Reading RGI0 9QR. Tel: 01734-341808. *General Secretary*, G. Nichols

INSTITUTION OF PROFESSIONALS, MANAGERS AND SPECIALISTS (81,015), 75–79 York Road, London SEI 7AQ. Tel: 0171-928 9951. *General Secretary*, W. Brett

IRON AND STEEL TRADES CONFEDERATION (51,000), Swinton House, 324 Gray's Inn Road, London WCIX 8DD. Tel: 0171-837 6691. *General Secretary*, D. K. Brookman

MANAGERIAL AND PROFESSIONAL OFFICERS (12,000), Terminus House, The High, Harlow, Essex CM20 ITZ. Tel: 01279-434444. *General Secretary*, G. Corless

MANUFACTURING, SCIENCE AND FINANCE UNION (MSF) (452,000), MSF Centre, 33–37 Moreland Street, London ECIV 8BB. Tel: 0171-505 3000. *General Secretary*, R. Lyons

MILITARY AND ORCHESTRAL MUSICAL INSTRUMENT MAKERS TRADE SOCIETY (61), 2 Whitehouse Avenue, Borehamwood, Herts WD6 IHD. *General Secretary*, F. McKenzie

MUSICIANS' UNION (32,304), 60–62 Clapham Road, London SW9 OJJ. Tel: 0171-582 5566. *General Secretary*, D Scard

NATFHE (THE UNIVERSITY AND COLLEGE LECTURERS UNION) (71,000), 27 Britannia Street, London WCIX 9JP. Tel: 0171-837 3636. *General Secretary*, J. Akker

NATIONAL ASSOCIATION OF COLLIERY OVERMEN, DEPUTIES AND SHOTFIRERS, Simpson House, 48 Nether Hall Road, Doncaster DNI 2PZ. Tel: 01302-368015. *Secretary*, P. McNestry

NATIONAL ASSOCIATION OF CO-OPERATIVE OFFICIALS (3,300), Coronation House, Arndale Centre, Manchester M4 2HW. Tel: 0161-834 6029. *General Secretary*, L. W. Ewing

NATIONAL ASSOCIATION OF LICENSED HOUSE MANAGERS (7,100), Carlton House, 7 Wilson Patten Street, Warrington, Cheshire WAI IPG. Tel: 01925-244888. *General Secretary*, P. Love

NATIONAL ASSOCIATION OF PROBATION OFFICERS (8,000), 3–4 Chivalry Road, London SWII IHT. Tel: 0171-223 4887. *Secretary*, Ms J. McKnight

NASUWT (NATIONAL ASSOCIATION OF SCHOOLMASTERS/UNION OF WOMEN TEACHERS) (157,146), 5 King Street, London WC2E 8HN. Tel: 0171-379 9499. *General Secretary*, N. de Gruchy

NATIONAL LEAGUE OF THE BLIND AND DISABLED (2,100), 2 Tenterden Road, London NI7 8BE. Tel: 0181-808 6030. *General Secretary*, J. Mann

NATIONAL UNION OF DOMESTIC APPLIANCES AND GENERAL OPERATIVES (2,406), 6–8 Imperial Buildings Corporation Street, Rotherham, S. Yorks S60 IPB. Tel: 01709-382820. *General Secretary*, A. McCarthy

NATIONAL UNION OF INSURANCE WORKERS (10,460), 27 Old Gloucester Street, London WCIN 3AF. Tel: 0171-405 6798. *General Secretary*, K. Perry

NATIONAL UNION OF JOURNALISTS (NUJ) (26,000), Acorn House, 314–320 Gray's Inn Road, London WCIX 8DP. Tel: 0171-278 7916. *General Secretary*, J. Foster

NATIONAL UNION OF KNITWEAR, FOOTWEAR AND APPAREL TRADES (40,000), 55 New Walk, Leicester LEI 7EB. Tel: 0116-255 6703. *General Secretary*, P. Gates

NATIONAL UNION OF LOCK AND METAL WORKERS (4,850), Bellamy House, Wilkes Street, Willenhall, W. Midlands WVI3 2BS. Tel: 01902-366651. *General Secretary*, R. Ward

NATIONAL UNION OF MARINE, AVIATION AND SHIPPING TRANSPORT OFFICERS (18,200), Oceanair House, 750–760 High Road, London EII 3BB. Tel: 0181-989 6677. *General Secretary*, B. Orrell

NATIONAL UNION OF MINEWORKERS (NUM) (10,814), Miners' Offices, 2 Huddersfield Road, Barnsley, S. Yorks S70 2LS. Tel: 01226-284006. *President*, A. Scargill

NATIONAL UNION OF RAIL, MARITIME AND TRANSPORT WORKERS (RMT) (68,000), Unity House, Euston Road, London NWI 2BL. Tel: 0171-387 4771. *General Secretary*, Knapp

NATIONAL UNION OF TEACHERS (NUT) (179,000), Hamilton House, Mabledon Place, London WCIH 9BD. Tel: 0171-388 6191. *General Secretary*, D. McAvoy

NORTHERN CARPET TRADES' UNION (695), 22 Clare Road, Halifax, W. Yorks HXI 2HX. Tel: 01422-360492. *General Secretary*, K. Edmondson

POWER LOOM CARPET WEAVERS' AND TEXTILE WORKERS' UNION (2,000), 148 Hurcott Road, Kidderminster, Worcs DYI0 2RL. Tel: 01562-823192. *General Secretary*, G. Rudd

PRISON OFFICERS' ASSOCIATION (28,061), Cronin House, 245 Church Street, London N9 9HW. Tel: 0181-803 0255. *General Secretary*, D. Evans

PROFESSIONAL FOOTBALLERS ASSOCIATION (2,191), 2 Oxford Court, Bishopsgate, Manchester M2 3WQ. Tel: 0161-236 0575. *Chief Executive*, G. Taylor

PUBLIC SERVICES, TAX AND COMMERCE UNION (160,000), New Bridgewater House, 5–13 Great Suffolk Street, London ons. Tel: 0171-960 3000. *Joint General Secretaries*, C. Brooke, J. Sheldon

THE ROSSENDALE UNION OF BOOT, SHOE AND SLIPPER OPERATIVES (1,330), Taylor House, 7 Tenterfield Street, Waterfoot, Rossendale, Lancs BB4 7BA. Tel: 01706-215657. *General Secretary*, M. Murray, MBE

SCOTTISH PRISON OFFICERS' ASSOCIATION (3,291), 21 Calder Road, Edinburgh EH11 3PF. Tel: 0131-443 8105. *General Secretary*, D. Turner

SCOTTISH UNION OF POWER-LOOM OVERLOOKERS (42), 3 Napier Terrace, Dundee DD2 2SL. Tel: 01382-612196. *Secretary*, J. D. Reilly

SHEFFIELD WOOL SHEAR WORKERS' UNION (12), 5 Collin Avenue, Sheffield S6 4ES. Tel: 0114-232 1821. *Secretary*, B. Bell

THE SOCIETY OF RADIOGRAPHERS (14,000), 2 Carriage Row, 183 Eversholt Street, London NW1 1BU. Tel: 0171-391 4500. *General Secretary*, S. Evans

SOCIETY OF TELECOM EXECUTIVES (19,000), 1 Park Road, Teddington, Middx TW11 0AR. Tel: 0181-943 5181. *General Secretary*, S. Petch

TRANSPORT AND GENERAL WORKERS' UNION (TGWU) (900,000), 16 Palace Street, London SW1E 5JD. Tel: 0171- 828 7788. *General Secretary*, W. Morris

TRANSPORT SALARIED STAFFS' ASSOCIATION (36,000), Walkden House, 10 Melton Street, London NW1 2EJ. Tel: 0171-387 2101. *General Secretary*, R. A. Rosser

UNDEB CENEDLAETHOL ATHRAWON CYMRU (NATIONAL ASSOCIATION OF TEACHERS OF WALES) (4,000), Pen Roc, Rhodfa'r Mor, Aberystwyth, Ceredigion SY23 2AZ. Tel: 01970-615577. *General Secretary*, G. W. James

UNIFI (47,606), Oathall House, Oathall Road, Haywards Heath, W. Sussex RH1 3DG. Tel: 01444-458811. *General Secretary*, J. P. S. Snowball

UNION OF CONSTRUCTION, ALLIED TRADES AND TECHNICIANS (UCATT) (110,000), UCATT House, 177 Abbeville Road, London SW4 9RL. Tel: 0171-622 2442. *Secretary*, G. Brumwell

UNION OF SHOP, DISTRIBUTIVE AND ALLIED WORKERS (USDAW) (280,901), Oakley, 188 Wilmslow Road, Fallowfield, Manchester M14 6LJ. Tel: 0161-224 2804. *Secretary*, D. G. Davies, CBE

UNION OF TEXTILE WORKERS (1,526), Foxlowe, Market Place, Leek, Staffs ST13 6AD. Tel: 01538-382068. *General Secretary*, A. Hitchmough

UNISON (1,400,000), 1 Mabledon Place, London WC1H 9AJ. Tel: 0171-388 2366. *General Secretary*, R. Bickerstaffe

UNITED ROAD TRANSPORT UNION (18,000), 76 High Lane, Chorlton-cum-Hardy, Manchester M21 9EF. Tel: 0161-881 6245. *General Secretary*, D. Higginbottom

WRITERS' GUILD OF GREAT BRITAIN (1,800), 430 Edgware Road, London W2 1EH. Tel: 0171-723 8074. *General Secretary*, Ms A. Gray

BRITISH DENTAL ASSOCIATION (15,000), 64 Wimpole Street, London W1M 8AL. Tel: 0171-935 0875. *Chief Executive*, J. M. G. Hunt

CHARTERED INSTITUTE OF JOURNALISTS (2,000), 2 Dock Offices, Surrey Quays Road, London SE16 2XU. Tel: 0171-252 1187. *General Secretary*, C. Underwood

GOVERNMENT COMMUNICATIONS STAFF FEDERATION (2,500), Room A0904A, Priors Road, Cheltenham, Glos GL52 5AJ. Tel: 01242-573906. *Chairman*, B. Moore

NATIONAL ASSOCIATION OF HEAD TEACHERS (NAHT) (39,900), 1 Heath Square, Boltro Road, Haywards Heath, W. Sussex RH16 1BL. Tel: 01444-458133. *General Secretary*, D. Hart, OBE

NATIONAL SOCIETY FOR EDUCATION IN ART AND DESIGN (2,500), The Gatehouse, Corsham Court, Corsham, Wilts SN13 0BZ. Tel: 01249-714825. *General Secretary*, Dr J. H. M. Steers

PATTERN WEAVERS SOCIETY (58), 20 Hayfield Avenue, Oakes, Huddersfield HD3 4FZ. Tel: 01484-656886. *Secretary*, D. Mellor

RETAIL BOOK, STATIONERY AND ALLIED TRADES EMPLOYEES' ASSOCIATION (8,000), 8–9 Commercial Road, Swindon SN1 5RB. Tel: 01793-615811. *President*, A. Willmott

ROYAL COLLEGE OF MIDWIVES (37,000), 15 Mansfield Street, London W1M 0BE. Tel: 0171-872 5100. *General Secretary*, Mrs J. Allison

SCOTTISH SECONDARY TEACHERS' ASSOCIATION (7,200), 15 Dundas Street, Edinburgh EH3 6QG. Tel: 0131-556 5919. *General Secretary*, A. M. Lamont

SECONDARY HEADS ASSOCIATION (8,500), 130 Regent Road, Leicester LE1 7PG. Tel: 0116-247 1797. *General Secretary*, J. Sutton

SOCIETY OF AUTHORS (5,900), 84 Drayton Gardens, London SW10 9SB. Tel: 0171-373 6642. *General Secretary*, M. Le Fanu

SOCIETY OF CHIROPODISTS AND PODIATRISTS (6,135), 53 Welbeck Street, London W1M 7HE. Tel: 0171-486 3381. *General Secretary*, J. G. C. Trouncer

NON-AFFILIATED TRADE UNIONS

ASSOCIATION OF TEACHERS AND LECTURERS (150,000), 7 Northumberland Street, London WC2N 5DA. Tel: 0171-930 6441. *General Secretary*, P. Smith

National Academies of Scholarship

THE BRITISH ACADEMY (1901)
20–21 Cornwall Terrace, London NW1 4QP
Tel 0171-487 5966

The British Academy is an independent, self-governing learned society for the promotion of historical, philosophical and philological studies. It supports advanced academic research in the humanities and social sciences, and is a channel for the Government's support of research in those disciplines. The Humanities Research Board is responsible for the administration of the majority of the Academy's grant programmes.

The Fellows are scholars who have attained distinction in one of the branches of study that the Academy exists to promote. Candidates must be nominated by existing Fellows. At 1 June 1996 there were 635 Fellows, 14 Honorary Fellows, and 306 Corresponding Fellows overseas.

President, Sir Keith Thomas, PBA
Vice-Presidents, Prof. P. Haggett, FBA; Prof. M. McGowen, FBA
Treasurer, J. S. Flemming, FBA
Foreign Secretary, Prof. B. E. Supple, FBA
Publications Officer, Prof. D. E. Luscombe, FBA
Chairman, Humanities Research Board, Prof. J. D. M. H. Laver, FBA
Secretary, P. W. H. Brown, CBE

THE ROYAL ACADEMY (1768)
Burlington House, London W1V 0DS
Tel 0171-439 7438

The Royal Academy of Arts is an independent, self-governing society devoted to the encouragement and promotion of the fine arts.

Membership of the Academy is limited to 80 Royal Academicians, all being painters, engravers, sculptors or architects. Candidates are nominated and elected by the existing Academicians. There is also a limited class of honorary membership and there were 14 honorary members as at mid-1996.

President, Sir Philip Dowson, CBE, PRA
Treasurer, M. Kenny, RA
Keeper, L. McComb, RA
Secretary, P. Rodgers

THE ROYAL ACADEMY OF ENGINEERING (1976)
29 Great Peter Street, London SW1P 3LW
Tel 0171-222 2688

The Royal Academy of Engineering was established as the Fellowship of Engineering in 1976. It was granted a Royal Charter in 1983 and its present title in 1992. It is an independent, self-governing body whose object is the pursuit, encouragement and maintenance of excellence in the whole field of engineering, in order to promote the advancement of the science, art and practice of engineering for the benefit of the public.

Election to the Fellowship is by invitation only from nominations supported by the body of Fellows. Fellows are chosen from among chartered engineers of all disciplines. At July 1996 there were 1,036 Fellows, 14 Honorary Fellows and 68 Foreign Members. The Duke of Edinburgh is the Senior Fellow and the Duke of Kent is a Royal Fellow.

President, Sir David Davies, CBE, FRS, F.Eng
Senior Vice-President, B. R. R. Butler, OBE, F.Eng
Vice-Presidents, Sir Gordon Higginson, F.Eng; R. J. Margetts, F.Eng; S. N. Mustow, CBE, F.Eng
Hon. Treasurer, D. Hanson
Hon. Secretaries, P. N. Paul, F.Eng (*Civil Engineering*); Dr J. R. Forrest, F.Eng (*Electrical Engineering*); P. C. Ruffles, F.Eng (*Mechanical Engineering*); G. Clerehugh, OBE, F.Eng (*Process Engineering*); B. R. R. Butler, OBE, F.Eng (*International Activities*); Sir Gordon Higginson, F.Eng (*Education, Training and Competence to Practise*)
Executive Secretary, J. R. Appleton

THE ROYAL SCOTTISH ACADEMY (1838)
The Mound, Edinburgh EH2 2EL
Tel 0131-225 6671

The Scottish Academy was founded in 1826 to arrange exhibitions for contemporary paintings and to establish a society of fine art in Scotland. The Academy was granted a Royal Charter in 1838.

Members are elected from the disciplines of painting, sculpture, architecture and printmaking. Elections are from nominations put forward by the existing membership. At mid-1995 there were 9 Senior Academicians, 36 Academicians, 43 Associates, three non-resident Associates and 21 Honorary Members.

President, W. J. L. Baillie, PRSA
Secretary, I. McKenzie Smith, RSA
Treasurer, J. Morris, RSA
Librarian, P. Collins, RSA
Administrative Secretary, B. Laidlaw

ROYAL SOCIETY (1660)
6 Carlton House Terrace, London SW1Y 5AG
Tel 0171-839 5561

The Royal Society is the United Kingdom academy of science. It is an independent, self-governing body under a Royal Charter, promoting and advancing all fields of physical and biological sciences, of mathematics and engineering, medical and agricultural sciences, their applications and place in society.

Election to Fellowship of the Royal Society is limited to those distinguished for original scientific work. Each year up to 40 new Fellows and six Foreign Members are elected from the most distinguished scientists. In addition, the Council can recommend for election members of the Royal family and, on average, one person each year for conspicuous service to the cause of science. At January 1996, there were 1,137 Fellows, 106 Foreign Members and six Royal Fellows or Patrons.

President, Sir Aaron Klug, OM, PRS
Treasurer, Sir John Horlock, FRS, F.Eng

Biological Secretary, Prof. P. J. Lachmann, FRS
Physical Secretary, Prof. J. S. Rowlinson, FRS, F.Eng
Foreign Secretary, Dr A. L. McLaren, DBE, FRS
Executive Secretary, Dr P. T. Warren

THE ROYAL SOCIETY OF EDINBURGH
(1783)
22–24 George Street, Edinburgh EH2 2PQ
Tel 0131-225 6057

The Royal Society of Edinburgh is Scotland's premier learned society. The Society was founded by Royal Charter in 1783 for 'the advancement of Learning and Useful Knowledge', and its principal role is the promotion of scholarship in all its branches. It provides a forum for

broadly-based interdisciplinary activity in Scotland, including organizing public lectures, conferences and specialist research seminars; providing advice to Parliament and government; administering a range of research fellowships held in Scotland; and publishing learned journals.

Fellows are elected by ballot after being nominated by at least four existing Fellows. At 31 May 1996 there were 1,125 Ordinary Fellows and 72 Honorary Fellows.
President, Dr T. L. Johnston
Treasurer, Sir Lewis Robertson, CBE, FRSE
General Secretary, Prof. V. B. Proudfoot
Executive Secretary, Dr W. Duncan

Royal Academicians

*Senior Academician

1989	Abrahams, Ivor	1979	Dowson, Sir Philip, CBE	1987	McComb, Leonard
1988	Ackroyd, Prof. Norman	1990	Draper, Kenneth	1993	MacCormac, Richard, CBE
1967	Adams, Norman	1959	*Dunstan, Bernard	1947	*Machin, Arnold, OBE
1978	Aitchison, Craigie	1994	Durrant, Jennifer	1995	Maine, John
1989	*Armfield, Diana	1976	Eyton, Anthony	1976	*Manasseh, Leonard, OBE
1994	*Armitage, Kenneth	1992	*Fedden, Mary	1994	Manser, Michael
1982	Ayres, Gillian, OBE	1987	Flanagan, Barry, OBE	1985	*Martin, Sir Leslie
1986	Bellany, John, CBE	1983	Foster, Sir Norman	1991	Mistry, Dhruva
1992	Berg, Adrian	1975	Fraser, Donald Hamilton	1994	Moon, Mick
1971	Blackadder, Elizabeth, OBE	1990	Freeth, Peter	1992	Neiland, Brendan
1974	Blake, Peter, CBE	1992	*Frost, Terry	1995	Orr, Christopher
1970	*Blamey, Norman	1995	*Gear, William	1979	Paolozzi, Sir Eduardo, CBE
1971	Blow, Sandra	1964	*Gore, Frederick, CBE	1980	Partridge, John, CBE
1970	Bowey, Olwyn	1971	Green, Anthony	1983	*Pasmore, Victor, CH, CBE
1974	Bowyer, William	1994	Grimshaw, Nicholas	1984	Phillips, Tom
1968	Brown, Ralph	1963	*Hayes, Colin	1972	Powell, Sir Philip, CH, OBE
1964	Butler, James	1990	*Herman, Josef, OBE	1969	*Roberts-Jones, Ivor, CBE
1971	*Cadbury-Brown, Prof. H. T., OBE	1985	Hockney, David	1978	Rogers, Sir Richard
		1974	*Hogarth, Paul, OBE	1990	Rooney, Michael
1974	Camp, Jeffery	1992	Hopkins, Sir Michael, CBE	1960	*Rosoman, Leonard, OBE
1962	*Casson, Sir Hugh, CH, KCVO	1983	Howard, Ken	1982	Sandle, Prof. Michael
1993	Caulfield, Patrick	1983	Hoyland, John	1975	Stephenson, Ian
1980	Christopher, Ann	1987	Huxley, Prof. Paul	1977	Sutton, Philip
1970	Clarke, Geoffrey	1989	Jacklin, Bill	1985	Tilson, Joe
1968	Clatworthy, Robert	1981	Jones, Allen	1973	Tindle, David
1965	Coker, Peter	1976	Kenny, Michael	1986	Titchell, John
1965	Cooke, Jean	1989	Kiff, Ken	1992	Tucker, William
1994	Cragg, Prof. Tony	1977	King, Prof. Phillip, CBE	1956	*Ward, John, CBE
1993	Craxton, John	1984	Kitaj, R. B.	1955	*Weight, Prof. Carel, CH, CBE
1989	Cullinan, Edward, CBE	1970	Kneale, Bryan	1980	Whishaw, Anthony
1969	Cuming, Frederick	1986	Koralek, Paul, CBE	1970	*Williams, Kyffin, OBE
1992	Cummins, Gus	1991	*Lasdun, Sir Dennis, CBE	1990	Wilson, Colin St J.
1977	*Dannatt, Prof. Trevor	1982	Lawson, Sonia	1983	Wragg, John
1970	Dickson, Jennifer	1975	Levene, Ben		

Royal Scottish Academy

SENIOR ACADEMICIANS

1958	Armour, Dr Mary
1974	Crosbie, William
1976	Malcolm, Ellen
1963	Morrocco, Alberto, OBE
1957	Patrick, J. McIntosh
1977	Robertson, R. Ross
1975	Wheeler, Sir Anthony, OBE
1977	Whiston, Peter

ROYAL SCOTTISH ACADEMICIANS

1979	Baillie, William
1972	Blackadder, Elizabeth, OBE
1993	Bryce, Gordon
1991	Buchan, Dennis
1986	Bushe, Fred
1977	Butler, Vincent
1981	Campbell, Alex
1974	Collins, Peter
1992	Donald, George
1989	Evans, David
1989	Fraser, Alexander
1989	Harvey, Jake
1972	Houston, John
1979	Knox, John
1973	Littlejohn, William
1991	Maclean, William
1971	McClure, David
1990	MacMillan, Andrew
1991	Merrylees, Andrew
1990	Metzstein, Izi
1972	Michie, David

1989	Morris, James
1992	Morrison, James
1990	Pelly, Frances
1991	Pottinger, Frank
1992	Rae, Barbara
1976	Reeves, Philip
1989	Richards, John, CBE
1989	Robertson, James
1984	Scott, Bill
1990	Shanks, Duncan
1987	Smith, Ian McKenzie
1985	Snowden, Michael
1979	Steedman, Robert
1982	Walker, Frances

ASSOCIATES

Arnott, Ian
Black, Robert
Boys, John
Brotherston, William
Busby, John
Bytautus, Alfons
Cairns, Joyce
Campbell, A. Buchanan
Clarke, Derek
Clifford, J. G.
Cocker, Douglas
Convery, Frank
Crowe, Victoria
Dean, Fiona
Docherty, Michael
Dunbar, Lennox
Fairgrieve, James

Fisher, Beth
The Earl Haig
Howard, Ian
Johnstone, John
Lamb, Elspeth
Low, Bet
McCulloch, Ian
McIntosh, Ian
MacPherson, George
Main, Kirkland
Mooney, John
Onwin, Glen
Page, David
Rayner, Martin
Renton, James, OBE
Rodger, Willie
Ross, Alastair
Squire, Geoffrey
Stenhouse, Andrew
Stiven, Fred
Watson, Arthur
Webster, Robin
Wedgwood, Roland
Wishart, Sylvia
Wisziewski, Adrian
Wyllie, George

NON-RESIDENT ASSOCIATES

Balmer, Barbara
Gasson, Barry
Morrocco, Leon

The Research Councils

The Government funds basic and applied civil science research, mostly through the seven research councils, which are supported by the Department of Trade and Industry. The councils support research and training in universities and other higher education establishments. They also receive income for research commissioned by government departments and the private sector.

GOVERNMENT SCIENCE BUDGET 1996–7

	£m
BBSRC	176.31
CCLRC	1.45
ESRC	63.08
EPSRC	375.95
MRC	281.89
NERC	164.65
PPARC	191.68

BIOTECHNOLOGY AND BIOLOGICAL SCIENCES RESEARCH COUNCIL (BBSRC)
Polaris House, North Star Avenue, Swindon SN2 1UH
Tel 01793-413200

The BBSRC promotes and supports research and post-graduate training relating to the understanding and exploitation of biological systems; advances knowledge and technology, and provides trained scientists to meet the needs of biotechnological-related industries; and provides advice, disseminates knowledge, and promotes public understanding of biotechnology and the biological sciences.
Chairman, Sir Alistair Grant
Chief Executive, Prof. R. Baker, FRS

INSTITUTES

BABRAHAM INSTITUTE
Director, Dr R. G. Dyer, Babraham Hall, Babraham, Cambridge CB2 4AT. Tel: 01223-832312

INSTITUTE FOR ANIMAL HEALTH
Director, Prof. F. J. Bourne, CBE, Compton, Newbury, Berks RG20 7NN. Tel: 01635-577238

BBSRC AND MRC NEUROPATHOGENESIS UNIT, Ogston Building, West Mains Road, Edinburgh EH9 3JF. Tel: 0131-667 5204/5. *Head,* Dr C. J. Bostock
COMPTON LABORATORY, Compton, Newbury, Berks RG20 7NN. Tel: 01635-578411. *Divisional Head in Charge,* Dr P. W. Jones
PIRBRIGHT LABORATORY, Ash Road, Pirbright, Woking, Surrey GU24 0NF. Tel: 01483-232441. *Head,* Dr A. I. Donaldson

INSTITUTE OF ARABLE CROPS RESEARCH
Director, Prof. B. J. Miflin, Rothamsted, Harpenden, Herts AL5 2JQ. Tel: 01582-763133
IACR – BROOM'S BARN, Higham, Bury St Edmunds, Suffolk IP28 6NP. Tel: 01284-810363. *Head,* Dr J. D. Pidgeon
IACR – LONG ASHTON RESEARCH STATION, Department of Agricultural Sciences, University of Bristol, Long Ashton, Bristol BS18 9AF. Tel: 01275-392181. *Head,* Prof. P. R. Shewry

IACR – ROTHAMSTED, Harpenden, Herts AL5 2JQ. Tel: 01582-763133. *Head,* Prof. B. J. Miflin.

INSTITUTE OF FOOD RESEARCH
Director, Prof. A. D. B. Malcolm, Earley Gate, Whiteknights Road, Reading RG6 6BZ. Tel: 01189-357055
NORWICH LABORATORY, Norwich Research Park, Colney Lane, Norwich NR4 7UA. Tel: 01603-255000. *Deputy Director and Head of Laboratory,* Prof. P. S. Belton
READING LABORATORY, Earley Gate, Whiteknights Road, Reading RG6 6BZ. Tel: 01189-357000. *Deputy Director and Head of Laboratory,* Prof. H. J. H. MacFie

INSTITUTE OF GRASSLAND AND ENVIRONMENTAL RESEARCH
Director, Prof. C. J. Pollock, Plas Gogerddan, Aberystwyth, Ceredigion SY23 3EB. Tel: 01970-828255
ABERYSTWYTH RESEARCH CENTRE, Plas Gogerddan, Aberystwyth, Ceredigion SY23 3EB. Tel: 01970-828255. *Officer-in-charge,* D. A. Davies
NORTH WYKE RESEARCH STATION, Okehampton, Devon EX20 2SB. Tel: 01837-82558. *Head,* Prof. R. J. Wilkins

JOHN INNES CENTRE
Director, Prof. R. B. Flavell, Norwich Research Park, Colney, Norwich NR4 7UH. Tel: 01603-452571
NITROGEN FIXATION LABORATORY, Norwich Research Park, Colney, Norwich NR4 7UH. Tel: 01603-452571. *Head,* Prof. B. E. Smith

ROSLIN INSTITUTE
Director, Prof. G. Bulfield, Roslin, Midlothian EH25 9PS. Tel: 0131-440 2726

SILSOE RESEARCH INSTITUTE
Director, Prof. B. J. Legg, Wrest Park, Silsoe, Bedford MK45 4HS. Tel: 01525-860000

INTERDISCIPLINARY RESEARCH CENTRES

ADVANCED CENTRE FOR BIOCHEMICAL ENGINEERING
Director, Prof. P. Dunnill, FENG., University College London, Torrington Place, London WC1E 7JE. Tel: 0171-380 7031
CENTRE FOR GENOME RESEARCH
Director (acting), Dr A. Smith, University of Edinburgh, King's Buildings, West Mains Road, Edinburgh EH9 3JQ. Tel: 0131-650 5890
OXFORD CENTRE FOR MOLECULAR SCIENCES
Director, Prof. J. E. Baldwin, FRS, New Chemistry Laboratory, University of Oxford, South Parks Road, Oxford OX1 3QT. Tel: 01865-275654
SUSSEX CENTRE FOR NEUROSCIENCE
Director, Prof. M. O'Shea, School of Biological Sciences, University of Sussex, Brighton BN1 9QG. Tel: 01273-678055

SCOTTISH AGRICULTURAL AND BIOLOGICAL RESEARCH INSTITUTES

HANNAH RESEARCH INSTITUTE, Ayr KA6 5HL. Tel: 01292-476013. *Director,* Prof. M. Peaker, FRS

MACAULAY LAND USE RESEARCH INSTITUTE,
Craigiebuckler, Aberdeen AB15 8QH. Tel: 01224-318611.
Director, Prof. T. J. Maxwell, FRSE
MOREDUN RESEARCH INSTITUTE, 408 Gilmerton Road,
Edinburgh EH17 7JH. Tel: 0131-664 3262. *Director,* Prof.
I. D. Aitken, OBE
ROWETT RESEARCH INSTITUTE, Greenburn Road,
Bucksburn, Aberdeen AB21 9SB. Tel: 01224-712751.
Director, Prof. W. P. T. James, CBE, FRSE
SCOTTISH CROP RESEARCH INSTITUTE (SCRI),
Invergowrie, Dundee DD2 5DA. Tel: 01382-562731.
Director, Prof. J. Hillman, FRSE
BIOMATHEMATICS AND STATISTICS SCOTLAND
(BioSS) (Administered by SCRI), University of
Edinburgh, James Clerk Maxwell Building, The King's
Buildings, Mayfield Road, Edinburgh EH9 3JZ. Tel: 0131-
650 4900. *Director,* R. A. Kempton

COUNCIL FOR THE CENTRAL LABORATORY OF THE RESEARCH COUNCILS (CCLRC)
Chilton, Didcot, Oxon OX11 0QX
Tel 01235-821900

The CCLRC was set up in April 1995 and is responsible for
the Daresbury and Rutherford Appleton Laboratories.
Chairman and Chief Executive, Dr P. R. Williams, CBE

DARESBURY LABORATORY, Daresbury, Warrington,
Cheshire WA4 4AD. Tel: 01925-603000. *Head,* Dr R. W.
Newport
RUTHERFORD APPLETON LABORATORY, Chilton, Didcot,
Oxon OX11 0QX. Tel: 01235-821900. *Head,* Dr T. G.
Walker

ECONOMIC AND SOCIAL RESEARCH COUNCIL (ESRC)
Polaris House, North Star Avenue, Swindon SN2 1UJ
Tel 01793-413000

The purpose of the ESRC is to promote and support
research and postgraduate training in the social sciences; to
advance knowledge and provide trained social scientists; to
provide advice on, and disseminate knowledge and
promote public understanding of, the social sciences.
Chairman, Dr B. Smith, OBE
Chief Executive, Prof. R. Amann

RESEARCH CENTRES

CAMBRIDGE GROUP FOR THE HISTORY OF POPULATION
AND SOCIAL STRUCTURE, 27 Trumpington Street,
Cambridge CB2 1QA. Tel: 01223-333186. *Director,* Dr
R. Smith
CENTRE FOR BUSINESS RESEARCH, Department of
Applied Economics, University of Cambridge, Sidgwick
Avenue, Cambridge CB3 9DE. Tel: 01223-335248.
Director, A. Hughes
CENTRE FOR ECONOMIC LEARNING AND SOCIAL
EVOLUTION, University College London, Gower
Street, London WC1E 6BT. Tel: 0171-387 7050. *Director,*
Prof. K. Binmore
CENTRE FOR ECONOMIC PERFORMANCE, London School
of Economics, Houghton Street, London WC2A 2AE. Tel:
0171-955 7048. *Director,* Prof. R. Layard
CENTRE FOR HOUSING RESEARCH AND URBAN STUDIES,
University of Glasgow, 25 Bute Gardens, Hillhead,
Glasgow G12 8RS. Tel: 0141-330 4615. *Director,*
Prof. D. MacLennan, PH.D.
CENTRE FOR FISCAL POLICY, Institute for Fiscal Studies,
7 Ridgmount Street, London WC1E 7AE. Tel: 0171-636
3784. *Director,* Prof. R. Blundell
CENTRE FOR INTERNATIONAL EMPLOYMENT RELATIONS
RESEARCH, School of Industrial and Business Studies,
University of Warwick, Coventry CV4 7AL. Tel: 01203-
524265. *Director,* Prof. K. Sisson
CENTRE FOR RESEARCH IN DEVELOPMENT, INSTRUCTION
AND TRAINING, Department of Psychology, University
of Nottingham, Nottingham NG7 2RD. Tel: 0115-951
5312. *Director,* Prof. D. J. Wood
CENTRE FOR RESEARCH IN ETHNIC RELATIONS,
University of Warwick, Coventry CV4 7AL. Tel: 01203-
523607. *Director,* Prof. Z. Layton-Henry
CENTRE FOR RESEARCH INTO ELECTIONS AND SOCIAL
TRENDS, Nuffield College, University of Oxford,
Oxford OX1 1NF. Tel: 01865-278537. *Director,* Dr A. F.
Heath; Social and Community Planning Research,
35 Northampton Square, London EC1V 0AX. Tel: 0171-
250 1866. *Director,* Prof. R. Jowell
CENTRE FOR RESEARCH ON INNOVATION AND
COMPETITIVE ENVIRONMENTS, Faculty of Economic
and Social Studies, University of Manchester M13 9PL.
Tel: 0161-275 2000. *Director,* Prof. S. Metcalfe;
Manchester School of Management, UMIST,
Manchester M60 1QD. Tel: 0161-236 3311. *Director,* Prof.
R. Coombs
CENTRE FOR SOCIAL AND ECONOMIC RESEARCH ON THE
GLOBAL ENVIRONMENT, School of Environmental
Sciences, University of East Anglia, Norwich NR4 7TJ.
Tel: 01603-593176; University College London, Remax
House, 31–32 Alfred Place, London WC1E 7DP. Tel: 0171-
380 7874. *Director,* Prof. D. Pearce
CENTRE FOR THE STUDY OF AFRICAN ECONOMIES,
Institute of Economics and Statistics, University of
Oxford, St Cross Building, Manor Road, Oxford OX1 3UL.
Tel: 01865-271084. *Director,* Prof. P. Collier
COMPLEX PRODUCT SYSTEM INNOVATION CENTRE,
SPRU, Mantell Building, University of Sussex, Brighton
BN1 9RF. Tel: 01273-686758. *Director,* Dr M. Hobday;
Business School, University of Brighton, Brighton BN2
4AT. Tel: 01273-600900. *Director,* H. Rush
FINANCIAL MARKETS CENTRE, London School of
Economics, Houghton Street, London WC2A 2AE. Tel:
0171-955 7002. *Director,* Prof. D. Webb
HUMAN COMMUNICATION RESEARCH CENTRE,
University of Edinburgh, 2 Buccleuch Place, Edinburgh
EH8 9LW. Tel: 0131-650 4444. *Director,* Prof. K. Stenning
RESEARCH CENTRE ON MICRO-SOCIAL CHANGE,
University of Essex, Wivenhoe Park, Colchester, Essex
CO4 3SQ. Tel: 01206-872957. *Director,* Prof. J. Gershuny
TRANSPORT STUDIES UNIT, Centre for Transport
Studies, University College London, Gower Street,
London WC1E 6BT. Tel: 0171-380 7009. *Director,* Dr
P. Goodwin

RESOURCE CENTRES

BUSINESS PROCESS RESOURCE CENTRE, Warwick
Manufacturing Group, University of Warwick,
Coventry CV4 7AL. Tel: 01203-523155. *Director,*
Dr D. Park
CENTRE FOR APPLIED SOCIAL SURVEYS, Social and
Community Planning Research, 35 Northampton
Square, London EC1V 0AX. Tel: 0171-250 1866. *Director,*
R. Thomas

CENTRE FOR ECONOMIC POLICY RESEARCH, 25–28 Old
Burlington Street, London WIX ILB. Tel: 0171-734 9110.
Director, Prof. R. Portes
ESRC DATA ARCHIVE, University of Essex, Wivenhoe
Park, Colchester, Essex CO4 3SQ. Tel: 01206-872001.
Director, Prof. D. Lievesley
INTERNATIONAL BIBLIOGRAPHY OF THE SOCIAL
SCIENCES, London School of Economics, Houghton
Street, London WC2A 2AE. Tel: 0171-955 7000. *Director,*
Ms L. Brindley
QUALITATIVE DATA ARCHIVAL RESOURCE CENTRE,
Department of Sociology, University of Essex,
Wivenhoe Park, Colchester, Essex CO4 3SQ. Tel: 01206-
873059. *Director,* Prof. P. Thompson
RESOURCE CENTRE FOR ACCESS TO DATA IN EUROPE,
Department of Geography, University of Durham,
Durham DHI 3LE. Tel: 0191-374 2452. *Director,* Prof. R.
Hudson; University of Essex, Wivenhoe Park,
Colchester CO4 3SQ. Tel: 01206-872001. *Director,* Prof. D.
Lievesley
SOCIAL SCIENCE INFORMATION GATEWAY, Centre for
Computing in the Social Sciences, University of Bristol,
Bristol BS8 ITN. Tel: 0117-928 8471. *Contact,* N. Ferguson

ENGINEERING AND PHYSICAL SCIENCES
RESEARCH COUNCIL (EPSRC)
Polaris House, North Star Avenue, Swindon SN2 IET
Tel 01793-444000

The purpose of the EPSRC is to encourage and support all
basic and strategic research and training in UK higher
education institutions in the natural and physical sciences
and engineering. It no longer has any research institutions.
Chairman, Dr A. Rudge, OBE, FRS, FEng.
Chief Executive, Prof. R. Brook, OBE

MEDICAL RESEARCH COUNCIL (MRC)
20 Park Crescent, London WIN 4AL
Tel 0171-636 5422

The purpose of the MRC is to promote medical and related
biological research. The council employs its own research
staff and funds research by other institutions and indivi-
duals, complementing the research resources of the
universities and hospitals.
Chairman, Sir David Plastow
Chief Executive, Prof. G. K. Radda, CBE, D.Phil., FRS
Chairman, Neurosciences and Mental Health Board,
Dr T. W. Robbins
Chairman, Molecular and Cellular Medicine Board, Prof.
L. K. Borysiewicz
Chairman, Physiological Medicine and Infections Board,
Prof. A. M. McGregor, MD, FRCP
Chairman, Health Services and Public Health Research Board,
Prof. A. Haines

NATIONAL INSTITUTE FOR MEDICAL RESEARCH, The
Ridgeway, Mill Hill, London NW7 IAA. Tel: 0181-959
3666. *Director,* Sir John Skehel, Ph.D., FRS
CLINICAL SCIENCES CENTRE, Royal Postgraduate
Medical School, Du Cane Road, London WI2 ONN. Tel:
0181-743 2030. *Director,* Prof. A. McNeish
LABORATORY OF MOLECULAR BIOLOGY, Hills Road,
Cambridge CB2 2QH. Tel: 01223-248011. *Director,*
Dr R. Henderson, FRS

RESEARCH UNITS

ANATOMICAL NEUROPHARMACOLOGY UNIT, Mansfield
Road, Oxford OXI 3TH. Tel: 01865-271865. *Hon. Director,*
Prof. A. D. Smith, D.Phil.
APPLIED PSYCHOLOGY UNIT, 15 Chaucer Road,
Cambridge CB2 2EF. Tel: 01223-355294. *Administrative
Director,* M. Davies, Ph.D.
BBSRC/MRC NEUROPATHOGENESIS UNIT, Ogston
Building, West Mains Road, Edinburgh EH9 3JF. Tel:
0131-667 5204. *Director,* vacant
BIOCHEMICAL AND CLINICAL MAGNETIC RESONANCE
UNIT, University Department of Biochemistry, South
Parks Road, Oxford OXI 3QU. Tel: 01865-275274. *Hon.
Director,* D. Styles, D.Phil.
BIOSTATISTICS UNIT, Institute of Public Health,
University Forvie Site, Robinson Way, Cambridge
CB2 2SR. Tel: 01223-330366. *Hon. Director,* Prof.
N. E. Day, Ph.D.
BRAIN METABOLISM UNIT, University Department of
Pharmacology, 1 George Square, Edinburgh EH8 9JZ.
Tel: 0131-650 3543. *Director,* Prof. G. Fink, MD, D.Phil.,
FRSE
CELL MUTATION UNIT, University of Sussex, Falmer,
Brighton BNI 9RR. Tel: 01273-678123. *Director,* Prof. B. A.
Bridges, Ph.D., FIBiol.
CELLULAR IMMUNOLOGY UNIT, Sir William Dunn School
of Pathology, Oxford OXI 3RE. Tel: 01865-275594.
Director (acting), D. W. Mason
CHILD PSYCHIATRY UNIT, Institute of Psychiatry, De
Crespigny Park, Denmark Hill, London SE5 8AF. Tel:
0171-703 5411. *Hon. Director,* Prof. Sir Michael Rutter,
CBE, MD, FRCP, FRCPsych, FRS
COGNITIVE DEVELOPMENT UNIT, 4 Taviton Street,
London WCIH OBT. Tel: 0171-387 4692. *Director,* Prof.
J. Morton, Ph.D.
COLLABORATIVE CENTRE, 1–3 Burtonhole Lane, Mill
Hill, London NW7 IAD. Tel: 0181-906 3811. *Director,*
C. C. G. Hentschel, Ph.D.
CYCLOTRON UNIT, MRC Clinical Sciences Centre,
RPMS Hammersmith Hospital, Du Cane Road, London
WI2 ONN. Tel: 0181-740 3162. *Director (acting),* T. Jones,
D.SC., MD
DUNN NUTRITION UNIT, Downhams Lane, Milton Road,
Cambridge CB4 IXJ. Tel: 01223-426356. *Director,*
R. G. Whitehead, CBE, Ph.D.
ENVIRONMENTAL EPIDEMIOLOGY UNIT, Southampton
General Hospital, Southampton SO9 4XY. Tel: 01703-
777624. *Director,* Prof. D. J. P. Barker, MD, Ph.D, FRCP,
FRCOG
EPIDEMIOLOGY AND MEDICAL CARE UNIT, Wolfson
Institute of Preventive Medicine, St Bartholomew's
Medical College, Charterhouse Square, London
ECIM 6BQ. Tel: 0171-982 6000. *Director,* Prof.
T. W. Meade, CBE, DM, FRCP
EXPERIMENTAL EMBRYOLOGY AND TERATOLOGY UNIT,
St George's Hospital Medical School, Cranmer Terrace,
London SWI7 ORE. Tel: 0181-672 9944 ext. 2824. *Director,*
Prof. D. G. Whittingham, D.SC., FRCVS, FIBIOL.
HUMAN BIOCHEMICAL GENETICS UNIT, The Galton
Laboratory, University College London, Wolfson
House, 4 Stephenson Way, London NWI 2HE. Tel: 0171-
387 7050. *Director,* Prof. D. A. Hopkinson, MD
HUMAN GENETICS UNIT, Western General Hospital,
Crewe Road, Edinburgh EH4 2XU. Tel: 0131-332 2471.
Director, Prof. N. D. Hastie, Ph.D., FRSE
HUMAN GENOME MAPPING PROJECT RESOURCE
CENTRE, Hinxton Hall, Hinxton, Cambridge CBIO IRQ.
Tel: 01223-494516. *Manager,* K. Gibson, Ph.D.

HUMAN MOVEMENT AND BALANCE UNIT, Institute of Neurology, National Hospital for Neurology and Neuro-surgery, Queen Square, London WC1 3BG. Tel: 0171-837 3611. *Hon. Director,* Prof. C. D. Marsden, D.SC., FRCP, FRS

IMMUNOCHEMISTRY UNIT, University Department of Biochemistry, South Parks Road, Oxford OX1 3QU. Tel: 01865-275354. *Director,* Prof. K. B. M. Reid, PH.D.

INSTITUTE OF HEARING RESEARCH, University of Nottingham, Nottingham NG7 2RD. Tel: 0115-922 3431. *Director,* Prof. M. P. Haggard, PH.D.

MAMMALIAN GENETICS UNIT, Harwell Site, Chilton, Didcot, Oxon OX11 0RD. Tel: 01235-834393. *Director (acting),* B. Cattanach, D.SC., FRS

MEDICAL SOCIOLOGY UNIT, 6 Lilybank Gardens, Glasgow G12 8QQ. Tel: 0141-357 3949. *Director,* Prof. S. Macintyre, PH.D.

MOLECULAR HAEMATOLOGY UNIT, Institute of Molecular Medicine, John Radcliffe Hospital, Headington, Oxford OX3 9DU. Tel: 01865-222359. *Hon. Director,* Prof. Sir David Weatherall, MD, FRCP, FRCPath., FRS

MOLECULAR IMMUNOPATHOLOGY UNIT, MRC Centre, University Medical School, Hills Road, Cambridge CB2 2QH. Tel: 01223-245133. *Hon. Director,* Prof. P. J. Lachmann, PH.D., SC.D., FRCP, FRCPath., FRS

MOUSE GENOME CENTRE, Harwell Site, Chilton, Didcot, Oxon OX11 0RD. Tel: 01235-834393. *Director,* Prof. S. Brown, PH.D.

MRC LABORATORIES, THE GAMBIA, PO Box 273, Banjul, The Gambia, W. Africa. *Director,* Prof. K. McAdam, FRCP

MRC LABORATORIES, JAMAICA, University of the West Indies, Mona, Kingston 7, Jamaica. *Director,* Prof. G. R. Serjeant, CMG, MD, FRCP

MUSCLE AND CELL MOTILITY UNIT, Division of Biomedical Sciences, King's College London, 26–29 Drury Lane, London WC2B 5RL. Tel: 0171- 465 5353. *Hon. Director,* Prof. R. M. Simmons, PH.D.

NEUROCHEMICAL PATHOLOGY UNIT, Newcastle General Hospital, Westgate Road, Newcastle upon Tyne NE4 6BE. Tel: 0191-273 5251. *Director,* Prof. J. A. Edwardson, PH.D.

PROTEIN FUNCTION AND DESIGN UNIT, Department of Chemistry, University of Cambridge, Lensfield Road, Cambridge CB2 1EW. Tel: 01223-336341. *Hon. Director,* Prof. A. R. Fersht, PH.D., FRS

PROTEIN PHOSPHORYLATION UNIT, Department of Biochemistry, Medical Sciences Institute, University of Dundee, Dundee DD1 4HN. Tel: 01382-307238. *Hon. Director,* Prof. P. Cohen, PH.D., FRS, FRSE

RADIATION AND GENOME STABILITY UNIT, Harwell Site, Chilton, Didcot, Oxon OX11 0RD. Tel: 01235-834393. *Director (acting),* D. Goodhead, D.Phil.

REPRODUCTIVE BIOLOGY UNIT, Centre for Reproductive Biology, 37 Chalmers Street, Edinburgh EH3 9EW. Tel: 0131-229 2575. *Director,* Prof. D. W. Lincoln, D.SC., FRSE

TOXICOLOGY UNIT, Hodgkin Building, University of Leicester, PO Box 138, Lancaster Road, Leicester LE1 9HN. Tel: 0116-252 5600. *Director,* L. Smith, PH.D.

TUBERCULOSIS AND RELATED INFECTIONS UNIT, MRC Clinical Sciences Centre, RPMS, Hammersmith Hospital, Du Cane Road, London W12 0NN. Tel: 0181-740 3161. *Director,* Prof. J. Ivanyi, MD, PH.D.

VIROLOGY UNIT, Institute of Virology, Church Street, Glasgow G11 5JR. Tel: 0141-330 4017. *Director,* Dr D. J. McGeoch

NATURAL ENVIRONMENT RESEARCH COUNCIL (NERC)

Polaris House, North Star Avenue, Swindon SN2 1EU
Tel 01793-411500

The purpose of the NERC is to promote and support research, survey, long-term environmental monitoring and related postgraduate training in terrestrial, marine and freshwater biology, and Earth, atmospheric, hydrological, oceanographic and polar sciences and Earth observation; to advance knowledge and technology, and to provide services and trained scientists and engineers; to provide advice, disseminate knowledge and promote public understanding in these fields.

Chairman, R. Malpas, CBE, FEng.
Chief Executive, Prof. J. R. Krebs, FRS
Director, Science and Technology, Dr D. J. Drewry

CENTRES/SURVEYS

BRITISH ANTARCTIC SURVEY, High Cross, Madingley Road, Cambridge CB3 0ET. Tel: 01223-251400. *Director,* Dr B. Heywood

BRITISH GEOLOGICAL SURVEY, Kingsley Dunham Centre, Nicker Hill, Keyworth, Nottingham NG12 5GG. Tel: 0115-936 3100. *Director,* Dr P. Cook, CBE

CENTRE FOR COASTAL AND MARINE SCIENCE
Director, Dr B. Bayne (based at Plymouth Marine Laboratory)
    PLYMOUTH MARINE LABORATORY, Prospect Place, West Hoe, Plymouth PL1 3DH. Tel: 01752-633100. *Director,* Prof. R. F. Mantoura
    PROUDMAN OCEANOGRAPHIC LABORATORY, Bidston Observatory, Birkenhead L43 7RA. Tel: 0151-653 8633. *Director,* Dr B. S. McCartney
    DUNSTAFFNAGE MARINE LABORATORY, PO Box 3, Oban, Argyll PA34 4AD. Tel: 01631-562244. *Director,* Dr G. B. Shimmield

CENTRE FOR ECOLOGY AND HYDROLOGY
Director, Prof. W. B. Wilkinson (based at Institute of Hydrology)
    INSTITUTE OF FRESHWATER ECOLOGY, The Ferry House, Far Sawrey, Ambleside, Cumbria LA22 0LP. Tel: 015394-42468. *Director,* Prof. A. D. Pickering
    INSTITUTE OF HYDROLOGY, Maclean Building, Crowmarsh Gifford, Wallingford, Oxon OX10 8BB. Tel: 01491-838800. *Director,* A. Debney
    INSTITUTE OF TERRESTRIAL ECOLOGY, Monks Wood, Abbots Ripton, Huntingdon PE17 2LS. Tel: 01487-773381. *Director,* Prof T. M. Roberts
    INSTITUTE OF VIROLOGY AND ENVIRONMENTAL MICROBIOLOGY, Mansfield Road, Oxford OX1 3SR. Tel: 01865-512361. *Director,* Dr P. Nuttall

SOUTHAMPTON OCEANOGRAPHY CENTRE, University of Southampton, Empress Dock, Southampton SO14 3ZH. Tel: 01703-596666. *Director,* Dr J. Shepherd

UNITS

SEA MAMMAL RESEARCH UNIT, Gatty Marine Laboratory, University of St Andrews, St Andrews, Fife KY16 8LB. Tel: 01334-463472. *Head,* J. Harwood, PH.D.

UNIT OF AQUATIC BIOCHEMISTRY, School of Natural Sciences, Stirling University, Stirling FK9 4LA. Tel: 01786-473171. *Director,* Prof. J. R. Sargent, FRSE

UNIT OF COMPARATIVE PLANT ECOLOGY, University of Sheffield, Sheffield S10 2TN. Tel: 0114-276 8555. *Director,* Prof. J. P. Grime

ENVIRONMENTAL SYSTEMS SCIENCE CENTRE, Department of Geography, Reading University, Whiteknights, Reading RG6 2AB. Tel: 01734-318741. *Director*, Prof. R. Gurney

CENTRE FOR POPULATION BIOLOGY, Imperial College, Silwood Park, Ascot, Berks SL5 7PY. Tel: 01344-294354. *Director*, Prof. J. Lawton, FRS

PARTICLE PHYSICS AND ASTRONOMY RESEARCH COUNCIL (PPARC)

Polaris House, North Star Avenue, Swindon SN2 1EU
Tel 01793-442000

The purpose of the PPARC is to support research into elementary particles and the fundamental forces of nature, planetary and solar research, including space physics, and astronomy, astrophysics and cosmology. It funds research in the universities and is responsible for funding both national and international facilities, including the European Laboratory for Particle Physics (CERN) and the European Space Agency.
Chairman, Dr P. Williams, CBE
Chief Executive, Prof. K. Pounds, CBE, FRS
ROYAL GREENWICH OBSERVATORY, Madingley Road, Cambridge CB3 0EZ. Tel: 01223-374000. *Director*, Dr J. V. Wall
ROYAL OBSERVATORY, EDINBURGH, Blackford Hill, Edinburgh EH9 3HJ. Tel: 0131-668 8100. *Director*, S. G. Pitt
ISAAC NEWTON GROUP OF TELESCOPES, Apartado de Coreos 321, Santa Cruz de la Palma, Tenerife 38780, Canary Islands. Tel: 00 3422-411048. *Head*, Dr S. Unger
JOINT ASTRONOMY CENTRE, 660 N A'ohoku Place, University Park, Hilo, Hawaii 96720. Tel: 00 808-961 3756. *Head*, Prof. I. Robson

---

Research and Technology Organizations

The following industrial and technological research bodies are members of the Association of Independent Research and Technology Organizations (AIRTO). Members' activities span a wide range of disciplines from life sciences to engineering. Their work includes basic research, development and design of innovative products or processes, instrumentation testing and certification, and technology and management consultancy. AIRTO publishes a directory to help clients identify the organizations which might be able to assist them.
AIRTO, PO Box 330, Cambridge CB5 8DU. Tel: 01223-467831. *Secretary-General*, J. Bennett
ADVANCED MANUFACTURING TECHNOLOGY RESEARCH INSTITUTE, Hulley Road, Macclesfield, Cheshire SK10 2NE. Tel: 01625-425421. *Managing Director*, D. Palethorpe
AIRCRAFT RESEARCH ASSOCIATION LTD, Manton Lane, Bedford MK41 7PF. Tel: 01234-350681. *Chief Executive*, B. Timmins
ASSOCIATION FOR INFORMATION MANAGEMENT (ASLIB), Information House, 20–24 Old Street, London EC1V 9AP. Tel: 0171-253 4488. *Chief Executive*, R. Bowes

BHR GROUP LTD (*Fluid mechanics and process technology*), Cranfield, Bedford MK43 0AJ. Tel: 01234-750422. *Chief Executive*, I. Cooper
BIBRA INTERNATIONAL (*Assessment of toxicity of food and chemicals to humans*), Woodmansterne Road, Carshalton, Surrey SM5 4DS. Tel: 0181-652 1000. *Director*, Dr S. E. Jaggers
BLC (THE LEATHER TECHNOLOGY CENTRE), Leather Trade House, Kings Park Road, Moulton Park, Northants NN3 6JD. Tel: 01604-494131. *Chief Executive*, Dr K. Alexander
BRITISH GLASS, Northumberland Road, Sheffield S10 2UA. Tel: 0114-268 6201. *Director-General*, Dr W. Cook
BRITISH MARITIME TECHNOLOGY LTD, Orlando House, 1 Waldegrave Road, Teddington, Middx TW11 8LZ. Tel: 0181-943 5544. *Chief Executive*, D. Goodrich
BRF INTERNATIONAL (*Alcoholic beverages*), Lyttel Hall, Coopers Hill Road, Nutfield, Surrey RH1 4HY. Tel: 01737-822272. *Director-General*, Prof. B. Atkinson
BRITISH TEXTILE TECHNOLOGY GROUP, Wira House, West Park Ring Road, Leeds LS16 6QL. Tel: 0113-259 1999; Shirley House, Didsbury, Manchester M20 8RX. Tel: 0161-445 8141. *Chief Executive*, A. King
BUILDING SERVICES RESEARCH AND INFORMATION ASSOCIATION, Old Bracknell Lane West, Bracknell, Berks RG12 7AH. Tel: 01344-426511. *Chief Executive*, G. J. Baker
CAMBRIDGE CONSULTANTS LTD (*Products, systems and manufacturing processes design and development*), Science Park, Milton Road, Cambridge CB4 4DW. Tel: 01223-420024. *Chief Executive*, Dr J. P. Auton
CAMBRIDGE REFRIGERATION TECHNOLOGY (CRT), 140 Newmarket Road, Cambridge CB5 8HE. Tel: 01223-365101. *Technical Director*, R. D. Heap
CAMPDEN AND CHORLEYWOOD FOOD RESEARCH ASSOCIATION, Chipping Campden, Glos GL55 6LD. Tel: 01386-842000; Chorleywood, Herts WD3 5SH. Tel: 01923-284111. *Director-General*, Prof. C. Dennis
CERAM (BRITISH CERAMIC RESEARCH LTD), Queen's Road, Penkhull, Stoke-on-Trent ST4 7LQ. Tel: 01782-845431. *Chief Executive*, Dr N. E. Sanderson
CIRIA (CONSTRUCTION INDUSTRY RESEARCH AND INFORMATION ASSOCIATION), 6 Storey's Gate, London SW1P 3AU. Tel: 0171-222 8891. *Director-General*, Dr P. L. Bransby
CRL (*Specialist products, technology licences, intellectual property rights services, research and development*), Dawley Road, Hayes, Middx UB3 1HH. Tel: 0181-848 9779. *Managing Director*, Dr J. White
CUTLERY AND ALLIED TRADES RESEARCH ASSOCIATION, Henry Street, Sheffield S3 7EQ. Tel: 0114-276 9736. *Director of Research*, R. C. Hamby
EA TECHNOLOGY (*Use and distribution of electricity*), Capenhurst, Chester CH1 6ES. Tel: 0151-339 4181. *Chief Executive*, Dr S. F. Exell
ERA TECHNOLOGY LTD (*Electronic, electrical, materials and structural engineering*), Cleeve Road, Leatherhead, Surrey KT22 7SA. Tel: 01372-367000. *Chief Executive*, M. J. Withers
FABRIC CARE RESEARCH ASSOCIATION, Forest House Laboratories, Knaresborough Road, Harrogate, N. Yorks HG2 7LZ. Tel: 01423-885977. *Managing Director*, C. Tebbs
FURNITURE INDUSTRY RESEARCH ASSOCIATION, Maxwell Road, Stevenage, Herts SG1 2EW. Tel: 01438-313433. *Company Secretary*, R. Morgan
HR WALLINGFORD GROUP LTD (*Hydroinformatics and engineering*), Howbery Park, Wallingford, Oxon OX10 8BA. Tel: 01491-835381. *Chief Executive*, Dr J. Weare, OBE

INTERNATIONAL RESEARCH AND DEVELOPMENT LTD
(*Materials, joining and electro-mechanical systems*), Shields
Road, Newcastle upon Tyne NE6 2YD. Tel: 0191-275
2800. *General Manager*, R. Potts

LEATHERHEAD FOOD RESEARCH ASSOCIATION, Randalls
Road, Leatherhead, Surrey KT22 7RY. Tel: 01372-376761.
Director, Dr M. P. J. Kierstan

MATERIALS ENGINEERING RESEARCH LABORATORY LTD,
Tamworth Road, Hertford SG13 7DG. Tel: 01992-500120.
Managing Director, Dr A. Stevenson

MOTOR INDUSTRY RESEARCH ASSOCIATION, Watling
Street, Nuneaton, Warks CV10 0TU. Tel: 01203-355000.
Managing Director, J. R. Wood

THE NATIONAL COMPUTING CENTRE LTD, Oxford
House, Oxford Road, Manchester M1 7ED. Tel: 0161-228
6333. *Managing Director*, C. Pearse

PAINT RESEARCH ASSOCIATION, 8 Waldegrave Road,
Teddington, Middx TW11 8LD. Tel: 0181-977 4427.
Managing Director, J. A. Bernie

PERA GROUP (*Multi-disciplinary research, design,
development and consultancy*), Middle Aston House,
Middle Aston, Oxon OX6 3PT. Tel: 01869-347755. *Chief
Executive*, R. A. Armstrong

PIRA INTERNATIONAL (*Paper and board, printing, publishing
and packaging*), Randalls Road, Leatherhead, Surrey KT22
7RU. Tel: 01372-802000. *Managing Director*, B. W.
Blunden, OBE

RAPRA TECHNOLOGY LTD (*Rubber and plastics*),
Shawbury, Shrewsbury SY4 4NR. Tel: 01939-250383;
North East Centre, 18 Belasis Court, Belasis
Technology Park, Billingham TS23 4AZ. Tel: 01642-
370406. *Chief Executive*, Dr M. Copley

SATRA FOOTWEAR TECHNOLOGY CENTRE, Satra
House, Rockingham Road, Kettering, Northants NN16
9JH. Tel: 01536-410000. *Chief Executive*, Dr R. E.
Whittaker

SIRA LTD (*Measurement, instrumentation, control and optical
systems technology*), South Hill, Chislehurst, Kent BR7 5EH.
Tel: 0181-467 2636. *Managing Director*, R. A. Brook

SMITH SYSTEM ENGINEERING LTD, Surrey Research
Park, Guildford, Surrey GU2 5YP. Tel: 01483-442000.
Managing Director, Dr T. Black

STEEL CONSTRUCTION INSTITUTE, Silwood Park, Ascot,
Berks SL5 7QN. Tel: 01344-23345. *Director*, Dr G. Owens

TRADA TECHNOLOGY LTD (*Timber and wood-based
products*), Stocking Lane, Hughenden Valley, High
Wycombe, Bucks. Tel: 01494-563091. *Managing
Director*, A. Abbott

THE WELDING INSTITUTE (TWI), Abington Hall,
Abington, Cambridge CB1 6AL. Tel: 01223-891162. *Chief
Executive*, A. B. M. Braithwaite, OBE

WRC PLC, (*Water, waste water and environmental management*),
PO Box 16, Marlow, Bucks SL7 2HD. Tel: 01491-571531.
Managing Director, Dr J. Moss

Sports Bodies

*Governing body for the sport

Sports Councils

CENTRAL COUNCIL OF PHYSICAL RECREATION, Francis House, Francis Street, London SW1P 1DE. Tel: 0171-828 3163. *General Secretary*, M. Denton

SCOTTISH SPORTS COUNCIL, Caledonia House, South Gyle, Edinburgh EH12 9DQ. Tel: 0131-317 7200. *Chief Executive*, F. A. L. Alstead, CBE

†THE SPORTS COUNCIL, 16 Upper Woburn Place, London WC1H 0QP. Tel: 0171-388 1277. *Chairman*, Sir Rodney Walker; *Chief Executive*, D. Casey

SPORTS COUNCIL FOR NORTHERN IRELAND, House of Sport, Upper Malone Road, Belfast BT9 5LA. Tel: 01232-381222. *Chief Executive*, E. McCartan

SPORTS COUNCIL FOR WALES, Sophia Gardens, Cardiff CF1 9SW. Tel: 01222-397571. *Chief Executive*, L. Tatham

Alpine Skiing

*BRITISH SKI FEDERATION, 258 Main Street, East Calder, Livingston, W. Lothian EH53 0EE. Tel: 01506-884343. *Chief Executive*, M. Jardine

Angling

*NATIONAL FEDERATION OF ANGLERS, Halliday House, Egginton Junction, Derbys DE65 6GU. Tel: 01283-734735. *Chief Administration Officer*, K. E. Watkins

Archery

*GRAND NATIONAL ARCHERY SOCIETY, 7th Street, National Agricultural Centre, Stoneleigh, Kenilworth CV8 2LG. Tel: 01203-696631. *Chief Executive*, J. S. Middleton

Association Football

*THE FOOTBALL ASSOCIATION, 16 Lancaster Gate, London W2 3LW. Tel: 0171-262 4542. *Chief Executive*, R. H. G. Kelly

*FOOTBALL ASSOCIATION OF WALES, Plymouth Chambers, 3 Westgate Street, Cardiff CF1 1DD. Tel: 01222-372325. *Secretary*, D. G. Collins

FOOTBALL LEAGUE LTD, 319 Clifton Drive South, Lytham St Annes, Lancs FY8 1JG. Tel: 01253-729421. *Secretary*, J. D. Dent

*IRISH FOOTBALL ASSOCIATION, 20 Windsor Avenue, Belfast BT9 6EE. Tel: 01232-669458. *General Secretary*, D. I. Bowen

IRISH FOOTBALL LEAGUE, 96 University Street, Belfast BT7 1HE. Tel: 01232-242888. *Secretary*, H. Wallace

*SCOTTISH FOOTBALL ASSOCIATION, 6 Park Gardens, Glasgow G3 7YF. Tel: 0141-332 6372. *Chief Executive*, J. Farry

SCOTTISH FOOTBALL LEAGUE, 188 West Regent Street, Glasgow G2 4RY. Tel: 0141-248 3844. *Secretary*, P. Donald

Athletics

AMATEUR ATHLETIC ASSOCIATION OF ENGLAND, 225A Bristol Road, Edgbaston, Birmingham B5 7UB. Tel: 0121-440 5000. *Chairman*, D. Cropper

ATHLETICS ASSOCIATION OF WALES, Morfa Athletics Stadium, Upper Bank, Landore, Swansea SA1 7DF. Tel: 01792-456237. *National Administrator*, Mrs B. Currie

---

† To be replaced by a UK Sports Council and an English Sports Council in autumn 1996

---

*BRITISH ATHLETIC FEDERATION, 225A Bristol Road, Edgbaston, Birmingham B5 7UB. Tel: 0121-440 5000. *Executive Chairman*, Prof. P. F. Radford

NORTHERN IRELAND AMATEUR ATHLETIC FEDERATION, House of Sport, Upper Malone Road, Belfast BT9 5LA. Tel: 01232-383817. *Secretary*, J. Allen

SCOTTISH ATHLETICS FEDERATION, Caledonia House, South Gyle, Edinburgh EH12 9DQ. Tel: 0131-317 7320. *Administrator*, N. F. Park

Badminton

*BADMINTON ASSOCIATION OF ENGLAND LTD, National Badminton Centre, Bradwell Road, Loughton Lodge, Milton Keynes MK8 9LA. Tel: 01908-568822. *Chief Executive*, G. Snowdon

*SCOTTISH BADMINTON UNION, Cockburn Centre, 40 Bogmoor Place, Glasgow G51 4TQ. Tel: 0141-445 1218. *Chief Executive*, Miss A. Smillie

*WELSH BADMINTON UNION, Fourth Floor, 3 Westgate Street, Cardiff CF1 1DD. Tel: 01222-222082. *Coaching Development Manager*, L. Williams

Baseball

*BRITISH BASEBALL FEDERATION, 66 Belvedere Road, Hessle, E. Yorks HU13 9JJ. Tel: 01482-643551. *Secretary*, Ms W. Macadam

Basketball

*BASKETBALL ASSOCIATION OF WALES, Connies House, Rhymney River Bridge Road, Cardiff CF3 7YZ. Tel: 01222-454395. *Administrator*, F. M. Daw

*ENGLISH BASKETBALL ASSOCIATION, 48 Bradford Road, Stanningley, Leeds LS28 6DF. Tel: 0113-236 1166. *Chief Executive*, S. Catton

*SCOTTISH BASKETBALL ASSOCIATION, Caledonia House, South Gyle, Edinburgh EH12 9DQ. Tel: 0131-317 7260. *President*, W. D. McInnes

Billiards

*WORLD LADIES BILLIARDS AND SNOOKER ASSOCIATION, 26 Welbeck Road, Wisbech, Cambs PE13 2JY. Tel: 01945-589589. *Chairman*, Ms M. Fisher

*WORLD PROFESSIONAL BILLIARDS AND SNOOKER ASSOCIATION, 27 Oakfield Road, Clifton, Bristol BS28 2AT. Tel: 0117-974 4491. *Company Secretary*, M. Veal

Bobsleigh

*BRITISH BOBSLEIGH ASSOCIATION, The Chestnuts, 85 High Street, Codford, Warminster, Wilts BA12 0ND. Tel: 01985-850064. *Secretary*, Ms H. Alderman

Bowls

*BRITISH ISLES BOWLING COUNCIL, 28 Woodford Park, Lurgan, Co. Armagh BT66 7HA. Tel: 01762-322036. *Hon. Secretary*, W. A. Gracey

*BRITISH ISLES INDOOR BOWLS COUNCIL, 9 Highlight Lane, Barry CF62 8AA. Tel: 01446-733978. *Secretary*, J. R. Thomas, MBE

*BRITISH ISLES WOMEN'S BOWLING COUNCIL, 2 Case Gardens, Seaton, Devon EX12 2AP. Tel: 01297-21317. *Hon. Secretary*, Mrs N. Colling

*BRITISH ISLES WOMEN'S INDOOR BOWLS COUNCIL, 16 Windsor Crescent, Radyr, Cardiff CF4 8AE. Tel: 01222-842391. *Hon. Secretary*, Mrs J. Johns

*ENGLISH BOWLING ASSOCIATION, Lyndhurst Road, Worthing, W. Sussex BN11 2AZ. Tel: 01903-820222. *Secretary*, G. D. Shaw

*English Indoor Bowling Association, David Cornwell House, Bowling Green, Leicester Road, Melton Mowbray, Leics LE13 0DA. Tel: 01664-481900. *Secretary*, D. N. Brown
*English Women's Bowling Association, 2 Case Gardens, Seaton, Devon EX12 2AP. Tel: 01297-21317. *Hon. Secretary*, Mrs N. Colling
*English Women's Indoor Bowling Association, 3 Scirocco Close, Moulton Park, Northampton NN3 6AP. Tel: 01604-494163. *Secretary*, Mrs M. E. Ruff

Boxing
*Amateur Boxing Association of England Ltd, Crystal Palace National Sports Centre, London SE19 2BB. Tel: 0181-778 0251. *Secretary*, C. Brown
*British Amateur Boxing Association, 96 High Street, Lochee, Dundee DD2 3AY. Tel: 01382-611412. *Chief Executive*, F. Hendry
*British Boxing Board of Control Ltd, Jack Petersen House, 52A Borough High Street, London SE1 1XW. Tel: 0171-403 5879. *General Secretary*, J. Morris

Canoeing
*British Canoe Union, Adbolton Lane, West Bridgford, Nottingham NG2 5AS. Tel: 0115-982 1100. *Chief Executive*, P. Owen

Chess
*British Chess Federation, 9A Grand Parade, St Leonards-on-Sea, E. Sussex TN38 0DD. Tel: 01424-442500. *Manager*, Mrs G. White

Clay Pigeon Shooting
*Clay Pigeon Shooting Association, Earlstrees Court, Earlstrees Road, Corby, Northants NN17 4AX. Tel: 01536-443566. *Director*, E. G. Orduna

Cricket
MCC, Lord's, London NW8 8QN. Tel: 0171-289 1611. *President*, A. C. D. Ingleby-Mackenzie; *Secretary*, R. Knight
*‡Test and County Cricket Board, Lord's, London NW8 8QZ. Tel: 0171-286 4405. *Chief Executive*, T. Lamb

Croquet
*Croquet Association, c/o The Hurlingham Club, Ranelagh Gardens, London SW6 3PR. Tel: 0171-736 3148. *Secretary*, L. W. D. Antenen

Cycling
*British Cycling Federation, National Cycling Centre, Stuart Street, Manchester M11 4DQ. Tel: 0161-230 2301. *Chief Executive*, J. Hendry
*Road Time Trials Council, 77 Arlington Drive, Pennington, Leigh, Lancs WN7 3QP. Tel: 01942-603976. *National Secretary*, P. Heaton

Diving
*Great Britain Diving Federation, PO Box 222, Batley, W. Yorks WF17 8XD. Tel: 01924-422322. *Director of Administration*, J. Cryer

Equestrianism
*British Equestrian Federation, British Equestrian Centre, Stoneleigh Park, Kenilworth, Warks CV8 2LR. Tel: 01203-696697. *Director-General*, Col. J. D. Smith-Bingham

Eton Fives
*Eton Fives Association, 74 Clarence Road, St Albans, Herts AL1 4NG. Tel: 01727-837099. *Secretary*, R. Beament

Fencing
*Amateur Fencing Association, 1 Baron's Gate, 33–35 Rothschild Road, London W4 5HT. Tel: 0181-742 3032. *Secretary*, Miss G. Kenneally

Gliding
*British Gliding Association, Kimberley House, Vaughan Way, Leicester LE1 4SE. Tel: 0116-253 1051. *Secretary*, B. Rolfe

Golf
*Ladies' Golf Union, The Scores, St Andrews, Fife KY16 9AT. Tel: 01334-475811. *Secretary*, Mrs. E. A. Mackie
*Royal and Ancient Golf Club, St Andrews, Fife KY16 9JD. Tel: 01334-472112. *Secretary*, M. F. Bonallack, OBE

Greyhound Racing
*National Greyhound Racing Club Ltd, 24–28 Oval Road, London NW1 7DA. Tel: 0171-267 9256. *Chief Executive*, F. Melville

Gymnastics
*British Amateur Gymnastics Association, Ford Hall, Lilleshall National Sports Centre, nr Newport, Shropshire TF10 9NB. Tel: 01952-820330. *General Secretary*, D. Minnery

Hockey
*All England Women's Hockey Association, The Stadium, Silbury Boulevard, Milton Keynes MK9 1NR. Tel: 01908-689290. *Administrator*, Miss B. Carter
*Hockey Association, The Stadium, Silbury Boulevard, Milton Keynes MK9 1HA. Tel: 01908-241100. *Chief Executive*, S. P. Baines
*Scottish Hockey Union, 48 Pleasance, Edinburgh EH8 9TJ. Tel: 0131-650 8170. *Chairman*, P. Monaghan
*Welsh Hockey Union, 80 Woodville Road, Cathays, Cardiff CF2 4ED. Tel: 01222-233257. *President*, Miss M. A. Ellis, MBE

Horseracing
*British Horseracing Board, 42 Portman Square, London W1H 0EN. Tel: 0171-396 0011. *Chief Executive*, R. T. Ricketts
The Jockey Club, 42 Portman Square, London W1H 0EN. Tel: 0171-486 4921. *Senior Steward*, Sir Thomas Pilkington, Bt.

Ice Hockey
*British Ice Hockey Association, Second Floor Suite, 517 Christchurch Road, Boscombe, Bournemouth BH1 4AG. Tel: 01202-303946. *Chief Executive*, D. Frame

Ice Skating
*National Ice Skating Association of the UK Ltd, 15–27 Gee Street, London EC1V 3RE. Tel: 0171-253 3824. *Chief Executive*, Ms C. Godsall

Judo
*British Judo Association, 7A Rutland Street, Leicester LE1 1RB. Tel: 0116-255 9669. *Office Manager*, Mrs S. Startin

Lacrosse
*English Lacrosse Association, 4 Western Court, Bromley Street, Digbeth, Birmingham B9 4AN. Tel: 0121-773 4422. *Chief Executive Officer*, D. Shuttleworth
*English Lacrosse Union, 70 High Road, Rayleigh, Essex SS6 7AD. Tel: 01268-770758. *Hon. Secretary*, R. Balls

Lawn Tennis
*Lawn Tennis Association, The Queen's Club, London W14 9EG. Tel: 0171-381 7000. *Secretary*, J. C. U. James

---

‡ To be replaced by the England and Wales Cricket Board in Jan. 1997

Lugeing
*GREAT BRITAIN LUGE ASSOCIATION, 1 Highfield House, Hampton Bishop, Hereford HR1 4JN. Tel: 01432-271982. *General Secretary*, J. G. Evans

Martial Arts
MARTIAL ARTS DEVELOPMENT COMMISSION, PO Box 381, Erith, Kent DA8 1TF. Tel: 01322-431440. *Office Administrator*, Mrs E. Jewell

Motor Sports
*AUTO-CYCLE UNION, ACU House, Wood Street, Rugby, Warks CV21 2YX. Tel: 01788-540519. *Chief Executive*, G. Wilson
BRITISH MOTORCYCLE CIRCUIT RACING CONTROL BOARD (MCRCB), PO Box 72, Castle Donington, Derby DE74 2ZQ. Tel: 01332-853822. *Manager*, D. R. Barnfield
*RAC MOTOR SPORTS ASSOCIATION LTD, Motor Sports House, Riverside Park, Colnbrook, Slough SL3 0HG. Tel: 01753-681736. *Chief Executive*, J. R. Quenby
*SCOTTISH AUTO CYCLE UNION LTD, Block 2, Unit 6, Whiteside Industrial Estate, Bathgate, W. Lothian EH48 2RX. Tel: 01506-630262. *Secretary*, A. M. Brownlie

Mountaineering
*BRITISH MOUNTAINEERING COUNCIL, 177–179 Burton Road, West Didsbury, Manchester M20 2BB. Tel: 0161-445 4747. *General Secretary*, R. Payne

Multi-Sport Bodies
BRITISH OLYMPIC ASSOCIATION, 1 Wandsworth Plain, London SW18 1EH. Tel: 0181-871 2677. *General Secretary*, R. Palmer, OBE
BRITISH UNIVERSITIES SPORTS ASSOCIATION, 8 Union Street, London SE1 1SZ. Tel: 0171-357 8555. *Chief Executive*, G. Gregory-Jones
COMMONWEALTH GAMES COUNCIL FOR ENGLAND, Tavistock House South, Tavistock Square, London WC1H 9JZ. Tel: 0171-388 6643. *General Secretary*, Miss A. Hogbin
COMMONWEALTH GAMES FEDERATION, Walkden House, 3–10 Melton Street, London NW1 2EB. Tel: 0171-383 5596. *Hon. Secretary*, D. Dixon, CVO

Netball
*ALL ENGLAND NETBALL ASSOCIATION LTD, Netball House, 9 Paynes Park, Hitchin, Herts SG5 1EH. Tel: 01462-442344. *Chief Executive*, Mrs E. M. Nicholl
*NORTHERN IRELAND NETBALL ASSOCIATION, Netball Office, House of Sport, Upper Malone Road, Belfast BT9 5LA. Tel: 01232-381222. *Secretary*, Mrs R. McWhinney
*SCOTTISH NETBALL ASSOCIATION, Kelvin Hall Sports Complex, Argyle Street, Glasgow G3 8AA. Tel: 0141-334 3650. *Administrator*, Ms S. McQueen
*WELSH NETBALL ASSOCIATION, 50 Cathedral Road, Cardiff CF1 9LL. Tel: 01222-237048. *President*, Miss P. Nicholas

Orienteering
*BRITISH ORIENTEERING FEDERATION, Riversdale, Dale Road North, Darley Dale, Matlock, Derbys DE4 2HX. Tel: 01629-734042. *Secretary-General*, N. Cameron

Polo
*THE HURLINGHAM POLO ASSOCIATION, Winterlake, Kirtlington, Kidlington, Oxon OX5 3HG. Tel: 01869-350044. *Secretary*, J. W. M. Crisp

Rackets and Real Tennis
*TENNIS AND RACKETS ASSOCIATION, c/o The Queen's Club, Palliser Road, London W14 9EQ. Tel: 0171-386 3447. *Chief Executive*, Brig. A. D. Myrtle, CB, CBE

Rifle Shooting
*NATIONAL RIFLE ASSOCIATION, Bisley Camp, Brookwood, Woking, Surrey GU24 0PB. Tel: 01483-797777. *Chief Executive*, Col. C. C. C. Cheshire, OBE
*NATIONAL SMALL-BORE RIFLE ASSOCIATION, Lord Roberts House, Bisley Camp, Brookwood, Woking, Surrey GU24 0NP. Tel: 01483-476969. *Secretary*, Lt.-Col. J. D. Hoare

Rowing
*AMATEUR ROWING ASSOCIATION LTD, The Priory, 6 Lower Mall, London W6 9DJ. Tel: 0181-748 3632. *National Manager*, Mrs R. Napp
HENLEY ROYAL REGATTA, Regatta Headquarters, Henley-on-Thames, Oxon RG9 2LY. Tel: 01491-572153. *Secretary*, R. S. Goddard
SCOTTISH AMATEUR ROWING ASSOCIATION, 18 Daniel McLauchlin Place, Kirkintilloch, Glasgow G66 2LH. Tel: 0141-775 0522. *Secretary*, Miss R. Clarke
*WELSH AMATEUR ROWING ASSOCIATION, 15 Kingfisher Close, St Mellons, Cardiff CF3 0DD. *Hon. Secretary*, M. Nhatiw

Rugby Fives
*RUGBY FIVES ASSOCIATION, The Old Forge, Sutton Valence, Maidstone, Kent ME17 3AW. Tel: 01622-842278. *General Secretary*, M. F. Beaman

Rugby League
*BRITISH AMATEUR RUGBY LEAGUE ASSOCIATION, West Yorkshire House, 4 New North Parade, Huddersfield HD1 5JP. Tel: 01484-544131. *Chief Executive*, M. F. Oldroyd
*THE RUGBY FOOTBALL LEAGUE, Red Hall, Red Hall Lane, Leeds LS17 8NB. Tel: 0113-232 9111. *Chief Executive*, M. P. Lindsay

Rugby Union
*IRISH RUGBY FOOTBALL UNION, 62 Lansdowne Road, Ballsbridge, Dublin 4, Republic of Ireland. Tel: 00 353-1-668 4601. *Secretary*, P. R. Browne
IRISH WOMEN'S RUGBY UNION, 140 Georgian Village, Castleknock, Dublin 15, Republic of Ireland. Tel: 00 353-1-821 4237. *Secretary*, Ms R. Hanley
*RUGBY FOOTBALL UNION, Twickenham TW1 1DZ. Tel: 0181-892 8161. *Secretary*, A. P. Hallett
RUGBY FOOTBALL UNION FOR WOMEN (ENGLAND), 33 Rice Mews, St Thomas, Exeter EX2 9AY. Tel: 01635-278177. *Secretary*, Ms. S. Eakers
*SCOTTISH RUGBY UNION, Murrayfield, Edinburgh EH12 5PJ. Tel: 0131-346 5000. *Chief Executive*, I. A. L. Hogg
SCOTTISH WOMEN'S RUGBY UNION, 11 Bavelaw Crescent, Penicuik, Midlothian EH26 9AX. Tel: 01968-673355. *Chairperson*, Ms M. Sharp
*WELSH RUGBY UNION, Cardiff Arms Park, PO Box 22, Cardiff CF1 1JL. Tel: 01222-390111. *Secretary*, R. Jasinski
WELSH WOMEN'S RUGBY UNION, 40 Wolseley Street, Pilwenlly, Newport NP9 2HP. Tel: 01633-220249. *Secretary*, Ms. F. Margerison

Snooker
*WORLD LADIES BILLIARDS AND SNOOKER ASSOCIATION, 26 Welbeck Road, Wisbech, Cambs PE13 2JY. Tel: 01945-589589. *Chairman*, Ms M. Fisher
*WORLD PROFESSIONAL BILLIARDS AND SNOOKER ASSOCIATION, 27 Oakfield Road, Clifton, Bristol BS28 2AT. Tel: 0117-974 4491. *Company Secretary*, M. Veal

Speedway
*SPEEDWAY CONTROL BOARD LTD, ACU Headquarters, Wood Street, Rugby, Warks CV21 2YX. Tel: 01788-540096. *Manager*, G. Reeve

Squash Rackets
*SCOTTISH SQUASH, Caledonia House, South Gyle,
Edinburgh EH12 9DQ. Tel: 0131-317 7343. *Secretary*, N.
Brydon
*SQUASH RACKETS ASSOCIATION, PO Box 1106, London
W3 0ZD. Tel: 0181-746 1616. *General Secretary*, N. T.
Moore
*WELSH SQUASH RACKETS FEDERATION, 7 Kymin
Terrace, Penarth, S. Glamorgan CF6 1AP. Tel: 01222-
704096. *Chairman*, S. Osborne

Sub-Aqua
*BRITISH SUB-AQUA CLUB, Telfords Quay, Ellesmere
Port, Cheshire L65 4FY. Tel: 0151-357 1951. *Chairman*,
C. Allen

Swimming
*AMATEUR SWIMMING ASSOCIATION, Harold Fern House,
Derby Square, Loughborough, Leics LE11 5AL. Tel:
01509-230431. *Chief Executive*, D. Sparkes
*SCOTTISH AMATEUR SWIMMING ASSOCIATION,
Holmhills Farm, Greenlees Road, Cambuslang,
Glasgow G72 8DT. Tel: 0141-641 8818. *Administration
Manager*, Mrs E. Mackenzie
*WELSH AMATEUR SWIMMING ASSOCIATION, Wales
Empire Pool, Wood Street, Cardiff CF1 1PP. Tel: 01222-
342201. *Hon. General Secretary*, G. Robins

Table Tennis
*ENGLISH TABLE TENNIS ASSOCIATION, Queensbury
House, Havelock Road, Hastings, E. Sussex TN34 1HF.
Tel: 01424-722525. *Chief Executive*, R. Yule

Volleyball
*ENGLISH VOLLEYBALL ASSOCIATION, 27 South Road,
West Bridgford, Nottingham NG2 7AG. Tel: 0115-
981 6324. *Chief Executive Officer*, Mrs G. Harrison
*SCOTTISH VOLLEYBALL ASSOCIATION, 48 Pleasance,
Edinburgh EH8 9TJ. Tel: 0131-556 4633. *Director*, N. S.
Moody
*WELSH VOLLEYBALL ASSOCIATION, Pencae Bleddyn,
Llanbedr, Crickhowell NP8 1SY. Tel: 01873-811357.
Secretary, Ms K. Falkner

Walking
*RACE WALKING ASSOCIATION, Hufflers, Heard's Lane,
Shenfield, Brentwood, Essex CM15 0SF. Tel: 01277-
220687. *Hon. Secretary*, P. J. Cassidy

Water Skiing
*BRITISH WATER SKI FEDERATION, 390 City Road,
London EC1V 2QA. Tel: 0171-833 2855. *Executive Officer*,
Ms. G. Hill

Weightlifting
*BRITISH AMATEUR WEIGHTLIFTERS ASSOCIATION, 3
Iffley Turn, Oxford OX4 4DU. Tel: 01865-200339. *Hon.
Secretary*, W. Holland, OBE

Wrestling
*BRITISH AMATEUR WRESTLING ASSOCIATION, 41 Great
Clowes Street, Salford, Manchester M7 1RQ. Tel: 0161-
832 9209. *National Development Officer*, R. Tomlinson

Yachting
*ROYAL YACHTING ASSOCIATION, RYA House, Romsey
Road, Eastleigh, Hants SO50 9YA. Tel: 01703-627400.
Secretary-General, R. Duchesne, OBE

Clubs

ALPINE CLUB (1857), 55 Charlotte Road, London
EC2A 3QT. Tel: 0171-613 0755. *Hon. Secretary,*
G. D. Hughes
AMERICAN WOMEN'S CLUB (1899), 68 Old Brompton
Road, London SW7 3LQ. Tel: 0171-589 8292. *Secretary,*
Ms. C. Galler
ANGLO-BELGIAN CLUB (1955), 60 Knightsbridge, London
SW1X 7LF. Tel: 0171-235 2121. *Secretary,* Baronne van
Havre
ARMY AND NAVY CLUB (1837), 36 Pall Mall, London
SW1Y 5JN. Tel: 0171-930 9721. *Secretary,*
Maj. D. B. Taylor
ARTS CLUB (1863), 40 Dover Street, London W1X 3RB. Tel:
0171-499 8581. *Secretary,* Ms. J. Downing
ARTS THEATRE CLUB (1927), 50 Frith Street, London
W1V 5TE. Tel: 0171-287 9236. *Hon. Secretary,* S. Labisko
THE ATHENAEUM (1824), 107 Pall Mall, London SW1Y 5ER.
Tel: 0171-930 4843. *Secretary,* R. T. Smith
AUTHORS' CLUB (1892), 40 Dover Street, London W1X 3RB.
Tel: 0171-499 8581. *Secretary,* Mrs. A. Carter
BEEFSTEAK CLUB (1876), 9 Irving Street, London
WC2H 7AT. Tel: 0171-930 5722. *Secretary,* Sir John Lucas-
Tooth, Bt.
BOODLE'S (1762), 28 St James's Street, London SW1A 1HJ.
Tel: 0171-930 7166. *Secretary,* R. J. Edmonds
BROOKS'S (1764), St James's Street, London SW1A 1LN. Tel:
0171-493 4411. *Secretary,* G. Snell
BUCK'S CLUB (1919), 18 Clifford Street, London W1X 1RG.
Tel: 0171-734 6896. *Secretary,* Capt. P. G. J. Murison, RN
CALEDONIAN CLUB (1891), 9 Halkin Street, London
SW1X 7DR. Tel: 0171-235 5162. *Secretary,* P. J. Varney
CANNING CLUB (1910), 94 Piccadilly, London W1V 0BP.
Tel: 0171-499 5163. *Secretary,* T. M. Harrington
CARLTON CLUB (1832), 69 St James's Street, London
SW1A 1PJ. Tel: 0171-493 1164. *Secretary,* R. N. Linsley
CAVALRY AND GUARDS CLUB (1893), 127 Piccadilly,
London W1V 0PX. Tel: 0171-499 1261. *Secretary,*
N. J. Walford
CHELSEA ARTS CLUB (1891), 143 Old Church Street,
London SW3 6EB. Tel: 0171-376 3311. *Secretary,*
D. Winterbottom
CITY LIVERY CLUB (1914), 20 Aldermanbury, London
EC2V 7HY. Tel: 0171-814 0200. *Hon. Secretary,*
B. L. Morgan, CBE
CITY OF LONDON CLUB (1832), 19 Old Broad Street,
London EC2N 1DS. Tel: 0171-588 7991. *Secretary,*
G. S. Jones
CITY UNIVERSITY CLUB (1895), 50 Cornhill, London
EC3V 3PD. Tel: 0171-626 8571. *Secretary,*
Miss R. C. Graham
EAST INDIA CLUB (1849), 16 St James's Square, London
SW1Y 4LH. Tel: 0171-930 1000. *Secretary,* J. G. F. Stoy
FARMERS CLUB (1842), 3 Whitehall Court, London
SW1A 2EL. Tel: 0171-930 3751. *Secretary,*
Gp Capt. G. P. Carson
FLYFISHERS' CLUB (1884), 69 Brook Street, London
W1Y 2ER. Tel: 0171-629 5958. *Secretary,* Cdr. N. T. Fuller
(retd)
GARRICK CLUB (1831), 15 Garrick Street, London
WC2E 9AY. Tel: 0171-379 6478. *Secretary,* M. J. Harvey

GREEN ROOM CLUB (1877), 9 Adam Street, London
WC2N 6AA. Tel: 0171-836 7453. *Secretary,* Ms J. Mander
GROUCHO CLUB (1985), 45 Dean Street, London W1V 5AP.
Tel: 0171-439 4685. *Company Secretary,* Miss Z. Noordin
HURLINGHAM CLUB (1869), Ranelagh Gardens, London
SW6 3PR. Tel: 0171-736 8411. *Secretary,* P. H. Covell
KEMPTON PARK CLUB (1878), Kempton Park Racecourse,
Sunbury-on-Thames, Middx TW16 5AQ. Tel: 01932-
782292. *Secretary,* Miss T. Alexander
KENNEL CLUB (1873), 1–5 Clarges Street, London W1Y 8AB.
Tel: 0171-493 6651. *Chief Executive,* R. French
LANSDOWNE CLUB (1934), 9 Fitzmaurice Place, London
W1X 6JD. Tel: 0171-629 7200. *Secretary,* Lt.-Cdr. T. P.
Havers (retd)
LONDON ROWING CLUB (1856), Embankment, Putney,
London SW15 1LB. Tel: 0181-788 1400. *Hon. Secretary,*
N. A. Smith
MCC (MARYLEBONE CRICKET CLUB) (1787), Lord's
Cricket Ground, London NW8 8QN. Tel: 0171-289 1611.
Secretary, R. D. V. Knight
NATIONAL CLUB (1845), c/o The Carlton Club, 69 St
James's Street, London SW1A 1PJ. Tel: 0171-493 1164.
Hon. Secretary, I. Nash
NATIONAL LIBERAL CLUB (1882), Whitehall Place,
London SW1A 2HE. Tel: 0171-930 9871. *Secretary,*
S. J. Roberts
NAVAL AND MILITARY CLUB (1862), 94 Piccadilly,
London W1V 0BP. Tel: 0171-499 5163. *Secretary,* Cdr. J. A.
Holt, MBE
NAVAL CLUB (1946), 38 Hill Street, London W1X 8DP. Tel:
0171-493 7672. *Chief Executive,* Capt. R. J. Husk, CBE, RN
(retd)
NEW CAVENDISH CLUB (1984), 44 Great Cumberland
Place, London W1H 8BS. Tel: 0171-723 0391. *Secretary,*
J. Malone-Lee
DEN NORSKE KLUB (1924), Norway House, 21–24
Cockspur Street, London SW1Y 5BN. Tel: 0171-930 4084.
Secretary, Ms J. P. Okkenhaug
ORIENTAL CLUB (1824), Stratford House, Stratford Place,
London W1N 0ES. Tel: 0171-629 5126. *Secretary,*
S. C. Doble
PORTLAND CLUB (1816), 42 Half Moon Street, London
W1Y 7RD. Tel: 0171-499 1523. *Secretary,* J. Burns, CBE
PRATT'S CLUB (1841), 14 Park Place, London SW1A 1LP. Tel:
0171-493 0397. *Secretary,* G. Snell
QUEEN'S CLUB (1886), Palliser Road, London W14 9EQ.
Tel: 0171-385 3421. *Secretary,* J. A. S. Edwardes
RAILWAY CLUB (1899), Room 208, 25 Marylebone Road,
London NW1 5JS. Tel: 0173-781 2175. *Hon. Secretary,*
A. G. Wells
REFORM CLUB (1836), 104–105 Pall Mall, London
SW1Y 5EW. Tel: 0171-930 9374. *Secretary,* R. A. M. Forrest
ROEHAMPTON CLUB (1901), Roehampton Lane, London
SW15 5LR. Tel: 0181-876 5505. *Chief Executive,* M. Yates
ROYAL AIR FORCE CLUB (1918), 128 Piccadilly, London
W1V 0PY. Tel: 0171-499 3456. *Secretary,* P. N. Owen
ROYAL AUTOMOBILE CLUB (1897), 89–91 Pall Mall,
London SW1Y 5HS. Tel: 0171-930 2345. *General Secretary,*
Col. N. A. Johnson, OBE, TD
ROYAL OCEAN RACING CLUB (1925), 20 St James's Place,
London SW1A 1NN. Tel: 0171-493 2248. *General Manager,*
D. J. Minords, OBE

ROYAL OVER-SEAS LEAGUE (1910), Over-Seas House, Park Place, St James's Street, London SW1A 1LR. Tel: 0171-408 0214. *Director-General*, R. F. Newell
ROYAL THAMES YACHT CLUB (1775), 60 Knightsbridge, London SW1X 7LF. Tel: 0171-235 2121. *Secretary*, Capt. D. Goldson, RN
ST STEPHEN'S CONSTITUTIONAL CLUB (1870), 34 Queen Anne's Gate, London SW1H 9AB. Tel: 0171-222 1382. *Secretary*, L. D. Mawby
SAVAGE CLUB (1857), 1 Whitehall Place, London SW1A 2HD. Tel: 0171-930 8118. *Hon. Secretary*, D. Stirling
SAVILE CLUB (1868), 69 Brook Street, London W1Y 2ER. Tel: 0171-629 5462. *Secretary*, N. Storey
SKI CLUB OF GREAT BRITAIN (1903), 118 Eaton Square, London SW1W 9AF. Tel: 0171-245 1033. *Chief Executive*, Ms I. Grimsey
THAMES ROWING CLUB (1860), Embankment, Putney, London SW15 1LB. Tel: 0181-788 0798. *Hon. Secretary*, J. McConnell
TRAVELLERS CLUB (1819), 106 Pall Mall, London SW1Y 5EP. Tel: 0171-930 8688. *Secretary*, M. S. Allcock
TURF CLUB (1868), 5 Carlton House Terrace, London SW1Y 5AQ. Tel: 0171-930 8555. *Secretary*, Col. J. G. B. Rigby, OBE
UNITED OXFORD AND CAMBRIDGE UNIVERSITY CLUB (1972), 71 Pall Mall, London SW1Y 5HD. Tel: 0171-930 5151. *Secretary*, G. R. Buchanan
UNIVERSITY WOMEN'S CLUB (1886), 2 Audley Square, South Audley Street, London W1Y 6DB. Tel: 0171-499 2268. *Secretary*, J. Robson
VICTORIA CLUB (1863), 1 North Court, Great Peter Street, London SW1P 3LL. Tel: 0171-222 2357. *Secretary*, Ms S. David
VICTORY SERVICES CLUB (1907), 63–79 Seymour Street, London W2 2HF. Tel: 0171-723 4474. *General Manager*, G. F. Taylor
WHITE'S (1693), 37–38 St James's Street, London SW1A 1JG. Tel: 0171-493 6671. *Secretary*, D. C. Ward
WIG AND PEN CLUB (1908), 229–230 Strand, London WC2R 1BA. Tel: 0171-583 7255. *Administrator*, J. Reynolds

---

CLUBS OUTSIDE LONDON

Bath: BATH AND COUNTY CLUB (1865), Queen's Parade, Bath BA1 2NJ. Tel: 01225-423732. *Secretary*, Mrs G. M. Jones
Birmingham: BIRMINGHAM CLUB (1872), Winston Churchill House, 8 Ethel Street, Birmingham B2 4BG. Tel: 0121-643 3357. *Hon. Secretary*, T. R. Pepper
ST PAUL'S CLUB (1859), 34 St Paul's Square, Birmingham B3 1QZ. Tel: 0121-236 1950. *Hon. Secretary*, E. A. Fellowes
Bishop Auckland: THE CLUB (1868), 1 Victoria Avenue, Bishop Auckland, Co. Durham DL14 7JH. Tel: 01388-603219. *Hon. Secretary*, R. Kellett
Blackburn: DISTRICT AND UNION CLUB (1849), Northwood, 1 West Park Road, Blackburn BB2 6DE. Tel: 01254-51474. *Hon. Secretary*, B. Haydock
Bristol: CLIFTON CLUB (1882), 22 The Mall, Clifton, Bristol BS8 4DS. Tel: 0117-973 5527. *Secretary*, M. G. Henry
Cambridge: AMATEUR DRAMATIC CLUB (1855), ADC Theatre, Park Street, Cambridge CB5 8AS. Tel: 01223-359547. *Secretary*, M. Mitchell
THE UNION (1815), Bridge Street, Cambridge CB2 1UB. Tel: 01223-361521. *House Manager*, J. C. Haslam
Canterbury: KENT AND CANTERBURY CLUB (1868), The Elms, 17 Old Dover Road, Canterbury CT1 3JB. Tel: 01227-462181. *Secretary*, H. V. Brown, LVO, QPM, CPM

Cheltenham: NEW CLUB (1874), Montpellier Parade, Cheltenham GL50 1UD. Tel: 01242-523285. *Hon. Secretary*, N. S. Parrack
Chichester: REGNUM CLUB (1862), 45A South Street, Chichester, W. Sussex PO19 1DS. Tel: 01243-780219. *Chairman*, M. Pearson
Durham: COUNTY CLUB (1890), 52 Old Elvet, Durham DH1 3HJ. Tel: 0191-384 8156. *Secretary*, Mrs C. Arnot
DURHAM UNION SOCIETY (1842), 24 North Bailey, Durham DH1 3EP. Tel: 0191-384 3724. *Secretary*, Mrs E. M. Hardcastle
Guildford: COUNTY CLUB, 158 High Street, Guildford GU1 3HJ. Tel: 01483-575370. *Hon. Secretary*, R. W. D. Hemingway
Henley-on-Thames: LEANDER CLUB (1818), Henley-on-Thames, Oxon RG9 2LP. Tel: 01491-575782. *Hon. Secretary*, J. Beveridge
PHYLLIS COURT CLUB (1906), Marlow Road, Henley-on-Thames, Oxon RG9 2HT. Tel: 01491-574366. *Secretary*, R. Edwards
Hove: HOVE CLUB (1882), 28 Fourth Avenue, Hove, E. Sussex BN3 2PJ. Tel: 01273-730872. *Secretary*, J. L. C. Young
Leamington Spa: TENNIS COURT CLUB (1846), 50 Bedford Street, Leamington Spa, Warks CV32 5DT. Tel: 01926-424977. *Hon. Secretary*, O. D. R. Dixon
Leeds: LEEDS CLUB (1850), 3 Albion Place, Leeds LS1 6JL. Tel: 0113-242 1591. *Manager*, Mrs C. Myers
Leicester: LEICESTERSHIRE CLUB (1873), 9 Welford Place, Leicester LE1 6ZH. Tel: 0116-254 0399. *Secretary*, T. M. Bedingfield
Liverpool: THE ATHENAEUM (1797), Church Alley, Liverpool L1 3DD. Tel: 0151-709 7770. *Secretary*, B. B. P. Kinsman
Macclesfield: OLD BOYS' AND PARK GREEN CLUB, 7 Churchside, Macclesfield, Cheshire SK10 1HG. Tel: 01625-423292. *Hon. Secretary*, M. J. Garrity
Manchester: ST JAMES'S CLUB, St James's House, Charlotte Street, Manchester M1 4DZ. Tel: 0161-236 2235. *Hon. Secretary*, H. J. J. Rylands
Newcastle upon Tyne: NORTHERN CONSTITUTIONAL CLUB (1882), 37 Pilgrim Street, Newcastle upon Tyne NE1 6QE. Tel: 0191-232 0884. *Hon. Secretary*, J. L. Browne
Northampton: NORTHAMPTON AND COUNTY CLUB (1873), George Row, Northampton NN1 1DF. Tel: 01604-32962. *Secretary*, J. Green
Norwich: NORFOLK CLUB (1770), 17 Upper King Street, Norwich NR3 1RB. Tel: 01603-610652. *Secretary*, G. G. Hardaker
Nottingham: NOTTINGHAM AND NOTTS UNITED SERVICES CLUB (1920), Newdigate House, Castle Gate, Nottingham NG1 6AF. Tel: 0115-941 8001. *Secretary*, K. Goodman
Oxford: FREWEN CLUB (1869), 98 St Aldate's, Oxford OX1 1BT. Tel: 01865-243816. *Hon. Secretary*, B. R. Boyt
VINCENT'S CLUB (1863), 1A King Edward Street, Oxford OX1 4HS. Tel: 01865-722984. *Steward*, H. Dean
Paignton: PAIGNTON CLUB (1882), The Esplanade, Paignton, Devon TQ4 6ED. Tel: 01803-559682. *Hon. Secretary*, P. Grafton
Shrewsbury: SALOP CLUB (1974), The Old House, Dogpole, Shrewsbury SY1 1EP. Tel: 01743-362182. *Secretary*, J. W. Rouse
Stourbridge: STOURBRIDGE OLD EDWARDIAN CLUB (1898), Drury Lane, Stourbridge, West Midlands DY8 1BL. Tel: 01384-395635. *Hon. Secretary*, D. J. Lucas
Teddington: ROYAL CANOE CLUB (1866), Trowlock Island, Teddington, Middx TW11 9QZ. Tel: 0181-977 5269. *Hon. Secretary*, Mrs J. S. Evans

WALES

Cardiff: CARDIFF AND COUNTY CLUB (1866), Westgate Street, Cardiff CFI IDA. Tel: 01222-220846. *Hon. Secretary,* Cdr. J. E. Payn, RD

SCOTLAND

Aberdeen: ROYAL NORTHERN AND UNIVERSITY CLUB (1854/ 1889, amal. 1979), 9 Albyn Place, Aberdeen AB10 IYE. Tel: 01224-583292. *Secretary,* Miss R. A. Black
Ayr: AYR COUNTY CLUB (1872), Savoy Park Hotel, Racecourse Road, Ayr KA7 2UT. Tel: 01292-266112. *Hon. Secretary,* G. A. Hay
Edinburgh: CALEDONIAN CLUB, 32 Abercromby Place, Edinburgh EH3 6QE. Tel: 0131-557 2675. *Secretary,* P. Walker
NEW CLUB (1787), 86 Princes Street, Edinburgh EH2 2BB. Tel: 0131-226 4881. *Secretary,* A. D. Orr Ewing
Glasgow: GLASGOW ART CLUB (1867), 185 Bath Street, Glasgow G2 4HU. Tel: 0141-248 5210. *Secretary,* L. J. McIntyre
ROYAL SCOTTISH AUTOMOBILE CLUB (1899), 11 Blythswood Square, Glasgow G2 4AG. Tel: 0141-221 3850. *Secretary,* J. C. Lord
WESTERN CLUB (1825), 32 Royal Exchange Square, Glasgow GI 3AB. Tel: 0141-221 2016. *Secretary,* D. H. Gifford

NORTHERN IRELAND

Belfast: ULSTER REFORM CLUB (1885), 4 Royal Avenue, Belfast BTI IDA. Tel: 01232-323411. *Secretary,* Miss M. P. Mackintosh
Londonderry: NORTHERN COUNTIES CLUB (1880), 24 Bishop Street, Londonderry BT48 6PP. Tel: 01504-262012. *Hon. Secretary,* N. Dykes

CHANNEL ISLANDS

Guernsey: UNITED CLUB (1870), Pier Steps, St Peter Port, Guernsey GYI 2LF. Tel: 01481-725722. *Hon. Secretary,* G. D. E. Chaloner
Jersey: VICTORIA CLUB (1853), Beresford Street, St Helier, Jersey JE2 4WN. Tel: 01534-23381. *Secretary,* Miss C. Rynd

---

YACHT CLUBS

Bembridge: BEMBRIDGE SAILING CLUB (1886), Embankment Road, Bembridge, IOW PO35 5NR. Tel: 01983-872237. *Secretary,* Lt.-Col. M. J. Samuelson, RM
Birkenhead: ROYAL MERSEY YACHT CLUB (1844), Bedford Road East, Rock Ferry, Birkenhead, Merseyside L42 ILS. Tel: 0151-645 3204. *Hon. Secretary,* P. A. Bastow
Bridlington: ROYAL YORKSHIRE YACHT CLUB (1847), 1 Windsor Crescent, Bridlington, E. Yorks YO15 3HX. Tel: 01262-672041. *Secretary,* J. H. Evans
Burnham-on-Crouch: ROYAL CORINTHIAN YACHT CLUB (1872), Burnham-on-Crouch, Essex CM0 8AX. Tel: 01621-782105. *Hon. Secretary,* B. Stanford
Chichester: CHICHESTER YACHT CLUB (1965), Chichester Yacht Basin, Birdham, Chichester, W. Sussex PO20 7EJ. Tel: 01243-512918. *Secretary,* Mrs V. A. Allan
Cowes: ROYAL YACHT SQUADRON (1815), The Castle, Cowes, IOW PO31 7QT. Tel: 01983-292191. *Secretary,* Maj. R. P. Rising, RM
Dover: ROYAL CINQUE PORTS YACHT CLUB (1872), 5 Waterloo Crescent, Dover, Kent CT16 ILA. Tel: 01304-206262. *Secretary,* Mrs C. A. Partridge

Fowey: ROYAL FOWEY YACHT CLUB (1881), Whitford Yard, Fowey, Cornwall PL23 IBH. Tel: 01726-833573. *Hon. Secretary,* M. E. J. Harrison
Harwich: ROYAL HARWICH YACHT CLUB (1843), Woolverstone, Ipswich IP9 IAT. Tel: 01473-780319. *Secretary,* Cdr. J. A. Adams, RD
Kingswear: ROYAL DART YACHT CLUB (1866), Priory Street, Kingswear, Dartmouth, Devon TQ6 0AB. Tel: 01803-752496. *Secretary,* N. Baxter
Leigh on Sea: ESSEX YACHT CLUB (1890), HQS Bembridge, Foreshore, Leigh-on-Sea, Essex SS9 IBD. Tel: 01702-78404. *Hon. Secretary,* A. Manning
London: THE CRUISING ASSOCIATION (1908), CA House, 1 Northey Street, Limehouse Basin, London E14 8BT. Tel: 0171-537 2828. *General Secretary,* Mrs. L. Hammett
ROYAL CRUISING CLUB (1880), c/o Royal Thames Yacht Club, 60 Knightsbridge, London SW1X 7LF. Tel: 01276-65946. *Hon. Secretary,* P. Price
ROYAL THAMES YACHT CLUB (1775), 60 Knightsbridge, London SW1X 7LF. Tel: 0171-235 2121. *Secretary,* Capt. D Goldson, RN
Lowestoft: ROYAL NORFOLK AND SUFFOLK YACHT CLUB (1859), Royal Plain, Lowestoft, Suffolk NR33 0AQ. Tel: 01502-566726. *Hon. General Secretary,* B. Falat
Lymington: ROYAL LYMINGTON YACHT CLUB (1922), Bath Road, Lymington, Hants SO41 3SE. Tel: 01590-672677. *Secretary,* Gp Capt. J. D. Hutchinson (retd)
Plymouth: ROYAL WESTERN YACHT CLUB OF ENGLAND (1827), Queen Anne's Battery, Plymouth PL4 0TW. Tel: 01752-660077. *Chief Executive,* J. Lewis
ROYAL PLYMOUTH CORINTHIAN YACHT CLUB (1877), Madeira Road, Plymouth PLI 2NY. Tel: 01752-664327. *Hon. Secretary,* V. J. De Boo
Poole: EAST DORSET SAILING CLUB (1875), 352 Sandbanks Road, Poole, Dorset BH14 8HY. Tel: 01202-706111. *Hon. Secretary,* Mrs T. Neely
PARKSTONE YACHT CLUB (1895), Pearce Avenue, Poole, Dorset BH14 8EH. Tel: 01202-743610. *Secretary,* D. E. Norman
POOLE HARBOUR YACHT CLUB (1949), 38 Salterns Way, Lilliput, Poole, Dorset BH14 8JR. Tel: 01202-707321. *Secretary,* J. N. J. Smith
POOLE YACHT CLUB (1865), New Harbour Road West, Hamworthy, Poole, Dorset BH15 4AQ. Tel: 01202-672687. *Secretary/Manager,* Miss L. Clark
Portsmouth: ROYAL NAVAL CLUB AND ROYAL ALBERT YACHT CLUB (1867), 17 Pembroke Road, Portsmouth PO1 2NT. Tel: 01705-824491. *Secretary,* Cdr. N. J. Stone, OBE
Ramsgate: ROYAL TEMPLE YACHT CLUB (1857), 6 Westcliff Mansions, Ramsgate, Kent CT11 9HY. Tel: 01843-591766. *Hon. Secretary,* G. F. Randell
Southampton: ROYAL AIR FORCE YACHT CLUB (1932), Riverside House, Rope Walk, Hamble, Southampton SO31 4HD. Tel: 01703-452208. *Secretary,* Mrs S. E. Fullwood
ROYAL SOUTHAMPTON YACHT CLUB, 1 Channel Way, Ocean Village, Southampton SO14 3QF. Tel: 01703-223352. *Secretary,* A. M. Paterson
ROYAL SOUTHERN YACHT CLUB (1837), Rope Walk, Hamble, Southampton SO31 4HB. Tel: 01703-453271. *Secretary,* Mrs. J. A. Atkins
Torquay: ROYAL TORBAY YACHT CLUB (1863), Beacon Hill, Torquay, Devon TQI 2BQ. Tel: 01803-292006. *Club Administrator,* R. Porteous
Westcliff-on-Sea: THAMES ESTUARY YACHT CLUB (1895), 3 The Leas, Westcliff-on-Sea, Essex SS0 7ST. Tel: 01702-345967. *Hon. Secretary,* D. Howard
Weymouth: ROYAL DORSET YACHT CLUB (1875), 11 Custom House Quay, Weymouth, Dorset DT4 8BG. Tel: 01305-786258. *Secretary,* Mrs K. Mead

Windermere: ROYAL WINDERMERE YACHT CLUB (1860),
Fallbarrow Road, Bowness-on-Windermere,
Windermere, Cumbria LA23 3DJ. Tel: 015394-43106.
Hon. Secretary, P. V. Barraclough
Yarmouth: ROYAL SOLENT YACHT CLUB (1878), Yarmouth,
IOW PO41 ONS. Tel: 01983-760256. *Secretary,*
Mrs S. Tribe

WALES

Beaumaris: ROYAL ANGLESEY YACHT CLUB (1802), 6–7
Green Edge, Beaumaris, Anglesey LL58 8BY. Tel: 01248-
810295. *Hon. Secretary,* J. E. de Leyland-Berry
Caernarfon: ROYAL WELSH YACHT CLUB (1847), Porth-Yr-
Aur, Caernarfon LL55 1SW. Tel: 01286-672599. *Hon.
Secretary,* J. H. Long
Penarth: PENARTH YACHT CLUB (1880), The Esplanade,
Penarth, Vale of Glamorgan CF64 3AU. Tel: 01222-
708196. *Hon. Secretary,* R. S. McGregor
Swansea: BRISTOL CHANNEL YACHT CLUB (1875), 744
Mumbles Road, Mumbles, Swansea SA3 4EL. Tel: 01792-
366000. *Hon. Secretary,* M. J. Snowdon

SCOTLAND

Dundee: ROYAL TAY YACHT CLUB (1885), 34 Dundee Road,
Broughty Ferry, Dundee DD5 1LX. Tel: 01382-477516.
Hon. Secretary, S. Buchanan
Edinburgh: ROYAL FORTH YACHT CLUB (1868), Middle Pier,
Granton Harbour, Edinburgh EH5 1HF. Tel: 0131-
552 8560. *Hon. Secretary,* A. R. Woods
Glasgow: ROYAL WESTERN YACHT CLUB (1875), Edenbank,
66 Colquhoun Street, Helensburgh, Argyll and Bute
G84 9JP. *Hon. Secretary,* D. W. Pritty
Oban: ROYAL HIGHLAND YACHT CLUB (1881), Ythan,
Ferryfield Road, Connel, Argyll PA37 1SR. Tel: 01631-
710738. *Secretary,* Mrs A. Wood
Rhu: ROYAL NORTHERN AND CLYDE YACHT CLUB (1824,
amal. 1978), Rhu, Helensburgh, Argyll and Bute
G84 8NG. Tel: 01436-820322. *Hon. Secretary,* B. C. Staig

NORTHERN IRELAND

Bangor: ROYAL ULSTER YACHT CLUB (1866), 101 Clifton
Road, Bangor, Co. Down BT20 5HY. Tel: 01247-270568.
Secretary, Mrs V. F. M. Boyd

CHANNEL ISLANDS

Jersey: ROYAL CHANNEL ISLANDS YACHT CLUB (1862), Le
Boulevard, Bulwarks, St Aubin, Jersey JE3 8GW. Tel:
01534-45783. *Hon. Secretary,* D. C. Dale

Societies and Institutions

Although this section is arranged in alphabetical order, organizations are usually listed by the keyword in their title. The date in parenthesis after the organization's title is the year of its foundation.

ABBEYFIELD SOCIETY (1956), Abbeyfield House, 53 Victoria Street, St Albans, Herts AL1 3UW. Tel: 01727-857536. Housing for elderly people. *Chief Executive*, F. Murphy

ACCOUNTANTS, CHARTERED ASSOCIATION OF CERTIFIED (1904), 29 Lincoln's Inn Fields, London WC2A 3EE. Tel: 0171-242 6855. *Chief Executive*, Mrs A. L. Rose

ACCOUNTANTS, INSTITUTE OF COMPANY (1974), 40 Tyndalls Park Road, Bristol BS8 1PL. Tel: 0117-973 8261. *Director-General*, B. T. Banks

ACCOUNTANTS, INSTITUTE OF FINANCIAL (1916), Burford House, 44 London Road, Sevenoaks, Kent TN13 1AS. Tel: 01732-458080. *Chief Executive*, J. M. Dean

ACCOUNTANTS IN ENGLAND AND WALES, INSTITUTE OF CHARTERED (1880), Chartered Accountants' Hall, PO Box 433, Moorgate Place, London EC2P 2BJ. Tel: 0171-920 8100. *Secretary*, A. J. Colquhoun

ACCOUNTANTS OF SCOTLAND, INSTITUTE OF CHARTERED (1854), 27 Queen Street, Edinburgh EH2 1LA. Tel: 0131-225 5673. *Chief Executive*, P. W. Johnston

ACCOUNTING TECHNICIANS, ASSOCIATION OF (1980), 154 Clerkenwell Road, London EC1R 5AD. Tel: 0171-837 8600. *Secretary*, Ms J. Scott Paul (from 1 January 1997)

ACE STUDY TOURS (formerly Association for Cultural Exchange), Babraham, Cambridge CB2 4AP. Tel: 01223-835055. *General Secretary*, P. B. Barnes

ACTION RESEARCH (1952), Vincent House, North Parade, Horsham, W. Sussex RH12 2DP. Tel: 01403-210406. *Director-General*, Mrs A.Luther

ACTORS' BENEVOLENT FUND (1882), 6 Adam Street, London WC2N 6AA. Tel: 0171-836 6378. *General Secretary*, Mrs R. Stevens

ACTORS' CHARITABLE TRUST (1896), 255–256 Africa House, 64–78 Kingsway, London WC2B 6BD. Tel: 0171-242 0111. *Chief Executive*, J. C. Dunn

ACTORS' CHURCH UNION (1899), St Paul's Church, Bedford Street, London WC2E 9ED. Tel: 0171-836 5221. *Senior Chaplain*, Canon W. Hall

ACTUARIES, INSTITUTE OF (1848), Staple Inn Hall, High Holborn, London WC1V 7QJ. Tel: 0171-242 0106. *Secretary-General*, A. G. Tait

ACTUARIES IN SCOTLAND, FACULTY OF (1856), 40 Thistle Street, Edinburgh EH2 1EN. Tel: 0131-220 4555. *Secretary*, W. W. Mair

ADMINISTRATIVE MANAGEMENT, INSTITUTE OF (1915), 40 Chatsworth Parade, Petts Wood, Orpington, Kent BR5 1RW. Tel: 01689-875555. *Chief Executive*, Prof. G. Robinson

ADULT SCHOOL ORGANIZATION, NATIONAL (1899), MASU Centre, Gaywood Croft, Cregoe Street, Birmingham B15 2ED. Tel: 0121-622 3400. *General Secretary*, S. B. Shuttleworth

ADVERTISING BENEVOLENT SOCIETY, NATIONAL (1913), 199–205 Old Marylebone Road, London NW1 5QP. Tel: 0171-723 8028. *Director*, Mrs D. K. Larkin

ADVERTISING, INSTITUTE OF PRACTITIONERS IN (1927), 44 Belgrave Square, London SW1X 8QS. Tel: 0171-235 7020. *Director-General*, N. Phillips

ADVERTISING STANDARDS AUTHORITY (1962), 2 Torrington Place, London WC1E 7HW. Tel: 0171-580 5555. *Director-General*, Mrs M. Alderson

AERONAUTICAL SOCIETY, ROYAL (1866), 4 Hamilton Place, London W1V 0BQ. Tel: 0171-499 3515. *Director*, R. J. Kennett

AFRICAN INSTITUTE, INTERNATIONAL (1926), SOAS, Thornhaugh Street, Russell Square, London WC1H 0XG. Tel: 0171-323 6035. *Hon. Director*, Prof. P. Spencer

AFRICAN MEDICAL AND RESEARCH FOUNDATION, 11 Old Queen Street, London SW1H 9JA. Tel: 0171- 233 0066. *Executive Director*, A. Heroys

AGE CONCERN CYMRU, 4th Floor, 1 Cathedral Road, Cardiff CF1 9SD. Tel: 01222-371566. *Director*, R. W. Taylor

AGE CONCERN ENGLAND (1940), Astral House, 1268 London Road, London SW16 4ER. Tel: 0181-679 8000. *Director-General*, Ms S. Greengross, OBE

AGE CONCERN NORTHERN IRELAND (1976), 3 Lower Crescent, Belfast BT7 1NR. Tel: 01232-245729. *Director*, C. J. Common

AGE CONCERN SCOTLAND (1943), 113 Rose Street, Edinburgh EH2 3DT. Tel: 0131-220 3345. *Director*, Ms M. O' Neill

AGEING, CENTRE FOR POLICY ON (1947), 25–31 Ironmonger Row, London EC1V 3QP. Tel: 0171-253 1787. *Director*, Dr G. Dalley

AGEING, RESEARCH INTO (1978), Baird House, 15–17 St Cross Street, London EC1N 8UN. Tel: 0171-404 6878. *Director*, Mrs E. Mills

AGRICULTURAL BENEVOLENT INSTITUTION, ROYAL (1860), Shaw House, 27 West Way, Oxford OX2 0QH. Tel: 01865-724931. *Chief Executive*, Air Cdre R. B. Duckett, CVO, AFC

AGRICULTURAL BENEVOLENT INSTITUTION, ROYAL SCOTTISH (1897), Ingliston, Edinburgh EH28 8NB. Tel: 0131-333 1023. *Director*, I. C. Purves-Hume

AGRICULTURAL ENGINEERS ASSOCIATION (1875), Samuelson House, Paxton Road, Orton Centre, Peterborough PE2 5LT. Tel: 01733-371381. *Director-General*, J. Vowles

AGRICULTURAL SOCIETY, EAST OF ENGLAND, East of England Showground, Peterborough PE2 6XE. Tel: 01733-234451. *Chief Executive*, T. Gibson, OBE

AGRICULTURAL SOCIETY OF ENGLAND, ROYAL (1838), National Agricultural Centre, Stoneleigh Park, Warks CV8 2LZ. Tel: 01203-696969. *Chief Executive*, C. Runge

AGRICULTURAL SOCIETY OF THE COMMONWEALTH, ROYAL (1957), 55 Sleaford Street, London SW8 5AB. Tel: 0171-978 1301. *Hon. Secretary*, F. R. Francis, CVO, MBE

AGRICULTURAL SOCIETY, ROYAL ULSTER (1826), The King's Hall, Balmoral, Belfast BT9 6GW. Tel: 01232-665225. *Chief Executive*, W. H. Yarr, OBE

716   Societies and Institutions

AIR LEAGUE, THE (1909), 4 Hamilton Place, London WIV OBQ. Tel: 0171-491 0470. *Director,* Gp Capt. E. R. Cox

ALCOHOLICS ANONYMOUS (1947), PO Box 1, Stonebow House, Stonebow, York YO1 2NJ. Tel: 01904-644026. *General Secretary,* J. Keeney

ALEXANDRA ROSE DAY (1912), 2A Ferry Road, Barnes, London SW13 9RX. Tel: 0181-748 4824. *National Director,* Mrs G. Greenwood

ALLIANCE PARTY OF NORTHERN IRELAND (1970), 88 University Street, Belfast BT7 1HE. Tel: 01232-324274. *Party Leader,* Dr J. T. Alderdice

ALLOTMENT AND LEISURE GARDENERS LIMITED, NATIONAL SOCIETY OF (1930), Hunters Road, Corby, Northants NN17 5JE. Tel: 01536-266576. *National Secretary,* G. W. Stokes

ALMSHOUSES, NATIONAL ASSOCIATION OF (1946), Billingbear Lodge, Wokingham, Berks RG11 5RU. Tel: 01344-52922. *Director,* D. M. Scott

ALZHEIMER'S DISEASE SOCIETY (1979), Gordon House, 10 Greencoat Place, London SW1P 1PH. Tel: 0171-306 0606. *Executive Director,* H. Cayton

AMNESTY INTERNATIONAL UNITED KINGDOM (1961), 99–119 Rosebery Avenue, London EC1R 4RE. Tel: 0171-814 6200. *Director,* D. Bull

ANAESTHETISTS OF GREAT BRITAIN AND IRELAND, ASSOCIATION OF (1932), 9 Bedford Square, London WC1B 3RA. Tel: 0171-631 1650. *Hon. Secretary,* Dr D. A. Saunders

ANCIENT BUILDINGS, SOCIETY FOR THE PROTECTION OF (1877), 37 Spital Square, London E1 6DY. Tel: 0171-377 1644. *Secretary,* P. Venning, FSA

ANCIENT MONUMENTS SOCIETY (1924), St Ann's Vestry Hall, 2 Church Entry, London EC4V 5HB. Tel: 0171-236 3934. *Secretary,* M. J. Saunders

ANGLO-ARAB ASSOCIATION (1961), The Arab British Centre, 21 Collingham Road, London SW5 0NU. Tel: 0171-373 8414. *Executive Director,* A. Lee

ANGLO-BELGIAN SOCIETY (1982), 45 West Common, Haywards Heath, W. Sussex RH16 2AJ. Tel: 01444-452183. *Hon. Secretary,* Mrs A. M. Woodhead

ANGLO-BRAZILIAN SOCIETY (1943), 32 Green Street, London W1Y 3FD. Tel: 0171-493 8493. *Secretary,* Mrs J. Byers

ANGLO-DANISH SOCIETY (1924), 25 New Street Square, London EC4A 3LN. Tel: 01753-884846. *Chairman,* H. Castenskiold, OBE

ANGLO-NORSE SOCIETY (1918), 25 Belgrave Square, London SW1X 8QD. Tel: 0171-235 7151. *Chairman,* Dame Gillian Brown, DCVO, CMG

ANIMAL CONCERN (1988), 62 Old Dumbarton Road, Glasgow G3 8RE. Tel: 0141-334 6014. *Organizing Secretary,* J. F. Robins

ANIMAL HEALTH TRUST (1942), PO Box 5, Newmarket, Suffolk CB8 7DW. Tel: 01638-661111. *Director,* A. J. Higgins, PH.D.

ANTHROPOLOGICAL INSTITUTE, ROYAL (1843), 50 Fitzroy Street, London W1P 5HS. Tel: 0171-387 0455. *Director,* J. C. M. Benthall

ANTHROPOSOPHICAL SOCIETY IN GREAT BRITAIN (1923), Rudolf Steiner House, 35 Park Road, London NW1 6XT. Tel: 0171-723 4400. *General Secretary,* N. C. Thomas

ANTIQUARIES OF LONDON, SOCIETY OF (1717), Burlington House, Piccadilly, London W1V 0HS. Tel: 0171-734 0193. *General Secretary,* D. Morgan Evans, FSA

ANTIQUARIES OF SCOTLAND, SOCIETY OF (1780), National Museums of Scotland, York Buildings, Queen Street, Edinburgh EH2 1JD. Tel: 0131-225 7534 ext 327/8. *Director,* Mrs F. Ashmore, FSA

ANTIQUE DEALERS' ASSOCIATION, BRITISH (1918), 20 Rutland Gate, London SW7 1BD. Tel: 0171-589 4128. *Secretary-General,* Mrs E. J. Dean

ANTI-SLAVERY INTERNATIONAL (1839), Unit 4, Stableyard, Broomgrove Road, London SW9 9TL. Tel: 0171-924 9555. *Director,* M. Dottridge

ANTI-VIVISECTION: BRITISH UNION FOR THE ABOLITION OF VIVISECTION (1898), 16A Crane Grove, London N7 8LB. Tel: 0171-700 4888. *Director (acting),* Dr M. Eames

ANTI-VIVISECTION SOCIETY, NATIONAL (1875), 261 Goldhawk Road, London W12 9PE. Tel: 0181-846 9777. *Director,* Ms J. Creamer

APOSTLESHIP OF THE SEA (1920), Stella Maris, 66 Dock Road, Tilbury, Essex RM18 7BX. Tel: 01375-845641. *National Director,* Revd J. Maguire, MHM

APOTHECARIES OF LONDON, SOCIETY OF (1617), 14 Black Friars Lane, London EC4V 6EJ. Tel: 0171-236 1189. *Clerk,* R. J. Stringer

ARBITRATORS, CHARTERED INSTITUTE OF (1915), 24 Angel Gate, City Road, London EC1V 2RS. Tel: 0171-837 4483. *Secretary-General,* K. Harding

ARCHAEOLOGICAL ASSOCIATION, CAMBRIAN (1846), The Laurels, Westfield Road, Newport NP9 4ND. Tel: 01633-262449. *General Secretary,* Dr J. M. Hughes

ARCHAEOLOGICAL INSTITUTE, ROYAL (1843), c/o Society of Antiquaries of London, Burlington House, Piccadilly, London W1V 0HS. *Secretary,* J. G. Coad, FSA

ARCHAEOLOGY, COUNCIL FOR BRITISH (1944), Bowes Morrell House, 111 Walmgate, York YO1 2UA. Tel: 01904-671417. *Director,* R. K. Morris

ARCHITECTS, ROYAL INSTITUTE OF BRITISH (1834), 66 Portland Place, London W1N 4AD. Tel: 0171-580 5533. *President,* Dr F. Duffy; *Director-General,* A. Reid, PH.D.

ARCHITECTS AND SURVEYORS INSTITUTE (1926), St Mary House, 15 St Mary Street, Chippenham, Wilts SN15 3WD. Tel: 01249-444505. *Chief Executive,* C. G. A. Nash, OBE

ARCHITECTS BENEVOLENT SOCIETY (1850), 43 Portland Place, London W1N 3AG. Tel: 0171-580 2823. *Hon. Secretary,* R. Roth

ARCHITECTS IN SCOTLAND, ROYAL INCORPORATION OF (1922), 15 Rutland Square, Edinburgh EH1 2BE. Tel: 0131-229 7545. *Secretary,* S. Tombs

ARCHITECTS REGISTRATION COUNCIL OF THE UNITED KINGDOM (1931), 73 Hallam Street, London W1N 6EE. Tel: 0171-580 5861. *Registrar,* D. W. Smart

ARCHITECTURAL ASSOCIATION INC. (1847), 34–36 Bedford Square, London WC1B 3ES. Tel: 0171-636 0974. *Secretary,* E. Le Maistre

ARCHITECTURAL HERITAGE FUND, THE (1976), 27 John Adam Street, London WC2N 6HX. Tel: 0171-925 0199. *Secretary,* Ms H. Weir

ARCHIVISTS, SOCIETY OF (1947), Information House, 20–24 Old Street, London EC1V 9AP. Tel: 0171-253 5087. *Executive Secretary,* P. S. Cleary

ARK ENVIRONMENTAL FOUNDATION, THE (1988), Suite 640–643, Linen Hall, 162–168 Regent Street, London W1R 5TB. Tel: 0171-439 4567. *Co-ordinator,* Ms N. Malone

ARLIS/UK AND IRELAND (THE ART LIBRARIES SOCIETY) (1969), 18 College Road, Bromsgrove, Worcs B60 2NE. Tel: 01527-579298. *Administrator*, Ms S. French

ARMY BENEVOLENT FUND (1944), 41 Queen's Gate, London sw7 5HR. Tel: 0171-581 8684. *Controller*, Maj.-Gen. G. M. G. Swindells, CB

ARMY CADET FORCE ASSOCIATION (1930), E Block, Duke of York's HQ, London sw3 4RR. Tel: 0171-730 9733/4. *General Secretary*, Brig. R. B. MacGregor-Oakford, CBE, MC

ART, ROYAL CAMBRIAN ACADEMY OF (1882), Crown Lane, Conwy, Conwy LL32 8BH. Tel: 01492-593413. *Curator and Secretary*, Ms V. Macdonald

ART COLLECTIONS FUND, NATIONAL (1903), Millais House, 7 Cromwell Place, London sw7 2JN. Tel: 0171-225 4800. *Director*, D. Barrie

ARTHRITIS AND RHEUMATISM COUNCIL FOR RESEARCH (1936), Copeman House, St Mary's Court, St Mary's Gate, Chesterfield, Derbys s41 7TD. Tel: 01246-558033. *Chief Executive*, J. Norton

ARTHRITIS CARE (1949), 18 Stephenson Way, London NW1 2HD. Tel: 0171-916 1500. *Secretary*, I. Robinson

ARTISTS, FEDERATION OF BRITISH, 17 Carlton House Terrace, London sw1Y 5BD. Tel: 0171-930 6844. *Chairman*, J. Walton

ARTISTS' GENERAL BENEVOLENT INSTITUTION (1814) and ARTISTS' ORPHAN FUND (1871), Burlington House, Piccadilly, London w1v 0DJ. Tel: 0171-734 1193. *Secretary*, Ms A. Connett-Dance

ARTS, NATIONAL CAMPAIGN FOR THE (1984), Francis House, Francis Street, London sw1P 1DE. Tel: 0171-828 4448. *Director*, Ms J. Edwards

ASIAN FAMILY COUNSELLING SERVICE (1985), 74 The Avenue, London w13 8LB. Tel: 0181-997 5749. *Co-ordinator*, Ms K. Randhawa

ASLIB (The Association for Information Management) (1924), Information House, 20–24 Old Street, London EC1V 9AP. Tel: 0171-253 4488. *Chief Executive*, R. Bowes

ASTHMA CAMPAIGN, NATIONAL (1927), Providence House, Providence Place, London N1 0NT. Tel: 0171-226 2260. *Chief Executive*, Ms M. Letts

ASTRONOMICAL ASSOCIATION, BRITISH (1890), Burlington House, Piccadilly, London w1v 9AG. Meetings at the Scientific Societies Lecture Theatre, 23 Savile Row, London w1X 1AB. *Assistant Secretary*, Miss P. M. Barber

ASTRONOMICAL SOCIETY, ROYAL (1820), Burlington House, Piccadilly, London w1v 0NL. Tel: 0171-734 4582/3307. *President*, Prof. Sir Martin Rees, FRS; *Executive Secretary*, J. E. Lane

ATS/WRAC BENEVOLENT FUNDS (1964), Block 10, AGC Centre, Worthy Down, Winchester, Hants so21 2RG. Tel: 01962-887612/478. *Secretaries*, Mrs A. H. S. Matthews; Maj. K. C. Jay

AUDIT BUREAU OF CIRCULATIONS LTD (1931), Black Prince Yard, 207–209 High Street, Berkhamsted, Herts HP4 1AD. Tel: 01442-870800. *Secretary*, J. Beadell

AUTHORS, SOCIETY OF (1884), 84 Drayton Gardens, London sw10 9SB. Tel: 0171-373 6642. *General Secretary*, M. Le Fanu, OBE

AUTOMOBILE ASSOCIATION (1905), Norfolk House, Priestley Road, Basingstoke, Hants RG24 9NY. Tel: 01256-20123. *Director-General (acting)*, R. Chase

AVICULTURAL SOCIETY (1894), c/o Bristol Zoological Gardens, Clifton, Bristol bs8 3HA. Tel: 0117-973 8951. *Hon. Secretary*, G. R. Greed

AYRSHIRE CATTLE SOCIETY OF GREAT BRITAIN AND IRELAND (1877), 1 Racecourse Road, Ayr KA7 2DE. Tel: 01292-267123. *Chief Executive*, S. J. Thomson

BACK PAIN ASSOCIATION, NATIONAL (1968), 16 Elmtree Road, Teddington, Middx TW11 8ST. Tel: 0181-977 5474. *Executive Director*, G. Thomas

BALTIC AIR CHARTER ASSOCIATION (1949), 6 The Office Village, Romford Road, London E15 4EA. Tel: 0181-519 3909. *Hon. Executive*, D. Shepherd

BALTIC EXCHANGE, THE (1903), St Mary Axe, London EC3A 8BH. Tel: 0171-623 5501. *Chief Executive*, J. Buckley

BALTIC EXCHANGE CHARITABLE SOCIETY (1978), 38 St Mary Axe, London EC3A 8BH. Tel: 0171-369 1643/4. *Secretary*, D. A. Painter

BALZAN FOUNDATION, INTERNATIONAL (1956), Piazzetta U Giordano 4, Milan, Italy 20122. Tel: 00 3902-7600 2212. Awards prizes for literature; moral sciences and the arts; physical, mathematical and natural sciences; medicine; humanity, peace and brotherhood. *Secretary-General*, Mrs P. Rognoni

BANKERS, CHARTERED INSTITUTE OF (1879), 90 Bishopsgate, London EC2N 4AS. Tel: 0171-444 7111. *Chief Executive*, G. Shreeve

BANKERS IN SCOTLAND, CHARTERED INSTITUTE OF (1875), 19 Rutland Square, Edinburgh EH1 2DE. Tel: 0131-229 9869. *Chief Executive*, Dr C. W. Munn

BAPTIST MISSIONARY SOCIETY (1792), Baptist House, PO Box 49, 129 Broadway, Didcot, Oxon OX11 8XA. Tel: 01235-512077. *General Director*, Revd Dr A. Brown

BAR ASSOCIATION FOR LOCAL GOVERNMENT AND THE PUBLIC SERVICE (1945), c/o Milton Keynes Borough Council, Civic Offices, 1 Saxon Gate East, Milton Keynes MK9 3HG. Tel: 01908-682205. *Chairman*, P. G. Stivadoros

BARNARDO'S (1866), Tanners Lane, Barkingside, Ilford, Essex IG6 1QG. Tel: 0181-550 8822. *Senior Director*, R. Singleton

BARONETAGE, STANDING COUNCIL OF THE (1898), The Church House, Bibury, Cirencester, Glos GL7 5NR. Tel: 0171-938 2955. *Chairman*, Sir Brian Barttelot, Bt.

BARRISTERS' BENEVOLENT ASSOCIATION (1873), 14 Gray's Inn Square, London WC1R 5JP. Tel: 0171-242 4761. *Secretary*, Mrs A. Ashley

BEECHAM TRUST, SIR THOMAS (1946), Denton House, Denton, Harleston, Norfolk IP20 0AA. Tel: 01986-788780. *Secretary*, Shirley, Lady Beecham

BEE-KEEPERS' ASSOCIATION, BRITISH (1874), National Agricultural Centre, Stoneleigh Park, Kenilworth, Warks CV8 2LZ. Tel: 01203-696679. *General Secretary*, A. C. Waring

BIBLE SOCIETY, BRITISH AND FOREIGN (1804), Stonehill Green, Westlea, Swindon SN5 7DG. Tel: 01793-418100. *Executive Director*, N. Crosbie

BIBLIOGRAPHICAL SOCIETY (1892), National Art Library, Victoria and Albert Museum, London sw7 2RL. Tel: 0171-938 9655. *Hon. Secretary*, D. Pearson

BIBLIOGRAPHICAL SOCIETY, EDINBURGH (1890), c/o Department of Special Collections, Edinburgh University Library, George Square, Edinburgh EH8 9LJ. Tel: 0131-650 3412. *Hon. Secretary*, Dr M. C. T. Simpson

BIOCHEMICAL SOCIETY (1911), 59 Portland Place, London WIN 3AJ. Tel: 0171-580 5530. *Executive Secretary*, G. D. Jones

BIOLOGY, INSTITUTE OF (1950), 20–22 Queensberry Place, London SW7 2DZ. Tel: 0171-581 8333. *General Secretary*, Dr R. H. Priestley

BIRMINGHAM AND MIDLAND INSTITUTE (1854) and PRIESTLEY LIBRARY (1779), Margaret Street, Birmingham B3 3BS. Tel: 0121-236 3591. *Administrator and General Secretary*, P. A. Fisher

BLIND, GUIDE DOGS FOR THE, *see* GUIDE DOGS FOR THE BLIND ASSOCIATION

BLIND, NATIONAL LIBRARY FOR THE (1882), Cromwell Road, Bredbury, Stockport, Cheshire SK6 2SG. Tel: 0161-494 0217. *Chief Executive*, Mrs P. M. Lynn

BLIND PEOPLE, ACTION FOR (1857), 14–16 Verney Road, London SE16 3DZ. Tel: 0171-732 8771. *Chief Executive*, S. Remington

BLIND, ROYAL LONDON SOCIETY FOR THE (1838), 105 Salusbury Road, London NW6 6RH. Tel: 0171-624 8844. *Chief Executive*, P. Talbot

BLIND, ROYAL NATIONAL COLLEGE FOR THE (1872), College Road, Hereford HR1 1EB. Tel: 01432-265725. *Principal*, C. Housby-Smith, PH.D.

BLIND, ROYAL NATIONAL INSTITUTE FOR THE, *see* ROYAL NATIONAL INSTITUTE FOR THE BLIND

BLIND, ROYAL SCHOOL FOR THE, *see* SEEABILITY

BLOOD SERVICE, NATIONAL (1948), Oak House, Reeds Crescent, Watford, Herts WD1 1QH. Tel: 01923-212121. *Chief Executive*, J. Adey

BLOOD TRANSFUSION ASSOCIATION, SCOTTISH NATIONAL (1940), c/o Scottish National Blood Transfusion Service, Ellen's Glen Road, Edinburgh EH17 7QT. Tel: 0131-664 2317. *Secretary*, W. Mack

BLUE CROSS (1897), Shilton Road, Burford, Oxon OX18 4PF. Tel: 01993-822651. *Secretary*, A. Kennard, MBE

BODLEIAN, FRIENDS OF THE (1925), Bodleian Library, Oxford OX1 3BG. Tel: 01865-277022/277234. *Secretary*, G. Groom

BOOK AID INTERNATIONAL (1954), 39–41 Coldharbour Lane, London SE5 9NR. Tel: 0171-733 3577. *Director*, Mrs S. Harrity

BOOKSELLERS ASSOCIATION OF GREAT BRITAIN AND IRELAND (1895), Minster House, 272 Vauxhall Bridge Road, London SW1V 1BA. Tel: 0171-834 5477. *Chief Executive*, T. E. Godfray

BOOK TRADE BENEVOLENT SOCIETY (1967), Dillon Lodge, The Retreat, Kings Langley, Herts WD4 8LT. Tel: 01923-263128. *Executive Secretary*, Mrs A. R. Brown

BOOK TRUST (1986), Book House, 45 East Hill, London SW18 2QZ. Tel: 0181-870 9055. *Executive Director*, B. Perman

BORN FREE FOUNDATION, THE (1984), Cherry Tree Cottage, Coldharbour, Dorking, Surrey RH5 6HA. Tel: 01306-712091. *Director*, W. Travers

BOTANICAL SOCIETY OF SCOTLAND, c/o Royal Botanic Garden, Inverleith Row, Edinburgh EH3 5LR. Tel: 0131-552 7171. *Hon. General Secretary*, R. Galt

BOTANICAL SOCIETY OF THE BRITISH ISLES (1836), The Natural History Museum, Cromwell Road, London SW7 5BD. Tel: 0171-938 5832. *Hon. General Secretary*, R. Gwynn Ellis

BOY SCOUTS ASSOCIATION, *see* SCOUT ASSOCIATION

BOYS' AND GIRLS' CLUBS OF NORTHERN IRELAND (1940), 2nd Floor, 38 Dublin Road, Belfast BT2 7HN. Tel: 01232-241924. *General Secretary*, K. Culbert

BOYS' BRIGADE (1883), Felden Lodge, Hemel Hempstead, Herts HP3 0BL. Tel: 01442-231681. *Brigade Secretary*, S. Jones, OBE

BREWING, INSTITUTE OF (1886), 33 Clarges Street, London W1Y 8EE. Tel: 0171-499 8144. *Chief Executive*, P. W. E. Istead

BRIDEWELL ROYAL HOSPITAL (1553), Witley, Godalming, Surrey GU8 5SG. Tel: 01428-682371. *Registrar*, Mrs J. Benyon

BRITAIN-NEPAL SOCIETY (1960), 3C Gunnersbury Avenue, London W5 3NH. Tel: 0181-992-0173. *Hon. Secretary*, Mrs P. Mellor

BRITAIN-RUSSIA CENTRE (1959), 14 Grosvenor Place, London SW1X 7HW. Tel: 0171-235 2116. *Director*, Dr I. Elliot

BRITISH AND FOREIGN SCHOOL SOCIETY (1808), Richard Mayo Hall, Eden Street, Kingston upon Thames, Surrey KT1 1HZ. Tel: 0181-546 2379. *Secretary*, New appointment awaited

BRITISH INSTITUTE IN EASTERN AFRICA (1959), 20–22 Queensberry Place, London SW7 2DZ. Tel: 0171-584 4653. *London Secretary*, Mrs J. Moyo

BRITISH INSTITUTE OF ARCHAEOLOGY AT ANKARA (1948), 31–34 Gordon Square, London WC1H 0PY. Tel: 0171-388 2361. *London Secretary*, Ms G. Coulthard

BRITISH INSTITUTE OF PERSIAN STUDIES (1961), 63 Old Street, London EC1V 9HX. Tel: 0171-490-4404. *Assistant Secretary*, Ms J. Dryden

BRITISH INTERPLANETARY SOCIETY (1933), 27–29 South Lambeth Road, London SW8 1SZ. Tel: 0171-735 3160. *Executive Secretary*, Ms S. A. Jones

BRITISH ISRAEL WORLD FEDERATION (1919), 8 Blades Court, Deodar Road, London SW15 2NU. Tel: 0181-877 9010. *Secretary*, A. E. Gibb

BRITISH LEGION, ROYAL (1921), 48 Pall Mall, London SW1Y 5JY. Tel: 0171-973 7200. *General Secretary*, Vacant

BRITISH LEGION SCOTLAND, ROYAL (1921), New Haig House, Logie Green Road, Edinburgh EH7 4HR. Tel: 0131-557 2782. *General Secretary*, Maj.-Gen. J. D. MacDonald, CB, CBE

BRITISH MEDICAL ASSOCIATION (1832), BMA House, Tavistock Square, London WC1H 9JP. Tel: 0171-387 4499. *Chairman*, Dr A. Macara; *Secretary*, Dr E. Armstrong

BRITISH NATIONAL PARTY (1982), PO Box 117, Welling, Kent DA16 3DW. Tel: 0374-454893. *Chairman*, J. Tyndall

BRITISH RED CROSS (1870), 9 Grosvenor Crescent, London SW1X 7EJ. Tel: 0171-235 5454. *Director-General*, M. R. Whitlam

BRITISH SCHOOL OF ARCHAEOLOGY IN JERUSALEM (1919), 21 Buccleuch Place (Top Flat), The University of Edinburgh, Edinburgh EH8 9LN. Tel: 0131-650 3975. *President*, P. R. S. Moorey, PH.D., FBA

BTCV (BRITISH TRUST FOR CONSERVATION VOLUNTEERS) (1970), 36 St Mary's Street, Wallingford, Oxon OX10 0EU. Tel: 01491-839766. *Chief Executive*, T. O. Flood

BTG (BRITISH TECHNOLOGY GROUP INTERNATIONAL) PLC, 101 Newington Causeway, London SE1 6BU. Tel: 0171-403 6666. *Chief Executive*, I. A. Harvey

BUDDHIST SOCIETY, THE (1924), 58 Eccleston Square, London SW1V 1PH. Tel: 0171-834 5858. *General Secretary*, R. C. Maddox

BUDGERIGAR SOCIETY, THE (1925), 49–53 Hazelwood Road, Northampton NN1 1LG. Tel: 01604-24549. *General Secretary*, D. Whittaker

BUILDING, CHARTERED INSTITUTE OF (1834), Englemere, King's Ride, Ascot, Berks SL5 8TB. Tel: 01344-23355. *Chief Executive*, K. Banbury

BUILDING ENGINEERS, ASSOCIATION OF (1925), Jubilee House, Billing Brook Road, Weston Favell, Northampton NN3 8NW. Tel: 01604-404121. *Chief Executive*, B. D. Hughes

BUILDING SERVICES ENGINEERS, CHARTERED INSTITUTE OF (1897), 222 Balham High Road, London SW12 9BS. Tel: 0181-675 5211. *Secretary*, A. V. Ramsay

BUILDING SOCIETIES ASSOCIATION (1936), 3 Savile Row, London W1X 1AF. Tel: 0171-437 0655. *Director-General*, A. Coles

BUSINESS AND PROFESSIONAL WOMEN UK LTD (1938), 23 Ansdell Street, London W8 5BN. Tel: 0171-938 1729. *General Secretary*, Mrs R. Bangle

BUSINESS ARCHIVES COUNCIL (1934), The Clove Building, 4 Maguire Street, London SE1 2NQ. Tel: 0171-407 6110. *Secretary-General*, Ms W. S. Quinn

BUSINESS IN THE COMMUNITY (1982), 44 Baker Street, London W1M 1DH. Tel: 0171-224 1600. *Chief Executive*, Ms J. Cleverdon, CBE

CADET FORCE ASSOCIATION, COMBINED (1952), E Block, The Duke of York's HQ, London SW3 4RR. Tel: 0171-730 9733/4. *Secretary*, Brig. R. B. MacGregor-Oakford, CBE, MC

CAFOD (CATHOLIC FUND FOR OVERSEAS DEVELOPMENT) (1962), Romero Close, Stockwell Road, London SW9 9TY. Tel: 0171-733 7900. *Director*, J. Filochowski

CALOUSTE GULBENKIAN FOUNDATION (1956), 98 Portland Place, London W1N 4ET. Tel: 0171-636 5313. *Director*, B. Whitaker

CAMBRIDGE PRESERVATION SOCIETY (1929), Wandlebury Ring, Gog Magog Hills, Babraham, Cambridge CB2 4AE. Tel: 01223-243830. *Secretary*, G. Brewster

CAMERON FUND, THE (1971), Tavistock House North, Tavistock Square, London WC1H 9HR. Tel: 0171-388 0796. *Secretary*, Mrs J. Martin

CAMPAIGN FOR NUCLEAR DISARMAMENT (CND) (1958), 162 Holloway Road, London N7 8DQ. Tel: 0171-700 2393. *Chair*, Ms J. Bloomfield

CANCER RELIEF MACMILLAN FUND (1911), Anchor House, 15–19 Britten Street, London SW3 3TZ. Tel: 0171-351 7811. *Chief Executive*, N. Young

CANCER RESEARCH CAMPAIGN, 10 Cambridge Terrace, London NW1 4JL. Tel: 0171-224 1333. *Director-General*, Prof. J. G. McVie

CANCER RESEARCH FUND, IMPERIAL (1902), PO Box 123, Lincoln's Inn Fields, London WC2A 3PX. Tel: 0171-242 0200. *Director-General*, Dr P. Nurse, FRS

CANCER RESEARCH: ROYAL CANCER HOSPITAL, INSTITUTE OF, 17A Onslow Gardens, London SW7 3AL. Tel: 0171-352 8133. *Chief Executive*, Prof. P. B. Garland

CANCER UNITED PATIENTS, BRITISH ASSOCIATION OF (BACUP) (1985), 3 Bath Place, Rivington Street, London EC2A 3JR. Tel: 0171-696 9003. Cancer Information Service: 0800-181199 or 0171-613 2121. *Chief Executive*, Ms J. Mossman

CARERS NATIONAL ASSOCIATION (1988), Ruth Pitter House, 20–25 Glasshouse Yard, London EC1A 4JS. Tel: 0171-490 8818. *Chief Executive*, Ms J. Pitkeathley, OBE

CARNEGIE DUNFERMLINE TRUST (1903), Abbey Park House, Dunfermline, Fife KY12 7PB. Tel: 01383-723638. *Secretary*, W. C. Runciman

CARNEGIE HERO FUND TRUST (1908), Abbey Park House, Dunfermline, Fife KY12 7PB. Tel: 01383-723638. *Secretary*, W. C. Runciman

CARNEGIE UNITED KINGDOM TRUST (1913), Comely Park House, Dunfermline, Fife KY12 7EJ. Tel: 01383-721445. *Secretary*, C. J. Naylor, OBE

CATHEDRALS FABRIC COMMISSION FOR ENGLAND (1949), Fielden House, Little College Street, London SW1P 3SH. Tel: 0171-222 3793. *Secretary*, Dr R. Gem

CATHOLIC CENTRAL LIBRARY (1914), St Francis Friary, 47 Francis Street, London SW1P 1QR. Tel: 0171-834 6128. *Director*, Brother J. Hand

CATHOLIC ENQUIRY OFFICE (1954), The Chase Centre, 114 West Heath Road, London NW3 7TX. Tel: 0181-458 3316. *Dean*, Revd M. Casey

CATHOLIC RECORD SOCIETY (1904), c/o 12 Melbourne Place, Wolsingham, Co. Durham DL13 3EH. Tel: 01388-527747. *Hon. Secretary*, Dr L. Gooch

CATHOLIC TRUTH SOCIETY (1868), 192 Vauxhall Bridge Road, London SW1V 1PD. Tel: 0171-834 4392. *General Secretary*, D. Murphy

CATHOLIC UNION OF GREAT BRITAIN (1872), St Maximilian Kolbe House, 63 Jeddo Road, London W12 9EE. Tel: 0181-749 1321. *Secretary*, P. H. Higgs, CBE

CATTLE ASSOCIATION, NATIONAL, 60 Kenilworth Road, Leamington Spa, Warks CV32 6JX. Tel: 01926-337378. *Secretary*, R. W. Kershaw-Dalby

CATTLE BREEDER'S CLUB LTD, BRITISH (1945), 16A Swan Street, Loughborough, Leics LE11 0BL. Tel: 01509-261810. *Secretary*, M. J. Peasnall

CENTRAL AND CECIL HOUSING TRUST (1926), 2 Priory Road, Kew, Richmond, Surrey TW9 3DG. Tel: 0181-940 9828/9. *Secretary*, G. Brighton

CENTRAL BUREAU FOR EDUCATIONAL VISITS AND EXCHANGES (1948), 10 Spring Gardens, London SW1A 2BN. Tel: 0171-389 4004. *Director*, A. H. Male

CENTREPOINT (1969), Bewlay House, 2 Swallow Place, London W1R 7AA. Tel: 0171-629 2229. *Chief Executive*, V. O. Adebowale

CHADWICK TRUST (1895), Department of Civil and Environmental Engineering, University College, Gower Street, London WC1E 6BT. Tel: 0171-380 7327/7766. For the promotion of health and prevention of disease. *Secretary to the Trustees*, I. K. Orchardson PH.D.

CHANTREY BEQUEST (1875), Royal Academy of Arts, Burlington House, Piccadilly, London W1V 0DS. Tel: 0171-439 7438. *Secretary*, P. Rodgers

CHARITIES AID FOUNDATION (1974), King's Hill, West Malling, Kent ME19 4TA. Tel: 01732-520000. *Executive Director*, M. Brophy

CHEMICAL ENGINEERS, INSTITUTION OF (1922), Davis Building, 165–189 Railway Terrace, Rugby, Warks CV21 3HQ. Tel: 01788-578214. *Chief Executive,* Dr T. J. Evans

CHEMISTRY, ROYAL SOCIETY OF, Burlington House, Piccadilly, London W1V OBN. Tel: 0171-437 8656. *Secretary-General,* Dr. T. D. Inch

CHESHIRE (LEONARD) FOUNDATION, *see* Leonard Cheshire Foundation

CHESS FEDERATION, BRITISH (1904), 9A Grand Parade, St Leonards-on-Sea, E. Sussex TN38 0DD. Tel: 01424-442500. *Manager,* Mrs G. White

CHEST, HEART AND STROKE ASSOCIATION, *see* STROKE ASSOCIATION

CHILDBIRTH TRUST, NATIONAL (1956), Alexandra House, Oldham Terrace, London W3 6NH. Tel: 0181-992 8637. *Director,* Ms C. Swarbrick

CHILDREN 1ST (ROYAL SCOTTISH SOCIETY FOR PREVENTION OF CRUELTY TO CHILDREN) (1884), Melville House, 41 Polwarth Terrace, Edinburgh EH11 1NU. Tel: 0131-337 8539. *Chief Executive,* A. M. M. Wood, OBE

CHILDREN'S SOCIETY, THE (1881), Edward Rudolf House, Margery Street, London WC1X 0JL. Tel: 0171-837 4299. *Chief Executive,* I. Sparks

CHINA ASSOCIATION, THE (1889), Swire House, 59 Buckingham Gate, London SW1E 6AJ. Tel: 0171-821 3220. *Executive Director,* Brig. B. G. Hickey, OBE, MC

CHIROPODISTS AND PODIATRISTS, SOCIETY OF (1945), 53 Welbeck Street, London W1M 7HE. Tel: 0171-486 3381. *General Secretary,* J. G. C. Trouncer

CHIROPRACTIC ASSOCIATION, BRITISH (1925), 29 Whitley Street, Reading, Berks RG2 0EG. Tel: 01734-757557. *Executive Director,* Miss S. A. Wakefield

CHOIRS SCHOOLS ASSOCIATION (1921), The Minster School, Deangate, York YO1 2JA. Tel: 01904-625217. *Administrator*

CHRISTIAN AID (1945), PO Box 100, London SE1 7RT. Tel: 0171-620 4444. *Director,* Revd M. H. Taylor

CHRISTIAN EDUCATION COUNCIL, NATIONAL (1809), 1020 Bristol Road, Selly Oak, Birmingham B29 6LB. Tel: 0121-472 4242. *General Secretary,* Revd J. Gear

CHRISTIAN EDUCATION MOVEMENT (1965), Royal Buildings, Victoria Street, Derby DE1 1GW. Tel: 01332-296655. *Director,* Revd Dr S. Orchard

CHRISTIAN EVIDENCE SOCIETY (1870), St Stephen's House, St Stephen's Crescent, Brentwood, Essex CM13 2AT. Tel: 01277-214623. *Administrator,* Mrs G. M. Ryeland

CHRISTIAN KNOWLEDGE, SOCIETY FOR PROMOTING (SPCK) (1698), Holy Trinity Church, Marylebone Road, London NW1 4DU. Tel: 0171-387 5282. *General Secretary,* P. Chandler

CHRISTIANS AND JEWS, COUNCIL OF (1942), Drayton House, 30 Gordon Street, London WC1H 0AN. Tel: 0171-388 3322. *Director,* P. Mendel

CHURCH ARMY (1882), Independents Road, London SE3 9LG. Tel: 0181-318 1226. *Chief Secretary,* Capt. P. Johanson

CHURCH BUILDING SOCIETY, INCORPORATED (1818), Fulham Palace, London SW6 6EA. Tel: 0171-736 3054. *Secretary,* M. W. Tippen

CHURCH EDUCATION CORPORATION, Bedgebury School, Goudhurst, Cranbrook, Kent TN17 2SH. Tel: 01580-211630. *Secretary,* Col. C. G. Champion

CHURCH HOUSE, THE CORPORATION OF (1888), Dean's Yard, London SW1P 3NZ. Tel: 0171-222 5261. *Secretary,* C. D. L. Menzies

CHURCH LADS' AND CHURCH GIRLS' BRIGADE (1891), 2 Barnsley Road, Wath upon Dearne, Rotherham, S. Yorks S63 6PY. Tel: 01709-876535. *General Secretary,* J. S. Cresswell

CHURCH MISSION SOCIETY (1799), Partnership House, 157 Waterloo Road, London SE1 8UU. Tel: 0171-928 8681. *General Secretary,* Ms D. K. Witts

CHURCH MUSIC, ROYAL SCHOOL OF (1927), Addington Palace, Croydon CR9 5AD. Tel: 0181-654 7676. *Chief Executive,* C. King

CHURCH OF ENGLAND PENSIONS BOARD (1926), 7 Little College Street, London SW1P 3SF. Tel: 0171-222 2091. *Secretary,* R. G. Radford

CHURCH UNION (1859), Faith House, 7 Tufton Street, London SW1P 3QN. Tel: 0171-222 6952. *House Manager,* Mrs J. Miller

CHURCHES, COUNCIL FOR THE CARE OF (1921), Fielden House, Little College Street, London SW1P 3SH. Tel: 0171-222 3793. *Secretary,* Dr T. Cocke

CHURCHES FOR BRITAIN AND IRELAND, COUNCIL OF (1942), Inter-Church House, 35–41 Lower Marsh, London SE1 7RL. Tel: 0171-620 4444. *General Secretary,* Revd J. P. Reardon

CHURCHES, FRIENDS OF FRIENDLESS (1957), St Ann's Vestry Hall, 2 Church Entry, London EC4V 5HB. Tel: 0171-236 3934. *Hon. Director,* M. Saunders

CHURCHES MAIN COMMITTEE (1941), Fielden House, Little College Street, London SW1P 3SH. Tel: 0171-222 4984. *Secretary,* D. Taylor Thompson, CB

CHURCHES TOGETHER IN ENGLAND (1990), Inter-Church House, 35–41 Lower Marsh, London SE1 7RL. Tel: 0171-620 4444. *General Secretary,* Revd Canon M. Reardon

CHURCHES TOGETHER IN SCOTLAND, ACTION OF (1990), Scottish Churches House, Kirk Street, Dunblane FK15 0AJ. Tel: 01786-823588. *General Secretary,* Revd M. Craig

CHURCHILL SOCIETY (1990), 18 Grove Lane, Ipswich IP4 1NR. Tel: 01473-221607. *Founder,* N. H. Rutherlyn

CITIZEN'S ADVICE BUREAUX, NATIONAL ASSOCIATION OF (1931), Myddelton House, 115–123 Pentonville Road, London N1 9LZ. Tel: 0171-833 2181. *Chief Executive,* Ms A. Abraham

CITY BUSINESS LIBRARY, Brewers Hall Garden, London EC2V 5BX. Tel: 0171-638 8215.

CITY PAROCHIAL FOUNDATION (1891), 6 Middle Street, London EC1A 7PH. Tel: 0171-606 6145. *Clerk,* T. Cook

CIVIC TRUST, THE (1957), 17 Carlton House Terrace, London SW1Y 5AW. Tel: 0171-930 0914. *Director,* M. Gwilliam

CIVIL ENGINEERS, INSTITUTION OF (1818), 1 Great George Street, London SW1P 3AA. Tel: 0171-222 7722. *Director-General,* R. S. Dobson, OBE

CIVIL LIBERTIES, NATIONAL COUNCIL FOR, *see* LIBERTY

CLASSICAL ASSOCIATION (1903), Department of Classics, University of Keele, Keele, Newcastle under Lyme, Staffs ST5 5BG. Tel: 01782-583048. *Hon. Treasurer,* R. Wallace

CLEAR AIR AND ENVIRONMENTAL PROTECTION,
NATIONAL SOCIETY FOR (1899), 136 North Street,
Brighton BN1 1RG. Tel: 01273-326313. *Secretary-General*,
Dr T. Crossett

CLERGY ORPHAN CORPORATION (1749), 57B Tufton
Street, London SW1P 3QL. Tel: 0171-222 1812. *Secretary*,
Miss J. Buncher

CLERKS OF WORKS OF GREAT BRITAIN INC., INSTITUTE OF
(1882), 41 The Mall, London W5 3TJ. Tel: 0181-579 2917/
8. *Secretary*, A. P. Macnamara

COACHING CLUB (1871), West Compton House, West
Compton, Shepton Mallet, Somerset BA4 4PD. Tel:
01749-890633. *Secretary*, D. H. Clarke

COLITIS AND CROHN'S DISEASE, NATIONAL
ASSOCIATION FOR (1979), PO Box 205, St Albans, Herts
AL1 1AB. Tel: 01727-844296. *Director*, R. Driscoll

COMMERCE, BRITISH CHAMBER OF (1860), 9 Tufton Street,
London SW1P 3QB. Tel: 0171-222 1555. *Director-General*, R.
G. Taylor, CBE

COMMERCE AND INDUSTRY, LONDON CHAMBER OF (1881),
Swan House, 33 Queen Street, London EC4R 1AP. Tel:
0171-248 4444. *Chief Executive*, S. G. Sperryn

COMMERCE AND MANUFACTURERS, EDINBURGH
CHAMBER OF (1786), 3 Randolph Crescent, Edinburgh
EH3 7UD. Tel: 0131-225 5851. *Chief Executive*, D. I. Brown

COMMERCE AND MANUFACTURES, GLASGOW CHAMBER
(1783), 30 George Square, Glasgow G2 1EQ. Tel: 0141-
204 2121. *Chief Executive*, G. Runcie

COMMERCE, ASSOCIATION OF SCOTTISH CHAMBERS OF,
Conference House, The Exchange, 152 Morrison Street,
Edinburgh EH3 8EB. Tel: 0313-477 8025. *Director*, L. Gold

COMMERCE, CANADA-UNITED KINGDOM CHAMBER OF
(1921), 3 Regent Street, London SW1Y 4NZ. Tel: 0171-
930 7711. *Executive Director*, M. Hall

COMMERCIAL TRAVELLERS' BENEVOLENT INSTITUTION
(1849), Gable End, Mill Hill Road, Arnesby, Leicester
LE8 3WG. Tel: 0116-247 8647. *Secretary*, M. N. Bown

COMMISSIONAIRES, THE CORPS OF (1859), Market House,
85 Cowcross Street, London EC1M 6BP. Tel: 0171-
490 1125. *Managing Director*, C. J. Salt

COMMONWEALTH TRUST (linking the Royal
Commonwealth Society and the Victoria League for
Commonwealth Friendship), Commonwealth House, 18
Northumberland Avenue, London WC2N 5BJ. Tel: 0171-
930 6733. *Director-General*, Sir David Thorne, KBE, CVO

COMMUNICATORS IN BUSINESS, BRITISH ASSOCIATION OF
(1949), 3 Locks Yard, High Street, Sevenoaks, Kent
TN13 1LT. Tel: 01732-459331. *Director*, A. F. Brobyn

COMPLEMENTARY AND ALTERNATIVE MEDICINE,
COUNCIL FOR (1985), 179 Gloucester Place, London
NW1 6DX. Tel: 0171-724 9103. *Secretary*, Ms C. Daglish

COMPLEMENTARY MEDICINE, INSTITUTE FOR (1856), PO
Box 194, London SE16 1QZ. Tel: 0171-237 5165. *Director*, A.
Baird

COMPOSERS' GUILD OF GREAT BRITAIN (1945), 34
Hanway Street, London W1P 9DE. Tel: 0171-436 0007.
General Secretary, Ms H. Rosenblatt

COMPUTER SOCIETY, BRITISH (1957), 1 Sanford Street,
Swindon SN1 1HJ. Tel: 01793-417417. *Chief Executive*,
G. Kirkpatrick

CONSERVATION OF HISTORIC AND ARTISTIC WORKS,
INTERNATIONAL INSTITUTE FOR (1950), 6 Buckingham
Street, London WC2N 6BA. Tel: 0171-839 5975. *Secretary-
General*, D. Bomford

CONSULTANTS BUREAU, BRITISH (1965), 1 Westminster
Palace Gardens, 1–7 Artillery Row, London SW1P 1RJ.
Tel: 0171-222 3651. *Director*, C. Adams, CBE

CONSULTING ECONOMISTS' ASSOCIATION,
INTERNATIONAL (1986), 3 St George's Court, Putney
Bridge Road, London SW15 2PA. Tel: 0181-875 9960.
Chairman, Ms H. Acton

CONSULTING ENGINEERS, ASSOCIATION OF (1913),
Alliance House, 12 Caxton Street, London SW1H 0QL. Tel:
0171-222 6557. *Chief Executive*, H. C. Woodrow

CONSULTING SCIENTISTS, ASSOCIATION OF (1958), Gaw
House, Alperton Lane, Wembley, Middx HA0 1WU. Tel:
0181-991 4883. *Hon. Secretary*, A. Brewster

CONSUMERS' ASSOCIATION (1957), c/o The Association
for Consumer Research, 2 Marylebone Road, London
NW1 4DF. Tel: 0171-830 6000. *Director*, Dr J. Beishon

CONTEMPORARY APPLIED ARTS (1948), 2 Percy Street,
London W1P 9FA. Tel: 0171-436 2344. *Director*,
Ms M. La Trobe-Bateman

CONVENIENCE STORES, ASSOCIATION OF (1890),
Federation House, 17 Farnborough Street, Farnborough,
Hants GU14 8AG. Tel: 01252-515001. *National Secretary*, T.
Dixon

CONVEYANCERS, COUNCIL FOR LICENSED (1986), 16
Glebe Road, Chelmsford, Essex CM1 1QG. Tel: 01245-
349599. *Director*, Mrs V. Eden

CO-OPERATIVE PARTY, Victory House, 10–14 Leicester
Square, London WC2H 7QH. Tel: 0171-439 0123. *Secretary*,
P. Clarke

CO-OPERATIVE UNION LTD (1869), Holyoake House,
Hanover Street, Manchester M60 0AS. Tel: 0161-
832 4300. *Chief Executive*, D. L. Wilkinson

CO-OPERATIVE WHOLESALE SOCIETY (CWS) LTD (1863),
PO Box 53, New Century House, Manchester M60 4ES.
Tel: 0161-834 1212. *Chief Executive*, D. Skinner

COPYRIGHT COUNCIL, BRITISH (1953), 29–33 Berners
Street, London W1P 4AA. *Secretary*, Mrs H. Rosenblatt

CORONERS' SOCIETY OF ENGLAND AND WALES (1846), 44
Ormond Avenue, Hampton, Middx TW12 2RX. Tel: 0181-
979 6805. *Hon. Secretary*, M. J. G. Burgess

CORPORATE TREASURERS, ASSOCIATION OF (1979), 12
Devereux Court, London WC2R 3JJ. Tel: 0171-936 2354.
Secretary, Ms R. Robinson

CORPORATE TRUSTEES, ASSOCIATION OF (1974), 43
Surrey Road, Westbourne, Bournemouth, Dorset
BH4 9HR. Tel: 01202-761112. *Secretary*, R. J. Payne

CORRESPONDENCE COLLEGES, ASSOCIATION OF BRITISH
(1955), 6 Francis Grove, London SW19 4DT. Tel: 0181-
544 9559. *Secretary*, Mrs H. Owen

CORRYMEELA COMMUNITY (1965), Corrymeela House, 8
Upper Crescent, Belfast BT7 1NT. Tel: 01232-325008.
Leader, Revd T. Williams

COTTON GROWING ASSOCIATION, BRITISH (1904),
Knowle Hill Park, Fairmile Lane, Cobham, Surrey
KT11 2PD. Tel: 01932-861000. *Managing Director*,
P. R. Walters

COUNCIL FOR THE PROTECTION OF RURAL ENGLAND, *see*
CPRE

COUNCIL SECRETARIES AND SOLICITORS, ASSOCIATION
OF (1974, merged 1996), 11 Rectory Road, Frampton
Cotterell, Bristol BS17 2BN. Tel: 01454-775883. *Hon.
Secretary*, R. King

COUNSEL AND CARE (1954), Twyman House, 16 Bonny Street, London NW1 9PG. Tel: 0171-485 1550. Advice Line: 0171-485 1566. *General Manager*, J. Smith

COUNTRY HOUSES ASSOCIATION (1955), 41 Kingsway, London WC2B 6UB. Tel: 0171-836 1624. *Chief Executive*, R. D. Bratby

COUNTRY LANDOWNERS ASSOCIATION (1907), 16 Belgrave Square, London SW1X 8PQ. Tel: 0171-235 0511. *Director-General*, J. Anderson

COUNTY CHIEF EXECUTIVES, ASSOCIATION OF (1974), PO Box 9, Shire Hall, Warwick CV34 4RR. Tel: 01926-412559. *Hon. Secretary*, I. G. Caulfield

COUNTY COUNCILS, ASSOCIATION OF (1890), Eaton House, 66A Eaton Square, London SW1W 9BH. Tel: 0171-201 1500. *Secretary*, R. G. Wendt, CBE

COUNTY EMERGENCY PLANNING OFFICERS' SOCIETY, *see* EMERGENCY PLANNING

COUNTY SECRETARIES, SOCIETY OF, *see* COUNCIL SECRETARIES AND SOLICITORS, ASSOCIATION OF

COUNTY SURVEYORS' SOCIETY (1884), c/o Director of Environment, Gloucestershire County Council, Shire Hall, Bearland, Glos GL1 2TH. Tel: 01452 426191. *Hon. Secretary*, D. T. Gardner

COUNTY TREASURERS, SOCIETY OF (1903), PO Box 4, County Hall, Chelmsford, Essex CM1 1JZ. Tel: 01245-431000. *Hon. Secretary*, K. D. Neale

CPRE (COUNCIL FOR THE PROTECTION OF RURAL ENGLAND) (1926), Warwick House, 25 Buckingham Palace Road, London SW1W 0PP. Tel: 0171-976 6433. *Director*, Ms F. Reynolds

CRAFTS COUNCIL (1971), 44A Pentonville Road, London N1 9BY. Tel: 0171-278 7700. *Director*, T. Ford

CRISIS (1967), 7 Whitechapel Road, London E1 1DU. Tel: 0171-377 0489. *Director*, M. Scothern

CROSSLINKS (1922), 251 Lewisham Way, London SE4 1XF. Tel: 0181-691 6111. *General Secretary*, Revd R. Bowen

CRUEL SPORTS, THE LEAGUE AGAINST (1924), 83–87 Union Street, London SE1 1SG. Tel: 0171-403 6155. *Executive Director*, G. Sirl

CRUELTY TO ANIMALS, SOCIETY FOR THE PREVENTION OF, *see* ROYAL and SCOTTISH

CRUELTY TO CHILDREN, SOCIETY FOR THE PREVENTION OF, *see* CHILDREN 1ST and NATIONAL

CRUSE - BEREAVEMENT CARE (1959), 126 Sheen Road, Richmond, Surrey TW9 1UR. Tel: 0181-940 4818. Bereavement Line: 0181-332 7227. *Director*, R. Pearce

CURWEN INSTITUTE (1875), 5 Bigbury Close, Styvechale, Coventry CV3 5AJ. Tel: 01203-413010. *Director*, J. Dowding

CWMNI URDD GOBAITH CYMRU (1922), Swyddfa'r Urdd, Aberystwyth, Dyfed SY23 1EN. Tel: 01970-623744. *Chief Executive*, J. O'Rourke

CYCLISTS' TOURING CLUB (1878), Cotterell House, 69 Meadrow, Godalming, Surrey GU7 3HS. Tel: 01483-417217. *Director*, A. Harlow

CYMMRODORION, THE HONOURABLE SOCIETY OF (1751), 30 Eastcastle Street, LONDON W1N 7PD. Tel: 0171-631 0502. *Hon. Secretary*, D. L. Jones

CYSTIC FIBROSIS TRUST (1964), Alexandra House, 5 Blyth Road, Bromley, Kent BR1 3RS. Tel: 0181-464 7211. *Executive Director*, G. J. Edkins

CYTUN (CHURCHES TOGETHER IN WALES) (1990), 21 St Helen's Road, Swansea SA1 4AP. Tel: 01792-460876. *General Secretary*, Revd N. A. Davies

DAIRY FARMERS, ROYAL ASSOCIATION OF BRITISH (1876), 60 Kenilworth Road, Leamington Spa, Warks CV32 6JX. Tel: 01926 887477. *Chief Executive*, P. M. Gilbert

DAIRY TECHNOLOGY, SOCIETY OF (1943), 72 Ermine Street, Huntingdon, Cambs PE18 6EZ. Tel: 01480-450741. *National Secretary*, Mrs R. Gale

DATA (DESIGN AND TECHNOLOGY ASSOCIATION), 16 Wellesbourne House, Walton Road, Wellesbourne, Warks CV35 9JB. Tel: 01789-470007. *Chairman*, Dr R. V. Peacock, OBE

D-DAY AND NORMANDY FELLOWSHIP (1968), 9 South Parade, Southsea, Hants PO5 2JB. Tel: 01705-812180. *Hon. Secretary*, Mrs L. R. Reed

DEAF, COMMONWEALTH SOCIETY FOR THE (1959), 134 Buckingham Palace Road, London SW1W 9SA. Tel: 0171-259 0200. *Chairman*, F. R. Rutter

DEAF ASSOCIATION, BRITISH (formerly British Deaf and Dumb Association) (1890), 1 Worship Street, London EC2A 2AB. Tel: 0171-588 3520. *Chief Executive*, J. McWhinney

DEAF CHILDREN, ROYAL SCHOOL FOR (1792), Victoria Road, Margate, Kent CT9 1NB. Tel: 01843-227561. *Secretary*, J. C. Gunnell, OBE

DEAF PEOPLE, FOLEY HOUSE RESIDENTIAL HOME FOR (1851), Foley House, 115 High Garrett, Braintree, Essex CM7 5NU. Tel: 01376-326652. *Director*, Mrs N. Hartard

DEAF PEOPLE, ROYAL ASSOCIATION IN AID OF (1841), 27 Old Oak Road, London W3 7HN. Tel: 0181-743 6187. *General Secretary*, B. Edmond

DEAF PEOPLE, ROYAL NATIONAL INSTITUTE FOR (1911), 19–23 Featherstone Street, London EC1Y 8SL. Tel: 0171-289 8000. *Chief Executive*, D. Alker

DEFENCE STUDIES, ROYAL UNITED SERVICES INSTITUTE FOR (1831), Whitehall, London SW1A 2ET. Tel: 0171-930 5854. *Director*, Rear-Adm. R. Cobbold, CB

DEMOCRATIC LEFT (1991), 6 Cynthia Street, London N1 9JF. Tel: 0171-278 4443. *Secretary*, Ms N. Temple

DENTAL ASSOCIATION, BRITISH (1880), 64 Wimpole Street, London W1M 8AL. Tel: 0171-935 0875. *Chief Executive*, J. M. G. Hunt

DENTAL COUNCIL, GENERAL (1956), 37 Wimpole Street, London W1M 8DQ. Tel: 0171-486 2171. *Registrar*, N. T. Davies, MBE

DENTAL HOSPITALS OF THE UNITED KINGDOM, ASSOCIATION OF (1942), Birmingham Dental Hospital, St Chad's Queensway, Birmingham B4 6NN. Tel: 0121-236 8611 ext.5732. *Hon. Secretary*, Mrs P. Harrington

DESIGN AND INDUSTRIES ASSOCIATION (1915), Business Design Centre, 52 Upper Street, London N1 0QH. Tel: 0171-288 6212. *Chairman*, G. Adams

DESIGNERS, CHARTERED SOCIETY OF (1930), 32–38 Saffron Hill, London EC1N 8FH. Tel: 0171-831 9777. *Director*, B. Lymbery

DESIGNERS FOR INDUSTRY, FACULTY OF ROYAL (1936), RSA, 8 John Adam Street, London WC2N 6EZ. Tel: 0171-930 5115. *Secretary*, P. Cowling

DIABETIC ASSOCIATION, BRITISH (1934), 10 Queen Anne Street, London W1M 0BD. Tel: 0171-323 1531. *Director-General*, M. Cooper

DICKENS FELLOWSHIP (1902), Dickens House, 48 Doughty Street, London WC1N 2LF. Tel: 0171-405 2127. *Hon. General Secretary*, E. G. Preston

DIRECTORS, INSTITUTE OF (1903), 116 Pall Mall, London SWIY 5ED. Tel: 0171-839 1233. *Director-General*, T. Melville-Ross

DIRECTORS OF PUBLIC HEALTH, ASSOCIATION OF (1982), Walsall Health Authority, Lichfield House, 27–31 Lichfield Street, Walsall, West Midlands WS1 1TE. Tel: 01922-720255. *Hon. Secretary*, Dr S. Ramaiah

DIRECTORY PUBLISHERS ASSOCIATION (1970), 93A Blenheim Crescent, London W11 2EQ. Tel: 0171-221 9089 *Secretary*, Mr R. Pettit

DISPENSING OPTICIANS, ASSOCIATION OF BRITISH (1925), 6 Hurlingham Business Park, Sulivan Road, London SW6 3DU. Tel: 0171-736 0088. *Registrar*, D. S. Baker

DISTRICT COUNCILS, ASSOCIATION OF (1974), 26 Chapter Street, London SW1P 4ND. Tel: 0171-233 6868. *Secretary*, G. Filkin

DISTRICT SECRETARIES, ASSOCIATION OF, *see* COUNCIL SECRETARIES AND SOLICITORS, ASSOCIATION OF

DITCHLEY FOUNDATION, Ditchley Park, Enstone, Chipping Norton, Oxon OX7 4ER. Tel: 01608-677346. *Director*, Sir Michael Quinlan, GCB

DOWNS SYNDROME ASSOCIATION (1970), 155 Mitcham Road, London SW17 9PG. Tel: 0181-682 4001. *Assistant Director*, Ms G. Rush

DOWSERS, BRITISH SOCIETY OF (1933), Sycamore Barn, Hastingleigh, Ashford, Kent TN25 5HW. Tel: 01233-750253. *Secretary*, M. D. Rust

DRAINAGE AUTHORITIES, ASSOCIATION OF (1937), The Mews, 3 Royal Oak Passage, High Street, Huntingdon, Cambs PE18 6EA. Tel: 01480-411123. *Secretary*, D. Noble

DRINKING FOUNTAIN AND CATTLE TROUGH ASSOCIATION, METROPOLITAN (1859), Oaklands, 5 Queensborough Gardens, Chislehurst, Kent BR7 6NP. Tel: 0181-467 1261. *Secretary*, R. P. Baber

DRIVING SOCIETY, BRITISH (1957), 27 Dugard Place, Barford, Warwick CV35 8DX. Tel: 01926-624420. *Secretary*, Mrs J. M. Dillon

DRUG DEPENDENCE, INSTITUTE FOR THE STUDY OF (ISDD) (1968), 32 Loman Street, London SE1 0EE. Tel: 0171-928 1211. *Director*, Ms A. Bradley

DUKE OF EDINBURGH'S AWARD SCHEME (1956), Gulliver House, Madeira Walk, Windsor, Berks SL4 1EU. Tel: 01753-810753. *Director*, M. F. Hobbs, CBE

DYERS AND COLOURISTS, SOCIETY OF (1884), PO Box 244, Perkin House, 82 Grattan Road, Bradford BD1 2JB. Tel: 01274-725138. *General Secretary*, J. D.Watson

DYSLEXIA INSTITUTE (1972), 133 Gresham Road, Staines, Middlesex TW18 2AJ. Tel: 01784-463851. *Executive Director*, Mrs E. J. Brooks

EARLY CHILDHOOD EDUCATION, BRITISH ASSOCIATION FOR (1923), 111 City View House, 463 Bethnal Green Road, London E2 9QY. Tel: 0171-739 7594. *Secretary*, Mrs B. Boon

ECCLESIASTICAL HISTORY SOCIETY (1961), Department of Medieval History, University of Glasgow, Glasgow G12 8QQ. Tel: 0141-330 5192. *Secretary*, M. J. Kennedy

ECCLESIOLOGICAL SOCIETY (1839), Underedge, Back Lane, Hathersage, Sheffield S30 1AR. Tel: 01433-650833. *Hon. Secretary*, Prof. K. H. Murta

EDITH CAVELL AND NATION'S FUND FOR NURSES (1917), Flints, Petersfield Road, Winchester, Hants SO23 0JD. Tel: 01962-860900. *Administrator*, Mrs A. Rich

EDITORS, GUILD OF (1946), Bloomsbury House, 74–77 Great Russell Street, London WC1B 3DA. Tel: 0171-636 7014. *Secretary*, Ms V. L. Hird

EDUCATION OFFICERS' SOCIETY, COUNTY (1889), Education Department, Northamptonshire County Council, PO Box 149, County Hall, Northampton NN1 1AU. Tel: 01604-236250. *Secretary*, J. R. Atkinson

EDUCATION OFFICERS, SOCIETY OF (1971), Boulton House, 17–21 Chorlton Street, Manchester M1 3HY. Tel: 0161-236 5766. *General Secretary*, A. Collier

EDUCATIONAL RESEARCH IN ENGLAND AND WALES, NATIONAL FOUNDATION FOR (1946), The Mere, Upton Park, Slough SL1 2DQ. Tel: 01753-574123. *Director*, Dr S. Hegarty

EGYPT EXPLORATION SOCIETY (1882), 3 Doughty Mews, London WC1N 2PG. Tel: 0171-242 1880. *Secretary*, Dr P. A. Spencer

ELECTORAL REFORM SOCIETY, 6 Chancel Street, London SE1 0UU. Tel: 0171-928 1622. *President*, Baroness Seear; *Office Manager*, P. Stock

ELECTRICAL ENGINEERS, INSTITUTION OF (1871), Savoy Place, London WC2R 0BL. Tel: 0171-240 1871. *Secretary*, J. C. Williams, PH.D., FENG.

ELGAR FOUNDATION (1973), 23 Meadow Hill Road, King's Norton, Birmingham B38 8DE. Tel: 0121-458 2747. *Secretary to the Trustees*, J. G. Hughes

ELGAR SOCIETY (1951), 29 Van Diemens Close, Chinnor, Oxon OX9 4QE. Tel: 01844-354096. *Secretary*, Ms W. Hillary

EMERGENCY PLANNING SOCIETY (1966), Emergency Planning Officer, London Borough of Brent, Pyramid House, Forthway, Wembley, Middx HA9 0LJ. Tel: 0181-908 7035. *Hon. Secretary*, K. D. Gosling

ENABLE (SCOTTISH SOCIETY FOR THE MENTALLY HANDICAPPED) (1954), 7 Buchanan Street, Glasgow G1 3HL. Tel: 0141-226 4541. *Director*, N. Dunning

ENERGY ASSOCIATION, BRITISH (1924), 34 St James's Street, London SW1A 1HD. Tel:0171-930 1211. *Director*, M. Jefferson

ENERGY, INSTITUTE OF (1927), 18 Devonshire Street, London W1N 2AU. Tel: 0171-580 7124. *Secretary*, J. E. H. Leach

ENERGY SAVING TRUST (1992), 11–12 Buckingham Gate, London SW1E 6LB . Tel: 0171-931 8401. *Chief Executive*, Dr E. Lees

ENGINEERING COUNCIL, THE (1981), 10 Maltravers Street, London WC2R 3ER. Tel: 0171-240 7891. *Public Affairs Director*, T. Miller

ENGINEERING DESIGNERS, INSTITUTION OF (1945), Courtleigh, Westbury Leigh, Westbury, Wilts BA13 3TA. Tel: 01373-822801. *Secretary*, M. J. Osborne

ENGINEERING INDUSTRIES ASSOCIATION (1941), 16 Dartmouth Street, London SW1H 9BL. Tel:0171-222 2367. *Director-General*, N. J. Harvey

ENGINEERS, INSTITUTION OF BRITISH (1928), Royal Liver Building, 6 Hampton Place, Brighton BN1 3DD. Tel: 01273-734274. *Secretary*, Ms J. Busby

ENGINEERS, THE SOCIETY OF (1854), Guinea Wiggs, Nayland, Colchester, Essex CO6 4NF. Tel:01206-263332. *Secretary*, Mrs L. C. A. Wright

ENGLISH ASSOCIATION, THE (1906), University of Leicester, University Road, Leicester LE1 7RH. Tel: 0116-252 3982. *Secretary*, Ms H. Lucas

ENGLISH FOLK DANCE AND SONG SOCIETY (1932), Cecil Sharp House, 2 Regent's Park Road, London NW1 7AY. Tel: 0171-485 2206. *Chief Executive*, N. Thompson

ENGLISH PLACE-NAME SURVEY (1923), Grey College, Durham DH1 3LG. Tel: 0191-374 2960. *Hon. Director*, V. E. Watts, FSA

ENGLISH-SPEAKING UNION OF THE COMMONWEALTH (1918), Dartmouth House, 37 Charles Street, London W1X 8AB. Tel: 0171-493 3328. *Director-General*, Mrs V. Mitchell

ENTOMOLOGICAL SOCIETY OF LONDON, ROYAL (1833), 41 Queen's Gate, London SW7 5HR. Tel: 0171-584 8361. *Registrar*, G. G. Bentley

ENVIRONMENTAL HEALTH, CHARTERED INSTITUTE OF (1883), Chadwick Court, 15 Hatfields, London SE1 8DJ. Tel: 0171-928 6006. *Chief Executive*, M. Cooke

ENVIRONMENT COUNCIL (1969), 21 Elizabeth Street, London SW1W 9RP. Tel: 0171-824 8411. *Chief Executive*, S. Robinson

EPILEPSY ASSOCIATION, BRITISH (1949), Anstey House, 40 Hanover Square, Leeds LS3 1BE. Tel: 0113-243 9393/ 0800-309030. *Chief Executive*, P. Lee

EPILEPSY, NATIONAL SOCIETY FOR (1892), Chalfont St Peter, Gerrards Cross, Bucks SL9 0RJ. Tel: 01494-873991. *Chief Executive*, Col. D. W. Eking

EQUESTRIAN FEDERATION, BRITISH (1972), British Equestrian Centre, Stoneleigh Park, Kenilworth, Warks CV8 2LR. Tel: 01203-696697. *Director-General*, Col. J. D. Smith-Bingham

ESPERANTO ASSOCIATION OF BRITAIN (1977), 140 Holland Park Avenue, London W11 4UF. Tel: 0171-727 7821. *Office Manager*, M. McClelland

ESTATE AGENTS, NATIONAL ASSOCIATION OF (1962), Arbon House, 21 Jury Street, Warwick CV34 4EH. Tel: 01926-496800. *Chief Executive*, H. Dunsmore-Hardy

ESTATE AGENTS, OMBUDSMAN FOR CORPORATE (1990), Beckett House, 4 Bridge Street, Salisbury, Wilts SP1 2LX. Tel: 01722-333306. *Ombudsman*, T. D. Quayle, CB

EUGENICS SOCIETY, *see* GALTON INSTITUTE

EVANGELICAL ALLIANCE (1846), Whitefield House, 186 Kennington Park Road, London SE11 4BT. Tel: 0171-582 0228. *General Director*, Revd C. R. Calver

EVANGELICAL LIBRARY, THE (1928), 78A Chiltern Street, London W1M 2HB. Tel: 0171-935 6997. *Librarian*, S. J. Taylor

EXPORT, INSTITUTE OF (1935), Export House, 64 Clifton Street, London EC2A 4HB. Tel: 0171-247 9812. *Director-General*, I. J. Campbell

EX-SERVICES LEAGUE, BRITISH COMMONWEALTH (1921), 48 Pall Mall, London SW1Y 5JG. Tel: 0171-973 7263. *Secretary-General*, Brig. M. J. Doyle, MBE

EX-SERVICES MENTAL WELFARE SOCIETY (1919), Broadway House, The Broadway, London SW19 1RL. Tel: 0181-543 6333. *Director*, Brig. A. K. Dixon

FABIAN SOCIETY (1884), 11 Dartmouth Street, London SW1H 9BN. Tel: 0171-222 8877. *General Secretary (acting)*, Ms G. Thornton

FAIR ISLE BIRD OBSERVATORY TRUST (1948), Fair Isle Bird Observatory, Fair Isle, Shetland ZE2 9JU. Tel: 01595-760258. *Administrator*, W. Christie

FAMILY HISTORY SOCIETIES, FEDERATION OF (1974), The Benson Room, Birmingham and Midland Institute, Margaret Street, Birmingham B3 3BS. *Administrator*, Mrs P. A. Saul

FAMILY MEDIATION, NATIONAL (The National Association of Family Mediation and Conciliation Services) (1982), 9 Tavistock Place, London WC1H 9SN. Tel: 0171-383 5993. *Director*, Ms T. Fisher

FAMILY PLANNING ASSOCIATION (1939), 2–12 Pentonville Road, London N1 9FP. Tel: 0171-837 5432. *Director*, Ms A. Weyman

FAMILY WELFARE ASSOCIATION (1869), 501–505 Kingsland Road, London E8 4AU. Tel: 0171-254 6251. *Director*, Ms L. Berry

FAUNA AND FLORA INTERNATIONAL (1903), Great Eastern House, Tenison Road, Cambridge CB1 2DT. Tel: 01223-461471. *Director*, M. Rose

FELLOWSHIP HOUSES TRUST (1937), Clock House, 192 High Road, Byfleet, Surrey KT14 7RN. Tel: 01932-343172. *Secretary*, Mrs A. J. Elliot

FIELD ARCHAEOLOGISTS, INSTITUTE OF (1982), University of Manchester, Oxford Road, Manchester M13 9PL. Tel: 0161-275 2304. *General Secretary*, Ms K. Sisson

FIELD SPORTS SOCIETY, BRITISH (1930), 59 Kennington Road, London SE1 7PZ. Tel: 0171-928 4742. *Director*, R. Hanbury-Tenison, OBE

FIELD STUDIES COUNCIL (1943), Preston Montford, Montford Bridge, Shrewsbury SY4 1HW. Tel: 01743-850674. *Director*, A. D. Thomas

FILM CLASSIFICATION, BRITISH BOARD OF (1912), 3 Soho Square, London W1V 6HD. Tel: 0171-439 7961. *Director*, J. Ferman

FIRE ENGINEERS, INSTITUTION OF (1918), 148 New Walk, Leicester LE1 7QB. Tel: 0116-255 3654. *General Secretary*, D. W. Evans

FIRE PROTECTION ASSOCIATION (1946), Melrose Avenue, Borehamwood, Herts WD6 2BJ. Tel: 0181-207 2345. *Director*, S. Kidd

FIRE SERVICES NATIONAL BENEVOLENT FUND (1943), Marine Court, Fitzalan Road, Littlehampton, W. Sussex BN17 5NF. Tel: 01903-736063. *General Manager*, C. W. Pile

FLAG INSTITUTE, THE (1971), 10 Vicarage Road, Chester CH2 3HZ. Tel: 01244-351335. *Director*, Dr W. G. Crampton

FLEET AIR ARM OFFICERS' ASSOCIATION (1957), 94 Piccadilly, London W1V 0BP. Tel: 0171-499 0360. *Chairman*, Capt. A. A. Hensher, MBE, RN

FOLKLORE SOCIETY, c/o University College, Gower Street, London WC1E 6BT. Tel: 0171-387 5894. *Hon. Secretary*, Dr J. Simpson

FOOD FROM BRITAIN (1983), 123 Buckingham Palace Road, London SW1W 9SA. Tel: 0171-233 5111. *Chairman*, G. John, CBE

FOOD SCIENCE AND TECHNOLOGY, INSTITUTE OF (1964), 5 Cambridge Court, 210 Shepherd's Bush Road, London W6 7NJ. Tel: 0171-603 6316. *Chief Executive*, Ms H. G. Wild

FORCES HELP SOCIETY AND LORD ROBERTS WORKSHOPS, *see* SSAFA FORCES HELP

FOREIGN PRESS ASSOCIATION IN LONDON (1888), 11 Carlton House Terrace, London SW1Y 5AJ. Tel: 0171-930 0445. *Secretary*, Ms D. Crole

FORENSIC SCIENCE SOCIETY (1959), Clarke House, 18A Mount Parade, Harrogate, N. Yorks HG1 1BX. Tel: 01423-506068. *Hon. Secretary*, Dr A. R. W. Forrest

FORENSIC SCIENCES, BRITISH ACADEMY OF (1959), Anaesthetic Unit, The Royal London Hospital, Whitechapel, London E1 1BB. Tel: 0171-377 9201. *Secretary-General*, Dr P. J. Flynn

FORESTERS, INSTITUTE OF CHARTERED (1982), 7A St Colme Street, Edinburgh EH3 6AA. Tel: 0131-225 2705. *Secretary*, Mrs M. W. Dick

FORESTRY ASSOCIATION, COMMONWEALTH (1921), c/o Oxford Forestry Institute, South Parks Road, Oxford OX1 3RB. Tel: 01865-275072. *Chairman*, P. J. Wood

FORESTRY SOCIETY OF ENGLAND, WALES AND NORTHERN IRELAND, ROYAL (1882), 102 High Street, Tring, Herts HP23 4AF. Tel: 01442-822028. *Director*, J. E. Jackson, PH.D.

FORESTRY SOCIETY, ROYAL SCOTTISH (1854), The Stables, Dalkeith County Park, Dalkeith, Midlothian EH22 2NA. Tel: 0131-660 9480. *Director*, M. Osborne

FOUNDRYMEN, INSTITUTE OF BRITISH (1904), Bordesley Hall, The Holloway, Alvechurch, Birmingham B48 7QA. Tel: 01527-596100. *Secretary*, G. A. Schofield

FRANCO-BRITISH SOCIETY (1924), Room 623, Linen Hall, 162–168 Regent Street, London W1R 5TB. Tel: 0171-734 0815. *Executive Secretary*, Mrs M. Clarke

FREE CHURCH FEDERAL COUNCIL (1940), 27 Tavistock Square, London WC1H 9HH. Tel: 0171-387 8413. *General Secretary*, Revd G. H. Roper

FREEDOM ASSOCIATION (1975), 35 Westminster Bridge Road, London SE1 7JB. Tel: 0171-928 9925. *Office Manager*, Mrs P. North

FREEMASONS, GRAND LODGE OF ANTIENT FREE AND ACCEPTED MASONS OF SCOTLAND (1736), Freemasons' Hall, 96 George Street, Edinburgh EH2 3DH. Tel: 0131-225 5304. *Grand Master Mason of Scotland*, The Lord Burton; *Grand Secretary*, C. M. McGibbon

FREEMASONS: UNITED GRAND LODGE OF ENGLAND (1717), Freemasons' Hall, Great Queen Street, London WC2B 5AZ. Tel: 0171-831 9811. *Grand Master*, HRH The Duke of Kent, KG, GCMG, GCVO; *Grand Secretary*, Cdr. M. B. S. Higham

FREEMEN OF ENGLAND AND WALES (1966), Glenrise, Churchfields, Stonesfield, Witney, Oxon OX8 8PP. Tel: 01993-891414. *President*, R. J. M. Bishop

FREEMEN OF THE CITY OF LONDON, GUILD OF (1908), PO Box No 153, 40A Ludgate Hill, London EC4M 7DE. Tel: 0171-223 7638. *Clerk*, Col. D. Ivy

FREEMEN OF THE CITY OF YORK, GILD OF (1953), 29 Albermarle Road, York YO2 1EW. Tel: 01904-653698. *Hon. Clerk*, R. Lee

FREEMEN'S GUILD, CITY OF COVENTRY (1946), 47 Brownshill Green Road, Coventry CV6 2AP. Tel: 01203-333980. *Hon. Clerk*, K. Talbot

FRIENDLY SOCIETIES, THE ASSOCIATION OF (1887), Royex House, Aldermanbury Square, London EC2V 7HR. Tel: 0171-606 1881. *General Secretary*, Miss M. Poole

FRIENDS OF CATHEDRAL MUSIC (1956), 26 Dumbrells Court, North End, Ditchling, W. Sussex BN6 8TG. Tel: 01273-842903. *Secretary*, V. Waterhouse

FRIENDS OF THE EARTH (1971), 26–28 Underwood Street, London N1 7JQ. Tel: 0171-490 1555. *Director*, C. Secrett

FRIENDS OF THE ELDERLY AND GENTLEFOLK'S HELP (1905), 42 Ebury Street, London SW1W 0LZ. Tel: 0171-730 8263. *Chief Executive*, Mrs S. Levett

FRIENDS OF THE NATIONAL LIBRARIES (1931), c/o The British Library, London WC1B 3DG. Tel: 0171-412 7559. *Hon. Secretary*, M. Borrie, OBE, FSA

FURNITURE HISTORY SOCIETY (1964), 1 Mercedes Cottages, St John's Road, Haywards Heath, W. Sussex RH16 4EH. Tel: 01444-413845. *Membership Secretary*, Dr B. Austen

GALLIPOLI ASSOCIATION (1915), Earleydene Orchard, Earleydene, Ascot, Berks SL5 9JY. Tel: 01344-26523. *Hon. Secretary*, J. C. Watson Smith

GALTON INSTITUTE, THE (1907), 19 Northfields Prospect, London SW18 1PE. Tel: 0181-874 7257. *General Secretary*, Mrs L. Brooks

GAMBLERS ANONYMOUS (1954), PO Box 88, London SW10 0EU. Tel: 0171-384 3040.

GAME CONSERVANCY TRUST (1969), Fordingbridge, Hampshire SP6 1EF. Tel: 01425-652381. *Director-General*, Dr G. R. Potts

GARDEN HISTORY SOCIETY (1965), 77 Cowcross Street, London EC1M 6BP. Tel: 0171-608 2409. *Membership Secretary*, Mrs A. Richards

GARDENERS' ASSOCIATION, THE GOOD (1968), Pinetum, Churcham, Glos GL2 8AD. Tel: 01452-750402. *Hon. Director*, D. Wilkin

GARDENERS' ROYAL BENEVOLENT SOCIETY, THE (1839), Bridge House, 139 Kingston Road, Leatherhead, Surrey KT22 7NT. Tel: 01372-373962. *Chief Executive*, C. R. C. Bunce

GARDENS SCHEME CHARITABLE TRUST, NATIONAL (1927), Hatchlands Park, East Clandon, Guildford, Surrey GU4 7RT. Tel: 01483-211535. *Director*, Lt.-Col. T. A. Marsh

GAS CONSUMERS COUNCIL (1986), 6th Floor, Abford House, 15 Wilton Road, London SW1V 1LT. Tel: 0171-931 0977. *Director*, I. W. Powe

GAS ENGINEERS, INSTITUTION OF (1863), 21 Portland Place, London W1N 3AF. Tel: 0171-636 6603. *Chief Executive*, Mrs S. M. Raine

GEMMOLOGICAL ASSOCIATION AND GEM TESTING LABORATORY OF GREAT BRITAIN (1931), 27 Greville Street, (Saffron Hill entrance), London EC1N 8SU. Tel: 0171-404 3334. *Director*, Dr R. R. Harding

GENEALOGICAL RESEARCH SOCIETY, IRISH (1936), c/o The Irish Club, 82 Eaton Square, London SW1W 9AJ. Tel: 0171-235 4164. *Hon. Librarian*, J. G. Chartres

GENEALOGISTS AND RECORD AGENTS, ASSOCIATION OF (1968), 29 Badgers Close, Horsham, W. Sussex RH12 5RU.

GENEALOGISTS, SOCIETY OF (1911), 14 Charterhouse Buildings, Goswell Road, London EC1M 7BA. Tel: 0171-251 8799. *Director*, A. J. Camp

GENERAL PRACTITIONERS, ROYAL COLLEGE OF (1952), 14 Princes Gate, London SW7 1PU. Tel: 0171-581 3232. *Secretary*, Dr W. Reith

GENTLEPEOPLE, GUILD OF AID FOR (1904), 10 St Christopher's Place, London W1M 6HY. Tel: 0171-935 0641. *Secretary*

GEOGRAPHICAL ASSOCIATION, 343 Fulwood Road, Sheffield S10 3BP. Tel: 0114-267 0666. *Senior Administrator*, Miss F. M. Soar

GEOGRAPHICAL SOCIETY, ROYAL (1830), 1 Kensington Gore, London SW7 2AR. Tel: 0171-589 5466. *President*, The Earl Jellicoe, KBE, DSO, MC, FRS, PC; *Director*, Dr R. Gardener

GEOGRAPHICAL SOCIETY, ROYAL SCOTTISH (1884), Graham Hills Building, 40 George Street, Glasgow G1 1QE. Tel: 0141-552 3330. *Director*, A. B. Cruickshank

GEOLOGICAL SOCIETY (1807), Burlington House, Piccadilly, London W1V 0JU. Tel: 0171-434 9944. *Executive Secretary*, R. M. Bateman

GEOLOGISTS' ASSOCIATION (1858), Burlington House, Piccadilly, London W1V 9AG. Tel: 0171-434 9298. *Executive Secretary*, Mrs S. Stafford

GEORGIAN GROUP (1937), 6 Fitzroy Square, London W1P 6DX. Tel: 0171-387 1720. *Secretary*, N. Burton

GIFTED CHILDREN, NATIONAL ASSOCIATION FOR (1966), Park Campus, Boughton Green Road, Northampton NN2 7AL. Tel: 01604-792300. *Executive Director*, P. Carey

GILBERT AND SULLIVAN SOCIETY (1924), 1 Nethercourt Avenue, Finchley, London N3 1PS. *Hon. Secretary*, Ms M. Bowden

GINGERBREAD, AN ASSOCIATION FOR ONE PARENT FAMILIES AND THEIR CHILDREN (1970), 16–17 Clerkenwell Close, London EC1R 0AA. Tel: 0171-336 8183. *Chief Executive*, K. Murphy

GIRL GUIDES, *see* GUIDE ASSOCIATION

GIRLS' BRIGADE, Girls' Brigade House, 62 Foxhall Road, Didcot, Oxon OX11 7BQ. Tel: 01235-510425. *Brigade Secretary*, Mrs S. P. Bunting

GIRLS' FRIENDLY SOCIETY IN ENGLAND AND WALES (1875), 126 Queens Gate, London SW7 5LQ. Tel: 0171-589 9628. *General Secretary*, Mrs H. Crompton

GIRLS' VENTURE CORPS AIR CADETS (1964), Redhill Aerodrome, Kings Mill Lane, South Nutfield, Redhill RH1 5JY. Tel: 01737-823345. *Corps Director*, Mrs M. A. Rowland

GLASS ENGRAVERS, GUILD OF (1975), 19 Wildwood Road, London NW11 6UL. Tel: 0181-731 9352. *Secretary*

GLASS TECHNOLOGY, SOCIETY OF (1916), Thornton, 20 Hallam Gate Road, Sheffield S10 5BT. Tel: 0114-266 3168. *Administration Manager*, Ms J. Costello

GLIDING ASSOCIATION, BRITISH (1930), Kimberley House, Vaughan Way, Leicester LE1 4SE. Tel: 0116-253 1051. *Secretary*, B. Rolfe

GOAT SOCIETY, BRITISH (1879), 34–36 Fore Street, Bovey Tracey, Newton Abbot, Devon TQ13 9AD. Tel: 01626-833168. *Secretary*, Ms S. Knowles

GRAPHOLOGISTS, BRITISH INSTITUTE OF (1983), 24–26 High Street, Hampton Hill, Middx TW12 1PD. *Chairman*, Dr C. Molander

GREEK INSTITUTE (1969), 34 Bush Hill Road, London N21 2DS. Tel: 0181-360 7968. *Director*, Dr K. Tofallis

GREEN PARTY, THE (1973), 1A Waterlow Road, London N19 5NJ. Tel: 0171-272 4474. *Office Manager*, Ms V. Olliver

GREENPEACE UK (1971), Canonbury Villas, London N1 2PN. Tel: 0171-865 8100. *Executive Director*, The Lord Melchett

GUIDE ASSOCIATION, THE (1910), 17–19 Buckingham Palace Road, London SW1W 0PT. Tel: 0171-834 6242. *Chief Commissioner*, Mrs M. Wright; *Chief Executive*, Ms H. Williams

GUIDE DOGS FOR THE BLIND ASSOCIATION (1931), Hillfields, Burghfield, Reading, Berks RG7 3YG. Tel: 01734-835555. *Director-General*, J. C. Oxley

GULBENKIAN FOUNDATION, *see* CALOUSTE GULBENKIAN FOUNDATION

HAEMOPHILIA SOCIETY (1950), 123 Westminster Bridge Road, London SE1 7HR. Tel: 0171-928 2020. *Director of Services and Development*, G. Barker

HAIG HOMES (1928), Alban Dobson House, Green Lane, Morden, Surrey SM4 5NS. Tel: 0181-648 0335. *General Secretary*, J. B. Holt

HAKLUYT SOCIETY (1846), c/o Map Library, The British Library, Great Russell Street, London WC1B 3DG. Tel: 01986-788359. *Hon. Secretary*, A. P. Payne

HANSARD SOCIETY FOR PARLIAMENTARY GOVERNMENT (1944), St Philips Building North, Sheffield Street, London WC2A 2EX. Tel: 0171-955 7478. *Director*, D. Harris

HARD OF HEARING, BRITISH ASSOCIATION OF THE (1948), 7–11 Armstrong Road, London W3 7JL. Tel: 0181-743 1110. *Director*, C. J. Meyer, OBE

HARVEIAN SOCIETY OF EDINBURGH (1782), Respiratory Medicine Unit, Department of Medicine, The Royal Infirmary, Edinburgh EH3 9YW. Tel: 0131-536 2351. *Joint Secretaries*, A. B. MacGregor; Prof. N. J. Douglas

HARVEIAN SOCIETY OF LONDON (1831), Lettson House, 11 Chandos Street, London W1M 0EB. Tel: 0171-580 1043. *Executive Secretary*, M. C. Griffiths, TD

HEALTH AUTHORITIES AND TRUSTS, NATIONAL ASSOCIATION OF (1974), Birmingham Research Park, Vincent Drive, Birmingham B15 2SQ. Tel: 0121-471 4444. *Director*, P. Hunt, OBE

HEALTH CARE ASSOCIATION, BRITISH (1931), 24A Main Street, Garforth, Leeds LS25 1AA. Tel: 0113-232 0903. *Chief Executive*, Mrs C. Bell

HEALTH EDUCATION, INSTITUTE OF (1962), Department of Oral Health and Development, University Dental Hospital, Higher Cambridge Street, Manchester M15 6FH. Tel: 0161-275 6610. *Hon. Secretary*, Prof. A. S. Blinkhorn

HEALTH, GUILD OF (1904), Edward Wilson House, 26 Queen Anne Street, London W1M 9LB. Tel: 0171-580 2492. *General Secretary*, Revd A. Lynn

HEALTH SERVICES MANAGEMENT, INSTITUTE OF (1902), 39 Chalton Street, London NW1 1JD. Tel: 0171-388 2626. *Director*, Ms K. Caines

HEART FOUNDATION, BRITISH (1963), 14 Fitzhardinge Street, London W1H 4DH. Tel: 0171-935 0185. *Director-General*, Maj.-Gen. L. F. H. Busk, CB

HEDGEHOG PRESERVATION SOCIETY, BRITISH (1982), Knowbury House, Knowbury, Ludlow, Shropshire SY8 3LQ. Tel: 01584-890287. *Founder*, Maj. A. H. Coles, TD

HELLENIC STUDIES, SOCIETY FOR THE PROMOTION OF (1879), 31–34 Gordon Square, London WC1H 0PP. Tel: 0171-387 7495. *Secretary*, Miss F. J. Fisher

HELP THE AGED (1960), St James's Walk, Clerkenwell Green, London EC1R 0BE. Tel: 0171-253 0253. *Director-General*, J. Mayo, OBE

HERALDIC AND GENEALOGICAL STUDIES, INSTITUTE OF (1961), 79–82 Northgate, Canterbury, Kent CT1 1BA. Tel: 01227-768664. *Registrar*, J. Palmer

HERALDRY SOCIETY, THE (1947), 44–45 Museum Street, London WC1A 1LY. Tel: 0171-430 2172. *Secretary*, Mrs M. Miles, MBE

HERPETOLOGICAL SOCIETY, BRITISH (1947), c/o Zoological Society of London, Regent's Park, London NW1 4RY. Tel: 0181-452 9578. *Secretary*, Mrs M. Green

HISPANIC AND LUSO BRAZILIAN COUNCIL (1943), Canning House, 2 Belgrave Square, London SW1X 8PJ. Tel: 0171-235 2303. *Director-General*, J. Amey

HISTORICAL ASSOCIATION, THE (1906), 59A Kennington Park Road, London SE11 4JH. Tel: 0171-735 3901. *Secretary*, Mrs M. Stiles

HISTORICAL SOCIETY, ROYAL (1868), University College London, Gower Street, London WC1E 6BT. Tel: 0171-387 7532. *Executive Secretary*, Mrs J. N. McCarthy

HISTORIC HOUSES ASSOCIATION (1973), 2 Chester Street, London SW1X 7BB. Tel: 0171-259 5688. *Director-General*, R. Wilkin

HOME FARM TRUST (1962), Merchants House, Wapping Road, Bristol BS1 4RW. Tel: 0117-927 3746. *Director-General*, C. Carey

HOMEOPATHIC ASSOCIATION, BRITISH (1902), 27A Devonshire Street, London W1N 1RJ. Tel: 0171-935 2163. *General Secretary*, Mrs E. Segall

HONG KONG ASSOCIATION (1961), Swire House, 59 Buckingham Gate, London SW1E 6AJ. Tel: 0171-821 3220. *Executive Director*, Brig. B. G. Hickey, OBE, MC

HOROLOGICAL INSTITUTE, BRITISH (1858), Upton Hall, Upton, Newark, Notts NG23 5TE. Tel: 01636-813795. *Secretary*, Ms H. Bartlett

HOROLOGICAL SOCIETY, ANTIQUARIAN (1953), New House, High Street, Ticehurst, Wadhurst, E. Sussex TN5 7AL. Tel: 01580-200155. *Secretary*, Mrs P. Hossbach

HORSE SOCIETY, BRITISH (incorporating The Pony Club) (1947), British Equestrian Centre, Stoneleigh Park, Kenilworth, Warks CV8 2LR. Tel: 01203-696697. *Chief Executive*, Col. T. Eastwood

HOSPITAL FEDERATION, INTERNATIONAL (1947), 4 Abbot's Place, London NW6 4NP. Tel: 0171-372 7181. *Director-General*, Dr E. N. Pickering

HOSPITALITY ASSOCIATION, BRITISH (1907), Queens House, 55–56 Lincoln's Inn Fields, London WC2A 3BH. Tel: 0171-404 7744. *Chief Executive*, J. Logie

HOSPITAL SATURDAY FUND (1873), 24 Upper Ground, London SE1 9PQ. Tel: 0171-928 6662. *Chief Executive*, K. R. Bradley

HOSPITAL SAVING ASSOCIATION, Hambleden House, Andover, Hants 1LQ. Tel: 01264-353211. *Chief Executive*, J. A. Young

HOTEL AND CATERING INTERNATIONAL MANAGEMENT ASSOCIATION (1971), 191 Trinity Road, London SW17 7HN. Tel: 0181-672 4251. *Chief Executive*, D. Wood

HOUSE OF ST BARNABAS-IN-SOHO (1846), 1 Greek Street, London W1V 6NQ. Tel: 0171-437 1894. For homeless women in London. *Director*, Ms S. Dixon

HOUSING, CHARTERED INSTITUTE OF, Octavia House, Westwood Business Park, Westwood Way, Coventry CV4 8JP. Tel: 01203-694433. *Chief Executive*, Ms C. Laird

HOUSING AID SOCIETY, CATHOLIC (1956), 209 Old Marylebone Road, London NW1 5QT. Tel: 0171-723 7273. *Director*, Ms R. Rafferty

HOUSING AND TOWN PLANNING COUNCIL, NATIONAL (1900), 14–18 Old Street, London EC1V 9AB. Tel: 0171-251 2363. *Director*, K. MacDonald

HOVERCRAFT SOCIETY, THE (1971), 24 Jellicoe Avenue, Alverstoke, Gosport, Hants PO12 2PE. Tel: 01705-601310. *Chairman*, N. MacDonald

HOWARD LEAGUE FOR PENAL REFORM (1866), 708 Holloway Road, London N19 3NL. Tel: 0171-281 7722. *Director*, Ms F. Crook

HUGUENOT SOCIETY OF GREAT BRITAIN AND IRELAND (1885), The Huguenot Library, University College, Gower Street, London WC1E 6BT. Tel: 0171-380 7094. *Hon. Secretary*, Mrs M. Bayliss

HUMANE RESEARCH TRUST (1974), Brook House, 29 Bramhall Lane South, Bramhall, Stockport, Cheshire SK7 2DN. Tel: 0161-439 8041. *Chairman*, K. Cholerton

HUMANIST ASSOCIATION, BRITISH (1963), 47 Theobald's Road, London WC1X 8SP. Tel: 0171-430 0908. *Administrator*, Ms A. Todd

HYDROGRAPHIC SOCIETY (1972), c/o University of East London, Longbridge Road, Dagenham, Essex RM8 2AS. Tel: 0181-597 1946. *Hon. Secretary*, R. Naylor

HYMN SOCIETY OF GREAT BRITAIN AND IRELAND (1936), St Nicholas Rectory, Glebe Fields, Curdworth, Sutton Coldfield, West Midlands B76 9ES. Tel: 01675-470384. *Secretary*, Revd M. Garland

ICAN (INVALID CHILDREN'S AID NATIONWIDE) (1888), Barbican Citygate, 1–3 Dufferin Street, London EC1Y 8NA. Tel: 0171-374 4422. *Director*, B. J. Jones

IMMIGRATION ADVISORY SERVICE (1970), County House, 190 Great Dover Street, London SE1 4YB. Tel: 0171-357 7511/24-hour line: 0181-814 1559. *Chief Executive*, K. Best

INDEPENDENT BRITAIN, CAMPAIGN FOR AN (1976), 81 Ashmole Street, London SW8 1NF. Tel: 0181-340 0314. *Hon. Secretary*, Sir Robin Williams, Bt.

INDEPENDENT SCHOOL BURSARS' ASSOCIATION (1933), Woodlands, Closewood Road, Denmead, Waterlooville, Hants PO7 6JD. Tel: 01705-264506. *Secretary*, D. J. Bird

INDEPENDENT SCHOOLS CAREERS ORGANIZATION (1942), 12A Princess Way, Camberley, Surrey GU15 3SP. Tel: 01276-21188. *National Director*, G. W. Searle

INDEPENDENT SCHOOLS INFORMATION SERVICE (1972), 56 Buckingham Gate, London SW1E 6AG. Tel: 0171-630 8793. *Director*, D. J. Woodhead

INDEPENDENT SCHOOLS JOINT COUNCIL (1974), Grosvenor Gardens House, 35–37 Grosvenor Gardens, London SW1W 0BS. Tel: 0171-630 0144. *General Secretary*, Dr A. G. Hearnden, OBE

INDEXERS, SOCIETY OF (1957), 38 Rochester Road, London NW1 9JJ. Tel: 0171-916 7809. *Secretary*, Mrs C. Shuttleworth

INDUSTRIAL SOCIETY, THE (1918), Robert Hyde House, 48 Bryanston Square, London W1H 7LN. Tel: 0171-262 2401. *Chief Executive*, T. Morgan

INDUSTRY AND PARLIAMENT TRUST, 1 Buckingham Place, London SW1E 6HR. Tel: 0171-976 5311. *Director*, F. R. Hyde-Chambers

INDUSTRY CHURCHES FORUM (formerly Industrial Churches Fellowship) (1877), 86 Leadenhall Street, London EC3A 3DH. Tel: 0171-283 6120. *Chairman*, Revd Canon B. Brown

INDUSTRY TRAINING ORGANIZATIONS, NATIONAL COUNCIL OF (1988), 10 Meadowcourt, Amos Road, Sheffield S9 1BX. Tel: 0114-261 9926. *Administrator*, J. Maisari

INFANT DEATHS, FOUNDATION FOR THE STUDY OF (1971), 35 Belgrave Square, London SW1X 8QB. Tel: 0171-235 0965. *Secretary-General*, Mrs J. Epstein

INFORMATION SCIENTISTS, INSTITUTE OF (1958), 44–45 Museum Street, London WC1A 1LY. Tel: 0171-831 8003. *Director*, E. Hyams

INNER WHEEL CLUBS IN GREAT BRITAIN AND IRELAND, ASSOCIATION OF (1934), 51 Warwick Square, London SW1V 2AT. Tel: 0171-834 4600. *Secretary*, Miss J. Dobson

INSOLVENCY, SOCIETY OF PRACTITIONERS OF (1990), 18–19 Long Lane, London EC1A 9HE. Tel: 0171-600 3375. *General Secretary*, R. M. Stancombe

INSURANCE AND INVESTMENT BROKERS' ASSOCIATION, BRITISH, BIIBA House, 14 Bevis Marks, London EC3A 7NT. Tel: 0171-623 9043. *Chairman*, A. Gavaghan

INSURANCE BROKERS REGISTRATION COUNCIL, 15 St Helen's Place, London EC3A 6DS. Tel: 0171-588 4387. *Registrar*, Miss E. J. Rees

INSURANCE INSTITUTE, CHARTERED (1897), 20 Aldermanbury, London EC2V 7HY. Tel: 0171-606 3835. *Director-General*, Dr D. E. Bland

INSURERS, ASSOCIATION OF BRITISH (1985), 51 Gresham Street, London EC2V 7HQ. Tel: 0171-600 3333. *Director-General*, M. Boléat

INTERCON (INTERCONTINENTAL CHURCH SOCIETY) (1823), 175 Tower Bridge Road, London SE1 2AQ. Tel: 0171-407 4588. *General Secretary*, Deaconess P. K. L. Schmiegelow

INTERNATIONAL AFFAIRS, ROYAL INSTITUTE OF (1920), Chatham House, 10 St James's Square, London SW1Y 4LE. Tel: 0171-957 5700. *Director*, Air Marshal Sir Timothy Garden, KCB (from 1 January 1997)

INTERNATIONAL FRIENDSHIP LEAGUE (1931), 3 Creswick Road, London W3 9HE. Tel: 0181-752 0055. *Secretary*, Ms. J. Nelson

INTERNATIONAL POLICE ASSOCIATION (British Section) (1950), 1 Fox Road, West Bridgford, Nottingham NG2 6AJ. Tel: 0115-981 3638. *Chief Executive Officer*, A. F. Carter

INTERNATIONAL STUDENTS HOUSE (1962), 229 Great Portland Street, London W1N 5HD. Tel: 0171-631 8300. *Executive Director*, P. Anwyl

INTERSERVE (1852), 325 Kennington Road, London SE11 4QH. Tel: 0171-735 8227. *National Director*, R. Clark

INTER VARSITY CLUBS, ASSOCIATION OF (1946), 2nd Floor, Grosvenor House, 94–96 Grosvenor Square, Manchester M1 7HL. Tel: 0161-273 2316. *Secretary*, D. Bousfield

INVALIDS-AT-HOME (1966), 17 Lapstone Gardens, Kenton, Harrow, Middx HA3 0EB. Tel: 0181-907 1706. *Executive Officer*, Mrs S. Lomas

INVISIBLES, BRITISH (1983), 6th Floor, Windsor House, 39 King Street, London EC2V 8DQ. Tel: 0171-600 1198. *Director-General*, The Hon. Mrs A. Wright

INVOLVEMENT AND PARTICIPATION ASSOCIATION (1884), 42 Colebrooke Row, London N1 8AF. Tel: 0171-354 8040. *Director*, B. C. Stevens

IRAN SOCIETY (1936), 2 Belgrave Square, London SW1X 8PJ. Tel: 0171-235 5122. *Hon. Secretary*, A. D. Ashmole

ITRI (formerly International Tin Research Institute) (1932), Kingston Lane, Uxbridge, Middlx UB8 3PJ. Tel: 01895-272406. *Director*, R. Bedder

JACQUELINE DU PRÉ MUSIC BUILDING APPEAL (1988), St Hilda's College, Oxford OX4 1DY. Tel: 01865-272803. *Chairman*, Dr J. H. Mellanby

JAPAN ASSOCIATION, THE (1950), Swire House, 59 Buckingham Gate, London SW1E 6AJ. Tel: 0171-821 3221. *Executive Director*, Brig. B. G. Hickey, OBE, MC

JERUSALEM AND THE MIDDLE EAST CHURCH ASSOCIATION (1887), 1 Hart House, The Hart, Farnham, Surrey GU9 7HA. Tel: 01252-726994. *Secretary*, Mrs V. Wells

JEWISH HISTORICAL SOCIETY OF ENGLAND (1893), 33 Seymour Place, London W1H 5AP. Tel: 0171-723 5852. *Hon. Secretary*, C. M. Drukker

JEWISH PEOPLE, CHURCH'S MINISTRY AMONG (1809), 30c Clarence Road, St Albans, Herts AL1 4JJ. Tel: 01727-833114. *General Director*, Revd Dr W. Riggans

JEWISH YOUTH, ASSOCIATION FOR (part of Norwood Child Care) (1899), 128 East Lane, Wembley, Middx HA0 3NL. Tel: 0181-908 4747. *Head*, E. Finestone

JOURNALISTS, CHARTERED INSTITUTE OF (1883), 2 Dock Offices, Surrey Quays Road, London SE16 2XU. Tel: 0171-252 1187. *General Secretary*, C. J. Underwood

JUSTICE (British Section of the International Commission of Jurists) (1957), 59 Carter Lane, London EC4V 5AQ. Tel: 0171-329 5100. *Director*, Ms A. Owers

JUSTICES' CLERKS' SOCIETY (1839), The Magistrates' Court, 107 Dale Street, Liverpool L2 2JQ. Tel: 0151-255 0790. *Hon. Secretary*, M. Marsh

KING EDWARD'S HOSPITAL FUND FOR LONDON (THE KING'S FUND) (1897), 11–13 Cavendish Square, London W1M 0AN. Tel: 0171-307 2400. *Chief Executive*, Dr R. J. Maxwell, CBE

KING GEORGE'S FUND FOR SAILORS (1917), 8 Hatherley Street, London SW1P 2YY. Tel: 0171-932 0000. *Director-General*, Capt. M. J. Appleton, RN

KIPLING SOCIETY, THE (1927), Tree Cottage, 2 Brownleaf Road, Brighton, E. Sussex BN2 6LB. Tel: 01273-303719. *Hon. Secretary*, J. W. M. Smith

LADIES IN REDUCED CIRCUMSTANCES, SOCIETY FOR THE ASSISTANCE OF (1886), Lancaster House, 25 Hornyold Road, Malvern, Worcs WR14 1QQ. Tel: 01684-574645. *Secretary*

LANDSCAPE INSTITUTE (1929), 6–8 Barnard Mews, London SW11 1QU. Tel: 0171-738 9166. *Director-General*, S. Royston

LAND-VALUE TAXATION AND FREE TRADE, INTERNATIONAL UNION FOR, 177 Vauxhall Bridge Road, London SW1V 1EU. Tel: 0171-834 4266. *Hon. Secretary*, Mrs B. P. Sobrielo

LANGUAGE LEARNING, ASSOCIATION FOR (1990), 150 Railway Terrace, Rugby CV21 3HN. Tel: 01788-546443. *Secretary-General*, Mrs C. Wilding

LAW REPORTING FOR ENGLAND AND WALES, INCORPORATED COUNCIL OF (1865), 3 Stone Buildings, Lincoln's Inn, London WC2A 3XN. Tel: 0171-242 6471. *Secretary*, B. Symondson

LEAGUE OF THE HELPING HAND (1908), Petersham Hollow, 226 Petersham Road, Petersham, Richmond, Surrey TW10 7AL. Tel: 0181-940 7303. *Secretary*, Mrs I. Goodlad

LEAGUE OF WELLDOERS (1893), 119–133 Limekiln Lane, Liverpool L5 8SN. Tel: 0151-207 1984. *Warden and Secretary*, Mrs C. Fell

LEATHER AND HIDE TRADES' BENEVOLENT INSTITUTION (1860), 60 Wickham Hill, Hurstpierpoint, Hassocks, W. Sussex BN6 9NP. Tel: 01273-843488. *Secretary*, Mrs G. M. Stapleton, MBE

LEGAL EXECUTIVES, INSTITUTE OF (1892), Kempston Manor, Kempston, Bedford MK42 7AB. Tel: 01234-841000. *Chief Executive*, R. Ball

LEONARD CHESHIRE FOUNDATION (1955), 26–29 Maunsel Street, London SW1P 2QN. Tel: 0171-828 1822. *Director-General*, J. Stanford

LEPROSY MISSION, THE (England and Wales) (1874), Goldhay Way, Orton Goldhay, Peterborough PE2 5GZ. Tel: 01733-370505. *Executive Director*, Revd J. A. Lloyd, PH.D.

LEUKAEMIA RESEARCH FUND (1962), 43 Great Ormond Street, London WC1N 3JJ. Tel: 0171-405 0101. *Executive Director*, D. L. Osborne

LIBERAL PARTY (1877; relaunched 1989), Gayfere House, 22 Gayfere Street, London SW1 3HP. Tel: 0171-233 2124. *Secretary-General*, N. Ashton

LIBERTY (NATIONAL COUNCIL FOR CIVIL LIBERTIES) (1934), 21 Tabard Street, London SE1 4LA. Tel: 0171-403 3888. *General Secretary*, A. Puddephatt

LIBRARY ASSOCIATION (1877), 7 Ridgmount Street, London WC1E 7AE. Tel: 0171-636 7543. *Chief Executive*, R. Shimmon

LIFEBOATS, *see* ROYAL NATIONAL LIFEBOAT INSTITUTION

LIGHT HORSE BREEDING SOCIETY, NATIONAL (1885), 96 High Street, Edenbridge, Kent TN8 5AR. Tel: 01732-866277. *Secretary*, G. W. Evans

LINGUISTS, INSTITUTE OF (1910), 24A Highbury Grove, London N5 2DQ. Tel: 0171-359 7445. *Director*, Ms E. H. F. Ostarhild

LINNEAN SOCIETY OF LONDON, THE (1788), Burlington House, Piccadilly, London W1V 0LQ. Tel: 0171-434 4479. *President*, Prof. B. G. Gardiner; *Executive Secretary*, Dr J. C. Marsden

LIONS CLUBS INTERNATIONAL (British Isles and Ireland) (1949), 257 Alcester Road South, Kings Heath, Birmingham B14 6BT. Tel: 0121-441 4544. *Office Manager*, Mrs J. Davis

LLOYD'S OF LONDON, 1 Lime Street, London EC3M 7HA. Tel: 0171-623 7100. *Chief Executive*, R. Sandler

LLOYD'S PATRIOTIC FUND (1803), Lloyd's, Lime Street, London EC3M 7HA. Tel: 0171-327 5925. *Secretary*, Mrs L. Harper

LLOYD'S REGISTER, 71 Fenchurch Street, London EC3M 4BS. Tel: 0171-709 9166.

LOCAL AUTHORITY CHIEF EXECUTIVES, SOCIETY OF (1974), PO Box 21, Archway Road, Huyton, Knowsley, Merseyside L36 9YU. Tel: 0151-443 3931. *Executive Officer*, Ms S. Rheinlander

LOCAL COUNCILS, NATIONAL ASSOCIATION OF (1947), 109 Great Russell Street, London WC1B 3LD. Tel: 0171-637 1865. *Secretary*, J. Clarke, OBE

LOCAL GOVERNMENT INTERNATIONAL BUREAU (1913), *also* Council of European Municipalities and Regions (British Section) and International Union of Local Authorities (British Section) (1951), 35 Great Smith Street, London SW1P 3BJ. Tel: 0171-222 1636. *Secretary-General*, J. Smith

LOCAL HISTORY, BRITISH ASSOCIATION FOR (1843), 24 Lower Street, Harnham, Salisbury, Wilts SP2 8EY. Tel: 01722-332158. *Administrator*, M. Cowan

LONDON APPRECIATION SOCIETY (1932), 14 Hill View, 2–4 Primrose Hill Road, London NW3 3AX. *Chairman*, Miss V. C. Colin-Russ

LONDON CITY MISSION (1835), 175 Tower Bridge Road, London SE1 2AH. Tel: 0171-407 7585. *General Secretary*, Revd J. McAllen

LONDON COURT OF INTERNATIONAL ARBITRATION (1892), 12 Carthusian Street, London EC1M 6EB. Tel: 0171-417 8228. *Executive Director*, Ms M. May, CBE

LONDON FLOTILLA (1937), 40 Endlesham Road, London SW12 8JL. Tel: 0181-673 1879. *Hon. Secretary*, Lt.-Cdr. H. C. R. Upton, RD, RNR

LONDON GOVERNMENT, ASSOCIATION OF (1964), 36 Old Queen Street, London SW1H 9SF. Tel: 0171-222 7799. *Secretary*, J. McDonnell

LONDON LIBRARY, THE (1841), 14 St James's Square, London SW1Y 4LG. Tel: 0171-930 7705. *Librarian*, A. S. Bell

LONDON MAGISTRATES' CLERKS' ASSOCIATION (1889), c/o Thames Magistrates' Court, 58 Bow Road, London E3 4DJ. Tel: 0181-980 1000 ext. 3708. *Hon. Secretary*, J. Mulreany

LONDON PLAYING FIELDS SOCIETY (1890), Boston Manor Playing Field, Boston Gardens, Brentford, Middx TW8 9LR. Tel: 0181-560 3667. *Secretary*, D. Northwood

LONDON SOCIETY, THE (1912), 4th Floor, Senate House, Malet Street, London WC1E 7HU. Tel: 0171-580 5537. *Hon. Secretary*, Mrs B. Jones

LORD'S DAY OBSERVANCE SOCIETY (1831), 6 Sherman Road, Bromley, Kent BR1 3JH. Tel: 0181-313 0456. *General Secretary*, J. G. Roberts

LOTTERIES COUNCIL (1979), Windermere House, Kendal Avenue, London W3 0XA. Tel: 0181-896 2333. *Hon. Secretary*, G. Wilson, CBE

LUNG FOUNDATION, BRITISH (1985), 78 Hatton Garden, London EC1N 8JR. Tel: 0171-831 5831. *Chief Executive*, I. J. Govendir

MAGISTRATES' ASSOCIATION, THE (1920), 28 Fitzroy Square, London W1P 6DD. Tel: 0171-387 2353. *Secretary*, Ms S. Dickson

MAILING PREFERENCE SERVICE (1983), 5 Reef House, Plantation Wharf, London SW11 3UF. Tel: 0345-034599. To limit direct mail: Freepost 22, London W1E 7EZ. *Chief Executive*, Ms K. Beckett

MAIL USERS' ASSOCIATION (1976), Pharos House, Wye Valley Business Park, Hay-on-Wye, Hereford HR3 5PG. Tel: 01497-821357. *President*, L. K. Morelli

MALAYSIAN RUBBER PRODUCERS' RESEARCH ASSOCIATION (1938), Tun Abdul Razak Research Centre, Brickendonbury, Hertford SG13 8NL. Tel: 01992-584966. *Director*, Dr C. S. L. Baker

MALCOLM SARGENT CANCER FUND FOR CHILDREN (1968), 14 Abingdon Road, London W8 6AF. Tel: 0171-937 4548. *Chief Executive*, Mrs D. Yeo

MANAGEMENT, INSTITUTE OF (1992), Management House, Cottingham Road, Corby, Northants NN17 1TT. Tel: 01536-204222. *Director-General*, R. Young

MANAGEMENT AND PROFESSIONAL STAFFS, ASSOCIATION OF (1972), Parkgates, Bury New Road, Prestwich, Manchester M25 0JW. Tel: 0161-773 8621. *Executive Secretary*, A. J. Casey

MANAGEMENT SERVICES, INSTITUTE OF, 1 Cecil Court, London Road, Enfield, Middx EN2 6DD. Tel: 0181-366 1261. *Secretary*

MANIC DEPRESSION FELLOWSHIP (1983), 8–10 High Street, Kingston upon Thames, Surrey KT1 1EY. Tel: 0181-974 6550. *Director*, Ms M. Fulford

MANORIAL SOCIETY OF GREAT BRITAIN (1906), 104 Kennington Road, London SE11 6RE. Tel: 0171-735 6633. *Hon. Chairman*, R. A. Smith

MANPOWER SOCIETY (1969), 39 Apple Tree Walk, Climping, Littlehampton, W. Sussex BN17 5QN. Tel: 01903-731728. *Administrator*, Mrs H. Gale

MARIE CURIE CANCER CARE (1948), 28 Belgrave Square, London SW1X 8QG. Tel: 0171-235 3325. Scottish Office: 21 Rutland Street, Edinburgh EH1 2AH. Tel: 0131-229 8332. *Director-General*, Maj.-Gen. M. E. Carleton-Smith, CBE

MARINE ARTISTS, ROYAL SOCIETY OF (1939), 17 Carlton House Terrace, London SW1Y 5BD. Tel: 0171-930 6844. *Secretary*, Ms S. Robinson

MARINE BIOLOGICAL ASSOCIATION OF THE UK (1884), Citadel Hill, Plymouth PL1 2PB. Tel: 01752-633331. *Secretary*, Prof. M. Whitfield

MARINE ENGINEERS, INSTITUTE OF (1889), The Memorial Building, 76 Mark Lane, London EC3R 7JN. Tel: 0171-481 8493. *Secretary*, J. E. Sloggett, OBE

MARINE SCIENCE, SCOTTISH ASSOCIATION FOR (1914), PO Box 3, Oban, Argyll PA34 4AD. Tel: 01631-562244. *Director*, Dr G. B. Shimmield

MARINE SOCIETY, THE (1756), 202 Lambeth Road, London SE1 7JW. Tel: 0171-261 9535. *General Secretary*, Lt. -Cdr. R. M. Frampton

MARIO LANZA EDUCATIONAL FOUNDATION (1976), 1 Kenton Gardens, Minster, Ramsgate, Kent CT12 4EN. Tel: 01843-822389. *Hon. Secretary*, Mrs W. Stilwell

MARKET AUTHORITIES, NATIONAL ASSOCIATION OF BRITISH (1948), NABMA House, 21 Tarnside Road, Orrell, Wigan, Lancs WN5 8RN. Tel: 01695-623860. *Secretary*, J. Edwards

MARKETING, CHARTERED INSTITUTE OF (1911), Moor Hall, Cookham, Maidenhead, Berks SL6 9QH. Tel: 01628-427500. *Director-General*, S. Cuthbert

MARK MASTER MASONS, GRAND LODGE OF (1856), Mark Masons' Hall, 86 St James's Street, London SW1A 1PL. Tel: 0171-839 5274. *Grand Master*, HRH Prince Michael of Kent, KVCO; *Grand Secretary*, P. G. Williams

MARRIAGE CARE (formerly the Catholic Marriage Advisory Council) (1946), Clitherow House, 1 Blythe Mews, Blythe Road, London W14 0NW. Tel: 0171-371 1341. *Chief Executive*, Mrs M. Corbett

MASONIC BENEVOLENT INSTITUTION, ROYAL (1842), 20 Great Queen Street, London WC2B 5BG. Tel: 0171-405 8341. *Chief Executive*, Ms J. Reynolds

MASONIC TRUST FOR GIRLS AND BOYS (1985), 31 Great Queen Street, London WC2B 5AG. Tel: 0171-405 2644. *Secretary*, Lt.-Col. J. C. Chambers

MASTERS OF WINE, INSTITUTE OF (1955), Five Kings House, 1 Queen Street Place, London EC4R 1QS. Tel: 0171-236 4427. *Executive Director*, J. F. Casson

MATERIALS, INSTITUTE OF (1985), 1 Carlton House Terrace, London SW1Y 5DB. Tel: 0171-839 4071. *Secretary*, Dr J. A. Catterall

MATERNAL AND CHILD WELFARE LTD, NATIONAL ASSOCIATION FOR (1911), 1st Floor, 40–42 Osnaburgh Street, London NW4 3ND. Tel: 0171-383 4117. *Administrator*, Mrs V. A. Farebrother

MATERNITY ALLIANCE, THE (1980), 15 Britannia Street, London WC1X 9JP. Tel: 0171-837 1265. *Chair*, A. Phillips

MATHEMATICAL ASSOCIATION (1871), 259 London Road, Leicester LE2 3BE. Tel: 0116-270 3877. *Executive Secretary*, Ms H. Whitby

MATHEMATICS AND ITS APPLICATIONS, INSTITUTE OF (1964), Catherine Richards House, 16 Nelson Street, Southend-on-Sea, Essex SS1 1EF. Tel: 01702-354020. *Executive Secretary*, Dr A. M. Lepper

ME ASSOCIATION (1976), Stanhope House, High Street, Stanford-le-Hope, Essex SS17 0HA. Tel: 01375-642466. *Director*, Ms P. Grenier

MEASUREMENT AND CONTROL, INSTITUTE OF (1944), 87 Gower Street, London WC1E 6AA. Tel: 0171-387 4949. *Secretary*, M. J. Yates

MECHANICAL ENGINEERS, INSTITUTION OF (1847), 1 Birdcage Walk, London SW1H 9JJ. Tel: 0171-222 7899. *Director-General*, Dr R. Pike

MEDIC-ALERT FOUNDATION, 12 Bridge Wharf, 156 Caledonian Road, London N1 9UU. Tel: 0171-833 3034. *Chief Executive*, Miss J. Friend

MEDICAL COUNCIL, GENERAL (1858), 178 Great Portland Street, London W1N 6JE. Tel: 0171-580 7642. *Registrar*, F. Scott, TD

MEDICAL SOCIETY OF LONDON (1773), Lettsom House, 11 Chandos Street, London W1M 0EB. Tel: 0171-580 1043. *Registrar*, M. Griffiths, TD

MEDICAL WOMEN'S FEDERATION (1917), Tavistock House North, Tavistock Square, London WC1H 9HX. Tel: 0171-387 7765. *Hon. Secretary*, Dr I. Weinreb

MEMORIAL FUND FOR DISASTER RELIEF, Europa House, 13–17 Ironmonger Row, London EC1V 3QN. Tel: 0171-250 1700. *Director*, D. Childs

MENCAP (THE ROYAL SOCIETY FOR MENTALLY HANDICAPPED CHILDREN AND ADULTS) (1946), 123 Golden Lane, London EC1Y 0RT. Tel: 0171-454 0454. *Chief Executive*, F. Heddell

MENSA LTD, BRITISH (1946), Mensa House, St Johns Square, Wolverhampton WV2 4AH. Tel: 01902-772771. *General Manager*, D. Chatten

MENTAL AFTER CARE ASSOCIATION (1879), 25 Bedford Square, London WC1B 3HW. Tel: 0171-436 6194. *Director*, B. G. Garner

MENTAL HEALTH FOUNDATION (1949), 37 Mortimer Street, London W1N 8JU. Tel: 0171-580 0145. *Director*, Ms J. McKerrow

MENTAL HEALTH, NATIONAL ASSOCIATION FOR, *see* MIND

MENTAL HEALTH, SCOTTISH ASSOCIATION FOR (1923), Atlantic House, 38 Gardeners Crescent, Edinburgh EH3 8DQ. Tel: 0131-229 9687. *Director*, R. Laing

MENTALLY HANDICAPPED, SCOTTISH SOCIETY FOR THE, *see* ENABLE

MERCHANT NAVY WELFARE BOARD (1948), 19–21 Lancaster Gate, London W2 3LN. Tel: 0171-723 3642. *General Secretary*, Capt. D. A. Parsons

METAL TRADES BENEVOLENT SOCIETY, ROYAL (1843), Brooke House, 4 The Lakes, Bedford Road, Northampton NN4 7YD. Tel: 01604-22023. *General Secretary*, A. N. Nisbet

METEOROLOGICAL SOCIETY, ROYAL (1850), 104 Oxford Road, Reading, Berks RG1 7LJ. Tel: 01734-568500. *Executive Secretary*, R. P. C. Swash

METROPOLITAN AND CITY POLICE ORPHANS FUND (1870), 30 Hazlewell Road, London SW15 6LH. Tel: 0181-788 5140. *Secretary*, R. Duff-Cole, BEM

METROPOLITAN AUTHORITIES, ASSOCIATION OF (1974), 35 Great Smith Street, London SW1P 3BJ. Tel: 0171-222 8100. *Secretary*, R. Brooke, CBE

METROPOLITAN HOSPITAL-SUNDAY FUND (1872), 45 Westminster Bridge Road, London SE1 7JB. Tel: 0171-922 0200. *Secretary*, H. F. Doe

MIDDLE EAST ASSOCIATION (1961), Bury House, 33 Bury Street, St James's, London SW1Y 6AX. Tel: 0171-839 2137. *Director-General*, J. R. Grundon

MIDWIVES, ROYAL COLLEGE OF (1881), 15 Mansfield Street, London W1M 0BE. Tel: 0171-872 5100. *General Secretary*, Mrs J. Allison

MIGRAINE ASSOCIATION, BRITISH (1858), 178A High
Road, Byfleet, West Byfleet, Surrey KT14 7ED. Tel: 01932-
352468. *Secretary*, Mrs B. M. Jones

MIGRAINE TRUST (1965), 45 Great Ormond Street,
London WCIN 3HZ. Tel: 0171-278 2676. *Director*,
Ms A. Rush

MILITARY HISTORICAL SOCIETY, National Army
Museum, Royal Hospital Road, London SW3 4HT. Tel:
0181-460 7341. *Hon. Secretary*, J. Gaylor

MIND (THE NATIONAL ASSOCIATION FOR MENTAL
HEALTH), Granta House, 15–19 Broadway, London
EI5 4BQ. Tel: 0181-519 2122. *National Director*,
Ms J. Clements

MINERALOGICAL SOCIETY (1876), 41 Queen's Gate,
London SW7 5HR. Tel: 0171-584 7516. *Hon. General
Secretary*, Dr B. A. Cressey

MINES OF GREAT BRITAIN, FEDERATION OF SMALL, 29
King Street, Newcastle under Lyme, Staffs ST5 IER. Tel:
01782-614618. *Secretary*, R. W. Bladen

MINIATURE PAINTERS, SCULPTORS AND GRAVERS, ROYAL
SOCIETY OF (1895), Burwood House, 15 Union Street,
Wells, Somerset BA5 2PU. Tel: 01749-674472. *Executive
Secretary*, Mrs S. M. Burton

MINING AND METALLURGY, THE INSTITUTION OF (1892),
44 Portland Place, London WIN 4BR. Tel: 0171-580 3802.
Secretary, M. J. Jones

MINING ENGINEERS, INSTITUTION OF (1889), Danum
House, 6A South Parade, Doncaster, S. Yorks DNI 2DY. Tel:
01302-320486. *Secretary*, Dr G. J. M. Woodrow

MISSING PERSONS HELPLINE, NATIONAL (1992), Roebuck
House, 284–286 Upper Richmond Road West, London
SW14 7JE. Tel: 0181-392 2000. *Co-Founders*, Ms M. Asprey;
Ms J. Newman

MISSION TO DEEP SEA FISHERMEN, ROYAL NATIONAL
(1881), 43 Nottingham Place, London WIM 4BX. Tel:
0171-487 5101. *Chief Executive*, A. D. Marsden

MISSIONS TO SEAMEN (1856), St Michael Paternoster
Royal, College Hill, London EC4R 2RL. Tel: 0171-
248 5202. *Secretary-General*, Revd Canon G. Jones

MODERN CHURCHPEOPLE'S UNION (1898), MCU Office,
25 Birch Grove, London W3 9SP. Tel: 0181-992 2333.
General Secretary, Revd N. P. Henderson

MONUMENTAL BRASS SOCIETY (1887), Lowe Hill House,
Stratford St Mary, Colchester, Essex CO7 6JX. Tel: 01206-
337239. *Hon. Secretary*, H. M. Stuchfield

MORAVIAN MISSIONS, LONDON ASSOCIATION IN AID OF
(1817), Moravian Church House, 5–7 Muswell Hill,
London NIO 3TJ. Tel: 0181-883 3409. *Secretary*, Ms J.
Morten

MOTHERS' UNION (1876), Mary Sumner House, 24 Tufton
Street, London SWIP 3RB. Tel: 0171-222 5533. *Chief
Executive*, Mrs A. Ridler

MOTOR INDUSTRY, INSTITUTE OF THE, Fanshaws,
Brickendon, Hertford SGI3 8PQ. Tel: 01992-511521.
Secretary, F. W. James

MOUNTBATTEN MEMORIAL TRUST (1979), 1 Grosvenor
Crescent, London SWIX 7EF. Tel: 0171-235 5231 ext 255.
Director, J. Boyd-Brent

MOUNTBATTEN TRUST, THE EDWINA (1960), 1
Grosvenor Crescent, London SWIX 7EF. Tel: 0171-
235 5231 ext 255. *Secretary*, J. Boyd-Brent

MULTIPLE SCLEROSIS SOCIETY (1953), 25 Effie Road,
London SW6 IEE. Tel: 0171-610 7171. *Helpline:* 0171-371
8000. *Chief Executive*, P. Cardy

MUNICIPAL ENGINEERS, ASSOCIATION OF, Institution of
Civil Engineers, Great George Street, London SWIP 3AA.
Tel: 0171-222 7722. *Director*, A. Bhogal

MUSEUMS ASSOCIATION (1889), 42 Clerkenwell Close,
London ECIR OPA. Tel: 0171-608 2933. *Director*,
M. Taylor

MUSIC HALL SOCIETY, BRITISH (1963), Brodie and
Middleton Ltd, 68 Drury Lane, London WC2B 5SP. Tel:
0171-836 3289/0. *Hon. Secretary*, Mrs D. Masterton

MUSICIANS BENEVOLENT FUND (1921), 16 Ogle Street,
London WIP 8JB. Tel: 0171-636 4481. *Secretary*,
Ms H. Faulkner

MUSICIANS, INCORPORATED SOCIETY OF (1882), 10
Stratford Place, London WIN 9AE. Tel: 0171-629 4413.
Chief Executive, N. Hoyle

MUSICIANS OF GREAT BRITAIN, ROYAL SOCIETY OF
(1738), 10 Stratford Place, London WIN 9AE. Tel: 0171-
629 6137. *Secretary*, Mrs M. Gibb

MUSIC INFORMATION CENTRE, BRITISH (1967), 10
Stratford Place, London WIN 9AE. Tel: 0171-499 8567.
Directors, M. Greenall; T. Morgan

MUSIC SOCIETIES, NATIONAL FEDERATION OF (1935),
Francis House, Francis Street, London SWIP IDE. Tel:
0171-828 7320. *Chief Executive*, R. Jones

NABC - CLUBS FOR YOUNG PEOPLE (1925), 371
Kennington Lane, London SEII 5QY. Tel: 0171-793 0787.
National Director, C. Groves

NACRO (NATIONAL ASSOCIATION FOR THE CARE AND
RESETTLEMENT OF OFFENDERS) (1966), 169 Clapham
Road, London SW9 OPU. Tel: 0171-582 6500. *Director
(acting)*, Ms H. Edwards

NATIONAL BENEVOLENT INSTITUTION (1812), 61
Bayswater Road, London W2 3PG. Tel: 0171-723 0021.
Secretary, Gp Capt. D. St J. Homer, MVO

NATIONAL COUNCIL FOR VOLUNTARY ORGANIZATIONS
(1919), Regent's Wharf, 8 All Saints Street, London
NI 9RL. Tel: 0171-713 6161. *Chief Executive*, S. Etherington

NATIONAL COUNCIL OF WOMEN OF GREAT BRITAIN
(1895), 36 Danbury Street, London NI 8JU. Tel: 0171-
354 2395. *President*, Mrs J. Clark

NATIONAL DEMOCRATS (formerly National Front) (1967),
PO Box 2269, London E6 3RF. Tel: 0181-471 6872.
Chairman, I. Anderson

NATIONAL EXTENSION COLLEGE (1963), 18 Brooklands
Avenue, Cambridge CB2 2HN. Tel: 01223-316644.
Director, Dr R. Morpeth

NATIONAL LISTENING LIBRARY, 12 Lant Street, London
SEI IQH. Tel: 0171-407 9417. *Executive Director*,
G. A. Hepworth

NATIONAL SOCIETY, THE (1811), Church House, Great
Smith Street, London SWIP 3NZ. Tel: 0171-222 1672. For
promoting religious education. *General Secretary*,
G. Duncan

NATIONAL SOCIETY FOR THE PREVENTION OF CRUELTY
TO CHILDREN (NSPCC) (1884), 42 Curtain Road,
London EC2A 3NH. Tel: 0171-825 2500. *Director*, J.
Harding

NATIONAL TRUST, THE (1895), 36 Queen Anne's Gate,
London SWIH 9AS. Tel: 0171-222 9251. *Chairman*, C.
Nunneley; *Director-General*, M. Drury

NATIONAL TRUST FOR SCOTLAND (1931), 5 Charlotte
Square, Edinburgh EH2 4DU. Tel: 0131-226 5922.
Chairman, H. L. Melville; *Director*, D. Dow, CB

NATIONAL UNION OF STUDENTS (1922), Nelson Mandela House, 461 Holloway Road, London N7 6LJ. Tel: 0171-272 8900. *National President*, J. Murphy

NATIONAL VIEWERS' AND LISTENERS' ASSOCIATION (1964), All Saints House, High Street, Colchester CO1 1UG. Tel: 01206-561155. *General Secretary*, N. Beyer

NATIONAL WOMEN'S REGISTER (1960), 3A Vulcan House, Vulcan Road North, Norwich NR6 6AQ. Tel: 01603-406767. *National Organizer*, Mrs B. Hicks

NATURALISTS' ASSOCIATION, BRITISH (1905), 1 Bracken Mews, London E4 7UT. *Hon. Membership Secretary*, Mrs Y. H. Griffiths

NATURE CONSERVATION, ROYAL SOCIETY FOR, *see* RSNC

NAUTICAL RESEARCH, SOCIETY FOR (1911), c/o National Maritime Museum, Greenwich, London SE10 9NF. *Hon. Secretary*, Lt.-Cdr. W. J. R. Gardner

NAVAL ARCHITECTS, ROYAL INSTITUTION OF (1860), 10 Upper Belgrave Street, London SW1X 8BQ. Tel: 0171-235 4622. *Secretary*, J. Rosewarn

NAVAL, MILITARY AND AIR FORCE BIBLE SOCIETY (1780), Radstock House, 3 Eccleston Street, London SW1W 9LZ. Tel: 0171-730 2155. *General Secretary*, J. M. Hines

NAVIGATION, ROYAL INSTITUTE OF (1947), 1 Kensington Gore, London SW7 2AT. Tel: 0171-589 5021. *Director*, Gp Capt. D. W. Broughton, MBE

NAVY RECORDS SOCIETY (1893), Barclays De Zoete Wedd Ltd, Ground Floor, Minster House, 12 Arthur Street, London EC4R 9AB. *Hon. Secretary*, A. J. McMillan

NCH ACTION FOR CHILDREN (1869), 85 Highbury Park, London N5 1UD. Tel: 0171-226 2033. *Chief Executive*, D. Mead

NEEDLEWORK, ROYAL SCHOOL OF (1872), Apartment 12A, Hampton Court Palace, East Molesey, Surrey KT8 9AU. Tel: 0181-943 1432. *Principal*, Mrs E. Elvin

NEWCOMEN SOCIETY (1920), The Science Museum, London SW7 2DD. Tel: 0171-589 1793. For the study of the history of engineering and technology. *Executive Secretary*, C. Ellam

NEWSPAPER PRESS FUND (1864), Dickens House, 35 Wathen Road, Dorking, Surrey RH4 1JY. Tel: 01306-887511. *Director*, P. W. Evans

NEWSTRAID BENEVOLENT SOCIETY (1839), PO Box 306, Dunmow, Essex CM6 1HY. Tel: 01371-874198. *President*, A. Cameron

NOISE ABATEMENT SOCIETY (1959), PO Box 518, Eynsford, Dartford, Kent DA4 0LL. Tel: 01322-862789. *Chairman*, J. Connell, OBE

NON-SMOKERS, NATIONAL SOCIETY OF, *see* QUIT

NORWOOD CHILD CARE (1795), Norwood House, Harmony Way, Victoria Road, London NW4 2DR. Tel: 0181-203 3030. *Executive Director*, S. Brier

NOTARIES' SOCIETY (1907), 7 Lower Brook Street, Ipswich IP4 1AF. Tel: 01473-214762. *Secretary*, A. G. Dunford

NUCLEAR ENERGY SOCIETY, BRITISH (1962), 1–7 Great George Street, London SW1P 3AA. Tel: 0171-222 7722. *Executive Officer*, A. Tillbrook

NUFFIELD FOUNDATION, THE (1943), 28 Bedford Square, London WC1B 3EG. Tel: 0171-631 0566. *Director*, A. Tomei

NUFFIELD PROVINCIAL HOSPITALS TRUST (1939), 59 New Cavendish Street, London W1M 7RD. Tel: 0171-485 6632. *Secretary*, Prof. A. Maynard

NURSES' NATIONAL HOME, RETIRED (1934), Riverside Avenue, Bournemouth BH7 7EE. Tel: 01202-396418. *Chairman*, G. J. Rowlett

NURSES, ROYAL NATIONAL PENSION FUND FOR, Burdett House, 15 Buckingham Street, London WC2N 6ED. Tel: 0171-839 6785. *General Manager*, V. G. West

NURSING, MIDWIFERY AND HEALTH VISITING, ENGLISH NATIONAL BOARD FOR, Victory House, 170 Tottenham Court Road, London W1P 0HA. Tel: 0171-388 3131. *Chief Executive Officer*, A. P. Smith

NURSING, MIDWIFERY AND HEALTH VISITING, UK CENTRAL COUNCIL FOR, 23 Portland Place, London W1N 4JT. Tel: 0171-637 7181. *Registrar and Chief Executive*, Ms S. Norman

NURSING, MIDWIFERY AND HEALTH VISITING, WELSH NATIONAL BOARD FOR, Floor 13, Pearl Assurance House, Greyfriars Road, Cardiff CF1 3AG. Tel: 01222-395535. *Chief Executive*, D. A. Ravey

NURSING, MIDWIFERY AND HEALTH VISITING FOR NORTHERN IRELAND, NATIONAL BOARD FOR, Centre House, 79 Chichester Street, Belfast BT1 4JE. Tel: 01232-238152. *Chief Executive*, Dr O. D'A. Slevin

NURSING, MIDWIFERY AND HEALTH VISITING FOR SCOTLAND, NATIONAL BOARD FOR, 22 Queen Street, Edinburgh EH2 1NT. Tel: 0131-226 7371. *Chief Executive*, Mrs L. Mitchell

NURSING, ROYAL COLLEGE OF (1916), 20 Cavendish Square, London W1M 0AB. Tel: 0171-409 3333. *General Secretary*, Miss C. Hancock

NUTRITION FOUNDATION, BRITISH (1967), High Holborn House, 52–54 High Holborn, London WC1V 6RQ. Tel: 0171-404 6504. *Director-General*, Dr B. A. Wharton

NUTRITION SOCIETY (1941), 10 Cambridge Court, 210 Shepherds Bush Road, London W6 7NJ. Tel: 0171-602 0228. *Hon. Secretary*, Dr R. F. Grimble

OBSTETRICIANS AND GYNAECOLOGISTS, ROYAL COLLEGE OF (1929), 27 Sussex Place, London NW1 4RG. Tel: 0171-262 5425. *President*, Dr N. Patel; *Secretary*, P. A. Barnett

OCCUPATIONAL HEALTH AND SAFETY AGENCY, 18–20 Hill Street, Edinburgh EH2 3NB. Tel: 0131-220 4177. *Chief Executive*, Dr E. C. McCloy

OCCUPATIONAL PENSIONS ADVISORY SERVICE (1982), 11 Belgrave Road, London SW1V 1RB. Tel: 0171-233 8080. *Chief Executive (acting)*, Mrs P. A. Green

OCCUPATIONAL SAFETY AND HEALTH, INSTITUTION OF (1946), The Grange, Highfield Drive, Wigston, Leics LE18 1NN. Tel: 0116-257 1399. *Chief Executive*, J. R. Barrell, OBE

OFFICERS' ASSOCIATION, THE (1920), 48 Pall Mall, London SW1Y 5JY. Tel: 0171-930 0125. *General Secretary*, Brig. P. D. Johnson

OFFICERS' PENSIONS SOCIETY (1946), 68 South Lambeth Road, London SW8 1RL. Tel: 0171-820 9988. *General Secretary*, Maj.-Gen. P. R. F. Bonnet, CB, MBE

OIL PAINTERS, ROYAL INSTITUTE OF (1883), 17 Carlton House Terrace, London SW1Y 5BD. Tel: 0171-930 6844. *Secretary*, B. Bennett

ONE-PARENT FAMILIES, NATIONAL COUNCIL FOR, 255 Kentish Town Road, London NW5 2LX. Tel: 0171-267 1361. *Director*, Ms K. Pappenheim

OPEN-AIR MISSION, THE (1853), 19 John Street, London WC1N 2DL. Tel: 0171-405 6135. *Secretary*, A. J. Greenbank

OPEN SPACES SOCIETY (1865), 25A Bell Street, Henley-on-Thames, Oxon RG9 2BA. Tel: 01491-573535. *General Secretary*, Miss K. Ashbrook

OPERATIC AND DRAMATIC ASSOCIATION, NATIONAL (1899), NODA House, 1 Crestfield Street, London WC1H 8AU. Tel: 0171-837 5655. *General Administrator*, M. Thorburn

OPSIS (National Association for the Education, Training and Support of Blind and Partially Sighted People) (1992), Gretton House, 43 Hatton Garden, London ECIN 8EE. Tel: 0171-405 6697. *Secretary-General*, Sir Anthony Walker, KCB

OPTICAL COUNCIL, GENERAL (1958), 41 Harley Street, London WIN 2DJ. Tel: 0171-580 3898. *Registrar*, R. Wilshin

OPTOMETRISTS, COLLEGE OF, 10 Knaresborough Place, London SW5 OTG. Tel: 0171-373 7765. *Secretary*, P. D. Leigh

ORDERS AND MEDALS RESEARCH SOCIETY (1942), 123 Turnpike Link, Croydon CRO 5NU. Tel: 0181-680 2701. *General Secretary*, N. G. Gooding

ORIENTAL CERAMIC SOCIETY (1921), 30B Torrington Square, London WC1E 7LJ. Tel: 0171-636 7985. *Secretary*, Mrs J. Martin

ORNITHOLOGISTS' CLUB, SCOTTISH (1936), 21 Regent Terrace, Edinburgh EH7 5BT. Tel: 0131-556 6042. *Secretary*, Ms S. Laing

ORNITHOLOGISTS' UNION, BRITISH (1858), c/o The Natural History Museum, Akeman Street, Tring, Herts HP23 6AP. Tel: 01442-890080. *Administrative Secretary*, Mrs G. Bonham

ORNITHOLOGY, BRITISH TRUST FOR (1932), The National Centre for Ornithology, The Nunnery, Thetford, Norfolk IP24 2PU. Tel: 01842-750050. *Director of Services*, A. Elvin

ORTHOPAEDIC ASSOCIATION, BRITISH (1918), c/o The Royal College of Surgeons, 35/43 Lincoln's Inn Fields, London WC2A 3PN. Tel: 0171-405 6507. *Hon. Secretary*, I. J. Leslie, FRCS

OSTEOPATHIC MEDICINE, LONDON COLLEGE OF, 8–10 Boston Place, London NW1 6QH. Tel: 0171-262 5250. *Clinic Manager*, Ms A. Dalby

OSTEOPATHS, GENERAL COUNCIL AND REGISTER OF (1936), 56 London Street, Reading, Berks RG1 4SQ. Tel: 01734-576585. *Secretary*, Dr D. C. Weeks

OSTEOPOROSIS SOCIETY, NATIONAL (1986), PO Box 10, Radstock, Bath BA3 3YB. Tel: 01761-432472. *General Secretary*, Miss H. Wollacott

OUTWARD BOUND TRUST (1941), PO Box 1219, Windsor, Berks SL4 1XR. Tel: 01753-730060. *Director*, M. Hobbs, CBE

OVERSEAS DEVELOPMENT INSTITUTE (1960), Regent's College, Inner Circle, Regent's Park, London NW1 4NS. Tel: 0171-487 7413. *Director*, Prof. J. Howell

OVERSEAS SERVICE PENSIONERS' ASSOCIATION (1960), 138 High Street, Tonbridge, Kent TN9 1AX. Tel: 01732-363836. *Secretary*, D. F. B. Le Breton, CBE

OVERSEAS SETTLEMENT (1925), Church of England Board for Social Responsibility, Great Smith Street, London SW1P 3NZ. Tel: 0171-222 9011. *Administration Secretary*, Miss P. J. Hallett

OXFAM (1942), 274 Banbury Road, Oxford OX2 7DZ. Tel: 01865-311311. *Director*, D. Bryer, CMG

OXFORD PRESERVATION TRUST (1927), 10 Turn Again Lane, St Ebbes, Oxford OX1 1QL. Tel: 01865-242918. *Secretary*, Mrs M. Haynes

OXFORD SOCIETY (1932), 41 Wellington Square, Oxford OX1 2JF. Tel: 01865-270088. *Secretary*, Mrs M. E. Russell

PAEDIATRIC ASSOCIATION, BRITISH (1928), 5 St Andrews Place, Regents Park, London NW1 4LB. Tel: 0171-486 6151. *Hon. Secretary*, Dr K. Dodd

PAINTER-PRINTMAKERS, ROYAL SOCIETY OF (1880), Bankside Gallery, 48 Hopton Street, London SE1 9JH. Tel: 0171-928 7521. *President*, Prof. D. Carpanini; *Secretary*, Miss J. Dixey

PAINTERS IN WATER COLOURS, ROYAL INSTITUTE OF (1831), 17 Carlton House Terrace, London SW1Y 5BD. Tel: 0171-930 6844. *Secretary*, R. Spurrier

PALAEONTOLOGICAL ASSOCIATION (1957), c/o Lapworth Museum, School of Earth Sciences, University of Birmingham, Edgbaston, Birmingham B15 2TT. Tel: 0121-414 4173. *Secretary*, Dr P. Smith

PARENTS AT WORK (1985), 45 Beech Street, Barbican, London EC2Y 8AD. Tel: 0171-628 3578. *Director*, Mrs L. Daniels

PARKINSON'S DISEASE SOCIETY (1969), 22 Upper Woburn Place, London WC1H ORA. Tel: 0171-383 3513. *Chief Executive*, B. A. Brooking

PARLIAMENTARY AND SCIENTIFIC COMMITTEE (1939), 16 Great College Street, London SW1P 3RX. Tel: 0171-222 7085. *Administrative Secretary*, Dr A. Whitehouse

PASTORAL PSYCHOLOGY, GUILD OF (1936), PO Box 1107, London W3 6ZP. Tel: 0181-993 8366. *Administrator*, Mrs N. Stanley

PATENT AGENTS, CHARTERED INSTITUTE OF (1882), Staple Inn Buildings, High Holborn, London WC1V 7PZ. Tel: 0171-405 9450. *Secretary*, M. C. Ralph

PATENTEES AND INVENTORS, INSTITUTE OF (1919), Suite 505A, Triumph House, 189 Regent Street, London W1R 7WF. Tel: 0171-434 1818. *Secretary*, R. Magnus

PATHOLOGISTS, ROYAL COLLEGE OF, 2 Carlton House Terrace, London SW1Y 5AF. Tel: 0171-930 5861. *President*, Prof. A. J. Bellingham; *Secretary*, K. Lockyer

PATIENTS ASSOCIATION (1963), 8 Guilford Street, London WC1N 1DT. Tel: 0171-242 3460. *Chief Executive*, G. Howland

PDSA (PEOPLE'S DISPENSARY FOR SICK ANIMALS) (1917), Whitechapel Way, Priorslee, Telford, Shropshire TF2 9PQ. Tel: 01952-290999. *Director-General*, M. R. Curtis, MBE

PEACE COUNCIL, NATIONAL (1908), 88 Islington High Street, London N1 8EG. Tel: 0171-354 5200. *Co-ordinator*, Ms L. Peck

PEAK AND NORTHERN FOOTPATHS SOCIETY (1894), 15 Parkfield Drive, Tyldesley, Manchester M29 8NR. Tel: 0161-790 4383. *Hon. General Secretary*, D. Taylor

PEARSON'S HOLIDAY FUND, PO Box 123, Bishops Waltham, Southampton SO32 1ZE. Tel: 01489-893260. *General Secretary*, R. Heasman

PEDESTRIANS ASSOCIATION (1929), 126 Aldersgate Street, London EC1A 4JQ. Tel: 0171-490 0750. *Chairman*, Ms F. Lawson

PEN, INTERNATIONAL (1921), 9–10 Charterhouse Buildings, Goswell Road, London EC1M 7AT. Tel: 0171-253 4308. English Centre, 7 Dilke Street, London SW3 4JE. Tel: 0171-352 6303. World association of writers. *International Secretary*, A. Blokh

PENSION FUNDS LTD, NATIONAL ASSOCIATION OF (1923), 12–18 Grosvenor Gardens, London SW1W ODH. Tel: 0171-730 0585. *Director-General*, Dr A. Robinson

PERFORMING RIGHT SOCIETY LTD (1914), 29–33 Berners Street, London WIP 4AA. Tel: 0171-580 5544. *Chief Executive*, J. Hutchinson

PERIODICAL PUBLISHERS ASSOCIATION LTD (1913), Queens House, 28 Kingsway, London WC2B 6JR. Tel: 0171-404 4166. *Chief Executive*, I. Locks

PESTALOZZI CHILDREN'S VILLAGE TRUST (1959), Sedlescombe, Battle, E. Sussex TN33 0RR. Tel: 01424-870444. *Director*, M. Phillips

PETROLEUM, INSTITUTE OF (1913), 61 New Cavendish Street, London WIM 8AR. Tel: 0171-467 7100. *Director-General*, I. Ward

PHARMACEUTICAL SOCIETY OF GREAT BRITAIN, ROYAL (1841), 1 Lambeth High Street, London SEI 7JN. Tel:0171-735 9141. *Secretary and Registrar*, J. Ferguson, OBE

PHARMACOLOGICAL SOCIETY, BRITISH (1931), 16 Angel Gate, City Road, London EC1V 2PT. Tel: 0171-417 0113. *Hon. General Secretary*, Prof. N. G. Bowery

PHILOLOGICAL SOCIETY (1842), School of Oriental and African Studies, University of London, Thornhaugh Street, London WC1H 0XG. Tel: 0171-637 2388. *Hon. Secretary*, Prof. R. J. Hayward

PHILOSOPHY, ROYAL INSTITUTE OF (1925), 14 Gordon Square, London WC1H 0AG. Tel: 0171-387 4130. *Director*, Prof. A. Phillips Griffiths

PHOTOGRAPHY, BRITISH INSTITUTE OF PROFESSIONAL (1901), Fox Talbot House, Amwell End, Ware, Herts SG12 9HN. Tel: 01920-464011. *Chief Executive*, A. Mair

PHYSICAL RECREATION, CENTRAL COUNCIL OF (1935), Francis House, Francis Street, London SWIP IDE. Tel: 0171-828 3163/4. *General Secretary*, M. Denton

PHYSICIANS, ROYAL COLLEGE OF (1518), 11 St Andrews Place, London 4LE. Tel: 0171-935 1174. *President*, Prof. Sir Leslie Turnberg; *Secretary*, D. B. Lloyd

PHYSICIANS AND SURGEONS OF GLASGOW, ROYAL COLLEGE OF (1599), 232–242 St Vincent Street, Glasgow G2 5RJ. Tel: 0141-221 6072. *President*, Prof. N. Mackay; *Hon. Secretary*, Dr S. Slater

PHYSICIANS OF EDINBURGH, ROYAL COLLEGE OF (1681), 9 Queen Street, Edinburgh EH2 1JQ. Tel: 0131-225 7324. *President*, Dr J. D. Cash; *Secretary*, Dr J. Thomas

PHYSICS AND ENGINEERING IN MEDICINE AND BIOLOGY, INSTITUTION OF, 4 Campleshon Road, York YO2 1PE. Tel: 01904 610821. *Hon. Secretary*, Dr D. Pearson

PHYSICS, INSTITUTE OF (1874), 76 Portland Place, London WIN 4AA. Tel: 0171-470 4800. *Chief Executive*, Dr A. D. W. Jones

PHYSIOLOGICAL SOCIETY (1876), PO Box 11319, London WC1E 7JF. Tel: 0171-631 1456. *Hon. Secretary*, Prof. P. Stanfield

PHYSIOTHERAPY, CHARTERED SOCIETY OF (1894), 14 Bedford Row, London WC1R 4ED. Tel: 0171-306 6666. *Secretary*, T. Simon

PIG ASSOCIATION, BRITISH (1884), 7 Rickmansworth Road, Watford WD1 7HE. Tel: 01923-234377/230421. *Chief Executive*, G. E. Welsh

PILGRIM TRUST (1930), Fielden House, Little College Street, London SW1P 3SH. Tel: 0171-222 4723. *Secretary*, Miss G. Nayler

PILGRIMS OF GREAT BRITAIN (1902), c/o 32 Old Queen Street, London SW1H 9HP. Tel: 0171-222 0232. *Hon. Secretary*, M. P. S. Barton

PLANT ENGINEERS, INSTITUTION OF, 77 Great Peter Street, London SW1P 2EZ. Tel: 0171-233 2855. *Secretary*, P. F. Tye

PLAYING FIELDS ASSOCIATION, NATIONAL (1925), 25 Ovington Square, London SW3 1LQ. Tel: 0171-584 6445. *Director*, Ms E. Davies

PLUNKETT FOUNDATION (1919), 23 Hanborough Business Park, Long Hanborough, Oxford OX8 8LH. Tel: 01993-883636. *Director*, E. Parnell

POETRY SOCIETY (1909), 22 Betterton Street, London WC2H 9BU. Tel: 0171-240 4810. *Director*, C. Meade

POLICY STUDIES INSTITUTE (1978), 100 Park Village East, London NW1 3SR. Tel: 0171-468 0468. *Director*, Ms P. Meadows

POLIO FELLOWSHIP, BRITISH (1939), Ground Floor, Unit A, Eagle Office Centre, The Runway, South Ruislip, Middx HA4 6SE. Tel: 0181-842 1898. *General Secretary*, M. Drake

POLITE SOCIETY, THE (1986), 6 Norman Avenue, Henley-on-Thames, Oxon RG9 1SG. Tel: 01491-572794. *Hon. Secretary*, Miss G. Mackenzie

PORTRAIT PAINTERS, ROYAL SOCIETY OF (1891), 17 Carlton House Terrace, London SW1Y 5BD. Tel: 0171-930 6844. *Secretary*, P. Brason

POST OFFICE USERS' NATIONAL COUNCIL (1970), 6 Hercules Road, London SE1 7DN. Tel: 0171-928 9458. *Secretary*, K. Hall

PRAYER BOOK SOCIETY (1975), St James Garlickhythe, Garlick Hill, London EC4V 2AL. Tel: 0181-958 8769. *Hon. Secretary*, Mrs M. Thompson

PRECEPTORS, COLLEGE OF (1846), Coppice Row, Theydon Bois, Epping, Essex CM16 7DN. Tel: 01992-812727. *Chief Executive Officer*, T. Wheatley

PRE-SCHOOL LEARNING ALLIANCE, 69 Kings Cross Road, London WC1X 9LL. Tel: 0171-833 0991. *Chief Executive Officer*, Ms M. Lochrie

PRESS UNION, COMMONWEALTH (1909), 17 Fleet Street, London EC4Y 1AA. Tel: 0171-583 7733. *Director*, R. MacKichan

PREVENTION OF ACCIDENTS, ROYAL SOCIETY FOR THE (1916), Edgbaston Park, 353 Bristol Road, Birmingham B5 7ST. Tel: 0121-248 2000. *Chief Executive*, A. Edwards

PRINCESS LOUISE SCOTTISH HOSPITAL (Erskine Hospital) (1916), Bishopton, Renfrewshire PA7 5PU. Tel: 0141-812 1100. For disabled ex-servicemen and women. *Chief Executive*, Col. M. F. Gibson, OBE

PRINCESS ROYAL TRUST FOR CARERS (1990), 16 Byward Street, London EC3R 5BA. Tel: 0171-480 7788. *Chief Executive*, Dr E. Nelson

PRINCE'S SCOTTISH YOUTH BUSINESS TRUST, THE (1989), 6th Floor, Mercantile Chambers, 53 Bothwell Street, Glasgow G2 6TS. Tel: 0141-248 4999. *Director*, D. W. Cooper

PRINCE'S TRUST, THE (1976) and THE ROYAL JUBILEE TRUSTS (1935, 1977), 18 Park Square East, London NW1 4LH. Tel: 0171-543 1234. *Director*, T. Shebbeare, CVO

PRINCE'S YOUTH BUSINESS TRUST, THE, 18 Park Square East, London NW1 4LH. Tel: 0171-543 1234. *Chief Executive*, R. Street

PRINTERS' CHARITABLE CORPORATION (1827), 7 Cantelupe Mews, Cantelupe Road, East Grinstead, W. Sussex RH19 3BG. Tel: 01342-318882. *Director*, H. J. Court

PRINTING HISTORICAL SOCIETY (1964), St Bride Institute, Bride Lane, London EC4Y 8EE. *Hon. Secretary*, J. H. Bowman

PRINTING, INSTITUTE OF (1961), 8 Lonsdale Gardens, Tunbridge Wells, Kent TN1 1NU. Tel: 01892-538118. *Secretary-General*, D. Freeland

PRISONERS ABROAD (1978), 72–82 Rosebery Avenue, London EC1R 4RR. Tel: 0171-833 3467. *Director*, C. Laurenzi

PRISON VISITORS, NATIONAL ASSOCIATION OF (1922), 46B Hartington Street, Bedford MK41 7RP. Tel:01234-359763. *General Secretary*, Mrs A. G. McKenna

PRIVATE LIBRARIES ASSOCIATION (1957), Ravelston, South View Road, Pinner, Middlx HA5 3YD. *Hon. Secretary*, F. Broomhead

PROCURATORS IN GLASGOW, ROYAL FACULTY OF (1600), 12 Nelson Mandela Place, Glasgow G2 1BT. Tel: 0141-552 3422. *Clerk*, A. J. Campbell

PROFESSIONAL CLASSES AID COUNCIL (1921), 10 St Christopher's Place, London W1M 6HY. Tel: 0171-935 0641. *Secretary*

PROFESSIONAL ENGINEERS, UK ASSOCIATION OF (1969), Hayes Court, West Common Road, Bromley BR2 7AU. Tel: 0181-462 7755. *National Secretary*, J. M. Dalgleish

PROFESSIONS SUPPLEMENTARY TO MEDICINE, COUNCIL FOR, Park House, 184 Kennington Park Road, London SE11 4BU. Tel: 0171-582 0866. *Registrar (acting)*, Dr P. Burley

PROFESSIONAL FOOTBALLERS' ASSOCIATION, 2 Oxford Court, Bishopsgate, Manchester M2 3WQ. Tel: 0161-236 0575. *Chief Executive*, G. Taylor

PROTECTION OF UNBORN CHILDREN, SOCIETY FOR THE (1967), Phyllis Bowman House, 5–6 St Matthew Street, London SW1P 2JT. Tel: 0171-222 5845. *National Director*, J. Smeaton

PROTESTANT ALLIANCE (1845), 77 Ampthill Road, Flitwick, Bedford MK45 1BD. Tel: 01525-712348. *General Secretary*, Dr S. J. Scott-Pearson

PSORIASIS ASSOCIATION (1968), 7 Milton Street, Northampton NN2 7JG. Tel: 01604-711129. *National Secretary*, Mrs L. Henley

PSYCHIATRISTS, ROYAL COLLEGE OF (1971), 17 Belgrave Square, London SW1X 8PG. Tel: 0171-235 2351. *President*, Dr R. Kendell; *Secretary*, Mrs V. Cameron

PSYCHICAL RESEARCH, SOCIETY FOR (1882), 49 Marloes Road, London W8 6LA. Tel: 0171-937 8984. *Secretary*, Ms E. J. O'Keeffe

PSYCHOLOGICAL SOCIETY, BRITISH (1901), St Andrews House, 48 Princess Road East, Leicester LE1 7DR. Tel: 0116-254 9568. *Executive Secretary*, C. V. Newman PH.D.

PUBLIC FINANCE AND ACCOUNTANCY, CHARTERED INSTITUTE OF (1885), 3 Robert Street, London WC2N 6BH. Tel: 0171-543 5600. *Director*, N. P. Hepworth, OBE

PUBLIC HEALTH AND HYGIENE, ROYAL INSTITUTE OF (1937), 28 Portland Place, London W1N 4DE. Tel: 0171-580 2731. *Secretary*, Gp Capt. R. A. Smith

PUBLIC RELATIONS, INSTITUTE OF (1948), The Old Trading House, 15 Northburgh Street, London EC1V 0PR. Tel: 0171-253 5151. *Executive Director*, J. B. Lavelle

PUBLIC TEACHERS OF LAW, SOCIETY OF (1908), Faculty of Law, Kings College London, Strand, London WC2R 2LS. Tel: 0171-836 5454. *Hon. Secretary*, Prof. D Hayton

PURCHASING AND SUPPLY, CHARTERED INSTITUTE OF (1967), Easton House, Easton on the Hill, Stamford, Lincs PE9 3NZ. Tel: 01780-56777. *Director-General*, P. Thomson

PURE WATER ASSOCIATION, NATIONAL (1960), Meridan, Cae Goody Lane, Ellesmere, Shropshire SY12 9DW. Tel: 01691-623015. *Secretary*, N. Brugge

QUAKER SOCIAL RESPONSIBILITY AND EDUCATION, Friends House, 173–177 Euston Road, London NW1 2BJ. Tel: 0171-387 3601. *General Secretary*, Ms B. Smith

QUALITY ASSURANCE, INSTITUTE OF, PO Box 712, 61 Southwark Street, London SE1 1SB. Tel: 0171-401 7227. *Secretary-General*, D. G. Campbell

QUARRIERS HOMES (1871), Bridge of Weir, Renfrewshire PA11 3SA. Tel: 01505-612224. *Director*, G. E. Lee

QUARRYING, INSTITUTE OF (1917), 7 Regent Street, Nottingham NG1 5BS. Tel: 0115-941 1315. *Secretary*, M. J. Arthur

QUEEN ELIZABETH'S FOUNDATION FOR DISABLED PEOPLE (1967), Leatherhead Court, Leatherhead, Surrey KT22 0BN. Tel: 01372-842204. *Director*, M. B. Clark, PH.D.

QUEEN'S ENGLISH SOCIETY, THE (1972), 104 Drive Mansions, Fulham Road, London SW6 5JH. Tel: 0171-371 7530. *Hon. Membership Secretary*, M. Plumbe

QUEEN'S NURSING INSTITUTE (1887), 3 Albemarle Way, London EC1V 4JB. Tel: 0171-490 4227. *Director*, Mrs P. Bagnall

QUEEN VICTORIA CLERGY FUND (1897), Church House, Dean's Yard, London SW1P 3NZ. Tel: 0171-222 5261. *Secretary*, C. D. L. Menzies

QUEEN VICTORIA SCHOOL (1908), Dunblane, Perthshire FK15 0JY. Tel: 01786-822288. *Headmaster*, B. Raine

QUEKETT MICROSCOPICAL CLUB (1865), Flat 3, Romagna, 101 Truro Road, London N22 4DL. *Hon. Business Secretary*, Miss P. Hamer

QUIT (1926), Victory House, 170 Tottenham Court Road, London W1P 0HA. Tel: 0171-388 5775. *Chief Executive*, P. McCabe

RADAR (ROYAL ASSOCIATION FOR DISABILITY AND REHABILITATION) (1977), 12 City Forum, 250 City Road, London EC1V 8AF. Tel: 0171-250 3222. *Director*, B. Massie, OBE

RADIOLOGISTS, ROYAL COLLEGE OF (1934), 38 Portland Place, London W1N 4JQ. Tel: 0171-636 4432. *President*, Dr M. J. Brindle; *Secretary*, A. J. Cowles

RADIOLOGY, BRITISH INSTITUTE OF (1897), 36 Portland Place, London W1N 4AT. Tel: 0171-580 4317. *Chief Executive*, Ms M. A. Piggott

RAIL USERS' CONSULTATIVE COMMITTEE, CENTRAL (1948), Clements House, 14–18 Gresham Street, London EC2V 7NL. Tel: 0171-505 9090. *Secretary*, M. Patterson

RAILWAY AND CANAL HISTORICAL SOCIETY, 17 Clumber Crescent North, The Park, Nottingham NG7 1EY. Tel: 0115-941 4844. *Hon. Secretary*, G. H. R. Gwatkin

RAILWAY BENEVOLENT INSTITUTION (1858), Pullman House, Railway Technical Centre, London Road, Derby DE24 8UP. Tel: 01332-264205. *Director*, R. B. Boiling

RAINER FOUNDATION (1876), 89 Blackheath Hill, London SE10 8TJ. Tel: 0181-694 9497. Provides community-based services for young people who are homeless, offending or in difficulty with their families. *Director*, Ms N. Varma

RAMBLERS' ASSOCIATION (1935), 1–5 Wandsworth Road, London SW8 2XX. Tel: 0171-582 6878. *Director,* A. Mattingly

RARE BREEDS SURVIVAL TRUST (1973), National Agricultural Centre, Kenilworth, Warks CV8 2LG. Tel: 01203-696551. *Executive Director,* G. L. H. Alderson

RATHBONE COMMUNITY INDUSTRY (1919), 1st Floor, The Excalibur Building, 77 Whitworth Street, Manchester MI 6EZ. Tel: 0161-236 5358. Advice Line: 0161-236 1877. Helps people with learning difficulties. *Chief Executive,* Ms A. Weinstock, CBE

RECORD SOCIETY, SCOTTISH (1897), Department of Scottish History, University of Glasgow, Glasgow G12 8QH. Tel: 0141-339 8855 ext 5682. *Hon. Secretary,* J. Kirk, PH.D.

RECORDS ASSOCIATION, BRITISH (1932), 18 Padbury Court, London E2 7EH. Tel: 0171-729 1415. *Hon. Secretary,* Mrs E. Hughes

RED CROSS SOCIETY, BRITISH, *see* BRITISH RED CROSS

RED POLL CATTLE SOCIETY (1888), The Market Hill, Woodbridge, Suffolk IP12 4LU. Tel: 01394-380643. *Secretary,* P. Ryder-Davies

REFRIGERATION, INSTITUTE OF (1899), Kelvin House, 76 Mill Lane, Carshalton, Surrey SM5 2JR. Tel: 0181-647 7033. *Secretary,* M. J. Horlick

REFUGEE COUNCIL, BRITISH (1981), Bondway House, 3/9 Bondway, London SW8 1SJ. Tel: 0171-820 3000. *Director,* M. Hardwick

REGIONAL STUDIES ASSOCIATION (1965), Wharfdale Projects, 15 Micawber Street, London N1 7TB. Tel: 0171-490 1128. *Director,* Mrs S. Hardy

REGULAR FORCES EMPLOYMENT ASSOCIATION (1885), 49 Pall Mall, London SW1Y 5JG. Tel: 0171-321 2011. *Chief Executive,* Maj.-Gen. M. F. L. Shellard, CBE

RELATE: NATIONAL MARRIAGE GUIDANCE (1938), Herbert Gray College, Little Church Street, Rugby, Warks CV21 3AP. Tel: 01788-573241. *Director,* Ms S. Bowler

RENT OFFICERS AND RENTAL VALUES, INSTITUTE OF (1966), Beaufort House, Hamble Lane, Bursledon, Southampton SO31 8BR. Tel: 01703-403716. *General Secretary,* A. E. Corcoran

RESEARCH DEFENCE SOCIETY (1908), 58 Great Marlborough Street, London WIV 1DD. Tel: 0171-287 2818. *Executive Director,* Dr M. Matfield

RESIDENTS' ASSOCIATIONS, NATIONAL UNION OF (1921), 35 Clement Way, Upminster, Essex RM14 2NX. Tel: 014024-42751. *General Secretary,* Mrs B. Reith

RETIREMENT PENSIONS ASSOCIATIONS, NATIONAL FEDERATION OF (1938), 14 St Peter Street, Blackburn BB2 2HD. Tel: 01254-52606. *General Secretary,* R. Stansfield

REVENUES, RATING AND VALUATION, INSTITUTE OF (1882), 41 Doughty Street, London WC1N 2LF. Tel: 0171-831 3505. *Director,* C. Farrington

RICHARD III SOCIETY (1924), 4 Oakley Street, London SW3 5NN. Tel: 0171-351 3391. *Secretary,* Miss E. M. Nokes

ROAD SAFETY OFFICERS, INSTITUTE OF (1971), 31 Heather Grove, Hollingworth, via Hyde, Cheshire SK14 8JL. Tel: 0161-474 4876. *Secretary,* B. Wilkinson

ROAD TRANSPORT ENGINEERS, INSTITUTE OF (1945), 22 Greencoat Place, London SW1P 1PR. Tel: 0171-630 1111. *Chief Executive,* A. F. Stroud

ROMAN STUDIES, SOCIETY FOR THE PROMOTION OF (1910), 31–34 Gordon Square, London WC1H 0PP. Tel: 0171-387 8157. *Secretary,* Dr H. M. Cockle

ROTARY INTERNATIONAL IN GREAT BRITAIN AND IRELAND (1914), Kinwarton Road, Alcester, Warks B49 6BP. Tel: 01789-765411. *Secretary,* D. Morehen

ROUND TABLES OF GREAT BRITAIN AND IRELAND, NATIONAL ASSOCIATION OF (1927), Marchesi House, 4 Embassy Drive, Edgbaston, Birmingham B15 1TP. Tel: 0121-456 4402. *General Secretary,* R. H. Renold

ROYAL AIR FORCE BENEVOLENT FUND (1919), 67 Portland Place, London W1N 4AR. Tel: 0171-580 8343. *Controller,* Air Chief Marshal Sir Roger Palin, KCB, OBE

ROYAL AIR FORCES ASSOCIATION (1943), 43 Grove Park Road, London W4 3RX. Tel: 0181-994 8504. *Secretary-General,* J. G. Hargreaves, CBE

ROYAL ALEXANDRA AND ALBERT SCHOOL (1758), Gatton Park, Reigate, Surrey RH2 0TW. Tel: 01737-642576. *Secretary,* Wg Cdr. N. J. Wright

ROYAL ALFRED SEAFARERS' SOCIETY (1865), Weston Acres, Woodmansterne Lane, Banstead, Surrey SM7 3HB. Tel: 01737-352231. *General Secretary,* A. R. Quinton

ROYAL ARMOURED CORPS WAR MEMORIAL BENEVOLENT FUND (1946), c/o RHQ RTR, Bovington Camp, Wareham, Dorset BH20 6JA. Tel: 01929-403331. *Secretary,* Maj. A. Henzie, MBE (retd)

ROYAL ARTILLERY ASSOCIATION, Artillery House, Front Parade, Royal Artillery Barracks, Woolwich, London SE18 4BH. Tel: 0181-781 3003. *General Secretary,* Lt.-Col. M. J. Darmody

ROYAL ASIATIC SOCIETY (1823), 60 Queen's Gardens, London W2 3AF. Tel: 0171-724 4741/2. *Secretary,* Miss L. Collins

ROYAL BRITISH LEGION, *see* BRITISH LEGION, ROYAL

ROYAL CALEDONIAN SCHOOLS (1815), Aldenham Road, Bushey, Watford, Herts WD2 3TS. Tel: 01923-226642. *Chief Executive,* J. Horsfield

ROYAL CELTIC SOCIETY (1820), 23 Rutland Street, Edinburgh EH1 2RN. Tel: 0131-228 6449. *Secretary,* J. G. Cameron, WS

ROYAL CHORAL SOCIETY (1871), Unit 9, 92 Lots Road, London SW10 0QD. Tel: 0171-376 3718. *Administrator,* G. Tonge

ROYAL ENGINEERS ASSOCIATION, RHQ Royal Engineers, Brompton Barracks, Chatham, Kent ME4 4UG. Tel: 01634-847005. *Controller,* Lt.-Col. J. W. Ray (retd)

ROYAL ENGINEERS, INSTITUTION OF (1875), Brompton Barracks, Chatham, Kent ME4 4UG. Tel: 01634-842669. *Secretary,* Col. R. I. Reive, OBE

ROYAL HIGHLAND AND AGRICULTURAL SOCIETY OF SCOTLAND (1784), Royal Highland Centre, Ingliston, Edinburgh EH28 8NF. Tel: 0131-333 2444. *Secretary,* J. R. Good

ROYAL HORTICULTURAL SOCIETY (1804), PO Box 313, 80 Vincent Square, London SW1P 2PE. Tel: 0171-834 4333. *Secretary,* D. P. Hearn

ROYAL HOSPITAL FOR NEURO-DISABILITY (1854), West Hill, London SW15 3SW. Tel: 0181-780 4500. *Chief Executive,* V. J. Beauchamp

ROYAL HUMANE SOCIETY (1774), Brettenham House, Lancaster Place, London WC2E 7EP. Tel: 0171-836 8155. *Secretary,* Maj.-Gen. C. Tyler, CB

ROYAL INSTITUTION, THE (1799), 21 Albemarle Street, London W1X 4BS. Tel: 0171-409 2992. *Director,* Prof. P. Day, FRS

ROYAL LIFE SAVING SOCIETY UK (1891), Mountbatten House, Studley, Warks B80 7NN. Tel: 01527-853943. *Director-General,* S. Lear

ROYAL LITERARY FUND (1790), 144 Temple Chambers, Temple Avenue, London EC4Y 0DA. Tel: 0171-353 7150. *Secretary,* Mrs F. M. Clark

ROYAL MEDICAL BENEVOLENT FUND (1836), 24 King's Road, London SW19 8QN. Tel: 0181-540 9194. *Secretary,* Mrs G. A. R. Wells

ROYAL MEDICAL SOCIETY (1737), Students Centre, 5/5 Bristo Square, Edinburgh EH8 9AL. Tel: 0131-650 2672. *Secretary,* C. Parsons

ROYAL MICROSCOPICAL SOCIETY (1839), 37–38 St Clements, Oxford OX4 1AJ. Tel: 01865-248768. *Administrator,* P. B. Hirst

ROYAL MUSICAL ASSOCIATION (1874), Department of Music, The University of Leeds, Leeds LS2 9JT. Tel: 0113-2332579. *President,* J. Rushton

ROYAL NATIONAL INSTITUTE FOR THE BLIND (1868), 224 Great Portland Street, London W1N 6AA. Tel: 0171-388 1266. *Director-General,* I. Bruce

ROYAL NATIONAL LIFEBOAT INSTITUTION (1824), West Quay Road, Poole, Dorset BH15 1HZ. Tel: 01202-663000. *Director,* B. Miles, CBE, RD

ROYAL NAVAL AND ROYAL MARINES CHILDREN'S TRUST (1834), HMS Nelson, Portsmouth PO1 3HH. Tel: 01705-817435. *Secretary,* Mrs M. Bateman

ROYAL NAVAL ASSOCIATION (1950), 82 Chelsea Manor Street, London SW3 5QJ. Tel: 0171-352 6764. *General Secretary,* Capt. R. McQueen

ROYAL NAVAL BENEVOLENT SOCIETY (1739), 1 Fleet Street, London EC4Y 1BD. Tel: 0171-353 4080 ext 471. *Secretary,* Cdr. P. J. F. Moore

ROYAL NAVAL BENEVOLENT TRUST (1922), Castaway House, 311 Twyford Avenue, Portsmouth PO2 8PE. Tel: 01705-690112. *Chief Executive,* Cdr. J. Owens

ROYAL NAVY OFFICERS, ASSOCIATION OF (1920), 70 Porchester Terrace, London W2 3TP. Tel: 0171-402 5231. *Secretary,* Lt.-Cdr. I. M. P. Coombes

ROYAL OVER-SEAS LEAGUE (1910), Over-Seas House, Park Place, St James's Street, London SW1A 1LR. Tel: 0171-408 0214. *Director-General,* R. F. Newell

ROYAL PATRIOTIC FUND CORPORATION (1854), 40 Queen Anne's Gate, London SW1H 9AP. Tel: 0171-233 1894. *Secretary,* Brig. T. G. Williams, CBE

ROYAL PHILATELIC SOCIETY (1869), 41 Devonshire Place, London W1N 1PE. Tel: 0171-486 1044. *Hon. Secretary,* Prof. B. S. Jay

ROYAL PHOTOGRAPHIC SOCIETY (1853), The Octagon, Milsom Street, Bath BA1 1DN. Tel: 01225-462841. *Secretary-General,* B. Lane

ROYAL PINNER SCHOOL FOUNDATION, 110 Old Brompton Road, London SW7 3RA. Tel: 0171-373 6168. *Secretary,* D. Crawford

ROYAL SAILORS' RESTS (1876), 5 St Georges Business Centre, St Georges Square, Portsmouth PO1 1EY. Tel: 01705-296096. *General Secretary,* A. A. Lockwood, MBE

ROYAL SIGNALS INSTITUTION (1950), 56 Regency Street, London SW1P 4AD. Tel: 0171-414 8421. *Secretary,* Col. A. N. de Bretton-Gordon

ROYAL SOCIETY FOR ASIAN AFFAIRS (1901), 2 Belgrave Square, London SW1X 8PJ. Tel: 0171-235 5122. *Secretary,* Mrs H. McKeag

ROYAL SOCIETY FOR THE ENCOURAGEMENT OF ARTS, MANUFACTURES AND COMMERCE (RSA) (1754), 8 John Adam Street, London WC2N 6EZ. Tel: 0171-930 5115. *Director,* P. Cowling

ROYAL SOCIETY FOR THE PREVENTION OF CRUELTY TO ANIMALS (RSPCA) (1824), Causeway, Horsham, W. Sussex RH12 1HG. Tel: 01403-264181. *Director-General,* P. R. Davies, CB

ROYAL SOCIETY FOR THE PROTECTION OF BIRDS (RSPB) (1889), The Lodge, Sandy, Beds SG19 2DL. Tel: 01767-680551. *Chief Executive,* Miss B. S. Young

ROYAL SOCIETY OF HEALTH (1876), RSH House, 38 St George's Drive, London SW1V 4BH. Tel: 0171-630 0121. *Chief Executive,* A. J. Byrne

ROYAL SOCIETY OF LITERATURE (1823), 1 Hyde Park Gardens, London W2 2LT. Tel: 0171-723 5104. *Secretary,* Miss M. Parham

ROYAL SOCIETY OF MEDICINE (1805), 1 Wimpole Street, London W1M 8AE. Tel: 0171-290 2901. *Chief Executive,* Dr J. T. Green

ROYAL SOCIETY OF ST GEORGE (1894), Dartmouth House, 37 Charles Street, London W1X 8AB. Tel: 0171-499 5430. *Chairman,* Admiral Sir Peter Herbert; *General Secretary,* Lt.-Cdr. D. Odell

ROYAL STAR AND GARTER HOME FOR DISABLED SAILORS, SOLDIERS AND AIRMEN (1916), Richmond upon Thames, Surrey TW10 6RR. Tel: 0181-940 3314. *Chief Executive,* I. Lashbrooke

ROYAL STATISTICAL SOCIETY (1834), 12 Errol Street, London EC1Y 8LX. Tel: 0171-638 8998. *Executive Secretary,* I. J. Goddard

ROYAL TANK REGIMENT BENEVOLENT FUND (1919), RHQ RTR, Bovington Camp, Wareham, Dorset BH20 6JA. Tel: 01929-403331. *Regimental Secretary,* Maj. A. Henzie, MBE

ROYAL TELEVISION SOCIETY (1927), Holborn Hall, 100 Gray's Inn Road, London WC1X 8AL. Tel: 0171-430 1000. *Executive Director,* M. Bunce

ROYAL UNITED KINGDOM BENEFICENT ASSOCIATION (1863), 6 Avonmore Road, London W14 8RL. Tel: 0171-602 6274. *Director,* W. Rathbone

RURAL ENGLAND, COUNCIL FOR THE PROTECTION OF, *see* CPRE

RURAL SCOTLAND, ASSOCIATION FOR THE PROTECTION OF (1926), 3rd Floor, Gladstone's Land, 483 Lawnmarket, Edinburgh EH1 2NT. Tel: 0131-225 7012/3. *Manager,* Mrs E. J. Garland

RURAL WALES, CAMPAIGN FOR THE PROTECTION OF (1928), Ty Gwyn, 31 High Street, Welshpool, Powys SY21 7JP. Tel: 01938-552525. *Director,* M. Williams

SAILORS' FAMILIES' SOCIETY (1821), Newland, Hull HU6 7RJ. Tel: 01482-342331. *Chief Executive,* G. J. Powell

SAILORS' SOCIETY, BRITISH AND INTERNATIONAL (1818), 3 Orchard Place, Southampton SO14 3AT. Tel: 01703-337333. *General Secretary,* G. Chambers

ST DEINIOL'S RESIDENTIAL LIBRARY (1902), Hawarden, Deeside, Flintshire CH5 3DF. Tel: 01244-532350. *Warden and Chief Librarian,* Revd Dr P. J. Jagger

ST DUNSTAN'S, PO Box 4XB, 12–14 Harcourt Street, London W1A 4XB. Tel: 0171-723 5021. For men and women blinded in the Services. *Secretary,* G. B. J. Frost

St John Ambulance (1887), 1 Grosvenor Crescent, London swix 7ef. Tel: 0171-235 5231. *Executive Director*, L. Martin

Sales and Marketing Management, Institute of (1966), Georgian House, 31 Upper George Street, Luton lui 2rd. Tel: 01582-411130. *Chief Executive*, D. G. Hales

Salmon and Trout Association (1903), Fishmongers' Hall, London Bridge, London ec4r 9el. Tel: 0171-283 5838. *Director*, C. W. Poupard

Saltire Society (1936), 9 Fountain Close, 22 High Street, Edinburgh eh1 itf. Tel: 0131-556 1836. *Administrator*, Mrs K. Munro

Samaritans, The (1953), 10 The Grove, Slough sl1 1qp. Tel: 01753-532713. Telephone numbers in local directories or ring 0345-909090. *Chief Executive*, S. Armson

Samuel Pepys Club (1903), 26 Gloucester Street, Faringdon, Oxon sn7 7hy. Tel: 01367-222537. *Secretary*, P. L. Gray

SANE: The Mental Health Charity (1986), 199–205 Old Marylebone Road, London nw1 5qp. Tel: 0171-724 6520. Saneline: 0345-678000. *Chief Executive*, Ms M. Wallace, mbe

Save Britain's Heritage (1975), 68 Battersea High Street, London sw11 3hx. Tel: 0171-228 3336. *Secretary*, Miss E. Phillips

Save the Children Fund (1919), 17 Grove Lane, London se5 8rd. Tel: 0171-703 5400. *Director-General*, M. Aaronson

Schizophrenia Fellowship, National (1970), 28 Castle Street, Kingston upon Thames, Surrey kt1 1ss. Tel: 0181-547 3937. *Chief Executive*, B. Mehta

School Library Association (1937), Liden Library, Barrington Close, Liden, Swindon sn3 6hf. Tel: 01793-617838. *Executive Secretary*, Ms V. Fea

Schoolmasters, Society of (1798), Dolton's Farm, Woburn, Milton Keynes mk17 9hx. Tel: 01525-290093. *Secretary*, Mrs B. A. Skipper

Schoolmistresses and Governesses Benevolent Institution (1843), Queen Mary House, Manor Park Road, Chislehurst, Kent br7 5py. Tel: 0181-468 7997. *Director*, L. I. Baggott

Science, British Association for the Advancement of (1831), 23 Savile Row, London w1x 2nb. Tel: 0171-973 3500. *Executive Secretary*, Dr P. Briggs

Science Education, Association for (1963), College Lane, Hatfield, Herts al10 9aa. Tel: 01707-267411. *General Secretary*, Dr D. S. Moore

SCOPE (formerly The Spastics Society) (1952), 12 Park Crescent, London w1n 4eq. Tel: 0171-636 5020. *Chief Executive*, R. P. Brewster

Scotch Whisky Association (1919), 20 Atholl Crescent, Edinburgh eh3 8hf. Tel: 0131-229 4383. *Director-General*, H. Morison

Scottish Chiefs, Standing Council of (1952), Hope Chambers, 52 Leith Walk, Edinburgh eh6 5hw. Tel: 0131-554 6321. *General Secretary*, G. A. Way of Plean

Scottish Church History Society (1922), St Serf's Manse, 1 Denham Green Terrace, Edinburgh eh5 3pg. Tel: 0131-552 4059. *Hon. Secretary*, Revd Dr P. H. Donald

Scottish Corporation, Royal (1611), 37 King Street, London wc2e 8js. Tel: 0171-240 3718. *Chief Executive*, Wg Cdr. A. Robertson

Scottish Country Dance Society, Royal (1923), 12 Coates Crescent, Edinburgh eh3 7af. Tel: 0131-225 3854. *Secretary*, Miss G. S. Parker

Scottish Genealogy Society (1953), Library and Family History Centre, 15 Victoria Terrace, Edinburgh eh1 2jl. Tel: 0131-220 3677. *Hon. Secretary*, Miss J. P. S. Ferguson

Scottish History Society (1886), Department of History, University of Aberdeen, Aberdeen ab9 2ub. Tel: 01224-272456. *Hon. Secretary*, Dr S. Boardman

Scottish Landowners' Federation (1906), 25 Maritime Street, Edinburgh eh6 5pw. Tel: 0131-555 1031. *Director*, B. N. J. Speed, obe

Scottish Law Agents Society, 79 West Regent Street, Glasgow g2 2aw. Tel: 0141-332 5537. *Secretary*, D. C. Clapham

Scottish National Institution for the War Blinded (1915), PO Box 500, Gillespie Crescent, Edinburgh eh10 4hz. Tel: 0131-229 1456. *Secretary*, J. B. M. Munro

Scottish National War Memorial (1927), The Castle, Edinburgh eh1 2yt. Tel: 0131-226 7393. *Secretary*, Lt.-Col. I. Shepherd

Scottish Society for the Prevention of Cruelty to Animals (1839), Braehead Mains, 603 Queensferry Road, Edinburgh eh4 6ea. Tel: 0131-339 0222. *Chief Executive*, J. Morris, cbe

Scottish Society for the Protection of Wild Birds (1927), Foremount House, Kilbarchan, Renfrewshire pa10 2ez. Tel: 01505-702419. *Secretary*, Dr J. A. Gibson

Scottish Wildlife Trust (1964), Cramond House, Kirk Cramond, Cramond Glebe Road, Edinburgh eh4 6ns. Tel: 0131-312 7765. *Director*, D. J. Hughes-Hallett

Scout Association (1907), Baden-Powell House, Queen's Gate, London sw7 5js. Tel: 0171-584 7030. *Chief Scout*, W. G. Purdy; *Chief Executive Commissioner*, Vacant

Scribes and Illuminators, Society of (1921), 6 Queen Square, London wc1n 3ar. Tel: 01483-894155. *Hon. Secretary*, Ms C. Turvey

Scripture Gift Mission Incorporated (1888), Radstock House, 3 Eccleston Street, London sw1w 9lz. Tel: 0171-730 2155. *International Director*, R. Kennedy

Scripture Union (1867), 207–209 Queensway, Bletchley, Milton Keynes mk2 2eb. Tel: 01908-856000. *General Director*, J. H. Simmons

Sea Cadets (1895), 202 Lambeth Road, London se1 7jf. Tel: 0171-928 8978. *General Secretary*, Cdr P. J. Grindal, cbe

Seamen's Boy's Home, British (1863), Grenville House, Berry Head Road, Brixham, Devon tq5 9af. Tel: 01803-882129. *Secretary*, Capt. E. M. Marks, rd, rnr

Seamen's Christian Friend Society (1846), 48 South Street, Alderley Edge, Cheshire sk9 7es. Tel: 01625-590010. *Director*, M. J. Wilson

Seamen's Pension Fund, Royal (1919), 65 High Street, Ewell, Epsom, Surrey kt17 1rx. Tel: 0181-393 5873. *Secretary*, D. Barker

Secretaries and Administrators, Institute of Chartered (1891), 16 Park Crescent, London w1n 4ah. Tel: 0171-580 4741. *Chief Executive*, M. J. Ainsworth

Secular Society Ltd, National (1866), Bradlaugh House, 47 Theobald's Road, London wc1x 8sp. Tel: 0171-404 3126. *General Secretary*, K. P. Wood

SEEABILITY (formerly Royal School for the Blind) (1799), 56–66 Highlands Road, Leatherhead, Surrey KT22 8NR. Tel: 01372-373086. *Chief Executive*, R. M. Perkins

SELDEN SOCIETY (1887), Faculty of Laws, Queen Mary and Westfield College, Mile End Road, London E1 4NS. Tel: 0171-975 5136. To encourage the study and advance the knowledge of the history of English law. *Secretary*, V. Tunkel

SENSE (THE NATIONAL DEAFBLIND AND RUBELLA ASSOCIATION) (1955), 11–13 Clifton Terrace, London N4 3SR. Tel: 0171-272 7774. *Chief Executive*, R. Clark

SHAFTESBURY HOMES AND *Arethusa* (1843), 3 Rectory Grove, London SW4 0DX. Tel: 0171-720 8709. *Director*, Capt. N. C. Baird-Murray, CBE, RN

SHAFTESBURY SOCIETY, THE (1844), 16 Kingston Road, London SW19 1JZ. Tel: 0181-239 5555. Provides care and education services to people with learning and/or physical disabilities, and support for poor or disadvantaged people. *Chief Executive*, Ms F. Beckett

SHELLFISH ASSOCIATION OF GREAT BRITAIN (1969), Fishmongers' Hall, London Bridge, London EC4R 9EL. Tel: 0171-283 8305. *Director*, E. Edwards, OBE, PH.D.

SHELTER (THE NATIONAL CAMPAIGN FOR HOMELESS PEOPLE) (1966), 88 Old Street, London EC1V 9HU. Tel: 0171-505 2000. *Director*, C. Holmes

SHERLOCK HOLMES SOCIETY OF LONDON (1951), 64 Graham Road, London SW19 3SS. Tel: 0181-540 7657. *General Secretary*, T. J. K. Owen

SHIPBROKERS, INSTITUTE OF CHARTERED (1911), 3 St Helen's Place, London EC3A 6EJ. Tel: 0171-628 5559. *Director*, Mrs B. Fletcher

SHIRE HORSE SOCIETY (1878), East of England Showground, Peterborough PE2 6XE. Tel: 01733-234451. *Secretary*, T. Gibson, OBE

SHRIEVALTY ASSOCIATION (1971), Office of the High Sheriffs, Duncombe Place, York YO1 2DY. Tel: 01904-634771. *Secretary*, J. H. N. Towers

SIGHT SAVERS INTERNATIONAL (Royal Commonwealth Society for the Blind) (1950), Grosvenor Hall, Bolnore Road, Haywards Heath, W. Sussex RH16 4BX. Tel: 01444-412424. *Executive Director*, R. Porter

SIMPLIFIED SPELLING SOCIETY (1908), Clare Hall, Tailours, High Road, Chigwell, Essex IG7 6DL. Tel: 0181-501 0405. *Chairman*, C. J. H. Jolly

SIR OSWALD STOLL FOUNDATION (1916), 446 Fulham Road, London SW6 1DT. Tel: 0171-385 2110. *Director*, R. C. Brunwin

SMALL BUSINESSES, FEDERATION OF (1974), Parliamentary Office, 140 Lower Marsh, Westminster Bridge, London SE1 7AE. Tel: 0171-928 9272. *National Chairman*, Mrs P. McAlester

SMALL FARMERS' ASSOCIATION (1979), PO Box 18, Woodbridge, Suffolk IP13 0QP. Tel: 0171-249 4790. *Chairman*, J. Morford

SOCIAL CONCERN, NATIONAL COUNCIL FOR, 59 Catherine Place, London SW1E 6DY. Tel: 0171-630 7046. *Director*, P. Carlin

SOCIALIST PARTY OF GREAT BRITAIN (1904), 52 Clapham High Street, London SW4 7UN. Tel: 0171-622 3811. *General Secretary*, Ms J. Carter

SOCIAL WORKERS, BRITISH ASSOCIATION OF (1970), 16 Kent Street, Birmingham B5 6RD. Tel: 0121-622 3911. *General Secretary*, D. N. Jones

SOIL ASSOCIATION (1946), 86 Colston Street, Bristol BS1 5BB. Tel: 0117-929 0661. *Director*, P. Holden

SOLDIERS' AND AIRMEN'S SCRIPTURE READERS ASSOCIATION (1838), Havelock House, Barrack Road, Aldershot, Hants GU11 3NP. Tel: 01252-310033. *General Secretary*, Lt.-Col. M. Hitchcott

SSAFA FORCES HELP (1885, merged 1997), 19 Queen Elizabeth Street, London SE1 2LP. Tel: 0171-403 8783. *Controller*, Maj.-Gen. P. Sheppard, CB, CBE

SOLDIERS' WIDOWS, ROYAL CAMBRIDGE HOME FOR (1851), 82–84 Hurst Road, East Molesey, Surrey KT8 9AH. Tel: 0181-979 3788. *Superintendent*, Mrs I. O. Yarnell

SOLICITORS IN THE SUPREME COURT OF SCOTLAND, SOCIETY OF (1784), SSC Library, Parliament House, 11 Parliament Square, Edinburgh EH1 1RF. Tel: 0131-225 6268. *Secretary*, I. L. S. Balfour

SOROPTIMIST INTERNATIONAL OF GREAT BRITAIN AND IRELAND (1923), 127 Wellington Road South, Stockport SK1 3TS. Tel: 0161-480 7686. *Executive Officer*, Ms K. Heward

SOS SOCIETY, see 2CARE

SOUTH AMERICAN MISSION SOCIETY (1844), Allen Gardiner House, Pembury Road, Tunbridge Wells, Kent TN2 3QU. Tel: 01892-538647. *General Secretary*, Rt Revd D. R. J. Evans

SOUTH WALES INSTITUTE OF ENGINEERS (1857), Empire House, Mount Stuart Square, Cardiff CF1 6DN. Tel: 01222-481726. *Hon. Secretary*, R. E. Lindsay

SPEAKERS CLUBS, ASSOCIATION OF (1971), 28 High Street, Auchterarder, Perthshire PH3 1DF. Tel: 01764-662457. *National Secretary*, D. Williams

SPINA BIFIDA AND HYDROCEPHALUS, ASSOCIATION FOR (ASBAH), 42 Park Road, Peterborough PE1 2UQ. Tel: 01733-555988. *Executive Director*, A. Russell

SPORTS MEDICINE, INSTITUTE OF (1963), Burlington House, Piccadilly, London W1V 0LQ. Tel: 0171-287 5269. *Hon. Secretary*, Dr W. T. Orton

SPURGEON'S CHILD CARE (1867), 74 Wellingborough Road, Rushden, Northants NN10 9TY. Tel: 01933-412412. *Chief Executive*, D. C. Culwick

STANDING CONFERENCE OF NATIONAL AND UNIVERSITY LIBRARIES (SCONUL) (1950), 102 Euston Street, London NW1 2HA. Tel: 0171-387 0317. *Secretary*, A. J. C. Bainton

STATISTICIANS, INSTITUTE OF, see ROYAL STATISTICAL SOCIETY

STATUTE LAW SOCIETY (1968), Onslow House, 9 The Green, Richmond, Surrey TW9 1PU. Tel: 0181-940 0017. *Hon. Secretary*, N. Frudd

STEWART SOCIETY (1899), 17 Dublin Street, Edinburgh EH1 3PG. Tel: 0131-557 6824. *Hon. Secretary*, Mrs M. Walker

STRATEGIC PLANNING SOCIETY (1967), 17 Portland Place, London W1N 3AF. Tel: 0171-636 7737. *General Manager*, T. Haddon

STRATEGIC STUDIES, INTERNATIONAL INSTITUTE FOR (1958), 23 Tavistock Street, London WC2E 7NQ. Tel: 0171-379 7676. *Director*, Dr J. Chipman

STROKE ASSOCIATION (1899), CHSA House, Whitecross Street, London EC1Y 8JJ. Tel: 0171-490 7999. *Director-General*, Dr S. McLauchlan

STRUCTURAL ENGINEERS, INSTITUTION OF (1908), 11 Upper Belgrave Street, London SW1X 8BH. Tel: 0171-235 4535. *Chief Executive*, Dr J. W. Dougill

STUDENT CHRISTIAN MOVEMENT (1889), Mary Burnie House, Westhill College, 14–16 Weoley Park Road, Selly Oak, Birmingham B29 6LL. Tel: 0121-471 2404. *Administrator*, Ms S. Cowley

SUFFOLK HORSE SOCIETY (1878), The Market Hill, Woodbridge, Suffolk IP12 4LU. Tel: 01394-380643. *Secretary*, P. Ryder-Davies

SURGEONS OF EDINBURGH, ROYAL COLLEGE OF (1505), Nicolson Street, Edinburgh EH8 9DW. Tel: 0131-527 1600. *Secretary*, Ms A. Campbell, FRCSEd.

SURGEONS OF ENGLAND, ROYAL COLLEGE OF (1800), 35–43 Lincoln's Inn Fields, London WC2A 3PN. Tel: 0171-405 3474. *Secretary*, R. H. E. Duffett

SURVEYORS, ROYAL INSTITUTION OF CHARTERED (1868), 12 Great George Street, London SWIP 3AD. Tel: 0171-222 7000. *Chief Executive*, Ms C. Makin

SURVIVAL INTERNATIONAL (1969), 11–15 Emerald Street, London WCIN 3QT. Tel: 0171-242 1441. *Director*, S. Corry

SUZY LAMPLUGH TRUST (1986), 14 East Sheen Avenue, London SW14 8AS. Tel: 081-392 1839. *Executive Secretary*, P. Lamplugh

SWEDENBORG SOCIETY (1810), 20–21 Bloomsbury Way, London WCIA 2TH. Tel: 0171-405 7986. *Secretary*, Ms M. G. Waters

TALKING BOOKS FOR THE HANDICAPPED AND HOSPITAL PATIENTS, *see* NATIONAL LISTENING LIBRARY

TAVISTOCK INSTITUTE, THE (1947), 30 Tabernacle Street, London EC2A 4DD. Tel: 0171-417 0407. *Secretary*, Ms C. Turnbull

TAXATION, CHARTERED INSTITUTE OF (1930), 12 Upper Belgrave Street, London SW1X 8BB. Tel: 0171-235 9381. *Secretary-General*, R. A. Dommett

TEACHERS OF HOME ECONOMICS AND TECHNOLOGY, NATIONAL ASSOCIATION OF (1896), Hamilton House, Mabledon Place, London WCIH 9BJ. Tel: 0171-387 1441. *Secretary*, G. Thompson

TEACHERS OF MATHEMATICS, ASSOCIATION OF (1952), 7 Shaftesbury Street, Derby DE3 8YB. Tel: 01332-346599. *Hon. Secretary*, Ms A. Gammon

TEACHERS OF THE DEAF, BRITISH ASSOCIATION OF (1977), 41 The Orchard, Leven, Beverley, E. Yorks HU17 5QA. Tel: 01964-544243. *Hon. Secretary*, Mrs A. Underwood

TEACHERS' UNION, ULSTER (1919), 94 Malone Road, Belfast BT9 5HP. Tel: 01232-662216. *General Secretary*, D. Allen

TELECOMMUNICATION USERS' ASSOCIATION (1965), Woodgate Studios, 2–8 Games Road, Cockfosters, Herts EN4 9HN. Tel: 0181-449 8844. *Executive Chairman*, W. E. Mieran

TEMPERANCE COUNCIL, NATIONAL UNITED (1880), Alliance House, 12 Caxton Street, London OQS. Tel: 0181-444 5004. *General Secretary*, Mrs G. O. Stretton

TEMPERANCE FRIENDLY SOCIETY, ORDER OF THE SONS OF (1855), 5 Ashbourne Road, Derby DE22 3FQ. Tel: 01332-341672. *Secretary*, D. Newbury

TEMPERANCE LEAGUE, BRITISH NATIONAL (1834), Westbrook Court, 2 Sharrow Vale Road, Sheffield SII 8YZ. Tel: 0114-267 9976. *Executive Director*, A. Willis

TEMPERANCE SOCIETY, ROYAL NAVAL (1876), 5 St George's Business Centre, St George's Square, Portsmouth POI 3EY. Tel: 01705-296096. *General Secretary*, A. A. Lockwood, MBE

TEMPLETON FOUNDATION (1973), 18 Eastgate Gardens, Taunton, Somerset TAI IRD. Tel: 01823-324522. *UK Representative*, Mrs N. Pearse

TERRENCE HIGGINS TRUST (1982), 52–54 Grays Inn Road, London WCIX 8JU. Tel: 0171-831 0330. *Helpline:* 0171-242 1010. *Chairman*, N. Partridge

TERRITORIAL, AUXILIARY AND VOLUNTEER RESERVE ASSOCIATIONS, COUNCIL OF (1908), Centre Block, Duke of York's HQ, London SW3 4SG. Tel: 0171-730 6122. *Secretary*, Maj.-Gen. W. A. Evans, CB

TEXTILE INSTITUTE, THE (1910), 10 Blackfriars Street, Manchester M3 5DR. Tel: 0161-834 8457. *Chief Executive*, R. G. Denyer

THEATRE RESEARCH, SOCIETY FOR (1948), c/o The Theatre Museum, 1E Tavistock Street, London WC2E 7PA. *Joint Hon. Secretaries*, Ms E. Cottis; Ms F. Dann

THEATRES TRUST, THE (1976), 22 Charing Cross Road, London WC2H OHR. Tel: 0171-836 8591. *Director*, P. Longman

THEATRICAL FUND, ROYAL (1839), 11 Garrick Street, London WC2E 9AR. Tel: 0171-836 3322. *Secretary*, Mrs R. M. Oliver

THEOSOPHICAL SOCIETY IN ENGLAND (1875), 50 Gloucester Place, London WIH 4EA. Tel: 0171-935 9261. *General Secretary*, Miss L. Storey

THISTLE FOUNDATION, THE (1945), Niddrie Mains Road, Edinburgh EH16 4EA. Tel: 0131-661 3366. *Director*, Ms J. Fisher

THOMAS CORAM FOUNDATION FOR CHILDREN (formerly The Foundling Hospital) (1739), 40 Brunswick Square, London WCIN IAZ. Tel: 0171-278 2424. *Director (acting)*, R. I. Wyber

TIDY BRITAIN GROUP (1953), The Pier, Wigan WN3 4EX. Tel: 01942-824620. *Director-General*, Prof. G. Ashworth, CBE

TOC H (1915), 1 Forest Close, Wendover, Aylesbury, Bucks HP22 6BT. Tel: 01296-623911. *Director*, M. Lyddiard

TOURIST BOARD, ENGLISH, Thames Tower, Black's Road, London W6 9EL. Tel: 0181-846 9000. *Chief Executive*, T. Bartlett

TOURIST BOARD, NORTHERN IRELAND, St Anne's Court, 59 North Street, Belfast BTI INB. Tel: 01232-231221. *Chief Executive*, I. G. Henderson

TOURIST BOARD, SCOTTISH (1969), 23 Ravelston Terrace, Edinburgh EH4 3EU. Tel: 0131-332 2433. *Chief Executive*, D. D. Reid

TOURIST BOARD, WALES, Brunel House, 2 Fitzalan Road, Cardiff CF2 IUY. Tel: 01222-499909. *Chief Executive*, J. French

TOWN AND COUNTRY PLANNING ASSOCIATION (1899), 17 Carlton House Terrace, London SW5AS. Tel: 0171-930 8903/4/5. *Secretary*, D. Hall, MBE

TOWN PLANNING INSTITUTE, ROYAL (1914), 26 Portland Place, London WIN 4BE. Tel: 0171-636 9107. *Secretary-General*, D. Rose

TOWNSWOMEN'S GUILDS (1929), Chamber of Commerce House, 75 Harborne Road, Birmingham B15 3DA. Tel: 0121-456 3435. *National Secretary*, Mrs P. Wilkes

TOYNBEE HALL (1884), 28 Commercial Street, London EI 6LS. Tel: 0171-247 6943. *Chief Executive*, A. Prescott

TRADE MARK AGENTS, INSTITUTE OF (1934), Canterbury House, 2–6 Sydenham Road, Croydon CRO 9XE. Tel: 0181-686 2052. *Secretary*, Mrs M. J. Tyler

TRADING STANDARDS ADMINISTRATION, INSTITUTE OF (1881), 3–5 Hadleigh Business Centre, 351 London Road, Hadleigh, Essex ss7 2BT. Tel: 01702-559922. *Chief Executive*, A. J. Street

TRANSLATION AND INTERPRETING, INSTITUTE OF (1986), 377 City Road, London EC1V 1NA. Tel: 0171-713 7600. *Chairman*, S. Slade

TRANSPORT ADMINISTRATION, INSTITUTE OF (1944), 32 Palmerston Road, Southampton SO14 1LL. Tel: 01703-631300. *Director*, Wg Cdr. P. F. Green

TRANSPORT, CHARTERED INSTITUTE OF (1919), 80 Portland Place, London W1N 4DP. Tel: 0171-636 9952. *Director*, Mrs S. Gross

TRAVEL AGENTS, ASSOCIATION OF BRITISH (ABTA) (1950), 55–57 Newman Street, London W1P 4AH. Tel: 0171-637 2444. *President*, C. Trigger

TREE COUNCIL (1974), 51 Catherine Place, London SW1E 6DY. Tel: 0171-828 9928. *General Secretary*, R. Osborne

TREE FOUNDATION, INTERNATIONAL (formerly Men of the Trees) (1922), Sandy Lane, Crawley Down, W. Sussex RH10 4HS. Tel: 01342-712536. *Chairman*, S. G. Keys

TROPICAL MEDICINE AND HYGIENE, ROYAL SOCIETY OF (1907), Manson House, 26 Portland Place, London W1N 4EY. Tel: 0171-580 2127. *Hon. Secretaries*, Dr D. C. Barker; Dr W. R. C. Weir

TURNER SOCIETY (1975), BCM Box Turner, London WC1N 3XX. *Chairman*, E. Joll

2CARE (formerly The SOS Society) (1929), 11–13 Harwood Road, London SW6 4QP. Tel: 0171-371 0118. Residential and nursing homes for the elderly, and psychiatric rehabilitation centres. *Chief Executive*, Miss E. C. R. O'Sullivan

UFAW (UNIVERSITIES FEDERATION FOR ANIMAL WELFARE) (1926), 8 Hamilton Close, South Mimms, Potters Bar, Herts EN6 3QD. Tel: 01707-658202. *Director*, Dr J. K. Kirkwood

UK INDEPENDENCE PARTY, 80 Regent Street, London W1R 5PE. Tel: 0171-434 4559. *Secretary*, G. Batten

UNITED KINGDOM ALLIANCE (1863), 176 Blackfriars Road, London SE1 8ET. Tel: 0171-928 1538. *General Secretary*, Revd B. Kinman

UNITED NATIONS ASSOCIATION OF GREAT BRITAIN AND NORTHERN IRELAND (1945), 3 Whitehall Court, London SW1A 2EL. Tel: 0171-930 2931. *Director*, M. C. Harper

UNITED REFORMED CHURCH HISTORY SOCIETY (1972), 86 Tavistock Place, London WC1H 9RT. Tel: 0171-916 2020. *Hon. Secretary*, Revd Dr S. Orchard

UNITED SOCIETY FOR CHRISTIAN LITERATURE (1799), Robertson House, Leas Road, Guildford, Surrey GU1 4QW. Tel: 01483-577877. *General Secretary*, Dr A. Marriage

UNITED SOCIETY FOR THE PROPAGATION OF THE GOSPEL (USPG) (1701), Partnership House, 157 Waterloo Road, London SE1 8XA. Tel: 0171-928 8681. *Secretary*, Revd Canon P. Price

UNIVERSITIES OF THE UNITED KINGDOM, COMMITTEE OF VICE-CHANCELLORS AND PRINCIPALS OF THE (1918), 29 Tavistock Square, London WC1H 9EZ. Tel: 0171-387 9231. *Chief Executive*, Ms D. Warwick

UNIVERSITY AND COLLEGE LECTURERS, ASSOCIATION OF (1973), 104 Albert Road, Southsea, Hants PO5 2SN. Tel: 01705-818625. *Chief Executive*, Ms C. Cheesman

VALUERS AND AUCTIONEERS, INCORPORATED SOCIETY OF (1968), 3 Cadogan Gate, London SW1X 0AS. Tel: 0171-235 2282. *Chief Executive*, H. Whitty

VEGAN SOCIETY (1944), Donald Watson House, 7 Battle Road, St Leonards-on-Sea, E. Sussex TN37 7AA. Tel: 01424-427393. *Information Officer*, Ms A. Rofe

VEGETARIAN SOCIETY OF THE UNITED KINGDOM LTD, Parkdale, Dunham Road, Altrincham, Cheshire WA14 4QG. Tel: 0161-928 0793. *Chief Executive*, Ms T. Fox

VENEREAL DISEASES, MEDICAL SOCIETY FOR THE STUDY OF (1922), c/o The Royal Society of Medicine, 1 Wimpole Street, London W1M 8AE. Tel: 0171-290 2968. *Hon. Secretary*, Dr T. McManus

VERNACULAR ARCHITECTURE GROUP (1953), 16 Falna Crescent, Coton Green, Tamworth, Staffs B79 8JS. Tel: 01827-69434. *Hon. Secretary*, R. A. Meeson

VETERINARY ASSOCIATION, BRITISH (1881), 7 Mansfield Street, London W1M 0AT. Tel: 0171-636 6541. *Chief Executive*, J. H. Baird

VETERINARY SURGEONS, ROYAL COLLEGE OF (1844), Belgravia House, 62–64 Horseferry Road, London SW1P 2AF. Tel: 0171-222 2001. *President*, D. J. Thompson, OBE; *Registrar*, P. E. Woolley, OBE

VICTIM SUPPORT (NATIONAL ASSOCIATION OF VICTIMS SUPPORT SCHEMES) (1979), National Office, Cranmer House, 39 Brixton Road, London SW9 6DZ. Tel: 0171-735 9166. *Director*, Ms H. Reeves, OBE

VICTORIA CROSS AND GEORGE CROSS ASSOCIATION, Room 028, The Old War Office, London SW1A 2EU. Tel: 0171-930 3506. *Chairman*, Col. B. S. T. Archer, GC, OBE

VICTORIA INSTITUTE (PHILOSOPHICAL SOCIETY OF GREAT BRITAIN), 41 Marne Avenue, Welling, Kent DA16 2EY. Tel: 0181-303 0465. *Chairman of Council*, T. C. Mitchell

VICTORIAN SOCIETY (1958), 1 Priory Gardens, Bedford Park, London W4 1TT. Tel: 0181-994 1019. *Director*, Dr W. Filmer-Sankey

VICTORY (SERVICES) ASSOCIATION LTD AND CLUB (1907), 63–79 Seymour Street, London W2 2HF. Tel: 0171-723 4474. *General Manager*, G. F. Taylor

VIKING SOCIETY FOR NORTHERN RESEARCH (1892), Department of Scandinavian Studies, University College, Gower Street, London WC1E 6BT. Tel: 0171-380 7176. *Hon. Secretaries*, Prof. M. P. Barnes; Dr J. Jesh

VOLUNTARY ORGANIZATIONS, NATIONAL COUNCIL FOR (1919), Regents Wharf, 8 All Saints Street, London N1 9RL. Tel: 0171-713 6161. *Chief Executive*, S. Etherington

VOLUNTARY ORGANIZATIONS, SCOTTISH COUNCIL FOR (1943), 18–19 Claremont Crescent, Edinburgh EH7 4QD. Tel: 0131-556 3882. *Director*, M. Sime

VSO (VOLUNTARY SERVICE OVERSEAS) (1958), 317 Putney Bridge Road, London SW15 2PN. Tel: 0181-780 2266. *Director*, D. Green

WAR ON WANT (1952), Fenner Brockway House, 37–39 Great Guildford Street, London SE1 0ES. Tel: 0171-620 1111. *Director*, Ms M. Lynch

WATER AND ENVIRONMENTAL MANAGEMENT, CHARTERED INSTITUTION OF (1987), 15 John Street, London WC1N 2EB. Tel: 0171-831 3110. *Executive Director*, R. A. Bispham

WATERCOLOUR SOCIETY, ROYAL (1804), Bankside Gallery, 48 Hopton Street, London SE1 9JH. Tel: 0171-928 7521. *Secretary*, Ms J. Dixey

WELL BEING (1964), 27 Sussex Place, London NW1 4SP. Tel: 0171-262 5337. *Director*, Mrs R. Barnes

WELLCOME TRUST (1936), The Wellcome Building, 183 Euston Road, London NW1 2BE. Tel: 0171-611 8888. *Director*, Dr B. M. Ogilvie

WELLS SOCIETY, H. G. (1961), English Department, Nene College, Moulton Park, Northampton NN2 7AL. Tel: 01604-735500 ext. 2133. *Hon. Secretary*, Dr S. Hardy

WESLEY HISTORICAL SOCIETY (1893), 34 Spiceland Road, Northfield, Birmingham B31 1NJ. Tel: 0121-475 4914. *General Secretary*, Dr E. D. Graham

WEST LONDON MISSION (1887), 19 Thayer Street, London W1M 5LJ. Tel: 0171-935 6179. *Superintendent*, Revd D. S. Cruise

WESTMINSTER FOUNDATION FOR DEMOCRACY (1992), Clutha House, 10 Storey's Gate, London SW1P 3AY. Tel: 0171-976 7565. *Chief Executive*, S. Cox

WES (WORLD-WIDE EDUCATION SERVICE LTD) (1888), Canada House, 272 Field End Road, Eastcote, Ruislip, Middx HA4 9NA. Tel: 0181-866 4400. *Head of Consultancy*, Mrs T. Mulder-Reynolds

WILDFOWL AND WETLANDS TRUST (1946), The New Grounds, Slimbridge, Glos GL2 7BT. Tel: 01453-890333. *Director-General*, Dr M. Owen

WILDLIFE TRUSTS, THE (1912), The Green, Witham Park, Waterside South, Lincoln LN5 7JR. Tel: 01522-544400. *Director-General*, Dr S. Lyster

WILLIAM MORRIS SOCIETY AND KELMSCOTT FELLOWSHIP (1918), Kelmscott House, 26 Upper Mall, London W6 9TA. Tel: 0181-741 3735. *Hon. Secretary*, D. Baker

WINE AND SPIRIT ASSOCIATION OF GREAT BRITAIN AND NORTHERN IRELAND (*c*. 1825), Five Kings House, 1 Queen Street Place, London EC4R 1XX. Tel: 0171-248 5377. *Director*, P. Lewis

WOMEN, SOCIETY FOR PROMOTING THE TRAINING OF (1859), The Rectory, Main Street, Great Casterton, Stamford, Lincs PE9 4AP. Tel: 01780-64036. *Hon. Secretary*, Revd B. Harris

WOMEN ARTISTS, SOCIETY OF (1855), Westminster Gallery, Westminster Central Hall, Storey's Gate, London SW1H 9NU. *President*, Prof. B. Tate

WOMEN GRADUATES, BRITISH FEDERATION OF (1907), 4 Mandeville Courtyard, 142 Battersea Park Road, London SW11 4NB. Tel: 0171-498 8037. *Secretary*, Mrs A. B. Stein

WOMEN'S ENGINEERING SOCIETY (1920), Imperial College of Science and Technology, Department of Civil Engineering, Imperial College Road, London SW7 2BU. Tel: 0171-594 6025. *Secretary*, Mrs C. MacGillivray

WOMEN'S INSTITUTES, NATIONAL FEDERATION OF (1915), 104 New Kings Road, London SW6 4LY. Tel: 0171-371 9300. *General Manager*, Ms J. Osborne

WOMEN'S INSTITUTES OF NORTHERN IRELAND, FEDERATION OF (1932), 209–211 Upper Lisburn Road, Belfast BT10 0LL. Tel: 01232-301506/601781. *General Secretary*, Mrs I. A. Sproule

WOMEN'S INTERNATIONAL LEAGUE FOR PEACE AND FREEDOM (British Section) (1915), Barton Hill Settlement, 43 Ducie Road, Bristol BS5 0AX

WOMEN'S NATIONWIDE CANCER CONTROL CAMPAIGN (1964), Suna House, 128–130 Curtain Road, London EC2A 3AR. Tel: 0171-729 4688/1735. Helpline: 0171-729 2229. *Administrator*, Miss J. Harding

WOMEN'S ROYAL NAVAL SERVICE BENEVOLENT TRUST (1942), 311 Twyford Avenue, Portsmouth PO2 8PE. Tel: 01705-655301. *General Secretary*, Mrs J. Russell

WOMEN'S ROYAL VOLUNTARY SERVICE (WRVS), 234–244 Stockwell Road, London SW9 9SP. Tel: 0171-416 0146. *National Chariman*, Lady Elizabeth Toulson

WOMEN'S RURAL INSTITUTES, SCOTTISH (1917), 42 Heriot Row, Edinburgh EH3 6ES. Tel: 0131-225 1724. *General Secretary*, Mrs A. Peacock

WOMEN'S TRANSPORT SERVICE (FANY) (1907), Mercury House, Duke of York's Headquarters, London SW3 4RX. Tel: 0171-730 2058. *Corps Commander*, Mrs A. Whitehead

WOODLAND TRUST, THE (1972), Autumn Park, Dysart Road, Grantham, Lincs NG31 6LL. Tel: 01476-74297. *Chief Executive*, J. D. James, OBE

WOOD PRESERVING AND DAMP-PROOFING ASSOCIATION, BRITISH (1930), 6 The Office Village, 4 Romford Road, London E15 4EA. Tel: 0181-519 2588. *Director*, Dr C. R. Coggins

WORKERS' EDUCATIONAL ASSOCIATION, Temple House, 17 Victoria Park Square, London E2 9PB. Tel: 0181-983 1515. *General Secretary*, R. Lochrie

WORLD EDUCATION FELLOWSHIP (1921), International Headquarters, 22 A Kew Gardens Road, Kew, Richmond, Surrey TW9 3HD. Tel: 0181-940 0131. *General Secretary*, Mrs R. Crommelin

WORLD ENERGY COUNCIL (1924), 34 St James's Street, London SW1A 1HD. Tel: 0171-930 3966. *Secretary-General*, I. D. Lindsay

WORLD MISSION, COUNCIL FOR (1977), Livingstone House, 11 Carteret Street, London SW1H 9DL. Tel: 0171-222 4214. *General Secretary*, D. P. Niles, PH.D.

WORLD SHIP SOCIETY (1946), 101 The Everglades, Hempstead, Gillingham, Kent ME7 3PZ. Tel: 01634-372015. *Secretary*, J. Poole

WORLD SOCIETY FOR THE PROTECTION OF ANIMALS (1981), 2 Langley Lane, London SW8 1TJ. Tel: 0171-793 0540. *Chief Executive*, A. Dickson

WRITERS TO HM SIGNET, SOCIETY OF (1532), 16 Hill Street, Edinburgh EH2 3LD. Tel: 0131-226 6703. *Clerk*, A. M. Kerr

WWF-UK (WORLD WIDE FUND FOR NATURE) (1961), Panda House, Weyside Park, Godalming, Surrey GU7 1XR. Tel: 01483-426444. *Director*, Dr R. Pellew

YEOMANRY BENEVOLENT FUND (1902), 10 Stone Buildings, Lincoln's Inn, London WC2A 3TG. Tel: 0171-831 6727. *Secretary*, Mrs C. W. Chrystie

YORKSHIRE AGRICULTURAL SOCIETY (1837), Great Yorkshire Showground, Harrogate, N. Yorks HG2 8PW. Tel: 01423-561536. *Chief Executive*, R. T. Keigwin

YORKSHIRE SOCIETY, THE (1812), 35 Waldorf Heights, Camberley, Surrey GU17 9JH. Tel: 01276-36342. Educational trust making grants to students of all ages. *Secretary*, G. G. Prince, TD

YOUNG FARMERS' CLUBS, NATIONAL FEDERATION OF, YFC Centre, National Agricultural Centre, Stoneleigh Park, Kenilworth, Warks CV8 2LG. Tel: 01203-696544. *Chief Executive*, B. Loughran

YOUNG MEN'S CHRISTIAN ASSOCIATION (YMCA) (1844), National Council of YMCAs, 640 Forest Road, London E17 3DZ. Tel: 0181-520 5599. *National Secretary*, N. Nightingale

Young Women's Christian Association of Great Britain (YWCA) (1855), 52 Cornmarket Street, Oxford OX1 3EJ. Tel: 01865-726110. *Chief Executive,* Ms G. Tishler

Youth Action, Northern Ireland (1944), Hampton, Glenmachan Park, Belfast BT4 2PJ. Tel: 01232-760067. *Director,* P. Graham

Youth Clubs UK (1911), 11 St Bride Street, London EC4A 4AS. Tel: 0171-353 2366. *Chief Executive,* J. Bateman

Youth Hostels Association (England and Wales) (1930), Trevelyan House, 8 St Stephen's Hill, St Albans, Herts AL1 2DY. Tel: 01727-855215. *Chief Executive,* C. Logan

Youth Hostels Association of Northern Ireland (1931), 22 Donegall Road, Belfast BT12 5JN. Tel: 01232-324733. *Hon. Secretary,* N. O'Reilly

Youth Hostels Association, Scottish (1931), 7 Glebe Crescent, Stirling FK8 2JA. Tel: 01786-451181. *General Secretary,* W. Forsyth

Zoological Society, North of England (1934), Chester Zoo, Upton by Chester, Chester CH2 1LH. Tel: 01244-380280. *Director,* Dr G. McGregor Reid

Zoological Society of London (1826), Regent's Park, London NW1 4RY. Tel: 0171-722 3333. *President,* Sir Martin Holdgate, CB, FIBIOL; *Clerk to the Council,* P. H. Denton

Zoological Society of Scotland, Royal (1913), Scottish National Zoological Park, Edinburgh Zoo, 134 Corstorphine Road, Edinburgh EH12 6TS. Tel: 0131-334 9171. *Director,* Prof. R. J. Wheater, OBE

LOCAL HISTORY AND ARCHAEOLOGICAL SOCIETIES

ENGLAND

Berkshire: Berkshire Archaeological Society. *Hon. Secretary,* L. J. Over, 43 Laburnham Road, Maidenhead, Berks SL6 4DE. Tel: 01628-31225.

Buckinghamshire: Buckinghamshire Archaeological Society. *Hon. Secretary,* Dr R. P. Hagerty, County Museum, Church Street, Aylesbury, Bucks HP20 2QP. Tel: 01296-20984.

Cambridgeshire: Cambridge Antiquarian Society. *Hon. Secretary,* Mrs S. Oosthuizen, 5 High Street, Great Eversden, Cambs CB3 7FN. Tel: 01223-264030.

Cheshire: Chester Archaeological Society. *Secretary,* Dr D. J. P. Mason, FSA, Ochr Cottage, Porch Lane, Hope Mountain, Caergwrle, Flintshire LL12 9LS. Tel: 01978-760834.

Cornwall: Cornwall Archaeological Society. *Hon. Secretaries,* Mr and Mrs B. Hammond, 7 Porthmeor Road, Holmbush, St Austell, Cornwall PL25 3LT. Tel: 01726-74763.

Cumberland and Westmorland: Cumberland and Westmorland Antiquarian and Archaeological Society. *Hon. Secretary,* R. Hall, 2 High Tenterfell, Kendal, Cumbria LA9 4PG. Tel: 01539-814405.

Derbyshire: Derbyshire Archaeological Society. *Hon. Secretary,* I. Mitchell, 68 Myrtle Avenue, Long Eaton, Nottingham NG10 3LY. Tel: 0115-972 9029.

Devonshire: Devon Archaeological Society. *Hon. Secretary,* H. Bishop, RAM Museum, Queen Street, Exeter, Devon EX4 3RX. Tel: 01392-265858.

Dorset: Dorset Natural History and Archaeological Society. *Secretary,* M. M. de Peyer, Dorset County Museum, Dorchester, Dorset DT1 1XA. Tel: 01305-262735.

Durham: Durham and Northumberland Architectural and Archaeological Society. *Hon. Secretary,* A. Lloyd-Wallis, 53 Brook Terrace, Darlington, Co. Durham DL3 6PJ. Tel: 01325-359772.

Essex: Essex Society for Archaeology and History. *Secretary,* Dr C. Thornton, Hollytrees Museum, High Street, Colchester CO1 1UG. Tel: 01206-271458.

Gloucestershire: Bristol and Gloucestershire Archaeological Society. *Hon. Secretary,* D. J. H. Smith, FSA, 22 Beaumont Road, Gloucester GL2 0EJ. Tel: 01452-302610.

Hampshire: Hampshire Field Club and Archaeological Society. *Hon. Secretary,* D. Allen, c/o Andover Museum, 6 Church Close, Andover, Hants SP10 1DP. Tel: 01264-366283.

Herefordshire: Woolhope Naturalists' Field Club. *Hon. Secretary,* J. W. Tonkin, FSA, Chy an Whyloryon, Wigmore, Leominster, Herefordshire HR6 9UD. Tel: 01568-770356.

Hertfordshire: East Hertfordshire Archaeological Society. *Hon. Secretary,* Mrs M. C. Readman, 1 Marsh Lane, Stanstead Abbots, Ware, Herts SG12 8HH. Tel: 01920-870664.

St Albans and Hertfordshire Architectural and Archaeological Society. *Hon. Secretary,* B. E. Moody, 24 Rose Walk, St Albans, Herts AL4 9AF. Tel: 01727-853204.

Isle of Wight: Isle of Wight Natural History and Archaeological Society. *Hon. Secretary,* Mrs T. Goodley, Island Countryside Centre, Rylstone Gardens, Shanklin, Isle of Wight PO37 6RG. Tel: 01983-867016.

Kent: Kent Archaeological Society. *Hon. General Secretary,* A. I. Moffat, Three Elms, Woodlands Lane, Shorne, Gravesend, Kent DA12 3HH. Tel: 01474-822280.

Leicestershire: Leicestershire Archaeological and Historical Society. *Hon. Secretary,* Dr A. D. McWhirr, The Guildhall, Leicester LE1 5FQ. Tel: 0116-270 3031.

London and Middlesex: City of London Archaeological Society. *Hon. Secretary,* Ms M. Bowen, 34 College Cross, London N1 1PR. Tel: 0171-609 2930.

London and Middlesex Archaeological Society. *Hon. Secretary,* M. Curtis, 34 Alexandra Road, Wimbledon, London SW19 7JZ. Tel: 0181-879 7109.

Norfolk: Norfolk and Norwich Archaeological Society. *Hon. General Secretary,* R. Bellinger, 30 Brettingham Avenue, Norwich NR4 6XG. Tel: 01603-455913.

Northumberland and Tyne and Wear: Society of Antiquaries of Newcastle upon Tyne. *Secretary,* N. Hodgson, Black Gate, Castle Garth, Newcastle upon Tyne NE1 1RQ. Tel: 0191-261 5390.

Sunderland Antiquarian Society. *Hon. Secretary,* Mrs V. M. Stevens, 16 Grizedale Court, Seaburn Dene, Sunderland SR6 8JP. Tel: 0191-548 7541.

Oxfordshire: Oxfordshire Architectural and Historical Society. *Hon. Secretary,* Dr A. J. Dodd, 53 Radley Road, Abingdon, Oxon OX4 3PN. Tel: 01235-525960.

Shropshire: Shropshire Archaeological and Historical Society. *Chairman,* J. B. Lawson, Westcott

Farm, Pontesbury, Shrewsbury sy5 0SQ. Tel: 01743-790531.

Somerset: SOMERSET ARCHAEOLOGICAL AND NATURAL HISTORY SOCIETY. *Hon. Secretary,* Dr I. J. Sinclair, Taunton Castle, Taunton, Somerset TA1 4AD. Tel: 01823-272429.

Staffordshire: CITY OF STOKE-ON-TRENT MUSEUM ARCHAEOLOGICAL SOCIETY. *Chairman,* E. E. Royle, City Museum and Art Gallery, Hanley, Stoke-on-Trent STI 3DW. Tel: 01782-202173.

Suffolk: SUFFOLK INSTITUTE OF ARCHAEOLOGY AND HISTORY. *Hon. Secretary,* E. A. Martin, Oak Tree Farm, Finborough Road, Hitcham, Ipswich IP7 7LS. Tel: 01449-741266.

Surrey: SURREY ARCHAEOLOGICAL SOCIETY. *Hon. Secretaries,* Mr and Mrs K. J. Graham, Castle Arch, Guildford, Surrey GU1 3SX. Tel: 01483-32454.

Sussex: SUSSEX ARCHAEOLOGICAL SOCIETY. *Chief Executive,* J. Manley, Bull House, 92 High Street, Lewes, E. Sussex BN7 1XH. Tel: 01273-486260.

Warwickshire: BIRMINGHAM AND WARWICKSHIRE ARCHAEOLOGICAL SOCIETY. *Hon. Secretary,* Miss S. Middleton, c/o Birmingham and Midland Institute, Margaret Street, Birmingham B3 3BS.

Wiltshire: WILTSHIRE ARCHAEOLOGICAL AND NATURAL HISTORY SOCIETY. *Secretary,* Cdr P. M. M. Coston, The Museum, 41 Long Street, Devizes, Wilts SN10 1NS. Tel: 01380-727369.

Worcestershire: WORCESTERSHIRE ARCHAEOLOGICAL SOCIETY. *Hon. Secretary,* T. J. Bridges, Queen Elizabeth House, Trinity Street, Worcester WR1 2PW. Tel: 01905-722369.

Yorkshire: HALIFAX ANTIQUARIAN SOCIETY. *Hon. Secretary,* Dr J. A. Hargreaves, 7 Hyde Park Gardens, Haugh Shaw Road, Halifax, W. Yorks HX1 3AH. Tel: 01422-250780.

THORESBY SOCIETY. *Hon. Secretary,* B. Harrison, Claremont, 23 Clarendon Road, Leeds LS2 9NZ. Tel: 0113-245 7910.

YORKSHIRE ARCHAEOLOGICAL SOCIETY. *Hon. Secretary,* Ms J. Heron, Claremont, 23 Clarendon Road, Leeds LS2 9NZ. Tel: 0113-245 7910.

SCOTLAND

AYRSHIRE ARCHAEOLOGICAL AND NATURAL HISTORY SOCIETY. *Hon. Secretary,* Dr T. Mathews, 10 Longlands Park, Ayr KA7 4RJ. Tel: 01292-441915.

DUMFRIESSHIRE AND GALLOWAY NATURAL HISTORY AND ANTIQUARIAN SOCIETY. *Hon. Secretary,* M. White, Smithy Cottage, Crocketford Road, Milton, Crocketford, Dumfries DG2 8QT

HAWICK ARCHAEOLOGICAL SOCIETY. *Hon. Secretary,* I. W. Landles, Orrock House, Stirches Road, Hawick, Roxburghshire TD9 7HF. Tel: 01450-375546.

INVERNESS FIELD CLUB. *Hon. Secretary,* Miss I. McLean, 6 Drumblair Crescent, Inverness IV2 4RG. Tel: 01463-234702.

WALES

Dyfed: CEREDIGION ANTIQUARIAN SOCIETY. *Hon. Secretary,* Mrs M. T. Burdett-Jones, Skomer, Llanbadarn Road, Aberystwyth, Ceredigion SY23 3QW. Tel: 01970-612342.

Powys: POWYSLAND CLUB. *Hon. Secretary,* Miss P. M. Davies, Llygad y Dyffryn, Llanidloes, Powys SY18 6JD. Tel: 01686-412277.

CHANNEL ISLANDS

SOCIÉTÉ JERSIAISE, ARCHAEOLOGICAL SECTION. *Hon. Secretary,* Mrs P. Syuret, La Hougue Bie Museum, Grouville, Jersey. Tel: 01534-58314.

International Organizations

ASSOCIATION OF SOUTH EAST ASIAN NATIONS
70 A. Jl. Sisingamangaraja Kebayoran Baru, Jakarta Selatan, PO Box 2072, Jakarta, Indonesia

The Association of South East Asian Nations (ASEAN) was formed in 1967 with the aims of fostering economic growth, social progress and cultural development, and ensuring regional stability.

The heads of government meeting, which convenes every three years, is ASEAN's highest authority. Its main policy-making body is the annual meeting of foreign ministers of the member countries, which appoints the secretary-general. The founding members are Indonesia, Malaysia, the Philippines, Singapore and Thailand. Brunei and Vietnam joined in 1984 and 1995 respectively, and Cambodia, Laos and Myanmar are expected to accede by 2000.

The heads of government summit in 1992 agreed to set up the ASEAN Free Trade Area (AFTA) in 2008, progress towards which began in 1993 with the introduction of a common preferential tariff. In 1994 it was decided to bring foward the date for AFTA implementation to 2003, with Vietnam likely to join by 2006.

At the 1995 annual summit, a South East Asia nuclear weapon-free zone was declared by ASEAN, Cambodia, Laos and Myanmar.

Secretary-General, Dato' Ajit Singh (Malaysia)

BANK FOR INTERNATIONAL SETTLEMENTS
Centralbahnplatz 2, 4002 Basle, Switzerland
Tel: Basle 280-8702

The objectives of the Bank for International Settlements (founded in 1930) are to promote co-operation between central banks; to provide facilities for international financial operations; and to act as trustee or agent in international financial settlements entrusted to it. The London agent is the Bank of England, and the Governor of the Bank of England is a member of the Board of Directors, in which administrative control is vested.

Chairman of the Board of Directors and President of the Bank for International Settlements, Dr W. F. Duisenberg (Netherlands)

CAB INTERNATIONAL
Wallingford, Oxon OX10 8DE
Tel 01491-832111

CAB International (formerly the Commonwealth Agricultural Bureaux) was founded in 1929. It generates, disseminates and applies scientific knowledge in support of sustainable development, with an emphasis on the needs of developing countries. The organization is owned and governed by its 40 member governments, each represented on an Executive Council. A Governing Board provides guidance to management on policy issues.

CABI has five institutes: mycology, entomology, parasitology, biological control and information science. These undertake taxonomic research, offer pest and disease diagnostic services, characterize biodiversity, develop sustainable crop protection practices, test new drugs against human diseases, and provide training and information services. The organization publishes books, journals and newsletters and produces bibliographic databases on agriculture, forestry, allied disciplines and aspects of human health. It also undertakes contracted scientific research and provides consultancy services and information support to developing countries.
Director-General, J. Gilmore

CARIBBEAN COMMUNITY AND COMMON MARKET
PO Box 10827, Georgetown, Guyana
Tel: Georgetown 692809

The Caribbean Community and Common Market (CARICOM) was established in 1973 with three objectives: economic co-operation through the Caribbean Common Market, the co-ordination of foreign policy among the member states, and the provision of common services and co-operation in matters such as health, education, culture, communications and industrial relations.

The supreme organ is the Conference of Heads of Government, which determines policy, takes strategic decisions and is responsible for resolving conflicts and all matters relating to the founding treaty. The Caribbean Community Council consists of ministers of government with special responsibility for CARICOM affairs and is responsible for the operational planning, resource allocation, development and smooth running of the Common Market and for the settlement of any problems arising out of its functioning. The principal administrative arms are the Secretariat, based in Guyana, and the Bureau of the Conference.

The 14 member states are Antigua and Barbuda, The Bahamas (which is not a member of the Common Market), Barbados, Belize, Dominica, Grenada, Guyana, Jamaica, Montserrat, St Christopher and Nevis, St Lucia, St Vincent and the Grenadines, Suriname and Trinidad and Tobago. The British Virgin Islands and the Turks and Caicos Islands are associate members. The Dominican Republic, Haiti, Mexico, Puerto Rico and Venezuela have observer status.
Secretary-General, Edwin W. Carrington

THE COMMONWEALTH

The Commonwealth is a voluntary association of 53 sovereign independent states together with their associated states and dependencies. All of the states were formerly parts of the British Empire or League of Nations (later UN) mandated territories, except for Mozambique which was admitted as a unique case because it was surrounded by Commonwealth nations.

The status and relationship of member nations were first defined by the Inter-Imperial Relations Committee of the 1926 Imperial Conference, when the six existing dominions (Australia, Canada, the Irish Free State, Newfoundland, New Zealand and South Africa) were described as 'autonomous Communities within the British Empire, equal in status, in no way subordinate one to another in any aspect of their domestic or external affairs, though united by a common allegiance to the Crown and freely associated as Members of the British Commonwealth of Nations'. This formula was given legal substance by the Statute of Westminster 1931.

This concept of a group of countries owing allegiance to a single Crown changed in 1949 when India decided to become a republic. Her continued membership of the Commonwealth was agreed by the other members on the basis of her 'acceptance of The King as the symbol of the free association of its independent member nations and as such the head of the Commonwealth'. This paved the way for other republics to join the association in due course. Member nations agreed at the time of the accession of Queen Elizabeth II to recognize Her Majesty as the new Head of the Commonwealth. However, the position is not vested in the British Crown.

THE MODERN COMMONWEALTH

As the UK's former colonies joined, initially with India and Pakistan in 1947, the Commonwealth was transformed from a grouping of all-white dominions into a multi-racial association of equal, sovereign nations. It increasingly focused on promoting development and racial equality, most notably imposing sanctions against South Africa in the 1970s over its policy of apartheid.

The new goals of advocating democracy, the rule of law, good government, human rights and social justice were enshrined in the Harare Commonwealth Declaration (1991), which formed the basis of new membership guidelines agreed in Cyprus in 1993. The heads of government meeting in Auckland, New Zealand, in 1995 adopted the Millbrook Commonwealth Action Programme to implement the Harare principles and suspended Nigeria for its anti-democratic behaviour. South Africa attended its first summit, having been readmitted.

MEMBERSHIP

Membership of the Commonwealth involves acceptance of the association's basic principles and is subject to the approval of existing members. There are 53 members at present. (The date of joining the Commonwealth is shown in parenthesis.)

*Antigua and Barbuda (1981)
*Australia (1931)
*The Bahamas (1973)
Bangladesh (1972)
*Barbados (1966)
*Belize (1981)
Botswana (1966)
Brunei (1984)
Cameroon (1995)
*Canada (1931)
Cyprus (1961)
Dominica (1978)
The Gambia (1965)
Ghana (1957)
*Grenada (1974)
Guyana (1966)
India (1947)
*Jamaica (1962)
Kenya (1963)
Kiribati (1979)
Lesotho (1966)
Malawi (1964)
Malaysia (1957)
The Maldives (1982)
Malta (1964)
Mauritius (1968)
Mozambique (1995)
Namibia (1990)
Nauru (1968)
*New Zealand (1931)
†Nigeria (1960)
Pakistan (1947)
*Papua New Guinea (1975)
*St Christopher and Nevis (1983)
*St Lucia (1979)
*St Vincent and the Grenadines (1979)
Seychelles (1976)
Sierra Leone (1961)
Singapore (1965)
*Solomon Islands (1978)
South Africa (1931)
Sri Lanka (1948)
Swaziland (1968)
Tanzania (1961)
Tonga (1970)
Trinidad and Tobago (1962)
*Tuvalu (1978)
Uganda (1962)
*United Kingdom
Vanuatu (1980)
Western Samoa (1970)
Zambia (1964)
Zimbabwe (1980)
*Realms of Queen Elizabeth II
†Suspended in 1995

Nauru and Tuvalu are special members, with the right to participate in all functional Commonwealth meetings and activities, but not to attend meetings of Commonwealth heads of government.

Countries which have left the Commonwealth
Fiji (1987)
Republic of Ireland (1949)
Pakistan (1972, rejoined 1989)
South Africa (1961, rejoined 1994)

Of the 53 member states, 16 have Queen Elizabeth II as head of state, 32 are republics, and five have national monarchies.

In each of the realms where Queen Elizabeth II is head of state (except for the UK), she is personally represented by a Governor-General, who holds in all essential respects the same position in relation to the administration of public affairs in the realm as is held by Her Majesty in Britain. The Governor-General is appointed by The Queen on the advice of the government of the state concerned.

INTERGOVERNMENTAL AND OTHER LINKS

The main forum for consultation is the Commonwealth heads of government meetings held biennially to discuss international developments and to consider co-operation among members. The UK is the venue of the October 1997 meeting. Decisions are reached by consensus, and the views of the meeting are set out in a communiqué. There are also annual meetings of finance ministers and frequent meetings of ministers and officials in other fields, such as education, health, labour, law, women's affairs, agriculture, youth and science. Intergovernmental links are complemented by the activities of some 300 Commonwealth non-governmental organizations linking professionals, sportsmen and sportswomen, and interest groups, forming a 'people's Commonwealth'. The Commonwealth Games take place every four years.

Assistance to other Commonwealth countries normally has priority in the bilateral aid programmes of the association's developed members (Australia, Britain, Canada and New Zealand), who direct about 30 per cent of their aid to other member countries. Developing Commonwealth nations also assist their poorer partners, and many Commonwealth voluntary organizations promote development.

Many of the smaller Commonwealth countries are party to the Lomé Convention, which accords preferential access to the European Union (EU) for developing countries of Africa, the Caribbean and the Pacific, and provides for them to receive EU aid.

COMMONWEALTH SECRETARIAT

The Commonwealth has a secretariat, established in 1965 in London, which is funded by all member governments. This is the main agency for multilateral communication between member governments on issues relating to the Commonwealth as a whole. It promotes consultation and co-operation, disseminates information on matters of common concern, organizes meetings including the biennial summits, co-ordinates Commonwealth activities, and provides technical assistance for economic and social development through the Commonwealth Fund for Technical Co-operation.

The Commonwealth Foundation was established by Commonwealth governments in 1966 as an autonomous body with a board of governors representing Commonwealth governments that fund the Foundation. It promotes and funds exchanges and other activities aimed at strengthening the skills and effectiveness of professionals and non-government organizations. It also promotes culture, rural development, social welfare and the role of women.

COMMONWEALTH SECRETARIAT, Marlborough House, Pall Mall, London SW1Y 5HX. Tel: 0171-839 3411. *Secretary-General*, Chief Emeka Anyaoku (Nigeria)
COMMONWEALTH FOUNDATION, Marlborough House, Pall Mall, London SW1Y 5HY. Tel: 0171-930 3783.
Director, Dr Humayun Khan (Pakistan)
COMMONWEALTH INSTITUTE, Kensington High Street, London W8 6NQ. Tel: 0171-603 4535. *Director-General*, S. Cox

COMMONWEALTH OF INDEPENDENT STATES

The Commonwealth of Independent States (CIS) is a multilateral grouping of 12 sovereign states which were formerly constituent republics of the USSR. It was formed by Russia, Ukraine and Belorussia on 8 December 1991, the remaining republics, apart from the Baltic states and Georgia, joining on 21 December. Georgia joined in December 1993. Azerbaijani and Moldovan membership effectively lapsed, because of non-ratification, until September 1993 and April 1994 respectively. The CIS charter, signed in 1993, formally established the functions of the organization and the obligations of its member states.

The CIS acts as a co-ordinating mechanism for foreign, defence and economic policies, and is a forum for addressing those problems which have specifically arisen from the break-up of the USSR. These matters are addressed in more than 50 inter-state, intergovernmental co-ordinating and consultative statutory bodies. The two supreme CIS bodies are the Council of Heads of State and the Council of Heads of Government. The Council of Heads of State is the highest organ of the CIS and meets not less than twice yearly; it is chaired by the heads of state of the members in (Russian) alphabetical order. The Council of Heads of Government meets not less than once every three months to co-ordinate military and economic activity. Other important bodies are the Council of Heads of Collective Security (defence ministers), the Joint Staff for co-ordinating military co-operation, the CIS Inter-Parliamentary Assembly, the Economic Arbitration Court and the Co-ordinating Consultative Committee. Administrative support is provided by the Executive Secretariat based in Minsk.

DEFENCE CO-OPERATION

On becoming member states of the CIS, the 11 original states agreed to recognize their existing borders, respect one another's territorial integrity and reject the use of military force or other forms of coercion to settle disputes between them. Agreement was also reached on fulfilling all the international treaty obligations of the former USSR, and on a unified central control for nuclear weapons and other strategic forces, together with the establishment of CIS joint armed forces.

The members agreed on a central CIS command for all nuclear weapons, the control over which was passed to CIS commander-in-chief Marshal Shaposhnikov in December 1991. All tactical nuclear weapons had been transferred to the Russian republic by May 1992. An agreement was reached with the USA in May 1992 by the four republics with strategic nuclear weapons (Russia, Ukraine, Belarus, Kazakhstan) on implementing the strategic arms reduction talks (START) treaty previously signed by the USA and USSR, and the START I treaty was ratified by the five parties between October 1992 and February 1994. Under this agreement Ukraine, Belarus and Kazakhstan agreed to eliminate all their strategic nuclear weapons over a seven-year period and Russia has agreed to reduce its strategic nuclear weapons over the same period to such an extent that there will be a 38 per cent reduction in the overall former Soviet arsenal. In June 1996, Ukraine completed the transferral of its nuclear weapons to Russia for disposal and reprocessing. In December 1994 Ukraine, Kazakhstan and Belarus signed the Nuclear Non-Proliferation Treaty.

A CIS high command and a joint conventional force were created in 1992 to operate in parallel with member states' own armed forces. In the same year, a Treaty on Collective Security was signed by six states and a joint peacemaking force, to intervene in CIS conflicts, was agreed upon by nine states. Deployment of these forces was made conditional on consensus in the Council of Heads of State. Fear of Russian domination by some states (Ukraine, Moldova, Turkmenistan) hampered defence co-operation and led to the downgrading of the high command into a joint staff for military co-operation in 1993. Russia responded by concluding bilateral and multilateral agreements with other CIS states under the supervision of the Council of Heads of Collective Security (established 1993). These have been gradually upgraded into CIS agreements under the umbrella of the Treaty on Collective Security, enabling Russia to station troops in ten of the other 11 CIS states (not Ukraine), and giving Russian forces *de facto* control of virtually all of the former USSR's external borders. Only Ukraine and Moldova remain outside the defence co-operation framework and have not signed the Treaty on Collective Security. In November 1995, the ten agreed to recreate a joint air defence system which Russia will, in effect, control and take financial responsibility for. In March 1996, a Joint Chiefs of Staff Committee, comprising the chiefs of staff of the member states' armed forces, was established to formulate a plan on the creation of a military security system.

ECONOMIC CO-OPERATION

As it became clear that the Soviet Union was disintegrating in October 1991, nine republics signed a treaty forming an economic community, and were joined by two other republics in November 1991. The principles of the treaty were embodied within the CIS and formed the basis of its economic co-operation in 1992 and the first half of 1993. Members agreed to refrain from economic actions that would damage each other and to co-ordinate economic and monetary policies. A Co-ordinating Consultative Committee, an economic arbitration court and an inter-state bank were established. A single monetary unit, the rouble, was originally agreed upon by all member states, and the members recognized that the basis of recovery for their economies was private ownership, free enterprise and competition. Throughout 1992 and early 1993 economic co-operation failed to function effectively because of the differing pace of economic reform and the introduction of separate currencies by member states.

Russia effectively forced the collapse of the rouble zone in July 1993 by withdrawing all pre-1993 roubles and forcing the remaining states using roubles to accept Russian monetary control or introduce their own currencies, which all did apart from Tajikistan. The resulting economic collapse of the non-Russian economies led to renewed interest in economic co-operation and the signing of a Treaty on Economic Union in September 1993. The 11 CIS members who have signed the Treaty (Ukraine is an associate member of the economic union) are committed to a common market without internal barriers to trade, common fiscal policies and an eventual currency union with currencies semi-fixed against the rouble. In order to facilitate faster economic integration 11 states (not Turkmenistan) agreed in October 1994 to establish an Interstate Economic Committee, and in May 1995 a monetary committee to facilitate payments in different currencies was agreed. Belarus has withdrawn its currency and rejoined Russia and Tajikistan in the rouble zone. A treaty creating a common market was signed by Kazakhstan, Kyrgyzstan, Russia and Belarus in March 1996, with other CIS states excluded from membership.

Originally the main advantage of economic co-ordination by the CIS members was the granting of large amounts of aid by Western countries and international organizations, which made it clear that economic aid was dependent on CIS co-ordination in accepting responsibility for the former USSR's debt, abiding by all the former USSR's international obligations (such as nuclear and conventional arms reductions), and having a secure, central control and command of nuclear weapons. As a result of CIS co-ordination members have gained extensive grants, loans, credits, trade agreements and technological, business and planning expertise and guidance.

THE COUNCIL OF EUROPE
67075 Strasbourg, France
Tel: Strasbourg 8841 2576

The Council of Europe was founded in 1949. Its aim is to achieve greater unity between its members, to safeguard their European heritage and to facilitate their progress in economic, social, cultural, educational, scientific, legal and administrative matters, and in the furtherance of pluralist democracy, human rights and fundamental freedoms.

The 39 members are Albania, Andorra, Austria, Belgium, Bulgaria, Cyprus, Czech Republic, Denmark, Estonia, Finland, France, Germany, Greece, Hungary, Iceland, the Republic of Ireland, Italy, Latvia, Liechtenstein, Lithuania, Luxembourg, Macedonia (Former Yugoslav Republic of), Malta, Moldova, the Netherlands, Norway, Poland, Portugal, Romania, Russia, San Marino, Slovakia, Slovenia, Spain, Sweden, Switzerland, Turkey, the UK and Ukraine. 'Special guest status' has been granted to Belarus and Bosnia-Hercegovina. Turkey's membership was suspended from April 1995 to September 1996 over its military offensive against Kurdish guerrillas in northern Iraq. The Council voted in May 1996 to block Croatia's accession until its human rights record improved.

The organs are the Committee of Ministers, consisting of the foreign ministers of member countries, who meet twice yearly, and the Parliamentary Assembly of 281 members, elected or chosen by the national parliaments of member countries in proportion to the relative strength of political parties. There is also a Joint Committee of Ministers and Representatives of the Parliamentary Assembly.

The Committee of Ministers is the executive organ. The majority of its conclusions take the form of international agreements (known as European Conventions) or recommendations to governments. Decisions of the Ministers may also be embodied in partial agreements to which a limited number of member governments are party. Member governments accredit Permanent Representatives to the Council in Strasbourg, who are also the Ministers' Deputies. The Committee of Deputies meets every month to transact business and to take decisions on behalf of Ministers.

The Parliamentary Assembly holds three week-long sessions a year. Its 13 permanent committees meet once or twice between each public plenary session of the Assembly. The Congress of Local and Regional Authorities of Europe each year brings together mayors and municipal councillors in the same numbers as the members of the Parliamentary Assembly.

One of the principal achievements of the Council of Europe is the European Convention on Human Rights (1950) under which was established the European Commission and the European Court of Human Rights, which were merged in 1993. The reorganized European Court of Human Rights sits in chambers of seven judges or exceptionally as a grand chamber of 17 judges. Litigants must exhaust legal processes in their own country before bringing cases before the court.

Among other conventions and agreements are the European Social Charter, the European Cultural Convention, the European Code of Social Security, the European Convention on the Protection of National Minorities, and conventions on extradition, the legal status of migrant workers, torture prevention, conservation, and the transfer of sentenced prisoners. Most recently, the specialized bodies of the Venice Commission and Demosthenes have been set up to assist in developing legislative, administrative and constitutional reforms in central and eastern Europe.

Non-member states take part in certain Council of Europe activities on a regular or ad hoc basis; thus the Holy See participates in all the educational, cultural and sports activities. The European Youth Centre is an educational residential centre for young people. The European Youth Foundation provides youth organizations with funds for their international activities.

Secretary-General, Daniel Tarschys (Sweden)
Permanent UK Representative, HE Roger Beetham, CMG, LVO, *apptd* 1993

THE ECONOMIC COMMUNITY OF WEST AFRICAN STATES
Secretariat Building, Asokoro, Abuja, Nigeria
Tel: Abuja 523 1858

The Economic Community of West African States (ECOWAS) was founded in 1975 and came into operation in 1977. It aims to promote the cultural, economic and social development of West Africa through mutual co-operation. A revised ECOWAS Treaty was signed in 1993 which also makes the prevention and control of regional conflicts an aim of ECOWAS. The Treaty also provides for the establishment of a regional parliament, an economic and social council, and a court of justice.

Measures undertaken by ECOWAS include the gradual elimination of barriers to the movement of goods, people and services between member states and the improvement of regional telecommunications and transport.

The supreme authority of ECOWAS is vested in the annual summit of heads of government of all 16 member states. A Council of Ministers, two from each member state, meets biannually to monitor the organization and make recommendations to the summit. ECOWAS operates through a Secretariat, headed by the Executive Secretary. In addition there is a financial controller, an external auditor, the Disputes Tribunal and the Defence Council.

A Fund for Co-operation, Compensation and Development, situated at Lomé, Togo, finances development projects and provides compensation to member states who have suffered losses as a result of ECOWAS's policies, particularly trade liberalization.

In 1989–90 ECOWAS attempted to mediate in the Liberian civil war and sent an ECOWAS Monitoring Group (ECOMOG) peacekeeping force to the country in 1990. The force succeeded in establishing an interim government and preventing further conflict in 1991 but fighting broke out again in late 1992. ECOMOG forces remained in the country charged with maintaining the buffer zones provided for in the 1994 cease-fire. When fighting resumed in December 1995 ECOMOG soldiers were unable to maintain control and became embroiled in the factional rivalry, suffering several fatalities.
Executive Secretary, Edouard Benjamin

THE EUROPEAN BANK FOR RECONSTRUCTION AND DEVELOPMENT
One Exchange Square, London EC2A 2EH
Tel 0171-338 6000

The charter of the European Bank for Reconstruction and Development (EBRD) was signed by 40 countries, the European Commission and the European Investment Bank in May 1990 and was inaugurated in April 1991.

The aim of the EBRD is to facilitate the transformation of the states of central and eastern Europe (Albania, Bulgaria, Czech Republic, Estonia, Hungary, Latvia, Lithuania, Poland, Romania, Slovakia, the republics of the former USSR and former Yugoslavia) from centrally-planned to free market economies, and to promote multi-party democracy, entrepreneurial initiative, and respect for human rights and the environment.

The EBRD provides technical assistance, training and investment in the upgrading of infrastructure; privatization; the strengthening of legal systems; gaining foreign direct investment; the creation of modern financial systems; nuclear safety; tourism; the exploitation of natural resources; and the restructuring of state industries. The EBRD's assistance is weighted towards the private sector; no more than 40 per cent of its investment can be made in state-owned concerns. It works in co-operation with its members, private companies, and international organizations such as the OECD, the IMF, the World Bank and the UN specialized agencies.

The EBRD has an initial subscribed capital of 10 billion ECU, which its shareholders agreed to double at their annual meeting in April 1996, of which 30 per cent is paid in. The EBRD is also able to borrow on world capital markets. Its major subscribers are the USA, 10 per cent; Britain, France, Germany, Italy and Japan, 8.5 per cent each; central and eastern European states, 11.9 per cent. The EBRD offers a range of financing instruments including loans, equity investments and guarantees. In 1995 the EBRD approved 134 projects, totalling ECU 2,855 million; the total number of projects approved since its establishment is 382, involving ECU 6,300 million of EBRD funds.

The EBRD has 59 members. The highest authority is the Board of Governors; each member appoints one Governor and one Alternate. The Governors delegate most powers to a 23-member Board of Directors; the Directors are responsible for the EBRD's operations and budget, and are appointed by the Governors for three-year terms. The Governors also elect the President of the Board of Directors, who acts as the Bank's president, for a four-year term. A Secretary-General liaises between the Directors and EBRD staff.
President of the Board of Directors, Jacques de Larosière (France)
UK Executive Director, Robert Graham-Harrison
Secretary-General, Antonio Maria Costa (Italy)

EUROPEAN FREE TRADE ASSOCIATION
9–11 rue de Varembé, 1211 Geneva 20, Switzerland
Tel: Geneva 749 1111
74 rue de Trèves, 1040 Brussels, Belgium

The European Free Trade Association (EFTA) was established in 1960, by Austria, Denmark, Norway, Portugal, Sweden, Switzerland and the UK, and was subsequently joined by Finland, Iceland and Liechtenstein. Six members have left to join the European Union: Denmark and the UK (1972), Portugal (1985), Austria, Finland and Sweden (1994). The remaining members are Iceland, Liechtenstein, Norway and Switzerland (not a European Economic Area (EEA) member).

The first objective of EFTA was to establish free trade in industrial goods between members; this was achieved in 1966. Its second objective was the creation of a single market in western Europe and in 1972 EFTA signed a free trade agreement with the EC covering trade in industrial goods; the remaining tariffs on industrial products were abolished in 1984.

Exploratory talks on the free movement of goods, services, capital and labour throughout the EC–EFTA area led to negotiations on the establishment of the EEA encompassing all 19 EC and EFTA countries. These concluded with the signing of the EEA Agreement in 1992. The EEA was intended to enter into force at the same time as the EC single market in 1993 but this proved impossible when the Swiss electorate rejected ratification of the EEA Agreement in a referendum in December 1992. The other EFTA states and the EC negotiated a protocol to the EEA Agreement which was signed in March 1993 and the EEA Agreement entered into force on 1 January 1994 for the remaining countries (except Liechtenstein, which joined on 1 May 1995 after adapting its customs union with Switzerland) after its ratification by all 18 states.

EFTA has expanded its relations with other non-EU states in recent years and free trade agreements have been signed with Turkey (1991), Israel, Poland and Romania (1992), Bulgaria, Hungary, the Czech Republic and Slovakia (1993), and Estonia, Latvia, Lithuania and Slovenia (1995). In addition, EFTA has signed declarations of economic co-operation with Albania (1992), and Egypt, Morocco and Tunisia (1995).

The EFTA Council is the principle organ of the Association. It generally meets twice a month at the level of heads of the permanent national delegations to the EFTA Secretariat in Geneva and twice a year at ministerial level. The chairmanship of the Council rotates every six months. Each state has a single vote and recommendations must normally be unanimous; decisions of the Council are binding on member countries.
Secretary-General, Kjartan Jóhannsson (Iceland)

EUROPEAN ORGANIZATION FOR NUCLEAR RESEARCH (CERN)
CH-1211 Geneva 23, Switzerland
Tel: Geneva 767 4101

The Convention establishing the European Organization for Nuclear Research (CERN) came into force in 1954. CERN promotes European collaboration in high energy physics of a scientific, rather than a military nature.

The member countries are Austria, Belgium, the Czech Republic, Denmark, Finland, France, Germany, Greece, Hungary, Italy, the Netherlands, Norway, Poland, Portugal, Slovakia, Spain, Sweden, Switzerland and the UK. Israel, Russia, Turkey, the EU Commission and UNESCO have observer status.

The Council is the highest policy-making body and comprises two delegates from each member state. There is also a Committee of the Council comprising a single delegate from each member state (who is also a Council member) and the chairmen of the scientific policy and finance advisory committees. The Council is chaired by the President who is elected by the Council in Session. The Council also elects the Director-General, who is responsible for the internal organization of CERN. The Director-General heads a workforce of approximately 3,000, including physicists, craftsmen, technicians and administrative staff. At present over 6,000 physicists use CERN's facilities.

The member countries contribute to the budget in proportion to their net national revenue. The 1996 budget was SFr 938 million.

President of the Council, Prof. Hubert Curien (France)
Director-General (1994–9), Prof. Christopher Llewellyn-Smith (UK)

EUROPEAN SPACE AGENCY
8–10 rue Mario Nikis, 75738 Paris, France
Tel: Paris 5369 7400

The European Space Agency (ESA) was created in 1975 by the merger of the European Space Research Organization (ESRO) and the European Launcher Development Organization (ELDO). Its aims include the advancement of space research and technology, the implementation of a long-term European space policy and the co-ordination of national space programmes.

The member countries are Austria, Belgium, Denmark, Finland, France, Germany, Republic of Ireland, Italy, Netherlands, Norway, Spain, Sweden, Switzerland and the UK. Canada is a co-operating state.

The agency is directed by a Council composed of the representatives of the member states; its chief officer is the Director-General.

Director-General, Jean-Marie Luton, *apptd* 1990

FOOD AND AGRICULTURE ORGANIZATION OF THE UNITED NATIONS
Viale delle Terme di Caracalla, 00100 Rome, Italy
Tel: Rome 52251

The Food and Agriculture Organization (FAO) is a specialized UN agency, established in 1945. It assists rural populations by raising levels of nutrition and living standards, and by encouraging greater efficiency in food production and distribution. It collects, analyses and disseminates information on agriculture and natural resources. The FAO also advises governments on national agricultural policy and planning; its Investment Centre, together with the World Bank and other financial institutions, helps to prepare development projects. The FAO's field programme covers a range of activities, including strengthening crop production, rural and livestock development, and conservation.

The FAO's top priorities are sustainable agriculture, rural development and food security. The Organization attempts to ensure the availability of adequate food supplies, stability in the flow of supplies and the securing of access to food by the poor. The FAO monitors potential famine areas. The Office for Special Relief Operations channels emergency aid from governments and other agencies, and assists in rehabilitation. The Technical Co-operation Programme provides schemes for countries facing agricultural crises.

The FAO had 175 members (174 states and the EU) and one associate member (Puerto Rico) as at May 1996. It is governed by a biennial conference of its members which sets a programme and budget. The budget for 1996–7 is US$650 million, funded by member countries in proportion to their gross national products. The FAO is also funded by the UN Development Programme, donor governments and other institutions.

The Conference elects a Director-General and a 49-member Council which governs between conferences. The Regular and Field Programmes are administered by a Secretariat, headed by the Director-General. Five regional, five sub-regional and 80 national offices help administer the Field Programme.

Director-General, Jacques Diouf (Senegal)
UK Representative, D. Sands Smith, British Embassy, Rome

INTERNATIONAL ATOMIC ENERGY AGENCY
Vienna International Centre, Wagramerstrasse 5, PO Box 100, 1400 Vienna, Austria
Tel: Vienna 2060

The International Atomic Energy Agency (IAEA) was established in 1957 as a consequence of the UN International Conference on the Peaceful Uses of Atomic Energy held the previous year. It operates under the aegis of, and reports annually to, the UN, but is not a specialized agency.

The IAEA aims to enhance the contribution of atomic energy to peace, health and prosperity, and to ensure that any assistance that it provides is not used for military purposes. It establishes atomic energy safety standards and offers services to its member states for the safe operation of their nuclear facilities and for radiation protection. It is the focal point for international conventions on the early notification of a nuclear accident, assistance in the case of a nuclear accident, civil liability for nuclear damage, physical protection of nuclear material, and nuclear safety. The IAEA also encourages research and training in nuclear power. It is additionally charged with drawing up safeguards and verifying their use in accordance with the Nuclear Non-Proliferation Treaty (NPT) 1968, the Treaty for the Prohibition of Nuclear Weapons in Latin America (Tlatelolco Treaty) 1968, the Treaty on a South Pacific Nuclear Free Zone (Rarotonga Treaty), and the African Nuclear Weapon-Free Zone Treaty (Pelindaba Treaty) 1996. Together with the Food and Agriculture

Organization and the World Health Organization, the IAEA established an International Consultative Group on Food Irradiation in 1983.

The IAEA has attempted to prevent North Korea from developing a nuclear weapons programme. In June 1994 the IAEA informed the UN Security Council that North Korea had violated its NPT obligations and all technical aid to North Korea was suspended. North Korea resigned from the IAEA in June 1994, but permitted IAEA inspections under the terms of an agreement with the USA which ended North Korea's nuclear weapons production and enabled the IAEA to resume safeguards inspections.

The IAEA had 123 members as at May 1996. A General Conference of all its members meets annually to decide policy, a programme and a budget (1996, US$219 million), as well as electing a Director-General and a 35-member Board of Governors. The Board meets four times a year to formulate policy which is implemented by the Secretariat under a Director-General.

Director-General, Hans Blix (Sweden)
Permanent UK Representative, C. Hulse, Jaurèsgasse 12, 1030
Vienna, Austria

INTERNATIONAL CIVIL AVIATION ORGANIZATION
1000 Sherbrooke Street West, Montreal, Quebec,
Canada H3A 2R2
Tel: Montreal 285 8221

The International Civil Aviation Organization (ICAO) was founded with the signing of the Chicago Convention on International Civil Aviation in 1944, and became a specialized agency of the United Nations in 1947. It sets international technical standards and recommended practices for all areas of civil aviation, including airworthiness, air navigation, traffic control and pilot licensing. It encourages uniformity and simplicity in ground regulations and operations at international airports, including immigration and customs control. The ICAO also promotes regional air navigation, plans for ground facilities, and collects and distributes air transport statistics worldwide. It is dedicated to improving safety and to the orderly development of civil aviation throughout the world.

The ICAO had 184 members as at 3 November 1995. It is governed by an assembly of its members which meets at least once every three years. A Council of 33 members is elected, which represents leading air transport nations as well as less developed countries. The Council elects the President, appoints the Secretary-General and supervises the organization through subsidiary committees, serviced by a Secretariat.

President of the Council, Dr Assad Kotaite (Lebanon)
Secretary-General, Dr Philippe Rochat (Switzerland)
UK Representative, D. S. Evans, CMG, Suite 928, 1000
Sherbrooke Street West, Montreal, Quebec, Canada
H3A 3G4

INTERNATIONAL CONFEDERATION OF FREE TRADE UNIONS
Boulevard Emile Jacqmain 155 B1, B-1210
Brussels, Belgium
Tel: Brussels 224 0211

The International Confederation of Free Trade Unions (ICFTU) was created in 1949. It aims to establish, maintain and promote free trade unions, and to promote peace with economic security and social justice.

Affiliated to the ICFTU are 194 individual unions and representative bodies in 136 countries and territories. There were 127 million members on 3 December 1995.

The Congress, the supreme authority of the ICFTU, convenes at least every four years. It is composed of delegates from the affiliated trade union organizations. The Congress elects an Executive Board of 49 members which meets not less than once a year. The Board establishes the budget and receives suggestions and proposals from affiliates as well as acting on behalf of the Confederation. The Congress also elects the General Secretary.

General Secretary, Bill Jordan (UK)
UK Affiliate, TUC, Congress House, 23–28 Great Russell
Street, London WC1B 3LS. Tel: 0171-636 4030

INTERNATIONAL CRIMINAL POLICE ORGANIZATION
200 Quai Charles de Gaulle, 69006 Lyon, France
Tel: Lyon 7244 7000

The International Criminal Police Commission (Interpol) was set up in 1923 to establish an international criminal records office and to harmonize extradition procedures. On 1 January 1996 the organization comprised 176 member states.

Interpol's aims are to promote co-operation between criminal police authorities, and to support government agencies concerned with combating crime, whilst respecting national sovereignty. It is financed by annual contributions from the governments of member states.

Interpol's policy is decided by the General Assembly which meets annually; it is composed of delegates appointed by the member states. The 13-member Executive Committee is elected by the General Assembly from among the member states' delegates, and is chaired by the President, who has a four-year term of office. The permanent administrative organ is the General Secretariat, headed by the Secretary-General, who is appointed by the General Assembly.

Secretary-General, Raymond Kendall, QPM (UK)
UK OFFICE, NCIS-Interpol, Spring Gardens, Tinworth
Street, London SE11 5EH. Tel: 0171-238 8000. *UK Representative,* A. Pacey, CBE, QPM

INTERNATIONAL ENERGY AGENCY
Chateau de la Muette, 2 rue André-Pascal, 75775
Paris, France
Tel: Paris 4524 9873

The International Energy Agency (IEA), founded in 1974, is an autonomous agency within the framework of the Organization for Economic Co-operation and Development (OECD). The IEA had 23 member countries at June 1996.

The IEA's objectives include improvement of energy co-operation world-wide, increased efficiency, development of alternative energy sources and the promotion of relations between oil producing and oil consuming countries. The IEA also maintains an emergency system to alleviate the effects of severe oil supply disruptions.

The main decision-making body is the Governing Board composed of senior energy officials from member countries. Various standing groups and special committees exist to facilitate the work of the Board. The IEA Secretariat, with a staff of energy experts, carries out the work of the Governing Board and its subordinate bodies. The Executive Director is appointed by the Board.

Executive Director, Robert Priddle (UK)

INTERNATIONAL FUND FOR AGRICULTURAL DEVELOPMENT
107 Via del Serafico, 00142 Rome, Italy
Tel: Rome 519 3328

The establishment of the International Fund for Agricultural Development (IFAD) was proposed by the 1974 World Food Conference and IFAD began operations as a UN specialized agency in 1977. Its purpose is to mobilize additional funds for agricultural and rural development projects in developing countries that benefit the poorest rural populations; provide employment and additional income for poor farmers; reduce malnutrition; and improve food distribution systems.

IFAD had 158 members as at 25 January 1996. Membership is divided into three categories: category I, with 22 members, the developed countries (OECD); category II, with 12 members, the oil-exporting developing countries (OPEC); and category III, with 124 members, the remaining developing countries. The three groups have equal voting rights in IFAD's governing structure. All powers are vested in a Governing Council of all member countries. It elects an 18-member Executive Board (with 17 alternate members) responsible for IFAD's operations. The Council meets annually and elects a President who is also chairman of the Board. He is assisted by a Vice-President and three Assistant Presidents.

At the end of December 1995 IFAD's loan portfolio comprised commitments of US$4,548 million for 429 approved projects in 104 developing countries. The operational budget for 1995 was US$455.3 million.

President, Fawzi H. Al-Sultan (Kuwait)

INTERNATIONAL LABOUR ORGANIZATION
4 route des Morillons, 1211 Geneva 22, Switzerland
Tel: 0171-828 6401

The International Labour Organization (ILO) was established in 1919 as an autonomous body of the League of Nations and became the UN's first specialized agency in 1946. The ILO aims to increase employment, improve working conditions, raise living standards and encourage democratic development. It sets minimum international labour standards through the drafting of international conventions. Member countries are obliged to submit these to their domestic authorities for ratification, and thus undertake to bring their domestic legislation in line with the conventions. Members must report to the ILO periodically on how these regulations are being implemented. The ILO plays a major role in helping developing countries achieve economic stability and job expansion through its wide-ranging programme of technical co-operation. The ILO is also the world's principal resource centre for information, analysis and guidance on labour and employment. The organization aims to improve working and living conditions throughout the world and to support the transition to democracy and market economics under way in many states.

The ILO had 173 members as at June 1996. It is composed of the International Labour Conference, the Governing Body and the International Labour Office. The Conference of members meets annually, and is attended by national delegations comprising two government delegates, one worker delegate and one employer delegate. It formulates international labour conventions and recommendations, provides a forum for discussion of world employment and social issues, and approves the ILO's programme and budget (1996–7, US$579.5 million).

The 56-member Governing Body, composed of 28 government, 14 worker and 14 employer members, acts as the ILO's executive council. Ten governments, including Britain, hold seats on the Governing Body because of their industrial importance. There are also various regional conferences and advisory committees. The International Labour Office acts as a secretariat and as a centre for operations, publishing and research.

Director-General, Michel Hansenne (Belgium)
UK Office, Vincent House, Vincent Square, London SW1P 2NB. Tel: 0171-828 6401

INTERNATIONAL MARITIME ORGANIZATION
4 Albert Embankment, London SE1 7SR
Tel: 0171-735 7611

The International Maritime Organization (IMO) was established as a UN specialized agency in 1948. Owing to delays in treaty ratification it did not commence operations until 1958. Originally it was called the Inter-Governmental Maritime Consultative Organization (IMCO) but changed its name in 1982.

The IMO fosters intergovernmental co-operation in technical matters relating to international shipping, especially with regard to safety at sea. It is also charged with preventing and controlling marine pollution caused by shipping and facilitating marine traffic. The IMO is responsible for convening maritime conferences and drafting marine conventions. It also provides technical aid to countries wishing to develop their activities at sea.

The IMO had 153 members as at May 1996. It is governed by an Assembly comprising delegates of all its members. It meets biennially to formulate policy, set a budget (1996–7, £36.6 million), vote on specific recommendations on pollution and maritime safety and elect the Council. The Council fulfils the functions of the Assembly between sessions and appoints the Secretary-General. It consists of 32 members: eight from the world's largest shipping nations, eight from the nations most dependent on seaborne trade, and 16 other members to ensure a fair geographical representation. The Maritime Safety Committee, through its sub-committees, makes reports and recommendations to the Council and the Assembly. There are a number of other specialist subsidiary committees, including one for marine environmental protection.

The IMO acts as the secretariat for the London Convention (1972) which regulates the disposal of land-generated waste at sea.

Secretary-General, William A. O'Neil (Canada)

INTERNATIONAL MOBILE SATELLITE ORGANIZATION
99 City Road, London ECIY IAX
Tel: 0171-728 1773

Inmarsat (the International Mobile Satellite Organization) was founded in 1979 as the International Maritime Satellite Organization and began operations in 1982. Inmarsat is an internationally-owned co-operative which operates a system of satellites to provide global mobile communications. Inmarsat satellite terminals are used world-wide on ships, in aircraft and on land for telephone, facsimile, telex and e-mail data, as well as maritime safety, position reporting and distress communications.

Inmarsat comprises three bodies: the Assembly, the Council and the Directorate. The Assembly is composed of representatives of the 79 member countries, each having one vote. It meets every two years to review activities and objectives, and to make recommendations to the Council. The Council is the main decision-making body and consists of representatives of the 18 members with the largest investment shares, and four members representing the interests of developing countries who are elected to the Council on the basis of geographical representation. Members have voting powers equal to their investment shares. The Council meets at least three times a year and oversees the activities of the Directorate, the permanent staff of Inmarsat.

Director-General, Warren Grace (Australia)

INTERNATIONAL MONETARY FUND
00 19th Street NW, Washington DC 20431, USA

The International Monetary Fund (IMF) was established in 1944, at the UN Monetary and Financial Conference held at Bretton Woods, New Hampshire. Its Articles of Agreement entered into force in 1945 and it began operations in 1946.

The IMF exists to promote international monetary co-operation, the expansion of world trade, and exchange stability, and to eliminate foreign exchange restrictions. The IMF advises members on their economic and financial policies; promotes policy co-ordination among the major industrial countries; and gives technical assistance in central banking, balance of payments accounting, taxation, and other financial matters. The IMF serves as a forum for members to discuss important financial and monetary issues and seeks the balanced growth of international trade and, through this, high levels of employment, income and productive capacity. As at April 1996 the IMF had 181 members. Sudan's and Zaire's voting rights have been suspended.

Upon joining the IMF, a member is assigned a 'quota', based on the member's relative standing in the world economy and its balance of payments position, that determines its capital subscription to the Fund, its access to IMF resources, its voting power, and its share in the allocation of Special Drawing Rights (SDRs). Quotas are reviewed every five years and adjusted accordingly. In the Ninth General Review of quotas in 1994, total Fund quotas stand at SDR 145.3 billion. The SDR, an international reserve asset issued by the IMF, is calculated daily on a basket of usable currencies and is the IMF's unit of account; on 30 April 1996, SDR 1 equalled US$1.45006. SDRs are allocated at intervals to supplement members'

reserves and thereby improve international financial liquidity.

IMF financial resources derive primarily from members' capital subscriptions, which are equivalent to their quotas. In addition, the IMF is authorized to borrow from official lenders. It may also draw on a line of credit of SDR 18.5 billion from various countries under the so-called General Arrangements to Borrow (GAB). Periodic charges are also levied on financial assistance. At the end of April 1996, total outstanding IMF credits amounted to SDR 36.3 billion.

The IMF is not a bank and does not lend money; it provides temporary financial assistance by selling a member's SDRs or other members' currencies in exchange for the member's own currency. The member can then use the purchased currency to alleviate its balance of payments difficulties. The IMF's credit under its regular facilities is made available to members in tranches or segments of 25 per cent of quota. For first credit tranche purchases, members are required to demonstrate reasonable efforts to overcome their balance of payments difficulties. There are no performance criteria and the total amount is repaid in three and a quarter to five years. Upper credit tranche purchases are normally associated with stand-by arrangements. These typically cover periods of one to two years. They focus on macroeconomic policies aimed at overcoming balance of payment difficulties and are required to meet certain performance criteria. Repurchases are made in three and a quarter to five years.

The IMF supports long-term efforts at economic reform and transformation, such as the re-establishment of market economies in the countries of eastern Europe and the former Soviet Union. In addition, the IMF supports medium-term programmes under the extended Fund facility, which generally runs for three years (sometimes up to four years) and is aimed at overcoming balance of payments difficulties stemming from macroeconomic and structural problems. Members experiencing a temporary balance of payments shortfall have access to the compensatory and contingency financing facility. The IMF also offers credits to low-income countries engaged in economic reform through its structural adjustment facility (SAF) and enhanced structural adjustment facility (ESAF). As at 30 April 1996, SDR 5.6 billion in SAF and ESAF loans is outstanding.

The IMF is headed by a Board of Governors, comprising representatives of all members, which meets annually. The Governors delegate powers to 24 Executive Directors, who are appointed or elected by member countries. The Executive Directors operate the Fund on a daily basis under a Managing Director, whom they elect. The appointed directors represent France, Germany, Japan, UK and USA.

Managing Director, Michel Camdessus (France)
UK Executive Director, Huw Evans, Room 11-120, IMF, 700 19th Street NW, Washington DC 20431

INTERNATIONAL RED CROSS AND RED CRESCENT MOVEMENT
17 avenue de la Paix, 1211 Geneva, Switzerland
Tel: 0171-201 5008

The International Red Cross and Red Crescent Movement is composed of three elements. The International Committee of the Red Cross (ICRC), the organization's founding body, was formed in 1863. It aims to negotiate between warring factions and to protect and assist victims of armed conflict. It also seeks to ensure the application of the Geneva Conventions with regard to prisoners of war and detainees.

The International Federation of Red Cross and Red Crescent Societies was founded in 1919 to contribute to the development of the humanitarian activities of national societies, to co-ordinate their relief operations for victims of natural disasters, and to care for refugees outside areas of conflict. There are Red Cross and Red Crescent Societies in 169 countries, with a total membership of 250 million.

The International Conference of the Red Cross and Red Crescent meets every four years, bringing together delegates of the ICRC, the International Federation and the national societies, as well as representatives of nations bound by the Geneva Conventions.

President of the ICRC, Cornelio Sommaruga
BRITISH RED CROSS, 9 Grosvenor Crescent, London SW1X 7EJ. *Director-General,* Michael R. Whitlam

---

INTERNATIONAL TELECOMMUNICATIONS SATELLITE ORGANIZATION
3400 International Drive NW, Washington DC 20008–3098, USA
Tel: Washington DC 944 7835

The International Telecommunications Satellite Organization (Intelsat) was formed in 1964. It owns and operates the world-wide commercial communications satellite system which is composed of over 20 satellites and more than 4,000 antennas which connect over 180 countries, territories and dependencies. Intelsat provides international and domestic voice/data and video services.

Each of the 139 member states contributes to the capital costs of the organization in proportion to its investment share, which is based on its relative usage of the system.

There is a four-tier hierarchy. The Assembly of Parties to the agreement meets every two years to consider long-term objectives and is composed of representatives of the member governments. The Meeting of Signatories annually considers the financial, technical and operational aspects of the system. The Board of Governors has 28 members; INTELSAT Management is the permanent staff of the organization and is headed by a Director-General who reports to the Board of Governors.

Director-General, Irving Goldstein (USA)

INTERNATIONAL TELECOMMUNICATION UNION
Place des Nations, 1211 Geneva 20, Switzerland

The International Telecommunication Union (ITU) was founded in Paris in 1865 as the International Telegraph Union and became a UN specialized agency in 1947. It promotes international co-operation and sets standards and regulations for the interconnection of telecommunications systems of all kinds. It assists the development of telecommunications in developing countries by providing technical assistance, management, investment financing and network installation. The ITU adopts international regulations and treaties to allocate the radio frequency spectrum and registers radio frequency assignments in order to avoid harmful interference between radio stations of different countries. It also governs and allocates the use of the geostationary-satellite orbit and collects and disseminates telecommunications information.

The ITU had 184 member states and 363 members (scientific and industrial companies, broadcasters, public and private operators, and international organizations) as at 30 January 1995. The supreme authority is the Plenipotentiary Conference, composed of representatives of all the members, which meets once every four years. It elects the Administrative Council of 46 members which meets annually to supervise the Union and set the budget (1995, SFr 164 million). The Conference also elects the Secretary-General, who heads the General Secretariat. The ITU is structured into three sectors: the radiocommunication sector, including world and regional radiocommunication conferences, radiocommunication assemblies and the Radio Regulations Board; the telecommunication standardization sector; and the telecommunication development sector.

Secretary-General, Dr P. Tarjanne (Finland)

LEAGUE OF ARAB STATES
Maidane Al-Tahrir, Cairo, Egypt

The purpose of the League of Arab States, founded in 1945, is to ensure co-operation among member states and protect their independence and sovereignty, to supervise the affairs and interests of Arab countries, to control the execution of agreements concluded among the member states, and to promote the process of integration among them. The League considers itself a regional organization and has observer status at the United Nations.

Member states are Algeria, Bahrain, Comoros, Djibouti, Egypt, Iraq, Jordan, Kuwait, Lebanon, Libya, Mauritania, Morocco, Oman, Palestine, Qatar, Saudi Arabia, Somalia, Sudan, Syria, Tunisia, United Arab Emirates and the Republic of Yemen.

Member states participate in various specialized agencies of the League whose role is to develop specific areas of co-operation between Arab states. These include the Arab Organization for Mineral Resources; the Arab Monetary Fund; the Arab Satellite Communication Organization; the Arab Academy of Maritime Transport; the Arab Bank for Economic Development in Africa; the Arab League Educational, Cultural and Scientific Organization, and the Council of Arab Economic Unity.

Secretary-General, Dr Ahmed Esmat Abdel-Meguid (Egypt)
UK OFFICE, 52 Green Street, London W1Y 3RH

NORDIC COUNCIL
Tyrgatan 7, Box 19506, Stockholm 10432, Sweden

The Nordic Council was established in March 1952 as an advisory body on economic and social co-operation comprising parliamentary delegates from Denmark, Iceland, Norway and Sweden. It was subsequently joined by Finland (1955), and representatives from the Faröe (1970), the Åland Islands (1970), and Greenland (1984).

Co-operation is regulated by the Treaty of Helsinki signed in 1962. This was amended in 1971 to create the Nordic Council of Ministers, which discusses all matters except defence and foreign affairs. Matters are given preparatory consideration by a Committee of Co-operation Ministers' Deputies and joint committees of official Decisions of the Council of Ministers, which are taken by consensus, are binding, although if ratification by member parliaments is required, decisions only become effective following parliamentary approval. The Council of Ministers is advised by the Nordic Council, to which it reports annually. There are Ministers for Nordic Co-operation in every member government.

The Nordic Council, comprising 87 voting delegates nominated from member parliaments and about 80 non-voting government representatives, meets twice a year in plenary sessions. The full Council chooses an 11-member Praesidium, comprising two delegates from each sovereign member and one party group-nominated delegate, which conducts business between sessions. A Secretariat, located in Stockholm and headed by a Secretary-General, liaises with the Council of Ministers and provides administrative support, as well as acting as a publishing house and information centre. The Council of Ministers has a separate Secretariat, based in Copenhagen.
Secretariat to the Nordic Council, Tyrgatan 7, S-10432 Stockholm, Sweden. *Secretary-General,* Anders Wenström (Sweden)
Secretariat of Nordic Council of Ministers, Store Strandgade 18, 1255 Copenhagen K, Denmark.
Secretary-General, Per Stenback (Finland)

NORTH ATLANTIC TREATY ORGANIZATION
Brussels 1110, Belgium
Tel: Brussels 728 4111

The North Atlantic Treaty (Treaty of Washington) was signed in 1949 by Belgium, Canada, Denmark, France, Iceland, Italy, Luxembourg, the Netherlands, Norway, Portugal, the UK and the USA. Greece and Turkey acceded to the Treaty in 1952, the Federal Republic of Germany in 1955 (the reunited Germany acceded in October 1990), and Spain in 1982.

The North Atlantic Treaty Organization (NATO) is the structural framework for a defensive political and military alliance designed to provide common security for its members through co-operation and consultation in political, military and economic as well as scientific and other non-military fields.

The North Atlantic Council, chaired by the Secretary-General, is the highest authority of the Alliance and is composed of permanent representatives of the 16 member countries. It meets at ministerial level (foreign ministers) at least twice a year. The permanent representatives (ambassadors) head national delegations of advisers and experts. Defence matters are dealt with by the Defence Planning Committee (DPC), composed of representatives of all member countries. The DPC also meets at ministerial level (defence ministers) at least twice a year. Nuclear matters are dealt with in the Nuclear Planning Group (NPG), composed of representatives of all countries except for France (Iceland being an observer). The NPG meets regularly at Permanent Representatives level and twice a year at ministerial level (defence ministers). The NATO Secretary-General chairs the Council, the DPC and the NPG.

The Council and DPC are forums for constant inter-governmental consultation and are the main decision-making bodies within the Alliance. They are assisted by an International Staff, divided into five divisions: political affairs; defence planning and policy; defence support; infrastructure, logistics and civil emergency planning; scientific and environmental affairs.

The senior military authority in NATO, under the Council and DPC, is the Military Committee composed of the Chief of Defence Staffs of each member country except Iceland, which has no military and may be represented by a civilian. The Military Committee, which is assisted by an integrated international military staff, also meets in permanent session with permanent military representatives and is responsible for making recommendations to the Council and DPC on measures considered necessary for the common defence of the NATO area and for supplying guidance on military matters to the major NATO commanders. The Chairman of the Military Committee, elected for a period of two to three years, represents the committee on the Council.

The strategic area covered by the North Atlantic Treaty is divided between two major NATO commands (MNCs), European and Atlantic; and three major subordinate commands (MSCs) within Allied Command Europe, South, Central and North-West. There is also a Regional Planning Group (Canada and the United States).

The major NATO commanders are responsible for the development of defence plans for their respective areas, for the determination of force requirements and for the deployment and exercise of the forces under their command. The major NATO commanders report to the Military Committee. From 1995 the reorganized NATO force structure consists of three components: the Allied Rapid Reaction Corps of four divisions, with air and sea components (the majority of which are British forces); the main defence force of four corps (one Danish-German, one Dutch-German, two US-German); and the augmentation forces of reserves and territorials.

In response to the new security environment arising from the demise of the Warsaw Pact and the end of the Cold War in 1990, NATO issued a Declaration of Peace and Co-operation in 1991, and published a new strategic concept which introduced organizational changes and force reductions of around 30 per cent. It also provided for a reduced dependence on nuclear weapons; greater mobility, flexibility and adaptability of forces; greater use of multinational formations; active involvement in international crisis management and peacekeeping operations; increased co-ordination with international institutions such as the UN, OSCE and WEU; and a streamlining of NATO's military command structure.

The North Atlantic Co-operation Council (NACC) was established in 1991 to foster closer security links with eastern European and former Soviet states. Its role is to facilitate closer official and informal ties on security and related issues between its 38 member states (Finland has observer status). The NACC focuses on peacekeeping, defence planning, defence industry conversion, defence management and force structuring, and the democratic concepts of civilian-military relations. It formed the basis for the Partnership for Peace (PFP) programme, launched in 1994, a form of associate membership offering increased security co-operation and consultation to non-NATO countries. Partners work towards transparency in defence budgeting, democratic control of defence ministries, joint planning and joint military exercises. NATO will consult with any PFP partner which perceives a direct threat to its territorial integrity, political independence or security. Most of the 27 PFP partners send liaison officers to NATO headquarters in Brussels and to the Partnership Co-ordination Cell in Mons, Belgium, and participate in joint military exercises co-ordinated by NATO. Russia and some other states have individual partnership programmes.

In 1994, NATO announced that it would consider admitting new members, and a summit scheduled for early 1997 will consider applications. The most likely new members are Poland, the Czech Republic and Hungary. Russian opposition to this proposed expansion was tempered by a North Atlantic Council meeting in June 1996, which agreed to a new military structure. It proposed the creation of combined joint task forces which would provide European NATO members with a framework for operations without US involvement, under the auspices of the WEU. The strengthened role for Europeans was also credited with prompting France to announce that it would re-establish a permanent military mission to NATO, which had been closed in 1966. A French representative attended a meeting of NATO defence ministers in June 1996.

From 1992 until the end of 1995, NATO provided support for UN peacekeeping efforts in the former Yugoslavia. With the signing of the Bosnian peace agreement in December 1995, a NATO-led multinational Implementation Force (IFOR) embarked on Operation Joint Endeavour to implement the peace accord. IFOR is due to leave Bosnia-Hercegovina in December 1996.

Secretary-General and Chairman of the North Atlantic Council, of the DPC and of the NPG, Javier Solana (Spain)
UK Permanent Representative on the North Atlantic Council, John Goulden, CMG
Chairman of the Military Committee, Gen. Klaus Naumann (Germany)
Supreme Allied Commander, Europe, Gen. George Joulwan (USA)
Supreme Allied Commander, Atlantic, Gen. John Sheehan (USA)

ORGANIZATION FOR ECONOMIC CO-OPERATION AND DEVELOPMENT
2 rue André-Pascal, 75116 Paris
Tel: Paris 4524 9820

The Organization for Economic Co-operation and Development (OECD) was formed in 1961 to replace the Organization for European Economic Co-operation. It is the instrument for international co-operation among industrialised member countries on economic and social policies. Its objectives are to assist its member governments in the formulation and co-ordination of policies designed to achieve high, sustained economic growth while maintaining financial stability, to contribute to world trade on a multilateral basis and to stimulate members' aid to developing countries.

The members are Australia, Austria, Belgium, Canada, the Czech Republic, Denmark, Finland, France, Germany, Greece, Hungary, Iceland, Republic of Ireland, Italy, Japan, Luxembourg, Mexico, the Netherlands, New Zealand, Norway, Portugal, Spain, Sweden, Switzerland, Turkey, the UK and the USA. The OECD is considering membership applications from Slovakia, Poland and the Republic of Korea.

The Council is the supreme body of the organization. It is composed of one representative for each member country and meets at permanent representative level under the chairmanship of the Secretary-General, or at ministerial level (usually once a year) under the chairmanship of a minister elected annually. Decisions and recommendations are adopted by the unanimous agreement of all members. An executive committee comprising 14 members of the Council is chosen annually, although most of the OECD's work is undertaken in over 200 specialized committees and working parties. Five autonomous or semi-autonomous bodies are associated in varying degrees to the Organization: the Nuclear Energy Agency, the International Energy Agency, the Development Centre, the Centre for Educational Research and Innovation, and the European Conference of Ministers of Transport. These bodies, the committees and the Council

are serviced by an international Secretariat headed by the Secretary-General.

Secretary-General, Donald Johnston (Canada)
UK Permanent Representative, HE Peter Vereker, 19 rue de Franqueville, Paris 75116

ORGANIZATION FOR SECURITY AND CO-OPERATION IN EUROPE
Kärntner Ring 5–7, A-1010 Vienna, Austria
Tel: Vienna 5143 6150

The Organization for Security and Co-operation in Europe (OSCE) was launched in 1975 (as the Conference on Security and Co-operation in Europe (CSCE)) under the Helsinki Final Act. This established agreements between NATO members, Warsaw Pact members, neutral and non-aligned European countries covering security in Europe; economic, scientific, technological and environmental co-operation; and humanitarian principles. Further conferences were held at Belgrade (1977–8), Madrid (1980–3) and Vienna (1986–9).

With the end of the Cold War, it was decided that the CSCE should be institutionalized to provide a new security framework for Europe. The Charter of Paris for a New Europe, signed on 21 November 1990, committed members to support multi-party democracy, free-market economics, the rule of law, and human rights. The signatories also agreed to regular meetings of heads of government, ministers and officials. The first institutionalized heads of state and government summit was held in Helsinki in December 1992, at which the Helsinki Document was adopted. This declared the CSCE to be a regional organization and defined the structures of the organization. The summit also appointed a High Commissioner on National Minorities. At its December 1994 summit the CSCE was renamed the Organization for Security and Co-operation in Europe.

Three structures have been established: the Ministerial Council of foreign ministers, the central decision-making and governing body, which meets at least once a year; the Senior Council, which prepares work for the Ministerial Council, carries out its decisions and is responsible for the overview, management and co-ordination of OSCE activities and meets at least three times a year; and the Permanent Council, which is responsible for the day-to-day operational tasks of the OSCE and is the regular body for political consultation, meeting weekly. The chairmanship of the Ministerial Council, Senior Council and Permanent Council rotates among participating states with the Senior Council meeting in Prague and the Permanent Council in Vienna.

The OSCE is also underpinned by four permanent institutions: a Secretariat (Vienna); a Forum for Security Co-operation (Vienna), which meets weekly to discuss arms control, disarmament and security-building measures; an Office for Democratic Institutions and Human Rights (Warsaw), which is charged with furthering human rights, democracy and the rule of law; and an office of the High Commissioner on National Minorities (The Hague) which identifies ethnic tensions that might endanger peace and promotes their resolution. There is also a documentation and conference centre in Prague, an OSCE Parliamentary Assembly with a secretariat based in Copenhagen, and a Court of Conciliation and Arbitration in Geneva.

In June 1991 the CSCE agreed upon new crisis prevention mechanisms to prevent or manage violent conflict between and within member countries. In an attempt to put these mechanisms into place, the OSCE has established monitoring missions in eight areas of potential or actual conflict, has sent an assistance group to Chechenia, and has a peacekeeping mission in Nagorno-Karabakh. There is an OSCE mission to Bosnia-Hercegovina which will supervise elections in September 1996. A Joint Consultative Group of the OSCE promotes the objectives and implementation of the Conventional Armed Forces in Europe (CFE) Treaty (1990) which limits conventional ground and air forces.

The OSCE has 55 participating states: Albania, Andorra, Armenia, Austria, Azerbaijan, Belarus, Belgium, Bosnia-Hercegovina, Bulgaria, Canada, Croatia, Cyprus, Czech Republic, Denmark, Estonia, Finland, France, Georgia, Germany, Greece, Hungary, Iceland, Ireland, Italy, Kazakhstan, Kyrgyzstan, Latvia, Liechtenstein, Lithuania, Luxembourg, Macedonia (Former Yugoslav Republic of), Malta, Moldova, Monaco, the Netherlands, Norway, Poland, Portugal, Romania, Russia, San Marino, Slovakia, Slovenia, Spain, Sweden, Switzerland, Tajikistan, Turkey, Turkmenistan, UK, Ukraine, USA, Uzbekistan, the Vatican and Yugoslavia (suspended from activities July 1992).

Chair of the OSCE: (1996), Switzerland; *(1997)*, Denmark
Secretary-General of the OSCE, Wilhelm Hoÿnck (Germany)
Director of the Office for Democratic Institutions and Human Rights, Audrey Glover (UK)
OSCE High Commissioner on National Minorities, Max van der Stoel (Netherlands)

ORGANIZATION OF AFRICAN UNITY
PO Box 3243, Addis Ababa, Ethiopia

The Organization of African Unity (OAU) was established in 1963 and has 53 members; Morocco suspended its participation in 1985 in protest at the Polisario-proclaimed Saharan Arab Democratic Republic (SADR), representing Western Sahara, being admitted as a member. The OAU aims to further African unity and solidarity, to co-ordinate political, economic, social and defence policies, and to eliminate colonialism in Africa.

The chief organs are the Assembly of heads of state or government, which is the supreme organ of the OAU and meets once a year to consider matters of common African concern and to co-ordinate the Organization's policies; the Council of foreign ministers, which is the Organization's executive body responsible for the implementation of the Assembly's policies, and which meets twice a year; and the Commission of Mediation, Conciliation and Arbitration which promotes the peaceful settlement of disputes between member countries. The main administrative body is the General Secretariat, based in Addis Ababa, headed by a Secretary-General who is elected by the Assembly for a four-year term.

Substantial budgetary arrears due to delays in the payment of national contributions has meant that the OAU continually faces difficulties in furthering its aims. Most OAU programmes were suspended in November 1994 after unpaid contributions reached US$77 million although arrears had dropped to US$38.3 million by June 1995. In June 1991 the Assembly adopted an African Economic Community Treaty which envisages establishment of the Economic Community after ratification by two-thirds of the OAU's membership. In June 1993 a mechanism was created for conflict prevention, management and resolution, and a peace fund was established.
Secretary-General, Salim Ahmed Salim (Tanzania)

ORGANIZATION OF AMERICAN STATES
17th Street and Constitution Avenue NW, Washington DC 20006, USA
Tel: Washington DC 458 3000

Originally founded in 1890 for largely commercial purposes, the Organization of American States (OAS) adopted its present name and charter in 1948. The charter entered into force in 1951 and was amended in 1967, 1985 and 1996; the 1992 Protocol of Washington will enter into force upon ratification by two-thirds of member states.

The OAS aims to strengthen the peace and security of the continent; to promote and consolidate representative democracy with due respect for the principle of non-intervention; to prevent possible causes of difficulties and to ensure the peaceful resolution of disputes arising among its member states; to provide for common action on the part of those states in the event of aggression; to seek the resolution of political, judicial and economic problems that may arise among them; to promote, by co-operative action, their economic, social and cultural development; and to achieve an effective limitation of conventional weapons so that resources can be devoted to economic and social development. The OAS is a regional organization within the UN.

Policy is determined by the annual General Assembly, which is the supreme authority and elects the Secretary-General for a five-year term. The Meeting of Consultation of ministers of foreign affairs considers urgent problems on an *ad hoc* basis. The Permanent Council, comprising one representative from each member state, promotes friendly inter-state relations, acts as an intermediary in case of disputes arising between states and oversees the General Secretariat, the main administrative body. The Inter-American Council for Integral Development was created in January 1996 by the ratification of the Protocol of Managua to promote sustainable development.

The 35 member states are Antigua and Barbuda, Argentina, Bahamas, Barbados, Belize, Bolivia, Brazil, Canada, Chile, Colombia, Costa Rica, Cuba, Dominica, Dominican Republic, Ecuador, Grenada, Guatemala, Guyana, Haiti, Honduras, Jamaica, Mexico, Nicaragua, Panama, Paraguay, Peru, St Christopher and Nevis, St Lucia, St Vincent and the Grenadines, El Salvador, Suriname, Trinidad and Tobago, Uruguay, USA and Venezuela. The European Union and 39 non-American states have permanent observer status.
Secretary-General, Dr César Gaviria Trujillo (Colombia)

ORGANIZATION OF ARAB PETROLEUM EXPORTING COUNTRIES
PO Box 20501, Safat 13066, Kuwait

The Organization of Arab Petroleum and Exporting Countries (OAPEC) was founded in 1968. Its objectives are to promote co-operation in economic activities, to safeguard members' interests, to unite efforts to ensure the flow of oil to consumer markets, and to create a favourable climate for the investment of capital and expertise.

The Ministerial Council is composed of oil ministers from the member countries and meets twice a year to determine policy, to direct activities and to approve the budgets and accounts of the General Secretariat and the Judicial Tribunal. The Judicial Tribunal is composed of seven part-time judges who rule on disputes between member countries and disputes between countries and oil companies. The executive organ of OAPEC is the General Secretariat.

The members are Algeria, Bahrain, Egypt, Iraq, Kuwait, Libya, Qatar, Saudi Arabia, Syria and the United Arab Emirates. Tunisia's membership has been inactive since 1987.

Secretary-General, Abdel-Aziz A. Al-Turki

ORGANIZATION OF THE ISLAMIC CONFERENCE
PO Box 178, Jeddah 21411, Saudi Arabia

The Organization of the Islamic Conference (OIC) was established in 1971 with the purpose of generating solidarity and co-operation between Islamic countries. It also has the specific aims of co-ordinating efforts to safeguard the Muslim holy places, supporting the formation of a Palestinian state, assisting member states to maintain their independence, co-ordinating the views of member states in international forums such as the UN, and improving co-operation in the economic, cultural and scientific fields.

The OIC has three central organs, supreme among them the Conference of the Heads of State which meets once every three years to discuss issues of importance to Islamic states. The Conference of Foreign Ministers meets annually to prepare reports for the Conference of Heads of State. The General Secretariat carries out administrative tasks. It is headed by a Secretary-General who is elected by the Conference of Foreign Ministers for a non-renewable four-year term.

In addition to this structure, the OIC has several subsidiary bodies and specialized bodies. These include the Islamic Solidarity Fund, to aid Islamic institutions in member countries, and the Islamic Development Bank, to finance development projects in poorer member states. An Islamic Court of Justice is planned. The OIC runs various offices to organize the economic boycott of Israel.

The achievement of the OIC's aims has often been prevented by political rivalry and conflicts between member states, such as the Iran-Iraq war and the Iraqi invasion of Kuwait. Egypt's membership was suspended from 1979 to 1984 because of its peace treaty with Israel. Saudi Arabia, the main source of funding, exercises great influence within the OIC. Since 1991 the OIC has become more united and has spoken out against violence against Muslims in India, the Occupied Territories and Bosnia-Hercegovina. From 1993 to 1995 the OIC co-ordinated the offering of troops to the UN by Muslim states to protect Muslim areas of Bosnia-Hercegovina.

The Organization has 52 members (51 sovereign Muslim states in Africa, the Middle East, central and south-east Asia and Europe, plus the Palestine Liberation Organization) and one observer, Turkish Northern Cyprus. It has an annual budget of £5 million.

Secretary-General, Hamid Algabid (Niger)

ORGANIZATION OF THE PETROLEUM EXPORTING COUNTRIES
Obere Donaustrasse 93, 1020 Vienna, Austria
Tel: Vienna 21112

The Organization of the Petroleum Exporting Countries (OPEC) was created in 1960 as a permanent intergovernmental organization with the principal aims of unifying and co-ordinating the petroleum policies of its members,

determining ways of protecting their interests individually and collectively, and ensuring the stabilization of prices in international oil markets with a view to eliminating unnecessary fluctuations. Since 1982 OPEC has attempted (only partially successfully) to impose overall production limits and production quotas in an attempt to maintain stable oil prices. In the first quarter of 1996 the overall production quota was 24,520,000 barrels per day.

The supreme authority is the Conference of Ministers of oil, mines and energy of member countries, which meets at least twice a year to formulate policy. The Board of Governors, nominated by member countries, directs the management of OPEC and implements conference resolutions. The Secretariat carries out executive functions under the direction of the Board of Governors.

The member states are Algeria, Gabon, Indonesia, Iran, Iraq, Kuwait, Libya, Nigeria, Qatar, Saudi Arabia, UAE and Venezuela. Ecuador withdrew in 1992.

Secretary-General, HE Dr Rilwanu Lukman (Nigeria)

SOUTH PACIFIC COMMISSION
BP D5, Nouméa Cedex, New Caledonia
Tel: Nouméa Cedex 262000

The South Pacific Commission is a technical assistance agency with programmes in agriculture and plant protection, fisheries and marine resources, community health, socio-economic and statistical services, and community education services. The organization is run by a management committee headed by the Secretary-General. The other committee members are the Director of Services and the Director of Programmes.

The South Pacific Commission (SPC) was established in 1947 by Australia, France, the Netherlands, New Zealand, the UK and the USA with the aim of promoting the economic and social stability of the islands in the region. The SPC now numbers 26 member states and territories: the four remaining founder states (the Netherlands and the UK have withdrawn), in which no programmes are run, and the other 22 states and territories of Melanesia, Micronesia and Polynesia.

The South Pacific Conference meets annually to discuss and adopt the SPC's work programme, to adopt the budget and to nominate the Commission's officers.

Secretary-General, Bob Dun (Australia)
Director of Programmes, Jimmie Rodgers (Solomon Islands)
Director of Services, Lourdes Pangelinan (Guam)

THE UNITED NATIONS
UN Plaza, New York, NY 10017, USA

The United Nations is an intergovernmental organization of member states, dedicated through signature of the UN Charter to the maintenance of international peace and security and the solution of economic, social and political problems through international co-operation. The UN is not a world government and has no right of intervention in the essentially domestic affairs of states.

The UN was founded as a successor to the League of Nations and inherited many of its procedures and institutions. The name 'United Nations' was first used in the Washington Declaration 1942 to describe the 26 states which had allied to fight the Axis powers. The UN Charter developed from discussions at the Moscow Conference of the foreign ministers of China, the UK, the USA and the Soviet Union in 1943. Further progress was made at

Dumbarton Oaks, Washington, in 1944 during talks involving the same states. The role of the Security Council was formulated at the Yalta Conference in 1945. The Charter was formally drawn up by 50 allied nations at the San Francisco Conference between April and 26 June 1945, when it was signed. Following ratification the UN came into effect on 24 October 1945, which is celebrated annually as United Nations Day. The UN flag is light blue with the UN emblem centred in white.

The principal organs of the UN are the General Assembly, the Security Council, the Economic and Social Council, the Trusteeship Council, the Secretariat and the International Court of Justice. The Economic and Social Council and the Trusteeship Council are auxiliaries, charged with assisting and advising the General Assembly and Security Council. The official languages used are Arabic, Chinese, English, French, Russian and Spanish. Deliberations at the International Court of Justice are in English and French only.

MEMBERSHIP

Membership is open to all countries which accept the Charter and its principle of peaceful co-existence. New members are admitted by the General Assembly on the recommendation of the Security Council. The original membership of 51 states has grown to 185:

Afghanistan	Cyprus
Albania	*Czech Republic
Algeria	*Denmark
Andorra	Djibouti
Angola	Dominica
Antigua and Barbuda	*Dominican Republic
Argentina	*Ecuador
Armenia	*Egypt
Australia	Equatorial Guinea
Austria	Eritrea
Azerbaijan	Estonia
The Bahamas	*Ethiopia
Bahrain	Federated States of
Bangladesh	Micronesia
Barbados	Fiji
Belarus	Finland
Belgium	*France
Belize	Gabon
Benin	Gambia
Bhutan	Georgia
Bolivia	Germany
Bosnia-Hercegovina	Ghana
Botswana	*Greece
Brazil	Grenada
Brunei	*Guatemala
Bulgaria	Guinea
Burkina	Guinea-Bissau
Burundi	Guyana
Cambodia	*Haiti
Cameroon	*Honduras
Canada	Hungary
Cape Verde	Iceland
Central African Rep.	*India
Chad	Indonesia
Chile	*Iran
China	*Iraq
Colombia	Ireland, Republic of
Comoros	Israel
Congo	Italy
Costa Rica	Jamaica
Côte d'Ivoire	Japan
Croatia	Jordan
Cuba	Kazakhstan

Kenya	Romania
Korea, D. P. Rep. (North)	*Russian Federation
Korea, Rep. of (South)	Rwanda
Kuwait	St Christopher and Nevis
Kyrgyzstan	St Lucia
Laos	St Vincent and the
Latvia	Grenadines
*Lebanon	*El Salvador
Lesotho	San Marino
*Liberia	São Tomé and Príncipe
Libya	*Saudi Arabia
Liechtenstein	Senegal
Lithuania	Seychelles
*Luxembourg	Sierra Leone
Macedonia (The Former	Singapore
Yugoslav Republic of)	*Slovakia
Madagascar	Slovenia
Malawi	Solomon Islands
Malaysia	Somalia
The Maldives	*South Africa
Mali	Spain
Malta	Sri Lanka
Marshall Islands	Sudan
Mauritania	Suriname
Mauritius	Swaziland
*Mexico	Sweden
Moldova	*Syria
Monaco	Tajikistan
Mongolia	Tanzania
Morocco	Thailand
Mozambique	Togo
Myanmar (Burma)	Trinidad and Tobago
Namibia	Tunisia
Nepal	*Turkey
*Netherlands	Turkmenistan
*New Zealand	Uganda
*Nicaragua	*Ukraine
Niger	United Arab Emirates
Nigeria	*United Kingdom
*Norway	*United States of America
Oman	*Uruguay
Pakistan	Uzbekistan
Palau	Vanuatu
*Panama	*Venezuela
Papua New Guinea	Vietnam
*Paraguay	Western Samoa
*Peru	Yemen
*Philippines	*Yugoslavia (suspended)
*Poland	Zaire
Portugal	Zambia
Qatar	Zimbabwe

*Original member (i.e. from 1945). From 25 October 1971 'China' was taken to mean the People's Republic of China. Czechoslovakia was an original member in 1945 and a member until 31 December 1992; the successor states of the Czech Republic and Slovakia were admitted as members in January 1993.

The Russian Federation took over the membership of the Soviet Union in the Security Council and all other UN organs on 24 December 1991. Belarus (formerly Belorussia) and the Ukraine on becoming independent sovereign states continued their existing memberships of the UN, both having been granted separate UN membership in 1945 as a concession to the Soviet Union.

OBSERVERS

Permanent observer status is held by the Holy See and Switzerland. The Palestine Liberation Organization has special observer status.

NON-MEMBERS

A number of countries are not members, usually due to their small size and limited financial resources. Notable exceptions include Switzerland, which follows a policy of absolute neutrality, and Taiwan, which was replaced by the People's Republic of China in 1971. The others are Kiribati, Nauru, Tonga, Tuvalu and the Holy See.

THE GENERAL ASSEMBLY
UN Plaza, New York, NY 10017, USA

The General Assembly is the main deliberative organ of the UN. It consists of all members, each entitled to five representatives but having only one vote. The annual session begins on the third Tuesday of September, when the President is elected, and usually continues until mid-December. Special sessions are held on specific issues and emergency special sessions can be called within 24 hours.

The Assembly is empowered to discuss any matter within the scope of the Charter, except when it is under consideration by the Security Council, and to make recommendations. Under the 'uniting for peace' resolution, adopted in 1950, the Assembly may also take action to maintain international peace and security when the Security Council fails to do so because of a lack of unanimity of its permanent members. Important decisions, such as those on peace and security, the election of officers, the budget, etc., need a two-thirds majority. Others need a simple majority. The Assembly has effective power only over the internal operations of the UN itself; external recommendations are not legally binding.

The work of the General Assembly is divided among six main committees, on each of which every member has the right to be represented: disarmament and international security; economic and financial; social, humanitarian and cultural; special political issues and decolonization (including non-self governing territories); administrative and budgetary; and legal. In addition, the General Assembly appoints ad hoc committees to consider special issues, such as human rights, peacekeeping, disarmament and international law. All committees consider items referred to them by the Assembly and recommend draft resolutions to its plenary meeting.

The Assembly is assisted by a number of functional committees. The General Committee co-ordinates its proceedings and operations, while the Credentials Committee verifies the credentials of representatives. There are also two standing committees, the Advisory Committee on Administration and Budgetary Questions and the Committee on Contributions, which suggests the scale of members' payments to the UN.
President of the General Assembly (1995), Diogo Freitas do Amaral (Portugal)

The Assembly has created a large number of specialized bodies over the years, which are supervised jointly with the Economic and Social Council. They are supported by UN and voluntary contributions from governments, non-governmental organizations and individuals. These organizations include:

THE CONFERENCE ON DISARMAMENT (CD)
Palais des Nations, 1211 Geneva 10, Switzerland
Established by the UN as the Committee on Disarmament in 1962, the CD is the single multilateral disarmament

negotiating forum. The present title of the organization was adopted in 1984. There were 40 members as at June 1994.

A Chemical Weapons Convention was agreed and opened for signing in Paris in 1993. The Convention will come into force six months after it has been ratified by 65 states. It bans the use, production, stockpiling and transfer of all chemical weapons. All US and Russian weapons must be destroyed within 15 years of the Convention entering into force and all other states' weapons must be destroyed within ten years.
Secretary-General, Vladimir Petrovsky (Russia)
UK Representative, N. C. R. Williams, CMG, 37–39 rue de Vermont, 1211 Geneva 20, Switzerland

THE UNITED NATIONS CHILDREN'S FUND (UNICEF)
3 UN Plaza, New York, NY 10017, USA
Established in 1947 to assist children and mothers in the immediate post-war period, UNICEF now concentrates on developing countries. It provides primary health-care and health education. In particular, it conducts programmes in oral hydration, immunization against leading diseases, child growth monitoring, and the encouragement of breast-feeding. Its operations are often conducted in co-operation with the World Health Organization (WHO).
Executive Director, Carol Bellamy (USA)

THE UNITED NATIONS DEVELOPMENT PROGRAMME (UNDP)
1 UN Plaza, New York, NY 10017, USA
Established in 1966 from the merger of the UN Expanded Programme of Technical Assistance and the UN Special Fund, UNDP is the central funding agency for economic and social development projects around the world. Much of its annual expenditure is channelled through UN specialized agencies, governments and non-governmental organizations.
Administrator, James G. Speth (USA)

THE UNITED NATIONS HIGH COMMISSIONER FOR REFUGEES (UNHCR)
Centre William Rappard, 154 rue de Lausanne, PO Box 2500, 1211 Geneva 2, Switzerland
Established in 1951 to protect the rights and interests of refugees, it organizes emergency relief and longer-term solutions, such as voluntary repatriation, local integration or resettlement.
High Commissioner, Sadako Ogata (Japan)
UK OFFICE, 76 Westminster Palace Gardens, London SW1P 1RL. Tel: 0171-222 3065

THE UN RELIEF AND WORKS AGENCY FOR PALESTINE REFUGEES IN THE NEAR EAST (UNRWA)
Vienna International Centre, Wagramerstrasse 5, PO Box 100, 1400 Vienna, Austria
Established in 1949 to bring relief to the Palestinian displaced by the Arab-Israeli conflict.
Commissioner-General, Ilter Turkman (Turkey)

THE UNITED NATIONS HIGH COMMISSIONER FOR HUMAN RIGHTS
Established in 1993 to secure respect for, and prevent violations of human rights by engaging in dialogue with governments and international organizations. Responsible for the co-ordination of all UN human rights activities.
High Commissioner, José Ayala Lasso (Ecuador)

Other bodies include:

THE UN CENTRE FOR HUMAN SETTLEMENTS (Habitat), PO Box 30030, Nairobi, Kenya

THE UN CONFERENCE ON TRADE AND DEVELOPMENT (UNCTAD), Palais des Nations, 1211 Geneva 10, Switzerland
THE DEPARTMENT OF HUMANITARIAN AFFAIRS (DHA), Palais des Nations, 1211 Geneva 10, Switzerland
THE INTERNATIONAL SEABED AUTHORITY, Kingston, Jamaica
THE UN ENVIRONMENT PROGRAMME (UNEP), PO Box 30552, Nairobi, Kenya
THE UN POPULATION FUND (UNFPA), 220 East 42nd Street, New York, NY 10017, USA
THE UN INSTITUTE FOR THE ADVANCEMENT OF WOMEN (INSTRAW), PO Box 21747, Santo Domingo, Dominican Republic
THE UN UNIVERSITY (UNU), Toho Seimei Building, 15–1, Shibuya, 2-Chome, Shibuya-ku, Tokyo 150, Japan
THE WORLD FOOD COUNCIL (WFC), Via delle Terme di Caracalla, 00100 Rome, Italy
THE WORLD FOOD PROGRAMME (WFP), Via delle Terme di Caracalla, 00100 Rome, Italy

BUDGET OF THE UNITED NATIONS

The budget adopted for the biennium 1996–7 was US$2,510 million. The scale of assessment contributions of 88 UN members is set at the minimum 0.01 per cent. The ten largest assessments are: USA, 25 per cent; Japan, 12.45; Germany, 8.93; Russia, 6.91; France, 6.00; UK, 5.02; Italy, 4.29; Canada, 3.11; Spain, 1.98; Australia, 1.51.

THE SECURITY COUNCIL
UN Plaza, New York, NY 10017, USA

The Security Council is the senior arm of the UN and has the primary responsibility for maintaining world peace and security. It consists of 15 members, each with one representative and one vote. There are five permanent members, China, France, Russia, the UK and the USA, and ten non-permanent members. Each of the non-permanent members is elected for a two-year term by a two-thirds majority of the General Assembly and is ineligible for immediate re-election. Five of the elective seats are allocated to Africa and Asia, one to eastern Europe, two to Latin America and two to western Europe and remaining countries. Procedural questions are determined by a simple majority vote. Other matters require a majority inclusive of the votes of the permanent members; they thus have a right of veto. The abstention of a permanent member does not constitute a veto. The presidency rotates each month by state in (English) alphabetical order. Parties to a dispute, other non-members and individuals can be invited to participate in Security Council debates but are not permitted to vote. In 1996 the ten non-permanent members were: Botswana, Germany, Honduras, Indonesia, Italy (*term expires 31 December 1996*), Chile, Egypt, Guinea-Bissau, Poland, Republic of Korea (*term expires 31 December 1997*).

The Security Council is empowered to settle or adjudicate in disputes or situations which threaten international peace and security. It can adopt political, economic and military measures to achieve this end. Any matter considered to be a threat to or breach of the peace or an act of aggression can be brought to the Security Council's attention by any member state or by the Secretary-General. The Charter envisaged members placing at the disposal of the Security Council armed forces and other facilities which would be co-ordinated by the Military Staff Committee, composed of military representatives of the five permanent members. The Security Council is also supported by a Committee of Experts, to advise on procedural and technical matters, and a Committee on Admission of New Members.

Owing to superpower disunity, the Security Council rarely played the decisive role set out in the Charter; the Military Staff Committee was effectively suspended from 1948 until 1990, when a meeting was convened during the Gulf Crisis on the formation and control of UN-supervised armed forces. However, at an extraordinary meeting of the Security Council in January 1992, heads of government laid plans to transform the UN in light of the changed post-Cold War world. The Secretary-General was asked to draw up a report on enhancing the UN's preventive diplomacy, peacemaking and peacekeeping ability. The report, *An Agenda for Peace*, was produced in June 1992 and centred on the establishment of a UN army composed of national contingents on permanent standby, as envisaged at the time of the UN's formation.

PEACEKEEPING FORCES

The Security Council has established a number of peacekeeping forces since its foundation, comprising contingents provided mainly by neutral and non-aligned UN members. Current forces include: the UN Truce Supervision Organization (UNTSO), Israel, 1948; the UN Military Observer Group in India and Pakistan (UNMOGIP), 1949; the UN Peacekeeping Force in Cyprus (UNFICYP), 1964; the UN Disengagement Observer Force (UNDOF), Golan Heights, Syria, 1974; the UN Interim Force in Lebanon (UNIFIL), 1978; the UN Iraq-Kuwait Observation Mission (UNIKOM), 1991; the UN Mission for the Referendum in Western Sahara (MINURSO), 1991; the UN Observer Mission in Georgia (UNOMIG), 1993; the UN Observer Mission in Liberia (UNOMIL), 1993; the UN Mission in Haiti (UNMIH), 1993; the UN Observer Mission in Guatemala (MINUGA), 1994; the UN Observer Mission in Tajikistan (UNMOT), 1994; the UN Preventive Deployment Force (UNPREDEP), Former Yugoslav Republic of Macedonia, 1995; eastern Slavonia, 1996.

THE ECONOMIC AND SOCIAL COUNCIL
UN Plaza, New York, NY 10017, USA

The Economic and Social Council is responsible under the General Assembly for the economic and social work of the UN and for the co-ordination of the activities of the 15 specialized agencies and other UN bodies. It makes reports and recommendations on economic, social, cultural, educational, health and related matters, often in consultation with non-governmental organizations, passing the reports to the General Assembly and other UN bodies. It also drafts conventions for submission to the Assembly and calls conferences on matters within its remit.

The Council consists of 54 members, 18 of whom are elected annually by the General Assembly for a three-year term. Each has one vote and can be immediately re-elected on retirement. A President is elected annually and is also eligible for re-election. One substantive session is held annually and decisions are reached by simple majority vote of those present.

The Council has established a number of standing committees on particular issues and several commissions. Commissions include: Statistical, Human Rights, Social Development, Sustainable Development, Status of Women, Crime Prevention and Criminal Justice, Narcotic Drugs, Science and Technology for Development, and Population; and Regional Economic Commissions for Europe, Asia and the Pacific, Western Asia, Latin America and Africa.

THE TRUSTEESHIP COUNCIL
UN Plaza, New York, NY10017, USA

The Trusteeship Council supervised the administration of territories within the UN Trusteeship system inherited from the League of Nations. It consists of the five permanent members of the Security Council. With the independence of the Republic of Palau in October 1994, all eleven trusteeships have now progressed to independence or merged with neighbouring states and the Trusteeship Council suspended its operations on 1 November 1994.

THE SECRETARIAT
UN Plaza, New York, NY 10017, USA

The Secretariat services the other UN organs and is headed by a Secretary-General elected by a majority vote of the General Assembly on the recommendation of the Security Council. He is assisted by an international staff, chosen to represent the international character of the organization. The Secretary-General is charged with bringing to the attention of the Security Council any matter which he considers poses a threat to international peace and security. He may also bring other matters to the attention of the General Assembly and other UN bodies and may be entrusted by them with additional duties. As chief administrator of the UN, the Secretary-General is present in person or via representatives at all meetings of the other five main organs of the UN. He may also act as an impartial mediator in disputes between member states.

The power and influence of the Secretary-General has been determined largely by the character of the office-holder and by the state of relations between the superpowers. The thaw in these relations since the mid-1980s has increased the effectiveness of the UN, particularly in its attempts to intervene in international disputes. It helped to end the Iran-Iraq war and sponsored peace in Central America. Following Iraq's invasion of Kuwait in 1990 the UN took its first collective security action since the Korean War. UN action to protect the Kurds in northern Iraq has widened its legal authority by breaching the prohibition on its intervention in the essentially domestic affairs of states. Currently the UN is involved in peacekeeping, aid distribution and negotiations in the former Yugoslavia; and is addressing the global problems of Aids and environmental destruction.
Secretary-General, Boutros Boutros-Ghali, apptd 1992 (Egypt)

UNDER-SECRETARIES-GENERAL
Internal Oversight Services, Karl-Theodor Paschke (Germany)
Political Affairs, Marrack Goulding (UK)
Peacekeeping Operations, Kofi Annan (Ghana)
Development Support and Management Services, Ji Chaozhu (China)
Legal Affairs, Hans Axel Valdemar-Corell (Sweden)
Humanitarian Affairs, Peter Hansen (Denmark)
Administration and Management, Joseph Connor (USA)
Policy Co-ordination and Sustainable Development, Nitin Desai (India)
Economic and Social Information and Policy Analysis, Jean-Claude Milleron (France)
Special Advisers to the Secretary-General, Ismat Kittani (Iraq); Chinmaya Gharekhan (India)

FORMER SECRETARIES-GENERAL
1946–53   Trygve Lie (Norway)
1953–61   Dag Hammarskjöld (Sweden)
1961–71   U Thant (Burma)
1971–81   Kurt Waldheim (Austria)
1981–91   Javier Pérez de Cuéllar (Peru)

INTERNATIONAL COURT OF JUSTICE
The Peace Palace, 2517 KJ The Hague, The Netherlands

The International Court of Justice is the principal judicial organ of the UN. The Statute of the Court is an integral part of the Charter and all members of the UN are *ipso facto* parties to it. The Court is composed of 15 judges, elected by both the General Assembly and the Security Council for nine-year terms which are renewable. Judges may deliberate over cases in which their country is involved. If no judge on the bench is from a country which is a party to a dispute under consideration, that party may designate a judge to participate *ad hoc* in that particular deliberation. If any party to a case fails to adhere to the judgment of the Court, the other party may have recourse to the Security Council.
President, Mohammed Bedjaoui (Algeria) (2000)
Vice-President, Stephen M. Schwebel (USA) (1997)
Judges, Geza Herczegh (Hungary) (2003); Rosalind Higgins (UK) (2000); Jens Evensen (Norway) (1997); Vladen S. Vereshchetin (Russia) (1997); Gilbert Guillaume (France) (2000); Mohammed Shahabuddeen (Guyana) (1997); Andrés Aguilar Mawdsley (Venezuela) (2000); Christopher G. Weeramantry (Sri Lanka) (2000); Raymond Ranjeva (Madagascar) (2000); Shi Jiuyong (China) (2003); Abdul Koroma (Sierra Leone) (2000); Carl-August Fleischauer (Germany) (2003)

INTERNATIONAL WAR CRIMES TRIBUNAL FOR THE FORMER YUGOSLAVIA
Churchill Plein 1, PO Box 13888, 2501 EW The Hague, The Netherlands

In February 1993, the Security Council voted to establish a war crimes tribunal for the former Yugoslavia to hear cases covering grave breaches of the Geneva Conventions and crimes against humanity. The Court was inaugurated in November 1993 in The Hague with 11 judges elected by the UN General Assembly from 11 states, divided into two trial chambers of three judges each and an appeal chamber of five judges. The court is unable to force suspects to stand trial but is empowered to pass verdicts in the absence of suspects and can put suspects under an 'act of accusation' which prevents them from leaving their own country.

The first indictment was issued by the court in November 1994 against a Bosnian Serb who was extradited from Germany to The Hague in April 1995 to stand trial along with 20 absent Bosnian Serbs on charges of murder torture and rape. In October 1995, the tribunal formally charged the Bosnian Serb leaders Radovan Karadzic and Gen. Ratko Mladic, and the Croatian Serb President Milar Martic and 21 others with genocide and crimes against humanity. As at May 1996, only three of the 57 suspected war criminals to be indicted have been taken into custody.
President, Antonio Cassese (Italy)
Chief Prosecutor, Louise Arbour (Canada)

INTERNATIONAL CRIMINAL TRIBUNAL FOR RWANDA
In November 1994, the UN Security Council voted to establish a tribunal to try those responsible for genocide and other violations of international humanitarian law in Rwanda between 1 January and 31 December 1994. The tribunal, based in Arusha, Tanzania, is empowered to try

the most senior people responsible for the massacre. It formally opened in November 1995 to consider 463 indictments.

Chief Prosecutor, Justice Goldstone (South Africa)

SPECIALIZED AGENCIES

Fifteen independent international organizations, each with its own membership, budget and headquarters, carry out their responsibilities in co-ordination with the UN under agreements made with the Economic and Social Council. An entry for each appears elsewhere in the International Organizations section. They are: the Food and Agriculture Organization of the UN; International Civil Aviation Organization; International Fund for Agricultural Development; International Labour Organization; International Maritime Organization; the International Monetary Fund; International Telecommunications Union; UN Educational, Scientific and Cultural Organization; UN Industrial Development Organization; Universal Postal Union; World Bank (International Bank for Reconstruction and Development, International Development Agency, International Finance Corporation); World Health Organization; World Intellectual Property Organization; and World Meteorological Organization. The International Atomic Energy Agency and the World Trade Organization are linked to the UN but are not specialized agencies.

UK MISSION TO THE UNITED NATIONS
One Dag Hammarskjöld Plaza, 885 Second Avenue, New York, NY 10017, USA
Permanent Representative to the United Nations and Representative on the Security Council, Sir John Weston, KCMG, *apptd* 1995
Deputy Permanent Representative, S. J. Gomersall

UK MISSION TO THE OFFICE OF THE UN AND OTHER INTERNATIONAL ORGANIZATIONS IN GENEVA
37–39 rue de Vermont, 1211 Geneva 20, Switzerland
Permanent UK Representative, N. C. R. Williams, CMG, *apptd* 1993
Deputy Permanent Representatives, Sir John Ramsden, Bt. (*Head of Chancery*); P. R. Jenkins (*Economic Affairs*)

UK MISSION TO THE INTERNATIONAL ATOMIC ENERGY AGENCY, THE UN INDUSTRIAL DEVELOPMENT ORGANIZATION AND THE UN OFFICE AT VIENNA
Jaurèsgasse 12, 1030 Vienna, Austria
Permanent UK Representative, C. Hulse, CMG, OBE, *apptd* 1993
Deputy Permanent Representative, S. H. Innes

UN OFFICE AND INFORMATION CENTRE
18 Buckingham Gate, London SW1E 6LB
Tel 0171-630 1981

UNITED NATIONS EDUCATIONAL, SCIENTIFIC AND CULTURAL ORGANIZATION
7 place de Fontenoy, 75352 Paris 07SP, France

The United Nations Educational, Scientific and Cultural Organization (UNESCO) was established in 1946. It promotes collaboration among its member states in education, science, culture and communication. It aims to further a universal respect for human rights, justice and the rule of law, without distinction of race, sex, language or religion, in accordance with the UN Charter.

UNESCO runs a number of programmes to improve education and extend access to it. It provides assistance to ensure the free flow of information and its wider and better balanced dissemination without any obstacle to freedom of expression, and to maintain cultural heritage in the face of development. It fosters research and study in all areas of the social and environmental sciences.

UNESCO had 183 member states as at July 1995. There are three associate members. The General Conference, consisting of representatives of all the members, meets biennially to decide the programme and the budget (1994–5, US$455,490,000). It elects the 51-member Executive Board, which supervises operations, and appoints a Director-General who heads a Secretariat responsible for carrying out the organization's programmes. In most member states national commissions liaise with UNESCO to execute its programme.

The UK withdrew from UNESCO in 1985. It was granted observer status in 1986.

Director-General, Federico Mayor Zaragoza (Spain)

UNITED NATIONS INDUSTRIAL DEVELOPMENT ORGANIZATION
Vienna International Centre, Wagramerstrasse 5, PO Box 300, A-1400 Vienna, Austria
Tel: Vienna 211 310

The United Nations Industrial Development Organization (UNIDO) was established as an organ of the UN General Assembly in 1966, replacing the Centre for Industrial Development. It became a UN specialized agency in 1985 with the aims of co-ordinating industrial activities within the UN system and promoting the industrialization of developing countries, with special emphasis upon the manufacturing sector. To this end it provides technical assistance and advice, provides investment promotion and helps with planning. UNIDO assists both public and private sectors and has made its services available to former centrally planned economies in transition to a market economy.

UNIDO had 169 members as at June 1996. It is funded by the UN, member states and non-governmental organizations. A General Conference of all the members meets biennially to discuss strategy and policy, set a budget (1996–7, US$181 million) and elect the Industrial Development Board. This executive body is composed of members from 53 member states and reviews implementation of the regular work programme and of General Conference decisions. There is a subsidiary Programme and Budget Committee. A Secretariat administers UNIDO under a Director-General, appointed by the Conference.

Director-General, Mauricio de Maria y Campos (Mexico)
Permanent UK Representative, C. Hulse, CMG, OBE, British Embassy, Vienna

UNIVERSAL POSTAL UNION
Weltpoststrasse 4, 3000 Berne 15, Switzerland
Tel: Berne 350 3111

The Universal Postal Union (UPU) was established by the Treaty of Berne 1874, taking effect from 1875, and became a UN specialized agency in 1948. The UPU is an intergovernmental organization which exists to form and regulate a single postal territory of all member countries for the reciprocal exchange of correspondence without discrimination. It also assists and advises on the improvement of postal services.

The UPU had 189 members as at May 1996. A Universal Postal Congress of all its members is the UPU's supreme authority and meets every five years to review the Treaty. A Council of Administration composed of 41 members was established by the 1994 Congress. It meets annually to ensure continuity between congresses, study regulatory developments and broad policies, approve the budget and examine proposed Treaty changes. A Postal Operations Council also meets annually to deal with specific technical and operational issues. The three UPU bodies are served by the International Bureau, a secretariat headed by a Director-General.

Funding is provided by members according to a scale of contributions drawn up by the Congress. The Council sets the annual budget (1996, SFr 33,376,400) within a five-year figure decided by the Congress.

Director-General, Thomas E. Leavey (USA)

WESTERN EUROPEAN UNION
4 rue de la Régence, 1000 Brussels, Belgium

The Western European Union (WEU) originated as the Brussels Treaty Organization (BTO) established under the Treaty of Brussels, signed in 1948 by Belgium, France, Luxembourg, the Netherlands and the UK, to provide collective self-defence and economic, cultural and social collaboration amongst its signatories. With the collapse of the European Defence Community and the decision of NATO to incorporate the Federal Republic of Germany into the Western security system, the BTO was modified to become the WEU in 1954 with the admission of West Germany and Italy. However, owing to the overlap with NATO and the Council of Europe, the Union became largely defunct.

From the late 1970s onwards efforts were made to add a security dimension to the EC's European Political Co-operation. Opposition to these efforts from Denmark, Greece and Ireland led the remaining EC countries, all WEU members, to decide to reactivate the Union in 1984. Members committed themselves to harmonizing their views on defence and security and developing a European security identity, while bearing in mind the importance of transatlantic relations. Portugal and Spain joined the WEU in 1988, and Greece became a full member in 1995.

After much debate about its future, the EU Maastricht Treaty designated the WEU as the future defence component of the European Union. WEU foreign ministers agreed in the Petersberg Declaration 1992 to assign forces to WEU command for 'peacemaking' operations in Europe. In November 1992 the WEU's role as the common security dimension of the EU was enhanced when WEU ministers signed a declaration with remaining European NATO members to give them various forms of WEU membership. Iceland, Norway and Turkey became associate members; Ireland, Denmark, Austria, Finland and Sweden became observer members. In 1994 the WEU reached agreements with nine eastern European states (Estonia, Latvia, Lithuania, Poland, Czech Republic, Slovak Republic, Hungary, Romania and Bulgaria) under which they all became associate partners.

The WEU acts in accordance with positions adopted within the Atlantic Alliance, and relations between the WEU and NATO are developing on the basis of transparency and complementarity. WEU foreign ministers stated in the Luxembourg Declaration 1993 that the WEU is ready to participate in the future work of the NATO Alliance as its European pillar, and to co-operate to prevent the duplication of WEU and NATO actions.

The formation of a 'Eurocorps' based on the Franco-German brigade as a force answerable to the WEU was announced in 1992. The 'Eurocorps' was inaugurated in 1993 and became fully operational in 1995 with 51,000 troops comprising French, German, Belgian, Luxembourg and Spanish forces.

A Council of Ministers (foreign and defence) meets biannually in the capital of the presiding country; the presidency rotates biannually. A Permanent Council of the member states' permanent representatives meets weekly in Brussels. Associate members have the right to attend Permanent Council meetings. The Permanent Council is chaired by the Secretary-General and serviced by the Secretariat. A planning cell has been established to draw up contingency plans in the areas of humanitarian relief, peacekeeping and crisis management. The Assembly of the WEU is composed of 115 parliamentarians of member states and meets twice annually in Paris to debate matters within the scope of the revised Brussels Treaty.

Presidency (1996), UK, Belgium; (1997), France, Germany
Secretary-General, José Cutileiro (Portugal)
UK Representative on the Permanent Council, Sir John Goulden, KCMG
ASSEMBLY, 43 avenue du Président Wilson, 75775 Paris Cedex 16, France

---

THE WORLD BANK
1818 H Street NW, Washington DC 20433, USA

The World Bank, more formally known as the International Bank for Reconstruction and Development (IBRD), is a specialized agency of the UN. It developed from the international monetary and financial conference held at Bretton Woods, New Hampshire, in 1944 and was established by 44 nations in 1945 to encourage economic growth in developing countries through the provision of loans and technical assistance to their respective governments. The IBRD now has 178 members.

The Bank is owned by the governments of member countries and its capital is subscribed by its members. It finances its lending primarily from borrowing in world capital markets, and derives a substantial contribution to its resources from its retained earnings and the repayment of loans. The interest rate on its loans is calculated in relation to its cost of borrowing. Loans generally have a grace period of five years and are repayable within 20 years. The loans made by the Bank since its inception to 30 June 1994 totalled US$333,806.8 million to 110 countries. Total capital is US$170,003 million.

Originally directed towards post-war reconstruction in Europe, the Bank has subsequently turned towards assisting less-developed countries with the establishment of two affiliates, the International Finance Corporation (IFC) in 1956 and the International Development Association (IDA) in 1960. The IFC aids developing member countries by promoting the growth of the private sector of their economies and by helping to mobilize domestic and foreign capital for this purpose. The IFC's subscribed share capital was US$2,251 million at 30 June 1994. It is also empowered to borrow up to two and a half times the amount of its unimpaired subscribed capital and accumulated earnings for use in its lending programme. At 30 June 1994, the IFC had committed financing totalling more than US$14,316,215 million in about 162 countries.

The IDA performs the same function as the World Bank but primarily to less developed countries and on terms that bear less heavily on their balance of payments than IBRD loans. Eligible countries typically have a per capita gross national product of less than US$835 (1994). Funds (called credits to distinguish them from IBRD loans) come mostly in the form of subscriptions and contributions from the IDA's richer members and transfers from the net income of the IBRD. The terms for IDA credits, which bear no interest and are made to governments only, are ten-year grace periods and 35- or 40-year maturities. By 30 June 1994, the IDA had extended development credits totalling US$87,880 million to 157 countries.

The IBRD and its affiliates are financially and legally distinct but share headquarters. The IBRD is headed by a Board of Governors, consisting of one Governor and one alternate Governor appointed by each member country. Twenty-four Executive Directors exercise all powers of the Bank except those reserved to the Board of Governors. The President, elected by the Executive Directors, conducts the business of the Bank, assisted by an international staff. Membership in both the IFC (162 members) and the IDA (157 members) is open to all IBRD countries. The IDA is administered by the same staff as the Bank; the IFC has its own personnel but draws on the IBRD for administrative and other support. All share the same President.

In 1988 a third affiliate, the Multilateral Investment Guarantee Agency (MIGA) was formed. MIGA encourages foreign investment in developing states by providing investment guarantees to potential investors and advisory services to developing member countries. At 30 December 1994 128 countries were members of MIGA.
President (IBRD, IFC, IDA, MIGA), James D. Wolfensohn (USA)
UK Executive Director, H. Evans, Room 11-120, IMF, 700 19th Street NW, Washington DC 20431
EUROPEAN OFFICE, 66 avenue d'Iena, 75116 Paris, France
JAPAN OFFICE, Kokusai Building 916, 1-1 Marunouchi 3-Chomse, Chiyoda-ku, Tokyo 100, Japan
UK OFFICE, New Zealand House, Haymarket, London SWIY 4TQ

THE WORLD COUNCIL OF CHURCHES
PO Box 2100, 1211 Geneva 2, Switzerland
Tel: Geneva 791 6152

The World Council of Churches (WCC) was constituted in 1948 to promote unity among Christian churches. The 330 member churches have adherents in more than 100 countries. With the exception of Roman Catholicism, virtually all Christian traditions are represented.

The policies of the Council are determined by delegates of the member churches meeting in Assembly, roughly every seven years; the seventh Assembly was held in Canberra, Australia, in February 1991 and the eighth Assembly is scheduled to be held in Harare, Zimbabwe, in September 1998. More detailed decisions are taken by a 151-member Central Committee which is elected by the Assembly and meets, with the eight WCC Presidents, annually. The Central Committee in turn appoints a smaller Executive Committee and also nominates commissions to guide the various programmes.
General Secretary, Dr Konrad Raiser (Germany)

WORLD HEALTH ORGANIZATION
20 avenue Appia, 1211 Geneva 27, Switzerland
Tel: Geneva 791 2888

The UN International Health Conference, held in 1946, established the World Health Organization (WHO) as a UN specialized agency, with effect from 1948. It is dedicated to attaining the highest possible level of health for all. It collaborates with member governments, UN agencies and other bodies to improve health standards, control communicable diseases and promote all aspects of family and environmental health. It seeks to raise the standards of health teaching and training, and promotes research through collaborating research centres worldwide. Its other services include the *International Pharmacopoeia*, epidemiological surveillance, and the collation and publication of statistics. WHO activities are orientated to achieving 'Health for All'.

WHO had 190 members as at May 1995. It is governed by the annual World Health Assembly of members which meets to set policy, approve the budget (1996-7, US$1,900 million), appoint a Director-General, and adopt health conventions and regulations. It also elects 32 members who designate one expert to serve on the Executive Board. The Board effects the programme, suggests initiatives and is empowered to deal with emergencies. A Secretariat, headed by the Director-General, supervises the activities of six regional offices.
Director-General, Dr H. Nakajima (Japan)

WORLD INTELLECTUAL PROPERTY ORGANIZATION
34 chemin des Colombettes, 1211 Geneva 20, Switzerland
Tel: Geneva 730 9246

The World Intellectual Property Organization (WIPO) was established in 1967 by the Stockholm Convention, which entered into force in 1970. In addition to that Convention, WIPO administers 18 treaties, the principal ones being the Paris Convention for the Protection of Industrial Property and the Berne Convention for the Protection of Literary and Artistic Works. WIPO became a UN specialized agency in 1974.

WIPO promotes the protection of intellectual property throughout the world through co-operation among states, and the administration of various 'Unions', each founded on a multilateral treaty and dealing with the legal and administrative aspects of intellectual property.

Intellectual property comprises two main branches: industrial property (inventions, trademarks, industrial designs and appellations of origin); and copyright (literary, musical, photographic, audiovisual and artistic works, etc.). WIPO also assists creative intellectual activity and facilitates technology transfer, particularly to developing countries.

The WIPO had 157 members as at June 1996. The biennial session of all its governing bodies sets policy, a programme and a budget (1996-7, SFr300 million). WIPO has three governing bodies: the General Assembly, composed of WIPO members who are also members of the Paris or Berne conventions; the Conference, composed of all WIPO members; and the Co-ordination Committee, composed of member states elected by members of WIPO and the Paris and Berne conventions. The General Assembly elects a Director-General, who heads the International Bureau (secretariat).

A separate International Union for the Protection of New Varieties of Plants (UPOV), established by convention in 1961, is linked to WIPO. It has 30 members.
Director-General, Dr Arpad Bogsch (USA)

WORLD METEOROLOGICAL ORGANIZATION
41 avenue Giuseppe Motta, PO Box 2300, 1211 Geneva 20, Switzerland

The World Meteorological Organization (WMO) was established as a UN specialized agency in 1950, succeeding the International Meteorological Organization founded in 1873. It facilitates co-operation in the establishment of networks for making meteorological, climatological, hydrological and geophysical observations, as well as their exchange, processing and standardization, and assists technology transfer, training and research. It also fosters collaboration between meteorological and hydrological services, and furthers the application of meteorology to aviation, shipping, environment, water problems, agriculture, etc.

The WMO had 178 member states and five member territories as at 30 June 1995. The supreme authority is the World Meteorological Congress of member states and member territories, which meets every four years to determine general policy, make recommendations and set a budget (1992–5, SFr236.1 million). It also elects 26 members of the 36-member Executive Council, the other members being the President and three Vice-Presidents of the WMO, and the Presidents of the six regional associations, who are ex-officio members. The Council supervises the implementation of Congress decisions, initiates studies and makes recommendations on matters needing international action. The WMO functions through six regional associations and eight technical commissions. Each of the regional associations has responsibility for co-ordinating meteorological activities within its region. The technical commissions study meteorological and hydrological problems, lay down the necessary methodologies and procedures, and make recommendations to the Executive Council and Congress. The Secretariat is headed by a Secretary-General, appointed by the Congress.
Secretary-General, G. O. P. Obasi (Nigeria)

WORLD TRADE ORGANIZATION
Centre William Rappard, 154 rue de Lausanne, 1211 Geneva 21, Switzerland
Tel: Geneva 739 5286

The World Trade Organization was established on 1 January 1995 as the successor to the General Agreement on Tariffs and Trade (GATT). GATT was established in 1948 as an interim agreement until the charter of a new international trade organization could be drafted by a committee of the UN Economic and Social Council and ratified by member states. The charter was never ratified and GATT became the only regime for the regulation of world trade, evolving its own rules and procedures.

GATT was dedicated to the expansion of non-discriminatory international trade and progressively extended free trade via 'rounds' of multilateral negotiations. Eight 'rounds' were concluded: Geneva (1947), Annecy (1948), Torquay (1950), Geneva (1956), Dillon (1960-1), Kennedy (1964-7), Tokyo (1973-9) and Uruguay (1986-94). By the time that the measures of the Uruguay Round are fully implemented in 2002 the average duties on manufactured goods will have been reduced from 40 per cent in the 1940s to 3 per cent. The Final Act of the Uruguay Round was signed by trade ministers from the

128 GATT negotiating states and the EU in Marrakesh, Morocco, on 15 April 1994. It established the World Trade Organization (WTO) to supersede GATT and implement the Uruguay Round agreements.

The WTO is the legal and institutional foundation of the multilateral trading system. It provides the contractual obligations determining how governments frame and implement trade policy and provides the forum for the debate, negotiation and adjudication of trade problems. The WTO's principal aims are to liberalize world trade and place it on a secure basis, and it seeks to achieve this partly by an agreed set of trade rules and market access agreements and partly through further trade liberalization negotiations. The WTO also administers and implements a further 29 multilateral agreements in fields such as agriculture, textiles and clothing, services, government procurement, rules of origin and intellectual property.

The highest authority of the WTO is the Ministerial Conference composed of all members which meets at least once every two years. The General Council meets as required and acts on behalf of the Ministerial Conference in regard to the regular working of the WTO. Composed of all members, the General Council also convenes in two particular forms: as the Dispute Settlement Body, dealing with disputes between members arising from the Uruguay Round Final Act; and as the Trade Policy Review Body, conducting regular reviews of the trade policies of members. A secretariat of 450 staff headed by a Director-General services WTO bodies and provides trade performance and trade policy analysis.

As at 15 June 1996 there were 122 WTO members, and a further 29 governments had applied to join the WTO. The WTO budget for 1996 was SFr115 million, with members' contributions calculated on the basis of their share of the total trade conducted by WTO members. The official languages of the WTO are English, French and Spanish.
Director-General, Renato Ruggiero (Italy)
Permanent UK Representative, N. C. R. Williams, CMG, 37–39 rue de Vermont, 1211 Geneva 20

The European Union

MEMBERS

State	Accession Date	Population (million)	GNP (US$ million)	GDP per head‡	Council Votes	EP Seats
Austria	1 January 1995	7.86	197,475	114	4	21
Belgium	1 January 1958*	10.05	231,051	114	5	25
Denmark	1 January 1973	5.17	145,384	116	3	16
Finland	1 January 1995	5.06	95,817	91	3	16
France	1 January 1958*	57.47	1,355,039	110	10	87
Germany	1 January 1958*†	80.69	2,075,452	111	10	99
Greece	1 January 1981	10.37	80,194	64	5	25
Ireland	1 January 1973	3.53	48,275	86	3	15
Italy	1 January 1958*	57.12	1,101,258	103	10	87
Luxembourg	1 January 1958*	0.4	15,973	163	2	6
Netherlands	1 January 1958*	15.28	338,144	105	5	31
Portugal	1 January 1986	9.84	92,124	70	5	25
Spain	1 January 1986	39.48	525,334	77	8	64
Sweden	1 January 1995	8.69	206,419	98	4	22
UK	1 January 1973	57.92	1,069,457	99	10	87
Total		368.93	7,577,396		87	626

* Acceded to the European Coal and Steel Community (ECSC) on its formation in 1952
† Federal Republic of Germany (West) 1952/1958; German Democratic Republic (East) acceded on German reunification (3 October 1990)
‡ Expressed as purchasing power parities: EU average = 100
EP European Parliament

DEVELOPMENT

1950 Robert Schuman (French foreign minister) proposes that France and West Germany pool their coal and steel industries under a supranational authority (Schuman Plan)

1951 Paris Treaty signed by France, West Germany, Belgium, Italy, Luxembourg and the Netherlands establishes the European Coal and Steel Community (ECSC)

1952 ECSC treaty enters into force

1957 25 March: Treaty of Rome signed by the six, establishes the European Economic Community (EEC) and the European Atomic Energy Authority (EURATOM). Treaty aims to create a customs union; remove obstacles to free movement of capital, goods, people and services; establish common external trade policy and common agricultural and fisheries policies; co-ordinate economic policies; harmonize social policies; promote co-operation in nuclear research

1958 1 January: EEC and EURATOM begin operation. Joint Parliament and Court of Justice established for all three communities, and the Commission, Council of Ministers, Economic and Social Committee and Investment Bank for the EEC

1962 Common Agricultural Policy (CAP) agreed (see pages 768–9)

1967 EEC, ECSC and EURATOM merge to form the European Communities (EC), with a single Council of Ministers and Commission

1968 EEC customs union completed
Implementation of CAP completed

1970 Foreign policy co-ordination begins

1971 The Common Fisheries Policy comes into operation

1972 European Social Fund established

1974 Regular heads of governments summits begin

1975 'Own resources' funding of EC budget introduced (see page 768)
UK renegotiates its terms of accession
European Regional Development Fund created

1979 European Monetary System (EMS) comes into operation (see page 769)
First direct elections to European Parliament (June)

1984 Fontainebleau summit settles UK annual budget rebate and agrees first major CAP reform
European Parliament elections (June)

1986 Single European Act (SEA) signed (see page 769)
European Political Co-operation (EPC) established (see page 769)

1988 Second major CAP reform

1989 European Parliament elections (June)

1991 Maastricht Treaty agreed (see page 770)

1992 31 December: Single internal market programme completed

1993 September: the exchange rate mechanism (ERM) of the EMS effectively suspended
1 November: The Maastricht Treaty enters into force, establishing the European Union (EU)

1994 1 January: European Economic Area (EEA) agreement comes into operation (see page 770)
Norway rejects EU membership in referendum

1995 Schengen Agreement enters into force

ENLARGEMENT AND EXTERNAL RELATIONS

The procedure for accession to the EU is laid down in the Treaty of Rome; states must be stable European democracies governed by the rule of law with free market economies. A membership application is studied by the Commission, which produces an Opinion. If the Opinion is positive, negotiations may be opened leading to an Accession Treaty which must be approved by all member state governments and parliaments, the European Parliament, and the applicant state's government and parliament. *Applicants:* Morocco (applied 1987/rejected 1987), Turkey (applied 1987/negative Opinion 1989), Cyprus (applied 1990/rejected 1993), Malta (applied 1990/negative Opinion 1993), Switzerland (applied 1992/no Opinion yet), Hungary (applied 1994/no Opinion yet), Poland (applied 1994/no Opinion yet), Bulgaria (applied 1995/no Opinion yet), Estonia (applied 1995/no Opinion yet), Latvia (applied 1995/no Opinion yet), Lithuania (applied 1995/no Opinion yet), Romania (applied 1995/no Opinion yet), Slovakia (applied 1995/no Opinion yet), the Czech Republic (applied 1996/no Opinion yet).

Apart from the EEA Agreement (*see* page 770), the EU has three types of agreements with other European and CIS states. 'Europe' Agreements commit the EU and signatory states to long-term political and economic integration, a free trade zone (apart from agriculture and labour movement) and eventual EU membership. Government representatives from the signatory states are entitled to attend one summit and two finance and foreign council meetings a year. 'Europe' agreements have been signed with Poland, Hungary (1991), Romania, Bulgaria, Czech Republic, Slovak Republic (1993), Estonia, Latvia and Lithuania (1995). Association agreements include a commitment to EU financial aid and to eventual membership; agreements have been signed with Malta (1971), Cyprus (1972), Turkey (1974) and Slovenia (1996). Partnership and co-operation agreements are based on regulating and improving political and economic relations and mutual trade concessions but exclude any possibility of membership. Agreements have been signed with Ukraine, Russia, Moldova (1994), Kyrgyzstan and Belarus (1995).

THE COMMUNITY BUDGET

The principles of funding the European Community budget were established by the Treaty of Rome and remain with modifications to this day. There is a legally binding limit on the overall level of resources (known as 'own resources') that the Community can raise from its member states; this limit is defined as a percentage of gross national product (GNP). Budget revenue and expenditure must balance and there is therefore no deficit financing. The own resources decision, which came into effect in 1975, states that there are four sources of Community funding under which each member state makes contributions: levies charged on agricultural imports into the Community from non-member states; customs duties on imports from non-member states; contributions based on member states' shares of a notional Community harmonized VAT base; and contributions based on member states' shares of Community GNP. The latter is the budget-balancing item and covers the difference between total expenditure and the revenue from the other three sources. Since 1984 the UK has had an annual rebate equivalent to 66 per cent of the difference between what the UK contributes to the budget and what it receives. This was introduced to compensate the UK for disproportionate contributions caused by its high proportion of agricultural and non-agricultural imports from non-member states and its relatively small receipts from the Common Agricultural Policy, the most important portion of Community expenditure.

BUDGET 1996

	Billion ECU*	As % of total
Agriculture	41.3	51.6
Regional and Social	26.0	32.5
External Action	4.5	5.6
Administration	4.1	5.1
Research and Technology	3.1	3.8
Consumer Protection, Industry, Internal Market	0.7	0.8
Energy and Environment	0.2	0.2
Foreign and Security Policy	0.1	0.1
TOTAL	80	99.7

EC BUDGET BY MEMBER STATE 1994 (*billion ECU**)

	Contributions		Receipts	Net gain‡
Germany	21.56	(31.4%)	7.73	− 13.83
France	12.73	(18.5%)	9.92	− 2.81
Italy	8.02	(11.7%)	5.22	− 2.80
UK	6.80	(10.0%)	5.26	− 1.54
Spain	4.83	(7.0%)	7.83	+ 3.00
Netherlands	4.23	(6.2%)	2.42	− 1.81
Belgium	2.82	(4.1%)	2.81	− 0.01
Denmark	1.30	(1.9%)	1.50	+ 0.20
Greece	1.03	(1.5%)	4.84	+ 3.81
Portugal	1.16	(1.7%)	3.04	+ 1.88
Ireland	0.66	(1.0%)	2.40	+ 1.74
Luxembourg	0.17	(0.2%)	0.42	+ 0.25
TOTAL	65.31	(95.2%)	53.39	

* 1 ECU = £0.81 as at 18 September 1996
‡ Net contributor (−)/net recipient (+)

Under the Edinburgh summit agreement (December 1992) the EC budget will rise in stages from 1.2 per cent of Community (Union) GNP in 1992 to 1.27 per cent in 1999

THE COMMON AGRICULTURAL POLICY

The Common Agricultural Policy (CAP) was established to increase agricultural production, provide a fair standard of living for farmers and ensure the availability of food at reasonable prices. This aim is achieved by a number of mechanisms:
− import levies (the EC sets a target price for a particular product in the Community, the world price is monitored and if it falls below the guide price, an import levy can be imposed equivalent to the difference between the two)
− intervention purchase (if the price of a product falls below the level indicated by the Council, member states must purchase supplies of the product, provided that they are of suitable quality)
− export subsidies (the EC pays a food exporter a subsidy equivalent to the difference between the price at which the product is bought in the EC and the lower sale price on the world market)

These measures stimulated production but also placed increasing demands on the EC budget which were exacerbated by the increase in EC members and yields enlarged by technological innovation; CAP now accounts for almost 50 per cent of EC expenditure. To surmount these problems reforms were agreed in 1984, 1988 and 1992.

The 1984 reforms created the system of co-responsibility levies; farm payments to the EC by volume of product sold. This system was supplemented by national quotas for particular products, such as milk. The 1988 reforms emphasized set aside, whereby farmers are given direct grants to take land out of production as a means of reducing surpluses. Originally aimed at cereal farmers, who were allowed to set aside between 15 per cent and 100 per cent of their land, the set aside reforms were extended in 1993 for another five years and to every farm in the EC, which must set aside at least 18 per cent of its land. The 1992 reforms are based on the reduction of target prices for cereals, beef and dairy produce. These are being reduced by 29 per cent, 15 per cent and 5 per cent respectively, and the amount of money spent by the EC on the three mechanisms will fall. By 1995 successive CAP reforms had virtually eliminated EU food mountains.

Under the Uruguay round agreement of GATT concluded in December 1993, the EU must, over a six-year period from 1 January 1995, reduce its import levies by 36 per cent, reduce its domestic subsidies by 20 per cent, reduce its export subsidies by 36 per cent in value, and reduce its subsidized exports by 21 per cent in volume.

COMMON FOREIGN AND SECURITY POLICY

The Common Foreign and Security Policy (CFSP) was created as a pillar of the EU by the Maastricht Treaty (*see* page 770). It adopted the machinery of the European Political Co-operation (EPC) framework which it replaced and was charged with providing a forum for member states and EU institutions to consult on foreign affairs.

The CFSP system is headed by the European Council, which provides general lines of policy, decided by unanimity. Specific policy decisions are taken by the Council of Foreign Ministers, which meets at least four times a year to determine areas for joint action. The foreign minister of the state holding the EU presidency initiates action, manages the CFSP and represents it abroad. He is supported by a secretariat based in Brussels and is advised by the past and future holders of the presidency, forming a so-called troika. The Council of Ministers is supported by the Political Committee which meets monthly, or within 48 hours if there is a crisis, to prepare for ministerial discussions. A group of correspondents, designated diplomats in each member's foreign ministry, provides day-to-day contact.

THE EUROPEAN MONETARY SYSTEM

The European monetary system (EMS) began operation in March 1979 with three main purposes. The first was to establish monetary stability in Europe, initially in exchange rates between EC member state currencies, and in the longer term to be part of a wider stabilization process, overcoming inflation and budget and trade deficits. The second purpose was to overcome the constraints resulting from the interdependence of EC economies, and the third was to aid the long-term process of European monetary integration. All EC member state currencies are members of the EMS.

The EMS has three components: the ECU; the exchange rate mechanism (ERM); and the credit mechanisms. The ECU is a monetary unit, the value of which is calculated as a basket of set amounts of each member state currency. The relative weighting given to each currency in the ECU basket is proportional to the size of an EU member's economy and the state's share of EU trade. The German Deutsche Mark (DM) has the largest weighting of 32 per cent. The ECU is used for officially fixing the central rates in the ERM and as a means of settlement among central banks in the EMS.

The ERM is the central component of the EMS. Officially all member currencies of the ERM have a central rate against the ECU, the anchor of the mechanism. In practice, the Deutsche Mark has become the anchor currency, with all other currencies' central rates expressed against the DM. Central banks are obliged to maintain their currencies within set margins of their central rate (either 2.25 per cent or 6 per cent above or below) by intervening in the foreign currency markets. Currencies may be revalued or devalued by up to 10 per cent by agreement with all other ERM members. To do this, central banks co-ordinate their actions and can use the credit mechanisms to borrow money from each other and from the Central European Monetary Co-operation Fund where they each deposit 20 per cent of their reserves. Financial assistance is available to central banks over very short-term, short-term and medium-term periods.

Five currencies (Deutsche Mark, French franc, Belgian franc, Dutch guilder, Danish krone) joined the ERM with 2.25 per cent fluctuation margins, and two currencies (Irish punt and Italian lira) with 6 per cent margins in 1979. Subsequently the punt and lira reduced to 2.25 per cent margins. The Spanish peseta (1989), UK pound sterling (1990) and Portuguese escudo (1992) joined the ERM with 6 per cent margins. The pound and the lira were forced out of the mechanism by speculation in September 1992. Speculation forced the widening of the fluctuation margins to 15 per cent from August 1993 for six of the remaining ERM member currencies (the Deutsche Mark and Dutch guilder remain within 2.25 per cent margins). By April 1994 the French franc, Belgian franc, Irish punt, Danish krone were informally operating within 2.25 per cent fluctuation margins again. The Austrian schilling joined the ERM in January 1995, operating within 15 per cent margins.

THE SINGLE MARKET

Throughout the 1970s and early 1980s, EC members became concerned at the slow growth of the European economy. Although tariffs and quotas had been removed between member states, the EC was still separated into a number of national markets by a series of non-tariff barriers. It was to overcome these internal barriers to trade that the concept of the Single Market was developed. The measures to be undertaken were outlined in the Cockfield report (1985) and codified in the Single European Act (SEA) 1986, which came into force in 1987 with a target date of 31 December 1992 for completion.

The SEA includes articles removing obstacles that distort the internal market: the elimination of frontier controls; the mutual recognition of professional qualifications; the harmonization of product specifications, largely by the mutual recognition of national standards; open tendering for public procurement contracts; the free movement of capital; the harmonization of VAT and excise duties; and the reduction of state aid to particular industries. The SEA changed the legislative process within the EC, particularly with the introduction of qualified majority voting in the Council of Ministers for some policy areas, and the introduction of the assent procedure in the European Parliament, requiring the approval of an absolute majority of MEPs for other policy areas. The SEA also extends EC competence into the fields of technology, the environment, regional policy, monetary policy and external policy. The Single Market came into effect on 1 January 1993 and is expected to result in at least a 5 per cent increase in the collective GNP of EC member states. The full implementation of the elimination of frontier controls and the harmonization of taxes have, however, been repeatedly delayed.

THE EUROPEAN ECONOMIC AREA (see also EFTA entry)

The EC Single Market programme spurred European non-member states to open negotiations with the EC on preferential access for their goods, services, labour and capital to the Single Market. Principal among these states were European Free Trade Association (EFTA) members who opened negotiations on extending the Single Market to EFTA by the formation of the European Economic Area (EEA) encompassing all 19 EC and EFTA states. Agreement was reached in May 1992 but the operation of the EEA was delayed by its rejection in a Swiss referendum, necessitating an additional protocol agreed by the remaining 18 states. The EEA came into effect on 1 January 1994 after ratification by 17 member states (Liechtenstein joined on 1 May 1995 after adapting its customs union with Switzerland).

Austria, Finland and Sweden joined the EU itself on 1 January 1995, leaving only Norway, Iceland and Liechtenstein as the non-EU EEA members. Under the EEA agreement, the three states are to adopt the EU's *acquis communautaire*, apart from in the fields of agriculture, fisheries, and coal and steel.

The EEA is controlled by regular ministerial meetings and by a joint EU-EFTA committee which extends relevant EU legislation to EEA states. Apart from single market measures, there is co-operation in education, research and development, consumer policy and tourism. An EFTA Court of Justice has been established in Luxembourg and an EFTA Surveillance Authority in Brussels to supervise the implementation of the EEA Agreement.

THE SCHENGEN AGREEMENT

The Schengen Agreement was signed by France, Germany, Belgium, Luxembourg and the Netherlands in 1990 to replace an accord on border controls agreed in Schengen, Luxembourg, in 1985. The Agreement committed the five states to abolishing internal border controls and erecting external frontiers against illegal immigrants, drug traffickers, terrorists and organized crime.

Subsequently signed by Spain and Portugal, the Agreement was ratified by the seven signatory states and entered into force in March 1995 with the removal of frontier, passport, customs and immigration controls. France reimposed border controls in June 1995 and pressed for an extension to the initial three-month trial period. This was rejected by the other member states who agreed to end passport and border controls permanently from July 1995. Austria joined the Agreement in April 1995, and Italy and Greece are to do so by the end of 1996.

Provisional agreement was reached in June 1995 between the signatory states and the Nordic Union on a merger of the two frontier-free zones, enabling Denmark, Finland and Sweden to achieve observer status in May 1996 as a prelude to full membership.

THE MAASTRICHT TREATY

The Treaty on European Union was agreed at a meeting of the European Council in Maastricht, the Netherlands, in December 1991. It was the result of intergovernmental conferences on political union and economic and monetary union, and came into effect in November 1993 following ratification by the member states.

Three 'pillars' formed the basis of the new treaty:
– the European Community with its established institutions and decision-making processes

– a Common Foreign and Security Policy (see page 769) with the Western European Union as the potential defence component of the EU
– co-operation in Justice and Home Affairs, with the Council of Ministers to co-ordinate policies on asylum, immigration, conditions of entry, cross-border crime, drug trafficking and terrorism

The Treaty established a common European citizenship for nationals of all member states and introduced the principle of subsidiarity whereby decisions are taken at the most appropriate level: national, regional or local. It extended EC competency into the areas of environmental and industrial policies, consumer affairs, health, and education and training, and extended qualified majority voting in the Council of Ministers to cover areas which had previously required a unanimous vote. The powers of the European Parliament over the budget and over the Commission were also enhanced and a co-decision procedure enabled the Parliament to override decisions made by the Council of Ministers (see below).

Timetables for economic and monetary union (EMU) and an eventual single currency (the Euro) were set in motion by the Treaty and fleshed out at the Madrid summit in December 1995. Founding members of EMU will be picked in 1998 on the basis of 1997 economic performance and must conform to the following criteria:
– the budget deficit must be less than 3 per cent of gross domestic product (GDP)
– total government debt must not exceed 60 per cent of GDP
– inflation must be a maximum of 1.5 per cent, and interest rates a maximum of 2 per cent above the average of the three best performing economies

The European Monetary Institute is to become the European Central Bank by 1 July 1998 and the Euro will be introduced by 1 January 1999.

A special protocol was agreed allowing the UK to 'opt out' of a single currency if it so wishes in January 1999. Denmark also secured an 'opt out' from the single currency, European citizenship, common defence policy, and the justice and interior affairs 'pillar' in order to obtain a vote in favour of ratifying Maastricht in a second referendum. A separate protocol on the Maastricht Treaty on social policy was adopted by 11 member states but not the UK. A year-long intergovernmental conference to review the Treaty opened in Turin, Italy, in March 1996.

THE LEGISLATIVE PROCESS

The core of the EU policymaking process is a dialogue between the Commission, which initiates and implements policy, and the Council of Ministers, which takes policy decisions. A degree of democratic control is exercised by the European Parliament.

The original legislative process is known as the consultative procedure. The Commission drafts a proposal which it submits to the Council and to the Parliament. The Council then consults the ESC, the Parliament and the Committee of the Regions; the Parliament may request that amendments are made. With or without these amendments, the proposal is then adopted by the Council and becomes law.

Under the Single European Act (SEA), changes were made to the legislative process, particularly in strengthening the role of the Parliament by the introduction of the co-operation procedure. The Parliament now has a second reading of proposals in some fields, and after the second reading its rejection of a proposal can only be overturned by a unanimous decision of the Council. The Maastricht Treaty extends the scope of the co-operation procedure, which now applies to Single Market laws and harmonization, trans-European networks, development policy, the social fund, and some aspects of transport, environment, research, social policy and competition policy.

The SEA introduced the assent procedure, whereby an absolute majority of the Parliament must vote to approve laws in certain fields before they are passed. Issues covered by the assent procedure include foreign treaties, accession treaties, international agreements with budgetary implications, citizenship, residence rights, the CAP, and regional and structural funds.

The Maastricht Treaty introduced the co-decision procedure; if, after the Parliament's second reading of a proposal, the Council and Parliament fail to agree, a conciliation committee of the two will reach a compromise. If a compromise is not reached, the Parliament can reject the legislation by the vote of an absolute majority of its members. This procedure applies in the areas of education and training, health, consumer protection, culture, research frameworks, general environment programmes and many Single Market issues.

The Council issues the following legislation:
- Regulations, which are binding in their entirety and directly applicable to all member states; they do not need to be incorporated into national law to come into effect
- Directives, which are less specific, binding as to the result to be achieved but leaving the method of implementation open to member states; a directive thus has no force until it is incorporated into national law
- Decisions, which are also binding but are addressed solely to one or more member states or individuals in a member state
- Recommendations
- Opinions, which are merely persuasive

The Council also has certain budgetary powers, including the power to reject the budget as a whole and to increase expenditure or redistribute money within sectors.

THE COUNCIL OF THE EUROPEAN UNION
175 rue de la Loi, 1048 Brussels, Belgium

The Council of the European Union (Council of Ministers) consists of ministers from the government of each of the member states. It formally comprises the foreign ministers of the member states but in practice the minister depends on the subject under discussion, e.g. when EC environment matters are under discussion, the meeting is informally known as the Environment Council. Council decisions are taken by qualified majority vote (in which members' votes are weighted), by a simple majority, or by unanimity. Council meetings are prepared by the Committee of Permanent Representatives (COREPER) of the member states, which acts as the 'gatekeeper' between national governments and the supranational EC, often negotiating on proposals with the Commission during the legislative process.

Unanimity votes are taken on issues such as taxation, budgets, foreign policy, the accession of new members, European Parliament electoral law, rights of free movement and residence, and some environment and transport policies. Qualified majority votes are taken on Single Market laws and harmonization, environment policy, health and safety, transport policy, overseas aid, research and development, culture, consumer protection, education and training, the development of a single currency and social policy. Member states have weighted votes in the Council loosely proportional to their relative population sizes (see introductory table), with a total of 87 votes. For a proposal from the Commission to pass, it must receive 62

votes; 26 votes are necessary to block a proposal, and 23 votes constitute a temporary blocking minority. For other proposals to be passed they must receive 62 votes cast by at least ten member states.

The European Council, comprising the heads of government of the member states, meets twice a year to provide overall policy direction. The presidency of the EC is held in rotation for six-month periods, setting the agenda for and chairing all Council meetings. The presidency provides the incumbent nation with an opportunity to pursue its own policy priorities. The European Council holds a summit in the country holding the presidency at the end of its period in office. The holders of the presidency for the years 1996–8 are:

1996 Italy, Ireland
1997 Netherlands, Luxembourg
1998 UK, Austria

OFFICE OF THE UNITED KINGDOM PERMANENT REPRESENTATIVE TO THE EUROPEAN COMMUNITIES
Rond-point Robert Schuman 6, 1040 Brussels, Belgium
Ambassador and UK Permanent Representative, HE Sir Stephen Wall, KCMG, LVO, *apptd* 1995
Minister and Deputy Permanent Representative, D. Bostock

THE EUROPEAN COMMISSION
200 rue de la Loi, 1049 Brussels, Belgium

The Commission consists of 20 Commissioners, two each from France, Germany, Italy, Spain and the UK, and one each from the remaining member states. The members of the Commission are appointed for five-year renewable terms by the agreement of the member states; the present Commission came into office on 23 January 1995 and in future the five-year term will run concurrently with the term of the European Parliament. The President and Vice-Presidents are elected by the Commissioners from among their number. The Commissioners pledge sole allegiance to the EC. The Commission initiates and implements EC legislation and is the guardian of the EC treaties. It is the exponent of Community-wide interests rather than the national preoccupations of the Council. Each Commissioner is supported by advisers and oversees whichever of the 24 departments, known as Directorates-General (DGs), is assigned to him. Each Directorate-General is headed by a Director-General. The Commission has a total staff of around 15,000 civil servants.

COMMISSIONERS *as at June 1996*

President

Secretariat-General; Forward Studies Unit; Inspectorate-General; Legal Services; Spokesman's Service; Joint Interpreting and Conference Service; Security Office; Overall responsibility for monetary matters, common foreign and security policy, institutional questions and intergovernmental conference, Jacques Santer (Luxembourg)

Vice-Presidents

External Relations with the Mediterranean, the Middle East, Latin America and parts of Asia, Manuel Marin (Spain)
External Relations with North America, Australia, Japan, New Zealand, China, South Korea, Taiwan, Hong Kong, Macao, Common Commercial Policy, Relations with the OECD and WTO, Sir Leon Brittan (UK)

Members

Industrial Affairs, Information Technology and Telecommunications, Martin Bangemann (Germany)

Immigration, Interior and Judicial Affairs, Financial Control, Anti-Fraud Measures, Relations with the Ombudsman, Anita Gradin (Sweden)
Agriculture and Rural Development, Franz Fischler (Austria)
Budget, Personnel and Administration, Translation, Erkki Liikanen (Finland)
Economic and Financial Affairs, Monetary matters, Credit and Investments, Statistical Office, Yves-Thibault de Silguy (France)
Energy and Euratom Supply Agency, Small and Medium Enterprises, Tourism , Christos Papoutis (Greece)
Institutional Questions, Intergovernmental Conference, Relations with the European Parliament, Culture and Audiovisual, Publications Office, Openness, Communications and Information, Marcelino Oreja (Spain)
Transport, Neil Kinnock (UK)
Regional Policy, Relations with the Committee of the Regions, Cohesion Fund, Monika Wulf-Mathies (Germany)
Science, Research and Development, Joint Research Centre, Human Resources, Education, Training and Youth, Edith Cresson (France)
Competition, Karel Van Miert (Belgium)
External Relations with Central and Eastern Europe, the former Soviet Union and other European states, Common Foreign and Security Policy, External Service, Hans van den Broek (Netherlands)
External Relations with African, Caribbean and Pacific states, Lomé Convention, João de Deus Pinheiro (Portugal)
Social Affairs and Employment, Relations with the Economic and Social Committee, , Padraig Flynn (Ireland)
Fisheries, Consumer Policy, EC Humanitarian Office, Emma Bonino (Italy)
Environment, Nuclear Safety, Ritt Bjerregaard (Denmark)

Internal Market, Financial Services, Customs, Taxation, Mario Monti (Italy)
Secretary-General, D. Williamson (UK)

THE EUROPEAN PARLIAMENT

The European Parliament (EP) originated as the Common Assembly of the ECSC; it acquired its present name in 1962. Members (MEPs) were initially appointed from the membership of national parliaments. Direct elections to the Parliament were first held in 1979. Elections to the Parliament are held on differing bases throughout the EC; British MEPs are elected on a first-past-the-post system, except in Northern Ireland which uses proportional representation. The latest elections were held in June 1994, when the Parliament expanded from 518 to 567 seats to include representatives from the former East Germany and concurrent increases in other member states' representatives. It expanded to 626 seats on 1 January 1995 with the accession of Austria, Finland and Sweden to the EU. For total number of seats per member and political groupings, *see* table below. MEPs serve on 20 committees, which scrutinize draft EC legislation and the activities of the Commission. A minimum of 12 plenary sessions a year are held in Strasbourg and Brussels, committees meet in Brussels, and the Secretariat's headquarters is in Luxembourg.

The EP has gradually expanded its influence within the EU through the Single European Act, which introduced the co-operation procedure, and the Maastricht Treaty, which extended the co-operation procedure and introduced the co-decision procedure (*see* Legislative Process).

EUROPEAN PARLIAMENT POLITICAL GROUPINGS

	PES	EPP	UFE	ELDR	EUL/NGL	Green	ERA	EN	Ind.	Total
Austria	8	6	–	1	–	1	–	–	5	21
Belgium	6	7	–	6	–	2	1	–	3	25
Denmark	3	3	–	5	1	–	–	4	–	16
Finland	4	4	–	6	1	1	–	–	–	16
France	15	12	16	1	7	–	13	12	11	87
Germany	40	47	–	–	–	12	–	–	–	99
Greece	10	9	2	–	4	–	–	–	–	25
Ireland	1	4	7	1	–	2	–	–	–	15
Italy	18	14	27	6	5	4	2	–	11	87
Luxembourg	2	2	–	1	–	–	1	–	–	6
Netherlands	8	10	–	10	–	1	–	2	–	31
Portugal	10	1	3	8	3	–	–	–	–	25
Spain	22	30	–	2	9	–	1	–	–	64
Sweden	7	5	–	3	3	4	–	–	–	22
UK	63	19	–	2	–	–	–	–	1	87
TOTAL	221	173	55	52	31	25	19	19	31	626

PES   Party of European Socialists (including British Labour Party, Northern Ireland Social Democratic and Labour Party, Italian Democratic Left Party) Socialist, Social Democratic and Labour parties

EPP   European People's Party (including British Conservative Party, Northern Ireland Official Unionist Party, Spanish Popular Party, French UDF, Irish Fine Gael, Swedish Moderate Party) Christian Democrats and Conservatives

UFE   Union for Europe (including Forza Italia Party, French Gaullists, Irish Fianna Fáil, Greek Political Spring Party, Portuguese Centre Party)

ELDR   European Liberal Democratic and Reformist Group (including British Liberal Democratic Party, Italian Northern League, Portuguese Social Democrats) centre and liberal parties

EUL/NGL   Confederal Group of the European United Left/Nordic Green Left (French, Greek, Spanish and Portuguese Communist Parties, Italian Refounded Communist Party, some Spanish regionalists, Danish, Swedish, Finnish Green/Left parties)

Green   Green and Ecologist parties

ERA   European Radical Alliance (Scottish National Party, French Radicals of the Left, Italian Radical Party, Belgian Flemish and Spanish regionalists)

EN   Europe of the Nations Group (French Other Europe Group, Dutch and Danish Euro-sceptics)

Ind   Independents (Italian National Alliance, French National Front, Belgian Vlaams Blok, Northern Ireland Democratic Unionist Party)

It has general powers of supervision over the Commission, and consultation and co-decision with the Council; it votes to approve a newly appointed Commission and can dismiss it at any time by a two-thirds majority. Under the Maastricht Treaty it has the right to be consulted on the appointment of the new Commission and can veto its appointment. It can reject the EU budget as a whole, alter non-compulsory expenditure not specified in the EU primary legislation, and can question the Commission's management of the budget and call in the Court of Auditors. Although the EP cannot directly initiate legislation, its reports can spur the Commission into action. In accordance with the Maastricht Treaty the EP appointed an Ombudsman in October 1995, to provide citizens with redress against maladministration by EU institutions.

The Parliament's organization is deliberately biased in favour of multi-national political groupings, recognition of a political grouping in the parliament entitling it to offices, funding, representation on committees and influence in debates and legislation. A political grouping with members from only one country needs a minimum of 29 members for recognition, whereas one with members from two countries needs 23 members, a grouping with members from three countries needs 18 members, and a grouping with members from four or more countries needs only 14 members.

PARLIAMENT, Palais de l'Europe, 67006 Strasbourg Cedex, France; 97–113 rue Belliard, 1047 Brussels, Belgium
SECRETARIAT, Centre Européen, Kirchberg, L-2929 Luxembourg
President, Klaus Hänsch (Germany)
Ombudsman, Jacob Söderman (Finland), 1 avenue du Président Robert Schuman, BP403, F-67001, Strasbourg, France
(For a full list of British MEPs, *see* pages 268–9)

THE ECONOMIC AND SOCIAL COMMITTEE
2 rue Ravenstein, 1000 Brussels, Belgium

The Economic and Social Committee (ESC) is an advisory and consultative body. The ESC has 222 members, who are nominated by member states. It is divided into three groups: employers, workers, and other interest groups such as consumers, farmers and the self-employed. It issues opinions on draft EC legislation and can bring matters to the attention of the Commission, Council and Parliament; it has a key role in providing specialist and technical input.
President, Carlos Ferrer (Spain)

THE COURT OF AUDITORS
12 rue A. De Gasperi, L-1615 Luxembourg

The Court of Auditors, established in 1977, is responsible for the audit of the legality and regularity as well as of the sound financial management of the resources managed by the European Communities and Community bodies. The Court may also submit observations on specific questions and deliver opinions. The Court draws up an annual report and a statement of assurance on the accounts and underlying operations of the Communities. The Maastricht Treaty designated the Court as a full institution of the European Union, enabling it to take other institutions to the Court of Justice. It has 15 members appointed for six-year terms by the Council of Ministers following consultation with the European Parliament.
President, Bernhard Friedmann (Germany)

COURT OF JUSTICE OF THE EUROPEAN COMMUNITIES
L–2925 Luxembourg

The European Court superseded the Court of Justice of the ECSC and is common to the three European Communities. It exists to safeguard the law in the interpretation and application of the Community treaties, to decide on the legality of decisions of the Council of Ministers or the Commission, and to determine violations of the treaties. Cases may be brought to it by the member states, the Community institutions, firms or individuals. Its decisions are directly binding in the member countries, and the Maastricht Treaty enhanced the Court's powers by permitting it to impose fines on member states. The 15 judges and nine advocates-general of the Court are appointed for renewable six-year terms by the member governments in concert. During 1995, 415 new cases were lodged at the court, 250 cases were concluded and 172 judgments were delivered.

Composition of the Court, in order of precedence, with effect from 7 October 1995:
G. C. Rodríguez Iglesias (*President*); C. N. Kakouris (*President of the 4th and 6th Chambers*); G. Tesauro (*First Advocate-General*); D. A. O. Edward (*President of the 1st and 5th Chambers*); J.-P. Puissochet (*President of the 3rd Chamber*); G. Hirsch (*President of the 2nd Chamber*); G. F. Mancini (*Judge*); C. O. Lenz (*Judge*); F. A. Schockweiler (*Judge*); J. C. Moitinho de Almeida (*Judge*); F. G. Jacobs (*Advocate-General*); P. J. G. Kapteyn (*Judge*); C. Gulmann (*Judge*); J. L. Murray (*Judge*); A. M. La Pergola (*Advocate-General*); G. Cosmas (*Advocate-General*); P. Léger (*Advocate-General*); M. B. Elmer (*Advocate-General*); P. Jann (*Judge*); H. Ragnelmalm (*Judge*); L. Sevón (*Judge*); N. Fennelly (*Advocate-General*); D. Ruiz-Jarabo Colomer (*Advocate-General*); M. Wathelet (*Judge*); R. Grass (*Registrar*)

COURT OF FIRST INSTANCE
L-2925 Luxembourg

Established under powers conferred by the Single European Act, the Court of First Instance started to exercise its functions at the end of October 1989. It had jurisdiction to hear and determine certain categories of cases brought by natural or legal persons, in particular cases brought by European Community officials, or cases on competition law. By a Council decision of 1993 the court had its jurisdiction enlarged to hear and determine all actions brought by natural or legal persons. During 1995, 253 new cases were lodged at the court, 198 cases were concluded and 98 judgments were delivered.

Composition of the Court, in order of precedence, for the judicial year 1995–6:
A. Saggio (*President of the Court and of the 1st Chamber*); H. Kirschner (*President of the 2nd Chamber*); R. Schintgen (*President of the 5th Chamber*); C. P. Briët (*President of the 3rd Chamber*); K Lenaerts (*President of the 4th Chamber*); B. Vesterdorf (*Judge*); R. García-Valdecasas y Fernandez (*Judge*); C. W. Bellamy (*Judge*); A. Kalogeropoulos (*Judge*); V. Tiili (*Judge*); P. Lindh (*Judge*); J. Azizi (*Judge*); A. Potocki (*Judge*); R. Moura-Ramos (*Judge*); J. D. Cooke (*Judge*); H. Jung (*Registrar*)

THE EUROPEAN INVESTMENT BANK
100 Boulevard Konrad Adenauer, L-2950 Luxembourg

The European Investment Bank (EIB) was set up in 1958 under the terms of the Treaty of Rome to finance capital investment projects promoting the balanced development of the European Community.

It grants long-term loans to private and public enterprises, public authorities and financial institutions, to finance projects which further the economic development of less advanced regions (Assisted Areas); improvement of European communications; environmental protection; attainment of the EU's energy policy objectives; modernization of enterprises, co-operation between undertakings in the different member states, and the activities of small and medium-sized enterprises.

EIB activities have also been extended outside member countries as part of the EU's development co-operation policy, under the terms of different association or co-operation agreements with 12 countries in the Mediterranean region, 11 in central and eastern Europe, 30 in Latin America and Asia, and, under the Lomé Conventions, 70 in Africa, the Caribbean and the Pacific.

The Bank's total financing operations in 1995 amounted to 21,400 million ECU, of which 18,600 million was for investment in the EU and 2,800 million for investment outside the EU. Between 1991 and 1995 the EIB made available a total of more than £9,100 million for investment in the UK.

The members of the EIB are the 15 member states of the EU, who have all subscribed to the Bank's capital of 62,013 million ECU. The bulk of the funds required by the Bank to carry out its tasks are borrowed on the capital markets of the EU and non-member countries, and on the international market.

As it operates on a non-profit-making basis, the interest rates charged by the EIB reflect the cost of the Bank's borrowings and closely follow conditions on world capital markets.

The Board of Governors of the EIB consists of one government minister nominated by each of the member countries, usually the finance minister, who lay down general directives on the policy of the Bank and appoint members to the Board of Directors (24 nominated by the member states, one by the European Commission), which takes decisions on the granting and raising of loans and the fixing of interest rates. A Management Committee, composed of the Bank's President and seven Vice-Presidents, also appointed by the Board of Governors, is responsible for the day-to-day operations of the Bank. The President and Vice-Presidents also preside as Chairman and Vice-Chairmen at meetings of the Board of Directors.
President, Sir Brian Unwin, KCB
Vice-Presidents, Wolfgang Roth; Panagiotis-Loukas Gennimatas; Massimo Ponzellini; Louis Martí; Ariane Obolensky; Rudolf de Korte; Claes de Neergaard
UK OFFICE: 68 Pall Mall, London SW1Y 5ES. Tel: 0171-343 1200

NEW INSTITUTIONS AND AGENCIES

The Maastricht Treaty, together with the 1993 Brussels Council summit, established a number of new institutions and agencies:

THE COMMITTEE OF THE REGIONS
2 rue Ravenstein, 1000 Brussels, Belgium

The Committee of the Regions (COR) is an advisory and consultative body established to redress the lack of a role for regional and local authorities in the EU democratic system. The COR is composed of 222 appointed and indirectly elected members, of whom half are from large regions and half are from small local authorities, who meet

five times each year for two days. The COR delivers opinions on policies affecting regions, such as trans-border transport links, economic and social cohesion, education and training, social policy, culture and regional policy.
President, Maragrll Emerr (Spain)

THE EUROPEAN MONETARY INSTITUTE
29 Kaiserstrasse, 60311 Frankfurt-am-Main, Germany

The European Monetary Institute was established to co-ordinate member states' monetary policy during stage II of economic and monetary union (EMU), which began on 1 January 1994; to oversee preparation for a transfer to a single currency; and to create the right conditions for the third and final stage of EMU. The EMI consists of the governors of the central banks of the 15 EU member states, who form the EMI Council, and support staff. The council meets monthly to assess how well member governments are meeting the criteria laid down by the Maastricht Treaty for achieving economic convergence.
President, Baron Alexandre Lamfalussy (Belgium)

THE EUROPEAN DRUGS AGENCY
Raamweg 47, 2596HN The Hague, The Netherlands

The European Drugs Agency (EUROPOL) was established as an information clearing house engaged in surveillance of drug trafficking. It is staffed by 80 personnel seconded from member states' police, gendarmeries and customs forces, housed in 15 national liaison offices linked to their respective national police computers; the working language is English. Its remit has been expanded from co-ordinating cross-border drug-trafficking investigations to include combating illegal immigration rackets, trade in nuclear materials, cross-border car theft and any associated money laundering. EUROPOL has no legal powers of its own and can only operate through member states' police and customs forces. At present it operates on an *ad hoc* basis as its convention has yet to be agreed and ratified by the member states.
Co-ordinator, Juergen Storbeck (Germany)

Other bodies include:
THE EUROPEAN MEDICINE EVALUATION AGENCY, London
THE EUROPEAN TRADEMARK OFFICE, Alicante
THE EUROPEAN AGENCY FOR HEALTH AND SAFETY AT WORK, Bilbao
THE EUROPEAN OFFICE FOR VETERINARY AND PLANT HEALTH INSPECTION, Dublin
THE EUROPEAN DRUGS OBSERVATORY, Lisbon
THE EUROPEAN FOUNDATION FOR TRAINING, Turin
THE EUROPEAN CENTRE FOR THE DEVELOPMENT OF VOCATIONAL TRAINING, Salonika
THE EUROPEAN ENVIRONMENT AGENCY, Copenhagen
THE EUROPEAN TRANSLATION AGENCY, Luxembourg

EUROPEAN COMMUNITY INFORMATION

EUROPEAN COMMISSION REPRESENTATIVE OFFICES
ENGLAND, 8 Storey's Gate, London SW1P 3AT. Tel: 0171-973 1992
WALES, 4 Cathedral Road, Cardiff CF1 9SG. Tel: 01222-371631
SCOTLAND, 9 Alva Street, Edinburgh EH2 4PH. Tel: 0131-225 2058
NORTHERN IRELAND, Windsor House, 9–15 Bedford Street, Belfast BT2 7EG. Tel: 01232-240708
REPUBLIC OF IRELAND, 39 Molesworth Street, Dublin 2

USA, 2100 M Street NW (Suite 707), Washington DC 20037; 1 Dag Hammarskjöld Plaza, 254 East 47th Street, New York, NY 10017
CANADA, Inn of the Provinces, Office Tower (Suite 1110), 350 Sparks Street, Ottawa, Ontario, KIR 7SA
AUSTRALIA, 18 Alakana Street, Yarralumia, ACT 2600, and a number of other cities

UK EUROPEAN PARLIAMENT INFORMATION OFFICE 2 Queen Anne's Gate, London SWIH 9AA. Tel: 0171-227 4300

There are European Information Centres, set up to give information and advice to small businesses, in 24 British towns and cities. A number of universities maintain European Documentation Centres.

Presidents of the USA

Name (with Native State)	Party	Born	Inauguration	Died	Age
George Washington, Va.	Federation	22 February 1732	1789	14 December 1799	67
John Adams, Mass.	Federation	30 October 1735	1797	4 July 1826	90
Thomas Jefferson, Va.	Republican	13 April 1743	1801	4 July 1826	83
James Madison, Va.	Republican	16 March 1751	1809	28 June 1836	85
James Monroe, Va.	Republican	28 April 1758	1817	4 July 1831	73
John Quincy Adams, Mass.	Republican	11 July 1767	1825	23 February 1848	80
Andrew Jackson, SC	Democrat	15 March 1767	1829	8 June 1845	78
Martin Van Buren, NY	Democrat	5 December 1782	1837	24 July 1862	79
William Henry Harrison†, Va.	Whig	9 February 1773	1841	4 April 1841	68
John Tyler (a), Va.	Whig	29 March 1790	1841	17 January 1862	71
James Knox Polk, NC	Democrat	2 November 1795	1845	15 June 1849	53
Zachary Taylor†, Va.	Whig	24 November 1784	1849	9 July 1850	65
Millard Fillmore (a), NY	Whig	7 January 1800	1850	8 March 1874	74
Franklin Pierce, NH	Democrat	23 November 1804	1853	8 October 1869	64
James Buchanan, Pa.	Democrat	23 April 1791	1857	1 June 1868	77
Abraham Lincoln†§, Ky.	Republican	12 February 1809	1861	15 April 1865	56
Andrew Johnson (a), NC	Republican	29 December 1808	1865	31 July 1875	66
Ulysses Simpson Grant, Ohio	Republican	27 April 1822	1869	23 July 1885	63
Rutherford Birchard Hayes, Ohio	Republican	4 October 1822	1877	17 January 1893	70
James Abram Garfield†§, Ohio	Republican	19 November 1831	1881	19 September 1881	49
Chester Alan Arthur (a), Vt.	Republican	5 October 1830	1881	18 November 1886	56
Grover Cleveland, NJ	Democrat	18 March 1837	1885	24 June 1908	71
Benjamin Harrison, Ohio	Republican	20 August 1833	1889	13 March 1901	67
Grover Cleveland, NJ	Democrat	18 March 1837	1893	24 June 1908	71
William McKinley†§, Ohio	Republican	29 January 1843	1897	14 September 1901	58
Theodore Roosevelt (a), NY	Republican	27 October 1858	1901	6 January 1919	60
William Howard Taft, Ohio	Republican	15 September 1857	1909	8 March 1930	72
Woodrow Wilson, Va.	Democrat	28 December 1856	1913	3 February 1924	67
Warren Gamaliel Harding†, Ohio	Republican	2 November 1865	1921	2 August 1923	57
Calvin Coolidge (a), Vt.	Republican	4 July 1872	1923	5 January 1933	60
Herbert Clark Hoover, Iowa	Republican	10 August 1874	1929	20 October 1964	90
Franklin Delano Roosevelt†‡, NY	Democrat	30 January 1882	1933	12 April 1945	63
Harry S. Truman (a), Missouri	Democrat	8 May 1884	1945	26 December 1972	88
Dwight David Eisenhower, Texas	Republican	14 October 1890	1953	28 March 1969	78
John Fitzgerald Kennedy†§, Mass.	Democrat	29 May 1917	1961	22 November 1963	46
Lyndon Baines Johnson (a), Texas	Democrat	27 August 1908	1963	22 January 1973	64
Richard Milhous Nixon, California	Republican	9 January 1913	1969	22 April 1994	81
Gerald Rudolph Ford (b), Nebraska	Republican	14 July 1913	1974		
James Earl Carter, Georgia	Democrat	1 October 1924	1977		
Ronald Wilson Reagan, Illinois	Republican	6 February 1911	1981		
George Herbert Walker Bush, Mass.	Republican	12 June 1924	1989		
William Jefferson Blythe IV Clinton, Ark.	Democrat	19 August 1946	1993		

† Died in office
(a) Elected as Vice-President
§ Assassinated
‡ Re-elected 5 November 1940, the first case of a third term; re-elected for a fourth term 7 November 1944
(b) Appointed under the provisions of the 25th Amendment

Nobel Prizes

For prize winners for the years 1901–92, *see* earlier editions of *Whitaker's Almanack*.

The Nobel Prizes are awarded each year from the income of a trust fund established by the Swedish scientist Alfred Nobel, the inventor of dynamite, who died on 10 December 1896 leaving a fortune of £1,750,000. The prizes are awarded to those who have contributed most to the common good in the domain of:

Physics – awarded by the Royal Swedish Academy of Sciences
Chemistry – awarded by the Royal Swedish Academy of Sciences
Physiology or Medicine – awarded by the Karolinska Institute
Literature – awarded by the Swedish Academy of Arts
Peace – awarded by a five-person committee elected by the Norwegian Storting
Economic Sciences (instituted 1969) – awarded by the Royal Swedish Academy of Sciences

The first awards were made in 1901 on the fifth anniversary of Nobel's death. The prizes are awarded every year on 10 December, the anniversary of Nobel's death.

The Trust is administered by the board of directors of the Nobel Foundation, Stockholm, consisting of five members and three deputy members. The Swedish Government appoints a chairman and a deputy chairman, the remaining members being appointed by the awarding authorities.

The awards have been distributed as follows:
Physics
American 60, British 20, German 19 (1948–90, West German 8), French 11, Soviet 7, Dutch 6, Swedish 4, Austrian 3, Danish 3, Italian 3, Japanese 3, Canadian 2, Chinese 2, Swiss 2, Indian 1, Irish 1, Pakistani 1
Chemistry
American 40, German 27 (1948–90, West German 10), British 23, French 7, Swiss 5, Swedish 4, Canadian 3, Dutch 3, Argentinian 1, Austrian 1, Belgian 1, Czech 1, Finnish 1, Hungarian 1, Italian 1, Japanese 1, Mexican 1, Norwegian 1, Soviet 1
Physiology or Medicine
American 74, British 23, German 15 (1948–90, West German 4), French 7, Swedish 7, Danish 5, Swiss 5, Austrian 4, Belgian 4, Italian 3, Australian 2, Canadian 2, Dutch 2, Hungarian 2, Russian 2, Argentinian 1, Japanese 1, Portuguese 1, South African 1, Spanish 1
Literature
French 12, American 10, British 8, Swedish 7, German 6 (1948–90, West German 1), Italian 5, Spanish 5, Danish 3, Irish 3, Norwegian 3, Soviet 3, Chilean 2, Greek 2, Japanese 2, Polish 2, Swiss 2, Australian 1, Belgian 1, Colombian 1, Czech 1, Egyptian 1, Finnish 1, Guatemalan 1, Icelandic 1, Indian 1, Israeli 1, Mexican 1, Nigerian 1, South African 1, Trinidadian 1, Yugoslav 1, Stateless 1
Peace
American 17, Institutions 17, British 10, French 9, Swedish 5, German 4 (1948–90, West German 1), South African 4, Belgian 3, Israeli 3, Swiss 3, Argentinian 2, Austrian 2, Norwegian 2, Soviet 2, Burmese 1, Canadian 1, Costa Rican 1, Danish 1, Dutch 1, Egyptian 1, Guatemalan 1, Irish 1, Italian 1, Japanese 1, Mexican 1, Palestinian 1, Polish 1, Tibetan 1, Vietnamese 1, Yugoslav 1
Economics
American 24, British 6, Norwegian 2, Swedish 2, Dutch 1, French 1, German 1, Soviet 1

Prize	1993	1994	1995
Physics	Dr R. Hulse (American) Dr J. Taylor (American)	Prof. B. Brockhouse (Canadian) Prof. C. Shull (American)	Dr M. Perl (American) Dr F. Reines (American)
Chemistry	Prof. M. Smith (Canadian) Dr K. Mullis (American)	Prof. G. Olah (American)	P. Crutzen (Dutch) Dr M. Molina (Mexican) Dr S. Rowland (American)
Physiology or Medicine	R. Roberts (British) Prof. P. Sharp (American)	Dr A. Gilman (American) Dr M. Rodbell (American)	Dr E. Lewis (American) Dr C. Nuesslein-Volhard (German) Dr E. Wieschaus (American)
Literature	Ms T. Morrison (American)	K. Oe (Japanese)	S. Heaney (Irish)
Peace	N. Mandela (South African) Pres. F. W. de Klerk (South African)	Y. Rabin (Israeli) Y. Arafat (Palestinian) S. Peres (Israeli)	Prof. J. Rotblat (British) The Pugwash Conference on Science and World Affairs
Economics	Prof. R. Fogel (American) Prof. D. North (American)	J. Harsanyi (American) J. Nash (American) R. Selten (German)	R. Lucas (American)

Countries of the World

WORLD AREA AND POPULATION

The total population of the world in mid-1990 was estimated at 5,292 million, compared with 3,019 million in 1960 and 2,070 million in 1930.

Continent, etc.	Area sq. miles '000	sq. km '000	Estimated population mid-1990
Africa	11,704	30,313	642,000,000
North America[1]	8,311	21,525	276,000,000
Latin America[2]	7,933	20,547	448,000,000
Asia[3]	10,637	27,549	3,113,000,000
Europe[4]	1,915	4,961	498,000,000
Former USSR	8,649	22,402	289,000,000
Oceania[5]	3,286	8,510	26,500,000
TOTAL	52,435	135,807	5,292,000,000

[1] Includes Greenland and Hawaii
[2] Mexico and the remainder of the Americas south of the USA
[3] Includes European Turkey, excludes former USSR
[4] Excludes European Turkey and former USSR
[5] Includes Australia, New Zealand and the islands inhabited by Micronesian, Melanesian and Polynesian peoples
Source: UN Demographic Yearbook 1990 (pub. 1992)

A United Nations report The Sex and Age Distribution of the World Populations (revised 1994) puts the world's population in the late 20th and the 21st centuries at the following levels (medium variant data):

1995	5,716.4m	2030	8,670.6m
2000	6,158.0m	2040	9,318.2m
2010	7,032.3m	2050	9,833.2m
2020	7,887.8m		

The population forecast for the years 2000 and 2050 is:

Continent, etc.	Estimated population (million) 2000	2050
Africa	831.596	2,140.844
North America[1]	306.280	388.997
Latin America[2]	523.875	838.527
Asia	3,753.846	5,741.005
Europe	729.803	677.764
Oceania	30.651	46.070
TOTAL	6,158.051	9,833.207

[1] Includes Bermuda, Greenland, and St Pierre and Miquelon
[2] Mexico and the remainder of the Americas south of the USA

AREA AND POPULATION BY CONTINENT

No complete survey of many countries has yet been achieved and consequently accurate area figures are not always available. Similarly, many countries have not recently, or have never, taken a census. The areas of countries given below are derived from estimated figures published by the United Nations. The conversion factors used are:
(i) to convert square miles to square km, multiply by 2.589988
(ii) to convert square km to square miles, multiply by 0.3861022
Population figures for countries are derived from the most recent estimates available. Accurate and up-to-date data for the populations of capital cities are scarce, and definitions of cities' extent differ. The figures given below are the latest estimates available, and where it is known that the figure applies to an urban agglomeration this is indicated.
*   latest census figure
Ψ   seaport
u.a.   urban agglomeration

AFRICA

COUNTRY/TERRITORY	AREA sq. miles	sq. km	POPULATION	CAPITAL	POPULATION OF CAPITAL
Algeria	919,595	2,381,741	26,722,000	Ψ Algiers	3,250,000
Angola	481,354	1,246,700	10,276,000	Ψ Luanda	3,000,000
Benin	43,484	112,622	5,215,000	Ψ Porto Novo	208,258
Botswana	224,607	581,730	1,326,796*	Gaborone	133,458*
Burkina Faso	105,869	274,200	9,682,000	Ouagadougou	441,514
Burundi	10,747	27,834	5,958,000	Bujumbura	235,440
Cameroon	183,569	475,442	12,600,000	Yaoundé	653,670
Cape Verde	1,557	4,033	370,000	Ψ Praia	57,748
Central African Republic	240,535	622,984	3,173,000	Bangui	473,817
Chad Republic	495,755	1,284,000	5,961,000	Ndjaména	402,000
The Comoros	838	2,171	585,000	Moroni	17,267
Congo	132,047	342,000	2,443,000	Brazzaville	600,000
Côte d'Ivoire	124,503	322,463	13,316,000	Yamoussoukro	106,786
Djibouti	8,494	22,000	520,000*	Ψ Djibouti	340,700
Egypt	386,662	1,001,449	58,978,000	Cairo	13,000,000
Equatorial Guinea	10,830	28,051	379,000	Ψ Malabo	30,418
Eritrea	36,170	93,679	3,500,000	Asmara	275,000
Ethiopia	471,778	1,221,900	51,859,000	Addis Ababa	3,500,000
Gabon	103,347	267,667	1,035,000	Ψ Libreville	251,000
Gambia	4,361	11,295	1,081,000	Ψ Banjul (u.a.)	44,536

Country/Territory	Area sq. miles	sq. km	Population	Capital	Population of Capital
Ghana	92,100	238,537	16,944,000	Ψ Accra (u.a.)	1,781,100
Guinea	94,926	245,857	6,501,000	Ψ Conakry	763,000
Guinea-Bissau	13,948	36,125	1,050,000	Ψ Bissau	109,486*
Kenya	224,961	582,646	26,017,000	Nairobi	1,400,000
Lesotho	11,720	30,355	1,943,000	Maseru	288,951*
Liberia	43,000	111,369	2,640,000	Ψ Monrovia	425,000
Libya	679,362	1,759,540	5,222,000	Ψ Tripoli	1,000,000
Madagascar	226,669	587,041	13,101,000	Antananarivo	1,250,000
Malawi	45,747	118,484	10,843,000	Lilongwe	223,973
Mali	478,791	1,240,000	9,524,000	Bamako	658,275*
Mauritania	397,955	1,030,700	2,217,000	Nouakchott	850,000
Mauritius	790	2,045	1,082,998	Ψ Port Louis	144,250
Mayotte (Fr.)	144	372	94,410*	Mamoundzou	12,000
Morocco	172,414	446,550	26,448,000	Ψ Rabat	1,494,000
Western Sahara	102,703	266,000	183,000	Laayoune	96,784*
Mozambique	309,495	801,590	16,500,000	Ψ Maputo	1,150,000
Namibia	318,261	824,292	1,500,000	Windhoek	110,000
Niger	489,191	1,267,080	8,846,000	Niamey	410,000
Nigeria	356,669	923,768	107,900,000	Abuja	378,671
Réunion (Fr.)	969	2,510	643,000	St Denis	122,000
Rwanda	10,169	26,338	7,750,000	Kigali	156,000
St Helena (UK)	47	122	5,644	Ψ Jamestown	1,332
Ascension Island	34	88	1,160	Ψ Georgetown	—
Tristan da Cunha	38	98	292	Ψ Edinburgh of the Seven Seas	—
São Tomé and Príncipe	372	964	125,000	Ψ São Tomé	25,000
Senegal	75,750	196,192	8,102,000	Ψ Dakar	1,000,000
Seychelles	108	280	73,000	Ψ Victoria	24,324
Sierra Leone	27,699	71,740	4,587,000	Ψ Freetown	470,000*
Somalia	246,201	637,657	9,077,000	Ψ Mogadishu	1,000,000
South Africa	471,445	1,221,031	40,049,000	{ Pretoria (u.a.) { Ψ Cape Town (u.a.)	822,925 1,911,521
Sudan	967,500	2,505,813	27,361,000	Khartoum (u.a.)	3,000,000
Swaziland	6,704	17,363	906,000	Mbabane	38,290
Tanzania	364,900	945,087	28,846,000	Dodoma	88,474
Togo	21,925	56,785	4,010,000	Ψ Lomé	366,476
Tunisia	63,170	163,610	8,815,000	Ψ Tunis	1,394,749
Uganda	91,259	236,036	18,592,000	Kampala (u.a.)	750,000
Zaïre	905,567	2,345,409	42,552,000	Kinshasa	2,778,281
Zambia	290,586	752,614	9,196,000	Lusaka (u.a.)	1,000,000
Zimbabwe	150,804	390,580	11,200,000	Harare	1,184,000

AMERICA

North America

Country/Territory	Area sq. miles	sq. km	Population	Capital	Population of Capital
Canada	3,849,670	9,970,599	29,606,100	Ottawa (u.a.)	313,987*
Greenland (Den.)	840,004	2,175,600	55,700	Ψ Godthåb	—
Mexico	761,605	1,972,547	91,858,000	Mexico City (u.a.)	14,987,051*
St Pierre and Miquelon (Fr.)	93	242	6,300	Ψ St Pierre	—
United States	3,787,318	9,809,108	259,681,000	Washington DC	585,221

Central America and the West Indies

Country/Territory	Area sq. miles	sq. km	Population	Capital	Population of Capital
Anguilla (UK)	35	91	8,960*	The Valley	1,400
Antigua and Barbuda	170	440	65,962*	Ψ St John's	30,000
Aruba (Neth.)	75	193	71,000	Ψ Oranjestad	25,000
Bahamas	5,380	13,935	269,000	Ψ Nassau	171,000*
Barbados	166	431	264,000	Ψ Bridgetown	108,000
Belize	8,867	22,965	205,000*	Belmopan	3,739*
Bermuda (UK)	20	53	60,075	Ψ Hamilton	2,277
Cayman Islands (UK)	100	259	33,600	Ψ George Town	17,500
Costa Rica	19,575	50,700	3,232,526	San José (u.a.)	86,178
Cuba	42,804	110,861	10,905,000	Ψ Havana	2,143,406
Dominica	290	751	71,000	Ψ Roseau	15,850
Dominican Republic	18,816	48,734	7,684,000	Ψ Santo Domingo (u.a.)	1,313,172*
Grenada	133	344	95,000	Ψ St George's	10,000
Guadeloupe (Fr.)	687	1,779	420,000	Ψ Basse Terre	14,000

Country/Territory	Area sq. miles	sq. km	Population	Capital	Population of Capital
Guatemala	42,042	108,889	10,332,000	Guatemala City	1,675,589
Haiti	10,714	27,750	7,035,000	Ψ Port-au-Prince	1,000,000
Honduras	43,277	112,088	5,493,900	Tegucigalpa	670,100
Jamaica	4,244	10,991	2,960,000	Ψ Kingston (u.a.)	696,300
Martinique (Fr.)	425	1,102	375,000	Ψ Fort de France	101,540
Montserrat (UK)	38	98	9,000	Ψ Plymouth	2,500
Netherlands Antilles (Neth.)	371	961	197,000	Ψ Willemstad	50,000
Nicaragua	50,193	130,000	4,275,000	Managua	615,000
Panama	29,762	77,082	2,631,013	Ψ Panama City	1,064,221
Puerto Rico (USA)	3,435	8,897	3,600,000	Ψ San Juan (u.a.)	437,745
St Christopher and Nevis	101	261	41,000	Ψ Basseterre	15,000
St Lucia	238	616	143,000	Ψ Castries	56,000
St Vincent and the Grenadines	150	388	110,000	Ψ Kingstown	33,694
El Salvador	8,124	21,041	5,641,000	San Salvador	497,644
Trinidad and Tobago	1,981	5,130	1,239,908	Ψ Port of Spain	50,878
Turks and Caicos Is. (UK)	166	430	19,000	Ψ Grand Turk	4,000
Virgin Islands:					
British (UK)	59	153	16,108*	Ψ Road Town	3,983
US (USA)	132	342	101,809	Ψ Charlotte Amalie	11,756

South America

Argentina	1,073,512	2,780,400	32,370,298	Ψ Buenos Aires	2,960,976
Bolivia	424,165	1,098,581	6,440,000*	La Paz	1,115,000
Brazil	3,286,488	8,511,965	156,275,000	Brasilia	1,596,274*
Chile	292,258	756,945	13,813,000	Santiago	5,443,000
Colombia	439,737	1,138,914	36,000,000	Bogotá	8,000,000
Ecuador	109,484	283,561	10,980,972	Quito	1,387,887
Falkland Islands (UK)	4,700	12,173	2,121	Ψ Stanley	1,643
French Guiana (Fr.)	35,135	91,000	140,000	Ψ Cayenne	41,000
Guyana	83,000	214,969	825,000	Ψ Georgetown	185,000
Paraguay	157,048	406,752	4,830,000	Asunción (u.a.)	729,307*
Peru	496,225	1,285,216	22,331,000	Lima (u.a.)	6,483,901*
South Georgia (UK)	1,580	4,092	—	—	—
Suriname	63,037	163,265	418,000	Ψ Paramaribo (u.a.)	110,000
Uruguay	68,037	176,215	3,116,802	Ψ Montevideo	1,383,660
Venezuela	353,857	916,490	21,378,000	Caracas (u.a.)	2,784,000

ASIA

Afghanistan	251,772	652,090	17,691,000	Kabul	1,424,400
Bahrain	240	622	539,000	Ψ Manama	108,684*
Bangladesh	55,598	143,998	108,000,000*	Dhaka	6,537,308*
Bhutan	18,147	47,000	650,000	Thimphu	15,000
Brunei	2,226	5,765	276,300	Bandar Seri Begawan	56,300
Cambodia	69,898	181,035	9,308,000	Ψ Phnom Penh	920,000
China[1]	3,705,408	9,596,961	1,200,000,000	Beijing (Peking)	6,560,000
Hong Kong (UK)	416	1,074	6,307,900	—	—
India	1,269,346	3,287,590	846,302,688*	Delhi	8,375,188
Indonesia	735,358	1,904,569	189,907,000	Ψ Jakarta	7,885,519
Iran	636,296	1,648,000	66,000,000	Tehran	6,042,584
Iraq	167,925	434,924	19,951,000	Baghdad	3,841,286
Israel[2]	8,019	20,770	5,090,000	Tel Aviv	1,781,500
West Bank and Gaza Strip	2,406	6,231	1,635,000	Gaza City	120,000
Japan	145,834	377,708	124,764,215	Tokyo (u.a.)	11,935,700
Jordan	37,738	97,740	4,095,579	Amman	1,270,000
Kazakhstan	1,049,155	2,716,626	16,963,600	Alma-Ata	1,500,000
Korea, D.P.R. (North)	46,540	120,538	23,472,000	Pyongyang	2,000,000
Korea, Rep. of (South)	38,025	98,484	44,563,000	Seoul	10,229,000
Kuwait	6,969	18,049	1,575,983*	Ψ Kuwait (city)	400,000
Kyrgyzstan	76,642	198,501	4,500,000	Bishkek	616,000
Laos	91,429	231,800	4,605,300*	Vientiane	120,000
Lebanon	4,015	10,400	2,806,000	Ψ Beirut	1,500,000
Macao (Port.)	6	16	395,000	Ψ Macao	—
Malaysia	127,317	329,749	20,103,000	Kuala Lumpur	1,231,500
Maldives	115	298	246,000	Ψ Malé	46,334
Mongolia	604,250	1,565,000	2,363,000	Ulan Bator	600,500

Country/Territory	Area sq. miles	sq. km	Population	Capital	Population of Capital
Myanmar (Burma)	261,218	676,552	45,555,000	Ψ Yangon (Rangoon) (*u.a.*)	3,973,872
Nepal	54,342	140,747	21,360,000	Kathmandu	300,000
Oman	82,030	212,457	2,000,000*	Ψ Muscat	400,000
Pakistan	341,026	883,254	126,284,000	Islamabad (*u.a.*)	350,000
Philippines	115,831	300,000	66,188,000	Ψ Manila	1,876,195
Qatar	4,247	11,000	537,000	Ψ Doha	220,000
Saudi Arabia	830,000	2,149,640	16,929,294*	Riyadh	2,000,000
Singapore	247	639	2,930,200	—	
Sri Lanka	25,332	65,610	17,619,000	Ψ Colombo	2,026,000
Syria	71,498	185,180	14,171,000	Damascus	1,451,000
Taiwan	13,800	35,742	20,944,066	Taipei	2,719,659
Tajikistan	55,251	143,100	5,513,400	Dushanbe	595,000
Thailand	198,457	514,000	58,336,072	Ψ Bangkok	5,572,712
Turkey[3]	301,382	780,576	60,771,000	Ankara	3,236,626
Turkmenistan	188,456	488,100	4,483,000*	Ashkhabad	407,000
United Arab Emirates	32,278	83,600	2,310,000	Abu Dhabi	450,000
Uzbekistan	172,742	447,229	21,206,800	Tashkent	2,073,000
Vietnam	127,242	329,556	72,500,000	Hanoi	2,150,000
Yemen	203,850	527,696	15,800,000*	Sana'a	972,000

[1] Including Tibet
[2] Including East Jerusalem, the Golan Heights and Israeli citizens on the West Bank
[3] Including Turkey in Europe

EUROPE

Country/Territory	Area sq. miles	sq. km	Population	Capital	Population of Capital
Albania	11,099	28,748	3,500,000	Tirana	244,153
Andorra	180	468	64,311	Andorra la Vella	22,821
Armenia	11,306	29,271	3,754,000	Yerevan	1,254,000
Austria	32,375	83,853	8,015,000	Vienna	1,539,848*
Azerbaijan	33,436	86,565	7,553,000	Baku	1,149,000
Belarus	80,300	207,897	10,265,000	Minsk	1,589,000
Belgium	11,781	30,513	10,100,631	Brussels (*u.a.*)	949,070
Bosnia-Hercegovina	19,735	51,129	2,900,000	Sarajevo	453,324
Bulgaria	42,823	110,912	8,472,000	Sofia	1,114,925
Croatia	21,823	56,538	4,784,265	Zagreb	867,865
Cyprus	3,572	9,251	740,000	Nicosia	185,000
Czech Republic	30,372	78,664	10,302,000*	Prague	1,215,076
Denmark	16,630	43,063	5,215,718	Ψ Copenhagen (*u.a.*)	1,339,395
Faroe Islands	540	1,399	43,700	Ψ Tórshavn	
Estonia	17,413	45,082	1,491,583	Talinn	434,763
Finland	130,500	338,000	5,098,754	Ψ Helsinki	515,765
France	211,208	547,026	57,218,000	Paris (*u.a.*)	9,318,800
Georgia	26,911	69,673	5,401,000	Tbilisi	1,260,000
Germany	137,738	365,755	81,075,000	Berlin	3,454,200
Gibraltar (*UK*)	2	6	28,051	Ψ Gibraltar	—
Greece	50,944	131,944	10,256,464	Athens (*u.a.*)	3,096,775*
Hungary	35,919	93,030	10,278,000	Budapest	2,004,000
Iceland	39,768	103,000	266,786	Ψ Reykjavik (*u.a.*)	103,036
Ireland, Republic of	27,136	70,283	3,621,035	Ψ Dublin	480,996*
Italy	116,304	301,225	57,154,000	Rome (*u.a.*)	2,693,383*
Latvia	24,695	63,935	2,529,600	Riga	840,000
Liechtenstein	61	157	31,000	Vaduz	5,072
Lithuania	26,173	67,761	3,724,000	Vilnius	579,000
Luxembourg	998	2,586	406,600	Luxembourg	75,800
Macedonia	9,925	25,713	1,936,877*	Skopje	448,229*
Malta	122	316	76,335*	Ψ Valletta	7,184*
Moldova	13,912	36,018	4,335,000	Kishinev	665,000*
Monaco	0.4	1	29,972	Monaco-Ville	1,151
Netherlands	15,770	40,844	15,391,000	Ψ Amsterdam (*u.a.*)	1,031,000
Norway[1]	125,181	324,219	4,348,410	Ψ Oslo	483,401
Poland	120,725	312,677	38,600,000	Warsaw	1,641,900
Portugal[2]	35,553	92,082	9,862,700*	Ψ Lisbon	2,128,000
Romania	91,699	237,500	22,760,449*	Bucharest	2,064,474*
Russia[3]	6,593,391	17,070,289	148,100,000	Moscow	8,700,000
San Marino	23	61	25,058	San Marino	—

Country/Territory	Area sq. miles	sq. km	Population	Capital	Population of Capital
Slovakia	18,932	49,035	5,336,455	Bratislava	448,785
Slovenia	7,816	20,251	1,989,477	Ljubljana	269,972
Spain[4]	194,897	504,782	38,872,268*	Madrid (u.a.)	4,947,555
Sweden	173,732	449,964	8,745,109*	Ψ Stockholm (u.a.)	1,532,803
Switzerland	15,943	41,293	7,127,000	Berne	135,600*
Ukraine	233,090	603,700	51,471,000*	Kiev	2,577,000
United Kingdom[5]	94,248	244,101	58,395,000	Ψ London (u.a.)	6,961,900
England	50,351	130,410	48,708,000	—	
Wales	8,015	20,758	2,913,000	Ψ Cardiff	300,000
Scotland	30,420	78,789	5,132,000	Ψ Edinburgh	444,000
Northern Ireland	5,461	14,144	1,642,000	Ψ Belfast (u.a.)	297,000
Vatican City State	0.2	0.44	1,000	Vatican City	—
Yugoslavia, Fed. Rep. of	39,506	102,350	10,410,000	Belgrade	1,455,000

[1] Excludes Svalbard and Jan Mayen Islands (approx. 24,101 sq. miles (62,422 sq. km) and 3,000 population)
[2] Includes Madeira (314 sq. miles) and the Azores (922 sq. miles)
[3] Includes Russia in Asia
[4] Includes Balearic Islands, Canary Islands, Ceuta and Melilla
[5] Excludes Isle of Man (221 sq. miles (572 sq. km), 69,788* population), and Channel Islands (75 sq. miles (194 sq. km), 142,949* population)

OCEANIA

Country/Territory	Area sq. miles	sq. km	Population	Capital	Population of Capital
American Samoa (USA)	76	197	46,773	Ψ Pago Pago	—
Australia	2,967,909	7,686,848	18,114,000	Canberra	328,000
Norfolk Island	14	36	1,912	Ψ Kingston	—
Fiji	7,055	18,274	758,000	Ψ Suva	69,665
French Polynesia (Fr.)	1,544	4,000	215,000	Ψ Papeete	24,200
Guam (USA)	212	549	133,152	Agaña	—
Kiribati	281	728	77,000	Tarawa	17,921
Marshall Islands	70	181	52,000	Majuro	20,000
Micronesia, Fed. States of	271	701	107,000	Palikir	—
Nauru	8	21	10,000	Ψ Nauru	—
New Caledonia (Fr.)	7,358	19,058	178,000	Ψ Noumea	65,000
New Zealand	103,736	268,676	3,494,300	Ψ Wellington (u.a.)	329,000
Cook Islands	91	236	18,300	Avarua	—
Niue	100	259	2,239	Alofi	—
Ross Dependency[1]	286,696	750,310	—	—	—
Tokelau	5	12.9	1,700	—	—
Northern Mariana Islands (USA)	184	476	43,345	Saipan	39,090
Palau (USA)	192	497	15,122*	Koror	10,493
Papua New Guinea	178,260	461,691	4,205,000	Ψ Port Moresby	173,500
Pitcairn Islands (UK)	1.9	5	54	—	—
Solomon Islands	10,983	28,446	328,723*	Ψ Honiara	40,000
Tonga	270	699	98,000	Ψ Nuku'alofa	30,000
Tuvalu	10	25	12,000	Ψ Funafuti	2,856
Vanuatu	4,706	12,190	159,800	Ψ Port Vila	26,100
Wallis and Futuna Islands (Fr.)	106	274	13,705	Ψ Mata-Utu	—
Western Samoa	1,097	2,842	158,000	Ψ Apia	36,000*

[1] Includes permanent shelf ice

THE ANTARCTIC

The Antarctic is generally defined as the area lying within the Antarctic Convergence, the zone where cold north-ward-flowing Antarctic sea water sinks below warmer southward-flowing water. This zone is at about latitude 50° S. in the Atlantic Ocean and latitude 55°–62° S. in the Pacific Ocean. The continent itself lies almost entirely within the Antarctic Circle, an area of about 14.25 million sq. km (5.5 million sq. miles), 99 per cent of which is permanently ice-covered. The average thickness of the ice is 2,450 m (7,100 ft) but in places exceeds 4,500 m (14,500 ft). Some mountains protrude, the highest being Vinson Massif, 4,897 m (16,067 ft). The ice amounts to some 30 million cubic km (7.2 million cubic miles) and represents more than 90 per cent of the world's fresh water.

Along one-third of the Antarctic coastline, land-ice flowing outwards forms extensive ice shelves, fragments of which break off to form tabular icebergs, leaving ice-cliffs up to 50 m (150 ft) high. Much of the sea freezes in winter, forming fast ice which breaks up in summer and drifts north as pack ice.

The most conspicuous physical features of the continent are its high inland plateau (much of it over 3,000 m (10,000 ft)), the Transantarctic Mountains (which together with the large embayments of the Weddell Sea and Ross Sea mark the approximate boundary between East and West Antarctica), and the mountainous Antarctic Peninsula and off-lying islands which extend northwards towards South America. The continental shelf averages about 32 km (20 miles) in width (half the global mean, and in places it is non-existent) and reaches exceptional depths (390–780 m (1,300–2,600 ft), which is three to six times the global mean).

CLIMATE

On land, summer temperatures range from just below freezing around the coast to −34° C (about −30° F) on the plateau, and in winter from −20° C (about −4° F) on the coast to −65° C (about −85° F) inland. Over a large area the maxima do not exceed −15° C (+5° F).

Precipitation is scant over the plateau but amounts to 25–76 cm (10–30 in) (water equivalent) along the coast and some scientific stations are permanently buried by snow. Some rain falls over the more northerly areas in summer. Gravity winds on the plateau slopes and cyclonic storms further north can both exceed 160 km/h (100 m.p.h.) and gusts have been known to reach 240 km/h (150 m.p.h.). Visibility can be reduced to zero in blizzards.

FLORA AND FAUNA

Although a small number of flowering plants, ferns and clubmosses occur on the sub-Antarctic islands, only two (a grass and a pearlwort) extend south of 60° S. Antarctic vegetation is dominated by lichens and mosses, with a few liverworts, algae and fungi. Most of these occur around the coast or on islands, but lichens and some mosses also occur inland.

The only land animals are tiny insects and mites with nematodes, rotifers, and tardigrades in the mosses, but large numbers of seals, penguins and other sea-birds go ashore to breed in the summer. The emperor penguin is the only species which breeds ashore throughout the winter. By contrast, the Antarctic seas abound with life, a wide variety of invertebrates (including krill) and fish providing food for the seals, penguins and other birds, and a residual population of whales.

In 1994 the International Whaling Commission agreed to establish a whale sanctuary around Antarctica in which commercial whaling will be banned for ten years. The sanctuary will cover all sea areas south of 60°S. latitude, apart from the south-west Atlantic and south-east Pacific where it will be south of 40°S. latitude.

POTENTIAL RESOURCES

In the 180 years from Captain James Cook's circumnavigation of the Antarctic in 1772–5 to the mid-1950s, expeditions to the Antarctic made major contributions to geographical and scientific knowledge of the area.

Increasing pressure on the world's food and mineral supplies has stimulated interest in the potential resources even in the extremely hostile polar environment. Minerals may be present in great variety but not in commercially exploitable concentrations in accessible localities. There are indications that off-shore hydrocarbons may be present but mostly below great depths of stormy, ice-infested seas.

Currently, the chief interest is in marine protein, including the shrimp-like krill already fished commercially by Japan and Poland. Research to ensure management of stocks of this organism is being continued by international groups, but it is estimated that they could sustain a yield equal to the present total annual world fish catch.

THE ANTARCTIC TREATY

The International Geophysical Year 1957–8 gave great impetus to Antarctic research, increasing the number of stations from 17 to 44 and the number of nations involved in research from four to 12 by 1957. The co-operative scientific effort proved so fruitful that the 12 nations involved (Argentina, Australia, Belgium, Chile, France, Japan, New Zealand, Norway, South Africa, the Soviet Union, the UK and the USA) pledged themselves to promote scientific and technical co-operation unhampered by politics, and the Antarctic Treaty was signed by the 12 states in 1959.

The 12 signatories to the treaty agreed to establish free use of the Antarctic continent for peaceful scientific purposes; to freeze all territorial claims and disputes in the Antarctic; to ban all military activities in the area; and to prohibit nuclear explosions and the disposal of radioactive waste. Since then additional agreements have been reached to promote conservation and restrict tourism, waste disposal and pollution.

The Antarctic Treaty was defined as covering areas south of latitude 60° S., excluding the high seas but including the ice shelves, and came into force in 1961. It has since been signed by a further 31 states, 14 of which are active in the Antarctic and have therefore been accorded consultative status, bringing the number of consultative parties to 26. In 1991 a protocol to the treaty was adopted by the signatory states which introduced a range of measures to protect Antarctica's environment and prohibit mineral exploitation and mining.

TERRITORIAL CLAIMS

Under the provisions of the Antarctic Treaty all territorial claims and disputes were frozen without the acceptance or denial of the claims of the various claimants. The US and Soviet governments also made it clear that although they had not made any specific territorial claims, they did not relinquish the right to make such claims.

Seven states have made claims in the Antarctic: Argentina claims the part of Antarctica between 74° W. and 25° W.; Chile that part between 90° W. and 53° W.; Britain claims the British Antarctic Territory, an area of 1,810,000 sq. km (700,000 sq. miles) between 20° and 80° W. longitude; France claims Adélie Land, 432,000 sq. km (166,800 sq. miles) between 136° and 142° E.; Australia claims the Australian Antarctic Territory, 6,120,000 sq. km (2,320,000 sq. miles) between 160° and 45° E. longitude excluding Adélie Land; Norway claims Queen Maud Land between 20° W. and 45° E.; and New Zealand claims the Ross Dependency, 450,000 sq. km (175,000 sq. miles) between 160° E. and 150° W. longitude. The Argentinian, British and Chilean claims overlap while the part of the continent between 90° W. and 150° W. is unclaimed by any state.

SCIENTIFIC RESEARCH

There are over 40 permanently occupied stations operated by the following nations: Argentina (6), Australia (4), Brazil (1), Chile (3), China (2), France (5), Germany (1), India (1), Japan (2), New Zealand (1), Poland (1), Russia (4), South Africa (3), South Korea (1), UK (2), Ukraine (1), Uruguay (1), USA (3, including one at the South Pole).

The staff of these stations and summer field-workers are the only people present on the continent and off-lying islands. There are no indigenous inhabitants.

LARGEST CITIES OF THE WORLD

In most cases figures refer to urban agglomerations (Ψ seaport)

	Population			Population
Mexico City, Mexico	14,987,051	Delhi, India		8,375,188
Cairo, Egypt	13,000,000	Bogotá, Colombia		8,000,000
Ψ Bombay, India	12,571,720	Ψ Jakarta, Indonesia		7,885,519
Tokyo, Japan	11,718,720	Ψ New York, USA		7,333,253
Ψ Calcutta, India	10,916,272	Ψ Istanbul, Turkey		7,309,190
Seoul, South Korea	10,229,000	Ψ Karachi, Pakistan		7,183,000
São Paulo, Brazil	9,480,427	Ψ London, UK		6,961,900
Paris, France	9,318,800	Beijing, China		6,560,000
Ψ Shanghai, China	8,760,000	Dhaka, Bangladesh		6,537,308
Moscow, Russia	8,700,000	Lima, Peru		6,483,901

784

Currencies of the World
AND EXCHANGE RATES AGAINST £ STERLING

Franc CFA = Franc de la Communauté financière africaine
Franc CFP = Franc des Comptoirs français du Pacifique

COUNTRY/TERRITORY	MONETARY UNIT	AVERAGE RATE TO £ 1 September 1995	AVERAGE RATE TO £ 30 August 1996
Afghanistan	Afghani (Af) of 100 puls	Af 6896.21	Af 7424.25
Albania	Lek (Lk) of 100 qindarka	Lk 177.063	Lk 170.523
Algeria	Algerian dinar (DA) of 100 centimes	DA 80.6524	DA 81.9872
American Samoa	Currency is that of USA	US$ 1.5525	US$ 1.5630
Andorra	French and Spanish currencies in use	—	—
Angola	Readjusted kwanza (Kzrl) of 100 lwei, replaced new kwanza (Nkz)	Nkz 5005.26	Kzrl 49678.4
Anguilla	East Caribbean dollar (EC$) of 100 cents	EC$ 4.1918	EC$ 4.2201
Antigua and Barbuda	East Caribbean dollar (EC$) of 100 cents	EC$ 4.1918	EC$ 4.2201
Argentina	Peso of 10,000 australes	Pesos 1.5517	Pesos 1.5609
Armenia	Dram of 100 couma	Dram 635.097	Dram 654.585
Aruba	Aruban florin	Florins 2.7790	Florins 2.7978
Australia	Australian dollar ($A) of 100 cents	$A 2.0714	$A 1.9754
Austria	Schilling of 100 Groschen	Schilling 15.9756	Schilling 16.2535
Azerbaijan	Manat of 100 gopik	Manat 6823.24	Manat 6727.15
Bahamas	Bahamian dollar (B$) of 100 cents	B$ 1.5525	B$ 1.5630
Bahrain	Bahrain dinar (BD) of 1,000 fils	BD 0.5853	BD 0.5893
Bangladesh	Taka (Tk) of 100 poisha	Tk 61.7895	Tk 65.4898
Barbados	Barbados dollar (BD$) of 100 cents	BD$ 3.1226	BD$ 3.1437
Belarus	Rouble of 100 kopeks	Roubles 17853.8	Roubles 26852.4
Belgium	Belgian franc (or frank) of 100 centimes (centiemen)	Francs 46.7225	Francs 47.5621
Belize	Belize dollar (BZ$) of 100 cents	BZ$ 3.1050	BZ$ 3.1260
Benin	Franc CFA	Francs 784.440	Francs 790.270
Bermuda	Bermuda dollar of 100 cents	$ 1.5525	$ 1.5630
Bhutan	Ngultrum of 100 chetrum (Indian currency is also legal tender)	Ngultrum 49.5403	Ngultrum 55.7523
Bolivia	Boliviano ($b) of 100 centavos	$b 7.5141	$b 8.0182
Bosnia-Hercegovina	Dinar of 100 paras		
Botswana	Pula (P) of 100 thebe	P 4.3551	P 5.4508
Brazil	Real of 100 centavos	Real 1.4740	Real 1.5888
British Virgin Islands	US dollar (US$) (£ sterling and EC$ also circulate)	US$ 1.5525	US$ 1.5630
Brunei	Brunei dollar of 100 sen (fully inter-changeable with Singapore currency)	$ 2.2061	$ 2.1995
Bulgaria	Lev of 100 stotinki	Leva 105.469	Leva 329.012
Burkina Faso	Franc CFA	Francs 784.440	Francs 790.270
Burundi	Burundi franc of 100 centimes	Francs 393.171	Francs 338.437
Cambodia	Riel of 100 sen	Riel 3570.75	Riel 3594.90
Cameroon	Franc CFA	Francs 784.440	Francs 790.270
Canada	Canadian dollar (C$) of 100 cents	C$ 2.0858	C$ 2.1386
Cape Verde	Escudo Caboverdiano of 100 centavos	Esc 128.811	Esc 129.682
Cayman Islands	Cayman Islands dollar (CI$) of 100 cents	CI$ 1.2858	CI$ 1.3303
Central African Republic	Franc CFA	Francs 784.440	Francs 790.270
Chad	Franc CFA	Francs 784.440	Francs 790.270
Chile	Chilean peso of 100 centavos	Pesos 610.676	Pesos 641.846
China	Renminbi Yuan of 10 jiao or 100 fen	Yuan 12.9156	Yuan 12.9828
Christmas Island	Currency is that of Australia	$A 2.0714	$A 1.9754
Cocos (Keeling) Islands	Currency is that of Australia	$A 2.0714	$A 1.9754
Colombia	Colombian peso of 100 centavos	Pesos 1474.56	Pesos 1628.65
Comoros	Franc CFA/Franc	Francs 588.476	Francs 593.921
Congo	Franc CFA	Francs 784.440	Francs 790.270
Cook Islands	Currency is that of New Zealand	NZ$ 2.3755	NZ$ 2.2644
Costa Rica	Costa Rican colón (C) of 100 céntimos	C 286.343	C 329.715
Côte d'Ivoire	Franc CFA	Francs 784.440	Francs 790.270
Croatia	Kuna of 100 lipas	Kuna 8.3241	Kuna 8.1782

COUNTRY/TERRITORY	MONETARY UNIT	AVERAGE RATE TO £ 1 September 1995	AVERAGE RATE TO £ 30 August 1996
Cuba	Cuban peso of 100 centavos	Pesos 1.5525	Pesos 1.5630
Cyprus	Cyprus pound (C£) of 100 cents	C£ 0.7114	C£ 0.7164
Czech Republic	Koruna (Kčs) of 100 haléřu	Kčs 41.8570	Kčs 40.5380
Denmark	Danish krone of 100 øre	Kroner 8.8252	Kroner 8.9275
Djibouti	Djibouti franc of 100 centimes	Francs 275.911	Francs 250.080
Dominica	East Caribbean dollar (EC$) of 100 cents	EC$ 4.1918	EC$ 4.2201
Dominican Republic	Dominican Republic peso (RD$) of 100 centavos	RD$ 21.4245	RD$ 21.7023
Ecuador	Sucre of 100 centavos	Sucres 3890.57	Sucres 5125.86
Egypt	Egyptian pound (£E) of 100 piastres or 1,000 millièmes	£E 5.2770	£E 5.3123
Equatorial Guinea	Franc CFA	Francs 784.440	Francs 790.270
Eritrea	Ethiopian currency is in use	EB 9.0045	EB 9.0654
Estonia	Kroon of 100 sents	Kroons 18.2251	Kroons 18.5316
Ethiopia	Ethiopian birr (EB) of 100 cents	EB 9.0045	EB 9.0654
Falkland Islands	Falkland pound of 100 pence	at parity with £ sterling	
Faroe Islands	Currency is that of Denmark	Kroner 8.8252	Kroner 8.9275
Fiji	Fiji dollar (F$) of 100 cents	F$ 2.1971	F$ 2.1799
Finland	Markka (Mk) of 100 penniä	Mk 6.8109	Mk 6.9845
France	Franc of 100 centimes	Francs 7.8444	Francs 7.9027
French Guiana	Currency is that of France	Francs 7.8444	Francs 7.9027
French Polynesia	Franc CFP	Francs 142.661	Francs 143.981
Gabon	Franc CFA	Francs 784.440	Francs 790.270
Gambia	Dalasi (D) of 100 butut	D 14.9040	D 15.3643
Georgia	Georgian Coupon	—	—
Germany	Deutsche Mark (DM) of 100 Pfennig	DM 2.2717	DM 2.3098
Ghana	Cedi of 100 pesewas	Cedi 1870.76	Cedi 2633.66
Gibraltar	Gibraltar pound of 100 pence	at parity with £ sterling	
Greece	Drachma of 100 leptae	Drachmae 365.723	Drachmae 369.415
Greenland	Currency is that of Denmark	Kroner 8.8252	Kroner 8.9275
Grenada	East Caribbean dollar (EC$) of 100 cents	EC$ 4.1918	EC$ 4.2201
Guadeloupe	Currency is that of France	Francs 7.8444	Francs 7.9027
Guam	Currency is that of USA	US$ 1.5525	US$ 1.5630
Guatemala	Quetzal (Q) of 100 centavos	Q 9.0919	Q 9.5038
Guinea	Guinea franc of 100 centimes	Francs 1536.04	Francs 1558.31
Guinea-Bissau	Guinea-Bissau peso of 100 centavos	Pesos 26001.3	Pesos 28190.3
Guyana	Guyana dollar (G$) of 100 cents	G$ 223.250	G$ 217.101
Haiti	Gourde of 100 centimes	Gourdes 29.4975	Gourdes 23.2178
Honduras	Lempira of 100 centavos	Lempiras 14.6867	Lempiras 18.8654
Hong Kong	Hong Kong dollar (HK$) of 100 cents	HK$ 12.0176	HK$ 12.0863
Hungary	Forint of 100 fillér	Forints 201.771	Forints 235.958
Iceland	Icelandic króna (Kr) of 100 aurar	Kr 101.906	Kr 103.471
India	Indian rupee (Rs) of 100 paisa	Rs 49.5403	Rs 55.7523
Indonesia	Rupiah (Rp) of 100 sen	Rp 3519.91	Rp 3660.55
Iran	Rial	Rials 4657.50	Rials 4689.00
Iraq	Iraqi dinar (ID) of 1,000 fils	ID 0.9315	ID 0.4860
Ireland, Republic of	Punt (IR£) of 100 pence	IR£ 0.9774	IR£ 0.9630
Israel	Shekel of 100 agora	Shekels 4.7219	Shekels 4.9060
Italy	Lira of 100 centesimi	Lire 2523.90	Lire 2358.53
Jamaica	Jamaican dollar (J$) of 100 cents	J$ 51.2325	J$ 53.5328
Japan	Yen of 100 sen	Yen 151.237	Yen 169.742
Jordan	Jordanian dinar (JD) of 1,000 fils	JD 1.1054	JD 1.1094
Kazakhstan	Tenge	—	Tenge 106.597
Kenya	Kenya shilling (Ksh) of 100 cents	Ksh 85.8533	Ksh 88.9348
Kiribati	Australian dollar ($A) of 100 cents	$A 2.0714	$A 1.9754
Korea, North	Won of 100 jun	Won 3.3379	Won 3.3605
Korea, South	Won of 100 jeon	Won 1200.32	Won 1280.49
Kuwait	Kuwaiti dinar (KD) of 1,000 fils	KD 0.4697	KD 0.4678
Kyrgyzstan	Som	—	—
Laos	Kip (K) of 100 at	K 1428.30	K 1437.96
Latvia	Lats of 100 santimes	Lats 0.8339	Lats 0.8502
Lebanon	Lebanese pound (L£) of 100 piastres	L£ 2504.96	L£ 2441.41
Lesotho	Loti (M) of 100 lisente	M 5.6802	M 7.0140
Liberia	Liberian dollar (L$) of 100 cents	L$ 1.5525	L$ 1.5630
Libya	Libyan dinar (LD) of 1,000 dirhams	LD 0.5519	LD 0.5557

Country/Territory	Monetary Unit	Average Rate to £ 1 September 1995	Average Rate to £ 30 August 1996
Liechtenstein	Swiss franc of 100 rappen (or centimes)	Francs 1.8588	Francs 1.8718
Lithuania	Litas	Litas 6.2100	Litas 6.2520
Luxembourg	Luxembourg franc (LF) of 100 centimes (Belgian currency is also legal tender)	LF 46.7225	LF 47.5621
Macao	Pataca of 100 avos	Pataca 12.3984	Pataca 12.4867
Macedonia, Former Yugoslav Rep.	Dinar of 100 paras	Dinars 61.0139	Dinars 63.2940
Madagascar	Franc malgache (FMG) of 100 centimes	FMG 6908.63	FMG 6017.55
Malawi	Kwacha (K) of 100 tambala	K 23.6878	K 23.9139
Malaysia	Malaysian dollar (ringgit) (M$) of 100 sen	M$ 3.8743	M$ 3.8978
Maldives	Rufiyaa of 100 laaris	Rufiyaa 18.2730	Rufiyaa 18.3965
Mali	Franc CFA	Francs 784.440	Francs 790.270
Malta	Maltese lira (LM) of 100 cents or 1,000 mils	LM 0.5559	LM 0.5594
Marshall Islands	Currency is that of USA	US$ 1.5525	US$ 1.5630
Martinique	Currency is that of France	Francs 7.8444	Francs 7.9027
Mauritania	Ouguiya (UM) of 5 khoums	UM 200.257	UM 214.233
Mauritius	Mauritius rupee of 100 cents	Rs 28.2788	Rs 31.6430
Mayotte	Currency is that of France	Francs 7.8444	Francs 7.9027
Mexico	Peso of 100 centavos	Pesos 9.7187	Pesos 11.8585
Moldova	Leu	Leu 7.0383	Leu 7.2445
Monaco	French franc of 100 centimes	Francs 7.8444	Francs 7.9027
Mongolia	Tugrik of 100 möngö	Tugriks 697.228	Tugriks 729.406
Montserrat	East Caribbean dollar (EC$) of 100 cents	EC$ 4.1918	EC$ 4.2201
Morocco	Dirham (DH) of 100 centimes	DH 13.3586	DH 13.4903
Mozambique	Metical (MT) of 100 centavos	MT 14908.7	MT 17412.6
Myanmar (Burma)	Kyat (K) of 100 pyas	K 8.8421	K 9.1519
Namibia	Namibian dollar of 100 cents	*at parity with SA Rand*	
Nauru	Australian dollar ($A) of 100 cents	$A 2.0714	$A 1.9754
Nepal	Nepalese rupee of 100 paisa	Rs 78.2305	Rs 87.5671
Netherlands	Gulden (guilder) or florin of 100 cents	Guilders 2.5461	Guilders 2.5893
Netherlands Antilles	Netherlands Antilles guilder of 100 cents	Guilders 2.7790	Guilders 2.7978
New Caledonia	Franc CFP	Francs 142.661	Francs 143.981
New Zealand	New Zealand dollar (NZ$) of 100 cents	NZ$ 2.3755	NZ$ 2.2644
Nicaragua	Córdoba (C$) of 100 centavos	C$ 11.9061	C$ 13.3918
Niger	Franc CFA	Francs 784.440	Francs 790.270
Nigeria	Naira (N) of 100 kobo	N 34.1519	N 34.3860
Niue	Currency is that of New Zealand	NZ$ 2.3755	NZ$ 2.2644
Norfolk Island	Currency is that of Australia	$A 2.0714	$A 1.9754
Northern Mariana Islands	Currency is that of USA	US$ 1.5525	US$ 1.5630
Norway	Krone of 100 øre	Kroner 9.9360	Kroner 10.0138
Oman	Rial Omani (OR) of 1,000 baiza	OR 0.5978	OR 0.6019
Pakistan	Pakistan rupee of 100 paisa	Rs 48.5758	Rs 55.6184
Palau	Currency is that of USA	US$ 1.5525	US$ 1.5630
Panama	Balboa of 100 centésimos (US notes are also in circulation)	Balboa 1.5525	Balboa 1.5630
Papua New Guinea	Kina (K) of 100 toea	K 2.1209	K 2.0512
Paraguay	Guaraní (Gs) of 100 céntimos	Gs 3046.78	Gs 3243.23
Peru	New Sol of 100 cénts	New Sol 3.5009	New Sol 3.8607
Philippines	Philippine peso (P) of 100 centavos	P 40.3185	P 40.9428
Poland	Złoty of 100 groszy	Złotys 3.8393	Złotys 4.2803
Portugal	Escudo (Esc) of 100 centavos	Esc 236.570	Esc 236.873
Puerto Rico	Currency is that of USA	US$ 1.5525	US$ 1.5630
Qatar	Qatar riyal of 100 dirhams	Riyals 5.6527	Riyals 5.6909
Réunion	Currency is that of France	Francs 7.8444	Francs 7.9027
Romania	Leu (Lei) of 100 bani	Lei 3221.44	Lei 4798.41
Russia	Rouble of 100 kopeks	Roubles 0.9717	Roubles 8384.71
Rwanda	Rwanda franc of 100 centimes	Francs 496.490	Francs 507.037
St Christopher and Nevis	East Caribbean dollar (EC$) of 100 cents	EC$ 4.1918	EC$ 4.2201
St Helena	St Helena pound (£) of 100 pence	*at parity with £ sterling*	

Country/Territory	Monetary Unit	Average Rate to £ 1 September 1995	Average Rate to £ 30 August 1996
St Lucia	East Caribbean dollar (EC$) of 100 cents	EC$ 4.1918	EC$ 4.2201
St Pierre and Miquelon	Currency is that of France	Francs 7.8444	Francs 7.9027
St Vincent and the Grenadines	East Caribbean dollar (EC$) of 100 cents	EC$ 4.1918	EC$ 4.2201
El Salvador	El Salvador colón (₡) of 100 centavos	₡ 13.5999	₡ 13.6841
San Marino	Italian currency is in circulation	Lire 2523.90	Lire 2358.53
São Tomé and Príncipe	Dobra of 100 centavos	Dobra 1953.56	Dobra 3727.96
Saudi Arabia	Saudi riyal (SR) of 20 qursh or 100 halala	SR 5.8229	SR 5.8621
Senegal	Franc CFA	Francs 784.440	Francs 790.270
Seychelles	Seychelles rupee of 100 cents	Rs 7.5110	Rs 7.7916
Sierra Leone	Leone (Le) of 100 cents	Le 1133.33	Le 1359.81
Singapore	Singapore dollar (S$) of 100 cents	S$ 2.2061	S$ 2.1995
Slovakia	Koruna (Kčs) of 100 haléřu	Kčs 47.2737	Kčs 47.8356
Slovenia	Tolar (SIT) of 100 stotin	Tolars 190.849	Tolars 205.460
Solomon Islands	Solomon Islands dollar (SI$) of 100 cents	SI$ 4.6488	SI$ 5.5526
Somalia	Somali shilling of 100 cents	Shillings 4067.55	Shillings 4095.06
South Africa	Rand (R) of 100 cents	R 5.6802	R 7.0140
Spain	Peseta of 100 céntimos	Pesetas 194.893	Pesetas 195.445
Sri Lanka	Sri Lankan rupee of 100 cents	Rs 78.4323	Rs 86.9029
Sudan	Sudanese dinar (SD) of 10 pounds	SD 80.8543	SD 225.072
Suriname	Suriname guilder of 100 cents	Guilders 763.831	Guilders 640.830
Swaziland	Lilangeni (E) of 100 cents (South African currency also in circulation)	E 5.6802	E 7.0140
Sweden	Swedish krona of 100 öre	Kronor 11.3549	Kronor 10.3397
Switzerland	Swiss franc of 100 rappen (or centimes)	Francs 1.8588	Francs 1.8718
Syria	Syrian pound (S$) of 100 piastres	S£ 65.1274	S£ 65.5679
Taiwan	New Taiwan dollar (NT$) of 100 cents	NT$ 42.6914	NT$ 42.9317
Tajikistan	Tajik rouble (TJR) of 100 tanga	—	TJR 83.8471
Tanzania	Tanzanian shilling of 100 cents	Shillings 939.263	Shillings 906.540
Thailand	Baht of 100 satang	Baht 38.8747	Baht 39.5518
Togo	Franc CFA	Francs 784.440	Francs 790.270
Tokelau	Currency is that of New Zealand	NZ$ 2.3755	NZ$ 2.2644
Tonga	Pa'anga (T$) of 100 seniti	T$ 2.0714	T$ 1.9754
Trinidad and Tobago	Trinidad and Tobago dollar (TT$) of 100 cents	TT$ 8.8570	TT$ 9.2860
Tunisia	Tunisian dinar of 1,000 millimes	Dinars 1.4746	Dinars 1.4974
Turkey	Turkish lira (TL) of 100 kurus	TL 74892.7	TL 135613.7
Turkmenistan	Manat	—	—
Turks and Caicos Islands	US dollar (US$)	US$ 1.5525	US$ 1.5630
Tuvalu	Australian dollar ($A) of 100 cents	$A 2.0714	$A 1.9754
Uganda	Uganda shilling of 100 cents	Shillings 1490.40	Shillings 1667.72
Ukraine	Karbovanets (Ka)	Ka 253057.7	Ka 275869.6
United Arab Emirates	UAE dirham of 100 fils	Dirham 5.7024	Dirham 5.7407
United Kingdom	Pound sterling (£) of 100 pence	£ 1.00	£ 1.00
United States of America	US dollar (US$) of 100 cents	US$ 1.5525	US$ 1.5630
Uruguay	New Uruguayan peso of 100 centésimos	Pesos 10.1223	Pesos 12.9651
Uzbekistan	Sum	—	—
Vanuatu	Vatu of 100 centimes	Vatu 174.269	Vatu 173.313
Vatican City State	Italian currency is legal tender	Lire 2523.90	Lire 2358.53
Venezuela	Bolívar (Bs) of 100 céntimos	Bs 263.591	Bs 742.425
Vietnam	Dông of 10 hào or 100 xu	Dông 17105.5	Dông 17223.5
Virgin Islands (US)	Currency is that of USA	US$ 1.5525	US$ 1.5630
Wallis and Futuna Islands	Franc CFP	Francs 142.661	Francs 143.981
Western Samoa	Tala (WS$) of 100 sene	WS$ 3.8968	WS$ 3.8069
Republic of Yemen	Riyal of 100 fils	Riyals 78.0132	Riyals 218.820
Yugoslavia, Federal Rep.	New dinar of 100 paras	—	New Dinars 7.6879
Zaïre	Zaïre of 100 makuta	Zaïre 8419.52	Zaïre 77999.2
Zambia	Kwacha (K) of 100 ngwee	K 1459.23	K 1985.01
Zimbabwe	Zimbabwe dollar (Z$) of 100 cents	Z$ 13.4408	Z$ 16.1615

Time Zones

Standard time differences from the
Greenwich meridian

+ hours ahead of GMT
− hours behind GMT
* may vary from standard time at
some part of the year (Summer
Time or Daylight Saving Time)
h hours
m minutes

	h	*m*
Afghanistan	+ 4	30
*Albania	+ 1	
Algeria	+ 1	
*Andorra	+ 1	
Angola	+ 1	
Anguilla	− 4	
Antigua and Barbuda	− 4	
Argentina	− 3	
Armenia	+ 4	
Aruba	− 4	
Ascension Island	0	
*Australia	+10	
Broken Hill area		
(NSW)	+ 9	30
Lord Howe Island	+10	30
Northern Territory	+ 9	30
*South Australia	+ 9	30
Western Australia	+ 8	
*Austria	+ 1	
Azerbaijan	+ 4	
*Azores	− 1	
*Bahamas	− 5	
Bahrain	+ 3	
Bangladesh	+ 6	
Barbados	− 4	
*Belarus	+ 2	
*Belgium	+ 1	
Belize	− 6	
Benin	+ 1	
*Bermuda	− 4	
Bhutan	+ 6	
Bolivia	− 4	
*Bosnia-Hercegovina	+ 1	
Botswana	+ 2	
Brazil		
Acre	− 5	
*eastern, including all coast		
and Brasilia	− 3	
Fernando de Norouha		
Island	− 2	
*western	− 4	
British Antarctic Territory	− 3	
British Indian Ocean		
Territory	+ 5	
Diego Garcia	+ 6	
British Virgin Islands	− 4	
Brunei	+ 8	
*Bulgaria	+ 2	
Burkina Faso	0	
Burundi	+ 2	
Cambodia	+ 7	
Cameroon	+ 1	
Canada		
*Alberta	− 7	
*British Columbia	− 8	
British Columbia NE	− 7	
*Labrador	− 4	

	h	*m*
*Manitoba	− 6	
*New Brunswick	− 4	
*Newfoundland	− 3	30
*Northwest Territories		
east of 68° W.	− 4	
68° W.–85° W.	− 5	
85° W.–102° W.	− 6	
west of 102° W.	− 7	
*Nova Scotia	− 4	
Ontario		
*east of 90° W.	− 5	
west of 90° W.	− 5	
*Prince Edward Island	− 4	
*Quebec		
east of 63° W.	− 4	
west of 63° W.	− 5	
*Saskatchewan	− 6	
*Yukon	− 8	
*Canary Islands	0	
Cape Verde	− 1	
Cayman Islands	− 5	
Central African Republic	+ 1	
Chad	+ 1	
*Chatham Island	+12	45
*Chile	− 4	
China	+ 8	
Christmas Island (Indian		
Ocean)	+ 7	
Cocos Keeling Islands	+ 6	30
Colombia	− 5	
Comoros	+ 3	
Congo	+ 1	
Cook Islands	− 10	
Costa Rica	− 6	
Côte d'Ivoire	0	
*Croatia	+ 1	
*Cuba	− 5	
*Cyprus	+ 2	
*Czech Republic	+ 1	
*Denmark	+ 1	
Djibouti	+ 3	
Dominica	− 4	
Dominican Republic	− 4	
Ecuador	− 5	
Galápagos Islands	− 6	
*Egypt	+ 2	
Equatorial Guinea	+ 1	
Eritrea	+ 3	
*Estonia	+ 2	
Ethiopia	+ 3	
*Falkland Islands	− 4	
*Faröe Islands	0	
Fiji	+12	
*Finland	+ 2	
*France	+ 1	
French Guiana	− 3	
French Polynesia	−10	
Marquesas Islands	− 9	30
Gabon	+ 1	
The Gambia	0	
*Georgia	+ 4	
*Germany	+ 1	
Ghana	0	
*Gibraltar	+ 1	
*Greece	+ 2	
Greenland	− 3	

	h	*m*
Danmarkshavn	0	
Mesters Vig	0	
*Scoresby Sound	− 1	
*Thule area	− 4	
Grenada	− 4	
Guadeloupe	− 4	
Guam	+10	
Guatemala	− 6	
Guinea	0	
Guinea-Bissau	0	
Guyana	− 4	
*Haiti	− 5	
Honduras	− 6	
Hong Kong	+ 8	
*Hungary	+ 1	
Iceland	0	
India	+ 5	30
Indonesia		
Bali	+ 8	
Flores	+ 8	
Irian Jaya	+ 9	
Java	+ 7	
Kalimantan (south and		
east)	+ 8	
Kalimantan (west and		
central)	+ 7	
Molucca Islands	+ 9	
Sulawesi	+ 8	
Sumatra	+ 7	
Sumbawa	+ 8	
Tanimbar	+ 9	
Timor	+ 8	
*Iran	+ 3	30
*Iraq	+ 3	
*Ireland, Republic of	0	
*Israel	+ 2	
*Italy	+ 1	
Jamaica	− 5	
Japan	+ 9	
*Jordan	+ 2	
*Kazakhstan	+ 6	
Kenya	+ 3	
Kiribati		
Banaba	+12	
Gilbert Islands	+12	
Kiritimati Island	−10	
Line Islands	+14	
Phoenix Islands	−13	
Korea, North	+ 9	
Korea, South	+ 9	
Kuwait	+ 3	
*Kyrgyzstan	+ 5	
Laos	+ 7	
*Latvia	+ 2	
*Lebanon	+ 2	
Lesotho	+ 2	
Liberia	0	
Libya	+ 2	
*Liechtenstein	+ 1	
*Lithuania	+ 2	
*Luxembourg	+ 1	
Macao	+ 8	
*Macedonia (Former Yug.		
Rep. of)	+ 1	
Madagascar	+ 3	
*Madeira	0	

	h	m
Malawi	+ 2	
Malaysia	+ 8	
Maldives	+ 5	
Mali	0	
*Malta	+ 1	
Marshall Islands	+12	
Ebon Atoll	−12	
Martinique	− 4	
Mauritania	0	
Mauritius	+ 4	
Mexico	− 6	
central	− 7	
western	− 8	
Micronesia		
Caroline Islands	+10	
Kosrae	+11	
Pingelap	+11	
Pohnpei	+11	
*Moldova	+ 2	
*Monaco	+ 1	
*Mongolia	+ 8	
Montserrat	− 4	
Morocco	0	
Mozambique	+ 2	
Myanmar	+ 6	30
*Namibia	+ 1	
Nauru	+12	
Nepal	+ 5	45
*Netherlands	+ 1	
Netherlands Antilles	− 4	
New Caledonia	+11	
*New Zealand	+12	
Nicaragua	− 6	
Niger	+ 1	
Nigeria	+ 1	
Niue	−11	
Norfolk Island	+11	30
Northern Mariana Islands	+10	
*Norway	+ 1	
Oman	+ 4	
Pakistan	+ 5	
Palau	+ 9	
Panama	− 5	
Papua New Guinea	+10	
*Paraguay	− 4	
Peru	− 5	
Philippines	+ 8	
*Poland	+ 1	
*Portugal	+ 1	
Puerto Rico	− 4	
Qatar	+ 3	
Réunion	+ 4	
*Romania	+ 2	
*Russia		
Zone 1	+ 2	
Zone 2	+ 3	
Zone 3	+ 4	
Zone 4	+ 5	
Zone 5	+ 6	
Zone 6	+ 7	
Zone 7	+ 8	
Zone 8	+ 9	
Zone 9	+10	
Zone 10	+11	
Zone 11	+12	
Rwanda	+ 2	
St Helena	0	
St Kitts and Nevis	− 4	

	h	m
St Lucia	− 4	
*St Pierre and Miquelon	− 3	
St Vincent and the		
Grenadines	− 4	
El Salvador	− 6	
Samoa, American	−11	
*San Marino	+ 1	
São Tomé and Príncipe	0	
Saudi Arabia	+ 3	
Senegal	0	
Seychelles	+ 4	
Sierra Leone	0	
Singapore	+ 8	
*Slovakia	+ 1	
*Slovenia	+ 1	
Solomon Islands	+11	
Somalia	+ 3	
South Africa	+ 2	
South Georgia	− 2	
*Spain	+ 1	
Sri Lanka	+ 5	30
Sudan	+ 2	
Suriname	− 3	
Swaziland	+ 2	
*Sweden	+ 1	
*Switzerland	+ 1	
*Syria	+ 2	
Taiwan	+ 8	
Tajikistan	+ 5	
Tanzania	+ 3	
Thailand	+ 7	
Togo	0	
Tonga	+13	
Trinidad and Tobago	− 4	
Tristan da Cunha	0	
Tunisia	+ 1	
*Turkey	+ 2	
Turkmenistan	+ 5	
*Turks and Caicos Islands	− 5	
Tuvalu	+12	
Uganda	+ 3	
*Ukraine	+ 2	
*Simferopol	+ 3	
United Arab Emirates	+ 4	
United States		
*Alaska, east of		
169° 30′ W.	− 9	
*Aleutian Islands, west		
of 169° 30′ W.	−10	
eastern time	− 5	
*central time	− 6	
Hawaii	−10	
*mountain time	− 7	
*Pacific time	− 8	
Uruguay	− 3	
Uzbekistan	+ 5	
Vanuatu	+11	
*Vatican City State	+ 1	
Venezuela	− 4	
Vietnam	+ 7	
Virgin Islands (US)	− 4	
Western Samoa	−11	
Yemen	+ 3	
*Yugoslavia (Fed. Rep. of)	+ 1	
Zaïre		
East	+ 2	
West	+ 1	

	h	m
Zambia	+ 2	
Zimbabwe	+ 2	

Source: reproduced with permission from data produced by HM Nautical Almanac Office

Countries of the World: A–Z

Sources: sources of statistical data specific to one country are credited in that country's entry. Sources of statistical data used throughout the Countries of the World section include *UN Demographic Yearbook*, *UN Statistical Yearbook* (pub. UN), *UNESCO Statistical Yearbook* (pub. UNESCO), *World Bank Atlas*, *World Bank World Tables* (pub. World Bank), *World Mineral Statistics* (pub. British Geological Survey), *The Military Balance* (pub. IISS).

Other sources of information include the Foreign and Commonwealth Office and the diplomatic representatives and information offices in London of overseas countries, whom Whitaker's wishes to thank for their assistance.

AFGHANISTAN
Da Afghanistan Jamhuriat

Afghanistan is bounded on the west by Iran, on the south by Pakistan, on the north by Tajikistan, Uzbekistan and Turkmenistan, and on the east by Pakistan and China. The estimated area is 251,772 sq. miles (652,090 sq. km).

Mountains, chief among which are the Hindu Kush, cover three-quarters of the country, the elevation being generally over 4,000 feet. There are three great river basins, the Oxus, Helmand, and Kabul. The climate is dry, with extreme temperatures.

The population is 17,691,000 (1993 UN estimate). It is estimated that 3.5 million refugees fled to Pakistan and two million to Iran during the Soviet occupation, and that one million died in the war between the mujahidin and the Soviet and Afghan armed forces. About 1.5 million refugees have returned since 1992. The most numerous race is the Pushtuns who form around half of the population and predominate in the south and west, the Tajiks, a Persian-speaking people, Uzbeks and Turkomans in the north, Hazaras in the centre, Baluchis in the south-west and Nuristanis, who live near the Chitral border. All are Sunni Muslims, except the Hazaras and Kizilbashes, who belong to the Shia sect.

Capital – Kabul (1,424,400 in 1988 but much reduced since due to fighting). The chief commercial centres are Kabul and Kandahar (225,500). Other provincial capitals are (UN estimates) Herat (177,300), Mazar-i-Sharif (130,600), Jalalabad (55,000).

Currency – Afghani (Af) of 100 puls.

Flag – Three horizontal stripes of green, white, black with the national arms in the centre in gold.

National Anthem – Soroud-e-Melli.

National Day – 19 August.

GOVERNMENT

The constitutional monarchy, introduced by the 1964 constitution, was overthrown by a coup in 1973. The country was ruled by presidential decree until 1977 when a constitution was approved and Mohammad Daoud was elected President. He was overthrown in 1978 by the armed forces and power was handed to the People's Democratic Party of Afghanistan (PDPA). In December 1979 Soviet troops invaded Afghanistan and installed Babrak Karmal as head of state. Armed Islamic resistance groups, the mujahidin, aided by western arms and Arab finance, fought against Soviet and Afghan armed forces

until the 1988 peace agreement which led to the withdrawal of Soviet troops. Mujahidin resistance to the Homeland Party (formerly PDPA) government continued until the government collapsed in April 1992. Mujahidin forces overran Kabul bringing an end to the war, and declared an Islamic state.

The Pakistan-based government-in-exile returned to Kabul and appointed Burhanuddin Rabbani as interim president. The mujahidin coalition divided over the election of a permanent president and fighting resumed in December 1992 between Hezb-i-Islami (mainly Pushtun), led by Gulbardin Hekmatyar, supported by the Hezb-i-Wahdat forces (Shia), and Jamiat-i-Islami of Ahmad Shah Massoud and Rabbani (mainly Tajik), which controlled Kabul. The fighting was interrupted with the signing of a power-sharing agreement under which Rabbani remained President and Hekmatyar became head of a transitional government. The cease-fire collapsed in October 1993 and Hekmatyar was forced out of Kabul in June 1994 despite forming an alliance with Uzbek militia leader Gen. Rashid Dostrum. In the winter of 1994–5, Hezb-i-Islami and Hezb-i-Wahdat suffered heavy defeats at the hands of the Taliban (armed Islamic students), which extended its power across half of the country, and took control of the city of Herat. By the end of 1995, the Taliban had laid siege to Kabul, devastating the city with daily rocket attacks. In March 1996, Hekmatyar signed an agreement with Rabbani to combine their forces against the Taliban. The coalition succeeded in forcing the Taliban to pull back from Kabul in May 1996. The agreement also provided for Hekmatyar to become prime minister and for Hezb-i-Islami to fill the defence and finance portfolios.

Heads of State and Government
President of the Islamic State of Afghanistan, Prof. Burhanuddin Rabbani, *elected* 30 December 1992
Prime Minister, Gulbardin Hekmatyar, *sworn in* 3 July 1996

Embassy of the Islamic State of Afghanistan
31 Prince's Gate, London SW7 1QQ
Tel 0171-589 8891
Ambassador Extraordinary and Plenipotentiary, new appointment awaited
Minister-Counsellor and Chargé d'Affaires, Ahmad Wali Masud

British Embassy
Karte Parwan, Kabul
Staff were withdrawn from post in February 1989. Ambassador is now resident in Islamabad.

DEFENCE

After the fall of the PDPA government the Afghan army disintegrated, with large numbers defecting to local mujahidin groups. The Northern Army Command was formed into the National Islamic Movement under the Uzbek militia leader General Dostum and numbers around 65,000 men. The Jamiat-i-Islami forces of Rabbani and Massoud number 60,000 men, while Hekmatyar's Hezb-i-Islami forces number 50,000. Five other Sunni Muslim mujahidin groups have forces of 113,000 personnel and the Shia Hezb-i-Wahdat coalition of forces have 116,000 men under arms. Taliban forces are roughly 25,000 strong. The former Air Force has been divided between Dostum's and Rabbani's forces.

ECONOMY

The economy has been devastated by the political upheavals of the last 15 years. Agriculture and sheep raising have been the principal industries. There are generally two crops a year, one of wheat (the staple food), barley or lentils, the other of rice, millet, maize and dal. Sugar beet and cotton are grown. Afghanistan is rich in fruits. Sheep, including the Karakuli, and transport animals are bred. Silk, woollen and hair cloths and carpets are manufactured. Salt, silver, copper, coal, iron, lead, rubies, lapis lazuli, gold, chrome, barite, uranium, and talc are found.

TRADE

Trade is currently limited but in the past exports have been mainly Persian lambskins (Karakul), dried fruits, nuts, cotton, raw wool, carpets, spice and natural gas, while the imports are chiefly oil, cotton yarn and piece goods, tea, sugar, machinery and transport equipment.

Trade with UK	1994	1995
Imports from UK	£7,830,000	£7,156,000
Exports to UK	4,096,000	415,000

COMMUNICATIONS

Main roads run from Kabul to Kandahar, Herat, Maimana via Mazar-i-Sharif and Faizabad via Khanabad. Roads cross the border with Pakistan at Chaman and via the Khyber Pass, and there are roads from Herat to the borders of Central Asia and Iran. A network of minor roads fit for motor traffic in fine weather links up important towns and districts.

In 1982 the Afghan and Uzbek shores of the River Oxus were linked by a road and rail bridge which joins the Afghan port of Hairatan and the Uzbek port of Termez.

CULTURE

The principal languages of the country are Dari (a form of Persian) and Pushtu, although a number of minority languages are also spoken in various provinces. All school-children learn both Persian and Pushtu. Education is free and nominally compulsory, elementary schools having been established in most centres; there are secondary schools in large urban areas and four universities, in Kabul (established 1932), Jalalabad (established 1962), Balkh and Herat (both established 1988).

ALBANIA
Republika Shqipërisë

Situated on the Adriatic Sea, Albania is bounded on the north by Montenegro, on the east by Serbia and Macedonia and on the south by Greece. The area is estimated at 11,099 sq. miles (28,748 sq. km), with a population (1993 UN estimate) of 3,500,000. After many years as an officially atheist country, the Albanian population is now estimated to be 65 per cent Muslim, 20 per cent Orthodox and 10 per cent Roman Catholic.

CAPITAL – Tirana, population (1990) 244,153.
CURRENCY – Lek (Lk) of 100 qindarka.
FLAG – Black two-headed eagle on a red field.
NATIONAL DAY – 28 November.

GOVERNMENT

Albania was under Turkish suzerainty from 1468 until 1912, when independence was declared. After a period of unrest, a republic was declared in 1925, and in 1928 a monarchy. The King went into exile in 1939 when the country was occupied by the Italians; Albania was liberated in November 1944. Elections in 1945 resulted in a Communist-controlled Assembly; the King was deposed in absentia and a republic declared in January 1946.

From 1946 to 1991 Albania was a one-party, Communist state. In March 1991 multiparty elections were held and were won by the Socialist Party (the renamed Communist Party of Labour). A coalition government was formed in June 1991, but in December 1991 the Democratic Party withdrew from the government and new elections were held in March 1992. These elections were won overwhelmingly by the Democratic Party, which formed a coalition government with the Social Democrat and Republican parties. In April 1992 the Democratic Party leader Dr Sali Berisha was elected by parliament as Albania's first non-Communist President. The general election on 26 May 1996 was marred by allegations of ballot-rigging and voter intimidation. A re-run on 16 June was boycotted by opposition parties, enabling the Democratic Party to remain in power with a large majority.

HEAD OF STATE
President, Dr Sali Berisha, *elected* April 1992

COUNCIL OF MINISTERS *as at July 1996*
Prime Minister, Aleksander Meksi
Deputy PM, Foreign Affairs, Tritan Shehu
Interior, Halit Shamata
Finance, Ridvan Bode
Defence, Safet Zhulali
Justice, Kristofor Peci
Industry, Transport and Trade, Suzana Panariti
Energy and Mineral Resources, Abdyl Xhaja
Public Works, Territorial Adjustment and Tourism, Albert Brojka
Health and Environment, Maksim Cikuli
Agriculture and Food, Bamir Topi
Education and Sport, Edmond Lulja
Higher Education and Scientific Research, Besnik Gjongecaj
Culture, Youth and Women, Teodor Laco
Labour and Social Affairs, Arlinda Keci
Privatization, Dylber Vrioni
Without Portfolio, Hasan Halili

EMBASSY OF THE REPUBLIC OF ALBANIA
4th Floor, 38 Grosvenor Gardens, London SW1W 0EB
Tel 0171-730 5709
Ambassador Extraordinary and Plenipotentiary, HE Pavli Qesku, apptd 1993

BRITISH EMBASSY
Rruga Vaso Pasha, 7–1, Tirana
Tel: Tirana 34973/4
Ambassador Extraordinary and Plenipotentiary, HE Andrew Tesorierre, apptd 1996

DEFENCE

Albania has a total active armed forces strength of some 73,000 personnel (22,800 conscripts). Conscripts serve for a term of 12 months. The Army has a strength of 60,000 (20,000 conscripts). The Navy has a strength of 2,500 (1,000 conscripts) and the Air Force has a strength of 10,000 personnel (1,800 conscripts).

ECONOMY

Much of the country is mountainous and nearly a half is covered by forest. There are fertile areas along the Adriatic coast and the Koritza Basin and there have been land reclamation and irrigation programmes. The main crops are wheat, maize, sugar-beet, potatoes and fruit. There are large chromium deposits.

The principal industries are agricultural product processing, textiles, oil products and cement. Exports include crude oil, minerals (bitumen, chrome, nickel, copper), tobacco, fruit and vegetables. The government is committed to economic reform, privatization and the creation of a market economy. Most agriculture has been privatized and land redistributed, with a consequent increase in production. Most housing and 2,780 small and medium-sized enterprises have been privatized.

Since April 1992, the government has imposed severe austerity measures in an attempt to reduce the budget deficit and to cut inflation, which stood at 23 per cent in 1994. The currency has stabilized, with economic growth of 8 per cent of GDP in 1994, signalling a recovery from the economic collapse of 1988–92. The country is now self-sufficient in food production, producing 470,000 tonnes of wheat in 1993. Remittances from 500,000 overseas workers remain an important source of revenue. Albania has received $1 billion in aid from Western donors.

Trade with UK	1994	1995
Imports from UK	£5,607,000	£7,555,000
Exports to UK	220,000	1,017,000

ALGERIA
Al-Jumhuriya al-Jazairiya ad-Dimuqratiya ash-Shabiya

Algeria lies between 8° 45′ W. and 12° E. longitude, 27° 6′ N. to a southern limit about 19° N. and has an area of 919,595 sq. miles (2,381,741 sq. km). The population (1987 census) was 22,971,558. A 1993 UN estimate gives a figure of 26,722,000.

Capital – ΨAlgiers, population 3,250,000 (approx). It is one of the principal ports of the Mediterranean as well as an important industrial centre. Other towns include ΨOran; Constantine; ΨAnnaba; Blida; Setif; Sidi-Bel-Abbès; Tlemcen; ΨMostaganem; ΨSkikda; ΨBejaia and Tizi Ouzou.

Currency – Algerian dinar (DA) of 100 centimes.

Flag – Divided vertically green and white with a red crescent and star over all in the centre.

National Anthem – Qassaman.

National Day – 1 November.

GOVERNMENT

Algeria was annexed to France in 1842, with the departments of Algiers, Oran and Constantine forming an integral part of France. President de Gaulle declared Algeria independent in July 1962 following an eight-year armed rebellion by the (Arab) Front de Libération Nationale (FLN), whose leader, Ben Bella, was elected President in 1963. Ben Bella was deposed in 1965 by a military junta presided over by Col. Boumediène, who was formally elected President in 1976. Boumediène died in 1978 and was succeeded by Chadli Bendjedid.

A new constitution agreed by referendum in 1989 moved Algeria towards a pluralist system. However, the 1991 legislative elections were abandoned in anticipation of the success of the opposition Islamic Salvation Front

(FIS), which had campaigned on a radical 'Islamist' platform. The Army forced President Bendjedid to resign and a military-backed Higher Committee of State (HCS), headed by former FLN veteran Mohammed Boudiaf, took power. The HCS declared a state of emergency in 1992 which was extended indefinitely in 1993. In 1992, the FIS was banned but continued to operate covertly and was suspected of assassinating Boudiaf in June 1992.

In 1993–4 the HCS and armed forces attempted unsuccessfully to reach agreement with non-Islamic political parties on a common anti-Islamic front. A national reconciliation conference in January 1994 was boycotted by the FIS and other political parties, but nevertheless it appointed General Liamine Zeroual as President to replace the HCS, which disbanded itself. Zeroual was elected President for a five-year term in November 1995. In May 1996 he proposed constitutional reforms which would limit the president to two terms in office, establish a supreme court and bicameral legislature, and ban religious and ethnic militant groups from politics. Legislative elections are due to be held in early 1997.

Insurgency

Since the abortive elections in 1992, the FIS-backed Islamic Salvation Army (AIS) and the more extreme Armed Islamic Group (GIA) have waged an armed campaign against the military regime in favour of an Islamic state. The two groups have targeted the military and security forces, their secular supporters in the population, and foreign expatriates; the military has killed and detained thousands of Islamic militants and sentenced hundreds to death. Some 40,000 have died in the fighting so far, including 97 foreigners.

Head of State
President, Gen. Liamine Zeroual, *elected* November 1995

Government *as at June 1996*
Prime Minister, Ahmed Ouyahia
Foreign Affairs, Ahmed Attaf
Justice, Mohammed Adami
Interior, Local Communities, Environment, Mustapha Benmansour
Finance, Ahmed Benbitour
Industry and Restructuring, Mourad Benachenhou
Energy and Mines, Amar Makhloufi
War Veterans, Said Abadou
National Education, Slimane Chikh
Communications and Culture, Mihoub Mihoubi
Higher Education and Scientific Research, Boubakeurr Benbouzid
Agriculture and Fisheries, Noureddine Bahbouh
Health, Yahia Guidoum
Social Affairs and Vocational Training, Hacene Laskri
Posts and Telecommunications, Mohand Salah Youyou
Religious Affairs, Ahmed Merani
Housing, Kamel Hakimi
Equipment and Urban Planning, Smain Dine
Housing, Kemal Hakimi
Youth and Sports, Mouldi Aissaoui
Small and Medium-Sized Enterprises, Abdelkader Hamitou
Commerce, Abdelkrim Harchaoui
Tourism and Handicrafts, Abdelaziz Ben Mhidi
Transport, Essaid Bendakir

ALGERIAN EMBASSY
54 Holland Park, London WII 3RS
Tel 0171-221 7800
Ambassador Extraordinary and Plenipotentiary, HE Ahmed
Benyamina, apptd 1996

BRITISH EMBASSY
7 Chemin des Glycines,
BP08, Alger-Gare 16000, Algiers
Tel: Algiers 692411
Ambassador Extraordinary and Plenipotentiary, HE Peter
Marshall, CMG, apptd 1995

DEFENCE

Algeria has a total active armed forces strength of 121,700
personnel, of which 90,000 are conscripts. Conscripts serve
only in the Army and for a period of 18 months.
The Army has a strength of 105,000 (90,000 conscripts)
with 960 main battle tanks, 1,375 armoured personnel
carriers and armoured infantry fighting vehicles, and 590
artillery pieces.
The Navy has a strength of 6,700. It is equipped with two
submarines, three frigates and 22 patrol and coastal vessels.
The Air Force has a strength of 10,000 personnel with 170
combat aircraft and 60 armed helicopters.
There are 41,200 personnel in the paramilitary Gendarmerie and National Security Forces.

ECONOMY

From 1965 to 1989 the economy was centrally planned and
state-controlled in most sectors. Economic reform, begun
in 1987, was speeded up in 1988 and now includes
industrial and financial sectors. In April 1994 the government finally accepted full economic reform and liberalization under a reform programme agreed with the IMF to
gain US$1,000 million necessary for balance of payments
support. The government has cut the budget deficit,
devalued the currency and freed price controls. In 1995,
the economy registered growth of 3.6 per cent of GDP,
although inflation remained above 30 per cent a year and
unemployment at 25 per cent. In April 1995 the IMF lent
Algeria a further US$1,800 million towards restructuring
the economy.
The main industry is the hydrocarbons industry. Oil and
natural gas are pumped from the Sahara to terminals on the
coast before being exported; the gas is first liquefied at
liquefaction plants at Skikda and Arzew, although pipelines serve Libya and Italy direct.
Other major industries include a steel industry, motor
vehicles, building materials, paper making, chemical
products and metal manufactures. Most major industrial
enterprises are still under state control.

TRADE WITH UK	1994	1995
Imports from UK	£47,257,000	£64,277,000
Exports to UK	182,853,000	244,279,000

Exports are worth around US$12,000 million annually,
mainly from crude oil and liquefied natural gas. The
country's external debt is US$29,500 million, which was
rescheduled with IMF agreement in May 1995 to halve the
debt service ratio.

COMMUNICATIONS

Algeria has a rapidly expanding network of roads and
railways. Considerable sums are also being spent on the
development of the state airline, the national shipping
company and telecommunications.

ANDORRA
Principat d'Andorra

A small, neutral principality formed by a treaty in 1278,
Andorra is situated on the southern slopes of the Pyrenees
between Spain and France. It is surrounded by mountains
of 6,500 to 10,000 feet. It has an approximate area of 175 sq.
miles (468 sq. km), and population (estimate 1994) of
84,311, less than one-quarter of whom are native Andor-
rans. The official language of the country is Catalan, but
French and Spanish (Castilian) are also spoken. The
established religion is Roman Catholicism.

CAPITAL – Andorra la Vella (population 22,821).
CURRENCY – French francs and Spanish pesetas are both in
use.
FLAG – Three vertical bands, blue, yellow, red; Andorran
coat of arms frequently imposed on central (yellow)
band but not essential.
NATIONAL DAY – 8 September.

GOVERNMENT

Under a new constitution promulgated in May 1993,
Andorra became an independent, democratic parliamentary co-principality, with sovereignty vested in the people
rather than in the two co-princes, as was previously the
case. The constitution enables Andorra to establish an
independent judiciary for the first time and to carry out its
own foreign policy, whilst its people may now join trade
unions and political parties. The two co-princes, the
President of the French Republic and the Spanish Bishop
of Urgel, remain heads of state but now only have the
power to veto treaties with France and Spain which affect
the state's borders and security. The co-princes are
represented by Permanent Delegates of whom one is the
French Prefect of the Pyrenees Orientales Department at
Perpignan and the other is the Spanish Vicar-General of
the Diocese of Urgel. They are in turn represented in
Andorra la Vella by two resident Viguiers known as the
Viguier Français and the Viguier Episcopal.
Andorra has a unicameral legislature of 28 members
known as the *Consell General de las Valls d'Andorra* (Valleys of
Andorra General Council). Fourteen members are elected
on a national list basis and 14 in seven dual-member
constituencies based on Andorra's seven parishes. The
Council appoints the head of the executive government,
who designates the members of his government.
The first elections under the new constitution were held
in December 1993, and on 20 January 1994 the first
sovereign government of Andorra took office.

Viguier Français, Jean Ive Caullet
Viguier Episcopal, Nemesi Marqués

EXECUTIVE COUNCIL *as at June 1996*
President, Marc Forné Molné
Foreign Affairs, Manel Mas Ribó
Economy, Joan Tomàs Roca
Finance, Susagna Arasanz Serra
Social Affairs and Culture, Pere Canturri Montanya
Education, Youth and Sports, Carme Sala Sansa
Territorial Administration, Lluis Montanya Tarrés
Interior, Olivier Montel Monteret
Health, Josep Maria Goicoechea Utrillo
Sindic (President) of General Council, Josep Dalleres

ANDORRAN DELEGATION, 63 Westover Road, London
SW18 2RF. Tel: 0181-874 4806

BRITISH AMBASSADOR – HE David Brighty, CMG, CVO, resident at Madrid

ECONOMY

The estimated national revenue (1993) was US$1,005 million, with a per capita income of US$15,411.

Potatoes are produced in the highlands and tobacco in the valleys. The mountain slopes have been developed for skiing, and it is estimated that 10 million tourists visit the valleys during the year. The economy is largely based on tourism, banking, commerce, tobacco, construction and forestry; a third of the country is classified as forest, in which pine, fir, oak, birch and box-tree predominate. Andorra has negotiated a customs union with the European Union which came into force in 1991. The economy is now diversifying rapidly into offshore financial services.

TRADE WITH UK	1994	1995
Imports from UK	£12,070,000	£13,043,000
Exports to UK	298,000	8,000

COMMUNICATIONS

A road into the valleys from Spain is open all year round, and that from France is closed only occasionally in winter. An airport at Seo d'Urgell just outside Andorra provides limited air connections. There are two radio stations in Andorra, one privately owned and Radio Andorra, operated by the government.

ANGOLA
República de Angola

Angola, which has an area of 481,354 sq. miles (1,246,700 sq. km), lies on the western coast of Africa. To the north and east lies Zaïre, to the east Zambia and to the south Namibia. The enclave of Cabinda is separated from the rest of Angola by Zaïre and also borders on the Congo. The population in 1993 was estimated by the UN at 10,276,000.

CAPITAL – ΨLuanda, population estimate 1993, 3,000,000.

CURRENCY – New Kwanza (Kz) of 100 lwei.

FLAG – Red and black with a yellow star, machete and cogwheel.

NATIONAL ANTHEM – Angola Avante.

NATIONAL DAY – 11 November (Independence Day).

GOVERNMENT

After a Portuguese presence of five centuries, and an anticolonial war since 1961, Angola became independent on 11 November 1975 in the midst of civil war. Soviet-Cuban military assistance to the Popular Movement for the Liberation of Angola (MPLA) enabled it to defeat its rivals early in 1976. However, the MPLA government remained under pressure from the National Union for the Total Independence of Angola (UNITA) guerrilla movement (led by Dr Jonas Savimbi) which by the mid-1980s was operating freely. In 1988 a cease-fire between South African, Cuban and Angolan forces took place and an agreement providing for the withdrawal of South African and Cuban troops by July 1991 was signed. A peace agreement was signed between the government and UNITA in 1991, and multiparty legislative and presidential elections took place in 1992, with the MPLA and its leader, Dos Santos, winning. UNITA refused to accept the results and the civil war resumed in 1993.

Fighting continued throughout most of 1993 and 1994, until UNITA and the MPLA government signed a peace

agreement (the Lusaka Protocol) under UN mediation in November 1994. By this stage UNITA's position had significantly deteriorated, so that it controlled only 20 per cent of the country and no major towns or cities. The process of demobilization of rebel forces proceeded slowly in 1995 and early 1996 despite the arrival of the UN operation (UNAVEM III), which was renewed, expanded and given a fresh mandate in February 1995. Dos Santos and Savimbi met on several occasions and agreed to form a 90,000-strong national army and a government of national unity by July 1996. Savimbi consented to serve as one of two vice-presidents in the new government.

The MPLA, formerly a Marxist-Leninist party, was the sole legal party until early 1991 when a multiparty system was adopted. The constitution declares Angola to be a democratic state and provides for a President, who appoints a Council of Ministers to assist him, and a 220-member National Assembly. The present MPLA-dominated government also includes several minor parties and was sworn in after the elections in November 1992. The Council of Ministers was dismissed in March 1996 and had not been reappointed at time of going to press.

SECESSION

In the northern enclave of Cabinda, the Front for the Liberation of the Cabinda Enclave (FLEC) fought a 20-year war of independence until the signing of a cease-fire with the government in September 1995, which was followed by the initialling of a peace agreement in April 1996. Cabinda is rich in oil and is separated from the rest of Angola by Zaïre.

HEAD OF STATE
President, José Eduardo Dos Santos, *re-elected* 30 September 1992

EMBASSY OF ANGOLA
98 Park Lane, London WIY 3TA
Tel 0171-495 1752
Ambassador Extraordinary and Plenipotentiary, HE Añtonio DaCosta Fernandes, apptd 1993

BRITISH EMBASSY
Rua Diogo Cão 4 (Caixa Postal 1244), Luanda
Tel: Luanda 334582
Ambassador Extraordinary and Plenipotentiary, HE Roger Hart, apptd 1995

DEFENCE

Under the 1994 Lusaka Protocol, UNITA's 75,000 guerrillas are to be partly demobilized and partly merged with government forces to form a 90,000-strong national army, which was due to be established before July 1996.

Existing government forces number 82,000. The Army has 75,000 personnel with 200 main battle tanks, 150 armoured infantry fighting vehicles and armoured personnel carriers and 300 artillery pieces. The Navy has a strength of 2,000 with 17 patrol and coastal craft. The Air Force has a strength of 5,500 personnel with 109 combat aircraft and 40 armed helicopters. There are 40,000 paramilitary internal security police.

ECONOMY

The government is attempting to reform the socialist economy by free market reforms but is making little progress, with high inflation and a collapsing economy, together with the loss of most diamond-producing areas to UNITA. The total foreign debt in 1994 was US$10,000 million. In September 1995, international donors pledged US$1 billion in aid.

Angola has valuable oil and diamond deposits and exports of these two commodities account for over 90 per cent of total exports.

Principal agricultural crops are cassava, maize, bananas, coffee, palm oil and kernels, cotton and sisal. Coffee, sisal, maize and palm oil are exported; exports also include mahogany and other hardwoods from the tropical rain forests in the north of the country.

TRADE WITH UK	1994	1995
Imports from UK	£23,681,000	£29,387,000
Exports to UK	12,173,000	22,408,000

ANTIGUA AND BARBUDA
State of Antigua and Barbuda

Antigua and Barbuda comprises the islands of Antigua (108 sq. miles (279 sq. km)), Barbuda (62 sq. miles (160 sq. km)) 25 miles north of Antigua, and Redonda (½sq. mile (1.2 sq. km)) 25 miles south-west of Antigua. Antigua is part of the Leeward Islands in the eastern Caribbean and lies 17° 3′ N. and 61° 48′ W. It is distinguished from the rest of the Leeward group by its absence of high hills and forest, and a drier climate than most of the West Indies. Barbuda, formerly a possession of the Codrington family, is very flat, mainly scrub-covered, with a large lagoon.

The total population (official census 1991) is 65,962; Antigua had a population of 64,562, Barbuda 1,400, and Redonda was uninhabited.

CAPITAL – ΨSt John's. Population, 30,000. The town of Barbuda is Codrington.

CURRENCY – East Caribbean dollar (EC$) of 100 cents.

FLAG – Red with an inverted triangle divided black over blue over white, with a rising gold sun on the white band.

NATIONAL ANTHEM – Fair Antigua and Barbuda.

NATIONAL DAY – 1 November (Independence Day).

GOVERNMENT

Antigua was first settled by the English in 1632, and was granted to Lord Willoughby by Charles II. It became internally self-governing in 1967 and fully independent on 1 November 1981, as a constitutional monarchy with The Queen as Head of State, represented by the Governor-General. There is a Senate of 17 appointed members and a House of Representatives of 17 members elected every five years. The Attorney-General may be appointed.

The Antigua Labour party won the general election of March 1994 and a fifth successive term of office with 11 seats in the House of Representatives compared to five seats for the United Progressive Party.

Governor-General, HE Sir James Carlisle, GCMG

CABINET *as at June 1996*

Prime Minister, Foreign Affairs, Social Affairs, Hon. Lester Bird

Justice, Legal Affairs and Attorney-General, Hon. Clare Roberts

Public Utilities, Public Works, Energy, Hon. Robin Yearwood

Agriculture, Lands, Fisheries, Planning and Co-operatives, Hon. John St Luce

Labour and Home Affairs, Hon. Adolphus Freeland

Trade, Industry, Commerce, Consumer Affairs, Hon. Hilroy Humphreys

Finance and Social Security, Molwyn Joseph

Tourism, Culture, Environment, Dr Rodney Williams

Education, Youth, Sports, Community Development, Hon. Bernard Percival

Prime Minister's Office, Hon. Henderson Simon

Health and Civil Service Affairs, Hon. Samuel Aymer

HIGH COMMISSION FOR ANTIGUA AND BARBUDA
15 Thayer Street, London WIM 5LD
Tel 0171-486 7073
High Commissioner, HE Ronald Sanders, apptd 1995

BRITISH HIGH COMMISSION
11 Old Parham Road (PO 483), St John's
Tel: St John's 462 0008/9
High Commissioner, HE Emrys Thomas Davies, CMG, resident at Bridgetown, Barbados
Resident Representative, M. Maxwell, MVO (*Acting High Commissioner*)

ECONOMY

Tourism is the main sector of the economy. Tourism and related services account for 60 per cent of GDP and employ 40 per cent of the workforce.

For many years sugar was the dominant crop but is no longer produced. Agricultural production includes livestock, sea island cotton, mixed market gardening and fishing.

FINANCE	1992*	1993*
Revenue	EC$251,331,799	EC$255,893,891
Expenditure (recurrent)	278,084,340	306,663,306
*estimated		

TRADE WITH UK	1994	1995
Imports from UK	£24,177,000	£23,272,000
Exports to UK	2,166,000	1,517,000

ARGENTINA
República Argentina

Argentina occupies the greater portion of the southern part of the South American continent, and extends from Bolivia to Cape Horn, a total distance of nearly 2,300 miles; its greatest breadth is about 930 miles. It is bounded on the north by Bolivia, on the north-east by Paraguay, Brazil and Uruguay, on the south-east and south by the Atlantic, on the west by Chile, from which it is separated by the Cordillera de los Andes. On the west the mountainous Cordilleras, with their plateaux, extend from the northern to the southern boundaries; on the east are the great plains. The area is 1,073,512 sq. miles (2,780,400 sq. km.), with a population (census 1991) of 32,370,298. The language is Spanish.

CAPITAL – ΨBuenos Aires, population (1991), metropolitan area 2,960,976; with suburbs, 10,686,163. Other large towns are: ΨRosario (894,645), Córdoba (1,148,305), ΨLa Plata (640,344), ΨMar del Plata (519,707), San Miguel de Tucumán (622,348), and Mendoza (773,559).

CURRENCY – Peso.

FLAG – Horizontal bands of blue, white, blue; gold sun in centre of white band.

NATIONAL ANTHEM – ¡Oid Mortales! (Hear, oh mortals!).

NATIONAL DAY – 25 May.

GOVERNMENT

The estuary of La Plata was discovered in 1515 by Juan Díaz de Solís and the region was subsequently colonized by the Spanish. Spain ruled the territory from the 16th century until 1810, when Spanish rule was defied. In 1816, after a long campaign of liberation conducted by General José de San Martín, the independence of Argentina was declared by the Congress of Tucumán.

President Juan Domingo Perón was overthrown in 1955, and there followed 18 years of political and economic instability until 1973 when he was recalled from exile. Perón died within a year and was succeeded by his widow, Vice-President María Estela Martínez de Perón. However, warring factions in the Perónist movement and increasing terrorist activity led to a coup and the establishment of a military junta in 1976. Following the Falkland Islands defeat in 1982 the President, Gen. Galtieri, resigned and the Army appointed Gen. Bignone as President. Elections for a civilian government were held in 1983 and a civilian President was elected. Presidential elections in 1989 were won by the Justicialist Party (Perónist) candidate Carlos Menem.

The 1853 constitution was amended by constitutional assembly in 1994. Power is vested in the President who appoints the Cabinet and is directly elected for a once-renewable four-year term. A presidential candidate must win at least 45 per cent of the vote, or 40 per cent with a 10 per cent lead over the nearest challenger, to gain victory. The legislature consists of a 72-member (three for each province) Senate and a 259-member Chamber of Deputies. A third of the Senate is elected every three years and half of the Chamber of Deputies is elected every two years. Senators serve for a nine-year term and Deputies for a four-year term. After the most recent elections in May 1995 the Justicialist Party held 135 seats in the Chamber of Deputies.

The republic is divided into 23 provinces, each with an elected Governor and legislature, and one federal district (Buenos Aires), with an elected mayor and autonomous government.

HEAD OF STATE
President, Dr Carlos Saúl Menem, *elected* May 1989, *re-elected* 14 May 1995
Vice-President, Dr Carlos Ruckauf

CABINET *as at June 1996*
Interior, Carlos Corach
Foreign Affairs, Dr Guido Di Tella
Labour, Armando Caro-Figueroa
Economy and Public Works, Dr Domingo Cavallo
Education and Culture, Susana Decibe
Defence, Dr Oscar Camillión
Health and Social Welfare, Dr Alberto Mazza
Justice, vacant

EMBASSY OF THE ARGENTINE REPUBLIC
53 Hans Place, London SWIX OLA
Tel 0171-584 6494
Ambassador Extraordinary and Plenipotentiary, HE Rogelio Pfirter, apptd 1995
Defence Attaché, Col. Hector José Gallardo
Minister (Economic and Commercial Affairs), Armando Maffei

BRITISH EMBASSY
Dr Luis Agote 2412, 1425 Buenos Aires
Tel: Buenos Aires 803-7070/1
Ambassador Extraordinary and Plenipotentiary, HE Sir Peter Hall, KBE, CMG, apptd 1994
Deputy Ambassador, Minister and Consul-General, David Reddaway, CMG
Defence and Military Attaché, Col. R. J. Lawson
First Secretary (Commercial), H. Wiles
Cultural Attaché and British Council Representative, Michael Potter, Marcelo T. de Alvear 590, 1058 Buenos Aires

BRITISH CHAMBER OF COMMERCE, Av. Corrientes 457, 10 piso, 1043 Buenos Aires

ECONOMY

The Menem government introduced an economic reform programme in 1991 involving the privatization of most state-owned industries, widespread deregulation, exchange-rate stabilization and lower trade barriers. This has led to economic growth (33 per cent of GDP in 1990–4), increased foreign investment (US$17 billion in 1993) and much lower inflation (5 per cent annually in 1994–5).

Argentina's foreign debt has been reduced from US$50,000 million in 1988 to US$32,000 million in 1995 by an April 1993 debt reduction agreement with creditors and by privatization receipts. Despite an austerity programme introduced in April 1995 in the wake of the Mexican economic crisis, the pace of growth slowed in 1995–6, unemployment remained high at 18.6 per cent in 1995, but inflation was under 5 per cent.

AGRICULTURE
Of a total land area of about 700 million acres, farmland occupies 425 million, of which 60 per cent is pasture, 10 per cent annual crops, 5 per cent permanent crops and the remaining 25 per cent forest and wasteland. A large proportion of the land is still held in large estates devoted to cattle raising but the number of small farms is increasing. The principal crops are wheat, maize, oats, barley, rye, linseed, sunflower seed, alfalfa, sugar, fruit and cotton. Argentina is pre-eminent in the production of beef, mutton and wool, and pastoral and agricultural products provide about 85 per cent of Argentina's exports.

MINERAL PRODUCTION
Oil is found in various parts of the republic and the production of oil is of great importance. Total petroleum output for 1991 was 484,000 b.p.d. There is a refinery in San Lorenzo (Santa Fé province). Natural gas is also produced in a number of provinces.

Coal, lead, zinc, tungsten, iron ore, sulphur, mica and salt are the other chief minerals being exploited. There are small worked deposits of beryllium, manganese, bismuth, uranium, antimony, copper, kaolin, arsenate, gold, silver and tin. Coal is produced at the Rio Turbio mine in the province of Santa Cruz. The output of other materials is not large but greater attention is now being paid to the development of these natural resources, especially copper, for which the government and private companies are carrying out exploration.

INDUSTRIES
Meat-packing is one of the principal industries; flour-milling, sugar-refining, and the wine industry are also important. In recent years progress has been made by the textile, plastic and machine tool industries and engineering, especially in the production of motor vehicles and steel manufactures.

TRADE WITH UK	1994	1995
Imports from UK	£224,942,000	£233,682,000
Exports to UK	170,970,000	252,265,000

COMMUNICATIONS

The 25,386 miles of railway are state-owned. Plans are in hand for complete reorganization of the railways in order to improve their operating efficiency and reduce a large financial deficit. The combined national and provincial road network totals approximately 137,000 miles of which 23,180 miles are surfaced.

DEFENCE

Total active armed forces number 67,300 personnel (18,100 conscripts). Reserves total 377,000. The Army numbers 40,400, including about 13,400 conscripts, and has 250,000 reserves.

The Navy numbers 18,000, including 3,500 conscripts and 4,000 marines, with a further 77,000 reserves. The Air Force has a strength of 8,900 (1,200 conscripts) with 50,000 reserves. There is a paramilitary gendarmeric of 18,000 personnel under Ministry of Defence control.

EDUCATION

Education is compulsory for the seven grades of primary school (six to 13). Secondary schools (14 to 17+) are available in and around Buenos Aires and in most of the important towns in the interior of the country. Most secondary schools are administered by the Central Ministry of Education in Buenos Aires, while primary schools are administered by the Central Ministry or by Provincial Ministries of Education. Private schools, of which there are many, are also loosely controlled by the Central Ministry. The total number of universities is over 50 with 24 national, 25 private and a small number of provincial universities.

CULTURE

The literature of Spain is part of the culture. There is little indigenous literature before the break from Spain, but all branches have flourished since the latter half of the 19th century. About 450 daily newspapers are published in Argentina, including seven major ones in the city of Buenos Aires. The English language newspaper is the *Buenos Aires Herald* (daily). There are several other foreign language newspapers.

ARMENIA

Hayastany Hanrapetoutioun

Armenia has an area of 11,306 sq. miles (29,800 sq. km) and lies between the Black and Caspian Seas, occupying the south-western part of the Caucasus region of the former Soviet Union. It is bordered on the east and south-west by Azerbaijan, on the north by Georgia, on the south by Iran and on the west by Turkey. It is very mountainous, consisting of several vast tablelands surrounded by ridges. The climate is continental, dry and cold, but the Ararat valley has a long, hot and dry summer.

The population (1996 estimate) is 3,754,000, concentrated in the low-lying part of Armenia, the Ararat valley and the Yerevan hollow. Armenians form 93.8 per cent of the population, Kurds 1.7 per cent and Russians 1.6 per cent. Azerbaijanis formed 2.6 per cent of the population, but most fled or were expelled after the outbreak of war with Azerbaijan. There are also Ukrainians, Greeks and Assyrians. The Armenian diaspora numbers some 5,300,000, including 1,500,000 in the former Soviet states, one million in the USA and 400,000 in France.

Armenian is the official language, though Russian is widely spoken and understood. The main religion is Armenian Orthodox Christian (Armenian Church centred in Etchmiadzin). Armenia adopted Christianity as its official religion in AD 301, the first state in the world to do so.

CAPITAL – Yerevan. Population 1,254,000 (1990).
CURRENCY – Dram of 100 louma.

FLAG – Three horizontal stripes of red, blue and orange.
NATIONAL DAY – 21 September (Independence Day).

GOVERNMENT

Armenia was first unified in 95 BC but was divided between the Persian and Byzantine Empires in AD 387 and then conquered in the 11th century by the Seljuk Turks and the Mongols. In the 16th century most of Armenia was incorporated into the Ottoman Empire. In 1639 the country was divided again, the eastern-most portions, now the republic of Armenia, becoming part of the Persian Empire. In 1828 eastern Armenia became part of the Russian Empire while western Armenia remained under Ottoman rule. The Ottomans launched pogroms against the Armenians from 1894 onwards, and in 1915 to 1918 massacred 1,500,000 Armenians.

Armenia declared its independence on 28 May 1918, but was crushed and divided between Turkish and Soviet forces in 1920, with the area under Soviet control proclaimed a Soviet Socialist Republic on 29 November 1920. The Soviet government was overthrown by a nationalist revolt in 1921 but reinstated by the Red Army a few months later. In early 1922 Armenia acceded to the USSR.

In 1987, demonstrations against industrial pollution and local Communist Party corruption developed into political opposition to Communist rule, focused by support for the self-determination of the autonomous region of Nagorny-Karabakh in Azerbaijan which has a predominantly Armenian population. The Soviet authorities were perceived as supporting Azerbaijan over Nagorny-Karabakh, and an Armenian nationalist movement evolved which swept to power in national elections in mid-1990. In a referendum in 1991, 99 per cent of the electorate voted for independence, which was declared on 21 September 1991.

The dispute between the (ethnic Armenian) Nagorno-Karabakh forces supported by Armenia and the Azeri government over Nagorny-Karabakh erupted into all-out war in May 1992, when Nagorno-Karabakh forces breached Azerbaijan's defences to form a land bridge to Armenia. By the end of summer 1992 all of Nagorny-Karabakh was under Armenian control. Continued victories over Azeri forces in 1992–3 brought all Azeri territory that separated Nagorny-Karabakh from Armenia and all mountainous Azeri territory around Nagorny-Karabakh, an estimated 10 per cent of Azeri territory, under the control of Nagorny-Karabakh Armenians. Armenia claims this territory as historically Armenian land arbitrarily given to Azerbaijan by Stalin in 1921–2. A cease-fire agreement between Armenia, Azerbaijan and Nagorny-Karabakh was reached in May 1994 and has held since.

In April 1995, a law was passed creating a 190-member National Assembly, to be elected every four years by a combined constituency and party-list system. In the first elections to the new body in July 1995, the ruling Republican coalition led by the Pan-Armenian National Movement won a majority of seats. A new constitution was approved by a referendum in July 1995.

Armenia is divided into 11 Administrative Regions.

HEAD OF STATE
President, Levon Ter-Petrosyan, *elected* 16 October 1991

CABINET *as at June 1996*
Prime Minister, Grant Bagratian
Interior, Vanik Sirodegyan
Foreign Affairs, Vagan Papazian
Defence, Vazgen Sargsyan

Finance, Levon Barhudaryan
Culture, Hakob Movses
Environment, Souren Avetissian
Industry, Ashot Safarian
Transport, Genrikh Kochinyan
Urban Planning and Construction, Felix Pirumyan
Economics, Vagram Avanesyan
Communications, Grigor Pokhpatyan
Information, Grach Tamrazyan
National Security, Serzh Sargsyan
Justice, Marat Alexanyan
Education and Science, Vardkes Gnuni
Public Health, Ara Babloyan
Regional Government Affairs, Ruben Barsegyan
Relations with the National Assembly, Arsen Kamalgan
*Relations with the CIS, EU and International Economic
  Organizations*, Gagik Shakhbazyan
Agriculture and Food Supplies, O. Tokmadzhan
Social Security, Employment and Refugees, Rafael Bagoyan
Trade Services and Tourism, Vagan Melkonyan
Power Industry, Gagik Martirosyan
Director, Statistics, State Register and Analysis Department,
  Eduard Agadzhanov
Director, the Department for Emergency Situations, Stephan
  Badalyan
Director, State Taxation Agency, Pavel Safryan
Secretary of Government, Sergei Manasaryan

Chairman of the Supreme Soviet, Babken Ararktsyan

EMBASSY OF THE REPUBLIC OF ARMENIA
25A Cheniston Gardens, London w8 6TG
Tel 0171-938 5415
Ambassador Extraordinary and Plenipotentiary, HE Dr Armen
  Sarkissian, apptd 1993

BRITISH EMBASSY
Armenia Hotel, 1 Vramshapouh Akra Str, Yerevan 375010
Ambassador Extraordinary and Plenipotentiary, HE David
  Miller, OBE, apptd 1995

DEFENCE

Armenia maintains an army of 51,800 regular personnel,
including conscripts who serve 18-month terms, and
paramilitary forces of some 1,000. The regular army has
101 main battle tanks, 218 armoured personnel carriers and
armoured infantry fighting vehicles, 225 artillery pieces,
six combat aircraft and seven armed helicopters.

Russia maintains 5,000 army personnel in Armenia. An
agreement on military co-operation with Russia was
signed in May 1996 which paved the way for joint military
exercises. A protocol was also signed on the establishment
of coalition troops in Transcaucasia and the planned use of
Russian and Armenian armed forces as part of coalition
troops in cases of mutual interest.

ECONOMY

The Armenian economy has been badly affected by the
1988 earthquake which devastated much of the country,
and by the Azeri and Turkish economic embargos which
have been in place since 1988. The main trade and
transportation routes now lie via Georgia and Iran.

Armenia has a strong agricultural sector in low-lying
areas, where industrial and fruit crops are grown. Grain is
grown in the hills and the country is also noted for its wine
and brandy. There are large copper ore and molybdenum
deposits and other minerals. The country also has developed chemicals, industrial vehicles and textiles
industries.

The government introduced a programme of economic
reforms in November 1994 with IMF support, including

the liberalization of prices, stabilization of the currency,
privatization, and reducing the budget deficit.

TRADE WITH UK	1994	1995
Imports from UK	£4,371,000	£918,000
Exports to UK	27,000	173,000

CULTURE

The Armenian alphabet was established in AD 405. Major
writers include the poets Frick (13th century), Nahapet
Kuchak (16th century) and Sayat-Nova (18th century).
The composer Aram Khachaturian (1903–78) was
Armenian.

AUSTRALIA
The Commonwealth of Australia

AREA AND POPULATION*

States and Territories	Area (sq. km)	Resident population 30 September 1995p
New South Wales (NSW)	801,600	6,135,000
Queensland (Qld.)	1,727,200	3,297,900
South Australia (SA)	984,000	1,474,700
Tasmania (Tas.)	67,800	473,300
Victoria (Vic.)	227,600	4,511,100
Western Australia (WA)	2,525,500	1,740,100
Australian Capital Territory (ACT)	2,400	304,900
Northern Territory (NT)	1,346,200	174,700
Total	7,682,300	18,114,000

* estimated
p preliminary

POPULATION OF ABORIGINAL AND TORRES STRAIT
ISLANDER ORIGIN (*1991 census*)

	Number	% of state population
New South Wales	70,019	1.20
Queensland	70,124	2.40
South Australia	16,232	1.14
Tasmania	8,885	0.20
Victoria	16,735	0.40
Western Australia	41,779	2.54
Australian Capital Territory	1,775	0.63
Northern Territory	39,916	22.70
Total	265,459	1.60

BIRTHS, DEATHS, MARRIAGES AND DIVORCES
Year ended 30 June

	1994	1995p
Births	259,359	257,706
Deaths	123,918	125,771
Marriages	110,716	111,063
Divorces	47,759	48,779

p preliminary

MIGRATION *year ended 30 June*

	1994	1995
Permanent arrivals	69,770	87,430
Permanent departures	27,280	26,950

GEOGRAPHY

Australia is a continent in the southern hemisphere. The
western half of the continent consists mainly of a great
plateau 300–600 metres in altitude. The interior lowland

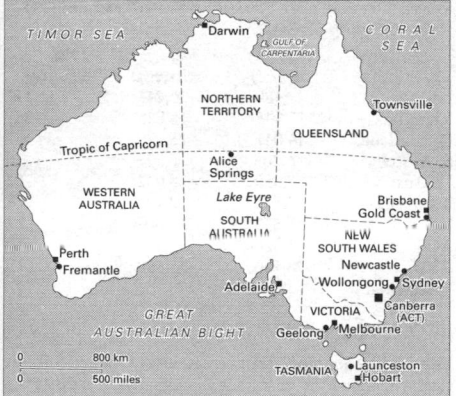

includes the channel country of south-west Queensland (drainage to Lake Eyre) and the Murray-Darling river system to the south. The eastern uplands consist of a broad belt of varied width extending from north Queensland to Tasmania and composed largely of tablelands, ranges and ridges with only a few mountain areas above 1,000 metres. The highest point is Mt. Kosciusko (2,228 m) and the lowest, Lake Eyre (–15 m).

Climatic conditions range from the alpine to the tropical. Two-thirds of the continent is arid or semi-arid although good rainfalls (over 800 mm annually) occur in the northern monsoonal belt and along the eastern and southern highland regions. Fifty per cent of Australia has a medium rainfall of less than 300 mm per year and 80 per cent has less than 600 mm. The effectiveness of the rainfall is greatly reduced by marked alternations of wet and dry seasons, unreliability from year to year, high temperatures and high potential evaporation.

FEDERAL CAPITAL – Canberra, in the Australian Capital Territory. Estimated population at 30 June 1994 was 328,000. It has been the seat of government since 1927. The Australian Capital Territory was surrendered by New South Wales to the Commonwealth Government in 1911.

CURRENCY – Australian dollar ($A) of 100 cents.

FLAG – The British Blue Ensign with five stars of the Southern Cross in the fly and the white Commonwealth Star of seven points beneath the Union Flag.

NATIONAL ANTHEM – Advance Australia Fair.

NATIONAL DAY – 26 January (Australia Day).

GOVERNMENT

The continent of Australia was discovered in the 18th century and was colonized by the British, initially as a penal colony. The Commonwealth of Australia was inaugurated on 1 January 1901, at which time Australia gained dominion status within the British Empire. Australia became independent within the British Commonwealth by the 1931 Statute of Westminster.

The government is that of a federal Commonwealth within the British Commonwealth, the executive power being vested in the Sovereign (through the Governor-General), assisted by a federal government. Under the constitution the federal government has acquired and may acquire certain defined powers as surrendered by the states, residuary legislative power remaining with the states. The right of a state to legislate on any matter is not abrogated except in connection with matters exclusively under federal control, but where a state law is inconsistent with a law of the Commonwealth the latter prevails to the extent of the inconsistency.

The 1993 Native Title Act restores land rights to the Aborigines which were lost after British settlement, establishing a system of tribunals that may give land title to indigenous people who can show customary use over the land.

GOVERNOR-GENERAL

Governor-General, HE Hon. Sir William Deane, AC, KBE, *assumed office* 16 February 1996

CABINET *as at July 1996*

Prime Minister, Hon. John Howard
Deputy Prime Minister, Trade, Hon. Tim Fischer
Treasurer, Hon. Peter Costello
Primary Industries and Energy, Hon. John Anderson
Leader of the Government in the Senate, Environment, Senator Hon. Robert Hill
Communications, Senator Hon. Richard Alston
Leader of the House, Industrial Relations, Hon. Peter Reith
Social Security, Minister Assisting the Prime Minister for the Status of Women, Senator Hon. Jocelyn Newman
Foreign Affairs, Hon. Alexander Downer
Industry, Science and Tourism, Hon. John Moore
Defence, Hon. Ian McLachlan
Transport and Regional Development, Hon. John Sharp
Health and Family Services, Hon. Dr Michael Wooldridge
Finance, Hon. John Fahey
Employment, Education, Training and Youth Affairs, Senator Hon. Amanda Vanstone

AUSTRALIAN HIGH COMMISSION

Australia House, Strand, London WC2B 4LA
Tel 0171-379 4334
High Commissioner, HE Hon. Neal Blewett, apptd 1994
Deputy High Commissioner, R. McGovern
Ministers, I. Wilcock (*Political*); R. Murray (*Economic*);
     D. Richard (*Commercial*); M. Fitzpatrick (*Industry, Science and Technology*)
Defence Adviser and Head of Defence Staff, Brig. P. L. McGuiness
Consul-General, Ms J. Harrhy (*Manchester*)

BRITISH HIGH COMMISSION

Commonwealth Avenue, Yarralumla, Canberra, ACT 2600
Tel: Canberra 270 6666
High Commissioner, HE Sir Roger John Carrick, KCMG, LVO, apptd 1995
Deputy High Commissioner, Head of Chancery, D. W. Fall
Counsellor, T. H. Byrne (*Director, Trade Promotion*)
Defence and Naval Adviser and Head of British Defence Liaison Staff, Cdre P. C. Wykeham-Martin, RN
Consuls-General, J. C. Durham, LVO (*Brisbane*); G. Finlayson (*Melbourne*); A. J. Abott (*Perth*); P. Morrice (*Sydney*)
Cultural Adviser and British Council Representative, J. Potts, OBE, Edgecliff Centre, 401/203 New South Head Road (PO Box 88), Edgecliff, Sydney, NSW 2027

LEGISLATURE

Parliament consists of The Queen, the Senate and the House of Representatives. The constitution provides that the number of members of the House of Representatives shall be, as nearly as practicable, twice the number of senators. Members of the Senate are elected for six years by universal suffrage, half the members retiring every third year. Each of the six states returns 12 senators, and the Australian Capital Territory and the Northern Territory two each. The House of Representatives, similarly elected for a maximum of three years, contains members proportionate to the population, with a minimum of five members for each state. There are now 148 members in the House of Representatives, including one member for the Northern Territory and two for the Australian Capital Territory.

President of the Senate, Senator Hon. Kerry Sibraa
Speaker, House of Representatives, Hon. Stephen Martin, MP

JUDICATURE

The High Court, composed of a Chief Justice and six Justices, exercises jurisdiction over all matters arising from the constitution, all matters arising between the states and between residents of different states, matters to which the Commonwealth of Australia is a party, and treaties and foreign representatives in Australia. The High Court also hears appeals from the Federal Court and from the Supreme Courts of states and territories.

The Federal Court of Australia was established in 1977 as a superior court of record. It has jurisdiction over important industrial, trade practices, intellectual property, administrative law and bankruptcy matters. It also acts as a court of appeal for decisions from the Australian Capital Territory Supreme Court and certain decisions of state Supreme Courts exercising federal jurisdiction.

Each state has its own judicature of supreme, superior and minor courts for criminal and civil cases.

Chief Justice of the High Court of Australia, Hon. Sir Gerard Brennan, AC, KBE
Chief Justice of the Federal Court of Australia, Hon. M. E. J. Black
Chief Justice of the Australian Capital Territory, Hon. J. A. Miles

DEFENCE

The total active armed forces number 56,100 personnel, with reserves numbering 38,250 personnel. All service is voluntary. The Army has a strength of 23,700 and has 28,900 reserves. Equipment includes 90 main battle tanks, 786 armoured personnel carriers and armoured infantry fighting vehicles, 383 artillery pieces, 22 aircraft and 126 helicopters, of which 25 are armed.

The Navy has a strength of 15,000 with a further 4,950 reservists, and has four main bases at Sydney, Cockburn Sound, Cairns and Darwin. It has four submarines, three destroyers, eight frigates and 16 patrol and coastal craft with 23 armed helicopters.

The Air Force has a strength of 17,425, together with 4,400 reserves, and 125 combat aircraft.

One Army infantry company and one Air Force detachment are stationed in Malaysia.

FINANCE

COMMONWEALTH GOVERNMENT FINANCE

Outlays and revenue of the Commonwealth Government were ($A million):

	1994–5	1995–6
Current outlays	121,602	128,913
Capital outlays	6,371	1,563
Total revenue	114,065	127,769

STATE GOVERNMENT FINANCE 1995–6* ($A million)

	Outlay (current and capital)	Revenue and grants received	Total financing
NSW	27,489	25,245	2,244
Victoria	17,945	18,825	−881
Queensland	14,041	13,979	62
S. Australia	6,205	6,575	−370
W. Australia	7,350	8,052	−702
Tasmania	2,518	2,400	118
NT	1,632	1,603	29
ACT	1,320	1,210	110
Total	78,500	77,889	611

* estimated

ECONOMY

In 1993, 59.9 per cent of land area consisted of agricultural establishments, the remainder being urban areas, state forests, mining leases and unoccupied land. Crop-growing areas constituted around 2.25 per cent of the total agricultural establishments, emphasizing the relative importance of the livestock industries (sheep in the warm, temperate, semi-arid lands and beef cattle in the tropics).

The wide range of climatic and soil conditions has resulted in a diversity of crops. Generally, cereal crops (excluding rice and sorghum) are widely grown, while other crops are confined to specific locations in a few states. However, scant or erratic rainfall, limited potential for irrigation and unsuitable soils or topography have restricted intensive agriculture.

GROSS VALUE OF AGRICULTURAL COMMODITIES 1992–3

	$A million
Crops	10,554.5
Livestock slaughterings and other disposals	6,023.5
Livestock products	5,205.3
Total agriculture	21,836.4

Significant mineral resources include bauxite, coal, copper, crude petroleum, gems, gold, ilmenite, iron ore, lead, limestone, manganese, nickel, rutile, salt, silver, tin, tungsten, uranium, zinc and zircon.

In 1993–4 the total value of all minerals produced was $A28,488 million. In 1993–4 mine production of coal was 177,874,000 tonnes, crude oil (including condensate) was 29,583 megalitres and natural gas 15,959 gigalitres. Production of principal metals in 1993–4 was (tonnes):

Iron ore	115,703,000
Copper	330,000
Lead	525,000
Gold	240

TRADE

Of total exports in the year 1994–5, the largest category was iron ore concentrates worth $A7,313 million followed by: coal, $A6,731 million; gold, $A4,623 million; and textile fibres, $A4,528 million.

The largest category of imports was transport equipment, worth $A8,268 million. This was followed by office and automatic data processing machines, $A5,414 million; road vehicles, $A4,593 million; industrial machinery $A4,063 million; and petrol and oils $A3,400 million.

	1994	1995
Imports	$A68,099m	$A77,491m
Exports	64,766m	71,548m

In 1995, 23 per cent of total exports went to Japan. The Republic of Korea received 8.5 per cent, New Zealand 7.4, USA 6.5, Singapore 5.4, Taiwan 4.6, China 4.4, Hong Kong 4 and UK 3.5.

Of total imports in 1995, 21.5 per cent came from the USA, 15.5 from Japan, 6.5 Germany, 6 UK, 5 China, 4.5 New Zealand and 3.5 Taiwan.

Trade with UK	1994	1995
Imports from UK	£1,914,442,000	£2,121,352,000
Exports to UK	1,063,253,000	1,110,118,000

COMMUNICATIONS

There are six government-owned railway systems, operated by the State Rail Authority of NSW, Victorian Railways, Queensland Government Railways, Western Australian Government Railways, the State Transport Authority of Southern Australia, and the Australian National Railways Commission. The ANRC incorporates the former Commonwealth Railways system, and the Tasmanian and non-metropolitan South Australian railways (urban rail services in Southern Australia remain the responsibility of the State Transport Authority).

THE NORTHERN TERRITORY

The Northern Territory has a total area of 519,770 sq. miles (1,346,200 sq. km), and lies between 129°–138° E. longitude and 11°–26° S. latitude. The estimated population in the Northern Territory in June 1994 was 171,134, of which about a quarter are Aboriginals.

GOVERNMENT

The administration was taken over by the Commonwealth on 1 January 1911 from the State of South Australia. The Northern Territory (Self-Government) Act 1978 established the Northern Territory as a body politic from 1 July 1978, with Ministers having control over and responsibility for Territory finances and the administration of the functions of government. Proposed laws passed by the Legislative Assembly in relation to a transferred function require the assent of the Administrator. Proposed laws in all other cases may be assented to by the Administrator or reserved by the Administrator for the Governor-General's pleasure. The Governor-General may disallow any laws assented to by the Administrator within six months of the Administrator's assent.

The Northern Territory elects one member to the federal House of Representatives and two members to the Senate.

The Aboriginal Land Rights (NT) Act of 1976 provides for the investigation and determination of Aboriginal traditional claims to vacant Crown land or land already owned by or on behalf of Aboriginals. Successful land claims to date have increased Aboriginal ownership to 42 per cent of the Northern Territory and a further 6 per cent is the subject of claims.

SEAT OF ADMINISTRATION – Darwin

Administrator, Hon. Austin Asche, AC, QC
Chief Minister, Hon. Shane Stone
Chief Justice of the Supreme Court of the Northern Territory,
 Hon. B. F. Martin

ECONOMY

Northern Territory's economy is based on the exploitation of its natural resources of minerals, land and fisheries and on tourist attractions. The agricultural and horticultural industries are also beginning to contribute an increasing amount to Territory output. The beef cattle industry continues to be the major user of pastoral lands.

Mining and energy resource development has played a major part in the development of the Northern Territory and in 1992–3 the total value of production was $A1.35 billion. The Territory is a leading uranium producer and contains 20 per cent of the developed world's low-cost uranium reserves. Large-scale production of zinc-lead concentrate commenced in 1994. In 1992–3 more than one million tonnes of manganese was sold, with a total value of about $A135 million. Gold production for 1992–3 was estimated at $A292 million. The value ex mines of bauxite sales exceeded $A131 million and alumina production was valued at $A392 million. The value of oil and gas production for 1992–3 was $A675 million.

Tourism is a major growth industry and generates over $A603 million annually.

COMMUNICATIONS

The Northern Territory has three main ports: Darwin, and the private mining ports of Gove and Groote Eylandt.

There is a standard gauge rail link between Southern Australia and Alice Springs. The link between Alice Springs and Darwin is provided by a rail-road service.

The main population centres are linked by the Stuart Highway, which connects Alice Springs to Darwin via Tennant Creek and Katherine. Most freight in the Northern Territory is moved by road trains. These are massive trucks hauling two or three trailers, having a net capacity of about 100 tonnes and measuring up to 45 metres in length.

EXTERNAL TERRITORIES

ASHMORE AND CARTIER ISLANDS

Ashmore Islands (known as Middle, East and West Islands) and Cartier Island are situated in the Indian Ocean 850 km and 790 km west of Darwin respectively. The islands are uninhabited.

Great Britain took formal possession of the Ashmores in 1878 and Cartier was annexed in 1909. In 1931 the islands were placed under the authority of the Commonwealth of Australia, and were accepted in 1933 under the name of the Territory of Ashmore and Cartier Islands. The territory is administered by the Commonwealth Government. In 1983 Ashmore Reef was declared a national nature reserve.

THE AUSTRALIAN ANTARCTIC TERRITORY

The Australian Antarctic Territory was established in 1933 by an Order in Council which placed under the government of the Commonwealth of Australia all the islands and territories, other than Adélie Land, which are situated south of the latitude 60° S. and lying between 160° E. longitude and 45° E. longitude. The Order came into force in 1936. The territory is administered by the Antarctic Division of the Department of the Environment, Sport and Territories, which, since 1948, has organized yearly expeditions to Antarctica, known as Australian National Antarctic Research Expeditions (ANARE).

Scientific research is carried out at Mawson Station in MacRobertson Land, Davis Station in Princess Elizabeth Land and Casey Station, and a station on Macquarie Island, about 900 miles north of the Antarctic Continent. Summer stations have been established at Cape Denison, Commonwealth Bay in the Bunger Hills, the Larsemann Hills, the Prince Charles Mountains, and on Heard Island.

CHRISTMAS ISLAND

Christmas Island is situated in the Indian Ocean about 1,408 km NW of North West Cape in Western Australia, and has an area of 135 sq. km. Population (1991 census) is 1,275, largely consisting of mineworkers and government employees. There is no indigenous population. The island became an Australian territory in 1958, having previously been administered as part of the colony of Singapore.

The Administrator is responsible to the Australian Minister for the Environment, Sport and Territories in Canberra. The Christmas Island Shire Council has nine elected members. The Council is responsible for municipal functions and services on the island.

The island had extensive deposits of phosphates, the extraction of which has traditionally been the major economic activity. The deposits of low grade phosphate ore are now being extracted by a private mining company, Phosphate Resources NL. The other major commercial activity is the operation of a casino and resort complex.

Administrator, M. Chilvers

COCOS (KEELING) ISLANDS

The Cocos (Keeling) Islands are two separate atolls (North Keeling Island and, 24 km to the south, the main atoll) comprising some 27 small coral islands with a total area of about 14 sq. km, situated in the Indian Ocean in latitude 12° 5' S. and longitude 96° 53' E. The main islands of the southern atoll are West Island (about 9 km in length) on which are the administrative centre, the aerodrome, and the Australia-based employees of government departments; Home Island, where the Cocos Malay community lives; Direction Island, Horsburgh and South Island. The population as at 30 June 1991 was 647.

The islands were declared a British possession in 1857. All land in the islands was granted to George Clunies-Ross and his heirs by Queen Victoria in 1886. In 1955 the islands, which had been governed through the British colonies of Ceylon (from 1878), the Straits Settlements (1886) and Singapore (1903), were accepted as a Territory of Australia. In 1978 the Australian Government purchased all Clunies-Ross land and property interests except for the family home and grounds. Between 1979 and 1984 most of the land was transferred to the Cocos (Keeling) Islands Council, the local government body established in 1979. In 1993 the federal government purchased the last of the remaining grounds.

The Cocos (Keeling) Islands Act 1955 provided the legal framework for the political and administrative arrangements in the territory. On 6 April 1984 the Cocos community, in a UN supervised Act of Self-Determination, chose to integrate with Australia. The islands are administered by the Australian Government through the Department of the Environment, Sport and Territories in Canberra.

The territory has a limited economic base. In 1986–7 the copra industry suffered severe losses and in 1987 ceased production. Tourism is being developed.

Administrator, Jarl Andersson

CORAL SEA ISLANDS TERRITORY

The Coral Sea Islands Territory lies east of Queensland between the Great Barrier Reef and longitude 156° 06' E., and between latitudes 12° and 24° S. It comprises scattered islands, spread over a sea area of 780,000 sq. km. The islands are formed mainly of coral and sand, and most are extremely small, with no permanent fresh water. There is a manned meteorological station in the Willis Group but the remaining islands are uninhabited. Large populations of sea birds breed in the area, and two national nature reserves were designated in the Territory in 1982.

The Australian Government bases its claim to the islands on numerous acts of sovereignty since early this century and enacted the Coral Sea Islands Act 1969 which declares the islands a territory of the Commonwealth of Australia. The Department of the Environment, Sport and Territories, Canberra, is responsible for the administration of the territory.

HEARD ISLAND AND McDONALD ISLANDS

The Heard and McDonald islands, about 4,100 km southwest of Fremantle, comprise all the islands and rocks lying between 52° 30' and 53° 30' S. latitude and 72° and 74° 30' E. longitude. Sovereignty over the islands was transferred by the UK to the Commonwealth of Australia in 1947. The Heard Island and McDonald Islands Act 1953 provides for the government of the islands as one territory. The islands are administered by the Department of the Environment, Sport and Territories.

NORFOLK ISLAND

Norfolk Island is situated in the South Pacific Ocean at latitude 29° 02' S. and longitude 167° 57' E. It is about 8 km long by 5 km wide, with an area of 3,455 hectares. The climate is mild and subtropical. Resident population at the 1991 census was 1,912.

The island, discovered by Captain Cook in 1774, served as a penal colony from 1788 to 1814 and 1825 to 1855. In 1856, 194 descendants of the *Bounty* mutineers accepted an invitation to leave Pitcairn and settle on Norfolk Island, which led to Norfolk Island becoming a separate settlement under the jurisdiction of the Governor of New South Wales. In 1897 Norfolk Island became a dependency of NSW and in 1914 a territory of Australia. From that date, Norfolk Island has been regarded as an integral part of Australia.

In 1979 Norfolk Island gained a substantial degree of self-government. Wide powers are exercised by a nine-member Legislative Assembly. The Act preserves the Commonwealth's responsibility for Norfolk Island as a territory under its authority, with the Minister for the Environment, Sport and Territories as the responsible Minister.

The island is a popular tourist resort, and a large proportion of the population depends on tourism and its ancillaries for employment.

The seat of government and administration offices are in Kingston.

Administrator, A. G. Kerr

AUSTRALIAN STATES

NEW SOUTH WALES

New South Wales is situated entirely between the 28th and 38th parallels of S. latitude and 141st and 154th meridians of E. longitude, and comprises an area of 309,433 sq. miles (801,427 sq. km) (exclusive of 939 sq. miles of Australian Capital Territory which lies within its borders). The preliminary estimated resident population at 30 June 1994 was 6,051,400.

STATE CAPITAL – ΨSydney, on the shores of Port Jackson. Sydney Harbour extends inland for 21 km; the total area of water is about 55 sq. km. The preliminary estimated resident population in 1994 of the Sydney statistical division was 3,738,500. The Newcastle and Wollongong statistical subdivisions contain populations of 460,210 and 251,390 respectively.

Towns – The populations of other principal municipalities are: Albury 41,450, Greater Taree 43,670, Hastings 53,850, Lismore 44,420, Shoalhaven 76,160, Wagga Wagga 56,670.

GOVERNMENT

New South Wales was first colonized as a British possession in 1788, and after progressive settlement a partly elective legislature was established in 1843. In 1855 responsible government was granted, the present constitution being founded on the Constitution Act of 1902. New South Wales federated with the other states of Australia in 1901.

The executive authority is vested in a Governor (appointed by the Crown), assisted by a Council of Ministers. The legislature consists of the Legislative Council of 42 members, elected by popular vote, and the Legislative Assembly of 99 members elected for a maximum period of four years. After the last by-election on 25 May 1996 the Assembly was composed of: Australian Labor Party 51, Liberal-National Alliance 45, Independents 3.

Governor of New South Wales, HE Hon. Gordon Samuels, AC, *assumed office* March 1996
Lt.-Governor and Chief Justice of NSW, Hon. Mr Justice Gleeson, AC
Premier, Hon. Bob Carr, MP
President of the Legislative Council, Hon. M. Willis, MLC
Speaker, Legislative Assembly, Hon. J. Murray, MP

NEW SOUTH WALES GOVERNMENT OFFICE IN LONDON, 75 King William Street, London EC4N 7HA. Tel: 0171-283 2166.

EDUCATION

Education is compulsory between the ages of six and 15 years. It is non-sectarian and free at all government schools. The enrolment in 1994 in 2,187 government and 862 non-government schools was 1,051,849. The nine universities, together with advanced education colleges, had an enrolment of 174,000 in 1993. Students enrolled in technical and further education colleges in 1993 numbered 423,600.

ECONOMY

A large area is suitable for sheep-raising, the principal breed of sheep being the merino, which was introduced in 1797.

The principal minerals are coal, lead, zinc, gold, rutile, copper and zircon. The total value of minerals extracted in 1993–4 was $A4,249 million. The average number of persons employed in the mining industry during 1993–4 was 19,483. In 1993–4, 84,014,000 tonnes of coal were produced.

In 1991–2 there were 9,588 manufacturing establishments (employing four or more persons). The number of persons employed at 30 June 1991 was 309,124.

LORD HOWE ISLAND

Lord Howe Island, which is part of New South Wales, is situated 702 kilometres north-east of Sydney, in 31° 33′ 4″ S. latitude and 159° 4′ 26″ E. longitude. Area 6.37 sq. miles (16.5 sq. km.). Population, 1994, 350. The island is of volcanic origin, Mount Gower reaching an altitude of 866 m. The affairs of the Island are administered by the Lord Howe Island Board.

QUEENSLAND

The state, including islands, is situated in 9° 14′–29° S. latitude and 138°–154° 7′ E. longitude and comprises the whole north-eastern portion of the Australian continent. Queensland possesses an area (including offshore islands) of 668,997 sq. miles (1,732,700 sq. km). At September 1995 the estimated resident population numbered 3,298,000.

STATE CAPITAL – ΨBrisbane is situated on the Brisbane River. The estimated resident population of the Brisbane statistical division at 30 June 1995 was 1,489,069. This area includes the cities of Brisbane (801,958), Ipswich (131,514), Logan (162,500) and Redcliffe (49,732).

CITIES – Other cities with population at 30 June 1995, are: ΨTownsville 124,925; Gold Coast 330,540; Toowoomba 124,925; ΨRockhampton 67,764; ΨCairns 100,891; ΨCaloundra 90,563; Mackay 70,466.

GOVERNMENT

Queensland was constituted a separate colony with responsible government in 1859, having previously formed part of New South Wales. The executive authority is vested in a Governor (appointed by the Crown), aided by an Executive Council of 18 members. Parliament consists of a Legislative Assembly of 89 members. The Assembly, as at 6 February 1996, was composed of: Australian Labor Party, 44; National Party of Australia, 29; Liberal Party of Australia, 15; Independent, 1. The National and Liberal parties formed a coalition government.

Governor of Queensland, HE Mary Marguerite Leneen Forde, AC
Premier, Hon. R. E. Borbider, MLA
Speaker, Legislative Assembly, Hon. N. J. Turner, MLA

AGENT-GENERAL'S OFFICE IN LONDON, 392 Strand, London WC2R 0LZ. Tel: 0171-836 1333. *Agent-General*, D. A. McManus

EDUCATION

Education is compulsory, secular and free between the ages of five and 15. At August 1995, there were 1,002 government primary schools, 73 primary/secondary, and 188 secondary schools with 264,567 primary students, and 140,983 secondary students. There were also 240 primary, 90 primary/secondary and 76 secondary non-government schools with 77,377 primary students and 73,185 secondary students.

Post-secondary education involves Technical and Further Education (TAFE) and higher education. During 1994, 261,232 students were enrolled in TAFE courses. In 1995, there were 57,010 full-time, 11,257 part-time, and 8,870 external students enrolled in university courses.

ECONOMY

Queensland is Australia's major beef-producing state. In March 1994, there were 9.7 million beef cattle in the state, which constituted 42 per cent of Australia's total meat cattle. In 1994–5, Queensland's overseas exports of beef were valued at $A1,661.7 million.

There were 6,187 manufacturing establishments in June 1993, with a total turnover of $A23,206.2 million in 1992–3, which contributed 13.7 per cent of total Australian manufacturing turnover.

In 1994–5, Queensland's coal, coke and briquette exports were valued at $A4,124.5 million. The major metallic minerals mined in 1994–5 were bauxite (9.3 million tonnes), copper concentrate (749,260 tonnes), gold bullion (41,770 kilograms) and lead concentrate (299,382 tonnes). The total value of all minerals produced in Queensland in 1994–5 was $A5,430.4 million.

In 1995, Queensland had 1.7 million overseas visitors and 3 million interstate visitors.

SOUTH AUSTRALIA

South Australia is situated between 26° and 38° S. latitude and 129° and 141° E. longitude, the total area being 380,070 sq. miles (984,376 sq. km). At 30 June 1995, the resident population was estimated to be 1,473,966.
STATE CAPITAL – ΨAdelaide, estimated resident population on 30 June 1995, 1,080,972 inclusive of suburbs. Other centres (with 1995 populations) are: ΨWhyalla (24,228); ΨMt Gambier (22,666); ΨPort Pirie (14,531); ΨPort Augusta (14,402).

GOVERNMENT

South Australia was proclaimed a British province in 1836, and in 1851 a partially elective legislature was established. The present constitution rests upon a law of 24 October 1856, the executive authority being vested in a Governor appointed by the Crown, aided by a Council of 13 Ministers.
Parliament consists of a Legislative Council of 22 members elected for eight years, one half retiring every four years; and a House of Assembly of 47 members, elected for a maximum duration of four years. Election is by ballot, with universal adult suffrage for both the Legislative Council and the House of Assembly. The representation in the House of Assembly is 36 Liberals and 11 Labor.

Governor of South Australia, HE Hon. Sir Eric Neal, AC, CVO, *assumed office* 1996
Lt.-Governor, The Hon. Dr Basil Hetzel, AC, *assumed office* 1992
Premier, Hon. Dean Craig Brown, MP
President of the Legislative Council, Hon. H. P. K. Dunn
Speaker of the House of Assembly, Hon. G. Gunn, MP

AGENT-GENERAL'S OFFICE IN LONDON, 115 Strand, London WC2R OAJ. *Agent-General*, G. Walls

EDUCATION

Education at the primary and secondary level is available at government schools controlled by the Education Department and at non-government schools, most of which are denominational. In 1995 there were 660 government schools with 78,471 students, and 193 independent schools with 66,321 students. Tertiary education is available through universities, and technical and further education colleges.
The three universities had, in 1994, a total enrolment of 47,277 students.

TASMANIA

Tasmania is an island state situated in the Southern ocean off the south-eastern extremity of the mainland. It is separated from the mainland by Bass Strait and incorporates King Island and the Furneaux group of islands which are in the strait. It lies between 40° 38'–43° 39' S. latitude and 144° 36'–148° 23' E. longitude, and has an area of 26,383 sq. miles (68,331 sq. km). Macquarie Island, situated at 54° 30' S. and 158° 57' E., about 900 miles north of the Antarctic Continent, is a dependency of Tasmania. The estimated resident population at 30 June 1994 was 472,357.
STATE CAPITAL – ΨHobart, founded 1804. Population (30 June 1994) (metropolitan area), 194,167. Other towns (with population at 30 June 1994) are ΨLaunceston (metropolitan area, 97,918); ΨBurnie-Devonport (79,035).

GOVERNMENT

The island was first settled by a British party from New South Wales in 1803, becoming a separate colony in 1825.

In 1851 a partly elective legislature was inaugurated, and in 1856 responsible government was established. In 1901 Tasmania became a state of the Australian Commonwealth. Executive authority is vested in a Governor appointed by the Crown, but is exercised by Cabinet Ministers responsible to the legislature, of which they are members. Parliament consists of a Legislative Council of 19 members, elected for six years (three retiring annually, in rotation, except in every sixth year, when four retire), and a House of Assembly of 35 members, elected by proportional representation for four years in five sevenmember constituencies. All Tasmanians of 18 years and over who have resided continuously in the State for at least six months may vote in elections to both houses. Elections for the Assembly are held every four years.
The February 1992 election resulted in a victory for the Liberal Party, with 19 Liberal, 11 Labor and 5 Tasmanian Green members of the House of Assembly. The state of the parties in the Legislative Council following the election was Independent 17, Liberal 1, Labor 1.
Governor of Tasmania, HE Gen. Sir Phillip Bennett, AC, KBE, DSO
Premier, Hon. Raymond J. Groom, MHA
President of the Legislative Council, vacant
Speaker of the House of Assembly, Hon. G. R. Page, MHA

EDUCATION

Government schools are of three main types: primary, secondary and secondary colleges. On 1 July 1994 there were 64,061 students enrolled in 233 government schools. There were also 68 independent schools with an enrolment of 21,298. The University of Tasmania with campuses in Hobart and Launceston, had 8,185 full-time students and 3,845 part-time students in 1994.

ECONOMY

Tasmania produces the most electrical energy per head of population of the Australian states. Most of it is derived from water power, with a total installed generator capacity of 2,435,000 kW at 30 June 1993. By reason of its low-cost electricity, Tasmania has large plants producing ferromanganese and newsprint. An aluminium plant is situated at Bell Bay and Tasmania is the source of the bulk of Australian requirements of zinc and fine papers.
The quantity of timber (excluding firewood) cut in 1993–4 was 4,349,200 cubic metres, including 3,448,800 cubic metres for woodchip and wood-pulp. The chief ores mined are those containing copper, tin, iron, silver, zinc and lead.
The chief manufactures for export are refined metals, agricultural products, textiles, paper, confectionery, wood chips and sawn timber. As at September 1994, 21,500 people were employed in manufacturing.

VICTORIA

Victoria comprises the south-east corner of Australia, at the part where its mainland territory projects furthest into the southern latitudes; it lies between 34°–39° S. latitude and 141°–150° E. longitude. Its area is 87,876 sq. miles (227,600 sq. km). The estimated resident population at December 1995 was 4,502,000.
STATE CAPITAL – ΨMelbourne had a resident population at December 1995 estimated at 3,189,201. Other urban centres are ΨGeelong 152,691; Ballarat 76,423; Bendigo 72,433.

GOVERNMENT

Victoria was originally known as the Port Phillip District of New South Wales and was created a separate colony in

1851, with a partially elective legislature. In 1855 responsible government was conferred.

The executive authority is vested in a Governor, appointed by the Crown, aided by an Executive Council of Ministers. Parliament consists of a Legislative Council of 44 members, elected for the 22 provinces for two terms of the Legislative Assembly, one half retiring every four years at a general election; and a Legislative Assembly of 88 members, elected for a maximum duration of four years. Voting is compulsory.

The state of parties in the Legislative Council (July 1996) is Liberal Party 28, Australian Labor Party 10, National Party 6. The state of parties in the Legislative Assembly (elected March 1996) is Liberal Party 49, Australian Labor Party 29, National Party 9, Independent 1.

Governor of Victoria, HE Hon. Richard E. McGarvie, *assumed office* 23 April 1992
Lt.-Governor, Hon. Sir John McIntosh Young, KCMG, AO, *apptd* 1974
Premier, Hon J. G. Kennett, MLA
President of the Legislative Council, Hon. Bruce Chamberlain, MLC
Speaker of the Legislative Assembly, Hon. J. Plowman

AGENT-GENERAL'S OFFICE IN LONDON, Victoria House, Melbourne Place, Strand, London WC2B 4LG. *Agent-General*, vacant

EDUCATION

State education is compulsory, secular and free between the ages of six and 15. In 1994 there were 2,410 schools, attended by 773,194 students. Victoria has 29 technical and further education colleges and nine universities.

ECONOMY

Minerals raised include oil and natural gas, brown coal, limestone, clays and stone for construction material. Production of brown coal in 1993–4 was 48,214 million tonnes. Production from Victorian natural gas and crude oil fields in 1993–4 was 17,221 megalitres of crude oil and 4,999 gigalitres of natural gas.

At 30 June 1993 there were 11,600 manufacturing establishments in which total employees numbered 281,000.

WESTERN AUSTRALIA

Western Australia includes all that portion of the continent west of 129° E. longitude, the most westerly point being in 113° 9′ E. longitude and from 13° 44′ to 35° 8′ S. latitude. Its area is 975,920 sq. miles (2,527,621 sq. km). At 30 June 1995 the estimated resident population was 1,731,723.

STATE CAPITAL – ΨPerth, on the north bank of the Swan River estuary, 12 miles from Fremantle. Estimated resident population (30 June 1995) of Perth statistical division, including the port of ΨFremantle, 1,262,569.

GOVERNMENT

Western Australia was first settled in 1829, and in 1870 it was granted a partially elective legislature. In 1890 responsible government was granted.

The executive is vested in a Governor appointed by the Crown and aided by a Council of Ministers. Parliament consists of a Legislative Council and a Legislative Assembly, elected by adult suffrage subject to qualifications of residence and registration. There are 34 members in the Legislative Council elected for a period of four years. The Legislative Assembly has 57 members, who are elected for a term of four years. The Legislative Assembly (elected 6 February 1993) is composed of Liberal Party 26, Austra-

lian Labor Party 23, National Party of Australia 6, Independent Liberal 2.

Governor of Western Australia, HE Maj.-Gen. Michael Jeffery, AO, MC
Lt.-Governor, Hon. D. K. Malcolm, AC
Premier, Hon. Richard Court, MLA
President of the Legislative Council, Hon. C. E. Griffiths, MLC
Speaker of the Legislative Assembly, Hon. J. Clarko, MLA

EUROPEAN OFFICE, Western Australia House, 115 Strand, London WC2R 0AJ *Agent-General*, W. R. B. Hassell

EDUCATION

In 1993 there were 766 government and 249 non-government primary and secondary school campuses with 222,451 and 74,288 full-time students respectively. The principal higher education institutions are the University of Western Australia (12,795 enrolments in 1994), Murdoch University (8,830), Curtin University (20,617) and Edith Cowan University (17,216).

ECONOMY

There were 3,386 manufacturing establishments at 30 June 1993. The total number of persons employed (including working proprietors) by these establishments at the end of June 1993 was 61,473.

The forests contain some of the finest hardwoods in the world. The total quantity of sawn timber produced during 1992–3 was 3,081,000 cubic metres.

The ex-mine value of all minerals (excluding construction materials) produced during 1993–4 was $A10,550 million.

AUSTRIA
Republik Österreich

Austria lies in central Europe, bounded on the north by the Czech Republic and Slovakia, on the south by Italy and Slovenia, on the east by Hungary, on the north-west by Germany and on the west by Switzerland and Liechtenstein. Its area is 32,375 sq. miles (83,853 sq. km), and its population is 8,015,000 (estimate 1994). The predominant religion is Roman Catholicism. The language is German, but the rights of the Slovene- and Croat-speaking minorities in Carinthia, Styria and Burgenland are protected.

CAPITAL – Vienna, on the Danube, population 1,539,848 (census 1991). Other larger towns are Graz (237,810), Linz (203,044), Innsbruck (118,112), Salzburg (143,978), and Klagenfurt (89,415).
CURRENCY – Schilling of 100 Groschen.
FLAG – Three equal horizontal stripes of red, white, red.
NATIONAL ANTHEM – Land der Berge, Land am Strome (Land of mountains, land on the river).
NATIONAL DAY – 26 October.

GOVERNMENT

The Republic of Austria was established in 1918 on the break-up of the Austro-Hungarian Empire. In March 1938, as a result of the *Anschluss*, Austria was incorporated into Nazi Germany under the name *Ostmark*. After the liberation of Vienna in 1945, the Republic of Austria was reconstituted within the frontiers of 1937 and a freely-elected government took office in December 1945. The country was divided at this time into four zones occupied respectively by the UK, USA, USSR and France, while Vienna was jointly occupied by the four Powers. In 1955 the Austrian State Treaty was signed in Vienna by the foreign ministers of the four Powers and of Austria. This treaty recognized the re-establishment of Austria as a sovereign, independent and democratic state, having the same frontiers as on 1 January 1938. Austria acceded to the European Union on 1 January 1995.

There is a bicameral national assembly; the lower house (*Nationalrat*) has 183 members and the upper house (*Bundesrat*) has 66 members. There is a 4 per cent qualification for parliamentary representation. After the general election of 17 December 1995 the Social Democrats and the People's Party formed a coalition government. The state of the parties in the Nationalrat as at May 1996 was: Social Democrat Party, 71; People's Party (Conservative), 53; Freedom Party (Liberal-Nationalist), 40; Green, 9; Liberal Forum, 10. In the Bundesrat in June 1996 the Social Democrat Party held 27 seats, the People's Party 26 and the Freedom Party 13.

There are nine provinces: Burgenland, Carinthia, Lower Austria, Upper Austria, Salzburg, Styria, Tyrol, Vienna, and Vorarlberg.

HEAD OF STATE
President of the Republic of Austria, Dr Thomas Klestil, *took office* 8 July 1992

CABINET *as at July 1996*
Chancellor, Franz Vranitzky (SPÖ)
Vice-Chancellor, Foreign Affairs, Wolfgang Schüssel (ÖVP)
Environment, Youth and Family, Martin Barteinstein (ÖVP)
Economic Affairs, Johann Farnleitner (ÖVP)
Interior, Caspar Einem (SPÖ)
Defence, Werner Fasslabend (ÖVP)
Environment, Martin Bartenstein (ÖVP)
Employment and Social Affairs, Franz Hums (SPÖ)
Science, Rudolf Scholten (SPÖ)
Education and Culture, Elisabeth Gehrer (ÖVP)
Women's Affairs, Helga Konrad (SPÖ)
Health, Sport and Consumer Protection, Christa Krammer (SPÖ)
Justice, Nikolaus Michalek (Ind.)
Agriculture and Forestry, Wilhelm Molterer (ÖVP)
Science, Transport and the Arts, Rudolf Schlögl (SPÖ)
SPÖ Social Democrats; ÖVP People's Party (Conservatives); Ind. Independent

AUSTRIAN EMBASSY
18 Belgrave Mews West, London swix 8HU
Tel 0171–235 3731
Ambassador Extraordinary and Plenipotentiary, new appointment awaited
Minister-Counsellor, Dr Herbert Krauss
Defence Attaché, Brig. H. Rüdiger Sulzgruber
Consul-General, G. R. Widor
Commercial Counsellor and Trade Commissioner, Dr Rudolf Engl

BRITISH EMBASSY
Jaurèsgasse 12, 1030 Vienna
Tel: Vienna 716130
Ambassador Extraordinary and Plenipotentiary, HE Sir Anthony Figgis, KCVO, CMG, apptd 1996
Deputy Ambassador, Counsellor and Consul-General, J. W. Forbes-Meyler, OBE
Defence Attaché, C. G. Stallard
First Secretary (Commercial), R. H. Williams

BRITISH CONSULAR OFFICES – There is a consular office at Vienna, and Honorary Consulates at Bregenz, Graz, Innsbruck and Salzburg.

BRITISH COUNCIL REPRESENTATIVE,David Handforth, Schenkenstrasse 4, A–1010 Vienna

EDUCATION

Education is free and compulsory between the ages of six and 15 and there are good facilities for secondary, technical and professional education. There are 12 state-maintained universities and six colleges of art with a combined registered student population of around 216,100 in 1994–5.

COMMUNICATIONS

Internal communications are partly restricted because of the mountainous nature of the country, although there is now a network of 1,567 km of *Autobahn* between major cities which also links up with the German and Italian networks. The railways (ÖBB) are state-owned and in 1993 had 5,605 km of track, 58.8 per cent of which is electrified. Of the 425 km of waterways, 350 km are navigable and there is considerable trade through the Danube ports by both local and foreign shipping. There are six commercial airports catering for 5,527,600 passengers in 1995.

There are four national radio and two national television channels, together with three national and twelve regional newspapers which have a combined daily circulation of 2,528,998.

DEFENCE

The total active strength of the armed forces numbers 55,750 (25,000 conscripts). In addition, there are 119,000 reserves ready at 72 hours notice. Conscripts serve for a minimum of seven months.

The Army has an active strength of 51,500 (22,000 conscripts) with 169 main battle tanks, 465 armoured personnel carriers, and 270 artillery pieces and anti-tank heavy guns. The Air Force has an active strength of 4,250 (3,400 conscripts) with 48 combat aircraft.

ECONOMY

The total value of GDP in 1995 was Schilling 2,360.1 billion.

Austria is self-sufficient in agricultural production, with about 267,444 agricultural units. The arable land produces wheat, rye, barley, oats, maize, potatoes, sugar beet, turnips, and miscellaneous crops. Many varieties of fruit trees flourish and the vineyards produce excellent wine. The pastures support horses, cattle and pigs and large numbers of chickens are also produced. Timber forms a valuable source of Austria's indigenous wealth, about 47 per cent of the total land area consisting of forest areas.

In 1995, 17,173,000 foreign tourists visited Austria. Foreign exchange receipts from tourism were a major contribution to the balance of payments.

FINANCE	1994	1995
Federal Budget (Schilling)		
Revenue	626,629m	646,678m
Expenditure	731,447m	764,581m

Total federal public debt in 1995 was Schilling 1,350.3 billion.

TRADE

Main exports are processed goods (iron and steel, other metal goods, textiles, paper and cardboard products), machinery and transport equipment, other finished goods (including clothing), raw materials, chemical products and foodstuffs. Main imports are machinery and transport equipment, processed goods, chemical products, foodstuffs, fuel and energy.

	1992	1993
Imports	Schilling 594,000m	564,909m
Exports	488,000m	467,171m

Over 80 per cent of trade is with other European countries, EU countries accounting for about 70 per cent, eastern Europe for about 8 per cent and EFTA members for 6 per cent. By far the most important trading partner is Germany, with which around 40 per cent of Austrian trade is conducted.

Trade with UK	1994	1995
Imports from UK	£1,034,899,000	£1,068,300,000
Exports to UK	1,017,879,000	883,900,000

AZERBAIJAN
Azarbaijchan Respublikasy

Azerbaijan has an area of 33,436 sq. miles (86,600 sq. km) and occupies the eastern part of the Caucasus region of the former Soviet Union, on the shore of the Caspian Sea. It is bordered on the south by Iran, on the west by Armenia and on the north by Georgia and Russia. The north-eastern part of the republic is taken up by the south-eastern end of the main Caucasus ridge, its south-western part by the smaller Caucasus hills, and its south-eastern corner by the spurs of the Talysh Ridge. Its central part is a depression irrigated by the River Kura and the lower reaches of its tributary the Araks. Sheltered by the mountains from the humid west winds blowing from the Black Sea, Azerbaijan has a continental climate.

Azerbaijan has 64 administrative districts and also includes the Nakhichevan Autonomous Republic, which is geographically separated from the rest of Azerbaijan by Armenia and borders on Iran and Turkey, and the Nagorno-Karabakh Autonomous Province.

According to a 1996 estimate, Azerbaijan has a population of 7,553,000, of which 83 per cent are Azeri, 6 per cent Russian and 6 per cent Armenian. There are also Kurds, Jews, Georgians and Turks. There are more Azeris in Iran than in Azerbaijan.

The population is predominantly Shia Muslim although it was heavily secularized during the Soviet era. Azeri in the Latin script was adopted as the official language in December 1992. Closely related to Turkish, Azeri was previously written in the Russian script.

CAPITAL – ΨBaku. Population 1,149,000 (1990).

CURRENCY – Manat of 100 gopik.

FLAG – Three horizontal stripes of blue, red and green with a white crescent and eight-pointed star in the centre.

NATIONAL DAY – 28 May (Independence Day).

GOVERNMENT

The territory that is now Azerbaijan was successively part of the Assyrian, Persian, Median and Greek empires. With the influx of Huns and Khazars in the first century BC, the Turkic Azerbaijani people evolved and formed an independent state. This was invaded by the Arab Caliphates in the seventh century AD and under their 300-year rule Islam was introduced and became the dominant religion. In the 16th century Azerbaijan was again invaded by Persia and became a Persian province. The country was divided during the Russo-Persian wars of the early 19th century, the northern portion (the present-day Azerbaijan) becoming part of the Russian Empire and the southern portion remaining Persian and subsequently Iranian.

A Soviet government was set up in Azerbaijan in 1918. This was overthrown by Allied forces a few months later but when Allied forces withdrew in 1920, the Soviet government was restored and Azerbaijan acceded to the USSR in 1922.

In January 1990, the Azerbaijani Popular Front took power from the local Communist Party and declared independence from the Soviet Union, partly because of the Soviet government's decision in 1989 to take control of the Nagorno-Karabakh region away from Azerbaijan and to impose direct rule upon it to stop Azeri-Armenian fighting. Soviet troops overthrew the Popular Front regime the day after it took power and restored the Communist regime under President Ayaz Mutalibov. This government declared Azerbaijan's independence in August 1991. Mutalibov won the presidential election held in September 1991, but he was forced to resign by widespread civil unrest at his perceived pro-Moscow stance and the poor conduct of the war with Armenia. At the presidential election in June 1992 the Popular Front leader Abulfaz Elchibey was elected.

Azerbaijan withdrew from the CIS in October 1992. The war (*see* Secession) continued to go badly in 1992–3, the defeats leading to political crisis. President Elchibey declared a state of emergency but discontent with his rule grew in parliament and military rebels seized power in June 1993. The former Azerbaijani Communist Party First Secretary Heidar Aliyev took over the presidency and the rebel leader Col. Husseinov the premiership. The new regime was confirmed in office in a referendum in August and Aliyev won the presidential election in October 1993.

The government has sought to tread a middle path between Russia, Turkey and other states interested in investing in its oil industry. It rejoined the CIS in September 1993. Internal tension over relations with Russia and Turkey led to unsuccessful coup attempts against President Aliyev's government in October 1994, March 1995, and August 1995.

In November 1995, elections were held to the *Milli Majlis* (parliament), which had been increased to 125 seats: 100 directly elected and 25 allocated by proportional representation. The pro-Aliyev New Azerbaijan party won 70 per cent of the vote and a majority of seats, although the OSCE declared the elections unfair.

A new constitution was approved by a referendum in November 1995, which created a presidential republic with executive power to be exercised by the president and with legislative power vested in the Milli Majlis.

SECESSION

In 1988 fighting broke out in the predominantly Armenian-populated region of Nagorny-Karabakh between Soviet Azerbaijani forces and ethnic Armenians demanding unification with Armenia. Fighting continued through the breakup of the Soviet Union and reached its peak in late 1993 when Nagorno-Karabakh forces captured all of the region, together with all Azeri territory separating the region from Armenia (20 per cent of Azeri territory). Azeri forces pushed back the Nagorno-Karabakh forces in early 1994 before a cease-fire agreement was signed in May 1994. The cease-fire has held since then and peace talks have been held under the auspices of the OSCE. Twenty per cent of Azeri territory remains under the control of Nagorno-Karabakh forces. Between 500,000 and one million Azeris have been displaced by the fighting.

HEAD OF STATE

President, Heidar Aliyev, *assumed office* 18 June 1993, *elected* 3 October 1993

GOVERNMENT *as at July 1996*
Prime Minister (acting), Fuad Guliev
Deputy Prime Ministers, Tofik Azizov; Izzyat Rustamov
Foreign Affairs, Gasan Gasanov
Interior, Ramil Usubov
Housing and Communal Services, Suddgedin Abdullaev
Foreign Economic Relations (acting), Nigat Kuliev
Culture, Byul-byul Polad
Press and Information, Rafel Mamedov
Labour and Social Security (acting), Ilgar Ragimov
Material Resources, Faruh Zeinalov
Land Improvement and Water Conservancy, Salekh Gadzhiyev
Local Industry, Agabba Abdulaev
Finance, Fikret Yusifov
Education, Lidiya Rasulova
National Security, Namig Abbasov
Defence, Lt.-Gen. Safar Abuyev
Communications, Sirus Abbasbeily
Agriculture and Foodstuffs, Ershad Aliev
Trade, Miri Ganbarov
Economics, Samed Sadyhov
Justice (acting), Sudaba Gasanova
Public Health, Ali Insanov
Chairman of the Supreme Soviet, Rasul Guliev

AZERBAIJANI EMBASSY
4 Kensington Court, London W8 5DL
Tel 0171-938 3412
Ambassador Extraordinary and Plenipotentiary, HE Mahmud
  Mamed-Kuliyev, apptd 1994

BRITISH EMBASSY
c/o 2 Izmir Street, Baku
Tel: Baku 985 558
Ambassador Extraordinary and Plenipotentiary, HE Thomas
  Young, apptd 1993

DEFENCE

The total active strength of the armed forces is 86,700 personnel, with conscripts serving 17-month terms. The Army has a strength of 73,300, with 325 main battle tanks, 831 armoured personnel carriers and armoured infantry fighting vehicles and 343 artillery pieces. The Navy is based at Baku, with a share of the former Soviet Caspian Fleet Flotilla, comprising two frigates and 15 patrol and coastal combatants, together with 2,200 personnel. The Air Force is 11,200 strong with 46 combat aircraft.

ECONOMY

Azerbaijan was heavily industrialized as part of the Russian Empire and is a major oil-producing centre. Industry is dominated by oil and natural gas extraction and related industries centred on Baku and Sumgait and the large oil deposits in the Caspian Sea, estimated at 3–4,000 million barrels. An agreement to explore and exploit three oilfields in the Caspian Sea was signed in September 1994 with a consortium of western oil firms, in which the consortium will gain a 70 per cent stake in the contract, Azerbaijan 20 per cent and the Russian Lukoil company 10 per cent. One pipeline will go through Russia, the other through Georgia.

    The republic is also rich in mineral resources, with iron, copper, lead and salt, and is important as a cotton-growing area and a silkworm breeding area.

    The Azeri economy was devastated by the war and inflation is still running at 15–20 per cent a year. The IMF approved a loan of US$132 million in November 1995 in support of government reforms, including the abolition of food subsidies and privatization of state enterprises.

TRADE WITH UK	1994	1995
Imports from UK	£5,803,000	£13,906,000
Exports to UK	1,517,000	6,080,000

CULTURE

Azerbaijan was the birthplace of the prophet Zoroaster, who founded one of the first monotheistic religions in the world. The country has witnessed a succession of three religions: Zoroastrianism, Christianity and Islam.

    Azeri is one of the Turkic languages. In the 18th and 19th centuries Azerbaijani literature produced the poets and dramatists Vagif, Vazekhi, Zakir, Akhundov and Vezirov.

THE BAHAMAS
The Commonwealth of The Bahamas

The Bahamas are an archipelago lying in the North Atlantic Ocean between 20° 55′–25° 22′ N. latitude and 72° 35′–79° 35′ W. longitude. They extend from the coast of Florida on the north-west almost to Haiti on the southeast. The group consists of 700 islands, of which 30 are inhabited, and 2,400 cays comprising an area of more than 5,832 sq. miles. The principal islands include: Abaco, Acklins, Andros, Berry Islands, Bimini, Cat Island, Crooked Island, Eleuthera, Exuma, Grand Bahama, Harbour Island, Inagua, Long Island, Mayaguana, New Providence (on which is located the capital, Nassau), Ragged Island, Rum Cay, San Salvador and Spanish Wells. San Salvador was the first landfall in the New World of Christopher Columbus on 12 October 1492. The population (UN estimate 1993) is 269,000.

CAPITAL – ΨNassau, population (census 1990) 171,000.
CURRENCY – Bahamian dollar (B$) of 100 cents.
FLAG – Horizontal stripes of aquamarine, gold and
  aquamarine, with a black equilateral triangle on the
  hoist.
NATIONAL ANTHEM – March on, Bahamaland.
NATIONAL DAY – 10 July (Independence Day).

GOVERNMENT

The Bahamas were settled by the British and became a Crown colony in 1717. Taken over in 1782 by the Spanish, the Treaty of Versailles in 1783 restored them to the British. The Bahamas gained independence on 10 July 1973. The head of state is HM Queen Elizabeth II, represented in the islands by a Governor-General. There is an appointed Senate of 16 members and an elected House of Assembly of 49 members which is to be reduced to 40 members before the general election due in August 1997. A general election held in August 1992 was won by the Free National Movement, defeating the Progressive Liberal Party, which had held power since independence. The Free National Movement won 33 seats in the House of Assembly and the Progressive Liberal Party 16 seats.

Governor-General, HE Sir Orville Turnquest, GCMG, QC,
  apptd 1994

CABINET *as at June 1996*
Prime Minister, Rt. Hon. Hubert A. Ingraham
Deputy Prime Minister, Tourism, Hon. Frank H. Watson
Foreign Affairs, Attorney-General, Hon. Janet G. Bostwick
Social Development, Hon. Maurice E. Moore
Education, Senator the Hon. Dame Ivy Dumont, DCMG
Public Safety and Immigration, Hon. Cornelius A. Smith

Transport, Hon. Tennyson R. G. Wells
Public Works, Hon. Arlington G. Butler
Youth and Culture, Hon. Algernon Allen
Health and Environment, Hon. Theresa M. Moxey-Ingraham
Finance and Planning, Hon. William C. Allen
Agriculture and Fisheries, Hon. Pierre V. Dupuch

President of the Court of Appeal, Sir Joaquim Gonsalves-Sabola, KCMG
Chief Justice, Hon. Sir Cyril Fountain, ILD

BAHAMAS HIGH COMMISSION
Bahamas House, 10 Chesterfield Street, London WIX 8AH
Tel 0171-408 4488
High Commissioner, HE Arthur A. Foulkes, apptd 1992

BRITISH HIGH COMMISSION
PO Box N-7516, Nassau
Tel: Nassau 325-7471/2/3
High Commissioner, HE Peter Young, OBE, apptd 1996

ECONOMY

Tourism employs about half of the labour force and provides about half of government revenue and about half the country's foreign exchange earnings. International banking and trust business is also important. The absence of any direct taxation and internal stability have enabled the country to become one of the world's leading offshore financial centres.

Agricultural production is mainly of fresh vegetables, fruit, meat and eggs for the domestic market, and crawfish, mostly for export. Reserves of aragonite, limestone and salt are being commercially exploited. Freeport is the country's leading industrial centre, with a pharmaceutical and chemicals plant, an oil trans-shipment and storage terminal, and port and bunkering facilities. There are also a brewery and a rum distillery on New Providence.

TRADE

The imports are chiefly foodstuffs, manufactured articles, building materials, vehicles and machinery, chemicals and petroleum. The chief exports are rum, petroleum, hormones, salt, crawfish and aragonite.

Trade with UK	1994	1995
Imports from UK	£30,580,000	£30,912,000
Exports to UK	25,628,000	33,029,000

EDUCATION

Education is compulsory between the ages of five and 14. More than 59,500 students are enrolled in Ministry of Education and independent schools in New Providence and the Family Islands.

COMMUNICATIONS

The main ports are Nassau (New Providence), Freeport (Grand Bahama), Matthew Town (Inagua). International air services are operated from Abaco, Bimini, Eleuthera, Exuma, Grand Bahama and New Providence. About 50 smaller airports and landing strips facilitate services between the islands, the services being mainly provided by Bahamasair, the national carrier. There are roads on the larger islands, and roads are under construction on the smaller islands. There are no railways.

BAHRAIN
Dawlet al-Bahrein

Bahrain consists of a group of low-lying islands situated about half-way down the Gulf, some 20 miles off the east coast of Saudi Arabia. The largest of these, Bahrain island, is about 30 miles long and 10 miles wide at its broadest, with the capital, Manama, situated on the north shore. The second largest, Muharraq, with the town and Bahrain International Airport, is connected to Manama by a causeway 1½ miles long. Bahrain is connected by causeway to Saudi Arabia.

The climate is humid all the year round, with rainfall of about 3 inches, concentrated in the mild winter months, December to March; in summer, May to October, temperatures can exceed 110°F (44°C).

The population (1993 UN estimate) is 539,000, of whom about 70 per cent are Bahraini. About 40 per cent of the Bahrainis are Sunni Muslims, the remaining 60 per cent being Shias; the ruling family and many of the most prominent merchants are Sunnis.

CAPITAL – ΨManama, population (1981 census) 108,684.
CURRENCY – Bahrain dinar (BD) of 1,000 fils.
FLAG – Red, with vertical serrated white bar next to staff.
NATIONAL DAY – 16 December.

GOVERNMENT

Bahrain has been a fully independent state since 1971, when British protectorate status was ended. Government takes the form of a constitutional monarchy, in which traditional consultative procedures continue to play an important role. The 1973 constitution provides for a National Assembly but this was dissolved in 1975. In December 1992 the Amir announced plans to set up a consultative council, which was established with 30 members in January 1993 and dominated by the business community. Since 1994, Shi'ite protestors demanding the re-establishment of the National Assembly have regularly clashed with security forces and Shi'ite leaders have been detained. In May 1996, the government arrested 29 people alleged to have been involved in an Iranian-backed coup attempt. Opponents of the government have engaged in a sustained bombing campaign.

HEAD OF STATE
HH The Amir of Bahrain, Shaikh Isa bin Sulman Al-Khalifa, GCMG, *born* 1932; *acceded* 16 December 1961
Crown Prince (and C.-in-C., Bahrain Defence Force), HE Shaikh Hamad bin Isa Al Khalifa, KCMG

CABINET *as at July 1996*
Prime Minister, HH Shaikh Khalifa bin Salman Al-Khalifa
Foreign Affairs, HE Shaikh Mohammed bin Mubarak Al-Khalifa
Justice and Islamic Affairs, HE Shaikh Abdulla bin Khalifa Al-Khalifa
Interior, HE Shaikh Mohammed bin Khalifa Al-Khalifa
Defence, HE Maj.-Gen. Shaikh Khalifa bin Ahmed Al-Khalifa
Transport, HH Shaikh Ali bin Khalifa bin Sulman Al-Khalifa
Housing, Municipalities and Environment, Shaikh Khalid bin Abdulla Al-Khalifa
Oil and Industry, HE Shaikh Isa bin Ali Al-Khalifa
Cabinet Affairs and Information, HE Mohammed Ebrahim Al-Mutawa
Agriculture and Public Works, HE Majid Jawad Al-Jishi

Finance and National Economy, HE Ebrahim Abdul-Karim Mohammed
Commerce, HE Ali Saleh Abdulla Al-Saleh
Education, HE Abdul-Aziz bin Mohammed Al-Fadhil
Health, HE Dr Faisal Radhi Al-Mousawi
Power and Water, HE Abdulla Mohammed Juma
Labour and Social Affairs, HE Abdul-Nabi Al-Shula
Minister of State, HE Jawad Salem Al-Urayed
Chairman of the Consultative Council, Ebrahim Mohammed Humaidan

EMBASSY OF THE STATE OF BAHRAIN
98 Gloucester Road, London SW7 4AU
Tel 0171–370 5132
Ambassador Extraordinary and Plenipotentiary, HE Shaikh Abdul-Aziz bin Mubarak Al-Khalifa, apptd 1996

BRITISH EMBASSY
21 Government Avenue, Manama 306, PO Box 114
Tel: Manama 534404
Ambassador Extraordinary and Plenipotentiary, HE Ian Lewty, apptd 1996

BRITISH COUNCIL REPRESENTATIVE, John Shorter, AMA Centre, PO Box 452, Manama 356

DEFENCE

Total active armed forces number 10,700. The army has 8,500 personnel and is equipped with 106 main battle tanks, 235 armoured personnel carriers and 49 artillery pieces. The 700-strong navy, based at Mina Sulman, is equipped with one frigate and four patrol craft. The air force has 1,500 personnel and is equipped with 24 combat aircraft and ten armed helicopters.

ECONOMY

The largest sources of revenue are oil production and refining. The Bahrain field, discovered in 1932, is wholly owned by the Bahrain National Oil Co. The Sitra refinery derives about 70 per cent of its crude oil by submarine pipeline from Saudi Arabia. Bahrain also has a half share with Saudi Arabia in the profits of the offshore Abu Sa'afa field. A reservoir of unassociated gas has recently been developed on Bahrain island.

Heavy industry is currently limited to the Aluminium Bahrain (ALBA) smelter, the Gulf Petrochemical Industries Co. (GPIC) producing ammonia and methanol, the Gulf Aluminium Rolling Mill (GARMCO), and the Arab Shipbuilding and Repair Yard (ASRY), operating dry dock facilities up to 500,000 tons. There are a number of small to medium-sized industrial units.

The state has developed as a financial centre. Apart from several commercial banks, many international banks have been licensed as offshore banking units; there are also money brokers and merchant banks.

TRADE WITH UK	1994	1995
Imports from UK	£150,378,000	£150,757,000
Exports to UK	25,380,000	26,379,000

COMMUNICATIONS

Bahrain International airport is one of the main air traffic centres of the Gulf; it is the headquarters of Gulf Air, and a stopping point on routes between Europe and Australia and the Far East for other airlines. A causeway links Bahrain to Saudi Arabia.

A world-wide telephone and telex service, by satellite and cable, is operated by Bahrain Telecommunications Company.

BANGLADESH
Ghana Praja Tantri Bangladesh

Bangladesh has an area of 55,598 sq. miles (143,998 sq. km) in the region of the Gangetic delta. The country is crossed by a network of rivers, including the eastern arms of the Ganges, the Jamuna (Brahmaputra) and the Meghna, flowing into the Bay of Bengal. The climate is tropical and monsoon; hot and extremely humid during the summer, and mild and dry during the short winter. The rainfall is heavy, varying from 50 inches to 135 inches in different districts and the bulk of it falls during the monsoon season from June to September.

The population (1991 census) was 108 million. The faith of 88 per cent of the population is Islam and 10.5 per cent Hinduism. Islam has been declared the state religion of Bangladesh.

The state language is Bengali. Use of Bengali is compulsory in all government departments. English is understood and is used widely as an unofficial second language.

CAPITAL – Dhaka, population (1991 census) 6,537,308.
CURRENCY – Taka (Tk) of 100 poisha.
FLAG – Red circle on a bottle-green ground.
NATIONAL ANTHEM – Amar Sonar Bangla.
NATIONAL DAY – 26 March (Independence Day).

GOVERNMENT

Prior to becoming East Pakistan, Bangladesh had been the province of East Bengal and the Sylhet district of Assam of British India. The territory acceded to Pakistan in October 1947, which became a republic on 23 March 1956. Bangladesh achieved its independence from Pakistan on 16 December 1971, following the conclusion of the Indo-Pakistan war. Pakistan and Bangladesh accorded one another mutual recognition in 1974.

In 1975 the constitution was amended and a one-party presidential system was introduced, with Prime Minister Sheikh Rahman assuming the presidency under martial law until he was assassinated in 1975. A presidential election in 1978 was won by Maj.-Gen. Zia Rahman, who lifted martial law and introduced a multiparty presidential system of government. Zia was assassinated in 1981. He was replaced by Justice Abdus Sattar, who was overthrown in 1982 in a coup led by the then Chief of Army Staff, Gen. Ershad. Following parliamentary elections in 1986, a civilian Cabinet was appointed and Gen. Ershad was elected President. Popular unrest forced Gen. Ershad's resignation in December 1990 and parliamentary elections were held in February 1991. The Bangladesh Nationalist Party (BNP) won the largest number of seats and the BNP leader, Begum Khaleda Zia, was sworn in as Prime Minister. In August 1991 Parliament approved a constitutional amendment returning Bangladesh to parliamentary rule. BNP nominee Abdur Rahman Biswas was elected President.

In December 1994, the opposition parties resigned from parliament and organized a series of mass rallies and strikes in demand of an independent caretaker government to oversee fresh elections. Public disorder persisted despite a general election in February 1996 which was won by the BNP, although turnout was a mere 5 per cent. In March 1996, Prime Minister Zia agreed to new elections, to be supervised by an interim 11-member ruling council led by former Supreme Court Chief Justice Muhammad Habibur Rahman. The fresh elections in June 1996 produced a majority for the Awami League under Prime Minister Sheikh Hasina.

There is a unicameral parliament (*Jatiya Sangshad*) of 330 members which can amend the constitution by a two-thirds majority. The country is divided into six administrative divisions, sub-divided into 64 districts.

HEAD OF STATE

President, Abdur Rahman Biswas, *sworn in* 8 October 1991

CABINET *as at July 1996*

Prime Minister, Defence, Environment, Tourism, Labour, Health, Sheikh Hasina
Foreign Affairs, Abdus Samad Azad
Local Government, Rural Development and Co-operatives, Mohammad Zillur Rahman
Finance, S. A. M. S. Kibria
Education, Science and Technology, A. S. H. K. Sadeque
Water Resources, Abdur Razzak
Commerce and Industry, Tofael Ahmed
Power, Energy and Mineral Resources, Lt.-Gen. (retd) Nooruddin Khan
Home Affairs, Maj. (retd) Rafiqul Islam Bir Uttam
Post and Telecommunications, Mohammad Nasim
Agriculture, Disaster Management and Relief, Matia Chowdhury
Communications, Anwar Hossain Manju
Health and Family Welfare, Salahuddin Yousuf
Shipping, A. S. M. Abdur Rob

BANGLADESH HIGH COMMISSION

28 Queen's Gate, London sw7 5AJ
Tel 0171–584 0081/2/3/4
High Commissioner, new appointment awaited
Deputy High Commissioner, S. Akhtar
Defence Adviser, Brig. A. M. Zaman
Minister, G. K. Chowdhury (*Economic*)

BRITISH HIGH COMMISSION

United Nations Road, Baridhara Dhaka
PO Box 6079, Dhaka-12
Tel: Dhaka 882705
High Commissioner, HE David Walker, apptd 1996
Deputy High Commissioner, J. R. Nicols
Defence Adviser, Col. J. M. Philips

BRITISH COUNCIL REPRESENTATIVE, K. Burd, OBE,
5 Fuller Road (PO Box 161), Dhaka 1000

EDUCATION

Primary education is free and planned to be universal by 2000. There are 50,314 primary schools, mostly managed by the Government. There are 11,094 secondary schools and 980 colleges offering general and technical education. There are 11 universities with a total enrolment of 52,620 students. In 1995 the literacy rate was estimated to be 38.1 per cent (49.4 per cent male and 26.1 per cent female).

COMMUNICATIONS

Principal seaports are Chittagong and Mongla. The Bangladesh Shipping Corporation has been set up by the Government to operate the Bangladesh merchant fleet. The principal airports are Dhaka (Zia International) and Chittagong. The international airline, Bangladesh Biman, serves Europe, the Middle East, South and South-East Asia, and an internal network.

There are about 680 miles of roads; 4,724 miles are metalled. There are 1,680 miles of railway track.

Radio Bangladesh is the main national broadcasting service. A television service was introduced in 1965 and colour transmissions began in 1980.

ECONOMY

Between 1991–5, the BNP government implemented an IMF economic reform plan which delivered stable prices and inflation, and reduced the budget deficit from 8 per cent of GDP in 1989 to 5.3 per cent in 1993. However, half of the population still lives in poverty. GNP per capita stood at US$230 in 1994, making Bangladesh one of the world's poorest countries.

Bangladesh is self-sufficient in food production. Agricultural products include rice, wheat, tobacco, tea, oil seeds, pulses and sugar cane. The chief industries are jute, cotton, tea, leather, pharmaceuticals, fertilizer, sugar, prawn fishing, natural gas. Garment manufacturing is the main export, earning £1,400 million in 1994–5, 63 per cent of total foreign exchange earnings. Remittances sent home by Bangladeshis abroad are of considerable significance to the economy.

Bangladesh is a major recipient of bilateral and multilateral development aid. The total aid pledged for 1995 from international donors formed into a consortium led by the World Bank was US$1,950 million.

TRADE WITH UK	1994	1995
Imports from UK	£55,678,000	£89,145,000
Exports to UK	156,004,000	231,644,000

BARBADOS

Barbados, the most easterly of the Caribbean islands, is situated in 13° 14′ N. latitude and 59° 37′ W. longitude with a total area of 166 sq. miles (430 sq. km); the land rises in a series of terraced tablelands to the highest point, Mt Hillaby (1,116 ft). Barbados is nearly 21 miles long by 14 miles broad. The annual average temperature is 26.6°C (79.8°F) with rainfall varying from a yearly average of 75 inches in the high central district to 50 inches in the low-lying coastal areas.

The population (1993 UN estimate) was 264,000. There are 11 administrative areas (parishes): St Michael, Christ Church, St Andrew, St George, St James, St John, St Joseph, St Lucy, St Peter, St Philip and St Thomas.

CAPITAL – ΨBridgetown (population, estimated 1990, 108,000) in the parish of St Michael. There are three other towns, Oistins in Christ Church, Holetown in St James and Speightstown in St Peter.
CURRENCY – Barbados dollar (BD$) of 100 cents.
FLAG – Three vertical stripes, dark blue, gold and dark blue, with a trident head on gold stripe.
NATIONAL ANTHEM – In Plenty and in Time of Need.
NATIONAL DAY – 30 November (Independence Day).

GOVERNMENT

The first inhabitants of Barbados were Arawak Indians but the island was uninhabited when first settled by the British in 1627. It was a Crown Colony from 1652 until it became an independent state within the Commonwealth on 30 November 1966. The legislature consists of the Governor-General, a Senate and a House of Assembly. The Senate comprises 21 Senators appointed by the Governor-General, of whom 12 are appointed on the advice of the Prime Minister, two on the advice of the Leader of the Opposition and seven by the Governor-General at his/her discretion to represent religious, economic or social interests. The House of Assembly comprises 28 members elected every five years by adult suffrage. The last general election took place on 6 September 1994 and seats in the

House of Assembly were distributed as follows: Barbados Labour Party 19, Democratic Labour Party 8, National Democratic Party 1.

Governor-General, HE Sir Clifford Husbands, GCMG, KA, apptd 1996

CABINET *as at June 1996*
Prime Minister, Finance and Economic Affairs, Civil Service, Rt. Hon. Owen Arthur
Deputy Prime Minister, Foreign Affairs, Tourism and International Transport, Hon. Billie Miller
Attorney-General and Home Affairs, Hon. David Simmons, QC
Agriculture and Rural Development, Hon. Rawle Eastmond
Education, Youth and Culture, Hon. Mia Mottley
Health and Environment, Hon. Elizabeth Thompson
Labour, Community Development and Sport, Hon. Rudolph Greenidge
Public Works, Transport and Housing, Hon. George Payne
Industry and Commerce, Sen. Hon. Reginald Farley
International Trade, Sen. Hon. Phillip Goddard
Minister of State, Prime Minister's Office, Sen. Hon. Glyne Murray
Minister of State, Foreign Affairs, International Transport and Tourism, Hon. Ronald Toppin

BARBADOS HIGH COMMISSION
1 Great Russell Street, London WC1B 3JY
Tel 0171–631 4975
High Commissioner, HE Peter Simmons, apptd 1995
Deputy High Commissioner, H. Yearwood
First Secretary (Commercial), K. Campbell

BRITISH HIGH COMMISSION
Lower Collymore Rock, PO Box 676, Bridgetown C
Tel: Bridgetown 436 6694
High Commissioner, HE Richard Thomas, CMG, apptd 1994
Deputy High Commissioner, P. J. Mathers, LVO
Defence Adviser, Capt. I. M. Hime, RN
First Secretary (Chancery), S. R. Morley

JUDICATURE

There is a Supreme Court of Judicature consisting of a High Court and a Court of Appeal. In certain cases a further appeal lies to the Judicial Committee of the Privy Council. The Chief Justice and Puisne Judges are appointed by the Governor-General on the recommendation of the Prime Minister and after consultation with the Leader of the Opposition.

Chief Justice, The Hon. Sir Denys Williams, KCMG

ECONOMY

Barbados is an upper-middle income country, with a GNP per capita of US$6,530 in 1994. Unemployment, however, was 24.2 per cent in 1993 and inflation was predicted to rise to 4 per cent in 1996.

The economy is based on tourism, sugar and light manufacturing. In 1995, 442,107 tourists visited Barbados and 484,670 cruise ship passengers. Chief exports are sugar and its by-products, chemicals, electronic components and clothing.

FINANCE	1993–4*
Current revenue	BD$1,009,900,000
Current expenditure	1,136,200,000
Deficit	126,300,000
*estimated	

TRADE WITH UK	1994	1995
Imports from UK	£30,992,000	£101,144,000
Exports to UK	15,906,000	25,639,000

EDUCATION

Education is free in government schools. There are 105 primary schools, 21 government secondary schools and 15 approved government secondary schools.

COMMUNICATIONS

Barbados has some 965 miles of roads, of which about 917 miles are asphalted. The Grantley Adams International airport is situated at Seawell, 12 miles from Bridgetown, and frequent scheduled services connect Barbados with the major world air routes. Bridgetown, the only port of entry, has a deep-water harbour with berths for eight ships, but oil is pumped ashore at Spring Garden and at an Esso installation on the West Coast. Barbados has a colour television service, three radio broadcasting services, and a wired broadcasting service.

BELARUS
Respublika Belarus

Belarus (formerly Byelorussia) has an area of 80,300 sq. miles (207,600 sq. km) and is situated in the western part of the European area of the former USSR. It is bordered on the north by Latvia and Lithuania, on the east by Russia, on the south by the Ukraine and on the west by Poland. Much of the land is a plain, with many lakes, swamps and marshy areas. The main rivers are the upper reaches of the Dnieper, of the Niemen and of the Western Dvina.

The climate is continental with mild, humid winters and relatively cool and rainy summers.

The population (1995 official estimate) is 10,265,000, of which 78 per cent are Belarusian, 13 per cent Russian, 4 per cent Polish and 3 per cent Ukrainian, with smaller numbers of Jews and Lithuanians. Most of the population are Belarusian Orthodox, with a minority of Roman Catholics.

Belarusian, one of the Slavonic family of languages, is the first official language; the alphabet is similar to the Russian one. Russian remains the dominant language and is the second official language.

CAPITAL – Minsk. Population 1,589,000 (1989). The city is the administrative centre of the CIS. Other important cities are Gomel, Vitebsk, Brest and Grodno.
CURRENCY – Rouble of 100 kopeks.
FLAG – Red with a green strip along the lower edge, and in the hoist a vertical red and white ornamental pattern.
NATIONAL ANTHEM – The former Soviet national anthem but with the words omitted.
NATIONAL DAY – 27 July (Independence Day).

HISTORY

In the ninth century AD the Kievan Rus state was a unified state encompassing all the Russian, Ukrainian and Belarusian populations. After being absorbed into Lithuania in the 13th and 14th centuries, the Belarusian nationality, language and culture flourished until it came under Polish rule in the mid-16th century. Two hundred years of Polish rule followed until Belarus was re-absorbed into the Russian Empire.

Much of Belarus was under German control at the time of the Russian revolution and it was not until German forces withdrew that a Byelorussian Soviet Socialist

Republic was declared on 1 January 1919. Western Belarus was ceded to Poland after the Soviet defeat in the Polish-Soviet war of 1919–20, and was not recovered until Soviet forces occupied the area under the 1939 Nazi-Soviet Pact. Belarus was devastated by the German invasion in the Second World War; 25 per cent of the population was killed and thousands deported.

Belarus issued a Declaration of State Sovereignty on 27 July 1990 and declared its independence from the Soviet Union after the failed coup in Moscow in August 1991.

GOVERNMENT

After the failed Moscow coup, Stanislav Shuskevich became Belarusian leader, at the head of an informal coalition of Communists and democrats. Until 1994, however, parliament and the government remained under the control of former Communists, who thwarted the economic and political reform efforts of Shuskevich and his democratic nationalist allies. Shuskevich was forced to resign in January 1994 and was replaced by Gen. Mecheslav Grib who pursued closer political, economic and trade relations with Russia. An economic and monetary union agreement with Russia collapsed, however.

Alexander Lukashenko defeated Gen. Grib in a July 1994 presidential election and appointed a reformist government. A referendum on 14 May 1995 overwhelmingly approved a renewed economic union with Russia, gave the Russian language equal official status and extended the President's powers over parliament. An agreement was signed with Russia in April 1996 to form a Commonwealth of Sovereign Republics paving the way for the introduction of a common currency, a common foreign policy and closer political integration.

Four rounds of legislative elections were held in 1995 in an attempt to produce a quorum in the Supreme Soviet, few candidates having obtained in the first ballot the majority of votes of a turnout of 50 per cent or more required to win a seat.

A new constitution came into effect on 30 March 1994 under which a directly elected President serving a maximum of two five-year terms was instituted. The President appoints the Cabinet and directs government policy. Legislative power is held by a directly elected 260-seat Supreme Soviet. The republic is divided into six regions: Brest, Gomel, Grodno, Minsk, Mogilev and Vitebsk.

HEAD OF STATE
President, Alexander Lukashenko, *elected* 10 July 1994

CABINET *as at June 1996*
Prime Minister, Mikhail Chigir
Deputy Prime Ministers, Sergei Ling; Uladzimir Garkun;
    Valeri Kokarav; Uladzimir Rusakevich; Leanid Sinitsyn;
    Vasili Dolgalev
Foreign Affairs, Uladzimir Syanko
Interior, Valyantsyn Agalets
Defence, Leanid Maltsav
Justice, Valyantsin Sukala
Trade, Pyotr Kazlov
Economy, Georgy Badzey
Finance, Pavel Dzik
Public Health, Inesa Drabyshevskaya
Information, Uladzimir Belski
Education, Vasil Strazhau
Culture, Alexander Sasnovski
Agriculture, Vasili Leonav
Transport and Communication, Alexander Lukashov
Social Welfare, Volga Dargel
Construction, Genadz Navitsky

EMBASSY OF THE REPUBLIC OF BELARUS
6 Kensington Court, London W8 5DL
Tel 0171-937 3288
Ambassador Extraordinary and Plenipotentiary, HE Uladzimir
    Shchasny, apptd 1995

BRITISH EMBASSY
37 Karl Marx Street, Minsk 220016
Tel: Minsk 292303/4/5
Ambassador Extraordinary and Plenipotentiary, HE Jessica
    Pearce, apptd 1995

DEFENCE

Belarus has on its territory 18 SS-25 Intercontinental Ballistic Missiles which it is obliged to return to Russia for destruction under the terms of the START 1 Treaty, which it ratified in 1993 along with the Nuclear Non-Proliferation Treaty.

The total active armed forces number 82,190 personnel. The Army has 45,214 personnel, the Air Force has 12,667 personnel (including 10,446 Air Defence). In addition there are 955 parliamentary border guards.

ECONOMY

The collapse of the Soviet centrally planned economic system hit Belarusian industry badly. Belarus had many factories manufacturing products such as tractors, textiles and metal workings from raw materials sent from the rest of the former USSR. The country could not afford to pay market prices for oil, gas and raw materials, bringing the economy close to collapse by mid-1994.

Since then economic reform and privatization have been introduced and in May 1995 a customs union agreement with Russia took effect under which Belarus will receive supplies of Russian oil and gas at subsidized prices. Belarus has also been given large-scale financial aid by Russia. A treaty was signed with Kazakhstan, Kyrgyzstan and Russia in March 1996 aimed at closer economic and social integration and the establishment of a single customs territory.

Belarusian agriculture, based on the meat and dairy industries, is relatively efficient and will cushion the republic from the worst of any food shortages, but rationing for some goods has been enforced since late 1992.

TRADE WITH UK	1994	1995
Imports from UK	£11,097,000	£22,570,000
Exports to UK	12,035,000	20,981,000

BELGIUM
Royaume de Belgique

Belgium has a total area of 11,781 sq. miles (30,513 sq. km) and is bounded on the north by the Netherlands, on the south by France, on the east by Germany and Luxembourg, and on the west by the North Sea. The Meuse and its tributary, the Sambre, divide it into two distinct regions, that in the west being generally level and fertile, while the tableland of the Ardennes, in the east, has mostly poor soil. The polders near the coast, which are protected by dykes against floods, cover an area of 193 sq. miles. The highest hill, Signal de Botranges, is 2,276 feet, but the mean elevation of the whole country does not exceed 526 feet. The principal rivers are the Scheldt and the Meuse.

The population (1994) was 10,100,631: Greater Brussels 949,070; Flanders 5,847,022; Wallonia 3,304,539, of whom 68,741 are German-speaking. The majority of Belgians are Roman Catholic.

Belgium is divided between those who speak Dutch (the Flemings) and those who speak French (the Walloons). Dutch is recognized as the official language in the northern areas and French in the southern (Walloon) area and there are guarantees for the respective linguistic minorities. Brussels is officially bi-lingual. There is a small German-speaking area (Eupen and Malmédy) along the German border, east of Liège.

CAPITAL – Brussels, population (1994) 949,070. Other towns are ΨAntwerp, the chief port (933,813); Liège (594,699); ΨGhent (490,285); Louvain (442,685); Charleroi (428,206); Namur (275,897); Mons (252,990); Bruges (267,172).
CURRENCY – Belgian franc of 100 centimes (centiemen).
FLAG – Three vertical bands, black, yellow, red.
NATIONAL ANTHEM – La Brabançonne.
NATIONAL DAY – 21 July (Accession of King Leopold I, 1831).

GOVERNMENT

The kingdom formed part of the Low Countries (Netherlands) from 1815 until 14 October 1830, when a National Congress proclaimed its independence. On 4 June 1831, Prince Leopold of Coburg was chosen as the hereditary king. The separation from the Netherlands and the neutrality and inviolability of Belgium were guaranteed by a Conference of the European powers, and by the Treaty of London 1839. On 4 August 1914 the Germans invaded Belgium, in violation of the terms of the treaty, and this led the Allies to declare war. Eupen and Malmédy were ceded by Germany under the Versailles Treaty 1919. The kingdom was again invaded by Germany in 1940 and was occupied by Nazi troops until liberated by the Allies in September 1944.

CONSTITUTION

According to the 1831 constitution Belgium is a constitutional representative and hereditary monarchy with a bicameral legislature, consisting of the King, the Senate and the Chamber of Deputies. The parliamentary term is four years. However, political tension between the Flemings and the Walloons since 1968 has led to constitutional amendments devolving power to the regions. The national government retains competence only in foreign and defence policies, the national budget and monetary policy, social security, and the judiciary, legal and penal systems. The Senate now has 71 seats, of which 40 are directly

elected, 21 indirectly elected and ten co-opted by the Flemish and Francophone Communities. The Chamber of Deputies now has 150 seats.
The last general election was held on 21 May 1995. The results were as follows (seats):
Chamber of Deputies: CVP 29; PS 21; VLD (Flemish Liberals and Democrats) 21; SP 20; PRL-FDF (Liberal Reform Party-Democratic Front (Francophone)) 18; PSC 12; Vlaams Blok (Flemish Nationalist Party) 11; Ecolo (Francophone Ecology Party) 6; Agalev (Flemish Environmental Party) 5; VU (Flemish People's Union) 5; Front National (FN) 2.
Senate: of the 40 seats directly elected, CVP 7; SP 6; VLD 6; PRL-FDF 5; PS 5; PSC 3; Vlaams Blok 3; VU 2; Ecolo 2; Agalev 1. A further 31 Senators are indirectly elected or co-opted (see above).

HEAD OF STATE
HM The King of the Belgians, King Albert II, born 6 June 1934; succeeded 9 August 1993; married 2 July 1959, Donna Paola Ruffo di Calabria, and has issue Prince Philippe (see below); Princess Astrid, b. 5 June 1962; Prince Laurent, b. 20 October 1963
Heir, HRH Prince Philippe Léopold Louis Marie, born 15 April 1960

CABINET as at July 1996
Prime Minister, Jean-Luc Dehaene (CVP)
Deputy Prime Minister, Economic Affairs, Elio Di Rupo (PS)
Deputy Prime Minister, Finance, Philippe Maystadt (PSC)
Deputy Prime Minister, Interior Affairs, Johan Vande Lanotte (SP)
Deputy Prime Minister, Budget, Herman Van Rompuy (CVP)
Scientific Policy, Yvan Ylieff (PS)
Defence, Jean-Pol Poncelet (PSC)
Pensions and Public Health, Marcel Colla (SP)
Foreign Affairs, Eric Derycke (SP)
Employment, Equal Opportunities, Miet Smet (CVP)
Social Affairs, Magda De Galan (PS)
Agriculture and Small- and Medium-Sized Enterprises, Karel Pinxten (CVP)
Transport, Michel Daerden (PS)
Justice, Stefaan De Clerck (CVP)
Civil Service, André Flahaut (PS)

CVP Christian Social Party (Flemish); PS Socialist Party (Francophone); SP Socialist Party (Flemish); PSC Christian Social Party (Francophone)

BELGIAN EMBASSY
103 Eaton Square, London SW1W 9AB
Tel 0171-470 3700
Ambassador Extraordinary and Plenipotentiary, HE Jonkheer Prosper Thuysbaert, apptd 1994
Minister-Counsellor, A. Querton (Political), J. M. Veranneman
Military, Naval and Air Attaché, Col. J. Bouzette
First Secretary (Economic), R. Van Lancker

BRITISH EMBASSY
rue d'Arlon 85, 1040 Brussels
Tel: Brussels 287 6211
Ambassador Extraordinary and Plenipotentiary, HE David Colvin, apptd 1993
Deputy Ambassador, Counsellor and Consul-General, E. C. Glover
Counsellor (Commercial), N. R. Jarrold
Defence and Military Attaché, Gp Capt. D. C. Hencken
There are British Consular Offices at Brussels, Antwerp and Liège.

British Council Representative to Belgium and Luxembourg – Dr Ken Churchill, OBE, rue de la Charite 15, Liefdadigheidstraat 15, 1210 Brussels.
British Chamber of Commerce for Belgium and Luxembourg (Inc.), rue Joseph II 30, 1040 Brussels

REGIONAL GOVERNMENT

The constitutional amendments of 1980, 1988 and 1993 make provision for four levels of sub-national government in Belgium: community, regional, provincial, and communal.

There are four communities: Flemish; Francophone; Brussels; Germanophone. Each community has its own assembly, which elects the community government. At this level, Flanders is covered by the Flemish Community Assembly; Brussels is covered by its Joint Community Commission as well as the Flemish and Francophone Community Assemblies; most of Walloonia is covered by the Francophone Community Assembly and the areas of Walloonia in the German-speaking communities of Eupen and Malmédy are covered by the Germanophone Community Assembly.

At regional level, Belgium is divided into the regions of Walloonia, Brussels and Flanders. Each region has its own assembly and government.

There are ten provinces; five French-speaking in Walloonia (Hainault, Liège, Luxembourg, Namur and French Brabant); and five Dutch-speaking in Flanders (Antwerp, East Flanders, West Flanders, Limbourg and Flemish Brabant). In addition, Belgium has 589 communes as the lowest level of local government.

The main consequence of the constitutional amendments has been the increase in power of the regional governments at the expense of both the community and national levels. The Francophone Community Assembly and Government is gradually losing power to the Walloon and Brussels regional governments, whilst the Flemish have amalgamated their community and regional governments to form one increasingly powerful Flanders government.

Minister-President of the Flemish Government, Luc Van den Brande (CVP)
Minister-President of the Walloon Regional Government, Robert Collignon (PS)

DEFENCE

The total active armed forces number 47,200 with 275,700 reservists. Conscription was abolished in 1995.

The Army has a strength of 30,100 with 334 main battle tanks, 597 armoured personnel carriers and armoured infantry fighting vehicles, 308 artillery pieces and 80 helicopters.

The Navy has a strength of 2,800 with two frigates and 11 mine warfare vessels. The Air Force is 12,300 strong with 133 combat aircraft and another 71 in store.

The headquarters of NATO, SHAPE and the Western European Union Military Planning Cell are in Belgium; 1,500 US personnel are stationed in the country.

ECONOMY

Belgium is a manufacturing country. With no natural resources except coal, production of which has now ceased, industry is based largely on the processing for re-export of imported raw materials. Principal industries are steel and metal products, chemicals and petrochemicals, textiles, glass, and foodstuffs.

In an attempt to meet the Maastricht Treaty criteria for economic and monetary union, the government introduced a series of austerity packages in 1993–6 to try to reduce Belgian public debt of 140 per cent of GDP, which is the highest in the developed world. The austerity measures have prompted public sector strikes. GNP per capita was US$22,920 in 1994.

FINANCE

Budget	1994	1995
Revenue	BFr.2,131,300m	BFr.2,200,000m
Expenditure	2,796,400m	1,942,700m

TRADE

External trade figures relate to Luxembourg as well as Belgium since the two countries formed an economic union in 1921.

	1993	1994
Total imports	BFr.4,021,000m	BFr.4,192,000m
Total exports	4,191,000m	4,580,000m

Trade with UK (Belgium and Luxembourg)

	1994	1995
Imports from UK	£7,111,693,000	£7,880,300,000
Exports to UK	6,886,191,000	7,631,300,000

CULTURE

The literature of France and the Netherlands is supplemented by an indigenous Belgian literary activity in both French and Dutch. Maurice Maeterlinck (1862–1949) was awarded the Nobel Prize for Literature in 1911. Emile Verhaeren (1855–1916) was a poet of international standing. Of contemporary Belgian writers, the most celebrated was Georges Simenon (1903–89).

EDUCATION

Nursery schools provide free education for children from two and a half to six years. There are over 4,000 primary schools (6 to 12 years), more than 1,000 secondary schools offering a general academic education slightly over half of which are free institutions (predominantly Roman Catholic but subsidized by the state) and the remainder official institutions. The official school-leaving age is 18.

COMMUNICATIONS

The railways are operated by the Belgian National Railways. Ship canals include Ghent-Terneuzen (18 miles, half in the Netherlands) by which ships up to 60,000 tons reach Ghent; Willebroek Rupel-Brussels (20 miles, by which ships drawing 18 ft reach Brussels from the sea); Bruges (from Zeebrugge on the North Sea to Bruges, 6½ miles); Albert (79 miles), Liège to Antwerp for barges up to 1,350 tons. The River Meuse from the Dutch to the French frontiers, the River Sambre betwen Namur and Monceau, the River Scheldt from Antwerp to Ghent and the Brussels-Charleroi Canal are being widened or deepened to take barges up to 1,350 tons. Most maritime trade is carried in foreign shipping.

In 1986 there were 14,260 km of trunk road, of which about 1,550 km were motorways. The Belgian national airline Sabena operates regular services between Brussels and European centres, as well as intercontinental services worldwide.

There were 33 daily newspapers in 1992.

BELIZE

Belize lies on the east coast of Central America, bounded on the north and north-west by Mexico, and on the west and south by Guatemala. The total area (including offshore islands) is about 8,867 sq. miles (22,965 sq. km.).

The coastal areas are mostly flat and swampy with many islets but the country rises gradually towards the interior, which is mainly forest. The northern and western districts are hilly, and in the south the Maya Mountains and the Cockscombs form the backbone of the country, reaching a height of 3,700 feet at Victoria Peak. The climate is subtropical, with a mean annual temperature of 20°C, but is tempered by sea breezes. There are two dry seasons (February–May and August–September) and occasional hurricanes.

The population is 205,000 (1993 census), of which the main racial groups are Mestizo (Maya-Spanish), 44 per cent; Creole, 30 per cent; Maya, 11 per cent; plus a number of East Indian and Spanish descent. The races are now inter-mixed. The majority of the population is Christian, about 58 per cent Catholic and 34 per cent Protestant. The official language and language of instruction is English. Spanish is also widely spoken and English Creole is the vernacular. There are also Garifuna and Maya speakers.

CAPITAL – Belmopan (1993 census 3,739). The largest city and former capital is ΨBelize City (1993 census 46,342). Other towns are Corozal (7,420), San Ignacio (9,417), Dangriga (6,761), Orange Walk (11,573).

CURRENCY – Belize dollar (BZ$) of 100 cents. The Belize dollar is tied to the US dollar, BZ$2 = US$1.

FLAG – Blue ground with red band along top and bottom edges, and in centre a white disc containing the coat of arms surrounded by a green garland.

NATIONAL ANTHEM – Land of the Free.

NATIONAL DAY – 21 September (Independence Day).

GOVERNMENT

Numerous ruins in the area indicate that Belize was heavily populated by the Maya Indians. The first British settlement was established in 1638 but was subject to repeated attacks by the Spanish, who claimed sovereignty until defeated by the Royal Navy and settlers in 1798. In 1871 the area was recognized by Britain as a colony and called British Honduras. In 1973 the colony was renamed Belize, and was granted independence on 21 September 1981. The long-standing territorial dispute with Guatemala was provisionally resolved in 1992 when the Guatemalan Congress and Supreme Court voted to recognize Belize and establish diplomatic relations. Guatemala still retains its claim, subject to arbitration by the International Court of Justice.

Queen Elizabeth II is head of state, represented in Belize by a Governor-General. There is a National Assembly, comprising a House of Representatives (29 members elected for five years) and a Senate (nine members appointed by the Governor-General). Executive power is vested in the Cabinet, which is responsible to the National Assembly.

The National Assembly was dissolved in June 1993 and in the ensuing elections the People's United Party government was defeated by the United Democratic Party.

Governor-General, HE Sir Colville Norbert Young, GCMG, apptd 17 November 1993

THE CABINET *as at July 1996*
Prime Minister, Finance and Economic Development, Rt. Hon. Manuel Esquivel
Deputy PM, National Security, Attorney-General, Foreign Affairs, Hon. Dean O. Barrow
Human Resources, Women's Affairs and Youth Development, Hon. Philip S. W. Goldson
Education, Public Service, Hon. Elodio Aragon
Health and Sports, Ruben Campos
Tourism and Environment, Hon. Henry Young
Trade and Industry, Hon. Salvador Fernandez
Natural Resources, Hon. Eduardo Juan
Housing, Urban Development and Co-operatives, Hon. Hubert Elrington
Agriculture and Fisheries, Hon. Russell Garcia
Works, Hon. Melvin Hulse jun.
Home Affairs and Labour, Hon. Elito Urbina sen.
Energy, Science, Technology and Transport, Hon. Joseph Cayetano

BELIZE HIGH COMMISSION
22 Harcourt House, 19 Cavendish Square, London WIM 9AD
Tel 0171- 499 9728
High Commissioner, HE Dr Ursula Barrow, apptd 1993

BRITISH HIGH COMMISSION
PO Box 91, Belmopan
Tel: Belmopan 22146/7
High Commissioner, HE Gordon Baker, apptd 1994

ECONOMY

About 30 per cent of the population is engaged in agriculture. Corn (maize), rice, red kidney beans, root crops and fruit are the main food crops, although the main agricultural exports are sugar, bananas and citrus products. The country is more or less self-sufficient in fresh beef, pork and poultry, but processed meat and dairy products are imported. About 25 per cent of timber production (mostly mahogany) is exported, and there is a large US market for lobster, conch and scale fish. Tourism is also a valuable source of income.

TRADE	1992	1993
Total imports	BZ$548.3m	BZ$545.3m
Total exports	231.1m	228.6m

Trade with UK	1994	1995
Imports from UK	£12,767,000	£14,261,000
Exports to UK	42,504,000	47,010,000

EDUCATION

Education is compulsory from six to 14 years of age. In 1992 primary education was provided by 241 schools, most of which are government-aided. Enrolment totalled 48,612. Secondary education is provided by 40 secondary and post-secondary institutions with an enrolment of 10,647. A University College of Belize has been established. The Government also offers scholarships for students to go abroad. There is an extra-mural faculty of the University of the West Indies, with a resident tutor.

COMMUNICATIONS

There is a government-operated radio service and three privately-owned radio stations but no official television service in the country. An automatic telephone service operated by Belize Telecommunications Ltd covers the whole country.

The principal airport is at Belize City and various airlines operate international flights to the USA and other Central American states. The main port is also Belize City, which has deep water quays. Several inland waterways are also navigable. There are 1,865 miles of road, including four main highways, but there is no railway system.

BENIN
République du Benin

A republic situated in West Africa, between 2° and 3° W. and 6° and 12° N., Benin (formerly known as Dahomey) has a short coastline of 78 miles on the Gulf of Guinea but extends northwards inland for 437 miles. It is flanked on the west by Togo, on the north by Burkina and Niger, and on the east by Nigeria. The four main regions, running horizontally, are a narrow sandy coastal strip, a succession of inter-communicating lagoons, a clay belt and a sandy plateau in the north. It has an area of 43,484 sq. miles (122,622 sq. km), and a population of 5,215,000 (UN 1993 estimate). The official language is French. Although poor in resources, Benin is one of the most heavily populated areas in West Africa, with a high standard of education.

CAPITAL – ΨPorto Novo, population (1982 estimate) 208,258. Principal commercial town and port, ΨCotonou (487,020).
CURRENCY – Franc CFA of 100 centimes.
FLAG – Two horizontal stripes of yellow over red with a vertical green band in the hoist.
NATIONAL DAY – 30 November.

GOVERNMENT

The country was placed under French administration in 1892 and became an independent republic within the French Community in December 1958; full independence outside the Community was proclaimed on 1 August 1960. Between 1963 and 1972 successive governments were overthrown by the military until a coup d'état in 1972 brought to power a Marxist-Leninist military government headed by Lt.-Col. Kerekou.

The government dropped Marxism-Leninism as the official ideology in 1989, revoked the constitution in March 1990 and changed the country's official name from the People's Republic of Benin to the Republic of Benin. The Revolutionary National Assembly (legislature) was replaced by a High Council of the Republic (HCR). A pluralistic constitution was adopted in December 1990 and legislative and presidential elections were held in 1991. Nicéphore Soglo was sworn in as President and appointed a Benin Resistance Party (PRB)-dominated provisional government which was dependent on an unstable alliance of independents in the 64-member National Assembly. Legislative elections to the 83-seat National Assembly in March 1995 gave the PRB and allies 32 seats and opposition parties 49 seats. Soglo was defeated by former military ruler Gen. Kerekou in a presidential election in March 1996.

HEAD OF STATE
President and Head of the Armed Forces, HE Gen. Mathieu Kerekou, *sworn in* 4 April 1996

CABINET *as at July 1996*
Prime Minister, Adrien Houngbedji
Defence, Séverin Adjovi
Foreign Affairs and Co-operation, Pierre Otcho
Justice, Ismael Djani-Cerpos
Finance, Moïse Mensah
Interior, Théophile Nda

Planning and Employment Promotion, Albert Tevoedjre
Rural Development, Jerome-Desiré Sakassina
Industry, Tourism and Handicrafts, Delphin Houngbedji
Energy and Water Resources, Emmanuel Golou
Public Works and Transport, Oumarou Fassassi
Environment and Housing, Saidou Binade Dango
Civil Service, Yacoubou Assouma
National Education, Leonard Djidjofon Kpadonou
Health, Marina D'Almeida
Communication, Culture and Information, Timothée Zanou
Youth and Sports, Zinsou Damien Alahata

EMBASSY OF THE REPUBLIC OF BENIN
87 Avenue Victor Hugo, 75116 Paris, France
Tel: Paris 4500 9882
Ambassador Extraordinary and Plenipotentiary, HE Richard Adjaho
HONORARY CONSULATE, 16 The Broadway, Stanmore, Middx HA7 4DW. Tel: 081–954 8800. *Honorary Consul*, L. Landau

BRITISH AMBASSADOR, HE J. T. Masefield CMG, resident at Lagos, Nigeria

ECONOMY

In early 1994 the IMF approved a three-year enhanced structural adjustment facility credit of US$72.6m to underpin economic reforms.

The principal exports are cotton, palm products, groundnuts, shea-nuts, and coffee. Small deposits of gold, iron and chrome have been found. Oil production started in 1983; 192,000 tonnes were produced in 1994.

TRADE WITH UK	1994	1995
Imports from UK	£30,352,000	£43,115,000
Exports to UK	3,820,000	1,012,000

BHUTAN
Druk-yul

Bhutan is a small kingdom in the Himalayas with Tibet to the north and India to the west, south and east. The total area is about 18,147 sq. miles (47,000 sq. km), with a mountainous northern region which is infertile and sparsely populated, a central zone of upland valleys where most of the population and cultivated land is found, and in the south the densely forested foothills of the Himalayas, which are mainly inhabited by Nepalese settlers and indigenous tribespeople.

The population is estimated at 650,000, about 80 per cent of whom are Buddhists. The remainder (mostly the Nepali Bhutanese) are Hindu. The official language, for administrative and religious purposes, is Dzongkha, a variant of Tibetan, which functions as a lingua franca amongst a variety of languages and dialects. From 1990 it has been government policy to make the study of Dzongkha compulsory in schools. However, Nepali remains a recognized language and English remains the medium of instruction and the working language of the administration.

CAPITAL – Thimphu, population estimate (1987) 15,000.
CURRENCY – Ngultrum (Nu) of 100 chetrums. Indian currency is also legal tender.
FLAG – Saffron yellow and orange-red divided diagonally, with dragon device in centre.
NATIONAL DAY – 17 December.

GOVERNMENT

Under a 1949 treaty Bhutan is guided by the advice of India in regard to its external relations. It retains its own diplomatic representatives and is a member of the UN. It also receives from India an annual payment of Rs500,000 as compensation for portions of its territory annexed by the British Government in India in 1864.

Bhutan has a 150-member National Assembly which meets twice a year. The ten-member Royal Advisory Council, nominated by the King and the National Assembly, acts as a consultative body when the National Assembly is not in session. The King is also assisted by a Council of Ministers. There are no political parties.

In January 1989 the King introduced a code of national etiquette designed to protect the national culture and language from Nepali encroachment. These measures, together with the granting of citizenship only to Nepalis settled in Bhutan before 1958, has led to an exodus of ethnic Nepalis to Nepal, where about 80,000 live in camps. A low-level insurgency has been waged in the south of the country against the King's policies by ethnic Nepalis since 1990. Talks between the Nepali and Bhutan governments continue in an attempt to resolve the fate of the refugees.

HEAD OF STATE

HM The King of Bhutan, Jigme Singye Wangchuk, *born* 11 November 1955; *succeeded his father* July 1972; *crowned* 2 June 1974

Heir, Crown Prince Jigme Gesar Namgyal Wangchuk, *designated* 31 October 1988

COUNCIL OF MINISTERS *as at June 1996*

Chairman of Council of Ministers, HM The King
Secretary, Foreign Affairs, Dawa Tsering
Agriculture, HRH Dechhen Wangmo Wangchuck
Finance, HRH Sonam Chhoden Wangchuck
Home Affairs, Namgyel Wangchuk
Social Services and Communications, Tashi Tobgyal
Trade, Industry and Tourism, Om Pradan

ECONOMY

The seventh five-year plan (1992–7) envisages a doubling of internal revenues to Nu2,000m. Economic emphasis is on the infrastructure, especially roads and telecommunications, and hydro-electric power.

The economy is based on agriculture and animal husbandry, which engage over 90 per cent of the workforce in what is largely a self-sufficient rural society. The principal food crops are rice, wheat, maize and barley. Vegetables and fruit are also produced. Bhutan is the world's largest producer of cardamom, which forms its principal export to countries other than India. Agriculture is, however, limited by the country's mountainous topography and 60 per cent forest cover. The mountains contain rich deposits of limestone, gypsum, dolomite and graphite and small amounts of coal, which are exported to India. A modest industrial base is being developed. A distillery and cement, chemicals and food-processing plants are in production; a forestry industries complex is being expanded. Tourism and postage stamps are increasingly important sources of foreign exchange.

TRADE

Over 90 per cent of foreign trade is with India. Principal exports are agricultural products, timber, cement and coal; main imports are textiles, cereals and consumer goods. Bhutan's airline, Druk Air, flies between Paro, New Delhi and Calcutta.

Trade with UK	1994	1995
Imports from UK	£1,631,000	£2,428,000
Exports to UK	857,000	492,000

BOLIVIA
República de Bolivia

Bolivia extends between 10° and 23° S. latitude and 57° 30′ and 69° 45′ W. longitude. It has an area estimated at 424,165 sq. miles (1,098,581 sq. km) and is landlocked.

The chief topographical feature is the great central plateau over 500 miles in length, at an average altitude of 12,500 feet above sea level, between the two great chains of the Andes, which traverse the country from south to north. The total length of the navigable rivers is about 12,000 miles, the principal rivers being the Itenez, Beni, Mamore and Madre de Dios.

The population (1992 census) was 6,440,000, of which 12 per cent is of white European descent, 30 per cent mestizo (mixed European-Indian), 25 per cent Quechua Indian and 17 per cent Aymará Indian. The official language is Spanish, which is spoken by around 60 per cent of the population, with Quechua spoken by 25 per cent and Aymará by 15 per cent. Roman Catholicism was the state religion until disestablishment in 1961.

CAPITAL – La Paz (population, 1,115,000). Other large centres are Cochabamba (512,000), Oruro (183,000), Santa Cruz (694,000), Potosí (112,000), Sucre, the legal capital and seat of the judiciary (131,000) and Tarija (90,000).

CURRENCY – Boliviano ($b) of 100 centavos.

FLAG – Three horizontal bands; red, yellow, green.

NATIONAL ANTHEM – Bolivianos, El Hado Propicio (Oh Bolivia, our long-felt desires).

NATIONAL DAY – 6 August (Independence Day).

GOVERNMENT

Bolivia won its independence from Spain in 1825 after a war of liberation led by Simon Bolivar (1783–1830), from whom the country derives its name. From 1964 to 1982 Bolivia was ruled by military juntas until civilian rule was restored. The constitution provides for a directly elected executive President who appoints the Cabinet. The legislature (Congress) consists of a 27-member Senate and a 130-member Chamber of Deputies. Both the President and Congress are elected for four-year terms.

Congressional and presidential elections were held in June 1993 with Gonzalo Sánchez of the opposition National Revolutionary Movement (MNR) winning the largest share of the vote in the presidential election but as no candidate won more than 50 per cent, the new President was chosen by Congressional vote in August, when Gonzalo Sánchez was elected. The MNR emerged as the largest party in Congress, winning 52 out of 130 seats, and formed a government in coalition with the Civic Solidarity Union (20 seats) and the Free Bolivia Movement (7 seats).

HEAD OF STATE

President of the Republic, Gonzalo Sánchez de Lozada, *inaugurated* 5 August 1993
Vice President, Victor Hugo Cardenas

CABINET *as at July 1996*

Foreign Affairs and Worship, Antonío Araníbar Quiroga
Interior, Carlos Sanchez Berzain
National Defence, Jorge Otasevic Toledo

Presidency, José Guillermo Justiniano
Economic Development, Jaime Villalovof
Education and Culture, Carlos Pimentel
Labour, Reynaldo Peters
Human Development, Freddy Teodovich
Information, Guillermo Richter
Justice, René Blattman
Privatization, Alfonso Revollo
Sustainable Development, Moises Jarmusz
Finanoo, Fernando Caudia
Health, Oscar Sandoval Moron

BOLIVIAN EMBASSY
106 Eaton Square, London SW1W 9AD
Tel 0171-235 2257/4248
Ambassador Extraordinary and Plenipotentiary, HE Carlos
    Morales-Landívar, apptd 1995

BRITISH EMBASSY
Avenida Arce 2732, (Casilla 694) La Paz
Tel: La Paz 357424
Ambassador Extraordinary and Plenipotentiary, HE David
    Ridgway, OBE, apptd 1995
Deputy Ambassador, Consul and First Secretary, I. Davies

There is an Honorary Consulate at Santa Cruz.

EDUCATION

Elementary education is compulsory and free and there are
secondary schools in urban centres. Provision is also made
for higher education; in addition to St Francisco Xavier's
University at Sucre, founded in 1624, there are seven other
universities, the largest being the University of San Andres
at La Paz, and ten private universities.

ECONOMY

Mining, natural gas, petroleum and agriculture are the
principal industries. The ancient silver mines of Potosí are
now worked chiefly for tin, but gold is obtained on the
Eastern Cordillera of the Andes. Tin output, together with
other minerals (copper, tungsten, antimony, lead, zinc,
asbestos, wolfram, bismuth salt and sulphur), provides over
one-third of exports. Small quantities of oil are produced
for internal consumption, and gas (currently providing
about a quarter of export income) is piped to Argentina;
there are plans to build a pipeline to São Paulo, Brazil.

The economy deteriorated badly in the late 1970s and
early 1980s, with a large external debt, and the collapse of
world tin prices. In the mid-1980s economic reforms were
introduced with privatization of some state-owned firms
and the encouragement of foreign investment. Tin prices
began to increase in 1989, but the industry remains
uneconomic. Many workers took to growing coca, which
has now become a significant export.

The peso was replaced in 1987 with the Boliviano of
1,000,000 old pesos in a successful effort to stem hyperinflation and had brought the inflation rate down to 9 per
cent in 1993. The economy and currency have stabilized
and the foreign debt (US$3,700 million in 1993) is being
repaid. GNP in 1994 was US$5,601 million. In December
1994 Bolivia received a US$147 million loan from the IMF.

TRADE

Mineral exports represent about 35 per cent of total trade.
Bolivia has now developed its own smelters and is
exporting metals. The chief imports are wheat and flour,
iron and steel products, machinery, vehicles and textiles.

Trade with UK	1994	1995
Imports from UK	£10,147,000	£17,042,000
Exports to UK	16,780,000	14,732,000

COMMUNICATIONS

There are 2,200 miles of railways in operation including
the lines from Corumbá to Santa Cruz. There is direct
railway communication to the sea at Antofagasta, Arica,
and Mollendo, and also to Buenos Aires. Communication
with Peru is by road from La Paz via Copacabana and
thence to the railhead at Puno. In 1993 Bolivia and Peru
signed an agreement granting Bolivia a concession of 162
hectares at the southern Peruvian port of Ilo for 98 years to
construct a free trade zone.

Commercial aviation is conducted by the national
airline, Lloyd Aereo Boliviano and Transporte Aereo
Militar between the major towns, and Lloyd Aereo
Boliviano and a number of foreign airlines provide international flights to the USA, South and Central America
and Europe.

Most towns have radio, telephone or telegraph communication with the main cities. There are 16 principal daily
newspapers.

BOSNIA-HERCEGOVINA

Bosnia-Hercegovina is bounded by Serbia on the east,
Montenegro on the south-east and Croatia on the north
and west, apart from a narrow 20 km coastline on the
Adriatic at Neum. The total area is 19,735 sq. miles (51,129
sq. km). The population (1991 census) was 4.4 million, of
whom some 44 per cent were Muslims, 31 per cent Serbs
and 17 per cent Croats. The 1995 population was estimated
to be 2.9 million of whom 1,270,000 were Muslims, 892,000
Serbs and 512,000 Croats.

CAPITAL – Sarajevo, population (1991) 453,324. Other
    major cities include Tuzla, Banja Luka, Zenica, Vitez
    and Mostar.
CURRENCY – Bosnian dinar.
FLAG – White flag bearing a blue shield with a white
    diagonal and six gold fleurs-de-lys.
NATIONAL DAY – 1 March (anniversary of 1992
    declaration of independence).

HISTORY

The country was settled by Slavs in the seventh century
and conquered by the Ottoman Turks in 1463. Ruled by
the Turks for over 400 years, the country came under
Austro-Hungarian control in 1878. Austria-Hungary's
annexation of Bosnia-Hercegovina in 1908 was never
accepted by Serbia because of the large ethnic Serb
population in the country, and the assassination of the
heir to the Austro-Hungarian throne in Sarajevo by an
ethnic Serb precipitated the First World War. Bosnia-
Hercegovina became part of the 'Kingdom of Serbs,
Croats and Slovenes' (renamed Yugoslavia in 1929) under
the Versailles Treaty 1919. It was occupied by German and
Axis forces between 1941 and 1945. At the end of the war
Bosnia-Hercegovina came under Communist rule as part
of the Socialist Federal Republic of Yugoslavia, which
eventually collapsed with the secession of Slovenia and
Croatia in 1991.

The Bosnia-Hercegovina government issued a declaration of sovereignty in October 1991 against the wishes of
the ethnic Serb Democratic Party. Independence was

declared on 1 March 1992 following a referendum which was boycotted by the Bosnian Serbs. Bosnia-Hercegovina was recognized as an independent state by the EC and USA in April 1992 and admitted to UN membership in May 1992.

THE WAR

Independence was supported by the Muslims and Croats in Bosnia but rejected by the Serbs, who wanted to form a Greater Serbia with the Serbian republic. Fighting be-tween Muslims and Serbs broke out in March 1992 and the Serb-dominated Federal Yugoslav Army (JNA) inter-vened against the poorly-armed Muslims, overrunning much of the republic and leaving Bosnian government forces besieged in Sarajevo and a few other enclaves. International pressure forced the JNA to withdraw but it handed over its weapons to Bosnian Serb forces. By August 1992, 70 per cent of Bosnia was controlled by Bosnian Serb forces and 20 per cent by Bosnian Croat forces, and the Bosnian government was in an uneasy alliance with Croatian and Bosnian Croat forces. The UN imposed a trade embargo on the rump Yugoslavia (Serbia and Montenegro) in May 1992 and deployed peacekeeping troops to distribute humanitarian aid the following winter.

A peace conference in London in August 1992 failed to reconcile the warring parties but was reconvened in Geneva in January 1993, when the joint UN-EU nego-tiating team presented the Vance-Owen plan. This was accepted by the Bosnian government, the Bosnian Croats, and the Bosnian Serb leader Radovan Karadzic, but rejected by the Bosnian Serb parliament.

In 1993 the Bosnian government was fighting both Bosnian Serb and Bosnian Croat forces. Bosnian Serb forces starved and shelled Muslim enclaves in eastern Bosnia and Sarajevo, causing the UN to declare the enclaves of Srebrenica, Zepa, Gorazde, Sarajevo, Tuzla and Bihac 'safe areas'. Fighting between the government and Bosnian Croat forces ended in February 1994 after a Muslim-Croat Federation was agreed (see below) and the two sides reformed their alliance of 1992 and early 1993. UN troops were dispatched to patrol the new cease-fire lines.

A three-month détente between the government and Bosnian Serbs collapsed in December 1993, leading to the shelling of Sarajevo and government-held enclaves. A Bosnian Serb artillery attack on a Sarajevo market in February 1994 killed 68 and prompted the UN and NATO to impose a heavy weapons exclusion zone around the city. Bosnian Serb forces captured most of the enclave of Gorazde in April despite NATO air strikes. NATO widened its threat of air strikes to all UN 'safe areas' and galvanized the USA, Britain, France, Germany and Russia to form the Contact Group (CG) to co-ordinate peace efforts. The CG brought about a cease-fire in June 1994 and presented a peace plan, proposing a 51:49 division of territory between the Muslim-Croat Federation and the Bosnian Serbs. The Bosnian Serbs rejected the plan and the CG attempted to isolate them, with the support of Serbia, which had agreed to blockade Bosnian Serb forces in exchange for a relaxation of sanctions.

NATO air strikes against Bosnian Serbs in December 1994 resulted in the seizure of 350 UN peacekeepers, who were released as part of a cease-fire agreement in January. Bosnian Serbs retaliating against a Federation offensive in March resumed artillery attacks on Sarajevo, prompting a NATO bombing campaign and a second hostage crisis.

Fighting intensified in 1995, climaxing in a land-grab during the final months of the war. Bosnian Serb forces overran the UN safe areas of Zepa and Srebrenica in July, allegedly massacring thousands of fleeing Muslims, and then laid siege to the Bihac 'safe area' together with Croatian Serbs and rebel Muslims. The Croatian army and Bosnian Croat forces attacked the area south of Bihac, driving Bosnian Serb civilians eastwards. Bosnian govern-ment and Croatian forces lifted the siege of Bihac in August, enabling a joint attack on Serb-held central Bosnia.

A Serb artillery attack on Sarajevo on 28 August which killed 37 people prompted NATO to take a tougher stance against the Bosnian Serbs. NATO bombed military and infrastructure targets and issued an ultimatum to the Bosnian Serbs to remove their heavy weapons from around Sarajevo; the ultimatum was met by 20 September, following coercion from President Milosevic of Serbia.

The foreign ministers of Bosnia, Croatia and Serbia (rump Yugoslavia) met in Geneva in September 1995 and agreed to a US-sponsored peace accord. A cease-fire agreement was signed on 5 October and observed from 22 October, delayed by a Federation advance in the west and north-west, and Bosnian Serbs overrunning Tuzla. See also Events of the Year.

THE PEACE AGREEMENT

The presidents of Bosnia, Serbia and Croatia met in Dayton, Ohio, USA, for negotiations which culminated in an agreement on 21 November 1995. The Dayton Peace Treaty was signed in Paris on 14 December. It was agreed to preserve Bosnia as a single state with a 51:49 division of territory between the Bosnian and Croat Federation and the Republika Srpska (Bosnian Serbs). A Republican (national) government, presidency and democratically elected institutions, based in Federation-controlled Sara-jevo, were provided for. The Bosnian Serbs agreed to return five Sarajevo suburbs to the Federation and were given access to the sea in a land-swap with Croatia. The Federation gained a land corridor between Sarajevo and Gorazde but was obliged to return Mrkonjic Grad to the Bosnian Serbs. The Dayton agreement provided for the deployment of a 60,000-strong NATO-led Peace Imple-mentation Force (IFOR) which took over from UNPRO-FOR on 20 December 1995 and was mandated until December 1996.

The peace agreement was supplemented by a Peace Implementation Conference in London on 8–9 December 1995, which agreed to appoint an EU High Representative, Carl Bildt; and by a reconstruction conference in Brussels on 12 April 1996 at which £800 million was pledged by international donors.

GOVERNMENT

In December 1990 Alija Izetbegovic (Muslim) was elected to lead a seven-man collective rotating presidency; in practice, he remained president throughout the war. The Bosnian Serbs under Radovan Karadzic declared their own 'Republika Srpska' in August 1992 with its capital at Pale, and the Bosnian Croats established the 'Republic of Herceg-Bosna' in August 1993 with its capital at Mostar. The predominantly Muslim Bosnian government remained in Sarajevo.

After a Muslim-Croat cease-fire in February 1994, the Bosnian, Bosnian Croat and Croatian governments agreed to form a Bosnian Muslim-Croat Federation, with a federal presidency, joint federal-republican government and constituent assembly. In practice the Federation's operation proved difficult, and the Muslims and Croats agreed to appoint an international arbiter to help resolve their differences in February 1995.

Under the Dayton peace agreement, the Bosnian republican (national) government was made responsible for foreign affairs, currency, citizenship and immigration. Executive authority was vested in a democratically elected presidential triumvirate comprising a representative from each community; the chairmanship is to rotate. Legislative authority was vested in a bicameral parliament, two-thirds of its members from the Federation and one-third from the Republika Srpska. The agreement stipulated that elections to the national presidency and parliament and to the Federation and Republika Srpska parliaments should be held within nine months, and these were scheduled for 14 September 1996. The Republican and Federation parliaments elected new governments on 30 and 31 January 1996 respectively. Indicted war criminals were barred from standing for election.

Mostar, which had been divided during the war between the Muslims and Croats of the Federation and administered by the European Union, held elections in June 1996 which were seen as a pilot for the September national elections. The (Muslim) Party for Social Democracy defeated the Croat Democratic Party although the ethnic composition of the town council had been predetermined as 16 Croats, 16 Muslims and 5 Serbs.

REPUBLICAN (NATIONAL) GOVERNMENT *as at July 1996*
Presidency Members, Alija Izetbegovic (current President); Tatjana Ljujic-Mijatovic; Mirko Pejanovic
Prime Minister, Hasan Muratovic
Finance, Mirsad Kikanovic
Foreign Affairs, Jadranko Prlic
Foreign Trade and International Communications, Neven Tomic
Justice and Administration, Hilmo Pasic
Refugees and Displaced Persons, Nudzeim Recica
Without Portfolio, Dragoljub Stojanov

FEDERATION GOVERNMENT *as at July 1996*
President, Kresimir Zubak
Vice President, Ejup Ganic
Prime Minister, Izudin Kapetanovic
Deputy Prime Minister, Drago Bilandzija
Agriculture, Water Management and Forestry, Ahmed Smajic
Defence, Vladimir Soljic
Education, Culture and Sports, Fahrudin Rizvanbegovic
Energy, Mining and Industry, Enver Kreso
Finance, Drago Bilandzija
Health, Bozo Ljubic

Interior, Avdo Hebib
Justice, Mate Tadic
Social Policy and Refugees, Ferid Alic
Town Planning and Environment, Ibrahim Morancic
Trade, Nikola Grabovac
Transport and Communications, Rasim Gacanovic
Without Portfolio, Nedeljko Despotovic; Martin Raguz

REPUBLIKA SRPSKA GOVERNMENT *as at July 1996*
Acting President, Biljana Plavsic
Vice-President, Nikola Koljevic
Prime Minister, Rajko Kasagic
Deputy PM Economy and Finances, Milomir Draganic
Deputy PM Social Affairs, Velibor Ostojic
Deputy PM Internal Policy, Miroslav Vjectica
Agriculture, Forestry and Waterworks, Djojo Arsenovic
Defence, Milan Ninkovic
Education, Science and Culture, Nedeljko Rasula
Finance, Novak Kondic
Foreign Affairs, Aleksa Buha
Health, Labour and Social Welfare, Dragan Kalinic
Industry and Energy, Milorad Skoko
Information, Dragan Bozanic
Interior, Dragan Kijac
Justice and Administration, Marko Arsenic
Refugees and Displaced Persons, Ljubisa Vladusic
Religious Affairs, Dragan Davidovic
Trade and Food Supplies, Spasoje Albijanic
Transportation and Communications, Nedeljko Lajic
Urban Affairs, Construction and Utilities, Ratko Misanovic
Veterans' Issues, Vojislav Radiskovic
Without Portfolio, Miroslav Toholj

EMBASSY OF THE REPUBLIC OF BOSNIA-HERCEGOVINA
4th Floor, Morley House, 314–22 Regent Street, London WI
Tel 0171-255 3758
Ambassador Extraordinary and Plenipotentiary, HE Prof. Muhamed Filipovic, apptd 1995

BRITISH EMBASSY
8 Tina Ujevica, Sarajevo
Tel: Sarajevo 444429
Ambassador Extraordinary and Plenipotentiary, HE Charles Crawford, apptd 1996

BRITISH COUNCIL REPRESENTATIVE, Sue Barnes

TRADE WITH UK	1994	1995
Imports from UK	£3,120,000	£4,084,000
Exports to UK	191,000	240,000

BOTSWANA
The Republic of Botswana

Botswana (formerly the British Protectorate of Bechuanaland) lies between 18° and 26° S. latitude and 20° and 28° W. longitude and is bounded by South Africa on the south and east, by Zimbabwe, the rivers Zambezi and Chobe (Linyanti) on the north and north-east, and by Namibia on the west. It has a total area of 224,607 sq. miles (581,730 sq. km).

A plateau at a height of about 4,000 feet divides Botswana into two main topographical regions. To the east of the plateau streams flow into the Marico, Notwani and Limpopo rivers; to the west lies a flat region comprising the Kgalagadi Desert, the Okavango Swamps and the Northern State Lands area. The climate is generally subtropical, but varies considerably with latitude and altitude.

Botswana has a population (1991 census) of 1,326,796. The national language is Setswana and the official language is English.

CAPITAL – Gaborone, population (1991 census) 133,458. Other centres are Francistown (55,244), Lobatse (26,052), and Selebi-Phikwe (39,772).
CURRENCY – Pula (P) of 100 thebe.
FLAG – Light blue with a horizontal black stripe fimbriated in white across the centre.
NATIONAL ANTHEM – Fatshe La Rona.
NATIONAL DAY – 30 September.

GOVERNMENT

On 30 September 1966, Bechuanaland became a republic within the Commonwealth under the name Botswana. The President is head of state and is elected by an absolute majority in the National Assembly. He appoints as Vice President a member of the National Assembly who is leader of government business in the National Assembly. The Assembly consists of the President, 40 members elected every five years on a basis of universal adult suffrage, four specially elected members, the Attorney-General (non-voting) and the Speaker. Presidential and legislative elections are held every five years. There is also a 15-member House of Chiefs which considers legislation affecting the constitution and chieftaincy matters. The last general election on 15 October 1994 was won by the Botswana Democratic Party with 26 seats to the Botswana National Front's 13 seats.

HEAD OF STATE
President, HE Sir Ketumile Masire, GCMG, *re-elected* 17 October 1994 for a third five-year term

CABINET *as at May 1996*
The President
Vice President, Finance and Development Planning, Hon. Festus Mogae
Presidential Affairs, Public Administration, Hon. Ponatshengo Kedikilwe
Local Government, Lands and Housing, Hon. Patrick Balopi
External Affairs, Hon. Lt.-Gen. Mompati Merafhe
Mineral Resources and Water, Hon. David Magang
Commerce and Industry, Hon. George Kgoroba
Agriculture, Hon. Roy Blackbeard
Works, Transport and Communications, Hon. Daniel Kwelagobe
Health, Hon. Chapson Butale
Education, Hon. Dr Gaositwe Chiepe
Labour and Home Affairs, Hon. Bahiti Temane
Assistant Ministers: Finance and Development Planning, Hon. J. Mothibamele; *Local Government, Housing and Lands*, Hon. B. Mokgothu, Hon. M. Nasha; *Agriculture*, Hon. R. Sebego

BOTSWANA HIGH COMMISSION
6 Stratford Place, London WIN 9AE
Tel 0171–499 0031
High Commissioner, new appointment awaited

BRITISH HIGH COMMISSION
Private Bag 0023, Gaborone
Tel: Gaborone 352841
High Commissioner, HE David Beaumont, apptd 1994

BRITISH COUNCIL REPRESENTATIVE , T. A. Jones, MBE, British High Commission Building, Queen's Road, The Mall, PO Box 439, Gaborone

ECONOMY

Agriculture is predominantly pastoral. The national herd is around 2.2 million cattle and one million sheep and goats. Cattle rearing accounts for about 85 per cent of agricultural output and livestock products, particularly beef, are a major source of foreign exchange earnings.

Mineral extraction and processing is now the major source of income following the opening of large mines for diamonds and copper-nickel. Botswana is one of the largest producers of diamonds in the world, with diamonds accounting for 70 per cent of export revenue since they were discovered in the early 1970s. Large deposits of coal have been discovered and are now being mined. In 1994, Botswana produced 900,298 tonnes of coal, 22,780 tonnes of copper and 15,538,000 carats (15 per cent of the world total) of diamonds. Manufacturing industry is growing but it is still a small sector of the economy. The economy expanded by an average 9 per cent a year in the 1980s.

FINANCE	1992–3	1993–4
Revenue	P4,114m	P3,907m
Expenditure	4,224m	4,476m

TRADE		
	1992	1993
Imports	P3,970m	P4,297m
Exports	3,675m	4,179m

Trade with UK	1994	1995
Imports from UK	£22,461,000	£25,837,000
Exports to UK	19,618,000	23,647,000

EDUCATION

There are 657 primary schools (enrolment 305,500), 163 community junior secondary schools (enrolment 62,634) and 23 government and government-aided senior secondary schools (enrolment 22,604). Total enrolment in the tertiary sector (teacher training establishments, colleges of education and the University of Botswana) numbers 6,923.

COMMUNICATIONS

The railway from Cape Town to Zimbabwe passes through eastern Botswana. The main roads are the north-south road, which closely follows the railway, and the road running east–west that links Francistown and Maun. A road from Nata to Kazungula provides a direct link to Zambia from Botswana. Air services are provided on a scheduled basis between the main towns.

BRAZIL
República Federativa do Brasil

Brazil is bounded on the north by the Atlantic Ocean, the Guianas, Colombia and Venezuela; on the west by Peru, Bolivia, Paraguay, and Argentina; on the south by Uruguay; and on the east by the Atlantic Ocean. It extends between 5° 16′ N. and 33° 45′ S. latitude and 34° 45′ and 73° 59′22″ W. longitude and has an area of 3,286,488 sq. miles (8,511,965 sq. km). The population (official estimate 1992) is 156,275,000. Portuguese is the language of the country, but Italian, Spanish, German, Japanese and Arabic are also spoken.

The north is mainly wide, low-lying, forest-clad plains. The central areas are principally plateau land and the east and south are traversed by successive mountain ranges interspersed with fertile valleys. The principal ranges are

Serra do Mar, the Serra da Mantiqueira and the Serra do Espinhaco along the east coast.

The River Amazon flows from the Peruvian Andes to the Atlantic. Its principal tributaries are the Rio Branco, Rio Negro, Japurá, Juruá, Purus, Madeira, Tapajós and Xingú. Other major rivers are the Tocatins, Araguaia, Parnaiba, São Francisco and Paraguai.

CAPITAL – Brasilia (inaugurated 1960). Population (1991 census) 1,596,274. Other important centres are São Paulo (9,480,427); the former capital ӱRio de Janeiro (5,336,179); Belo Horizonte (2,048,861); ӱRecife (1,290,149); ӱSalvador (2,056,013); ӱFortaleza (1,758,334).

CURRENCY – Real of 100 centavos.

FLAG – Green with a yellow lozenge containing a blue sphere studded with white stars, and crossed by a white band with the motto *Ordem e Progresso*.

NATIONAL ANTHEM – Ouviram do Ipirangasàs Margens Placidas (From peaceful Ypiranga's banks).

NATIONAL DAY – 7 September (Independence Day).

GOVERNMENT

Brazil was discovered by the Portuguese navigator Pedro Alvares Cabral in 1500 and colonized by Portugal in the early 16th century. In 1822 it became independent under Dom Pedro, son of King Joao VI of Portugal, who had been forced to flee to Brazil during the Napoleonic Wars. In 1889, Dom Pedro II was dethroned and a republic was proclaimed. In 1985 Brazil returned to democratic rule after two decades of military government.

The Federative Republic of Brazil is composed of the federal district and 26 states. Under the 1988 constitution the President, who heads the executive, is directly elected for a single four-year term. The Congress consists of an 81-member Senate (three senators per state elected for an eight-year term) and a 517-member Chamber of Deputies which is elected every four years; the number of deputies per state depends upon the state's population. Each state has a Governor, and a Legislative Assembly with a four-year term.

Fernando Cardoso of the Social Democratic Party, part of the Liberal Front coalition, was elected outright in the presidential election of October 1994. In the November 1994 legislative elections the Liberal Front won 33 Senate seats, 175 seats in the Chamber of Deputies and nine state governorships.

HEAD OF STATE

President, Fernando Henrique Cardoso, *sworn in* 1 January 1995

Vice President, Marco Antonio de Oliveira Maciel

CABINET *as at July 1996*

External Relations, Luiz Felipe Lampreia
Justice, Nelson Jobim
Finance, Pedro Malan
Agriculture, Arlindo Porto
Land Reform, Raul Jungmann
Labour, Paulo Paiva
Administration, Luiz Carlos Bresser
Education, Paulo Renato de Souza
Sports, Edson Arantes do Nascimento (Pelé)
Health, Adib Domingos Jatene
Social Security, Reinhold Stephanes
Communications, Sérgio Roberto Vieira da Motta
Transport, Odacir Klein
Planning and Budget, vacant
Mines and Energy, Raimundo Mendes de Brito
Culture, Francisco Correa Weffort

Environment, Water Resources and Amazonia, Gustavo Krause Gonçalves Sobrinho
Industry, Trade and Tourism, Francisco Dornelles
Political Co-ordination, Luiz Carlos Santos
Navy, Admiral Mauro Cesar Rodrigues Pereira
Armed Forces, Gen. Benedito Onofre Bezerra Leonel
Army, Gen. Zenildo Gonzaga Zoroastro de Lucena
Air Force, Air Chief Marshal Brigadier Lélio Viana Lobo
Minister Chief of Staff of the Presidency, Gen. Alberto Mendes Cardoso
Minister for the Civilian Cabinet, Clóvis de Barros Carvalho

BRAZILIAN EMBASSY
32 Green Street, London WIY 4AT
Tel 0171-499 0877
Ambassador Extraordinary and Plenipotentiary, HE Rubens Antonio Barbosa, LVO, apptd 1994
Military Attaché, Fernando Drubski de Campos
Counsellor (Commercial Affairs), Marcos Bezerva Abbott Galvão

There is also a Brazilian Consulate-General in London and honorary consular offices at Cardiff and Glasgow.

BRITISH EMBASSY
Setor de Embaixadus Sul, Quadra 801, Conjunto K, CEP 70.408 Brasilia DF
Tel: Brasilia 225–2710
Ambassador Extraordinary and Plenipotentiary, HE Keith Haskell, CMG, CVO, apptd 1995
Deputy Ambassador, Consul-General, P. R. Jenkins
Defence Attaché, Col. D. M. Black
First Secretary (Commercial), M. A. Patterson

There are British Consulates-General at Rio de Janeiro and São Paulo.

BRITISH COUNCIL REPRESENTATIVE, Patric Early, OBE, SCRN, 708/9 Bloco F Nos 1/3 (Caixa Postal 6104), 70740-780 Brasilia DF. Regional directors in Recife, Rio de Janeiro and São Paulo

BRITISH AND COMMONWEALTH CHAMBER OF COMMERCE IN SÃO PAULO, Rua Barão de Itapetininga 275, 7th Floor, 01042, São Paulo (*Postal Address*, PO Box 1621, 01000 São Paulo) and Rua Real Grandeza 99, 22281 Rio de Janeiro

DEFENCE

The total strength of the active armed forces is 295,000 (132,000 conscripts). Conscripts serve for 12 months and there are 400,000 reservists subject to immediate recall.

The Army has a strength of 195,000, of which 125,000 are conscripts. The Navy has a strength of 50,000 personnel (2,000 conscripts) including 15,000 marines, with one aircraft carrier, five submarines, five destroyers, 15 frigates and 29 patrol and coastal craft, together with some 33 armed helicopters.

The Air Force is 50,000 strong (5,000 conscripts). It deploys 273 combat aircraft and 29 armed helicopters. In addition there is the 385,600-strong Public Security Forces paramilitary unit.

ECONOMY

Since the return to civilian rule in 1985 successive Brazilian governments have attempted to curb high inflation and large budget deficits. In February 1994 the government and Congress agreed the first balanced budget in 20 years and created a US$16 billion social emergency fund. An interim currency pegged to the US dollar, known as the Real Unit Value, was introduced in March 1994 and replaced by a new non-inflationary currency, the real, in

July 1994. By mid-1995 inflation had been reduced to two per cent a month, bringing economic stabilization and an increase in foreign exchange reserves to US$40,000 million. The privatization programme was reactivated and the oil industry, telecommunications, electricity supplies, gas distribution and coastal shipping have been opened to private investment. In 1994 Brazil signed an agreement to reschedule its US$52,000 million debt to 750 foreign commercial banks.

There are large mineral deposits including iron ore (hematite), manganese, bauxite, beryllium, chrome, nickel, tungsten, cassiterite, lead, gold, monazite (containing rare earths and thorium) and zirconium. Diamonds and precious and semi-precious stones are also found. The iron ore deposits of Minas Gerais are exceeded by those of the Amazon region, principally in the Carajás areas where deposits are estimated at 35,000 million tonnes.

Electric power production in 1994 was 52,000 m Kwh. In 1994, the total output of pig iron was 25.4 million tonnes and production of crude petroleum was 34.7 million tonnes. Brazil is the world's largest producer of coffee; the other main agriculture products are cassava, maize, soya, rice, wheat, black beans, potatoes, cotton, cocoa, tobacco and peanuts.

TRADE

Principal imports are fuel and lubricants, machinery, mineral products, chemicals, wheat, metals and metal manufactures. Principal exports are industrial goods, coffee, iron ore, soya, meat, steel and orange juice. In 1994 the Brazilian automobile industry produced 1,400,000 vehicles. Of these, 374,000 vehicles were exported.

	1993	1994
Total imports	US$25,500m	US$33,168m
Total exports	38,600m	43,558m

Trade with UK	1994	1995
Imports from UK	£525,240,000	£674,502,000
Exports to UK	919,360,000	986,520,000

EDUCATION

The education system includes both public and private institutions. Public education is free at all levels. In 1990, 28.2 million students attended compulsory primary education, although illiteracy remained at 17 per cent.

COMMUNICATIONS

There are 1,670,148 km of highways and the route-length of railways is 30,129 km. There are ten international airports and internal air services are highly developed. There are 21,944 miles of navigable inland waterways. Rio de Janeiro and Santos are the two leading ports.

BRUNEI
Negara Brunei Darussalam

Brunei is situated on the north-west coast of the island of Borneo, and has a total area of 2,226 sq. miles (5,765 sq. km). The population is 276,300 (1993), of whom 67 per cent are of Malay, 5 per cent Chinese and 6 per cent indigenous races. The majority are Sunni Muslims. The country has a humid tropical climate.

CAPITAL – Bandar Seri Begawan, with a population of 56,300 (1993).

CURRENCY – Brunei dollar (B$) of 100 sen. It is fully interchangeable with the currency of Singapore.

FLAG – Yellow with diagonal stripes of white over black and the arms in red all over the centre.
NATIONAL ANTHEM – Allah Peliharakan Sultan (God Bless His Majesty).
NATIONAL DAY – 23 February.

GOVERNMENT

In 1959 the Sultan promulgated the first written constitution, which provides for a Privy Council, a Council of Ministers and a Legislative Council. On 1 January 1984 Brunei resumed full independence from Britain. A ministerial system of government was established with ministers being appointed by the Sultan and responsible to him. The Sultan presides over the Privy Council and the Council of Ministers. The Legislative Council was disbanded in 1984. The Sultan effectively rules by decree as a state of emergency has been in effect since a revolt in 1962.

HEAD OF STATE
HM The Sultan of Brunei, HM Sultan Haji Hassanal Bolkiah Mu'izzaddin Waddaulah, Sultan and Yang Di-Pertuan, GCB, *acceded* 1967, *crowned* 1 August 1968

THE COUNCIL OF MINISTERS *as at July 1996*
Prime Minister, Defence, HM The Sultan
Foreign Affairs, HRH Prince Mohamed
Finance, HRH Prince Jefri
Special Adviser to the Sultan and Minister for Home Affairs, Pehin Dato Haji Isa
Education, Pehin Dato Abdul Aziz
Law, Pengiran Bahrin
Industry and Primary Resources, Pehin Dato Abdul Rahman
Religious Affairs, Pehin Dato Mohammed Zain
Development, Pengiran Dato Dr Ismail
Culture, Youth and Sports, Pehin Dato Haji Hussein
Health, Dato Dr Johar
Communications, Dato Haji Zakaria

BRUNEI DARUSSALAM HIGH COMMISSION
19–20 Belgrave Square, London SWIX 8PG
Tel 0171-581 0521
High Commissioner, HE Dato Kassim Daud, apptd 1993

BRITISH HIGH COMMISSION
Hong Kong and Shanghai Bank Building (3rd Floor), Jalan Pemancha, PO Box 2197 Bandar Seri Begawan
Tel: Bandar Seri Begawan 222231
High Commissioner, HE Ivan Callan, CMG, apptd 1994

BRITISH COUNCIL REPRESENTATIVE , Susan Mathews, PO Box 3049, Bandar Seri Begawan 1930

ECONOMY

The economy is based on the production of oil and natural gas by Brunei Shell Petroleum. Royalties and taxes from these operations form the bulk of government revenue and have enabled the construction of free health, education and welfare services. The country has eight hospitals, 350 schools and one university. Brunei's main road connects the capital with Kuala Belait in the centre of the oil fields. Royal Brunei Airlines operates scheduled flights to the UK, Australia and throughout the Far East. Radio Television Brunei broadcasts one colour television and three radio channels from the capital.

TRADE WITH UK	1994	1995
Imports from UK	£417,540,000	£254,282,000
Exports to UK	294,186,000	125,918,000

BULGARIA
Republika Bulgaria

Bulgaria is bounded on the north by Romania, on the west by Serbia and the former Yugoslav republic of Macedonia, on the east by the Black Sea, and on the south by Greece and Turkey. The total area is 42,823 sq. miles (110,912 sq. km), with a population (UN estimate 1993) of 8,472,000. The predominant religion is the Greek Orthodox Church.

The language is Bulgarian, a Southern Slavonic tongue closely allied to Serbo-Croat and Russian with local admixtures of modern Greek, Albanian and Turkish words. The alphabet is Cyrillic.

CAPITAL – Sofia, population (1992), 1,114,925. Other important centres are ΨVarna (308,432), on the Black Sea; ΨBourgas (195,686), on the Black Sea; Plovdiv (341,058), Rousse (170,038), Pleven (130,812), Stara Zagora (150,518), Sliven (106,212) and Dobrich (104,494).
CURRENCY – Lev of 100 stotinki.
FLAG – 3 horizontal bands, white, green, red.
NATIONAL DAY – 3 March.

HISTORY

A principality of Bulgaria was created by the Treaty of Berlin 1878. In 1908 the country was declared an independent kingdom.

In September 1944 a coup d'état gave power to the Fatherland Front, a coalition of Communists, Agrarians and Social Democrats. In August 1945, the main body of Agrarians and Social Democrats left the government. A referendum in September 1946 led to the abolition of the monarchy and the setting up of a republic.

The post-war period was dominated by the Communist Party (BCP), led by Todor Zhivkov. He was forced to resign in November 1989, and in January 1990 the National Assembly voted to abolish the BCP's constitutional guarantee of power. Multiparty elections to a Grand National Assembly (parliament) were held in June 1990 and won by the BCP, renamed the Bulgarian Socialist Party, which formed a government which lasted two months. A multiparty government was formed in December 1990 which began to implement a programme of economic and political reform.

GOVERNMENT

A new constitution, enshrining democracy and the free market was adopted by the Grand National Assembly on 12 July 1991.

After legislative elections in October 1991 a coalition government of the Union of Democratic Forces (UDF) and the Turkish Movement for Rights and Freedom Party (MRF) was formed with a pledge to stabilize the economy and defeat inflation. The government was brought down in a vote of no confidence and replaced in December 1992 by a weak government of non-party technocrats which also collapsed. The BSP won the ensuing general election in December 1994 and formed a government with the Agrarian National Union (ANU). The state of the parties in the 240-seat National Assembly is BSP 125, UDF 69, ANU 18, MRF 15, Bulgarian Business Block (BBB) 13.

HEAD OF STATE
President, Zhelyu Zhelev, *elected* 1 August 1990, *re-elected* 19 January 1992

COUNCIL OF MINISTERS *as at July 1996*
Prime Minister, Jan Videnov
Deputy PM, Territorial Development and Construction, Doncho Konakchiev
Deputy PM, Agriculture and Food Industry, Svetoslav Shivarov
Deputy PM, Economic Development, Roumen Gechev
Foreign Affairs, Georgi Pirinski
Trade and Foreign Economic Co-operation, Atanas Paparizov
Home Affairs, Lyubomir Nachev
Health, Mimi Virkova
Culture, Georgi Kostov
Education, Science and Technologies, Ilcho Dimitrov
Environment, Georgi Georgiev
Defence, Dimiter Pavlov
Justice, Mladen Chervenyakov
Industry, Kliment Vuchev
Transport, Stamen Stamenov
Labour and Social Welfare, Mincho Koralski
Finance, Dimiter Kostov

EMBASSY OF THE REPUBLIC OF BULGARIA
186–188 Queen's Gate, London SW7 5HL
Tel 0171–584 9400/9433
Ambassador Extraordinary and Plenipotentiary, HE Stefan Tafrov, apptd 1995
Counsellor (Commercial/Economic), D. Georgiev
Military, Air and Naval Attaché, Capt. Ivan Mladenov Yordanov

BRITISH EMBASSY
Boulevard Vassil Levski 65–67, Sofia 1000
Tel: Sofia 492 3361/2
Ambassador Extraordinary and Plenipotentiary, HE Roger Short, MVO, apptd 1994
Deputy Ambassador, Consul and First Secretary, J. F. Gunn
Defence Attaché, Col. M. I. V. Dore
First Secretary (Commercial), M. J. Carbine

BRITISH COUNCIL REPRESENTATIVE, David Stokes, 7 Tulovo Street, 1504, Sofia

DEFENCE

Bulgaria has a total active armed forces strength of 101,900, including 51,300 conscripts who serve for 18 months. The Army has a strength of 51,600 personnel, including 33,300 conscripts. The Navy has a strength of 3,000 personnel (2,000 conscripts). The Air Force has a strength of 21,600 (16,000 conscripts). In addition, there are 12,000 paramilitary border guards.

EDUCATION

Education is free and compulsory for children from seven to 15 years inclusive. In 1993, there were 2,770 primary schools attended by 839,419 pupils. There are three universities (at Sofia, Plovdiv and Veliko Turnovo), an American University and 21 higher educational establishments.

ECONOMY

Under Communism about 90 per cent of the country's agriculture was turned over to co-operatives. Land is currently being handed over to its previous owners. The principal crops are wheat, maize, beet, tomatoes, tobacco, oleaginous seeds, fruit, vegetables and cotton. The livestock includes cattle, sheep, goats, pigs, horses, asses, mules and water buffaloes.

There is a substantial engineering industry and considerable production of ferrous and non-ferrous metals.

There are mineral deposits of varying importance. Heavy industry includes steel, chemicals, petro-chemical and metallurgical centres.

Privatization has proceeded slowly, with only 30 to 40 large- and medium-sized enterprises being privatized by 1995. However, 1,227 enterprises were due to be privatized in 1996 by means of a voucher system.

The overall lack of radical economic reform has hampered the economy; annual inflation in 1994–5 was 120 per cent and unemployment 20 per cent. In the first half of 1996, the lev lost 70 per cent of its value and food shortages were experienced in some cities. The government responded by adopting a radical reform package including the closure of 70 state companies.

TRADE

Since 1989 the European Union and industrialized nations have replaced the Soviet bloc as Bulgaria's most important trade partners. In 1993 Bulgaria signed an Association Agreement with the EU, and EU duties on Bulgarian industrial goods were abolished by 1995 and levies on agricultural goods significantly lowered.

The principal imports are fuels, minerals and metals, engineering goods and industrial equipment. The principal exports are agricultural produce, engineering goods and industrial equipment, industrial consumer goods, chemicals and fuels, minerals and metals.

Trade with UK	1994	1995
Imports from UK	£86,138,000	£104,224,000
Exports to UK	69,927,000	118,550,000

BURKINA FASO

Burkina Faso (formerly Upper Volta) is an inland savannah state in West Africa, situated between 9° and 15°N. latitude and 2°E. and 5°W. longitude, with an area of 105,869 sq. miles (274,200 sq. km). It borders Mali on the west, Niger and Benin on the east and Togo, Ghana and the Côte d'Ivoire on the south.

The population (UN estimate 1993) is 9,682,000. The largest tribe is the Mossi whose king, the Moro Naba, still wields a certain moral influence. The official language is French.

CAPITAL – Ouagadougou (441,514). Other principal towns: Bobo-Dioulasso (228,668) and Koudougou (30,000).

CURRENCY – Franc CFA.

FLAG – Equal bands of red over green, with a yellow star in centre.

NATIONAL DAY – 11 December.

GOVERNMENT

Burkina Faso was annexed by France in 1896 and between 1932 and 1947 was administered as part of the Colony of the Ivory Coast. It decided on 11 December 1958 to remain an autonomous republic within the French Community; full independence outside the Community was proclaimed on 5 August 1960.

The 1960 constitution provided for a presidential form of government with a single chamber National Assembly, but in 1966 the Army assumed power. A new constitution allowing for a partial return to civilian rule but with the Army still in effective control was adopted in 1970, but in 1974 this was suspended. Full legislative and presidential elections were held again in 1978.

Following a number of military coups, Capt. Blaise Compaoré seized power in 1987. A new constitution was adopted in 1991. Presidential elections were held in December 1991 and won by Capt. Compaoré in the face of a boycott by the main opposition parties, who were unhappy with the new constitution. Opposition parties also boycotted the legislative elections held in May 1992, which were won by Compaoré's Organization for Popular Democracy-Labour Movement (ODP-MT) party; it formed the government in coalition with several smaller parties.

HEAD OF STATE
President, Capt. Blaise Compaoré, assumed office October 1987, elected December 1991

COUNCIL OF MINISTERS as at May 1996
Prime Minister, Kadre Desire Ouedraogo
Water and Environment, Salif Diallo
Integration and African Solidarity, Hermann Yameogo
Economy and Finance, Zephirin Diabre
External Relations, Ablasse Ouedraogo
Defence, Col. Badaye Fayama
Justice, Yarga Larba
Territorial Administration and Security, Yero Boli
Trade, Industry and Cottage Industry, Dominique Talata Kafando
Industry, Energy and Mines, Eli Ouedraogo
Secondary and Higher Education, Scientific Research, Maurice Melegue Traore
Basic and Mass Education, Seydou Baworo Sanou
Public Works, Housing, Town Planning, Joseph Kabore
Relations with Parliament, Thomas Sanou
Employment, Labour, Social Security, Soulemane Zibare
Civil Service and Administrative Organization, Juliette Bonkougou
Agriculture and Animal Resources, Michel Koutaba
Communications and Culture, Claude Nourchior Somda
Health, Christophe Dabire
Youth and Sports, Joseph André Tiendrebeogo
Transport and Tourism, Viviane Yolande Ouedraogo
Social Affairs and Family, Bana Ouandaogo

EMBASSY OF BURKINA FASO
16 Place Guy d'Arezzo, 1060 Brussels, Belgium
Tel: Brussels 345 9912
Ambassador Extraordinary and Plenipotentiary, HE Youssouf Ouedraogo, apptd 1995, resident in Brussels
HONORARY CONSULATE, 5 Cinnamon Row, Plantation Wharf, London SW11 3TW. Tel: 0171-738 1800. Honorary Consul-General, S. G. Singer

BRITISH AMBASSADOR, HE Margaret Rothwell, CMG, resident at Abidjan, Côte d'Ivoire

ECONOMY

The principal industry is the rearing of cattle and sheep and the chief exports are livestock, groundnuts, millet and sorghum. Small deposits of gold, manganese, copper, bauxite and graphite have been found.

TRADE WITH UK	1994	1995
Imports from UK	£6,107,000	£8,881,000
Exports to UK	851,000	398,000

BURUNDI
République de Burundi

Situated on the east side of Lake Tanganyika, Burundi has an area of 10,747 sq. miles (27,834 sq. km). The population (UN estimate 1993) is 5,958,000, 83 per cent Hutu and 15 per cent Tutsi. The official languages are Kirundi, a Bantu language, and French. Kiswahili is also used.

CAPITAL – Bujumbura (formerly Usumbura), with 235,440 (1990 estimate) inhabitants. Kitega (18,000 inhabitants) is the only other sizeable town.
CURRENCY – Burundi franc of 100 centimes.
FLAG – Divided diagonally by a white saltire into red and green triangles; on a white disc in the centre three red six-pointed stars edged in green.
NATIONAL DAY – 1 July.

GOVERNMENT

Formerly a Belgian trusteeship under the United Nations, Burundi became independent as a constitutional monarchy on 1 July 1962. However, the monarchy was overthrown in 1966 and the country became a republic. In 1987 the government was overthrown by a Military Committee of National Redemption led by Maj. Pierre Buyoya.

Although most of the population is Hutu, political and military power has traditionally rested with the Tutsi minority. Hutu attempts to overthrow Tutsi rule resulted in ethnic massacres in 1965, 1969, 1972 and 1988. It was against a background of continuing Tutsi-Hutu violence that the National Unity and Progress Party (UPRONA) government attempted to introduce multi-party non-tribal politics in 1991–2. This was approved by national referendum in March 1992.

Tutsi dominance appeared to be broken by the election of Melchior Ndadaye, a Hutu, as President in June 1993 and the success of the opposition Front for Democracy in Burundi (FRODEBU) in the legislative elections the same month. However, the identification of the FRODEBU government with Hutu interests led the Tutsi-dominated army to attempt a coup in October 1993 in which President Ndadaye and six Cabinet ministers were killed. The remainder of the government survived and regained control in December but two months of inter-racial fighting left 50,000–100,000 dead and 500,000, mainly Hutu, refugees in neighbouring states. Ndadye was succeeded by Cyprien Ntaryamira (Hutu), but he was killed in a rocket attack on the plane of President Habyarimana of Rwanda in April 1994.

FRODEBU and UPRONA agreed to form a coalition government in February 1994 with a Tutsi as Prime Minister, and interim President Ntibantunganya (Hutu) was appointed to the post permanently by a convention of government in September 1994. The convention incorporated into the constitution a provision that the 25-member Cabinet must include ten Tutsi, ten Hutu and five neutral ministers. However, the government has been unable to halt attacks by the Tutsi-dominated army and Hutu militias on each other. The fighting claimed 200,000 lives in 1993–5 and more than 100 lives a week in 1996. *See also* Events of the Year.

HEAD OF STATE
President, Sylvestre Ntibantunganya, *sworn in* 1 October 1994

COUNCIL OF MINISTERS *as at December 1995*
Prime Minister, Antoine Nduwayo (UPRONA)
External Relations and International Co-operation, Venerand Bakevyumusaya (FRODEBU)
Interior, Antoine Baza
Justice, Gerard Ngendabanka
Defence, Lt.-Col. Firmin Sinzoyiheba
Finance, Salvator Toyi (FRODEBU)
Planning, Development and Reconstruction, Gerard Niyibigira (UPRONA)
Reintegration and Resettlement of Displaced and Repatriated Persons, Claudine Matuturu (UPRONA)
Territorial Development and Environment, Patrice Nsabagannwa
Communal Development, Severin Mfatiye (FRODEBU)
Agriculture and Livestock, Pierre Claver Nahimana (FRODEBU)
Trade and Industry, Astere Nzisibira
Labour and Professional Training, Vedaste Ngendanganya
Civil Service, Vincent Ndikumasabo (UPRONA)
Primary Education and Literacy, Nicephore Ndimurukundo
Secondary and Higher Education, Liboire Ngendahayo (FRODEBU)
Human Rights and Women's Development, Marcienne Mujawaha (FRODEBU)
Youth, Sport and Culture, Christophe Ndikuriyo
Health, Charles Batungwanayo (FRODEBU)
Communication, Germain Nkeshimana (FRODEBU)
Public Works, Bernard Barandereka (UPRONA)
Telecommunications, Posts and Transport, Leonce Sinzinkayo (FRODEBU)
Energy and Mines, Idi Buhanga Precede
Relations with the National Assembly, Terence Sinunguruza (UPRONA)

EMBASSY OF THE REPUBLIC OF BURUNDI
Square Marie Louise 46, 1040 Brussels, Belgium
Tel: Brussels 2304535
Ambassador Extraordinary and Plenipotentiary, new appointment awaited (resident in Brussels)
BRITISH AMBASSADOR, HE Edward Clay, CMG, resident at Kampala, Uganda

ECONOMY

The chief crop is coffee, representing about 80 per cent of export earnings. Cotton is the second most important crop. Mineral, tea, hide and skin exports are also important.

TRADE WITH UK	1994	1995
Imports from UK	£3,288,000	£3,339,000
Exports to UK	4,251,000	3,670,000

CAMBODIA

Cambodia is situated in Indochina, with Thailand to the west and north, Laos to the north, Vietnam to the east and south, and the Gulf of Thailand to the south-west. The area is 69,898 sq. miles (181,035 sq. km), of which 50 per cent is forest or jungle. Around the Tonlé Sap lake and along the Mekong river, which traverses the country, there is ample fertile land. The climate is tropical monsoon with a rainy season from May to October.

The population (UN estimate 1993) is 9,308,000. The state religion is Buddhism of the 'Little Vehicle' which was suppressed by the Khmer Rouge. The national language is Khmer.

CAPITAL – Phnom Penh, population 920,000 (1993 estimate).

CURRENCY – Riel of 100 sen.

FLAG – Three horizontal stripes of blue, red, blue, with the blue of double width and containing a representation of the temple of Angkor in white.

NATIONAL ANTHEM – Nokoreach.

NATIONAL DAY – 9 November (Independence Day).

HISTORY

Cambodia became a French protectorate in 1863 and was granted independence within the French Union as an Associate State in 1949. Full independence was proclaimed on 9 November 1953. From 1955 the political life of the country was dominated by Prince Norodom Sihanouk, first as king, then as head of government after he had abdicated in favour of his father and finally (following his father's death in 1960) as head of state. In March 1970 Prince Sihanouk was deposed and a Khmer Republic was declared in October 1970.

In April 1975 Phnom Penh fell to the North Vietnamese-backed Khmer Rouge after a five-year civil war. A new constitution was promulgated in 1976, a government led by Pol Pot, the leader of the Khmer Rouge (Communist) party, was appointed and the state was renamed Democratic Kampuchea. During Khmer Rouge rule hundreds of thousands of Cambodians fled into exile and an estimated two million were killed.

In December 1978 Vietnamese troops invaded Cambodia, capturing Phnom Penh on 7 January 1979. The following day the Cambodian National United Front for National Salvation established a People's Revolutionary Council. The state was renamed The People's Republic of Kampuchea (PRK); in April 1989 it became the State of Cambodia (SOC). With support from the Vietnamese army, PRK forces won control of most of the country from the forces of the Coalition Government of Democratic Kampuchea (CGDK), formed in June 1982 by the Khmer Rouge and two non-Communist groups. Following the Vietnamese withdrawal in 1989, the resistance forces regained ground inside Cambodia.

In September 1990, the SOC and the CGDK established a Supreme National Council. A permanent cease-fire

began on 23 June and peace agreements were signed on 23 October 1991. In March 1992 the United Nations Transitional Authority for Cambodia (UNTAC) assumed authority from the SOC government in the run-up to the May 1993 elections.

GOVERNMENT

Multiparty elections under UNTAC supervision were held in May 1993 for 120 seats in a National Assembly. Prince Sihanouk brokered a coalition government agreement between FUNCINPEC and the Cambodian People's Party (CPP) (the former SOC party) under which he became head of state and FUNCINPEC and CPP leaders Prince Ranariddh and Hun Sen became co-prime ministers of the coalition government. In September 1993 the National Assembly adopted a new constitution under which Cambodia became a pluralist liberal democracy with a constitutional monarchy and the UN force departed. Prince Sihanouk was elected king and he appointed a new government. Legislative power is vested in the National Assembly, executive power in the Royal Government, with the King having the power only to make appointments and declare a state of emergency, in consultation with the government.

The Khmer Rouge remain unreconciled to the new government and continue their guerrilla campaign, mainly in the north and east of the country, where they control 10 per cent of territory along the border with Thailand. In July 1994 the Royal Government outlawed the Khmer Rouge, which responded by declaring a provisional government. A government amnesty ended in January 1995 with the defection of around half of the Khmer Rouge personnel, leaving it with about 7,000 guerrillas. A fresh offensive against the Khmer Rouge was launched in early 1996.

HEAD OF STATE
HM The King of Cambodia, Norodom Sihanouk, *elected by the Council of the Throne* 23 September 1993

GOVERNMENT *as at July 1996*

First Prime Minister, Prince Norodom Ranariddh (F)
Second Prime Minister, Hun Sen (C)
Vice-PM, Minister of State, Public Works, Ing Kieth (F)
Vice-PM, Interior and National Security, Sar Kheng (C)
Ministers of State, Keat Chhon (*Finance*) (C); Ung Phan (F);
  Van Moulyvan (C); Chem Snguon (*Justice*) (C)
Agriculture, Forests and Fisheries, Tao Seng Hour (F)
Commerce, Cham Prasidh (C)
Defence, Gen. Tea Banh (C); Tea Champat (F)
Education, Youth and Sport, Tol Lah
Finance and Economy, Keat Chhon (C)
Foreign Affairs, Ung Huot (F)
Health, Chea Thain (C)
Industry, Mines and Energy, Pou Southirak (F)
Information, Ieng Mouly (B)
Interior and National Security, You Hokry (F)
Planning, Chea Chanto (C)
Trade and Industry, Var Huot (C)

Chairman of the National Assembly, Chea Sim

B Buddhist Liberal Democratic Party; C Cambodian
People's Party; F FUNCINPEC

BRITISH EMBASSY
29, Street 75, Phnom Penh
Tel: Phnom Penh 855 2327124
Ambassador Extraordinary and Plenipotentiary, HE Paul
  Reddicliffe, apptd 1994

ECONOMY

The economy is based on agriculture, fishing and forestry.
In addition to rice, which is the staple crop, the major
products are rubber, livestock, maize, timber, pepper, palm
sugar, fresh and dried fish, kapok, beans, soya and tobacco.
Rice and rubber used to be the main exports, though
production was brought to a standstill by the hostilities.

Under the Khmer Rouge, the urban population was
forced to work on the land, and re-establish plantations
producing such crops as cotton, rubber and bananas.
Following the Vietnamese invasion of 1978 the towns
were repopulated and factories, in particular textile mills,
iron smelting works and cement works, were put back in
production.

Cambodia is heavily dependent on foreign aid to rebuild
its economy and US$1,350 million has been given since the
1991 Paris peace agreements and a further US$2,280
million pledged. In addition, all Cambodia's debts to the
IMF have been paid by other states and US$160 million of
debt was written off in February 1995. Foreign investors
have been unenthusiastic because of insecurity, corruption, and the lack of a firm legal basis for business.

TRADE WITH UK	1994	1995
Imports from UK	£2,327,000	£2,989,000
Exports to UK	1,672,000	7,531,000

COMMUNICATIONS

The country had over 5,000 kilometres of roads, of which
nearly half were hard-surfaced and passable in the rainy
season, although now in a state of disrepair. There are two
railways, one from Phnom Penh to the Thai border, the
other from Phnom Penh to Kampot and Sihanoukville
(Kompong Som), but operations and repairs are hindered
by occasional Khmer Rouge attacks. Phnom Penh is on a
river capable of receiving ships of up to 2,500 tons all the
year round. The deep water port at Sihanoukville (Kompong Som) on the Gulf of Thailand can receive ships up to
10,000 tons. The port is linked to Phnom Penh by a
modern highway.

CAMEROON
République du Cameroun

Cameroon lies on the Gulf of Guinea between Nigeria to
the west, Chad and the Central African Republic to the east
and Congo and Gabon and Equatorial Guinea to the south.
It has an area of 183,569 sq. miles (475,442 sq. km).

The population is 12,600,000 (UN estimate 1993).
French and English are both official languages and enjoy
equal status.

CAPITAL – Yaoundé, population estimate (1986) 653,670.
ΨDouala (1,029,736) is the commercial centre.
CURRENCY – Franc CFA of 100 centimes.
FLAG – Vertical stripes of green, red and yellow with
single five-pointed yellow star in centre of red stripe.
NATIONAL ANTHEM – O Cameroun, Berceau de Nos
Ancêtres (O Cameroon, thou cradle of our forefathers).
NATIONAL DAY – 20 May.

GOVERNMENT

The German colony of the Cameroons, established in
1884, was captured by British and French forces in 1916
and divided into the League of Nations-mandated territories (later UN trusteeships) of East (French) and West
(British) Cameroon. On 1 January 1960 East Cameroon
became independent as the Republic of Cameroon. This
was joined on 1 October 1961 by the southern part of West
Cameroon after a plebiscite held under United Nations
auspices; the northern part joined Nigeria. Cameroon
became a federal republic with separate East and West
Cameroon state governments. After a plebiscite held in
1972, Cameroon became a unitary republic and a one-
party state.

After extensive unrest, multiparty elections were held
in March 1992, although they were boycotted by two of the
main opposition parties. The ruling People's Democratic
Movement emerged short of a parliamentary majority but
formed a coalition government with a small opposition
party, the Movement for the Defence of the Republic.

Presidential elections were held in October 1992 and
won by the incumbent Paul Biya. The results were
disputed by the runner-up Fru Ndi, two opposition parties
and foreign observers, who accused the authorities of
widespread malpractice. In November a new coalition
government was formed with the addition of the Union for
Democracy and Progress and the Union of Peoples of
Cameroon. In May 1993 President Biya published a draft
bill on constitutional reform providing for a Council of
State, Senate and a Constitutional Court but rejecting a
return to a federal state. In December 1995, a constitutional amendment was passed extending the president's
term in office from five to seven years and authorizing a
maximum of two terms. A Senate was also created.

Cameroon joined the Commonwealth in November
1995.

HEAD OF STATE
President and Commander in Chief of the Armed Forces, Paul
  Biya, *acceded* 6 November 1982, *elected* 14 January 1984,
  re-elected 24 April 1988, 10 October 1992, *sworn in* 3
  November 1992

CABINET *as at May 1996*

Prime Minister, Simon Achidi Achu
Deputy PM, Territorial Administration, Gilbert Andze-
  Tsoungui

Deputy PM, Housing and Town Planning, Hamadou
  Mustapha
Minister of State, Posts and Telecommunications, Dakole
  Daissala
*Minister of State, Agriculture, Planning and Regional
  Development*, Augustin Frederic Kodock
Minister of State, Communications, Augustin Koutchou
  Kouomegni
Defence, Edouard Akame Mfoumou
External Relations, Ferdinand Leopold Oyono
Justice, Douala Moutome
Animal Husbandry and Fisheries, Hamadjoda Adjoudi
Higher Education, Peter Agbortabi
Public Health, Joseph Owona
Labour and Social Insurance, Simon Mbila
Industrial and Commercial Development, Pierre Eloundou
  Mani
Economy and Finance, Justin Naioro
Women and Social Affairs, Aissatou Yaou
Public Works, Jean-Baptiste Bokam
Scientific Research, Joseph Mbede
Tourism, Pierre Souman
Environment and Forests, Dr Djingoer Bava
Youth and Sports, Joseph Marie Bipoun Woum
National Education, Dr Robert Mbella
Mines, Water Resources and Energy, Andre Bello Mbelle
Transport, Issa Bakary Tchiroma
Culture, Toko Mangan

EMBASSY OF THE REPUBLIC OF CAMEROON
84 Holland Park, London WII 3SB
Tel 0171–727 0771/3
Ambassador Extraordinary and Plenipotentiary, HE Samuel
  Libock Mbei, apptd 1995

BRITISH HIGH COMMISSION
Avenue Winston Churchill, BP 547 Yaoundé
Tel: Yaoundé 220545
High Commissioner, HE Nicholas McCarthy, MBE, apptd
  1996
There is also a British Consulate at Douala.

BRITISH COUNCIL DIRECTOR, Terrence Humphreys,
Avenue Charles de Gaulle (BP 818), Yaoundé

ECONOMY

Principal products are cocoa, coffee, bananas, cotton,
timber, groundnuts, aluminium, rubber and palm products. There is an aluminium smelting plant at Edéa with
an annual capacity of 50,000 tons. Crude petroleum is also
one of Cameroon's principal products, although production dropped from 8.3 million tonnes in 1990 to 6.5 million
tonnes in 1994.
  In 1993 most foreign donors suspended aid after an IMF
structural adjustment plan lapsed in 1992. The IMF agreed
to resume support of an improved economic reform
programme with the approval of standby credits totalling
US$214 million in 1994–5. GNP per capita was US$820 in
1993; inflation rose to over 25 per cent in 1995.

TRADE WITH UK	1994	1995
Imports from UK	£15,452,000	£25,234,000
Exports to UK	34,889,000	31,328,000

CANADA

AREA AND POPULATION

Provinces or Territories (with official contractions)	Area (sq. miles)	Population estimate 1995
Alberta (AB)	255,290	2,747,000
British Columbia (BC)	365,950	3,766,000
Manitoba (MB)	250,950	1,137,500
New Brunswick (NB)	28,360	760,100
Newfoundland and Labrador (NF)	156,650	575,400
Nova Scotia (NS)	21,420	937,800
Ontario (ON)	412,580	11,100,300
Prince Edward Island (PE)	2,180	136,100
Quebec (QC)	594,860	7,334,200
Saskatchewan (SK)	251,870	1,015,600
Yukon Territory (YT)	186,660	30,100
Northwest Territories (NT)	1,322,900	65,800
Total	3,849,670	29,606,100

Area figures include land and water area

PHYSIOGRAPHY

Canada occupies the whole of the northern part of the
North American continent, with the exception of Alaska,
from 49° N. latitude to the North Pole and from the Pacific
to the Atlantic Ocean. In eastern Canada, the southernmost point is Middle Island in Lake Erie, at 41° 41′ N.
  Canada has six main physiographic divisions: the
Appalachian-Acadian region, the Canadian shield, the St
Lawrence-Great Lakes lowland, the interior plains, the
Cordilleran region and the Arctic archipelago.
  The Canadian shield comprises more than half the
country. The interior as a whole is an undulating, low
plateau (general level 1,000 to 1,500 feet), with water or
muskeg-filled depressions separated by irregular hills and
ridges, 150 to 200 feet in elevation. The St Lawrence-
Great Lakes lowland varies from 500 feet in the east to
1,700 feet south of Georgian Bay. The interior plains,
comprising the Pacific provinces, slope eastward and
northward a few feet per mile. The descent from west to
east is made from 5,000 feet to less than 1,000 feet in three
distinct levels, each marked by an eastward-facing conteau
or scarp.
  The Cordilleran region has coastal ranges, largely above
5,000 feet with deep fjords and glaciated valleys; an interior
plateau, around 3,500 feet and comparatively level; the
Selkirk ranges, largely above 5,000 feet; the Rocky
Mountains with their chain of 10,000 to 12,000 feet peaks;
and the Peace River or Tramontane region with its rolling
diversified country.
  The Arctic archipelago, with its plateau-like character
has an elevation between 500 and 1,000 feet, though in
Baffin Land and Ellesmere Island the mountain ranges rise
to 8,500 and 9,500 feet. Two tremendous waterway
systems, the St Lawrence and the Mackenzie, occupy a
broad area of lowland with their dominant axis following
the edge of the shield.
  The climate of the eastern and central portions presents
greater extremes than in corresponding latitudes in
Europe, but in the south-western portion of the prairie
region and the southern portions of the Pacific slope the
climate is milder.

FEDERAL CAPITAL – Ottawa, on the south bank of the
  Ottawa river, and connected with Lake Ontario by the
  Rideau Canal. The city population was 313,987 at the
  1991 census and the population of the metropolitan area
  of Ottawa–Hull was estimated at 1,024,657 in 1995.

CURRENCY – Canadian dollar (C$) of 100 cents.
FLAG – Red maple leaf with 11 points on white square, flanked by vertical red bars one-half the width of the square.
NATIONAL ANTHEM – O Canada.
NATIONAL DAY – 1 July (Dominion Day).

HISTORY

Canada was originally discovered by Cabot in 1497 but its history dates from 1534, when the French took possession of the country. The first permanent settlement at Port Royal (now Annapolis), Nova Scotia, was founded in 1605, and Quebec was founded in 1608. In 1759 Quebec was captured by British forces under General Wolfe and in 1763 the whole territory of Canada became a possession of Great Britain by the Treaty of Paris 1763. Nova Scotia was ceded in 1713 by the Treaty of Utrecht, the provinces of New Brunswick and Prince Edward Island being subsequently formed out of it. British Columbia was formed into a Crown colony in 1858, having previously been a part of the Hudson Bay Territory, and was united to Vancouver Island in 1866.

The constitution of Canada has its source in the British North America Act of 1867 which formed a Dominion, under the name of Canada, of the four provinces of Ontario, Quebec, New Brunswick and Nova Scotia. To this federation the other provinces have subsequently been admitted: Manitoba (1870), British Columbia (1871), Prince Edward Island (1873), Alberta and Saskatchewan (1905) and Newfoundland (1949). In 1982, the constitution was patriated (severed from the British parliament) with the approval of all provinces except Quebec. In 1985, the federal Prime Minister and the provincial premiers concluded the Meech Lake Accord which provided for Quebec to be recognized as a distinct society within Canada. However, two provincial legislatures withheld approval and the accord did not come into force. In Quebec, a referendum calling for sovereignty and a new political and economic partnership was defeated in October 1995.

GOVERNMENT

Executive power is vested in a Governor-General appointed by the Sovereign on the advice of the Canadian government.

Parliament consists of a Senate and a House of Commons. The Senate consists of 104 members, nominated by the Governor-General, the seats being distributed between the various provinces.

The House of Commons has 295 members and is elected every five years at longest. Representation by provinces is at present: Newfoundland 7, Prince Edward Island 4, Nova Scotia 11, New Brunswick 10, Quebec 75, Ontario 99, Manitoba 14, Saskatchewan 14, Alberta 26, British Columbia 32, Yukon 1, Northwest Territories 2.

The state of the parties in the Senate as at July 1996 was Liberals 51, Progressive Conservatives 50, Independent 3.

The Liberal Party defeated the Progressive Conservative Party in the federal general election on 25 October 1993. The state of parties in the House of Commons as at July 1996 was Liberals 174, Bloc Québécois 53, Reform Party 51, New Democracy 9, Progressive Conservatives 2, Independents 5, vacant 1.

GOVERNOR-GENERAL
Governor-General and Commander-in-Chief, HE the Rt. Hon. Roméo Le Blanc, CC, CMM, CD

CABINET *as at July 1996*
Prime Minister, Rt. Hon. Jean Chrétien
Deputy Prime Minister, Heritage, Hon. Sheila Copps
Agriculture and Agri-Food, Hon. Ralph Goodale
Atlantic Canada Opportunities Agency, Hon. Lawrence Macaulay
Citizenship and Immigration, Hon. Lucienne Robillard
Environment, Hon. Sergio Marchi
Federal Office of Regional Development-Quebec, Hon. Martin Cauchon
Finance, Hon. Paul Martin
Fisheries and Oceans, Hon. Fred Mifflin
Foreign Affairs, Hon. Lloyd Axworthy
Health, Hon. David Dingwall

Human Resources Development, Hon. Douglas Young
Indian Affairs and Northern Development, Hon. Ron Irwin
Industry, Hon. John Manley
Infrastructure, Hon. Marcel Masse
Intergovernmental Affairs, Hon. Stephane Dion
International Co-operation and the Francophonie, Hon. Pierre
    Pettigrew
International Trade, Hon. Arthur Eggleton
Justice and Attorney General, Hon. Allan Rock
Labour, Hon. Alfonso Gagliano
National Defence, Hon. David Collenette
National Revenue, Hon. Jane Stewart
Natural Resources, Hon. Anne McLellan
Public Works and Government Services, Hon. Diane Marleau
Transport, Hon. David Anderson
Veterans Affairs, Hon. David Collenette
Western Economic Diversification, Hon. Jon Gerrard
Speaker of the Senate, Hon. Gildais Molgat
Speaker of the House of Commons, Hon. Gilbert Parent, MP

CANADIAN HIGH COMMISSION
Macdonald House, 1 Grosvenor Square, London WIX OAB
Tel 0171-258 6600
High Commissioner, HE Roy MacLaren, apptd 1996
Deputy High Commissioner, Jacques Bilodeau
Minister, Gilles Landry (*Commercial/Economic*)
Defence Adviser, Cdre D. Miller
Counsellors, G. Berry (*Economic*); D. Stimpson (*Consular*);
    J.-M. Roy; G. des Rivières; C. MacLain

BRITISH HIGH COMMISSION
80 Elgin Street, Ottawa KIP 5K7
Tel: Ottawa 237 1530
High Commissioner, HE A. M. Goodenough, KCMG, apptd
    1996
Deputy High Commissioner, L. J. Duffield
Counsellor, W. B. McCleary (*Economic*)
Defence and Military Adviser, Brig. A. P. Naughton
There are also Consulates-General at Montreal, Toronto,
    and Vancouver and Consulates at Halifax, St John's and
    Winnipeg
BRITISH COUNCIL DIRECTOR, J. Harniman, OBE (*Cultural
    Attaché*)
BRITISH COUNCIL REPRESENTATIVE IN QUEBEC,
    S. Dawbarn, 1000 ouest rue de la Gauchetière,
    Montreal, Quebec H3B 4W5

JUDICATURE

The judicature is administered by judges following the
civil law in Quebec province and common law in other
provinces. Each province has a Court of Appeal. All
superior, county and district court judges are appointed by
the Governor-General, the others by the Lieutenant-
Governors of the provinces.

The highest federal court is the Supreme Court of
Canada, which exercises general appellate jurisdiction
throughout Canada in civil and criminal cases, and which
usually holds three sessions each year. There is one other
federally constituted court, the Federal Court of Canada,
which has jurisdiction on appeals from its trial division,
from federal tribunals and reviews of decisions and
references by federal boards and commissions. The trial
division has jurisdiction in claims by or against the Crown,
its officers or servants or federal bodies. It also deals with
inter-provincial and federal-provincial disputes.

Chief Justice of Canada, Rt. Hon. A. Lamer
Chief Justice, Federal Court, Hon. J. Isaac

FINANCE

Federal government gross general revenue and expenditure was:

	1994–5	1995–6*
Total revenue	C$136,982m	C$145,453m
Total expenditure	174,216m	177,703m
*estimated		

	1994	1995
DEBT		
Gross public debt	C$558,701m	C$599,268m
Net public debt	503,766m	541,128m

DEFENCE

The Canadian armed forces are unified and organized into
three functional commands: Mobile Command; Maritime
Command; Air Command. The Canadian armed forces
number 70,500 personnel and are an all-volunteer force.

Land forces comprise 20,300 personnel with 114 main
battle tanks, 1,858 armoured personnel carriers and 364
artillery pieces.

Maritime forces number 10,000 personnel with four
destroyers, 12 frigates, three submarines and 12 patrol and
coastal craft. Air forces number 17,100 personnel with 140
combat aircraft and 128 armed helicopters. In addition,
there are 23,100 personnel not identified in any of the
above three services.

ECONOMY

About 7.3 per cent of the total land area is farmed. Over 60
per cent of this is under cultivation, the remainder being
predominantly classified as unimproved pasture. More
than 80 per cent of the cultivated land is in the prairie
region of western Canada.

Farm cash receipts from the sale of farm products in
1995 were C$26,782 million. Livestock and animal prod-
ucts contributed C$12,934 million; field crops C$12,769
million; grain and oilseed C$9,300 million.

Canada in 1994–5 produced pelts valued at C$57
million. Wildlife pelts made up 45.2 per cent of the total,
with a value of C$26 million.

The marketed value of fish catches in 1993 was C$3,017
million (preliminary).

About 42 per cent of the total land area is considered as
inventoried forest area. The value of shipments and other
revenue from forestry-related industries in 1993 was:
logging $9,030.9 million; sawmill and planing mill prod-
ucts $12,246.5 million; shingle and shake $283.7 million;
veneer and plywood $1,225.4 million; and paper and allied
products $15,630.6 million.

In 1994, Canada was the world's largest producer of zinc,
potash and uranium, the second largest of nickel, asbestos,
cadmium and elemental sulphur. The country is also rich
in gold, copper, lead, molybdenum, platinum group
metals, gypsum, cobalt, titanium concentrates, and aluminium. The total value of mineral production in 1995 was
C$43,367.7 million.

Production of gold was 145,980,000 kg in 1994* and
of silver 774,506 kg. Uranium production in 1992 was
9,057,000 kg.

TRADE

Merchandise imports in 1995 were valued at C$225,493
million and merchandise exports (including re-exports) at
C$263,696 million. The main exports in 1995 were
passenger automobiles and chassis, other machinery and
equipment, lumber and sawmill products, newsprint
paper, metals and alloys, chemicals, plastics and fertilizers.
Trade with the USA accounts for about 79 per cent of total
trade in merchandise.

Trade with UK	1994	1995
Imports from UK	£1,916,664,000	£1,811,964,000
Exports to UK	1,880,941,000	2,379,624,000

COMMUNICATIONS

The total track of railways in operation on 31 December 1991, was 85,563 km. In 1991 freight transportation was 261 billion tonne-kilometres, and the balance of property accounts at end 1991 was C$18,635m.

The registered shipping on 1 January 1991 including inland vessels, was 43,787 vessels with gross tonnage 4,956,845. The volume of international shipping handled at Canadian ports in 1991 was 168,030,334 metric tonnes loaded and 65,863,148 metric tonnes unloaded.

The bulk of canal shipping in Canada is handled through the two sections of the St Lawrence Seaway, which provide access to the Great Lakes for ocean-going ships. In 1992, transits on the Montreal-Lake Ontario section numbered 2,493 for a total of 31,400,000 cargo tonnes; transits in the Welland Canal section numbered 3,140 for a total of 33,200,000 cargo tonnes. Principal commodities carried were iron ore, wheat, corn, barley, soybeans, manufactured iron and steel, coal and salt.

EDUCATION

Education is under the control of the provincial governments, the cost of the publicly controlled schools being met by local taxation, aided by provincial grants. In 1992–3 there were 16,063 elementary and secondary schools with 5,287,730 pupils. Of these, 1,515 were private schools with 256,140 pupils; 383 federal schools with 55,600 pupils and 19 special schools for the blind and deaf with 2,330 pupils.

In 1992–3 there were 69 degree-granting universities with a full-time enrolment of 572,900, as well as 348,400 students in 203 other post-secondary, non-university institutions.

Source: for financial and economic statistics, Statistics Canada

YUKON TERRITORY

The area of the Territory is 205,346 sq. miles (531,842 sq. km), with a population (1991 census) of 27,797. Minerals, government and tourism are the chief industries, followed by transportation, communications and other utilities industries.

SEAT OF GOVERNMENT – Whitehorse, population (1991 census) 17,925.

The Yukon Act 1970, as amended, provides for the administration of the Territory by a Commissioner acting under instructions given by the Governor-in-Council or the Minister of Indian Affairs and Northern Development. Legislative powers, analogous to those of a provincial government, are exercised by a Legislative Assembly of 17 members elected from electoral districts in the Territory. The Executive Council of the Assembly consists of the government leader as chairman and five elected members.

Commissioner, J. Gingell
Premier, Hon. John Ostashek

NORTHWEST TERRITORIES

The area of the Northwest Territories is 1,322,900 sq. miles (3,426,389 sq. km), with a population (1991 census) of 57,649. The Northwest Territories are subdivided into the regions of Baffin, Fort Smith, Inuvik, Keewatin, Kitikmeot. The chief industry is mining, particularly lead, zinc, gold, silver and oil exploration and natural gas.

SEAT OF GOVERNMENT – Yellowknife, population (1991 census) 15,179.

The Northwest Territories Act 1979, as amended, provides for a Legislative Assembly of 24 elected members, of which the Executive Council under the chairmanship of the government leader is the senior decision-making body of the government in the Territory.

In 1992 a referendum approved a plan to divide the Territories into two and to establish in one part a self-governing autonomous Inuit (Eskimo) populated territory known as Nunavat. Nunavat will comprise the present regions of Baffin, Keewatian and Kitikmeot and will be phased in over six years up to 1999. The territory will have its own government and legislature, though neither will have provincial status. It has a population of some 22,000, of which 80 per cent are Inuit, and covers some 850,000 sq. miles (2,201,500 sq. km). The agreement has yet to be ratified by the Federal Parliament.

Commissioner, H. Makasgak
Government Leader, Hon. D. McKin

CANADIAN PROVINCES

ALBERTA

Alberta has an area of 661,185 sq. km (255,285 sq. miles), including about 6,485 sq. miles of water (16,796 sq. km), with a population (July 1995) of 2,576,500.

PROVINCIAL CAPITAL – Edmonton, city population (1995) 626,999, metropolitan area, 888,500. Other centres are Calgary (749,073), Lethbridge (64,938), Red Deer (60,023), Medicine Hat (45,892), St Albert (45,895).

GOVERNMENT

The Government is vested in a Lieutenant-Governor and Legislative Assembly composed of 83 members, elected for five years. As at July 1996, the Progressive Conservative Party holds 54 seats and the Liberal Party 29 seats.

Lt.-Governor, Hon. H. A. Olson
Premier, President of Executive Council, Hon. Ralph Klein, MLA
Chief Justice, Court of Appeal, Hon. C. A. Fraser

ECONOMY

The total GDP at factor cost in 1995 amounted to C$77,458 million. Preliminary estimates for mineral production in 1995 came to C$21,085 million. Of this total, crude oil amounted to C$10,653 million, and natural gas and its by-products to C$9,351 million.

The total value of manufacturing shipments (1995) was C$27,160 million. The leading industrial products are refined petroleum and coal products, meat and meat products, chemicals and chemical products, fabricated metal products, non-metallic mineral products and primary metals.

FINANCE

	1994–5	1995–6
Revenue	C$16,068m	C$15,572m
Expenditure	15,396m	14,440m

BRITISH COLUMBIA

British Columbia has a total area estimated at 952,263 sq. km (367,669 sq. miles), with a population of 3,764,200 (July 1995).

PROVINCIAL CAPITAL – ΨVictoria, metropolitan population (1995) 316,492. Other principal cities are ΨVancouver (metropolitan population (1995) 1,819,745), Prince George, Kamloops, Kelowna and Nanaimo.

GOVERNMENT

The government consists of a Lieutenant-Governor and an Executive Council together with a Legislative Assembly of 75 members.

The New Democratic Party formed a government after a general election on 28 May 1996. The present standing in the Assembly is New Democratic Party 39, Liberal Party 33, Reform Party 2, Progressive Democratic Alliance 1.
Lt.-Governor, Hon. David C. Lam
Premier, Hon. Glen Clark, MLA
Chief Justice, Supreme Court, Hon. W. A. Esson

AGENT-GENERAL'S OFFICE IN LONDON, British Columbia House, 1 Regent Street, London SW1Y 4NS.
Agent-General, Paul King

FINANCE	1995–6	1996–7
Estimated revenue	C$20,300m	C$20,659m
Estimated expenditure	20,186m	20,572m

ECONOMY

Service industries generate 72 per cent of provincial GDP and account for over 76 per cent of employment. Manufacturing activity is based largely on the processing of the output of the logging, mineral, fishing and agriculture industries. The principal manufacturing centres are Vancouver, Burnaby, Richmond, Surrey, Kamloops, Victoria, North Vancouver and Kelowna. British Columbia is the leading provincial producer of timber and sawmill products. Mining, the second most important non-service activity, is based on copper, zinc, lead, iron concentrates, molybdenum, coal, natural gas, crude petroleum, asbestos, gold and silver. Molybdenum production is approximately 96 per cent of the Canadian total.

The production levels for important industries for 1995 were: lumber 32,611,000 cu. metres; paper 2,850,000 tonnes; pulp 4,572,000 tonnes; coal 24,555,000 tonnes; natural gas 21,338,000,000 cu. metres. Solid mineral production for 1995 is estimated to be valued at C$3,463 million.

The most important agricultural products are livestock, eggs and poultry, fruits and dairy products. In 1995 farm cash receipts were valued at C$1,521.3 million. Salmon accounts for approximately 56 per cent of the value of fisheries.

An estimated 55–60 per cent of industrial production is exported to foreign markets. Manufacturing shipments in 1995 were valued at C$33,442 million.

MANITOBA

Manitoba, originally the Red River settlement, is the central province of Canada. The province has a large area of prairie land but also has 645 kilometres (401 miles) of coastline on Hudson Bay, large lakes and rivers covering an area of 101,592 sq. km (39,225 sq. miles). The total area is 649,947 sq. km (250,946 sq. miles), with a population (1994 estimate) of 1,131,100.

PROVINCIAL CAPITAL – Winnipeg, population 652,355 (1991). Other cities are Brandon (38,567), Thompson (14,977), Portage la Prairie (13,186) and Flin Flon (7,119).

GOVERNMENT

The Lieutenant-Governor is The Queen's representative in Manitoba. There is a Legislative Assembly of 57 members, of which the Executive Council of Ministers are all members.

The Progressive Conservatives formed a majority government after a general election held on 25 April 1995. The standing in the House at July 1995 was: Progressive Conservatives 31, New Democratic Party 23, Liberal 3.
Lt.-Governor, Hon. W. Yvon Dumont
Premier, Hon. Gary A. Filmon, MLA
Chief Justice, Court of Appeal, Hon. Richard J. Scott

ECONOMY

The projected revenue in the fiscal year 1995–6 was C$5,504 million while expenditures were forecast at C$5,455 million.

Of the total land area, 19,126,517 acres are in occupied farms. The gross value of agriculture production in 1994 was estimated at C$2,383 million.

The chief manufacturing centres are Winnipeg, Brandon, Selkirk and Portage la Prairie. The largest manufacturing industry is the food and beverage industry, followed by transportation equipment and primary metal industries.

NEW BRUNSWICK

New Brunswick is one of the eastern maritime provinces and is situated between 45°–48° N. latitude and 63° 47'–69° W. longitude. It has a total area of 73,439 sq. km (28,355 sq. miles), with a population (1996) of 761,400.

PROVINCIAL CAPITAL – Fredericton, population (1991), 71,869. Other cities are ψSaint John (124,981); Moncton (106,503); Bathurst (36,167); Edmundston (22,478); Campbellton (17,183).

GOVERNMENT

Government is administered by a Lieutenant-Governor, an Executive Council, and an elected Legislative Assembly of 55 members. The last provincial election was held on 11 September 1995. As of May 1996 the party standing was Liberals 48, Progressive Conservatives 6, New Democratic Party 1.
Lt-Governor, Hon. Margaret McCain
Premier, Hon. Frank McKenna, MLA
Chief Justice, Court of Appeal, Hon. William Hoyt

ECONOMY

The estimated revenue for the year ending 31 March 1995 was C$4,015,682,573 and ordinary expenditure, $3,924,837,537.

New Brunswick's largest manufacturing sectors are the paper and allied industries and the food and wood industries. Together these accounted in 1995 for 55.4 per cent of the total value of manufacturing shipments of C$7,868 million. Saint John has an ice-free port and is the principal manufacturing centre of the province.

Farmland amounted to 926,820 acres in 1991. Dairy products and potatoes are the leading agricultural products. Farm cash receipts in 1995 totalled C$295,867,000. Fishing is an important industry, employing about 8,800 fishermen. Landings reached 125,651 tonnes valued at C$143,592,000 in 1994.

Zinc, lead, copper and coal deposits are mined in New Brunswick, which is the largest zinc producer in Canada. Antimony and potash are also produced. Total mineral production was valued at C$1,001,964,000 in 1994.

NEWFOUNDLAND AND LABRADOR

The island of Newfoundland is situated between 46° 37'–51° 37' N. latitude and 52° 44'–59° 30' W. longitude, on the north-east side of the Gulf of St Lawrence, and is separated from the North American continent by the Straits of Belle Isle on the north-west and by Cabot

Strait on the south-west. The island is about 510 km long and 508 km broad and is triangular in shape. It comprises an area of 111,390 sq. km (43,008 sq. miles). The population (1995 estimate) (inclusive of Labrador) is 575,400.

Labrador forms the most easterly part of the North American continent, and extends from Point St Charles, at the north-east entrance to the Straits of Belle Isle on the south, to Cape Chidley, at the eastern entrance to Hudson's Straits on the north. It has an area of 294,328 sq. km (113,641 sq. miles), with a population (1991 census) of 30,375.

PROVINCIAL CAPITAL – ΨSt John's (population 1991 census, Greater St John's 171,859) is North America's oldest city. It is the principal port for the island of Newfoundland. Newfoundland's second city of Corner Brook (population 1991 census, 22,410) is situated on the west coast.

GOVERNMENT

The government is administered by a Lieutenant-Governor, aided by an Executive Council and a Legislative Assembly of 48 members elected for a term of five years. A general election was held on 22 February 1996. The standings in the current House of Assembly are: Liberals 37; Progressive Conservatives 19, New Democrats 1, Independent 1.
Lt.-Governor, Hon. Frederick W. Russell
Premier, Hon. Brian Tobin, MHA
Chief Justice, Court of Appeal, Hon. James Gushue

ECONOMY

The estimated gross capital and current account revenues for 1996–7 are C$3,393,033,000 and the gross current and capital account expenditures C$3,437,805,000.

The main primary industries are fishing, forestry and mining. In 1995 shipments of fish products were valued at C$400 million; newsprint shipments at C$673 million; and mining (mainly iron ore) plus structural materials shipments at C$940 million. Total manufacturing shipments were valued at C$1,485 million. The hydro-electric plant on the Churchill river is the largest underground plant in the world, with a capacity of 5,225,000 kW.

Over 139 wells have been drilled off Newfoundland since 1965. Oil was discovered in 1979 on the Grand Banks. Oil production is expected to begin in the late 1990s, with a peak production of 125,000 barrels of oil a day.

NOVA SCOTIA

Nova Scotia is a peninsula between 43° 25′–47° N. latitude and 59° 40′–66° 25′ W. longitude, and is connected to New Brunswick by a low isthmus about 28 km wide. It has an area of 55,490 sq. km (21,425 sq. miles), including 2,650 sq. km of lakes and rivers and 10,424 km of shoreline. No place is more than 56 km from the Atlantic Ocean. Population (1996 estimate) 941,173.

Cape Breton Island has been part of Nova Scotia since 1819. It is the centre of the steel manufacturing and coal mining industries.

PROVINCIAL CAPITAL – ΨHalifax, including the neighbouring city of Dartmouth, has a population of 182,253. The harbour, ice-free all year round, is the main Atlantic winter port of Canada. Other cities and towns include ΨSydney (26,063), ΨGlace Bay (19,501).

GOVERNMENT

The government consists of a Lieutenant-Governor and a 52-member elected Legislative Assembly, from which the Executive Council is selected. The party standings in June

1996 were Liberals 40, Progressive Conservatives 9, New Democratic Party 3.

The Lieutenant-Governor represents The Queen and is appointed by the Governor-in-Council.
Lt.-Governor, Hon. J. James Kinley
Premier, Hon. John Savage, MLA
Speaker of the House of Assembly, Hon. Paul MacEwan, MLA
Chief Justice, Supreme Court, Hon. Constance R. Glube

ECONOMY

The revenue for the fiscal year ending 31 March 1996 was C$4,241.5 million and expenditure was C$4,539.6 million. Provincial GDP in 1995 was C$16,290 million, of which 11.7 per cent was produced by manufacturing.

The value of commodity production in 1995 was: minerals C$566,000,000; fish and shellfish C$481,803,000; farm production C$334,728,000. The total value of manufacturing shipments was C$6,210 million.

Forest land covers 73 per cent of the land area and most is privately owned. Forest-based industries employed an average of 9,700 in 1995, and contributed C$1,117 million to the Nova Scotia economy.

ONTARIO

Ontario has a total area of 1,068,472 sq. km (412,578 sq. miles), with a population (1993 estimate) of 10,746,000.

PROVINCIAL CAPITAL – ΨToronto (metropolitan, census 1991, 3,893,046). Other major urban areas are: Ottawa, the national capital (313,987); ΨHamilton (599,760); London (381,522); ΨWindsor (262,075); Kitchener (356,421) and Sudbury (157,613).

GOVERNMENT

The government is vested in a Lieutenant-Governor and a Legislative Assembly of 130 members elected for five years.

The last legislative election was held on 8 June 1995 and won by the Progressive Conservatives who formed a government. The state of the parties at July 1995 was: Progressive Conservatives 82, Liberals 30, New Democrats 17, Independent 1.
Lt.-Governor, Hon. Henry N. R. Jackman
Premier, Hon. Michael Harris, MPP
Chief Justice, Court of Appeal, Hon. C. L. Dubin

ECONOMY

Ontario is the chief manufacturing province in Canada, producing 50 per cent of all manufactured goods. Major industries are iron and steel, metal fabrication, machinery, electricals and chemicals. Toronto is also a major centre of finance and service industry.

Agricultural production had a gross value of C$6,030 million and total net farm income was C$1,180 million. Productive forested lands cover 39.9 million hectares. Paper and allied industries are by far the most important sector of Ontario's forest industry.

Ontario's natural resources include basic minerals such as copper, iron ore, zinc, sulphur, gold, nickel and platinum. Total value of the mineral production in 1992 was estimated at C$4,800 million.

PRINCE EDWARD ISLAND

Prince Edward Island lies in the southern part of the Gulf of St Lawrence, between 46°–47° N. latitude and 62°–64° 30′ W. longitude. It is about 225 km in length, and from 6 to 64 km in breadth; its area is 5,659 sq. km (2,185 sq. miles), and its population (1994 estimate) 131,600.

PROVINCIAL CAPITAL – ΨCharlottetown (30,436), on the shore of Hillsborough Bay, which forms a good harbour.

GOVERNMENT

The government is vested in a Lieutenant-Governor, an Executive Council, and Legislative Assembly of 32 members elected for a term of up to five years, 16 as Councillors and 16 as Assemblymen. After the election of 29 March 1993 there were 31 Liberals and 1 Progressive Conservative.

Lt.-Governor, Hon. Gilbert R. Clements
Premier, Hon. Catherine S. Callbeck, MLA
Speaker of the Legislative Assembly, Hon. Nancy Guptill, MLA
Chief Justice, Appeal Division, Hon. Norman H. Carruthers

ECONOMY

The ordinary revenue of the province in 1994–5 was C$702.2 million and the expenditure C$774.2 million.

Approximately 46 per cent of the total area of the province is farmland. The value of farm cash receipts in 1995 was C$308.5 million, of which 47 per cent was from the sale of potatoes. Dairy, beef and hogs are also important agriculture products. Fish landings were valued at C$116 million in 1995 of which 68 per cent was of lobster.

The total value of manufacturing shipments was C$687.5 million in 1995, of which 68.5 per cent was in the food products industry. A major summer economic activity is tourism. Non-resident tourists spent C$141.4 million in the province in 1995.

QUEBEC

Quebec has an estimated area of 1,540,667 sq. km (594,855 sq. miles) with a population (1996 estimate) of 7,361,300, of which 83 per cent are French-speaking.

PROVINCIAL CAPITAL – ΨQuebec. Population (1991 census) 167,517. Other important cities are ΨMontreal (1,017,666); Laval (314,398); Sherbrooke (76,429); Montreal-Nord (85,516); La Salle (73,804); Longueuil (129,874) and Gatineau (92,284).

GOVERNMENT

The government of the province is vested in a Lieutenant-Governor, a Council of Ministers and a National Assembly of 125 members elected for five years. The last provincial election on 12 September 1994 was won by the Parti Québécois. At June 1996 the state of the parties was: Parti Québécois 75, Liberals 47, Québec Democratic Action Party 1, Independent 2.

Lt.-Governor, Hon. Martial Asselin
Prime Minister, Hon. Lucien Bouchard
Chief Justice, Court of Appeal, Hon. Pierre Michaud

AGENT-GENERAL'S OFFICE IN LONDON, 59 Pall Mall, London SW1Y 5JH. *Agent-General,* Richard Guay

ECONOMY

The revenue for the year 1994–5 was C$36,431.1 million; expenditure amounted to C$42,143.5 million.

Total estimated value of shipments in the manufacturing industries in 1995 was C$93,656 million. Value of 1995 shipments in the chief industries was accounted for by paper and allied industries, C$11,403 million; transport equipment, C$10,978 million; food, C$10,162 million; primary metal equipment, C$9,622 million.

Forest lands cover 655,376 sq. km, of which 527,650 sq. km are productive. In 1995 total farm receipts were: crops, C$1,001,216,000; livestock and livestock products, C$2,859,203,000; other farm receipts, C$522,206,000. In

1994 51,230 tonnes of fish, to the value of C$130,026,000 were landed.

Minerals to the value of C$3,091,243,000 were mined in 1995. This included copper, C$423,937,000; asbestos, C$232,800,000; and gold, C$663,578,000.

SASKATCHEWAN

Saskatchewan lies between Manitoba to the east and Alberta to the west and has an area of 652,324 sq. km (251,864 sq. miles), of which the land area is 570,269 sq. km, or 220,182 sq. miles. The population (estimated 1995) is 1,018,800. Saskatchewan extends along the Canada–USA boundary for 632 km (393 miles) and northwards for 1,224 km (761 miles). Its northern width is 440 km (276 miles).

PROVINCIAL CAPITAL – Regina. Population (estimated 1995), 178,726. Other cities: Saskatoon (189,745), Moose Jaw (33,803), Prince Albert (33,507) and Yorkton (15,574).

GOVERNMENT

The government is vested in the Lieutenant-Governor, with a Legislative Assembly of 58 members. There is an Executive Council of 19 members. The Legislative Assembly is elected for five years and the state of the parties in June 1996 was: New Democratic Party 42; Liberal 10; Progressive Conservative 5; Independent 1.

Lt.-Governor, Hon. Jack Wiebe
Premier, Hon. Roy Romanow, QC
Chief Justice, Court of Appeal, Hon. E. D. Bayda

FINANCE

General Revenue Fund revenue for year ending March 1997 is C$5,345,400,000 and expenditure C$4,987,602,000.

CAPE VERDE
República de Cabo Verde

Cape Verde, off the west coast of Africa, consists of two groups of islands, Windward (Santo Antão, São Vicente, Santa Luzia, São Nicolau, Boa Vista and Sal) and Leeward (Maio, São Tiago, Fogo and Brava) with a total area of 1,557 sq. miles (4,033 sq. km). The population (UN estimate 1993) was 370,000, the majority of whom are Roman Catholic.

CAPITAL – ΨPraia, population (1980) 57,748.
CURRENCY – Escudo Caboverdiano of 100 centavos.
FLAG – Blue with three horizontal stripes of white, red, white near the bottom; over all on these near the hoist a ring of ten yellow stars.
NATIONAL DAY – 5 July (Independence Day).

GOVERNMENT

The islands, colonized *c.*1460, achieved independence from Portugal on 5 July 1975 under the nationalist party of Guinea Bissau and Cape Verde. A federation of the islands with Guinea Bissau was planned but this was dropped following the 1980 coup in Guinea Bissau.

The republic was a one-party state under the African Party for the Independence of Cape Verde (PAICV) until the constitution was amended in 1990. Multiparty elections, held in January 1991, were won by the opposition Movement for Democracy (MPD). The MPD government was re-elected in December 1995 with 50 of the 72 seats in the National Assembly. President António Mascarenhas Monteiro was re-elected unopposed in February 1996.

HEAD OF STATE
President, António Mascarenhas Monteiro, *assumed office* 22 March 1991, *re-elected* 18 February 1996

COUNCIL OF MINISTERS *as at July 1996*
Prime Minister, Carlos Wahnon Veiga
Economic Co-ordination, António Gualberto do Rosário
Foreign Affairs, Amilcar Spencer Lopes
Education, Science and Culture, José Luís Livramento Monteiro Alves de Brito
Adjoint-Minister of the Prime Minister, José António dos Reis
National Defence, Minister of Presidence of the Ministers' Council, Ulpio Napoleão Fernandes
Justice and Internal Administration, Simão Monteiro
Sea, Helena Semedo
Infrastructure and Transport, Armindo Ferreira
Agriculture, Alimentation and Environment, José António Pinto Monteiro
Health and Social Promotion, João Medina
Secretary of State, Finance, José Ulisses Correia e Silva
Secretary of State, Foreign Affairs and Co-operation, José Luís de Jesus
Secretary of State, Culture, António Jorge Delgado
Secretary of State, Public Administration, Paula Almeida
Secretary of State, Youth and Sports, Victor Osório

EMBASSY OF THE REPUBLIC OF CAPE VERDE
44 Konninginnegracht, 2514 AD, The Hague, The Netherlands
Tel: The Hague 3469623
Ambassador Extraordinary and Plenipotentiary, new appointment awaited

BRITISH AMBASSADOR, HE Alan E. Furness, CMG, resident at Dakar, Senegal
There is a British Consulate on São Vicente.

ECONOMY

The islands have little rain and agriculture is mostly confined to irrigated inland valleys. The chief products are bananas and coffee (for export), maize, sugar-cane and nuts. Fish and shellfish are important exports. Salt is obtained on Sal, Boa Vista and Maio; volcanic rock is also mined for export.

In January 1993 the government announced a programme of reform to institute a change to a market economy and to privatize most industry within four years. GNP per capita was US$910 in 1994. External debt totalled US$157.4 million in 1993.

The main ports are Praia and Mindelo, and there is an international airport on Sal.

TRADE WITH UK	1994	1995
Imports from UK	£3,763,000	£4,465,000
Exports to UK	484,000	584,000

CENTRAL AFRICAN REPUBLIC
République Centrafricaine

The Central African Republic lies just north of the Equator between Cameroon, Chad, the southern part of Sudan, and Zaire. The area is 240,535 sq. miles (622,984 sq. km), and the population (UN estimate 1992) is 3,173,000.

CAPITAL – Bangui, near the border with Zaire, population (1984 estimate) 473,817.
CURRENCY – Franc CFA of 100 centimes.

FLAG – Four horizontal stripes, blue, white, green, yellow, crossed by central vertical red stripe with a yellow five-pointed star in top left-hand corner.
NATIONAL DAY – 1 December.

GOVERNMENT

In December 1958 the French colony of Ubanghi Shari elected to remain within the French Community and adopted the title of the Central African Republic. It became fully independent on 17 August 1960. The first President David Dacko was overthrown in 1966 by the then Col. Bokassa. In December 1976, President Bokassa proclaimed himself Emperor and a new constitution was introduced, the country being known as the Central African Empire. In 1979 Bokassa was deposed by Dacko in a bloodless coup and the country reverted to a republic. President Dacko surrendered power in 1981 to Gen. André Kolingba, who instituted military rule until 1985, when a civilian-dominated Cabinet was appointed. In November 1986 a referendum was held which approved a new constitution and the establishment of a one-party state.

Multiparty presidential and legislative elections were held in October 1992 but were annulled due to irregularities. President Kolinga formed a coalition government in December 1992 and another in February 1993. Presidential and legislative elections held in 1993 were won by Ange-Felix Patasse (MPLC), and the Central African People's Liberation Party (MPLC). The MPLC formed a coalition government in October 1993.

Constitutional reforms were passed in a national referendum in December 1994 which created a constitutional court, introduced elected local assemblies, extended the presidential mandate to a maximum of two six-year terms and subordinated the government to the President.

HEAD OF STATE
President, Ange-Felix Patasse, *elected* 19 September 1993

COUNCIL OF MINISTERS *as at May 1996*
Prime Minister, Gabriel Koyambounou
Finance and Budget, Emmanuel Dokouna
Defence and War Veterans, Jean Mette-Yapende
Foreign and Francophone Affairs, Prof. Simon Bedaya-Ngaro
Justice and Law Reform, Betty Maras
Education, Research and Technology, Albert Mberyo
Public Health and Population, Gabriel Fio Ngaindiro
Government Spokesman, Energy Resources and Minerals, Charles Massi
Agriculture and Livestock, Gabriel Badekara
Water, Forests, Hunting, Fishing, Laurent Ngom Baba
Industry, Commerce and Crafts, Joseph Agbo
Civil Service, Social Security and Training, Eloi Anguimate
Post and Telecommunications, Vincent Sakanga
Transport, Albert Yomba-Yambo
Youth and Sport, Fidele Ogbami
Women's Affairs and Social Action, Marie-Noelle Koyara
Relations with Parliament, Nestor Kombot-Naguemo
Communications, Arts and Culture, Maurice Saragba
Economy, Planning and Co-operation, Dogonendji Be
Public Works, Housing and Territorial Development, Dieudonné Beket
Territorial Administration and National Security, Thierry Kiandji
Decentralization, Gerard Gaba
Environment and Tourism, Daniel Emery Dede

EMBASSY OF THE CENTRAL AFRICAN REPUBLIC
30 rue des Perchamps, 75016, Paris
Tel: Paris 42244256

Ambassador Extraordinary and Plenipotentiary, new appointment awaited
BRITISH AMBASSADOR, HE Nicholas McCarthy, OBE, resident at Yaoundé, Cameroon
Honorary Consul, M. A. G. Perreard, PO Box 728, Bangui

ECONOMY

In an effort to revive an ailing economy, the government began in 1986 to streamline the civil service, increase tax revenues, and reduce price controls. The IMF approved a US$23 million credit to support economic reform in 1994. Cotton, diamonds, coffee and timber are the major exports.

GNP per capita was US$370 in 1994; external debt was US$904.3 million in 1993.

TRADE WITH UK	1994	1995
Imports from UK	£1,056,000	£638,000
Exports to UK	151,000	192,000

CHAD REPUBLIC
République du Tchad

Situated in north-central Africa, the Chad Republic extends from 23° to 7° N. latitude and is flanked by Niger and Cameroon on the west, by Libya on the north, by the Sudan on the east and by the Central African Republic on the south. It has an area of 495,755 sq. miles (1,284,000 sq. km) and a population (UN estimate 1992) of 5,961,000.

The Aouzou strip was claimed by Libya, which occupied the area from 1973 to 1994. A war over the territory ended in 1987. In 1990 Chad and Libya presented their claims to the International Court of Justice, which in 1994 awarded jurisdiction over the whole of the strip to Chad.

CAPITAL – Ndjaména, south of Lake Chad (402,000).
CURRENCY – Franc CFA of 100 centimes.
FLAG – Vertical stripes, blue, yellow and red.
NATIONAL DAY – 13 April.

GOVERNMENT

Chad became a member state of the French Community in 1958, and was proclaimed fully independent on 11 August 1960. The constitution was suspended in 1975 when President Tombalbaye was killed in a coup by Gen. Felix Malloum, who was overthrown in 1979. A Transitional Government of National Unity was replaced in 1982 by the government of Hissène Habré, but this was overthrown in 1990 in a coup led by Idriss Déby. Déby announced the adoption of a multiparty system, allowing the legalization of political parties in 1991 and 1992. A sovereign national conference held in 1993 elected a Higher Transitional Council (CST) to serve as the transitional legislature and appointed a transitional government in conjunction with President Déby until multiparty elections are held. The CST has twice extended the transitional period by one year to allow sufficient time to organize elections. In March 1996, the government concluded the Franceville agreement with opposition parties which provided for a national cease-fire and an independent commission to oversee the election. A new constitution, establishing a unified, democratic state, was confirmed by a referendum. Initial results indicated that Déby had won the first multiparty presidential elections held on 2 June 1996.

HEAD OF STATE
President, Idriss Déby, *took power* December 1990

TRANSITIONAL GOVERNMENT *as at July 1996*
Prime Minister, Djimasta Koibla
Justice, Maldoum Bada Abbas
Foreign Affairs, Ahmat Abderamane Haggar
Territorial Administration, Mahamat Nouri
Finance, Mahamat Ahmat Alhabo
Planning and Co-operation, Nassour Owaido
Public Works and Transport, Gali Gata Nghote
National Education, Djibrine Hissein Grinky
Rural Development, Mahamat Zene Ali Fadel
Commerce and Industrial Production, Yantebaye
Livestock and Water Resources, Mahamat Nour Mallaye
Environment and Tourism, Paul Mbainodoum
Public Health, Ngare Ada
Mines, Energy and Oil, N'Gargos Mosda
Communications, Youssouf Mbodou
Social Affairs and Women, Achta Selguet
Civil Service and Labour, Salibou Garba
Armed Forces, Youssouf Togoimi
Posts and Telecommunications, Moktar Nganassou
Culture, Youth and Sports, Mahamat Seid Farah

EMBASSY OF THE REPUBLIC OF CHAD
Boulevard Lambermont 52, 1030 Brussels, Belgium
Tel: Brussels 2151975
Ambassador Extraordinary and Plenipotentiary, HE Ramadane Barma, apptd 1994
BRITISH AMBASSADOR, HE John Masefield, CMG, resident at Lagos/Abuja, Nigeria
Honorary Consul, E. Abtour, BP877, Avenue Charles de Gaulle, Ndjaména

ECONOMY

About 90 per cent of the workforce is occupied in agriculture, fishing and forestry. There is an oilfield in Kanem and salt is mined around Lake Chad, but the most important activities are cotton growing (mostly in the south) and animal husbandry (in central areas). Raw cotton and meat are the main exports.

The IMF approved a loan of US$74 million in 1995 in support of an economic and structural reform programme initiated by the government. In 1994 GNP per capita was US$190; external debt in 1993 was US$757 million.

TRADE WITH UK	1994	1995
Imports from UK	£1,924,000	£1,939,000
Exports to UK	1,113,000	3,173,000

CHILE
República de Chile

Chile lies between the Andes (5,000 to 15,000 feet above sea level) and the shores of the South Pacific, extending coastwise from the arid north around Arica to Cape Horn, between 17° 15′ and 55° 59′ S. latitude and 66° 30′ and 75° 48′ W. longitude. The extreme length of the country is about 2,800 miles, with an average breadth, north of 41°, of 100 miles. The total area is 292,258 sq. miles (756,945 sq. km).

Island possessions include the Juan Fernandez group (three islands) about 360 miles from Valparaiso; one of these islands is the reputed scene of Alexander Selkirk's (Robinson Crusoe) shipwreck. Easter Island (27° 8′ S. and 109° 28′ W.), about 2,000 miles away in the South Pacific Ocean, contains stone platforms and hundreds of stone figures.

The population (UN estimate 1993) is 13,813,000. There are four main groups: indigenous Araucanian Indians, Fuegians, and Changos; Spanish settlers and their descendants; mixed Spanish Indians; and European immigrants. Because of extensive intermarriage only a few indigenous Indians are racially separate. The main religion is Roman Catholicism. The language is Spanish, with admixtures of local words of Indian origin.

CAPITAL – Santiago, population (1993 estimate) 5,443,000 (Greater Santiago). Other large towns are: ΨValparaíso (608,000), Concepción (311,000), Temuco (249,000), ΨAntofagasta (110,000), ΨValdivia (70,000). ΨPunta Arenas (50,000), on the Straits of Magellan, is the southernmost city in the world.

CURRENCY – Chilean peso of 100 centavos.

FLAG – Two horizontal bands, white, red; in top sixth a white star on blue square, next staff.

NATIONAL ANTHEM – Canción Nacional de Chile.

NATIONAL DAY – 18 September (National Anniversary).

GOVERNMENT

Chile was discovered by Spanish adventurers in the 16th century and remained under Spanish rule until 1810, when a revolutionary war secured independence.

A Marxist, Salvador Allende, was elected President in 1970, but was overthrown in a military coup in 1973.

In 1981, Gen. Pinochet was sworn in to serve as President until 1989; a plebiscite to permit a second eight-year term of office was rejected in 1988. Presidential and congressional elections were held in 1989, beginning the transition to full democracy. Gen. Pinochet remains Commander-in-Chief of the Armed Forces until 1997, which has led to political friction between the government and armed forces.

Executive power is held by the President, legislative power is exercised by a Congress which comprises a Senate of 47 Senators (38 elected and nine appointed) and a Chamber of Deputies of 120 elected members.

Presidential and legislative elections were held in 1993. Eduardo Frei won the presidential election and his ruling Coalition for Democracy (centre and centre-left parties) won 70 Chamber of Deputies seats and 22 of the Senate seats. A joint session of Congress in 1994 reduced the presidential term from eight to six years with no possibility of re-election.

Chile is divided into 12 regions and the Metropolitan Area.

HEAD OF STATE
President of the Republic, Eduardo Frei Ruíz-Tagle, *elected* 11 December 1993, *sworn in* 11 March 1994

CABINET *as at July 1996*
Agriculture, Emiliano Ortega
Central Planning, Luis Maira
Defence, Edmundo Pérez Yoma
Education, Sergio Molina
Finance, Eduardo Aninat
Foreign Affairs, José Miguel Insulza
Secretary-General of the Government, José Joaquín Brunner
Secretary-General of the Presidency, Genaro Arriagada
Transport, Narciso Irureta
Housing, Eduardo Hermosilla
Interior, Carlos Figueroa
Justice, Soledad Alvear
Labour and Social Security, Jorge Arrate
Mining, Benjamín Teplisky
National Properties, Adriana del Piano
Public Health, Carlos Massad

Public Works, Ricardo Lagos
Trade and Industry, Alvaro García
Promotion and Business, Felipe Sandoval
Women's Affairs, Josefina Bilbao
Energy, Alejandro Jadresic

EMBASSY OF CHILE
12 Devonshire Street, London WIN 2DS
Tel 0171–580 6392
Ambassador Extraordinary and Plenipotentiary, HE Mario Artaza, apptd 1996

BRITISH EMBASSY
Avenida El Bosque Norte 0125
Casilla 72-D, Santiago 9
Tel: Santiago 2313737
Ambassador Extraordinary and Plenipotentiary, HE Frank B. Wheeler, CMG, apptd 1993
Counsellor, Head of Chancery and Consul-General, P. L. Hunt
Defence, Naval and Military Attaché, Capt. R. F. Johns, OBE, RN
First Secretary (Commercial), D. H. Cairns
There are British Consular Offices at Antofagasta, Arica, Concepción, Santiago, Punta Arenas, Valparaíso.

BRITISH COUNCIL DIRECTOR, W. Campbell (*Cultural Attaché*), Eliodoro Yañez 832, Casilla 115 Correa 55, Santiago
BRITISH-CHILEAN CHAMBER OF COMMERCE, Av. Suecia 155-C, Casilla 536, Santiago

ECONOMY

Economic reforms during the late 1970s and 1980s, with large-scale privatization and deregulation, have made Chile the most successful economy in Latin America. The economy has grown by 50 per cent in ten years, with economic growth averaging 7 per cent a year in 1987–94. In 1994 inflation was down to single figures from 30 per cent in 1990, unemployment is 5 per cent, and the country has attracted considerable foreign investment and an annual foreign trade surplus.

Cereals, vegetables, fruit, tobacco, hemp and vines are grown extensively and livestock accounts for nearly 40 per cent of agricultural production. Sheep farming predominates in the extreme south. There are large timber tracts in the central and southern zones which produce timber, cellulose and wood for export. Industrial-scale fishing makes Chile the fifth largest producer in terms of catch.

Chile is rich in copper-ore, iron-ore and nitrates, and has the only commercial production of nitrate of soda (Chile saltpetre) from natural resources in the world. There are large deposits of high grade sulphur. Oil and natural gas are produced in the Magallanes area, but domestic production is now declining. Production figures for 1994 were: coal 1,528,414 tonnes; copper 2,135,937 tonnes; crude oil 651,409 tonnes; natural gas 2,100,000 cu. metres.

Foreign debt at 28 February 1994 was US$21,598 million, including Central Bank obligations with the IMF of US$438 million.

TRADE
The principal exports are minerals, timber and metal products, fish products, vegetables, fruit and wool. The principal imports are sugar and other food products, industrial raw materials, machinery, equipment and spares, oil fuels, lubricants and transportation equipment.

840 Countries of the World

	1994	1995
Total imports	US$11,149m	US$14,903m
Total exports	11,644m	16,453m

Trade with UK	1994	1995
Imports from UK	£152,839,000	£170,949,000
Exports to UK	194,555,000	299,959,000

COMMUNICATIONS

With the improvement of the roads an increasing share of internal transportation is moving by road and rail, although shipping is still important. The road system is about 65,000 km in length.

A railway line (*the Longitudinal*) runs from La Calera, just north of Santiago, to Iquique. Another rail line runs from Valparaíso through La Calera and Santiago to Puerto Montt. With the completion of a section of 435 miles from Corumba, Brazil, to Santa Cruz, Bolivia, the Trans-Continental Line will link the Chilean Pacific port of Arica with Rio de Janeiro on the Atlantic. A line runs from Antofagasta to Salta (Argentina).

Chile is served by over 20 international airlines. Domestic traffic is carried by Linea Aerea Nacional (LAN) and LADECO, which also operate internationally, and smaller regional carriers.

DEFENCE

Military service is compulsory for one year (Army) or two years (Navy and Air Force). The total active armed forces strength is 99,000, including 31,000 conscripts. The Army consists of 54,000 personnel (27,000 conscripts). Naval strength is 31,000 (3,000 conscripts) including 3,000 marines and 1,500 coastguard personnel. The Air Force numbers 14,000 personnel (1,000 conscripts) with 110 combat aircraft. There is a paramilitary Carabineros police force of 31,000 personnel.

EDUCATION AND CULTURE

Elementary education is free and compulsory. There are eight universities (three in Santiago, two in Valparaíso, one each in Antofagasta, Concepción and Valdivia). Recent efforts have reduced illiteracy.

The Nobel Prize for Literature was awarded in 1945 to Gabriela Mistral, for Chilean verse and prose, and in 1971 to the poet Pablo Neruda. There are over 100 newspapers and a large number of periodicals.

CHINA
Zhonghua Renmin Gongheguo – The People's Republic of China

The area is 3,705,408 sq. miles (9,596,961 sq. km).

A census (the fourth) was held in 1990 and recorded a total population of 1,130 million. The estimated population for 1994 was 1,200 million.

POPULATION OF THE PROVINCES (1991 estimates)

Anhui	57,610,000
Beijing	10,940,000
Fujian	30,790,000
Gansu	22,850,000
Guangdong	64,390,000
Guangxi Zhuang Autonomous Region	43,240,000
Guizhou	33,150,000
Hainan	6,740,000
Hebei	62,200,000
Heilongjiang	35,750,000
Henan	87,630,000
Hubei	55,120,000
Hunan	62,090,000
Jiangsu	68,440,000
Jiangxi	38,650,000
Jilin	25,090,000
Liaoning	39,900,000
Inner Mongolia Autonomous Region	21,840,000
Ningxia Hui Autonomous Region	4,800,000
Qinghai	4,540,000
Shaanxi	33,630,000
Shandong	85,700,000
Shanghai	13,400,000
Shanxi	29,420,000
Sichuan	108,970,000
Tianjin	9,090,000
Tibet Autonomous Region	2,260,000
Xinjiang Uygur Autonomous Region	15,550,000
Yunnan	37,820,000
Zhejiang	42,020,000
Armed Forces	2,700,000

About 6 per cent of the population belong to around 55 ethnic minorities. Among the largest are the Zhuang of Guangxi, the Uygurs of Xinjiang, the Tibetans and the Mongols.

The indigenous religions are Confucianism, Taoism and Buddhism. There are also Muslims (officially estimated at about 12 million) and Christians (unofficially estimated at about 50 million).

CAPITAL – Beijing (Peking), population (1993) 6,560,000.
MAJOR CITIES – Population of major cities in 1993 was:

ΨShanghai	8,760,000	Harbin	3,100,000
Tianjin	4,970,000	Chengdu	2,670,000
Shenyang	3,860,000	Nanjing	2,430,000
Wuhan	3,860,000	Changchun	2,400,000
Chongqing	3,780,000	Xian	2,360,000
Guangzhou	3,780,000	Dalian	2,330,000
(Canton)	3,560,000	Qingdao	2,240,000

CURRENCY – The currency is called Renminbi (RMB). The unit of currency is the yuan of 10 jiao or 100 fen.
FLAG – Red, with large gold five-point star and four small gold stars in crescent, all in upper quarter next staff.
NATIONAL ANTHEM – March of the Volunteers.
NATIONAL DAY – 1 October (Founding of People's Republic).

HISTORY

China was ruled by imperial dynasties for over 20 centuries until revolutionaries led by Sun Yat-sen forced the Emperor to abdicate on 10 October 1911. Neither the new Nationalist Party (Kuomintang (KMT)) government nor the emergent Chinese Communist Party (CCP) were able to unify China, or to agree on the basis for further reform. Warlord infighting rendered China weak, enabling Japan to occupy Manchuria and all the important northern and coastal areas of China by 1939. Japan's occupation was ended by its defeat by the allies in 1945.

The Communists' initial five-year co-operation with the KMT ended in 1927, although the KMT was unable to suppress the CCP. The CCP had successfully politicized the rural population, setting up a 'Soviet Republic' in Jiangxi in the early 1930s, but were forced to flee by the KMT and began the 'Long March' to Shanxi in 1934. The Communists established control over large areas of China in the early 1940s, seizing the territory abandoned by Japan in 1945. Civil war lasted until 1949 when the CCP, led by Mao Zedong (Mao Tse-tung), inaugurated the People's

Republic of China (PRC), and the KMT under Chiang K'ai-shek went into exile in Taiwan. The USA continued to recognize the Chiang Kai-shek regime as the rightful government of China until 1971, when the PRC took over China's membership of the United Nations from Taiwan.

Under Mao Zedong China was ruled on the basis of four 'cardinal principles': Marxist–Leninist–Maoist thought, the Socialist Road, the dictatorship of the proletariat, and the leadership of the CCP. Mao's 'Great Leap Forward' (1958–61) was an attempt to industrialize rural areas which resulted in a famine in which 30–40 million people died. The country was plunged into chaos during the cultural revolution (1966–70) when the Red Guards were used to rid the country of 'rightist elements'.

GOVERNMENT

Following the death of Mao Zedong in 1976, the disgraced Deng Xiaoping was recalled. In 1977 he was elected Vice-Chairman of the CCP, becoming the dominant force within the party by eliminating leftist influence, rehabilitating fallen leaders and promoting an 'open door' policy of economic liberalization. The Congresses of 1982 and 1987 reaffirmed Deng's policies, and in 1987 most of the revolutionary generation were replaced in the top posts by younger, more liberal supporters of reform.

Student-led pro-democracy demonstrations in April and May 1989, centred on Tiananmen Square in Beijing, ended on 3–4 June when the army took control of Beijing, killing thousands of protesters. This strengthened the position of hardliners within the leadership, who re-adopted policies of centralization based on Marxist ideology. Deng retired from his last official post in November 1989 but retained effective control until late 1994, when he was incapacitated by ill health.

At Deng's instigation during 1992 the emphasis switched back to economic reform and the power of the hardliners waned. The 14th Party Congress in 1992 endorsed Deng's calls for faster, bolder economic reforms and his 'socialist market economy'. However, austerity measures to combat inflation have seen official unemployment rise to around five million, with a further 50–100 million migrant labourers unemployed, causing peasant unrest. A degree of central control has been reasserted over the free-market coastal regions, especially their tax revenues, in an attempt to prevent a repetition of the political unrest of 1989.

CONSTITUTION

Under the 1982 constitution, the National People's Congress is the highest organ of state power. It is elected for a term of five years and is supposed to hold one session a year. It is empowered to amend the constitution, make laws, select the President and Vice-President and other leading officials of the state, approve the national economic plan, the state budget and the final state accounts, and to decide on questions of war and peace. The State Council is the highest organ of the state administration. It is composed of the Premier, the Vice-Premiers, the State Councillors, heads of Ministries and Commissions, the Auditor-General and the Secretary-General. Command over the armed forces is vested in the Central Military Commission.

Deputies to Congresses at the primary level are 'directly elected' by the voters 'through a secret ballot after democratic consultation'. This is now extended to county level. These Congresses elect the deputies to the Congress at the next higher level. Deputies to the National People's Congress are elected by the People's Congresses of the provinces, autonomous regions and municipalities directly under the central government, and by the armed forces.

Local government is conducted through People's Governments at provincial, municipal and county levels. Autonomous regions, prefectures and counties exist for national minorities and are described as self-governing.

HEAD OF STATE

President of the People's Republic of China, Jiang Zemin, *elected* April 1993

Vice President, Rong Yiren
Chairman of the Standing Committee of the Eighth National People's Congress, Qiao Shi
Chairman of the Central Military Commission, Jiang Zemin

STATE COUNCIL *as at May 1996*
Premier, Li Peng
Vice-Premiers, Qian Qichen; Li Lanqing; Zhu Rongji; Zou
  Jiahua; Wu Bangguo; Jiang Chunyun
State Councillors, Li Tieying; Chi Haotian; Song Jian; Li
  Guixian; Ismail Amat; Peng Peiyun; Luo Gan; Chen
  Junsheng

MINISTERS
Agriculture, Jiang Chunyun
Chemical Industry, Gu Xiulian
Civil Affairs, Doje Cering
Coal Industry, Wang Senhao
Communications, Huang Zhendong
Construction, Hou Jie
Culture, Liu Zhongde
Electronics Industry, Hu Qili
Finance, Liu Zhongli
Foreign Affairs, Qian Qichen
Foreign Trade and Economic Co-operation, Wu Yi
Forestry, Xu Youfang
Geology and Mineral Resources, Sun Ruixiang
Internal Trade, Chen Bangzhu
Justice, Xiao Yang
Labour, Li Boyong
Machine Industry, He Guangyuan
Metallurgical Industry, Liu Qi
National Defence, Chi Haotian
Personnel, Song Defu
Posts and Telecommunications, Wu Jichuan
Power Industry, Shi Dazhen
Public Health, Chen Minzhang
Public Security, Tao Siju
Radio, Film and Television, Sun Jiazheng
Railways, Han Zhubin
State Security, Jia Chunwang
Supervision, Cao Qingze
Water Resources, Niu Maosheng

MINISTERS IN CHARGE OF STATE COMMISSIONS
Economics and Trade, Wang Zhongyu
Education, Zhu Kaixuan
Family Planning, Peng Peiyun
Nationalities Affairs, Ismail Amat
Physical Culture and Sports, Wu Shaozu
Planning, Chen Jinhua
Restructuring Economy, Li Tieying
Science, Technology and Industry for National Defence, Ding
  Henggao
Science and Technology, Song Jian
Auditor-General, Lu Peijian
Secretary-General, Luo Gan

President of the People's Bank of China, Dai Xianglong

THE CHINESE COMMUNIST PARTY
General Secretary, Jiang Zemin
Politburo Standing Committee, Jiang Zemin; Li Peng; Qiao
  Shi; Li Ruihuan; Zhu Rongji; Liu Huaqing; Hu Jintao
Politburo of the Central Committee, Tian Jiyun; Qiao Shi; Jiang
  Zemin; Li Tieying; Li Ruihuan; Liu Huaqing; Zhu
  Rongji; Hu Jintao; Ding Guangen; Qian Qichen; Jiang
  Chunyun; Li Lanqing; Wei Jianxing; Wu Bangguo; Xie
  Fei; Yang Baibing; Zou Jiahua; Li Peng; Huang Ju (*full
  members*); Wen Jiabao; Wang Hanbin (*alternate members*)
Secretariat of the Central Committee, Jiang Zemin; Ding
  Guangen; Hu Jintao; Wei Jiangxing; Ren Jianxin; Wen
  Jiabao; Wu Bangguo; Jiang Chunyun (*full members*)

Discipline Inspection Commission, Wei Jianxing (*Secretary*); Xu
  Qing; Hou Zongbin; Chen Zuolin; Wang Deying
  (*Deputy Secretaries*)
Membership, 52,000,000 (1993)

EMBASSY OF THE PEOPLE'S REPUBLIC OF CHINA
49–51 Portland Place, London WIN 3AH
Tel 0171–636 9375/5726
Ambassador Extraordinary and Plenipotentiary, HE Jiang
  Enzhu, apptd 1995
Minister-Counsellor, Lu Kexing (*Commercial*)
Defence Attaché, Maj.-Gen. Han Kaihe
Cultural Attaché, Fan Zhonghui

BRITISH EMBASSY
11 Guang Hua Lu, Jian Guo Men Wai, Beijing 100 600
Tel: Beijing 5321961/5
Ambassador, HE Sir Leonard Appleyard, KCMG, apptd 1994
Minister, Consul-General and Deputy Head of Mission,
  J. W. Hodge
Counsellors, N. Cox (*Political*); S. D. R. Brown (*Commercial*);
  M. Davidson (*Cultural, and British Council Representative*)
Defence, Military and Air Attaché, Col. K. O. Winfield
There is also a Consulate-General in Shanghai.

DEFENCE

All three military arms are parts of the People's Liberation
Army (PLA), which is estimated to have approximately
2,930,000 personnel under arms (1,275,000 conscripts),
with a further 1,200,000 reserves. Military service is
selective, with conscripts serving three years in the Army
and four years in the Air Force and the Navy.

China has 17 intercontinental and 70 intermediate range
land-based, and 12 submarine-launched nuclear ballistic
missiles. The Army has a strength of 2,200,000 (around
1,075,000 conscripts), with some 8,000 main battle tanks,
2,000 light tanks, 4,500 armoured personnel carriers and
armoured infantry fighting vehicles, and 14,500 artillery
pieces.

The Navy has a strength of 260,000 (40,000 conscripts),
50 submarines, 18 destroyers, 32 frigates, 870 patrol and
coastal craft, one marine brigade of 5,000 men, 880 combat
aircraft and 68 armed helicopters. The Air Force numbers
470,000 (160,000 conscripts) and some 4,970 combat
aircraft.

ECONOMY

Economic liberalization in the early 1980s reduced central
planning and broadened the role of the market, which has
led to an explosion in manufacturing, concentrated in
China's coastal regions. Foreign direct investment, especially from Hong Kong and Taiwan, has mushroomed and
enabled the construction of a significant industrial base
and transport infrastructure. In the coastal regions the
economy has become a free market in all but name, with
several stock markets and Shanghai's emergence as a
financial centre. The economy is prone to bouts of 'over-
heating', fuelled by excessive investment in capital construction, which has required austerity measures in
1993–5 in an attempt to control inflation (14.8 per cent in
1995). By 1994, 50–60 per cent of industrial output was
produced by private or collective firms which employed a
total of 120 million people.

Agriculture remains of great importance, with 70
per cent of the population still living in rural areas.
Agricultural policies have devolved responsibility for
agricultural production to individual households.

Cereals, with peas and beans, are grown in the northern
provinces, and rice, tea and sugar in the south. Rice is the
staple food of the inhabitants. Cotton (mostly in valleys of

the Yangtze and Yellow Rivers), tea (in the west and south), with hemp, jute and flax, are the most important crops. Livestock is raised in large numbers. Sericulture is one of the oldest industries. Cottons, woollens and silks are manufactured in large quantities.

Coal, iron ore, tin, antimony, wolfram, bismuth and molybdenum are abundant. Oil is produced in several northern provinces, particularly in Heilongjiang and Shandong, and off-shore deposits are being sought in co-operation with western and Japanese companies.

In 1996, the government announced that its aim of quadrupling the 1980 GDP by 2000 had been achieved five years ahead of schedule. GDP had reached Yuan 5.76 billion and was forecast to grow by 8 per cent between 1996 and 2000. A new five-year plan for the same period focuses on directing investment to inland regions, decreasing unemployment, and reducing the losses of state-owned enterprises.

TRADE

Foreign trade and external economic relations have grown enormously since 1978. In 1995, foreign trade increased more than 18 per cent over 1994, to US$281 billion; exports increased by 23 per cent and imports by 14.2 per cent. Import tariffs were cut to an average 23 per cent in line with China's attempts to join the World Trade Organization. The principal exports are animals and animal products, oil, textiles, ores, metals, tea, electronics and manufactured goods. The principal imports are motor vehicles, machinery, chemical fertilizer, plants, aircraft, books, paper and paper-making materials, chemicals, metals and ores, and dyes.

Trade with UK	1994	1995
Imports from UK	£844,865,000	£824,403,000
Exports to UK	1,641,798,000	1,937,869,000

COMMUNICATIONS

There are more than 53,400 km of railway lines and 1,041,100 km of highway (1991). In addition, internal civil aviation has been developed, with routes totalling more than 471,900 km.

In the past the principal means of communication east to west was by the rivers, the most important of which are the Yangtze (Changjiang) (3,400 miles), the Yellow River (Huanghe) (2,600 miles) and the West River (Xihe) (1,650 miles). These, together with the network of canals connecting them, are still much used but their overall importance has declined. Coastal port facilities are being improved and the merchant fleet expanded.

Postal services and telecommunications have developed in recent years and it is claimed that 95 per cent of all rural townships are on the telephone and that postal routes reach practically every production brigade headquarters.

EDUCATION

Primary education lasts five years, and enrolment (1993) was 124,212,400. Secondary education lasts five years (three years in junior middle school and two years in senior middle school). There were 53,837,300 middle school pupils in 1993. There are over 1,000 universities, colleges and institutes with an enrolment (1993) of 2,642,288 students. In 1995, an estimated 18.5 per cent of the population was illiterate.

CULTURE

The Chinese language has many dialects, notably Cantonese, Hakka, Amoy, Foochow, Changsha, Nanchang, Wu (Shanghai) and the northern dialect. The Common Speech or *putonghua* (often referred to as Mandarin) is based on the northern dialect. The Communists have promoted it as the national language and it is taught throughout the country. As *putonghua* encourages the use of the spoken language in writing, the old literary style and ideographic form of writing has fallen into disuse. Since 1956 simplified characters have been introduced to make reading and writing easier. In 1958 the National People's Congress adopted a system of romanization known as pinyin.

Chinese literature is one of the richest in the world. Paper has been employed for writing and printing for nearly 2,000 years. The Confucian classics which formed the basis of traditional Chinese culture date from the Warring States period (fourth to third centuries BC), as do the earliest texts of Taoism. Histories, philosophical and scientific works, poetry, literary and art criticism, novels and romances survive from most periods.

The most important among the newspapers and magazines are the *People's Daily* and the twice-monthly *Qiushi*, which replaced *Red Flag* as the CCP's mouthpiece in 1989.

TIBET

Tibet is a plateau seldom lower than 10,000 feet, which forms the northern frontier of India (boundary imperfectly demarcated), from Kashmir to Burma, but is separated therefrom by the Himalayas. The area is estimated at 463,000 sq. miles with a population of 2,260,000 in 1991.

From 1911 to 1950, Tibet was virtually an independent country though its status was never officially so recognized. In 1950 Chinese Communist forces invaded eastern Tibet. In 1951 an agreement was reached whereby the Chinese army was allowed entry into Tibet, and a Communist military and administrative headquarters was set up. A series of revolts against Chinese rule culminated in 1959 in a rising in Lhasa. Fighting continued for several days before the rebellion was crushed and military rule was imposed. The Dalai Lama fled to India where he and his followers were granted political asylum and established a government in exile.

In 1964 the Dalai Lama was declared a traitor, and both he and the Panchen Lama were dismissed, marking the end of co-operation between the Chinese government and the traditional religious authorities. Tibet became an Autonomous Region of China in 1965. Martial law was declared in Tibet in 1989 after serious unrest, and sporadic outbursts of unrest continue.

The Panchen Lama died in 1989. China rejected the Dalai Lama's choice of successor, who is believed to have been executed, and enthroned its own candidate.

COLOMBIA
República de Colombia

Colombia lies in the extreme north-west of South America, having a coastline on both the Caribbean Sea and Pacific Ocean. It is situated between 4° 13′ S. to 12° 30′ N. latitude and 68° to 79° W. longitude, with an area of 440,714 sq. miles (1,141,748 sq. km).

The country is divided by the Cordillera de los Andes into a coastal region in the north and west and extensive plains in the east. The eastern range of the Colombian Andes is a series of vast tablelands. This temperate region is the most densely peopled portion of the country. The principal rivers are the Magdalena, Guaviare, Cauca, Atrato, Caquetá, Putumayo and Patia.

The population (UN estimate 1995) is 36,000,000. The language is Spanish. Roman Catholicism is the established religion.

CAPITAL – Bogotá, population (1992 estimate) 8,000,000. Other centres are Medellín (2,400,000); Cali (1,800,000); ΨBarranquilla (1,400,000), the major port on the Caribbean; ΨCartagena (700,000), Bucaramanga (350,000); ΨBuenaventura (130,000), the major port on the Pacific.

CURRENCY – Colombian peso of 100 centavos.

FLAG – Broad yellow band in upper half, surmounting equal bands of blue and red.

NATIONAL ANTHEM – Oh gloria inmarcesible.

NATIONAL DAY – 20 July (National Independence Day).

GOVERNMENT

The Colombian coast was visited in 1502 by Columbus, and in 1536 a Spanish expedition penetrated the interior and established a government. The country remained under Spanish rule until 1819 when Simón Bolivar (1783–1831) established the Republic of Colombia, consisting of the territories now known as Colombia, Panama, Venezuela and Ecuador. In 1829–30 Venezuela and Ecuador withdrew, and in 1831 the remaining territories formed the Republic of New Granada. The name was changed to the Granadine Confederation in 1858, to the United States of Colombia in 1861 and to the Republic of Colombia in 1866. Panama seceded in 1903.

During the early 1950s Colombia suffered a period of virtual civil war between the supporters of the Conservative and the Liberal parties. From 1957 to 1974 the country was governed under the 'National Front' agreement with an alternating presidency and equal numbers of ministerial posts. The alternation of the presidency ended in 1974 and parity in appointments in 1978. Thereafter, the constitution lays down that government portfolios and administrative appointments shall be divided proportionally among the two major parties in Congress.

Elections to a constitutional convention were held in 1990, in which the former guerrilla movement M19 gained 30 per cent of the vote and a new constitution was promulgated in 1991. Congressional elections to the 102-seat Senate and 163-seat House of Representatives were last held in March 1994 and saw the re-emergence of the traditional parties. The Liberal Party won 89 seats, the Social Conservative Party (PSC) 56 seats and M19 two seats. In the Senate elections the Liberal Party won 52 seats, the PSC 21 seats and M19 one seat. In the second round of the 1994 presidential election the Liberal candidate Ernesto Samper narrowly defeated the PSC candidate. President Samper appointed a Liberal–PSC coalition government in August 1994.

INSURGENCY

Colombia is dogged by insurgency from left-wing guerrillas and from the drugs cartels centred on Cali. In 1989–94 the government reached peace agreements with four left-wing guerrilla groups, including M19 and the Current of Socialist Revolution (CRS), although the Simón Bolivar National Guerrilla Co-ordinating Board remains active. The security threat from the Medellín drugs cartel effectively ended with the death of Pablo Escobar, the cartel leader, in December 1993. In 1993–6 the government had captured or killed six of the seven cartel members. In 1995, the government came under suspicion of having links with the cartel and President Samper was accused of authorizing the use of cartel money to fund his 1994 election campaign.

HEAD OF STATE
President, Dr Ernesto Samper-Pizano, *elected* 19 June 1994, *sworn in* 7 August 1994

CABINET *as at July 1996*
Interior, Horacio Serpa Uribe
Foreign Affairs, Rodrígo Pardo Garcia-Peña
Finance, José Antonio Ocampo
Justice, Carlos Eduardo Medellín
National Defence, Juan Carlos Esguerra
Transport, Carlos Hernán López
Labour, Orlando Obregón
Agriculture, Cecilia López Montaño
Health, Maria Teresa Forero de Sade
Mines and Energy, Rodrigo Villamizar
Communications, Juan Manuel Turbay
Education, Maria Emma Mejia
Development, Rodrigo Marin Bernal
Foreign Trade, Maurice Hars Meyer
Planning, vacant
Environment, José Vicente Mogollón

COLOMBIAN EMBASSY
Flat 3A, 3 Hans Crescent, London SWIX OLR
Tel 0171–589 9177/5037
Ambassador Extraordinary and Plenipotentiary, HE Dr Carlos Lemos-Simmonds, apptd 1996

BRITISH EMBASSY
Torre Propaganda Sancho, Calle 98 No. 9–03 Piso 4, Bogotá
Tel: Bogotá 2185111
Ambassador Extraordinary and Plenipotentiary, HE Arthur L. Coltman, CMG, apptd 1994
There are British Consular Offices at Barranquilla, Bogotá, Cali and Medellín.

BRITISH COUNCIL DIRECTOR, Kate Board, Calle 87 No. 12–79, Bogotá DE
COLOMBO-BRITISH CHAMBER OF COMMERCE, Apartado Aereo 054 728, Av. 39 No. 13–62, Bogotá DE

DEFENCE

The total active strength of the armed forces is 146,400 personnel (67,300 conscripts). Service is compulsory and lasts between one and two years.

The Army's strength is some 121,000 (63,800 conscripts) with 12 light tanks, 156 armoured personnel carriers and 130 artillery pieces. The Navy, with 18,100 personnel including 8,800 marines, has 12 frigates, 40 patrol and coastal craft and two submarines. The Air Force, with 7,300 personnel (3,500 conscripts), has a strength of 74 combat aircraft and 75 armed helicopters. There is also a paramilitary police force of 87,000.

ECONOMY

Coal, natural gas and hydro-electricity resources are largely unexploited, although development of coal is being given priority. Coal production in 1993 was 17.6 million tonnes; oil exports were 550,000 b.p.d. Since 1993 oil reserves of 1,000 million barrels and large gas reserves have been discovered.

The hydrocarbon sector accounts for over half of the mining output, precious metals (gold, platinum and silver) and iron ore accounting for the remainder. Other mineral deposits include nickel, bauxite, copper, gypsum, limestone, phosphates, sulphur and uranium. Colombia is also the world's largest producer of emeralds and has deposits of other precious and semi-precious stones.

A wide variety of crops are grown, principally coffee. Other major cash crops are sugar, bananas, cut flowers and cotton. Cattle are raised in large numbers, and meat and cured skins and hides are also exported.

The government has encouraged diversification to reduce dependence on coffee as the major export and this has led to the growth of new export-orientated industries, particularly textiles, paper products and leather goods. Stimulus to the economy has been provided by loans from the World Bank and IADB for project development, particularly in the power sector (in which hydroelectric projects have predominated) and for telecommunications.

Since the late 1980s the government has introduced trade liberalization and privatization measures which have effectively freed foreign exchange transactions, increased foreign competition, ended protectionism and reduced inflation. In 1995 GDP growth was 5.3 per cent.

TRADE

Principal exports are petroleum and derivatives, coffee, bananas, cut flowers, clothing and textiles, ferro-nickel and coal. Principal trading partners are USA, the EU and Latin America.

Trade with UK	1994	1995
Imports from UK	£231,445,000	£145,244,000
Exports to UK	191,449,000	174,109,000

COMMUNICATIONS

The Andes make surface transport difficult so air transport is used extensively. There are daily air services between Bogotá and all the principal towns, as well as frequent services to other countries. The 'Atlantic Railway' links the departmental lines running down to the River Magdalena, and completes the connection between Bogotá and Santa Marta. Although the railways are in a poor state, there are about 2,600 miles of rail in use at present. The road network consists of 105,201 km of roads of all types, of which 21,800 km are classified as main trunk and transversal roads. A canal to link the Pacific Ocean and the Caribbean Sea has been planned.

There are over 450 radio stations and three national television channels.

CULTURE

State education is free. Efforts have been made to reduce illiteracy, which was estimated at 8.7 per cent in 1995. There are 27 universities. There is a flourishing press in urban areas and a national literature supplements the rich inheritance from the time of Spanish colonial rule.

THE COMOROS
République Fédérale Islamique des Comores

The Comoro archipelago includes the islands of Great Comoro, Anjouan, Mayotte and Moheli and certain islets in the Indian Ocean with an area of 838 sq. miles (2,171 sq. km) and a population (UN estimate 1992) of 585,000, most of whom are Muslim.

CAPITAL – Moroni, on Great Comoro (pop. 17,267).
CURRENCY – Comorian franc of 100 centimes. The Comoros also uses the Franc CFA of 100 centimes.
FLAG – Green with a white crescent and four white stars in the centre, tilted towards the lower fly.
NATIONAL DAY – 6 July (Independence Day).

GOVERNMENT

The islanders voted for independence from France in December 1974 and three islands became independent on 6 July 1975. The island of Mayotte opposed independence and has remained under French administration.

A new constitution was adopted by referendum in 1992 which provides for a President directly elected for a five-year term which is renewable once only; an elected 42-member legislative assembly with a four-year term; a 15-member Senate (five from each island) chosen by an electoral college for six-year terms; and the appointment of a prime minister from the largest party in the legislative assembly. A transitional administration governed until a legislative election in December 1993 which brought President Djohar's PDR party to power. Djohar was temporarily ousted in a coup attempt by mercenaries led by former French colonel Bob Denard in September 1995 which was thwarted by French troops. While Djohar was abroad for medical attention, the Prime Minister of the newly installed unity government, Caabiel Yachroutou, declared himself interim President and refused to acknowledge Djohar's authority, resulting in the formation of a rival government. Djohar returned to the Comoros in January 1996 but was prohibited from contesting the March 1996 presidential election, which was won by Mohammad Taki Abdoulkarim of the National Union for Democracy in the Comoros. Taki dissolved the National Assembly and set elections for October 1996; a constitutional referendum was also proposed.

Each island is administered by a Governor, assisted by up to four Commissioners whom he appoints, and has an elected Legislative Council.

HEAD OF STATE
President, Mohammad Taki Abdoulkarim, *sworn in 25 March 1996*

GOVERNMENT *as at July 1996*
Prime Minister, Tajiddine Ben Said Massonde
Agricultural Production and the Environment, Said Ali Mohamed
Defence, Mouhdar Ahmed Charif
Education, Professional Training, Francophone Affairs, Culture, Youth, Sports and Scientific Research, Mouzaoir Abdallah
Finance, Economy, Budget and Internal Trade, Said Ali Kemal
Foreign Affairs, Co-operation and External Trade, Said Omar Said Ahmed
Industry, Works and Mining Research, Madi Ahmada
Interior and Information, Said Mohamed Said Hassan
Justice and Islamic Affairs, Mohamed Abdul Wahab
Territorial Development, Housing and Town Planning, Soidri Salim Madi
Public Health, Population and Social Affairs, Halidi Abderenane Ibrahim
Tourism, Transport, Posts and Telecommunications, Omar Tamou

BRITISH AMBASSADOR, HE Robert Dewar, resident at Antananarivo, Madagascar

ECONOMY

The most important products are vanilla, copra, cloves and essential oils, which are the principal exports; cacao, sisal and coffee are also cultivated. Great Comoro is well forested and produces some timber.

Trade with UK	1994	1995
Imports from UK	£1,272,000	£2,021,000
Exports to UK	52,000	13,000

CONGO
République du Congo

The Congo lies on the Equator between Gabon on the west and Zaire on the east, the River Congo and its tributary the Ubangui forming most of the eastern boundary of the state. It has a short Atlantic coastline. The area is 132,047 sq. miles (342,000 sq. km), with a population of 2,443,000 (UN estimate 1993).

CAPITAL – Brazzaville (600,000); ΨPointe Noire (350,000).
CURRENCY – Franc CFA of 100 centimes.
FLAG – Divided diagonally into green, yellow and red bands.
NATIONAL DAY – 15 August.

GOVERNMENT

Formerly the French colony of Middle Congo, the Congo became a member state of the French Community on 28 November 1958 and fully independent on 17 August 1960.
In 1968, a National Council of army officers took power and created the Parti Congolais du Travail (PCT) and the People's Republic of the Congo the following year. After popular pressure, the PCT abandoned its monopoly of power and renounced Marxism in 1990. A transitional government was formed in January 1991 and a national conference suspended the constitution, stripped President Sassou-Nguesso of all powers and formed itself into the Higher Council of the Republic (CSR). In December 1991 the CSR adopted a new multiparty constitution with a directly-elected President and a bicameral parliament. The new constitution was approved by a referendum in March 1992 and in the ensuing presidential and legislative elections the Pan-African Union for Social Democracy (UPADS) emerged as the largest party in both the Senate and the National Assembly. The lack of a parliamentary majority forced President Lissouba to call fresh elections in May and June 1993. These too were won by the UPADS but the results were disputed by opposition groups and violence broke out between the armed forces and armed supporters of the URD (Union for Democratic Renewal)-PCT opposition alliance. In a rerun of elections for 11 seats in the 125-seat National Assembly, the majority were won by the URD-PCT but UPADS still retained a parliamentary majority. Fighting resumed until February 1994, when it was agreed to call in an international panel to examine the 1993 election results. The panel annulled the results in nine seats, for which by-elections were held in April 1995, most being won by opposition parties. A new UPADS-dominated government was appointed in January 1995 which included URD members who had left the opposition alliance. Fighting ended in December 1995 when the government and opposition parties agreed to disband all militias.

HEAD OF STATE
President, Pascal Lissouba, *elected* 16 August 1992

CABINET *as at July 1996*
Prime Minister, Jacques-Joachim Yhombi Opango
Minister of State, Development, Martin M'Beri
Minister of State, National Defence, Maurice-Stephane Bongho-Nouarra
Minister of State, Interior, Security, Regional Development, Col. Philippe Bikinkita
Justice and Administration, Joseph Ouabari
Foreign and Francophone Affairs and Co-operation, Arsene-Destin Tsaty-Bongou

Economy and Finance, N'Guila Moungounga Nkombo
Industrial Development, Mines and Energy, Posts and Telecommunications, Jean Itadi
Equipment and Public Works, Lambert Galibali
Agriculture, Fisheries and Animal Husbandry, Jean-Prosper Koyo
Transport and Civil Aviation, Séraphin Gompe
Commerce and Small and Medium-sized Enterprises, Marius Mouambenga
Health and Social Welfare, Jean Mouyabi
Civil Service, Labour and Social Security, Anaclet Tsomambet
Hydrocarbons, Benoit Koukebene
Culture, Arts, Tourism and Environment, Gabriel Matsiona
Communications, Government Spokesman, Albertine Lipou-Massala
Education, Research and Technology, Martial de Paul Ikounga
Women's Development, Marie Thérèse Avemeka
Youth and Sports, Gen. Claude-Emmanuel Eta-Onka

EMBASSY OF THE REPUBLIC OF CONGO
37 bis rue Paul Valéry, 75116 Paris, France
Tel: Paris 45006057
Ambassador Extraordinary and Plenipotentiary, HE Pierre-Michel Nguimbi, apptd 1996

HONORARY CONSULATE, Alliance House, 12 Caxton Street, London SWIH OQS. Tel: 0171-222 7575. *Honorary Consul*, L. Muzzu

BRITISH AMBASSADOR, Marcus Hope, resident at Kinshasa, Zaire
There are Honorary Consulates in Brazzaville and Pointe Noire.

ECONOMY

Congo has its own oil deposits, producing about 9 million tonnes annually. It also produces lead, zinc and gold. The principal agricultural products are timber, cassava, sugar cane and yams. Imports are mainly of machinery.

TRADE WITH UK	1994	1995
Imports from UK	£14,649,000	£18,426,000
Exports to UK	4,061,000	5,229,000

COSTA RICA
República de Costa Rica

Costa Rica extends across the Central American isthmus between 8° 17' and 11° 10' N. latitude and from 82° 30' to 85° 45' W. longitude. It has an area of 19,575 sq. miles (50,700 sq. km). The republic lies between Nicaragua and Panama, and between the Caribbean Sea and the Pacific Ocean. The coastal lowlands have a tropical climate but the interior plateau, with a mean elevation of 4,000 feet, enjoys a temperate climate.
The population (1994 estimate) is 3,232,526, mainly of European origin. The language is Spanish.

CAPITAL – San José, population (estimate 1994) 86,178; Alajuela (44,358); ΨPuntarenas (37,390); ΨLimón (67,784).
CURRENCY – Costa Rican colón (₡) of 100 céntimos.
FLAG – Five horizontal bands, blue, white, red, white, blue (the red band twice the width of the others with emblem near staff).
NATIONAL ANTHEM – Himno Nacional de Costa Rica
NATIONAL DAY – 15 September.

GOVERNMENT

For nearly three centuries (1530–1821) Costa Rica was under Spanish rule. In 1821 the country obtained its independence, although from 1824 to 1839 it was one of the United States of Central America.

In 1948 the Army was abolished, the President declaring it unnecessary. Executive power is vested in the President, who is head of state and government, with legislative power vested in the 57-member Legislative Assembly. Under the constitution both the President and the members of the Legislative Assembly are elected for a single four-year term and may not be re-elected. The main political parties are the Social Christian Unity Party (PUSC) and the National Liberation Party (PLN). The last presidential and legislative elections were held on 6 February 1994 when PLN candidate José Maria Figueres won the presidential election, and the PLN won 28 seats and the PUSC 25 seats in the Legislative Assembly.

HEAD OF STATE
President, José Maria Figueres Olsen, *took office* 8 May 1994

MINISTERS *as at July 1996*

Vice-President, Minister for the Presidency, Rodrigo Oreamuno
Foreign Affairs, Dr Fernando Naranjo
Interior, Justice, Maureen Clark
Finance, Francisco de Paula Gutierrez
Agriculture, Roberto Solorzano
Economy, Industry and Commerce, Marcos Vargas
Foreign Trade, José Rossi
Natural Resources, Energy and Mines, Rene Castro
Special Projects, Dr Longino Soto
National Co-ordination, Sergio Quiros
Public Works and Transport, Bernardo Arce
Education, Eduardo Doryam
Health, Dr Herman Weinstok
Culture, Youth and Sports, Dr Arnoldo Mora
Labour, Farid Ayales
Planning, Dr Leonardo Garnier
Housing, Edgar Arroyo
Security, Juan Diego Castro
Science and Technology, Eduardo Sibaja
Information, Alejandro Soto
Tourism, Carlos Roesch
State Reorganization, Mario Carvajal

COSTA RICAN EMBASSY
Flat 1, 14 Lancaster Gate, London W2 3LH
Tel 0171-706 8844
Ambassador Extraordinary and Plenipotentiary, HE Jorge Borbón, apptd 1994

BRITISH EMBASSY
Apartado 815, Edificio Centro Colón (11th Floor), San José 1007
Tel: San José 2215566
Ambassador Extraordinary and Plenipotentiary and Consul-General, HE Richard Michael Jackson, CVO, apptd 1995

ECONOMY

Agriculture is the chief industry and the principal products are coffee, bananas, sugar and cattle (for meat). Other crops are cocoa, rice, maize, potatoes, hemp, pineapple, cassava, ginger, chaw chaw, melon and flowers. Industrial activity is principally in the manufacturing sector and manufactured goods include foodstuffs, textiles and clothing, plastic goods, pharmaceuticals, fertilizers and electrical equipment. Tourism is of growing importance and became the main source of foreign exchange revenue in 1992.

TRADE

The chief exports are manufactured goods and other products, coffee, bananas, cocoa and sugar. The chief imports are machinery, including transport equipment, manufactures, chemicals, fuel and mineral oils and foodstuffs.

	1992	1993
Total imports	US$2,461.7m	US$2,936.8m
Total exports	1,828.4m	2,064.3m
Trade with UK	1994	1995
Imports from UK	£20,930,000	£23,271,000
Exports to UK	76,795,000	78,515,000

COMMUNICATIONS

The chief ports are Limón on the Atlantic coast, through which passes most of the coffee exported, and Caldera on the Pacific coast. The railway system is 500 miles long and nationalized. LACSA is the national airline, operating flights throughout Central and South America, the Caribbean and USA, besides internal flights to local airports by SANSA.

CÔTE D'IVOIRE
République de Côte d'Ivoire

Côte d'Ivoire is situated on the Gulf of Guinea between 5° and 10° N. latitude and 3° and 8° W. longitude. It is flanked on the west by Guinea and Liberia, on the north by Mali and Burkina, and on the east by Ghana. It has an area of 124,503 sq. miles (322,463 sq. km). The climate is equatorial in the south and west, which are mainly forested; tropical in the centre and east, which are savannah regions with trees; dry and tropical in the north, which is a grassy savannah region.

The population of 13,316,000 (UN estimate 1993) is divided into a large number of ethnic and tribal groups. The official language is French. Some 39 per cent of the population is Muslim, 28 per cent Christian (mainly Roman Catholic) and 17 per cent maintain traditional beliefs.

CAPITAL – Yamoussoukro (population 106,786) has been the political and administrative capital since 1983. The economic and financial capital remains Abidjan (population 2,700,000), which is also the largest city and main port.
CURRENCY – Franc CFA of 100 centimes.
FLAG – Three vertical stripes, orange, white and green.
NATIONAL ANTHEM – L'Abidjanaise.
NATIONAL DAY – 7 August.

GOVERNMENT

Although French contact was made in the first half of the 19th century, Côte d'Ivoire became a colony only in 1893 and was finally pacified in 1912. It decided on 5 December 1958 to remain an autonomous republic within the French Community; full independence outside the Community was proclaimed on 7 August 1960.

Côte d'Ivoire has a presidential system of government and a single-chamber National Assembly of 175 members. Although the constitution provides for a multiparty system, it was not until 1990 that any party other than the ruling PDCI party was authorized. The PDCI won multiparty elections held in November 1990 amid allegations of electoral fraud; opposition protests continue. After having been President since independence in 1960, President Houphouët-Boigny died in December 1993 and was replaced as president by the parliamentary speaker Henri Konan-Bédié. Konan-Bédié was elected by an overwhelming majority following an opposition party boycott in the October 1995 presidential election. The PDCI won 148 of the 175 seats in the November 1995 elections to the National Assembly.

HEAD OF STATE
President, Henri Konan-Bédié, *took office* 7 December 1993, *elected* 22 October 1995

CABINET *as at May 1996*
Prime Minister, Planning and Industrial Development, Daniel Kablan Duncan
Relations with Institutions, Ahoua N'Guetta Timothee
National Solidarity, Laurent Dona-Fologo
Religious Affairs and Dialogue with the Opposition, Leon Konan Koffi
Foreign Affairs, Amara Essy
Interior and National Integration, Emile Constant Bombet
Defence, Bandama N'Gatta
Justice and Public Freedom, Faustin Kouame
Agriculture and Animal Resources, Lambert Kouassi Konan
Raw Material, Guy-Alain Emmanuel Gauze
Economy and Finance, Niamien N'Goran
Economic Infrastructure, Ezan Akele
Higher Education, Scientific Research and Technological Innovation, Saliou Toure
National Education and Basic Training, Pierre Kipre
Technical Education and Professional Training, Zakpa Komenan
Security, Gaston Ouassenan Koné
Public Health, Maurice Kacou Guikahue
Mines and Petroleum Resources, Lamine Fadiga
Employment and Civil Service, Social Welfare, Atchi Atsin
Commerce, Ferdinand Kacou Angora
Housing, Living Conditions and Environment, Albert Kacou Tiapani
Communications, Government Spokesperson, Danielle Boni-Claverie
Culture, Bernard Zadi Zahourou
Family and Women's Promotion, Albertine Gnanazan Epie
Youth Promotion and Civil Education, Vlami Bi Dou
Sports, Guei Robert
Tourism and Handicrafts, Lancine Gon Coulibaly
Yamoussoukro, Jean Konan Banny

EMBASSY OF THE REPUBLIC OF CÔTE D'IVOIRE
2 Upper Belgrave Street, London SW1X 8BJ
Tel 0171–235 6991
Ambassador Extraordinary and Plenipotentiary, HE Gervais Yao Attoungbré, apptd 1989

BRITISH EMBASSY
Immeuble Les Harmonies, 01 BP 2581, Abidjan 01
Tel: Abidjan 226850
Ambassador Extraordinary and Plenipotentiary, HE Margaret I. Rothwell, CMG, apptd 1990

ECONOMY

Côte d'Ivoire became wealthy in the 1970s because of the high prices of its two principal export earners, coffee and cocoa. In the late 1980s the economy contracted considerably as its exports deteriorated in competitiveness and its rivals devalued their currencies while the franc CFA remained pegged to the French franc. In early 1995 Côte d'Ivoire had a relatively large foreign debt of US$13,100 million incurred by the infrastructure programmes of the 1970s and 1980s. An economic reform and stabilization

programme began in 1989 under IMF auspices which has brought down inflation, increased investment and led to GDP growth. The devaluation of the CFA franc in January 1994 has increased exports considerably and restored a trade surplus. For the 1994–6 period Côte d'Ivoire has received US$467 million in credit support from the IMF.

The principal exports are coffee, cocoa, timber, palm oil, sugar, rubber, pineapples, bananas, and cotton. There are a few deposits of diamonds and minerals including manganese and iron. Oil and gas deposits began to be exploited in 1995.

TRADE WITH UK	1994	1995
Imports from UK	£27,057,000	£49,428,000
Exports to UK	65,958,000	101,737,000

CROATIA

Croatia is bounded by Slovenia, Hungary, the rump Federal Yugoslav state and Bosnia-Hercegovina; it has an area of 21,823 sq. miles (56,538 sq. km). It is divided into three major geographic regions: the Pannonian region in the north, the central mountain belt, and the Adriatic coast region of Istria and Dalmatia which has 1,185 islands and islets and 1,104 miles (1,778 km) of coastline.

The population (1991 census) was 4,784,265, of which 78 per cent were Croats, 12 per cent Serbs, 2 per cent Yugoslavs and 1 per cent Muslims. The remaining minorities were Hungarians, Italians, Albanians, Czechs, Ukrainians and Jews. Croatia is host to some 500,000 refugees from Bosnia-Hercegovina.

About 77 per cent of the population is Roman Catholic, 11 per cent Serbian Orthodox and 1 per cent Muslim. The majority language is Croatian in the Latin script. Serbs use Serbian in the Cyrillic script.

CAPITAL – Zagreb, population 867,865. Other major cities are Split (200,000), Rijeka (200,000) and Osijek (160,000).
CURRENCY – Kuna of 100 lipas.
FLAG – Three horizontal stripes of red, white, blue, with the national arms over all in the centre.
NATIONAL ANTHEM – Lijepa naša domovina (Our Beautiful Homeland).
NATIONAL DAY – 30 May (Statehood Day).

HISTORY

Croatia was part of the Austro-Hungarian Empire from 1526 to 1918. On 29 October 1918 the Croatian parliament declared Croatia independent and soon after Croatia joined with Slovenia, Bosnia-Hercegovina, Serbia and Montenegro to form the 'Kingdom of Serbs, Croats and Slovenes' (renamed Yugoslavia in 1929). From 1941 to 1945 Yugoslavia was occupied by the Axis powers, with Italy and Hungary annexing parts of Croatia and a pro-Nazi Croat puppet state being established in the remainder of Croatia and Bosnia-Hercegovina. The armed extremists of this state (Ustashe) engaged in fierce fighting with Serbian royalists, Communist partisans and pro-Allied Croat partisans.

At the end of the war Yugoslavia was re-established as a federal republic under Communist rule but gradually disintegrated following the death of the wartime partisan leader Josep Tito in 1980. When Croatia informed Belgrade of its independence in June 1991, the Federal Yugoslav Army (JNA) intervened against local defence forces to prevent the disintegration of the federation. Croatia's ethnic Serb minority, which rejected Croatia's independence, formed itself into armed groups and began fighting with the Croat defence forces. By September 1991 this had escalated into war between Croatia and Serbia, which had assumed control of the JNA.

The war in Croatia continued until January 1992 when a cease-fire was declared. The JNA and Serb forces had secured control of virtually all ethnic Serb areas in Croatia. Four UN protected areas, Northern and Southern Krajina and Eastern and Western Slavonia, were created from the Serb-controlled areas in Croatia and UN troops arrived to police the areas. The JNA withdrew from Croatia but the ethnic Serb forces refused to disarm.

GOVERNMENT

In April and May 1990 Croatia's first free, democratic elections were won by the Croatian Democratic Union (HDZ) of Dr Franjo Tudjman. A new constitution was adopted by parliament in December 1990 and a referendum in May 1991 backed independence from Yugoslavia. Croatia declared its independence on 30 May 1991.

Executive power is vested in a President and government. The President is directly elected for five-year terms. Legislative power is vested in the bicameral parliament, comprising the 63-member Chamber of Districts and the 138-member Chamber of Deputies.

Croatia is divided into 21 counties; each county elects three members to the Chamber of Districts. Counties are composed of groups of districts and function both as units of local government and as regional offices for the central administration. There are 102 districts.

The HDZ won a majority of seats in the October 1995 elections to the Chamber of Deputies. The state of the parties in July 1996 is: Croatian Democratic Union (HDZ) 75; Croatian Social Liberal Party (HSLS) 12; Croatian Peasant Party (HSS) 10; Party of Democratic Change (SDP) 10; Croatian Party of the Rights (HSP) 4; Others 16.

Croatia's ethnic Serbs voted to establish a Republic of Serbian Krajina (RSK) in 1993 and elected President Milan Martic and a legislature in January 1994. Following an agreement with the Croatian government in November 1995, a 5,000-strong UN force arrived in Eastern Slavonia in early 1996 to oversee the formation· of a two-year transitional government. In April 1996, the regional council of Eastern Slavonia, the sole remaining component of the RSK, appointed Goran Hadzic as president. The council was dissolved and replaced by a regional assembly based in Vukovar.

SECESSION

Fighting between Croatian Serbs and government troops in the UN-protected areas of Slavonia and Krajina resumed until a cease-fire agreement was concluded in April 1994. The Croatian government accused the UN of failing to disarm Serb forces and refused to extend the UN mandate in March 1995. A new mandate was agreed for the UN Confidence Rebuilding Operation (UNCRO) but was annulled in Western Slavonia following the capture of the area by Croatian forces in May 1995. The government forces advanced southwards seizing the whole of Krajina in August 1995 and prompting the withdrawal of 10,000 UNCRO peacekeepers and the flight of 150,000 Serbs. The last Croatian Serb-held area of Eastern Slavonia agreed in November 1995 to its eventual reintegration into Croatia in 1997–8. A 5,000-strong UN force was dispatched to the area in 1996. *See also* Events of the Year.

HEAD OF STATE

President, Franjo Tudjman, *elected* May 1990, *re-elected* 2 August 1992

CABINET *as at July 1996*

Prime Minister, Zlatko Matesa
Deputy PM, Economy and Finance, Borislav Skegro
Deputy PM, Foreign Affairs, Dr Mate Granic
Deputy PM, Reconstruction and Development, Dr Jure Radic
Deputy PM, Humanitarian Issues and Science, Dr Ivica Kostovic
Deputy PM, Interior and Social Affairs, Ljerka Mintas-Hodak
Defence, Gojko Susak
Interior, Ivan Jarnjak
Finance, Bozo Prka
Economy, Davor Stern
Privatization, Ivan Penic
Agriculture and Forestry, Matej Jankovic
Maritime Affairs, Transport and Communications, Zeljko Luzavec
Health, Dr Andrija Hebrang
Culture, Bozo Biskupic
Education and Sport, Ljilja Vokic
Tourism, Nico Bulic
Labour and Social Welfare, Joso Skara
Construction and Housing, Marina Dropulic-Matulovic
Justice, Miroslav Separovic
Administration, Davorin Mlakar
Co-ordination and Emigration, Marijan Petrovic
Without Portfolio, Branko Mocibob

EMBASSY OF THE REPUBLIC OF CROATIA
21 Conway Street, London WIP 5HL
Tel 0171-387 2022
Ambassador Extraordinary and Plenipotentiary, HE Dr Ante Čičin-Šain, apptd 1994

BRITISH EMBASSY
Vlaska 121/III Floor, PO Box 454, 4100 Zagreb
Tel: Zagreb 334245
Ambassador Extraordinary and Plenipotentiary, HE Gavin Hewitt, CMG, apptd 1994
There are British Consulates in Split and Dubrovnik.
BRITISH COUNCIL DIRECTOR, I. Stewart, PO Box 55, 10001, Zagreb

DEFENCE

The armed forces number 105,000 active and 180,000 reserve personnel, with conscripts serving for ten months. The Army has some 99,600 personnel (65,000 conscripts), with 176 main battle tanks, 150 armoured personnel carriers and 949 artillery pieces. The Air Force has 4,300 personnel, mainly air defence forces, with 28 aircraft and five armed helicopters. The Navy has 1,100 personnel with one submarine and eight patrol and coastal combatants. Paramilitary personnel include 40,000 armed police and 5,000 members of the nationalist Croatian Party of Rights (HSP) armed wing (HOS).

ECONOMY

Production was severely hampered during the conflict in 1991–5; the material damage was estimated by the government to be US$27 billion, with the loss of 13,583 lives. Large areas of farmland were destroyed and the tourist industry, which provided one third of total foreign exchange earnings in 1990, was decimated. Annual inflation was 1,150 per cent at the height of the conflict in 1993 but had dropped to 3.7 per cent in late 1995 as the result of a stabilization programme. During the same period unemployment dropped from 17.4 per cent to 12.8 per cent. GDP was US$17.2 billion in 1995.

Shipbuilding and fishing are major industries on the Adriatic coast. Inland there is a light manufacturing sector, food-processing industries, bauxite deposits, thermal mineral springs, hydro-electric potential, and agriculture based on grain, horticulture, livestock and tobacco. In April 1996, Croatia agreed to pay 29.5 per cent of Yugoslavia's debt, totalling US$1.45 billion.

TRADE

	1994	1995
Total imports	US$5,229m	US$7,509.9m
Total exports	4,260m	4,632.7m
Trade with UK	1994	1995
Imports from UK	£142,332,000	£231,512,000
Exports to UK	41,238,000	36,725,000

CUBA
República de Cuba

Cuba, the largest island in the Caribbean, lies between 74° and 85° W. longitude, and 19° and 23° N. latitude, with a total area of 42,804 sq. miles (110,861 sq. km). The population (1993 UN estimate) was 10,905,000. The language is Spanish.

CAPITAL – ΨHavana, population estimate (1991) 2,143,406; other towns are ΨSantiago (425,787), Santa Clara (202,190), Camagüey (291,122), Holguín (241,100) and Guantánamo (204,836).
CURRENCY – Cuban peso of 100 centavos.
FLAG – Five horizontal bands, blue and white (blue at top and bottom) with red triangle, close to staff, charged with five-point star.
NATIONAL ANTHEM – Al Combate, Corred Bayameses (To battle, men of Bayamo).
NATIONAL DAY – 1 January (Day of Liberation).

GOVERNMENT

The island was visited by Columbus in 1492. Early in the 16th century the island was conquered by the Spanish, and for almost four centuries remained under Spanish rule. Separatist agitation culminated in the closing years of the 19th century in open warfare. In 1898 the USA intervened and demanded the evacuation of Cuba by Spanish forces. The Spanish–American war led to the abandonment of the island, which came under American military rule from 1899 until 1902, when an autonomous government was inaugurated with an elected president, and bicameral legislature.

A revolution led by Dr Fidel Castro overthrew the government of Gen. Batista in 1959. In 1965 the Communist Party of Cuba was formed to succeed the United Party of the Socialist Revolution; it is the only authorized political party. A new Socialist constitution came into force in 1976 and indirect elections to the National Assembly of People's Power were subsequently held. The first direct elections to the 589-member National Assembly were held in February 1993; all candidates were officially approved by the Communist Party and ran for election unopposed. The 14 provincial assemblies were elected in the same manner.

HEAD OF STATE
President of Council of State, Dr Fidel Castro Ruz, *appointed* 2 November 1976, *re-elected* 15 March 1993 for a five-year term

COUNCIL OF STATE *as at May 1996*
President, Dr Fidel Castro Ruz
First Vice-President, Raúl Castro Ruz
Vice-President, Carlos Lage Dávila

COUNCIL OF MINISTERS *as at May 1996*
President, Dr Fidel Castro Ruz
First Vice-President, Raúl Castro Ruz
Vice-Presidents, Dr Carlos Rafael Rodríguez; Antonio Esquivel Yedra; José Ramón Fernández Alvarez; José Luis Rodríguez García; Jaime Crombet Hernández-Baquero; Adolfo Diaz Suárez
Secretary, Carlos Lage Dávila
Ministers, Alfredo Jordan Morales (*Agriculture*); Marcos J. Portal Leon (*Heavy Industry*); Gen. Silvano Colás Sanchez (*Communications*); Juan M. Junco del Pino (*Construction*); José M. Cañete Alvarez (*Construction Materials Industry*); Armando Enrique Hart Dávalos (*Culture*); Barbara Castillo Cuesta (*Domestic Trade*); José Luis Rodríguez García (*Economy and Planning*); Luis Ignacio Gomez Gutierrez (*Education*); Manuel Millares Rodriguez (*Finance and Prices*); Orlando Felipe Rodriguez Romay (*Fishing*); Alejandro Roca Iglesias (*Food Industry*); Ernesto Meléndez Bachs (*Foreign Investment and Economic Co-operation*); Roberto Robaina (*Foreign Relations*); Ricardo Cabrisas Ruiz (*Foreign Trade*); Fernando Vecino Alegret (*Higher Education*); Gen. Abelardo Colomé Ibarra (*Interior*); Ignacio González Planas (*Iron and Steel, Machine and Electronics Industries*); Carlos Amat Forés (*Justice*); Salvador Valdes Mesa (*Labour and Social Security*); Jesus Perez Othon (*Light Industry*); Carlos Dotres Martinez (*Public Health*); Raul Castro Ruz (*Revolutionary Armed Forces*); Rosa Elena Simeón Negrín (*Science, Technology and Environment*); Nelson Torres Perez (*Sugar Industry*); Osmany Cienfuegos Gorriarán (*Tourism*); Gen. Senén Casas Regueiro (*Transport*); Wilfredo Lopez Rodriguez (*Minister without Portfolio*)
President of the National Bank, Francisco Soberon Valdez

EMBASSY OF THE REPUBLIC OF CUBA
167 High Holborn, London WC1V 6PA
Tel 0171–240 2488
Ambassador Extraordinary and Plenipotentiary, Rodney Alejandro Lopez Clemente, apptd 1995

BRITISH EMBASSY
e7 ma Y 17, Miramar, Havana.
Tel: Havana 33 1771
Ambassador Extraordinary and Plenipotentiary, HE Philip McLean, CMG, apptd 1994

DEFENCE

Cuba has a total active armed forces strength of 105,000 personnel, including 74,500 conscripts who serve for two years. There are 135,000 ready reserves who serve for 45 days a year and a territorial militia of 1,300,000 personnel. Paramilitary Ministry of Interior personnel number 15,000.

The Army numbers 85,000 and uses reservists to man many units. The Navy has a strength of 5,000 (3,000 conscripts), including two marine battalions. The Air Force has 15,000 personnel.

The last former Soviet combat personnel left Cuba in 1993, but 810 Russian military advisers remain to operate military intelligence facilities. The United States has 2,550 naval personnel at Guantánamo Bay Naval Base, which has been leased since before the 1959 revolution.

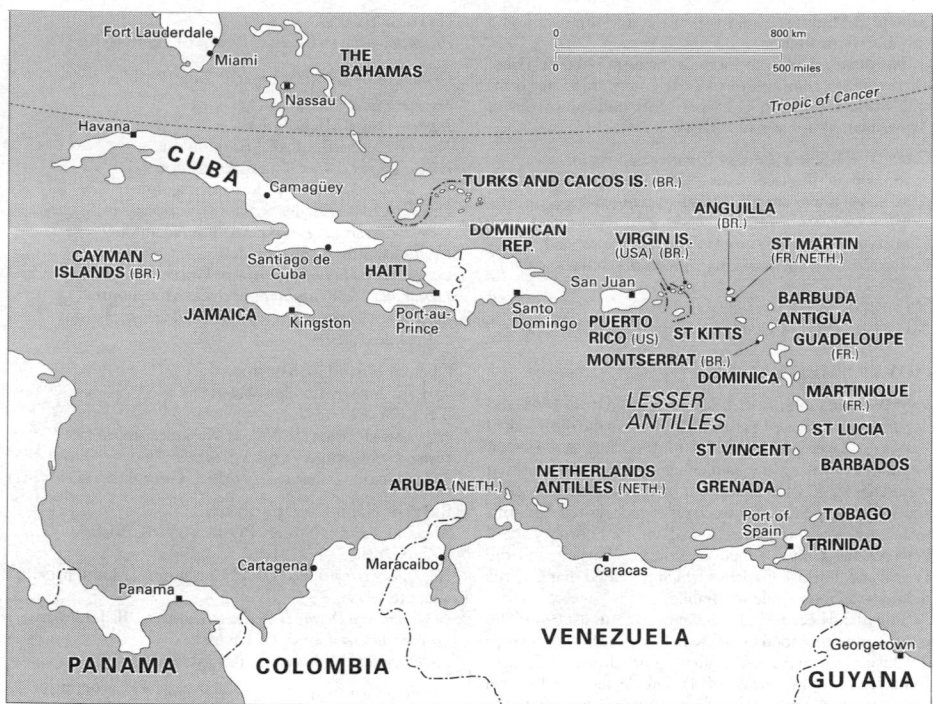

ECONOMY

After the revolution virtually all land and industrial and commercial enterprises were nationalized. Following the curtailing of Cuba's privileged trading relationships with the Soviet bloc in 1989, the economy deteriorated sharply. GDP fell by 75 per cent between 1989 and 1994, and the government was forced to introduce reforms. Since 1993, the government has legalized the holding of US dollars by private individuals, permitted private enterprise, cut subsidies to loss-making state industries, allowed prices for some goods and services to rise, and introduced income tax. State farms have been transformed into co-operatives run by private individuals and permitted to sell 20 per cent of produce on the open market, but remain relatively unproductive. In 1995, foreign investors were permitted to buy property and own Cuban-based companies, with British and Canadian firms becoming involved in the oil and mining industries. However, further foreign investment may be deterred by the 'Helms-Burton' bill, signed by US President Clinton in March 1996, which aims to punish foreign firms benefiting from US properties confiscated by Cuba.

Austerity measures imposed in 1993 enabled the economy to grow by 0.7 per cent in 1994 and 2.5 per cent in 1995; 5 per cent growth is forecast for 1996. Sugar is still the mainstay of the economy and the principal source of foreign exchange; production dropped from 8.04 million tons in 1989–90 to 4 million tons in 1993–4. The 1996 sugar harvest was predicted to be 5 million tons, the highest since the collapse of the Soviet Union. Domestic oil production is rising and reached 1.2 million tonnes in 1994.

The tourism industry has expanded since 1986. In 1993 544,000 tourists visited Cuba, generating US$700 million in gross income. The total foreign debt stands at US$16,000 million.

TRADE

Cuba's exports dropped from US$8.1 billion in 1989 to US$1.7 billion in 1993 while imports declined by 73 per cent. Trade between Cuba and the former socialist economies of Europe is now less than 10 per cent of pre-1989 levels. A trade deal was signed with Russia in 1995 providing for the exchange of sugar for oil. The US trade and economic embargo remains in force. Principal exports are sugar, nickel, seafood, citrus fruits, tobacco and rum.

Trade with UK	1994	1995
Imports from UK	£26,456,000	£19,160,000
Exports to UK	10,634,000	8,184,000

There are 12,700 km of railway track, of which 5,000 km are in public service. In 1986 there were 13,247 km of road. At present scheduled international air services run to Central and South American countries and Europe.

CULTURE

Education is compulsory and free. In 1964 illiteracy was officially declared to be eliminated. The press and broadcasting are under the control of the government.

CYPRUS
Kypriaki Dimokratia / Kibris Cumhuriyeti

Cyprus has an area of 3,572 sq. miles (9,251 sq. km). Its greatest length is 140 miles and greatest breadth 60 miles, situated at 35°N. latitude and 33° 30'E. longitude. It is about 40 miles from the nearest point of Asia Minor. The climate is Mediterranean, with a hot dry summer and a variable warm winter.

The population in 1995 was estimated at 740,000. There are two major communities, Greek Cypriots (84 per cent) and Turkish Cypriots (12.5 per cent), and minorities of Armenians, Maronites and others.

CAPITAL – Nicosia (Lefkosia), with a population of 185,000 (in the government-controlled area); the other principal towns are ΨLimassol, ΨFamagusta, ΨLarnaca, Paphos and Kyrenia.

CURRENCY – Cyprus pound (C£) of 100 cents.

FLAG – White with a gold map of Cyprus above a wreath of olive.

NATIONAL ANTHEM – Ode to Freedom.

NATIONAL DAY – 1 October (Independence Day).

GOVERNMENT

Cyprus came under British administration from 1878, and was formally annexed to Britain in 1914 on the outbreak of war with Turkey. From 1925 to 1960 it was a Crown Colony. Following the launching in 1955 of an armed campaign by EOKA in support of union with Greece, a state of emergency was declared which lasted for four years. An agreement was signed on 19 February 1959 between the United Kingdom, Greece, Turkey, and the Greek and Turkish Cypriots which provided that Cyprus would be an independent republic.

The island became independent on 16 August 1960. The constitution provided for a Greek Cypriot President and a Turkish Cypriot Vice-President. The House of Representatives was to consist of 35 Greek and 15 Turkish members. The constitution proved unworkable and led to intercommunal trouble. The UN Peace-Keeping Force in Cyprus (UNFICYP) was set up in 1964.

A general election was held for the House of Representatives (expanded to 56 Greek Cypriot and 24 vacant Turkish Cypriot seats) on 26 May 1996, resulting in the parties gaining the following seats: Democratic Rally-Liberal Party 20; AKEL (Communist) 19; Democratic Party (DIKO) 10; EDEK (Socialist) 5; Free Democrats 2. The last presidential election was held in 1993 and won by Glafcos Clerides of the Democratic Rally-Liberal Party.

DIVISION

In 1974, mainland Greek officers under instructions from the military junta in Athens launched a coup against President Makarios and installed a former EOKA member, Nikos Sampson, in his place. Turkey invaded northern Cyprus and occupied over a third of the island. In 1975 a 'Turkish Federated State of Cyprus' under Rauf Denktash was declared in this area, its constitution being approved by referendum. In 1983 a 'Declaration of Statehood' was issued which purported to establish the 'Turkish Republic of Northern Cyprus'. The declaration was condemned by the UN Security Council and only Turkey has recognized the new 'state'. In 1985 a referendum in the north of Cyprus approved a constitution for the 'Turkish Republic of Northern Cyprus', Denktash was elected President of the 'state' and a general election was held. Denktash was re-elected in 1990 and April 1995, and general elections were held in 1990 and 1993.

Since 1974 attempts to reach a settlement have focused on intercommunal talks under the auspices of the UN. Although a UN plan for a bizonal bi-communal federal state was approved by the UN Security Council and in principle by the Greek community in 1992, it was rejected by the Turkish.

HEAD OF STATE
President, Glafcos Clerides, *elected* 14 February 1993

COUNCIL OF MINISTERS *as at July 1996*
Foreign Affairs, Alecos Michaelides
Interior, Dinos Michaelides
Finance, Christodoulos Christodoulou
Education and Culture, Claire Angelidou
Justice and Public Order, Alecos Evangelou
Defence, Costas Eliades
Communications and Works, Adamos Adamides
Health, Manolis Christophides
Commerce and Industry, Kyriacos Christophi
Labour and Social Insurance, Andreas Moushouttas
Agriculture, Environment and Natural Resources, Costas Petrides

CYPRUS HIGH COMMISSION
93 Park Street, London W1Y 4ET
Tel 0171-499 8272
High Commissioner, HE Vanias Markides, apptd 1995
Counsellors, George Vyrides (*Consular Affairs*); Klitos Avgoustinos (*Cultural Affairs*); A. Georgiades (*Commerce*)

BRITISH HIGH COMMISSION
Alexander Pallis Street (PO Box 1978), Nicosia
Tel: Nicosia 2-473131
High Commissioner, HE David Christopher Madden, CMG, apptd 1994
Counsellor and Deputy High Commissioner, C. B. Jennings
Defence Adviser, Col. A. C. Taylor
First Secretary (Commercial), P. J. Newman

BRITISH COUNCIL DIRECTOR, Robert Frost, PO Box 5654, 3 Museum Street, 1097 Nicosia

BRITISH SOVEREIGN AREAS
The UK retained full sovereignty and jurisdiction over two areas of 99 square miles in all: Akrotiri–Episkopi–Paramali and Dhekelia–Pergamos–Ayios Nicolaos–Xylophagou. The British Administrator of these areas is appointed by The Queen and is responsible to the Secretary of State for Defence. The combined total of army and RAF personnel stationed in the areas is 3,900.
Administrator of the British Sovereign Areas, Air Vice-Marshal P. Millar

ECONOMY

Agriculture still occupies a prime position in the economy, employing 12 per cent of the workforce and producing 31 per cent of exports. Main products are citrus fruits, grapes and vine products, meat, milk, potatoes and other vegetables. Manufacturing, construction, distribution and other service industries are other major employers. Tourism is the main growth industry with two million tourists producing C£1,200 million in foreign exchange earnings in 1995; it contributed 25 per cent of GDP and employed 25 per cent of the workforce. Over 5,000 foreign firms and individuals have registered as offshore companies in Cyprus, and 20 per cent of the world's ships are Cypriot registered.

Britain continues to be the most important trading partner, taking 29 per cent of exports in 1994 and supplying 12 per cent of imports. Cyprus is seeking to diversify its export markets away from the Middle East towards the EU.

TRADE

There is a large visible trade deficit which is offset by invisible earnings, particularly from tourism.

	1994	1995
Imports	C£1,482.6m	C£1,670.4m
Exports	476.0m	555.6m

Trade with UK	1994	1995
Imports from UK	£245,192,000	£307,438,000
Exports to UK	120,857,000	156,451,000

CZECH REPUBLIC
Česká Republika

The Czech Republic, composed of Bohemia and Moravia, has an area of 30,441 sq. miles (78,664 sq. km). Bohemia is surrounded by mountain ranges while Moravian land stretches to the Danubian basin. The republic is bordered by Poland in the north-east, Germany in the west and north-west, Austria in the south and Slovakia in the south-east.

The population (1991 census) is 10,302,000, of which 95 per cent is Czech and 3 per cent Slovak. The majority are Roman Catholic, with a small Protestant minority. Czech is the official language.

CAPITAL – Prague (Praha) on the Vltava (Moldau), with a population (1991) of 1,215,076. Other major cities are Brno (Brün) (391,093), Ostrava (331,241) and Plzeň (174,676).

CURRENCY – Koruna (Kc) or Czech crown of 100 Haléřů (Heller).

FLAG – White over red horizontally with a blue triangle extending from the hoist to the centre of the flag. (The Czech Republic retained the former Czechoslovak federal flag.)

NATIONAL ANTHEM – Kde Domov Můj (Where is my Motherland).

NATIONAL DAY – 28 October.

HISTORY

The area which is now the Czech Republic came under the rule of the Habsburg dynasty in 1526 and remained part of the Austro-Hungarian Empire until 1918. Austrian attempts to Germanize the Czech lands in the 18th and 19th centuries led to the rise of Czech nationalism in the late 19th century. The independence of Czechoslovakia was proclaimed on 28 October 1918 following an amalgamation of Bohemia, Moravia, Slovakia and Ruthenia and was confirmed by the Versailles Peace Conference in 1919. Czechoslovakia was forced to cede the ethnic German Sudetenland to Nazi Germany in 1938 after the Munich Agreement. German forces invaded the Czech Republic in March 1939 and incorporated it into Germany while Slovakia became a puppet state. The Czech Republic was liberated by Soviet and American forces in May 1945. The pre-war democratic Czechoslovak state was re-established in 1945, having ceded Ruthenia to the Soviet Union, with the Communist Party in a strong political position. The Communists took power in a coup in 1948 and remained in power until 1989.

In 1968 the Communist Party under Alexander Dubček embarked on a political and economic reform programme (the Prague Spring). The reforms were suppressed following an invasion by Warsaw Pact troops on the night of 20 August 1968, and were abandoned when Gustáv Husák became leader of the Communist Party in 1969.

Opposition to Communist Party rule gathered pace in the late 1980s and mass protests in November 1989 led to the resignation of the Communist Party Central Committee. The Communist Party was forced to concede its monopoly of power and on 10 December a new government was appointed in which only half the ministers were Communists. Husák resigned as President and was replaced by the dissident writer Václav Havel. Free elections were held in June 1990 in which the Communist Party was defeated.

GOVERNMENT

Legislative elections in June 1992 returned the Civic Democratic Party and the Movement for a Democratic Slovakia as the dominant parties in the Czech and Slovak republics respectively. Talks between Czech and Slovak leaders on continuing the federation broke down because of the insistence of Vladimir Meciar, the Slovak leader, on a declaration of Slovak sovereignty. An interim federal government was sworn in in July 1992 and in late 1992 the leaders of the Czech and Slovak republics agreed to dissolve the federation and form two sovereign states; this took effect on 1 January 1993.

The elections of June 1992 had returned the Civil Democratic Party (ODS) as the largest party in the Czech parliament, and it formed a coalition government with three other centre-right parties in July 1992 which was sworn in as the government of the Czech Republic on 1 January 1993. The former federal President Havel was elected President. Following the general election of 31 May 1996, the ODS and its coalition partners, two seats short of a majority, agreed to slow the rate of privatization in return for support from the opposition Social Democrats.

The Czech constitution vests legislative power in the bicameral parliament, comprising a 200-member Chamber of Deputies elected for a four-year term and an 81-member Senate elected for a six-year term, one-third being renewed every two years. The President is elected by parliament for a five-year term. Executive power is held by the Prime Minister and Council of Ministers. A two-thirds majority in parliament is necessary to amend the constitution, and federal laws remain in place unless superseded by Czech ones. A Constitutional Court has been established comprising 15 judges nominated by the President for ten-year terms with Senate approval.

HEAD OF STATE
President, Václav Havel, elected 26 January 1993, sworn in 2 February 1993

COUNCIL OF MINISTERS as at July 1996
Prime Minister, Václav Klaus (ODS)
Foreign Affairs, Josef Zieleniec (ODS)
Finance, Ivan Kocarnik (ODS)
Agriculture, Josef Lux (KDU-CSL)
Justice, Jan Kalvoda (ODA)
Interior, Jan Ruml (ODS)
Industry and Trade, Vladimir Dlouhy (ODA)
Environment, Jiri Skalicky (ODA)
Health, Jan Strasky (ODS)
Culture, Jaromir Talir (KDU-CSL)
Labour and Social Affairs, Jindrich Vodicka (ODS)
Education, Ivan Pilip (ODS)
Defence, Miloslav Vyborny (KDU-CSL)
Transport, Martin Riman (ODS)
Development of Regions, Towns and Municipalities, Jaromir Schneider (KDU-CSL)
Without Portfolio, Pavel Bratinka (ODA)

ODS Civic Democratic Party; KDU-CSL Christian Democratic Union-Czech People's Party; ODA Civic Democratic Alliance

EMBASSY OF THE CZECH REPUBLIC
26–30 Kensington Palace Gardens, London w8 4QY
Tel 0171–243 1115
Ambassador Extraordinary and Plenipotentiary, HE Karel
   Kühnl, apptd 1993
Minister-Counsellor, Milan Jakobec
Military Attaché, Maj.-Gen. S. Thurnvald
Counsellor (Commercial), J. Žabža
BRITISH EMBASSY
Thunovská 14, 11800 Prague 1
Tel: Prague 10439
Ambassador Extraordinary and Plenipotentiary, HE Sir
   Michael Burton, KCVO, CMG, apptd 1994
Deputy Head of Mission, J. M. Cresswell
Defence and Military Attaché, Col. W. E. Nowosielski-
   Slopowron
First Secretary (Commercial), M. L. Connor
Cultural Attaché, W. Jefferson, OBE *(British Council Director)*

DEFENCE

Total active military personnel number 86,400, including 40,400 conscripts who serve one-year terms. The army has a strength of 37,400 with 1,011 main battle tanks, 1,501 armoured personnel carriers and armoured infantry fighting vehicles and 893 artillery pieces. The Air Force has a strength of 18,500, with 224 combat aircraft and 36 attack helicopters. There are 5,600 paramilitary personnel.

ECONOMY

Under Communist rule industry was state-owned and nearly all agricultural land was cultivated by state or co-operative farms. An economic reform programme began in 1990 to produce a free-market economy, and the government of the Czech Republic has continued to follow the policies of the former federal government. This has necessitated a restrictive monetary policy to stem inflation and a restructuring of industry to be competitive, and these were major reasons for the break with Slovakia. As a result, foreign investment (US$4,000 million in 1989–94) and private enterprises have grown and reliance on trade with the former Soviet bloc countries has ended. Unemployment has risen but is still low (3 per cent), and a trade-liberalizing association agreement with the EU is in operation. The Czech Republic applied for membership of the EU in January 1996.

Privatization of state enterprises began in May 1993 and by late 1995 over 90 per cent of the economy had been privatized, with two-thirds of the population owning shares. Overall output has grown since 1993, as has GDP (5 per cent growth in 1994) although inflation remains at 8.5 per cent. The budget was balanced in 1996, foreign debt is small, and foreign currency reserves had risen to US$5,300 million by late 1994.

A customs union between the Czech and Slovak Republics is in place but separate currencies were introduced in February 1993 following speculation. The Koruna was made fully convertible in October 1995.

The Czech Republic is not rich in minerals, although significant quantities of coal and lignite are mined. Principal agricultural products are sugar-beet, potatoes and cereal crops; the timber industry is also very important. Having been the major industrial area of the Austro-Hungarian Empire, the country has long been industrialized, and machinery, industrial consumer goods and raw materials are major exports.

TRADE WITH UK	1994	1995
Imports from UK	£374,453,000	£567,923,000
Exports to UK	278,301,000	321,497,000

CULTURE

The Reformation gave a widespread impetus to Czech literature, the writings of Jan Hus (martyred in 1415 as a religious and social reformer) familiarizing the people with Wyclif's teaching. This lasted until the close of the 17th century when Jan Amos Komensky or Comenius (1592–1670) was expelled from the country. Under Austrian rule and with the pursuit of Germanization, there was a period of stagnation until the national revival in the 19th century. Authors of international reputation include Jaroslav Hašek (1883–1923), Jaroslav Seifert (1901–86, Nobel Prize for Literature, 1985), Václav Havel (b. 1936) and Milan Kundera (b. 1929).

EDUCATION

Education is compulsory and free for all children from the ages of six to 16. There are seven universities of which the oldest and most famous is Charles University in Prague (founded 1348).

DENMARK
Kongeriget Danmark

Denmark is a kingdom, consisting of the islands of Zealand, Funen, Lolland, etc., the peninsula of Jutland, the outlying island of Bornholm in the Baltic, and the Faröes and Greenland. It is situated between 54° 34' and 57° 45' N. latitude and 8° 4'–15° 12' E. longitude, with an area of 16,630 sq. miles (43,063 sq. km), and a population (official estimate 1995) of 5,215,718.

CAPITAL – ΨCopenhagen, population (1992) 464,566; Greater Copenhagen 1,339,395; ΨAarhus 204,139; ΨOdense 140,886; ΨAalborg 114,970; ΨEsbjerg 72,205; ΨRanders 55,358.
CURRENCY – Danish krone (Kr) of 100 øre.
FLAG – Red, with white cross.
NATIONAL ANTHEMS – Kong Kristian and Det er et yndigt land.
NATIONAL DAY – 5 June (Constitution Day).

GOVERNMENT

The legislature consists of one chamber, the *Folketing*, of not more than 179 members, including two for the Faröes and two for Greenland, which is elected for a four-year term. The voting age is 18 with voting based on a proportional respresentation system with a 2 per cent threshold for parliamentary representation.

On 25 January 1993 a coalition government of the Social Democrat, Centre Democrat, Social Liberal and Christian People's Party was sworn in after the previous Conservative-Liberal coalition had resigned. After the last parliamentary election on 21 September 1994, a new coalition government of the Social Democrat, Social Liberal and Centre Democrat parties was formed. The state of the parties in the Folketing is: Social Democrat Party (SD) 63; Liberals (L) 44; Conservatives (C) 28; Socialist People's Party (SP) 13; Progress Party (P) 10; Social Liberal Party (SL) 8; Red-Green Alliance 6; Centre Democrat Party (CD) 5; Independent 1.

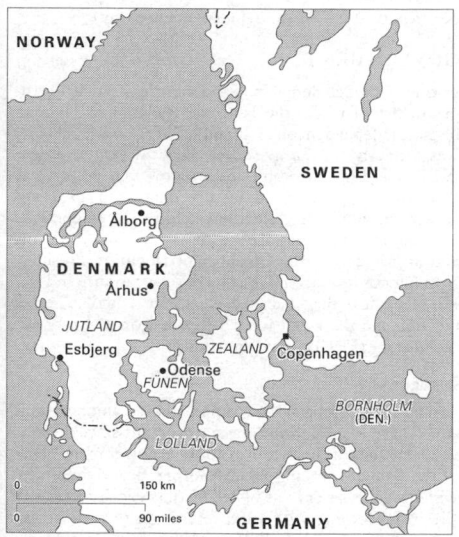

NORWAY

SWEDEN

Ålborg

DENMARK
Århus•

JUTLAND
Esbjerg   ZEALAND Copenhagen
         •Odense
      FÜNEN
                    BORNHOLM
                    (DEN.)
       LOLLAND

0   150 km

0   90 miles
                GERMANY

HEAD OF STATE

HM *The Queen of Denmark*, Queen Margrethe II, KG, *born* 16 April 1940, *succeeded* 14 January 1972, *married* 10 June 1967, Count Henri de Monpezat (Prince Henrik of Denmark), and *has issue* Crown Prince Frederik (*see* below); Prince Joachim, *born* 7 June 1969
Heir, HRH Crown Prince Frederik, *born* 26 May 1968

CABINET *as at July 1996*

Prime Minister, Poul Nyrup Rasmussen (SD)
Business and Industry, Mimi Jakobsen (CD)
Economic Affairs and Nordic Co-operation, Marianne Jelved (SL)
Finance, Mogens Lykketoft (SD)
Foreign Affairs, Niels Helveg Petersen (SL)
Agriculture and Fisheries, Henrik Dam Christensen (SD)
Environment and Energy, Svend Auken (SD)
Education, Ole Vig Jensen (SL)
Housing and Building, Ole Løvig Simonsen (SD)
Development Co-operation, Poul Nielson (SD)
Interior and Ecclesiastical Affairs, Birthe Weiss (SD)
Labour, Jytte Andersen (SD)
Taxation, Carsten Koch (SD)
Defence, Hans Haekkerup (SD)
Cultural Affairs, Jytte Hilden (SD)
Social Affairs, Karen Jespersen (SD)
Transport, Jan Trøjborg (SD)
Justice, Bjørn Westh (SD)
Health, Yvonne Herløv Andersen (CD)
Research, Frank Jensen (SD)

ROYAL DANISH EMBASSY
55 Sloane Street, London SWIX 9SR
Tel 0171–333 0200
Ambassador Extraordinary and Plenipotentiary, HE Ole Lønsmann Poulsen, apptd 1996
Counsellor (Commercial), Jorgen Gulev
Defence Attaché, Capt. P. Grooss

BRITISH EMBASSY
36–40 Kastelsvej, DK-2100 Copenhagen Ø
Tel: Copenhagen 35 264600
Ambassador Extraordinary and Plenipotentiary, HE Andrew Bache, CMG, apptd 1996
Counsellor and Deputy Head of Mission, F. X. Gallagher, OBE

Defence Attaché, Cmdr. W. T. Wiseman, RN
First Secretary (Commercial), D. T. Cox
There are Consulates at Aabenraa, Aalborg, Aarhus, Esbjerg, Fredericia, Herning, Odense, Rønne (Bornholm); at Tórshavn (Faröe Islands); and Nuuk (Godthåb) (Greenland).

BRITISH COUNCIL REPRESENTATIVE, Len Tyler, Gammel Mont 123, 1117 Copenhagen K

DEFENCE

Total active armed forces number 34,400 (8,300 conscripts). Conscripts serve for up to two years. Reserves number 68,000 personnel.

Army personnel number 17,700 but the 42,300 reservists reinforce peacetime units. Equipment includes 411 main battle tanks, 637 armoured personnel carriers and armoured infantry fighting vehicles and 553 artillery pieces.

The Navy has 4,500 personnel with three frigates, five submarines, 29 patrol and coastal craft and eight armed helicopters.

The Air Force numbers 5,700 personnel with 66 combat aircraft.

ECONOMY

Of the labour force, in 1995 37.7 per cent was employed in the private retailing sector; 30.5 per cent in the public sector; 21 per cent in manufacturing and building and 4.7 per cent in agriculture. The chief agricultural products are pigs, cattle, dairy products, poultry and eggs, seeds, cereals and sugar beet; manufactures are mostly based on imported raw materials but there are also considerable imports of finished goods. Denmark is self-sufficient in oil and natural gas.

GDP grew by 2.6 per cent in 1995, and was forecast to grow by 1.1 per cent in 1996. The rate of unemployment was 8.8 per cent in March 1996, a 2.3 per cent drop from May 1995. The inflation rate was roughly 2 per cent in 1996 and falling.

FINANCE

Budget estimates	1994	1995
Revenue	Kr334,533m	Kr588,000m
Expenditure	388,901m	605,000m

TRADE

Denmark's balance of payments on current account showed a deficit for 1995 of Kr8,000 million. The foreign debt was Kr263,000 million.

The principal imports are industrial raw materials, consumer goods, construction inputs, machinery, raw materials, vehicles and textile products. The chief exports are manufactured articles, agricultural and dairy products.

Trade with UK	1994	1995
Imports from UK	£1,771,309,000	£1,996,100,000
Exports to UK	2,107,577,000	2,075,200,000

COMMUNICATIONS

In 1996, the Danish mercantile fleet numbered 584 ships of more than 100 gross tonnage. There were 3,000 km of railway, 85 per cent of which belonged to the state and 15 per cent to privately-owned companies.

EDUCATION AND CULTURE

Education is free and compulsory. Special schools are numerous, commercial, technical and agricultural predominating. There are universities at Copenhagen (founded in 1479), Aarhus (1928), Odense (1966), Roskilde (1972) and Aalborg (1974).

The Danish language is akin to Swedish and Norwegian. Danish literature, ancient and modern, embraces all forms of expression, familiar names being Hans Christian Andersen (1805–75), Søren Kierkegaard (1813–55) and Karen Blixen (1885–1962). Some 38 newspapers are published in Denmark; eight daily papers are published in Copenhagen.

THE FARÖES

The Faröes, or Sheep Islands have an area of 540 sq. miles (1,399 sq. km) and a population (1995) of 43,700. The capital is Tórshavn.

Since 1948 the Faröes have had a degree of home rule. The islands are governed by a *Løgting* of 32 members and a *Landsstyre* of four members which deals with special Faröes affairs, and send two representatives to the *Folketing* at Copenhagen. The Faröes are not part of the EU.

The main industries are agriculture, fishing, fish-farming, whaling and the public sector; tourism is growing in importance.

Prime Minister, Edmund Joensen

Trade with UK	1994	1995
Imports from UK	£10,747,000	£8,334,000
Exports to UK	67,936,000	79,435,000

GREENLAND

Greenland has a total area of 2,175,600 sq. km, of which about 16 per cent is ice-free, and a population (1995) of 55,700. It is divided into three provinces: West, North and East. The capital is Nuuk (Godthåb).

Greenland attained a status of internal autonomy in May 1979 and a government (*Landsstyre*) was established. It has a *Landsting* of 31 members and sends two representatives to the *Folketing* at Copenhagen. Greenland negotiated its withdrawal from the EU, without discontinuing relations with Denmark, and left on 1 February 1985.

The traditional industries of fishing, sealing, whaling and reindeer herding are the most important sectors of the economy, together with public services and administration. Mineral and oil prospecting revealed deposits of lead, zinc, iron ore, oil, gas and uranium. Commercial exploitation of these resources has begun. The trade of Greenland is mainly under the management of the Grønlands Handel. The USA has acquired certain rights to maintain air bases in Greenland.

Premier, Lars Emil Johansen

Trade with UK	1994	1995
Imports from UK	£927,000	£1,884,000
Exports to UK	11,295,000	9,549,000

DJIBOUTI
Jumhouriyya Djibouti

Djibouti is situated on the north-east coast of Africa and borders Eritrea, Ethiopia and Somalia. It has an area of 8,494 sq. miles (22,000 sq. km.). The climate is harsh and much of the country is semi-arid desert. It has a population (1991 census) of 520,000, most of which is either Afar or Issas.

Capital – Ψ Djibouti, population (1991) 340,700.
Currency – Djibouti franc of 100 centimes.
Flag – Blue over green with white triangle in the hoist containing a red star.

National Day – 27 June (Independence Day).

GOVERNMENT

Formerly French Somaliland and then the French Territory of the Afars and the Issas, the Republic of Djibouti became independent on 27 June 1977. The sole legal party was formerly the *Rassemblement Populaire pour le Progrès* (RPP, the Popular Rally for Progress). A multiparty constitution was adopted by referendum in 1992 and subsequent multiparty elections held in December 1992 were won by the ruling RPP with 77 per cent of the vote and all 65 seats in the Chamber of Deputies. President Aptidon was re-elected for a fourth six-year term in 1993. However, less than half the electorate voted in either election and the Front for the Restoration of Unity and Democracy (FRUD) boycotted both.

INSURGENCY

Armed FRUD rebels, their support based among ethnic Afars, have been fighting the government since 1991 in protest at the concentration of political power in the hands of the Somali-speaking Issas. A formal peace agreement with the government was signed by the majority faction of FRUD in December 1994 and FRUD was recognized as a political party in March 1996. A minority faction has condemned the agreement and continues to fight.

Head of State
President, Hassan Gouled Aptidon, *elected* 1977, *re-elected* 1981, 1987 and 9 May 1993

Cabinet as at July 1996
Prime Minister, Planning and Territorial Administration, Barkat Gourad Hamadou
Justice and Islamic Affairs, Hassan Farah Miguil
Foreign Affairs and International Co-operation, Mohamed Moussa Chehem
Interior and Decentralization, Idriss Harbi Farah
National Defence, Abdallah Chirwa Djibril
Finance and Economy, Mohamed Ali Mohamed
Ports, Transport and Telecommunications, Saleh Omar Hildid
National Education, Ahmed Guirreh Waberi
Youth and Sports and Culture, Abdou Bolock Abdou
Public Health and Social Affairs, Ali Mohamed Daoud
Civil Service and Administrative Reform, Mohamed Dini Farah
Public Works, Construction and Housing, Atteyeh Ismael Waiss
Industry, Energy and Mines, Abdi Farah
Labour and Professional Organizations, Osman Robleh Daach
Agriculture and Water Resources, Ougoure Kifle Ahmed
Commerce and Tourism, Rifki Abdoulkader

Embassy of the Republic of Djibouti
26 rue Emile Ménier, 75116 Paris, France
Tel: Paris 47274922
Ambassador Extraordinary and Plenipotentiary, HE Ahmed Omar Farah, apptd 1991

British Ambassador, HE Duncan Christopher, resides at Addis Ababa, Ethiopia

British Consulate
PO Box 81, 9–11 Rue de Geneve, Djibouti
Honorary Consul, J. McCauley

The French continue to maintain army, navy and air force bases in Djibouti, with a total strength of 3,400 personnel. Djibouti has an excellent port, an international airport, and a railway line runs to Addis Ababa.

Trade with UK	1994	1995
Imports from UK	£13,701,000	£13,699,000
Exports to UK	373,000	62,000

DOMINICA
The Commonwealth of Dominica

Dominica, in the Lesser Antilles, lies in the Windward Group, between 15° 12' and 15° 39' N. latitude and 61° 14' and 61° 29' W. longitude, 95 miles south of Antigua. It is about 29 miles long and 16 miles wide, with an area of 289 sq. miles (748.5 sq. km). The island is of volcanic origin and very mountainous, and the soil is very fertile. The temperature varies, according to the altitude, from 13° to 29°C. The population is 71,000 (1993 UN estimate).

CAPITAL – ΨRoseau, on the south-west coast, population 15,850. The other principal town is Portsmouth, population 3,620.

CURRENCY – East Caribbean dollar (EC$) of 100 cents.

FLAG – Green ground with a cross overall of yellow, black and white stripes, and in the centre a red disc charged with a Sisserou parrot in natural colours within a ring of ten green stars.

NATIONAL ANTHEM – Isle of Beauty.

NATIONAL DAY – 3 November (Independence Day).

GOVERNMENT

The island was discovered by Columbus in 1493, when it was a stronghold of the Caribs, who remained virtually the sole inhabitants until the French established settlements in the 18th century. It was captured by the British in 1759 but passed back and forth between France and Britain until 1805, after which British possession was not challenged. From 1871 to 1939 Dominica was part of the Leeward Islands Colony, then from 1940 the island was a unit of the Windward Islands group. Internal self-government from 1967 was followed on 3 November 1978 by independence as a republic.

Executive authority is vested in the President, who is elected by the House of Assembly for not more than two terms of five years. Parliament consists of the President and the House of Assembly (21 representatives elected by universal adult suffrage for a five-year term) and nine Senators, five of whom are appointed on the advice of the Prime Minister and the other four on the advice of the Leader of the Opposition.

The last general election was held on 12 June 1995 and won by the Dominica United Workers' Party, which captured 11 seats, with five seats each going to the Dominica Freedom Party and the Dominica Labour Party.

HEAD OF STATE
President, HE Crispin Sorhaindo, OBE, *elected* 4 October 1993, *took office* 25 October 1993

CABINET *as at July 1996*
Prime Minister, External Affairs, Legal Affairs and Labour, Hon. Edison James
Finance, Industry and Planning, Hon. Julius Timothy
Tourism, Ports and Employment, Sen. Hon. Norris Prevost
Health and Social Security, Hon. Doreen Paul
Trade and Marketing, Hon. Norris Charles
Community Development and Women's Affairs, Hon. Gertrude Roberts
Communications, Works and Housing, Hon. Earl Williams
Agriculture and the Environment, Hon. Peter Carbon
Education, Sports and Youth Affairs, Hon. Ronald Green

HIGH COMMISSION FOR THE COMMONWEALTH OF DOMINICA
1 Collingham Gardens, London SW5 0HW
Tel 0171–370 5194/5
High Commissioner, HE Ashworth Elwin, apptd 1992

BRITISH HIGH COMMISSIONER, HE Richard Thomas, CMG, resides at Bridgetown, Barbados

BRITISH CONSULATE
PO Box 6, Roseau
Honorary Consul, R. W. Duckworth

ECONOMY

Agriculture is the principal occupation, with tropical and citrus fruits the main crops. Products for export are bananas, lime juice, lime oil, bay oil, copra and rum. Forestry, fisheries and agro-processing are being encouraged. The only commercially exploitable mineral is pumice, used chiefly for building purposes. Manufacturing consists largely of the processing of agricultural products.

TRADE WITH UK	1994	1995
Imports from UK	£8,055,000	£9,038,000
Exports to UK	18,892,000	15,324,000

DOMINICAN REPUBLIC
República Dominicana

The Dominican Republic, the eastern part of the island of Hispaniola (Haiti is the western part), is the oldest European settlement in America. The island lies between Cuba on the west and Puerto Rico on the east and the Dominican Republic covers an area of 18,816 sq. miles (48,734 sq. km). The climate is tropical in the lowlands and semi-tropical to temperate in the higher altitudes. The population (1994 UN estimate) is 7,684,000. Spanish is the language of the republic.

CAPITAL – Ψ Santo Domingo, population of the Capital District (1981 census) 1,313,172. Other centres, with populations (1981 census): Santiago de los Caballeros (550,372); La Vega (385,043); San Francisco De Macoris (235,544); San Juan (239,957); San Cristóbal (446,132).

CURRENCY – Dominican Republic peso (RD$) of 100 centavos.

FLAG – Divided into blue and red quarters by a white cross.

NATIONAL ANTHEM – Quisqueyanos Valientes, Alcemos (Brave men of Quisqueya, let's raise our song).

NATIONAL DAY – 27 February (Independence Day 1844).

GOVERNMENT

Santo Domingo was discovered by Columbus in 1492, and was a Spanish colony until 1821. In 1822 it was subjugated by the neighbouring Haitians who remained in control until 1844, when the Dominican Republic was proclaimed. The country was occupied by American marines from 1916 until 1924. Gen. Rafael Trujillo ruled from 1930 until 1961.

President Juan Bosch held office from December 1962 to September 1963, when he was deposed by a military junta. A left-wing revolt in favour of ex-President Bosch in April 1965 developed into civil war lasting until September the same year when Bosch's supporters were defeated by the arrival of US troops and a provisional president was elected. A presidential election in May 1994 was won by the incumbent President Balaguer. Balaguer was replaced by opposition Dominican Liberation Party (PLD) candidate, Leonel Fernández, who defeated the ruling Christian Social Reform Party (PRSC) candidate, Jacinto Peynado, in a run-off election on 30 June 1996.

Executive power is vested in the president, who is directly elected for four-year terms and appoints the Cabinet. Legislative power is exercised by the Congress, which has a term of four years concurrent with the presidency. The Congress comprises the Senate of 30 senators, one for each province and one for Santo Domingo, and the 120-member Chamber of Deputies.

HEAD OF STATE
President, Leonel Fernández, *elected* 30 June 1996

CABINET *as at May 1996*
Presidency, Rafael Bello Andino
Foreign Affairs, Carlos Morales Troncoso
Armed Forces, Rear-Adm. Ivan Vargas Cespedes
Interior, Atilio Gúzman Fernández
Education, José Andres Aybar Sanchez
Agriculture, Virgilio Alvarez Bonilla
Labour, Rafael Alberqueque de Castro
Health and Social Welfare, Victoriano de Jesus Garcia Santos
Public Works and Communications, Ricardo Canalda Carbajal
Industry and Commerce, José Ramon González Pérez
Sports, Francisco José Torres
Finance, Roberto Martinez Villanueva
Tourism, Frank Jorge Elias
Without Portfolio, Domingo Gutierrez; Licelotte Marte de Barrios; Luis Toral Cordova; Francisco Augusto Lora; Joaquin Ricardo García; Donald Reid Cabral

EMBASSY OF THE DOMINICAN REPUBLIC
17 rue La Fontaine, 75016 Paris, France
Tel: Paris 45206841
Ambassador Extraordinary and Plenipotentiary, HE Dr Alfonso Canto Dinzey, apptd 1994

HONORARY CONSULATE
6 Queen's Mansions, Brook Green, London W6 7ED
Tel 0171-602 1885
Honorary Consul, J. de Wardener

BRITISH AMBASSADOR, HE John Gerrard Flynn, CMG, resident at Caracas, Venezuela

BRITISH CONSULATE
Abraham Lincoln 552, Santo Domingo DR
Tel: Santo Domingo 540 3132
Honorary Consul, M. Tejeda, OBE

COMMUNICATIONS

There are over 4,000 miles of roads and a direct road from Santo Domingo to Port-au-Prince, the capital of Haiti, but that part of it in the border area has fallen into disuse. The frontier has been closed since 1967, except for the section crossed by the main road linking the two capitals. A telephone system connects all the principal towns and there is a telegraph service to all parts of the world. There are more than 90 commercial broadcasting stations and six television stations.

There are two national airlines with an international airport 18 miles to the east of the capital and one near Puerto Plata on the north coast.

ECONOMY

Since 1990 the government has successfully reduced inflation from 100 per cent to 3 per cent a year and has increased output substantially. Large amounts of foreign debt have been paid off but unemployment remains high at 30 per cent. State subsidies were ended in 1995 in an attempt to reduce the budget deficit. GNP per capita was US$1,320 in 1994 and inflation stood at 8 per cent.

Sugar, coffee, cocoa, and tobacco are the most important crops. Other products are peanuts, maize, rice, bananas, molasses, salt, cement, ferro-nickel, gold, silver, cattle, sisal products, honey and chocolate. Light industry produces beer, tinned foodstuffs, glass products, textiles, soap, cigarettes, construction materials, plastic articles, shoes, papers, paint, rum, matches, peanut oil and other products.

TRADE
The chief imports are machinery, foodstuffs, iron and steel, cotton textiles and yarns, mineral oils (including petrol), motor vehicles, chemical and pharmaceutical products, electrical equipment and accessories, construction material, paper and paper products, and rubber and rubber products. The chief exports are sugar, coffee, cocoa, tobacco, chocolate, molasses, bauxite, ferro-nickel and gold.

	1992	1993
Imports	RD$2,174.6m	RD$2,115.5m
Exports	562.4m	530.4m
Trade with UK	1994	1995
Imports from UK	£24,708,000	£27,946,000
Exports to UK	20,687,000	24,343,000

ECUADOR
República del Ecuador

Ecuador is an equatorial state of South America, extending from 1° 38' N. to 4° 50' S. latitude, and between 75° 20' and 81° W. longitude, comprising an area of about 109,484 sq. miles (283,561 sq. km). It extends across the Western Andes, the highest peaks being Chimborazo (20,408 ft) and Ilinza (17,405 ft) in the Western Cordillera; and Cotopaxi (19,612 ft) and Cayambe (19,160 ft) in the Eastern Cordillera. Ecuador is watered by the Upper Amazon, and by the rivers Guayas, Mira, Santiago, Chone, and Esmeraldas on the Pacific coast. There are extensive forests.

The population (UN estimate 1993) is 10,980,972, descendants of the Spanish, aboriginal Indians, and Mestizos. Spanish is the principal language but Quechua is also a recognized language and is spoken by the majority of Indians.

CAPITAL – Quito, population (1991 estimate) 1,387,887; ΨGuayaquil (1,531,229) is the chief port; Cuenca (332,117).
CURRENCY – Sucre of 100 centavos.
FLAG – Three horizontal bands, yellow, blue and red (the yellow band twice the width of the others); emblem in centre.
NATIONAL DAY – 10 August (Independence Day).

GOVERNMENT

The former kingdom of Quito was conquered by the Incas of Peru in the 15th century. Early in the 16th century Pizarro's conquests led to the inclusion of the present territory of Ecuador in the Spanish Vice-royalty of Quito. Independence was achieved in a revolutionary war which culminated in the battle of Mount Pichincha 1822.

After seven years of military rule, Ecuador returned to democracy in 1979. The 1978 constitution provides for an elected president and vice-president who serve for a single four-year term. There is a unicameral National Congress which meets for two months a year and has 77 members, 12 of whom are elected on a national basis every four years and 65 on a provincial basis every two years. Voting is compulsory for all literate and voluntary for all illiterate citizens over the age of 18. The republic is divided into 21 provinces.

In the 1992 legislative election a loose coalition of parties enabled President Ballén to introduce a programme of economic reform, financial liberalization and privatization. This, together with reductions in state spending, caused social unrest in 1992–4 and led to the government's defeat in the May 1994 legislative elections. In the July 1996 elections the ruling Social Christian Party won a majority of seats. A populist, Abdala Bucaram, was elected President in July 1996, and appointed a coalition government.

The border with Peru was demarcated by a 1942 treaty which was partly revoked by Ecuador in 1960 in relation to a disputed 50-mile stretch. An inconclusive four-week border war was fought with Peru in February 1995 until a cease-fire was signed on 1 March 1995. A 54-mile demilitarized zone was agreed in July 1995.

HEAD OF STATE

President, Abdala Bucaram, *elected* 8 July 1996
Vice-President, Roslia Arteaga de Cordova

CABINET *as at August 1996*

Government Affairs, Gen. Frank Vargas
Foreign Affairs, Dr Galo Leoro Franco
Finance, Pablo Concha Ledergerber
Public Works, Vicente Estrada Velasquez
Public Welfare, Adolfo Bucaram
Agriculture, Hugo Enrique Encalada
Defence, Gen. Victor Manuel Bayas Garcia
Housing, Dr Victor Hugo Sicourte
Industry, Jorge Marun Rodriguez
Tourism, Napoleon Ycaza
Energy and Mines, Alfredo Adum Ziade
Education, Dr Sandra Correa
Labour, Dr Guadalupe Leon
Health, Dr Marcelo Cruz

EMBASSY OF ECUADOR

Flat 3B, 3 Hans Crescent, London SWIX OLS
Tel 0171–584 1367
Ambassador Extraordinary and Plenipotentiary, HE Patricio Maldonado, apptd 1994

BRITISH EMBASSY

Av. González Suárez, 111 (Casilla 314), Quito
Tel: Quito 560670
Ambassador Extraordinary and Plenipotentiary, HE Richard Lavers, apptd 1993

There are British Consular Offices at Cuenca, Galápagos and Guayaquil.

BRITISH COUNCIL REPRESENTATIVE, Anthony Deyes, Av. Amazonas 1646, Orellana (Casilla 17078829), Quito

ECONOMY

Agriculture is the most important sector of the economy, supporting nearly 50 per cent of the population and contributing 14.5 per cent of GDP and 19.5 per cent of exports. The main products for export are fish, bananas, which provide a third of agricultural exports, cocoa and coffee. Other important crops are sugar, corn, soya, rice, cotton, African palm, vegetables, fruit and timber. The main imports are manufactured goods and machinery.

The economy was transformed by the discovery in 1972 of major oil fields in the Oriente area which are evacuated by a trans-Andean pipeline to the port of Balao. Ecuador withdrew from OPEC in 1992 in order to raise its production to 19,303,000 tonnes in 1994. The total foreign debt, estimated at US$12,500 million in early 1994, was rescheduled and reduced by the IMF in May 1994 and a US$184 million loan was also agreed.

TRADE WITH UK	1994	1995
Imports from UK	£65,290,000	£52,825,000
Exports to UK	22,891,000	20,390,000

COMMUNICATIONS

There are 23,256 km of permanent roads and 5,044 km of roads which are only open during the dry season. There are about 750 miles of railway. Ten commercial airlines operate international flights and there are internal services between all important towns. Two daily newspapers are published at Quito and four at Guayaquil.

EDUCATION

More than 90 per cent of the population are now literate. Elementary education is free and compulsory. There are ten universities (three at Quito, three at Guayaquil, and one each at Cuenca, Machala, Loja and Portoviejo), polytechnic schools at Quito and Guayaquil and eight technical colleges in other provincial capitals.

GALÁPAGOS ISLANDS

The Galápagos (Giant Tortoise) Islands, forming the province of the Archipelago de Colón, were annexed by Ecuador in 1832. The archipelago lies in the Pacific, about 500 miles from the mainland. There are 12 large and several hundred smaller islands with a total area of about 3,000 sq. miles and an estimated population (1982) of 6,119. The capital is San Cristóbal, on Chatham Island. Although the archipelago lies on the equator, the temperature of the surrounding water is well below equatorial average owing to the Humboldt current. The province consists for the most part of National Park Territory, where unique marine birds, iguanas, and the giant tortoises are conserved. There is some local subsistence farming; the main industry, apart from tourism, is tuna and lobster fishing.

EGYPT

Al-Jumhuriyat Misr al-Arabiya

Egypt comprises Egypt proper, the peninsula of Sinai and a number of islands in the Gulf of Suez and Red Sea, of which the principal are Jubal, Shadwan, Gafatin and Zeberged (or St John's Island). This territory lies between 22° and 32° N. latitude and 24° and 37° E. longitude. Egypt borders the Mediterranean in the north, Sudan in the south and Libya in the west. The eastern border (of Sinai) borders on the Gaza Strip and Israel between Rafah and the Gulf of Aqaba. The total area is 386,662 sq. miles (1,001,449 sq. km).

The country is mainly flat but there are mountainous areas in the south-west, along the Red Sea coast and in the south of the Sinai peninsula; the highest peak is Mt Catherina (8,668 ft). Most of the land is desert and the Nile valley and delta were the only fertile areas until the opening of the Aswan Dam allowed areas of desert to be reclaimed by irrigation and fertilization. West of the Nile Valley is the Western desert, containing some depressions whose springs irrigate oases of which the principal are Kharga, Dakhla, Farafra, Baharia and Siwa. The Eastern Desert between the Nile and the mountains along the Red Sea coast is mostly plateaux dissected by wadis (dry watercourses).

The population (official estimate 1995) is 58,978,000. The largest, or 'Egyptian' element, is a Hamito-Semite race. A second element is the *Bedouin,* or nomadic Arabs of the Western and Arabian deserts, who are now mainly semi-sedentary tent-dwellers. The third element is the *Nubian* of the Nile Valley of mixed Arab and Negro blood. Over 90 per cent of the population are Muslims of the Sunni denomination, and most of the rest Coptic Christians.

CAPITAL – Cairo (population, 1994 official estimate, 13 million), stands on the Nile about 14 miles from the head of the delta.

Other cities and towns are: ΨAlexandria (population, 1994 official estimate, 3,419,000), founded 332 BC by Alexander the Great, was for over 1,000 years the capital of Egypt and a centre of Hellenic culture; Ismailia (400,000); ΨPort Said (526,000); Asyût (300,000); Faiyûm (180,000); ΨSuez (458,000).

CURRENCY – Egyptian pound (£E) of 100 piastres and 1,000 millièmes.

FLAG – Horizontal bands of red, white and black, with an eagle in the centre of the white band.

NATIONAL DAY – 23 July (Anniversary of Revolution in 1952).

HISTORY

The unification of the kingdoms of Lower and Upper Egypt under the Pharaohs *c.*3100 BC marked the establishment of the Egyptian state, with Memphis as its capital. Egypt was ruled for nearly 2,800 years by a succession of 31 Pharaonic dynasties which built the pyramids at Gizeh. A period of Hellenic rule began in 332 BC, followed by a period of rule by Rome (30 BC to AD 324) and then by the Byzantine Empire. In AD 640 Egypt was subjugated by Arab Muslim invaders. In 1517 the country was incorporated in the Ottoman Empire, under which it remained until the early 19th century. A British Protectorate over Egypt lasted from 1914 to 1922, when Sultan Ahmed Fuad was proclaimed King of Egypt. In 1953 the monarchy was deposed and Egypt became a republic.

In 1956, as a result of Egypt's trade agreements with Communist countries, Britain and USA withdrew offers of financial aid and in retaliation President Nasser seized the assets of the Suez Canal Company. Egyptian occupation of the Canal Zone while repulsing an Israeli attack was used as a pretext for military action by Britain and France in support of their Suez Canal Company interests. A cease-fire and Anglo-French withdrawal were negotiated by the UN.

The Israeli invasion of 1956 overran the Sinai peninsula but six months later Israel withdrew. However, mounting tension culminated in a second invasion of Sinai (the Six Day War in June 1967) and occupation of the peninsula by Israel. Egypt's attempt to recapture the territory (the Yom Kippur War in October 1973) was unsuccessful but Sinai was returned to Egypt in 1982 under the treaty of 1979 which resulted from the Camp David talks and formally terminated a 31-year-old state of war between the two countries.

GOVERNMENT

The constitution of 1971 provides for an executive President who appoints the Council of Ministers and determines government policy. The President is elected by the legislature every six years. The legislature is the People's Assembly which has 454 members, 444 of whom are elected, the remaining ten nominated by the President. The Shura Council or Consultative Assembly (258 members) has an advisory role.

The ruling National Democratic Party won the general election held in November and December 1995. President

Mubarak was nominated by the legislature to run unopposed for a third six-year term in July 1993, and was elected in October.

INSURGENCY

Militant Muslim fundamentalists re-emerged in 1992, carrying out attacks on Coptic Christians, tourists, government ministers, civil servants and the security forces. Attacks have continued in 1993–6 and are concentrated in Upper Egypt and the Cairo area. The government has reacted vigorously to the armed campaign with the arrest of 20,000 militants.

HEAD OF STATE

President, Muhammad Hosni Mubarak, *elected* 1981, *re-elected* 1987, 13 October 1993

COUNCIL OF MINISTERS *as at July 1996*

Prime Minister, Planning, Dr Ahmed Kamal al Ganzouri
Deputy PM, Agriculture and Land Reclamation, Yousef Amin Wali
Social Affairs and Social Insurance, Dr Amal Abdel Rehim Othman
Transport and Communications, Soliman Metwalli Soliman
Electricity and Energy, Mohammad Maher Othman Abaza
Information, Mohammad Safwat el-Sharif
Defence and Military Production, Field Marshal Mohammad Hussein Tantawi Soliman
Foreign Affairs, Amr Mahmoud Moussa
Public Enterprise, Administrative Development and Environment, Dr Atef Mohammad Mohammad Ebeid
Justice, Farouk Seif el-Nasr
Culture, Farouk Hosni Abdel Aziz
Local Government, Dr Mahmoud el-Sherif Sayeed Ahmad
Oil, Dr Hamdi Abdel Wahab Al Banbi
Manpower and Emigration, Ahmad Ahmad Al Amawy
Supply and Trade, Dr Ahmed Ahmad Gowaili
Finance, Dr Mohieddin Abu Bakr Al Ghareeb
Planning, Dr Zafer Selim Al Beshri
Cabinet Affairs, Tala'at Sayyed Ahmad Hammad
Religious Affairs (Waqfs), Dr Mahmoud Hamdi
Health, Dr Ismail Awadallah Sallam
Economy and International Co-operation, Dr Nawal Abdel Monein al-Tatawi
Education, Dr Hussein Kamel Bahael Din
Interior, Hassan Mohamed Al Alfi
Minister of State at the Council of Ministers, Dr Yussef Boutros Ghali
Minister of State for the People's Assembly and Shura Council, Kamal Mohammed Al Shazli
Tourism, Dr Mamdouh Ahmad Al-Beltagui
Public Works and Water Resources, Mohamed Abdel Hadi Abdel Hamid Radi
Housing and Public Utilities, Mohamed Ibrahim Soliman
Scientific Research, Dr Venice Kamel Gouda
Military Production, Dr Mohammad Al-Ghamrawi Daoud Hassan

EMBASSY OF THE ARAB REPUBLIC OF EGYPT
26 South Street, London WIY 8EL
Tel 0171-499 2401
Ambassador Extraordinary and Plenipotentiary, HE Mohamed I. Shaker, apptd 1988
Ministers Plenipotentiary, Gehad Mahdy (*Deputy Chief of Mission*); Hassan Salem (*Consul-General*); Ahmed Abdel Hameed Nafeh; Amr Osman El Menshawi (*Commercial*)
Defence Attaché, Comm. Nour Eldin Negm
Cultural Counsellor, Samir Youssef Elsayed

BRITISH EMBASSY

Ahmed Ragheb Street, Garden City, Cairo
Tel: Cairo 3540850
Ambassador Extraordinary and Plenipotentiary, HE David
Blatherwick, CMG, OBE, apptd 1995
Counsellors, R. E. Makepeace (*Deputy Head of Mission*); J. B.
MacPherson
Defence and Military Attaché, Col. A. W. G. Snook, OBE
First Secretaries, J. M. Taylor (*Consul*); A. D. F. Henderson
(*Commercial*)

There are British consular offices at Luxor, Suez and Port
Said, and a Consulate-General at Alexandria.

BRITISH COUNCIL REPRESENTATIVE, Howard
Thompson, OBE, 192 Sharia el Nil, Agouza, Cairo.

DEFENCE

The armed forces number 436,000 active personnel
(222,000 conscripts). Selective conscription for three-
year terms operates.

The Army numbers 310,000 (200,000 conscripts) with
3,500 main battle tanks, 4,914 armoured infantry fighting
vehicles and armoured personnel carriers, and 1,247
artillery pieces.

The Navy has 16,000 personnel (12,000 conscripts) with
one destroyer, six frigates, four submarines, 43 patrol and
coastal craft, and 14 armed helicopters. The Air Force has
30,000 personnel (10,000 conscripts) with 564 combat
aircraft and 103 armed helicopters. There are also 174,000
paramilitary Security Forces.

ECONOMY

Egypt's foreign debt to western governments stood at
US$14 billion in mid-1994, having been reduced from
US$20 billion the previous year by write-offs tied to an
IMF economic and financial reform programme. Economic growth has improved under the programme to 4.5 per
cent of GDP in 1994–5 while inflation stood at roughly 10
per cent a year in 1995.

Despite increasing industrialization, agriculture remains the most important economic activity, employing
over 45 per cent of the labour force and producing 17 per
cent of exports. Output has been increased by land
reclamation, more efficient methods of irrigation, fertilization and increasing mechanization. Egypt is still a net
importer of foodstuffs, especially grain, and a food security
programme has been set up with the aim of achieving self-
sufficiency. The main cash crop is cotton, of which Egypt is
one of the world's main producers. Other important crops
are maize, rice, sugar cane, wheat, beans, citrus fruit and
other fruits and vegetables are also grown.

With its considerable reserves of petroleum and natural
gas, and the hydro-electric power produced by the Aswan
and High Dams, Egypt is self-sufficient in energy. Electricity has been provided to almost all of the country and
there are plans to extend the natural gas network to all
major cities. The production of petroleum provides 60–65
per cent of total exports, and supports a refining industry.
The major manufacturing industries are food processing,
motor cars, electrical goods, steel, chemical products,
yarns and textiles.

TRADE

The main imports are wheat, flour, wood and trucks. The
main exports are crude petroleum, cotton, cotton yarn,
oranges, rice and cotton textiles.

Trade with UK	1994	1995
Imports from UK	£368,000,000	£383,541,000
Exports to UK	252,203,000	246,619,000

COMMUNICATIONS

The road and rail networks link the Nile valley and delta
with the main development areas east and west of the river.
The Suez Canal was reopened in 1975 and a two-stage
development project begun to widen and deepen the canal
to allow the passage of larger shipping and to permit two-
way traffic. Port Said and Suez have been reconstructed
and the port of Alexandria is being improved.

EQUATORIAL GUINEA
República de Guinea Ecuatorial

Equatorial Guinea consists of the island of Bioko, in the
Bight of Biafra about 20 miles from the west coast of Africa,
Annonbón Island in the Gulf of Guinea, the Corisco Islands
(Corisco, Elobey Grande and Elobey Chico), and Rio
Muni, a mainland area between Cameroon and Gabon. It
has a total area of 10,830 sq. miles (28,051 sq. km), and a
population (UN estimate 1993) of 379,000.

CAPITAL – ΨMalabo, on the island of Bioko, population
(1983 estimate) 30,418. ΨBata is the principal town and
port of Rio Muni.
CURRENCY – Franc CFA of 100 centimes.
FLAG – Three horizontal bands, green over white over
red; blue triangle next staff; coat of arms in centre of
white band.
NATIONAL DAY – 12 October.

GOVERNMENT

Formerly colonies of Spain, the territories now forming
Equatorial Guinea were constituted as two provinces of
Metropolitan Spain in 1959, became autonomous in 1963
and fully independent in 1968.

In 1979 President Macias was deposed by a revolutionary military council headed by Col. Obiang Nguema.
Constitutional amendments in 1982 provided for legislative elections, which were held in 1983 and 1988, but all
candidates were presidential nominees.

A multiparty political system under a new constitution
was approved by a referendum in 1991 and ten opposition
parties have been legalized, operating alongside the ruling
Equatorial Guinea Democratic Party (PDGE). A National
Pact was agreed and signed in March 1993 but when
legislative elections were held in November they were
boycotted by most of the electorate and opposition parties.
The PDGE won 68 out of 80 National Assembly seats and
formed a government. In the February 1996 election, the
President claimed to have won more than 99 per cent of the
vote. Most opposition parties boycotted the ballot.

HEAD OF STATE
*President of the Supreme Military Council and Minister of
Defence,* Brig.-Gen. Teodoro Obiang Nguema Mbasogo,
took office August 1979, *re-elected* June 1989, February
1996

MINISTERS *as at July 1996*
Prime Minister, Angel Serafin Seriche Dougan
Deputy P.M, Civil Service and Administrative Reform,
Francisco Javier Ngomo Mbengono
Missions, Alejandro Evuna Owono Asangono
Foreign Affairs and Co-operation, Miguel Oyono Ndong
Mifumu
Interior and Local Communities, Júlio Ndong Ela Mangue
Youth and Sports, Francisco Pascual Eyegue Obama Asue
Labour and Social Security, Carmelo Modu Akune

Planning and Economic Resources, vacant
Government Secretary-General, Salomon Nguema Owono
Relations with Parliament and Legislative Co-ordination,
    Antonio Pascual Oko Ebobo
Transport and Communications, Elias Ovono Nguema
Justice, Ignacio Minlane Ntang
Education, Ricardo Mangue Obama Nfue
Health, Dario Tadeo Ndong Olomo
Mines and Energy, Juan Olo Mba Nseng
Public Works, Housing and Town Planning, Pedro Nze Obama
    Angono
Agriculture and Livestock, Vidal Djoni Becoba
Information, Santos Pascual Bikomo Nanguande
Industry, Small- and Medium-Sized Enterprises, Constantino
    Ekong Zue
Culture and Francophone Affairs, Pedro Cristino Bueriberi
Social and Women's Affairs, Margarita Alene Mba
Economy and Finance, Marcelino Oyono Ntutumu

EMBASSY OF THE REPUBLIC OF EQUATORIAL GUINEA
6 Rue Alfred de Vigny, 75008, Paris
Tel: Paris 47664433
Ambassador Extraordinary and Plenipotentiary, new
    appointment awaited

BRITISH AMBASSADOR, HE William Ernest Quantrill,
    resident at Yaoundé, Cameroon

ECONOMY

The chief products are cocoa, coffee and wood (which is exported almost entirely from Rio Muni). Production has declined and except for cocoa there is little commercial agriculture. The economy is heavily dependent on outside aid, principally from Spain. Oil and gas deposits exist but remain largely unexploited. Equatorial Guinea entered the 'franc zone' in 1985.

TRADE WITH UK	1994	1995
Imports from UK	£387,000	£347,000
Exports to UK	—	94,000

ERITREA

Eritrea is bordered on the north and north-west by Sudan, on the south and south-west by Ethiopia, on the south-east by Djibouti and on the north-east and east borders on the Red Sea. Included in its territory are the Dahlak Islands in the Red Sea. Eritrea claims the three Hanish Islands in the Red Sea, the largest of which, Hanish al Kabir, was seized from Yemen in December 1995. The land border with Djibouti is also disputed. Eritrea has an area of 36,170 sq. miles (93,679 sq. km) and rises from a long, narrow, low-lying coastal strip to highlands in the centre and north which are 2,000–3,000 m (6,500–9,800 ft) high.

The population is 3,500,000 (1991 official estimate). About 50 per cent are Coptic Christian and 50 per cent Muslim. The majority of highlanders are Christian and the majority of lowlanders are Muslim. The two main languages are English and Arabic. There are also nine indigenous language groups: Afar; Bilen; Hadareb; Kunama; Nara; Rashida; Saho; Tigre; Tigrinya.

CAPITAL – Asmara (275,000) in the central highlands.
ΨMassawa and ΨAssab are the two main ports and other major towns.
CURRENCY – The Ethiopian birr of 100 cents remains in use at present.

FLAG – Divided into three triangles; the one based on the hoist is red and bears a gold olive wreath; the upper triangle is green and the lower one light blue.
NATIONAL DAY – 24 May (Independence Day).

GOVERNMENT

Eritrea was colonized by Italy in the late 19th century and was the base for the 1936 Italian invasion of Abyssinia (Ethiopia). After the Italian defeat in East Africa in 1941 by British and Commonwealth forces, Eritrea became a British protectorate. This lasted until 15 September 1952 when Eritrea was federated with Ethiopia. The Ethiopian Emperor Haile Selassie incorporated Eritrea as a province of Ethiopia in 1962. An armed campaign for independence began in the 1970s, first against Emperor Haile Selassie's forces and from 1974 against the Mengistu regime.

In May 1991 the Mengistu government was overthrown by the Eritrean People's Liberation Front (EPLF) and the Ethiopian People's Revolutionary Democratic Front (EPRDF). In July 1991 the new EPRDF-led government in Ethiopia agreed to an Eritrean referendum on independence which was held in April 1993 and recorded a 99 per cent vote in favour. Independence was declared on 24 May 1993.

At independence the provisional government became the transitional government of Eritrea to govern for a maximum of four years while a new constitution is drafted. At the end of the transition period multiparty elections are to be held. During the transition period legislative power is vested in the National Assembly and executive power in the State Council appointed and chaired by the President. In 1994 the EPLF transformed itself into a political party, the People's Front for Democracy and Justice (PFDJ), and the National Assembly was changed for the remainder of the transition period to comprise 75 PFDJ central council members and 75 elected members. The 700,000 refugees who fled to Sudan during the war have been repatriated.

HEAD OF STATE
President, Chairman of the National Assembly, Issaias Afewerki,
    elected by National Assembly 22 May 1993

STATE COUNCIL *as at May 1996*
Chairman, The President
Local Government, Mahmoud Ahmed Sherifo
Internal Affairs, Ali Said Abdella
Health, Sebhat Ephrem
Justice, Fozia Hashim
Defence, Mesfin Hafos
Foreign Affairs, Petros Soloman
Culture and Information, Baraki Gebresalassie
Finance and Development, Haile Weldetensae
Trade and Industry, Ekuba Abraha
Agriculture, Tesfai Ghermazien
Marine Resources, Saleh Meki
Construction, Abraha Asfaha
Energy, Mining and Water Resources, Tesfay Gebraselassie
Education, Osman Saleh Muhammed
Transport, Giorgis Tekle Mikael
Tourism, Worku Tesfa Mikael

EMBASSY OF THE STATE OF ERITREA
382 avenue Louise, 1050 Brussels, Belgium
Tel: Brussels 644 2401
Ambassador Extraordinary and Plenipotentiary, HE Andebrhan
    Weldegiorgis, apptd 1996

Consulate
96 White Lion Street, London ni 9pf
Tel: 0171-713 0096

British Ambassador, HE Duncan Christopher, resides
at Addis Ababa, Ethiopia

British Consulate
c/o Mitchell Cotts Building, Emperor Yohanes Ave 54,
PO Box 5584, Asmara
Tel: Asmara 120145
Honorary Consul, Dr R. B. Hicks
British Council Director – Dr Negusse Araya, PO
Box 997, Asmara

ECONOMY

The economy was devastated by the war of independence
and the scorched earth policy of the retreating Ethiopian
forces. Since 1991 the government has directed all its
efforts into rebuilding industry, agriculture and infrastructure, especially in the highlands, where the Ethiopian
army uprooted nearly all the trees. Some 22 million tree
seedlings are being grown for planting. As the agricultural
and industrial sectors producing sorghum, livestock, salt,
cement, fish, hides and potash are rebuilt, the government
has directed large numbers of the population into infrastructure rebuilding schemes in return for daily food. The
focus of the rebuilding programme are the ports of
Massawa and Assab, the roads from the ports to Ethiopia,
and the railway from Massawa to Sudan via Asmara. Before
1962 Eritrea was one of the most industrialized areas of
Africa and some industry remains, producing textiles and
footwear. The government hopes to base the rebuilding of
the economy on the return of well-educated exiles,
international aid and investment, the development of
tourism along the coast, and the diversification of the
economy away from agriculture. The reconstruction
programme has, however, been hampered severely by
food shortages in late 1993 and early 1994.

Trade with UK	1994	1995
Imports from UK	£912,000	£768,000
Exports to UK	—	41,000

ESTONIA
The Republic of Estonia

Estonia is situated on the eastern coast of the Baltic Sea. To
the north lies the Gulf of Finland, to the east Russia, and to
the south Latvia. Estonia lies between 57°30′ and 59°49′N.,
and between 21°46′ and 28°13′E. and has an area of 17,458
sq. miles (45,125 sq. km) including 1,500 islands in the
Baltic Sea and the Gulf of Riga. Forests cover roughly 20
per cent of the country, which also has many lakes. The
climate is mild and maritime.

The population is 1,491,583 (1995 estimate), of which
64.2 per cent are Estonian, 28.7 per cent Russian, 2.7 per
cent Ukrainian, 1.5 per cent Belarusian. The majority
religion is Lutheran, with Russian Orthodox and Baptist
minorities. Estonian is the first language of 64.2 per cent
and Russian of 28.7 per cent.

Capital – Tallinn (population 434,763). Other cities are
Tartu (104,907); Narva (77,770); Kohtla-Järve (55,415);
Pärnu (1,526).
Currency – Kroon (Crown) of 100 sent.
Flag – Three horizontal stripes of blue, black, white.
National Anthem – Mu Isamaa, mu õnn ja rõõm (My
Native Land, My Joy, Delight).
National Day – 24 February (Independence Day).

HISTORY

Estonia, a former province of the Russian Empire, declared
its independence on 24 February 1918. A war of independence was fought against the German army until November 1918, and then against Soviet forces until the peace
treaty of Tartu was signed in 1920. By this treaty the Soviet
Union recognized Estonia's independence.

The Soviet Union annexed Estonia in 1940 under the
terms of the Molotov-Ribbentrop pact with Germany.
Estonia was occupied when Germany invaded the Soviet
Union during the Second World War. In 1944 the Soviet
Union recaptured the country from Germany and con-
firmed its annexation.

The Estonian Supreme Soviet in November 1989
declared the republic to be sovereign and its 1940 annexation by the Soviet Union to be illegal. In February 1990 the
leading role of the Communist Party was abolished, and
following multiparty elections in March 1990 a period of
transition to independence was inaugurated. Independence was supported by an overwhelming majority in a
referendum and was declared on 20 August 1991.

GOVERNMENT

Under the 1992 constitution, legislative power is exercised
by the unicameral *Riigikogu* of 101 members elected by
proportional representation every four years. The president is elected for a five-year term by the Riigikogu by a
two-thirds majority or, if no candidate receives this
majority after three rounds of voting, by an electoral body
composed of Riigikogu members and local government
officials. Executive authority is vested in a prime minister
and government formed from a governing majority within
the parliament.

Presidential and legislative elections were held in
September 1992 on the basis of special provisions different
from the 1992 constitution. The President was directly

elected for a four-year term and the Riigikogu for a three-year one. A radical right-wing coalition government was elected which held power until losing a parliamentary vote of no confidence in September 1994. At the legislative election of March 1995 a centre-left government of the Coalition Party and Rural People's Union (KMÜ) and the Centre Party was formed; the government collapsed following a phone-tapping scandal in October 1995. A new coalition government formed by the KMÜ and the Reform Party was sworn in on 3 November 1995.

Estonia is divided into 46 towns and 15 districts for local administration purposes.

HEAD OF STATE
President, Lennart Meri, *elected* 5 October 1992

GOVERNMENT *as at July 1996*
Prime Minister, Tiit Vähi (KMÜ)
Foreign Affairs, Siim Kallas (R)
Justice, Paul Varul (KMÜ)
Interior, Märt Rask (R)
Economic Affairs, Andres Lipstok (R)
Finance, Mart Opmann (KMÜ)
Social Affairs, Toomas Vilosius (R)
Defence, Andrus Öövel (KMÜ)
Education, Jaak Aaviksoo (R)
Culture, Jaak Allik (KMÜ)
Agriculture, Ilmar Mändmets (KMÜ)
Environment, Villu Reiljan (KMÜ)
Transport and Communications, Kalev Kukk (R)
EU, Endel Lippmaa (KMÜ)
Regional Affairs, Tiit Kubri (KMÜ)
KMÜ Coalition Party and Rural People's Union;
R Reform Party

EMBASSY OF THE REPUBLIC OF ESTONIA
16 Hyde Park Gate, London SW7 5DG
Tel 0171-589 3428
Ambassador Extraordinary and Plenipotentiary, new appointment awaited

BRITISH EMBASSY
Kentmanni 20, Tallinn EE0100
Tel: Tallinn 6313353
Ambassador Extraordinary and Plenipotentiary, HE Charles De Chassiron, apptd 1994
BRITISH COUNCIL REPRESENTATIVE, Colin Campbell, Vana Posti 7, Talinn

DEFENCE

The Estonian army has 3,958 active personnel. Conscripts serve 12 months and reserve forces number 2,660. In addition there are 2,000 paramilitary and maritime border guards. The last Russian combat troops withdrew on 31 August 1994 and the last specialist support troops in September 1995.

ECONOMY

Since 1992 the government has introduced free-market reforms, privatization and restructuring. In support of these reforms and a strong and fully convertible currency, the IMF has provided credits worth US$94 million. Having in 1992 established a stable currency pegged to the Deutsche Mark, the economy has stabilized, with unemployment of only 2 per cent, although double-digit inflation has persisted. Output is recovering from the fall experienced in 1990–2 with GDP growth of 5 per cent in 1995. Privatization, started in 1992, has gained momentum with foreign direct investment quadrupling in 1994. Estonia has no outstanding debt to Russia but is still dependent on Russian natural gas supplies.

Agriculture and dairy-farming are a major sector of the economy, the main products being rye, oats, barley, flax, potatoes, meat, milk, butter and eggs.

Light industry is the other major sector, concentrating on textiles, clothing and footwear, forestry, wood and paper products, and food and fish processing. Some heavy industry exists, mostly chemicals and the manufacture of power equipment.

TRADE

Although Estonia signed a free trade deal with Russia in 1992, it has greatly reduced its trade with the former Soviet states. In 1994 over 70 per cent of trade was with EU and EFTA states and Estonia's trade rose by 50 per cent. Free trade and association agreeements with the EU came into effect in 1995; Estonia applied for membership of the EU in December 1995.

Trade with UK	1994	1995
Imports from UK	£15,285,000	£29,665,000
Exports to UK	58,830,000	111,840,000

COMMUNICATIONS

Freedom of the press is guaranteed in the constitution, and the state monopoly on television and radio ended soon after independence. All newspapers have been privatized and broadcasting channels are in the process of being privatized. Russian-language news and programmes are provided on Estonian Television. There are five Estonian and three Russian-language daily newspapers.

EDUCATION

Estonia has a three-tier education system, consisting of primary level (four years), secondary level (six years) and university level (four to six years). Primary- and secondary-level education is compulsory.

ETHIOPIA
Federal Democratic Republic of Ethiopia

Ethiopia is in north-eastern Africa, bounded on the north-west by the Sudan, on the south by Kenya, on the east by Djibouti and Somalia, and on the north-east by Eritrea. The area is 435,608 sq. miles (1,128,221 sq. km).

A large central plateau (average height, 6,000–7,000 ft) rises to nearly 15,000 ft at Ras Dashan in the north. The plateau drops to the Nile basin in the west, to the Ogaden desert in the east and to Eritrea and the Red Sea in the north. The chief river is the Blue Nile, issuing from Lake Tana; the Atbara and many other tributaries of the Nile also rise in the Ethiopian highlands.

The population (UN estimate 1993) is 51,859,000. About one-third are of Semitic origin (Amharas and Tigreans) and the remainder mainly Oromos (about 40 per cent of the population), Somalis and Afar. Those of Semitic origin and many of the Oromos, are Ethiopian Orthodox Christians, whose current Patriarch is Abuna Paulos Gebre-Yohannis. The Afar people in the north and the Somalis in the south-east, as well as some Oromos, are Muslim.

There are eight major ethnic groups speaking a total of 70 languages, of which the most widely used is Amharic.

CAPITAL – Addis Ababa (population, 1994 estimate, 3,500,000). Dire Dawa is the most important commercial centre after Addis Ababa.
CURRENCY – Ethiopian birr (EB) of 100 cents.
FLAG – Three horizontal bands: green, yellow, red.

NATIONAL ANTHEM – Ityopya, Ityopya Kidemi.
NATIONAL DAY – 28 May.

GOVERNMENT

The Hamitic culture was heavily influenced by Semitic immigration from Arabia at about the time of Christ. Christianity was introduced in the fourth century. The empire attained its zenith in the sixth century under the Axum rulers but was checked by Islamic expansion from the east. Modern Ethiopia dates from 1855 when Theodore established supremacy over the various tribes. The last emperor was Haile Selassie who reigned from 1930 until 1974, when he was deposed by the armed forces. After ten years of military rule, a Workers' Party on the Soviet model was formed with Lt.-Col. Mengistu Haile Mariam as General Secretary. The People's Democratic Republic of Ethiopia was established under a new constitution in 1987 with Lt.-Col. Mengistu as president. Armed insurgencies by the Eritrean People's Liberation Front (EPLF) and the Ethiopian People's Revolutionary Democratic Front (EPRDF), originating in Tigre, brought down Mengistu's government in May 1991.

A transitional administration comprising the EPRDF and other opposition groups formed a Council of Representatives which governed until 1995 under President Meles Zenawi. In 1994, the Council agreed on a draft federal constitution which was adopted by an elected Constituent Assembly on 8 December 1994. The constitution provided for a federal government responsible for foreign affairs, defence and economic policy, and for nine regional administrations (Tigre, Afar, Amara, Oromia, Somai, Benshangui, Gambela, Harer and Southern), with a degree of autonomy and the right to secede. Multiparty elections in May and June 1995 were won by the EPRDF, which gained 80 per cent of the seats in the newly-created 526-seat Council of People's Representatives; a 117-member Federal Council to represent the 22 ethnic groups was also created. The Council of People's Representatives elected Dr Negasso Gidaola to the non-executive office of President and Meles Zenawi as Prime Minister. The Federal Democratic Republic of Ethiopia was proclaimed on 22 August 1995.

HEAD OF STATE
President, Dr Negasso Gidada, *elected by the Council of People's Representatives* 22 August 1995

FEDERAL GOVERNMENT *as at August 1996*
Prime Minister, Meles Zenawi
Deputy PM, Defence, Tamirat Layne
Deputy PM, Economic Affairs, Kassu Illala
Foreign Affairs, Seyoum Mesfin
Justice, Mahteme Solomon
Finance, Sufiyan Ahmed
Economic Development and Co-operation, Girma Birru
Trade and Industry, Kasahun Ayele
Agriculture, Dr Tekedel Forsido
Water Resources, Shiferaw Jarso
Works and Urban Development, Haile Assegde
Transport and Communications, Abdulmejid Hussien
Mines and Energy, Ezedin Ali
Labour and Social Affairs, Hassan Abdela
Education, Genet Zewdie
Health, Dr Adem Ibrahim
Information and Culture, Michael Chamo

EMBASSY OF ETHIOPIA
17 Prince's Gate, London SW7 1PZ
Tel 0171-589 7212/3/4/5
Ambassador Extraordinary and Plenipotentiary, HE Dr Solomon Gidada, apptd 1992
Counsellor, Laine Kahsu (*Commercial*)

BRITISH EMBASSY
Fikre Mariam Abatechan Street (PO Box 858), Addis Ababa
Tel: Addis Ababa 611235 4
Ambassador Extraordinary and Plenipotentiary, HE Duncan R. Christopher, apptd 1994
Deputy Ambassador and First Secretary, C. O. Pigott
BRITISH COUNCIL REPRESENTATIVE, Michael Sargent, Artistic Building, Adwa Avenue (PO Box 1043), Addis Ababa

ECONOMY

The post-Mengistu government implemented a programme of free-market economic reform which reduced government spending and inflation. The currency was devalued, the civil service reduced and the army cut by two-thirds. Western states have responded with debt relief and loans; the IMF approved a three-year loan of US$70 million in 1992. An agreement waiving customs levies was concluded with Eritrea in April 1995.

Thousands of peasant farmers resettled by the Mengistu regime in barren areas have returned to their own areas. Farms remain in state ownership but farmers have been granted security of tenure for life and agricultural policy is now market-based. Agriculture accounts for approximately 40 per cent of GDP, 85 per cent of exports and 80 per cent of total employment. The major food crops are teff, maize, barley, sorghum, wheat, pulses and oil seeds. Coffee generates over 50 per cent of export earnings. Famine conditions, which attracted world attention in 1984–5, recurred to a lesser extent in 1992. However, agricultural liberalization has led to dramatic progress in food production and produced a record harvest of 7.7 million tonnes of grain and pulses in 1993.

Manufacturing industry accounts for less than 9 per cent of GDP and is heavily dependent on agriculture. Ethiopia's known, but as yet largely unexploited, natural resources include gold, platinum, copper and potash. Traces of oil and natural gas have been found.

TRADE
The chief imports by value are machinery and transport equipment, manufactured goods and chemicals; the principal exports by value are coffee, oil seeds, hides and skins, and pulses.

Trade with UK	1994	1995
Imports from UK	£48,236,000	£53,337,000
Exports to UK	13,128,000	15,928,000

COMMUNICATIONS

A network of roads has been built in rural areas and links the major cities with each other, with the Sudanese and Kenyan borders and through Eritrea to the Red Sea coast. The Ethiopian and Eritrean governments negotiated an agreement in 1992 which guarantees Ethiopia access to the Red Sea via the ports of Assab and Massawa. Transport links suffered during the secessionist wars and under the heavy burden of famine relief traffic.

There is a railway link from Addis Ababa to Djibouti. Ethiopian Airlines maintains regular services from Addis

Ababa to many provincial towns, throughout Africa and to Europe.

EDUCATION

Elementary education is provided by government schools in the main centres of population; there are also mission schools. Government secondary schools are found in Addis Ababa and the provincial capitals. The National University (founded 1961) co-ordinates the institutions of higher education. There is a separate university at Alemaya (agricultural).

Amharic was the official language of instruction, with English as the first foreign language and main language of instruction from secondary level upwards. Arabic is taught in Koran schools; and Ge'ez (ancient Ethiopic) in Christian church schools. Language policy is now under review by the post-Mengistu government.

FIJI
Matanitu Ko Viti – Republic of Fiji

Fiji is composed of roughly 332 islands (about 100 permanently inhabited) and over 500 islets in the South Pacific, about 1,100 miles north of New Zealand. The group extends 300 miles from east to west and 300 miles north to south between 15° 45' and 21° 10' S. latitude and 176° E. and 178° W. longitude. The International Date Line has been diverted to the east of the island group. Its area is 7,055 sq. miles (18,274 sq. km). The largest islands are Viti Levu and Vanua Levu. The main groups of islands are Lomaiviti, Lau and Yasawas. Most of the larger islands are mountainous, but also have areas of flat land and many of the rivers have built extensive deltas. The climate is tropical without extremes of heat and temperatures rarely exceed 32°C or fall below 15°C.

The population (census 1986) was 715,373, comprising 48.6 per cent Indians, 46.2 per cent Fijians, and 5.2 per cent other races. A UN estimate (1993) gives a total figure of 758,000. Since the 1987 coup many ethnic Indians have left and by 1994 Melanesian Fijians formed the largest population group.

Capital – ΨSuva, on the island of Viti Levu. Population (1986) 69,665.

Currency – Fiji dollar (F$) of 100 cents.

Flag – Light blue ground with Union flag in top left quarter and the shield of Fiji in the fly.

National Anthem – God Bless Fiji.

National Day – 10 October (Fiji Day).

GOVERNMENT

Fiji was a British colony from 1874 until 10 October 1970 when it became an independent state and a member of the Commonwealth.

A left-wing coalition under Dr Timoci Bavadra won a general election in April 1987, but was overthrown in a military coup on 14 May by Lt.-Col. Sitiveni Rabuka. An Advisory Council was set up as an interim government, but it too was overthrown on 25 September 1987. On 7 October Rabuka declared Fiji a republic; the Governor-General resigned on 15 October; Fiji's Commonwealth membership lapsed and another interim government was formed.

A new constitution, promulgated in 1990, established the political dominance of the Melanesian community within the judiciary and a bicameral parliament. The parliament consists of a Senate of 34 members appointed by the President, of which 24 seats are reserved for Melanesian Fijians, one for the Polynesian island of Rotuma and nine for other races. The House of Representatives has 70 seats; 37 reserved for Melanesians, 27 for Indians, one for Rotuma, and five for other races. The presidency and the premiership can only be held by Melanesians. The President is elected by the (Melanesian) Great Council of Chiefs. The Fijian Political Party led by Rabuka won the general elections in May 1992 and February 1994 and has formed a coalition government with the General Voters Party.

Head of State
President, Ratu Sir Kamisese Mara, GCMG, KBE, *inaugurated* 18 January 1994

Cabinet *as at August 1996*
Prime Minister, Fijian Affairs, Multi-ethnic Affairs, Regional Development, Maj.-Gen. Sitiveni Rabuka, OBE
Attorney-General, Justice, Ratu Etuate Tavai
Finance and Economic Development, Berenado Vunibobo, CBE
Lands, Mining and Energy, Ratu Timoci Vesikula
Health, Leo Smith
Home Affairs, Col. Paul Manueli, OBE
Agriculture, Fisheries and Forests, Militoni Leweniqila
Foreign Affairs, Filipe Bole, CBE
Information, Broadcasting, Television and Telecommunications, Ratu Jo Nacola
Public Works and Infrastructure, Ratu Inoke Kubuabola
Commerce, Trade and Industry, Isimeli Bose
Education, Women and Culture, Taufa Vakatale
Urban Development, Housing and Environment, Vilisoni Cagimaivei
Tourism, Transport and Civil Aviation, David Pickering
Labour and Industrial Relations, Vincent Lobendahn
Youth, Employment Opportunities and Sports, Jim Ah Koy, OBE

Embassy of the Republic of Fiji
34 Hyde Park Gate, London SW7 5DN
Tel 0171-584 3661
Ambassador Extraordinary and Plenipotentiary, HE Filimone Jitoko, apptd 1996

British Embassy
Victoria House, 47 Gladstone Road, PO Box 1355, Suva
Tel: Suva 311033
Ambassador Extraordinary and Plenipotentiary, HE Michael Peart, CMG, LVO, apptd 1995

ECONOMY

The economy is primarily agrarian. The principal cash crop is sugar cane, which is the main export, followed by coconuts, ginger and copra. A variety of other fruit, vegetables and root crops are also grown, and self-sufficiency in rice is a major aim. Forestry, fishing and beef production are being encouraged in order to diversify the economy. The processing of agricultural, marine and timber products are the main industries, along with gold mining and textiles. Tourism is second only to sugar as a money-earner.

Finance	1993	1994
Public income	F$643m	F$685m
Public expenditure	679m	650m

Trade

The chief imports are foodstuffs, machinery, mineral fuels, chemicals, beverages, tobacco and manufactured articles. Chief exports are sugar, coconut oil, gold, lumber, garments, molasses, ginger and canned fish.

	1993	1994
Total imports	F$938m	F$1,209m
Total exports	653m	800m

Trade with UK	1994	1995
Imports from UK	£6,179,000	£6,770,000
Exports to UK	80,642,000	82,020,000

COMMUNICATIONS

Fiji is one of the main aerial crossroads in the Pacific, providing services to New Zealand, Australia, Tonga, Western Samoa, Vanuatu, the Solomon Islands, Kiribati, Tuvalu, New Caledonia and American Samoa. Fiji has three ports of entry, at Suva, Lautoka and Levuka. There are 5,100 km of roads.

FINLAND
Suomen Tasavalta

Finland is situated on the Gulfs of Finland and Bothnia, with a total area of 130,500 sq. miles (338,000 sq. km), of which 69 per cent is forest, 8 per cent cultivated land and 10 per cent lakes. The population (1994 estimate) is 5,098,754. The population is predominantly Lutheran. Finnish and Swedish are both official languages, 93.6 per cent speaking Finnish as their first language and 6.2 per cent Swedish. Lapp is spoken by the Lapps who number about 2,500 and live in the far north of the country. Both Finnish and Swedish are used for administration and education.

The Åland archipelago (Ahvenanmaa), a group of small islands at the entrance to the Gulf of Bothnia, covers about 572 square miles, with a population (1994) of 25,158 (95.2 per cent Swedish-speaking). The islands have semi-autonomous status.

CAPITAL – ΨHelsinki (Helsingfors), population (1994) 515,765; other towns are Tampere (Tammerfors), 179,251; ΨTurku (Åbo), 162,370; Espoo (Esbo), 186,507; Vantaa (Vanda), 164,379; ΨOulu (Oleåborg), 106,419; Lahti (Lahtis), 94,706; ΨPori (Björneborg), 76,561.

CURRENCY – Markka (Mk) of 100 penniä.

FLAG – White with blue cross.

NATIONAL DAY – 6 December (Independence Day).

GOVERNMENT

Finland was part of the Swedish Empire from the middle ages until it was ceded to Russia in 1809 and became an autonomous grand duchy of the Russian Empire. Finland became independent after the Russian revolution of 1917, but was forced to cede around one-tenth of its land to the Soviet Union and to resettle 10 per cent of its population under the Treaty of Paris 1947, thereby losing access to the Arctic Ocean and to Lake Ladoga. A Soviet-Finnish Co-operation Treaty forced Finland to demilitarize its Soviet border, to enter into a barter trade agreement and to adopt a stance of neutrality. These terms lasted until the demise of the Soviet Union in 1991.

Under the constitution there is a unicameral legislature, the *Eduskunta*, composed of 200 members elected by universal suffrage. The highest executive power is held by the President who is directly elected for a period of six years. The first direct elections for the presidency were held in 1994, the president having previously been elected by an electoral college.

The present government took office in April 1995 after legislative elections in March. The five parties in the ruling coalition are the Social Democratic Party, the National Coalition Party (conservative), the Left-wing Alliance, the Swedish People's Party, and the Green League, with a total of 145 out of 200 seats.

Finland joined the European Union on 1 January 1995 following a referendum in October 1994 in which accession was approved by 57 per cent in Finland and by 74 per cent in a separate Åland Islands referendum.

HEAD OF STATE
President, Martti Ahtisaari, *inaugurated* 1 March 1994

CABINET *as at August 1996*
Prime Minister, Paavo Lipponen (SDP)
Deputy PM, Finance, Sauli Niinistö (NCP)
Foreign Affairs, Tarja Halonen (SDP)
Europe, Ole Norrback (SPP)
Interior, Jan-Erik Enestam (SPP)
Administration, Jouni Backman (SDP)
Defence, Anneli Taina (NCP)
Finance, PM's Office, Arja Alho (SDP)
Education, Olli-Pekka Heinonen (NCP)
Culture, Youth, Universities, Science, Claes Andersson (LA)
Agriculture and Forestry, Kalevi Hemilä (Ind.)
Transport, Tuula Linnainmaa (NCP)
Trade and Industry, Antti Kalliomäki (SDP)
Social Affairs and Health, Housing and Building, Sinikka Mönkäre (SDP)
Labour Protection, Social and Health Services, Equality Affairs, Terttu Huttu (LA)
Labour, Liisa Jaakonsaari (SDP)
Environment, Development Co-operation, Pekka Haavisto (Green)
Justice, Kari Häkämies (NCP)

SDP Social Democratic Party; NCP National Coalition Party; LA Left-wing Alliance; SPP Swedish People's Party; Green Green League

EMBASSY OF FINLAND
38 Chesham Place, London SW1X 8HW
Tel 0171-838 6200

Ambassador Extraordinary and Plenipotentiary, HE Leif
Blomqvist, GCVO, apptd 1991
Minister, L. Korpinen, CMG
Counsellor (Commercial), Olli Anttila
Defence Attaché, Col. H. Strang

BRITISH EMBASSY
Itäinen Puistotie 17, 00140 Helsinki
Tel: Helsinki 661293
Ambassador Extraordinary and Plenipotentiary, HE David
Burns, CMG, apptd 1995
Deputy Ambassador and Counsellor, D. J. Gowan
First Secretary (Commercial), H. B. Formstone, OBE
Defence Attaché, Lt.-Col. S. W. L. Strickland
There are British Consular offices at Helsinki, Jyväskylä,
Kotka, Kuopio, Oulu, Pori, Tampere, Turku, Vaasa and
Mariehamn.

BRITISH COUNCIL REPRESENTATIVE, Tuija Talvitie,
Hakaniemenkatu 2, 00530 Helsinki

DEFENCE

Total active armed forces number 31,100 personnel,
including 23,900 conscripts, who serve for eight to 11
months. However, total mobilization strength is based on
the 700,000 reservists, who are obliged to undergo between
40 and 100 days training up to age 50.

The Army has a strength of 25,700 (21,600 conscripts)
with 232 main battle tanks, 900 armoured infantry fighting
vehicles and armoured personnel carriers, and 715 artillery
pieces. The Navy has 2,500 personnel (1,000 conscripts)
with 21 patrol and coastal craft. The Air Force has 2,900
personnel (1,300 conscripts) and 108 combat aircraft.
There are also 3,500 Ministry of Interior Frontier Guards.

ECONOMY

Finland is an industrialized country producing a wide
range of capital and consumer goods. Timber and timber-
based products account for a third of exports, but the
importance of metal-working, shipbuilding and engineering has grown. The textile industry is well developed and
the glass, ceramics and furniture industries enjoy international reputations. Other important industries are
rubber, plastics, chemicals and pharmaceuticals, footwear,
foodstuffs and electronic equipment.

The Finnish economy was adversely affected by declining trade with the former Soviet bloc, together with the
world-wide economic recession, causing GDP to fall by 15
per cent, and output by 13 per cent, in 1990–3 before
exports and the currency strengthened in 1994–5. Unemployment rose to 20 per cent in 1993 before declining to 16
per cent in 1996; inflation in 1996 was under 1 per cent.
GDP growth was 4.2 per cent in 1995, but forecast to drop
in 1996. The government has introduced austerity
measures, raising taxes, and reducing health and social
welfare spending and the large overseas development
budget in order to curb the growth of public debt (60 per
cent of GDP in 1994).

TRADE

The principal imports are raw materials, machinery and
manufactured goods. The value of exports in 1994 was
dominated by wood and paper products (38 per cent) and
metal and engineering products (44 per cent). The special
barter-trade relationship with the former Soviet Union
collapsed in 1991 and exports to the countries of the former
Soviet Union fell from 20 per cent of the total in the early
1980s to 5 per cent in 1994.

Trade with UK	1994	1995
Imports from UK	£1,297,265,000	£1,630,900,000
Exports to UK	2,253,250,000	2,345,200,000

COMMUNICATIONS

There are 9,000 km of railroad, railway connections with
Sweden and Russia, and passenger boat connections with
Sweden, Germany, Poland, Russia and the Baltic states.
There are also passenger/cargo services between Britain
and Helsinki, Kotka and other Finnish ports. External air
services are maintained by most European airlines. The
merchant fleet at the end of 1993 totalled 1,429,052 tons
gross.

EDUCATION

Primary education (co-educational comprehensive
school) is free and compulsory for children from seven to
16 years. In 1993, there were 580,800 students in comprehensive schools, 127,700 in senior secondary schools,
211,200 in vocational and professional education institutions, and 124,000 in 21 universities or other schools of
similar academic level.

CULTURE

Newspapers, books, plays and films appear in both Finnish
and Swedish. There is a vigorous modern literature. F. E.
Sillanpää, who died in 1964, was awarded the Nobel prize
for Literature in 1939. In 1994 there were 60 daily
newspapers (12 Swedish).

FRANCE
La République Française

France extends from 42° 20′ to 51° 5′ N. latitude, and from
7° 85′ E. to 4° 45′ W. longitude. Its area is estimated at
211,208 sq. miles (547,026 sq. km), divided into 95 departments, including the island of Corsica, in the Mediterranean off the west coast of Italy. The principal rivers are the
Seine, Loire, Garonne and Rhône. The population,
according to the 1992 official estimate, is 57,218,000
(Metropolitan France), and 58,745,000 when overseas
departments are included.

POPULATION OF THE REGIONS 1992
Names of Departments in brackets

Alsace (Bas-Rhin, Haut-Rhin)	1,640,000
Aquitaine (Dordogne, Gironde, Landes, Lot-et-Garonne, Pyrénées-Atlantiques)	2,825,000
Auvergne (Allier, Cantal, Haute-Loire, Puy-de-Dôme)	1,318,000
Basse-Normandie (Calvados, Manche, Orne)	1,399,000
Bourgogne (Côte-d'Or, Nièvre, Saône-et-Loire, Yonne)	1,613,000
Bretagne (Côtes-du-Nord, Finistère, Ille-et-Vilaine, Morbihan)	2,816,000
Centre (Cher, Eure-et-Loir, Indre, Indre-et-Loire, Loir-et-Cher, Loiret)	2,397,000
Champagne-Ardenne (Ardennes, Aube, Marne, Haute-Marne)	1,348,000
Corse (Corse-du-Sud, Haute-Corse)	251,000
Franche-Comté (Doubs, Haute-Saône, Jura, Territoire-de-Belfort)	1,104,000

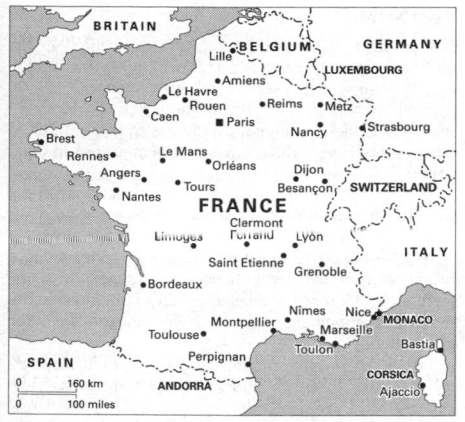

Haute-Normandie (Eure, Seine-Maritime)   1,751,000
Île-de-France (Essonne, Hauts-de-Seine,
  Seine-et-Marne, Seine-St-Denis, Val-de-
  Marne, Val-d'Oise, Ville de Paris,
  Yvelines)   10,822,000
Languedoc-Roussillon (Aude, Gard, Hérault,
  Lozère, Pyrénées-Orientales)   2,161,000
Limousin (Corrèze, Creuse, Haute-Vienne)   720,000
Lorraine (Meurthe-et-Moselle, Meuse,
  Moselle, Vosges)   2,298,000
Midi-Pyrénées (Ariège, Aveyron, Haute-
  Garonne, Gers, Lot, Hautes-Pyrénées,
  Tarn, Tarn-et-Garonne)   2,458,000
Nord-Pas-de-Calais (Nord, Pas-de-Calais)   3,974,000
Pays de la Loire (Loire-Atlantique, Maine-et-
  Loire, Mayenne, Sarthe, Vendée)   3,093,000
Picardie (Aisne, Oise, Somme)   1,834,000
Poitou-Charentes (Charente, Charente-
  Maritime, Deux-Sèvres, Vienne)   1,609,000
Provence-Alpes-Côte d'Azur (Alpes-de-
  Haute-Provence, Alpes-Maritimes,
  Bouches-du-Rhône, Hautes-Alpes, Var,
  Vaucluse)   4,344,000
Rhône-Alpes (Ain, Ardèche, Drôme, Isère,
  Loire, Rhône, Savoie, Haute-Savoie)   5,442,000
CAPITAL – Paris, on the Seine. Population (census 1990)
  2,152,400 (city); 9,318,800 (incl. suburbs).
The largest conurbations (populations 1990) are Lyon
(1,262,000); ΨMarseille (1,231,000); Lille (959,000);
ΨBordeaux (696,000); Toulouse (650,000); Nice
(516,000); Nantes (496,000); Toulon (437,000);
Grenoble (404,000); Strasbourg (388,000).
The chief towns of Corsica are ΨAjaccio (58,315) and
ΨBastia (52,446).
CURRENCY – French franc of 100 centimes.
FLAG – The tricolour, three vertical bands, blue, white, red
(blue next to flagstaff).
NATIONAL ANTHEM – La Marseillaise.
NATIONAL DAY – 14 July (Bastille Day 1789).

HISTORY

There are dolmens and menhirs in Brittany, prehistoric
remains and cave drawings in Dordogne and Ariège, and
throughout France various megalithic monuments erected
by primitive tribes, predecessors of Iberian invaders from
Spain (now represented by the Basques), Ligurians from
northern Italy and Celts or Gauls from the valley of the
Danube. Julius Caesar found Gaul 'divided into three

parts' and described three political groups: Aquitanians
south of the Garonne, Celts between the Garonne and the
Seine and Marne, and Belgae from the Seine to the Rhine.
Roman remains are plentiful throughout France in the
form of aqueducts, arenas, triumphal arches, etc. The
celebrated Norman and Gothic cathedrals, including
Notre Dame in Paris and those of Chartres, Reims,
Amiens, Bourges, Beauvais, Rouen, etc., have survived
invasions and bombardments with only partial damage,
and many of the Renaissance and the 17th- and 18th-
century chateaux survived the French Revolution.

GOVERNMENT

The legislature consists of the National Assembly of 577
deputies (555 for Metropolitan France and 22 for the
overseas departments and territories) and the Senate of 321
Senators (296 for Metropolitan France, 13 for the overseas
departments and territories and 12 for French citizens
abroad). One-third of the Senate is indirectly elected every
three years.
  The Prime Minister is appointed by the President, as is
the Council of Ministers on the Prime Minister's recommendation. They are responsible to the legislature, but as
the executive is constitutionally separate from the legislature, ministers may not sit in the legislature and must
hand over their seats to a substitute.
  The state of the parties in the Senate at August 1996 was:
Rassemblement pour la république (RPR) 102; Socialists
78; Centrist Union (UDC) 64; Republican and Independent Union (RI) 47; Democratic and European Rally
(RDE) 26; Communists 15; Independents 9.
  The last elections to the National Assembly in March
1993 were won by the right-wing alliance of the Gaullist
Rassemblement pour la république (RPR) and the Union
pour la démocratie française (UDF) parties. At August
1996 the state of parties was: RPR 259; UDF 206; Socialists
(PS) and allies 63; Communists (PCF) 23; Independent 2;
vacant 1.

HEAD OF STATE
President of the French Republic, Jacques Chirac, *elected* 7 May
  1995, *took office* 17 May 1995

COUNCIL OF MINISTERS *as at August 1996*
Prime Minister, Alain Juppé (RPR)
Justice, Jacques Toubon (RPR)
National and Further Education, Research, François Bayrou
  (UDF)
Defence, Charles Millon (UDF)
Transport, Tourism, Housing and Capital Works, Bernard Pons
  (RPR)
Foreign Affairs, Hervé de Charette (UDF)
Labour and Social Affairs, Jacques Barrot (UDF)
Interior, Jean-Louis Debré (RPR)
Economic and Finance, Jean Arthuis (UDF)
Relations with Parliament, Roger Romani (RPR)
Environment, Corinne Lepage (Ind.)
Culture, Philippe Douste-Blazy (UDF)
Industry, Post and Telecommunications, Franck Borotra (RPR)
Agriculture, Fisheries and Food, Philippe Vasseur (UDF)
Town and Country Planning, Urban Affairs and Integration,
  Jean-Claude Gaudin (UDF)
*Small- and Medium-Sized Enterprises, Trade and Artisan
  Activities,* Jean-Pierre Raffarin (UDF)
Civil Service, Administrative Reform and Decentralization,
  Dominique Perben (RPR)

President of the Senate, René Monory
President of the National Assembly, Philippe Séguin
President of the Constitutional Council, Roland Dumas

FRENCH EMBASSY
58 Knightsbridge, London SWIX 7JT
Tel 0171-201 1004
Ambassador Extraordinary and Plenipotentiary, HE Jean
Gueguinou, apptd 1993
Minister-Counsellor, J. P. Taix
Defence Attaché, Contre-Amiral Y. de Kersauson
Cultural Counsellor, O. P. D'Arvor
Minister-Counsellor (Economic and Commercial Affairs),
O. Louis

BRITISH EMBASSY
35 rue du Faubourg St Honoré, 75383 Paris Cedex 08
Tel: Paris 4451 3100
Ambassador Extraordinary and Plenipotentiary, HE Michael
Jay, CMG, apptd 1996
Minister, The Hon. Michael Pakenham, CMG
Defence and Air Attaché, Air Cdre P. H. Eustace
Counsellor, (Finance and Economic), P. F. Ricketts
First Secretary and Consul-General, K. C. Moss

BRITISH CONSULAR OFFICES – at Bordeaux, Biarritz,
Toulouse, Lille, Boulogne, Calais, Dunkirk, Lyon,
Marseille, Nice, Paris, Cherbourg, Le Havre, Nantes
and St Malo in Metropolitan France, and overseas in
Cayenne (French Guiana), Papeete (French Polynesia),
Fort de France (Martinique), Pointe à Pitre
(Guadeloupe) and St Denis (Réunion).

BRITISH COUNCIL DIRECTOR, D. Ricks, OBE, 9 rue de
Constantine, 75007 Paris
FRANCO-BRITISH CHAMBER OF COMMERCE, 8 rue
Cimarosa, 75116 Paris. *President,* R. Lyon. *Vice-President,*
B. Cordery, OBE

DEFENCE

The total active armed forces number 409,000 personnel
(189,200 conscripts). Conscripts serve for ten months.
Reserves total 337,000. Strategic nuclear forces consist of
80 submarine-launched ballistic missiles on five nuclear-
powered submarines, 18 land-based intermediate range
ballistic missiles, 15 nuclear-capable Mirage IVP aircraft
and 45 Mirage 2000N aircraft, both with medium-range
nuclear air-to-surface missiles.

The Army has a strength of 241,400 (136,800 conscripts)
with 15 Hadès short-range nuclear missile launchers, 1,016
main battle tanks, 4,688 armoured personnel carriers and
armoured infantry fighting vehicles, 1,479 artillery pieces
and 645 helicopters.

The Navy has a strength of 64,200 (18,600 conscripts)
with 24 Super Etendard aircraft (with 22 in store), capable
of carrying short-range nuclear air-to-surface missiles,
13 submarines, two aircraft carriers, one cruiser, four
destroyers, 36 frigates, 52 other combat aircraft and 40
armed helicopters.

The Air Force has a strength of 89,200 (33,800 conscripts) and some 682 combat aircraft.

France deploys 48,938 armed forces personnel abroad;
15,000 in Germany; 21,700 in French Overseas Departments and Territories; 8,300 in former French colonies in
Africa; and 3,938 on UN and peacekeeping duties.

There is also a paramilitary Gendarmerie with 93,400
personnel (11,900 conscripts) and 139,000 reserves.

In February 1996, the government announced a major
defence review, proposing the creation of a professional
army, with conscription to be phased out over six years,
beginning in 1997; a reduction in personnel to around
350,000; the retention of only six overseas bases; and the
scrapping of all land-based nuclear weapons.

ECONOMY

Government expenditure (ordinary and capital) in the
1995 general budget was F1,615,900 million, of which the
largest components were: local government F327,100
million, education F262,200 million, defence F243,400
million. In 1995 the budget deficit was equivalent to 3.55
per cent of GDP with an unemployment rate of 11.6 per
cent.

In 1993 the conservative government announced the
privatization of most public sector companies, which was
expected to generate F300,000 million over five years.

In 1994 the government established the independence
of the central bank, the Banque de France, with the
formation of a nine-member monetary policy council to
define and implement monetary policy independent of the
government.

In 1995–6, the government sought to introduce austerity measures to enable France to meet the Maastricht
criteria for European monetary union in 1999. Cost-
cutting reforms targeted the welfare budget, provoking a
series of strikes by public-sector workers and students in
December 1995 and early 1996. Concessions to the unions,
tax cuts, and a high level of public debt make it unlikely
that France will reduce the budget deficit to the required 3
per cent in 1997. Unemployment reached 12.4 per cent in
June 1996 with 1 per cent growth in GDP predicted for
1996.

Approximately 30,139,000 hectares of land is used for
agricultural purposes; 15,885,500 hectares is forested.
Production in 1995 included wheat, 30,000,000 tonnes;
maize, 12,500,000 tonnes; and sugar beet 29,000,000
tonnes.

Viniculture is extensive, regions famous for their wines
including Bordeaux, Burgundy and Champagne. Production of wine in 1995 was 5,300,000 tonnes. Cognac,
liqueurs and cider are also important products.

Oil is produced from fields in the Landes area, but
France is a net importer of crude oil, for processing by its
important oil-refining industry. Natural gas is produced in
the foothills of the Pyrenees. Electricity production was
453,000m kW in 1995.

Heavy industries include oil-refining and the production of iron and steel, and aluminium. In 1993
production of steel was 14,732,000 tonnes and cement
21,600,000 tonnes. Other important industries produce
chemicals, tyres, aluminium, textiles, paper products and
processed food. Engineering products include motor
vehicles, and television and radio sets.

TRADE

The principal imports are raw materials for the heavy and
manufacturing industries (e.g. oil, minerals, chemicals),
machinery and precision instruments, agricultural products and vehicles. Raw materials, semi-manufactured and
manufactured goods are also the principal exports. Other
EU countries are France's main trading partners.

	1993	1994
Imports	F1,095,456m	F1,683,900m
Exports	1,186,656m	1,522,900m

Trade with UK	1994	1995
Imports from UK	£13,121,021,000	£14,442,200,000
Exports to UK	14,611,129,000	15,498,400,000

COMMUNICATIONS

The length of roads in 1996 was 964,356 km, of which
7,396 km were motorways.

The railroad system is extensive. The length of lines
open for traffic in 1996 was 31,940 km.

The French mercantile marine consisted in 1995 of 208 ships of a total of 4,300,000 tonnes which transported 91,500,000 tonnes of freight.

EDUCATION

The educational system is highly centralized and is administered by the Ministry of National Education. Education is compulsory, free and secular from six to 16. Schools may be single-sex or co-educational. Primary education is given in nursery schools, primary schools and *collèges d'enseignement général* (four-year secondary modern course); secondary education in *collèges d'enseignement technique*, *collèges d'enseignement secondaire* and *lycées* (seven-year course leading to one of the five *baccalauréats*). Special schools are numerous.

There are many *grandes écoles* in France which award diplomas in many subjects not taught at university, especially applied science and engineering. Most of these are state institutions but have a competitive system of entry, unlike universities. There are universities in 24 towns including 13 in Paris and the immediate area.

In 1992–3 enrolment in pre-school and primary schools was 6,610,000; in secondary schools 5,458,800, and in post-secondary education 1,951,994.

In 1993 the government gave German official parity with French in Alsace schools.

CULTURE

French is the official language. The work of the French Academy, founded in 1635, has established *le bon usage*, equivalent to 'The Queen's English' in Britain. French authors have been awarded the Nobel Prize for Literature on 12 occasions and include R. F. A. Sully-Prudhomme (1901), Anatole France (1921), André Gide (1947), François Mauriac (1952), Albert Camus (1957), Jean Paul Sartre (1964) and Claude Simon (1985).

OVERSEAS DEPARTMENTS

Greater powers of self-government were granted to French Guiana, Guadeloupe, Martinique and Réunion in 1982. These former colonies had enjoyed departmental status since 1946 and the status of regions since 1974. Their directly-elected Assemblies operate in parallel with the existing, indirectly constituted Regional Councils. The French government is represented by a Prefect in each.

FRENCH GUIANA – Situated on the north-eastern coast of South America, French Guiana is flanked by Suriname on the west and by Brazil on the south and east. Area, 34,749 sq. miles (90,000 sq. km). Population (1994) 140,000. Capital, ΨCayenne (41,000). Under the administration of French Guiana is a group of islands (St Joseph, Ile Royal and Ile du Diable), known as Iles du Salut.
Prefect, P. Dartout

Trade with UK	1994	1995
Imports from UK	£6,483,000	£3,734,000
Exports to UK	927,000	591,000

GUADELOUPE – A number of islands in the Leeward Islands group of the West Indies, consisting of the two main islands of Guadeloupe (or Basse-Terre) and Grande-Terre, with the adjacent islands of Marie-Galante, La Désirade and Îles des Saintes, and the islands of St Martin and St Barthélemy over 150 miles to the north-west. Area, 687 sq. miles (1,779 sq. km). Population (1994) 420,000. Capital ΨBasse Terre (14,000) in Guadeloupe. Other towns are ΨPointe à Pitre (26,000) in Grande-Terre and ΨGrand Bourg (6,611) in Marie-Galante.
Prefect, M. Diefenbacher

Trade with UK	1994	1995
Imports from UK	£5,772,000	£6,896,000
Exports to UK	63,000	211,000

MARTINIQUE – An island situated in the Windward Islands group of the West Indies, between Dominica in the north and St Lucia in the south. Area, 425 sq. miles (1,102 sq. km). Population (1994) 375,000. Capital ΨFort de France (101,540). Other towns are ΨTrinité (11,214) and ΨMarin (6,104).
Prefect, J-F Cordet

Trade with UK	1994	1995
Imports from UK	£17,417,000	£13,839,000
Exports to UK	35,000	14,000

RÉUNION – Réunion, which became a French possession in 1638, lies in the Indian Ocean, about 569 miles east of Madagascar and 110 miles south-west of Mauritius. Area, 969 sq. miles (2,510 sq. km). Population (1994) 643,000. Capital, St Denis (122,000). Other towns are Saint-Paul (71,669) and Saint-Pierre (58,846). The smaller, uninhabited islands of Bassas da India, Europa, Îles Glorieuses, Juan de Nova and Tromelin are administered from Réunion.
Prefect, P. Steinmetz

Trade with UK	1994	1995
Imports from UK	£14,096,000	£15,345,000
Exports to UK	1,410,000	2,278,000

TERRITORIAL COLLECTIVITÉS

MAYOTTE – Area, 144 sq. miles (372 sq. km). Population (1991 census) is 94,410. Capital, Mamoundzou (12,000). Part of the Comoros Islands group, Mayotte remained a French dependency when the other three islands became independent as the Comoros Republic in 1975. Since 1976 the island has been a *collectivité territoriale*, an intermediate status between Overseas Department and Overseas Territory.
Prefect, A. Weil

Trade with UK	1994	1995
Imports from UK	£11,086,000	£5,064,000
Exports to UK	72,000	312,000

ST PIERRE AND MIQUELON – Area 93 sq. miles (242 sq. km). Population (1990) 6,300. Two small groups of islands off the coast of Newfoundland. Became a *collectivité territoriale* in 1985.
Prefect, R. Maurice

Trade with UK	1994	1995
Imports from UK	£584,000	£561,000
Exports to UK	—	25,000

OVERSEAS TERRITORIES

FRENCH POLYNESIA – Five archipelagos in the south Pacific, comprising the Society Islands (Windward Islands group includes Tahiti, Moorea, Makatea, Mehetia, Tetiaroa, Tubuai Manu; Leeward Islands group includes Huahine, Raiatea, Tahaa, Bora-Bora, Maupiti), the Tuamotu Islands (Rangiroa, Hao, Turéia, etc.), the Gambier Islands (Mangareva, etc.), the Tubuai Islands (Rimatara, Rurutu, Tubuai, Raivavae, Rapa, etc.) and the Marquesas Islands (Nuku-Hiva, Hiva-Oa, Fatu-Hiva, Tahuata, Ua Huka, etc.). Area, 1,544 sq. miles (4,000 sq. km). Population (1994) 215,000. Capital, ΨPapeete (24,200) in Tahiti. Economy based on tourism and exports of copra, coffee, vanilla, citrus fruits and cultured pearls.
High Commissioner, P. Roncière

Trade with UK	1994	1995
Imports from UK	£4,028,000	£6,078,000
Exports to UK	52,000	235,000

NEW CALEDONIA – A large island in the western Pacific, 700 miles east of Queensland. Dependencies are the Isles of Pines, the Loyalty Islands (Mahé, Lifou, Urea, etc.), the Bélep Archipelago, the Chesterfield Islands, the Huon Islands and Walpole. New Caledonia was discovered in 1774 and annexed by France in 1854; from 1871 to 1896 it was a convict settlement. A referendum in 1987 on the question of independence was boycotted by the indigenous Kanaks, and New Caledonia therefore voted to remain French. However, a new independence referendum has been promised for 1998. In 1995, the territory was divided into three provinces, each with a provincial assembly which combined form the Territorial Assembly. In elections in July 1995, Kanaks won majorities in North province and the Loyalty Islands, whereas pro-French settlers won a majority in the South province. Area, 7,358 sq. miles (19,058 sq. km). Population (1994) 178,000. Capital ΨNoumea (65,000). It is one of the world's largest producers of nickel.
High Commissioner, D. Cultiaux

Trade with UK	1994	1995
Imports from UK	£7,012,000	£9,006,000
Exports to UK	12,910,000	9,534,000

SOUTHERN AND ANTARCTIC TERRITORIES – Created in 1955 from former Réunion dependencies, the territory comprises the islands of Amsterdam (25 sq. miles) and St Paul (2.7 sq. miles), the Kerguelen Islands (2,700 sq. miles) and Crozet Islands (116 sq. miles) archipelagos and Adélie Land (116,800 sq. miles) in the Antarctic continent. The only population are members of staff of the scientific stations.
WALLIS AND FUTUNA ISLANDS – Two groups of islands (the Wallis Archipelago and the Îles de Hoorn) in the central Pacific, north-east of Fiji. Area, 106 sq. miles (274 sq. km). Population (1990 census) 13,705. Capital, Mata-Utu on Uvea, the main island of the Wallis group.
Supreme Administrator, L.-A. Legrand

Trade with UK	1994	1995
Imports from UK	£4,000	£17,000
Exports to UK	—	—

THE FRENCH COMMUNITY

The constitution of the Fifth French Republic, promulgated in 1958, envisaged the establishment of a French Community of States. A number of the former French states in Africa have seceded from the Community but for all practical purposes continue to enjoy the same close links with France as those that remain formally members. Most former French African colonies are closely linked to France by financial, technical and economic agreements.
Source for statistical data: *Tableaux de l'Economie Française 1995–6.*

GABON
République Gabonaise

Gabon lies on the Atlantic coast of Africa at the Equator and is flanked on the north by Equatorial Guinea and Cameroon, and on the east and south by Congo. It has an area of 103,347 sq. miles (267,667 sq. km) and a population (UN estimate 1994) of 1,035,000.

CAPITAL – ΨLibreville (251,000).
CURRENCY – Franc CFA of 100 centimes.
FLAG – Horizontal bands, green, yellow and blue.
NATIONAL ANTHEM – La Concorde.
NATIONAL DAY – 17 August.

GOVERNMENT

Gabon elected on 28 November 1958 to remain an autonomous republic within the French Community and gained full independence on 17 August 1960. The constitution provides for an executive President directly elected for a seven-year term, who appoints the Council of Ministers. There is a 120-member unicameral National Assembly.

Following popular unrest, a national conference was held in March 1990 which demanded the legalization of opposition parties. Multiparty elections held in autumn 1990 were won by the ruling Parti Démocratique Gabonais (PDG), amid allegations of fraud. The PDG formed a coalition government, although the other parties left the government in 1991 in protest at PDG domination. A presidential election in 1993 was won by the incumbent, President Bongo of the PDG, amid accusations of corruption, which led to riots in Libreville. In September 1994, the government and opposition parties signed the Paris Agreement, which provided for a new coalition government and parliamentary elections which were scheduled for, but not held in, early 1996. The democratic reforms proposed in the Agreement were approved in a referendum on 23 July 1995.

HEAD OF STATE
President, El Hadj Omar Bongo, *assumed office* December 1967, *re-elected* 1973, 1979, 1986 and 5 December 1993

COUNCIL OF MINISTERS *as at August 1996*
Prime Minister, Dr Paulin Obame-Nguema
Minister of State, Equipment and Construction, Zacharie Myboto
Minister of State, Justice, Max Remondo
Minister of State, Foreign Affairs and Co-operation, Casimir Oye Mba
Minister of State, Lands, Housing, Welfare, Jean-François Ntoutoume-Emane
Minister of State, Labour, Human Resources and Training, Jean-Rémy Pendy Bouyiki
Minister of State, Planning and Territorial Administration, Pierre-Claver Maganga Moussavou
Minister of State, Agriculture, Livestock and Rural Economy, Emmanuel Ondo Methogo
Public Health and Population, Dr Serge Mba Bekale
National Defence, Gen. Idriss Ngari
Communication, Culture, Arts, Education, Human Rights, Alexandre Sambat
Transport, Tourism, Merchant Marine and Fisheries, Antoine Mboumbou Miyakou
Finance, Economy and Participation, Marcel Doupambi Matoka
Civil Service and Administrative Reform, Max Mebale
Commerce and Industry, André-Dieudonné Berre
Mining, Energy and Oil, Paul Toungui
Higher Education and Scientific Research, Gaston Mozogo Ovono
Forestry, Posts and Telecommunications, Environment, Martin-Fidèle Magnaga
Youth and Sports, Women's Affairs, Government Spokesperson, Paulette Missambo
Social Affairs, Sebastien Mamboundou Mouyama

EMBASSY OF THE REPUBLIC OF GABON
27 Elvaston Place, London SW7 5NL
Tel 0171–823 9986
Ambassador Extraordinary and Plenipotentiary, HE Honorine
   Dossou-Naki, apptd 1996

BRITISH AMBASSADOR, HE N. M. McCarthy, OBE, resident
   in Yaoundé, Cameroon

ECONOMY

The economy is heavily dependent on oil and, to a much lesser extent, other mineral resources, including manganese and uranium. Gabon has considerable timber reserves (particularly Okoumé) with 80 per cent of the country still forested, although production has stagnated in recent years.

The economy experienced considerable growth in real terms from the mid-1970s onwards but after 1986 was adversely affected by the fall in oil prices. Revenue has increased in the 1990s following oil exploitation at Rabi-Kounga. Gabon is a full member of OPEC. The IMF approved a US$85 million credit in 1994 and a three-year credit of US$165 million in 1995. Total external debt was $US3,818 million in 1993, 80 per cent of GNP.

TRADE WITH UK	1994	1995
Imports from UK	£26,900,000	£25,358,000
Exports to UK	3,851,000	5,948,000

THE GAMBIA
The Republic of the Gambia

The Gambia is named after the Gambia River, which it straddles for over 200 miles inland from the west coast of Africa. It is a narrow strip, surrounded by Senegal, except at the coast, lying between 13° 10′–13° 45′ N. and 13° 90′–16° 50′ W. The area is 4,361 sq. miles (11,295 sq. km), of which one-fifth is the river. The climate is Sahelian, with a dry season between October and May and heavy rainfall in July and August (32–40 inches a year).

The population (UN estimate 1994) was 1,081,000, mainly Wolof, Mandinka and Fula peoples who originally migrated from the north and east.

CAPITAL – ΨBanjul. Population (1983 census) of the island of Banjul was 44,536; including adjacent Kombo St Mary 147,394.

CURRENCY – Dalasi (D) of 100 butut.

FLAG – Horizontal stripes of red, blue and green, separated by narrow white stripes.

NATIONAL ANTHEM – For The Gambia, Our Homeland.

NATIONAL DAY – 18 February (Independence Day).

HISTORY

The Gambia River basin was part of the region dominated in the tenth to 16th centuries by the Songhai and Mali kingdoms centred on the upper Niger. The Portuguese reached the Gambia River in 1447; English merchants began to trade along the river from 1588. Merchants from France, Courland (now Latvia) and the Netherlands also established trading posts. In 1816 the British stationed a garrison on an island at the river mouth which became the capital of a small British-administered colony. In 1889 France agreed that the British rights along the upper river should extend 10 km on either bank. British administration was extended from the Colony to this Protectorate. The Gambia became independent within the Commonwealth on 18 February 1965, and a republic on 24 April 1970.

The relationship with Senegal remains an important factor in political and economic policy. Moves towards a closer association were accelerated after an abortive coup in 1981 was put down with the help of Senegalese troops. In 1982 the Senegambia Confederation was instituted but following disagreements it was dissolved in 1989. A treaty of friendship and co-operation was signed with Senegal in 1991.

GOVERNMENT

The constitution is democratic and parliamentary, with an executive President elected for five years. The House of Representatives has 35 elected members, five elected Chiefs' Representatives and up to eight nominated members plus the Attorney-General (ex-officio). The Vice-President and other ministers are appointed by the President. Parliament must be dissolved after five years.

The last general elections were held in 1992. In July 1994 junior army officers launched a military coup in protest at not being paid and at government corruption, which was blamed for squandering foreign aid. The President and some of his government fled to Senegal and the army officers formed a ruling military council. The coup leader, Lt. (later Capt.) Jammeh, assumed the presidency, the constitution was suspended and a civilian-military government was formed to rule in conjunction with the Ruling Military Council. A coup attempt in November 1994 led by Vice-President Lt. Sabally was defeated. Presidential and legislative elections are scheduled for September and December 1996 respectively.

HEAD OF STATE
President, Chairman of the Ruling Military Council, Capt. Yayah
   Jammeh, *took power* 23 July 1994
Vice-President, Capt. Edward Singatey

RULING MILITARY COUNCIL *as at August 1996*
Capt. Yayah Jammeh, Capt. Edward Singatey, Capt.
   Yankuba Touray, Capt. Monofou Bajo, M. B. Wadda,
   Mawdo Touray

CABINET *as at August 1996*
The President
Vice-President and Defence, Capt. Edward Singatey
Interior, Capt. Kaba Barjo
Finance and Economic Affairs, Bala Garba-Jahumpa
Attorney-General, Justice, vacant
External Affairs, Baboucarr Blaise Jagne
Trade, Industry and Employment, Dominick Mendy
Tourism and Culture, Susan Waffa-Ogoo
Health, Social Welfare and Women's Affairs, Nyimasata
   Sanneh-Bojang,
Education, Satang Jow
Works, Communication and Information, Ebrima Ceesay
Agriculture and National Resources, Musa Mbenga
Youth and Sports, Amina Faal-Sonko

GAMBIA HIGH COMMISSION
57 Kensington Court, London W8 5DG
Tel 0171-937 6316
High Commissioner, new appointment awaited

BRITISH HIGH COMMISSION
48 Atlantic Road, Fajara (PO Box 507), Banjul
Tel: Banjul 95133
High Commissioner, HE J. Wilde, apptd 1995

ECONOMY

Agriculture accounts for 75 per cent of employment and contributes 40 per cent of GDP. The chief product, groundnuts, is also the most important export item, forming over 80 per cent of domestic exports. Other crops are rice, millet, sorghum, maize and cotton. Fishing and livestock industries are being developed. Thirty per cent of the country's basic food requirements are imported. There are no significant deposits of minerals.

Manufactures are limited to groundnut processing, minor metal fabrications, paints, furniture, soap and bottling. Tourism is developing quickly. Trade through The Gambia, re-exporting imported goods to neighbouring countries, is an important element in the economy. Total external debt was US$386,300,000 in 1993, 25 per cent of GNP. GNP per capita was US$360 in 1994.

TRADE WITH UK	1994	1995
Imports from UK	£16,521,000	£13,591,000
Exports to UK	4,638,000	3,119,000

COMMUNICATIONS

There is an international airport at Yundum, 17 miles from Banjul, with scheduled services flying to other West African states and to the UK and Belgium. Banjul is the main port. Internal communication is by road and river. There are three broadcasting stations and a UHF telephone service linking Banjul with the principal towns in the provinces. There is no television service.

EDUCATION

There are 24 secondary schools (eight high and 16 technical) with a total enrolment of 15,635 students. Two high schools provide A-level education. Gambia College provides post-secondary courses in education, agriculture, public health and nursing. There are seven vocational training institutions with a total enrolment of 1,400. Higher education and advanced training courses are taken outside The Gambia, currently by over 200 students. In 1992, only 30 per cent of adults were literate.

GEORGIA
Sakartvelos Respublika

Georgia has an area of 26,911 sq. miles (69,700 sq. km) and occupies the north-western part of the Caucasus region of the former Soviet Union. It is bordered on the north by Russia, on the south-east by Azerbaijan, on the south by Armenia, on the south-west by Turkey, and on the west by the Black Sea. It contains the two autonomous republics of Abkhazia and Adjaria and the disputed region of South Ossetia (Tskhinvali).

Georgia is mountainous, with the Greater Caucasus in the north and the Lesser Caucasus in the south. The relatively low-lying land between these two ranges is divided into western and eastern Georgia by the Surz Ridge. Western Georgia has a mild and damp climate, eastern Georgia is more continental and dry. The Black Sea shore and the Rioni lowland are subtropical.

According to a 1995 estimate, Georgia has a population of 5,401,000, of which 70 per cent are Georgian, 8 per cent Armenian, 6 per cent Russian, 6 per cent Azerbaijani and 3 per cent Ossetians, together with smaller groups of Abkhazians, Greeks, Ukrainians, Jews and Kurds. The majority religion is the Georgian Orthodox Church. There is also a small Muslim minority.

Georgian, Russian and Armenian are the most commonly used languages. Georgian is one of the oldest languages in the world to have been continually in use, the alphabet having emerged in the third century BC.

CAPITAL – Tbilisi. Population 1,260,000 (1989). Other major cities are Sukhumi (capital of Abkhazia) (125,000) and Batumi (150,000).
CURRENCY – The Lari, introduced in October 1995.
FLAG – Cherry red with a canton in the upper hoist divided black over white.
NATIONAL DAY – 26 May (Independence Day).

HISTORY

The Georgians formed two states, Colchis and Iberia, on the edge of the Black Sea around 1000 BC. After centuries of invasions by Arabs, Turks and Khazars, Georgia entered its 'Golden Age' in the 12th century AD when trade, irrigation and communications were developed. Invasions by the Khazars and Mongols led to the division of Georgia into several states. These struggled against the Turkish and the Persian Empires from the 16th to the 18th centuries, gradually turning to the Russian Empire for protection and support. Eastern Georgia signed a treaty of alliance with Russia which recognized Russian supremacy in 1783 and joined the Russian Empire in 1801, followed soon after by Western Georgia.

In the late 19th century nationalist and Marxist movements competed for limited political influence under autocratic Russian rule. One of the most prominent Marxist activists was Iosif Dzhugashvili (Josef Stalin). After the Russian revolution of 1917, a nationalist government came to power in Georgia supported by allied intervention forces. In 1921 Soviet forces occupied Tbilisi, and in 1922 Georgia joined the Soviet Union as part of the Transcaucasian Soviet Socialist Republic.

In March 1990 the Georgian Supreme Soviet declared illegal the treaties of 1921–2 by which Georgia had joined the Soviet Union. The Communist Party's monopoly on power was abolished and in multiparty elections held in October and November 1990 the nationalist leader Zviad Gamsakhurdia was elected President. Georgia declared its independence from the Soviet Union in May 1991 and was admitted to UN membership on 31 July 1992.

GOVERNMENT

After independence Gamsakhurdia's government faced armed opposition from 1991 onwards. Defeat in the ensuing civil war in Tbilisi led to Gamsakhurdia's overthrow in January 1992, with a military council taking power until March 1992, when a state council was appointed with the former Soviet foreign minister Eduard Shevardnadze as chairman. Fighting continued throughout 1992 and 1993. In October 1992 Shevardnadze was elected head of state and Chairman of the Parliament, and a loose alliance of pro-Shevardnadze parties formed a government.

Gamsakhurdia returned to western Georgia in September 1993, a month after economic chaos had forced the government to resign. President Shevardnadze assumed full executive powers at the head of an emergency council, but failed to prevent the advance of Gamsakhurdia's rebels because most government forces were engaged in Abkhazia. Shevardnadze was forced to accept Russian armaments and troops to defeat the rebellion and in return agreed to join the CIS. Russian influence in Georgia was further increased by the signing of a ten-year Treaty of Friendship and Co-operation in February 1994 under which Russia gained a decisive say in Georgian economic policy and maintains four major military bases in the country. The Georgian parliament ratified CIS membership on 1 March 1994.

A new constitution was promulgated on 24 August 1995 which provided for a federal republic with a unicameral legislature; and a popularly elected president who serves a maximum of two five-year terms. Presidential and legislative elections, held on 5 November 1995, were won by President Shevardnaze and his Citizens' Union of Georgia party.

SECESSION

In late 1990 the South Ossetians took up arms against Georgian rule in an attempt to join North Ossetia, itself part of Russia. The South Ossetian provincial parliament voted in November 1992 to secede from Georgia and join Russia. The province's status remains unresolved since June 1992 when fighting stopped and a joint Russian-Georgian-Ossetian peacekeeping force was dispatched.

Representatives of the South Ossetian and Georgian governments met in April 1996 to agree security and confidence-building measures. South Ossetia was renamed Tskhinvali under Georgia's 1995 constitution.

In July 1992 the Abkhazian republican parliament declared Abkhazia independent. Fighting broke out between Georgian forces and Abkhazian separatists supported by Russian arms and irregulars; Georgian forces were defeated and were forced to withdraw in September 1993. Negotiations under Russian auspices led to an Abkhaz-Georgian cease-fire and separation of forces agreement being signed in May 1994 and the deployment of 2,500 Russian UN peacekeepers on the Abkhaz-Georgian border. In November 1994 the Abkhaz Supreme Soviet declared Abkhazia's independence again and elected Vladislav Ardzinba as President. Abkhazia was given autonomous republic status under the 1995 constitution; this was rejected by the republican parliament.

HEAD OF STATE

President, Eduard Shevardnadze, *elected* 11 October 1992, *re-elected* 5 November 1995

CABINET *as at August 1996*

Chairman of the Supreme Soviet, Zurab Zhvanian
Minister of State, Nicoloz Lekishvili
Education, Tamaz Kvachantiradze
Environment, Nino Chkobadze
Economy, Vladimer Papava
Trade and Foreign Economic Relations, Konstantine Zaldastanishvili
Defence, Vardiko Nadibaidze
Communications and Post, Fridon Injia
Culture, Valeri Asatiani
Refugees, Valeri Vashakidze
Urbanization and Building, Merab Chkhenkeli
Foreign Affairs, Irakli Menagarishvili
State Security, Shota Kviraia
State Property Management, Avtandil Silagadze

Agriculture, Bakur Gulua
Social Security, Tengiz Gazdeliani
Finance, David Iakobidze
Interior Affairs, Kakha Targamadze
Health, Avtandil Jorbenadze

GEORGIAN AMBASSADOR, HE Teimuraz Mamatsashvili, apptd 1995

BRITISH AMBASSADOR, HE Stephen Nash, apptd 1995

ECONOMY

The economy was brought to the brink of collapse by civil and secessionist wars and the ending of former Soviet trading relationships. Industrial production fell by 70 per cent between 1991 and 1995 and foreign aid forms a large part of the budget. The IMF loaned Georgia US$40 million in 1994 and US$157 million in 1995. Although Georgia has deposits of coal, they have not been exploited and it is desperately short of energy supplies. There were little or no supplies of gas, electricity and heating in the winter of 1994–5; shortages were pre-empted the following winter by humanitarian aid of fuel and grain from Russia. A large proportion of production is stolen by black marketeers, whilst the tourist industry on the Black Sea coast has been destroyed by the fighting. The only productive sector of the economy is agriculture, with a concentration on viniculture, tea and tobacco-growing and citrus fruits.

Economic performance improved in 1995 with inflation dropping from 7,500 per cent in 1994 to 2 per cent per month in 1995. Reforms included the launch of a coupon privatization scheme in March 1995, the introduction of a new currency in October 1995, and new legislation permitting the private ownership of arable land and stricter bank regulation. GNP per capita was US$580 in 1993; GDP has experienced negative growth since the late 1980s.

TRADE WITH UK	1994	1995
Imports from UK	£6,392,000	£2,842,000
Exports to UK	143,000	1,185,000

GERMANY
Bundesrepublik Deutschland – Federal Republic of Germany

The area is approximately 138,000 sq. miles (357,050 sq km). The estimated population (March 1993) is 81,075,000, of whom 65,400,000 live in the former West and 15,700,000 in the former East Germany. In 1992 there were 28,875,000 Protestants, 27,663,000 Roman Catholics, and 1,900,000 Muslims. The number of Jews was estimated to be 41,000 in 1993.

CAPITAL – Berlin. The seat of government and parliament is to be transferred from Bonn, West Germany's postwar capital, to the historical capital, Berlin. The move is scheduled for completion by 2000.

OTHER CITIES AND TOWNS – populations (1992):

Berlin	3,454,200	Stuttgart	596,900
Hamburg	1,675,200	Düsseldorf	577,400
Munich	1,241,300	Bremen	553,200
Cologne	958,600	Duisberg	538,300
Frankfurt am		Hanover	520,900
Main	660,800	Leipzig	500,000
Essen	627,800	Nuremberg	498,500
Dortmund	600,700	Dresden	483,400

CURRENCY – Deutsche Mark (DM) of 100 Pfennig.
FLAG – Horizontal bars of black, red and gold.

NATIONAL ANTHEM – Einigkeit und Recht und Freiheit (Unity and right and freedom).
NATIONAL DAY – 3 October (Anniversary of 1990 Unification).

HISTORY

The term 'deutsch' (German) was probably first used in the eighth century and described the language spoken in the eastern part of the Frankish realm. The first German realm was the Holy Roman Empire, established in AD 962 when Otto I of Saxony was crowned Emperor. The Empire endured until 1806, but the achievement of a national state was prevented by fragmentation into small principalities and dukedoms.

The Empire was replaced by a loose association of sovereign states known as the German Confederation, which was dissolved in 1866 and replaced by the Prussian-dominated North German Federation. Prussia had translated its earlier economic predominance into political hegemony by the annexation of the duchies of Schleswig and Holstein from Denmark in 1864 and a decisive defeat of Austria in 1866 (the Seven Weeks' War). After the Franco-Prussian War of 1870–1, which resulted in the defeat of France and the cession of Alsace and part of Lorraine, the south German principalities united with the northern federation to form a second German Empire, the King of Prussia being proclaimed Emperor in 1871.

Defeat in the First World War led to the abdication of the Emperor, and the country became a republic. The Treaty of Versailles 1919 returned Alsace–Lorraine to France, and large areas in the east were lost to Poland. The world economic crisis of 1929 contributed to the collapse of the Weimar Republic and the subsequent rise to power of the National Socialist movement of Adolf Hitler, who became Chancellor in 1933.

After concluding a Treaty of Non-Aggression with the Soviet Union in August 1939, Germany invaded Poland (1 September 1939), precipitating the Second World War, which lasted until 1945. Hitler committed suicide on 30 April 1945. On 8 May 1945, Germany unconditionally surrendered.

THE POST-WAR PERIOD

After the surrender, Germany was divided into American, French, British and Soviet zones of occupation. Supreme authority was exercised by the respective Commanders-in-Chief, and jointly through the Control Council of the four Commanders, with Berlin under joint administration. The USSR withdrew from the Control Council in 1948 and the rift divided Germany *de facto* into east and west.

The Federal Republic of Germany (FRG) was created out of the three western zones in 1949 when a federal government took office in Bonn and the Basic Law (federal constitution) came into force. A Communist government was established in the Soviet zone (henceforth the German Democratic Republic (GDR)). The Bonn/Paris Conventions in 1955 restored federal German autonomy subject to the reservation of Three Power rights and responsibilities relating to Berlin and to Germany as a whole.

In 1961 the Soviet zone of Berlin was sealed off, and the Berlin Wall was built along the zonal boundary, partitioning the western sectors of the city from the eastern.

Soviet-initiated reform in eastern Europe during the late 1980s led to unrest in the GDR. The mass exodus of its citizens to the west via Hungary and Czechoslovakia culminated in the opening of the Berlin Wall in November 1989 and the collapse of Communist government there. The 'Treaty on the Final Settlement with Respect to Germany', concluded between the FRG, GDR and the four former occupying powers in September 1990, unified Germany with effect from 3 October 1990 as a fully sovereign state occupying the territory of the former two Germanies and Berlin. Economic and monetary union preceded formal union on 1 July 1990. Unification is constitutionally the accession of Berlin and the five reformed *Länder* of the GDR to the FRG, which remains in being. The first government of the new Germany took office in January 1991 following all-German elections on 2 December 1990.

GOVERNMENT

The Basic Law provides for a President, elected by a Federal Convention (electoral college) for a five-year term, a lower house (*Bundestag*) of 672 members elected by direct universal suffrage for a four-year term of office, and an upper house (*Bundesrat*) composed of 79 members appointed by the governments of the *Länder* in proportion to *Länder* populations, without a fixed term of office.

The distribution of seats following the last election for the Bundestag on 16 October 1994 was: Christian Democratic Union, 244; Social Democrats, 252; Free Democrats, 47; Christian Social Union, 50; Democratic Socialists, 30; The Greens, 49.

HEAD OF STATE
Federal President, Professor Roman Herzog, *born* 1934, *elected* 23 May 1994, *sworn in* 1 July 1994

CABINET *as at August 1996*

Federal Chancellor, Dr Helmut Kohl (CDU)
Foreign Affairs and Deputy Chancellor, Dr Klaus Kinkel (FDP)
Federal Chancellery, Friedrich Bohl (CDU)
Interior, Manfred Kanther (CDU)
Economy, Dr Günter Rexrodt (FDP)
Justice, Dr Edzard Schmidt-Dortzing (FDP)
Finance, Dr Theodor Waigel (CSU)
Agriculture, Jochen Borchert (CDU)
Labour and Social Affairs, Dr Norbert Blüm (CDU)
Defence, Volker Rühe (CDU)
Health, Horst Seehofer (CSU)
Family and Elderly, Women and Youth, Claudia Nolte (CDU)
Transport, Matthias Wissmann (CDU)

Environment, Dr Angela Merkel (CDU)
Posts and Telecommunications, Dr Wolfgang Bötsch (CSU)
Regional Planning, Housing and Urban Development, Prof.
Klaus Töpfer (CDU)
Education, Research and Technology, Dr Jürgen Rüttgers
(CDU)
Economic Co-operation and Development, Carl-Dieter
Spranger (CSU)

CDU Christian Democratic Union; CSU Christian Social
Union; FDP Free Democratic Party.

EMBASSY OF THE FEDERAL REPUBLIC OF GERMANY
23 Belgrave Square, London SWIX 8PZ
Tel 0171-824 1300
Ambassador Extraordinary and Plenipotentiary, HE Dr Jürgen
Osterhelt, apptd 1995
Minister, Peter von Butler
First Counsellors, Dr R. W. Ehni (Cultural Affairs); B. Westphal
(Economic Affairs)
Defence Attaché, Brig.-Gen. Ecuard Fischer

BRITISH EMBASSY
Friedrich-Ebert-Allée 77, 53113 Bonn
Tel: Bonn 91670
Ambassador Extraordinary and Plenipotentiary, HE Sir Nigel
Broomfield, KCMG, apptd 1993
Minister, J. A. Shepherd, CMG
Defence Attaché, Col. P. P. Rawlens, MBE
Counsellor (Economic), Dr P. Collecott
Counsellor (Management and Consular), S. C. Johns

BRITISH EMBASSY OFFICE, BERLIN
Unter den Linden 32/34, 0-10117 Berlin
Tel: Berlin 201 840
Minister and Head of Mission, R. J. Spencer, CMG
Counsellor, Deputy Head of Mission, D. L. Corner
First Secretary (Commercial), P. Bateman

There are British Consulates-General at Berlin, Düsseldorf, Frankfurt, Hamburg, Munich and Stuttgart and
Consulates at Bremen, Hanover, Kiel and Nuremberg.

BRITISH COUNCIL REPRESENTATIVE, K. Dobson, OBE,
Hahnenstrasse 6, 50667 Köln. Offices at Berlin, Leipzig,
Hamburg and Munich and British Council libraries at all
five centres.

BRITISH CHAMBER OF COMMERCE, Neumarkt 14,
D-5000 Köln 1. Director, Herr Heumann

REGIONAL GOVERNMENT

Germany is a federal republic composed of 16 states
(Länder) (ten from the former West, five from the former
East and Berlin). Each Land has its own directly elected
legislature and government led by Minister-Presidents
(Prime Ministers) or equivalents. The 1949 Basic Law
vests executive power in the Länder governments except in
those areas reserved for the federal government.

Land	Popu-lation (1995)	Minister-President (August 1996)
Baden-Württemberg	10.3m	Erwin Teufel (CDU)
Bavaria	11.9m	Edmund Stoiber (CSU)
Berlin	3.5m	Eberhard Diepgen (CDU)*
Brandenburg	2.5m	Manfred Stolpe (SPD)
Bremen	0.7m	Dr Henning Scherf
Hamburg	1.7m	Henning Voscherau (SPD)*
Hesse	6.0m	Hans Eichel (SPD)
Lower Saxony	7.7m	Gerhard Schröder (SPD)

Land	Popu-lation (1995)	Minister-President (August 1996)
Mecklenburg–Western Pomerania	1.8m	Berndt Seite (CDU)
North Rhine-Westphalia	17.8m	Johannes Rau (SPD)
Rhineland-Palatinate	4.0m	Kurt Beck (SPD)
Saarland	1.1m	Oskar Lafontaine (SPD)
Saxony	4.8m	Kurt Biedenkopf (CDU)
Saxony-Anhalt	2.8m	Reinhard Höppner (SPD)
Schleswig-Holstein	2.7m	Heidi Simonis (SPD)
Thuringia	2.5m	Bernhardt Vogel (CDU)

*Berlin, Govening Mayor; Bremen, Mayor; Hamburg, First
Mayor.

JUDICATURE

Judicial authority is exercised by the Federal Constitutional Court, the federal courts provided for in the Basic
Law and the courts of the Länder. The death sentence has
been abolished.
President of Federal Constitutional Court, Jutta Limbach

DEFENCE

Under the terms of the Treaty of Unification, the German
armed forces have been limited to 370,000 active personnel since the end of 1994. The actual strength is 339,900
(137,300 conscripts), with a term of conscription of 12
months.
The Army has a strength of 234,300 including 112,800
conscripts. It deploys 2,695 main battle tanks, 2,228
artillery pieces, 6,480 armoured personnel carriers and
armoured infantry fighting vehicles, and 653 helicopters.
The Navy has a strength of 28,500 including 5,800
conscripts, with 20 submarines, 13 principal surface
combatants and 54 combat aircraft and 17 armed helicopters. The Air Force has a strength of 75,300 including
18,700 conscripts, with 488 combat aircraft.
There remain 137,450 NATO personnel in Germany
(USA 86,600; UK 28,600; Belgium 4,250; France 15,000;
Netherlands 3,000). The number is to be reduced to
110,000 by 2000; all remaining Russian forces left on 31
August 1994.
During 1993 both the Constitutional Court and the
Bundestag agreed that German armed forces may operate
outside Germany and the NATO area in UN and other
peacekeeping operations for the first time since 1945. In
1994 the Constitutional Court ruled that German forces
could serve in armed peacemaking missions.

ECONOMY

After a mini-boom generated by new East German demand
in 1990 and 1991, Germany entered its most severe
recession since the war induced by the costs of reunification. In 1993 a 'Solidarity Pact' was agreed by federal and
länder governments, opposition parties, and employers
and trade unions, to take effect from 1995. The pact lays
down the basis of future funding transfers to the East based
on a 7.5 per cent rise in income taxes, wage restraint in the
West, more private investment in the East, and the
distribution of the funding burden between the federal
and länder governments. The pact was supplemented in
August 1993 by reductions in Western social security
payments for the 1994–6 period, and by a petrol tax levy.
The economy returned to export-led growth in 1994 with
a GDP growth rate of 2.8 per cent but re-entered recession
in May 1996 when unemployment also surpassed four
million (10.8 per cent), having averaged 9.4 cent in 1995.

GDP growth of no more than 1 per cent was predicted for 1996. The government, under pressure to meet the criteria for European monetary union in 1999, announced proposed spending cuts of 2.5 per cent for 1996, which met strong disapproval from the unions.

PRODUCTION

Germany has a predominantly industrial economy. Principal industries are coal mining, iron and steel production, machine construction, the electrical industry, the manufacture of steel and metal products, chemicals, automobile production, electronics, textiles, and the processing of foodstuffs.

In 1994, Germany produced 54,344,000 tonnes of hard coal; 207,134,000 tonnes of brown coal; and 2,936,000 tonnes of crude petroleum.

In 1994 total area of farmland was 17.3 million hectares, of which 11.8 million hectares were arable land. Forest areas cover 10.4 million hectares. Milk production in 1994 was 27,866,000 tonnes; total yield of fisheries was 143,527 tonnes.

FINANCE

	1994	1995p
Expenditure	DM478 billion	DM484 billion
Revenue	408 billion	425 billion
p planned		

TRADE

	1994	1995
Total imports	DM611,138m	DM641,114m
Total exports	685,267m	732,251m

France, the Netherlands and Italy are Germany's main trading partners.

Trade with UK	1994	1995
Imports from UK	£16,827,931,000	£19,224,100,000
Exports to UK	21,349,900,000	24,889,600,000

COMMUNICATIONS

In 1995 the state-owned railways measured 40,209 km of which 17,054 km were electrified, and the privately owned railways totalled approximately 2,807 km. Classified roads measured 228,604 km in 1995, of which motorways were 11,143 km. Merchant shipping under the German flag in 1994, amounted to 5,696,088 tonnes gross. Inland waterways are 6,929 km long.

EDUCATION

School attendance is compulsory between the ages of six and 18 and comprises nine years full-time education at primary and main schools and three years of vocational education on a part-time basis. In 1993 there were 24,095 primary and main schools (*Grund und Hauptschulen*) with 4,626,400 pupils. Secondary modern schools (*Realschulen*) numbered 3,527 with 1,106,000 pupils. There were 4,099 other general secondary schools (*Gymnasien* including *Gesamtschulen*) with 2,624,000 pupils.

There were also 3,389 special schools (*Sonderschulen*) for physically and mentally handicapped and socially maladjusted children with 372,200 pupils.

The secondary school leaving examination (*Abitur*) entitles the holder to a place of study at a university or another institution of higher education.

Children below the age of 18 who are not attending a general secondary or a full-time vocational school have compulsory day-release at a vocational school. In 1993 there were 3,327 full- and part-time vocational schools (*Berufsschulen*) with 1,613,700 pupils and 211 vocational extension schools (*Berufsaufbauschulen*) with 5,600 pupils, 2,627 full-time vocational schools (*Berufsfachschulen*) with 285,500 pupils, 1,337 schools for secondary technical studies (*Fachoberschulen/Fachgymnasien*) with 235,400 students.

In 1993–4 there were a total of 1,874,938 students at institutions of higher education, of whom 1,296,231 were attending universities. The largest universities are in Munich, Berlin, Hamburg, Bonn, Frankfurt and Cologne.

CULTURE

Modern (or New High) German has developed from the time of the Reformation to the present day, with differences of dialect in Austria, Alsace, Luxembourg, Liechtenstein and the German-speaking cantons of Switzerland.

The literary language is usually regarded as having become fixed by Luther and Zwingli at the Reformation, since which time many great names occur in all branches, notably philosophy, from Leibnitz (1646–1716) to Kant (1724–1804), Fichte (1762–1814), Schelling (1775–1854) and Hegel (1770–1831); drama, from Goethe (1749–1832) and Schiller (1759–1805) to Gerhart Hauptmann (1862–1946); and poetry, Heine (1797–1856). Seven German authors have received the Nobel Prize for Literature: Theodor Mommsen (1902), R. Eucken (1908), P. Heyse (1909), Gerhart Hauptmann (1912), Thomas Mann (1929), N. Sachs (1966) and Heinrich Böll (1972).

GHANA
The Republic of Ghana

Ghana is situated on the Gulf of Guinea, between 3° 07′ W. and 1° 14′ E. longitude, and extends 441 miles north from Cape Three Points (4° 45′ N.) to 11° 11′ N. It is bounded on the north by Burkina, on the west by the Côte d'Ivoire, on the east by Togo, and on the south by the Atlantic Ocean. Although tropical, Ghana is cooler than many countries in similar latitudes. It has a total area of 92,099 sq. miles (238,537 sq. km).

The population (UN estimate 1994) was 16,944,000. Most are Sudanese Negroes, although Hamitic strains are common in the north. The official language is English. The principal indigenous language group is Akan, of which Twi and Fanti are the most commonly used. Ga, Ewe and languages of the Mole-Dagbani group are common in certain regions. Most Ghanaians are Christians, although there is a substantial Muslim minority in the north.

CAPITAL – ΨAccra. Population of the Greater Accra Region (including Tema) was (1990 estimate) 1,781,100. Other towns are Kumasi, Tamale, ΨSekondi-Takoradi, ΨCape Coast, Sunyani, Ho, Koforidua, Wa and ΨWinneba.

CURRENCY – Cedi of 100 pesewas.

FLAG – Equal horizontal bands of red over gold over green; five-point black star on gold stripe.

NATIONAL ANTHEM – God Bless our Homeland Ghana.

NATIONAL DAY – 6 March (Independence Day).

GOVERNMENT

First reached by Europeans in the 15th century, the constituent parts of Ghana came under British administration at various times, the original Gold Coast Colony being constituted in 1874; Ashanti in 1901; and the Northern Territories Protectorate in 1901. The territory of Trans-Volta-Togoland, part of the former German colony of Togo, was mandated to Britain by the League of

Nations after the First World War, and remained under British administration as a United Nations Trusteeship after the Second World War. After a plebiscite in 1956, under UN auspices, the territory was integrated with the Gold Coast Colony. The former Gold Coast Colony and associated territories became the independent state of Ghana on 6 March 1957 and became a republic in 1960.

Since 1966 Ghana has experienced long periods of military rule (1966–9, 1972–9, 1982–92) interspersed with short-lived civilian governments. A coup in 1979 led to the formation of an Armed Forces Revolutionary Council chaired by Flt. Lt. Jerry Rawlings. Civilian rule was restored in 1979 but overthrown on 31 December 1981, when another coup brought Flt. Lt. Rawlings back to power.

A referendum in April 1992 approved a new multiparty constitution and the legalization of political parties. The National Democratic Congress (NDC) was established as a political party from the ruling Provisional National Defence Council. Flt. Lt. Rawlings won the presidential election in November 1992 and the NDC won parliamentary elections in December 1992, which were boycotted by most opposition parties and most of the electorate. The Fourth Republic was declared on 7 January 1993 and a new government nominated by the President and approved by parliament took office in March 1993. As executive President, Flt. Lt. (retd) Rawlings also chairs the Cabinet. The presidential term is four years, renewable only once.

For political and administrative purposes Ghana is divided into ten regions, each headed by a Regional Minister who is the representative of the central government.

HEAD OF STATE

President, Flt. Lt. (retd) Jerry John Rawlings, *took power* 31 December 1981, *elected* 3 November 1992
Vice-President, Kow Nkensen Arkaah

CABINET *as at August 1996*

The President
The Vice-President
Defence, Mahama Iddrisu
Finance and Economic Planning, Mines and Energy, Richard Kwame Peprah
Foreign Affairs, Acting Attorney-General and Justice, Dr Obed Asamoah
Information, Kofi Quakyi
Parliamentary Affairs, J. H. Owusu-Acheampong
Interior, Col. (retd) E. M. Osei-Owusu
Trade and Industries, Ibrahim Issaka Adam
Transport and Communications, Edward Salia
Education, Harry Sawyer
Local Government and Rural Development, Kwamena Ahwoi
Food and Agriculture, Cdre (retd) Steve Obimpeh
Employment and Social Welfare, David Boateng
Environment, Christine Amoaka-Nuamah
Health, Eunice Brookman-Amissah
Lands and Forestry, Dr Kwabena Adjei
Minister of State, Without Portfolio, Maj. (retd) Emmanuel Tetteh
Works and Housing, Ebenezer Kwabene Foso

GHANA HIGH COMMISSION
104 Highgate Hill, London N6 5HE
Tel 0181-342 8686
High Commissioner, new appointment awaited
Acting High Commissioner, Patrick Hayford
Defence Adviser, Brig. H. W. K. Agbevey
Counsellor, A. K. Budu-Amoako (*Trade*)

BRITISH HIGH COMMISSION
PO Box 296, Osu Link, Accra
Tel: Accra 221665
High Commissioner, HE Ian Mackley, CMG, apptd 1996
Deputy High Commissioner, D. Wyatt
Defence Adviser, Lt.-Col. A. R. Gale, MBE
First Secretary (Commercial), W. F. Somerset

BRITISH COUNCIL DIRECTOR, T. Cowin, Liberia Road (PO Box 771), Accra. There is also an office in Kumasi.

ECONOMY

Agriculture is the basis of the economy, employing 70 per cent of the work-force. Crops include cocoa, the largest single source of revenue, rice, cassava, avocado pears, oranges and pineapples, groundnuts, corn, millet, oil palms, yams, maize and vegetables. Livestock is raised in uncultivated areas. Attempts are being made to diversify agricultural production, with cash crops such as coffee and tobacco being cultivated for export. Fishing is important in coastal areas and in the Volta lake and river system.

Manganese production ranks among the world's largest, with 238,430 tonnes of ore being produced in 1994; diamonds and bauxite are also produced. The Ashanti Goldfields Corporation is one of the world's largest producers and was privatized in 1994 with estimated gold reserves of 20.3 million ounces. Some 30,000 persons are employed by the mining companies.

Small-scale traditional industries include tailoring, goldsmithing and carpentry. Priority has been given in recent years to establishing a number of manufacturing industries and a modern industrial complex has developed in the Accra-Tema area. Tourism is also of importance.

Since 1966 the Volta Dams at Akosombo and Kpong have generated hydro-electric power for the processing of bauxite and fed a power transmission network for most of Ghana, Togo and Benin.

Under the Economic Recovery Programme (ERP) in place since 1983, the Ghanaian economy has achieved a growth rate of 6 per cent a year for the past decade and paid off a large proportion of its foreign debt; debt servicing had fallen to 23 per cent of export earnings in 1993. Total external debt was US$4,589 million in 1993. IMF and World Bank support for the ERP's free market and deregulatory restructuring has gained Ghana US$3,858 million in soft loans and grants in the past decade. GDP growth was forecast at 5 per cent for 1996.

TRADE

Principal exports are cocoa, timber, minerals and gold. Principal imports are road vehicles, manufacturing equipment, petroleum and raw materials.

Trade with UK	1994	1995
Imports from UK	£190,625,000	£240,081,000
Exports to UK	138,814,000	163,812,000

COMMUNICATIONS

The Kotoka Airport at Accra is an international airport and Ghana Airways is the national airline. There are also internal airports at Takoradi, Kumasi, Sunyani, and Tamale.

There are 20,000 miles of motorable roads, of which 2,335 miles are bitumenized. There are 600 miles of railway, linking Accra and the principal ports of Takoradi and Tema with their hinterlands, the mining centres and with each other.

Takoradi Harbour consists of seven quay berths: one is leased specially for manganese exports. Tema Harbour has ten berths for larger ocean-going vessels and the largest dry dock on the West African coast. An oil berth has also been built to serve the refinery at Tema.

GREECE
Elliniki Dimokratia

Greece is a maritime state in the south-east of Europe, bounded on the north by Albania, the Former Yugoslav Republic of Macedonia and Bulgaria, on the south and west by the Ionian and Mediterranean seas, and on the east by Turkey and the Aegean Sea. It has an estimated area of 50,944 sq. miles (131,944 sq. km).

The main areas are: Macedonia (which includes Mt Athos and the island of Thasos), Thrace (including the island of Samothrace), Epirus, Thessaly, Continental Greece (which includes the island of Euboea and the Sporades), Crete and the Peloponnese. The main island groups are the Sporades (of which the largest is Skyros), the Dodecanese or Southern Sporades (Rhodes, Astypalaia, Karpathos, Kassos, Nisyros, Kalymnos, Leros, Patmos, Kos, Symi, Khalki, Tilos), the Cyclades (about 200, including Syros, Andros, Tinos, Mykonos, Naxos, Paros, Santorini, Milos and Serifos), the Ionian Islands (Corfu, Paxos, Levkas, Ithaca, Cephalonia, Zante and Cerigo), the Aegean Islands (Chios, Lesbos, Limnos and Samos). In Crete from about 3000 to 1400 BC a civilization flourished which spread its influence throughout the Aegean, and the ruins of the palace of Minos at Knossos afford evidence of astonishing comfort and luxury.

The population at the 1991 census was 10,256,464. Over 97 per cent are adherents of the Greek Orthodox Church, which is the state religion.

CAPITAL – Athens, population (including ΨPiraeus and suburbs), 3,096,775 (1991 census). Other large towns are (1991) ΨThessaloniki (Salonika) (739,998); ΨPatras (172,763); ΨHeraklion (Crete) (127,600); ΨVolos (115,732); Larissa (113,426); ΨCanea (Crete) (65,519); ΨKavalla (58,576); ΨRhodes (43,619).

CURRENCY – Drachma of 100 leptae.

FLAG – Blue and white stripes with a white cross on a blue field in the canton.

NATIONAL ANTHEM – Imnos Eis Tin Eleftherian (Hymn to Freedom).

NATIONAL DAY – March 25 (Independence Day).

GOVERNMENT

Greece was under Turkish rule from the mid 15th century until a war of independence (1821–7) led to the establishment of a Greek kingdom in the Peloponnese in 1829. The remainder of Greece gradually became independent until the Dodecanese were returned by Italy in 1947. After heavy resistance to the Nazi German occupation of 1941–4, a civil war between monarchist and Communist groups lasted from 1946 to 1949, and tension between right-wing and radical groups continued after 1949. In 1967 right-wing elements in the army seized power and established a military regime (the 'Greek Colonels'). The King went into voluntary exile in 1967; in 1974 the monarchy was abolished and a republic established.

Unrest in Athens in 1973–4 intensified after the government was involved in the overthrow of President Makarios of Cyprus in July 1974, and led the Colonels to surrender power. Konstantinos Karamanlis (Prime Minister 1955–63) returned from exile to form a provisional government, and the first elections for ten years were held in 1974. The constitutional position of the King, who was still in exile, remained unsettled until 8 December, when the restoration of the monarchy was rejected by referendum and Greece became a republic.

A new constitution came into force in 1975. In 1986 most executive power was transferred from the president to the government and the president became a ceremonial figure. The unicameral 300-member Chamber of Deputies is elected for a four-year term by universal adult suffrage under a system of proportional representation, with a three per cent threshold for parliamentary representation.

The most recent general election was held on 22 September 1996* with the Panhellenic Socialist Party (PASOK) winning 162 seats, the New Democracy Party (Christian Democrats) 108 seats, the Communist Party 11 seats, the Coalition of the Left and Progress ten seats, and the Democratic Social Movement nine seats.

A dispute with the Former Yugoslav Republic of Macedonia over its alleged territorial claim to northern Greece was settled in September 1995 when an accord was signed normalizing relations.

HEAD OF STATE
President of the Hellenic Republic, Constantine Stephanopoulos, *elected by parliament* 8 March 1995

CABINET *as at August 1996*

Prime Minister, Kostas Simitis
Foreign Affairs, Theodoros Pangalos
Interior, Public Administration and Decentralization, Akis Tsohatzopoulos
National Defence, Gerasimos Arsenis
Justice, Evangelos Venizelo
National Economy, Yiannos Papantoniou
Merchant Marine, Kosmas Sfiriou
Agriculture, Stephanos Tzoumakas
Finance, Alexandros Papadoupoulos
Labour and Social Security, Evangelos Yannopoulos
Health and Welfare, Athanassios Peponis
Education and Religious Affairs, Georgios Papandreou
Culture, Stavros Benos
Public Order, Kostas Geitonas
Macedonia and Thrace, Philip Petsalnikos
Aegean, Antonis Kotsakas
Environment, Town Planning and Public Works, Kostas Laliotis
Development, Vasso Papandreou

Transport and Communications, Athanassious Tsouras
Press and Media, Dimitri Reppas

EMBASSY OF GREECE
1A Holland Park, London WII 3TP
Tel 0171-229 3850
Ambassador Extraordinary and Plenipotentiary, HE Vassilis
Zafiropoulos, apptd 1996
Defence Attaché, Capt. A. Economou
Minister (Consular Affairs), G. Costoulas
Counsellor, A. Missa-Kerkentzes (*Economic Affairs*)

There are Honorary Consulates at Belfast, Birmingham,
Edinburgh, Falmouth, Glasgow, Leeds and Southampton.

BRITISH EMBASSY
1 Ploutarchou Street, 10675 Athens
Tel: Athens 7236211
Ambassador Extraordinary and Plenipotentiary, HE Sir
Michael Llewellyn Smith, KCVO, CMG, apptd 1996
Deputy Head of Mission, Counsellor and Consul-General, C. J.
Denne, CMG
Defence and Military Attaché, Brig. W. A. McMahon
First Secretary (Commercial), G. G. Thomas

BRITISH CONSULAR OFFICES – There are British
Consular Offices at Athens, Corfu, Patras, Kos, Rhodes,
Salonika, Heraklion (Crete) and Syros.

BRITISH COUNCIL DIRECTOR, Dr J. L. Munby, OBE, 17
Plateia Philikis Etairias (PO Box 3488), Kolonaki
Square, Athens 10210. There is also an office at Salonika.

BRITISH-HELLENIC CHAMBER OF COMMERCE, 25 Vas.
Sofias Avenue, GR-106 74 Athens. Tel: 72 10 361

DEFENCE

The total active armed forces number 171,300 personnel
(114,000 conscripts); conscripts serve between 19 and 23
months. The strength of the Army is 125,000 (98,000
conscripts), in addition there are 34,000 in the National
Guard. Equipment includes 2,268 main battle tanks, 2,668
armoured personnel carriers and armoured infantry fighting vehicles, and 2,168 artillery pieces. The Navy consists
of 19,500 men (1,600 conscripts) and is equipped with eight
submarines, four destroyers and nine frigates with 16
armed helicopters. The Air Force consists of 26,800 men
(14,400 conscripts) and has a total of 351 combat aircraft.
Greece maintains 2,250 army personnel in Cyprus.
There is also a paramilitary Gendarmerie of 26,500
personnel. Some 550 US personnel are stationed in Greece.

ECONOMY

The 1989–93 New Democracy government followed an
IMF-recommended austerity programme of privatization
and reduction of the public sector. This has been partially
reversed by the PASOK government, which has slowed
privatization. The economy is improving although it
remains in poor condition, with inflation at 8.1 per cent,
the budget deficit 9.2 per cent of GDP, public debt at 112
per cent of GDP, large-scale tax evasion and a huge black
economy.
Though there has been a substantial measure of
industrialization, agriculture still employs about a fifth of
the working population and contributes 12 per cent of
GDP. The most important agricultural products are
tobacco, wheat, cotton, sugar, rice, fruit (olives, peaches,
vines, oranges, lemons, figs, almonds and currant-vines).
Export of fresh fruit, currants and vegetables are an
important contributor to the economy.
The principal minerals are nickel, bauxite, iron ore, iron
pyrites, manganese magnesite, chrome, lead, zinc and

emery, and prospecting for petroleum is being carried on.
The chief industries are textiles (cotton, woollen and
synthetics), chemicals, cement, glass, metallurgy, shipbuilding, domestic electrical equipment and footwear, the
production of aluminium, nickel, iron and steel products,
tyres, chemicals, fertilizers and sugar (from locally-grown
beet). Food processing and ancillary industries are also
growing.
The development of the country's electric power
resources, irrigation and land reclamation schemes, and
the exploitation of lignite resources for fuel and industrial
purposes are also being carried out. Tourism has developed rapidly, with over 10 million visitors in 1994.

TRADE	1993	1995
Total imports	US$17,615m	US$22,854m
Total exports	5,034m	5,774m
Trade with UK	1994	1995
Imports from UK	£908,837,000	£990,200,000
Exports to UK	347,634,000	403,900,000

COMMUNICATIONS

The 2,650 km of railways are state-owned, with the
exception of the Athens–Piraeus Electric Railway. Roads
total over 35,500 km, of which about 25 per cent are
national highways and just under 30,000 km are provincial
roads. The Greek mercantile fleet numbers 1,864 ships
over 100 tons gross with a total tonnage of 53,778,128 tons
gross. Athens has direct airline links with Australasia,
North America, most countries in Europe, Africa and the
Middle East.

EDUCATION

Education is free and compulsory from the age of six to 15
and is maintained by state grants. There are ten universities: Athens, Thessaloniki, Patras, Thrace, Ioannina, Piraeus, Aegean, Ionian, Thessaly and Crete. There are
several other institutes of higher learning, mostly in
Athens.

CULTURE

Greek civilization emerged *c.* 1300 BC and the poems of
Homer, which were probably current *c.* 800 BC, record the
struggle between the Achaeans of Greece and the
Phrygians of Troy (1194 to 1184 BC).
The spoken language of modern Greece is descended
from the Common Greek of Alexander the Great's empire.
Katharevousa, a conservative literary dialect evolved by
Adamantios Corais (Diamant Coray) (1748–1833) and
used for official and technical matters, has been phased out.
Novels and poetry are mostly in *dimotiki,* a progressive
literary dialect which owes much to John Psycharis
(1854–1929). The poets Solomos, Palamas, Cavafy and
Sikelianos have won a European reputation. George
Seferis (1963) and Odysseus Elytis (1979) have won the
Nobel Prize for Literature.

GRENADA
The State of Grenada

Grenada is situated between 12°13′–11° 58′ N. latitude and
61° 20′–61° 35′ W. longitude, and is about 90 miles north of
Trinidad, 68 miles south-south-west of St Vincent, and
about 120 miles south-west of Barbados. The island is
about 21 miles long and 12 miles wide, with an area of 133
sq. miles (344 sq. km). Also a part of Grenada are some of

the Grenadines islets, the largest of which is Carriacou, 13 square miles in area. The country is mountainous.
The population is 95,000 (1992 census).

CAPITAL – ΨSt George's (population 10,000) on the south-west coast, has a good harbour.
CURRENCY – East Caribbean dollar (EC$) of 100 cents.
FLAG – Divided diagonally into yellow and green triangles within a red border containing six yellow stars, a yellow star on a red disc in the centre and a nutmeg on the green triangle in the hoist.
NATIONAL DAY – 7 February (Independence Day).

GOVERNMENT

Discovered by Columbus in 1498, and named Conception, Grenada was originally colonized by France and was ceded to Great Britain by the Treaty of Versailles 1783. It became an Associated State in 1967 and an independent nation within the Commonwealth on 7 February 1974.

The government was overthrown in 1979 by the New Jewel Movement and a People's Revolutionary Government was set up. In October 1983 disagreements within the PRG led to the death of Prime Minister Maurice Bishop, whose government was replaced by a Revolutionary Military Council. These events prompted the intervention of Caribbean and US forces. The Governor-General installed an advisory council to act as an interim government until a general election was held in December 1984. A phased withdrawal of US forces was completed by June 1985.

The Queen is head of state and is represented by a Governor-General. Legislative power is vested in a bicameral parliament consisting of an elected 15-member House of Representatives and a nine-member Senate appointed by the Governor-General. The general election held on 20 June 1995 was won by the New National Party led by Dr Keith Mitchell, with eight seats in the House of Representatives to the National Democratic Congress's five seats.

Governor-General, HE Daniel Williams, QC, apptd 1996

CABINET *as at August 1996*

Prime Minister, Finance, Trade and Industry, External Affairs, National Security, Dr Hon. Keith Mitchell
Tourism, Civil Aviation, Women's Affairs, Co-operatives and Social Security, Hon. Grace Duncan
Education, Hon. Lourina Waldron
Youth, Sports, Culture and Community Development, Hon. Adrian Mitchell
Labour, Legal Affairs, Local Government and CARICOM Affairs, Sen. Hon. Lawrence Joseph
Agriculture, Forestry, Lands and Fisheries, Sen. Hon. Joslyn Whiteman
Communications, Works and Public Utilities, Sen. Hon. Gregory Bowen
Health, Housing and Environment, Hon. Mark Isaacs
Without Portfolio, Dr Hon. Raphael Fletcher
Ministers of State, Hon. Patrick Bubb (*Finance*); Hon. Willan Drewsbury (*Youth*); Hon. Oliver Archibald (*Works*)

GRENADA HIGH COMMISSION
1 Collingham Gardens, London sw5 0HW
Tel 0171-373 7809
High Commissioner, HE June Lendore, apptd 1996

BRITISH HIGH COMMISSIONER, HE Richard Thomas, CMG, resides at Bridgetown, Barbados

JUDICIARY

Justice is administered by the Organization of Eastern Caribbean States (OECS) Supreme Court, which is composed of a High Court of Justice and a two-tier Court of Appeals, and by Magistrates' Courts. The final court of appeal remains the UK Privy Council.

ECONOMY

The economy is principally agrarian, with cocoa, nutmegs and bananas the major crops. Fruit and vegetables are grown and a little livestock raised for domestic consumption. The fishing industry is being developed. Manufacturing consists of processing agricultural products and the production of textiles, concrete, aluminium and handicrafts.

Tourism has prospered since the opening of the Point Salines International Airport in 1984 and is the main foreign exchange earner. A hotel expansion programme is taking place. The number of cruise ship calls to Grenada in 1995 was 438, bringing 249,879 out of a total of 357,836 tourists.

TRADE

In 1993 total exports amounted to US$20.4 million, of which 84 per cent were agricultural products, mainly nutmeg, cocoa, bananas and mace. Total imports were US$118.4 million, mainly machinery and manufactured goods. The total external debt in 1993 was US$66.4 million.

Trade with UK	1994	1995
Imports from UK	£7,335,000	£7,582,000
Exports to UK	2,707,000	3,311,000

GUATEMALA
República de Guatemala

Guatemala, in Central America, is situated in 13° 45' to 17° 49' N. latitude and 88° 12' 49" to 92°13' 43" W. longitude and has an area of 42,042 sq. miles (108,889 sq. km). The country is traversed from west to east by mountains containing volcanic summits rising to 13,000 feet above sea level; earthquakes are frequent. There are numerous rivers. The climate is hot and malarial near the coast, temperate in the higher regions.

The population (estimate 1994) is 10,322,000. The language is Spanish, but 40 per cent of the population speak an Indian language.

CAPITAL – Guatemala City, population estimate (1990), 1,675,589. Quezaltenango has a population of over 100,000. Other towns are ΨPuerto Barrios (23,000), Mazatenango (21,000), and Antigua (30,000).
CURRENCY – Quetzal (Q) of 100 centavos.
FLAG – Three vertical bands, blue, white, blue; coat of arms on white stripe.
NATIONAL ANTHEM – Guatemala Feliz (Guatemala be praised).
NATIONAL DAY – 15 September.

GOVERNMENT

Guatemala was under Spanish rule from 1524 until 1821 when it became independent. It formed part of the Confederation of Central America from 1823 to 1839.

After military coups in 1963, 1982 and 1983, civilian rule was restored with the election of a Constituent Assembly in 1984 and the promulgation of a new constitution in 1985

In May 1993 President Serrano partially suspended the constitution and attempted to rule by decree but was effectively ousted by the army on 1 June. Ramiro de León Carpio, was elected President by Congress to serve out Serrano's term to January 1996.

President de León continued the attempt to curb political corruption and in November 1993 forced Congress and the Supreme Court to dissolve themselves and to agree to constitutional changes, including reducing the presidential term to four years, which were ratified by a referendum in January 1994. Legislative elections to a smaller 80-seat National Congress were held in August 1994 and the new Congress elected 13 new Supreme Court judges in October 1994. Elections to the National Congress on 12 November 1995 were won by the National Advancement Party (PAN) which won 43 seats to the Guatemalan Republican Front's 21. The presidential election in January 1996 was won by Alvaro Arzú of the PAN.

Executive power is vested in the directly elected president, who appoints the Cabinet and is assisted by the vice-president. Legislative authority is vested in the National Congress.

The republic is divided into 22 departments.

INSURGENCY

Since 1960 the armed forces have been fighting insurgency by the left-wing, mainly Mayan Indian, guerrillas of the Guatemalan Revolutionary National Unity Movement (URNG). Some 100,000 have been killed in the fighting, which climaxed in the Army's 1979–82 counter-insurgency campaign. Government-URNG negotiations began in 1991 and have continued since, leading to a reduction in fighting and agreements in 1993. In March 1994 a human rights accord was reached under which a 300-strong UN Observer Mission (MINUGUA) was established in November 1994 to supervise the implementation of government–URNG accords. An accord recognizing the rights of the indigenous population was signed in March 1995. Peace talks continue and the URNG has shrunk to around 2,000 guerrillas.

HEAD OF STATE

President, Alvaro Arzú Irigoyen, *sworn in* 14 January 1996
Vice-President, Luis Flores Asturias

GOVERNMENT *as at August 1996*
The President
The Vice-President
Foreign Affairs, Eduardo Stein
Interior, Rodolfo Mendoza
Defence, Gen. Julio Balconi
Finance, José Alejandro Arevalo
Economy, Juan Mauricio Wurmser
Communications, Fritz García Gallont
Education, Arabella Castro
Energy, Leonel López Rodas
Agriculture, Luis Reyes Mayen
Public Health and Social Security, Marco Tulio Sosa
Labour, Arnoldo Ortiz Moscoso

EMBASSY OF GUATEMALA
13 Fawcett Street, London SW10 9HN
Tel 0171-351 3042
Ambassador Extraordinary and Plenipotentiary, HE Edmundo Nanne, apptd 1992

BRITISH EMBASSY
Edificio Centro Financiero (7th Floor), Seventh Avenue 5–10, Zone 4, Guatemala City
Tel: Guatemala City 321601

Ambassador Extraordinary and Plenipotentiary, HE Peter Newton, apptd 1995
There is also a consulate at Puerto Barrios.

ECONOMY

The central government revenue in 1992 was Quetzales 5,483 million, and expenditure Quetzales 5,756 million. Agriculture provides 25 per cent of GDP. The principal export is coffee, other articles being manufactured goods, sugar, bananas, cotton, beef and essential oils. The chief imports are petroleum, vehicles, machinery and foodstuffs.

The chief seaports are San José de Guatemala and Champerico on the Pacific and Santo Tomás de Castilla and Puerto Barrios on the Atlantic side.

TRADE WITH UK	1994	1995
Imports from UK	£22,686,000	£31,103,000
Exports to UK	14,683,000	14,898,000

GUINEA
République de Guinée

Formerly part of French West Africa, Guinea has a coastline on the Atlantic Ocean between Guinea-Bissau and Sierra Leone, and in the interior is adjacent to Senegal, Mali, Côte d'Ivoire, Liberia and Sierra Leone. The area is 94,926 sq. miles (245,857 sq. km). The population (UN estimate 1994) is 6,501,000, mostly of the Fullah, Malinké and Soussou tribes.

CAPITAL – ΨConakry (763,000). Other towns are Kankan, which is connected with Conakry by a railway, Kindia, N'Zérékoré, Mamou, Siguiri and Labé.
CURRENCY – Guinea franc of 100 centimes.
FLAG – Three vertical stripes of red, yellow and green.
NATIONAL DAY – 2 October (Anniversary of Proclamation of Independence).

GOVERNMENT

Guinea was separated from Senegal in 1891 and administered by France as a separate colony until 1958. On 2 October 1958 Guinea became an independent republic.

M. Sékou Touré assumed office as head of the new government, and was elected President in 1961. The death of President Sékou Touré in 1984 was followed by a military coup. Guinea was ruled by a military government directed by a Military Committee for National Recovery (CMRN). A new constitution, providing for the end of military rule and the introduction of a two-party system within five years, was approved by referendum in 1990.

In January 1991 the CMRN was dissolved and a mixed civilian-military Transitional Committee for National Recovery (CTRN) was established which appointed a new government. Disturbances throughout 1991 led by trade unions and opposition parties caused the government to introduce a full multiparty system in April 1992, since when 40 opposition parties have been legalized. A presidential election held in 1993 was won by the incumbent President Conté with 51 per cent of the vote amid opposition claims of electoral fraud. Legislative elections in June 1995 were won by President Conté's Party of Unity and Progress (PUP), which gained 71 of the 114 National Assembly seats. An unsuccessful military coup was staged in February 1996.

HEAD OF STATE

President, Maj.-Gen. Lansana Conté, *took power* 3 April 1984, *elected* 19 December 1993

COUNCIL OF MINISTERS *as at June 1996*
The President
Foreign Affairs, Kozo Zomanigui
Interior, Alseny René Gomez
Defence, Maj. Abdourahmane Diallo
Justice, Salifou Sylla
Planning and Co-operation, Michekl Kamano
Finance, El Hadj Camara
Economic and Financial Control, Kazaliou Balde
Mines and Geology, Facinet Fofana
Energy and Environment, Assifat Dorank
Urban Affairs and Housing, Lt.-Col. Jean Traore
Health, Kandjoura Drame
Administrative Reform, Germaine Dualamu
Youth, Arts and Sport, Toumani Dakoum Sako
Secondary Education, Aicha Bah Diallo
Higher Education and Scientific Research, Alioune Banire Diallo
Public Works, Cellou Dalen Diallo
Trade and Industry, Seku Konate
Transport, Maj. Ibrahima Sylla
Agriculture, Makale Camara
Fishing, Mamadi Diare
Labour and Social Affairs, Josephine Guilavo
Childhood, Yvonne Conde
Post and Telecommunications, Emmanuel Gnan
High Commissioner for Information, Alpha Camara
High Commissioner for Tourism, Sidi Cissoko
Secretary-General to the President, Rene Loua Fassou

EMBASSY OF THE REPUBLIC OF GUINEA
51 rue de la Faisanderie, 75061 Paris, France
Tel: Paris 47048148
Ambassador Extraordinary and Plenipotentiary, HE Lamine Kamara, apptd 1994

BRITISH CONSULATE
BP 834 Conakry, Guinea
British Ambassador, HE Alan Furness, CMG, resident at Dakar, Senegal

ECONOMY

The principal products are bauxite, alumina, iron ore, palm kernels, millet, rice, coffee, bananas, pineapples and rubber. At Sangaredi in the mountainous hinterland large deposits of bauxite are mined. Deposits of iron ore, gold, diamonds and uranium have also been discovered. Principal imports are cotton goods, manufactured goods, tobacco, petroleum products, sugar, rice, flour and salt; exports, bauxite, alumina, iron ore, diamonds, coffee, hides, bananas, palm kernels and pineapples.

TRADE WITH UK	1994	1995
Imports from UK	£22,307,000	£16,643,000
Exports to UK	1,675,000	2,983,000

GUINEA-BISSAU
República da Guiné-Bissau

Guinea-Bissau, formerly Portuguese Guinea, lies in western Africa, between Senegal and Guinea; it has an area of 13,948 sq. miles (36,125 sq. km), and a population (UN estimate 1994) of 1,050,000. The main ethnic groups are the Balante, Malinké, Fulani, Mandjako and Pepel.

CAPITAL – ΨBissau, population (census 1979) 109,486, is also the chief port.
CURRENCY – Guinea-Bissau peso of 100 centavos.

FLAG – Horizontal bands of yellow over green with vertical red band in the hoist charged with a black star.
NATIONAL DAY – 24 September (Independence Day).

GOVERNMENT

Guinea-Bissau achieved independence on 24 September 1974. Following a coup led by Maj. (now Brig.-Gen.) Vieira in 1980, the Assembly was suspended and a Revolutionary Council was established. Under a new constitution adopted in 1984, the Revolutionary Council became a 15-member Council of State and an Assembly of 150 members was set up. The ruling African Party for the Independence of Guinea and Cape Verde (PAIGC) voted to introduce a multiparty system in January 1991. Ten opposition parties have been legalized since November 1991. Legislative elections to a new 100-seat legislature were held on 3 July 1994 and won by the PAIGC, which took 64 seats. Brig.-Gen. Vieira won the second round of the presidential election on 7 August 1994 with 52 per cent of the vote.

HEAD OF STATE
Chairman of the Republic, C.-in-C. of the Armed Forces, Brig.-Gen. João Bernardo Vieira, *took power* November 1980, *elected* June 1989, *re-elected for a five-year term* 7 August 1994

COUNCIL OF MINISTERS *as at August 1996*
Prime Minister, Manuel Saturnino da Costa
Cabinet Chair and Parliamentary Affairs, Helder Proença
National Defence, Zeca Martins
Foreign Affairs, Fernando Delfim da Silva
Interior, Amaro Correia
Territorial Administration, Raimundo Pereira
War Veterans, Arafan Mane
Commerce, Luis Oliveira Sanca
Education, Paulo Silva
Youth, Culture and Sport, Ibrahim Sow
Civil Service and Labour, Abubacar Balde
Public Works, Armando Antonio Napoco
Transport and Communications, Ansumane Mane
Tourism, Crafts and Environment, Cipriano Casama
Planning and International Development, Aristides Gomes
Justice, Daniel Ferreira
Finance, Rui Dia de Sousa
Rural Development and Agriculture, Antonio Issac Monteiro
Natural Resources, Energy and Industry, João Gomes Cardoso
Fishing, Artur Silva
Health, Eugenia Saldanha Araujo
Social and Women's Affairs, Nharebat Ninçaia N'Tchasso
Secretaries of State, Francisco Correia (*Treasury*); Ibrahima Dieme (*Planning*); Carlos Pinho Brandao (*Energy*)

EMBASSY OF THE REPUBLIC OF GUINEA-BISSAU
94 Rue St Lazare, Paris 9, France
Tel: Paris 45261851
Ambassador Extraordinary and Plenipotentiary, HE Leonel Sebastiao Vieira, apptd 1995

BRITISH CONSULATE
Mavegro Int., CP100, Bissau
British Ambassador, HE Alan Furness, CMG, resident at Dakar, Senegal

ECONOMY

The country produces rice, coconuts, groundnuts and palm oil products. Cattle are raised, and there are bauxite deposits in the south. The government has started to introduce free market reforms to the economy and in January 1995 agreed a three-year loan of US$14 million with the IMF to support continuing reforms.

Trade with UK	1994	1995
Imports from UK	£4,016,000	£1,889,000
Exports to UK	4,000	60,000

GUYANA
The Co-operative Republic of Guyana

Guyana (formerly British Guiana) is situated on the north-east coast of South America, bordering Venezuela, Brazil and Suriname. It has a total area of 83,000 sq. miles (214,969 sq. km).

There is a narrow alluvial coastal belt ten to 40 miles deep, mainly below sea level, which is drained and irrigated by canals constructed by the Dutch. Mountainous dense rain forest lies behind this, reaching its highest point at Mount Roraima (9,000 ft) on the junction of the Guyana–Brazil–Venezuela borders. In the south-west lies the open savanna of the Rupununi. The country is intersected by numerous large rivers and has many waterfalls, notably the Kaieteur Fall on the Potaro River, the Horse Shoe Falls on the Essequibo and the Marina Fall on the Ipobe. There are two dry seasons: mid-February to end April and mid-August to end November.

The population (UN estimate 1994) is 825,000.

CAPITAL – ΨGeorgetown. Estimated population, including environs, 185,000. Other towns are: Linden (29,000); ΨNew Amsterdam (23,000); Corriverton (17,000).

CURRENCY – Guyana dollar (G$) of 100 cents.

FLAG – Green with a yellow, white-bordered triangle based on the hoist and surmounted by a red, black-bordered triangle.

NATIONAL ANTHEM – Dear Land of Guyana.

NATIONAL DAYS – 26 May (Independence Day); 23 February (Republic Day).

GOVERNMENT

Guyana became independent on 26 May 1966, with a Governor-General appointed by The Queen. It became a republic on 23 February 1970. The Independence constitution was replaced by a new constitution promulgated in 1980. It provides for an executive president who serves a five-year term, a first vice-president and prime minister, and a National Assembly of 65 members, of which 53 are elected nationally by proportional representation and 12 are regional representatives.

Presidential and general elections were held on 5 October 1992 after proper voter registration lists and electoral machinery had finallly been established after many years. In the presidential election Dr Cheddi Jagan defeated the incumbent Desmond Hoyte and in the legislative election Jagan's People's Progressive Party (PPP) defeated the People's National Congress (PNC) which had governed since independence. In the National Assembly the state of the parties at August 1994 was: PPP 36, PNC 26, Working People's Alliance 2, United Force 1.

HEAD OF STATE
Executive President, Dr Cheddi Bharrat Jagan, *elected* 5 October 1992, *sworn in* 9 October 1992

CABINET *as at August 1996*
The Executive President
First Vice-President, Prime Minister, Mining, Samuel Hinds
Foreign Affairs, Clement Rohee
Finance, Bharrat Jagdeo
Attorney-General, Justice, Bernard de Santos

Home Affairs, Feroze Mohamed
Agriculture, Reepu Daman Persaud
Education, Dale Bisnauth
Labour, Henry Jeffrey
Health, Gail Teixera
Cabinet Secretary, Roger Luncheon
Ministers of State, Clinton Collymore (*Agriculture*); Harry Nokta Persaud (*Public Works, Communications and Regional Development*); Michael Shree Chand (*Trade*); Vilbert de Souza (*Amerindian Affairs*)

GUYANA HIGH COMMISSION
3 Palace Court, Bayswater Road, London W2 4LP
Tel 0171-229 7684
High Commissioner, HE Laleshwar Singh, apptd 1993

BRITISH HIGH COMMISSION
44 Main Street (PO Box 10849), Georgetown
Tel: Georgetown 65881/4
High Commissioner, HE David J. Johnson, CMG, CVO, apptd 1993

JUDICATURE

The Supreme Court of Judicature consists of a Court of Appeal and a High Court. There are also Courts of Summary Jurisdiction. The Court of Appeal consists of the Chancellor as President, the Chief Justice and Justices of Appeal.

The High Court consists of the Chief Justice, as President, and nine Puisne Judges. It is a court with unlimited jurisdiction in civil matters and exercises exclusive jurisdiction in probate, divorce and admiralty, and certain other matters.

Chancellor, K. M. George
Chief Justice, Aubrey Bishop

ECONOMY

The economy is based almost entirely on the main export items of Demerara sugar, rice, bauxite and alumina. Diamonds and gold are also mined, timber and rum are produced. There is some cattle ranching in the savanna country, and oil deposits have been found there. The fishing industry is being expanded. Industry is fairly small-scale. Much emphasis is now being placed on eco-tourism.

Trade with UK	1994	1995
Imports from UK	£26,922,000	£33,946,000
Exports to UK	71,717,000	72,821,000

COMMUNICATIONS

Georgetown and New Amsterdam are the principal ports, though bauxite ships also sail to Linden, on the Demerara, and Everton, on the Berbice. There are no public railways and the few roads are confined mainly to the coastal areas. Air transport is the easiest form of communication between the coast and the interior.

There is a state-owned radio broadcasting station which operates two channels and a fledgling television service.

EDUCATION

The government assumed total control of the education system in 1976 and made education free. The government trains teachers for primary and secondary schools at its own institutions.

Approximately 1,800 students were enrolled at the University of Guyana in degree programmes and certificate and diploma courses in 1990. The government instituted fees for study at the University in 1994.

There are several technical and vocational institutions, as well as some 30 adult education schools (with an enrolment of 13,500). There are also a number of technical and vocational institutions not under the aegis of the Ministry of Education.

HAITI
République d'Haiti

The Republic of Haiti occupies the western third of the Caribbean island of Hispaniola. The area, including off-shore islands, is 10,714 sq. miles (27,750 sq. km), of which about three-quarters is mountainous. The climate is tropical with high humidity and an almost constant temperature.

The population (UN estimate 1994) is 7,035,000, of which 90 per cent are black and 10 per cent mulatto (mixed race). Both French and Creole are regarded as official languages. French is the language of government and the press but it is only spoken by the educated mulatto minority. The usual language is Creole.

CAPITAL – ΨPort-au-Prince. Population estimated at about 1 million. Other centres are: ΨCap Haitien (54,691); Gonaives (36,736); Les Cayes (27,222); Jérémie (25,117).
CURRENCY – Gourde of 100 centimes.
FLAG – Horizontally blue over red.
NATIONAL ANTHEM – La Dessalinienne.
NATIONAL DAY – 1 January.

GOVERNMENT

Haiti was a French slave colony under the name of Saint-Domingue from 1697 until 1791, when French rule was overthrown in a revolt led by Toussaint L'Ouverture, who made himself Governor-General. French rule was restored by Napoleon in 1802 but in 1803 French forces surrendered to a British naval blockade and on 1 January 1804 the colony was declared independent as Haiti by Jean Jacques Dessalines. Dessalines became Emperor of Haiti but was assassinated in 1806.

Haiti was under US military occupation from 1915 to 1934. Dr François 'Papa Doc' Duvalier was elected in 1957 and became life President in 1964. He was succeeded in 1971 by his son Jean-Claude 'Baby Doc' Duvalier who continued his father's brutal methods of maintaining power. Jean-Claude Duvalier fled to France in 1986 in the face of sustained popular unrest. Five years of political instability and military government followed until Father Jean-Bertrand Aristide, leader of the National Front for Change and Democracy, won a free presidential election in 1990.

Aristide fled to the USA following a military coup in September 1991. The UN and OAS led efforts to force the military to accept Aristide's return by imposing an oil and arms embargo and freezing the military élite's foreign assets, which forced the regime to negotiate the Governor's Island Agreement in July 1993. The Agreement provided for Aristide's return and led to the lifting of UN sanctions, but in September 1993 the military reneged on the agreement and the UN reimposed sanctions, and imposed a naval blockade and a total economic, trade and travel ban. As the USA began preparations for a UN-sponsored invasion, President Clinton sent a negotiating team to Haiti which on 18 September 1994 reached an agreement with the military regime on President Aristide's return and the flight of the military junta members abroad. The UN

sanctions were lifted and Aristide returned on 15 October and appointed a new government. The Army and police were retrained by US personnel. UN forces of the UNMIH (UN Mission in Haiti) took over responsibility for internal security and retraining Army personnel on 31 March 1995. The last US soldiers left in April 1996. Elections to the 27-member Senate and 83-member Chamber of Deputies in June to August 1995 were won by the pro-Aristide Lavalas party. The presidential election on 17 December 1995 was won by the Lavalas candidate René Préval.

HEAD OF STATE
President, René Préval, *sworn in* 7 February 1996

CABINET *as at August 1996*
Prime Minister, Rony Smarth
Foreign Affairs, Fritz Longchamp
Interior, Jean-Joseph Moliere
Economy and Finance, Fred Joseph
Commerce, Fresel Germain
Agriculture, Gérald Mathurin
Social Affairs, Pierre-Denis Amédée
Women's Affairs, Ginette Cherubin
Culture, Raoul Peck
Education, Jacques Edouard Alexis
Planning, Jean-Erick Dérice
Environment, Yves Andre Wainright
Justice, Pierre Max Antoine
Public Health and Population, Rudolphe Malebranche
Haitians Abroad, Paul Dejean
Secretaries of State, Astide Foucher Gardere (*Judicial Reform*); Adeline Chancy (*Literacy*); Robert Manuel (*Public Security*); Maryse Penette (*Tourism*); Evans Lescouflair (*Youth and Sport*)

BRITISH AMBASSADOR, HE A. R. Thomas, CMG, resident at Kingston, Jamaica

ECONOMY

UN sanctions led to a sharp decline in economic activity, with industry particularly badly hit by the shortage of fuel. US aid increased dramatically, however, under the September 1994 agreement with the military regime, with US$550 million in emergency aid for food and fuel and the establishment of a US$1,000 million reconstruction fund. The new government has initiated a programme of economic reform supported by an IMF loan of US$31 million. A privatization scheme was unveiled in March 1996.

Agricultural production declined after the ending of the colonial plantation scheme. Measures had been taken with the aim of a gradual restoration of productivity. Coffee accounts for about 32 per cent of total exports. Cocoa is the second largest export earner. Corn, sorghum and rice are also grown. Increased production of tropical fruits and vegetables is being encouraged.

Items such as leather goods, textiles, electronic components and sports equipment are manufactured, using imported raw materials, for re-export. Principal imports are raw materials for the export assembly sector, foodstuffs, machinery, vehicles, mineral oils and textiles.

TRADE WITH UK	1994	1995
Imports from UK	£7,754,000	£13,466,000
Exports to UK	539,000	1,254,000

COMMUNICATIONS

The main roads are asphalted and secondary roads are fair. Air services are maintained between the capital and the principal provincial towns and to the USA and Caribbean and South American countries. The principal towns and villages are connected by telephone and/or telegraph. There are several commercial radio stations and two television stations at Port-au-Prince. Most services remain disrupted and are under reconstruction.

EDUCATION

Education is free but estimates of illiteracy are as high as 85 per cent.

HOLY SEE, see VATICAN CITY STATE

HONDURAS
República de Honduras

Honduras, in Central America, lies between 13° and 16° 30′ N. latitude and 83° and 89° 41′ W. longitude, with a seaboard of about 375 miles on the Caribbean Sea and 63 miles on the Pacific. It borders on Guatemala, Nicaragua and El Salvador and has a total area of 43,277 sq. miles (112,088 sq. km). The country is mountainous, being traversed by the Cordilleras, with peaks rising to 1,500 and 2,400 metres above sea level. Rainfall is seasonal, May to October being wet and November to April dry.

The population is 5,493,900 (1994 estimate) and of mixed Spanish and Indian blood. The Garifunas in the north are of West Indian origin. The language is Spanish, although English is the first language of many in the islands and on the north coast.

Capital – Tegucigalpa, population (1991 estimate) 670,100; other towns are San Pedro Sula (325,900), ψLa Ceiba (77,100), ψPuerto Cortes (32,500), Choluteca (63,200) and ψTela (24,000).

Currency – Lempira of 100 centavos.

Flag – Three horizontal bands, blue, white, blue (with five blue stars on white band).

National Anthem – Tu Bandera Es Un Lampo De Cielo (Your flag is a heavenly light).

National Day – 15 September.

GOVERNMENT

Discovered and settled by the Spanish in the 16th century, Honduras formed part of the Spanish American dominions until 1821 when independence was proclaimed. Under military government from 1972, Honduras returned to civilian rule in 1981 with an executive Presidency, a 128-seat unicameral Congress, and a multiparty system based on the Liberal Party and the National Party. The last presidential and legislative elections were held on 28 November 1993 and won by the Liberal Party, which formed a new government in January 1994.

The country is divided into 18 departments.

Head of State
President of the Republic, Carlos Roberto Reina, *elected* 28 November 1993, *sworn in* 27 January 1994
Vice-Presidents, Walter López Reyes; Juan de la Cruz Avelar; Guadalupe Jerezano

Cabinet *as at August 1996*
Interior and Justice, Efraín Moncada Silva
Foreign Affairs, Delmer Urbizo Panting
Defence, Col. José Luis Núñez Beneth
Education, Zenobia Rodas de León Gómez
Finance, Juan Ferrera
Economic Planning, Guillermo Molina Chocano

Communications and Public Works, Germán Aparicio
Health, Dr Enrique Samayoa
Labour and Social Security, Cecilio Zavala Méndez
Natural Resources, Dr Ramón Villeda Bermúdez
Culture, Rodolfo Pastor Fasquelle
Economy, Fernando García
Environment, Carlos Medina
President of the Central Bank of Honduras, Dr Hugo Noé Pino

Embassy of Honduras
115 Gloucester Place, London WIH 3PJ
Tel 0171-486 4880
Ambassador Extraordinary and Plenipotentiary, new appointment awaited

British Embassy
Apartado Postal 290, Tegucigalpa
Tel: Honduras 32–0612/18
Ambassador Extraordinary and Plenipotentiary, HE P. R. Holmes, apptd 1995
There is a British Consulate in San Pedro Sula.

ECONOMY

Three-quarters of the country is covered by pine forests. Agriculture and cattle raising is mainly confined to the fertile coastal plain on the Caribbean and the extensive valleys in the Comayagua and Olancho regions of the interior. The Mosquitia tropical forest covers the area from the coast to the border with Nicaragua and provides valuable reserves of timber. Lead, zinc and silver are mined on a small scale.

The chief exports are coffee, bananas, frozen meat and timber, the most important woods being pine, mahogany and cedar. Other products are tobacco, beans, maize, rice, cotton, palm oil, sugar cane, cement, shrimps, lobsters and tropical fruits.

In July 1994 the IMF approved a three-year loan of US$58 million in support of the government's 1992–5 economic reform programme.

Trade with UK	1994	1995
Imports from UK	£13,861,000	£15,537,000
Exports to UK	19,157,000	18,130,000

COMMUNICATIONS

There are about 1,004 km of railway in operation, chiefly to serve the banana plantations and the Caribbean ports. There are 17,947 km of roads, of which 2,613 km are paved. There are 33 smaller airstrips and four international airports, Tegucigalpa, San Pedro Sula, La Ceiba and Roatan (Bay Island).

The chief ports are Puerto Cortes, Tela and La Ceiba on the north coast, through which passes the bulk of the trade with the USA and Europe. Puerto Castilla is being developed as a deep-water container port, and San Lorenzo is also experiencing rapid growth.

EDUCATION

Primary and secondary education is free, primary education being compulsory, and the government has launched a campaign to eradicate illiteracy.

HUNGARY
Magyar Köztársaság

Hungary lies in eastern Europe and is bordered by the Slovak Republic to the north, Ukraine and Romania to the east, the rump Yugoslav Federal state and Croatia to the south, and Slovenia and Austria to the west. The area is 35,919 sq. miles (93,030 sq. km) with a population (1993) of 10,278,000. There are minorities of gypsies (4.8 per cent), ethnic Germans (1.9 per cent) and Slovaks (0.9 per cent). About two-thirds of the population are Roman Catholic and the remainder mostly Calvinist.

CAPITAL – Budapest, on the Danube; population (1992) 2,004,000. Other large towns are: Miskolc (192,000); Debrecen (215,000); Szeged (177,000) and Pécs (169,000).

CURRENCY – Forint of 100 fillér.

FLAG – Red, white, green (horizontally).

NATIONAL ANTHEM – Isten Aldd Meg A Magyart (God Bless the Hungarians).

NATIONAL DAYS – 15 March, 20 August, 23 October.

GOVERNMENT

Hungary, reconstituted as a kingdom in 1920 after having been declared a republic on 17 November 1918, joined the Anti-Comintern Pact in February 1939 and entered the Second World War on the side of Germany in 1941. On 20 January 1945 a Hungarian provisional government of liberation signed an armistice under the terms of which the frontiers of Hungary were withdrawn to the 1937 limits.

After the liberation, a coalition of parties carried out land reform and nationalization. By 1949 the Communists had succeeded in gaining a monopoly of power and by 1952 practically the entire economy had been 'socialized'.

Divisions within the Communist Party and popular demand for free elections and Soviet troop withdrawals grew from July 1956 onwards. An uprising on 23 October involving fighting between demonstrators and factory workers, and the State Security Police was quelled by Soviet forces the following morning. By 30 October the Soviets had withdrawn from Budapest and on 3 November an all-party coalition government under Imre Nagy was formed. This government was overthrown and the attempted revolution suppressed by a renewed attack by Soviet forces on Budapest on 4 November. The formation of a new Hungarian Revolutionary Worker Peasant (Communist) government under János Kádár was announced the same day.

From 1968 the government gradually introduced economic reforms and some political liberalization. Kádár was forced to resign in May 1989. In October 1989 the National Assembly (*Országgyülés*) approved an amended constitution which described Hungary as an independent, democratic state. The 386-seat National Assembly is elected on a mixed first past the post and proportional representation basis with a five per cent threshold for representation. The first free multiparty elections took place in March and April 1990 and were won by the (conservative) Hungarian Democratic Forum.

The last general election in May 1994 was won by the former ruling Communist Party, reconstituted as the Hungarian Socialist Party. A coalition government of the Hungarian Socialist Party and the Alliance of Free Democrats was sworn in on 15 July 1994. The composition of the National Assembly in August 1995 was: Hungarian Socialist Party (HSP) 209, Alliance of Free Democrats (AFD) 70, Hungarian Democratic Forum 21, Independent Smallholders Party 26, Christian Democratic People's Party 22, Federation of Young Democrats-Hungarian Civic Party 20, Hungarian Democratic People's Party 15.

HEAD OF STATE
President, Árpád Göncz, *sworn in* 3 August 1990, *re-elected by parliament* 19 June 1995

CABINET *as at August 1996*
Prime Minister, Gyula Horn (HSP)
Deputy Prime Minister, Interior, Gábor Kuncze (AFD)
Agriculture, László Lakos (HSP)
Justice, Pál Vastagh (HSP)
Industry and Trade, Imre Dunai (Ind.)
Transport, Telecommunications and Water Management, Károly Lotz (AFD)
Foreign Affairs, László Kovács (HSP)
Defence, György Keleti (HSP)
Environment and Regional Policy, Dr Ferenc Baja (HSP)
Labour, Péter Kiss (HSP)
Education and Culture, Bálint Magyar (AFD)
Health and Public Welfare, György Szabó (HSP)
Finance, Péter Medgyessy (HSP)
Without Portfolio, István Nikolits (HSP) (*Civil Secret Services*); Tamas Suchman (HSP) (*Privatization*)

HSP Hungarian Socialist Party; AFD Alliance of Free Democrats

EMBASSY OF THE REPUBLIC OF HUNGARY
35 Eaton Place, London SW1X 8BY
Tel 0171–235 4048/7191
Ambassador Extraordinary and Plenipotentiary, HE Tádé Alföldy, apptd 1995
Minister Plenipotentiary, József Hajgató
Counsellor and Consul-General, P. Kallós
Commercial Counsellor, Dr J. Hámori
Defence and Military Attaché, Col. L. Hajdú

BRITISH EMBASSY
Harmincad Utca 6, Budapest V
Tel: Budapest 266–2888
Ambassador Extraordinary and Plenipotentiary, HE Christopher Long, CMG, apptd 1995
Counsellor and Deputy Head of Mission, C. Prentice, CVO
Defence Attaché, Col. H. Stephens
First Secretary (Commercial), D. Taylor
First Secretary (Management) and Consul, I. H. Davies

BRITISH COUNCIL DIRECTOR, Dr John Grote, OBE, Benczur Utca 26, H–1068 Budapest VI

DEFENCE

Hungary has a total armed forces active strength of 70,500 (47,500 conscripts). Conscripts serve for 12 months. The Army has a strength of 53,700 (36,300 conscripts) with 1,016 main battle tanks, 1,598 armoured personnel carriers and armoured infantry fighting vehicles and 894 artillery pieces. The Air Force has a strength of 16,800 (11,200 conscripts), with 147 combat aircraft. In addition there are 700 paramilitary border guards and 1,800 internal security forces.

ECONOMY

The economy has suffered from the loss of export markets in the Soviet Union and the former Yugoslavia, and the transition to a market economy. The 1990–4 government embarked upon the privatization of state-owned concerns, the deregulation of the command economy and the return of nationalized land to its former owners. In 1992–5 the IMF twice suspended a three-year loan of US$1,621 million because of government overspending and delays to the privatization and economic reform programmes. The HSP-AFD government finally introduced an austerity budget cutting the equivalent of 3 per cent of GDP and devaluing the forint by 9 per cent in March 1995.

The budget deficit reached 7.2 per cent of GDP in 1995, with GDP falling substantially in 1991–3 before beginning to rise in 1994, and unemployment at 10.8 per cent and inflation at 19 per cent in mid-1995. Privatization and the establishment of small businesses proved successful in 1990–4, aided by large-scale foreign investment of US$7,000 million in 1990–4. Some 40 per cent of state enterprises have been privatized and they produced 55 per cent of GDP in 1994. Hungary joined the OECD in March 1996.

Industry is mainly based on imported raw materials but Hungary has its own coal (mostly brown), bauxite, considerable deposits of natural gas (some not yet under full exploitation), some iron ore and oil. Output figures in 1993 were (1,000 tons): coal 14,121; aluminium 6,328; rolled steel 1,835; crude oil 1,709. Natural gas production totalled 5,325 million cubic metres.

Agriculture accounts for 14 per cent of GDP and 23 per cent of exports. In 1993, 6 per cent of the land area was owned by state farms and 47 per cent was within co-operative farms, which will remain a feature of Hungarian agriculture. Production is concentrated on maize, wheat, sugar beet, barley, rye and oats.

TRADE (Forints)	1993	1994
Imports	1,162,500m	1,395,000m
Exports	819,900m	967,482m

Trade with UK	1994	1995
Imports from UK	£259,189,000	£295,859,000
Exports to UK	240,075,000	371,571,000

EDUCATION

There are five types of schools under the Ministry of Education: kindergartens for age three to six, general schools for age six to 14 (compulsory), vocational schools (15–18), secondary schools (15–18), universities and adult training schools (over 18).

CULTURE

Magyar, or Hungarian, is one of the Finno-Ugrian languages. Hungarian literature began to flourish in the second half of the 16th century. Among the greatest writers of the 19th and 20th centuries are Mihály Vörösmarty (1800–55), Sándor Petöfi (1823–49), János Arany (1817–82), Imre Madách (1823–64), Kálmán Mikszáth (1847–1910), Endre Ady (1877–1918), Attila József (1905–37), Mihály Babits (1883–1941), Dezsö Kosztolányi (1885–1936), Gyula Illyes (1902–83), János Pilinszky (1921–81) and Sándov Weöres (1913–89).

ICELAND
Island

Iceland is a large volcanic island in the North Atlantic Ocean, extending from 63° 24′ to 66° 33′ N. latitude, and from 13° 30′ to 24° 35′ W. longitude, with an estimated area of 39,756 sq. miles (103,000 sq. km). The population was 266,786 on 1 December 1994. Some 92.2 per cent of the population are members of the (Lutheran) Church of Iceland.

CAPITAL – ΨReykjavík, population (1 December 1994), 103,036. Other centres are ΨAkureyri, Kópavogur, ΨHafnarfjördur, Keflavík, Westmann Islands, Akranes, Isafjördur and ΨSiglufjördur.
CURRENCY – Icelandic króna (Kr) of 100 aurar.
FLAG – Blue, with white-bordered red cross.
NATIONAL ANTHEM – O Gud Vors Lands (Our Country's God).
NATIONAL DAY – 17 June.

GOVERNMENT

Iceland was uninhabited before the ninth century, when settlers came from Norway. For several centuries a form of republican government prevailed, with an annual assembly of leading men called the *Althing*, but in 1262 Iceland became subject to Norway, and later to Denmark. During the colonial period, Iceland maintained its cultural integrity but a deterioration in the climate, together with frequent volcanic eruptions and outbreaks of disease, led to a serious drop in living standards and to a decline in the population to little more than 40,000. In the 19th century a struggle for independence led to home rule in 1918 and to independence as a republic in 1944.

The parliamentary (*Althing*) elections on 8 April 1995 gave the Independence Party 25 seats, Progressives 15, Social Democratic Party 7, People's Alliance 9, Awakening of the Nation 4, and Women's Alliance 3. A coalition government of the Independence Party and the Progressive Party was formed after the election.

HEAD OF STATE
President, Olafur Ragnar Grimsson, *elected* 29 June 1996

CABINET *as at August 1996*
Prime Minister, Minister for the Statistical Bureau of Iceland, David Oddsson (IP)
Foreign Affairs and External Trade, Halldór Ásgrímsson (PP)
Finance, Fridrik Sophusson (IP)
Fisheries, Justice and Ecclesiastical Affairs, Thorsteinn Pálsson (IP)
Education and Culture, Björn Bjarnason (IP)
Social Affairs, Páll Pétursson (IP)
Health and Social Security, Ingibjörg Pálmadóttir (PP)
Trade and Industry, Finnur Ingólfsson (PP)
Communications, Halldór Blöndal (IP)
Agriculture and Environment, Gudmundur Bjarnason (PP)

IP Independence Party; PP Progressive Party

EMBASSY OF ICELAND
1 Eaton Terrace, London SW1W 8EY
Tel 0171–730 5131/2
Ambassador Extraordinary and Plenipotentiary, HE Benedikt Ásgeirsson, apptd 1995

BRITISH EMBASSY
Laufásvegur 49, 101 Reykjavík
Tel: Reykjavík 551 15883/4
Ambassador Extraordinary and Plenipotentiary and Consul-General, HE James McCulloch, apptd 1996

There is also a consulate at Akureyri.

ECONOMY

Iceland has considerable resources of hydro-electric and geothermal energy. It is estimated that exploitation of these two resources (4,540 Gigawatt hours in 1992) represents only about 9 per cent of that economically exploitable. Heavy industry includes an aluminium smelter, a nitrogen fertilizer factory, a cement factory, a diatomite plant and a ferro-silicon plant.

In 1994 Iceland had a total labour force of 149,000. The major sectors of the economy are fishing and fish processing, manufacturing, agriculture, energy production, government and the public sector, and tourism, which is of growing importance with 157,926 visitors in 1993.

As a member of the European Free Trade Association (EFTA), Iceland has become a member of the European Economic Area (EEA) which extends most of the provisions of the EU's single market to EFTA states.

TRADE

The principal exports are frozen fish fillets, salt fish, stock fish, fresh fish on ice, frozen scampi, fishmeal and oil, ferrosilicon and aluminium; the chief imports are consumer durables, capital goods, petroleum products, transport equipment, textiles, foodstuffs, animal feeds, timber, and alumina.

	1992	1993
Exports	Kr87,833m	Kr94,569m
Imports	96,895m	91,307m
Trade with UK	1994	1995
Imports from UK	£109,693,000	£138,103,000
Exports to UK	239,275,000	251,887,000

COMMUNICATIONS

At 1 January 1992, the mercantile marine consisted of 1,107 registered vessels (187,217 gross tons), of which 1,000 (140,349 gross tons) are decked fishing vessels. There are regular shipping services between Reykjavík and Felixstowe, Humber ports, Europe and the USA.

A regular air service is maintained by Icelandair between Glasgow and London and Reykjavík. There are also air services to Scandinavia, USA, Germany, France and Luxembourg.

Road communications are adequate in summer but greatly restricted by snow in winter. Only roads in town centres and key highways are metalled, the rest being of gravel, sand and lava dust. The climate and terrain make first-class surfaces for highways out of the question. There are no railways.

There are three television channels (one public, two private) and several private and public radio stations.

CULTURE

The ancient Norraena (or Northern tongue) has close affinities to Anglo-Saxon and as spoken and written in Iceland today differs little from that introduced into the island in the ninth century. There is a rich literature with two distinct periods of development, from the mid-11th to the late 13th century and from the early 19th century to the present.

INDIA
The Republic of India

India has an area of 1,269,346 sq. miles (3,287,590 sq. km), and three well-defined regions: the mountain range of the Himalayas, the Indo–Gangetic plain, and the southern peninsula. The main mountain ranges are the Himalayas (over 29,000 feet) and the Western and Eastern Ghats (over 8,000 feet). Major rivers include the Ganges, Indus, Krishna, Godavari and Mahanadi.

Temperatures vary over the country between averages of about 10°C and 33°C, reaching over 38°C in some parts during the hot season. There are similar variations in rainfall, from only a few inches a year falling in the western Thar Desert to over 400 inches in Meghalaya.

The population at the 1991 census was 846,302,688. The majority are Hindu (82.6 per cent), the rest being Muslim (11.4 per cent), Christian (2.4 per cent), Sikh (2.0 per cent), Buddhist (0.7 per cent) and Jain (0.5 per cent).

The official languages are Hindi in the Devanagari script and English, though 17 regional languages also are recognized for adoption as official state languages.

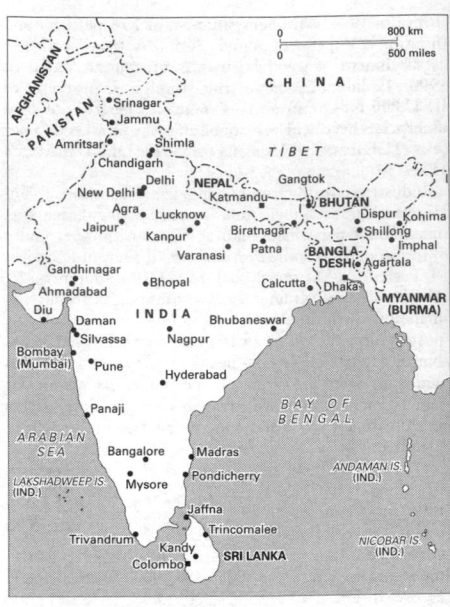

CAPITAL – Delhi (population in 1991 was 8,375,188). Populations of other principal cities (1991 figures) were Ahmadabad 3,297,655; Bangalore 4,086,548; ΨBombay (Mumbai) 12,571,720; ΨCalcutta 10,916,272; Hyderabad 4,280,261; Kanpur 2,111,284; Lucknow 1,642,134; ΨMadras 5,361,468; Pune 2,485,014.
CURRENCY – Indian rupee (Rs) of 100 paisa.
FLAG – A horizontal tricolour with bands of deep saffron, white and dark green in equal proportions. In the centre of the white band appears an Asoka wheel in navy blue.
NATIONAL ANTHEM – Jana-gana-mana.
NATIONAL DAY – 26 January (Republic Day).

HISTORY

The Indus civilization was fully developed by *c.*2500 BC but collapsed *c.*1750 BC, and was replaced by an Aryan civilization from the west. Arab invasions of the northwest began in the seventh century and Muslim, Hindu and Buddhist states developed until the establishment of the Mogul dynasty in 1526. The British East India Company established settlements throughout the 17th century; clashes with the French and native princes led to the British government taking control of the company in 1784 and gradually extending sovereignty over the whole subcontinent. The separate dominions of India and Pakistan became independent within the Commonwealth on 15 August 1947 and India became a republic in 1950.

India and Pakistan have fought three major wars since independence, in 1947–8, 1965 and 1971. Since 1985 they have continued a low-level war at altitude for control of the Siachen glacier in Kashmir.

GOVERNMENT

Under the 1950 constitution, executive power is vested in the President, elected for a five-year term by an electoral college consisting of the elected members of the Union and State legislatures. The President appoints the prime minister and, on the latter's advice, the ministers, and can dismiss them. The Council of Ministers is collectively responsible to the *Lok Sabha* (lower house). The Vice-

President is ex-officio chairman of the *Rajya Sabha* (upper house).

Legislative power rests with the President, the Rajya Sabha (245 members serving six-year terms) and the Lok Sabha (545 members). Twelve members of the Rajya Sabha are presidential nominees, the rest are indirectly elected representatives of the State and Union Territories. The 530 members of the Lok Sabha representing the States are directly elected by universal adult franchise, and 15 representatives of the Union Territories are chosen, for a maximum term of five years.

Between 1947 and 1996, India was ruled by the Congress (I) Party for all but four years (March 1977–January 1980, November 1989–June 1991). Congress (I) has been led by members of the Nehru-Gandhi dynasty for most of the post-independence period: Prime Ministers Jawaharlal Nehru (1947–64), Indira Gandhi (1966–1977, 1980–84) and Rajiv Gandhi (1984–89). Indira Gandhi was assassinated by Sikh extremists seeking an independent Sikh state in Punjab; her son Rajiv was assassinated by Sri Lankan Tamils.

The last parliamentary elections to the Lok Sabha in April and May 1996, were won by the Hindu nationalist Bharatiya Janata Party (BJP) which formed a government under Prime Minister Atal Behari Vajpayee. The BJP government lasted 13 days before resigning on 28 May in the face of an imminent vote of no confidence. A United Front coalition of Communist and low-caste parties led by H. D. Deve Gowda assumed office on 1 June 1996, winning a vote of confidence 11 days later thanks to Congress (I) support.

SECESSION

The Hindu Maharaja of Kashmir signed his state's instrument of accession to India in October 1947, two months after India and Pakistan became independent. This was disputed by Pakistan, on the basis that the majority of the state's population was Muslim, and the UN Security Council ordered a plebiscite but this never was held. After three Indian-Pakistani wars, a line of control was agreed under the 1972 Simla agreement (China has also occupied some of Kashmir since the 1962 Sino-Indian war). The line was rejected by armed groups which have waged a campaign of violence against the Hindu population and against Indian troops and police in the state. Kashmir was placed under direct rule in 1990 but state assembly elections are scheduled for August 1996. Since 1989, more than 12,000 people have died in the fighting, including 3,400 militants.

HEAD OF STATE

President of the Republic of India, Dr Shankar Dayal Sharma, *elected* 16 July 1992
Vice-President, K. R. Narayanan, *elected* 19 August 1992

COUNCIL OF MINISTERS *as at August 1996*

Prime Minister, Urban Affairs and Employment, Personnel Grievances and Pensions, Atomic Energy, Unassigned Portfolios, H. D. Deve Gowda
Finance and Company Affairs, Palaniappan Chidambaram
Defence, Mulayam Singh Yadav
External Affairs, I. K. Gujaral
Home Affairs, Indrajit Gupta
Agriculture, Chaturanan Mishra
Railways, Ram Vilas Paswan
Human Resource Development, S. R. Bommai
Industry, Murasoli Maran
Food, Civil Supplies, Consumer Affairs and Public Distribution, Devendra Prasad Tadav
Labour, M. Arunachalam

Welfare, Balwant Singh Ramoowalia
Civil Aviation and Tourism, Information and Broadcasting, C. M. Ibrahim
Surface Transport, T. G. Venkataraman
Rural Areas and Employment, Yarram Naidu
Parliamentary Affairs and Tourism, Srikant Kumar Jena
Steel and Mines, Birendra Prasad Baishya
Water Resources, Janeshwar Mishra
In addition there are 17 ministers of state and ministers of state with independent charge.

INDIAN HIGH COMMISSION

India House, Aldwych, London WC2B 4NA
Tel 0171–836 8484
High Commissioner, HE Dr L. M. Singhvi, apptd 1991
Deputy High Commissioner, P. K. Singh
Ministers, A. Bhatnagar (*Economic*); R. Banerji (*Consular*), Dr A. R. Basu (*Culture*)
Military Adviser, Brig. R. Dhir
There are Consulate-Generals in Birmingham and Glasgow.

BRITISH HIGH COMMISSION

Chanakyapuri, New Delhi 110021
Tel: New Delhi 872161
High Commissioner, HE Hon. David Gore-Booth, CMG, apptd 1996
Deputy High Commissioner and Minister, H. N. H. Synnott
Deputy High Commissioners, T. D. Curran (*Bombay*); A. B. N. Morey, CBE (*Calcutta*); S. H. Palmer (*Madras*)
Defence and Military Adviser, Brig. R. A. Draper, OBE
Counsellor (Economic and Commercial), W. Morris
Minister for Cultural Affairs and British Council Representative, A. P. Thomas, OBE
Offices also at Bombay, Calcutta and Madras. There are British Council libraries at these four centres and British libraries at Ahmadabad, Bangalore, Bhopal, Hyderabad, Lucknow, Patna, Pune and Trivandrum.

STATES AND TERRITORIES OF THE UNION

There are 25 States and seven Union Territories. Each state is headed by a Governor, who is appointed by the President and holds office for five years, and by a Council of Ministers. All states have a Legislative Assembly, and some have also a Legislative Council, elected directly by adult suffrage for a maximum period of five years.

The Union Territories are administered, except where otherwise provided by Parliament, by the President acting through an Administrator or Lieutenant-Governor, or other authority appointed by him.

(Capital in parenthesis)	Area (sq. km)	Population (1991 census)
STATES		
Andhra Pradesh (Hyderabad)	275,100	66,304,854
Arunachal Pradesh (Itanagar)	83,700	858,392
Assam (Dispur)	78,400	22,414,322
Bihar (Patna)	173,900	86,374,465
Goa (Panaji)	3,700	1,168,622
Gujarat (Gandhinagar)	196,000	41,309,582
Haryana (Chandigarh)	44,200	16,463,648
Himachal Pradesh (Shimla)	55,700	5,170,877
Jammu and Kashmir*		
(Srinagar/Jammu)	222,200	5,987,389
Karnataka (Bangalore)	191,800	44,977,201
Kerala (Trivandrum)	38,900	29,011,237
Madhya Pradesh (Bhopal)	443,500	66,135,862
Maharashtra (Bombay)	307,700	78,937,187

Manipur (Imphal)	22,300	1,826,714
Meghalaya (Shillong)	22,400	1,774,778
Mizoram (Aizawl)	21,100	686,217
Nagaland (Kohima)	16,600	1,209,549
Orissa (Bhubaneswar)	155,700	31,659,736
Punjab (Chandigarh)	50,400	20,190,795
Rajasthan (Jaipur)	342,200	44,005,990
Sikkim (Gangtok)	7,100	405,550
Tamil Nadu (Madras)	130,100	55,638,318
Tripura (Agartala)	10,500	2,744,827
Uttar Pradesh (Lucknow)	294,400	139,112,287
West Bengal (Calcutta)	88,800	67,982,732
UNION TERRITORIES		
Andaman and Nicobar Is.		
(Port Blair)	8,200	280,661
Chandigarh	114	642,015
Dadra and Nagar Haveli		
(Silvassa)	500	138,477
Daman and Diu	112	101,586
Delhi	1,500	9,420,644
Lakshadweep (Kavaratti)	30	51,681
Pondicherry	500	807,785

* The area figure includes those parts occupied by Pakistan and China, which are claimed by India, but the population figure excludes the population of these areas, where the census was not taken. The state's capital is at Srinagar in summer and Jammu in winter.

JUDICATURE

The Supreme Court consists of the Chief Justice and not more than 25 other judges, appointed by the President. It is the highest court in respect of all constitutional matters and the final Court of Appeal and is situated in New Delhi. Each state or group of states also has a High Court with a hierarchy of subordinate courts. The judges of the High Court of a state are appointed by the President.
Chief Justice, A. M. Ahmadi

DEFENCE

Total active armed forces strength numbers 1,245,000. Service is voluntary. India exploded its first nuclear weapon in 1974 and is since believed to have acquired a stockpile of nuclear arms. In 1993–4 India successfully test-fired its intermediate-range 'Agni' and 'Prithvi' ballistic missiles.

The Army has a total strength of 980,000, with 2,400 main battle tanks; 1,057 armoured infantry fighting vehicles and armoured personnel carriers; 4,255 artillery pieces and 199 helicopters.

The Navy has a strength of 55,000 personnel and consists of two aircraft carriers, 15 submarines, five destroyers, 18 frigates, 41 patrol and coastal craft, 68 combat aircraft and 75 armed helicopters. The Air Force has a strength of 110,000 with 844 combat aircraft and 32 armed helicopters.

In addition, there are 1,507,500 personnel in 13 paramilitary organizations.

ECONOMY

Agriculture is the chief industry, supporting about 65 per cent of the population, and providing nearly 29 per cent of GDP. The area under cultivation has been increased by irrigation schemes but most holdings are less than five acres. Production has grown by 2.6 per cent each year since 1951, remaining slightly ahead of the 2 per cent increase necessary to keep pace with the rising population. Food crops occupy three-quarters of the total cultivated area. The main food crops are rice, cereals (principally wheat)

and pulses. The major cash crops include sugar cane, jute, cotton and tea. Other products include oil seeds, spices, groundnuts, soya bean, tobacco, rubber and coffee. Livestock is raised, principally for dairy purposes or for the hides.

Industry is based on the exploitation and processing of mineral resources, principally coal, oil and iron, and on the production of textiles. The coal industry reached an output in 1994 of 257 million tonnes; production of crude oil was about 32.4 million tonnes. Steel production is mainly in the hands of the public sector, with five public and one private sector integrated steel plants producing 18.2 million tonnes of ingot steel in 1994. The engineering industry, heavy and light, is increasingly being privatized.

The manufacture of paper, cement, pharmaceuticals, chemicals, fertilizers, petrochemicals, motor vehicles and commercial vehicles has been expanded. Other principal manufactures are those derived from agricultural products, textiles, jute goods, sugar, leather, which along with tea, tobacco, rubber, fish, and iron ore and concentrates are major exports.

Faced with the need to obtain loans from the World Bank and assistance from the IMF, India abandoned 40 years of centralized planning in 1991 and introduced free market reforms. Subsidies were cut, state corporations privatized and the economy opened up to foreign competition and investment. To integrate India into the international trading system proper, the 1993–5 budgets floated the rupee, cut interest rates and duties on imports, reduced subsidies to farmers, restructured the taxation system, removed industrial controls and dismantled protectionist structures. The budgets are in line with IMF proposals and have prompted foreign donors to pledge more than US$20,000 million between 1993 and 1996. The reforms have been successful, producing US$10,000 million in foreign investment since 1991, a fall in inflation from 17 to 5 per cent in January 1996, a 24 per cent increase in exports, a rise in foreign currency reserves from US$1,000 million to US$16,000 million in 1996, an average GDP growth of 6 per cent per year, improved agricultural efficiency and an increase in the average annual industrial growth rate from 1 per cent to 12 per cent.

FINANCE

The budget estimates for 1996–7 placed total expenditure at Rs 2,020,240 million. Total revenue (excluding states' shares) was Rs 1,271,620 million.

TRADE WITH UK	1994	1995
Imports from UK	£1,311,495,000	£1,682,709,000
Exports to UK	1,288,939,000	1,435,481,000

COMMUNICATIONS

The International Airports Authority manages five international airports: Palam (Delhi), Sahar (Bombay), Dum Dum (Calcutta), Meenambakkam (Madras) and Trivandrum. The other 88 aerodromes are controlled and operated by the Civil Aviation Department of the government. The national airlines are Indian Airlines (internal) and Air India (international).

The railways are grouped into nine administrative zones, Southern, Central, Western, Northern, North-Eastern, North-East Frontier, Eastern, South-Eastern and South-Central with a total track length of 62,462 km, about 18 per cent of which is electrified. The total length of the road network is 2,065,209 km of which 964,072 km is surfaced.

The chief seaports are Bombay, Calcutta, Haldia, Madras, Mormugao, Cochin, Visakhapatnam, Kandla, Paradip, Mangalore and Tuticorin; these handled a cargo of 179.3 million tonnes in 1993–4. There are 139 minor working ports with varying capacity. On 31 August 1995, ships totalling 6,840,000 gross tons were on the Indian Register.

INDONESIA
Republik Indonesia

Indonesia is situated between 6° N. and 11° S. latitude and between 95° and 141° E. longitude, and comprises the islands of Java, Madura, Sumatra, the Riouw-Lingga archipelago, Bangka and Billiton, part of the island of Borneo (Kalimantan), Sulawesi (formerly Celebes) Island, the Molucca Islands, the islands of Bali, Lombok, Sumbawa, Sumba, Flores, Timor and others comprising the provinces of East and West Nusa Tenggara and the western half of the island of New Guinea (Irian Jaya), with a total area of 735,358 sq. miles (1,904,569 sq. km), and a population (UN estimate 1994) of 189,907,000.

CAPITAL – ΨJakarta (population 7,885,519). Other important centres are: (Java) ΨSurabaya (2,027,913), ΨSemarang (1,026,671), Bandung (1,462,637); (Sumatra) Palembang (787,187), Medan (1,378,955); (Sulawesi) ΨUjung Pandang (709,038); (Kalimantan) Banjarmasin (381,286), ΨPontianak (304,778), (Moluccas) Ambon (208,898); (Nusa Tenggara) Kupang (329,371); (Irian Jaya) Jayapura (107,164).
CURRENCY – Rupiah (Rp) of 100 sen.
FLAG – Equal bands of red over white.
NATIONAL ANTHEM – Indonesia Raya (Great Indonesia).
NATIONAL DAY – 17 August (Anniversary of Proclamation of Independence).

GOVERNMENT

From the early part of the 17th century much of the Indonesian archipelago was under Dutch rule. Following the Second World War, during which the archipelago was occupied by the Japanese, a strong nationalistic movement formed and after sporadic fighting all the former Dutch East Indies except western New Guinea became independent as Indonesia on 27 December 1949. Western New Guinea became part of Indonesia in 1963 under the name West Irian (now Irian Jaya), this interpretation being confirmed in an 'Act of Free Choice' in July 1969, of which the United Nations took note in November 1969.

Following a three-week period of unrest and violent student demonstrations, the Army Minister Gen. Suharto assumed effective political power in March 1966. Gen. Suharto was appointed President in 1968 and has been reappointed by the People's Consultative Assembly (composed of the House of People's Representatives together with 500 government, regional and party appointees) at each presidential election since. The House of People's Representatives is composed of 400 elected members and 100 military appointees. The military has effectively ruled since 1966 through its political organization Golkar.

Only three parties may legally contest elections. In the 1992 general election, Golkar obtained 281 seats, the Muslim United Development Party (PPP) 63 seats and the Indonesian Democratic Party (PDI) 56 seats. In June 1996, the daughter of former President Sukarno, Megawati Sukarnoputri, was ousted from the leadership of the PDI by a government-backed party congress. She has since become the focus of popular opposition to the Suharto regime. The next presidential election is scheduled to be held in 1998.

SECESSION

Besides East Timor (*see* page 894), there are two armed secessionist movements based on ethnic and nationalist groups, which are fighting perceived Javanese domination. In Irian Jaya government forces are fighting the Papua Independent Organization (OPM) guerrillas who claim the 1969 referendum was rigged and oppose Indonesian settlement. In northern Sumatra the Free Aceh Movement is active.

HEAD OF STATE
President, Gen. Suharto, *appointed Acting President* March 1967; *confirmed as President* 28 March 1968, *re-elected* 1973, 1978, 1983, 1988 and March 1993
Vice-President, Try Sutrisno, *elected* March 1993

CABINET *as at June 1996*
Co-ordinating Ministers, Gen. (retd) Soesilo Soedarman (*Political and Security Affairs*); Saleh Afiff (*Economy*); Maj.-Gen. Azwar Anas (*Public Welfare*); Ir Hartarto (*Production and Distribution*)
Ministers, Lt.-Gen. (retd) Yogi Memet (*Internal Affairs*); Ali Alatas (*Foreign Affairs*); Gen. Edi Sudrajat (*Defence and Security*); Oesman Oetojo (*Justice*); Mr Harmoko (*Information*); Mar'ie Muhammad (*Finance*); Satrio Yudono (*Trade*); Tungki Arinibowo (*Industry*); Sjarifuddin Baharsyah (*Agriculture*); Lt.-Gen. Ida Bagus Sujana (*Mines and Energy*); Radinal Mochtar (*Public Works*); Haryanto Dhanutirto (*Communications*); Abdul Latief (*Manpower*); Siswono Yudohusodo (*Transmigration*); Joop Ave (*Tourism, Posts and Telecommunications*); Wardiman Joyonegoro (*Education and Culture*); Dr Suyudi (*Health*); Tarmizi Taher (*Religious Affairs*); Prof. Endang Suweno (*Social Affairs*); Jamaludin Suryohadikasumo (*Forestry*); Subiakto Cakrawerdaya (*Co-operatives and Small Businesses*); Dr Murdiono (*Minister and State Secretary*)
In addition there are 14 ministers of state.

INDONESIAN EMBASSY
38 Grosvenor Square, London WIX 9AD
Tel 0171–499 7661
Ambassador Extraordinary and Plenipotentiary, HE Junus Habibie, apptd 1993
Minister, H. Sudirman (*Deputy Chief of Mission*)
Commercial Attaché, Andreas Anugerah

BRITISH EMBASSY
Jalan M. H. Thamrin 75, Jakarta 10310
Tel: Jakarta 330904
Ambassador Extraordinary and Plenipotentiary, HE Graham Burton, CMG, apptd 1994
Deputy Ambassador, Counsellor and Consul-General, Q. M. Quayle
Counsellor (Commercial/Development), P. J. Johnstone
Defence Attaché, Col. I. J. Hellberg, OBE

BRITISH CONSULAR OFFICES – There are British Consular Offices at Jakarta, Medan and Surabaya.
BRITISH COUNCIL DIRECTOR, Dr Neil Kemp, S Widjojo Centre, Jalan Jenderal Sudirman 71, Jakarta 12190.

DEFENCE

The armed forces have a total active strength of 274,500 with selective conscription of two years. The Army has a strength of 214,000 with 305 light tanks, 579 armoured personnel carriers, 181 artillery pieces and 36 helicopters. The Navy has 40,500 personnel (including 12,000 marines), two submarines, 13 frigates, 44 patrol and coastal craft, 24 combat aircraft and 14 armed helicopters. The Air

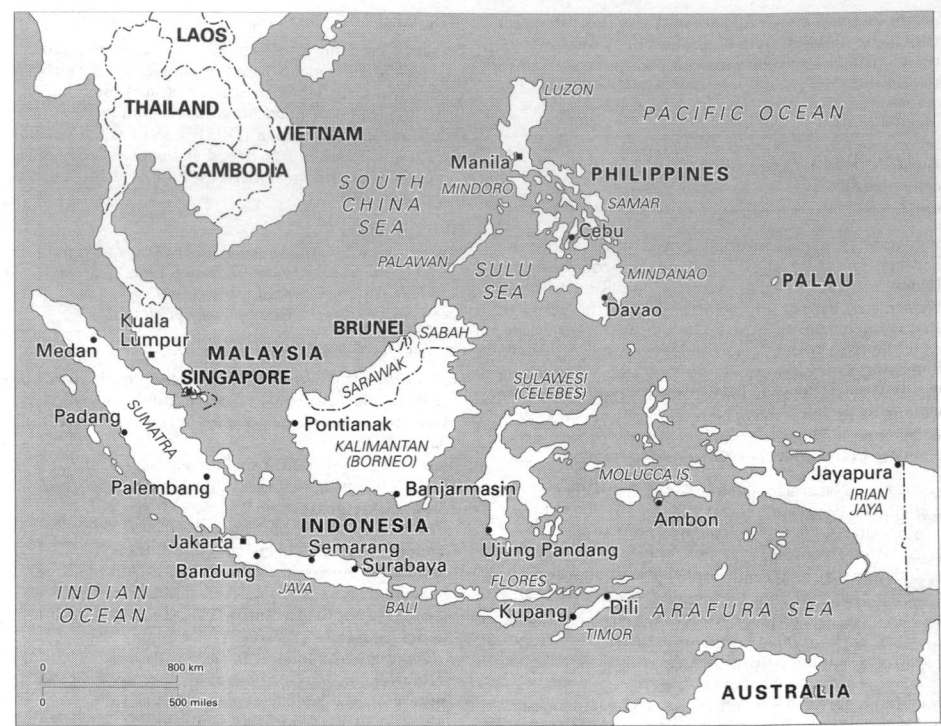

Force has 20,000 personnel and 73 combat aircraft. There are 174,000 paramilitary police personnel.

ECONOMY

Nearly 70 per cent of the population is engaged in agriculture and related production. Copra, kapok, nutmeg, pepper and cloves are produced, mainly by smallholders; palm oil, sugar, fibres and cinchona are produced by large estates. Rubber, tea, coffee and tobacco are produced by both in large quantities. Rice is a staple food and Java, Sulawesi and Sumatra are important producers. Production has risen rapidly in recent years and the country is now self-sufficient.

Oil and liquefied natural gas are the most important assets, the export of which constitutes around 80 per cent of export earnings. However, dependence on these has made the economy vulnerable to depressed international markets and weak oil prices. Timber is the second largest foreign exchange earner after oil.

Indonesia is rich in minerals, particularly tin, of which the country is the world's third biggest producer; coal, nickel and bauxite are the other principal mineral products. There are also considerable deposits of gold, silver, manganese phosphates and sulphur. Aid to Indonesia is channelled through the Indonesian Consultative Group (ICG). Indonesia received about US$5,400 million in 1994–5.

Indonesia is aiming to diversify its economy to reduce its dependence on oil and gas exports, with particular emphasis on agriculture, heavy engineering (shipbuilding) and high technology (aerospace). The past decade has been economically successful, with annual average GDP growth rates of 6 per cent. However, public and private sector debt has grown substantially to around US$90,000 million.

Principal exports are oil and natural gas, rubber, timber, non-ferrous metals, clothing, tea, coffee, spices, vegetable oils and fats. Imports are mainly of machinery, transport equipment, electrical equipment and chemicals.

Trade with UK	1994	1995
Imports from UK	£366,035,000	£525,499,000
Exports to UK	782,546,000	903,867,000

COMMUNICATIONS

There are railway systems in Java and Sumatra linking the main towns. There are about 50,000 miles of roads.

Sea communications are maintained by the state-run shipping companies Djakarta-Lloyd (ocean-going) and Pelni (coastal and inter-island) and other small concerns. Transport by small craft on the rivers of the larger islands plays an important part in trade.

Air services are operated by Garuda Indonesian Airways and other local airlines, and Jakarta is served by various international services.

EAST TIMOR

East Timor was a Portuguese colony from 1702 until Portuguese control collapsed following the 1974 coup in Portugal. An independence war waged by the Marxist Fretilin (Revolutionary Front for an Independent East Timor) developed into a civil war between Fretilin and local conservative forces in 1975. After gaining control, Fretilin declared East Timor independent on 27 November 1975 and this was recognized by Portugal. Indonesian forces invaded East Timor on 7 December 1975 and declared East Timor Indonesia's 27th province.

Since 1975 Fretilin has waged an armed campaign for independence; resistance has left 200,000 East Timorese dead. About 150,000 Muslims have been settled in East

Timor alongside the predominantly Roman Catholic population (80 per cent in 1975). The UN does not recognize the annexation and considers Portugal to exercise sovereignty still. A massacre of pro-independence demonstrators in the capital, Dili, in 1991 provoked international outrage. Fighting between Fretilin and the Indonesian army continues despite the imprisonment of Fretilin's leader, Xanana Gusmao in 1993. Sporadic demonstrations and strikes against Indonesian rule continue.

IRAN
Jomhuri-e-Islami-e-Iran

Iran has an area of 636,296 sq. miles (1,648,000 sq. km). It is mostly an arid tableland, encircled, except in the east, by mountains, the highest in the north rising to 18,934 ft. The central and eastern portion is a vast salt desert.

The population (1995 estimate) is 66,000,000, of which 99 per cent are Muslims (Shia 91 per cent and Sunni 8 per cent) with small minorities of Zoroastrians, Bahais, Jews, and Armenian and Assyrian Christians.

Persian or Farsi is an Indo-European language with many Arabic elements added; the alphabet is mainly Arabic, with writing from right to left. Among the great names in Persian literature are those of Abu'l Kásim Mansúr, or Firdausi (AD 939–1020), Omar Khayyám, the astronomer-poet (died AD 1122), Muslihu'd-Din, known as Sa'di (born AD 1184), and Shems-ed-Din Muhammad, or Hafiz (died AD 1389).

CAPITAL – Tehran, population (1990 UN estimate) 6,042,584. Other large towns are Tabriz, Esfahan, Mashhad, Shiraz, Resht, Kerman, Hamadan, Yazd, Kermanshah and Ahvaz.

CURRENCY – Rial.

FLAG – Three horizontal stripes of green, white, red, with the slogan *Allahu Akbar* repeated 22 times along the edges of the green and red stripes, and the national emblem in the centre.

NATIONAL ANTHEM – Sorood-e Jomhoori-e Eslami.

NATIONAL DAY – 11 February.

GOVERNMENT

Iran was ruled from the end of the 18th century by Shahs of the Qajar dynasty. In 1925 the last of the dynasty, Sultan Ahmed Shah, was deposed in his absence by the National Assembly, which handed executive power to Prime Minister Reza Khan. Reza Khan was elected Shah as Reza Shah Pahlavi by the Constituent Assembly in December 1925. In 1941 Reza Shah abdicated in favour of the Crown Prince, who ascended the throne as Mohammed Reza Shah Pahlavi.

In January 1979, the Shah left Iran, handing over power to the Prime Minister, who was ousted by Ayatollah Khomeini, the spiritual leader of the Shia Muslims, on his return from exile on 1 February. Following a national referendum, an Islamic Republic was declared on 1 April 1979. A new constitution, providing for a president, prime minister, Consultative Assembly, and leadership by Ayatollah Khomeini, was approved by referendum in December 1979. In June 1989 Khomeini died and President Khamenei was appointed Leader of the Islamic Republic. Rafsanjani was elected President in July 1989, and the post of prime minister was abolished. In the 1992 elections to the Majlis (consultative assembly), candidates supporting President Rafsanjani won over 200 of the 270

seats. However, in the 1993 presidential election, President Rafsanjani received only 63 per cent of the vote (compared with 94 per cent in 1989) and only 56 per cent of the electorate voted. The elections in March and April 1996 saw the conservative Society of Combatant Clergy lose overall control of the Majlis due to gains by the Servants of Iran's Construction.

Iran was at war with Iraq following the Iraqi invasion of Iran in September 1980. International efforts to end the fighting resulted in a cease-fire in August 1988. In August 1990 Iraq accepted Iran's conditions for settling the conflict, including a return to the 1975 border, but a formal peace treaty has not been signed.

Leader of the Islamic Republic, Ayatollah Seyed Ali Khamenei, *appointed* June 1989
President, Hojjatoleslam Ali Akbar Hashemi Rafsanjani, *elected* 28 July 1989, *re-elected* 11 June 1993
First Vice-President, Hassan Ebrahim Habibi

COUNCIL OF MINISTERS *as at June 1996*

Vice-Presidents, Seyed Ataollah Mohajerani (*Legal and Parliamentary Affairs*); Reza Amrollahi (*Atomic Energy*); Massoud Razavi (*State Employment and Administrative Affairs*); Mohammad Hashemi (*Executive Affairs*); Mehdi Manafi (*Environmental Protection*); Seyyed Mostafa Hashemi-Taba (*Physical Education*)
Agriculture, Issa Kalantari
Commerce, Yahya Al-Eshaq
Construction Crusade, Gholam Reza Forouzesh
Defence, Mohammed Forouzandeh
Economy and Finance, Morteza Mohammed Khan
Education, Mohammad Ali Najafi
Culture and Higher Education, Dr Hashemi Golpeygani
Energy, Bizhan Namdar Zanganeh
Islamic Culture and Guidance, Mostafa Mir-Salim
Foreign Affairs, Ali Akbar Velayati
Health, Ali Reza Marandi
Housing and Urban Development, Abbas Ahmad Akhundi
Industries, Mohammad Reza Nematzadeh
Intelligence, Ali Fallahian
Interior, Ali Mohammad Besharati
Justice, Mohammad Esmail Shoushtari
Labour and Social Affairs, Hossein Kamali
Mines and Metals, Mohammad Hossein Mahloujchi
Oil, Gholamreza Aghazadeh
Posts, Telephones and Telegraphs, Mohammad Gharrazi
Roads and Transport, Ali Akbar Torkan
Co-operatives, Gholem Reza Shafei

EMBASSY OF THE ISLAMIC REPUBLIC OF IRAN
16 Prince's Gate, London SW7 1PT
Tel 0171-225 3000
Chargé d'Affaires, G. Ansari

BRITISH EMBASSY
143 Ferdowsi Avenue, PO Box 11365–4474, Tehran 11344
Tel: Tehran 675011
Counsellor and Chargé d'Affaires, Jeffrey R. James, CMG, apptd 1993
First Secretary (Commercial), A. F. Bedford

DEFENCE

The Iranian armed forces number 513,000 active personnel. The conscription term is 24 months, with conscripts serving almost exclusively in the Army. The Army has a strength of 345,000 (including 250,000 conscripts) with 1,440 main battle tanks, 950 armoured personnel carriers and armoured infantry fighting vehicles, 2,948 artillery pieces and 100 attack helicopters.

The Navy is 18,000 strong, with two submarines, two destroyers, three frigates, 38 patrol and coastal craft, and nine armed helicopters. The Air Force has 30,000 personnel, with some 295 combat aircraft, of which only about 50 per cent are serviceable due to the US armaments embargo, in operation since 1979.

The Islamic Revolutionary Guards Corps numbers some 120,000, of which 100,000 are ground and 20,000 naval forces.

EDUCATION

Since 1943 primary education has been compulsory and free. There are 57 universities in Iran. The educational system has been reformed following the revolution. The literacy rate is 72 per cent.

ECONOMY

The economy has been badly affected by the recent fall in world oil prices, which has exacerbated the hardship caused by the loss of subsidies on all but the most basic foodstuffs following free market reforms. Privatization began in 1991 but since 1993 its pace has been reduced by the government because of the job losses it caused. Iran's support for international terrorism and its alleged nuclear weapons programme prompted the USA to impose a full trade and investment embargo in June 1995, and to impose sanctions on foreign companies investing more than £26 million a year in Iran's energy sector, in July 1996. However, in August 1996, Turkey signed a £13 billion deal to buy Iranian gas and for the construction of a gas pipeline. In 1994 the total foreign debt reached US$30,000 million, with inflation at 60 per cent in 1995.

Agricultural output rose following the end of the Iran–Iraq war and an attempt is being made to reduce dependence on food imports. Wheat is the principal crop; other important crops are barley, rice, cotton, sugar beet, fruit, nuts and vegetables. Wool is also a major product.

The oilfields, which lie in south-western Iran, were nationalized in 1951. From 1957 until the 1979 revolution a consortium of eight foreign oil companies was responsible for the production, refining and sale of oil but in July 1979 the National Iranian Oil Company assumed full control. Oil production is around 3.6 million b.p.d., of which some 2.5 million b.p.d. is exported. Iran is a member of OPEC.

Apart from oil, the principal industrial products are carpets, textiles, sugar, cement and other construction materials, ginned cotton, vegetable oil and other food products, leather and shoes, metal manufactures, pharmaceuticals, motor vehicles, fertilizers and plastics. Industrial output was severely curtailed by the 1979 revolution, and by the Iran–Iraq war, but the private sector is now being encouraged again.

TRADE

Over 80 per cent of export earnings come from oil, but an effort is being made to increase non-oil exports. The level of finance for imports depends largely on the international oil price and Iran has recently had a deficit in foreign trade partly because of the depressed state of world oil prices. Tighter import controls were introduced in 1994.

Imports are mainly industrial and agricultural machinery, motor vehicles and motor vehicle components for assembly, iron and steel (including manufactures), electrical machinery and goods, meat, various other foods, and certain textile fabrics and yarns.

The principal exports, apart from oil, are cotton, carpets, dried fruit, nuts, hides and skins, mineral ores, wool, gums, caviare, cumin seed and spices. Germany and Japan are Iran's leading suppliers.

Trade with UK	1994	1995
Imports from UK	£289,062,000	£332,614,000
Exports to UK	132,650,000	125,834,000

COMMUNICATIONS

Tehran is the centre of a network of highways linking the major towns, ports, the Caspian Sea and the national frontiers.

The Trans-Iranian Railway runs from Bandar Turcoman, on the Caspian Sea, via Tehran to Bandar Khomeini, on the Persian Gulf. Other lines link Tehran with Tabriz and Mashhad; Tabriz to Julfa; Zahedan to Quetta; Ahvaz to Khorramshahr; Qom to Kerman; and Bandar Turcoman to Gorgan. The rail system is linked to the Turkish system via Van. A track between Mashhad and Tedzhen in Turkmenistan, opened in May 1996, has re-established the ancient Silk Road between China and the Mediterranean.

There is an international airport at Tehran (Mehrabad), and airports at all the major provincial centres. The national airline, Iranair, is government-owned and operates international and domestic routes.

IRAQ
Al-Jumhouriya al-'Iraqia

Iraq extends between $37\frac{1}{4}°$ to $48\frac{1}{2}°$ E. longitude, and $37\frac{1}{4}°$ to 30° N. latitude, from Turkey on the north and north-east to the Gulf on the south and south-east, and from Iran on the east to Syria and the Arabian Desert on the west. In 1993 the border between Iraq and Kuwait was formally demarcated, moving a few hundred metres northwards and giving part of the port of Umm Qasr to Kuwait. The area of Iraq is 167,925 sq. miles (434,924 sq. km), of which 37 per cent is desert. The rivers Euphrates (1,700 miles) and Tigris (1,150 miles) rise in Turkey and traverse Iraq to their junction at Qurna, from where the Euphrates flows the 70 miles to the Gulf.

The population at the census of October 1987 was 16,278,316. The 1994 UN estimate was 19,951,000. The official language is Arabic. Minority languages include Kurdish (about 15 per cent), Turkic and Aramaic.

CAPITAL – Baghdad. Population of the governorate (1987 census) 3,841,286. Other towns of importance are ΨBasra, Mosul and Kirkuk.

CURRENCY – Iraqi dinar (ID) of 1,000 fils.

FLAG – Three horizontal stripes of red, white, black; on the white stripe three stars and the slogan *Allahu Akbar* all in green.

NATIONAL DAY – 17 July (Revolution Day).

HISTORY

Iraq is the site of the remains of several ancient civilizations: one site at Tel Hassuna, near Shura, dates back to 5000 BC; Tel Abu Shahrain near 'Ur of the Chaldees' is the site of the Sumerian city of Eridu; the ancient city of Hillah, 70 miles south of Baghdad, is near the site of Babylon and the Tower of Babel. Mosul governorate covers a great part of the ancient kingdom of Assyria, the ruins of Nineveh, the Assyrian capital, being visible on the banks of the Tigris, opposite Mosul. Qurna, at the junction of the Tigris and Euphrates, is traditionally supposed to be the site of the Garden of Eden.

Under the Treaty of Lausanne 1923, Turkey renounced sovereignty over Mesopotamia. A provisional government was set up in 1920, and in 1921 the Emir Faisal was elected

King of Iraq. The country was a monarchy until July 1958, when King Faisal II was assassinated. From 1958 Iraq has been under the rule of the Ba'ath Party.

Iraq invaded Iran in September 1980 and was at war until the August 1988 cease-fire. In 1990 Iraq accepted Iran's conditions for peace, including a return to the 1975 border, but a formal peace treaty has not been signed.

Iraq invaded Kuwait on 2 August 1990 and declared Kuwait a province of Iraq. The UN Security Council declared the annexation void. After months of diplomatic attempts to secure an Iraqi withdrawal from Kuwait, an alliance of NATO and Middle East countries launched an offensive in January 1991 and liberated Kuwait in February 1991.

GOVERNMENT

According to the provisional constitution, the highest state authority is the Revolutionary Command Council (RCC), which elects the president from among its members. A constitutional amendment approved in September 1995 provided for the confirmation of the RCC's choice of president by the National Assembly and by a popular referendum. The president appoints the Council of Ministers. Legislative authority is shared by the RCC and the 250-member National Assembly, which is elected every four years by universal adult suffrage. The Arab Ba'ath Socialist Party held a majority of Assembly seats following the 1989 elections; no party affiliations were ascribed in the results of the most recent election, held on 24 March 1996. Following the amendment to the constitution, a referendum on a further seven-year term for President Saddam was approved by a claimed 99.96 per cent of voters on 15 October 1995.

Since Iraq's aborted attempt to seize Kuwait, there have been several attempts to oust President Saddam. At least three coup plots were uncovered in 1995–6; an army rebellion was foiled in June 1995; and an assassination attempt by elite Republican Guards failed in July 1996.

Secession (*See also* Events of the Year)

Following the allied victory in Kuwait in February 1991, rebellion broke out in the Kurdish north and the Shi'ite south. Although the revolt was quickly suppressed, Iraqi attacks on Kurdish civilians led Western governments to set up a security zone and a UN safe haven in northern Iraq to protect them. An air exclusion zone north of the 36th parallel was also established. Saddam Hussein withdrew his administration from Kurdish northern Iraq in October 1991, enabling the Kurds to establish a *de facto* administration with its capital at Arbil and control over an area with a population of 3.5 million. In 1992 the Kurds voted in free elections for a 100-seat parliament and a 'political leader'. The Kurdish Democratic Party (KDP) and the Patriotic Union of Kurdistan (PUK) both gained 50 seats and a Kurdish government was formed with the two party leaders jointly in control. Trading difficulties, fuel and food shortages, and land disputes led to fighting between the two parties for most of 1994 and 1995, leaving 3,000 dead and the administration defunct. Peace talks led to a cease-fire in September 1995 and a provisional agreement to hold legislative elections, although fighting resumed in August 1996 before a ballot could be held.

Although the Shi'ite revolt in southern Iraq was defeated in April 1991, a low-level insurgency continued in the southern marshlands. Continued Iraqi bombing of Shi'ite refugees in these areas led to an air exclusion zone being established south of the 32nd parallel in August 1992, patrolled by US, British and French aircraft. Since then the Iraqi regime has systematically drained the southern marshes by canal construction and river diversion; with continued ground offensives, this had effectively ended the Shi'ite rebellion by late 1994.

Head of State
President, Chairman of the Revolutionary Command Council, Prime Minister, Saddam Hussein, *assumed office* 16 July 1979, *reappointed* 17 October 1995
Vice Presidents, Taha Yassin Ramadhan; Taha Mohieddin Maaruf

Revolutionary Command Council
Chairman, Saddam Hussein
Vice-Chairman, Izzat Ibrahim
Head of the Presidential Office, Ahmed Hussein Khudayyir
Members, Taha Yassin Ramadhan; Tariq Aziz; Mohammed Hamza al-Zubeidi; Gen. Ali Hassan al-Majeed; Mizban Khider Hadi; Taha Mohieddin Maaruf

Cabinet *as at August 1996*
Prime Minister, Saddam Hussein
Deputy Prime Ministers, Tariq Aziz; Taha Yassin Ramadhan; Mohammed Hamza al-Zubeidi
Interior, Muhammad Zimam Abdul-Razzaq
Defence, Gen. Sultan Hashim Ahmed
Foreign Affairs, Mohammed Saaed al-Sahhaf
Finance, Hikmat Mezban Ibrahim
Culture and Information, Abd-al-Ghani Abd-al-Ghafur
Justice, Shabib al-Maliki
Agriculture and Irrigation, Abdulillah Hameed Mahmoud Saleh
Industry and Minerals, Adnan Abdul-Majeed Jassim
Oil, Lt.-Gen. Amir Muhammad Rashid
Education, Abduljabbar Tawfig Mohammed
Labour and Social Affairs, Latif Nassif Jassem
Health, Umeed Madhat Mubarak
Irrigation, Mohamoud Diyab al-Ahmad
Higher Education and Scientific Research, Humam Abdel-Khaliq Ghafuras
Housing and Construction, Maan Abdullah Sarsam
Transport and Communications, Ahmed Murtada Ahmed Khalil
Religious Endowments and Religious Affairs, Abdul-Muneim Ahmed Saleh
Trade, Muhammed Mahdi Salih
Ministers of State, Gen. Abdel-Jabbar Shanshal (*Military Affairs*); Arshad al-Zibbari, Abdul Wahab Omar Mirza al-Atrushi (*Without Portfolio*)

Iraqi Diplomatic Mission in London
Since Iraq's breach of diplomatic relations with Britain in February 1991, the Jordanian Embassy has handled Iraqi interests in the UK.

British Diplomatic Representation
The British Embassy was closed in January 1991. The Russian Embassy has since handled British interests in Iraq.

DEFENCE

The Iraqi armed forces were decimated in the defeat by the allied coalition which drove them from Kuwait but have reorganized and now have around 382,500 active personnel (compared to a pre-war total of one million). Reservists number 650,000 personnel, of whom around 100,000 are on permanent recall to the Army. Conscripts serve 18 to 24 months.

The Army has a strength of around 350,000, with around 2,700 main battle tanks (5,300 pre-war); 4,400 reconnaissance vehicles, armoured personnel carriers and armoured infantry fighting vehicles (6,300 pre-war); 1,980 artillery pieces (3,150 pre-war) and 120 armed helicopters. The Army is organized into eight Republican Guard and 19 regular divisions with 10 specialized counterinsurgency brigades. The Navy has a strength of around 2,500 with one frigate and 7 patrol and coastal craft. The Air Force has a strength of around 30,000 with 320 combat aircraft (570 pre-war). In addition, there are 24,800 paramilitary frontier guards and security troops.

Since the end of the war, UN weapons inspection teams have destroyed or dismantled nuclear, chemical and biological weapons, Scud missiles and their launchers, and the superguns. By mid-1995 it was believed that nearly all these weapons and their means of production had been destroyed and a long-term monitoring operation was under way to ensure production did not restart.

In opposition to Iraqi forces there are 37,500 armed Kurdish guerrillas, with a further 36,000 support personnel. These are armed with captured Iraqi tanks, artillery and mortars, and small arms. There is also a brigade-sized armed Shi'ite opposition force based in Iran.

In 1991, the UN demanded the destruction of all weapons of mass destruction and their means of production as a prerequisite for the lifting of sanctions. Inspection teams sent to monitor compliance have met sustained resistance although in 1993 Iraq agreed to the dismantling of nuclear, chemical and biological weapons, Scud missiles and their launchers, and superguns. In late 1995, evidence of a ballistic missile programme and large biological weapons stockpiles was discovered.

ECONOMY

In August 1990, the UN imposed economic sanctions on Iraq, including a world-wide ban on its oil exports. In May 1996, Iraq agreed to a UN-proposed 'oil-for-food' deal, permitting the sale of £2.6 billion of oil a year to buy food and medicine, which received US approval in August 1996. Thirty per cent of the revenue will pay for reparations to Gulf War victims, up to 15 per cent will provide aid to Iraqi Kurds.

Apart from oil revenues, agricultural production is also important, with two harvests usually gathered in a year, depending on rainfall. Salinity and soil erosion, caused by a high water table, inadequate irrigation and drainage, and traditional farming methods are the major problems being addressed by development planners.

Increasing industrialization is taking place but industrial production has been greatly reduced because of war damage and sanctions. Iraq's major industry is oil production. It was nationalized in 1972 and usually accounts for approximately 98 per cent of the total government revenue and 45 per cent of GNP. Production was 3.5 million barrels per day in 1979 but has been reduced by war damage from the Iran–Iraq and Gulf wars, the closure of Syrian, Turkish and Saudi pipelines and UN economic sanctions.

TRADE

The principal imports are normally iron and steel, cement and other building materials, mechanical and electrical machinery, motor vehicles, textiles and clothing, essential foodstuffs, grain, tinned foods and raw industrial materials. The chief exports are normally crude petroleum, dates, raw wool, raw hides and skins and raw cotton.

Trade with UK	1994	1995
Imports from UK	£9,581,000	£5,044,000
Exports to UK	122,000	164,000

COMMUNICATIONS

The port of Basra has not been used since the outbreak of hostilities with Iran in 1980. Continuous dredging of the Shatt-al-Arab has also been suspended by hostilities and the channel has seriously silted. The port of Umm Qasr on the Kuwaiti border, which was developed for freight and sulphur handling and includes a container terminal, was opened in late 1993. All external borders, except that of Jordan, are closed to Iraqi traffic.

There is an international airport at Baghdad. Iraqi Airways provided flights between Baghdad and London, and other international airlines operated to Europe. Iraqi Republican Railways provided regular passenger and goods services between Basra, Baghdad and Mosul. There is also a metre gauge rail line connecting Baghdad with Khanaqin, Kirkuk and Arbil.

Iraqi communications were greatly affected by the Gulf War; large numbers of bridges were destroyed and the railway system extensively disrupted.

IRELAND

Ireland lies in the Atlantic Ocean between 51° 26' and 55° 21' N. latitude and 5° 25' and 10° 30' W. longitude. It is separated from Scotland by the North Channel and from England and Wales by the Irish Sea and St George's Channel. The area is 32,588 sq. miles (84,402 sq. km). The greatest length of the island, from north-east to south-west (Torr Head to Mizen Head), is 302 miles, and the greatest breadth, from east to west (Dundrum Bay to Annagh Head), is 174 miles. On the north coast of Achill Island (Co. Mayo) are the highest cliffs in the British Isles, 2,000 feet sheer above the sea.

The island is mostly a central plain with an elevation 50 to 350 ft above mean sea level, and with isolated mountain ranges near the coastline. The highest point is Carrantuohill (3,414 ft). The principal river is the Shannon (240 miles), which drains the central plain. The Slaney flows into Wexford Harbour, the Liffey to Dublin Bay, the Boyne to Drogheda, the Lee to Cork Harbour, the Blackwater to Youghal Harbour, and the Suir, Barrow and Nore to Waterford Harbour.

The principal hydrographic feature is the loughs; the Shannon chain of Allen, Boderg, Forbes, Ree and Derg, and the Erne chain of Gowna, Oughter, Lower Erne, and Erne; Melvin, Gill, Gara and Conn in the north-west; and Corrib and Mask (joined by a hidden channel) in the west. In Co. Kerry are the famous lakes of Killarney.

In the later Bronze Age a Celtic race of Goidels appears to have invaded Ireland, and in the early Iron Age Brythons from south Britain are believed to have settled in the south-east, while Picts from north Britain settled in the north. Towards the close of the Roman occupation of Britain, the dominant tribe in the island was the Scoti, who afterwards established themselves in Scotland.

Hibernia was visited by Roman merchants but never by Roman legions, and little is known of the history of the country until the invasions of Northmen (Norwegians and Danes) towards the close of the eighth century AD. The outstanding events in the encounters with the Northmen are the Battle of Tara (980), at which the Hy Neill king Maelsechlainn II defeated the Scandinavians of Dublin and the Hebrides under the king Amlaib Cuarán; and the Battle of Clontarf (1014) by which the Scandinavian power was completely broken.

After Clontarf the supreme power was disputed by the O'Briens of Munster, the O'Neills of Ulster, and the

O'Connors of Connaught, with varying fortunes. In 1152 Dermod MacMurrough (Diarmit MacMurchada), the deposed king of Leinster, sought assistance in his struggle with Rauidhri O'Connor (the high king of Ireland) from Henry II of England. Henry authorized him to obtain armed support in England for the recovery of his kingdom, and Dermod enlisted the services of Richard de Clare, the Norman Earl of Pembroke afterwards known as Strongbow, who landed at Waterford in 1170 with 200 knights and 1,000 other troops for the reconquest of Leinster, where he eventually settled after marriage with Dermod's daughter. In 1172 Henry II himself landed in Ireland. He received homage from the Irish kings and established his capital at Dublin. The invaders subsequently conquered most of the island and a feudal government was created. In the 14th and 15th centuries, the Irish recovered most of their lands, while many Anglo-Irish lords became virtually independent, royal authority being confined to the Pale, a small district round Dublin. Though, under Henry VII, Sir Edward Poynings, as Lord Deputy, had passed at the Parliament of Drogheda (1494) the act later known as Poynings' Law, subordinating the Irish legislature to the Crown, the Earls of Kildare retained effective power until Henry VIII began the reconquest of Ireland in 1534. Parliament in 1541 recognized him as King of Ireland and by 1603 English authority was supreme.

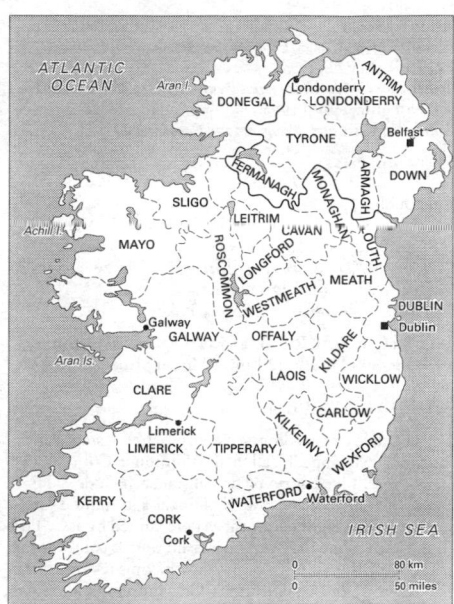

REPUBLIC OF IRELAND
Poblacht Na hEireann

The Republic of Ireland has a land area of 27,136 sq. miles (70,283 sq. km), divided into four provinces of 26 counties: Leinster (Carlow, Dublin, Kildare, Kilkenny, Laoighis, Longford, Louth, Meath, Offaly, Westmeath, Wexford and Wicklow); Munster (Clare, Cork, Kerry, Limerick, Tipperary and Waterford); Connacht (Galway, Leitrim, Mayo, Roscommon and Sligo); and part of Ulster (Cavan, Donegal and Monaghan).

The population of the Republic (1996 census) was 3,621,035. At the census of 1991 religious adherence was: Roman Catholic, 3,228,327; Church of Ireland, 89,187; Presbyterians, 13,199; Methodists, 5,037; others, 189,969. Irish is the first official language and English is recognized as a second official language, but is more commonly used.

CAPITAL – ΨDublin (*Baile Atha Cliath*), population (1996 census) 480,996. Other county boroughs, with their population figures at the 1996 census, are ΨCork (127,092); ΨLimerick (52,042); ΨWaterford (42,516); and Ψ Galway (57,095).
CURRENCY – Punt (Irish pound) of 100 pence.
FLAG – Equal vertical stripes of green, white and orange.
NATIONAL ANTHEM – Amhrán na BhFiann (The Soldier's Song).
NATIONAL DAY – 17 March (St Patrick's Day).

GOVERNMENT

The 1937 constitution declares the national territory to be the whole island of Ireland, but that pending the reintegration of the national territory, laws enacted by Parliament will apply in the area which constituted the Irish Free State, i.e. not in the six counties of Northern Ireland.

The president (*Uachtarán na hEireann*) is directly elected for a term of seven years, and is eligible for a second term. The president is aided and advised by a Council of State.

The National Parliament (*Oireachtas*) consists of the president, House of Representatives (*Dáil Éireann*) and Senate (*Seanad Éireann*). Dáil Éireann is composed of 166 members elected for a five-year term by adult suffrage on a basis of proportional representation by means of the single transferable vote. Seanad Éireann is composed of 60 members, of whom 11 are nominated by the Taoiseach and 49 are elected, six by institutions of higher education and 43 from panels of candidates established on a vocational basis.

Executive power is vested in the government subject to the constitution. The government is responsible to the Dáil. The taoiseach is appointed by the president on the nomination of the Dáil. The other members of the government are appointed by the president on the nomination of the taoiseach with the previous approval of the Dáil. The taoiseach appoints a member of the government to be his deputy (the *tánaiste*).

The last general election was on 25 November 1992. The composition of the Dáil Eireann in August 1996 was: Fianna Fáil 67; Fine Gael 47; Labour 32; Progressive Democrats 8; Democratic Left 6; Green 1; Independent 4. The present coalition government was formed by Fine Gael (FG), the Labour Party (L) and the Democratic Left (DL) on 15 December 1994.

HEAD OF STATE
President, Mary Robinson, *assumed office* 3 December 1990

CABINET *as at August 1996*

Taoiseach (*PM*), John Bruton (FG)
Tánaiste (*Deputy PM*), *Foreign Affairs*, Dick Spring (L)
Finance, Ruarí Quinn (L)
Employment and Enterprise, Richard Bruton (FG)
Justice, Nora Owen (FG)
Agriculture, Forestry and Food, Ivan Yates (FG)
Social Welfare, Proinsias De Rossa (DL)
Environment, Brendan Howlin (L)
Health, Michael Noonan (FG)
Education, Niamh Bhreathnach (L)
Defence and Marine, Sean Barrett (FG)
Transport, Energy and Communications, Michael Lowry (FG)
Tourism and Trade, Enda Kenny (FG)
Equality and Law Reform, Mervyn Taylor (L)
Arts, Culture and the Gaeltacht, Michael Higgins (L)

IRISH EMBASSY
17 Grosvenor Place, London SWIX 7HR
Tel 0171-235 2171
Ambassador Extraordinary and Plenipotentiary, HE Edward
  Barrington, apptd 1995
Counsellor, J. Timbs (*Economic and Commercial*)

BRITISH EMBASSY
31 Merrion Road, Dublin 4
Tel: Dublin 2053700
Ambassador Extraordinary and Plenipotentiary, HE Veronica
  Sutherland, CMG, apptd 1995
Counsellor and Deputy Head of Mission, R. I. Clarke
Defence Attaché, Col. S. D. Lambe, CBE
First Secretary (Commercial), R. N. J. Baker

BRITISH COUNCIL REPRESENTATIVE, Harold Fish, OBE,
  Newmount House, 22 Lower Mount Street, Dublin 2

JUDICIAL SYSTEM

The judicial system comprises courts of first instance and a
court of final appeal called the Supreme Court (*Cúirt
Uachtarach*). The courts of first instance include a High
Court (*Ard-Chúirt*) and courts of local and limited juris-
diction, with a right of appeal as determined by law. The
High Court alone has original jurisdiction to consider the
question of the validity of any law having regard to the
provisions of the constitution. The Supreme Court has
appellate jurisdiction from decisions of the High Court.
Chief Justice, Hon. Liam Hamilton
President of the High Court, Hon. Declan Costello
Attorney-General, Dermot Gleeson

DEFENCE

There is a Permanent Defence Force in which enlistment
is voluntary. The minimum term of enlistment is five
years, followed by seven years in the Reserve Defence
Force. Enlistment in the Reserve Defence Force is also
voluntary; minimum term of enlistment is three years. The
defence estimate for the year ending 31 December 1996
provides for an expenditure of IR£385,400,000.

The total active armed forces number 12,584 personnel
with 16,651 reserves. The Army has a strength of 10,449
personnel. The Navy has a strength of 1,037, with seven
patrol and coastal vessels. The Air Corps has a strength of
1,098, with 25 combat aircraft and 15 armed helicopters.
Ireland deploys an infantry battalion of 650 troops with
UN forces in South Lebanon.

ECONOMY

Although industry has expanded greatly since Ireland's
entry into the European Community in 1973, agriculture
remains of importance to the economy; in 1995, 11 per cent
of the workforce was employed in agriculture. The main
crops are wheat, barley, potatoes and sugar beet. Animal
products, dairy products and livestock, especially pigs and
cows, are major exports. Agriculture has benefited considerably from the EU Common Agricultural Policy and
support funds, which have been used to modernize farming
methods and machinery, but agriculture has suffered from
the drift of the rural population to urban areas and abroad.

Industry accounted for about 35 per cent of GNP and
about 28 per cent of employment in 1995. The traditional
brewing, spirits and food-processing sectors have expanded and have been joined by the manufacture of
textiles, chemical, pharmaceuticals, electronics, office
machinery and transportation equipment. The services
sector is currently the fastest-growing sector of the
economy and accounted for over 50 per cent of GNP and

over 60 per cent of employment in 1995. Tourism is the
most important part of the service sector and in recent
years has provided substantial revenue, with over four
million visitors in 1995.

The difficulties posed by the lack of energy resources
have been transformed over the past 15 years by the
discovery of two natural gas fields off the south coast,
which now supply all the country's natural gas needs but
are expected to be depleted by around 2000, and by the
opening of seven government-funded milled peat power-
generating stations. Hydro-electric power from the
Shannon barrage and other schemes is also important but
Ireland still imports 54 per cent of oil and coal for power
generation.

Metal content of ores raised (1995) was lead, 46,100
tonnes; zinc, 184,100 tonnes; silver 13,700,000 grammes.
An estimated 15,500 persons were employed in the
fisheries in 1995. Total value of all fish landed in 1995 was
IR£129.92 million.

FINANCE

	1995	1996
Total current revenue	IR£11,667m	IR£12,434m
Total current expenditure	12,029m	12,516m

The gross debt at end 1995 was IR£30,210 million.

TRADE	1994	1995
Imports	IR£17,283,400,000	IR£20,154,100,000
Exports	22,753,400,000	27,296,700,000
Trade balance	5,470,100,000	7,142,700,000

Trade with UK	1994	1995
Imports from UK	£6,947,834,000	£7,331,300,000
Exports to UK	5,647,543,000	6,651,500,000

EDUCATION

Primary education is directed by the state, with the
exception of 68 private primary schools with an enrolment
of 8,026 in 1994–5. There were 3,319 state-aided primary
schools with an enrolment of 491,256.

In 1994–5 there were 452 recognized secondary schools
with 225,490 pupils under private management (mainly
religious orders), and 247 vocational schools with 94,907
pupils. There were 16 state comprehensive schools in
1994–5 with a total enrolment of 9,292 students, and 60
community schools with an enrolment of 41,541 students.
Total full-time enrolment at second-level for 1994–5 was
375,457.

Third-level education is catered for by seven university
colleges, and also by third-level courses offered by the
technical colleges and regional technical colleges and
other third-level institutions. There were 92,595 full-time
third-level students in 1993–4, of whom 50,662 were
attending university courses.

The estimated state expenditure on education in 1996,
excluding administration and inspection, is: first-level
IR£775,600,000; second-level IR£672,147,000. The vote
for third-level education amounted to IR£453,629,000.

COMMUNICATIONS

In the year ended 31 December 1995, there were 1,945 km
of railway operated by *Iarnród Eireann;* the receipts were
IR£86,372,000 and expenditure IR£192,205,000.

In 1995 the number of ships with cargo which arrived at
Irish ports was 15,890 (45,968,000 net registered tons); of
these 2,438 (7,962,000 net registered tons) were of Irish
nationality.

Shannon Airport, Co. Limerick, is on the main transatlantic air route. In 1995 the airport handled 1,571,385
passengers. Dublin Airport serves the cross-channel and

European services operated by the Irish national airline Aer Lingus and other airlines. In 1995 the airport handled 8,024,894 passengers. In 1995 Cork Airport handled 971,319 passengers.

ISRAEL
Medinat Israel

Israel lies at the eastern edge of the Mediterranean Sea, between 29° 30′ to 33° 15′ N. latitude and 34° 15′ to 35° 40′ E. longitude. It is bordered by Lebanon on the north, Syria on the north-east, Jordan and the West Bank on the east, and the Gaza Strip and the Egyptian province of Sinai on the south-west. The area is estimated at 8,019 sq. miles (20,770 sq. km).

Israel comprises the hill country of Galilee and parts of Judea and Samaria, rising to heights of nearly 4,000 ft; the coastal plain from the Gaza strip to north of Acre, including the plain of Esdraelon running from Haifa Bay to the south-east which divides the hill region; the Negev, a semi-desert triangular-shaped region, extending from a base south of Beersheba, to an apex at the head of the Gulf of Aqaba; and parts of the Jordan valley, including the Hula region, Tiberias and the south-western extremity of the Dead Sea.

The principal river is the Jordan, which rises from three main sources in Israel, the Lebanon and Syria, and flows through the Hula valley, Lake Tiberias/Kinneret (Sea of Galilee) and the Jordan Valley into the Dead Sea, falling 1,517 ft from Hulata to the Dead Sea. The other principal rivers are the Yarkon and Kishon. The Dead Sea is a lake (shared between Israel, the West Bank and Jordan), 1,286 ft below sea-level; it has no outlet, the surplus being carried off by evaporation.

The climate is variable, modified by altitude and distance from the sea, with hot summers and rainy winters.

The population (estimate 1992) including East Jerusalem and Jewish settlers in the Occupied Territories is 5,090,000. Of these 4,175,000 are Jewish (82 per cent); 700,000 Arab Muslims (13.8 per cent); 130,000 Christians (2.5 per cent), of which 90 per cent are Arab, and 85,000 Druze (1.7 per cent). During the upheavals of 1948–9 a large number of Arabs left the country as refugees and settled in neighbouring countries and the Occupied Territories.

Since independence Israel has had a policy of granting an immigration visa to every Jew who expresses a desire to settle in Israel. Between 1948 and 1992, 2.3 million immigrants had entered Israel from over 100 different countries.

Hebrew and Arabic are the official languages. Arabs are entitled to transact all official business with government departments in Arabic.

CAPITAL – Most of the government departments are in Jerusalem, population (1993 estimate) 556,400. A resolution proclaiming Jerusalem as the capital of Israel was adopted by the *Knesset* in 1950. It is not, however, recognized as the capital by the UN because East Jerusalem is part of the Occupied Territories captured in 1967. The UN and international law continues to reject the Israeli annexation of East Jerusalem and considers the pre-1950 capital Tel Aviv (population, with district, 1,781,500) to be the capital. Other principal towns (1990) are ΨHaifa and district (432,900) and Beersheba and district (122,000).

CURRENCY – New Shekel of 100 agora.

FLAG – White, with two horizontal blue stripes, the Shield of David in the centre.

NATIONAL ANTHEM – Hatikvah (The Hope).

GOVERNMENT

The Ottoman Empire province of Palestine was captured by British forces in 1917, the same year that the British Government issued the Balfour Declaration which 'viewed with favour the establishment of a national home for the Jewish people in Palestine'. The Balfour Declaration's terms were enshrined in Britain's League of Nations mandate over Palestine, leading to steady Jewish immigration in the inter-war years and a post-1945 flood by Nazi concentration camp survivors. The Arab Palestinian population revolted against Jewish immigration from 1936 onwards, while Jewish groups conducted a terrorist campaign against the British administration from 1945 onwards.

In 1947 Britain announced its withdrawal from Palestine with effect from May 1948, handing over to the UN responsibility for resolving the conflict between Arabs and Jews. Both sides ignored the UN partition plan; on the withdrawal of British forces on 14 May 1948 the State of Israel was proclaimed and the first Arab-Israeli war began. By the time of the January 1949 cease-fire Israeli forces controlled all of the former mandate territory apart from the West Bank (and East Jerusalem) and the Gaza Strip, which had come under Jordanian and Egyptian control respectively.

During the 1967 Six-Day War Israel captured the West Bank and the Gaza Strip, together with Sinai from Egypt and the Golan Heights from Syria, and annexed East Jerusalem. Israel held onto its gains in the 1973 Yom Kippur War. The Golan Heights were annexed in 1981;

Sinai was returned to Egypt in 1982 in accordance with the 1979 Israeli–Egyptian peace treaty, and the South Lebanon Security Zone was established after the 1982–5 invasion of Lebanon. The annexations of East Jerusalem and the Golan Heights remain unrecognized internationally.

Israel is a sovereign democratic republic with executive power vested in a prime minister and Cabinet, and legislative power in a unicameral legislature (*Knesset*) of 120 members elected by proportional representation for a maximum term of four years. The president is head of state and is elected by the Knesset for a maximum of two five-year terms.

The Labour leader of the coalition government formed after the 1992 general election, Yitzhak Rabin, was assassinated by a Jewish extremist on 4 November 1995, and was replaced by Foreign Minister Shimon Peres. A general election on 29 May 1996, the first to have separate ballots for the prime minister and legislature, was won by Likud leader Benjamin Netanyahu, although no party gained outright control of the Knesset. Netanyahu formed an eight-party coalition government which commanded 66 seats in the Knesset.

A peace process started in October 1991 in Madrid led to agreements with the Palestine Liberation Organization (*see* page 903), and with Jordan on 14 September 1993. A full peace agreement with Jordan was signed on 26 October 1994 and provides for the return to Jordan of land occupied by Israel since 1967 in the southern Araba valley (completed 9 February 1995); the establishment of full diplomatic and economic relations; the prevention of terrorist attacks on each other; the sharing of the Jordan and Yarmouk rivers; and King Hussein's custodianship of Muslim sites in Jerusalem. Direct telephone links have been established, the first border crossing has opened, and agreements have been concluded on trade and transport.

Intermittent peace talks with Syria have stumbled over control of the Golan Heights and Israel's role in southern Lebanon.

HEAD OF STATE

President of Israel, Ezer Weizmann, *elected* 24 March 1993, *inaugurated* 13 May 1993

CABINET *as at August 1996*

Prime Minister, Construction and Housing, Religious Affairs, Benjamin Netanyahu
Deputy PM, Foreign Affairs, David Levy
Deputy PM, Agriculture and Rural Development, Environment, Rafael Eitan
Deputy PM, Education, Culture and Sport, Zevulun Hammer
Deputy PM, Tourism, Moshe Katzav
Science, Binyamin Ze'ev Begin
Immigrant Absorption, Yuli Edelstein
Public Security, Avigdor Kahalani
Transportation, Yitzhak Levy
Communications, Limor Livnat
Finance, Dan Meridor
Defence, Yitzhak Mordechai
Justice, vacant
Industry and Trade, Natan Sharansky
National Infrastructure, Ariel Sharon
Interior, Eli Suissa
Labour and Social Affairs, Eli Yishai

EMBASSY OF ISRAEL
2 Palace Green, Kensington, London W8 4QB
Tel 0171–957 9500
Ambassador Extraordinary and Plenipotentiary, HE Moshe Raviv, apptd 1993
Minister Plenipotentiary, A. Magid

Defence Attaché, Brig.-Gen. A. Nevo
Minister, M. Bar-On (*Consular*)
Counsellor, A. Wohl (*Commercial*)

BRITISH EMBASSY
192 Hayarkon Street, Tel Aviv 63405
Tel: Tel Aviv 5249171
Ambassador Extraordinary and Plenipotentiary,
  HE David G. Manning, CMG, apptd 1995
Counsellor, Consul-General and Deputy Ambassador,
  C. J. White
Defence and Military Attaché, Col. C. S. Wakelin, OBE
First Secretary (Commercial), W. W. Magor
There are British consular offices in Tel Aviv and Eilat and a Consulate-General in East Jerusalem (Occupied Territories).

BRITISH COUNCIL DIRECTOR, Harley Brookes,
  140 Hayarkon Street, PO Box 3302, Tel Aviv 61032.
There are also libraries in West Jerusalem and Nazareth.

ISRAEL-BRITISH CHAMBER OF COMMERCE, 76 IBN
  Guirol Street, Tel Aviv 64162

DEFENCE

The Israeli defence forces have a total active strength of 172,000 (including 138,500 conscripts). Since its inception, however, Israel has based its defence on a large and highly-trained reserve, which numbers at present 430,000 personnel. Conscripts serve for periods of up to four years. Israel is widely believed to have a nuclear capacity of around 100 warheads which could be delivered by aircraft and Jericho I and II missiles.

The Army has an active strength of 134,000 (114,700 conscripts) and a strength of 598,000 on mobilization, with 4,095 main battle tanks, 9,480 armoured personnel carriers and 1,550 artillery pieces.

The Navy has an active strength of 7,000 (3,000 conscripts) and 12,000 on mobilization, with three submarines and 55 patrol and coastal craft. The Air Force has a strength of 32,000 (21,800 conscripts) and 37,000 on mobilization, with 449 combat aircraft and 116 armed helicopters. The Air Force comprises 16 ground attack/fighter and four ground attack squadrons, together with one transport wing and reconnaissance, airborne early warning, tanker and training units. There is also a paramilitary force of 6,000 border police.

EDUCATION AND CULTURE

Education from six to 16 years is free and compulsory. The law also provides for working youth age 16–18, who for some reason have not completed their education, to be exempted from work in order to do so. There are seven universities including two engineering and technological institutes.

Important historic sites in Israel include: *Jerusalem* – the Church of the Holy Sepulchre, the Al Aqsa Mosque and Dome of the Rock standing on the remains of the Temple Mount of Herod the Great of which the Western (wailing) Wall is a fragment, the Church of the Dormition and the Coenaculum on Mount Zion, Ein Karem, Church of the Visitation, Church of St John the Baptist; *Galilee* – the Sea, Church and Mount of the Beatitudes, ruins of Capernaum and other sites connected with the life of Christ; *Mount Tabor* – Church of the Transfiguration; *Nazareth* – Church of the Annunciation, and other Christian shrines associated with the childhood of Christ; there are also numerous sites dating from biblical and medieval days, such as Ascalon, Caesarea, Atlit, Massada, Megiddo and Hazor.

COMMUNICATIONS

Israel State Railways serves Haifa, Tel Aviv, Jerusalem, Lod, Nahariya, Beersheba, Dimona, Ashdod and intermediate stations with a network of 528 km. There were 12,823 km of paved road in 1986. A major road building programme has been underway in the West Bank since 1992.

Israel's merchant marine had reached a total of 2,805,000 tons deadweight by December 1985. The chief ports are Haifa and Ashdod on the Mediterranean, and Eilat on the Red Sea; Acre has an anchorage for small vessels. The chief international airport is Ben Gurion between Tel Aviv and Jerusalem.

ECONOMY

The country is generally fertile with crops ranging from the temperate to the subtropical. Water supply for irrigation limits greater production. The area under cultivation is 1.1 million acres, of which 0.6 million is under irrigation. Agriculture accounts for 5 per cent of GNP and 4 per cent of exports.

The famous 'Jaffa' orange is produced in large quantities for export, along with other summer fruits, seasonal vegetables and glasshouse crops, such as flowers, tomatoes and strawberries. Olives are cultivated, mainly for the production of oil. The main winter crops are wheat, barley and various kinds of pulses, while in summer sorghum, millet, maize, sesame and summer pulses are grown. Beef, cattle and poultry farming have been developed and the production of mixed vegetables and dairy produce has greatly increased. Tobacco and medium staple cotton are now grown. Fishing production (mostly from fish farms) was 12,200 tons in 1993.

In value polished diamonds account for about 23 per cent of total exports. Amongst the most important industries are textiles, foodstuffs, chemicals (mainly fertilizers and pharmaceuticals). Metal-working and science-based industries are sophisticated and technologically advanced and include the aircraft and military industries. Other important manufacturing industries include plastics, rubber, cement, glass, paper and oil refining. Industry accounts for 30 per cent of GNP and 60 per cent of exports.

TRADE

The principal imports are foodstuffs, crude oil, machinery and vehicles, iron, steel and manufactures thereof, and chemicals. The principal exports are metal machinery, electronic goods, chemicals, rubber, plastics, textiles, food and beverages, minerals, citrus produce and polished diamonds.

Trade with UK	1994	1995
Imports from UK	£1,031,644,000	£1,108,455,000
Exports to UK	572,375,000	692,156,000

PALESTINIAN AUTONOMOUS AREAS

The total area is 2,406 sq. miles (6,231 sq. km). The area which is fully autonomous is 159 sq. miles (412 sq. km), of which the Gaza Strip is 136 sq. miles (352 sq. km) and the Jericho enclave 23 sq. miles (60 sq. km). The partially autonomous area is the remainder of the West Bank, some 2,247 sq miles (5,819 sq. km). The UN and the international community also recognize East Jerusalem as part of the Occupied Territories.

The population (1992 estimate) is 1,635,000, of whom 660,000 live in the Gaza Strip, 40,000 in Jericho, and 935,000 in the remainder of the West Bank. In addition there are 141,000 Jewish settlers in the West Bank and 4,000 in the Gaza Strip who remain under Israeli administration and jurisdiction. Some 90 per cent of Palestinians are Muslim (the vast majority Sunni) and 10 per cent are Christians.

CAPITAL – Although Palestinians claim East Jerusalem as their capital, the administrative capital has been established in Gaza City (120,000). Other major towns are Khan Yunis and Rafah in the Gaza Strip and Nablus, Hebron, Jericho, Ramallah and Bethlehem on the West Bank.

FLAG – Three horizontal stripes of black, white, green with a red triangle based on the hoist (the PLO flag).

NATIONAL ANTHEM – Biladi, Biladi (My Country, My Country).

GOVERNMENT

Israel captured the Gaza Strip, East Jerusalem and the West Bank during the 1967 Six-Day War and annexed East Jerusalem. After the war the Israeli government began to establish settlements in the Occupied Territories. Palestinian resistance to Israeli rule was led by the Palestine Liberation Organization (PLO) established in 1964, which carried out armed attacks, bombings and aircraft hijackings against Israeli targets around the world. Frustration at continued Israeli occupation led to the start of the *intifada* in 1987, a campaign of sustained unrest which left 1,400 Palestinians and 230 Jews dead by early 1995. When the 1991 Madrid peace process stalled, Israeli and PLO officials engaged in secret negotiations in Norway which led to the signing of the 'Declaration of Principles on Interim Self-Government Arrangements' on 13 September 1993. Under this agreement the PLO renounced terrorism and recognized Israel's right to exist in secure borders, while Israel recognized the PLO as the legitimate representative of the Palestinian people.

The Declaration of Principles established a timetable for progress towards a final settlement: negotiations leading to an Israeli military withdrawal from the Gaza Strip and Jericho by 13 April 1994, when power was to be transferred to a nominated Palestinian National Authority (PNA); elections to a new Palestinian Council, which would also exercise control over six policy areas in the rest of the West Bank (culture, tourism, health, education, social welfare, direct taxation), and the Israeli military administration dissolved by 13 July 1994; negotiations on a permanent settlement, including Jewish settlers and East Jerusalem, to begin by 13 April 1996; and a permanent settlement to be in place by 13 April 1999.

The timetable has slipped, with the Israeli military not finally redeploying in the Gaza Strip and withdrawing from Jericho until 18 May 1994, when the five-year period of interim self-government under the PNA began.

Israel and the Palestinians struggled to reach agreement on the extension of self-rule until 28 September 1995, when the 'Oslo B' or Taba Accord was signed which provided for Israeli withdrawal from six towns and 85 per cent of Hebron; the extension of self-rule to most of the West Bank by 1998; the release of 5,300 Palestinian prisoners; and the striking out of the demand for Israel's destruction from the PLO's charter. On 29 December 1995 an agreement was reached on the transfer of 17 areas of civilian power to the PNA in Hebron.

Implementation of the agreement began with the release of 1,100 Palestinian prisoners in October 1995; Israeli troops left Ramallah, the last of the six West Bank towns, on 27 December 1995 and the inaugural Palestinian National Council meeting on 23 April 1996 voted to amend the PLO charter. The final element of the Declaration of Principles, the 'final status talks' opened in Taba, Egypt, on 5 May 1996 to decide the final status of the West Bank, Gaza and

Jerusalem. Prospects of a final agreement were dampened by the election of a Likud-led government which vowed to prevent the establishment of a fully-fledged Palestinian state and continued to delay withdrawal from Hebron.

The Oslo B accord also laid down the political structure of the nascent Palestinian state. Executive authority is vested in the Palestinian National Authority which is headed by a popularly elected leader (*rais*). Legislative authority is vested in the 88-member Palestinian Council which is directly elected by means of a first-past-the-post system, and itself elects the four-fifths of the PNA not appointed by the leader.

Legislative elections on 20 January 1996 were won by the mainstream al-Fatah faction of the PLO, with its leader Yasser Arafat winning 88.1 per cent of the vote to become the leader.

PALESTINIAN NATIONAL AUTHORITY *as at August 1996*

Leader, Yasser Arafat
Tourism, Ilyas Furayj
Religious Trusts and Religious Affairs, Hasan Tahbub
Planning and International Co-operation, Nabil Shaath
Social Affairs, Intisar al-Wazir
Trade and Economy, Mahir al-Masri
Local Government, Sa'ib Urayqat
Justice, Furayh Abu Middayn
Health, Riyad al-Za'nun
Civil Affairs, Jamil al-Tarifi
Industry, Bashir al-Barghuthi
Transport, Ali al-Qawasimi
Supplies, Abu Ali Shahin
Housing, Abd al-Rahman Hamad
Communications, Imad al-Faluji
Public Works, Azzam al-Ahmad
Agriculture, Abd al-Jawad Salih
Finance, Muhamad Zuhdi al-Nashashibi
Education, Yasir Amru
Higher Education, Hanan Ashwari
Culture, Yasir Abd Ar-Rabbuh
Labour, Samir Ghawshah
Jerusalem, Faisal Husseini
Secretary-General of the Presidency, Tayyib Abd al-Rahim
Secretary-General of the Council of Ministers, Ahmed Abd al-Rahman
Adviser for Refugee Affairs, Abdullah Hurani
Adviser to the Health Ministry, Abd al-Aziz al-Hajj Ahmad
Adviser, Abd al-Hafiz al-Ashhab

BRITISH CONSULATE-GENERAL
19 Nashashibi Street, PO Box 19690, East Jerusalem 97200
Consul-General, R. J. Dalton

BRITISH COUNCIL DIRECTOR, Peter Skelton (*Cultural Attaché*), Al-Nuzha Building, 2 Abu Obeida Street, PO Box 19136, Jerusalem.

ITALY
Repubblica Italiana

Italy consists of a peninsula, the islands of Sicily, Sardinia, Elba and about 70 other small islands. It is bounded on the north by Switzerland and Austria, on the south by the Mediterranean Sea, on the east by the Adriatic Sea and Slovenia, and on the west by France and the Ligurian and Tyrrhenian Seas. The total area is about 116,304 sq. miles (301,225 sq. km).

The peninsula is for the most part mountainous, but between the Apennines, which form its spine, and the east

coastline are two large fertile plains: Emilia/Romagna in the north and Apulia in the south. The Alps divide Italy from France, Switzerland, Austria and Slovenia. Partly within the Italian borders are Monte Rosa (15,217 ft), the Matterhorn (14,780 ft) and several peaks from 12,000 to 14,000 ft. The chief rivers are the Po (405 miles), flowing through Piedmont, Lombardy and the Veneto; the Adige (Trentino and Veneto); the Arno (Florentine plain); the Tiber (flowing through Rome to Ostia).

The population (UN estimate 1994) was 57,154,000. The language is Italian, a Romance language derived from Latin. It is spoken in its purest form in Tuscany, but there are numerous dialects, showing variously French, German, Spanish and Arabic influences. Sard, the dialect of Sardinia, is accorded by some authorities the status of a distinct Romance language.

CAPITAL – Rome. Population of the commune (1991 census) 2,693,383. The Eternal City was founded, according to legend, by Romulus in 753 BC. It was the centre of Latin civilization and capital of the Roman Republic and Roman Empire. The other principal cities and towns (population of the commune, 1991 census) are Milan 1,371,008; ΨNaples 1,054,601; Turin 961,916; ΨGenoa 675,639; Bologna 404,322; Florence 402,316; Sicily, ΨPalermo 697,162; Sardinia, ΨCagliari 203,254.
CURRENCY – Lira of 100 centesimi.
FLAG – Vertical stripes of green, white and red.
NATIONAL ANTHEM – Inno di Mameli.
NATIONAL DAY – 2 June.

HISTORY

Italian unity was accomplished under the House of Savoy after a struggle from 1848 to 1870 in which Mazzini (1805–72), Garibaldi (1807–82) and Cavour (1810–61) were the principal figures. It was completed when Lombardy was ceded by Austria in 1859 and Venice in 1866, and through the evacuation of Rome by the French in 1870. In 1871 the King of Italy entered Rome, and that city was declared to be the capital.

A fascist regime came to power in 1922 under Benito Mussolini, known as *Il Duce* (The Leader), who was prime minister from 1922 until 25 July 1943, when the regime was abolished. Mussolini was captured by Italian partisans while attempting to escape across the Swiss frontier and killed on 28 April 1945.

In fulfilment of a promise given in April 1944 that he would retire when the Allies entered Rome, a decree was signed in June 1944 by King Victor Emmanuel III under which Prince Umberto, his son, became Lieutenant-General of the Realm. The King remained head of the House of Savoy and retained the title King of Italy until his abdication in May 1946, when he was succeeded by the Crown Prince. A general election was held in June 1946, together with a referendum on the future of the monarchy, in which a majority favoured a republic and the royal family left the country.

GOVERNMENT

The 1947 constitution provides for the election of the president for a seven-year term by an electoral college which consists of the two houses of the parliament (the Chamber of Deputies and the Senate) sitting in joint session, together with three delegates from each region (one in the case of the Valle d'Aosta). The president, who must be over 50 years of age, has numerous carefully defined powers, the main one of which is the right to dissolve one or both houses after consultation with the Speakers. Members of both houses were elected wholly by proportional representation until 1993. Now 75 per cent (232) of the 315 elected seats in the Senate are elected on a first-past-the-post basis and the remaining elected seats are filled by proportional representation. In addition there are 11 life senators, who are past presidents and prime ministers. In the Chamber of Deputies 75 per cent (472) of seats are elected on a first-past-the-post basis, and 25 per cent (158) by proportional representation, with a 4 per cent threshold for parliamentary representation.

Political instability (50 governments since 1947) and widespread corruption, often with Mafia links, led to public disenchantment with the major political parties. Their support collapsed in the April 1992 general election, which produced an increase in support for Northern League and anti-Mafia parties. The so-called 'clean hands' investigation into corruption and Mafia links that began in Milan in February 1992 has led to the arrest by magistrates of thousands of politicians and businessmen.

The first general election under the new electoral system, on 27–28 March 1994, resulted in victory for the right-wing Freedom Alliance composed of the new Forza Italia party, the Northern League and the National Alliance. The Forza Italia leader and millionaire business-man Silvio Berlusconi formed a government in May 1994. The coalition government proved unstable and collapsed on 21 December 1994 when the majority of the Northern League ministers withdrew from the government over Berlusconi's indictment on charges of bribery and corruption. The independent Treasury minister Lamberto Dini formed a government of technocrats in January 1995 which was mandated to make extensive cuts to public spending. Dini resigned on 11 January 1996 and his designated successor, Antonio Maccanico, was unable to form a coalition government forcing another general election. The election of 21 April 1996 was won by the left-wing Olive Tree alliance led by the Democratic Party of the Left, whose leader, Romano Prodi, became prime minister. The government won 157 seats in the Senate and 284 seats in the Chamber of Deputies where it required the support of the Communist Refoundation to win a vote of confidence.

HEAD OF STATE
President, Oscar Luigi Scalfaro, *elected by electoral college*
25 May 1992

COUNCIL OF MINISTERS *as at August 1996*
Prime Minister, Romano Prodi (IPP)
Deputy PM, Culture, Walter Veltroni (DPL)
Foreign Affairs, Lamberto Dini (IR)
Defence, Beniamino Andreatta (IPP)
Interior, Giorgio Napolitano (DPL)
Justice, Giovanni Maria Flick (Ind.)
Finance, Vincenzo Visco (DPL)
Treasury, Budget, Carlo Azeglio Ciampi (Ind.)
Public Works, Antonio di Pietro (Ind.)
Labour, Tiziano Treu (IR)
Regional Affairs, Franco Bassanini (DPL)
Industry, Pierluigi Bersani (DPL)
Transport, Claudio Burlando (DPL)
Education, Luigi Berlinguer (DPL)
Post and Telecommunications, Antonio Maccanico (IPP)
Foreign Trade, Augusto Fantozzi (IR)
Environment, Edo Ronchi (Green)
Family and Social Affairs, Livia Turco (DPL)
Health, Rosaria Bindi (DPL)
Equal Opportunities, Anna Finocchiaro (DPL)
Agriculture, Michele Pinto (IPP)
DPL Democratic Party of the Left; IPP Italian Popular Party; IR Italian Renewal

ITALIAN EMBASSY
14 Three Kings Yard, Davies Street, London WIY 2EH
Tel 0171-312 2200
Ambassador Extraordinary and Plenipotentiary,
HE Dr Paolo Galli, apptd 1995
Minister-Counsellor, A. Armellini
Defence Attaché, P. Rizzo
Cultural Attaché, Prof. B. Bini
Consul-General, L. Brofferio
First Counsellor, G. Ardizzone (*Commercial*)
There are also consular offices in Bedford, Edinburgh and Manchester.

BRITISH EMBASSY
Via XX Settembre 80A, 00187 Rome
Tel: Rome 482-5441
Ambassador Extraordinary and Plenipotentiary,
HE Thomas L. Richardson, CMG, apptd 1996
Minister, D. H. Colvin, CMG
Defence and Military Attaché, Brig. J. H. Thoyts
Director-General for British Trade Development in Italy and Consul-General, R. J. Chase (*Milan*)
Counsellor (Economic and Commercial), T. G. Paxman

BRITISH CONSULAR OFFICES – There are Consulates-General at Milan and Naples and Consulates offices at Rome, Genoa, Florence, Venice, Trieste, Bari and Turin.

BRITISH COUNCIL REPRESENTATIVE, R. Alford, OBE, Palazzo del Drago, Via Quattro Fontane 20, 00184 Rome. There are British Council Offices at Milan, Bologna and Naples, each with a library.

BRITISH CHAMBER OF COMMERCE, Via San Paolo 7, 20121 Milan.

DEFENCE

Total active armed forces personnel number 328,700 (including 174,700 conscripts who serve for 12 months). Reserves number 584,000, with an obligation to age 25 or 45 (Air Force), 34 (Army), 39 or 73 (Navy).

The Army has a strength of 175,000 (131,600 conscripts), with 1,319 main battle tanks, 3,031 armoured personnel carriers and 1,946 artillery pieces.

The Navy has a strength of 44,000 (including 17,600 conscripts), with nine submarines, one helicopter carrier, one cruiser, four destroyers and 26 frigates with 30 armed helicopters. The Air Force has a strength of 67,800 (25,500 conscripts) with 369 combat aircraft.

In addition to the regular armed forces there is the 111,800-strong paramilitary Carabinieri.

ECONOMY

The governments of 1992 to 1994 introduced measures to reduce corruption, the budget deficit and national debt by reforming the pensions system, civil service and health service, and launching large-scale privatization. One of the economy's major problems is the large budget deficit which in 1995 was still around 8 per cent of GDP despite four successive austerity budgets from 1993 to 1995. In June 1996, the Prodi government outlined a proposed mini-budget aimed at stabilizing the budget deficit at 5.9 per cent of GDP, and predicted a drop to 4.4 per cent in 1997, 1 per cent outside the EU's Maastricht criteria for monetary union. Unemployment remains high at 12 per cent but inflation has dropped below 4 per cent.

The state-owned sector of Italian industry is still important, dominated by the holding companies IRI (mechanical, steel, airlines), ENI (petrochemicals), STET (telecommunications) and ENEL (electricity). Industry accounted for 30.2 per cent of GDP in 1991. It is centred around Milan (steel, machine tools, motor cars), Turin (motor cars, steel, roller bearings, textiles), Rome (light industries), Venice (shipbuilding, paper, mechanical equipment, electrical goods, woollens), Bologna/Florence (food industry, footwear and textiles, reproduction furniture, glassware, pottery, ceramics), Naples, Bari (valves, vehicle bodies, tyres), Taranto (steel, oil refining), Trieste (shipbuilding) and Cagliari (aluminium production, petrochemicals).

Italy is generally poor in mineral resources but deposits of natural methane gas and oil have been discovered, mainly south of Sicily, and rapidly exploited. Production of lignite has also increased. Other minerals include iron ores and pyrites, mercury (over one-quarter of the world production), lead, zinc and aluminium. Rich gold veins were discovered in Sardinia in May 1996. Marble is a traditional product of the Massa Carrara district.

Agriculture accounted for 3.8 per cent of GDP in 1991. Production is concentrated in Tuscany, Emilia-Romagna, Sicily and the whole of the southern third of the country. The principal products are wine, tobacco, citrus fruits, tomatoes, almonds, sugar beet, wheat and maize.

Tourism is a major sector of the economy, with over 50 million foreign tourists a year. Tourism is centred on Rome, Florence, Venice, the Alps, Sicily, the Adriatic coast and the Bay of Naples. The commercial and banking services are concentrated in Rome and in Milan, where the stock market is located.

Trade with UK	1994	1995
Imports from UK	£6,617,827,000	£7,436,500,000
Exports to UK	7,181,993,000	7,834,300,000

COMMUNICATIONS

The main railway system is state-run by the *Ferrovia dello Stato*. A network of motorways (*autostrade*) covers the country, built and operated mainly by the IRI state holding company and ANAS, the state highway authority. Alitalia, the principal international and domestic airline, is also state-controlled by the IRI group. Other smaller companies, including ATI (an Alitalia subsidiary) and Air Mediterranea, operate on domestic routes. Genoa is the

major port, handling about one-third of Italy's foreign trade.

CULTURE

Florence, the capital of Tuscany, was one of the greatest cities in Europe from the 11th to the 16th centuries, and the cradle of the Renaissance. Under the Medici family in the 15th century flourished many of the greatest names in Italian art, including Filippo Lippi, Botticelli, Donatello and Brunelleschi, and in the 16th century Michelangelo and Leonardo da Vinci.

Italian literature (in addition to Latin literature, which is the common inheritance of western Europe) is one of the richest in Europe, particularly in its golden age (Dante, 1265–1321; Petrarch, 1304–74; Boccaccio, 1313–75) and in the Renaissance (Ariosto, 1474–1533; Machiavelli, 1469–1527; Tasso, 1544–95). Notable in modern Italian literature are Manzoni (1785–1873), Carducci (1835–1907) and Gabriele d'Annunzio (1864–1938). The Nobel Prize for Literature has been awarded to Italian authors on five occasions: G. Cariducci (1906), Signora G. Deledda (1926), Luigi Pirandello (1934), Salvatore Quasimodo (1959) and Eugenio Montale (1975).

EDUCATION

Education is free and compulsory between the ages of six and 14; this comprises five years at primary school and three in the 'middle school', of which there are about 8,000. Pupils who obtain the middle school certificate may seek admission to any 'senior secondary school', which may be a lyceum with a classical or scientific or artistic bias, or an institute directed at technology (of which there are eight different types), trade or industry (including vocational schools), or teacher-training. Courses at the lyceums and technical institutes usually last for five years and success in the final examination qualifies for admission to university. In 1990–1 there were 3,056,000 students at elementary school, 2,266,000 at middle school and 2,861,000 at senior secondary school.

There are 35 state and 14 private universities, some of ancient foundation; those at Bologna, Modena, Parma and Padua were started in the 12th century. University education is not free, but entrants with higher qualifications are charged reduced fees according to a sliding scale. In 1990–1 there were 1,381,000 students at university.

In general, schools, lyceums and universities are financed by local taxation and central government grants.

ISLANDS

PANTELLERIA ISLAND (part of Trapani Province) in the Sicilian Narrows; area 31 sq. miles; population 9,601.

THE PELAGIAN ISLANDS (Lampedusa, Linosa and Lampione) are part of the province of Agrigento; area 8 sq. miles; population 4,811.

THE TUSCAN ARCHIPELAGO (including Elba); area 293 sq. km; population 31,861.

PONTINE ARCHIPELAGO, including Ponza; area 10 sq. km; population 2,515.

FLEGREAN ISLANDS, including Ischia; area 60 sq. km; population 51,883.

CAPRI.

EOLIAN ISLANDS, including Lipari; area 116 sq. km; population 18,636.

TREMITI ISLANDS; area 3 sq. km; population 426.

JAMAICA

Jamaica is situated in the Caribbean Sea south-east of Cuba and lies between 17° 43′ and 18° 32′ N. latitude and 76° 11′ and 78° 21′ W. longitude. It is 4,244 sq. miles (10,991 sq. km) in area and is divided into three counties (Surrey, Middlesex and Cornwall) and 14 parishes. The island consists mainly of coastal plains, divided by the Blue Mountain range in the east and the hills and limestone plateaux in the central and western areas of the interior. The central chain of the Blue Mountains is over 6,000 feet above sea level, and the Blue Mountain Peak is 7,402 feet.

The population (UN estimate 1994) was 2,960,000.

CAPITAL – ΨKingston, the largest town and seaport (estimated population of the corporate area of Kingston and St Andrew in 1982, 696,300). Other main towns are ΨMontego Bay, Ocho Rios, Spanish Town, Mandeville and May Pen.
CURRENCY – Jamaican dollar (J$) of 100 cents.
FLAG – Gold diagonal cross forming triangles of green at top and bottom, triangles of black at hoist and in fly.
NATIONAL ANTHEM – Jamaica, Land We Love.
NATIONAL DAY – First Monday in August (Independence Day).

GOVERNMENT

The island was discovered by Columbus in 1494, and occupied by Spain from 1509 until 1655 when a British expedition under Admiral Penn and General Venables captured the island. In 1670 it was formally ceded to England by the Treaty of Madrid. Jamaica became an independent state within the Commonwealth on 6 August 1962.

HM Queen Elizabeth II is the head of state, represented by the Governor-General. The legislature consists of a Senate of 21 nominated members and a House of Representatives consisting of 60 members elected by universal adult suffrage.

At the general election of 30 March 1993, the People's National Party won 52 seats and the Jamaica Labour Party won 8.

Governor-General, HE Howard Felix Hanlon Cooke, apptd 1991

CABINET *as at August 1996*
Prime Minister, Defence, Rt. Hon. Percival J. Patterson, QC
Deputy Prime Minister, Foreign Affairs and Trade, Hon. Seymour Mullings
Tourism, Hon. John Junior
Public Utilities, Transport and Energy, Hon. Robert Pickersgill
Housing and the Environment, Hon. Easton Douglas
Industry, Investments and Commerce, Hon. Dr Paul Robertson
Education, Youth and Culture, Hon. Burchell Whiteman
Health, Sen. the Hon. Peter Phillips
Labour, Social Security and Sports, Hon. Portia Simpson
Local Government and Works, Hon. Roger Clarke
National Security and Justice, Hon. K. D. Knight
Without Portfolio, Hon. Maxine Henry-Wilson
Legal Affairs, Hon. David Coore
Agriculture and Mining, Hon. Horace Clarke
Finance and Planning, Hon. Omar Davies

JAMAICAN HIGH COMMISSION
1–2 Prince Consort Road, London SW7 2BZ
Tel 0171-823 9911
High Commissioner, HE Derek Heaven, apptd 1994

Deputy High Commissioners, O. Singh; J. K. Pringle, CBE (*Trade*)
Minister-Counsellor, W. Gregory (*Consular Affairs*)
Defence Adviser, B. Blake
BRITISH HIGH COMMISSION
PO Box 575, Trafalgar Road, Kingston 10
Tel: Kingston 926 9050
High Commissioner, HE Richard Thomas, CMG, apptd 1995
Deputy High Commissioner, A. White
Defence Adviser, Col. J. J. Dumas, OBE
First Secretary (Management/Consular), J. McLeod
BRITISH COUNCIL REPRESENTATIVE IN THE CARIBBEAN, Andrew Norris, 4th Floor, PCMB Building, 64 Knutsford Boulevard, PO Box 575, Kingston 5.

JUDICATURE

Chief Justice, Hon. Lemley Wolfe
President of the Court of Appeal, Hon. Carl Rattray
Judges of the Court of Appeal, Hons. M. L. Wright; I. X. Forte; H. E. Downer; U. D. Gordon; B. H. Carey; C. Patterson

ECONOMY

Since 1989 the PNP government has introduced economic reforms including the abolition of price subsidies, the removal of foreign exchange controls and the introduction of a 10 per cent consumption tax. The IMF in 1992 approved a credit facility of US$153 million for a three-year period. Jamaica is a popular tourist resort, attracting 1,563,097 visitors during 1992. Actual foreign exchange receipts from tourism amounted to US$850 million in 1992.

Alumina, bananas, bauxite and sugar are the main exports. Earnings from sugar in 1992 amounted to US$82.5 million, bauxite and alumina US$560 million and bananas US$39.6 million. Other exports include garments, processed food products, limestone and ornamental horticultural products.

TRADE	1993	1994
Imports	US$5,158.7m	US$5,141m
Exports	3,530.4m	3,726m

Trade with UK	1994	1995
Imports from UK	£56,354,000	£69,771,000
Exports to UK	133,963,000	149,076,000

COMMUNICATIONS

There are several excellent harbours, Kingston being the principal port. The island has 2,944 miles of main roads and 7,264 miles of subsidiary roads.

There are two international airports, the Norman Manley International Airport on the south coast serving Kingston, and Sangster Airport on the north coast serving the major tourist areas. In addition there are licensed aerodromes at Port Antonio, Ocho Rios, Mandeville and Negril. There are 16 privately owned, seven public and two military airstrips. Air Jamaica, the national airline, operates international services; Air Jamaica Express and Tropical Airways operate scheduled internal and regional services.

JAPAN
Nihon Koku – Land of the Rising Sun

Japan consists of four large islands: *Honshū* (or Mainland) 88,839 sq. miles (230,448 sq. km), *Shikoku,* 7,231 sq. miles

(18,757 sq. km), *Kyūshū*, 16,170 sq. miles (42,079 sq. km), *Hokkaido*, 30,265 sq. miles (78,508 sq. km), and many small islands (including Okinawa) situated in the north Pacific Ocean between 128° 6' and 145° 49' E. longitude and between 26° 59' and 45° 31' N. latitude, with a total area of 145,834 sq. miles (377,708 sq. km).

The interior is very mountainous, and crossing the mainland from the Sea of Japan to the Pacific is a group of volcanoes, mainly extinct or dormant. Mount Fuji, the most sacred mountain of Japan, is 12,370 ft high and has been dormant since 1707, but volcanoes which are active include Mount Aso in Kyūshū. There are frequent earthquakes, mainly along the Pacific coast near the Bay of Tokyo. The climate varies from sub-tropical in the south to cool temperate in the north.

The population (1993 estimate) is 124,764,215. The principal religions are Mahayana Buddhism and Shinto. About 1 per cent of Japanese are Christians.

CAPITAL – Tokyo, population (December 1989) 11,718,720. The other chief cities had the following populations (1994): ΨYokohama (3,265,000); ΨOsaka (2,481,000); ΨNagoya (2,091,000); Sapporo (1,719,000); ΨKobé (1,479,000); Kyoto, the ancient capital (1,391,000); ΨFukuoka (1,221,000).

CURRENCY – Yen of 100 sen.

FLAG – White, charged with sun (red).

NATIONAL ANTHEM – Kimigayo.

NATIONAL DAY – 23 December (the Emperor's Birthday).

GOVERNMENT

According to tradition, Jimmu, the first Emperor of Japan, ascended the throne on 11 February 660 BC. Under the *Meiji* constitution (1889), the monarchy is hereditary in the male heirs of the Imperial house.

After the unconditional surrender to the allied nations (14 August 1945), Japan was occupied by Allied forces under General MacArthur. A Japanese peace treaty became effective on 28 April 1952. Japan then resumed her status as an independent power.

Under the 1947 constitution, legislative authority rests with the elected Diet, which is bicameral, consisting of a 511-member House of Representatives and a 252-member House of Councillors. The House of Councillors, whose powers are subordinate to the House of Representatives, elects half its members every three years. Executive authority is vested in the Cabinet which is responsible to the legislature.

The (conservative) Liberal Democratic Party (LDP) governed Japan almost without interruption from the Second World War until 1993. During the 1990s growing public disgust at political corruption led to a loss of support for the LDP and in 1992 and 1993 three splinter parties were formed: Japan New Party (JNP), Japan Renewal Party (JRP) (Shinseito) and the Sakigate (Harbinger) Party. Support for the new parties caused the LDP to lose its majority at the election in July 1993, following which the three new parties formed a coalition with the opposition Komeito, Social Democratic (SDPJ), Democratic Socialist (DSP) and United Social Democratic (USDP) (Shaminren) parties. The new government was sworn in on 9 August 1993.

The seven-party coalition government led by Morihiro Hosokawa (JNP) reached a compromise with the LDP-controlled House of Councillors in January 1994 to pass laws limiting corporate donations to individual MPs' funds and to ban them after five years, introducing state subsidies for political parties, and changing the first-past-the-post electoral system with multi-member constituencies to a system with 200 MPs elected by proportional representa-

tion and 300 single-member, first-past-the-post constituencies. After corruption scandals and coalition manoeuvrings the governments of Hosokawa and his successor Tsutoma Hata were brought down and the LDP returned to power in June 1994 in coalition with the SDPJ and Sakigate parties, with SDPJ leader Tomiichi Murayama becoming Japan's first socialist Prime Minister. The five reformist opposition parties (JNP, JRP, Komeito, DSP, USDP) merged in November 1994 to form the New Frontier Party (NFP) (Shinshinto) as a rival centre-right conservative party to the LDP. Murayama resigned as Prime Minister on 5 January 1996 and was replaced by LDP leader Ryutaro Hashimoto.

In August 1996 the strength of the parties in the House of Representatives was: Liberal Democratic Party 206; New Frontier Party (Shinshinto) 169; Social Democratic Party 63; Sakigate 23; Japanese Communist Party 15; Independents 6; others 12.

In August 1996 the strength of the parties in the House of Councillors was: Liberal Democratic Party 110; Heisei-kai 68; Social Democratic Party 36; Japanese Communist Party 14; Independents 3; others 21.

HEAD OF STATE

His Imperial Majesty The Emperor of Japan, Emperor Akihito, *born* 23 December 1933; *succeeded* 8 January 1989; *enthroned* 12 November 1990; *married* 10 April 1959, Miss Michiko Shoda, and has *issue*: the Crown Prince; Prince Fumihito, *born* 30 November 1965; and Princess Sayako, *born* 18 April 1969

Heir, HRH Crown Prince Naruhito Hironomiya, *born* 23 February 1960, *married* 9 June 1993 Miss Masako Owada

CABINET *as at August 1996*

Prime Minister, Ryutaro Hashimoto (LDP)

Deputy PM, Finance, Wataru Kubo (SDPJ)

Justice, Ritsuko Nagao (Ind.)

Foreign Affairs, Yukihiko Ikeda (LDP)

Education, Mikio Okuda (LDP)

Health and Welfare, Naoto Kan (Sakigate)

Agriculture, Forestry and Fisheries, Ichizo Ohara (LDP)

International Trade and Industry, Shunpei Tsukahara (LDP)

Transport, Yoshiyuki Kamei (LDP)

Posts and Telecommunications, Ichiro Hino (SDPJ)

Labour, Takanobu Nagai (SDPJ)

Construction, Eiichi Nakao (LDP)

Home Affairs, Hiroyuki Kurata (LDP)

MINISTERS OF STATE

Chief Cabinet Secretary, Seiroku Kajiyama (LDP)

Director-General, Hokkaido and Okinawa Development Agencies, Saburo Okabe (LDP)

Director-General, Defence Agency, Hideo Usui (LDP)

Director-General, Science and Technology Agency, Hidenao Nakagawa (LDP)

Director-General, Environment Agency, Sukio Iwatare (SDPJ)

Director-General, Economic Planning Agency, Shusei Tanaka (Sakigate)

Director-General, National Land Agency, Kazumi Suzuki (SDPJ)

Director-General, Management and Co-ordination Agency, Sekisuke Nakanishi (SDPJ)

SDPJ Social Democratic Party of Japan; LDP Liberal Democratic Party; Ind. Independent.

EMBASSY OF JAPAN

101–104 Piccadilly, London W1V 9FN

Tel 0171-465 6500

Ambassador Extraordinary and Plenipotentiary, HE Hiroaki Fujii, apptd 1994

Ministers, S. Numata; M. Amano (*Commercial*); Y. Matsuo (*Financial*); M. Kohno (*Consul-General*) *Defence Attaché*, Capt. M. Shimada *Counsellor* (*Culture*), M. Muto

BRITISH EMBASSY
No. 1 Ichiban-cho, Chiyoda-ku, Tokyo 102
Tel: Tokyo 5211-1100
Ambassador Extraordinary and Plenipotentiary, HE David J. Wright, KCMG, LVO, apptd 1996
Ministers, C. T. W. Humfrey; J. E. W. Kirby (*Financial*) *Counsellors*, D. A. Warren (*Commercial*); P. V. Rollitt (*Management and Consul-General*)
Defence and Naval Attaché, Capt. N. D. V. Robertson
There are British Consulates General at Tokyo and Osaka, and Honorary Consulates at Fukuoka, Hiroshima and Nagoya.

BRITISH COUNCIL REPRESENTATIVE, Michael Barrett, OBE (*Cultural Attaché*), 2 Kagurazaka 1-Chome, Shinjuku-ku, Tokyo 162. There is also an office and library in Kyoto.

BRITISH CHAMBER OF COMMERCE, No. 16 Kowa Building, 1–9–20 Akasaka, Minato-ku, Tokyo 107

ECONOMY

Owing to the mountainous nature of the country less than 20 per cent of its area can be cultivated and only 14 per cent is used for agriculture; 67 per cent is wooded. The soil is only moderately fertile but intensive cultivation secures good crops. Tobacco, tea, potatoes, rice, maize, wheat and other cereals are all cultivated. Rice is the staple food of the people, about 13,255,000 tonnes being produced in 1992. Fruit is abundant and pigs and chickens are widely reared.

The country has mineral resources, including gold, silver, copper, lead, zinc, iron chromite, white arsenic, coal, sulphur, petroleum, salt and uranium. However, iron ore, coal and crude oil are among the principal imports to supply deficiencies at home.

Japan is one of the most highly industrialized nations in the world, with the whole range of modern light and heavy industries, including steel, aerospace, computers, office machinery, motor vehicles, electronics, metals, machinery, chemicals, textiles (cotton, silk, wool and synthetics), cement, pottery, glass, rubber, lumber, paper, oil refining and shipbuilding.

The labour force in 1993 (average) was 64,500,000, of which around 2.5 per cent were unemployed. Of the total labour force, over 15 per cent are over 65 and this rate is increasing. Industrial, manufacturing and services workers numbered 60,694,000 and agricultural, forestries and fisheries workers 3,806,000 in 1993. In 1992 primary industry accounted for 2.2 per cent of GDP, manufacturing, mining and construction for 41.1 per cent of GDP, and services for 59.1 per cent. Japan's GDP of US$4,190,399 million in 1993 made its economy the second largest in the world. GDP growth was predicted to rise above 3 per cent in 1997, following sluggish growth of 0.9 per cent in 1995.

FINANCE

The 1996–7 budget of Yen 75,105,000 million was passed on 10 May 1996, despite opposition from Shinshinto, which objected to the allocation of funds to rescue seven mortgage companies.

TRADE

Being deficient in natural resources, Japan has had to develop a complex foreign trade. Principal imports in 1993 consisted of machinery and equipment (19.4 per cent), foodstuffs (16.4 per cent), petroleum (11.6 per cent), chemicals (7.5 per cent), metal ores and scrap (2.9 per cent). Principal exports consist of machinery and equipment (76 per cent, of which motor vehicles comprise 16.1 per cent), iron and steel (4.0 per cent), chemicals (5.6 per cent), textile goods (2.3 per cent) and ships (1.4 per cent).

	1992	1993
Total imports	US$232,698m	US$240,670m
Total exports	339,762m	360,911m

	1994	1995
Trade with UK		
Imports from UK	£2,991,159,000	£3,782,955,000
Exports to UK	8,841,577,000	9,613,810,000

COMMUNICATIONS

Japan National Railways was privatized in 1987 and is known as Japan Railways (JR). There are six regional companies and one goods company. Shinkansen (bullet train) tracks are currently being expanded. The opening in 1988 of the Seikan rail tunnel and the Seto Ohashi rail bridge means that the four major islands are now linked for the first time.

The merchant fleet had a shipping capacity of 25.4 million gross tons and 10,091 vessels in 1992, making it the largest in the world in terms of number of vessels and third in terms of tonnage.

DEFENCE

The constitution prohibits the maintenance of armed forces, although internal security forces were created in 1950 and 1952. In 1954 the mission of the forces was extended to include the defence of Japan against direct and indirect aggression. Legislation passed in 1992 allows a maximum of 2,000 troops to take part in UN peacekeeping missions overseas, limited to non-front line activities; legislation passed in 1994 allows the armed forces to enter foreign conflicts in order to rescue Japanese nationals.

The total active armed forces strength is 239,500. The Ground Self-Defence Force (GSDF) has a strength of 151,200. Equipment includes 1,160 main battle tanks 930 armoured personnel carriers and infantry fighting vehicles, 810 artillery pieces and 80 attack helicopters.

The Maritime Self-Defence Force (MSDF) has a strength of 43,700 personnel, with 18 submarines and 63 destroyers and frigates, 110 combat aircraft and 99 armed helicopters.

The Air Self-Defence Force (ASDF) has a strength of 44,600 personnel with 450 combat aircraft.

The USA at present stations 45,500 personnel in Japan: Army 2,000; Navy 7,300; Marines 21,000; Air Force 15,200.

EDUCATION

Education at elementary (six-year course) and lower secondary (three-year course) schools is free, compulsory and co-educational. The (three-year) upper secondary schools are attended by 96.7 per cent of the age group. They have courses in general, agricultural, commercial, technical, mercantile marine, radio communication and home economics education, etc.

Of the population aged between 18 and 21, 32.7 per cent were enrolled in higher education in 1992. There are two-or three-year junior colleges and four-year universities. Some of the universities have graduate schools. In 1993 there were 1,129 universities and junior colleges, the vast majority of which are privately maintained. The most prominent universities are the seven state universities of Tokyo, Kyoto, Tohoku (Sendai), Hokkaido (Sapporo), Kyushu (Fukuoka), Osaka and Nagoya, and the two private universities of Keio and Waseda.

CULTURE

Japanese is said to be one of the Uro-Altaic group of languages and remained a spoken tongue until the fifth to seventh centuries AD, when Chinese characters came into use. Japanese who have received school education (99.8 per cent of the population) can read and write the Chinese characters in current use (about 1,800 characters) and also the syllabary characters called Kana. English is the best known foreign language. It is taught in all middle and high schools and universities. There are 125 daily newspapers.

JORDAN
Al-Mamlaka al Urduniya al-Hashemiyah

The Hashemite Kingdom of the Jordan, which covers 37,738 sq. miles (97,740 sq. km), is bounded on the north by Syria, on the west by Israel, on the south by Saudi Arabia and on the east by Iraq.

The population on the East Bank of the Jordan (1994 census) was 4,095,579. The majority are Sunni Muslims and Islam is the religion of the state; however, freedom of belief is guaranteed by the constitution.

CAPITAL – Amman, population (1994 estimate) 1,270,000.
CURRENCY – Jordanian dinar (JD) of 1,000 fils.
FLAG – Three horizontal stripes of black, white, green and a red triangle based on the hoist, containing a seven-pointed white star.
NATIONAL ANTHEM – Long Live the King.
NATIONAL DAY – 25 May (Independence Day).

HISTORY

After the defeat of Turkey in the First World War, the Amirate of Transjordan was established in the area east of the River Jordan as a state under British mandate. The mandate was terminated after the Second World War and the Amirate, still ruled by its founder the Amir Abdullah, became the Hashemite Kingdom of Jordan. Following the 1948–9 war between Israel and the Arab states, that part of Palestine remaining in Arab hands (the West Bank and East Jerusalem, but excluding Gaza) was, with Palestinian agreement, incorporated into the Hashemite Kingdom. King Abdullah was assassinated in 1951; his son Talal ruled briefly but abdicated in favour of King Hussein in 1952.

The West Bank has been under Israeli occupation since its capture from Jordan in the 1967 war, and East Jerusalem was annexed by Israel in 1967. In 1988 Jordan severed its legal and administrative ties with the occupied West Bank, but did not formally renounce sovereignty over the area. As a result of the wars of 1948–9 and 1967 there are about one million Palestinian refugees and displaced persons living in East Jordan, about 200,000 of whom live in refugee and displaced persons camps established by the UN Relief and Works Agency (UNRWA). In addition there are 300,000 self-supporting Palestinians in East Jordan.

GOVERNMENT

The 1952 constitution provides for a senate of 40 members (all appointed by the King) and an elected House of Representatives. Until 1988, the House of Representatives had 60 members representing both the East and West Banks. Legislation passed in 1989 stipulated that in future elections seats would be contested on the East Bank only. The first parliamentary elections since 1967 took place in 1989 to a new 80-member House of Representatives. The

House was dissolved by King Hussein on 17 August 1996, after opposition parties had used it as a platform for criticizing the government in the wake of riots over increased bread prices.

The King appoints the members of the Council of Ministers. Crown Prince Hassan normally acts as regent when King Hussein is abroad. In 1991 a new national charter was agreed between the King and political parties in a National Conference which lifted the ban on political parties, imposed in 1957 after a left-wing coup attempt, in return for allegiance to the monarchy. The first multiparty parliamentary elections since 1956 were held in 1993, traditionalists and centrists winning 59 seats and the Islamic Action Front 16 seats.

The Middle East peace process begun in 1991 led to Jordan signing an agreement on a 'common agenda' for peace with Israel in 1993. Intensive bilateral negotiations continued throughout 1993–4 with Israel agreeing to return two narrow strips of territory in the Arava desert seized in 1967. On 25 July 1994 King Hussein and the Israeli Prime Minister signed a framework agreement for peace which ended the state of war existing since 1948. The first Israeli–Jordanian border crossing was opened between Eilat and Aqaba in August 1994. A full peace treaty was signed on 26 October 1994 which established full diplomatic and economic relations between the two states. It included agreements on sharing water from the Jordan and Yarmouk rivers; co-operating in the fields of commerce, transport, tourism, communications, energy and agriculture; and granted King Hussein custodianship of Islamic holy sites in Jerusalem. Israeli forces completed their withdrawal from Jordanian land in the Arava valley on 9 February 1995.

HEAD OF STATE

His Majesty The King of the Jordan, King Hussein, GCVO, *born* 14 November 1935, *succeeded* on the abdication of his father, King Talal, 11 August 1952, *assumed constitutional powers*, 2 May 1953, on coming of age
Crown Prince, Prince Hassan, third son of King Talal of Jordan, *born* 1947, *appointed Crown Prince*, 1 April 1965

COUNCIL OF MINISTERS *as at August 1996*

Prime Minister, Defence, Foreign Affairs, Abdul Karim Kabariti
Higher Education, Abdullah Ensour
Interior, Awad Khleifat
Public Works and Housing, Abdul Hadi al Majali
Justice, Abdul Karim al Dughmi
Post and Telecommunications, Jamal Sarayireh
Water and Irrigation, Samir Kawar
Industry and Trade, Ali Abul Ragheb
Tourism and Antiquities, Saleh Irsheidat
Municipal, Rural and Environmental Affairs, Abdul Razzaq Tbeishat
Health, Aref Bataineh
Religious Affairs, Abdul Salam al-Abbadi
Planning, Rima Khalaf-Hneidi
Energy and Mineral Resources, Hashem Dabbas
Social Development, Hammad Abu Jamous
Supply, Munir Sobar
Labour, Abdul Hafez Shakhanbeh
Culture, Ahmad Qudah
Agriculture, Mustafa Shneikat
Youth, Mohammed Daoudieh
Education, Dr Munther al-Masri
Finance, Marwan Awad
Information, Marwan Muasher
Administrative Development, Kamal Nasser
Transport, Naser al-Lawzi

EMBASSY OF THE HASHEMITE KINGDOM OF JORDAN
6 Upper Phillimore Gardens, London W8 7HB
Tel 0171-937 3685
Ambassador Extraordinary and Plenipotentiary, HE Fouad
   Ayoub, apptd 1991
Defence Attaché, Maj.-Gen. Abdel Jalil Ma'Aytah
Information Bureau: 11–12 Buckingham Gate, London SW1E
   6LB. Tel: 0171-630 9277

BRITISH EMBASSY
Abdoun (PO Box 87), Amman
Tel: Amman 823100
Ambassador Extraordinary and Plenipotentiary, HE Peter R. M.
   Hinchcliffe, CMG, CVO, apptd 1994
Counsellor, S. P. Collis (*Deputy Head of Mission and Consul-
   General*)
Defence Attaché, Col. T. R. Dumas, OBE
First Secretary, D. G. Tunstall (*Management*)
BRITISH COUNCIL DIRECTOR, Dr David Burton,
   Rainbow Street (PO Box 634), Amman 11118

DEFENCE

The total active armed forces strength is 98,600 personnel,
with selective conscription of two-year terms in operation.
Reserves number a further 35,000. The Army has a
strength of 90,000, with 1,141 main battle tanks, 1,135
armoured personnel carriers and armoured infantry fighting vehicles, and 485 artillery pieces.
   The Navy has 600 personnel in its Aqaba base with five
patrol craft. The Air Force has a strength of 8,000
personnel with 82 combat aircraft and 24 armed helicopters. In addition, there is a paramilitary civil militia of
200,000 personnel.

ECONOMY

The main agricultural areas are the Jordan Valley, the hills
overlooking the valley, and the flatter country to the south
of Amman and around Madaba and Irbid. However, several
large farms, which depend for irrigation on water pumped
from deep aquifers, have been established in the southern
desert area. The rest of the country is desert and semi-
desert. The principal crops are wheat, barley, vegetables,
olives and fruit (mainly grapes and citrus fruits). Agricultural production has increased considerably in recent years
due to improvements in production and irrigation techniques, and exports are increasing.
   Important industrial products are raw phosphates (1994,
4.2 million tons) and potash (1994, 1.6 million tons), most of
which is exported, together with fertilizers and pharmaceuticals. The Trans-Arabian oil pipeline (Tapline) runs
through north Jordan from Saudi Arabia to the Lebanese
port of Sidon. A branch pipeline, together with oil trucked
by road from Iraq, feeds a refinery at Zerqa (production
1994, 2.9 million tons) which meets most of Jordan's
requirements for refined petroleum products. Sufficient
reserves of natural gas have been discovered in the north-
east to produce electricity for the national grid since 1989.
No significant reserves of oil have been found.
   Tourism has steadily developed, principally in Amman,
Aqaba, Zerka Ma'in and on the shores of the Dead Sea. The
peace agreement with Israel has enabled planning to begin
of new coastal resorts spanning the border between Aqaba
and Israel. Following the peace agreement, the US and UK
governments wrote off most of the bilateral debt owed by
Jordan.
   The peace with Israel, including a preferential trade
agreement signed in October 1995, has created a mini-
boom, with a 40 per cent rise in tourism and 25 per cent rise
in exports. In 1994–5, GDP grew at a rate of 6 per cent,

inflation remained below 3.5 per cent, but unemployment
remained high at 15 per cent. The IMF approved a loan of
US$295 million in February 1996 to support economic
reforms, including privatization.

TRADE WITH UK	1994	1995
Imports from UK	£114,716,000	£119,597,000
Exports to UK	24,034,000	24,894,000

COMMUNICATIONS

The trunk road system is good. Amman is linked to Aqaba,
Damascus, Baghdad and Jeddah by roads which are of
considerable importance in the overland trade of the
Middle East.
   The former Hejaz Railway runs from Syria through
Jordan, and is used mainly for freight between Amman and
Damascus. The Aqaba railway carries phosphate rock from
the mines of al Hasa and al Abiad to Aqaba. A total of 2,485
vessels called at Aqaba in 1994, and 10,572,300 tons of cargo
were handled.
   The Royal Jordanian Airline operates from Amman to
Aqaba and has an extensive network of routes to the Middle
East, Europe, North America and the Far East.

KAZAKHSTAN
Kazak Respublikasy

Kazakhstan has an area of 1,049,155 sq. miles (2,717,300 sq.
km) and occupies the northern part of what was Soviet
Central Asia. It stretches from the Volga and the Caspian
Sea in the west to the Altai and Tienshan mountains in the
east. It is bordered on the west by the Caspian Sea and
Russia, on the south by Turkmenistan, Uzbekistan and
Kyrgyzstan, on the east by China and on the north by
Russia. The country consists of arid steppes and semi-
deserts, flat in the west, hilly in the east and mountainous in
the south-east (Southern Altai and Tienshan mountains).
The main rivers are the Irtysh, the Ural, the Syr-Darya and
the Ili. The climate is continental and very dry.
   The population (1994 estimate) is 16,963,600, of which
43 per cent are Kazakhs, 36 per cent Russians, 5 per cent
Ukrainians and 4 per cent ethnic Germans, with smaller
numbers of Tatars, Uzbeks, Koreans and Belarusians. The
Russian population is concentrated in the north of the
country, where it forms a significant majority, and in Alma-
Ata.
   The majority of ethnic Kazakhs are Sunni Muslims, and
this is the main religion of the republic. Kazakh (one of the
Turkic languages) became the official language in 1993
and Russian was given a special status as the 'social
language between peoples'. Otherwise each ethnic group
uses its own language.

CAPITAL – Alma-Ata (Almaty). Population 1,500,000
   (1994). The Kazakh parliament in 1994 voted to move
   the capital to the central town of Akmola by 2000. The
   other major city is Chimkent, population 400,000
   (1992).
CURRENCY – Tenge.
FLAG – Dark blue with a sun and a soaring eagle in the
   centre all in gold, and a red vertical ornamentation
   stripe near the hoist.
NATIONAL DAY – 16 December (Republic Day).

HISTORY

Kazakhstan was inhabited by nomadic tribes before being
invaded by Ghenghiz Khan and incorporated into his

empire in 1218. After his empire disintegrated, feudal towns emerged based on large oases. These towns affiliated and established a Kazakh state in the late 15th century which engaged in almost continuous warfare with the marauding Khanates on its southern border. After appealing to Russia for aid and protection, in 1731 Kazakhstan acceded to the Russian Empire under a voluntary act of accession.

The First World War brought privation to Kazakhstan, leading to an uprising in 1916 against the conscription of male Kazakhs. After the 1917 Russian revolution, Kazakhstan came under the control of White Russian forces until 1919. On 26 August 1920 a constitution was signed under which Kazakhstan became a Soviet Socialist Republic. Under Soviet rule in the 1920s and 1930s there was rapid industrial development and the traditional nomadic way of life disappeared. The Kazakhs suffered greatly in the Stalinist purges, the merchant and religious classes being murdered and thousands dying in the desert on collective farms. Other nationalities, such as Tatars and Germans, were forceably transported to Kazakhstan by Stalin. Kazakhstan was the last of the former USSR republics to declare its independence (16 December 1991).

GOVERNMENT

Under the constitution adopted on 28 January 1993, executive power is vested in the president and government. The president must be a Kazakh speaker and has the power to appoint the prime minister, other senior ministers and all ambassadors. The parliament does not have the power to impeach the president but the president can dissolve parliament.

A new constitution approved by referendum on 30 August 1995 granted the President the power to dissolve the legislature and to rule by decree. It also nominated Kazakh as the sole official language; prohibited dual citizenship; and created a new bicameral legislature composed of a 40-member Senate and a 67-member Majlis. The Constitutional Court, which opposed the new constitution, was replaced by a Constitutional Council which was made subject to presidential veto. The changes resulted from a power struggle between the Court and the President over the March 1994 legislative elections won by the Communist-derived Congress of People's Unity of Kazakhstan (SNEK) which the Court had ruled invalid. The President responded by dissolving the Supreme Kenges in March 1995. Elections to the new legislature were held in December 1995; the requirement for candidates to achieve an absolute majority made run-offs necessary. A referendum on 29 April 1995 extended President Nazarbayev's term until 2000.

HEAD OF STATE
President, Nursultan Nazarbayev, *elected* 1 December 1991, *confirmed in office until 2000 by referendum* 29 April 1995

GOVERNMENT *as at August 1996*
Prime Minister, Akezhan Kazhegeldin
First Vice-Premier, Nigmatzhan Isingarin
Vice-Premiers, Zhanybek Karibzhanov; Nikolai Makiyevsky; Viktor Sobolev; Imangali Tasmagambetov; Nagashbai Shaikenov
Internal Affairs, Kairbek Suleimenov
Geology and Mineral Resources, Serikbek Daukeyev
Health, Vassily Devyatko
Foreign Affairs, Kasymzhomart Tokayev
Culture, Talgat Mamashev
Science, Vladimir Shkolnik
Oil and Gas, Nurlan Balgimbayev
Education, Murat Zhurinov

Defence, Gen. Alibek Kasymov
Youth Affairs, Tourism, Physical Culture and Sport, Temerkan Dosmukhambetov
Industry and Trade, Garry Shtoik
Agriculture, Serik Akhymbekov
Social Protection, Seitsultan Aimbetov
Construction and Housing, Askar Kulibayev
Transport and Communications, Yury Lavrinenko
Labour, Pyotr Krepak
Finance, Alexander Pavlov
Ecology and Biological Resources, Nikolai Bayev
Economics, Umirzak Shukeyev
Power Engineering and Coal, Viktor Khrapunov
Justice, Konstantin Kolpakov

EMBASSY OF THE REPUBLIC OF KAZAKHSTAN
114A Cromwell Road, London SW7 4ES
Tel 0171-244 0011
Ambassador Extraordinary and Plenipotentiary,
  HE Nurtay Abykaev, apptd 1995

BRITISH EMBASSY
U1 Furmanova 173, Alma-Ata
Tel: Alma-Ata 506191
Ambassador Extraordinary and Plenipotentiary,
  HE Douglas B. McAdam, apptd 1996

BRITISH COUNCIL DIRECTOR, Elizabeth White, Panfilov 158, 480046

DEFENCE

In 1993–4 Kazakhstan established its own armed forces from forces that were formerly under joint CIS control with Russia. An agreement signed with Russia in January 1995 provides for eventual reunification of the two states' armed forces. The CIS mutual defence treaty of 1993, to which Kazakhstan is a signatory, retains a common air defence force, while Kazakh forces also take part in the CIS peacekeeping force along the Tajikistan-Afghanistan border. Kazakhstan ratified the Start 1 Treaty in 1992 and signed the Nuclear Non-Proliferation Treaty in December 1994. By 1996, all nuclear warheads had been returned to Russia although Kazakhstan retained 48 SS-18 intercontinental ballistic missiles.

The army numbers 25,000 personnel with 624 main battle tanks, 1,850 artillery pieces and 1,200 armoured combat vehicles. The Caspian Sea Flotilla, which Kazakhstan shares with Russia and Turkmenistan, operates under Russian command. The air force has a strength of 15,000 personnel, with 133 combat aircraft and 44 attack helicopters. In addition, paramilitary internal security, border guard and republican guard forces number 34,500.

ECONOMY

In March 1993 the government announced a three-year privatization programme under which most state-owned enterprises were to be sold by means of a voucher system. Small businesses and retail outlets have been sold at auction since 1992. Foreign investment from western states has been significant since 1992, with US$500 million invested so far. Foreign aid has exceeded US$1,000 million, including US$436 million from the USA to dismantle nuclear weapons and US$255 million from the IMF to aid the transformation to a market economy. The economy was weakened by the ending of preferential trading links to other CIS states at the break-up of the Soviet Union although a single market was formed with Kyrgyzstan and Uzbekistan in 1994. A treaty on further economic and humanitarian co-operation, as well as a customs union, was signed with Belarus, Kyrgyzstan and Russia in March 1996.

Kazakhstan is rich in minerals, with copper, lead, gold, uranium, chromium, silver, zinc, iron ore, coal, oil and natural gas. In 1994 production of coal was 104 million tonnes and iron ore was 1.3 million tonnes, while reserves of gold were estimated at 60 million tonnes. The oil and gas industry, concentrated in the west of the country, is being expanded by western investment, which is also being used to explore two large fields in the Caspian Sea: Karachaganak (gas), with reserves of 16,000 million cubic feet, and Tengiz (oil), with reserves of 6,000–9,000 million barrels. An agreement was signed with Russia, Oman and eight oil companies in April 1996 to begin construction of a pipeline between Russia and Kazakhstan. Oil production in 1994 was 19 million tonnes. Industry is dominated by food processing and mining and metals production; textiles, steel and tractors are also produced. The main centres of the metal industry are in the Altai mountains, in Chimkent, north of Lake Balkhash and in central Kazakhstan.

Agriculture, including stock-raising, is highly developed, particularly in the central and south-west of the republic. Grain is grown in the north and north-east, and cotton and wool produced in the south and south-east. A record grain crop was grown in 1992 and 1.5 million tonnes of meat produced in 1993.

Trade with UK	1994	1995
Imports from UK	£40,699,000	£26,561,000
Exports to UK	70,576,000	48,902,000

KENYA
Jamhuri ya Kenya

Kenya is bisected by the equator and extends approximately from 4° N. to 4° S. latitude and from 34° E. to 41° E. longitude. The Indian Ocean and Somalia lie to the east, Ethiopia to the north, Sudan to the north-west, Uganda and Lake Victoria to the west, and Tanzania to the south. The total area is 224,961 sq. miles (582,646 sq. km), including 5,171 square miles of water. The country is divided into eight provinces (Central, Coast, Eastern, Nairobi, Nyanza, North Eastern, Rift Valley, Western).

The population is 26,017,000 (1994 UN estimate). The main tribal groups are the Kikuyu, Luhya, Luo, Kalenjin, Kamba and Masai. The official languages are Swahili, which is generally understood throughout Kenya, and English; numerous indigenous languages are also spoken.

CAPITAL – Nairobi, population 1,400,000 (1989 estimate).
CURRENCY – Kenya shilling (Ksh) of 100 cents.
FLAG – Horizontally black, red and green with the red fimbriated in white, and with a shield and crossed spears all over in the centre.
NATIONAL ANTHEM – Kenya, Land of the Lion.
NATIONAL DAY – 12 December (Independence Day).

GOVERNMENT

Kenya became an independent state and a member of the British Commonwealth on 12 December 1963 and a republic in 1964. In 1982 the government introduced amendments to the constitution making the country a one-party state, with Kenya African National Union (KANU) as the ruling party. In December 1991 the government yielded to internal and international pressure and introduced a multiparty democracy.

Multiparty presidential and legislative elections were held in December 1992 which were won by President Moi and KANU respectively, amid opposition claims that the elections were not free and fair which were supported by the Commonwealth observers. In the unicameral National Assembly of 200 seats, KANU has 107 seats (95 elected and 12 nominated by the President) and the three major opposition parties have 85 seats between them. KANU formed a new government on 13 January 1993 and parliament reopened on 22 March 1993 but was boycotted by two of the main opposition parties for three months.

Ethnic clashes in the Rift Valley since 1991 between the Kikuyu, the Luo and the Luhya tribes on the one hand, who mainly support opposition parties, and the smaller government-supporting tribes of the Kalenjin, Masai and Pokot have left some 1,500 dead and 300,000 displaced.

HEAD OF STATE
President and C.-in-C. Armed Forces, Hon. Daniel T. arap Moi, *took office* 14 October 1978, *re-elected* 1979, 1983, 1988 and 29 December 1992

CABINET *as at August 1996*
The President
Vice-President and Minister for Planning and National Development, Hon. Prof. George Saitoti
Foreign Affairs, Hon. Stephen Musyoka
Finance, Hon. Wycliffe Mudavadi
Agriculture, Livestock Development and Marketing, Hon. Simon Nyachae
Land Reclamation, Regional and Water Development, Hon. Hussein Maalim Mohammed
Environment and Natural Resources, Hon. John Sambu
Transport and Communication, Hon. Wilson Ndolo Ayah
Energy, Hon. Darius Mbela
Commerce and Industry, Hon. Kirugi M'mukindia
Education, Hon. Joseph Kamotho
Tourism and Wildlife, Hon. Katana Ngala
Health, Hon. Joshua Angatia
Local Government, Hon. William Ntimana
Home Affairs and National Heritage, Hon. Francis Lotodo
Lands and Urban Planning, Hon. Jackson Mulinge
Labour and Manpower Development, Hon. Phillip Masinde
Information and Broadcasting, Hon. Johnstone Makau
Cultural and Social Services, Hon. Nyiva Mwendwa
Co-operative Development, Hon. Kamwithi Munyi
Public Works and Housing, Hon. Jonathan N'geno
Research and Technical Training, Hon. Zachary Onyonka
Attorney-General, Hon. Dr Amos Wako

KENYA HIGH COMMISSION
45 Portland Place, London WIN 4AS
Tel 0171-636 2371
High Commissioner, HE Mwanyengela Ngali, apptd 1996
Defence Attaché, Col. E. Sifuma
Commercial Attaché, D. Mbogua

BRITISH HIGH COMMISSION
Bruce House, Standard Street, PO Box 30465 Nairobi
Tel: Nairobi 335944
High Commissioner, HE Simon Nicholas Hemans, CMG, CVO, apptd 1995
Deputy High Commissioner, Dr R. A. Pullen
Defence and Military Adviser, Col. R. D. Vellacott, OBE
First Secretary (Commercial), S. Martin
First Secretary (Consular), J. Dunlop
There are consular offices in Nairobi, Mombasa and Malindi.

BRITISH COUNCIL REPRESENTATIVE, Bill Harvey, (PO Box 40751) ICEA Building, Kenyatta Avenue, Nairobi. There are offices at Kisumu and Mombasa.

ECONOMY

Kenya has had a turbulent relationship with international donors. The government's failure to implement economic reform and curb corruption prompted the suspension of IMF aid from November 1991 to May 1993. In April 1996, the IMF approved a loan of US$216 million, withheld since late 1994. GDP per capita was US$270 in 1993; the inflation rate was 10.6 per cent a year, and the total external debt was US$6,993.7 million.

Agriculture provides about 52 per cent of total export earnings (excluding processed oil products). The great variation in altitude and ecology provides conditions under which a wide range of crops can be grown. These include wheat, barley, pyrethrum, coffee, tea, sisal, coconuts, cashew nuts, cotton, maize and a wide variety of tropical and temperate fruits and vegetables. The total area of well-farmed land on which concentrated mixed farming can be practised is small and the remainder is arid or semi-arid country but population pressure and the need to increase agricultural production for export has led to attempts to develop such areas.

Mineral production consists of soda ash, salt and limestone. Hydro-electric power has been developed, particularly on the Upper Tana River. Kenya is now almost self-sufficient in electric power generation but the connection with Owen Falls in Uganda is still in being.

There has been considerable industrial development over the last 15 years and Kenya has a variety of industries processing agricultural produce and manufacturing products from local and imported raw materials. New industries are steel, textile mills, dehydrated vegetable processing and motor tyre manufacture. Smaller schemes have added to the country's consumer goods manufacturing base. There is an oil refinery in Mombasa supplying both Kenya and Uganda, and a fuel pipeline now connects Mombasa and Nairobi.

TRADE

Principal exports are coffee and tea, which account for 33 per cent of total export earnings. Also exported are fruit, vegetables, and crude animal and vegetable material. Petroleum products account for about 37 per cent of imports; other imports are manufactured goods, particularly machinery, transport equipment, metals, pharmaceuticals and chemicals.

Trade with UK	1994	1995
Imports from UK	£195,880,000	£244,347,000
Exports to UK	167,152,000	162,198,000

COMMUNICATIONS

The Kenya Railways Corporation has 1,700 miles of railway open to traffic. There are also 39,000 miles of road, of which 5,000 are bitumen surfaced. Trans-border links with Tanzania were reopened in 1985 with rail services for freight and steamer services for passengers and freight.

The principal port is Mombasa, operated by the Kenya Ports Authority. International air services operate from airports at Nairobi and Mombasa.

KIRIBATI
Ribaberikin Kiribati

Kiribati, the former Gilbert Islands, became an independent republic in 1979. Kiribati comprises 36 islands, the Gilberts Group (17) including Banaba (formerly Ocean Island), the Phoenix Islands (8), and the Line Islands (11),

which are situated in the south-west central Pacific around the point at which the International Date Line cuts the Equator. The total land area of 281 sq. miles (728 sq. km) is spread over some 2 million square miles of ocean. Few of the atolls are more than half a mile in width or more than 12 feet high. The vegetation consists mainly of coconut palms, breadfruit trees and pandanus. The population (UN estimate 1994) is 77,000, and predominantly Christian.

CAPITAL – Tarawa, population estimated at 17,921.
CURRENCY – Kiribati uses the Australian dollar ($A) of 100 cents.
FLAG – Red, with blue and white wavy lines in base, and in the centre a gold rising sun and a flying frigate bird.
NATIONAL ANTHEM – Teirake Kain Kiribati (Stand Kiribati).
NATIONAL DAY – 12 July (Independence Day).

GOVERNMENT

The president is head of state as well as head of government and is elected nationally. There is a House of Assembly of 41 members (39 elected and two appointed: the Attorney-General and a representative of Banaba Island). Executive authority is vested in the Cabinet. The last legislative election was held in July 1994, and the last presidential election, on 30 September 1994, was won by Teburoro Tito.

HEAD OF STATE
President, Teburoro Tito, *sworn in* 1 October 1994
Vice-President, Tewareka Tentoa

CABINET *as at August 1996*
President, Foreign Affairs, Trade, Teburoro Tito
Vice-President, Home Affairs, Rural Development, Tewareka Tentoa
Education, Science and Technology, Willie Tokataake
Finance and Economic Planning, Benjamina Tinga
Environment and Natural Resources, Anote Tong
Health, Family Planning and Social Welfare, Katoike Tekee
Transport, Communications and Tourism, Manroai Kaiea
Commerce, Industry and Employment, Tanieru Awerika
Works and Energy, Emile Schutz
Line and Phoenix Islands, Teiraoi Tetabea

HONORARY CONSULATE
The Great House, Penpergwn, near Abergavenny, Gwent NP7 9UY
Tel 0171-222 6952
Honorary Consul, M. Walsh

BRITISH HIGH COMMISSIONER, HE Michael Peart, CMG, LVO, apptd 1995, resident at Suva, Fiji.

ECONOMY

Most people still practise a semi-subsistence economy, the main staples of their diet being coconuts and fish.

The principal imports are foodstuffs, consumer goods, machinery and transport equipment. The principal exports are copra and fish. Total value of exports in 1990 was $A3,681,000.

TRADE WITH UK	1994	1995
Imports from UK	£300,000	£431,000
Exports to UK	13,000	3,000

COMMUNICATIONS

Air communication exists between most of the islands and is operated by Air Tungaru, a statutory corporation. Air Marshall Islands operates a weekly service between Majuro, Tarawa, Funafuti and Nandi, and Air Nauru between Tarawa, Nauru and Nandi. Inter-island shipping is operated by a statutory corporation, the Shipping Corporation of Kiribati.

SOCIAL WELFARE

The government maintains a teacher training college and a secondary school. Five junior secondary schools are maintained by missions. Throughout the republic there are about a hundred primary schools. The total enrolment of children of school age is about 16,000. The Marine Training School at Tarawa trains seamen for service with overseas shipping lines.

There is a general hospital at Tarawa. The other inhabited islands have dispensaries.

KOREA

Korea is situated between 124° 11″ and 130° 57′ E. longitude, and between 33° 7′ and 43° 1″ N. latitude. It has an area of 84,565 sq. miles (219,022 sq. km).

The population (UN estimate 1994) is 68,035. The southern and western coasts are fringed with innumerable islands, of which the largest, forming a province of its own, is Cheju. The Korean language is of the Ural-Altaic Group. Its script, Hangul, was invented in the 15th century; prior to this Chinese characters alone were used. Despite the great cultural influence of the Chinese, Koreans have developed and preserved their own cultural heritage.

HISTORY

The last native dynasty (Yi) ruled from 1392 until 1910 when Japan formally annexed Korea. The country remained part of the Japanese Empire until the defeat of Japan in 1945, when it was occupied by troops of the USA and the USSR, the 38th parallel being fixed as the boundary between the two zones of occupation.

Attempts to reunite Korea failed and the issue was referred to the UN General Assembly. The UN in November 1947 resolved that elections should be held for a National Assembly which, when elected, should set up a government. The Soviet government refused to comply and a UN commission was only allowed to operate south of the 38th parallel.

A general election was held on 10 May 1948, and the first National Assembly met in Seoul on 31 May. The Assembly passed a constitution on 12 July and on 15 August 1948 the republic was formally inaugurated and American military government came to an end. Meanwhile, in the Soviet-occupied zone north of the 38th parallel the Democratic People's Republic had been established with its capital at Pyongyang. A Supreme People's Soviet was elected in September 1948, and a Soviet-style constitution adopted.

THE KOREAN WAR

Korea remained divided along the 38th parallel until June 1950, when North Korean forces invaded South Korea. In response to Security Council recommendations, 16 nations, including the USA and the UK, came to the aid of the Republic of Korea. China entered the war on the side of North Korea in November 1950. The fighting was ended by an armistice agreement signed on 27 July 1953. By this agreement (which was not signed by the Republic of Korea), the line of division between North and South Korea remained close to the 38th parallel, and a Military Armistice Commission (MAC) was established to monitor

the cease-fire. North Korea and China withdrew from the MAC in 1994.

Talks between North and South Korea on the reunification of the country have taken place intermittently. A non-aggression accord was signed between the North and South in 1991 and an agreement on the denuclearization of the Korean peninsula was reached in 1992. A summit of North and South Korean Presidents was scheduled for July 1994 but Kim Il-sung died before it could take place.

REPUBLIC OF KOREA
Daehanminkuk

The Republic of Korea was not officially recognized by any former Communist bloc country until 1989, and not by the People's Republic of China until 1992.

The population (UN estimate 1994) is 44,563,000. There is freedom of religion; the largest religion is Buddhism (13 million), with large minorities of Christians (8 million Protestants, 2.2 million Roman Catholics) and Confucianists (4.7 million).

CAPITAL – Seoul, population (1995) 10,229,000. Other main centres are ΨPusan (3,814,000), Taegu (2,449,000) and ΨInchon (2,308,000).
CURRENCY – Won of 100 jeon.
FLAG – White with a red and blue yin-yang in the centre, surrounded by four black trigrams.
NATIONAL ANTHEM – Aegukka.
NATIONAL DAY – 15 August (Independence Day).

GOVERNMENT

A new constitution was adopted in 1988 following a year of political unrest. The president, who is head of state, chief of the executive and commander-in-chief of the Armed Forces, is directly elected for a single term of five years. He appoints the prime minister with the consent of the National Assembly, and members of the State Council (Cabinet) on the recommendation of the prime minister. The president is also empowered to take wide-ranging measures in an emergency, including the declaration of martial law, but must obtain the agreement of the National Assembly. The National Assembly of 299 members is directly elected for a four-year term.

The most recent elections to the National Assembly in April 1996 produced no outright majority although the ruling New Korea Party (formerly Democratic Liberal Party) was able to form a government following defections from opposition parties. In the most recent presidential election of December 1992, long-time opposition leader Kim Young-sam was victorious. In February 1993 he named the first wholly civilian government in 32 years.

HEAD OF STATE
President, Kim Young-sam, *elected* 18 December 1992, *took office* 25 February 1993

CABINET *as at August 1996*

Prime Minister, Lee Soo-sung
Deputy PM, Finance, Economic Planning Board, Rha Woong-bae
Deputy PM, National Unification, Kwan O-kie
Foreign Affairs, Gong Ro-myung
Home Affairs, Kim Woo-suk
Justice, An U-man
Defence, Yi Yang-ho
Education, Ahn Byung-young
Agriculture and Fisheries, Choi In-kee

Environment, Kim Chung-wi
Trade and Industry, Pak Chae-yun
Construction and Transportation, Oh Myung
Health and Social Affairs, So Sang Mok
Labour, Yi Hong-ku
Information and Communications, Lee Suk-chae
Culture and Sports, Chu Ton-sik
Information, Oh In-hwan
Government Administration, So Sok-chae
Science and Technology, Chung Kun-mo
Patriot's and Veteran's Administration, Hwang Chang-pyung
First Minister for Political Affairs, Kim Yun-hwan
Second Minister for Political Affairs, Kim Chang-suk
Director, National Security Planning Agency, Kwon Yong-Lae

EMBASSY OF THE REPUBLIC OF KOREA
60 Buckingham Gate, London SW1E 6AJ
Ambassador Extraordinary and Plenipotentiary, HE Choi
Dong-jin, apptd 1996
Defence Attaché, Capt. Jang Kil Joo
Consul, Han Gon Lee
Commercial Attaché, Young Sang Yoo

BRITISH EMBASSY
No. 4, Chung-Dong, Chung-Ku, Seoul 100
Tel: Seoul 735–7341/3
Ambassador Extraordinary and Plenipotentiary,
HE Thomas George Harris, CMG, apptd 1994
Counsellor (Economic), Consul-General and Deputy Ambassador,
T. C. Holmes
Defence and Military Attaché, Brig. C. D. Parr, OBE
First Secretary (Commercial), A. C. Stephens

There is a Trade Office and an Honorary British Consul at
Pusan.

BRITISH COUNCIL REPRESENTATIVE, Terry Toney, 1st
Floor, Anglican Church Building, 3–7 Chung Dong,
Choong-ku, Seoul 100–120. There is also an office at
Pusan.

BRITISH CHAMBER OF COMMERCE, c/o Chartered Bank,
1st and 2nd Floors, Samsung Building, 50, 1-Ka Ulchi
Ro, Chung-Ku, Seoul.

DEFENCE

The Republic of Korea has total active armed forces of
633,000 personnel. Conscripts serve for 26 months (army)
or 30 months (navy and air force) and then in reserve forces
until age 33. Reserves number 4,500,000 personnel.

The army has a strength of 520,000 personnel, with
2,050 main battle tanks, 2,460 armoured personnel carriers
and armoured infantry fighting vehicles, 4,500 artillery
pieces and 143 armed helicopters.

The navy has a strength of 60,000 (19,000 conscripts)
including 25,000 marines, with three submarines, seven
destroyers and 33 frigates, 122 patrol and coastal craft, 23
combat aircraft and 47 armed helicopters. The air force has
a strength of 53,000, with 461 combat aircraft.

The USA maintains 36,450 personnel in the country,
divided into 27,500 army and 8,950 air force personnel.

ECONOMY

The soil is fertile but arable land is limited by the
mountainous nature of the country. Staple agricultural
products are rice, barley and other cereals, beans, tobacco
and hemp. Fruit-growing, sericulture and the growing of
the medicinal root ginseng are also practised. The fishing
industry is a major contributor to both food supply and
exports.

The Republic of Korea is deficient in mineral resources,
except for deposits of coal on the east coast and tungsten.
There are some prospects of discovering oil in the sea
between Korea and Japan.

Land redistribution and US aid (US$6,000 million from
1945 to 1978) enabled the rapid industrialization of South
Korea in the 1950s and 1960s. Former land owners formed
chaebols (industrial conglomerates) which benefited from a
highly-educated workforce and protectionist and import
substitution policies. From 1961 to 1979 export-led growth
averaged 10 per cent a year. Despite a decline in aid and a
brief slowdown in the early 1980s and early 1990s, growth
has been maintained, averaging 7.8 per cent in 1985 to
1994. Major industries now include shipbuilding, construction, iron and steel, textiles, electrical and electronic
goods, footwear, passenger vehicles and railway rolling
stock. The 1994–8 five-year economic plan includes the
liberalization of foreign exchange rates and capital
markets, the deregulation of interest rates and the easing
of regulations on foreign exchange holdings by companies.

FINANCE

The 1995 budget totals Won 75,247,200 million. From
1962 a series of successful five-year plans resulted in real
economic growth averaging around 10 per cent a year.
However, GDP growth fell to 5.1 per cent in 1992
before rising to 9 per cent in 1995. Annual per capita
GNP is US$10,076 (1995).

TRADE WITH UK	1994	1995
Imports from UK	£970,978,000	£1,153,116,000
Exports to UK	1,096,209,000	1,561,775,000

COMMUNICATIONS

In 1989 there were 37,493 km of paved road. Seoul and
Pusan have subway systems and there are 6,000 km of
railway lines. Korean Air operates regular flights to
Europe, the USA, the Middle East and south-east Asia.
Pusan and Inchon are the major ports with Pusan serving
the industrial areas of the south-east. Inchon, 28 miles from
Seoul, serves the capital, but development and operation at
Inchon are hampered by a tidal variation of 9–10 metres.

EDUCATION

Primary education is compulsory for six years from the age
of six. Secondary and higher education is extensive with
the option of middle school to age 15 and high school to age
18. The national illiteracy rate is among the lowest in Asia.

DEMOCRATIC PEOPLE'S REPUBLIC OF KOREA
Chosun Minchu-chui Inmin Kongwa-guk

The area is 46,540 sq. miles (120,538 sq. km), with a
population (UN estimate 1994) of 23,472,000.

CAPITAL – Pyongyang, approximate population,
2,000,000.
CURRENCY – Won of 100 chon.
FLAG – Red with white fimbriations and blue borders at
top and bottom; a large red star on a white disc near the
hoist.
NATIONAL ANTHEM – A Chi Mun Bin No Ra I Gang San
(Shine bright, oh dawn, on this land so fair).
NATIONAL DAY – 16 February (Kim Jong-il's birthday).

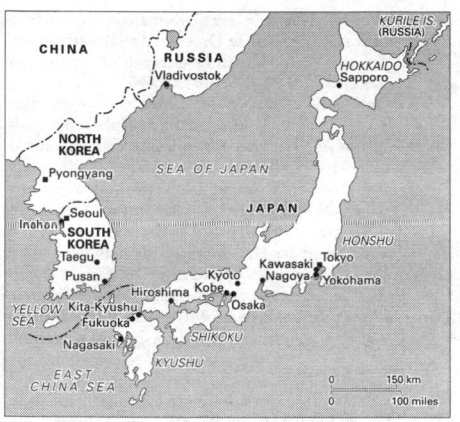

GOVERNMENT

The constitution of the Democratic People's Republic of Korea provides for a Supreme People's Assembly, presently consisting of 687 deputies, which is elected every five years by universal suffrage. The Assembly elects a president for a five-year term, and the Central People's Committee. In turn, the Central People's Committee directs the Administrative Council which implements the policy formulated by the Committee. The Administrative Council (51 members), the government of North Korea, includes the prime minister and various ministers. In practice, however, the country is ruled by the Korean Workers' Party which elects a Central Committee; this in turn appoints a Politburo. The senior ministers of the Administrative Council are all members of the Communist Party Central Committee and the majority are also members of the Politburo. Kim Il-sung, who had been head of the state, party and military since the country's inception in 1948, died on 8 July 1994. His son Kim Jong-il has not yet assumed his father's positions but is expected to do so in 1997.

HEAD OF STATE

President, vacant
Vice-Presidents, Kim Yong-ju; Kim Pyong-sik; Pak Song-ch'ol; Yi Chong-ok

Politburo of the Central Committee, Kim Jong-il (*full member and member of the presidium*); Kim Yong-ju; Yi Chong-ok; Pak Song-chol; Kim Yong-nam; Kye Ung-tae; Kang Song-san; So Yun-sok; Chon Pyong-ho; Choe Kwang; Han Song-yong (*full members*); Li Son-sil; Hong Song-nam; Choe Tae Pok; Kim Chol-man; Choe Yong-nim; Ying Hyong-sop; Yon Hyong-muk; Hong Sok-hyong (*alternate members*)

ADMINISTRATION COUNCIL *as at August 1996*

Prime Minister, Kang Song-san
Deputy Prime Ministers, Hong Song-nam; Kim Yun-hyok; Kim Chang-ju; Kong Jin-tae (*Chairman, Public Welfare Commission*); Chang Chol (*Culture and Art*); Kim Yong-nam (*Foreign Affairs*); Kim Bok-sin (*Chairman, Light Industry Commission*); Kim Hwan (*Chemical Industry*); Choe Yong-rim (*Metals Industry*)

MINISTERS

Atomic Energy Industry, Choe Hak-gun
Building Materials Industry, Li Dong-chun
City Management, Li Chol-bong
Coal Industry, Kim Ri-ryong

Commerce, Han Jang-gun
Construction, Cho Yun-hui
Defence, Choe Kwang
External Economic Affairs, Chong Song-nam
Finance, Yun Gi-jong
Forestry, Li Chun-sok
Labour Administration, Li Jae-yun
Local Industry, Kim Song-gu
Machine Building Industry, Kwak Pom-gi
Marine, O Song-ryol
Mining Industry, Kim Phyong-gil

DEFENCE

The total active armed forces number remains high, at 1,128,000 personnel, and is a destabilizing factor in the region. Conscripts serve for three to four years (air force), five to eight years (army) or five to ten years (navy), followed by service in the reserves to age 40 and the Red Guard to age 60.

The army has an active strength of 1 million personnel, with 3,400 main battle tanks, 2,200 armoured personnel carriers and 7,500 artillery pieces. Reserves number 1,200,000. The navy is 46,000 strong, with 25 submarines, three frigates and 413 patrol and coastal vessels. The air force has a strength of 82,000 personnel, with 509 combat aircraft and 80 armed helicopters. In addition, paramilitary troops of the Ministry of Public Security number 115,000 personnel.

Between 1992 and 1994 North Korea embarked on a clandestine nuclear weapons programme despite being a signatory of the Nuclear Non-Proliferation Treaty (NPT). The NPT's enforcing arm, the International Atomic Energy Authority (IAEA), was repeatedly refused access to inspect military installations. North Korea threatened to withdraw from the NPT, carrying out its threat in June 1994 following an IAEA report that North Korea was attempting to reprocess plutonium for use in nuclear weapons. An agreement was signed with the USA on 21 October 1994 under which North Korea vowed to remain a party to the NPT; to permit IAEA inspections; and to switch to light-water reactors unsuitable for plutonium production. In return the USA agreed to establish diplomatic and economic relations and to pay for interim energy requirements. The IAEA verified the halting of North Korea's nuclear programme in November 1994 although a final settlement was only achieved in June 1995.

ECONOMY

North Korea is rich in minerals and industry was developed, but the economy has stagnated owing to poor planning and a shortage of foreign exchange. The current economic crisis was precipitated by the curtailment of barter trade with the Soviet Union after 1991, and the end of subsidized oil and grain from China. Industrial output has collapsed, with industry operating at one-third of capacity. The economy has been sustained by foreign exchange sent by ethnic Koreans in Japan.

In 1995–6, a slump in agricultural production was exacerbated by widespread flooding which devastated the rice harvest and threatened potential famine. South Korea, Japan, the USA and China offered food aid in response to a North Korean government announcement that food would run out before the October 1996 harvest.

Under the nuclear agreement, North Korea is to receive 500,000 tons of oil a year and is hoping to export manganese to the USA; it has lifted the embargo on the import of US commodities.

TRADE WITH UK	1994	1995
Imports from UK	£23,134,000	£22,266,000
Exports to UK	158,000	173,000

KUWAIT
Dowlat al- Kuwait

Kuwait extends along the shore of the Persian Gulf from Iraq to Saudi Arabia, with an area of 6,969 sq. miles (18,049 sq. km). In 1993 the UN settled the dispute between Kuwait and Iraq, moving the border some few hundred metres northwards. Kuwait has since completed a 130-mile ditch, sand wall and barbed wire system along its border.

Kuwait has a dry, desert climate with summer extending from April to September. The mean temperature varies between 29–45°C in summer, and 8–18°C in winter. Humidity rarely exceeds 60 per cent except in July and August.

At the 1995 census the population was 1,575,983, of whom 41.6 per cent were Kuwaiti citizens, the remainder being other Arabs, Iranians, Indians and Pakistanis. The total Western population was 14,240.

Islam is the official religion, though religious freedom is constitutionally guaranteed. The official language is Arabic, and English is widely spoken as a second language.

CAPITAL – Ψ Kuwait, population (excluding suburbs) 400,000.
CURRENCY – Kuwaiti dinar (KD) of 1,000 fils.
FLAG – Three horizontal stripes of green, white and red, with black trapezoid next to staff.
NATIONAL DAY – 25 February.

GOVERNMENT

Although Kuwait had been independent for some years, the 'exclusive agreement' of 1899 between the Sheikh of Kuwait and the British government was formally abrogated by an exchange of letters dated 19 June 1961. Iraq invaded Kuwait on 2 August 1990 and it was liberated on 26 February 1991 by an alliance of Western and Arab forces. Iraq built up its armed forces on Kuwait's border in October 1994, until it was deterred by the arrival of US and British forces. Iraq formally recognized the sovereignty and territorial integrity of Kuwait as well as the UN-demarcated border in November 1994. Roughly 600 Kuwaitis are still held in Iraq.

Under the constitution legislative power is vested in the Amir and the 50-member National Assembly, and executive power in the Amir and the Cabinet. The sixth National Assembly was dissolved in July 1986. Following popular pressure after the liberation, elections for the National Assembly were held on 5 October 1992; the next elections will be in October 1996. The electorate consists of all Kuwaiti male nationals over 21 whose families have lived in the Emirate since before 1921.

HEAD OF STATE
HH The Amir of Kuwait, Sheikh Jabir al-Ahmad al Jabir Al-Sabah, *born* 1928, acceded 31 December 1977
Crown Prince, HH Sheikh Saad al-Abdullah al-Salim al-Sabah

CABINET *as at August 1996*
Prime Minister, HH The Crown Prince
First Deputy PM, Foreign Affairs, Sheikh Sabah al-Ahmad al-Jabir al-Sabah

Second Deputy PM, Finance, Nasir al-Rowdhan
Education and Higher Education, Dr Ahmad al-Rubie
Defence, Sheikh Ahmad Hamoud al-Jabir al-Sabah
Interior, Sheikh Ali Sabah al-Salim al-Sabah
Information, Sheikh Saoud Nasir al-Sabah
Social Affairs and Labour, Ahmed Khalid al-Kulaib
Communications, Electricity and Water, Jasim Muhammed al-Awn
Public Health, Dr Abdul Rahman Saleh al-Mehilan
Public Works and Housing, Habib Jawhar Hayat
Oil, Abdel-Mohsen al-Mudej
Awqaf and Islamic Affairs, Dr Ali Fahd al-Zumai
Commerce and Industry, Hilal Meshari al-Mutairi
Planning and Cabinet Affairs, Abdul-Aziz al-Dakheel
Justice and Administrative Affairs, Mishari Jassim al-Anjari
Speaker of the National Assembly, Ahmad Abdul-Aziz al-Saadoun

EMBASSY OF THE STATE OF KUWAIT
45–46 Queen's Gate, London SW7 5JN
Tel 0171-589 4533
Ambassador Extraordinary and Plenipotentiary, HE Khaled al-Duwaisan, GCVO, apptd 1993
Attachés, Derar Al-Najran (Consular Affairs); Prof. Ibraheem Al-Rifai (Cultural)

BRITISH EMBASSY
PO Box 2 Safat, 13001 Safat, Kuwait
Tel: Kuwait 2403334/6
Ambassador Extraordinary and Plenipotentiary, HE Graham H. Boyce, CMG, apptd 1996
Counsellor and Deputy Ambassador, J. Jenkins, LVO
First Secretaries, F. Thompson (Management and Consul); M. Hurley (Commercial)
Defence Attaché, Col. T. V. Merritt, OBE
BRITISH COUNCIL REPRESENTATIVE, A. Broderick, 2 al Arabi Street (PO Box 345), 13004 Safat, Mansouriyah.

ECONOMY

Despite the desert terrain, 8.4 per cent of land is under cultivation, fruit and vegetables being the main crops. Shrimp fishing is becoming important.

The oil industry was brought into government ownership in 1975. Since reorganization in 1980, the national industry has been run by the Kuwait Petroleum Corporation. The centre of oil production is at Burgan, south of Kuwait City. Oil is also lifted in the Kuwait/Saudi Arabia Partitioned Zone (Wafra) south of the state. Oil is exported through a specially constructed port at Mina al Ahmadi.

Oil installations were extensively damaged when Iraqi forces set light to 727 oil wells prior to their retreat. Oil exports were resumed in July 1991 and production (including output from the neutral zone) reached 2,000,000 barrels per day in December 1993, in line with the quota allocated by OPEC (compared to a production capacity of 2,200,000 barrels per day before the Iraqi invasion. Capacity is 2,500,000 barrels per day.

Before the Iraqi invasion Kuwait had six power stations capable of generating 7,200 MW of electricity. Associated desalination capacity, on which the country largely depends for water, was 118 million gallons a day; reserves stored up to 2,000 million barrels. All six power stations were damaged during the Iraqi occupation. Essential services were restored after liberation and after substantial investment electricity and water distillation capacity was restored to pre-invasion levels in 1995.

FINANCE

Expected revenue for the financial year 1995–6 was KD2,910 million and expenditure KD4,230 million. Oil revenues constitute about 90 per cent of total revenue. The cost of paying allied nations for the war and of rebuilding the country (now complete) has severely affected public finances, but the government aims to balance the budget by 2000 by raising indirect taxes and privatizing assets. The banking system is controlled by the Central Bank of Kuwait.

TRADE

Oil is the major export. Non-oil exports, mainly to Asian countries and the Indian sub-continent, have included chemical fertilizers, ammonia and other chemicals, metal pipes, shrimps and building materials. Re-exports to neighbouring states traditionally accounted for a major proportion of non-oil exports but were brought to a halt by the Iraqi invasion. Major trading partners are Japan, the USA and Western Europe.

Trade with UK	1994	1995
Imports from UK	£312,037,000	£550,870,000
Exports to UK	239,359,000	151,377,000

COMMUNICATIONS

Ports and airport were damaged during the Iraqi occupation, but have reopened since liberation. There is a network of dual-carriageway roads and more are under construction. Telecommunications and postal services are conducted by the government. Its earth satellite station and telecommunications network were severely damaged during the Iraqi occupation but domestic and international telephone services have been fully restored.

SOCIAL WELFARE

The government invested its considerable oil revenues in comprehensive social services. Education and medical treatment are free. Kuwait University opened in 1966, and in 1987–8 had 15,602 students. In 1987–8 there were over 489,000 pupils at government and private schools. These numbers have declined along with the total population since the Iraqi invasion and a number of schools did not reopen after Kuwait's liberation.

KYRGYZSTAN
Kyrgyz Respublikasy

Kyrgyzstan (formerly Kirghizia) has an area of 76,642 sq. miles (198,500 sq. km) and occupies the central eastern part of the former Soviet Central Asia. It is bordered on the north by Kazakhstan, on the east by China, on the south and south-west by Tajikistan and on the west by Uzbekistan. The country is mountainous, the major part being covered by the ridge of the Central Tienshan, while the Pamir-Altai system occupies its southern part. There are a number of spacious mountain valleys, the Alai, Susamyr and others. Kyrgyzstan is divided into six administrative regions.

The population (1994 estimate) is 4,500,000, of which 52.4 per cent are Kirghiz (Turkic origin), 21.5 per cent are Russian and 12.9 per cent Uzbek, with smaller numbers of Ukrainians, Germans, Tatars and Kazakhs. The majority of the population is concentrated in plains lying at the foot of the mountains. Islam is the main religion.

Kirghiz is a Turkic language which was given an alphabet in the 1930s and became the official language after independence. Russian is an equal official language in the fields of science, industry and the health service, and in all regions where there is a large Russian population. Otherwise the ethnic groups use their own languages.

CAPITAL – Bishkek. Population 616,000 (1989 census).
CURRENCY – Som (introduced on 10 May 1993 at rate of 1:200 against the Rouble).
FLAG – Red with a rayed sun containing a representation of a yurt, all in gold.
NATIONAL DAY – 31 August (Independence Day).

GOVERNMENT

The Kirghiz people were first mentioned in Chinese chronicles in the second millennium BC. They are a merger of two ethnic groups, a Turkic-speaking people driven into the area by the Mongols from the River Yenisei area of Central Asia, and indigenous peoples who spoke a similar language. After a long period under Mongol, Chinese and Persian rule, the Kirghiz became part of the Russian Empire in the 1860s and 1870s. Kyrgyzstan became part of the Soviet Union in 1920 and underwent some industrialization.

Kyrgyzstan declared independence just after the failed Moscow coup on 31 August 1991. A new constitution was adopted on 5 May 1993 by the *Uluk Kenesh* (parliament) which requires the country's adherence to moral and international principles of law and human rights and to the values of Islam. President Akaev transferred the role of head of government from himself to the prime minister although a referendum in February 1996 gave the president the power to appoint all senior officials except the Prime Minister, whose appointment requires legislative approval.

Ethnic tensions between the rural nomadic Kirghiz, the urban Russians and the wealthy Uzbeks who own many businesses and form the majority in the second largest town of Osh, are never far from the surface. By presidential decree the sphere of official usage of the Russian language has been expanded to encourage Russians to remain, and a treaty on dual citizenship has been signed with Russia. The government is also committed to the fair representation of ethnic Russians in the civil service.

President Akaev had difficulty in introducing economic reforms because of obstruction by the bureaucracy and the Uluk Kenesh over the reforms enshrined in the constitution. The President won a referendum on his plans for greater economic reform in January 1994. A second referendum in October 1994 overwhelmingly supported the abolition of the Uluk Kenesh and its replacement by a smaller bicameral parliament composed of a 35-member Legislative Assembly and a 70-member People's Assembly. Elections to the new parliament, the *Zhogorku Kenesh*, were held in February 1995. A new government was appointed by the President in February 1996 in the wake of the referendum enhancing his powers.

HEAD OF STATE
President, Askar Akaev, *elected* 12 October 1991, *re-elected* 24 December 1995

GOVERNMENT *as at August 1996*
Prime Minister, Apas Jumagulov
First Deputy PM, Abdyzhapar Tagayev
Deputy PMs, Mira Jangarachova (*Sociocultural Policy*); Amangeldy Muraliyev (*Industrial Policy*); Bekbolot Talgarbekov (*Agrarian Policy*)
Foreign Affairs, Roza Otunbayeva
Interior, Omurbek Kutuyev
Architecture and Construction, Alexander Moiseyev
Finance, Kemelbek Nanayev
Water Conservancy, Zhenishbek Bekbolotov
Geology and Mineral Resources, Baisent Tursungaziyev
Defence, Murzakan Subanov

National Security, Anarbek Bakayev
Environmental Protection, Kulubek Bokonbayev
Co-operation with CIS States, Yan Fisher
Emergency Situations and Civil Defence, Mambetzhunus
    Abylov
Industry and Entrepreneurship, Andrei Iordan
Communications, Abdyzhapar Tagayev
Agriculture and Foodstuffs, Karimshar Abdimomunov
Transport, Toktorbek Azhikeyev
Tourism and Sport, Myrza Kaparov
Justice, Larisa Gutnichenko
Economy, Talaibek Koichumanov
Labour, Zafar Khakimov
Health, Naken Kasiyev
Culture, Cholponbek Basarbayev
Chairman of the Legislative Assembly, Almanbet Matubraimov

BRITISH AMBASSADOR, HE Douglas B. McAdam; resident
    at Alma-Ata, Kazakhstan.

ECONOMY

The government introduced the som in May 1993 to break
the link with the depreciating rouble, the cause of high
inflation in 1992 and early 1993. The IMF has provided a
US$62 million credit to support the currency reform and a
loan of US$26 million to support privatization. In July
1994 the IMF announced a further three-year loan of
US$104 million to support the 1994–7 economic and
financial reform programme. The President and government have also made the Central Bank independent of
government and parliamentary control. However, the
country needs direct foreign investment desperately and
has had most of its trading links with other Central Asian
republics reduced because of their refusal to accept
payments in soms, although this has been ameliorated by
the signing of an economic union agreement with Kazakhstan and Uzbekistan in February 1994. Subsidized goods
supplies from Russia have also been reduced. In March
1996, a treaty was signed with Belarus, Kazakhstan and
Russia enhancing economic co-operation and working
towards a single customs territory.

Agriculture is the main sector of the economy, with
sugar beet, cotton and sheep the main products. Industry is
concentrated in the food-processing, textiles, timber and
mining fields. Hydro-electric power is abundant and
Kyrgyzstan has reserves of gold, coal, mercury and
uranium, although only gold has so far been exploited and
is the country's largest export.

TRADE WITH UK	1994	1995
Imports from UK	£6,729,000	£4,086,000
Exports to UK	2,600,000	846,000

CULTURE

Until the 1930s the Kirghiz language had an oral tradition
of literature which included the epic poem *Manas,* which
tells the history of the Kirghiz people. Internationally, one
of the best-known writers of the former Soviet Union is the
Kirghiz writer Chingiz Aitmatov (1928–).

LAOS

Satharanarath Pasathipatai Pasason Lao

Laos is in the northern part of Indo-China, with China and
Vietnam on the north and east, Myanmar (Burma) and
Thailand on the west, and Cambodia to the south. The area
of the country is 91,429 sq. miles (231,800 sq. km), with a
population (1995 census) of 4,605,300.

CAPITAL – Vientiane, population (estimated 1984)
    120,000.
CURRENCY – Kip (K) of 100 at.
FLAG – Blue background with a central white circle,
    framed by two horizontal red stripes.
NATIONAL DAY – 2 December.

GOVERNMENT

The kingdom of Lane Xang, the Land of a Million
Elephants, was founded in the 14th century but broke up
at the beginning of the 16th century into the separate
kingdoms of Luang Prabang and Vientiane and the
principality of Champassac, which together came under
French protection in 1893. In 1945 the Japanese staged a
coup and suppressed the French administration. In 1947
Laos became a constitutional monarchy under King
Sisvang Vong, and an independent sovereign state in
1953. The next 22 years in Laos were marked by power
struggles and civil war, eventually won by the North
Vietnamese-backed Pathet Lao, a Communist-dominated
organization.

The Lao People's Democratic Republic was proclaimed
in December 1975 following victory by the Pathet Lao and
the abdication of the King. A President and Council of
Ministers were installed, and a 45-member Supreme
People's Council was appointed to draft a constitution,
which was approved in 1991. The Lao People's Revolutionary Party (LPRP) is the sole legal political organization. A general election to the 85-member National
Assembly established by the 1991 constitution was held
on 20 December 1992; all the candidates were approved by
the LPRP. The President, Prime Minister and Council of
Ministers were confirmed in their posts by the National
Assembly on 22 February 1993.

HEAD OF STATE
President, Nouhak Phonmsavan, *elected by Supreme People's
    Assembly* 25 November 1992

COUNCIL OF MINISTERS *as at August 1996*
Prime Minister, Gen. Khamtai Siphandone
Deputy PM, Khamphoui Keobounalapha
Deputy Prime Minister, Bounnhang Vorachit
*National Defence and Supreme Commander of the Lao People's
    Army,* Lt.-Gen. Choummali Saygnasone
Minister, and Head of the Office of the Council of Ministers,
    Khamsai Souphanouvong
Foreign Affairs, Somsavat Lengsavat
Interior, Lt.-Gen. Asang Laoli
Justice, Khamouane Boupha
Health, Dr Pommeck Daraloy
Agriculture and Forestry, Dr Siene Saphangthong
Industry, Soulivong Dalavong
Communications, Transport, Posts and Construction, Phao
    Bounnaphol
Finance, Saysomphone Phonvihane
Education, Phimmasone Leuangkhamma
Commerce, Sompadith Volasane
Information and Culture, Osakan Thammatheva
Governor of the National Bank, Boutsabong Souvannavong
Labour and Social Welfare, Thongloun Sisoulith
Head of the President's Office, Thongdam Chanthapon
President of the Supreme People's Assembly, Samane Vignaket

EMBASSY OF THE LAO PEOPLE'S DEMOCRATIC REPUBLIC
74 Avenue Raymond-Poincaré 75116 Paris
Tel: Paris 45530298

Ambassador Extraordinary and Plenipotentiary, HE Kamphan Simmalavong, apptd 1995

BRITISH AMBASSADOR, HE Christian Adams, CMG, resident at Bangkok, Thailand

ECONOMY

A 'new economic mechanism' programme was introduced in 1986 which began the liberalization of the economy, with greater autonomy for state enterprises, the relaxation of price controls and the encouragement of private business and investors. These reforms have produced a market-orientated economic system which has produced economic growth of 8 per cent in 1995, and a decline in inflation from 68 per cent in 1989 to 12 per cent in 1993. The economy is dominated by the agricultural sector, which contributed 60 per cent of real GDP in 1994, when 1.5 million tons of paddy rice was produced. Although Laos has a balance of payments problem, exports have recently been increasing.

Although Laos is one of the poorest states in the world, there is potential for increased hydro-electric power exports to Thailand and there are unexploited deposits of iron ore, gold, bauxite and lignite. Foreign capital investment in infrastructure began with the 1994 opening of the Friendship Bridge over the Mekong river border with Thailand which links road routes from Singapore to China. Hydroelectric power is the main export, followed by wood.

TRADE WITH UK	1994	1995
Imports from UK	£1,308,000	£3,472,000
Exports to UK	1,804,000	13,993,000

LATVIA
The Republic of Latvia

Latvia is situated in northern Europe on the eastern coast of the Baltic sea. To the north lies Estonia, to the south Lithuania and Belarus, and to the east the Russian Federation. The area is 63,935 sq. km (24,695 sq. miles). Latvia is low-lying with occasional chains of hills. Forests cover more than 20 per cent of the total territory. The climate is continental and temperate, influenced by maritime winds.

The population is 2,529,600 (1995), of which 54.8 per cent is Latvian, 32.8 per cent Russian, 4.0 per cent Belarusian, with small Ukrainian and Polish minorities. The main religions are Lutheran, Roman Catholic and Russian Orthodox.

The majority (54.8 per cent) have Latvian as their first language and 32.8 per cent Russian. Education is in Latvian and Russian. Public sector employees must pass language tests in Latvian to a level commensurate with the nature of their employment. The right of minorities to use their mother tongue has been acknowledged.

CAPITAL – Riga (population (1995) 840,000). Other major cities are: Daugavpils (120,200); Liepaja (100,200); Jelgava (71,100); Jurmala (59,300); and Ventspils (47,000).

CURRENCY – Lats of 100 santimes.

FLAG – Crimson, with a white horizontal stripe across the centre.

NATIONAL ANTHEM – Dievs, svētī Latviju (God bless Latvia).

NATIONAL DAY – 18 November (Independence Day 1918).

HISTORY

Latvia came under the control of the German Teutonic Knights at the end of the 13th century. During the next few centuries the country endured sporadic invasions by the Swedes, Poles and Russians. By 1795 Latvia was entirely under Russian control. On 18 November 1918 Latvia declared its independence and this was confirmed by the Versailles Treaty in 1919. Several years of fighting with the new Soviet Russia ensued until a peace treaty was signed under which Soviet Russia renounced all claims to Latvian territory.

The Soviet Union annexed Latvia in 1940 under the terms of the Molotov–Ribbentrop pact with Germany. Latvia was invaded and occupied when Germany invaded the Soviet Union during the Second World War. In 1944 the Soviet Union recaptured Latvia from Germany and confirmed its annexation, though this was never accepted as legal by most states.

In 1988 the Popular Front of Latvia was formed to campaign for greater sovereignty and democracy for Latvia. It won the elections to the Supreme Council in 1989, and on 4 May 1990 the Supreme Council declared the independent republic of Latvia to be, *de jure*, still in existence. Agitation in Latvia against Soviet rule led in 1990 and early 1991 to clashes between independence supporters and Latvian Communists and the Soviet military. Violence reached a peak in January 1991 with deaths caused by Soviet Interior Ministry troops and attacks on Baltic border posts. A national referendum was held in March 1991 in which 73 per cent voted in favour of independence, and this was declared on 21 August 1991. The State Council of the Soviet Union recognized the independence of Latvia on 10 September 1991.

GOVERNMENT

Democratic government and a unicameral parliament were restored after multiparty elections in June 1993. The 1922 constitution was restored in July 1993 and the laws of the pre-war republic are gradually being restored. Executive authority is vested in a prime minister and Cabinet of Ministers. Legislative power is exercised by the unicameral parliament (*Saeíma*), which consists of 100 deputies elected for three-year terms by proportional representation with a 4 per cent threshold for parliamentary representation. The deputies elect a president of state, who in turn appoints the prime minister. The prime minister appoints, and the Saeíma approves, the Cabinet of Ministers. The electorate and citizenship had been restricted to descendants of Latvian citizens before the 1940 Soviet occupation and to those who can pass the required Latvian language tests, until 1994 when a law was passed enabling naturalization of long-term residents..

After the 31 September – 1 October 1995 general election nine political parties were represented in the Saeíma. No party had a clear majority, but a coalition of Saimnieks, Latvia's Way and six other parties formed a government.

Latvia applied for membership of the EU in October 1995 and was admitted to the Council of Europe in February 1995.

HEAD OF STATE
President, Guntis Ulmanis, *elected* 7 July 1993, *re-elected* 18 June 1996

COUNCIL OF MINISTERS *as at August 1996*
Prime Minister, Andris Šķēle
Deputy PM, Education and Science, Māris Grīnblats
Deputy PM, Agriculture, vacant

*Deputy PM, Environmental Protection and Regional
  Development*, Māris Gailis
Deputy PM, Defence, Andrejs Krastiņš
Deputy PM, Ziedonis Čevers
Foreign Affairs, Valdis Birkavs
Economy, Guntars Krasts
Finance, Aivars Guntis Kreituss
Interior, Dainis Turlais
Transport, Vilis Krištopāns
Welfare, Vladimirs Makarovs
Justice, Dzintars Rasnačs
Culture, Ojārs Spārītis
EU Affairs, Aleksandrs Kiršteins
Local Government, Ernests Jurkāns

EMBASSY OF THE REPUBLIC OF LATVIA
45 Nottingham Place, London WIM 3FE
Tel 0171-312 0040
Ambassador Extraordinary and Plenipotentiary, HE Jānis Lūsis,
  apptd 1992

BRITISH EMBASSY
5, Alunana Iela Street, Riga LV1010
Tel: Riga 7338 126
Ambassador Extraordinary and Plenipotentiary, HE Nicholas
  R. Jarrold, apptd 1996

BRITISH COUNCIL DIRECTOR, Arthur Sanderson, MBE,
  Lazaretes iela 3, Riga LV-1010

DEFENCE

Total active armed forces number 6,950 personnel with
conscripts serving for 18 months. The army has 1,500
personnel, and the army reserve of the Home Guard
numbers 18,000. The navy is 1,000 strong, with 14 patrol
craft. The air force is 150 strong, with a few transport
aircraft and helicopters. The paramilitary border guard
numbers 4,300 personnel.

All remaining Russian forces withdrew from Latvia on
31 August 1994 except for those stationed at the anti-
ballistic missile early-warning radar at Skrunda, which will
continue to operate until 1999.

ECONOMY

Attempts to move from a command economy to a market
economy resulted in low growth and high unemployment
in the early 1990s. Economic independence from the CIS
was largely achieved, however. The government has
initiated a privatization process which has made many
industrial facilities available for purchase both by Latvian
and foreign private investors. By the end of 1993 20 per cent
of economic production and 40 per cent of agricultural
production had been privatized.

Latvia is an agricultural exporter, specializing in cattle
and pig breeding, dairy farming and crops, including sugar
beet, flax, cereals and potatoes. Natural resources include
limestone, gypsum, peat and timber.

Industry was organized to contribute to the centralized
Soviet economy and is specialized in certain areas. These
include the production of electric and diesel trains,
telephones, telephone exchange equipment, food processing, agricultural machinery, and timber and paper
products.

Tourism is being developed, capitalizing on its beach
resorts, nature reserves and parks. Latvia is also geographically well-placed for the development of transport
services.

TRADE

Russia remains one of the most important trading partners
for Latvia. In 1994, 41 per cent of exports went to the CIS,
40 per cent to the EU and EFTA states, and 6 per cent to
Lithuania and Estonia. Of total imports, 38 per cent came
from the CIS, 17 per cent from the EU, 13 per cent from
Lithuania and Estonia, 11 per cent from EFTA states. The
main imports are oil and energy, and the main exports are
wood and wood products, artificial fibres, meat, dairy
products and rolled ferrous metals.

Trade with UK	1994	1995
Imports from UK	£30,696,000	£40,058,000
Exports to UK	222,378,000	170,411,000

COMMUNICATIONS

Latvia has a reasonably well-developed railway (2,397 km)
and road (18,834 km) system, along which a significant
proportion of exports from CIS republics are transported
to western Europe. Latvia is also being developed as a
transportation route from Scandinavia to central and
southern Europe. Several warm-water ports exist, of which
two, Riga and Ventspils, are developed for commercial
transport. The national airline, Latvijas Aviolinijas,
operates regular flights to Russia, Scandinavia and Europe.

CULTURE

The Latvian language belongs to the Baltic branch of the
Indo-European languages, and as such is distinct from
Russian. The Latin alphabet is used. Independent Latvian
literature appeared in the late 18th and early 19th centuries
and played a role in the fight for independence in 1918.

There are 15 higher education institutions, of which
four are universities.

LEBANON
Al-Jumhouriya al-Lubnaniya

Lebanon forms a strip about 120 miles long and between 30
and 35 miles wide along the Mediterranean littoral. It
extends from the Israeli frontier in the south to the Nahr al
Kebir (15 miles north of Tripoli) in the north; its eastern
boundary runs down the Anti-Lebanon range and then
down the great central depression, the *Beqa'a*, from which
flow the rivers Orontes and Litani. It is divided into six
districts, North Lebanon, Mount Lebanon, Beirut, South
Lebanon, Nabatiah and Beqaa. The seaward slopes of the
mountains have a Mediterranean climate and vegetation.
The inland range of Anti-Lebanon has the characteristics
of steppe country. The area is 4,015 sq. miles (10,400
sq. km).

The population (UN estimate 1993) was 2,806,000. It is
a mixture of Christians, Muslims and Druses. Arabic is the
official language, and French and English are also widely
used.

CAPITAL – Ψ Beirut (population 1,500,000). Other towns
  are Ψ Tripoli (200,000), ΨSidon (100,000), Ψ Tyre
  (70,000), Zahlé (30,000).
CURRENCY – Lebanese pound (L£) of 100 piastres.
FLAG – Horizontal bands of red, white and red with a
  green cedar of Lebanon in the centre of the white band.
NATIONAL ANTHEM – Kulluna Lil Watan Lil'ula Lil'alam
  (We all belong to the homeland).
NATIONAL DAY – 22 November.

TURKEY

CYPRUS
Nicosia
Famagusta
Limassol

MEDITERRANEAN
SEA

SOUTH LEBANON
SECURITY ZONE

ISRAEL
Tel Aviv
Jerusalem
GAZA STRIP
Beersheba

EGYPT

Eilat
Aqaba

• Aleppo

Latakia
Hama

Tripoli
LEBANON
Beirut
Sidon
Tyre
Haifa

• Damascus
GOLAN HEIGHTS

Homs

SYRIA

• Palmyra

Nablus
WEST BANK
Jericho
Dead Sea

JORDAN

Amman

SAUDI
ARABIA

IRAQ

0   160 km
0   100 miles

GOVERNMENT

Lebanon became an independent state in 1920, administered under French mandate until 22 November 1943. Powers were transferred to the Lebanese government from January 1944 and French troops were withdrawn in 1946.

In 1975, fighting broke out in Beirut between Maronite, Sunni and Shia factions, the latter supported by Palestinian guerrillas based in Lebanon. In 1976 the Arab Deterrent Forces, composed mainly of Syrian troops, imposed a cease-fire but fighting resumed and continued until the end of the civil war in 1990. In 1978 Israeli forces invaded but withdrew some months later, handing over their positions, except for a belt in the south, to the UN Interim Force in Lebanon (UNIFIL). In 1982 Israeli forces again invaded, penetrating as far as Beirut. Following negotiations, Palestinian officials and fighters left Beirut for various Arab countries. Although the bulk of Israeli troops withdrew from southern Lebanon in 1985, a buffer zone controlled by the Israeli-backed South Lebanon Army (SLA), a Christian militia, was established along the Israeli–Lebanon border. Syrian forces are deployed in west Beirut and in the north and the east of the country.

The Taif Accord 'for national conciliation', drawn up by an Arab League-appointed committee, gained the approval of most Lebanese MPs in 1989, but was resisted by Gen. Aoun, who insisted on an immediate withdrawal of the 35,000 Syrian troops in Lebanon. The Lebanese government with the backing of Syrian troops ousted Gen. Aoun in October 1990 and a new government incorporating the main militia leaders was formed in December 1990. Since then the government has attempted to clear the militias from the Greater Beirut area and restore its authority throughout most of the country. The Beqa'a valley remains under Syrian control and the South Lebanon Security Zone under Israeli control. All militias have been disarmed apart from Hezbollah and the SLA. Since 1993 the Lebanese Army has deployed in southern villages alongside UNIFIL forces but has not disarmed Hezbollah forces, who are financed, armed and trained by Syria and Iran to continue fighting against Israel and the

SLA. Low-level fighting continued throughout 1993–5. On 11 April 1996, Israel began a two-week missile bombardment of Hezbollah targets in Beirut and southern Lebanon. The mission, code-named 'Grapes of Wrath', was in retaliation for Hezbollah strikes against Israel's northern cities, and suicide bombers who killed 59 Israelis prior to the operation. More than 150 Lebanese were killed during the operation, including 110 civilians sheltering at the UNIFIL headquarters in Qana. An agreement was reached on 15 April to confine hostilities to southern Lebanon.

The first parliamentary elections since 1972 were held between August and October 1992. The 128-seat National Assembly was directly elected by universal suffrage and divided equally between Christians and Muslims. The polls were widely boycotted in Christian areas because of the continuing presence of Syrian troops, in breach of the Taif Accord. A government was formed under Prime Minister Rafiq Hariri in October 1992 which has focused on the economy and reconstruction. National Assembly elections have been scheduled for August and September 1996.

In October 1991 Lebanon began to participate in the bilateral sessions of the Middle East peace talks, but so far has, with Syria, boycotted the multilateral rounds.

HEAD OF STATE
President of the Republic of Lebanon, Elias Hrawi, *took office* 25 November 1989 (term extended by three years by National Assembly on 19 October 1995)

CABINET *as at August 1996**
Prime Minister and Finance, Rafiq Hariri
Deputy P.M., Interior, Michel Murr
Foreign and Expatriate Affairs, Fares Bouez
Justice, Bahij Tabbara
Health, Marwan Hamadeh
Defence, Mohsen Dalloul
Labour, Ali Hrajli
Posts and Telecommunications, El-Fadl Chalak
Education, Youth and Sports, Robert Ghanem
Economy and Trade, Yassin Jaber
Information, Farid Mkari
Agriculture, Chawki Fakhoury
Public Works, Assaad Hardan
Industry and Oil, Chahe Barsoumian
Municipal and Rural Affairs, Hagop Demirdjian
Refugee Affairs, Walid Jumblatt
Housing and Co-operatives, Mohammad Abu Hamdan
Tourism, Nicolas Fattoush
Hydroelectricity Resources, Ilyas Hubayqah
Culture and Higher Education, Michel Edde
Transport, Omar Meskaoui
Vocational and Technical Education, Abdel-Rahim Mrad
Environment, Pierre Pharaon
Emigrants, Ali El-Khalil
Social Affairs, Estephan Doueyhi
* The government may change following the general elections in August and September 1996

National Assembly Speaker, Nabih Berri

LEBANESE EMBASSY
21 Kensington Palace Gardens, London w8 4QM
Tel 0171–229 7265/6
Ambassador Extraordinary and Plenipotentiary, HE Mahmoud Hammoud, apptd 1990

BRITISH EMBASSY
Autostrade Jal El Dib, Coolrite Building (PO Box 60180), Beirut
Tel: Beirut 406330

Ambassador Extraordinary and Plenipotentiary,
HE David MacLennan, apptd 1996
BRITISH COUNCIL DIRECTOR, Ann Malamah-Thomas,
    MBE, Sidani Street, Azar Building, Beirut

DEFENCE

Total active military personnel number 44,300, with conscripts serving one-year terms. The Army has a strength of 43,000, with 300 main battle tanks, 740 armoured personnel carriers and 200 artillery pieces. The Navy has 500 personnel, with 13 patrol and inshore craft. The Air Force has a strength of 800, with three combat aircraft and four armed helicopters. Internal security force personnel number 13,000.

There are a 4,963-strong UN peacekeeping force, 35,000 Syrian troops and 150 Iranian Revolutionary Guards operating in Lebanon.

ECONOMY

A ten-year plan has been initiated to repair war damage and to restore Lebanon's position as a regional financial services and light industrial centre. The 1993–2002 reconstruction plan is estimated to cost US$12,900 million in total, of which US$7,600 million is to come from foreign loans and grants and US$5,300 million from budget surpluses. It is to concentrate on rebuilding housing, transport, utilities, services, education and health services, and aiding industry and agriculture.

Economic recovery has been impressive, with GDP growth of 6 per cent in 1994, inflation reduced to 9 per cent (from 131 per cent in 1992) and foreign exchange reserves increased to US$4,000 million. A plan to reconstruct the commercial centre of Beirut has been started, with the issue in January 1994 of US$650 million shares in the US$1,800 million Solidère company which will reconstruct the 400-acre site. The government has also obtained US$1,600 million in loans and grants for its national reconstruction programme, mainly from Arab states and international agencies.

Operation 'Grapes of Wrath' halted the resurgence of business confidence in Beirut and set back the redevelopment of the infrastructure. The World Bank provided US$50 million to compensate for the damage caused by the operation.

Fruits are the most important products and include citrus fruit, apples, grapes, bananas and olives. There is some light industry, mostly for the production of consumer goods, but most factories are still in need of reconstruction because of the civil war.

TRADE

Principal imports are gold and precious metals, machinery and electrical equipment, textiles and yarns, vegetable products, iron and steel goods, and motor vehicles. There had been a gradual decline in the overall amount of imports as a result of continued instability.

Principal exports include gold and precious metals, fruits and vegetables, textiles, building materials, furniture, plastic goods, foodstuffs, tobacco and wine.

At one time there was a considerable transit trade through Beirut into the Arab hinterland. Lebanon is the terminal for two oil pipelines, one formerly belonging to the Iraq Petroleum Company, debouching at Tripoli, the other belonging to the Trans Arabian Pipeline Company, at Sidon. These lines have not functioned for some years.

Trade with UK	1994	1995
Imports from UK	£138,616,000	£175,616,000
Exports to UK	7,282,000	14,198,000

COMMUNICATIONS

The railways are not functioning as a result of the civil war. There is an international airport at Beirut, served by the national carrier MEA and other airlines. An internal service operates from Beirut to Tripoli.

ARCHAEOLOGY

Lebanon has some important historical remains, notably Baalbek (Heliopolis) which contains the ruins of first- to third-century Roman temples and Jbeil (Byblos), one of the oldest continuously inhabited towns in the world, and ancient Tyre.

EDUCATION

There are six universities in Beirut, the American and the French universities, and the Lebanese National University, the Beirut University College, the Kaslik Saint Esprit University and the Arab University, with the University of Balamand situated near Tripoli. There are several institutions for vocational training, and there is a good provision throughout the country of primary and secondary schools, among which are a great number of private schools.

LESOTHO
'Muso oa Lesotho

Lesotho is a landlocked mountainous state entirely surrounded by South Africa. Of the total area of 11,720 sq. miles (30,355 sq. km), about one-third, in the west and south, is lowland, between 5,000 and 6,000 ft above sea level. The remaining two-thirds are foothills and highlands, rising to 11,425 ft. The population (UN estimate 1993) is 1,943,000.

CAPITAL – Maseru, population (1986 census) 288,951.
CURRENCY – Loti (M) of 100 lisente.
FLAG – Diagonally white over blue over green with the white of double width, and an assegai and knobkerrie on a Basotho shield in brown in the upper hoist.
NATIONAL ANTHEM – Pina ea Sechaba.
NATIONAL DAY – 4 October (Independence Day).

GOVERNMENT

Lesotho (formerly Basutoland) became a constitutional monarchy within the Commonwealth on 4 October 1966. The independence constitution was suspended in 1970 and the country was governed by a Council of Ministers headed by Leabua Jonathan until the establishment of a nominated National Assembly in 1974.

Jonathan's government was overthrown in 1986, and executive and legislative powers were conferred on the King, to be advised by the Military Council and Council of Ministers led by Maj.-Gen. Justin Lekhanya. In March 1990 King Moshoeshoe II's powers were formally revoked and in November the King was deposed and replaced by his son, who assumed the title of Letsie III. Maj.-Gen. Lekhanya was overthrown in 1991 in a coup led by Col. Elias Ramaema. Elections promised for 1992 were eventually held in March 1993 and the Basotho Congress Party (BCP) won all 65 seats in the new National Assembly. The BCP government led by Ntsu Mokhele was sworn in on 2 April 1993, at which time King Letsie III swore allegiance to a new multiparty democratic constitution and the Military Council was dissolved.

Sections of the military remained opposed to the BCP government and launched two unsuccessful coup attempts in 1994 which were defeated after heavy fighting. On 17 August 1994 King Letsie III and sections of the military mounted a coup attempt and announced the dismissal of the government and the dissolution of parliament until new elections. After mediation, the government, which had refused to leave office, was restored by the King. King Letsie also announced his intention to abdicate in favour of his father, Moshoeshoe II, who was restored on 25 January 1995. When King Moshoeshoe II died in a car crash on 15 January 1996 King Letsie III again ascended to the throne.

The country is divided into ten administrative districts. In each district there is a district secretary who co-ordinates all government activity in the area, working in co-operation with hereditary chiefs.

HEAD OF STATE
HM The King of Lesotho, King Letsie III, *acceded* February 1996

COUNCIL OF MINISTERS *as at August 1996*
Prime Minister, Defence, Public Service, Dr Ntsu Mokhehle
Deputy PM, Home Affairs, Local Government, Rural and Urban Development, Pakalitha Mosisili
Foreign Affairs, Kelebone Albert Maope
Education, Lesao Lehohla
Trade and Industry, Lira Motete
Agriculture, Co-operatives and Youth Affairs, Mopshatla Mabitle
Health and Social Welfare, Tefo Mabote
Natural Resources, Shakhane Robong Mokhehle
Transport and Communications, Mamoshebi Kabi
Justice, Human Rights, Law and Constitutional Affairs, Sephiri Motanyane
Works, Mohaila Mohale
Information and Broadcasting, Pakane Khala
Labour and Employment, Not'si Victor Molopo
Tourism, Sport and Culture, Pasho Mochesane
Finance and Development Planning, Viktor Ketlo

HIGH COMMISSION FOR THE KINGDOM OF LESOTHO
7 Chesham Place, London SW1X 8HN
Tel 0171-235 5686
High Commissioner, HE Benjamin Masilonyane Masilo, apptd 1996

BRITISH HIGH COMMISSION
PO Box 521, Maseru 100
Tel: Maseru 313961
High Commissioner, HE Peter J. Smith, CBE, apptd 1996

BRITISH COUNCIL REPRESENTATIVE, P. Thompson, Hobson's Square, PO Box 429, Maseru 100

JUDICIARY

The courts of law consist of the court of appeal, the High Court, magistrates' courts, judicial commissioners' court, central and local courts. Magistrates' and higher courts administer the law and also adjudicate appeals from the judicial commissioners' and subordinate courts.
Chief Justice, Hon. J. L. Kheola

ECONOMY

The economy is based on agriculture and animal husbandry, and the adverse balance of trade (mainly consumer and capital goods) is offset by the earnings of the large numbers of the population who work in South Africa. Apart from some diamonds, Lesotho has few natural resources and only small-scale industrial development. The Lesotho National Development Corporation was set up to promote the development of industry, mining, trade and tourism. Work has commenced on the Highlands

Water Scheme designed to provide water for the Vaal industrial zone in South Africa and hydroelectricity for Lesotho. Drilling is being carried out for oil. A National Park has been established at Sehlabathebe in the Maluti mountains. A number of light manufacturing and processing industries have recently been established.

The main sources of revenue are customs and excise duty. The IMF approved a US$12 million loan in September 1994 to support the government's 1994–5 economic reform programme. A further US$11 million was pledged in July 1995.

TRADE WITH UK	1994	1995
Imports from UK	£665,000	£1,324,000
Exports to UK	1,605,000	399,000

COMMUNICATIONS

A tarred road links Maseru to several of the main lowland towns, and this is being extended in the south of the country. The mountainous areas are linked by tarred, gravelled and earth roads and tracks. Roads link border towns in South Africa with the main towns in Lesotho. Maseru is also connected by rail with the main Bloemfontein–Natal line of the South African Railways. Scheduled international air services are operated daily between Maseru and Johannesburg and other scheduled international flights are to Gabarone, Harare, Manzini and Maputo. There are around 30 airstrips. Internal scheduled services are operated by the Lesotho Airways Corporation.

The telephone network is fully automated in all urban centres. Radio telephone communication is used extensively in the remote rural areas.

EDUCATION

Most schools are mission-controlled, the government providing grants for salaries and buildings. There are over 1,000 primary and over 100 secondary schools; few areas lack a school and there is a literacy rate of about 70 per cent. Increasing emphasis is being laid on agricultural and vocational education. The National University of Lesotho at Roma was established as a university in 1975.

LIBERIA
Republic of Liberia

An independent republic of West Africa, occupying the territory between Sierra Leone and Côte d'Ivoire which is between the rivers Mano in the north-west and Cavalla in the south-east, a distance of about 350 miles, and extending to the interior to latitude 8° 50', a distance of 150 miles from the seaboard. The area is about 43,000 sq. miles (111,369 sq. km). The population at the census of 1974 was 1,481,524; a 1993 UN estimate put the figure at 2,640,000. The official language is English. Over 16 ethnic languages are spoken.

CAPITAL – ΨMonrovia, population estimate (1984) 425,000. Other ports are ΨBuchanan, ΨGreenville (Sinoe) and ΨHarper (Cape Palmas).
CURRENCY – Liberian dollar (L$) of 100 cents.
FLAG – Alternate horizontal stripes (five white, six red), with five-pointed white star on blue field in upper corner next to flagstaff.
NATIONAL ANTHEM – All Hail, Liberia, Hail.
NATIONAL DAY – 26 July.

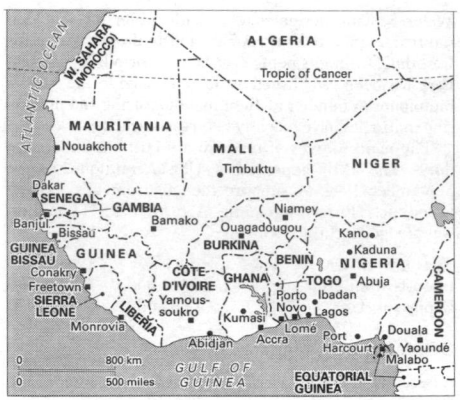

GOVERNMENT

Liberia was founded by the American Colonization Society in 1822 as a colony for freed American slaves, and has been recognized since 1847 as an independent state.

William V. S. Tubman, President since 1944, died in 1971 and was succeeded by Dr Tolbert. The constitution was suspended following a military coup in 1980 during which Tolbert was killed. M/Sgt. Samuel Doe assumed power as chairman of a military council. A new constitution was endorsed by a referendum in 1984. Doe and his party, the National Democratic Party of Liberia (NDPL) won the elections held in 1985, amid allegations of electoral fraud, and a civilian government was formally installed in 1986.

Civil War

A rebel incursion in 1989 by the National Patriotic Front of Liberia (NPFL) led by Charles Taylor developed into a full-scale civil war in 1990. A five-nation ECOWAS peacekeeping force (known as ECOMOG) landed in Monrovia in an effort to end the conflict but in September 1990 President Doe was killed, having refused to step down. The Interim Government of National Unity (IGNU) was formed in August 1990 in The Gambia and arrived in Monrovia in November. An agreement to establish a cease-fire and confine troops to barracks under ECOMOG supervision broke down in October 1992 when the NPFL attempted to seize Monrovia. In response ECOMOG was enlarged to 15,000 personnel and assumed a more offensive role, driving NPFL forces out of Monrovia's suburbs. By March 1993 the NPFL had been driven into eastern parts of Liberia and peace negotiations between the warring factions had begun. Under UN-sponsored negotiations a peace agreement was signed by the IGNU, NPFL and another rebel group ULIMO on 25 July 1993 which brought about a cease-fire on 1 August. Interim President Amos Sawyer was due to be replaced within one month by a five-member Council of State to govern the country during a transitional period, together with a 35-member transitional legislature including members from all three factions. The Council of State and legislature did not take power until March 1994 and the transitional government of IGNU, NPFL and ULIMO members not until May 1994. Continued fighting and the fracturing of the three factions led to further negotiations and an agreement in December 1994 on a new Council of State. A Council of State comprising the faction leaders was inaugurated on 1 September 1995 and a transitional government formed. Fighting resumed in April 1996,

however, following the dismissal of ULIMO-J leader Roosevelt Johnson from the Council. Legislative elections originally planned for November 1995 were rescheduled for May 1997 in the wake of a new cease-fire agreed on 31 July 1996.

Embassy of the Republic of Liberia
2 Pembridge Place, London W2 4XB
Tel 0171-221 1036
Minister-Counsellor, Chargé d'Affaires, Ishmael Grant

British Embassy
The British Embassy in Monrovia was closed in March 1991.

ECONOMY

Before the civil war began principal exports were iron ore, crude rubber, timber, uncut diamonds, palm kernels, cocoa and coffee, but the civil war has resulted in the suspension of most economic activity.

	1994	1995
Trade with UK		
Imports from UK	£8,510,000	£8,456,000
Exports to UK	254,000	544,000

COMMUNICATIONS

The artificial harbour and free port of Monrovia was opened in 1948. There are nine ports of entry, including three river ports. Robertsfield International Airport is under NPFL control and not yet in use. Spriggs Payne airfield, on the outskirts of Monrovia, normally used for internal flights, is currently being used for flights to other West African countries.

LIBYA
Al-Jamahiriya Al-Arabiya
Al-Libiya Al-Shabiya Al-Ishtirakiya Al-Uthma

Libya, on the Mediterranean coast of Africa, is bounded on the east by Egypt and Sudan, on the south by Chad and Niger, and on the west by Algeria and Tunisia. It consists of the three former provinces of Tripolitania, Cyrenaica and the Fezzan, with an area of 679,362 sq. miles (1,759,540 sq. km).

Vast sand and rock deserts, almost completely barren, occupy the greater part of Libya. The southern part of the country lies within the Sahara Desert. There are few rivers and as rainfall is irregular outside parts of Cyrenaica and Tripolitania, good harvests are rare.

The population (UN estimate 1994) is 5,222,000. The people of Libya are principally Arab with some Berbers in the west and some Tuareg tribesmen in the Fezzan. Islam is the official religion of Libya, but other religions are tolerated. The official language is Arabic.

The ancient ruins in Cyrenaica, at Cyrene, Ptolemais (Tolmeta) and Apollonia, are outstanding, as are those at Leptis Magna, 70 miles east, and at Sabratha, 40 miles west of Tripoli. An Italian expedition found in the south-west of the Fezzan a series of rock-paintings more than 5,000 years old.

Capital – ΨTripoli, population estimate (1991) 1,000,000. The principal towns are: ΨBenghazi (500,000); ΨMisurata (200,000); Sirte (100,000).
Currency – Libyan dinar (LD) of 1,000 dirhams.
Flag – Libya uses a plain emerald green flag.
National Day – 1 September.

GOVERNMENT

Libya was occupied by Italy in 1911–12 in the course of the Italo-Turkish War, and under the Treaty of Ouchy 1912 sovereignty over the province was transferred by Turkey to Italy. In 1939 the four provinces of Libya (Tripoli, Misurata, Benghazi and Derna) were incorporated in the national territory of Italy as *Libia Italiana*. After the Second World War Tripolitania and Cyrenaica were placed provisionally under British and the Fezzan under French administration, and in conformity with a resolution of the UN General Assembly in 1949, Libya became on 24 December 1951 the first independent state to be created by the UN. The monarchy was overthrown by a revolution in 1969 and the country was declared a republic. It was ruled by the Revolutionary Command Council (RCC) under the leadership of Colonel Muammar Gadhafi.

In 1977 a new form of direct democracy, the 'Jamahiriya' (state of the masses) was promulgated and the official name of the country was changed to Socialist People's Libyan Arab Jamahiriya. At local level authority is now vested in about 1,500 Basic and 14 Municipal People's Congresses which appoint Popular Committees to execute policy. Officials of these congresses and committees, together with representatives from unions and other organizations, form the General People's Congress, which normally meets for about a week each year. In addition, a number of extraordinary sessions are held throughout the year. This is the highest policy-making body in the country.

The General People's Congress appoints its own General Secretariat and the General People's Committee, whose members head the government departments which execute policy at national level. The Secretary of the General People's Committee has functions similar to those of a prime minister.

Since a reorganization in 1979 neither Col. Gadhafi nor his former RCC colleagues have held formal posts in the administration. Gadhafi continues to hold the ceremonial title 'Leader of the Revolution'.

Leader of the Revolution and Supreme Commander of the Armed Forces, Col. Muammar al-Gadhafi

SECRETARIAT OF THE GENERAL PEOPLE'S CONGRESS *as at August 1996*

Secretary, Zanati Muhammad al-Zanati
Assistant Secretary, Mahmud al-Hadyi
Secretary, Affairs of People's Congresses,
    Ahmed Ibrahim Mansur
Secretary, Affairs of People's Committees, Ali al Sha'iri
Secretary, Trade Unions, Ali al-Shamikh
Secretary, Women's Affairs, Thuriya Ramadan Abu Tabrika
Secretary, Foreign Affairs, Sa'ad Mujbir

GENERAL PEOPLE'S COMMITTEE (CABINET)

Secretary-General (Premier), Abd al-Majid al-Qa'ud
Foreign Liaison, Omar al-Muntasir
Unity, Jum'a al-Mahdi al-Fazzani
Justice and Public Order, Mohammed Mahmud al-Hijazi
Animal Resources, Messaoud Abousoud
Information and Culture, Fawzia Bashir Challabi
Marine Resources, Bachir Ramadhan Boujenah
Industry and Mining, Mufta Azzouz
Energy, Abdullah Salem al-Badri
Finance, Dr Muhammad Bayt al Mal
Education, Youth and Sports, Training and Scientific Research,
    Ma'tug Muhammad Ma'tug
Health and Social Security, Dr Baghdadi Ali al-Mahmudi
Public Works and Housing, Mubarak Abdullah al-Shamikh
Public Accounting and Control, Mahmud Badji
Planning, Economy and Trade, Abdel Hafidh Zlitini

Transport and Communications, Izz al-Din al-Hinshiri
Great Man-Made River Project, Jadallah Azzouz el-Talhi
Tourism, Boukhari Hawda
Agrarian Reform, Ali Ben Romdhan
Control and Follow-up, Mahmud Badi

LIBYAN DIPLOMATIC MISSION IN LONDON

Since the break of diplomatic relations with Libya in April 1984, the Royal Embassy of Saudi Arabia has handled Libyan interests in Britain.

BRITISH EMBASSY

British interests are currently handled by the British Interests Section of the Italian Embassy, Sharia Uahran 1 (PO Box 4206), Tripoli.

DEFENCE

Libya has a total active armed forces of 80,000, with selective conscription of two years. The army has a strength of 50,000 (25,000 conscripts), with 2,210 main battle tanks, 1,990 armoured infantry fighting vehicles and armoured personnel carriers, and some 1,770 artillery pieces. The navy has a strength of 8,000 personnel, with four submarines, two frigates, 36 patrol and coastal vessels, and 30 armed helicopters. The air force has 22,000 personnel, with 417 combat aircraft and 52 armed helicopters.

Libya is alleged to have built at least one chemical weapons plant. The USA claims that a plant at Rabta, closed in 1990, was reopened in 1995, and that a plant has been constructed near Tahunah, south of Tripoli.

As part of the UN economic sanctions imposed in April 1992 there is a total embargo on arms sales to Libya.

ECONOMY

Economic sanctions were imposed on Libya in April 1992 by the UN Security Council following Libya's failure to hand over two suspects in the bombing of Pan-Am flight 103 over Lockerbie, Scotland, in 1988. The UN imposed additional sanctions in December 1993, including freezing assets abroad and restricting imports of spare parts and equipment for the oil and aviation sectors. All the sanctions remain in place and are renewed every 120 days. The USA also enacted legislation in July 1996 penalizing foreign companies that invest more than £26 million a year in Libya's energy sector.

Agriculture is confined mainly to the coastal areas of Tripolitania and Cyrenaica, where barley, wheat, olives, almonds, citrus fruits and dates are produced, and to the areas of the oases, many of which are well supplied with springs supporting small fertile areas. Among the important oases are Jaghbub, Ghadames, Jofra, Sebha, Murzuq, Brak, Ghat, Jalo and the Kufra group in the south-east.

The main industry is oil and gas production. There are pipelines from Zelten to the terminal at Mersa Brega, from Dahra to Ras-es-Sider, from Amal to Ras Lanuf, and from the Intisar field to Zuetina. In 1995 66.6 million tonnes of crude oil was produced. A major petrochemical complex has been built at Ras Lanuf where a refinery and ethylene plant began operations in 1985. The construction of an iron and steel plant at Misurata has been completed. Economic constraints have delayed some projects, particularly since Libya decided in 1983 to go ahead with a major irrigation scheme, the 'Great Man-Made River'.

Libya has technical assistance agreements with a number of countries, and also employs large numbers of foreign labourers and experts.

TRADE

Exports are dominated by crude oil, but some wool, cattle, sheep and horses, olive oil, and hides and skins are also exported. Principal imports are foodstuffs, including sugar, tea and coffee, and most construction materials and consumer goods. After the revolution the private sector was virtually eliminated and Libya became a state trading country with imports controlled by state monopolies. In 1988, however, reforms were implemented which have allowed a small private sector to be re-established.

Trade with UK	1994	1995
Imports from UK	£194,905,000	£227,369,000
Exports to UK	148,151,000	131,787,000

COMMUNICATIONS

The coastal road running from the Tunisian frontier through Tripoli to Benghazi, Tobruk and the Egyptian border serves the main population centres. Main roads also link the provincial centres, and the oil-producing areas of the south with the coastal towns.

There are airports at Tripoli and Benghazi (Benina), Tobruk, Mersa Brega, Sebha, Ghadames and Kufra regularly used by commercial airlines. Since April 1992 a UN embargo on air links with Libya has been in force.

LIECHTENSTEIN
Fürstentum Liechtenstein

Liechtenstein is a principality on the Upper Rhine, between Vorarlberg (Austria) and Switzerland, with an area of 61 sq. miles (158 sq. km), and a population in 1994 of 31,000. The language of the principality is German.

CAPITAL – Vaduz, population (1993) 5,072.
CURRENCY – Swiss franc of 100 rappen (or centimes).
FLAG – Equal horizontal bands of blue over red; gold crown on blue band near staff.
NATIONAL ANTHEM – Oben am Jungen Rhein (High on the Rhine).
NATIONAL DAY – 15 August.

GOVERNMENT

The Patriotic Union and Progressive Citizens' parties have governed the country in coalition since 1938. There is a threshold of 8 per cent for parties to gain representation in the Landtag. At the general election on 24 October 1993 the Progressive Citizens' Party won 11 seats, the Patriotic Union Party 13 seats and the Free List (Environmentalist) grouping, 1 seat.

HEAD OF STATE
HSH *The Prince of Liechtenstein,* Hans Adam II, *born* 14 February 1945; *succeeded* 13 November 1989; *married* 30 July 1967, Countess Marie Kinsky; and has *issue*: Prince Alois (*see* below); Prince Maximilian, *b.* 16 May 1969; Prince Constantin, *b.* 15 March 1972; Princess Tatjana, *b.* 10 April 1973
Heir, HSH Prince Alois, *b.* 11 June 1968, *married* 1993 Duchess Sophie of Bavaria; and has *issue*: Prince Wenzel, *b.* 24 May 1995

MINISTRY *as at August 1996*
Prime Minister, Dr Mario Frick (*Head of Government* 'Presidium', Finance, Justice)
Deputy PM, Thomas Büchel (*Interior, Agriculture, Forestry and Environment, Education*)

Government Councillors, Cornelia Gassner-Matt (*Construction, Traffic*), Andrea Willi (*Foreign Affairs, Culture, Youth and Sport*), Michael Ritter (*Economy, Family, Welfare, Health*)

DIPLOMATIC REPRESENTATION
Liechtenstein is represented in diplomatic and consular matters in the United Kingdom by the Swiss Embassy.

BRITISH AMBASSADOR, David Beattie, CMG, resident at Berne, Switzerland

ECONOMY

The main industries are high and ultra-high vacuum engineering, the semi-conductor industry, roller bearings, fastenings and securing systems, artificial teeth, heating and hot water equipment, synthetic fibres, woollen and homespun fabrics.

In 1991 Liechtenstein became a member of the European Free Trade Association, and as such is a party to the European Economic Area (EEA) Agreement with the EU which came into force on 1 January 1994. In December 1992 in separate referenda, Switzerland voted against EEA membership while Liechtenstein voted in favour. After adapting its customs union with Switzerland, and again voting in favour of joining the EEA in a referendum on 9 April 1995, Liechtenstein joined the EEA on 1 May 1995.

FINANCE	1993
Revenue	F449,165,116
Expenditure	441,383,850

LITHUANIA
Lietuva

Lithuania lies on the eastern coast of the Baltic Sea between 53° 54′ and 56° 27′ N., and 20° 56′ and 26° 51′ E. To the north lies Latvia, to the east and south lies Belarus, to the south-west lie Poland and the Kaliningrad region of the Russian Federation. The area is 25,170 sq. miles (65,200 sq. km).

Lithuania lies in the middle and lower basin of the river Nemunas. Along the coast is a lowland plain which rises inland to form uplands in east and central Lithuania. These uplands, the Middle Lowlands, give way to the Baltic Highlands in east and south-east Lithuania; the highest point is 294 m (965 ft). There is a network of rivers and over 2,800 lakes, which mainly lie in the east of the country. The climate varies between maritime and continental.

The population is 3,724,000 (1994), of which 80.6 per cent are Lithuanian, 8.7 per cent Russian, 7.1 per cent Polish, 1.6 per cent Belarusian, 1.1 per cent Ukrainian. The majority are Roman Catholic, with Russian Orthodox and Lutheran minorities. Lithuanian is the state language, spoken by 80 per cent, with Russian, Polish and Belarusian minorities.

CAPITAL – Vilnius (population 579,000). Other major cities are Kaunas (419,000), Klaipéda (203,000), Siauliai (147,000).
CURRENCY – Litas.
FLAG – Three horizontal stripes of yellow, green, red.
NATIONAL ANTHEM – Tautiška Giesmé (The National Song).
NATIONAL DAY – 16 February (Independence Day).

HISTORY

The first independent Lithuanian state emerged as the Kingdom of Lithuania in 1251, and over the next few centuries acted as a buffer state between Germans to the west and Mongols and Tartars to the east. After forming a joint Commonwealth and Kingdom with Poland in 1561, Lithuania was taken over by the Russian Empire in the partitions of Poland that occurred in 1772, 1792 and 1795.

Lithuania declared its independence from the Russian Empire on 16 February 1918 and then fought against German and Soviet forces until its independence was recognized by the Versailles Treaty 1919 and the peace treaty signed with the Soviet Union on 12 July 1920. The Soviet Union annexed Lithuania in 1940 under the terms of the Molotov–Ribbentrop pact with Germany. Lithuania was invaded and occupied when Germany invaded the Soviet Union during the Second World War. In 1944 the Soviet Union recaptured the country and confirmed its annexation, though this was never accepted as legal by most states.

In December 1989 public pressure forced the Lithuanian Communist Party to agree to multiparty elections, which were held in February 1990. These were won by the nationalist Sajudis movement, and the Supreme Council (parliament) declared the restoration of independence on 11 March 1990. Clashes occurred throughout 1990 between Lithuanians and Soviet military forces. Over 90 per cent of the population voted for independence in a referendum in February 1991. The Soviet Union recognized the independence of Lithuania on 10 September 1991.

GOVERNMENT

Under the 1992 constitution, executive authority is vested in the government, consisting of the prime minister, who is appointed by the president with the approval of the Seimas, and ministers appointed upon the recommendation of the prime minister. The government is accountable to the Seimas, and presidential powers are under strict parliamentary control.

Legislative power is exercised by the Seimas, which is a unicameral parliament of 141 members elected for four-year terms. Seventy-one members are elected in first-past-the-post constituencies and 70 by proportional representation, with a 5 per cent threshold for representation. The constitution bans an alignment of Lithuania with any post-Soviet eastern alliance.

Lithuania applied for membership of the EU in December 1995; a treaty of association with the EU was ratified by parliament on 20 June 1996.

In the parliamentary elections of October and November 1992, a majority of seats in the Seimas were won by the Lithuanian Democratic Labour Party (DLP) (the former Lithuanian Communist Party), which formed a government under Bronislovas Lubys. The DLP leader Algirdas Brazauskas was elected Chairman of the Seimas and acting President of Lithuania until direct presidential elections, which he won in February 1993. The Sajudis leader and former Chairman of the Supreme Council, (President) Vytautas Landsbergis, became leader of the opposition in Parliament. On 10 March 1993 President Brazauskas appointed as Prime Minister Adolfas Šleževičius, who formed a new government on 16 March. Šleževičius was forced to resign in February 1996, having been implicated in a banking scandal, and was replaced by the former Minister for Administrative Reform and Municipal Affairs Laurynas Stankevičius. A legislative election is scheduled for October 1996.

LOCAL GOVERNMENT

Lithuania is divided into 11 cities and 44 rural districts. Each has a municipal council elected by the local population for a period of five years.

HEAD OF STATE
President, Algirdas Brazauskas, *elected* 14 February 1993 for a five-year term

GOVERNMENT *as at August 1996*
Prime Minister, Laurynas Mindaugas Stankevičius
Agriculture, Vytautas Einoris
Communications and Information, Vaidotas Abraitis
Culture, Juozas Nekrošius
Defence, Linas Linkevičius
Education and Science, Vladislavas Domarkas
Energy, Saulius Kutas
Environmental Protection, Bronius Bradauskas
Finance, Algimantas Križinauskas
Foreign Affairs, Povilas Gylys
Administrative Reform and Municipal Affairs, Petras Popovas
Health, Antanas Vinkus
Housing and Urban Development, Aldona Baranauskiene
Industry and Trade, Kazimieras Klimašauskas
Interior, Virgilijus Bulovas
Justice, Albertas Valys
Social Security and Labour, Mindaugas Mikaila
Transport, Jonas Biržiškis
Economy, Zenonas Antanas Kaminskas
Forestry, Albertas Vasiliauskas

EMBASSY OF LITHUANIA
84 Gloucester Place, London WIH 3HN
Tel 0171-486 6401
Ambassador Extraordinary and Plenipotentiary, new appointment awaited

BRITISH EMBASSY
2 Antakalnio, 2055 Vilnius
Tel: Vilnius 2222070
Ambassador Extraordinary and Plenipotentiary, HE Thomas Macan, apptd 1994

BRITISH COUNCIL REPRESENTATIVE, Virginija Ziukiene, Vilniaus 39/6,2600 Vilnius

JUDICIAL SYSTEM

The judicial system comprises the Constitutional Court (consisting of nine judges appointed for terms of nine years), the Supreme Court, Court of Appeal, district and local courts. For the investigation of administrative, labour, family and other litigations, specialized courts may be established pursuant to law. Supreme legal supervision is exercised by the Prosecutor-General and by local prosecutors under his supervision.

DEFENCE

Total active armed forces personnel stands at 8,900. Authorized conscription for 12-month terms operates and the reserve National Guard numbers a further 12,000 personnel. The army has an active strength of 4,300 personnel. The navy numbers 350 personnel with two frigates and ten patrol and coastal craft. The air force has 250 personnel, whilst the paramilitary border guard numbers 4,000. The last Russian troops withdrew on 31 August 1993.

ECONOMY

The economy was largely agricultural prior to rapid industrialization during the Soviet era. The transition from a centralized to a free-market economy has taken place against the background of a decline in GDP in 1992 of 35 per cent. GDP began to grow again in 1994 and reached 5 per cent growth in 1995, although inflation was 30 per cent. A privatization programme begun in 1991 ran into difficulties over the restitution of agricultural land and the modernization of state-owned industries, but progress in the sale of small enterprises has been quick and successful. By the end of 1993 nearly all housing and agricultural enterprises had been privatized. In October 1994 the IMF approved a three-year loan of US$201 million to support economic stabilization and reform.

In 1994, agriculture and forestry accounted for 8.1 per cent of GDP, the chief products being beef, pork, rye, oats, wheat, flax, barley, sugar beet and potatoes. The main industries are chemicals and petrochemicals, food processing, wood products, building materials, textiles, leather goods, machinery, machine tools and household appliances.

TRADE

In 1994 trade with western states (51.4 per cent) overtook trade with the CIS (48.6 per cent). In 1995, there was a trade surplus for the first time in five years. The Lithuanian economy is still heavily dependent on Russian supplies of oil, gas and metals. Lithuania agreed to repay a US$32 million debt to the Russian gas monopoly in April 1996, thereby avoiding a threatened disruption of supply.

Trade with UK	1994	1995
Imports from UK	£24,080,000	£49,435,000
Exports to UK	155,387,000	173,387,000

COMMUNICATIONS

Lithuania has a relatively well-developed railway system of 1,240 miles (2,000 km) running east-west and north-south and linking the major towns with Vilnius and Klaipéda, the main international port. Vilnius has an international airport and there are smaller ones at Kaunas, Palanga and Siauliai.

CULTURE

Lithuanian culture and literature are closely linked to the national liberation movements of the 19th and early 20th centuries, and the underground literature of the Soviet occupation era.

There are national television and radio stations and several privately-owned radio stations.

SOCIAL WELFARE

Lithuania re-established a national education system in 1990. There are 2,147 schools of general education with 517,000 pupils (1991). Education begins at age 6–7 years, with the system comprising elementary schools (four years), nine-year schools (five years), and secondary schools (three years). The language of instruction is predominantly Lithuanian, but there are also Russian and Polish schools. There are 105 vocational schools and 65 colleges. Lithuania has six universities and eight other institutes of higher education. Vilnius University, founded in 1579, is one of the oldest universities in eastern Europe.

In 1993 there were 198 hospitals with 43,600 beds, 16,622 physicians and 39,896 paramedical personnel. A national social security system exists which comprises compulsory state social insurance, and social benefits provided by the state. The retirement age is 60 years for men and 55 years for women.

LUXEMBOURG
Grand-Duché de Luxembourg

Luxembourg is a grand duchy in western Europe, bounded by Germany, Belgium and France. The area is 998 sq. miles (2,586 sq. km), the population of 406,600 (1995) is nearly all Roman Catholic. The officially designated 'national language' is Letzebuergesch (Luxembourgish), a mainly spoken language which is a dialect of German with many French admixtures. French and German are the official languages for written purposes, and French is the language of administration.

CAPITAL – Luxembourg, population (1993) 75,800, is a dismantled fortress.
CURRENCY – Luxembourg franc (LF) of 100 centimes. Belgian currency is also legal tender. The Luxembourg franc is linked in a currency union with the Belgian franc.
FLAG – Three horizontal bands, red, white and blue.
NATIONAL ANTHEM – Ons Hémécht (Our homeland).
NATIONAL DAY – 23 June.

GOVERNMENT

Established as an independent state under the sovereignty of the King of the Netherlands as Grand Duke by the Congress of Vienna in 1815, Luxembourg formed part of the Germanic Confederation from 1815 to 1866, and was included in the German 'Zollverein'. In 1867 the Treaty of London declared it a neutral territory. On the death of the King of the Netherlands in 1890 it passed to the Duke of Nassau.

The territory was invaded and overrun by the Germans at the beginning of the war in 1914 but was liberated in 1918. By the Treaty of Versailles 1919, Germany renounced its former agreements with Luxembourg and in 1921 an economic union was formed with Belgium. The Grand Duchy was again invaded and occupied by Germany in 1940, and liberated in 1944.

The constitution was modified in 1948 and the stipulation of permanent neutrality was abandoned. Luxembourg is now a signatory of the Brussels and North Atlantic Treaties, and also a member of the EU. Luxembourg is a member of the Belgium-Netherlands-Luxembourg Customs Union (Benelux 1960).

There is a Chamber of 60 deputies, elected by universal suffrage for five years. Legislation is submitted to the Council of State. The last general election was held on 12 June 1994 and a coalition government was installed.

HEAD OF STATE
HRH The Grand Duke of Luxembourg, Grand Duke Jean, KG, *born* 5 January 1921; *succeeded* (on the abdication of his mother) 12 November 1964; *married* 9 April 1953 Princess Joséphine-Charlotte of Belgium, and has *issue*, three sons and two daughters
Heir, HRH Prince Henri, *born* 16 April 1955, *married* 14 February 1981, Maria Teresa Mestre, and has *issue*, Prince Guillaume, *b.* 11 November 1981; Prince Felix, *b.* 3 June 1984; Prince Louis, *b.* 3 August 1986; Princess Alexandra, *b.* 2 February 1991; Prince Sébastien, *b.* 16 April 1992.

CABINET *as at August 1996*
Prime Minister, Minister of State, Employment, Finance and Treasury, Jean-Claude Juncker (CD)
Deputy PM, Foreign Affairs, Trade, Overseas Aid and Development, Jacques Poos (SOC)

Agriculture, Rural Development, Small Businesses, Housing and Tourism, Fernand Boden (CD)
Justice, Budget, Relations with Parliament, Marc Fischbach (CD)
Family, Women and the Disabled, Marie-Josée Jacobs (CD)
Education, Cultural and Religious Affairs, Erna Hennicot-Schoepges (CD)
Home Affairs, Civil Service and Administrative Reforms, Michel Wolter (CD)
Economy, Public Works, Energy, Robert Goebbels (SOC)
Environment, Health, Johny Lahure (SOC)
Land Planning, Defence, Youth and Sports, Alex Bodry (SOC)
Social Security, Transport, Post and Communication, Mady Delvaux-Stehres (SOC)
CD Christian Social People's Party; SOC Luxembourg Socialist Workers' Party

EMBASSY OF LUXEMBOURG
27 Wilton Crescent, London SW1X 8SD
Tel 0171-235 6961
Ambassador Extraordinary and Plenipotentiary, HE Joseph Weyland, apptd 1993

BRITISH EMBASSY
14 Boulevard F. D. Roosevelt, L-2450 Luxembourg Ville
Tel: Luxembourg 229864
Ambassador Extraordinary and Plenipotentiary, HE John N. Elam, CMG, apptd 1994

DEFENCE

Luxembourg has a total active armed forces strength of 800 personnel organized into one light infantry battalion. For legal reasons, NATO's squadron of 18 E-3A Sentry airborne early warning aircraft is registered in Luxembourg. The paramilitary gendarmerie number 560 personnel.

ECONOMY

The country has an important iron and steel industry and is an important financial centre. Government revenue for 1995 was estimated at LF 145.1 million, expenditure LF 146.4 million.

TRADE WITH UK
(Belgium and Luxembourg)

	1994	1995
Imports from UK	£7,111,693,000	£7,880,300,000
Exports to UK	6,886,191,000	7,631,300,000

MACEDONIA (FORMER YUGOSLAV REPUBLIC OF)

Macedonia is a mountainous landlocked country situated in the southern Balkans and bordered on the north by the Federal Republic of Yugoslavia (Serbia), on the east by Bulgaria, on the south by Greece and on the west by Albania. It has an area of 9,925 sq. miles (25,713 sq. km).

According to the 1994 census the population is 1,936,877, of whom 66.5 per cent are Macedonian, 22.9 per cent Albanian, 4.0 per cent ethnic Turks, 2.3 per cent gypsies, 2.3 per cent Serbs and 0.4 per cent Vlachs. The census results are disputed by the ethnic Albanians and Serbs.

Macedonian Orthodox Christianity is the majority religion, with a Muslim minority. The main language is Macedonian (a south Slavic language), which is written in the Cyrillic script.

CAPITAL – Skopje, population (1991 census) of 448,229. Other major towns are Bitola (84,002), Prilep (70,152) and Kumanov (69,231).
CURRENCY – Macedonian Denar.
FLAG – Red with an eight-rayed sun displayed over the whole field.
NATIONAL ANTHEM – Today over Macedonia.

GOVERNMENT

From the ninth to the 14th centuries AD Macedonia was ruled alternately by the Bulgars and the Byzantine Empire. In the middle of the 14th century the area was conquered by the Turks and remained under the Ottoman Empire for over 500 years. After the defeat of Turkey in the two Balkan wars of 1912–13 the geographical area of Macedonia was divided, the major part becoming Serbian (the areas of the present-day Macedonia) and the remainder given to Greece and Bulgaria. In 1918 on the formation of the Kingdom of the Serbs, Croats and Slovenes (later Yugoslavia), Serbian Macedonia was incorporated into Serbia as South Serbia. When Yugoslavia was reconstituted in 1944 as a Communist federal republic under President Tito, Macedonia became a constituent republic.

Multiparty elections for the 120-seat assembly held in November and December 1990 produced the first non-Communist government since the Second World War. The electorate overwhelmingly approved Macedonian sovereignty and independence in a referendum on 8 September 1991 and independence was declared on 18 September 1991. A new constitution was adopted in November 1991 and then amended at the EC's request to make it clear that Macedonia had no territorial claim on its neighbours. Macedonia applied for EC recognition in December 1991 but was refused because of Greece's objections to the state's name, flag and currency which, according to the Greek government, amounted to a territorial claim on the Greek province of Macedonia. The peaceful withdrawal of the Yugoslav Army (JNA) from Macedonia was completed in April 1992.

Tensions between Macedonia and its neighbours grew in late 1992, with Greece imposing a virtual economic blockade and Albania alleging discrimination against ethnic Albanians. Fearing conflict, the UN sent 1,000 peacekeepers in 1992–3 to man border posts with Serbia and Albania. A full UN peacekeeping force, the UN Preventive Deployment Force (UNPREDEP) was established in March 1995; its mandate has been extended until December 1996.

Macedonia gained UN membership on 8 April 1993 following a compromise with Greece by which it is temporarily known as the 'Former Yugoslav Republic of Macedonia' (FYROM). Greece subsequently reopened its border to Macedonian trade in September 1993, but reimposed its economic blockade in February 1994 after the majority of EU states established diplomatic relations with Macedonia. An agreement was signed in September 1995 under which Greece agreed to lift the embargo on 15 October 1995 in exchange for Macedonia removing the contentious Star of Vergina from its flag.

Presidential and parliamentary elections were held in October 1994, and the presidential election were won by the incumbent, Kiro Gligorov. The parliamentary elections to the 120-seat *Sobranie* (National Assembly) were marred by allegations of ballot-rigging and partially boycotted by the Democratic Party and the nationalist UMRO party. The elections were won by the ruling Alliance for Macedonia (a coalition of the Social Democrat, Liberal and Socialist parties) with 95 seats; the ethnic Albanian parties won 19 seats, and independents six. A coalition government was formed in December 1994 by the Alliance for Macedonia and the Party of Democratic Prosperity of Albanians in Macedonia.

Despite the coalition government, ethnic tensions continue between Macedonians and Albanians over the constitution, which Albanians claim to be discriminatory; the 1994 census, which ethnic Albanians partially boycotted; the forbidding of the use of the Albanian language on identity cards and passports; and the Albanian-language university at Tetovo which opened in February 1995 but was forcibly closed by the government, leading to violent clashes.

HEAD OF STATE
President, Kiro Gligorov, *elected* 27 January 1991, *re-elected* 16 October 1994

GOVERNMENT *as at August 1996*
Prime Minister, Branko Crvenovski
Deputy Prime Ministers, Ljube Trpeski; Jane Miljovski
Foreign Affairs, Ljubomir Frckovski
Economy, Bekjir Zuta
Defence, Blagoja Handziski
Interior, Tomislav Cokrevski
Justice, Vlado Popovski
Urbanism, Civil Engineering, Traffic and Environment, Jorgo Sundovski
Transport, Dimitar Buzlevski
Health, Dr Ilija Filipce
Finance, Taki Fiti
Agriculture, Nikola Parakeov
Education and Physical Culture, Dr Sofija Todorova
Culture, Slobodan Unkovski
Development, Abdelmenaf Bedzeti
Labour and Social Policy, Naser Ziberi
Science, Aslan Selmani
Without Portfolio, Vlado Naumovski, Dzemail Hajdari

EMBASSY OF THE FORMER YUGOSLAV REPUBLIC OF MACEDONIA
10 Harcourt House, 19A Cavendish Square, London WIM 9AD
Tel 0171-499 5152
Ambassador Extraordinary and Plenipotentiary, HE Risto Nikovski, apptd 1994

BRITISH EMBASSY
Veljko Vlahović 26, 9100 Skopje
Tel: Skopje 116 772
Ambassador Extraordinary and Plenipotentiary, HE Tony Millson, apptd 1994

ECONOMY

Economic activity was decimated by the UN trade sanctions against the rump Yugoslavia (from May 1992 until November 1995), with which Macedonia had conducted 60 per cent of its trade. The Greek economic blockade (from February 1994 until October 1995) deprived Macedonia of most of its oil supplies and industry survived on imports from Turkey and Bulgaria. Macedonia is attempting to transform its economy to a market-orientated one and introduce privatization under an IMF stabilization programme which began in 1994 with loans totalling US$97 million. Foreign debt, mostly inherited from the former Yugoslavia, stands at US$866 million, although Western donors have paid off debts to the World Bank. In early 1995 unemployment was 45 per cent and annual inflation 57 per cent. Output and GDP have fallen significantly since 1990. Foreign investment has been minimal because of the lack of international recognition.

In 1991 41.2 per cent of GDP was produced by industry and mining and 14 per cent by agriculture. Mineral resources include nickel, lead, zinc, manganese and iron ore. The main industrial sectors are basic metal industries, chemicals, textiles and food processing. Important agricultural crops are wheat, tobacco, rice, wine, lamb, cotton and sugar beet.

TRADE WITH UK	1994	1995
Imports from UK	£14,166,000	£18,079,000
Exports to UK	5,897,000	5,323,000

MADAGASCAR
Repoblika n'i Madagaskar

Madagascar lies 240 miles off the east coast of Africa and is the fourth largest island in the world. It has an area of 226,662 sq. miles (587,041 sq. km), and a population (UN estimate 1994) of 13,101,000. The people are of mixed Malayo-Polynesian, Arab and African origin. There are sizeable French, Chinese and Indian communities. The official languages are Malagasy and French.

CAPITAL – Antananarivo, population estimate 1,250,000. Other main towns are the chief port ΨToamasina (230,000); ΨMahajanga (200,000); Fianarantsoa (300,000); ΨAntsiranana (220,000).
CURRENCY – Franc Malgache (Malagasy franc) (FMG) of 100 centimes.
FLAG – Equal horizontal bands of red (above) and green, with vertical white band by staff.
NATIONAL DAY – 26 June (Independence Day).

GOVERNMENT

Madagascar (known from 1958 to 1975 as the Malagasy Republic) became a French protectorate in 1895, and a French colony in 1896 when the former queen was exiled. Republican status was adopted on 14 October 1958, and independence was proclaimed on 26 June 1960.

The post-independence civilian government was replaced by a military government in 1975 and the following month martial law was declared. A Supreme Council of the Revolution under Capitaine de Frégate (subsequently Admiral) Didier Ratsiraka was established.

In November 1991, after six months of strikes and agitation against his one-party socialist rule, President Ratsiraka relinquished executive power to a new Prime Minister, Guy Razanamasy. However, the President retained his official position and the main opposition grouping, the *Forces Vives*, established a rival government led by Albert Zafy. In December 1991 a transitional government including Forces Vives and Razanamasy supporters was formed to draft a new constitution, which was approved by referendum in August 1992. Presidential elections were held in two rounds in November 1992 and February 1993, Albert Zafy emerging victorious with 67 per cent of the vote. He became the first President of the Third Republic, which also came into being at the same time. A legislative election held in June 1993 was won by Forces Vives and allied parties, with Forces Vives member Francisque Ravony being elected Prime Minister by parliament in August 1993. The new constitution declares Madagascar to be a unitary state and reduces the executive powers of the president, although the president acquired the power to appoint the prime minister following a referendum in September 1995. Prime Minister Ravony resigned after the referendum and a new administration was formed in November 1995 under Prime Minister

Rakotovahiny. Rakotovahiny resigned in May 1996 following criticism of the government by the IMF. The new Prime Minister, Norbert Ratsirahonana vowed to reach agreement with the IMF.

HEAD OF STATE
President, Professor Albert Zafy, *elected* 10 February 1993

COUNCIL OF MINISTERS *as at August 1996*
Prime Minister, Norbert Ratsirahonana
Deputy P.M, Social and Cultural Affairs, Radesa François De Sales
Armed Forces, Gen. Marcel Ranjeva
Interior and Decentralization, Manahira Noharisoa Wilfred
Foreign Affairs, Jacques Sylla
Justice, Hussein Abdallah
National Police, Leon Arsene Belalahy
Finance, Farhaoudin Mohamed
Industry, Craftsmanship and Trade, Julien Razafimbevalo
Transport and Meteorology, André Rasolo
Energy and Mining, Bruno Betiana
Tourism, Elyette Rasendratsirofo
Agriculture and Rural Development, Evariste Marson
Fishing and Fish Stocks, Mady Abdulanziz
Public Works and Town and Country Planning, Sylvain Randrianaivo
Posts and Telecommunications, Ny Hasina Andriamanjato
National Education, Fulgence Fanony
Higher Education, Pierre Andrianatenaina
Health, Damasy Andriambao
Population and Social Recovery, Jean-René Randriamanjaka
Youth and Sport, Theodore Ranjivason
Civil Service, Labour and Social Legislation, Richard Randafison
Culture, Communications and Relations with Institutions, Henri Rakotonirainy
Secretaries of State, Col. Andriamanantsoa (*National Gendarmerie*); Auguste Paraina (*Economy and Planning*); Rabemanantsoa (*Environment*); Johnson Randrianiaina (*Budget*); Gen. Soja (*Commissioner-General for Integrated Development of the South*)

EMBASSY OF THE REPUBLIC OF MADAGASCAR
4 avenue Raphael, 75016 Paris, France
Tel: Paris 45046211
Ambassador Plenipotentiary and Extraordinary, new appointment awaited

HONORARY CONSULATE OF THE REPUBLIC OF MADAGASCAR
16 Lanark Mansions, Pennard Road, London W12 8DT
Tel 0181-746 0133
Honorary Consul, Stephen Hobbs

BRITISH EMBASSY
1st Floor, Immeuble 'Ny Havana', Cite de 67 Ha,
BP 167, Antananarivo
Tel: Antananarivo 277 49
Ambassador Extraordinary and Plenipotentiary, HE Robert S. Dewar, apptd 1996

ECONOMY

The economy is still largely based on agriculture, which accounts for three-quarters of its exports. Development plans have placed emphasis on increasing agricultural and livestock production, the improvement of communications, the exploitation of mineral deposits and the creation of small industries.

TRADE WITH UK	1994	1995
Imports from UK	£7,881,000	£7,203,000
Exports to UK	18,785,000	15,236,000

MALAWI
Dziko La Malawi

Malawi lies in south-eastern Africa. Its neighbours are Tanzania to the north-east, Zambia to the west, and Mozambique, which surrounds the southern part of the country. Much of the eastern border of Malawi is formed by Lake Malawi (formerly Lake Nyasa), which covers nearly half of the north of the country. The valley of the River Shire runs south from the lake, its watershed with the Zambezi lying on the western border with Mozambique and its tributary, the Ruo, with lakes Chinta and Chirwa, lying on the eastern border with Mozambique. The north and centre are plateaux, and the south highlands. The total area is 45,747 sq. miles (118,484 sq. km).

According to a UN estimate (1994), the population was 10,843,000. The official languages are Chichewa and English.

CAPITAL – Lilongwe, population (1987) 223,973. The city of Blantyre in the south, incorporating Blantyre and Limbe (population (1987) 331,588), is the major commercial and industrial centre. Other main centres are: Mzuzu, Thyolo, Mulanje, Mangochi, Salima, Dedza and Zomba, the former capital.
CURRENCY – Kwacha (K) of 100 tambala.
FLAG – Horizontal stripes of black, red and green, with rising sun in the centre of the black stripe.
NATIONAL ANTHEM – O God Bless Our Land of Malawi.
NATIONAL DAY – 6 July (Independence Day).

GOVERNMENT

Malawi (formerly Nyasaland) assumed internal self-government on 1 February 1963, and became independent on 6 July 1964. It became a republic on 6 July 1966.

There is a Cabinet consisting of the President and ministers. The National Assembly consists of 177 members, each elected by universal suffrage, and usually meets three times a year. A new multiparty constitution took effect on 17 May 1994. It ends the idea of the Life Presidency, reduces presidential powers, establishes the posts of First and Second Vice-President and provides for a Senate, to come into being by May 1999.

In 1991–2 Life President Hastings Banda, who had ruled since independence, came under increasing pressure to introduce a multiparty democratic system of government. In May 1992 aid donors tied new loans to improvements in the human rights record and moves to multiparty democracy. A referendum was held on the adoption of a multiparty democracy in June 1993 and approved by 63 per cent of voters. President Banda and the Malawi Congress Party refused to resign but parliament passed a law to amend the constitution to allow multiparty politics and Banda announced a political amnesty to allow exiles to return. Multiparty presidential and legislative elections were held in May 1994 and won by Bakili Muluzi and the United Democratic Front (UDF) respectively. Foreign and multilateral aid has since been restored. A coalition UDF-AFORD government was formed although AFORD withdrew from the coalition in June 1996. The state of the parties in parliament following the election was United Democratic Front (UDF) 84 seats, Malawi Congress Party (MCP) 55 seats, Alliance for Democracy (AFORD) 36 seats.

HEAD OF STATE
President, Bakili Muluzi, *elected* 17 May 1994, *sworn in* 21 May 1994

First Vice-President, Justin Malewezi
Second Vice-President, Chakufwa Chihana

CABINET *as at August 1996*
The President
Defence, The First Vice-President
Finance, Economic Planning and Development, Hon. Aleke
  Banda
Transport and Civil Aviation, Hon. Harry I. Thomson
Irrigation and Water Development, Hon. E. C. Bwanali
Information, Broadcasting, Posts and Telecommunications, Hon.
  Brown Mpinganjira
Local Government, Hon. Dr Matembo Mzunda
Home Affairs, Hon. Wenham Nakanga
Education, Hon. Prof. Dr Donton Mkandawire
Foreign Affairs, Hon. Dr George Nga Ntafu
Tourism, Hon. Patrick Mbewe
Agriculture and Livestock Development, Hon. Dr Mapopa
  Chipeta
Lands and Valuation, Hon. Peter Pachi
Physical Planning and Surveys, Hon. Edda Chitalo
Works and Supplies, Hon. A. Pillane
Health and Population, Hon. Ziliro Chibambo
Attorney-General, Justice, Hon. C. Chilumpha
Housing, Hon. Tim Mangwazu
Natural Resources, Hon. M. Moyo
Research and Environmental Affairs, Hon. Mayinga
  Mkandawire
Youths, Sports and Culture, Hon. Kamangadazi Chambalo
Energy and Mining, Hon. Revd Dr Dumbo Lemani
Relief and Rehabilitation, Hon. Richard J. Sombereka
Labour and Manpower Development, Hon. D. Kaliyoma
  Phumisa
Commerce and Industry, Hon. Chakakala Chaziya
*Women, Children's Affairs, Community Development and Social
  Welfare*, Hon. Lilian Patel

MALAWI HIGH COMMISSION
33 Grosvenor Street, London WIX ODE
Tel 0171-491 4172/7
High Commissioner, HE Jake Muwamba, apptd 1995

BRITISH HIGH COMMISSION
PO Box 30042, Lilongwe 3
Tel: Lilongwe 782400
High Commissioner, HE John Francis Martin, CMG, apptd
1993

BRITISH COUNCIL REPRESENTATIVE, James Kennedy,
  Plot No. 13/20, City Centre, PO Box 30222,
  Lilongwe 3.

ECONOMY

The economy is largely agricultural, with maize the main
subsistence crop. Tobacco, sugar, tea, groundnuts and
cotton are the main cash crops and principal exports. There
are two sugar mills. A number of light manufacturing
industries have been established, mainly in agricultural
processing, clothing/textiles and building materials. In
November 1994 the IMF approved a US$22 million loan to
support economic reform; a further credit of US$69
million was pledged for 1995–8 in October 1995.

TRADE WITH UK	1994	1995
Imports from UK	£19,594,000	£13,449,000
Exports to UK	25,816,000	16,188,000

COMMUNICATIONS

A single-track railway runs from Mchinji on the Zambian
border, through Lilongwe and Salima on Lake Malawi
(itself served by two passenger and a number of cargo
boats) through to Blantyre. The route south to the
Mozambique port of Beira was severed by the Mozambican civil war, but the route to Nacala in Mozambique is
open again. There are 12,215 km of roads in Malawi of
which about 21.8 per cent are bituminized. There is an
international airport 26 km from Lilongwe, which handles
regional and intercontinental flights.

EDUCATION

Primary education is the responsibility of local authorities
in both urban and rural areas, although policy, curricula
and inspection are the responsibility of the Ministry of
Education and Culture. The Ministry is also responsible
for secondary schools, technical education and primary
teacher training. Religious bodies, with government assistance, still play an important part in these fields. The
University of Malawi was opened in 1965 and has five
constituent colleges. Illiteracy was estimated at 43.6 per
cent of the population in 1995.

MALAYSIA
Persekutuan Tanah Malaysia

Malaysia, comprising the 11 states of peninsular Malaya
plus Sabah and Sarawak, lies between 1° and 7° N. latitude
and 100° and 119° E. longitude. It occupies two distinct
regions, the Malay peninsula which extends from the
isthmus of Kra to the Singapore Strait, and the north-west
coastal area of the island of Borneo. Each is separated from
the other by the South China Sea. The total area of
Malaysia is about 127,317 sq. miles (329,749 sq. km).

The year is commonly divided into the south-west and
north-west monsoon seasons. Rainfall averages about 100
inches throughout the year. The average daily temperature varies from 21° C to 32° C, though in higher areas
temperatures are lower and vary widely.

The population was 16,921,300 (1988 census),
20,103,000 official estimate (1995). The principal racial
groups are the Malays (53 per cent), the Chinese (35 per
cent), and those of Indian and Sri Lankan origin, as well as
the indigenous races of Sarawak and Sabah. Bahasa
Malaysia (Malay) is the sole official language, but English,
various dialects of Chinese, and Tamil are also widely
spoken. There are a few indigenous languages widely
spoken in Sabah and Sarawak.

Islam is the official religion of Malaysia, each ruler being
the head of religion in his state (except in Sabah and
Sarawak). The Yang di-Pertuan Agung is the head of
religion in Melaka and Penang. The constitution guarantees religious freedom.

CAPITAL – Kuala Lumpur was proclaimed federal
  territory in 1974. Its population (1990) is 1,231,500.
CURRENCY – Malaysian dollar (ringgit) (M$) of 100 sen.
FLAG – Equal horizontal stripes of red (seven) and white
  (seven); 14-point yellow star and crescent in blue
  canton.
NATIONAL ANTHEM – Negara-Ku.
NATIONAL DAY – 31 August (*Hari Kebangsaan*).

GOVERNMENT

The Federation of Malaya became an independent country within the Commonwealth on 31 August 1957. On 16 September 1963 the federation was enlarged by the accession of the states of Singapore, Sabah (formerly British North Borneo) and Sarawak, and the name of Malaysia was adopted from that date. On 9 August 1965 Singapore seceded from the federation.

The constitution provided a strong federal government and a degree of autonomy for the state governments. It created a constitutional Supreme Head of the Federation (HM the *Yang di-Pertuan Agung*) and a Deputy Supreme Head (HRH *Timbalan Yang di-Pertuan Agung*) to be elected for a term of five years by the rulers from among their number. The Malay rulers are either chosen or succeed to their position in accordance with the custom of the particular state. In other states of Malaysia, choice of the head of state is at the discretion of the Yang di-Pertuan Agung after consultation with the Chief Minister of the state.

The Federal Parliament consists of two houses, the Senate and the House of Representatives. The Senate (*Dewan Negara*) consists of 68 members, 26 elected by the Legislative Assemblies of the States (two from each) and 42 appointed by the Yang di-Pertuan Agung. The House of Representatives (*Dewan Rakyat*) consists of 192 members elected by universal adult suffrage with a common electoral roll.

According to the constitution, each state shall have its own constitution not inconsistent with the federal constitution, with the ruler or governor acting on the advice of an Executive Council appointed on the advice of the Chief Minister and a single-chamber Legislative Assembly. The Legislative Assemblies are fully elected on the same basis as the Federal Parliament.

The National Front (Barisan Nasional) Coalition led by Dr Mahathir Muhammad won a fourth term in office in a general election held on 25 April 1995, winning 162 of the 192 seats.

HEAD OF STATE

Supreme Head of State, HM Tuanku Jaafar Ibni Al-Marhum Tuanku Abdul Rahman (Yang Dipertuan Besar of Negeri Sembilan), *sworn in* 26 April 1994, *crowned* 22 September 1994

Deputy Supreme Head of State, HRH Sultan Salahuddin Abdul Aziz Shah Al-Haj ibni Almarhum Sultan Hishamuddin Alam Shah Al-Haj (Sultan of Selangor)

CABINET *as at August 1996*

Prime Minister, Minister of Home Affairs, Hon. Datuk Seri Dr Mahathir Muhammad
Deputy Prime Minister, Minister for Finance, Hon Datuk Seri Anwar Ibrahim
Transport, Hon. Datuk Seri Dr Ling Liong Sik
Energy, Telecommunications and Posts, Hon. Datuk Leo Moggie Anak Irok
Primary Industries, Hon. Datuk Seri Dr Lim Keng Yaik
Works, Hon. Datuk Seri S. Samy Vellu
International Trade and Industry, Hon. Datuk Seri Rafidah Aziz
Education, Hon. Datuk Seri Najib Tun Razak
Agriculture, Hon. Datuk Dr Sulaiman Daud
Rural Development, Senator Datuk Haji Annuar bin Musa
Domestic Trade and Consumer Affairs, Hon. Datuk Haji Abu Hassan bin Haji Omar
Health, Hon. Chua Jui Meng
Foreign Affairs, Hon. Datuk Abdullah bin Haji Ahmad Badawi
Defence, Hon. Datuk Syed Hamid Albar

Information, Hon. Datuk Mohamed bin Rahmat
Culture, Arts and Tourism, Hon. Datuk Sabbaruddin Chik
National Unity and Community Development, Hon. Datin Paduka Zaleha Ismail
Entrepreneur Development, Hon. Datuk Mustapa Mohamed
Human Resources, Hon. Datuk Lim Ah Lek
Science, Technology and Environment, Hon. Datuk Law Hieng Ding
Housing and Local Government, Hon. Datuk Dr Ting Chew Peh
Land and Co-operative Development, Hon. Osu bin Haji Sukam
Youth and Sports, Hon. Tan Sri Muhyiddin Yassin
Prime Minister's Department, Hon. Datuk Abang Abu Bakar bin Datu Bandar Abang Haji Mustapha; Hon. Dr Abdul Hamid Othman; Senator Datuk Chong Kah Kiat

NOTE: Tunku/Tengku, Tun, Tan Sri, and Datuk are titles. Tunku/Tengku is equivalent to Prince. Tun denotes membership of the highest order of Malaysian chivalry and Tan Sri and Datuk (Datuk Seri in Perak and Datu in Sabah) are each the equivalent of a knighthood. The wife of a Tun is styled Toh Puan, that of a Tan Sri is styled Puan Sri and of a Datuk, Datin. The honorific Tuan or Encik is equivalent to Mr and the honorific Puan is equivalent to Mrs.

MALAYSIAN HIGH COMMISSION

45 Belgrave Square, London SWIX 8QT
Tel 0171-235 8033
High Commissioner, HE Dato Kamarudin Abu, apptd 1992
Deputy High Commissioner, Jasmi Muhammad Yusoff
Defence Attaché, Col. Muhammad Yunus
Counsellor (Commercial), Z. M. Perai

BRITISH HIGH COMMISSION

185 Jalan Ampang (PO Box 11030), 50450 Kuala Lumpur
Tel: Kuala Lumpur 2482122
High Commissioner, HE David Moss, CMG, apptd 1994
Deputy High Commissioner, T. N. Byrne
Counsellor (Commercial/Economic), I. R. Murray, OBE
Defence Adviser, Col. J. L. Seddon-Brown

BRITISH COUNCIL DIRECTOR, T. Edmundson, PO Box 10539, Jalan Bukit Aman, Kuala Lumpur 50916. There are also offices at Johore Bahru, Kota Kinabalu (Sabah) and Kuching (Sarawak), and a library in Penang.

STATES

The 13 states of the Federation of Malaysia are:

State	Capital	Population (1988 census)
ΨJohore	Johore Bahru	2,007,300
Kedah	Alor Setar	1,353,500
Kelantan	Kota Bahru	1,150,400
ΨMelaka	Melaka	560,700
Negri Sembilan	Seremban	694,100
ΨPahang	Kuantan	1,001,200
ΨPenang	Georgetown	1,103,200
Perak	Ipoh	2,143,200
Perlis	Kangar	179,700
ΨSabah	Kota Kinabalu	1,371,000
ΨSarawak	Kuching	1,591,000
ΨSelangor	Shah Alam	1,878,300
ΨTerengganu	Kuala Terengganu	705,200

Federal Territories

Kuala Lumpur		} 1,182,700
Labuan		

JUDICATURE

The judicial system consists of a Federal Court and two High Courts, one in peninsular Malaysia and one for Sabah and Sarawak. The Federal Court comprises a President, the two Chief Justices of the High Courts and other judges. It possesses appellate, original and advisory jurisdiction.

Each of the High Courts consists of a Chief Justice and not less than four other judges. In peninsular Malaysia the subordinate courts consist of the sessions courts and the magistrates' courts. In Sabah/Sarawak the magistrates' courts constitute the subordinate courts.

DEFENCE

Total active armed forces personnel number 114,500, with volunteer service in operation. The Army has a strength of 90,000 personnel, with 26 light tanks, 816 armoured personnel carriers and 186 artillery pieces. Reserve army personnel number 55,000. The Royal Malaysian Navy has a strength of 12,000, with four frigates, 37 patrol and coastal craft and 12 armed helicopters. The Royal Malaysian Air Force has a strength of 102 combat aircraft and 12,500 personnel.

The paramilitary police field force has a strength of 18,000 personnel in 21 battalions, together with marine police (2,100) and air wing units. Border scouts in Sabah and Sarawak number 1,200.

Australia maintains an infantry company and an air force detachment in Malaysia.

ECONOMY

From being an agriculturally-based economy reliant on raw materials exports at independence, Malaysia has undergone an industrialization programme and now produces clothing, textiles, rubber goods, electronics, office equipment, cars, household appliances, semiconductors, food processing and chemicals. Under the New Economic Policy of 1970–90, the economy grew at an average rate of 6.7 per cent a year. The National Development Policy 1990–2000 is seen as the second stage in making Malaysia a fully-developed industrial state by 2020. Economic growth in 1990–5 has averaged 8.0 per cent a year. The 1996–2000 five-year plan aims to achieve 8 per cent GDP growth and to keep unemployment at no more than 2.8 per cent. In 1995 44 per cent of GDP was produced by services, 35 per cent by manufacturing and 13 per cent by agriculture.

FINANCE	1994	1995*
Revenue	M$49,446m	M$50,380m
Expenditure	45,038m	49,794m
*estimated		

TRADE

Malaysia is the largest exporter of natural rubber, tin, palm oil and tropical hardwoods. Other major export commodities are manufactured and processed products, petroleum, oil, and other minerals, palm kernel oil, tea and pepper. Exports of major commodities were (1995): manufactured goods 78 per cent, agricultural products 12 per cent, minerals, oil and gas 6 per cent. Imports consist mainly of machinery and transport equipment, manufactured goods, foods, mineral fuels, chemicals and inedible crude materials.

	1994	1995
Imports (c.i.f.)	M$155,919m	M$196,516m
Exports (f.o.b.)	153,688m	186,869m

Trade with UK	1994	1995
Imports from UK	£1,305,201,000	£1,189,582,000
Exports to UK	1,204,026,000	1,487,884,000

THE MALDIVES
Divehi Jumhuriya

The Maldives are a chain of coral atolls 400 miles to the south-west of Sri Lanka, stretching north for about 600 miles from just south of the Equator. There are about 20 coral atolls comprising over 1,200 islands, 202 of which are inhabited. The total area of the islands is 115 sq. miles (298 sq. km). No point in the entire chain of islands is more than 8 feet above sea-level.

The population of the islands (official estimate 1994) is 246,000. The people are Sunni Muslims and the Maldivian (Dhivehi) language is akin to Elu or old Sinhalese.

CAPITAL – ΨMalé, population (1985) 46,334. There is an international airport at Malé.

CURRENCY – Rufiyaa of 100 laaris.

FLAG – Green field bearing a white crescent, with wide red border.

NATIONAL ANTHEM – Qawmee Salaam.

NATIONAL DAY – 26 July.

GOVERNMENT

Until 1952 the islands were a sultanate under the protection of the British Crown. Internal self-government was achieved in 1948 and full independence in 1965. The Maldives became a special member of the Commonwealth in 1982 and a full member in 1985.

The Maldives form a republic which is elective. There is a legislature, the *Citizens' Majlis*, with representatives elected from all the atolls. The life of the Majlis is five years. The government consists of a Cabinet, which is responsible to the Majlis.

HEAD OF STATE
President, HE Maumoon Abdul Gayoom, *elected* 1978, *re-elected* 1983, 1989, 1 October 1993

CABINET *as at August 1996*
Defence and National Security, The President
Foreign Affairs, Fathulla Jameel
Justice and Islamic Affairs, Mohamed Rasheed Ibrahim
Home Affairs, Abdulla Jameel
Education, Mohamad Latheef
Health and Welfare, Ahmed Abdullah
Fisheries and Agriculture, Hassan Sobir
Atolls Administration, Abdul Rasheed Hussain
Trade and Industries, Abdulla Yameen
Tourism, Ibrahim Hussain Zaki
Planning and Environment, Ismail Shafeeu
Transport and Communications, Ahmed Zahir
Construction and Public Works, Umar Zahir
Information and Culture, Ibrahim Maniku
Youth, Women's Affairs and Industries, Rashida Yoosuf
Attorney-General, Mohamed Munawar
Ministers of State, Anbaree Abdul Sattar (*Defence and National Security*); Arif Hilmy (*Finance and Treasury*)
Speaker of the Citizens' Majlis, Abdulla Hameed

BRITISH HIGH COMMISSIONER, HE David Tatham, CMG, resident at Colombo, Sri Lanka

ECONOMY

The vegetation of the islands is coconut palms with some scrub. Hardly any cultivation of crops is possible and nearly all food to supplement the basic fish diet has to be imported. The principal industry is fishing and considerable quantities of fish and dried fish are exported to Japan and Sri Lanka. The tourist industry is expanding rapidly (278,000 visitors in 1994). Fishing and tourism together account for about 30 per cent of GDP. The Maldives National Ship Management Ltd (MNSML) has a fleet of nine merchant ships.

TRADE WITH UK	1994	1995
Imports from UK	£2,580,000	£3,850,000
Exports to UK	7,404,000	8,879,000

MALI
République du Mali

Mali, an inland state in north-west Africa, has an area of 478,791 sq. miles (1,240,000 sq. km), and a population (UN estimate 1994) of 9,524,000. The principal rivers are the Niger and the Senegal.

CAPITAL – Bamako (1987 census, 658,275). Other towns are Gao, Kayes, Mopti, Sikasso, Segou and Timbuktu (all regional capitals).
CURRENCY – Franc CFA of 100 centimes.
FLAG – Vertical stripes of green (by staff), yellow and red.
NATIONAL DAY – 22 September.

GOVERNMENT

Formerly the French colony of Soudan, the territory elected on 24 November 1958 to remain an autonomous republic within the French Community. It associated with Senegal in the Federation of Mali, which was granted full independence on 20 June 1960. The Federation was effectively dissolved in August 1960 by the secession of Senegal. The title of the Republic of Mali was adopted in September 1960.

The regime of Modibo Keita was overthrown in 1968 by a group of army officers who formed a National Liberation Committee and appointed a Prime Minister. Moussa Traoré assumed the functions of head of state. A new civil constitution came into being in 1979.

President Traoré was overthrown in March 1991 by troops led by Lt.-Col. Toure. A military National Reconciliation Committee joined with democratic parties to form a Transitional Committee for the Salvation of the People which suspended the constitution and dissolved the Mali People's Democratic Union (UPDM), formerly the sole party. A transitional government was formed in April 1991. A new constitution was approved by a national referendum in January 1992. The new constitution provided for a multiparty political system, and legislative elections were held in February and March 1992 with the Alliance for Democracy in Mali (ADEMA) emerging victorious. Alpha Konaré, the ADEMA leader, won the presidential elections in April 1992 and appointed a government dominated by ADEMA members. The government resigned in April 1993 after political unrest in Bamako. On 12 April the President appointed a new Cabinet, again dominated by ADEMA, but this was replaced by another ADEMA-dominated Cabinet in February 1994.

HEAD OF STATE
President, Alpha Oumar Konaré, *elected* 28 April 1992, *sworn in* 8 June 1992

CABINET *as at August 1996*

Prime Minister, Ibrahim Boubacar Keita
Minister of State, Foreign Affairs, Malians Abroad and African Integration, Dioncounda Traore
Mines, Energy and Water Resources, Cheickna Seydou Diawara
Civil Service, Labour and Employment, Boubacar Diarra
Public Works and Transport, Mohamed Ag Erlaf
Finance and Commerce, Soumeyla Cisse
Youth and Sports, Boubacar Coulibaly
Tourism and Crafts, Fatou Haidara
Health, Solidarity and Pensioners, Modibo Sidibe
Territorial Administration and Security, Lt.-Col. Sada Samake
Primary Education, Adama Sammassekou
Rural Development and Environment, Modibo Traore
Justice, Cheikna Kamissoko
Secondary and Higher Education and Scientific Research, Moustapha Dicko
Culture and Communications and Government Spokesman, Bakary Koniba Traore
Armed Forces and Veterans, Momedou Ba
Urbanization and Housing, Sy Kadiatou Sow

EMBASSY OF THE REPUBLIC OF MALI
Avenue Molière 487, 1060 Brussels, Belgium
Tel: Brussels 3457432
Ambassador Extraordinary and Plenipotentiary, HE N'Tiji Traoré, apptd 1993; resident at Brussels
BRITISH AMBASSADOR, HE Alan Furness, CMG, resident at Dakar, Senegal
There is a Consulate in Bamako.

ECONOMY

Mali's principal exports are gold, groundnuts, cotton fibres, meat and dried fish. Mali rejoined the CFA Franc Zone in 1984. In March 1994 the IMF approved a US$41 million credit to support a free market economic reform programme; it was supplemented by loans of US$46 million in April 1995, and a three-year loan of US$91 million in April 1996.

TRADE WITH UK	1994	1995
Imports from UK	£10,841,000	£24,074,000
Exports to UK	477,000	225,000

MALTA
Repubblika Ta'Malta

Malta lies in the Mediterranean Sea, 58 miles (93 km) from Sicily and about 180 miles (288 km) from the African coast. It is about 17 miles (27 km) in length and 9 miles (14.5 km) in breadth, and has an area of 94.9 sq. miles (246 sq. km). Malta also includes the islands of Gozo (area 25.9 sq. miles (67 sq. km)), Comino and minor islets.

The population (census 1995) was 376,335. The Maltese are mainly Roman Catholic. The Maltese language is of Semitic origin and held by some to be derived from the Carthaginian and Phoenician tongues. Maltese and English are the official languages of administration. Maltese is the official language in all the courts of law and the language of general use in the islands.

CAPITAL – ΨValletta. Population (census 1995), 7,184.
CURRENCY – Maltese lira (LM) of 100 cents and 1,000 mils.
FLAG – Two equal vertical stripes, white at the hoist and red at the fly. A representation of the George Cross is carried edged with red in the canton of the white stripe.
NATIONAL ANTHEM – L-Innu Malti.
NATIONAL DAYS – 31 March (Freedom Day); 8 September (Lady of Victories); 7 June; 21 September (Independence Day); 13 December (Republic Day).

GOVERNMENT

Malta was in turn held by the Phoenicians, Carthaginians, Romans and Arabs. In 1090 it was conquered by Count Roger of Normandy and in 1530 handed over to the Knights of St John. In 1565 it sustained the famous siege, when the Turks were successfully withstood by Grandmaster La Valette. The Knights fortified the islands and built Valletta before being expelled by Napoleon in 1798. The Maltese rose against the French garrison soon afterwards and the island was subsequently blockaded by the British fleet. The Maltese people requested the protection of the British Crown in 1802 on condition that their rights would be respected. The islands were finally annexed to the British Crown by the Treaty of Paris in 1814.

Malta was again besieged during the Second World War. From June 1940 to the end of the war, 432 members of the garrison and 1,540 civilians were killed by enemy aircraft, and about 35,000 houses were destroyed or damaged. The island was awarded the George Cross for gallantry on 15 April 1942.

On 21 September 1964 Malta became an independent state within the Commonwealth, and on 13 December 1974 a republic within the Commonwealth.

Elections to the unicameral Parliament of 65 members are held every five years by a system of proportional representation.

Malta applied for EC membership in 1990 and in June 1993 the Commission issued its Opinion that Malta should be accepted as a member subsequent to the implementation of a series of economic reforms. In June 1995 the European Council confirmed that most of the reforms were being carried out successfully and that accession negotiations would be opened in 1997.

HEAD OF STATE
President, Dr Ugo Mifsud Bonnici, *took office* 4 April 1994

CABINET *as at August 1996*
Prime Minister, Dr Edward Fenech Adami
Deputy PM and Minister of Foreign Affairs, Prof. Guido de Marco
Education and Human Resources, Michael Falzon
Social Development, Dr Louis Galea
Economic Services, Prof. Josef Bonnici
Environment, Dr Francis Zammit Dimech
Food, Agriculture and Fisheries, Censu Galea
Home Affairs, Tonio Borg
Justice and the Arts, Dr Michael Refalo
Transport, Communications and Technology, Dr Michael Frendo
Gozo, Anton Tabone
Finance, John Dalli

MALTA HIGH COMMISSION
Malta House, 36–38 Piccadilly, London WIV OPQ
Tel 0171-292 4800
High Commissioner, HE Victor Camilleri, apptd 1996

BRITISH HIGH COMMISSION
7 St Anne Street, Floriana (PO Box 506)
Tel: Floriana 233134/8
High Commissioner, HE Graham Archer, apptd 1995
BRITISH COUNCIL REPRESENTATIVE, Anne Bradley, c/o British High Commission

ECONOMY

Agriculture and fisheries contributed 2.8 per cent of GDP in 1994. Principal products are animal products, vegetables, fruit (especially grapes), flowers and cuttings.

The island's leading industry is the state-owned Malta Drydocks, employing about 3,329 people. The main port of Grand Harbour handled traffic of 1.75 million tonnes in 1993. Malta Freeport was opened in 1990 in the southern port of Marsaxlokk and comprises a container distribution centre, an oil products terminal and warehouse facilities. A second container terminal is being built.

In 1994 manufacturing employed 22.1 per cent of the workforce and accounted for 24 per cent of GDP. Industries include food processing, textiles, footwear and clothing, plastics and chemical products, electronic equipment, machinery and components. The gross output of the manufacturing industry in 1994 was LM739.9 million, of which LM537.6 million (72.7 per cent) were export sales.

Tourism has assumed primary importance, with 1,176,223 tourists visiting the island in 1994. The number of cruise liners calling at the Grand Harbour has increased considerably. Gross income from tourism stood at LM241.6 million in 1994. In 1994 2,565,000 passengers passed through Malta airport.

FINANCE	1994	1995
Revenue	LM486,926,000	LM520,505,000
Expenditure	472,703,000	522,820,000

TRADE
The principal imports are foodstuffs (mainly wheat, meat and bullocks, milk and fruit), fodder, beverages and tobacco, fuels, chemicals, textiles and machinery (industrial, agricultural and transport). The chief exports are processed food, electronics, textiles, and other manufactures.

	1994	1995
Imports	LM918.8m	LM1,042.5m
Exports	587m	672m
Trade with UK	1994	1995
Imports from UK	£205,463,000	£284,346,000
Exports to UK	75,096,000	79,790,000

EDUCATION

Education is compulsory between the ages of five and 16 and is free at all levels. In October 1995, 6,210 children were enrolled in state kindergartens and 23,368 children attended six-year primary education courses in 80 state schools. Secondary education in state schools is provided in secondary schools, junior lyceums and trade schools. In 1995–6 there were 10 junior lyceums with 8,859 students; 18 secondary schools with 9,133 students, five centres catering for 1,522 low achievers while there were 3,139 students enrolled in trade schools.

A Junior College, administered by the University of Malta, prepares students specifically for a university course. About 2,920 students attended state higher secondary educational institutions, while 1,703 students attended the Junior College. Tertiary education is available at the University of Malta, which had 6,000 students in October 1995. There were also 18,033 students attending schools administered by the Catholic Church while 7,310 students attended private schools.

MARSHALL ISLANDS
Republic of the Marshall Islands

The Republic of the Marshall Islands consists of 29 atolls and five islands in the central Pacific Ocean lying between 4° and 19° N., and 160° and 175° E. The islands and atolls are scattered over 1,294,500 sq. km (500,000 sq. miles), forming two parallel chains running north-west to south-east: the Ratak (Sunrise) chain and the Ralik (Sunset) chain. The total land area is 70 sq. miles (181 sq. km). The largest atoll is Kwajalein in the Ralik chain. The atolls are coral and the islands are volcanic. None of the islands rises more than a few metres above sea level. The climate is hot and humid with little seasonal variation in temperature. The typhoon season lasts from December to March.

The population is 52,000 (1994 UN estimate), of which 99 per cent are Micronesian. Over half the population is under 15. About 60 per cent of the population is concentrated on the two atolls of Majuro and Kwajalein.

The population is Christian, primarily Protestant but with a substantial Catholic minority. The principal Protestant denomination is the United Church of Christ. Marshallese and English are the official languages.

CAPITAL – Majuro (population 20,000). The other major town is Ebeye (9,200).
CURRENCY – US Dollar.
FLAG – Blue with a diagonal ray divided white over orange running from the lower hoist to the upper fly; in the canton a white sun.
NATIONAL DAY – 21 October (Compact Day).

GOVERNMENT

The Marshall Islands were claimed by Spain in 1592 but were left undisturbed by the Spanish Empire for 300 years. In 1886 the Marshall Islands formally became a German protectorate. On the outbreak of the First World War in 1914, Japan took control of the islands on behalf of the Allied powers, and after the war administered the territory as a League of Nations mandate. During the Second World War US armed forces seized the islands from the Japanese after intense fighting. In 1947 the USA entered into agreement with the UN Security Council to administer the Micronesia area, of which the Marshall Islands are a part, as the UN Trust Territory of the Pacific Islands.

The islands became internally self-governing in 1979, and the US Trusteeship administration came to an end on 21 October 1986, when a Compact of Free Association between the USA and the Republic of the Marshall Islands came into effect. By this agreement the USA recognized the Republic of the Marshall Islands as a fully sovereign and independent state. The UN Security Council terminated the UN Trust Territory of the Pacific in relation to the Marshall Islands and recognized its independence in December 1990.

The republic is a democracy based on a parliamentary system of government. Under the 1979 constitution, the executive is headed by the President, who is elected by the *Nitijela* from among its members. The President serves for a four-year term. The legislature has two chambers, the Council of Iroij of 12 members and the Nitijela of 33 members. The Nitijela is the law-making chamber, to which the President and government are accountable. The Council of Iroij has an advisory role.

There are 24 local government districts, each of which usually consists of an elected council, a mayor and appointed local officials.

The Republic of the Marshall Islands has no defence forces. The Compact of Free Association places full responsibility for defence of the Marshall Islands on the USA. The US Department of Defence retains control of islands within Kwajalein Atoll where it has a missile test range.

HEAD OF STATE
President, Hon. Amata Kabua, *elected* 1979, *re-elected* 1984, 1988, 1992, 1995

THE GOVERNMENT *as at August 1996*
The President
Finance, Ruben Zachkras
Foreign Affairs, Thomas Kijiner
Transport and Communications, Kunio Lemari
Resources and Development, Amsa Jonathan
Education, Phillip Muller
Social Services, Christopher Loeak
Public Works, Antonio Eliu
Health and Environment, Henchi Balos
Justice, Luckner Abner
Internal Affairs, Brenson Wase

BRITISH AMBASSADOR, HE Michael Peart, CMG, LVO, resident at Suva, Fiji

ECONOMY

The economy is a mixture of subsistence and a service-based sector. About half the working population is engaged in agriculture and fishing, with coconut oil and copra production comprising 90 per cent of total exports. The service sector is based in Majuro and Ebeye and concentrated in banking and insurance, construction, transportation and tourism. Direct US aid under the Compact accounts for two-thirds of the islands' budget. The islands charge large foreign (mainly Japanese) fishing fleets licences for fishing tuna in the waters around the islands. Japanese fleets pay some US$3 million a year. The USA and Japan are the major trading partners.

The GNP was (1994) US$88 million and GNP per capita (1994) was US$1,610.

TRADE WITH UK	1994	1995
Imports from UK	£2,403,000	£3,271,000
Exports to UK	76,000	364,000

COMMUNICATIONS

Air Marshall Islands provides air services within the islands and to Hawaii. Continental Air Micronesia serves Majuro and Kwajalein with flights to Hawaii and Guam. Majuro also has shipping links to Hawaii, Australia, Japan and throughout the Pacific.

SOCIAL WELFARE

The state school system provides education up to age 18, but only 25 per cent of students proceed beyond elementary level because of inadequate resources.

Majuro and Ebeye have hospitals run by the government with aid from the US Public Health Service. Each outer island community has a health assistant.

MAURITANIA
République Islamique de Mauritanie

Mauritania lies on the north-west coast of Africa. It is bounded on the south by Senegal, on the south and east by Mali, and on the north by Algeria and the Western Sahara. The area is 397,955 sq. miles (1,030,700 sq. km). The population (UN estimate 1994) is 2,217,000. The official languages are French and Arabic.

CAPITAL – Nouakchott (850,000).
CURRENCY – Ouguiya of 5 khoums.
FLAG – Yellow star and crescent on green ground.
NATIONAL DAY – 28 November.

GOVERNMENT

Mauritania elected on 28 November 1958 to remain within the French Community as an autonomous republic. It became fully independent on 28 November 1960. In 1972 Mauritania left the Franc Zone.

Mauritania and Morocco occupied the Western Sahara territory in February 1976 when Spain formally relinquished it and in April 1976 agreed on a new frontier dividing the territory between them. In August 1979, Mauritania relinquished all claim to the southern sector of the Western Sahara after a three-year war against Polisario Front guerrillas.

After a military coup in 1978, Mauritania was ruled by a Military Committee for National Salvation (CMSN). Having previously rejected reform, in April 1991 President Ould Taya announced a political amnesty and a referendum on the constitution, followed by multiparty elections for a reconvened Senate and National Assembly. The constitution was approved in July 1991. Multiparty elections to the Senate and National Assembly were held in March 1992 and won by the Republican Democratic and Social Party (PRDS) led by President Ould Taya. The President appointed a Cabinet of PRDS members in April 1992 but the legitimacy of the new government was undermined by the boycott of the elections by the main opposition grouping, the Union of Democratic Forces (UDF). Tension continues between the Arab-dominated government and the African minority in the south of the country.

HEAD OF STATE
President, Col. Maaouya Ould Sidi Ahmed Taya, *took power* 12 December 1984, *elected* 17 January 1992

CABINET *as at August 1996*
Prime Minister, Cheihk el Avia Ould Mohamed Khouna
Foreign Affairs and Co-operation, Lemrabott Sidi Mahmoud Ould Cheikh Ahmed
Defence, Abdallahi Ould Abdi
Justice, Ethmane Ould Sid' Ahmed Ould Yessa
Interior, Posts and Telecommunications, Dah Ould Abdel Jelil
Finance, Camara Ali Gueladio
Education, Baba Ould Sidi
Health and Social Affairs, Abou Demba Sow
Planning, Mohammed Ould Amar
Fisheries and Maritime Economy, Abdallahi Ould Nem
Commerce, Handicrafts and Tourism, Boidiel Ould Houmeid
Mines and Industry, N'gaide Lemine Kayou
Civil Service, Labour, Youth and Sports, Sidi Mohamed Ould Mohamed Vall
Equipment and Transport, Mohamed Deina Sow
Rural Development and the Environment, Mohamed Lemine Ch'bih Ould Cheick Melainine
Water and Energy, Mohamed Lemine Ould Ahmed
Communications and Relations with Parliament, Rachid Ould Saleh
Culture, Islamic Affairs, Mohamed Ould Mboirick

EMBASSY OF THE ISLAMIC REPUBLIC OF MAURITANIA
5 rue de Montevideo, Paris XVIe, France
Tel: Paris 45048854
Ambassador Extraordinary and Plenipotentiary, new appointment awaited

BRITISH AMBASSADOR, HE William H. Fullerton, CMG, resident at Rabat, Morocco

ECONOMY

The main source of potential wealth lies in rich deposits of iron ore around Zouérate, in the north of the country, and rich fishing grounds off the coast.

In October 1992 Mauritania agreed a four-year economic restructuring programme with the IMF to reduce inflation and the country's external debt. In late 1992 the IMF announced a US$47 million loan to support the government's economic and financial reform programme up to September 1995, with further loans of US$23 million announced in January 1994 and US$63 million in January 1995.

TRADE WITH UK	1994	1995
Imports from UK	£9,949,000	£6,026,000
Exports to UK	10,978,000	14,579,000

MAURITIUS

Mauritius is an island group lying in the Indian Ocean, 550 miles east of Madagascar, between 57° 17′ and 57° 46′ E. longitude and 19° 58′ and 20° 33′ S. latitude. Mauritius and Rodrigues with the other outer islands comprise an area of 790 sq. miles (2,045 sq. km). The climate is sub-tropical and maritime, with a wide range of rainfall and temperature resulting from the mountainous nature of the island. Humidity is high throughout the year.

The population (1994 estimate, excluding Rodrigues and the outer islands) was 1,082,998, made up of Asiatic races (Hindus 51.8 per cent, Muslims 16.5 per cent, Chinese 2.8 per cent), and persons of European (mainly French) extraction, mixed and African descent (28.6 per cent). English is the official language but French may be used in the National Assembly and lower law courts. Creole is the most commonly used language and several Indian languages are also used.

CAPITAL – ΨPort Louis, population (1993) 144,250; other centres are Beau Bassin-Rose Hill (95,966); Curepipe (76,133); Vacoas-Phoenix (92,846) and Quatre Bornes (72,999).
CURRENCY – Mauritius rupee of 100 cents.
FLAG – Red, blue, yellow and green horizontal stripes.
NATIONAL ANTHEM – Glory to thee, Motherland.
NATIONAL DAY – 12 March.

GOVERNMENT

Mauritius was discovered in 1511 by the Portuguese; the Dutch visited it in 1598 and named it Mauritius after Prince Maurice of Nassau. From 1638 to 1710 it was held as a Dutch colony and in 1715 the French took possession but did not settle it until 1721. Mauritius was taken by a British force in 1810 and became a Crown Colony. It became an independent state within the Commonwealth on 12 March 1968 and a republic on 12 March 1992.

The President is head of state and is elected by the members of the National Assembly. The Prime Minister, appointed by the President, is the member of the National Assembly who appears to the President best able to command the support of the majority of members of the Assembly. Other ministers are appointed by the President acting in accordance with the advice of the Prime Minister.

The National Assembly has a normal term of five years and consists of 62 elected members (the island of Mauritius is divided into 20 three-member constituencies and Rodrigues returns two members), and eight specially-elected members. Of the latter, four seats go to the 'best loser' of whichever communities in the island are under-represented in the Assembly after the general election and the four remaining seats are allocated on the basis of both party and community.

The last general election was held on 20 December 1995. The present government is a coalition of the Partides Travailleurs Mauricien (PTM) and the Militant Mauritian Movement (MMM) which won all 62 elected seats, ousting the Mauritian Socialist Movement (MSM) government.

HEAD OF STATE
President, Cassam Uteem, *elected* June 1992

COUNCIL OF MINISTERS *as at August 1996*

Prime Minister, Defence and Internal Security, Civil Service, Rodrigues and Outer Islands, Reform Institutions, Housing, Lands and Town and Country Planning, Hon. Navin Ramgoolam
Deputy PM, Foreign Affairs and Co-operation, Hon. Paul Raymond Berenger
Economic Planning, Information and Telecommunications, Hon. Rajkeswur Purryag
Industry, Technology, Research and Handicrafts, Hon. Jayakrishna Cuttaree
Employment and Training, Hon. Ahmed Rashid Beebeejaun
Finance, Hon. Rundheersing Bheenick
Justice and Industrial Relations, Hon. Abdool Razack Mahomed Peeroo
Local Government, Hon. Rajesh Anand Bhagwan
Education and Science, Hon. James Burty David
Social Security, Hon. Marie-Thérèse Minerve
Trade and Shipping, Hon. Dhurma Gian Nath
Agriculture and Natural Resources, Hon. Arvin Boolell
Arts, Culture and Leisure, Hon. Tsang Fan Hin Kin
Fisheries and Marine Resources, Hon. Louis Steven Obeegadoo
Tourism, Hon. José Arunasalon
Women and Family Welfare, Hon. Indira Savitree Sidaya
Works, Hon. Siddick Mohammed Chady
Co-operatives, Hon. Motee Ramdass
Health, Hon. Ramsamy Chedumbarum Pillay
Energy and Water Resources, Hon. Devenand Virahswamy
Environment, Hon. Samioullah Lauthan
Youth and Sport, Hon. Sachindev Mahess Soonarane

MAURITIUS HIGH COMMISSION
32–33 Elvaston Place, London SW7 5NW
Tel 0171-581 0294
High Commissioner, HE Sir Satcam Boolell, QC, apptd 1996

BRITISH HIGH COMMISSION
Les Cascades Building, Edith Cavell Street, Port Louis (PO Box 1063)
Tel: Port Louis 211 1361
High Commissioner, HE John Clive Harrison, apptd 1993

BRITISH COUNCIL DIRECTOR, Michael Bootle, PO Box 111, Rose Hill.

ECONOMY

About 55 per cent of the total sugar crop is produced on plantations, while smaller owners (cultivating less than ten acres) cultivate about 24 per cent of the land under cane. Tea and tobacco are also grown commercially but on a smaller scale than sugar. Production in 1994 was: sugar, 500,209 tonnes; tea (manufactured), 5,089 tonnes; tobacco (leaves), 1,025 tonnes. In 1994 production of molasses, mainly for export, was 138,421 tonnes. Other products include alcohol, rum, denatured spirits, perfumed spirits and vinegar.

The bulk of the island's requirements in manufactured products still has to be imported. However, the Mauritius Export Processing Zone (MEPZ) scheme, introduced in 1971, has attracted investment from overseas and the number of export-orientated enterprises had risen from ten in 1971 to 509 at the end of 1994, employing 83,862 people. The biggest firms are in clothing manufacture, particularly woollen knitwear, but the range of goods produced includes toys, plastic products, leather goods, diamond cutting and polishing, watches, television sets and telephones.

Tourism is a major source of income, with an estimated 400,000 tourists in 1994. Earnings from tourism in 1994 are estimated to be Rs.6,052 million. France is the most important source of tourists, followed closely by the neighbouring French island of Réunion.

FINANCE

The main sources of government revenue are private and company income tax, customs and excise duties, mainly on imports but also on sugar exports.

	1993–4	1994–5
Public revenue	Rs.12,937m	Rs.13,800m
Public expenditure (recurrent)	13,250m	14,290m

TRADE

Most foodstuffs and raw materials have to be imported from abroad. Apart from local consumption (about 36,500 tonnes a year), the sugar produced is exported, mainly to Britain.

	1993	1994
Total imports	Rs.30,319m	Rs.34,473m
Total exports	23,522m	24,697m

Trade with UK	1994	1995
Imports from UK	£75,182,000	£71,018,000
Exports to UK	292,504,000	345,149,000

COMMUNICATIONS

Port Louis, on the north-west coast, handles the bulk of the island's external trade. A bulk sugar terminal capable of handling the total crop began operating in 1980. The international airport is located at Plaisance about five miles from Mahébourg. There are four daily newspapers and 15 weeklies, mostly in French, and two Chinese daily papers and one weekly paper. The Mauritius Broadcasting Corporation operates television and radio broadcasting in the country. There is a satellite communications ground station near Port Louis.

EDUCATION

Primary and secondary education are free and primary education is compulsory. In 1994, 212,748 children were in education, with 123,167 children at 279 primary schools. At secondary level there were a total of 89,581 students attending 127 secondary schools; fees and teachers' salaries in the private secondary schools are paid by government. There are a number of training facilities offering vocational training. The Institute of Education is responsible for training primary and secondary schoolteachers and for curriculum development. The University of Mauritius had 2,186 students in 1994–5. Estimated expenditure on education in 1994–5 was Rs.2,062,875,000.

RODRIGUES AND DEPENDENCIES

Rodrigues, formerly a dependency but now part of Mauritius, is about 350 miles east of Mauritius, with an area of 40 square miles. Population (1994) 34,652. Cattle, salt fish, sheep, goats, pigs, maize and onions are the principal exports. The island is administered by an Island Secretary.

Island Secretary, B. Juggoo

The islands of Agalega and St Brandon are dependencies of Mauritius. Total population (1989) 500.

MEXICO
Estados Unidos Mexicanos

Mexico occupies the southern part of North America, with an extensive seaboard to both the Atlantic and Pacific Oceans, extending from 14° 33′ to 32° 43′ N. latitude and 86° 46′ to 117° 08′ W. longitude. It covers an area of 761,605 sq. miles (1,972,547 sq. km).

The Sierra Nevada, known in Mexico as the Sierra Madre, and Rocky Mountains continue south from the northern border with the USA, running parallel to the west and east coasts. The interior consists of an elevated plateau between the two ranges. In the west is the peninsula of Lower California, separated from the mainland by the Gulf of California. The main rivers are the Rio Grande (Rio Bravo) del Norte, which forms part of the northern boundary and is navigable for about 70 miles from its mouth in the Gulf of Mexico, and the Rio Grande de Santiago, the Rio Balsas and Rio Papaloapan.

At the 1990 census, the population was 81,140,922; a 1994 UN estimate gives a figure of 91,858,000. Spanish is the official language and is spoken by about 95 per cent of the population. In addition, there are five main groups of Indian languages (Náhuatl, Maya, Zapotec, Otomí, Mixtec) and 59 dialects derived from them.

CAPITAL – Mexico City, population of metropolitan area (1990 census) 14,987,051. Other cities (1990 census) are:

Guadalajara	2,846,000	Puebla	1,454,526
Monterrey	2,521,697	León	956,070
Torreón	876,456	Ciudad Juarez	797,679
Toluca	827,339	Tijuana	742,686

CURRENCY – Peso of 100 centavos.

FLAG – Three vertical bands in green, white, red, with the Mexican emblem (an eagle on a cactus devouring a snake) in the centre.

NATIONAL ANTHEM – Mexicanos, Al Grito De Guerra (Mexicans, to the war cry).

NATIONAL DAY – 16 September (Proclamation of Independence).

HISTORY

Present-day Mexico and Guatemala were once the centre of a civilization which flowered in the periods from AD 500 to 1100 and 1300 to 1500 and collapsed before the army of Spanish adventurers under Hernán Cortés in the years following 1519. Pre-Columbian Mexico was divided between different Indian cultures, each of which has left distinctive archaeological remains. The best-known of these are Chichén Itzá, Uxmal, Bonampak and Palenque, in Yucatán and Chiapas (Maya); Teotihuacán, renowned for the Pyramid of the Sun in the Valley of Mexico (Teotihuacáno); Monte Albán and Mitla, near Oaxaca (Zapotec); El Tajín in the state of Veracruz (Totonac); and Tula in the state of Hidalgo (Toltec). The last and most famous Indian culture, the Aztec, based on Tenochtitlán, suffered more than the others at the hands of the Spanish and very few Aztec monuments remain.

After the conquest, the Spanish appointed a Viceroy to rule their new dominions, which they called New Spain. The country was largely converted to Christianity and a distinctive colonial civilization, representing a marriage of Indian and Spanish traditions, developed. In 1810 a revolt began against Spanish rule. This was finally successful in 1821, when a precarious independence was proclaimed.

Friction with the USA led to the war of 1845–8, at the end of which Mexico was forced to cede the northern provinces of Texas, California and New Mexico. In 1862 Mexican insolvency led to invasion by French forces which installed Archduke Maximilian of Austria as Emperor. The empire collapsed with the execution of the Emperor in 1867 and the austere reformer Juárez restored the republic. Juárez's death was followed by the dictatorship of Porfirio Díaz, which saw an enormous increase in foreign, particularly British and American, investment in the country. In 1910 began the Mexican Revolution which reformed the social structure and the land system, curbed the power of foreign companies and ushered in the independent industrial Mexico of today. In 1986 Mexico joined GATT and began a liberalization programme of privatization and administrative reform.

GOVERNMENT

Under the 1917 constitution (as subsequently amended), Congress consists of a Senate of 128 members, elected for six years, and of a Chamber of Deputies, at present numbering 500, elected for three years. The chief executive of the government is the President, who is elected for a six-year term and may not be re-elected.

There are nine registered political parties, of which the largest is the Partido Revolucionario Institucional (PRI) which has constituted the governing party for more than 60 years. The main opposition parties are Partido de Acción Nacional (PAN) and Partido de la Revolución Democrática (PRD). After the 1994 elections the state of the parties in the Chamber of Deputies was: PRI 302, PAN 123, PRD 69, other parties six. In the Senate the state of the parties was PRI 95, PAN 25, PRD 8.

In 1988–94 President Salinas de Gortari reformed Mexico's political, economic and social systems. Economic reforms have brought about significant economic growth, whilst political reform has reduced corruption and autocracy. However, certain sections of the population remain untouched by the reforms. An armed revolt of Zapatista peasant Indians in the southern state of Chiapas in January 1994 highlighted continuing charges against the PRI of corruption and fraud at national and local level, and these continued up to the 21 August 1994 presidential and Congressional elections. Although irregularities in the elections were confirmed, they were considered to be on a much smaller scale than in the past. PRI candidate Ernesto Zedillo won the presidential election with 51 per cent of the vote.

A further armed revolt by the Zapatista National Liberation Army (ZNLA) in Chiapas from December 1994 to February 1995 caused a political and economic crisis. President Zedillo responded by introducing political reforms agreed with the PAN and PRD, making the electoral commission fully independent and providing for the re-examination of contentious elections by impartial observers. Negotiations with the Zapatistas produced a preliminary agreement on indigenous rights in February 1996 and are still ongoing

The country is divided into 31 states and the federal district of Mexico City.

HEAD OF STATE

President, Dr Ernesto Zedillo Ponce de León, *elected* 4 June 1994, *took office* 1 December 1994

CABINET *as at August 1996*

Interior, Emilio Chuayffet Chemor
Foreign Affairs, José Angel Gurría
Finance and Public Credit, Guillermo Ortiz Martínez
Defence, Gen. Enrique Cervantes Aguirre
Navy, Adm. José Ramón Lorenzo Franco
Energy, Jesús Reyes Heroles
Trade and Industry, Herminio Blanco Mendoza
Agriculture, Livestock and Rural Development, Francisco Labastida Ochoa
Communications and Transport, Carlos Ruiz Sacristán
Education, Miguel Limón Rojas
Social Development, Carlos Rojas
Health, Juan Ramón de la Fuente Ramírez
Employment and Social Welfare, Javier Bonilla
Agrarian Reform, Arturo Warman
Tourism, Silvia Hernández
Fishing, Environment and Natural Resources, Julia Carabias
Attorney-General, Antonio Lozano
Attorney-General of the Federal District, José Antonio Fernández
Comptroller-General, Arsenio Farell Cubillas
Mayor of Mexico City, Oscar Espinosa Villareal

MEXICAN EMBASSY

42 Hertford Street, London WIY 7TF
Tel 0171-499 8586
Ambassador Extraordinary and Plenipotentiary, HE Andrés Rozental, apptd 1995
Minister, Deputy Ambassador, J. Brito-Moncada
Military Attaché, Gen. F. A. Meza-Castro
Minister, Consul-General, J. Ibarra
Counsellor, F. Estandía-González (*Commercial*)

BRITISH EMBASSY

Calle Río Lerma 71, Colonia Cuauhtémoc, 06500 Mexico City
Tel: Mexico City 207 20 89
Ambassador Extraordinary and Plenipotentiary, HE Adrian John Beamish, CMG, apptd 1994
Deputy Ambassador, Minister-Counsellor and Consul-General, G. Berg, MVO
Defence Attaché, Col. S. R. Daniell
First Secretary (*Commercial*), M. H. McIntosh

There are British Consular Offices at Mexico City, Acapulco, Cancun, Guadalajara, Mérida, Monterrey, Tampico, Tijuana, Veracruz, and Ciudad Juarez.

BRITISH COUNCIL DIRECTOR, Dr Frank Edwards, Maestro Antonio Caso 127, Col. San Rafael, Delegación Cuauhtemoc, (PO Box 30-588), Mexico 06470 DF.

BRITISH CHAMBER OF COMMERCE, British Trade Centre, Rio de la Plata 30, Col. Cuauhtemoc, CP 06500, Mexico City DF, *Manager*, Stephen Grant.

DEFENCE

The total armed forces number some 175,000, including 60,000 conscripts. Conscription is decided by lottery and is for a one-year period. The Army has a strength of 130,000 (including 60,000 conscripts), with 110 armoured personnel carriers and 118 artillery pieces.

The Navy has a strength of 37,000 personnel, including 8,600 marines, with three destroyers, two frigates, 105 patrol and coastal vessels, and nine combat aircraft. The Air Force is 8,000 strong, with 101 combat aircraft and 25 armed helicopters.

ECONOMY

Political and economic uncertainty in late 1994 caused a crisis of confidence in the economy by foreign investors and a run on the peso. Insolvency and defaulting on the foreign debt was only averted by a US$50,000 million loan package from the USA and international institutions. Since January 1995 the government has introduced two austerity packages, increasing interest rates and petrol taxes, curbing pay levels and reducing public expenditure in an attempt to keep inflation and debt levels under control and to rein back a runaway trade deficit. Inflation has risen to 50 per cent a year (from 7 per cent in 1994) and unemployment is rising. GDP growth fell by 6.9 per cent in 1995 and foreign debt reached US$100,900 million. Mexico joined the OECD in 1994.

In 1995, 23.3 per cent of GDP was produced by commerce, 23 per cent by manufacturing, 30 per cent by services, 4.6 per cent by construction, 7.6 per cent by agriculture, 3.6 per cent by mining and 7.9 per cent by transportation and communications. Direct foreign investment at the end of 1995 was a cumulative US$55.9 billion, of which 62.7 per cent was American. Privatization has been successful, with only 208 public enterprises remaining in 1991 (1,155 in 1982). Agriculture has been reformed to allow communal farmers to buy and sell their own plots.

The principal crops are maize, beans, rice, wheat, sugar cane, coffee, cotton, tomatoes, chillies, tobacco, chick-peas, groundnuts, sesame, alfalfa, vanilla, cocoa and many kinds of fruit. The maguey, or Mexican cactus, yields several fermented drinks, mezcal and tequila (distilled) and pulque (undistilled). Another species of the plant supplies sisal-hemp (henequen). The forests contain mahogany, rosewood, ebony and chicle trees. Agriculture employs an estimated 20 per cent of the working population.

The principal industries are mining and petroleum, although there has been considerable expansion of both light and heavy industries; exports of manufactured goods now average about 56 per cent of total exports. The steel industry expanded steadily until recently and current production is around 7.9 million tons. In 1995, 931,000 motor vehicles were produced, of which 779,000 were for export.

The mineral wealth is great, and principal minerals are gold, silver, copper, lead, zinc, quicksilver, iron and sulphur. Substantial reserves of uranium have been found. Mexico produces 25 per cent of the world's supply of fluorspar.

Oil exports were 1.5 million barrels per day in 1996. Daily production of natural gas is approximately 3 billion cubic feet. Oil reserves have increased substantially due to discoveries in the Gulf of Campeche. A refinery at Tula is the nation's largest; and new refineries in Monterrey, State of Nuevo León, and Salina Cruz, State of Oaxaca, are under construction.

TRADE

Major imports include computers, auto assembly material, electrical parts, auto and truck parts, powdered milk, corn and sorghum, transport, sound-recording and power-generating equipment, chemicals, industrial machinery, pharmaceuticals and specialized appliances. Principal exports include oil, automobiles, auto engines, fruits and vegetables, shrimps, coffee, computers, cattle, glass, iron and steel pipes, and copper. The main trading partners are the USA (65.6 per cent), EU (15 per cent), Latin America (5.2 per cent) and Japan (5 per cent). The North American Free Trade Agreement, to which Mexico is a signatory, came into effect on 1 January 1994, significantly increasing Mexico's trade.

Trade with UK	1994	1995
Imports from UK	£389,299,000	£276,753,000
Exports to UK	239,740,000	298,124,000

COMMUNICATIONS

Veracruz, Tampico and Coatzacoalcos are the chief ports on the Atlantic, and Guaymas, Mazatlán, Puerto Lázaro Cárdenas, Acapulco, Salina Cruz and Puerto Madero on the Pacific. Work is proceeding on the reorganization and re-equipment of the whole rail system. Total track length of the railways was 240,186 km in 1990. Mexico City may be reached by at least three highways from the USA, and from the south from Yucatán as well as on two principal highways from the Guatemalan border.

There are 1,113 airports and landing fields in Mexico, of which 18 are equipped to handle long-distance flights. There are 166 airline companies, including two of the major, now private, national airlines, Mexicana de Aviación and Aeroméxico.

Teléfonos de México, now privatized, controls about 98 per cent of all telephone services.

EDUCATION

Education is divided into primary, secondary and superior levels. In 1993 there were 14,469,450 students in the first level, 6,977,086 in the second and 1,358,271 in the third.

FEDERATED STATES OF MICRONESIA

The Federated States of Micronesia comprise more than 600 islands extending 2,900 km (1,800 miles) across the archipelago of the Caroline Islands in the western Pacific Ocean. The islands are located between the Equator and 9° N., and 138° and 168° E. Pohnpei island is 4,670 km (2,900 miles) south-west of Honolulu and 1,610 km (1,100 miles) south-east of Guam. The area is 700 sq. km (270 sq. miles). The islands vary geologically from mountainous islands to low coral atolls. The climate is tropical. Storms are common between August and December, and typhoons between July and November.

The population (1994 UN estimate) of 107,000 is Micronesian and predominantly Christian.

Pohnpei: population, 31,000; capital, Kolonia

Chuuk (Truk): population, 52,000; capital, Moen

Yap: population, 12,000; capital, Colonia

Kosrae: population, 6,500; capital, Lelu

English (official) and eight other languages are used in different parts of the Federated States: Yapese, Ulithian, Woleaian, Ponapean, Nukuoran, Kapingamarangi, Trukese and Kosraen.

CAPITAL – The federal capital is Palikir, on Pohnpei island.

FLAG – United Nations blue with four white stars in the centre.

HISTORY

The Spanish Empire claimed sovereignty over the Caroline Islands until 1899, when Spain withdrew from her Pacific territories and sold her possessions in the Caroline Islands to Germany. The Caroline Islands became a German protectorate until the outbreak of the First World War in 1914, when Japan took control of the islands on behalf of the Allied powers. After the war Japan continued to administer the territory under a League of Nations mandate. During the Second World War, US armed forces took control of the islands from the Japanese. In 1947 the USA entered into agreement with the UN Security Council to administer the Micronesia area, of which the Federated States of Micronesia were a part, as the UN Trust Territory of the Pacific Islands.

The US Trusteeship administration came to an end on 3 November 1986, when a Compact of Free Association between the USA and the Federated States of Micronesia came into effect. By this agreement the USA recognized the Federated States of Micronesia as a fully sovereign and independent state. The independence of the Federated States of Micronesia was recognized by the UN in December 1990.

GOVERNMENT

The Federated States of Micronesia is a federal republic of four constituent states: Chuuk, Kosrae, Pohnpei and Yap. The constitution separates the executive, legislative and judicial branches. There is a bill of rights and provision for traditional rights.

The executive comprises a federal President and Vice-President, both of whom must be chosen from amongst the four nationally-elected senators. There is a single-chamber Congress of 14 members, four members elected on a nation-wide basis and ten members elected from congressional districts apportioned by population.

Each of the constituent states has its own government and legislative system.

The Compact of Free Association places full responsibility for the defence of the Federated States of Micronesia on the USA.

HEAD OF STATE

President, Bailey Olter (Pohnpei), *elected by Congress* 11 May 1991, *re-elected* May 1995

Vice-President, Jacob Nina (Kosrae)

CABINET *as at August 1996*

Administrative Services, Kapily Capelle

Budget, Aloysius Tuuth

Education, Catalino Cantero

External Affairs, Asterio Tuuth

Finance, Patrick Mackenzie

Human Resources, Eliuel Pretrick

Planning and Statistics, Bermin Weilbacher

Resources and Development, Sabastian Anefal

Transport and Communications, Robert Weilbacher

Attorney-General, Camillo Noket

BRITISH AMBASSADOR, HE Michael Peart, CMG, LVO, resident at Suva, Fiji

JUDICIARY

The judiciary is headed by the Supreme Court, which is divided into trial and appellate divisions. Below this, each state has its own judicial system.

ECONOMY

The economy is dependent mainly on subsistence agriculture and government spending. Copra and fish are the two main exports. The majority of the working population is engaged in government administration, subsistence farming, fishing, copra production and the growing tourist industry.

TRADE WITH UK	1994	1995
Imports from UK	£106,000	£105,000
Exports to UK	—	30,000

MOLDOVA
Republica Moldovenească

Moldova has an area of 13,912 sq. miles (33,700 sq. km) and occupies the extreme south-western corner of the former USSR. To the north, east and south-east it is bordered by Ukraine, and to the west by Romania. The border with Romania is formed by the Pruth (Prut) river, but the main river is the Dniester, navigable along its whole course. The north consists of flat steppe lands, in the centre there are woody hills, and in the south low-lying steppe lands. Forests skirt the Dniester. The climate is moderate.

The population (official estimate 1996) is 4,335,000, of which 65 per cent are Moldovan, 14.2 per cent Ukrainian and 13 per cent Russian, together with smaller numbers of Gagauz (ethnic Turks), Jews and Bulgarians. Most of the population are adherents of the Romanian Orthodox Church.

Moldovan was made the official language (written in the Latin script) in 1989 but the use of Russian and Ukrainian in official business is permitted.

CAPITAL – Kishinev. Population 665,000 (1989 census).
CURRENCY – Leu (plural lei) which replaced the rouble in November 1993.
FLAG – Vertical stripes of blue, yellow, red, with the national arms in the centre.
NATIONAL DAY – 27 August (Independence Day).

GOVERNMENT

A Moldovan feudal state was established in the 14th century when Slavic tribes who had previously lived under Roman and Byzantine rule integrated with Slavic tribes from further east. In the 15th century a Moldovan principality was formed which entered into military and political alliances with Muscovy before being absorbed into the Turkish Empire in the 16th century. Moldova became the site of many Russo-Turkish battles and skirmishes in the 18th century before the area between the Dniester and Prut rivers (later known as Bessarabia) was annexed to the Russian Empire by the Bucharest Peace Treaty of 1812.

After the Russian Revolution in 1917, Bessarabia came under the control of White Russian forces and was annexed to Romania under the Versailles Peace Treaty in 1919. In 1924 the Moldavian Autonomous Soviet Socialist Republic (ASSR) was established on the east bank of the Dniester river as part of Soviet Ukraine. In August 1940 the Soviet Union forced Romania to cede Bessarabia and the Moldavian Soviet Socialist Republic was formed from the fusion of the majority of Bessarabia (the southernmost parts were incorporated into the Ukraine) with the Moldavian ASSR.

When Moldova (formerly Moldavia) declared its independence from the USSR in August 1991, the majority ethnic Romanian (Moldovan) population expressed a wish to rejoin Romania. This alienated the ethnic Ukrainian and Russian populations, who form a majority east of the Dniester. After failed negotiations and several armed clashes, the Ukrainian and Russian populations declared their independence from Moldova as the Transdniester republic in December 1991. The Moldovan government refused to recognize this and in the first half of 1992 a war was waged between government forces and Transdniester forces, who were supported by the 30,000-strong former Soviet 14th Army stationed in Transdniester and by Cossack volunteers from Russia.

A mainly Russian CIS peacekeeping force (later changed to a joint Russian-Moldovan-Transdniester force) was deployed in July 1992 and a cease-fire has held since August 1992. Although no political solution has been finalized and a state of armed truce remains, the Moldovan government in February 1994 agreed to a CSCE plan for the Transdniester area to have a high degree of autonomy within Moldova but no independent or federal status. In October 1994 the Russian and Moldovan presidents signed an agreement on the withdrawal of the 14th Army over a three-year period, the first troops leaving in February 1996.

Reunification with Romania was defeated in a referendum on 6 March 1994, following which the Moldovan parliament voted to join the CIS. In July 1994 the Moldovan parliament adopted a new constitution which defines Moldova as a 'presidential parliamentary republic' based on political pluralism. It also provides for autonomous status for the Gagauz and Transdniester regions, with the Gagauz region having its own elected National Assembly. A referendum in Transdniester on 24 December 1995 approved independence.

The Moldovan Popular Front government, which came to power in the 1990 legislative elections to the 380-seat Supreme Soviet, was replaced in July 1992 by a government of national accord led by the Peasant Democratic Party. The former Communists of the Agrarian Democratic Party were brought back to power in the legislative election of February 1994 and formed a coalition government with the Socialist Party. President Snegur left the Agrarian Democratic Party in August 1995 following a disagreement over the pace of reform and formed the Party of Revival and Conciliation. Parliament now has 104 seats and is elected by proportional representation.

HEAD OF STATE
President, Mircea Snegur, *elected* 8 December 1991

GOVERNMENT *as at August 1996*
Prime Minister, Andrei Sangeli
Deputy PMs, Ion Gutzu, Grigoire Ojugu, Valeriu Bulgar, Valentin Kunev
Minister of State, Gheorghe Gusac
National Economy, Valerian Boboutac
Agriculture and Foodstuffs, Vitali Gorincioi
Industry, Grigore Triboi
Transport and Roads, Vasile Iouv
Foreign Economic Relations, Andrei Keptine
Information, Science and Communications, Ion Cassian
Public Health, Timofei Mosneaga
Culture, Mihail Cebotari
Justice, Vasile Sturza
Internal Affairs, Maj.-Gen. Constantin Antoci
Foreign Affairs, Mihai Popov

National Security, Col. Vasile Calmoi
Defence, Maj.-Gen. Pavel Creanga
Finance, Valeriu Chitan
Education, Pavel Gauges
Utilities, Mihai Severovan
Social Protection, Dumitru Nidelcu
Privatization, Ceslav Ciobanu
Power Engineering, Valentin Chumak

MOLDOVAN AMBASSADOR, HE Tudor Botnaru, resident
at Brussels
BRITISH AMBASSADOR, HE Andrew Wood, CMG, resident
at Moscow

ECONOMY

The main sector is agriculture, especially viniculture, fruit-growing and market gardening. Industry is small and concentrated east of the Dniester. Severe drought in 1992, the severance of most trading ties with former Soviet republics, war damage and reductions in Russian fuel deliveries paralysed the economy from 1992 to 1994. Entry into the CIS and its economic union in April 1994 should, however, improve trading ties with other former Soviet republics and increase Russian fuel supplies. An economic reform programme began in summer 1993 and is being supported by IMF credits of US$420 million. A privatization programme, completed in November 1995, sold off 1,132 large enterprises and 613 shops by means of voucher auctions.

TRADE WITH UK	1994	1995
Imports from UK	£1,686,000	£2,248,000
Exports to UK	793,000	301,000

MONACO
Principauté de Monaco

A small principality on the Mediterranean, with land frontiers joining France at every point, Monaco is divided into the districts of Monaco-Ville, La Condamine, Fontvielle and Monte Carlo. The principality comprises a narrow strip of land about two miles long with an area of approximately 195 hectares, and 29,972 inhabitants (1992).

CAPITAL – Monaco-Ville, population (1992) 1,151.
CURRENCY – The French franc is legal tender.
FLAG – Two equal horizontal stripes, red over white.
NATIONAL ANTHEM – Hymne Monegasque.
NATIONAL DAY – 19 November.

GOVERNMENT

The principality, ruled by the Grimaldi family since the late 13th century, was abolished during the French Revolution and re-established in 1815 under the protection of the kingdom of Sardinia. In 1861 Monaco came under French protection.

The 1962 constitution, which can be modified only with the approval of the National Council, maintains the traditional hereditary monarchy and guarantees freedom of association, trade union freedom and the right to strike. Legislative power is held jointly by the Prince and a unicameral, 18-member National Council elected by universal suffrage. Executive power is exercised by the Prince and a four-member Council of Government, headed by a Minister of State. The judicial code is based on that of France.

HEAD OF STATE
HSH *The Prince of Monaco*, Prince Rainier III Louis-Henri-Maxence Bertrand, *born* 31 May 1923, *succeeded* 9 May 1949; *married* 19 April 1956, Miss Grace Patricia Kelly (died 14 September 1982) and *has issue* Prince Albert (*see* below); Princess Caroline Louise Marguerite, *born* 23 January 1957; and Princess Stephanie Marie Elisabeth, *born* 1 February 1965
Heir, HRH Prince Albert Alexandre Louis Pierre, *born* 14 March 1958

President of the Crown Council, Jean-Charles Marquet
President of the National Council, Dr Jean-Louis Campora
Minister of State, Paul Dijoud, *appointed* 1994

CONSULATE-GENERAL OF MONACO
4 Cromwell Place, London SW7 2JE
Tel 0171-225 2679
Consul-General, I. B. Ivanovic.

BRITISH CONSUL-GENERAL, P. Yarnold, apptd 1995,
resident at Marseilles, France

ECONOMY

The whole available ground is built over so that there is no cultivation, though there are some notable public and private gardens. The economy is based on real estate revenues, the financial sector and tourism (over 250,000 visitors a year). Monaco has a small harbour (30 ft alongside quay) and the import duties are the same as in France.

MONGOLIA
State of Mongolia

Mongolia lies in northern Asia, bordered by Russia to the north and China to the south. Its area is 604,250 sq. miles (1,565,000 sq. km). Mongolia, which is almost entirely at least 1,000 metres above sea level, forms part of the central Asiatic plateau and rises towards the west in the mountains of the Mongolian Altai and Hangai ranges. The Hentai range, situated to the north-east of the capital Ulan Bator, is lower. The Gobi region covers much of the southern half of the country and contains sand deserts interspersed with semi-desert. There are several long rivers and many lakes but good water is scarce as much of the lake water is salty. The climate is harsh, with a short mild summer giving way to a long winter when temperatures can drop as low as −50°C.

The population (1994 estimate) is 2,363,000; this total constitutes only part of the Mongolians of Asia, a number of whom are to be found in China and in the neighbouring regions of Russia, especially the Mongolian Buryat Autonomous Region.

CAPITAL – Ulan Bator (Ulaanbaator), population (1993) 600,500.
CURRENCY – Tugrik of 100 möngö.
FLAG – Vertical tri-colour red, blue, red and in the hoist the traditional Soyombo symbol in gold.
NATIONAL DAY – 11 July.

GOVERNMENT

Mongolia, under Genghis Khan the conqueror of China and much of Asia, was for many years a buffer state between Tsarist Russia and China, although it was under general Chinese suzerainty. The Chinese Revolution in 1911 led to a declaration of autonomy under Chinese suzerainty which was confirmed by the Sino-Russian Treaty of

Kiakhta 1915 but cancelled by a unilateral Chinese declaration in 1919. Later the country became a battleground of the Russian civil war, and Soviet and Mongolian troops occupied Ulan Bator in 1921; this was followed by another declaration of independence. In 1924 the Soviet Union in a treaty with China again recognized the latter's sovereignty over Mongolia, but this was never properly exercised because of China's preoccupation with internal affairs and later by the war with Japan. The Mongolian People's Republic was formally established in 1924. Under the Yalta Agreement, President Chiang Kai-shek of China agreed to a plebiscite, held in 1945, in which the Mongolians declared their desire for independence and this was formally recognized by China.

The Mongolian People's Revolutionary Party (MPRP) was the sole political party from 1924 to 1990. Demonstrations in favour of political and economic reform began in December 1989 and led to changes in the MPRP leadership in March 1990. The MPRP's constitutionally guaranteed monopoly of power was subsequently relinquished, and the introduction of a multiparty system was approved by the Great People's Hural (parliament). The MPRP won the first multiparty elections, held in July 1990. Since then, and following Moscow's lead, Mongolia has embarked on a programme of political and economic reforms.

A new constitution was approved in January 1992 which enshrines the concepts of democracy, a mixed economy, free speech and neutrality in foreign affairs. The Great and Little Hurals were abolished, and a new unicameral Great Hural became the legislative body of the country. Members of the Great Hural are elected for four-year terms by a simple majority amounting to at least 25 per cent of the votes cast. Elections were held in June 1992 which were won by the MPRP with 57 per cent of the vote and 71 out of 76 seats. The most recent legislative election, held on 30 June 1996, was won by the Democratic Union Coalition (Mongolian National Democratic Party and Mongolian Social Democratic Party) which won 50 seats. The country's first direct presidential election was held in 1993 and won by the incumbent Punsalmaagiyn Ochirbat, who stood as an opposition candidate after the MPRP refused to endorse him as its candidate.

The last remaining former Soviet armed forces personnel were withdrawn in late 1992.

The country and three city districts (Ulan Bator, Darkhan and Erdenet) are divided into 21 *aimaks* (provinces) and beneath these into 258 *somons* (districts), and these form the basis of the state organization of the country.

HEAD OF STATE
President, Punsalmaagiyn Ochirbat, *elected* June 1993

CABINET *as at August 1996*
Prime Minister, External Relations, Mendsaihany Enkhsahan
Environment, T. Adiyasuren
Defence, D. Dorligjav
Finance, P. Tsagaan
Infrastructure Development, G. Nyamdavaa
Justice, J. Amarsanaa
Health and Social Security, L. Zorig
Education, C. Lhagvajav
Agriculture and Industry, L. Nyamsambuu
Chairman of the Great Hural, Radnaasumbereliin Gonchigdorj

EMBASSY OF MONGOLIA
7 Kensington Court, London W8 5DL
Tel 0171-937 0150

Ambassador Extraordinary and Plenipotentiary, HE Gendengiin Nyamdoo, apptd 1995

BRITISH EMBASSY
30 Enkh Taivny Gudamzh (PO Box 703), Ulan Bator 13
Tel: Ulan Bator 358133
Ambassador Extraordinary and Plenipotentiary, HE Ian Sloane, apptd 1994

ECONOMY

The country has been experiencing transitional problems in its attempt to establish a market economy, with food and fuel shortages, inflation, and unemployment. Western countries, Japan and the IMF have provided loans of US$287 million in 1993–5 to aid its economic restructuring. In April 1994 Mongolia signed a treaty of friendship and mutual assistance with China to gain aid and economic and technological co-operation.

Traditionally the Mongolians led a nomadic life tending flocks of sheep, goats, horses, cows and camels. With the coming of the Communist regime, and especially after 1952, great efforts were made to settle the population but a proportion still live nomadically or semi-nomadically in the traditional *ger* (circular tent). Collectivization at the end of the 1950s into huge *negdels* (co-operatives) and state farms hastened the process of settlement, but within these the herdsmen and their families still move with their *gers* from pasture to pasture as the seasons change. Total livestock was 25 million in 1993.

The semi-desert areas of the Gobi region provide pasture for sheep, goats, camels, horses and some cattle. In the steppe areas to the north of the Gobi pasturage is better and livestock more abundant. Even further north, in the better-watered provinces, grain, fodder and vegetable crops are grown.

Although the economy remains predominantly pastoral, factories have started up, coal, copper and molybdenum are mined and the electricity industry has been developed. Ulan Bator and Darkhan are the main seats of industry, which includes lime, cement and building materials, a flour mill and a power station. Choibalsan is also being developed industrially.

Mongolia's economic difficulties stem from its small labour force, and its undeveloped infrastructure. Communication is still difficult as there are very few tarmac roads and horses are still the characteristic means of transport for the rural population. The trans-Mongolian railway links Mongolia with both China and Russia.

TRADE
Foreign trade was formerly dominated by the Soviet Union and other eastern bloc countries. Following the collapse of the COMECON trading system, trade with Western countries, Japan and South Korea is increasing. Since January 1991, trade is in hard currency, causing particular strain. The principal exports are animal by-products (especially wool, hides and furs) and cattle.

Trade with UK	1994	1995
Imports from UK	£2,637,000	£3,023,000
Exports to UK	1,680,000	1,960,000

MOROCCO
Al-Mamlaka Al-Maghrebia

Morocco is situated in the north-west of the African continent between 27° 40′ and 36° N. latitude and 1° and 13° W. longitude with an area estimated at 172,414 sq.

miles (446,550 sq. km). It is traversed in the north by the Rif mountains and, in a south-west to north-east direction, by the Middle Atlas, the High Atlas, the Anti-Atlas and the Sarrho ranges. Much of the country is desert. The north-westerly point of Morocco is the peninsula of Tangier dominated by the Jebel Mousa which, with the rocky eminence of Gibraltar, was known to the ancients as the Pillars of Hercules, the western gateway of the Mediterranean.

The population (1994 estimate) is 26,448,000. Arabic is the official language. Berber is the vernacular, mainly in the mountain regions. French and Spanish are also spoken, mainly in the towns. Islam is the state religion.

CAPITAL – ΨRabat, population (including Salé) 1,494,000. Regional capitals, with municipal population figures as at 1991, are: ΨCasablanca (2,990,000); Marrakesh (644,000); Fez (719,000); Oujda (646,000); Meknes (484,000); ΨAgadir (420,000).
CURRENCY – Dirham (DH) of 100 centimes.
FLAG – Red, with green pentagram (the Seal of Solomon).
NATIONAL DAY – 3 March (Anniversary of the Throne).

GOVERNMENT

Morocco became an independent sovereign state in 1956, following joint declarations made with France on 2 March 1956 and with Spain on 7 April 1956. The Sultan of Morocco, Sidi Mohammad ben Youssef, adopted the title of King Mohammad V.

The 1992 constitution states that Morocco is a democratic constitutional monarchy. The King nominates the Prime Minister and, on the latter's recommendation, appoints the members of the Council of Ministers. The government is responsible both to parliament and to the King. The unicameral legislature (Chamber of Representatives) has 333 members, 222 elected by direct universal suffrage (including five representing overseas workers) and 111 members elected by electoral colleges representing local government, industry, agriculture, professional and trade union groups. The replacement of the Chamber of Representatives with a directly-elected bicameral legislature has been proposed by the King.

Effective political power remains with the King despite the constitutional changes of October 1992 enhancing the Prime Minister's and legislature's powers. Legislative elections were held in June–September 1993, with the centre-right four-party Entente National coalition winning 154 seats and the leftist six-party Bloc Démocratique winning 120 seats. After both coalitions had been unable to form a government, King Hassan appointed a government of technocrats and independents in November 1993. In February 1995 the King replaced this with a government of the Entente National and technocrats. Diplomatic relations with Israel were opened in September 1994.

HEAD OF STATE
HM The King of Morocco, King Hassan II (Moulay Hassan Ben Mohammed), born 9 July 1929; acceded 3 March 1961
Heir, HRH Crown Prince Sidi Mohamed, born 21 August 1963

COUNCIL OF MINISTERS as at June 1996

Prime Minister, Foreign Affairs and Co-operation, Abdellatif Filali
Minister of State, Moulay Ahmed Alaoui
Interior, Driss Basri
Justice, Abderrahmane Amalou
National Education, Rachid Ben Mokhtar
Public Health, Ahmed Alami

Religious Endowments and Islamic Affairs, Abdelkebir Alaoui M'Daghri
Public Works, Abdelaziz Meziane Belfkih
Finance and Foreign Investments, Mohamed Kabbaj
Transport, Said Ameskane
Energy and Mines, Abdelatif Gurraoui
Youth and Sport, Ahmed Meziane
Sea Fisheries and the Merchant Marine, Mustapha Sahel
Secretary-General of the Government, Abdessadek Rabiah
Culture, Abdellah Azmani
Housing, Said Fassi
Posts and Telecommunications, Hamza Kettani
Agriculture and Agricultural Investment, Hassan Abouyoub
Trade, Industry and Handicrafts, Driss Jettou
Employment and Social Affairs, Amine Demnati
Foreign Trade, Mohammad Alami
Tourism, Mohammad Alaoui M'Hamdi
Communications, Government Spokesman, Driss Alaoui M'daghri
Privatization, Abderrahmane Saaidi
Higher Education and Scientific Research, Driss Khalil
Environment, Dr Noureddine Benomar Alami
Vocational Training, Abdessalam Beroual

EMBASSY OF THE KINGDOM OF MOROCCO
49 Queen's Gate Gardens, London SW7 5NE
Tel 0171–581 5001/4
Ambassador Extraordinary and Plenipotentiary, HE Khalil Haddaoui, apptd 1991

BRITISH EMBASSY
17 Boulevard de la Tour Hassan (BP 45), Rabat
Tel: Rabat 7209 05/6
Ambassador Extraordinary and Plenipotentiary, HE William H. Fullerton, CMG, apptd 1996
There is a British Consulate-General/Commercial Office at Casablanca and Consulates at Agadir, Marrakesh and Tangier.

BRITISH COUNCIL DIRECTOR, Tony O'Brien, BP 427, 36 rue Tanger, Rabat
BRITISH CHAMBER OF COMMERCE, 1st Floor, 185 Boulevard Zerktouni, Casablanca. Tel: 256920

DEFENCE

The armed forces have a total active strength of 195,500, including authorized conscripts who serve 18-month terms. Total reserves number 150,000. The Army has a strength of 175,000 (100,000 conscripts), the majority of whom have been deployed in southern Morocco and Western Sahara fighting the Polisario Front. It is equipped with 524 main battle tanks, 100 light tanks, 900 armoured infantry fighting vehicles and armoured personnel carriers, and 331 artillery pieces.

The Navy has a strength of 7,000, with one frigate, and 27 patrol and coastal combatant craft, together with a marine battalion. The Air Force has a strength of 13,500, with 99 combat aircraft and 24 armed helicopters. In addition, there are a paramilitary Gendarmerie Royale of 12,000 and an Auxiliary Force of 30,000 paramilitaries.

Morocco deploys 2,000 troops in the United Arab Emirates. The UN has some 398 personnel in Western Sahara pending the referendum. Polisario deploys 3,000–6,000 troops in Western Sahara with Algerian-supplied and captured Moroccan tanks, armoured personnel carriers, anti-tank and anti-aircraft weapons.

ECONOMY

Morocco's main sources of wealth are agricultural and mineral. The latest development plan (1987 onwards) emphasizes social improvement, industrial development, agriculture, fisheries and tourism. Economic reform has also been implemented to reduce debt and inflation. A large-scale privatization programme has attracted substantial foreign investment, but inflation remains high.

Agriculture employs more than 40 per cent of the working population. The main agricultural exports are fruit and vegetables, with cereals and sugar beet produced and sheep reared for domestic consumption. Cork and wood-pulp are the most important commercial forest products. Esparto grass is also produced. There is a fishing industry and substantial quantities of canned fish, mainly sardines and fishmeal, are exported.

For a developing country Morocco has a large industrial sector. The main sectors are chemicals, textiles and leather goods, food processing and cement production. Manufacturing industries are centred in Casablanca, Fez, Tangier and Safi.

Morocco's mineral exports are phosphates, fluorite, barite, manganese, iron ore, lead, zinc, cobalt, copper and antimony. Morocco possesses nearly three-quarters of the world's estimated reserves of phosphates. There are oil refineries at Mohammedia and Sidi Kacem handling about four million tonnes of crude oil a year.

Tourism is of increasing importance to the economy, with development concentrated in Agadir and Marrakesh. In 1993, 2,945,700 foreign tourists visited Morocco. Workers' remittances, US$1,959 million in 1993, are also very important to the economy.

TRADE

The main imports are petroleum products, motor vehicles, building materials, agricultural and other machinery, chemical products, sugar, green tea and other foodstuffs. The EU, with which an association agreement was signed in November 1995, is Morocco's largest trading partner. The main exports are textiles, phosphates and phosphoric acid, fertilizers, citrus fruits, and fish and seafoods.

	1993	1994
Imports	US$6,643m	US$6,600m
Exports	3,680m	4,000m
Trade with UK	1994	1995
Imports from UK	£193,665,000	£271,114,000
Exports to UK	200,583,000	253,752,000

COMMUNICATIONS

Railroads cover 1,175 miles (1,893 km), linking the major towns. An extensive network of 9,880 miles (15,900 km) of well-surfaced roads covers all the main towns. There are air services between Casablanca, Tangier, Agadir (seasonal), Marrakesh and London, and also between Tangier and Gibraltar connecting with London. Royal-Air-Maroc operates internal services and services to 36 states in Europe, Africa and Asia.

EDUCATION

There are government primary, secondary and technical schools. In 1991 there were 4,890 government schools with a total of 3,608,757 pupils. At Fez there is a theological university of great repute in the Muslim world. There is a secular university at Rabat. A total of 206,725 students studied at 13 universities in 1991. Schools for special denominations, Jewish and Catholic, are permitted and may receive government grants. American schools operate in Rabat and Casablanca.

WESTERN SAHARA

Formerly the Spanish Sahara, the territory was split between Morocco and Mauritania in 1976 after Spain withdrew in December 1975. In 1976 the Polisario Front (Frente Popular para la Liberación de Saguia y Río de Oro) declared Western Sahara to be an independent state, the Saharan Arab Democratic Republic, and formed a government led by Bouchraya Bayoune which remains in exile. The Polisario Front has been recognized as the legitimate government of Western Sahara by over 70 states and the Organization of African Unity. In 1979 Mauritania renounced its claim to its share of the territory, which was added by Morocco to its area.

In 1988, Morocco and the Polisario Front accepted a UN peace plan under which a cease-fire came into effect in September 1991. A referendum to determine the future of the area was to have been held in January 1992 but has not yet taken place because the Moroccan government and Polisario have not agreed on the referendum terms or voter eligibility. The UN Security Council intervened to break the impasse, passing a resolution which stipulates that the referendum should be a straight choice between independence or integration with Morocco. A further resolution provided for the drawing up of a new voter registration list. Voter identification began in August 1994 but the failure to agree on eligibility prompted the UN to threaten the suspension of the UN Mission for the Referendum in Western Sahara (MINURSO), which had been deployed since 1991.

MOZAMBIQUE
República de Moçambique

Mozambique lies on the east coast of Africa, and is bounded by Swaziland in the south, South Africa in the south and west, Zimbabwe in the west, Zambia and Malawi in the north-west and Tanzania in the north. It has an area of 309,495 sq. miles (801,590 sq. km), with a population (1995 estimate) of 16,500,000. The official language is Portuguese.

CAPITAL – Ψ Maputo, estimated population (1990), 1,150,000. Other main ports are ΨBeira and ΨNacala.
CURRENCY – Metical (MT) of 100 centavos.
FLAG – Horizontally green, black, yellow with white fimbriations; a red triangle based on the hoist containing the national emblem.
NATIONAL DAY – 25 June (Independence Day).

GOVERNMENT

Mozambique, discovered by Vasco da Gama in 1498 and colonized by Portugal, achieved independence on 25 June 1975. It was a Marxist one-party (Frelimo) state until a multiparty system was adopted in 1990. The legislative assembly has 250 members.

Following two years of negotiations, the Frelimo government and rebel Mozambican National Resistance (Renamo) signed a peace agreement in October 1992 which ended 16 years of civil war. Under the peace agreement, demobilization of government and Renamo troops was due to begin within one month of parliamentary ratification of the peace accord (which occurred on 9 October 1992) although the belated arrival of the UN Operation for Mozambique (ONUMOZ) delayed demobilization until 1994.

Presidential and legislative elections, which had been scheduled for June 1993, were finally held on 27–29

October 1994, with a Renamo boycott only being rescinded on the 28th. The incumbent, Joaquim Chissano of Frelimo, won the presidential election in the first round with 53 per cent of the vote. Frelimo also won the legislative election, gaining 129 seats to Renamo's 112 seats and the Democratic Union's 9 seats. President Chissano was sworn in for a five-year term on 23 December with his new Frelimo government. The last ONUMOZ troops left in January 1995.

Mozambique was admitted to the Commonwealth on 13 November 1995 as a special case, because of its close links with Commonwealth countries.

HEAD OF STATE
President, Joaquim Alberto Chissano, *sworn in* November 1986, *elected* 29 October 1994

COUNCIL OF MINISTERS *as at August 1996*

Prime Minister, Pascoal Mocumbi
Foreign Affairs and Co-operation, Leonardo Simão
National Defence, Aguiar Real Mazula
State Administration, Alfredo Gamito
Education, Arnaldo Nhavoto
Interior, Manuel Macananda
Transport and Communications, Paulo Muxanga
Finance, Tomas Salomao
Health, Aurelio Zihao
Agriculture and Fisheries, Carlos Rosario
Industry, Trade and Tourism, Oldemiro Baloi
Mineral Resources and Energy, John Kachamila
Justice, José Abudo
Culture, Youth and Sports, José Mateus Katupha
Labour, Guilherme Mavila
Environment, Bernardo Ferraz
Social Affairs, Alcinda de Abreu
Public Works and Housing, Roberto White
Ministers in the President's Office, Eneias Comiche (*Economic and Social Affairs*); Francisco Madeira (*Parliamentary Affairs*); Almerindo Manhenje (*Defence and Security Affairs*)

HIGH COMMISSION FOR THE REPUBLIC OF MOZAMBIQUE
21 Fitzroy Square, London WIP 5HJ
Tel 0171–383 3800
High Commissioner, HE Dr Eduardo José Baciao Koloma, apptd 1996

BRITISH HIGH COMMISSION
Av. Vladimir I Lenine 310, CP 55, Maputo
Tel: Maputo 420111/2/5/6/7
High Commissioner, HE Bernard J. Everett, apptd 1996

BRITISH COUNCIL DIRECTOR, Gail Liesching, PO Box 4178, Maputo

ECONOMY

The basis of the economy is subsistence agriculture, but there is an industrial sector based mainly in Beira and Maputo. There are substantial coal deposits in Tete province and an offshore gas field at Pande. After giving priority to the development of collective farms and state enterprises in all sectors, the government launched an economic rehabilitation programme in 1987 to attract foreign investment and boost production. Economic subsidies have been removed and an IMF reform programme is being implemented. The economy is still heavily dependent on aid. A three-year loan of US$110 million was approved by the IMF in June 1996 to supplement loans of US$65 million from the EU in May 1995, and US$780 million from the Paris club of donor states in March 1995. GDP growth was an estimated 4.3 per cent in 1994 and

forecast to grow, although inflation was roughly 50 per cent and external debt reached US$5,300 million in 1993. An agreement on non-aggression and good neighbourliness with South Africa was signed in 1984 (the Nkomati Accord), and in June 1994 a joint Mozambican-South African Chamber of Commerce was formed. A five-year plan has been launched with the priorities of rural development, education, health and land reform.

TRADE
The main exports are shellfish, cotton, sugar, cashew nuts, copra, tea and sisal. Exports totalled US$150 million in 1994 and imports US$1,000 million. Mozambique's main trading partners are Portugal, Spain and France.

Trade with UK	1994	1995
Imports from UK	£35,489,000	£13,274,000
Exports to UK	2,903,000	1,922,000

MYANMAR
Pyidaungsu Myanma Naingngandaw – Union of Myanmar

Myanmar (Burma) forms the western portion of the Indo-Chinese part of Asia, lying between 9° 58′ and 28° N. latitude and 92° 11′ and 101° 9′ E. longitude, with an extreme length of approximately 1,200 miles and an extreme width of 575 miles. It has a sea coast on the Bay of Bengal to the south and west, and a frontier with Bangladesh along the Naaf River and with India to the north-west. In the north and east the country borders China and there is a short frontier with Laos in the east, while the long finger of Tenasserim stretches southwards along the west coast of the Malay peninsula, forming a frontier with Thailand to the east. The total area is 261,218 sq. miles (676,552 sq. km).

Mountains enclose Myanmar on three sides. The principal river systems are the Kaladan-Lemro in Arakan, the Irrawaddy-Chindwin and the Sittang in central Myanmar, and the Salween which flows through the Shan Plateau.

The population (1994 estimate) is 45,555,000. The indigenous inhabitants are of similar racial types and speak languages of the Tibeto-Burman, Mon-Khmer and Thai groups. The three significant non-indigenous elements are Indians, Chinese and those from Bangladesh. Burmese is the official language, but minority languages include Shan, Karen, Chin, Kayah and the various Kachin dialects. English is spoken in educated circles.

Buddhism is the religion of 85 per cent of the people, with 5 per cent Animists, 4 per cent Muslims, 4 per cent Hindus and less than 3 per cent Christians.

CAPITAL – ΨYangon (Rangoon). Population (1983): Yangon District 3,973,872; city population 2,458,712. The other major cities are Mandalay, population (1983): Mandalay district 4,580,923; city 532,985; Mawlamyine (Moulmein) 219,991 and Pathein (Bassein) 144,092. Pagan, on the Irrawaddy, contains many sacred buildings.

CURRENCY – Kyat (K) of 100 pyas.

FLAG – Red, with a canton of dark blue, inside which are a cogwheel and two rice ears surrounded by 14 white stars.

NATIONAL DAY – 4 January.

GOVERNMENT

The Union of Burma (the name was officially changed to the Union of Myanmar in 1989) became an independent republic outside the British Commonwealth on 4 January

INDIA

BANGLADESH

CHINA

Mandalay

MYANMAR

Akyab

LAOS

Prome

Pegu

Pathein

Yangon

THAILAND

Mawlamyine

BAY OF
BENGAL

Dawei

ANDAMAN
ISLANDS
(INDIA)

0   500 km

0   300 miles

1948 and remained a parliamentary democracy for 14 years. In 1962 the army took power and suspended the parliamentary constitution. A Revolutionary Council of senior officers under Gen. Ne Win instituted a socialist state.

After months of popular demonstrations and a series of presidents during 1988, Gen. Saw Maung, leader of the armed forces, assumed power in September 1988. The People's Assembly, the Council of State and the Council of Ministers were abolished and replaced by the State Law and Order Restoration Council (SLORC). The constitution was effectively abrogated.

A People's Assembly Election Law was published in 1989 committing the SLORC to hold multiparty elections. These were held on 27 May 1990, resulting in a majority for the National League for Democracy (NLD) even though its leader Aung San Suu Kyi had been under house arrest since July 1989. The SLORC refused to transfer power to a civilian government and large numbers of NLD MPs and supporters were detained. Others fled to the border areas with Thailand where an exile government led by Sein Win, the National Coalition Government of the Union of Burma (NCGUB), was set up. However, following the replacement of Saw Maung by Than Shwe as SLORC Chairman and Prime Minister in April 1992, the government began a dialogue with some elements of the opposition. A Constitutional Convention of delegates appointed by the SLORC to discuss a future constitution convened in January 1993 and has continued fitfully since, but with minimal progress. The SLORC has released about 2,000 political detainees including on 10 July 1995 Aung

San Suu Kyi (who won the Nobel Peace Prize in 1991), but many others remain in detention or under house arrest.

Myanmar is comprised of seven states (Chin, Kachin, Kayin (Karen), Kayah, Mon, Rakhine, Shan) and seven divisions (Irrawaddy, Magwe, Mandalay, Pegu, Yangon (Rangoon), Sagaing, Tenasserim).

INSURGENCY

Since independence in 1948 the government has fought various armed insurgent groups, the largest of which were derived from the Kachin, Karen, Karenni, and Wa ethnic groups but the Shan, Mon, Arakan and Chin ethnic minorities have also formed armed groups.

Since 1992, as a result of government offensives, 15 ethnic groups have signed cease-fire agreements with the government, including the Kachin Independence Army, the Karenni National People's Liberation Front and the Shan State Liberation Organization in 1994, and Mon rebels in July 1995. In 1995–6, government forces launched successful offensives against the Karen National Union, the Karenni National Progressive Party and the Mong Tai army, whose leader, the drugs warlord Khun Sa, surrendered in January 1996.

STATE LAW AND ORDER RESTORATION COUNCIL

Chairman, Gen. Than Shwe
Vice-Chairman, Lt.-Gen. Maung Aye
Members, Vice-Adm. Maung Maung Khin; Lt.-Gen. Tin Tun; Lt.-Gen. Aung Ye Kyaw; Lt.-Gen. Phone Mying; Lt.-Gen. Sein Aung; Lt.-Gen. Chit Swe; Lt.-Gen. Kyaw Ba; Lt.-Gen. Maung Thint; Lt.-Gen. Nyan Lin; Lt.-Gen. Myint Aung; Lt.-Gen. Mya Thinn; Lt.-Gen. Tun Kyi; Lt.-Gen. Aye Thaung; Lt.-Gen. Myo Nyunt; Lt.-Gen. Maung Hla; Lt.-Gen. Kyaw Min; Lt.-Gen. Khin Nyunt; Lt.-Gen. Tin U

CABINET *as at June 1996*

Deputy PMs, Vice-Adm. Maung Maung Khin; Lt.-Gen. Tin Tun
Prime Minister's Office, Brig.-Gen. Lun Maung; Col. Pe Thein; Brig.-Gen. Myo Thant; U Than Shwe; U Khin Maung Yin
Foreign Affairs, U Ohn Gyaw
Home Affairs, Lt.-Gen. Mya Thinn
National Planning and Economic Development, Brig.-Gen. David Abel
Religious Affairs, Lt.-Gen. Myo Nyunt
Finance and Revenue, Brig.-Gen. Win Tin
Culture, U Aung San
Co-operatives, U Than Aung
Industry, Lt.-Gen. Sein Aung; Maj.-Gen. Kyaw Than
Forestry Affairs, Lt.-Gen. Chit Swe
Agriculture, Maj.-Gen. Myint Aung
Information, Maj.-Gen. Aye Kyaw
Social Welfare, Relief and Resettlement, Lt.-Gen. Sor Myinh
Immigration and Population, Lt.-Gen. Maung Hla
Energy, U Khin Maung Thein
Railways, U Win Sein
Construction, Maj.-Gen. Saung Tun
Communication, Posts and Telecommunications, U Soe Tha
Education, U Pan Aung
Transport, Lt.-Gen. Thein Win
Trade, Lt.-Gen. Tun Kyi
Tourism, Lt.-Gen. Kyaw Ba
Development of Border Areas and National Races, Lt.-Gen. Maung Thint
Labour, Maj.-Gen. Saw Lwin
Health, U Saw Tun
Livestock Breeding and Fisheries, U Aung Thaung
Minister in the Deputy PM's Office, Brig.-Gen. Maung Maung

Mines, Lt.-Gen. Kyaw Min
Minister in the Office of the SLORC Chairman, Lt.-Gen. Min
    Thein

EMBASSY OF THE UNION OF MYANMAR
19A Charles Street, Berkeley Square, London WIX 8ER
Tel 0171-629 6966
Ambassador Extraordinary and Plenipotentiary, new
    appointment awaited

BRITISH EMBASSY
80 Strand Road (Box No. 638), Yangon
Tel: Yangon 95300
Ambassador Extraordinary and Plenipotentiary, HE Robert A.
    E. Gordon, OBE, apptd 1995
Cultural Attaché and British Council Director, Chris Harrison

DEFENCE

Total active armed forces number 286,000 personnel. The
Army has a strength of 265,000, with 26 main battle tanks,
170 armoured personnel carriers and 246 artillery pieces.
The Navy has a strength of 12,000–15,000 (including 800
naval infantry), with 56 patrol and coastal combatants.
Paramilitary personnel number 85,250.

ECONOMY

The chief sources of revenue are profits on state trading,
taxes and duties; the chief heads of expenditure are
defence, education and police. The budget estimates for
1992–3 were: revenue K53,867 million; expenditure,
K57,203 million.

Three-quarters of the population depend on agriculture; the chief products are rice, oilseeds (sesamum and
groundnut), maize, millet, cotton, beans, wheat, grain, tea,
sugar-cane, tobacco, jute and rubber.

Myanmar is rich in minerals, including petroleum, lead,
silver, tungsten, zinc, tin, wolfram and gemstones. Of these,
petroleum products are the most important. Oil is produced from oilfields in Myanaung, Prome and Shwepyitha
and at Chauk, Yenangyaung, Mann, and Letpando. Production of crude oil in 1994 totalled 765,000 tonnes. There
are refineries at Chauk, the main oilfield, Syriam and
Mann. Major reserves of natural gas have been discovered
in the Martaban Gulf, production of which totalled 1,290
million cubic metres in 1994–5. Timber production is also
an important industry and timber is a major export.

All industrial activity of any size is in the public sector.
Under development plans, projects completed or under
construction with overseas financial and technical assistance include the production of cement, bricks and tiles,
sheet glass, steel sections, jute bags and twine, cotton yarns
and cloth, pharmaceuticals, sugar, paper, plywood, urea
fertilizers, soda ash, tractors and tyres; also a hydroelectric
scheme and various irrigation works.

A new ministry was established in 1992 with the task of
attracting 500,000 tourists; less than 10,000 visited in 1991
but visitors and revenues are increasing.

In 1993 the military government began to open the
economy to foreign investment, signing 50 joint ventures
in the fields of oil and gas exploration, hotel construction
and forestry. Mild economic liberalization, including the
legalization of small-scale private enterprises, has so far
failed to gain the country IMF loans, but the first foreign
hotels have opened in Yangon and Mandalay.

In July 1996, ASEAN agreed to grant Myanmar
observer status.

TRADE WITH UK	1994	1995
Imports from UK	£13,011,000	£15,244,000
Exports to UK	14,004,000	9,283,000

COMMUNICATIONS

The Irrawaddy and its chief tributary, the Chindwin, are
important waterways, the main stream being navigable 900
miles from its mouth and carrying much traffic. The chief
seaports are Yangon (Rangoon), Mawlamyine (Moulmein), Akyab (Sittwe) and Pathein (Bassein).

The railway network covers 2,764 route miles, extending to Myitkyina on the Upper Irrawaddy. There are 2,452
miles of highways and 11,767 miles of other main roads.
The airport at Mingaladon, about 13 miles north of Yangon
(Rangoon), only handles limited international air traffic.

EDUCATION

The literacy rate is high compared to other Asian countries. Most children attend primary school, and about six
million are currently enrolled; in middle and high schools,
enrolment is about two million. There are five universities,
at Yangon (Rangoon), Mandalay, Taunggyi, Sagaing and
Mawlamyine (Moulmein). Under the universities are
three affiliated degree colleges and the Workers' College,
Yangon. There are also 14 two-year colleges affiliated to
the universities, spread throughout the country.

Vocational training is provided at 16 teachers' training
institutes, seven government technical institutes, 14 technical high schools, 15 agricultural institutes and schools,
and 34 vocational schools for handicrafts, etc.

NAMIBIA
The Republic of Namibia

Namibia lies on the south-west coast of Africa. It is
bordered in the north by Angola (17° 23′ S. latitude), in the
south by the Northern Cape region of South Africa, in the
east by Botswana, and on the west lies the Atlantic Ocean.
In addition the Caprivi Strip in the north-east of the
country borders on Zambia and Zimbabwe. Namibia has an
area of 318,261 sq. miles (824,292 sq. km), including the
area of Walvis Bay (434 sq. miles). The average rainfall
over 70 per cent of the country is below 400 mm a year.

The population was estimated at 1,500,000 in 1994. The
main population groups are: Ovambo (587,000), Kavango
(110,000), Damara (89,000), Herero (89,000), whites
(78,000), Nama (57,000), coloured (48,000), Caprivians
(44,000), Bushmen (34,000), Rehoboth Baster (29,000),
Tswana (7,000). English is the official language, with
Afrikaans, German and local languages also in use.

CAPITAL – Windhoek (population, 1987 estimate,
    110,000). Other major towns are Grootfontein,
    ΨWalvis Bay, ΨLüderitz, Karasburg and
    Keetmanshoop.
CURRENCY – Namibian Dollar of 100 cents, introduced in
    September 1993 at parity to South African rand (the
    previous currency).
FLAG – Divided diagonally blue, red and green with the
    red fimbriated in white; a gold twelve-rayed sun in the
    upper hoist.
NATIONAL DAY – 21 March (Independence Day).

HISTORY

The German protectorate of South West Africa from 1880
to 1915, Namibia was administered until the end of 1920 by
the Union of South Africa. Under the terms of the Treaty of
Versailles, the territory was entrusted to South Africa with
full powers of administration and legislation over the
territory. After the dissolution of the League of Nations

and in the absence of a trusteeship agreement, South Africa informed the UN that it would continue to administer South West Africa.

In 1971 the International Court of Justice at The Hague delivered a majority opinion that the continued presence of South Africa was illegal. The South African government rejected this opinion, but accepted the principle that the territory should attain independence. In 1977 the five Western members of the UN Security Council drew up a plan, later incorporated into Security Council Resolution 435, for a peaceful settlement. Implementation began in April 1989 and elections for 72 seats in Namibia's first nationally elected body took place under UN supervision on 7–11 November 1989. The South West Africa People's Organization (SWAPO) won 41 seats, the Democratic Turnhalle Alliance 21 seats, the United Democratic Front 4 seats, Action Christian National 3, Namibia Patriotic Front 1, Federal Convention of Namibia 1, and Namibia National Front 1. Independence was declared on 21 March 1990. Namibia joined the Commonwealth upon independence.

Previously a British and South African colony separate from German South West Africa/Namibia, Walvis Bay was governed from August 1992 by the joint South African-Namibian Walvis Bay Administrative Body until 28 February 1994, when South Africa renounced its claim to sovereignty over the enclave and it became part of Namibia.

GOVERNMENT

Constitutionally defined as a multiparty, secular, democratic republic, Namibia has an executive President as head of state who exercises the functions of government with the assistance of a Cabinet headed by a Prime Minister. The President is directly elected for a maximum of two five-year terms. Legislative authority lies with the National Assembly, which is the lower house of a bicameral parliament; an upper house (National Council) representing regional councils was elected in November 1992 and inaugurated in January 1993. Each of the 13 regional councils appoints two representatives to the National Council. The main function of the National Council is to review and consider legislation from the National Assembly. Under a system of proportional representation, elections to the National Assembly are to take place every five years, or earlier if decided by the President. Members of the National Council hold their seats for six years. The constitution can only be changed by a two-thirds majority in the National Assembly.

Presidential and legislative elections were held on 7–8 December 1994 and won by the incumbent, Sam Nujoma, and by SWAPO respectively. In the 72-seat National Assembly SWAPO has 53 seats, the Democratic Turnhalle Alliance 15 seats, and other parties four seats.

HEAD OF STATE
President, Dr Sam Nujoma, *elected* 16 February 1990, *re-elected* 8 December 1994

CABINET *as at August 1996*
Prime Minister, Hage Geingob
Deputy PM, Revd. Hendrik Witbooi
Foreign Affairs, Theo-Ben Gurirab
Home Affairs, Jerry Ekandjo
Labour and Manpower Development, Moses Garoeb
Mines and Energy, Andimba Toivo ya Toivo
Information and Broadcasting, Ben Amadhila
Tertiary Education and Vocational Training, Nahas Angula
Basic Education and Culture, John Mutorwa
Justice, Ngarikutuke Tjiriange

Regional and Local Government and Housing, Libertine Amadhila
Trade and Industry, Hidipo Hamutenya
Health and Social Services, Nick Iyambo
Environment and Tourism, Gert Hanekom
Works, Transport and Communication, Hampie Plichta
Fisheries and Marine Resources, Hifikepunye Pohamba
Lands, Resettlement and Rehabilitation, Richard Kapelwa-Kabajani
Finance, Helmut Angula
Youth and Sport, Pendukeni Ithana
Agriculture, Water and Rural Development, Nangolo Mbumba
Prisons and Correctional Services, Marco Hausiku
Defence, Philemon Malima

HIGH COMMISSION OF THE REPUBLIC OF NAMIBIA
6 Chandos Street, London WIM OLQ
Tel 0171-636 6244
High Commissioner, HE Benjamin Ulenga, apptd 1996

BRITISH HIGH COMMISSION
116 Robert Mugabe Avenue, Windhoek 9000
Tel: Windhoek 223022
High Commissioner, HE Robert H. G. Davies, apptd 1996

BRITISH COUNCIL REPRESENTATIVE, Dr Phillip Mitchell, PO Box 24224, 74 Bülowstrasse, Windhoek 9000

ECONOMY

GDP growth in 1995 was 2 per cent compared with 5.8 per cent in 1994. GDP per capita was US$1,660 in 1993. The government's 'First National Development Plan' envisages growth of 5 per cent a year from 1995 to 2000.

Mining (mainly diamonds and uranium), agriculture and fisheries account for over 40 per cent of GDP. Most of the labour force is employed in the agricultural sector. Large deposits of diamonds along the coast and offshore along the sea bed are estimated at between 1,500 and 3,000 million carats. Walvis Bay and Lüderitz are the main ports.

TRADE WITH UK	1994	1995
Imports from UK	£4,530,000	£5,983,000
Exports to UK	26,723,000	26,635,000

NAURU
The Republic of Nauru

Nauru is an island 8.2 sq. miles (21 sq. km) in area, situated in 166° 55′ E. longitude and 0° 32′ S. of the Equator. It had a population (census 1983) of 8,042: Nauruans 4,964; other Pacific Islanders 2,134; Asians 682; Caucasians 262. The UN estimated a total population of 10,000 in 1993. About 43 per cent of Nauruans are adherents of the Nauruan Protestant Church and there is a Roman Catholic mission on the island. The main languages are English and Nauruan.

CURRENCY – Nauru uses the Australian dollar ($A) of 100 cents as legal tender.
FLAG – Twelve-point star (representing the 12 original Nauruan tribes) below a gold bar (representing the Equator), all on a blue ground.
NATIONAL DAY – 31 January (Independence Day).

GOVERNMENT

From 1888 until the First World War Nauru was administered by Germany. In 1920 it became a British Empire-mandated territory under the League of Nations, administered by Australia. A trusteeship superseding the mandate was approved in 1947 by the UN and Nauru continued to be administered by Australia until it became independent on 31 January 1968. It was announced in November 1968 that a special form of membership of the Commonwealth had been devised for Nauru at the request of its government.

Parliament has 18 members including the Cabinet and Speaker. Voting is compulsory for all Nauruans over 20 years of age, except in certain specified instances. Elections are held every three years. The Cabinet is chosen by the President, who is elected by the Parliament from amongst its members, and comprises not fewer than five nor more than six members including the President.

HEAD OF STATE

President and Minister for External Affairs, Island Development and Industry, Civil Aviation Authority and the Public Service, Lagumot Harris, *elected by parliament* November 1995

CABINET *as at August 1996*

Education, Kennan Adeang
Finance, Minister Assisting the President, Reuben Kun
Health, Clinton Benjamin
Justice, Anthony Audoa
Works, Community Services, Roy Degoregore

BRITISH HIGH COMMISSIONER, HE Michael Peart, CMG, CVO, resident at Suva, Fiji

JUDICIARY

A Supreme Court of Nauru is presided over by the Chief Justice. The District Court, which is subordinate to the Supreme Court, is presided over by a Resident Magistrate. Both the Supreme Court and the District Court are courts of record. The Supreme Court exercises both original and appellate jurisdiction.

ECONOMY

The only fertile areas are the narrow coastal belt and local requirements of fruit and vegetables are mostly met by imports. The economy is heavily dependent on the extraction of phosphate, of which the island has one of the world's richest deposits. About one million tonnes of phosphate are mined each year, providing employment for over 1,000 people. The industry has been run since 1970 by the Nauru Phosphate Corporation. Considerable investments have been made abroad with the royalties on phosphate exports to provide for a time when production declines. In 1993 an agreement was signed with Australia for compensation to cover damage caused by phosphate mining during the Australian mandate and trusteeship periods. The compensation package is worth some £50 million (a portion of which will be paid by the UK and New Zealand governments), composed of a £33 million payment and a 20-year package of health and education programmes.

The Nauru Pacific Line owns six ships; the government-owned Air Nauru operates air services throughout the Pacific region and to Australia, New Zealand, Japan, Singapore and the Philippines.

TRADE WITH UK	1994	1995
Imports from UK	£837,000	£1,195,000
Exports to UK	—	134,000

SOCIAL SERVICES

Nauru has a hospital service and other medical and dental services. There is also a maternity and child welfare service.

Education is available in nine primary and two secondary schools on the island with a total enrolment of about 1,600 pupils receiving primary education and 500 secondary education.

NEPAL

Nepal lies between India and the Tibet Autonomous Region of China on the slopes of the Himalayas, and includes Mount Everest (29,028 ft). It has a total area of 54,342 sq. miles (140,747 sq. km).

The southern region, the Terai, was covered with jungle but has been more widely cultivated recently. It forms about 23 per cent of the total land area and nearly 44 per cent of the population live there. The central belt is hilly, but with many fertile valleys, leading up to the snowline at about 16,000 feet. The hills account for 42 per cent of the area and about 48 per cent of the population. The remainder of the country, the Himalayan region, consists of high mountains which are sparsely inhabited. The country is drained by three great river systems rising within and beyond the Himalayan mountain ranges and eventually flowing into the Ganges in India.

The population (UN estimate 1994) was 21,360,000. The inhabitants are of mixed stock, with Mongolian characteristics prevailing in the north and Indian in the south. The official religion is Hinduism: 89.5 per cent of the population are Hindus and 6 per cent are Buddhist. Gautama Buddha was born in Nepal.

CAPITAL – Kathmandu, population (1989) 300,000. Other towns of importance are Biratnagar (94,000), Lalitpur (81,000), Bhaktapur (50,500), and Pokhara (48,500).

CURRENCY – Nepalese rupee of 100 paisa.

FLAG – Double pennant of crimson with blue border on peaks; white moon with rays in centre of top peak; white quarter sun, recumbent in centre of bottom peak.

NATIONAL ANTHEM – May Glory Crown Our Illustrious Sovereign.

NATIONAL DAYS – 18 February (National Democracy Day); 28 December (The King's Birthday).

GOVERNMENT

Nepal was originally divided into numerous hill clans and petty principalities but emerged as a nation in the middle of the 18th century when it was unified by the warrior Raja of Gorkha, Prithvi Narayan Shah, who founded the present Nepalese dynasty. In 1846 power was seized by Jung Bahadur Rana after a massacre of nobles, and he was the first of a line of hereditary Rana Prime Ministers who ruled Nepal for 104 years. During this time the role of the monarchs was mainly ceremonial.

In 1950–1 a revolutionary movement broke the hereditary power of the Ranas and restored the monarchy to its former position. After ten years, during which various parties and individuals tried their hand at government, King Mahendra proscribed all political parties and assumed direct powers in 1960, with the object of leading a united country to democracy. In 1962 he introduced a new constitution embodying a tiered, partyless system of panchyat (council) democracy.

Mass agitation for political reform led in April 1990 to the lifting of the ban on political parties and the abolition of the panchyat system. A new constitution was promulgated in November 1990 establishing a multiparty, parliamentary system of government and a constitutional monarchy. The King retains joint executive power with the Council of Ministers. A bicameral legislature was set up, consisting of a 205-member House of Representatives and a 60-member National Council, including ten royal nominees. Elections in May 1991 were won by the Nepali Congress Party, which formed a government. This was brought down by a no-confidence vote in July 1994. Elections in November 1994 produced no overall control for any party and the United Marxist Leninist Party formed a minority government as the largest party. This government was brought down by a no confidence vote in June 1995 and was replaced by a coalition government of the Congress Party, right-wing Rashtriya Prajatrantra and royalist Sandbhavana Parishad parties.

HEAD OF STATE
HM The King of Nepal, King Birendra Bir Bikram Shah Dev, *born* 28 December 1945; *succeeded* 31 January 1972; *crowned* 24 February 1975; *married* February 1970, HM Queen Aishwatya Rajya Laxmi Devi Shah
Heir, HRH Crown Prince Dipendra Bir Bikram Shah Dev, *born* 27 June 1971

CABINET *as at June 1996*
Prime Minister, Palace Affairs, Defence, Sher Bahadur Deuba
Industry, Dhindi Raj Shastri
Home Affairs, Khum Bahadur Khadka
Supplies, Gajendra Narayan Singh
Local Development, Rajiv Parajuli
Labour, Bal Bahadur Rai
Forestry and Conservation, Shaikh Idris
Agriculture, Mahendra Raya
Information and Communications, Chirajibi Wagle
Housing and Planning, Shanti Shumsher Rana
Education, Govinda Raj Joshi
Water Resources, Sarbendra Nath Sukla
Tourism and Civil Aviation, Chakra Prasad Bastola
Finance, Ram Sharan Mahat
Foreign Affairs, Prakas Chandra Lohani
Works and Transport, Bijaya Gachhedar
Health, Arjun Narsingh
Law and Justice, Prasad Pahadi
Commerce, Phatteh Singh Tharu
Land Reform and Management, Prem Bahadur Bhandari
Women and Social Services, Vila Koirala
Youth, Sports and Culture, Bal Bahadur Kesi
General Administration, Dimal Nendra Nevi
Population and Environment, Prakash Man Singh
Parliamentary Affairs, Nara Hari Achari

ROYAL NEPALESE EMBASSY
12A Kensington Palace Gardens, London W8 4QU
Tel 0171–229 1594/6231
Ambassador Extraordinary and Plenipotentiary, HE Surya Prasad Shrestha, apptd 1992

BRITISH EMBASSY
Lainchaur Kathmandu, PO Box 106
Tel: Kathmandu 410583
Ambassador Extraordinary and Plenipotentiary, HE Lloyd B. Smith, CMG, apptd 1996

BRITISH COUNCIL REPRESENTATIVE, Sarah Ewans, (PO Box 640), Kantipath, Kathmandu

ECONOMY

The budget for the fiscal year 1995–6 is estimated at NRs. 52,894.6 million, of which NRs. 22,342.8 million was allocated to regular and NRs. 30,551.7 million to development expenditures. Revenue was estimated at NRs. 31,782.5 million, foreign aid and grants NRs. 14,573.6 million, and domestic borrowing NRs. 2,300 million.

In October 1992 the IMF approved a three-year loan of US$49 million; in April 1996, the Paris club pledged US$993 million for 1996–7.

Nepal exports carpets, jute, handicrafts, garments, hides and skins, medicinal herbs, cardamom, pulses, tea, etc., and imports textiles, machinery and parts, transport equipment, medicine, construction materials etc. Tourism is the single largest commercial earner of foreign exchange.

Trade with UK	1994	1995
Imports from UK	£9,119,000	£7,618,000
Exports to UK	6,877,000	4,562,000

COMMUNICATIONS

The total length of roads is 6,525 km. Most of the major roads have been built since the 1960s, often with aid from India and China. Kathmandu is connected by road with India and Tibet. Internally, the road network links Kathmandu to Kodari and Pokhara, and Pokhara to Sunauli. A road between Mugling and Naryanghat has further improved communications between Kathmandu and the Terai. The East–West Highway (Mahendra Raj Marg) running along the entire length of the country is complete except for the Banbasa-Mahakali section.

Royal Nepal Airlines operates an extensive network of domestic flights, and there are international flights to Europe, the Middle East and throughout Asia.

Telecommunication services, both domestic and international, are available. Television was introduced in 1984.

THE NETHERLANDS
Koninkrijk der Nederlanden

The kingdom of the Netherlands is a maritime country of western Europe, situated on the North Sea, in 50° 46′ to 53° 34′ N. latitude and 3° 22′ to 7° 14′ E. longitude, consisting of 12 provinces (Eastern and Southern Flevoland being amalgamated to form the twelfth province) and containing a total area of 15,770 sq. miles (40,844 sq. km). The land is generally flat and low, intersected by numerous canals and connecting rivers. The principal rivers are the Rhine, Maas, Yssel and Scheldt.

The population (1994 estimate) is 15,391,000. The language is Dutch, a West Germanic language of Saxon origin closely akin to Old English and Low German. It is spoken in the Netherlands and the northern part of Belgium (Flanders). It is also used in the Netherlands Antilles.

CAPITAL – ΨAmsterdam, population 1,031,000 (urban agglomeration), 713,407 (city) (1992).
SEAT OF GOVERNMENT – The Hague (Den Haag or, in full, 's-Gravenhage), population 445,287 (1992).
Other principal cities (1992) ΨRotterdam 589,707; Utrecht, 232,705; Eindhoven, 193,966; Haarlem 149,788; Groningen 169,387; Tilburg 160,618.
CURRENCY – Netherlands guilder of 100 cents.
FLAG – Three horizontal bands of red, white and blue.
NATIONAL ANTHEM – Wilhelmus.

GOVERNMENT

In 1815 the Netherlands became a constitutional kingdom under King William I, a descendant of the house of Orange-Nassau.

The States-General consists of the *Eerste Kamer* (First Chamber) of 75 members, elected for four years by the Provincial Council; and the *Tweede Kamer* (Second

Chamber) of 150 members, elected for four years by voters of 18 years and upwards. Members of the *Tweede Kamer* are paid. The most recent election to the Second Chamber was held on 3 May 1994 and resulted in a three-party centre-left coalition of the Labour Party, People's Party and Democrats 66. The state of the parties as at August 1996 was: Labour Party (PvdA) 37; Christian Democratic Appeal (CDA) 34; People's Party for Freedom and Democracy (VVD) 31; Democrats 66 (D66) 24; Green Left 5; others 19.

HEAD OF STATE

HM The Queen of the Netherlands, Queen Beatrix Wilhelmina Armgard, KG, GCVO, *born* 31 January 1938; *succeeded* 30 April 1980, upon the abdication of her mother Queen Juliana; *married* 10 March 1966, HRH Prince Claus George Willem Otto Frederik Geert of the Netherlands, Jonkheer van Amsberg; and has *issue*, Prince Willem (*see* below); Prince Johan Friso, *b.* 25 September 1968; Prince Constantijn Christof, *b.* 11 October 1969

Heir, HRH Prince Willem Alexander, *b.* 27 April 1967

CABINET *as at August 1996*

Prime Minister, Minister of General Affairs, Wim Kok (PvdA)
Deputy PM and Home Affairs, Hans Dijkstal (VVD)
Deputy PM and Foreign Affairs, Hans van Mierlo (D66)
Finance, Gerrit Zalm (VVD)
Development Co-operation, Jan Pronk (PvdA)
Defence, Netherlands Antilles and Aruba Affairs, Joris Voorhoeve (VVD)
Economic Affairs, G. J. Wijers (D66)
Justice, Winnie Sorgdrager (D66)
Agriculture, Nature Management and Fisheries, J. van Aartsen (VVD)
Education, Culture and Science, Dr Jo Ritzen (PvdA)
Social Affairs and Employment, Ad Melkert (PvdA)
Transport and Public Works, Annemarie Jorritsma-Lebbink (VVD)
Housing, Physical Planning and Environment, M. De Boer (PvdA)
Welfare, Health and Sport, Dr E. Borst-Eilers (D66)

VVD People's Party for Freedom and Democracy; D66 Democrats 66; PvdA Labour Party

ROYAL NETHERLANDS EMBASSY
38 Hyde Park Gate, London SW7 5DP
Tel 0171–584 5040
Ambassador Extraordinary and Plenipotentiary, HE Jan Herman van Roijen, apptd 1995
Ministers Plenipotentiary, G. C. M. van Pallandt; R. Brouwer (*Economic*)
Consul-General, H. Nijenhuis
Defence, Naval and Air Attaché, Capt. J. J. Blok

BRITISH EMBASSY
Lange Voorhout 10, The Hague, 2514 ED
Tel: The Hague 427 0427
Ambassador Extraordinary and Plenipotentiary, HE Sir David Miers, KBE, CMG, apptd 1993
Counsellors, P. S. Dimond (*Deputy Head of Mission*); C. W. Robins (*Commercial and Consul-General*)
Defence and Naval Attaché, Capt. P. J. Organ, RN
There is a Consulate-General at Amsterdam, a Consulate at Willemstad (Curaçao) and a Vice-Consulate at Philipsburg (St Maarten) (both Netherlands Antilles).

BRITISH COUNCIL DIRECTOR, Tim Butchard, Keizersgracht 343, 1016 EH Amsterdam

NETHERLANDS-BRITISH CHAMBER OF COMMERCE, The Dutch House, 307–308 High Holborn, London WC1V 7LS

UK OFFICE IN THE HAGUE, Holland Trade House, Bezuidenhoutseweg 181, 2594 AH The Hague

DEFENCE

The armed forces are almost entirely committed to NATO. Total armed forces number 74,400, which includes 27,700 conscripts. In addition there are 130,600 reservists. There is compulsory military service of nine months. In 1993 the government announced plans to abolish conscription in 1998.

The Army has a strength of 43,200 (24,700 conscripts) with 740 main battle tanks, 1,975 armoured infantry fighting vehicles and armoured personnel carriers, and 581 artillery pieces.

The Navy has a strength of 14,300, including 2,900 marines and 1,000 conscripts. It maintains a force of four submarines, four destroyers, four frigates with 33 patrol and coastal craft, 13 combat aircraft and 22 armed helicopters. The Air Force has a strength of 12,500 (2,000 conscripts), with 183 combat aircraft.

There is also a paramilitary Royal Military Constabulary of 3,600 personnel (500 conscripts).

ECONOMY

Of a total GNP of US$338,144 million in 1994, industry accounted for around 19.2 per cent, agriculture for 3.5 per cent and services 60.4 per cent. Inflation was 2 per cent in 1996; the unemployment rate was 7 per cent.

The chief agricultural products are potatoes, wheat, rye, barley, sugar beet, cattle, pigs, milk and milk products, cheese, butter, poultry, eggs, beans, peas, vegetables, fruit, flower bulbs, plants and cut flowers and there is an important fishing industry.

Among the principal industries are engineering, electronics, nuclear energy, petrochemicals and plastics, road vehicles, aircraft and defence equipment, shipbuilding repair, steel, textiles of all types, electrical appliances, metal ware, furniture, paper, cigars, sugar, liqueurs, beer, clothing etc.

TRADE

The Dutch are traditionally a trading nation. Trade, banking and shipping are of particular importance to the economy. The geographical position of the Netherlands, at the mouths of the Rhine, Meuse and Scheldt, brings a large volume of transit trade to and from the interior of Europe to Dutch ports. Principal trading partners are Germany, Belgium/Luxembourg and France.

	1993	1994
Imports	Guilders 231,612.9m	Guilders 256,430.9m
Exports	258,342.5m	287,452m

Trade with UK	1994	1995
Imports from UK	£9,314,331,000	£11,639,300,000
Exports to UK	9,745,362,000	10,854,300,000

COMMUNICATIONS

The total extent of navigable rivers including canals is 5,052 km. The total length of the railway system is 2,757 km, of which 1,991 km are electrified. The mercantile marine in 1995 consisted of 385 ships of total 2,903,000 gross registered tons. The total of kilometres flown by KLM (Royal Dutch Airlines) in 1991–2 was 188 million km.

There are six national papers, four of which are morning papers, and there are many regional daily papers.

EDUCATION

Primary and secondary education is given in both denominational and state schools. Attendance at primary school is compulsory.

The principal universities are at Leiden, Utrecht, Groningen, Amsterdam (two), Nijmegen, Maastricht and Rotterdam, and there are technical universities at Delft, Eindhoven, Enschede and Wageningen (agriculture).

OVERSEAS TERRITORIES

ARUBA

Aruba covers an area of 75 sq. miles (193 sq. km) and has a population (1994) of 71,000. The island was from 1828 part of the Dutch West Indies and from 1845 part of the Netherlands Antilles. On 1 January 1986 it became a separate territory within the Kingdom of the Netherlands. The 1983 Constitutional Conference agreed that Aruba's separate status would last for ten years from 1986, after which the island would become fully independent. In 1994 this decision was changed and it was decided that Aruba will retain its separate status within the Kingdom of the Netherlands.
Governor, O. L. Koolman
Prime Minister, J. H. A. Eman

CAPITAL – ΨOranjestad (population 25,000); and Sint Nicolaas (17,000).
CURRENCY – Aruban florin.

ECONOMY – The economy of Aruba is based largely on tourism. In 1995 there were 612,916 tourists.

Trade with UK	1994	1995
Imports from UK	£47,748,000	£58,816,000
Exports to UK	5,417,000	3,605,000

NETHERLANDS ANTILLES

The Netherlands Antilles comprise the islands of Curaçao, Bonaire, part of St Martin, St Eustatius, and Saba in the West Indies. The islands cover an area of 308 sq. miles (800 sq. km) with a population (1993) of 197,000 (Curaçao 146,800, Bonaire 11,400, St Martin 35,800, St Eustatius 1,840, Saba 1,180). The Netherlands Antilles, which have a 22-member federal parliament, are largely self-governing under the terms of the Realm Statute which took effect in 1954.
Governor, Dr Jaime Saleh
Prime Minister, Miguel Pourier

CAPITAL – ΨWillemstad (on Curaçao) (pop. 50,000).
CURRENCY – Netherlands Antilles guilder of 100 cents.

ECONOMY – The economy of the Netherlands Antilles is based on small manufacturing industries. The soil is too poor to permit large-scale agriculture and most products for consumption and industrial raw materials must be imported. Tourism is also important, with 753,000 tourists and 866,000 cruise-ship day trippers in 1993.

Trade with UK	1994*	1995*
Imports from UK	£17,831,000	£18,615,000
Exports to UK	28,633,000	14,378,000
*Curaçao		

NEW ZEALAND

New Zealand consists of a number of islands in the South Pacific Ocean, and also has administrative responsibility for the Ross Dependency in Antarctica. The two larger islands, North Island and South Island, are separated by a relatively narrow strait. The remaining islands are much smaller and widely dispersed. The boundaries, inclusive of the most outlying islands and dependencies, range from 33° to 53° S. latitude, and from 162° E. longitude to 173° W. longitude.

Much of the North and South Islands is mountainous. The principal range is the Southern Alps, extending the entire length of the South Island and having its culminating point in Mount Cook (12,349 ft). The North Island mountains include several volcanoes, two of which are active. Of the numerous glaciers in the South Island, the Tasman (18 miles long by 1¼ wide), the Franz Josef and the Fox are the best known. The North Island is noted for its hot springs and geysers. The more important rivers include the Waikato (270 miles in length), Wanganui (180), and Clutha (210) and lakes include Taupo, 234 sq. miles in area; Wakatipu, 113; and Te Anau, 133.

New Zealand includes, in addition to North and South Islands: Chatham Islands (Chatham, Pitt, South East Islands and some rocky islets, combined area, 965 sq. km (373 sq. miles), largely uninhabited); Stewart Island (area 1,746 sq. km (674 sq. miles), largely uninhabited); the Kermadec Group (Raoul or Sunday, Macaulay, Curtis Islands, L'Esperance, and some islets; population 9–10, all government employees at a meteorological station); Campbell Island, used as a weather station; the Three Kings (discovered by Tasman on the Feast of the Epiphany); Auckland Islands; Antipodes Group; Bounty Islands; Snares Islands and Solander.

New Zealand has a temperate marine climate, but with abundant sunshine. The mean temperature ranges from 15°C in the north to about 9°C in the south. Rainfall in the North Island ranges from 35 to 70 inches and in the South Island from 25 to 45 inches.

AREA AND POPULATION

Islands	Area (sq. miles)	Population at 31 March 1993
North Island	44,281	2,604,200
South Island	58,093	890,100
Other islands	1,362	
Total	103,736	3,494,300

Territories		
Tokelau	5	1,700 (a)
Niue	100	2,239
Cook Islands	93	18,300 (b)
Ross Dependency	175,000	

(a) 1994
(b) 1991

Of the total population of New Zealand, some 79 per cent is of European stock, 13 per cent Maori and 5 per cent other Pacific Islanders.

The main religion is Christianity. In 1991 the principal denominations were Anglican 22.1 per cent, Presbyterian 16.3 per cent, Roman Catholic 15 per cent, Methodist 4.2 per cent, Baptist 2.1 per cent.

CAPITAL – ΨWellington, in the North Island. Population (March 1994 estimate) of Wellington urban area, 329,000. Other large urban areas: ΨAuckland 929,300; ΨChristchurch 318,100; ΨDunedin 112,400; Hamilton 153,800; Ψ Napier-Hastings 110,200.
CURRENCY – New Zealand dollar (NZ$) of 100 cents.
FLAG – Blue ground, with Union Flag in top left quarter, four five-pointed red stars with white borders on the fly.
NATIONAL ANTHEM – God Save The Queen/God Defend New Zealand.
NATIONAL DAY – 6 February (Waitangi Day).

GOVERNMENT

The discoverers and first colonists of New Zealand were Polynesian people, ancestors of the modern-day Maori. The ninth century is generally considered to be the date of the first settlement; by the 13th or 14th century there were well-established settlements. The first European to discover New Zealand was a Dutch navigator, Abel Tasman, who sighted the coast in 1642 but did not land. It was the British explorer James Cook who circumnavigated New Zealand and landed in 1769. Largely as a result of increased British emigration, the country was annexed by the British government in 1840. The British Lieutenant-Governor, William Hobson, proclaimed sovereignty over the North Island by virtue of the Treaty of Waitangi, signed by him and many Maori chiefs, and over the South Island and Stewart Island by right of discovery.

In 1841 New Zealand was created a separate colony distinct from New South Wales. In 1907 the designation was changed to 'The Dominion of New Zealand'. The constitution rests upon the Constitution Act 1852 and other imperial statutes. A 1986 Constitution Act brought a number of statutory constitutional provisions. The Statute of Westminster was formally adopted by New Zealand in 1947.

The executive authority is entrusted to a Governor-General appointed by the Crown and aided by an Executive Council, within a unicameral legislature, the House of Representatives. The House of Representatives consists of 99 members elected for three years. There are four Maori electorates. In a referendum in 1992 the electorate voted in favour of the introduction of a mixed-member proportional representation system to replace the first-past-the-

post system. From the October 1996 election onwards there will be 120 House of Representatives seats, of which 65 will be elected by the first-past-the-post system and 55 by proportional representation on a party list basis. The number of Maori electorates will be increased to five.

Following the general election of 6 November 1993, the state of the parties in the House of Representatives is National 42, Labour 42, United 7, The Alliance 2, New Zealand First 2, Christian Democrats 1, Conservative 1, Independent 1, vacant 1. The National Party signed a pact with the newly-formed United Party in February 1996 to form a coalition government with a one-seat majority.

In 1994 the government offered NZ$1,000 million over a ten-year period to Maori tribes to settle outstanding land claims.

GOVERNOR-GENERAL
Governor-General and Commander-in-Chief, HE Sir Michael Hardie Boys, KCMG, *sworn in* March 1996

THE EXECUTIVE COUNCIL *as at August 1996*
The Governor-General
Prime Minister, Minister in Charge of the New Zealand Security Intelligence Service, Rt. Hon. J. B. Bolger
Deputy PM, Foreign Affairs and Trade, Pacific Island Affairs, Leader of the House, Rt. Hon. D. C. McKinnon
Finance, Rt. Hon. W. F. Birch
Health and Women's Affairs, Hon. Jenny Shipley
Attorney-General, Hon. Paul East
Agriculture, Hon. Dr Lockwood Smith
Employment, Education, Hon. Wyatt Creech
Foreign Affairs, Trade Negotiations, State-Owned Enterprises, Railways, Hon. Philip Burdon
Environment, Research, Science and Technology, Hon. Simon Upton
Local Government, Tourism, Recreation and Sport, Hon. John Banks
Social Welfare, Senior Citizens, Hon. Peter Gresham
Defence, Interior, Hon. Warren Cooper
Justice, Disarmament and Arms Control, Treaty of Waitangi Negotiations, Culture, Hon. Douglas Graham
Forestry, Racing, Hon. John Falloon
Labour, Fisheries and Energy, Hon. Doug Kidd
Housing, Customs, Hon. Murray McCully
Lands, Hon. Denis Marshall
Police, Maori Affairs, Hon. John Luxton
Transport, Communications, Broadcasting, Statistics, Hon. Maurice Williamson
Revenue, Internal Affairs, Hon. Peter Dunne
Crown Health Enterprises, Hon. Bill English

Speaker of the House of Representatives, Hon. Peter Tapsell

NEW ZEALAND HIGH COMMISSION
New Zealand House, Haymarket, London SW1Y 4TQ
Tel 0171-930 8422
High Commissioner, HE John Collinge, apptd 1994
Deputy High Commissioner, M. Chilton
Minister, J. Waugh (*Commercial*)
Head, Defence Staff, Cdre J. Peddie
First Secretary, G. Rush (*Cultural Affairs*)

BRITISH HIGH COMMISSION
44 Hill Street (PO Box 1812), Wellington 1
Tel: Wellington 4726-049
High Commissioner, HE Robert Alston, CMG, apptd 1994
Deputy High Commissioner, C. H. Salvesen
Counsellor, A. W. Turquet
Defence Adviser, Col. P. R. Barry, CBE
First Secretary, M. A. Capes (*Commercial*)
Consul-General and Director of Trade Promotion, J. Smith-Laittan (*resides at Auckland*)

There is a Consulate-General at Auckland and a Consulate in Christchurch.

BRITISH COUNCIL DIRECTOR, Paul Smith

BRITISH CHAMBER OF COMMERCE FOR AUSTRALIA AND NEW ZEALAND, PO Box 141, Manuka, ACT 2603, Australia; UK OFFICE, Suite 615, 6th Floor, The Linen Hall, 162–168 Regent Street, London WIR 5TB.

JUDICATURE

The judicial system comprises a High Court, a Court of Appeal and district courts having both civil and criminal jurisdiction.

Chief Justice, Rt. Hon. Sir Thomas Eichelbaum, GBE, PC.
President, Court of Appeal, Rt. Hon. Sir Ivor Lloyd Morgan Richardson.

DEFENCE

The total active armed forces personnel is 10,050, with a further 6,650 reserves. The Army has a strength of 4,500 personnel, with 26 light tanks, 78 armoured personnel carriers and 43 artillery pieces. The Navy has a strength of 2,200, with four frigates, four patrol and support craft, and five armed helicopters. The Air Force has a strength of 3,350 personnel with 37 combat aircraft. A support unit of 20 troops is maintained in Singapore.

FINANCE

Revenue and expenditure for the year ended 30 June 1994 was: revenue NZ$29,598 million, expenditure NZ$29,174 million. Taxation receipts in 1993–4 for all purposes amounted to NZ$28,203 million. The principal items of expenditure were social services NZ$10,528 million, education NZ$4,631 million, health NZ$4,103 million, debt services NZ$3,557 million and administration NZ$2,979 million.

ECONOMY

Since 1984 economic reforms have changed the economy from a highly regulated, nationalized and protected economy with a large welfare state to an economy at the forefront of market economics. Finance market and labour market deregulation, privatization, VAT reform, the introduction of private sector principles in the civil service, health service and education, the ending of agricultural subsidies and the near elimination of import tariffs have all occurred. The Reserve Bank has been made independent, with a contract to keep inflation below 2 per cent. Centralized wage-bargaining has ended and widespread means-testing has been introduced throughout the welfare state, so that only the very poor receive free or subsidized healthcare and other benefits. In 1994 economic growth was 5 per cent and the net public debt began to be reduced after public spending had been brought under control during the previous few years. Growth was predicted to slow to 2.6 per cent in 1996–7.

Agricultural production is dominated by cattle- and sheep-rearing, for meat, wool, dairy products and other by-products, such as skins, leather, etc. Gross agricultural production in 1992 was NZ$9,014 million, of which NZ$2,203 million was from dairy products, NZ$1,423 million from cattle and NZ$782 million from wool. Livestock on farms at 30 June 1994 included 3.6 million dairy cattle, 4.8 million beef cattle and 1.5 million deer and goats. Sheep numbered 50 million.

The output of sawn timber for 1993–4 was 2,800,000 cubic metres, of which 90 per cent was radiata pine.

Non-metallic minerals such as coal, clay, limestone and dolomite are more important than metallic ones. Coal output in 1994 was 2,800,000 tonnes. Of the metals, the most important are gold and ironsand. Natural gas deposits in the offshore Taranaki Maui field and onshore fields are increasingly being exploited and used for electricity generation and as a premium fuel. Hydroelectric power is used to generate 96 per cent of the country's electricity.

Manufacturing has become increasingly important to the economy over the past decade and is based on food processing, machinery production, motor vehicle assembly, chemicals, electrical and electronic goods, and paper and printing. Tourism is the fastest growing sector of the economy, with 1,263,000 visitors in 1993–4 earning NZ$3,500 million in foreign exchange.

TRADE	1992–3	1993–4
Imports (c.i.f.)	NZ$17,333m	NZ$18,469m
Exports (f.o.b.)	18,971m	19,808m

New Zealand's largest trading partners are Australia, Japan, USA and the UK. New Zealand exports to the UK include butter and cheese, wool, lamb, hides, skins and leather.

Trade with UK	1994*	1995*
Imports from UK	£412,865,000	£437,451,000
Exports to UK	539,830,000	576,587,000
*Includes Niue, Tokelau and Cook Islands		

COMMUNICATIONS

The national railway system is owned and operated by the privately-owned New Zealand Rail Ltd. In March 1993, there were 4,251 route km of railway in operation.

During 1991–2 the vessels entered from overseas ports numbered 3,282 (gross tonnage 27,983,000) and those cleared for overseas 3,298 (gross tonnage 27,508,000).

Domestic flights in 1990 carried 4,502,000 passengers and 47,700 tonnes of freight. International flights carried 3,129,000 passengers, 134,074 tonnes of freight and 5,082 tonnes of mail.

EDUCATION

Schools are free and attendance is compulsory between the ages of six and 15. In 1991 there were 403,435 pupils attending public primary schools, and 12,649 pupils attending registered private primary schools. Secondary education is carried on in 314 state secondary schools and 21 registered private secondary schools. The total number of pupils receiving full-time secondary education in July 1992 was 227,912. There were seven universities with a total of 93,182 students in 1992.

TERRITORIES

TOKELAU (OR UNION ISLANDS)

Tokelau is a group of atolls, Fakaofo, Nukunonu and Atafu, with a total land area of 5 sq. miles and a population of 1,700 (1994). It was proclaimed part of New Zealand as from 1 January 1949. A Council of Faipule, composed of one elected representative from each atoll, was established in August 1992 to govern Tokelau when the council of elders (General Fono) was not in session. The position of *Ulu-o-Tokelau* (leader) was also established in 1992 and is rotated among the three Faipale members annually. Administrative responsibility for Tokelau lies with the Administrator but in January 1994 his powers were delegated to the General Fono and Council of Faipale. The Tokelau Amendment Act, passed by the New Zealand Parliament in 1996, conferred legislative power on the General Fono.

New Zealand provides substantial aid (NZ$5.0 million in year ended 30 June 1994), to meet administrative, social, economic and development requirements. Tokelau receives revenue from the granting of fishing rights in its economic zone.
Administrator, Lindsay Watt
Ulu-o-Tokelau (1997) Falima Teao

THE ROSS DEPENDENCY

The Ross Dependency, placed under the jurisdiction of New Zealand in 1923, is defined as all the Antarctic islands and territories between 160° E. and 150° W. longitude which are situated south of the 60° S. parallel, including Edward VII Land and portions of Victoria Land. Since 1957 a number of research stations have been established in the Dependency.

ASSOCIATED STATES

COOK ISLANDS

Included in the realm of New Zealand since June 1901, the Cook Islands group consists of the islands of Rarotonga, Aitutaki, Mangaia, Atiu, Mauke, Mitiaro, Manuae, Takutea, Palmerston, Penrhyn or Tongareva, Manihiki, Rakahanga, Suwarrow, Pukapuka or Danger, and Nassau. The total population of the group was 18,300 in 1991.

The Queen has a representative on the islands, as does the New Zealand government. Since 1965 the islands have been in free association with New Zealand and enjoyed complete internal self-government, executive power being in the hands of a Cabinet consisting of the Prime Minister and eight other ministers. There is a 25-member Legislative Assembly. New Zealand has residual responsibility for foreign affairs and defence. The New Zealand citizenship of the Cook Islanders is embodied in the constitution.

The chief industries are tourism, financial services, clothing, agriculture, and black pearls. The New Zealand Government continues to give development aid to the Cook Islands.
HM Representative, Apenera Short, OBE
Prime Minister, Sir Geoffrey Henry, KBE
New Zealand High Commissioner, Darryl Dunn

NIUE

The population of Niue was 2,239 at the November 1991 census. A New Zealand High Commissioner is stationed at Niue, which since 1974 has been self-governing in free association with New Zealand. New Zealand is responsible for external affairs and defence, and continues to give financial aid. Executive power is in the hands of a Premier and a Cabinet of three drawn from the Assembly of 20 members. The Assembly is the supreme legislative body.
New Zealand High Commissioner, W. Searell

NICARAGUA
República de Nicaragua

Nicaragua is the largest state of Central America, with a long seaboard on both the Atlantic and Pacific Oceans, situated between 10° 45' and 15° N. latitude and 83° 40' and 87° 38' W. longitude. It has an area of 50,193 sq. miles (130,000 sq. km).

There is a population (UN estimate 1994) of 4,275,000, of whom about three-quarters are of mixed blood. Another 15 per cent are white, mostly of pure Spanish descent, and the remaining 10 per cent are West Indians or Indians. The latter group includes the Misquitos, who live on the

Atlantic coast. The official language is Spanish and the majority are Roman Catholic, although the English language and the Moravian Church are widespread on the Atlantic coast.

CAPITAL – Managua, population 615,000. Other centres are León, 158,577; Granada, 72,640; Masaya, 78,308; Chinandega, 144,291.
CURRENCY – Córdoba (C$) of 100 centavos.
FLAG – Horizontal stripes of blue, white and blue, with the Nicaraguan coat of arms in the centre of the white stripe.
NATIONAL ANTHEM – Salve A Ti Nicaragua (Hail, Nicaragua).
NATIONAL DAY – 15 September.

GOVERNMENT

The eastern coast of Nicaragua was touched by Columbus in 1502, and was overrun by Spanish forces in 1518. It formed part of the Spanish Captaincy-General of Guatemala until 1821, when its independence was secured. In 1927 Augusto Cesar Sandino began a guerrilla war against the occupation of Nicaragua by US Marines, which continued until they were expelled in 1933. Sandino was assassinated by Anastasio Somoza, director of the National Guard, and in 1936 Somoza assumed the presidency. He was succeeded by his sons Luis and Anastasio Somoza, until 1979 when the family and the National Guard were overthrown by guerrillas of the Sandinista National Liberation Front (FSLN).

After ten years in power and a ten-year civil war against US-backed Contra guerrillas, the Sandinistas lost their parliamentary majority in elections held in February 1990. A coalition of former opposition parties, Unión Nacional de Opositora (UNO), gained 51 seats to the Sandinistas' 39 seats in the 92-seat National Assembly and formed a government, with UNO leader Violeta Chamorro as President. With the defeat of the Sandinistas, the civil war came to an end.

President Chamorro and the UNO were forced to compromise with the Sandinistas, who controlled the trade unions, and to leave the armed forces and police under Sandinista control. Resentment among the UNO coalition members came to a head in December 1992 when UNO deputies tried to oust Chamorro from power. Chamorro ordered the police to seize the National Assembly and negotiated a new governing majority in the National Assembly of 39 Sandinistas and nine loyal UNO deputies, forcing the remaining 42 UNO deputies and Vice-President Godoy into opposition. A further 19 UNO deputies formed the Democratic Christian Union (UDC) in January 1994, which joined the governing coalition. A deadlock over constitutional reforms was broken in July 1995 when President Chamorro conceded the curbing of presidential powers. The President's term of office was reduced from six to five years with a maximum of two terms. Power over taxation and international treaties is to be transferred to the National Assembly after President Chamorro leaves office. Presidential and legislative elections are due to be held in October 1996.

HEAD OF STATE
President, Violeta Barrios de Chamorro, *inaugurated* 25 April 1990
Vice-President, Julia Mena Rivera

COUNCIL OF MINISTERS *as at August 1996*
Defence, The President
Minister to the Presidency, Julio Cárdenas
External Relations, Ernesto Leal

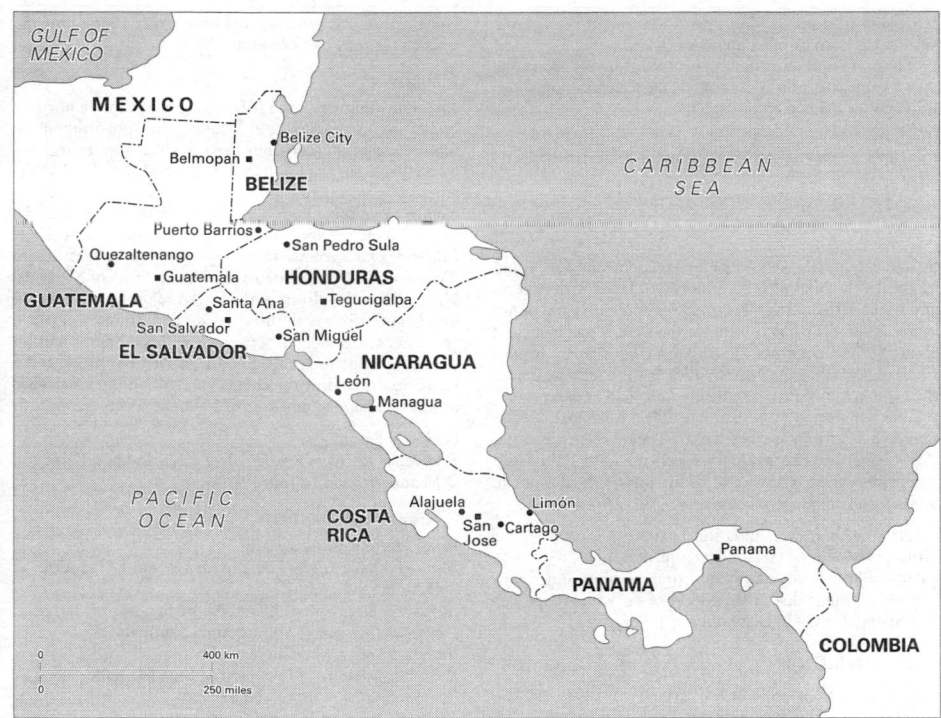

Interior, Sergio Narvaez
Finance, Emilio Pereira
Foreign Co-operation, Erwin Krugger
Construction and Transport, Pablo Vigil
Health, Dr Federico Muñoz Fernández
Agriculture, Dionisio Cuadra
Labour, Francisco Rosales
Economy and Planning, Pablo Pereira
Education, Humberto Belli Pereira
Tourism, Fernando Guzmán
Environment and Natural Resources, Claudio Gutierrez

EMBASSY OF NICARAGUA
2nd Floor, 36 Upper Brook Street, London WIY IPE
Tel 0171-409 2536
Ambassador Extraordinary and Plenipotentiary, HE Verónica
   Lacayo de Gómez, apptd 1995

BRITISH EMBASSY
PO Box A-169, Plaza Churchill, Reparto 'Los Robles',
Managua
Tel: Managua 780014
Ambassador and Consul-General, HE John Howard Culver,
   apptd 1992

DEFENCE

Under the Sandinista government, Nicaragua maintained
armed forces of over 120,000 personnel. Since 1990, active
armed forces personnel has fallen to 12,000 and service is
now voluntary. The Army has 10,000 personnel. The Navy
has a strength of 800, with 12 patrol and coastal vessels. The
Air Force has 1,200 personnel and 15 armed helicopters.
Conscription was ended in July 1995.

ECONOMY

Since the end of the civil war the UNO government has
begun to transform the Sandinistas' socialist economy into
a free-market one. An agreement was reached with the
IMF in April 1994 which provided US$662 million in
credits; the Paris club pledged US$1.5 billion in June 1995.
   The country is mainly agricultural. The major crops are
peanuts, cotton, coffee, sugar-cane, tobacco, sesame and
bananas. Beans, rice, maize and ipecacuanha, livestock and
timber production are also important. However, fishing,
forestry, grain and cattle production are still recovering
from the civil war in the main growing areas. Nicaragua
possesses deposits of gold and silver.

TRADE

Considerable quantities of foodstuffs are imported as well
as cotton goods, jute, iron and steel, machinery and
petroleum products. The chief exports are peanuts, sesame
seed, cotton, coffee (30 per cent of total export earnings),
beef, gold, sugar, cottonseed and bananas.

Trade with UK	1994	1995
Imports from UK	£3,969,000	£7,334,000
Exports to UK	5,185,000	8,265,000

COMMUNICATIONS

Transport, except on the Pacific slope, is still difficult but
many new roads have been opened. The Inter-American
Highway runs between the Honduras and the Costa Rican
borders; the inter-oceanic highway runs from the Corinto
on the Pacific coast via Managua to Rama, where there is a
natural waterway to Bluefields on the Atlantic. The main
airport is at Managua. The chief port is Corinto on the
Pacific. There are 252 miles of railway, all on the Pacific
side of the country. There are 51 radio stations and five

television stations in Managua. An automatic telephone system has been installed in major cities.

There are four daily newspapers published at Managua, apart from the official Gazette (*La Gaceta*). There are universities at León and Managua.

NIGER
République du Niger

Situated in central west Africa, between 12° and 24° N. and 0° and 16° E., Niger has common boundaries with Algeria and Libya in the north, Chad in the east, Nigeria and Benin in the south, Mali and Burkina in the west. It has an area of about 489,191 sq. miles (1,267,000 sq. km). Apart from a small region along the Niger Valley in the south-west near the capital, the country is entirely savannah or desert.

The population (UN estimate 1994) is 8,846,000. The main ethnic groups are the Hausa (54 per cent) in the south, the Songhai and Djerma in the south-west, the Fulani, the Beriberi–Manga, and the nomadic Tuareg in the north. The official language is French.

CAPITAL – Niamey, population 410,000.
CURRENCY – Franc CFA of 100 centimes.
FLAG – Three horizontal stripes, orange, white and green with an orange disc in the middle of the white stripe.
NATIONAL DAY – 18 December.

GOVERNMENT

The first French expedition arrived in 1891 and the country was fully occupied by 1914. It decided on 18 December 1958 to remain an autonomous republic within the French Community; full independence outside the Community was proclaimed on 3 August 1960.

The 1960 constitution provided for a presidential system of government and a single-chamber National Assembly. In 1974 Lt.-Col. Seyni Kountché seized power, suspended the constitution, dissolved the National Assembly and suppressed all political organizations. He set up a Supreme Military Council with himself as President. President Kountché died in 1987 and was succeeded by his cousin, Col. Ali Saibou.

In August 1991, a national conference of all groups voted to suspend the constitution and stripped President Saibou of all powers. A transitional government held office until a legislative election was held in February 1993. The former ruling party, the National Movement for a Development Society (MNSD), emerged as the largest party, with 29 seats in the 83-seat National Assembly. The opposition Alliance of Forces for Change (AFC) gained 50 seats, however, and formed the government. Mahamane Ousmane of the AFC won the presidential election in March, when the Third Republic also came into being.

The defection of one of the main AFC parties from the government in late 1994 led to a parliamentary election in January 1995 which was won by the MNSD and allied parties, with 43 seats to the AFC's 40 seats. Political deadlock followed until Hama Amadou of the MNSD was able to form a government in February 1995. The President and government were overthrown by a military coup led by Col. Ibrahim Barre Mainassara on 27 January 1996. Power was assumed by a National Salvation Council, which suspended the constitution, appointed a civilian Cabinet and created a transitional legislature until presidential and parliamentary elections could be held in July. Brig.-Gen. Mainassara was elected President on 8 July 1996, despite opposition claims of vote-rigging. A new constitution was promulgated on 12 May 1996 following endorsement by a referendum.

INSURGENCY

An ethnic Tuareg-based insurgency began in the north of Niger in November 1991, leading the government to impose a state of emergency in April 1992. The insurgency by the Front for the Liberation of Aïr and Azawad (FLAA) aimed to gain greater local autonomy for the Tuaregs, a change to regional boundaries, the demilitarization of the north and the teaching of the Tuareg language, Tamashek. In 1993 two groups, the Front for the Liberation of Tamoust (FLT) and the Revolutionary Army of Northern Niger (RANN) split from the FLAA in protest at its entry into negotiations with the government. An interim peace agreement was signed between the government and all Tuareg groups in Ouagadougou in October 1994, and a peace accord ending the conflict and providing for a peace process was signed on 24 April 1995.

HEAD OF STATE
President of the Third Republic, Brig.-Gen. Ibrahim Barre Mainassara, *elected* July 1996

CABINET *as at June 1996*
Prime Minister, Boukary Adji
Minister of State, Higher Education and Research, Hamidou Harouna Sidicou
Minister of State, Foreign Affairs, André Salifou
Finance and Planning, Almoustapha Soumaila
National Defence, Mahamane Dobi
Rural Development and Environment, Brah Mamane
External Relations, Mohamed Bazoum
National Education, Moumouni Aissata
Trade, Transport and Tourism, Jacques Nignon
Justice and Human Rights, Boube Oumarou
Communications, Culture, Youth and Sports, Government Spokesman, Inoussa Ousseni
Boukar Mines, Industry and Technology, Mai Manga
Interior and Territorial Development, Idi Ango Omar
Public Health and Social Affairs, Aloua Moussa
Civil Service, Labour and Employment, Seini Ali Gado
Equipment and Infrastructure, Cherif Chako
Secretary of State, Budget, Ibrahim Koussou
Secretary of State, Interior, Attaher Abdoulmoumine
Women's and Children's Promotion, Hima Mariama

EMBASSY OF THE REPUBLIC OF NIGER
154 rue de Longchamp, 75116, Paris
Tel: Paris 45048060
Ambassador Extraordinary and Plenipotentiary, HE Sandi Yacouba, apptd 1990

BRITISH AMBASSADOR, HE Margaret Rothwell, CMG, resident at Abidjan, Côte d'Ivoire

ECONOMY

The IMF approved a three-year loan of US$83 million in June 1996. The cultivation of groundnuts and the production of livestock are the main industries and provide two of the main exports. A company formed by the government, the French Atomic Energy Authority and private interests is exploiting uranium deposits at Arlit, and this is the main export. There is also some oil exploration which has found signs of oil in the eastern desert. Gold deposits exist north-west of Niamey.

TRADE WITH UK	1994	1995
Imports from UK	£3,853,000	£3,809,000
Exports to UK	4,312,000	14,000

NIGERIA
Federal Republic of Nigeria

Nigeria is situated on the west coast of Africa. It is bounded on the south by the Gulf of Guinea, on the west by Benin, on the north by Niger and on the east by Cameroon. It has an area of 356,669 sq. miles (923,768 sq. km). A belt of mangrove swamp forest lies along the entire coastline. North of this there is a zone of tropical rain forest and oil-palms. North of the rain forest, the country rises and the vegetation changes to open woodland and savannah. In the extreme north the country is semi-desert. The Niger, Benue, and Cross are the main rivers. The climate is tropical. The rainy season is from about April to October. During the dry season the cool *harmattan* wind blows from the desert.

The population (UN estimate 1994) is 107,900,000; Nigerian census result (1991) 88,514,501. The main ethnic groups are Hausa/Fulani, Yoruba and Ibo, and the principal languages are English, Hausa, Yoruba and Ibo. Over half the population are Muslim, these being concentrated in the north and west. In the southern areas in particular there are many Christians.

CAPITAL – Ψ Abuja, estimated population 378,671, declared the federal capital in December 1991. Other important towns are the former capital Lagos, Ibadan, Kaduna, Kano, Benin City, Enugu and Ψ Port Harcourt.
CURRENCY – Naira (N) of 100 kobo.
FLAG – Three equal vertical bands, green, white and green.
NATIONAL ANTHEM – Arise, O Compatriots.
NATIONAL DAY – 1 October (Independence Day).

GOVERNMENT

The Federation of Nigeria attained independence as a member of the Commonwealth on 1 October 1960 and became a republic in 1963. Originally regional in structure, the Federation is now divided into 30 states and the Federal Capital Territory.

In 1966 the military took power; in 1979 civil rule was restored after elections at national and state level. After similar elections in 1983 the new administration was overthrown by the military on 31 December, this regime itself being overthrown in August 1985. A 28-member Armed Forces Ruling Council (AFRC) was sworn in and governed in conjunction with a Council of Ministers until January 1993, when they were replaced by a National Defence and Security Council (NDSC) and a civilian Transitional Council respectively to govern the country until a handover to civilian government. A presidential election on 11 June is generally believed to have been won by Chief Moshood Abiola of the Social Democratic Party but the military government declared the election invalid. The military government resigned on 26 August, handing power to the Transitional Council.

Continued instability led Defence Minister Gen. Sanni Abacha to launch a military coup on 17 November 1993 and install himself as head of state. A (military) Provisional Ruling Council and (civilian) Federal Executive Council were established to govern the country until a new constitution is passed. Strikes and pro-democracy demonstrations continued in support of Chief Moshood Abiola, who returned from exile in June 1994 to establish a rival government, for which he has been imprisoned.

The National Constitutional Conference (NCC) convened by Gen. Abacha in June 1994 announced in January 1995 that Gen. Abacha should have an open-ended term of office. An attempted coup was defeated in March 1995 and political activity was restored in June, when the NCC presented the draft of a new constitution to Gen. Abacha. The military regime vowed to hand over power to an elected government in October 1998.

Nigeria was suspended from the Commonwealth on 11 November 1995, following the execution of nine human rights activists.

HEAD OF STATE
*Chairman of the Provisional Ruling Council and Federal
Executive Council, Commander-in-Chief of the Armed Forces,*
Gen. Sanni Abacha, *took power* 17 November 1993

FEDERAL EXECUTIVE COUNCIL *as at August 1996*
Chairman, Minister of Defence, Gen. Sanni Abacha
Vice-Chairman, Chief of General Staff, Lt.-Gen. D. O. Diya
Federal Capital Territory, Lt.-Gen. J. Useni
Education, Mohammad Liman
Industries, Lt.-Gen. Muhammadu Haladu
Works and Housing, Maj.-Gen. Abdulkarim Adisa
Finance, Chief Anthony Ani
Petroleum Resources, Chief Dan Etete
Power and Steel, Bashir Dalhatu
Health, Ikechukwa Madubuike
Foreign Affairs, Chief Tom Ikimi
Interior, Babagana Kingibe
Communications, Maj.-Gen. Tajudeen Olarenwaju
Labour, Uba Ahmed
Agriculture, Gambo Jimata
Information and Culture, Walter Ofonagoro
Justice and Attorney-General, Michael Agbamuche
Commerce and Tourism, Rear Adm. J. O. Ayinla
Aviation, Air Cdre. Isa Ibrahima
Water Resources, Aliyu Yelwa
Science and Technology, Brig.-Gen. Samuel Momah
Planning, Ayo Ogunlade
Solid Mineral Resources, Kaloma Ali
Transport, Maj.-Gen. Ibrahim Gumel
Women's and Social Affairs, Judith Attah
Youth and Sports, Chief Jim Nwobodo

NIGERIA HIGH COMMISSION
9 Northumberland Avenue, London WC2N 5BX
Tel 0171-839 1244
Acting High Commissioner, U. O. Okeke
Ministers, A. A. Ella; A. K. Sambo
Defence Attaché, vacant
Information Attaché, G. Ehiobuche
Head of Commerce/Trade, A. A. Ella

BRITISH HIGH COMMISSION
Shehu Shangari Way (North), Maitama, Abuja
Tel: Abuja 5232011
11 Eleke Crescent, Victoria Island, Lagos
Tel: Lagos 2619531
High Commissioner, HE John Thorold Masefield, CMG,
apptd 1994
Deputy High Commissioner and Counsellor (Political),
G. S. Hand
Counsellor (Economic and Commercial), D. D. Pearey
There are liaison offices at Kaduna, Kano, Port Harcourt and Ibadan.

BRITISH COUNCIL DIRECTOR, Dr John Hawkins, 11 Kingsway Road, Ikoyi (PO Box 3702), Lagos. Branch offices at Enugu, Ibadan, Kaduna and Kano City.

DEFENCE

Nigeria has a total active armed forces of 77,100 personnel, all of whom are volunteers. The Army is 62,000 strong, with 210 main battle tanks, 380 armoured personnel carriers and 462 artillery pieces. The Navy has 5,600 personnel, with one frigate, 53 patrol and coastal vessels and two armed helicopters. The Air Force numbers 9,500 personnel, with 92 combat aircraft and 15 armed helicopters.

EDUCATION

A programme was introduced in 1976 intended to achieve universal primary education. There are 37 universities (24 federal, 12 state and one military). Illiteracy was 48 per cent in 1992.

COMMUNICATIONS

The Nigerian railway system, which is controlled by the Nigerian Railway Corporation, has 2,178 route miles of lines. The principal international airlines operate from Lagos, Kano and Port Harcourt. A network of internal air services connects the main centres. The principal seaports are served by a number of shipping lines, including the Nigerian National Line. A nationwide television and radio network is being developed, with each state eventually having its own television and radio station.

ECONOMY

Nigeria was a predominantly agricultural country until the early 1970s when oil became the principal source of export revenue (over 90 per cent). Since 1981 oil revenues have fallen to half their peak level and austerity measures were introduced in 1982. Recent governments have attempted to stimulate greater self-reliance by encouraging non-oil exports and the use of local rather than imported raw materials. Even so Nigeria has a foreign debt of US$32,585 million (126 per cent of GNP). The 1994 budget deficit was equivalent to 12 per cent of GDP, while inflation in 1994 was 70 per cent. In response to these problems the government introduced economic reforms in January 1995, including lifting exchange controls and ending foreign investment controls in Nigerian or jointly-owned firms. Economic recovery has been hampered by the suspension of aid and development programmes following the execution of nine human rights activists in November 1995. Growth of 4.94 per cent has been forecast for 1996.

Three oil refineries are in operation at Port Harcourt, Warri and Kaduna, and steel plants at Warri and Ajaokuta. Other projects include natural gas liquifaction, petrochemicals, fertilizers, power stations and irrigation schemes. Tin and calumbite mining on the Jos plateau, textiles and coal mining are also important.

TRADE

The principal exports are oil, groundnuts, palm products, tin, cocoa, rubber and timber.

Trade with UK	1994	1995
Imports from UK	£457,916,000	£431,502,000
Exports to UK	124,577,000	181,038,000

NORWAY
Kongeriket Norge

Norway is a kingdom in the northern and western part of the Scandinavian peninsula, 1,752 km in length, its greatest width about 430 km. The length of the coastline is 2,650 km, and the frontier between Norway and the neighbouring countries of Sweden, Finland and Russia is

2,542 km. It has an area of 149,405 sq. miles (386,958 sq. km), of which Svalbard and Jan Mayen have a combined area of 24,355 sq. miles (63,080 sq. km).

The coastline is deeply indented with numerous fjords and fringed with rocky islands. The surface is mountainous, consisting of elevated and barren tablelands separated by deep and narrow valleys. At the North Cape the sun does not appear to set from the second week in May to the last week in July, causing the phenomenon known as the Midnight Sun; conversely, there is no apparent sunrise from about 18 November to 23 January. During the long winter nights are seen the Northern Lights or Aurora Borealis.

The population (1995) is 4,348,410. The Norwegian language in both its present forms is closely related to other Scandinavian languages. Independence from Denmark (1814) and resurgent nationalism led to the development of 'new Norwegian' based on dialects, which now has equal official standing with 'bokmål', in which Danish influence is more obvious. This was formed in the time of the Reformation. Ludvig Holberg (1684–1754) is regarded as the father of Norwegian literature, though the modern period begins with the writings of Henrik Wergeland (1808–45). Some of the famous names are Henrik Ibsen (1828–1906), Bjørnstjerne Bjørnson (1832–1910), Nobel Prizewinner in 1903, and the novelists Jonas Lie (1833–1908), Alexander Kielland (1849–1906), Knut Hamsun (1859–1952) and Sigrid Undset (1882–1949), the latter two also Nobel Prizewinners. Old Norse literature is among the most ancient and richest in Europe.

CAPITAL – ΨOslo (including Aker), population (1995) 483,401. Other towns are ΨTrondheim 142,927; ΨBergen 221,717; ΨStavanger 103,590; ΨKristiansand 68,609.

CURRENCY – Krone of 100 øre.
FLAG – Red, with white-bordered blue cross.
NATIONAL ANTHEM – Ja, Vi Elsker Dette Landet (Yes, we love this country).
NATIONAL DAY – 17 May (Constitution Day).

GOVERNMENT

The kingdom of Norway was founded in AD 872. From 1397 to 1814 Norway was united with Denmark and from 1814 with Sweden. The union with Sweden was dissolved on 7 June 1905 when Norway regained complete independence. Under the 1814 constitution, the 165-member *Storting* elects one-quarter of its members to constitute the *Lagting* (Upper Chamber), the other three-quarters forming the *Odelsting* (Lower Chamber).

The centre-right coalition government collapsed in October 1990 because of a dispute over whether to apply for membership of the European Community and was replaced by a minority Labour government. This was returned to power in the general election held on 13 September 1993. The state of the parties as at August 1996 was Labour 67, Centre Party 32, Conservatives 28, Christian Democrats 13, Socialist Left 13, Progress Party 10, Liberal Party 1, Red Electoral Alliance 1.

The Storting voted in November 1992 to apply to join the European Community. Negotiations with the EU concluded on 1 March 1994 with a proposed accession date of 1 January 1995, subject to parliamentary and national referendum ratifications. However, in a national referendum on 28 November 1994 the electorate voted against joining the EU by 52.4 per cent to 47.6 per cent.

HEAD OF STATE

HM *The King of Norway*, King Harald V, GCVO, *born* 21 February 1937; *succeeded* 17 January 1991, on the death of his father King Olav V; *married* 29 August 1968, Sonja Haraldsen, and has *issue*, Prince Haakon Magnus (*see* below), and Princess Martha Louise, *born* 22 September 1971
Heir, HRH Crown Prince Haakon Magnus, *born* 20 July 1973

CABINET *as at August 1996*

Prime Minister, Gro Harlem Brundtland
Foreign Affairs, Bjørn Tore Godal
Industry, Petroleum and Energy, Jens Stoltenberg
Defence, Jørgen Kosmo
Local Government and Labour, Gunnar Berge
Government Administration, Nils Olav Totland
Agriculture, Gunhild Øyangen
Justice, Grete Faremo
Fisheries, Jan Henry Olsen
Environment, Thorbjørn Berntsen
Transport and Communications, Kjell Opseth
Health, Gudmund Hernes
Church, Education and Research, Reidar Sandal
Trade and Shipping, Grete Knudsen
Family and Children's Affairs, Grete Berget
Cultural Affairs, Åse Kleveland
Finance, Sigbjørn Johnsen
Development Co-operation, Kari Nordheim-Larsen
Social Affairs, Hill-Marta Solberg

ROYAL NORWEGIAN EMBASSY
25 Belgrave Square, London SWIX 8QD
Tel 0171-235 7151
Ambassador Extraordinary and Plenipotentiary, HE Kjell Colding, apptd 1996
Defence Attaché, Capt. T. Seim
First Secretary, Inger Brusell (*Consular*)

Counsellor, S. Lindtvedt (*Commercial*)

BRITISH EMBASSY
Thomas Heftyesgate 8, 0244 Oslo
Tel: Oslo 22 55 24 00
Ambassador Extraordinary and Plenipotentiary, HE Mark Elliott, CMG, apptd 1994
Counsellor, E. J. Hughes (*Deputy Head of Mission and Consul-General*)
First Secretary, N. S. Archer (*Economic and Commercial*)
Defence and Naval Attaché, Lt-Col P. D. T. Irvine, OBE
BRITISH CONSULAR OFFICES – There is a British Consular Office at Oslo and Honorary Consulates at Bergen, Tromsø, Alesund, Kristiansund (North), Stavanger, Trondheim, Kristiansand (South), Haugesund and Harstad.

BRITISH COUNCIL REPRESENTATIVE, Rosalind Olsen, Fridtjof Nansens Plass 5, 0160, Oslo 1

DEFENCE

Norway is a member of NATO and the headquarters of Allied Forces Northern Europe is situated near Oslo. The total active armed forces number 30,000 (16,900 conscripts). Reserve forces number 255,000. The Army has a strength of 14,700 (9,200 conscripts), with 170 main battle tanks, 223 armoured infantry fighting vehicles and armoured personnel carriers, and 402 artillery pieces. The Navy has a strength of 6,400, including 3,600 conscripts, with 12 submarines, four frigates, and 30 patrol and coastal combatants. The Air Force has a strength of 7,900 (4,100 conscripts), with 80 combat aircraft. The period of compulsory national service is 12 months.

ECONOMY

The cultivated area is about 10,826 sq. km, 3.5 per cent of the total surface area. Forests cover nearly 23 per cent; the rest consists of highland pastures or uninhabitable mountains. The chief agricultural products are grain, potatoes, root vegetables, milk, furs and timber.

The Gulf Stream causes the sea temperature to be higher than the average for the latitude, which brings shoals of herring and cod into the fishing grounds. The quantity of fish caught by Norwegian fishing vessels is greater than that of any other European country except Russia. In 1993 the total catch amounted to 2,374,840 tonnes.

The chief industries are oil production and transport, construction, electricity supply, manufactures, agriculture and forestry, fisheries, mining, production of metals and ferro-alloys, and shipping. Industries providing both manufactured products and services for the development of North Sea oil and gas resources have become increasingly important. In 1994 129,321,000 tons of crude oil were produced, of which 111,336,000 tons were exported. Manufactures are aided by great resources of hydro-electric power. Actual production in 1994 amounted to 113,482 GWh. In 1994, the total workforce was 2,035,000 of which 5.6 per cent were employed in agriculture, forestry and fishing, 22.5 per cent in industry, construction and mining, and 71.6 in services.

FINANCE	1994	1995
Total revenue	K344,521m	K416,657m
Total expenditure	373,443m	431,434m

TRADE

The chief imports are raw materials, motor vehicles, chemicals, ships and machinery, foods and textiles. Exports consist chiefly of crude oil and gas, manufactured goods, fish and fish products (as canned fish, whale oils), pulp, paper, iron ore and pyrites, nitrate of lime, stone, calcium carbide, aluminium, ferro-alloys, zinc, nickel, cyanamides, etc. Norway's major trading partners are members of the EU.

	1993	1994
Total imports	K267,800m	K282,436m
Total exports	317,600m	334,746m

Trade with UK	1994	1995
Imports from UK	£2,020,878,000	£1,998,499,000
Exports to UK	3,709,666,000	4,325,432,000

EDUCATION

Education from seven to 16 is free and compulsory in the 'basic schools', and free from 16 to 19 years. The majority of the pupils receive post-compulsory schooling at 'upper secondary' schools, regional colleges akin to polytechnics (98), universities (five) and seven other university-level specialist colleges. In 1994–5 there were 160,000 students at universities and university-level institutions.

COMMUNICATIONS

The total length of railways open at the end of 1994 was 4,023 km, excluding private lines. There are 90,174 km of public roads in Norway (including urban streets). Scheduled internal air services are operated by Scandinavian Airlines System (SAS) on behalf of Det Norske Luftfartselskap (DNL), by Braathens South American and Far East Airtransport (SAFE), and by Widerões Flyveselskap AS. The mercantile marine in 1994 consisted of 1,642 vessels of 21,745,000 gross tons (vessels above 100 gross tons, excluding fishing boats, floating whaling factories, tugs, salvage vessels, icebreakers and similar types of vessel). In 1993 there were 149 daily newspapers.

TERRITORIES

SVALBARD

The Svalbard archipelago lies between 74° and 81° N. and between 10° and 35° E., with an estimated area of 24,295 sq. miles. The archipelago consists of the main island, Spitsbergen (15,200 sq. miles), North East Land, the Wiche Islands, Barents and Edge Islands, Prince Charles Foreland, Hope Island, Bear Island and many islands in the neighbourhood of the main group. Glaciers cover 60 per cent of the land area. South Cape is 355 miles from the Norwegian coast. Transit from Tromsø to Green Harbour takes two to three days.

The sovereignty of Norway over the archipelago was recognized by other nations in 1920 and in 1925 Norway assumed sovereignty. The 3,700 inhabitants are mainly engaged in coal-mining, but the islands are also visited by hunters for seals, foxes and polar bears.

JAN MAYEN ISLAND

Jan Mayen, an island in the Arctic Ocean (70° 49' to 71° 9' N. and 7° 53' to 9° 5' W.) was joined to Norway by law in 1930.

NORWEGIAN ANTARCTIC TERRITORIES

BOUVET ISLAND (54° 26' S. and 3° 24' E.) was declared a dependency of Norway in 1930.
PETER THE FIRST ISLAND (68° 48' S. and 90° 35' W.), was declared a dependency of Norway in 1931.
PRINCESS RAGNHILD LAND (from 70° 30' to 68° 40' S. and 24° 15' to 33° 30' E.) has been claimed as Norwegian since 1931.

QUEEN MAUD LAND – In 1939 the Norwegian Government declared the area between 20° W. and 45° E., adjacent to Australian Antarctica, to be Norwegian territory.

OMAN
The Sultanate of Oman

Oman lies at the eastern corner of the Arabian peninsula, bordered on the west by Yemen, Saudi Arabia and the UAE. To the north lies the Gulf of Oman and to the east the Arabian Sea, giving a coastline of nearly 1,000 miles. Sharjah and Fujairah (UAE) separate the main part of Oman from the northernmost part of the state, a peninsula extending into the Strait of Hormuz. The area has been estimated at 82,030 sq. miles (212,457 sq. km).

The north and the south of Oman are divided by nearly 400 miles of desert. The Batinah, the coastal plain, is fertile. The Hajjar is a mountain spine running from north-west to south-east and for the most part barren, but valleys penetrate the central massif which is irrigated by wells or a system of underground canals called *falajs* which tap the water table. The two plateaus leading from the western slopes of the mountains descend to the Empty Quarter of the Arabian Desert. Dhofar, the southern province, is the only part of the Arabian peninsula to be touched by the south-west monsoon. Temperatures are more moderate than in the north.

The population (1992 census) is 2,000,000. The inhabitants of the north are mostly Arab, though there are large communities of Hindus, Khojas and Baluch, in addition to Omanis of Zanzibari origin, especially around Salalah. However, in the mountains the inhabitants are either of pure Arab descent or belong to tribes of pre-Arab origin, the Qarra and Mahra, who speak their own dialects of Semitic origin.

CAPITAL – Ψ Muscat, estimated population 400,000. The commercial centre has grown around Mutrah, three miles away and the main port, and Ruwi. The main towns on the northern coast are ΨSur, ΨBarka and ΨSohar. The main town of Dhofar is Salalah.
CURRENCY – Rial Omani (OR) of 1,000 baiza.
FLAG – Red with a white panel in the upper fly and a green one in the lower fly; in the canton the national emblem in white.
NATIONAL DAY – 18 November.

GOVERNMENT

A State Consultative Council established in 1981 was replaced by Sultanic decree in 1991 by a *Majlis A' shura*, or State Advisory Council. This body, meeting twice a year, consists of a representative from each of the 59 wilayats, or governorates, of the Sultanate. The Council has the right to review legislation, question ministers and make policy proposals. Effective political power remains with the Sultan, who rules by decree and is advised by the Cabinet, which he appoints.

HEAD OF STATE

HM The Sultan of Oman, Sultan HM Qaboos Bin-Said, *succeeded* on deposition of Sultan Said bin Taimur, 23 July 1970

COUNCIL OF MINISTERS *as at August 1996*
Prime Minister, Foreign Affairs, Defence and Finance, The Sultan
Personal Representative of HM The Sultan, HH Sayyid Thuwainy bin Shihab Al Said

Deputy PM for Security and Defence, HH Sayyid Fahr bin Taimur al Said
Deputy PM for Cabinet Affairs, HH Sayyid Fahad bin Mahmood al Said
Minister of State for Legal Affairs, HE Mohammed bin Ali al Alawi
Minister of State and Governor of Dhofar, HE Sayyid Mussellam bin Ali Al Busaidi
Minister of State and Governor of Muscat, HE Sayyid Al Mutassim bin Hamoud Al Busaidi
Minister of State for Development Affairs, HE Mohammed bin Moosa al Yousef
National Heritage and Culture, HH Sayyid Faisal bin Ali al Said
Agriculture and Fisheries, HE Mohammed bin Abdallah bin Zaher al Hinai
Electricity and Water, HE Shaikh Mohammed bin Ali Al Qatabi
Water Resources, HE Hamed bin Said Al Aufi
Justice, Awqaf and Islamic Affairs, HE Hamoud bin Abdullah Al Harthi
Health, HE Dr Ali bin Mohammed bin Moosa
Petroleum and Minerals, HE Said bin Ahmed bin Said al Shanfari
Housing, HE Malik bin Suleiman al Ma'amari
Civil Service, HE Shaikh Abdullaziz bin Matar al-Azizi
Communications, HE Salim bin Abdullah Al Ghazali
Education, HE Saud bin Ibrahim bin Saud al-Busa'idi
Higher Education, HE Yahya bin Mahfoodh al Manthri
Interior, HE Sayyid Badr bin Sa'oud bin Hareb al Busaidi
Information, HE Abdul Aziz bin Mohammed al Rowas
Regional Municipalities and Environment, HE Shaikh Amer bin Shuwain al Hosni
Minister of State for Foreign Affairs, HE Yousuf bin Alawi bin Abdullah
Commerce and Industry, HE Maqbool bin Ali bin Sultan
Social Affairs and Labour, HE Ahmed bin Mohammed bin Salim Al Isa'ee
National Economy, HE Ahmed bin Abdul Nabi Macki
Posts, Telegraphs and Telephones, HE Ahmed bin Sweidan al Baluchi
Secretary-General to the Cabinet, HE Sayyid Hamoud bin Faisal bin Said
Diwan of Royal Court, HE Sayyid Saif bin Hamed bin Sa'oud
Palace Office Affairs, HE Gen. Ali bin Majid Al Ma'amari

EMBASSY OF THE SULTANATE OF OMAN
167 Queen's Gate, London SW7 5HE
Tel 0171-225 0001
Ambassador Extraordinary and Plenipotentiary, HE Hussain Ali Abdullatif, apptd 1995
Minister Plenipotentiary, Ghassan Ibrahim Shaker
Military Attaché, Col. Said Hassan Al-Shedad

BRITISH EMBASSY
PO Box 300, Muscat
Tel: Muscat 693-77
Ambassador Extraordinary and Plenipotentiary, HE Richard John Muir, CMG, apptd 1994
Counsellor, N. J. Guckian (*Deputy Head of Mission*)
Defence and Military Attaché, Brig. M. I. Keun
First Secretary (Commercial), P. Williams
Consul, Mrs G. Brown

BRITISH COUNCIL DIRECTOR, Clive Bruton, PO Box 73, Muscat, Oman. There are also offices at *Salalah* and *Sohar.*

DEFENCE

The total active armed forces strength is 43,500 personnel. Service is voluntary. The Army has a strength of 25,000 personnel, with 91 main battle tanks, 37 light tanks and 102 artillery pieces. The Navy has 4,200 personnel, and 12 patrol and coastal vessels. The Air Force has 4,200 personnel and 46 combat aircraft. The Royal Household has 6,500 personnel formed into a Royal Guard brigade, two special forces regiments, the Royal Yacht Squadron and the Royal Flight. In addition there is the paramilitary home guard (*Firqat*) of 4,000 personnel. Some 3,700 hired and seconded personnel (many British) serve in the Omani armed forces.

ECONOMY

Although there is considerable cultivation in the fertile areas and cattle are raised on the mountains, the backbone of the economy is the oil industry. Petroleum Development (Oman) Ltd (owned 60 per cent by Oman Government and 34 per cent by Shell) began exporting oil in 1967. Concessions (off and on shore) are held by several major international companies. The current level of oil production is about 650,000 barrels per day, planned to increase to 700,000.

A gas turbine power station operates at Rusail, where there is also a 200-plot industrial estate. There is a power station and a desalination plant near Muscat and flour, animal feed, cement and copper production facilities.

TRADE

Trade is mainly with the UAE, UK, Japan, the Netherlands, USA, Germany, France and India. Chief imports are machinery, cars, building materials, food and telecommunications equipment.

Trade with UK	1994	1995
Imports from UK	£362,129,000	£447,922,000
Exports to UK	78,273,000	74,232,000

COMMUNICATIONS

Port Qaboos at Matrah has eight deep-water berths which have been constructed as part of the harbour facilities. A modern telecommunications service to the main population centres and an international service are operated by the General Telecommunications Organization. There are good tarmac roads linking most main population centres of the country with the coast and with the towns of the UAE, though only a trunk road links the north and south of Oman.

SOCIAL WELFARE

For many years the Sultanate was a poor country but the advent of oil revenues and the change of regime in 1970 led to the initiation of a wide-ranging development programme, especially concerned with health, education and communications. There are now nearly 50 hospitals with around 3,400 beds; 823 schools, with 387,000 pupils, were in operation in 1992.

PAKISTAN
Islami Jamhuriya-e-Pakistan

Pakistan is situated in the north-west of the Indian subcontinent, bordered by Iran, Afghanistan, China, the disputed territory of Kashmir, and India. It covers a total area (including Pakistan-controlled Kashmir) of 341,026 sq. miles (883,254 sq km). Running through Pakistan are five great rivers, the Indus, Jhelum, Chenab, Ravi and

Sutlej. The upper reaches of these rivers are in Kashmir, and their sources in the Himalayas.

The census in 1981 showed a population figure of 83,780,000 (1994 UN estimate, 126,284,000). Of these, about 95 per cent are Muslims, 3.5 per cent Christians, about 1 per cent Hindus, and 0.5 per cent Buddhists. Urdu is the national language, but is only spoken by a small minority of the population. The most widely used language is Punjabi, followed by Sindi and Pushto. English is used in business, government and higher education.

CAPITAL – Islamabad, population 350,000. ψKarachi (estimated population 7,183,000) is the largest city and seaport; Lahore has a population of 4,072,000.

CURRENCY – Pakistan rupee of 100 paisa.

FLAG – Green with a white crescent and star, and a white vertical strip in the hoist

NATIONAL ANTHEM – Quami Tarana.

NATIONAL DAYS – 23 March (Pakistan Day), 14 August (Independence Day).

GOVERNMENT

Pakistan was constituted as a Dominion under the Indian Independence Act 1947, becoming a republic on 23 March 1956. Until 1972 Pakistan consisted of two geographical units, West and East Pakistan, separated by about 1,100 miles of Indian territory. East Pakistan's insistence on complete autonomy led to civil war, which broke out on 25 March 1971 and continued until December 1971 when a cease-fire was arranged. The independence of East Pakistan as Bangladesh was proclaimed in April 1972. Under the 1972 Simla Agreement with India, a line of control was established in Kashmir; Pakistan controls an area of 33,653 sq. miles (87,159 sq. km) to the north and west of the line.

The armed forces under Gen. Zia-ul-Haq assumed power in 1977 and martial law was in force from July 1977 to March 1985. Gen. Zia declared himself President in September 1978, but was killed in a plane crash in August 1988. The Pakistan People's Party (PPP) won the election to the National Assembly and Benazir Bhutto became Prime Minister. In August 1990 the President dissolved the National Assembly and dismissed the Bhutto Cabinet. Elections were held in October 1990 and won by the Islamic Democratic Alliance, led by Mian Muhammad Nawaz Sharif.

In July 1993, the Army intervened to end a power struggle between President Ishaq Khan and Prime Minister Sharif by replacing them with a caretaker administration until new elections were held in October. These were won by the PPP and Benazir Bhutto resumed the premiership. The PPP candidate Farooq Leghari was elected President by an electoral college of the National and provincial assemblies.

INSURGENCY

Since early 1994 there has been civil disorder in Sind province, especially in Karachi, in two conflicts: armed militants of the Mohajir Qaumi Movement (MQM) Party, which represents Urdu-speaking Indian Muslims who fled from India at partition and their descendants, are fighting for an autonomous Karachi province; and there is an armed conflict between Shia and Sunni fundamentalists. More than 2,000 people died in politically-inspired violence in Karachi in 1995, despite government attempts to negotiate with the MQM.

HEAD OF STATE

President, Farooq Ahmad Khan Leghari, *elected* 13 November 1993

FEDERAL CABINET *as at August 1996*

Prime Minister, Minister of Finance, Benazir Bhutto
Defence, Aftab Shahban Mirani
Foreign Affairs, Aseff Ahmad Ali
Industries and Production, Brig. (retd) Muhammad Asghar
Interior, Maj.-Gen. (retd) Nasirullah Khan Babar
Kashmir and Northern Affairs, Muhammad Afzal Khan
Law and Justice, Prof. N. D. Khan
Social Welfare and Special Education, Dr Sher Afghan Khan Niazi
Petroleum and Natural Resources, Anwar Saifullah Khan
Information and Broadcasting, Khalid Ahmad Khan Kharal
Education, Khurshid Ahmed Shah
Works, Makhdoom Mohammed Amin Fahim
Food, Agriculture and Livestock, Mohammed Yousef Talpur
Water and Power, Ghulam Mustafa Khar
Commerce, Chaudhry Ahmed Mukhtar
Population Welfare, Julius Salik
Minister without Portfolio, Abdul Qadir Jilani
Narcotics Control, Arbab Muhammad Jehangir Khan
Sports and Tourism, Sikandar Iqbal
Science and Technology, Muhammad Nawaz
Political and Religious Affairs, Jehangir Bader
Industries, Abdul Sattar
Human Rights, Iqbal Haider
Investment, Asif Ali Zardari
Privatization, Syed Naveed Qamar
Ministers of State, Makhdoom Shahabuddin (*Finance*); Ghulam Akbar Lasi (*Labour and Manpower*); Abdul Qayyum Khan (*States and Frontier Region*); Raza Rabbani (*Law and Justice*); Shah Mahmood Qureshi (*Parliamentary Affairs*); Muhammad Nazeer Sultan (*Foreign Affairs*); Nauraiz Shakoor Khan (*Youth*); Muhammad Nasir Baig (*Sports*); Muhammad Afaque Khan Shahid (*Works*); Manzoor Hussain Wassan (*Water*); Muhammad Ayub Jattak (*Food*); Muhammad Yaqub Khan (*Local Government and Rural Development*)

HIGH COMMISSION FOR PAKISTAN
35–36 Lowndes Square, London SWIX 9JN
Tel 0171-235 2044
High Commissioner, HE Wajid Shamsul Hassan, apptd 1994
Deputy High Commissioner, M. J. Naim
Minister, K. Shafi
Consul-General, M. Nisar
Defence and Naval Attaché, A. U. Khan
Counsellor, M. A. Tahir (*Commercial*)

BRITISH HIGH COMMISSION
Diplomatic Enclave, Ramna 5, PO Box 1122, Islamabad
Tel: Islamabad 822131/5
High Commissioner, HE Sir Christopher MacRae, KCMG, apptd 1994
Deputy High Commissioners, J. W. Watt (*Islamabad*); E. W. Callway (*Karachi*)
Counsellor (Economical and Commercial), S. N. Evans, OBE
Counsellor, A. J. C. Boyd
Defence and Military Adviser, Brig. R. D. O'Lone

There is a British Deputy High Commission at Karachi and a Consulate at Lahore.

BRITISH COUNCIL REPRESENTATIVE, Peter Elborn, OBE, PO Box 1135, Islamabad. There are offices at Karachi, Lahore and Peshawar.

DEFENCE

In August 1994 former Prime Minister Nawaz Sharif stated that Pakistan had constructed a nuclear weapon, although the government denies US allegations that China is assisting in the manufacture of a medium-range missile system.

Pakistan has a total armed forces active strength of 587,000 personnel, with a further 513,000 reserves. The Army has a strength of 520,000 personnel, with 2,050 main battle tanks, 1,019 armoured personnel carriers, 1,806 artillery pieces and 20 attack helicopters. The Navy has 22,000 personnel, with nine submarines, three destroyers, eight frigates, 13 patrol and coastal vessels, four combat aircraft and 13 armed helicopters. The Air Force has 45,000 personnel, and 430 combat aircraft. In addition, there are 257,000 paramilitary personnel in four organizations.

ECONOMY

The economy is based on agriculture. The principal crops are cotton, rice, wheat, sugar cane. Pakistan has one of the longest irrigation systems in the world. The total area irrigated is 42.5 million acres. There are large deposits of rock salt.

Pakistan also produces hides and skins, leather, wool, fertilizers, paints and varnishes, soda ash, paper, cement, fish, carpets, sports goods, surgical appliances and engineering goods, including switchgear, transformers, cables and wires.

An agreement was reached in 1993 with the IMF for a three-year loan of US$1,320 million on implementation of an austerity and structural adjustment programme. This has led to the lowering of the foreign debt, inflation and the budget deficit (5.5 per cent of GDP in 1994–5). Privatization and economic deregulation begun under Bhutto's 1988–90 government has continued. The IMF suspended the agreement in February 1995 after the government announced its proposed budget, although a US$596 million standby credit was negotiated in December 1995, before austerity measures were reintroduced.

TRADE

Principal imports are petroleum products, machinery, fertilizers, transport equipment, edible oils, chemicals and ferrous metals. Principal exports are raw cotton, cotton yarn and cloth, carpets, rice, petroleum products, synthetic textiles, leather, and fish.

Trade with UK	1994	1995
Imports from UK	£355,058,000	£340,382,000
Exports to UK	358,879,000	363,068,000

COMMUNICATIONS

The main seaport is Karachi. The main airports are at Karachi, Islamabad, Lahore, Peshawar and Quetta. Pakistan International Airlines operates air services between the principal cities as well as abroad. There are 179,752 km of roads and 8,163 km of rail track.

EDUCATION

Education consists of five years of primary education (five to nine years), three years of middle or lower secondary (general or vocational), two years of upper secondary, two years of higher secondary (intermediate) and two to five years of higher education in colleges and universities. Education is free to upper secondary level. Illiteracy was 64 per cent in 1992.

PALAU
Republic of Palau

The Republic of Palau consists of 340 islands and islets in the western Pacific Ocean, of which eight are inhabited. Part of the Caroline Islands group, the Palau archipelago stretches over 400 miles (644 km) between 2° and 8°N., and 131° and 138°E. Koror island is about 810 miles (1,300 km) south-west of Guam and about 530 miles (852 km) south-east of Manila. The total land area is 177 sq. miles (458 sq. km), and Babelthaup is by far the largest island. The islands vary in terrain from the highly mountainous to low coral atolls. The climate is tropical with a rainy season lasting from June to October; the average temperature is 27°C (80°F).

The population (1990 census) is 15,122, of which 13,900 live on Koror and Babelthaup. The population is Micronesian, and predominantly Roman Catholic with a Protestant minority. Both Palauan and English are official languages.

CAPITAL – Koror, population 10,493.
CURRENCY – US dollar.
FLAG – Light blue with a yellow disc set neat the hoist.

HISTORY

Spain acquired sovereignty over the Caroline Islands, of which the Palau archipelago is part, in 1886. After defeat in the Spanish-American war of 1898, Spain sold its remaining Pacific possessions, including Palau, to Germany in 1899. On the outbreak of the First World War in 1914 Japan took control of Palau on behalf of the Allied powers, and Japanese administration was confirmed in a League of Nations mandate in 1921. During the Second World War Allied forces gained control of the archipelago after intense fighting. In 1947 the USA entered into agreement with the UN Security Council to administer the Micronesia area, including Palau, as the UN Trust Territory of the Pacific Islands.

In July 1978 the Palau electorate voted in a referendum not to join the new Federated States of Micronesia and instead became a separate part of the UN Trust Territory. A Compact of Free Association was signed with the USA in 1982, which allowed the entry of US nuclear waste and weapons into Palau in contravention of the 1979 constitution. A referendum in November 1993 amended the constitution to enable the implementation of the Compact on 1 October 1994. Under this agreement the USA recognized the Republic of Palau as a fully sovereign and independent state and the UN Trust Territory of the Pacific Islands was terminated. Palau was admitted to UN membership in December 1994.

GOVERNMENT

Under the 1981 constitution, Palau is a democracy with separate executive, legislative and judicial branches of government. Executive power is vested in the President and Vice-President, who are elected for four-year terms; the President appoints the Cabinet. There is a bicameral legislature (*Olbiil Era Kekulau*) composed of the 16-member House of Delegates (one member elected from each of the 16 constituent states) and the 14-member Senate. There is also a Council of Chiefs to advise the President on matters concerning traditional law and customs. The judiciary consists of a Supreme Court, a National Court and lesser courts. Each of the 16 component states have their own elected governors and legislatures. The last presidential and legislative elections were held in November 1992.

Palau maintains no defence forces. The Compact of Free Association places responsibility for the defence of Palau on the USA for 50 years.

HEAD OF STATE
President, Kuniwo Nakamura, *elected* 4 November 1992
Vice-President, Tommy Remengesau

ECONOMY

The economy remains heavily dependent on US financial support, which the USA is committed to giving under the Compact. Fisheries, tourism, subsistence agriculture and government service are the main areas of employment. Agricultural products include coconuts and copra, and Palau earns significant revenue from the sale of fishing licences to foreign fleets fishing for tuna. Tourism is being developed; there were 26,000 visitors in 1989.

The USA carried out an infrastructure improvement programme in the 1970s and 1980s. There are now three airports on Koror, Peleliu and Angaur which have daily flights from Guam operated by Continental Air Micronesia. Ocean freight services to Palau are provided by two shipping lines to the port at Koror. A communications centre on Arakabesang Island handles international telephone, telex, cable and facsimile communications. There is a privately owned television station and a government-operated radio station.

SOCIAL WELFARE

There is a free public school system which, together with independent missionary schools, provides primary and secondary education. A tertiary technical school has been established on Koror since 1969. General medical and dental care is provided by a public hospital and a medical clinic.

PANAMA
República de Panama

Panama lies on the isthmus of that name which connects North and South America. The area is 29,762 sq. miles (77,082 sq. km), the population (1995 estimate) 2,631,013. Spanish is the official language.

CAPITAL – ΨPanama City, population (1990) 1,064,221.
CURRENCY – Balboa of 100 centésimos (at parity with the US dollar). US$ notes are also in circulation.
FLAG – Four quarters; white with blue star (top, next staff), red (in fly), blue (below, next staff) and white with red star.
NATIONAL ANTHEM – Alcanzamos Por Fin La Victoria (Victory is ours at last).
NATIONAL DAY – 3 November.

GOVERNMENT

After a revolt in 1903, Panama declared its independence from Colombia and established a separate government. After 1968, control of Panama was increasingly taken over by Gen. Omar Torrijos, commander of the National Guard, following a military coup. In 1978 Gen. Torrijos withdrew from the government, and Dr Aristides Royo was elected President by the Assembly of Representatives.

An attempt in February 1988 by President Delvalle to remove Gen. Noriega as Commander of the Defence Forces failed. Noriega ousted Delvalle and replaced him

with Manuel Solis Palma. Presidential elections were held in May 1989 but Noriega annulled the results, which appeared to give victory to the opposition and on 15 December he assumed power formally as head of state. On 20 December US troops invaded Panama to oust Noriega. Guillermo Endara, believed to have won the May elections, was installed as President. In December 1991 the Legislative Assembly approved a change to the constitution which abolished the armed forces.

Legislative power is vested in a unicameral Legislative Assembly of 72 members; executive power is held by the President, assisted by two elected Vice-Presidents and an appointed Cabinet. Elections are held every five years under a system of universal and compulsory adult suffrage. The last presidential election was held on 8 May 1994 and won by Ernesto Pérez Balladares of the Democratic Revolutionary Party (PRD) who appointed the government.

HEAD OF STATE
President, Ernesto Pérez Balladares, *elected* 8 May 1994, *sworn in* 1 September 1994
First Vice-President, Tomas Gabriel Altamirano Duque
Second Vice-President, Felipe Alejandro Virzi

CABINET *as at August 1996*
Interior and Justice, Raúl Montenegro
Foreign Affairs, Ricardo A. Arias
Public Works, Luis Blanco
Finance and Treasury, Olmedo Miranda
Education, Dr Pablo Thalassinos
Labour and Social Welfare, Mitchell Doens
Health, Aida de Rivera
Commerce and Industry, Nitzia de Villareal
Housing, Dr Francisco Sánchez Cárdenas
Agricultural Development, Carlos Sousa-Lennox
Economy and Planning, Dr Guillermo Chapman
Presidency, Raúl Arango

EMBASSY OF THE REPUBLIC OF PANAMA
48 Park Street, London WIY 3PD
Tel 0171-493 4646
Ambassador Extraordinary and Plenipotentiary, HE Aquilino Boyd de la Guardia, apptd 1994

BRITISH EMBASSY
Torre Swiss Bank, Calle 53 (Apartado 889) Zona 1, Panama City, Panama 1
Tel: Panama City 269-0866
Ambassador Extraordinary and Plenipotentiary, HE William B. Sinton, apptd 1996

ECONOMY

GDP was US$5,496.4 million in 1991, of which 71 per cent was contributed by services, 17 per cent by industry and 12 per cent by agriculture. GDP grew by almost 4 per cent in 1994, although external debt remained high at US$6,802.2 million.

The soil is moderately fertile, but nearly one-half of the land is uncultivated. The chief crops are bananas, sugar, coconuts, cacao, coffee and cereals. The shrimping industry plays an important role in the economy. In 1992 tourism became the principal foreign currency earner, ahead of bananas. A railway joins the Atlantic and Pacific oceans.

Education is compulsory and free from seven to 15 years.

TRADE

Imports are mostly manufactured goods, machinery, lubricants, chemicals and foodstuffs. Exports are bananas, petroleum products, shrimps, sugar, meat and fishmeal.

Republic of Panama	1992	1993
Imports	US$2,108,424m	US$2,187,376m
Imports	480,912m	507,606m
Colon Free Zone		
Imports	US$4,364,054m	US$4,495,687m
Re-Exports	4,826,386m	5,150,552m
Trade with UK†	1994	1995
Imports from UK	£48,614,000	£67,975,000
Exports to UK	7,139,000	2,553,000

†Including Colon Free Zone

THE PANAMA CANAL ZONE

With effect from 1 October 1979 the Canal Zone (647 sq. miles) was disestablished, with all areas of land and water within the Zone reverting to Panama. By the 1977 treaty with the USA, the USA is allowed the use of operating bases for the Panama Canal, together with several military bases, but the Republic of Panama is sovereign in all such areas. Control of the Canal will revert to Panama at noon on 31 December 1999.

DEPENDENCIES

Taboga Island (area 4 sq. miles) is a popular tourist resort some 12 miles from the Pacific entrance to the Panama Canal.

Tourist facilities have also been developed in the Las Perlas Archipelago in the Gulf of Panama, particularly on the island of Contadora.

There is a penal settlement at Guardia on the island of Coiba (area 19 sq. miles) in the Gulf of Chiriqui.

PAPUA NEW GUINEA

Papua New Guinea extends from the Equator to Cape Baganowa in the Louisiade Archipelago at 11° S. latitude and from the border with Irian Jaya to 160° E. longitude. The total area is 178,260 sq. miles, (461,691 sq. km), of which approximately 152,420 sq. miles form the mainland on the island of New Guinea. The country has many island groups, principally the Bismarck Archipelago, a portion of the Solomon Islands, the Trobriands, the D'Entrecasteaux Islands and the Louisiade Archipelago. The main islands of the Bismarck Archipelago are New Britain, New Ireland and Manus. Bougainville is the largest of the Solomon Islands within Papua New Guinea.

Papua New Guinea lies within the tropics and has a typically monsoonal climate. Temperature and humidity are uniformly high throughout the year.

The population in 1994 (UN estimate) was 4,205,000.

CAPITAL – ΨPort Moresby. Estimated population (1990), 173,500. Other major towns are Lae, Rabaul, Madang, Wewak, Goroka and Mount Hagen.

CURRENCY – Kina (K) of 100 toea.

FLAG – Divided diagonally red (fly) and black (hoist); on the red a soaring Bird of Paradise in yellow and on the black five white stars of the Southern Cross.

NATIONAL ANTHEM – Arise All You Sons.

NATIONAL DAY – 16 September (Independence Day).

GOVERNMENT

New Guinea was sighted by Portuguese and Spanish navigators in the early 16th century, but remained largely isolated from the rest of the world. In 1884 a British Protectorate, British New Guinea, was proclaimed over the southern coast of New Guinea (Papua) and the adjacent islands, which were annexed outright in 1888. In 1906 the Territory of British New Guinea was placed under the authority of Australia.

In 1884 Germany had formally taken possession of certain northern areas, later known as the Trust Territory of New Guinea. In 1914 the German areas were occupied by Australian troops and remained under military administration until 1921, when they became a League of Nations mandate administered by Australia. New Guinea was administered under the mandate and Papua under the Papua Act until the invasion by the Japanese in 1942 when the civil administration was suspended until the Japanese surrendered in 1945.

From 1970 there was a gradual assumption of powers by the Papua New Guinea government, culminating in formal self-government in December 1973. Papua New Guinea achieved full independence within the Commonwealth on 16 September 1975.

Elections are held every five years. The Parliament comprises 109 elected members, 20 from regional electorates, the remainder from open electorates. The Governor-General is appointed by Parliament for a six-year term. Provincial governments were abolished in August 1995, and replaced with councils combining local and national politicians and headed by an appointed governor.

SECESSION

Separatist aspirations, dormant since independence, re-emerged in 1989 when the Bougainville Revolutionary Army (BRA) mounted a successful insurrection. Government security forces withdrew from the island, enabling the BRA to declare an independent republic in May 1990. A peace accord was signed in January 1991, although the question of Bougainville's status was left unresolved. Fighting resumed and government forces returned to the island in October 1992, subsequently capturing 90 per cent of rebel-held territory. The government launched a new offensive in June 1996 after peace talks failed to produce a breakthrough. At least 7,000 people, mostly civilians, have died as a result of the insurrection.

Governor-General, HE Sir Wiwa Korowi, GCMG, *appointed* 18 November 1991

NATIONAL EXECUTIVE COUNCIL *as at August 1996*

Prime Minister, Foreign Affairs and Trade, Rt. Hon. Sir Julius Chan, GCMG, KBE
Deputy PM, Planning, Hon. Chris Haiveta
Administrative Services, Hon. Paul Tohian
Agriculture and Livestock, Hon. David Mai
Civil Aviation, Culture, and Tourism, Hon. Michael Nali
Commerce and Industry, Hon. Nakikus Konga
Communications, Hon. Joseph Egilio
Correctional Services, Hon. Paul Wanjik
Defence, Hon. Mathias Ijape
Education, Hon. John Waiko
Environment, Hon. Paul Mambei
Fisheries and Marine Resources, Hon. Titus Philemon
Foreign Affairs and Trade, Hon. Kilroy Genia
Forests, Hon. Andrew Baing
Heath, Hon. Philemon Embel
Home Affairs, Hon. David Unagi
Housing, Hon. Robert Nagle
Industrial Relations, Hon. Samson Napo
Justice, Hon. Arnold Marsipal
Lands, Hon. Sir Albert Kipalan, KBE
Mining and Petroleum, Hon. John Giheno, CMG
National Planning, Hon. Moi Avei
Police, Hon. Castan Maibawa

Provincial and Local Governments, Hon. Peter Barter
Public Service, Hon. Joseph Onguglo
Transport and Works, Hon. Peter Yama
Minister of State, Hon. Parry Zeipi

PAPUA NEW GUINEA HIGH COMMISSION
3rd Floor, 14 Waterloo Place, London SWIR 4AR
Tel 0171-930 0922/7
High Commissioner, HE Sir Kina Bona, KBE, apptd 1995

BRITISH HIGH COMMISSION
PO Box 212, Waigani NCD 131, Port Moresby
Tel: Port Moresby 251677
High Commissioner, HE Robert Low, CBE, apptd 1994

ECONOMY

Until the 1970s the economy was based almost entirely on agriculture, principally copra, cocoa, tea, coffee, palm oil, rubber, groundnuts, spices and timber. A variety of commercial agricultural developments co-exist with the traditional rural economy. In 1995, the government initiated an austerity programme intended to reduce the budget deficit, privatize state assets and eliminate trade tariffs. The IMF approved a US$111 million credit to support the programme in July 1995.

There are extensive mineral deposits throughout Papua New Guinea, including copper, gold, silver, nickel, chromite, bauxite and possibly commercial deposits of oil and gas. In 1972, Bougainville Copper Pty Ltd (BCL) began mining in the North Solomons province, producing copper, silver and gold. The Bougainville copper mine closed indefinitely in 1989 because of the unrest on the island. The most important new developments are the exploitation of large copper and gold deposits on the Ok Tedi, in the Western province and the development of a gold mine on Lihir island with an estimated reserve of 42.5 million ounces, where production is planned to begin in 1998.

Industry includes processing of primary products, and brewing, bottling and packaging, paint, plywood, and metal manufacturing and the construction industries.

TRADE WITH UK	1994	1995
Imports from UK	£9,074,000	£10,849,000
Exports to UK	56,981,000	97,391,000

COMMUNICATIONS

Air Niugini operates regular air services to other countries in the region. Internal air services are operated by Air Niugini, Douglas Airways, and Talair. Several shipping companies operate cargo services to Australia, Europe, the Far East and USA. There are very limited cargo and passenger services between Papua New Guinea main ports, outports, plantations and missions. Road communications are very limited, the most important road being that linking Lae with the populous highlands. Papua New Guinea is linked by international cable to Australia, Guam, Hong Kong, Kota Kinabalu, the Far East and USA. Telecommunications are widely available.

PARAGUAY
República del Paraguay

Paraguay is an inland subtropical state of South America, situated between Argentina, Bolivia and Brazil. The area is estimated at 157,048 sq. miles (406,752 sq. km). It is a country of grassy plains and forested hills. In the angle formed by the Paraná-Paraguay confluence are extensive marshes, one of which, known as Neembucú (or endless) is drained by Lake Ypoa, a large lagoon south-east of the capital. The Chaco, lying between the rivers Paraguay and Pilcomayo and bounded on the north by Bolivia, is a flat plain, rising uniformly towards its western boundary to a height of 1,140 feet; it suffers much from floods and still more from drought, but the building of dams and reservoirs has converted part of it into good pasture for cattle.

The population (1994 UN estimate) is 4,830,000. Spanish is the official language of the country but outside the larger towns Guaraní, the language of the largest single group of original Indian inhabitants, is widely spoken, and is also an official language.

CAPITAL – Asunción, population (1985 census) 729,307; other centres are Ciudad del Este (98,491); Encarnación (31,445); Concepción (25,607); P. Juan Caballero (41,475).

CURRENCY – Guaraní (Gs) of 100 céntimos.

FLAG – Three horizontal bands, red, white, blue with the National seal on the obverse white band and the Treasury seal on the reverse white band.

NATIONAL ANTHEM – Paraguayos, República O Muerte (Paraguayans, republic or death).

NATIONAL DAY – 15 May.

GOVERNMENT

In 1535 Paraguay was settled as a Spanish possession. In 1811 it declared its independence from Spain.

The constitution provides for a two-chamber legislature consisting of a 45-member Senate and an 80-member Chamber of Deputies. Deputies are elected on a regional basis, the number of seats allocated to each regional department being directly proportional to the department's population. Voting is compulsory for all citizens over 18. The President is elected for a five-year term and may not be re-elected. The Vice-President may only contest the presidency if he resigns his post six months before the election. The President appoints the Cabinet, which exercises all the functions of government.

Gen. Alfredo Stroessner, dictator from 1954, was overthrown in February 1989 by Gen. Andrés Rodríguez, who was elected President in May 1989. In May 1991, the first free municipal elections were held, and elections to the parliament were held in December 1991. Amendments to the constitution came into effect in June 1992. The last presidential and legislative elections were held on 9 May 1993. The presidential election was won by Juan Carlos Wasmosy (Colorado Party). In the legislative election, the distribution of seats in the senate was: the ruling Colorado Party (ANR-PC) 20; Authentic Radical Liberal Party (PLRA) 17; National Encounter (EN) eight. In the Chamber of Deputies, the distribution of seats was: ANR-PC 40, PLRA 32, EN eight. An attempt by Gen. Lino Oviedo to oust the President was thwarted in April 1996.

HEAD OF STATE
President, Juan Carlos Wasmosy, *elected* 9 May 1993, *sworn in* 15 August 1993

CABINET *as at August 1996*
Foreign Affairs, Ruben Melgarejo Lan
Interior, Juan Morales
Finance, Carlos Facetti
Education, Nicanor Duarte Frutos
Agriculture and Livestock, Juan Borgognon
Public Works and Communications, Gustavo Pedrozo
National Defence, Hugo Estigarribia Elizeche
Public Health and Social Welfare, Andrés Vidovich
Justice and Labour, Sebastian Gonzalez
Industry and Commerce, Ubaldo Scavone

EMBASSY OF PARAGUAY
EMBASSY OF PARAGUAY
Braemar Lodge, Cornwall Gardens, London SW7 4AQ
Tel 0171-937 1253
Ambassador Extraordinary and Plenipotentiary, HE
 Washington Ashwell, apptd 1995

BRITISH EMBASSY
Calle Presidente Franco 706 (PO Box 404), Asunción
Tel: Asunción 444472
*Ambassador Extraordinary and Plenipotentiary and Consul-
General*, HE Graham Pirnie, apptd 1995

ECONOMY

President Rodríguez introduced an economic liberalization programme which has been continued by the
Wasmosy government. This has reduced foreign debt and
attracted foreign investment. About three-quarters of the
population are engaged in agriculture and cattle raising.
Cassava, sugar cane, soya, corn, cotton and wheat are the
main agricultural products. The forests contain many
varieties of timber which find a good market abroad.

Paraguay's rivers give it considerable hydroelectric
capacity. There is a hydroelectric power station at Acaray
which exports surplus power to Argentina and Brazil. Joint
projects have been undertaken with Brazil, on a hydro-
electric dam at Itaipú (the largest in the world), and with
Argentina, at Yacyretá.

TRADE

The chief imports are machinery; fuels and lubricants;
transport and accessories; and drinks and tobacco. The
chief exports are soya bean, cotton fibres, meat and coffee.

Trade with UK	1994	1995
Imports from UK	£48,935,000	£66,430,000
Exports to UK	3,321,000	3,468,000

COMMUNICATIONS

There are direct shipping services from Asunción to
Europe and the USA, and river steamer services for
internal transport and to Argentina. Eight airlines operate
services from Asunción. There are 27,741 km (1990) of
asphalted roads in Paraguay, connecting Asunción with
São Paulo (26 hours) via the Bridge of Friendship and Foz
de Yguazú, and with Buenos Aires (24 hours) via Puerto
Pilcomayo, and about 4,050 miles of earth roads liable to be
closed or to become impassable in wet weather. A 1,000 km
road links Asunción with the Bolivian border. Rail services,
with train ferries, provide internal and international links.
Four daily and five weekly newspapers are published in
Asunción.

EDUCATION

Education is free and compulsory. In 1993 there were 5,172
primary schools with 798,981 pupils and 33,061 teachers.
There were 214,272 pupils undergoing secondary edu-
cation and 20,793 teachers. The National University in
Asunción had 20,343 students in 1984. The Catholic
University had 10,971 students.

PERU
República del Peru

Peru is a maritime republic of South America, situated
between 0° 00′ 48″ and 18° 21′ 00″ S. latitude and between
68° 39′ 27″ and 81° 20′ 13″ W. longitude. The area is
496,225 sq. miles (1,285,216 sq. km). The country is
traversed throughout its length by the Andes, running
parallel to the Pacific coast. There are three main regions,
the Costa, west of the Andes, the Sierra or mountain ranges
of the Andes, which include the Punas or mountainous
wastes below the region of perpetual snow, and the
Montaña or Selva, which is the vast area of jungle
stretching from the eastern foothills of the Andes to the
eastern frontiers of Peru. The coastal area, lying upon and
near the Pacific, is not tropical though close to the Equator,
being cooled by the Humboldt Current.

The population (1994 estimate) is 22,331,000. Spanish,
the language of the original Spanish stock from which the
governing and professional classes are mainly recruited is
an official language, together with Quechua and Aymará.
Quechua and Aymará are spoken by more than half the
population.

CAPITAL – Metropolitan Lima (including ΨCallao),
 population census (1993) 6,483,901. Other major cities
 are: Arequipa (820,471) and Trujillo (508,715).
CURRENCY – Nuevo Sol 100 cents.
FLAG – Three vertical stripes of red, white, red.
NATIONAL ANTHEM – Somos Libres, Seámoslo Siempre
 (We are free, let us remain so forever).
NATIONAL DAY – 28 July (Anniversary of
 Independence).

GOVERNMENT

Peru was conquered in the early 16th century by Francisco
Pizarro (1478–1541). He subjugated the Incas (the ruling
caste of the Quechua Indians), who had started their rise to
power some 500 years earlier, and for nearly three
centuries Peru remained under Spanish rule. A revolutionary war of 1821–4 established its independence,
declared on 28 July 1821. A military junta ruled Peru
from 1968 until 1980 when civilian government was
restored. In April 1992 President Fujimori, faced with
increasing terrorist violence, suspended the constitution,
dissolved Congress and began to govern by decree. A
programme of market-orientated economic reform, new
anti-terrorist measures, and a streamlining of the executive, legislative and judicial institutions was undertaken. In
November 1992 a legislative election was held to an 80
seat Democratic Constituent Congress (CCD) which was
installed as an interim legislature and constituent assembly
to write a new constitution. Parties supporting Fujimori's
suspension of the constitution gained a majority in the
CCD. In January 1993 the 1979 constitution was re-
established and the CCD declared Fujimori constitutional
head of state. The CCD produced a new constitution
which was endorsed in a national referendum in October
1993. The constitution, promulgated in December 1993,
provides for the President to be able to serve two terms
rather than one, as previously; the introduction of the
death penalty for terrorists; and the formation of a new
120-member unicameral Congress. A constitutional panel
approved a Bill in August 1996, allowing President
Fujimori to stand for a third term in office.

Parliamentary and presidential elections were held on 9
April 1995, with President Fujimori winning the first
round of the presidential election outright and his Cambio
90-Nueva Mayoría Party winning 67 out of 120 seats in the
new Congress.

INSURGENCY

Since the late 1970s the government has faced violence
from drug organizations and insurgencies from two leftist
guerrilla movements, the Maoist Sendero Luminoso
(Shining Path) and the Movimiento Revolucionario Tapac
Amaru (MRTA). Some areas of the country remain under

states of emergency, but the capture of the leaders of both groups in 1992 and the anti-terrorist clampdown from 1992 to 1994 has reduced violence considerably. The Shining Path continues to launch attacks on security forces and infrastructure and has engaged in mass intimidation and execution campaigns in rural areas, with fighting having left 30,000 dead. In mid-1995 the Shining Path joined forces with drugs organizations in the north of the country as a means of continuing to fund their guerrillas.

HEAD OF STATE

President of the Republic, Alberto Fujimori, *assumed office* 28 July 1990, *re-elected* 9 April 1995, *sworn in* 28 July 1995

CABINET *as at August 1996*

Prime Minister, Minister of Fisheries, Alberto Pandolfi Arbulú
Foreign Affairs, Francisco Tudela Van Breugel-Douglas
Energy and Mines, Daniel Hokama Tokashiki
Agriculture, Rodolfo Muñante Sanguinetti
Transport, Communications, Housing and Construction, Elsa Carrera de Escalante
Justice, Eduardo Hermoza Moya
Education, Domingo Palermo Cabrejos
Labour and Social Promotion, Jorge González Izquierdo
Health, Marino Costa Bauer
Industry, Tourism, Integration and International Trade Negotiations, Liliana Canale Novella
Economy and Finance, Jorge Camet Dickman
Defence, Gen. (retd) Tomás Guillermo Castilla Meza
Interior, Gen. Juan Briones Dávila
Minister of the Presidency, Jaime Yoshiyama Tanaka

EMBASSY OF PERU
52 Sloane Street, London SWIX 9SP
Tel 0171-235 1917/2545/3802
Ambassador Extraordinary and Plenipotentiary, HE Eduardo Ponce-Vivanco, apptd 1995

BRITISH EMBASSY
Edificio El Pacifico Washington, Piso 12, Plaza Washington (PO Box 854), Lima 100
Tel: Lima 334735
Ambassador Extraordinary and Plenipotentiary, HE John Illman, apptd 1995

There is a British Consular Office at Lima and Honorary Consulates in Arequipa, Cusco, Iquitos, Piura and Trujillo.

BRITISH COUNCIL DIRECTOR, Chris Brown, PO Box No. 14-0114, Calle Alberto Lynch 110, San Isidro, Lima 27

DEFENCE

The armed forces have a total active strength of 115,000 (65,500 conscripts), with selective conscription of two years duration. The Army has a strength of 75,000 (50,000 conscripts). It has 300 main battle tanks, 110 light tanks, 276 armoured personnel carriers and 234 artillery pieces. The Navy has 25,000 personnel (13,500 conscripts). It has a strength of six submarines, two cruisers, five destroyers and four frigates, seven patrol and coastal vessels, seven combat aircraft and 14 armed helicopters. The Air Force has a strength of 15,000 personnel (2,000 conscripts), with 90 combat aircraft and 14 armed helicopters. There is also a 60,000-strong paramilitary National Police.

ECONOMY

Since 1990 the government has launched a radical free-market restructuring programme which has rebuilt the foreign exchange reserves from virtually zero, reduced inflation from 7,600 per cent a year in 1990 to 10 per cent in 1995, cut subsidies and import tariffs, freed interest rates, privatized most state firms, and seen the economy grow by 8 per cent of GDP in 1995. Foreign investment has been encouraged and has grown dramatically. In March 1993 Peru cleared its arrears with the World Bank and IMF of US$1,700 million, enabling it to gain access to a new IMF loan of US$1,395 million over three years. In October 1995 Peru reached agreement with its creditors to reschedule US$10,000 million in debt; US$940 million in loans was pledged for 1996.

The chief products of the coastal belt are cotton, sugar and petroleum. There are large tracts of land suitable for cultivation and stock-raising (cattle, sheep, llamas, alpacas and vicuñas) on the eastern slopes of the Andes, and in the mountain valleys maize, potatoes and wheat are grown. The jungle area is a source of timber and petroleum. Other major crops are fruit, vegetables, rice, barley, grapes and coffee. The mountains contain rich mineral deposits and mineral exports include lead, zinc, copper, iron ore and silver. Peru is normally the world's largest exporter of fishmeal.

TRADE

The principal imports are machinery and chemicals and pharmaceutical products. The chief exports are minerals and metals, fishmeal, sugar, cotton and coffee.

Trade with UK	1994	1995
Imports from UK	£44,580,000	£57,500,000
Exports to UK	112,911,000	122,645,000

COMMUNICATIONS

In recent years the coastal and sierra zones have been opened up by means of roads and air routes. There is air communication, as well as communication by protracted land routes, with the tropical and eastern zones which lie east of the Andes towards the borders of Brazil. The Andean Highway forms a link between the Pacific, the Amazon and the Atlantic. The Pan-American Highway runs along the Peruvian coast connecting it with Ecuador and Chile. The Inter-Ocean Corridor linking the port of Matarani and Buenos Aires will be opened soon.

The railway is administered by the government. There is also steam navigation on the Ucayali and Huallaga, and in the south on Lake Titicaca. Air services are maintained throughout Peru, and many international services call at Lima.

EDUCATION

Education is compulsory and free between five and 16. Illiteracy was 14 per cent in 1992.

THE PHILIPPINES
Repúblika ng Pilipinas

The Philippines is situated between 21° 20′–4° 30′ N. latitude and 116° 55′–126° 36′ E. longitude, and is about 500 miles from the south-east coast of the continent of Asia. The total land area of the country is 115,831 sq. miles (300,000 sq. km). There are eleven larger islands and 7,079 other islands. The principal islands are:

	sq. miles		sq. miles
Luzon	40,422	Mindoro	3,759
Mindanao	36,538	Leyte	2,786
Samar	5,050	Cebu	1,703
Negros	4,906	Bohol	1,492
Palawan	4,550	Masbate	1,262
Panay	4,446		

Other groups are the Sulu islands (capital, Jolo), Babuyanes and Batanes; the Calamian islands; and Kalayaan Islands.

The population (UN estimate 1994) is 66,188,000. The inhabitants are basically of Malay stock, with a considerable admixture of Spanish and Chinese blood in many localities. The Chinese minority is estimated at 500,000, with smaller numbers of Spanish, American and Indian. About 90 per cent are Christian, predominantly Roman Catholics. Most of the remainder are Muslims, in the south, and indigenous animists, mainly in Luzon and parts of Mindanao.

The official languages are Filipino and English. Filipino is based on Tagalog, one of the Malay–Polynesian languages and is spoken by 29.66 per cent of the total number of households (and understood by nearly 90 per cent of the population), but local languages and dialects are strong and Cebuano is spoken by 24.2 per cent of total households. English, which is the language of government and of instruction in secondary and university education, is spoken by at least 44 per cent of the population. Spanish, which ceased to be an official language in 1973, is now spoken by a very small minority. Eighty-nine per cent of the population are literate.

CAPITAL – ѰManila, on the island of Luzon, estimated population (1990) City area 1,876,195; Manila with suburbs (incl. Quezon City, Pasay City, Caloocan City, Makati, Parañaque, San Juan Mandaluyong, Malabon, Valenzuela, Peteros, Las Piñas, Taguig, Muntinlupa

and Navotas) 6,720,050. The next largest cities are (1989 estimate) ѰCebu (613,184), ѰDavao (819,525), ѰIloilo (287,711), ѰZamboanga (433,328), and Bacolod (328,648).

CURRENCY – Philippine peso (P) of 100 centavos.

FLAG – Equal horizontal bands of blue (above) and red; gold sun with three stars on a white triangle next to staff.

NATIONAL ANTHEM – Bayang Magiliw.

NATIONAL DAY – 12 June (Independence Day 1898).

GOVERNMENT

The Portuguese navigator Magellan came to the Philippines in 1521 and was killed by the natives of Mactan, a small island near Cebu. In 1565 Spain undertook the conquest of the country, which was named Filipinas after Philip II of Spain. In 1896 the Filipinos revolted against Spanish rule and declared their independence on 12 June 1898. In the Spanish–American War of 1898, Manila was captured by American troops with the help of Filipinos and the islands were ceded to the USA by the Treaty of Paris in 1898. Despite a rebellion against US rule between 1899 and 1902, the Americans remained in control of the country until 1946. The Republic of the Philippines came into existence on 4 July 1946.

Ferdinand Marcos was President from 1965 to 1986. Although he gained a majority of votes in the official count of a presidential election in February 1986, the election was marred by widespread electoral abuse and his rival, Mrs Corazon Aquino, launched a campaign of non-violent civil disturbance which gained wide support. On 25 February Marcos fled to Hawaii. Mrs Aquino took over as President and survived seven coup attempts.

A new constitution was approved by referendum in 1987 and came into force that July. Legislative authority is vested in a bicameral elected Congress comprising a House of Representatives of 250 members and a 24-member Senate. Fidel Ramos was elected President on 11 May 1992 and has overcome the problems that plagued President Aquino, namely military coup attempts and legislative obstructiveness. Legislative elections to both houses of Congress were held on 8 May 1995 when the coalition of the Lakas ng Edsa, National Union of Christian Democrats and Laban ng Demokratikong Pilipino won majorities in both houses. Leban ng Demokratikong Pilipino subsequently withdrew from the ruling coalition

INSURGENCY

In August 1996, the government reached agreement with the Moro National Liberation Front (MNLF) on the creation of an autonomous Muslim state in the Mindanao region, ending a 24-year rebellion which had left more than 120,000 people dead. The Moro Islamic Liberation Front (MILF), a radical breakaway group, threatened an upsurge in violence to disrupt the agreement. The Communist New People's Army (NPA) maintains a presence in eastern Mindanao, Negros, Samar, Bicol, the mountains of northern Luzon and Bataan. The NPA signed a cease-fire agreement with the government in December 1993; peace talks are continuing. The 900-strong Islamic fundamentalist Abu Sayyaf group killed over 100 people in an attack on Ipil in April 1995.

HEAD OF STATE

President, Fidel V. Ramos, *assumed office* 30 June 1992

Vice-President, Joseph Estrada

CABINET SECRETARIES *as at August 1996*

Foreign Affairs, Domingo Siazon

Finance, Roberto de Ocampo

Justice, Teofisto Guingona

Agriculture, Salvador Escudero
Public Works and Highways, Gregorio Vigilar
Education, Culture and Sport, Ricardo Gloria
Labour and Employment, Leonardo Quisumbing
National Defence, Gen. Renato de Villa
Health, Carmencita Reodica
Trade and Industry, Cesar Bautista
Social Welfare and Development, Lina Laigo
Agrarian Reform, Ernesto Garilao
Interior and Local Government, Robert Barbers
Tourism, Eduardo Pilapil
Environment and Natural Resources, Victor Ramos
Budget and Management, Salvador Enriquez
Transport and Communications, Jesus Garcia
Science and Technology, William Padolina
Director-General, Socio-Economic Planning Authority, Cielito
  Habito
Energy, Francisco Viray
Press and Presidential Spokesman, Hector Villanueva

EMBASSY OF THE PHILIPPINES
9A Palace Green, London w8 4QE
Tel 0171-937 1600
Ambassador Extraordinary and Plenipotentiary, HE Jesus P.
  Tambunting, apptd 1993
Defence Attaché, Col. E. Abu
Counsellor and Consul-General, E. Castro
Commercial Counsellor, P. Sales

BRITISH EMBASSY
Locsin Building, 6752 Ayala Avenue, Corner Makati
Avenue, 1226 Makati, Metro Manila (PO Box 2927
MCPO)
Tel: Manila 816-7116
Ambassador Extraordinary and Plenipotentiary, HE Adrian
  Thorpe, apptd 1995
Deputy Ambassador, D. B. Merry
Defence Attaché, Gp Capt. P. G. Wildman
First Secretary, C. B. Glynn (*Commercial*)

BRITISH COUNCIL DIRECTOR, Dr Kate Bailey, 10F
  Taipan Place, Emerald Avenue, Ortigas Complex,
  Pasig City, Manila

DEFENCE

The Philippine armed forces number 106,500 active
personnel with a further 131,000 reserves. The Army has
an active strength of 68,000 personnel, with 41 light tanks,
415 armoured personnel carriers and armoured infantry
fighting vehicles and 242 artillery pieces. The Navy has
23,000 personnel, including 8,500 marines, and deploys
one frigate, 47 patrol and coastal vessels, eight combat
aircraft and ten marine battalions. The Air Force has some
15,500 personnel, with 43 combat aircraft and 104 armed
helicopters. The paramilitary Philippine National Police
number 40,500 personnel and there is a part-time militia of
60,000 personnel.

ECONOMY

The Philippines has been bypassed by the economic
growth of most of the rest of south-east Asia since the
1960s, mainly because of the incompetence and corruption
of the Marcos regime. President Ramos has, however,
restored economic growth, which was over 5 per cent in
1995, and increased electricity generation to resolve the
energy crisis. An economic reform programme of liberalization, privatization and deregulation has also been put in
place and has led to increased exports, increased foreign
investment, a reduction in inflation to 5.1 per cent in 1994,
and brought the debt service ratio down to 16 per cent of

GDP. Total foreign debt in 1995 was US$41,600 million. In
June 1994 the IMF approved a US$684 million loan over
three years to support the economic reform programme.

The Philippines is predominantly agricultural, the chief
products being rice, coconuts, maize, coffee, sugar-cane,
abaca (manila hemp), fruits, tobacco and lumber. There is,
however, an increasing number of manufacturing industries and it is the policy of the government to diversify its
economy. There are also deposits of nickel, iron, copper,
gold and silver.

TRADE
Principal exports are sugar, coconut oil, copper concentrate, lumber and copra, together with increasingly important manufactured exports such as electronics products
and clothing. The major trading partners are the USA,
Japan, Taiwan and Hong Kong.

	1992	
Total imports	US$10,580m	
Total exports	7,150m	

Trade with UK	1994	1995
Imports from UK	£355,131,000	£432,397,000
Exports to UK	244,346,000	352,425,000

COMMUNICATIONS

The highway system covers about 161,709 kilometres. The
Philippine National Railway used to operate 1,282 km of
track, but a greater part of this is being rebuilt. There are 94
ports of entry and 164,404 vessels of various types totalling
50,467,000 tons are engaged in inter-island traffic. There
are 82 national airports and 137 privately operated airports. Philippine Air Lines have regular flights throughout
the Far East, to the USA and Europe, in addition to inter-
island services.

EDUCATION

Secondary and higher education is extensive and there are
37 private universities recognized by the government,
including the Dominican University of Santo Tomas
(founded in 1611). There are also 296 state-supported
colleges and universities, including the University of the
Philippines, founded 1908.

POLAND
Rzeczpospolita Polska

Poland adjoins Germany in the west, the boundary being
formed by the rivers Oder and Neisse, the Czech Republic
and Slovakia in the south, and Belarus, Ukraine, Lithuania
and the Kaliningrad region of Russia in the east. To the
north is the Baltic Sea. Poland has an area of 120,725 sq.
miles (312,677 sq. km), and a population (official estimate
1995) of 38,600,000. Roman Catholicism is the religion of
95 per cent of the inhabitants.

CAPITAL – Warsaw, on the Vistula, population (1994)
  1,641,900. Other large towns are Lódź (831,300);
  Kraków (745,800); Wroclaw (643,100); Poznan
  (582,800); Gdansk (463,600); Szczecin (418,300);
  Katowice (359,000); Bydgoszcz (385,400).
CURRENCY – New Zloty of 100 groszy (equal to 10,000
  old Zloty). Both old and new are legal tender until 31
  December 1996.
FLAG – Equal horizontal stripes of white (above) and red.

National Anthem – Jeszcze Polska Nie Zginela (Poland has not yet been destroyed).
National Day – 3 May.

GOVERNMENT

The Polish Commonwealth ceased to exist in 1795 after three successive partitions in 1772, 1793 and 1795 in which Prussia, Russia and Austria shared. The Republic of Poland, reconstituted within the limits of the old Polish Commonwealth, was proclaimed at Warsaw in November 1918, and its independence guaranteed by the signatories of the Treaty of Versailles.

German forces invaded Poland on 1 September 1939; on 17 September, Russian forces invaded eastern Poland, and on 21 September 1939 Poland was declared by Germany and Russia to have ceased to exist. At the end of the war a coalition government was formed in which the Polish Workers' Party played a large part. In December 1948, the Polish Workers' Party and the Polish Socialist Party merged to form the Polish United Workers' Party (PUWP). A new constitution modelled on the Soviet constitution was adopted in 1952, and was modified in 1976.

Steep price rises in 1980 prompted strikes which forced the government to allow independent trade unions, including 'Solidarity' led by Lech Walesa. The unions agitated for further reforms although their activities were suspended when martial law was in force from December 1981 until July 1983.

A wave of strikes resulted in talks between Walesa and the PUWP early in 1989. Multiparty parliamentary elections were held in the summer of 1989, following which the PUWP ceased to be the ruling party. The post-Communist governments have introduced a market economy but economic difficulties and a fragmented Parliament have led to a succession of short-lived governments. Elections held on 19 September 1993 resulted in six parties gaining representation in the 460-seat Sejm: Democratic Left Alliance (SLD) 171 seats; Polish Peasant Party (PSL) 132 seats; Freedom Union (UW) 74 seats; Labour Union (UP) 41 seats; Confederation for an Independent Poland (KPN) 22 seats; Reform Bloc 16 seats; German minority parties 4 seats. In the 100-member Senate the results were: SLD 37; PSL 36; Solidarity 10; UW 4; others 13. The SLD (dominated by reformist Communists) returned to power after four years by forming a coalition government with the PSL and UP parties.

The cohabitation of a left-wing government and anti-Communist President Lech Walesa produced tension over the scale and pace of economic reform in 1993–5. PSL Prime Minister Waldemar Pawlak was forced to resign in February 1995 because he was considered to be obstructing economic reform. He was replaced by Józef Oleksy of the SLD, who resigned in February 1996 over espionage charges. The election of former SLD leader Aleksander Kwaśniewski as President is likely to reduce intergovernmental conflict.

In November 1992 President Walesa signed a 'small constitution' which defines the division of powers between the President and government. The President appoints the Prime Minister and has the right to be consulted over the appointment of the foreign, defence and interior ministers. There is a 5 per cent threshold for representation for parties in the Sejm and 8 per cent for alliances (except for minority groups). The Senate is elected on a provincial basis.

Head of State
President, Aleksander Kwaśniewski, *elected* 19 November 1995, *sworn in* 23 December 1995

Council of Ministers *as at August 1996*
Prime Minister, Wlodzimierz Cimoszewicz (SLD)
Deputy PM, Agriculture, Roman Jagieliński (PSL)
Deputy PM, Head of the Central Planning Office, Miroslaw Pietrewicz (PSL)
Deputy PM, Finance, Prof. Grzegorz Kolodko (Ind.)
Defence, Stanislaw Dobrzánski (PSL)
Foreign Affairs, Dariusz Rosati (Ind.)
Interior, Zbigniew Siemiatikowski (SLD)
Labour and Social Policy, Andrzej Baczkowski (Ind.)
Regional Planning and Construction, Barbara Blida (SLD)
Foreign Economic Relations, Jacek Buchacz (PSL)
Privatization, Wieslaw Kaczmarek (SLD)
Justice, Leszek Kubicki (Ind.)
Transport and Maritime Economy, Boguslaw Liberadzki (Ind.)
Head of the Council of Ministers, Leszek Miller (SLD)
Culture, Zdzislaw Podkański (PSL)
Industry and Trade, Klemens Ścierski (PSL)
National Education, Jerzy Wiatr (SLD)
Communications, Andrzej Zieliński (Ind.)
Environmental Protection, Natural Resources and Forestry, Stanislaw Zelichowski (PSL)
Health, Ryszard Zochowski (PSL)
Head of the Scientific Research Committee, Alexsander Luczak (PSL)

PSL Polish Peasant Party; SLD Democratic Left Alliance; Ind Independent

Embassy of the Republic of Poland
47 Portland Place, London win 4jh
Tel 0171-580 4324/9
Ambassador Extraordinary and Plenipotentiary, HE Ryszard Stemplowski, apptd 1994
Defence Attaché, Cdr. R. Szlegier
Consul-General, J. Starośćiak
Minister, P. Kozerski (*Commercial*)

British Embassy
No. 1 Aleja Róz, 00-556 Warsaw
Tel: Warsaw 6281001
Ambassador Extraordinary and Plenipotentiary, HE Christopher O. Hum, cmg, apptd 1996
Counsellor, W. A. Harrison (*Deputy Head of Mission*)
Defence and Air Attaché, Gp Capt H. Delve, mbe
First Secretary (*Commercial and Consul-General*), A. J. Gooch
There are Honorary Consulates at Katowice, Poznan and Gdansk.

British Council Director, Edward Pugh, Al. Jerozolimskie 59, 00–697 Warsaw

DEFENCE

The total active armed forces number 278,600 personnel (158,100 conscripts) with a further 465,500 reserves. Conscripts serve in all services for 18 months. The Army numbers 188,200 (108,100 conscripts) with 2,787 main battle tanks, 1,553 armoured infantry fighting vehicles and armoured personnel carriers and 1,725 artillery pieces. The Navy has a strength of 17,800 including 12,400 conscripts, with three submarines, one destroyer, one frigate, 33 patrol and coastal vessels, 35 combat aircraft and 11 armed helicopters. The Air Force is 72,600 strong (40,300 conscripts), with 412 combat aircraft and 30 attack helicopters. The Paramilitary Border Guards and Police Prevention Units number 23,400 personnel (1,400 conscripts).

ECONOMY

In 1990, the government embarked upon a series of measures designed to introduce a free-market economy, including legal reforms, privatization, trade liberalization and the creation of a social security system. However, growth did not resume until 1992 and the public backlash against rising food prices and unemployment prompted the government to overstep the budgetary limits agreed with international creditors. The IMF prescribed a 'shock therapy' of allowing bankruptcy and ending of state subsidies to reduce the deficit. Further IMF credits followed the passing of an austerity budget and the introduction of a mass privatization bill for 600 state-owned firms in 1993.

The transition to a market economy has been painful, with unemployment rising from 6.3 per cent in 1990 to 14.9 per cent in late 1995. Industrial output has improved and the rate of growth of GDP has increased, reaching 6.5 per cent in 1995, although inflation remains high (26.8 per cent in 1995). In September 1995 Poland's foreign debt totalled US$42,800 million, agreements having been reached to cancel US$39,900 million in 1994. Of the 8,441 state enterprises registered in 1990, 4,920 had been privatized by 1994.

Poland is well endowed with mineral resources; there are large reserves of brown coal (14,100 million tons) in central and south-western Poland and hard coal (65 million tons) in Upper Silesia and the Walbrzych and Lublin regions; sulphur, copper, zinc, lead, natural gas and salt are also produced. In 1994, there were 18.6 million hectares of arable land, 73 per cent of which was privately owned.

Poland's major imports are petroleum, textiles, industrial and electrical equipment. Its major exports are fruits and vegetables, clothing, coal, non-ferrous metals, iron and steel, furniture and transport equipment. Germany is Poland's main trading partner.

TRADE WITH UK	1994	1995
Imports from UK	£702,711,000	£944,672,000
Exports to UK	544,928,000	638,077,000

EDUCATION

Elementary education (ages seven to 15) is compulsory and free. Secondary education is optional and free. There are universities at Kraków, Warsaw, Poznan, Lódź, Wroclaw, Lublin and Toruń and a number of other towns.

CULTURE

Polish is a western Slavonic tongue, the Latin alphabet being used. Major writers include Henryk Sienkiewicz (1846–1916), Nobel Prizewinner for Literature in 1905; Boleslaw Prus (1847–1912); Stanislaw Reymont (1868–1925), Nobel Prizewinner in 1924; Czeslaw Milosz, Nobel Prizewinner in 1980.

The state monopoly on radio and television broadcasting ended in October 1992.

PORTUGAL
República Portuguesa

Portugal occupies the western part of the Iberian Peninsula, covering an area of 34,317 sq. miles (88,880 sq. km). It lies between 36° 58' and 42° 12" N. latitude and 6° 11' 48" and 9° 29' 45" W. longitude. It is 362 miles in length from north to south, and averages about 117 miles in breadth from east to west.

The population (census 1991) is 9,862,700 (including the Azores and Madeira). The language is Portuguese, a Romance language with admixtures of Arabic and other idioms.

CAPITAL – ΨLisbon, population estimate (1989) 2,128,000. ΨOporto 1,683,000.
CURRENCY – Escudo (Esc) of 100 centavos.
FLAG – Divided vertically into unequal parts of green and red with the national emblem over all on the line of division.
NATIONAL ANTHEM – A Portuguesa.
NATIONAL DAY – 10 June.

GOVERNMENT

Portugal was a monarchy from the 12th century until 1910, when an armed rising in Lisbon drove King Manuel II into exile and a republic was set up. A period of political instability ensued until the military stepped in and abolished political parties in 1926. The constitution of 1933 gave formal expression to the corporative 'Estado Novo' (New State) which was personified by Dr Salazar, Prime Minister 1932–68. Dr Caetano succeeded Salazar as Prime Minister in 1968 but his failure to liberalize the regime or to conclude the wars in the African colonies resulted in his government's overthrow by a military coup on 25 April 1974. There was great political turmoil between April 1974 and July 1976 but with the failure of an attempted coup by the extreme left in November 1975 the situation stabilized.

Under the 1976 constitution, amended in 1982 and 1989, the President, elected for a five-year term by universal adult suffrage, appoints the Prime Minister and, on the latter's recommendation, the members of the Council of Ministers. Legislative authority is vested in the 230-member Assembly of the Republic, elected by a system of proportional representation every four years. The President retains certain limited powers to dismiss the government, dissolve the Assembly or veto laws.

In the general election held on 1 October 1995, the Socialist Party (PS) won 112 seats, the Social Democrats (PSD) 88 seats, the Christian Democrats (CDS/PP) 15 seats, and the Communist Coalition (CDU) 15 seats. The Socialist candidate, Jorge Sampaio, won the January 1996 presidential election.

HEAD OF STATE
President of the Republic, Jorge Sampaio, *elected* 1996, *inaugurated* 9 March 1996

COUNCIL OF MINISTERS *as at August 1996*
Prime Minister, António Guterres
Defence, António Vitorino
Foreign Affairs, Jaime Gama
Finance, Sousa Franco
Economy, Augusto Mateus
Employment, Maria João Rodrigues
Social Security, Ferro Rodrigues
Agriculture, Food and Fisheries, Gomes da Silva
Culture, Manuel Maria Carrilho
Education, Marçal Grilo
Science and Technology, Mariano Gago
Home Affairs, Alberto Costa
Justice, José Vera Jardim
Health, Maria de Belém Roseira
Planning and Territorial Administration, João Cravinho
Environment, Elisa Ferreira
Assistant to the PM, Jorge Coelho

PORTUGUESE EMBASSY
11 Belgrave Square, London swix 8pp
Tel 0171-235 5331
Ambassador Extraordinary and Plenipotentiary, HE António
Costa-Lobo, apptd 1995
Minister-Plenipotentiary and Consul-General, A. de Almeida
Ribeiro
Minister-Counsellor, F. Xavier-Esteves
Defence Attaché, Capt. A. Bettencourt
Counsellors, M. Quartin-Bastos, LVO (*Economic*); M. do Céu
Hespanha (*Commercial*)

BRITISH EMBASSY
Rua de S. Bernardo 33, 1200 Lisbon
Tel: Lisbon 3924000
Ambassador Extraordinary and Plenipotentiary, HE Roger
Westbrook, CMG, apptd 1995
Counsellor, A. F. Smith (*Deputy Head of Mission*)
Defence Attaché, Cdr. R. Wykes-Sneyd, AFC
First Secretaries, P. Shaw (*Commercial*); D. J. Ferguson
(*Consul*)

There are British Consulates in Oporto, Portimão,
Funchal (Madeira), Ribeira Grande (Azores) and Macao

BRITISH COUNCIL DIRECTOR, Bill Jefferson, OBE, Rua de
Sao Marçal 174, 1294 Lisbon. There are also offices at
Cascais, Coimbra and Oporto.
BRITISH PORTUGUESE CHAMBER OF COMMERCE, Rua da
Estrela 8, 1200 Lisbon and Rua Sa de Bandeira
784–20E, Frente, 4000 Oporto.

DEFENCE

The armed forces have a total active strength of 54,200
(17,600 conscripts) with reserves of 210,000. Conscripts
serve four to 18 months. The present strength of the Army
is 29,700 (15,000 conscripts), with 198 main battle tanks,
350 armoured personnel carriers and 318 artillery pieces.
The Navy consists of 12,500 personnel (800 conscripts),
including 2,100 marines, with three submarines, 11 frigates
and 30 patrol and coastal vessels. The strength of the Air
Force is 7,300 (1,800 conscripts), with 97 combat aircraft.
The paramilitary National Republican Guard, Public
Security Police and Border Security Force number a total
of 49,800 personnel.
Lisbon is the base of the NATO Iberian Atlantic
Command and the USA maintains 1,155 personnel in
mainland Portugal and on the Azores.

ECONOMY

Since joining the EC (EU) in 1986 Portugal has been
adjusting its economy to the European single market, and
to the economic and monetary union criteria laid down in
the Maastricht Treaty. The escudo joined the ERM in
April 1992 and the budget deficit has been reduced to 5.8
per cent of GDP in 1995; inflation was under 5 per cent and
unemployment 8 per cent.
The chief agricultural products are cork, potatoes,
maize, wheat, rice, vegetables, olives, olive oil, figs, citrus
fruits, almonds, timber, port wine and table wines. There
are extensive forests of pine, cork, eucalyptus and chestnut
covering about 20 per cent of the total area of the country.
The principal mineral products are pyrites, wolfram,
uranium, iron ores, copper and sodium and calcium
minerals.
The country is moderately industrialized. The principal manufactures are textiles, clothing and footwear,
machinery (including electric machinery and transport
equipment), pulp and paper, pharmaceuticals, foodstuffs,
chemicals, fertilizers, wood, cork, furniture, cement, glassware and pottery. There are a modern steelworks and two

large shipbuilding and repair yards at Lisbon and Setúbal,
working mainly for foreign shipowners. There are several
hydroelectric power stations and a new thermal power
station.

TRADE

The principal imports are cereals, meat, raw and semi-
manufactured iron and steel, industrial machinery, chemicals, crude oil, motor vehicles and raw materials for
textiles. The principal exports are textiles, footwear,
timber, pulp, automotive parts, cork, electrical and other
machinery, and chemicals.

	1992	1993
Total imports	Esc4,087,577,000m	Esc3,882,777,000m
Total exports	2,475,202,000m	2,474,401,000m
Trade with UK	1994	1995
Imports from UK	£1,226,872,000	£1,391,300,000
Exports to UK	1,253,541,000	1,397,200,000

COMMUNICATIONS

There are international airports at Lisbon and Oporto, and
at Faro in the Algarve. Four morning and one evening daily
newspapers are published in Lisbon and four morning
newspapers in Oporto, and six main weekly newspapers.

EDUCATION

Education is free and compulsory for nine years from the
age of six. Secondary education is mainly conducted in
state lyceums, commercial and industrial schools, but there
are also private schools. There are also military, naval,
technical, polytechnic and other special schools. There are
universities at Coimbra (founded in 1290), Oporto, Lisbon,
Braga, Aveiro, Vila Real, Faro, Evora and in the Azores.

AUTONOMOUS REGIONS

Madeira and The Azores are two administratively autonomous regions of Portugal, having locally elected assemblies and governments.

MADEIRA

Madeira is a group of islands in the Atlantic Ocean about
520 miles south-west of Lisbon, and consists of Madeira,
Porto, Santo and three uninhabited islands (Desertas). The
total area is 314 sq. miles (813 sq. km), with a population of
271,400 (1989). ΨFunchal in Madeira, the largest island
(270 sq. miles), is the capital (population 44,111); Machico
(10,905).

THE AZORES

The Azores are a group of nine islands (Flores, Corvo,
Terceira, São Jorge, Pico, Faial, Graciosa, São Miguel and
Santa Maria) in the Atlantic Ocean, with a total area of
922 sq. miles (2,387 sq. km), and a population of 255,100
(1989). ΨPonta Delgada, on São Miguel, is the capital of
the group (population 137,700). Other ports are ΨAngra,
in Terceira (55,900) and ΨHorta (16,300).

OVERSEAS TERRITORY

MACAO

Macao, situated at the mouth of the Pearl River, comprises
a peninsula and the islands of Coloane and Taipa, having an
area of six sq. miles (15.5 sq. km), with a population (UN
estimate 1994) of 395,000. Macao became a Portuguese
colony in 1557; in a Sino-Portuguese treaty of 1887 China
recognized Portugal's sovereignty over Macao. An agreement to transfer the administration of Macao to the
Chinese authorities was signed on 13 April 1987. Macao

will become a 'special administrative region' (SAR) of China when transferred on 20 December 1999. The final session of the Macao SAR Basic Law Drafting Committee was held in Beijing in January 1993 and approved the Basic Law which will serve as Macao's constitution after 1999.

Macao is subject to Portuguese constitutional law but otherwise enjoys autonomy. The Governor is appointed by the Portuguese President and there is a 23-member legislative assembly, which has a three-year term. The assembly comprises seven members appointed by the Governor; eight directly elected, and eight indirectly elected by business associations.

Macao's major industry is textile manufacturing, which accounts for 62 per cent of all exports. Most government revenue, however, comes from gambling. Port Macao is served by British, Portuguese and Dutch shipping lines and has regular services to Hong Kong, some 35 miles away.

Governor, Rocha Vieira.

TRADE WITH UK	1994	1995
Imports from UK	£15,591,000	£15,963,000
Exports to UK	55,208,000	55,079,000

QATAR
Dawlat Qatar

The state of Qatar covers the peninsula of Qatar in the Gulf from approximately the northern shore of Khor al Odaid to the eastern shore of Khor al Salwa. The area is about 4,247 sq. miles (11,000 sq. km).

The population (UN estimate 1994) is 537,000. Most of the population is concentrated in the urban district of Doha. Only a small minority still pursue the traditional life of the semi-nomadic tribesmen and fisherfolk.

CAPITAL – ΨDoha, population (estimated) 220,000. Other towns include Khor, Dukhan, Wakra and ΨUmm Said.

CURRENCY – Qatar riyal of 100 dirhams.

FLAG – White and maroon, white portion nearer the mast; vertical indented line comprising 17 angles divides the colours.

NATIONAL DAY – 3 September.

GOVERNMENT

Qatar was one of nine independent emirates in the Gulf in special treaty relations with the UK until 1971. On 2 April 1970 a provisional constitution for Qatar was proclaimed, providing for the establishment of a Council of Ministers and for the formation of a Consultative Council to assist the Council of Ministers in running the affairs of the state. There are no political parties or legislature. The Amir, who had ruled since 22 February 1972, was overthrown on 27 June 1995 by his son and heir, who assumed power as Amir the same day. A coup attempt was thwarted in February 1996.

HEAD OF STATE
HH Amir of Qatar, Sheikh Hamad bin Khalifa Al Thani, KCMG, *assumed power* 27 June 1995

COUNCIL OF MINISTERS *as at August 1996*

Prime Minister, Minister of Defence and Commander-in-Chief of Armed Forces, The Amir
Deputy PM, Interior, HH Sheikh Abdullah bin Khalifa Al-Thani
Minister of State, Amiri Diwan Affairs, HE Sheikh Hamad bin Suhaim Al-Thani

Finance, Economy and Trade, HE Sheikh Mohamed bin Khalifa Al-Thani
Foreign Affairs, HE Sheikh Hamad bin Jassem bin Jabr Al-Thani
Minister of State, HE Sheikh Ahmed bin Saif Al-Thani
Minister of State for Defence Affairs, Deputy C.-in-C. of Armed Forces, HE Sheikh Hamad bin Abdullah Al-Thani
Endowments and Islamic Affairs, HE Sheikh Abdulla bin Khalid Al-Thani
Municipal Affairs and Agriculture, HE Sheikh Ahmed bin Hamad Al-Thani
Minister of State, Cabinet Affairs, HE Sheikh Mohamed bin Khalid Al-Thani
Communication and Transport, HE Abdulla Saleh Al-Manei
Education, HE Abdulaziz Abdullah Turki
Electricity and Water, HE Ahmed Mohamed Ali Al-Subaie
Energy and Industry, HE Abdulla bin Hamad Al-Attiyah
Information and Culture, HE Dr Hamad Abdulaziz Al-Kawari
Public Health, HE Ali Saeed Al-Khayareen
Justice, HE Dr Najib Mohamed Al-Nuaimi
Minister of State for Foreign Affairs, HE Ahmed Abdulla Al-Mahmoud

EMBASSY OF THE STATE OF QATAR
1 South Audley Street, London W1Y 5DQ
Tel 0171-493 2200
Ambassador Extraordinary and Plenipotentiary, HE Ali Al-Jaidha, apptd 1993

BRITISH EMBASSY
PO Box 3, Doha
Tel: Doha 421991
Ambassador Extraordinary and Plenipotentiary, HE Patrick F. Wogan, CMG, apptd 1993

BRITISH COUNCIL DIRECTOR, Brian Austin, Ras Abu Aboud Road (PO Box 2992), Doha

ECONOMY

Although Qatar is a desert country, there are gardens and smallholdings near Doha and to the north, and encouragement is being given to the development of agriculture.

The Qatar General Petroleum Corporation is the state-owned company controlling Qatar's interests in oil, gas and petrochemicals. The corporation is responsible for Qatar's oil production onshore and offshore. The production level for Qatar agreed in OPEC is currently 364,000 b.p.d. The large reserves of natural gas in the North Field came into production in September 1991. A 50,000 b.p.d. oil refinery was commissioned in 1984 to increase domestic refinery capacity.

Current industries include a steel mill, a fertilizer plant, a cement factory, a petrochemical complex and two natural gas liquids plants. With the exception of the cement works at Umm Bab, all these industries are at Umm Said, about 30 miles south of Doha. Qatar is also expanding its infrastructure, including electrical generation and water distillation, roads, houses, and government buildings, although reduced demand for crude oil in international markets has led to a downturn in the economy and a slower rate of development than hitherto.

TRADE WITH UK	1994	1995
Imports from UK	£127,575,000	£146,289,000
Exports to UK	7,499,000	14,950,000

COMMUNICATIONS

Regular air services provided by Gulf Air and Qatar Airways connect Qatar with the other Gulf states, the Middle East, the Indian sub-continent, Africa and Europe.

The Qatar Broadcasting Service transmits on medium, shortwave, and VHF. Regular television transmissions in colour began in 1974 and a second channel opened in 1982.

ROMANIA
România

Romania is a republic of central Europe, formerly the classical Dacia and Scythia Pontica. The area is 91,699 sq. miles (237,500 sq. km).

The population (1992 census) is 22,760,449. Romanians number 21,559,910 (88 per cent), there is a Hungarian minority of 1,714,000 (7.9 per cent), a dwindling German minority of 359,000 (1.6 per cent) and 227,000 gypsies (1.1 per cent). The leading religion is that of the Romanian Orthodox Church; the Roman Catholic and some Protestant denominations are of importance numerically.

Romanian is a Romance language with many archaic forms and with admixtures of Slavonic, Turkish, Magyar and French words. There is a wealth of folk-songs and folklore, transmitted orally through many centuries and collected in the 19th century.

CAPITAL – Bucharest, on the Dimbovita, population (1992 census) 2,064,474.

Other large towns are:

Braşov	323,835	Ψ Galati	325,788
Constanţa	350,476	Craiova	303,520
Cluj-Napoca	328,008	Ploiesti	252,073
Iasi	342,994	Ψ Brăila	234,706
Timisoara	334,278		

CURRENCY – Leu (*plural* Lei) of 100 bani.
FLAG – Three vertical bands, blue, yellow, red.
NATIONAL ANTHEM – Desteapta-te, romane.
NATIONAL DAY – 1 December.

GOVERNMENT

Romania has its origin in the union of the Danubian principalities of Wallachia and Moldavia under the Treaty of Paris in 1856. Although under nominal Turkish suzerainty, the principalities achieved effective unification and independence in 1859 when Alexander Cuza had himself proclaimed ruler of both principalities. The new country adopted the name Romania in 1862. By the Treaty of Berlin in 1878 the principality was recognized as an independent state, and part of the Dobrudja (which had been occupied by the Romanians) was incorporated; on 27 March 1881 it was recognized as a kingdom. The First World War added Bessarabia, the Bukovina, the Banat and Crisana-Maramures, these additions being confirmed by the Versailles Treaty in 1919. Following the break-up of the Austro-Hungarian Empire, a National Assembly was held in Transylvania on 1 December 1918 which proclaimed the union of all Romanians in one state. In 1920 Transylvania was formally acquired from Hungary under the Treaty of Trianon. In 1940, Bessarabia and Northern Bukovina were ceded to the Soviet Union, and the portion of southern Dobrudja taken from Bulgaria in 1913 was returned.

In 1947 King Michael was forced to abdicate and Romania became 'The Romanian People's Republic'. The leading political force from the Second World War until 1989 was the Romanian Communist Party. A revolution in December 1989 led to the overthrow of Nicolae Ceauşescu, President since 1965. A provisional government abolished the leading role of the Communist Party and held free elections in May 1990. A new constitution adopted in 1991 formally makes Romania a multiparty democracy and endorses human rights and a market economy. There is a Senate of 143 members and a 341-member Assembly of Deputies (of which 13 seats are reserved for ethnic minorities other than Hungarians).

Presidential and parliamentary elections took place in September and October 1992. President Iliescu was re-elected and his Democratic National Salvation Front (DNSF), renamed the Social Democracy Party of Romania (PSDR) in July 1993, gained the largest number of seats in both houses of parliament and formed a minority government. The worsening economic situation caused the PSDR to seek political support and in March 1994 it formed a coalition government with the nationalist Party of Romanian National Unity (PRNU). In January 1995 a protocol was signed by these two parties and the Greater Romanian Party (GRP) and the ex-Communist Socialist Labour Party (SLP), although the GRP left the government in October 1995. Legislative elections are due to be held on 3 November 1996.

HEAD OF STATE
President of the Republic, Ion Iliescu, *elected* May 1990, *re-elected* 11 October 1992

GOVERNMENT *as at August 1996*
Prime Minister, Nicolae Vacaroiu
Minister of State, Foreign Affairs, Teodor Melescanu
Minister of State, Finance, Florin Georgescu
Minister of State, Labour and Social Protection, Dan Popescu
Minister of State, Economic Reform and Strategy, Mircea Cosea
Defence, Gheorghe Tinca
Industry, Alexandru Stanescu
Interior, Ioan Taracila
Justice, Iosif Chiuzbaian
Communications, Ovidiu Iuliu Muntean
Parliamentary Relations, Valer Dorneanu
Public Works and Physical Planning, Marin Cristea
Research and Technology, Doru Palade
Education, Liviu Maior
Culture, Viorel Marginean
Agriculture and Food Industry, Valeriu Tabara
Environment, Forestry and Water, Aurel Ilie
Health, Iulian Mincu
Tourism, Matei Dan
Trade, Petru Crisan
Transport, Aurel Novac
Youth and Sports, Alexandru Mironov

EMBASSY OF ROMANIA
Arundel House, 4 Palace Green, London W8 4QD
Tel 0171-937 9666
Ambassador Extraordinary and Plenipotentiary, HE Sergiu Celac, apptd 1990
Defence Attaché, Lt.-Col. Vasile Huică
First Secretary, C. Turturea (*Economic*)
Third Secretary, A. Gheorghe (*Consular*)

BRITISH EMBASSY
24 Strada Jules Michelet, 70154 Bucharest
Tel: Bucharest 3120 303
Ambassador Extraordinary and Plenipotentiary, HE Christopher D. Crabbie, CMG, apptd 1996
Counsellor, Deputy Head of Mission, R. M. Publicover
Defence Attaché, Lt.-Col. R. J. F. Owen, OBE
First Secretary (Commercial), N. U. Sheppard

BRITISH COUNCIL DIRECTOR, Claus Henning, OBE, Calea Dorobantilor 14, Bucharest

DEFENCE

Romania has a total active armed forces strength of 217,400 personnel (104,700 conscripts) with a further 427,000 reserves. Conscripts serve 12 months (Army and Air Force) and 18 months (Navy). The Army has a strength of 128,800 (84,700 conscripts) with 1,843 main battle tanks, 160 assault guns, 2,210 armoured infantry fighting vehicles and armoured personnel carriers and 2,341 artillery pieces. The Navy has a strength of 19,000 personnel (10,000 conscripts) including 1,000 coastal defence and 8,000 marines. It deploys one submarine, one destroyer, five frigates and 77 patrol and coastal vessels. The Air Force has 54,000 personnel (10,000 conscripts) with 402 combat aircraft and 17 attack helicopters. Paramilitary Border Guards, Security Guards and Gendarmerie number 79,100 personnel.

ECONOMY

Wallachia, Moldavia and Transylvania are among the most fertile areas in Europe, and agriculture employs 35 per cent of the workforce and contributes 20 per cent of GDP. The principal cereal crops are vegetables, flax and hemp. Vines and fruits are also grown. The forests of the mountainous regions are extensive, and the timber industry is important.

There are plentiful supplies of natural gas, together with various mineral deposits including coal, iron ore, bauxite, lead, zinc, copper and uranium in quantities which allow a substantial part of the requirements of industry to be met from local resources. Production of crude oil was 6,716,000 tonnes in 1994.

The economy faced increasing problems from the late 1970s as a result of over-investment in heavy industry and neglect of agriculture, aggravated by global recession and high interest rates. The Ceauşescu government sought to repay the heavy foreign debt by reducing borrowing, cutting imports and increasing exports.

After the 1989 revolution the government pursued only a limited programme of economic reform. Subsidies for fuel, food and other goods continued, as did those for uneconomic state firms, wages were indexed to prices and privatization delayed. In early 1994, after inflation had surpassed 300 per cent annually and unemployment 10 per cent, Romania agreed to implement an IMF austerity package to gain loans of US$700 million. Most consumer subsidies and price controls have since been lifted, interest and exchange rates have been freed and the restructuring of state enterprises has begun. A strong economic recovery has resulted, with GDP growth of 3.5 per cent in 1994 likely to increase. Unemployment was still above 10 per cent in 1995, however, and foreign debt was US$5,500 million and rising. In July 1994 the government announced a mass privatization programme. Progress towards the aim of privatizing enterprises has been slow.

TRADE

Imports are chiefly semi-manufactured goods, foodstuffs, raw materials, fuel, machinery and metals. Exports consist principally of textiles and footwear, metals, mineral products and chemicals. Germany is Romania's main trading partner.

Trade with UK	1994	1995
Imports from UK	£127,059,000	£176,770,000
Exports to UK	146,375,000	173,844,000

COMMUNICATIONS

In 1990 there were 11,348 km of railway open for traffic. The mercantile marine had a gross tonnage of 12,140,000 tons in 1990. The principal ports are Constanta (on the Black Sea), Sulina (on the Danube Estuary), Galati, Braila, Giurgiu and Turnu Severin. The Danube and the Black Sea are linked by a canal completed in 1984.

EDUCATION

Education is free and nominally compulsory. There are state universities in seven cities, 66 private universities, six polytechnics, two commercial academies, and five agricultural colleges.

An education bill adopted in July 1995 was opposed by the ethnic Hungarian community who claimed that it would reduce the provision for education in the Hungarian language agreed in 1993.

RUSSIA
Rossiiskaya Federatsiya – Russian Federation

Russia has an area of 6,593,391 sq. miles (17,075,400 sq. km) and occupies three-quarters of the land area of the former Soviet Union. In the west it is bordered by Norway, the Gulf of Finland, Finland, Estonia, Latvia, Belarus and Ukraine; the Kaliningrad enclave borders Lithuania and Poland. To the south Russia is bordered in Europe by Georgia, Azerbaijan, the Black Sea and the Caspian Sea, and in Asia by Kazakhstan, China, Mongolia and North Korea. In the east it meets the North Pacific (where its nearest point is only a few miles from Japan), and the Bering Strait (where its nearest point is only a few miles from Alaska). To the north is the Arctic Ocean and the Barents Sea.

The Russian Federation comprises 89 members: 49 regions (*oblast*) – Amur, Archangel, Astrakhan, Belgorod, Bryansk, Chelyabinsk, Chita, Irkutsk, Ivanovo, Kaliningrad, Kaluga, Kamchatka, Kemerovo, Kirov, Kostroma, Kurgan, Kursk, Lipetsk, Magadan, Moscow, Murmansk, Nizhny-Novgorod, Novgorod, Novosibirsk, Omsk, Orel, Orenburg, Penza, Perm, Pskov, Rostov, Ryazan, St Petersburg, Sakhalin, Samara, Saratov, Smolensk, Sverdlovsk, Tambov, Tomsk, Tula, Tver, Tyumen, Ulyanovsk, Vladimir, Volgograd, Vologda, Voronezh, Yaroslavl; six autonomous territories (*krai*) – Altai, Khabarovsk, Krasnodar, Krasnoyarsk, Primorye, Stavropol; 21 republics – Adygeia, Altai, Bashkortostan, Buryatia, Chechen, Chuvash, Daghestan, Ingush, Kabardino-Balkar, Kalmykia, Karachaevo-Cherkess, Karelia, Khakassia, Komi, Mari-El, Mordovia, North Ossetia (Alania), Sakha, Tatarstan, Tyva, Udmurt; ten autonomous areas – Agin-Buryat, Chukot, Evenki, Khanty-Mansi, Komi-Permyak, Koryak, Nenets, Taimyr, Ust-Orda-Buryat, Yamal-Nenets; two cities of federal status – Moscow, St Petersburg; and one autonomous Jewish region, Birobijan.

There are three principal geographic areas: a low-lying flat western area stretching eastwards up to the Yenisei and divided in two by the Ural ridge; the eastern area between the Yenisei and the Pacific, consisting of a number of tablelands and ridges; and a southern mountainous area. Russia has a very long coast-line, including the longest Arctic coastline in the world (about 17,000 miles). The most important rivers are the Volga, the Northern Dvina and the Pechora, the Neva, the Don and the Kuban in the European part, and in the Asiatic part, the Ob, the Irtysh, the Yenisei, the Lena and the Amur, and, further north, the Khatanga, Olenek, Yana, Indigirka, Kolyma and Anadyr. Lakes are abundant, particularly in the north-west. The huge Lake Baikal in eastern Siberia is the deepest lake in the world. There are also two large artificial water reservoirs within the Greater Volga canal system, the

Moscow and Rybinsk 'Seas'. Climatically, Russia extends from Arctic and tundra belts to the subtropical in the south.

The 1996 estimate gave a population of 148,100,000, of which about 87.5 per cent is Russian, 3.5 per cent Tatar, 2.7 per cent Ukrainian, 1.3 per cent ethnic German, 1.1 per cent Chavash, 0.9 per cent Bashkir, 0.7 per cent Belarusian and 0.7 per cent Mordovian. There are another six minorities with populations of over half a million and more than 130 nationalities in total.

The Russian Orthodox Church is the predominant religion, though the Tatars are Muslims and there are Jewish communities in Moscow and St Petersburg.

Russian is a branch of the Slavonic family of languages and is written in the Cyrillic script.

CAPITAL – Moscow (population 8,700,000 (1994)), founded about 1147, became the centre of the rising Moscow principality and in the 15th century the capital of the whole of Russia (Muscovy). In 1325 it became the seat of the Metropolitan of Russia. In 1703 Peter the Great transferred the capital to St Petersburg, but on 14 March 1918 Moscow was again designated as the capital. ΨSt Petersburg (from 1914 to 1924 Petrograd and from 1924 to 1991 Leningrad) has a population of 4,952,000 (1993).

Other towns with populations (1990) exceeding one million are:

Nizhny-Novgorod (Gorky)	1,438,000
Novosibirsk (Novonikolayevsk)	1,436,000
Yekaterinburg (Sverdlovsk)	1,367,000
Samara (Kuibyshev)	1,257,000
Omsk	1,148,000
Chelyabinsk	1,143,000
Ufa	1,083,000
Perm (Molotov)	1,091,000
Kazan	1,094,000
Rostov-on-Don	1,020,000

CURRENCY – Rouble of 100 kopeks.
FLAG – Three horizontal stripes of white, blue, red.
NATIONAL ANTHEM – The Patriotic Song.
NATIONAL DAY – 12 June (Independence Day).

HISTORY

The Gregorian calendar was not introduced until 14 February 1918. For the events surrounding the 1917 revolutions the dates given here are the Gregorian calendar dates in use in the rest of the world at the time, with the dates in the Julian calendar (os) in parenthesis.

Russia was formally created from the principality of Muscovy and its territories by Tsar Peter I (The Great) (1682–1725), who initiated its territorial expansion, introduced western ideas of government and founded St Petersburg. By the end of Peter the Great's reign, the Baltic territories (modern-day Estonia and Latvia) had been annexed from Sweden and Russia had become the dominant military power of north-eastern Europe. In the 18th century the partitions of Poland and wars with Turkey brought the territories of modern-day Lithuania, Belarus, Ukraine and the Crimea under Russian control, and the colonization of Siberia east of the Urals began in earnest. Russia overran the Caucasus region (modern-day Armenia, Azerbaijan and Georgia) in the early 19th century, seized Finland from Sweden in 1809 and Bessarabia from Turkey in 1812. Throughout the remainder of the 19th century Russia subdued and annexed the independent Muslim states which later formed the five Central Asian republics.

It was as a multinational empire covering a huge geographical area, in which the monarch and nobility held almost absolute power (an ineffectual parliament, the Duma, was created in 1905), that the Russian Empire entered the First World War in 1914. Discontent caused by autocratic rule, the poor conduct of the military campaign and wartime privation led to a revolution which broke out on 12 March (27 February os) 1917. Tsar Nicholas II abdicated three days later and a provisional government was formed; a republic was proclaimed on 14 September (1 September os) 1917. A power struggle ensued between the provisional government and the Bolshevik Party which controlled the Soviets (councils) set up by workers, soldiers and peasants. This led to a second revolution on 7 November (25 October os) 1917 in which the Bolsheviks, led by Lenin, seized power.

The Bolshevik (Communist) Party withdrew from the First World War under the Treaty of Brest-Litovsk (March 1918), surrendering large areas of territory. Armed resistance to Communist rule developed into an all-out civil war between 'red' Bolshevik forces and 'white' monarchist and anti-Communist forces which lasted until the end of 1922. During the civil war, Russia had been declared a Soviet Republic and other Soviet republics had been formed in Ukraine, Byelorussia and Transcaucasia. These four republics merged to form the Union of Soviet Socialist Republics (USSR) on 30 December 1922.

The Nazi-Soviet pact of August 1939 and the Second World War resulted in further territorial expansion, regaining much of the territory lost in or after 1918, as well as extending Soviet influence to the countries of eastern Europe liberated by Soviet troops. The USSR lost 26 million combatants and civilians in the war.

After an internal Communist Party power struggle following Lenin's death in 1924, Joseph Stalin emerged in 1928 as the undisputed party leader. He initiated a series of reorganizations of the USSR, introduced a policy of rapid industrialization under a series of five-year plans, brought all sectors of industry under government control, abolished private ownership and enforced the collectivization of agriculture. He eliminated potential political opponents through purges and show trials, and total political repression lasted until his death in 1953.

Repression lessened under Khrushchev and Brezhnev, but the Communist Party remained dominant in all walks of life. This was the state of affairs when Mikhail Gorbachev became Soviet leader in March 1985. Gorbachev introduced the policies of *perestroika* (complete restructuring) and *glasnost* (openness) in order to revamp the economy, which had stagnated since the 1970s, to root out corruption and inefficiency, and to end the Cold War and its attendant arms race. Private ownership was allowed, individual expression and limited private enterprise were tolerated, political prisoners released and the guaranteed leading role of the Communist Party abolished. The political openness and the retreat from total control by the Communist Party unleashed ethnic and nationalist tensions. Events came to a head on 19 August 1991 when a coup was attempted against President Gorbachev by hardline elements of the Communist Party, the armed forces and the state security service (KGB) in order to reimpose Communist control on the USSR. The coup was defeated by reformist and democratic political groupings with mass support, who staged demonstrations under the leadership of Russian President Yeltsin. The coup leaders were arrested, and Mikhail Gorbachev returned to Moscow. However, it became clear that effective political power was in the hands of the republican leaders, especially Russian President Yeltsin, and the Soviet Union began to break up as the constituent republics declared their independence. Mikhail Gorbachev resigned as Soviet President on 25 December 1991 and on 26 December 1991 the USSR formally ceased to exist.

GOVERNMENT

Russia was recognized as an independent state by the EC and USA in January 1992, and it inherited the Soviet Union's seat at the UN on 24 December 1991.

A new Russian Federal Treaty was signed on 13 March 1992 between the central government and the autonomous republics. Tatarstan refused to sign the Treaty and in April 1992 declared its 'independence'. In February 1994 Tatarstan signed its own agreement with the federal government on the basis of being a 'state united with Russia'. Similarly, after declaring its 'independence' in March 1992, Bashkortostan signed a treaty with the Federation in August 1994 giving it considerable legislative and economic autonomy. In November 1992 President Yeltsin imposed direct rule in the autonomous republics of Ingush and North Ossetia after Ingush forces attacked North Ossetia; a state of emergency was declared by President Yeltsin in the two autonomous republics in March 1993; it remains in place.

Throughout 1992–3 President Yeltsin's government and reformist political groups faced opposition to constitutional political and economic reform from the bureaucracy, some of the military, influential heads of major state enterprises and the Supreme Soviet and the Congress of People's Deputies, led by its speaker Ruslan Khasbulatov. Despite an overwhelming victory for President Yeltsin in an April 1993 referendum on continuing socio-economic reform, parliamentary hardliners continued to block reform. Events came to a head on 21 September 1993 when President Yeltsin dissolved parliament and called new elections. The hardline parliamentary forces led by Khasbulatov and Rutskoi declared the move a coup d'état, formed a rival government and occupied the White House. After several days of fighting in Moscow between parliamentary and government forces, the parliamentary hardline forces attempted a coup which was put down by the army. President Yeltsin's government suspended the constitutional court, clamped down on broadcasting and press organizations that had supported the coup attempt, and held new elections in all 89 regions and republics.

Elections to the Federal Assembly were held on 12 December 1993 and resulted in the pro-reform Russia's Democractic Choice bloc emerging as the largest party in the State Duma. The strong showing of the anti-reform Communist and Agrarian parties led to a more centrist government being formed and the ending of radical economic reforms. The state of the parties in the State Duma following the December 1995 election was: Communist Party 157 seats (34.9 per cent); Our Home is Russia 55 (12.2 per cent); Liberal Democratic Party 51 (11.3 per cent); Yabloko 45 (10 per cent); Agrarian Party 20 (4.4 per cent); Russia's Democratic Choice 9 (2 per cent); Power to the People 9 (2 per cent); Congress of Russian Communities 5 (1.1 per cent); Independents 77 (17.1 per cent); others 22 (5 per cent). The first round of voting in the presidential election on 16 June 1996 gave President Yeltsin a marginal (2.69 per cent) lead over Communist Party candidate Gennadi Zyuganov. President Yeltsin offered the third-placed candidate, Gen. Aleksandr Lebed, the position of National Security Adviser and secretary of the presidential Security Council. Gen. Lebed accepted and stepped down from the presidential race, enabling President Yeltsin to win the second ballot on 3 July 1996 by 53.8 per cent to Zyuganov's 40.3 per cent.

CONSTITUTION

The present constitution came into force on 22 December 1993 after approval in a national referendum. It enshrines the right to private ownership and the freedoms of press, speech, association, worship and travel, and states that Russia is a multiparty democracy. The President is given strong powers under the constitution, being head of state, head of government, head of the Security Council and commander-in-chief of the armed forces. The President is pre-eminent in foreign and defence policies and may declare war on foreign states or declare a state of emergency or martial law in Russia (subject to confirmation by the Federation Council). He may chair Cabinet meetings, determine basic government policy, veto parliamentary legislation, issue decrees and directives, call referendums, dismiss the government, nominate senior judges, the prosecutor-general and the Central Bank Governor. The President nominates the Prime Minister and Deputy Prime Ministers, who must be approved by the State Duma. If the President's nominees are rejected once or twice by the State Duma he may ignore it; on the third rejection he may dismiss the State Duma and call new elections. The President is directly elected for a maximum of two four-year terms, and may only be impeached on the grounds of treason or serious crime after rulings in both the Supreme and Constitutional Courts and two-thirds majorities in both houses of parliament. The Prime Minister takes over from the President in the event that he is unable to fulfil his duties.

Legislative power is vested in the Federal Assembly, comprising the Federation Council (upper house) of 178 members, two elected by each of the 89 members of the Russian Federation; the State Duma (lower house) of 450 members, of which 225 are elected by constituencies on a first-past-the-post basis and 225 by proportional representation, with a 5 per cent threshold for representation. State Duma deputies may not serve as ministers. The Federation Council maintains jurisdiction over central-local government matters, and its approval is needed for economic and defence legislation to be passed. The Council is composed of two representatives from each constituent territory of the Federation: the head of the legislative and the head of the executive body. Elections for the latter are due to be held by December 1996. The State Duma, elected for four-year terms, oversees government appointments, has the power to reject the government's fiscal and monetary policies, may pass votes of no confidence in the government (which the President may ignore on the first vote), and cannot be dissolved less than one year after its election.

The main clauses of the constitution may only be changed with the agreement of the President and with a three-quarters vote in the Federation Council, a two-thirds vote in the State Duma, and the agreement of two-thirds of the Russian Federation's 89 members.

The judicial system consists of a Constitutional Court of 19 members appointed for a 12-year term which protects and interprets the constitution and decides if laws are compatible with it. The Supreme Court adjudicates in criminal and civil laws cases. The Arbitration Court deals with commercial disputes between companies. The new code of civil law came into force in January 1995.

SECESSION

The Chechen republic declared its 'independence' in November 1991 after a nationalist coup in the republic which brought former Soviet Air Force General Dudayev to power as republican President. Chechenia refused to sign the Russian Federal Treaty in March 1992 and a constitutional stalemate ensued. Civil war began in early 1994 between Gen. Dudayev's forces and armed opposition forces of the 'Provisional Chechen Council', tacitly supported by the Russian government. After Russian forces surrounded Chechenia in September 1994 to stop the conflict overspilling the borders, President Yeltsin ordered the laying down of arms by the rival groups on 29 November. When this request was refused Russian aircraft began to bomb the Chechen capital Grozny and on 9 December President Yeltsin ordered the Russian military to retake the republic. Russian army and interior ministry forces entered Chechenia two days later. Chechen forces were finally forced out of Grozny in early February.

The Chechens continued low-level attacks, including the seizure of over 1,000 hostages in the southern Russian town of Budyonnovsk on 14 June 1995. A cease-fire agreement on 22 June 1995 was followed by a peace accord, signed on 30 July 1995, which provided for the disarming of rebels and the withdrawal of Russian troops. The agreement collapsed in October 1995, however, and a state of emergency was declared by the Russian government. The Russian-approved candidate Doku Zavgayev was elected head of state of Chechenia and member of the State Duma of the Russian Federation on 17 December

1995 and concluded an autonomy accord with Russia giving the region autonomous status within the Federation. The rebels rejected the accord and intensified their insurrection, briefly seizing Chechenia's second town, Gudermes, in December 1995, instigating a second hostage crisis in Kizlyar, Dagestan, in January 1996, and attacking Grozny in March 1996. With public resentment of the war growing in Russia and a presidential election looming, President Yeltsin launched a new peace initiative and a cease-fire agreement was reached in May 1996 which lasted until July, just after President Yeltsin's re-election. Following an intensive rebel counter-attack on Grozny, President Yeltsin's new National Security Adviser, Gen. Aleksandr Lebed, resumed negotiations with the rebels in August, reaching an agreement to cease hostilities and to delay a decision on Chechenia's final status until 2001. (*See also* Events of the Year).

HEAD OF STATE

President, Boris Yeltsin, *elected* 12 June 1991, *re-elected* 3 July 1996, *inaugurated* 9 August 1996

GOVERNMENT *as at August 1996*

Prime Minister, Viktor Chernomyrdin
First Deputy PMs, Vladimir Potanin (*Economy*); Viktor Ilyushin (*Social Affairs*); Alexei Bolshakov (*Ministries and Departments*)
Deputy PMs, Oleg Davydov (*Foreign Economic Relations*); Alexander Zaveryukha (*Agribusiness and Environmental Protection*); Valery Serov (*Co-operation with the CIS, Federal, Regional and Legal Policies*); Vladimir Babichev (*Chief of Staff*); Alexander Livshits (*Finance*); Vitaly Ignatenko; Oleg Lobov
Construction, Yefim Basin
Communication, Vladimir Bulgak
General and Vocational Education, Vladimir Kinelev
Justice, Valentin Kovalev
Interior, Anatoly Kulikov
Labour and Social Development, Gennady Melikyan
Atomic Energy, Viktor Mikhailov
Nationalities and Federal Affairs, Vyacheslav Mikhailov
Defence Industry, Zinovy Pak
Foreign Affairs, Yevgeni Primakov
Defence, Igor Rodionov
Agriculture and Food, Viktor Khlystun
Transport, Nikolai Tsakh
Civil Defence, Disaster Relief, Sergei Shoigu
Economy, Yevgeny Yasin
Fuel and Energy, Pyotr Rodionov
Railways, Anatoly Zaitsev
Industry, Yury Bespalov
Natural Resources, Viktor Orlov
CIS Affairs, Aman Tuleyev
Health, Tatyana Dmitriyeva
Culture, Yevgeny Sidorov

EMBASSY OF THE RUSSIAN FEDERATION
13 Kensington Palace Gardens, London W8 4QX
Tel 0171-229 3628
Ambassador Extraordinary and Plenipotentiary, HE Anatoly Adamishin, apptd 1994
Minister-Counsellors, Aleksandr Kudinov; G. Gventsadze
Defence Attaché, Lt.-Gen. V. N. Pronin
Trade Representative, N. B. Teliatnikov.

BRITISH EMBASSY
Sosiiskaya Naberezhnaya 14, Moscow 10972
Tel: Moscow 9567200
Ambassador Extraordinary and Plenipotentiary, HE Sir Andrew Wood, KCMG, apptd 1995
Minister and Deputy Head of Mission, A. Carter, CMG

Minister-Counsellor, M. B. Nicholson
Defence and Air Attaché, Air Cdre M. L. Freenan, CBE
Counsellor (Commercial), A. R. Brenton
Consuls-General: I. Kydd (Moscow); J. W. Guy, OBE (St Petersburg)
There is a British Consulate-General in St Petersburg.

BRITISH COUNCIL DIRECTOR, Mark Evans, CVO, Ul Nikoloyamskaya 1, Moscow 109189. There is also an office at St Petersburg.

DEFENCE (see also CIS entry, pages 747–8)

Since the demise of the Soviet Union the Russian armed forces have been considerably reduced but remain some of the most powerful in the world. The total active armed forces number 1,520,000 personnel (including 400,000 conscripts serving two-year periods and 220,000 Ministry of Defence staff). Reserves number 20,000,000 personnel.

The Strategic Nuclear Forces are centrally controlled, number 149,000 personnel and have 684 nuclear missiles in 45 submarines; 928 land-based inter-continental ballistic missiles; 95 long-range nuclear bombers; 100 anti-ballistic missiles with related satellites, radar and long-range early warning systems.

The Navy has a strength of 200,000 personnel (including 40,000 conscripts, 30,000 naval aviation and 24,000 coastal defence personnel). It deploys 138 tactical submarines; one fixed-wing and one V/STOL aircraft carriers; 25 cruisers; 22 destroyers; 102 frigates; 143 patrol and coastal craft; 188 mine warfare vessels; and 596 support ships. Naval Aviation has 783 combat aircraft and 251 armed helicopters whilst the coastal defence force deploys 500 main battle tanks, 1,500 armoured vehicles and 806 artillery pieces.

The Army numbers 670,000 personnel (210,000 conscripts) organized into 80 divisions and 152 brigades. Equipment includes 19,000 main battle tanks; 33,000 armoured infantry fighting vehicles and armoured personnel carriers; 20,650 artillery pieces; 600 surface-to-surface missiles; 1,000 attack helicopters. The Air Force has a strength of 130,000 personnel (including 40,000 conscripts) with 130 long-range bombers, 750 ground attack aircraft, 425 air defence fighters, 350 transport aircraft, 200 reconnaissance aircraft and 1,670 training aircraft. Paramilitary forces number 280,000, including 100,000 Frontier Forces and 180,000 internal security troops.

The Russian withdrawal from eastern Europe was completed on 31 August 1994, except for 600 troops in Latvia to operate and then dismantle the Skrunda radar base over five and a half years; 200 troops left Estonia on 27 September 1995, having dismantled the Paldiski nuclear submarine base. In the rest of the CIS, Russia maintains a joint air defence force with the five Central Asian republics, maintains joint armed forces of 11,000 personnel with Turkmenistan, and was due to establish a joint armed forces with Kazakhstan by the end of 1995. It also deploys forces in Armenia (9,000), Georgia (22,000), Moldova (6,400), Tajikistan (12,000).

ECONOMY

Under the Soviet regime, an essentially agrarian economy in 1917 was transformed by the early 1960s into the second strongest industrial power in the world. However, by the early 1970s the concentration of resources on the military-industrial complex was causing the civilian economy to stagnate. This was exacerbated by the bureaucratic inefficiency of the centrally planned economic system and the poor distribution system. It was in an attempt to solve these problems that Gorbachev introduced economic restruc-

turing (perestroika). Free market reforms were introduced, including the legalization of small private businesses, the reduction of state control over the economy, and de-nationalization and privatization. In May 1992 most state subsidies were abolished and price liberalization was introduced. The first stage of mass privatization of state industries began in October 1992 and the central distribution system was abolished with effect from 1 January 1993.

However, the abolition of central planning before a fully free market system was in place, and continued disagreement over reform within the government in 1992–4 resulted in economic confusion. By the end of the first stage of mass privatization in June 1994 an estimated 35–40 per cent of enterprises had been privatized (about 85,000, including 15,000 large and medium-sized enterprises employing 70 per cent of industrial workers); 45 per cent of the workforce worked in the private sector, which produced 40 per cent of GDP; and an estimated 40 million Russians owned shares. This added to the 30,000 small enterprises and shops and 184,000 agricultural holdings privatized in 1992. On 27 October 1993 President Yeltsin issued a decree allowing the unrestricted buying and selling of land for the first time since 1917. The second stage of mass privatization was launched on 1 July 1994 and consists of the sale of residual government shares in most companies. By February 1996, 80 per cent of the economy had been privatized.

While privatization has been a success, the restructuring of state enterprises has not. In January 1992 the radical reform government introduced economic 'shock therapy' to end hyperinflation and restore government reserves by liberalizing prices and restructuring firms to end their reliance on state subsidies. The policy was only partially implemented in 1992–4 due to parliamentary insistence on large budget deficits to support bankrupt enterprises. The result was that industrial production declined (18 per cent in 1992, 15.5 per cent in 1993), hyperinflation (900 per cent in 1993) continued and the rouble fell further (90 per cent against the US dollar in 1992–4) than necessary. In early 1994 the economic situation stabilized, with industrial output growing, inflation at 8 per cent a month, a budget deficit of 6 per cent of GDP, and a trade surplus of US$20,900 million for 1993, which had helped to raise government foreign currency reserves to US$10,000 million. GDP in 1993 was 170,320,000 million roubles and foreign investment was US$5,000 million.

From 1994 to 1996, the economy began to stabilize with economic reforms judged to have become irreversible, despite the election of a Communist-dominated State Duma, and the costs of the Chechen war. Industrial output and GDP fell by 3 per cent and 4 per cent respectively in 1995, compared with 21 per cent and 18.6 per cent in 1994, a result of the government having finally gained control of the money supply following the resignation of Central Bank governor Viktor Geraschenko in October 1994. Inflation has dropped from 800 per cent a year in 1993 to 131 per cent in 1995. The purchasing power of the rouble compared with the US dollar grew by over 70 per cent, and the budget deficit was reduced by 20 per cent. Agricultural production declined by more than 10 per cent in 1995, whereas arms sales grew by 62 per cent, rising to US$6,000 million from US$3,700 million in 1994. Overall, the economy shrank by 4 per cent in 1995 but is expected to grow by up to 3 per cent in 1996. The main economic battle of 1994–5 was over the budget; the government finally forced the legislature to pass an IMF-approved budget which keeps the budget deficit down to 7.8 per cent of GDP and aims for an inflation rate of 2 per cent per month. The foreign trade surplus in 1994 was US$19,800 million, while by February 1995 the total official and commercial debt owed by Russia to foreign creditors had risen to US$120,000 million. GDP in 1994 was 630,000,000 million roubles.

Russia has received considerable international aid since 1993. In April 1993 a rescheduling of Russia's US$80 billion foreign debt was announced, which saved US$15 billion in repayments. A further US$39.5 billion was rescheduled in 1994–5. The G7 summit in Tokyo in April 1994 pledged aid of US$43 billion for structural reform and rouble stabilization, conditional on political and economic reforms. Since 1992 the IMF has provided US$4,000 million under its systemic transformation facility to bring about a market economy. In 1995 the IMF provided US$6,800 million in standby credit to cover part of the budget deficit. A further three-year credit of US$10,087 million, granted in February 1996, was made conditional on the government maintaining spending limits.

Russia has some of the richest mineral deposits in the world. Coal is mined in the Kuznetsk area, in the Urals, south of Moscow, in the Donets basin and in the Pechora area in the north. Oil is produced in the northern Caucasus, between the Volga and the Urals, and in western Siberia, which also has large deposits of natural gas. Coal and gas deposits in Siberia and the far east (especially Yakutia) are currently being developed. The Ural mountains contain high-quality iron ore, manganese, copper, aluminium, gold, platinum, precious stones, salt, asbestos, pyrites, coal, oil, etc. Iron ore is also mined near Kursk, Tula, Lipetsk, in several areas in Siberia and in the Kola Peninsula. Nonferrous metals are found in the Altai, in eastern Siberia, in the northern Caucasus, in the Kuznetsk basin, in the far east and in the far north.

The vast area and the great variety in climatic conditions is reflected in the structure of agriculture. In the far north reindeer breeding, hunting and fishing are predominant. Further south, timber industry is combined with grain growing. In the southern half of the forest zone and in the adjacent forest-steppe zone, the acreage under grain crops is larger and the structure of agriculture more complex. Between the Volga and the Urals cericulture is predominant (particularly summer wheat), followed by cattle breeding. Beyond the Urals is another important grain-growing and stock-breeding area in the southern part of the western Siberian plain. The southern steppe zone is the main wheat granary of Russia, containing also large acreages under barley, maize and sunflowers. In the extreme south cotton is cultivated. Vine, tobacco and other southern crops are grown on the Black Sea shore of the Caucasus.

Moscow and St Petersburg are still the two largest industrial centres in the country, but new industrial areas have been developed in the Urals, the Kuznetsk basin, in Siberia and the far east. Most of the oil produced in the former USSR came from Russia; half the annual output comes from Tyumen Oblast in western Siberia. All industries are represented in Russia, including iron and steel and engineering.

TRADE

Trade from January to November 1995 was worth US$112,500 million, 20.6 per cent more than the same period in 1994. Exports were US$7,170 million, a 21.4 per cent increase on 1994, and imports were US$40,800 million, a 19.2 per cent increase.

Trade with UK	1994	1995
Imports from UK	£707,599,000	£870,387,000
Exports to UK	804,817,000	965,870,000

COMMUNICATIONS

The European area of Russia is well served by railways, St Petersburg and Moscow being the two main focal points of rail routes. The centre and south have a good system of north-south and east-west lines, but the eastern part (the Volga lands), traversed by trunk lines between Europe and Asia, lacks north-south routes. In Asia, there are still large areas, notably in the far north and Siberia, with few or no railways. In the northern part of European Russia, the North Pechora Railway has been completed, while in the far east a second Trans-Siberian line (the Baikal-Amur Railway) is partially in use; it follows a more northerly alignment than the earlier Trans-Siberian and terminates in the Pacific port of Sovetskaya Gavan.

The most important ports (Taganrog, Rostov and Novorossiisk) lie around the Black Sea and the Sea of Azov. The northern ports (St Petersburg, Murmansk and Archangel) are, with the exception of Murmansk, icebound during winter. Several ports have been built along the Arctic Sea route between Murmansk and Vladivostok and are in regular use every summer. The far eastern port of Vladivostok, the Pacific naval base of Russia, is kept open by icebreakers all the year round.

Inland waterways, both natural and artificial, are of great importance in the country, although some of them are icebound in winter (from two and a half months in the south to six months in the north). The great rivers of European Russia flow outwards from the centre, linking all parts of the plain with the chief ports, an immense system of navigable waterways which carried about 690 million tons of freight in 1988. They are supplemented by a system of canals which provide a through traffic between the White, Baltic, Black and Caspian Seas. The most notable are the White Sea-Baltic Canal, the Moscow-Volga Canal and the Volga-Don Canal linking the Baltic and the White Seas in the north to the Caspian Sea, the Black Sea and the Sea of Azov in the south.

CULTURE

Before the westernization of Russia under Peter the Great (1682–1725), Russian literature consisted mainly of folk ballads (byliny), epic songs, chronicles and works of moral theology. The 18th and 19th centuries saw the development of poetry and fiction. Poetry reached its zenith with Alexander Pushkin (1799–1837), Mikhail Lermontov (1814–41), Alexander Blok (1880–1921), the 1958 Nobel Prize laureate Boris Pasternak (1890–1960), Vladimir Mayakovsky (1893–1930) and Anna Akhmatova (1888–1966). Fiction is associated with the names of Nikolai Gogol (1809–52), Ivan Turgenev (1818–83), Fyodor Dostoevsky (1821–81), Leo Tolstoy (1828–1910), Anton Chekhov (1860–1904), Maxim Gorky (1868–1936), Ivan Bunin (1870–1953), Mikhail Bulgakov (1891–1940), Mikhail Sholokhov (1905–84) and Alexander Solzhenitsyn (b. 1918).

Great names in music include Glinka (1804–57), Borodin (1833–87), Mussorgsky (1839–81), Rimsky-Korsakov (1844–1908), Rubinstein (1829–94), Tchaikovsky (1840–93), Rachmaninov (1873–1943), Skriabin (1872–1915), Prokofiev (1891–1953), Stravinsky (1882–1971), Shostakovich (1906–75) and Alfred Schnittke (b. 1934).

RWANDA
Republika y'u Rwanda

Rwanda, formerly part of the Belgian-administered trust-eeship of Ruanda-Urundi, has an area of 10,169 sq. miles (26,338 sq. km), and a population (UN estimate 1994) of 7,750,000, mainly of the Hutu tribe (90 per cent), with Tutsi (9 per cent) and Twa (pygmy) (1 per cent) minorities. Kinyarwanda, French and English are the official languages.

CAPITAL – Kigali (156,000).
CURRENCY – Rwanda franc of 100 centimes.
FLAG – Three vertical bands, red, yellow and green with letter R on yellow band.
NATIONAL DAY – 1 July.

GOVERNMENT

The majority Hutu population rebelled against Tutsi feudal rule (under the Belgian colonial authority) in 1959–61, leading to the massacre of thousands of Tutsis. Large numbers fled into exile in Uganda. A referendum held in September 1961 showed the majority of the population were opposed to the retention of the monarchy, which was abolished in October 1961. Rwanda became an independent republic on 1 July 1962, with Gregoire Kayibanda as head of state. He was deposed in 1973 and replaced by a military government under Maj.-Gen. Juvénal Habyarimana, who established a one-party state.

Armed Tutsi exiles repeatedly attempted to invade Rwanda in the 1960s and 1970s but were defeated by the predominantly Hutu army. Continued Hutu-Tutsi conflict left thousands dead over a period of 30 years. In October 1990 Rwanda was invaded by the Rwandan Patriotic Front (RPF) of exiled Tutsis and moderate Hutus, who forced the one-party MRND (National Revolutionary Movement for Development) government to end its monopoly of power and introduce a multiparty constitution in 1991. After the government reneged on a 1992 peace agreement, the RPF advanced on Kigali and forced the government to restart negotiations, which led to the August 1993 Arusha peace accord. The accord provided for a transitional period under a broad-based government including the RPF until the 1995 elections, with UN forces in the country throughout the period.

During the transitional period, President Habyarimana, who had retained the interim presidency, died on 6 April 1994 in a plane crash widely believed to have been caused by a rocket attack by extremist sections of the Hutu army. The Hutu army and armed militia, the *interahamwe*, then carried out a preplanned act of genocide against the Tutsi minority and moderate Hutus; 500,000 people were massacred in three months. The civil war restarted and the RPF gradually re-established its control over the country, forcing the defeated government forces and two million Hutu refugees into exile, while another 1.2 million Hutus fled to the French 'safe zone' in the south-west. On 18 July 1994 the RPF declared victory and established a broad-based government of national unity in which moderate Hutus were given the presidency and premiership and the RPF took eight of the 22 seats.

Some 50,000–60,000 Hutu refugees died of disease in refugee camps in eastern Zaïre in August–September 1994. The remainder have since been prevented from returning to Rwanda by the Hutu army and militia forces. French troops withdrew from their 'safe zone' in the south-west of Rwanda in September 1994 and were replaced by RPF forces who gradually returned most refugees in the zone to their homes. UN forces (UNAMIR II) were deployed to deter revenge attacks by Tutsis on Hutus, although their mandate expired in March 1996.

In April 1995 200,000 Hutu refugees remained in camps in the south-west controlled by armed Hutu militia members. RPF forces attacked the camps and broke the militia control in fighting which killed hundreds of people before the return of refugees was completed. In August the Zaïrean government began the forcible repatriation of some of the over one million Hutu refugees who, it felt, were destabilizing eastern Zaïre. However, after thousands had fled to the countryside rather than return to Rwanda, international pressure forced the Zaïrean government to agree to a voluntary repatriation programme organized by the UN High Commissioner for Refugees (UNHCR). In November 1994 the UN Security Council established the International Criminal Tribunal for Rwanda to prosecute those responsible for genocide and other international humanitarian law violations between 1 January and 31 December 1994. An estimated 200,000 Tutsi refugees who fled to Uganda in the 1960s and 1970s have returned to Rwanda. By December 1995, 500,000 refugees remained in Tanzania, and one million in Zaïre

The 70-member Transitional National Assembly provided for by the Arusha agreement began operation on 12 December 1994 with the extremist Hutu MRND excluded. However, tensions between Tutsis and moderate Hutus in the government remain, with Prime Minister Twagiramungu and four other ministers being dismissed in August 1995 after criticizing the lack of power-sharing by the RPF and the security situation in the country. (*See also* Events of the Year).

HEAD OF STATE
President, Pasteur Bizimungu, *sworn in* 19 July 1994
Vice-President, Gen. Paul Kagame

GOVERNMENT OF NATIONAL UNITY *as at June 1996*
The President
Defence, The Vice-President
Prime Minister, Pierre Claver Rwigema
Deputy PM, Interior and Communal Development, Col. Alex Kanyarengwe
Foreign Affairs, Anastase Gasana
Justice, Marthe Mukamurenzi
Agriculture and Livestock, Augustin Iyamuremye
Primary and Secondary Education, Laurien Ngirabanzi
Higher Education and Scientific Research, Joseph Nsengimana
Finance, Marc Rugenera
Information, Jean-Pierre Bizimana
Commerce, Industry and Handicrafts, Prosper Higiro
Planning, Jean-Berchmans Birara
Health, Col. Joseph Karemera
Transport and Communications, Charles Muligande
Labour and Social Affairs, Pie Mugabo
Public Works and Energy, Charles Ntakiruntinka
Environment and Tourism, Jean-Nepomucene Nayinzira
Family and Women's Development, Aloysia Inyumba
Youth, Jacques Bihozagara
Repatriation and Reconstruction, Patrick Mazimpaka
Civil Service, Abdul Karim Harerimana

EMBASSY OF THE REPUBLIC OF RWANDA
42 Aylmer Road, London N2
Ambassador Extraordinary and Plenipotentiary, Dr Zac Nsenga, apptd 1996

BRITISH EMBASSY
Parcelle No. 1071, Kimihurara, Kigali
Tel: Kigali 84098
Ambassador Extraordinary and Plenipotentiary, HE Kaye W.
 Oliver, OBE, apptd 1996

ECONOMY

Coffee, tea and sugar are grown. Tin, hides, bark of quinine
and extract of pyrethrum flowers are also exported.
In 1991 total imports were valued at US$267 million;
total exports, US$94 million. Coffee accounted for 90 per
cent of export earnings in 1989.

Trade with UK	1994	1995
Imports from UK	£2,542,000	£4,825,000
Exports to UK	1,666,000	1,841,000

ST CHRISTOPHER AND NEVIS
The Federation of St Christopher and Nevis

The state of St Christopher and Nevis is located at the
northern end of the eastern Caribbean. It comprises the
islands of St Christopher (St Kitts) (68 sq. miles) and Nevis
(36 sq. miles). The central area of St Christopher, 17° 18' N.
and 62° 48' W., is forest-clad and mountainous, rising to the
3,792 ft. Mount Liamuiga. Nevis, 17° 10' N. and 62° 35' W.,
is separated from the southern tip of St Christopher by a
strait two miles wide and is dominated by Nevis Peak,
3,232 ft. The combined population (UN estimate 1994)
was 41,000.

CAPITAL – ΨBasseterre (estimated population, 15,000).
 The chief town of Nevis is ΨCharlestown (population
 1,200), which is a port of entry.
CURRENCY – East Caribbean dollar (EC$) of 100 cents.
FLAG – Three diagonal bands, green, black and red; each
 colour separated by a stripe of yellow. Two white stars
 on the black band.
NATIONAL ANTHEM – Oh Land of Beauty.
NATIONAL DAY – 19 September (Independence Day).

GOVERNMENT

St Christopher was the first island in the British West
Indies to be colonized (1623). The Territory of St
Christopher and Nevis became a State in Association with
Britain in 1967. The State of St Christopher and Nevis
became an independent nation on 19 September 1983.
 Under the constitution, The Queen is head of state,
represented in the islands by the Governor-General.
There is a central government with a ministerial system,
the head of which is the Prime Minister of St Christopher
and Nevis, and a National Assembly located on St
Christopher. The National Assembly is composed of the
Speaker, three senators (nominated by the Prime Minister
and the Leader of the Opposition) and 11 elected repres-
entatives. On Nevis there is a Nevis Island Administration,
the head being styled Premier of Nevis, and a Nevis Island
Assembly of five elected and three nominated members.
 In the July 1995 election to the National Assembly, the
Labour Party won seven seats, and the People's Action
Movement won one seat. Of the three seats reserved for
Nevis, the Concerned Citizens Movement won two seats
and the Nevis Reformation Party won one seat.

Governor-General, HE Sir Cuthbert Montraville Sebastian,
 GCMG, OBE, apptd 1996

CABINET *as at August 1996*
Prime Minister and Minister of Finance, National Security,
 Planning, Information and Foreign Affairs, Hon. Dr Denzil
 Douglas
Deputy PM, Trade and Industry, Caricom Affairs, Youth, Sports
 and Community Affairs, Hon. Sam Condor
Agriculture, Lands and Housing, Hon. Timothy Harris
Health and Women's Affairs, Hon. Dr Earl Asim Martin
Culture, Environment and Tourism, Hon. G. A. Dwyer
 Astaphan
Education, Labour and Social Security, Hon. Rupert Herbert
Communications, Works, Public Utilities and Posts, Hon. Cedric
 Liburd
Attorney-General, Hon. Delano Bart

HIGH COMMISSION FOR ST CHRISTOPHER AND NEVIS
10 Kensington Court, London W8 5DL
Tel 0171-937 9522
High Commissioner for the Eastern Caribbean States, HE Aubrey
 Hart, apptd 1994

BRITISH HIGH COMMISSIONER, HE Richard Thomas,
 CMG, resident at Bridgetown, Barbados

ECONOMY

The economy of the islands has been based on sugar for
over three centuries. Tourism (210,000 visitors in 1994)
and light industry, concentrating on brewing, food processing, clothing and electronics, are now being developed.
The economy of Nevis centres on small peasant farmers,
but a sea-island cotton industry is being developed for
export.
 The main exports are sugar, lobsters and electrical
equipment. Foodstuffs, energy, machinery and transport
equipment are the main imports. GDP was estimated at
US$162 million in 1994, a drop of 3 per cent on 1993.

FINANCE	1991	1992
Revenue	EC$93,300,000	EC$108,900,000
Expenditure	97,500,000	105,000,000

TRADE WITH UK	1994	1995
Imports from UK	£6,915,000	£9,104,000
Exports to UK	6,505,000	8,671,000

COMMUNICATIONS

Basseterre is a port of registry and has deep water harbour
facilities. Golden Rock airport, on St Kitts, can take most
large jet aircraft; Newcastle airstrip on Nevis can take
small aircraft and has night landing facilities. The sea ferry
route from Basseterre to Charlestown is 11 miles.

ST LUCIA

St Lucia, the second largest of the Windward group,
situated in 13° 54' N. latitude and 60° 50' W. longitude, is
27 miles in length, with an extreme breadth of 14 miles. It
comprises an area of 238 sq. miles (616 sq. km), with a
population of 143,000. It is mountainous, its highest point
being Mt Gimie (3,145 ft) and for the most part it is covered
with forest and tropical vegetation.

CAPITAL – ΨCastries (population 1989, 56,000).
CURRENCY – East Caribbean dollar (EC$) of 100 cents.
FLAG – Blue, bearing in centre a device of yellow over
 black over white triangles having a common base.
NATIONAL ANTHEM – Sons and Daughters of Saint
 Lucia.
NATIONAL DAY – 22 February (Independence Day).

GOVERNMENT

Possession of St Lucia was fiercely disputed and it constantly changed hands between the British and the French. It became independent within the Commonwealth on 22 February 1979. The head of state is The Queen, represented in the island by a St Lucian Governor-General, and there is a bicameral legislature. The Senate has 11 members, six appointed by the ruling party, three by the Opposition and two by the Governor-General. The House of Assembly, which has a life of five years, has 17 elected Members and a Speaker, who may be elected from outside the House.

Governor-General, HE George Mallet, apptd 1996

CABINET *as at August 1996*

Prime Minister, Minister for Finance, Planning, Development, Foreign Affairs, Home Affairs and Information, Dr Hon. Vaughan Lewis, CBE

Deputy PM and Minister for Education, Culture, Labour and Broadcasting, Hon. Louis George

Tourism, Public Utilities, National Mobilization and Civil Aviation, Hon. Romanus Lansiquot

Health, Hon. Stephenson King

Communications, Works and Transport, Hon. Gregory Avril

Agriculture, Lands, Fisheries and Forestry, Hon. Ira D'Auvergne

Community Development, Social Affairs, Youth, Sports, Co-operatives and Local Government, Hon. Desmond Braithwaite

Attorney-General, Legal Affairs and Women's Affairs, Senator Lorraine Williams

Trade, Senator Dunstan DuBoulay, MBE

Minister in the Ministry of Community Development, Social Affairs, Youth, Sports, Co-operatives and Local Government, Hon. Edward Innocent

Minister in the Ministry of Agriculture, Lands, Fisheries and Forestry, Hon. Peter Josie

Minister in the Office of the Prime Minister with responsibility for Housing, Urban Renewal and Financial Services, Senator Michael Pilgrim

Minister in the Office of the Prime Minister with responsibility for the Public Service, Senator Leton Thomas, CBE

Senior Minister, Rt. Hon. John G. M. Compton

ST LUCIA HIGH COMMISSION
10 Kensington Court, London W8 5DL
Tel 0171-937 9522

High Commissioner for the Eastern Caribbean States, HE Aubrey Hart, apptd 1994

OFFICE OF THE BRITISH HIGH COMMISSION
Derek Walcott Square, PO Box 227, Castries
Tel: Castries 4522484

High Commissioner, HE Richard Thomas, CMG, resident at Bridgetown, Barbados

Acting High Commissioner, B. Robertson

ECONOMY

The economy is mainly agrarian, with manufacturing based on the processing of agricultural products. Principal crops are bananas, coconuts, cocoa, mangoes, avocado pears, breadfruit, spices, root crops such as cassava and yams, and citrus fruit. Attempts are being made to diversify the economy, in particular through greater industrialization. Tourism is also of increasing importance, with 204,000 visitors to the island in 1989. The economy grew by 2.2 per cent in 1994; external debt totals roughly US$122 million.

TRADE

The principal exports are bananas, coconut products (copra, edible oils, soap), cardboard boxes, beer, and textile manufactures. The chief imports are flour, meat, machinery, building materials, motor vehicles, cotton piece goods, petroleum and fertilizers.

Trade with UK	1994	1995
Imports from UK	£42,496,000	£70,076,000
Exports to UK	41,294,000	45,993,000

ST VINCENT AND THE GRENADINES

The territory of St Vincent includes certain of the Grenadines, a chain of small islands stretching 40 miles across the Caribbean Sea between Grenada and St Vincent, some of the larger of which are Bequia, Canouan, Mayreau, Mustique, Union Island, Petit St Vincent and Prune Island. The whole territory extends 150 sq. miles (388 sq. km). The main island, St Vincent, is situated between 13° 6' and 14° 35' N. latitude and 61° 6' and 61° 20' W. longitude. The island has an area of 133 sq. miles (344 sq. km), and a population of 110,000.

CAPITAL – ΨKingstown, estimated population 33,694.
CURRENCY – East Caribbean dollar (EC$) of 100 cents.
FLAG – Three vertical bands, of blue, yellow and green, with three green diamonds in the shape of a 'V' mounted on the yellow band.
NATIONAL ANTHEM – St Vincent, Land So Beautiful.
NATIONAL DAY – 27 October (Independence Day).

GOVERNMENT

St Vincent was discovered by Christopher Columbus in 1498. It was granted by Charles I to the Earl of Carlisle in 1627 and after subsequent grants and a series of occupations alternately by the French and English, it was finally restored to Britain in 1783. St Vincent achieved full independence within the Commonwealth as St Vincent and the Grenadines on 27 October 1979.

The Queen is head of state, represented by a Governor-General. The House of Assembly consists of 15 elected members and four Senators appointed by the government and two by the Opposition. It is presided over by a Speaker elected by the House from within or without it. The governing New Democratic Party won 12 seats and the United Labour Party three seats at the election held in February 1994.

Governor-General, HE Sir David Jack, GCMG, MBE, *sworn in* 20 September 1989.

CABINET *as at August 1996*

Prime Minister, Minister of Finance and Planning, Rt. Hon. Sir James Mitchell, KCMG

Deputy PM, Attorney-General and Minister of Justice, Ecclesiastical Affairs and Information, Hon. Carlisle Dougan, QC

Culture, Education and Women's Affairs, Hon. John Horne

Agriculture and Labour, Hon. Allan Cruickshank

Foreign Affairs and Tourism, Hon. Alpian Allen

Health and the Environment, Hon. Yvonne Francis-Gibson

Trade, Industry and Consumer Affairs, Hon. Bernard Wyllie

Housing, Local Government, Community Development, Youth and Sports, Hon. Louis Jones

Communications and Works, Hon. Monty Roberts

Minister of State in the PM's Office, Hon. Stephanie Browne

Parliamentary Secretaries, Hon. Stuart Nanton (*Foreign Affairs and Tourism*), Hon. Alfred Bynoe (*Housing, Local Government, Community Development, Youth and Sports*)

ST VINCENT AND THE GRENADINES HIGH COMMISSION
10 Kensington Court, London W8 5DL
Tel 0171-937 9522
High Commissioner for the Eastern Caribbean States, HE Aubrey Hart, apptd 1994

BRITISH HIGH COMMISSION
Granby Street (PO Box 132), Kingstown
Tel: St Vincent 4571701
High Commissioner, HE Richard Thomas, CMG, resident at Bridgetown, Barbados
Acting High Commissioner, B. Robertson

ECONOMY

This is based mainly on agriculture but tourism (155,068 visitors in 1992) and manufacturing industries have been expanding. The main products are bananas, arrowroot, coconuts, cocoa, spices and various kinds of food crops. The main imports are foodstuffs (meat, rice, beverages), textiles, lumber, cement and other building materials, fertilizers, motor vehicles and fuel.

TRADE WITH UK	1994	1995
Imports from UK	£7,652,000	£7,215,000
Exports to UK	14,312,000	22,242,000

EL SALVADOR
República de El Salvador

El Salvador extends along the Pacific coast of Central America for 160 miles, with an area of 8,124 sq. miles (21,041 sq. km). The surface of the country is very mountainous, many of the peaks being extinct volcanoes. Much of the interior has an average altitude of 2,000 feet. The climate varies from tropical to temperate. There is a wet season from May to October, and a dry season from November to April. Earthquakes have been frequent, the most recent being in October 1986.

The population (UN estimate, 1994) was 5,641,000. The language is Spanish.

CAPITAL – San Salvador (497,644, 1989 estimate). Estimated population of metropolitan area, 2,000,000. Other towns are Santa Ana (417,000), San Miguel (157,838), Ψ La Union (Cutuco), Ψ La Libertad and Ψ Acajutia.

CURRENCY – El Salvador colón (₡) of 100 centavos.

FLAG – Three horizontal bands, sky blue, white, sky blue; coat of arms on white band.

NATIONAL ANTHEM – Saludemos La Patria Orgullosos (Let us proudly hail the Fatherland).

NATIONAL DAY – 15 September.

GOVERNMENT

El Salvador was conquered in 1526 by Pedro de Alvarado, and formed part of the Spanish viceroyalty of Guatemala until 1821. It is divided into 14 Departments.

Decades of military rule ended in March 1982 when a Constituent Assembly was elected. Subsequent presidential and parliamentary elections were boycotted by the FMLN (Farabundo Martí National Liberation Front) guerrilla movement. Conflict between the guerrillas and the government continued throughout the 1980s until negotiations culminated in a peace plan signed in January 1992. A cease-fire took effect on 1 February and began a nine-month transition period which ended in December 1992 when the FMLN finished its disarmament and became a political party. A 'Truth Commission', established under UN auspices to investigate human rights abuses in the 1980–91 period, reported in March 1993. The report caused a political crisis when it declared that 15 senior army commanders should be removed. The government was reluctant to do so but came under economic pressure from the USA, which withheld aid for reconstruction until the officers were dismissed on 1 July 1993.

The UN Observer Mission in El Salvador (ONUSAL) monitored the 1992–4 transition process, overseeing the final destruction of FMLN arms in August 1993 and the presidential, parliamentary and local elections held in March and April 1994. Armando Calderón Sol of the ruling right-wing ARENA party won the presidential election, defeating the FMLN's Ruben Zamora. ARENA won 39 of the Legislative Assembly's 84 seats and formed a government with other right-wing parties; the FMLN won 21 seats.

HEAD OF STATE
President, Armando Calderón Sol, *assumed office* 1 June 1994
Vice-President, Enrique Borgo Bustamante

CABINET *as at August 1996*
Minister of the Presidency, The Vice President
Foreign Affairs, Oscar Alfredo Santamaria
Planning, Ramón González
Interior, Roberto Angulo Samayoa
Justice, Dr Rubén Antonio Mejía Peña
Economy, Eduardo Zablah Touche
Education, Cecilia Gallardo de Cano
Labour and Social Security, Eduardo Tomasino
Agriculture, Oscar Gutiérrez
Public Health, Dr Eduardo Interiano
Public Works, Jorge Sansivirini
Finance, Manuel Hinds
Defence and Public Security, Gen. Jaime Guzmán Morales

EMBASSY OF EL SALVADOR
5 Great James Street, London WC1N 3DA
Tel 0171-430 2141
Ambassador Extraordinary and Plenipotentiary, HE Manuel Gutiérrez Ruiz, apptd 1996

BRITISH EMBASSY
PO Box 1591, San Salvador
Tel: San Salvador 2981763
Ambassador Extraordinary and Plenipotentiary, HE Ian Gerken, LVO, apptd 1995

ECONOMY

El Salvador has received substantial aid to rebuild the country's war-damaged infrastructure and services. The USA has written off 75 per cent of El Salvador's debt and in May 1993 the IMF agreed a standby credit facility for El Salvador of US$49 million over 10 months. A further IMF standby credit of US$58 million was approved in July 1995. Average annual growth was 5.5 per cent between 1993 and 1995, with inflation averaging ten per cent.

The principal cash crops are coffee, cotton, chemical products, sugar-cane and shrimps. However, cotton and sugar production have decreased as a result of the civil war. Also cultivated are maize, sesame, indigo, rice, balsam, etc. In the lower altitudes towards the east, sisal is produced and used in the manufacture of coffee and cereal bags. The Salvadorean Coffee Company, sugar exports and the banking system are being privatized.

Existing factories make textiles, clothing, constructional steel, furniture, cement and household items. In 1995 GDP amounted to US$9,659.9 million.

TRADE

Chief exports are coffee, cotton, sugar, shrimps, sisal, balsam, meat, towels, hides and skins. The chief imports are chemicals, fertilizers, pharmaceutical goods, petroleum, manufactured goods, industrial and electronic machinery and equipment, vehicles and consumer goods. Exports were estimated at US$1,661.3 million in 1995, and imports at US$3,352.4 million.

Trade with UK	1994	1995
Imports from UK	£19,217,000	£22,737,000
Exports to UK	7,200,000	3,419,000

COMMUNICATIONS

The Executive Autonomous Port Commission (CEPA) administers the ports of Cutuco, La Unión, Acajutla, and the railways through FENADESAL. There are 6,089 miles (9,800 km) of paved roads. There are good roads between Acajutla and the capital (60 miles), and between the capital and Guatemala City. The Pan-American Highway from the Guatemalan frontier follows this route and continues to the Honduran frontier. The El Salvador international airport can receive jet aircraft with daily flights to other Central American capitals, Mexico, and five US cities. There are 100 broadcasting stations and six television stations. Five daily newspapers are published in San Salvador and four in the provinces.

EDUCATION

The literacy rate is 72.3 per cent. Primary education is nominally compulsory, but the number of schools and teachers available is too small to enable education to be given to all children of school age.

SAN MARINO
Repubblica di San Marino

San Marino is a small republic in the hills near Rimini, on the Adriatic, founded, it is said, by a pious stonecutter of Dalmatia in the fourth century. The republic resisted Papal claims and those of neighbouring dukedoms during the 15th to 18th centuries, and its integrity and sovereignty is recognized and respected by Italy. The area is approximately 23 sq. miles (61 sq. km.) and the population (1995) is 25,058.

CITY – San Marino, on the slope of Monte Titano, has three towers, a fine church and Government palace, a theatre and museums.
CURRENCY – San Marino and Italian currencies are in circulation.
FLAG – Two horizontal bands, white, blue (with coat of arms of the republic in centre).
NATIONAL DAY – 3 September.

The republic is governed by a Congress of State of ten members, under the presidency of two heads of state, who are elected at six-monthly intervals (every March and September). The Great and General Council, a legislative body of 60 members, is elected by universal suffrage for a term of five years. A Council of Twelve forms in certain cases a Supreme Court of Justice. A coalition government of the Christian Democratic Party and the Socialist Party

took office in March 1992, and was returned in the general election of 31 May 1993.

The principal products are wine, cereals, and fruits, and the main industries are tourism, metals, machinery, textiles and food.

HEADS OF STATE
Regents, Two 'Capitani Reggenti'

CONGRESS OF STATE *as at August 1996*
Foreign and Political Affairs, Gabriele Gatti
Finance and Budget, Planning and Information, Clelio Galassi
Internal Affairs, Antonio Lazzaro Volpinari
Environment and Agriculture, Emma Rossi
Industry and Handicrafts, Fiorenzo Stolfi
Education, Justice and Culture, Pier Menicucci
Labour and Co-operation, Claudio Podeschi
Health and Social Security, Sante Canducci
Communications, Transport, Tourism and Sport, Augusto Casali
Commerce and Relations with Local Councils, Ottaviano Rossi

CONSULATE-GENERAL IN LONDON
166 High Holborn, London WCIV 6TT
Tel 0171-836 7744
Consul-General, vacant

BRITISH CONSUL-GENERAL, R. J. Griffiths, OBE, resident at Florence, Italy

TRADE

Trade with UK	1994	1995
Imports from UK	£4,312,000	£5,091,000
Exports to UK	711,000	2,285,000

SÃO TOMÉ AND PRÍNCIPE
República Democrática de São Tomé e Príncipe

The islands of São Tomé and Príncipe are situated in the Gulf of Guinea, off the west coast of Africa. They have an area of 372 sq. miles (964 sq. km), and a population (UN estimate 1994) of 125,000.

CAPITAL – ΨSão Tomé (25,000).
CURRENCY – Dobra of 100 centavos.
FLAG – Horizontal stripes of green, yellow, green, the yellow of double width and bearing two black stars; and a red triangle in the hoist.
NATIONAL DAY – 12 July (Independence Day).

GOVERNMENT

The islands became independent on 12 July 1975. A multi-party constitution was approved by referendum in August 1990. The Movement for the Liberation of São Tomé and Príncipe-Social Democratic Party (MLSTP-PSD), which had been the sole legal party since independence, was defeated by the opposition Democratic Convergence Party (PCD) in legislative elections held on 20 January 1991. Miguel Trovoada, an independent, was elected President on 3 March 1991. The President dismissed governments in 1992 and 1994 because of mounting criticism of economic reforms. A legislative election on 2 October 1994 was won by the MLSTP-PSD with 27 seats in the 55-seat National Assembly to the PCD's 14 seats. The MLSTP-PSD formed a government but this was dismissed on 15 August 1995 after five junior army officers launched a bloodless military coup, arrested the President and suspended parliament and the constitution. The EU threatened to suspend all aid and the officers relinquished power on 21 August after Angolan mediation. The President, government, parliament and constitution were restored and the officers were granted an amnesty. A government of national unity incorporating opposition party members, was appointed on 5 January 1996. Prime Minister Almeida tendered his resignation on 29 March 1996, but agreed to continue until a presidential election, due by 3 April 1996, could be held. The National Assembly extended President Trovoada's term for five months enabling an election to be held in June. President Trovoada was re-elected and reappointed Prime Minister Almeida.

HEAD OF STATE
President and Commander-in-Chief of the Armed Forces,
    Miguel Trovoada, *elected* 3 March 1991, *re-elected* June
    1996, *inaugurated* 3 September 1996

COUNCIL OF MINISTERS *as at August 1996*
Prime Minister, Armindo Vaz Almeida
Foreign Affairs, Guilherme Posser da Costa
Justice, Public and Local Administration, Gabriel Costa
Finance and Planning, Rafael Branco
Health, Family and Women, Fernanda de Azevedo Roncon
Education and Sport, Guilherme Octaviano Viegas d'Abreu
Defence and Internal Security, C. Silva
Agriculture and Fisheries, Julio Silva
Industry, Trade and Tourism, Arlindho Carvelho

EMBASSY OF THE DEMOCRATIC REPUBLIC OF SÃO TOMÉ
AND PRÍNCIPE
42 avenue Brugman, Brussels 1060, Belgium
Tel: Brussels 3475375
Ambassador Extraordinary and Plenipotentiary, new
    appointment awaited

HONORARY CONSULATE
42 North Audley Street, London WIA 4PY
Tel 0171-499 1995
Honorary Consul, Willie S. Wilder

BRITISH CONSULATE
Residencial Avenida, Av. Da Independencia CP 257
British Ambassador, HE Roger D. Hart, resident at Luanda,
    Angola
Honorary Consul, J. Gomes

ECONOMY

The economy is heavily dependent on tourism and agriculture, with cacao being the main product. In 1995 the total foreign debt was US$255 million, annual inflation was 40 per cent and unemployment 38 per cent.

TRADE WITH UK	1994	1995
Imports from UK	£2,313,000	£2,297,000
Exports to UK	3,000	85,000

SAUDI ARABIA
Al Mamlaka al Arabiya as-Sa'udiyya

Saudi Arabia comprises almost the whole of the Arabian peninsula, with the exception of Yemen in the extreme south, Oman and the UAE in the south-east and Qatar in the east. In the north-west it borders Jordan and in the north-east Iraq and Kuwait, while to the west lies the Red Sea and to the east the Gulf where a causeway links the Eastern Province with Bahrain. The Nejd ('plateau') extends over the centre of the peninsula, including the Nafud and Dahna deserts. The Hejaz ('the boundary')

extends along the Red Sea coast to Asir and contains the holy towns of Mecca (Makkah) and Medina (Madinah). Asir ('inaccessible') is so named for its mountainous terrain, and, with the coastal plain of the Tihama, lies along the southern Red Sea coast from the Hejaz to the border with Yemen. It is the only region to enjoy substantial rainfall. The east and south-east of the country are lower-lying and largely desert. The total area is about 830,000 sq. miles (2,149,640 sq. km), with a population (1992 census) of 16,929,294. Islam is the only permitted religion.

Mecca (Al-Makkah), about 60 km east of Jeddah, is the birthplace of the Prophet Muhammad, and contains the Great Mosque, within which is the Kaaba (*Ka'abah*) or sacred shrine of the Muslim religion. This is the focus of the annual Hajj ('pilgrimage'). Medina (Al-Madinah) Al Munawwarah ('The City of Light'), some 300 km north of Mecca, is celebrated as the first city to embrace Islam and as the Prophet Muhammad's burial place.

CAPITAL – Riyadh, population (1992) about 2 million.
    Other major centres are Jeddah (estimated population
    1.5 million), Buraydah, Dammam, Hofuf, Mecca,
    Medina and Tabuk.
CURRENCY – Saudi riyal (SR) of 20 qursh or 100 halala.
FLAG – Green oblong, white Arabic device in centre:
    'There is no God but God and Muhammad is the
    Prophet of God,' and a white scimitar beneath the
    lettering.
NATIONAL ANTHEM – Long live our beloved King.
NATIONAL DAY – 23 September (proclamation and
    unification of the Kingdom, 1932).

GOVERNMENT

In the 18th century Nejd was an independent state governed from Diriya, and the stronghold of the Wahhabis, a puritanical Islamic sect. It subsequently fell under Turkish rule; in 1913 Abdul Aziz Ibn Saud threw off Turkish rule and captured the Turkish province of Al Hasa. In 1920 he captured the Asir and in 1921 the Jebel Shammar territory of the Rashid family. In 1925 he completed the conquest of the Hejaz. Great Britain recognized Abdul Aziz Ibn Saud as an independent ruler, King of the Hejaz and of Nejd and its Dependencies, in 1927. The name was changed to the Kingdom of Saudi Arabia in September 1932.

Saudi Arabia is a hereditary monarchy, ruled by the sons and grandsons of Abdul Aziz Ibn Saud, in accordance with the *Shari'ah* law of Wahhabi Islam. The line of succession passes from brother to brother according to age, although several sons of Ibn Saud renounced their right to the throne. All sons and grandsons of Ibn Saud must be consulted before a new king accedes the throne.

In 1992 King Fahd announced a new Basic Law for the system of government based on *Shari'ah* law and including rules to protect personal freedoms. The constitution is defined as the Holy Koran (*Qur'an*) and the *Sunnah* (the teachings and sayings of the Prophet Muhammad). The King and the Council of Ministers (established in 1953) retain executive power. A consultative council (*Majlis-al-Shura*) of a chairman and 60 members appointed by the King was set up to share power with, and question, the government and to make recommendations to the King. The Majlis-al-Shura began meeting in December 1993 and debates government policy in the areas of the budget, defence, foreign and social affairs. Members of the ruling Al-Saud family are excluded from membership of the Council, which has a four-year term and takes decisions by majority vote. Cabinet ministers have terms of four years, with the possibility of a two-year extension.

Opposition to the Al-Saud regime has been growing, fuelled by the economic downturn. Attacks on government and US military targets, including a bomb which killed 19 people at a US Air Force base in June 1996, have been blamed on Islamic militants.

In 1993 the country was reorganized into 13 provinces: Riyadh; Mecca (Makkah); Medina (Madinah); Al Qasim; Eastern; Asir; Tabuk; Hail; Northern Border; Jizan; Najran; Baha; Jouf. Each province has a governor appointed by the King and a council of prominent local citizens to advise the governor on local government, budgetary and planning issues.

The judicial system is based on the *Shari'ah* (Islamic law), administered by the Justice Ministry through the *Shari'ah* courts: general courts, courts of first instance, the High *Shari'ah* Court and the Appeals Court. Labour, social affairs and commercial disputes may be dealt with by the Board of Grievances or by special courts. The highest court of appeal is the Council of Ministers whose decision, signed by the King, is final and absolute.

HEAD OF STATE
Custodian of the Two Holy Mosques and HM The King of Saudi Arabia, King Fahd bin Abdul Aziz Al Saud, *born* 1921, *ascended the throne* 1 June 1982
HRH Crown Prince, Prince Abdullah bin Abdul Aziz Al Saud

COUNCIL OF MINISTERS *as at August 1996*
Prime Minister, HM The King
First Deputy Prime Minister and Commander of the National Guard, HRH The Crown Prince
Second Deputy Prime Minister, Defence and Aviation, HRH Prince Sultan bin Abdul Aziz Al Saud
Public Works and Housing, HRH Prince Mit'ab bin Abdul Aziz Al Saud
Interior, HRH Prince Naif bin Abdul Aziz Al Saud
Foreign Affairs, HRH Prince Saud al-Faisal bin Abdul Aziz
Finance and National Economy, Dr Ibrahim bin Abdul Aziz Al Assaf
Agriculture and Water, Dr Abdullah bin Abdul Aziz bin Muammar
Municipal and Rural Affairs, Mohammed bin Ibrahim al-Jarallah
Justice, Dr Abdallah bin Ibrahim Al Shaikh
Commerce, Osama bin Jaafar al Faqih
Communications, Dr Nasser bin Mohammed Al Salloum

Petroleum and Mineral Resources, Ali bin Ibrahim al-Nouaimi
Planning, Dr Abdul Wahab al-Attar
Labour and Social Affairs, Mousaed bin Mohammed al-Sulaymi
Information, Dr Fouad bin Abdul-Salam Farisi
Health, Osama bin Abdul-Majid Aziz Shobokshi
Islamic Affairs, Awqafs and Guidance, Dr Abdul Mohsen Al-Turki
Pilgrimage, Dr Mahmoud Safr
Education, Mohammed bin Ahmad al-Rashid
Higher Education, Dr Khalid al-Angari
Posts, Telegraphs and Telecommunications, Ali bin Talal al-Jehani
Industry and Electricity, Dr Hashem bin Abdullah Yamani
Ministers of State, Dr Mohammed bin Abdul Azziz Al Skeikh; Dr Mutlib bin Abdullah Al Nafisa; Dr Abdul Azziz bin Ibrahim Al Manie; Dr Musaid bin Mohammed Al Aiban; Dr Madani bin Abdulqadir Alaqi; Dr Abdul Azziz bin Abdullah Al Khwaiter

ROYAL EMBASSY OF SAUDI ARABIA
30 Charles Street, London WIX 7PM
Tel 0171-917 3000
Ambassador Extraordinary and Plenipotentiary, HE Dr Ghazi Algosaibi, apptd 1992
Minister Plenipotentiary, Dr Mohammed Rajah Al-Hussainy
Defence Attaché, Brig. A. H. Al-Bassam
Cultural Attaché, A. M. Al-Nasser
Commercial Attaché, M. A. Al-Sheddi

BRITISH EMBASSY
PO Box 94351, Riyadh 11693
Tel: Riyadh 488 0077
Ambassador Extraordinary and Plenipotentiary, HE Andrew F. Green, CMG, apptd 1996
Counsellors, W. C. Patey (*Deputy Head of Mission and Consul-General*); C. M. J. Segar (*Commercial*); J. H. Bunney
Defence and Military Attaché, Brig. W. E. Strong
First Secretary and Consul, T. C. Lamb

CONSUL-GENERAL, L. E. Walker, OBE, LVO, PO Box 393, Jeddah 21411. There is also a trade office in Dhahran/Al Khobar (PO Box 88, Dhahran Airport 31932).

BRITISH COUNCIL DIRECTOR, Anthony Lewis, Olaya Main Road, Al Mousa Centre, Tower B (PO Box 58012), Riyadh 11594. There are also offices in Jeddah, Dammam and Jubail.

DEFENCE

Total active armed forces number 105,500 personnel, service being voluntary. The Army numbers 70,000 personnel, with 1,055 main battle tanks, 2,820 armoured infantry fighting vehicles and armoured personnel carriers and 438 artillery pieces. The Navy has 13,500 personnel including two battalions of 1,500 marines. It deploys eight frigates, 29 patrol and coastal combatants and 23 armed helicopters. The Air Force has 22,000 personnel, including 4,000 air defence forces, and deploys 295 combat aircraft of US and UK manufacture. The National Guard, which is directly under royal command, has 57,000 active personnel and 20,000 tribal levies, with 1,100 armoured personnel carriers and 70 artillery pieces. In addition, the para-military Frontier Force and Coast Guard number 15,000 personnel. Saudi Arabia is base to the Gulf Co-operational Council Peninsula Shield Force of 7,000 troops. The USA, UK and France station aircraft and support units in the country to patrol the air exclusion zone in southern Iraq.

ECONOMY

Saudi Arabia's revenue has been lower since the drop in world oil prices from the mid-1980s onwards, and in the 1990s financial reserves have been used up to meet budget deficits. In addition the country has had the cost of the 1990–1 Gulf War, estimated at US$60,000 million. The 1995 budget was in deficit by SR15,000 million, or 4.0 per cent of GDP, following spending cuts of 20 per cent in 1994 and increases in local petrol and utilities prices in an attempt to achieve a balanced budget. The 1996 budget deficit was estimated at SR18,500 million. GDP in 1992 was US$113,000 million.

Outside the manufacturing centres which have grown up around many towns, most of the population are engaged in agriculture. The productivity of traditional dryland farming is supplemented by extensive irrigation, desalination and use of aquifers, so that agricultural production has increased greatly over the past 20 years.

The principal industry is oil extraction and processing, which produced 33 per cent of GDP in 1992. Oil was first found in commercial quantities in 1938. About 97 per cent of the total is extracted by Saudi Aramco, formerly the Arabian–American Oil Company. Aramco's 66-year lease will terminate in 1999 but the company was effectively nationalized in 1980. Proven oil reserves of 260,100 million barrels account for about one-quarter of the world's proven reserves. The country is the world's largest oil exporter and supplied 12 per cent of world demand in 1993. Recoverable gas reserves of 181.65 trillion cubic feet, in fields, associated with crude oil and those separate from it, are beginning to be exploited. Mineral exploitation of gold, silver, copper and other minerals is also beginning, with gold production of 5.1 tonnes in 1995.

The government, in a series of five-year development plans since 1970, has actively encouraged the establishment of manufacturing industries in the country. Industries have developed in the fields of construction materials, metal fabrication, simple machinery and electrical equipment, food and beverages, textiles, chemicals and plastics. Investment in industrial gases, intermediate petrochemicals, light engineering and machinery is encouraged.

Eight industrial centres have been established, the principal ones at Jubail and Yanbu, financed by the state agency Saudi Arabian Basic Industries Corporation. Linked by gas and oil pipelines, both have petrochemical complexes producing ethylene and methanol; six of the seven plants on-stream are joint ventures with American and Japanese companies.

The state agency Petromin operates nine refineries with a capacity of 1,800,000 b.p.d., producing petrol, fuel and diesel oil, liquefied petroleum gas, jet fuel, kerosene and asphalt.

TRADE

Oil remains the main source of receipts in the balance of payments. The leading suppliers of imports are USA, Japan, Germany, the UK, Italy and France and the chief customers for exports are Japan, France, USA and Singapore. There is a total ban on the importation of alcohol, pork products, firearms, and items regarded as non-Islamic or pornographic.

Trade with UK	1994	1995
Imports from UK	£1,515,252,000	£1,644,356,000
Exports to UK	£739,601,000	£720,783,000

COMMUNICATIONS

There is one railway line from Dammam on the Gulf to Riyadh which was opened in 1951 and is operated by the Saudi Government Railway Organization, carrying around 400,000 passengers and 1.8 million tons of goods per year. The line is being extended to the port of Jubail on the Gulf. A network of 80,000 miles of roads, including an expressway system, connects all the cities and main towns. There are 21 ports, of which the five major ones are Dammam and Jubail (Gulf) and Jeddah, Yanbu and Jizan (Red Sea). The total of 179 berths moved 73 million tons of cargo in 1992. The 15.5 mile-long King Fahd Causeway completed in 1986 connects the Eastern Province to the state of Bahrain.

The government-owned Saudi Arabian Airlines (Saudia) operate scheduled services to 22 domestic airports. There are international airports at Dhahran (King Fahd), Jeddah (King Abdul Aziz), and Riyadh (King Khalid). Saudia have an extensive overseas operation, and a large number of international airlines operate into the country.

Telecommunications are being rapidly expanded with 1.64 million telephone lines in 1992 and seven earth stations linked to the Intelsat system, allowing direct dialling to 185 countries.

EDUCATION

With the exception of a few schools for expatriate children, all schools are government-supervised and are segregated for boys and girls. There are universities in Jeddah, Mecca, Riyadh (branches in Abha and Qassim), Dammam (branch at Hofuf) and Dhahran, and there are Islamic universities in Medina and Riyadh together with 83 tertiary colleges with a total of 142,000 students. There is great emphasis on vocational training, provided at literacy and artisan skill training centres and more advanced industrial, commercial and agricultural education institutes. Education from kindergarten to university is free, with 18,000 schools and 926,000 pupils in 1992.

SENEGAL
République du Sénégal

Senegal lies on the west coast of Africa between Mauritania in the north, Mali in the east, and Guinea-Bissau and Guinea in the south. It entirely surrounds the Gambia, except for its sea-coast. Senegal has an area of 75,750 sq. miles (196,192 sq. km), and a population (UN estimate 1994) of 8,102,000.

CAPITAL – ΨDakar (1,000,000).
CURRENCY – Franc CFA of 100 centimes.
FLAG – Three vertical bands, green, yellow and red; a green star on the yellow band.
NATIONAL DAY – 4 April.

GOVERNMENT

Formerly a French colony, Senegal elected in 1958 to remain within the French Community as an autonomous republic. It became independent as part of the Federation of Mali in June 1960 and seceded to form the Republic of Senegal in September 1960. A border dispute with Mauritania was defused in early 1992 when the border was reopened and diplomatic relations restored. There is an insurgent separatist movement (Movement of Democratic Forces of Casamance (MFDC)) in the southern Casamance region. A cease-fire between the government and MFDC was signed in July 1993 but a political agreement has still to be reached and clashes continue.

In 1963 a new constitution was approved giving executive powers to the President. There are 16 officially recognized political parties. A general election for the National Assembly of 120 seats (70 elected by proportional representation and 50 on a majority basis) is held every five years. The President announced on 31 December 1995 that a Senate would be created to serve as an upper house.

President Diouf was re-elected in the first round of presidential elections in February 1993 with 58.4 per cent of the vote. The legislative election in May 1993 was won by the ruling Parti Socialiste (PS), which secured 84 seats, with the Parti Démocratique Sénégalais (PDS) winning 27 seats, and other parties nine seats. A coalition PS-PDS government was formed in March 1995 to settle political instability.

HEAD OF STATE
President, Abdou Diouf, *installed* 1981, *re-elected* 1988, 21 February 1993

GOVERNMENT *as at August 1996*
Prime Minister, Habib Thiam
Ministers of State, Moustapha Niasse (*Foreign Affairs and Expatriates*); Robert Sagna (*Agriculture*); Ousmane Dieng (*Presidential Services*); Abdoulaye Wade (*Presidency*)
Justice, Jacque Baudin
Interior, Abdourahmane Sow
Armed Forces, Cheikh Hamidou Kane
Economy, Finance and Planning, Papa Sakho
Environment and Protection of Nature, Abdoulaye Bathily
National Education, André Sonko
Energy, Mines and Industry, Magued Diouf
Modernization, Babacar Néné Mbaye
Communications, Serigne Diop
Culture, Abdoulaye Kane
Public Health and Social Action, Ousmane Ngom
Employment, Labour and Professional Training, Assane Diop
Commerce and Handicrafts, Idrissa Seck
Women, Children and Family Welfare, Aminata Mbengue Ndiaye
Equipment and Land Transport, Landing Sané
Youth and Sports, Ousmane Paye
Fisheries and Sea Transport, Alassane Dialy N'diaye
Tourism and Air Transport, Tidiane Sylla
Water Resources, Mamadou Faye
Towns, Daour Cisse
Scientific Research and Technology, Marie-Louise Corea

EMBASSY OF THE REPUBLIC OF SENEGAL
2nd Floor, Norway House, 21–24 Cockspur Street, London SWIY 5BN
Tel 0171-930 7606
Ambassador Extraordinary and Plenipotentiary, HE Gabriel Alexandre Sar, apptd 1993

BRITISH EMBASSY
BP 6025, Dakar
Tel: Dakar 237392
Ambassador Extraordinary and Plenipotentiary, HE Alan Furness, CMG, apptd 1993

BRITISH COUNCIL REPRESENTATIVE, John Whitehead, 34–36 Blvd. de la Republique, Immeuble Sonatel, BP 6232, Dakar

TRADE

Senegal's principal exports are groundnuts (raw and processed) and phosphates. Tourism is also of growing importance as a revenue earner.

Trade with UK	1994	1995
Imports from UK	£20,933,000	£32,217,000
Exports to UK	7,625,000	8,485,000

SEYCHELLES
The Republic of Seychelles

Seychelles, in the Indian Ocean, consists of 115 islands with a total land area of 176 sq. miles (456 sq. km), spread over 400,000 sq. miles of ocean. There is a relatively compact granitic group, 32 islands in all, with high hills and mountains (highest point about 2,972 ft), of which Mahé is the largest and most populated (90 per cent of the population live on Mahé); and the outlying coralline group, for the most part only a little above sea-level. Although only 4° S. of the Equator, the climate is pleasant though tropical.

The population is 73,000 (1994 UN estimate).

CAPITAL – ΨVictoria (population, 1987, 24,324), on Mahé.
CURRENCY – Seychelles rupee (Rs) of 100 cents.
FLAG – Five rays extending from the lower hoist over the whole field, coloured blue, yellow, green, white and red.
NATIONAL ANTHEM – Fyer Seselwa (Proud Seychellois).
NATIONAL DAY – 5 June.

GOVERNMENT

Proclaimed French territory in 1756, the Mahé group was settled as a dependency of Mauritius from 1770, was captured by a British ship in 1794, and changed hands several times between 1803 and 1814, when it was finally assigned to Great Britain. In 1903 these islands, together with the coralline group, were formed into a separate colony. On 29 June 1976, the islands became an independent republic within the Commonwealth. A coup d'état took place in 1977. Seychelles was a one-party state from 1979 until 1991, when a multiparty democratic system was proposed by the President. A new constitution was adopted in a referendum in June 1993. Under the new constitution multiparty politics was institutionalized, a National Assembly of 33 members (22 elected by constituencies, 11 by proportional representation) was established and the presidential mandate was set at five years, renewable three times. In presidential and legislative elections held in July 1993, President René was re-elected and the Seychelles People's Progressive Front formed a government after winning 27 of the National Assembly seats, to the Democratic Party's five.

HEAD OF STATE
President, France Albert René, *assumed office* 5 June 1977; *elected* 1979; *re-elected* 1984, 1989, 27 July 1993

COUNCIL OF MINISTERS *as at August 1996*
Finance, Communication and Defence, James Michel
Administration and Manpower, Joseph Belmont
Industry, Ralph Adam
Environment, Planning and Foreign Affairs, Danielle de St Jorre
Health, Jacquelin Dugasse
Agriculture and Fisheries, Esmé Juneau
Employment and Social Affairs, William Herminie
Tourism and Transport, Simone de Comarmond
Local Government, Youth and Sports, Sylvette Frichot
Education and Culture, Patrick Pillay
Community Development, Dolor Ernesta

SEYCHELLES HIGH COMMISSION
Box No. 4PE, 2nd Floor, Eros House, 111 Baker Street, London WIM IFE
Tel 0171-224 1660
High Commissioner, HE John P. Mascarenhas, apptd 1993

BRITISH HIGH COMMISSION
Victoria House, PO Box 161 Victoria, Mahé
Tel: Victoria 225225
High Commissioner, HE Peter Thomson, CVO, apptd 1994

ECONOMY

The economy is based on tourism, fishing, small-scale agriculture and manufacturing, and the re-export of fuel for aircraft and ships. Deep sea tuna fishing by foreign fleets under licence, improved trans-shipment and other port facilities at Victoria, exports from a tuna canning factory and the export of fresh and frozen fish, attract growing revenues. The government is attempting to reduce the reliance on tourism, which generates 70 per cent of foreign exchange earnings, by promoting the country as an offshore haven for financial services.

TRADE

The principal imports are foodstuffs, beverages, tobacco, mineral fuels, manufactured items, building materials, machinery and transport equipment.

Trade with UK	1994	1995
Imports from UK	£20,065,000	£19,217,000
Exports to UK	9,159,000	9,827,000

SIERRA LEONE
The Republic of Sierra Leone

Sierra Leone, with a total land area of 27,699 sq. miles (71,740 sq. km), is on the west coast of Africa, between Guinea and Liberia.

The population (1994 UN estimate) is 4,587,000. The south is inhabited by peoples whose languages fall into the Mende group; the north by the Temne and smaller groups such as the Limba, Loko, Koranko and Susu.

CAPITAL – ΨFreetown (population, 1985 census, 470,000).
CURRENCY – Leone (Le) of 100 cents.
FLAG – Three horizontal stripes of leaf green, white and cobalt blue.
NATIONAL ANTHEM – High We Exalt Thee, Realm of the Free.
NATIONAL DAY – 27 April (Independence Day).

GOVERNMENT

In the late 18th century a project was begun to settle destitute Africans from England on Freetown peninsula. In 1808 the settlement was declared a Crown colony and became the main base in West Africa for enforcing the 1807 Act outlawing the slave trade. The colony was also used as a settlement for Africans from North America and the West Indies, and Africans rescued from slave ships also settled there. In 1896 a Protectorate was declared over the hinterland.

In 1951 a new constitution was set up that united the colony of Freetown and the Protectorate and on 27 April 1961 Sierra Leone became a fully independent state within the Commonwealth. In 1971 a republican constitution was adopted and Dr Siaka Stevens became the first Executive President. In 1978 Sierra Leone became a one-party state, following approval by Parliament and a referendum.

In September 1991 a new multiparty constitution was adopted and an interim government formed until a general election could be held. This government was overthrown by a coup on 29 April 1992. Captain Valentine Strasser

became head of state, the House of Representatives was dissolved and all political activity was suspended. A Cabinet was appointed to govern the country until promised multiparty elections. In July 1992 Strasser abolished the Cabinet and appointed a Council of State Secretaries to co-ordinate the day-to-day running of government. Capt. Strasser was ousted in a bloodless coup on 16 January 1996 by his deputy, Brig.-Gen. Julius Maada Bio. The military government finally surrendered power to a civilian government on 29 March 1996, following legislative elections on 26–27 February and a run-off election for the presidency on 15 March. The Sierra Leone People's Party (SLPP) won 27 seats to the 68-member National Assembly, eight short of a majority, and formed a government with the support of the People's Democratic Party and the Democratic Centre Party. Six parties exceeded the 4.8 per cent minimum to gain legislative representation. The SLPP's candidate, Ahmad Tejan Kabbah, won the presidential contest, attracting 59.4 per cent of the vote.

INSURGENCY

Since May 1991 government forces have been fighting the Revolutionary United Front (RUF) led by Foday Sankoh whose aim is to force all foreigners out of the country and to nationalize the mining sector. Talks between the RUF and the new civilian government produced an interim cease-fire on 23 April 1996, and a 'final cease-fire' in May. The civil war has claimed more than 10,000 lives and displaced more than half the population.

HEAD OF STATE
President, Ahmad Tejan Kabbah, *elected* 15 March 1996
Vice-President, Albert Demby

CABINET *as at June 1996*
Parliament and Public Affairs, Abu Aiah Koroma
Special Adviser to the President, R. E. S. Lagawo
Finance, Thaimu Bangura
Foreign Affairs, Maigore Kallon
Attorney-General, Justice, Solomom Berewa
National Resettlement and Rehabilitation, Momodu Yillah
Development and Economic Planning, vacant
Transport, Communications and Environment, Sulaiman Tejan Jalloh
Mineral Resources, Prince A. Harding
Internal Affairs, Kemoh Salia-Bao
Education, Alpha Wurie
Health and Sanitation, Mohamed K. Turay
Agriculture and Natural Resources, Harry Will
Information and Broadcasting, George Banda-Thomas
Gender and Children's Affairs, Amy Smythe
Employment and Industrial Relations, Mohammed Gassama
Energy and Power, Yembeh Mansaray
Trade and Industry, Abdul Thorllu-Bangura
Maritime Resources, Lawrence Kamara
Works and Technical Maintenance, Emmanuel O. Grant
Local Government and Community Development, George K. Saffa
Social Welfare, Youth and Sports, Sheku B. Saccoh
Lands, Housing and Country Planning, Abdul Rahman Kamara
Tourism and Culture, Shirley Gbujama
Permanent Representative at the UN, James Jonah

SIERRA LEONE HIGH COMMISSION
33 Portland Place, London WIN 3AG
Tel 0171-636 6483/4/5/6
High Commissioner, new appointment awaited

BRITISH HIGH COMMISSION
Spur Road, Freetown
Tel: Freetown 223961
High Commissioner, HE Ian McCluney, CMG, apptd 1993
BRITISH COUNCIL DIRECTOR, Peter Hilken, OBE, PO Box
124, Tower Hill, Freetown

ECONOMY

The military government cracked down on corruption, liberalized the foreign exchange system and reduced inflation from 120 per cent to 25 per cent. The government's economic and financial reform programme for 1994–6 has been approved by the IMF, which has provided a credit of US$163 million to support it.

On the Freetown peninsula, farming is largely confined to the production of cassava and crops such as maize and vegetables for local consumption. In the hinterland the principal agricultural product is rice, which is the staple food of the country, and cash crops such as cocoa, coffee, palm kernels and ginger.

The economy depends largely on mineral exports, mainly diamonds, gold, bauxite and rutile, the production of which has been disrupted by the insurgency. Diamond exports provided Le1,254.5m in 1989. Total imports for 1989 were to the value of Le10,901.8m and exports were Le8,269.5m.

TRADE WITH UK	1994	1995
Imports from UK	£20,241,000	£26,319,000
Exports to UK	19,743,000	4,774,000

COMMUNICATIONS

Since the phasing out of the railway system in 1974 the road network has been developed considerably and there are now 5,000 miles of roads in the country, over 2,000 miles being surfaced. A bridge has been constructed over the Mano River linking Sierra Leone and Liberia.

The Freetown international airport is situated at Lungi. The main port is Freetown, which has one of the largest natural harbours in the world, and where there is a deep water quay. There are smaller ports at Pepel, Bonthe and Niti.

Radio is operated by the government. Broadcasts are made in several of the indigenous languages, in addition to English and French.

EDUCATION

In 1992 there were 2,042 primary schools and 215 secondary schools. Technical education is provided in the two government technical institutes, situated in Freetown and Kenema, in two trade centres and in the technical training establishments of the mining companies. Teacher training is carried out at the University of Sierra Leone, six colleges in the provinces and in the Milton Margai Training College near Freetown.

SINGAPORE

Singapore consists of the island of Singapore and 59 islets, covering a total area of 244 sq. miles (639 sq. km). Singapore island is 26 miles long and 14 miles in breadth and is situated just north of the Equator off the southern extremity of the Malay peninsula, from which it is separated by the Straits of Johore. A causeway crosses the three-quarters of a mile to the mainland. The climate is hot and humid. Rainfall averages 240 cm a year and temperature ranges from 24° to 32° C (76°–89° F).

In 1994 the population was 2,930,200, which comprised 2,269,600 (77.5 per cent) Chinese, 415,900 (14.2 per cent) Malays, 209,400 (7.1 per cent) Indians (including those of Pakistani, Bangladeshi and Sri Lankan origin) and 35,300 (1.2 per cent) from other ethnic groups. Malay, Mandarin, Tamil and English are the official languages. At least eight Chinese dialects are used. Malay is the national language and English is the language of administration.

CURRENCY – Singapore dollar (S$) of 100 cents.
FLAG – Horizontal bands of red over white; crescent with five five-point stars on red band near staff.
NATIONAL ANTHEM – Majulah Singapura.
NATIONAL DAY – 9 August.

GOVERNMENT

Singapore, where Sir Stamford Raffles first established a trading post under the East India Company in 1819, was incorporated with Penang and Malacca to form the Straits Settlements in 1826. The Straits Settlements became a Crown colony in 1867. Singapore fell into Japanese hands in 1942 and civil government was not restored until 1946, when it became a separate colony. Internal self-government was introduced in 1959. Singapore became a state of Malaysia in September 1963, but left Malaysia and became an independent sovereign state within the Commonwealth on 9 August 1965. Singapore adopted a republican constitution from that date.

There is a Cabinet collectively responsible to an 87-member (81 elected and six nominated by the President) Parliament. In November 1991 the constitution was amended to provide for a directly-elected President, elected for a six-year term, with enlarged powers and the ability to veto government decisions relating to internal security, the budget, financial reserves and the appointment of senior civil servants. The President appoints the Prime Minister and, on his advice, the members of the Cabinet.

After the general election of 31 August 1991 the People's Action Party (PAP) had 77 seats in Parliament. The Singapore Democratic Party (SDP) won three seats and the Workers' Party won one seat.

HEAD OF STATE
President, Ong Teng Cheong, *elected* 28 August 1993, *took office* 2 September 1993

CABINET *as at August 1996*
Prime Minister, Hon. Goh Chok Tong
Senior Minister, PM's Office, Hon. Lee Kuan Yew, GCMG, CH
Deputy PM, Foreign, Trade, Hon. Lee Hsien Loong
Deputy PM, Defence, Hon. Dr Tony Tan
Trade and Industry, Hon. Yeo Cheow Tong
Education, Hon. Lee Yock Suan
Communications, Hon. Mah Bow Tan
Law and Foreign Affairs, Hon. Prof. S. Jayakumar
Finance, Hon. Dr Richard Tsu Tau Hu
Labour, Hon. Dr Lee Boon Yang
Muslim Affairs and Community Development, Hon. Abdullah Tarmugi
Health, Information and the Arts, Hon. George Yeo
Home Affairs, Hon. Wong Kan Seng
National Development, Hon. Lim Hng Kiang
Environment, Teo Chee Hean
Without Portfolio, Hon. Lim Boon Heng

HIGH COMMISSION FOR THE REPUBLIC OF SINGAPORE
9 Wilton Crescent, London SW1X 8SA
Tel 0171-235 8315

High Commissioner, HE J. Y. Pillay, apptd 1996
Counsellor (Defence Procurement), Col. Hung Khiang Puah
First Secretary, F. Tay (*Commercial*)

BRITISH HIGH COMMISSION
Tanglin Road, Singapore 247919
Tel: Singapore 4739333
High Commissioner, HE Gordon Duggan, CMG, apptd 1990
*Deputy High Commissioner and Counsellor (Economic/
Commercial)*, J. P. Freeman
Defence Adviser, Gp Capt J. M. Collier

BRITISH COUNCIL DIRECTOR, J. Davies, 30 Napier Road,
Singapore 1025

ECONOMY

Historically Singapore's economy was based on the sale
and distribution of raw materials from surrounding
countries and on entrepot trade in finished products. An
industrialization programme was launched in 1968 and
manufacturing industries have been established, including shipbuilding and repairing, iron and steel, transport
equipment, textiles, footwear, wood products, micro-
electronics, televisions, computers, telecommunications
equipment, office machinery, audio equipment, scientific
instruments, detergents, confectionery, pharmaceuticals,
petroleum products, etc. Singapore has also become an
important financial services centre with significant insurance and foreign exchange markets, a stock exchange, 132
commercial banks and 75 merchant banks and an oil-
refining centre. The economy grew by 10.1 per cent of
GDP in 1994. Singapore's major trading partners are the
USA, Malaysia, the EU, Hong Kong and Japan.

FINANCE	1993	1994
Revenue	S$19,527m	S$23,280m
Expenditure	12,600m	14,100m

TRADE	1993	1994
Total imports	S$137,603m	S$156,000m
Total exports	119,473m	147,000m

Trade with UK	1994	1995
Imports from UK	£1,768,541,000	£2,068,581,000
Exports to UK	1,896,892,000	2,205,799,000

COMMUNICATIONS

Singapore is one of the largest and busiest seaports in the
world, with six terminals, deep water wharves and ship
repairing facilities. Ships also anchor in the roads, unload-
ing into lighters. In 1994, the total volume of cargo handled
was 290,100,000 tonnes. More than 500 shipping lines use
the port, with 101,107 ship arrivals in 1994.

The international airport is at Changi, in the east of the
island, with Singapore Airlines operating flights to 40
countries and 21,644,677 passengers using the airport in
1994. There are 67 km of metre gauge railway connected
to the Malaysian rail system by the causeway across the
Straits of Johore, and 3,027 km of roads.

There are nine radio and three television channels
operated by the Singapore Broadcasting Corporation in
the four official languages, and three private broadcasting
stations.

SLOVAKIA
Slovenská Republika – The Republic of Slovakia

Slovakia has an area of 18,940 sq. miles (49,035 sq. km). It is
situated in central Europe and is bordered to the north by

Poland, to the east by Ukraine, to the south by Hungary, to
the south-west by Austria and to the west by the Czech
Republic. The Tatry (Tatras) mountains in the centre and
north of the country reach heights of 2,600 m (8,530 ft).
The major river is the Váh which flows from the Tatry
mountains to join the Danube at the Hungarian border.
The climate is continental.

The population (1993) is 5,336,455, of which 85.7 per
cent are ethnic Slovaks, 10.8 per cent ethnic Hungarians,
1.4 per cent gypsy, 1.1 per cent Czech, with smaller
numbers of Ruthenians, Ukrainians and Germans. The
population is mainly Christian, some 60 per cent Roman
Catholic and 6 per cent Protestant.

The main languages are Slovak, Hungarian and Czech.
A bill was passed in November 1995 making Slovak the
only official language and limiting the use of minority
languages.

CAPITAL – Bratislava, on the Danube, population (1993)
448,785. Other major cities are: Košice (238,454); Žilina
(86,373); Prešov (92,013); Banská Bystríca (78,321).
CURRENCY – Slovak Koruna (SK) (Crown).
FLAG – Three horizontal stripes of white, blue, red with
the arms all over near the hoist.
NATIONAL ANTHEM – Nad Tatrou sa blýska (Storm over
the Tatras).
NATIONAL DAYS – 1 January (Establishment of Slovak
Republic); 5 July (Day of the Slav Missionaries);
29 August (Slovak National Uprising); 1 September
(Constitution Day).

GOVERNMENT (*see also* Czech Republic)

At the end of the 11th century Slovakia became part of the
Hungarian state when the Magyars gained control of the
area. After the Hungarians were defeated at the battle of
Moháč in 1526, most of Hungary (including part of Slovakia) was occupied by the Turks, with the remainder of
Hungary and Slovakia being incorporated into the Austrian Empire. With the establishment of the Austro-
Hungarian monarchy in 1867, Slovakia again came under
Hungarian control. The attempted Magyarization of
Slovakia gave impetus to the national revival which had
begun in 1848–9, and when the First World War came
many Slovaks fought with the allies. Amalgamated into the
republic of Czechoslovakia on 28 October 1918, Slovakia
became independent in March 1939 as a Nazi puppet state
when Germany invaded the Czech lands. Slovakia was
liberated by Soviet forces in 1945 and returned to
Czechoslovakia. The formation of a federal republic
between the Czech lands and Slovakia was the only Prague
Spring reform to survive the Soviet invasion of 1968.
Following the collapse of Communist rule at federal and
republic level in 1989, nationalist feeling grew even
stronger and the Czech and Slovak republics began to
negotiate the dissolution of the federation into two
sovereign states in 1992. Dissolution took effect on
1 January 1993.

The constitution vests legislative power in the National
Council of 150 members elected for a four-year term by
proportional representation with a five per cent threshold
for parliamentary representation. The President is elected
for a five-year term by the National Council; executive
power is held by the Prime Minister and Cabinet. Minority
rights are enshrined in the constitution but discrimination
is claimed by the ethnic Hungarian population.

A coalition government of the Movement for a Democratic Slovakia (HZDS) and Slovak National Party (SNS)
was sworn in on 12 January 1993 but lost its majority in
the National Council when the SNS left the government. Increasing criticism of the economic policy and

authoritarian style of the HZDS government led ten HZDS members to form a new party which, in alliance with three other parties, brought down the government by a no-confidence vote in March 1994. The four-party coalition then formed a government which was approved by President Kováč on 16 March 1994.

Legislative elections on 30 September and 1 October 1994, however, returned the HZDS to power at the head of a three-party coalition with the Association of Slovak Workers (ZRS) and the Slovak National Party (SNS) which took office on 13 December 1994. Antagonism between President Kováč and Prime Minister Mečiar resulted in transferral of the role of Commander-in-Chief of the Armed Forces from the President to the government in June 1995.

The state of the parties in the National Council following the 1994 election was: HZDS 61; Democratic Left Party (SDL) 18; Christian Democratic Movement (KDH) 17; Hungarian Coalition 17; Democratic Union (DU) 15; ZRS 13; SNS 9.

HEAD OF STATE
President, Michal Kováč, *elected* 15 February 1993

GOVERNMENT *as at August 1996*
Prime Minister, Vladimír Mečiar (HZDS)
Deputy PM, Legislature and Media, Katarína Tóthová (HZDS)
Deputy PM, Economy and Finance, Sergej Kozlík (HZDS)
Deputy PM, Social, Industrial and Trade Union Relations, Jozef Kalman (ZRS)
Foreign Affairs, Juraj Schenk (HZDS)
Defence, Ján Sitek (SNS)
Economy, Ján Ducký (HZDS)
Privatization, Peter Bisák (ZRS)
Interior, Ľudovít Hudek (HZDS)
Labour, Social Affairs and Family, Oľga Keltošová (HZDS)
Culture, Ivan Hudec (HZDS)
Justice, Jozef Liščák (ZRS)
Education and Science, Eva Slavkovská (SNS)
Health, Ľubomír Javorský (HZDS)
Agriculture, Peter Baco (HZDS)
Transport and Communications, Alexander Rezeš (HZDS)
Environment, Jozef Zlocha (ZRS)
Construction and Public Works, Ján Mráz (ZRS)

HZDS Movement for a Democratic Slovakia; ZRS Association of Slovak Workers; SNS Slovak National Party

Chairman, Slovak National Council, Ivan Gašparovič.

EMBASSY OF THE SLOVAK REPUBLIC
25 Kensington Palace Gardens, London W8 4QY
Tel 0171-243 0803
Ambassador Extraordinary and Plenipotentiary, new appointment awaited

BRITISH EMBASSY
4th Floor, Grösslingova 35, 81109 Bratislava
Tel: Bratislava 364420
Ambassador Extraordinary and Plenipotentiary, HE Peter Harborne, apptd 1995
BRITISH COUNCIL DIRECTOR, Susan Wallace-Shaddad, PO Box 68, Panská 17, 81499 Bratislava

DEFENCE

Total active armed forces number 47,000; conscripts serve for 18 months. The Army has a strength of 33,000, with 912 main battle tanks, 1,043 armoured personnel carriers and armoured infantry fighting vehicles and 808 artillery pieces. The Air Force has a strength of 14,000, with 111 combat aircraft and 19 attack helicopters. There are 3,950 paramilitary personnel.

ECONOMY

From independence until mid-1994 Slovakia faced economic difficulties because of the structure of its centrally-planned and inefficiently managed economy, reliant on state-subsidized heavy industries with low productivity, and because of the ambivalent attitude to reform of the HZDS government. The HZDS faced increasing problems in 1993 as output, exports and foreign currency reserves fell and unemployment and inflation increased. In July 1993 the Slovak Crown was devalued by 10 per cent in return for an IMF loan of US$89 million. Economic reform policies, including macro-economic stabilization, price liberalization, currency convertibility and extensive privatization were continued, though at a slower rate than in the Czech Republic. Firms have been privatized by a voucher system, transfer, public auction, restoration to former owners, or transformation into joint-stock companies.

In mid-1994, however, the economic situation stabilized as the Moravčik government, more committed to reform, implemented a second round of privatization. The budget deficit was brought down to 3.8 per cent of GDP, the trade balance was brought into surplus, while the foreign debt was reduced and foreign exchange reserves increased significantly. In 1994 unemployment (15 per cent) and inflation (11.7 per cent) were reduced and foreign investment is increasing and beginning to offset the loss of subsidies from the former Czechoslovak federation. In July 1994 the IMF approved a US$263 million credit to support the economic reform programme. GDP grew by four per cent in 1994, but the election of a new HZDS-led government in October 1994 has slowed the pace of reform. The previous government's privatization contracts were cancelled by the National Council in November 1994 and the government suspended the privatization programme the following month. The average inflation rate was 10 per cent in 1995, and the unemployment rate was 13.7 per cent. Natural resources include brown coal, natural gas, iron ore, antimony, lead, zinc and magnesite.

TRADE WITH UK	1994	1995
Imports from UK	£44,666,000	£76,764,000
Exports to UK	56,654,000	67,509,000

SLOVENIA
Republika Slovenija

Slovenia is a small mountainous state which is the most northerly of the former Yugoslav republics. It has an area of 7,819 sq. miles (20,251 sq. km) and is bordered on the north by Austria, on the north-east by Hungary, on the east and south by Croatia and on the west by Italy. The two major rivers are the Sava and the Drava. There is a short coastline in the south-west 29 miles (46 km) in length on the Adriatic. The climate is a mixture of Mediterranean, continental and alpine.

The population (1994) is 1,989,477 and is mostly Slovenian. There are small Hungarian (0.5 per cent) and Italian (0.1 per cent) minorities, together with a Romany population. About 30,000 refugees from the former Yugoslavia remain in Slovenia.

The main religion is Roman Catholicism. Slovene is the official language, together with Hungarian and Italian in ethnically mixed regions.

CAPITAL – Ljubljana, population (1994) 269,972. Other major towns (1994) are: Maribor (103,113); Celje (39,782); Kranj (36,770) and ΨKoper (24,495), the only port.

CURRENCY – Slovene Tolar (SIT) of 100 stotin.

FLAG – Three horizontal stripes of white, blue, red, with the arms in the upper hoist.

NATIONAL ANTHEM – Zdravljica (A Toast).

NATIONAL DAY – 25 June (Statehood Day).

GOVERNMENT

The area that is now Slovenia came under the control of the Habsburg Empire in the 15th century and remained so until the defeat of the Austro-Hungarian Empire in 1918. On 27 October 1918 Slovenia became part of the state of Slovenes, Croats and Serbs (later Yugoslavia) and this was confirmed by the Versailles Treaty 1919. Slovenia was reduced in size, however, by the Italian annexation of the western third of the country and the Austrian annexation of parts of the north. In 1941 Yugoslavia was invaded by German forces and Slovenia was divided between Germany, Italy and Hungary. Slovenia was reformed as a constituent republic of the federal Yugoslav state in May 1945. After a dispute with Italy and nine years of international administration, the Adriatic coast and hinterland were returned to Slovenia in 1954 and Italy retained Trieste.

Slovenian fears of Serbian dominance led the Slovene Assembly in 1989 to amend the republican constitution to lay the basis of a sovereign state. The first democratic elections, held in April 1990, were won by the pro-independence 'Demos' coalition. In a referendum in December 1990, 88 per cent of the electorate voted for independence, which was declared on 25 June 1991. A ten-day war with the Yugoslav National Army followed before the Army called off hostilities and withdrew.

A new constitution was adopted in December 1991. Executive power is vested in the Prime Minister and Cabinet of Ministers. Legislative authority is held by a bicameral parliament, composed of the 90-member National Assembly (lower house) and 40-member National Council (upper house). The National Assembly is elected on a proportional representation basis, with one seat each reserved for the Italian and Hungarian minorities. The National Council has 22 elected and 18 appointed members (six by non-profit making organizations, four by employers, four by employees and four by farmers, small businessmen and independent professionals). Presidential and legislative elections were held on 6 December 1992, with incumbent President Milan Kučan being re-elected and the Liberal Democratic Party emerging as the largest party in parliament. A coalition government led by the Liberal Democrats was formed in January 1993. The Associated List of Social Democrats (ZLSD) and the United List (ZL) withdrew from the government in January 1996.

Slovenia signed an association agreement and applied for membership of the EU in June 1996.

HEAD OF STATE
President, Milan Kučan, *elected* April 1990, *re-elected for a five-year term* 6 December 1992

CABINET *as at August 1996*

Prime Minister, Janez Drnovšek (LDS)
Foreign Affairs, Dr Davorin Kračun (LDS)
Finance, Mitja Gaspari (LDS)
Economy, Development, Janko Deželak (SKD)
Education and Sports, Slavko Gaber (LDS)
Justice, Meta Zupančič (Ind.)
Internal Affairs, Andrej Šter (SKD)

Transport and Communications, Igor Umek (SKD)
Agriculture and Forestry, Jože Osterc (SKD)
Health, Božidar Voljč (LDS)
Science and Technology, Dr Andrej Umek (SKD)
Labour, Family and Social Affairs, Tone Rop (LDS)
Culture, Dr Janez Dular (SKD)
Economic Activities, Metod Dragonja (Ind.)
Environment, Dr Pavle Gantar (LDS)
Defence, Jelko Kacin (LDS)

LDS Liberal Democracy of Slovenia; SKD Slovenian Christian Democrats.

EMBASSY OF SLOVENIA
11–15 Wigmore Street, London WIH 9LA
Tel 0171-495 7775
Ambassador Extraordinary and Plenipotentiary, HE Matjaž Šinkovec, apptd 1992

BRITISH EMBASSY
4th Floor, Trg Republike 3, 61-000 Ljubljana
Tel: Ljubljana 1257191
Ambassador Extraordinary and Plenipotentiary, HE Gordon Johnston, OBE, apptd 1992

BRITISH COUNCIL DIRECTOR, Francis King, Štefanova 1/III, 61000 Ljubljana

ECONOMY

Slovenia's economy has emerged as the most stable of the former Yugoslav economies and the least affected by the end of central planning. Although it has lost its captive export market and cheap supplies of raw materials from Serbia, Slovenia is one of the richest former Communist countries. It has successfully re-orientated its exports towards Western markets, with 70 per cent of exports going to EU states in 1994. By mid-1995, 88 per cent of companies were in the private sector. Trade surpluses were recorded from 1992 to 1994 (US$475 million in 1994), with foreign currency reserves of US$3.2 billion in mid-1995 and foreign debt at US$2.49 billion. Slovenia has agreed to assume 18 per cent of the former Yugoslavia's debt of US$4,700 million. Inflation has been gradually reduced to around 18 per cent and the tolar is stable and convertible, while GDP grew in 1993 and 1994.

In 1994 GDP was US$14,037 million, of which agriculture, forestry and fishing produced 5 per cent. The main products are potatoes, wheat, corn, apples, wine, meat and milk. Mining and manufacturing produced 55 per cent of GDP, the major sectors being metal-working, electronics, textiles, automotive parts, chemicals, glass products and food-processing. Tourism (worth US$750 million in 1993) and transport are major export earners, with 1,400,000 tourists visiting in 1991. Foreign investment is being attracted, with US$1,300 million invested by the end of 1993.

TRADE WITH UK	1994	1995
Imports from UK	£89,690,000	£122,397,000
Exports to UK	93,529,000	113,956,000

COMMUNICATIONS

Important road and rail communications cross the country from west to east (Milan–Ljubljana–Budapest), and north to south (Munich–Ljubljana–Zagreb–Belgrade–Athens). There are international airports at Ljubljana, Maribor and Portoroz (Adriatic Coast). The port of Koper is an important shipment point for goods from Austria, Hungary, the Czech Republic and Slovakia.

EDUCATION

Education is compulsory and free between the ages of seven and 14. There are 821 primary schools (age seven–14), 152 secondary or middle schools (age 14–19), 30 colleges and two universities (Ljubljana and Maribor).

SOLOMON ISLANDS

Forming a scattered archipelago of mountainous islands and low-lying coral atolls, the Solomon Islands stretches about 900 miles in a south-easterly direction from the Shortland Islands to the Santa Cruz islands. The archipelago covers an area of about 249,000 sq. miles, with a land area of 10,938 sq. miles (28,446 sq. km), between 155° 30' and 170° 30'E. longitude and 5° 10' and 12° 45'S. latitude. The six biggest islands are Choiseul, New Georgia, Santa Isabel, Guadalcanal, Malaita and Makira. They are characterized by thickly-forested mountain ranges intersected by deep, narrow valleys.

The total population was 328,723 at the 1991 census. English is the official language; there are over 80 local languages.

CAPITAL – ΨHoniara, population (1991) 40,000.
CURRENCY – Solomon Islands dollar (SI$) of 100 cents.
FLAG – Blue over green divided by a diagonal yellow band, with five white stars in the top left quarter.
NATIONAL ANTHEM – God Bless our Solomon Islands.
NATIONAL DAY – 7 July (Independence Day).

GOVERNMENT

The origin of the present Melanesian inhabitants is uncertain. European interest in the islands began in the mid-16th century and continued intermittently for about 300 years, when the inauguration of sugar plantations in Queensland and Fiji (which created a need for labour) and the arrival of missionaries and traders led to increased European interest in the region. Great Britain declared a Protectorate in 1893 over the Southern Solomons, adding the Santa Cruz group in 1898 and 1899. The islands of the Shortland groups were transferred from Germany to Great Britain by treaty in 1900.

The Solomon Islands achieved internal self-government in 1976, and became independent in July 1978. The Solomon Islands is a constitutional monarchy, The Queen being represented locally by the Governor-General. Legislative power is vested in a unicameral National Parliament of 47 members, elected for a four-year term. Executive authority is exercised by the Cabinet. A four-party National Coalition government led by Francis Billy Hilly took power after winning 24 of the 47 seats in the legislative election of 26 May 1993. Hilly was, however, forced to resign as Prime Minister in October 1994 after his coalition lost its parliamentary majority. On 7 November the National Parliament elected Solomon Mamaloni as Prime Minister and he formed a new government.

Governor-General, HE Sir Moses Pitakaka, GCMG, apptd 1994

CABINET *as at June 1996*

Prime Minister, Hon. Solomon Mamaloni
Home Affairs, Hon. Nathaniel Supa
Agriculture and Fisheries, Hon. Edmond Adresen
Commerce, Employment and Trade, Hon. George Luilamo
Development Planning, Hon. David Sitai
Culture and Tourism, Hon. William Haomae
Education and Training, Hon. Alfred Maitia
Finance, Hon. Christopher Abe
Health and Medical Services, Hon. Gordon Mars
Foreign Affairs, Hon. Danny Philip

Justice, Hon. Oliver Zapo
Provincial Government and Rural Development, Hon. Allan Qurucu
Post and Communication, Hon. John Masuota
Transport, Works and Utilities, Hon. John Fieango
Lands and Housing, Hon. Francis Orodani
Forestry, Environment and Conservation, Hon. Allan Kemakeza
Energy, Minerals and Mines, Hon. David Vuza
Sports, Youth and Women's Development, Hon. Brown Beu
Police and National Security, Hon. Victor Ngele

HIGH COMMISSION OF THE SOLOMON ISLANDS
Avenue de l'Yser 13, BTE 3, 1040 Brussels
Tel: Brussels 2732 7085
High Commissioner, new appointment awaited

HONORARY CONSULATE
19 Springfield Road, London SW19 7AL
Tel 0181-296 0232
Honorary Consul, Edward Nielsen, OBE

BRITISH HIGH COMMISSION
Telekon House, Mendana Avenue (PO Box 676), Honiara
Tel: Honiara 21705/6
High Commissioner, HE Brian N. Connelly, apptd 1996

COMMUNICATIONS

Solomon Airlines operates international services to other Pacific states and Australia. Air Niugini flies from Port Moresby to Honiara. There are about 52 miles of secondary and minor roads in the urban areas of Honiara, Auki and Gizo. In the rural areas there are some 800 miles of road, including those in private plantations, forestry areas and roads built and maintained by councils. Telekom, a company jointly owned by Cable and Wireless and the Solomon Islands government, operates the international and domestic telephone circuits from a ground station in Honiara via the Intelsat Pacific Ocean communication satellite.

TRADE

The main imports are foodstuffs, consumer goods, machinery and transport materials. Principal exports are timber, fish, copra, and palm oil. Fisheries exports for 1992 totalled SI$88.1m, timber SI$110.4m and copra SI$22.7m. Other exports include cocoa and marine shells.

Trade with UK	1994	1995
Imports from UK	£1,059,000	£1,014,000
Exports to UK	2,719,000	8,602,000

SOMALIA
Jamhuuriyadda Diimoqraadiga ee Soomaaliya

Somalia occupies part of the north-east horn of Africa, with a coastline on the Indian Ocean extending from the boundary with Kenya (2° S. latitude) to Cape Guardafui (12° N.), and on the Gulf of Aden to the boundary with Djibouti. Somalia is bounded on the west by Djibouti, Ethiopia and Kenya and covers an area of about 246,201 sq. miles (637,657 sq. km). The population, of which a large proportion is nomadic, is 9,077,000 (UN estimate 1994).

CAPITAL – ΨMogadishu, population (estimated 1987), 1,000,000. Other towns are Hargeisa (20,000), Boroma (65,000), ΨKisimayu (60,000), ΨBerbera (15,000) and Burao (15,000).
CURRENCY – Somali shilling of 100 cents.

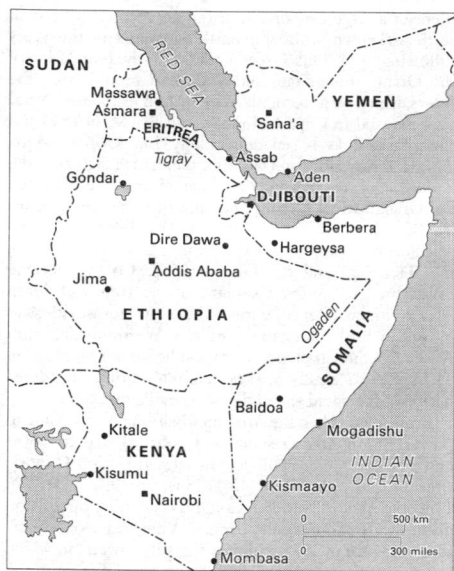

FLAG – Five-pointed white star on blue ground.
NATIONAL DAY – under review.

GOVERNMENT

British rule in Somaliland lasted from 1887 until 1960, except for a short period in 1940–1 when the Protectorate was occupied by Italian forces. Somalia, formerly an Italian colony, was occupied by British forces in 1941. In 1950 it was placed under Italian administration by a resolution of the UN; this trusteeship lasted until the British protectorate and the trust territory became independent as the Somali Democratic Republic on 1 July 1960. In 1969, the armed forces seized power and established a ruling Revolutionary Council under Siad Barre's leadership.

Siad Barre was overthrown by rebels in January 1991, sparking civil war between rival clan-based movements. The United Somali Congress (USC) seized control in Mogadishu and formed an interim administration under Ali Mahdi Mohammed, which was contested by the Somali Salvation Democratic Front (SSDF), the Somali Patriotic Movement (SPM) and the Somali Democratic Movement (SDM). In the north, the Somali National Movement (SNM) formed a rival administration under its leader, Abourahman Ahmed Ali. Fighting between the USC and supporters of the Somali National Alliance (SNA) of Gen. Mohammed Aideed devastated Mogadishu and large parts of the south, exacerbating famine conditions. The UN Operation in Somalia (UNOSOM) proved ineffective in securing aid distribution routes and was replaced on 9 December 1992 by a UN-approved, US-led, United Task Force (UNITAF) which, having secured distribution routes, attempted to confiscate weapons, provoking retaliatory attacks from the factions.

On 4 May 1993, UNITAF handed over to a 28,000-strong UN force (UNOSOM). Clashes between the UN force, attempting to broker a settlement, and the SNA left 90 UN troops and 2,000 Somalis dead between June and November 1993. Western troops withdrew from the UN operation in March 1994, leaving UN troops from India, Pakistan and Egypt, which were easily overrun by the Somali factions.

The UN Security Council voted to withdraw its troops in March 1995, enabling Gen. Aideed's militia to take control of the city's port and airport amid heavy fighting. On 12 June 1995, Gen. Aideed was ousted as SNA leader by a joint USC-SNA congress which nominated Osman Ali Ato as its leader. Gen. Aideed responded by declaring himself President on 15 June 1995. Low-level fighting between the two factions has continued. Gen. Aideed died of gunshot wounds in July 1996 and was replaced by his son, Hussein Aideed. About 350,000 are believed to have died from starvation or in the fighting.

SECESSION

Civil war broke out in May 1988 between the government and the opposition Somali National Movement (SNM) in the north of the country. With the downfall of Siad Barre, the SNM took control of the north-west (the former British Somaliland Protectorate) and in May 1991 declared unilateral independence as the 'Somaliland Republic'. A government and legislature was formed which elected Mohamed Ibrahim Egal as President in May 1993.

SOMALI DIPLOMATIC REPRESENTATION
The Embassy closed in January 1992.

BRITISH DIPLOMATIC REPRESENTATION
The British Embassy in Mogadishu closed in January 1991.

ECONOMY

Livestock raising is the main occupation and there is a modest export trade in livestock, skins and hides. Italy, the Gulf States and Saudi Arabia import the bulk of the banana crop, the second biggest export. Due to UN aid and pacification of the countryside, the harvest improved from 10 per cent of normal in 1992 to 50 per cent in 1993.

TRADE WITH UK	1994	1995
Imports from UK	£7,502,000	£3,714,000
Exports to UK	1,508,000	23,000

SOUTH AFRICA
Republiek van Suid-Afrika – Republic of South Africa

South Africa occupies the southernmost part of the African continent from the courses of the Limpopo, Marico, Molopo, Nosop and Orange Rivers (34° 50′ 22 S.) to the Cape of Good Hope, with the exception of Lesotho, Swaziland and the extreme south of Mozambique. It has a total area of 471,445 sq. miles (1,221,031 sq. km) and borders on Namibia in the north-west, Botswana and Zimbabwe in the north, Mozambique and Swaziland in the north-east, and Lesotho, which it completely surrounds. To the west, east and south lie the south Atlantic and southern Indian Oceans. Some 1,192 miles (1,920 km) to the south-east of Capetown lie Prince Edward and Marion Islands, part of South Africa since 1947.

Ranges of hills run parallel to the coast along much of the southern and eastern coastline, rising in steps towards the interior. Most of the ranges are of no great height, the exception being the Drakensberg (11,000 ft) running south-west to north-east in the east of the country. Between the ranges of hills and in the interior in the north-east are plateaux, such as the Great Karoo in the south. In the north and centre are grassy plains with occasional hills or kopjes. The Orange, with its tributary the Vaal, is the principal river, rising in the Drakensberg and flowing into the Atlantic near the border with Namibia. The Limpopo, or Crocodile River, in the north, rises in the Transvaal and flows into the Indian Ocean through Mozambique. Most of the remaining rivers are furious torrents after rain, with partially dry beds at other seasons.

The climate is subtropical, dry and sunny moderated by the warm temperate winds from the Atlantic and Indian Oceans. Moist hot air masses from the Indian Ocean are the chief source of rainfall for most of the country.

The official population estimate for 1993, excluding Bophuthatswana, Ciskei, Transkei and Venda, was 32,589,000, comprising 23,016,000 Blacks, 5,149,000 Whites, 3,402,000 Coloureds, and 1,022,000 Indians. The population of the four homelands (now reincorporated into South Africa) was 7,460,000, which was overwhelmingly black, giving a total estimated population of 40,049,000. The population in May 1995 was estimated as: 75.6 per cent Black; 13 per cent White; 8.7 per cent Coloured; 2.7 per cent Indian.

The interim constitution designates 11 official languages: Afrikaans; English; Ndebele; Sesotho sa Leboa; Sesotho; Si Swati (Swazi); Tsonga; Tswana; Venda; Xhosa; Zulu. Afrikaans and English are to remain the languages of record although any citizen may correspond official business in his own language. Afrikaans is descended from old Dutch and is the language of the Afrikaner and Coloured populations.

CAPITAL – The administrative seat of the government is Pretoria, Gauteng; population (1985 estimate) 822,925; the seat of the legislature is ΨCape Town, Western Cape, population (1985) 1,911,521; the seat of the judiciary is Bloemfontein, Orange Free State (232,984). Other large towns (1985 figures) are Johannesburg, Gauteng (1,609,408); ΨDurban, Kwazulu/Natal, the largest seaport (634,301); ΨPort Elizabeth, Eastern Cape (651,993); ΨEast London, Eastern Cape (167,992); and Pietermaritzburg, Kwazulu/Natal (192,417).

CURRENCY – Rand (R) of 100 cents.

FLAG – Divided red over blue by a horizontal white-fimbriated green Y; in the hoist a black triangle fimbriated in yellow.

NATIONAL ANTHEMS – Die Stem Van Suid-Afrika (The Call of South Africa); Nkosi Sikelel'i Afrika (God Bless Africa).

NATIONAL DAY – 27 April (Freedom Day).

HISTORY

The colony of the Cape of Good Hope was founded by the Dutch at Cape Town in 1652 and remained a Dutch colony until Britain took possession of it in 1795. Restored to Dutch rule in 1803, it was again taken by Britain in 1806 and this was confirmed by the London Convention of 1814. Increasing Anglicization of the colony led to the move-

ment of a large proportion of the descendants of Dutch settlers (known as Boers) north-eastwards in the years following 1834. This 'Great Trek' led to the foundation of the Orange Free State and Transvaal republics by the Boers, which were recognized by Britain in 1853–4. Natal was annexed to Cape Colony by the British in 1844 and then formed as a separate colony in 1856, to which Zululand was added in 1897 after the British victory in the Zulu wars. Transvaal and the Orange Free State (renamed the Orange River Colony) became British colonies after the Boer defeat in the Second Boer War 1899–1902. The self-governing colonies of the Cape of Good Hope, Natal, the Transvaal and the Orange River Colony became united in 1910 under the name of the Union of South Africa. Independence within the Commonwealth was gained in 1931 under the Statute of Westminster. South Africa left the Commonwealth and became a republic on 31 May 1961, largely as a result of international condemnation of apartheid and of the Sharpeville massacre.

From 1948, when the Afrikaner National Party came to power, South Africa's social and political structure was based on apartheid, a policy of racial segregation. Opposition protests culminated in the Sharpeville massacre in 1960; the African National Congress and other opposition groups were subsequently banned. A new wave of opposition climaxed in 1976 with uprisings in Soweto, in which hundreds were shot dead. In 1984 renewed rioting in the black townships and continuing unrest led to the declaration of a state of emergency in July 1985 in 36 districts, and nationwide from 12 June 1986; it was renewed annually until 1990.

As part of its policy of apartheid, the government established a number of black 'homelands'. Six areas (Gazankulu, Lebowa, KwaNdebele, KaNgwane, Qwaqwa and KwaZulu) were designated as self-governing states. A further four (Bophuthatswana, Ciskei, Transkei and Venda) were regarded as independent republics by the South African government but never recognized as such by the UN.

MOVES TO DEMOCRACY

The first moves to reform apartheid came into effect in 1984, when a new constitution extended the franchise to the Coloured and Indian populations. Coloureds and Indians elected members to a three-chamber parliament, Coloured and Indian houses being added to the existing white chamber. However, whites retained effective political power and blacks remained excluded.

In 1989, F. W. de Klerk became President of South Africa and accelerated the process of reform. In 1990, the ban on the ANC and restrictions on other anti-apartheid groups were lifted; Nelson Mandela, the main ANC political detainee, was released. In 1991 the laws implementing apartheid were effectively abolished. In 1992 a referendum amongst the white electorate on continued political reform and a new constitution reached by negotiation was approved by 69 per cent to 31 per cent.

On 20 December 1991, the Convention on a Democratic South Africa (CODESA) talks between the government, ANC, Inkatha Freedom Party and other political, business and church groups, opened. Despite increasing intercommunal violence, which prompted the temporary withdrawal of the ANC in June 1992, CODESA reached agreement on the establishment of an inter-racial administration and the formation of a five-year coalition government following a multiracial election. On 7 September 1993, the delegates agreed to form a multiparty Transitional Executive Council (TEC), which became effective in December 1993. An interim constitution was agreed on 17 November and adopted by parliament on 22 December.

GOVERNMENT

The interim constitution establishes a democratic, multi-party state, and will remain in force until 1999, when the final constitution will take effect. The final constitution, agreed by the Constituent Assembly (composed of the National Assembly and Senate) on 8 May 1996, retains the existing political structure but replaces the Senate with a National Council of Provinces, rejects the representation of minority parties in the Cabinet and incorporates a Bill of Rights.

Under the interim constitution the ten homelands have been reincorporated in South Africa. Executive power is vested in a President and Cabinet, with the President elected by parliament; two deputy Presidents appointed by parties with over 20 per cent of the vote; and a Cabinet and government of national unity to last five years composed of all parties gaining over 5 per cent of the vote. Legislative power is vested in a bicameral parliament, a directly elected 400-member National Assembly elected by proportional representation, and an indirectly elected 90-member Senate composed of ten members elected by each of the nine regional legislatures.

The four former provinces (Cape Province, Natal, Orange Free State, Transvaal) have been replaced by nine new regions (Western Cape, Northern Cape, Eastern Cape, Free State, North-West, KwaZulu/Natal, Gauteng, Northern Province, Eastern Transvaal). Each region has its own Prime Minister, a legislature of between 30 and 100 seats elected by proportional representation, and its own constitution. At local government level, new multiracial municipal councils have their seats allocated on a 30 per cent white, 30 per cent non-white and 40 per cent non-racial basis.

The interim constitution also established, in February 1995, a constitutional court of 11 members to adjudicate in disputes between the three tiers of government, to inter-pret and certify amendments to the constitution, to ensure that all executive, legislative and judicial actions conform to the new Bill of Rights, to decide on the validity of the final constitution, and to protect all rights and freedoms.

In the country's first multiracial general election held on 26–29 April 1994 the results in the National Assembly were (seats): African National Congress (ANC) 62.7 per cent (252), National Party (NP) 20.4 per cent (82), Inkatha Freedom Party (IFP) 10.5 per cent (43), Freedom Front (FF) 2.2 per cent (9), Democratic Party (DP) 1.7 per cent (7), Pan Africanist Congress (PAC) 1.3 per cent (5), African Christian Democratic Party 0.4 per cent (2). In the Senate the ANC gained 60 seats, the NP 17, IFP 5, FF 5, DP 3. In the regional elections the ANC won control of seven regional legislatures: Gauteng, Northern Transvaal, East-ern Transvaal, North-West Northern Cape, Eastern Cape, Orange Free State. The NP won control in the Western Cape and the IFP in KwaZulu/Natal but the NP withdrew from all provincial governments and the government of national unity in June 1996.

The new Parliament has passed two significant pieces of legislation to settle the legacy of the apartheid era. In November 1994 the Restitution of Land Rights Act was passed which established a Land Claims Commission and a Land Claims Court to restore the rights of those dispos-sessed of their land since the 1913 Land Act. In June 1995 the Promotion of National Unity and Reconciliation Act was passed which established a Truth Commission cover-ing the apartheid era, with a remit to assess confessions, grant amnesties for political crimes and set compensation for victims. The first hearing opened on 15 April 1996.

ANC-IFP violence in KwaZulu/Natal has left 15,000 people dead since the mid-1980s, although local elections, held on 26 June 1996, were relatively peaceful.

HEAD OF STATE
President, Nelson Rolihlahla Mandela, OM, *elected by parliament* 9 May 1994, *sworn in* 10 May 1994
Executive Deputy President, Thabo Mbeki (ANC)

CABINET *as at August 1996*
Justice, Dullah Omar (ANC)
Defence, Joe Modise (ANC)
Safety and Security, Sydney Mufamadi (ANC)
Education, Prof. Sibusiso Bengu (ANC)
Trade and Industry, Alec Erwin (ANC)
Foreign Affairs, Alfred Nzo (ANC)
Labour, Tito Mboweni (ANC)
Post, Telecommunications and Broadcasting, Jay Naidoo (ANC)
Health, Dr Nkosazana Zuma (ANC)
Transport, Mac Maharaj (ANC)
Provincial Affairs and Constitutional Development, Mohammed Valli Moosa (ANC)
Land and Agriculture, Derek Hanekom (ANC)
Public Enterprises, Stella Sigcau (ANC)
Public Services and Administration, Dr Zola Skweyiya (ANC)
Housing, S. D. Mthembi-Mahanyele (ANC)
Public Works, Jeff Radebe (ANC)
Correctional Services, Dr Sipho Mzimela (IFP)
Finance, Trevor Manuel (ANC)
Sports and Recreation, Steve Tshwete (ANC)
Home Affairs, Dr Mangosuthu Buthelezi (IFP)
Water and Forestry, Prof Kader Asmal (ANC)
Environmental Affairs and Tourism, Dr Pallo Jordan (ANC)
Mines and Energy, Penwell Maduna (ANC)
Welfare and Population Development, Geraldine Fraser-Moleketi (ANC)
Arts, Culture, Science and Technology, Dr Ben Ngubane (IFP)

HIGH COMMISSION OF THE REPUBLIC OF SOUTH AFRICA
South Africa House, Trafalgar Square, London WC2N 5DP
Tel 0171-930 4488
High Commissioner, HE Mendi Msimang, apptd 1995
Deputy High Commissioner, G. J. Grobler
Minister (Economic), S. Pretorius
Counsellors, B. C. Barn; D. Seals; L. Hanekom (*Consul-General*)
Defence Attaché, Brig. G. A. Hallowes

BRITISH HIGH COMMISSION
255 Hill Street, Pretoria 0002
Tel: Pretoria 433121
91 Parliament Street, Cape Town 8001
Tel: Cape Town 4617220
High Commissioner, HE Maeve Fort, CMG, apptd 1996
Counsellor, Deputy High Commissioner, M. J. Lyall-Grant
Counsellor (Political), A. Hardie, OBE
Defence Attaché, Brig. J. W. Parker, CBE
Consul-General and Director of Trade Promotion (Johannesburg), P. Longworth

There is a British Consulate-General at Johannesburg (PO Box 10101, Johannesburg 2000), Consulates at Cape Town and Durban, and Honorary Consuls at Port Elizabeth and East London.

Cultural Attaché and British Council Representative, Les Phillips, OBE, 76 Juta Street, (PO Box 30637), Braamfontein 2017, Johannesburg. There is also an office in Cape Town.

DEFENCE

The armed forces are engaged in the formation of a new South African National Defence Force (SANDF) from the merger of the South African Defence Forces (SADF), the Umkhonto we Sizwe (MK) armed wing of the ANC, the Azanian People's Liberation Army (APLA) of the PAC, and the defence forces of the four former independent homelands. White conscription is being phased out and the SANDF will be a fully professional force.

The total active armed forces number 136,900. Total reserves number 890,000 personnel. The active Army strength is 118,000 personnel. Equipment includes 250 main battle tanks, 3,160 armoured personnel carriers and armoured infantry fighting vehicles and 550 artillery pieces.

The Navy has a strength of 4,500 with three submarines and 12 patrol and coastal combatants. The Air Force has a strength of 9,000 with 243 combat aircraft and 14 armed helicopters. In addition the paramilitary South African Police number 140,000 personnel, with 37,000 reserves.

COMMUNICATIONS

There are international airports at Johannesburg, Durban and Cape Town. South African Airways operates international services to Europe, South America, the Far East, Africa, Australia and the USA, and it is the principal operator of domestic flights. The largest seaport is Durban, Natal. Other major ports are Cape Town, Port Elizabeth, East London, Saldanha Bay and Mossel Bay in Cape Province and Richards Bay, Natal. The national railway system, and most long-distance passenger and freight road transport are run by independent companies. The six landlocked states of Botswana, Lesotho, Swaziland, Zimbabwe, Zambia and Malawi make extensive use of South African Railways for foreign trade.

ECONOMY

The economy has suffered from recession, industrial unrest, drought, the fall in the world gold price and foreign disinvestment. The price of gold has recovered slightly and the drought ended but industrial unrest continues because of black workers' increased expectations. An austerity programme launched in 1985 reduced the national debt to 70 per cent of GDP and enabled the government in September 1993 to announce the repayment of the US$5,000 million foreign debt over an eight-year period.

The first budget of the new government in June 1994 included a one-off 5 per cent levy on corporations and wealthy individuals. Although the budget was well-received, argument over the cost of the ANC's reconstruction and development programme (RDP), including increased spending on education, health care, new homes and electrification, led to a run on the rand and a crisis in foreign exchange and gold reserves, necessitating a scaling-down of expenditure. Some R2,500 million has been spent on the RDP in 1994–5, with a projected R119,000 million to be spent over ten years. The March 1996 budget envisaged expenditure of R173,700 million and revenue of 144,900 million, and a budget deficit of 5.1 per cent of GDP. The economy grew by 3 per cent in 1995 with a surge of foreign capital and investment and fewer industrial strikes. Foreign exchange reserves have been increased and inflation kept down to 9 per cent, but unemployment remains high at 45 per cent.

The rand fell by 20 per cent against the US dollar in April and May 1996, following the withdrawal of the National Party from the government and the appointment of the ANC's first Finance Minister, Trevor Manuel. In June 1996, Manuel unveiled the government's economic strategy, which sought to generate 6 per cent growth and 40,000 jobs a year, and to restore confidence in the currency. Manuel vowed to reduce the budget deficit to 3 per cent of GDP by 2000.

Mining is of great importance, producing 10.0 per cent of GDP and 60 per cent of exports in 1993 and minerals to the value of R39,376 million. The principal minerals produced are gold, coal, diamonds, copper, iron ore, manganese, lime and limestone, uranium, platinum, fluorspar, andalusite, zinc, zirconium, vanadium, titanium, nickel, lead and chrome ore. South Africa is the world's largest producer of gold, platinum, diamonds, chrome ore, manganese and vanadium, and has the world's largest reserves of chrome ore, manganese, vanadium and andalusite.

Agriculture, forestry and fishing account for about 5 per cent of GDP. Over 50 per cent of land is pasture so livestock farming is widespread and meat and wool important products. Principal crops are maize, sugar-cane, fruits and vegetables, wheat, sorghum, sunflower seed and groundnuts. Cotton is widely grown because of its suitability to the climate, and viticulture is also widespread.

Industries, concentrated most heavily around Johannesburg, Pretoria and the major ports, process foodstuffs, metals and non-metallic mineral products, produce oil from coal, and also produce beverages and tobacco, motor vehicles, chemicals and chemical products, machinery, textiles and clothing, and paper and paper products. Manufacturing industry contributed 24.0 per cent of GDP in 1994.

Energy production is based upon coal and natural gas and the production of synthetic liquid fuel from coal. One nuclear power station is in operation and others are planned. South Africa exports electricity through its electric grid connections to all states in southern Africa.

TRADE

Principal exports are gold, base metals and metal products, coal, diamonds, food (especially fruit), chemicals, machinery and transport equipment, and wool. Principal imports are machinery, chemicals, motor vehicles, metals and metal products, food, inedible raw materials and textiles.

American and EU sanctions, in place since 1986, were lifted in July 1991 and January 1992 respectively. The longer-standing UN finance, oil and arms embargoes were lifted in October 1993, December 1993 and April 1994 respectively.

Trade with UK	1994	1995
Imports from UK	£1,410,878,000	£1,830,397,000
Exports to UK	970,718,000	1,113,064,000

SPAIN
España

Spain occupies most of the Iberian Pensinsula, between 36° and 43° 45′ N., and 4° 25′ E. and 9° 20′ W. It is bounded on the south and east by the Mediterranean, on the west by the Atlantic and Portugal, and on the north by the Bay of Biscay and France. It comprises a total area of 194,897 sq. miles (504,782 sq. km), with a population (1991 census) of 38,872,268.

The interior of the Iberian peninsula consists of an elevated tableland surrounded and traversed by mountain ranges: the Pyrenees, the Cantabrian Mountains, the Sierra Guadarrama, Sierra Morena, Sierra Nevada, Montes de Toledo, etc. The principal rivers are the Duero, the Tajo, the Guadiana, the Guadalquivir, the Ebro and the Miño.

CAPITAL – Madrid, population (1991) 4,947,555. Other large cities are ΨBarcelona (4,654,407), ΨValencia (2,117,972), Seville (1,619,703), Alicante (1,292,563), ΨMálaga (1,160,843), Bilbao (1,179,148); Murcia (1,045,601).

CURRENCY – Peseta of 100 céntimos.

FLAG – Three horizontal stripes of red, yellow, red, with the yellow of double width.

NATIONAL ANTHEM – Marcha Real Española.

NATIONAL DAY – 12 October.

GOVERNMENT

Spain was a monarchy until 1931, when King Alfonso XIII left the country and a republic was proclaimed. A provisional government, drawn from the various republican and socialist parties, was formed. In July 1936 a counter-revolution broke out in military garrisons in Spanish Morocco and spread throughout Spain. The principal leader was Gen. Franco, leader of the Military-Fascist fusion, or *Falange*. Civil war ensued until March 1939, when the Popular Front governments in Madrid and Barcelona surrendered to the Nationalists (as Gen. Franco's followers were then named). Gen. Franco became President and ruled the country until his death in 1975, when, according to his wishes, he was succeeded as head of state by Prince Juan Carlos of Bourbon (grandson of Alfonso XIII) and Spain again became a monarchy. The first free election was held on 15 June 1977.

Under the 1978 constitution there is a bicameral *Cortes Generales* comprising a 350-member Congress of Deputies elected for a maximum term of four years, which elects the Prime Minister; and a Senate consisting of 208 directly elected representatives of the provinces, islands, and Ceuta and Melilla, and 44 representatives appointed by the assemblies of the autonomous regions. The general election of June 1993 was won by the PSOE (Spanish Socialist Workers' Party), which formed a minority government with the support of the Catalan and Basque nationalists. The withdrawal of nationalist support following the government's embroilment in the anti-terrorist GAL scandal forced Prime Minister González to call an early general election, on 3 March 1996. The Popular Party (PP) won 156 seats (38.9 per cent) in the Congress of Deputies, defeating the PSOE which won 141 seats (37.5 per cent). The PP formed a minority government with the support of the Catalan nationalists.

REGIONS

Since the promulgation of the 1978 constitution, 17 autonomous regions have been established, with their own parliaments and governments. These are Andalucia, Aragon, Asturias, Balearics, the Basque country, Canaries, Castilla-La Mancha, Castilla-Leon, Cantabria, Cataluña, Extremadura, Galicia, Madrid, Murcia, Navarre, La Rioja and Valencia. The Basque country, incorporating the three provinces of Álava, Guipúzcoa and Vizcaya, has the authority to raise taxes and is responsible for social services, culture and the Basque language within the region. In addition Madrid and Barcelona have special autonomous status, but not the same degree of autonomy as the autonomous regions. In February 1995 statutes of autonomy for Ceuta and Melilla were approved by the Cortes, giving them similar autonomous status to Madrid and Barcelona. They will each have a mayor, a council of government and an elected legislative assembly.

SECESSION

The Basque separatist terrorist organization ETA (*Euzkadi ta Azkatasuna* – Basque Nation and Liberty) has since its formation in 1959 carried out a terrorist campaign of bombings, shootings and kidnappings against the Spanish state and its security forces in an attempt to gain independence for the Basque country. ETA rejected regional autonomy for the Basque country in 1979 as insufficient and continued its campaign, but increased co-operation between French and Spanish security forces and an alleged illegal anti-terrorist campaign organized by the Spanish state under the acronym GAL (*Grupos Antiterroristas de Liberación*) had greatly weakened ETA by the early 1990s. Most of its leaders were caught and jailed in 1992; the conflict has left 700–800 dead and 600 ETA members in jail.

HEAD OF STATE

HM The King of Spain, King Juan Carlos I de Borbón y Borbón, KG, GCVO, *born* 5 January 1938, *acceded to the throne* 22 November 1975, *married* 14 May 1962, Princess Sophie of Greece *and has issue* Infante Felipe (*see* below); Infanta Elena Maria Isabel Dominga, *born* 20 December 1963; and Infanta Cristina Federica Victoria Antonia, *born* 13 June 1965

Heir, HRH The Prince of the Asturias (Infante Felipe Juan Pablo Alfonso y Todos los Santos), *born* 30 January 1968

CABINET *as at August 1996*

Prime Minister, José María Aznar López
Deputy PM, Presidency, Francisco Alvárez-Cascos Fernández
Deputy PM, Economy and Finance, Rodrigo de Rato y Figaredo
Foreign Affairs, Abel Matutes Juan
Justice, Margarita Mariscal de Gante
Defence, Eduardo Serra Rexach
Interior, Jaime Mayor Oreja
Development, Rafael Arias-Salgado y Montalvo
Education and Culture, Esperanza Aguirre y Gil de Biedma
Labour and Social Affairs, Javier Arenas Bocanegra
Industry and Energy, Josep Piqué i Camps
Agriculture, Food and Fisheries, Loyola de Palacio del Valle-Lersundi
Public Administration, Mariano Rajoy Brey
Health and Consumer Affairs, José Manuel Romay Beccaría
Environment, Isabel Tocino Biscarolasaga

SPANISH EMBASSY
39 Chesham Place, London SW1X 8SB
Tel 0171-235 5555
Ambassador Extraordinary and Plenipotentiary, HE Don
   Alberto Aza Arias, apptd 1993
Minister Counsellor, Don Pablo Barrios Almanzor
Defence Attaché, Lt.-Col. D. L. Diaz-Ripoll
Minister, Dr D. de Lario (*Cultural*)
Minister, Don L. E. Valera (*Consul*)
Counsellor, Don J. García-Valverde (*Commercial*)

BRITISH EMBASSY
Calle de Fernando el Santo 16, 28010 Madrid
Tel: Madrid 319 0200
Ambassador Extraordinary and Plenipotentiary, HE Anthony
   David Brighty, CMG, CVO, apptd 1994
Minister, Deputy Head of Mission, J. A. Drew
Counsellors, M. H. Conner (*Commercial*); C. J. Ingham
   (*Economic and Community Affairs*); D. C. Ankerson
Defence and Naval Attaché, Capt. J. Gozzard RN
Consuls-General, D. G. Alexander, MBE (*Madrid*);
   J. R. Cowling (*Barcelona*); M. McLoughlin (*Bilbao*)

There are Consulates-General in Madrid, Barcelona,
Bilbao; Consulates in Tenerife, Alicante, Seville, Malaga,
Palma de Mallorca, Las Palmas; Vice-Consulates in Ibiza
and Menorca; Honorary Consulates in Santander,
Tarragona, Vigo.

BRITISH COUNCIL DIRECTOR, Peter Taylor, OBE, Paseo
   del General Martinez, Campos 31, 28100 Madrid.
   There are offices in Barcelona, Bilbao, Las Palmas,
   Palma, Segovia, Seville and Valencia.

BRITISH CHAMBER OF COMMERCE, Plaza de Santa Barbara
   10, 1st Floor, 28004 Madrid; Paseo de Gracia 11,
   Barcelona 7; Alameda de Mazarredo 5, Bilbao 1.

DEFENCE

The armed forces have a total active strength of 206,000
(126,000 conscripts). Conscription has been reduced to six
months; a professional army is to be formed by 2003. The
Army has 144,700 personnel (97,000 conscripts), with 668
main battle tanks, 2,092 armoured personnel carriers, 1,292
artillery pieces, and 28 combat helicopters. The Army is
organized into eight regional commands.

The Spanish Navy has a strength of 31,900 (16,900
conscripts), including 7,000 marines, and consists of eight
submarines, one aircraft carrier, 17 frigates, 31 patrol and
coastal combatants, 25 armed helicopters and 20 Harrier
aircraft. The Air Force has a strength of 29,400 (12,100
conscripts) and has 161 combat aircraft. The paramilitary
Guardia Civil with 72,000 personnel (2,200 conscripts)
operates as a gendarmerie in rural areas under the control
of the Ministry of Defence and has been actively engaged
in combating Basque terrorism.

The USA maintains 4,500 naval and 400 air force
personnel in Spain.

ECONOMY

The expansion of the economy and accession to the EU
have led to changes in Spanish agriculture. It accounts for
over 5 per cent of GDP and employs over 10 per cent of the
working population. The country is generally fertile, and
olives, oranges, lemons, almonds, pomegranates, bananas,
apricots, tomatoes, peppers, cucumbers and grapes are
cultivated. Other agricultural products include wheat,
barley, oats, rice, hemp and flax. The vine is cultivated
widely; in the south-west, around Jerez, sherry and tent
wines are produced. The fishing industry is important.

Spain's mineral resources of coal, iron, wolfram, copper,
zinc, lead and iron ores are exploited. Output of coal in

1994 was 29.5 million tonnes; output of steel (1988) 11.9
million tonnes.

The principal industrial goods are cars, steel, ships,
manufactured goods, textiles, chemical products, footwear
and other leather goods. Tourism is a major industry; in
1993 an estimated 57,259,000 tourists visited Spain.

The government is attempting to reform the economy
so that it will meet the convergence criteria laid down for
entry into a future EU economic and monetary union. The
budget deficit was reduced from 6.7 per cent of GDP in
1994 to 5.8 per cent in 1995. The weak peseta had to be
devalued by 7 per cent in the exchange rate mechanism in
March 1995. The new PP government announced spending cuts of £1,000 million and froze public sector workers'
wages in an attempt to reduce spending to 3 per cent of
GDP by 1997. The unemployment rate was 22.5 per cent
in March 1996.

TRADE

The principal imports are cotton, tobacco, cellulose,
timber, coffee and cocoa, food products, fertilizers, dyes,
machinery, motor vehicles and agricultural tractors, wool
and petroleum products. The principal exports include
cars, petroleum products, iron ore, cork, salt, vegetables,
fruits, wines, olive oil, potash, mercury, pyrites, tinned
fruit and fish, tomatoes and footwear.

Trade with UK	1994	1995
Imports from UK	£4,996,135,000	£4,123,900,000
Exports to UK	3,630,298,000	5,800,100,000

EDUCATION

Education is free for those aged six to 18, and compulsory
up to the age of 14. Private schools (30 per cent of primary
and 60 per cent of secondary schools) have to fulfill certain
criteria to receive government maintenance grants. There
are 33 public sector universities, the oldest of which,
Salamanca, was founded in 1218. Other ancient foundations are Valladolid (1346), Barcelona (1430), Zaragoza
(1474), Santiago (1495), Valencia (1500), Seville (1505),
Madrid (1508), Granada (1531), Oviedo (1604). Private
universities are Deusto in Bilbao, Navarra in Pamplona,
one in Madrid and one in Salamanca. Student numbers in
the universities in 1989–90 totalled 1,067,874.

CULTURE

Castilian is the language of more than three-quarters of the
population of Spain. Basque, said to have been the original
language of Iberia, is spoken in Vizcaya, Guipuzcoa and
Alava. Catalan is spoken in Provençal Spain, and Galician,
spoken in the north-western provinces, is akin to Portuguese. The governments of these regions actively encourage use of their local languages.

The literature of Spain is one of the oldest and richest in
the world, the *Poem of the Cid*, the earliest of the heroic songs
of Spain, having been written about 1140. The outstanding
writings of its golden age are those of Miguel de Cervantes
Saavedra (1547–1616), Lope Felix de Vega Carpio
(1562–1635) and Pedro Calderón de la Barca (1600–81).
The Nobel Prize for Literature has five times been
awarded to Spanish authors: J. Echegaray (1904), J.
Benavente (1922), Juan Ramón Jiménez (1956), Vicente
Aleixandre (1977) and Camilo José Cela (1989).

ISLANDS AND ENCLAVES

The Balearic Isles form an archipelago off the east coast of
Spain. There are four large islands (Majorca, Minorca,
Ibiza and Formentera), and seven smaller (Aire, Aucanada,
Botafoch, Cabrera, Dragonera, Pinto and El Rey). The total
area is 1,935 sq. miles (5,011 sq. km), with a population of

685,088. The archipelago forms a province of Spain, the capital being ΨPalma in Majorca, pop. 304,422.

The Canary Islands are an archipelago in the Atlantic, off the African coast, consisting of seven islands and six mostly uninhabited islets. The total area is 2,807 sq. miles (7,270 sq. km), with a population of 1,444,626. The Canary Islands form two provinces of Spain: Las Palmas, comprising Gran Canaria, Lanzarote (38,500), Fuerteventura (19,500) and the islets of Alegranza, Roque del Este, Roque del Oeste, Graciosa, Montaña Clara and Lobos, with seat of administration at ΨLas Palmas (366,454) in Gran Canaria; and Santa Cruz de Tenerife, comprising Tenerife, La Palma (76,000), Gomera (31,829), and Hierro (10,000), with seat of administration at ΨSanta Cruz in Tenerife, population estimate 190,784.

Isla de Faisanes is an uninhabited Franco-Spanish condominium, at the mouth of the Bidassoa in La Higuera bay.

ΨCeuta is a fortified post on the Moroccan coast, opposite Gibraltar. The total area is 5 sq. miles (13 sq. km), with a population of 70,864.

ΨMelilla is a town on a rocky promontory of the Rif coast, connected with the mainland by a narrow isthmus. Population 58,449. Ceuta and Melilla are parts of Metropolitan Spain.

OVERSEAS TERRITORIES

Spanish settlements on the Moroccan seaboard are:
Peñón de Alhucemas, a bay including six islands, population 366
Peñón de la Gomera (or *Peñón de Velez*), a fortified rocky islet, population 450
The Chaffarinas (or Zaffarines), a group of three islands near the Algerian frontier, population 610

SRI LANKA
Sri Lanka Prajatantrika Samajawadi Janarajaya

Sri Lanka (formerly Ceylon) is an island in the Indian Ocean, off the southern tip of India and separated from it by the narrow Palk Strait. Situated between 5° 55' and 9° 50' N. latitude and 79° 42' and 81° 52' E. longitude, it has an area of 25,332 sq. miles (65,610 sq. km), including 33 sq. miles of inland water. Forests, jungle and scrub cover the greater part of the island. In areas over 2,000 ft above sea level grasslands (*patanas* or *talawas*) are found. One of the highest peaks in the central massif is Adam's Peak (7,360 ft), a place of pilgrimage for Buddhists, Hindus and Muslims.

The climate is warm throughout the year, with a high relative humidity. The two main monsoon seasons are mid-May to September (south-west) and November to March (north-east).

The population (1993 estimate) was 17,619,000, of which 74 per cent were Sinhalese, 12.6 per cent Sri Lanka Tamils, 5.6 per cent Indian Tamils, 7.1 per cent Sri Lankan Moors and 0.7 per cent Burghers, Malays and others. The religion of the majority is Buddhism (69.3 per cent), then Hinduism (15.5 per cent), Islam (7.6 per cent), and Christianity (7.5 per cent). The national languages are Sinhala, Tamil and English.

CAPITAL – ΨColombo, population (1993) 2,026,000.
    Other principal towns are ΨJaffna (879,000), Kandy (1,269,000), ΨGalle (971,000), and ΨTrincomalee (323,000).
CURRENCY – Sri Lankan rupee (Rs) of 100 cents.

FLAG – On a dark red field, within a golden border, a golden lion passant holding a sword in its right paw, and a representation of a *bo*-leaf, issuing from each corner; and to its right, two vertical stripes of saffron and green also placed within a golden border, to represent the minorities of the country.
NATIONAL ANTHEM – Namo Namo Matha (We all stand together).
NATIONAL DAY – 4 February (Independence Day).

GOVERNMENT

The Portuguese landed in Ceylon in the early 16th century and founded settlements, eventually conquering much of the country. Portuguese rule lasted 150 years; in 1658 it gave way to that of the Dutch East India Company until 1796. The maritime provinces of Ceylon were ceded by the Dutch to the British in 1798, becoming a British Crown Colony in 1802. With the annexation of the Kingdom of Kandy in 1815, all Ceylon came under British rule.

Ceylon became a self-governing state and a member of the British Commonwealth on 4 February 1948. A republican constitution was adopted in 1972 and the country was renamed Sri Lanka (meaning 'Resplendent Island'). In 1978 a new constitution introduced a system of proportional representation. Legislative power is exercised by the Parliament, executive power being exercised by the President and Cabinet.

Eight provincial councils were set up in 1988 under the Indo-Sri Lankan peace accord in an attempt to diffuse ethnic tension. Since then, except for the temporarily merged North-East province, all provinces have had elected provincial councils.

In the general election of 16 August 1994 the ruling United National Party (UNP) was defeated by the opposition People's Alliance led by Chandrika Bandaranaike Kumaratunga. The People's Alliance, a coalition of seven parties, won 105 seats; the UNP 94 seats; and other parties, mainly Muslim and moderate Tamils, 26 seats. The People's Alliance formed a government with the support of the Sri Lankan Muslim Congress and moderate Tamil parties. Prime Minister Kumaratunga won the presidential election on 9 November 1994 with 62 per cent of the vote after the UNP candidate Gamini Dissanayake was assassinated by Tamil Tiger terrorists. President Kumaratunga handed over the premiership to her mother, the former Prime Minister Sirimavo Bandaranaike.

In August 1995 the government proposed constitutional changes intended to form a federal state with eight autonomous regions (one covering the Tamil north-east). Each region would have its own elected legislature, executive and judicial branch of government, a police force, and powers devolved from the central government. The package must be passed by a two-thirds parliamentary majority and a national referendum.

SECESSION

The Liberation Tigers of Tamil Eelam (LTTE) guerrilla group has been fighting Sri Lankan forces for control of the Tamil majority areas in the north and east of the country since 1983. Some 40,000–50,000 have been killed in 13 years of fighting.

The People's Alliance government came to power on a platform of negotiating a peaceful settlement, to include full autonomy for the Tamil-majority areas. Peace negotiations opened in September 1994, leading to a formal cease-fire with the LTTE which began on 8 January 1995. Fighting resumed in April 1995 after the LTTE had unilaterally broken the cease-fire and negotiations had broken down. A government offensive, launched in October 1995, forced the LTTE to retreat, enabling the government to regain control of Jaffna town in December. The rebels rejected the offer of an amnesty and devolution and heavy fighting and bomb attacks continued. A second government offensive in April 1996 gained control over almost the entire northern Jaffna peninsula, although the rebels counter-attacked, briefly seizing a government military base in July 1996. The LTTE has a strength of up to 10,000 personnel.

HEAD OF STATE

President, Chandrika Bandaranaike Kumaratunga, *elected* 9 November 1994, *sworn in* 12 November 1994

CABINET *as at August 1996*

Buddha Sasana, Defence, Finance, Planning, Ethnic Affairs and National Integration, The President
Prime Minister, Sirimavo Bandaranaike
Public Administration, Local Government, Plantations and Parliamentary Affairs, Ratnasiri Wickremanayake
Power and Energy, Irrigation, Col. Anuruddha Ratwatte
Indigenous Medicine, Provincial Councils and Co-operatives, Amarasiri Dodangoda
Foreign Affairs, Lakshman Kadirgamar
Cultural and Religious Affairs, Lakshman Jayakody
Science, Technology and Human Resources Development, Bernard Soysa
Agriculture, Lands and Forests, D. M. Jayaratne
Labour and Vocational Training, Mahinda Rajapakse
Shipping, Ports, Rehabilitation and Reconstruction, M. H. M. Ashroff
Information, Tourism and Aviation, Dharmasiri Senanayake
Justice and Constitutional Affairs, G. L. Peiris
Industrial Development, C. V. Gunaratne
Education and Higher Education, Richard Pathirana
Housing, Construction and Public Utilities, Nimal Siripala De Silva
Posts and Telecommunications, Mangala Samaraweera
Youth Affairs, Sports and Rural Development, D. S. M. B. Dissanayaka
Transport, Highways, Environment and Women's Affairs, Srimani Athulathmudali
Internal and External Trade, Commerce and Food, Kingsley Wickremeratne
Health, Highways and Social Services, A. H. M. Fowzie
Fisheries, Indika Gunawardena
Livestock Development and Rural Industries, S. Thondaman

HIGH COMMISSION FOR THE DEMOCRATIC SOCIALIST REPUBLIC OF SRI LANKA
13 Hyde Park Gardens, London W2 2LU
Tel 0171-262 1841
High Commissioner, HE Sarath Wickremesinghe, apptd 1995
Deputy High Commissioner, G. S. Munasinghe
Ministers, S. Rajapakse (*Consular*); K. J. Weerasinghe (*Commercial*)
First Secretary, G. H. Indradasa (*Defence*)

BRITISH HIGH COMMISSION
Galle Road 190, Kollupitiya (PO Box 1433), Colombo 3
Tel: Colombo 437336
High Commissioner, HE David Tatham, CMG, apptd 1996
Deputy High Commissioner, P. C. Gregory-Hood
Defence Adviser, Lt.-Col. T. J. O'Donnell, MBE
First Secretary (*Commercial*), I. M. Dallas

BRITISH COUNCIL DIRECTOR, Peter Ellwood, 49 Alfred House Gardens, PO Box 753, Colombo 3. Library also in Kandy.

DEFENCE

Total active military personnel number 125,300; there are 4,200 reserves. The Army has a strength of 105,000, with 25 main battle tanks, 153 armoured personnel carriers and armoured infantry fighting vehicles and 50 artillery pieces. The 10,300-strong Navy has 40 patrol and coastal vessels.

The Air Force has a strength of 10,000, with 27 combat aircraft and 26 armed helicopters. There is a paramilitary police force of 80,000; additional paramilitary personnel number 30,200.

ECONOMY

The staple products of the island are tea, rubber, copra, spices and gems. There is increasing emphasis on local production of food, especially rice, and plans for the large-scale production of sugar-cane, cotton and citrus fruits.

The manufacturing sector has grown considerably over the past few years and produces ceramic ware, vegetable oils and by-products, paper, tobacco, tanning and leather goods, plywood, cement, chemicals, beverages, sugar, flour, salt, textiles and garments, ilmenite, tiles, tyres, fertilizers, clothing, jewellery and hardware and there is a petroleum refinery. Foreign investment in manufacturing is increasing considerably and, together with the tourism sector (400,000 visitors in 1994), has contributed to an average economic growth rate of 5 per cent since 1991. GDP per capita was US$713 in 1995.

Since regaining control of Jaffna, the government has requested £178 million in foreign aid to fund a three-year programme of reconstruction.

TRADE WITH UK	1994	1995
Imports from UK	£153,850,000	£156,409,000
Exports to UK	185,784,000	205,652,000

COMMUNICATIONS

There are over 15,660 miles of roads in Sri Lanka and a government-run railway system with 984 miles of lines. A satellite earth station at Padukka provides telecommunication links world-wide. The principal airport is at Katunayake, 19 miles north of Colombo. Air Lanka operates 69 flights weekly to the Gulf States, the Maldives, western Europe and throughout the Far East.

SUDAN
Al-Jamhuryat es-Sudan Al-Democratia

Sudan lies in north-east Africa, between 22° and 3°36′ N. latitude, and 21° 49′ and 38° 35′ E. longitude. To the north lies Egypt, to the east the Red Sea, Eritrea and Ethiopia, to the south Kenya, Uganda and Zaire, and to the west the Central African Republic, Chad, and Libya. The area is about 967,500 sq. miles (2,505,813 sq. km).

The White Nile, as the Bahr el Jebel, flows through Sudan from Nimule to Wadi Halfa. The Blue Nile flows from Lake Tana on the Ethiopian plateau through Sudan to join the White Nile at Khartoum. The next confluence of importance is at Atbara where the main Nile is joined by the River Atbara. Between Khartoum and Wadi Halfa lie five of the six cataracts.

The population is 27,361,000 (UN estimate 1994). Arab and Nubian peoples populate the north and centre, Nilotic and Negro peoples the south. Arabic is the official language and Islam the state religion, although the Nilotics of the Bahr el Ghazal and Upper Nile valleys are generally Animists or Christians.

CAPITAL – Khartoum. The combined population of Khartoum, Khartoum North and Omdurman (excluding refugees and displaced people) is estimated at 3,000,000.

CURRENCY – Sudanese Dinar of 10 pounds.

FLAG – Three horizontal stripes of red, white and black with a green triangle next to the hoist.

NATIONAL ANTHEM – Nahnu Djundullah (We are the army of God).

NATIONAL DAY – 1 January (Independence Day).

GOVERNMENT

The Anglo-Egyptian Condominium over Sudan was established in 1899 and ended when the Sudan House of Representatives, on 19 December 1955, declared Sudan a fully independent sovereign state. A republic was proclaimed on 1 January 1956, and was recognized by Great Britain and Egypt. Sudan was under military rule from 1958 to 1964; under the rule of a revolutionary council headed by Col. Gaafar Mohamed El Nimeri from 1969 until April 1985 when the army command deposed Nimeri; and experienced a third military coup in June 1989 when the civilian government, in power since 1986, was overthrown by Brig.-Gen. Omar Hassan Ahmad al-Bashir. The constitution was suspended and parliament was replaced by a 15-member ruling junta (Revolutionary Command Council) who exercised control over a Cabinet. The ruling junta appointed Gen. al-Bashir as head of state on 16 October 1993 and then dissolved itself. Presidential and legislative elections were held in March 1996. President al-Bashir was elected with 75.7 per cent of the vote having faced no serious contender. Hassan al-Tourabi of the fundamentalist National Islamic Front was elected President of the 269-member National Assembly, although political parties had officially been banned from contesting the elections.

The government has developed close relations with Iran and is believed by western states to support international terrorism and have Iranian Revolutionary Guards' bases on its territory. Supported and dominated by the NIF, the government has since 1989 turned Sudan into an Islamic state. In August 1993 the USA placed Sudan on a list of countries sponsoring terrorism and suspended all trade apart from humanitarian goods. In 1995 Sudan's relations with its neighbours, notably Egypt, Eritrea and Uganda, deteriorated as they consider that Sudan is arming Islamic and insurgent groups in their states. In April 1996 the UN imposed sanctions on Sudan for failing to extradite three people suspected of attempting to assassinate President Mubarak of Egypt in Ethiopia in June 1996.

SECESSION

Nearly 17 years of insurrection in the southern provinces ended in 1972 with the signing of an agreement recognizing southern regional autonomy within the Sudanese state. However, insurrection resumed in 1983 and since then there has been civil war in the regions of Eastern and Western Equatoria in the south of the country between government forces and the Christian and Animist majority in the area, organized into the Sudan People's Liberation Army (SPLA). Although the Islamic government has officially stated that it is not attempting to introduce Sharia law in the south, the Sharia affects the two million Christians in northern areas. Between 1991 and 1994 the SPLA was split into four factions based on tribal groups. The two principal factions were SPLA-Torit led by the original SPLA leader John Garang, and SPLA-United led by Riek Machar. The SPLA lost the control that it had exercised over most of the south to government forces because of fighting between the SPLA factions, three of whom were armed by government forces to fight the SPLA-Torit faction. By early 1994 government forces controlled most of the towns and roads in the region and launched the largest offensive since 1983, forcing the SPLA factions to resort to guerrilla tactics. Garang's SPLA-Torit faction, suspected of receiving support from Uganda, Tanzania and Eritrea, made considerable advances against government forces in late 1995 and early 1996. In April 1996, the government signed a peace treaty with the South Sudan Independence Movement and SPLA-United who agreed to relinquish any hope of independence. SPLA-Torit rejected the agreement.

The warfare has left an estimated 1.3 million dead, including 300,000 who died in the war-induced famine in 1988 and thousands in a similar situation in 1994. Some three million refugees have fled the fighting, either to the north, to neighbouring states or to the far south near the Ugandan border. The fighting has left large areas of the south desolate and uninhabitable.

HEAD OF STATE

President, Minister of Defence, Lt.-Gen. Omar Hassan Ahmad al-Bashir, *appointed* 16 October 1993, *elected* 17 March 1996

First Vice-President, Maj.-Gen. Zubir Mohammed Saleh

Second Vice-President, George Kongor Arop

CABINET *as at August 1996*

Agriculture and Forests, Nafie Ali Nafie

Animal Resources, Musa Mek Kur

Aviation, Tigani Adam Al-Tahir

Cabinet Affairs, Salah-Eddin Mohamed Ahmed Karrar

Culture and Information, Brig. Al-Tayeb Ibrahim Mohamed Khair

Defence, Lt.-Gen. Hasan Abdel-Rahman Ali

Education, Dr Kabshour Kuku

Energy and Mining, Awad Ahmed Al-Jaz

Environment and Tourism, Mohamed Tahir Eila

External Trade, Osman Al-Hadi

Federal Rule Chamber, Ali Al-Haj Mohammad

Finance, Abdel Wahhab Osman

Foreign Affairs, Ali Osman Mohammad Taha

Health, Ihsan al-Ghabshawi

Higher Education and Scientific Research, Abdel-Wahab Abdel-Rahim Bob

Industry, Badr Al-Din Suleiman

Interior and Adviser to the President, Brig. Bakri Hassan Salih

Irrigation and Water Resources, Yacoub Musa Abu-Shora

Justice, Abdel Basit Sabdrat

Parliamentary Affairs, Abul Gazim Mohammad Ibrahim

Presidential Affairs, Brig. Abdel-Rahim Mohammad Hussein

Public Service, Labour, Administrative Reform, Angelo Beda

Roads and Communications, al-Hadi Bushra

Social Planning, Mohammad Osman Al-Khalifa

Survey and Architectural Development, Col. Gatlouk Deng

Transport, Albino Akol Akol

EMBASSY OF THE REPUBLIC OF THE SUDAN

3 Cleveland Row, London SWIA IDD

Tel 0171-839 8080

Ambassador Extraordinary and Plenipotentiary, HE Sayed Omer Yousif Bireedo, apptd 1995

BRITISH EMBASSY

(PO Box 801), Khartoum

Tel: Khartoum 777105

Ambassador Extraordinary and Plenipotentiary, HE Alan Goulty, apptd 1995

BRITISH COUNCIL DIRECTOR, Don Sloan, 14 Abu Sin Street (PO Box 1253), Khartoum.

ECONOMY

Agriculture provides employment for over half the labour force and contributes over one-third of GDP. It is based on large and medium-sized public sector irrigation projects with small-scale private irrigation schemes providing mostly fruit and vegetables. Mechanized and traditional agriculture is practised in areas of sufficient rainfall. The principal grain crops are *dura* (great millet) and wheat, the staple food of the population. Sesame and groundnuts are other important food crops, which also yield an exportable surplus, and a promising start has been made with castor seed. The principal export crop is cotton, both long-staple cotton and short and medium-staple cotton. Sudan also produces the bulk of the world's supply of gum arabic. Sugar is an increasingly important crop, although Sudan still has to achieve self sufficiency in its production.

Livestock is the mainstay of the nomadic Arab tribes of the desert and the Negro tribes of the swamp and wooded grassland country in the south. Production has been affected by drought, famine and civil war.

The manufacturing sector contributes less than 8 per cent to GDP and provides employment for 4 per cent of the work-force. The main manufacturing enterprises are food processing, textiles, shoes, cigarettes and batteries.

TRADE

The principal exports are cotton, livestock, gum arabic and other agricultural produce. The chief imports are petroleum goods and other raw materials, machinery and equipment, transport and equipment, medicines and chemicals.

Trade with UK	1994	1995
Imports from UK	£45,603,000	£44,222,000
Exports to UK	7,301,000	10,183,000

COMMUNICATIONS

The railway system, adversely affected by the civil war, has a route length of about 3,200 miles. Nile river services between Khartoum and Juba have been interrupted by the southern insurrection. Port Sudan is the country's main seaport. Sudan Airways flies services from Khartoum to other parts of the Sudan and to other African states, Europe and the Middle East.

EDUCATION

School education is free for most children but not compulsory, beginning with six years of primary education, followed by three years of secondary education at general secondary schools, the more academic higher secondary schools or vocational schools. The medium of instruction is Arabic. English is no longer taught in schools since new Arabization legislation came into effect in 1991.

Khartoum University has ten faculties. There is a branch of Cairo University in Khartoum, an Islamic University at Omdurman and universities at Wad Medani and Juba. In addition to the universities there are various technical post-secondary institutes as well as professional and vocational training establishments.

SURINAME
Republiek Suriname

Suriname is situated on the north coast of South America and is bounded by the Atlantic in the north, French Guiana in the east, Brazil in the south and Guyana in the west. It has an area of 63,037 sq. miles (163,265 sq. km), with a population (UN 1994 estimate) of 418,000. The official language is Dutch, the native language Sranang Tongo, and other widely-used languages are Hindustani and Javanese.

CAPITAL – ΨParamaribo, population (1971) 110,000.
CURRENCY – Suriname guilder (gulden) of 100 cents.
FLAG – Horizontal stripes of green, white, red, white, green, with a five-pointed yellow star in the centre.
NATIONAL DAY – 25 November.

GOVERNMENT

Formerly known as Dutch Guiana, Suriname remained part of the Netherlands West Indies until 25 November 1975, when it achieved complete independence. The civilian government was ousted in 1980 by the military who appointed a predominantly civilian government in 1982. According to the 1987 constitution, a National Assembly of 51 members elects the President.

President Shankar was overthrown in a military coup, instigated by Lt.-Col. Desi Bouterse, in December 1990; Johan Kraag, a supporter of Bouterse, was installed as President. Elections to the National Assembly were held in May 1991. The New Front for Democracy and Development, a coalition comprising opposition groups, won 30 of the 51 seats, but failed to gain the necessary two-thirds majority to appoint the President. In September 1991 a special sitting of a United People's Assembly elected New Front leader Ronald Venetiaan as President and he formed a government which amended the constitution in April 1992 to limit the power of the military. In August 1992 the government and the two largest guerrilla groups signed a peace agreement under which the guerrillas will be integrated into the police force.

The New Front won the most seats in the elections to the National Assembly on 23 May 1996 but failed to win a majority sufficient to appoint the President, and a coalition government headed by the National Democratic Party was formed.

HEAD OF STATE
President, Jules Wijdenbosch, *inaugurated* 14 September 1996
Vice-President, Pretaapnarain Radhakishun

CABINET *as at September 1996*
Internal Affairs, Sonny Kertowidjojo
Foreign Affairs, Errol Alibuks
Finance, Motilal Mungra
Trade and Industry, Robby Dragman
Planning and International Co-operation, Ernie Brunings
Agriculture, Animal Husbandry and Fisheries, Saimin Redjosentono
Regional Development, Yvonne Raveles-Resida
Social Affairs and Housing, Soewarto Moestadja
Education, Tjan Gobardhan
Labour, Errol Snijders
Public Health, Elias Khodabaks
Public Works, Richard Kalloe
Justice and Police, Paul Sjak Sie
Transportation, Communication and Tourism, Dick De Bie
Defence, Ramon Dwarka-Panday

EMBASSY OF THE REPUBLIC OF SURINAME
2 Alexander Gogelweg, The Hague, The Netherlands
Tel: The Hague 3650844
Ambassador Extraordinary and Plenipotentiary, HE Evert Guillaume Azimullah, apptd 1994

BRITISH AMBASSADOR, HE David Johnson, CVO, resident at Georgetown, Guyana

BRITISH CONSULATE, c/o VSH United Buildings, Van't Hogerhuystraat, PO Box 1300, Paramaribo. *Honorary Consul*, J. J. Healy, MBE

ECONOMY

Suriname has large timber resources. Rice and sugar-cane are the main crops. Bauxite is mined, and is the principal export. Principal trading partners are the Netherlands, USA and Norway.

TRADE WITH UK	1994	1995
Imports from UK	£9,163,000	£7,536,000
Exports to UK	17,447,000	22,992,000

SWAZILAND
Umbuso we Swatini

Swaziland is a small, land-locked country surrounded by South Africa on its northern, western and southern borders and by Mozambique to the east. The broken mountainous Highveld along the western border, with an average altitude of 4,000 ft, is densely forested, mainly with conifers and eucalyptus; the Middleveld, averaging about 2,000 ft, is a mixed farming area including cotton and pineapples; and the Lowveld in the east was mainly scrubland until the introduction of large sugar-cane plantations. Four rivers, the Komati, Usutu, Mbuluzi and Ngwavuma, flow from west to east. The total area is 6,704 sq. miles (17,363 sq. km), and the population (UN estimate 1994) is 906,000.

CAPITAL – Mbabane (population 1986, 38,290). Other main townships are Manzini (estimated population, 30,000), Big Bend, Mhlambanyati, Mhlume, Nhlangano, Pigg's Peak and Simunye.

CURRENCY – Lilangeni (E) of 100 cents. South African currency is also in circulation. Swaziland is a member of the Common Monetary Area and its unit of currency *Emalangeni* (singular *Lilangeni*) has a par value with the South African rand.

FLAG – Blue with a wide crimson horizontal band bordered in yellow across the centre, bearing a shield and two spears horizontally.

NATIONAL ANTHEM – Ingoma Yesive.

NATIONAL DAY – 6 September (Independence Day).

GOVERNMENT

The Kingdom of Swaziland came into being on 25 April 1967 under a self-government constitution and became an independent kingdom, headed by HM Sobhuza II, in membership of the Commonwealth on 6 September 1968.

A new government system was introduced in 1978 and amended in 1992–3 under which the King, assisted by his appointed Cabinet, holds considerable executive, legislative and judicial authority. In addition, there is a bicameral legislative body comprising a Senate and a House of Assembly. Each of the 55 traditional *Tinkhundla* (chieftaincies) are directly elected and become members of the House of Assembly. The King appoints ten members to the House of Assembly, making 65 in all, who then elect ten members of their own number to the Senate. To these are added 20 senators appointed by the King, bringing the full membership of the Senate to 30. All political parties are banned under the 1978 constitution. Pro-democracy protests, including a week-long general strike in January 1996, drew concessions from King Mswati III, who promised to review the ban on political parties and to establish a People's Parliament and a National Council, although their functions were not defined.

HEAD OF STATE
King of Swaziland, HM King Mswati III, *inaugurated* 25 April 1986

CABINET *as at August 1996*
Prime Minister, Rt. Hon. Barnabus S. Dlamini
Deputy Prime Minister, Hon. Dr Sishayi Nxumalo
Foreign Affairs, Hon. Solomon Dlamini
Justice, Hon. Chief Maweni Simelane
Home Affairs, Hon. Prince Sobandla
Finance, Hon. Dr Derek von Wissel
Education, Hon. Arthur Khoza
Works and Construction, Hon. Prince Mahlalengangeni
Health, Hon. Muntu Mswane
Agriculture and Co-operatives, Hon. Chief Dambuza Lukhele
Commerce and Industry, Hon. Majehenkhaba Dlamini
Labour and Public Service, Hon. Albert Shabangu
Natural Resources and Energy, Hon. Revd Absalom Dlamini
Housing and Urban Development, Hon. John Carmichael
Economic Planning and Development, Hon. Themba Masuku
Transport and Communications, Hon. Ephraem Magagula
Broadcasting, Information and Tourism, Hon. Prince Khuzulwandle

KINGDOM OF SWAZILAND HIGH COMMISSION
20 Buckingham Gate, London SW1E 6LB
Tel 0171-630 6611
High Commissioner, HE Revd Percy S. Mngomezulu, apptd 1994

BRITISH HIGH COMMISSION
Allister Miller Street, Mbabane
Tel: Mbabane 42581
High Commissioner, HE John F. Doble, OBE, apptd 1996

BRITISH COUNCIL DIRECTOR, Dr Patrick Brazier (*Cultural Attaché*)

ECONOMY

In the 1989–90 budget, total expenditure, including debt repayment, was projected at E447 million. A surplus of E12.5 million was predicted due to increase in revenue. Manufacturing was announced to have replaced agriculture as the dominant sector in 1988. The 1996–7 budget forecast total expenditure of E1,790 million and a deficit of E140 million.

TRADE WITH UK	1994	1995
Imports from UK	£3,287,000	£3,033,000
Exports to UK	42,034,000	39,714,000

COMMUNICATIONS

Swaziland's railway is about 150 miles long and connects with the Mozambique port of Maputo and the South African railway network to Richards Bay. A rail line to the north-west border provides a link to Komatipoort. Most passenger and goods traffic is carried by privately-owned motor transport services. There are scheduled air services by Royal Swazi National Airways to southern and eastern Africa. International telecommunications and television services are provided through a satellite earth station, and there is also a national telephone network.

SWEDEN
Konungariket Sverige

Sweden occupies the eastern area of the Scandinavian peninsula in north-west Europe with a total area of 173,732 sq. miles (449,964 sq. km), and population of

1014　Countries of the World

8,745,109 (1993 census). The state religion is Lutheran Protestant, to which over 95 per cent officially adhere.

CAPITAL – ΨStockholm. Population (1993): City 692,954; Greater Stockholm, 1,532,803; ΨGothenburg (Göteborg) (437,313); ΨMalmö (237,438); Uppsala (178,011).

CURRENCY – Swedish krona of 100 öre.

FLAG – Yellow cross on a blue ground.

NATIONAL ANTHEM – Du Gamla, Du Fria (Thou ancient, thou freeborn).

NATIONAL DAY – 6 June (Day of the Swedish Flag).

GOVERNMENT

Sweden is a constitutional monarchy, with the monarch retaining purely ceremonial functions as head of state. Under the Act of Succession 1810 (with amendments) the throne is hereditary in the House of Bernadotte. The constitution is based upon the Instrument of Government 1974, which amended the 1810 Act and removed from the monarch the roles of appointing the Prime Minister and signing parliamentary bills into law. A 1979 amendment vested the succession in the monarch's eldest child irrespective of sex.

Executive power is vested in the Prime Minister and Council of Ministers. There is a unicameral legislature (*Riksdag*) of 349 members elected by universal suffrage on a proportional representation basis (with a 4 per cent threshold for representation) for four years. The Council of Ministers (*Statsråd*) is responsible to the *Riksdag*. In the general election held on 18 September 1994 the four-party centre-right coalition of the Moderate, Liberal, Centre and Christian Democratic Parties was defeated by the Social Democrats, who formed a minority government. (The Social Democratic Party has been in government, either alone or in coalition, continuously since 1932, apart from 1936, 1976–82 and 1991–4.) Prime Minister Ingvar Carlsson retired in March 1996, and was replaced by Göran Persson.

Sweden applied for EU membership in July 1991 and negotiations on entry were successfully concluded on 1 March 1994. The Accession Treaty was ratified in a national referendum on 13 November 1994 by 52.3 per cent to 46.8 per cent and by a parliamentary vote on 15 December, enabling Sweden to accede to the EU on 1 January 1995.

Sweden is divided into 24 counties (*län*) and 288 municipalities (*kommun*).

HEAD OF STATE

HM The King of Sweden, Carl XVI Gustaf, KG, *born* 30 April 1946, *succeeded* 15 September 1973, *married* 19 June 1976 Fräulein Silvia Renate Sommerlath and has *issue*, Crown Princess Victoria (*see* below); Prince Carl Philip Edmund Bertil, Duke of Värmland, *born* 13 May 1979; Princess Madeleine Thérèse Amelie Josephine, Duchess of Hälsingland and Gästrikland, *born* 10 June 1982

Heir, HRH Crown Princess Victoria Ingrid Alice Désirée, Duchess of Västergötland, *born* 14 July 1977

COUNCIL OF MINISTERS *as at August 1996*

Prime Minister, Göran Persson
PM's Office, Leif Pagrotsky
Justice, Laila Freivalds
Foreign Affairs, Lena Hjelm-Wallén
Defence, Thage Peterson
Health and Social Affairs, Maj-Inger Klingvall
Transport and Communications, Ines Uusmann
Finance, Erik Åsbrink

Education and Science, Carl Tham
Agriculture, Food and Fisheries, Annika Ahnberg
Labour, Margareta Winberg
Culture, Marita Ulvskog
Industry and Commerce, Anders Sundström
Home Affairs, Jörgen Andersson
Environment, Anna Lindh

SWEDISH EMBASSY
11 Montagu Place, London WIH 2AL
Tel 0171-917 6400
Ambassador Extraordinary and Plenipotentiary, HE Lars-Åke Nilsson, apptd 1995
Minister (Economic), Mårten Grunditz
Defence and Military Attaché, Col. G. Diurlin
Consul-General, G. Dannerljung
Trade Commissioner, A. Lundwall

BRITISH EMBASSY
Skarpögatan 6–8, S115 93 Stockholm
Tel: Stockholm 671 9000
Ambassador Extraordinary and Plenipotentiary, HE Robert Bone, CMG, apptd 1995
Counsellor, Consul-General and Deputy Head of Mission, E. C. Robson
Counsellor (Economic and Commercial), A. R. Murray
Defence and Air Attaché, Wg Cdr. P. McCullum

There are British Consular Offices at Stockholm and Gothenburg, and Honorary Consulates at Gothenburg, Malmö and Sundsvall.

BRITISH COUNCIL REPRESENTATIVE, Ann Hellström, Strandagen 57A, S-115 23 Stockholm
BRITISH-SWEDISH CHAMBER OF COMMERCE, Grevgatan 34, 11453 Stockholm.

DEFENCE

Sweden has a policy of non-alignment in peace and neutrality in war, and it maintains a 'total defence' which includes peacetime organizations for civil, economic and psychological defence. All men aged 18–47 are eligible for conscription, with the initial term being seven to 15 months for the Army and Navy and eight to 12 months for the Air Force. Men are obliged to serve in the reserves until age 47.

The armed forces have a total active strength of 64,000 (31,600 conscripts), with reserves of 729,000. The Army has a strength of 43,500 (27,000 conscripts). Equipment includes 708 main battle tanks, 210 light tanks, 795 armoured infantry fighting vehicles and armoured personnel carriers and 634 artillery pieces. The Navy has 13 submarines, 41 patrol and coastal vessels, 29 mine warfare craft, two coast artillery brigades and a strength of 9,000 (4,100 conscripts). The Air Force has 393 combat aircraft and a strength of 11,500 (5,500 conscripts).

ECONOMY

Following the election of a centre-right government in 1991 there was drastic change in the Swedish socio-economic system. Free market economic policies of privatization, deregulation, the ending of state subsidies, trade union legislation, floating the exchange rate, central bank independence, tax reform, and welfare and spending cuts have been introduced. Austerity packages were introduced in November 1992 and April 1993 to overcome budget deficits, improve competitiveness and stabilize the currency. The restructuring of industry, together with the world recession, caused unemployment to rise to 9.5 per cent (together with a further 4 per cent on workfare schemes) in 1994, before falling to 8.3 per cent in 1995; manufacturing output fell 15 per cent between 1989 and

1992, and GDP fell by 5 per cent from 1990 to 1993. The 1995 budget deficit remained high at 11.2 per cent of GDP, with the national debt reaching 90 per cent of GDP in the same year. Further budget cuts and reductions in the public sector, local government, and the welfare state, together with tax increases, were announced in the new Social Democratic government's first budget in January 1995. The aim is to reduce the unsustainable levels of public spending and reduce the budget deficit to 5 per cent of GDP by 1998. The government announced in June 1996 measures intended to boost the economy and cut unemployment. GDP grew by 3 per cent in 1995.

Industrial prosperity is based on natural resources: forests, mineral deposits and water power. The forests cover about half the total land surface and sustain timber, finished wood products, pulp and paper milling industries. The mineral resources include iron ore, lead, zinc, sulphur, granite, marble, precious and heavy metals (the latter not exploited) and extensive deposits of low grade uranium ore. Industries based on mining are important but it is the general engineering industry that provides the basis of Sweden's exports, especially specialized machinery and systems, motor vehicles, aircraft, electrical and electronic equipment, pharmaceuticals, plastics and chemical industries. The relative importance of agriculture has declined and in 1993 only 3.5 per cent of the labour force was engaged in farming, compared to 26 per cent in mining, manufacturing and construction, 41 per cent in services and 29.5 per cent in government.

Apart from water power (hydroelectricity supplies 15 per cent of energy needs) Sweden has no significant indigenous resources of conventional hydrocarbon fuels and relies for 50 per cent of its energy needs upon imported oil and coal. Around half of Sweden's electricity is generated by nuclear power but as a result of a referendum in 1980 the nuclear programme is to be discontinued in the future. Small supplies of natural gas are imported from Denmark into southern Sweden, with the pipeline being extended to Gothenburg.

FINANCE	1993	1994
Revenue	Kronor 878,600m	Kronor 895,700m
Expenditure	1,071,600m	1,063,900m

TRADE

About 45 per cent of industrial output is exported, mainly in the form of cars, trucks, machinery, electrical and communications equipment. Sweden conducts 70 per cent of its trade with EFTA and the rest of the EU.

	1993	1994
Imports	Kronor 420,500m	Kronor 397,741m
Exports	473,100m	471,217m

Trade with UK	1994	1995
Imports from UK	£3,348,029,000	£4,286,400,000
Exports to UK	4,159,883,000	3,894,800,000

COMMUNICATIONS

The total length of railroads is 11,745 km. The road network is over 400,000 km in length. The mercantile marine amounted in 1992 to 3,037,000 gross tonnage. Regular domestic air traffic is maintained by the Scandinavian Airlines System and by Linjeflyg. Regular European and inter-continental air traffic is maintained by the Scandinavian Airlines System.

EDUCATION

The state system provides nine years' free and compulsory schooling from the age of seven to 16 in the comprehensive elementary schools. Over 90 per cent continue into further education of two to four years' duration in the upper secondary schools and a unified higher education system administered in six regional areas containing one of the universities: Uppsala (founded 1477); Lund (1668); Stockholm (1878); Gothenburg (1887); Umeå (1963) and Linköping (1967). At present there are 33 institutions of higher education including three technical universities in Stockholm, Gothenburg and Luleå, and the Karolinska Institute in Stockholm, which specializes in medicine and dentistry.

CULTURE

Swedish belongs, with Danish and Norwegian, to the North Germanic language group. Swedish literature dates back to King Magnus Eriksson, who codified the old Swedish provincial laws in 1350. With his translation of the Bible, Olaus Petri (1493–1552) formed the basis for the modern Swedish language. Literature flourished during the reign of Gustavus III, who founded the Swedish Academy in 1786. Notable Swedish writers include Almquist (1795–1866), Strindberg (1849–1912) and Lagerlöf (1858–1940), Nobel Prizewinner in 1909. Contemporary authors include Lagerquist (1891–1974), Nobel Laureate in 1951, Martinson (1904–78) and Johnson (1900–76), Nobel Laureates jointly in 1974. The Swedish scientist Alfred Nobel (1833–96) founded the Nobel Prizes for literature, science and peace.

SWITZERLAND
Schweizerische Eidgenossenschaft – Confédération Suisse – Confederazione Svizzera

Switzerland, the Helvetia of the Romans, lies in central Europe, situated between 45° 50′ and 47° 48′ N. latitude and 5° 58′ and 10° 30′ E. longitude. It comprises a total area of 15,943 sq. miles (41,293 sq. km), with a population (1994 estimate) of 7,127,000. Of the total population in 1991, 46.1 per cent was Roman Catholic, 40 per cent Protestant, 5 per cent other religions and 8.9 per cent without religion. The official languages are German (the first language of 63.7 per cent), French (19.2 per cent), Italian (7.6 per cent) and Romansch (0.6 per cent).

Switzerland is the most mountainous country in Europe. The Alps, from 5,000 to 15,217 ft in height, occupy its southern and eastern frontiers and the chief part of its interior; the Jura mountains rise in the north-west. The Alps occupy 61 per cent, and the Jura mountains 12 per cent of the country. The highest peak, Mont Blanc, Pennine Alps (15,782 ft) is partly in France and Italy; Monte Rosa (15,217 ft) and Matterhorn (14,780 ft) are partly in Switzerland and partly in Italy. The highest wholly Swiss peaks are Dufourspitze (15,203 ft), Finsteraarhorn (14,026), Aletschhorn (13,711), Jungfrau (13,671), Mönch (13,456), Eiger (13,040), Schreckhorn (13,385), and Wetterhorn (12,150) in the Bernese Alps, and Dom (14,918), Weisshorn (14,803) and Breithorn (13,685). The Swiss lakes include Lakes Maggiore, Zürich, Lucerne, Neuchâtel, Geneva, Constance, Thun, Zug, Lugano, Brienz and the Walensee. There are also many artificial lakes.

CAPITAL – Berne, population (1991 census) 135,600 (city). Other large towns are (1991) Zürich (345,200), Basle (173,800), Geneva (169,600), Lausanne (124,800), Winterthur (86,800), St Gallen (74,500), Lucerne (60,500).
CURRENCY – Swiss franc of 100 centimes or rappen.
FLAG – Square and red, bearing a couped white cross.

NATIONAL ANTHEM – Trittst im Morgenrot Daher (Radiant in the morning sky).
NATIONAL DAY – 1 August.

GOVERNMENT

Switzerland is a federal republic. There are 23 cantons, three of which are subdivided, making 26 in all. Each canton has its own government.

The federal government consists of the Federal Assembly of two chambers, a National Council (*Nationalrat*) of 200 members, and a States Council (*Ständerat*) of 46 members (two from each canton and one from each demi-canton). Members of the National Council are elected for four years, elections taking place in October. The executive power is in the hands of a Federal Council (*Bundesrat*) of seven members, elected for four years by the Federal Assembly and presided over by the President of the Confederation. Each year the Federal Assembly elects from the Federal Council the President and the Vice-President. Not more than one of the same canton may be elected a member of the Federal Council; however, there is a tradition that Italian- and French-speaking areas should between them be represented on the Federal Council by at least two members. On 22 October 1995, the ruling coalition, comprising the Social Democrats, the Swiss People's Party, the Radical Democratic Party and the Christian Democrats, in power since 1959, was re-elected with 162 of the 200 seats in the National Council.

The Federal Council voted in 1992 to apply for European Community membership. The European Economic Area (EEA) Treaty between the EC and EFTA, which extends the provisions of the EC single internal market to EFTA states, was defeated in a national referendum on 6 December 1992. Switzerland is consequently the only EFTA state outside the EEA.

FEDERAL COUNCIL

President of the Swiss Confederation (1996) *and Head of Economic Affairs*, Jean-Pascal Delamuraz
Vice-President (1996) *and Justice*, Arnold Koller
Transport, Communications and Energy, Moritz Leuenberger
Foreign Affairs, Flavio Cotti
Military, Adolf Ogi
Home Affairs, Ruth Dreifuss
Finance, Kaspar Villiger

EMBASSY OF SWITZERLAND
16–18 Montagu Place, London WIH 2BQ
Tel 0171-616 6000
Ambassador Extraordinary and Plenipotentiary, HE François Nordmann, apptd 1994

Minister, R. Reich
Defence Attaché, Col. Walter Ritzmann
Consul-General, K. Müller
Counsellor, J. de Watteville (*Economic and Financial*)

There is a Swiss Consulate-General in Manchester.

BRITISH EMBASSY
Thunstrasse 50, 3005 Berne
Tel: Berne 3525021/6
Ambassador Extraordinary and Plenipotentiary, HE David Beattie, CMG, apptd 1992
Counsellor and Deputy Head of Mission, I. Knight-Smith
Consul-General and Director of British Export Promotion, D. M. Bell (*Zurich*)
Consul-General, J. R. Nichols (*Geneva*)
Defence Attaché, Lt.-Col. The Lord Crofton

BRITISH COUNCIL DIRECTOR , Caroline Morrissey, Thunstrasse 50, PO Box 265, Berne 15

BRITISH CONSULAR OFFICES – There is a Consular section at the Embassy in Berne; Consulates-General at Zürich and Geneva and Consular offices at Lugano, Valais and Montreux. The Directorate of British Export Promotion in Switzerland is in the Consulate-General Office, Dufourstrasse 56, 8008 Zürich.

BRITISH-SWISS CHAMBER OF COMMERCE, Freiestrasse 155, 8032 Zürich
SWISS-BRITISH SOCIETIES: Berne, *President*, Dr H. Beriger; Zürich, *President*, J.-P. Müller; Basle, *President*, Dr C. Grey

DEFENCE

All Swiss males must undertake military service in the Army or the Air Corps, which is part of the Army. The total active armed forces number some 1,800 regulars with 28,000 each year for recruit training. Conscription takes the form of 17 weeks of recruit training at age 20 and 30 weeks of regular reservist refresher training up to age 42, with some 390,000 reservists attending training each year. The Army has a strength on mobilization of 396,364 with 869 main battle tanks, 1,353 armoured personnel carriers and armoured infantry fighting vehicles, and 1,115 artillery pieces. The Air Corps has a strength on mobilization of 32,500 with 153 combat aircraft. In addition, there are the paramilitary civil defence forces, with 300,000 personnel.

ECONOMY

Agriculture is followed chiefly in the valleys and the central plateau, where cereals, flax, hemp, and tobacco are produced, and fruits and vegetables as well as grapes are grown. Dairying and stock-raising are the principal industries, about 3,000,000 acres being under grass for hay and 2,000,000 acres pasture. The forests cover about 28 per cent of the whole surface.

The chief manufacturing industries comprise engineering and electrical engineering, metal-working, chemicals and pharmaceuticals, textiles, watchmaking, woodworking, foodstuffs, printing and publishing, and footwear. Banking, insurance and tourism are major industries.

Some 5.9 per cent of the work-force is employed in agriculture, 34.7 per cent in industry and 59.4 per cent in services.

FINANCE	1994	1995
Revenue	SFr36,239m	SFr36,319m
Expenditure	41,341m	42,399m

TRADE

The principal imports are machinery, electrical and electronic equipment, textiles, motor vehicles, non-ferrous metals, chemical elements, clothing, food, medicinal and pharmaceutical products. The principal exports are machinery, chemical elements, non-ferrous metals, watches, electrical and electronic equipment, textiles, dyeing, tanning and colouring equipment.

	1993	1994
Total imports	SFr89,830m	SFr92,608m
Total exports	93,289m	95,827m
† *Trade with UK*	1994	1995
Imports from UK	£2,455,847,000	£2,759,325,000
Exports to UK	4,817,153,000	5,157,507,000

†Including Liechtenstein

COMMUNICATIONS

There were in 1993, 5,029 km of railway tracks (Swiss Federal Railways, 2,990 km; privately owned railways 2,039 km). At the end of 1993 the total length of motorways was 1,530 km. The merchant marine consisted at June 1990 of 20 vessels with a total gross tonnage of 287,487 tonnes. In 1989, goods handled at Basle Rhine ports amounted to 8,845,162 tonnes. In 1990, 163 lake and river vessels (excluding the Rhine) transported 12 million passengers and 500 tonnes of freight. Swiss airlines have a network covering 348,762 km (1990) and in 1990 carried 17,100,000 passengers. Swissair, the national airline, flies to and from the airports at Zürich, Geneva and Basle.

The Swiss electorate voted in a February 1994 referendum for a ban on foreign lorries using alpine roads, which will be phased in over ten years. From 2005 onwards foreign lorries will have to use two new north-south road-rail tunnels.

EDUCATION

Education is controlled by cantonal and communal authorities. Primary education is free and compulsory. School age varies, generally seven to 14, with secondary education from age 12 to 15. Special schools make a feature of commercial and technical instruction. Universities are Basle (founded 1460), Berne (1834), Fribourg (1889), Geneva (1873), Lausanne (1890), Zürich (1832), and Neuchâtel (1909), the technical universities of Lausanne and Zürich and the economics university of St Gall.

CULTURE

There are four national languages: French, German, Italian and Romansch. German is the dominating language in 19 of the 26 cantons; French in Fribourg, Jura, Geneva, Neuchâtel, Valais and Vaud; Italian in Ticino; and Romansch in parts of the Grisons.

Modern authors who have achieved international fame include Karl Spitteler (1845–1924) and Hermann Hesse (1877–1962), awarded the Nobel Prize for Literature in 1919 and 1946 respectively.

In 1993 there were 96 daily newspapers published (78 German, 17 French, four Italian).

SYRIA
Al-Jamhouriya Al-Arabia as-Souriya

Syria is in the Levant, bounded by the Mediterranean and Lebanon on the west, Israel and Jordan on the south-west, Iraq on the east and Turkey on the north. It has an estimated area of 71,498 sq. miles (185,180 sq. km). The Orontes flows northwards from the Lebanon range across the northern boundary to Antakya (Antioch, Turkey). The Euphrates crosses the northern boundary near Jerablus and flows through north-eastern Syria to the boundary of Iraq.

The population (UN estimate 1994) is 14,171,000, most of whom are Muslim. Arabic is the principal language, but Kurdish, Turkish and Armenian are spoken among significant minorities and a few villages still speak Aramaic, the language spoken by Christ and the Apostles. English has taken over from French as the main foreign language.

The region is rich in historical remains. Damascus (Dimishq ash-Sham) is said to be the oldest continuously inhabited city in the world (although Aleppo disputes this claim), having existed as a city for over 4,000 years. The city contains the Omayed Mosque, the Tomb of Saladin, and the 'street which is called Straight' (Acts 9:11), while to the north-east is the Roman outpost of Dmeir and further east is Palmyra. On the Mediterranean coast at Amrit are ruins of the Phoenician town of Marath, and also ruins of Crusaders' fortresses at Markab, Sahyoun, and Krak des Chevaliers. At Tartous the cathedral of Our Lady of Syria, built by the Knights Templars in the 12th and 13th centuries, has been restored as a museum. One of the oldest alphabets in the world has been discovered at Ugarit (Ras Shamra), a Phoenician village near the port of Latakia. Hittite cities dating from 2000 to 1500 BC, have been explored on the west bank of the Euphrates at Jerablus and Kadesh.

CAPITAL – Damascus, population (1992 estimate) 1,451,000. Other important towns are Aleppo, Homs and Hama, and the principal port is ΨLatakia.

CURRENCY – Syrian pound (S£) of 100 piastres.

FLAG – Red over white over black horizontal bands, with two green stars on central white band.

NATIONAL DAY – 17 April.

GOVERNMENT

Once part of the Ottoman Empire, Syria came under French mandate after the First World War. Syria became an independent republic during the Second World War; the first independently elected Parliament met in August 1943, but foreign troops were in occupation until April 1946. Syria remained an independent republic until 1958, when it became part, with Egypt, of the United Arab Republic. It seceded from the United Arab Republic in September 1961.

A new constitution was promulgated in 1973. This declared that Syria is a democratic, popular socialist state, and that the Arab Socialist Renaissance (Ba'ath) Party, which has been the ruling party since 1963, is the leading party in the state and society. Elections to the 250-seat People's Council in August 1994 resulted in a large majority for the National Progressive Front which won 167 seats and is dominated by the Ba'ath Party, its allies being the Arab Socialist Union, Socialist Unionist Movement, Arab Socialist Party and Syrian Communist Party. Independents won 83 seats.

HEAD OF STATE
President, Lt.-Gen. Hafez el Assad, *assumed office* 14 March 1971, *re-elected* 1978, 1985, 3 December 1991
Vice-Presidents, Abdul Halim Khaddam, Rifaat Al Assad, Zuhair Mashariqa

MINISTERS *as at June 1996*
Prime Minister, Mahmoud Al Zubi
Deputy PM and Minister for Defence, Gen. Mustafa Tlass

Deputy PM for Public Services, Rashid Akhtarini
Deputy PM for Economic Affairs, Dr Salim Yassin
Education, Ghassan Halabi
Higher Education, Salha Sankar
Interior, Mohammad Harbah
Transport, Mufeed Abdul-Karim
Information, Mohammad Salman
Local Administration, Yahya Abu Asali
Supply and Internal Trade, Nadim Akkash
Economy and Foreign Trade, Mohammad al-Imadi
Culture, Najah al-Attar
Foreign Affairs, Farooq al-Shara
Tourism, Danhu Dawud
Health, Iyad al-Shatti
Waqfs (Religious Endowments), vacant
Irrigation, Abd ar-Rahman Madani
Electricity, Munib Daher
Oil and Mineral Resources, Nadir Nabulsi
Construction, Majid Ezzou Ruhaybani
Housing and Utilities, Hosam al-Safadi
Agriculture and Agrarian Reform, As'ad Mustafa
Finance, Khaled al-Mahayni
Industry, Ahmad Nizan al-Din
Communications, Redwan Martini
Justice, Hussein Hassun
Presidential Affairs, Wahib Fadil
Labour and Social Affairs, Ali Khalil

EMBASSY OF THE SYRIAN ARAB REPUBLIC
8 Belgrave Square, London SW1X 8PH
Tel 0171-245 9012
Ambassador Extraordinary and Plenipotentiary, HE
    Mohammed Khodor, apptd 1991

BRITISH EMBASSY
Kotob Building, 11 rue Mohammad Kurd Ali, Malki,
Damascus (PO Box 37)
Tel: Damascus 3712561
Ambassador Extraordinary and Plenipotentiary, HE Adrian
    John Sindall, CMG, apptd 1994
There is also a consulate in Aleppo.

BRITISH COUNCIL DIRECTOR, Dr Peter Clark, OBE,
    Ground Floor, Tasheen Tabaa' Building, Abd Almalek
    Bin Marwan Street, Malki, PO Box 33105, Damascus.

DEFENCE

The total active armed forces have a strength of 423,000.
There is a conscription period of 30 months, with a reserve
commitment to age 45; reserves number 1,300,000 personnel. The Army has a strength of 315,000 (250,000 conscripts), with 4,600 main battle tanks, 3,810 armoured
personnel carriers and armoured infantry fighting vehicles
and 3,298 artillery pieces. The Navy has a strength of 8,000
personnel, with three submarines, two frigates, 29 patrol
and coastal combatants and 29 armed helicopters. The Air
Force (including the Air Defence Command) has a
strength of some 100,000, with 579 combat aircraft and
100 armed helicopters of Soviet manufacture, together
with 25 Air Defence brigades with surface-to-air missiles.
Syria maintains a force of some 35,000 men in Lebanon;
1,036 UN troops are deployed on the Golan Heights.

ECONOMY

Agriculture is the principal source of production; wheat
and barley are the main cereal crops, but the cotton crop is
the highest in value. Tobacco is grown in the maritime
plain in Sahel, the Sahyoun and the Djebleh district of
Latakia. Large areas are coming under cultivation in the
north-east of the country as a result of irrigation from the

Thawra dam. There are an increasing number of light
assembly plants as Syria's industrialization programme
develops. Skins and hides, leather goods, wool and silk,
textiles, cement, vegetable oil, glass, soap, sugar, plastics
and copper and brass utensils are produced. Oil has been
found at Karachuk and other parts in the north-eastern
corner of the country and production of high quality
reserves is proceeding in the region of Deir ez Zor. Syria
produces nearly 400,000 barrels per day at present. A
pipeline has been built to the Mediterranean port of Banias,
via Homs. Two oil refineries are in production at Homs
and Banias. Syria also has gas reserves, deposits of
phosphate and rock salt, and produces asphalt.

TRADE

The principal imports are foodstuffs (fruit, vegetables,
cereals, meat and dairy products, tea, coffee and sugar),
mineral and petroleum products, yarn and textiles, iron
and steel manufactures, machinery, chemicals, pharmaceuticals, fertilizers and timber. Exports include raw
cotton, oil, cereals, fruit, phosphates, cement, livestock
and dairy products, other foodstuffs, textiles and raw wool.

Trade with UK	1994	1995
Imports from UK	£101,988,000	£84,593,000
Exports to UK	97,990,000	89,768,000

COMMUNICATIONS

Although railway lines run from Damascus to both Beirut
and Amman, train services go only to Amman as much of
the Lebanese line has been dismantled. A track has been
opened connecting Homs with Damascus. A track links
Homs, Hamah, Aleppo, Deir ez Zor and Qamishliye to the
Iraq frontier. Branch lines connect the ports of Tartous and
Latakia to the system and another line runs from Aleppo
down the Euphrates valley to Deir ez Zor and thence north
to Qamishliye, with a branch going to the Euphrates dam.
All the principal towns in the country are connected by
roads which vary from modern dual carriageways to
narrow country lanes. An internal air service operates
between all major towns. The main international airport is
at Damascus and there are also flights from Aleppo.

There are three daily newspapers and several periodicals in Arabic published in Damascus, and also a daily
newspaper in English.

EDUCATION

Education is under state control and although a few of the
schools are privately owned, they all follow a common
syllabus. Elementary education is free at state schools and
is compulsory from the age of seven. Secondary education
is not compulsory and is free only at the state schools.
There are universitites at Damascus, Aleppo, Tishrin,
Latakia and the Ba'ath University, Homs.

TAIWAN (REPUBLIC OF CHINA)
Chung-hua Min-kuo

An island of some 13,800 sq. miles (35,742 sq. km) in the
China Sea, Taiwan, formerly Formosa, lies 90 miles east of
the Chinese mainland in 21° 45' to 25° 56' N. latitude. The
eastern part of the main island is mountainous and forested.
Mt Morrison (Yu Shan) (13,035 ft) and Mt Sylvia
(Tz'ukaoshan) (12,972 ft) are the highest peaks. The
western plains are watered by many rivers.

Territories include the Pescadores Islands (50 sq. miles),
some 35 miles west of Taiwan, as well as Quemoy (68 sq.

miles) and Matsu (11 sq. miles) which are only a few miles from mainland China.

The population (1996) is 20,944,066, almost entirely Chinese. About two million mainlanders came to the island with Chiang Kai-shek in 1947–9. Mandarin Chinese has been the official language since 1949. Now Taiwanese, spoken by 85 per cent of the population, is growing in importance.

CAPITAL – Taipei, population (1990) 2,719,659. Other towns are ΨKaohsiung (1,386,723); Tainan (667,622); Taichung (730,376); and ΨKeelung (348,672).

CURRENCY – New Taiwan dollar (NT$) of 100 cents.

FLAG – Red, with blue quarter at top next staff, bearing a 12-point white sun.

NATIONAL DAY – 10 October.

GOVERNMENT

Settled for centuries by the Chinese, the island was ceded by China to Japan in 1895 and remained part of the Japanese empire until Japan's defeat in 1945. Nationalist Kuomintang (KMT) leader Gen. Chiang Kai-shek withdrew to Taiwan in 1949, towards the end of the war against the Communist regime in mainland China, after which the territory continued under his presidency until his death in 1975. He was succeeded as President by his son Gen. Chiang Ching-kuo who ruled until his death in 1988, when Vice-President Lee Teng-hui was appointed President. Taiwan (Nationalist China) held China's seat on the UN Security Council until 25 October 1971 when it was replaced by the People's Republic of China. Martial law was lifted in 1987 after 38 years.

In 1991, President Lee announced that the 'period of Communist rebellion' on the Chinese mainland was over, recognizing *de facto* the People's Republic of China. The announcement also ended emergency measures which had frozen political life on Taiwan since 1949. In 1991–2 power shifted away from mainlanders to native Taiwanese with the forcible retirement of the 'Senior Parliamentarians' who had retained their seats since being elected on the mainland in 1948. The new parliament, the Legislative Yuan, gained control of the budget, of law-making and of the appointment of the Prime Minister. A general election to the Legislative Yuan in December 1995 was won by the KMT with 85 of the 164 seats; the pro-independence Democratic Progressive Party won 54 seats, the pro-reunification New Party won 21 seats; and independents and minor parties the remaining 4 seats.

Constitutional reforms passed by the Legislative Yuan in July 1994 provide for the President and Vice-President to be directly elected for four-year terms (previously the President was elected by parliament). The incumbent, President Lee, won the first democratic presidential election on 23 March 1996, with 54 per cent of the vote. His running-mate, former Prime Minister Lien Chan, was reappointed and holds the posts of Vice-President and Prime Minister concurrently. Mainland China conducted large-scale military exercises in the Taiwan Strait during both the legislative and presidential elections.

HEAD OF STATE
President, Lee Teng-hui, *appointed* 13 January 1988, *elected by parliament* 21 March 1990, *elected* 23 March 1996
Vice-President, Lien Chan

EXECUTIVE YUAN *as at August 1996*

Prime Minister, Lien Chan
Deputy PM, Hsu Li-teh
Ministers of State, Shirley W. Y. Guo, Lin Chen-kuo, Ma Ying-jeou, Yang Shih-chien, Tu Teh-chi, Yeh Chin-fong, Tsai Cheng-wen

Interior, Lin Fong-cheng
Foreign Affairs, Chang Hsiao-yen
National Defence, Chiang Chung-ling
Finance, Paul Chiu
Education, Wu Jin
Justice, Liao Cheng-hao
Economic Affairs, Wang Chih-kang
Health, Chang Po-ya
Transport and Communication, Tsay Jaw-yang
Directorate-General of Budget, Accounting and Statistics, Wei Duan
Central Personnel Administration, Cheng Kang-chin
Government Information Office, Su Chi

Chairs of Councils:
Atomic Energy, Hu Ching-piao
Science, Liu Chao-shiuan
Youth, Wu Wan-lan
Mongolian and Tibetan Affairs, Lee Hou-kao
Overseas Chinese Affairs, James Chu
Cultural Affairs, Lin Cheng-chih
Environmental Protection Administration, Tsai Hsung-hsiung
Mainland Affairs, Chang King-yuh
Economic Planning and Development, Chiang Pin-kung
Construction, Ou Chin-der
Labour Affairs, Hsieh Shen-san
Agriculture, Tiju Mau-ying
Research, Huang Ta-chou

TAIPEI REPRESENTATIVE OFFICE, 50 Grosvenor Gardens, London, SWIW OEB.

BRITISH COUNCIL REPRESENTATIVE, Tom Buchanan, 7th Floor, Fu Key Building, 99 Jen Ai Road, Section 2, Taipei 10625.

DEFENCE

The total active armed forces number 376,000 personnel, with conscripts serving for two-year terms. Reserves number 1,657,500 with an obligation until the age of 30. The Army is 240,000 strong with 570 main battle tanks, 905 light tanks, 1,175 armoured infantry fighting vehicles and armoured personnel carriers, 1,175 artillery pieces and 192 helicopters. The Navy has a strength of 68,000, including 30,000 marines, with four submarines, 22 destroyers, 12 frigates, 98 patrol and coastal combatants, 32 combat aircraft and 22 armed helicopters. The Air Force has 68,000 personnel, with 430 combat aircraft. Paramilitary security groups number 25,000 personnel.

ECONOMY

Over the past 30 years Taiwan has transformed itself from a mainly agricultural country to one of the fastest growing industrial economies in Asia. A series of six-year plans has expanded the industrial base; important sectors are steel, shipbuilding, chemicals, cement, machinery, plastic and rubber goods, electrical equipment and textiles. In 1990–4 economic growth averaged 6 per cent and inflation 3.6 per cent. GNP in 1994 was US$244,200 million. Continued trade surpluses have led to one of the largest foreign exchange reserves of any country in the world (US$97,930 million in early 1995).

The soil is very fertile, producing sugar, rice, sweet potatoes, tea, bananas, pineapples and tobacco. Mineral resources are meagre. Taiwan produces one-tenth of its coal needs and some natural gas. There are important fisheries. The principal seaports are ΨKeelung and ΨKaohsiung situated in the north and south of the island.

TRADE

The principal exports are electronic goods, machinery, metal goods, textiles, plastic products and toys and games. The main imports are oil, chemicals, machinery and natural resources. The main trading partners are the USA, Japan, Hong Kong, Germany, UK, Canada.

Trade with UK	1994	1995
Imports from UK	£735,287,000	£961,933,000
Exports to UK	1,580,880,000	1,726,761,000

TAJIKISTAN
Respublika i Tojikiston

Tajikistan has an area of 55,251 sq. miles (143,100 sq. km) and occupies the extreme south-east of former Soviet Central Asia. It is bordered on the west and north-west by Uzbekistan, on the north-east by Kyrgyzstan, on the east by China and on the south by Afghanistan. The republic includes the Gorno-Badakhstan Autonomous Province and the Kulyab, Kurgan-Tyubinsk and Khodzhent Provinces. The country is mountainous with the Pamir highlands in the east and the high ridges of the Pamir-Altai system in the centre. Plains are formed by wide stretches of the Syr-Darya valley in the north and of the Amu-Darya in the south. The country has areas prone to earthquakes, and a continental climate.

The population (1989 census) is 5,093,000, of which 62 per cent are Tajiks, 23 per cent Uzbeks and 8 per cent Russians, with smaller numbers of Tatars, Kirghiz, Germans and Ukrainians. The estimated population in 1996 was 5,513,400. The people are predominantly Sunni Muslim. The main languages are Tajik (62 per cent), Uzbek (23 per cent), Russian (8 per cent). Tajik is close to the Farsi spoken in Iran.

CAPITAL – Dushanbe. Population 595,000 (1989).

CURRENCY – Rouble of 100 kopeks.

FLAG – Three horizontal stripes of red, white and green with the white of double width and charged with a crown and seven stars, all in gold.

NATIONAL DAY – 9 September (Independence Day).

GOVERNMENT

The area that is now Tajikistan was invaded and conquered by Alexander the Great in the fourth century BC. The area remained under Greek and Greco-Persian rule for 200 years until the Kingdom of Kusha was established, based on Bacharia (Bukhara). Tajikistan was invaded by the Arabs in the seventh century AD and by the Samanid Persians in the ninth century AD. The Tajik cities of Bukhara and Samarkand became two of the most important cultural and educational centres in the Islamic world.

The Tajiks lived under the control of various feudal emirates until the area was subsumed within the Russian Empire in 1868. At the time of the Russian revolution in 1917 the central Asian emirates attempted to re-establish their independence. Soviet power was re-established in northern Tajikistan by 1 April 1918, when the Turkestan Soviet Socialist Republic was formed, and the Bukhara emirate was overthrown by Soviet forces in 1920. In 1924 the Tajikistan Autonomous Soviet Socialist Republic was formed as part of the Uzbek Republic before Tajikistan was given full republican status within the Soviet Union in 1929. Stalin deprived the Tajiks of Bukhara and Samarkand, which remained in Uzbekistan, and during Soviet rule 1,000,000 Uzbeks and 800,000 Russians were settled in Tajikistan.

Tajikistan declared independence from the Soviet Union on 9 September 1991 and became a UN member on 2 March 1992. Tension between President Nabiev's supporters and the opposition Islamic and democratic groups led to armed clashes in 1992 and Nabiev was forced to resign on 7 September 1992 as he tried to flee the capital. The Islamic-Democratic alliance formed a government in September but civil war broke out as forces loyal to the former Communist regime rebelled against the new government. By early November pro-Communist forces controlled virtually all the country and the Supreme Soviet installed Imamali Rakhmonov as its Speaker and head of state. Fighting continued but by March 1993 the Islamic-Democratic forces had been defeated by government and Russian Army units and driven across the border into Afghanistan.

Fighting resumed in July between Russian and Tajik government forces and the Afghan-based rebels, leading to the establishment of a CIS peacekeeping force on the Tajik-Afghan border to contain continuing rebel attacks. Throughout 1993–4 fighting continued along the border and there were terrorist and guerrilla attacks inside Tajikistan. Negotiations between the government and opposition began in April 1994 in Moscow, bringing about a cease-fire in October 1994 to allow for presidential and parliamentary elections. The elections were boycotted by most opposition groups and fighting restarted along the Afghan border in early 1995, with rebel attacks on Russian and Tajik border posts. In retaliation Russian forces launched air attacks on rebel bases in Afghanistan in April. Heavy fighting in August 1996 shattered a cease-fire sponsored by the UN a month earlier. Islamic rebels claimed to have taken control of Tavildara, in addition to two other towns seized in January.

A new democratic constitution which re-established the presidency was approved by parliament in July 1994 and by the electorate in a national referendum on 6 November 1994. On the same day the presidential election was won by acting head of state Imamali Rakhmonov amid a boycott by most opposition parties. Legislative elections to the new 181-seat Supreme Assembly (*Madjlisi Oli*) were held on 26 February 1995 and won by the ruling (former Communist) People's Party of Tajikistan amid another opposition boycott. The election was condemned as undemocratic by the OSCE monitoring team. Administratively Tajikistan is divided into two regions and one autonomous region.

HEAD OF STATE

President, Imamali Rakhmonov, *elected by Supreme Soviet* 19 November 1992, *elected* 6 November 1994

GOVERNMENT *as at August 1996*

Prime Minister, Yakhia Azimov
First Deputy PM, Makhmasaid Ubaidullaev
Deputy PMs, Okil Okilov; Kholisjon Temurjanov; Jamoliddin Mansurov; Kadriddin Giasov; Yuri Ponasov
Interior, Saidamir Zukhurov
Foreign Affairs, Talbak Nazarov
Culture and Information, Bobkhon Makhmadov
Defence, Sherali Khairullayev
Industry, Shavkat Umarov
Finance, Anvarzho Muzaffarov
Justice, Shavkat Ismailov
Agriculture, Kurbon Turaiev
Economy and Foreign Economic Relations, Rustam Mirzoiev
Communications, Ibrahim Usmanov
Transport, Fariddun Muhiddinov
Trade and Material Resources, Khakim Saliyev

Health, Alamkhon Ahmedov
Environmental Protection, Ismail Davlatov
Land Improvement and Water Conservancy, Ismat Eshmirzoev
Social Security, Saidanvar Kamolov
Chair of State Property Committee, Davlatov
Ambassador to Russia, Ramazan Mirzoyev
Education, Munira Inoyatova
Labour, Shukurgan Zukhurov
Bakery, Bekmurod Urakov

BRITISH AMBASSADOR, HE Barbara Hay, MBE, apptd 1995, resident in Tashkent, Uzbekistan

ECONOMY

In January 1994 Tajikistan entered into a monetary union with Russia and exchanged its old roubles for post-1993 new Russian roubles. Effectively monetary control was handed over to the Russian central bank and a large amount of economic sovereignty to the Russian government in exchange for a US$100 million loan from Russia. This was needed to prevent an economic collapse caused by 40 per cent of the budget being spent on the civil war. The Tajik rouble was introduced to replace the Russian rouble in May 1995. The economy is being reformed and privatization undertaken in order to attract foreign investment. The IMF approved a standby credit of US$22,000,000 in May 1996.

Agriculture is the major sector of the economy, concentrating on cotton-growing and cattle-breeding. Tajikistan also has rich mineral deposits of lead, zinc and oil, is a source of uranium, and has estimated gold reserves of 16 million ounces. Industry specializes in the production of clothing and textiles.

TRADE WITH UK	1994	1995
Imports from UK	£4,266,000	£4,754,000
Exports to UK	142,000	138,000

TANZANIA
Jamhuri ya Muungano wa Tanzania

Tanzania comprises Tanganyika, on the mainland of east Africa between 1° and 11° 45′ S. latitude and 29° 20′ and 40° 38′ E. longitude, and the island of Zanzibar. The mainland part is bounded on the north by Kenya and Uganda; on the south by Mozambique; on the south-west by Lake Malawi, Malawi and Zambia; on the west by Rwanda, Burundi and Zaire; and on the east by the Indian Ocean. Tanzania has an area of 364,900 sq. miles (945,087 sq. km). The greater part of the country is occupied by the central African plateau from which rise, among others, Mt Kilimanjaro (19,340 ft), the highest point on the continent of Africa, and Mt Meru (14,974 ft). The Serengeti National Park covers an area of 6,000 sq. miles in the Arusha, Mwanza and Mara Regions.

Zanzibar was formerly ruled by the Sultan of Zanzibar and was a British Protectorate until 10 December 1963. It consists of the islands of Zanzibar, Pemba and Mafia. The area is 2,461 sq. km, and the population (1992 estimate), is 687,634. ΨZanzibar (population, 133,000) is the chief town and seaport of the island.

The total population was (UN estimate 1994) 28,846,000. Africans form a large majority, with European, Asian, and other non-African minorities. The African population consists mostly of tribes of mixed Bantu race. Swahili is the national and official language. The use of English is widespread both for educational and government purposes.

CAPITAL – Dodoma (population 88,474, 1988 estimate). The economic and administrative centre is ΨDar es Salaam (population 1,096,000, 1985 estimate). Other towns (1985 population) are ΨTanga (172,000), Mwanza (252,000), Mbeya (194,000).
CURRENCY – Tanzanian shilling of 100 cents.
FLAG – Green (above) and blue; divided by diagonal black stripe bordered by gold, running from bottom (next staff) to top (in fly).
NATIONAL ANTHEM – Mungu Ibariki Afrika (God Bless Africa).
NATIONAL DAY – 26 April (Union Day).

GOVERNMENT

Tanganyika became an independent state and a member of the British Commonwealth on 9 December 1961, and a republic within the Commonwealth on 9 December 1962. On 10 December 1963, Zanzibar became an independent state within the Commonwealth and on 26 April 1964, Tanganyika united with Zanzibar to form the United Republic of Tanzania.

The President and Vice-President are directly elected and may only serve two terms. The National Assembly contains 275 members, of whom 182 are elected from mainland constituencies and 50 from Zanzibar, 37 seats are reserved for women and are distributed to parties in ratio to their share of seats, five are nominated by the Zanzibar government and one is reserved for the Attorney-General. The Speaker may either be elected from among the members or be an additional member. Constituency members are elected by popular vote at a general election held at a maximum of five-yearly intervals.

Although Zanzibar has its own President, government and 50-member House of Representatives, Tanganyika is governed by the government of the Union. The sole legal political party from 1977 to 1992 was the Chama Cha Mapinduzi (CCM). In 1992 President Mwinyi and the CCM leadership agreed to amend the constitution to allow multiparty politics. In June 1992 President Mwinyi endorsed a bill legalizing multiparty politics, with the stipulation that all parties must be active in both the mainland and in Zanzibar and that parties must not be formed on regional, religious, tribal or racial grounds. The first multiparty presidential and parliamentary elections were held in October and November 1995. The CCM's candidate, Salmin Amour, was elected President of Zanzibar with 50.2 per cent of the vote and his party won 26 seats in the Zanzibar House of Representatives. The Civic United Front gained 24 seats. Benjamin Mkapa of the CCM was elected Union President with 61 per cent of the vote, all other candidates having retired, accusing the CCM of ballot-rigging. The CCM won 186 of the 232 elected seats in the National Assembly. The President of Zanzibar is also a member of the Union Cabinet.

HEAD OF STATE
President of the United Republic, HE Hon. Benjamin William Mkapa, *elected* 23 November 1995
Vice-President, Hon. Dr Omar Ali Juma

CABINET *as at August 1996*
The President
The Vice-President
Prime Minister, Hon. Frederick Sumaye
Ministers of State, President's Office, Hon. Daniel Yona Ndihira; Hon. Mateo Karesi (*Planning*)
Minister of State, Vice-President's Office, Hon. Mohammed Seif Khatib

Ministers of State, PM's Office, Hon. Bakari Mbonde; Hon.
Mussa Nkhanngaa; Hon. Kigunga Mgombale Mwiru
Defence, Hon. Edgar Maokola Majogo
Home Affairs, Hon. Ali Ameir Mohammed
Finance, Hon. Prof. Simon Mbilinyi
Industries and Trade, Hon. Dr Abdallah Omar Kigoda
Communication and Transport, Hon. William Kusila
Agriculture and Co-operatives, Hon. Paul Kimiti
Health, Hon. Zakia Meghji
Foreign Affairs and International Co-operation, Hon. Mrisho
Jakaya Kikwette
Education, Hon. Juma Athumani Kapuya
Energy and Mineral Resources, Hon. William Shija
Water and Livestock Development, Hon. Pius Ng'wandu
Natural Resources and Tourism, Hon. Juma Ngasongwa
Lands, Hon. Gideon Cheyo
Science, Technology and Higher Education, Hon. Jackson
Makweta
Works, Hon. Anna Abdallah
Labour and Youth Development, Hon. Sebastian Rukiza
Kinyondo
Community Development, Women's Affairs and Children, Hon.
Mary Nagu
Justice and Constitutional Affairs, Hon. Bakari Mwapachu

HIGH COMMISSION FOR THE UNITED REPUBLIC OF
TANZANIA
43 Hertford Street, London WIY 8DB
Tel 0171-499 8951/2/3/4
High Commissioner, HE Dr Abdulkader A. Shareef, apptd
1995

BRITISH HIGH COMMISSION
Hifadhi House, Samora Avenue (PO Box 9200), Dar es
Salaam
Tel: Dar es Salaam 29601-5
High Commissioner, HE Alan Montgomery, CMG, apptd 1995
BRITISH COUNCIL DIRECTOR, Robert Sykes, Ohio
Samora Avenue (PO Box 9100), Dar es Salaam

ECONOMY

The economy is based mainly on the production and
export of primary produce and the growing of foodstuffs
for local consumption. The islands of Zanzibar and Pemba
produce a large part of the world's supply of cloves and
clove oil; and coconuts, coconut oil and copra are also
produced. The mainland's chief export crops are coffee,
cotton, sisal, tea, tobacco, cashew nuts and diamonds. The
most important minerals are diamonds. Hides and skins are
another valuable export. Industry is largely concerned
with the processing of raw material for either export or
local consumption. There are also secondary manufacturing industries, including factories for the manufacture of
leather and rubber footwear, knitwear, razor blades,
cigarettes and textiles, and a wheat flour mill.

TRADE WITH UK	1994	1995
Imports from UK	£82,312,000	£87,412,000
Exports to UK	22,452,000	27,480,000

COMMUNICATIONS

The main ports are Dar es Salaam, Tanga, Mtwara,
Zanzibar, Mkoani and Wete, in addition to Mwanza,
Musoma and Bukoba on Lake Victoria and Kigoma on
Lake Tanganyika. Coastal shipping services connect the
mainland to Zanzibar, and lake services are operated on
Lake Tanganyika and Lake Malawi with neighbouring
countries. The principal international airports are Dar es
Salaam and Kilimanjaro. Other airports include Zanzibar,
Arusha, Mwanza and Tanga. There are two railway

systems; one connecting Dar es Salaam to Zambia, and the
second having two main lines running from Dar es Salaam,
one to northern Tanzania and Kenya and the other to
Lakes Tanganyika and Victoria.

EDUCATION

The school system is administered in Swahili but the
government is making efforts to improve English standards
for the purposes of secondary and higher education. All
Tanzanian secondary schools are expected to include
practical subjects in the basic course. For higher education
Tanzanian students go to the University of Dar es Salaam,
Sokoine University of Agriculture in Morogoro, other
African universities, or to universities and colleges outside
Africa.

THAILAND
Prathes Thai

Thailand, formerly known as Siam, has an area of 198,457
sq. miles (514,000 sq. km). It has a common boundary with
Malaysia in the south, is bounded on the west by Myanmar
(Burma) and on the north-east and east by Laos and
Cambodia. Thailand is divided geographically into four:
the centre is a plain; to the north-east there is a plateau area
and to the north-west mountains. The south of Thailand
consists of a narrow mountainous peninsula. The principal
rivers are the Chao Phraya in the central plains, and the
Mekong on the northern and north-eastern borders.

The population (1993 census) is 58,336,072. The
principal language is Thai, a monosyllabic, tonal language
of the Indo-Chinese linguistic family, with a vocabulary
strongly influenced by Sanskrit and Pali. It is written in an
alphabetic script derived from ancient Indian scripts.
Significant minorities speak Chinese (in urban areas), Lao
(in the north-east), Khmer (in the east) and Malay (in the far
south).

The principal religion is Buddhism (94.37 per cent),
with 3.95 per cent Muslims, 0.53 per cent Christians and
1.15 per cent other religions.

CAPITAL – ΨBangkok, at the mouth of the River Chao
Phraya, population (metropolitan area) (1993)
5,572,712. Other centres are Chiang Mai, Phitsanulok,
Chon Buri, Korat, Khon Kaen, Surat Thani, Hat Yai and
ΨPhuket.
CURRENCY – Baht of 100 satang.
FLAG – Five horizontal bands, red, white, dark blue, white,
red (the blue band twice the width of the others).
NATIONAL ANTHEM – Pleng Chart.
NATIONAL DAY – 5 December (The King's Birthday).

GOVERNMENT

Thailand became a constitutional monarchy in 1932. The
1978 constitution (as amended) provides for a National
Assembly consisting of a 260-member Senate appointed by
the Prime Minister and a 391-member House of Representatives elected by universal adult suffrage for a term of
four years. Following a military coup in February 1991, a
new constitution was approved in December 1991 under
which the military would appoint the members of the
Senate and so enshrine its place in Thai politics. Parties
aligned with the military won the general election in
March 1992, but opposition to the military-controlled
government grew and mass demonstrations held in Bangkok from 17 to 20 May eventually, with the help of the
King, forced the government from power. Military power

was curbed, the 1978 constitution was restored and the interim government sacked military chiefs.

Parliamentary elections in September 1992 resulted in a majority for 'democratic parties', i.e. those not allied with the military. Chuan Leekpai became Prime Minister at the head of a five-party governing coalition which implemented a series of reforms in education, land tenure and the constitution. Some 600,000 families have been granted land title rights, the voting age has been reduced to 18, the appointed Senate reduced to a maximum of two-thirds of the number of House of Representatives' seats and anticorruption laws introduced. However, the coalition government lost power in May 1995 when one of the main parties withdrew over corruption allegations. In the ensuing general election on 2 July 1995 the opposition and military-aligned Chart Thai party emerged as the largest party and formed a coalition government with six other parties. The Prachakorn Thai party withdrew from the coalition in June 1996. On 22 March 1996, Prime Minister Banharn Silpa-Archa became the first democratically elected Prime Minister to appoint the Senate, of whose 260 members only 39 are serving military officers.

HEAD OF STATE
HM The King of Thailand, King Bhumibol Adulyadej, *born* 1927; *succeeded his brother* 9 June 1946; *married* 28 April 1950 Princess Sirikit Kitiyakara; *crowned* 5 May 1950; and has *issue*, Princess Ubolratana, *born* 6 April 1951; Crown Prince Vajiralongkorn (*see* below); Princess Maha Chaki Sirindhorn, *born* 2 April 1955; Princess Chulabhorn, *born* 4 July 1957
Heir, HRH Crown Prince Vajiralongkorn, *born* 28 July 1952; *married* 3 January 1977 Soamsawali Kitiyakra

CABINET *as at August 1996*
Prime Minister, Minister of the Interior, Banharn Silpa-Archa (CT)
Deputy PM, Defence, Gen. Chavalit Yongchaiyudh (NA)
Deputy PM, Foreign Affairs, Amnuay Viravan (NT)
Deputy PMs, Samak Sundarave (PT), Montree Pongpanit (SA), Air Chief Marshal Somboon Rahong (CT)
Ministers to the Prime Minister's Office, Pongpol Adireksarn (CT), Ruangvit Leeke (CT), Piyanat Watcharaporn (CT), Chatchai Earsakul (NA), Boonpun Kaevatana (SA), Bhokin Bhalakula (CT)
Agriculture and Co-operatives, Suwit Khunkitti (SA)
Commerce, Shucheep Hansaward (CT)
Education, Sukavich Rangsitpol (NA)
Finance, Bodi Chunnanon (CT)
Industry, Chaiwat Sinsuwong (PD)
Justice, Chalerm Ubumrung (M)
Public Health, Sanoh Thienthong (CT)
Science, Technology and Environment, Yingpan Manasikarn (PT)
Transport and Communication, Wan Muhamadnoor Matha (NA)
University Affairs, Boonchoo Treethong (CT)
Labour and Social Welfare, Prasong Boonpong (NA)
CT Chart Thai; NA New Aspiration; SA Social Action; PT Prachakorn Thai; NT Nam Thai; M Muanchon

ROYAL THAI EMBASSY
1–3 Yorkshire House, Grosvenor Crescent, London SWIX 7EP
Tel 0171-259 5005
Ambassador Extraordinary and Plenipotentiary, HE Vidhya Rayananonda, apptd 1994
Minister and Deputy Head of Mission, A. Chabchitrchaidol
Defence Attaché, Gp Capt. A. Ganchanahirun
Minister Counsellor, S. Jaovisidha (*Commercial*)

BRITISH EMBASSY
Thanon Witthayu, Bangkok 10330
Tel: Bangkok 253 0191 9
Ambassador Extraordinary and Plenipotentiary, HE James Hodge, apptd 1996
Deputy Ambassador and Counsellor, R. T. Fell
Defence Attaché, Col. J. D. Fielden, MBE
Counsellor (Commercial), M. J. Greenstreet
Consul, B. P. Kelly
There is a British Consulate at Chang Mai

BRITISH COUNCIL DIRECTOR, Dr John Richards, 428 Rama 1 Road, Siam Square Soi 2, Pathumwan, Bangkok 10330. There is also an office in Chiang Mai

BRITISH CHAMBER OF COMMERCE, BP Building 18th Floor, Unit 1810, 54 Asoke Road (Sukhumvit 21) Bangkok 10110

DEFENCE
Total active armed forces number 259,000 personnel, with conscription terms of two years. Reserves number a further 200,000 personnel. The Army numbers 150,000 (80,000 conscripts) with 200 main battle tanks, 404 light tanks, 940 armoured personnel carriers and 409 artillery pieces. The Navy has 66,000 personnel (15,000 conscripts), with ten frigates, 62 patrol and coastal combatants, 49 combat aircraft, eight armed helicopters and a 20,000-strong marine division. The Air Force has 43,000 personnel, with 197 combat aircraft. Six paramilitary forces, including four police forces, have a total strength of 161,500 personnel.

ECONOMY
The agricultural sector provides just under half the national income and employs 67.5 per cent of the labour force. Rice remains the most important crop, accounting for 60 per cent of the area planted. The other main crops are sugar, maize, sorghum, cassava, rubber, tobacco, kenaf and jute. In recent years the production of livestock and poultry, especially pigs and chickens for export, has gained importance. There is a large fishing industry with more than 20,000 vessels registered. Fish and prawn farming is popular in many inland areas. A ban on hardwood export has resulted in the decline of the forestry industry.

Onshore oil and offshore gas were discovered in the late 1970s; crude oil production began in 1983. The predicted surplus of natural gas has led the government to designate an area on the east coast as the future centre of the petrochemical industry. Another energy resource is lignite, which is found mainly in the north and is being used increasingly for electricity production. Mineral resources are mainly tin, tungsten, lead, antimony and iron. Among these tin is the most important. In addition, a zinc refinery was opened in 1984.

Since 1960 the government has actively promoted industrial investment by means of tax relief and other incentives to local and foreign investors; in 1985, 74.6 per cent of this investment was in Thai projects. Initially industries established under this scheme were importsubstituting but the emphasis has shifted now to exportoriented industries. Important sectors are textiles, transportation vehicles and equipment, construction materials, brewing, petroleum refining, electrical appliances, plastics, computers and parts, and integrated circuits. Manufacturing now accounts for about 21.8 per cent of the national income, and the rapid growth of manufacturing exports since 1985 meant that by 1994 manufacturers provided 81 per cent of exports. The service sector is large, the banking system contributing greatly to the economy, and since 1982 tourism has been the main foreign exchange earner.

In 1995 the economy grew by 8.6 per cent, inflation was 5.8 per cent, the government budget had a surplus of 2.7 per cent of GDP and foreign currency reserves stood at US$36,200 million.

TRADE

Thailand's main exports are rice, tapioca and tapioca products, garments, rubber, computers and parts, cars, integrated circuit boards, precious stones, pearls and other ornaments, maize, canned sea food, fabrics, sugar and tin. Main imports are crude oil, chemicals and pharmaceuticals, electrical and non-electrical machinery and spare parts, industrial machinery, iron and steel, diesel oil and other fuel oil, vehicle and transport equipment.

	1994	1995
Total imports	Bhat 1,352,425m	Bhat 1,630,000m
Total exports	1,088,073m	1,360,000m

Trade with UK	1994	1995
Imports from UK	£745,587,000	£836,622,000
Exports to UK	913,135,000	1,039,849,000

EDUCATION

Primary education is compulsory and free, and secondary education in government schools is free. Private universities and colleges are playing an increasing role in higher education. Out of 43 universities and other similar higher institutes of learning, 21 are private.

COMMUNICATIONS

The road network, totalling 56,903 km in 1993, reaches all parts of the country. Most of the smaller towns and bigger villages are now served by paved roads. Navigable waterways have a length of about 1,100 km in the dry season and 1,600 km in the wet season. About 4,450 km of state-owned railways were open to traffic in 1989. Main lines run from Bangkok to the Cambodian border, the ferry terminal on the River Mekong opposite Vientiane, Chiang Mai and to Hat Yai, whence lines run down both sides of the Malay peninsula to Singapore. A new line to Sattahip on the east coast is being constructed. Bangkok is the international airport, though airports at Chiang Mai, Phuket and Hat Yai also receive international flights. Most major provincial towns have airports. A mass transit system has been planned for Bangkok.

There are two important ports in the country. Bangkok, which is a river port, can serve vessels up to 27 ft draught. The deep-sea port at Sattahip caters for larger vessels. Phuket and Songkhla deep-water ports have already been completed and are the first to be managed privately under a ten-year concession. Construction of Laem Chabang deep-water port started in 1988.

TOGO

République Togolaise

Togo is situated in West Africa between 0° and 2° W. and 6° and 11° N., with a coastline 35 miles long on the Gulf of Guinea. It extends northwards inland for 350 miles and is flanked on the west by Ghana, on the north by Burkina and in the east by Benin. It has an area of 21,925 sq. miles (56,785 sq. km), and a population (UN estimate 1994) of 4,010,000, including people of several African races. The official language is French; Ewe is spoken by about 47 per cent.

CAPITAL – ΨLomé, population (1983) 366,476.

CURRENCY – Franc CFA of 100 centimes.

FLAG – Five alternating green and yellow horizontal stripes; a quarter in red at top next staff bearing a white star.

NATIONAL DAY – 13 January (National Liberation Day).

GOVERNMENT

The first President of Togo, Sylvanus Olympio, was assassinated in 1963. His successor was overthrown by an army coup d'état in 1967 and the army commander Lt.-Col. (later Gen.) Eyadéma named himself President. President Eyadéma came under increasing popular pressure to introduce reforms in 1990 and in October the Rassemblement du peuple togolais (RPT), the sole legal party, approved plans for a new constitutional conference after pro-democracy riots. Riots broke out again in March 1991 in protest at the slow pace of reform, and in April the government was forced to concede a political amnesty, the introduction of a multiparty constitution and a national conference. In August 1991 the national conference stripped President Eyadéma of all powers, banned the RPT and elected Kokou Koffigoh as Prime Minister of an interim government. The national conference set a date of 9 February 1992 for a referendum on a new constitution.

From the second half of 1991 onwards the political situation became progressively more unstable. Troops loyal to President Eyadéma three times attempted to overthrow the Koffigoh government (October, November and December 1991) but were frustrated by pro-democracy supporters. Continued political violence in 1992 between the army and pro-democracy groups and among rival opposition parties forced the postponement of the referendum until September 1992, when a new multiparty constitution was agreed. In November Eyadéma, who had regained the position of head of state in August 1992, ordered the Army to crush civil unrest and a general strike against his rule. In February 1993, as political violence continued, Koffigoh and Eyadéma agreed on the formation of a crisis government, which the national conference and the Collective Democratic Opposition-2 (COD-2) declared illegal.

President Eyadéma won a presidential election in August 1993 that was boycotted by opposition parties and declared rigged by international monitors. Legislative elections to the 81-seat National Assembly were held in February 1994 and won by the opposition alliance of the Action Committee for Renewal (CAR) (36 seats) and the Togolese Union for Democracy (UTD) (7 seats), while the RPT and allied parties won 38 seats. However, Eyadéma persuaded UTD leader Edem Kodjo to form a coalition UTD-RPT government in April 1994, the RPT retaining a majority of Cabinet seats. The CAR returned to the National Assembly in August 1995, following a nine-month boycott prompted by a Supreme Court decision invalidating the election of some CAR candidates.

HEAD OF STATE
President, Gen. Gnassingbé Eyadéma, *assumed office* 14 April 1967; *re-elected* 1986, August 1993

GOVERNMENT *as at June 1996*

Prime Minister, Edem Kodjo
Foreign Affairs and Co-operation, Barry Moussa Barque
Economy and Finance, Elome Kwami Dadzie
National Defence, Bitokotipou Yagninim
Interior and Security, Col. Seyi Memene
Justice, Elliot Lattevi Atcho Lawson
Industry and State Enterprises, Payadowa Boukpessi
Rural Development, Yao Do Felli
Relations with the National Assembly, Atsutse Agbobli

Works, Mines and Energy, Tchamdja Andjo
Education and Scientific Research, François Benissan
Technical Education, Bamouni Somolou Stanislas Baba
Planning and Regional Development, Kwassi Klutse
Youth and Sports, Kouami Agbogboli Ihoul
Communications and Culture, Solitoki Esso
Public Health, Jean-Pierre Amedon
Environment and Tourism, Ayitou Singo
Commerce and Transport, Kodjo Messan Joffre Appoh
Employment, Labour and Civil Service, Liwoibe Sambiani
Social Welfare and Women's Affairs, Kissem Tchangai-Walla
Human Rights and Rehabilitation, Ephrem Dorkenoo

EMBASSY OF TOGO
The Embassy of Togo closed in September 1991

BRITISH AMBASSADOR, HE Ian Mackley, CMG, resident in Accra, Ghana
There is a Consulate (BP 20050) and a Commercial Office (BP 60958 BE) in Lomé.

ECONOMY

Although the economy remains largely agricultural, exports of phosphates have superseded agricultural products as the main source of export earnings. Other exports include palm kernels, copra and manioc. The production of phosphates entirely for export was taken over completely by the government in February 1974. The IMF approved a loan of US$95 million in September 1994 to support the 1994–7 economic reform programme. In May 1995, France cancelled US$33.68 million of Togo's debt and rescheduled a further US$37.64 million.

TRADE WITH UK	1994	1995
Imports from UK	£7,278,000	£11,781,000
Exports to UK	3,176,000	2,671,000

TONGA
Kingdom of Tonga

Tonga, or the Friendly Islands, comprises a group of islands situated in the southern Pacific some 450 miles east-south-east of Fiji, with an area of 270 sq. miles (699 sq. km), and population (1994 UN estimate) of 98,000. The largest island, Tongatapu, was discovered by Tasman in 1643. Most of the islands are of coral formation, but some are volcanic (Tofua, Kao and Niuafoou or 'Tin Can' Island). The limits of the group are between 15° and 23° 30′ S., and 173° and 177° W.

CAPITAL – ΨNuku'alofa (population estimate 30,000), on Tongatapu.
CURRENCY – Pa'anga (T$) of 100 seniti.
FLAG – Red with a white canton containing a couped red cross.
NATIONAL ANTHEM – E, 'Otua Mafimafi (Oh, Almighty God Above).
NATIONAL DAY – 4 June (Emancipation Day).

GOVERNMENT

The Kingdom of Tonga is an independent constitutional monarchy within the Commonwealth. Prior to 4 June 1970 it had been a British-protected state for 70 years. The constitution provides for a government consisting of the Sovereign, an appointed privy council which functions as a Cabinet, a legislative assembly and a judiciary. The 30-member legislative assembly comprises the King, the 11-member privy council, nine hereditary nobles elected by

their peers, and nine popularly elected representatives who hold office for three years. The most recent election took place in January 1996 and up to seven of the nine seats were won by candidates wishing to reduce the power of the King and nobles and to strengthen democracy.

HEAD OF STATE
King of Tonga, HM King Taufa'ahau Tupou IV, GCMG, GCVO, KBE, *born* 4 July 1918, *acceded* 16 December 1965
Heir, HRH Crown Prince Tupouto'a

CABINET *as at August 1996*
Prime Minister, Minister of Agriculture, Fisheries, Forests, and Marine, Baron Vaea of Houma
Deputy P.M., Minister of Education and Civil Aviation, Hon. Dr S. Langi Kavaliku
Police, Prisons and Fire Services, Hon. Clive Edwards
Health, Hon. Dr S. Tapa
Foreign Affairs and Defence, HRH Crown Prince Tupouto'a
Attorney-General, Justice, Hon. Tevita P. Tupou
Minister without Portfolio, Hon. Ma'afu Tuku'i'aulahi
Lands, Survey, and Natural Resources, Finance, Governor of Ha'apai, Hon. Tutoatasi Fakafanua
Works and Disaster Relief, Hon. J. C. Cocker
Labour, Commerce and Industry, Hon. Giulio Masaso Paunga
Governor of Vava'u, Hon. Tu'i'afitu

TONGA HIGH COMMISSION
36 Molyneux Street, London WIH 6AB
Tel 0171-724 5828
High Commissioner, HE Akosita Fineanganofo, apptd 1996

BRITISH HIGH COMMISSION
PO Box 56, Nuku'alofa
Tel: Nuku'alofa 21020
High Commissioner, HE Andrew James Morris, apptd 1994

ECONOMY

The economy is primarily agricultural; the main crops are coconuts, bananas, vanilla, yams, taro, cassava, groundnuts, squash pumpkins and other fruits. Fish is an important staple food, though recent shortfalls have led to canned fish being imported. Industry is based on the processing of agricultural produce, and the manufacture of foodstuffs, clothing and sports equipment.

TRADE
The principal exports are copra, squash, other coconut products, tropical root crops, bananas, knitwear, leather goods and fibreglass boats.

Trade with UK	1994	1995
Imports from UK	£686,000	£3,010,000
Exports to UK	341,000	113,000

TRINIDAD AND TOBAGO
The Republic of Trinidad and Tobago

Trinidad, the most southerly of the West Indian islands, lies seven miles off the north coast of Venezuela. The island is situated between 10° 2′ and 11° 12′ N. latitude and 60° 30′ and 61° 56′ W. longitude, and is about 50 miles in length by 37 miles in width, with an area of 1,864 sq. miles (4,828 sq. km). Two mountain systems, the Northern and Southern Ranges, stretch across almost its entire width and a third, the Central Range, lies diagonally across its middle portion; otherwise the island is mostly flat.

Tobago lies between 11° 9′ and 11° 21′ N. latitude and between 60° 30′ and 60° 50′ W. longitude, 19 miles north-east of Trinidad. The island is 32 miles long at its widest point, and 11 wide, and has an area of 116 sq. miles (300 sq. km).

Corozal Point and Icacos Point, the north-west and south-west extremities of Trinidad, enclose the Gulf of Paria. West of Corozal Point lie several islands, of which Chacachacare, Huevos, Monos and Gaspar Grande are the most important.

The climate is tropical. There is a dry season from December to May, and a wet season from June to November broken by a short dry season (the *Petite Careme*) in September and October.

The population (1992 estimate) was 1,239,908; Tobago's population is about 45,000. The language is English. Roman Catholicism, Protestantism, Hinduism and Islam are all practised.

CAPITAL – ΨPort of Spain (population (1990) 50,878) is the administrative centre of the islands. San Fernando (population 34,300) is emerging as the industrial centre of Trinidad. The main town of Tobago is ΨScarborough.

CURRENCY – Trinidad and Tobago dollar (TT$) of 100 cents.

FLAG – Black diagonal stripe bordered with white stripes, running from top by staff, all on a red field.

NATIONAL DAYS – 31 August (Independence Day); 24 September (Republic Day).

GOVERNMENT

Trinidad was discovered by Columbus in 1498, was colonized in 1532 by the Spaniards, capitulated to the British in 1797, and was ceded to Britain under the Treaty of Amiens 1802. Tobago was discovered by Columbus in 1498. Dutch colonists arrived in 1632; Tobago subsequently changed hands numerous times until it was ceded to Britain by France in 1814 and amalgamated with Trinidad in 1888.

The Territory of Trinidad and Tobago became an independent state and a member of the British Commonwealth on 31 August 1962, and a republic in 1976. The President is elected for five years by all members of the Senate and the House of Representatives. The House of Representatives has 36 members, elected by universal adult suffrage, and the Senate has 31, of whom 16 are appointed on the advice of the Prime Minister, six on the advice of the Leader of the Opposition and nine at the discretion of the President. Legislation was passed in September 1980 which afforded Tobago a degree of self-administration through the 15-member Tobago House of Assembly.

The most recent general election on 6 November 1995 produced 17 seats each for the ruling People's National Movement (PNM) and the United National Congress (UNC). The UNC formed a coalition government with the Alliance for Reconstruction (NAR) which held the remaining two seats.

HEAD OF STATE
President, HE Noor Mohammed Hassanali, *elected* 1987, *re-elected* February 1992

CABINET *as at August 1996*
Prime Minister, Hon. Basdeo Panday
Adviser to the PM, Tobago Affairs, Relations with the UN and International Organizations, Hon. A. N. Robinson
Attorney-General, Hon. Kamla Persad-Bissessar
Finance, Hon. Brian Kuei Tung

Foreign Affairs, Hon. Ralph Maraj
Planning and Development, Hon. Trevor Sudama
Public Administration and Information, Hon. Wade Mark
Labour and Co-operatives, Hon. Harry Partap
Public Utilities, Hon. Ganga Singh
Sport and Youth Affairs, Hon. Pamela Nicholson
Trade, Industry and Consumer Affairs, Hon. Mervyn Assam
National Security, Hon. Joseph Theodore
Education, Hon. Dr Adesh Nanan
Works and Transport, Hon. Sadeeq Baksh
Agriculture, Lands and Marine Resources, Hon. Dr Reeza Mohammed
Energy, Hon. Finbar Ganga
Housing, Hon. John Humphrey
Health, Hon. Dr Hamza Rafeeq
Local Government, Hon. Dhanraj Singh
Social Development, Hon. Manohar Ramsaran
Culture and Women's Affairs, Hon. Daphne Phillips

HIGH COMMISSION OF THE REPUBLIC OF TRINIDAD AND TOBAGO
42 Belgrave Square, London SWIX 8NT
Tel 0171-245 9351
High Commissioner, HE Sheelagh de Osuna, apptd 1996

BRITISH HIGH COMMISSION
19 St Clair Ave, St Clair, Port of Spain
Tel: Port of Spain 6222748
High Commissioner, HE Leo G. Faulkner, apptd 1996

ECONOMY

Trinidad and Tobago's main source of revenue is from oil. Production of domestic crude was 55 million barrels in 1990. Trinidad has large reserves of natural gas, and reserves are estimated to be in the region of 100 years at the current rates of production. An integrated steel plant, an anhydrous ammonia plant and a methanol plant have been constructed at Point Lisas. An industrial complex, including an iron and steel production plant, is developing around San Fernando.

Fertilizers, tyres, clothing, soap, furniture and foodstuffs are manufactured locally while motor vehicles, radios, TV sets, and electro-domestic equipment are assembled from parts, mainly from Japan. The main agricultural products are sugar, cocoa, coffee, horticultural products, and teak.

TRADE	1991	1992
Imports	TT$7,084.8m	TT$6,081.1m
Exports	8,436.4m	7,942.9m
Trade with UK	1994	1995
Imports from UK	£72,270,000	£103,434,000
Exports to UK	48,287,000	43,600,000

EDUCATION

Education is free at all state-owned and government-assisted denominational schools and certain faculties at the University of the West Indies. In addition there are various private teaching establishments. Attendance is compulsory for children aged six to 12 years, after which attendance at free secondary schools is determined by success in the common entrance examination at 11 years. There are three technical institutes, two teachers' training colleges, and one of the three branches of the University of the West Indies is located in Trinidad. A medical teaching complex at Mt Hope operates in collaboration with the University of the West Indies.

COMMUNICATIONS

There are some 6,436 km of all-weather roads in Trinidad and Tobago. The only general cargo port is Port of Spain but there are specialized port facilities elsewhere for crude oil, refinery products, sugar, bauxite and cement. Regular shipping services call and many inter-island craft use the port. Another rapidly growing port is at Port Lisas where new industries powered by local natural gas are located. International scheduled airlines, including the national airline, Trinidad and Tobago Airways (BWIA) Corporation, use Piarco International Airport, Port of Spain. The airline also flies between Piarco and Crown Point Airport in Tobago.

Three commercial broadcasting stations and one commercial television station operate in Trinidad and Tobago. The internal telephone system and the external telephone and telegraph connections are operated by partly state-owned companies.

TUNISIA
Al-Djoumhouria Attunusia

Tunisia lies between Algeria and Libya and extends southwards to the Sahara Desert, with a total area of 164,150 sq. km, and a population (UN estimate 1994) of 8,815,000.

CAPITAL – Ψ Tunis had a population (1984) of 1,394,749. The ruins of ancient Carthage lie a few miles from the city. Other towns of importance are: Ψ Sfax (577,992); Ψ Sousse (322,491); Ψ Bizerta (394,670); Kairouan; Gabes; Menzel Bourguiba.
CURRENCY – Tunisian dinar of 1,000 millimes.
FLAG – Red with a white disc containing a red crescent and star.
NATIONAL ANTHEM – Himat Al Hima.
NATIONAL DAY – 20 March.

GOVERNMENT

A French Protectorate from 1881 to 1956, Tunisia became an independent sovereign state on 20 March 1956. In 1957 the Constituent Assembly abolished the monarchy and elected M. Bourguiba President of the Republic. In March 1975 the National Assembly proclaimed M. Bourguiba as President for life but he was deposed on 7 November 1987 and succeeded by President Zine el-Abidine Ben Ali. Presidential and legislative elections were held in April 1989. The Rassemblement Constitutionnel Démocratique (RCD) won all 141 seats in the National Assembly, which were contested by seven parties; President Ben Ali was elected with 99 per cent of the vote. Electoral changes enacted in September 1993 provide for opposition parties to be represented in the National Assembly; the Assembly has been expanded to 163 seats, 19 of which are reserved, on a proportional basis, for those parties not winning any of the 144 first-past-the-post seats. Presidential and legislative elections held in March 1994 were won by President Ben Ali, the only candidate, and the RCD, which won all 144 constituency seats. Diplomatic relations were opened with Israel in October 1994.

The country is divided into 23 regions (*gouvernorats*) each administered by a governor.

HEAD OF STATE
President, Zine el-Abidine Ben Ali, *took office* 7 November 1987, *elected* 2 April 1989, *re-elected* 21 March 1994

CABINET *as at August 1996*
Prime Minister, Hamed Karoui
Minister of State, National Defence, Abdallah Kallel
Justice, Sadok Chaabane
Director of Presidential Office, Mohamed el Jeri
Foreign Affairs, Habib ben Yahia
Defence, Abdelaziz Ben Dhia
Interior, Mohammed Jegham
Finance, Nouri Zorgati
Economic Development, Taoufik Baccar
International Co-operation and Foreign Investment, Mohammed Ghannouchi
Agriculture, M'Hamed Ben Rajab
State Property, Mustapha Bouaziz
Equipment and Housing, Ali Chaouch
Transport, Sadok Rabeh
Tourism and Handicrafts, Slaheddine Maaoui
Communications, Habib Ammar
Education, Hatem Ben Othman
Culture, Abdelbaki Hermassi
Health, Hedi Mhenni
Social Affairs, Chedli Neffati
Environment and Land Development, Mohamed Mehdi Melika
Vocational Training and Employment, Moncer Rouissi
Youth and Childhood Welfare, Abderrahim Zouari
Secretary-General of the Government, Ridha Grira
Religious Affairs, Ali Chebbi
Higher Education, Dali Jazi
Family and Women's Affairs, Neziha Zarrouk
Trade, Mondher Zenaidi
Industry, Slaheddine Bouguerra

TUNISIAN EMBASSY
29 Prince's Gate, London SW7 1QG
Tel 0171-584 8117
Ambassador Extraordinary and Plenipotentiary, new appointment awaited

BRITISH EMBASSY
5 Place de la Victoire, Tunis 1015 RP
Tel: Tunis 1341444
Ambassador Extraordinary and Plenipotentiary and Consul-General, HE Richard J. S. Edis, CMG, apptd 1995
First Secretary, B. England (*Deputy Head of Mission*)
There is a Consulate at Sfax.

BRITISH COUNCIL DIRECTOR, C. Stevenson (*Cultural Attaché*)

ECONOMY

The valleys of the northern region support large flocks and herds and contain rich agricultural areas in which wheat, barley, and oats are grown. Vines and olives are extensively cultivated. Some oil has been discovered and crude oil production in 1994 was 4.5 million tons. Gas has also been discovered off the east coast but is only exploited in small quantities. Tourists numbered 3,540,000 in 1992 and tourism is the main foreign exchange earner.

TRADE

The chief exports are crude oil, phosphates, olive oil, finished textiles, and fruit. The chief imports are machinery and equipment, foodstuffs, petroleum products, and textiles. France remains the main trading partner.

Tunisia became an associate of the EC early in 1969 and signed a new agreement with the EC in 1976. In May 1995 a new EU-Tunisian partnership agreement was signed which aims to modernize Tunisia's economy and improve its competitiveness with a view to creating a future free trade zone with the EU.

Trade with UK	1994	1995
Imports from UK	£81,056,000	£83,667,000
Exports to UK	46,000,000	55,690,000

TURKEY
Türkiye Cumhuriyeti

Turkey lies partly in Europe and partly in Asia. The total area is 814,578 sq. km, of which 790,200 sq. km is in Asia and 24,378 sq. km is in Europe. Turkey in Europe consists of Eastern Thrace, including the cities of Istanbul and Edirne, and is separated from Asia by the Bosporus at Istanbul and by the Dardanelles (about 40 miles in length with a width varying from one to four miles), the political neighbours being Greece and Bulgaria on the west. Turkey in Asia comprises the whole of Asia Minor or Anatolia and extends from the Aegean Sea to the western boundaries of Georgia, Armenia and Iran, and from the Black Sea to the Mediterranean and the northern boundaries of Syria and Iraq.

Population at the 1990 census was 56,473,035. The 1994 UN estimate is 60,771,000. Islam ceased to be the state religion in 1928 but 98.99 per cent of the population are Muslim. The main religious minorities, which are concentrated in Istanbul and on the Syrian frontier, are Greek Orthodox, Armenian, Syrian Christian, and Jewish.

CAPITAL – Ankara (Angora), in Asia, population (1990) 3,236,626. Ankara (or Ancyra) was the capital of the Roman Province of *Galatia Prima*, and a marble temple (now in ruins), dedicated to Augustus, contains the *Monumentum (Marmor) Ancyranum*, inscribed with a record of the reign of Augustus Caesar. ΨIstanbul (7,309,190), in Europe, is the former capital. The Roman city of Byzantium, it was selected by Constantine the Great as the capital of the Roman Empire about AD 328 and renamed Constantinople. Istanbul contains the celebrated church of St Sophia, which, after becoming a mosque, was made a museum in 1934. It also contains Topkapi, former palace of the Ottoman Sultans, which is also a museum. Other cities are ΨIzmir (2,694,770); Adana (1,934,907); Bursa (1,603,137); Gaziantep (1,140,549); and Konya (1,750,303).

CURRENCY – Turkish lira (TL) of 100 kurus.
FLAG – Red, with white crescent and star.
NATIONAL ANTHEM – Istiklal Marşi (The Independence March).
NATIONAL DAY – 29 October (Republic Day).

GOVERNMENT

On 29 October 1923 the National Assembly declared Turkey a republic and elected Gazi Mustafa Kemal (later known as Kemal Ataturk) President. In 1945 a multiparty system was introduced but in 1960 the government was overthrown by the armed forces. A new constitution was adopted in 1961 and a civilian government took office. Civilian governments remained in power until September 1980 when mounting problems with the economy and terrorism led to a military takeover.

A new constitution, extending the powers of the President, was approved in 1982. It provided for the separation of powers between the legislature, executive and judiciary, and the holding of free elections to the unicameral Grand National Assembly, which now has 550 members elected every five years. Following the general election in November 1983 the military leadership handed

over power to a civilian government. Following the election held in October 1991, Süleyman Demirel, leader of the True Path Party, formed a coalition government with the Social Democrat Populist Party. President Özal died on 17 April 1993 leading to the election by parliament of Süleyman Demirel as President. Tansu Çiller was elected party chairman by the True Path Party and formed a government which was sworn in on 25 June by President Demirel, when Çiller became the first woman Turkish Prime Minister. The Social Democrat Populist Party merged with the Republican People's Party (CHP) in February 1995 when the CHP became the junior coalition party. The CHP withdrew from the government, forcing Çiller to resign on 20 September 1995. The True Path Party formed a minority government with the Democratic Left Party and the National Action Party on 6 October but was forced to resign following a vote of no-confidence ten days later. The True Path–CHP coalition was re-formed on 30 October until elections could be held on 24 December 1995. The Islamist Welfare Party (Refah Partisi (RP)) won the most seats but was unable to form a government, enabling the True Path Party and the Motherland Party to form a coalition. The administration lasted until 24 May 1996 when True Path withdrew following corruption allegations against its leader, Tansu Çiller. The RP and True Path Party formed a coalition government on 28 June 1996, having agreed to rotate the premiership between Tansu Çiller and the RP leader Necmettin Erbakan. The RP has 158 seats in the Grand National Assembly, the True Path Party 135, the Motherland Party 132, the Democratic Left Party 76, and the National Action Party 49.

Turkey is divided for administrative purposes into 76 *il* with subdivisions into *ilçe* and *nahiye*. Each *il* has a governor (*vali*) and elective council.

SECESSION

Since 1984 Turkey has been fighting armed guerrillas of the Marxist Kurdish Workers Party (PKK) in the south-east of the country where Kurds are the majority population. The PKK has an estimated strength of 10,000 operating from bases in Lebanon, northern Iraq and Syria, with the latter giving tacit support and finance. The south-east remains under martial law and about 15,000 have died in the 11 years of warfare. Since the end of a two-month PKK cease-fire in May 1993, the Turkish army has attempted to destroy the PKK by launching land and air raids against PKK bases in Syria and northern Iraq. The largest land incursion occurred in northern Iraq from March to May 1995 when 35,000 Turkish troops, backed by tanks and aircraft, destroyed PKK bases and supply routes and killed about 500 guerrillas. In June 1996, 4,000 Turkish troops returned to northern Iraq and the Turkish government said it intended to establish a six-mile deep buffer zone on the border to deter incursions by PKK rebels. The PKK has unsuccessfully attempted to gain the Kurdish population's support by intimidating and executing hundreds of those who oppose it. Turkish security forces have razed villages suspected of harbouring PKK guerrillas. Some 1,500,000 Kurds have been driven from their homes by the fighting and 200,000 Turkish troops are engaged in the conflict.

HEAD OF STATE
President, Süleyman Demirel, *elected by parliament for a seven-year term* 16 May 1993

GOVERNMENT *as at August 1996*
Prime Minister, Necmettin Erbakan (RP)
Deputy PM, Foreign Affairs, Prof. Tansu Çiller (DYP)
Justice, Şevket Kazan (RP)

National Defence, Turhan Tayan (DYP)
Interior, Mehmeet Ağar (DYP)
Finance and Customs, Abdullatif Şener (RP)
Education, Mehmet Sağlam (DYP)
Public Works and Housing, Cevat Ayhan (RP)
Health, Yildirim Aktuna (DYP)
Agriculture and Rural Affairs, Musa Demirci (RP)
Labour and Social Security, Necati Çelik (RP)
Trade and Industry, Yalim Erez (DYP)
Energy and Natural Resources, Recai Kutan (RP)
Culture, Ismail Kahraman (RP)
Tourism, Bahattin Yocel (DYP)
Forestry, Halit Dağli (DYP)
Environment, Ziyaettin Tokar (RP)
Transport, Ömer Barutçu (DYP)
Ministers of State, Fehim Adak, Nevzat Ercan, Abdullah
    Gül, Işilay Saygin, Sabri Tekir, Nafiz Kurt, Mehmet
    Altinsoy, N. Kemal Zeybek, Lütfü Esengül, Salim
    Ensarioğlu, Ahmet Cemil Tunç, Bekir Aksoy, Gürcan
    Dağdaş, Ufuk Söylemez, Teoman Riza Güneri, Ayfer
    Yilmaz, Sacit Günbey, Bahattin Şeker, Ahmet Demircan
DYP True Path Party; RP Welfare Party

TURKISH EMBASSY
43 Belgrave Square, London SWIX 8PA
Tel 0171-393 0202
Ambassador Extraordinary and Plenipotentiary, HE Özdem
    Sanberk, apptd 1995
Minister Counsellor, Çinar Aldemir

BRITISH EMBASSY
Sehit Ersan Caddesi 46/A, Cankaya, Ankara
Tel: Ankara 4686230
Ambassador Extraordinary and Plenipotentiary, HE Sir Kieran
    Prendergast, KCVO, CMG, apptd 1995
Counsellor, Deputy Head of Mission, N. A. Ling
First Secretary, A. T. MacDermott (*Commercial*)
Defence and Military Attaché, Brig. A. V. Twiss
Consul-General (Istanbul), M. E. Cook

BRITISH CONSULAR OFFICES, There is a Consulate-
    General at Istanbul, a Vice-Consulate at Izmir and
    Honorary Consulates at Antalya, Bodrum, Iskenderun,
    Mersin and Marmaris.

BRITISH COUNCIL DIRECTOR, David Marler, OBE,
    Kirklangic Sokak 9, Gazi Osman Pasa, Ankara 06700.
    There is also a centre and library at Istanbul.

BRITISH CHAMBER OF COMMERCE OF TURKEY INC.,
    Mesrutiyet Caddessi No. 34, Tepebasi Beyoğlu,
    Istanbul (*postal address*, PO Box 190 Karaköy, Istanbul).

DEFENCE

The armed forces have a total active strength of 507,800
(415,200 conscripts), with a term of conscription of 18
months. Reserves number 378,700 with commitment to
age 41. The Army has an active strength of 400,000
(352,000 conscripts) with 4,280 main battle tanks, 3,711
armoured personnel carriers and 4,341 artillery pieces.
The Navy has 51,000 personnel (34,500 conscripts)
including 3,100 marines, with 16 submarines, 5 destroyers,
16 frigates, 44 patrol and coastal craft, nine combat aircraft
and 14 armed helicopters. The Air Force has a strength of
56,800 (28,700 conscripts), with 447 combat aircraft.
Paramilitary Gendarmerie and National Guard forces
number 180,000 active and 50,000 reserve personnel.
    Between 150,000 and 200,000 troops are stationed in the
south-east of the country fighting Kurdish guerrillas.
    Since its invasion of Cyprus in 1974, Turkey has
maintained forces in the north of the island and at present
has 30,000 men stationed there.

As a member of NATO, Turkey is host to the Headquarters Allied Land Forces South-Eastern Europe and the
Sixth Allied Tactical Air Force Headquarters. US (2,900
personnel), UK (260 personnel) and French (150 personnel) air force detachments are based at Incirlik air base in
southern Turkey to patrol the air exclusion zone over
northern Iraq.

ECONOMY

Agricultural production accounts for some 16 per cent of
GDP at constant factor prices. About 50 per cent of the
working population are in the rural sector. The principal
crops are wheat, barley, rice, tobacco, sugar beet, tea,
olives, grapes, figs and hazelnuts. With the exception of
wheat, which is mostly grown on the arid central Anatolian
plateau, most of the crops are grown on the fertile littoral.
Tobacco, sultana and fig cultivation is centred around
Izmir, where substantial quantities of cotton are also
grown. The main cotton area is in the Cukurova plain
around Adana. The forests which lie between the littoral
plain and the Anatolian plateau contain beech, pine, oak,
elm, chestnut, lime, plane, alder, box, poplar and maple. In
1990 28 per cent of the land area was forest.
    After agriculture, Turkey's most important industry is
based on the considerable mineral wealth which is, however, comparatively unexploited. The main export minerals are chromite and boron. Production in 1994 was
(tonnes):

Coal	50,000,000
Crude petroleum	4,038,000
Iron Ore	6,684,000

The bulk of the country's requirements in sugar, cotton,
woollen and silk textiles, and cement, is produced locally.
Other industries include vehicle assembly, paper, glass and
glassware, iron and steel, leather and leather goods, sulphur
refining, canning and rubber goods, soaps and cosmetics,
pharmaceutical products, and prepared foodstuffs.
    Steep rises in oil prices from 1973 onwards led to a
succession of economic crises culminating in January 1980
in the introduction of an economic stability programme.
Exports have since risen dramatically, topping US$11,846
million in 1988, but since 1988 imports have risen
dramatically too, creating a significant trade gap. Inflation
remains high (60 per cent in 1993). GNP growth for 1992
was 5.2 per cent and unemployment remains high. The
total foreign debt in 1992 stood at US$54,700 million and
the budget deficit in 1993 was equivalent to 9 per cent of
GDP.
    The Çiller government has announced radical measures
to deregulate, liberalize and transform the economy. The
government effectively gained the power to issue decrees
to run the economy without parliamentary approval in
June 1992. About 100 large state-owned firms are debt-
ridden and seen as a source of inflation, which reached an
annual rate of 130 per cent in 1995. A large-scale
privatization programme is under way, which is designed
to raise some US$26,000 million in revenue. An austerity
package of price rises, new taxes and job cuts in state
industries was introduced in April 1994 to curb inflation
and reduce the budget deficit. At the same time a standby
agreement was reached with the IMF for loans of US$690
million over three years in return for a devaluation of the
lira by 28 per cent; a further loan of US$742 million was
approved in July 1994 in support of the 1994–5 economic
reform programme.
    A customs union with the EU came into force on 1
January 1996 which was expected to boost the economy,
although Greece succeeded in suspending an EU aid
package of US$480 million in February 1996. A gas deal

worth £14,800 million was signed with Iran in August 1996 which provided for a 20-year supply of Iranian gas.

TRADE

The main imports are machinery, crude oil and petroleum products, iron and steel, vehicles, medicines and dyes, chemicals, fertilizers and electrical appliances. Agricultural commodities (cotton, tobacco, fruits, nuts, livestock) represent 47 per cent of total exports. Other exports are minerals, textiles, glass and cement.

	1993	1994
Total imports	US$29,428m	US$23,270m
Total exports	15,345m	18,105m

Trade with UK	1994	1995
Imports from UK	£813,522,000	£1,157,777,000
Exports to UK	628,109,000	794,890,000

COMMUNICATIONS

The rail network is run by the State Railways Administration. The total length of lines in operation (1993) is 10,386 km. In 1993, there were 59,770 km of roads. The Bosporus is spanned by two bridges; plans are being drawn up for a third fixed link between the two continents. By the end of 1988 the number of ships over 18 gross tons was 3,805. The state airline (THY) operates all internal services and has services to Europe, the Far East, Africa, North America and the Middle East. Most of the leading European airlines operate services to Istanbul and some also to Ankara.

EDUCATION

Education is free, secular and compulsory at primary level. There are elementary, secondary and vocational schools. There are 27 universities in Turkey, including six in Istanbul, five in Ankara, two in Izmir, and one each in Erzurum and Trabzon.

CULTURE

Turkish was written in Arabic script until 1926 when a version of the Roman alphabet reflecting Turkish phonetics was substituted for use in official correspondence and in 1928 for universal use, with Arabic numerals as used throughout Europe. The revolution of 1908 led to the introduction of native literature free from foreign influences and adapted to the understanding of the people.

The leading Turkish newspapers are centred in Istanbul and Ankara, although most provincial towns have their own daily papers. There are foreign language papers in French, Greek, Armenian and English and numerous magazines and weeklies.

TURKMENISTAN
Turkmenostan Respublikasy

Turkmenistan has an area of 188,456 sq. miles (488,100 sq. km) and occupies the extreme south of the former Soviet Central Asia between the Caspian Sea and the Amu-Darya river. To the west it is bordered by the Caspian Sea, to the south by Iran, to the south-east by Afghanistan, to the east and north by Uzbekistan and to the north-west by Kazakhstan. The republic comprises five regions: Ashkhabad; Chardjou; Krasnovodsk; Mary; and Tashauz. The country is a low-lying plain fringed by hills in the south. Ninety per cent of the plain is taken up by the Obe Kara-Kum (Black Sands) desert. The climate is hot and dry.

The population (1996 census) is 4,483,000, of which 77 per cent are Turkomans, 6.7 per cent Russians and 9.2 per cent Uzbeks, together with smaller numbers of Kazakhs, Tatars, Ukrainians and Armenians. Most of the population are Sunni Muslims. The main languages are Turkmenian (72 per cent), Russian (9 per cent), Uzbek (9 per cent). Turkmenian is one of the Turkic languages.

CAPITAL – Ashkhabad. Population 407,000 (1990).
CURRENCY – Manat.
FLAG – Green with a vertical carpet pattern near the hoist in black, white and wine-red; in the upper hoist a crescent and five stars, all in white.
NATIONAL DAY – 27 October (Independence Day).

GOVERNMENT

Situated at the cross-roads of Central Asia, the area that is now Turkmenistan has been invaded and occupied by many empires: Persian; Greek under Alexander the Great; Parthian; Mongol. A Turkmenian nation was established in the 15th century but remained riven with dissent and divided between warring emirates. From the early 19th century until 1886 Turkmenistan was gradually incorporated into the Russian Empire. Soviet control over Turkmenistan was established on 30 April 1918 when it became an Autonomous Soviet Socialist Republic. The banks, cotton refineries and oil and gas fields were nationalized before a civil war broke out in July 1918, sparked by the intervention of British troops from Iran and India. The war ended in 1920 with the withdrawal of the interventionist forces; Turkmenistan became a full republic of the Soviet Union in February 1925.

Turkmenistan declared its independence from the Soviet Union on 27 October 1991 and gained UN membership on 2 March 1992. The constitution passed on 18 May 1992 declares the President head of state and government and provides for a bicameral legislature of the existing Supreme Soviet (renamed the *Majlis*) and a 60-member (50 directly elected and ten appointed) supervisory upper house, the *Khalk Maslakhaty* (People's Council).

The autocratic government of President Niyazov has prevented any effective political opposition or free press through harassment and the continuation of authoritarianism. The political leadership has rejected political pluralism and instead a cult of personality has developed around President Niyazov. The Supreme Soviet voted on 30 December 1993 to extend the term of President Niyazov to 2002 and this was confirmed by a 99.99 per cent vote in a referendum on 15 January 1994. The Communist Party, renamed the Democratic Party, remains in power. Legislative elections to the *Khalk Maslakhaty* were won by the Democratic Party.

In 1992 joint Turkmen–Russian armed forces of 34,000 army and air force personnel were established and remain in operation. In late 1993 Turkmen–Russian agreements were signed allowing Russian troops to protect the borders with Iran and Afghanistan; Russian citizens to undergo military training in Turkmenistan; Turkmen officers to train in Russia; and Turkmenistan to bear the cost of Russian forces in the country. Agreement on dual citizenship for ethnic Russians in Turkmenistan was also reached. In December 1993 Turkmenistan signed the CIS charter to become a full CIS member and in January 1994 became a member of the CIS economic union.

HEAD OF STATE

President, Saparmurad Niyazov, *elected* 27 October 1990, *re-elected* 21 June 1992, *appointed head of government* 18 May 1992, *elected by referendum for an eight-year term* 15 January 1994

COUNCIL OF MINISTERS *as at June 1996*
Prime Minister, The President
Deputy PM, Foreign Affairs, Boris Shikmuradov
Deputy PM, Construction, Transport and Communications,
Yagmur Ovezov
Deputy PMs, Orasgeldy Ajdogdyev; Matkarim Rajapov;
Reedjep Saparov; Klekhim Ishanov; Batyr Ovezov;
Mukhamed Abalakov; Amanazar Ilamanov; Valery
Otchertsov; Ilaman Shykhyiev
Interior, Kurbanmukhamed Kasymov
Defence, Dangatar Kopekov
Trade, Halnazar Agakhanov
Economy and Finance, Valery Otchertsov
Justice, Tagandurdy Khallyev
Culture and Tourism, Soltan Pirmukhamedov
Health, Chary Kuliev
Communications, Amanmurad Djummiev
Oil and Gas, Aman Ezenov
Agriculture and Foodstuffs, Ata Nabadov
Social Affairs, Khalykberdy Ataiev
Construction and Architecture, Allaberdy Tekaiev
Education, Mukhamed Abalakov
Water Conservancy, Amannazar Ilamanov
Automobile Transport and Roads Maintenance, Senkuly
Rakhmanov
Foreign Economic Relations, Mired Orazov
Environment, Dortkuli Kurbanov
Industry, Khalmukhamed Orazsakhatov
Consumer Goods, Begerich Nepesov
Grain Products, Amageldy Chariyarov
Power Engineering and Industry, Saparmurad Nuryev

BRITISH EMBASSY
Suite 220, Ashkhabad Business Centre, Berzengi,
Ashkhabad
Ambassador Extraordinary and Plenipotentiary, HE Neil Hook,
MVO, apptd 1995

ECONOMY

The large reserves of natural gas and the foreign revenue
that they earn make the country economically viable and
have enabled the government to maintain low stable prices
for all basic commodities and utilities.

Cotton cultivation, stock-raising and mineral extraction are the principal industries, together with the natural
gas production and the long-established silk industry.
Some fisheries exist along the Caspian sea coast. Arable
land is irrigated by the Niyazov canal, which cuts through
the Kara Kum desert. There are estimated reserves of some
700 million tonnes of oil and 8,000,000 million cubic
metres of natural gas. Natural gas is exported by pipeline to
Ukraine and western Europe and another pipeline is being
built through Iran and Turkey to Europe.

A new railroad links Turkmenistan with Iran.

TRADE WITH UK	1994	1995
Imports from UK	£4,382,000	£3,902,000
Exports to UK	837,000	738,000

TUVALU

Tuvalu comprises nine coral atolls situated in the south-
west Pacific around the point at which the International
Date Line cuts the Equator. The total land area is about 10
sq. miles. Few of the atolls are more than 12 ft above sea
level or more than half a mile in width. The vegetation
consists mainly of coconut palms.

The resident population in 1985 was 8,229, but it is
estimated that about 1,500 Tuvaluans work overseas,
mostly in Nauru, or as seamen. The UN estimated that
the population was 12,000 in 1992. The people are almost
entirely Polynesian. The principal languages are Tuva-
luan and English. The entire population is Christian,
predominantly Protestant.

CAPITAL – ΨFunafuti, estimated population 2,856. The
capital has a grass strip airfield from which a service
operates regularly to Fiji and Kiribati, and is also the
only port.
CURRENCY – Tuvalu uses the Australian dollar ($A) of 100
cents as legal tender. In addition there are Tuvalu dollar
and cent coins in circulation.
FLAG – Unequal horizontal stripes of blue, white, red,
white and blue with a pattern of eight white stars over all
in the fly, in the hoist a white triangle bearing the
national arms.
NATIONAL ANTHEM – Tuvalu Mo Te Atua (Tuvalu for
the Almighty).
NATIONAL DAY – 1 October (Independence Day).

GOVERNMENT

Tuvalu, formerly the Ellice Islands, formed part of the
Gilbert and Ellice Islands Colony until 1 October 1975,
when separate constitutions came into force. Separation
from the Gilbert Islands was implemented on 1 January
1976. On 1 October 1978 Tuvalu became a fully independent state within the Commonwealth.

The constitution provides for a Prime Minister and four
other Ministers, who must be members of the 12-member
elected Parliament. The Prime Minister presides at meetings of the Cabinet, which consists of the five Ministers,
and is attended by the Attorney-General. Local government services are provided by elected Island Councils.

Governor-General, HE Toomu Sione

CABINET *as at August 1996*
Prime Minister, Foreign Affairs and Economic Planning, Rt.
Hon. Kamuta Lataasi
*Deputy Prime Minister, Natural Resources, Home Affairs and
Rural Development,* Hon. Otinielu Tausi
Labour, Works and Communications, Hon. Houati Iele
Health and Human Resource Development, Hon. Faimalaga
Luka, OBE
Finance, Trade, Commerce, Public Corporations, Koloa Talake
BRITISH HIGH COMMISSIONER, HE Michael Peart, CMG,
LVO, resides at Suva, Fiji

SOCIAL WELFARE

There are eight primary schools in Tuvalu and a church
secondary school run jointly with the government. A
maritime training school caters for 60 boys a year. There is
a 30-bed hospital at Funafuti. All islands are served by a
dispensary and a primary school.

ECONOMY

Most people still practise a subsistence economy, the main
staples of the diet being coconuts and fish. The main
imports are foodstuffs, consumer goods and building
materials. The only export is copra, though philatelic sales
provide a major source of revenue and handicraft sales are
increasing. However, Tuvalu is almost entirely dependent
on foreign aid.

TRADE WITH UK	1994	1995
Imports from UK	£134,000	£268,000
Exports to UK	£1,000	—

UGANDA
Republic of Uganda

Uganda is situated in eastern Africa, flanked by Zaire, Sudan, Kenya and on the south by Tanzania and Rwanda. Large parts of Lakes Victoria, Edward and Albert (Mobuto) are within its boundaries, as are Lakes Kyoga, Kwania, George and Bisina (formerly Salisbury) and the course of the River Nile from its outlet from Lake Victoria to the Sudan border at Nimule. Uganda has an area of 91,259 sq. miles (236,036 sq. km) (water and swamp 16,400 sq. miles) and a population (1994 UN estimate) of 18,592,000. The official language is English. The main local vernaculars are of Bantu, Nilotic and Hamitic origins. Ki-Swahili is generally understood.

Despite its tropical location, the climate is tempered by its situation some 3,000 ft above sea level, and well over that altitude in the highlands of the Western and Eastern Regions. Uganda has three National Parks and a fourth (Lake Mburo) has been designated.

CAPITAL – Kampala (estimated population of Greater Kampala, 1990, 750,000). Other principal towns are Jinja (45,000), Mbale (28,000) and Masaka (29,000).
CURRENCY – Uganda shilling of 100 cents.
FLAG – Six horizontal stripes of black, yellow, red, with a white disc in the centre containing the badge of a crested crane.
NATIONAL ANTHEM – Oh Uganda.
NATIONAL DAY – 9 October (Independence Day).

GOVERNMENT

Uganda became an independent state within the Commonwealth on 9 October 1962, after some 70 years of British rule. A republic was instituted in 1967, under an executive President assisted by a Cabinet of Ministers.

Early in 1971 an army coup took place and Maj.-Gen. Idi Amin, the army commander, proclaimed himself head of state. In 1979, following uprisings and military intervention by Tanzania, President Amin was overthrown. Dr Milton Obote became President in 1980 but was ousted by a military coup in 1985. A military council was installed but the National Resistance Movement led by Yoweri Museveni captured Kampala in January 1986, securing control of the rest of the country in the following few months. Yoweri Museveni was sworn in as President in January 1986.

A Constituent Assembly was elected in March 1994 to draft a new constitution. The constitution, promulgated on 8 October 1995, endorsed the existing non-party political system. The National Resistance Council, the legislature, was replaced by a new 276-seat National Assembly. President Museveni won the first direct presidential election on 9 May 1996 with 74.2 per cent of the vote. Supporters of the President won a majority of seats in legislative elections on 27 June. The ban on political party activity in the interest of stability will continue until 2000.

HEAD OF STATE
President, Yoweri Museveni, *sworn in* 29 January 1986, *elected* 9 May 1996
Vice-President, Speciosa Wandira Kazibwe

CABINET *as at August 1996*
Prime Minister, Kintu Musoke
First Deputy PM, Foreign Affairs, Eriya Kategaya
Second Deputy PM, Tourism, Wildlife and Antiquities, Brig. Moses Ali
Third Deputy PM, Labour and Social Services, Paul Orono Etiang
Agriculture, Animal Industry and Fisheries, The Vice-President
Educational and Sports, Amanya Mushega
Finance, Joash Mayanja-Nkangi
Gender and Community Development, Hajati Janeti B. Mukwaya
Health, Dr Crispus W. C. B. Kiyonga
Information, Dr Ruhakana-Rugunda
Internal Affairs, Maj. Tom Butime
Attorney-General, Justice, Bart Katureebe
Lands, Housing and Urban Development, Francis Ayume
Local Government, Bidandi-Ssali
Natural Resources, Gerald Ssendaula
Public Services, Prof. A. Nsibambi
Trade and Industry, Henry Muganwa Kajura
Works, Transport and Communications, John Nasasira
Planning and Economic Development, Richard Kaijuka
Minister Without Portfolio, Kirunda Kivejjinja

UGANDA HIGH COMMISSION
Uganda House, 58–59 Trafalgar Square, London WC2N 5DX
Tel 0171–839 5783
High Commissioner, HE Prof. George Kirya, apptd 1990
Deputy High Commissioner, D. Ssozi
Minister Counsellor, A. Nyerwanire
Financial Attaché, A. Bamweyana

BRITISH HIGH COMMISSION
10–12 Parliament Avenue, PO Box 7070, Kampala
Tel: Kampala 257054/9
High Commissioner, HE Edward Clay, CMG, apptd 1993
Deputy High Commissioner, J. O. Atkinson
Defence Adviser, Lt.-Col. N. P. C. Lewis, MBE
First Secretary (Commercial), D. W. Seddon

BRITISH COUNCIL DIRECTOR, Roger Wilkins (*Cultural Attaché*)

EDUCATION

Education is a joint undertaking by the government, local authorities and voluntary agencies. In 1988 Uganda had an estimated 7,905 primary schools with 2,638,100 children, 774 secondary schools with 240,834 students; and 7,291 students in various technical training institutions. There are four universities, Makerere University in Kampala, the Uganda Martyrs University, and at Mbale and Mbarara.

COMMUNICATIONS

There is an international airport at Entebbe, and eight other airfields around the country. Having no sea coast, Uganda is dependent upon rail and road links to Mombasa and Dar es Salaam for its trade. Over 5,000 km of the country's roads are currently being rehabilitated. A railway network joins the capital to the western, eastern and northern centres.

ECONOMY

Since 1988 the government has been successful in implementing an IMF recovery programme. The civil service and army have been reduced in size, foreign investment encouraged, and property returned to Asians expelled by

Idi Amin. Annual growth since 1988 has averaged 6 per cent, inflation has been reduced to 3 per cent a year and aid donors in June 1993 gave £550 million of aid. In October 1994 the IMF approved a US$175 million loan to support the government's economic reform programme over the next three years. In February 1995 the Paris Club of bilateral official aid donors agreed to write off two-thirds of Uganda's debt to them.

The principal export earner is coffee, over 90 per cent of all exports. Attempts are being made to increase production of tobacco, cocoa, cotton and tea for export. Hydro-electricity is produced from the Owen Falls power station, some of which is exported to Kenya. The principal food crops are plantains, bananas, cassava, sweet potatoes, potatoes, maize and sorghum; livestock raising and inshore fishing are also important.

TRADE WITH UK	1994	1995
Imports from UK	£40,779,000	£49,105,000
Exports to UK	15,491,000	11,136,000

UKRAINE
Ukraina

Ukraine has an area of 233,090 sq. miles (603,700 sq. km) and lies in the south-west of the European part of the former Soviet Union. It is bordered on the north by Belarus and Russia, on the east by Russia, on the south by the Black Sea, on the south-west by Romania and Moldova and on the west by Hungary, Slovakia and Poland. The area of the present Ukraine is larger than that of the Ukrainian Soviet Republic formed in 1917–19 because of the westward territorial expansion of the former Soviet Union in the 1939–45 period and the addition of the Crimea from Russia in 1954. Ukraine now consists of 25 regions: Cherkassy, Chernigov, Chernovtsy, Crimea, Dneproptrovsk, Donetsk, Ivano-Frankovsk, Kharkov, Kherson, Khmelnitsky, Kiev, Kirovograd, Lugansk, Lvov, Nikolayev, Odessa, Poltava, Rovno, Sumy, Ternopol, Transcarpathia, Vinnitsa, Volhynia, Zaporozhye and Zhitomir.

Most of Ukraine forms a plain with small elevations. The Carpathian mountains lie in the south-western part of the republic. The main rivers are the Dnieper with its tributaries, the Southern Bug and the Northern Donets (a tributary of the Don). The climate is moderate with relatively mild winters (particularly in the south-west) and hot summers.

The population (1989 census) was 51,471,000, of which 73 per cent are Ukrainian and 22 per cent Russian, with smaller numbers of Jews, Belarusians, Moldovans, Tatars, Poles, Hungarians and Greeks. The 1996 estimate put the population at 52,100,000.

The two main religions are Roman Catholicism and Orthodox. The Orthodox rite is divided between the Russian Orthodox Church with its Patriarch in Moscow and the Autocephalous Orthodox Church of the Ukraine with its own Patriarch in Kiev. There are also large numbers of Reformed Protestants in the Transcarpathian region and a sizeable Jewish community in Kiev.

The main languages are Ukrainian (73 per cent) and Russian (22 per cent). Ukrainian is an Eastern Slavonic language related to Russian and Belarusian.

CAPITAL – Kiev. Population 2,577,000 (1989). Other major cities (1990) are Kharkov (1,611,000); Dnepropetrovsk (1,179,000); ΨOdessa (1,115,000); Donetsk (1,110,000).

CURRENCY – Coupons called Karbovanets were introduced in November 1992 and are fully convertible to the rouble.
FLAG – Two horizontal stripes of blue over yellow.
NATIONAL DAY – 24 August (Independence Day).

GOVERNMENT

The earliest Russian state was formed in the middle reaches of the Dnieper River with its capital at Kiev in the ninth century AD. The state united the two large Slav states of Kiev and Novgorod and established the first common Russian language and nationality. The state lasted until Kiev fell to the Mongols in 1240. For the next four centuries Ukraine was invaded and ruled by Tatars, Turks, Poles, Hungarians and Lithuanians. In 1648 the Ukrainians threw off Polish rule to become independent and increasingly allied with Russia (formerly Muscovy). During the reign of Catherine the Great of Russia (1763–96) Ukraine and the Crimea came under Russian control.

By the time of the Treaty of Brest-Litovsk in March 1918, most of Ukraine had been occupied by German and Austrian forces. The Treaty forced the Soviet government in Moscow to cede parts of western Ukraine to Germany and Austria-Hungary and accept the independence of the remainder. After the defeat of Germany in 1918, Ukraine became a battleground in the Russian civil war before the imposition of Soviet rule in 1922. Ukraine became a constituent republic of the USSR on 30 December 1922. The 1920s saw the collectivization of agriculture, which led to a famine in which millions died, and the Stalinist purges caused thousands more to be killed. Ukraine was again devastated in the Second World War and millions of Ukrainians died. The country was rebuilt and heavily industrialized in the post-war period.

Ukraine declared itself independent of the Soviet Union, subject to a referendum, after the failed Moscow coup in August 1991. The referendum was held on 1 December 1991 and 90 per cent of the electorate voted for independence. Simultaneously, the former Ukrainian Communist leader Leonid Kravchuk was elected President of the Republic. Political power in Ukraine in 1991–4 rested with the former Communists, led by the President, in loose alliance with the Rukh nationalist party. This has limited political and economic change, although Leonid Kuchma, Prime Minister 1992–3, began to introduce economic reforms in December 1992, with privatization and the partial liberalization of price controls. Kuchma resigned in September 1993 after the Supreme Council obstructed his reform programme and President Kravchuk effectively took over the government. Economic chaos due to strikes forced the President to call early legislative and presidential elections.

In the legislative elections to the 450-seat Supreme Council in March to November 1994, the western regions of Ukraine voted for nationalist and reformist candidates while the eastern regions voted for Communist and allied ones; the result was a majority of Communist and allied candidates, plus 'independents' who were mainly agricultural and industrial managers tied to the status quo. In the June 1994 presidential election Kuchma defeated President Kravchuk.

A power struggle over who should appoint the Cabinet and over economic reform soon developed between President Kuchma and the Supreme Council. Kuchma inherited the government of his predecessor President Kravchuk and was only able to appoint his own government in March 1995. This reformist government lost a no confidence vote in the Supreme Council but President Kuchma refused to dismiss it, and in June 1995 secured the passing of a 'constitutional treaty' by the Supreme Council. This gives the President the power to appoint and dismiss the government without reference to the Supreme Council and allows greater presidential power to rule by decree. These changes were incorporated into a new constitution adopted by the Supreme Council on 28 June 1996. The constitution also provides for the Supreme Council to be renamed the People's Council (*Narodna Rada*) and for the holding of legislative elections in March 1998 and a presidential election in October 1999.

The Crimean parliament voted to make Crimea an autonomous republic in September 1991, which was accepted by Kiev, but then voted for independence in May 1992, which was not accepted and was suspended. A Russian nationalist, Yuri Meshkov, was elected President of Crimea in January 1994 and the Crimean parliament in May 1994 restored the suspended 1992 constitution declaring sovereignty. A constitutional and political crisis in Crimea caused by a power struggle between President Meshkov and the Crimean parliament from September 1994 onwards was resolved by Ukrainian intervention in March 1995. Direct presidential rule over Crimea was imposed in April 1995, to be lifted in August following elections to the Crimean parliament which saw a dramatic drop in support for pro-Russian parties. Arkady Demydenko was appointed Prime Minister of Crimea on 26 February 1996.

A referendum in June 1994 in the Donbass region of eastern Ukraine in favour of closer economic ties with Russia and making Russian an official language was overwhelmingly passed, as was one in the Crimea in favour of dual Russian–Ukrainian citizenship.

HEAD OF STATE
President, Leonid Kuchma, *elected* 10 July 1994, *sworn in* 19 July 1994

CABINET *as at June 1996*
Prime Minister, Pavlo Lazarenko
First Deputy PM, Security Issues and Emergency Situations, Vasyl Durdynets
Deputy PM, Industrial Policy Issues, Anatoliy Kinakh
Deputy PM, Humanitarian Issues, Ivan Kuras
Deputy PM, Economic Issues, Roman Shpek
Deputy PM, Economic Reform Issues, Victor Pynzenyk
Deputy PM, Fuel and Energy Complex, Vasyl Yevtukhov
Foreign Affairs, Gennadi Udovenko
Defence, Valeriy Shmarov
Foreign Economic Relations and Trade, Serhiy Osyka
Minister of the Cabinet, Valeriy Pustovoitenko
Interior, Yuriy Kravchenko
Economy, Vasyl Gureyev
Culture, Dmytro Ostapenko
Health, Yevhen Korolenko
Communications, Valeriy Yefremov
Forestry, Valeriy Samoplavsky
Power and Electrification, Yuri Bochkaryov
Machine Building, Military Industrial Complex and Conversion, Valeriy Maleyev
Industry, Valeriy Mazur
Environmental Protection and Nuclear Safety, Yuriy Kostenko
Statistics, Mykola Borysenko
Management of Consequences of Chernobyl Accident, Volodymyr Kholosha
Finance, Valentin Koronevsky
Justice, Serhiy Holovaty
Transport, Ivan Dankevich
Youth and Sports, Valeriy Borzov
Social Security, Arkadiy Yershov
Labour, Mykhailo Kaskevich

Education, Mykhailo Zgurovsky
Coal Industry, Victor Poltavets
Nationalities, Migration and Religion Issues, vacant
Food and Agriculture, Anatolii Korishko
Press and Information, Mykhailo Onufriychuk
Fisheries, Mykola Shvedenko

Chairman of the Supreme Council, Alexander Moroz

UKRAINIAN EMBASSY
78 Kensington Park Road, London WII 2PL
Tel 0171-727 6312
Ambassador Extraordinary and Plenipotentiary, HE Prof. Sergui Komisarenko, apptd 1992
Minister-Counsellor, Prof. M. Bilousov
Counsellor (Economic and Commercial), Dr B. Savchuk

BRITISH EMBASSY
252025 Kiev Desyatinna 9
Tel: Kiev 462 0011
Ambassador Extraordinary and Plenipotentiary, HE Roy Reeve, apptd 1995
Consul-General and Deputy Head of Mission, R. T. Jenkins, OBE
Defence Attaché, Capt. L. P. C. Merrick, RN
First Secretary (Commercial), T. M. V. Abbott-Watt
BRITISH COUNCIL DIRECTOR – John Day, 9/1 Bessarabska Ploshcha, Flat 9, Kiev 252004.

DEFENCE

Since the demise of the Soviet Union, Russia and Ukraine have clashed over defence issues. All strategic nuclear weapons were placed under a central CIS command in December 1991, but on the abolition of the central command in July 1993 the government claimed possession of all nuclear weapons on its territory. Despite international pressure, the Supreme Council only ratified the START I Treaty in February 1994 and the Nuclear Non-Proliferation Treaty in November 1994.

Under a January 1994 USA–Russia–Ukraine Treaty, Ukraine agreed to transfer its nuclear arsenal to Russia for dismantling over a seven-year period. This was completed in May 1996. In return Ukraine has received a territorial guarantee from Russia, a cancellation of a large part of its debt to Russia, and nuclear security guarantees from Russia and the USA. Ukraine will also receive low-grade uranium from Russia for use in its power stations; economic and technical aid from the USA; US$340 million from the USA to pay for dismantling the weapons; and US$1,000 million to buy some of the enriched uranium from the warheads.

Agreement between Ukraine and Russia over the division of the former Soviet Black Sea Fleet was reached in June 1995. The fleet is to be divided 82:18 Russian: Ukrainian, with Russia retaining the use of and the control of the fleet base at Sevastopol but paying rent in the form of debt relief and energy supplies.

The total armed forces number 452,000 personnel (including 71,000 central staff but excluding the Black Sea Fleet and strategic nuclear forces), with conscripts serving 24 months. The Army numbers 212,600 personnel, with 4,775 main battle tanks, 5,170 armoured personnel carriers and armoured infantry fighting vehicles and 3,685 artillery pieces. The Air Force and air defence forces have 151,000 personnel, with 846 combat aircraft, 24 attack helicopters and 825 surface-to-air missiles. The paramilitary National Guard and Border Guard number 66,000 personnel.

ECONOMY

Throughout 1991–4 the Communist-led government and legislature obstructed economic reform and economic mismanagement resulted. The economy came close to collapse because of hyperinflation caused by the printing of money to support uneconomic enterprises and to pay strikers' wage demands. Industrial output and GDP fell considerably, while Russia threatened to cut all oil and gas supplies as Ukraine could not pay in hard currency. Ukraine has joined the CIS economic union as an associate member and is likely to seek full membership for access to better trading relations with Russia. In March 1995 Ukrainian debt to Russia was US$5,000 million.

President Kuchma has, since September 1994, introduced a wide-ranging economic reform programme. Price controls on food and rents have been lifted, as have currency and export controls; subsidies to industries are being reduced; agricultural reform has begun; mass privatization has started. Ukraine has received large amounts of foreign aid in support of its economic reform programme and for the closure of the Chernobyl nuclear plant which suffered a partial melt-down in 1986. In May 1995 the IMF approved a standby loan of US$867 million; in December 1995 the G7 countries and the IAEA agreed to grant Ukraine US$500 million in exchange for the closure of Chernobyl by 2000; and the USA granted US$1,200 million in February 1996.

A large proportion of Ukraine's debt to Russia has been paid by granting Russian enterprises shares in Ukrainian firms which are to be privatized; the remainder of the debt has been rescheduled. Under economic reform the exchange rate has stabilized and inflation has fallen to 10 per cent a month. Some 8,000 enterprises are to be privatized in 1995–6; President Kuchma issued a decree to privatize most of the remaining enterprises in March 1996.

The southern part of the country contains a coal-mining and iron and steel industrial area which was the largest in the former Soviet Union. Ukraine also contains engineering and chemical industries and ship-building yards on the Black Sea coast. Ukrainian agricultural production is good with large areas under cultivation with wheat, cotton, flax and sugar beet; stock-raising is very important. There are large deposits of coal and salt in the Donets Basin, of iron ore in Krivoy Rog and near Kerch in the Crimea, of manganese in Nikopol, and of quicksilver in Nikitovka.

The major ports are Odessa, Nikolayev, Kerch and Sevastopol.

TRADE WITH UK	1994	1995
Imports from UK	£86,284,000	£111,106,000
Exports to UK	18,072,000	22,941,000

UNITED ARAB EMIRATES
Al-Imarat Al-Arabiya Al-Muttahida

The United Arab Emirates is situated in the south-east of the Arabian peninsula. Six of the emirates lie on the shore of the Gulf between the Musandam peninsula in the east and the Qatar peninsula in the west while the seventh, Fujairah, lies on the Gulf of Oman. The climate varies between hot and humid in May to September and mild with erratic rainfall in October to April. The approximate area is 32,278 sq. miles (83,600 sq. km), and the population (1993 estimate) is 2,310,000, of which 75 per cent are expatriates. The official language is Arabic, and English is widely spoken. The established religion is Islam.

CAPITAL – Abu Dhabi. Population (city) 450,000.

CURRENCY – UAE dirham (Dh) of 100 fils.
FLAG – Horizontal stripes of green over white over black with vertical red stripe in the hoist.
NATIONAL DAY – 2 December.

GOVERNMENT

The United Arab Emirates (formerly the Trucial States) is composed of seven emirates (Abu Dhabi, Ajman, Dubai, Fujairah, Ras al-Khaimah, Sharjah and Umm al-Qaiwain) which came together as an independent state on 2 December 1971 when they ended their individual special treaty relationships with the British government (Ras al-Khaimah joined the other six on 10 February 1972). On independence the Union Government assumed full responsibility for all internal and external affairs apart from some internal matters that remained the prerogative of the individual emirates.

Overall authority lies with the Supreme Council of the seven emirate rulers, each of whom also governs in his own territory. The President and Vice-President are elected every five years by the Supreme Council from among its members. The Supreme Council appoints the Council of Ministers. A 40-member Federal National Council, drawn proportionately from each emirate and composed of appointees of the rulers, studies draft laws referred to it by the Council of Ministers. Each emirate also has its separate government, with Abu Dhabi having an executive council chaired by the Crown Prince.

The legal system consists of both secular and religious courts guided by the Islamic philosophy of justice. Individual emirates retain their own penal codes and courts alongside a federal court system and penal code.

Relations with Iran remain strained over Iran's illegal occupation of three UAE islands in the Gulf (Abu Musa and the Two Tunbs).

HEAD OF STATE
President, HH Sheikh Zayed bin Sultan al-Nahyan (*Abu Dhabi*), *elected* 1971, *re-elected* 1976, 1981, 1986, October 1991
Vice-President, HH Sheikh Maktoun bin Rashid al-Maktoum (*Dubai*), *elected* October 1991

SUPREME COUNCIL *as at August 1996*
President, HH Sheikh Zayed bin Sultan al-Nahyan (*Abu Dhabi*)
Vice-President, HH Sheikh Maktoun bin Rashid al-Maktoum (*Dubai*)
HH Sheikh Sultan bin Mohammed al-Qassimi (*Sharjah*)
HH Sheikh Saqr bin Mohammed al-Qassimi (*Ras Al-Khaimah*)
HH Sheikh Hamid bin Mohammed al-Sharqi (*Fujairah*)
HH Sheikh Humaid bin Rashid al-Nuaimi (*Ajman*)
HH Sheikh Rashid bin Ahmed al-Mualla (*Umm al-Qaiwain*)

COUNCIL OF MINISTERS *as at August 1996*
The President
Prime Minister, The Vice-President
Deputy Prime Minister, Sheikh Sultan bin Zayed al-Nahyan
Finance and Industry, HH Sheikh Hamdan bin Rashid al-Maktoum
Defence, HH Gen. Sheikh Mohammed bin Rashid al-Maktoum
Interior, Lt.-Gen. Dr Mohammed Saeed al-Badi
Foreign Affairs, Rashid Abdullah al-Nuaimi
Communications, Mohammed Saeed al-Mulla
Planning, Sheikh Humaid bin Ahmed al-Mu'alla
Islamic Affairs and Endowments, Sheikh Mohammed bin Ahmed al Khazraji

Water and Electricity, Humaid bin Nasser al-Owais
Economy and Commerce, Saeed Ghobash
Agriculture and Fisheries, Saeed al-Ragabani
Labour and Social Affairs, Seif al-Jarwan
Information and Culture, Khalfan bin Mohammed al-Roumi
Education, Hamad Abdul Rahman al-Madfa
Higher Education, HH Sheikh Nahyan bin Mubarak al-Nahyan
Justice, Dr Abdullah Omran Taryam
Health and Environment, Hamad Abdul Rahman al-Madfa
Petroleum and Mineral Resources, Rakkad bin Salem bin Rakkad
Public Works and Housing, Rakkad bin Salem bin Rakkad
Youth and Sports, Sheikh Faisal bin Khaled al-Qassimi
Minister of State for Cabinet Affairs, Saeed al-Gaith
Minister of State for Financial and Industrial Affairs, Ahmed bin Humaid al-Tayer
Minister of State for Foreign Affairs, Sheikh Hamdan bin Zayed al-Nahyan
Minister of State for Supreme Council Affairs, Sheikh Mohammed bin Saqr al-Qassimi

EMBASSY OF THE UNITED ARAB EMIRATES
30 Prince's Gate, London SW7 1PT
Tel 0171–581 1281
Ambassador Extraordinary and Plenipotentiary, HE Easa Saleh Al-Gurg, CBE, apptd 1991
Minister-Plenipotentiary, Khalid Abdul-Latif Al-Bassam
Military Attaché, Col. B. S. B. Al-Noaimi
Cultural Attaché, A. A. M. Al-Marri

BRITISH EMBASSIES
PO Box 248, Abu Dhabi
Tel: Abu Dhabi 326600
Ambassador Extraordinary and Plenipotentiary, HE Anthony David Harris, CMG, LVO, apptd 1994
First Secretary, Consul and Deputy Head of Mission, P. Morgan
First Secretary (Commercial), J. P. R. Girdlestone
Defence and Military Attaché, Col. C. J. Copeland

PO Box 65, Dubai
Tel: Dubai 521070
Counsellor and Consul-General, C. E. J. Wilton
Deputy Head of Post, Consul and First Secretary (Commercial), J. C. Fisher

BRITISH COUNCIL REPRESENTATIVES
Abu Dhabi – David Latta (*Cultural Attaché*)
Dubai – A. Mackay, PO Box 1636, Dubai

DEFENCE

The armed forces of the emirates were merged in 1976, although Dubai still retains some independent units. The total active armed forces strength is 65,000, of which around 30 per cent are hired or seconded foreign nationals. The Army is 65,000 strong including 15,000 Dubai forces, and is equipped with 133 main battle tanks, 76 light tanks, 728 armoured personnel carriers and armoured infantry fighting vehicles and 172 artillery pieces. The Navy has a strength of 1,500 personnel, with 19 patrol and coastal vessels. The Air Force is 3,500 strong, with 97 combat aircraft and 42 armed helicopters. Some 2,000 Moroccan troops are stationed in the UAE.

ECONOMY

The UAE is the Gulf's third largest oil producer after Saudi Arabia and Iran, producing 3 million barrels per day (bpd) in 1993, and with oil reserves of 200,000 million barrels and gas reserves of 200,000,000 million cubic feet. Oil production in 1993 accounted for 40 per cent of GDP. Other important sectors of the economy are government,

re-exporting, construction, manufacturing (aluminium, cement, chemicals, fertilizers, ship repair), finance and insurance services, and transport and communications. Tourism is growing in importance. Agricultural production (vegetables, dates, fruit, milk, eggs, poultry, flowers, olives, animal husbandry) has increased significantly due to large-scale water desalination and irrigation projects, with 280,000 hectares of agricultural land in 1993. There is no personal or corporate taxation apart from on oil companies and foreign banks.

Fourteen major ports, of which nine are modern container terminals, handled 35 million tonnes of cargo in 1993. Six international airports (Dubai, Abu Dhabi, Sharjah, Ras al-Khaimah, Fujairah, Al Ain) are in operation.

Oil revenues over the past 30 years have enabled the government to invest heavily in education, health and social services, housing, transport and communications infrastructure, and agriculture, and enabled the UAE's citizens to have one of the highest GDPs per capita in the world.

TRADE		1993
Exports		Dhs 85,200m
Imports		67,700m

Trade with UK	1994	1995
Imports from UK	£1,113,578,000	£1,184,136,000
Exports to UK	230,670,000	281,041,000

SOCIAL WELFARE

In 1993 there were 300,000 pupils studying at the 580 government schools, where education is free; some 150,000 (many expatriates) attended 300 private schools. The Emirates University at Al Ain (Abu Dhabi) had 10,900 students in 1993, and the three Colleges of Technology (Abu Dhabi, Dubai, Al Ain) had 1,800 students. There are 29 government and six private hospitals, 96 government health centres and 500 private clinics with a total of 4,300 beds.

ABU DHABI

Abu Dhabi is by far the largest emirate, with an area of 30,888 sq. miles (80,000 sq. km) stretching from Khor al-Odaid in the west to the borders with Dubai in the Jebel Ali area. It includes six villages in the Buraimi oasis, the other three being part of the Sultanate of Oman, and a number of settlements in the Liwa oasis system. Following negotiations with Saudi Arabia, some adjustment of the border has now been made in the Khor al-Odaid region, but the agreement has not yet been ratified. The population of the Emirate (1990) is 889,000.

The Abu Dhabi government controls oil, gas and petrochemical operations in the emirate through the Supreme Petroleum Council. This body in turn issues instructions to the Abu Dhabi National Oil Company (ADNOC) which has majority shareholdings in the oil operating and gas treatment companies, and in oil industry-related companies covering drilling, refining, distribution, chemical manufacture and investment. Production began offshore in 1962 and onshore in 1963. Crude oil production in 1992 was approximately 91.28 million tonnes. With its oil wealth the emirate has seen a period of growth (which is currently slowing down), in Abu Dhabi, Al-Ain in the Buraimi oasis and in the new petrochemical city at Ruwais.

AJMAN AND UMM AL-QAIWAIN

Ajman (100 sq. miles, 259 sq. km) and Umm al-Qaiwain (300 sq. miles, 777 sq. km) are the smallest emirates in area; they have populations (1990) of 92,000 and 21,000 respectively. Both lie on the Gulf coast although Ajman has two inland enclaves at Manama and Masfut. Exploration work continues in both emirates for oil and gas but so far only Umm al-Qaiwain has experienced any success, with the offshore discovery of natural gas, but the field has yet to be commercially developed. The discovery of onshore gas in nearby Sharjah has increased hopes of similar discoveries in both Ajman and Umm al-Qaiwain.

DUBAI

Dubai is the second largest emirate both in size (1,506 sq. miles, 3,900 sq. km) and in population, which is (1990) 559,000. The town of Dubai is the main port for the UAE. Dubai's prosperity was established by this trade long before the discovery of oil in 1966; production began in 1969. The producer in Dubai's offshore oilfields is Dubai Petroleum Company, operated by CONOCO. Production is in excess of 350,000 b.p.d. In 1982 an extensive gas and condensate field was discovered onshore. A small amount of condensate is produced from the onshore Margam field. Oil income has been used to finance Dubai's infrastructure. The port of Jebel Ali, at the heart of an industrial complex, and its immediate area is a free trade zone which is expected to attract more industry.

FUJAIRAH

Fujairah, with an area of 502 sq. miles (1,300 sq. km) and a population (1990) of 76,000, is the most remote of the seven emirates, lying on the Gulf of Oman coast and only connected by a metal road to the rest of the country. Largely agricultural, its population is spread between the slopes of the inland Hajar mountain range and the town of Fujairah itself, together with a number of smaller settlements on the comparatively fertile plain on the coast. Although exploration work continues, there have been no hydrocarbon discoveries in the emirate. However, there are some chrome and other mineral deposits and a free trade zone has been established.

RAS AL-KHAIMAH

Ras al-Khaimah has an area of 656 sq. miles (1,700 sq. km) and a population (1990) of 159,000, of whom more than half live in the town. An ancient sea-port, near to which archaeological remains have been found, Ras al-Khaimah is the most agricultural of the emirates, producing vegetables, dates, fruit and tobacco. In 1982 oil and gas were discovered offshore and this field currently produces approximately 5,000 b.p.d. An industrial area has been developed to the north of the emirate, and the infrastructure has been developed.

SHARJAH

Sharjah, with an area of 1,004 sq. miles (2,600 sq. km) and a population (1990) of 377,000, has declined from its former position as principal town in the area. Oil production began in 1974 and gas discoveries were made in 1982; production now stands at about 55,000 b.p.d. Sharjah is connected by metalled roads to all the other northern emirates. A container port has been constructed on the Gulf of Oman at Khor Fakkan. A free trade zone has been established.

UNITED STATES OF AMERICA

The United States of America occupies nearly all of the North American continent between the Atlantic and Pacific Oceans, in 25° 07' to 49° 23' N. latitude and 66° 57' to 124° 44' W. longitude, its northern boundary adjoining Canada and the southern boundary Mexico. The separate state of Alaska reaches a latitude of 71° 23' N., at Point Barrow. The coastline has a length of about 2,069 miles on the Atlantic, 7,623 miles on the Pacific, 1,060 miles on the Arctic, and 1,631 miles on the Gulf of Mexico.

The principal river is the Mississippi-Missouri-Red (3,710 miles long), traversing the whole country to its mouth in the Gulf of Mexico; its main affluents are the Yellowstone, Platte, Arkansas, and Ohio rivers. The chain of the Rocky Mountains separates the western portion of the country from the remainder. West of these, bordering the Pacific coast, the Cascade Mountains and Sierra Nevada form the outer edge of a high tableland, consisting in part of stony and sandy desert and partly of grazing land and forested mountains, and including the Great Salt Lake, which extends to the Rocky Mountains. In the eastern states large forests still exist, the remnants of the forests which formerly extended over all the Atlantic slope. The highest point is Mount McKinley (20,320 ft) in Alaska, and the lowest point of dry land is in Death Valley (Inyo, California), 282 ft below sea-level.

AREA AND POPULATION

	Total land area 1990 (sq. miles)	Population census 1990
The United States (a)	3,536,278	248,709,873
Outlying areas under US jurisdiction	4,043	3,847,309
Territories	4,027	3,847,116
Puerto Rico	3,427	3,522,037
Guam	210	133,152
US Virgin Islands	134	101,809
American Samoa	77	46,773
Northern Mariana Is.	179	43,345
Other possessions	16	193
Population abroad (b)	–	925,845
TOTAL	3,540,321	253,483,027

(a) the 50 states and the Federal District of Columbia
(b) excludes US citizens temporarily abroad on business

The total population was estimated at 259,681,000 on 1 January 1994

VITAL STATISTICS

In 1993 live births were 4,000,240, a rate of 15.5 per 1,000 of population. Deaths were 2,268,553, a rate of 8.8 per 1,000 of population. In 1993 (provisional figures) marriages were 2,334,000, a rate of 9.0 per 1,000 of population. Divorces were approximately 1,187,000, a rate of 4.6 per 1,000 of population.

RESIDENT POPULATION BY RACE 1990 (*Thousands*)

White	199,686.1
Black	29,986.1
*American Indian	1,959.2
Chinese	1,645.5
Filipino	1,406.8
Japanese	847.6
Asian Indian	815.4
Korean	798.8
Vietnamese	614.5
Other Asian	780.0
Pacific Islander	365.0
All other races	9,804.8
†Hispanic origin	22,354.1
Cuban	1,043.9
Mexican	13,495.9
Puerto Rican	2,727.8
Other Hispanic	5,086.4
TOTAL	248,709.9

*Includes Eskimo and Aleut
†Persons of Hispanic origin may be of any race

IMMIGRATION

From 1820 to 1995, 62,224,327 immigrants were admitted to the United States. Total number of immigrants in 1995 was 720,461, of which 277,192 came from North and South America (89,932 from Mexico), 267,931 from Asia and 128,185 from Europe.

LARGEST CITIES *1994 estimate*

ΨNew York, NY	7,333,253
ΨLos Angeles, California	3,448,613
ΨChicago, Illinois	2,731,743
ΨHouston, Texas	1,702,086
ΨPhiladelphia, Pennsylvania	1,524,249
ΨSan Diego, California	1,151,977
Phoenix, Arizona	1,048,949
Dallas, Texas	1,022,830
ΨDetroit, Michigan	992,038
San Antonio, Texas	968,905

Ψ seaport

CAPITAL

The federal capital is the City of Washington in the District of Columbia. It is situated on the west central edge of Maryland, opposite the state of Virginia, on the left bank of the Potomac at its confluence with the Anacostia. The area of the District of Columbia (with which the City of Washington is considered co-extensive) is 61 sq. miles, with a resident population (mid-1992 estimate) of 585,221. The population of the metropolitan area in 1992 was estimated at 4,360,349. The District of Columbia is governed by an elected mayor and City Council.

CURRENCY – The dollar ($) of 100 cents.

FLAG – Thirteen horizontal stripes, alternately red and white, with blue canton in the fly showing 50 white stars in nine horizontal rows of six and five alternately (known as the Star-Spangled Banner).

NATIONAL ANTHEM – The Star-Spangled Banner.

NATIONAL DAY – 4 July (Independence Day).

GOVERNMENT

The United States of America is a federal republic consisting of 50 states and the federal District of Columbia and of organized territories. Of the present 50 states, 13 are original states, seven were admitted without previous organization as territories, and 30 were admitted after such organization.

THE STATES OF THE UNION

STATE (with date and *order* of admission)	LAND AREA sq. m.	POPULATION (1990 census)	CAPITAL	GOVERNOR (term of office in years, and expiry year)	
Alabama (Ala.) (1819) *(22)*	50,750	4,040,587	Montgomery	Fob James *(R)*	(4 – 1999)
Alaska (1959) *(49)*	570,374	550,043	Juneau	Tony Knowles *(D)*	(4 – 1998)
Arizona (Ariz.) (1912) *(48)*	113,642	3,665,228	Phoenix	Fife Symington *(R)*	(4 – 1999)
Arkansas (Ark.) (1836) *(25)*	52,075	2,350,725	Little Rock	Mike Huckabee *(R)*	(? – 1999)
California (Calif.) (1850) *(31)*	155,973	29,760,021	Sacramento	Pete Wilson *(R)*	(4 – 1999)
Colorado (Colo.) (1876) *(38)*	103,729	3,294,394	Denver	Roy Romer *(D)*	(4 – 1999)
Connecticut (Conn.) § (1788) *(5)*	4,845	3,287,116	Hartford	John Rowland *(R)*	(4 – 1999)
Delaware (Del.) § (1787) *(1)*	1,955	666,168	Dover	Tom Carper *(D)*	(4 – 1997)
Florida (Fla.) (1845) *(27)*	53,997	12,937,926	Tallahassee	Lawton Chiles *(D)*	(4 – 1999)
Georgia (Ga.) § (1788) *(4)*	57,919	6,478,216	Atlanta	Zell Miller *(D)*	(4 – 1999)
Hawaii (1959) *(50)*	6,423	1,108,229	Honolulu	Ben Cayetano *(D)*	(4 – 1998)
Idaho (1890) *(43)*	82,751	1,006,749	Boise	Phil Barr *(R)*	(4 – 1999)
Illinois (Ill.) (1818) *(21)*	55,593	11,430,602	Springfield	Jim Edgar *(R)*	(4 – 1999)
Indiana (Ind.) (1816) *(19)*	35,870	5,544,159	Indianapolis	Evan Bayh *(D)*	(4 – 1997)
Iowa (1846) *(29)*	55,875	2,776,755	Des Moines	Terry Branstad *(R)*	(4 – 1999)
Kansas (Kan.) (1861) *(34)*	81,823	2,477,574	Topeka	Bill Graves *(R)*	(4 – 1999)
Kentucky (Ky.) (1792) *(15)*	39,732	3,685,296	Frankfort	Paul Patton *(D)*	(4 – 1999)
Louisiana (La.) (1812) *(18)*	43,566	4,219,973	Baton Rouge	Murphy Foster *(R)*	(4 – 2000)
Maine (Me.) (1820) *(23)*	30,865	1,227,928	Augusta	Angus King *(I)*	(4 – 1999)
Maryland (Md.) § (1788) (7)	9,775	4,781,468	Annapolis	Paris Glendening *(D)*	(4 – 1999)
Massachusetts (Mass.) § (1788) *(6)*	7,838	6,016,425	Boston	William Weld *(R)*	(4 – 1999)
Michigan (Mich.) (1837) *(26)*	56,809	9,295,297	Lansing	John Engler *(R)*	(4 – 1999)
Minnesota (Minn.) (1858) *(32)*	79,617	4,375,099	St Paul	Arne Carlson *(R)*	(4 – 1999)
Mississippi (Miss.) (1817) *(20)*	46,914	2,573,216	Jackson	Kirk Fordice *(R)*	(4 – 2000)
Missouri (Mo.) (1821) *(24)*	68,898	5,117,073	Jefferson City	Mel Carnahan *(D)*	(4 – 1997)
Montana (Mont.) (1889) *(41)*	145,556	799,065	Helena	Marc Raciot *(R)*	(4 – 1997)
Nebraska (Neb.) (1867) *(37)*	76,878	1,578,385	Lincoln	Ben Nelson *(D)*	(4 – 1999)
Nevada (Nev.) (1864) *(36)*	109,806	1,201,833	Carson City	Robert J. Miller *(D)*	(4 – 1999)
New Hampshire (NH) § (1788) *(9)*	8,969	1,109,252	Concord	Steve Merrill *(R)*	(2 – 1997)
New Jersey (NJ) § (1787) *(3)*	7,419	7,730,188	Trenton	Christine Whitman *(R)*	(4 – 1998)
New Mexico (NM) (1912) *(47)*	121,365	1,515,069	Santa Fé	Gary Johnson *(R)*	(4 – 1999)
New York (NY) § (1788) *(11)*	47,224	17,990,455	Albany	George Pataki *(R)*	(4 – 1999)
North Carolina (NC) § (1789) *(12)*	48,718	6,628,637	Raleigh	James B. Hunt, jun. *(D)*	(4 – 1997)
North Dakota (ND) (1889) *(39)*	68,994	638,800	Bismarck	Edward Schafer *(R)*	(4 – 1997)
Ohio (1803) *(17)*	40,953	10,847,115	Columbus	George Voinovich *(R)*	(4 – 1999)
Oklahoma (Okla.) (1907) *(46)*	68,679	3,145,585	Oklahoma City	Frank Keating *(R)*	(4 – 1999)
Oregon (Ore.) (1859) *(33)*	96,003	2,842,321	Salem	John Kitzhaber *(D)*	(4 – 1999)
Pennsylvania (Pa.) § (1787) *(2)*	44,820	11,881,643	Harrisburg	Tom Ridge *(R)*	(4 – 1999)
Rhode Island (RI) § (1790) *(13)*	1,045	1,003,464	Providence	Lincoln Almond *(R)*	(2 – 1997)
South Carolina (SC) § (1788) *(8)*	30,111	3,486,703	Columbia	David Beasley *(R)*	(4 – 1999)
South Dakota (SD) (1889) *(40)*	75,896	696,004	Pierre	William Janklow *(R)*	(4 – 1999)
Tennessee (Tenn.) (1796) *(16)*	41,220	4,877,185	Nashville	Don Sundquist *(R)*	(4 – 1999)
Texas (1845) *(28)*	261,914	16,986,510	Austin	George W. Bush *(R)*	(4 – 1999)
Utah (1896) *(45)*	82,168	1,722,850	Salt Lake City	Mike Leavitt *(R)*	(4 – 1999)
Vermont (Vt.) (1791) *(14)*	9,249	562,758	Montpelier	Howard Dean *(D)*	(2 – 1997)
Virginia (Va.) § (1788) *(10)*	39,598	6,187,358	Richmond	George Allen *(R)*	(4 – 1998)
Washington (Wash.) (1889) *(42)*	66,581	4,866,692	Olympia	Mike Lowry *(D)*	(4 – 1997)
West Virginia (W. Va.) (1863) *(35)*	24,087	1,793,477	Charleston	Gaston Caperton *(D)*	(4 – 1997)
Wisconsin (Wis.) (1848) *(30)*	54,314	4,891,769	Madison	Tommy Thompson *(R)*	(4 – 1999)
Wyoming (Wyo.) (1890) *(44)*	97,105	453,588	Cheyenne	Jim Geringer *(R)*	(4 – 1999)
Dist. of Columbia (DC) (1791)	61	606,900	—	Marion Barry *(D)* *(Mayor)*	

OUTLYING TERRITORIES AND POSSESSIONS

American Samoa	77	46,773	Pago Pago	A. P. Lutali *(D)*	(4 – 1997)
Guam	210	133,152	Agaña	Carl Gutierrez *(D)*	(4 – 1999)
Northern Mariana Islands	179	43,345	Saipan	Froilan C. Tenorio *(D)*	(4 – 1998)
Puerto Rico	3,427	3,522,037	San Juan	Dr Pedro J. Rossello *(PNP)*	(4 – 1997)
US Virgin Islands	134	101,809	Charlotte Amalie	Roy Schneider *(I)*	(4 – 1999)

§The 13 original states
D Democratic Party; *I* Independent; *PNP* New Progressive Party; *R* Republican Party

By the constitution of 17 September 1787 (to which amendments were added in 1791, 1798, 1804, 1865, 1868, 1870, 1913, 1920, 1933, 1951, 1961, 1964, 1967, 1971 and 1992), the government of the United States is entrusted to three separate authorities: the executive (the President and Cabinet), the legislature (Congress) and the judicature.

The President is indirectly elected every four years. There is also a Vice-President, who, should the President die, becomes President for the remainder of the term. The tenure of the presidency is limited to two terms.

The President, with the consent of the Senate, appoints the Cabinet officers and all the chief officials. He makes recommendation of a general nature to Congress, and when laws are passed by Congress he may return them to Congress with a veto. But if a measure so vetoed is again passed by both Houses of Congress by two-thirds majority in each House, it becomes law, notwithstanding the objection of the President. The President must be at least 35 years of age and a native citizen of the United States.

Presidential elections

Each state elects (on the first Tuesday after the first Monday in November of the year preceding the year in which the presidential term expires) a number of electors, equal to the whole number of Senators and Representatives to which the state may be entitled in the Congress. The electors for each state meet in their respective states on the first Monday after the second Wednesday in December following, and vote for a President by ballot. The ballots are then sent to Washington, and opened on 6 January by the President of the Senate in the presence of Congress. The candidate who has received a majority of the whole number of electoral votes cast is declared President for the ensuing term. If no one has a majority, then from the highest on the list (not exceeding three) the House of Representatives elects a President, the votes being taken by states, the representation from each state having one vote. A presidential term begins at noon on 20 January.

President of the United States, William Jefferson Blythe IV Clinton, *born* 19 August 1946, *sworn in* 20 January 1993. Democrat

Vice-President, Albert Gore, jun., *born* 31 March 1948, *sworn in* 20 January 1993

The Cabinet *as at August 1996*

Secretary of State, Warren Christopher
Secretary of the Treasury, Robert Rubin
Secretary of Defence, Dr William Perry
Attorney-General, Janet Reno
Secretary of the Interior, Bruce Babbit
Secretary of Agriculture, Daniel Glickman
Secretary of Commerce, Mickey Kantor
Secretary of Labour, Robert Reich
Secretary of Health and Human Services, Donna Shalala
Secretary of Housing and Urban Development, Henry Cisneros
Secretary of Transportation, Federico Pena
Secretary of Energy, Hazel O'Leary
Secretary of Education, Richard Riley
Secretary of Veterans' Affairs, Jesse Brown
Ambassador to the UN, Madeleine Albright
US Trade Representative, Charlene Barshefsky
Administrator, Environmental Protection Agency, Carol Browner
Director, Office of Management and Budget, Franklin Raines
National Security Adviser, Anthony Lake
White House Chief of Staff, Leon Panetta

Other senior positions:
Director of CIA, John Deutch

Director, Office of National Drug Control Policy, Gen. Barry McCaffrey
Director of FBI, Louis Freeh
Chairman, Federal Reserve Board of Governors, Alan Greenspan

UNITED STATES EMBASSY
24 Grosvenor Square, London WIA IAE
Tel 0171-499 9000
Ambassador Extraordinary and Plenipotentiary, HE The Honourable Adm. William J. Crowe, jun., apptd 1994
Deputy Chief of Mission, R. Bradtke
Defence and Naval Attaché, Capt. J. E. Hart
Minister-Counsellors, L. M. Dent, jun. (*Administrative*); C. A. Ford (*Commercial*); M. N. Robinson (*Consular*)

BRITISH EMBASSY
3100 Massachusetts Avenue NW, Washington DC 20008
Tel: Washington DC 462 1340
Ambassador Extraordinary and Plenipotentiary, HE Sir John Kerr, KCMG, apptd 1995
Ministers, H. P. Evans (*Economic*); S. Webb (*Defence Equipment*); D. B. Logan, CMG; C. H. Mak, E. B. Wiggam, CBE (*Hong Kong Economic and Trade Affairs*)
Head of British Defence Staff and Defence Attaché, Rear-Adm. D. A. Blackburn, LVO, RN
Counsellor, H. Parkinson (*Management and HM Consul-General*)
Consul-General (*New York*) *and Director-General of Trade and Investment*, Jeffrey Ling, CMG
Cultural Attaché and British Council Director, David Evans

BRITISH CONSULATES-GENERAL – Atlanta, Boston, Chicago, Houston, Los Angeles, New York and San Francisco.

BRITISH CONSULATES – Anchorage, Charlotte, Cleveland, Dallas, Denver, Kansas City, Miami, Minneapolis, New Orleans, Orlando, Philadelphia, Portland, St Louis, Salt Lake City, Seattle and Puerto Rico.

BRITISH-AMERICAN CHAMBER OF COMMERCE, 275 Madison Avenue, New York 10016; UK OFFICE, Suite 201, High Holborn, London WCIV 6RR

THE CONGRESS

Legislative power is vested in two houses, the Senate and the House of Representatives. The Senate has 100 members, two Senators from each state, elected for the term of six years, and each Senator has one vote. Representatives are chosen in each state, by popular vote, for two years.

The House of Representatives consists of 435 Representatives, a resident commissioner from Puerto Rico and a delegate each from American Samoa, the District of Columbia, Guam and the Virgin Islands.

Members of the 104th Congress were elected on 2 November 1994. The 104th Congress is constituted as follows:

Senate – Republicans 53; Democrats 47; total 100
House of Representatives – Republicans 235; Democrats 198; Independent 1; Vacant 1; total 435 (August 1996)

President of the Senate, The Vice-President
Senate Majority Leader, Trent Lott (*R*), *Mississippi*
Speaker of the House of Representatives, Newton Gingrich (*R*), *Georgia*
Secretary of the Senate, Kelly D. Johnson, *Virginia*
Clerk of the House of Representatives, Robin H. Carle, *Virginia*

THE JUDICATURE

The federal judiciary consists of three sets of federal courts: the Supreme Court at Washington DC, consisting of a

Chief Justice and eight Associate Justices, with original jurisdiction in cases where a state is a party to the suit, and with appellate jurisdiction from inferior federal courts and from the judgments of the highest courts of the states; the United States Courts of Appeals, dealing with appeals from district courts and from certain federal administrative agencies, and consisting of 168 circuit judges within 13 circuits; the 94 United States district courts served by 575 district court judges.

THE SUPREME COURT
US Supreme Court Building, Washington DC 20543

Chief Justice, William H. Rehnquist, *Arizona*, apptd 1986

Associate Justices
John Paul Stevens, *Illinois*, apptd 1975
Sandra Day O'Connor, *Arizona*, apptd 1981
Antonin Scalia, *Virginia*, apptd 1986
Anthony M. Kennedy, *California*, apptd 1988
David H. Souter, *New Hampshire*, apptd 1990
Clarence Thomas, *Georgia*, apptd 1991
Ruth Bader Ginsburg, *New York*, apptd 1993
Stephen Breyer, *Massachusetts*, apptd 1994

Clerk of the Supreme Court, William K. Suter

CRIMINAL STATISTICS *Number of offences*

	1993	1994
Murder and non-negligent manslaughter	24,526	23,305
Forcible rape	106,014	102,096
Robbery	659,757	618,817
Aggravated assault	1,135,099	1,119,950
Burglary	2,834,808	2,712,156
Larceny – theft	7,820,909	7,876,254
Thefts of motor vehicles	1,561,047	1,539,097
Total	14,142,160	13,991,675

DEFENCE

Each military department is separately organized and functions under the direction, authority and control of the Secretary of Defence. The Air Force has primary responsibility for the Department of Defence space development programmes and projects.

Secretary of Defence (in the Cabinet), Dr William Perry
Chairman, Joint Chiefs of Staff, Gen. John Shalikashvili

STRENGTHS *as at 30 May 1995*
The US Army had a strength of 527,514. The strength of the Navy was 445,902 active duty personnel. The strength of the Marine Corps was 171,928 active duty personnel. The Air Force had 409,127 officers and airmen on active duty.

DEPLOYMENT

Under strategic command the USA has 384 submarine-launched ballistic missiles, 597 inter-continental ballistic missiles and 195 heavy nuclear-capable bombers, together with multiple intelligence satellites, radars and early warning systems throughout the world. The Army deploys 12,245 main battle tanks, 123 light tanks, 30,587 armoured infantry fighting vehicles and armoured personnel carriers, 8,624 artillery pieces, 361 aircraft and 1,595 armed helicopters. The Navy deploys 16 strategic submarines, 82 tactical submarines, 12 aircraft carriers, 32 cruisers, 46 destroyers, 49 frigates, 21 patrol and coastal combatants, 155 amphibious and support ships, 1,634 combat aircraft and 301 armed helicopters. The Marine Corps has 271 main battle tanks, 1,322 amphibious armoured vehicles, 584 artillery pieces, 478 combat aircraft and 189 armed helicopters. The Air Force deploys 204 long-range and 2,655 tactical combat aircraft and 3,075 transport, tanker and training aircraft. The major deployments of US personnel overseas are: Germany (86,600); UK (11,450); Italy (14,890); Mediterranean (16,500); Japan (45,500); South Korea (36,450); Panama (9,120); Spain (3,130); Turkey (2,950).

FINANCE

BUDGET

	1994	1995
Total receipts	$1,257.2 bn	$1,350.6 bn
Total outlay	1,460.6 bn	1,514.4 bn
Defence	281.5 bn	272.2 bn
Social security	319.6 bn	335.8 bn
Income security	214.0 bn	220.2 bn
Debt interest	203.0 bn	232.2 bn

SOCIAL WELFARE EXPENDITURE 1992

	Total	*Per capita*
Social insurance	$616,975 m	$2,369
Education	292,199 m	1,126
Public aid	207,945 m	801
Health and medical	71,035 m	274
Veterans' programmes	34,767 m	130
Other social welfare	21,532 m	83
Housing	20,617 m	79
TOTAL	1,265,070 m	4,863

PUBLIC DEBT
At the end of September 1992 the total gross federal debt stood at US$4,002,815 million.

ECONOMY

GROSS DOMESTIC PRODUCT BY INDUSTRY 1994

	US$ millions
Private industries	6,000,021
Agriculture, forestry, fisheries	117,848
Mining	90,058
Construction	269,232
Manufacturing	1,197,098
Transportation and public utilities	606,354
Wholesale trade	461,863
Retail trade	609,908
Finance, insurance, and real estate	1,273,678
Services	1,342,720
Government and government enterprises	931,336
Statistical discrepancy	31,262
TOTAL	12,931,378

AGRICULTURE
The total number of farms in 1996 was 2,063,010, with a total area of land in farms of 968,048,000 acres, and an average acreage per farm of 469 acres. The total number of people employed on farms during the week of 9–15 April 1996 was 2,906,000, of whom 455,000 were unpaid workers, 780,000 hired workers and 207,000 agricultural service workers. Principal crops are corn for grain, soybeans, wheat hay, cotton, tobacco, grain sorghums, potatoes, oranges and barley.

Livestock on farms on 1 January 1995 and 1996 was:

	1995	1996
Cattle and calves	102,755,000	103,819,000
Milk cows	9,487,000	9,412,000
Sheep and lambs	8,886,000	8,457,000
Hogs and pigs	59,990,000	58,700,000
Chickens	383,829,000	384,241,000

Gross income from farming in 1995 was US$210,399 million, of which cash receipts from marketing were US$185,750 million and government payments US$7,252 million. Cash income from all crops in 1995 was US$98,906 million and from livestock and livestock products US$86,844 million.

MINERALS

The value of non-fuel raw mineral production in 1993 totalled an estimated US$31,844 million compared with US$32,012 million in 1992. Mineral exports in 1993 were valued at US$26,904 million, and imports at US$41,583 million.

Production ('000 metric tons)	1993	1994
Iron ore	55,661	58,400
Phosphate rock	35,494	41,100
Zinc ore	488	570
Refined copper	1,801	1,830
Refined lead	328	340

ENERGY

Production in 1994 was 70.62 quadrillion BTU, principally coal, natural gas and crude oil. Coal accounted for almost half of energy exports of 4.12 quadrillion BTU. Imports were 22.71 quadrillion BTU, of which crude oil was 15.34 quadrillion BTU, to meet consumption of 88.9 quadrillion BTU (quadrillion=10^{15}).

LABOUR

The civilian labour force was 133,699,000 in June 1996. Unemployment was estimated at 7,060,000 in June 1996 (5.3 per cent) (5.6 per cent in June 1995).

TRADE	1991	1992
General imports		
c.i.f. value	US$510,168m	US$553,335m
customs value	488,453	532,665
Exports and re-exports		
†f.a.s. value	421,853	447,471
Trade balance		
f.a.s. exports: c.i.f. imports	−88,315	−105,864
f.a.s. exports: customs imports	−65,723	−84,501

†excluding military aid

Principal sources of imports were Asian countries (of which Japan contributed 41 per cent), north and central America (of which Canada 68 per cent), Europe (of which EC countries 83 per cent). Principal destinations for exports and re-exports were Asian states (of which Japan took 34 per cent), north and central America (of which Canada 63 per cent), Europe (of which EC 83 per cent).

Trade with UK	1994	1995
Imports from UK	£16,792,741,000	£17,949,473,000
Exports to UK	17,728,209,000	20,268,863,000

COMMUNICATIONS

Revenue, etc., of class I line-haul railroads (US$ thousands):

	1993	1994
Operating revenue	28,824,852	30,808,977
Operating expenses	24,516,966	25,511,105
Railroad track (miles)	186,288	183,685
Employees	193,000	190,000

In 1994 there were 3.9 million miles of public roads and streets, of which 3.09 million miles were in rural areas and 813,591 miles were in urban areas. Surfaced roads and streets account for 59.8 per cent of the total. An estimated total of US$90,074 million was spent in 1994 on roads and streets in the United States. In 1994 there were 40,676 deaths caused by motor vehicle accidents. The death rate per 100 million vehicle-miles of travel was 1.72 in 1994 compared with 1.75 in 1993.

The ocean-going merchant marine on 1 April 1995 consisted of 540 vessels of 1,000 gross tons and over, of which 351 were privately-owned and 189 were government-owned ships. There were 138 ships in the National Defence Reserve Fleet of inactive government-owned vessels.

According to preliminary figures, US domestic and international scheduled airlines in 1995 carried 547,432,082 passengers over 540,366,065 revenue passenger-miles. Air cargo ton-miles were distributed as follows: freight and express 20,649,503,543; and air mail 2,610,209,968. Total operating revenues of all US scheduled airlines were US$94,169,120,402 in 1995. Total operating expenses rose to US$88,279,585,679 in 1995. Scheduled operations showed a net operating profit of US$5,889,534,723 in 1995, compared with a net operating profit of US$2,710,058,686 in 1994.

EDUCATION

All the states and the District of Columbia have compulsory school attendance laws. In general, children are obliged to attend school from seven to 16 years of age. In the autumn of 1995, 50,362,000 children were enrolled in regular elementary and secondary day schools, of whom 5.7 million or 11.3 per cent attended private schools.

During the 1993−4 school year, the average daily attendance in regular public elementary and secondary day schools was 40,146,393. In the 1994−5 school year 2,288,000 students graduated from regular public high schools and 264,000 graduated from private high school. In addition an estimated 498,000 received high school equivalency certificates. Public school teachers numbered 2,551,712, with an average salary of US$36,802.

Most of the revenue for public elementary and secondary school purposes comes from federal, state, and local governments. Less than three per cent comes from gifts and from tuition and transportation fees. Revenue receipts during 1993−4 amounted to US$260,142 million; 7 per cent from the federal government, 45.2 per cent from state governments, and 45.1 per cent from local sources. Estimated current expenditure in the 1993−4 school year was US$231,522 million; for sites, buildings, furniture and equipment expenditures US$23,747 million; for interest on school debt US$5,335 million.

HIGHER EDUCATION

In the autumn of 1995, total enrolment in universities, colleges, professional schools, and two-year schools numbered 14,210,000.

During 1993−4 the major fields for bachelor's degrees were business and management (246,654), social sciences (133,680), education (107,600) and engineering (62,220). First-profession degrees in law (40,044) and medicine (15,368) predominated. Master's degrees were heavily concentrated in education (98,938) and business and management (93,437). The most popular fields of study for doctorates were education (6,908) and engineering (5,963). Total expenditures for colleges and universities during the 1993−4 academic year were US$191,584 million.

Among the better-known universities are: Harvard, founded at Cambridge, Mass. in 1636, and named after John Harvard of Emmanuel College, Cambridge, England, who bequeathed to it his library and a sum of money in 1638; Yale, founded at New Haven, Connecticut, in 1701; Princeton, NJ, founded 1746.

US TERRITORIES, ETC

Responsibility for territorial affairs generally is centred in the Office of the Assistant Secretary, Territorial and International Affairs, Department of the Interior, Washington DC.

As well as the territories mentioned below, the USA also exercises sovereignty over the following:

Johnston Atoll – two small islands, less than 1 sq. mile in area, to the south-west of Hawaii; administered by the US Air Force.

Midway Islands – two islands (area, 3 sq. miles), at the western end of the Hawaiian chain; administered by the US Navy.

Wake Islands – area about 3 sq. miles and average elevation of less than 3 metres, lying about 2,300 miles west of Hawaii; administered by the US Air Force.

Certain small guano islands, rocks or keys, considered as appertaining to the USA.

THE COMMONWEALTH OF PUERTO RICO

Puerto Rico (Rich Port) is an island of the Greater Antilles group in the West Indies, and lies between 17° 50′ and 18° 30′ N. latitude and 65° 30′ and 67° 15′ W. longitude, with a total area of 3,427 sq. miles (8,875 sq. km), and a population (1994 estimate) of 3,600,000. The 1990 census put the population at 3,522,037. The majority of the inhabitants are of Spanish descent, and Spanish and English are the official languages.

Puerto Rico was discovered in 1493 by Columbus and explored by Ponce de León in 1508. It was a Spanish possession until 1898, when the USA took formal possession as a result of the Spanish-American War.

The 1952 constitution establishes the Commonwealth of Puerto Rico with full powers of local government. The Legislative Assembly consists of two elected houses; the Senate of 27 members and the House of Representatives of 51 members. The term of the Legislative Assembly is four years. The Governor is popularly elected for a term of four years. Residents of Puerto Rico are US citizens. Puerto Rico is represented in Congress by a Resident Commissioner, elected for a term of four years, who has a seat in the House of Representatives but not a vote, although he has a right to vote on those committees of which he is a member. A plebiscite on the future constitutional status of Puerto Rico was held on 14 November 1993 in which 48 per cent voted to maintain the existing Commonwealth status, 46 per cent voted for full US statehood and 4 per cent for independence. The existing Commonwealth status continues which gives Puerto Rico the benefit of a common market with the USA and leaves it without the burden of federal taxes.

Preliminary 1994–5 figures for the Commonwealth government's budget were receipts, US$16,629 million. Manufacturing added US$16,614 million to net Commonwealth income in 1994–5 (preliminary figures), trade US$4,045 million, finance, insurance and real estate US$4,563 million and agriculture US$425 million. Principal crops are sugar cane, coffee, vegetables, fruits and tobacco. Most valuable areas of manufacturing are chemicals and allied products, metal products and machinery, and food processing.

CAPITAL – ΨSan Juan, population of the municipality (1990), 437,745; Other major towns are: Bayamón (220,262); ΨPonce (187,749); and Carolina (177,806).

Governor, Dr Pedro J. Rossello

TRADE	1993–4	1994–5
Total Imports	US$16,654m	US$18,817m
Total Exports	21,753m	23,811m

Trade with UK	1994	1995
Imports from UK	£309,154,000	£466,196,000
Exports to UK	77,236,000	81,961,000

GUAM

Guam, the largest of the Mariana Islands in the north Pacific Ocean, lies in 13° 26′ N. latitude and 144° 39′ E. longitude and has an area of about 210 sq. miles (544 sq. km). The population (1990 estimate) is 133,152, mostly of Chamorro stock mingled with Filipino and Spanish blood. The Chamorro language belongs to the Malayo-Polynesian family, but with considerable admixture of Spanish. Chamorro and English are the official languages and most residents are bilingual.

Guam was occupied by the Japanese in December 1941 but was recaptured by US forces in 1944. Under the Organic Act of Guam 1950, Guam has statutory powers of self-government, and Guamanians are US citizens. A 21-member unicameral legislature is elected biennially. The Governor and Lieutenant-Governor are popularly elected. A non-voting Delegate is elected to serve in the US House of Representatives. There is also a District Court of Guam, with original jurisdiction in cases under federal law.

Guam's two main sources of revenue are tourism and US military spending.

CAPITAL – Agaña. Port of entry, ΨApra.

Governor, Carl Gutierrez
Lt.-Governor, Frank Blas

AMERICAN SAMOA

American Samoa consists of the islands of Tutuila, Anu'u, Ofu, Olesega, Ta'u, Rose and Swains Islands, with a total area of 77 sq. miles (199 sq. km). Tutuila, the largest of the group, has an area of 52 sq. miles and a magnificent harbour at Pago Pago. The remaining islands have an area of about 24 sq. miles. The population (1990 estimate) is 46,773. Tuna and copra are the chief exports.

American Samoans are US nationals, but some have acquired citizenship through service in the United States armed forces or other naturalization procedure. The 1960 constitution grants American Samoa a measure of self-government, with certain powers reserved to the US Secretary of the Interior. There is a bicameral legislature with popularly elected Representatives and Governors and a popularly elected Governor. A non-voting Delegate is elected to serve in the US House of Representatives.

SEAT OF GOVERNMENT – Fagatogo.

Governor, A. P. Lutali
Lt.-Governor, Tauese P. Sunia

THE VIRGIN ISLANDS

The US Virgin Islands were purchased from Denmark and proclaimed US territory in 1917. The total area of the islands is 134 sq. miles (347 sq. km), with a population (1990) of 101,809. There are three main islands, St Thomas (28 sq. miles), St Croix (84 sq. miles), St John (20 sq. miles) and about 50 small islets or cays, mostly uninhabited.

Under the provisions of the Revised Organic Act of the Virgin Islands 1954, legislative power is vested in the Legislature, a unicameral body composed of 15 senators popularly elected for two-year terms. The Governor is popularly elected. Virgin Islanders are US citizens. A non-voting Delegate is elected to serve in the US House of Representatives. A referendum is to take place at a future date to determine the future political status of the islands.

CAPITAL – ΨCharlotte Amalie on St Thomas. Population (1980) 11,756.

Governor, Roy Schneider
Lt.-Governor, Derek M. Hodge

TRADE WITH UK	1994	1995
Imports from UK	£178,500,000	£4,018,000
Exports to UK	365,000	95,000

NORTHERN MARIANA ISLANDS

The land area of the Northern Mariana Islands is 179 sq. miles (464 sq. km) with an estimated population (1990) of 43,345. The USA administered the islands as part of a UN Trusteeship until the trusteeship agreement was terminated in 1986 bringing fully into effect a 1976 congressional law establishing a commonwealth of the Northern Mariana Islands. Most of the residents became US citizens. There is a popularly elected bicameral legislature and a popularly elected Governor.

SEAT OF GOVERNMENT – Saipan.
Population (1990 estimate) 39,090.

Governor, Froilan C. Tenorio
Lt.-Governor, Benjamin M. Manglona

THE PANAMA CANAL

As a result of the Panama Canal Treaty 1977, the Canal Zone was disestablished, with all jurisdiction over the former Canal Zone reverting to Panama with effect from 1 October 1979. Under the treaty, the United States is allowed the use of operating areas for the Panama Canal, together with several military bases, although the Republic of Panama is sovereign in all such areas. The Panama Canal Commission, an arm of the US Government, will continue to operate the canal until noon on 31 December 1999.

In the fiscal year 1994, the total number of transits by ocean-going commercial traffic was 12,337; canal net tons totalled 194,289,433; cargo tons totalled 170,538,437.

URUGUAY
República Oriental del Uruguay

Uruguay is situated on the east coast of the Rio de la Plata in South America, in 30° to 35° S. latitude and 53° 15' to 57° 42' W. longitude, with an area of 68,037 sq. miles (176,215 sq. km). The country consists mainly of undulating grassy plains. The principal river is the Rio Negro (with its tributary the Yi), flowing from north-east to south-west into the Rio Uruguay. The climate is temperate.

The population (1992) is 3,116,802, predominantly of Spanish and Italian descent. Spanish is the official language. Many Uruguayans are Roman Catholics. There is no established church.

CAPITAL – ΨMontevideo, population (1992) 1,383,660. Other centres are Salto, ΨPaysandu, Mercedes, Minas, Melo, Rivera and Punta del Este.
CURRENCY – New Uruguayan peso of 100 centésimos.

FLAG – Four blue and five white horizontal stripes surcharged with sun on a white ground in the top corner, next flagstaff.
NATIONAL ANTHEM – Orientales, La Patria O La Tumba (Uruguayans, the fatherland or death).
NATIONAL DAY – 25 August (Declaration of Independence, 1825).

GOVERNMENT

Uruguay (or the *Banda Oriental,* as the territory lying on the eastern bank of the Uruguay River was then called) resisted all attempted invasions of the Portuguese and Spanish until the early 17th century; 100 years later the Portuguese settlements were captured by the Spanish. From 1726 to 1814 the country formed part of Spanish South America. In 1814 the armies of the Argentine Confederation captured the capital and annexed the province; afterwards it was annexed by Portugal and became a province of Brazil. In 1825, the country threw off Brazilian rule. This action led to war between Argentina and Brazil which was settled by the mediation of the United Kingdom, Uruguay being declared an independent state in 1828. In 1830 a republic was inaugurated.

Under the constitution the President (who may serve only a single term) appoints a council of 11 ministers and a Secretary (Planning and Budget Office), and the Vice-President presides over Congress. The Congress consists of a Chamber of 99 deputies and a Senate of 30 members (plus the Vice-President), elected for five years by proportional representation. General elections held in 1984 marked the return to civilian rule after 11 years of presidential rule with military support. The first fully free presidential and legislative elections since 1971 were held in 1989, and were won by the Partido Nacional Blanco. After the 1994 elections a coalition government of the Colorado Party and the Partido Nacional Blanco was appointed by President Sanguinetti (Colorado Party).

The republic is divided into 19 Departments, each with an elected governor and legislature.

HEAD OF STATE
President, Dr Julio Maria Sanguinetti, *elected* 27 November 1994, *took office* 1 March 1995
Vice-President, Dr Hugo Batalla

CABINET *as at August 1996*

Interior, Dr Didier Operti
Foreign Affairs, Alvaro Ramos
Economy and Finance, Luis Mosca
Transport and Public Works, Lucio Caceres
Public Health, Dr Alfredo Solari
Labour and Social Security, Ana Lía Piñeyrua
Livestock, Agriculture and Fisheries, Carlos Gasparri
Education and Culture, Samuel Lichtensztejn
National Defence, Dr Raúl Iturria
Industry and Energy, Federico Slinger
Tourism, Benito Stern
Housing, Territorial Regulation and Environment, Juan Chiruchi
Secretary, Planning and Budget Office, Ariel Davrieux

EMBASSY OF THE ORIENTAL REPUBLIC OF URUGUAY
2nd Floor, 140 Brompton Road, London SW3 1HY
Tel 0171-584 8192; *Consulate* 0171-589 8835
Ambassador Extraordinary and Plenipotentiary, HE Juan Enrique Fischer, apptd 1993

BRITISH EMBASSY
Calle Marco Bruto 1073, Montevideo 11300 (PO Box 16024)
Tel: Montevideo 623650
Ambassador Extraordinary and Plenipotentiary, HE Robert Hendrie, apptd 1994

BRITISH-URUGUAYAN CHAMBER OF COMMERCE,
Avenida Labertador Brig. Gen., Lavalleja 1641, P2-OF 201, Montevideo

ECONOMY

The economy is based on agriculture, primarily livestock. There are just over 9 million cattle and just under 24 million sheep. Wheat, barley, maize, linseed, sunflower seed and rice are cultivated. In addition to wool, meat packing, other foodstuffs (citrus, wine, beer), fishing and textile industries are of importance.

Industrial development continues and, in addition to the greatly augmented textile industry, includes tyres, sheet-glass, three-ply wood, cement, leather-curing, beet-sugar, plastics, household consumer goods, edible oils and the refining of petroleum and petroleum products. There are some ferrous minerals, not extracted at present. Non-ferrous exploited minerals include clinker, dolomite, marble and granite.

The external debt in 1993 was US$4,200 million. Central Bank reserves (1992) were US$1,711 million, while GNP was (1991) US$9,480,000m, inflation (1995) 35 per cent, unemployment (1992) 8.3 per cent and budget deficit (1992) was 0.7 per cent of GDP. The IMF approved a credit of US$148 million in March 1996.

FINANCE	1991	1992
Revenue	US$1,839,075m	US$1,990,373m
Expenditure	1,800,733m	1,959,930m

TRADE

The major exports are meat and by-products, wool and by-products, hides and bristle and agricultural products. The principal imports are raw materials, construction materials, oils and lubricants, automotive vehicles, kits and machinery. Principal trading partners are Brazil, USA and Argentina.

	1992	1993
Total exports	US$1,702,500m	US$2,324,000m
Total imports	$2,058,000m	1,645,000m

Trade with UK	1994	1995
Imports from UK	£51,546,000	£56,833,000
Exports to UK	52,173,000	62,379,000

COMMUNICATIONS

There are about 11,300 km of national highways, and 2,993 km of standard gauge railway in use. Passenger rail services were cancelled in 1988 and services are now limited to cargo transport; services are state-run. A state-owned airline, PLUNA, provides international services, and internal passenger and limited freight services are provided by TAMU, another state-owned airline, using principally military aircraft and personnel. The international airport of Carrasco lies 12 miles outside Montevideo. The River Uruguay is navigable from its estuary to Salto, 200 miles north, and the Negro is also navigable for a considerable distance.

Six daily newspapers are published in Montevideo and most of them are distributed throughout the country.

EDUCATION

Primary and secondary education is compulsory and free, and technical and trade schools and evening courses for adult education are state controlled. The university at Montevideo (founded in 1849) has ten faculties and a new university has been built at Salto.

UZBEKISTAN
Ozbekiston Respublikasy

Uzbekistan has an area of 172,742 sq. miles (447,400 sq. km) and occupies the south-central part of former Soviet Central Asia, lying between the high Tienshan Mountains and the Pamir highlands in the east and south-east and sandy lowlands in the west and north-west. It is bordered on the north by Kazakhstan and the Aral Sea, on the east by Kyrgyzstan and Tajikistan, on the south by Afghanistan and Turkmenistan, and on the west by Kazakhstan. Uzbekistan consists of the Kara-Kalpak Autonomous Republic and 12 regions: Andizhan, Bokhara, Dzhizak, Ferghana, Kashkadar, Khorezm, Namangan, Navoi, Samarkand, Surkhan-Darya, Syr-Darya and Tashkent. Most of the country is a plain with huge waterless deserts, and several large oases which form the main centres of population and economic life. The climate is continental and dry.

The population (1995 estimate) is 21,206,800, of which 71 per cent are Uzbeks, 8 per cent Russians, 5 per cent Tajiks and 4 per cent Kazakhs, with smaller numbers of Tatars, Kara-Kalpaks, Koreans, Ukrainians and Kirghiz. The predominant religion is Sunni Muslim. Islam is tolerated within strict bounds; it is allowed to play no part in politics.

The principal language is Uzbek (71 per cent) with Russian (8 per cent), Tajik (5 per cent) and Kazakh (4 per cent). Uzbek is one of the Turkic group of languages. In June 1994 the government approved a six-year programme for the transfer of the Uzbek language to a Latin script.

CAPITAL – Tashkent. Population 2,073,000 (1992). Samarkand (388,000) contains the Gur-Emir (Tamerlane's Mausoleum) completed 1400 by Ulugbek, Tamerlane's astronomer grandson.
CURRENCY – Sum (Som) of 100 tiyin.
FLAG – Three horizontal stripes of blue, white, green, with the white fimbriated in red; on the blue near the hoist a crescent and twelve stars, all in white.
NATIONAL DAY – 1 September (Independence Day).

GOVERNMENT

Between the sixth and fourth centuries BC the area that is now Uzbekistan was under the control of the Persians and then Alexander the Great. In the 14th century the area became the centre of a great Muslim empire under Tamerlane and then his grandson Ulugbek, following whose murder the state disintegrated. By the beginning of the 19th century three independent Khanates, Khiva, Kokand and Bukhara, existed in what is now Uzbekistan. These were gradually annexed to the Russian Empire by the middle of the 19th century. In November 1917 a Communist revolution broke out in Tashkent and parts of Uzbekistan were included in the Turkestan Soviet Republic at its formation in 1918. The remainder of Uzbekistan was under the rule of the independent states of Khiva and Bukhara, which had re-emerged in 1918, until they were defeated by the Red Army and Soviet rule was established throughout the area in 1921. Under Soviet rule a massive land irrigation programme was implemented to allow the cultivation of cotton.

Uzbekistan declared its independence from the Soviet Union on 1 September 1991 after the failed Moscow coup. Its independence was confirmed in a referendum on 29 December and recognized internationally. A new constitution was adopted by the Supreme Soviet in December 1992 under which the President and government hold executive power. The President may serve a maximum of two five-year terms and has the power to dissolve the 250-member Supreme Assembly (*Oliy Majilis*), which may not remove or impeach the President. Elections to the new *Oliy Majilis* were held on 25 December 1994 and won by the ruling People's Democratic Party and its allies with a total of 205 seats.

The government of President Karimov is formed by the former Communist Party, which has renamed itself the People's Democratic Party. Despite the constitutionally guaranteed freedom of religion and thought, and respect for human rights and multiparty democracy, censorship is still widely used and little political opposition is tolerated. The main opposition parties, Erk (Freedom) and Birlik (Unity) nationalist party, have been continually banned since the introduction of the multiparty constitution in December 1992. In March 1995 President Karimov's hold on power was confirmed when his term of office was extended to 2000 by a national referendum. Uzbek forces have been deployed in Tajikistan since late 1992 to help maintain the government and defeat the Islamic forces.

Uzbek nationalism has caused violent clashes with Tajiks in the Ferghana valley in recent years. The ability to speak Uzbek is now a condition of appointment to government posts. This has severely disrupted the civil service and public sector, mostly staffed by ethnic Russians. President Karimov is attempting to form close ties with Turkey in the cultural and business spheres, and in 1994 began to strengthen economic ties with Russia again.

HEAD OF STATE
President, Islam Karimov, *elected* 29 December 1991, *elected by referendum for a five-year term* 26 March 1995.

CABINET *as at July 1996*
Chairman of the Cabinet, The President
Prime Minister, Utkir Sultanov
First Deputy Prime Minister, Ismail Djurabekov
Deputy PMs, Dilbar Gulamova (*Women*); Kayim Khakkulov (*Industry, Fuel and and Power*); Bakhtiyar Khamidov (*Finance and Economy*); Viktor Chzhen (*State Property and Privatization*); Uktam Ismailov; Saidmukhtar Saidkasymov; Mirabror Usmanov; Rustam Yunusov; Rim Giniyatullin
Interior, Zokirjon Almatov
Foreign Affairs, Abdulaziz Kamilov
Defence, Lt.-Gen. Rustam Akhmedov
Justice, Srodidin Mustafayev
Health, Shavkat Karimov
Education, Djura Yuldashev
Agriculture, Marx Jumaniyazov
Communications, Tokhir Rakhimov
Labour, Akildzhan Abidov
Higher Education, Akil Salimov
Public Utilities, Viktor Mikhailov
Culture, Erkin Khaitbaiev
Social Security, Bakhodir Umarzakov
Power Engineering, Valeri Ataiev
Emergency Situations, Ismail Djurabekov

Chairman of the Oliy Majilis, Erkin Khalilov

EMBASSY OF THE REPUBLIC OF UZBEKISTAN
72 Wigmore Street, London WIH 9DL
Tel: 0171-935 1899
Ambassador Extraordinary and Plenipotentiary, new appointment awaited

BRITISH EMBASSY
Flats 84–85, Murtazaeva Street 6, Tashkent
Tel: Tashkent 891288
Ambassador Extraordinary and Plenipotentiary, HE Barbara Hay, MBE, apptd 1995

ECONOMY
Uzbekistan is attempting to integrate its economy with that of Kazakhstan, with which it signed an economic agreement in January 1994 to allow the free circulation of goods, services and capital and the co-ordination of credit and finance policies, budgets, taxation and customs duties. Uzbekistan is also a member of the CIS economic union and in March 1994 signed an economic treaty with Russia to provide for mutually convertible currencies and enhance private business links. In 1994–5 the government has also embarked on an economic reform programme under which subsidies on foodstuffs and transport were abolished and those on public utilities reduced. Peasant farmers have been granted private plots of land and inflation has been reduced. In January 1995 the IMF approved a US$75 million loan to support the economic reform programme. A further IMF loan of US$150 million was approved in December 1995.

Uzbekistan's economy is based on intensive agricultural production, and especially cotton production, made possible by extensive irrigation schemes. In addition there are some agricultural and textile machinery plants and several chemical combines. Large and previously underdeveloped mineral resources have begun to be exploited; these include gold, natural gas, oil, copper, lead, zinc and coal. A sizeable oilfield was discovered in the Ferghana Valley in 1992. The Muruntao mine is the largest open-cast gold mine in the world, producing 75 million tonnes per year. Foreign direct investment of US$2,000 million has been pledged in the fields of mining, exploration and vehicle assembly plants.

TRADE WITH UK	1994	1995
Imports from UK	£17,297,000	£15,073,000
Exports to UK	3,493,000	1,611,000

VANUATU
Ripablik Blong Vanuatu

Vanuatu is situated in the South Pacific Ocean, between 13° and 21° S. and 166° and 170° E. It includes 13 large and some 70 small islands, of coral and volcanic origin, including the Banks and Torres Islands in the north, and has a total land area of 4,706 sq. miles (12,190 sq. km). The principal islands are Vanua Lava, Espiritu Santo, Maewo, Pentecost, Ambae, Malekula, Ambrym, Epi, Efate, Erromango, Tanna and Aneityum. Most islands are mountainous and there are active volcanoes on several. The climate is oceanic tropical, moderated by the south-east trade winds which blow between May and October. At other times winds are variable and cyclones may occur.

The population (1993 estimate) is 159,800. About 95 per cent are Melanesian, the rest being mostly Micronesian, Polynesian and European. The national language is Bislama, but English and French are also official languages.

SEAT OF ADMINISTRATION – ΨPort Vila, Efate, population (1993) 26,100. The only other town is Luganville (population, 1993, 8,800), on Espiritu Santo.
CURRENCY – Vatu of 100 centimes.
FLAG – Red over green with a black triangle in the hoist, the three parts being divided by fimbriations of black and yellow, and in the centre of the black triangle a boar's tusk overlaid by two crossed fern leaves.
NATIONAL ANTHEM – Nasonal sing sing blong Vanuatu.
NATIONAL DAY – 30 July (Independence Day).

GOVERNMENT

Vanuatu, the former Anglo-French Condominium of the New Hebrides, became an independent republic within the Commonwealth on 30 July 1980. Parliament consists of 46 members elected for a term of four years. A Council of Chiefs advises on matters of custom. Executive power is held by the Prime Minister (elected from and by parliament) and a Council of Ministers who are responsible to parliament. The President is elected for a five-year term by the presidents of the six provincial governments and the members of parliament.

HEAD OF STATE
President, HE Jean-Marie Leye, *elected* 2 March 1994

COUNCIL OF MINISTERS *as at June 1996*
Prime Minister, Hon. Maxime Carlot Korman
Deputy PM, Education, Hon. Donald Kalpokas
Finance, Hon. Barak Sope
Foreign Affairs, Hon. Amos Bangabiti
Home Affairs, Charley Nako
Transport and Public Works, Hon. Amos Andeng
Lands, Hon. William Edgell
Health, Hon. Cyriaque Metmetsan
Agriculture, Hon. Vincent Boulekone
Justice, Hon. Joe Natuman
Commerce, Hon. Sela Molisa
Civil Aviation, Tourism, Telecommunications and Meteorology, Albert Ravutia

HIGH COMMISSIONER TO GREAT BRITAIN, vacant, resident at Port Vila, Vanuatu

BRITISH HIGH COMMISSION
PO Box 567, Port Vila
Tel: Vila 23100
High Commissioner, HE James Daly, CVO, apptd 1995

ECONOMY

Most of the population is employed on plantations or in subsistence agriculture. Subsistence crops include yams, taro, manioc, sweet potato and breadfruit; principal cash crops are copra, cocoa and coffee. Large numbers of cattle are kept on the plantations and beef is the second largest export. Principal exports are copra, meat (frozen, tinned and chilled), timber and cocoa.

Tourism is an important revenue earner, and the absence of direct taxation has led to growth in the finance and associated industries.

TRADE WITH UK	1994	1995
Imports from UK	£383,000	£277,000
Exports to UK	1,618,000	1,162,000

VATICAN CITY STATE
Stato della Città del Vaticano

The office of the ecclesiastical head of the Roman Catholic Church (Holy See) is vested in the Pope, the Sovereign Pontiff. For many centuries the Sovereign Pontiff exercised temporal power but by 1870 the Papal States had become part of unified Italy. The temporal power of the Pope was in suspense until the treaty of 1929 which recognized the full and independent sovereignty of the Holy See in the City of the Vatican. The area of the Vatican City is 108 acres and its population in 1989 was about 1,000.

CURRENCY – Italian currency is legal tender.
FLAG – Square flag; equal vertical bands of yellow (next staff), and white; crossed keys and triple crown device on white band.
NATIONAL DAY – 22 October (Inauguration of present Pontiff).

Sovereign Pontiff, His Holiness Pope John Paul II (Karol Wojtyla), *born* at Wadowice (Krakow, Poland), 18 May 1920, *elected* Pope in succession to Pope John Paul I, 16 October 1978
Secretary of State, Cardinal Angelo Sodano, *appointed* December 1990

APOSTOLIC NUNCIATURE
54 Parkside, London SW19 5NF
Tel 0181-946 1410
Apostolic Nuncio, HE Archbishop Luigi Barbarito, apptd 1986

BRITISH EMBASSY TO THE HOLY SEE
91 Via Condotti, I–00187 Rome
Tel: Rome 678 9462
Ambassador Extraordinary and Plenipotentiary, HE Maureen Macglashen, apptd 1995

TRADE WITH UK	1994	1995
Imports from UK	£1,138,000	£1,528,000
Exports to UK	1,000	—

VENEZUELA
República de Venezuela

Venezuela is a South American republic, situated approximately between 0° 45′ S. and 12° 12′ N. latitude and 59° 45′ and 73° 09′ W. longitude. It has a total area of 353,857 sq. miles (916,490 sq. km) and is bounded on the north by the Caribbean Sea, west by Colombia, east by Guyana, and south by Brazil. Included in the area of the republic are 72 islands off the coast, with a total area of about 14,650 sq. miles, the largest being Margarita (area, about 400 sq. miles), which is politically associated with Tortuga, Cubagua and Coche to form the state of Nueva Esparta. The mountains are the Eastern Andes and Maritime Andes, running south-west to north-east. The main range is known as the Sierra Nevada de Mérida, and contains Pico Bolivar (16,411 ft) and Picacho de la Sierra (15,420 ft). The principal river is the Orinoco, with innumerable affluents, the main river exceeding 1,600 miles in length. The upper waters of the Orinoco are united with those of the Rio Negro (a Brazilian tributary of the Amazon) by a natural river or canal, known as the Casiquiare. The coastal regions contain many lagoons and lakes, of which Maracaibo (area 8,296 sq. miles) is the largest lake in South America. The climate is tropical, except where modified by altitude or tempered by sea breezes.

The population (UN estimate 1994) is 21,378,000, of which 67 per cent are Mestizo, 21 per cent white, 10 per cent black and 2 per cent Indian. Spanish is the language of the country. About 96 per cent of the population is Roman Catholic.

CAPITAL – Caracas, population 2,784,000. Other principal towns are ΨMaracaibo (1,364,000), Barquisimeto (602,000), Valencia (903,000), Maracay (354,000), San Cristóbal (230,000), Cumaná (212,000) and Ciudad Guayana (536,506).

CURRENCY – Bolivar (BS) of 100 céntimos.

FLAG – Three horizontal stripes of yellow, blue, red with an arc of seven white stars on the blue stripe.

NATIONAL ANTHEM – Gloria Al Bravo Pueblo (Glory to the brave people).

NATIONAL DAY – 5 July.

GOVERNMENT

Venezuela gained independence from Spain in 1830. Under the 1961 constitution, executive power is held by the President, who also appoints the Council of Ministers. Legislative power is exercised by a bicameral National Congress, comprising a 204-member Chamber of Deputies and a Senate of 49 elected members plus the former presidents of constitutional governments as life members. The President and National Congress are directly elected for concurrent five-year terms.

Carlos Andrés Pérez of the (Social Democratic) Democratic Action (AD) party won the December 1988 presidential election and the AD emerged as the largest party in both houses in the Congressional elections. President Pérez's government successfully introduced a series of free market economic reforms which led to impressive economic growth but increasing social problems. Two military coup attempts in 1992 were defeated but President Pérez resigned in May 1993 after the Supreme Court indicted him on corruption charges. Former President Rafael Caldera won the ensuing presidential election in December 1993 but his National Convergence coalition of 17 parties failed to gain majorities in either house of Congress, where the traditional AD and COPEI (Social Christian) parties remained strong. President Caldera took office with his new government in February 1994 and announced an economic austerity programme and the revival of privatization.

Venezuela is divided into 22 states, one federal territory and a federal district.

HEAD OF STATE
President, Rafael Caldera Rodríguez, *elected* 5 December 1993, *sworn in* 2 February 1994

COUNCIL OF MINISTERS *as at August 1996*
Interior, José Guillermo Andueza
Foreign Affairs, Miguel Angel Burelli
Finance, Luis Raul Matos
Defence, Pedro Nicolas Valencia
Transport and Communications, Antonio Corrales
Urban Development, Freddy Rojas Parra
Energy and Mines, Erwin José Arrieta
Environment and Natural Resources, Roberto Pérez Lecuna.
Health and Social Security, Pedro Rincon Gutiérrez
Agriculture and Livestock, Raul Alegrett
Education, Antonio Luis Cardenas
Family Affairs, Carlos Altimari Gásperi
Justice, Henrique Meier
Presidential Secretariat, Asdrúbal Aguiar Aranguren

Decentralization, José Guillermo Andueza
Culture, Oscar Sambrano
Urban Development, Francisco Gonzalez
Minister, Guyana Corporation of Venezuela, Elias Nadim Inaty
Federal District Governor, Abdón Vivas Terán
Labour and Employment, Juan Garrido
Central Planning Office, Teodoro Petkoff
Venezuelan Tourist Corporation, Hermann Soriano
Information, Fernando Egaña
Science and Technology, Guido Arnal Arroyo
Venezuelan Investment Fund, Alberto Poleto
State Reform, Ricardo Combellas

VENEZUELAN EMBASSY
1 Cromwell Road, London SW7 2HW
Tel 0171-584 4206/7
Ambassador Extraordinary and Plenipotentiary, HE Dr Roy Chaderton-Matos, apptd 1996
Defence Attaché, Capt. A. Sanchez

BRITISH EMBASSY
Apartado 1246, Caracas 1010–A
Tel: Caracas 9934111
Ambassador Extraordinary and Plenipotentiary, HE John G. Flynn, CMG, apptd 1993
Counsellor, P. Ware, LVO (*Deputy Head of Mission*)
Defence Attaché, Capt. K. Ridland, RN
First Secretary (Commercial), A. F. N. Goodworth

There are British Consular Offices at Caracas, Maracaibo, Margarita and Mérida.

BRITISH COUNCIL DIRECTOR, Paul de Quincey, Apartado 65131, Caracas 1065

BRITISH-VENEZUELAN CHAMBER OF COMMERCE, Apartado 5713, Caracas 1010. Torre Británica, Piso 10, Letra E, Av. José Félix Sosa, Altamira Sur, Caracas 1060

DEFENCE

The total active armed forces strength is 79,000 personnel, including 31,000 conscripts, who serve for 30 months. Conscription is selective. The Army has 34,000 personnel (27,000 conscripts), with 70 main battle tanks, 161 light tanks, 290 armoured personnel carriers, 107 artillery pieces and five attack helicopters. The Navy has 15,000 personnel (4,000 conscripts), including 5,000 marines, with two submarines, six frigates, six patrol and coastal vessels, four combat aircraft and eight armed helicopters. The Air Force is 7,000 strong, with 119 combat aircraft and 27 armed helicopters. The National Guard has 23,000 internal security personnel, with 194 armoured infantry fighting vehicles and armoured personnel carriers, mortar, aircraft, helicopters and inshore patrol craft.

EDUCATION

Education is free and compulsory between the ages of five and 14. There are more than ten universities in Venezuela, five in Caracas and the others in Maracaibo, Mérida, Valencia, Cumaná and Barquisimeto.

ECONOMY

The government of President Caldera has promised to moderate the free market reforms which provided impressive GDP growth in 1990–2 but saw recession in 1993–4. The oil industry accounted for 21.3 per cent of GNP in 1992, manufacturing 16.8 per cent, commerce 11.7 per cent, government 8.7 per cent and construction 7.4 per cent. A banking crisis in 1994 which necessitated a government rescue of private banks caused the budget deficit to increase drastically, inflation to soar and the currency to collapse. In response, the government announced a two-year economic stabilization programme in September 1994, reintroducing exchange and currency controls, raising taxes and domestic petrol prices, attracting foreign investment, reactivating the privatization programme and reducing government spending. The programme failed to rejuvenate the economy, compelling President Caldera to launch a second stabilization plan in April 1996 as a means of securing an IMF standby credit of US$1,000 million. The programme introduced large increases in petrol prices and the total dismantling of foreign exchange controls.

Products of the tropical forest region include orchids, wild rubber, timber, mangrove bark, balata gum and tonka beans. Agricultural products include corn, bananas, cocoa beans, coffee, cotton, rice, maize, sugar, sesame, groundnuts, potatoes, tomatoes, other vegetables, sisal and tobacco. There is an extensive beef and dairy farming industry. Despite substantial improvements in agriculture, Venezuela is heavily reliant upon food imports, which constitute about 60 per cent of total consumption.

The principal industry is that of petroleum, although daily production in the oilfields (nationalized 1976) has steadily declined since 1973 in line with Venezuela's conservation policies. There are eight refineries. The Orinoco heavy oil belt is being developed; estimates put recoverable resources at 70,000 million barrels in the Orinoco region.

Aluminium is the second highest source of foreign exchange after petroleum. The Venezuelan state holds the majority stake in both the principal producing companies, Venalum and Alcasa, and is moving towards a consolidation of the industry. Rich iron ore deposits in eastern Venezuela have been developed. The government-owned steel mill at Matanzas uses local iron ore and obtains its electric power from hydro-electric installations on the Caroni River. A mill at Ciudad Guayana produces centrifugally-cast iron pipe. Other industry includes a wide variety of manufacturing and component assembly, principally petrochemicals, gold, diamonds, clothing and foodstuffs.

TRADE

Apart from oil the main exports are bauxite, iron ore, agricultural products and basic manufactures. The main imports are machinery and transport equipment, chemicals and foodstuffs. Some 50 per cent of trade is conducted with the USA.

	1993	1994
Total imports	US$11,013m	US$11,631m
Total exports	14,226m	18,278m
Trade with UK	1994	1995
Imports from UK	£196,787,000	£178,784,000
Exports to UK	133,589,000	204,167,000

COMMUNICATIONS

There are about 93,471 km of roads, 29,954 km of them paved. The state has now acquired all but a very few of the railway lines, whose total length is only some 363 km. Road and river communications have made railways of negligible importance in Venezuela except for carrying iron ore in the south-east, though the government is expanding the network.

The Orinoco is navigable for ocean-going ships (up to 40 ft draught) for 150 miles upstream, by large steamers for 700 miles, and by smaller vessels some 900 miles upstream. There are seven Venezuelan airlines which between them have a comprehensive network of internal and international flights. There are ten television stations, one of which is government controlled.

VIETNAM
Công Hòa Xã Hôi Chu Nghĩa Việt Nam

Vietnam has an area of 127,242 sq. miles (329,556 sq. km), and an estimated population (1994) of 72,500,000. It is bordered on the north by China and the west by Laos and Cambodia.

CAPITAL – Hanoi, population (1993) 2,150,000. Other cities are Ho Chi Minh City (3,169,000) and Hai Phong (456,000).
CURRENCY – Dông of 10 hao or 100 xu.
FLAG – Red, with yellow five-point star in centre.
NATIONAL ANTHEM – Tien Quan Ca (The troops are advancing).
NATIONAL DAY – 2 September.

GOVERNMENT

Following the end of the war in Vietnam in 1975, North and South Vietnam were reunified in 1976 under the name of the Socialist Republic of Vietnam. The national flag, anthem and capital of North Vietnam were adopted, and Saigon was renamed Ho Chi Minh City. Effective power lies with the Vietnamese Communist Party (VCP), its highest executive body being the Central Committee, elected by a Party Congress on a national basis. The Politburo and the Secretariat of the Central Committee exercise the real power.

A new constitution was adopted in June 1992 which reaffirmed Communist Party rule but also formalized free market economic reforms. The constitution increased the powers of the President and replaced the Council of Ministers by a Prime Minister and Cabinet. A new National Assembly of 365 members was elected in August 1992 and convened in September when it elected Le Duc Anh as President and, in October, approved the composition of the new government headed by Vo Van Kiet.

HEAD OF STATE
President, Le Duc Anh, *elected by National Assembly* 23 September 1992
Vice President, Nguyen Thi Binh

CABINET *as at August 1996*
Prime Minister, Vo Van Kiet
First Deputy PM, Phan Van Khai
Deputy PMs, Nguyen Kanh; Tran Duc Luong
National Defence, Doan Khue
Foreign Affairs, Nguyen Manh Cam
Interior, Bui Thien Ngo
Planning and Investment, Do Quoc Sam
Youth Work, Ha Quang Du
Ethnic Minorities and Mountain Regions, Hoang Duc Nghi
Minister in Charge of Government Office, Le Xuan Trinh
Finance, Ho Te
Governor, State Bank, Cao Sy Kiem
Commerce and Tourism, Le Van Triet
Labour, War Invalids and Social Affairs, Tran Dinh Hoan
Construction, Ngo Xuan Loc
Communications and Transport, Bui Danh Luu
Industry, Dang Vu Chu
Energy, Thai Phung Ne
Agriculture, Nguyen Cong Tan
Chief Justice, Pham Hung
General Inspector of State Inspectorate, Ta Huu Thanh

Culture and Information, Tran Hoan
Public Health, D. Nguyen Phuong
Education and Training, Tran Hong Quan
Science, Technology and Environment, Dang Huu
Population and Family Planning, Mai Ky
Children, Nguyen Thi Thanh Thanh

VIETNAMESE COMMUNIST PARTY

Politburo of the Central Committee, Do Muoi (*General
    Secretary*); Le Duc Anh; Vo Van Kiet; Nong Duc Manh;
    Le Kha Phieu; Doan Khue; Phan Van Khai; Nguyen
    Manh Cam; Nguyen Duc Binh; Nguyen Van An; Pham
    Van Tra; Tran Duc Luong; Nguyen Thi Xuan My;
    Truong Tan Sang; Le Xuan Tung; Le Minh Huong;
    Pham The Duyet; Nguyen Tan Dung (*full members*)

EMBASSY OF THE SOCIALIST REPUBLIC OF VIETNAM
12–14 Victoria Road, London W8 5RD
Tel 0171-937 1912/8564
Ambassador Extraordinary and Plenipotentiary, HE Huynh
    Ngoc An, apptd 1994

BRITISH EMBASSY
16 Pho Ly Thuong Kiet, Hanoi
Tel: Hanoi 25 2349
Ambassador Extraordinary and Plenipotentiary, HE Peter
    Williams, CMG, apptd 1990
There is also a Consulate-General in Ho Chi Minh City.

BRITISH COUNCIL DIRECTOR, Muriel Kirton (*Cultural
    Attaché*)

DEFENCE

Total active armed forces number 572,000 personnel, with
conscripts serving between two and three years. Reserves
number three to four million. The Army has 500,000
personnel, with 1,300 main battle tanks, 600 light tanks,
1,400 armoured infantry fighting vehicles and armoured
personnel carriers and 2,330 artillery pieces. The Navy is
42,000 strong, including 30,000 naval infantry, and deploys
seven frigates and 57 patrol and coastal vessels. Air Force
strength is 15,000, with 190 combat aircraft and 33 armed
helicopters. The Air Defence Force has 15,000 personnel,
with surface-to-air missiles.

ECONOMY

Vietnam experienced economic difficulties following the
imposition of socialist reforms in the south after 1975.
These were exacerbated by reductions in western aid as a
result of Vietnam's invasion and occupation of Cambodia,
border hostilities with China, and the allocation of
resources to military expenditure. The economy has also
been adversely affected by the sharp decrease in aid from
the former Soviet Union. However, economic reforms,
known as 'Doi Moi' liberalization, were instituted after the
Sixth Party Congress (1986) and have had significant
success. Inflation had been brought down to 4 per cent a
year in 1994, but rose to 14 per cent in 1995; the exchange
rate has been rationalized, subsidies removed, much greater private economic activity allowed and average economic growth of 7 per cent a year in 1991–3 attained (9.5
per cent in 1995). The state's share of control has fallen to
60 per cent of industry, 40 per cent of services and 2 per cent
of agriculture, which is now mainly run by family farms.
This has led to a significant improvement in agricultural
production, with Vietnam becoming a major rice exporter.
    Foreign investment has been actively encouraged, with
US$5,300 million invested in 1988–93. This level is
growing since the USA dropped its opposition to IMF and
World Bank loans and aid to Vietnam in July 1993 and
ended its trade embargo in February 1994. Investment was
further boosted by the US decision in July 1995 to establish
full diplomatic and economic relations and by Vietnam's
accession to ASEAN in August 1995. International aid
donors, the IMF and the World Bank approved a loan and
grant package of US$1,860 million in November 1993 and
US$2,535 million in November 1994 to support economic
reform. The London Club agreed to restructure US$900
million of commercial debt in May 1996. A bankruptcy law
has been passed, which has led to increasing unemployment and fears for social stability. Oil production (mainly
offshore) has increased to 110,000 barrels per day and large
natural gas reserves have been found offshore, though
these are also claimed by China.

TRADE WITH UK	1994	1995
Imports from UK	£62,915,000	£60,442,000
Exports to UK	66,389,000	106,943,000

WESTERN SAMOA
Malotuto'atasi o Samoa i Sisifo

Western Samoa lies in the south Pacific Ocean between 13°
and 15° S. latitude and 171° and 173° W. longitude. It
consists of the islands of Savai'i (662 sq. miles), Upolu,
Apolima, Manono, Fanuatapu, Namua, Nuutele, Nuulua
and Nuusafee, and has an area of 435 sq. miles (1,714 sq.
km). All the islands are mountainous. Upolu, the most
fertile, contains the harbours of Apia and Mulifanua, and
Savai'i the harbour of Salelologa.
    The population (1989 census) was 162,000, the largest
numbers being on Upolu (114,980) and Savai'i (43,150); a
1992 UN estimate put the figure at 158,000. The Samoans
are a Polynesian people, though the population also
includes other Pacific Islanders, Euronesians, Chinese and
Europeans. The main languages are Samoan and English.
The islanders are Christians of different denominations.

CAPITAL – ΨApia, on Upolu (population, 1989 census,
    36,000). Robert Louis Stevenson died and was buried at
    Apia in 1894.
CURRENCY – Tala (WS$) of 100 sene.
FLAG – Red with a blue canton bearing five white stars of
    the Southern Cross.
NATIONAL ANTHEM – The Banner of Freedom.
NATIONAL DAY – 1 June (Independence Day).

GOVERNMENT

Formerly administered by New Zealand (latterly with
internal self-government), Western Samoa became fully
independent on 1 January 1962. The state was treated as a
member country of the Commonwealth until its formal
admission on 28 August 1970.
    The 1962 constitution provides for a head of state to be
elected by the 49-member legislative assembly, the *Fono,*
for a five-year term. Initially two of the four Paramount
chiefs jointly held the office of head of state for life. When
one of the chiefs died in April 1963, Malietoa Tanumafili II
became head of state for life. The head of state's functions
are analogous to those of a constitutional monarch.
Executive government is carried out by a Cabinet of
Ministers.
    Suffrage was made universal following a referendum
held in 1990. After elections held on 26 April 1996, the seats
in the *Fono* were: Human Rights Protection Party 26;
Samoan National Development Party 13; Independents 10.

HEAD OF STATE

Head of State for Life, HH Malietoa Tanumafili II, GCMG, CBE, since 15 April 1963
Deputy Head of State, Hon. Mataafa Faasuamaleaui Puela

CABINET *as at August 1996*
Prime Minister, Minister for Foreign Affairs, Hon. Tofilau Eti Alesana
Finance, Hon. Tuilaepa S. Malielegaoi
Justice, Youth, Sports and Culture, Hon. Luagalau L. Kamu
Education, Hon. Fiame Naomi
Health, Hon. Misa Telefoni
Post and Telecommunications, Hon. Tolofua F. Leiataua
Agriculture, Fisheries and Transport, Hon. Molioo Teofilo
Public Works, Hon. Leafa Vitale
Lands and Environment, Hon. Tuala Kerslake
Transport, Hon. Joe Keil
Women's Affairs, Hon. Leniu Avamagalo
Internal Affairs, Hon. Leota Lu II
Labour, Polataivao Fosi

WESTERN SAMOA HIGH COMMISSION
Avenue Franklin D. Roosevelt 123, 1050 Brussels
Tel: Brussels 6608454
High Commissioner, HE Afamasaga Toleafoa, apptd 1990

BRITISH HIGH COMMISSIONER, HE Robert Alston, CMG, resident at Wellington, New Zealand
There is an Honorary Consulate (PO Box 2029) in Apia.

ECONOMY

Agriculture is the basis of the economy, the principal cash crops (and exports) being coconuts (copra), cocoa and bananas. Other agricultural exports include coffee, timber, tropical fruits and seeds. Efforts are being made to develop fishing on a commercial scale. Manufacturing is very small in scope and concerned largely with processing agricultural products, but is being encouraged by the government. Tourism is increasing rapidly.

TRADE WITH UK	1994	1995
Imports from UK	£1,115,000	£567,000
Exports to UK	12,000	16,000

REPUBLIC OF YEMEN
Al-Jamhuriya Al-Yamaniya

Yemen lies in the extreme south-west of the Arabian peninsula. Bounded on the west by the Red Sea, on the north by Saudi Arabia, on the east by Oman and on the south by the Gulf of Aden, Yemen has an estimated area of 203,850 sq. miles (527,969 sq. km) and a population (1995 census) of 15,800,000. Included in the state are the offshore islands of Perim and Kamaran in the Red Sea, and Socotra in the Gulf of Aden. The border with Saudi Arabia is unclear and remains in dispute; only the north-west corner of it is delineated, by the 1934 Taif Accord. The highlands and central plateau, and the highest portions of the maritime range in the south, form the most fertile part of Arabia, with abundant but irregular rainfall. The north is largely composed of mountains and desert, and rainfall is generally scarce.

CAPITAL – Sana'a, population (1995) 972,000. Ψ Aden (562,000) is the other main city and the former capital of South Yemen.
CURRENCY – Yemeni Riyal of 100 fils.
FLAG – Horizontal bands of red, white and black.
NATIONAL DAY – 22 May.

GOVERNMENT

Turkish occupation of North Yemen (1872–1918) was followed by the rule of the Hamid al-Din dynasty until a revolution in 1962 overthrew the monarchy and the Yemen Arab Republic was declared. The People's Republic of South Yemen was set up in 1967 when the British government ceded power to the National Liberation Front, bringing to an end 129 years of British rule in Aden and some years of protectorate status in the hinterland. Negotiations towards merging the two states began in 1979 and unification was proclaimed on 22 May 1990. The constitution was approved by referendum in May 1991. A five-member Presidential Council comprising former senior government figures of the separate states was formed for the period of transition.

A general election for the House of Representatives took place on 27 April 1993. Of the total of 301 seats, 122 were won by the General People's Congress (GPC, former ruling party in the North), 62 by the Islamic Islah (Alliance for reform) party and 56 by the Yemeni Socialist Party (YSP, former ruling party in the South). The three parties formed a coalition government and the House of Representatives asked the Presidential Council to remain in office.

Continued political tensions and a power struggle between the former Northern and Southern Yemen elites in mid-1993, coupled with arguments over the distribution of oil revenues and the alleged assassination of Southern ministers led YSP leaders to withdraw to Aden in August 1993. A reconciliation pact signed in February 1994 by President Saleh and Vice-President al-Beedh was never implemented and, after sporadic clashes, a civil war broke out on 5 May 1994 between the unmerged Northern and Southern forces. The Southern leadership declared secession on 20 May but fled when Aden was captured by victorious Northern forces on 7 July, bringing the civil war to an end.

After the civil war a coalition government of the General People's Congress and the Islamic Islah was formed, an amnesty for the secessionists declared (with the exception of key YSP leaders) and the constitution amended. The Presidential Council was abolished and will be replaced from 1999 with a directly elected President. Gen. Saleh was elected President by the House of Representatives for a five-year term. Multiparty democracy, a free market economy and Shari'a-based Islamic law are enshrined in the constitution.

HEAD OF STATE
President, Gen. Ali Abdullah Saleh, *took office* 22 May 1990, *elected* 1 October 1994
Vice-President, Maj. Gen. Abd Rabbah Mansour Hadi

COUNCIL OF MINISTERS *as at August 1996*
Prime Minister, Abdel Aziz Abdel-Ghani
Deputy PM, Abdel-Wahab Ali al-Ounsi
Deputy PM, Foreign Affairs, Abdul Ali Karim al-Iryani
Deputy PM, Oil and Mineral Resources, Mohammed Said al-Attar
Deputy PM, Planning and Development, Abdul-Qader Ba Jammal
Interior, Col. Hussein Mohammed Arab
Finance, Mohammed Ahmad al-Junayd
Information, Abdurahman al-Akawaa
Transport, Ahmad Musa'id Husayn
Communications, Ahmad Mohammed al-Unsi
Culture and Tourism, Yahya Husayn al-Arashi
Social Affairs and Labour, Mohammed Abdullah al-Batani
Legal and Parliamentary Affairs, Abdullah Ahmad Ghanim
Civil Administration, Sadiq Amin Abu Ras

Supply and Trade, Abdulrahman Mohammed Ali Othman
Health, Najib Ghanem
Local Government, Mohammed Hassan Damaj
Religious Guidance, Ghaleb Abdul-Kafi al-Quirshi
Fisheries, Abdul-Rahman al-Qadar Bafadl
Justice, Abd al-Wahhab Lufti al-Daylami
Defence, Brig. Abd al-Malik Ali al-Sayyani
Industry, Ahmed Mohammed Sofan
Agriculture and Water Resources, Ahmad Salim al-Jabali
Housing and Urban Planning, Ali Hamid Sharaf
Education, Abduh Ali al-Qudati
Youth and Sports, Abd al-Wahhab Rawih
Electricity and Water, Abdallah Muhsin al-Akwa
Speaker of the House of Representatives, Shaikh Abdullah bin Husain al-Ahmar

EMBASSY OF THE REPUBLIC OF YEMEN
57 Cromwell Road, London SW7 2ED
Tel 0171-584 6607
Ambassador Extraordinary and Plenipotentiary, HE Dr Hussein Abdullah Al-Amri, apptd 1995

BRITISH EMBASSY
PO Box 1287, Sana'a
Tel: Sana'a 264 081
Ambassador Extraordinary and Plenipotentiary, HE Douglas Scrafton, apptd 1995

BRITISH COUNCIL DIRECTOR, Brendan McSharry, MBE, As-Sabain Street No. 7 (PO Box 2157), Sana'a

DEFENCE

Total active armed forces number 39,500, including 25,000 conscripts who serve for three-year terms. The 37,000-strong Army has 40,000 reserves and is equipped with 1,125 main battle tanks, 830 armoured personnel carriers and armoured infantry fighting vehicles and 508 artillery pieces.
  The Navy has a strength of 1,500, with ten patrol and coastal vessels. The Air Force has a strength of 1,000 personnel, with 69 combat aircraft and eight attack helicopters. Paramilitary personnel number 30,000.

ECONOMY

The civil war has seriously damaged the country's economy, already weakened since 1991 by the loss of US$2,000 million in annual remittances from 800,000 Yemeni workers in Saudi Arabia, who were sent home because of Yemen's support for Iraq in the Gulf War. However, the war had little effect on oil production, which averages 180,000 barrels per day (bpd) from the Marib field and 150,000 bpd from the Masila field, on stream since August 1993. The refinery at Aden was damaged in the civil war and is working at reduced capacity. An agreement was signed with the French oil company Total in September 1995 for the exploitation of liquefied natural gas over a 25-year period and the construction of a gas liquefication plant by 2000. Despite the production of oil Yemen remains one of the poorest states in the world. The critical economic situation obliged the government in 1995 to begin implementing a series of IMF and World Bank-prescribed reforms to combat the 55 per cent inflation (1995), 50 per cent unemployment and US$9,000 million external debt. The IMF approved a 15-month standby credit of US$193 million in March 1996.
  Agriculture is the main occupation of the inhabitants. This is largely of a subsistence nature, sorghum, sesame and millets being the chief crops, with wheat and barley widely grown at the higher elevations. Exports include cotton, coffee, hides and skins.

TRADE WITH UK	1994	1995
Imports from UK	£74,177,00	£66,825,000
Exports to UK	5,081,000	4,113,000

YUGOSLAVIA
Federativna Republika Jugoslavije – Federal Republic of Yugoslavia

The area of the two remaining Yugoslav republics (Serbia and Montenegro) is 39,506 sq. miles (102,350 sq. km). The rump Federal Yugoslav state, which is not internationally recognized as the successor state to the former Socialist Federal Republic of Yugoslavia, is bordered to the north by Hungary, to the east by Romania and Bulgaria, to the south by the Former Yugoslav Republic of Macedonia, to the south-west by Albania and the Adriatic Sea, and to the west by Bosnia-Hercegovina and Croatia. The climate is continental. Montenegro and southern Serbia are extremely mountainous, while the north is dominated by the low-lying plains of the Danube. The major rivers are: the Danube, which flows through the north of Serbia to Romania and Bulgaria; the Sava, which flows eastwards from Bosnia to join the Danube at Belgrade; the Drina, which flows along most of the Serbian–Bosnian border to join the Sava; and the Morava, which flows from the extreme south to join the Danube in the north.
  The last (federal) estimate of 1988 gave a population of 10,410,000, of which 66 per cent are Serbs and Montenegrins, 18 per cent Albanian, 8 per cent Muslim, 4 per cent Hungarian, with smaller numbers of Yugoslavs (no ethnic group), Croats and Bulgarians. The majority religion is Serbian Orthodox, with significant Muslim and small Roman Catholic minorities.
  The main language is Serbian (Serbo-Croat) (74 per cent), with Albanian and Hungarian minorities. Serbo-Croat is a South Slav language written in the Cyrillic script.

CAPITAL – (federal and Serbian) Belgrade, on the Danube (population 1,455,000). Other major cities are (1981): Novi Sad (257,685); Niš (230,711); Priština (210,040); Kragujevac (164,823); Subotica (154,611); Podgorica (132,290), the capital of Montenegro.
CURRENCY – Dinar of 100 paras.
FLAG – Three horizontal stripes of blue, white, red.
NATIONAL ANTHEM – Hej, Slaveni, Jošte Živi Reő Naših Dedova (Oh! Slavs, our ancestors' words still live).
NATIONAL DAY – 29 November.

GOVERNMENT

Serbia emerged from the rule of the Byzantine Empire in the 13th century to form a large and prosperous state in the Balkans. Defeat by the Turks in 1389 led to almost 500 years of Turkish rule. After gaining autonomy within the Ottoman Empire in 1815, Serbia became fully independent in 1878 and a kingdom in 1881. Montenegro was part of the Serbian state before it was conquered by the Turks in 1355; it became independent in 1851. At the end of the First World War Serbia and Montenegro joined with the former Austro-Hungarian provinces of Slovenia, Croatia and Bosnia-Hercegovina to form the 'Kingdom of Serbs, Croats and Slovenes' which was proclaimed on 1 December 1918 under the rule of the Serbian royal house. The state was renamed Yugoslavia in 1929. In 1941–5 Yugoslavia was occupied by Axis forces which were fought by Communist and royalist Chetnik partisans supplied by Allied forces. In 1945 with the defeat of Nazi Germany,

Yugoslavia was reformed as a Communist federal republic under the presidency of partisan leader Josip Tito.

Increasing pressure from the non-Serbian nationalities for more political power were met by Tito in the post-war period by new constitutions in 1963 and 1974 which devolved power to the republics (Slovenia, Croatia, Bosnia-Hercegovina, Serbia, Montenegro and Macedonia). Tito died in 1980 and the delicate political balance of a rotating federal presidency was unable to contain the growing nationalist movements after his death. Efforts by the six republican Presidents to negotiate a new federal or confederal structure for the country failed in 1991. On 25 June 1991 Slovenia and Croatia declared their independence from Yugoslavia. Intervention by the Federal Yugoslav Army (JNA) against local defence forces to prevent the disintegration of the federation failed and within two months the ethnically homogeneous Slovenia had negotiated its independence.

In Croatia the ethnic Serb minority refused to accept Croatia's independence and fighting began in July 1991 between Croat Defence Forces and Serbian guerrillas backed by the JNA. By September 1991 this had escalated into war between Croatia and Serbia. The war in Croatia continued until January 1992 when the EU and the UN were able to bring about a cease-fire (*see* Croatia).

Bosnia-Hercegovina adopted a memorandum on state sovereignty on 15 October 1991 and independence was affirmed in a referendum on 1 March 1992. Independence was supported by the ethnic Muslims and Croats but rejected by the ethnic Serbs and fighting between Muslims and Serbs broke out in March 1992. The JNA intervened against the Muslims but in May 1992 withdrew to Serbia and Montenegro.

On 27 April 1992 the two remaining republics of the former Socialist Federal Republic of Yugoslavia, Serbia and Montenegro, announced the formation of a new Yugoslav federation, which they invited Serbs in Croatia and Bosnia-Hercegovina to join. The new federation remains unrecognized internationally. Continued Serbian aid and supplies to the ethnic Serb forces in the Bosnian war led to increasing international pressure and the imposition by the UN in May 1992 of a trade embargo, economic sanctions and a ban on air and sporting links. In April 1993 a total blockade was imposed.

President Milosevic severed all political and economic ties to the Bosnian Serb leadership in July 1994 under the threat of further sanctions and in September 1994 closed the Yugoslav-Bosnian border to all trade except food and medicines, leading the UN Security Council to suspend the ban on sporting, cultural, air and sea links with Yugoslavia in October. The remaining UN sanctions

were lifted on 22 November 1995, following the initialling of the Dayton Peace Accord on Bosnia the previous day. President Milosevic attended the negotiations in Dayton, Ohio, USA, and signed the agreement on behalf of the Bosnian Serbs.

The Federal Republic has a bicameral parliament with a 138-seat (108 Serbian, 30 Montenegrin) lower house, the Chamber of Citizens, and a 40-seat (20 Serbian, 20 Montenegrin) upper house, the Chamber of Republics. Executive power is vested in a Federal President and government but has effectively been usurped by the authoritarian Serbian Socialist (former Communist) Party leader and Serbian President Slobodan Milosevic. The last federal legislative elections were held in December 1992 and were universally considered flawed and unfair. The Serbian Socialist Party emerged as the largest party in the federal legislature and formed a coalition government with the extreme nationalist Serbian Radical Party. This government was replaced in March 1993 by a coalition of the Serbian Socialist Party and the Montenegrin Social Democratic Party.

HEAD OF STATE
Federal President, Zoran Lilic, *elected by parliament* 25 June 1993

FEDERAL GOVERNMENT *as at August 1996*
Prime Minister, Radoje Kontic
Deputy Prime Ministers, Jovan Zebic; Nikola Sainovic
Justice, Vladimir Krivokapic
Finance, Tomica Raicevic
Economy, Rade Filipovic
Foreign Affairs, Milan Milutinovic
Interior, Vukasin Jokanovic
Defence, Pavle Bulatovic
Transport and Communications, Zoran Vujovic
Labour, Health and Social Policy, Miroslav Ivanesevic
Development, Science and Environment, Janko Radulovic
Information, Dragutin Brcin
Trade, Djordje Siradovic
Agriculture, Tihomir Vrebalov
Sport, Zoran Bingulac
Human and Minority Rights, Margit Savovic
Ministers Without Portfolio, Margit Savovic; Zoran Bingulac; Dragutin Brcin
Government Secretary-General, Mladen Vukcevic

EMBASSY OF YUGOSLAVIA
5 Lexham Gardens, London W8 5JJ
Tel 0171-370 6105
Chargé d'Affaires, R. Bogojevic
Defence Attaché, Capt. M. Ladicorbic
Consul-General, R. Jengic

BRITISH EMBASSY
Generala Ždanova 46, 11000 Belgrade
Tel: Belgrade 645055
Ambassador Extraordinary and Plenipotentiary, and Consul-General, HE I. A. Roberts, CMG
Defence and Military Attaché, Col. J. H. Crosland, MC
First Secretaries (Political), A. Crombie; T. G. Bradley, OBE
First Secretary (Commercial), D. A. Slinn

BRITISH COUNCIL REPRESENTATIVE, J. McGrath, Generala Ždanova 34-Mazanin (Post Fah 248), 11001 Belgrade

MONTENEGRO
Montenegro has an area of 5,331 sq. miles (13,812 sq. km) and a population of 615,000, of whom 62 per cent are Montenegrins, 14.5 per cent Muslims, 6.5 per cent Albanians and 3 per cent Serbs. The capital is Podgorica with a

population (1981) of 132,290. The Montenegrin Social Democrat Party (former Communists) won multiparty elections in December 1992 for the 85-seat republican assembly and formed a government.

President, Momir Bulatovic, *elected* 11 January 1993
Prime Minister, Milo Djukanović

SERBIA

Serbia has a total area of 34,175 sq. miles (88,538 sq. km) and a total population of 9.3 million, of whom 66 per cent are Serbs. The capital is Belgrade with a population (1981) of 1,455,000. It includes the provinces of Kosovo (population 1.6 million), of great historic importance to Serbs, and Vojvodina (population 2 million); the autonomy of both was ended in September 1990. Kosovo, with its capital at Priština, is predominantly Albanian (90 per cent). In defiance of the Serbian authorities, ethnic Albanians held parliamentary and presidential elections in May 1992, which were won respectively by the Democratic League of Kosovo and its leader Ibrahim Rugova. Tension between Albanians and Serbs remains very high. Vojvodina, with its capital at Novi Sad, has a large Hungarian minority (21 per cent).

The Socialist Party of Serbia (SPS) (formerly the Communists) emerged as the largest party in multiparty elections for the 250-seat National Assembly, held in December 1992 and formed a coalition government with the extreme nationalist Serbian Radical Party (SRS). The coalition broke down in September 1993 when the SRS called for a parliamentary vote of no confidence in the government, forcing President Milosevic to dissolve parliament. In the ensuing parliamentary election on 19 December 1993 the SPS gained 123 seats; the People's Assembly Party (NSS) 45 seats; SRS 39 seats; Democratic Party 29 seats; Democratic Party of Serbia 7 seats; Democratic Community of Hungarians in the Vojvodina 5 seats; Albanian coalition 2 seats. The SPS, three seats short of a majority, formed a minority government in March 1994, and has unsuccessfully sought the support of centrist opposition parties.

President, Slobodan Milosevic, *elected* 20 December 1992
Prime Minister, Mirko Marjanovic

DEFENCE

Total active armed forces number 126,500, including 60,000 conscripts who serve terms of up to 15 months; reserves number 400,000. The Army has a strength of 90,000, with 639 main battle tanks, 629 armoured personnel carriers and armoured infantry fighting vehicles and 1,449 artillery pieces. The Navy has a strength of 6,000 (including 900 Marines), with four submarines, four frigates and 41 patrol and coastal combatants. The Air Force comprises 29,000 personnel, 282 combat aircraft and 110 armed helicopters. The UN voted to phase out the arms embargo on all the former Yugoslav republics in November 1995.

ECONOMY

Since 1991 the economy has been devastated by the wars in Croatia and Bosnia-Hercegovina, by the UN economic sanctions and trade embargo, and because of the lack of free-market reforms. Most factories have closed. Only the evasion of UN sanctions and the country's agricultural self-sufficiency have kept it alive. In 1993 hyperinflation became rampant because the government continued to print money to finance the wars and subsidize industries. By December 1993 inflation had reached 21,000 per cent a month, the tax system had collapsed, output was one-third

of pre-war levels, industry was working at one-quarter of capacity and the dinar had been devalued ten times. In January 1994 a successful economic stabilization package was introduced with a new superdinar pegged at one-to-one parity with the Deutsche Mark. This reduced monthly inflation from 313 million per cent in January to 1 per cent in February. The UN voted to lift economic sanctions on 22 November 1995 following the conclusion of the Dayton Peace Accord on Bosnia. Industrial production remains extremely low and unemployment high.

TRADE WITH UK	1994	1995
Imports from UK	£4,253,000	£9,970,000
Exports to UK	44,000	560,000

ZAIRE
République du Zaïre

Situated between 12° and 31° E. longitude and 5° N. and 13° S. latitude, Zaïre comprises an area of 905,567 sq. miles (2,345,409 sq. km). Apart from the coastal district in the west which is fairly dry, the rainfall averages between 60 and 80 inches. The average temperature is about 27°C, but in the south the winter temperature can fall nearly to freezing point. Extensive forest covers the central districts.

The population was 34,671,607 at the 1985 census. A 1994 UN estimate put it at 42,552,000. It is composed almost entirely of Bantu groups, divided into semi-autonomous tribes. Minorities include Sudanese, Nilotes, Pygmies and Hamites, as well as refugees from Angola.

Swahili, a Bantu dialect with an admixture of Arabic, is the nearest approach to a common language in the east and south, while Lingala is the language of a large area along the river and in the north, and Kikongo of the region between Kinshasa and the sea. French is the language of administration.

CAPITAL – Kinshasa (formerly Leopoldville), population (1985 census) 2,778,281. Principal towns, Lubumbashi (formerly Elisabethville) (403,623); Kisangani (formerly Stanleyville) (310,705); Likasi (146,394); Kananga (601,239); ΨMatadi (143,598); and Mbandaka (134,495).
CURRENCY – Zaïre of 100 makuta.
FLAG – Dark brown hand and torch with red flame in yellow roundel on green background.
NATIONAL DAY – 24 November.

GOVERNMENT

The state of the Congo, founded in 1885, became a Belgian colony in 1908 and was administered by Belgium until independence in 1960. Mobutu Sésé Seko, formerly commander-in-chief of the Congolese National Army, came to power in a coup in 1965 and was elected President in 1970. Legislative power was vested in a unicameral National Legislative Council, elected for a five-year term by compulsory direct and universal suffrage with candidates proposed by the sole legal political party, Mouvement Populaire de la Révolution (MPR).

Political reforms were announced in April 1990 and President Mobutu called a National Conference to draft a new constitution in April 1991. The conference convened in August but the government refused to grant it sovereign status, causing the main opposition parties to form a 'Sacred Union' to bring down the transitional government. Mobutu accepted an opposition-dominated government under Prime Minister Etienne Tshisekedi in October 1991. His attempts to replace this with MPR-dominated governments failed and the National Conference confirmed the Tshisekedi government as legitimate in August 1992.

From 1992 to 1995 President Mobutu and the opposition were locked in a power struggle. In January 1994 President Mobutu dissolved the pro-Mobutu government and endorsed the formation of a High Council of the Republic–Parliament of Transition (HCR–PT) with a mandate of choosing a new Prime Minister. On 9 April 1994 President Mobutu promulgated a Transitional Constitutional Act endorsed by the HCR–PT which regulated a 15-month period of transition to democracy. During the period the HCR–PT oversees the activities of a transitional government while a constitutional referendum and presidential and legislative elections are held. On 17 June 1994 President Mobutu appointed Kengo Wa Dondo as Prime Minister after he had been elected by the HCR–PT; Tshisekedi's candidacy was excluded, leading to opposition unrest. Prime Minister Dondo named a Cabinet and government equally divided between opposition parties and Mobutu-supporting MPR members, but Tshisekedi's supporters refused to join the government. In July 1995 the HCR–PT voted to extend the transition period by a further two years. A constitutional referendum has been scheduled for December 1996, and presidential and legislative elections for May 1997.

There are 11 regions, each under a Governor and provincial administration: Bas-Zaïre (provincial capital, Matadi); Bandundu (Bandundu); Equateur (Mbandaka); Haut-Zaïre (Kisangani); Kinshasa (Kinshasa); Maniema (Kindu); Nord-Kivu (Goma); Sud-Kivu (Bukavu); Shaba (Katanga) (Lubumbashi); East Kasai (Mbuji-Mayi); West Kasai (Kananga).

SECESSION

Since 1992 ethnic Katangans have been forcing ethnic Kasai mineworkers and their families out of the southern region of Shaba (Katanga) in a wave of ethnic violence which is a repeat of the Katanga secessionist war in 1960. In December 1993 the Governor of Shaba declared total autonomy from the rest of Zaïre and announced the reversion of the region's name to Katanga.

HEAD OF STATE
President of the Republic and National Security, Marshal Mobutu Sésé Séko, *assumed office* 25 November 1965; *elected* 5 November 1970; *re-elected* 1977, 1984, *remained in power when term ended* 1991

CABINET *as at August 1996*
Prime Minister, Leon Kengo Wa Dondo
Deputy PMs, Kamanda Wa Kamanda (*Interior and Decentralization*); Adm. Mavua Mudima (*National Defence*); Kititwa Tumansi Benga Ntundu (*Foreign Affairs*); Mutomba Bafawa Nsenda (*Mines*)
International Co-operation, Landu Kavidi
Justice, N'Singa Udjuu
Information and Media, Boguo Makeli
Planning, Mambu Ma Khenzu
Finance, Kiakwama Kiakiziki
Budget, Idambitwo Bakaato Dimbisa
Agriculture, Tshikung Nawej
Economy, Banguli N'Sambwe
Energy, Mpetshi Ilonga
Public Works, Thambwe Mwamba
Transport and Communications, Mwando Nsimba
External Trade, Kasongo Mwindinge
Land Affairs, Kayumba Bin Amani
Higher Education, Mushobekwa Kalimba Wa Katana
Primary, Secondary and Vocational Education, Sekimonyo Wa Mangango

Health, Kasongo Numbi
Social Affairs, Lumbu-Lumbu Musavuli
Labour, Omba Pene Djunga
Civil Service, Tshipasa Vangi Sivavi
Communications, Gifuza Ginday
Environment and Tourism, Tshibanda Ntungamulongo
Youth, Sports and Leisure, Kisomba Kiaku Mwisi
Culture and Arts, Epee Ngambwa
Minister Without Portfolio, Mboso Nkodia Mpuanga

EMBASSY OF THE REPUBLIC OF ZAIRE
26 Chesham Place, London SWIX 8HH
Tel 0171-235 6137
Ambassador Extraordinary and Plenipotentiary, new appointment awaited

BRITISH EMBASSY
Avenue des Trois 'Z', Gombe, Kinshasa
Tel: Kinshasa 34775
Ambassador Extraordinary and Plenipotentiary, Marcus L. H. Hope, apptd 1996

There is a British Consulate at Kisangani.

ECONOMY

The cultivation of oil palms is widespread, palm oil being the most important agricultural cash product though it is no longer exported. Coffee, rubber, cocoa and timber are the most important agricultural exports. The production of cotton, pyrethrum and copal is increasing. The country is rich in minerals, particularly Shaba (Katanga) province. Copper is widely exploited, and industrial diamonds and cobalt are also produced. Oil deposits are exploited off the Zaïre estuary and reef-gold is mined in the north-east of the country.

There is a wide variety of small secondary industries, the main products being foodstuffs, beverages, tobacco, textiles, leather, wood products, cement and building materials, metallurgy, small river craft and bicycles. There are reserves of hydro-electric power and the Inga dam on the river Zaïre supplies electricity to Matadi, Kinshasa and Shaba.

Rampant hyper-inflation and corruption have left the economy and the state's finances in a parlous state. Multilateral and bilateral aid has also been greatly reduced because of President Mobutu's refusal to leave office. In June 1994 Zaïre's voting rights at the IMF were suspended over its failure to pay its financial arrears.

TRADE

The chief exports are copper, crude oil, coffee, diamonds, rubber, cobalt, gold, cassiterite, zinc and other metals.

Trade with UK	1994	1995
Imports from UK	£12,058,000	£15,671,000
Exports to UK	10,973,000	11,350,000

COMMUNICATIONS

There are approximately 20,500 km of roads (earth-surfaced) of national importance, and 6,000 km of railways. The country has four international and 40 principal airports.

ZAMBIA
Republic of Zambia

Zambia lies on the plateau of Central Africa between 22° and 33° 33′ E. longitude and 8° 15′ and 18° S. latitude. It has an area of 290,586 sq. miles (752,614 sq. km) and a population (UN estimate, 1994) of 9,196,000. With the exception of the valleys of the Zambezi, the Luapula, the Kafue and the Luangwa rivers, and the Luano valley, elevations vary from 3,000 to 5,000 feet above sea level, but in the north-east the plateau rises to occasional altitudes of over 6,000 feet. Although Zambia lies within the tropics, and fairly centrally in the African land mass, its elevation relieves it from extremely high temperatures and humidity.

CAPITAL – Lusaka, population (1989 estimate) 1 million. Other centres are Livingstone, Kabwe, Chipata, Mazabuka, Mbala, Kasama, Solwezi, Mongu, Mansa, Ndola, Luanshya, Mufulira, Chingola, Chililabombwe, Kalulushi and Kitwe, the last six towns being the main centres on the copper belt.

CURRENCY – Kwacha (K) of 100 ngwee.

FLAG – Green with three small vertical stripes, red, black and orange (next fly); eagle device on green above stripes.

NATIONAL ANTHEM – Stand and Sing of Zambia, Proud and Free.

NATIONAL DAY – 24 October (Independence Day).

GOVERNMENT

Northern Rhodesia came under British rule in 1889. It achieved internal self-government when the Federation of Rhodesia and Nyasaland was dissolved in 1963 and became an independent republic within the Commonwealth on 24 October 1964 under the name of Zambia.

Zambia was a one-party state (the United National Independence Party) from 1973 until 1990, when pressure from opposition groups led to a new constitution (August 1991) and multiparty legislative and presidential elections in October 1991. The Movement for Multiparty Democracy (MMD) won 125 of the 150 seats in parliament, and the MMD candidate Frederick Chiluba defeated Kaunda, who had ruled since independence, in the presidential election. The MMD government has begun the transformation of the state-controlled economy into a free market system with the sale and privatization of large sectors of the economy. Aid and investment have poured into the country, foreign exchange controls have been removed, the Kwacha floated and prices freed. A state of emergency was in force between March and May 1993 after the discovery of a coup plot by UNIP. Continued allegations of corruption by government ministers led first to the resignation of 15 MMD MPs from the party and then ministerial resignations, under pressure from foreign aid donors in 1993–4. A constitutional amendment was approved by the President in May 1996 requiring presidential candidates to be third-generation Zambians, thereby excluding former President Kenneth Kaunda who had returned to politics in June 1995. Elections are due in October 1996.

HEAD OF STATE
President, Hon. Frederick J. Chiluba, *elected* 31 October 1991
Vice-President, Hon. Brig. Godfrey Miyanda

CABINET *as at August 1996*
Defence, Hon. Benjamin Mwila
Foreign Affairs, Hon. Gen. Christon Tembo
Finance, Hon. Ronald Penza
Home Affairs, Hon. Chitalu Sampa
Local Government and Housing, Hon. Ben Mwiinga
Health, Hon. Dr Katele Kalumba
Education, Hon. Alfeyo Hambayi

Commerce, Trade and Industry, Dr S. K. Syamujaye
Community Development and Social Welfare, Hon. Paul Kaping'a
Labour and Social Security, Hon. Newstead Zimba
Communications and Transport, Hon. Dawson Lupunga
Energy and Water Development, Hon. Edith Nawakwi
Agriculture, Food and Fisheries, Hon. Suresh Desai
Lands, Hon. Luminzu Shimaponda
Environment and Natural Resources, Hon. William Harrington
Information and Broadcasting, Hon. Amusa Mwanawambwa
Mines and Mineral Development, Hon. Kelly Walubita
Technical Education and Vocational Training, Hon. Dr Kabunda Kayongo
Sport, Youth and Child Development, Hon. Samuel Miyanda
Tourism, Hon. Gabriel Maka
Works and Supply, Hon. Lt.-Gen. Patrick Kafumukacho
Legal Affairs, Hon. Dr Remmy K. K. Mushota
Minister Without Portfolio, Hon. Michael Sata

HIGH COMMISSION FOR THE REPUBLIC OF ZAMBIA
2 Palace Gate, London W8 5LS
Tel 0171-589 6655
High Commissioner, HE Love Mtesa, apptd 1992
Defence Adviser, Brig.-Gen. M. G. Lisita
First Secretary, J. Chikwenda (*Information/Tourism*)

BRITISH HIGH COMMISSION
Independence Avenue (PO Box 50050), 15 101 Ridgeway, Lusaka
Tel: Lusaka 251133
High Commissioner, HE Patrick Nixon, CMG, OBE, apptd 1993
Deputy High Commissioner, B. S. Jones, LVO
First Secretary (Commercial/Consular), R. Clark

BRITISH COUNCIL DIRECTOR, Adrian Greer, Heroes Place, Cairo Road (PO Box 34571), Lusaka. There is also a library in Ndola.

ECONOMY

The free market economic reforms introduced since 1991 by the MMD government have revolutionized the economy, which had been highly regulated and protected from competition. Price subsidies and tariffs have been lowered or abolished and public sector wages frozen but inflation and interest rates have increased, causing hardships. Increased imports have affected manufacturing and agricultural production.

Principal products are maize, sugar, groundnuts, cotton, livestock, vegetables and tobacco. Mineral production was valued at K8,390 million in 1987, of which copper production (of 483,100 tonnes) accounted for K6,870 million.

Following the reforms initiated by the government, the US government wrote off K59,000 million of debt in April 1993. The IMF lifted its suspension of Zambia, in place since September 1987; loans worth US$1,300 million were subsequently approved. However, the constitutional amendment approved in May 1996 establishing qualifications for presidential candidacy prompted foreign donors to suspend aid.

TRADE WITH UK	1994	1995
Imports from UK	£44,523,000	£49,819,000
Exports to UK	13,038,000	19,460,000

ZIMBABWE
Republic of Zimbabwe

Zimbabwe, the former Southern Rhodesia, lies south of the Zambezi river and borders Zambia and Mozambique on the north, South Africa and Botswana on the south and west, and Mozambique on the east. It has a total area of 150,804 sq. miles (390,580 sq. km), and a population (1994 estimate) of 11,200,000. The 1992 census recorded 10,400,000 people.

CAPITAL – Harare (formerly Salisbury) situated on the Mashonaland plateau, population (1992) 1,184,000. Bulawayo is the largest town in Matabeleland, population (1992) 621,000. Other centres are Chitungwiza, Mutare, Gweru, Kadoma, Kwe Kwe, Masvingo and Hwange.

CURRENCY – Zimbabwe dollar (Z$) of 100 cents.

FLAG – Seven horizontal stripes of green, yellow, red, black, red, yellow, green; a white, black-bordered, triangle based on the hoist containing the national emblem.

NATIONAL ANTHEM – Ngaikomberarwe Nyika Ye Zimbabwe (Blessed be the country of Zimbabwe).

NATIONAL DAY – 18 April (Independence Day).

GOVERNMENT

Southern Rhodesia was granted responsible government in 1923. An illegal declaration of independence on 11 November 1965 was finally terminated on 12 December 1979. Following elections in February 1980 the country became independent on 18 April 1980 as the Republic of Zimbabwe, a member of the British Commonwealth.

The independence constitution was amended in 1987, making the presidency an executive post. The President is popularly elected for a six-year term, appoints the Cabinet and can veto parliamentary bills. The legislature became unicameral in 1990 and the House of Assembly has 150 members, 120 elected, eight provincial governors, ten traditional chiefs and 12 others appointed by the President. A merger agreement between the ZANU (PF) and ZAPU parties was signed in 1987 with a view to the eventual creation of a one-party state. The new party is known as ZANU-PF. The latest general election was held in April 1995 and ZANU-PF won 118 of the 120 elective seats, although it lost a by-election in November 1995. President Mugabe was re-elected for a six-year term in March 1996, following the withdrawal of the other two contenders. Turnout was 31.7 per cent.

The country is divided into eight provinces: Manicaland, Masvingo, Matabeleland North, Matabeleland South, Midlands, Mashonaland West, Central and East.

HEAD OF STATE

Executive President, Hon. Robert Gabriel Mugabe, *elected* 30 December 1987, *re-elected* March 1990, March 1996

CABINET *as at August 1996*

The President
Vice-Presidents, Hon. Simon Muzenda; Hon. Dr Joshua Nkomo
National Security, Hon. Dr Sidney Sekeramayi
Finance, Hon. Dr Herbert M. Murerwa
Planning, Hon. Richard Hove
National Affairs, Employment Creation and Co-operatives, Hon. Florence Chitauro
Local Government, Rural and Urban Development, Hon. John Nkomo

Agriculture, Hon. Dennis Norman
Foreign Affairs, Hon. Dr Stanislaus Mudenge
Justice, Legal and Parliamentary Affairs, Hon. Emmerson Mnangagwa
Defence, Hon. Moven Mahachi
Higher Education, Hon. Ignatius Chombo
Education, Hon. Edmund Garwe
Home Affairs, Hon. Dumiso Dabengwa
Public Construction and National Housing, Hon. Enos Chikowore
Lands and Water Resources, Hon. Kumbirai Kangai
Information, Posts and Telecommunications, Hon. Joyce Mujuru
Labour, Public Service and Social Welfare, Hon. Florence L. Chitauro
Industry and Commerce, Hon. Dr Nathan M. Shamuyarira
Mines, Hon. Dr Swithun T. Mombeshora
Transport and Energy, Hon. Simon Moyo
Health and Child Welfare, Hon. Dr Timothy Stamps
Environment and Tourism, Hon. Chenhamo Chimutingwende
Sports, Recreation and Culture, Hon. Dr Witness Mangwende
President's Office, Hon. Cephas Msipa
Ministers Without Portfolio, Dr Eddison J. M. Zvobgo; Joseph Msika

HIGH COMMISSION OF THE REPUBLIC OF ZIMBABWE
Zimbabwe House, 429 Strand, London WC2R 0SA
Tel 0171-836 7755
High Commissioner, HE Dr Ngoni Togarepi Chideya, apptd 1993
Minister-Counsellors, A. Nyazika; J. Mupamhanga
Defence Adviser, Lt.-Col. E. Zabanyana
Counsellor, Dr S. Undenge (*Commercial*)

BRITISH HIGH COMMISSION
Corner House, Samora Machel Avenue (PO Box 4490), Harare
Tel: Harare 793781
High Commissioner, HE Martin J. Williams, CVO, OBE, apptd 1995
Deputy High Commissioner, T. J. David
Defence Adviser, Col. A. R. Screen, OBE
First Secretaries, A. R. Ashcroft (*Commercial*); G. M. Johnson (*Consular*)

BRITISH COUNCIL DIRECTOR, Dr Jerry Eyres, OBE, 23 Jason Moyo Avenue (PO Box 664), Harare. There is also a library at Bulawayo.

ECONOMY

Ten years of socialism and central planning in 1980–90, coupled with a period of drought, brought the economy to crisis point before free market economic reforms were introduced in 1990 under the auspices of a World Bank-enhanced structural adjustment programme. This has involved the removal of food subsidies, the floating of the currency, opening the market to imports, and reducing subsidies. The programme has been partly implemented but the economy remains highly regulated and the civil service and armed forces have not been reduced sufficiently, leading to a budget deficit of around 13 per cent of GDP. The foreign debt is £2,000 million and costs one-third of export revenue to service. Inflation remains high at 20 per cent and the economic restructuring programme has caused unemployment to rise to 40 per cent as the government lays off public sector workers. The compulsory purchase of white-owned commercial farms by the government in 1993–4 has caused a scandal as the land has been given to senior government officials rather than the landless black peasants it was intended for, and the farmers given compensation in worthless government bonds. The Supreme Court approved government plans to seize 12 million acres of white-owned farmland in June 1996.

The country is endowed with minerals, water, forests, wildlife and other resources. The agricultural sector is well-developed, accounts for 68 per cent of GDP and employs 70 per cent of the workforce. Tobacco remains the most important crop in terms of export (Zimbabwe is the largest exporter in the world), and maize the most important for domestic consumption. Agriculture has diversified in recent years with horticultural products (especially roses and tulips), fruit and vegetables becoming important export earners. Other crops include wheat, cotton, and sugar. Beef is exported to the EU.

The manufacturing sector is very dependent on the agricultural sector for raw materials. Industry is also dependent on imports e.g. fuel oil, steel products and chemicals, as well as heavy machinery and items of transport. The mining sector, although contributing a relatively small portion to GDP, is important to the economy as a foreign exchange earner. Almost all mineral production is exported. Gold is the most important mineral, others are asbestos, diamonds, silver, nickel, copper, chrome ore, tin, iron ore and cobalt. There is a successful ferro-chrome industry and a substantial steel works which has been heavily subsidized by government. Platinum mining is about to begin following a £160 million investment by an Australian firm.

Tourism is of growing importance, with more than 1,000,000 visitors in 1995.

Trade with UK	1994	1995
Imports from UK	£104,690,000	£87,696,000
Exports to UK	145,640,000	149,344,000

EDUCATION

Since independence, a policy of free primary education and accelerated expansion at secondary level has resulted in rapidly expanding enrolment. Over 80 per cent of schools are government-aided schools. The University of Zimbabwe was founded in 1955.

British Dependent Territories

ANGUILLA

Anguilla is a flat coralline island, about 16 miles in length, three and a half miles in breadth at its widest point and its area is about 35 sq. miles (91 sq. km). It lies approximately 18° N. latitude and 63° W. longitude, to the north of the Leeward Islands group. The island is covered with low scrub and fringed with white coral-sand beaches. The climate is pleasant, with temperatures in the range of 24-30° C throughout the year.

POPULATION – The population (1992 census) is 8,960.
CAPITAL – The Valley (population 1,400).
CURRENCY – East Caribbean dollar (EC$) of 100 cents.
FLAG – British Blue Ensign with the coat of arms and three dolphins in the fly.

GOVERNMENT

Anguilla has been a British colony since 1650. For much of its history it was linked administratively with St Christopher, but three months after the Associated State of Saint Christopher (St Kitts)-Nevis-Anguilla came into being in 1967, the Anguillans repudiated government from St Kitts. A Commissioner was installed in 1969 and in 1976 Anguilla was given a new status and separate constitution. Final separation from St Kitts and Nevis was effected on 19 December 1980 and Anguilla reverted to a British dependency. A new constitution was introduced in 1982, providing for a Governor, an Executive Council comprising four elected Ministers and two ex-officio members (the Attorney-General and Permanent Secretary, Finance), and an 11-member legislative House of Assembly presided over by a Speaker.

The 1982 Constitution (Amendment) Order 1990 came into operation on 30 May 1990. Among the new constitutional provisions are a Deputy Governor (who replaces the Permanent Secretary (Finance) in the Executive Council and the Legislature), a Parliamentary Secretary, Leader of Opposition and Deputy Speaker.

Governor, HE Alan Hoole, OBE, *apptd* 1995
Deputy Governor, Henry McCrory, LVO, OBE, *apptd* 1991

EXECUTIVE COUNCIL *as at June 1996*
Chairman, The Governor
Chief Minister and Minister of Tourism, Lands, Agriculture and Fisheries, Hon. Hubert Hughes
Social Services, Hon. Edison Baird
Communications, Public Utilities and Works, Hon. Albert Hughes
Finance and Economic Development, Hon. Victor Banks
Attorney-General, Hon. Kurt De Freitas
Member, The Deputy Governor

ECONOMY

Low rainfall limits agricultural output and export earnings are mainly from sales of fish and lobsters. Tourism has developed rapidly in recent years and accounts for most of the island's economic activity. In 1995 there were 38,531 tourists and a further 68,555 day visitors.

FINANCE	1994	1995
Revenue	EC$41,746,351	EC$46,403,084
Expenditure	38,602,637	43,752,307

TRADE WITH UK	1994	1995
Imports from UK	£1,320,000	£2,059,000
Exports to UK	86,000	14,000

ASCENSION
— *see* St Helena

BERMUDA

The Bermudas, or Somers Islands, are a cluster of about 100 small islands (about 20 of which are inhabited) situated in the west of the Atlantic Ocean, in 32° 18′ N. latitude and 64° 46′ W. longitude, the nearest point of the mainland being Cape Hatteras in North Carolina, about 570 miles distant. The total area is approximately 20.59 sq. miles (53 sq. km), which includes 2.3 sq. miles leased to the USA.

POPULATION – The civil population (1994) is 60,075.
CAPITAL – ΨHamilton (population 1993, 2,277).
CURRENCY – Bermuda dollar of 100 cents.
FLAG – British Red Ensign with the shield of arms in the fly.

GOVERNMENT

The colony derives its name from Juan Bermudez, a Spaniard, who sighted it before 1515. No settlement was made until 1609 when Sir George Somers, who was shipwrecked there on his way to Virginia, colonized the islands.

Internal self-government was introduced in 1968. There is a Senate of 11 members and an elected House of Assembly of 40 members. The Governor retains responsibility for external affairs, defence, internal security and the police, although administrative matters for the police service have been delegated to the Minister of Labour, Home Affairs and Public Safety. Independence from the UK was rejected in a referendum in August 1995.

The last general election was held on 5 October 1993. The United Bermuda Party holds 22 seats, and the Progressive Labour Party 18 seats.

Governor and Commander-in-Chief, HE John Kelly, *apptd* 1996
Deputy Governor, Peter Willis

CABINET *as at June 1996*
Premier, Hon. David J. Saul
Deputy Premier, Education and Human Affairs, Hon. C. Jerome Dill
Labour, Home Affairs and Public Safety, Hon. Quinton L. Edness
Works and Engineering, Parks and Housing, Hon. Leonard O. Gibbons
Environment, Planning and Natural Resources, Hon. Pamela F. Gordon
Transport and Aviation Services, Hon. Wayne L. Furbert
Finance, Hon. Dr E. G. Grant Gibbons
Health and Social Services, Harry W. Soares

Legislative Affairs and Women's Issues, Hon. Lynda Milligan-Whyte
Tourism and Marine Services, Hon. A. David Dodwell
Youth Development, Sports and Recreation, Hon. M. Timothy Smith
Technology and Information, Hon. John Barritt
Community and Cultural Affairs, Hon. Yvette V. A. Swan

President of the Senate, Hon. A. S. Jackson, CBE
Speaker of the House of Assembly, Hon. Ernest DeCouto
Chief Justice, Hon. Austin Ward, QC

ECONOMY

The islands' economic structure is based on tourism, the major industry, and international company business, attracted by the low level of taxation and sophisticated telecommunications system. In 1995 a total of 589,855 visitors arrived by air and cruise ship.

Locally manufactured concentrates, perfumes, cut flowers and pharmaceuticals are the colony's leading exports. Little food is produced except vegetables and fish, other foodstuffs being imported.

In November 1995, the US, UK and Canadian governments handed over 1,500 acres of land (roughly 10 per cent of the colony), to the government. The land, which had been used for military bases, included an airport on St David's Island.

FINANCE	1994–5	1995–6
Public revenue	$385,112,000	$426,065,000
Public expenditure	358,112,000	390,448,000
TRADE WITH UK	1994	1995
Imports from UK	£23,512,000	£17,316,000
Exports to UK	6,309,000	3,085,000

COMMUNICATIONS

One daily and two weekly newspapers are published in Bermuda. Three commercial companies operate radio and television services, including a cable-television system which started service in July 1988. The Bermuda Telephone Company and Cable and Wireless provide telecommunications links to more than 140 countries.

EDUCATION

Free elementary education was introduced in 1949. Free secondary education was introduced in 1965 for those children in the aided and maintained schools who were below the upper limit of the statutory school age of 18 (from 1969 onwards).

THE BRITISH ANTARCTIC TERRITORY

The British Antarctic Territory was designated in 1962 and consists of the areas south of 60°S. latitude which were previously included in the Falkland Islands Dependencies. The territory lies between longitudes 20° and 80°W., south of latitude 60°S. and includes the South Orkney Islands, the South Shetland Islands, the mountainous Antarctic Peninsula (highest point Mount Jackson, 13,620 ft, in Palmer Land) and all adjacent islands, and the land mass extending to the South Pole. The territory has no indigenous inhabitants and the British population consists of the scientists and technicians who man the British Antarctic Survey stations. The number averages about 60 to 70 in winter, but increases considerably in the summer

months with the arrival of field workers. Argentina, Brazil, Chile, China, Korea (South), Poland, USA, Russia, Spain, Ukraine and Uruguay also have scientific stations in the territory.

The first two British Antarctic Survey stations were established in the South Shetland Islands in 1944, and by 1956 the number of stations had risen to 12. Due to the completion of field work in some areas and increased mobility, the number has now been reduced to four. These are Rothera (Adelaide Island), Halley (Caird Coast) and, in summer only, Fossil Bluff (George VI Sound) and Signy Island (South Orkney Islands). Fifteen other stations have been established but are at present unoccupied.

The territory is administered by a Commissioner, resident in London.

Commissioner (non-resident), Anthony J. Longrigg, *apptd* 1995

THE BRITISH INDIAN OCEAN TERRITORY

The British Indian Ocean Territory was established by an Order in Council in 1965 and included islands formerly administered from Mauritius and the Seychelles. The islands of Farquhar, Desroches and Aldabra became part of the Seychelles when it became independent in 1976; since then the Territory has consisted of the islands of the Chagos Archipelago only.

The Chagos Archipelago consists of six main groups of islands situated on the Great Chagos Bank and covering some 21,000 sq. miles (54,389 sq. km). The largest and most southerly of the Chagos Islands is Diego Garcia, a sand cay with a land area of about 17 sq. miles approximately 1,100 miles east of Mahé, used as a joint naval support facility by Britain and the USA.

The other main island groups of the archipelago, Peros Banhos (29 islands with a total land area of 4 sq. miles) and Salomon (11 islands with a total land area of 2 sq. miles) are uninhabited. The islands have a tropical maritime climate, with average temperatures between 25° C and 29° C in Diego Garcia, and rainfall in the whole archipelago of 90–100 inches a year.

FLAG – Divided horizontally into blue and white wavy stripes, with the Union Flag in the canton and a crowned palm-tree over all in the fly.

Commissioner, David Ross MacLennan, *apptd* 1994
Administrator, D. J. Smith

TRADE WITH UK	1994	1995
Imports from UK	£1,557,000	£1,924,000
Exports to UK	5,000	—

THE BRITISH VIRGIN ISLANDS

The Virgin Islands are situated at the eastern extremity of the Greater Antilles, divided between the UK and the USA. Those of the group which are British number 46, of which 11 are inhabited, and have a total area of about 59 sq. miles (153 sq. km). The principal islands are Tortola, the largest (situated in 18° 27′ N. lat. and 64° 40′ W. long., area, 21 sq. miles), Virgin Gorda (8¼ sq. miles), Anegada (15 sq. miles) and Jost Van Dyke (3½ sq. miles).

Apart from Anegada, which is a flat coral island, the British Virgin Islands are hilly, being an extension of the

Puerto Rico and the US Virgin Islands archipelago. The highest point is Sage Mountain on Tortola which rises to a height of 1,780 feet.

The islands lie within the trade winds belt and possess a sub-tropical climate. The average temperature varies from 22°–28° C in winter to 26°–31° C in summer. Average annual rainfall is 53 inches.

POPULATION – The 1991 census showed a total population of 16,108: Tortola (13,225); Virgin Gorda (2,431); Anegada (162); Jost Van Dyke (140); and other islands (144).

CAPITAL – ΨRoad Town, on the south-east of Tortola. Population 3,983.

CURRENCY – The US dollar (US$) of 100 cents is legal tender.

FLAG – British Blue Ensign with the shield of arms in the fly.

GOVERNMENT

Under the 1977 constitution the Governor, appointed by the Crown, remains responsible for defence and internal security, external affairs and the civil service but in other matters acts in accordance with the advice of the Executive Council. The Executive Council consists of the Governor as Chairman, one ex-officio member (the Attorney-General), the Chief Minister and three other ministers. The Legislative Council consists of a Speaker chosen from outside the Council, one ex-officio member (the Attorney-General), and 13 elected members returned from ten electoral districts.

Governor, HE David Patrick Mackilligin, CMG, *apptd* 1995
Deputy Governor, M. Elton Georges, OBE

EXECUTIVE COUNCIL *as at 30 June 1996*
Chairman, The Governor
Chief Minister and Minister of Finance, Hon. Ralph O'Neal, OBE
Natural Resources and Labour, Hon. Oliver Cills
Communications and Works, Hon. Alvin Christopher
Health, Education and Welfare, Hon. Alred Frett
Attorney-General, Hon. Dancia Penn

Puisne Judge (resident), Justice Ephraim Georges

ECONOMY

Tourism is the main industry but the financial centre is growing steadily in importance. Other industries include a rum distillery, three stone-crushing plants and factories manufacturing concrete blocks and paint. The major export items are fresh fish, gravel, sand, fruit and vegetables; exports are largely confined to the US Virgin Islands. Chief imports are building materials, machinery, cars and beverages.

FINANCE	1994	1995
Revenue	US$77,125,000	US$100,041,697
Expenditure	76,475,000	85,476,778

TRADE WITH UK	1994	1995
Imports from UK	£5,935,000	£5,399,000
Exports to UK	3,716,000	994,000

COMMUNICATIONS

The principal airport is on Beef Island, linked by bridge to Tortola, and an extended runway of 3,600 ft enables larger aircraft to call. There is a second airfield on Virgin Gorda and a third on Anegada. There are direct shipping services to the UK and the USA and fast passenger services connect the main islands by ferry.

THE CAYMAN ISLANDS

The Cayman Islands, between 79° 44′ and 81° 26′ W. and 19° 15′ and 19° 46′ N., consist of three islands, Grand Cayman, Cayman Brac, and Little Cayman, with a total area of 100 sq. miles (259 sq. km). About 150 miles south of Cuba, the islands are divided from Jamaica, 180 miles to the south-east, by the Cayman Trench, the deepest part of the Caribbean. The nearest point on the US mainland is Miami in Florida, 450 miles to the north. Cooled by trade winds, the annual average temperature and rainfall are 27.2° C and 50.7 inches respectively.

POPULATION – Population (estimate 1995) 33,600, of which most live on Grand Cayman.

CAPITAL – ΨGeorge Town, in Grand Cayman, population (estimate 1995) 17,500.

CURRENCY – Cayman Islands dollar (CI$) of 100 cents, which is fixed at CI$ = US$1.20.

FLAG – British Blue Ensign with the arms on a white disc in the fly.

GOVERNMENT

The colony derives its name from the Carib word for the crocodile, 'caymanas', which appeared in the log of the first English visitor to the islands, Sir Francis Drake. Although tradition has it that the first settlers arrived in 1658, the first recorded settlers arrived in 1666–71. The first recorded permanent settlers followed the first land grant by Britain in 1734. The islands were placed under direct control of Jamaica in 1863. When Jamaica became independent in 1962, the islands opted to remain under the British Crown.

The constitution provides for a Governor, a Legislative Assembly and an Executive Council, and effectively allows a large measure of self-government. Unless there are exceptional reasons, the Governor accepts the advice of the Executive Council, which comprises three official members and five ministers elected from the 15 elected members of the Assembly. The official members also sit in the Assembly. The Governor has responsibility for the police, civil service, defence and external affairs. The Governor handed over the presidency of the Legislative Assembly to the Speaker in 1991. The normal life of the Assembly is four years, with a general election next due in November 1996.

Governor, HE John Wynne Owen, MBE, *apptd* 1995

EXECUTIVE COUNCIL *as at 30 June 1996*
President, The Governor
Chief Secretary, Hon. J. Ryan, MBE
Attorney-General, Hon. R. H. Coles
Financial Secretary, Hon. G. A. McCarthy, OBE
Tourism, Aviation and Commerce, Hon. T. C. Jefferson, OBE
Community Development, Sports, Women's and Youth Affairs and Culture, Hon. W. M. Bush
Education and Planning, Hon. T. M. Bodden, OBE
Health, Drug Abuse Prevention and Rehabilitation, Hon. A. S. Eden
Agriculture and Environment, Communications, Works, Hon. J. McLean, OBE

Speaker of Legislative Assembly, Mrs S. I. McLaughlin, MBE
CAYMAN ISLANDS GOVERNMENT OFFICE, 6 Arlington Street, London SW1A 1RE. Tel: 0171-491 7772.
Government Representative, T. Russell, CMG, CBE

ECONOMY

With a complete absence of direct taxation, the Cayman Islands has become successful over the past 25 years as an offshore financial centre. With representation from 62 countries, there were, at the end of 1995, 564 banks and trust companies, of which local offices were maintained by 107. In addition, there were 543 licensed insurance companies and 34,000 registered companies at the end of 1995. Tourism, with an emphasis on scuba diving, has also been developed successfully. There were 361,400 visitors by air and 682,900 cruise ship callers in 1995.

The two industries support a heavy imbalance in trade resulting from the need to import most of what is consumed and used on the islands, and have created a thriving local economy in which the GDP reached US$913.9 million (US$28,622 per capita) in 1994. Import duty and fees from financial centre operations have provided revenue enabling the government to undertake heavy investment in education (which is provided free to all four- to 16-year olds), health and other social programmes.

FINANCE	1995*	1996
Revenue	CI$172.0m	CI$201.5m
Expenditure	178.0m	202.7m
*estimated		

TRADE	1994	1995
Total imports	CI$270.0m	CI$335.0m
Total exports	2.0m	2.0m

TRADE WITH UK	1994	1995
Imports from UK	£6,780,000	£10,621,000
Exports to UK	2,575,000	1,330,000

FALKLAND ISLANDS

The Falkland Islands, the only considerable group in the South Atlantic, lie about 300 miles east of the Straits of Magellan, between 52° 15'–53° S. latitude and 57° 40'– 62° W. longitude. They consist of East Falkland (area 2,610 sq. miles; 6,759 sq. km), West Falkland (2,090 sq. miles; 5,413 sq. km) and over 100 small islands. Mount Usborne (E. Falkland), the loftiest peak, rises 2,312 feet above sea level. The islands are chiefly moorland.

The climate is cool. At Stanley the mean monthly temperature varies between 9° C in January and 2° C in July.

POPULATION – The population, excluding the British garrison, was 2,121 at 5 March 1991.

CHIEF TOWN – ΨStanley, population (1991) 1,643.

Stanley is about 8,103 miles from Britain.

CURRENCY – Falkland pound of 100 pence.

FLAG – British Blue Ensign with the arms on a white disc in the fly.

GOVERNMENT

The Falklands were sighted first by Davis in 1592, and then by Hawkins in 1594; the first known landing was by Strong in 1690. A settlement was made by France in 1764; this was subsequently sold to Spain, but the latter country recognized Great Britain's title to a part at least of the group in 1771. After Argentina declared independence from Spain, the Argentine government in 1820 proclaimed its sovereignty over the Falklands and a settlement was founded in 1826. The settlement was destroyed by the Americans in 1831. In 1833 occupation was resumed by the

British for the protection of the seal-fisheries, and the islands were permanently colonized. Argentina continued to claim sovereignty over the islands (known to them as las Islas Malvinas), and in pursuance of this claim invaded the islands on 2 April 1982 and also occupied South Georgia. A naval and military force dispatched from Great Britain recaptured South Georgia on 25 April and after landing at San Carlos Bay on 21 May, recaptured the islands from the Argentines, who surrendered on 14 June 1982. A British naval and military garrison of 1,700 personnel remains in the area. A military zone of 55 miles (previously 80) remains around the islands within which Argentinian naval and air forces may not intrude.

Under the 1985 constitution, the Governor is advised by an Executive Council consisting of three elected members of the Legislative Council and two ex-officio members, the Chief Executive and the Financial Secretary. The Legislative Council consists of eight elected members and the same two ex-officio members.

Governor and Chairman of the Executive Council, HE Richard Peter Ralph, CVO, *apptd* 1996
Chief Executive, Hon. A. M. Gurr
Financial Secretary, Hon. D. F. Howatt
Commander, British Forces, Falkland Islands, Cdr. A. S. Backus
Attorney-General, D. G. Lang, QC
FALKLAND ISLANDS GOVERNMENT OFFICE, Falkland House, 14 Broadway, London SW1H OBH. Tel: 0171-222 2542. *Government Representative*, Miss S. Cameron

ECONOMY

The economy was formerly based solely on agriculture, principally sheep-farming with a little dairy farming for domestic requirements and crops for winter fodder. Since the 1982 war the UK government has provided some £46 million to restore the economy. Since the establishment of an interim conservation and management fishing zone around the islands and the consequent introduction in 1987 of a licensing regime for vessels fishing within the 200-mile zone, the economy has diversified and income from the associated fishing activities, mainly for illex squid, is now the largest source of revenue. The dramatic increase in government revenue from fishing licences has led to the establishment of a substantial health, education and welfare system with a well-equipped hospital in Stanley, free education until the age of 16 and further education in the UK paid for by the Falklands government. The islands are now self-financing except for defence. Chief imports are provisions, alcoholic beverages, timber, clothing and hardware. Tourism is a small but expanding industry.

In 1993 the Falkland Islands government announced a 200-mile oil exploration zone around the islands. In September 1995 the UK and Argentina signed an agreement which provided for a joint commission to co-ordinate exploration of the oil field. The Falkland Islands' government agreed to use the revenue from exploration licences to pay for the British military garrison and the costs of the 1982 defence of the islands by the UK. The first licensing round for oil exploration opened in October 1995, with bids for exploration rights to be made in July 1996.

FINANCE	1993–4	1994–5
Public revenue	£38,000,000	£36,980,123
Expenditure	33,500,000	28,435,544

TRADE WITH UK	1994	1995
Imports from UK	£9,360,000	£15,665,000
Exports to UK	4,516,000	4,721,000

GIBRALTAR

Gibraltar is a rocky promontory with a total area of 2½ sq. miles (6.5 sq km) and a height of 1,396 ft at its greatest elevation. It juts southwards from the south-east coast of Spain, with which it is connected by a low isthmus. It is about 20 miles (32 km) from the opposite coast of Africa. The town stands at the foot of the promontory on the west side.

POPULATION – The population at the end of 1993 was 28,051.

CURRENCY – Gibraltar pound of 100 pence.

FLAG – White with a red stripe along the lower edge; over all a red castle with a key hanging from its gateway.

GOVERNMENT

Gibraltar was captured in 1704, during the war of the Spanish Succession, by a combined Dutch and English force, and was ceded to Great Britain by the Treaty of Utrecht 1713. Several attempts have been made to retake it, the most celebrated being the great siege of 1779 to 1783, when General Eliott held it for three years and seven months against a combined French and Spanish force. The Treaty of Utrecht stipulates that if Britain ever relinquishes its colonial rights over Gibraltar the colony would return to Spain. In a 1967 referendum on the colony's status, 12,000 voted to remain a British Dependent Territory and 44 voted to join Spain. Spain closed the border with Gibraltar from 1969 to 1985 and refused to engage in any trade.

The 1969 constitution makes provision for certain domestic matters to devolve on a local government of ministers appointed from among elected members of the House of Assembly. The House of Assembly consists of an independent Speaker, 15 elected members, the Attorney-General and the Financial and Development Secretary.

The Governor retains responsibility for external affairs, defence, internal security and financial security, while the local government is responsible for other domestic matters. However, the Gibraltar government has recently been agitating for more local autonomy and responsibility, especially in the colony's relations with the EU, and this has led to tension with the UK and Spanish governments. Gibraltar is part of the EU (with the UK government responsible for enforcing EU directives affecting Gibraltar) but is not a fully-fledged member. In recent years Spain has insisted on excluding Gibraltar's airport from the air liberalization directive of the EC Single Market programme, while the Gibraltar government has been slow in implementing EU directives against drug and tobacco smuggling and money-laundering, which has primarily impacted on Spain. After an ultimatum from the British government in May 1995 that it would use its residual constitutional power to assume executive power, the Gibraltar government agreed to act against tobacco smuggling and money-laundering and implement the directives.

Governor and Commander-in-Chief, HE Adm. Sir Hugo Moresby White, GCB, CBE
Flag Officer, Gibraltar, and Admiral Superintendent, HM Naval Base, Gibraltar, Maj.-Gen. S. J. Pack
Deputy Governor, Hon. M. Robinson, CMG
Financial and Development Secretary, Hon. B. Traynor
Attorney-General, Hon. K. Dawson
Chief Justice, D. Schoffield
Chief Minister, Hon. Peter Caruana
Speaker, Hon. J. Alcantara

ECONOMY

Gibraltar has an extensive shipping trade and is a popular shopping centre and tourist resort. The chief sources of revenue are the port dues, the rent of the Crown estate in the town, and duties on consumer items. The free port tradition of Gibraltar is still reflected in the low rates of import duty. A financial services industry is expanding, based on Gibraltar's status as an offshore financial centre. However, many jobs have been lost as a result of reductions in the British naval and military presence.

A total of 4,026 merchant ships (53.5 million gross registered tons aggregate) entered the port during 1994. There are 49.9 km of roads.

FINANCE	1993–4	1994–5
Revenue	£69,850,000	£71,287,000
Expenditure	71,998,000	70,416,000

TRADE	1994	1995
Total imports	£420.2m	£460.0m
Total exports	175.6m	180.0m

TRADE WITH UK	1994	1995
Imports from UK	£74,866,000	£79,579,000
Exports to UK	4,819,000	10,598,000

EDUCATION

Education is compulsory and free for children between the ages of four and 15 whose parents are ordinarily resident in Gibraltar. Scholarships are available for higher education in Britain. The total enrolment in government schools was 4,696 in December 1994.

HONG KONG

Hong Kong, consisting of more than 230 islands and of a portion of the mainland (Kowloon and the New Territories) on the south-east coast of China, is situated at the eastern side of the mouth of the Pearl River, between 22° 9′ and 22° 37′ N. latitude and 113° 52′–114° 30′ E. longitude. The total area of the territory (including recent reclamation) is 418 sq. miles (1,083 sq. km).

Hong Kong Island is about 11 miles (18 km) long and from two to eight miles (three to eight km) broad, with a total area of 30 sq. miles (77.6 sq. km); at the eastern entrance to the harbour it is separated from the mainland by a narrow strait.

The climate is sub-tropical, tending towards the temperate for nearly half the year. The mean monthly temperature ranges from 16° C to 29° C. The average annual rainfall is 2,214 mm, of which nearly 80 per cent falls between May and September. Tropical cyclones occur between May and November, causing high winds and heavy rain.

POPULATION – Population at the end of 1995 was 6,307,900.

CURRENCY – Hong Kong dollar (HK$) of 100 cents.

FLAG – British Blue Ensign with the arms on a white disc in the fly (until 30 June 1997); red with a white bauhinia flower of five petals each containing a red star (effective 1 July 1997).

GOVERNMENT

Hong Kong Island was first occupied by Great Britain in 1841 and formally ceded by the Treaty of Nanking in 1842. Kowloon was acquired by the Peking Convention of 1860 and the New Territories, consisting of a peninsula in the southern part of the Guangdong province together with adjacent islands, by a 99-year lease signed on 9 June 1898.

Hong Kong is administered by the Hong Kong government, headed by the Governor, who is aided by an Executive Council and a Legislative Council. The Executive Council consists of three ex-officio members (the Chief Secretary, the Financial Secretary and the Attorney-General) together with ten other members, including one official appointed by the Governor with the approval of the British Foreign Secretary. The Legislative Council consists of 60 members, all of whom were elected in September 1995 in accordance with Governor Patten's reforms. Twenty were directly elected, 30 were elected by functional constituencies and ten were indirectly elected by regional and urban councillors. The pro-reform Democratic Party formed the largest group in the legislature with 19 seats, the pro-China Democratic Alliance for the Betterment of Hong Kong secured only six seats. The President of the Legislative Council is elected by the members.

The Urban Council provides services relating to public health and sanitation, culture and recreation in the urban area. From the March 1995 elections, the Urban Council consists of 41 members, of whom 32 are directly elected from district constituencies and nine are representative members from the urban district boards. A Regional Council was set up in 1986 to provide similar services in the New Territories. Of the 39 Regional Council seats, 27 are directly elected from district constituencies and nine are elected as representatives of the nine district boards within the Regional Council area. The remaining three are ex-officio members, being the chairman and the two vice-chairmen of the Heung Yee Kuk (a statutory advisory body which represents the indigenous population of the New Territories). There are also 18 district boards (nine in the urban areas and nine in the New Territories) which are statutory bodies that provide a forum for public consultation and participation in the administration of the districts. There are 346 directly elected members and 27 ex-officio members who are rural committee chairmen.

HANDOVER TO CHINA

Under the terms of the Joint Declaration of the British and Chinese governments, which came into force on 27 May 1985, Hong Kong will become, with effect from 1 July 1997, a Special Administrative Region (SAR) of the People's Republic of China. However, the social and economic systems in the SAR will remain unchanged for 50 years. The Declaration guarantees: the free movement of goods and capital; the retention of Hong Kong's free port status, separate customs territory and freely convertible currency; the protection of property rights and foreign investment; the right of free movement to and from Hong Kong; Hong Kong's autonomy in the conduct of its external commercial relations and its own monetary and financial policies; and judicial independence. The British and Chinese governments have, since the entry into force of the agreement, been involved in consultations on the implementation of the agreement via the Joint Liaison Group.

In the run-up to the 1997 transfer of sovereignty, the Chinese government's insistence on a greater say in the running of the colony and Governor Patten's plan for an extension of democracy have prompted acrimonious disputes. Patten's proposals, first put forward in 1992, were for all 60 members of the Legislative Council to be elected; the Chinese government maintained that it had agreed to only 20 elected seats when it signed the 1985 Joint Declaration. The reforms, passed by the Legislative Council in 1994, established the constituencies, and direct and indirect elections to the Legislative, Regional and Urban Councils for the 1995 elections (*see* above); introduced single-member constituencies; reduced the voting age from 21 to 18; replaced corporate voting by individual voting in the existing functional constituencies; and established independent boundary and election commissions.

The Chinese government has refused to accept the reforms and has vowed to replace the Legislative Council with a provisional legislature of 60 people chosen by a 400-strong selection panel of local residents. The panel will itself be chosen by the preparatory committee, a 150-member body including 94 pro-China Hong Kong people and headed by Chinese Foreign Minister Qian Qichen, which was inaugurated in January 1996. The selection panel will also recommend a Chief Executive for appointment by China to replace the existing Governor. The Chief Executive-designate will select the principal officials of the SAR at least six months before the handover date.

Governor, HE The Rt. Hon. Christopher Patten, *sworn in* 9 July 1992
Chief Justice, vacant

CIVIL ESTABLISHMENT *as at June 1996*
Chief Secretary, Mrs Anson Chan, CBE
Commander, British Forces, Maj.-Gen. B. Dutton, CBE
Financial Secretary, Donald Tsang, OBE
Attorney-General, J. F. Mathews, CMG
Civil Service, Michael Sze, ISO
Constitutional Affairs, Nicholas Ng
Planning, Environment and Lands, Bowen Leung
Transport, Haider Barma, ISO
Education and Manpower, Joseph Wong
Economic Services, Gordon Siu
Home Affairs, Michael M. Y. Suen
Health and Welfare, Mrs Katherine Fok, OBE
Security, Peter Lai
Financial Services and Economic Analysis, Rafael Hui
Recreation and Culture, Chau Tak-hay, CBE
Trade and Industry, Denise Yue
Works, Kwong Hon-sang
Political Adviser, Robert Peirce
Commissioner of Police, Eddie Hui Ki-on
Treasury, Kwong Ki-chi
*ex-officio member of the Executive Council

BRITISH COUNCIL REPRESENTATIVE, T. Buchanan, Easey Commercial Building, 225 Hennessy Road, Wanchai, Hong Kong.
HONG KONG GOVERNMENT OFFICE, 6 Grafton Street, London WIX 3LB. Tel: 0171-499 9821. *Commissioner*, Sir David Ford, KBE, LVO, *apptd* 1993

ECONOMY

Hong Kong is one of the world's major trade, manufacturing and financial centres. In 1995 it had an unemployment rate of 3.5 per cent and a per capita GDP of HK$179,552. Increasingly tied economically to China, Hong Kong firms are the largest investors in China and China has invested some HK$20 billion in Hong Kong, which is also the main trade and investment entry point into China.

The main economic sector is the services industry, especially financial services, and it employs about 75 per cent of the workforce. The manufacturing sector contributes about 9.3 per cent to the GDP and accounts for about 18.9 per cent of total employment. Up to 80 per cent of manufacturing output is eventually exported. Light consumer goods, such as electronics, plastics, electrical products, watches and clocks, accounted for 31 per cent of total domestic exports in 1995. Textiles and clothing, Hong Kong's traditional leading industries, accounted for 60 per cent of exports in 1995.

Diversification in terms of products and markets continues to be the main feature of recent industrial development, as are industrial partnerships with overseas companies. The economy is based on export rather than the domestic market.

FINANCE	1994–5	1995–6
Public revenue	HK$173,561m	HK$175,000m
Public expenditure	170,852m	143,200m

TRADE

Hong Kong's visible trade account had in 1995 a deficit of HK$147,000 million. Taking visible and invisible trade together, there was a combined deficit of HK$20,700 million, compared with a surplus of HK$18,739 million in 1994. In 1995, Hong Kong's principal customers for its domestic products, in order of value of trade, were China, USA, Singapore, Germany and Japan. China was its principal supplier.

	1994	1995
Total exports	HK$1,170,013m	HK$1,344,100m
Total imports	1,250,709m	1,491,100m

Trade with UK	1994	1995
Imports from UK	£2,297,561,000	£2,656,583,000
Exports to UK	3,079,611,000	3,538,821,000

COMMUNICATIONS

Hong Kong has one of the world's finest natural harbours, and it is the busiest container port in the world, with eight terminals, as well as large modern cargo and liner terminals. Dockyard facilities include eight floating drydocks, the largest being capable of docking vessels up to 150,000 tonnes deadweight. In 1995 ocean-going vessels loaded and discharged more than 128 million tonnes of cargo at Hong Kong. A new 17-berth container port will open in stages between 1997 and 2003.

Hong Kong International Airport, Kai Tak, situated to the east of the Kowloon peninsula, is regularly used by over 63 international airlines, providing nearly 3,000 scheduled passenger and cargo services each week. During 1995, over 21 million passengers and 1,458,000 tonnes of freight arrived and departed by air. A new international airport is being built on reclaimed land off Lantau Island at Chek Lap Kok and is planned to become operational by April 1998. It will be capable of handling 35 million passengers and 1.5 million tonnes of cargo annually.

EDUCATION

In the school year 1994–5 there were 2,355 day schools with 1,157,219 pupils. Free education for children up to the age of 15 is compulsory. Post-secondary education is provided by six universities and one college; total student numbers were 72,154 in December 1994. The Open Learning Institute of Hong Kong provides university education to about 18,400 students. There are also seven technical institutes and the Hong Kong Institute of Education.

MONTSERRAT

Situated in 16° 45′ N. latitude and 61° 15′ W. longitude, 27 miles south-west of Antigua, Montserrat is about 11 miles long and seven miles wide, with an area of 38 sq. miles (98 sq. km). Fertile and green, it is volcanic with several hot springs. About two-thirds of the island is mountainous, the rest capable of cultivation.

POPULATION – Population (estimate 1996) was 9,000.
CHIEF TOWN – ΨPlymouth, population 2,500.
CURRENCY – East Caribbean dollar (EC$) of 100 cents.
FLAG – British Blue Ensign with the shield of arms in the fly.

GOVERNMENT

Discovered by Columbus in 1493, Montserrat became a British colony in 1632. The first settlers were predominantly Irish indentured slaves from St Kitts. Montserrat was captured by the French in 1664, 1667 and 1782 but the island reverted to Britain within a few years on each occasion and was finally assigned to Great Britain in 1783.

A ministerial system was introduced in Montserrat in 1960. The Executive Council is presided over by the Governor and is composed of four elected members (the Chief and three other Ministers) and two ex-officio members (the Attorney-General and the Financial Secretary). The four Ministers are appointed from the members of the political party holding the majority in the Legislative Council. The Legislative Council consists of the Speaker, two ex-officio members (the Attorney-General and the Financial Secretary), two nominated members and seven elected members.

The southern half of Montserrat, including Plymouth, was evacuated because of volcanic activity for the third time in April 1996. Government departments were temporarily relocated in the north of the island and about 4,500 people were forced to vacate their homes.

Governor, HE Frank Savage, CMG, LVO, OBE, *apptd* 1993

EXECUTIVE COUNCIL *as at June 1996*
President, The Governor
Chief Minister and Minister of Finance and Economic Development, Hon. Reuben T. Meade
Communications and Works, Hon. Nowell Tuitt
Agriculture, Trade and the Environment, Hon. Charles T. Kirnon
Education, Health, Community Services and Labour, Hon. Lazelle Howes
Attorney-General, Hon. Gertel Thom
Financial Secretary, Hon. C. T. John, OBE

Speaker of the Legislative Council, Dr The Hon. H. A. Fergus, CBE

ECONOMY

The economy is dominated by tourism, related construction activities and offshore business services. There is some light industry and efforts are being made to increase agricultural exports and establish an agro-processing industry.

FINANCE	1991	1992
Revenue	EC$44,443,000	EC$39,273,000
Expenditure	39,216,000	39,056,000

TRADE WITH UK	1994	1995
Imports from UK	£2,651,000	£2,554,000
Exports to UK	15,000	4,720,000

PITCAIRN ISLANDS

Pitcairn, a small volcanic island 1.9 sq. miles (5 sq. km) in area, is the chief of a group of islands situated about midway between New Zealand and Panama in the South Pacific Ocean at longitude 130° 06′ W. and latitude 25° 04′ S. The island rises in cliffs to a height of 1,100 feet and access from the sea is possible only at Bounty Bay, a small rocky cove, and then only by surf boats. The other three islands of the group (Henderson lying 105 miles east-north-east of Pitcairn, Oeno lying 75 miles north-west and Ducie lying 293 miles east) are all uninhabited.

Mean monthly temperatures vary between 66° F (19° C) in August and 75° F (24° C) in February and the average annual rainfall is 80 inches. With an equable climate, the island is very fertile and produces both tropical and sub-tropical trees and crops.

POPULATION – At 31 December 1995 the population was 54. Since 1887 the islanders have all been adherents of the Seventh-day Adventist Church.

FLAG – British Blue Ensign with the arms in the fly.

GOVERNMENT

First settled in 1790 by the Bounty mutineers and their Tahitian companions, Pitcairn was left uninhabited in 1856 when the entire population was resettled on Norfolk Island. The present community are descendants of two parties who, not wishing to remain on Norfolk, returned to Pitcairn in 1859 and 1864 respectively.

Pitcairn became a British settlement under the British Settlement Act 1887, and was administered by the Governor of Fiji from 1952 until 1970, when the administration was transferred to the British High Commission in New Zealand and the British High Commissioner was appointed Governor. The local Government Ordinance of 1964 provides for a Council of ten members of whom six are elected.

Governor of Pitcairn, Henderson, Ducie and Oeno Islands, HE Robert John Alston, CMG (*British High Commissioner to New Zealand*)
Island Magistrate and Chairman of Island Council, J. Warren

ECONOMY

The islanders live by subsistence gardening and fishing. Wood carvings and other handicrafts are sold to passing ships and to a few overseas customers. Other than small fees charged for gun and driving licences there are no taxes and government revenue is derived almost solely from the sale of postage stamps and income from investments. Communication with the outside world is maintained by cargo vessels travelling between New Zealand and Panama which call at irregular intervals, and by means of a satellite service providing telephone, telex and fax facilities.

SOCIAL WELFARE

Education is compulsory between the ages of five and 15. Secondary education in New Zealand is encouraged by the administration, which provides scholarships and bursaries. Medical care is provided by a registered nurse when a doctor is not present.

ST HELENA AND DEPENDENCIES

ST HELENA

St Helena is situated in the South Atlantic Ocean, 955 miles south of the Equator, 702 miles south-east of Ascension, 1,140 miles from the nearest point of the African continent, 1,800 miles from the coast of South America, 1,694 miles from Cape Town, in 15° 55′ S. latitude and 5° 42′ W. longitude. It is 10½ miles long, 6½ broad, and encloses an area of 47 sq. miles (122 sq. km).

St Helena is of volcanic origin, and consists of numerous rugged mountains, the highest rising to 2,700 feet (820 m), interspersed with picturesque ravines. Although within the tropics, the south-east trade winds keep the temperature mild and equable.

POPULATION – The population (1987) is 5,644.
CAPITAL– ΨJamestown. Population (1987) 1,332.
CURRENCY – St Helena pound (£) of 100 pence.
FLAG – British Blue Ensign with the shield of arms in the fly.

GOVERNMENT

St Helena was discovered by the Portuguese navigator, Juan da Nova Castella, in 1502 (probably on St Helena's Day) and remained unknown to other European nations until 1588. It was used as a port of call for vessels of all nations trading to the East until it was annexed by the Dutch in 1633. It was never occupied by them, however, and the English East India Company seized it in 1659. From 1815 to 1821 the island was lent to the British government as a place of exile for the Emperor Napoleon Bonaparte who died in St Helena on 5 May 1821, and in 1834 it was ceded to the British Crown.

The government of St Helena is administered by a Governor, with the aid of a Legislative Council, consisting of a Speaker, three ex-officio members (Chief Secretary, Financial Secretary and Attorney-General) and 12 elected members. Five committees of the Legislative Council are responsible for general oversight of the activities of government departments and have in addition a wide range of statutory and administrative functions. The Governor is also assisted by an Executive Council of the three ex-officio members and the chairmen of the Council committees.

Governor, HE David Leslie Smallman, LVO, *apptd* 1995
Chief Secretary, J. G. Perrott
Financial Secretary, M. J. Young
Attorney-General, vacant
Deputy Secretary, E. C. Yon
Chief Medical Officer, Dr J. L. Sharp
Chief Agriculture and Forestry Officer, C. Lomas
Chief Education Officer, J. T. Price
Chief Engineer, vacant
Chief Social Services and Employment Officer, J. Young
Chief Personnel Officer, S. I. Ellick
Chief Development Officer, K. M. Thomas
Chief Finance Officer, D. H. Wade
Chief Justice, G. W. Martin, OBE
Postmistress, D. G. Fagan
Chief Auditor, K. G. Jones
Chief of Police, G. F. Henry

ECONOMY

The only significant export is canned and frozen fish. The other exports are a small amount of high quality coffee and cottage industry products (including lace, decorative woodwork and beadwork). St James's Bay, on the north-west of the island, possesses a good anchorage. There is as yet no airport or airstrip.

FINANCE	1993–4	1994–5
Local revenue	£7,253,922	£6,524,731
Budgetary	3,495,000	3,225,000
Recurrent expenditure	9,646,824	10,463,029
Development aid	1,396,019	1,413,935
TRADE	1992–3	1993–4
Total imports	£6,100,400	£7,753,329
Total exports	169,525	265,853
TRADE WITH UK	1994	1995
Imports from UK	£10,423,000	£9,144,000
Exports to UK	496,000	446,000

ASCENSION

The small island of Ascension lies in the South Atlantic (7° 56′ S., 14° 22′ W.) some 750 miles north-west of the island of St Helena. It is a rocky peak of purely volcanic origin. The highest point (Green Mountain), some 2,817 ft, is covered with lush vegetation and has a farm of some ten acres, producing vegetables and livestock. The island is a breeding area for turtles and for the sooty tern, or wideawake. Other wildlife includes feral donkeys and cats, and francolin partridge.

POPULATION – The resident population in March 1996 totalled 1,160, of whom 757 were from St Helena, 185 from the UK and 218 from the USA. The residents consist of the employees and families of the British organizations, of the contractors of the US Air Force (Computer Sciences Raytheon) and of the St Helena government.

British forces returned to the island in April 1982 in support of operations in the Falkland Islands. At present there are over 150 RAF personnel on the island supporting the air link to the Falklands.

CAPITAL – Georgetown.

GOVERNMENT

Ascension is said to have been discovered by Juan da Nova Castella on Ascension Day 1501 and two years later was visited by Alphonse d'Albuquerque, who gave the island its present name. It was uninhabited until the arrival of Napoleon in St Helena in 1815 when a small British naval garrison was stationed on the island. It remained under the supervision of the Board of Admiralty until 1922, when it was made a dependency of St Helena.

The British Foreign Secretary appoints the Administrator who is responsible to the Governor resident in St Helena. There is a small police force and post office. The British organizations through Ascension Island Services (AIS) provide and operate various common services for the island (school, hospital, public works etc).

Administrator, Roger Huxley, *apptd* 1995

COMMUNICATIONS

Cable and Wireless PLC operates the international telephone and cable services and maintains an internal telephone service. The BBC opened its Atlantic relay station broadcasting to Africa and South America in 1967. There is a monthly shipping service and two flights a week by RAF Tristars which transit Ascension en route to the Falkland Islands.

TRISTAN DA CUNHA

Tristan da Cunha is the chief island of a group of islands in the South Atlantic which lies in latitude 37° 0′ S. and longitude 12° 2′ W., some 1,260 nautical miles (2,333 km)

south-south-west of St Helena. It has an area of 38 sq. miles (98 sq. km). Inaccessible Island lies 20 nautical miles south-west and has an area of 4 sq. miles (10 sq. km), and the three Nightingale Islands lie 20 nautical miles south of Tristan da Cunha and have an area of three-quarters of a sq. mile (2 sq. km). Gough Island lies some 230 nautical miles south-south-east of Tristan da Cunha in latitude 40° 20′ S. and longitude 9° 58′ W. and has an area of 35 sq. miles (91 sq. km).

All the islands are volcanic and steep-sided with cliffs or narrow beaches. Tristan itself has a single volcanic cone rising to 6,760 feet (2,060 m) and a narrow north-western coastal plain on which the settlement of Edinburgh is situated.

Inaccessible Island is a lofty mass of rock with sides two miles in length; the island is the resort of penguins and sea-birds. Cultivation was started in 1937 but has been abandoned.

The Nightingale Islands are three in number, of which the largest is one mile long and three-quarters of a mile wide, and rises in two peaks, 960 and 1,105 feet above sea level respectively. The smaller islands, Stoltenhoff and Middle Isle, are little more than huge rocks. Seals, penguins, and sea-birds visit these islands.

Gough Island is about eight miles long and four miles broad. It is the resort of penguins, sea-elephants, fur seals and sea-birds and has valuable guano deposits.

Gough and Inaccessible islands are nature reserves and access is strictly limited.

The islands have a warm-temperate oceanic climate which is damp and windy. Rainfall averages 66 inches a year on the coast of Tristan da Cunha.

POPULATION – Population in 1996 was 292, in the settlement of Edinburgh on Tristan da Cunha. In addition, there is a meteorological station maintained on Gough Island by the South African government. Inaccessible Island and the Nightingale Islands are uninhabited.

CAPITAL – Edinburgh of the Seven Seas.

CURRENCY – Pound sterling.

HISTORY

Tristan da Cunha was discovered in 1506 by a Portuguese admiral (Tristão da Cunha) after whom it was named. In 1760 a British naval officer visited the islands and gave his name to Nightingale Island. In 1816 the group was annexed to the British Crown and a garrison was placed on Tristan da Cunha, but this force was withdrawn in 1817. Corporal William Glass remained at his own request with his wife and two children. This party, with two others, formed a settlement. In 1827 five women from St Helena, and afterwards others from Cape Colony, joined the party.

Due to its position on a main sailing route the colony thrived, with an economy based on trading with whalers, sealers and other passing ships. However, the replacement of sail by steam and the opening of the Suez Canal in the late 19th century led to decline.

In October 1961 a volcano, believed to have been extinct for thousands of years, erupted and the danger of further volcanic activity led to the evacuation of inhabitants to the UK. An advance party returned to Tristan da Cunha in 1963 and subsequently the main body of the islanders returned to the island.

GOVERNMENT

In 1938 Tristan da Cunha and the neighbouring islands of Inaccessible, Nightingale and Gough were made dependencies of St Helena. They are administered by the Governor of St Helena through a resident Administrator, with headquarters at Edinburgh. Under a constitution introduced in 1985, the Administrator is advised by an

Island Council of eight elected members, of whom one must be a woman, and three appointed members. There is universal suffrage at 18.

Administrator, Brendan Dalley, *apptd* 1994

ECONOMY

The island is financially self-sufficient. The main industries are crayfish fishing, fish-processing and agriculture, with the shore-based fishing industry having been developed with the construction of the boat harbour in 1967 and the re-establishment of the lobster factory in 1966. There are no taxes, income being derived from the royalties from the rock lobster fishery around the islands, interest from the reserve fund, and the sales of stamps and handicrafts. Apart from the fishing industry, the other main employer is the administration itself. There is one hospital with a resident medical officer, and a school catering for children up to age 15. Healthcare and education are free for the islanders.

COMMUNICATIONS

Scheduled visits to the island are restricted to about six calls a year by fishing vessels from Cape Town and annual calls of the RMS *St Helena* and the *SA Agulhas*, also from Cape Town. A wireless station on the island is in daily contact with Cape Town and a radio-telephone service was established in 1969, the same year that electricity was introduced to all the islanders' homes. A marine satellite system providing direct dialling telephone, telex and fax facilities was installed in 1992.

SOUTH GEORGIA AND THE SOUTH SANDWICH ISLANDS

South Georgia is an island 800 miles east-south-east of the Falkland group, with an area of 1,450 sq. miles. The population comprises a small military garrison and a civilian harbour master at King Edward Point, and staff of the British Antarctic Survey at Bird Island, to the north-west of South Georgia.

The South Sandwich Islands lie some 470 miles south-east of South Georgia. The group is a chain of uninhabited, actively volcanic islands about 150 miles long, with a wholly Antarctic climate.

The present constitution came into effect in 1985. It provides for a Commissioner who, for the time being, is the officer administering the government of the Falkland Islands.

In 1993 the UK government decreed an extension of Crown sovereignty and jurisdiction from 12 miles around South Georgia and the South Sandwich Islands to 200 miles around each in order to preserve marine stocks.

Commissioner for South Georgia and the South Sandwich Islands, Richard Ralph, CVO, *apptd* 1996

TURKS AND CAICOS ISLANDS

The Turks and Caicos Islands are situated between 21° and 22° N. latitude and 71° and 72° W. longitude, about 50 miles south-east of the Bahamas of which they are geographically an extension. There are over 30 islands, of which eight are inhabited, covering an estimated area of 166 sq. miles (430 sq. km). The principal island and seat of government is Grand Turk.

The islands lie in the trade wind belt. The average temperature varies from 24°–27° C in the winter to 29°–32° C in the summer and humidity is generally low. Average rainfall is 21 inches a year.

POPULATION – The population in 1995 was estimated to be 19,000 (Grand Turk 4,000).

FLAG – British Blue Ensign with the shield of arms in the fly.

GOVERNMENT

A constitution was introduced in 1988, and amended in 1993, which provides for an Executive Council and a Legislative Council. The Executive Council is presided over by the Governor and comprises the Chief Minister and five elected Ministers, together with the ex-officio Chief Secretary and Attorney-General.

At the general election of 31 January 1995, the People's Democratic Movement won eight seats and the Progressive National Party five seats in the Legislative Council.

Governor, HE Martin Bourke, *apptd* 1993

EXECUTIVE COUNCIL *as at June 1996*

President, The Governor
Chief Secretary, Hon. R. Cousins
Attorney-General, Hon. D. F. Ballantyne
Chief Minister, Hon. D. H. Taylor
Other Ministers, Hon. S. Harvey; Hon. O. Skippings; Hon. H. Ewing; Hon. C. Selver; Hon. S. Rigby

ECONOMY

FINANCE	1993–4*	1995
Local revenue	US$25,981,350	US$31,814,219
Expenditure	28,615,287	30,385,502
*estimate		

The most important industries are fishing, tourism and offshore finance. The islands were visited by 79,000 tourists in 1995.

TRADE WITH UK	1994	1995
Imports from UK	£1,492,000	£1,437,000
Exports to UK	104,000	58,000

COMMUNICATIONS

The principal airports are on the islands of Grand Turk, Providenciales and South Caicos. Air services link Providenciales and Grand Turk with Miami, the Bahamas, Haiti and the Dominican Republic. An internal air service provides a twice daily service between the principal islands. There are direct shipping services to the USA (Miami). A comprehensive telephone and telex service is provided by Cable and Wireless (WI) Ltd.

Events of the Year

1 September 1995 to 31 August 1996

SEPTEMBER 1995

8. David Trimble was elected leader of the Ulster Unionists. 11. The TUC conference opened in Brighton; it was addressed by the President of the European Commission, Jacques Santer. 14. Kevin McNamara resigned as Labour's Civil Service spokesman over the approach of the Labour leader (Tony Blair) to the Northern Ireland peace process and in particular Mr Blair's support for the Government over the decommissioning of IRA weapons. Nuclear Electric was fined £250,000 for serious lapses in safety procedures after an accident at the Wylfa power station in Anglesey in July 1993. 18. The Liberal Democrat party conference opened in Glasgow. 20. A commission headed by the Bishop of Durham recommended changes in the organization of the Church of England, including the establishment of a National Council. 27. Britain and Argentina signed an agreement on the joint exploration for and exploitation of oil around the Falkland Islands.

OCTOBER 1995

1. Metrication became compulsory in the UK for the sale of pre-packed food, petrol and other goods. 2. The Labour Party conference opened in Brighton. 7. The Conservative MP and former minister Alan Howarth resigned from the Conservative Party and said that he would take the Labour whip in the House of Commons. 9. The former Prime Minister Lord Home of the Hirsel died. The Conservative Party conference opened in Blackpool. Lloyds Bank and the TSB announced that they were to merge. 15. A bridge linking the Isle of Skye to the mainland of Scotland was opened. 16. Derek Lewis was sacked as director-general of the Prison Service after the publication of a highly critical report on security in the service following a review by Gen. Sir John Learmont. Mr Lewis later sued the Home Secretary (Michael Howard) for unfair dismissal. 17. President Ahtisaari of Finland arrived in Britain for a four-day state visit. A junior minister at the Home Office, Nicholas Baker, resigned on health grounds. 19. The Shadow Cabinet was reshuffled. 26. A Canadian chat show host posing as the Canadian prime minister, Jean Chrétien, held a telephone conversation with The Queen about the independence referendum in Quebec; he then broadcast an edited tape of the conversation on a Montreal radio station. 29. Anti-nuclear protesters clashed with police in the grounds of Chequers before a visit by the French

President, Jacques Chirac. On 30 October Mr Major and M. Chirac reached agreement on defence, naval and nuclear issues. 31. The education association appointed by the Government in July 1995 to run Hackney Downs school, London, recommended that the school should be closed down.

NOVEMBER 1995

1. The Queen arrived in New Zealand for a tour including the Commonwealth heads of government meeting in Auckland and signed her assent to an Act compensating a Maori tribe for lands confiscated by British colonists in 1863. 6. The Prince of Wales, the Prime Minister (John Major), the Leader of the Opposition (Tony Blair) and the leader of the Liberal Democrats (Paddy Ashdown) attended the funeral of the assassinated Israeli Prime Minister Yitzhak Rabin in Jerusalem. In the House of Commons an Opposition amendment requiring MPs to disclose how much they earn from outside consultancies was passed by 322 votes to 271. 7. The last Royal Navy ships left Rosyth naval base on the Firth of Forth. 10. At the Commonwealth heads of government meeting in Auckland John Major attacked a statement condemning French nuclear tests which had been agreed by all the other heads of government. 11. Nigeria was suspended from membership of the Commonwealth following the execution of the writer Ken Saro-Wiwa. Thousands of people observed an Armistice Day two-minute silence at 11 a.m. 13. The Prince of Wales left Britain for a five-day official visit to Germany and Latvia. 15. The state opening of Parliament took place. Demonstrators threw paint and flour at the Conservative Party chairman, Brian Mawhinney, at College Green, Westminster. 16. Queen Elizabeth the Queen Mother underwent a hip replacement operation. 20. The Princess of Wales was interviewed on the BBC1 programme *Panorama*; she talked frankly about her unhappiness during her marriage and her husband's affair with Camilla Parker Bowles, and admitted that she had also had an extra-marital affair. She said that members of the Royal Household had waged a campaign against her since her separation from the Prince of Wales, that she did not want a divorce and that she did not know if her husband would become King. She also said that she would like to be an ambassador for Britain and a 'queen in people's hearts'. Her press secretary, Geoffrey Crawford, resigned because the Princess had given the interview without his knowledge. 21. Buckingham Palace officials said in a press statement that they would be talking to the Princess of Wales to see how they could help her define her

future role and continue to support her as a member of the Royal Family. **28.** The Chancellor of the Exchequer (Kenneth Clarke) presented his Budget to the House of Commons (*see* page 1154). **29.** President Clinton started a three-day visit to the British Isles; he held talks with John Major at Downing Street and then addressed both Houses of Parliament. On 30 November he became the first serving US president to visit Northern Ireland, and on 1 December he visited Dublin and received the freedom of the city. **30.** The Queen became the first reigning monarch for more than 400 years to attend a Roman Catholic service in an official capacity when she attended a service at Westminster Cathedral to mark the centenary of its foundation.

DECEMBER 1995

7. Beef prices fell sharply because of public fears over conflicting reports of a link between bovine spongiform encephalopathy (BSE) in cattle and Creutzfeld-Jakob disease (CJD) in humans; the Prime Minister said in the House of Commons that there was no scientific evidence of a link. **8.** An official at the British embassy in Colombia who had been kidnapped by left-wing guerrillas on 26 August was released unharmed. **12.** The Defence Secretary (Michael Portillo) announced plans to send more than 13,000 British troops to join the NATO force implementing the peace settlement in Bosnia. **13.** Rioting broke out in Brixton, London, during a demonstration over the death of a man in police custody. Bank base rates cut by a quarter of a per cent to 6.5 per cent. **16.** Eighteen-year-old Leah Betts died four days after taking an Ecstasy tablet at her birthday party; her parents warned other teenagers of the dangers of taking the drug. **15.** The Court of Appeal ruled that the rail franchising director (Roger Salmon) had acted illegally in setting minimum service requirements which were lower than those already in existence for five of the new companies set up as part of the privatization of British Rail. On 18 December the Transport Secretary (Sir George Young) said that the instructions to the franchising director would be clarified to ensure that franchise holders would be able to adjust commercial services while operating core services at a broadly similar level to those in operation immediately before franchising. **19.** A government motion on European fish quotas was defeated in the House of Commons; two Conservative MPs voted with the Opposition and 11 abstained. The first franchise to be awarded as part of the privatization of British Rail was won by the bus company Stagecoach. **20.** Buckingham Palace confirmed that The Queen had written to the Prince and Princess of Wales expressing her view that an early divorce was desirable. **21.** The Prince of Wales said that he had no intention of remarrying. **24–28.** Strong winds and heavy snow brought down power lines in many parts of Scotland; a state of emergency was declared in Shetland on 26 December. **29.** The Conservative MP Emma Nicholson resigned from the Conserva-

tive Party and said that she would take the Liberal Democrat whip in the House of Commons.

JANUARY 1996

1–2. Thousands of households in Wales, Scotland, Northern Ireland and northern England were left without water supplies when pipes burst in the rapid thaw following the cold snap. **3.** Eleven-year-old David Kearney, who had been savaged by two rottweilers near his home in Darwen, Lancs, on 23 December, died. **4.** The chief executive of the Stock Exchange, Michael Lawrence, was dismissed. **8.** An industrial tribunal ruled that the Labour Party's policy of women-only shortlists in marginal parliamentary seats was illegal. **11.** Baroness Thatcher gave a lecture in London in which she said that pro-European One-Nation Conservatives were 'No Nation Conservatives' and said that the Government was unpopular because it had let down its middle class supporters. **11.** The Prince of Wales, the Prime Minister and the Leader of the Opposition attended a requiem mass for François Mitterrand, the former President of France, in Paris. **17.** Sir Richard Body, MP, accepted the Conservative whip; he had resigned it in November 1994. **18.** Bank base rates were cut to 6.25 per cent. The Home Secretary said that the policy of chaining pregnant women prisoners in hospital would be discontinued. **22.** The private secretary to the Princess of Wales, Patrick Jephson, resigned. **23.** Forte shareholders voted to accept a £3,800 million hostile take-over bid from Granada. **25.** Results showed that more than 50 per cent of 11-year-olds failed to reach the expected standard in English and mathematics in the first national school tests taken in May 1995. **30.** The Princess Royal arrived in the Falkland Islands for a five-day official visit.

FEBRUARY 1996

1. The Hemsworth by-election took place (*see* page 235). **5.** The first privatized rail services began running on South West Trains and Great Western routes; the privatization of the London, Tilbury and Southend line was cancelled because of an alleged fraud relating to ticket revenue arrangements. **6.** British Gas announced that it would split into two companies, and that its chief executive, Cedric Brown, would retire in April 1996. **7.** Tony Blair said that a Labour government would remove the voting rights of hereditary peers in the House of Lords. **8.** The Prince of Wales arrived in Split for a two-day official visit to Croatia and Bosnia. **15.** The report of the Inquiry into Exports of Defence Equipment and Dual-Use Goods to Iraq headed by Sir Richard Scott and set up after the collapse of the Matrix Churchill trial in 1992 was published (*see* below). The Chief Secretary to the Treasury and former Foreign Office minister (William Waldegrave) and the Attorney-General (Sir Nicholas Lyell) rejected calls by Opposition MPs for their resignations. On 26 February the Government won a vote on the Scott report by one vote. **22.** The Conservative MP

Peter Thurnham resigned the party whip. **28.** The Princess of Wales said that she had agreed to a divorce from Prince Charles and announced the basic terms of the settlement; the Queen said that she was interested to hear that the princess had agreed to a divorce but that no settlement details had been discussed.

Main findings and recommendations of the Scott inquiry:
– there had been a deliberate failure to inform Parliament of a secret relaxation of the guidelines on sales of equipment to Iraq because ministers feared public opposition
– the Attorney-General had been wrong to advise ministers that it was their duty to sign public interest immunity certificates which could have affected the outcome of the Matrix Churchill trial
– the then Foreign Office minister (William Waldegrave) had known the facts that made untrue his statements to the effect that there had been no change in policy; however Mr Waldegrave had not intended to mislead Parliament
– there had been no organized conspiracy between ministers to affect the outcome of the trial or cover up the Government's actions
– new guidelines should be drawn up on the issuing of public interest immunity certificates, which should not be used again in criminal cases
– written procedures should be put in place to avoid systematic failures to pass on intelligence to relevant government departments
– ministers should never withhold information in order to avoid political embarrassment
– if the Government intends to use export controls to pursue foreign policy objectives, this should be stated in legislation and open to public debate
– a new export licensing system should be introduced
– the use of 'waivers' by HM Custom and Excise should cease

MARCH 1996

7. An earthquake registering 3.2 on the Richter scale hit Shropshire. **8.** Bank base rates were cut to 6 per cent. **12.** The Government published a White Paper on Europe (*see* pages 1168–9). **20.** The Health Secretary (Stephen Dorrell) said that the most likely cause of a new strain of CJD that had recently been identified was beef from cows with BSE eaten before some types of offal were banned in 1989. On 21 March five European countries banned the import of British beef and prices at cattle markets fell as consumers boycotted British beef and beef products. More European countries banned the import of British beef on 22 March, and on 23 March the fast food chain McDonald's suspended the sale of British beef products in all its outlets. **24.** The Queen with the Duke of Edinburgh arrived in Warsaw at the start of a week-long state visit to Poland and the Czech Republic. **25.** The Government's Spongiform Encephalopathy Advisory Committee (SEAC) said that children were no more susceptible

than adults to infection by BSE. **28.** The Agriculture Minister (Douglas Hogg) announced a ban on the sale of meat from newly-slaughtered cattle over 30 months old. **29.** The Home Office agreed to settle the unfair dismissal claim of the former director-general of the Prison Service, Derek Lewis, who was sacked in October 1995.

APRIL 1996

2–3. Emergency legislation introduced by the Government to strengthen anti-terrorism laws passed through all its parliamentary stages; the Liberal Democrats and some Labour MPs protested at the guillotine imposed to limit debate on the measure. **3.** EU agriculture ministers agreed to provide financial assistance for British measures to eradicate BSE in cattle but refused to lift the worldwide export ban. A British aid worker was shot dead in Angola. The Home Secretary (Michael Howard) published a White Paper on crime and criminal justice, including proposals for radical reforms to sentencing (*see* pages 1169–70). **11.** Labour won the Staffordshire South East by-election (*see* page 235). **16.** The Government said that it would challenge the EU ban on the export of British beef and beef products in the European Court of Justice. The Agriculture Minister (Douglas Hogg) announced a package of measures to help cattle farmers and the beef industry, including £550 million to slaughter and destroy cattle over 30 months old to prevent them from entering the food chain. **18.** Thousands of fishermen held a rally in central London and burned an EU flag in protest at Britain's participation in the common fisheries policy. **21.** The Queen celebrated her 70th birthday. **23.** The Prince of Wales arrived in Canada for an eight-day official visit. **24.** The Government announced plans to slaughter up to 40,000 cattle. The Home Secretary and the Scottish Secretary (Michael Forsyth) announced a firearms amnesty to run from 3 June to 30 June.

MAY 1996

2. The Conservative Party lost hundreds of council seats in local elections held in 150 authorities in England. **3.** Royal Insurance and Sun Alliance announced that they were to merge. **6.** An earthquake registering 2.8 on the Richter scale hit parts of Staffordshire and south Cheshire. **7.** The Register of MPs' Interests was published in the House of Commons; 12 Conservative and two Labour MPs had refused to disclose full details of their outside earnings resulting from their membership of Parliament as required by new rules introduced as a result of the Nolan inquiry. **9.** In a district auditor's report Dame Shirley Porter, the former leader of Westminster Council, and five other council officers were ordered to pay a total surcharge of £31.6 million for their wilful misconduct in attempting to gerrymander the allocation of council homes to increase the Conservative vote in marginal wards in the late 1980s. **14.** President Chirac of France arrived in Britain for a three-day state visit. **15.**

Nine hostages, including four British students, who were kidnapped in Indonesia on 8 January were freed in a rescue operation mounted by Indonesian special forces; two Indonesian hostages and eight kidnappers were killed. **17.** Four British diplomats were expelled by Russia for alleged espionage activities; Britain responded by expelling four Russian embassy staff on the same grounds. **20.** Trading in Railtrack shares began. **21.** In an emergency statement in the House of Commons the Prime Minister said that Britain would use its veto to block all further EU policy initiatives until progress was made on lifting the ban on British beef exports. Eleven-year-old Jaymee Bowen, who was refused experimental treatment for leukaemia on the NHS in 1995 and whose treatment was subsequently paid for by a private donor, died. **26.** The Ministry of Agriculture, Fisheries and Food said that phthalates, chemicals used to soften plastic, had been found in baby formula milk; the Ministry refused to name the brands containing higher levels on the grounds that there was no danger to babies' health. **30.** The Duke and Duchess of York were granted a divorce. **31.** A visit by the Queen to the University of Wales, Aberystwyth, was curtailed because of threatened protests by Welsh language activists.

JUNE 1996

2. Rod Richards, a junior Welsh Office minister, resigned after newspaper allegations of an extramarital affair. **4–7.** The President of the Republic of Ireland, Mary Robinson, made an official visit to Britain, the first Irish president to do so since the foundation of the Republic of Ireland. **7.** Two women were bitten by a rabid bat in Newhaven, E. Sussex. **11.** In the House of Commons, 78 Conservative MPs supported the introduction of a bill calling for a referendum on Britain's future in the EU. **19.** Britain accepted a framework plan drawn up by the European Commission that detailed the measures required from Britain, including an increased cattle cull, to lead to a gradual removal of the beef export ban; at an EU summit meeting in Florence on 21 June the framework was agreed by member states and Britain ended its policy of non-co-operation. **20.** The House of Commons trade and industry select committee cleared the former Cabinet minister Jonathan Aitken of involvement in the illegal export of arms to Iraq in the 1980s. **21.** Postal workers held a 24-hour strike over pay and conditions. **25.** The Prince of Wales began a three-day visit to Northern Ireland. The Government published an education White Paper including proposals for greater selection in schools (*see* page 1170). **26.** Violence broke out in central London, Bradford and other areas after England's defeat by Germany in the European football championships. **27–8.** Postal workers held another 24-hour strike.

JULY 1996

3. The Prime Minister said that the Stone of Scone would be returned to Scotland. **5.** In a speech in the House of Lords, the Archbishop of Canterbury (Dr George Carey) deplored the current tendency towards 'privatized morality' and called on schools to reinstate the daily act of worship. **8.** President Nelson Mandela of South Africa arrived in Britain at the start of a four-day state visit. On 9 July he was welcomed by crowds on Horse Guards parade and in the Mall, and a state banquet was held at Buckingham Palace. On 10 July he received eight honorary degrees in a ceremony at Buckingham Palace, held talks with Mr Major at Downing Street and addressed business executives in the City of London. On 11 July he addressed both Houses of Parliament and attended a concert at the Royal Albert Hall. On 12 July he visited Brixton and addressed crowds outside the South African embassy in Trafalgar Square. **10.** MPs voted in favour of awarding themselves a 26 per cent pay increase. **12.** The Prince and Princess of Wales reached agreement over a divorce settlement; a decree nisi was pronounced on 15 July. **15.** Shares in British Energy began trading on the Stock Exchange. **20.** Up to 45 British tourists were injured when a bomb planted by Basque separatists exploded at Reus airport, near Barcelona, Spain. **22.** The Paymaster-General, David Heathcoat-Amory, resigned from the Government in protest at its policy towards the European Union and in particular its failure to rule out British participation in a single European currency. **23.** The Prime Minister reshuffled some junior ministerial posts. **27.** A British aid worker was kidnapped in Chechnya; he was released unharmed on 21 August.

AUGUST 1996

1. The Central Veterinary Laboratory published evidence showing that BSE can be transmitted from cow to calf. **6.** The Government suspended the Post Office's monopoly on letter delivery for one month because of a series of one-day strikes over new working practices. **22.** The Home Secretary (Michael Howard) announced that a voluntary identity card would be introduced in Britain. The Prison Service released hundreds of prisoners affected by a change in the legal interpretation of sentencing guidelines relating to time spent on remand by prisoners subsequently given consecutive sentences; on 23 August the Home Secretary suspended further releases. After a legal challenge in the High Court the revised interpretation was deemed to be an 'absurdity' and the Home Secretary's decision was upheld. **28.** The Prince and Princess of Wales were divorced.

NORTHERN IRELAND AFFAIRS

SEPTEMBER 1995

5. A summit meeting between John Major and John Bruton planned for 6 September was postponed at the request of the Irish government on the grounds that agreement could not be reached on the terms of reference of an international commission to oversee the decommissioning of terrorist arms. **6.** John Adair was sentenced in Belfast to 16 years' imprisonment for directing the terrorist activities of the UFF. **7.** John Bruton called on the British government to invite Sinn Fein to join all-party talks. **10.** Rioting broke out between loyalists and nationalists in Dunloy, Co. Antrim. **19.** The new leader of the Ulster Unionists (David Trimble) met John Major at Downing Street. The leader of the Ulster Democratic Party (Gary McMichael) met John Bruton in Dublin, the first formal meeting between a loyalist leader and an Irish Prime Minister. **22.** David Trimble called for the setting-up of a directly-elected assembly for Northern Ireland. **29.** The IRA ruled out any decommissioning of weapons in advance of a political settlement.

October 1995

2. David Trimble held talks with John Bruton in Dublin.

November 1995

2. The Secretary of State for Northern Ireland (Sir Patrick Mayhew) announced the departure of a third army unit from Northern Ireland. **6.** The Irish government sanctioned the early release of four IRA prisoners from Portlaoise prison, including Nessan Quinlivan and Pearse McCauley who escaped while on remand in London in 1991; the British government started proceedings for their extradition. **10.** A vehicle carrying a 1,000 lb bomb was intercepted by police near Carrickmacross, Co. Monaghan. **11.** John Bruton called on the British government to open all-party talks in advance of decommissioning of arms by the IRA; on 12 November John Major said that this would be a 'reckless short-term gesture'. **15.** Unionist leaders called on John Major to set a date for elections to a constituent assembly. **17.** Eighty-four republican and loyalist prisoners were released from prison under the Northern Ireland (Remission of Sentences) Act 1995. **28.** John Major and John Bruton agreed to set up a three-member international body chaired by a former US senator George Mitchell to advise both governments on suitable methods of arms decommissioning; they also set a target date of the end of February 1996 for the beginning of all-party talks. **30.** President Clinton became the first serving US president to visit Northern Ireland and was greeted by large crowds in Belfast and Londonderry; he met leading political figures and urged Northern Ireland to become 'a model of peace through tolerance'.

December 1995

1. Sir Patrick Mayhew invited leaders of all the political parties to join preliminary talks on a separate basis to establish an agenda for full negotiations. On 5 December David Trimble refused to join talks involving the Irish government. **4.** The leader of the SDLP (John Hume) and David Trimble held their first formal talks since Mr Trimble's election. **8.** The IRA said there was no question of surrendering any weapons before the start of all-party talks. **15.** The international arms decommissioning body met for the first time. **21.** The Prime Minister visited Northern Ireland and attacked Sinn Fein for claiming that Sinn Fein and the IRA were totally separate organizations. He later met John Bruton in Dublin. The planned release of ten IRA prisoners in the Republic of Ireland was cancelled because of the alleged involvement of the IRA in the murders of three suspected drug dealers in Belfast during December by a group calling itself Direct Action Against Drugs. **27.** A man was shot dead in west Belfast.

January 1996

1. A man was shot in Lurgan, Co. Armagh; he died on 2 January. **2.** Sir Patrick Mayhew said that the murders carried out by Direct Action Against Drugs could put the planned all-party talks in jeopardy. **24.** The international advisory body on the decommissioning of paramilitary weapons said that no weapons would be decommissioned before the start of all-party talks and that a compromise agreement was necessary under which weapons would be decommissioned during negotiations. It set out proposals for the decommissioning process and six principles to which all parties should adhere (*see* below). John Major endorsed the principles and proposed that elections should be held in the spring to provide a pool of representatives to conduct all-party talks. **25.** John Bruton said that the question of elections should be resolved during, not before, all-party talks. Sir Patrick Mayhew proposed a Grand Committee for Northern Ireland pending a political settlement. **26.** Gerry Adams said that Sinn Fein was implacably opposed to elections. **30.** The alleged leader of the INLA, Gino Gallagher, was shot dead near the Falls Road, Belfast.

Principles set out by the disarmament body:
- democratic and exclusively peaceful means of resolving political issues
- the total disarmament of all paramilitary organizations
- agreement for the disarmament to be independently verified
- renunciation of the use of force to influence the outcome of all-party talks
- agreement to abide by the terms of any agreement reached in all-party talks
- the cessation of 'punishment' killings and beatings

February 1996

1. President Clinton met Gerry Adams at the White House. **2.** Shots were fired at the home of an RUC reserve officer in Moy, Co. Tyrone. **7.** The Irish foreign minister, Dick Spring, proposed a two-day summit meeting to help to bring about all-party talks. **9.** The IRA announced at 6 p.m. that it was calling off its cease-fire; at 7 p.m. two people were killed, more than 100 injured, and extensive damage was caused when a bomb exploded at South Quay in

London's docklands. 12. In a televised broadcast, John Major said that the peace process would continue but that ministers would not meet Sinn Fein until IRA violence ended. Thousands of people attended a peace rally in Belfast. 15. An IRA bomb was defused in central London. Five hundred troops were flown to Northern Ireland. 18. An IRA member was killed and at least nine people were injured when a bomb exploded on a bus in central London; police said that the bus was not believed to have been the intended target. 21. The Ulster Unionists issued proposals for an elected 'peace convention'; they were rejected by Sinn Fein. 23. Security patrols resumed on the streets of Belfast. 26. More troops were flown to Northern Ireland. 28. John Major and John Bruton met at Downing Street and announced that intensive multilateral consultations would start on 4 March aimed at reaching agreement on the processes for elections to be held in May and the basis for all-party talks to begin on 10 June; they said that Sinn Fein would be admitted to the talks if the IRA resumed its cease-fire. They also agreed to consider whether parallel referendums on a peaceful political settlement should be held in Northern Ireland and the Republic.

MARCH 1996

9. A small IRA bomb exploded in west London. 12. The Combined Loyalist Military Command said that if IRA bombing continued it would be matched 'blow for blow'. 15. The British and Irish governments issued a consultative document on the framework for all-party talks. 21. John Major outlined the processes for elections to a peace forum to be held on 30 May. 22. The INLA said that its units had been placed on stand-by.

APRIL 1996

4. The IRA issued a statement in which it reaffirmed its commitment to 'the armed struggle' but said that it was ready to help to develop the conditions which would allow negotiations to proceed. 8. Violence broke out in the Lower Ormeau Road, Belfast, when a crowd gathered to protest at the re-routing of an Apprentice Boys' march. 16. A draft bill on the proposed elections in Northern Ireland was published. 17. A small IRA bomb exploded in Kensington, London. 19. Gerry Adams said that all the nationalist parties should ignore the forthcoming elections. 24. The detonator of a 30 lb IRA bomb exploded under Hammersmith Bridge, London; it failed to ignite the bomb. 24. Gerry Adams said that Sinn Fein would take part in the forthcoming elections but would not sit in the forum.

MAY 1996

16. John Major said that he would not let the issue of arms decommissioning block progress on political negotiations. 20. Gerry Adams said that he was prepared to agree to the six principles set out by the Mitchell report (see above) within the context of all-party talks. 25. A member of an INLA breakaway

group was shot dead in Belfast. 30. In elections to the peace forum the Ulster Unionist Party won 30 seats, the Democratic Unionist Party 24, the SDLP 21, Sinn Fein 17, the Alliance Party 7, the UK Unionist Party 3, the Progressive Unionist Party 2, the Ulster Democratic Party 2, the Women's Coalition 2 and Labour 2; the turnout was 64.52 per cent.

JUNE 1996

6. The framework for all-party talks was agreed by the British and Irish governments. 7. An Irish special branch detective was shot dead in Adare, Co. Limerick; the IRA said that its members were responsible but that the murder had been unauthorized. 9. A member of an INLA breakaway group was shot dead in Belfast. 10. All-party talks opened at Stormont Castle, Belfast; Sinn Fein delegates were turned away because the IRA had failed to call a cease-fire. Unionist delegates objected to the appointment of the former US senator George Mitchell as chairman of the talks. Disputes over the chairmanship continued but Mr Mitchell was appointed temporary chairman on 12 June. 14. The elected Northern Ireland forum opened in Belfast under the interim chairmanship of John Gorman, a Roman Catholic Unionist. Sinn Fein members boycotted the forum. 15. More than 200 people were injured and extensive damage was caused when an IRA bomb exploded in central Manchester. 28. Three IRA mortar bombs were fired at a British military base in Osnabrück, Germany; there were no injuries but several buildings were badly damaged.

JULY 1996

7. Thousands of Orangemen refused to accept a police ban on their marching through a predominantly Roman Catholic area of Portadown, Co. Armagh; a stand-off ensued. 8. A Roman Catholic taxi driver was found murdered near Lurgan, Co. Armagh, loyalist demonstrators blocked major roads throughout Northern Ireland and sectarian incidents occurred in Belfast. 9–10. Trouble continued and two extra infantry battalions were sent to Northern Ireland. 11. The Orangemen were allowed to march through the disputed area; petrol bombs were thrown by nationalists and police fired plastic bullets to scatter them. 12. Three RUC officers were shot and wounded in the Ardoyne area of Belfast. Rioting broke out in Belfast, Londonderry and Armagh, and shots were fired at a police station in west Belfast. John Bruton accused John Major of yielding to pressure and failing to treat the two communities in Northern Ireland impartially. 13. A Roman Catholic man died after being crushed by a security vehicle during disturbances in Londonderry. Rioting continued and the SDLP withdrew from the Northern Ireland Forum. 14. Seventeen people were injured when a bomb, believed to have been planted by a republican group, destroyed a hotel in Enniskillen, Co. Fermanagh. Disturbances continued in Belfast and Londonderry. 15. Police

raided houses in Peckham and Tooting, London, and discovered 36 bombs under construction. **29.** The all-party talks at Stormont Castle were suspended for six weeks after disagreements over the issue of decommissioning arms.

AUGUST 1996

7. Part of the city wall of Londonderry overlooking the Bogside was sealed off by police and troops to prevent an Apprentice Boys march using the route on 10 August.

ACCIDENTS AND DISASTERS

SEPTEMBER 1995

5–6. Twelve people were killed and widespread damage was caused when Hurricane Luis hit Antigua and St Martin in the Caribbean. **8.** One person was killed and at least five injured when the diesel tank fell off an inter-city train and set carriages on fire outside Maidenhead station, Berks. **17.** At least nine people were killed and widespread damage was caused when Hurricane Marilyn hit the US Virgin Islands and Puerto Rico. **19.** The cross-channel Sealink ferry *Stena Challenger* ran aground outside Calais; it was refloated on 20 September. **23.** Mount Ruapehu in New Zealand's North Island began erupting.

OCTOBER 1995

1. At least 68 people were killed and 200 injured when an earthquake registering 6.0 on the Richter scale hit western Turkey. Twenty-nine people were killed when a typhoon hit the Philippines. **5.** At least 11 people were killed and widespread damage was caused when Hurricane Opal hit Florida, USA. **7.** At least 20 people were killed when an earthquake registering 7.0 on the Richter scale hit central Sumatra. **9.** At least 48 people were killed when an earthquake registering 7.5 on the Richter scale hit western Mexico. Schools and offices were closed in Redcar, Cleveland, after a major fire at an ICI chemical plant. **24.** At least 29 people were killed when an earthquake registering 6.5 on the Richter scale hit Yunnan province, south-west China. **29.** At least 300 people were killed in a fire on an underground train in Baku, Azerbaijan. About 100 people were killed when a tropical storm hit the central Philippines.

NOVEMBER 1995

2–3. At least 66 people were killed and thousands of homes were destroyed when Typhoon Angela hit the Philippines. **12.** At least 50 people were killed in avalanches near Mount Everest.

DECEMBER 1995

21. At least 140 people were killed when an American Airlines plane crashed in the Andes near Cali, Colombia. **22.** Three men were killed in an explosion at a gas production platform in Howden, Tyne and Wear. **23.** At least 425 people, most of them children and teenagers, were killed in a fire at a school in Dabwali, northern India. **25.** At least 135 people were killed when the River Umsindusi burst its banks in Edendale township near Pietermaritzburg, South Africa. **28.** An 11-year-old girl and two men who tried to rescue her died after being trapped under ice on a frozen lake at Hemsworth park, W. Yorks.

JANUARY 1996

17. About 500 workmen were evacuated when the NatWest tower in the City of London caught fire; no-one was injured. **19.** At least 200 people died when a ferry capsized off the north coast of Indonesia.

FEBRUARY 1996

3. At least 240 people were killed when an earthquake registering 7.0 on the Richter scale hit Lijiang, south-west China.

MARCH 1996

8. One person was killed and at least 20 injured when a freight train and a mail train crashed head-on in Stafford. **18.** At least 150 people were killed in a fire in a disco in Manila, the Philippines. **29.** About 62 people were killed when an earthquake hit Pujili, central Ecuador.

APRIL 1996

3. Thirty-three people, including the US Commerce Secretary Ron Brown, were killed when their plane crashed outside Dubrovnik, Croatia. **11.** At least 16 people were killed when fire broke out in a flower shop at Düsseldorf airport, Germany. **18.** Sixty people were killed when two trains crashed head-on in northern India.

MAY 1996

11. A plane crashed in the Florida Everglades, USA, killing 109 people. **21.** About 600 people were presumed drowned when a ferry sank in Lake Victoria, Tanzania.

JULY 1996

18. All 230 people aboard a TWA jumbo jet were killed when it exploded soon after take-off from J. F. Kennedy airport, New York, *en route* to Paris. About 50 children were injured when the roof was torn off their double-decker school bus as it went under a low bridge in Murdishaw, Runcorn. **22.** The death toll from flooding in central and eastern China since early 1996 reached 800.

AUGUST 1996

8. A woman was killed and more than 60 people were injured when two trains crashed head-on near Watford Junction station, Herts. At least 83 people were killed when flash floods swept away a camp-site in the Spanish Pyrenees. **11.** Five teenagers were killed in a car crash near Ingoldmells, Lincs. **19.** Two children disappeared from a beach at Holme next the Sea, Norfolk; they were later found drowned. **29.** All 141 people on board a Russian airliner were reported to have been killed when it crashed in Spitsbergen in the Arctic Circle. **31.** The death toll from flooding during the monsoon season in Nepal reached 244.

ARTS, SCIENCE AND MEDIA

SEPTEMBER 1995

20. The Jerwood Prize for modern art, worth £30,000, was awarded jointly to Patrick Caulfield and Maggi Hambling. **26.** Penguin, HarperCollins and Random House announced that they would pull out of the Net Book Agreement from 1 October; on 28 September the Publishers' Association announced that it could no longer enforce the terms of the agreement.

OCTOBER 1995

5. Seamus Heaney was awarded the Nobel Prize for Literature. **19.** The Department of Health warned that seven brands of contraceptive pill were more likely than others to cause thrombosis; the advice was described as premature by the doctor leading the research. **27.** The Independent Television Commission awarded the licence for Britain's fifth and final terrestrial television channel to Channel 5 Broadcasting, a consortium led by the Pearson and MAI media groups.

NOVEMBER 1995

7. Pat Barker was awarded the Booker Prize for *The Ghost Road*. **17.** *Today* newspaper was published for the last time. **20.** The Kirklees sports stadium in Huddersfield, W. Yorks, won the 1995 RIBA Building of the Year Award. **28.** Damien Hirst won the Turner Prize for modern art.

DECEMBER 1995

7. The Galileo spacecraft successfully launched a probe into Jupiter's atmosphere and transmitted data back to NASA. **13.** The managing director of the Royal Philharmonic Orchestra, Paul Findlay, was sacked. **22.** The Millennium Commission rejected an application for a £50 million grant for a new Cardiff Bay Opera House.

JANUARY 1996

9. Sir Christopher Bland was appointed chairman of the BBC from April 1996. **29.** La Fenice opera house in Venice was destroyed by fire.

FEBRUARY 1996

6. Sir Simon Rattle said that he would resign as music director of the City of Birmingham Symphony Orchestra in 1998. **13.** The pop group Take That split up. **19.** Oasis won the Brit awards for best band, best album and best video; Jarvis Cocker, the lead singer of Pulp, disrupted a performance by Michael Jackson during the awards ceremony in London. **26.** The actor Haing Ngor was shot dead in Los Angeles.

MARCH 1996

6. Trevor Nunn was appointed director of the National Theatre from October 1997. **25.** Emma Thompson became the first person to win Oscars for both acting and writing when she won the award for best adapted screenplay for *Sense and Sensibility*. **31.** Rafal Payne was named the BBC Young Musician of the Year.

APRIL 1996

24. The Press Complaints Commission upheld a complaint from The Queen over an article in the magazine *BusinessAge* that presented an inaccurate and speculative estimation of her wealth.

MAY 1996

15. Helen Dunmore won the first Orange prize for women's fiction, worth £30,000. **17.** The Victoria and Albert Museum unveiled plans for a glass extension seven storeys high.

JUNE 1996

2. More than 1 million people went to the cinema for £1 on National Cinema Day. **4.** The European Ariane 5 space rocket, which had taken more than ten years to develop and was carrying cargo worth £500 million, veered off course after take-off from French Guiana on its maiden flight and was blown up for safety reasons. **7.** The BBC announced a radical restructuring of its operations. **17.** London City Ballet went into liquidation. **23.** A farewell gala was held at Sadler's Wells Theatre, London, to mark its closure; in July 1996 work began on a new theatre on the site. **24.** Hundreds of people complained to the *Daily Mirror* over its use of Second World War imagery in its articles about the run-up to the European Championships semi-final between England and Germany.

JULY 1996

3. A 12th-century reliquary casket believed to have held the blood and bones of St Thomas à Becket was sold at Sotheby's to a private collector for £4.18 million. On 4 July the National Heritage Secretary (Virginia Bottomley) made an unprecedented intervention to prevent the casket from leaving the country without an export licence. On 11 July the collector withdrew and the bid from the National Heritage Memorial Fund was accepted.

AUGUST 1996

6. Scientists announced that a meteorite which was found in Antarctica and was believed to have been ejected from Mars millions of years ago, contained structures likely to be microfossils of bacteria, thus providing the first evidence of life on the planet. On 7 August President Clinton said that further missions to Mars would be launched to investigate the discovery. **9.** Doctors said that a woman in Birmingham who had received fertility treatment was pregnant with eight babies. **14.** NASA scientists said that images taken by the spacecraft Galileo of Europa, one of Jupiter's moons, showed that icy floes on its surface could be floating on slush or water. **21.** A re-creation of Shakespeare's Globe Theatre in Southwark, London, opened with a production of *Two Gentlemen of Verona*. **23.** Classic FM was taken over by the radio group GWR. **26.** The rock group R.E.M. signed a record £51.6 million deal with Warner Brothers Records. **28.** The Advertising Standards Authority ruled that a Conservative Party advertisement depicting the Labour leader, Tony Blair, with demonic eyes broke its code of practice and should be withdrawn.

CRIMES AND LEGAL AFFAIRS

SEPTEMBER 1995

10. Eighteen-year-old Rachel Lean was found stabbed to death near RAF Coltishall, Norfolk; a woman was charged with the murder. **11.** James Doyle was sentenced at the Central Criminal Court to 24 years' imprisonment for masterminding a series of armed robberies in London in 1991-2. **16.** Fifteen-year-old Naomi Smith was found murdered near her home in Nuneaton, Warks. **19.** In the first successful private prosecution for rape in England and Wales, Christopher Davies was sentenced in Maidstone to 14 years' imprisonment for raping two women in 1991 and 1992. **24.** Lee Tyson was sentenced in Winchester to life imprisonment for the murder in October 1994 of a woman manager in the company for which he worked. A 16-year-old boy killed 12 people and wounded eight others near Toulon, France; he then shot himself. **27.** The European Court of Human Rights ruled that Britain had breached the Human Rights Convention over the shooting of three IRA members in Gibraltar in 1988. Paul Hickson, a former Olympic swimming coach, was sentenced in Cardiff to 17 years' imprisonment for the rape and indecent assault of girls he trained between 1976 and 1991.

OCTOBER 1995

3. The former American footballer and actor O. J. Simpson was acquitted in Los Angeles of murdering his former wife and her friend in June 1994. **4.** The trial of Geoffrey Knights, the partner of the actress Gillian Taylforth, was halted because of what Judge Sanders called 'unlawful, misleading, scandalous and malicious' reporting of the case by eight tabloid newspapers. **12.** The Home Secretary (Michael Howard) announced plans to end the automatic

early release of prisoners and ensure longer prison terms for habitual criminals; the Lord Chief Justice (Lord Taylor of Gosforth) said that longer sentences would not deter criminals and that mandatory minimum sentences were inconsistent with the interests of justice. An elderly couple and their daughter and granddaughter were found murdered at their home in London. **17.** Keith Moore, an accountant, was sentenced in Southwark to six years' imprisonment for stealing £6 million from the rock musician Sting for whom he worked. **21.** A stable-girl was found beaten to death at National Hunt stables at Buckfastleigh, Devon; on 22 October a man was charged with the murder. **27.** In a landmark judgment, the High Court ruled that the former owner of an asbestos factory near Leeds was liable to compensate people who had lived near the factory and developed cancer caused by asbestos dust. The Home Secretary banned the leader of the Moonies religious cult from entering Britain; on 1 November the High Court ruled that the Home Secretary had acted unlawfully because he had failed to follow rules of procedural fairness before taking the decision. **31.** Badrul Miah was sentenced at the Central Criminal Court to life imprisonment for the murder of 15-year-old Richard Everitt in a racial attack in north London in August 1994. Members of the insolvent Lloyds Syndicate 418, which made heavy losses in the 1980s and early 1990s, won a libel action in the High Court against the syndicate, its agents and its auditors.

NOVEMBER 1995

7. The convictions of four businessmen in 1992 for illegally exporting defence equipment to Iraq through their company Ordtec were ruled by the Court of Appeal to be 'unsafe and unsatisfactory' because of the failure of the Government to disclose documents vital to the defence case. Graeme Souness, the former Liverpool and Glasgow Rangers football manager, accepted £100,000 libel damages from Mirror Group Newspapers in place of the £750,000 he was awarded in the High Court in June 1995. **10.** At Southwark coroner's court an inquest jury found that Richard O'Brien, who died in April 1994 after being arrested and pinned to the ground by five police officers, was unlawfully killed. **19.** Four people died in a fire started deliberately in a block of flats in Shepherd's Bush, London. **20.** Sam Hill, who was sentenced in 1988 to life imprisonment for murder, was released after the Court of Appeal found that his conviction was unsafe and unsatisfactory. **21–22.** Rosemary West was convicted in Winchester of murdering ten young women and girls, including her daughter and step-daughter, between 1971 and 1987; she was sentenced to ten terms of life imprisonment. The Lord Chancellor (Lord Mackay of Clashfern) started an inquiry into payments which had been made or promised by newspapers to prosecution witnesses in the trial. **26.** The Liberal Democrat leader, Paddy Ashdown, was threatened at knifepoint in his constituency at

Yeovil, Somerset. 30. The European Court of Justice ruled that Britain's procedures for implementing exclusion orders under the Prevention of Terrorism Act were unlawful because they infringed the right of free movement for EU nationals guaranteed by the Treaty of Rome.

DECEMBER 1995

1. Nick Leeson, the trader who precipitated the collapse of Barings Bank, pleaded guilty in Singapore to two charges of fraud and forgery in return for nine other charges being dropped; on 2 December he was sentenced to six and a half years' imprisonment. Two British women, Susan Hagan and Sally-Anne Croft, were each sentenced in Portland, Oregon, to five years' imprisonment for their part in a plot to murder the US Attorney for Oregon in 1985. 4. A diamond necklace and bracelet belonging to the Duchess of York were stolen on a flight from the USA; they were recovered in New York on 5 December and a baggage handler was arrested. 7. Three men believed to have been involved in drug dealing were shot dead in a country lane in Essex. 8. Philip Lawrence, the headmaster of St George's Roman Catholic School in Maida Vale, London, was stabbed to death outside the school after going to the aid of one of his pupils who was being attacked by a gang; a 15-year-old boy was charged with the murder. 12. Victor Willoughby was sentenced at the Central Criminal Court to five terms of life imprisonment for raping five women in 1993–4. The Court of Appeal reduced libel damages of £350,000 awarded to the rock star Elton John against the publishers of the *Sunday Mirror* in November 1993 to £75,000, and said that judge and counsel could in future give guidance to juries on the level of libel damages. 13. The conviction of Sara Thornton, who was released on bail in July 1995 after serving five years of a life sentence for the murder of her husband, was quashed by the Court of Appeal; following a retrial Thornton was convicted on 30 May 1996 of manslaughter on the grounds of diminished responsibility and sentenced to five years' imprisonment; she did not return to prison as she had already served the period of the sentence. 14. Stephen Wilkinson, a paranoid schizophrenic, was convicted in Leeds of the manslaughter of 12-year-old Nikki Conroy, who was stabbed to death at her school in Cleveland in March 1994; he was ordered to be detained indefinitely in a mental hospital. 15. Dr Simon Heighes, an Oxford don, was sentenced in Oxford to two years' imprisonment for stealing rare books from university libraries and selling them. 19. The Conservative MP David Ashby lost a libel action in the High Court against the *Sunday Times* over an article published in January 1994 that said that he was a homosexual, a liar and a hypocrite. 20. Gordon Wardell was sentenced in Oxford to life imprisonment for the murder of his wife in September 1994; he had faked a robbery at the building society where she worked and claimed that she had been kidnapped by a gang

who had also attacked him. 23. The bodies of 16 members of the Solar Temple cult were found near Grenoble, France. 29. The body of 19-year-old Celine Figard, a French student who was last seen hitching a lift from a lorry driver on 19 December, was found in a lay-by near Hawford, Worcs. Ten people were stabbed by a shop assistant at a food store in Birmingham.

JANUARY 1996

3. Nineteen-year-old Anthony Erskine was kicked to death after going to the aid of his father who was being taunted by a gang of youths outside his home in Stratford-upon-Avon, Warks. Four people were stabbed by a woman at a Jobcentre in Bexleyheath, south-east London. 4. A man was found tied to his bed at his home in north London after being burgled on 26 December; he died the next day. 14. The body of a British tourist, Johanne Masheder, who had been missing since mid December 1995, was found in a ravine near Kanchanaburi, Thailand; a Thai monk was charged with murder and sentenced to death. 19. Kevin and Ian Maxwell, the sons of the late publisher Robert Maxwell, were cleared at the Central Criminal Court of conspiring to defraud Mirror Group Newspapers pensioners of £122 million; on 26 January the Serious Fraud Office said that Kevin Maxwell and other former executives of the company would face further charges. 20. A woman and four of her children were murdered in incidents in Birmingham and Bristol. 25. An inquest jury found that a Nigerian asylum seeker who had died in a struggle with two police officers in east London in December 1994 was unlawfully killed. 29. A man who suffered severe burns in the fire at King's Cross underground station in London in 1987 was awarded £650,000 damages in an out-of-court settlement with London Regional Transport.

FEBRUARY 1996

2. Paddy Ashdown's car was destroyed by a petrol bomb outside his home in Somerset. 9. Lord Brocket was sentenced at Luton Crown Court to five years' imprisonment for a £4.5 million insurance fraud involving four classic cars. 17. The body of 18-year-old Louise Smith, who went missing early on Christmas morning 1995, was found in a quarry near her home in Chipping Sodbury. 19. Richard Whyte was sentenced at the Central Criminal Court to life imprisonment for the rape and murder of Caroline Williams in August 1994. 21. The European Court of Human Rights ruled that the role of the Home Secretary and the Parole Board in reviewing the continued detention after completion of their minimum sentence of juveniles convicted of murder and detained 'at Her Majesty's pleasure' failed to meet the requirements of an independent assessment and therefore breached the human rights of the juvenile offenders. 28. Steven Grieveson was sentenced at Leeds Crown Court to three terms of life imprisonment for the murders of three teenagers in Sunderland in 1993–4. A British woman,

Sandra Gregory, was sentenced at a court in Bangkok to 25 years' imprisonment for smuggling heroin out of Thailand in February 1993.

MARCH 1996

4. The body of five-year-old Rosemary McCann, who went missing on 14 January, was found in Oldham. A British woman, Caroline Beale, pleaded guilty in New York to the reckless manslaughter of her new-born baby in September 1994; she received permission to return to Britain for psychiatric treatment. **9.** The body of a woman was found in the River Ely, Cardiff; she had been attacked while walking her dogs. **13.** Sixteen children and their teacher were shot dead and a further 12 children and two teachers were injured at Dunblane primary school, Perthshire, by a gunman, Thomas Hamilton, who then shot himself. On 14 March a public inquiry into the killings, to be headed by Lord Cullen, was announced. On 15 March John Major and Tony Blair visited Dunblane. On 17 March a minute's silence was observed throughout Britain and the Queen and the Princess Royal visited the town. **29.** Three British soldiers were sentenced in Cyprus to life imprisonment for the abduction, attempted rape and manslaughter of a Danish tour guide in September 1994.

APRIL 1996

2. Brendan O'Donnell was sentenced at the Central Criminal Court in Dublin to three terms of life imprisonment for the murders of a woman, her three-year-old son and a priest in Co. Clare in 1994. **3.** A Greek businessman who had been kidnapped, drugged and locked in a cupboard for nine days in Maida Vale, London, was freed by police. A High Court judge gave doctors permission to switch off the life support machine of a three-month old baby girl with severe brain damage; he refused, however, to lay down guidelines for such decisions. **6.** A 74-year-old man was beaten and robbed when he stopped his car to ask directions in Chapeltown, Leeds; he later died of a heart attack. **10.** Scotland Yard disclosed that a blackmailer had been sending explosive devices to branches of Barclays Bank since December 1994; on 20 April a small bomb exploded outside a branch of the bank in west London. The Lord Advocate said that doctors in Scotland who stopped treating coma patients deemed to be incapable of recovery would be granted immunity from prosecution when the patient died. **17.** Robin Pask was sent to a psychiatric hospital for an indefinite period for the manslaughter of an Open University lecturer, Elizabeth Howe, at a summer school in York in July 1992. **19.** John Scripps, a Briton who had been convicted of murdering a tourist in Singapore in March 1995, was hanged at Changi jail, Singapore. **19.** A rugby player who was paralysed after a scrum collapsed in a match in 1991 was awarded damages against the referee for his failure to exercise reasonable skill in preventing scrum collapses during the match. **25.** Jonathan Jones, who

was sentenced in April 1995 to two terms of life imprisonment for the murder of his girlfriend's parents, was released when the Appeal Court found that his conviction was unsafe. A private murder prosecution at the Central Criminal Court brought by the parents of Stephen Lawrence, a black teenager who was murdered in London in April 1993, collapsed when the judge ruled that the evidence of a key witness was unsafe and could not be put before the jury. The Appeal Court ruled that Customs and Excise had wrongly charged retailers VAT on interest-free credit deals since the tax was introduced in 1973; Customs and Excise said it would contest the judgement in the House of Lords. **28.** Thirty-two people were shot dead by a man at a tourist centre in Port Arthur, Tasmania. He then took three people hostage in a guest-house; the hostages died when the guest-house was destroyed by fire, but the man survived and was charged with the murders. **29.** Darren Carr was convicted at Birmingham Crown Court of the manslaughter of a woman and her two daughters by setting their home on fire in Abingdon, Oxon, in June 1995. **30.** Thirteen-year-old Louise Allen was kicked to death after trying to break up a fight in Corby, Northants; two girls aged 12 and 13 were charged with her manslaughter.

MAY 1996

1. A man was shot dead in Liverpool in what was believed to be the latest of a series of revenge attacks. **2.** The High Court ruled that the Home Secretary (Michael Howard) had acted unlawfully in fixing a 15-year minimum sentence for the two boys who murdered two-year-old James Bulger in February 1993. Matthew Simmons was fined £500 at Croydon magistrates' court and banned from going to football matches for a year for using threatening words and behaviour towards the Manchester United footballer Eric Cantona at a match in January 1995; he was also sentenced to seven days' imprisonment for attacking the prosecuting solicitor. The Lord Chief Justice, Lord Taylor of Gosforth, announced his early retirement owing to ill-health. **5.** Four children were killed in a house fire started deliberately in Southampton. **7.** Steven Heaney was sentenced at Liverpool Crown Court to two terms of life imprisonment for the murders of two boys, Paul Barker and Robert Gee, at fishing ponds at Eastam Rake, Cheshire, in July 1995. **9.** Eighteen-year-old Helen Martin was found beaten to death near Symonds Yat, Herefordshire. **14.** The Home Secretary said in a written answer in the House of Commons that equipment used since 1989 to test for traces of explosives in evidence presented in terrorist trials had been contaminated with the explosive RDX, and that about 12 convictions would be reviewed. **16.** Timothy Morss and Brett Tyler were sentenced at the Central Criminal Court to life imprisonment for sexually assaulting and murdering nine-year-old Daniel Handley in October 1994. **19.** A man was stabbed to death by another driver on a slip-road of the M25 in Kent. **22.** The businessman Owen Oyston was sentenced at Liverpool Crown Court to six years' imprisonment for raping a 16-year-old model in 1992. **23.** An 11-year-old boy was convicted at Leeds Crown Court of the manslaughter of an elderly woman who was hit by a concrete block he had pushed off the roof of a block of flats in Leeds in August 1995; he was freed under a three-year-supervision order. **28.** A German woman on holiday in Britain was shot dead in an attempted robbery at a hotel in Bedford. **30.** A man was shot dead during a row about a minor traffic accident in London.

JUNE 1996

3. In an out-of-court settlement 14 police officers accepted a total of £1.2 million in compensation for the psychological trauma they suffered attempting to rescue victims of the Hillsborough football stadium disaster in 1989. **24.** An elderly couple were found murdered at their home in Fulham, London. **26.** Ray Lee was sentenced at the Central Criminal Court to ten years' imprisonment for the manslaughter of PC Phillip Walters in April 1995.

JULY 1996

2. The Government published a White Paper proposing radical reforms to the legal aid system (*see* page 1170). **4.** Simon Smith was sentenced in Stafford to three terms of life imprisonment for suffocating three of his children in separate incidents between 1989 and 1994. **7.** Nine-year-old Jade Matthews was found beaten to death on a railway line near her home in Bootle, Merseyside; a 13-year-old boy was charged with the murder. **8.** Three children and four adults were injured when a man with a machete attacked them in the playground of an infants' school in Wolverhampton. **10.** A woman and her six-year-old daughter were found beaten to death in a field near Nonington, Kent; her nine-year-old daughter was seriously injured in the attack. **18.** Howard Hughes was sentenced in Chester to three terms of life imprisonment for the rape and murder of seven-year-old Sophie Hook in Llandudno in July 1995. **19.** Thirteen-year-old Caroline Dickinson, who was on a school trip to Brittany, was raped and murdered at a youth hostel in Pleine-Fougères. **26.** The Master of the Rolls (Lord Woolf) published proposals for a radical reform of the civil justice system in England and Wales. **27.** Two people were killed and about 110 injured when a bomb exploded in the Centennial Olympic Park in Atlanta, Georgia. **31.** Michael Brookes was sentenced at the Central Criminal Court to life imprisonment for the murder of 16-year-old Lynn Siddons in 1978. The former Test cricketers Ian Botham and Allan Lamb lost a High Court libel action in which they claimed that the former Pakistan captain Imran Khan had described them as racist and lower class and had accused Botham of ball-tampering.

AUGUST 1996

8. The fashion designer Ossie Clark was stabbed to death at his home in London; his former lover was charged with the murder. **13.** A vicar was stabbed to death outside his church in Anfield, Liverpool. **14.** Richard Humphrey was sentenced at the Central Criminal Court to four terms of life imprisonment for the murder in May 1995 of a woman in south London, three attempted murders, and robbery and firearms offences. **17.** Belgian police launched investigations into a suspected international paedophile ring after the bodies of two children were found in the garden of a house in Sars-la-Buissière, Belgium. **20.** Sixteen-year-old Lucy Burchell, who had been working as a prostitute, was found murdered in Ladywood, Birmingham. **22.** The Home Office said that it would be examining the trial of Ralston Edwards, who was convicted at the Central Criminal Court on two charges of rape; because he had elected to defend himself, he had cross-examined his victim over a period of six days during the trial. **26.** Fourteen-year-old Caroline Glachan was found murdered at Bonhill, Dumbarton. **27.** A hijacked Sudanese airliner with 200 people on board landed at Stansted airport, Essex. Over a period of eight hours all the passengers and crew were released; one person had been injured. The Iraqi hijackers surrendered and sought political asylum in Britain.

ENVIRONMENT

SEPTEMBER 1995

4. Foresters acting on the orders of the Duke of Edinburgh began to fell 28 ancient oak trees on Queen Anne's Ride, Windsor Great Park. After protests from conservationists the felling was halted, and on 9 October the Crown Estate Commissioners said that the remaining 20 oak trees would be preserved. Greenpeace apologized to Shell UK for miscalculating the pollution risk posed by the Brent Spar oil rig. **5.** France carried out the first of a series of underground nuclear tests at Mururoa atoll in the south Pacific. **13.** The Welsh Secretary (William Hague) rejected a scheme to build a barrage across the River Usk. **22.** The UN agreed formally to ban the export of toxic waste from developed to developing countries. **23.** A 30-mile slick formed off Flamborough Head; the oil was believed to have been discharged from a tanker. **24.** A leaked government report disclosed that more than half the wetland nature reserves in Britain had been damaged or seriously threatened in the past five years. The Ramblers' Association held a series of rallies to demand the 'right to roam' in the British countryside.

OCTOBER 1995

17. The Government published a White Paper on the English countryside (*see* page 1168). 20. The Secretary of State for Scotland (Michael Forsyth) announced proposals to sell 109,000 hectares of Crown land in the Scottish Highlands to crofters; he also encouraged lairds to sell their land to crofters. The National Trust for Scotland revoked the ban on fox-hunting on its land which had been imposed in February 1995,

DECEMBER 1995

11. British Energy abandoned plans to build two new nuclear power stations.

JANUARY 1996

9–11. Anti-road protesters prevented contractors from undertaking clearance work for the construction of the Newbury bypass; on 12 January 34 people were arrested for aggravated trespass.

FEBRUARY 1996

15. The Liberian-registered tanker *Sea Empress* ran aground at the entrance to Milford Haven harbour, south Wales. On 17 February the tanker's crew was lifted to safety by helicopter after a salvage attempt failed; nearby homes were evacuated and Milford Haven port was closed. On 20 February another salvage attempt failed. On 21 February the tanker was refloated; about 65,000 tons of crude oil had leaked into the sea. 21. Coalite Products was fined £150,000 and ordered to pay an estimated £300,000 costs for knowingly burning large quantities of chemical waste at a low temperature and emitting dioxins into the atmosphere in 1990 and 1991. 29. Bailiffs began to evict protesters from camps set up on the site of the Newbury bypass.

MARCH 1996

21. The European Court of Justice ruled that Britain had acted illegally in 1993 in excluding part of the Lappel Bank reserve on the River Medway, Kent, from Special Protection Area listing under the EU's Birds Directive, thereby favouring economic interests over the interests of the environment.

MAY 1996

15. The Government published a strategy for protecting the rarest and most threatened life forms in Britain.

JUNE 1996

5. The Prince of Wales opened the £330 million second Severn crossing. 19. Some of the prehistoric stones at Avebury were damaged by being daubed with painted symbols. 23–4. Greenpeace vessels clashed with Danish boats involved in the industrial fishing of sand eels in the Firth of Forth.

JULY 1996

2. The European Commission ordered an emergency 50 per cent cut in the North Sea herring catch.

13. The *Sunday Telegraph* published details of a leaked Ministry of Defence document concerning the contamination of parts of Berkshire by radioactive fall-out after a fire at the Greenham Common air base in 1958. 18. Chris Green resigned as chief executive of English Heritage over alleged administrative irregularities.

AUGUST 1996

5. Severn Trent Water Authority was fined £175,000 for leaking chemicals into the River Wye, killing 33,000 young salmon. 20. The Environment Secretary (John Gummer) announced a national air quality strategy, including new targets for reducing the level of eight hazardous pollutants in the atmosphere by 2005.

SPORT

SEPTEMBER 1995

2. Frank Bruno won the WBC world heavyweight boxing championship when he defeated Oliver McCall on points at Wembley. 7. The Rugby Football Union announced that the sport below international level would remain amateur for the 1995–6 season. The jockey Lester Piggott announced his retirement. 18. Eleven leading rugby union clubs passed a vote of no confidence in the RFU commission set up to establish guidelines in the open era; on 8 November the commission published proposals for the future structure and management of the sport. 21. The England rugby union player Rob Andrew joined Newcastle United Sporting Club as rugby development director; on 19 October he announced his retirement from international rugby after being dropped by his club Wasps. 24. Europe's golfers won the Ryder Cup for the first time since 1989.

OCTOBER 1995

7. Middlesbrough signed the Brazilian midfielder Juninho for £4.75 million. 11. The Scotland and Everton footballer Duncan Ferguson was jailed after losing his appeal against a three-month sentence imposed in May 1995 for head-butting a player while playing for Glasgow Rangers in April 1994. 12. Three players were sent home from the rugby league world cup after testing positive for drugs. 13. The boxer James Murray collapsed in the final round of a British bantamweight title fight against Drew Docherty in Glasgow; he died on 14 October. Rioting broke out in the hall at the end of the fight. 16. The former world boxing champion Chris Eubank announced his retirement. The England cricketer Devon Malcolm accepted substantial undisclosed damages in the High Court over an article in *Wisden Cricket Monthly* that questioned his commitment to the national team because he was born and brought up in the West Indies.

Phillip DeFreitas later won libel damages over the same article and Chris Lewis received an apology from the magazine. **18.** The three-times Grand National winner Red Rum died and was buried at Aintree racecourse. **25.** The British Boxing Board of Control proposed a 12-point plan to make the sport safer. **31.** After six years playing rugby league the former rugby union international Jonathan Davies signed for Cardiff rugby union club.

NOVEMBER 1995

10. The Formula 1 racing driver Mika Häkkinen was seriously injured after losing control of his car during the qualifying session for the Australian Grand Prix in Adelaide. **16.** The first cricket Test match between England and South Africa in South Africa since 1965 opened in Pretoria. **22.** Colin McRae became the first Briton to win the world motor rallying championship. **27.** Graeme Le Saux and David Batty of Blackburn Rovers were fined by the club after exchanging blows during a match on 22 November. **28.** The Football League agreed a £125 million five-year deal with Sky television to broadcast Endsleigh League and Coca Cola Cup matches.

DECEMBER 1995

1. Sarah Hardcastle won the 800 metres freestyle gold medal at the world short-course championships. **3.** The England wicketkeeper Jack Russell became the first cricketer to take 11 catches in a Test match in the game against South Africa in Johannesburg. **3–4.** The England cricket captain Mike Atherton was 185 not out after batting for 10¾ hours to force a draw in the second Test against South Africa. **8.** A former press officer of the International Amateur Athletic Federation (IAAF) claimed that the result of the 1994 female athlete of the year award had been rigged. **10.** Jonathan Edwards was named BBC Sports Personality of the Year. **13.** ITV bought the rights to screen all Formula One grand prix from 1997. **17.** The European Court of Justice ruled that football clubs of different EU member states should not be able to charge transfer fees for players whose contracts have expired, and that the limit of three foreign players in a team was illegal. On 22 December the Premier League abandoned its limit on the number of EU players clubs can field. **21.** Jack Charlton resigned as manager of the Republic of Ireland football team. **22.** The Norwegian adventurer Borge Ousland reached the South Pole and became the first person to ski alone and unaided to both Poles.

JANUARY 1996

4. St Helens beat Warrington 80–0 in the rugby league Regal Trophy semi-final; on 5 January Warrington's coach, Brian Johnson, resigned. **5.** David Hempleman-Adams became the first Briton to walk solo and unsupported to the South Pole. **6.** In Liverpool's 7–0 defeat of Rochdale at Anfield, Ian Rush scored a record 42nd goal in an FA Cup match.

10. The England football coach Terry Venables said that he would resign after the European Championships in June 1996 in order to concentrate on several pending legal cases. **12.** UEFA banned Tottenham Hotspur and Wimbledon from their European tournaments for one year, with the suspension active for five years, for fielding under-strength teams in the 1995 InterToto Cup; on 26 January the ban was rescinded and replaced by fines. **14.** At a special general meeting, members of the Rugby Football Union voted to hold a second meeting to decide whether rugby union in England should become open. **15.** The England cricketer Devon Malcolm strongly criticized his treatment by the chairman of selectors, Ray Illingworth. **16.** The British champion skier Kirsteen McGibbon was killed in a fall while training in Austria. Wigan won the Rugby League championship for the seventh successive season.

FEBRUARY 1996

1. The Leyton Orient footballer Roger Stanislaus was banned for one year by the FA for testing positive for a performance-enhancing drug in November 1995; on 6 February he was sacked by Leyton Orient. **5.** Mick McCarthy was appointed manager of the Republic of Ireland football team. **6.** The House of Lords passed an amendment to the Broadcasting Bill preventing satellite television from obtaining exclusive coverage of major sporting events. On 4 March the National Heritage Secretary (Virginia Bottomley) said that the right of terrestrial channels to show live coverage of eight major events would be safeguarded. **11.** The jockey Walter Swinburn was badly injured in a fall in Hong Kong. **12.** The World Boxing Organization heavyweight champion Tommy Morrison was suspended after confirmation that he is HIV positive. **29.** At the cricket world cup in India, the West Indies were beaten by the amateur Kenyan team. On 5 March the West Indies captain Richie Richardson announced that he would retire from international cricket after the world cup and a new captain, team coach and team manager were appointed.

MARCH 1996

6. At the cricket world cup in Kandy, Sri Lanka scored a record one-day total of 398 runs in their match against Kenya. **9.** Will Carling announced his resignation as England rugby union captain. **13.** The cricket world cup semi-final between India and Sri Lanka in Calcutta was halted by crowd rioting; Sri Lanka was awarded the match by default. **24.** The IAAF decided to allow prize money to be awarded at major championships. **25.** The British athlete Diane Modahl, who was suspended in August 1994 after a positive drugs test, was cleared by the IAAF. Ray Illingworth resigned as manager of the England cricket team; on 29 March David Lloyd was appointed its coach. **27.** Frans Botha was stripped of his IBF world heavyweight boxing title after testing positive for steroids.

APRIL 1996

2. The Sri Lankan cricketer Sanath Jayasuriya scored the fastest-ever century in a one-day international when he reached 100 in 48 balls against Pakistan in Singapore; he also hit a record 11 sixes in his innings and made a record 29 runs in one over. **9.** The Rugby Football Union confirmed that there would be a ten-club first division in the 1996–7 season, and reasserted its right as a governing body to control the game in England. **11.** The twenty leading rugby union clubs in England said that they would not take part in RFU competitions in the 1996–7 season and put forward their own proposals for a competition structure. **18.** David Graveney and Graham Gooch were elected to the selection committee for the England cricket team, defeating six other candidates including Ian Botham. **26.** Shaun Pollock took four wickets in four balls in his début for Warwickshire. **27.** A football match between Brighton and York was abandoned after 16 minutes when Brighton fans invaded the pitch in protest at plans to sell the Goldstone Ground and ground-share with Portsmouth for a season; on 30 April the club announced that it would remain at the ground for one more season. **29.** Ronnie O'Sullivan was fined £20,000 and banned from snooker tournaments for two years, the ban being suspended for two years, for assaulting a press officer at the world championships in Sheffield. **30.** The Newcastle United striker Faustino Asprilla was fined £20,000 and suspended for one match by the FA for elbowing and head-butting the Manchester City captain Keith Curle during a match in February.

MAY 1996

2. Glen Hoddle was appointed coach of the England football team from July 1996. **4.** In the Pilkington Cup final at Twickenham the referee awarded a last-minute penalty try against Leicester which gave Bath victory. The Leicester flanker Neil Back pushed the referee over at the end of the match; he later said that he had mistaken him for a Bath player. On 13 May he was banned for six months by the RFU. **5.** Manchester United won the Premiership for the third time in four years. **6.** Stephen Hendry won the world snooker championship for the sixth time in seven years. **7.** Rugby Union in England officially became professional. **8.** In the first intercode rugby match between club sides for more than 100 years, Wigan beat Bath 82–6 in a match played under league rules at Maine Road; on 25 May Bath beat Wigan 44–19 in a match played under union rules at Twickenham. **11.** Manchester United became the first team to win the FA Cup and League championship in the same year for a second time when they beat Liverpool to win the FA Cup. The rugby league club Wigan won the rugby union Middlesex Sevens tournament at Twickenham. **24.** The RFU and the leading clubs reached agreement on the future operation of the sport. **28.** Cathay Pacific said that members of the England football squad had caused damage on the flight back from a tour to China and Hong Kong; on 3 June the England coach (Terry Venables) said that the squad took collective responsibility for the incident and that fines had been imposed.

JUNE 1996

6. Premier League football clubs agreed a £743 million four-year television deal with BSkyB and the BBC. **8.** The European football championships opened at Wembley stadium, London. Alex Greaves became the first woman to ride in the Derby. **10.** The RFU signed an exclusive five-year £87.5 million television deal with BSkyB which put the future of the Five Nations championship in jeopardy. **23.** Michael Johnson broke the world 200 metres record, set in 1979, with a time of 19.66 seconds. **26.** In the semi-finals of the European championships Germany beat England 6–5 on penalties at Wembley after sudden-death extra time. **28.** At Wimbledon two British men (Tim Henman and Luke Milligan) met in a singles match on Centre Court for the first time since 1938. **30.** In the final of the European Championships Germany beat the Czech Republic 2–1 at Wembley after sudden-death extra time.

JULY 1996

1. Tim Henman became the first British man to reach the quarter-finals at Wimbledon for 23 years when he beat Magnus Gustafsson in straight sets. On 4 July he was beaten in straight sets by Todd Martin, the only original seed to reach the semi-finals of the men's championship. **4.** The Italian striker Fabrizio Ravanelli joined Middlesbrough for £7 million. **6.** Steffi Graf won the ladies' singles championship at Wimbledon for the seventh time. **7.** In the men's singles final at Wimbledon Richard Krajicek beat the unseeded MaliVai Washington in straight sets. **8.** Fifteen-year-old Martina Hingis became the youngest-ever Wimbledon champion when she won the ladies' doubles championship with Helena Sukova. **13.** England were excluded from the 1997 Five Nations' rugby union championship. **19.** The Olympic Games opened in Atlanta, Georgia. The National Hunt jockey Richard Davis died after being crushed by his horse in a fall at Southwell racecourse. **21.** Tom Lehman became the first American since 1926 to win the Open golf championship. **24.** The Prime Minister said that a national Academy of Sport would be set up. **27.** At the Olympic Games Donovan Bailey set a new world record of 9.84 seconds in the final of the 100 metres; Linford Christie was disqualified from the race after two false starts. Steve Redgrave won his fourth successive Olympic gold medal in his event when he won the coxless pairs with Matthew Pinsent. **29.** The Blackburn Rovers striker Alan Shearer was transferred to Newcastle United for a world record fee of £15 million. **30.** Carl Lewis won the Olympic long jump gold medal, his fourth successive Olympic gold medal in the event.

AUGUST 1996

1. Michael Johnson set a new world record of 19.32 for the 200 metres and became the first man to win Olympic gold medals for both the 200 metres and the 400 metres. **12.** Bruce Rioch was sacked as manager of Arsenal FC. **15.** The paralympics opened in Atlanta, Georgia. **20.** The fast bowler Ed Giddins was banned from professional cricket until April 1998 by the TCCB for cocaine use. **21.** Kenny Dalglish resigned as director of football at Blackburn Rovers. **26.** St Helens won the inaugural rugby league Stones Super League championship. Alan Ball resigned as manager of Manchester City FC. **28.** Chris Boardman set a new world record of 4 minutes 13.353 seconds when he won the 4,000 metres individual pursuit world cycling championship. **30.** The former world boxing champion Frank Bruno announced his retirement.

APPOINTMENTS AND RESIGNATIONS

In addition to those mentioned above, the following appointments and resignations were announced:

1995

1 September: Phil Hall was appointed editor of the *News of the World*

29 September: Max Hastings, the editor of the *Daily Telegraph*, was appointed editor of the London *Evening Standard* from January 1996

18 October: Charles Moore was appointed editor of the *Daily Telegraph*; Dominic Lawson, the editor of *The Spectator*, was appointed editor of the *Sunday Telegraph* in his place

19 October: Frank Johnson was appointed editor of *The Spectator*

30 October: Bill Cockburn, the chief executive of the Post Office, was appointed chief executive of W. H. Smith

1 November: Sir Nicholas Lloyd resigned as editor of the *Daily Express*

3 November: Robert Ayling was appointed chief executive of British Airways

13 November: Ian Hargreaves resigned as editor of the *Independent*

15 November: Peter Middleton resigned as chief executive of Lloyd's of London; he was replaced by Ron Sandler

24 November: Richard Addis was appointed editor of the *Daily Express*; Peter Bonfield was appointed chief executive of British Telecom from January 1996

8 December: Steve Platt resigned as editor of the *New Statesman and Society*

1996

19 February: Liz Forgan resigned as managing director of BBC Network Radio

29 March: Will Hutton was appointed editor of the *Observer* in the place of Andrew Jaspan

26 April: Andrew Marr was appointed editor of the *Independent*

4 July: Genista McIntosh was appointed general director of the Royal Opera House from early 1997

29 July: Sir Peter Hall was appointed artistic director of the Old Vic theatre from January 1997

AFRICA

SEPTEMBER 1995

11. Rwandan government soldiers killed over 100 Hutu villagers in the north-west of the country in retaliation for attacks on army units by Hutu militias based in Zaire. **28.** Mercenaries led by a former French colonel launched a coup d'état in the Comoros in which President Djohar was arrested and replaced by a Military Transition Council.

OCTOBER 1995

1. Islamic militants killed 18 people in an attack on a bus in southern Algeria. **4.** French forces landed in the Comoros, releasing President Djohar and arresting the coup leaders. **15.** The leader of Zimbabwe's only parliamentary opposition party, Revd Ndabaningi Sithole, was arrested in connection with an alleged assassination attempt on President Mugabe. **22.** In the presidential election in Côte d'Ivoire, President Konan-Bédié was returned to office with an overwhelming majority following an opposition boycott. **29.** A car bomb planted by Islamic fundamentalists exploded at a police barracks on the outskirts of Algiers, killing 11 people. **29.** The first free democratic national election for the Tanzanian presidency was won by Benjamin Mkapa of the Chama Cha Mapinduzi ruling party.

NOVEMBER 1995

7. Rwandan government troops attacked a Hutu base on the Zaire border, killing 171. **10.** Ken Saro-Wiwa and eight other human rights activists were executed in Nigeria despite Commonwealth pleas for clemency. **11.** Nigeria's membership of the Commonwealth was suspended. **16.** The Algerian presidential election was won by President Liamine Zeroual. **23.** An Egyptian military court jailed 54 members of the Islamic fundamentalist Muslim Brotherhood for aiding the armed campaign against the government.

DECEMBER 1995

10–14. Algerian security forces killed 36 Islamic militants and captured caches of arms in a series of raids. **25.** Fourteen people were killed in KwaZulu/Natal, South Africa, in continuing communal violence. **26.** Ten people were killed in fighting between Inkatha and ANC supporters in KwaZulu/Natal.

JANUARY 1996

15. King Moshoeshoe II of Lesotho was killed in a car accident. 16. Sierra Leone's president, Capt. Valentine Strasser, was overthrown in a military coup led by his deputy, Capt. Julius Bio. 27. President Ousmane of Niger was overthrown in a coup by the armed forces, who established a National Salvation Committee. 29. Ten people were killed when seven unidentified gunmen opened fire on a queue of 2,000 people seeking employment outside a factory near Johannesburg, South Africa.

FEBRUARY 1996

7. King Letsie was sworn in as king of Lesotho. 11. Eighteen people were killed by two car bombs planted by Islamic fundamentalists in Algiers. 18. Twelve people were killed by two car bombs in Algiers.

MARCH 1996

4. The former South African defence minister Gen. Magnus Malan went on trial in Durban charged with collusion in the murders of 13 people massacred in Natal in 1987. 8. The mandate for the deployment of UN forces in Rwanda ended and the remaining troops began to leave. 17. Robert Mugabe was re-elected President of Zimbabwe in an election in which only 31 per cent of the electorate voted and the two opposition candidates, Bishop Abel Muzorewa and Revd Ndabaningi Sithole, withdrew, claiming the election was unfair. 21. Ten ANC sympathisers and one child were shot dead in KwaZulu/Natal on the first day of campaigning for local elections. 28. Thousands of Zaïrean-born Tutsis began crossing the border into Rwanda as a result of a pogrom by Hutu militia and Zaïrean soldiers. 29. The military government in Sierra Leone handed over power to President Kabbah. 30. Libyan government forces were sent to Benghazi to put down a fundamentalist uprising which had begun ten days earlier with the escape of 400 prisoners.

APRIL 1996

3. Five members of the South African neo-Nazi Afrikaner Resistance Movement (AWB) were each sentenced to 26 years' imprisonment for a bombing campaign which killed 20 people in April 1994. 6. Fighting broke out in Monrovia, Liberia, following the dismissal from the government of Roosevelt Johnson. 10. Warring factions in Liberia agreed to a cease-fire. 11. Forty-nine African countries signed the Treaty of Pelindaba which declared the continent a nuclear-free zone. 18. Islamic militants opened fire on a hotel in Cairo, Egypt, killing 17 Greek tourists and one Egyptian. 21. The US sent a diplomatic mission to Liberia in an attempt to negotiate peace; militia gunmen released 127 peo-

ple, including 71 foreigners. 23. Seven people died in a shoot-out between Egyptian police and two men suspected of massacring Greek tourists.

MAY 1996

1. Fighting resumed in Liberia. 2–3. Sixteen people died in communal violence in KwaZulu/Natal. 3. Roosevelt Johnson was smuggled out of Liberia for peace talks in Ghana. 4–5. Nigerian and Cameroonian forces clashed in a struggle for control of the mineral-rich Bakassi peninsula. 8. The South African Constituent Assembly adopted a new constitution. 9. The National Party said it would withdraw from South Africa's Government of National Unity. 11. In the presidential election in Uganda, President Museveni was returned to power for a second five-year term. 14. A freighter carrying 3,500 Liberian refugees docked in Ghana, having spent ten days at sea. 19. Two hundred soldiers mutinied in the Central African Republic, killing three people and taking a minister and an Army Chief of Staff hostage; on 27 May the mutineers released their hostages and were returned to barracks by French troops. 28. France suspended military co-operation with Burundi after 51 Tutsi refugees were killed by Hutu rebels.

JUNE 1996

4. Kudirat Abiola, wife of the jailed Nigerian opposition leader, Chief Moshood Abiola, was murdered. 13. Nigeria agreed to receive a Commonwealth task force to discuss a return to democracy. Burundian soldiers massacred at least 70 Hutu civilians in central Burundi. 17. Nineteen people died in pre-election violence in KwaZulu/Natal, South Africa. 18. A Russian trawler carrying 400 refugees returned to Liberia after three weeks at sea. 20. The Rwandan government began issuing new passports, thereby invalidating those held by Hutu refugees in exile. 22. Eight people were killed in fighting between rival factions in Mogadishu, Somalia.

JULY 1996

4. Sixty people were reported to have been killed near Bujumbura, Burundi, bringing the total number of deaths to 1,060 during the week. Twelve people were killed in clashes between police and anti-government rebels in Benghazi, Libya. 14. Fifty people died when security forces opened fire on spectators at a football match in Libya after the crowd began chanting anti-Gadhafi slogans. 20–21. At least 300 Tutsis were massacred by Hutus at Bugendana, Burundi. 23. Tutsi mourners attacked the helicopter carrying President Ntibantaganya of Burundi, who was attempting to attend the funeral of the victims of the Bugendana massacre. 25. The army overthrew President Ntibantaganya of Burundi and installed a moderate Tutsi, Maj. Pierre Buyoya, as transitional head of state. 31. The leaders of six African nations, meeting in Tanzania, decided to impose economic sanctions against Burundi's

military government. Fifteen people were trampled to death in a South African railway station as security guards attempted to deter fare dodgers with electric cattle prods. The leaders of Liberia's warring factions agreed to an immediate cease-fire and withdrawal of troops.

AUGUST 1996

2. The Somali warlord Gen. Mohammed Aideed died from gunshot wounds. 10–11. Ethiopian forces attacked Muslim fundamentalist militia in northern Somalia.

THE AMERICAS

SEPTEMBER 1995

7. Senator Robert Packwood (Republican) resigned from the US Senate after the ethics committee voted to expel him for sexual harassment of women over a 20-year period. 19. The *Washington Post* in agreement with the *New York Times* published the 35,000-word manifesto of the 'Unabomber' so that he would end his terrorist campaign. 20. The US Senate approved an amended version of the House of Representatives' welfare reform bill. 29. Pete Wilson, the governor of California, withdrew from the campaign for the Republican Party nomination for the 1996 presidential election.

OCTOBER 1995

1. The Egyptian cleric Sheikh Omar Abderahman and nine co-defendants were convicted in New York of bombing the World Trade Centre in 1993; on 17 January the Sheik was sentenced to life imprisonment and his co-defendants to terms of between 25 and 35 years each. 6. The USA relaxed restrictions on travel to Cuba and ended the restrictions on US news organizations opening offices in Cuba. 9. A suspected terrorist bomb derailed a train in Arizona, killing one person and injuring 100. 16. An estimated 400,000 black men gathered in Washington DC to listen to an address by Louis Farrakhan, the extremist leader of the Nation of Islam. 31. A referendum on sovereignty for Quebec was defeated by 50.6 per cent to 49.4 per cent.

NOVEMBER 1995

8. Gen. Colin Powell announced that he would not run for the US presidency in 1996. 13. President Clinton vetoed a borrowing bill proposed by Congress because of the budget cuts it contained, leading to a partial closure of government agencies as the federal government ran out of funding. 15. The US Treasury borrowed US$61,000 million from two government pension schemes to pay US$25,000 million due to holders of US securities. 19. President Clinton and Congress reached a temporary budget compromise to allow federal

government operations to continue until 15 December.

DECEMBER 1995

6. President Clinton vetoed a bill which would have balanced the federal budget in seven years by reducing projected spending and cutting taxes. 12. The Senate committee investigating the Whitewater affair claimed a breakthrough when files relating to Hillary Clinton's involvement in the land and banking scandal were found in the basement of one of her associates. 13. President Clinton refused to comply with a Senate subpoena to release unconditionally documents relating to the Whitewater affair. 15. The Senate Whitewater committee rejected President Clinton's conditional offer to release Whitewater documents and voted to take the administration to court over the subpoena. 16. The US federal government laid off non-essential employees as government agencies were again closed down because of the budget stalemate between President Clinton and Congress. 17. Rene Préval won the Haitian presidential election. 21. President Clinton agreed to release unconditionally documents relating to the Whitewater affair after the Senate voted to take the administration to the Supreme Court to force it to hand over the documents. 22. The White House surrendered to the Senate Whitewater committee subpoenaed documents which showed that administration officials had tried to obtain confidential information about independent inquiries into the Whitewater affair.

JANUARY 1996

5. President Clinton and Congress reached a budget compromise which allowed federal government agencies to resume work until 26 January. Under congressional pressure the White House released two confidential memos which implicated Hillary Clinton in the decision in 1993 to dismiss seven White House travel staff and transfer the White House travel contract to a business partly-owned by a friend. 9. An appeal court in St Louis, Missouri, ruled that President Clinton should face a civil trial while he was in office over an alleged sexual advance to a woman in 1991. 22. The special prosecutor investigating the Whitewater affair subpoenaed Hillary Clinton to appear before a federal grand jury to answer questions over the legal work that she had done for Madison Guaranty, the bank at the centre of the scandal; Mrs Clinton appeared before the jury four days later. 26. President Clinton and Congress agreed on a compromise short-term budget plan to keep the US federal government functioning until mid-March.

FEBRUARY 1996

6. President Clinton was subpoenaed by an Arkansas judge to appear as a defence witness in the trial of his former business partner Susan McDougal. 7. Patrick Buchanan won the Louisiana state primary vote for

the Republican presidential nomination. Twenty-seven current and former officials of the Clinton administration were subpoenaed to testify to a House of Representatives' committee about the dismissal of White House travel office officials; the Justice Department was ordered to release all the documents on the affair that it possessed. 13. Senator Robert Dole won the Iowa state primary vote for the Republican presidential nomination. 14. The Colombian Attorney-General charged President Samper with using money from the Cali drugs cartel to finance his 1994 election campaign and also with obstruction of investigations into electoral fraud. 20. Patrick Buchanan won the New Hampshire state primary vote. 24. Cuban Air Force fighters shot down over international waters two US-based civilian light aircraft operated by Cuban exile organizations who were searching for Cuban refugees fleeing to Florida. Two days later President Clinton increased US sanctions against Cuba. 25. Steve Forbes won the Delaware primary vote for the Republican presidential nomination. 27. Senator Robert Dole won the North and South Dakota primary votes but lost the Arizona vote to Steve Forbes.

MARCH 1996

2. Senator Robert Dole won the South Carolina state primary vote. 5. Senator Robert Dole won the state primary votes in Maine, Vermont, Connecticut, Rhode Island, Massachusetts, Maryland, Colorado and Georgia. 6. Republican candidates Lamar Alexander and Senator Richard Lugar withdrew from the presidential campaign. 8. Senator Robert Dole won the New York state primary vote. 12. Senator Robert Dole won the primary votes in Texas, Florida, Mississippi, Tennessee, Louisiana, Oregon, and Oklahoma. 14. The Republican candidate Steve Forbes withdrew from the presidential campaign. 19. Senator Robert Dole won the state primary votes in Michigan, Ohio, Illinois and Wisconsin. 22. The House of Representatives voted to lift a ban on the public ownership of assault weapons. 27. Senator Robert Dole won the California, Washington and Nevada state primary votes, clinching the Republican presidential nomination. 28. Congress approved a bill enabling the President to exercise a 'line-item veto' over legislation.

APRIL 1996

2. David Hale, a witness in the Whitewater trial, alleged that President Clinton had agreed to accept a covert loan of £98,684 while governor of Arkansas. 3. Theodore Kaczynski, thought to be the Unabomber, was detained in Montana. 3. Five thousand people were evacuated from the south of Montserrat as a volcano erupted on the island. 10. President Clinton vetoed a bill that would have prohibited a form of late-term abortion. 23. Gen. Lino Oviedo complied with a request from President Wasmosy of Chile to resign as head of the army, having refused the previous day. 24. President Clinton reached

agreement with Congress on a spending bill which would end the dispute over the budget.

MAY 1996

1. President Clinton ordered the release of 12 million barrels of petroleum onto the market in an attempt to curb rising fuel prices. 3. The Attorney-General of Columbia, Orlando Vasquez Velasqez, was arrested on drugs and corruption charges. 9. President Clinton, giving evidence via videotape at the trial of his former business partners in Arkansas, denied involvement in procuring an illegal loan. 15. Republican presidential nominee Robert Dole resigned his seat in the Senate. 16. The top US naval officer Adm. Jeremy 'Mike' Boorda committed suicide, having allegedly worn medals he had not been awarded. 28. President Clinton's former business partners Jim and Susan McDougal and the governor of Arkansas, Jim Guy Tucker, were found guilty of conspiracy and fraud. 30. President Clinton surrendered documents relating to the dismissal of members of the White House travel office which had been subpoenaed by a congressional committee.

JUNE 1996

13. President Samper was cleared of drug corruption charges by Colombia's House of Representatives. An 81-day siege by the FBI of a white supremacist militia group at a ranch in Montana ended peacefully. 14. An FBI report criticized President Clinton for obtaining 408 confidential files on Republican officials. 17. Hillary Clinton sent an affidavit to the Senate Whitewater committee in an attempt to refute accusations of corruption. 18. The Senate Whitewater committee issued a report accusing Hillary Clinton of involvement in a fraudulent land deal whilst her husband was governor of Arkansas. Theodore Kaczynski, the alleged Unabomber, was charged on ten counts, including four bombings. 24. The US Supreme Court agreed to delay a sexual harassment lawsuit against President Clinton until after the November presidential election. 25. President Clinton agreed to allow congressional investigators to view subpoenaed documents relating to the dismissal of members of the White House travel office. 26. The director of President Clinton's personal security office, Craig Livingstone, resigned, accepting responsibility for ordering FBI files on Republican officials.

JULY 1996

8. Abdala Bucaram was elected President of Ecuador. 16. President Clinton announced that any lawsuits relating to the Helms-Burton Act, penalizing foreign companies benefiting from American property seized by Cuba, would be delayed for six months. 23. The US House of Representatives approved a bill designed to impose sanctions on foreign companies investing in oil and gas fields in Libya and Iran.

AUGUST 1996

1. Two Arkansas bankers were acquitted of concealing funds donated to President Clinton's 1990 gubernatorial campaign. 2. Coca farmers in Colombia staged violent protests against a government plan to destroy their crops. 5. Republican presidential candidate Robert Dole unveiled an election manifesto in which he called for tax cuts of 15 per cent. 9. Jack Kemp was chosen to be Robert Dole's presidential running mate. 11. The Republican Party convention to nominate formally the party's presidential candidate opened; Robert Dole was officially nominated on the 15th. 18. Ross Perot was nominated as the presidential candidate of the Reform Party. 22. President Clinton signed a bill ending the guarantee of federal aid to the poor. 23. President Clinton signed an executive order classifying nicotine as an addictive drug. 25. The Democratic Party convention to nominate formally the party's presidential candidate opened in Chicago; President Clinton embarked on a four-day train journey to the convention. 29. President Clinton delivered his key-note speech to the Democratic convention; Dick Morris, a senior aide to President Clinton, resigned amid allegations that he had had an affair with a prostitute.

ASIA

SEPTEMBER 1995

4. A car bomb in the Kashmiri capital Srinagar killed 15 people. Taliban, the fundamentalist Islamic students movement, captured Afghanistan's second city Herat and the surrounding province from government forces. 10. The Nepali Prime Minister Man Mohan Adhikari resigned after his government lost a parliamentary vote of confidence. 18. In elections to Hong Kong's Legislative Council, the Democratic Party and its allies won 29 seats, pro-China parties won seven seats, and independents and liberals won 24 seats.

OCTOBER 1995

2. Sri Lankan forces began an offensive to recapture the Jaffna peninsula from the Tamil Tiger guerrillas. 20. Tamil Tiger guerrillas blew up the two main oil storage depots in Colombo. 22–26. Tamil Tiger guerrillas killed 127 civilians in eastern Sri Lanka.

NOVEMBER 1995

14. Sri Lankan government forces advanced to within one mile of the centre of Jaffna and captured the Tamil Tigers' political headquarters. 19. Sixteen people were killed and the Egyptian embassy was destroyed by a car bomb planted by Islamic extremists in the Pakistani capital Islamabad. The annual meeting of heads of government of the Asia-Pacific Economic Co-operation (APEC) Forum

ended with agreement on a mutual opening of markets to each other's products by 2020. 20. Sri Lankan troops surrounded Jaffna and captured the nearby town of Nallur.

DECEMBER 1995

3. The Sri Lankan army captured Jaffna. The ruling Kuomintang party won Taiwan's legislative election. 13. After a closed trial, the Chinese pro-democracy activist Wei Jingsheng was jailed for 14 years for allegedly attempting to overthrow the government. 22. A car bomb exploded in Peshawar, Pakistan, killing 60 people. 28. The Chinese National People's Congress approved the establishment and membership of the 150-member Hong Kong Preparatory Committee to choose the territory's first post-1997 government.

JANUARY 1996

5. The Japanese coalition government resigned following the resignation of the Prime Minister, Tomiichi Murayama, who stated that the position was beyond his capability. 11. A new coalition government under Ryutaro Hashimoto was approved by the Japanese parliament. 17. Three Indian Cabinet ministers and the leader of the country's main opposition party resigned after police charged them with bribery and corruption. 31. A Tamil Tiger lorry bomb exploded in the centre of Colombo, killing 81 people.

FEBRUARY 1996

3. The International Committee of the Red Cross began an airlift of food and medicines into the Afghan capital Kabul after supplies in the besieged city had been exhausted. 20. Two more Indian Cabinet ministers resigned after being implicated in bribery and corruption.

MARCH 1996

7. During military manoeuvres, China began to test-fire surface-to-surface missiles off the coast of Taiwan. 10. China began naval and military exercises along the coast opposite Taiwan and in the Taiwan Strait. US battle groups were ordered to Taiwan. 15. The first direct talks between the Indian government and representatives of Kashmiri secessionist groups took place in New Delhi. 18. China began a second series of military and naval exercises in the Taiwan Strait and warned the USA not to send its carrier battle groups into the strait. 23. President Lee Teng-hui won the first democratic presidential elections in Taiwan. 24. China announced that Hong Kong's existing Legislative Council would be wound up 1 July 1997 and replaced by a Provisional Legislative Council. Kashmiri separatists killed 11 of the 2,000 troops besieging a mosque which they had seized. 25. China ended its military exercises in the Taiwan Strait. 30. Muhammad Habibur Rahman was installed as head of a caretaker government following the dissolution of Bangladesh's parliament. 30. Indian troops killed 22 Kashmiri rebels in

BRITISH BEEF CRISIS
Fears about BSE in British beef caused beef consumption to plummet across Europe in 1996, damaging farmers' livelihoods (*Associated Press*)

NORTHERN IRELAND
Huge crowds greeted President Clinton on his visit to Ireland in November 1995, when he encouraged hopes of progress in the peace process (*PA News*)

NORTHERN IRELAND
Sinn Fein representatives were barred from the Northern Ireland peace talks at Stormont in June 1996 (above; *Pacemaker Press*) after the IRA broke, and failed to reinstate, their cease-fire with bombings in London and Manchester (*Rex Features*)

NORTHERN IRELAND
Tension rose in Northern Ireland in July and August 1996 as the Orange Order lodges held their
traditional marches, some in nationalist areas (*PA News*)

ROYAL DIVORCE
Princess Diana gave an unprecedentedly frank interview on the BBC's *Panorama* programme in November 1995. The Prince and Princess of Wales were divorced in August 1996 (*BBC TV*)

DUNBLANE SHOOTING TRAGEDY
Sixteen children and a teacher were shot dead at a primary school in Dunblane in March 1996 (above; *Rex Features*). The Queen and the Princess Royal visited the injured and bereaved on 17 March, when a minute's silence was held nation-wide (*PA News*)

MANDELA STATE VISIT
President Mandela of South Africa attracted huge crowds wherever he went during his state visit to Britain
in July 1996 (*PA News*)

PRIME MINISTER ASSASSINATED
The Israeli Prime Minister Yitzhak Rabin was assassinated in November 1995, raising fears for the future of the Middle East peace process (*Rex Features*)

TWA FLIGHT 800
A Paris-bound jumbo jet exploded shortly after take-off from New York in July 1996, killing all on board (*PA News*)

RUSSIA
Fighting in the separatist republic of Chechenia ended with a cease-fire agreement in August 1996 and Russian forces began to withdraw (*Associated Press*)

Boris Yeltsin was re-elected President of Russia in July 1996 despite ill-health but subsequently was hardly seen in public. He announced in September that he needed heart surgery, creating a power vacuum in Russia (*Rex Features*)

VOLCANIC ACTIVITY IN NEW ZEALAND
Mount Ruapehu began erupting in autumn 1995 (*Rex Features*)

THE GLOBE THEATRE
A reconstruction, complete with thatched roof, of the theatre at which many of Shakespeare's plays were first performed, was opened on London's Bankside in August 1996 (*Rex Features*)

OBITUARIES

Deaths included (left to right): (top) François Mitterrand, Yitzhak Rabin, Ella Fitzgerald, Sir Kingsley Amis; (bottom) Dean Martin, Andreas Papandreou, George Burns, Lord Home (Sir Alec Douglas-Home) (*Rex Features*)

Gene Kelly, dancer, actor, choreographer and film director, died in February 1996 (*Kobal*)

THE OLYMPIC GAMES
Michael Johnson achieved a unique 200 metre and 400 metre double at the Games, as well as setting a new world record in the 200 metres (*Richard Pelham/The Sun*)

Matthew Pinsent and Steve Redgrave won Britain's only gold medal, Redgrave achieving the rare feat of winning the gold medal in his event at four consecutive Olympic Games (*Allsport*)

EURO '96
Germany's football team celebrate their winning goal in the European Championship final (*Allsport*)

BRITISH TENNIS HOPE
Tim Henman reached the quarter-finals at Wimbledon in 1996, the first British man to do so for 23 years, and won Olympic silver in the men's doubles in August (*Allsport*)

Srinagar. **31.** Tamil Tiger rebels attacked a military base in eastern Sri Lanka, killing 54 people.

APRIL 1996

1. Myanmar's Constitutional Convention decided guidelines for choosing the president, including a 20-year residency requirement, which would exclude the opposition leader Aung San Suu Kyi. **3.** The Hong Kong government released 207 Vietnamese boat people who had been detained illegally. Two Indian ministers resigned in protest at Congress (I)'s alliance with a small party led by an actress. **5–7.** North Korean soldiers made three incursions into the demilitarized zone on the border with South Korea. **8.** President Kumaratunga of Sri Lanka extended the 11-year-old state of emergency across the country, increasing police and military powers and curtailing civil liberties. **11.** The ruling New Korea Party won 139 of the 253 seats in the South Korean National Assembly, 11 short of a majority. **16.** A peace plan for the Korean peninsular, announced by US President Clinton, was rejected by North Korea. **17.** The USA and Japan issued a joint declaration reaffirming their commitment to a joint defence strategy in East Asia; the USA pledged to maintain 100,000 troops in the region, including 47,000 in Japan, but to close 11 military bases in Japan. **19.** Nearly 20,000 Sri Lankan troops embarked on a fresh offensive against Tamil Tiger rebels in the Jaffna peninsula. **20.** A bomb, jointly planted by Punjabi and Kashmiri separatists in a hotel in New Delhi, India, killed 17 people. **23.** Shoko Asahara, the leader of the Aum Shinrikyo cult in Japan, went on trial accused of mass murder. **28.** Fifty-two people were killed by a bomb planted on a bus in Lahore, Pakistan. **30.** Human rights activist Liu Gang escaped from China to the USA.

MAY 1996

6. Eleven people were shot dead during voting in Assam, India. **8.** North Korea requested 3,000 tonnes of rice from the USA to cope with expected food shortages. Eight people died in an explosion on a bus in Lahore, Pakistan. **10.** The Prime Minister of India, Narashima Rao, resigned as it became clear that his Congress (I) party had lost the general election. **13.** More than 500 people were killed by a tornado in Bangladesh. Hezb-i-Islami troops returned to Kabul following an accord with the Afghan government. **14.** Chinese troops clashed with monks in Tibet who had refused to remove pictures of the Dalai Lama. **15.** The Bharatiya Janata Party (BJP) was invited to form the next government after emerging as the largest party in India's general election. **16.** Atal Behari Vajpayee was appointed Prime Minister of India. The Sri Lankan army ousted Tamil Tiger rebels from their last remaining stronghold. **17.** Seven North Korean soldiers entered the demilitarized zone on the border with South Korea. **20.** Soldiers loyal to the sacked army chief Gen. Abu Saleh Muhammad Nasim mutinied in Bangladesh. **21.** A bomb planted by Kashmiri separatists exploded in Delhi, India, killing 25 people. **22.** Gen. Abu Saleh Muhammad Nasim was detained and charged with sedition. A bomb blast in Rajhastan, India, killed 14 people. **26–28.** The National League for Democracy, led by Aung San Suu Kyi, held a meeting of its members in Myanmar despite the arrest of 262 supporters. **28.** The Prime Minister of India, Atal Vajpayee, resigned. The Sri Lankan government offered an amnesty to Tamil Tiger rebels. **30.** Four people died during the second round of voting in Kashmir.

JUNE 1996

1. H. D. Deve Gowda became Prime Minister of India at the head of a United Front coalition government. **13.** Following the general election in Bangladesh, the opposition Awami League emerged as the largest party, but without an overall majority. **19.** The Indian government abandoned its austerity programme, which had threatened to split the 13-party coalition. **20.** Soldiers and police broke up a 5,000-strong demonstration by opposition party supporters in Jakarta, Indonesia. **23.** China invited President Lee Teng-hui of Taiwan to visit Beijing for talks on reunification, with the proviso that he would not be treated as a head of state.

JULY 1996

1. The Democratic Union coalition defeated the ruling Mongolian People's Revolutionary Party to win Mongolia's general election. **4.** A Tamil Tiger suicide bomber killed 21 people in Jaffna, Sri Lanka. **18.** More than 4,000 Tamil Tigers overran the Mullaitivu military garrison in northern Sri Lanka, killing 1,200 soldiers. **19.** A Tamil Tiger suicide boat sank a Sri Lankan government naval ship. **22.** A bomb exploded in Lahore, Pakistan, killing 20 people. **24.** Two bombs exploded on a train in Columbo, Sri Lanka, killing 70 people; Sri Lankan troops retook the military garrison in Mullaitivu. Opposition parties in Pakistan formed an alliance in an attempt to oust the government. A national emergency was declared in Japan following the outbreak of a food poisoning epidemic which had affected 8,230 people and killed seven. **26.** The Sri Lankan army launched an attack on the town of Killinochchi, held by the Tamil Tigers. **27–28.** Two people died during anti-government riots in Jakarta, Indonesia. **29.** China exploded a nuclear device underground and immediately declared a moratorium on nuclear tests.

AUGUST 1996

1. The attempt by Megawati Sukarnoputri, daughter of Indonesia's former President, to have her removal from the leadership of the opposition Indonesian Democracy Party by a rebel party conference in June 1995 ruled invalid, was postponed by an Indonesian court; pro-democracy demonstrations were broken up by riot police. **4–5.** Sri Lankan government troops attacked the Tamil Tiger headquarters in Killinochchi, killing 200 guerrillas. **8.** A Khmer Rouge commander, Ieng Sary, and two generals were reported to have defected to the Cambodian government. **9.** Megawati Sukarnoputri was interrogated by Indonesian police. **14.** Prime Minister Hashimoto of Japan apologized for the abuse of Asian 'comfort women' by Japanese soldiers during the Second World War. **19.** The Philippines government held talks with the Moro National Liberation Front on the creation of an autonomous state in the Muslim Mindanao region. **20.** South Korean riot police ended a nine-day demonstration by students demanding reunification with North Korea. **26.** Former South Korean president Chun Doo-hwan was sentenced to death and his successor, Roh Tae-woo, was imprisoned after both had been found guilty of mutiny and treason for seizing power in a coup in 1979 and ordering the military to attack pro-democracy demonstrators. **29.** British forces began withdrawing from Hong Kong.

AUSTRALASIA AND THE PACIFIC

SEPTEMBER 1995

1. French commandos seized two Greenpeace ships which had entered the exclusion zone around the nuclear test site at the Muroroa atoll in French Polynesia. **5.** France carried out the first of a series of underground nuclear tests at Muroroa. **6.** Anti-nuclear protesters set light to the terminal at Tahiti's international airport in a riot which was dispersed by French police. The following day the rioting escalated, with looting and burning of shops and offices in Papeete. **10.** French commandos seized the yacht *La Ribaude* after it sailed into the exclusion zone around Muroroa, arresting eight MPs from four countries who were on board. **22.** The International Court of Justice rejected on technical grounds New Zealand's attempt to reopen its 1973 legal action to stop France conducting nuclear tests in French Polynesia.

OCTOBER 1995

1. France carried out its second nuclear test at Fangataufa atoll. **27.** France carried out its third nuclear test at Muroroa.

NOVEMBER 1995

2. The Queen signed the Waikato-Raupatu Claims Settlement, which compensates the Tainui federation of Maori tribes in New Zealand's North Island for the confiscation of their land by British settlers in 1863. **21.** France carried out its fourth nuclear test at Muroroa.

DECEMBER 1995

27. France carried out its fifth nuclear test at Muroroa.

JANUARY 1996

27. France carried out its sixth nuclear test at Fangataufa. **29.** President Chirac announced that the series of nuclear tests was complete.

MARCH 1996

2. In Australia's general election the Labor party was defeated by the opposition Liberal-National coalition. **25.** The trial opened of Ivan Milat, accused of murdering seven backpackers in Australia; he was found guilty and sentenced to life imprisonment on 26 July.

APRIL 1996

28. A gunman killed 35 people in Tasmania, Australia (*see also* Crimes and Legal Affairs).

MAY 1996

10. Australian state and territory governments agreed to ban all automatic and semi-automatic weapons. **29.** The Australian government launched an inquiry into allegations that its diplomats had sexually abused Asian children.

JUNE 1996

19. Papua New Guinea security forces executed eight former secessionist guerrillas on the island of Bougainville. **20.** Papua New Guinea armed forces launched an offensive against Bougainville Revolutionary Army rebels.

JULY 1996

1. Euthanasia was legalized in Australia's Northern Territory.

AUGUST 1996

19. Students, Aborigines and trade unionists stormed Parliament House in protest at the Australian government's austerity budget.

EUROPE

SEPTEMBER 1995

3. Four people were slightly injured by a terrorist bomb, which failed to explode properly, in Paris. **6.** A bomb exploded in a Lyon suburb. **8.** France deployed armed troops at tourist sites, schools, public buildings, railway stations, airports and borders because of the bombings. **10.** The Catalan Nationalist Party withdrew its parliamentary support of the Spanish socialist government because of continuing allegations that the government had organized illegal anti-terrorist squads. **11.** French security forces arrested 40 suspected Islamic extremists and recovered armaments, forged documents and suspect vehicles in a series of raids around Paris and Grenoble. **13.** Greece and the Former Yugoslav Republic of Macedonia (FYROM) signed an agreement normalizing diplomatic relations under which

Greece would end its economic embargo and FYROM would change its flag. **20.** The Turkish Prime Minister Tansu Çiller resigned after the Republican People's Party withdrew from her coalition government; President Demirel asked her to form a new government the next day. **26.** The trial of the former Italian Prime Minister Giulio Andreotti on charges of collusion with the Mafia opened in Palermo, Sicily. **29.** French gendarmes shot dead Khaled Kelkal, a French-Algerian wanted for the attempted bombing of the Paris to Lyon railway in August, after he opened fire on them.

OCTOBER 1995

1. The Socialist Party won the Portuguese general election. **6.** A bomb exploded near a Paris Metro station, injuring 13 people. **10.** Public sector workers held a one-day nation-wide strike in France in protest at a public sector wage freeze and planned job cuts. **15.** A bomb exploded in a Paris suburb. The Turkish Prime Minister Tansu Çiller resigned after her new minority government lost a parliamentary vote of confidence. **17.** A bomb planted by the Algerian Armed Islamic Group exploded on a Paris Metro train, injuring 29 people; on 19 October the French government deployed an extra 2,500 troops in the country's major cities. **27.** The former Italian Prime Ministers Bettino Craxi and Arnaldo Forlani, former foreign minister Gianni de Michelis and the Northern League leader Umberto Bossi were sent to prison for terms of between six months and four years after being found guilty of corruption.

NOVEMBER 1995

2. French police and security forces arrested ten suspected Islamic terrorists and seized bomb-making equipment in raids in three cities. **5.** A new Turkish coalition government of the True Path and Republican People's Parties under Tansu Çiller was approved by the Turkish parliament. Giulio Andreotti was charged with ordering the murder in 1979 of an investigative journalist because of information that the journalist had obtained about the murder of Prime Minister Aldo Moro in 1978. **7.** The French Prime Minister Alain Juppé resigned and was immediately reappointed by President Chirac in a reshuffle which reduced the number of government ministers from 25 to 16. **13.** The trial began of six former leaders of the East German politburo, including former Communist Party leader Egon Krenz, on charges of manslaughter and attempted manslaughter arising from the East German government's policy of shooting to kill people attempting to cross the border to the west. **19.** A former Communist minister, Aleksander Kwasniewski, won the second round of the Polish presidential election, defeating the incumbent President Lech Walesa. **24.** A nation-wide strike by French public sector workers in protest at government measures to reform the social welfare system closed down most of the country's transport system. **25.** In a referendum the electorate of the Irish Republic voted to amend the constitution to legalize divorce.

DECEMBER 1995

5. More French public sector workers, and civil servants and students joined the two-week long transport strike. **7.** A strikers' march in France ended in violent clashes with the police. **11.** A car bomb planted by the Basque separatist group ETA exploded in Madrid, killing six people. **15.** French public sector and transport workers began to return to work after the government conceded some of the strikers' demands. **17.** The Austrian coalition government was returned to power in the general election. **19.** A public sector strike in Belgium affected the state-owned railways and airline; it was in protest at proposed government austerity measures. **21.** The outgoing President of Poland, Lech Walesa, accused Prime Minister Jozef Oleksy of supplying secrets to Russian secret services. **24.** The Islamic Refah (Welfare) Party won the most seats in the Turkish general election. **30.** The Italian President refused to accept the resignation of Prime Minister Lamberto Dini and his government of technocrats and ordered the government to remain in office until parliament could debate the formation of another government.

JANUARY 1996

8. The former French President François Mitterrand died. **11.** The Italian Prime Minister Lamberto Dini tendered his resignation for the second time in two weeks; the President reserved judgement on whether to accept it. **14.** Jorge Sampaio won the Portuguese presidential election. **15.** Andreas Papandreou resigned as Prime Minister of Greece after two months of serious illness; Constantine Simitis was elected Prime Minister on 18 January. **17.** The former Italian Prime Minister Silvio Berlusconi went on trial in Milan, charged with corruption. **18.** A hostel in Lubeck, northern Germany, was destroyed in a suspected arson attack which left ten people dead. **25.** The Spanish Supreme Court charged a former Interior minister, José Barrionuevo, with organizing illegal anti-terrorist squads in the 1980s. **26.** The Polish Prime Minister Jozef Oleksy resigned after an investigation was launched into allegations that he had passed national secrets to the KGB and its successors; Oleksy was succeeded five days later by Wlodzimierz Cimoszewicz. **30–31.** Greek and Turkish forces confronted each other over the uninhabited islet of Imia in the eastern Aegean Sea until the US government intervened to diffuse the situation.

FEBRUARY 1996

1. President Scalfaro appointed Antonio Maccanico as Italy's Prime Minister. **14.** A Spanish judge was assassinated by the ETA. **16.** President Scalfaro dissolved parliament and called parliamentary elections after Antonio Maccanico was unable to form a government. **19.** French police arrested 24 suspected Islamic extremists in the Paris region in a series of raids.

MARCH 1996

3. The Popular Party won the most votes in Spain's general election but failed to achieve a parliamentary majority. 6. President Demirel of Turkey approved the formation of a coalition government of the Motherland and True Path parties, with the premiership to rotate between the two party leaders. 15. The ruling Swedish Social Democratic Party elected finance minister Goran Persson as its new leader, and he became Prime Minister three days later. 22. Erik Asbrik was appointed finance minister of Sweden. 26. Slovakia ratified a treaty with Hungary recognizing their mutual border and the rights of Slovakia's ethnic Hungarian community. 28. The former Polish head of state, Wojciech Jaruzelski, was charged with ordering troops to fire on protesters, killing 44 people, in 1970.

APRIL 1996

2. The Belgian government's plan to cut 300 teaching jobs in Wallonia provoked violent clashes between demonstrators and the police. 6. Turkish troops launched a combined air and ground assault on Kurdish rebels in the south-east of Turkey. 11. The trial opened in Italy of former Prime Minister Giulio Andreotti. 16. Former Italian Prime Minister Bettino Craxi was fined £15 million and sentenced to eight years' imprisonment in absentia for corruption. 22. The left-wing Olive Tree alliance led by Romano Prodi won the Italian general election. 24. The Turkish parliament voted to investigate corruption charges against former Prime Minister Tansu Çiller. 26. The Catalan Nationalist Party in Spain agreed to support the Popular Party of José Maria Aznar, enabling him to form a government with a 16-seat majority.

MAY 1996

5. Voters in Brandenburg rejected unification of their state with Berlin. 6. Spain threatened to close its border with Gibraltar unless Britain cracked down on smuggling from the colony. 7. The new Spanish government announced spending cuts of £1 billion and a reorganization of the country's intelligence services. 8. Erich Priebke, a former SS captain, went on trial in Italy for his alleged role in the murder of 335 people in 1944. 13. The Belgian parliament passed a law giving Prime Minister Dehaene extensive powers to cut government spending. Corsican nationalists embarked on a terrorist campaign in response to a police crackdown on drug dealing and smuggling. 17. The Gibraltar Social Democrats, led by Peter Caruana, were elected to office. 18. President Demirel of Turkey survived an assassination attempt. 19. Turkish troops killed 60 Kurdish Workers Party (PKK) guerrillas. 20. A Spanish soldier was killed by a bomb believed to have been planted by the ETA. 20–21. More than 100,000 German public service employees took strike action in protest at government austerity measures. 24. Turkey's True Parth party withdrew from the ruling coalition. 25. King Simeon II returned to Bulgaria after 50 years in exile. 26. The opposition Socialist Party withdrew from Albania's general election in protest at alleged ballot rigging and intimidation. 27. In Cyprus the Democrat Rally-Liberal Party coalition government won the general election with a majority of one. The ruling Democratic Party claimed to have won 100 of the 140 seats contested in Albania's parliamentary election. 28. Members of Albania's Socialist Party clashed with police while protesting against the May 26 election, which international observers declared unfair. President Chirac of France announced that military conscription would be phased out from January 1997. 31. The leaders of Albania's opposition Socialist Party went on hunger strike to demand fresh elections.

JUNE 1996

4. The ruling Civic Democratic Party won the Czech parliamentary election, but were two seats short of a majority. 6. Prime Minister Yilmaz of Turkey resigned a day before his government was due to face a vote of confidence. 15. More than 30,000 German trade unionists demonstrated against the government's austerity programme. 16. The ruling Democratic Party of Albania won the rerun of the disputed general election after opposition parties boycotted it. 18. President Ulmanis was elected for a second term by the Latvian parliament. 27. Turkish troops entered northern Iraq in an offensive against Kurdish guerrillas. 28. Necmettin Erbakan, leader of the Islamist Welfare Party, was sworn in as Prime Minister of Turkey at the head of a coalition government which included the True Path party, whose leader, Tansu Çiller, was appointed deputy prime minister. 30. Prime Minister Simitis of Greece was elected leader of the Panhellenic Socialist Party (PASOK), following the death of former leader Andreas Papandreou.

JULY 1996

3. The German Constitutional Court ruled that former slave labourers used by companies during the Nazi regime would be allowed to claim compensation. 17. France announced the disbanding of a quarter of its military regiments as part of a plan to create a purely professional army by 2002. 18. The president of the French state railway, Loïk Le Floch-Prigent, was remanded in custody on charges of corruption; Michel Mouillot, the mayor of Cannes, was also arrested. 20–21. The ETA planted five bombs in the Costa Dorada region of Spain. 23. French police arrested six ETA members, including Julián Atxurra Egurola, alias Pototo, believed to be a senior ETA leader; a further three members were arrested the following day. 25. The Belgian Senate passed three laws enabling Prime Minister Dehaene to rule by decree as a means of imposing austerity measures.

AUGUST 1996

1. Erich Priebke, a former SS officer, was found guilty of complicity in the murder of 335 civilians in 1944, but was released because he was following orders; he was rearrested the same day pending an application for extradition from Italy to Germany. **9.** French police began investigating corruption allegations against former directors of the state-owned bank Crédit Lyonnais. **10.** One man was killed when Greek Cypriot motor cyclists attempted to cross the buffer zone into Turkish-controlled northern Cyprus, in a protest at the division of the island. **14.** A Greek Cypriot was shot dead by Turkish troops while demonstrating in the Cyprus buffer zone. **23.** French police rounded up 300 African illegal immigrants who had occupied a church in Paris for seven weeks, including ten who had been on hunger strike for 50 days.

THE COMMONWEALTH OF INDEPENDENT STATES

SEPTEMBER 1995

10. Russian and Chechen negotiators agreed a schedule for the disarmament of Chechen guerrillas, a partial withdrawal of Russian forces and a prisoner exchange. **13.** A rocket-propelled grenade was fired at the US Embassy in Moscow. **21.** Russian commandos freed 18 hostages and captured two gunmen when they stormed a bus which had been hijacked in the Dagestan republic in southern Russia.

OCTOBER 1995

6. The commander of Russian forces in Chechenia, Gen. Anatoly Romanov was seriously wounded in a bomb attack in Grozny. **9.** The Russian government said that it was to stop observing the July cease-fire with Chechen rebels as the rebels had not disarmed and fighting was increasing. **15.** Russian special forces stormed a hijacked bus in central Moscow, killing the hijacker who had held South Korean tourists hostage. **26.** President Yeltsin suffered his second heart attack in three months.

NOVEMBER 1995

5. The incumbent, Eduard Shevardnadze, won the presidential election in Georgia.

DECEMBER 1995

4. A car bomb exploded in Grozny, killing 11 people. Russian aircraft bombed rebel positions in Chechenia in retaliation. **8.** The Russian government and the Russian-supported government in the Chechen republic signed an autonomy agreement allowing the republic its own consulates and trade missions abroad, an amnesty for guerrillas who laid down their arms, and the right of Chechen conscripts in the Russian armed forces to serve only in Chechenia. **11.** Chechen guerrillas attacked the Russian military headquarters in Grozny. **14–23.** Russian troops and Chechen guerrillas fought for control of the city of Gudermes, which the Russian forces eventually retook. **17.** In parliamentary elections to the State Duma in Russia, the Communist Party won the largest number of seats. **26.** President Yeltsin returned home after spending two months recovering from his heart attack in October.

JANUARY 1996

9. Chechen separatists broke through Russian positions on the Russian-Chechen border and took some 2,000 civilians hostage in the hospital in the Russian town of Kizlyar. **10.** The Chechen rebels left Kizlyar in a fleet of buses with over 100 Russian hostages and headed for Chechenia but were stopped at the border village of Pervomayskiy by Russian forces, who surrounded the convoy. **14.** The Russian government gave the Chechen rebels in Pervomayskiy a 24-hour deadline to free their hostages. **15.** After their ultimatums were ignored, Russian forces attacked the Chechen rebels in Pervomayskiy, capturing the village on the 18th and releasing 82 hostages; some Chechen rebels escaped to Chechenia with an unknown number of hostages. **16.** As fighting continued in Pervomayskiy, a group of armed Chechens seized Russian power workers in Grozny and another group seized a Turkish ferry with mainly Russian passengers in Trabzon. **19.** The Chechen gunmen on the Turkish ferry surrendered to Turkish police and released their hostages. **24.** Chechen rebels who had escaped from Pervomayskiy released 45 Russian hostages in exchange for the bodies of Chechens killed in the village.

FEBRUARY 1996

20. After five days of fighting, Russian forces captured the town of Novogroznensky from Chechen rebels. **22.** The IMF agreed to lend US$10,000 million to Russia to support economic reforms and cover part of the budget deficit.

MARCH 1996

6–10. Russian forces repulsed attacks by Chechen guerrillas attempting to infiltrate Grozny. **8.** Four Chechen gunmen hijacked a Turkish Cypriot aircraft with 109 passengers and crew on board and forced it to fly to Munich; the gunmen surrendered the next day. **29.** Russia, Belarus, Kazakhstan, and Kyrgyzstan signed an agreement to form a common market and customs union and to create an interstate council. **31.** President Yeltsin announced a cease-fire and partial troop withdrawal from Chechenia.

APRIL 1996

1. Chechen rebels killed 28 Russian soldiers. **2.** The presidents of Russia and Belarus signed a treaty to form a Commonwealth of Sovereign States; the treaty provided for co-operation on foreign and defence policy and a single currency by the end of 1997. **3.** Russian aircraft bombed Shalazhi, one of the 156 Chechen towns and villages which had signed a peace agreement with the Russian military. 4. Chechen rebels shot down a Russian military aircraft. 16. More than 70 Russian soldiers died in an ambush of their convoy by Chechen rebels. 23. The Chechen rebel leader Dzhokhar Dudayev was reported to have been killed by a Russian missile on the 21st.

MAY 1996

4. Chechen rebels attacked government offices in Grozny. 5. The rebel leader Zelimkhan Yandarbiyev rejected negotiations with Russia; a Russian aircraft was shot down over southern Chechenia. 16. President Yeltsin vowed to abolish conscription in the Russian army by 2000, including voluntary service only in Chechenia to take immediate effect. 22. Forty Russian soldiers were killed attempting to storm a Chechen stronghold at Bamut. 27. President Yeltsin met Zelimkhan Yandarbiyev; an immediate three-day cease-fire was declared as a prelude to the permanent cessation of hostilities on 1 June. President Kuchma of Ukraine sacked Prime Minister Evgeny Marchuk, whom he blamed for the country's worsening economic situation. 28. President Yeltsin visited Grozny. 29. President Yeltsin announced a power-sharing treaty under which Chechenia would become a sovereign state within the Russian Federation.

JUNE 1996

1. Twenty-six Russian soldiers were captured by Chechen rebels south-west of Grozny. 2. Four Russian soldiers were killed by a mine in Grozny. 10. Russia signed an agreement with Chechen rebels agreeing to withdraw all forces, apart from two brigades, by September. 16. President Yeltsin won the first round of voting in Russia's presidential election. 18. Gen. Aleksandr Lebed, the third-placed candidate in the Russian presidential election, was appointed National Security Adviser and secretary of the presidential Security Council by President Yeltsin; defence minister Gen. Pavel Grachev resigned. 20. President Yeltsin dismissed his security advisor, the head of the Federal Security Service and the First Deputy Prime Minister, after they had allegedly arranged for the arrest of two members of Yeltsin's campaign team.

JULY 1996

4. Boris Yeltsin was re-elected President of Russia. 9. The Russian army attacked a village in Chechenia, believed to be the location of the Chechen leader Zelimkhan Yandarbiyev, in violation of the May cease-fire. 11. A bomb exploded in central Moscow; a Russian general was killed in Chechenia. 12. A second bomb exploded in central Moscow. 15. Russian troops in Chechenia destroyed a base at Mekhketi believed to be the headquarters of Zelimkhan Yandarbiyev. 16. Prime Minister Lazarenko of Ukraine survived an assassination attempt when a bomb exploded beneath his car.

AUGUST 1996

6. Chechen rebels launched a counterattack against Russian troops, seizing parts of Grozny and two other towns. 22. A cease-fire was agreed by Russian troops and Chechen rebels. President Yeltsin returned to work at the Kremlin following two weeks' recuperation from the demands of the presidential election campaign. 25. Russian troops began withdrawing from Grozny. 27. Russian and Chechen commanders signed a cease-fire agreement. 31. Gen. Aleksandr Lebed signed an agreement with the Chechen leader Aslan Maskhadov designed to end the conflict in Chechenia by delaying a decision on the region's status until 2001.

THE FORMER YUGOSLAVIA

SEPTEMBER 1995

1. NATO aircraft ended their bombing operations but UN artillery continued to bombard Bosnian Serb artillery and missile sites around Sarajevo. 3. UN peacekeepers opened a road into Sarajevo for a convoy of lorries bringing aid into the city and breaking its siege. 5. After the Bosnian Serbs failed to comply with an ultimatum to withdraw all their heavy weapons from within 12½ miles of Sarajevo, halt attacks on safe areas, allow Sarajevo airport to reopen, and allow UN forces freedom of movement, NATO aircraft recommenced bombing Bosnian Serb artillery positions, ammunition dumps, and communication centres. Bosnian Serb forces shelled Sarajevo in response. 8. The foreign ministers of Bosnia, Croatia and the rump Yugoslav state (negotiating on behalf of the Bosnian Serbs) reached agreement in Geneva that Bosnia-Hercegovina would be recognized as existing within its present borders and comprising the Muslim-Croat Federation, holding 51 per cent of the land and the (Bosnian Serb) Republica Srpska, holding the remaining 49 per cent. 10. The USS *Normandy* destroyed Bosnian Serb ground-to-air missile sites around Banja Luka with cruise missiles after Bosnian Serb Gen. Mladic rejected UN demands that the Bosnian Serbs withdraw heavy weapons from around Sarajevo. NATO aircraft bombed Bosnian Serb positions around Tuzla from which the Bosnian Serbs had been shelling Tuzla airport. 11. NATO aircraft bombed Bosnian Serb military and communications installations throughout Bosnia and widened the range of targets to include bridges and supply routes. 12. NATO aircraft destroyed the Bosnian Serbs' main munitions dump at Vogosca near Sarajevo. Bosnian government and Bosnian Croat forces began an advance in western Bosnia. 14. NATO suspended its bombing campaign after US envoy Richard Holbrooke brokered an agreement between President Milosevic of Serbia and Bosnian Serb leaders under which the Bosnian Serbs would withdraw their heavy weapons from around Sarajevo over a six-day period. Bosnian government, Bosnian Croat and Croatian army forces captured the towns of Donji Vakuf, Drvar, Jajce and Sipovo in central and

western Bosnia from Bosnian Serb forces. **15.** Bosnian government and Bosnian Croat forces captured Bosanki Petrovac. Sarajevo airport re-opened for the first time in five months. **17.** Bosnian Serb forces began to withdraw their heavy weapons from the exclusion zone around Sarajevo. Bosnian government, Bosnian Croat and Croatian forces captured Kljuc; 90,000 Bosnian Serb refugees fled to Banja Luka. **20.** NATO indefinitely suspended air strikes against the Bosnian Serbs after it had confirmed that most of the Bosnian Serbs' heavy weapons had been removed from the Sarajevo exclusion zone and that air and land routes into the city had been opened. **26.** Foreign ministers from Bosnia-Hercegovina, Croatia and the rump Yugoslav state reached agreement in New York on a set of constitutional principles for Bosnia-Hercegovina.

OCTOBER 1995

3. President Gligorov of the former Yugoslav Republic of Macedonia was seriously injured in a car bomb attack in Skopje. Bosnian government forces launched artillery attacks from within Sarajevo on Bosnian Serb positions around the city and were rebuked by the UN, which refused a Bosnian Serb request to be allowed to move their heavy weapons back into the exclusion zone around the city. **4.** NATO aircraft fired missiles at Bosnian Serb missile batteries in Bosnia after the batteries had 'locked on' to the aircraft. **5.** President Izetbegovic of Bosnia and the Bosnian Serb leaders Radovan Karadzic and Gen. Ratko Mladic signed a US-brokered nation-wide cease-fire agreement, to become effective five days later provided that gas and electricity supplies to Sarajevo had been restored. **8.** Bosnian Serb forces launched artillery attacks on a Muslim refugee camp near Tuzla, and an air attack on the government-held town of Tesanjika. **9.** The Bosnian government postponed the implementation of the cease-fire agreement because gas and electricity had yet to be restored to Sarajevo and Bosnian Serb artillery had shelled Tuzla airport. NATO aircraft bombed a Bosnian Serb command post near Tuzla in retaliation. **10.** Bosnian government forces captured the western Bosnian town of Mrkonjic Grad. **12.** The nation-wide Bosnian cease-fire came into effect. Bosnian government and Bosnian Croat forces captured the town of Sanski Most. Bosnian Serb forces forced 6,000 Muslims out of the Banja Luka region, the men being taken into concentration camps. UN troops were prevented from opening a road from Sarajevo to Gorazde by Bosnian Serb forces. **13.** In defiance of the cease-fire, Bosnian government and Bosnian Croat forces shelled Prijedor and advanced on Banja Luka. **15.** Bosnian government forces uncovered evidence of the massacre of Muslims by Bosnian Serb forces in Sanski Most. **22.** The fighting in northern Bosnia between government and Bosnian Serb forces ended. **29.** The Croatian Democratic Union (HDZ) won the Croatian parliamentary elections.

NOVEMBER 1995

1. Bosnian peace negotiations opened at Dayton, Ohio, USA between delegations led by President Izetbegovic of Bosnia, President Tudjman of Croatia and President Milosevic of Serbia. President Tudjman and President Milosevic signed a US-brokered agreement to resolve peacefully the dispute over the Croatian region of eastern Slavonia held by ethnic Serbs. **9.** The International War Crimes Tribunal for the former Yugoslavia issued its first indictments against three Yugoslav Army officers, charging them with the murder of 261 Croatian men in Vukovar in 1991. A report by the UN special investigator for human rights in the former Yugoslavia accused Croatian forces of carrying out attacks on Serb civilians during their Krajina offensive in August. **12.** The Croatian government and Croatian Serb leaders in the Serb-held region of eastern Slavonia signed an agreement providing for the return of the region to Croatian rule after a one-year transition period and the return of 100,000 refugees. **13.** The International War Crimes Tribunal issued indictments against six Bosnian Croat political, military and police leaders. **21.** President Izetbegovic, President Tudjman and President Milosevic initialled a peace settlement for Bosnia-Hercegovina in Dayton, Ohio. **22.** The UN Security Council voted to lift the sanctions imposed on the rump Yugoslav state and also voted to lift gradually the arms embargo on all the former Yugoslav states.

DECEMBER 1995

4. The first troops of NATO's Peace Implementation Force (IFOR) began arriving in Bosnia-Hercegovina to enforce the Dayton peace agreement. **8.** The Bosnian Peace Implementation Conference opened in London; it closed the following day having established a framework for civilian police and aid organizations to operate in Bosnia, and appointed the EU envoy Carl Bildt as High Representative in charge of all civilian operations. **12.** Two French airmen held by the Bosnian Serbs since 30 August were released. **14.** President Izetbegovic, President Tudjman and President Milosevic signed the Paris Peace Treaty ending the war in Bosnia and creating the Union of Bosnia-Hercegovina. **20.** The UNPROFOR peacekeeping operation in Bosnia-Hercegovina ended and responsibility for implementing the Dayton Peace Agreement was transferred to IFOR. **26.** The NATO commander in Bosnia-Hercegovina, Adm. Leighton Smith, refused a request by the Bosnian Serb leadership that their forces be allowed to remain in Bosnian Serb-held areas of Sarajevo until September 1996. **27.** Bosnian government and Bosnian Serb forces withdrew from their frontline positions in and around Sarajevo.

JANUARY 1996

2. The Bosnian government protested to IFOR after 17 Bosnian civilians travelling through Bosnian Serb-held suburbs of Sarajevo were abducted by

Bosnian Serb forces. **4.** Sixteen of the abducted civilians were freed after the intervention of IFOR commanders in Sarajevo, but the Bosnian government stated that three more civilians had been abducted. **9.** Bosnian Serbs fired a rocket-propelled grenade at a tram in Sarajevo, killing one person; NATO forces returned fire. **15.** The Bosnian government refused to participate in an exchange of prisoners until it received information from the Bosnian Serbs about 24,000 missing Muslims. The UN Security Council voted to send 5,000 peace-keepers to the Croatian region of eastern Slavonia held by Croatian Serbs. **19.** Bosnian government, Bosnian Serb and Bosnian Croat forces withdrew 2 km either side of cease-fire lines and transferred military authority in the 4 km-wide zones of separation to IFOR. **28.** Three British soldiers serving with IFOR were killed when their tank hit a mine near Gornji Vakuf. Bosnian government and Bosnian Serb forces released about 500 of 650 remaining prisoners.

FEBRUARY 1996

3. Five Bosnian Serb-held suburbs of Sarajevo and a land corridor from Sarajevo to Gorazde were transferred nominally to Bosnian government control, though Bosnian Serb police officers remained until the 19th; land around the western Bosnian town of Mrkonjic Grad was transferred to Bosnian Serb control. **5.** Bosnian government forces detained eight Bosnian Serb soldiers as suspected war criminals. **9.** Bosnian Serb military and civilian authorities severed all communications with IFOR until the eight detained Bosnian Serbs were released. **12.** The two senior Bosnian Serb officers detained by the Bosnian government, Gen. Djordje Djukic and Col. Aleksa Krsmanovic, were flown to the Hague to appear before the International War Crimes Tribunal. **17.** President Izetbegovic, President Tudjman and President Milosevic attended a two-day US-organized summit in Rome and agreed that communications with IFOR by the Bosnian Serbs would resume. **20.** At the instigation of the Bosnian Serb leadership, thousands of Bosnian Serbs began to leave the suburbs of Sarajevo which were being transferred to Bosnian government control. **23.** The Bosnian government took control of the first of five Bosnian Serb-held suburbs of Sarajevo. **27.** The UN suspended sanctions against the Bosnian Serbs after IFOR certified that the Bosnian Serbs had withdrawn from all zones of confrontation.

MARCH 1996

1. Gen. Djordje Djukic was charged with crimes against humanity and violation of the laws and customs of war by the International War Crimes Tribunal. **7.** The International War Crimes Tribunal requested that Serbia hand over two Bosnian Serb soldiers who had been arrested by Serbian police after admitting in an interview with a newspaper to participating in a massacre of Muslims from Srebrenica in July 1995. **12.** Bosnian government

forces took control of a second Sarajevo suburb; most of the buildings had been destroyed by Bosnian Serbs as they left. **19.** Land transfers throughout Bosnia were completed and Sarajevo was reunited under Bosnian government control. Three suspected war criminals were arrested in Germany and Austria. **22.** The UN confirmed that 3,000 Muslims had been killed by Bosnian Serb forces in Srebrenica in July 1995. **31.** Bosnian Muslims and Croats agreed on a joint flag and a customs union.

APRIL 1996

5. A *Los Angeles Times* report claimed that the US government had approved the covert shipment of Iranian arms to Bosnia in 1994 despite the arms embargo. The Bosnian government released 18 Serb prisoners of war. **7.** President Chirac of France admitted that he had approved the sale of weapons to the Bosnian Serbs in order to secure the release of two French pilots shot down over Pale in August 1995. **8.** The Federal Republic of Yugoslavia signed a treaty with the Former Yugoslav Republic of Macedonia normalizing relations. **10.** Bosnian Serbs released three prisoners of war and promised to send files on 16 others to the International War Crimes Tribunal, thereby becoming eligible to participate in the conference for reconstruction. **12–13.** Fifty-five states attended an international aid conference in Brussels and pledged £800 million for the reconstruction of Bosnia; Bosnian Serbs refused to attend as part of the Bosnian delegation and were told to expect little aid until their war leaders were banned from office. **24.** The International War Crimes Tribunal released Gen. Djordie Djukic because he was suffering from terminal cancer. **26.** The Pentagon confirmed that the USA would maintain peacekeeping troops in Bosnia beyond the 20 December deadline agreed at the Dayton peace talks. **29.** Three Muslims were killed attempting to return to their homes in a Serb-held area.

MAY 1996

7. Dusan Tadic, a Serb accused of killing 16 Bosnian Muslims, went on trial at the International War Crimes Tribunal. **8.** The International War Crimes Tribunal announced that it had detained Zejnil Delalic, a Bosnian Muslim officer accused of murder. **13.** An alleged war criminal, Goran Lajic, was handed over to the International War Crimes Tribunal by German authorities. **15.** Radovan Karadzic sacked the prime minister of the Republika Srpska, Rajko Kasagic. **22.** The Bosnian government threatened to boycott the general election set for September unless Bosnian Serb leaders were tried for war crimes. **23.** Elections due to be held in Mostar on 31 May were postponed until 31 June. **30.** Carl Bildt, the EU's mediator in Bosnia, said he would not co-operate with Biljana Plavsic, who had been appointed to represent the Republika Serpska in its dealings with the international community. **31.** Drazen Erdemovic, a Croat who served in the

Bosnian Serb army, pleaded guilty to murdering 70 Muslims after the fall of Srebrenica in July 1995.

JUNE 1996

2. The USA warned that sanctions might be reimposed on Serbia unless the Bosnian Serb leaders Radovan Karadzic and Gen. Ratko Mladic were removed from office. 6. The president of the International War Crimes Tribunal asked for sanctions to be reimposed on the Bosnian Serbs and Serbia, for failing to hand over Karadzic and Mladic. 13. An international conference to review the Dayton peace accord opened in Florence, Italy. NATO defence ministers endorsed a plan to give IFOR increased powers. 14. Delegates at the Florence summit agreed that elections should go ahead in Bosnia despite the absence of full democracy; an arms limitation agreement was also signed. 16. Separatist Croats in Bosnia announced a government for their breakaway state of Herceg-Bosna. 18. The UN arms embargo on the former Yugoslavia was lifted. 27. The International War Crimes Tribunal began preliminary hearings into the Karadzic and Mladic cases. 28. Gen. Mladic was reported to have suffered a stroke. 29. The Group of Seven (G7) nations threatened to reimpose trade sanctions on Bosnia unless Karadzic retired from political office. 30. Karadzic said that he was transferring his presidential powers to a deputy, Biljana Plavsic, but would retain the title of President of Republika Srpska; the Party for Social Democracy defeated the Croat Democratic Party in municipal elections in Mostar.

JULY 1996

7. War crimes investigators began exhuming the bodies of Muslims thought to have been massacred following the capture of Srebrenica by Bosnian Serbs in July 1995. 8. The Organization for Security and Co-operation in Europe warned that it would ban the Serb Democratic Party from contesting the election in September unless Radovan Karadzic resigned as party leader. 9. The Muslim-Croat Federation parliament in Bosnia passed a law unifying Muslim and Croat forces in a single Federation army. UN investigators unearthed the bodies of ten people believed to have been murdered by Bosnian Serbs as they fled the enclave of Srebrenica in July 1995. 11. The International War Crimes Tribunal issued arrest warrants for Radovan Karadzic and Gen. Ratko Mladic. 15. Former American chief negotiator Richard Holbrooke began a special mission to Serbia in an attempt to have Karadzic and Mladic removed from power in Republika Srpska. 19. Radovan Karadzic resigned as President of the Republika Srpska and as leader of the ruling Serb Democratic Party. 23. Bosnian Croats blocked the adoption of a new mandate for the EU administration in Mostar and boycotted the first sitting of the city council. 24. The EU threatened to withdraw from Mostar unless Bosnian Croats participated in the city council. 31. Bosnian

Muslims and Croats agreed a plan to dismantle the Croat breakaway state of Herceg-Bosna.

AUGUST 1996

6. Bosnian Croats in Mostar agreed to recognize the results of the municipal election pending a ruling from the Supreme Court. 12. A NATO inspection team was refused access to the Han Pijesak military complex east of Sarajevo where Gen. Ratko Mladic was thought to be. 13. NATO was permitted access to the Han Pijesak military complex. 23. Croatia and Yugoslavia formally established diplomatic relations. 27. Bosnia's municpal elections were postponed.

EUROPEAN UNION

SEPTEMBER 1995

3. The official in charge of the European Monetary System (EMS) unit of the European Commission denounced a future single currency as a dangerous confidence trick and a threat to peace between France and Germany. The EU Reflection Group of ministers and representatives of the European Parliament and Commission held their first meeting to draw up an agenda for the Intergovernmental Conference in 1996. 17. Sweden held its first election to the European Parliament. 30. EU finance ministers and central bank governors unanimously agreed that stage three of economic and monetary union would begin in 1999 with the introduction of a single currency.

OCTOBER 1995

13. Latvia applied for EU membership. 17. The European Court of Justice ruled in a test case that positive discrimination favouring women over men in employment matters was illegal.

NOVEMBER 1995

14. The president of the Court of Auditors refused to approve the accounts for the 1994 budget because expenditure of £4,200 million was not properly documented and at least £410 million had been lost through fraud and a failure to collect payments. 28. The EU and 12 Mediterranean states signed an agreement in Barcelona to create an economic and political partnership leading to a free trade zone by 2010.

DECEMBER 1995

4. Estonia applied for EU membership. 13. The European Parliament approved the creation from 1 January 1996 of a customs union between the EU and Turkey. 16. The European Council summit in Madrid approved the name 'euro' for the single currency and confirmed that it would come into operation on 1 January 1999.

FEBRUARY 1996

21. The Schengen Agreement signatory states agreed to increase co-operation over the extradition of terrorist suspects.

MARCH 1996

22. Following an announcement by the British government on 20 March that BSE in cattle might be the cause of a new strain of CJD in humans, the EU's Scientific Veterinary Committee recommended tighter safety measures for British beef, including a cull of older cattle. 25. The EU banned the export of British beef and beef products world-wide; the ban was officially confirmed on 27 March. France announced that it would open its borders with Germany and Spain in accordance with the Schengen Agreement but retain controls at borders with the Benelux countries because of concerns about drug trafficking. 29. The Intergovernmental Conference opened in Turin, Italy.

APRIL 1996

3. At an emergency meeting in Luxembourg EU agriculture ministers agreed to provide financial assistance for British measures to eradicate BSE in cattle but refused to lift the world-wide export ban. 13. EU finance ministers met in Verona, Italy, to discuss a new exchange rate mechanism (ERM) to link countries inside the single currency area to those outside it, obliging governments to enact legislation to cut their country's deficit should it exceed 3 per cent of GNP and establishing a two-year ERM-membership requirement for single currency entry. 14. The European agriculture commissioner (Franz Fischler) said that the ban on British beef and beef products had been imposed to ensure that the European beef market did not collapse.

MAY 1996

8. The European Commission reported that £880 million, 1.4 per cent of the EU budget, had been lost through crime in 1995. 9. Spain signed an informal agreement with France promising support in all EU negotiations in return for tougher action against terrorism. 20. EU veterinary experts voted to continue the total ban on British beef exports in opposition to a Commission recommendation that the ban on beef products should be lifted. 21. Britain said it would block all EU decisions until progress was made on lifting the beef ban. The EU struck a deal with Spain to waive a fine of £230 million for breaching agricultural regulations. 29. The European Commission announced a £52 million compensation package for farmers and a 40 per cent reduction in the EU fishing fleet. The President of the European Commission, Jacques Santer, lambasted Britain for its policy of non-co-operation.

JUNE 1996

3. EU finance ministers agreed to drop the two-year membership of ERM as a precondition for entry into economic and monetary union in 1999. EU agricultural ministers voted in favour of lifting the ban on the export of British beef products, but by too small a majority for the ban to be lifted immediately. 5. The European Commission authorized the partial lifting of the ban on the export of British beef products and warned Britain to end its policy of non-co-operation. 18. The European Commission endorsed a plan for lifting the world-wide ban on British beef exports provided the UK government ended its policy of non-co-operation with the EU. 19. EU veterinary experts approved the phased lifting of the ban on British beef, but insisted on the slaughter of up to 67,000 cattle in addition to the 150,000 already being culled. 21. The UK ended its policy of non-co-operation after agreement was reached at the EU summit in Florence for a gradual lifting of the beef ban.

JULY 1996

12. The European Court of Justice rejected an attempt by the British government to obtain an interim injunction temporarily lifting the ban on British beef exports. 24. The EU Commission authorized a £588 million subsidy to Air France by the French government. 30. The EU Commission threatened to fine European companies co-operating with the USA's Helms-Burton law punishing foreign companies which benefit from US property seized by Cuba.

AUGUST 1996

2. Germany called for the reimposition of a total ban on the export of British beef following the publication of a study suggesting that BSE might be transmitted from cow to calf.

THE MIDDLE EAST

SEPTEMBER 1995

28. Israel and the PLO signed an agreement extending Palestinian autonomy on the West Bank.

OCTOBER 1995

6. The Israeli Knesset voted by 61 votes to 59 to approve the agreement on the second stage of Palestinian autonomy. 10. Several hundred Palestinian prisoners refused to leave Israeli jails, as agreed under the Israeli-PLO autonomy agreement, in protest at the Israelis' refusal to release four female Palestinian prisoners. 11. The UN special commission overseeing Iraqi disarmament presented a report to the UN Security Council which stated that Iraq had manufactured more chemical and biological weapons material than it had previously admitted and had not destroyed most of it. 13. Three Israeli soldiers were killed in a bomb attack by the Hezbollah militia on an Israeli convoy in the South Lebanon Security Zone. 15. Six Israeli soldiers were

killed in a bomb attack by Hezbollah militia on their convoy in south Lebanon; Israel retaliated with artillery and air attacks. 15. Saddam Hussein won 99.96 per cent of the vote in a referendum in Iraq nominating him for a seven-year presidential term. 25. Israeli troops began their withdrawal from Palestinian towns in the West Bank. 29. The leader of the militant Islamic Jihad movement, Fathi Shiqaqi, was assassinated in Malta, allegedly by agents of the Israeli secret service Mossad.

NOVEMBER 1995

2. Eleven Israeli settlers in the Gaza Strip were injured in two suicide car bomb attacks by Palestinian militants. 4. The Israeli Prime Minister Yitzhak Rabin was assassinated at a peace rally in Tel Aviv by an extremist Jew opposed to the Palestinian peace process; the gunman, Yigal Amir, was arrested immediately. 9. Israeli police arrested five suspects involved in a suspected conspiracy to murder Yitzhak Rabin and uncovered a cache of illegally-held arms. 13. A car bomb exploded at a joint US-Saudi military base in Riyadh, killing six people. Israeli forces completed their withdrawal from the West Bank town of Jenin and control of the town was handed over to the Palestinian National Authority (PNA).

DECEMBER 1995

10. Israeli forces completed their withdrawal from the West Bank town of Tulkarm. 11. Israeli forces withdrew from Nablus. 15–18. Eritrean forces landed on the disputed island of Greater Hanish in the Red Sea and seized control from Yemeni forces after a three-day battle. 18. Yemeni aircraft attacked Greater Hanish. 21. Israeli forces completed their withdrawal from Bethlehem. 27. Syrian and Israeli delegations began three days of preliminary peace negotiations at Wye Plantation, Maryland, USA. Israeli forces completed their withdrawal from West Bank town of Ramallah.

JANUARY 1996

1. King Fahd of Saudi Arabia transferred the management of government affairs to Crown Prince Abdullah whilst he was recovering from illness. 5. Yehiya Ayyash, believed to have masterminded the Hamas bombing campaign against Israel, was killed by the Israeli secret services in the Gaza Strip; on the 7th Israel imposed an indefinite ban on Palestinian workers entering Israel from the West Bank and Gaza Strip in an attempt to stop retaliatory bombings. 10. King Hussein of Jordan made his first official visit to Israel; Israel released 800 Palestinian prisoners. 16. Two Israeli soldiers were killed when their vehicle was attacked by suspected Islamic militants near Hebron. 19. Three members of Hamas were shot dead at an Israeli checkpoint near Jenin. 20. Elections were held in the West Bank, Gaza Strip and East Jerusalem for a Palestinian leader and a Palestinian Council; the leadership election was won by Yasser Arafat.

FEBRUARY 1996

12. Yasser Arafat was sworn in as the first elected Palestinian leader or president. 20. Lt.-Gen. Hussein Hassan and Col. Saddam Kamel, two sons-in-law of President Saddam Hussein of Iraq who had defected to Jordan in August 1995, returned to Iraq after being pardoned by the President. They were killed on the 23rd after having been divorced by their wives. 21. King Fahd of Saudi Arabia resumed full control of government affairs. 25. Two Hamas suicide bombers killed 25 Israelis when they exploded bombs in Jerusalem and Ashkelon.

MARCH 1996

3. A Hamas suicide bomber killed 18 people with a bomb on a bus in Jerusalem; in response Yasser Arafat outlawed the military wings of Hamas and Islamic Jihad. 4. A Hamas suicide bomber exploded a bomb in Tel Aviv, killing 14 people. The Israeli government responded by announcing that it would mount military operations against Hamas in Palestinian Autonomous Areas. 8. Iraqi officials prevented UN weapons inspectors from searching a building in Baghdad which they suspected housed parts for ballistic missiles. 13. Western and Middle Eastern heads of state and government held a one-day anti-terrorism summit in Egypt in support of the Israeli-Palestinian peace process. 24. Iraqis elected 220 members to the 250-member National Assembly in a poll in which 93 per cent of the electorate allegedly participated. 26. The execution of a man convicted of murdering a police officer sparked unrest among the Shi'ite community in Bahrain. 27. Yigal Amir, who assassinated the Israeli Prime Minister Yitzhak Rabin, was sentenced life imprisonment.

APRIL 1996

11. Seven people died in Israeli air strikes on a Hezbollah base in Beirut which were launched in response to rocket attacks on northern Israel. 12. Israel intensified its attacks on Hezbollah targets in Lebanon following further rocket attacks on Israel's northern cities; about 400,000 Lebanese and 11,000 Israelis fled the affected areas. 16. The USA announced a peace plan designed to end the conflict between Hezbollah and Israel and revive Israeli negotiations with Syria and Lebanon. 17. Hezbollah rejected the US peace plan. 18. An Israeli shell fell on a UN base in Qana, south Lebanon, killing 109 people. 21. The Society of Combatant Clergy won 120 of the 270 seats in Iran's consultative assembly, although no group won overall control. 24. The PLO National Council voted to eliminate from its charter clauses calling for the destruction of the Israeli state. 25. The Israeli Labour Party formally ended its opposition to a Palestinian state. 26. Israel and Hezbollah agreed a cease-fire, to come into effect the following day.

MAY 1996

5. Israel and the PLO began talks on a final peace settlement in Taba, Egypt. Nine bombs exploded in Bahrain. 9. Fighting resumed in south Lebanon between Israel and Hezbollah. 13. A gunman shot dead a Jewish settler north of Jerusalem. 15. Israel imposed a total military blockade of the West Bank and Gaza Strip. 18. Hassan Salameh, a leading member of Hamas, was shot and detained by Israeli soldiers. 19. Two Hezbollah members were killed by Israeli soldiers in south Lebanon; a civilian was injured, prompting claims that Israel had broken the cease-fire. 20. Iraq accepted a UN deal permitting the sale of oil to fund humanitarian aid. 31. The Likud leader Binyamin Netanyahu was confirmed as Israel's prime minister having narrowly defeated the incumbent, Shimon Peres.

JUNE 1996

4. The government of Bahrain foiled an Iranian-backed coup attempt and arrested 44 people. 10. Five soldiers and two settlers were killed in attacks by Hezbollah and a suspected Palestinian gunman in Israel. 13. Iraq barred UN inspectors from visiting three military sites. 20. The Israeli government rejected the offer of a conditional cease-fire by the military wing of Hamas. 21. UN inspectors in Iraq destroyed a biological weapons factory. 22. Iraq agreed to allow UN weapons inspectors unconditional access to military sites. 25. Nineteen people died in a bomb explosion at a US air force base near Dhahran, Saudi Arabia.

JULY 1996

1. The USA objected to Iraq's attempts to resume oil exports under an agreement with the UN, claiming that Iraq would use the revenue to import unauthorized equipment. 12. President Saddam Hussein of Iraq was reported to have foiled a coup attempt by 50 military officers. 16. Israel announced the easing of the 19-week blockade of the West Bank and Gaza Strip, imposed following a spate of terrorist attacks. 17. Public sector workers in Israel went on strike in protest at the government's proposed cuts in government spending. 19. UN inspectors abandoned an attempt to inspect an Iraqi military installation after being refused unconditional access. In a deal with Hezbollah, Israel exchanged 45 Lebanese prisoners and the corpses of 123 Hezbollah fighters for the remains of two Israeli soldiers. 25. Israel offered to withdraw from southern Lebanon in exchange for peace along the northern border and the disarming of Hezbollah. 26. Israel sealed off the West Bank and Gaza Strip following the shooting of two Israelis. 28–29. Iranian troops launched an offensive against Kurdish guerrillas in northern Iraq.

AUGUST 1996

2. Palestinians rioted in the West Bank, broke into a prison and released ten political prisoners; Israel submitted a secret peace proposal to Syria via the USA. 4. Hamas called for Palestinians to launch an uprising against the Palestinian National Authority and its leader Yasser Arafat, amid continuing unrest. 7. Syria rejected the Israeli peace proposal and demanded the return of the Golan Heights. 8. Israeli jets bombed Hezbollah targets in southern Lebanon in response to the killing of an Israeli soldier in a shelling attack. 16. Demonstrators in the city of Karak in southern Jordan clashed with police in a protest at an increase in the price of bread; rioting spread to other cities. 17. King Hussein of Jordan dissolved the House of Representatives. 27. The Israeli government approved the construction of 1,800 homes in the West Bank. 28. Yasser Arafat urged Palestinians to rebel against Israeli authority. 29. Palestinians staged a four-hour strike in protest at renewed Israeli settlement on the West Bank. 31. Iraqi troops seized the Kurdish city of Arbil in the UN-designated safe haven in northern Iraq.

INTERNATIONAL RELATIONS

SEPTEMBER 1995

4. The fourth UN world conference on women opened in Beijing, China, with speeches by President Finnbogadóttir of Iceland, Prime Minister Benazir Bhutto of Pakistan and Prime Minister Khaleda Zia of Bangladesh. The conference closed on 15 September with the adoption of a non-binding conference paper which advocated sexual freedom and denounced violence against women; parts of this were rejected by several delegations and governments. 27. The Council of Europe's European Court of Human Rights overturned the verdict of the Commission of Human Rights and declared that the killing of three IRA terrorists by the SAS in Gibraltar in 1988 was a breach of international conventions.

OCTOBER 1995

13. The NATO Secretary-General Willy Claes was questioned by a Belgian parliamentary committee about corruption charges involving two defence contracts signed in 1988 when he was Belgium's economics minister; the committee voted to agree to his legal indictment. 19. The Belgian parliament voted to revoke Claes's immunity and send him for trial on corruption charges; Claes resigned his NATO post the next day.

NOVEMBER 1995

1. Cameroon became a member of the Commonwealth. 9. The Commonwealth heads of government meeting began in Auckland, New Zealand. 10. The Commonwealth heads of government meeting issued a communiqué condemning France's nuclear tests, despite British objections; the British delegation issued a separate statement supporting nuclear deterrence and nuclear tests. 11. Nigeria's membership of the Commonwealth was suspended follow-

ing the execution of Ken Saro-Wiwa and eight other human rights activists. 12. Mozambique, a former Portuguese colony, became a member of the Commonwealth as 'a unique and special case'. 17. Russia failed to meet the deadline for completion of its agreed reductions in military equipment under the Conventional Forces in Europe (CFE) Treaty 1989, refusing to reduce the forces on its northern and southern borders. 28. The Czech Republic became a member of the OECD. 30. The Euro-corps, comprising troops from Germany, France, Spain, Belgium and Luxembourg, became fully operational.

DECEMBER 1995

1. The Spanish foreign minister Javier Solana Madariaga was appointed Secretary-General of NATO. 5. France announced that it was upgrading its involvement in NATO by rejoining the Military Committee. 12. The International Criminal Tribunal for Rwanda charged eight Hutu leaders with genocide and crimes against humanity. 20. Ukraine agreed to close down the Chernobyl nuclear power station by 2000 in exchange for financial help from the G7 nations.

JANUARY 1996

5. The UN set a deadline of 31 January for member states to pay their outstanding debts of £1,600 million, of which £774 million was owed by the USA.

FEBRUARY 1996

28. Russia was admitted by the Council of Europe as a member on condition that it reform its legal and penal systems, protect its ethnic minorities and abolish the death penalty.

MARCH 1996

10. The former Prime Minister Baroness Thatcher gave a speech at Fulton, Missouri, in which she warned of the growing threat to the West's security from the development of weapons of mass destruction and ballistic missiles by rogue states. 29. Hungary became a member of the OECD.

APRIL 1996

1. The UN announced an 8 per cent cut in staff and a £168 million cut in its budget in 1996–7. 23. A Commonwealth task force agreed measures to tighten sanctions against Nigeria. 24. The Council of Europe voted to admit Croatia. 25. President Yeltsin of Russia and President Jiang of China signed a strategic partnership accord. 26. China, Kazakhstan, Kyrgyzstan, Russia and Tajikistan signed a security pact affirming their common borders. 30. Israel and the USA signed a counter-terrorism accord.

MAY 1996

3. A UN conference in Geneva ended, having failed to conclude a total ban on land mines. 5. Talks aimed

at concluding a comprehensive nuclear test ban opened in Geneva. 14. Russia threatened to form a military alliance with Belarus if NATO pursued plans to admit former Communist countries. 15. NATO's North Atlantic Council approved the formation of combined joint task forces under European control. The USA announced tariffs on Chinese imports in retaliation for alleged copyright infringements; China imposed retaliatory sanctions on American goods. The USA agreed to ban certain land mines in line with the UN conference in Geneva. 17. Russia expelled four British diplomats accused of spying; Britain expelled four Russian diplomats in retaliation. 31. The Council of Europe refused Croatia accession until its human rights record improved.

JUNE 1996

3. Habitat II, a UN conference on human settlements opened in Istanbul, Turkey. NATO members agreed a new alliance arrangement with a greater role for the Western European Union. 4. Russia said it was willing to compromise on the enlargement of NATO. 17. China closed down 15 pirate compact disc factories, narrowly averting a trade war with the USA over copyright violations. 20. The USA said that it would use its veto to prevent UN Secretary-General Boutros Boutros Ghali from standing for a second term in office. 23. Arab leaders issued a final communiqué at the end of their summit warning Israel not to renege on its existing agreements and demanding withdrawal from all territory seized since 1967. 25. Following two days of talks with a Nigerian delegation in London, a Commonwealth ministerial action group on human rights decided not to impose sanctions on Nigeria for its human rights abuses. 28. The UN-sponsored conference on disarmament ended without the conclusion of a comprehensive test ban treaty for nuclear weapons.

JULY 1996

17. Angola, Brazil, Cape Verde, Guinea-Bissau, Mozambique, Portugal and São Tomé and Príncipe formed the Community of Portuguese-Speaking Countries to preserve cultural links and foster political co-operation. 19. Myanmar was given observer status in ASEAN. 30. The G7 nations agreed 25 measures to counter terrorism. Turkey agreed to renew the mandate for the international military operation to protect the Kurds in northern Iraq.

AUGUST 1996

5. President Clinton signed legislation imposing sanctions on foreign companies that invest more than £25 million annually in the energy sectors in Libya and Iran. 7. The USA approved the sale of £1.3 billion of Iraqi oil over six months, the revenue to be used to purchase food and humanitarian aid. China agreed to sign a comprehensive test ban treaty for nuclear weapons.

Obituaries

Adams, Charles, CMG, British ambassador to Thailand since 1992, aged 57 – 10 July 1996

Adams, Donald, opera and operetta singer, aged 67 – 8 April 1996

Aidid, Gen. Muhammad, leader of the Somali National Alliance, aged 59 – 1 August 1996

Airedale, 4th Baron, a Deputy Speaker of the House of Lords since 1962, aged 80 – 19 March 1996

Amis, Sir Kingsley, CBE, novelist and poet, aged 73 – 22 October 1995

Appleby, Barry, cartoonist, creator of the Gambols, aged 86 – 11 March 1996

Armstrong, Rt. Hon. Ernest, Labour MP for Durham North West 1964–87 and junior government minister 1974–9, aged 81 – 8 July 1996

Ashbrook, 10th Viscount, KCVO, MBE, aged 90 – 5 December 1995

Atholl, 10th Duke, aged 64 – 27 February 1996

Avonside, Lord (Ian Shearer), PC, QC, Senator of the College of Justice of Scotland 1964–84, aged 81 – 22 February 1996

Barrow, Dame Nita, GCMG, Governor-General of Barbados since 1990, aged 79 – 19 December 1995

Bearsted, 4th Viscount, MC, TD, merchant banker, aged 84 – 9 June 1996

Bebb, Dewi, Welsh rugby player and sports commentator, aged 57 – 14 March 1996

Berghaus, Ruth, German stage director and choreographer, aged 68 – 25 January 1996

Blackwood, Caroline, novelist, aged 64 – 14 February 1996

Bottomley, Lord (Arthur), OBE, PC, Labour MP for Chatham 1945–50, Rochester and Chatham 1950–9, and Middlesbrough East 1962, Secretary of State for Commonwealth Relations 1964–6, Minister of Overseas Development 1966–7, aged 88 – 3 November 1995

Boyne, 10th Viscount, KCVO, Lord Lieutenant of Shropshire since 1994 and a Lord-in-Waiting to The Queen since 1981, aged 64 – 14 December 1995

Brand, Lord, Solicitor-General for Scotland 1970–2, Senator of the College of Justice 1972–89, aged 72 – 14 April 1996

Brett, Jeremy, actor, aged 59 – 12 September 1995

Broccoli, Cubby, film producer, aged 87 – 27 June 1996

Brodkey, Harold, American author, aged 65 – 26 January 1996

Brodsky, Joseph, Russian Jewish poet, winner of the Nobel prize for literature in 1987, aged 55 – 28 January 1996

Broughshane, 2nd Baron, aged 92 – 22 September 1995

Brown, Ronald, US Secretary for Commerce, aged 54, in an air crash – 3 April 1996

Bruce, Brenda, OBE, actress, aged 76 – 19 February 1996

Burke, Admiral Arleigh, American naval commander in Second World War, aged 94 – 1 January 1996

Burns, George, American comedian, aged 100 – 9 March 1996

Burton, Beryl, OBE, British and international cycling champion, aged 58 – 5 May 1996

Cadell, Simon, actor, aged 45 – 6 March 1996

Caine, Marti, comedienne, aged 50 – 4 November 1995

Cairncross, John, Foreign Office and Treasury official dismissed in 1952 for passing information to Soviet spy Guy Burgess, aged 82 – 8 October 1995

Cameron, Sir John (Hon. Lord Cameron), KT, DSC, Senator of the College of Justice and Lord of Session 1955–85, aged 96 – 30 May 1996

Cargill, Patrick, actor and dramatist, aged 77 – 23 March 1996

Carlill, Vice-Adm. Sir Stephen, KBE, CB, DSO, last British commander of the Indian Navy, aged 93 – 9 February 1996

Cherkassky, Shura, Russian concert pianist, aged 84 – 27 December 1995

Chermayeff, Serge, architect, aged 95 – 8 May 1996

Chukovskaya, Lydia, Russian writer, aged 88 – 7 February 1996

Clark, Prof. Sir Grahame, CBE, FBA, archaeologist, aged 88 – 12 September 1995

Clark, Ossie, fashion designer, aged 54 – 7 August 1996

Clay-Jones, 'Clay', OBE, chairman of *Gardeners' Question Time* 1985–93, aged 71 – 3 July 1996

Clough, Gordon, radio journalist, aged 61 – 6 April 1996

Colbert, Claudette, American actress, aged 92 – 30 July 1996

Collison, Lord (Harold), CBE, trade unionist, and chairman of the Supplementary Benefits Commission 1969–75, aged 86 – 29 December 1995

Colyton, 1st Baron (Henry Hopkinson), CMG, PC, Conservative MP for Taunton 1950–6 and Minister of State for Colonial Affairs 1952–5, aged 94 – 6 January 1995

Condon, Richard, American thriller-writer, aged 81 – 9 April 1996

Courtenay, Margaret, actress, aged 72 – 15 February 1996

Davie, Prof. Donald, poet and critic, aged 73 – 18 September 1995

Davies, Robertson, Canadian author, aged 82 – 4 December 1995

Diamond, Harry, Republican Labour MP for Lower Falls, Belfast 1945–69 in the Parliament of Northern Ireland, aged 87 – May 1996

Dickson, Dorothy, actress and musical comedy star, aged 102 – 25 September 1995

Dormer, 16th Baron, aged 81 – 21 December 1995

Drew, Dame Jane, DBE, architect, aged 85 – 27 July 1996

Dudayev, Gen. Dzhokhar, president of Chechenia since 1991, aged 52 – 21 April 1996

Dunmore, 11th Earl, aged 82 – 28 September 1995

Duras, Marguerite, French novelist, aged 81 – 3 March 1996

Eddington, Paul, CBE, actor, aged 68 – 4 November 1995

Edwards, Percy, MBE, bird and animal impersonator, aged 88 – 7 June 1996

Effingham, 6th Earl, aged 90 – 22 February 1996

Ellis, Vivian, CBE, songwriter and composer, aged 91 – 19 June 1996

Enright, Derek, MP, Labour MP for Hemsworth since 1991 and MEP for Leeds 1979–84, aged 60 – 31 October 1995

Evans, Very Revd Eric, KCVO, Dean of St Paul's Cathedral since 1988, aged 68 – 17 August 1996

Ewart, Gavin, poet, aged 79 – 23 October 1995

Factor, Max, jun., make-up artist and cosmetics company executive, aged 91 – 7 June 1996

Faithfull, Baroness, OBE, organizer of childcare in local and central government from 1930s to 1974, President of the

National Children's Bureau since 1984, aged 85 –
13 March 1996

Fitzgerald, Ella, American jazz singer, aged 78 – 15 June
1996

Fleetwood, Susan, actress, aged 51 – 29 September 1995

Fraser of Kilmorack, Lord, CBE, director of the Conservative Research Department 1951–64, deputy chairman of
the Conservative Party Organization 1964–75, aged 80 –
1 July 1996

Garfield, Leon, writer, aged 74 – 2 June 1996

Garson, Greer, actress, aged 92 – 6 April 1996

Glendevon, 1st Baron (Lord John Hope), ERD, PC, Conservative MP for Northern Midlothian and Peebles
1945–64 and Minister for Works 1959–62, aged 83 –
18 January 1996

Goetz, Walter, cartoonist, aged 83 – 13 September 1995

Gould, Morton, American composer, conductor and
pianist, aged 82 – 21 February 1996

Gridley, 2nd Baron, colonial administrator, businessman,
conservationist, aged 90 – August 1996

Griffiths, Edward, Labour MP for Sheffield Brightside
1968–74, aged 66 – 18 October 1995

Grinkov, Sergei, Russian Olympic pairs figure skating
champion, aged 28 – 20 November 1995

Gryn, Hugo, CBE, rabbi and broadcaster, aged 66 –
18 August 1996

Guerin, Veronica, Irish journalist, aged 33 – assassinated
26 June 1996

Haden-Guest, 4th Baron, ballet dancer 1935–9, UN
administrator 1946–72, aged 82 – 8 April 1996

Haldane, Brodrick, society photographer, aged 83 –
3 February 1996

Hamilton, Geoff, gardening broadcaster and journalist,
aged 59 – 4 August 1996

Harris, 6th Baron, aged 75 – 17 September 1995

Harris, 7th Baron, aged 79 – 30 June 1996

Harrison, Kathleen, actress, aged 103 – 7 December 1995

Hawkes, Jacquetta, OBE, archaeologist and author, aged 85
– 18 March 1996

Hayward, Ron, CBE, general secretary of the Labour Party
1972–82, aged 78 – 22 March 1996

Hemingway, Margot, American actress and model, aged 41
– 1 July 1996

Heward, Air Chief Marshal Sir Anthony, KCB, OBE, DFC and
bar, AFC, aged 77 – 27 October 1995

Hills, Dick, comedy writer, aged 70 – 6 June 1996

Home of the Hirsel, Lord (former 14th Earl of Home), KT,
PC, Prime Minister (as Sir Alec Douglas-Home) 1963–4,
Foreign Secretary 1960–3 and 1970–4, a Conservative
MP 1931–51 and a Minister of State in the Lords
1951–60, aged 92 – 9 October 1995

Houghton of Sowerby, Lord (Douglas), CH, PC, Labour MP
for Sowerby 1949–74, Cabinet minister 1964–8, chairman of the Parliamentary Labour Party 1968–74, aged
97 – 2 May 1996

Hulme, Maj.-Gen. Jerrie, CB, Director-General of Ordnance Services 1988–90, senior logistics officer to UN
High Commissioner for Refugees in the former Yugoslavia since 1992, aged 60 – 20 September 1995

Hyson, Dorothy, film and stage actress, aged 81 – 23 May
1996

Iliffe, 2nd Baron, newspaper proprietor, aged 88 –
15 February 1996

Jacques, Lord, chairman of the Co-operative Union
1964–70, aged 90 – 20 December 1995

Jay, Lord (Douglas), PC, Labour MP for Battersea 1946–83,
President of the Board of Trade 1964–7, aged 88 –
6 March 1996

Jellicoe, Sir Geoffrey, CBE, RA, landscape architect, aged 95
– 17 July 1996

Jenco, Revd Lawrence, American hostage in Beirut
1985–6, aged 61 – 19 July 1996

Jewel, Jimmy, comedian and actor, aged 82 – 3 December
1995

Jones, Air Marshal Sir Laurence, KCB, AFC, Lieutenant
Governor of the Isle of Man since 1990, aged 62 –
23 September 1995

Kanyon, Prof. John, FBA, historian, aged 68 – 6 January
1996

Keane, Molly (M. J. Farrell), author, aged 91 – 22 April
1996

Kelly, Gene, American dancer, actor, choreographer and
film director, aged 83 – 2 February 1996

Kieslowski, Krzysztof, Polish film-maker, aged 54 –
12 March 1996

Killearn, 2nd Baron, businessman, aged 76 – 27 July 1996

Kirstein, Lincoln, founder and general director of New
York City Ballet, aged 88 – 5 January 1995

Lanigan, John, Australian-born opera singer, aged 75 –
1 August 1996

Lawrence, William, chief constable of South Wales
Constabulary since 1989, aged 53 – 21 May 1996

Laye, Evelyn, CBE, actress and singer, aged 95 – 17 February 1996

Learoyd, Wing Cdr Roderick, VC, aged 82 – 24 January
1996

Leary, Timothy, clinical psychologist and writer, 1960s
drugs proselytizer, aged 75 – 31 May 1996

Leathers, 2nd Viscount, shipping executive, aged 87 –
21 January 1996

Lenihan, Brian, Irish politician and Deputy Prime Minister
1987–90, aged 64 – 1 November 1995

Lightbown, Sir David, MP, Conservative MP for Staffordshire South East since 1983, aged 63 – 12 December 1995

Lindwall, Ray, MBE, Australian fast bowler, aged 74 –
23 June 1996

Luke, 2nd Baron, KCVO, businessman, aged 90 – 25 May
1996

MacCaig, Norman, OBE, poet, aged 85 – 23 January 1996

McCluskie, Sam, general secretary of the National Union
of Seamen 1986–90, aged 63 – 15 September 1995

McClymont, J. M., GC – 10 June 1996

MacDermot, Niall, CBE, QC, Labour MP for Lewisham
North 1957–9 and Derby North 1962–70, Financial
Secretary to the Treasury 1964–7, and secretary-
general, International Commission of Jurists 1970–90,
aged 79 – 22 February 1996

McFadzean, Lord, KT, chairman of BICC 1954–73 and
deputy chairman of Midland Bank 1968–77, aged 92 –
14 January 1996

McKaig, Adm. Sir John, KCB, CBE, UK Military Representative to NATO 1973–5, aged 73 – 7 January 1996

McKay, Margaret, Labour MP for Clapham 1964–70, aged
85 – 1 March 1996

Mackay Brown, George, OBE, poet and story-writer, aged
74 – 13 April 1996

Maclean of Dunconnell, Sir Fitzroy, Bt., KT, CBE, diplomat,
soldier, traveller, author and historian, Conservative MP
for Lancaster 1941–59 and Argyll and North Bute
1959–74, aged 85 – 15 June 1996

Madge, Charles, poet, sociologist and co-founder of Mass
Observation, aged 83 – 17 January 1996

Malle, Louis, French film director, aged 63 – 23 November
1995

Mann, Jackie, CBE, DFM, Battle of Britain fighter pilot and
from 1989–91 a hostage in Beirut, aged 81 – 12 November 1995

Margadale, 1st Baron, TD, Conservative MP for Salisbury
1942–64, chairman of the 1922 committee 1955–64,
aged 89 – 25 May 1996

Marks, Alfred, OBE, comedian, actor and singer, aged 75 – 1 July 1996

Marshall of Goring, Lord, CBE, FRS, chairman of the Atomic Energy Authority 1981–2 and of the Central Electricity Generating Board 1982–9, aged 63 – 20 February 1996

Martin, Dean, American singer, comedian and actor, aged 78 – 25 December 1995

Matthews, Lord, former deputy chairman and group chief executive of Trafalgar House, aged 76 – 5 December 1995

Maxwell, James, actor, and an artistic director of the Royal Exchange Theatre, Manchester, aged 66 – 18 August 1995

Mazar, Prof. Benjamin, Israeli archaeologist, excavator of the Temple Mount in Jerusalem, aged 89 – 9 September 1995

Meade, Prof. James, CB, FBA, economist and Nobel laureate 1977, aged 88 – 22 December 1995

Mersey, Katherine, Dowager Viscountess, and Lady Nairne (12th in line), aged 83 – 20 October 1995

Milne, Christopher, the Christopher Robin of the Winnie the Pooh books, aged 75 – 20 April 1996

Mitchell, Colin ('Mad Mitch'), soldier and Conservative MP for West Aberdeenshire 1970–4, aged 70 – 20 July 1996

Mitford, Jessica, writer, aged 78 – 23 July 1996

Mitterrand, François, President of France 1981–95, aged 79 – 8 January 1996

Moshoeshoe II, King of Lesotho 1966–90 and since 1995, aged 57 – 15 January 1996

Mott, Prof. Sir Nevill, CH, FRS, physicist and Nobel laureate 1977, aged 90 – 8 August 1996

Mullard, Arthur, comic actor, aged 83 – 11 December 1995

Muskie, Edmund, US Senator 1959–80 and Secretary of State 1980–1, aged 81 – 26 March 1996

Niarchos, Stavros, Greek shipowner and financier, aged 86 – 15 April 1996

Nix, Frank, GC, aged 82 – 8 August 1996

Norfolk, Lavinia, Duchess of, LG, CBE, Lord Lieutenant of West Sussex 1975–90, aged 79 – 10 December 1995

Northumberland, 11th Duke, aged 42 – 31 October 1995

O'Brien of Lothbury, Lord, GBE, PC, Governor of the Bank of England 1966–73, aged 87 – 24 November 1995

Packard, David, co-founder of Hewlitt Packard in 1939, aged 83 – March 1996

Paisley, Bob, footballer, manager of Liverpool Football Club 1974–83, aged 77 – 14 February 1996

Papandreou, Andreas, prime minister of Greece 1981–9 and 1993–6, aged 77 – 23 June 1996

Pargeter, Edith (Ellis Peters), OBE, BEM, novelist, aged 82 – 14 October 1995

Parsons, Sir Anthony, GCMG, MVO, MC, diplomat, aged 73 – 12 August 1996

Patton, John, GC, OBE, aged 80 – 13 May 1996

Pearsall, Phyllis, MBE, founder of Geographer's A–Z Map Company, aged 89 – 28 August 1996

Peierls, Sir Rudolf, CBE, FRS, physicist, aged 88 – 19 September 1995

Pertwee, Jon, actor, aged 76 – 20 May 1996

Piratin, Philip, Communist MP for Stepney, Mile End 1945–50, aged 88 – 10 December 1995

Pritchard, Lord, businessman, aged 85 – 16 October 1995

Rabin, Yitzhak, Prime Minister of Israel 1974–7 and since 1992, Defence Minister 1984–90, Army Chief of Staff 1964–7, aged 73 – assassinated 4 November 1995

Rahi, Sultan, Pakistani film actor, aged 57 – 9 January 1996

Red Rum, winner of the Grand National 1973, 1974 and 1977, aged 30 – 18 October 1995

Rimmer, Reginald, GC, aged 93 – 21 February 1996

Robinson, Rt. Hon. Sir Kenneth, Labour MP for St Pancras North 1949–70, Minister of Health 1964–8, chairman of the Arts Council 1977–82 and of London Transport Executive 1975–8, aged 84 – 16 February 1996

Rotherwick, 2nd Baron, shipping magnate, aged 83 – 11 June 1996

Rudolph, Arthur, German rocket scientist, aged 89 – 1 January 1996

Saro-Wiwa, Ken, Nigerian novelist and playwright, aged 54 – executed 10 September 1995

Scott, Annie, Britain's oldest person, aged 113 – 21 April 1996

Shawe-Taylor, Desmond, CBE, chief music critic of the *Sunday Times* 1959–83, aged 88 – 1 November 1995

Shotter, Winifred, actress, aged 91 – 4 April 1996

Siegel, Jery, creator of Superman, aged 81 – 28 January 1996

Sinclair, Jean, founder of the Black Sash anti-apartheid movement in South Africa, aged 87 – 6 June 1996

Sinden, Jeremy, actor, aged 45 – 29 May 1996

Skelton, Barbara, writer, aged 79 – 27 January 1996

Smythe, Pat, OBE, international showjumper, aged 67 – 27 February 1996

Snagge, John, OBE, broadcaster, aged 91 – 25 March 1996

Stair, 13th Earl, KCVO, MBE, aged 89 – 26 February 1996

Stedman, Baroness, OBE, Labour councillor and a junior minister, leader of the SDP in the House of Lords 1988–91, aged 79 – 8 June 1996

Stephens, Sir Robert, actor, aged 64 – 12 November 1995

Sylvester, W. G., GC – 23 February 1996

Thirkettle, Joan, ITN news reporter, aged 48 – 11 May 1996

Tran Van Tra, Gen., Vietnamese army general in Vietnam War, aged 77 – 20 April 1996

Travers, P. L., OBE, author, creator of Mary Poppins, aged 96 – 23 April 1996

Tweedsmuir, 2nd Baron, CBE, CD, FRSE, soldier, explorer, writer and businessman, aged 84 – 20 June 1996

Walker, Patric, astrologer, aged 64 – 8 October 1995

Warner, Sir Frederick, GCVO, KCMG, former ambassador and Conservative MEP 1979–84, aged 77 – 30 September 1995

Warnock, Sir Geoffrey, philosopher, Principal of Hertford College, Oxford 1971–88 and Vice-Chancellor of the University of Oxford 1981–5, aged 72 – 8 October 1995

Warrell, Charles, creator of the I–Spy books, aged 106 – 26 November 1995

Warwick, 8th Earl, aged 61 – 20 January 1996

Watkinson, 1st Viscount, CH, PC, Conservative MP for Woking 1950–64, Minister of Transport 1955–9 and Minister of Defence 1959–62, aged 85 – 19 December 1995

Webb, Kaye, MBE, children's book publisher and founder of the Puffin Club, aged 81 – 16 January 1996

Weeks, Alan, sports commentator, aged 72 – 11 June 1996

White, Wilfred, OBE, show jumper, aged 91 – 21 November 1995

Whittle, Air Cdre Sir Frank, OM, KBE, CB, FRS, FEng., inventor of the jet engine, aged 89 – 8 August 1996

Wingate Gray, Brig. Michael, OBE, MC and bar, a former director of the SAS, aged 74 – 3 November 1995

Worlock, Most Revd Archbishop Derek, CH, Roman Catholic Archbishop of Liverpool since 1976, aged 76 – 8 February 1996

Worsnip, Glyn, television presenter and actor, aged 57 – 6 June 1996

Archaeology

One of the most important archaeological events during the year under review was not an excavation but the opening at the end of January 1996 of the new Roman London gallery at the Museum of London. The new gallery reflects the changes both in knowledge of Roman London and in museum display techniques since the Museum first opened. Museums have a fundamental duty to interpret the results of archaeological excavations, presenting a synthesis of material from old and new investigations in as lively and exciting a way as possible. The concepts behind the new Roman London gallery are explained by Jenny Hall, curator of the Roman collection in the Museum of London, in *Minerva* (volume 7, no. 4) for July/August 1996.

The rise and fall of Roman London is presented in both a chronological sequence and with objects illustrating daily life in appropriate settings. Reviewing previous interpretations is a crucial function of the museum archaeologist; this has led to a reconsideration of the interpretation of the Temple of Mithras, excavated in 1954–5, and it is now being argued that the Temple was rededicated in about AD 350 to Bacchus. The new gallery also allows for a reinterpretation of the nature of the settlement at Southwark, previously seen as a small suburb. 'Ongoing work on excavations conducted in Southwark over the last 20 years is now revealing that the area may have been as important as the main settlement. Substantial buildings of high status have been excavated in Southwark, as at Winchester Palace, as well as timber warehouses in Park Street and a possible inn (*mansio*) in Southwark Street.'

The archaeological investigation of Roman London continues, and in the same issue of *Minerva* Kenneth E. Jermy describes the finding in an excavation by the Museum of London Archaeology Service of 'fragmentary but important evidence of a massive late fourth-century building at the top of Tower Hill in the City of London', dated by pottery 'as later than AD 350'. It is an aisled construction and 'the probability that this was an ecclesiastical building comes from the very close parallels with the cathedral of St Tecla in Milan, said to have been built by the architect St Ambrose. Both had wells in the nave, and both were double-aisled, in the tradition of St Peter's and St Paul Without-the-Walls in Rome. Both edifices could have been built from the same plan.' Being an obvious landmark on a low hill near the waterfront, 'the main significance of this building is that it continued the importance of London, adding to its administrative and religious functions when commercial activity began to decline. This is a pattern which is found in other cities of the Western Empire. So far, large urban churches have not been identified in England and Wales, but this may well be because they simply have not been recognized. There were certainly fourth-century bishops, who could well have been attached to urban cathedrals.'

BRONZE AGE LEWISMAN

The application to archaeology of techniques developed by other specialisms is always of interest and in an article entitled 'A Face from the Past' in *Current Archaeology* (no. 147, April 1996) Iain MacLeod and Trevor Cowie describe how techniques of facial reconstruction used by police forces were applied in 1995 to human remains found after being exposed by wind erosion, in a burial cyst on a beach in Lewis in 1992. 'The grave contained the flexed skeleton of a man, accompanied by a plain pottery vessel. A sample of bone provided a radiocarbon date indicating that the burial took place about the middle of the second millennium BC.' Upon examination it was found that the burial was that of an adult male of between 35 to 40 years of age and some 5ft 4in tall, but 'what was of particular interest was evidence of healed but extensive injuries to the right side of the face, in particular a severe fracture of the cheekbone. The injuries are consistent with a severe blow with a blunt object; one possibility is that the man had been savagely clubbed on the side of the face. Infection in the fractured bone ends resulted in further complications. He would have had limited jaw movement and this in turn led him to favour a softer diet, resulting in increased dental caries and abscesses.'

The authors go on to explain that the purpose of their project in 1995 'was to produce a facial likeness of the individual with the help of "state of the art" medical technology. The more conventional method has been to take an impression from the actual skull in order to create a plaster model; however this runs the risk of damaging the fragile skeletal remains, so instead we produced a plastic replica of the skull as the basis for the modelling process. This is a procedure that is being developed as an aid for plastic/maxillofacial surgeons to assess procedures for operating on the face, but it has not in any significant way been used in archaeology.' At the end of the project, after all the specialist tasks had been completed, there was a head ready to be displayed in the museum at Stornoway. 'Although the facial wounds had healed, maxillofacial surgeons confirmed that the man would have been left scarred; the model shows the puckering of the skin of the cheek characteristic of such injuries. Obviously, certain features – the shape of the ears, his nose, the cut of his hair and the length of his beard – are simply guesswork.'

Towards the end of their paper the authors speculate that many visitors to the museum on seeing the model 'will simply flinch at the thought of having to endure those injuries and all that subsequent discomfort in the absence of painkillers and medical care'. This comment prompted correspondence in *Current Archaeology* (no. 148, June 1996); John Clemence asks 'how far north the ubiquitous opium poppy, *Papaver somniferum*, grows. It was found around round houses associated with the Dartmoor reaves.' He is not sure that ancient man did suffer pain with no relief, given the existence of 'the three main poisonous plants with powerful narcotic uses, the painkiller poppy, major sedative deadly nightshade, and strong heart stimulant foxglove, from which are made opium/morphine, belladonna and digitalis respectively. In less quantity, the red field poppy also contains opium, although bleeding that species would be laborious to the level of pointlessness … an alternative lesser painkiller was hemp, again ubiquitous … Pain must have been very familiar to ancient people; but the control of pain is probably just as old, and would have included alcoholic drinks. Our ancestors did not always suffer helplessly in silence.'

FOOT NOTES

The study of skeletal remains to deduce nutritional and environmental information about the dead is a well-established part of archaeological science. Hitherto, the bones of the feet have not received any special attention. However, Phyllis Jackson, a retired chiropodist, is studying the bones of the human foot as recovered by archaeological excavation, as she explains in *Current Archaeology* (no. 144, August/September 1995). As a practising chiropodist she 'gradually came to realize that pain was more frequently caused not so much by wearing unsuitable footwear as by anomalies in the bone structure'. The deduction was that in isolated rural areas repeated intermarriage 'had turned these slight deformities into a recognizably typical and strongly hereditary shape of foot. This prevails not just in the direct family line but could be perceived in a wider circle of cousins twice removed.' This prompted the reflection that 'in the isolated groups of people in the prehistoric days, inbreeding was inevitable and any anomaly would soon be locked into the strong genetic and therefore tribal shape'. In addition to the regional shape, Phyllis Jackson was able to identify a foot structure different from that 'which is generally regarded as the traditional English foot – for which all shoe manufacturers in this country design their footwear'. This broad English foot may be contrasted to the Scots–Irish type which 'is slim in structure, the longitudinal arch (the one that goes flat!) is much longer than its English counterpart. The toe-line is rather level, unlike the English foot where the structure is such that the toes make quite a steep angle from the first to the fifth.' In contrasting the different types the crucial diagnostic feature is the 'cuboid' bone, the one on the outside of the foot between the heel-bone and the little toe.

By examining excavated material from a number of sites, Phyllis Jackson was able to distinguish in the Saxon cemetery at Lechlade, Glos, the Saxon newcomers from the descendants of the citizens of Corinium. Working on material from the Iron Age hill-fort at Danebury, Phyllis Jackson noted that 'the Danebury feet were also very interesting in another way: except for one woman, they were all very worn, indicating the incredibly hard work done by these people. The status of these Danebury burials has always been doubtful as they were found buried in disused storage pits, but judging by their feet, I think it highly probable that their short lives were terminated as much by overwork as by disease.' When compared with the remains of those people from the wealthy farming community at Owslebury in the same locality 'it was interesting to find the signs of wear were not so intense and that the bones of the Owslebury people, although similar in size, weighed more heavily and the texture was more robust. I do not think posthumous conditions had affected this.'

ROMAN SMALL TOWNS

'One of the biggest excavations ever to have taken place in this country has been that at the Romano-British small town at Heybridge near Maldon in Essex. Maldon lies at the head of the estuary of the River Blackwater; the Saxon town of Maldon is on the south bank and the Roman town of Heybridge is on the north.' Thus began an article on the excavation of Elms Farm, Heybridge, in *Current Archaeology* (no. 144, August/September 1995). In advance of housing development, the excavations were funded in part by the developer and partly by English Heritage who gave a grant of over £1 million towards the excavation of a 13 hectare area in 1994, at the time the largest single grant ever received by a field project. Excavation was undertaken by the Essex County Council Planning Department's Field Archaeology Group, directed by Mark Atkinson.

Although much work remains to be done, the site yielded a number of surprises. 'It had long been held that this was an undefended trading settlement where goods were transhipped for the nearby Roman town of Chelmsford, for Maldon marks the spot where the River Chelmer joins the River Blackwater. But the first surprise is that there is no obvious evidence for a direct trade link with the Continent … if transhipment took place, nothing was left behind, or else a waterfront lies along the River Chelmer. The second surprise is that the settlement originated in the late pre-Roman Iron Age. Indeed, its great period of prosperity appears to have straddled the late Iron Age and early Roman periods (*c.* 50 BC to AD 200) … The big surprise was that at the heart of the town there appeared to be a temple complex. This began in the late Iron Age when a large circular building was erected inside a square enclosure with an entrance to the east.' The article goes on to explain the subsequent changes to the site. Although this town appeared to be divided into a number of zones, with a temple area, a market area, and an industrial area to the south and east, it was not clear whether the centre of the town had yet been found; if the temple is not at the centre, then the latter could lie in an unexcavated area to the south-west and nearer the river. The whole settlement was abandoned by the later fifth century AD, the inhabitants having made an effort from the second century onwards to raise surface levels. This may explain why there was little evidence of Saxon occupation and why the Saxons apparently moved to the higher gravel terrace to the north. When analysis is complete 'the results of the Heybridge excavation seem set to make a significant contribution to late Iron Age and Roman settlement studies and with an estimated potsherd count in excess of a quarter of a million fragments, should help refine the ceramic chronology and typology of late Iron Age/early Roman transitional period for the region.'

Though the location of the administrative centre of Heybridge is still unclear, this is not the case at Tripontium 'a Roman roadside settlement, a small posting station situated on the Watling Street near Rugby. It is indeed the first posting station to the south from Venonae or High Cross, where the Watling Street crosses the Fosse Way, which is often taken to be the centre of England.' Described in *Current Archaeology* (no. 145, November 1995) 'the excavations of Jack Lucas and Rugby Archaeological Society have now made Tripontium into a prime example of a Romano-British small town'. The finds are impressive, which is appropriate because 'Tripontium is one of the towns named in the Antonine Itinerary which are often assumed to be the posting stations of the imperial posting system. The principal buildings in such towns – and often the only building in stone – is the *mansio*, the place from which the post service – the *cursus publicus* – was organized: it is often translated as "inn" but it was often rather more than that.' The report concludes by arguing that 'we must begin to reconsider the interpretation of the courtyard building as being an inn or hotel. The impression given is very much more of an administrative centre, comparable perhaps to the forum and baths in a major town. We should note that the buildings are well away from the line of the Watling Street itself, lying 150 yards back from the known line of the Roman road and the other side of what is today a small stream. No doubt the organization of the *cursus publicus* may have been the main task of the officials who had their offices in the rectangular building; but is it not time to reconsider the function of the *mansio* and the role that such *mansiones* played in the small towns of Roman Britain?'

CATTERICK RACECOURSE

Catterick is generally well-known for its associations with the Army and horse-racing, and equally well-known to archaeologists for its archaeological significance. The excavation there by the West Yorkshire Archaeology Service under Colm Moloney of an Iron Age settlement is described in *Current Archaeology* (no. 148, June 1996). The ultimate consequence of the excavation was the discovery of a late Neolithic/early Bronze Age cairn which had been reused by the Romans to form the bank of a previously unknown amphitheatre probably constructed towards the end of the second century AD. Nor was that all: 'the site which began life as a Neolithic cairn and then became part of the Roman Empire later went through a further transformation. At the end of the Roman Empire it became an Anglican cemetery when burials were placed up against the outside of the abandoned amphitheatre. Some 44 inhumations were revealed, mainly adult although a number of juveniles were recovered also. The majority of the adults appeared to be female on the basis of the associated grave goods although a number of male burials were present. Grave goods were of a high quality and included objects of glass, amber, various metals and ceramics. The "female" assemblage appears to consist of glass and amber necklaces, assorted bronze brooches and fasteners, girdle hangers, rings, knives and buckles. The "male" assemblage was less elaborate and consisted of knives, spearheads, buckles and in one grave a shield from which the boss survived. A gaming piece and a spindle whirl fashioned from Samian ware were also recovered. Burials did not appear to conform to any specific orientation. The bodies were crouched, extended, slightly flexed or in a few examples face down. The brooches had been dated typologically to between AD 450 and AD 550. This was probably part of a huge cemetery. Anglian finds have been recorded on and off ever since recording began in the area and numerous Anglian graves and structures have been identified in the area; Catterick was a major site in the Dark Ages, the site of the disastrous battle recorded in the Gododdin, the oldest surviving poem of the British language which records the defeat of the Britons by the Angles at Catraeth which is generally taken to be Catterick: could this cemetery have belonged to the victorious Anglians?'

ANGLO-SAXON LONDON

In *Minerva* (March/April 1996) David Keys reports that 'archaeologists have unearthed the remains of Anglo-Saxon London's first purpose-built port facility, constructed in the 880s when Alfred the Great took the first steps towards the refurbishment of London as England's capital'. Found near Southwark Bridge on the north bank of the Thames was a 'massive quay which protrudes 20 feet into the river, and together with a suspected second quay up to 50 feet to the west, would have created a small harbour capable of affording shelter to at least three partially beached trading vessels. It is likely that trade was conducted on the port site, as archaeologists have recently unearthed three silver pennies minted by Alfred in London.' Other discoveries during this excavation, directed by Julian Ayre of the Museum of London, included 'fragments of a tenth-century Viking or Anglo-Saxon longboat, a Dutch trading ship built in c.960 and held together with willow-wood nails, and a wooden building, possibly an Anglo-Saxon palace or church. Although only a few timbers of the building have been recovered – reused as part of a tenth- or eleventh-century renovation of the Anglo-Saxon port facility – archaeologists believe that parts of the original building were constructed in a distinctly Arab style.' Part of a three-tier arcade, these Arab-style pieces are noted as being 'the only examples of sophisticated wooden architectural elements known from that period in western Europe'.

In *The London Archaeologist* (spring 1996) Gabriel Pepper drew attention to the significance of the name Tothill Street, Westminster, explaining that 'the word *Tot-hyl*, from which the street takes its name, means "a watch-hill", and is directly related to a system of Anglo-Saxon beacons found in south-east England'. Noting that this place-name element is rare in Greater London, the only other one being a field name in Hendon, Gabriel Pepper writes that 'evidence from charters suggests that *Tot-hyl* and other beacon sites, are linked into an integrated system of Anglo-Saxon civil defence, by a system of routeways called *herepaths*, meaning literally "army-roads". Studies in Dorset, Hampshire and Wiltshire have illustrated the complexities of the *herepath* network extending from Beaford in north Devon, straight into Oxford Street in central London where a charter records a *here-strete*.' In addition to the place-name evidence, Gabriel Pepper finds the *Tot* mound suggested on Rocque's 18th-century map of London. 'It is set well back on the line of the original land surface, and commands an excellent view of both the city and Westminster ... Traces of the site exist to the present day. There is the slight rise of Regency Place – the junction of Rutherford Street, Horseferry Road, Maunsel Street and Ayneway Street. A more pronounced slope occurs at the western end of Page Street.'

A MEDIEVAL DONKEY

The usefulness of the study of animal bones from archaeological sites has been recognized for a number of years and the remains of horses are common on archaeological sites of all periods from the Iron Age onwards. The remains of donkeys and mules, however, are much rarer and are often discovered in such a state that their identification is not clear. 'Thus' argues Ian Baxter in *Current Archaeology* (no. 144, August/September 1995), 'the excavation of a relatively complete donkey skeleton must count as being a "first".' The beast in question was found in 1994 and properly excavated in 1995 at Medbourne, near Market Harborough, Leics. The donkey was found in a medieval pit containing pottery of 14th/15th-century date which had been cut into the remains of a Roman villa. 'The donkey was lying on his back with his hind legs fallen forward across his body. The skeleton is largely complete, the only major elements missing being the forefeet and hooves of all legs, destroyed when the pit was truncated. The donkey was male and between seven and 11 years old when it died.'

MEDIEVAL THATCH

According to *Current Archaeology* (no. 146, January 1996), following a report in *The Times* of 12 August 1995, English Heritage is funding John Letts, a botanist, to study the early seed content of thatched roofs. Because thatchers in previous centuries did not strip off the bottom layers of straw when rethatching buildings, medieval grain and seeds have survived, especially in buildings open to the roof, where smoke from the hearth has stopped seeds rotting. Nowadays thatchers tend to strip the straw totally, replacing it with reed; it is estimated that 'there are only 250 English houses with remains of 14th/15th-century thatch still in position and the greater majority of these are in Devon. Obviously, the seeds found in the thatch are no longer viable but can be used as a source of DNA if this is required. Of the cultivated species, he [Letts] has found one, rivet wheat, which was introduced by the Normans but is no longer grown.'

TREASURE TROVE

In the annual report of the treasure trove reviewing committee of the Department of National Heritage for 1994–5, Lord Inglewood, Under-Secretary of State for National Heritage, mentioned in his fore-word that all but five of the 27 cases of treasure trove recorded were found by the use of metal detectors. A summary of the report by Peter Clayton was published in *Minerva* (March/April 1996). 'During the year the detailed reports and valuations by the British Museum of the Hoxne Roman treasure trove hoard of coins, jewellery and plate were made public alongside the summaries of the reports of the three independent external experts consulted. At £1.75 million, it is the highest valuation ever made for a treasure trove find, and it was reassuring to note that all four of the separately conducted and independent valuations fell within 7 per cent of each other – which is notable considering the unique nature of some of the material.' Although coin hoards formed most of the finds declared as treasure trove, two exceptions out of the 27 cases 'were a bar-twisted gold torc of the middle Bronze Age (c.1350–1000 BC) found at Cissbury, West Sussex, and two late Bronze Age plain, pennanular gold bracelets (c.1000–700), found at Birstall, Leicestershire.' Amongst the coin finds 'the Middle-ham hoard, which was concealed in several pottery jars, consisted of 5,099 coins from the reigns of Edward VI to Charles I and is the largest coin hoard found from the period of the English Civil War. An interesting aspect of its contents was the large number of coins of the Spanish Netherlands (245) present, as well as coins of Scotland (31), Ireland (10) and two of Spanish America. The hoard also contained 39 forgeries.'

In addition to the report of the treasure trove reviewing committee, efforts to update the law on treasure trove resulted in the passing of the Treasure Act, which will not, however, come into force until a code of practice for dealing with finds has been drawn up. According to the *Museums Journal* (August 1996) 'the new Act defines treasure as objects that are at least 300 years old and contain at least 10 per cent gold or silver. Coins will only count as treasure if they are found in hoards, but this could mean as few as two coins being discovered at the same site. Anyone who fails to report a treasure find within 14 days of the discovery will be liable to a £5,000 fine or three months' imprisonment, or both. Any museum wishing to acquire an item declared treasure by a coroner must pay a reward to the finder.'

HERITAGE LOTTERY FUND

In November 1995 the first annual report of the Heritage Lottery Fund covering the year 1994–5 was published. Although the National Heritage Memorial Fund (NHMF) and the new Heritage Lottery Fund are governed by the same trustees, there are important differences in their responsibilities, as the annual report explains: 'NHMF will continue to work as an emergency fund for projects of outstanding national importance. The Heritage Lottery Fund, though it may also consider projects at national level, has the important extra responsibility of supporting initiatives which may be of regional or local importance only.' Applicants to the Heritage Lottery Fund will need 'to demonstrate the historical value, quality and public benefit of their project, which may fall within any of the Fund's five broad areas of interest. These are: land; buildings; museums, galleries and their collections; manuscripts, books and special library collections; industrial, transport and maritime history. Public access will usually be a condition of grant approval, as will the project's long-term financial viability.' There can be little doubt that the injection of National Lottery money will have a beneficial effect on the public appreciation of archaeology. So far the Heritage Lottery Fund has made a grant of £40,000 to the West Runton Elephant Project in Norfolk which has the aim of saving from the sea on the north Norfolk coast the remains of a fossil elephant, which, once excavated, will be placed on display in the Castle Museum, Norwich.

TOWER OF LONDON MOAT

The advent of the National Lottery has meant that for the first time money could be available in sufficient quantity to fund schemes that could not be contemplated before. In *The London Archaeologist* (winter 1995) Geoffrey Parnell reports that 'The National Heritage Memorial Fund announced that the Historic Royal Palaces Agency [HRPA] has been awarded £500,000 of Lottery money to finance technical studies into proposed improvements to the surroundings to the Tower of London.

A further £500,000 has been provided by the Tower Environs Consortium, which includes Tower Hamlets Council, Taylor Woodrow and the Port of London Authority. The centrepiece of the HRPA's Millennium project, with an estimated cost of £23,350,000, is the excavation and reflooding of the Tower moat and associated works to the gardens.' The moat to the Tower was originally dug between 1275 and 1281 and 'is the single most expensive item revealed in the great works of Edward I which gave the Tower the concentric pattern it retains to this day'. Geoffrey Parnell reviews the subsequent history of the Tower moat, including various efforts to improve, clean and renew it and its defining works.

As a result of his study Geoffrey Parnell is less than impressed by the HRPA's suggested scheme: 'Looking at the proposals put together by Historic Royal Palaces and their consultants in the Millennium project report, what is so depressing is the absence of any understanding or appreciation of the prevailing landscape, coupled with the suggested removal of features which the authors have not even bothered to date. The futility of trying to "restore" the moat to any particular pre-1843 period is compounded by a proposed "towpath", which may prove to be a necessary means of underpinning repaired sections of the retaining wall that rests on the infill, or are weakened by its removal ... Given that the Tower is a World Heritage Site, and one of the country's most important scheduled monuments, why not explain to the visitor what he or she sees now, rather than invest large sums of money in new creations? Surely to avoid the sort of damage that historic buildings and sites have suffered in the past, when accretions deemed to have no aesthetic value were removed or concealed, preservation rather than alteration should be the goal.'

ROMAN NUMERALS

1	I	11	XI	30	XXX	400	CD
2	II	12	XII	40	XL	500	D
3	III	13	XIII	50	L	600	DC
4	IV	14	XIV	60	LX	700	DCC
5	V	15	XV	70	LXX	800	DCCC
6	VI	16	XVI	80	LXXX	900	CM
7	VII	17	XVII	90	XC	1000	M
8	VIII	18	XVIII	100	C	1500	MD
9	IX	19	XIX	200	CC	1900	MCM
10	X	20	XX	300	CCC	2000	MM

Examples

43	XLIII	988	CMLXXXVIII
66	LXVI	996	CMXCVI
98	XCVIII	1674	MDCLXXIV
339	CCCXXXIX	1962	MCMLXII
619	DCXIX	1997	MCMXCVII

A bar placed over a numeral has the effect of multiplying the number by 1,000, e.g.

6,000	$\overline{\text{VI}}$	160,000	$\overline{\text{CLX}}$
16,000	$\overline{\text{XVI}}$	666,000	$\overline{\text{DCLXVI}}$

Architecture

ROYAL ARMOURIES MUSEUM
Clarence Dock, Leeds
Architect: Derek Walker Associates

The Royal Armouries collection has historically been based at the Tower of London, but the restrictions on space there have always resulted in only a tiny proportion of the total collection being on display at any one time. Despite much well-publicized opposition, the decision was taken to expand the opportunities for displaying the thousands of artefacts held in store; selected items were sent to other venues for display and an appropriate site was sought for a completely new museum in the north of England.

The selected location was at Clarence Dock in Leeds, as this offered a site of visual prominence relatively close to the city centre and with excellent connections to local and regional transport routes. The Leeds development corporation and Leeds City Council were keen to see such a potential tourist attraction brought to the city to boost its image, generate employment and set the tone for the subsequent development of the area, and they contributed development grants totalling some £8.5 million.

The building itself has something of the rugged austerity and commanding presence of a historic fort, with large expanses of blank masonry walls, occasional slit-like and sharply angled windows, and a tall faceted tower standing sentinel at the water's edge. With the exception of the tower, the building is arranged over three deep plan and double-height storeys. The two-storey high base is clad in a dark grey granite, sub-divided with narrow light-grey granite band courses, and the upper parts are clad in a dark gun-metal blue engineering brick with light-grey string courses at each of the main and intermediate floor levels and a wider grey parapet and capping course.

The octagonal tower element is entirely glazed above the granite base, which here is given a noticeable batter to accentuate the feeling of fortress-like mass. The tower contains the staircase, the major circulation route, winding up around a solid-walled internal light-well illuminated from the top by means of a projecting octagonal lantern structure. At night the warm red-ochre walls of the central core are illuminated.

The tower signals the termination of a six-storey high 'street' which cuts right through the building and is aligned on the axis of the main entrance on the opposite side. The main entrance doors are tucked beneath a tall diagonally-braced and glazed metal framework, standing clear within the massive portal formed by the blank striated granite walls of two escape staircases. The tone set by this strong

symbolic reference to medieval bastions and the portcullis is immediately impressive.

Once inside, the unremitting severity of the exterior is lightened by the dusky red walls of the interior street, punctuated at all levels by rows of rectangular openings giving onto the surrounding balcony walkways and galleries, and pleasantly top-lit by a continuous rooflight. The lower two floors of the building are devoted to a restaurant, café and bar, a 240-seat lecture hall, a shop, a library and an exhibition hall.

These activities help to generate revenue, an important factor in view of the procurement arrangements for the building, which have involved partial private funding as part of the Government's Private Finance Initiative, the first public arts building to use this programme. With £14 million of private investment from a funding consortium named Royal Armouries International, it was essential that returns were worthwhile. Both the consortium and the Royal Armouries have therefore been at pains to ensure that a wide range of display techniques, utilizing up-to-date methods of staged presentation and computer visualizations, are available to ensure that public understanding and enjoyment of the exhibits are maximized.

The museum proper is located on the first and second floors and their respective mezzanine levels. The galleries are set out on a 9.6-metres-square tartan grid with structural columns divided into clusters of four sub-columns, each enclosing a small square riser space used for services distribution. The tartan grid finds its expression on the external elevations with pairs of columns freestanding in front of the public area windows at ground floor, and framing the V-shaped projecting oriel windows on the upper floors. Each pair of sub-columns carries a pair of beams, with the space between them sub-divided to carry air handling and cable runs through the galleries at floor and ceiling levels. The routing of the services within the tartan grid enables the concrete floor slabs to be expressed as a decorative coffered waffle slab five bays square. The exposed structure is part of a carefully worked out regime for energy consumption which minimizes variations in internal temperature and humidity and enables the heat given off by people and lights to be controlled by a low velocity air diffusion system.

The historic artefacts are assembled in dramatic and visually stimulating displays and include several sizeable set-pieces, as well as film displays and re-enactments of historic battles which can be controlled by computers. Mezzanine gallery levels form ideal balcony viewing points for the regularly staged presentations that are enacted amongst the exhibits. The emphasis throughout is on action, and there are also spaces in the grounds for duelling and jousting displays.

One of the most dramatic features is the staircase tower. The visitor approaching at ground floor level is suddenly confronted by a breathtaking view up the top-lit six-storey octagonal shaft, lined from top to bottom with the serried ranks of medieval pikes, halberds, helmets and breastplates.

The creation of the £42.5 million museum has achieved a thoroughly satisfactory blend of visually stimulating exhibits with a building that is welcoming and pleasurable internally and dignified, austere and powerful outside. The designers are to be congratulated on a fine achievement that provides a worthy setting for such a historically significant collection.

UNIVERSITY LAW FACULTY
Cambridge
Architect: Sir Norman Foster and Partners

Cambridge University decided in 1990 to create new purpose-built accommodation for its law faculty on a site in the centre of the arts faculties campus bounded by Sigdwick Avenue, Queens Road and West Road. The site is not large and offered a testing architectural challenge for potential designers, being bounded on the west side by James Stirling's notorious history faculty building of 1968, and on the south side by Casson Conder's raised faculty building of 1959–61. To the north and east the site overlooks a landscape of lawns, mature trees and the gardens of the 19th-century houses fronting onto West Road.

A limited architectural competition was held for a two-phase project to house the law faculty and the Institute of Criminology. The brief for the new faculty building required a total of 9,000 square metres of accommodation to house the former Squire Law Library, seminar rooms, four lecture theatres, the Moot Court, senior and junior common rooms, faculty administration offices and associated service facilities. The building also had to satisfy the most up-to-date technical demands and user requirements. Sir Norman Foster and Partners were selected on the basis of an L-shaped design of two pavilions set in the landscape, with the major part of the law faculty housed in the longer of the two buildings in the first phase.

The completed building displays great technical assurance, and, while adopting an uncompromisingly bold and unusual geometric form, it goes some way to reflect its immediate architectural context as well as the landscape setting. The form is dominated by a huge, curved, glazed barrel-vault along the north side, which soars up over the internal floors for the entire length of the building, supported on triangulated vierendeel trusses. Like a huge greenhouse, it combines the functions of windows, walls and roof in one element.

However the vaulted enclosure does not complete a full semi-circle, as the semi-cylindrical volume is sliced away along the south side to create a simple vertical elevation of four storeys. This closely parallels the height and alignment of the raised faculty building on the other side of the pedestrian street that is now formed, and is clad partly in reconstituted Portland stone and partly with a pale Cambridge blue translucent glazing system, interspersed with clear-glazed vision strips and opening windows for natural ventilation.

The simplicity of this form is given added dramatic impetus by the 45° angle of the west elevation, which is intended to pick up the diagonal line established by the central bay of the history faculty's glazed atrium only a few yards away. Both east and west walls are glazed, and the resolution of the triangular barrel vault geometry with the 45° slice of the west end of the building has resulted in the western glazed wall adopting a sinusoidal curve on plan. This results in the diagonal line emerging from the north end in a long rising curve before straightening into the dramatically pointed prow under an overhanging section of the curved roof. At the logical point of climax of the whole three-dimensional composition, where north and west elevations should meet under the pointed curve of the roof, the wall planes have been deliberately drawn back into the volume, forming a rectangular recess for the main entrance. A solitary freestanding slender metal column spanning four storeys, but of no structural significance, marks the focal point of the entire building envelope.

The vault naturally provides the maximum amount of daylight for the interior. Passing through the main entrance, the curving line of the glazed wall creates a tapering atrium space which rises from basement level right through the building. From the triangular foyer, staircases are daringly cantilevered into the space. Further intriguing spatial effects are revealed as one progresses towards the base of the vault at ground level. From here the floors appear as a series of receding terraces, each open to the space beneath the glazed vault. Reading tables are placed along each of the levels, from which views are possible out through the sloping glazed panels to the landscape beyond. Bookstack areas and the enclosed spaces of the seminar rooms are confined to the central portion of each floor, while the vertical elevation to the south provides either the blank stone wall to lavatories and escape staircases, or the glazed window walls to the faculty offices and study carrels on the upper floors.

The ziggurat-like section of the upper floors is dramatically emphasized by the sharply raked angle of the line of internal structural columns running along the north side. Passing through successive floors at an angle of 60° to the horizontal, the concrete columns achieve jointless panels of great consistency of finish. White cement and Scottish granite aggregate were used for all the exposed surfaces, and a light grit-blasting was performed on the curved concrete to produce a natural-looking appearance. The concept of physical separation of the floors from the vaulted enclosure is pursued even where the ground floor extends right out to its base. Here a continuous band of glazed floor has been introduced, allowing daylight to flow down into the basement level where the principal lecture theatres are sited in the central zone.

It is possible to question whether the building will function satisfactorily as a traditional library when so many areas of it are effectively open to the noise and bustle of activity in other areas. There is evidence to suggest, however, that study patterns may be changing with the increased use of computers, and the workings of the building thus far would seem to reinforce this view. Certainly this is a design of originality and conviction, its formal simplicity leavened by an intricacy and refinement of detail, and one which also demonstrates a positive response to its surroundings within the constraints of the relative severity of its architectural vocabulary.

INTERNATIONAL CONFERENCE CENTRE
Edinburgh
Architect: Terry Farrell and Partners

Until now Edinburgh has lacked a purpose-built conference facility capable of accommodating major conferences and equipped with all the latest technology. The opportunity to develop such a facility arose in 1989 when four hectares of railway land became available with the closure of the Caledonian Station. The site lay close to Edinburgh's West End, in an area designated for the city's planned financial district. A competition was held in 1989 for a master plan for the new financial district, to be known as the Exchange, under the direction of a client body (EICC) formed by Edinburgh District Council, Lothian and Edinburgh Enterprise and Lothian Regional Council. It was won by a developer consortium of Greycoat, Sheraton Securities and Sheraton Caltrust with a design team headed by Terry Farrell. In the event the initial scheme had to be revised, but EICC retained the same team to rethink the master plan and to develop a design for the new conference centre.

The brief for the new centre required a 1,200-seat auditorium with the flexibility for subdivision into smaller halls while maintaining full sound insulation and all necessary technical facilities. Flexibility in seating arrangements is the key to the financial success of conference centres. With a technical innovation new to Europe (though there are numerous examples in North America) this new centre displays a high degree of flexibility, with a 1,200-seat tiered auditorium that at the turn of a switch can be transformed into three independent and fully serviced auditoria, seating 600, 300 and 300 respectively.

This is achieved by incorporating within the overall volume of the main hall two 300-seat revolving auditoria, each located to one side of a central entrance and to the rear of the remaining

fixed 600-seat section. Each revolve can be operated independently, generating seating combinations of 1,200, 900 and 300, or 600 and two 300s. The revolves, at 18.5 metres in diameter and with turntable loadings of some 150 tonnes, are amongst the largest ever built and can achieve their 180° rotation in no more than four minutes. Each 300-seat turntable also carries with it a half-circle of the rear wall, finished in the auditorium's American cherry wood panels on both sides, so that the rotation of the seating also results in the visual and acoustical separation of the smaller space from the main auditorium. Simultaneously the movement of the wall reveals a smaller stage area located to the rear, so that completion of the manoeuvre results in a completely independent 300-seat tiered auditorium with its own stage and its own independent access from the main crush bar foyer at first floor level.

Access to all the auditorium spaces is at the main first floor level, which is raised over a double-height reception hall. A semi-circular range of interlinking mezzanine-level committee rooms is placed over the main entrance, and a series of three interconnecting segment-shaped and flat-floored halls is tucked under the main auditorium. The basement is predominantly given over to an exhibition and banqueting hall, and associated kitchen facilities, capable of accommodating up to 800 people. This space is rectangular, with access from the ground floor via staircase and escalators at one end, kitchens and services plant rooms to either side, and access to a loading bay at the rear with vehicular access directly from the road.

The external form of the building takes its cue from the circular motif of the two revolving auditoria, with the conference hall spaces expressed as a grand stone-clad rotunda crowned with a dramatic black metal cantilevered cornice pierced with circles and punctuated by radiating metal ribs. The building plot is an irregular rectangle following the curving lines of Morrison Street and Western Approach Road on two sides. The central drum, almost touching every side, creates four unequal and irregular spaces at the corners, which are occupied by blocks housing services and secondary vertical circulation. These cubical forms reflect the height and scale of the neighbouring tenement blocks and office buildings, and act as a foil to the scale and grandeur of the rotunda.

The external cladding of the central drum is strongly modelled, being divided into horizontal bands by heavily accentuated movement joints, each band being divided by thin glass-block windows rising the full height of the band. The bands become progressively shallower as they rise up the building, an effect which, while increasing the feeling of height, also lightens the apparent mass and effectively leads the eye upwards to the dominant oversailing cornice. The glass-block windows also become slightly narrower at each successive level, the window slots in each ring being staggered like the vertical joints in bonded brick-work. The effect contributes to a strong feeling of rotational movement that cleverly expresses the internal workings of the building.

At the lowest level the structure is clad in a natural gritstone from Derbyshire, selected for its close colour match to the buff sandstone of the 19th-century tenement buildings in the area. The upper levels are clad in precast concrete panels with a buff-coloured sandstone mix to match the natural stone of the base, both materials being deeply scored with rustication to add a feeling of solidity and detail akin to the classical masonry of the New Town.

The main public entrance, on Morrison Street, adds a spectacular and somewhat bizarre touch to the street scene, with an exuberant display in steel, glass and tensile fabric. A series of double curved steel beams sweeps down from the central drum and out over the pavement, each one supported on the tips of upward-canted tapering steel struts project-ing from the tops of four cylindrical columns, freestanding in front of the glazed screen to the foyer areas. The columns have rusticated stone shafts surmounted by an unusual fretted steelwork upper part, with diagonal ties back to the externally expressed tubular steel supports of the main glazed frontage. In each bay between the sweeping wave-form ribs of the canopy roof, a tensile fabric sun-screen tapers down to a point, where a heavy arrow-shaped boss is suspended over the pavement and linked by a wave-shaped tubular metal tie-back to each of the columns. Tapering sail-like banners are suspended between the wave-form steel ribs and stone bollards set into the pavement.

Since opening for business in September 1995 the £35 million centre has already shown that the investment which it represents will be amply rewarded. It is reportedly fully booked until 2005, and is providing many opportunities for spin-off revenue in the city.

JUDGE INSTITUTE OF MANAGEMENT STUDIES
Cambridge
Architect: John Outram Associates in Association with Fitzroy Robinson Ltd

The Judge Institute, Cambridge University's new home for the School of Management Studies, has been created from the former Addenbrookes Hos-pital, which had been under threat of demolition. The original building, designed by Digby Wyatt, was listed Grade II and this led to proposals for its conversion.

The long narrow wing of the original building has been cleared of some unsightly 20th-century accretions, and the main façade facing onto Trump-ington Street has been restored to reveal the polychromatic brickwork and the forceful arcaded treatment of the original elevation. The two ward blocks either side of the central entrance have been converted into use as library, computer and seminar rooms, exploiting the high ceilings and good day-light provided by the generous storey heights.

The central section of the hospital behind the retained façade has been rebuilt to house common rooms and seminar rooms on the upper floors, and is linked to two new buildings at the rear of the site. All three are linked by enclosing the space between them to form an enormous atrium, called the Gallery. This rises to a height of 24 metres, with a solid roof supported on two rows of massive circular columns. Light filters in through glazed screens at each end placed on the diagonal plane to the main axis of the Gallery. The Gallery is intended to function as the main social focus of the complex; it is surrounded by arcades with projecting balconies, and criss-crossed by bridges and staircases.

The two new buildings are contrasting both in form and architectural treatment and have acquired names derived from the architect's personal philo-sophy.

'The Ark' is a long narrow building, equal in length to the ward block's central section and placed parallel to and in symmetry with it. It is four storeys in height, but these are lower, corresponding with only two storeys of the original building. It accom-modates individual study rooms flanking a central corridor, with spaces overlooking the Gallery as well as views to the outside. 'The Castle' closely abuts the Ark to one side and is square on plan. It is slightly higher than the Ark and accommodates two lecture theatres, one over the other, as well as further study rooms, offices and the storage and refuse-handling areas.

The distinctive visual quality of the building has its roots in the way the designer has combined traditional classical architecture with the functional arrangement of services and engineering elements to create a completely new giant order – a form which the architect calls the 'robot order'. The combination of functions is what determines the particularly large scale of the primary architectural elements, the giant columns. At 1.6 metres in diameter, these are large enough to contain not only the structural elements but also the mechan-ical and electrical services, ventilation ducts and drainage and water services, with sufficient room also for access ladders and crawlways, hatches and other service and maintenance devices.

The two major rows of 'robot' columns define the edges of the Gallery space between the two lines of buildings. The hollow columns constitute a closely spaced range of vertical risers from which short branches radiate, as with the necklace of supply air nozzles projecting from the air-handling columns at ground level. The Gallery provides a source of controlled natural daylight through the glazed end walls and the soaring clerestorey along the length of the Ark building. It also performs a key role in the provision of natural ventilation by utilizing the stack effect within the atrium space to circulate and control the amounts of warm and fresh air, and to draw in air flows from openable windows on the perimeter.

The Gallery, Ark and Castle elements each have their own individual architectural style, yet all are derived in some manner from the notion of the giant 'robot order'. The Gallery is perhaps the simplest, visually, of the three. Its giant plain circular columns are expressed as powerful red brick cylinders externally and white blockwork cylinders, with reddish-brown and blue banding, internally. They rise to glazed black capitals that support an intriguing entablature arrangement of circular blue concrete beams and grey-green concrete brackets.

The Ark features an extensive use of diaper patterned brickwork, with wide flat pilaster strips on the column lines and slightly projecting spandrel panels trimmed with white bull-nosed concrete strips at window sill and head positions. The diapering spreads across pilasters and spandrels, with large buff diamond shapes set on a darker ochre ground, with a 'zipper' pattern of red and blue bricks highlighting the undulating diamond patterns. At the foot of the pilasters the brickwork patterning is intensified in colour, a dark X-shape contrasting with a white ground to simulate the effect of the traditional pedestal column base. A double string course of bull-nosed white concrete containing a further narrow strip of patterned brickwork forms the cornice, beneath an undulating wave-form blue concrete parapet rail over a diagonal pierced trellis, which forms the enclosure to a roof garden accessible from the balcony walkway of the Gallery.

The Castle is heavily modelled, its giant columns emphasized by the recessing of the infill panels, and the feeling of mass accentuated by the oversized bull-nosed moulding at the base of the columns and the battered base storey of grey brickwork. The column base comprises a frame of white concrete enclosing either a louvred or plain grey concrete panel. The shaft has white concrete framing enclosing panels of red brick and plain grey concrete or louvres. The capitals are a four-square version of the circular glazed black capitals to the Gallery. The recessed panels between the columns feature large circular windows with radiused brick surrounds framed between secondary buttress-like projections with roll-top mouldings at the head.

Finally, the fourth storey of the original ward block has been significantly remodelled by reconfiguring the earlier undistinguished elevation with a colourful and generously scaled cornice and attic order. This incorporates several of the architectural motifs of the other parts of the building.

The principal external materials are brick and brightly coloured concrete, which is still in the innovative and developmental stage. A number of intricate and inventive techniques have been employed in this project, for which the architect has coined novel names such as 'doodlecrete' and 'blitzcrete', but whether the intoxicating range of the colour scheme is to everyone's taste remains to be seen. The underlying symbolism of the archi-

tect's vision may remain largely unappreciated, but this is a thoroughly modern, technically efficient and well thought-out piece of construction which should be welcomed for its sheer exuberance.

RAC REGIONAL SUPERCENTRE
Bristol
Architect: Nicholas Grimshaw and Partners

The Royal Automobile Club's highly distinctive £16 million regional control centre is located at Bradley Stoke, near Bristol, where the M4 motorway crosses the M5. It handles all RAC emergency and membership calls from south-west England, and accommodates administration departments, offices for national sales and marketing, a legal department and customer telecentres.

Local land levels have been manipulated so that the building sits within a landscaped depression. The building takes the form of a triangular doughnut. Each apex is smoothly curved rather than pointed, and the complete perimeter follows a continuously varying complex curving line. The 7,000 square metres of accommodation is arranged over three floors, around a central atrium whose form mirrors that of the outside. The atrium contains a tripartite arrangement of staircases providing access to the ground and upper floors. It has a glazed roof, and a series of meeting rooms arranged around its edge. The curved external façade is made more distinctive by being canted outwards from the ground level upwards, with a glass skin cladding the upper two floors while the glazing line at the ground floor is placed vertically and recessed to reveal a series of sturdy reinforced concrete legs tapering inwards towards the base.

From the leading edge of each concrete column a tapered steel column rises within the building volume to support the shallow curved steel roof beams that create a gently rising domed roof shape around the perimeter, clad with a standing seam aluminium sheet system. The outward leaning steel columns support bracketed tubular steel transom members, from which are cantilevered cruciform ball-jointed glazing support brackets. At the upper levels, projecting cleats form a support for a continuous horizontal aluminium bris-soleil that shades the glazed elevations from the glare of the sun and also provides maintenance access.

The outer edges are supported by a system of steel suspension rods and ties spanning between the roof eaves member and the head of the ground floor columns. These slim perforated metal shades run right round the building at two intermediate levels beneath a similarly profiled aluminium gutter and nose section at the eaves, dividing the black glazed band into three narrow layers and providing a completely horizontal emphasis to the modelling of the façades. A dramatic double-masted tower and 'crow's nest' structure soars upwards from the centre of the building to a height of 65 metres.

Two bright blue columns support a glazed lift shaft providing a dramatic ascent from the central atrium into a V-shaped glazed enclosure containing a customer visitor centre. A freestanding clear-glazed staircase tower rises to the same level. It is anchored to the projecting ends of the crow's-nest support spars and linked to the rear of the enclosure by a short glazed link. Above the visitor centre enclosure, the thick blue columns taper back into thinner sections, with cross-beams linking the masts, and culminate in a white panel displaying the RAC logo.

Each of the three internal floors has its own character and the spacial arrangement reflects the subdivision apparent in the external façade. The ground floor accommodates some open-plan office space and also houses the restaurant, which looks out over a circular landscaped garden and water feature, as well as plant rooms and a gymnasium.

The principal office accommodation is at first floor level (the main entrance level). It is laid out with open-plan work space around the outer perimeter and a number of enclosed spaces around the atrium, separated by partially acid-etched glass screens. The concrete floors are expressed with a detailed arrangement of coffers, and banks of suspended halogen uplighters bounce light off the white painted soffits.

Deep suspended floors accommodate all other services requirements, including ducted air and electrical and communications cabling, enabling the structural concrete floors to be exposed to the office space and to play a valuable part in the environmental control of the building. Air circulation is by a displacement ventilation system, treated air being supplied at floor level through directional floor slots set into circular metal discs. Solar heat gain is controlled by the external sun-shades and by the use of sealed double glazing units.

At the second-floor level the structure is withdrawn from the glazed exterior façade so that in effect the first and second floor spaces are combined. At this level there are fewer enclosed spaces, increasing the general availability of views out over surrounding areas. The ceiling is a series of suspended fabric panels following the curve of the roof beams, with lights mounted at soffit level and soft lighting transmitted through the translucent material.

The office workers can therefore benefit from a carefully engineered environment in this landmark headquarters building.

The Seven Wonders of the World

I The Pyramids of Egypt

The pyramids are found from Gizeh, near Cairo, to a southern limit 60 miles (96 km) distant. The oldest is that of Zoser, at Saqqara, built c.2650 BC. The Great Pyramid of Cheops (built c.2580 BC) covers 13.12 acres (756 × 756 ft (230.4 × 230.4 m) at the base) and was originally 481 ft (146.6 m) in height

II The Hanging Gardens of Babylon

These adjoined Nebuchadnezzar's palace, 60 miles (96 km) south of Baghdad. The terraced gardens, ranging from 75 ft to 300 ft (25–90 m) above ground level, were watered from storage tanks on the highest terrace

III The Tomb of Mausolus

Built at Halicarnassus, in Asia Minor, by the widowed Queen Artemisia about 350 BC. The memorial originated the term mausoleum

IV The Temple of Artemis at Ephesus

Ionic temple erected about 350 BC in honour of the goddess and burned by the Goths in AD 262

V The Colossus of Rhodes

A bronze statue of Apollo, set up about 280 BC. According to legend it stood at the harbour entrance of the seaport of Rhodes

VI The Statue of Zeus

Located at Olympia in the plain of Elis, and constructed of marble inlaid with ivory and gold by the sculptor Phidias, about 430 BC

VII The Pharos of Alexandria

A marble watch tower and lighthouse on the island of Pharos in the harbour of Alexandria, built c.270 BC

Bequests to Charity

The list below represents some of the principal charitable bequests from wills published since the last edition. Prior bequests, which are not always identifiable in value, such as properties, shares and chattels, and inheritance tax, which is never published, have to be deducted from the net figure given for each estate, which makes the exact value of residuary bequests uncertain.

The largest in terms of size of estate, and therefore size of charitable gift, is the estate of Angela Hobbins, who left £2,000,000 to follow the trusts of a settlement made in 1987 and the residue of her £10.5 million estate to 'the Will Charitable Trust'. Arthur Southon left £9.2 million, and included large individual bequests to three charities, half the residue to the Institute of Cancer Research and the other half between the RNIB and Fight for Sight. John Bargetto left the residue of his £3.1 million estate to the Cancer Research Campaign, and Diana Taylor left the residue of her £2.8 million estate to Chailey Heritage in East Sussex. Vivian Fletcher, Beryl Summers and Dorothy Thomson all left over £2 million and the residues of their respective estates among a number of charities. Violet Evans left nearly all her £3.9 million estate to charity, including two-thirds of the residue to the Save the Children Fund, 'in appreciation of the work done for that fund by the Princess Royal'.

This year's list includes several large bequests to charitable trusts, many sharing the surname of the testator. John Pilling, a company director, left most of his £7.9 million estate to the Pilling Trust Fund; John Brunton left the bulk of his £5.5 million estate to the Jack Brunton Charitable Trust; George Schiff left the residue of his £1.8 million estate to the Schiff Foundation; and Lavinia, Duchess of Norfolk left £100,000 from her £4 million estate to the charitable trust she had established in 1984. William Wrigley, of Kinver, Staffs, left virtually all his £835,728 estate to form the Ken Wrigley Memorial Charity, which was to be used for the benefit of people in the town. Frederic Plaxton made a similar gift of the residue of his £9.7 million estate, by leaving the income to a sister for life and then for charities to benefit the residents of his home town of Scarborough or its improvement, including the allocation of money for a new lifeboat there in memory of his father Frederick. Another North Yorkshire resident, Doris Wilkinson left the residue of her £1.1 million estate to be divided between ten local charities as her trustees decided, while Ivy MacFie left a number of local charitable bequests and the rest of her £1.3 million estate for charities in England and Wales to be selected by her trustees. Malcolm Knight, a retired dentist, left most of his £1 million estate between five named national charities, plus one animal charity to be selected by his trustees having regard to its efficiency and expense ratios.

Samuel Gorley Putt, a former Fellow of Christ's College, Cambridge, left the residue of his £1 million estate to the University to form the Gorley Putt Fund, to provide either a Professor, Reader, Lecturer or Assistant Lecturer in English Literary History in the Faculty of English. Mary Lascelles, a former Reader in English Literature at Oxford University, left the residue of her £534,151 estate to four charities, including the Friends of the Bodleian Library. Joseph Needham, the scientist, Sinologist and former Master of Gonville and Caius College, Cambridge, left the residue of his £871,856 estate to the East Asian History of Science Trust, for the completion and updating of his work *Science and Civilization in China*. He also hoped that the sermons he had given in the College chapel and at Thaxted Church would be prepared for publication and left his trustees up to £3,000 for that purpose.

Winifred Ferrier, sister of the famous contralto Kathleen Ferrier, left a large part of her £194,471 estate between the Kathleen Ferrier Society, the Kathleen Ferrier Chair of Clinical Oncology at Middlesex Hospital, London, and the Corporation of Blackburn, to exhibit and maintain its collection of Ferrier memorabilia. Baroness Faithfull, who had been chairman of the all-party parliamentary group for children, president of the National Children's Bureau and director of Oxford City Council social services department, left most of her £531,057 estate between 22 charities, most of them concerned with children and the local community in Oxford. Hilda Mann left nearly all her £1.2 million estate to the Derek Prince Ministries at Enfield, Middlesex, and Yvonne Fish left the residue of her £1.4 million estate to the Royal Society of Chemistry, to assist contributors to its conferences for seven years after her death and then to be used to advance knowledge in that subject. Cecil Betts left most of his £760,077 estate to charity, including £30,000 and one-eighth of the residue to the Severn Valley Railway at Bridgnorth in Shropshire, and £15,000 and one-eighth of the residue each to the Questors Theatre in west London, and the Tree Council.

The record for the greatest complexity in disposing of a residue must surely belong to Charles Burne, who lived near Stone, Staffs; he left £327,371 and instructed that two-fifths of the residue of his estate be divided into 244,750 parts, to be shared by 34 different local and national organizations in varying proportions ranging from 625 parts to two local charities up to 26,750 parts to the National Health Service!

John Raymond Bargetto, of Edmunds Walk, London N2, £3,119,397 (the residue to the Cancer Research Campaign)

Coralia Margaret Bellefontaine, of Alcombe, Somerset, £410,154 (her entire estate equally between the Somerset Trust for Nature Conservation, World Wide Fund for Nature, Bible Lands Society and the N. C. Bellefontaine Charitable Trust)

Cecil Holman Elkington Betts, of Hanger Lane, London W5, £760,007 (£30,000 and one-eighth of the residue to the Severn Valley Railway, £25,000 and one eighth of the residue each to the National Trust, World Wide Fund for Nature, PDSA and 'SPARKS', London, £20,000 and one-eighth of the residue to the RNIB and £15,000 and one-eighth of the residue each to the Questors Theatre, London W5, and the Tree Council)

Joan Mary Bosdet, of Thame, Oxon, £357,805 (her entire estate to the Carers Association)

Marian Rosina Bourne, of Bromley, Kent, £529,216 (the residue to the National Trust)

Aranka Braun, of Sheffield Terrace, London W8, £586,182 (the residue to Tel Aviv University Trust, mostly for a scholarship for needy students of the Medical Faculty)

John Greville Brunton, of Nunthorpe, Cleveland, £5,502,009 (the residue to the Jack Brunton Charitable Trust)

Lydia Marjorie Clare, of Chichester, W. Sussex, £392,096 (an oil painting by Clerisseau and the residue to King Edward VII Hospital, Midhurst)

Barbara Close Close, of Fremington, Richmond, N. Yorks, £1,092,014 (the residue equally between the Cancer Research Campaign and British Heart Foundation)

Lucy Joan Clough, of Morecambe, Lancs, £564,014 (her entire estate to the National Trust)

Leonard Stanley Collinson, of Middleton in Teesdale, Co. Durham, £325,783 (the residue to the Guide Dogs for the Blind Association)

Brian Cooper, of Coventry, £524,850 (the residue to the Charities Aid Foundation, for such charities as they determine or indicated by him in writing)

Dorothy Grace Craven, of Castlebar Park, London W5, £665,138 (the residue to the Salvation Army, for homes for the poor and disabled)

Eric Cronshaw, of Wilpshire, Lancs, £1,217,236 (the residue equally between St Silas Church, Blackburn, St Leonard's Church, Balderstone, the East Lancashire Hospice, Blackburn, Blackburn and District Children's Homes, Blackburn and Darwen Society for the Blind, the Mary Cross Trust, Preston, Derian House, Fulwood, Action for Blind People, Royal London Society for the Blind, Sight Savers, NSPCC, RSPCA, Barnardo's, Marie Curie Cancer Care, Age Concern England, Save the Children Fund, Spastics Society, Shelter, Salvation Army, Multiple Sclerosis Society, Motor Cycle Traders Benevolent Fund, RNLI, British Heart Foundation, Arthritis and Rheumatism Council, British Diabetic Association and Lepra)

Hyman Davidson, of Clarence Terrace, London NW1, £1,096,874 (70 per cent of the residue to Jewish Care, for homes for elderly Jews in memory of his parents, and 15 per cent of the residue each to Norwood Child Care and the Jewish Blind and Physically Handicapped Society)

John Lamprell Davies, of Eastbourne, E. Sussex, £442,999 (the residue equally between St Christopher's Hospice, London SE26, St Wilfrid's Hospice, Eastbourne, RNLI, British Association for the Hard of Hearing and the British Lung Foundation)

Susan Mary Dean, of Graffham, W. Sussex, £625,535 (two-thirds of the residue to King Edward VII Hospital, Midhurst, and one-sixth of the residue each to the Animal Welfare Trust and World Wildlife Fund)

Doreen Dennison, of Sidmouth, Devon, £302,121 (her entire estate to the RSPCA)

Lily Katharine Duff, of East Molesey, Surrey, £683,049 (the residue equally between the London Library Trust, Royal Botanic Gardens, Kew, and Newnham College, Cambridge)

Ruth Kathrina Frances Ericson, of Lyndhurst Road, London NW3, £777,561 (the residue to the Uniting Church in Australia Frontier Services, Sydney, for student accommodation)

Violet Elizabeth Beatrice Evans, of Bexhill, E. Sussex, £3,971,912 (two-thirds of the residue to the Save the Children Fund, in appreciation for the work done by the Princess Royal, and one-third of the residue equally between the Royal London Society for the Blind, Royal Commonwealth Society for the Blind, Age Concern England and the Salvation Army)

Baroness (Lucy) Faithfull, OBE, of Oxford, £531,057 (one quarter of the residue each to Barnardo's, Barkingside, and the Caldecott Community, Mersham le Hatch, Kent, one quarter of the residue equally between Bessels Leigh School for Maladjusted Children, Abingdon, Talbot Heath School, Bournemouth, the Family Courts Campaign, Birmingham Settlement, and the Conciliation Council, Swindon, and one quarter of the residue equally between the Church Army, Oxford, Simon Community, Oxford, the Oxfordshire Conciliation Service, St Mary the Virgin Church, Oxford, the Gracewell Institute, Moseley, Birmingham, and the Oxford branches of Cruse Bereavement Care, Barnardo's, NSPCC, Parent Line, Crossroads, Alzheimers Disease Society and British Dyslexia Association)

Eric James Feltham, of Kew, Surrey, £641,682 (the residue to the Cancer Research Campaign)

Winifred Margaret Ferrier, of North Hill, London N6, £194,471 (one-third of the residue each to Blackburn Corporation, to maintain and exhibit the collection of items relating to Kathleen Ferrier, the Kathleen Ferrier Chair of Clinical Oncology at Middlesex Hospital, London, and the Kathleen Ferrier Society)

Yvonne Angela Fish, of Petersham Place, London SW7, £1,446,461 (the residue to the Royal Society of Chemistry)

Doris Kathleen Fisher, of Throapham, S. Yorks, £517,337 (her entire estate equally between the Royal Hallamshire Hospital, Sheffield, for heart research, and Jessops Hospital Trust Fund, Sheffield)

Vivian Wellesley Fletcher, of Surbiton, Surrey, £2,181,660 (the residue equally between the RNLI, RUKBA, Royal Star and Garter Home, Richmond, and the Iris Fund for the Prevention of Blindness)

Anna Mai Freedman, of Hove, E. Sussex, £1,660,575 (a sum up to £200,000 to Brighton and Hove Jewish Welfare Board for a housing unit for the poor, and the residue equally between the Magen David Adom Organization, for an ambulance in Israel, the British Council of the Shaare Zedek Hospital, Jerusalem, for multiple sclerosis research, Jewish Welfare Board, Jewish Blind Society, Jewish Home and Hospital, Tottenham, the Multiple Sclerosis Society, Copper Cliff Nursing Home, Brighton, Nightingale House Home for Aged Jews, London SW12, the Bright Heart Support Trust at the Department of Cardiology of Royal Sussex County Hospital, Brighton, the Tarner Home, Brighton, British Red Cross Society, for use in Brighton and Hove, and the League of Hospital Friends, Hove)

Freda Mary Staniforth Gate, of Uckfield, E. Sussex, £631,090 (the residue equally between the Salvation Army, the Friends of the Lake District, East Sussex Association for the Blind, Shelter, Crisis, Rainbow Trust, Royal School for Deaf Children, Margate, Marie Curie Cancer Care, Motor Neurone Disease Association and Voluntary Service Overseas)

Audrey May Gilbert, of Putney Heath, London SW15, £2,592,000 (£200,000 each to the National Trust, to be spent on the Llanerchaeron estate, Aberaeron, Dyfed, and the Salvation Army)

Katharine Margaret Gill, of Walton on the Hill, Surrey, £1,783,816 (the residue equally between the RNLI, RNIB, RSPCA, RSPB, Afghanaid, and the Danilo Dolchi Trust, Sicily)

Margery Glennie, of Bovey Tracey, Devon, £1,315,708 (half the residue equally between the PDSA, RSPCA, Help the Aged, Cancer Research Campaign, Aged in Distress and St Dunstan's)

Michael Barrie Goulden, of Aldridge, West Midlands, £191,276 (his entire estate to the charity known as the Crystal Group, Fairwarp, E. Sussex)

Pamela Joy Eugenie Hall, of Ewell, Surrey, £1,601,431 (the residue to the Salvation Army)

Mary Elizabeth Harris, of Winscombe Hill, Avon, £677,507 (the residue equally between the Bristol Royal Society for the Blind, Bristol Children's Help Society, Muller Homes for Children, Bristol, Save the Children Fund, Oxfam, Cancer Research Campaign, British Heart Foundation and the Children's Society)

Susan Oakes Hiscock, MBE, of Yarmouth, Isle of Wight, £1,565,873 (the residue to the RNLI, for a new lifeboat to be named *Wanderer*)

Angela Mary Hobbins, of Stebbing, Essex, £10,537,919 (the residue to 'the Will Charitable Trust')

Antony Laurence Jones, of Worthing W. Sussex, £796,466 (the residue equally between St Barnabas Hospice, Worthing, the RSPB and the Nature Conservancy Council)

Millicent Dora Kaye, of Oswestry, Salop, £449,272 (the residue to Christ's College, Cambridge, for a prize in connection with cancer research)

Malcolm Charles Knight, of Pebmarsh, Essex, £1,034,985 (one-sixth of the residue each to the PDSA, 'Imperial Cancer Research Campaign', Royal Marsden Hospital Cancer Fund, London, the Atlantic Salmon Trust, the Scottish Salmon and Trout Association, and an animal charity to be chosen by his trustees)

Lily Klein, of Llandaff, Cardiff, £164,206 (her entire estate to the Weizmann Institute Foundation, for research into chemical water treatment in Israel)

Doris Josephine Larsen, of Clevelands, London W13, £465,839 (her entire estate equally between the Hospital for Sick Children, Great Ormond Street, London, and the Royal Marsden Hospital, London)

Mary Madge Lascelles, of Cromer, Norfolk, £534,151 (the residue equally between the Friends of the Bodleian Library, Oxford, the NSPCC, RNLI, and Royal Star and Garter Home, Richmond)

Leo Frederick Leffman, of St Johns Wood Park, London NW8, £3,160,958 (£250,000 to the Jewish Blind Society, £100,000 equally between Battersea Dogs Home, National Canine Defence League and Blue Cross, and £30,000 each to the Ravenswood Foundation, Cancer Relief Macmillan Fund and RAF Benevolent Fund)

Ivy Mary MacFie, of Ely, Cambs, £1,322,588 (the residue for such charities in England and Wales as her trustees appoint)

Hilda Catherine May Mann, of Leatherhead, Surrey, £1,219,891 (the residue to the Derek Prince Ministries, Enfield, Middx)

Marjorie Martin, of Burnham, Bucks, £1,020,177 (the residue equally between the RSPCA, National Trust, RSPB, International League for the Protection of Horses, RNID, RNIB and RUKBA)

Constance Alice Mutton, of Prentis Road, London SW16, £1,042,487 (the residue equally between the Animal Defence Trust, Save the Children Fund, Shaftesbury Society, Abbeyfield Society, WRVS, and John Groom's Association for the Disabled)

(Noel) Joseph (Montgomery) Needham, CH, FRS, of Cambridge, £871,856 (the residue to the East Asian History of Science Trust)

Lavinia, Duchess of Norfolk, LG, CBE, of Arundel, W. Sussex, £4,050,712 (£100,000 to her charitable trust established in 1964)

Agnes Gray Campbell Pilbeam, of Chipstead, Surrey, £1,176,382 (£100,000 each to the Royal Marsden Hospital, London, for equipment, and the RNLI, and £50,000 to the Multiple Sclerosis Society)

John Robert Makin Pilling, of Burrow, Lancs, £7,943,003 (the residue to the charitable trust known as the Pilling Trust Fund)

Frederic William Plaxton, of Scarborough, N. Yorks, £9,779,144 (the residue, on the death of his sister Gladys, for such charitable purposes as his trustees select, desiring that they should benefit the inhabitants of Scarborough or improve the town, including a new lifeboat in memory of his father)

William Pearson Powell, of Brough, E. Yorks, £7,692,503 (one-twentieth of the residue equally between the Charles Sykes Trust, Harrogate, Dove House Hospice, Hull, the Royal Naval Benevolent Society and the National Trust)

Maurice Leonard David Pryor, of Plymouth, £1,251,497 (the residue equally between St Dunstan's, Imperial Cancer Research Fund, Salvation Army Social Services, Mental Health Foundation, Save the Children Fund and the Stroke Association)

Samuel Gorley Putt, OBE, of Cambridge, £1,007,297 (the residue to Cambridge University, to fund either a Professor, Reader, Lecturer or Assistant Lecturer in English literary history)

Marjorie Beryl Ratcliffe, of Fixby, W. Yorks, £2,293,149 (half the residue equally between the Yorkshire Cancer Research Campaign, Barnardo's, RNLI and the Motor Neurone Disease Association)

Kathleen Faith Rayner, of South Ewell, Surrey, £465,114 (her entire estate to the RSPCA)

Harry Ridehalgh, CBE, of Stevenage Road, London SW6, £1,482,621 (one-fortieth of his estate each to the parish of St Mary, Ipsden, Oxon, the British Heart Foundation, Royal Marsden Hospital Cancer Fund, London, and the London Clinic)

George Schiff, of Elstree, Herts, £1,834,747 (the residue to the charity known as the Schiff Foundation)

Lillie Sheldrake, of Rastrick, W. Yorks, £828,033 (£100,000 to the RSPB, £50,000 each to the NSPCC, RSPCA, National Trust and World Wildlife Fund, and the residue to the Arthritis and Rheumatism Council)

Neil Anthony Smith, of Helensburgh, Argyll and Bute, £5,671,994 (£950,000 to the Newby Trust)

Arthur Charles Southon, of Canford Cliffs, Dorset, £9,284,336 (£250,000 to the Royal Bournemouth Hospital for the Eye Unit, £200,000 each to the International Glaucoma Association and the Calibre Cassette Library of Recorded Books, half the residue to the Institute of Cancer Research, and one quarter of the residue each to the RNIB and Fight for Sight)

Marie Vera Steele, of South Normanton, Derbys, £1,095,946 (the residue equally between the Friends Trust, Bradford School of Peace Studies, the Cheshire Home, Alfreton, the Hospice Fund at Kings Mill Hospital, Sutton in Ashfield, Notts, and the Ashgate Hospice, Chesterfield)

Beryl Marguerite Summers, of Teangue, Isle of Skye, £2,379,365 (the residue equally between the Imperial Cancer Research Fund, Arthritis and Rheumatism Council, National Trust, Church of England Central Church Fund, RAF Benevolent Fund and SSAFA)

Diana Margaret Taylor, of Babcary, Somerset, £2,837,965 (the residue to the Chailey Heritage, Lewes, E. Sussex)

Margaret Philothea Thompson, of Woodstock, Oxon, £445,936 (the residue to the National Trust)

Dorothy Isobel Thomson, of Southbourne, Dorset, £2,457,135 (the residue equally between the NSPCC, Spastics Society, RSPCA, Help the Aged, Cancer Research Campaign, Save the Children Fund and RNIB)

Mary Hay McEwen Thomson, of Sidmouth, Devon, £969,984 (the residue equally between the National Trust and Sidmouth Hospicare)

Arthur Sidney Thorn, of Balham High Road, London SW17, £1,353,387 (the residue to the Cancer Research Campaign)

Daphne Amelia van Deuren, of Breakspears Road, London SE4, £264,387 (her entire estate to the Cancer Research Campaign)

Kenneth William Varley, of Blackpool, £200,305 (his entire estate equally between Chethams School of Music, Manchester, the RSPCA and the Marie Curie Foundation)

Irene Maria Warrener, of Worksop, Notts, £691,784 (£5,000 and one-tenth of the residue to the Bassetlaw Hospice of the Good Shepherd, Worksop, and one-tenth of the residue each to the Royal Sheffield Institution for the Blind, St Luke's Hospice, Sheffield, the Dukeries Cheshire Home, Retford, the Sheffield Kidney Research Foundation, Yorkshire Cancer Research Campaign, Royal College of Surgeons, Skin Disease Research Fund, British Heart Foundation and Sue Ryder Foundation)

Ronald Ormande Gordon Waterall, of Elm Row, London NW3, £1,502,856 (the residue equally between the Actors Charitable Trust for the Denville Hall Fund, the Terrence Higgins Trust and the Cancer Research Campaign)

Violet Iva Weldon, of Eastbourne, E. Sussex, £845,231 (the residue equally between RUKBA and the National Trust)

Doris Ena Wilkinson, of Borrowby, Thirsk, N. Yorks, £1,180,530 (the residue to be divided between ten local charities as her trustees decide)

Rose Catherine Wilson, of Leamington Spa, Warwickshire, £755,476 (three-eighths of the residue each to Battersea Dogs Home and Animal Health Trust and one-eighth of the residue each to the Guide Dogs for the Blind Association, Leamington Spa, and the Royal College of Veterinary Surgeons)

Russell Edward Wray, of Frinton-on-Sea, Essex, £1,270,097 (the residue to St Helena Hospice, Colchester)

William Kenton Wrigley, of Kinver, Staffs, £835,728 (the residue to form the Ken Wrigley Memorial Charity for the benefit of the people of Kinver)

Broadcasting

TELEVISION

The year was widely regarded as the period when multi-channel television finally came of age in Britain. By July 1996 one in four homes had access to the ever-growing number of channels provided by satellite and cable transmission. For the first time the non-terrestrial television stations achieved more than a 10 per cent share of viewing. However, concern continued about the low quality of what the new stations were offering and the Independent Television Commission implied that if cable were to grow further it needed to put more effort into making good programmes. The UK's first experiment in pay-per-view, when subscribers to British Sky Broadcasting paid up to £14.99 to watch exclusive coverage of the boxing match between Frank Bruno and Mike Tyson, was a commercial success. Nevertheless, the ability of traditional broadcasting to set the national agenda was demonstrated in November 1995 when the BBC's *Panorama* screened an exclusive interview with the Princess of Wales.

This old-fashioned journalistic scoop, by reporter Martin Bashir, was unquestionably the television event of the year. The programme was watched by 22.8 million viewers, the third highest figure for a BBC programme since the present system of measuring audiences was introduced in 1981. Critics were divided over the princess's performance but everyone agreed that as television, the interview was in a class of its own. No member of the British royal family had ever spoken so freely or openly to the media. As the camera whirred, the princess admitted to adultery, spoke at length of her eating disorder and hinted darkly of a palace conspiracy to silence her.

The fall-out from the interview continued to be felt months after transmission. Marmaduke Hussey, who retired as BBC chairman in March 1996, made it known in a subsequent radio interview that he was unhappy at not being consulted over the broadcast. There was newspaper speculation that the decision by John Birt, the BBC's director-general, not to give Mr Hussey advance warning of the *Panorama* scoop was evidence of a rift between the two men. In July 1996 the decision by Buckingham Palace to end the arrangement whereby The Queen's Christmas broadcast was filmed exclusively by the BBC was seen as a direct reprisal for the *Panorama* interview. In future, filming of The Queen's Christmas message will alternate between the BBC and ITN.

BBC CONFIDENCE

In a year in which the BBC continued to build on its past achievements, the *Panorama* interview with the princess was another sign of the corporation's renewed confidence and what was widely regarded as a particularly strong portfolio of factual programmes. Throughout the year the BBC scored with a strong line-up of documentaries. The most ambitious was *People's Century*, eyewitness accounts of key events from the last 100 years. The first batch of the 26-part series was shown in autumn 1995. If *People's Century* failed to make the impact of such earlier documentary epics as *The Great War* or *The World At War*, it was probably because audiences have to cope with an ever-increasing weight of programming, much of it based on personal testimony.

The critics were kinder to BBC2's *The Death of Yugoslavia*, a five-part series that succeeded in making sense of a highly complex war. *The Gulf War* marked another milestone for BBC2 in recording recent history. In a different vein, the channel also scored with *The House*, a fly-on-the-wall account of life inside the Royal Opera House at Covent Garden. This warts-and-all portrait of an institution under siege was so revealing that some commentators felt Jeremy Isaacs, the director-general, had been naive in allowing the film-makers such unrestricted access. A new BBC2 documentary series, *Modern Times*, the successor to *Forty Minutes*, gave reviewers another reason to hail 1995–6 as a vintage year for the documentary; by taking such everyday topics as a swimming pool in south London or the John Lewis Partnership, *Modern Times*, it was agreed, extended the scope of subjects covered by television documentaries and enabled viewers to look at the familiar with fresh eyes.

In recent years BBC Television has not found it easy to satisfy all constituencies with its drama offerings. In 1995–6 it performed well in most areas and in Peter Flannery's nine-part *Our Friends In The North*, BBC2 finally came up with a blockbuster serial that had audiences coming back for more week after week. The story followed the lives of four Newcastle friends from 1964 through to middle age 30 years later. The critical reaction to this epic saga, some 14 years in gestation, was not wholly favourable but most reviewers agreed that as a snapshot of three decades of British life, *Our Friends In The North* had a lot to offer. The performance of veteran actor Peter Vaughan was outstanding.

Less controversial was the BBC's adaptation of Jane Austen's *Pride and Prejudice*, starring Jennifer Ehle and Colin Firth as the reluctant lovers Elizabeth Bennet and Mr Darcy. Originally rejected by ITV, this exquisitely crafted six-part serialization drew audiences of more than 12 million in autumn 1995, although for some, inevitably, the serial represented a travesty of the novel. *Pride and Prejudice* certainly won fewer awards than the BBC anticipated; in a newly created People's Award presented by the British Academy of Film and Television Arts (BAFTA) in April, *Pride and Prejudice* was runner-up to the American science-fiction hit *The X Files*. But *Pride and Prejudice* confirmed the BBC's skill at making costume drama. It was this programme, more than any of the other recent BBC period serials, that encouraged ITV to start making its own versions of literary classics once again. The results of this shift in policy will not be seen until autumn 1996.

HIT DRAMA

Meanwhile *Ballykissangel*, a comedy drama set in Ireland and featuring Stephen Tompkinson as a newly arrived English priest, gave BBC1 its biggest fiction hit for years; more than 14 million tuned in regularly. BBC1 also scored with *Silent Witness*, clearly inspired by ITV's acclaimed *Cracker*, and starring Amanda Burton as a forensic pathologist with a difficult personal life. Its grim accounts of gruesome crimes added nothing new to the television mix but most reviewers agreed it was well-made and creditably acted.

Judged by the pre-transmission hype, dramatist Dennis Potter's final pair of television plays, *Karaoke* and its sequel *Cold Lazarus*, both shown in the spring, should have been the drama event of the decade, let alone the year. In an unprecedented gesture of co-operation made as a promise to Potter when he was dying of cancer, the serials were screened simultaneously by BBC1 and Channel 4. After expending a lot of energy during his latter years railing against the people who run British television, most critics agreed that Potter had exacted his revenge by landing the two networks with work that did not justify this kind of exposure. Despite a fine performance by Albert Finney, the consensus was that neither *Karaoke* nor *Cold Lazarus* was vintage Potter. Judging by the ratings, most viewers agreed. Another disappointment for BBC1 was *The Final Cut*, the concluding part of the *House of Cards* trilogy starring Ian Richardson as the scheming Prime Minister Francis Urquhart. Despite some sexually explicit scenes, the series lacked the impact of the previous Urquhart adventures.

While the BBC made advances in most areas of television drama, the corporation still lacked a new early evening weekday hit capable of taking on the opposition. *EastEnders* continued to perform strongly but compared with ITV's trio of *Coronation Street*, *The Bill* and a revived *Emmerdale*, BBC1 looked vulnerable during this important time of the schedule. *This Life*, a spicy yarn about a group of young lawyers, was the nearest the BBC came to launching a successful new soap. However, the bedroom scenes were too graphic for the early

evening and *This Life* lacked enough popular appeal to merit a transfer from BBC2 to BBC1.

The latest Rowan Atkinson sitcom, *The Thin Blue Line*, set in a police station, did give BBC1 a pre-9 p.m. hit despite a hostile reception from the critics. Other BBC comedy successes were the spoof chat show *Mrs Merton*, *The Fast Show*, and a new sitcom, *Oh, Dr Beeching!*, from the veteran writer David Croft. *Men Behaving Badly*, Simon Nye's show based on the activities of two amiable lager louts, was another of BBC1's comic hits.

ITV SLIDES

In spring 1996, ITV launched an advertising campaign highlighting its continued popularity. Under the headline 'Britain's most popular button' *Coronation Street* characters Jack and Vera Duckworth, and Wolf and Hunter from *Gladiators* drew attention to the network's popularity. But anyone who scrutinized ITV's overall performance knew that the hype concealed a station struggling with falling ratings and desperately in need of new hits. In the first quarter of 1996 ITV's share of viewing fell to 36.5 per cent of the audience, a reduction of 1.5 per cent on the previous year.

To outsiders the decrease may appear small but in 1993 the corresponding figure was 40.9 per cent. While BBC1's audience share was static (a considerable achievement in a multi-channel market) and BBC2's actually increasing, ITV's audience was gradually being eroded. The main reason was the increasing number of satellite stations. During the year, BSkyB's audience share climbed from 5.3 per cent to 9.3 per cent, aided by additional channels including the Playboy Channel, the Disney Channel and Sky Sports Gold.

The weakest part of ITV's schedule was what had once been its traditional strength – entertainment programmes. High-profile Saturday night shows failed to please audiences or critics. A new, much-publicized game show *Raise The Roof*, in which contestants could win a house, was axed not long after its autumn debut. Two other new ITV entertainment shows were hammered by the critics – *Man O Man*, hosted by Chris Tarrant, and *The Sean Ritchie Experience*. In the latter, three couples competed to get married on screen. *Man O Man* was even tackier; the show featured an all-female audience who chose their ideal man from ten competitors. Unsuccessful candidates were pushed into a swimming pool by vampish female beauties. *Man O Man* was designed to stop viewers switching over to watch the National Lottery results on BBC1 but failed to accomplish this.

It is easy to understand why the Independent Television Commission's viewer consultative councils criticized ITV's weekend offerings, 'particularly the rather tired entertainment-led Saturday evening schedule'. An attempt to launch the relatively untried comic Jack Dee in his own Saturday night show backfired when the ITC accused ITV of putting the programme on at a time when many of the audience were offended by the comedian's 'robust' material.

The heavily publicized *The Beatles Anthology*, a six-part documentary chronicling the life and times of the Fab Four, occupied a prime position in the autumn 1995 schedule. ITV paid an estimated £4 million for the rights to the series in an auction with the BBC but the show did not win high ratings. Some critics regarded *The Beatles Anthology* as little more than a blatant plug for the group's newly released albums of outtakes and discarded tracks.

For many critics, too much of ITV's programming was based on crime stories, real or fictionalized. In autumn 1995 the network's obsession with the police and policing plunged to new depths when a live, two-hour documentary 'special' following police activity in several urban locations on a Saturday night failed to discover anything worth filming. Even ITV's largely successful portfolio of drama series attracted criticism for their dispiriting depiction of violent worlds, in series such as *Cracker*, *Band Of Gold* and *The Governor*.

Bruce Gyngell, the maverick head of Yorkshire Tyne-Tees Television, caught the public mood when speaking at the Royal Television Society in June 1996. He said mainstream television was in danger of sinking into a mire of sleaze and violence. The *Daily Mirror*'s former television critic Jaci Stephen made a similar point in a *Guardian* article published in March 1996. She claimed the high incidence of small-screen violence, not exclusively an ITV problem, was one reason she had decided to stop reviewing. 'The body count is growing,' she wrote, 'and for the first time TV executives are expressing concern about increasing levels of violence on the screen.'

While home-produced drama continued to gain strong ratings for ITV, *Savannah*, a new American soap opera from Aaron Spelling, the creator of *Dynasty*, proved that British audiences had not lost their appetite for glamorous American imports. The pulling power of television soap was demonstrated in October 1995 when more than 17 million viewers tuned in to watch the departure of Bet Gilroy (played by actress Julie Goodyear) from *Coronation Street*.

BBC Children's Television celebrated its 50th anniversary in 1996, adding a third weekly edition of *Blue Peter* to mark this milestone. Ironically, children's programmes were the one area where ITV got the better of its rivals, winning high audiences and praise from commentators. But the single most-talked-about children's programme of 1995–6 was the latest Wallace and Gromit adventure from Bristol-based Aardman Animation, *A Close Shave*, screened on BBC2 over Christmas. The film, which also delighted adults, won the pair of plasticine heroes another Oscar.

CHANNEL 4

The year 1995–6 was one of mixed fortunes for Channel 4. The station's statutory obligation to innovate and cater for audiences from all walks of life provoked fierce debate in the press, particularly in the *Daily Mail*, which wasted no time in attacking Channel 4's new Friday night youth entertainment programme, *The Girlie Show*. But it was not only the *Mail*, always a fierce critic of Channel 4, that attacked what many reviewers regarded as a coarse, predictable programme. The Broadcasting Standards Council condemned *The Girlie Show* for being preoccupied with 'scatological, sexual or generally tasteless behaviour'. The critics also turned on another new Channel 4 programme, *The Gaby Roslin Show*, a botched attempt to resuscitate the traditional Saturday night talk show. Even Ms Roslin's admirers agreed the programme was a mistake. 'Gaby is too genuine to walk down a staircase with musical accompaniment. It looked and felt wrong,' wrote Stephen Pile in the *Daily Telegraph*.

Chris Evans's latest Channel 4 vehicle, *TFI Friday*, was widely seen as a success, although it was decided to stop live transmission after several incidents involving the use of bad language. Both Evans and Gaby Roslin became Channel 4 personalities through their exposure on *The Big Breakfast* but minus the duo the programme struggled to retain its popularity. During 1995–6 *The Big Breakfast* experimented with a number of new presenters, including Julia Carling, estranged wife of the England rugby star Will Carling, and Gillian Taylforth, the *EastEnders* actress. However, a complete revamp of the programme seemed likely as breakfast rival *GMTV* overtook *The Big Breakfast* in the ratings.

One of the station's most successful shows of the year was *Father Ted*, a surreal sitcom written by Arthur Mathews and Graham Linehan, which was voted best comedy at the BAFTA awards. Featuring three wayward Catholic priests on a remote island off the Irish coast, *Father Ted*, it was agreed, managed to be irreverent about the Catholic Church without causing undue offence. Reviewers also responded well to a new adult animation series, *Crapston Villas*, made by the Spitting Image team.

The latest television drama from Alan Bleasdale, *Jake's Progress*, shown during autumn 1995, failed to match expectations despite fine performances from Julie Walters and Robert Lindsay, who played a dysfunctional couple attempting to raise a difficult child. Film On Four continued to make waves, notably with *Trainspotting* and Mike Leigh's latest film *Secrets And Lies*, winner of the Palme d'Or at Cannes.

The year saw the launch of a new Channel 4 soap, *Hollyoaks*, from the makers of *Brookside*. Set in leafy Cheshire, *Hollyoaks* was an attempt to produce a British *Neighbours*, the clean-cut Australian serial shown in Britain by the BBC. Many critics derided the poor quality of the acting but after a shaky start *Hollyoaks* established itself and there are plans to add an extra weekly episode from autumn 1996. Another new Channel 4 soap, *Annie's Bar*, set in the House of Commons and made by Prince Edward's production company Ardent, was less successful and was not recommissioned.

There was, however, praise for a lavish £13 million production of *Gulliver's Travels*, starring Ted Danson in the title role, which was shown over Easter. 'I consider it to be the small-screen event of my entire nine years as your TV critic,' gushed the *Mail's* Peter Paterson. The veteran Channel 4 soap *Brookside* continued to win high ratings and attract controversy, notably for a storyline involving an incestuous relationship. Channel 4's documentary programmes were generally well-received. *The Factory*, the latest fly-on-the-wall film from Paul Watson, told the grim story of a Liverpool gas fire manufacturer attempting to survive against the odds. *The Battle of Goose Green*, examining the final push that secured victory in the Falklands for the British in 1982, generated much press debate but most critics welcomed the new evidence shown in the programme.

Despite much to commend on Channel 4, the feeling persisted that commissioning decisions at the station were sometimes more concerned with gaining publicity than satisfying viewer expectations. In some quarters it was felt that the station was not giving enough coverage to the arts, although at Christmas chief executive Michael Grade made a late addition to the schedule by televising the acclaimed Glyndebourne production of Janáček's *The Makropoulos Case*.

Meanwhile, Mr Grade continued his campaign to end the complex funding arrangement that led to his station handing over £74 million to ITV in 1996. By the summer his efforts to end the 'funding formula' appeared to have succeeded, although another threat emerged with the possibility that the Government might privatize Channel 4, at present a non-profit making corporation.

RADIO

The year 1995–6 was a turbulent period for BBC Radio despite good news in May 1996 when figures were published showing that, contrary to the corporation's own predictions, the BBC had reclaimed the majority share of radio listening in the UK, achieving 50.4 per cent compared with commercial radio's 47.6 per cent. In November 1995 Liz Forgan, BBC Radio's managing director, had forecast that the corporation's share would decrease from 47.8 per cent to 30 per cent in three years as audiences fragmented because of the growing number of commercial stations. However, many in the industry regarded these statistics as an aberration, and figures published in August 1996 gave a more realistic picture, showing BBC Radio with a 48.6 per cent share of the radio audience.

The biggest upset of the year was Ms Forgan's surprise departure. She shocked colleagues and commentators in February 1996 when she announced her decision to leave the BBC. Her going indicated the extent of her rift with John Birt. Ms Forgan was known to be angry at plans to move radio's news and current affairs department from its traditional headquarters at Broadcasting House in central London to White City in west London. Further light was thrown on her departure in June when it emerged that Mr Birt was planning a radical reorganization of the entire BBC. Many critics argued the restructuring, probably the most far-reaching in the BBC's history, indicated that radio would in future come a long way behind television in the corporation's list of priorities.

Mr Birt and the new BBC chairman Sir Christopher Bland, who succeeded Marmaduke Hussey in April 1996, denied the reforms signified a lack of commitment to radio or any diminution of its role; commentators were not convinced. Writing in *The Times*, Brenda Maddox said: 'It is now obvious that Liz Forgan could not stay in an organization where radio is to lose its corporate identity.' Under the Birt–Bland blueprint, a newly centralized structure appeared to signal the end of radio's historic independence from television. In future, the bulk of the BBC's programming activities would be based around two new entities, BBC Broadcast and BBC Production. The former would take charge of scheduling and commissioning all the BBC's television and radio services in the UK and around the world; BBC Production would make programmes for BBC Broadcast, except news and current affairs programmes, which would be the responsibility of BBC News. Some, including the *Daily Telegraph's* Gillian Reynolds, saw the changes as a recipe for disaster. 'Programmes ... will be built to order,' she wrote. 'This is probably an excellent system for setting up a food manufacturing business. It is the kiss of death to programmes.'

However, Mr Birt argued that the plan, seen by some critics as further evidence of the director-general's 'totalitarian' approach to management, would enable the corporation to meet the challenge of digital broadcasting, both at home and overseas. In May 1996 Mr Birt had announced a scheme, planned to start in 18 months' time, to launch a number of digital services, including a 24-hour television news channel, digital radio services with CD-quality sound, extra regional options, and interactive educational services. Also envisaged were several pay-television themed channels covering drama, natural history, science and learning.

Even more controversial than the merger of radio and television was Mr Birt's apparent willingness to diminish the importance of the World Service, seen by many as symbolic of the BBC's public service role. The head of the World Service would no longer have a seat on the BBC's board of management, which would itself be scrapped and replaced by a smaller management team. The move, insisted critics, would further undermine the World

Service's role within BBC Worldwide, the corporation's commercial arm.

John Tusa, a former World Service managing director, described the plan as 'the greatest act of bureaucratic vandalism ever committed against the World Service'. Baroness James of Holland Park (the novelist P. D. James), until recently a BBC governor, accused Mr Birt and Sir Christopher of 'extraordinary arrogance' in announcing the changes without consulting either their employees or the public. A Save the World Service Campaign was launched by staff and supported by several public figures, including former Beirut hostages Terry Waite and John McCarthy, broadcaster Mark Tully, Booker Prize winner Ben Okri and Liberal Democrat MP Charles Kennedy; the *Guardian* mounted its own Save the World Service Campaign. The uproar forced Mr Birt, whose contract had been extended until 2000, and Sir Christopher to attend a meeting of MPs in July 1996 to explain their actions. Both insisted the World Service was safe in their hands and there was no intention of compromising the World Service's traditions or underestimating its importance as an international provider of unbiased news and information to millions of listeners world-wide.

RADIO 3'S SHOCK JOCK

Compared with the World Service row, other controversies involving BBC Radio were less spectacular, but still generated considerable debate. One such was the future of Radio 3, which became a 24-hour service in May. Much of the concern involved controller Nicholas Kenyon's abortive attempt to broaden the network's appeal by shunting *Composer of the Week* to a later time to make way for a new 9 a.m. show *Morning Collection*, hosted by ex-Radio 1 DJ Paul Gambaccini.

Recruiting Mr Gambaccini from Radio 3's commercial rival Classic FM provoked outrage from many of Radio 3's small but vociferous band of fans, who disliked his sugary commentaries and mid-Atlantic accent. One listener complained that 'he sounds as if he's selling raspberry ripple'. After six months on air it was announced that Mr Gambaccini was being dropped. Some critics claimed this was less to do with objections from the newly founded Save Radio 3 Campaign than the fact that the new presenter had failed to improve ratings. Mr Birt was uncomfortably aware that Radio 3 spends almost a quarter of BBC Radio's budget while delivering only 3 per cent of the radio audience; year-on-year, audiences had decreased by 200,000. Meanwhile, Classic FM was thriving.

Brian Kay, another new recruit to Radio 3 denounced by network diehards, was voted music presenter of the year at the Sony Awards in April 1996. Radio 3 also collected a prize for its 12-month season of British music and culture *Fairest Isle*, featuring the work of 650 British composers. Also outstanding, critics agreed, was *The Unknown Coleridge*, a programme exploring the life of the romantic poet. On Radio 4, *This Sceptred Isle*, a year-long history of Britain that ended in June, drew praise from critics. The *Sunday Times'* Paul Donovan described the aural epic as 'one of the greatest treats for listeners in recent years'. There was disappointment when John Tusa had to relinquish the role of presenting *20/20: A View of the Century*, a history series conceived by the late Brian Redhead, because Mr Tusa's new job running London's Barbican Centre did not allow him enough time to complete the project. His successor, Michael Ignatieff, according to one reviewer, failed to match the quality of Mr Tusa's commentaries.

TODAY'S EXITS

Radio 4's early morning current affairs show *Today* continued to set the daily news agenda for much of the nation. The programme was the subject of headlines when the BBC failed to renew the contract of its longest-serving presenter Peter Hobday, a *Today* regular for 14 years. The *Today* item 'Thought for the Day' came under scrutiny in the spring when it was announced that seven of its regular presenters were being 'rested'. One of these was the Bishop of Oxford, the Rt. Revd Richard Harries, a 'Thought for the Day' contributor for 24 years. The bishop has been an outspoken opponent of government policies on taxation and overseas aid but the BBC denied *Today* was acting because of pressure from Whitehall. The decision was made, explained a spokeswoman, simply to 'refresh' the programme.

During the year three Radio 4 stalwarts turned 50: *Woman's Hour*, *From Our Own Correspondent* and *Letter From America*. Another of the network's institutions, *The Archers*, attracted attention when the veteran serial ran a storyline portraying domestic violence; Shula was struck by her partner Simon. In the summer it was announced that a new Radio 4 controller, James Boyle, would take over in September 1996 following the retirement of Michael Green.

Radio 2 came under new management in 1995–6 with James Moir, a former head of BBC Television light entertainment, succeeding Frances Line as the station's controller. In common with Radio 3, Radio 2 faced growing competition and needed to attract new listeners without alienating traditional audiences. By playing more music from the 1960s and 1970s, Radio 2 attempted to woo listeners in their forties who previously had tuned in to Radio 1. In April Mr Moir announced several new signings, including Steve Wright, Debbie Thrower and Michael Parkinson.

The success in repositioning Radio 1 as a genuinely youth-orientated station continued during 1995–6. The once flagging network was now so fashionable that the station's blacklisting of a new recording by the Beatles, *Real Love*, released in March 1996, added to its credibility. Overall, Radio 1 attracted 800,000 new listeners, giving it a weekly audience of more than 13 million. The increase was largely attributed to the popularity of Chris Evans's breakfast show. Mr Evans was voted broadcaster of the year at the Sony Awards but his irreverent style was becoming too much for some people. Controversial segments included an item entitled 'I'm In Bed With My Boyfriend' in which female callers recited a poem while 'sucking their boyfriend's lollipop'. This was not the only element of Mr Evans's approach to cause offence. As the *Daily Telegraph*'s Tom Leonard remarked: 'More recently his style has shifted from smutty innuendo to a startling vindictiveness towards fellow celebrities. Evans increasingly seems to use his show to attack anyone he does not like.' On one occasion Mr Evans was docked a day's pay (reputed to be £7,000) when he failed to turn up for work because he was suffering from a hangover.

The BBC's newest national station, Radio 5 Live, went from strength to strength in 1995–6 despite the occasional problem in juggling schedules to meet the conflicting demands of those listeners who wanted sports coverage and those who preferred news. In April 1996, Radio 5 Live was voted station of the year at the Sony Awards.

INDEPENDENTS

In the commercial sector there were signs of growing confidence at Classic FM, boosted further by a clause in the Broadcasting Act enabling the station to keep its licence for another 14 years provided its programmes were judged satisfactory by the Radio Authority. Classic FM's advertising revenue grew from £8 million in 1992–3 to £18 million in 1995–6. Programme highlights included a day-long 'operathon' in May 1996, staged with Welsh National Opera, and exclusive coverage of a July concert by the Three Tenors in London.

Talk Radio, which celebrated its first birthday in February, experienced difficulties in 1995–6. In September 1995 a shift in emphasis was signalled when Talk abandoned its 'shock jock' policy, sacking DJs Terry Christian and Caesar the Geezer, a Greek nightclub bouncer from Essex. Jerry Thomas, Talk's programme director, said he wanted to turn the station into 'the GMTV of the airwaves'. This was easier said than done. Early in 1996 several of Talk's high-profile presenters, including Jeremy Beadle and Vanessa Feltz, left the network. There were complaints that the service was failing to live up to the terms of its contract by not broadcasting drama and readings. Mr Thomas was himself replaced by Jason Bryant in April 1996. By the summer a new general manager, former BBC Radio executive Paul Robinson, was attempting to increase Talk's ratings, stuck at around two million a week, and to improve its financial prospects. Talk was said to be losing up to £1 million a month.

The number of regional commercial stations continued to increase. Seven new stations began broadcasting in 1995–6. In London there were around 20 different services, with more to come. In July 1996, 25 groups applied for what was likely to be the last London FM station. Not all the fledgling services, however, were successful. Viva, the all-women station launched in the capital in summer 1995, recorded disastrously low audience figures and at the time of going to press was preparing for a late 1996 relaunch.

TELEVISION AWARD WINNERS

BAFTA AWARDS 1996
Best single drama – *Persuasion*
Best drama series – *Cracker*
Best drama serial – *The Politician's Wife*
Best light entertainment – *The Mrs Merton Show*
Best comedy – *Father Ted*
Best actor – Robbie Coltrane, *Cracker*
Best actress – Jennifer Ehle, *Pride and Prejudice*
Best comedy performance – Martin Clunes, *Men Behaving Badly*
Best light entertainment performance – Rory Bremner, *Rory Bremner – Who Else?*
Best factual series – *The Death of Yugoslavia*
Best arts programme (Huw Wheldon award) – *Children of the Revolution*
Best children's factual programme – *Short Change*
Best children's fictional programme – *Coping With Christmas*
Flaherty documentary award – *The Betrayed*
Best news coverage – Channel 4 news coverage of war crimes in former Yugoslavia
Best sports/events coverage – VE Day coverage
Best talk show – *Panorama* interview with the Princess of Wales
People's vote for favourite programme – *The X Files*
BAFTA Fellowship – John Schlesinger
Richard Dimbleby award (for most important personal contribution in factual television) – Jeremy Paxman
The Dennis Potter award – Roy Clark

ROYAL TELEVISION SOCIETY AWARDS 1995
Entertainment – *Shooting Stars*
Situation Comedy – *Men Behaving Badly*
Single Documentary – *True Stories: The Betrayed*
Documentary Series – *The Factory*
Presenter – John Tusa
Male Actor – Robert Carlyle, *Hamish MacBeth* and *Love Bites – Go Now*
Female Actor – Helen McCrory, *Streetlife*
Single Drama – *11 Men Against 11*
Drama Serial – *Hearts and Minds*
Drama Series – *Preston Front*
TV Performance – Caroline Hook
Sports Coverage – Sky Sports, *Super Sunday*
Sports News – BBC *Nine O'Clock News*, England fans riot in Dublin
Sports Documentary – BBC TV Sport, *Ayrton Senna*
Sports Presenter – Steve Rider (BBC)
Live Event – BBC Television, VJ50: The Final Tribute
News International – ITN, The Fall of Grozny
Home News – *Newsnight* (BBC), The Scott Report
News Event – BBC, Rabin's Assassination
Current Affairs International – Lauderdale Production for Channel 4, *The Dying Rooms*
Current Affairs Home – TVF Productions for Channel 4, *Dispatches: The Torture Trail*
Television Journalist of the Year – Martin Bashir (BBC)
The Gold Medal – Bill Cotton

Conservation and Heritage

THE NATURAL ENVIRONMENT

THE NEWBURY BYPASS

Early in 1996 preparatory tree clearance work began on the Newbury bypass. Press attention was attracted by the protesters, who successfully delayed operations and ensured that the work would be headline news, and also very expensive in terms of security arrangements. Local opinion is evenly divided; the local MP, David Rendel, and many residents and businesses in Newbury, favour the bypass (really a strengthening of the A34 'Euroroute') in the belief that it will ease traffic congestion in the town. The construction work is expected to cost some £101 million.

The 11 km route was chosen after two lengthy public inquiries. It runs west of the town through attractive countryside, and will damage parts of the Kennet and Lambourn valleys, as well as two battlefields, numerous archaeological sites and a wooded part of Snelsmore Common. Press attention was focused on an obscure snail, *Vertigo moulinsiana*, which had been found in river marshes in the path of the bypass in March 1996, and which, fortuitously, is a protected species under European legislation. A group of protesters took a case to the High Court in an attempt to legalize their presence on the grounds that they were protecting the snail. Although the judge disallowed this appeal, he did recommend that the Secretary of State for the Environment (John Gummer) should undertake to minimize damage to the habitat of the snails. In consequence, English Nature was able to propose a series of measures reducing the extent of habitat loss, 'creating' new areas of habitat elsewhere, and even locating and moving some of the tiny snails from the path of the road. Unfortunately English Nature's main recommendation – to build a viaduct in place of an earth embankment and bridge – was ignored.

Although the fuss about a little-known snail has its element of farce, it proved a useful legal instrument for those who oppose the bypass. For most people, though, it is the destruction of one of the prettiest remaining corners of rural Berkshire that is the real significance of the Newbury bypass.

According to the Wildlife Trusts, proposed road schemes threaten some 718 British wildlife sites nation-wide, including 76 SSSIs and 31 ancient woods. The main habitats affected are woodland, species-rich grassland and wet places, especially along river valleys. Some 70 of these have been reprieved by cuts in the Department of Transport road programme. The most contentious remaining schemes include the Salisbury bypass, which threatens water meadows by the River Avon; the M4 relief road in South Wales, which runs along the edge of the Gwent Levels; and numerous places affected by the widening of the A1 and M25. A Green Paper on transport, published by the Government in April 1996, acknowledged the public disquiet caused by road building, but proposed few solutions.

BIODIVERSITY

The UK Biodiversity Action Plan, which was published in December 1995, received formal government approval in May 1996. The plan was prepared by the Biodiversity Action Plan steering group, a unique collaboration between government departments, farmers, industry, local government, research institutes and conservation bodies. It sets targets for the conservation of 116 declining or endangered species of wild animals, birds, insects and plants, and for 14 'priority wildlife habitats'. The plan is one of four UK official strategies prepared in response to the 'Earth Summit', held in Rio de Janeiro in 1992, the others being Sustainable Development, Climatic Change and Sustainable Forestry.

The targets set by the Biodiversity plan are very precise. For example, one aim is to raise the declining population of bitterns from 15 'booming males' (the only practicable method of assessing numbers) to 50 by the year 2010. To achieve this, a group of conservation bodies is creating new reed beds in the Norfolk Broads and elsewhere by digging out pools and old dykes, and raising water levels. The Government hopes that industry and private enterprise will 'champion' some of the listed species. Conservation bodies are sponsoring others: the charity Plantlife acts as fairy godmother to the endangered starfruit plant, while the RSPB is launching a campaign to save the skylark.

The action plan has successfully united land-users, politicians and conservationists in a common cause, and cleverly borrowed the Government's own language of targets and strategies. But the planners may have been carried into a world of make-believe, where nature is a product, and skylarks and starfruits can be created on a production line. Already there are local biodiversity plans springing up, each with their own quantified targets, but with few resources. The Government is happy with the venture, since it involves mainly private sector finance.

One of the more solid recommendations of the steering group was for a UK Biodiversity Database to form a national centre and information service for biological records in Britain. Although a limited service exists at the Biological Records Centre at

Monkswood, most UK species records are organized on a local basis, and so the information is
widely dispersed and frequently inaccessible. The
Joint Nature Conservation Committee intends to
seek National Lottery funds for the project through
the Millennium Fund.

NATURE CONSERVATION AGENCIES

Since their creation in 1991, the four government
agencies responsible for nature conservation have
been subjected to an apparently endless series of
reviews. The overall loser is the Joint Nature
Conservation Committee (JNCC), which none of
the other three bodies support, and which was only
forced on the Government by the House of Lords.
An internal review was completed in May 1996, and
was predictably savage. The JNCC's core workforce has been cut and more of its activities
contracted out; on the other hand, the JNCC has
been made more aware of its precise purpose.

The review of Scottish Natural Heritage (SNH)
resulted in a budget cut of £4.3 million (14 per cent).
It is to spend proportionately less time on public
access and 'wider countryside' matters, such as
transport policy and agriculture, and more on
routine statutory site safeguard. It is said that the
Scottish Office was not amused at SNH's robust
opposition last year to a super-quarry on the island
of Harris.

English Nature underwent a financial management and policy review, and decided that it too
could contract out more of its work. Its budgetary
reduction, amounting to 8 per cent, will reduce
grant-aid, which some outsiders regard as this
body's most useful purpose, and staff training.

The happiest of the four bodies is the Countryside Council for Wales (CCW). Cut to the bone in
1995 by the then Secretary of State for Wales (John
Redwood), the Council has since been a model of
good housekeeping and has made intelligent use of
EU funding opportunities. Its annual grant-in-aid
has been increased by 20 per cent under Redwood's
more emollient successor, William Hague.

OTTER RECOVERY

The most recent national survey of the otter shows a
continued increase in the numbers of this elusive
animal as it moves back into river systems left vacant
since the 1950s. The survey, carried out between
1991 and 1994, was the third since monitoring began
in 1977. It shows relatively healthy populations in
the otter's strongholds in Scotland, mid-Wales and
Devon, a significant increase in East Anglia, where
otters have been released by the Vincent Wildlife
Trust, and a steady advance into the Midlands from
the north and west.

It is clear now that the main reason for the decline
of the otter in the 1950s and 1960s was the widespread use of organochlorine pesticides, such as
DDT and dieldrin, as seed dressings. These poisonous chemicals got into the water supply, and so into
the fish eaten by otters. Recovery has been slow,

possibly because of the continued use of PCB
pesticides. The mink, often pilloried as a cause of
the otter's decline, may be an 'innocent' party.
Observations have shown that although the two
mammals do compete for food, more often than not
the otter wins, and it may be displacing its smaller
rival as it continues to increase in numbers. Don
Jefferies, co-author of the survey report, cites
evidence that otters on occasion fight and kill mink.
It is probable that the otter and mink will co-exist,
but that the latter will be reduced in numbers. If so,
this may be good news for the water vole, whose
numbers have dropped sharply, apparently because
too many have fallen victim to mink.

THE NEW FOREST

A report by a recently-retired conservation officer
for the New Forest, Colin Tubbs, criticized Forestry Enterprise (an arm of the Forestry Commission which manages its forests) for its practices in the
New Forest. The nub of the problem is that
although the New Forest is one of the premier
wildlife sites in Europe, the Commission, which has
been responsible for the Forest under the Crown
since 1919, has consistently placed timber production objectives ahead of those of amenity and
conservation. Although Forestry Enterprise is now
committed, under government policy, to conserve
the traditional character of the Forest, Tubbs lists
many examples of contrary practice. These include
heavy thinning, the cutting and felling of ancient
trees, and a potentially damaging forward programme of 'silvicultural cleansing' of non-profitable
trees. He concludes that Forestry Enterprise's
programme falls foul of the 1877 New Forest Act, a
view which echoes that of a parliamentary commission in 1980, and he calls for the withdrawal of the
programme.

Whether the commercial foresters who run the
New Forest are fit guardians for such a place is
doubted by many. This concern was underlined
early in 1996 when a businessman, David Bills, was
appointed director-general of the Forestry Commission. Bills made his name and fortune cutting
down virgin forests in Tasmania, and opposed the
designation of parts of the forests as World Heritage
Areas.

FUNICULAR RAILWAY AT CAIRN GORM

A scheme to build a funicular railway to the summit
of Cairn Gorm in the Scottish Highlands was
approved by the local planning authority despite
opposition by conservation bodies. Since the 1960s,
Cairn Gorm has been the main centre for organized
downhill skiing in Britain, but the 50,000 summer
visitors have had to rely on a ski-tow to convey them
to the summit. A rope-drawn (funicular) railway
will greatly increase the numbers of summer
tourists; the Cairngorm Chairlift Company hopes
to attract some 200,000 visitors each year. The
project will cost £17 million, two-thirds of which
will come from the public purse.

The proposal heightens the evidently insoluble conflict between commercial and protection interests in the Cairngorms, which is Britain's premier area of mountain wilderness and a potential world heritage site. Nevertheless, Scottish Natural Heritage withdrew its initial objection to the scheme, provided that the company produces an acceptable 'visitor management plan' to safeguard the fragile mountain plateau. SNH's deputy chairman, the social historian Christopher Smout, dissented publicly from his colleagues, complaining that the proposal was 'thoroughly unsatisfactory' and wholly inappropriate in such an area.

Opposition to the scheme has been led by the RSPB, which has a large nature reserve in the area and is concerned at disturbance to rare nesting birds, such as dotterel and snow bunting. It has produced a counter proposal for a 'mountain ride experience', which makes greater use of the more robust lower slopes and closes the existing car park in summer. Unless the Scottish Secretary decides to intervene, however, the chairlift company will be free to build a highly intrusive structure in one of the finest mountain landscapes in Britain.

SEA EMPRESS DISASTER

On 15 February 1996 the tanker *Sea Empress* ran aground off St Anne's Head, Pembrokeshire. Over the next few days most of its cargo of oil, some 72,000 tonnes, spilled into the sea, producing a huge slick that contaminated 200 km of scenic cliffs, sandy bays and offshore islands. The *Sea Empress* was a thin-skinned, single-hulled tanker. No heavy-duty tug was available to tow it to port, and the salvage operation seems to have been bungled, perhaps in a desire to save the ship at the expense of the coastal environment. The Department of Transport rejected calls for an independent inquiry; instead, a report will be produced by its own Marine Accident Investigation Branch. Up to July, the clean-up operation had cost some £11 million, exclusive of compensation paid.

The spill blackened some 26 Sites of Special Scientific Interest (SSSIs) between St David's Head and the Twyi estuary, including the islands of Skomer and Lundy, both Marine Nature Reserves. About 7,000 seabirds were found dead or oiled, and the RSPB estimates the total number of bird victims at 25,000. The most prominent were about 4,000 common Scoter ducks, which gather in Carmarthen Bay in early spring before dispersing to nesting sites in the far north. Most of the remainder were guillemots and razorbills. There was widespread pollution to rock pools and shore life, which may or may not have long-term consequences. It may be that the 445 tonnes of dispersants used in a hurried attempt to clean the beaches before the holiday season began caused as much damage as the slick itself. However, it now appears that the more pessimistic forecasts of environmental catastrophe, given much prominence by the press, were ill-founded.

Apart from the oiled seabirds, the main impact was commercial. Local trawling and shellfish enterprises were closed by a fishing ban, and the hotel trade was badly hit. The recovery of the coastal wildlife is being monitored, with particular attention given to the health of grey seals using this part of the coast.

LAPPEL BANK TEST-CASE

The Government's decision to omit an important site for birds from its proposed Special Protection Area (SPA) in the Medway estuary resulted in a test case in the European Court. Lappel Bank, an erstwhile area of mudflats and shingle at the mouth of the Medway, was scheduled for development as part of an improvement of cargo-holding facilities for the Medway ports. It also happened to be used by shore birds on migration in sufficient numbers to warrant protection under EU legislation.

The RSPB took the case to the European Court and won. The Court found that the Government had acted illegally by taking economic factors into account when defining the boundaries of the Special Protection Area. However, the Court said that it might have been legal to damage the area after due scheduling, under certain circumstances. This ruling does not save Lappel Bank, which has already disappeared under concrete and is now a storage area for imported Japanese cars. The case does, however, have implications for development projects throughout the EU, not least in Britain, where there are similar conflicts between commerce and conservation at the Ipswich and Southampton docks, in the Humber estuary, and elsewhere. The RSPB intends to ask the Government to create new shoreline habitat in compensation for the loss of 65 ha at Lappel Bank.

METAL POLLUTION IN AVON GORGE

The rare rock plants of Avon Gorge, near Bristol, may be contaminated by heavy metal pollution following restoration work on Clifton suspension bridge. The bridge crosses the gorge at St Vincent's rocks, which is the only mainland British site of round-headed leek (*Allium sphaerocephalon*) and holds a significant proportion of plants of Bristol rock-cress (*Arabis scabra*) and Western spiked speedwell (*Veronica spicata*).

During summer 1995 the bridge was shot-blasted with copper slag to remove the old paint. Some months later, a botanist noticed large quantities of this material on rocks beneath the bridge, and a dusting of finer grains further down the gorge. The contractors had claimed that the material was 'inert'. Laboratory sampling proved that this was not the case, and that the fall-out contains high levels of zinc, cadmium and other toxic metals. Moreover, up to 100 tonnes had been used, and it is impracticable to remove it from the precipitous cliffs and ledges where the rare plants grow.

The contamination has the potential to pollute the soils for years to come, and many plants are likely to die in consequence, although the full impact of the accident cannot be predicted. The operation seems to have slipped through the various safety nets – SSSI, National Nature Reserve, proposed Special Area for Conservation, etc. – protecting the gorge and its rare flora. It appears that English Nature accepted the owning trust's assurance that the material was harmless, and that no-one thought to test it first.

DAMAGE TO SSSIs

One of the duties of the Joint Nature Conservation Committee is to monitor damage to SSSIs. This is usually divided into short-term damage, meaning that recovery is thought possible, and long-term damage, where recovery is probably not possible. A third category, 'partial damage', means that part of the site has been obliterated. The JNCC's most recent report outlined an apparent dramatic decrease in short-term damage, from 82,849 ha in 1991 to only 920 ha in 1995. Unfortunately, closer inspection reveals that the monitoring system was changed in 1994 so that the two sets of figures are not comparable. By apparent contrast, partial loss increased from only 38 ha in 1994 to an all-time high of 242 ha in 1995. As for long-term damage, some 1,267 ha on 48 SSSIs was lost. These figures do not take account of insidious damage from pollutants and acid precipitation.

Because of imperfections in the monitoring systems, and a tendency to move the goal posts every few years, the government agencies have failed to show whether damage to protected sites is in fact increasing or decreasing. This failing is something of a blessing to developers.

THE BUILT ENVIRONMENT

In 1995 the Heritage Lottery Fund, which distributes the proceeds from the National Lottery allocated to the national heritage, received £250 million for distribution, and the prediction for 1996 is that it will receive at least £260 million. All 'heritage' causes stand to benefit, including buildings, land, works of art, archives and museums. Even so, the Lottery promises to double or treble the amount available for the upkeep and conversion of historic buildings when compared with the funds available through English Heritage, which offered in 1994–5 grants to the value of £33.9 million. In addition, many projects which cannot be helped by English Heritage (or indeed Historic Scotland or Cadw) are eligible for lottery funding, for example Grade II listed buildings outside a conservation area. On the other hand, the ownership of the historic building in question can severely limit its eligibility for lottery funding. No private individual or commercial company can currently receive a lottery grant; this restriction does not apply to grants offered by English Heritage and other quangos.

However, both the Government and the Labour Party promised in 1996 to consider a relaxation of these restrictions.

LOTTERY GRANTS

By July 1996 the Heritage Lottery Fund had supported a total of 382 projects, with grants totalling £256.7 million; of this total, £4 million had been spent in Northern Ireland (2 per cent); £4.2 million in Wales (2 per cent); £35.4 million in Scotland (14 per cent) and the remainder in England (82 per cent). More than half the grants were for under £100,000.

An extraordinary variety of projects received assistance, including the Church of St Mary in the Castle, Hastings (£1.4 million), to complete a conversion scheme that has saved it from demolition; the Tower of London (£500,000), towards improvements to its setting; the Lowfield Heath Windmill at Charlwood, Surrey (£35,000); Clevedon Pier at Clevedon, Avon (£475,000); 10 Brunswick Square, Hove (£39,000), which is to become a House Museum along the lines of those already established in Bath and Edinburgh; the Watts Memorial Chapel at Compton, Surrey (£220,000), one of the most extraordinary buildings of High Victorian England; Wick Court, Glos (£330,000), to permit this Grade II* listed building to be taken over by Farms for City Children; Croome Park, Worcs (£4.917 million), to allow this outstanding landscape by Capability Brown to be passed to the National Trust; the Garnethill Synagogue, Glasgow (£59,000), built in 1859 and still in use for worship but also the home of the Scottish Jewish Archives Centre; Cheetham's Library, Manchester (£1.814 million), to endow and to repair 'the oldest surviving public library in the country with a history of continuous use for 340 years'; St George's Market, Belfast (£2.045 million), to repair and diversify the use of this remarkable late 19th-century complex; the Captain Cook Birthplace Museum in Middlesbrough, Cleveland (£800,000), to improve its facilities; Christ Church, in Spitalfields, London (£2.441 million), to complete the repair of Hawksmoor's masterpiece; and the Handel House Museum at 23–25 Brook Street, Mayfair (£500,000), to repair two unoccupied Georgian houses and establish a museum to the most famous resident of no. 25, George Frederic Handel, who lived there from 1723 until his death in 1759.

English Heritage itself was among the beneficiaries, receiving help for a number of schemes, including £112,000 to re-establish the cascade in the grounds of Chiswick House, London. A total of £50 million between 1996 and 1999 was allocated towards the regeneration of urban parks.

GOVERNMENT FUNDING CUTS

The income from the National Lottery may have exceeded almost all expectations, but the longer-established state agencies faced cuts in their funding in 1996, with the prospect of more to come. Among clients of the Department of National Heritage, only tourism and the Historic Royal Palaces Agency escaped virtually unscathed, although the increase to the Agency of £1 million in 1996–7, to £12.7 million, was mainly to allow the completion of the new Royal Armouries Museum in Leeds and will not be reflected in future years.

The grant for English Heritage was set at £103 million in 1996–7, falling to £101 million by 1998–9. The Heritage Memorial Fund received only £8 million in 1996–7, falling to £7.5 million by 1998–9. The Royal Commission on the Historical Monuments of England experienced an 8.2 per cent cut in its operational budget for 1996–7, which forced it to reduce the number of its permanent staff from 260 in June 1995 to 242 by April 1996.

English Heritage and equivalent bodies are being forced by the cuts to maximize their income from other sources, including gate receipts and fees from the Heritage Lottery Fund for expert advice.

HERITAGE BODIES

In 1994–5 English Heritage offered over £32 million in grants, of which £14 million went to places of worship. Its annual report for the year confirms that Conservation Area Partnerships have been formed with a quarter of all local authorities. Its total membership is now 340,000. More people signed on as members at the newly-opened Brodsworth Hall near Doncaster than at any other site. Alongside Brodsworth, Eltham Palace in south London was the most prestigious new English Heritage attraction.

The success of the National Trust continued unabated in the period under review. It has responsibility for 233 historic buildings open to the public in England, and its total expenditure in 1994–5 was £127.6 million. Its membership total stood at 2.21 million, more than that of all political parties put together. In 1995–6 it took some bold decisions on acquisitions, going beyond the archetypes of aristocratic country houses and tracts of unspoilt land. Its new purchases included 20 Forthlin Road, Liverpool, 'a typical 1950s mid-terrace house with a concrete tiled roof' which from 1955 to 1964 was the family home of Paul McCartney, member of the Beatles. Another 'shrine' taken into Trust hands in the course of the year was 2 Willow Road, Hampstead, London, another modest 20th-century house but one built and furnished by the leading modernist architect Erno Goldfinger. The Trust also explored the possibility of taking into care the Bedminster Union Workhouse near Bristol, to create 'a museum on the lives of the poor and the destitute'.

LISTING

In 1994, 4,129 historic buildings were added to the statutory lists in England, with a further 2,056 in 1995, bringing the total in December 1995 to 448,835. Of these, 6,090 were in the virtually sacrosanct Grade I category, some 23,000 were Grade II* and the remainder were Grade II. (An analysis by English Heritage in 1994 of structures in the Grade I category had renumbered the total to 11,600, an increase largely explained by itemizing terraces in their constituent units. However, that figure is not in government use.) Places of worship accounted for 40 per cent of the total.

By December 1995 the number of conservation areas in England reached 8,435, compared with 5,194 in April 1983 and 1,930 in October 1975. By December 1995, 16,023 sites had been scheduled as ancient monuments, the great majority being buried remains, ruins or monuments of industrial archaeology.

The Department of National Heritage has carried forward a programme of consultations prior to listing, something which has never hitherto been attempted. This democratization of the process is intended to involve interested members of the public as well as the owner of the property in question. In summer 1996 the Government confirmed its disposition to limit such consultations to the more controversial areas of post-war listing and the thematic surveys of historic buildings by type. This suggestion was included in a Green Paper *Protecting our Heritage*, which was issued for a three-month consultation period and which also asked for views on other proposed changes, particularly the delegation of scheduled monument consent procedures to local planning authorities, the introduction of a form of provisional listing for post-war buildings, and greater use of the Certificate of Immunity from Listing.

Additions to the statutory lists in the period under review included the memorial of 1924 to the novelist Joseph Conrad in Canterbury city cemetery, the soup kitchen of 1872 built in Hereford by the Hereford Society for Aiding the Industrious, and the Queen's Arms public house of 1828 at Patricroft, Greater Manchester, described as 'the first railway pub in the world'.

Listing does not mean that the building has to be preserved in perpetuity; it establishes a presumption in favour of retention, but that presumption can be set aside. Listed building consent for total demolition was granted in respect of 92 buildings in England in 1994, and in respect of 51 buildings in 1995. Important buildings still face demolition, but in recent years proposals for extension or reconstruction have proved just as controversial. Undoubtedly the most problematic case in 1995–6 was the proposed rebuilding of the Grade I listed medieval St Ethelburga's church in the City of London, where the west wall and roof were destroyed in the IRA bomb explosion in 1993. The radical rebuilding scheme, supported by the Bishop of London and his architectural assessors, was refused planning consent by the Corporation of London in summer 1996.

NOVELTIES

In 1995–6 a number of historic buildings opened to the public for the first time. These included

Crownhill Fort, Plymouth; Wingfield Manor at South Wingfield, Derbyshire; the Galleries of Justice in Nottingham; Taplow Court, Bucks; and the workhouse at Ripon, N. Yorks, as the Museum of Yorkshire Poor Law. Houghton House, the great Palladian mansion in Norfolk, reopened after two years' closure for restoration, whilst an appeal was launched to save and open to the public the garden created by the architect Sir Frederick Gibberd at Harlow. Perhaps the single most exciting discovery, although it is not yet open to the public, was the truncated remains of Britain's only surviving medieval synagogue, dating from c.1180, found in a shop basement at Guildford, Surrey.

The capacity of enthusiasts to come together with the like-minded to pursue their interests resulted in the launch of a number of new organizations. These included a Society for Church Archaeology; the Friends of Adam in London, established to campaign for the works of Robert Adam in the capital; the Pugin Society, dedicated eponymously to the man who more than any other gave the Gothic revival its philosophical base; 'Save Our Parsonages'; and the Village Lock Up Association.

The year also saw the launch of the new and prestigious NPI National Heritage Awards. The public were invited to vote for the historic attraction they most enjoyed visiting in 1995; categorization was by owner. The winner among National Trust properties was Fountains Abbey, and that for the National Trust for Scotland was Culzean Castle, Ayrshire. Chatsworth was the winner among privately-owned properties, and from among English Heritage's holding the winner was Bolsover Castle, Derbyshire.

WALES

The 1994–5 annual report of Cadw: Welsh Historic Monuments noted that the total number of listed buildings in Wales had risen to 17,164 by 31 March 1995, an increase of 1,076 over the previous year. In the same period 19 applications were lodged for total demolition of a listed building. Grants totalling £2.594 million were offered to outstanding secular buildings, £617,000 to outstanding buildings in use for worship and £830,000 for schemes within conservation areas. A further £361,000 was allocated towards the repair of eight cathedrals. Beneficiaries included the fishing lakes (1817–24) at Gyrn Castle, Llanasa, Clwyd; the war memorial designed by Clough Williams Ellis in 1922 at Llanfrothen, Gwynedd; and the house of 1914 in Swansea which was the birthplace and childhood home of Dylan Thomas.

SCOTLAND

Historic Scotland reported in the same period that the total of listed buildings had passed 42,000, whilst that for scheduled monuments stood at 6,720. It awarded £12.4 million in repair grants and welcomed 2.5 million visitors to sites it owned where an entry charge was levied. In December 1995 its

efforts were rewarded with the designation of the Old and New Towns of Edinburgh as a World Heritage Site, the first such designation in mainland Scotland.

Dance

The controversy over the award in July 1995 of £55 million of National Lottery proceeds to the Royal Opera House towards its redevelopment continued in the year under review. The situation was unintentionally exacerbated by the broadcast of a fly-on-the-wall television documentary series about the Royal Opera House. As one journalist wrote, it captured 'both the mundane and sublime madness that goes into creating high art'; it also showed a state of such administrative, artistic and financial ineptitude that it seems extraordinary that any successful productions ever reach the stage. It was perhaps fortunate for Jeremy Isaacs (who received a knighthood in the Queen's Birthday honours list), that he had already announced his intention to resign as director-general in 1997. The announcement that he will be replaced by Genista McIntosh, the executive director of the National Theatre, was widely welcomed.

The principle of public subsidy for the arts, and in particular for opera (since commentators frequently ignore the presence of ballet at the Royal Opera House) came into question. An unexpectedly eloquent defender was the Royal Ballet principal dancer Deborah Bull, who spoke at the Oxford Union against a motion deploring the use of Lottery money for the 'elitist' arts. She emphasized that human beings have spiritual as well as physical needs and that it is vital to support 'artistic performance at its peak'. She questioned the patronizing assumption that people can only enjoy what they have immediately to hand, and pointed out that the great artistic institutions must be 'both museum and laboratory' – preserving the artistic heritage while creating the heritage of the future. She said that artistic achievements could be argued to be an integral part of a stable culture, and that 'the art that we create today will speak for us in the future'. The motion was defeated.

London City Ballet, which survived for 18 years with minimal public funding, went into liquidation in June 1996. The company maintained consistently high standards in both its dancers and its productions, and toured to small venues throughout Britain which could not receive the larger-scale productions of other classical companies. In a year when millions of pounds of Lottery funding were awarded, it seems inexplicable that the relatively small sums that would have been needed to keep the company afloat could not be found. It has already been recognized that it makes no sense to confine Lottery funding to capital projects and to building new theatres while closing down companies. It is still necessary to insist that Lottery money should be in addition to and not a replacement for government funding for the arts. However, the guidelines for distribution have now been partially relaxed to encompass access to dance, working conditions for dancers and, possibly, training initiatives; they will have to be relaxed further if the money is to be wisely used. In August 1996 Harold King, the artistic director of London City Ballet, secured sufficient funding from Lloyds Bank and an anonymous benefactor to relaunch the company as the City Ballet of London, but further support was urgently needed to make the new company viable.

A happier outcome of Lottery funding was the award of £30 million to Sadler's Wells Theatre in north London towards a completely new state-of-the-art theatre to be built on the same site. The current theatre was built in 1931 and has many historic associations; it saw the birth of the future Royal Ballet companies and of English National Opera, and hosted many notable events, including the première of Benjamin Britten's *Peter Grimes* in 1945. It has been particularly associated with dance and has presented many important visiting companies, but the small size of the stage and the poor facilities both backstage and in the front of house were serious problems. A nostalgic but celebratory farewell gala was held on 23 June 1996 and the theatre closed on 30 June 1996; the new building is promised for 1998.

Meanwhile the Royal Opera House failed to find an appropriate home for its two companies during the planned closure of the theatre for two years from the summer of 1997. The original idea of using a purpose-built 'temporary' theatre on the south bank of the River Thames fell through because of problems over planning permission, and by the time this had happened all the other potential venues were unavailable. The Royal Ballet is therefore going to spend much of the time in short seasons at different London theatres and on extended 'Dance Bites' tours (as well as touring abroad). There are exciting possibilities here to broaden the audience for ballet, but also the danger of losing top artists to overseas companies. Moreover the Royal Ballet has been painstakingly built and nurtured over many decades and any fragmentation could be disastrous. It was somewhat ironic that the company should have marked the 50th anniversary of the reopening of the Opera House after the war at a time of such uncertainty about its immediate future. Darcey Bussell led a gala performance of *The Sleeping Beauty* on 20 February 1996, in honour of the performance of the same ballet led by Margot Fonteyn in February 1946. Leslie Edwards, who won the 1995 *Evening Standard* Award for Dance for his 'outstanding lifetime achievement', was one of many former stars of the company who took part in the gala.

WEAK WORLDLY-WISE

In artistic terms the Royal Ballet continued to struggle. Its much-trumpeted new work of the season was a full-length piece by the American choreographer Twyla Tharp, to Rossini extracts. Tharp spans the ballet-modern dance divide; *Mister Worldly-Wise* was surprisingly classical, and even in some ways traditional (one critic described it as '*Pilgrim's Progress* meets Petipa'), but failed to exploit the real strengths of the Royal Ballet dancers. It was witty and enjoyable but dramatically weak; it received a very mixed reception from the critics but audiences were largely enthusiastic. The other main new work was Matthew Hart's *Dances with Death*, a one-act work intended to depict the suffering caused by the Aids virus. A worthy aim, especially in the context of the ballet world, but with an unfortunately banal and superficial result.

The company also mounted a new production of Kenneth MacMillan's *Anastasia* with some choreographic adjustments and new designs. The production served mainly to confirm opinions of the work as impressive but flawed; the first two acts set in Imperial Russia are insufficiently eventful to sustain their length and do not gel artistically with the searingly powerful last act, which was created separately, in which Anna Anderson struggles with her identity in a lunatic asylum. The most successful new work of the season was in fact Matthew Hart's *Peter and the Wolf*, a delightful offering originally created for the Royal Ballet School's annual performance at the Opera House in the summer of 1995, with Anthony Dowell taking the roles of both the Grandfather and the Narrator with his usual dramatic brilliance. At the end of the season Matthew Hart left the Royal Ballet to join Rambert Dance Company; this was a major disappointment for the company, as it had placed great hopes in his developing choreographic talent. The company will also miss the dramatic powers of Stephen Jefferies, who left in the middle of the season to take on the artistic directorship of Hong Kong Ballet, and the versatility of Viviana Durante, who left at the end of the season for a year's leave of absence. It will, however, cope without the presence of Zoltan Solymosi, who was sacked over 'irreconcilable differences' with Anthony Dowell. Dowell's former partner at the Royal Ballet, Antoinette Sibley, who is now president of the Royal Academy of Dancing which celebrated its 75th anniversary in the year under review, received a DBE in the New Year's Honours.

One of the Royal Ballet's leading men, Adam Cooper, spent much of the season on leave of absence to perform in probably the biggest hit of the year, the all-male version of *Swan Lake* choreographed by Matthew Bourne for Adventures in Motion Pictures. This was intended as a serious reworking of the ballet rather than a Lindsay Kemp-style camp extravaganza, and it succeeded in producing a convincing and beautiful alternative to traditional productions. While sometimes confus-

ing in its mixture of comedy and gravity, it achieved a real poignancy, and Adam Cooper gave a tremendous performance as the Swan – one critic described him as 'the most fabulous sight on the London stage … wild, angelic, shockingly erotic'. The production won an Olivier award and returned for a run in London's West End in the autumn of 1996.

Birmingham Royal Ballet celebrated the 50th anniversary of the Royal Ballet's touring company in 1996. The 1995–6 season was the company's first under the directorship of David Bintley. Bintley created a full-length ballet, *Far from the Madding Crowd*, and a one-act work, *Carmina Burana*, as well as mounting five company premières and strengthening the company's roster of dancers. This was perhaps an over-ambitious programme for his first season. He seems to be going all out to please audiences – a worthy aim, but it is to be hoped that his intelligence will lead him back to the quality of choreography that he was producing until a few years ago. Both his new works were disappointing, but he did succeed in securing a Jerome Robbins work (*The Cage*) for the repertoire, a notoriously difficult feat, and he also imported two major Balanchine works, *Agon* and *Mozartiana*. Agnes Oaks and Thomas Edur, the stars of English National Ballet, are joining Birmingham Royal Ballet from the 1996–7 season, together with Ambra Vallo, another talented ENB dancer, and this bodes well for the status and future of the company.

English National Ballet had another busy and largely successful season, and has secured the London Coliseum as its Christmas 'home' in place of the Royal Festival Hall, which has always been unsatisfactory for ballet. The standard of dancing in the company is now excellent, although Agnes Oaks and Thomas Edur will be badly missed. Derek Deane mounted a production of *Alice in Wonderland* which was cleverly and imaginatively designed but choreographically moribund. However, a new production of *Cinderella* choreographed by Michael Corder, who has been absent from the British dance scene for too long, was a triumph. Corder's severely classical choreography is beautiful, musical and expressive, and is well complemented by David Walker's stylish designs; this is an important production which deserves to remain in circulation for many years. A new work by the ice-skating star Christopher Dean, entitled *Encounters* and set to songs by Paul Simon, turned out to be a professional and enjoyable if rather bland first choreographic effort. Kenneth MacMillan's *My Brother, My Sisters* also entered the company's repertoire and is a welcome indicator of Derek Deane's artistic judgement.

Scottish Ballet continued to make steady progress and undertook its usual far-reaching tour of Scotland. The recruitment of Mark Baldwin as resident choreographer in the summer of 1995 augurs well; he created two works for the company, both of which were well-received. Northern Ballet Theatre mounted yet another new production of

Don Quixote, with undistinguished choreography by Christopher Gable (who received a CBE in the Queen's Birthday honours list) and Michael Barrett-Pink, and excellent designs by Tim Goodchild. Before its untimely demise, London City Ballet had mounted an ambitious production of *Cinderella* by Matthew Hart which was rich with promise, and brought MacMillan's bitter-sweet *Solitaire* into the repertoire. The company also suffered the sudden death of leading dancer Jack Wyngaard at the age of 37.

CONTEMPORARY DANCE

Rambert Dance Company is looking in fine form. Christopher Bruce is now clearly in charge as artistic director and is putting into practice his twin aims of bridging the gap between classical and contemporary dance, and preserving Rambert's (and modern dance's) heritage as well as enriching it. He has put together a mostly new company of outstanding dancers and is achieving considerable success; he is also developing a valuable musical collaboration with London Musici under Mark Stephenson. In October 1995 Bruce brought a seminal British modern dance work, *Stabat Mater*, into the repertoire. *Stabat Mater* was created to Vivaldi's score of the same name by Robert Cohan in 1975 for London Contemporary Dance Theatre. It is a powerful work which expresses the grief of the Virgin Mary at the Cross and in so doing expresses all human grief. Bruce created two works for the company during the season. The second, *Quicksilver*, was made to celebrate the company's 70th anniversary – 1926 saw the première of Ashton's *A Tragedy of Fashion*, the first collaboration between Ashton and the company's founder, Marie Rambert. The company gave a season in London for the first time for four years in July 1996, becoming the first British contemporary dance company to perform at the London Coliseum, and proved a great success.

There is now a number of contemporary dance seasons in London each year. Dance Umbrella is still the largest and most ambitious. The 18th Umbrella, held in autumn 1995, featured Siobhan Davies, Merce Cunningham, Steve Paxton, Dana Reitz, DV8 Physical Theatre, Richard Alston, Hervé Robb and many others. Merce Cunningham presented several British premières and held an 'Event' at Riverside Studios – an evening of fragments of Cunningham works with a painted backdrop by Robert Rauschenberg. DV8's *Enter Achilles* was, as usual with the company's works, both amusing and disturbing. Other festivals included Spring Loaded, Resolution! and The Turning World. As part of The Turning World festival, the Trisha Brown Company visited Britain from the USA for the first time for five years and gave a season at the Queen Elizabeth Hall before touring Britain.

Siobhan Davies created two works in the year under review, both of them highly praised. On 2–4 February 1996 a contemporary dance marathon was held at the Royal Festival Hall and The Place

Theatre and featured work by Siobhan Davies, Mark Baldwin and others. Another notable contemporary dance event was Richard Alston's contribution to the Harrison Birtwistle retrospective held at the Queen Elizabeth Hall in May 1996; his *Bach Measures* was particularly successful. Jonathan Burrows, who won the 1995 Prudential Award for Dance, presented another pioneering work, *The Stop Quartet*. Anna Teresa de Keersmaeker became the first contemporary choreographer to brave the Royal Festival Hall, with a large-scale work to Mozart selections in July 1996.

In April 1996 the Arts Council of England published *The Policy for Dance of the English Arts Funding System*. It outlined the framework within which various elements of the funding system could develop action plans to meet specific local, regional and national needs. It also set out a range of strategies focusing on the support of dance, dancers, audiences, creativity, the national infrastructure and the 'dance economy'. The policy also expressed a welcome commitment to the establishment of a National Dance House – in the long term.

Among the losses in the dance world during the year were Lincoln Kirstein, the co-founder of New York City Ballet, who died on 5 January 1996; one of the 'baby ballerinas' of the 1930s, Tamara Toumanova, who died on 29 May 1996; and the man who inspired many dancers to take up the profession, Gene Kelly, who died on 2 February 1996.

PRODUCTIONS

ROYAL BALLET
Founded 1931 as the Vic-Wells Ballet
Royal Opera House, Covent Garden, London WC2E 9DD

World premières:
Mister Worldly-Wise (Twyla Tharp), 9 December 1995. A full-length work. Music, Rossini; design, David Roger. Cast led by Irek Mukhamedov (Mister Worldly-Wise), Darcey Bussell (Mistress Truth-on-Toe), Tetsuya Kumakawa (Master Bring-the-Bag), Leanne Benjamin, Deborah Bull, Stuart Cassidy, William Trevitt
Dances with Death (Matthew Hart), 7 February 1996. A one-act work. Music, Britten; design, Ian McNicholl. Cast led by Belinda Hatley, Jonathan Cope, Adam Cooper, Darcey Bussell. Solo violin, Vasko Vassilev
…now languorous, now wild… (Ashley Page), 7 February 1996. A *pas de deux*. Music, Liszt; design, Antony McDonald. Dancers, Viviana Durante, Irek Mukhamedov. Solo piano, Anthony Twiner
Signed in Red (Emma Diamond), 18 March 1996 at the Wycombe Swan, High Wycombe. A one-act work for four couples. Music, Wojciech Kilar; design, Allen Jones
Souvenir (Christopher Wheeldon), 18 March 1996 at the Wycombe Swan, High Wycombe. A one-act work for four couples. Music, Tchaikovsky; design, Angela Kostritzky
Odalisque (Tom Sapsford), 18 March 1996 at the Wycombe Swan, High Wycombe. A solo. Score, Fabienne Audéoud; design, Kitty Percy. Dancer, Gillian Revie
Sleeping with Audrey (Ashley Page), 18 March 1996 at the Wycombe Swan, High Wycombe. A one-act work. Score,

Orlando Gough; design, Ashley Page. Cast led by Laura Morera

Company première:
Peter and the Wolf (Matthew Hart), 22 December 1995. Music, Prokofiev; design, Ian Spurling. Cast led by Anthony Dowell (Narrator/Grandfather)

Full-length ballets from the repertoire: *Swan Lake* (Petipa/Ivanov, prod. Dowell 1987), *Manon* (MacMillan, 1974), *The Sleeping Beauty* (Petipa, prod. Dowell 1994), *Giselle* (Coralli/Perrot, prod. Wright 1985), *Anastasia* (MacMillan, 1971, new production realized by Deborah MacMillan with new designs by Bob Crowley).

One-act ballets and *pas de deux* from the repertoire: *Apollo* (Balanchine, 1928), *Side Show* (MacMillan, 1972), *Duo Concertant* (Balanchine, 1972), *Fearful Symmetries* (Page, 1994), *Les Patineurs* (Ashton, 1937), *Tales of Beatrix Potter* (Ashton, adapted for the stage by Dowell, 1992), *Rhapsody* (Ashton, 1980, with new designs by Patrick Caulfield), *The Invitation* (MacMillan, 1960), *Illuminations* (Ashton, 1950), *Symphonic Variations* (Ashton, 1946), *The Dream* (Ashton, 1964), *Le Corsaire pas de deux* (after Petipa, 1899), *Grand Pas Classique* (Gsovsky, 1949), *Tchaikovsky pas de deux* (Balanchine, 1960), *Herman Schmerman* (Forsythe, 1992), *A Month in the Country* (Ashton, 1976), *Steptext* (Forsythe, 1985), *Winter Dreams pas de deux* (MacMillan, 1991).

In addition to performances at the Royal Opera House, the company toured to Norway (Bergen), Denmark (Copenhagen), Greece (Athens), Argentina (Buenos Aires) and Israel (Caesaria and Tel Aviv) in May–June 1996. The repertoire on the tour was *Mr Worldly-Wise, Manon, The Dream, Rhapsody, A Month in the Country, Fearful Symmetries, The Sleeping Beauty, divertissements, The Invitation* and *Swan Lake*. On 31 May 1996 Darcey Bussell and Adam Cooper danced the *Winter Dreams pas de deux* at a gala at the Royal Danish Theatre, Copenhagen.

A group of Royal Ballet dancers performed in Bath, Blackpool, High Wycombe and Sheffield in March 1996 on the third 'Dance Bites' tour. They performed the world premières of *Signed in Red, Souvenir, Odalisque* and *Sleeping with Audrey*, together with … *now langourous, now wild* … and *Steptext*.

BIRMINGHAM ROYAL BALLET

Founded 1946 as the Sadler's Wells Opera Ballet
Birmingham Hippodrome, Thorp Street, Birmingham B5 4AU

World premières:
Carmina Burana (David Bintley), 27 September 1995. A one-act work. Music, Carl Orff; design, Philip Prowse. Cast led by Catherine Batcheller, Joseph Cipolla, Michael O'Hare, Yuri Zhukov
Far from the Madding Crowd (David Bintley), 21 February 1996. A full-length work. Score, Paul Reade; design, Hayden Griffin. Cast led by Leticia Müller (Bathsheba Everdene), Michael O'Hare (Gabriel Oak), Wolfgang Stollwitzer (Sergeant Troy), Joseph Cipolla (William Boldwood), Chenca Williams (Libby Smallbury)

Company premières:
Birthday Offering (Ashton), 27 September 1995. Music, Glazunov; design, Peter Farmer. Cast led by Jennifer Gelfand, Sergiu Po.bereznic, Asya Verzhibinsky, Ann Marie Little, Sandra Madgwick, Leticia Müller, Jessica Clarke
The Cage (Jerome Robbins), 28 February 1996. Given as part of Birmingham's 'Towards the Millennium' festival, a celebration of the 1950s. Music, Stravinsky; costumes, Ruth Sabotka; décor, Jean Rosenthal. Cast led by Monica Zamora, Joseph Cipolla, Catherine Batcheller, Sergiu Po.bereznic

Agon (Balanchine), 28 February 1996. Given as part of Birmingham's 'Towards the Millennium' festival. Music, Stravinsky.
Mozartiana (Balanchine), 2 May 1996. Music, Mozart; design, Rouben Ter-Arutunian. Cast led by Sabrina Lenzi
'Still Life' at the Penguin Café (David Bintley), 8 May 1996. Music, Simon Jeffes; design, Hayden Griffin

Full-length ballets from the repertoire: *Hobson's Choice* (Bintley, 1989), *Swan Lake* (Petipa/Ivanov, prod. Wright and Samsova 1981), *The Nutcracker* (Ivanov, prod. Wright, additional choreography by Vincent Redmon, 1990), *Coppélia* (Petipa, Cecchetti and Peter Wright, prod. Wright 1995), *La fille mal gardée* (Ashton, 1960).

One-act ballet from the repertoire: *Theme and Variations* (Balanchine, 1947).

On 2–4 May 1996 a choreographic project was presented at the Birmingham Hippodrome on a bill with *Mozartiana*. It involved a collaboration between 11 choreographers from within the company, who staged Mozart's *Mass in C Minor* (a score chosen by David Bintley). Students from the theatre design course at the University of Central England provided sets, costumes and lighting, and the work was sung by Ex Cathedra chamber choir.

In addition to five seasons at the Birmingham Hippodrome, the company toured to Plymouth (two seasons), Bristol (two seasons), Sunderland, Liverpool, Southampton and London (the Royal Opera House). It also toured to Japan in October–November 1995 with a repertoire of *Coppélia* and *Swan Lake*, and to Sicily in June 1996 with *La fille mal gardée*.

ENGLISH NATIONAL BALLET

Founded 1950 as London Festival Ballet
Markova House, 39 Jay Mews, London SW7 2ES

World premières:
Alice in Wonderland (Derek Deane), 19 October 1995. A full-length work. Music, Tchaikovsky, arranged by Carl Davis; design, Sue Blane; illusions, Paul Kieve. Cast led by Alice Crawford (Alice), Agnes Oaks, Thomas Edur
Cinderella (Michael Corder), 14 February 1996. A full-length work. Music, Prokofiev; design, David Walker. Cast led by Lisa Pavane (Cinderella), Greg Horsman (The Prince), Michael Coleman (Cinderella's Father), Emma Greenhalgh (Fairy Godmother), Elisabeth Miegge and Monica Perego (Stepsisters), David Peden (Dancing Master)
Encounters (Christopher Dean), 7 May 1996. A one-act work. Music, Paul Simon; design, Fotini Dimou. Cast, Thomas Edur, Greg Horsman, Agnes Oaks, Belinda Hernandez, Joanne Clarke, Monica Perego, Simona Ferrazza
Unrequited Moments (Patrick Lewis), 7 May 1996. A one-act work. Music, William Walton; design, Tim Hatley. Cast, Lisa Pavane, Greg Horsman, Dimitri Gruzdyev, Monica Perego

Company première:
My Brother, My Sisters (Kenneth MacMillan), 1 May 1996. Music, Schoenberg, Webern; design, Yolanda Sonnabend. Cast led by Rebecca Sewell, Josephine Jewkes, Robert Marshall

Full-length ballets from the repertoire: *The Nutcracker* (Ivanov, prod. Stevenson 1972), *Swan Lake* (Petipa/Ivanov, prod. Struchkova 1993), *Giselle* (Coralli/Perrot, prod. Deane 1994).

One-act ballets and *pas de deux* from the repertoire: *Symphonic Dances* (Bigonzetti, 1995), *Graduation Ball* (Lichine, 1940), *Nutcracker pas de deux* (Ivanov, prod.

Stevenson 1972), *Grand Pas* from *Paquita* (Petipa/Deane), *Square Dance* (Balanchine, 1957).

The full company toured to Southampton (three seasons), Liverpool, Manchester (two seasons), Leeds, Nottingham, London (two seasons each at the Royal Festival Hall and the London Coliseum), and Bristol. In May 1996 the company split into two groups; one group toured *Symphonic Dances*, *My Brother, My Sisters* and *Graduation Ball* to Dartford, Paignton, Basingstoke, Crawley and High Wycombe; the other group toured *Encounters*, *Unrequited Moments*, and *pas de deux* from *The Nutcracker*, *Cinderella*, *Alice in Wonderland* and *Swan Lake* to Cambridge, Barnstaple, Preston, Barrow-in-Furness and Crewe. In June 1996 the company gave one performance of *Swan Lake* in Greece (Athens).

RAMBERT DANCE COMPANY
Founded 1926 as the Marie Rambert Dancers
94 Chiswick High Road, London W4 1SH

World premières:
Small Hours (Sarah Warsop), 6 December 1995. Music, Patsy Kline
    Quicksilver (Christopher Bruce), 28 June 1996. Music, Michael Nyman; design, Marian Bruce

Company premières:
Stabat Mater (Robert Cohan), 3 October 1995. Music, Vivaldi; design, Robert Cohan. Cast led by Sara Matthews
    Moonshine (Christopher Bruce), 8 May 1996. Music, Bob Dylan; design, Walter Nobbe

Works from the repertoire: *Banter Banter* (Baldwin, 1994), *Swansong* (Bruce, 1987), *Rooster* (Bruce, 1991), *Dancing Attendance on the Cultural Chasm* (Hawkins, 1995), *Jupiter is Crying* (Jonsson, 1995), *Petite Mort* (Kylian, 1991), *Axioma 7* (Naharin, 1991), *Meeting Point* (Bruce, 1995), *Kol Simcha* (Veldman, 1995), *Dark Elegies* (Tudor, 1937).

The company performed in Carlisle, Glasgow, High Wycombe, Sheffield, Liverpool, Plymouth, Dartford, Cardiff, Bournemouth, Blackpool, Brighton, Northampton, Oxford, Canterbury, Swansea, Nottingham, Swindon, Ashton-under-Lyne, Leeds, Birmingham, Edinburgh, and London (the London Coliseum). Dancers from the company also took part in a gala performance by London Musici at St John's Smith Square, London, on 6 December 1995; works included *Odi et Amo* (Panufnik, 1995) and *Meeting Point*. A 'Music Song and Dance' matinée was held with London Musici at the London Coliseum on 13 July 1996; works included *Kol Simcha*.

The company also toured to China (Beijing) in January 1996, with a repertoire of *Petite Mort*, *Small Hours*, *Stabat Mater* and *Meeting Point*. It performed in Austria (Vienna) in March 1996, with a repertoire of *Axioma 7*, *Stabat Mater*, *Rooster*, *Swansong* and *Meeting Point*. In May – June 1996 the company performed *Axioma 7*, *Stabat Mater*, *Swansong* and *Rooster* at an international dance festival in Germany (Leverkusen, Cologne, Düsseldorf and Duisburg).

RICHARD ALSTON DANCE COMPANY
Founded 1994
The Place, 17 Duke's Road, London WC1H 9AB

All works danced by the company are choreographed by Richard Alston.

World premières:
Sometimes I Wonder, 3 October 1995. Music, Hoagy Carmichael (lyrics, Mitchell Parish); design, Belinda Ackerman
    Bach Measures, 4 May 1996. Created in collaboration with Harrison Birtwistle as part of a retrospective of the composer at the Queen Elizabeth Hall, London. Music,

Bach, arranged by Harrison Birtwistle; costumes, Fotini Dimou; set, Peter Mumford
    Orpheus Singing and Dreaming, 4 May 1996. Also created as part of the Birtwistle retrospective. Music, Harrison Birtwistle; costumes, Fotini Dimou; stage design, Peter Mumford. Cast led by Darshan Singh Bhuller, Samantha Smith. Soprano/narrator, Nicole Tibbels
    Secret Theatre, 4 May 1996. Also created as part of the Birtwistle retrospective. Music, Harrison Birtwistle

Company première:
Rainbow Bandit, 3 October 1995. Text-sound composition, Charles Amirkhanian; costumes, Belinda Ackermann

Work from the repertoire: *Lachrymae* (1994).

The company performed in Leicester, London (the Queen Elizabeth Hall), Coventry, Newcastle upon Tyne, Manchester, Horsham, Swindon, Blackpool, Oxford and at Snape Maltings. It also toured to Indonesia and the Philippines in October 1995, performing *Lachrymae*, *Rainbow Bandit* and the world première of *Sometimes I Wonder*.

SCOTTISH BALLET
Founded 1956 as the Western Theatre Ballet
261 West Princes Street, Glasgow G4 9EE

World premières:
Ae Fond Kiss (Mark Baldwin), 7 March 1996. A one-act work. Music, Stravinsky; design, Jacqueline Hancher. Cast led by Rupert Jowett, Nicci Theis
    More Poulenc (Mark Baldwin), 23 May 1996. A one-act work. Music, Poulenc; design, Andrew Flint-Shipman. Dancers, Preston Clare, Catherine Evers, Rupert Jowett, Anne Christie

Full-length ballets from the repertoire: *A Midsummer Night's Dream* (Cohan, 1993), *Coppélia* (Wright after Petipa/ Cecchetti, 1979), *Peter Pan* (Lustig, 1989), *La Sylphide* (Bournonville, prod. Hans Brenaa 1973).

One-act ballets and *pas de deux* from the repertoire: *That Certain Feeling* (Prokovsky, 1984, under the title *The Aquarium*), *Shoals of Herring pas de deux* (Maldoom, 1983), *Belong* (Vesak, 1972), *La Esmeralda pas de six* (Petipa, 1866).

The full company performed in Aberdeen (two seasons), Glasgow (three seasons), Edinburgh (three seasons), Newcastle upon Tyne (two seasons), Hull (two seasons) and Inverness (two seasons). In May – June 1996 it split into two groups and toured a repertoire of *More Poulenc*, *Belong*, *La Esmeralda pas de six*, *Shoals of Herring pas de deux* and *That Certain Feeling* to Dumfries, Dumbarton, Dunfermline, Alloa, Ayr, Dundee, Aberdeen, Fort William, Irvine, Wick, Greenock, Dornoch, Motherwell, Dunoon, Perth, Elgin, Stranraer, Inverurie, Peterhead, Montrose and Cumbernauld.

OTHER NEW WORKS
Other new works created during the season included: *Enter Achilles* (DV8 Physical Theatre under the direction of Lloyd Newson), 15 September 1995. Score, Adrian Johnston; design, Ian MacNeil. Dancers, Gabriel Castillo, Jordi Cortes-Molina, David Emanuel, Ross Hounslow, Jeremy James, Juan Kruz Diaz de Garaio Esnaola, Liam Steel, Robert Tannion
    Cinderella (Matthew Hart, for London City Ballet), 21 September 1995. A full-length work. Music, Prokofiev; design, Johan Engel and John Stevenson. Cast led by Tracey Newham Alvey (Cinderella), Michael Nunn (The Prince), Kim Miller and Jane Sanig (Stepsisters), Laura Hussey (Fairy Godmother), Avril Hurwitz (Stepmother), Paul Watson (Buttons)
    The Art of Touch (Siobhan Davies, for Siobhan Davies

Dance Company), 25 October 1995. Music, Scarlatti and Matteo Fargion; design, David Buckland

Swan Lake (Matthew Bourne, for Adventures in Motion Pictures), 9 November 1995. Music, Tchaikovsky; design, Lez Brotherston. Cast led by Adam Cooper (The Swan), Andrew Walkinshaw (The Young Prince), Fiona Chadwick (The Queen), Scott Ambler (The Prince), Emily Piercy (Prince's Girlfriend), Barry Atkinson (Private Secretary)

Don Quixote (Christopher Gable and Michael Barrett-Pink after Petipa, for Northern Ballet Theatre), 4 March 1996. Music, Minkus; design, Tim Goodchild. Cast led by Steven Wheeler (Don Quixote), Jeremy Kerridge (Sancho Panza)

Trespass (Siobhan Davies, for Siobhan Davies Dance Company), 10 May 1996. Music, Gerald Barry; design, David Buckland

---

FILM AWARD WINNERS

ACADEMY AWARDS 1995

Best picture – *Braveheart*
Best director – Mel Gibson, *Braveheart*
Best actor – Nicolas Cage, *Leaving Las Vegas*
Best actress – Susan Sarandon, *Dead Man Walking*
Best supporting actor – Kevin Spacey, *The Usual Suspects*
Best supporting actress – Mira Sorvino, *Mighty Aphrodite*
Best original screenplay – Christopher McQuarrie, *The Usual Suspects*
Best adapted screenplay – Emma Thompson, *Sense and Sensibility*
Best foreign language film – *Antonia's Line* (Netherlands)
Best original musical or comedy score – Alan Menken, Stephen Schwartz, *Pocahontas*
Best original dramatic score – Luis Bacalov, *Il Postino*
Best original song – Alan Menken, Stephen Schwartz, 'Colours of the Wind', *Pocahontas*
Best cinematography – John Toll, *Braveheart*
Best art direction – Eugenio Zanetti, *Restoration*
Best costume design – James Acheson, *Restoration*
Best film editing – Mike Hill, Dan Hanley, *Apollo 13*
Best sound – Rick Dior, Steve Pederson, Scott Millan, David MacMillan, *Apollo 13*
Best sound effects editing – Lon Bender, Per Hallberg, *Braveheart*
Best visual effects – Scott E. Anderson, Charles Gibson, Neal Scanlan, John Cox, *Babe*
Best make-up – Peter Frampton, Paul Pattison, Lois Burwell, *Braveheart*
Best animated short – *A Close Shave*
Best documentary feature – *Anne Frank Remembered*
Best short documentary – *One Survivor Remembers*
Best live action short – *Lieberman in Love*
Special achievement award – John Lasseter, *Toy Story*
Honorary awards – Kirk Douglas, Chuck Jones

BAFTA AWARDS 1996

Best film – *Sense and Sensibility*
Best director – Michael Radford, *Il Postino*
Best actor – Nigel Hawthorne, *The Madness of King George*
Best actress – Emma Thompson, *Sense and Sensibility*
Best supporting actor – Tim Roth, *Rob Roy*
Best supporting actress – Kate Winslet, *Sense and Sensibility*
Alex Korda award (British film of the year) – *The Madness of King George*
Best film not in English – *Il Postino*
People's vote for favourite film – *Braveheart*

CANNES FESTIVAL 1996

Palme d'Or – *Secrets and Lies*
Best director – Joel Coen, *Fargo*
Best actor – Daniel Auteuil, Pascal Duquenne, *The Eighth Day*
Best actress – Brenda Blethyn, *Secrets and Lies*
Grand Jury prize – *Breaking the Waves*
Special Jury Prize – *Crash*

BERLIN FESTIVAL 1996

Best film (Golden Bear) – *Sense and Sensibility*
Special Jury prize – *All Things Fair*
Best director – Yim Ho, *The Sun Has Ears*; Richard Loncraine, *Richard III*
Best actor – Sean Penn, *Dead Man Walking*
Best actress – Anouk Grinberg, *Mon Homme*

VENICE FESTIVAL 1996

Golden Lion – *Michael Collins*
Special Jury prize – *Brigands*
Best actor – Liam Neeson, *Michael Collins*
Best actress – Victoire Thivisol, *Ponette*

Film

A year of paradox, confusion and contradiction, 1995–6 saw Hollywood produce a spate of sleazy, dark, violent films, followed by a series of block-busters so mild-mannered and inoffensive that Disney's animated *The Hunchback of Nôtre Dame* looked like the most risqué film of the summer. Popular entertainments relied increasingly on special effects, becoming more and more expensive in the process, yet the most successful film of the year, in terms of profits relative to cost, was the independent comedy *The Brothers McMullen*, which took more than 67 times its budget at the box-office. It was a year in which the Academy ignored the most respected directors in Hollywood – Oliver Stone, Martin Scorsese, Michael Mann – and rewarded instead actor-director Mel Gibson (*Braveheart*), his fellow Australian Chris Noonan for a film about a talking pig, *Babe*, British nominees Mike Figgis and Mike Radford (*Leaving Las Vegas* and *Il Postino* respectively), the Taiwanese Ang Lee (*Sense and Sensibility*), and another thespian turned director, Tim Robbins (*Dead Man Walking*).

The firm pre-ceremony favourite at the Oscars was Ron Howard's *Apollo 13*, a bland but efficient mainstream film about NASA's failed moon mission with Tom Hanks as astronaut Jim Lovell. A box-office hit and a very American story ('a tragedy with a happy ending', as one critic put it), this had all the credentials the Academy usually looks for in a best picture contender, as well as Hanks coming off a two-year winning streak after *Philadelphia* and *Forrest Gump*. Against this, *Leaving Las Vegas* and *Dead Man Walking* both looked unhealthy contenders. Worthy films, certainly (the former a tale of alcoholism, the latter concerning the relationship between a death row convict and his spiritual advisor), but somehow not quite edifying enough to merit consideration for the main prize. It probably did not help that they were made outside the studio system, on relatively meagre budgets of less than $10 million.

This was also the case with Radford's charming Italian love story *Il Postino*, but this was a labour of love for star Massimo Troisi, who died of a heart attack the day after completing his performance and who was honoured with a posthumous nomination. This sentimental angle helped its American distributors, Miramax, to make the film the most successful foreign language film ever released in the USA. *Babe* was another underdog which performed well above expectations both with critics and at the box-office. A clever, charming children's film made from a young porker's point of view, it threatened to do for bacon sales what BSE was doing for British beef.

Braveheart

In the event, the other major studio film, Twentieth Century Fox's *Braveheart* won the Oscars for best film and best director. Gibson's epic about the Scottish warrior William Wallace looked splendid and featured some of the most visceral battle scenes ever mounted, but the Academy must have responded to its scope and its heart, not its simple-minded politics, narcissistic rhetoric and uneven tone. Like a previous winner, *Dances with Wolves*, *Braveheart* is credited as much for those films it emulates as for anything it actually accomplishes in its own right; here, the list would probably include David Lean's *Doctor Zhivago*, Orson Welles's *Chimes at Midnight*, and Stanley Kubrick's *Spartacus*.

The independent films were in fact superior. Susan Sarandon won the best actress Oscar for her portrait of Sister Helen Prejean, the nun whose book inspired Robbins' *Dead Man Walking*. A rigorous anti-capital punishment film that ultimately is more than an issue movie, it transformed the facts of Prejean's account into a worst-case scenario, with Sean Penn as an unapologetic rapist and murderer, and a racist to boot, whom the Sister gently guides to some painful acceptance of spiritual grace. As a director Robbins is occasionally self-conscious, but there was no faulting the two central performances, nor the integrity of the piece.

Leaving Las Vegas was even more remarkable. The film was shot on Super 16 mm film when Mike Figgis could not raise enough money for 35 mm, and even then it was only completed with a boost from his friend Sting (who also contributed a couple of songs to the soundtrack). Nicolas Cage earned an Oscar for the performance of his career as the alcoholic failed screenwriter who holes up in Vegas intent on drinking himself to death. Elisabeth Shue, an actress formerly wasted in faceless 'girl' parts in such films as *Cocktail* and *Back to the Future*, was the wounded hooker who becomes a soulmate on the condition that she never asks him to stop drinking. Figgis eschews the melodrama and the moralizing with which Hollywood traditionally sanitizes these topics in favour of a bitter, edgily funny and pathetic paean to the lonely romance of self-destruction.

Overlooked

Apollo 13 was the big loser on the night. Oddly, the Academy also failed to recognize the more ambitious pictures from within its own fold, including three three-hour epics from acclaimed film-makers. Martin Scorsese's highly touted *Casino* was the most notable example, rightly, perhaps, given its extreme violence, its over-reliance on voice-over, and its gratuitous duplication of themes, situations and characters from *Goodfellas*. It did boast a revelatory performance from Sharon Stone as the abused, exploitative wife of mobster Robert de Niro, but Scorsese failed to develop her role sufficiently. Oliver Stone's *Nixon* met with generous reviews for investing the Republican *bête noire* with tragic pathos, if not grandeur, although some found Anthony Hopkins's portrait of the former president problematic. A remarkable ensemble of look-alike actors included Paul Sorvino as Kissinger, Joan Allen as Pat Nixon, and James Woods as Erlichman. An expensive, prestigious film timed to coincide with the opening salvoes in the 1996 presidential campaign, *Nixon* proved a colossal flop at the box-office.

Although it was given short shrift by most American reviewers, the best American film of the year may have been Michael Mann's *Heat*. A thriller pitting a perfectionist criminal against an equally obsessive cop, it was not particularly original – in fact Mann had made it before himself, as a television film called *LA Takedown* – but the director's pinpoint expressionism and spare, laconic dialogue achieve an unexpected sensitivity and insight regarding male psychology. Consummate professionals living by a strict code, these men are nevertheless as lost and deluded as the Nic Cage character in *Leaving Las Vegas*. There was no more resonant scene this year than the coffee-shop meeting between the two antagonists – the first time Robert de Niro and Al Pacino have ever shared the screen.

Heat and *Casino* were two notable examples of the brief but pronounced flirtation with the seedy side of life with which Hollywood concluded 1995. Others in this ilk included Kathryn Bigelow's provocative *Strange Days*, a millennial thriller in which Ralph Fiennes investigates a series of rapes and murders recorded on a new sensory device. This ambitious, flawed film divided critics on both sides of the Atlantic and failed to find an audience anywhere, unlike David Fincher's brilliant, purgatorial *Seven*, with Brad Pitt and Morgan Freeman tracking a serial killer inspired by the deadly sins; this was a film so dark that some spectators were left groping for their flashlights. William Friedkin's *Jade*, scripted by the reliably meretricious Joe Eszterhas, and Paul Verhoeven's striptease saga *Showgirls*, also scripted by Eszterhas, both made headlines by hinting that they would push back censorship boundaries in the USA, but audiences were unimpressed with the results and the critics slated them. *From Dusk Till Dawn*, directed by Robert Rodriguez from a screenplay by Quentin Tarantino, took a killers-on-the-road scenario and transformed it into a full-scale vampire gore festival, but no matter how many severed limbs flew about, its tongue remained firmly in its cheek.

DYING A DEATH

The blockbuster films of 1996, by contrast, were mostly a benign lot. Admittedly Terry Gilliam's time-bending dystopian fantasy *12 Monkeys* wiped out five billion people – but all in the name of eco-awareness and post-modern conundrums. There was a comparable death toll in the year's most monolithic hit, *Independence Day*, effectively a re-make of H. G. Wells's *War of the Worlds*, which had

audiences cheering as aliens blitzkrieged Western civilization – including the White House, Los Angeles, St Paul's Cathedral and the Eiffel Tower. Director Roland Emmerich was careful not to show blood or pain, so the apocalypse felt as clean as a computer video game. Extraterrestrials, meanwhile, proved the perfect politically correct villain for the global market, an intergalactic locust even liberals could hate with a clear conscience.

With even the end of the world served up as feel-good entertainment, untrammelled escapism was definitely in. A specious effects film if ever there was one, *Twister* threw half-a-dozen tornadoes at its audience but could barely find the heart to kill off a single character. *Mission: Impossible* was as bloodless as the television series it rejigged, and John Woo rendered nuclear warheads harmless in the comic-book heroics of *Broken Arrow*. These films, alongside slick children's fare like *The Hunchback of Nôtre Dame*, *Toy Story* and *Babe*, and innocuous comedies like *Clueless*, *Get Shorty*, *The Nutty Professor* and *The American President* dominated the bullish US box-office in 1996. Depressingly, just two films, *Twister* and *Mission: Impossible*, took more than 50 per cent of the US market in June, with *Independence Day* approaching saturation levels in July and August. Such blanket success for a handful of blockbusters inevitably translates into less exposure for smaller films and a philosophy in Hollywood catering to the lowest common denominator. (Although the studios are obsessed with box-office records, new research which takes inflation into account revealed that *Gone with the Wind* is still box-office champion of champions, more than fifty years after its release.)

If mainstream films looked increasingly superficial as the year went on – and things do not get much more superficial than Demi Moore in *Striptease* or Matthew McConaughey, Sandra Bullock and Samuel Jackson in *A Time to Kill* – at least the independent sector continues to produce more challenging views of American culture. If the studios have an eye on international export, the independents are revelling in parochial peculiarity. Gus Van Sant was back on form with the New England small-town satire *To Die For*, the Coen brothers came up with a deliciously deadpan mid-Western morality tale in *Fargo* (set in their native Minnesota), while Wayne Wang collaborated rewardingly with novelist Paul Auster for two Brooklyn character pieces, the intricately-structured *Smoke*, and its spontaneous *alter ego*, *Blue in the Face*. Edward Burns' Woody Allenish *The Brothers McMullen* never left his own backyard (Long Island, New Jersey), and Todd Haynes' intriguingly understated *Safe* took housewife Julianne Moore from the poisonous ambience of 20th century California to the sterile environs of a new age sanctuary.

TEEN SHOCKER

But the most talked-about independent film of the year was *kids*. Directed by 53-year-old photographer Larry Clark, based on a script he worked up with 19-year-old Harmony Korine, this fiction aped *cinema-verité* fly-on-the-wall techniques to expose every parent's nightmare: a teen culture rife with promiscuity, drugs and alcohol. The film cuts between the libidinous Telly, a self-styled 'virgin surgeon', and a former conquest, Jennie, who discovers she is HIV-positive and desperately tries to alert him to the danger before he claims another victim. She fails, and, comatose after taking drugs, is raped by Telly's best friend Casper. For some critics the film was a masterpiece; others were more sceptical about its claims to credibility, and it was reviled as child pornography in some quarters. Unlike the Hollywood productions cited above, *kids* was censored by the British Board of Film Classification, which cut approximately 40 seconds and gave it an 18 certificate. In France, you had to be 12 years old to see the uncut film; 16 was the permitted age in Germany and the Netherlands; and in the USA any child could see it if accompanied by an adult.

In Britain, *kids* was measured against a home-grown *succès de scandale, Trainspotting.* The second film from the writer, producer and director team that made *Shallow Grave* (John Hodge, Andrew Macdonald and Danny Boyle), *Trainspotting* adapted from the cult novel by Irvine Welsh and made on a relatively low budget (£1.5 million) for Channel Four. It was an unlikely project, given that Welsh virtually dispensed with plot altogether, throwing together sketches, monologues and fantasies involving half-a-dozen Scottish youths growing up on heroin and the dole in the early 1980s. Written in an uncompromising vernacular, and not flinching from the harrowing details of a drug addict's life, the book seemed to defy adaptation, yet the film caught its essence in an exhilaratingly stylized, breathtakingly exuberant demonstration of cinematic verve. The film punches up the black comedy, and dares to show the rush of a drug hit ('Take the best orgasm you ever had. Multiply it by a thousand. You're still nowhere near it') before ramming home the dire, desperate straits addiction leads to. Predictably, the film was controversial, but this time the BBFC did not require any cuts, and supported by a massive marketing campaign (which cost the equivalent of half the film's budget again), *Trainspotting* went on to take over £11 million in the UK, the best takings for a British-made film since the rather different *Four Weddings and a Funeral;* it also created a potential new international star in Ewan McGregor.

REALLY EXCITING

Trainspotting was important because it showed a way forward for young British film-makers: it tackled the kind of grim, depressing subject matter associated with realists like Ken Loach, but did so in a style as exciting as anything coming from America. That excitement translated around the world. At the Cannes festival, where it was shown out of competition, *Trainspotting* became the film to see, and it was soon topping the box-office charts in countries as different as Australia and Sweden. In the USA, Miramax rerecorded some of the dialogue and acquiesced in fractional cuts; at the time of writing, the film had taken $3 million in three weeks from just a handful of screens. Even before they made *Trainspotting,* Boyle, Hodge and Macdonald were fielding lucrative offers from Hollywood, and it was encouraging that instead they chose to stick together and take on such volatile subject-matter. Like most film-makers, they are keen to gain access to the American market, but so far at least, they are doing it on their own terms.

Hollywood's lure for international directors remains undiminished. Most of the films in contention at the Oscars this year had foreign-born directors; Roland Emmerich, who directed *Independence Day,* is German; British film-makers such as Stephen Frears, Paul Anderson, Tony Scott and Antonia Bird all released US films this year. Meanwhile, the Taiwanese Ang Lee became the latest convert to the British Heritage school of cinema, with a witty, sensitive version of *Sense and Sensibility.* Although a Hollywood production, the film was quintessentially English, starring Emma Thompson, the promising newcomer Kate Winslet, Hugh Grant and Alan Rickman, and was based on Emma Thompson's own screenplay. Thompson picked up two Oscar nominations for her efforts and won the award for best adapted screenplay. Winslet also received a nomination for best supporting actress.

The English literary tradition is one of the mainstays for British film-making, and Jane Austen proved particularly fashionable this year. The BBC's *Pride and Prejudice* and *Persuasion* were popular both in the UK and abroad. *Emma* became a vehicle for Gwyneth Paltrow and Ewan McGregor, and, suitably updated, inspired Amy Heckerling's valley-girl satire *Clueless.* Shakespeare was also much in evidence. Kenneth Branagh went from the modest black and white comedy *In the Bleak Midwinter* (a behind-the-scenes farce at a makeshift production of *Hamlet*) to a four-hour, uncut, 70 mm all-star version of *Hamlet,* with a stop-off on the set of *Othello,* where he played Iago to Laurence Fishburne's Moor. Ian McKellen won further praise for his 1930s fascist vision of *Richard III,* directed with some zip by Richard Loncraine, and films of *Twelfth Night* and *Romeo and Juliet* are imminent.

SECRETS AND LIES

Good as some of these films may be, the most heartening development for British cinema in the past year has been the imaginative resource of directors engaging with contemporary experience: films like Gillies Mackinnon's *Small Faces,* Hettie Macdonald's *Beautiful Thing,* and, best of all, Mike Leigh's *Secrets and Lies,* the Palme d'Or winner at Cannes. This heartbreaking melodrama concerned a young black woman's discovery that her real mother is in fact a lonely white Londoner (Brenda Blethyn). Surprisingly, perhaps, Leigh underplays the multicultural aspect of the story, but focuses on the little evasions which permeate family life with such disastrous ramifications. For Leigh, the tragic and the banal are never far apart. This is his most mature and sympathetic film to date, and it was another local favourite at the box-office.

It was an excellent year for Channel Four, which had a stake in most of the best British films this year, and which announced plans for significantly increased investment. The BBC and ITV are both anxious to follow suit. If Britain can be said to have a film industry, then it owes it to television. Calls for tax incentives to boost local production continued, but the Government showed little sign of paying heed. Local studio facilities and technicians were again in heavy demand.

The British Film Institute announced ambitious plans to enter the digital age under the banner 'BFI 2000'. This 'radical new vision' included moving the National Film Theatre to a West End site and expanding the Museum of the Moving Image on the South Bank, with an IMAX screen to boost attendance figures. There are plans to double the budget of BFI production and for an interactive digital service, 'The Imagination Network', a fibre optic information highway providing access to the BFI's collections of film and television materials, and a filmographic database, to be located at universities, regional film theatres and arts centres, with new efforts to transfer the film archive to digital formats. Largely bankrolled by National Lottery grants, the BFI 2000 proposals coincided with a round of redundancies at the Institute and had a mixed response in the press. Just months after the plan was announced, it was beginning to look as if it would have to be modified beyond recognition.

Britain celebrated the centenary of cinema in 1996, though you could have been forgiven for missing it. The centrepiece was a day in which cinemas dropped their ticket price to just £1 – a welcome idea warmly received by the public. Classic films were revived throughout the regions, plaques went up at historic buildings around the country, a handful of exhibitions came and went, and the Royal Mail issued a set of commemorative stamps; in other words, the UK's traditionally dubious regard for the cinema was duly confirmed. At least cinema admissions went back up, after the disappointing drop in 1995.

PARISIAN RIOTS

In the non-English speaking world, only a handful of films stood out. Continental directors no longer command the respect they once did, and local industries everywhere are overshadowed by Hollywood. French cinema is probably the most rewarding in the world at the moment. It produced a thrilling, controversial picture to put beside *kids* and *Trainspotting*. *La Haine* is the second feature by the 26-year-old Mathieu Kassovitz, who may be the most gifted director to emerge in the last few years. Set against 24 hours of rioting in a housing project

outside Paris, *La Haine* has an urgent, emphatic virtuosity that reveals the influence of Spike Lee and Martin Scorsese. Kassovitz captures the dangerous edge of boredom and disaffection, the spiral of institutional racism and neglect into suppressed rage and finally just rage. But it is also a very funny film. We warm to Kassovitz's three heroes (an African, a Jew and an Arab) not because they are rebels, but because they're hopelessly, irrefutably human; missing the last train home, they break into a car and then realize that none of them can drive.

Kassovitz was unambiguous about his motives. 'This is an anti-police film,' he said, 'And that's how I want it understood.' When it was screened at the 1995 Cannes festival, the security guards in attendance turned their backs in protest, but Kassovitz went on to win the prize for best director and the film became a huge hit.

La Haine was the most talked-about of a new cycle of youthful, social conscience French films dubbed '*banlieue*' films; however, while young film-makers embraced previously ignored sectors of society, their older colleagues proved that France had not changed beyond all recognition. Claude Sautet's *Nelly and Monsieur Arnaud* was a subtle, compassionate companion piece to his *Un Coeur en Hiver*; Claude Lelouch returned to form with his epic updating of *Les Misérables*; and Eric Rohmer produced his most charming philosophical romance in years in *A Summer's Tale*. The extraordinarily rich fantasy *City of Lost Children*, by Jeunet et Caro, and Josiane Balasko's shrewd sex farce *French Twist* (*Gazon Maudit*) show the breadth of talent and interest currently at work in France.

Meanwhile, French producers are offering support to maverick film-makers. These include the Sarajevan Emir Kusturica, whose Yugoslav fable *Underground* took the top prize at Cannes in 1995 but was subsequently, and simplistically, tainted as Serbian propaganda; the Greek Theo Angelopoulos, whose own meditation on the war in the former Yugoslavia, *Ulysses's Gaze*, was far more idiosyncratic; and the Vietnamese Tran Ahn Hung, whose lacerating *Cyclo* triumphed at the Venice festival. France also came up with the most exciting of the cinema centenary events: a feature film consisting of 39 one-minute films shot on the original Lumière Kinematograph, the all-in-one camera, developer and projector which started everything in 1895. In *Lumière and Company*, the world's top directors were invited to make their own film with this camera, under the same conditions that the Lumière brothers made their first films, i.e. silent, using only natural light, and lasting no longer than 52 seconds. Angelopoulos, Spike Lee, Lasse Hallstrom, John Boorman, Jacques Rivette, David Lynch, Merchant/Ivory, Liv Ullman, Claude Lelouch, Wim Wenders and Zhang Yimou were just some of the modern masters who accepted the challenge, with spellbinding results: a felicitous reminder of cinema's power to illuminate, move and transform.

Literature

Possibly the most dramatic development in the British book trade this century was the demise in autumn 1995 of the Net Book Agreement (NBA), the arrangement by which retail prices for books were maintained at the level set by publishers for six months after publication; the NBA came into force 95 years ago. Discounts on books are nothing new in the USA and some other countries, but here the move gave rise to prophecies of doom, some of which soon appeared to be justified. This development will ultimately affect the kinds of books available in the shops, as well as their prices and the nature of the outlets in which they are sold. Some of the repercussions have yet to be seen.

What prompted the demise of the agreement was the action of a number of publishers who 'denetted' the price of their books. This process began with the Reed group in 1991; most other major publishers resisted the move until late September 1995, when Random House and HarperCollins, working with the powerful book retailer W. H. Smith, launched a discounting campaign in the pre-Christmas period. The Publishers Association, a staunch defender of the NBA in the past, withdrew its vehement support, maintenance of the NBA having become untenable as more and more publishers denetted their books. The Publishers Association decided against the 'complete abrogation' of the NBA and formally it still exists, but in practice it is no longer observed. Its disappearance caused an immediate flurry of discounts in the bookshops, with complicated consequences.

There are two schools of thought about the agreement. The pro-NBA school believes that abolition of the NBA disadvantages small independent bookshops, which do not have the volume of sales to negotiate large discounts from publishers and so are unable to compete with the big retail chains and supermarkets, and so could be forced out of business. This lobby believes also that the concentration of discounts on bestsellers will force up the prices of more specialist volumes, to protect publishers' margins, and that bestsellers will cease to subsidize the 'worthier' parts of a publisher's list. The range of books published then become narrower, there are fewer bookshops, and ultimately books become more expensive. By spring of 1996 there was some evidence to support this view; the total volume of book sales had declined and prices, on average, had risen.

The anti-NBA lobby believes, however, that times were so hard for the book trade that drastic measures were needed. Discounts, they argued, would expand readership and inspire new initiatives in new outlets. If the number of books published were reduced, they contended, an undesirable excess would be whittled away. Small bookshops, they said, would have to concentrate on the advantages of personal service, local convenience, and specialization.

The demise of the NBA also presents potential problems for authors. With bookshops demanding greater discounts, publishers might try to recoup their losses by cutting authors' royalties, reducing authors' income from their work.

Some observers, such as Tony Lacey, an executive at Penguin, believe that the abolition of the NBA will lead in the long term to a 'much more mass market culture'. 'It pushes one,' he says, 'into buying bigger books [i.e. obvious bestsellers]. It is tougher to nurture authors ...' And Christopher Sinclair-Stevenson, publisher-turned-agent, believes that the abolition of the NBA might become an excuse not to publish. 'Publishers might use it as a weapon – "If only the NBA were still there we would be happy to ...".' He suspects that children's writers and first novelists ('if not ... obviously exceptional') may be affected. 'Post-NBA, agents and authors will have a tougher time and will be inclined to concentrate on the obvious big books.'

Dan Franklin, publisher at Cape (part of the Random House group) also thinks the downfall of the NBA will 'probably accelerate a trend that is happening anyway – that small books are more difficult to publish ... You can get books off from a standing start but only with a lot of promotional muscle ... Wonderful books are dying on the vine because the publisher has decided not to spend £20,000 promoting them. Now it's very hard to publish a book well on enthusiasm alone, which didn't used to be the case. The loss of the NBA will have the knock-on effect of pressure to publish only the big books.'

JUICY ROWS

The past year saw a new initiative to encourage and celebrate reading in the form of the biggest fiction prize yet. It caused a stir, though, because it was open only to women (albeit, unlike the Booker, all women writing in English and therefore open to Americans). The Orange Prize is worth £30,000 to the winner, and was established by a group of women publishers, writers and critics. An original sponsorship deal crumbled after Simon Jenkins in *The Times* described the prize as 'sexist'. However, an anonymous benefactress stepped in and donated the prize money, and a new sponsorship deal was struck with the Orange telecommunications company. Detractors continued to call the prize patronizing and unnecessary, and one author, Anita Brookner, asked not to be entered because she disapproved of 'positive discrimination'. But one of the instigators of the prize, the publisher Liz Calder of Bloomsbury, summed up the mood of its founders: 'Let this be just for women. Let us have a big beautiful prize that will encourage women to write, that will encourage publishers to publish their work, and booksellers to sell it and readers to read it.'

Even with sponsorship and other difficulties resolved, however, trouble was not over. The judges (Kate Mosse, Val Hennessy, Susan Hill, Lorna Sage and Margaret Lally) suggested that the year was 'middling' rather than exceptional for women's fiction. Hill and Hennessy were said to be 'ashamed' by the 'drivel' that was submitted. The final prize-giving, preceded by a national author tour for five of the six shortlisted authors, was nevertheless characterized by a feeling of defiant celebration, and the prize was won by Helen Dunmore for *A Spell of Winter*. The administrators also secured £35,000-worth of sponsorship from the Government's pairing scheme to fund an initiative to promote reading through secondary schools.

Perhaps the greatest headline-grabbing book story of the year was the courtroom battle between the actress Joan Collins and her American publisher, Random House. Random House wanted Ms Collins to repay a $1.2 million advance for a novel it had commissioned but on delivery judged was too poor to publish. The jury ruled that Ms Collins had submitted a 'complete manuscript' and could keep her advance. The case prompted a lot of colourful copy and caused publishers to look carefully at their contracts. In the USA most contracts, though not Collins's, have a 'satisfactory clause', which specifies that the complete advance will be paid only if the delivered manuscript is of an acceptable standard. In the UK, some publishers' contracts stipulate 'delivery and acceptance' before all the advance is payable. Many agents have fought to delete this from contracts, and Joan Collins's agent (the late 'Swifty' Lazar) had deleted it from hers. The upshot was that the paperback publication of Ms Collins's previous novel *Too Damn Famous* was brought forward, and her autobiographical *Second Act* (published in September 1996) included her account of the court battle.

Another, less disputed, case of an author being asked to return an advance involved the commissioning of a sequel to Alexandra Ripley's *Scarlett*, the highly successful sequel to Margaret Mitchell's *Gone With the Wind*. Emma Tennant was commissioned to follow on from *Scarlett* in a $4.5 million deal for world rights with American publisher St Martin's Press. However, when the manuscript of Tennant's *Tara* arrived, St Martin's Press did not like it. Backed by the Mitchell estate, they objected to the characterization, story, setting and style, and refused to publish, preferring to seek another author for the task. Millions of dollars worth of deals with foreign publishers fell through because St Martin's had vetoed the book, and even the aspiring British publisher, who was very enthusiastic about Tennant's book, was unable to bring it to the public. Readers will never be able to make their own judgement.

The vogue for sequels, though past its peak, did not entirely wane in the last year. With much fanfare Hodder and Stoughton signed up a new author to carry on Ian Fleming's James Bond stories, following the resignation from this role of John Gardner. Gardner has written 14 Bond novels, and two novelizations of 007 films (*Goldeneye* and *Licence to Kill*) since 1981. Before him, in 1968, Kingsley Amis wrote one Bond novel, *Colonel Sun*, under the pen name of Robert Markham. Fleming himself wrote 12 Bond novels and two collections of Bond short stories. The new successor to Fleming, Raymond Benson, is, incredibly, a man who has never written any novels before, though he has been a Bond fan since the age of nine, has an encyclopaedic knowledge of the character and is the author of *The James Bond Bedside Companion*. He also served on the board of directors of the Ian Fleming Foundation. Benson is a computer game designer from Chicago whose games have included James Bond role-playing adventures; his first contribution to the Bond series will be published in 1997.

Also hitting the headlines was the discovery of not one, but two purportedly lost novels by Charlotte Brontë; both were found by a Scottish bookseller, Ian King. The first, a novella entitled *Sad Times*, came into his Edinburgh bookshop and King trawled the National Library of Scotland to verify or disprove its origins. In the process he came across another 19th-century novel, published as *Miss Miles* by one Mary Taylor, which aroused his suspicions. Using computerized comparisons of vocabulary and content, King came to the conclusion that both *Sad Times* and *Miss Miles* (which he renamed *Sarah Miles* because of Brontë's habit of using her heroines' Christian names in her titles) must be by the same hand that wrote *Jane Eyre* and *Shirley*. The Brontë biographer Juliet Barker reacted with scorn, and much debate was triggered in the press. The experts were not persuaded. At best, they agreed that authorship could not be proved either way.

Despite this, and bizarrely for books that were long out of copyright, publication rights were then sold in America and Britain for considerable sums of money. This occurred because a professor of history, Angus Calder, who chanced to live opposite Ian King's bookshop, on hearing about the discoveries, put King in touch with his own agent, Giles Gordon. Gordon was impressed by the efforts King had made to find out the truth, found his case convincing and advised him to write a full introduction giving an account of his discoveries and his research. The book was then sold as two novels in one volume, with King's introduction, appendix and footnotes. The amount of money King will make depends, however, on the number of rival editions other publishers put out, which they may do without charge.

There was also much speculation in the press about a novel entitled *Primary Colors*, which was a bestseller in both the USA and Britain but was published anonymously. It was set in a thinly disguised Clinton administration, and led readers to infer that it was written by a Clinton insider. The names of many possible authors were put forward, before a computer, analysing the style, came to the conclusion that the book was written by a *New York Times* journalist called Joe Klein. Klein denied authorship, but after a deal had been struck for a sequel, a manuscript was found with corrections in Klein's handwriting, thus blowing his cover.

WINNERS AND LOSERS

Salman Rushdie, still living under the shadow of the *fatwa* after more than six years, was voted author of the year at the British Book Awards, and made his first pre-announced public appearance in September 1995. His participation in the Times and Dillons debate on Writers Against the State was announced in *The Times* and on BBC Radio 4's *Today* programme on the morning of the event, which swelled the audience at the Westminster Central Hall to 500. In the course of his contribution, Mr Rushdie expressed his support for an economic boycott of Iran.

Rushdie's novel *The Moor's Last Sigh*, a tale centred around the life of an Indian merchant, was shortlisted for the Booker Prize but pipped at the post by Pat Barker's First World War elegy *The Ghost Road* (the third part of a trilogy), suggesting that the judges had resisted the temptation Howard Jacobson drew attention to in the television coverage of the prize-giving, to consider Rushdie's predicament rather than his book. *The Moor's Last Sigh* was generally held, however, to be Barker's nearest rival on the shortlist. A similar fate met Rushdie at the Whitbread Prize, where his book won the novel category but was beaten to the overall prize by the winner of the first novel category – the second time this has happened to Rushdie; in 1988 *The Satanic Verses* lost out to Paul Sayer's *The Comforts of Madness*. The winner, Kate Atkinson's *Behind the Scenes at the Museum* was an epic family chronicle which was relished by the critics for its humour and its light touch, and went on to enjoy impressive sales. Fortune favoured Rushdie, however, when he sold his next novel, *The Ground Beneath Her Feet*, on the basis of a 20-page outline for a sum reported to be £1 million. The book is described as a story of 'love, death and music, the tale of an Indian Orpheus in the Western "underworld" of rock 'n' roll.'

Among the literary novels that received critical acclaim or notable sales were Graham Swift's *Last Orders*, the story of five Londoners driving to Margate Sands to scatter the ashes of a friend. It was widely tipped as a contender for the 1996 Booker Prize. Julian Barnes also brought out a collection of short stories, *Crossing the Channel*, that capped the Anglo-Frenchness of all his *oeuvre* to date. Meanwhile, *A Debt to Pleasure*, a first novel by John Lanchester, was held by critics to be one of the few novels of recent years to bear comparison with Swift's *Waterland*, Barnes's *Flaubert's Parrot* and Martin Amis's *Money*.

The one literary novel that was conspicuously absent from the 1995 Booker shortlist, as it was from the bestseller lists, was Martin Amis's tale of literary rivalry *The Information*. Along with a collection of short stories, the novel had commanded a much publicized advance of £500,000 from its British publisher, HarperCollins. Critical response was mixed. Furthermore, the paperback was brought out with a jacket that displayed only a letter 'i', which seems to have been too elliptical for most book buyers. Despite an ambitious but rather obscure advertising campaign which incorporated this letter into such slogans as 'What is it?', estimates suggest that the paperback sold no more than 20,000 copies, considerably less than was necessary to recoup the advance. Neither the subject – likely to appeal to a rather limited circle of literati – nor the marketing campaign fired the public imagination.

A bad year for Martin Amis continued with the newspaper serialization after his father Sir Kingsley Amis's death, of diaries written by Kingsley Amis's rejected official biographer Eric Jacobs; these painted an unflattering picture of the distinguished author in his last years.

Subsequently, the partnership between Amis's American agent Andrew Wylie and his British partner Gillon Aitken ended, a split which some surmised (although this was denied by the protagonists) was triggered by the fact that Aitken had acted for Eric Jacobs in the sale of his serialization. The reason Aitken gave was that Andrew Wylie was pursuing 'global domination', which was a characteristic of a year in which literary agents thought big. Wylie set up his own office in London, causing a stir in the British publishing world because of his reputation for actively trying to entice other agents' authors.

This underlined one of the issues of the year – the right of authors to unrestrained choice about the handling of their affairs – and in one case the issue came to court. The literary agent Giles Gordon came into conflict with his former employer, Sheil Land Associates, when he left his job after 22 years to set up his own agency based in Edinburgh. Most of his clients (who include Sue Townsend, Peter Ackroyd, Barry Unsworth and Vikram Seth) wanted to go with him. But Sheil Land issued an injunction restraining him from 'canvassing, soliciting, approaching or enticing away or causing to be canvassed, solicited, approached, any client of Sheil Land in relation to the business of providing literary agency services'. Gordon's authors reacted indignantly. The High Court judged that authors should have the freedom to choose their agent.

CHEAP TASTERS

One of the most remarkable trends of the past year was the continued publication of slim, cheap editions of books in the wake of Penguin's phenomenally successful *60s* series, sixty little books for 60p published to celebrate the publishers' 60th anniversary, originally as a one-off commemorative gesture. The public turned out to have an un-expected appetite for tasters of the likes of Tacitus and Nietzsche, and the series improbably put Marcus Aurelius on the bestseller lists. Penguin produced further sets of *60s* in the genres of cookery, biography, travel, classics and children's books: in all, a total of 180 titles which sold 13 million copies altogether. Phoenix House responded with a similar series, Faber introduced a 60 pence poetry list, and Bloomsbury celebrated its tenth birthday with Bloomsbury Birthday Quids, short stories by its top authors for £1 each. Orion published 20 £1 poetry books, with 40 more planned for next year, as well as 25 cookery books at 99p called Masterchefs. Words-worth Editions, which had in fact preceded the *60s* with something very similar under £1 – as had Dover Thrift Editons, imported by Constable pub-lishers from America – introduced a new Classics of the World series at £2. But the fashion for cheap classy snippets may be past its heyday. The shops even began to discount these tiny bargains. Sales flattened out for Penguin during the year enough for the company to declare that the ten *60s* published for Christmas 1996 would be the last it would produce in this format. But their success will no doubt help towards the rumoured £1 million salary awarded to Penguin's new corporate boss, 36-year-old Michael Lynton, formerly president of Disney's Hollywood Pictures, who was appointed in August 1996.

Chiming with this fashion for publishing bite-size chunks was the issue of Stephen King's latest novel, *The Green Mile*, in six paperback chapters, a month at a time, at £1.99 each. The experiment seemed to work; the instalments of this tale of dreadful crimes and ghastly punishments on Death Row were bestsellers individually. The author, inspired by Dickens, also claimed that the end was not written when he began, and that he would take responses into account as he wrote (although in fact the publishing schedule meant that at least the first three chapters were written by the time the first chapter was published). Publication in one volume will follow. Meanwhile King's new hardback, *Rose Madder*, coincided with the latter chapters of *The Green Mile* on the bestseller lists.

Delia Smith's name was hardly absent from the bestseller lists all year, first with her *Winter Collection* and then with her *Summer Collection*, the runaway successes of the year. There were two other salient categories of books in the lists and among pub-lishers' new commissions: books about the SAS, following the success of Andy McNab's *Bravo Two-Zero*, which continued to be a bestseller in paper-back; and spin-offs from the television series *The X-Files*. The greatest SAS successes were Chris Ryan's *The One That Got Away*, and Andy McNab's new book *Immediate Action*. Hopeful commissions in-cluded *SAS: The Illustrated History* by Barry Davies, and *The SAS; Who Cares Who Wins* by Will Buckley and Paul Dornan; there was even an ambitiously marketed account from a wife's point of view, *Biting the Bullet: Married to the SAS* by Jenny Simpson. The

X-Files prompted two bestselling series: Jane Gold-man's *The X-Files Book of the Unexplained*, books 1 and 2, and four books by Les Martin (*X Marks the Spot* and *Darkness Falls*) and Kevin Anderson (*Ground Zero* and *Ruins*).

Besides these, outstanding sellers of the year included *Sophie's World* by Jostein Gaarder, the history of philosophy made simple, which was originally written for teenagers and published in Norway in 1992. It quickly became a bestseller throughout Scandinavia, where it topped the chil-dren's list in Norway and the adults' list in Denmark. It has since been translated into 25 languages and sold in 38 countries, and was a huge success, particularly in Germany and Japan. It was published in hardback in Britain at the beginning of 1995 and sold over 300,000 copies. The paperback came out in March 1996 and superseded the hardback with 23 weeks in the bestseller lists.

Books that also succeeded as well in paperback as in hardback included Robert Harris's story of code-breaking during the Second World War, *Enigma*. This matched the success of his previous novel *Fatherland*, a fantasy of Britain under Nazi occupa-tion, and went on to become a BBC Book at Bedtime. Nick Hornby's romantic comedy steeped in the history of pop music, *High Fidelity*, made a similar transition from hardback to paperback success, while paperback sales persisted throughout the year of Hornby's portrait of the artist as a football fan, *Fever Pitch*, even as the Channel 4 film of the book was being shot in North London. Nicholas Evans' tale of equine psychology and human self-discovery, *The Horse Whisperer*, which commanded much publicized advances and record sums for film rights, galloped off the shelves in both hard and soft editions, despite an unenthusiastic critical response. And Tom Sharpe, who broke through his lengthy writer's block to produce *Granchester Grind* was rewarded with sustained sales in both formats. Last year's surprise triumph, David Guterson's court-room drama of the Puget Sound, *Snow Falling on Cedars*, continued to be a paperback frontrunner well into the spring of 1996, and *Trainspotting*, Irvine Welsh's demotic comedy of Scottish drug addiction, was reinstated on the bestseller lists by the release of the film of the book.

Newly published books by commercial main-stays included John Grisham's *The Runaway Jury*, which followed hot on the heels of *The Rainmaker*, and Jilly Cooper's titillator about passions in an orchestra, *Appassionata*. Roddy Doyle's new book *The Woman Who Walked Into Doors*, the narrative of a battered wife, was liked by the critics and made a respectable, though not especially sustained, show-ing on the bestseller lists. And following the success of Stephen Fry's *The Liar* and *The Hippopotamus*, his partner in comedy, Hugh Laurie, made a successful fiction debut with *The Gun Seller*, a novel submitted anonymously to an agent. Fellow comedian Ben Elton's latest offering, *Popcorn*, about a film-maker held captive by a serial killer determined to make him admit his responsibility for the murders, was received with great enthusiasm by reviewers and reached the Booker Prize long-list.

RICHES

Some astonishingly large advances were paid for books that had yet to be published at the time of going to press. The Duchess of York's life story was acquired for a reported $1.3 million by Simon and Schuster, which bought world English rights for simultaneous publication in the USA, the UK and Canada in autumn 1996. The publishers promised an account of the Duchess and her experiences 'as they were, rather than as they have been portrayed'; however, there were expectations in some quarters that the book would be a bland account because of the confidentiality agreement the Duchess signed as part of her divorce settlement with Prince Andrew. The US publisher no doubt has high hopes; it is the same company that sold 600,000 copies of Andrew Morton's *Diana: Her Story.*

The chief prosecutor in the O. J. Simpson trial, Marcia Clark, sold her account of it in the USA and the UK for a reputed $5.7 million. And an author writing under the *nom de plume* of Christopher Creighton was paid £500,000 for world rights in a book (co-written with Duff Hart-Davis) that claimed that Hitler's henchman Martin Bormann lived in Surrey until 1989. Jeffrey Archer's next three novels were sold in a deal rumoured to be worth $25 million, while his account of rivalry between two newspaper magnates, based on the lives of Robert Maxwell and Rupert Murdoch, flourished under the title *The Fourth Estate*, chosen for it by *Sunday Times* readers.

In the world of children's books, Terry Pratchett landed on his *Feet of Clay*, which was an instant success. The winner of the prestigious Carnegie Medal caused a rumpus in the literary circles by arguing that the talent for story-telling in adult fiction had died with E. M. Forster. Philip Pullman's prizewinning book *Northern Lights* is an astonishing 400-page epic, the first part of a trilogy *His Dark Materials*, which owes something to *Paradise Lost.* Pullman contended that only in children's fiction these days did stories take precedence over style or ideas, and that it was in stories that real wisdom lay. The likes of A. S. Byatt, he implied, should hang their heads.

LITERARY PRIZEWINNERS

Nobel Prize 1995 – Seamus Heaney
Commonwealth Writers Prize 1995 – Louis de Bernières, *Captain Corelli's Mandolin*
Prix Goncourt 1995 – Andrei Makine, *Le Testament Français*
Booker Prize 1995 – Pat Barker, *The Ghost Road*
Whitbread Prize 1995: overall winner – Kate Atkinson, *Behind the Scenes at the Museum*
    Novel – Salman Rushdie, *The Moor's Last Sigh*
    First novel – Kate Atkinson, *Behind the Scenes at the Museum*
    Biography – Lord Jenkins of Hillhead, *Gladstone*
    Poetry – Bernard O'Donoghue, *Gunpowder*
    Children's novel – Michael Morpurgo, *The Wreck of the Zanzibar*
David Higham Prize 1995 – Vikram Chandra, *Red Earth and Pouring Rain*
Forward Prize 1995 (poetry) – Sean O'Brien, *Ghost Train*
    First collection – Jane Duran, *Breathe Now, Breathe*
Catherine Cookson Prize 1995 – not awarded
William Hill Sports Book of the Year 1995 – John Feinstein, *A Good Walk Spoiled*
Smarties Prize 1995 (children's books) – Jacqueline Wilson, *Double Act*
    Age 0–5 – Jill Murphy, *The Last Noo-Noo*
    Age 6–8 – Jill Paton Walsh, *Thomas and the Tinners*
    Age 9–11 – Lesley Howarth, *Weather Eye;* Jacqueline Wilson, *Double Act*
Crime Writers Association 1995:
    Gold Dagger (fiction) – Val McDermid, *The Mermaids Singing*
    Silver Dagger (fiction) – Peter Lovesey, *The Summons*
British Books Awards 1996 – Delia Smith, *Delia Smith's Winter Collection*
Orange Award 1996 (women writers) – Helen Dunmore, *A Spell of Winter*
NCR Award (non-fiction) – Eric Lomax, *The Railway Man*
Somerset Maugham Prize 1996 – Katherine Pierpoint, *Truffle Beds;* Alan Warner, *Morven Caller*
Betty Trask Prize 1996 – John Lanchester, *The Debt to Pleasure*
McKitterick Prize 1996 (first novel by a writer over 40) – Stephen Blanchard, *Gagarin and I*
Hawthornden Prize 1996 – Hilary Mantel, *An Experiment in Love*
W. H. Smith Prize 1996 – Andrew Klaven, *True Crime*
Mail on Sunday/John Llewellyn Rhys Prize 1996 – Melanie McGrath, *Motel Nirvana*
Encore Prize 1996 (second novel) – A. L. Kennedy, *So I Am Glad*
Cholmondeley Award 1996 (poetry) – Elizabeth Bartlett; Dorothy Nimmo; Peter Scupham; Iain Crichton Smith
Romantic Novel of the Year 1996 – Rosamunde Pilcher, *Coming Home*
Carnegie Prize 1996 (children's) – Philip Pullman, *His Dark Materials: Book 1, Northern Lights*
Kate Greenaway 1996 (children's illustrated) – P. J. Lynch, *The Christmas Miracle of Jonathan Toomey* by Susann Wojciechowski

Opera

The redevelopment of the Royal Opera House, Covent Garden, finally got under way in the year under review, with preliminary work beginning south of the theatre on excavation of basements and laying of foundations. When the Opera House closes at the end of the 1996–7 season, a substantial amount of work will have been done. During the two-year closure the Royal Opera will use a number of venues in London, such as the Royal Albert Hall and the Barbican Centre, and go on tour in Britain and abroad. Nearly 300 backstage staff will be made redundant.

Jeremy Isaacs, the general director of the Royal Opera House, was awarded the KBE in the Queen's Birthday honours list. He is due to retire in 1997 and his successor is to be Genista McIntosh, at present executive director at the Royal National Theatre. She will take up her position as chief executive of the Royal Opera House by the end of 1996. Nicholas Payne, director of the Royal Opera, and Sir Anthony Dowell, director of the Royal Ballet, will retain full artistic control of their companies but they will be ultimately answerable to Genista McIntosh.

Meanwhile the Royal Opera, despite stringent economies, was able to offer another successful season artistically. New productions included the world première of Alexander Goehr's opera *Arianna*, a modern setting of the 17th-century libretto by Ottavio Rinuccini written for Monteverdi's *Arianna* in 1608. The controversial *Ring* cycle directed by Richard Jones and designed by Nigel Lowery was completed with *Götterdämmerung*. Paul Hindemith's *Mathis der Maler* received its first production at Covent Garden to mark the centenary of the birth of the composer; directed by Peter Sellars, *Mathis der Maler* deservedly won the Royal Philharmonic Society's Opera Award for the conductor, Esa-Pekka Salonen.

A new production of Sir Michael Tippett's *The Midsummer Marriage* was mounted in honour of the 91-year-old composer. Massenet's *Hérodiade* had to be cancelled for financial reasons, and the proposed staging of *Il corsaro* during the Verdi Festival was replaced by two concert performances. The festival did include the premières of new productions of *Nabucco*, in association with Welsh National Opera, *Giovanna d'Arco*, in association with Opera North, and *Don Carlos*, in association with Théâtre du Châtelet, Paris, and three other theatres. *Don Carlos*, a very full edition of the original five-act French version, conducted by Bernard Haitink, was musically much admired but dramatically disappointing and inferior to the 1958 Luchino Visconti production which it replaced.

In June 1996 English National Opera received an advance draft of a feasibility study, commissioned with money from the National Lottery, examining options for the future of the company and of the London Coliseum. The Board was still considering the options – whether to remain at the Coliseum, which needs extensive structural repairs as well as refurbishment, or to move elsewhere – when the season ended. Meanwhile dramatic changes were taking place in the company management. In November 1995 Sian Edwards, the music director, announced her resignation after only two years in the post. It had been obvious for some time that she was not happy with ENO. Her successor is to be Paul Daniel, at present the highly successful music director of Opera North, who will take up the position at the beginning of the 1997–8 season.

ENO's 1995–6 season opened with a successful new production of Bizet's *Carmen*. Purcell's tricentenary was celebrated by *The Fairy Queen*, imaginatively staged and superbly sung by a fine cast headed by soprano Yvonne Kenny. New productions of *Fidelio* and *Salome* were well-received, but the most interesting event of the season was the first staging by a British company of *The Prince of Homburg* by Hans Werner Henze. Although Nicholas Lehnhoff's production, imported from Munich, was disappointing, the opera was well conducted by Elgar Howarth. The accidental death in June 1996 of Nicholas John, ENO's literary manager, aged only 42, cast a shadow over the end of the season.

Triumphant Hamlet

Opera North's season in Leeds opened with a new production of Ambroise Thomas's *Hamlet*, long despised in Britain for its 'happy ending' (Hamlet becomes king, though Ophelia dies), but the title role offers magnificent opportunities to a high dramatic baritone, opportunities which Anthony Michaels-Moore grasped with spectacular success. He won the Royal Philharmonic Society Award in the singing category. Paul Daniel conducted Janáček's *Jenůfa*, with Josephine Barstow taking the role of the Kostelnička, and Cherubini's *Medea*, with Barstow in the title role. He also conducted a fine new production of Verdi's *Luisa Miller*.

The first British stage production of Kurt Weill's *Love Life*, a vaudeville originally produced in New York in 1948, offered audiences a long overdue opportunity to hear some of Weill's finest songs (with lyrics by Alan Jay Lerner, who also wrote the book) in their proper context. Caroline Gawn's clever staging was not popular with everyone; however, her new production of *The Marriage of Figaro*, which ended a very successful season for Opera North, caught the public imagination.

Despite the disappointment of having its application to the Lottery Fund for money to build a new opera house in Cardiff turned down, Welsh National Opera celebrated its 50th anniversary in style. The company's opening performance in April 1946 was a double bill of *Cavalleria rusticana* and *Pagliacci*, followed by Gounod's *Faust*, and admirable productions of these works were mounted for the anniversary; the double bill was conducted by Carlo Rizzi, the present music director, and *Faust* by Sir Charles Mackerras, the previous music director. WNO also staged Stravinsky's *The Rake's Progress* for the first time; this production and the double bill were subsequently brought to Covent Garden where they were received with great enthusiasm. WNO's final anniversary celebration was the world première of *The Doctor of Myddfai*, commissioned from Sir Peter Maxwell Davies, with libretto by David Pountney, who also directed the production. The text is derived from the Welsh legend of Llyn y Fan Fach, in which the descendants of a shepherd and a mysterious girl who emerged from a lake are endowed with the power of healing and become the Doctors of Myddfai. Significant roles are provided for the fine chorus, the backbone of the company since its foundation. The conductor was Richard Armstrong, once music director of WNO.

Edinburgh Highlights

Richard Armstrong, now music director of Scottish Opera, also conducted the world première of *Inès de Castro*, with music and libretto by James MacMillan, which was presented by Scottish Opera at the Edinburgh International Festival in August 1996. The composer's first full-length opera, based on the play of the same name by John Clifford, *Inès de Castro* tells of the tragic love between Prince Pedro, heir to the Portuguese throne, and his Spanish mistress Inès, executed by order of Pedro's father King Alfonso IV. Other operas at the Edinburgh Festival included Virgil Thompson's *Four Saints in Three Acts*, the setting of a libretto by Gertrude Stein, performed by Houston Grand Opera and staged by Robert Wilson.

Glyndebourne Festival Opera's new productions this year were Handel's *Theodora* and Berg's *Lulu*. *Theodora*, though filled with wonderful music, remains stubbornly an oratorio; neither the skills of director Peter Sellars nor the superb conducting of the Orchestra of the Age of Enlightenment by William Christie, or the best efforts of a splendid cast, could turn it into music drama. Conversely *Lulu*, given in the complete three-act version, is dramatic from first note to last. Graham Vick's clear production shed light on the intricacies of Wedekind's text, Andrew Davis's conducting illuminated Berg's score, magnificently played by the London Philharmonic, and Christine Schäfer made a notable Lulu.

Lulu was among the operas performed at the Proms in 1996. Other operas included the Covent Garden *Don Carlos*, sung in Italian, Weill's *Der Silbersee*, Beethoven's *Leonore*, the original version of *Fidelio*, which was staged in the central arena of the Hall, and Handel's *Semele*, with William Christie conducting his choral and orchestral ensemble, Les

Arts Florissants; this was enthusiastically received by the large audience.

Anya Silja won the 1995 Evening Standard Award for Outstanding Performance in Opera, for her portrayal of Emilia Marty in Janáček's *The Makropulos Affair* at Glyndebourne. Felicity Lott, whose inimitable interpretations of Richard Strauss's Arabella, the Marschallin in *Der Rosenkavalier*, Christine Storch in *Intermezzo* and Countess Madeleine in *Capriccio* were first sung at Glyndebourne, was made a Dame in the 1996 Queen's Birthday honours list.

The bass Donald Adams, who took part in several Glyndebourne productions, notably *Katya Kabanova* in which he sang Dikoj, died in April 1996 at the age of 67. After appearing with the D'Oyly Carte Company for many years, he turned to opera, and sang at Covent Garden and with Scottish, English National and Welsh National Operas. He scored a personal triumph with WNO as Baron Ochs in *Der Rosenkavalier*; his best roles included Mozart's and Rossini's Dr Bartolo, Don Pasquale, Schigolch in *Lulu*, and Peter Quince and Nick Bottom in *A Midsummer Night's Dream*.

John Lanigan

John Lanigan, the Australian-born tenor who sang for 30 years with the Royal Opera, died in August 1996, aged 75. After ten years of singing lyric roles such as the Duke in *Rigoletto*, Rudolfo in *La Bohème*, Pinkerton in *Madama Butterfly* and Tamino in *The Magic Flute*, he became a superb character tenor. As Flute in Britten's *A Midsummer Night's Dream*, the Rector in *Peter Grimes*, Mime in Wagner's *Ring*, and, above all, as Shuisky in *Boris Godunov*, his most effective role, he was frequently outstanding. He created parts in two of Tippett's operas, Jack in *The Midsummer Marriage* (1955) and Hermes in *King Priam* (1962), as well as Mr Jones in Richard Rodney Bennett's *Victory* (1970) and the Cardinal and Archbishop in Peter Maxwell Davies' *Taverner* (1972).

The London-born composer Alan Bush, who died in October 1995, aged 94, was a dedicated Communist; he wrote several operas, including *The Men of Blackmoor* (1956), *The Sugar Reapers, or Guyana Johnny* (1966) and *Joe Hill – the man who never died* (1970), all with librettos by his wife Nancy, which were successfully produced in the then East Germany but were largely ignored in Britain. His best-known stage work, *Wat Tyler*, an account of the peasants' revolt of 1381, was premièred at Leipzig in 1953 and performed at Sadler's Wells Theatre in 1974.

Sadler's Wells Theatre closed its doors in June 1996; it is to be pulled down and a new theatre built in its place, funded by a £30 million National Lottery award. The first theatre on the Islington site was built in 1765; the current building opened in 1931 under the management of Lilian Baylis and was home to Sadler's Wells Opera (now ENO) until 1968, when the company moved to the Coliseum. In recent years the theatre served as a London stage for touring opera and ballet companies, both British and international, and the new theatre will perform the same function. During the two years scheduled for the redevelopment, the Peacock Theatre (previously the Royalty) off Kingsway, which is owned by the London School of Economics, will be used jointly by LSE and Sadler's Wells.

Sadler's Wells Theatre has a secure place in operatic history. Since the war, the premières of Britten's *Peter Grimes*, Lennox Berkeley's *Nelson*, John Gardner's *The Moon and Sixpence* and Richard Rodney Bennett's *The Mines of Sulphur* have taken place there, as well as the first British stage performances of Verdi's *Simon Boccanegra*, Dvořák's *Rusalka*, Prokofiev's *The Fiery Angel*, Shostakovich's *The Nose*, Szymanowski's *King Roger*, Janáček's *Katya Kabanova*, *The Makropulos Affair* and *The Cunning Little Vixen*, and Weill's *Rise and Fall of the City of Mahagonny*.

PRODUCTIONS

In the summaries of company activities shown below, the dates in brackets indicate the year that the current production entered the company's repertory.

ROYAL OPERA
Founded 1946
Royal Opera House, Covent Garden, London WC2E 9DD

Productions from the repertory: *Le nozze di Figaro* (1987), *Tosca* (1964), *Fedora* (1994), *Aida* (1994), *Semele* (1982), *La traviata* (1994), *Arabella* (1965), *Die Entführung aus dem Serail* (1987).

New productions:
Arianna (Alexander Goehr), 15 September 1995 (world première). Conductor, Ivor Bolton; director, Francesca Zambello; designer, Alison Chitty. Susan Graham (Ariadne), Anna Maria Panzarella (Amor), Sheila Nadler (Venus/Dorilla), Axel Kohler (Bacchus/Soldier/Fisherman), Patrick Raftery (Theseus), Christopher Ventris (Ambassador/Soldier), David Wilson-Johnson (Counsellor)
Götterdämmerung (Wagner), 16 November 1995. Conductor, Bernard Haitink; director, Richard Jones; designer, Nigel Lowery. Deborah Polaski (Brünnhilde), Vivian Tierney (Gutrune), Jane Henschel (Waltraute), Siegfried Jerusalem (Siegfried), Alan Held (Gunther), Ekkehard Wlaschilha (Alberich), Kurt Rydl (Hagen)
Mathis der Maler (Hindemith), 16 November 1995. Conductor, Esa-Pekka Salonen; director, Peter Sellars; designers, George Tsypin (sets), Dunya Ramikova (costumes). Inga Nielsen (Ursula), Christiane Oelze (Regina), Yvonne Minton (Countess von Helfenstein), Stig Andersen (Cardinal Albrecht), Wolfgang Fassler (Hans Schwalb), Alan Titus (Mathis), Gwynne Howell (Riedinger)
The Midsummer Marriage (Tippett), 16 January 1966. Conductor, Bernard Haitink; director, Graham Vick; designer, Paul Brown. Cheryl Barker (Jenifer), Lillian Watson (Bella), Eiddwen Harrhy (She-Ancient), Catherine Wyn-Rogers (Sorostris), Stephen O'Mara (Mark), Christopher Ventris (Jack), John Tomlinson (King Fisher), Peter Rose (He-Ancient)
Nabucco (Verdi), 9 April 1996. Conductor, Wladimir Jurowsky; director, Tim Albery; designer, Antony

McDonald. Nina Rautio (Abigaille), Leah-Marian Jones (Fenena), Dennis O'Neill (Ismaele), Alexander Agache (Nabucco), Samuel Ramey (Zaccariah)
Don Carlos (Verdi), 13 June 1996. Conductor, Bernard Haitink; director, Luc Bondy; designers, Gilles Aillaud (sets), Moidele Bickel (costumes). Karita Mattila (Elisabeth de Valois), Martine Dupuy (Princess Eboli), Anna Maria Panzarella (Thibault), Roberto Alagna (Don Carlos), Thomas Hampson (Marquis de Posa), Jose Van Dam (King Philip II), Kurt Rydl (Grand Inquisitor)
Giovanna d'Arco (Verdi), 24 June 1996. Conductor, Daniele Gatti; director and designer, Philip Prowse. June Anderson (Giovanna), Dennis O'Neill (Carlo VII), Vladimir Chernov (Giacomo)

ENGLISH NATIONAL OPERA
Founded 1931
London Coliseum, St Martin's Lane, London WC2N 4ES

Productions from the repertory: *Così fan tutte* (1994), *Rusalka* (1983), *The Barber of Seville* (1987), *The Pearl Fishers* (1987), *The Magic Flute* (1988), *Tosca* (1987), *Don Pasquale* (1993), *Orfeo* (1981), *Ariodante* (1993), *La Bohème* (1993).

New productions:
Carmen (Bizet), 13 September 1995. Conductor, Sian Edwards; director, Jonathan Miller; designers, Peter J.Davison (sets), Sue Blane (costumes). Janice Watson (Micaela), Louise Winter (Carmen), Robert Brubaker (Don José), Robert Hayward (Escamillo), Mark Richardson (Zuniga)
The Fairy Queen (Purcell), 19 October 1995. Conductor, Nicholas Kok; director, David Pountney; designers, Robert Israel (sets), Dunya Ramicova (costumes). Yvonne Kenny (Titania), Mary Hegarty, Janis Kelly (Fairies), Yvonne Barclay (Caroline), Michael Chance (Dick), Thomas Randle (Oberon), Jonathan Best (Drunken poet)
Turandot (Puccini), 22 November 1995. Conductor, David Atherton; director, Christopher Alden; designer, Paul Steinberg. Sophia Larson (Turandot), Janice Watson (Liu), Edmund Barham (Calaf), John Fryatt (Altoum), Roberto Salvatori (Ping), John Daszak (Pang), Anthony Mee (Pong), Andrew Greenan (Timur)
La belle Vivette (Offenbach), 11 December 1995. Conductor, James Holmes; director, Ian Judge; designers, John Gunter (sets), Deirdre Clancy (costumes). Lesley Garrett (Vivette), Neill Archer (Berger), Ryland Davies (Ploc), Harry Nicoll, John Graham Hall (Gonfleur brothers), Andrew Shore (Calcul)
Tristan and Isolde (Wagner), 10 February 1996. Conductor, Mark Elder; director, David Alden; designer, Charles Edwards. Elizabeth Connell (Isolde), Susan Parry (Brangaene), George Gray (Tristan), Jonathan Summers (Kurwenal), Gwynne Howell (King Mark)
Fidelio (Beethoven), 24 April 1996. Conductor, Richard Hickox; director Graham Vick; designer, Paul Brown. Kathryn Harries (Leonore), Mary Plazas (Marzelline), Philip Sheffield (Jacquine), Anthony Rolfe Johnson (Florestan), Peter Sidhom (Don Pizarro), Gwynne Howell (Rocco), John Connell (Don Fernando)
Salome (R. Strauss), 25 May 1996. Conductor, Andrew Litton; director, David Leveaux; designer, Vicki Mortimer. Kristine Ciesinski (Salome), Sally Burgess (Herodias), Ethna Robinson (Page), Alan Woodrow (Herod), Robert Hayward (Jokanaan)
The Prince of Homburg (Henze), 22 June 1996 (first performance by a British company). Conductor, Elgar Howarth; director, Nikolaus Lehnhoff; designer, Gottfried Pilz. Susan Bullock (Princess Natalie), Susan Bickley (Elector's Wife), William Cochrane (Elector), Peter Coleman-Wright (Prince Friedrich)

OPERA NORTH
Founded 1978
Grand Theatre, 46 New Briggate, Leeds LS1 6NU

Productions from the repertory: *The Pearl Fishers* (1995), *La Bohème* (1993), *The Duenna* (1992).

New productions:
  Hamlet (Thomas), 21 September 1995. Conductor, Oliver von Dohnanyi; director, David McVicar; designer Michael Vale. Rebecca Caine (Ophelia), Linda Finnie (Gertrude), Anthony Michaels-Moore (Hamlet), Alan Oke (Laertes), Jan Galla (Claudius)
  Jenufa (Janáček), 11 October 1995. Conductor, Paul Daniel; director/designer, Tom Cairns. Stephanie Friede (Jenufa), Josephine Barstow (Kostelnička), Pauline Tinsley (Grandmother Buryjovka), Neill Archer (Števa), Julian Gavin (Laca)
  Luisa Miller (Verdi), 22 December 1995. Conductor, Paul Daniel; director, Tim Albery; designer, Stewart Laing. Susannah Glanville (Luisa), Ethna Robinson (Federica), Arthur Davies (Rodolfo), Alan Opie (Miller), Matthew Best (Count Walter)
  Love Life (Kurt Weill), 25 January 1996 (British première). Conductor, Wyn Davies; director, Caroline Gawn; designers, Charles Edwards (sets), Nicky Gillibrand (costumes). Margaret Preece (Susan), Alan Oke (Sam), Geoffrey Dolton (Magician)
  Medea (Cherubini), 15 April 1996. Conductor, Paul Daniel; director, Phyllida Lloyd; designer, Anthony Ward. Josephine Barstow (Medea), Nicola Sharkey (Glauce), Anne Wilkens (Neris), Thomas Randle (Jason), Norman Bailey (Creon)
  The Marriage of Figaro (Mozart), 3 June 1996. Conductor, Richard Farnes; director, Caroline Gawn; designer, Alice Purcell. Janis Kelly (Countess Almaviva), Linda Kitchen (Susanna), Ann Taylor-Morley (Cherubino), Jeffrey Lloyd-Roberts (Don Basilio), Clive Bailey (Figaro), William Dazelely (Count Almaviva), Andrew Shore (Doctor Bartolo)
  Performances were given in the Grand Theatre, Leeds, and on tour at Manchester, Nottingham, Hull, Sheffield, Sunderland and Norwich.

SCOTTISH OPERA
Founded 1962
39 Elmbank Crescent, Glasgow G2 4PT

Production from the repertory: *La traviata* (1989).

New productions:
  The Jacobin (Dvořák), 2 September 1995. Conductor, Richard Armstrong; director, Christine Mielitz; designers, Reinhart Zimmermann (sets), Eleonore Kleiber (costumes). Rita Cullis (Julie), Claire Rutter (Terinka), Richard Coxon (Jiri), Peter Sidhom (Bohus), Alasdair Elliott (Benda), Donald Maxwell (Filip), Stafford Dean (Count Vilem)
  Don Giovanni (Mozart), 6 September 1995. Conductor, Nicholas McGegan; director, John Cox; designer, Peter Howson. Peter Mattei (Don Giovanni), Francesca Pedaci (Donna Anna), Joan Rodgers (Donna Elvira), Lisa Milne (Zerlina), Neill Archer (Don Ottavio), Yanni Yannissis (Leporello), Neal Davies (Masetto), Andrea Silvestrelli (Commendatore)
  La Belle Hélène (Offenbach), 25 October 1995. Conductor, Emmanuel Joel; directors, Patrice Caurier, Moshe Leiser; designers, Christian Ratz (sets), Agostino Cavalca (costumes). Anne Howells (Helen), Ann Taylor-Morley (Orestes), Tracey Welborn (Paris), John Mitchinson (Menelaus), Jonathan Veira (Calchas), Andrew Slater (Agamemnon)

Hansel and Gretel (Humperdinck), 12 January 1996. Conductor, Guido Ajmone-Marsan; director, Mark Tinkler; designer, Richard Aylwin. Clair Bradshaw (Hansel), Catriona Smith (Gretel), Anne Mason (Mother), Elizabeth Vaughan (Witch), Lisa Milne (Dew Fairy), Ann Archibald (Sandman), Russell Smythe (Father)
  Alceste (Gluck), 2 April 1996. Concuctor, Nicholas McGegan; director/designer, Yannis Kokkos. Isabelle Vernet (Alceste), Mark Padmore (Admète), Nathan Berg (Hercules/Herald), Matthew Best (High Priest/Apollo)
  Turandot (Puccini), 14 May 1996. Conductor, Richard Armstrong; director, Christopher Alden; designer, Paul Steinberg. Kathleen Broderick (Turandot), Francesca Pedaci (Liu), Deng (Calaf), Stephen Gadd (Ping), Stafford Dean (Timur)
  Performances were given in the Theatre Royal, Glasgow, and on tour at Newcastle upon Tyne, Edinburgh, Aberdeen, and Inverness.

WELSH NATIONAL OPERA
Founded 1946
John Street, Cardiff CF1 4SP

Productions from the repertory: *Madama Butterfly* (1978), *Idomeneo* (1991).

New productions:
  Nabucco (Verdi), 12 September 1995. Conductor, Carlo Rizzi; director, Tim Albery; designer Antony McDonald; Janice Cairns (Abigaille), Sara Fulgoni (Fenena), Gwyn Hughes Jones (Ismaele), Jonathan Summers (Nabucco), Willard White (Zaccharia)
  The Rake's Progress (Stravinsky), 17 February 1996. Conductor, Mark Wigglesworth; director, Matthew Warchus; designer, Laura Hopkins. Alwyn Mellor (Anne), Yvonne Lea (Mother Goose), Claire Powell (Baba the Turk), Paul Nilon (Tom Rakewell), Bryn Terfel (Nick Shadow), Neil Jenkins (Sellem), Jonathan Best (Truelove)
  Cavalleria rusticana (Mascagni), 5 March 1996. Conductor, Carlo Rizzi; director, Elijah Moshinsky; designer, Michael Yeargan. Anne-Marie Owens (Santuzza), Leah Marian Jones (Lola), Menai Davies (Mamma Lucia), Dennis O'Neill (Turiddu), Peter Sidhom (Alfio)
  Pagliacci (Leoncavallo), 5 March 1996. Conductor, Carlo Rizzi; director, Elijah Moshinsky; designer, Michael Yeargan. Rosalind Sutherland (Nedda), Dennis O'Neill (Canio), Anthony Mee (Beppo), Peter Sidhom (Tonio), Jason Howard (Silvio)
  Faust (Gounod), 16 April 1996. Conductor, Charles Mackerras; director, Christopher Alden; designer, Bruno Schwengl. Janice Watson (Marguerite), Pamela Helen Stephen (Sièbel), Susan Gorton (Martha), Paul Charles Clarke (Faust), Jason Howard (Valentin), Alastair Miles (Mephistophélès)
  The Doctor of Myddfai (Peter Maxwell Davies), 5 July 1996 (world première). Conductor, Richard Armstrong; director, David Pountney; designers, Huntley/Muir. Lisa Tyrrell (The Child), Elizabeth Vaughan (First Official), Ann Howard (Second Official), Nan Christie (Third Official), Paul Whelan (The Doctor), Gwynne Howell (The Ruler)
  Performances were given in the New Theatre, Cardiff, and on tour at Bristol, Oxford, Swansea, Birmingham, Southampton, Plymouth, Liverpool, London (Royal Opera House, Covent Garden) and Llandudno.

GLYNDEBOURNE FESTIVAL OPERA
Founded 1934
Glyndebourne, Lewes, East Sussex BN8 5UU

The Festival ran from 17 May to 25 August 1996. *Così fan tutte* (1991), *Yevgeny Onyegin* (1994), *Arabella* (1984) and *Ermione* (1995) were revived.

New productions:
Theodora (Handel), 17 May 1996. Conductor, William Christie; director, Peter Sellars; designers, George Tsypin (set), Duna Ramicova (costumes). Dawn Upshaw (Theodora), Lorraine Hunt (Irene), David Daniels (Didymus), Richard Croft (Septimus), Frode Olsen (Valens)

Lulu (Berg), 15 July 1996. Conductor, Andrew Davis; director, Graham Vick; designer, Paul Brown. Christine Schäfer (Lulu), Kathryn Harries (Countess Geschwitz), Patricia Bardon (Wardrobe Mistress/Schoolboy/Groom), David Kuebler (Alva), Stephen Drakulich (Painter), Neil Jenkins (Prince/Manservant/Marquis), Norman Bailey (Schigolch), Wolfgang Schöne (Dr Schön/Jack the Ripper), Donald Maxwell (Animal Trainer/Acrobat), Jonathan Veira (Stage Manager/Banker/Medical Specialist/Professor)

GLYNDEBOURNE TOURING OPERA performed *La traviata* (1987), *Le nozze di Figaro* (1994) and *Theodora* (1996) at Glyndebourne, Southampton, Oxford, Norwich, Plymouth, Woking and Manchester between 12 October and 7 December 1996.

ENGLISH TOURING OPERA
Founded 1980 as Opera 80

The Barber of Seville and *Werther* were toured to Richmond, Basingstoke, High Wycombe, Buxton, Southsea, Crewe, Canterbury, Dartford, York and Bath from 18 October to 9 December 1995.

Rigoletto and *Werther* were toured to London (Sadler's Wells), Poole, Swindon, Reading, Brighton, Lowestoft, Crawley, Yeovil, Exeter, Coventry, Cambridge, Lincoln, Southend, Ipswich, Ulverston, Preston, Darlington and Carlisle from 20 February to 1 June 1996.

OPERA FACTORY
Founded 1982
South Bank Centre, London SE1

Curlew River (Britten) and *Dido and Aeneas* (Purcell), 1 September 1995. Conductor, Nicholas Kok; director, David Freeman; designer, Karin Suss. Nigel Robson (Madwoman), Geoffrey Dolton (Ferryman), Jozic Koc (Traveller), René Linnenbank (Abbot). Marie Angel (Dido/Sorceress), Sally Harrison (Belinda), Jozic Koc (Aeneas). The double bill was performed at the Queen Elizabeth Hall, London, and toured to Oxford, Reading, Malvern and Zurich.

OPERA NORTHERN IRELAND
Founded 1982
181A Stranmillis Road, Belfast BT9 5DU

Autumn season 1995 at the Grand Opera House, Belfast: *The Cunning Little Vixen* (Janáček), 16 September 1995. Conductor, Kenneth Montgomery; director, Clare Venables; designer, Tim Reed. Louise Walsh (Vixen), Kate McCarney (Fox), Christopher Purves (Forester), Nicholas Folwell (Poacher), Gerard O'Connor (Badger/Priest)

For the spring season (March 1996) at the Grand Opera House, Belfast, *The Marriage of Figaro* (1991) was revived.

Masters of the Queen's (King's) Music

'Master of the King's Music' was the title given to the official who presided over the court band during the reign of Charles I. The first Master was appointed in 1626. Today the Master is expected to organize the music for state occasions and to write new music for them, although there are no fixed duties. The post is held for life and the Master receives an annual honorarium of £100.

Nicholas Lanier (1588–1666), appointed 1626
Louis Grabu (?–1674), appointed 1666
Nicholas Staggins (1650–1700), appointed 1674
John Eccles (1668–1735), appointed 1700
Maurice Greene (1695–1755), appointed 1735
William Boyce (1710–79), appointed 1755

John Stanley (1713–86), appointed 1779
Sir William Parsons (1746–1817), appointed 1786
William Shield (1748–1829), appointed 1817
Christian Kramer (?–1834), appointed 1829
François (Franz) Cramer (1772–1848), appointed 1834
George Anderson (?–1870), appointed 1848
Sir William Cusins (1833–93), appointed 1870
Sir Walter Parratt (1841–1924), appointed 1893
Sir Edward Elgar (1857–1934), appointed 1924
Sir Henry Walford Davies (1869–1941), appointed 1934
Sir Arnold Bax (1883–1953), appointed 1941
Sir Arthur Bliss (1891–1975), appointed 1953
Malcolm Williamson (1931–), appointed 1975

Parliament

Both Houses of Parliament returned from the summer recess on 16 October 1995 and opened with tributes to Lord Home of the Hirsel, the former Prime Minister, who had died on 9 October. On 16 October in the Commons, the Home Secretary (Michael Howard) announced the publication of the report by Gen. Sir John Learmont into prison security, in the light of escapes from Whitemoor and Parkhurst prisons, and of the report by HM Inspector of Prisons (Judge Stephen Tumim) into Parkhurst prison. He announced that the director-general of the Prison Service (Derek Lewis) had been sacked from his post. Labour's home affairs spokesperson (Jack Straw) accused the Home Secretary of 'scapegoating anybody and everybody to ensure that the buck stops anywhere but with himself'. This led to an Opposition debate on 19 October deploring the unwillingness of the Home Secretary to accept responsibility for serious operational failures in the Prison Service, which was defeated by 280 votes to 231. On 18 October there was an Opposition debate introduced by Labour's transport spokesperson (Michael Meacher) calling on the Government to abandon the sale of Railtrack, which was defeated by 288 votes to 259. On 19 October the Minister for Health (Gerald Malone) made a statement on the arrangements for prescription rate exemption for men over the age of 60 in the light of the ruling by the European Court of Justice in the Richardson case that the UK government was guilty of discrimination contrary to EC directives by charging men under 65 for prescriptions but allowing them free to women over 60. The Government accepted the ruling, allowing men aged 60 to 64 to obtain prescriptions without charge from 20 October and, where appropriate, obtain reimbursement of charges already paid.

On 23 October the Secretary of State for Health (Stephen Dorrell) made a statement about the steps taken the previous week to inform women of the latest evidence about the safety of certain contraceptives, on the advice of the Committee on the Safety of Medicines. Labour's health spokesperson (Harriet Harman) claimed that it was 'wholly unsatisfactory that GPs and doctors in family planning were not informed in advance'. On 26 October the Northern Ireland Secretary (Sir Patrick Mayhew) presented the Northern Ireland (Remission of Sentences) Bill, to bring the terms for remission in Northern Ireland in line with the rest of the UK. The bill was rushed through all its stages before prorogation and was not amended, with all

---

THE QUEEN'S SPEECH 1995

Legislation proposed in the Queen's Speech included measures:
– on media ownership and digital licensing to encourage a free market approach (Broadcasting Bill)
– to provide for a high-speed rail link between London and the Channel Tunnel (Channel Tunnel Rail Link Bill)
– to give borrowing powers to grant-maintained schools and to introduce a nation-wide system of vouchers for pre-school provision for 4-year-olds (Nursery Education and Grant-Maintained Schools Bill)
– to allow students to borrow from banks on the same terms as from the Student Loans Company (Education (Student Loans) Bill)
– to reform education and training in Scotland (Education (Scotland) Bill)
– to allow disabled people to receive cash to choose equipment and services themselves rather than rely on local authorities to provide them (Community Care (Direct Payments) Bill)
– on homelessness, to improve the allocation of social housing and extend private sector investment (Housing Bill and Housing Grants, Construction and Regeneration Bill)
– to allow the Security Service to support the police against organized crime and the international drugs trade (Security Service Bill)
– to reduce the burdens from existing criminal procedures and to speed up court procedures (Criminal Procedure and Investigation Bill)

– to streamline the handling of asylum claims and tighten up the enforcement of immigration laws (Asylum and Immigration Bill)
– to bring the law governing military reserves up-to-date (Reserve Forces Bill)
– to re-enact temporarily the 1991 Northern Ireland emergency legislation to ensure that the necessary safeguards remain in place until a lasting peace is established (Northern Ireland (Emergency Provisions) Bill)
– to implement the requirements of the Chemical Weapons Convention, to allow the UK to ratify the Convention (Chemical Weapons Bill)
– to reform divorce law by the provision of family mediation as part of the divorce process, to provide protection to one member of the family against violence from another, and to regulate the occupation of the family home where a relationship has broken down (Family Law Bill)
Also proposed but dependent on the legislative time available were bills to reform the law on:
– defamation: to simplify existing procedures
– trusts of land: to provide a new, simplified method of holding land on trust
– damages: to structure settlements in personal injury claims to the needs of the injured party

the Commons stages being taken on 30 October and all the Lords stages completed on 2 November; the bill received royal assent on 8 November.

On 26 October the Commons approved the draft Ministerial and Other Salaries Order 1995, with increases of 2.7 per cent, without division. The Lords approved the measure on 30 October. On 31 October during consideration of Lords amendments to the Disability Discrimination Bill, the Commons overturned government defeats in the Lords to clause 12 (discrimination in relation to goods, facilities and services) by 285 votes to 250. The Lords accepted these reverses on 6 November. On 1 November the Commons agreed to the carry-over motion for the Channel Tunnel Rail Link Bill. On 2 November various minor changes to parliamentary procedure, covering Law Commission bills, the Statutory Instrument committee, Friday sittings/Wednesday morning sittings, and short speeches were approved.

On 6 November both Houses paid tribute to the assassinated Israeli Prime Minister Yitzhak Rabin. In the Commons there was a debate on the report of the select committee on standards in public life, set up to consider the recommendations of the Nolan Committee. A motion to ban paid advocacy was passed by 587 votes to two, with an amendment to declare income received passed by 322 votes to 271. Other motions relating to public inspection, recording of deputations in the register of interests and participation in delegations were also passed. A motion to approve the appointment of Sir Gordon Downie as the first Parliamentary Commissioner for Standards was approved by 231 votes to 71. On 7 November the Lords approved a motion relating to the declaration and registration of their interests. In the Commons Diana Maddock (LD) presented the Family Homes and Domestic Violence (No. 2) Bill to replace the government bill which had been withdrawn the previous week after pressure from Conservative MPs who felt that the provisions covering non-married couples and rights to evictions, etc., from homes went against traditional Conservative family values; there was insufficient parliamentary time for the bill to make any progress.

THE QUEEN'S SPEECH

The 1994–5 parliamentary session ended on 8 November. The Queen opened the 1995–6 session of Parliament on 15 November. The Queen's Speech outlined 15 major bills, including measures to increase competition in broadcasting, increase access to nursery education, extend the involvement of the Security Service in fighting crime and reform the divorce law (see page 1152).

In the debate on The Queen's Speech the Prime Minister (John Major) said, 'our legislative programme will allow us to build on the successes of the past and to meet the challenges ahead ... we have served our nation well and we have built up a strong economy ... our legislative programme is the right programme for the country; it will also be a litmus test for the Opposition ... we will pursue our objectives for the economy, for choice, for opportunity and for a safe and secure United Kingdom. That is what lies at the heart of our programme ... No other party can put the interests of this country first as this Conservative Government do.' The Leader of the Opposition (Tony Blair) thought the content was 'utterly irrelevant to the interests of Britain. It is a programme of a party that has ceased to have any real vision or purpose in government at all. It is about the interests of the Tory party, cobbling together any old bric-à-brac of legislation that can keep the Conservative Party in one piece ... There is nothing about jobs, nothing about reducing inequality and insecurity and nothing about helping those in poverty. Indeed, there is the opposite.' He did, however, pledge the Labour Party to continue to back the Government in their efforts to secure peace in Northern Ireland and to do so 'even when progress is difficult'. The Liberal Democrat leader (Paddy Ashdown) said, 'a glance at this programme tells us, frankly, all we need to know about the Government. It tells us that they are no longer a Government of direction, let alone any kind of long-term vision. They cannot be saved by new policies, because they have none – they ran out of those years ago. They cannot be saved by another relaunch ... They cannot be saved by another lurch to the right. The Queen's Speech is a charade – a pantomime ... The country cannot wait for the Government to be out of office.' During the usual six days of debate, a Labour amendment regretting the lack of references to education and crime in the Speech was defeated by 297 votes to 268; and a further Labour amendment noting the Government's broken promises on taxes was defeated by 298 votes to 271. A Liberal Democrat amendment regretting the measures included on housing and immigration as adding to the divisions within society was also defeated, by 297 votes to 32. The Speech itself was approved without division.

On 20 November the Home Secretary outlined the proposals to be included in the Asylum and Immigration Bill designed to deal with bogus asylum seekers and other illegal immigrants by strengthening the legislation, streamlining decisions and appeals, and discouraging unfounded claims. The bill would designate selected countries of origin as not giving rise to serious risk of persecution, would make appeals against return to a safe third country exercisable only after removal, and would remove a number of obstacles to the effective operation of the Asylum and Immigration Appeals Act 1993. In addition it would make it a criminal offence to employ a person not entitled to work in the UK. Jack Straw expressed concern that the proposals might damage race relations and may not work effectively.

On 27 November the Health Secretary outlined revised proposals from the National Blood Authority for the future of the blood service, minimizing unnecessary administrative and support costs with a

THE BUDGET 1995

FISCAL OUTLOOK

Government spending plans in 1996-7 to be reduced by £3,300 million, with further reductions of £3,700 million in 1997-8 (*see* page 594)

Public spending as a share of GDP reduced by 3.75 per cent

Control total reduced to £255,500 million in 1995-6 (down £800 million on November 1994 forecast), but to rise to £260,200 million in 1996-7 (down £3,200 million on 1994 forecast) (*see* page 594)

Social security spending higher than planned but covered by unallocated reserve of £3,000 million within control total

Taxes and social security revenues projected to rise from £254,200 million in 1995-6 to £268,700 million in 1996-7

Budget cuts taxes overall by £3,250 million, mostly in direct taxes

General government receipts to rise from £271,900 million in 1995-6 to £284,800 million in 1996-7 (*see* page 594)

PSBR to fall from £29,000 million in 1995-6 to £22,400 million in 1996-7 (*see* page 595) and to be in balance by the end of the decade

SPENDING

Public sector pay: tight controls to be maintained and increases in pay to be offset by increased efficiency

Central government: provision for running costs reduced by £270 million in 1996-7 and £380 million in 1997-8

Social security: real growth to rise by 1 per cent in each of the next three years. New restrictions on benefits especially over fraud and asylum seekers. Gap between lone parents' benefit rates and those paid to other families to be narrowed. Housing benefit to single people under 25 to be restricted

Privatization: housing corporations loans book and Ministry of Defence married quarters estate to be privatized

Education: spending on schools to rise by £878 million in 1996-7, the bulk being channelled through the local authorities. Spending on higher and further education remains as planned and will finance an increase of 50,000 students in further education. Private funding to add £430 million in 1996-7 for higher and further education and grant-maintained schools

Health: spending on NHS to rise by more than £1,000 million in 1996-7. Cost savings of £650 million to be ploughed back into patient care. Private Finance Investment of £700 million over three years

Home Office: increased spending to allow for 5,000 additional police officers over next three years, more closed-circuit television cameras in town centres and some 4,000 additional prison places

Transport: spending plans on national roads and central government support for local roads and transport reduced. Plans for over £4,000 million a year of publicly financed spending, with £1,000 million a year of investment under the Private Finance Initiative on transport infrastructure

Private Finance Initiative: private finance to provide £2,000 million in investment each year for the next three years; expected to raise £14,000 million by the end of 1998-9

Long-term care: several measures to help those in need of long-term care, including: level of capital below which people become eligible for help for care in homes doubled to £16,000; level below which they need make no contribution out of their capital increased to £10,000; benefits from a range of long-term care insurance policies exempted from tax

TAXATION

Small companies' rate of corporation tax reduced to 24 pence

Employers' National Insurance contributions cut by 0.2 per cent from April 1997, to be financed by a tax on waste disposal in landfill sites, coming into effect on 1 October 1996

Real increases in business rates to be capped at 7.5 per cent for large and 5 per cent for small properties

Basic rate of income tax reduced to 24 pence. Basic rate limit increased by £1,200

Personal allowances rise by £240

Married couple's allowance increased by £700

Tax on savings income cut from 25 pence to 20 pence

Inheritance tax threshold increased to £200,000

Capital gains tax relief extended

Measures to boost share ownership, including a new tax relief for company share option schemes to allow companies to grant share options worth up to £20,000 with no income tax to be payable when the options are exercised; minimum amount which may be saved in a monthly savings-related share option scheme reduced from £10 to £5

Road fuel duties to be increased by 5 per cent a year in real terms; petrol and diesel go up by 3.5 pence a litre, and super-unleaded fuel to go up by another 4 pence a litre in May 1996. Vehicle Excise Duty (VED) increased to £140 but road tax for lorries frozen. Cars older than 25 years to be exempt from VED

Tobacco duties to be increased by 3 per cent a year in real terms on cigarettes; duty on hand-rolling tobacco frozen

No change in duty on beer and wine. Duty on strong cider up by 8 pence a pint. Duty on spirits reduced by 4 per cent

General betting duty reduced by 1 per cent, and a 5 per cent cut in pool betting duty, with a possible further 1 per cent reduction in May 1996 to offset the effect of the National Lottery

FORECAST

Rate of inflation remains low and on course to meet the target rate of 2.5 per cent by the end of the current Parliament. Forecast to be 3 per cent in 1995 and to fall to 2.5 per cent in 1996

GDP expected to rise by 2.75 per cent in 1995 and by 3 per cent in 1996. Treasury forecasts a current account deficit of 1 per cent of GDP (£6,500 million) in 1995, narrowing to 0.75 per cent (£5,000 million) in 1996

---

new computer system to allow stocks to be managed on a national basis and with the existing 13 administrative centres being concentrated at three centres in Leeds, Bristol and London. Processing and testing would also cease at Lancaster, Oxford, Cambridge, Liverpool and Plymouth. Harriet Harman felt that the proposals would 'make the service more expensive and less able to respond quickly to the need for blood'.

THE BUDGET

The Chancellor (Kenneth Clarke) presented his third Budget on 28 November, in a speech lasting one hour and ten minutes (*see* above). He said that the Budget was designed to 'help the economy work better by improving incentives for individuals, ensuring better value for money from public spending and delivering services more efficiently in partnership with the private sector' and to 'ensure that the Public Sector Borrowing Requirement continues to decline'.

Mr Clarke also said the Budget would, 'put Britain on course to be the enterprise centre of Europe; a Britain that creates more jobs and more wealth in which we can all share because business can flourish here in a secure climate of low borrowing, low taxation, deregulation and free trade ... I have achieved the hat trick of controlling spending, downward borrowing and cutting taxes only because the Government have followed a consistent economic policy ... We are aiming at borrowing to fall to zero; public spending below 40 per cent of national income; inflation below 2.5 per cent; and a 20 per cent basic rate of income tax. This Budget puts us on the path to meet all those goals.'

Tony Blair christened it the '7 pence up, 1 pence down Budget' and concluded that, 'What was extraordinary about the Budget speech was that it gave no sense of a great strategic vision for the country's future. There was nothing – no all-encompassing horizon of achievement for this nation ... The Government wanted to hail the Budget as a turning point, but the British people know better. It is another milestone on the Government's road to defeat.' Paddy Ashdown thought the Government's message in the Budget was simple and brutally clear: 'Please can we buy your vote for a 1 pence cut in income tax? We have nothing further to offer you, but we believe that that will be enough to fool you into voting for us again ... It is not a Budget for Britain's future, but for the Conservative Party's survival and it will not work.'

On the second day of the debate on the Budget the Shadow Chancellor (Gordon Brown) confirmed that the Opposition would not vote against the proposed 1 pence reduction in income tax. On the fifth day of debate the deputy leader of the Labour Party (John Prescott) moved an amendment to reduce VAT on fuel to 5 per cent; this was defeated by 307 votes to 290. The Budget itself was passed by 315 votes to 285. Specific votes were taken on excise duties (passed by 305 votes to 40); betting/pool duty (passed by 305 votes to 41); 1 pence off income tax (passed by 313 votes to 38 – ten Labour MPs defied their whip and voted against); and a Labour amendment on public expenditure was defeated by 310 votes to 257.

On 29 November, the day US President Clinton visited Parliament, the Prime Minister made a statement on developments in the Northern Ireland peace process. The UK had agreed with the government of the Irish Republic to establish an international body to provide an independent assessment of the decommissioning issue. It would consist of three members under the chairmanship of US Senator George Mitchell and would report back by the middle of January 1996. This so-called twin-track approach was the best hope for a lasting settlement. Tony Blair welcomed the statement and gave credit to the Prime Minister and the Taoiseach for their perseverance and dedication. On the same day the Secretary of State for Social Security (Peter Lilley) made the annual benefits uprating state-

ment, reiterating the details of the Budget about benefits for single parents and housing benefit for the under-25s being frozen. Labour's social security spokesperson (Chris Smith) said that the statement 'has not protected the vulnerable. It does not come anywhere near a coherent benefit-to-work strategy. It deepens the divisions in a divided Britain.' The Scottish Secretary (Michael Forsyth) also made a statement on plans to enhance the government of Scotland. He rejected the idea of a devolved Parliament but would build on the recently ex-panded role of the Scottish Grand Committee. All Scottish bills would have a second reading in Scotland and a third reading in the Grand Com-mittee. There would be increased use of the special standing committee procedure and all government ministers could now be called to the committee. Labour's Scottish affairs spokesperson (George Robertson) derided the proposals and suggested that 'the "do nothing" policy of the Government has now been replaced by the "do as little as possible" policy'. On 30 November the Welsh Secretary (William Hague) made a statement on increased powers for the Welsh Grand Committee in its scrutiny of government business, to include a Question Time, more short debates and adjourn-ment debates, and the ability to call on all ministers of the Crown. It would meet more frequently and in various cities, not just Cardiff. Labour's Welsh affairs spokesperson (Ron Davies) welcomed the admission of the inadequacies of the current ar-rangements but hoped for the day when more far-reaching democratic reforms for the government of Wales would be introduced by a Labour govern-ment.

The Criminal Procedure and Investigations Bill to reform the law on prosecution and defence disclosure had an unopposed second reading in the Lords on 27 November. On the second day of the report stage on 5 February, the Government was defeated when a new clause 90, moved by Lord Ackner (Ind.), on indemnification of justices and justices' clerks was approved by 80 votes to 72. The bill received an unopposed second reading in the Commons on 27 February. The committee stage was delayed until May and it had an unopposed third reading on 12 June. It received royal assent on 4 July.

FAMILY LAW BILL

The bill to reform the rules governing divorce, with greater use of mediation, reintroduced elements of the domestic violence measure lost in the previous session. The new bill had an unopposed second reading in the Lords on 30 November. In five days in committee the bill was not amended. However, the Government was defeated on 29 February, the second day of the report stage, when an amendment to clause 4 moved by Baroness Hollis of Heigham (Lab.), with all-party support, to allow for the splitting of pensions between couples at the time of divorce was passed by 178 votes to 150. An amendment moved by Baroness Young (C.) to retain the principle of fault in divorce was rejected by 118 votes to 65. An amendment moved by Baroness Young on the third reading on 11 March, to increase the period of reconciliation before divorce from 12 months to 18, was defeated by 157 votes to 109. On the second reading in the Commons on 25 March, the Chancellor of the Duchy of Lancaster (Roger Freeman) said the Government was ready to accept the principle of splitting pensions between divorcing couples and would not seek to overturn the defeat in the Lords, but it would not be feasible to introduce this provision in the present bill. The second reading was passed by 280 votes to 13; nine Conservative MPs led by former Cabinet minister John Patten defied their whip and voted against (the Opposition abstained). It was agreed that the controversial clauses 5 and 7 would be taken on the floor of the House before Easter and that free votes would be taken on matters of conscience.

In committee of the whole House on 24 April an amendment moved by Edward Leigh (C.) to reintroduce the concept of fault was defeated by 257 votes to 137 in a free vote; 16 ministers voted against. An amendment to allow a cooling-off period of 18 months rather than one year was passed by 200 votes to 196 in a free vote, against the wishes of the Lord Chancellor (Lord Mackay of Clashfern). Four Cabinet ministers (Messrs Dorrell, Hague, Howard and Lilley) voted for the amendment, as did 30 others on the so-called 'payroll vote'. In committee the bill was amended against the Government's wishes to extend the cooling-off period to 21 months. This defeat was subsequently overturned by the Government during the remaining stages debate on 17 June, when an amendment to restore the period to 18 months was passed by 312 votes to 154 in a free vote; five Cabinet ministers (Messrs Dorrell, Forsyth, Hague, Howard and Lang) and 15 other ministers voted against. The Government accepted an Opposition amendment giving the Lord Chancellor the power to amend the legislation to effect pension division between divorcing couples. The third reading was passed by 427 votes to nine; four Conservative MPs voted against the Government. The Lords accepted the Commons amendments on 27 June and the bill received royal assent on 4 July.

The Community Care (Direct Payments) Bill, to enable individuals to be given cash to purchase their care directly, was given a unopposed second reading in the Lords on 7 December. The second reading in the Commons on 6 March was also unopposed. In committee the Government was defeated on clause 11 when provision for special grants for disabled people over the age of 65 was added to the bill. In discussion on remaining stages in the Commons on 10 June, the Government reversed this defeat, when the Parliamentary Under-Secretary at the Department of Health (John Bowis) promised to review the legislation as drafted after one year. One Conservative MP (Sir Andrew Bowden) and the

Independent Conservative MP Peter Thurnham voted against the Government. The third reading was passed without division and the bill received royal assent on 4 July.

On 7 December there was an adjournment debate in the Commons on the European Union and the Foreign Secretary (Malcolm Rifkind) confirmed that the Government would be producing a white paper on plans for the Inter-Governmental Conference (see pages 1168–9). In the Lords the Government was defeated when a motion moved by Lord Allen of Abbeydale (Ind.) to ensure that proposed reforms of the probation system would lead to a professional qualification of a high standard and be subject to external validation (effectively annulling the Government's draft order) was passed against the Government's wishes by 108 votes to 85.

ASYLUM AND IMMIGRATION BILL

The bill to strengthen the procedure to deal more swiftly with claims, to combat immigration racketeering and to reduce economic incentives that encourage false applications was given a second reading in the Commons on 11 December. A Liberal Democrat amendment declining a second reading on the grounds that the measure would adversely affect genuine asylum seekers was defeated by 319 votes to 285. An Opposition motion to commit the bill to a special standing committee was defeated by 319 votes to 284. The second reading itself was passed by 314 votes to 287. The third reading in the Commons was passed by 280 votes to 250 on 22 February.

The bill had its second reading in the Lords on 14 March. The Government was defeated in committee in the Lords on 23 April, when an amendment to clause 1 moved by the Bishop of Liverpool to exempt those who had been the victims of torture or might reasonably expect to be subjected to torture was passed by 143 votes to 124. The bill was recommitted to the committee on 1 July to reconsider clauses 9 to 12 following a ruling by the Court of Appeal that the regulations made in February cutting benefits to asylum seekers were illegal. (The Social Security Secretary had told the Commons on 24 June that he would be seeking to restore the fundamental policy by introducing the relevant amendments to this bill to tighten the law.) Government amendments were proposed by the Minister of State at the Home Office (Baroness Blatch) but they suffered a defeat when an Opposition amendment moved by Baroness Hollis of Heigham (Lab.) to a new government clause, to allow would-be immigrants a period of three days to claim refugee status and so qualify for benefit, was passed by 158 votes to 155. The Lords did, however, vote by 153 to 140 to reinstate rules denying welfare benefits to those who failed to claim asylum on arrival in the UK, thus overturning the High Court ruling. The Government was then defeated on the first day of the third reading (taken on the same day) when an amendment to clause 8, to exempt domestic staff who had been abused or exploited from new employment regulations on illegal immigrants, moved by Lord Hylton (Ind.), was passed by 90 votes to 76. The Government overturned the defeat on the three-day time period in the Commons on 15 July, when their amendment restoring the rule that immigrants should not get benefits unless they apply for asylum as soon as they arrive was approved by 295 votes to 274. One Conservative MP (Sir Patrick Cormack) voted against the Government. Attempts in the Lords to reverse this on 22 July failed when an all-party amendment moved by Lord McIntosh of Haringey (Lab.) was defeated by 182 votes to 168. The bill received royal assent on 24 July.

The Education (Scotland) Bill, to allow for the setting up of a Scottish Qualifications Authority and making provision in the area of pre-school education, school boards and placing requests, had an unopposed second reading in the Lords on 11 December. Under the new procedures it was considered in committee by a Scottish select committee on 25 and 26 March before committee consideration off the floor of the House on 23 and 24 April. The second reading in the Commons was on 4 June and an Opposition amendment declining a second reading, on the grounds that it would allow for the introduction of nursery vouchers in Scotland, was defeated by 276 votes to 253; the second reading was approved by 268 votes to 244. On 26 June a motion was passed by 349 votes to five (four SNP MPs and one Labour MP) to allow the chairman of the committee considering the Education (Scotland) Bill to have the assistance of the Serjeant-at-Arms to remove MPs who were not members of that committee from the room; SNP MPs Alex Salmond and Roseanna Cunningham had already disrupted the committee the previous Tuesday. The third reading was approved on 10 July by 278 votes to 255, and the bill received royal assent on 18 July.

On 13 December the Chancellor of the Duchy of Lancaster made a statement in the Commons on proposals for the privatization of Her Majesty's Stationery Office (HMSO) under the name of 'Stationery Office', by means of a competitive tender offer. A small residual body called HMSO would be retained to cover Crown and parliamentary copyright. Labour denounced this proposal as 'being driven not by the interests of the HMSO but by Tory dogma' and asked for proposals for HMSO to operate more commercially in the public sector to be produced instead.

The Armed Forces Bill, to renew the various discipline acts for the three forces, had an unopposed second reading in the Commons on 13 December. During the remaining stages debate on 9 May, Edwina Currie (C.) tried to move a new clause to provide that the armed forces should not discriminate on the grounds of sexual orientation, but this was defeated by 188 votes to 120. Seven other Conservative MPs voted with Mrs Currie and

eight Labour MPs voted with the Government. The second reading in the Lords was on 3 June, with the committee stage taken off the floor of the House on 19 June and the bill received royal assent on 24 July.

On 18 December the Prime Minister reported on the outcome of the European Council meeting held in Madrid on 15–16 December, which had concentrated on economic and monetary union (EMU) and enlargement. Heads of government had agreed on the name of 'euro' for the single currency and that the third stage of EMU would come into effect on 1 January 1999, with decisions on which countries would take part to be taken as early as possible in 1998. Tony Blair welcomed much of the statement but said it was time for serious and well-informed national debate on EMU to begin: 'The Government's European policy ... is still in tatters and uncertain. Rebuilding that policy is essential for Britain's credibility.' The Secretary of State for Transport (Sir George Young) made a statement on the future of rail privatization following a Court of Appeal judgement on 15 February against the Director of Passenger Rail Franchising over the passenger service requirements (PSRs) for the London Tilbury and Southend Rail (LTSR) and four other franchises. Sir George had clarified the instructions to the Director, who would be pressing ahead with the first three franchises (including LTSR) and would be developing the PSRs for the award of future franchises. Labour's transport spokesperson (Clare Short) asked the minister to halt the privatization and review progress to date in the light of these developments: 'his duty is to protect the national interest – and that requires him to halt the process of rail privatization'.

On 19 December there was a short debate in the Commons to take note of a Ministry of Agriculture, Fisheries and Food memorandum on EU fish quotas, introduced by Michael Forsyth. An Opposition amendment was moved by Labour's agriculture spokesperson (Gavin Strang) on access to the Irish 'box' by Spanish fishermen and calling for reform of the Common Fisheries Policy (CFP). The Government announced the restoration of the £2 million National Harbour Grant scheme and the reinstatement of a separate scheme to promote fish marketing. The Opposition amendment was defeated by 305 votes to 297. The Government motion, however, was also defeated, by 299 votes to 297. Two Conservative MPs (Bill Cash and Michael Carttiss) voted against the Government and a further 25 did not vote with the Government (11 probably abstaining deliberately). After the defeat the Agriculture Minister (Douglas Hogg) said that the Government would give due weight to the vote in the discussions in the Fisheries Council later in the week. On 20 December the National Heritage Secretary (Virginia Bottomley) responded to a Private Notice Question from her Labour Shadow (Dr Jack Cunningham) on her decision to back the director-general of the Office of the National Lottery (Peter Davis) and retain him in post despite pressures surrounding his decision to accept free flights from the American company GTech, part of the successful Camelot consortium, on a visit to the USA. Dr Cunningham felt the whole episode 'exposed an abysmal lack of judgement'.

When the Commons returned from the Christmas recess on 9 January the Minister of State at the Home Office (Ann Widdecombe) replied to a Private Notice Question from Jack Straw on government policy on manacling pregnant prisoners in labour, following a Channel 4 television programme on this issue. She emphasized that it was policy to secure all prisoners under escort but where medical treatment was concerned, restraints were removed. Mr Straw said her statement was 'completely unacceptable and that in a civilized society it is inhuman, degrading and unnecessary for a prisoner to be shackled at any stage of labour'. On 15 January Miss Widdecombe made a personal statement to the House apologizing for misleading MPs during her earlier statement when she had wrongly claimed that the hospital concerned in the incident (Whittington) had not submitted any concerns to the Prison Service. She had received a letter from the Whittington NHS Trust on 11 January saying that she had herself been misinformed about the hospital's position and that the chief executive had in fact written to the Prison Service about this issue on 31 August. On 18 January the Home Secretary announced that the practice of shackling female prisoners attending hospital to give birth had been ended.

The Northern Ireland (Emergency Provisions) Bill to extend the emergency provisions in Northern Ireland when the current Act expired in August 1996 had its second reading in the Commons on 9 January. The Northern Ireland Secretary (Sir Patrick Mayhew) regretted that 'this is not the time when we can sensibly say that the need for special provisions in Northern Ireland has passed'. An Opposition amendment declining a second reading on the grounds that the bill took no account of the review by John Rowe of current legislation on such issues as internment was defeated by 295 votes to 206, and the second reading was passed by 295 votes to 205. The third reading in the Commons was passed without division on 19 February and the second reading in the Lords on 21 March was unopposed. The bill received royal assent on 16 June.

The bill to allow the Security Service to assist the police against organized crime had an unopposed second reading in the Commons on 10 January. The bill was not amended in the Lords when it had its second reading on 14 May and received royal assent on 18 July.

On 11 January the Social Security Secretary made a statement in the Commons on the regulations which had been laid down to reform benefit arrangements for asylum seekers. Following a critical report from the Social Security Advisory Committee, benefits would be restored to up to 13,000 current asylum seekers but there would be curbs on future asylum seekers, with a new cut-off date of 5 February. One of Labour's social security team (Keith Bradley) said, 'the Opposition clearly support proper measures to stop fraudulent asylum seekers but surely tackling appalling administrative delays in the procedures would be far more effective than this indiscriminate attack on applicants?'

The Finance Bill implementing the proposals in the Budget was given a second reading on 15 January. An Opposition amendment declining a second reading on the grounds that the bill failed to address the needs of the country was defeated by 309 votes to 251; the second reading was passed by 309 votes to 274. The committee of the whole House on 23 and 25 January dealt with clauses relating to landfill tax, share options, self-assessment for income tax and mis-selling of pensions. During the remaining stages debate on 27 and 28 March new government clauses relating to hydrocarbon oil, landfill tax, life assurance business and personal pension schemes were added. An Opposition amendment on VAT relief for energy-saving materials was defeated by 280 votes to 279. The third reading was passed without division. The Lords considered the bill on 24 April and it received royal assent on 29 April.

BROADCASTING BILL

The bill proposed to amend the regulatory structure of the 1990 Act to allow the development of new digital terrestrial broadcasting and to amend existing media ownership rules to allow greater cross-holdings between newspapers, television and radio companies (for provisions, see page 670). It had an unopposed second reading in the Lords on 16 January. The Government was defeated in committee on 6 February when an amendment introduced by Lord Howell (Lab.) to prevent various sporting events from being shown exclusively on satellite television was passed by 233 votes to 106. On report on 5 March, the Under-Secretary of State at the Department of National Heritage (Lord Inglewood) announced that the Government had agreed to preserve eight top sporting events on terrestrial television but refused to accept a further amendment extending the provision to edited highlights from all top sporting events. On 7 March he announced the ending of the funding formula under which Channel 4 paid an annual levy to independent television (ITV) in return for a safety net. On the third reading on 18 March Lord Howell withdrew his amendments relating to televised sport after Lord Inglewood had agreed to a compromise by drawing up a voluntary code under which broadcasters who bought the live rights to major events would offer highlights to other stations. An Opposition objection to the second reading in the Commons on 16 April on the grounds that the bill failed to provide the necessary incentives for rapid development of digital terrestrial television, contained no satisfactory safeguards for sporting events, and treated newspaper groups unfairly, was defeated by 297 votes to 267. In committee during May the Government introduced amendments to the rules on cross-media ownership and the third reading was passed without division on 2 July; the bill received royal assent on 24 July.

On 19 January John Butterfill (C.) introduced the British Time (Extra Daylight) Bill, which had come top of the Private Members' Bill ballot; it proposed to advance by one hour the time for general purpose throughout the year but was blocked on its second reading in the Commons. The Government remained neutral on the issue but many Scottish and northern MPs spoke against the bill. A closure motion was passed by 93 votes to 82 but as fewer than 100 MPs voted in favour, the debate lapsed. Andrew Hunter's Dogs (Fouling of Land) Bill received a procedural second reading. It completed its Commons stages on 22 March and had an unopposed second reading in the Lords on 8 May. It was not amended and received royal assent on 16 June.

The Nursery Education and Grant-Maintained Schools Bill proposed to provide for the expansion of the education of the under-fives with the provision of nursery school vouchers (with trials to take place in four pilot schemes); to remove the statutory bar preventing grant-maintained schools from borrowing on the commercial market; and to focus on improvement in standards of achievement and encouragement of parental choice, diversity and the aspirations of all parents and children. It had its second reading in the Commons on 22 January by 285 votes to 253; the third reading was approved by 272 votes to 238 on 19 March. The second reading in the Lords on 20 May was unopposed but the Government was defeated in committee on 17 June when an amendment to clause 1 was moved by Labour's education spokesperson in the Lords, Lord Morris of Castle Morris, with support from Liberal Democrat and cross-bench peers. The amendment required ministers to report back to Parliament with an evaluation of the workings of the four pilot schemes in their first year before extending the scheme nation-wide and was passed by 92 votes to 58. This would have delayed the implementation of the scheme nationally until after the next general election. This defeat was overturned in the Commons on 17 July by 275 votes to 251, and the bill received royal assent on 24 July.

On 23 January a move by the Labour Party to annul the Social Security (Persons from Abroad) Miscellaneous Regulations 1996 as 'simply inhumane' was defeated by 279 votes to 264. On 24 January the Prime Minister made a statement on the report of the Mitchell Commission on the decommissioning of arms in Northern Ireland, which had set out six principles embodying the path of democracy and non-violence (*see* page 1073), but had concluded that, on the basis of its discussions, the paramilitaries would not decommission any arms prior to all-party negotiations. As

he was not prepared to accept that any one group should, through its intransigence, stand in the way of peace and a comprehensive settlement for the people of Northern Ireland, Mr Major said that he was therefore taking up one of the ideas mentioned in the report of an election as a means of getting all parties together for talks. The Government was ready to introduce legislation in order to allow such an elective process to go ahead as soon as may be practicable and he hoped this would attract support right across the House. Tony Blair endorsed the six principles set out in the report and agreed that the elective process deserved serious consideration: 'we offer again today our unqualified support in pursuing peace in Northern Ireland'. On 26 January Alun Michael's Wild Mammals (Protection) Bill, to protect wild animals from torture and other cruel acts, completed all its Commons stages. Taken up by Baroness Nichol (Lab.) in the Lords, it received royal assent on 29 February. Lady Olga Maitland's Offensive Weapons Bill, to make it easier for the police to detain those carrying knives, also received a second reading. On 27 February the Parliamentary Under-Secretary of State at the Home Office (Timothy Kirkhope) introduced a motion to extend the scope of the bill to include supplying blades to those under the age of 16 and also having such a blade on school premises. This bill was adopted by the Earl of Lauderdale (C.) in the Lords and received royal assent on 4 July.

HOUSING BILL

The bill to extend the opportunities for people to own their own homes received a second reading in the Commons on 29 January by 290 votes to 259. In committee the Government was defeated when David Ashby (C.) voted with the Opposition to allow all tenants with leases over 21 years to buy their freeholds regardless of rent. In the remaining stages debate on 30 April the Government narrowly avoided defeat on their compromise solution reversing this defeat, when their amendment proposing that anyone with a lease of more than 50 years would qualify automatically but those with leases between 21 and 50 years would have to undergo a low rent test was passed by 289 votes to 287. The Government also overturned a defeat in committee that would have enabled leaseholders to remove the right to manage from a landlord irrespective of whether he was good, bad or indifferent when its new clause 15 (appointment of manager: transfer of jurisdiction to leasehold valuation tribunal) was passed by 288 votes to 279. The third reading was passed by 286 votes to 256. An unopposed second reading in the Lords on 16 May was followed by three days of report in July and the Government was nearly defeated on 11 July when a new clause was moved by Baroness Park of Monmouth (C.) demanding consultation on the proposed sale of armed forces married quarters, in an attempt to delay the sale indefinitely. This was defeated by 256 votes to 176, following the imposition of the first three-line whip in the Lords since 1993. The Government was defeated again on the third reading on 18 July when an amendment moved by Viscount Bledisloe (Ind.) to clause 83 (determination of reasonableness of service charges) to ensure that the amount of fees charged would be the same as for similar proceedings in the county court, was passed by 136 votes to 119. The Government overturned these defeats in the Commons on 22 July by 265 votes to 217, by substituting a figure of £500. An attempt by the Opposition to amend the low rent test qualifying period from 50 years to 35 was defeated by 239 votes to 119. The bill received royal assent on 24 July.

In the Lords on 30 January a move to annul the Social Security (Persons from Abroad) (Miscellaneous) Amendment Regulations 1996 by various Opposition peers led by Baroness Hollis of Heigham was defeated and the regulations were approved by 175 votes to 126. On 2 February John Marshall's Sexual Offences (Conspiracy and Incitement) Bill, to make it an offence to conspire or to incite a person to commit certain sexual offences abroad against children, had an unopposed second reading. Adopted by Lord Pilkington of Oxenford (C.) in the Lords, it received royal assent on 4 July.

On 5 February Sir George Young made a statement in the Commons in response to a Private Notice Question from Sir Teddy Taylor (C.) on the future management of LTSR following the delaying of the transfer of the franchise after the discovery of pricing irregularities in the sale of tickets; an investigation was underway. Clare Short asked for assurances that such fraud would not take place in companies that had already been franchised. On 6 February the Minister for Energy (Tim Eggar), responding to a Private Notice Question from Labour's trade and industry spokesperson (Margaret Beckett), made a statement on the newly announced British Gas Schedule 5 Transfer Scheme, splitting the company into two, and on the announcement of the early retirement of chief executive Cedric Brown. Mrs Beckett asked for 'absolute assurance that the interests of customers will be protected'. On 7 February there was an Opposition debate expressing concern at the grave allegations of fraud in the privatized rail sector but a government amendment applauding the progress of the privatization programme was passed instead by 298 votes to 262. Another debate on an Opposition motion, opposing any moves to privatize the Post Office, was also defeated by 289 votes to 255. Two Private Members' Bills completed all their Commons stages: the Non-Domestic Rating (Information) Bill introduced by Allan Stewart (C.) and the Law Reform (Year and a Day Rule) Bill introduced by Doug Hoyle (Lab.). Another, the Prisoners' Earnings Bill introduced by Hartley Booth (C.), had a procedural second reading. All three went on to gain royal assent.

On 12 February the Prime Minister made a statement on the IRA bomb explosion in London's Docklands on 9 February, the declared end to the IRA cease-fire and the implications for security and the peace process. Mr Major said, 'The Government will not be deterred by terrorism ... I will leave no stone unturned in the search for peace.' Tony Blair joined the Prime Minister in condemning the atrocity without reservation: 'Whatever the political differences between myself and the Prime Minister, on this matter we shall stand foursquare together in the cause of peace.'

THE SCOTT REPORT

On 15 February the President of the Board of Trade (Ian Lang) made a statement on the publication of the report by Sir Richard Scott into the sale of arms to Iran. He said that the report had shown that government ministers had not conspired to imprison innocent people nor had they wilfully misled Parliament. Labour's foreign affairs spokesperson (Robin Cook) said that he 'did not recognize the report from the statement the House has just heard ... it documents how ministers changed the guidelines but were more worried that Members of Parliament and the public might find out than they were about what Saddam Hussein might do with the weapons'. In the debate on the report on 26 February the Opposition forced a division, although the motion was on the adjournment of the House, which the Government won by one vote (320 to 319). The Independent Conservative MP Peter Thurnham voted against the Government, as did two Conservative MPs (Quentin Davies and Richard Shepherd). The three Democratic Unionist Party MPs abstained but all the other parties voted with the Opposition. In the debate in the Lords on the same day the former Prime Minister Baroness Thatcher defended the role of the two ministers most under attack, Sir Nicholas Lyell and William Waldegrave, by stressing that the guidelines on the sale of arms to Iraq had not been changed and Parliament had not been misled. On 16 February Harry Greenway's Noise Bill to amend the law on noise at night and make provision for the forfeiture and confiscation of equipment used to make noise unlawfully, had an unopposed second reading. It was adopted by Baroness Gardner of Parkes (C.) in the Lords and received royal assent on 18 July. Mark Robinson's Railway Heritage Bill also received an unopposed second reading. Adopted by Lord Finsberg (C.) in the Lords, it received royal assent on 18 July.

On 19 February the Secretary of State for Education and Employment (Gillian Shephard) made a statement in the Commons on higher education, announcing the setting up of a committee of inquiry, chaired by Sir Ron Dearing, to make recommendations on how the shape, structure, size and funding of higher education, including support for students, should develop to meet the needs of the UK over the next 20 years. Labour's education spokesperson (David Blunkett) welcomed the statement and commended the Secretary of State for her approach to a national inquiry. Sir

George Young made a statement on the operation to salvage the oil tanker *Sea Empress*, aground off the port of Milford Haven, and the Marine Accident Investigation Branch (MAIB) inquiry into the incident. Clare Short pressed for a fuller inquiry, possibly under Lord Donaldson, to review the problems that remained following the implementation of his earlier report into the *Braer* incident. Sir George told the Commons on 22 February that he had asked the Chief Inspector of the MAIB to extend the scope of the investigation to include the salvage operations as well as the cause of the incident itself. On 20 February Stephen Dorrell made a statement about the future of mental health services, announcing the publication of the report on the ministerial review of mental health (launched in August 1995), the publication of a document, *The Spectrum of Care*, setting out the range of services that should constitute a modern mental health service, the detailed application criteria for the Mental Health Challenge Fund, and details of the arrangements for the mental illness specific grant (increased by 23 per cent). Harriet Harman felt the statement 'offers no new money, no new rights and no new policy directions ... he has not taken the action to tackle the problems'.

On 28 February the Prime Minister reported on the outcome of the Anglo-Irish summit and progress in the peace process. All-party negotiations would begin on 10 June after elections, the details of which were still to be worked out and agreed. The possibility of a referendum would also be discussed. Sinn Fein could only join the talks if the IRA ceasefire was reinstated. The first item on the agenda of these negotiations would be decommissioning arms. Tony Blair welcomed the statement and 'the determination to try to put the peace process back on track'. On 29 February Sir George Young announced the award of the contract for the construction and running of the Channel Tunnel rail link to London and Continental Railways. Government financial support of £1,400 million would be provided, along with further debt write-offs. Clare Short welcomed the announcement but suggested that, but for delays caused by the Government, 'the project could have been started in 1989 at a cost of less than £1,000 million to public funds'.

On 6 March Douglas Hogg responded to a Private Notice Question from Gavin Strang on the effect of the 'Factortame' judgement on compensation for Spanish fishing vessels to be paid by the British taxpayer. He said that the Government would be pursuing treaty or other changes at the EU Inter-Governmental Conference to enable member states to ensure that fishing opportunities arising from their national quota provided real benefits to their own fishing communities and not to others. Gavin Strang called the judgement 'another demonstration of the indefensible workings of the common fisheries policy'. On 8 March Sir Anthony Grant's Treasure Bill, to amend the law on treasure

trove, was given an unopposed second reading. The bill was taken up in the Lords by the Earl of Perth (C.) and received royal assent on 4 July. In the Lords the Government was defeated when, on a motion to take note of the Government's plans for the future privatization of the Recruitment and Assessment Services, an amendment calling for the abandonment of the plan moved by Lord Bancroft (Ind.) was passed by 124 votes to 64.

The Defamation Bill, to give effect to the Law Commission report on defamation, was given an unopposed second reading in the Lords on 8 March. In committee on 3 April Lord Hoffman (Ind.) spoke to, but then withdrew, an amendment covering evidence concerning proceedings in Parliament, which would allow individual MPs to waive parliamentary privilege (amending the 1689 Bill of Rights) to sue newspapers over reports of their parliamentary activities. On report on 16 April Lord Finsberg (C.) had intended to move an amendment on behalf of Lord Hoffman, but when the division was called no-one either voted or spoke so the amendment was not made. The second reading in the Commons on 21 May was unopposed but in committee the amendment was finally added. During the remaining stages debate on 24 June a move to block this new clause was defeated by 264 votes to 201. The Government had officially remained neutral over the original amendment. The bill received royal assent on 4 July.

On 14 March the Scottish Secretary made a statement on the shooting of 16 primary school children and a teacher at Dunblane primary school the day before. He announced the setting up of an inquiry under Lord Cullen, the details of which would be announced once they had been agreed.

BSE CRISIS

On 20 March the Health Secretary made a statement in the Commons on the latest advice received from the Spongiform Encephalopathy Advisory Committee (SEAC) that a new strain of Creutzfeldt Jakob disease (CJD) had been uncovered which could possibly be linked to bovine spongiform encephalopathy (BSE) in animals. The committee had therefore recommended that a series of measures be taken to reduce further the risk to human and animal health and that further research should be carried out urgently. It had concluded that the risk from eating beef was extremely small and there was also no need to revise its advice on the safety of milk. Harriet Harman asked Mr Dorrell 'to confirm that we are dealing not with absolute risks but with relative risks, and that the aim is to achieve the difficult feat of balancing the interests of the economy and the meat industry with those of health'. This was followed by a statement by Douglas Hogg on the actions to be taken to minimize the risk; carcasses of animals over the age of 30 months must be deboned in specially licensed plants and trimmings kept out of the food chain, and the use of mammalian meat and bonemeal in feed for all farm animals was to be banned. Gavin Strang asked what advice the Government was 'giving to people about whether they, their children and their grandchildren should be eating beef and beef products'. Mr Hogg felt 'there should be no loss of confidence in beef.' On 21 March the Prime Minister made a statement on the proposed elections to the all-party negotiations in Northern Ireland. Elections would be held on 30 May and the life of the elected forum would be 12 months.

On 25 March Stephen Dorrell made a further statement on BSE developments, with the latest advice from SEAC that if human infection with the BSE agent did indeed occur, infants and children were no more likely to be susceptible to infection than adults. The Government would not therefore be advising schools to remove beef from their menus. SEAC did not believe that any additional precautionary measures were justified at this stage but the situation needed to be kept under careful review. Harriet Harman accused the Government of 'reckless disregard for public health and their dogma on deregulation that have swept us into this crisis'. Douglas Hogg also added to his earlier statement, announcing new measures recommended by SEAC to deal with the treatment of trimmings from cattle over 30 months of age, on meat and bonemeal, and on the status of the heads of animals over six months old. Gavin Strang asked him to recognize that his prime responsibility was 'to ensure that the food in our shops is safe to eat'. In a debate on BSE on 28 March, Mr Hogg announced that meat from newly slaughtered cattle aged over 30 months would be banned as part of an £85 million package to restore public confidence. He also announced the removal of further parts of cows from the food chain and concluded, 'British beef is safe and can be eaten with confidence.'

On 1 April the Prime Minister reported on the outcome of the European Council meeting in Turin on 29 March, where the purpose had been to launch the Inter-Governmental Conference. He had underlined the UK's stance on subsidiarity, the role of national parliaments, opposition to any extension of qualified majority voting and the need for reforms of the European Court of Justice. He had continued to resist any suggestion that the treaty be amended to cover employment issues. As a separate issue they had also discussed the Europe-wide crisis in the beef market and had agreed to the European Union bearing a share of the financial burden. Negotiations would continue in the Agriculture Council on the measures needed to restore confidence. Tony Blair felt the lesson of the weekend had been 'that Britain gains most from Europe by a spirit not of perpetual isolationism but constructive co-operation and that that is the only way for Britain to lead in Europe'. Michael Howard made a statement on the need to amend the Prevention of Terrorism Act to strengthen the ability of the police to protect the public against the threat from terrorism, with the real threat of a continued IRA campaign. With the

agreement of the Opposition he would be introducing a bill the next day with the hope of receiving royal assent before the Easter recess. It would give new powers to the police to search pedestrians in a designated area, to search listed non-residential premises, to search freight at ports, and to impose cordons and temporary parking bans. The Prevention of Terrorism (Additional Powers) Bill was presented on 2 April and all its Commons stages were taken that day; the official Opposition line was to abstain. All Lords stages were taken on 3 April and the bill received royal assent the same day.

On 3 April Douglas Hogg reported on the emergency meeting of the EU Agriculture Council in Luxembourg from which he had just returned. Despite some progress the propositions on the table at the end of the meeting did not meet the UK's central requirement that the export ban be lifted: 'the sweeping ban on our exports is unjustified and the Government will continue to work by every means possible to get that ban lifted'. Gavin Strang felt that 'the deal he has brought back ... is the worst of all worlds and that, once again, a weak Government who are isolated in Europe have failed completely to represent effectively Britain's interests in Europe'.

Returning from the Easter recess on 16 April, John Bowis responded to a Private Notice Question from Simon Hughes (LD) on the reliability of the Abbott tests for HIV/Aids over the preceding 12 months and the need to retest some 25,000 cases following the withdrawal of the test kit. Douglas Hogg made a statement on BSE, explaining that the Government would be challenging the EU ban on beef exports in the courts and announcing a further package of measures worth £938 million to support the domestic livestock industry in the current year, with a further £550 million in following years. Gavin Strang said, 'While the Government have announced some useful measures, four weeks later there is still a crisis and thousands of livelihoods are at stake.' On 17 April in the Lords there was a debate on the beef industry, while in the Commons an Opposition motion calling for the withdrawal of the plans for the privatization of Railtrack was defeated by 306 votes to 287.

On 25 April Douglas Hogg responded to a Private Notice Question from one of Labour's agriculture team, Elliot Morley, on the revised proposals for the slaughter of cattle that the UK was submitting to the European Commission. The scheme would involve limited numbers of individual animals, not the slaughter of whole herds, and was conditional on plans for lifting the EU ban on British beef. The issue was debated again at the Agriculture Council the following week and on 1 May Mr Hogg reported on the outcome. The Agriculture Council had concluded that the current export ban was temporary and that the measures already in place and foreseen were part of a process which should allow the ban to be lifted step-by-step. The lifting of the ban on by-products (tallow, gelatin and semen) would be addressed by the EU Standing Veterinary Committee shortly. The so-called 30-month slaughter scheme would be launched on 2 May with more than 60 abattoirs and 80 livestock markets acting as collection centres.

On 7 May the Minister of State for Agriculture, Fisheries and Food (Tony Baldry) responded to a Private Notice Question from Paul Tyler (LD) on progress with the 30-month cattle disposal scheme. Slaughtering had begun in Scotland on 3 May and elsewhere in the UK on 7 May. Some 104 markets and 72 abattoirs had been approved as collection centres. Paul Tyler said, 'a great industry in our rural areas is being held at gunpoint by the dither and delay of this Government'. On 9 May the Environment Secretary (John Gummer) made a statement in response to a Private Notice Question from Peter Brooke (C.) on the publication of the report of the district auditor (John Magill) on Westminster City Council and his decision to surcharge six Conservative councillors the sum of £31 million, on a charge of gerrymandering. Three other councillors, including the Conservative MP Barry Legg, had been cleared. Mr Gummer refused to comment on the findings as it was his understanding that the six intended to appeal. Frank Dobson condemned the six and called for a public inquiry to establish the involvement of Conservative Central Office and the Government in the scandal. An Opposition motion deploring the 'scandalous conduct of Tory flagship Westminster Council' was defeated by 288 votes to 267 on 14 May.

On 15 May the French President (Jacques Chirac) addressed both Houses of Parliament. The Home Secretary responded to a Private Notice Question from Jack Straw on the discovery of contaminated equipment at the Forensic Explosives Laboratory in Sevenoaks. An independent review under Prof. Brian Caddy had been set up to look into the circumstances and, in the light of the findings of that review, decisions would be made on whether particular cases, where prosecution had hinged on evidence from the laboratory, should be referred to the Court of Appeal. There was a row over the annual debate on the Common Agricultural Policy on 15 and 16 May when the Government tabled a motion for the adjournment of the House rather than a motion to take note, thus denying the Opposition any opportunity to table a substantive amendment. Gavin Strang announced that Labour would divide the House anyway. During the second day of the debate Tony Baldry announced an immediate interim payment to farmers of £300 for cattle caught in the backlog for culling. The Government instructed its MPs not to vote in the division called by the Labour Party, so the motion 'that the House do now adjourn' was passed by 252 votes to one and the rest of the day's business was lost. The vote against was from Conservative MP David Atkinson who stood to lose his adjournment debate if the motion was passed.

On 21 May John Major made a statement on the continuing efforts to get the EU ban on British beef and beef products lifted and on the implications for the UK's wider European policy. He thanked those countries and the Commission which had supported the UK position but expressed regret at the failure of the Standing Veterinary Council to lift the ban on secondary products. As a result, he declared a policy of non-co-operation with EU partners; with immediate effect Britain would use its veto to block the passage of all EU directives requiring unanimity and would adopt a policy of non-co-operation at meetings of the Inter-Governmental Conference. He was prepared to carry this on to the next EU summit at Florence, when he would refuse to sign the communiqué, so turning it into a legal nullity. Tony Blair pledged to 'support the Government in any sensible moves to ensure that the negotiations [on lifting the ban] are successful ... but before passing judgement on the policy of non-co-operation, we must know exactly what is meant by it'. Douglas Hogg then made a statement on the outcome of the Agriculture Council meeting on 20 and 21 May, when the European Commission had agreed to put the proposal for lifting the ban on secondary products, which the Veterinary Council had refused to endorse (although technically passed by 48 votes to 39, this was an insufficient majority), to the Council at its next meeting in June, when a simple majority would be all that was required to pass it.

On 11 June Bill Cash (C.) was given permission to introduce his Referendum Bill to allow for the holding of a referendum on the need for changes to the treaty on European Union affecting the UK's continuing membership of the EU and its participation in EMU and a single currency by 95 votes to one; 74 Conservative backbench MPs voted for the measure (with the four tellers, all Conservative, also in favour) and one (Robert Banks) against. However, lack of parliamentary time prevented the bill from making further progress.

On 17 June the Welsh Secretary (William Hague) announced plans for a public inquiry into child abuse in residential homes in Clwyd and Gwynedd in the 1970s and 1980s. He also announced that the Health Secretary had asked the Children's Safeguards Review under Sir William Utting to examine whether existing safeguards at residential institutions for children were the most effective that could be realistically designed. On 24 June the Prime Minister reported on the outcome of the European Council held in Florence on 21 and 22 June, which had covered the easing of the beef crisis and had enabled the lifting of the UK's policy of non-co-operation on EU business. Tony Blair asked for a definite date when the beef export ban would end and, in the absence of one, called it 'an object lesson in the Government's capacity to turn any crisis into a catastrophe'. A Liberal Democrat motion on 25 June calling for the salary of the

Agriculture Minister to be cut due to his mishandling of the beef crisis was defeated by 144 votes to 38.

MPs' PAY

On 10 July motions to approve the recommendations of the independent review body on parliamentary and ministerial salaries were introduced by the Leader of the House (Tony Newton). A government motion recommending limiting the increase to 3 per cent was defeated by 317 votes to 168. The 'payroll vote' (some 126 government members) had been instructed to vote for this option but some 16 failed to do so, including six Cabinet ministers; Tony Blair and 42 other Labour MPs voted for the motion but 12 members of the Shadow Cabinet voted against. A motion to accept the full increase of 26 per cent was approved by 279 votes to 154; it provoked widespread outrage and condemnation outside Parliament. Ministers' salary increases (an extra £8,000 a year) were approved by 253 votes to 49; the recommended mileage allowance reduction was approved by 376 votes to 39; and new office cost allowances were approved by 215 votes to 189.

On 11 July the South African President (Nelson Mandela) addressed both Houses of Parliament. On 15 July Sir Patrick Mayhew made a statement on the deteriorating situation in Northern Ireland following the Orange Order march down the Garvagy Road, Drumcree, and the bombing of the Killyhelvin Hotel in Enniskillen. He announced the establishment of a review to examine the existing arrangements for handling parades and marches in Northern Ireland. He stressed the need for the UK and Irish governments to continue to discuss mutual security interests. On 16 July an Opposition motion criticizing the Government's sale of Ministry of Defence married quarters was defeated by 307 votes to 275.

On 22 July Ian Lang made a statement in the Commons on plans to suspend the Post Office's statutory monopoly on the delivery of letters of less than £1 from 26 July for a period of one month unless the Communications Workers Union called off its planned strike. He said that if disruption of postal services was to continue, he would be proposing a further suspension of three months thereafter. Margaret Beckett called this 'a piece of transparent dishonesty ... the Government are trying yet again to pursue the folly of Post Office privatization by any means or excuse'. On 24 July Douglas Hogg made a statement on the outcome of the Agriculture Council meeting on 22 July and the recommendation of the SEAC that the brains of sheep over six months old should be removed from the human food chain. He reiterated that there was no direct threat to human health. Gavin Strang suggested that 'in view of the trade in lamb throughout Europe it clearly makes sense that any measures of this nature should be implemented across all members of the European Union'. There was a debate that evening on the accelerated slaughter programme on which the Liberal Democrats forced a vote but it was passed by 188 votes to 22. A motion to approve the third report of the committee on standards and privileges, in particular the code of conduct proposed in it, was passed without division. On 25 July the Parliamentary Under-Secretary of State at the Ministry of Defence (Earl Howe) made a statement on the placing of three new RAF procurement contracts, valued at £4,000 million, for a conventionally armed stand-off missile, an air-launched anti-armour missile and for a replacement for the Nimrod anti-submarine aircraft. There was a row earlier in the day when this long-awaited announcement was released as a written answer to a parliamentary question, and the leader of the Labour peers, Lord Richard, insisted on an oral statement.

The Commons rose for the summer recess on 24 July and the Lords rose on 25 July.

PUBLIC ACTS OF PARLIAMENT

This list is of those Public Acts which received the royal assent after August 1995. The date stated after each Act is the date on which it came into operation; c. indicates the chapter number of each Act

Atomic Energy Authority Act 1995, c. 37, 8 November 1995
Provides for the transfer of property rights and liabilities of the UK Atomic Energy Authority to other persons

Civil Evidence Act 1995, c. 38, day or days to be appointed
Provides for the admissibility of hearsay evidence, proof of certain documentary evidence and the admissibility of official actuarial tables in civil proceedings

Criminal Law (Consolidation) (Scotland) Act 1995, c. 39, 1 April 1996
Consolidates the statutes relating to Scottish criminal procedure

Criminal Procedure (Consequential Provisions) (Scotland) Act 1995, c. 40, 1 April 1996
Provides for the repeals, consequential amendments, transitional and transitory matters and savings in connection with the consolidation of enactments in the Criminal Procedure (Scotland) Act 1995, the Proceeds of Crime (Scotland) Act 1995 and the Criminal Law (Consolidation) (Scotland) Act 1995

Law Reform (Succession) Act 1995, c. 41, 8 November 1995

Introduces rules with regard to persons dying on or after 1 January 1996 relating to the distribution of estates on intestacy in England and Wales, and alters the effect on a will of the testator's divorce or the annulment of his marriage

Private International Law (Miscellaneous Provisions) Act 1995, c. 42, Part II on 8 January 1996, the rest on days to be appointed
Reforms three areas of conflict of law rules: payment of interest on judgment debts and arbitral awards expressed in a foreign currency; the validity within this jurisdiction of potentially polygamous marriages; the choice of law to be applied in tort or delict cases involving a foreign element

Proceeds of Crime (Scotland) Act 1995, c. 43, 1 April 1996
Consolidates certain enactments in Scotland relating to the confiscation of the proceeds of and the forfeiture of property used in crime

Statute Law (Repeals) Act 1995, c. 44, 8 November 1995
Provides for the repeals of various enactments which are no longer of practical utility

Gas Act 1995, c. 45, various dates
Introduces a new licensing framework for the British Gas Industry

Criminal Procedure (Scotland) Act 1995, c. 46, 1 April 1996
Consolidates certain enactments relating to Scottish criminal procedure

Northern Ireland (Remission of Sentences) Act 1995, c. 47, 17 November 1995
Permits the release on licence of persons serving sentences under the Northern Ireland (Emergency Provisions) Act 1991, s. 14

Charities (Amendment) Act 1995, c. 48, 8 November 1995
Provides that two or more charities sharing the same charity trustees may be treated as a single charity for the purposes of the Charities Act 1993

Town and Country Planning (Cost of Inquiries etc.) Act 1995, c. 49, 8 November 1995
Makes provision to enable the Secretary of State to recover payments from local authorities in respect of administrative costs of certain local inquiries and other hearings relating to town and country planning

Disability Discrimination Act 1995, c. 50, various dates, some to be appointed
Makes it illegal to discriminate against disabled persons in relation to employment, the provision of goods, facilities and services, and the management of premises; establishes a National Disability Council

Medical (Professional Performance) Act 1995, c. 51, various dates, some to be appointed
Amends the Medical Act 1983 to make provision relating to the professional performance of registered medical practitioners and the voluntary removal of names from the register of those practitioners; and for connected purposes

Mental Health (Patients in the Community) Act 1995, c. 52, 1 April 1996
Provides for the introduction of a system of supervision of the care in the community of certain mentally disordered patients following their release from hospital. Separate provision is made for England and Wales and for Scotland

Criminal Injuries Compensation Act 1995, c. 53, 8 November 1995
Provides for the establishment of a scheme for determining compensation payable for criminal injuries

Humber Bridge (Debts) Act 1996, c. 1, 29 February 1996
Confers power on the Secretary of State to provide that any sum payable to him by the Humber Bridge Board shall not be so payable

Hong Kong (Overseas Public Servants) Act 1996, c. 2, 29 February 1996
Confers power to grant payments to and to permit the early retirement of certain Hong Kong overseas public servants; and for connected purposes

Wild Mammals (Protection) Act 1996, c. 3, 29 April 1996
Provides for the protection of wild mammals from certain acts of cruelty; extends the protection of the Act to any wild mammal not otherwise protected by UK legislation and which is not a domestic or captive animal

Consolidated Fund Act 1996, c. 4, 21 March 1996
Applies certain sums out of the Consolidated Fund to the service of the years ending 31 March 1995 and 1996

Health Service Commissioners (Amendment) Act 1996, c. 5, 1 April 1996
Makes provision about the Health Service Commissioners, e.g. to make them subject to investigation; and for purposes connected with health

Chemical Weapons Act 1996, c. 6, day or days to be appointed
Promotes the control of chemical weapons and of certain toxic chemicals and precursors; and for connected purposes

Prevention of Terrorism (Additional Powers) Act 1996, c. 7, 3 April 1996
Extends powers of search in connection with acts of terrorism and terrorist investigations; confers powers on constables in relation to areas on which police cordons are imposed; and confers powers to impose prohibitions and restrictions in relation to vehicles on roads

Finance Act 1996, c. 8, 29 April 1996
Grants certain duties, alters others and amends the law relating to the national debt and the public revenue, e.g. it brings in a new tax relating to landfill, removes the requirement to pay road tax under certain conditions where the vehicle is over 25 years

old, imposes stamp duty reserve tax on paperless share transactions and brings in a new tax scheme relating to company loan relationships

Education (Student Loans) Act 1996, c. 9, 29 April 1996
Makes new provision for, and in consequence of, the payment of subsidy in respect of private sector student loans

Audit (Miscellaneous Provisions) Act 1996, c. 10, 29 April 1996
Extends the functions of the Audit Commission for Local Authorities and the NHS in England and Wales; alters the financial year of that Commission and the Accounts Commission in Scotland; and for other purposes connected with those Commissions

Northern Ireland (Entry to Negotiations, etc.) Act 1996, c. 11, 29 April 1996
Makes provision for elections in Northern Ireland for the purpose of providing delegates from among whom participants in negotiations may be drawn; for a forum constituted by those delegates; for referendums; and for connected purposes

Rating (Caravans and Boats) Act 1996, c. 12, 29 April 1996
Makes provision about liability for non-domestic rates in England and Wales in relation to certain caravans and boats

Non-Domestic Rating (Information) Act 1996, c. 13, 22 May 1996
Makes provision for and in connection with the disclosure by persons who are valuation officers or assessors to other such persons of information connected with non-domestic rating

Reserve Forces Act 1996, c. 14, day or days to be appointed
Makes provision with respect to the reserve forces of the Crown and persons liable to be recalled for permanent service, and for connected purposes

National Health Service (Residual Liabilities) Act 1996, c. 15, 22 May 1996
Makes provision with respect to the transfer of liabilities of certain NHS bodies (e.g. a NHS trust) in the event of their ceasing to exist

Police Act 1996, c. 16, part on day or days to be appointed, the balance on 22 August 1996
Consolidates the 1964 Act, Part IX of the Police and Civil Evidence Act 1984, Chapter I of Part I of the Police and Magistrates' Court Act 1994 and certain other enactments relating to the police

Industrial Tribunals Act 1996, c. 17, 22 August 1996
Consolidates enactments relating to industrial tribunals and the Employment Appeal Tribunal

Employment Rights Act 1996, c. 18, 22 August 1996
Consolidates enactments relating to employment rights

Law Reform (Year and a Day Rule) Act 1996, c. 19, 17 August 1996

Abolishes the 'year and a day rule' and in consequence imposes a restriction on the institution in certain circumstances of proceedings for a fatal offence

Dogs (Fouling of Land) Act 1996, c. 20, 17 August 1996
Makes provision with respect to the fouling of land by dogs

London Regional Transport Act 1996, c. 21, 17 August 1996
Extends and facilitates the exercise of the powers of LRT to enter into and carry out agreements

Northern Ireland (Emergency Provisions) Act 1996, c. 22, 25 August 1996
Re-enacts, with omissions and amendments, the 1991 Act

Arbitration Act 1996, c. 23, day or days to be appointed
Restates and improves the law relating to an arbitration agreement; makes other provision relating to arbitration and awards

Treasure Act 1996, c. 24, day or days to be appointed
Abolishes treasure trove and makes fresh provision in relation to treasure (which, *inter alia,* includes any item which would have been treasure trove under those rules)

Criminal Procedure and Investigations Act 1996, c. 25, 4 July 1996
Makes provision about criminal procedure and investigations

Offensive Weapons Act 1996, c. 26, various dates, some to be appointed
Makes provision about persons having knives and similar weapons; and about selling knives, etc., to persons under the age of 16

Family Law Act 1996, c. 27, various dates, some to be appointed
Makes provision with respect to divorce and separation; legal aid in family disputes; transfers of tenancies between spouses; and many connected matters

Commonwealth Development Corporation Act 1996, c. 28, 4 September 1996
Amends the 1978 Act to confer further powers on the Commonwealth Development Corporation

Sexual Offences (Conspiracy and Incitement) Act 1996, c. 29, day or days to be appointed
Makes provision about conspiracy or incitement to commit certain sexual acts outside the UK; the Act is designed to deter sex, etc., with juveniles

Community Care (Direct Payments) Act 1996, c. 30, day or days to be appointed
Enables local authorities responsible for community care services to make payments to persons to secure the provision of those services

Defamation Act 1996, c. 31, various dates, some to be appointed

Amends the law of defamation and the law of limitation with respect to actions for defamation or malicious falsehood

Trading Schemes Act 1996, c. 32, day to be appointed
Makes provision in respect of certain trading schemes

Prisoners' Earnings Act 1996, c. 33, day or days to be appointed
Authorizes deductions from or levies on prisoners' earnings and provides for their application

Marriage Ceremony (Prescribed Words) Act 1996, c. 34, day to be appointed
Provides alternative forms of wording for the declaration and words of contract prescribed by law for marriage ceremonies in registered buildings and register offices and on approved premises

Security Service Act 1996, c. 35, day to be appointed
Gives the Security Service the function of acting in support of the prevention and detection of serious crime

Licensing (Amendment) (Scotland) Act 1996, c. 36, day to be appointed
Amends the 1976 Act to require licensing boards to attach to licences conditions relating to certain events involving music and dancing; and for connected purposes

Noise Act 1996, c. 37, day or days to be appointed
Makes provision about noise emitted from dwellings at night; and about forfeiture and confiscation of equipment used to make noise unlawfully

Energy Conservation Act 1996, c. 38, day or days to be appointed
Makes further provision for energy conservation

Civil Aviation (Amendment) Act 1996, c. 39, 18 July 1996
Amends the 1982 Act so as to provide for the prosecution of persons committing offences on foreign aircraft while in flight to the UK

Party Wall, etc., Act 1996, c. 40, day or days to be appointed
Makes provision with respect to party walls and excavation and construction in proximity to certain buildings or structures

Hong Kong (War Wives and Widows) Act 1996, c. 41, 18 July 1996
Provides for the acquisition of British citizenship of certain women who are Hong Kong citizens

Railways Heritage Act 1996, c. 42, 18 September 1996
Makes further provision for and in connection with the preservation of railway records and artefacts

Education (Scotland) Act 1996, c. 43, day or days to be appointed
Provides for the establishment of the Scottish Qualification Authority; and for purposes connected therewith and with education

Deer (Amendment) (Scotland) Act 1996, c. 44, 18 October 1996
Amends the 1959 Act

Appropriation Act 1996, c. 45, 24 July 1996
Applies a sum out of the Consolidated Fund to the service of the year ending 31 March 1997; appropriates the supplies granted in this session of Parliament; repeals certain Consolidated Fund and Appropriation Acts

Armed Forces Act 1996, c. 46, day or days to be appointed
Continues the Army Act 1955, the Air Force Act 1955 and the Naval Discipline Act 1957; amends those Acts and other Acts relating to the armed forces; and makes various other provisions relating to the armed forces

Trusts of Land and Appointment of Trustee Act 1996, c. 47, day to be appointed
Makes new provision about trusts of land, including provision for phasing out the Settled Land Act 1925, abolishing the doctrine of conversion and otherwise amending the law relating to trusts for sale of land; amends the law relating to the appointment and retirement of trustees; and for connected purposes

Damages Act 1996, c. 48, 24 September 1996
Makes new provision in relation to damages for personal injury, including death

Asylum and Immigration Act 1996, c. 49, day or days to be appointed
Amends and supplements the Immigration Act 1971 and the Asylum and Immigration Appeals Act 1993, and immigration control; and for connected purposes

Nursery Education and Grant-Maintained Schools Act 1996, c. 50, day or days to be appointed
Provides for the making of grants in respect of nursery education; and permits borrowing by grant-maintained schools

Social Security (Overpayments) Act 1996, c. 51, 24 July 1996
Amends the provisions in the Social Security Administration Act 1992 and its equivalent in Northern Ireland relating to the recovery of overpayments

Housing Act 1996, c. 52

Housing Grants Construction and Regeneration Act 1996, c. 53, various dates, some to be appointed
Makes provision for grants and other assistance for housing purposes and about action in relation to unfit housing; and for other purposes connected with housing

Statutory Instruments (Production and Sale) Act 1996, c. 54, 24 July 1996
Makes retrospective provision for the printing and sale of statutory instruments and for their issue and reception in evidence of lists of such instruments

Broadcasting Act 1996, c. 55, various dates, some to be appointed

Provides for the broadcasting in digital form of television and sound programme services; abolishes the Broadcasting Complaints Commission and the Broadcasting Standards Council and establishes a Broadcasting Standards Commission; and for other purposes connected with broadcasting

Education Act 1996, c. 56, various dates, some to be appointed

Consolidates the Education Act 1944 and other enactments relating to education with amendments

to give effect to recommendations of the Law Commission

School Inspections Act 1996, c. 57, 1 November 1996

Consolidates provisions of the Education (Schools) Act 1992 and Part V of the Education Act 1993 with amendments to give effect to recommendations of the Law Commission

Deer (Scotland) Act 1996, c. 58, 18 November 1996

Consolidates the law relating to deer in Scotland

WHITE PAPERS, ETC.

Rural England: a Nation Committed to a Living Countryside was presented to Parliament by the Secretary of State for the Environment (John Gummer) on 17 October 1995. It described developments in the English countryside and analysed the issues facing rural areas. It made a series of recommendations, including the following:
– the Cabinet environment committee to examine the impact on the countryside of all government policies; a national forum on land management and a new steering group to monitor 'green' farming schemes to be set up
– reform of the EU common agricultural policy, especially production subsidies, to be advocated
– the amount of woodland in England to be doubled over the next 50 years
– surplus Ministry of Defence land rather than greenfield sites to be used for housing and commercial development
– fewer new trunk roads to be built in the countryside, with more spending on improving existing motorways and building village bypasses
– parish councils to take a more active role in community transport schemes
– rural householders to be encouraged to rent out rooms and private sector bodies to provide cheap rural housing
– small villages to be exempt from the Government's right-to-buy grant scheme
– planning controls on the conversion of rural buildings for business use to be relaxed
– a new business rates relief scheme to be introduced for village shops and post offices and 'community post offices' to be encouraged
– schools to be integrated more into village life and closures to be approved only when a range of factors have been taken into account
– local planning authorities to be encouraged to value a locally-based approach to building design
– a new good practice handbook to be produced for rural hospitals, health authorities and social services

Making Waste Work was presented to Parliament by the Secretary of State for the Environment (John Gummer) on 12 December 1995. It outlined the

Government's strategy for sustainable waste management in England and Wales and included the following new targets:
– to reduce the amount of controlled waste going to landfill to 60 per cent by 2005
– to recover 40 per cent of municipal waste by 2005
– 40 per cent of domestic properties with a garden to carry out home composting by 2000
– to have easily accessible recycling facilities for 80 per cent of households by 2000

Rural Scotland: People, Prosperity and Partnership was presented to Parliament by the Scottish Office Agriculture and Environment Minister (Lord Lindsay) on 15 December 1995. Its main proposals were:
– a Scottish Rural Partnership to be set up, comprising local partnerships of agencies with responsibilities in rural areas, a National Partnership Group co-ordinating advice and assistance to the local partnerships, and a £2.5 million Partnership Fund
– a business rate relief scheme to be introduced for shops providing services to isolated communities
– new research to be undertaken on rural crime, the management of small schools, the use of the planning system, forestry strategies, natural heritage designations, the Scottish coast and the design of rural housing

A Partnership of Nations: the British Approach to the European Union Inter-Governmental Conference was presented to Parliament by the Prime Minister (John Major) on 12 March 1996. It set out government policy in relation to the European Union in 18 discussion areas. It said that the role of the UK as a leading member of the EU was vital to the national interest but it rejected the concept of a 'United States of Europe', stating that national parliaments must remain the central focus of democratic legitimacy. It advocated flexibility but rejected the idea of a two-tier Europe. The main proposals were:
– a major reform of the weighted vote system in the Council of the EU and no extension of qualified majority voting
– no new powers for the European Parliament, and

a possible slimming down of the European Commission as the EU expands
- the powers of the European Court of Justice to be limited and an internal appeals procedure to be set up
- a minimum period for national parliaments to scrutinize EU documents to be instituted
- a single person to be appointed to represent EU foreign policy to the rest of the world; the UK not to be constrained by collective foreign policy decisions which it does not support; NATO to be reinforced as the bedrock of European security and the WEU's operational capabilities to be developed
- greater co-operation in home affairs areas, including the development of a Europol police office, but no supranational solutions to be imposed on member states
- the UK's opt-out from the social chapter to be retained
- reform of the Common Fisheries Policy
- EU regulations to be automatically scrapped or reviewed after a fixed period
- a commitment to animal welfare to be incorporated in the Treaty of Rome
- no new powers to be given to the EU in the areas of citizens' rights, employment, energy, civil protection or tourism

A Working Countryside for Wales was presented to Parliament by the Secretary of State for Wales (William Hague) on 18 March 1996. It included the following proposals:
- a new rate relief scheme for village shops and post offices
- more part-time community post offices
- more low-cost housing in villages
- derelict farm buildings to be converted into workshops and industrial premises
- a food strategy to encourage more rural food processors to source their raw materials locally
- diversification into forestry and tourism
- regional innovation grants for small firms wishing to develop new products or processes
- the self-employed to be encouraged to employ an assistant
- teleworking to be encouraged

Protecting the Public: the Government's Strategy on Crime in England and Wales was presented to Parliament by the Home Secretary (Michael Howard) on 3 April 1996. It outlined proposals for reforms in the following main areas:
- an automatic life sentence to be imposed for a second conviction for a serious violent or sex offence, unless there are 'genuinely exceptional circumstances'
- a minimum sentence of seven years to be imposed on those convicted of trafficking in a Class A substance who have two or more previous convictions for similar offences
- a minimum sentence of three years to be imposed on those convicted of domestic burglary who

have two or more previous convictions for similar offences
- automatic early release and parole to be abolished; offenders to serve the full term imposed by the court, with up to 20 per cent remission available as a reward for good behaviour

Foundations for Policing was presented to Parliament by the Secretary of State for Northern Ireland (Sir Patrick Mayhew) on 1 May 1996. It proposed reforms to the tripartite structure of policing in Northern Ireland comprising the Secretary of State, the chief constable of the Royal Ulster Constabulary and the Police Authority for Northern Ireland (PANI). The main proposals were:
- the Secretary of State to set the Government's key objectives for policing in Northern Ireland in the context of the Government's priorities in the UK
- the PANI to set Northern Ireland-wide objectives
- the chief constable to prepare an annual strategic plan taking account of the objectives and outlining medium-term goals
- the PANI to advise the Secretary of State on the RUC's annual expenditure proposals, take delivery of the money and monitor the achievement of objectives, with day-to-day responsibility for financial management delegated to the chief constable
- the chief constable and the PANI to publish annual reports
- the PANI to obtain the views of the community on policing
- a more open and flexible appointment process to the PANI

Crime and Punishment was presented to Parliament by the Secretary of State for Scotland (Michael Forsyth) on 17 June 1996. It invited views on proposals relating to sex offenders, mentally disordered offenders, criminal legal aid and the sentencing powers of sheriffs, and made the following main proposals:
- a life sentence to be imposed automatically on an offender convicted for the second time of a serious violent or sexual offence
- parole to be abolished and the maximum period of early release to be one-sixth of sentence; any prisoner granted early release to be liable to serve the whole period if s/he reoffends within the supervision or licence period
- the courts to be given a power to impose 'curfew orders' monitored by electronic 'tags'
- the courts to be given new powers to deal with mentally disordered offenders
- community service to be strengthened
- the Crown right to appeal against lenient sentences to be extended
- a Criminal Justice Forum to be established
- a new, privately financed, prison to be built at Bowhouse, Kilmarnock

– the police to be given powers to confiscate alcohol from underage drinkers in public places

– the Scottish Legal Aid Board to be able to enter into contracts with solicitors to carry out a certain volume of work at a fixed price

Spectrum Management: Into the 21st Century was presented to Parliament by the President of the Board of Trade (Ian Lang) on 17 June 1996. It announced the Government's intention of introducing legislation to permit the use of pricing as an aid to effective management of the radio spectrum, and set out proposals on how spectrum pricing should be applied, including the use of auctions and administrative pricing. It requested views on the proposals by 25 October 1996.

On the Record was presented to Parliament by the Home Secretary (Michael Howard) on 19 June 1996. It proposed the establishment of a Criminal Records Agency to provide criminal record checks for job applicants and potential employers. It said that no records would be provided without the applicant's agreement and that there would be a code of practice for employers. Checks would be available at three levels.

Self Government for Schools was presented to Parliament by the Secretary of State for Education (Gillian Shephard) on 25 June 1996. Its main proposals were:

– grant-maintained schools to be allowed to select up to 50 per cent of their pupils

– local authority schools to be allowed to select up to 20 per cent of their pupils

– schools to be required to make a decision annually on whether to introduce selection

– up to 75 schools to specialize in sport or the arts from 1997; specialist schools to be allowed to select up to 30 per cent of their pupils

– oversubscribed grant-maintained schools to be allowed to increase their numbers by 50 per cent

– the Funding Agency for Schools to be allowed to establish grammar schools in any area where there is a demand for extra places

– grant-maintained schools to be allowed to open nurseries or sixth forms

– future school ballots on opting out to be scrutinized by independent monitors

– state boarding schools to be allowed to recruit pupils from outside the European Union and charge them tuition as well as boarding fees

– 95 per cent of education budgets to be devolved to schools by local authorities

Development and Training for Civil Servants: A Framework for Action was presented to Parliament by the Chancellor of the Duchy of Lancaster (Roger Freeman) on 1 July 1996. Its main targets and recommendations were:

– by 1 April 1997, 65 per cent of civil servants to be working in organizations which are either recognized as Investors in People or have a formal action plan for achieving the standard

– by 1 April 1998 all civil servants to be working in such organizations

– by 2000 all civil servants to be working in organizations recognized as Investors in People

– better use to be made of specialists

– a more flexible approach to recruitment to be adopted at all levels

– civil servants to be given greater responsibility for their own development and careers within a supportive framework

Striking the Balance: the Future of Legal Aid in England and Wales was presented to Parliament by the Lord Chancellor (Lord Mackay of Clashfern) on 2 July 1996. Its main proposals were:

– cash limits to be imposed on the legal aid scheme

– legal services to be provided under contract and within a fixed budget by a range of sources

– more stringent merit tests to be introduced for assessing whether a case should be legally-aided

– a flat rate payment to be introduced in civil and family cases, payable by everyone including those receiving benefits; further contributions to be decided by means testing

– legally-aided litigants to be liable for their opponent's costs if they lose the case, with a fair level of costs to be decided by the courts; the Legal Aid Board to have the power to recoup costs from the future sale of a legally-aided person's home

– a flat rate payment to be introduced for the early stages of criminal cases, with contributions for further hearings to be decided by means testing and the payments to be refunded if the defendant is acquitted; those on benefits to be entitled to free advice and representation in the early stages of a case

Science and Discovery

LIFE ON MARS?

Hard on the heels of the discovery in Antarctica of meteorites from the Moon and Mars (*see* below) came the sensational claim that scientists in America had identified minute globules containing fossilized micro-organisms in a meteorite thought to have originated on Mars. The meteorite, labelled ALH 84001, weighs 1.9 kg and was collected in 1984 from the Allan Hills region of Antarctica. It is thought that the meteorite was broken off Martian rocks some 15 million years ago by the impact of an asteroid or comet, the force of the explosion causing the fragment to be blown clear of Mars and to land in Antarctica about 13,000 years ago.

NASA investigators say that the theory is controversial and that there will be disagreement. Nevertheless, the team are convinced that the tiny structures in the meteorite are evidence of primitive life on Mars. Their claim is based on globules of carbonate scattered in the fissures which run through the meteorite. With the help of high-powered microscopes and chemical analysis involving laser-based techniques, the team made three important discoveries: markings resembling the outlines of tiny cells, crystals containing iron similar to ones produced by some types of bacteria found on Earth, and organic molecules never seen before in a Martian meteorite. Images taken with a scanning electron microscope show tiny features on the surface of the globules. Some are round and others long and thin. They are all very small, the longest measuring 200 nanometres. It is these that have been interpreted as microfossils. In addition, the particles of magnetite and iron sulphide found in the globules have the same shape and composition as those produced by micro-organisms found on Earth. Chemical analysis at Stanford University identified polycyclic aromatic hydrocarbons (PAHs), oily molecules often produced as terrestrial micro-organisms decay.

These results are preliminary, however, and there is some years of work to be done before the discoveries can be regarded as conclusive proof that life has at some time existed in another part of our solar system.

METEORITE FINDS

Meteorites have been found on Earth which are known to have originated on Mars or the Moon; the total number of known Martian meteorites is now 12, and the total of known lunar meteorites is 15. These include three recent discoveries, made in the Queen Alexandra Range in Antarctica in 1995.

One, labelled QUE 94201, weighs 12 g and contains minerals normally found in volcanic basalts. Brian Mason of the Smithsonian Institution, Washington, comments that the overall composition of the meteorite is similar to that of shergottites, a class of meteorites recognized as originating in the lava flows on Mars before being thrown into space by some impact. The Martian meteorites are known as SNC-meteorites, an acronym derived from three of their types, shergottite, nakhlite and chassignite. They are similar in many respects to the igneous rocks which form the floors of the Earth's ocean basins.

The other two Antarctic specimens have different compositions. QUE 94269 is a small chip from rocks believed to originate in the lunar highlands. It has an identical composition to a specimen discovered in 1993 and it is thought that they arrived on Earth at the same time. The third specimen, QUE 94281, weighs 23.4 g and is a mixture of different rock types, but Mason says that the rich ratio of iron to manganese implies a lunar origin.

SPACE EXPLORATION

After a six-year journey of more than 3,800 million km, the space probe *Galileo* reached Jupiter in 1995. During its journey, problems arose; in April 1991, its main antenna failed to open properly; in summer 1995, a valve in the propellant-pressurization system would not close after firing the orbiter's main engine; in October 1995 the tape recorder started to play up. Despite these technological problems, on 7 December 1995 the scientific exploration of Jupiter and its moons began and some sensational data was sent back to Earth.

On 13 July 1995, the spacecraft had released an atmospheric probe and on 7 December this plunged into Jupiter's atmosphere at 38 km per second. Its seven instruments transmitted data for 58 minutes before succumbing to Jupiter's hostile conditions. Initial results published in January 1996 show far less helium in Jupiter's atmosphere than expected; revised figures show that the ratio of helium to hydrogen is roughly the same as that on the Sun. This implies that the bulk composition of Jupiter has not changed substantially since its formation. The amount of methane, carbon, nitrogen and sulphur recorded may indicate the effect of meteorite and comet impacts over the years. Winds of over 700 km per hour were recorded at levels well below one of the cloud layers, suggesting that they are formed by internal heating. Lightning activity was less than expected, although individual strikes are ten times more energetic than on Earth. The amount of water is about 20 per cent less than expected, and has caused some surprise. It has been suggested that the dearth may reflect conditions at the location where the probe entered the atmosphere rather than more generally.

Retro-rockets on board the orbiter section of the spacecraft fired successfully, putting it into an elliptical orbit round the planet. This orbit allows *Galileo* to make low passes over the main satellites of Jupiter. In December 1995 the probe passed close to the moon Io. Although no photographs of the moon were taken, Doppler shifts were recorded from the gravitational pull of the moon on the probe. This has enabled scientists to plot Io's gravitational field and from it deduce its internal structure. It is concluded that Io has a large metallic core, possibly a mixture of iron and iron sulphide, and that there was sufficient heat during its evolution for the silicates to rise to the surface.

In June 1996 the spacecraft flew within 835 km of another of Jupiter's moons, Gannymede. It detected a magnetic field about five times larger than could have been formed by the magnetic field of Jupiter. This suggests a field originating from within Gannymede, implying that the moon has a molten core; future close passes of the moon should produce more definite data.

With recent, more sophisticated spacecraft delivering more detailed, and often sensational, data about the solar system, the achievements of earlier probes which are still sending data back to Earth can get overlooked. In the early 1970s *Pioneers 10* and *11* made the first fly-bys of the outer planets. *Pioneer 10*, launched in March 1972, flew past Jupiter the following year and crossed the orbit of Neptune in 1983. On 22 September 1990 it became the first probe to travel 50 astronomical units (AU) from the Sun, and it is now heading towards the star Aldebaran at a speed of 2.7 AU per year. It is still sending back data and may have sufficient power to last until 1999.

Pioneer 11, launched in 1973, reached Jupiter in December 1994, passing within 40,000 km of Jupiter's cloud tops. The probe received an intense bombardment from the planet's radiation belt and it was only the high speed of the fly-by that saved its electronics from severe damage. The probe flew past Saturn in September 1979 and crossed the orbit of Neptune in February 1990. During its passage by Saturn it discovered two new moons and a new ring, and charted the magnetosphere, magnetic field and structure of the planet. The gravity assist from the fly-by enabled the probe to leave the plane of the planets and travel right across the solar system. During its transit of the solar system, *Pioneer 11* provided the first data on the shape of the Sun's magnetic field outside the ecliptic; this region is now being studied in greater detail by the *Ulysses* spacecraft. Unfortunately, the power plant on board *Pioneer 11* has now fallen too low to operate the instruments and transmit data. In September 1995 NASA stopped contacting the probe, although it will continue to listen for two hours every two to four weeks to see if any information can be collected. Although the instruments on board the probe are working well, the probe cannot be aligned for its antennae to point accurately towards the Earth.

COMET HYAKUTAKE

Comet Hyakutake was discovered on 30 January 1996 by a Japanese amateur astronomer, Yuji Hyakutake, as a 10th magnitude object 1.8 AU from the Earth. Within a few days it was realized that the comet was moving directly towards the Earth, and it flew by the Earth on 24 March at a distance of only 15.4 million km, passing over the North Pole. Prior to its nearest approach it became a spectacular object, by far the brightest comet for many years. The coma had a diameter of over 1° and a fairly bright gas tail extending over 12°. At nearest approach observers near cities or in heavily polluted areas were prevented from seeing the full extent of the tail, but observers situated in darker locations such as Arizona reported lengths of up to 100°. After passing the North Pole, the comet presented a brilliant object in the north-west sky at dusk, with a straight dust tail pointing directly upwards. It faded and shrank in size as it moved towards the Sun, but the tail seemed to increase as it approached perihelion (the nearest point to the Sun).

As the comet sped away from the Earth, a team of German and American astronomers recorded the biggest surprise of all. On 27 March it came into the field of view of ROSAT, an X-ray astronomy satellite. In the 24 hours available for studying the comet, it recorded very strong X-ray emission from the comet. Such high energy emissions are normally associated with much hotter sources. The intensity of the emission was comparable with that received from bright X-ray stars. The emission did not originate from the comet's coma but from a crescent-shaped region some 30,000 km from the nucleus, in the direction of the Sun.

Several theories have been put forward to explain the phenomenon but only one seems to explain all the known facts. It is suggested that the collision between the solar wind and material evaporating from the comet compresses the gas and magnetic lines of force; this would accelerate any charged particles to high energies and these could be responsible for the emission. Not all the data has yet been analysed but this, together with other data collected by ROSAT, may produce a more definite explanation.

NEW PLANETARY SYSTEMS

For years there has been speculation that planets may circle nearby stars. No evidence to substantiate this had been found until the past year, when astronomers have identified four cases. Astronomers at the Geneva Observatory announced in October 1995 that they had detected a wobble in the motion of the star 51 Pegasi, which lies about 42 light years away. Using a 1.9 m telescope at Haute Provence in France, they reported that the oscillations on the Doppler shift in the star's spectrum indicate that the star is being circled every four days by an object with roughly the mass of Jupiter. This means that the planet is exceptionally close to the parent star.

Geoff Marcy of the San Francisco State University and colleagues at the University of California, Berkeley, using the same method, found two more planetary systems, 70 Vir in the constellation of Virgo, and 47 UMa in Ursa Major. The planets lie about 35 light years away. The stars themselves are visible to the naked eye. In the case of 47 UMa, it is thought that the mass of the planet is about 2.3 times that of Jupiter and that it orbits the star in a position equivalent to the region lying between Mars and Jupiter. The 70 Vir planet has a mass at least 6.5 times that of Jupiter and is much closer to the parent star.

The fourth case has been identified in the dusty disc surrounding the star Beta Pictoris, by Chris Burrows of the Space Telescope Science Institute. The planet around Beta Pictoris lies 50 light years away and its effect has been identified in an image taken last year by the Hubble Space Telescope. The photograph shows a slight warp in the disc and dust surrounding the star and Burrows is convinced that this distortion is due to a planet.

BLACK HOLE IN VIRGO

Evidence of the existence of a black hole in the centre of the elliptical galaxy NGC4261 in the constellation of Virgo has grown in recent years, and the likelihood is greater because of the jets of X-ray emissions from the galaxy and the highly luminous core seen by radio astronomers. In addition, images taken by the Hubble Space Telescope showed a large disc of dust at a right angle to the direction of the radio jets. These observations support the belief that matter is spiralling into a black hole from the surrounding accretion disc.

Using data gathered by the Faint Object Spectrograph on board the Hubble Space Telescope, scientists from Leiden Observatory and Johns Hopkins University, Baltimore, measured the line of sight motions of the ionized nitrogen within the innermost arcsecond of the galaxy. They were able to determine the rotational speed of matter within 130 light years of the nucleus. From the rate at which the velocities increased with decreasing radius, it was deduced that a mass about 1,200 million times that of the Sun lies within a region less than 50 light years across.

This information proves almost conclusively that a black hole exists in the region. If such a dense concentration of matter existed temporarily as a cluster of stars, nothing could prevent its eventual collapse into a black hole. It is the second largest black hole known at the present time.

BROWN DWARFS FOUND

The discovery of brown dwarf stars, stars with a mass between that of Jupiter and normal stars, has been reported twice in the last few years, but there have been some doubts about whether the correct interpretation was being placed on the discoveries. Both candidates are relatively large and hot, and so there was a possibility that the objects are normal

but extremely faint stars. However, recent studies of the spectra of the stars have revealed the existence of lithium, an indication that they cannot be burning hydrogen, and this strengthens the claims for them being brown dwarfs.

Although star formation theories predict the existence of brown dwarfs, they have been difficult to detect. If they are at least 12 times the mass of Jupiter, their cores will be sufficiently compressed and heated to burn the most easily ignited thermonuclear fuel, deuterium; they are too small to sustain hydrogen–helium fusion, the process that exists on the Sun. Brown dwarfs, therefore, are initially faint and then cool, making them difficult to see.

The discovery of the existence of a third brown dwarf has been claimed by astronomers at the California Institute of Technology in Pasadena and the Johns Hopkins University in Baltimore. They found the brown dwarf by looking at 100 of the nearest stars using an instrument which blocks the light from the star by creating an artificial eclipse; this enables the scientists to probe for faint objects nearby which would normally be obscured by the light of the main star. Their work led to the discovery of such an object close to a cool red star 19 light years away in the constellation of Lepus. The dwarf is about as far away from the primary as Pluto is from the Sun. It emits 100 times less radiation than the smallest known star. Studies of its infra-red spectrum show that its atmosphere contains methane, which can exist only at temperatures lower than 1000 K.

The positive identification of three brown dwarfs should lead to further discoveries in the near future.

THE GREAT ATTRACTOR

In 1987 astronomers found that nearby galaxies seemed to be attracted towards a region in the southern hemisphere of our sky. This implied that they were being dragged gravitationally in that direction by a large mass ('the Great Attractor'), but at that time no such large mass could be distinguished. Later studies recognized the existence of an accumulation of galaxies, though these are spread over a large area and not in the sort of concentration predicted by theoretical astronomers.

Renée Kraan-Korteweg of the University of Paris-Meudon and Patrick Woudt of the University of Cape Town have made a study of photographic plates of the southern sky, visually scanning the plates through a microscope. Their aim was to identify faint smudges covering only 0.2 arcminutes, a fifth of the size searched in earlier surveys. Their scan revealed a concentration of more than 600 galaxies in the constellation Norma, the right place for the theoretical Great Attractor to be located.

This galaxy cluster, known as Abell 3627, is much larger than previously thought, as large as the giant galactic cluster in Coma which lies 450 million light years away. The centre of Abell 3627 is 300 million light years from the Earth, a figure based on data from the measured red shifts of 90 galaxies within the cluster.

Like the Coma cluster, Abell 3627 appears to be the main feature in a larger 'wall' of galaxies arranged in filaments. It seems to extend into a region obscured by dust in our galaxy. Plans are being made to probe this region using the 64 m Parkes Radio Telescope in Australia.

THE SUN'S BOW WAVE

Amateur astronomers are allowed observing time on the Hubble Space Telescope, and the work of William Alexander of West Virginia has provided data on the bow wave generated by the Sun as it rushes through space at 26 km per second. Alexander collaborated with Jeffrey Linsky and Brian Wood of the University of Colorado to produce evidence for a hydrogen wall around the Sun. Alexander took ultraviolet spectra for the purpose of determining the ratios of different hydrogen isotopes in the interstellar medium. Data from the spectra of Alpha-Centauri showed an absorption apparently caused by a curtain of hydrogen heated to about 30,000 K.

As the Sun travels through space, a hydrogen wall is generated where the solar wind of charged particles meets the interstellar medium, an effect similar to the bow wave produced by a ship travelling through water. Theory had predicted that the collisions of the particles would heat the hydrogen atoms to between 20,000 and 40,000 K. The wall around the Sun lies about 150 AU from the Sun, five times the distance of Neptune.

Linsky has shown that similar hydrogen walls exist around Epsilon Indi and Lambda Andromedae. Linsky said that detection of such walls on stars which are moving directly towards the Sun depends at present on the velocity of the gas in the wall differing sufficiently from that of the interstellar medium for the spectral absorption to be visible. Epsilon Indi is moving nearly four times as fast as the Sun, causing the hydrogen to be heated to 100,000 K. Lambda Andromedae is moving faster than the Sun, resulting in a higher temperature.

GAMMA RAY BURSTS

Bursts of gamma rays have been recorded for years but no satisfactory explanation has been given for them. If they were concentrated in the plane of the Milky Way, it would imply that the bursts originated within our galaxy. However, the bursts appear to originate from all over the sky, suggesting that the sources must lie in other galaxies. If this is the case, the events which cause the bursts must release a colossal amount of energy for the bursts to be recorded by instruments orbiting the Earth.

Some astronomers have suggested that the bursts are due to neutron stars colliding, but others argue that such events would not be powerful enough. Another suggestion is that the cause may be due to the collapse of a neutron star. Neutron stars are the remnants of a supernova explosion. They have a mass about that of the Sun but are only a few kilometres in diameter. Neutron stars spin rapidly, initially at about 50 revolutions per second. With such a high rotational speed, the surface layers are supported by centrifugal force. Over a period of millions of years the spin gradually slows down, so that the outer layers collapse inwards and the pressure at the centre of the star increases. The neutrons are then crushed until they merge into a soup of quarks. Feng Ma and Bingrong Xie of the University of Texas at Austin have examined the process and calculate that on rare occasions this process can happen suddenly. They believe that when the pressure is high enough for a tiny part of the core to collapse into a quark soup, it can trigger off a process that causes the radius of the star to fall from 12 km to less than 10 km. Half the neutron star's mass would then be transformed into an explosive burst of energy. Much of this would be dissipated as neutrinos, leaving a small fraction in the form of gamma rays. According to the astronomers, this situation can only happen with neutron stars within a narrow range of mass, roughly one in a million, but this would be sufficient to account for the number of gamma ray bursts detected.

IMPACT SITES

At Sudbury, Ontario, there is an oval crater measuring 60 × 27 km which is the second largest feature caused by the impact of a meteoroid from space. The huge deposits of metalliferous ores, in particular those of nickel, have made it economically important. Since its identification as an impact structure a few decades ago, the crater has been of interest in particular for the structure and composition of its rocks. A few years ago Luann Becker and Jeffrey Bada of the Scripps Institution of Oceanography in San Diego discovered large numbers of buckyballs (scientifically known as fullerenes). These molecules can easily be produced under laboratory conditions but the scientists were puzzled by their presence in the crater; they wondered how such molecules could be formed by natural processes in the Earth's crust or, if the molecules arrived with the meteoroid, how they could have survived the impact.

When the molecules were found at Sudbury, it was suggested that the compounds were formed by the heat generated at the time of the impact. However, further work has implied an extraterrestrial origin. The buckyballs have hollow structures and atoms or small molecules can be trapped inside them at the time that they are formed. Robert Poreda of the University of Rochester, New York, identified helium within the molecules and the ratio of the helium isotopes shows that the helium was not captured from the Earth's atmosphere but that the buckyballs were formed outside the solar system.

The most likely source is a red giant, a star that contains large amounts of helium and carbon. The researchers are of the opinion that the buckyballs were formed before the solar system and were swept up into a comet or asteroid, travelling through space for billions of years before entering the solar system. At the time of the impact at Sudbury, some part of the comet or asteroid must have broken away, remaining much cooler than the main mass which hit the Earth producing temperatures in excess of 5000°C. If this theory is correct it supports the idea put forward by Fred Hoyle and others (*see* Molecules From Space, below) that the first amino acids and other organic molecules arrived on Earth from space.

The Yucatan crater is increasingly believed to have a meteoritic origin. It is thought that a body about 10 km in diameter crashed into the Yucatan peninsula 65 million years ago, causing the conditions that led to the extinction of the dinosaurs. The impact threw up an immense cloud of dust and vapour that eventually settled as a layer of iridium-rich sediments, known as the K/T boundary layer. Recent evidence shows that fragments of the original meteorite still exist. Frank Kyte of the University of California at Los Angeles, during an examination of dark-brown clay taken from the bed of the north-west Pacific Ocean by an international ocean drilling project, identified a coarse-grained pebble about 2.5 mm long which contained chromium, iron and iridium in proportions similar to those found in meteorites. The pebble was found at the base of the K/T boundary, about 9,000 km west of the impact site. The fragment could have been produced by being thrown out at the time of the explosion or by breaking off from the meteorite prior to impact. Another possibility is that the fragment could have been a dust particle from the tail of a comet.

A team of NASA scientists has been sifting through rocks from the crater itself. If the asteroid had been completely vapourized on impact, the distribution of the iridium would be relatively even, but this is not the case. The scientists made a close study of the rocks which contained iridium to try to find the minerals that contained the metal. Using a scanning electron microscope they found exceptionally small fragments of virtually pure iridium. Some meteorites contain small nuggets of metals but nothing as pure as the Yucatan samples. It is thought that the other metals were vapourized on impact, leaving the iridium, which vapourizes only at a much higher temperature.

Interest in impact sites has increased considerably since the collision of fragments of Comet Shoemaker-Levy 9 with Jupiter in 1994. There are indications that the Earth was subjected to a similar bombardment several hundred million years ago, creating a chain of craters in Africa and America, though these are believed to have been formed separately. At the March 1996 meeting of the Lunar and Planetary Science Conference in Houston, Adriana Ocampo of the Jet Propulsion Laboratory, Pasadena, reported that the 12.6 km diameter crater at Aorounga in northern Chad has associated with it two, and possibly three, more craters, lying to the

north-north-east. Although buried beneath the sand of the Sahara Desert, space-borne imaging radar on board a Shuttle flight in 1994 revealed four impact sites lying in a line less than 100 km long. The largest of these features has a diameter of 17 km. The craters lie in rocks which are 360 million years old and the craters are thought to have a similar age.

In north America a line of eight craters stretching over 700 km from Kansas to Illinois and originally thought to be of volcanic origin, are now thought to be impact features. The lack of vulcanism in the whole area and evidence collected by geologists at two of the craters indicate that any volcanic theory can be ruled out. It is estimated that the impacts which created each chain of craters occurred between 330 and 310 million years ago.

MOLECULES FROM SPACE

Just over 40 years ago the British astronomer Fred Hoyle suggested that some of the organic molecules found on Earth came from space. This idea was dismissed by many scientists but there has been mounting evidence since that there may be some truth in the idea. Over the years astronomers have identified blips in the spectra of radiation emitted by interstellar dust clouds caused by a variety of organic molecules. Only two years ago the amino acid glycine was discovered in clouds of gas near to the centre of our galaxy. American scientists have now identified polycyclic aromatic hydrocarbons (PAHs) in meteorites. Scientists from Washington University in St Louis and Stanford University in California identified aromatic hydrocarbons such as naphthalene in 89 out of 124 sooty grains contained in some meteorites. When the carbon was re-examined to identify the particular isotopes, 58 contained unusually low or extraordinary high percentages of carbon-13. These isotope ratios showed conclusively that the grains were not formed in the neighbourhood of the Sun. It is thought that the grains were formed in clouds of gas and dust near distant stars. If so, this means that complex organic molecules have been found on the Earth which originated in regions outside the solar system, supporting the idea put forward by Hoyle.

NEW STATE OF MATTER

Over 70 years ago Albert Einstein and an Indian physicist Satyendra Nath Bose postulated that if certain types of gas were cooled to a fraction of a degree above absolute zero, they would stop behaving as a collection of individual particles and would behave as a single entity; the particles' wave functions would expand until they overlapped completely, to produce what is known as a Bose-Einstein condensate. This prediction could not be tested until recently because it was not possible to cool the gas sufficiently, to less than one millionth of a degree kelvin.

In 1995 a team from the National Institute of Standards and Technology at Boulder and the University of Colorado used a combination of laser and magnetic fields to cool a sample of rubidium until about 2,000 atoms coalesced to form a Bose-Einstein condensate. Unfortunately, it was too small to observe directly but a subsequent study as the gas expanded when the trap was turned off showed that the condensate existed.

Subsequent experiments carried out at the Massachusetts Institute of Technology produced a larger condensate using about five million sodium atoms. This lasted for about 20 seconds, and was about 8 micrometres wide and 150 micrometres long. They were able to see the condensate by measuring the deflection of a laser beam from it. Research will now be carried out to produce larger condensates and to solve some of the other problems associated with this strange state of matter.

NACREOUS CLOUD DISPLAY

The clear skies during the afternoon and evening of 16 February 1996 brought a spectacular display of nacreous clouds over the British Isles. Such clouds are normally formed in the Arctic and Antarctic regions, thought to be the sites of the chemical reactions associated with ozone depletion, and are sometimes referred to as polar stratospheric clouds. Also often referred to as mother of pearl clouds, nacreous clouds show iridescence, the iridescence being produced by diffraction of sunlight around small particles of clouds which form in the stratosphere between 21 and 30 km above the Earth's surface. The formation of clouds at these heights is rare because of the relative lack of moisture. The iridescence produced in these clouds is striking. It may show differing colours on one cloud, the colours being purer and resembling in some ways the colours of the rainbow. Because the iridescence is strong, it is not unusual for observers to think that the colours are produced by an auroral display.

Nacreous clouds, which are normally seen during winter months just after sunset or before sunrise, should not be confused with high noctilucent clouds, which can be seen in the northern sky during the summer months when the Sun is between about 6° and 16° below the horizon. Noctilucent clouds are formed at heights in the region of 80 km and cannot be seen in daylight. They form thin tenuous clouds which have a superficial resemblance to cirrus and often shine with a nearly white or electric blue colour. Nacreous clouds, however, are highly coloured.

LUNAR TIDES

The gravitational pull of the Moon on the Earth's seas and oceans, producing the twice daily rise and fall of the tides, has been understood since ancient times. But it is only recently that scientists have been able to measure the effect of the lunar gravitational force on the Earth itself, using NASA's Topex/Poseidon satellite (1992 52A), a satellite designed to measure sea surface topography with high resolution by timing the echoes of radar bounced off the surface of the water.

The lunar gravitational force distorts the shape of the Earth, producing two daily bulges of about 30 cm on opposite sides of the Earth. These bulges travel round the Earth as the Earth rotates. Because the Earth is not perfectly elastic, there is a time delay in this distortion. After extracting the effect of the oceanic tides, which tend to swamp all the measurements, scientists have been able to measure this time delay. They found that the delay is about 20 seconds, in which time the Earth rotates about 0.08 degrees. The length of the delay can be used to measure how much of the energy of this tidal motion is dissipated as heat; this was 83,000 megawatts, i.e. twice the output of Britain's electricity generators.

The results of these studies are of interest to geologists researching the structure of the Earth's interior. The tidal ripples reach down to the core and can provide data on the Earth's average viscosity.

BROKEN PLATES AND RISING ROCKS

The theory of plate tectonics, that the Earth's crust consists of a series of plates which move independently, is well-established. Where two plates are separating, a ridge is produced, e.g. the Mid-Atlantic Ridge. Where two plates are sliding by each other, as in California, faults such as the San Andreas Fault occur. However, two plates meeting each other more or less head-on causes one of the plates to be subducted under the other, throwing up mountain ranges, e.g. the Andes or the Himalayas and the Tibetan plateau. The stress to the Australian-Indian plate as it moves northwards has caused the plate to break into two parts.

American geologists had theorized that the Indo-Australian plate, once thought to be a single plate, was in fact two plates, with the Australian component circling anticlockwise around the Indian plate at a rate of about one degree every three million years. From mathematical models and indirect measurements, they predicted that the pivot was located some 1,000 km south of India. This theory has been confirmed by work at the Lamont-Doherty Observatory of Columbia University, New York, and by French geophysicists. They calculated the amount of compression east of the suspected pivot where the sea floor had buckled by analysing sonar images of the Indian Ocean taken in 1986 and 1991. At each point where the ocean floor had buckled, they calculated how long the section would have been when laid flat. This experiment was carried out over two 800 km transects, one just east of the suspected pivot and another some 300 km further east. The values for the compression were 11.2 km near to the pivot and 27.4 at the more easterly point. Although it was not possible to detect vertical buckling of less than 10 metres, the results are fairly conclusive. It is thought that the plate began to break up about eight million years ago.

Although the theory of plate tectonics has become generally accepted, understanding of the mechanisms is still developing. Recent evidence suggests that the mechanism is not as straightforward as was once thought. At a crustal collision, rocks from one plate are thought to be pushed down through a subduction zone into the underlying mantle, where they remain. Recent work by geologists from the University of California, Riverside, has identified in Switzerland a section of crust, tens of kilometres in length, that has risen from a depth of more than 300 km.

Earlier this year, work by other scientists had identified a tiny fleck of a mineral called staurolite which survived subduction by being trapped inside another crystal and then rose to the surface from a depth of 120 km. This specimen was found in the Dokolwayo diamond deposits in Swaziland, but pales into insignificance compared with the huge mass of rock found in the southern Swiss Alps, particularly the large chunk of peridotite, hundreds of metres across, contained in a large mass of gneiss. The crystal structure of another mineral within the gneiss, ilmenite, shows that it must have been formed at least 300 km into the Earth. The geologists think that the gneiss was taken into the mantle when it got caught between colliding plates and became embedded in a mass of denser mantle rock. As this heavier mass sank deeper, the gneiss freed itself and floated upwards. Further work is currently being carried out in the area; it might produce results that will lead to the revision of ideas about the behaviour of subducted rocks.

Earthquake Prediction

A reliable means of predicting earthquakes has been a high priority for research, especially at establishments near to active seismic zones. So far little positive progress has been made, though some of the investigations have shown promising possibilities, such as a study of creep, very small fault movements which are too slight to be recorded by a standard seismograph. The creep is measured by monitoring the deformation of a wire across the fault plane.

These small movements occur in the upper two kilometres of the fault planes and are common on some sections of large strike-slip faults (where two tectonic plates are sliding past each other). Clifford Thurber of the University of Wisconsin in Madison has monitored a segment of the section of the San Andreas Fault at a point south of the section which ruptured and produced the 1906 earthquake in San Francisco. He monitored five creep events where the fault moved about 3 mm in a day. On each occasion he predicted that there would be a tremor greater than magnitude 3.3 within five days. He was correct in four cases, and in the fifth, the tremor came just over five days later. During the time of the experiment there were also two unpredicted earthquakes. All the tremors had magnitudes of between 3.3 and 5 and occurred between 2 km and 10 km below the surface.

Although the experiments are promising, there are limitations. Thurber found that the creep-quake correlation worked only during periods of unusually high seismic activity, and then only in about half the cases. He believes that the link is of value only when the fault is about to rupture. Another limitation is that the method can only be used where faults are visible on the surface. Nevertheless, Thurber hopes that further work along similar lines in other parts of the world may produce results of value in predicting major tremors.

Antarctic Lake

Surveys have shown that there are 77 lakes under the Antarctic ice sheet; these were found in the 1970s using radio echo techniques. However, it is only recently that the size of one of the lakes has been appreciated. It covers more than 14,000 sq. km and has been named Lake Vostok because it lies beneath Russia's ice-drilling station. Using data supplied by the European Space Agency's ERS-1 satellite, the Scott Polar Research Institute at the University of Cambridge has shown that the lake lies under a 4 km layer of ice and is about 125 metres deep. The manner in which the lake supports the overlying ice-sheet indicates that the ice is salty and not fresh. It is thought that the lake was formed during the build-up of ice over a period of about one million years. The ice-sheet acted as a blanket, enabling the water in the lake to warm up to about −2°C. The ice layer provides a pressure of about 300 to 400 atmospheres, allowing the water in the lake to remain in liquid form.

The team hopes to be able to explore the biology of the lake; they believe the sediments at the bottom may contain unique micro-organisms. If so, the organisms will have had no contact with the outside world for over half a million years and might have evolved in a manner different from those outside the lake because of the low temperature, crushing pressures and almost total lack of nutrients. However, the engineering problems involved in successfully retrieving any micro-organisms are immense, and have been likened to bringing back samples from Mars.

Early Birds

Archaeopteryx has been regarded as the earliest known bird for over a century. However, recent work suggests that it was not the ancestor of modern birds but an evolutionary dead end, a 'feathered dinosaur'. Fossils from north-east China, found by scientists from the Institute of Vertebrate Palaeontology and Palaeoanthropology in Beijing, are thought to date from the late Jurassic period, the period *Archaeopteryx* is believed to have lived and which ended 140 million years ago. One of the new discoveries is of a bird, the holy Confucius bird (*Confuciusornis sactus*), which, unlike *Archaeopteryx*, has a modern looking beak; beaks were not believed to have evolved until 75 million years after *Archaeopteryx*. The team identified three such creatures in ancient lake sediments near the Chinese frontier with Korea. Although it is difficult to date accurately, it is thought that *Confuciusornis* lived about 10 million years after *Archaeopteryx*, which lived about 145 million years ago. In many respects the two birds are similar, e.g. their wings carried long claws. But, unlike *Archaeopteryx*, the new discovery did not have teeth but a modern-type beak.

Other fossils dating from the same period, still unnamed, show a warbler-sized bird with a well-developed keel, the ridge along its breastbone where flight muscles were attached. This suggests a strong flight ability, unlike *Archaeopteryx* and *Confuciusornis* which managed relatively short clumsy bursts of flight. The structure of the legs of the warbler-sized creature, long below the knee and short above it, indicates that it lived and fed on tree trunks in a similar manner to the modern woodpecker. There are fossils of a variety of birds in the same sedimentary deposits so it would appear that birds were already diverse as early as the late Jurassic period.

Shark-Toothed Dinosaur

In a cliff face on the northern edge of the Sahara Desert in Morocco, palaeontologists from the University of Chicago have discovered fragments of the skull of what could be the largest carnivorous dinosaur yet known. Although the skull was broken into about 350 fragments, the scientists have made casts of the fragments and fitted them together to form a model of the complete head. The head is 160 cm long, the largest dinosaur skull yet found, although examination shows that the brain was only the size of a tennis ball. It is estimated that the animal, named *Carcharodontosaurus saharicus* (shark-toothed reptile from the Sahara), measured about 13.5 m in length, over a metre longer than *Tyrannosaurus rex*. This newly discovered dinosaur lived about 90 million years ago and would have dominated the area which is now the Sahara Desert, although 94 to 88 million years ago the region was an area of lush river deltas and plains.

It is possible that *Carcharodontosaurus saharicus* was an even more formidable predator than *T. rex*. Whereas *T. rex* would have grabbed, punctured and ripped its prey, studies have shown that this new reptile, having knife-shaped teeth with razor-sharp blades, would have been able to slash and slice its victim. Its stocky neck would have allowed it to gulp down huge chunks of meat. It was very agile for its size. It stood about 3.5 m at the hip and weighed about 8 tons but was still able to run at about 20 mph. One of its sources of food would have been the larger vegetarian long-necked Sauropod.

Ancient Anemones

Life at the bottom of the oceans has not been investigated in great detail to date and so research is continually bringing valuable information to light. Researchers at the University of California have used radio-carbon dating to find the ages of three specimens of Gerardia, an anemone that lives some 620m below the surface of the ocean in the Bahamas. They found that the anemones had been alive for between 1,500 and 2,000 years, longer than any other known marine creature.

It is arguable that Gerardia can be considered as a single animal. As with corals, they are colonies of tiny animals, known as polyps, living together on a branching skeleton which they deposit in successive layers. They develop into a structure resembling a tree, with trunk and branches. Carbon-14 is known to decay at a recognized rate and radio-carbon testing of various parts of the structure, including the innermost layers of the trunk, enables the team to calculate the time lapse since the layers were deposited.

The little research that has been carried out on the life spans of reef corals suggests that life spans of a few hundred years are feasible, and one zoologist has said that he would not be surprised if some fossils had lived for thousands of years. The longevity of these creatures is a real bonus for scientists. The carbon found in the skeletons came from food, possibly plankton or organic debris descending from the surface, absorbed at the time that that part of the skeleton was deposited. Consequently the anemones provide data on the ocean's productivity over the last few thousand years.

Brachiopod Rings

Brachiopods are evolutionary leftovers from Palaeozoic times (250 million years ago). Although generally they have been replaced by clams, brachiopods still exist in our seas, often at great depths, and there are large numbers in the cold waters of the Southern Ocean. Lloyd Peck of the British Antarctic Survey at Cambridge and Thomas Brey of the Alfred Wegener Institute for Polar and Marine Research in Bremerhaven, Germany, have studied the rings visible on brachiopods' shells, as they were not convinced that these are annual growth rings. They measured the shells of brachiopods and then repeated the experiment two years later; the results suggested that the growth of the brachiopods was much slower than previously thought. The team then used radio-carbon dating to calculate the time lapse in the ring growth. Atom bomb tests, because they release significant quantities of carbon-14 into the atmosphere, provide a means of precise dating.

Analysis has shown that the rings are not laid down annually but in a cycle averaging 1.84 years. This means that the brachiopods live for longer than was thought, possibly for about 100 years. Shell fish build up their shells in minute daily increments, the size of which can vary over the year according to lunar cycles and fluctuations of water temperature, but the researchers cannot explain the peculiar value for the time taken to form a ring. It might reflect a two-year reproduction cycle affected by an unknown environmental factor. The team are now carrying out similar studies in other parts of the world to see if the pattern is common to all brachiopods.

CROWS MAKE TOOLS

The use of tools by early man is well documented but recent studies of the behaviour of crows on the island of New Caledonia show that they are as technologically advanced as early man. Work carried out by Gavin Hunt of Massey University in Palmerston North, New Zealand, has revealed that the birds make tools out of leaves and twigs which they use to reach insects in dead wood.

Hunt reports that on three sites on the island each type of tool is fashioned in the same manner regardless of the raw material. He claims that such a standardization only emerged in humans of the Lower Palaeolithic age (two million years ago). The crows construct their tools from hooked twigs and cut leaves; a bird would break off a hooked twig, fly to a perch, transfer the twig to its feet and then spend several minutes reshaping the hook with its bill, removing all leaves and bark. Hunt also found strong tapered leaves from which the birds had removed sections to create a harpoon-shaped tool with barbs facing away from the point, though so far he has not observed any birds making these tools. He has seen the birds using the tools to catch their prey. They use rapid back and forth movements when the insects are partially hidden and slow careful movements when the insects become visible.

Christophe Boesch of the University of Basle has questioned the thought mechanism associated with the making of the tools. The standard method of construction could be the result of trial and error, but he thinks that if the standardization is the result of mental planning, many of our basic ideas of the differences between humans and animals may have to be revised.

ORIGINS OF ÖTZI

The 5,000-year-old remains of a man, nicknamed Ötzi, were discovered in 1991 in the Otztaler Alps on the border between Italy and Austria. Much of the detail of the man's life style has been deduced from his remains, but it has proved difficult to establish where he came from. DNA comparisons seem to indicate that Ötzi was closely related to the modern inhabitants of central and northern Europe. However, his clothes and tools suggest that he was from the more advanced neolithic settlements which existed in Italy.

Research by scientists at the University of Glasgow, the University of Innsbruck and English Nature supports the more southerly origin. There is a general belief that because so much moss was found on the body, Ötzi may have used mosses for packing and for extra insulation in his clothing. In addition, the use of moss as toilet paper would be in line with its use at other neolithic and Roman sites. Since many of the mosses and liverworts attached to Ötzi's clothing grow only at lower altitudes, they must have been brought there. The present distribution of these mosses and liverworts was investigated. Of particular significance is the distribution of two species of moss, *Neckera complanata* and *Neckera*

crispa. These grow on sheltered rock faces in an area 20 km to the south of where Ötzi died, the nearest point to the north where both species exist being twice this distance; the researchers believe that the distribution of these mosses would have been more or less the same 5,000 years ago. If Ötzi lived in Vinschgau, to the south, a fit man could walk to where he died in a few hours but if he lived in Inntal, to the north, it would have taken him several days. It is therefore concluded that Ötzi came from the lowlands south of the pass where he died.

ANCIENT PAINTINGS IN AMAZON

More sophisticated techniques and greater ease of access to areas which have not been systematically explored before are providing information which in some cases contradicts established ideas. Dating of the oldest inhabited human site and paintings has had to be revised following excavations by archaeologists from the Field Museum of Natural History, Chicago. These have revealed an unknown ancient culture in the heart of the Amazon jungle, together with paintings 13,000–14,000 years old, older than any previously recorded in the New World. The paintings, dated by thermoluminescence and by calibrated radio-carbon techniques, show fish, birds and deer, and humans apparently masquerading as insects, stars and comets. One of the paintings shows a figure with an insect-like head and body but human limbs, whilst another portrays a human with a giant eye falling from the sky, with rays radiating from its head. Others illustrate women giving birth and hunters with spears. Similar paintings have been identified at hundreds of sites along a 30-mile stretch of the Amazon.

The archaeologists have also identified one of the oldest confirmed sites of human occupation, about 14,000 years old, at Pedra Pintada. It is thought that the occupants were among the first human colonists of South America. The other sites of the paintings are thought to be of a similar age. The discovery suggests that large areas of forest in Africa, southeast Asia and America may have been inhabited earlier than was previously thought. The Amazon sites are also the first to demonstrate that preagricultural Stone Age Man was able to survive in equatorial rain forests. The team plans to search for more sites, including some which may now be submerged under the Amazon.

THE GREAT WALL OF CHINA

Radar imaging from orbiting satellites has enabled Chinese scientists to study sections of the Great Wall of China which have been eroded and buried by sand. Sections of the Wall were first built in the 3rd century BC by the Warring States to protect the country from invaders from the north. From the images, Dr Guo Huadong of the Chinese Academy of Sciences in Beijing has identified various stages in the building of the Wall. The wall built in the Ming dynasty is about 600 years old but another, built some 400 years earlier during the Sui dynasty, is clearly visible. In subsequent centuries construction concentrated on linking a number of these older walls. Its present line is, broadly speaking, that of the Ming period, but different parts of it are built along alignments of walls built during earlier periods.

The satellite radar images are black and white, each frame showing a section two miles long. Usually it is not possible to find the sections from ground-based studies. The images show distinctly the differing generations of construction because the steep smooth sides (15 to 25 ft high at present) provide a prominent surface which reflects the radar beam very efficiently. Easily identified are the parts built during the Sui dynasty, which have been intermittently covered by wind-blown sand. This section was originally made of loose stones, soil and mud rather than bricks and rocks.

The synthetic aperture pictures were taken early in 1996 from the space shuttle. The scan was not one of the original objectives of the mission but it is a very efficient method for this type of work. The techniques are now being used to study the Angkor site in Cambodia, the lost city of Wabar in the Rub 'al Khali Desert, Oman, and the Silk Road through the north-west desert of China.

Periods of Gestation or Incubation

The table shows approximate periods of gestation or incubation for some common animals and birds. In some cases the periods may vary and where doubt arises professional advice should be sought.

Species	Shortest period (days)	Usual period (days)	Longest period (days)
Human	240	273	313
Horse	305	336	340
Cow	273	280	294
Goat	147	151	155
Sheep	140	147–50	160
Pig	109	112	125
Dog	55	63	70
Cat	53	56	63
Rabbit	30	32	35
Goose	28	30	32
Turkey	25	28	28
Duck	28	28	32
Chicken	20	21	22
Pigeon	17	18	19
Canary	12	14	14
Guinea Pig	63	–	70
Rat	21	–	24
Mouse	18	–	19
Elephant		21–22 months	
Zebra		56 weeks	
Camel		45 weeks	

Astronomers Royal

Instituted in 1675, the title of Astronomer Royal was given to the director of the Royal Greenwich Observatory until 1975. Currently it is an honorary title for an outstanding astronomer, who receives a stipend of approximately £100 a year.

John Flamsteed (1646–1719), appointed 1675
Edmund Halley (1656–1742), appointed 1720
James Bradley (1693–1762), appointed 1742
Nathaniel Bliss (1700–64), appointed 1762
Nevil Maskelyne (1732–1811), appointed 1765
John Pond (1767–1836), appointed 1811
Sir George Airy (1801–92), appointed 1835
Sir William Christie (1845–1922), appointed 1881
Sir Frank Dyson (1868–1939), appointed 1910
Sir Harold Jones (1890–1960), appointed 1933
Sir Richard Woolley (1906–86), appointed 1955
Sir Martin Ryle (1918–84), appointed 1972
Sir Francis Graham-Smith (1923–), appointed 1982
Sir Arnold Wolfendale (1927–), appointed 1991
Sir Martin Rees (1942–), appointed 1995

Theatre

In August 1996 the doors of Shakespeare's Globe finally opened, 300 yards from the site of the original Globe theatre in Southwark, London, with a production of *Two Gentlemen of Verona*. Sam Wanamaker's seemingly impossible dream of building a replica of the theatre in which so many of Shakespeare's plays received their first performance was at last realized. Wanamaker spent the latter part of his life fighting, against considerable hostility, to raise enough money and obtain planning permission to get the theatre built. Sadly he died in 1993, just as the builders began work. Academics and theatre people have been closely involved in the design of the thatched building and it is as accurate as possible, given the scanty information about the original. Members of the audience either sit on benches in the galleries or stand on the floor in front of the stage under the open sky. Although aiming for authenticity, the pristine theatre (which does have toilets) is not as dirty or crowded as the original would have been; and bear baiting, whores and cutpurses are also missing. Fire regulations restrict the capacity to 1,500, whereas the capacity in the 16th century would have been about 3,000.

It remains to be seen whether audiences will visit the theatre regularly or whether a visit will be a novelty to be experienced once before returning to the comfort of indoor theatres. Much will depend on the quality of productions under the artistic directorship of Mark Rylance and much will be learnt from the initial production. The stage itself is only a temporary structure at present so that final decisions can be made in the light of experience before the stage is carved in green oak. The whole complex, including the neighbouring Inigo Jones theatre, opens on 21 September 1999, the 400th anniversary of the first recorded performance at Shakespeare's Globe.

Nunn to the National

It was announced in March 1996 that Trevor Nunn would take over from Richard Eyre as artistic director of the Royal National Theatre in September 1997. The choice was unexpected. In all the speculation about Eyre's possible successor, Nunn was never considered as a contender for the post by journalists or by those who work in the theatre; Sam Mendes, artistic director of the Donmar Warehouse, and Stephen Daldry, artistic director of the Royal Court, were believed to be the frontrunners. The surprise was that Nunn, having already run one major company, the Royal Shakespeare Company (RSC), should be interested in running another. Now 56, Nunn was Peter Hall's chosen successor at the RSC in 1968 at the exceptionally young age of 28. Some of his productions for the RSC are

legendary: *The Alchemist, Nicholas Nickleby, Macbeth* with Sir Ian McKellen and Dame Judi Dench, and *All's Well That Ends Well*. Although very different plays, each production revealed a rare combination of scholarship, showmanship and humanity. Subsequently Nunn appeared to lose interest in the RSC and was frequently absent from Stratford; members of the company, fed up with his absences, once wrote to the television programme *Jim'll Fix It* to try to arrange a meeting with him. Instead Nunn took to directing musicals – *Cats, Les Misérables, Chess, Starlight Express*, and *Sunset Boulevard* – becoming a multi-millionaire in the process. His only previous connection with the National Theatre was a production of Tom Stoppard's *Arcadia*, which he directed with a restraint and discipline that Stoppard's plays often lack.

Later in 1996 Nunn was in the headlines again, when he complained about the squalor in the West End and called for the restoration of a single London authority. He claimed that the West End, 'looks like a garbage strike in its second month; gutters are clogged with litter, pavements are sticky with beer, urine and vomit', and that this put people off going to the theatre in London. Another discouragement was the resumption of hostilities by the IRA in February 1996. The Royal Exchange Theatre in Manchester was seriously damaged by a bomb in the city centre in June and the company was forced to find a temporary home elsewhere. Later the theatre was awarded £3.2 million of National Lottery money towards repairs. In London the return of bomb scares caused havoc to performances.

National Lottery

The National Lottery generated considerable sums for capital projects, i.e. buildings, while the freezing of Arts Council grants meant that less money was available for productions. Typical of the imbalance was the award to RADA, one of the country's leading drama schools, of £22 million to repair its building at a time when many young people are finding it impossible to obtain a local authority grant to study there. There were also complaints that the largest sums of money appeared to be going to London institutions: Sadler's Wells was awarded £30 million; the Royal National Theatre £31 million; and the Royal Court £16 million. Many people in the arts world campaigned for lottery funds to subsidize the product as well as the container. The Secretary of State for National Heritage (Virginia Bottomley) set up an inquiry into the possibility of expanding the use of lottery money to new work, young people's theatre and access. The Royal Court Theatre will close in autumn 1996 for two years for much-needed repairs to the dilapidated building in Sloane Square. The total cost will be £21 million. When given lottery funds, artistic director Stephen Daldry claimed, 'The theatre is in such a terrible state that without this funding it would not have been able to survive more than about 18 months.' While the work takes place, the company will move into the Ambassadors and the Duke of York's theatres in the West End.

The Donmar Warehouse announced on the opening night of *The Glass Menagerie* that it could no longer survive without subsidy. The strength of Sam Mendes's production, plus an exceptional number of Laurence Olivier nominations, helped the company's cause and eventually the theatre managed to raise enough money to continue, including a grant of £150,000 from the Arts Council, a sponsorship deal with Mercury Communications, and donations amounting to £80,000.

Sir Robert Stephens

Sir Robert Stephens died in November 1995 after a long illness. Stephens was a popular, flamboyant actor, whose talent was for playing flawed characters. He came to prominence in John Osborne's *Epitaph for George Dillon* in 1958, a part he later played on Broadway. He was then invited by Laurence Olivier to become a member of the new National Theatre Company at the Old Vic, where he created the part of Atahualpa in Peter Shaffer's *The Royal Hunt of the Sun*. He married another of the National's young stars, Maggie Smith, in 1967. The marriage was not a success and it broke up during a 1972 revival of *Private Lives* in which they both starred. Stephens's career subsequently floundered, only recovering in 1991 when Adrian Noble invited him to play Falstaff at the RSC. This was followed by King Lear but when the production came to London, his health began to decline rapidly and he had to withdraw from the role. He was knighted in 1995.

Prodigals Return

Producing a musical in the West End is an expensive and risky business. Sir Cameron Mackintosh and Sir Andrew Lloyd Webber have reaped massive rewards; many more have fallen by the wayside but there is no shortage of producers prepared to have a go. The most anticipated and, at £3.75 million, the most expensive new production this year was *Martin Guerre*, a new musical by Alain Boublil and Claude-Michel Schönberg that opened in the Prince Edward in July. Boublil and Schönberg were also responsible for the world-wide hits *Les Misérables* and *Miss Saigon;* as with their previous work, *Martin Guerre* was produced by Cameron Mackintosh. Declan Donnellan and Nick Ormerod from the highly respected touring company Cheek by Jowl were director and designer respectively.

Two films, *The Return of Martin Guerre* and *Sommersby*, have been based on the true story of a man who was tried and executed in Toulouse in the 16th century after arriving in the village of Artigat and claiming to be the long-absent Martin Guerre,

convincing even Guerre's wife. The true story is powerfully enigmatic but the musical wanders a long way from its source to incorporate themes of identity, religious hatred between Protestants and Catholics, and the life of the community. Most importantly, all suspense is lost when Iain Glen's Arnaud immediately confesses to Juliette Caton's Bertrande that he is not her long-lost husband in the show's most memorable number 'Tell Me To Go'. Audiences at the first previews found the plot so difficult to follow that extensive revisions were made and by the first night the plot had been simplified, but the show still suffered from a thematic overload. It is not clear yet whether *Martin Guerre* will be as popular as its predecessors but there is much to admire: Schönberg's soaring music; Bob Avian's stirring, foot-stamping choreography; and David Hersey's liquid lighting. The production also introduced the latest in design technology. Instead of running on tracks or being pushed manually, the sets are controlled by computers and, once programmed, can travel anywhere across the stage. The only drawback is the need for a steady supply of electricity; without this the whole set grinds to a halt and the show has to be cancelled. Fluctuations in the supply provoked a dispute between Mackintosh and the London Electricity Board.

Should *Martin Guerre* fail to succeed, Boublil and Schönberg can always try reworking and reviving it in 20 years time. In 1975 Andrew Lloyd Webber produced his one and only flop, *Jeeves*, based on the stories of P. G. Wodehouse, with a book and lyrics by Alan Ayckbourn. This failure clearly rankled, and Lloyd Webber and Ayckbourn got together again to transform *Jeeves* into *By Jeeves*, with which Ayckbourn opened the new Stephen Joseph Theatre in Scarborough in May 1996. Announcing that he thought the days of the high-tech musical might well be numbered, Lloyd Webber then brought this small-scale musical into the Duke of York's Theatre in London. The setting, a village hall in which a concert is supposed to be taking place, ensures that there is no elaborate set; rather, cars are created out of old sofas and cardboard boxes, and the sound effects are performed by members of the cast. With an amusing plot, masterminded by Malcolm Sinclair's impeccable Jeeves, and pretty, pastiche numbers from Lloyd Webber, *By Jeeves* makes for an undemanding but delightful evening.

A complete contrast is *Tommy*, which arrived from Broadway where it has won five Tony awards. Pete Townshend's rock opera was originally written for The Who in the 1960s. There have previously been unsuccessful attempts to turn the record into a stage musical and Ken Russell directed a bizarre and outrageous film version. From the single, crashing chord with which it opens, Des McAnuff's production never lets up, introducing all the technology of the 1990s to the story of the blind, deaf and dumb kid who 'sure plays a mean pinball'. McAnuff clarifies the story-line but can do little about the superficiality of characters who were never intended to appear on stage. Paul Keating was rescued from stacking supermarket shelves to play Tommy, but John Arnone's set, with its gantries, video screens, photomontage sequences and shattering glass, is the star of the evening, making the actors, including Kim Wilde as Tommy's mother, seem insignificant.

SONDHEIM TRIO

It was Stephen Sondheim's year in the West End in 1995–6. Sean Mathias's revival of *A Little Night Music* broke box-office records at the National Theatre and one of Judi Dench's two Olivier awards this year was for her performance as Desiree, the actress who sings Sondheim's most famous number 'Send in the Clowns'. Based on Ingmar Bergman's *Smiles of a Summer Night*, the musical is a curious mix of Swedish angst and Manhattan sophistication. The mood of wistful regret and loneliness is immediately set in the opening number, in which the entire company drift onto the Olivier stage to waltz on their own. Stephen Brimson Lewis's designs, consisting of floating, white drapes hanging from ceiling to floor, also enhance the atmosphere. In a strong cast, Patricia Hodge plays the elegant, abandoned Countess to whom was restored the understandably bitter number 'My Husband the Pig'.

The smaller Donmar Warehouse revived Sondheim's earlier musical *Company*, with its witty, astringent book by George Furth. Adrian Lester's own sweet elusive personality enhanced the role of the 35-year-old bachelor hero who cannot quite commit himself to marriage, to the bafflement of his married friends. Sheila Gish gave a raucous rendering of 'The Ladies who Lunch', while Sophie Thompson brilliantly expressed total terror in the panic-stricken 'Getting Married Today'. The production later transferred to the Albery.

The last of the trio was the London première of *Passion* at the Queen's Theatre. It was received with much less enthusiasm in spite of an accomplished production by Jeremy Sams and an astonishing performance by Maria Friedman. Set in 1863, *Passion* is the gothic story of an ugly woman called Fosca and her abject passion for a handsome soldier (played by Michael Ball) who finally succumbs to her love. What impressed most was Maria Friedman's vocally extraordinary Fosca, which she combined with a creepy intensity. It may not be Sondheim's best musical but *Passion* gave Friedman the opportunity to show her astonishing vocal and dramatic range.

Rivalling *Martin Guerre* as the other major new British musical of the year was Francis Essex and Rob Bettinson's *Jolson*, the story of the American crooner, played by Brian Conley. Unlike other musical biographies of singers, *Jolson* is not just a series of songs with snippets of narrative in between. It has a proper script which tells the story of one of Broadway's less attractive characters, ruthlessly determined to succeed, quarrelling with anybody who got close to him, yet with a magnetic voice that

won followers all round the world with such saccharine classics as 'Sonny Boy' and 'Mammy'. Conley, who, like Jolson, makes his first entrance down the centre aisle of the auditorium, gives an impeccable impersonation and barnstorming performance as the brash singer.

Jerry Herman and Michael Stewart's *Mack and Mabel*, first seen on Broadway in 1974, has long had a following among musical *aficionados* in Britain, especially since the music was used by Torvill and Dean in their 1982 championship-winning ice-dance routine. However, it was only in November 1995 that a production opened in London. Like *Jolson*, *Mack and Mabel* is a showbiz biography and is based on the lives of Mack Sennett, the silent movie director who invented the Keystone Cops, and his leading star Mabel Normand. Great liberties are taken with the details of their lives but without making their personalities more appealing to the audience. Paul Kerryson's production, which opened in Leicester before coming to the West End, lasted little more than six months at the Piccadilly.

Ned Sherrin had some success with his revival of Julian Slade's whimsical 1954 musical *Salad Days*. Some found its charming naïvety too dated to enjoy; others revelled in the camp nostalgia of it. It is a long way from the operatic sweep of *Martin Guerre*, yet if Cameron Mackintosh had not been taken backstage after seeing a production of *Salad Days* as a child and shown how the magic piano worked, then he might never have become hooked on musicals. On such slender foundations did the rise of the British musical in the 1980s depend!

STARS SHINE

In a year in which the Royal National Theatre was, unusually, more notable for its revivals than its new plays, Richard Eyre's production of *John Gabriel Borkman* was outstanding. Eyre's regime at the National has been distinguished by many good things but not for stellar productions of the classics. *Borkman* saw the return of Paul Scofield to the stage after an absence of almost five years and also, surprisingly, marked the debut of Vanessa Redgrave on the National stage. Looking a little like Ibsen himself, Scofield's performance as the disgraced Borkman was a triumph of artifice distinguished by his famous sonorous voice; very much the self-made man still waiting after years of ignominy to be recognized by others as the great man he believes himself to be. As he paces in his study above, his rancorous wife and her sister, the woman he once loved but sacrificed to his ambition, fight below over his son as they once fought over him. Eyre's production, using a sardonic new translation by Nicholas Wright, served the actors well and enhanced Ibsen's theme that our dreams are constantly undermined by reality. It was a remarkable display of classical acting of a kind rarely seen today.

The National produced other surprises during the year. In 1995 Dame Diana Rigg abandoned her usual glamorous roles to drag Mother Courage's cart onto the Olivier stage. The elegant, urbane Rigg transformed herself into a hard-boiled grimy trader, jaw jutting and vowels severely flattened. Above all, she had the drive, energy and sardonic humour to drive the play forward. Jonathan Kent's production was by no means a slave to Brecht's politics and the modernist spin was not admired by all. But, as in *Medea*, Rigg once more proved that her range extends far beyond Emma Peel in *The Avengers*.

Another surprise was the invitation to the beautiful French film actress Isabelle Huppert to play Mary Stuart in Friedrich Schiller's romantic tragedy of the same name. The British theatre is often criticized for ignoring the German playwright but *Mary Stuart*, famous for introducing a confrontation between Mary Stuart and Elizabeth I which never occurred, is more often performed than his other plays. Both women in Schiller's play are imprisoned: Mary Stuart literally, and Elizabeth by the demands of the state. Schiller's sympathies, writing in 1800, lay with the impulsive doomed Mary rather than the calculating, dessicated Elizabeth. However, in Howard Davies' production, which mingled costumes of Schiller's time with those of the 16th century, it was Anna Massey as Elizabeth who triumphed, with her steely presence and controlled delivery, rather than Huppert, whose French accent compounded her problems in playing a role in a foreign language.

In the West End Sir Peter Hall invited Alan Bates to play Solness, the ageing architect who lives in fear of the younger generation, in Ibsen's autobiographical *The Master Builder*. Although Bates was praised for his performance of a man riven by the conflict between desire and duty, guilt and happiness, it was Victoria Hamilton who was most admired, as the 23-year-old Hilde who brings him new life before sending him to his death. This young actress was heralded as one of the most remarkable talents to emerge in years. She won the Critics' Circle Award for the most promising newcomer; an opinion confirmed later when she appeared in Stratford as Cressida in *Troilus and Cressida*.

Peter Hall had a busy year. His celebrated production of *An Ideal Husband* returned to the West End with a new cast while the original company went to Broadway. But he had less success with his and Nikki Frei's version of the Feydeau farce *Occupe-toi d'Amélie*. Frei and Hall had difficulty fixing on a title, switching on tour from *Emily Needs Attention* to *Mind Millie for Me*. Felicity Kendal played the chambermaid who has slept her way to the top, becoming Paris's leading cocotte. For all Kendal's vast following, the heavy-handed production failed to make the audience roll in its seats, let alone in the aisles, and brought to a close Hall's occupation of the Haymarket. The indefatigable director refused to be daunted, however, and later it was announced that he would move to the Old Vic. There, Hall plans to create a permanent company, a

rarity these days, to perform a season of plays. He will direct the classics and he has invited Dominic Dromgoole, who has made such a success of the tiny Bush Theatre, to direct the new plays.

The Royal Court Theatre paved the way for its temporary move to the West End while the theatre in Sloane Square is refurbished, by launching a season of Royal Court Classics at the Duke of York's Theatre. The season opened with Ron Hutchinson's *Rat in the Skull*, first seen at the Royal Court in 1984. Daldry and his designer removed many of the seats from the West End theatre and placed Rufus Sewell, as the suspected IRA bomber, and Tony Doyle, as the RUC interrogator, on a diamond-shaped platform in the centre of what would normally be the stalls. The audience sat in the circle, the boxes and on the stage. In retrospect the reviews make sad reading, many concentrating on whether the play was still relevant in the light of the IRA cease-fire. *Rat in the Skull* was followed by revivals of *Hysteria* and *The Changing Room*. There were some quibbles that these plays were being given the status of classics rather early in their career, but none with the quality of the productions.

At the National and the RSC, another recent playwright to be given classic status was Dennis Potter. His *Blue Remembered Hills* was revived at the National in a production by Patrick Marber, while *Son of Man* played in the Pit with Joseph Fiennes as Jesus Christ. Both these productions were better received than Potter's posthumous television plays.

At the Donmar Warehouse, Sam Mendes revived Tennessee Williams's *The Glass Menagerie*. An impeccable cast included Zöe Wanamaker as an unusually youthful Amanda, forever dreaming of a romantic past, and Claire Skinner in an award-winning performance as the impossibly shy Laura. Designer Rob Howell introduced a fire escape that sprawled across the auditorium, heightening the sense of the family's isolation from the rest of the world. The production later transferred to the Comedy. At the Young Vic, the Theatre Royal, Plymouth came triumphantly to London with a production of Eugene O'Neill's *Long Day's Journey into Night* with Richard Johnson as James Tyrone and Penelope Wilton as his addicted wife. At the Comedy, Harold Pinter directed *Twelve Angry Men*, Reginald Rose's 1950s jury drama, first seen on television but most famous for the film with Henry Fonda. Kevin Whately, Peter Vaughan, Timothy West and Tony Haygarth challenged, with varying degrees of success, their Hollywood predecessors.

Major revivals of Shakespeare were thin on the ground. The RSC was preoccupied with its administrative changes, announcing in June 1996 that its fourth base would be Plymouth when the company reduces its season at the Barbican from a year to six months. In Stratford, Joseph Fiennes and Victoria Hamilton played the young lovers in *Troilus and Cressida*, and Tim Supple won much praise for his simple and truthful production of *A Comedy of Errors*. Most notable was the rash of Scottish plays that came in very different guises. The RSC at Stratford went for European expressionism, in which rhetoric was abandoned for a measured, thoughtful delivery, too slow for many members of the audience. At Greenwich, Mark Rylance dressed his *Macbeth* in Hare Krishna costumes, and Jane Horrocks as Lady Macbeth achieved notoriety by urinating on stage. The highly regarded English Touring Company's version was more traditional, while the Tricycle's mixed race production, lit by torches, was a fiery affair with rising star Helen McCrory as Lady Macbeth and Lennie James as the Scottish usurper.

NEW PLAYS

The past year was one in which revivals overshadowed new plays and the most exciting new plays were often written by the youngest writers and appeared in the smallest spaces. In particular, there was a flurry of Irish drama, most often to be seen at the Royal Court, where Sebastian Barry's *The Steward of Christendom* first played in the Royal Court Theatre Upstairs and later moved downstairs. Drawing on the true story of his grandfather, who was the Catholic head of the Dublin Metropolitan Police before Irish Independence in 1922, Barry's play shows his protagonist Thomas Dunne, now in a mental asylum, painfully trawling through his past mistakes. Barry and director Max Stafford-Clark were fortunate to cast Donal McCann as Dunne, who, with his shaven head and grimy long johns, looked like an early Christian martyr as he struggled to make sense of his life. Both McCann and Barry won awards and the production will move to New York in 1997. Also opening in the Theatre Upstairs was Martin McDonagh's *The Beauty Queen of Leenane*, presented by Druid Theatre Company. This was heralded as an outstanding debut for the 25-year-old playwright, whose blackly comic play is set in a dingy kitchen in Galway where the middle-aged Maureen looks after her ghastly, hypochondriac mother. Marina Carr's *Portia Coughlan*, on the main stage at the Royal Court, marked the English debut of Derbhle Crotty as the despairing, angry Portia who has never recovered from the suicidal drowning of her twin brother.

In the West End new plays struggled to make headway against musicals and glossy revivals. Zöe Wanamaker, in her second appearance in the West End in a year, demonstrated her versatility by playing a cute little pooch in A. R. Gurney's sentimental comedy *Sylvia*; this and Ray Cooney's farce *Funny Money* were the only new plays of the year that could be described as traditional West End fare. While Wanamaker was remarkable, straining at the leash and rolling over to have her tummy tickled, even dog lovers could not be persuaded to fill the theatre. More controversially, Harry Gibson's adaptation of Irvine Welsh's best-selling novel *Trainspotting*, moved into the West End just before Christmas. Not exactly Christmas entertainment, it nevertheless attracted a young and very different audience to its depiction of a group of drug addicts in Edinburgh who recount their adventures in a series of stomach-churning turns. Welsh's refusal to moralize about his characters pleased some but disturbed others.

The most successful new play at the National was Pam Gems's *Stanley*, an account of the tortured life of the painter Stanley Spencer, whose paintings covered the walls of the Cottesloe Theatre. In spite of living in rural seclusion in Cookham, Spencer's life was so eventful, as he switched between his devoted wife and the rapacious lesbian Patricia Preece who persuaded him to sign over his house to her, that Gems could hardly fail. The play was written for Antony Sher, a painter himself, who, with a floppy fringe and buck teeth, transformed his appearance for the role.

Stephen Poliakoff popped up at Hampstead directing his own unsettling piece *Sweet Panic*, with Harriet Walter as a child psychiatrist and Saskia Reeves as her nemesis, 'the mother from hell'. Hampstead also saw the opening of John Godber's *Lucky Sods*, a play memorable only in that it was the first in London to deal with the National Lottery.

REGIONS

Starved of funds, the regions were mostly dedicated to reworking old favourites rather than coming up with anything new. The biggest event was the opening of the new Stephen Joseph Theatre in Scarborough. Created out of an Odeon cinema dating from 1938, it has two spaces, a 400-seat theatre in the round called simply The Round, and a smaller 165 foot stage that opened with Alan Bennett's *Forty Years On*. Jude Kelly at the West Yorkshire Playhouse continued to produce interesting work, most notably enticing Warren Mitchell north to have a crack at King Lear, which he played in khaki uniform with a vast snowy beard. In York, there was an outcry when it was announced that the role of God in the 1996 York Mystery Plays cycle, performed once every four years, would be played by a woman. Topically, Bill Alexander at the Birmingham Rep produced *Divine Right*, a new play by Peter Whelan set in 2000 which anticipated a republican Britain. At Chichester Alan Bates appeared in a new play by Simon Gray called *Simply Disconnected*, and Maggie Smith performed for the first time on stage *A Bed among the Lentils* from Alan Bennett's television monologues *Talking Heads*. An acclaimed production of *Uncle Vanya* with Derek Jacobi, Trevor Eve and Alec McCowen also opened in the Minerva as part of the 1996 Chichester Festival and is expected to transfer to the West End in autumn 1996.

PRODUCTIONS
September 1995 to August 1996

LONDON PRODUCTIONS

ADELPHI, WC2. *Sunset Boulevard*, since July 1993
ALBERY, WC2 (2 February 1996) *The Long and the Short and*

the Tall (Willis Hall) with Mark Arden, Bert Kwouk; director, Paul Jerricho. (13 March) *Company*, transferred from the Donmar

ALDWYCH, WC2 (31 January 1996) *The Fields of Ambrosia* (Martin Silvestri, Joel Higgins) with Joel Higgins, Christine Andreas; director, Gregory S. Hurst. (27 February) *Present Laughter* (Coward) with Peter Bowles, Deborah Grant, Caroline Langrishe; director, Richard Olivier. (30 April) *Tolstoy* (James Goldman) with F. Murray Abraham, Gemma Jones; director, Jack Hofsiss

ALMEIDA, N1 (5 September 1995) *Gangster No. 1* (David Scinto, Louis Mellis) with Peter Bowles, Richard Johnson; director, Jonathan Kent. (16 October) *Venice Preserved* (Otway) with David Bark-Jones, Alice Krige, John Woodvine; director, Ian McDiarmid. (12 December) *The Tower* (Dumas, trans. Charles Wood) with Sinead Cusack, Adrian Dunbar; director, Howard Davies. (14 February 1996) *1953* (Racine's *Andromache*, adapt. Craig Raine) with Pooky Quesnel, Emma Fielding, Jason Isaacs, Adam Kotz; director, Patrick Marber. (1 April) *A Week's Worth* with Irene Worth, Peter Eyre. (23 April) *Tartuffe* (Molière) with Tom Hollander, Ian McDiarmid; director, Jonathan Kent. (18 June) *(Uncle) Vanya*, transferred from Leicester Haymarket. (31 July) *Murder in the Cathedral* (Eliot), an Art-Inter Odeon, Romania, production

AMBASSADORS, WC2 (October 1995) *Burning Blue*, transferred from the Theatre Royal, Haymarket. (15 December) *Trainspotting* (Irvine Welsh, adapt. Harry Gibson) with Paul Ireland, Michelle Gomez, Peter Ireland, Gavin Marshall; director, Harry Gibson. (29 May 1996) *Dames at Sea* (Jim Wise, George Halmsohn, Robin Miller) with Joanne Farrell, Jason Gardiner, Kim Criswell, Sara Crowe; director, John Gardyne

APOLLO, W1 (20 May 1996) *Sylvia* (A. R. Gurney) with Zöe Wanamaker, Robin Ellis, Maria Aitken; director, Michael Blakemore. (13 August) *Dial M for Murder* (Frederick Knott) with Peter Davidson, Catherine Rabett, Brian Deacon; director, Peter Wilson

APOLLO VICTORIA, SW1. *Starlight Express*, since 1984

ARTS, WC2 (12 February 1996) *Heaven By Storm* with the Umbilical Brothers. (25 March) *Brothers of the Bush* (Jimmy Murphy) with Stuart Graham, Phelim Drew, Darragh Kelly, Vinnie McCabe; director, Lynne Parker. (25 July) *Two Boys in a Bed on a Cold Winter's Night* (James Edwin Parker) with Steven Brand, Richard Laing; director, Julian Woolford

BARBICAN, EC2 (5 September 1995) *Henry V* (Shakespeare) with Iain Glenn; director, Matthew Warchus. (18 October) *A Patriot for Me* (Osborne) with James Wilby; director, Peter Gill. (7 December) *A Christmas Carol*, revival of 1994 production. (30 January 1996) *Les Enfants du Paradis* (Jacques Prévert, adapt. Simon Callow) with Helen McCrory, James Faulkner, Joseph Fiennes, Rupert Graves, James Purefoy; director, Simon Callow. (15 February) *Twelfth Night*, revival of 1994 production. (6 March) *Observe the Sons of Ulster Marching Towards the Somme* (Frank McGuinness), an Abbey Theatre, Dublin, production. (9 April) *The Taming of the Shrew* (Shakespeare) with Josie Lawrence, Michael Siberry; director, Gale Edwards. (23 April) *Romeo and Juliet* (Shakespeare) with Lucy Whybrow, Zurbin Varla; director, Adrian Noble. (23 May) *Julius Caesar* (Shakespeare) with John Nettles, Julian Glover, Hugh Quarshie, Christopher Benjamin; director, Peter Hall. (27 June) *Richard III* (Shakespeare) with David Troughton; director, Steven Pimlott

THE PIT (12 September 1995) *The Park* (Botho Strauss) with Louise Jameson, Adrian Lukas; director, David

Fielding. (17 October) *Son of Man* (Dennis Potter) with Joseph Fiennes; director, Bill Bryden. (14 December) *Cain* (Byron) with Marcus D'Amico, John Carlisle, Linford Brown; director, John Barton. (25 January 1996) *Slaughter City* (Naomi Wallace) with Olwen Fouéré, Robert Langdon Lloyd, Linal Haft, Sophie Stanton, Alexis Daniel; director, Ron Daniels. (10 April) *The Relapse* (Vanbrugh) with Leigh Lawson, Kate Duchene, Victor Spinetti, Lorraine Ashbourne; director, Ian Judge. (24 April) *The Devil Is An Ass* (Jonson) with John Dougall, David Troughton, John Nettles, Jules Melvin; director, Matthew Warchus. (21 May) *The Painter of Dishonour* (Calderón) with John Carlisle, Sara Mair-Thomas; director, Laurence Boswell. (26 June) *The Phoenician Women* (Euripides) with Lorraine Ashbourne, Lucy Whybrow; director, Katie Mitchell

BUSH, W12 (8 September 1995) *Two Lips Indifferent Red* (Tamsin Oglesby) with Saffron Burrow, Ian Gelder, Peter Darling, Fiona Mollison; director, Vicky Featherstone. (20 October) *One Flea Spare* (Naomi Wallace) with Robert Langdon Lloyd, Sheila Reid; director, Dominic Dromgoole. (30 November) *Knives in Hens* (David Harrower) with Pauline Knowles, Michael Nardone, Lewis Howden; director, Philip Howard. (6 January 1996) *Goldhawk Road* (Simon Bent) with Trevor Martin, John Simm, Neil Stuke, Danny Webb, Jack Carr; director, Paul Miller. (February) *Serving It Up* (David Elderidge) with Eddie Marsan, Jake Wood, Arbel Jones, Christopher Ettridge; director, Jonathan Lloyd. (2 April) *Clocks and Whistles* (Samuel Adamson) with John Light, Neil Stuke, Kate Beckinsale, Michael Cashman; director, Dominic Dromgoole. (10 May) *Resurrection* (Maureen Lawrence) with Malcolm Rennie, Tyrone Huggins; director, Penny Ciniewicz. (6 June) *Who Shall Be Happy...?* (Trevor Griffiths) with Stanley Townsend, Kulvinder Ghir; director, Trevor Griffiths. (5 July) *This Lime Tree Bower* (Conor McPherson) with Ian Cregg, Conor Mullen, Niall Shanahan; director, Conor McPherson

CAMBRIDGE, WC2. *Fame: the Musical*, since June 1995

COMEDY, WC2 (3 October 1995) *The Hothouse*, transferred from Chichester. (11 December) *The Glass Menagerie*, transferred from the Donmar. (20 March 1996) *Disgracefully Yours* (Richard O'Brien) with Richard O'Brien. (22 April) *Twelve Angry Men*, transferred from the Old Vic, Bristol

CRITERION, W1 (19 December 1995) *Rupert Street Lonely Hearts Club*, transferred from the Donmar. (7 March 1996) *The Complete Works of William Shakespeare (Abridged)*, with the Reduced Shakespeare Company. (12 March) *The Complete History of America (Abridged)* with the Reduced Shakespeare Company

DOMINION, WC1. *Grease*, since July 1993

DONMAR WAREHOUSE, WC2 (13 September 1995) *The Glass Menagerie* (Tennessee Williams) with Zöe Wanamaker, Claire Skinner, Ben Chaplin, Mark Dexter; director, Sam Mendes. (8 November) *Rupert Street Lonely Hearts Club* (Jonathan Harvey) with Scot Williams, Tom Higgins, Elizabeth Berrington, Lorraine Brunning, James Bowers; director, John Burgess. (13 December) *Company* (Sondheim) with Adrian Lester, Sheila Gish; director, Sam Mendes. (4 March 1996) *The King of Prussia* (Nick Darke), a Kneehigh Theatre production. (12 March) *Buddleia* (Paul Mercier), a Passion Machine Company production. (19 March) *Song from a Forgotten City* (Edward Thomas), an Y Cwmni production. (28 March) *Bondagers* (Sue Glover), an Edinburgh Traverse Theatre production. (17 April) *Endgame* (Beckett) with Alun Armstrong, Stephen Dillane, Eileen Nicholas, Harry

Jones; director, Katie Mitchell. (5 June) *Habeas Corpus* (Alan Bennett) with Jim Broadbent, Brenda Blethyn, Imelda Staunton; director, Sam Mendes. (1 August) *Hedda Gabler* (Ibsen) with Alexandra Gilbreath; director, Stephen Unwin

DRURY LANE THEATRE ROYAL, WC2. *Miss Saigon,* since 1989

DUCHESS, WC2. *Don't Dress for Dinner,* since 1992

DUKE OF YORK'S, WC2 (11 October 1995) *Rat in the Skull* (Ron Hutchinson) with Rufus Sewell, Tony Doyle; director, Stephen Daldry. (30 November) *Hysteria* (Terry Johnson) with Henry Goodman, Tim Potter, Aisling O'Sullivan, Fred Pearson; director, Phyllida Lloyd. (7 February 1996) *The Changing Room* (David Storey) with Brendan Coyle, David Hargreaves, Ewan Hooper, Philip Whitchurch, Simon Wolfe; director, James Macdonald. (2 July) *By Jeeves* (Ayckbourn, Lloyd Webber), transferred from Scarborough

FORTUNE, WC2. *The Woman in Black,* since 1989. (Sunday matinees from October 1995) *Marie* (Steve Trafford) with Elizabeth Mansfield; director, Annie Castledine

GARRICK, WC2 (24 October 1995) *An Inspector Calls,* the 1992 National Theatre production

GATE, WII (29 September 1995) *Don Juan Comes Back From the War* (von Horvath) with Patricia Kathleen Boyer; director, Joseph Blatchley. (27 October) *Silverface* (Ramon del Valle Inclan) with Tony Curran, Donald Sumpter, Peter Marinker, Tonia Chauvet; director, David Farr. (1 December) *Ballad of Wolves* (Ramon del Valle Inclan) with Donald Sumpter; director, David Farr. (January 1996) *Blood Knot* (Athol Fugard) with Wilbert Johnson, Chris Lailey; director, Jonathan Lloyd. (February) *Cat and Mouse (Sheep)* (Gregory Motton); *Services (or They All Do It)* (Elfriede Jelinek). (28 February) *Sisters, Brothers* (Stig Larsson) with Gabrielle Dellal, Emily Best; director, David Farr; *The Oginski Polonaise* (Nikolai Kolyada) with Victoria Worsley; director, Pat Kiernan. (28 March) *Sugar Dollies* (Klaus Chatten) with Katrina Levon, Nina Conti; director, Indhu Rubasingham; *After the Rain* (Sergi Belbel) with Steven Elder, Nicholas Bolton, Bonnie Engstrom; director, Gaynor Macfarlane. (16 April) *Miss Julie* (Strindberg) with Kate Fenwick, Peter Lindford, Kristin Hewson; director, Nick Philippou. (20 May) *Phaedra's Love* (Sarah Kane) with Philippa Williams, Cas Harkins; director, Sarah Kane. (21 June) *The Invisible Woman* (Paul Godfrey) with Claudia Boulton. (23 July) *The Decameron* (Boccaccio, adapt. Nick Ward) with Ioan Gruffudd, Matt Patresi; director, Nick Ward

GIELGUD, WI (19 February 1996) *Chapter Two* (Neil Simon) with Tom Conti, Sharon Gless; director, David Gilmore

GLOBE, SEI (24 August 1996) *Two Gentlemen of Verona* (Shakespeare) with Stephanie Roth, Lennie James, Mark Rylance; director, Jack Shepherd

GREENWICH, SE10 (25 September 1995) *Macbeth* (Shakespeare) with Mark Rylance, Jane Horrocks; director, Mark Rylance. (6 November) *The Country Girl* (Clifford Odets) with Corin Redgrave, Kika Markham, Daniel Stewart; director, Annie Castledine. (18 December) *Privates on Parade* (Peter Nichols) with Tony Slattery, Nicholas Le Prevost; director, Paul Clayton. (12 February 1996) *East Lynne* (Mrs Henry Wood, adapt. Lisa Evans) with Rachel Power, Robin Lermitte, Lloyd Owen; director, Philip Franks. (1 April) *The Last Romantics* (Nigel Williams) with Mark Kingston, Maggie Stead, Robert Langdon Lloyd; director, Matthew Francis. (13 May) *What Now, Little Man?* (Hans Fallada, adapt. Julian Forsyth) with Clive Walton, Sharon Small, Anita Dobson;

director, Margaret Forsyth. (8 July) *Northanger Abbey* (Austen, adapt. Matthew Francis) with Sarah Jane Holm; director, Matthew Francis. (29 August) *The Heidi Chronicles* (Wendy Wasserstein) with Susannah Harker; director, David Taylor

HACKNEY EMPIRE (15 November 1995) *King Lear,* transferred from the West Yorkshire Playhouse

HAMPSTEAD, NW3 (22 September 1995) *Lucky Sods* (John Godber) with Christine Cox, Iain Rogerson, Janet Dibley, Nicholas Lane, director, John Godber. (8 November) *Jeffrey Dahmer is Unwell* (Alan Francis, Mike Hanley) with Alan Francis, Mike Hanley; director, Anthony Neilson. (22 November) *Ten Women in a One-Frock Show* with Geraldine McNulty; *Heart and Sole* with Lynn Ferguson. (11 December) *According to Hoyle* (William Gaminara) with Nick Dunning, Peter-Hugo Daly, Trevor Cooper, Jonathan Coy, Robert Glenister; director, Robin Lefevre. (8 February 1996) *Sweet Panic* (Stephen Poliakoff) with Saskia Reeves, Harriet Walter; director, Stephen Poliakoff. (11 April) *Some Sunny Day* (Martin Sherman) with Cheryl Campbell, Sara Kestelman, Rupert Everett, Corin Redgrave; director, Roger Michell. (11 June) *Song At Sunset* with Niall Buggy; director, Shivaun O'Casey. (16 July) *The Memory of Water* (Shelagh Stephenson) with Mary Jo Randle, Haydn Gwynne, Jane Booker, Matilda Ziegler; director, Terry Johnson

HAYMARKET THEATRE ROYAL, SWI (13 October 1995) *The Master Builder* (Ibsen) with Alan Bates, Victoria Hamilton, Gemma Jones; director, Peter Hall. (17 January 1996) *An Ideal Husband* (Wilde) with David Yelland, Anna Carteret, Pennie Downie, Martin Shaw; director, Peter Hall. (7 May) *Mind Millie For Me* (Feydeau's *Occupe-toi d'Amélie*) with Felicity Kendal, Neil Pearson, Nicholas Le Prevost; director, Peter Hall. (26 June) *The Odd Couple* (Neil Simon) with Tony Randall, Jack Klugman; director, Harvey Midlinsky

HER MAJESTY'S, SWI. *The Phantom of the Opera,* since 1986

LONDON PALLADIUM, WCI. *Oliver!,* since December 1994

LYRIC, WI (11 October 1995) *Hobson's Choice,* transferred from Chichester. (12 December) *The Miser,* transferred from Chichester. (12 August 1996) *Ferry 'Cross the Mersey,* transferred from Liverpool Playhouse

LYRIC, W6 (11 September 1995) *The Letter* (Somerset Maugham) with Joanna Lumley, Tim Pigott-Smith, Neil Stacy; director, Neil Bartlett. (31 October) *The Cabinet of Doktor Caligari,* transferred from Nottingham Playhouse. (8 December) *Hansel and Gretel* (Grimm), a Red Shift and Pop Up companies co-production. (15 January 1996) *Macbeth* (Shakespeare) with Paul Higgins, Hilary Lyon; director, Stephen Unwin. (March) *The Threepenny Opera* (Brecht, Weill) with Laurence Taylor, Jessica Watson; director, Mark Pattenden. (9 April) *La Dolce Vita* (Fellini), a David Glass Ensemble production. (7 May) *Three Sisters* (Chekhov), a Bristol Old Vic production. (4 June) *Claustrophobia* (Susan Glaspell), a Maly Theatre of St Petersburg production. (12 June) *Jude the Obscure,* a Method and Madness production transferred from Theatre Clwyd, Mold. (17 June) *Private Lives* (Coward), a Method and Madness production. (24 June) *Flesh and Blood* (Philip Osment), a Method and Madness production

LYRIC STUDIO (5 September 1995) *Macario,* a Tottering Bipeds production. (25 September) *Stop Calling Me Vernon,* a Right Size production. (1 November) *'Tis Pity She's a Whore* (Ford), a Talawa Black Theatre production. (23 November) *The Modern Husband* (Fielding), an Actors Touring Company production. (8 December) *Soup* (Michael Mears) with Michael Mears. (5 January 1996) *Fav'rite Nation* (Robin Brooks), an Empty Space production. (25 January) *Comic Cuts* (Jack Shepherd) with

Gavin Richards, Carla Mondonçça; director, Jonathan Church. (28 March) *Lady Into Fox* (David Garnett, adapt. Neil Bartlett, Nicolas Bloomfield) with Louise Gold, Dale Rapley; director, Leah Hausman. (22 May) *Road Movie* (Godfrey Hamilton) with Mark Pinkosh. (15 July) *Birdy* (William Wharton, adapt. Naomi Wallace) with Tam Williams, Adam Garcia; director, Kevin Knight

MERMAID, EC4 (23 October 1995) *Vivat! Vivat Regina!* (Robert Bolt) with Janet McTeer, Barbara Flynn; director, Roy Marsden. (5 December) *Treasure Island* (R. L. Stevenson, adapt. Glyn Robbins) with Roy Marsden, Paul Basson; director, Phil Wilmott. (12 June 1996) *Coriolanus* (Shakespeare) with Steven Berkoff, Faith Brook; director, Steven Berkoff

NEW END, NW3 (14, 16 and 18 November 1995) *The Holocaust Trilogy* (Julia Pascal): *Theresa* with Ruth Posner, Thomas Kampe; director, Julia Pascal; *A Dead Woman on Holiday* with Claire Marchionne; director, Jon Harris; *The Dybbuk*; director, Julia Pascal. (January 1996) *Romeo and Juliet* (Shakespeare) with Joanne Mitchell, Matthew Lewis; director, Simon Parry. (4 April) *Victoriana* (David Hart) with Jonathan Elsom, Jon Harris; director, Jon Harris. (3 May) *Maria* (Anna Maria Grabania) with Fenella Fielding; director, Andrew Visnevski. (24 May) *Freiwild* (Schnitzler), a Moving Theatre production. (25 July) *The Yellow Wallpaper* (Charlotte Perkins Gilman) with Patricia Boyer; director, Judith Roberts. (15 August) *Love in a Wood* (Wycherley), a London Classic Theatre Company production

NEW LONDON, WC2. *Cats*, since 1981

OLD VIC, SE1 (29 November 1995) *The Wind in the Willows*, revival of 1990 National Theatre production. (7 May 1996) *An Ideal Husband*, transferred from the Theatre Royal, Haymarket

OPEN AIR, Regent's Park, NW1 (28 May 1996) *Comedy of Errors* (Shakespeare) with David Cardy, Peter Forbes, Debra Beaumont, Paula Wilcox, Gavin Muir, Philip Fox; director, Ian Talbot. (13 June) *The Tempest* (Shakespeare) with Denis Quilley, Debra Beaumont, Ellen O'Grady; director, Patrick Garland. (26 July) *Paint Your Wagon* (Lerner, Loewe) with Chook Sibtain, Claire Carrie, Tony Selby, John Berlyne; director, Ian Talbot

PALACE, WC2. *Les Misérables*, since 1985

PHOENIX, WC1. *Blood Brothers*, since 1991

PICCADILLY, W1 (7 November 1995) *Mack and Mabel*, transferred from Leicester

PLAYHOUSE, (2 October 1995) *Funny Money* (Ray Cooney) with Ray Cooney, Charlie Drake, Sylvia Syms, Henry McGee; director, Ray Cooney

PRINCE EDWARD, W1 (10 July 1996) *Martin Guerre* (Alain Boublil, Claude-Michel Schönberg) with Iain Glen, Juliette Caton; director, Declan Donnellan

PRINCE OF WALES, W1 (9 October 1995) *What a Show!* with Tommy Steele. (15 April 1996) *Elvis* (Jack Good, Ray Cooney) with P. J. Proby, Alexander Bar, Tim Whitnall; directors, Keith Strachan, Carole Todd

QUEENS, W1 (30 October 1995) *Prisoner Cell Block H* (Don Battye, Peter Pinne) with Lily Savage, Maggie Kirkpatrick; director, David McVicar. (26 March 1996) *Passion* (Sondheim, James Lapine) with Michael Ball, Maria Friedman, Helen Hobson; director, Jeremy Sams

RIVERSIDE STUDIOS, W6 (28 September 1995) *Mephisto* (Mann, adapt. Glen Neath) with Philippe Benninkmeyer; director, Katrin Magrowitz. (4 October) *Oh! What a Bloody Circus* (Ionesco) with Roger Monk, Colette Makindi; director, John Burton. (1 November) *Abundance* (Beth

Henley) with Maryam d'Abo, Myriam Cyr; director, Lisa Forrell. (9 May 1996) *Duet for One* (Tom Kempinski) with Anton Rodgers, Elizabeth Garvie

ROYAL COURT, SW1 (5 September 1995) *The Steward of Christendom*, revival of April 1995 Theatre Upstairs production. (9 November) *Waiting Room Germany* (Klaus Pohl) with Robin Soans, Maureen Beattie, Neil Dudgeon, Freda Dowie; director, Mary Peate. (28 November) *The Break of Day*, transferred from the Bristol Old Vic. (5 February 1996) *Valley Song* (Athol Fugard) with Athol Fugard, Esmeralda Bihl; director, Athol Fugard. (27 March) *Harry and Me* (Nigel Williams) with Ron Cook, Sheila Hancock, Dudley Sutton; director, James Macdonald. (14 May) *Portia Coughlan* (Marina Carr) with Derbhla Crotty; director, Garry Hynes. (10 June) *The Trick Is To Keep Breathing* (Janice Galloway, adapt. Michael Boyd) with Jennifer Black, Siobhan Redmond, Tracy Wiles. (22 July) *The Lights* (Howard Korder) with Lee Ross, Emily Mortimer, Deirdre Harrison; director, Ian Rickson

THEATRE UPSTAIRS, SW1 (31 August 1995) *Not a Game for Boys* (Simon Block) with Christopher Fairbank, Neil Stuke, Peter Wight; director, Richard Georgeson. (18 October) *Pale Horse* (Joe Penhall) with Ray Winstone, Kacey Ainsworth; director, Ian Rickson. (21 November) *Bruises* (Judy Upton) with Stephanie Buttle, Billy Carter, Ian Redford; director, Jane Howell. (30 January 1996) *Sweetheart* (Nick Grosso) with Joe Duttine, Kate Beckinsale; director, Roxana Silbert. (5 March) *The Beauty Queen of Leenane* (Martin McDonagh), a Druid Theatre Company production. (2 April) *The Thickness of Skin* (Clare McIntyre) with Elizabeth Garvie, Rupert Frazer, Amelia Bullmore, Mark Strong; director, Hettie Macdonald. (30 April) *Mules* (Winsome Pinnock) with Abi Eniola, Clare Perkins, Sheila Whitfield; director, Roxana Silbert

ROYAL NATIONAL THEATRE, SE1, COTTESLOE (25 October 1995) *Cyrano* (Rostand, trans. Ranjit Bolt), a Tara Arts production. (15 January 1996) *Violin Time* (Ken Campbell) with Ken Campbell, Teo-Wa Vuong; director, Colin Watkeys. (1 February) *Stanley* (Pam Gems) with Antony Sher, Deborah Findlay, Anna Chancellor; director, John Caird. (29 February) *The Ends of the Earth* (David Lan) with Michael Sheen, Samantha Bond, Tom Mannion; director, Andrei Serban. (15 March) *Frogs* (Aristophanes) with Richard Henders, Nicholas Tigg, Clive Hayward; director, Fiona Laird. (24 April) *The Designated Mourner* (Wallace Shawn) with Miranda Richardson, Mike Nichols, David de Keyser; director, David Hare. (25 June) *War and Peace* (Tolstoy, adapt. Helen Edmundson), a co-production with Shared Experience Theatre.

LYTTELTON (7 September 1995) *Wild Oats* (John O'Keeffe) with Anton Lesser, Sarah Woodward, James Bolam, Alan Cox; director, Jeremy Sams. (19 October) *The Way of the World* (Congreve) with Fiona Shaw, Roger Allam, Geraldine McEwan; director, Phyllida Law. (14 December) *Rosencrantz and Guildenstern are Dead* (Stoppard) with Simon Russell Beale, Adrian Scarborough; director, Matthew Francis. (21 March 1996) *Mary Stuart* (Schiller, trans. Jeremy Sams) with Isabelle Huppert, Anna Massey; director, Howard Davies. (2 May) *Blue Remembered Hills* (Dennis Potter) with Matt Bardock, Steve Coogan, Debra Gillett, Robert Glenister, Gerard Horan, Geraldine Somerville; director, Patrick Marber. (11 July) *John Gabriel Borkman* (Ibsen) with Paul Scofield, Vanessa Redgrave, Eileen Atkins; director, Richard Eyre

OLIVIER (26 September 1995) *A Little Night Music* (Sondheim) with Judi Dench, Sian Phillips, Patricia Hodge, Lambert Wilson, Laurence Guittard; director, Sean Mathias. (14 November) *Mother Courage and Her Children* (Brecht) with Diana Rigg; director, Jonathan Kent. (19 April 1996) *The Prince's Play* (Victor Hugo's *Le Roi s'Amuse*, trans. Tony Harrison) with Ken Stott, Arlene Cockburn, David Westhead; director, Richard Eyre. (1 August) *The Red Balloon* (Albert Lamorisse, adapt. Anthony Clark) with Nicky Adams; director, Anthony Clark

ST MARTINS, WC2. *The Mousetrap*, since 1974

SADLER'S WELLS, ECI (23 May 1996) *Calamity Jane* (Sammy Fain, Paul Webster) with Gemma Craven, Stephen McGann; director, Paul Kerryson

SAVOY, WC2 (20 September 1995) *Dead Funny* (Terry Johnson) with Belinda Lang, Kevin McNally; director, Terry Johnson. (29 January 1996) *Communicating Doors*, transferred from the Gielgud

SHAFTESBURY, WC2 (19 December 1995) *Return to the Forbidden Planet* (Bob Carlton), transferred from Coventry. (5 March 1996) *The Who's Tommy* (Pete Townshend, Des McAnuff) with Paul Keating, Kim Wilde; director, Des McAnuff

STRAND, WC2 (7 October 1995) *Buddy*, transferred from the Victoria Palace

THEATRE ROYAL, E15 (13 September 1995) *Jelly Roll!* (Vernel Bagneris) with Vernel Bagneris, Morten Gunnar Larsen; director, A. Dean Irby. (October) *Marabi* (Modikwe Dikobe), a Junction Avenue Theatre Company production. (November) *Funny Black Woman on the Edge* (Angie Le Mar) with Angie Le Mar. (21 February 1996) *Gulp Fiction* (Trish Cooke) with Eddie Nestor, Robbie Gee; director, Trish Cooke. (18 March) *The Soldier's Song* (Bryan James Ryder) with Billy Carter, Anne Carroll, Sarah Howe, Colin Tarrant, Mary MacLeod; director, John Dove. (April) *What a Bleeding' Liberty* (Tom Kempinski) with Kate Williams, Eric Richard; director, Philip Hedley. (May) *The 'No Boys' Cricket Club* (Roy Williams)

TRICYCLE, NW6 (25 September 1995) *Bedfellows* (David Anderson, David MacLennan), a Wildcat Theatre Company production. (25 October) *Macbeth* (Shakespeare) with Lennie James, Helen McCrory; director, Nicolas Kent. (22 November) *Desire Under the Elms* (O'Neill), a Shared Experience Theatre production. (19 December) *Tales From Home*, with the Besht Tellers. (29 January 1996) *Two Trains Running* (August Wilson) with George Harris, Stefan Kalipha, Tony Armatrading, Jenny Jules; director, Paulette Randall. (4 March) *20-52* with Stephanie Lightfoot-Bennett; director, Jeremy Weller. (8 May) *Responses: Haiti* (Keith Reddin); *Reel Rwanda* (Femi Osofisan); *Ex-Yu* (Goran Stefanovski) and *Nuremberg* (Richard Norton-Taylor) with Jeremy Clyde, William Hoyland, Moira Govan, Michael Cochrane, Michael Culver, Hoyland Keitel, Thomas Wheatley, Richard Heffer; director, Nicolas Kent. (10 June) *Truth Omissions* with Pieter-Dirk Uys. (11 July) *Roll With the Punches: the songs of Randy Newman*, with Belinda Lang, George Costigan, Paul J. Medford; director, Chris Bond

VAUDEVILLE, WC2 (13 November 1995) *The Shakespeare Revue* (Christopher Luscombe, Malcolm McKee) with Susie Blake, Janie Dee, Martin Connor, Christopher Luscombe, Malcolm McKee. (28 February 1996) *A Talent to Amuse* with Peter Greenwell. (18 April) *Salad Days* (Julian Slade) with Nicola Fulljames, Simon Connelly, Kit Hesketh-Harvey, Richard Sisson; director, Ned Sherrin

VICTORIA PALACE, SW1 (26 October 1995) *Jolson* (Francis Essex, Rob Bettinson) with Brian Conley, Sally Ann Triplett; director, Rob Bettinson

WHITEHALL, (October 1995) *Only The Lonely: the Roy Orbison Story*, transferred from the Piccadilly Theatre. (14 March 1996) *Trainspotting*, revival of December 1995 production at the Ambassadors Theatre. (22 July) *Voyeurz* (Michael Lewis, Peter Rafelson) with Sally Anne Marsh, Krysten Cummings, Natasha Kristie, Fem 2 Fem; director, Michael Lewis

WYNDHAM'S, WC2 (28 September 1995) *Three Tall Women* (Albee) with Maggie Smith, Sara Kestelman, Samantha Bond; director, Anthony Page. (2 January 1996) *The Duchess of Malfi* (Webster), a Cheek by Jowl production. (20 February) *Skylight*, transferred from the Royal National Theatre. (30 April) *Present Laughter*, transferred from the Aldwych. (1 July) *The Aspen Papers* (Henry James, adapt. Michael Redgrave) with Daniel J. Travanti, Hannah Gordon, Moira Lister; director, Auriol Smith

YOUNG VIC, SEI (4 September 1995) *Peer Gynt* (Ibsen) with Alex Jennings, Haydn Gwynne; director, John Barton. (17 October) *Making The Future: Mirad, A Boy From Bosnia* (Ad de Bont), *Hitler's Childhood* (Niklas Rådström), *Grace* (Ignace Cornellssen), Oxford Stage Company productions. (5 December) *The Jungle Book* (Kipling, adapt. Tim Supple) with Ronny Jhutti, Clive Mendus, Sarah C. Cameron, Andy Williams; director, Tim Supple. (13 February 1996) *The Misanthrope* (Molière) with Ken Stott, Elizabeth McGovern; director, Lindsay Posner. (29 March) *Miss Julie* (Strindberg) with Susan Lynch, John Hannah, Cara Kelly; director, Polly Teale. (29 April) *Foe*, transferred from Leeds. (14 June) *Cordelia*, a Theater la Balance production. (28 June) *Rain Snakes* (P. O. Enquist) with Jason Morell, Sian Thomas, Robert David MacDonald; director, Kim Dambaek. (5 July) *A Long Day's Journey Into Night*, transferred from Plymouth

OUTSIDE LONDON

BIRMINGHAM: REPERTORY (19 September 1995) *Macbeth* (Shakespeare) with Jeffery Kissoon, Lucy Cohu; director, Bill Alexander. (31 October) *The Way of the World* (Congreve) with James Purefoy, Rakie Ayola, Linda Spurrier; director, Bill Alexander. (8 December) *Toad of Toad Hall* (Grahame, adapt. A. A. Milne) with Geoffrey Freshwater, David Phelan, Ian Pepperell, Jack Smethurst; director, Gwenda Hughes. (6 February 1996) *The Entertainer* (Osborne) with David Ross; director, Anthony Clark. (12 March) *The Winslow Boy* (Rattigan); director, Gwenda Hughes. (23 April) *Divine Right* (Peter Whelan) with William Mannering; director, Bill Alexander. (21 May) *Gentlemen Prefer Blondes* (Anita Loos) with Lucy Akhurst; director, Anthony Clark. (2 July) *Dr Jekyll and Mr Hyde* (R. L. Stevenson, adapt. David Edgar) with David Schofield; director, Bill Alexander

BRISTOL: OLD VIC (September 1995) *Three Sisters* (Chekhov) with Anita Dobson, Catherine Russell, Kate Ashfield, David Fielder, Nigel Terry; director, Max Stafford-Clark. (September) *The Break of Day* (Timberlake Wertenbaker) with Catherine Russell, Nigel Terry, Maria Friedman, Brian Protheroe, Anita Dobson, David Fielder; director, Max Stafford-Clark. (March 1996) *Twelve Angry Men* (Reginald Rose) with Kevin Whately, Timothy West, Peter Vaughan; director, Harold Pinter

CHICHESTER: FESTIVAL (21 September 1995) *The Visit* (Dürrenmatt) with Lauren Bacall, Joss Ackland; director, Terry Hands. (May 1996) *Love for Love* (Congreve) with Jenny Quayle, Richard Garnett, Gary Olsen, Leslie Phillips, David Weston; director, Ian Judge. (4 June)

Mansfield Park (Austen, adapt. Willis Hall) with Lucy Scott, Mark Jax, Tony Britton, Liza Goddard; director, Michael Rudman. (6 June) *Beethoven's Tenth* (Ustinov) with Peter Ustinov, Liz Robertson, John Neville; director, Joe Harmston. (30 July) *When We Are Married* (Priestley) with Dawn French, Alison Steadman, Annette Badland, Roger Lloyd-Pack, Peter Copley, Gary Waldhorn, Dora Bryan, Leo McKern, Shirley-Ann Field; director, Jude Kelly. (6 August) *Hedda Gabler* (Ibsen) with Harriet Walter; director, Lindy Davies. (27 August) *Fortune's Fool* (Turgenev) with Alan Bates, Rachel Pickup, Desmond Barrit; director, Gale Edwards

MINERVA (19 September 1995) *Monsieur Amilcar* (Yves Jamiaque) with Keith Michell, Penelope Keith; director, Tim Luscombe. (13 May 1996) *Simply Disconnected* (Simon Gray) with Alan Bates, Benedick Bates, Gawn Grainger, Charles Kay; director, Richard Wilson. (10 June) *Talking Heads* (Alan Bennett): *Bed Among the Lentils* with Maggie Smith; *Soldiering On* with Margaret Tyzack; director, Alan Bennett. (9 July) *Uncle Vanya* (Chekhov) with Derek Jacobi, Trevor Eve, Alex McCowen, Frances Barber, Imogen Stubbs; director, Bill Bryden. (28 August) *Beatrix* (Judy Taylor, Patrick Garland) with Patricia Routledge; director, Patrick Garland

EDINBURGH: ROYAL LYCEUM (15 September 1995) *Our Country's Good* (Timberlake Wertenbaker) with Tom McGovern; director, Caroline Hall. (16 October) *The Caucasian Chalk Circle* (Brecht); director, Gerard Murphy. (10 November) *Hamlet* (Shakespeare) with Tom McGovern; director, Kenny Ireland. (8 December) *Merlin the Magnificent* (Stuart Paterson). (12 February 1996) *The Steamie* (Tony Roper); director, Caroline Hall. (9 February) *Of Mice and Men* (Steinbeck) with Tom McGovern, Bob Barrett; director, Kenny Ireland. (8 March) *Montrose* (Robert Forrest) with Liam Brennan, Laurie Ventry; director, Kenny Ireland. (12 April) *Pygmalion* (Shaw) with Emily Winter, Michael Mackenzie; director, Hugh Hodgart. (7 June) *Rough Crossing* (Tom Stoppard) with Briony McRoberts, John Bett; director, Kenny Ireland. (5 July) *Blithe Spirit* (Coward); director, Kenny Ireland

GLASGOW: CITIZENS (31 August 1995) *Ebb Tide* (Stevenson, adapt. Robert David MacDonald). (September) *Don Carlos* (Schiller) with Giles Havergal, Benedick Bates, Julie Saunders; director, Philip Prowse. (6 October) *Shadow of a Gunman* (O'Casey); director, Jon Pope. (2 November) *Lanark* (Alasdair Gray), a TAG Theatre Company production. (26 January 1996) *Travels with my Aunt* (Graham Greene); director, Giles Havergal. (29 February) *In the Bar of a Tokyo Hotel* (Tennessee Williams) with Colin Wells, Ellen Sheean, Johnny Brunel; director, Philip Prowse. (1 March) *Marabou Stork Nightmares* (Irvine Welsh, adapt. Harry Gibson) with James Cunningham, Joanna Macleod; director, Harry Gibson

LEEDS: WEST YORKSHIRE PLAYHOUSE (28 September 1995) *King Lear* (Shakespeare) with Warren Mitchell; director, Jude Kelly. (2 November) *Lucky Sods* (John Godber) with Polly Hemingway, Andrew Livingston; director, Noreen Kershaw. (4 January 1996) *Peter Pan* (Barrie) with John Padden, David Bamber, Morag Hood; director, Matthew Warchus. (15 February) *The Government Inspector* (Gogol) with Toby Jones, Bob Mason; director, Phelim McDermott. (7 March) *Foe* (J. M. Coetzee, adapt. Mark Wheatley), a Théâtre de Complicité production. (27 March) *The Entertainer*, transferred from Birmingham Repertory Theatre. (July) *Loot* (Orton) with John Alderton, Alan Cowan, Rebecca Lacey, Ifan Meredith, Mark Dexter; director, Alan Strachan

COURTYARD (12 September 1995) *With Every Beat* (Richard Cameron) with Denzil Kilvington; director, Mike Bradwell. (31 October) *The Beatification of Area Boy* (Wole Soyinka) with Tyrone Huggins; director, Jude Kelly. (December) *The World Goes 'Round* (Kander, Ebb) with Fiona Hendley, Pepsi Lawrie Demacque, Antony Corriette, RJC; director, Jude Kelly. (February 1996) *Trainspotting* (Irving Welsh). (10 April) *She Knows, You Know!* (Jean Fergusson) with Jean Fergusson; director, Alfred Hickling. (29 May) *The Hypochondriac* (Molière) with Paul Shelley; director, Toby Jones.(2 July) *Exquisite Sister: The Diaries of Dorothy Wordsworth* with Kelly Hunter; director, Simon Usher

LEICESTER: HAYMARKET (19 September 1995) *Mack and Mabel* (Jerry Herman, Michael Stewart) with Howard McGillin, Caroline O'Connor; director, Paul Kerryson. (20 November) *Guys and Dolls* (Loesser) with Fiona Sinnott, David Leonard, Geraldine Fitzgerald, Peter Forbes; director, Paul Kerryson. (13 March 1996) *The Homecoming* (Pinter) with Julia Lane, George Sewell; director, Ben Barnes. (23 April) *(Uncle) Vanya* (Howard Barker) with William Armstrong, Victoria Wicks, Edward Jewesbury, Thomas Lockyer; director, Howard Barker

LIVERPOOL: PLAYHOUSE (12 February 1996) *Ferry 'Cross the Mersey: The Musical* with Gerry Marsden, Carl Kirshner; director, Bill Kenwright

MANCHESTER: ROYAL EXCHANGE (7 September 1995) *Tartuffe* (Molière) with Roger Lloyd Pack, Hugh Ross; director, Robert Delamere. (19 October) *Miss Julie* (Strindberg) with Amanda Donohoe, Patrick O'Kane; director, Braham Murray. (23 November) *An Experienced Woman Gives Advice* (Iain Heggie) with Siobhan Redmond; director, Matthew Lloyd. (21 December) *Animal Crackers* (Gregory S. Kaufman, Morrie Ryskind) with Ben Keaton, Joseph Alessi, Toby Sedgwick; directors, Emil Wolk, Gregory Hersov. (8 February 1996) *The Rivals* (Sheridan) with Annabel Mullion, Maureen Lipman, Dominic Rowan, Tony Britton; director, Braham Murray. (28 March) *Tess of the D'Urbervilles* (Hardy, adapt. Michael Fry) with Elli Garnett; director, Dilys Hamlett. (9 May) *Misfits* (Alex Finlayson) with Lisa Eichhorn, Christian Burgess, James Clyde, Ray Lonnen, Stephen Yardley; director, Gregory Hersov. (6 June) *Hindle Wakes* (Stanley Houghton) with Sophie Stanton, Nicholas Gleaves, Ewan Hooper; director, Helena Kaut-Howson. (11 July) *The Philadelphia Story* (Philip Barry) with Jordan Baker, Tom Mannion, Una Stubbs, Richard Hawley; director, Josephine Abady

MOLD: THEATR CLWYD (October 1995) *The Tempest*, transferred from Nottingham Playhouse. (17 November) *The Daughter-in-Law* (D. H. Lawrence). (5 December) *Gulliver's Travels* (Swift, adapt. Humphrey Carpenter) with Jack Klaff; director, Roger Redfarn. (March 1996) *The Government Inspector* (Gogol) with Ian Hughes; director, Michael Bogdanov. (29 March) *A Family Affair* (Ostrovsky); director, Phelim McDermott. (30 April) *The Deep Blue Sea* (Rattigan); director, Janet Suzman. (21 May) *Double Indemnity* (James M. Cain) with Barry Foster; director, Edward Thomas. (29 May) *Jude the Obscure* (Hardy, adapt. Mike Alfreds), a Method and Madness production

NOTTINGHAM: PLAYHOUSE (8 September 1995) *The Tempest* (Shakespeare) with Michael Fitzgerald, Saira Todd, Stephen Mangan; director, Silviu Purcarete. (6 October) *The Cabinet of Doktor Caligari* (Barry Simner) with Matthew Kelly, John Ramm; director, Martin Duncan. (3 November) *Party Tricks* (Crispin Whittell) with Rob Spendlove, Alexander Armstrong; director, Martin Clunes. (26 February 1996) *All In The Timing* (David Ives)

with Steve Punt, Hugh Dennis; director, Hugh
Wooldridge. (25 March) *Delicate Balance* (Albee) with
Eleanor Bron, Michael J. Shannon, Sandra Voe, Gary
Raymond; director, Tom Cairns. (19 April) *Happy End*
(Brecht, Hauptmann, Weill) with Tataa Hugo, Ray Shell,
Graham Kent; director, Martin Duncan. (21 May)
Claustrophobia (Susan Glaspell), a Maly Theatre of St
Petersburg production

PLYMOUTH: THEATRE ROYAL (21 June 1996) *A Long Day's
Journey Into Night* (O'Neill) with Richard Johnson,
Penelope Wilton, Paul Rhys, Mark Lambert; director,
Laurence Boswell

SCARBOROUGH: STEPHEN JOSEPH (26 September 1995)
Talking Heads (Alan Bennett) with Elizabeth Kelly,
Christopher Webber, Marlene Sidaway; director,
Malcolm Hebden. (1 November) *Hard Times* (Dickens,
adapt. Stephen Jeffrey); director, Kate Valentine. (30
November) *Grimm Tales* (adapt. Tim Supple), the 1994
Young Vic production; director, Kate Valentine. (11
January 1996) *Just Between Ourselves* (Ayckbourn);
director, Robin Herford. (1 May) *By Jeeves* (Lloyd
Webber, Ayckbourn) with Steven Pacey, Malcolm
Sinclair; director, Alan Ayckbourn. (11 June) *Wild Honey*
(Chekhov) with Richard Derrington, Dorothy Atkinson,
Joanna van Gysegham; director, Alan Ayckbourn. (16
July) *A Going Concern* (Stephen Jeffreys); director, Robin
Herford. (20 August) *It Could Be Any One of Us* (Ayckbourn)
with Juliet Mills, Jon Strickland; director, Alan
Ayckbourn

SHEFFIELD: CRUCIBLE (8 September 1995) *Blue
Remembered Hills* (Dennis Potter) with Charles Dale, Steve
Nicolson, Ken Bradshaw, Roger Morlidge, Tristan
Sturrock, Poppy Miller, Morag Siller; director, Deborah
Paige. (3 November) *Macbeth* (Shakespeare) with Duncan
Bell, Siobhan Stanley; director, Philip Franks. (December)
Badenheim 1939 (Sian Evans) with Lucy Burge, Christian
Burgess, Linda Dobell, Philippe Giraudeau; director, Ian
Spink. (April 1996) *Way Upstream* (Ayckbourn) with Derek
Hutchinson, Sophie Thursfield, Pip Donaghy, Carolyn
Pickles, Nicholas Clay; director, Deborah Paige

SOUTHAMPTON: NUFFIELD (9 November 1995) *All's Well
That Ends Well* (Shakespeare) with Alexandra Mathie, Paul
Barnhill, Zena Walker, Granville Saxton; director, Patrick
Sandford. (12 December) *The Count of Monte Cristo*
(Dumas, adapt. Ken Hill). (13 February 1996) *Dead White
Males* (David Williamson) with Claire Price, Jeremy
Clyde, John Woodvine, Gabrielle Lloyd; director, Patrick
Sandford. (April) *The Price of Meat* (Michele Celeste) with
Joanna Monro; director, Patrick Sandford. (23 May)
Charley's Aunt (Brandon Thomas)

STRATFORD: MEMORIAL (6 September 1995) *Richard III*
(Shakespeare) with David Troughton; director, Steven
Pimlott. (25 April 1996) *As You Like It* (Shakespeare) with
Niamh Cusack, Rachel Joyce, Liam Cunningham, John
Woodvine, Joseph Fiennes, Victoria Hamilton; director,
Steven Pimlott. (16 May) *Macbeth* (Shakespeare) with
Roger Allam, Brid Brennan; director, Tim Albery. (24
July) *Troilus and Cressida* (Shakespeare) with Joseph
Fiennes, Victoria Hamilton, Clive Francis, Philip Voss;
director, Ian Judge

SWAN (9 September 1995) *Faust* (Goethe, adapt. Howard
Brenton) with Michael Feast, Hugh Quarshie, Sophie
Heyman; director, Michael Bogdanov. (26 April 1996)
The White Devil (Webster) with Jane Gurnett, Ray Fearon,
Stephen Boxer, Richard McCabe; director, Gale Edwards.
(15 May) *Three Hours After Marriage* (Gay, Pope,
Arbuthnot) with Clive Francis, Richard McCabe, Adam
Godley, Jane Gurnett; director, Richard Cottrell. (23

July) *The General From America* (Richard Nelson) with
James Laurenson, Corin Redgrave, Jay McInnes;
director, Howard Davies

THE OTHER PLACE (24 October 1995) *The Phoenician
Women* (Euripides) with Lorraine Ashbourne, Sean
Murray, Dermot Kerrigan, Lucy Whybrow; director,
Katie Mitchell. (22 May 1996) *The Herbal Bed* (Peter
Whelan) with Teresa Banham, Joseph Fiennes, Liam
Cunningham; director, Michael Attenborough. (3 July)
The Comedy of Errors (Shakespeare) with Robert Bowman,
Simon Coates, Sarah C. Cameron, Thusitha Jayasundera,
Ursula Jones; director, Tim Supple. (25 July) *The Learned
Ladies* (Molière) with Jane Gurnett, Niamh Cusack,
Alison Fiske, Caroline Blakiston, Roger Allam, John
Quayle; director, Steven Pimlott

THEATRE AWARD WINNERS

OLIVIER AWARDS 1996

Best Actor – Alex Jennings, *Peer Gynt*
Best Actress – Judi Dench, *Absolute Hell*
Best Actor in a Musical – Adrian Lester, *Company*
Best Actress in a Musical – Judi Dench, *A Little Night Music*
Best Director – Sam Mendes, *Company* and *The Glass
Menagerie*
Best Play – *Skylight* (David Hare)
Best Musical – *Jolson* (Francis Essex, Rob Bettinson)
Best Comedy – *Mojo* (Jez Butterworth)
Best Supporting Performance – Simon Russell Beale,
Volpone
Best Supporting Performance in a Musical – Sheila Gish,
Company

REGIONAL THEATRE AWARDS 1995

Best Actor – Anthony Sher, *Titus Andronicus* (West
Yorkshire Playhouse)
Best Actress – Kelly Hunter, *As You Like It* (English
Touring Theatre)
Best Director – Barrie Rutter, *The Cracked Pot* (West
Yorkshire Playhouse) and *The Midsummer Night's Dream*
(Northern Broadside tour)
Overall Production – *Titus Andronicus* (Market Theatre,
Johannesburg, and the Royal National Theatre Studio)
Best New Play – *Trainspotting* (Harry Gibson)
Best Musical – *Moll Flanders* (Theatre Royal, York)
Best Touring Production – *A Night in November*
(Dubbeljoint Productions)
Best Show for Children/Young People – *The Red Balloon*
(Birmingham Repertory Theatre)
Best Supporting Actor – Paul Copley, *The Servant*
(Birmingham Repertory Theatre)
Best Supporting Actress – Alexandra Mathie, *Twelfth Night*
(Nottingham Playhouse)
Most Outstanding Contribution – Paul Elliott

Weather

JULY 1995

Rainfall totals were below normal, except in Northern Ireland and south-west Scotland, but there were periods of heavy rain and thunderstorms in places. On the 2nd thunderstorms affected southern England and rain or showers fell over Scotland on the 5th. The 10th–11th brought thunderstorms to many areas; 48 mm (1.89 in) of rain fell at Cynwyd (Clwyd) on the 10th and 46.6 mm (1.81 in) fell at Machrihanish (Strathclyde) on the 11th. Lightning destroyed a new telephone exchange at Pontybodkin (Clwyd), flooding occurred throughout Britain and power was cut off in many areas. A man was killed by lightning near Preston (Lancs). Widespread thunderstorms occurred on the 14th, when 45 mm (1.77 in) of rain fell at Pendennis Point (Cornwall). Heavy rain occurred in western areas on the 17th, when 71.6 mm (2.82 in) fell at Nantmor (Gwynedd). The 18th brought rain generally, and rain fell over Scotland on the 19th and 20th and over northern England on the 21st; on the 19th, 79 mm (3.5 in) fell at Onich (Highland). Thunderstorms occurred over southern England on the 26th, with flooding in London. Scattered light rain fell during the rest of the month.

Monthly mean temperatures were above normal everywhere; it was the fourth hottest July since 1659 and the third hottest this century. The temperature reached 30.7°C (87.3°F) at Kinloss on the Moray Firth on the 31st and 32.0°C (89.6°F) at Heathrow (Greater London) on the 10th, but the highest temperature was 33.4°C (92.1°F) at Babworth (Cambs) on the 29th. The lowest temperature was −2.0°C (28.4°F) at Tomatin (Highland) on the 1st.

Sunshine totals were generally above normal. The highest daily total was 16.0 hours at Kirkwall (Orkney) on the 18th and the highest monthly total was 303 hours at Hemsby (Norfolk).

AUGUST 1995

Rainfall totals were below normal almost everywhere; it was the driest August on record over Northern Ireland and the fourth driest over England and Wales. Thunderstorms occurred in south-western areas on the 2nd, when 85 mm (3.35 in) of rain fell at Cardiff. On the 7th a whirlwind took the roof off a garden centre near Woodstock (Oxon). Rain fell mainly in western areas on the 12th. Drought orders were in force in many areas. On the 22nd 34.0 mm (1.34 in) of rain fell at Pendennis Point (Cornwall).

Monthly mean temperatures were above normal everywhere. It was the warmest August since 1659 over England and Wales and the warmest on record over Northern Ireland. The temperature reached 30.6°C (87.1°F) at Tandragee (Co. Armagh) on the 2nd, an August record for Northern Ireland. Onich (Highland) recorded 32.1°C (89.8°F) on the 1st. Forest and moorland areas were set ablaze in the heat. The highest temperature was 34.9°C (94.8°F) at Kew Gardens (London) on the 1st and the lowest was 0.0°C (32.0°F) at Culterty (Grampian) on the 8th.

Sunshine totals were above normal everywhere. It was the sunniest August on record over England and Wales. The highest daily total was 15.0 hours at Ronaldsway (Isle of Man) on the 6th and the highest monthly total was 322 hours at Poole (Dorset).

SEPTEMBER 1995

Rainfall totals were above normal except in Northern Ireland and a few places in western Britain. Totals were particularly high in Grampian, where Kinloss had over five times the normal amount. Rain fell in northern Scotland on the 1st, when Kinloss recorded 50.1 mm (1.97 in). The 2nd brought rain or thunderstorms to most areas and 19 people were injured by lightning at a football match at Aylesford (Kent). Thunderstorms were widespread on the 4th, when 40.3 mm (1.58 in) of rain fell at Aughton (Lancs). Flooding occurred in Merseyside, the Isle of Man, Wales and East Anglia. The 5th brought rain in the north and thunder in the south with further flooding. Heavy rain fell over England and Wales on the 6th and everywhere on the 7th, when 50.8 mm (2.0 in) fell at Linton-on-Ouse (N. Yorks). A gust of 55 knots (63 mph) was recorded at Plymouth (Devon) on the 6th and a whirlwind damaged property in Barrow (Suffolk). Rain fell in the north and east on the 8th, when Tyneside was flooded, and two people were killed when they were swept out to sea by freak waves at Langton Maltravers (Dorset) and Saltdean (E. Sussex). The 9th brought rain to Scotland, with 51.9 mm (2.05 in) falling at Glenlivet (Grampian). Heavy rain fell over England and Wales on the 10th, when 74.7 mm (2.94 in) fell at Tiverton (Somerset). A tornado damaged houses at Grouville (Jersey) and roads were closed by floods and landslides in north-east Scotland. The 11th brought heavy rain, mainly in eastern areas, and 76.5 mm (2.31 in) fell at Lossiemouth (Grampian). Flooding occurred in Grampian and farm losses were estimated at £26 million. The 12th brought thunderstorms to England and Wales. Heavy rain fell in England and Wales on the 14th when 61.1 mm (2.4 in) fell at Hayling Island (Hants). By the 15th there was flooding in many southern areas. A whirlwind caused damage in Prestatyn (Clwyd) on the 16th. Heavy rain fell over southern England on the 18th, with 39.0 mm (1.54 in) at Maidstone and East Malling (Kent). The 23rd brought heavy rain to northern areas, spreading south on the 25th. Flooding occurred in the Isle of Skye. Heavy rain fell over southern areas on the 25th. The 30th was wet everywhere.

Monthly mean temperatures were near normal everywhere. The highest temperature was 25.1°C (77.2°F) at Falmouth (Cornwall) on the 1st and the lowest was −3.0°C (26.6°F) at Carnwath (Strathclyde) on the 28th.

Sunshine totals were above average except in north-east Scotland. The highest daily total was 11.9 hours at Falmouth (Cornwall) on the 1st and Eastbourne (E. Sussex) on the 4th. The highest monthly total was 201.6 hours at Dale Fort (Dyfed).

OCTOBER 1995

Rainfall totals were above normal over Northern Ireland and Scotland but below normal over England and Wales. Glasgow had its wettest October for over a century. Rain fell over Scotland on the 1st and 2nd, when 56 mm (2.2 in) fell at Lochawe (Strathclyde). Heavy rain fell over northern England and Wales on the 3rd, with 39.3 mm (1.55 in) falling at Nantmor (Gwynedd). The 4th and 5th brought rain to many areas and heavy rain fell generally on the 6th and 7th. Rain fell in Northern Ireland and Scotland from the 11th to the 13th. The 14th was foggy, dense in places. Heavy rain fell over Scotland on the 16th and in western areas on the 17th. Rain fell in Scotland and Northern Ireland on the 19th. Heavy rain fell over Scotland on the 21st, when 42.4 mm (1.67 in) fell at Greenock (Strathclyde), and the 22nd when 43.4 mm (1.71 in) fell at Eskdalemuir (Dumfries and Galloway). Rain fell in Scotland on the 23rd. The 24th brought heavy rain and gales to western areas; 50.0 mm (1.97 in) of rain fell at Kilmory (Highland) and flooding occurred in the Midlands and Northern Ireland. Wind speeds reached 52 knots (60 mph) in the West Country and 82.5 knots (95 mph) in the Cairngorms. A North Sea oil rig was evacuated for a time as a barge broke from its moorings. The 25th was wet in Scotland and the 26th brought heavy rain to many areas; 40.7 mm (1.60 in) fell at Salsburgh (Strathclyde). Heavy rain fell over Scotland on the 30th and 31st.

Monthly mean temperatures were above normal everywhere. It was the warmest October since 1659 over England and Wales and the fourth warmest this century over Northern Ireland. The temperature reached 22.5°C (72.5°F) at Stirling (Central) on the 8th. The highest temperature recorded was 25.6°C (78.1°F) at Hawarden Bridge (Clwyd) on the 8th and Santon Downham (Suffolk) on the 9th. The lowest was −4.4°C (24.1°F) at Carnwath (Strathclyde) on the 21st.

Sunshine totals were above normal except in south-west Scotland. The highest daily total was 10.8 hours at Torquay (Devon) on the 8th and the highest monthly total was 167.7 hours at Hunstanton (Norfolk).

NOVEMBER 1995

Rainfall totals were above normal in south-west and north-east England, Northern Ireland and south-east Scotland, but below normal elsewhere. Rain fell mainly in western areas on the 7th and 8th, with general rain on the 9th becoming heavy on the 10th, when 37.6 mm (1.48 in) fell at Dunkeswell (Devon), and the 11th, when 40 mm (1.57 in) fell at Teignmouth (Devon). Rain fell in western areas on the 12th and heavy rain fell in many areas on the 14th and 15th; 57.6 mm (2.26 in) fell at Newcastle upon Tyne on the 15th. Snow fell in the Highlands. Snow fell in the north east on the 16th and as far south as Suffolk on the 17th. Flooding occurred in Edinburgh, Tyneside, Co.Durham, Cleveland and Ballymena (Co. Antrim). Rain fell over Northern Ireland and Scotland on the 20th. Rain fell generally on the 21st and over Scotland on the 22nd and 23rd. On the 24th, 25th and 27th rain was widespread, with flooding in Hampshire.

Monthly mean temperatures were slightly above normal everywhere. On the 18th a severe frost caused 'black' ice on roads everywhere. Snow lay 6 in deep over the North York moors and the eastern Pennines. The highest temperature was 17.6°C (63.7°F) at Falmouth (Cornwall) on the 13th and the lowest was −7.1°C (19.2°F) at Carnwath (Strathclyde) on the 18th.

Sunshine totals were above normal except in northern and eastern Scotland, north-east England and the coasts of East Anglia and south-east England. The highest daily total was 9.5 hours at Leeming (Yorks) on the 2nd and the highest monthly total was 108.3 hours at Gorey Castle (Jersey).

DECEMBER 1995

Rainfall totals were above normal in southern and north-east England and in north and east Scotland. North-west England and west and central Scotland were very dry. The month started with rain almost everywhere which turned to snow on the 5th. Three people were killed on icy roads in Nottinghamshire. In many areas 4−6 in (10−15 cm) of snow fell. A woman was killed in Carmarthen and about 3,000 motorists were stranded overnight on the M25 in Kent. Snow continued on the 6th and 7th. Flights from Heathrow were cancelled and a girl was killed in Berkshire on icy roads. Snow fell over northern England on the 8th. Freezing fog affected England and Wales on the 10th and five people were killed in car crashes. Rain was widespread on the 13th and 14th. Snow fell over southern England on the 15th and rain fell in the south-west on the 16th, spreading to Wales and southern England on the 17th. Heavy rain fell over Cornwall on the 18th and over most of England and Wales on the 19th, when 48.6 mm (1.91 in) fell at Tivington (Somerset). Rain continued in the south on the 20th, with snow further north. The 21st brought snow to many areas, with heavy rain in the south-west. At Cilfynydd (Mid Glamorgan) 40.9 mm (1.61 in) of rain fell and the river Avon burst its banks in Wiltshire. Heavy rain fell everywhere on the 22nd. The 23rd brought rain to the south and snow in the north. Heavy snow fell over Scotland on the 24th, when 48.0 mm (1.89 in) water equivalent fell at Lerwick (Shetland). Gales in the north gave blizzard conditions, with gusts of 86 knots (99 mph) at Butt of Lewis (Hebrides), 73 knots (84 mph) at Kirkwall (Orkney) and 82 knots (94 mph) at Fair Isle (Shetland). Snow fell in northern areas on the 25th, when 54.3 mm (2.35 in) water equivalent fell at Fylingdales (N. Yorks). Snow fell in the south-east on the 26th and southern England on the 27th, with snow and freezing fog in Northern Ireland. Two people were killed in Co. Durham, one in Paisley and one in Northern Ireland. Freezing fog formed on the 28th and 29th, while the 30th brought rain to southern England and snow to Wales. Parts of Shetland were under 30 ft (9 m) of snow, with many people cut off. The 31st brought freezing fog and rain to many places, with snow from the Midlands to southern Scotland.

Monthly mean temperatures were below normal everywhere. In central Scotland temperatures were 4°C (7.2°F) below normal. The highest temperature was 15.2°C (59.4°F) at Penzance (Cornwall) on the 3rd and the lowest was −27.0°C (−16.6°F) at Altnahara (Highland) on the 30th.

Sunshine totals were above normal in parts of western Scotland, Northern Ireland and Wales, but below normal elsewhere. The highest daily total was 7.7 hours at Bognor Regis (W. Sussex) on the 26th and the highest monthly total was 77.2 hours at Machrihanish (Strathclyde).

The Year 1995

The year will be remembered for the long drought in many areas, with water restrictions causing hardship to thousands of people and deep bitterness towards the water companies. January and February were wet and windy with extensive flooding. March was wet in Scotland and Northern Ireland. Snow and gales caused havoc in many areas, with extensive flooding and rail cancellations. April was the first dry month, except in the far north of Scotland, but there were some wet and thundery days. May was dry except in the far north of Scotland, but there were some wet days and the river Wye burst its banks in Gloucestershire on the 17th. A temperature of 28.4°C (83.1°F) was recorded at Southampton (Hants) on the 6th. June was mainly dry but with flooding in Tayside on the 3rd. Glasgow had its sunniest June since 1920 and a temperature of 33.8°C (92.8°F) was recorded at Barbourne (Worcs) on the 30th. July was dry and the third hottest this century, but thunderstorms caused havoc in some places. August was also dry, and water restrictions were extended to even the Seathwaite area of Cumberland, normally the wettest place in England. It was the warmest August over England and Wales since 1659. September was wet, particularly in eastern Scotland, with lightning and flooding in many areas. The heavy rain did nothing, however, to relieve the water shortages. October was wet and windy over Northern Ireland and Scotland. It was the warmest October over England and Wales since

1659, and the year November 1994 to October 1995 was the warmest such period ever recorded. November was wet around Tyneside but very dry in the Thames estuary. Snow caused road chaos in northern areas in the middle of the month and flooding occurred in some areas. December was mainly wet and very cold. Ice, snow and freezing fog caused many accidents.

January 1996

Rainfall totals were below normal except in the West Country and parts of Wales and Northern Ireland. South Down (Co. Down) had its wettest January on record. The 1st brought rain and snow to Scotland and Northern Ireland. The 1st, 2nd and 3rd were foggy, while the 4th brought heavy rain to mainly western areas. Heavy rain continued on the 5th and 6th and gales swept northern areas. Rain fell almost everywhere on the 7th and 8th, with 33.7 mm (1.33 in) falling at Bastreet (Cornwall) on the 8th. Gales continued in the north and west and heavy seas breached the sea-wall at Dawlish (Devon), causing widespread flooding. Heavy rain fell over southern England on the 9th, with flooding in many areas. Rain fell almost everywhere on the 11th and 12th. The 13th and 14th were wet in the west and 47.2 mm (1.86 in) of rain fell at Bastreet (Cornwall) on the 13th. The 15th to 17th brought fog, often persistent, over England and Wales. Rain fell, mainly in the west, on the 19th, when 36.0 mm (1.42 in) fell at Falmouth (Cornwall). The 21st brought snow to northern England. Heavy rain fell in southern areas on the 23rd, with snow in Wales. The 24th brought rain and snow to the West Country, and snow fell in many areas on the 25th with gales in the west. Minehead (Somerset) was flooded by high seas. At Porthmadog football ground (Gwynedd), a 500-seater stand was blown down. The 26th brought heavy snow to many areas, with up to 6 in in Sussex and Essex. Many accidents occurred and the M4 was closed. Snow fell on the 27th and gales affected western areas. Snow fell in the south-west on the 29th and 30th.

Monthly mean temperatures were generally above normal in spite of the cold spells. The highest temperature was 13.9°C (57.0°F) at Culdrose (Cornwall) on the 8th. The lowest was −13.4°C (7.9°F) at Dumnadrochit (Highland) on the 11th.

Sunshine totals were below normal except in the Highland region of Scotland. It was the dullest January over Northern Ireland since 1940. The highest daily total was 8.1 hours at Margate (Kent) on the 31st and the highest monthly total was 63.2 hours at Bognor Regis (W. Sussex).

February 1996

Rainfall totals were generally above normal, with parts of Scotland receiving more than twice the average. Heavy rain fell on the 5th, with snow in the west; 44.2 mm (1.74 in) fell at Bastreet (Cornwall). Drifts up to 10 ft (3 m) deep brought Jersey (Channel Isles) to a halt. Heavy snow spread east on the

6th, leaving thousands of motorists stranded. Snow fell in many places on the 7th and 8th but the 9th brought heavy rain and gales to most places with 160 mm (6.3 in) of rain falling at Dumfries. Heavy rain fell in most areas on the 11th when 50 mm (1.97 in) fell at Lochranza (Isle of Arran). On the 10th–11th 70.4 mm (2.8 in) fell at Aberdeen, causing extensive flooding. The 12th was wet, and a gust of 76 knots (87 mph) occurred at Torbay (Devon). Whirlwinds damaged houses at Royston (Herts), Camberley (Surrey) and Oswestry (Shropshire) and heavy snow caused chaos in north-east England. The 15th and 16th brought rain to northern areas while the 17th brought heavy rain generally. A gust of 71 knots (82 mph) occurred at Cairngorm (Grampian) and 41 mm (1.61 in) of rain fell at Rachwick (Orkney). On the 18th 80 mm (3.15 in) of rain fell at Knockanrock (Highland) and a gust of 65 knots (75 mph) was recorded at Middle Wallop (Hants). The 19th brought snow and gales everywhere. In north Norfolk sea defences were breached and many roads were blocked by snow; 13 cm (5 in) of snow fell in areas of southern England. Snow fell over England on the 20th. Flooding occurred in Deal (Kent) and Spurn Head (Humberside) was cut off from the mainland by high tides. Rain and snow fell on the 21st and 22nd and rain fell, mainly in the west, on the 23rd. The 24th and 25th brought rain to England and Wales. Fog formed in many areas on the 27th to 29th, with rain over northern Scotland.

Monthly mean temperatures were below normal everywhere. The highest temperature recorded was 14.4°C (57.9°F) at Barbourne (Worcs) on the 16th and the lowest was −14.2°C (6.4°F) at Camps Reservoir (Strathclyde) on the 2nd.

Sunshine totals were above normal except in northern Scotland. Braemar (Grampian) had its sunniest February this century. The highest daily total was 10.7 hours at Sandown (Isle of Wight) on the 29th and the highest monthly total was 151.1 hours at Penzance (Cornwall).

MARCH 1996

Rainfall totals were below normal except in a few places in south-west England and over the east coast of Scotland. Scattered showers fell from the 5th to 7th and rain fell over southern areas on the 8th, with snow in the West Country. The 11th was wet everywhere, with snow over northern England and the Midlands. The 12th brought snow everywhere except south-eastern England and strong winds made driving hazardous. There were floods in Cumbria and gusts of 75 knots (86 mph) at Fair Isle (Shetland) and 89 knots (102.5 mph) at Cairngorm (Highland) were recorded. Many roads were impassable and electricity supplies were cut over wide areas. Snow fell up to 7 in deep over the Pennines. The 14th brought wintry showers to Scotland, Northern Ireland and south-west England. Rain fell in western areas on the 15th and generally on the 16th, with snow over northern England and southern Scotland; 68 mm (2.7 in) of rain fell at Cairn-

gorm (Highland). The 17th and 18th brought rain to the west and north while the 19th saw fog over most of England and rain in Scotland. Heavy rain fell in southern areas on the 20th, when 41 mm (1.6 in) fell at Yarner Wood (Devon). Rain fell almost everywhere on the 21st and mostly in the south on the 22nd. Heavy rain fell in the south on the 25th. Rain, drizzle and snow fell in many places on the 26th and rain fell in Scotland on the 27th.

Monthly mean temperatures were below normal everywhere. The highest temperature was 16.7°C (62.1°F) at Margate (Kent) on the 23rd and the lowest was −15.0°C (5.0°F) at Cairngorm (Highland) on the 11th.

Sunshine totals were below normal almost everywhere. It was the dullest March on record over Northern Ireland, the Orkney Islands and the Isle of Man. The highest daily total was 11.5 hours at Lyneham (Wilts) on the 27th and the highest monthly total was 152.5 hours at Gorey Castle (Jersey).

APRIL 1996

Rainfall totals were above normal everywhere except south Devon. At Prestwick (Strathclyde) it was the wettest April since records began in 1942. The first significant rain fell on the 9th in far western areas. On the 4th the relative humidity fell to 16 per cent in London, the second-lowest figure ever recorded. The 10th brought rain to most areas and the 11th brought heavy rain to the west and persistent fog in places. Heavy rain and snow fell in most areas on the 12th. Snow fell over Wales and northern England on the 13th, and heavy rain fell in western areas on the 14th and over southern Scotland and Northern Ireland on the 15th. The 16th brought heavy rain to western areas. On the 20th there were thunderstorms over the Midlands and northern England with rain over Scotland and Northern Ireland. Rain fell in Scotland and the west on the 21st, with 38 mm (1.5 in) falling at Prestwick (Strathclyde). Heavy rain fell over England and Wales on the 22nd, and in northern England and Scotland on the 23rd. The 25th brought rain to northern areas. Rain fell in Scotland on the 26th and 27th. The 29th was showery with thunderstorms over southern Scotland. Heavy rain fell in Northern Ireland, southern Scotland and northern England on the 30th, with 29.6 mm (1.6 in) falling at Longframlington (Northumberland).

Monthly mean temperatures were above normal almost everywhere and Inverness (Highland) had its warmest April since 1914. The highest temperature was 23.7°C (74.7°F) at South Raynham (Norfolk) on the 21st and the lowest temperature was −8.8°C (16.2°F) at Grendon Underwood (Bucks) on the 4th.

Sunshine totals were below normal except in southern England and East Anglia. It was the dullest April since 1911 at Eskdalemuir (Dumfries and Galloway). The highest daily total was 14.5 hours at Bastreet (Cornwall) on the 27th and the highest monthly total was 215.4 hours at Folkestone (Kent).

MAY 1996

Rainfall totals were below normal, except in western areas and parts of eastern Scotland. The 1st was generally wet, with snow in southern Scotland, and 72 mm (2.8 in) of rain fell at Dunstaffnage (Strathclyde). Rain fell over England and Wales on the 2nd, with 41 mm (1.6 in) falling at Ventnor (Isle of Wight). Rain fell over northern areas on the 5th and 6th. The 10th brought rain to most of England and Wales, extending to Northern Ireland and southern Scotland on the 11th. The 16th and 17th brought heavy rain to south and south-east England. Heavy rain fell over England and Wales and northern Scotland on the 18th, when 43 mm (1.7 in) fell at St Mary's (Scilly Isles). The 19th was generally wet, with strong winds in southern areas. Walkers on Dartmoor had to be rescued by helicopter. Rain fell generally on the 20th and 21st, with thunderstorms in central areas. The 22nd was wet with strong winds. The 23rd was wet over England and Wales, when 52 mm (2.1 in) of rain fell at Moel Cynedd (Powys) and 48.3 mm (1.9 in) fell at Davidstow Moor (Cornwall). Heavy rain fell over southern areas on the 24th. The 26th brought general rain. Rain, heavy over Scotland, fell on the 28th, when 26.6 mm (1.1 in) fell at Kilmory (Highland). Rain fell over Wales and central England on the 29th and over Northern Ireland and Scotland on the 30th. On the 31st gusts of 96 knots (110.5 mph) at Fort William (Highland) and 103 knots (118.6 mph) at Cairngorm (Highland) were recorded.

Monthly mean temperatures were below normal everywhere. The highest temperature was 26.1°C (78.98°F) at Heathrow (Greater London) on the 30th and the lowest was −5.8°C (21.6°F) at Leadhills (Strathclyde) on the 18th.

Sunshine totals were above average in Scotland, Northern Ireland, Wales and south-west England but below normal elsewhere. The highest daily total was 15.4 hours at Kirkwall (Orkney) on the 21st and the highest monthly total was 284 hours at Tiree (Strathclyde).

JUNE 1996

Rainfall totals were below normal except in western Scotland. Heavy rain fell in western areas on the 3rd. The 5th brought heavy rain to Northern Ireland and western Scotland. Thunderstorms were widespread over England and Wales on the 7th, causing flooding across southern England. Hailstones the size of golfballs fell over a wide area. Thunderstorms affected England and the Channel Islands on the 8th. The 9th and 10th brought heavy rain to western areas, and the 11th was wet everywhere except south-east England. The 19th and 20th brought rain across southern England; 43 mm (1.7 in) fell at Bournemouth (Dorset) on the 19th. Heavy rain fell over Scotland and Northern Ireland on the 25th and more general rain fell on the 26th. Rain fell over Scotland and Northern Ireland on the 27th and almost everywhere on the 28th. On the 29th 46 mm (1.8 in) fell at Lairg (Highland).

Monthly mean temperatures were around normal everywhere. The highest temperature was 33.1°C (91.6°F) at St James's Park (London) on the 7th and the lowest was −5.4°C (22.3°F) at Mepal (Cambs) on the 4th.

Sunshine totals were above normal except in the Highlands and Islands of Scotland. The highest daily total was 16 hours at Tiree (Hebrides) on the 15th and the highest monthly total was 334.8 hours at Gorey Castle (Jersey).

BUCHAN'S WEATHER PERIODS

Dr Alexander Buchan, FRS, secretary of the Scottish Meteorological Society, published in 1867 a paper in the journal of the Society entitled *Interruptions in the regular rise and fall of temperature in the course of the year*. In this paper Buchan claimed the existence of tendencies for short spells of relatively cold and warm weather to occur at certain times of the year. His claims were based on his examination of the mean daily temperature as recorded at stations in Scotland over long periods.

Buchan gave six cold periods and three warm periods:

Cold periods	Warm periods
7–14 February	12–15 July
11–14 April	12–15 August
9–14 May	3–14 December
29 June–4 July	
6–11 August	
6–13 November	

Since Buchan's time, these smaller fluctuations of weather superimposed on the normal seasonal changes have been examined from the aspect of tendencies to stormy or anticyclonic spells over the British Isles and have been referred to as 'singularities'. Stormy periods are relatively warm in winter and cool in summer.

The following tendencies have been given:

5–17 January	stormy
18–24 January	anticyclonic
24 January–1 February	stormy
8–16 February	anticyclonic
21–25 February	cold
26 February–9 March	stormy
12–19 March	anticyclonic
24–31 March	stormy
10–15 April	stormy
23–26 April	unsettled
1–21 June	summer monsoon
10–24 July	warm
20–30 August	stormy
1–17 September	anticyclonic
17–24 September	stormy
24 September–4 October	anticyclonic
5–12 October	stormy
16–20 October	anticyclonic
24 October–13 November	stormy
15–21 November	anticyclonic
24 November–14 December	stormy
18–24 December	anticyclonic
25 December–1 January	stormy

AVERAGE AND GENERAL VALUES 1994–6 (June)

	Rainfall (mm)				Temperature (°C)				Bright Sunshine (hrs per day)			
	Average 1961–90	1994	1995	1996	Average 1961–90	1994	1995	1996	Average 1961–90	1994	1995	1996
ENGLAND AND WALES												
January	77	123	161	63	3.8	5.7	4.8	4.4	1.6	2.1	1.6	0.8
February	55	82	115	113	3.8	3.3	6.5	2.7	2.3	2.3	2.7	3.1
March	63	96	67	44	5.6	7.5	5.5	4.4	3.5	3.7	5.2	2.1
April	53	74	27	49	7.7	8.1	8.9	8.4	4.9	5.8	5.9	4.6
May	56	62	49	57	10.9	10.6	11.6	9.1	6.2	5.1	6.8	6.0
June	58	36	23	29	13.9	14.3	14.0	14.2	6.4	7.1	6.8	2.9
July	56	47	40	–	15.7	17.6	18.3	–	6.0	7.2	7.4	–
August	68	72	10	–	15.6	15.9	18.9	–	5.7	5.6	9.3	–
September	70	106	113	–	13.6	12.8	13.7	–	4.5	3.8	4.6	–
October	77	97	58	–	10.7	10.4	13.1	–	3.2	3.9	4.0	–
November	81	86	83	–	6.6	10.0	7.8	–	2.2	1.5	2.3	–
December	82	142	84	–	4.7	6.6	2.6	–	1.5	1.7	1.4	–
YEAR	796	1023	828	–	9.4	10.2	10.5	–	4.0	4.1	4.8	–
SCOTLAND												
January	117	215	227	89	3.1	3.4	2.9	4.7	1.3	1.1	1.3	0.9
February	78	96	205	198	3.1	2.3	3.9	2.5	2.3	2.2	2.4	2.7
March	94	250	143	60	4.6	4.8	3.6	4.0	3.2	3.1	3.3	2.1
April	60	133	67	107	6.5	6.4	7.0	7.4	4.8	4.5	4.4	3.5
May	67	29	84	77	9.3	8.7	9.4	7.7	5.6	7.1	5.8	6.0
June	67	110	43	65	12.1	11.8	12.4	12.3	5.6	4.8	7.4	4.3
July	74	67	86	–	13.6	14.7	15.1	–	4.9	5.1	6.2	–
August	92	101	34	–	13.5	13.3	16.1	–	4.6	4.4	7.8	–
September	111	103	198	–	11.5	10.9	11.9	–	3.5	3.8	3.5	–
October	120	110	228	–	9.1	8.5	11.0	–	2.6	2.6	2.8	–
November	118	156	126	–	5.3	8.5	6.9	–	1.7	1.4	1.7	–
December	116	245	56	–	3.9	4.8	1.5	–	1.0	1.2	1.6	–
YEAR	1114	1615	1497	–	7.9	8.2	8.5	–	3.4	3.4	4.0	–

Source: data provided by the Met Office

WEATHER RECORDS

WORLD RECORDS

Maximum air temperature	57.8°C/136°F
San Louis, Mexico, 11 August 1933	
Minimum air temperature	−89.2°C/−128.56°F
Vostok, Antarctica, 21 July 1983	
Greatest rainfall in one day	1870 mm/73.62 in
Cilaos, Isle de Réunion, 16 March 1952	
Greatest rainfall in one calendar month	9300 mm/366.14 in
Cherrapunji, Assam, July 1861	
Greatest annual rainfall total	22,990 mm/905.12 in
Cherrapunji, Assam, 1861	
Fastest gust of wind	201 knots/231 mph
Mt Washington Observatory, USA, 12 April 1934	

UNITED KINGDOM RECORDS

Maximum air temperature	37.1°C/98.8°F
Cheltenham, Glos, 3 August 1990	
Minimum air temperature	−27.2°C/−17°F
Braemar, Grampian, 11 February 1895 and 10 January 1982	
Greatest rainfall in one day	280 mm/11 in
Martinstown, Dorset, 18 July 1955	
Greatest annual rainfall total	6528 mm/257 in
Sprinkling Tarn, Cumbria, 1954	
Fastest gust of wind	150 knots/173 mph
Cairngorm, Highland, 20 March 1986	
Fastest low-level gust*	123 knots/141.7 mph
Fraserburgh, Grampian, 13 February 1989	
Highest mean hourly speed	92 knots/106 mph
Great Dun Fell, Cumbria, December 1974	
Highest low-level mean hourly speed*	72 knots/83 mph
Shoreham-by-Sea, Sussex, 16 October 1987	

* below 200 m/656 ft

WIND FORCE MEASURES

The *Beaufort Scale* of wind force has been accepted internationally and is used in communicating weather conditions. Devised originally by Admiral Sir Francis Beaufort in 1805, it now consists of the numbers 0–17, each representing a certain strength or velocity of wind at 10 m (33 ft) above ground in the open.

Scale no.	Wind Force	mph	knots
0	Calm	1	1
1	Light air	1–3	1–3
2	Slight breeze	4–7	4–6
3	Gentle breeze	8–12	7–10
4	Moderate breeze	13–18	11–16
5	Fresh breeze	19–24	17–21
6	Strong breeze	25–31	22–27
7	High wind	32–38	28–33
8	Gale	39–46	34–40
9	Strong gale	47–54	41–47
10	Whole gale	55–63	48–55
11	Storm	64–72	56–63
12	Hurricane	73–82	64–71
13	–	83–92	72–80
14	–	93–103	81–89
15	–	104–114	90–99
16	–	115–125	100–108
17	–	126–136	109–118

TEMPERATURE, RAINFALL AND SUNSHINE
At selected climatological reporting stations, July 1995–June 1996 and calendar year 1995

	Ht m	July 1995 °C	July 1995 Rain mm	July 1995 Sun hrs	August 1995 °C	August 1995 Rain mm	August 1995 Sun hrs	September 1995 °C	September 1995 Rain mm	September 1995 Sun hrs	October 1995 °C	October 1995 Rain mm	October 1995 Sun hrs
Abbotsinch (Glasgow)	5	16.3	94	6.4	17.2	18	8.2	12.5	121	4.1	11.7	249	2.8
Aberporth	134	17.5	37	7.3	18.7	8	9.4	13.5	77	5.3	13.1	87	3.9
Aldergrove	68	16.7	70	5.4	17.7	12	7.4	12.9	66	4.8	12.2	143	3.2
Aspatria	61	16.9	73	7.4	17.3	15	9.1	12.7	73	4.4	12.7	95	3.4
Auchincruive	48	16.3	93	–	16.7	24	–	12.5	91	–	12.1	203	–
Bala	163	16.6	70	5.3	16.9	11	8.0	11.7	69	4.1	11.7	69	3.8
Bognor Regis	7	18.9	40	9.4	19.9	1	10.3	14.8	142	6.0	14.4	21	4.4
Boulmer	23	15.3	22	6.7	15.9	11	8.7	12.5	95	4.2	12.1	34	4.0
Bradford	134	18.1	17	6.7	17.8	7	7.7	13.1	68	3.6	12.0	23	3.7
Braemar	339	14.5	47	–	15.1	20	7.6	10.3	181	2.6	9.1	146	2.6
Bristol	42	19.5	18	7.4	21.2	6	9.6	14.8	132	4.9	14.4	70	3.6
Bude	15	17.8	43	7.5	18.9	13	9.1	14.3	97	5.5	14.3	68	3.7
Buxton	307	17.0	69	7.3	16.7	25	8.6	11.7	93	3.7	10.9	45	3.9
Cambridge	24	19.6	27	7.6	19.4	5	7.9	14.2	105	3.8	13.5	13	4.8
Cheltenham	65	20.3	27	–	21.3	5	–	14.2	125	–	13.7	64	–
Dale Fort	33	17.4	33	7.7	19.2	39	10.1	14.7	73	6.7	14.3	64	3.5
Dundee (Mylnefield)	30	15.8	27	6.3	16.9	11	7.3	12.7	123	4.0	11.5	91	3.0
Durham	102	16.7	25	6.8	17.2	14	8.1	12.7	86	4.1	11.8	25	4.0
Dyce (Aberdeen)	65	15.4	40	7.3	16.1	12	7.6	12.3	235	3.2	11.0	65	3.3
East Malling	33	19.6	38	8.5	20.0	3	9.1	14.3	156	4.3	13.3	10	4.1
Edinburgh	26	15.8	40	6.4	16.7	12	7.7	12.6	147	4.3	12.1	93	3.7
Elmdon (Birmingham)	98	18.6	23	8.1	19.2	9	9.1	13.5	99	4.3	12.5	37	4.5
Eskdalemuir	242	14.7	104	5.5	15.6	24	8.0	11.1	118	3.7	10.5	335	1.9
Hastings	45	18.7	40	8.9	19.9	3	9.7	14.7	122	5.8	14.3	28	4.4
Heathrow (London)	25	20.7	20	8.0	21.3	0	9.5	14.9	95	4.7	14.3	19	4.2
Hurn (Bournemouth)	10	19.0	15	7.9	19.9	5	9.7	14.0	171	5.0	13.5	52	3.8
Inverness	4	16.2	16	6.1	17.5	17	7.3	12.6	236	2.8	11.3	67	3.5
Jersey	84	18.3	54	8.4	19.6	31	9.5	15.3	106	5.9	14.7	31	4.8
Leeming	32	18.1	31	6.6	17.9	15	7.9	13.4	117	4.2	12.4	20	3.9
Lerwick	82	11.6	55	5.3	12.7	49	4.3	11.1	139	3.5	9.3	114	2.8
Long Sutton	145	18.9	23	7.4	19.5	8	8.9	13.7	134	4.2	13.1	42	4.0
Lowestoft	25	18.7	54	8.5	18.7	18	8.9	14.7	74	5.3	13.7	6	4.5
Manston	44	19.5	28	9.3	19.7	14	9.6	14.7	94	5.4	13.6	8	4.5
Morecambe	7	18.3	57	6.6	18.7	13	8.9	13.7	59	4.9	13.1	63	3.3
Oxford	63	19.5	38	8.0	20.1	4	9.2	14.3	99	4.5	13.8	33	4.5
Penzance	19	17.9	43	–		48	–	15.1	111	–	14.5	96	–
Presteigne	175	17.3	73	6.6	17.5	6	9.3	12.5	89	4.8	11.9	56	3.7
Rettendon	16	19.7	31	8.7	19.6	5	8.7	14.5	95	4.6	13.5	4	4.1
Rhoose	65	18.4	40	6.9	19.7	20	10.5	14.0	126	5.5	13.7	87	3.8
Ringway (Manchester)	75	18.9	40	7.7	19.2	18	9.1	13.6	86	4.0	12.9	24	4.0
Ronaldsway	16	16.3	73	6.5	17.7	9	9.1	13.8	55	6.0	13.1	58	3.0
St Mawgan	103	17.9	20	7.8	19.7	21	8.9	14.3	113	6.1	13.9	79	3.9
Shawbury	72	18.3	34	7.5	18.7	13	8.8	12.9	84	4.3	12.3	32	4.4
Sheffield	131	18.9	23	7.4	18.8	12	8.3	13.7	76	3.9	12.7	22	3.2
Skegness	5	18.1	30	8.1	17.6	2	8.2	14.0	79	5.2	13.3	26	4.9
Slapton	32	17.7	117	6.6	19.2	17	9.1	14.9	123	5.4	14.2	79	3.3
Stornoway	15	13.2	67	5.7	14.7	32	6.3	11.6	131	3.3	10.3	191	2.8
Sutton Bonnington	48	18.9	11	7.2	18.9	6	7.9	13.5	83	3.7	12.5	21	4.3
Terrington St Clement	2	18.9	9	8.7	18.7	3	8.5	14.1	100	4.7	13.1	16	5.0
Tiree	9	14.7	90	5.6	15.6	34	7.7	12.6	86	5.9	11.8	195	2.8
Torquay	8	18.5	31	8.1	20.1	5	9.6	15.3	135	5.3	14.5	91	3.5
Valley	10	17.3	45	6.4	19.0	11	8.9	14.1	65	6.6	13.5	89	3.5
Ventnor	135	18.5	33	8.7	20.3	3	10.1	15.1	135	5.9	14.7	17	4.0
Waddington	68	19.0	12	8.2	18.6	6	8.4	13.7	56	4.4	12.9	16	4.6
Weymouth	35	18.0	14	7.9	19.8	7	9.8	15.3	104	5.3	14.7	45	3.5
Whitby	41	17.1	25	–	17.0	5	–	13.0	110	–	12.6	18	–

Ht   height (in metres) of station above mean sea level
°C   mean air temperature
Rain   total monthly rainfall
Sun   mean daily bright sunshine (hours)
Source: data provided by the Met Office

	November 1995			December 1995			The Year 1995			January 1996			February 1996		
	°C	Rain mm	Sun hrs	°C	Rain mm	Sun hrs	°C	Rain mm	Sun hrs	°C	Rain mm	Sun hrs	°C	Rain mm	Sun hrs
Abbotsinch (Glasgow)	6.9	63	2.2	0.5	37	1.9	9.2	1119	4.5	5.3	63	0.5	2.8	92	3.6
Aberporth	8.3	117	2.7	3.9	96	2.2	10.5	832	5.0	5.1	75	1.6	3.5	67	4.0
Aldergrove	7.9	117	1.8	3.4	42	1.8	9.8	808	4.1	5.9	117	0.8	3.0	70	3.2
Aspatria	7.5	69	2.3	1.4	33	1.5	9.5	808	4.7	5.1	41	1.2	2.3	85	3.3
Auchincruive	7.4	46	–	1.5	22	–	9.3	928	–	4.7	27	–	2.9	60	–
Bala	6.6	93	1.8	1.6	65	1.0	9.1	1023	4.0	4.1	77	0.4	1.7	132	2.2
Bognor Regis	8.5	36	3.1	3.5	79	1.8	11.5	698	6.0	5.6	72	2.0	3.3	65	4.2
Boulmer	7.7	102	2.1	−1.6	108	1.3	8.7	653	4.8	4.5	26	0.3	3.3	47	3.2
Bradford	7.1	42	1.8	2.0	57	0.9	9.7	648	4.2	3.5	41	0.3	2.3	67	2.6
Braemar	4.9	78	0.9	−1.9	59	0.9	6.8	–	–	2.6	–	0.4	0.0	97	2.8
Bristol	9.2	92	3.0	3.5	94	1.1	11.9	862	4.9	5.7	54	0.8	4.1	65	3.2
Bude	9.1	84	2.7	5.1	78	2.1	11.3	869	5.0	6.7	71	1.5	4.8	78	4.3
Buxton	6.3	72	2.1	0.7	77	1.2	8.6	1057	4.5	2.3	62	0.1	0.8	138	2.1
Cambridge	7.9	29	2.2	1.9	64	0.9	10.7	495	4.6	3.7	33	0.7	2.2	48	2.9
Cheltenham	8.1	101	–	2.1	89	–	11.6	803	–	4.5	56	–	2.8	88	–
Dale Fort	10.2	118	2.5	5.0	117	2.1	11.3	821	5.3	5.6	131	1.5	4.9	93	4.1
Dundee (Mylnefield)	7.1	80	1.7	1.9	81	1.2	9.1	–	4.4	4.9	68	0.4	2.9	57	3.4
Durham	7.0	116	1.6	1.8	88	1.0	9.3	604	4.5	3.5	30	0.3	2.5	67	3.1
Dyce (Aberdeen)	6.5	70	1.4	1.3	94	1.3	8.5	873	4.4	4.6	69	0.3	3.2	125	2.8
East Malling	8.0	24	2.2	3.1	89	1.5	11.3	629	5.0	4.8	59	0.6	3.0	47	2.9
Edinburgh	7.5	74	2.1	2.3	41	1.4	9.4	–	4.6	5.1	24	0.6	3.3	30	–
Elmdon (Birmingham)	7.1	61	2.5	1.7	77	1.9	10.3	583	5.0	3.7	41	0.4	2.1	59	2.7
Eskdalemuir	5.6	104	1.8	−0.1	55	1.8	7.7	1582	3.9	3.3	118	0.3	0.9	201	2.5
Hastings	9.3	39	2.8	3.7	91	1.7	11.4	676	5.6	4.9	52	1.6	3.3	46	3.3
Heathrow (London)	8.5	29	2.5	3.4	83	1.4	11.9	539	5.1	5.1	41	0.8	3.4	49	3.5
Hurn (Bournemouth)	7.9	122	2.8	3.5	81	1.6	11.1	838	5.2	5.8	75	1.0	2.9	94	3.8
Inverness	4.5	63	–	0.8	26	–	9.1	–	–	4.7	7	–	2.9	–	–
Jersey	9.7	57	3.5	5.9	107	1.6	12.0	898	5.4	6.7	43	1.8	4.9	97	3.3
Leeming	7.4	55	1.9	1.9	58	1.3	9.9	570	4.5	3.8	29	0.5	2.9	68	2.6
Lerwick	6.3	110	1.0	2.5	232	0.9	7.0	1279	3.7	4.8	45	0.4	2.4	119	1.5
Long Sutton	7.7	66	2.3	2.2	107	1.3	10.6	753	4.9	4.3	73	0.5	2.4	78	3.4
Lowestoft	8.7	28	1.9	3.3	57	0.9	10.7	540	5.0	3.9	11	0.7	2.7	36	2.6
Manston	8.5	20	2.1	3.5	76	1.7	11.1	492	5.3	4.3	29	1.1	2.7	34	2.5
Morecambe	8.3	51	2.5	3.0	35	1.5	10.5	772	4.7	5.3	34	0.9	2.7	70	3.3
Oxford	8.2	98	2.6	2.4	100	1.3	11.3	683	5.1	4.9	34	0.9	3.1	71	3.6
Penzance	10.4	90	2.7	7.5	112	1.7	–	1029	–	8.1	180	1.5	2.6	111	5.2
Presteigne	6.1	141	2.3	1.3	99	1.2	9.4	943	4.9	3.4	110	0.3	1.8	102	3.0
Rettendon	7.9	22	2.0	2.9	89	1.3	11.0	550	5.0	4.1	44	0.7	2.7	37	3.3
Rhoose	8.6	93	3.0	3.1	106	1.8	11.0	895	5.0	4.7	48	0.7	3.3	68	4.0
Ringway (Manchester)	7.7	45	2.6	2.5	37	1.8	10.0	646	5.0	4.8	16	0.7	2.5	62	2.5
Ronaldsway	9.5	93	2.3	5.1	56	1.9	11.0	689	5.0	6.3	63	0.6	4.3	91	4.0
St Mawgan	9.3	97	2.7	5.6	95	2.1	11.0	915	5.1	6.7	207	1.6	4.8	109	4.9
Shawbury	6.7	32	2.1	1.6	83	1.5	10.0	607	4.9	4.3	32	0.4	1.9	57	2.9
Sheffield	7.5	61	1.2	1.9	70	0.7	10.4	669	4.3	3.5	67	0.2	2.5	75	1.9
Skegness	8.2	39	2.4	3.1	48	1.4	10.3	481	4.9	3.7	30	0.9	2.7	47	3.2
Slapton	9.7	125	2.9	6.1	163	0.7	–	–	–	7.0	110	0.6	4.9	108	3.8
Stornoway	7.7	122	1.7	3.7	45	1.8	8.3	1242	3.5	6.2	69	1.2	3.9	74	2.0
Sutton Bonnington	7.5	53	2.3	1.9	73	1.3	10.4	490	4.3	3.8	26	0.5	2.5	46	2.6
Terrington St Clement	7.7	39	2.1	2.2	53	1.4	10.4	462	4.9	3.7	33	0.8	2.4	48	3.1
Tiree	8.7	103	2.0	4.3	44	2.0	9.3	1170	4.4	6.5	89	1.1	4.5	129	3.3
Torquay	9.7	171	3.0	5.9	146	0.9	12.1	1085	5.3	7.3	140	0.6	5.0	109	4.2
Valley	9.1	67	2.5	4.2	71	2.3	10.9	711	4.9	5.8	46	1.4	4.1	69	3.7
Ventnor	10.3	59	3.3	4.9	84	1.5	12.0	700	5.8	5.9	53	1.4	4.3	71	4.5
Waddington	7.3	52	2.2	1.9	57	1.6	10.2	439	4.9	3.2	35	0.6	2.3	44	2.9
Weymouth	10.3	107	3.0	4.9	88	1.3	11.9	755	5.3	6.4	66	0.8	4.5	90	4.0
Whitby	8.1	69	1.9	3.0	114	0.9	9.8	608	–	4.3	45	0.3	3.1	58	2.7

TEMPERATURE, RAINFALL AND SUNSHINE *contd.*

	March 1996			April 1996			May 1996			June 1996		
	°C	Rain mm	Sun hrs	°C	Rain mm	Sun hrs	°C	Rain mm	Sun hrs	°C	Rain mm	Sun hrs
Abbotsinch (Glasgow)	4.3	56	2.8	7.9	83	3.4	8.7	45	5.9	13.3	37	8.7
Aberporth	5.2	45	3.0	8.0	56	5.0	8.6	69	8.1	12.7	27	8.4
Aldergrove	5.0	49	1.7	8.4	116	4.3	8.5	74	6.4	13.3	32	6.8
Aspatria	4.3	24	3.5	8.1	62	3.6	8.5	53	7.3	12.9	28	8.5
Auchincruive	4.4	19	–	8.0	93	–	8.3	42	–	12.7	56	–
Bala	4.1	42	1.9	7.3	63	3.6	7.5	83	4.9	12.2	43	6.5
Bognor Regis	5.4	37	2.9	8.9	23	6.0	9.9	51	6.6	14.7	19	10.1
Boulmer	3.9	20	1.5	7.3	50	4.3	8.3	33	7.1	12.7	13	8.2
Bradford	3.4	39	1.4	8.3	55	–	8.7	49	4.7	13.5	65	–
Braemar	1.3	41	2.3	6.0	81	3.9	6.1	–	4.8	–	16	–
Bristol	6.1	60	2.0	9.7	53	4.6	10.5	74	6.1	16.2	14	9.6
Bude	6.3	43	3.4	8.7	74	5.1	9.5	80	6.8	–	–	–
Buxton	2.3	42	1.2	7.2	59	3.3	7.6	83	5.2	12.7	53	7.1
Cambridge	4.3	19	1.9	8.7	5	5.0	9.1	20	5.0	15.5	12	7.5
Cheltenham	5.3	73	–	9.5	66	–	10.1	41	–	16.3	35	–
Dale Fort	6.2	47	2.2	8.6	80	5.4	9.5	79	7.7	13.3	32	7.7
Dundee (Mylnefield)	3.9	57	1.7	7.9	71	3.3	8.5	44	5.8	–	–	–
Durham	3.3	26	0.9	7.7	34	3.7	8.3	36	6.1	13.1	9	7.2
Dyce (Aberdeen)	3.7	91	1.3	7.5	50	4.8	7.7	70	6.9	12.9	30	7.3
East Malling	4.7	32	2.5	8.7	12	5.2	9.7	34	5.2	15.1	20	9.0
Edinburgh	4.1	22	2.1	8.3	45	3.5	8.8	43	6.3	13.9	15	7.8
Elmdon (Birmingham)	4.1	24	1.6	8.3	39	4.6	8.9	35	5.7	14.3	29	9.0
Eskdalemuir	2.5	45	1.9	5.9	147	2.0	8.7	58	4.9	11.5	86	6.7
Hastings	5.1	35	3.2	8.9	10	6.8	9.8	62	6.4	14.5	23	9.1
Heathrow (London)	5.3	31	2.5	9.9	25	4.9	10.5	26	5.9	16.9	12	9.4
Hurn (Bournemouth)	5.1	55	2.7	8.5	36	5.0	9.5	54	6.2	14.1	36	9.8
Inverness	5.1	24	–	9.3	41	–	8.5	48	–	–	–	–
Jersey	6.7	26	4.5	9.5	22	6.2	10.3	65	6.3	15.6	12	10.4
Leeming	3.8	30	1.1	8.1	30	3.5	8.7	44	6.0	13.3	58	7.1
Lerwick	3.5	71	1.8	6.1	59	3.7	6.3	52	6.5	10.1	33	3.9
Long Sutton	3.9	46	1.7	8.3	44	4.8	8.9	49	5.5	14.7	13	8.5
Lowestoft	3.7	17	2.8	8.5	3	6.4	9.5	31	5.2	14.7	5	6.9
Manston	4.3	16	3.0	8.9	5	6.1	9.8	45	6.7	15.1	11	8.8
Morecambe	4.8	35	3.0	8.6	62	3.3	9.4	43	6.2	13.7	41	7.9
Oxford	5.1	29	2.5	9.3	49	4.9	9.9	36	6.0	15.7	31	9.6
Penzance	7.5	61	3.4	–	70	5.4	–	97	7.0	–	28	8.6
Presteigne	3.9	96	1.6	8.0	79	4.3	8.3	80	5.6	13.3	30	8.9
Rettendon	4.4	25	2.1	8.6	7	4.8	9.3	26	5.9	15.3	8	8.9
Rhoose	5.3	59	2.1	8.3	73	5.1	9.7	88	6.8	14.3	16	9.2
Ringway (Manchester)	4.9	24	2.5	8.9	42	3.2	9.3	59	5.6	14.1	47	7.5
Ronaldsway	5.5	67	1.9	7.9	59	3.9	8.8	63	7.4	12.5	37	9.0
St Mawgan	6.5	45	3.7	8.9	71	5.7	9.6	92	6.9	14.3	26	8.7
Shawbury	4.1	47	1.8	–	59	3.6	8.7	50	5.8	13.5	29	8.4
Sheffield	3.7	53	1.3	8.7	38	–	9.1	39	–	14.5	30	8.1
Skegness	3.9	16	2.1	7.1	10	5.3	9.5	21	6.5	14.1	26	8.7
Slapton	6.3	80	2.7	8.7	58	4.2	9.7	97	6.9	14.1	22	8.5
Stornoway	5.1	45	3.0	7.4	86	3.5	7.6	68	7.6	11.4	58	4.7
Sutton Bonington	4.1	25	1.5	8.3	32	4.3	9.1	20	5.0	14.1	31	6.5
Terrington St Clement	4.1	21	2.2	8.4	10	5.4	9.3	22	6.3	14.1	18	8.2
Tiree	5.5	50	3.0	7.9	100	4.8	8.1	56	9.2	11.9	73	7.3
Torquay	6.7	83	2.6	9.0	63	4.9	10.4	72	7.1	14.8	32	9.3
Valley	5.6	51	3.2	8.3	57	4.1	9.2	50	8.5	13.2	30	8.5
Ventnor	5.7	39	2.9	8.9	32	6.1	10.1	103	6.8	14.8	32	9.9
Waddington	3.7	16	1.9	8.3	24	5.0	9.3	32	5.6	14.5	20	7.9
Weymouth	5.9	63	3.2	8.5	49	5.1	9.9	61	6.5	14.3	41	9.1
Whitby	3.9	29	1.2	8.3	28	4.9	9.0	41	6.6	13.8	26	7.3

METEOROLOGICAL OBSERVATIONS London (Heathrow)

Temperature maxima and minima cover the 24-hour period 9–9 h; mean wind speed is 10 m above the ground; rainfall is for the 24 hours starting at 9 h on the day of entry; sunshine is for the 24 hours 0–24 h; averages are for the period 1961–90. *Source:* data provided by the Met Office

JULY 1995

Day	Temperature Max. °C	Min. °C	Wind knots	Rain mm	Sun hrs
1	22.9	13.6	9.6	0.0	7.2
2	20.4	11.4	4.4	12.2	0.7
3	20.1	13.0	3.3	0.0	2.3
4	23.3	12.4	5.5	0.0	9.8
5	24.5	16.1	5.2	0.0	5.0
6	25.1	12.6	7.4	0.0	10.1
7	24.0	17.7	5.4	0.0	3.7
8	28.8	13.0	5.5	0.0	10.1
9	29.1	14.9	8.5	0.0	9.8
10	32.0	16.0	8.3	Trace	6.7
11	27.8	18.7	5.7	1.0	7.0
12	26.9	15.4	6.5	1.0	12.0
13	23.9	15.4	5.8	1.0	4.4
14	24.4	15.9	10.7	2.0	13.0
15	23.2	14.6	10.0	0.4	6.3
16	24.0	14.3	7.4	0.6	2.8
17	23.0	13.4	7.7	Trace	3.4
18	26.5	16.1	10.0	0.0	1.9
19	26.7	19.2	4.8	0.0	0.7
20	31.8	15.6	5.3	0.0	14.8
21	29.8	17.9	6.0	0.0	10.3
22	23.1	12.6	5.7	0.0	15.1
23	26.0	11.2	5.2	0.0	13.5
24	28.5	12.9	4.7	0.0	14.5
25	28.6	15.5	11.3	0.0	13.9
26	26.3	18.3	6.9	1.5	7.9
27	24.9	16.3	6.3	0.4	6.3
28	26.2	16.3	7.3	0.0	2.3
29	30.6	16.8	4.6	0.0	14.3
30	31.2	16.2	3.3	Trace	7.3
31	32.6	17.8	4.8	0.0	10.0
Total	–	–	–	20.3	247.1
Mean	26.4	15.2	6.6	0.7	7.8
Temp °F	79.5	59.4	–	–	–
Average	22.5	13.1	7.4	46.0	194.5

AUGUST 1995

Day	Temperature Max. °C	Min. °C	Wind knots	Rain mm	Sun hrs
1	34.3	19.0	6.3	Trace	12.3
2	33.0	21.2	8.7	0.0	12.5
3	32.2	20.0	9.8	0.0	13.9
4	27.5	15.5	7.9	0.0	11.9
5	27.9	13.3	6.4	0.0	13.2
6	26.6	14.5	5.8	Trace	12.8
7	22.8	15.4	8.2	0.0	2.0
8	22.2	13.7	6.5	0.0	4.8
9	26.3	11.1	5.8	0.0	11.3
10	29.3	14.2	8.3	0.0	13.5
11	31.8	16.2	4.4	0.0	12.9
12	31.3	16.7	6.5	Trace	11.7
13	25.9	18.0	5.8	0.0	8.8
14	25.4	14.5	3.5	0.0	8.7
15	29.9	14.2	3.1	0.0	12.7
16	30.6	17.6	3.5	0.0	12.5
17	27.9	17.6	7.0	0.0	13.1
18	29.8	17.8	5.6	0.0	9.1
19	30.7	17.0	4.3	0.0	10.0
20	30.2	17.3	4.6	0.0	12.4
21	30.6	15.3	4.1	0.0	13.4
22	28.9	15.8	2.8	0.0	12.4
23	23.3	17.0	3.4	0.1	0.2
24	24.9	12.2	6.0	0.1	6.3
25	25.9	17.3	9.8	Trace	6.5
26	24.9	16.8	7.3	Trace	6.6
27	20.9	15.8	8.5	0.1	8.9
28	20.3	11.0	6.7	Trace	12.0
29	18.9	12.3	4.2	Trace	0.1
30	22.1	10.6	3.7	Trace	8.7
31	20.8	15.3	5.8	Trace	0.1
Total	–	–	–	0.3	295.3
Mean	27.1	15.7	6.0	0.01	9.5
Temp °F	80.8	60.3	–		
Average	22.1	12.8	7.2	51.0	186.7

SEPTEMBER 1995

Day	Temperature Max. °C	Min. °C	Wind knots	Rain mm	Sun hrs
1	19.9	14.4	3.9	2.3	0.2
2	19.1	15.1	3.4	2.4	3.3
3	20.9	7.2	4.1	0.0	9.0
4	22.0	8.8	3.0	Trace	8.9
5	20.8	10.8	4.7	4.3	6.4
6	21.0	11.8	7.0	5.3	2.9
7	19.6	13.9	10.0	7.8	1.1
8	20.3	15.0	7.4	Trace	1.6
9	22.4	12.5	7.1	Trace	7.7
10	18.4	11.7	5.4	13.7	0.6
11	21.9	13.0	7.6	1.5	7.4
12	19.2	12.2	5.2	3.1	5.9
13	19.8	9.5	2.6	0.0	7.1
14	19.7	9.5	5.3	5.2	4.2
15	18.4	10.6	3.4	Trace	2.0
16	18.4	12.6	4.5	17.0	0.6
17	20.0	12.9	4.3	4.1	2.2
18	19.9	12.4	7.7	3.1	1.4
19	18.7	14.9	8.7	0.0	0.7
20	18.4	11.5	6.1	0.3	6.1
21	19.6	6.9	2.5	0.0	10.6
22	20.2	10.0	4.0	Trace	6.6
23	18.9	11.3	5.1	2.8	9.7
24	16.5	10.9	10.0	1.2	4.0
25	17.2	5.4	7.6	Trace	5.1
26	18.4	10.3	7.6	19.9	0.0
27	16.3	11.1	8.7	Trace	8.0
28	15.6	5.0	5.6	0.1	6.9
29	17.2	4.5	3.5	0.0	9.2
30	18.1	6.2	4.3	0.9	3.0
31					
Total	–	–	–	95.0	142.4
Mean	19.3	10.8	5.7	3.2	4.7
Temp °F	66.7	51.4	–	–	–
Average	19.3	10.8	7.1	51.0	144.7

OCTOBER 1995

Day	Temperature Max. °C	Min. °C	Wind knots	Rain mm	Sun hrs
1	20.9	10.8	9.3	0.0	7.8
2	18.5	8.8	7.3	0.0	3.6
3	18.7	10.0	6.4	0.7	2.6
4	17.8	14.5	10.0	6.0	0.5
5	18.4	10.0	6.7	0.0	9.5
6	17.9	11.5	12.5	3.1	0.2
7	19.0	14.5	7.4	Trace	0.0
8	24.6	11.9	5.4	0.0	9.4
9	23.7	12.6	4.1	Trace	9.5
10	20.5	12.6	2.2	0.0	2.1
11	22.2	12.1	5.0	Trace	4.1
12	21.0	14.5	2.8	Trace	2.5
13	21.1	13.8	3.0	0.0	6.5
14	21.1	12.5	4.1	0.0	2.1
15	19.2	12.3	4.0	Trace	2.7
16	20.1	10.5	4.7	0.0	2.9
17	18.2	12.5	6.9	Trace	0.0
18	15.1	10.8	3.4	0.0	1.3
19	17.3	7.8	4.7	0.0	3.3
20	14.2	8.6	3.8	0.5	1.4
21	16.0	5.6	3.7	0.0	8.5
22	15.9	6.6	5.2	0.0	5.4
23	16.5	6.2	4.9	0.0	0.8
24	20.5	9.8	14.8	7.2	6.9
25	16.1	10.5	11.6	0.2	7.8
26	17.9	11.6	9.8	1.5	0.0
27	15.8	13.6	6.9	Trace	4.4
28	13.4	3.5	2.0	0.0	6.9
29	14.7	4.5	3.4	0.0	2.9
30	15.6	6.7	4.1	0.0	6.3
31	15.2	4.2	2.1	Trace	8.0
Total	–	–	–	19.2	129.9
Mean	18.3	10.2	5.9	0.6	4.2
Temp °F	64.9	50.4	–	–	–
Average	15.4	8.0	7.2	58.0	107.2

NOVEMBER 1995

	Temperature Max. °C	Min. °C	Wind knots	Rain mm	Sun hrs
Day 1	14.0	5.2	4.5	0.0	0.4
2	12.2	2.8	4.3	0.0	4.3
3	12.0	3.7	5.6	0.0	5.6
4	11.3	1.6	3.8	0.0	8.6
5	9.7	1.4	6.6	0.0	8.3
6	11.6	−1.9	2.9	0.0	8.0
7	11.1	1.4	2.0	0.0	0.1
8	14.1	3.2	2.0	Trace	0.3
9	13.9	9.5	3.5	6.4	0.0
10	11.7	9.5	5.4	1.0	2.3
11	15.0	8.3	7.8	1.2	0.0
12	15.0	11.2	4.7	0.6	0.0
13	15.4	10.5	2.4	Trace	3.5
14	13.5	6.3	4.1	1.9	2.4
15	14.7	8.9	4.4	0.9	3.1
16	12.0	9.4	5.8	0.8	0.4
17	5.4	0.5	5.3	0.0	6.2
18	7.6	−2.3	3.1	0.0	7.8
19	10.0	−0.2	5.4	Trace	7.0
20	10.2	−0.1	4.1	Trace	3.9
21	10.8	1.3	6.3	0.1	0.0
22	12.7	8.5	2.6	Trace	0.5
23	12.3	4.5	5.6	Trace	0.2
24	13.4	7.9	10.9	0.2	0.1
25	13.1	10.6	7.3	5.8	0.0
26	11.2	9.2	6.3	4.6	0.8
27	12.4	6.7	8.7	3.7	2.4
28	12.0	5.1	7.7	1.2	1.8
29	12.1	7.8	8.2	0.1	0.5
30	8.3	3.8	9.3	0.0	0.0
31					
Total	–	–	–	28.5	76.2
Mean	12.0	5.2	5.4	0.9	2.5
Temp °F	53.6	41.4	–	–	–
Average	10.4	4.1	8.0	55.0	68.1

DECEMBER 1995

	Temperature Max. °C	Min. °C	Wind knots	Rain mm	Sun hrs
Day 1	11.7	4.6	7.9	0.6	0.0
2	13.1	7.6	3.6	0.8	0.0
3	12.2	10.3	4.2	6.2	0.0
4	6.6	6.3	9.7	0.1	0.0
5	3.5	2.4	8.4	2.0	2.2
6	0.8	−2.4	6.1	1.7	0.0
7	1.8	−0.6	4.4	0.2	0.8
8	5.0	−0.3	3.7	0.0	5.2
9	6.2	−2.3	2.1	0.0	6.8
10	2.3	−4.1	1.8	0.1	0.2
11	7.9	−3.9	2.6	Trace	4.9
12	7.3	1.3	4.5	0.1	0.0
13	8.2	4.7	6.1	0.3	0.0
14	5.5	3.8	10.6	Trace	1.1
15	4.5	2.3	11.4	0.6	0.0
16	6.1	1.8	11.0	Trace	0.0
17	5.3	3.8	4.4	2.2	0.0
18	5.4	3.5	2.7	0.0	0.0
19	6.1	3.4	4.5	27.8	0.0
20	5.5	1.7	6.0	1.3	1.8
21	12.6	0.7	6.0	12.8	0.0
22	13.6	0.7	7.8	8.4	1.0
23	6.3	5.9	4.6	6.2	0.0
24	5.8	2.9	3.1	0.1	0.8
25	3.5	−2.1	3.7	0.0	3.6
26	2.1	−5.0	3.3	0.4	5.5
27	0.7	−3.7	3.3	0.0	0.0
28	0.3	−3.8	4.1	0.0	3.5
29	2.9	−4.6	9.1	0.0	7.3
30	2.6	−3.6	12.3	9.9	0.0
31	4.2	−1.2	2.9	Trace	0.0
Total	–	–	–	82.8	44.7
Mean	5.8	1.0	5.7	2.7	1.4
Temp °F	42.4	33.8	–	–	–
Average	8.0	2.3	8.1	57.0	46.2

JANUARY 1996

	Temperature Max. °C	Min. °C	Wind knots	Rain mm	Sun hrs
Day 1	6.3	1.2	3.5	0.1	0.0
2	6.8	2.7	2.4	0.0	0.0
3	6.4	3.6	7.3	Trace	0.0
4	7.6	3.2	9.8	4.1	0.9
5	8.6	4.6	7.5	3.1	0.0
6	10.6	5.8	10.0	6.6	0.1
7	11.3	5.7	8.0	0.4	2.0
8	12.6	6.8	11.6	20.6	0.0
9	11.6	7.8	7.8	0.3	0.3
10	11.9	4.7	3.6	0.0	0.8
11	10.8	6.1	10.3	0.9	0.0
12	11.5	7.4	13.1	0.7	0.3
13	12.4	9.7	8.6	Trace	2.0
14	12.7	7.0	7.7	0.0	4.1
15	10.2	3.7	3.4	0.1	0.5
16	7.3	5.0	2.1	Trace	0.1
17	11.2	4.7	5.2	Trace	2.9
18	6.6	3.6	6.6	Trace	0.0
19	8.2	3.3	7.2	0.0	0.0
20	4.4	4.0	11.7	Trace	0.0
21	4.4	1.5	12.0	0.0	0.0
22	6.7	1.7	12.7	Trace	0.0
23	4.5	3.5	12.7	4.4	0.0
24	4.8	1.9	12.6	0.0	0.0
25	0.1	−0.6	14.1	Trace	0.0
26	−1.2	−3.2	12.4	0.1	1.1
27	2.5	−5.3	6.0	0.1	3.4
28	1.8	−4.4	13.1	Trace	0.0
29	2.2	0.0	10.7	Trace	0.0
30	3.5	−0.3	7.7	0.0	0.0
31	5.6	1.0	6.6	0.0	6.8
Total	–	–	–	41.5	25.3
Mean	7.3	3.2	8.7	1.3	0.8
Temp °F	45.1	37.8	–	–	–
Average	7.1	1.4	8.5	52.0	51.7

FEBRUARY 1996

	Temperature Max. °C	Min. °C	Wind knots	Rain mm	Sun hrs
Day 1	5.2	−2.2	4.2	0.0	7.7
2	3.0	−2.0	5.0	0.0	2.6
3	5.2	−1.2	6.0	Trace	4.5
4	4.7	−0.6	3.4	0.0	3.1
5	1.6	−4.3	11.2	0.6	0.9
6	1.0	−1.8	8.0	0.4	0.0
7	1.9	−3.5	5.6	0.1	0.0
8	6.7	−2.9	4.2	0.3	6.6
9	7.2	−2.0	11.7	8.9	0.0
10	10.5	3.5	10.4	0.7	1.9
11	9.2	5.6	10.3	10.1	0.6
12	5.7	3.2	11.8	0.6	1.5
13	5.8	2.8	11.9	Trace	0.1
14	6.0	1.8	6.4	0.0	3.1
15	6.9	−2.5	4.5	0.0	0.1
16	13.1	0.2	8.3	0.0	5.1
17	10.4	5.6	9.9	5.4	2.3
18	9.1	5.0	14.2	0.8	6.5
19	3.8	0.9	15.9	2.4	4.2
20	1.8	−2.3	16.4	Trace	4.7
21	2.9	−1.9	6.3	1.3	5.4
22	5.9	−4.6	3.5	0.1	0.4
23	8.6	−0.5	6.7	3.3	4.6
24	9.4	2.7	10.6	10.3	0.1
25	7.6	4.8	6.3	3.4	0.2
26	10.1	0.9	5.1	0.3	7.4
27	11.2	−2.0	2.4	0.0	9.2
28	9.9	−0.5	4.7	0.0	7.9
29	11.3	−0.3	4.2	0.0	9.6
30					
31					
Total	–	–	–	49.0	100.3
Mean	6.8	0.1	7.9	1.7	3.5
Temp °F	44.2	32.2	–	–	–
Average	7.5	1.5	8.8	35.0	63.3

MARCH 1996

Day	Temperature Max. °C	Min. °C	Wind knots	Rain mm	Sun hrs
1	8.6	1.1	7.0	0.5	0.0
2	7.4	3.4	6.0	0.4	0.0
3	8.1	4.1	8.6	0.8	0.0
4	8.0	4.2	7.3	Trace	0.2
5	7.5	5.6	7.1	Trace	0.1
6	10.2	4.2	4.8	0.0	1.2
7	4.7	2.6	12.5	Trace	1.5
8	7.6	2.6	12.1	9.9	1.1
9	7.0	-0.5	5.6	0.3	1.1
10	10.0	2.7	5.7	0.0	9.0
11	7.3	-3.7	6.0	0.2	4.3
12	3.6	-0.3	14.6	0.0	0.0
13	4.5	-1.2	16.6	0.0	5.7
14	5.5	-0.7	13.5	0.0	2.9
15	12.3	0.5	7.4	Trace	5.1
16	6.9	3.3	3.7	0.9	0.0
17	11.5	-0.7	4.1	0.0	5.9
18	11.3	1.1	8.9	Trace	4.1
19	9.1	2.1	7.3	Trace	1.8
20	7.1	1.0	11.8	3.6	0.0
21	9.6	1.6	8.3	1.9	0.0
22	11.4	6.7	4.1	5.9	0.0
23	15.1	7.0	4.8	0.0	0.5
24	9.0	7.6	11.5	0.0	0.0
25	11.7	4.9	11.2	6.9	0.3
26	6.5	4.0	11.0	0.1	0.0
27	7.7	0.2	8.1	0.0	8.9
28	9.6	-1.6	5.9	Trace	4.9
29	10.3	-0.1	5.2	Trace	9.3
30	8.8	-0.7	4.5	0.0	8.0
31	7.0	3.2	2.6	0.0	0.0
Total	–	–	–	31.4	75.9
Mean	8.6	2.1	8.0	1.0	2.5
Temp °F	47.5	35.8	–	–	–
Average	10.3	2.7	8.9	47.0	110.1

APRIL 1996

Day	Temperature Max. °C	Min. °C	Wind knots	Rain mm	Sun hrs
1	8.5	0.1	6.3	Trace	7.4
2	9.1	-1.5	5.1	0.0	7.9
3	9.4	-1.0	5.9	0.0	11.2
4	11.6	-0.9	6.7	0.0	11.6
5	13.3	0.9	7.6	0.0	9.4
6	9.4	2.5	4.7	Trace	0.1
7	11.1	5.8	2.4	0.0	0.0
8	16.2	2.5	4.8	0.0	4.9
9	15.6	9.0	4.0	Trace	0.9
10	11.6	7.5	3.6	0.7	0.1
11	16.1	6.5	4.7	2.1	2.7
12	6.6	5.6	11.6	11.5	0.0
13	10.7	1.6	9.5	0.0	10.7
14	12.4	2.8	3.9	Trace	0.1
15	17.1	5.9	6.3	Trace	3.2
16	18.5	8.6	6.5	Trace	2.2
17	16.4	9.8	7.0	0.0	6.3
18	13.8	7.0	12.2	0.4	0.3
19	15.3	9.5	7.3	Trace	0.2
20	23.5	9.4	5.2	Trace	6.4
21	22.2	9.4	9.5	0.1	10.4
22	11.6	8.0	4.1	8.0	0.0
23	13.5	9.0	6.8	0.2	0.4
24	16.1	7.2	8.0	Trace	9.3
25	16.4	6.2	5.5	0.0	10.0
26	20.3	6.5	4.1	0.0	5.4
27	20.7	7.2	4.1	0.0	13.5
28	15.0	9.7	7.2	0.0	4.7
29	13.2	4.6	4.9	1.8	3.4
30	13.4	4.5	6.1	0.2	4.6
31					
Total	–	–	–	25.0	147.5
Mean	14.3	5.5	6.2	0.8	4.9
Temp °F	57.7	41.9	–	–	–
Average	13.1	4.7	8.5	45.0	146.9

MAY 1996

Day	Temperature Max. °C	Min. °C	Wind knots	Rain mm	Sun hrs
1	13.9	7.2	7.6	2.2	2.9
2	11.5	6.5	10.5	Trace	0.7
3	12.4	5.0	9.3	0.0	6.4
4	12.0	1.2	4.1	0.0	10.0
5	12.4	1.5	2.3	0.0	3.0
6	15.6	2.6	5.7	0.0	13.1
7	15.2	3.3	10.6	0.0	12.3
8	14.1	2.4	10.4	0.0	14.1
9	13.5	3.1	10.1	0.0	9.7
10	11.8	4.3	8.2	0.1	6.6
11	12.6	2.1	3.3	0.0	1.8
12	15.0	6.4	3.3	0.0	8.5
13	17.9	3.5	3.8	0.0	13.3
14	15.9	5.2	7.5	0.0	7.6
15	16.9	4.1	7.7	0.0	8.4
16	10.4	3.0	9.9	3.3	1.2
17	9.6	3.4	7.3	0.9	0.1
18	9.8	4.4	8.3	6.0	0.0
19	13.4	5.4	16.3	Trace	3.0
20	15.6	5.3	9.3	0.5	9.8
21	17.0	6.8	7.5	0.4	9.3
22	14.5	9.2	11.8	3.6	0.0
23	17.2	10.0	11.7	1.9	3.5
24	14.4	11.3	11.7	4.5	0.0
25	18.5	6.6	6.5	Trace	8.2
26	15.8	7.0	8.7	2.2	0.2
27	16.5	10.6	7.3	0.2	2.3
28	17.3	4.5	9.0	Trace	2.0
29	21.1	12.3	9.0	Trace	0.4
30	26.1	12.8	10.5	0.0	11.6
31	20.5	12.9	12.2	Trace	12.6
Total	–	–	–	25.8	182.6
Mean	15.2	6.0	8.5	0.8	5.9
Temp °F	59.4	42.8	–	–	–
Average	17.0	8.0	8.1	51.0	193.7

JUNE 1996*

Day	Temperature Max. °C	Min. °C	Wind knots	Rain mm	Sun hrs
1	18.7	9.4	–	0.2	10.2
2	19.4	7.3	–	0.0	7.4
3	20.5	7.6	–	Trace	9.0
4	23.1	12.5	–	0.0	13.7
5	27.7	11.0	–	0.0	14.5
6	30.6	14.4	–	0.0	14.5
7	31.8	19.2	–	9.9	14.2
8	21.1	14.4	–	Trace	4.2
9	23.0	10.7	–	0.0	14.9
10	24.1	11.2	–	Trace	6.7
11	22.8	12.6	–	Trace	1.4
12	21.2	12.3	–	0.0	13.7
13	22.1	8.9	–	0.0	15.5
14	22.5	10.3	–	0.0	15.4
15	23.9	9.0	–	0.0	15.7
16	26.4	9.4	–	0.0	15.3
17	28.5	13.0	–	0.0	14.6
18	22.4	12.0	–	0.0	12.1
19	22.7	11.0	–	Trace	11.4
20	15.5	10.2	–	Trace	0.0
21	17.4	9.8	–	0.0	6.9
22	17.0	2.5	–	Trace	4.9
23	21.7	7.7	–	0.0	11.6
24	22.1	10.2	–	0.0	7.4
25	25.7	11.8	–	0.0	10.0
26	26.0	11.8	–	Trace	9.2
27	24.1	16.1	–	0.2	1.8
28	19.7	13.5	–	1.7	1.5
29	18.2	10.9	–	Trace	1.4
30	22.6	10.7	–	0.0	3.6
31					
Total	–	–	–	12.0	282.7
Mean	22.8	11.3	–	0.4	9.4
Temp °F	73.0	52.3	–	–	–
Average	20.4	11.0	7.6	50.0	198.5

*Wind values for June were not available at the time of going to press

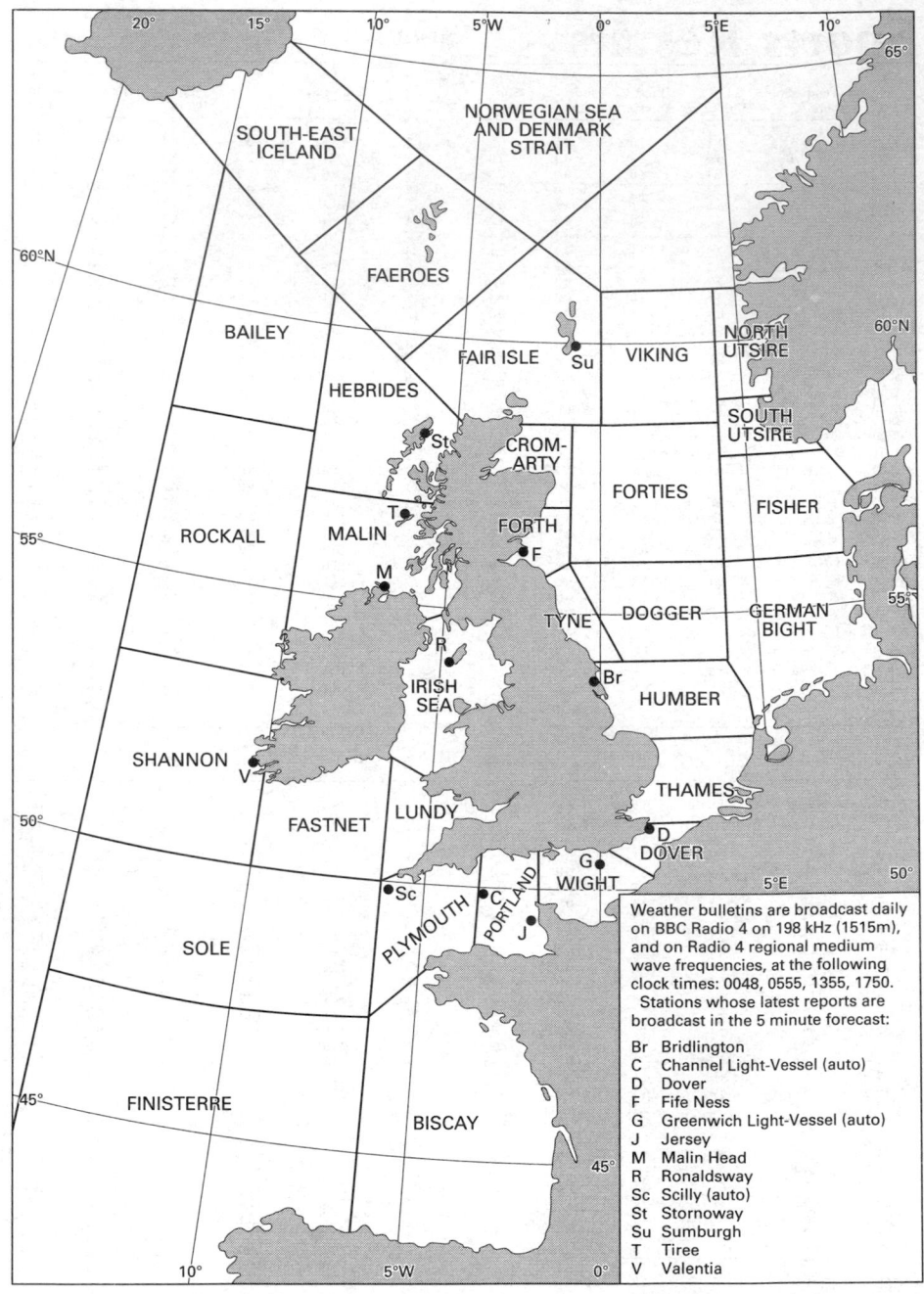

Weather bulletins are broadcast daily on BBC Radio 4 on 198 kHz (1515m), and on Radio 4 regional medium wave frequencies, at the following clock times: 0048, 0555, 1355, 1750.
  Stations whose latest reports are broadcast in the 5 minute forecast:

Br Bridlington
C   Channel Light-Vessel (auto)
D   Dover
F   Fife Ness
G   Greenwich Light-Vessel (auto)
J   Jersey
M   Malin Head
R   Ronaldsway
Sc Scilly (auto)
St Stornoway
Su Sumburgh
T   Tiree
V   Valentia

Sports Results

For 1997 sports fixtures, *see* pages 12–13

ALPINE SKIING

WORLD CUP 1995–6

MEN

Downhill: Luc Alphand (France), 577 points
Slalom: Sebastien Amiez (France), 539 points
Giant Slalom: Michael Von Grünigen (Switzerland), 738 points
Super Giant Slalom: Atle Skaardal (Norway), 312 points
Overall: Lasse Kjus (Norway), 1,216 points

WOMEN

Downhill: Picabo Street (USA), 640 points
Slalom: Elfi Eder (Austria), 580 points
Giant Slalom: Martina Ertl (Germany), 485 points
Super Giant Slalom: Katja Seizinger (Germany), 545 points
Overall: Katja Seizinger (Germany), 1,472 points

Nations Cup: Austria, 11,071 points

WORLD CHAMPIONSHIPS 1996
Sierra Nevada, Spain, February

MEN

Downhill: Patrick Ortlieb (Austria)
Slalom: Alberto Tomba (Italy)
Giant Slalom: Alberto Tomba (Italy)
Super Giant Slalom: Atle Skaardal (Norway)
Combined Event: Marc Girardelli (Luxembourg)

WOMEN

Downhill: Picabo Street (USA)
Slalom: Pernilla Wiberg (Sweden)
Giant Slalom: Deborah Compagnoni (Italy)
Super Giant Slalom: Isolde Kostner (Italy)
Combined Event: Pernilla Wiberg (Sweden)

AMERICAN FOOTBALL

XXX American Superbowl 1996 (Tempe, Arizona, 28 January): Dallas Cowboys beat Pittsburgh Steelers 27–17
World Bowl 1996 (Murrayfield): Scottish Claymores beat Frankfurt Galaxy 32–27
British League Division 1 final 1996: Leicester Panthers beat Milton Keynes Pioneers 10–6

ANGLING

NATIONAL COARSE CHAMPIONSHIPS 1995
Division: 1
Venue: Gloucester Canal; *no. of teams:* 85
Individual winner: S. Tyler (ABC), 25.250 kg
Team winners: Barnsley and District AA, 807 points

Division: 2
Venue: Grand Union Canal; *no. of teams:* 81
Individual winner: S. Joy (Chelmsford AA), 8.310 kg
Team winners: Avon Bait, 766 points

Division: 3
Venue: Bridgewater Canal; *no. of teams:* 80
Individual winner: G. Barclay (Oxford Pyrotec), 6.420 kg
Team winners: Birkenhead Centre AC, 794 points

Division: 4
Venue: River Thames; *no. of teams:* 80
Individual winner: B. Wallace (East Grinstead AS), 13.900 kg
Team winners: Hounslow Angling Centre, 765 points

Division: 5
Venue: River Trent; no. of teams: 86
Individual winner: R. Howe (Godalming AS), 12.420 kg
Team winners: Goole Avengers, 879 points

Ladies' Championship
Venue: Bridgewater Canal; *no. of competitors:* 138
Winner: W. Lythgoe, 6.040 kg

WORLD CHAMPIONSHIPS 1996
Peschiera, Italy, September

Individual winner: Alan Scotthorne (England), 10.076 kg
Team winners: Italy, 36 points

ASSOCIATION FOOTBALL

LEAGUE COMPETITIONS 1995–6

ENGLAND AND WALES
Premiership
1. Manchester United, 82 points
2. Newcastle United, 78 points
Relegated: Manchester City, 38 points; Queen's Park Rangers, 33 points; Bolton Wanderers, 29 points

Division 1
1. Sunderland, 83 points
2. Derby County, 79 points
Third promotion place: Leicester City
Relegated: Milwall, 52 points; Watford, 48 points; Luton Town, 45 points

Division 2
1. Swindon Town, 92 points
2. Oxford United, 83 points
Third promotion place: Bradford City
Relegated: Carlisle United, 49 points; Swansea City, 47 points; Brighton and Hove Albion, 40 points; Hull City, 31 points

Division 3
1. Preston North End, 86 points
2. Gillingham, 83 points
3. Bury, 79 points
Fourth promotion place: Plymouth Argyle
Bottom: Torquay United, 29 points

GM Vauxhall Conference
Champions: Stevenage Borough, 91 points (not promoted
  because the necessary improvements to their ground
  had not been made by 31 December 1995)
Relegated: Dover, 40 points; Runcorn, 35 points; Dagenham
  and Redbridge, 33 points

League of Wales: Barry Town, 97 points
Women's Premier League: Croydon

SCOTLAND
Premier Division
1. Rangers, 87 points
2. Celtic, 83 points
Relegated: Partick Thistle, 30 points; Falkirk, 24 points

Division 1
1. Dunfermline Athletic, 71 points
2. Dundee United, 67 points
Relegated: Hamilton Academicals, 36 points; Dumbarton,
  11 points

Division 2
1. Stirling Albion, 81 points
2. East Fife, 67 points
Relegated: Forfar Athletic, 40 points; Montrose, 20 points

Division 3
1. Livingston, 72 points
2. Brechin City, 63 points
Bottom: Albion Rovers, 29 points

NORTHERN IRELAND
Irish League Championship: Portadown, 56 points

CUP COMPETITIONS

ENGLAND
FA Cup final 1996 (Wembley, 11 May): Manchester United
  beat Liverpool 1–0
Coca Cola (League) Cup final 1996: Aston Villa beat Leeds
  United 3–0
Auto Windscreens Shield final 1996: Rotherham United beat
  Shrewsbury Town 2–1
Anglo-Italian Cup final 1996: Genoa beat Port Vale 5–2
FA Vase final 1996: Brigg Town beat Clitheroe 3–0
FA Trophy final 1996: Macclesfield Town beat Northwich
  Victoria 3–1
Arthur Dunn Cup final 1996: Lancing beat Brentwood 4–1
Charity Shield 1996: Manchester United beat Newcastle
  United 4–0
Women's FA Cup final 1996: Croydon 1, Liverpool 1 a.e.t.
  Croydon won 3–2 on penalties
Women's League Cup final 1996: Wembley 2, Doncaster
  Belles 2. Wembley won 5–3 on penalties

WALES
Welsh FA Cup final 1996: Llansantffraid 3, Barry Town 3
  a.e.t. Llansantffraid won 3–2 on penalties
League of Wales Cup final 1996: Connah's Quay Nomads
  beat Ebbw Vale 1–0

SCOTLAND
Scottish FA Cup final 1996 (Hampden Park, 18 May):
  Rangers beat Heart of Midlothian 5–1
Coca Cola (League) Cup final 1995: Aberdeen beat Dundee
  2–0
League Challenge Cup final 1995: Dundee United 0,
  Stenhousemuir 0 a.e.t. Stenhousemuir won 5–4 on
  penalties

NORTHERN IRELAND
Irish Cup final 1996: Glentoran beat Glenavon 1–0

EUROPE
European Champions' Cup final 1996 (Rome): Ajax
  Amsterdam 1, Juventus 1. Juventus won 4–2 on
  penalties
European Cup-Winners' Cup final 1996 (Brussels): Paris St
  Germain beat Rapid Vienna 1–0
UEFA Cup final 1996: Bayern Munich beat Bordeaux 5–1
  on agg.

African Nations Cup final 1996: South Africa beat Tunisia
  2–0

INTERNATIONALS

WORLD CUP QUALIFYING MATCHES
1996

2 June	San Marino	San Marino 0, Wales 5
31 Aug	Vienna	Austria 0, Scotland 0
	Cardiff	Wales 6, San Marino 0
	Belfast	N. Ireland 0, Ukraine 1
1 Sept	Kishinev	Moldova 0, England 3

EUROPEAN CHAMPIONSHIPS QUALIFYING MATCHES
1995

11 Oct	Cardiff	Wales 1, Germany 2
	Eschen	Liechtenstein 0, N. Ireland 4
15 Nov	Tirana	Albania 1, Wales 1
	Glasgow	Scotland 5, San Marino 0
	Belfast	N. Ireland 5, Austria 3

FRIENDLIES
1995

11 Oct	Oslo	Norway 0, England 0
	Stockholm	Sweden 2, Scotland 0
15 Nov	Wembley	England 3, Switzerland 1
12 Dec	Wembley	England 1, Portugal 1

1996

24 Jan	Terni	Italy 3, Wales 0
27 March	Wembley	England 1, Bulgaria 0
	Glasgow	Scotland 1, Australia 0
	Belfast	N. Ireland 0, Norway 2
24 April	Wembley	England 0, Croatia 0
	Copenhagen	Denmark 2, Scotland 0
	Lugano	Switzerland 2, Wales 0
	Belfast	N. Ireland 1, Sweden 2
18 May	Wembley	England 3, Hungary 0
23 May	Beijing	China 0, England 3
26 May	New Britain	USA 2, Scotland 1
29 May	Belfast	N. Ireland 1, Germany 1
30 May	Miami	Colombia 1, Scotland 0

EUROPEAN CHAMPIONSHIPS 1996
England, 8–30 June

FIRST ROUND
Group A: England 7 points; Holland 4 points; Scotland 4
  points; Switzerland 1 point
Group B: France 7 points; Spain 5 points; Bulgaria 4 points;
  Romania 0 points
Group C: Germany 7 points; Czech Republic 4 points; Italy
  4 points; Russia 1 point
Group D: Portugal 7 points; Croatia 6 points; Denmark 4
  points; Turkey 0 points

England 0, Spain 0 a.e.t. (England won 4–2 on penalties);
France 0, Holland 0 a.e.t. (France won 5–4 on penalties);
Germany 2, Croatia 1; Portugal 0, Czech Republic 1

SEMI-FINALS
France 0, Czech Republic 0 a.e.t. (Czech Republic won 6–5
on penalties); Germany 1, England 1 a.e.t. (Germany won
6–5 on penalties)

FINAL
Wembley, 30 June
Germany 2, Czech Republic 1 a.e.t.

ATHLETICS

EUROPEAN CROSS-COUNTRY CHAMPIONSHIPS
Alnwick, 10 December 1995

MEN
Individual: Paulo Guerra (Portugal), 26 min. 40 sec.
Team result: Spain, 32 points

WOMEN
Individual: Annemari Sandell (Finland), 13 min. 52 sec.
Team result: Russia, 20 points

GREAT BRITAIN v. RUSSIA (INDOORS)
Birmingham, 27 January 1996

MEN

	min.	sec.
60 *metres:* Jason Gardener (GB)		6.55
200 *metres:* Solomon Wariso (GB)		21.03
400 *metres:* Mark Hylton (GB)		46.96
800 *metres:* Andrei Loginov (Russia)	1	50.54
1,500 *metres:* Anthony Whiteman (GB)	3	39.47
3,000 *metres:* Vener Kashayev (Russia)	7	57.79
60 *metres hurdles:* Sergei Vetrov (Russia)		7.85
4 × 400 *metres relay:* Great Britain	3	08.47

	metres
High jump: Dalton Grant (GB)	2.34
Pole vault: Yevgeni Smiryagin (Russia)	5.55
Long jump: Kiril Sosunov (Russia)	8.06
Triple jump: Andrei Kurennoy (Russia)	16.49
Shot: Shaun Pickering (GB)	19.10

Team points: Great Britain 69, Russia 68

WOMEN

	min.	sec.
60 *metres:* Natalya Anisimova (Russia)		7.37
200 *metres:* Svetlana Goncharenko (Russia)		23.28
400 *metres:* Yelena Andreyeva (Russia)		53.49
800 *metres:* Irina Korzh (Russia)	2	05.32
1,500 *metres:* Irina Biryukova (Russia)	4	13.05
3,000 *metres:* Sonia McGeorge (GB)	9	28.04
60 *metres hurdles:* Clova Court (GB)		8.35
4 × 400 *metres relay:* Russia	3	31.88

	metres
High jump: Natalya Golodnova (Russia)	1.95
Pole vault: Svetlana Abramova (Russia)	4.00
Long jump: Denise Lewis (GB)	6.45
Triple jump: Natalya Kayukova (Russia)	13.90
Shot: Judy Oakes (GB)	18.63

Team points: Russia 80, Great Britain 57

AAA INDOOR CHAMPIONSHIPS
Birmingham, 3–4 February 1996

MEN

	min.	sec.
60 *metres:* Michael Roswess (Birchfield)		6.68
200 *metres:* Douglas Turner (Cardiff)		21.06
400 *metres:* Mark Hylton (Windsor)		46.45
800 *metres:* Martin Steele (Longwood)	1	51.21
1,500 *metres:* Terry West (Morpeth)	3	49.90
3,000 *metres:* Matthew Skelton (Tonbridge)	8	00.48
60 *metres hurdles:* Neil Owen (Belgrave)		7.81

	metres
High jump: Michael Robbins (Rotherham)	2.19
Pole vault: Nick Buckfield (Crawley)	5.61
Long jump: Chris Davidson (Newham)	7.60
Triple jump: Francis Agyepong (Shaftesbury)	16.55
Shot: Shaun Pickering (Haringey)	17.88

WOMEN

	min.	sec.
60 *metres:* Marcia Richardson (Windsor)		7.34
200 *metres:* Catherine Murphy (Shaftesbury)		23.69
400 *metres:* Melanie Neef (Glasgow)		52.50
800 *metres:* Vicki Sterne (Birchfield)	2	06.41
1,500 *metres:* Angela Davies (Basingstoke)	4	16.24
60 *metres hurdles:* Jackie Agyepong (Shaftesbury)		8.17

	metres
High jump: Michelle Dunkley (Kettering)	1.85
Pole vault: Kate Staples (Essex Ladies)	3.70
Long jump: Ann Brooks (Hull)	6.01
Triple jump: Michelle Griffith (Windsor)	13.18
Shot: Judy Oakes (Croydon)	18.57

Birmingham, 18 February 1996

	min.	sec.
3,000 *metres:* Sonia McGeorge (Brighton)	9	04.69

GREAT BRITAIN v. FRANCE (INDOORS)
Glasgow, 24 February 1996

MEN

	min.	sec.
60 *metres:* Jason John (GB)		6.62
200 *metres:* John Regis (GB)		20.88
400 *metres:* Du'aine Ladejo (GB)		46.39
800 *metres:* Jean-Christophe Vialettes (France)	1	50.35
1,500 *metres:* Abdelkader Chekhemani (France)	3	46.35
3,000 *metres:* Eric Dubus (France)	7	58.47
60 *metres hurdles:* Dan Philibert (France)		7.71
4 × 400 *metres relay:* Great Britain	3	07.72

	metres
High jump: Dalton Grant (GB)	2.26
Pole vault: Alain Andji (France)	5.60
Long jump: Romuald Ducros (France)	7.69
Triple jump: Francis Agyepong (GB)	16.92
Shot: Mark Proctor (GB)	18.09

Team points: Great Britain 72, France 68

WOMEN

	min.	sec.
60 *metres:* Beverley Kinch (GB)		7.33
200 *metres:* Fabe Dia (France)		23.77
400 *metres:* Sally Gunnell (GB)		53.28
800 *metres:* Patricia Djate (France)	2	03.43
1,500 *metres:* Debbie Gunning (GB)	4	17.02
3,000 *metres:* Laurence Duquennoy (France)	9	05.44
60 *metres hurdles:* Monique Tourret (France)		8.09
4 × 400 *metres relay:* France	3	36.25

	metres
High jump: Debbie Marti (GB)	1.89
Pole vault: Kate Staples (GB)	3.85
Long jump: Denise Lewis (GB)	6.48
Triple jump: Michelle Griffith (GB)	13.51
Shot: Judy Oakes (GB)	18.59

Team points: France 70, Great Britain 70

EUROPEAN INDOOR CHAMPIONSHIPS
Stockholm, 8–10 March 1996

MEN

	min.	sec.
60 *metres:* Marc Blume (Germany)		6.62
200 *metres:* Erik Wijmeersch (Belgium)		21.04
400 *metres:* Du'aine Ladejo (GB)		46.12
800 *metres:* Roberto Parra (Spain)	1	47.74
1,500 *metres:* Mateo Canellas (Spain)	3	44.50
3,000 *metres:* Anacleto Jiminez (Spain)	7	50.06
60 *metres hurdles:* Igor Kazunov (Latvia)		7.59

	metres
High jump: Dragutin Topic (Yugoslavia)	2.35
Pole vault: Dmitri Markov (Belarus)	5.85
Long jump: Mattias Sunneborn (Sweden)	8.06
Triple jump: Maris Bruzhiks (Latvia)	16.97
Shot: Paolo Dal Soglio (Italy)	20.50
Heptathlon: Erki Nool (Estonia)	6,188 points

WOMEN

	min.	sec.
60 *metres:* Ekaterini Thanou (Greece)		7.15
200 *metres:* Sandra Myers (Spain)		23.15
400 *metres:* Grit Breuer (Germany)		50.81
800 *metres:* Patricia Djaté-Taillard (France)	2	01.71
1,500 *metres:* Carla Sacramento (Portugal)	4	08.95
3,000 *metres:* Fernanda Ribeiro (Portugal)	8	39.49
60 *metres hurdles:* Patricia Girard (France)		7.89

	metres
High jump: Alina Astafei (Germany)	1.98
Pole vault: Vala Flosadottir (Iceland)	4.16
Long jump: Renata Nielsen (Denmark)	6.76
Triple jump: Iva Prandzheva (Bulgaria)	14.54
Shot: Astrid Kumbernuss (Germany)	19.79
Pentathlon: Yelena Lebendenko (Russia)	4,685 points

NATIONAL CROSS-COUNTRY CHAMPIONSHIPS
Newark, 9 March 1996

MEN (14 km)
Individual: John Nuttall (Preston), 40 min. 35 sec.
Team: Bingley Harriers, 105 points

WOMEN (6 km)
Individual: Nnenna Lynch (USA/Oxford University),
    21 min. 54 sec.
Team: Parkside, 52 points

INTERNATIONAL CROSS-COUNTRY CHAMPIONSHIPS
Cape Town, 23 March 1996

MEN (12.15 km)
Individual: Paul Tergat (Kenya), 33 min. 44 sec.
Team: Kenya, 33 points

WOMEN (6.35 km)
Individual: Gete Wami (Ethiopia), 20 min. 12 sec.
Team: Kenya, 24 points

LONDON MARATHON
21 April 1996

Men: Dionicio Ceron (Mexico), 2 hr. 10 min. 00 sec.
Women: Liz McColgan (GB), 2 hr. 27 min. 54 sec.

EUROPEAN CUP
Madrid, 1–2 June 1996

MEN

	min.	sec.
100 *metres:* Linford Christie (GB)		10.04
200 *metres:* Linford Christie (GB)		20.25
400 *metres:* Uwe Jahn (Germany)		45.64
800 *metres:* Roberto Parra (Spain)	1	44.97
1,500 *metres:* Fermin Cacho (Spain)	3	40.24
3,000 *metres:* Pieter Baumann (Germany)	7	57.19
5,000 *metres:* Gennaro Di Napoli (Italy)	13	52.34
3,000 *metres steeplechase:* Steffen Brand (Germany)	8	30.09
110 *metres hurdles:* Florian Schwarthoff (Germany)		13.20
400 *metres hurdles:* Fabrizio Mori (Italy)		
4 × 100 *metres relay:* Ukraine		38.53
4 × 400 *metres relay:* Great Britain	3	03.38

	metres
High jump: Arturo Ortiz (Spain)	2.27
Pole vault: Pyotr Bochkaryov (Russia)	5.70
Long jump: Simone Bianchi (Italy)	8.25
Triple jump: Jonathan Edwards (GB)	17.79
Shot: Paolo Dal Soglio (Italy)	20.72
Discus: David Martinez (Spain)	62.38
Hammer: Karsten Kobs (Germany)	78.18
Javelin: Raymond Hecht (Germany)	88.86

Team points: Germany 142, Great Britain 125, Italy 110,
    Spain 106, Russia 103, France 93½, Ukraine 84, Sweden
    75½, Finland 53

WOMEN

	min.	sec.
100 *metres:* Marina Trandenkova (Russia)		11.14
200 *metres:* Marie-José Pérec (France)		22.34
400 *metres:* Grit Breuer (Germany)		50.22
800 *metres:* Svetlana Masterkova (Russia)	1	57.87
1,500 *metres:* Olga Churbanova (Russia)	4	09.57
3,000 *metres:* Blandine Bitzner (France)	8	59.82
5,000 *metres:* Kathrin Wessel (Germany)	15	40.36
100 *metres hurdles:* Nadezhda Bodrova (Ukraine)		12.89
400 *metres hurdles:* Sally Gunnell (GB)		56.84
4 × 100 *metres relay:* Russia		42.55
4 × 400 *metres relay:* Germany	3	26.19

	metres
High jump: Alina Astafei (Germany)	1.98
Long jump: Iva Prandzheva (Bulgaria)	6.84
Triple jump: Ashia Hansen (GB)	14.57
Shot: Astrid Kumbernuss (Germany)	20.05
Discus: Ilke Wyludda (Germany)	65.66
Javelin: Oksana Ovchinnikova (Russia)	65.72

Team points: Germany 115, Russia 97, Belarus 79, Ukraine 78, France 75, Great Britain 73, Spain 49, Bulgaria 46

AAA CHAMPIONSHIPS
Birmingham, 14–16 June 1996

MEN

	min.	sec.
100 *metres:* Linford Christie (TVH)		10.04
200 *metres:* John Regis (Belgrave)		20.54
400 *metres:* Roger Black (Solent)		44.39
800 *metres:* Curtis Robb (Liverpool)	1	47.61
1,500 *metres:* John Mayock (Cannock)	3	37.03
5,000 *metres:* John Nuttall (Preston)	13	48.35
10,000 *metres:* Rob Denmark (Basildon)	28	20.80
3,000 *metres steeplechase:* Justin Chaston (Belgrave)	8	29.19
110 *metres hurdles:* Colin Jackson (Cardiff)		13.13
400 *metres hurdles:* Jon Ridgeon (Belgrave)		49.16
10,000 *metres walk:* Steve Partington (Manx)	42	29.73

	metres
High jump: Steve Smith (Liverpool)	2.31
Pole vault: Nick Buckfield (Crawley)	5.71
Long jump: Darren Ritchie (Sale)	7.86
Triple jump: Francis Agyepong (Shaftesbury)	17.12
Shot: Matthew Simson (Thurrock)	18.82
Discus: Rob Weir (Birchfield)	60.02
Hammer: Dave Smith (Belgrave)	72.58
Javelin: Nick Nieland (Shaftesbury)	83.06

WOMEN

	min.	sec.
100 *metres:* Stephanie Douglas (Sale)		11.55
200 *metres:* Simmone Jacobs (Shaftesbury)		23.11
400 *metres:* Phylis Smith (Sale)		51.74
800 *metres:* Kelly Holmes (Army)	1	57.84
1,500 *metres:* Kelly Holmes (Army)	4	08.14
5,000 *metres:* Paula Radcliffe (Bedford)	15	28.46
10,000 *metres:* Louise Watson (GEC)	33	21.46
100 *metres hurdles:* Angela Thorp (Wigan)		13.26
400 *metres hurdles:* Sally Gunnell (Essex Ladies)		54.65
5,000 *metres walk:* Vicky Lupton (Sheffield)	23	04.57

	metres
High jump: Debbie Marti (Bromley)	1.94
Pole vault: Kate Staples (Essex Ladies)	3.80
Long jump: Denise Lewis (Birchfield)	6.55
Triple jump: Ashia Hansen (Shaftesbury)	14.25
Shot: Judy Oakes (Croydon)	18.65
Discus: Jacqui McKernan (Lisburn)	54.12
Hammer: Lyn Sprules (Hounslow)	54.16
Javelin: Tessa Sanderson (Hounslow)	62.88

GRAND PRIX 1996 FINAL RESULTS

MEN
100 *metres:* Dennis Mitchell (USA)
400 *metres:* Michael Johnson (USA)
1,500 *metres:* Hicham El Guerrouj (Morocco)
5,000 *metres:* Daniel Komen (Kenya)
400 *metres hurdles:* Derrick Adkins (USA)
High jump: Patrik Sjoberg (Sweden)
Triple jump: Jonathan Edwards (GB)
Shot: John Godina (USA)
Hammer: Lance Deal (USA)
Overall winner: Daniel Komen (Kenya)

WOMEN
100 *metres:* Merlene Ottey (Jamaica)
400 *metres:* Cathy Freeman (Australia)
1,500 *metres:* Svetlana Masterkova (Russia)

5,000 *metres:* Roberta Brunet (Italy)
100 *metres hurdles:* Ludmila Engquist (Sweden)
Long jump: Inessa Kravets (Ukraine)
Discus: Ilke Wyludda (Germany)
Javelin: Tanja Damaske (Germany)
Overall winner: Ludmila Engquist (Sweden)

BADMINTON

Thomas Cup final 1996 (Men's World Team Championship): Indonesia beat Denmark 5–0
Über Cup final 1996 (Women's World Team Championship): Indonesia beat China 4–1

ENGLISH NATIONAL CHAMPIONSHIPS 1996
Norwich, April

Men's Singles: Darren Hall beat Peter Knowles 9–15, 15–3, 15–0
Women's Singles: Tanya Groves beat Julia Mann 11–5, 11–6
Men's Doubles: Simon Archer and Chris Hunt beat James Anderson and Ian Pearson 15–5, 15–10
Women's Doubles: Julie Bradbury and Jo Wright beat Joanne Davies and Emma Chaffin 15–12, 15–5
Mixed Doubles: Julie Bradbury and Simon Archer beat Jo Wright and Nick Ponting 17–14, 15–6

SCOTTISH NATIONAL CHAMPIONSHIPS 1996
Edinburgh, February

Men's Singles: Jim Mailer beat Bruce Flockhart 14–17, 18–16, 15–13
Women's Singles: Anne Gibson beat Elinor Middlemiss 11–3, 11–4
Men's Doubles: Alastair Gatt and Craig Robertson beat David Gilmour and Gordon Haldane 10–15, 17–16, 15–9
Women's Doubles: Jillian Haldane and Elinor Middlemiss beat Alexis Blanchflower and Sandra Watt 15–8, 15–2
Mixed Doubles: Elinor Middlemiss and Kenny Middlemiss beat Jillian Haldane and Gordon Haldane 15–3, 10–15, 15–11

WELSH NATIONAL CHAMPIONSHIPS 1996
Welshpool, February

Men's Singles: Richard Vaughan beat John Leung 18–16, 18–16
Women's Singles: Kelly Morgan beat Katy Howell 11–0, 11–0
Men's Doubles: Andrew Groves-Burke and Geraint Lewis beat Dayle Blencowe and Peter Hybart 15–12, 15–10
Women's Doubles: Kelly Morgan and Rachael Phipps beat Sarah Williams and Natasha Groves-Burke 15–10, 15–3
Mixed Doubles: Kelly Morgan and Richard Vaughan beat Rachael Phipps and Dayle Blencowe 15–10, 15–7

ALL-ENGLAND CHAMPIONSHIPS 1996
Birmingham, March

Men's Singles: Poul-Erik Hoyer-Larsen (Denmark) beat Rashid Sidek (Malaysia) 15–7, 15–6
Women's Singles: Bang Soo-Hyun (S. Korea) beat Ye Zhaoying (China) 11–1, 11–1
Men's Doubles: Rexy Mainaky and Ricky Subagdja (Indonesia) beat Cheah Soon Kit and Yap Kim Hock (Malaysia) 15–6, 15–5
Women's Doubles: Ge Fei and Gu Jun (China) beat Helene Kirkegaard and Rikke Olsen (Denmark) 15–7, 15–3

Mixed Doubles: Ra Kyung-Min and Park Joo-Bong (S. Korea) beat Julie Bradbury and Simon Archer (England) 15–10, 15–10

BASKETBALL

MEN

Championship play-off final 1996: Birmingham Bullets beat London Towers 78–72
League Trophy final 1996: London Towers beat Worthing Bears 90–84
National Cup final 1996: London Towers beat Sheffield Sharks 70–58
National League Championship 1996: London Towers

WOMEN

Championship play-off final 1996: Sheffield Hatters beat Birmingham Quality Cats 73–62
National Cup final 1996: Sheffield Hatters beat Barking and Dagenham 72–54
National League Championship 1996: Sheffield Hatters

BILLIARDS

World Professional Championship 1996: Mike Russell (England) beat Geet Sethi (India) 2,534–1,848
World Matchplay Championship 1996: Mike Russell (England) beat Peter Gilchrist (England) 7–5
UK Professional Championship 1996: Mike Russell (England) beat David Causier (England) 1,690–1,277
British Open Championship 1996: Roxton Chapman (England) beat Mike Russell (England) 1,616–772

BOWLS – INDOOR (MEN)

WORLD CHAMPIONSHIPS 1996
Preston, February
Singles: David Gourlay, jun. (Scotland) beat Hugh Duff (Scotland) 2–7, 7–5, 7–6, 3–7, 7–1
Pairs: Ian Schuback and Kelvin Kerrow (Australia) beat Gary Smith and Andy Thomson (England) 7–5, 2–7, 7–6, 4–7, 7–4

NATIONAL CHAMPIONSHIPS 1996
Melton Mowbray, April
Singles: Mark Bantock (Desborough) beat John Ottaway (Wymondham Dell) 21–17
Pairs: Nottingham beat Grantham 18–14
Triples: Stanley beat Whiteknights 18–7
Fours: Cyphers beat Great Aycliffe 18–15

BRITISH ISLES CHAMPIONSHIPS 1996
Auchinleck, March
Singles: John Price (Wales) beat Ian Bond (England) 21–13
Pairs: Scotland beat England 26–18
Triples: Wales beat England 17–11
Fours: Scotland beat Ireland 23–17

Hilton Trophy (Home International Championship) 1996: Scotland
Liberty Trophy (Inter-County Championship) final 1996: Wiltshire beat Cornwall 134–120

BOWLS – INDOOR (WOMEN)

WORLD CHAMPIONSHIPS 1996
Guernsey, April
Singles: Sandy Hazell (England) beat Jean Baker (England) 21–6

NATIONAL CHAMPIONSHIPS 1996
Southampton, March
Singles: Sandy Hazell (Mote Park) beat Jean Baker (South Forest) 21–8
Pairs: Peterborough beat Riverain 21–17
Triples: Padbrook Park beat Bassetlaw 16–14
Fours: Cherwell beat Egham 22–19

BRITISH ISLES CHAMPIONSHIPS 1996
Llanelli, March
Singles: Joyce Lindores (Scotland) beat Brenda Brown (England) 21–10
Pairs: England beat Wales 25–17
Triples: Scotland beat Wales 21–8
Fours: Wales beat England 19–16

Home International Championship 1996: England
Atherly Trophy (Inter-County Championship) final 1996: Surrey beat Norfolk 120–96

BOWLS – OUTDOOR (MEN)

WORLD CHAMPIONSHIPS 1996
Adelaide, March
Singles: Tony Allcock (England) beat Jeff Rabkin (Israel) 25–15
Pairs: Ireland beat Scotland 21–19
Triples: Scotland beat New Zealand 26–5
Fours: England beat Wales 20–9

NATIONAL CHAMPIONSHIPS 1996
Worthing, August
Singles: John Ottaway (Wymondham Dell, Norfolk) beat Andrew Kirtland (Hundens Park, Darlington) 21–12
Pairs: Bank House Hotel, Worcester, beat Cheltenham 20–19
Triples: British Cellophane beat Cowes Medina 21–17
Fours: March Conservatives beat Carlisle Courtfield 20–18

BRITISH ISLES CHAMPIONSHIPS 1996
Ulster Transport and Carrickfergus, July
Singles: Noel Graham (Ireland) beat John Leeman (England) 21–13
Pairs: Scotland beat England 25–12
Triples: Scotland beat England 16–14
Fours: Ireland beat Wales 24–8

Home International Championship 1996: Scotland
Middleton Cup (Inter-County Championship) final 1996: Lincolnshire beat Worcestershire 112–102

BOWLS – OUTDOOR (WOMEN)

WORLD CHAMPIONSHIPS 1996
Royal Leamington Spa, August
Singles: Carmelita Anderson (Norfolk Island) beat Wendy Line (England) 25–9

Pairs: Ireland beat Jersey 21–19
Triples: South Africa beat Australia 19–12
Fours: Australia beat South Africa 18–15

NATIONAL CHAMPIONSHIPS 1996
Royal Leamington Spa, August–September

Singles (four woods): Margaret Price (Burnham, Bucks) beat Kath Hawes (Oxford City and County) 21–17
Singles (two woods): Margaret Ashford-Hull (Beccles, Suffolk) beat Catherine Anton (Peterborough and District) 14–12
Pairs: Haynes Park, Hornchurch beat Bridport 181–3
Triples: Oxford City and County beat Lincoln Park 18–11
Fours: Burnham, Bucks beat Park Avenue, Grimsby 19–17

BRITISH ISLES CHAMPIONSHIPS 1996
Royal Leamington Spa, June

Singles: Margaret Johnston (Ireland) beat Nina Shipperlee (Wales) 25–18
Pairs: Wales beat Scotland 21–18
Triples: England beat Scotland 21–12
Fours: Ireland beat Wales 24–9

Home International Championship 1996: Scotland
Johns Trophy (Inter-County Championship) final 1996: Somerset beat Norfolk 118–81

BOXING

PROFESSIONAL BOXING
as at 1 September 1996

WORLD BOXING COUNCIL (WBC) CHAMPIONS
Heavy: Mike Tyson (USA)
Cruiser: Marcello Dominguez (Argentina)
Light-heavy: Fabrice Tiozzo (France)
Super-middle: Vincenzo Nardiello (Italy)
Middle: Keith Holmes (USA)
Super-welter: Terry Norris (USA)
Welter: Pernell Whitaker (USA)
Super-light: Oscar De La Hoya (USA)
Light: Jean-Baptiste Mendy (France)
Super-feather: Azumah Nelson (Ghana)
Feather: Luisito Espinosa (Philippines)
Super-bantam: Daniel Zaragoza (Mexico)
Bantam: Wayne McCullough (GB)
Super-fly: Hiroshi Kawashima (Japan)
Fly: Yuri Arbachakov (Russia)
Light-fly: Saman Sorjaturong (Thailand)
Straw: Ricardo Lopez (Mexico)

WORLD BOXING ASSOCIATION (WBA) CHAMPIONS
Heavy: Bruce Seldon (USA)
Cruiser: Nate Miller (USA)
Light-heavy: Virgil Hill (USA)
Super-middle: Frank Liles (USA)
Middle: William Joppy (USA)
Junior-middle: Julio Cesar Vasquez (Argentina)
Welter: Ike Quartey (Ghana)
Junior-welter: Frankie Randall (USA)
Light: Olzubek Nazarov (Kyrgyzstan)
Junior-light: vacant
Feather: Wilfredo Vasquez (Puerto Rico)
Junior-feather: Antonio Ceremeno (Venezuela)
Bantam: Nana Konadu (Ghana)
Junior-bantam: Alimi Goitia (Venezuela)
Fly: Saen Sor Ploenchit (Thailand)
Light-fly: Keiji Yamaguchi (Japan)
Straw: Rosendo Alvarez (Nicaragua)

INTERNATIONAL BOXING FEDERATION (IBF) CHAMPIONS
Heavy: Michael Moorer (USA)
Cruiser: vacant
Light-heavy: Henry Maske (Germany)
Super-middle: Roy Jones, jun. (USA)
Middle: Bernard Hopkins (USA)
Super-welter: Terry Norris (USA)
Welter: Felix Trinidad (Puerto Rico)
Super-light: Konstantin Tszyu (Australia)
Light: Philip Holiday (S. Africa)
Super-feather: Arturo Gatti (USA)
Feather: Tom Johnson (USA)
Super-bantam: Vuyani Bungu (S. Africa)
Bantam: Mbulelo Botile (S. Africa)
Super-fly: Harold Grey (Colombia)
Fly: Mark Johnson (USA)
Light-fly: Michael Carbajal (USA)
Straw: Ratanapol Sovorapin (Thailand)

BRITISH CHAMPIONS
Heavy: Scott Welch
Cruiser: Terry Dunstan
Light-heavy: Crawford Ashley
Super-middle: Joe Calzaghe
Middle: Neville Brown
Light-middle: Ensley Bingham
Welter: Kevin Lueshing
Light-welter: Andy Holligan
Light: Michael Ayers
Super-feather: P. J. Gallagher
Feather: Colin McMillan
Super-bantam: Richie Wenton
Bantam: Drew Docherty
Fly: Micky Cantwell

EUROPEAN CHAMPIONS
Heavy: Zeljko Mavrovic (Croatia)
Cruiser: Akim Tafer (France)
Light-heavy: Eddy Smulders (Holland)
Super-middle: Frederic Seillier (France)
Middle: Alexander Zaitsev (Russia)
Light-middle: vacant
Welter: Patrick Charpentier (France)
Light-welter: Soren Sondergaard (Denmark)
Light: Angel Mona (France)
Super-feather: Anatoly Alexandrov (Russia)
Feather: Billy Hardy (GB)
Super-bantam: Salim Nedjkoune (France)
Bantam: Johnny Bredahl (Denmark)
Fly: Jesper Yensen (Denmark)

COMMONWEALTH CHAMPIONS
Heavy: Scott Welch (GB)
Cruiser: Chris Okoh (GB)
Light-heavy: Nicky Piper (GB)
Super-middle: Henry Wharton (GB)
Middle: Robert McCracken (GB)
Light-middle: Steve Foster (GB)
Welter: Andrew Murray (Guyana)
Light-welter: Andy Holligan (GB)
Light: David Tetteh (Ghana)
Super-feather: Justin Juuko (Uganda)
Feather: Billy Hardy (GB)
Super-bantam: Neil Swain (GB)
Bantam: vacant
Fly: Peter Culshaw (GB)

1212   The Year 1995–6

AMATEUR BOXING

AMATEUR BOXING ASSOCIATION (ABA) CHAMPIONSHIP WINNERS 1996

Super-heavy (91+ kg): Danny Watts
Heavy (91 kg): Tony Oakey
Light-heavy (81 kg): Courtney Fry
Middle (75 kg): John Pearce
Light-middle (71 kg): Scott Dann
Welter (67 kg): Jawaid Khaliq
Light-welter (63.5 kg): Carl Wall
Light (60 kg): Kevin Wing
Feather (57 kg): Tony Mulholland
Bantam (54 kg): Lee Eedle
Fly (51 kg): Danny Costello
Light-fly (48 kg): Ray Mercer

CHESS

PCA World Championship 1995: Garry Kasparov (Russia) beat Vishy Anand (India) 10.5–7.5
FIDE World Championship 1996: Anatoly Karpov (Russia) beat Gata Kamsky (USA) 10.5–7.5
Women's World Champion 1996: Zsusza Polgar (Hungary)
British Champion 1996: Christopher Ward
British Women's Champion 1996: Harriet Hunt

CRICKET

TEST SERIES

SOUTH AFRICA V. ENGLAND

First Test (Centurion, 16–20 November 1995): Match drawn. England 381–9 dec. (match curtailed by rain)
Second Test (Johannesburg, 30 November–4 December 1995): Match drawn. South Africa 332 and 346–9 dec.; England 200 and 351–5
Third Test (Durban, 14–18 December 1995): Match drawn. South Africa 225; England 152–5 (match curtailed by rain)
Fourth Test (Port Elizabeth, 26–30 December 1995): Match drawn. South Africa 428 and 162–9 dec.; England 263 and 189–3
Fifth Test (Cape Town, 2–4 January 1996): South Africa won by 10 wickets. England 153 and 157; South Africa 244 and 70–0

ENGLAND V. INDIA

First Test (Edgbaston, 6–8 June 1996): England won by 8 wickets. India 214 and 219; England 313 and 121–2
Second Test (Lord's, 20–24 June 1996): Match drawn. England 344 and 278–9; India 429
Third Test (Trent Bridge, 4–9 July 1996): Match drawn. India 521 and 211; England 564–9

ENGLAND V. PAKISTAN

First Test (Lord's, 25–29 July 1996): Pakistan won by 164 runs. Pakistan 340 and 352–5 dec.; England 285 and 243
Second Test (Headingley, 8–12 August 1996): Match drawn. Pakistan 448 and 242–7 dec.; England 501
Third Test (The Oval, 22–26 August 1996): Pakistan won by 9 wickets. England 326 and 242; Pakistan 521–8 dec. and 48–1

OTHER TEST SERIES

Zimbabwe v. South Africa (October 1995): South Africa won 1–0
India v. New Zealand (October–November 1995): India won 1–0; two matches drawn
Australia v. Pakistan (November–December 1995): Australia won 2–1
New Zealand v. Pakistan (December 1995): Pakistan won 1–0
Australia v. Sri Lanka (December 1995–January 1996): Australia won 3–0
New Zealand v. Zimbabwe (January 1996): Two matches, both drawn
West Indies v. New Zealand (April–May 1996): West Indies won 1–0; one match drawn
Sri Lanka v. Zimbabwe (September 1996): Sri Lanka won 2–0

ONE-DAY INTERNATIONALS

SOUTH AFRICA V. ENGLAND

Cape Town (9 January 1996): South Africa won by 6 runs. South Africa 211–8; England 205
Blomfontein (11 January 1996): England won by 5 wickets. South Africa 262–8; England 265–5
Johannesburg (13 January 1996): South Africa won by 3 wickets. England 198–8; South Africa 199–7
Centurion (14 January 1996): South Africa won by 7 wickets. England 272–8; South Africa 276–3
Durban (17 January 1996): South Africa won by 5 wickets. England 184; South Africa 185–5
East London (19 January 1996): South Africa won by 14 runs. South Africa 129; England 115
Port Elizabeth (21 January 1996): South Africa won by 64 runs. South Africa 218–9; England 154
Rawalpindi (25 February 1996): South Africa won by 78 runs. South Africa 230; England 152

ENGLAND V. INDIA

The Oval (23–24 May 1996): Match abandoned due to rain. England 291–8; India 96–5
Headingley (25 May 1996): England won by 6 wickets. India 158; England 162–4
Old Trafford (26–27 May 1996): England won by 4 wickets. India 236–4; England 239–6

ENGLAND V. PAKISTAN

Old Trafford (29 August 1996): England won by 5 wickets. Pakistan 225–5; England 226–5
Edgbaston (31 August 1996): England won by 107 runs. England 292–8; Pakistan 185
Trent Bridge (1 September 1996): Pakistan won by 2 wickets. England 246; Pakistan 247–8

WORLD CUP 1996

FIRST ROUND

Group A

	P	W	L	NR	Pts
Sri Lanka	5	5	0	0	10
Australia	5	3	2	0	6
India	5	3	2	0	6
West Indies	5	2	3	0	4
Zimbabwe	5	1	4	0	2
Kenya	5	1	4	0	2

Group B

	P	W	L	NR	Pts
South Africa	5	5	0	0	10
Pakistan	5	4	1	0	8
New Zealand	5	3	2	0	6
England	5	2	3	0	4
United Arab Emirates	5	1	4	0	2
Holland	5	0	5	0	0

QUARTER-FINALS

Sri Lanka beat England by 5 wickets. England 235–8; Sri Lanka 236–5

India beat Pakistan by 39 runs. India 287–8; Pakistan 248–9

Australia beat New Zealand by 6 wickets. New Zealand 286–9; Australia 289–4

West Indies beat South Africa by 19 runs. West Indies 264–8; South Africa 245

SEMI-FINALS

Sri Lanka beat India by 131 runs; rioting stopped play. Sri Lanka 251–8; India 120–8

Australia beat West Indies by 5 runs. Australia 207–8; West Indies 202

FINAL

Lahore, 17 March

Sri Lanka beat Australia by 7 wickets. Australia 241–7; Sri Lanka 245–3

OTHER INTERNATIONAL CUPS

World Series Cup final 1996: Australia beat Sri Lanka 2–0

Sharjah Champions Trophy final 1995: Sri Lanka beat West Indies by 50 runs. Sri Lanka 273; West Indies 223

Sharjah Cup final: South Africa beat India by 38 runs. South Africa 287–5; India 249–9

SOUTH AFRICA v. ENGLAND 1995–6 (Test Averages)

SOUTH AFRICA BATTING

	I	NO	R	HS	Av.
D. J. Cullinan	6	0	307	91	51.16
G. Kirsten	7	1	303	110	50.50
B. M. McMillan	6	1	224	100*	44.80
D. J. Richardson	6	1	168	84	33.60
J. N. Rhodes	6	0	165	57	27.50
S. M. Pollock	6	1	133	36*	26.60
A. A. Donald	6	3	68	32	22.66
A. C. Hudson	7	1	124	45	20.66
W. J. Cronje	6	0	113	48	18.83
P. R. Adams	3	1	29	29	14.50
C. R. Matthews	3	0	20	15	6.66
J. H. Kallis	2	0	8	7	4.00

Played in one match: M. W. Pringle, 10,2; C. E. Eksteen, 13,2

*Not out

SOUTH AFRICA BOWLING

	O	M	R	W	Av.
S. M. Pollock	149.5	44	377	16	23.56
A. A. Donald	173.5	45	497	19	26.15
P. R. Adams	107.1	37	231	8	28.87
C. E. Eksteen	63	25	88	3	29.33
B. M. McMillan	111.3	30	247	8	30.87
C. R. Matthews	81	35	165	4	41.25
B. N. Schultz	16	5	47	1	47.00
M. W. Pringle	40	9	98	2	49.00

Also bowled: G. Kirsten, 6–4–2–0; J. H. Kallis, 4–2–2–0; W. J. Cronje, 16–11–16–0

ENGLAND BATTING

	I	NO	R	HS	Av.
M. A. Atherton	8	1	390	185*	55.71
G. A. Hick	8	2	293	141	48.83
R. A. Smith	7	0	254	66	36.28
A. J. Stewart	8	0	235	81	29.37
R. C. Russell	7	2	140	50*	28.00
G. P. Thorpe	8	1	184	59	26.28
R. K. Illingworth	2	0	28	28	14.00
D. G. Cork	6	1	69	23*	13.80
A. R. C. Fraser	4	2	10	5*	5.00
M. R. Ramprakash	3	0	13	9	4.33
P. J. Martin	3	0	13	9	4.33
D. E. Malcolm	3	2	1	1	1.00
D. Gough	2	0	2	2	1.00
M. C. Ilott	1	1	0	0*	–

Played in one match: J. E. R. Gallian, 28,14; M. Watkinson, 11,0

*Not out

ENGLAND BOWLING

	O	M	R	W	Av.
P. J. Martin	105	37	218	11	19.81
R. K. Illingworth	90.5	27	187	9	20.77
D. G. Cork	189.2	48	485	19	25.52
M. Watkinson	19	3	59	2	29.50
D. E. Malcolm	57	13	195	6	32.50
M. C. Ilott	44.4	10	130	4	32.50
A. R. C. Fraser	66	21	187	4	46.75
G. A. Hick	45.4	6	117	1	117.00

Also bowled: J. E. R. Gallian, 2–0–6–0; M. R. Ramprakash, 4–0–19–0; D. Gough, 27–4–112–0

ENGLAND v. INDIA 1996 (Test Averages)

ENGLAND BATTING

	I	NO	R	HS	Av.
N. Hussain	5	1	318	128	79.50
M. A. Atherton	5	1	263	160	65.75
G. P. Thorpe	5	1	193	89	48.25
A. J. Stewart	3	0	136	66	45.33
R. C. Russell	4	0	162	124	40.50
C. C. Lewis	4	1	78	31	26.00
R. C. Irani	3	0	76	41	25.33
M. M. Patel	2	0	45	27	22.50
A. D. Mullally	4	3	15	14*	15.00
D. G. Cork	4	1	37	32*	12.33
G. A. Hick	4	0	35	20	8.75

Played in one match: M. A. Ealham, 51,0; N. V. Knight, 27,14; P. J. Martin, 23,4

* Not out

ENGLAND BOWLING

	O	M	R	W	Av.
M. A. Ealham	43	14	111	6	18.50
C. C. Lewis	131.4	33	356	15	23.73
A. D. Mullally	129	40	298	12	24.83
D. G. Cork	120.4	26	369	10	36.90
R. C. Irani	21	7	74	2	37.00
P. J. Martin	34	10	70	1	70.00
M. M. Patel	46	8	180	1	180.00

Also bowled: G. P. Thorpe, 1–0–3–0; G. A. Hick, 19–6–51–0

INDIA BATTING

	I	NO	R	HS	Av.
S. Ganguly	3	0	315	136	105.00
S. R. Tendulkar	5	0	428	177	85.60
R. S. Dravid	3	0	187	95	62.33
P. L. Mhambrey	3	1	58	28	29.00
S. V. Manjrekar	4	0	105	53	26.25
N. R. Mongia	5	0	107	45	21.40
J. Srinath	5	0	76	52	15.20
V. Rathore	4	0	46	20	11.50
B. K. V. Prasad	5	3	17	13	8.50
M. Azharuddin	5	0	42	16	8.40
A. Kumble	5	0	36	15	7.20
A. D. Jadeja	3	0	16	10	5.33

Played in one match: S. Joshi, 12,12; S. L. V. Raju, 1*,0
* Not out

INDIA BOWLING

	O	M	R	W	Av.
S. Ganguly	37.5	4	125	6	20.83
B. K. V. Prasad	142.3	39	375	15	25.00
J. Srinath	152.1	37	433	11	39.36
A. Kumble	147	36	334	5	66.80
P. L. Mhambrey	43	6	148	2	74.00
S. L. V. Raju	43	12	76	1	76.00

Also bowled: S. R. Tendulkar, 9–1–29–0

ENGLAND v. PAKISTAN 1996 (Test Averages)

ENGLAND BATTING

	I	NO	R	HS	Av.
A. J. Stewart	5	0	396	170	79.20
J. P. Crawley	3	0	178	106	59.33
N. V. Knight	5	0	190	113	38.00
N. Hussain	3	0	111	51	37.00
M. A. Atherton	5	0	162	64	32.40
G. P. Thorpe	5	0	159	77	31.80
R. C. Russell	3	1	51	41*	25.50
I. D. K. Salisbury	4	1	50	40	16.66
D. G. Cork	5	0	58	26	11.60
A. D. Mullally	5	1	39	24	9.75
C. C. Lewis	3	0	18	9	6.00

Played in one match: M. A. Ealham, 25,5; S. J. E. Brown,
10*,1; R. D. B. Croft, 6,5; G. A. Hick, 4,4; A. R. Caddick, 4
* Not out

ENGLAND BOWLING

	O	M	R	W	Av.
M. A. Atherton	7	1	20	1	20.00
A. R. Caddick	57.2	10	165	6	27.50
D. G. Cork	131	23	434	12	36.16
A. D. Mullally	150.3	36	377	10	37.70
G. A. Hick	13	2	42	1	42.00
R. D. B. Croft	47.4	10	125	2	62.50
S. J. E. Brown	33	4	138	2	69.00
M. A. Ealham	37	8	81	1	81.00
I. D. K. Salisbury	61.2	8	221	2	110.50
C. C. Lewis	71	10	264	1	264.00

Also bowled: G. P. Thorpe, 13–4–19–0

PAKISTAN BATTING

	I	NO	R	HS	Av.
Moin Khan	3	1	158	105	79.00
Ijaz Ahmed	6	1	344	141	68.80
Salim Malik	5	2	195	100*	65.00
Inzamam-ul-Haq	5	0	320	148	64.00
Saeed Anwar	6	0	362	176	60.33
Aamir Sohail	3	1	77	46	38.50
Asif Mujtaba	3	0	90	51	30.00
Wasim Akram	5	1	98	40	24.50
Shadab Kabir	4	0	87	35	21.75
Mushtaq Ahmed	5	1	44	20	11.00
Waqar Younis	3	1	11	7	5.50
Ata-ur-Rehman	2	2	10	10*	–

Played in one match: Rashid Latif, 45
* Not out

PAKISTAN BOWLING

	O	M	R	W	Av.
Mushtaq Ahmed	195	52	447	17	26.29
Waqar Younis	125	25	431	16	26.93
Wasim Akram	128	29	350	11	31.81
Ata-ur-Rehman	48.4	6	173	5	34.60
Mohammad Akram	22	4	71	1	71.00

Also bowled: Salim Malik, 1–0–1–0; Asif Mujtaba,
7–5–6–0; Shadab Kabir, 1–0–9–0; Aamir Sohail,
11–3–24–0

COUNTY CHAMPIONSHIP TABLE 1996

Order for 1995 in brackets	P	W	L	D	Bt	Bl	Pts
Leicestershire (7)	17	10	1	6	57	61	296
Derbyshire (14)	17	9	3	5	52	58	269
Surrey (12)	17	8	2	7	49	64	262
Kent (18)	17	9	2	6	47	52	261
Essex (5)	17	8	5	4	58	57	255
Yorkshire (8)	17	8	5	4	50	58	248
Worcestershire (10)	17	6	4	7	45	60	222
Warwickshire (1)	17	7	6	4	39	55	218
Middlesex (2)	17	7	6	4	30	59	213
Glamorgan (16)	17	6	5	6	50	43	207
Somerset (9)	17	5	6	6	38	61	197
Sussex (15)	17	6	9	2	36	58	196
Gloucestershire (6)	17	5	7	5	23	59	177
Hampshire (13)	17	3	7	7	41	56	166
Lancashire (4)	17	2	6	9	49	52	160
Northamptonshire (3)	17	3	8	6	36	57	159
Nottinghamshire (11)	17	1	9	7	42	52	131
Durham (17)	17	0	12	5	22	60	97

FIRST CLASS BATTING AVERAGES 1996

	I	NO	R	HS	Av.
S. Ganguly	14	6	762	136	95.25
Saeed Anwar	19	1	1,224	219*	68.00
G. A. Gooch	30	1	1,944	201	67.03
H. H. Gibbs	14	1	867	183	66.69
A. J. Hollioake	29	6	1,522	129	66.17
Inzamam-ul-Haq	14	2	792	169*	66.00
M. G. Bevan	22	3	1,225	160*	64.47
S. R. Tendulkar	11	0	707	177	64.27
G. P. Thorpe	29	4	1,569	185	62.76
M. P. Maynard	30	4	1,610	214	61.92
S. Lee	25	4	1,300	167*	61.90
S. G. Law	26	1	1,545	172	61.80
M. J. Walker	13	3	606	275*	60.60
K. M. Curran	28	7	1,242	150	59.14
D. N. Crookes	11	1	566	155*	56.60
P. V. Simmons	24	2	1,244	171	56.54
H. Morris	32	2	1,666	202*	55.53
W. S. Kendall	23	4	1,045	145*	55.00
J. J. Whitaker	23	3	1,093	218	54.65
N. H. Fairbrother	20	0	1,068	204	53.40

*Not out

FIRST CLASS BOWLING AVERAGES 1996

	O	M	R	W	Av.
Saqlain Mushtaq	166.5	43	456	29	15.72
C. E. L. Ambrose	284.4	80	717	43	16.67
C. A. Walsh	526.3	145	1,432	85	16.84
P. V. Simmons	364.4	87	1,021	56	18.23
Mushtaq Ahmed	325	85	861	41	21.00
M. A. Ealham	401.4	130	995	47	21.17
Waqar Younis	195.1	42	654	30	21.80
C. A. Connor	362.4	99	1,071	49	21.85
P. C. R. Tufnell	839.1	273	1,712	70	21.94
D. Gough	573.3	142	1,535	67	22.91
J. D. Lewry	302	59	942	41	22.97
D. J. Millns	538.1	133	1,659	72	23.04
G. D. Rose	393.2	98	1,218	50	24.36
M. W. Alleyne	458.1	123	1,316	54	24.37
Wasim Akram	271.5	67	787	32	24.59
M. P. Bicknell	568.1	146	1,633	66	24.74
M. J. McCague	590	120	1,897	76	24.96
E. S. H. Giddins	367.4	66	1,204	48	25.08
A. F. Giles	633.3	191	1,615	64	25.23
L. Klusener	232.2	44	783	31	25.25

Source for averages and county championship table: TCCB/PA Cricket
Record

OTHER RESULTS 1996

Benson and Hedges Cup final: Lancashire beat
Northamptonshire by 31 runs. Lancashire 245–9;
Northamptonshire 214

NatWest Trophy final: Lancashire beat Essex by 129 runs.
Lancashire 186; Essex 57

Sunday League Champions: Surrey

MCC Trophy (Minor Counties knockout final): Cheshire beat
Bedfordshire by 6 wickets. Bedfordshire 253–7;
Cheshire 254–4

Minor Counties Championship final: Devon beat Norfolk by
168 runs. Devon 251–6 dec.; Norfolk 177

National Club Championship final: Walsall beat Chorley by
25 runs. Walsall 152–7; Chorley 127

National Village Championship final: Caldy beat Langleybury
by 6 runs. Caldy 222–5; Langleybury 216

Varsity Match: Cambridge beat Oxford by 103 runs.
Cambridge 321–6; Oxford 218

CYCLING

World Cup series overall winner 1995: Johan Museeuw
(Belgium), 199 points

Tour of Italy 1996: Pavel Tonkov (Russia)

Tour de France 1996: Bjarne Riis (Denmark)

Tour of Spain 1996: Alex Zülle (Switzerland)

World Professional Road Race Championship 1995: Abraham
Olano (Spain)

World Amateur Road Race Championship 1995: Danny
Nelissen (Netherlands)

World Open Cyclo-Cross Championship 1996: Adri van der
Poel (Netherlands)

British Open Road Race Championship 1996: David Rand
(Team Energy)

British Open Cyclo-Cross Championship 1996: Nick Craig
(Diamond Back)

Women's World Road Race Championship 1995: Jeannie Longo
(France)

Women's National Road Race Championship 1996: Maria
Lawrence (Team Ambrosia)

Women's British Open Cyclo-Cross Championship 1996:
Caroline Alexander (BMW/Klein)

EQUESTRIANISM

SHOW JUMPING

World Cup final 1996: Hugo Simon on ET (Austria)

British Jumping Derby 1996 (Hickstead): Nelson Pessoa on
Loro Piana Vivaldi (Brazil)

THREE-DAY EVENTING

Badminton Horse Trials 1996: Mark Todd on Bertie Blunt
(New Zealand)

British Open Horse Trials 1996 (Gatcombe Park): Mary
King on King William (GB)

Burghley Horse Trials 1996: Mary King on Star Appeal (GB)

ETON FIVES

County Championship final 1996: Middlesex beat Kent 3–0

Amateur Championship (Kinnaird Cup) 1996: Edward Wass
and James Halstead beat Robin Mason and Jonathan
Mole 3–0

Holmwoods Schools' Championship 1996: Eton I

Barber Cup final 1996: Old Cholmeleians beat Old
Salopians 3–0

League Championship (Douglas Keeble Cup) 1996: Old
Harrovians

FENCING (MEN)

BRITISH CHAMPIONS 1996

Foil: Harry Lancaster (Sussex House)

Epée: Quentin Berriman (Cardiff)

Sabre: James Williams (Salle Frohlich)

Team Foil: Sussex House

Team Epée: LTFC

International Epée World Cup Series 1996: Jean-François di
Martino (France)

Corble Cup 1996 (international sabre tournament):
Guillaume Galvez (France)

Cole Cup 1996 (international sabre tournament): Kirk
Zavieh (England)

FENCING (WOMEN)

BRITISH CHAMPIONS 1996

Foil: Lucy Harris (Salle Paul)

Epée: Sheila Pearce (Leicester)

Sabre: Sue Benny (Glastonbury)

Team Foil: Salle Paul

Team Epée: Team Eclipse

Ipswich Cup 1996 (international epée world cup series):
Oksana Jermakova (Estonia)

Cole Cup 1996 (international sabre tournament): Sue Benny
(England)

GOLF (MEN)

THE MAJOR CHAMPIONSHIPS 1996

US Masters (Augusta, Georgia, 11–14 April): Nick Faldo
(GB), 276

US Open (Oakland Hills, Detroit, 13–16 June): Steve Jones (USA), 278
The Open (Royal Lytham and St Annes, 18–21 July): Tom Lehman (USA), 271
US PGA Championship (Louisville, Kentucky, 8–11 August): Mark Brooks (USA), 277*

PGA EUROPEAN TOUR 1995
German Masters (Motzener See): Anders Forsbrand (Sweden), 264
World Matchplay Championship (Wentworth): Ernie Els (S. Africa) beat Steve Elkington (Australia) 2 and 1
Volvo Masters (Valderrama): Alexander Cejka (Germany), 282
European Tour Order of Merit 1995: 1. Colin Montgomerie (GB); 2. Sam Torrance (GB); 3. Bernhard Langer (Germany)
World Championship 1995 (Montego Bay): Fred Couples (USA), 279*
World Cup 1995 (Shenzhen): Davis Love III (USA), 267
World Open Championship 1995 (Atlanta, Georgia): Frank Nobilo (New Zealand), 208
World Championship of Golf 1995 (Scottsdale, Arizona): Barry Lane (GB)

PGA EUROPEAN TOUR 1996
Johnnie Walker Classic (Tanah Merah Club, Singapore): Ian Woosnam (GB), 272*
Heineken Classic (Perth): Ian Woosnam (GB), 277
South African PGA Championship (Johannesburg): Sven Strüver (Germany), 202
Players' Championship (Durban): Wayne Westner (S. Africa), 270
Catalan Open (Tarragona): Paul Lawrie (GB), 135
Moroccan Open (Rabat): Peter Hedblom (Sweden), 281
Dubai Desert Classic (Emirates Club): Colin Montgomerie (GB), 270
Portuguese Open (Lisbon): Wayne Riley (Australia), 271
Madeira Island Open (Santo de Serra): Jarmo Sandelin (Sweden), 279
Cannes Open: Raymond Russell (GB), 272
Turespaña Masters (Valencia): Diego Borrego (Spain), 271*
Italian Open (Bergamo): Jim Payne (GB), 275
Spanish Open (Madrid): Padraig Harrington (Ireland), 272
International Open (The Oxfordshire): Stephen Ames (Trinidad and Tobago), 283
PGA Championship (Wentworth): Costantino Rocca (Italy), 274
Open Championship (Hamburg): Frank Nobilo (New Zealand), 270
English Open (Forest of Arden): Robert Allenby (Australia), 278
Northumberland Challenge (Slaley Hall): Retief Goosen (S. Africa), 277
International Open (St Eurach, Germany): Marc Farry (France), 132
French Open (Paris): Robert Allenby (Australia), 272
Irish Open (Druid's Glen): Colin Montgomerie (GB), 279
Scottish Open (Carnoustie): Ian Woosnam (GB), 289
Dutch Open (Hilversum): Mark McNulty (Zimbabwe), 266
Scandinavian Masters (Gothenburg): Lee Westwood (GB), 281*
Austrian Open (Litschau): Paul McGinley (Ireland), 269
Czech Open (Marianske Lazne): Jonathan Lomas (GB), 272
German Open (Stuttgart): Ian Woosnam (GB),193
British Masters (Collingtree): Robert Allenby (Australia), 284*
European Masters (Crans-sur-Sierre): Colin Montgomerie (GB), 260

Lancôme Trophy (Paris): Jesper Parnevik (Sweden), 268
Loch Lomond World Invitational: Thomas Bjorn (Denmark), 277
European Open (K Club, Co. Kildare): Per-Ulrik Johansson (Sweden), 277

MAJOR TEAM EVENTS
Alfred Dunhill Cup final 1995 (St Andrews, 19–22 October): Scotland beat Zimbabwe 2–1
World Cup 1995 (Shenzhen): USA, 543

AMATEUR CHAMPIONSHIPS
British Amateur Championship 1996 (Turnberry): Warren Bladon (Kenilworth)
English Amateur Championship 1996 (Hollinwell): Shaun Webster (Ifield)
Welsh Amateur Championship 1996 (Ashburnham): Yestyn Taylor (Brynhill)
Scottish Amateur Championship 1996 (Dunbar): Michael Brooks (Carluke)
Brabazon Trophy (English Open Strokeplay) 1996 (Royal St George's): Peter Fenton (Huddersfield), 297
Welsh Open Strokeplay 1996 (Tenby): Matthew Blackey (Hayling), 276
Scottish Open Strokeplay 1996 (Cardross and Helensburgh): Alastair Forsyth (Ralston), 279
Lytham Trophy 1996 (Royal Lytham and St Anne's): Matt Carver (West Kent), 284
Berkshire Trophy 1996 (The Berkshire): Gary Wolstenholme (Bristol and Clifton), 274*
International Match 1996 (Sunningdale): France beat England 15–9
Home International Championship 1996 (Moray): England
European Amateur Championship 1996 (Karlstad): Daniel Olsson (Sweden), 276
President's Putter 1996 (Rye): Charlie Rotheroe beat Neil Pabari at 2nd extra hole
Halford Hewitt Trophy 1996 (for public schools' old boys) (Deal): Radley beat Malvern 3–2
Varsity Match 1996 (Royal West Norfolk): Oxford beat Cambridge 8½–6½

* After a play-off

GOLF (WOMEN)

US Women's Open 1996 (Southern Pines, N. Carolina): Annika Sorenstam (Sweden), 272
Women's World Championship 1995 (Cheju Island, S. Korea): Annika Sorenstam (Sweden), 282

WPG EUROPEAN TOUR 1995
French Open (St Endreol): Marie-Laure de Lorenzi (France), 210
Spanish Open (La Manga): Rachel Hetherington (Australia), 202
European Tour Order of Merit 1995: 1. Annika Sorenstam (Sweden); 2. Laura Davies (GB); 3. Karrie Webb (Australia)

WPG EUROPEAN TOUR 1996
Welsh Open (Chepstow): Lisa Hackney (GB), 289
Costa Azul Open (Lisbon): Shani Waugh (Australia), 214
Danish Open (Vejle): Nadene Gole (Australia), 209
Swiss Open (Geneva): Sophie Gustafson (Sweden), 280
Evian Masters: Laura Davies (GB), 274
Austrian Open (Gutenhof): Martina Koch (Germany), 213

Hennessy Cup (Cologne): Helen Alfredsson (Sweden), 280*
Irish Open (Dublin): Alison Nicholas (GB), 277
WPGA Championship (Gleneagles): Tina Fischer
  (Germany), 278
British Open (Woburn): Emilee Klein (USA), 277
Trygg–Hansa Open (Haninge, Sweden): Annika Sorenstam
  (Sweden), 279
Compaq Open (Orebro, Sweden): Federica Dassu (Italy),
  280*
European Open (Ware): Trish Johnson (GB), 274
English Open (The Oxfordshire): Laura Davies (GB), 273
German Open (Hamburg): Joanne Morley (GB), 281

MAJOR TEAM EVENTS

Solheim Cup 1996 (St Pierre, 20–22 September): USA beat
  Europe 17–11
Curtis Cup 1996 (amateur) (Killarney): Great Britain and
  Ireland beat USA $11\frac{1}{2}$–$6\frac{1}{2}$

AMATEUR CHAMPIONSHIPS

British Open Championship 1996 (Royal Liverpool): Kelli
  Kuehne (USA)
English Amateur Championship 1996 (Silloth): Joanne
  Hockley (Felixstowe Ferry)
Welsh Amateur Championship 1996 (Tenby): Lisa Dermott
  (Royal Liverpool)
Scottish Amateur Championship 1996 (Royal Dornoch): Anne
  Laing (Vale of Leven)
British Strokeplay 1996 (Conwy): Christina Kuld
  (Denmark), 289
English Strokeplay 1996 (Little Aston): Sarah Gallagher
  (Trentham Park), 290
Welsh Strokeplay 1996 (Whitchurch, Cardiff): Emma
  Duggleby (Malton and Norton), 223
Scottish Strokeplay 1996 (Royal Troon): Joanne Hockley
  (Felixstowe Ferry), 219
Home International Championship 1996 (Longniddry):
  England
Home International Championship 1995 (Wrexham): England
European Amateur Championship 1996 (Fureso, Denmark):
  S. Cavalleri (Italy), 288
* After a play-off

GREYHOUND RACING

Cesarewitch 1995 (Catford): Ballarue Minx
St Leger 1995 (Wembley): Ken's Dilemma
Oaks 1995 (Wimbledon): Sadler's Return
Grand Prix 1996 (Walthamstow): Suncrest Sail
Television Trophy 1996 (Walthamstow): Suncrest Sail
Grand National 1996 (Hall Green): Dynamic Display
Derby 1996 (Wimbledon): Shanless Slippy
Scurry Gold Cup 1996 (Catford): Come On Royal
The Masters 1996 (Reading): Doyou Getit
The Regency 1996 (Brighton): Restless Lass
Gold Collar 1996 (Catford): Alan's Rose

GYMNASTICS (MEN)

WORLD CHAMPIONSHIPS 1995
Sabae, Japan, October
World Champion: Li Xiaoshuang (China)
Individual Apparatus Champions:
Floor: Vitaly Scherbo (Belarus)
Pommel Horse: Li Donghua (Switzerland)

Rings: Yuri Chechi (Italy)
Vault: = Grigori Misutin (Ukraine) and Alexei Nemov
  (Russia)
Parallel Bars: Vitaly Scherbo (Belarus)
High Bar: Andreas Wecker (Germany)
World Team Champions 1995: China

WORLD CHAMPIONSHIPS 1996
San Juan, Puerto Rico, April

Individual Apparatus Champions:
Floor: Vitaly Scherbo (Belarus)
Pommel Horse: Gil Su Pae (S. Korea)
Rings: Yuri Chechi (Italy)
Vault: Alexei Nemov (Russia)
Parallel Bars: Rustan Sharipov (Ukraine)
High Bar: Jesus Carballo (Spain)

BRITISH CHAMPIONSHIPS 1995
Nottingham, November
British Champion: Marvin Campbell (City of Liverpool)
Individual Apparatus Champions:
Floor: Austin Woods (Gymworld)
Pommel Horse: Dominic Brindle (City of Leeds)
Rings: Lee McDermott (Sutton)
Vault: Craig Heap (North Tyne)
Parallel Bars: Lee Ricketts (unattached)
High Bar: Craig Heap (North Tyne)
British Team Champions 1996 (Adam Shield): City of
  Liverpool

GYMNASTICS (WOMEN)

WORLD CHAMPIONSHIPS 1995
Sabae, Japan, October
World Champion: Lilia Podkopayeva (Ukraine)
Individual Apparatus Champions:
Floor: Gina Gogean (Romania)
Beam: Mo Huilan (China)
Vault: = Lilia Podkopayeva (Ukraine) and Simona
  Amanar (Romania)
Assymetric Bars: Svetlana Chorkina (Russia)
World Team Champions 1995: Romania

WORLD CHAMPIONSHIPS 1996
San Juan, Puerto Rico, April

Individual Apparatus Champions:
Floor: = Gina Gogean (Romania) and Yuan Yuan Kui
  (China)
Beam: Dina Kochetkova (Russia)
Vault: Gina Gogean (Romania)
Assymetric Bars: Svetlana Chorkina (Russia)

World Rhythmics Team Champions 1996: Bulgaria

British Team Champions 1996: Heathrow
British Rhythmics Champion 1996: Alison Deehan (City of
  Coventry)

HOCKEY (MEN)

National League 1996: Cannock
Hockey Association Cup final 1996: Reading 2, Old
  Loughtonians 2. Reading won 3–2 on penalties
National Indoor Club Championship final 1996: Old
  Loughtonians beat Hull 6–5
County Championship final 1996: Surrey beat Lancashire 3–2

European Club Championship final 1996: Uhlenhorst
(Germany) beat Amsterdam (Netherlands) 3-0
European Indoor Club Championship final 1996: Rot-Weiss
Cologne (Germany) beat Bohemians Prague (Czech
Republic) 10-5
European Cup Winners' Cup final 1996: Durkheimer
(Germany) 2, HDM (Netherlands) 2. Durkheimer won
3-2 on penalties
Varsity Match 1996: Oxford beat Cambridge 4-1

HOCKEY (WOMEN)

National League 1996: Hightown
AEWHA Cup final 1996: Ipswich 0, Clifton 0. Ipswich won
3-0 on penalties
National Indoor League 1996: Slough
County Championship final 1996: Surrey 0, Suffolk 0. Surrey
won 4-3 on penalties
European Club Championship final 1996: Slough (England) 2,
SV Kampong (Netherlands) 2. SV Kampong won 3-0
on penalties
European Indoor Club Championship final 1996: Russelsheim
(Germany) beat Berliner (Germany) 7-4
European Cup Winners' Cup final 1996: Hightown (England)
beat Berliner (Germany) 2-1
European Indoor Nations Cup final 1996: England 2, Germany
2. England won 4-3 on penalties

HORSERACING

STATISTICS

WINNING OWNERS 1995

Hamdan Al-Maktoum	£2,586,055
Sheikh Mohammed	1,843,438
Godolphin	963,991
Saeed Maktoum Al-Maktoum	783,260
Maktoum Al-Maktoum	702,755
Khalid Abdulla	610,000
Mollers Racing	436,073
HRH Prince Fahd Salman	435,223
Cheveley Park Stud	412,986
Lord Weinstock and Simon Weinstock	412,686

WINNING TRAINERS 1995

John Dunlop	£2,010,756
Saeed bin Suroor	1,877,486
Michael Stoute	1,354,615
Richard Hannon	1,230,971
Mark Johnston	1,160,614
John Gosden	1,112,911
Barry Hills	994,188
Henry Cecil	973,491
Paul Cole	888,688
Clive Brittain	799,837

LEADING BREEDERS 1995

	Value
Gainsborough Stud Management Ltd	£1,450,528
Shadwell Estate Co. Ltd and Shadwell Farm Inc.	1,405,403
Sheik Mohammed	683,238
Juddmonte Farms	659,552
Ballymacoll Stud Farm Ltd	367,830
Cyril Humphries	316,280
Dene Investments NV	286,595
Lord Victor Matthews	280,668
Cheveley Park Stud Ltd	275,539
Lord Halifax	269,869

WINNING SIRES 1995

	Horses	Races won	Total value
Sadler's Wells (1981) by Northern Dancer	32	45	£920,764
Nijinsky (1967) by Northern Dancer	2	4	799,019
Salse (1985) by Topsider	25	36	738,255
Indian Ridge (1985) by Ahonoore	20	44	598,285
Rainbow Quest (1981) by Blushing Groom	26	35	536,283
Warning (1985) by Known Fact	21	34	536,224
Riverman (1969) by Never Bend	8	10	531,624
Cadeaux Genereux (1985) by Young Generation	31	50	497,755
Night Shift (1980) by Northern Dancer	26	40	494,548
Mtoto (1983) by Busted	15	27	482,660

WINNING FLAT JOCKEYS 1995

	1st	2nd	3rd	Unpl.	Total mts
Frankie Dettori	216	164	139	485	1,004
Kevin Darley	148	125	123	517	913
Jason Weaver	144	135	127	552	958
Willie Carson	139	91	94	391	715
Pat Eddery	125	79	74	368	646
Richard Quinn	111	97	109	520	837
Ray Cochrane	104	100	101	526	831
John Reid	101	96	84	412	693
Kieren Fallon	92	107	91	367	657
Willie Ryan	87	89	68	318	562

WINNING NATIONAL HUNT JOCKEYS 1995-6

	1st	2nd	3rd	Unpl.	Total mts
Tony McCoy	175	131	89	364	759
David Bridgwater	131	95	70	305	601
Richard Dunwoody	101	77	77	237	492
Peter Niven	84	62	37	222	405
Mick Fitzgerald	68	75	62	286	491
Tony Dobbin	67	42	40	178	327
Lorcan Wyer	66	46	43	194	349
Adrian Maguire	61	54	55	140	310
Carl Llewellyn	57	51	42	276	426
Jamie Osborne	53	46	36	178	313
†Richard Johnson	53	61	64	299	477

† Conditional (apprentice) jockey
The above statistics are the copyright of *The Sporting Life*

THE CLASSICS

ONE THOUSAND GUINEAS
(1814) Rowley Mile, Newmarket, for three-year-old fillies

Year	Winner	Betting	Owner	Jockey	Trainer	No. of Runners
1993	Sayyedati	4–1	Mohamed Obaida	W. Swinburn	C. Brittain	12
1994	Las Meninas	12–1	R. Sangster	J. Reid	T. Stack	15
1995	Harayir	5–1	H. Al-Maktoum	R. Hills	R. Hern	14
1996	Bosra Sham	10–11	Wafic Said	P. Eddery	H. Cecil	13

Record time: 1 minute 36.71 seconds, 1994

TWO THOUSAND GUINEAS
(1809) Rowley Mile, Newmarket, for three-year-olds

Year	Winner	Betting	Owner	Jockey	Trainer	No. of Runners
1993	Zafonic	5–6	K. Abdulla	P. Eddery	A. Fabre	14
1994	Mister Baileys	16–1	P. Venner	J. Weaver	M. Johnston	23
1995	Pennekamp	9–2	Sheikh Mohammed	T. Jarnet	A. Fabre	11
1996	Mark of Esteem	8–1	Godolphin	F. Dettori	Saeed bin Suroor	13

Record time: 1 minute 35.08 seconds, 1994

THE DERBY
(1780) Epsom, 1 mile and about 4 f, for three-year-olds

The first winner was Sir Charles Bunbury's Diomed in 1780. The owners with the record number of winners are Lord Egremont, who won in 1782, 1804, 1805, 1807, 1826 (also won five Oaks); and the late Aga Khan, who won in 1930, 1935, 1936, 1948, 1952. Other winning owners are: Duke of Grafton (1802, 1809, 1810, 1815); Mr J. Bowes (1835, 1843, 1852, 1853); Sir J. Hawley (1851, 1858, 1859, 1868); the 1st Duke of Westminster (1880, 1882, 1886, 1899); and Sir Victor Sassoon (1953, 1957, 1958, 1960).

Record times are: 2 min. 32.31 sec. by Lammtarra in 1995; 2 min. 33.80 sec. by Mahmoud in 1936; 2 min. 33.84 sec. by Kahyasi in 1988; 2 min. 33.9 sec. by Reference Point in 1987.

The Derby was run at Newmarket in 1915–18 and 1940–5.

Year	Winner	Betting	Owner	Jockey	Trainer	No. of Runners
1993	Commander In Chief	15–2	K. Abdulla	M. Kinane	H. Cecil	16
1994	Erhaab	7–2	H. Al-Maktoum	W. Carson	J. Dunlop	25
1995	Lammtarra	14–1	S. M. Al-Maktoum	W. Swinburn	Saeed bin Suroor	15
1996	Shaamit	12–1	Khalifa Dasmal	M. Hills	W. Haggas	20

THE OAKS
(1779) Epsom, 1 mile and about 4 f, for three-year-old fillies

Year	Winner	Betting	Owner	Jockey	Trainer	No. of Runners
1993	Intrepidity	5–1	Sheikh Mohammed	M. Roberts	A. Fabre	14
1994	Balanchine	6–1	M. Al-Maktoum	F. Dettori	H. Ibrahim	10
1995	Moonshell	3–1	M. Al-Maktoum/Godolphin	F. Dettori	Saeed bin Suroor	10
1996	Lady Carla	100–30	Wafic Said	P. Eddery	H. Cecil	11

ST LEGER
(1776) Doncaster, 1 mile and about 6 f, for three-year-olds

Year	Winner	Betting	Owner	Jockey	Trainer	No. of Runners
1993	Bob's Return	3–1	Mrs J. Smith	P. Robinson	M. Tompkins	9
1994	Moonax	40–1	Sheikh Mohammed	P. Eddery	B. Hills	8
1995	Classic Cliche	100–30	Godolphin	F. Dettori	Saeed bin Suroor	10
1996	Shantou	8–1	Sheikh Mohammed	F. Dettori	J. Gosden	11

Record time: 3 minutes 1.60 seconds, 1926 and 1934

RESULTS

Cambridgeshire Handicap
(1839) Newmarket, 1 mile

1992 Rambo's Hall (7y), (9st 3lb), D. McKeown
1993 Penny Drops (4y), (7st 13lb), D. Harrison
1994 Halling (3y), (8st 8lb), F. Dettori
1995 Cap Juluca (3y), (9st 10lb), R. Hughes

Prix de L'Arc de Triomphe
(1920) Longchamp, 1½ miles

1992 Subotica (4y), (9st 4lb), T. Jarnet
1993 Urban Sea (4y), (9st 1lb), E. Saint-Martin
1994 Carnegie (3y), (8st 11lb), T. Jarnet
1995 Lammtarra (3y), (8st 11lb), F. Dettori

Cesarewitch
(1839) Newmarket, 2 miles and about 2 f

1992 Vintage Crop (5y), (9st 6lb), W. Swinburn
1993 Aahsaylad (7y), (8st 12lb), J. Williams
1994 Captain's Guest (4y), (9st 9lb), A. Clark
1995 Old Red (5y) (7st 11lb), L. Charnock

Champion Stakes
(1877) Newmarket, 1 mile, 2 f

1992 Rodrigo de Triano (3y), (8st 12lb), L. Piggott
1993 Hatoof (4y), (9st), W. Swinburn
1994 Dernier Empereur (4y), (9st 4lb), S. Guillot
1995 Spectrum (3y), (8st 10lb), J. Reid

*Hennessy Gold Cup
(1957) Newbury, 3 miles and about 2½ f

1992 Sibton Abbey (7y), (10st), A. Maguire
1993 Cogent (9y), (10st 8lb), D. Fortt
1994 One Man (6y), (10st), A. Dobbin
1995 Couldn't Be Better (8y), (10st 8lb), D. Gallagher

*King George VI Chase
(1937) Kempton, about 3 miles

1992 The Fellow (7y), (11st 10lb), A. Kondrat
1993 Barton Bank (7y), (11st 10lb), A. Maguire
1994 Algan (6y), (11st 10lb), P. Chevalier
†1995 One Man (8y), (11st 10lb), R. Dunwoody

*Champion Hurdle
(1927) Cheltenham, 2 miles and about ½ f

1993 Granville Again (7y), (12st), P. Scudamore
1994 Flakey Dove (8y), (11st 9lb), M. Dwyer
1995 Alderbrook (6y), (12st), N. Williamson
1996 Collier Bay (6y), (12st), G. Bradley

*Queen Mother Champion Chase
(1959) Cheltenham, about 2 miles

1993 Deep Sensation (8y), (12st), D. Murphy
1994 Viking Flagship (7y), (12st), A. Maguire
1995 Viking Flagship (8y), (12st), C. Swan
1996 Klairon Davis (7y), (12st), F. Woods

*Cheltenham Gold Cup
(1924) 3 miles and about 2½ f

1993 Jodami (8y), (12st), M. Dwyer
1994 The Fellow (9y), (12st), A. Kondrat
1995 Master Oats (9y), (12st), N. Williamson
1996 Imperial Call (7y), (12st), C. O'Dwyer

Lincoln Handicap
(1965) Doncaster, 1 mile

1993 High Premium (5y), (8st 8lb), K. Fallon
1994 Our Rita (5y), (8st 5lb), D. Holland
1995 Roving Minstrel (4y), (8st 3lb), K. Darley
1996 Stone Ridge (4y), (8st 12lb), D. O'Neill

*Grand National
(1837) Liverpool, 4 miles and about 4 f

1993 Race declared void. Esha Ness (J. White) first past post
1994 Miinnehoma (11y), (10st 8lb), R. Dunwoody
1995 Royal Athlete (9y), (11st 10lb), J. Titley
1996 Rough Quest (10y), (10st 7lb), M. Fitzgerald

Record times: 8 minutes 47.8 seconds by Mr Frisk in 1990; 9 minutes 1.9 seconds by Red Rum in 1973

*Whitbread Gold Cup
(1957) Sandown, 3 miles and about 5 f

1993 Topsham Bay (10y), (10st), R. Dunwoody
1994 Ushers Island (8y), (10st), C. Swan
1995 Cache Fleur (9y), (9st 10lb), R. Dunwoody
1996 Life of A Lord (10y), (11st 10lb), C. Swan

Jockey Club Stakes
(1894) Newmarket, 1½ miles

1993 Zinaad (4y), (8st 9lb), W. Swinburn
1994 Silver Wisp (5y), (8st 9lb), M. Hills
1995 Only Royale (6y), (8st 11lb), F. Dettori
1996 Riyadian (4y), (8st 9lb), T. Quinn

Kentucky Derby
(1875) Louisville, Kentucky, 1½ miles

1993 Sea Hero, J. Bailey
1994 Go for Gin, C. McCarron
1995 Thunder Gulch, G. Stevens
1996 Grindstone, J. Bailey

Prix du Jockey Club
(1836) Chantilly, 1½ miles

1993 Hernando (9st 2lb), C. Asmussen
1994 Celtic Arms (9st 2lb), G. Mossé
1995 Celtic Swing (9st 2lb), K. Darley
1996 Ragmar (9st 2lb), G. Mossé

Ascot Gold Cup
(1807) Ascot, 2 miles and about 4 f

1993 Drum Taps (7y), (9st 2lb), F. Dettori
1994 Arcadian Heights (6y), (9st 2lb), M. Hills
1995 Double Trigger (4y), (9st), J. Weaver
1996 Classic Cliché (4y), (9st), M. Kinane

Irish Sweeps Derby
(1866) Curragh, 1½ miles, for three year olds

1993 Commander In Chief (9st), P. Eddery
1994 Balanchine (8st 11lb), F. Dettori
1995 Winged Love (9st), O. Peslier
1996 Zagreb (9st), P. Shanahan

Eclipse Stakes
(1886) Sandown, 1 mile and about 2 f

1993 Opera House (5y), (9st 7lb), M. Kinane
1994 Ezzoud (5y), (9st 7lb), W. Swinburn
1995 Halling (4y), (9st 7lb), W. Swinburn
1996 Halling (5y), (9st 7lb), J. Reid

King George VI and Queen Elizabeth Diamond Stakes
(1952) Ascot, 1 mile and about 4 f

1993 Opera House (5y), (9st 7lb), M. Stoute
1994 King's Theatre (3y), (8st 9lb), M. Kinane
1995 Lammtarra (3y), (8st 9lb), F. Dettori
1996 Pentire (4y), (9st 7lb), M. Hills

*National Hunt
†Run on 6 January 1996 because of bad weather

GOODWOOD CUP
(1812) Goodwood, about 2 miles

1993   Sonus (4y), (9st 3lb), P. Eddery
1994   Tioman Island (4y), (9st 5lb), T. Quinn
1995   Double Trigger (4y), (9st 5lb), J. Weaver
1996   Grey Shot (4y), (9st), P. Eddery

ICE HOCKEY

World Championship final 1996: Czech Republic beat
  Canada 4–2
British Championship final 1996: Sheffield Steelers 3,
  Nottingham Panthers 3 a.e.t. Sheffield Steelers won 2–1
  on penalties
League Championship 1996, Premier Division: Sheffield
  Steelers
Benson and Hedges Cup final 1995: Sheffield Steelers beat
  Nottingham Panthers 5–2
Stanley Cup final 1996: Colorado Avalanche beat Florida
  Panthers 4–0

ICE SKATING

BRITISH CHAMPIONSHIPS 1995
Basingstoke, November

Men: Steven Cousins
Women: Stephanie Main
Pairs: Marika Humphreys and Philip Askew
Ice Dance: Lesley Rogers and Michael Aldred

EUROPEAN CHAMPIONSHIPS 1996
Sofia, January

Men: Viacheslav Zagarodniuk (Ukraine)
Women: Irina Slutskaya (Russia)
Pairs: Oksana Kazakova and Artur Dmitriev (Russia)
Ice Dance: Oksana Gritschuk and Evgeny Platov (Russia)

WORLD CHAMPIONSHIPS 1996
Edmonton, March

Men: Todd Eldredge (USA)
Women: Michelle Kwan (USA)
Pairs: Marina Eltsova and Andrei Bushkov (Russia)
Ice Dance: Oksana Gritschuk and Evgeny Platov (Russia)

JUDO

BRITISH NATIONAL CHAMPIONSHIPS 1995
Bangor, Co. Down, December

MEN

Heavyweight (over 95 kg): Nick Kokotaylo
Light-heavyweight (95 kg): Keith Davies
Middleweight (86 kg): Gary Edwards
Light-middleweight (78 kg): Chris Johnson
Lightweight (71 kg): Paul Leishman
Featherweight (65 kg): Jean-Paul Bell
Bantamweight (60 kg): John Buchanan

WOMEN

Heavyweight (over 72 kg): Jane Morris
Light-heavyweight (72 kg): Joanne Melen
Middleweight (66 kg): Karen Powell
Light-middleweight (61 kg): Cheryl Peel
Lightweight (56 kg): Ceri Richards

Featherweight (52 kg): Debbie Allan
Bantamweight (48 kg): Kim Dunkley

LAWN TENNIS

MAJOR CHAMPIONSHIPS 1996

AUSTRALIAN OPEN CHAMPIONSHIPS
Melbourne, 15–28 January

Men's Singles: Boris Becker (Germany) beat Michael
  Chang (USA) 6–2, 6–4, 2–6, 6–2
Women's Singles: Monica Seles (USA) beat Anke Huber
  (Germany) 6–4, 6–1
Men's Doubles: Stefan Edberg (Sweden) and Petr Korda
  (Czech Republic) beat Sebastian Lareau (Canada) and
  Alex O'Brien (USA) 7–5, 7–5, 4–6, 6–1
Women's Doubles: Chanda Rubin (USA) and Arantxa
  Sánchez Vicario (Spain) beat Lindsay Davenport and
  Mary Joe Fernandez (USA) 7–5, 2–6, 6–4
Mixed Doubles: Larissa Neiland (Latvia) and Mark
  Woodforde (Australia) beat Nicole Arendt and Luke
  Jensen (USA) 4–6, 7–5, 6–0

FRENCH OPEN CHAMPIONSHIPS
Paris, 27 May–9 June

Men's Singles: Yevgeny Kafelnikov (Russia) beat Michael
  Stich (Germany) 7–6, 7–5, 7–6
Women's Singles: Steffi Graf (Germany) beat Arantxa
  Sánchez Vicario (Spain) 6–3, 6–7, 10–8
Men's Doubles: Yevgeny Kafelnikov (Russia) and Daniel
  Vacek (Czech Republic) beat Guy Forget (France) and
  Jakob Hlasek (Switzerland) 6–2, 6–3
Women's Doubles: Lindsay Davenport and Mary Joe
  Fernandez (USA) beat Gigi Fernandez (USA) and
  Natasha Zvereva (Belarus) 6–2, 6–1
Mixed Doubles: Patricia Tarabini and Javier Frana
  (Argentina) beat Nicole Arendt (USA) and Luke Jensen
  (USA) 6–2, 6–2

ALL-ENGLAND CHAMPIONSHIPS
Wimbledon, 24 June–8 July

Men's Singles: Richard Krajicek (Netherlands) beat
  MaliVai Washington (USA) 6–3, 6–4, 6–3
Women's Singles: Steffi Graf (Germany) beat Arantxa
  Sánchez Vicario (Spain) 6–3, 7–5
Men's Doubles: Todd Woodbridge and Mark Woodforde
  (Australia) beat Grant Connell (Canada) and Byron
  Black (Zimbabwe) 4–6, 6–1, 6–3, 6–3
Women's Doubles: Martina Hingis (Switzerland) and Helena
  Sukova (Czech Republic) beat Meredith McGrath
  (USA) and Larissa Neiland (Latvia) 5–7, 7–5, 6–1
Mixed Doubles: Helena Sukova and Cyril Suk (Czech
  Republic) beat Larissa Neiland (Latvia) and Mark
  Woodforde (Australia) 1–6, 6–3, 6–2

US OPEN CHAMPIONSHIPS
New York, 26 August–8 September

Men's Singles: Pete Sampras (USA) beat Michael Chang
  (USA) 6–1, 6–4, 7–6
Women's Singles: Steffi Graf (Germany) beat Monica Seles
  (USA) 7–5, 6–4
Men's Doubles: Todd Woodbridge and Mark Woodforde
  (Australia) beat Jacco Eltingh and Paul Haarhuis
  (Netherlands) 4–6, 7–6, 7–6
Women's Doubles: Gigi Fernandez (USA) and Natasha
  Zvereva (Belarus) beat Jana Novotna (Czech Republic)
  and Arantxa Sánchez Vicario (Spain) 1–6, 6–4, 6–4

Mixed Doubles: Lisa Raymond and Patrick Galbraith (USA) beat Manon Bollegraf (Netherlands) and Rick Leach (USA) 7–6, 7–6

Grand Slam Cup 1995: Goran Ivanisevic (Croatia) beat Todd Martin (USA) 7–6, 6–3, 6–4

TEAM CHAMPIONSHIPS
Davis Cup final 1995: USA beat Russia 3–2
Fed Cup final 1995: Spain beat USA 3–2
Fed Cup final 1996: USA beat Spain 5–0
LTA County Cup 1996:
Men: Surrey
Women: Essex

NATIONAL CHAMPIONSHIPS 1995
Telford, October–November

Men's Singles: Tim Henman beat Greg Rusedski 1–6, 6–3, 6–2

Women's Singles: Clare Wood beat Sam Smith 6–2, 6–2

Men's Doubles: Jeremy Bates and Tim Henman beat Miles Maclagan and Andrew Richardson 6–3, 1–6, 13–11

Women's Doubles: Shirli–Ann Siddall and Amanda Wainwright beat Julie Pullin and Lorna Woodroffe 6–4, 6–2

MOTOR CYCLING

---

500 cc GRAND PRIX 1995
Catalonian: Alex Criville (Spain), Honda
Riders' Championship 1995: 1. Michael Doohan (Australia), Honda, 248 points; 2. Daryl Beattie (Australia), Suzuki, 215 points; 3. Luca Cadalora (Italy), Yamaha, 176 points

500 cc GRAND PRIX 1996
Malaysian (Kuala Lumpur): Luca Cadalora (Italy), Honda
Indonesian (Jakarta): Michael Doohan (Australia), Honda
Japanese (Suzuka): Norifumi Abe (Japan), Yamaha
Spanish (Jerez): Michael Doohan (Australia), Honda
Italian (Mugello): Michael Doohan (Australia), Honda
French (Le Castellet): Michael Doohan (Australia), Honda
Dutch (Assen): Michael Doohan (Australia), Honda
German (Nurburgring): Luca Cadalora (Italy), Honda
British (Donington Park): Michael Doohan (Australia), Honda
Austrian (Zeltweg): Alex Criville (Spain), Honda
Czech (Brno): Alex Criville (Spain), Honda
San Marino (Imola): Michael Doohan (Australia), Honda
Catalonian: Carlos Checa (Spain), Honda

Senior Manx Grand Prix 1996: Ricky Mitchell (Honda)
Senior TT 1996, Isle of Man: Phillip McCallen (Honda)
Junior TT 1996, Isle of Man: Phillip McCallen (Honda)

MOTOR RACING

FORMULA ONE GRAND PRIX 1995
Pacific (Aida, Japan): Michael Schumacher (Germany), Benetton-Renault
Japanese (Suzuka): Michael Schumacher (Germany), Benetton-Renault
Australian (Adelaide): Damon Hill (GB), Williams-Renault

Drivers' World Championship 1995: 1. Michael Schumacher (Germany), Benetton-Renault, 102 points; 2. Damon Hill (GB), Williams-Renault, 69 points; 3. David Coulthard (GB), Williams-Renault, 49 points

Constructors' World Championship 1995: 1. Benetton-Renault, 137 points; 2. Williams-Renault, 112 points; 3. Ferrari, 73 points

FORMULA ONE GRAND PRIX 1996
Australian (Melbourne): Damon Hill (GB), Williams-Renault
Brazilian (São Paulo): Damon Hill (GB), Williams-Renault
Argentine (Buenos Aires): Damon Hill (GB), Williams-Renault
European (Nurburgring): Jacques Villeneuve (Canada), Williams-Renault
San Marino (Imola): Damon Hill (GB), Williams-Renault
Monaco (Monte Carlo): Olivier Panis (France), Ligier-Mugen Honda
Spanish (Barcelona): Michael Schumacher (Germany), Ferrari
Canadian (Montreal): Damon Hill (GB), Williams-Renault
French (Magny-Cours): Damon Hill (GB), Williams-Renault
British (Silverstone): Jacques Villeneuve (Canada), Williams-Renault
German (Hockenheim): Damon Hill (GB), Williams-Renault
Hungarian (Budapest): Jacques Villeneuve (Canada), Williams-Renault
Belgian (Spa-Francorchamps): Michael Schumacher (Germany), Ferrari
Italian (Monza): Michael Schumacher (Germany), Ferrari
Portuguese (Estoril): Jacques Villeneuve (Canada), Williams-Renault

Indianapolis 500 1996: Buddy Lazier (USA), Reynard-Ford
Le Mans 24-hour Race 1996: Manuel Reuter (Germany), Alexander Würz (Austria) and Davy Jones (USA), TWR Porsche

---

MOTOR RALLYING

1995
Hong Kong–Beijing Rally: Kenneth Eriksson (Sweden), Mitsubishi Lancer
Catalonia Rally: Carlos Sainz (Spain), Subaru Impreza
RAC Rally: Colin McRae (GB), Subaru Impreza
Drivers' World Championship 1995: Colin McRae (GB), Subaru Impreza, 90 points
Manufacturers' World Championship 1995: Subaru, 350 points

Rally of Thailand: Tommi Makinen (Finland), Mitsubishi Lancer

1996
Granada–Dakar Rally: Pierre Lartigue (France), Citroen
Swedish Rally: Tommi Makinen (Finland), Mitsubishi Lancer
Safari Rally: Tommi Makinen (Finland), Mitsubishi Lancer
Indonesian Rally: Carlos Sainz (Spain), Ford Escort
Acropolis Rally: Colin McRae (GB), Subaru Impreza
Argentine Rally: Tommi Makinen (Finland), Mitsubishi Lancer
New Zealand Rally: Richard Burns (GB), Mitsubishi Lancer

1,000 Lakes Rally (Jyvaskyla, Finland): Tommi Makinen (Finland), Mitsubishi Lancer
Australian Rally: Tommi Makinen (Finland), Mitsubishi Lancer

Monte Carlo Rally: Patrick Bernardini (France), Ford Escort
Rally of Thailand: Colin McRae (GB), Subaru Impreza

NETBALL

TEST MATCHES

1995
4 Nov	Wembley Arena	England 52, Cook Islands 44
8 Nov	Gateshead	England 42, Cook Islands 50
9 Nov	Cleveland	Wales 24, Cook Islands 53
11 Nov	Manchester	England 51, Cook Islands 48

INTERNATIONALS

1996
27 Jan	Dublin	Rep. of Ireland 30, Wales 57
	Cardiff	Wales 44, N. Ireland 48
24 Feb	Portsmouth	England 50, N. Ireland 40
23 Mar	Bedford	England 50, Wales 32
	Belfast	N. Ireland 76, Rep. of Ireland 33

Inter-County Championship final 1996: Essex Metropolitan beat Middlesex 13–10
National Clubs Championship final 1996: Floaters (Essex) beat Falcons (Notts) 79–58
English Counties League Championship 1996: Essex Metropolitan
National Clubs League Championship 1996: Linden

POLO

Prince of Wales's Trophy final 1996: Alcatel beat Les Lions 9–8
Queen's Cup final 1996: Ellerston White beat Alcatel 8–6
Warwickshire Cup final 1996: Ellerston White beat Black Bears 9–8
Gold Cup (British Open) final 1996: CS Brooks beat Ellerston White 14–13
Coronation Cup 1996: England beat Brazil 8–4
Prince Philip Trophy 1996: Ellerston White beat CS Brooks 11–10
Varsity Match 1996: Cambridge beat Oxford 7–2

RACKETS

World Singles Challenge 1995: James Male (GB) beat Neil Smith (GB) 6–2
World Doubles Challenge 1996: Neil Smith and Shannon Hazell (GB) beat James Male and John Prenn (GB) 5–0
Professional Singles Championship final 1996: Neil Smith beat David Makey 3–0
British Open Singles Championship final 1996: James Male (GB) beat Neil Smith (GB) 4–0
British Open Doubles Championship final 1996: Willie Boone and Tim Cockroft (GB) beat James Male and John Prenn (GB) (scratched), walkover
Amateur Singles Championship final 1995: James Male beat Willie Boone 3–0

Amateur Doubles Championship final 1996: Willie Boone and Tim Cockroft beat James Male and John Prenn 4–1
National League 1996: Old Wellingtonians
Noel Bruce Cup final 1995 (public schools' old boys' doubles championship): Radley (James Male and Julian Snow) beat Eton (Willie Boone and Mark Hue Williams) 4–2
Public Schools' Singles Championship final 1995: Neil Bailey (Eton) beat Guy Smith-Bingham (Eton) 3–1
Public Schools' Doubles Championship final 1996: Eton (Neil Bailey and Patrick Wigan) beat Winchester (Edward Craig and Harry Lloyd Owen) 4–0
Varsity Match 1996: Oxford beat Cambridge 3–0

REAL TENNIS

World Singles Challenge 1996: Robert Fahey (Australia) beat Wayne Davies (Australia) 7–1
Professional Singles Championship final 1996: Wayne Davies (Australia) beat Paul Tabley (Australia) 3–0
Professional Doubles Championship final 1996: Chris Bray and Mike Gooding (GB) beat Nick Wood and Adam Phillips (GB) 3–1
British Open Singles Championship final 1995: Robert Fahey (Australia) beat Lachie Deuchar (Australia) 3–0
British Open Doubles Championship final 1995: Robert Fahey and Frank Filippelli (Australia) beat Chris Bray and Mike Gooding (GB) 3–2
Amateur Singles Championship final 1996: Julian Snow (GB) beat Mark Howard (GB) 3–0
Amateur Doubles Championship final 1996: Julian Snow (GB) and Sam Howe (USA) beat Nigel Pendrigh and James Acheson-Gray (GB) 3–1
Henry Leaf Cup final 1996 (public schools' old boys' doubles championship): Haileybury I (Ruaraidh Gunn and William Hollington) beat Charterhouse I (Nigel Pendrigh and Alex Roberts-Miller) 2–0
Varsity Match 1996: Oxford beat Cambridge 5–1
Women's British Open Singles Championship final 1996: Penny Lumley (GB) beat Alex Garside (GB) 2–0
Women's British Open Doubles Championship final 1995: Penny Lumley and Sue Haswell (GB) beat Alex Garside and Sally Jones (GB) 2–1

ROAD WALKING

BAF MEN'S 20 KM WALK
Cardiff, 21 April 1996
Individual: Darrell Stone (Steyning), 1 hr. 26 min. 44 sec.
Team: Manx Harriers, 25 points

BAF WOMEN'S 10 KM WALK
Cardiff, 21 April 1996
Individual: Vicky Lupton (Sheffield), 47 min. 48 sec.
Team: Sheffield, 18 points

MEN'S NATIONAL 20 MILES WALK
Bolton, 6 July 1996
Individual: Chris Cheeseman (Surrey), 2 hr. 35 min. 15 sec.
Team: Coventry, 13 points

WOMEN'S NATIONAL 5,000 METRES WALK
Bolton, 6 July 1996
Individual: Vicky Lupton (Sheffield), 23 min. 05 sec.
Team: Sheffield, 14 points

MEN'S NATIONAL 50 KM WALK
Horsham, 7 September 1996
Individual: Chris Cheeseman (Surrey), 4 hr. 22 min. 12 sec.
Team: York, 21 points

WOMEN'S NATIONAL 20 KM WALK
Horsham, 7 September 1996
Individual: Vicky Lupton (Sheffield), 1 hr. 46 min. 43 sec.
Team: Sheffield, 10 points

ROWING

WORLD CHAMPIONSHIPS 1996
Strathclyde, August

MEN

Coxed pairs: France
Coxed fours: Romania

WOMEN

Coxless fours: USA

For the remaining senior heavyweight events, *see*
Olympic Games results, pages 1229–30

NATIONAL CHAMPIONSHIPS 1996
Holme Pierrepont, July

MEN

Coxed pairs: Oxford University/University of London
Coxless pairs: Imperial College/Queen's Tower
Coxed fours: Nottinghamshire County
Coxless fours: Nottinghamshire County B
Single sculls: Simon Goodbrand (Rob Roy)
Double sculls: Hexham/Glasgow
Quad sculls: London/University of London/Walton
Eights: London/Notts County

WOMEN

Coxless pairs: Kingston/Thames
Coxed fours: University of London
Coxless fours: Bedford/Kingston/University of London/
Staines
Single sculls: Rachel Kinninmonth (Thames)
Double sculls: Henley/Tideway Scullers' School
Quad sculls: Tideway Scullers' School
Eights: Bedford/Kingston/University of London/Staines/
Thames Tradesmen

THE 142nd UNIVERSITY BOAT RACE
Putney–Mortlake, 4 miles 1 f, 180 yd, 6 April 1996

Cambridge beat Oxford by 2¾ lengths; 16 min. 58 sec.
Cambridge have won 72 times, Oxford 68 and there has
been one dead heat. The record time is 16 min. 45 sec.,
rowed by Oxford in 1984

WOMEN'S BOAT RACE 1996 (Henley): Cambridge beat
Oxford by 4 lengths; 6 min. 12 sec.

HENLEY ROYAL REGATTA 1996

Grand Challenge Cup: Imperial College, London/Queen's
Tower beat Skadi/Argo (Holland) by 2 lengths
Ladies' Challenge Plate: Goldie beat Leander by 3½ lengths
Thames Challenge Cup: Neptune (Ireland) beat Wallingford
by ¾ length
Temple Challenge Cup: Yale University (USA) beat Imperial
College, London A by 1¾ lengths

Princess Elizabeth Challenge Cup: Brentwood College School
(Canada) beat St Edward's School easily
Stewards' Challenge Cup: Nottinghamshire County/London
beat Goldie by 4 lengths
Prince Philip Challenge Cup: Berlin (Germany) beat
Potomac/Arco Training Center (USA) by ¾ length
Queen Mother Challenge Cup: Mainz/Neuss (Germany) beat
Ratzeberger (Germany) by ¾ length
Visitors' Challenge Cup: Argo (Netherlands) beat Isis by ½
length
Wyfold Challenge Cup: Queen's Tower beat Molesey A by ¾
length
Britannia Challenge Cup: Oxford Brookes University beat
University of London by ¾ length
Fawley Challenge Cup: Windsor Boys' School/Poplar,
Blackwall and District beat Marlow/Nottinghamshire
County by 4½ lengths
Silver Goblets and Nickalls' Challenge Cup: Andreas Nader and
Hermann Bauer (Wiking Linz, Austria) beat B. Schmidt
and C. Codoni (Seeclub Zürich, Switzerland) by 4½
lengths
Double Sculls Challenge Cup: Greg Walker and Greg Lewis
(Potomac/National Training Center, USA) beat
Günter Schneider and Jürg Habermayr (Thalwil/
Thun, Switzerland) by 3 lengths
Diamond Challenge Sculls: Merlin Vervoorn (Proteus-
Eretes, Netherlands) beat A. Bihrer (Grasshopper Club
Zürich, Switzerland) by 1½ lengths
Women's Single Sculls: Maria Brandin (Kungälvs, Sweden)
beat C. Lüthi (Reuss Lucerne, Switzerland) by 4¾
lengths

OTHER ROWING EVENTS

Oxford Torpids 1996: Men, Oriel; *Women,* Osler Green
Cambridge Lents 1996: Men, Downing; *Women,* Trinity Hall
Oxford Summer Eights 1996: Men, Oriel; *Women,* Osler Green
Cambridge Mays 1996: Men, Downing; *Women,* Emmanuel
Head of the River 1996: Men, Leander I; *Women,* Kingston/
Thames/Tideway Scullers/Marlow
Doggett's Coat and Badge 1996: Robert Coleman (Poplar,
Blackwall and District)
Wingfield Sculls 1996: Peter Haining (Auriol Kensington)
Thames World Sculling Challenge 1995: Peter Haining (GB)

RUGBY FIVES

National Singles Championship final 1995: Wayne Enstone
beat Neil Roberts 15–8, 15–9
National Doubles Championship final 1996: Wayne Enstone
and Neil Roberts beat David Hebden and Ian Fuller
15–11, 15–12
National Club Championship final 1996: Manchester YMCA
beat RFA Club 90–72
National Schools' Singles Championship final 1996: Adam
Strang (Merchiston Castle) beat John Welch (St
Dunstan's) 11–7, 11–5
National Schools' Doubles Championship final 1996: Sedbergh
(James Lofthouse and Ian McKerrow) beat Bradfield
(Patrick Lord and Jeremy Sinton) 11–7, 11–7
Varsity Match 1996: Oxford beat Cambridge 292–152

RUGBY LEAGUE

WORLD CUP 1995
7–28 October

FIRST ROUND

Group 1: England, 6 points; Australia, 4 points; Fiji, 2 points; S. Africa, 0 points

Group 2: New Zealand, 4 points; Papua New Guinea, 1 point; Tonga, 1 point

Group 3: Wales, 4 points; W. Samoa, 2 points; France, 0 points

SEMI-FINALS

England 25, Wales 10; Australia 30, New Zealand 20 a.e.t.

FINAL

Wembley, 28 October

England 8, Australia 16

INTERNATIONAL MATCHES 1996

5 June	Carcassonne	France 14, Wales 34
12 June	Gateshead	England 73, France 6
26 June	Cardiff	Wales 12, England 26

TEST MATCH

| 28 Sept | Lae | Papua New Guinea 30, Great Britain 32 |

OTHER COMPETITIONS

Challenge Cup final 1996 (Wembley, 27 April): St Helens beat Bradford Bulls 40–32

Regal Trophy final 1996 (Huddersfield, 13 January): Wigan beat St Helens 25–16

Premiership Trophy final 1996 (Old Trafford, 8 September): Wigan beat St Helens 44–14

Divisional Premiership final 1996: Salford beat Keighley 19–6

Stones Super League (inaugural)1996: St Helens, 40 points

League Division 1 Championship (inaugural)1996: Salford, 36 points

League Division 2 Championship (inaugural)1996: Hull Kingston Rovers, 42 points

Stones Bitter Championship 1996: Wigan, 36 points

Stones Bitter Division 1 Championship 1996: Salford, 35 points

Stones Bitter Division 2 Championship 1996: Hull Kingston Rovers, 36 points

Varsity Match 1996: Cambridge beat Oxford 42–18

AMATEUR RUGBY LEAGUE 1995–6

County Championship: Cumbria

National Inter-League Open Age Shield Competition: Allerdale

National Cup Open Age Competition: Skirlaugh

National League Premier Division Champions: Woolston

RUGBY UNION

FIVE NATIONS' CHAMPIONSHIP 1996

20 Jan	Paris	France 15, England 12
	Dublin	Ireland 10, Scotland 16
3 Feb	Twickenham	England 21, Wales 15
	Murrayfield	Scotland 19, France 14
17 Feb	Cardiff	Wales 14, Scotland 16
	Paris	France 45, Ireland 10
2 Mar	Murrayfield	Scotland 9, England 18
	Dublin	Ireland 30, Wales 17
16 Mar	Twickenham	England 28, Ireland 15
	Cardiff	Wales 16, France 15

	P	W	D	L	Points		Total
					F	A	
England	4	3	0	1	79	54	6
Scotland	4	3	0	1	60	56	6
France	4	2	0	2	89	57	4
Wales	4	1	0	3	62	82	2
Ireland	4	1	0	3	65	106	2

OTHER INTERNATIONALS

1995

11 Nov	Cardiff	Wales 19, Fiji 15
18 Nov	Twickenham	England 14, S. Africa 24
	Murrayfield	Scotland 15, W. Samoa 15
	Dublin	Ireland 44, Fiji 8
16 Dec	Twickenham	England 27, W. Samoa 9

1996

6 Jan	Atlanta	USA 18, Ireland 25
16 Jan	Cardiff	Wales 31, Italy 26
8 June	Brisbane	Australia 56, Wales 25
15 June	Dunedin	New Zealand 62, Scotland 31
22 June	Auckland	New Zealand 36, Scotland 12
	Sydney	Australia 42, Wales 3
25 Sept	Cardiff	Wales 33, France 40

European Club Cup final 1996 (inaugural): Toulouse beat Cardiff 21–18 a.e.t.

International Challenge Cup final 1996 (inaugural): Agen beat Leicester 28–22

DOMESTIC COMPETITIONS

English League: Division 1, Bath, 31 points; *Division 2,* Northampton, 36 points; *Division 3,* Coventry, 30 points; *Division 4,* Exeter, 28 points; *Division 5 (north),* Wharfedale, 24 points; *Division 5 (south),* Lydney, 23 points

County Championship final 1996: Gloucestershire beat Warwickshire 17–13

Pilkington Cup final 1996: Bath beat Leicester 16–15

Scottish Premiership: Division 1, Melrose, 19 points; *Division 2,* Currie, 22 points; *Division 3,* Glasgow Academicals, 24 points; *Division 4,* Kilmarnock, 25 points

Scottish Cup final 1996: Hawick beat Watsonians 17–15

Welsh League: Division 1, Neath, 72 points; *Division 2,* Dunvant, 60 points; *Division 3,* Blackwood, 61 points; *Division 4,* Merthyr, 59 points; *Division 5,* Kidwelly, 65 points

Welsh Challenge (Swalec) Cup final 1996: Pontypridd beat Neath 29–22

Irish League: Division 1, Shannon, 16 points; *Division 2,* Old Crescent, 19 points; *Division 3,* Monkstown, 18 points; *Division 4,* Portadown, 16 points

Ulster Cup final 1996: Dungannon beat Malone 22–10

Hospitals' Cup final 1996: Charing Cross/Westminster beat St Mary's 26–22

Services Championship 1996: Royal Navy beat Army 9–6; Army beat Royal Air Force 31–23

Varsity Match 1995: Cambridge beat Oxford 21–19

Middlesex Sevens final 1996: Wigan beat Wasps 38–15

SHOOTING

127TH NATIONAL RIFLE ASSOCATION IMPERIAL MEETING
Bisley, July 1996

Queen's Prize: Alain Marion, 298.51 v-bulls

Grand Aggregate: Andrew Gent, 597.86 v-bulls

Prince of Wales Prize: Anton Aspin, 75.1 v-bulls

St George's Vase: James Lewis, 149.19 v-bulls

Allcomers Aggregate: Andrew Gent, 323.50 v-bulls

National Trophy: England, 2060.271 v-bulls
Kolapore Cup: Great Britain, 1100.93 v-bulls
Chancellor's Trophy: Cambridge University, 1148.119
v-bulls
Musketeers Cup: Bath University, 585.84 v-bulls
Vizianagram Trophy: House of Commons, 741.43 v-bulls
County Long-Range Championship: County of London,
441.54 v-bulls
Mackinnon Challenge Cup: Australia, 1160.143 v-bulls
The Ashburton: Sedbergh School CCF, 461 points
The Elcho: England, 1661.163 v-bulls
The Albert: William Meldrum, 214.17 v-bulls
Hopton Challenge Cup: James McAllister, 971.105 v-bulls

CLAY PIGEON SHOOTING

World Sporting Championship 1996: Carl Bloxham (England),
203
International Cup (Down-the-Line) 1996: England, 5933/
6000
British Open Down-the-Line Championship 1996: A. Evans,
100/300*
Mackintosh Trophy 1996: England
British Open Skeet Championship 1996: Martin Elworthy,
100*
British Open Sporting Championship 1996: Martin Elworthy,
83*
Coronation Cup 1996: John Timmins, 376
* After a shoot-off

SNOOKER

1995
Thailand Classic: John Parrott (England) beat Nigel Bond
(England) 9–6
Skoda Grand Prix: Stephen Hendry (Scotland) beat John
Higgins (Scotland) 9–5
Rothmans Grand Prix: Peter Ebdon (England) beat John
Higgins (Scotland) 7–4
UK Professional Championship: Stephen Hendry (Scotland)
beat Peter Ebdon (England) 10–3
1996
German Open: John Higgins (Scotland) beat Ken Doherty
(Ireland) 9–3
Welsh Open: Mark Williams (Wales) beat John Parrott
(England) 9–3
Benson and Hedges Masters: Stephen Hendry (Scotland)
beat Ronnie O'Sullivan (England) 10–5
International Open: John Higgins (Scotland) beat Rod
Lawler (England) 9–3
European Open: John Parrott (England) beat Peter Ebdon
(England) 9–7
Thailand Open: Alan McManus (Scotland) beat Ken
Doherty (Ireland) 9–8
Irish Masters: Darren Morgan (Wales) beat Steve Davis
(England) 9–8
British Open: Nigel Bond (England) beat John Higgins
(Scotland) 9–8
World Championship: Stephen Hendry (Scotland) beat Peter
Ebdon (England) 18–12
European League: Ken Doherty (Ireland) beat Steve Davis
(England) 10–5
Regal Masters: Peter Ebdon (England) beat Alan McManus
(Scotland) 9–6

Women's Scottish Regal Masters 1995: Kim Shaw (England)
beat Lynette Horsburgh (England) 4–3
Women's Scottish Regal Masters 1996: Kelly Fisher (England)
beat Lynette Horsburgh (England) 4–1

SPEEDWAY

GRAND PRIX 1996
Polish (Wroclaw): Tommy Knudsen (Denmark)
Italian (Lonigo): Hans Nielsen (Denmark)
German (Pocking): Hans Nielsen (Denmark)
Swedish (Linkoping): Billy Hamill (USA)
British (London): Jason Crump (Australia)
Danish (Vojens): Billy Hamill (USA)
World Team Cup final 1996: Poland, 27 points
World Championship, Overseas final 1996: Chris Manchester
(USA)
British League Riders' Championship 1996: Joe Screen
(Bradford)
British Premier League Champions 1995: Eastbourne
British Premier League Knock-Out Cup final 1995: Bradford
beat Belle Vue 111–97 on agg.

SQUASH RACKETS

World Mixed Team Cup final 1996 (inaugural): Australia beat
England 3–0

MEN
World Open Championship final 1995: Jansher Khan
(Pakistan) beat Del Harris (England) 3–1
World Team Championship final 1995: England beat Pakistan
2–1
European Team Championship final 1996: England beat
Scotland 3–1
European Club Championship 1996: Linköping (Sweden)
British Open Championship final 1996: Jansher Khan
(Pakistan) beat Rodney Eyles (Australia) 3–0
National Championship final 1996: Peter Nicol (Scotland)
beat Mark Chaloner (England) 3–0

WOMEN
World Open Championship final 1995: Michelle Martin
(Australia) beat Sarah FitzGerald (Australia) 3–0
European Team Championship final 1996: England beat
Germany 3–0
European Club Championship 1996: Herentals (Belgium)
British Open Championship final 1996: Michelle Martin
(Australia) beat Sarah FitzGerald (Australia) 3–1
National Championship final 1996: Suzanne Horner
(England) beat Linda Charman (England) 3–1

SWIMMING

NATIONAL CHAMPIONSHIPS 1996
Leeds, July

MEN
50 metres freestyle: Nicholas Osborn (Portsmouth Northsea)
100 metres freestyle: Gavin Meadows (City of Leeds)
200 metres freestyle: Gavin Meadows (City of Leeds)
400 metres freestyle: Ian Wilson (City of Leeds)
1,500 metres freestyle: Ian Wilson (City of Leeds)
50 metres backstroke: Simon Handley (City of Bristol)
100 metres backstroke: Tim Riley (Manchester United
Salford)
200 metres backstroke: Simon Militis (Regent Tiger)
50 metres breaststroke: Andrew Cooper (Rochdale
Aquabears)

100 metres breaststroke: Andrew Cooper (Rochdale Aquabears)
200 metres breaststroke: Jonathan Tunstall (City of Liverpool)
50 metres butterfly: David Jones (Ealing)
100 metres butterfly: Stephen Parry (City of Liverpool)
200 metres butterfly: Stephen Parry (City of Liverpool)
200 metres medley: David Warren (City of Leeds)
400 metres medley: David Warren (City of Leeds)
4 × 100 metres freestyle relay: City of Bristol
4 × 200 metres freestyle relay: City of Leeds
4 × 100 metres medley relay: City of Leeds

WOMEN

50 metres freestyle: Rosalind Brett (Hull Olympic)
100 metres freestyle: Jessica Craig (Haverhill)
200 metres freestyle: Sarah Collings (City of Bradford)
400 metres freestyle: Sarah Collings (City of Bradford)
800 metres freestyle: Sarah Collings (City of Bradford)
50 metres backstroke: Sarah Price (Barnet Copthall)
100 metres backstroke: Kathy Osher (Ealing)
200 metres backstroke: Kathy Osher (Ealing)
50 metres breaststroke: Jo Hocking (Truro City)
100 metres breaststroke: Jo Hocking (Truro City)
200 metres breaststroke: Linda Hindmarsh (City of Leeds)
50 metres butterfly: Sarah Massey (City of Bradford)
100 metres butterfly: Sarah Massey (City of Bradford)
200 metres butterfly: Margaretha Pedder (Portsmouth Northsea)
200 metres medley: Kathy Osher (Ealing)
400 metres medley: Jodie Swallow (Brentwood)
4 × 100 metres freestyle relay: City of Bradford
4 × 200 metres freestyle relay: City of Bradford
4 × 100 metres medley relay: City of Leeds

TABLE TENNIS

Women's World Cup final 1996: Deng Yaping (China) beat Yang Ying (China) 3–0

European Nations Cup final 1996: France beat Germany 3–1

ENGLISH NATIONAL CHAMPIONSHIPS 1996
Brighton, March

Men's Singles: Alan Cooke beat Carl Prean 3–0
Women's Singles: Alison Broe beat Andrea Holt 3–2
Men's Doubles: Alan Cooke and Desmond Douglas beat Bradley Billington and Jonathan Taylor 2–0
Women's Doubles: Nicola Deaton and Alison Broe beat Andrea Holt and Sue Collier 2–1
Mixed Doubles: Nicola Deaton and Alan Cooke beat Carol Giles and Paul Giles 2–0

VOLLEYBALL

MEN

World League final 1996: Holland beat Italy 3–2
National League Championship 1996: Mizuno Malory Lewisham
National Cup final 1996: Mizuno Malory Lewisham beat Tooting Aquila 3–0

WOMEN

World Grand Prix 1996: Brazil
National League Championship 1996: Britannia Music City

National Cup final 1996: London Malory beat Britannia Music City 3–0

YACHTING

See Olympic Games results, page 1231

The Olympic Games

ARCHERY (MEN)
Individual: Justin Huish (USA)
Team: USA

ARCHERY (WOMEN)
Individual: Kim Kyung-Wook (S. Korea)
Team: S. Korea

ATHLETICS (MEN)

	hr.	min.	sec.
100 *metres:* Donovan Bailey (Canada)			9.94
200 *metres:* Michael Johnson (USA)			19.32
400 *metres:* Michael Johnson (USA)			43.49
800 *metres:* Vebjorn Rodal (Norway)		1	42.58
1,500 *metres:* Noureddine Morceli (Algeria)		3	35.78
5,000 *metres:* Venuste Nyongabo (Burundi)		13	07.96
10,000 *metres:* Haile Gebrsilassie (Ethiopia)		27	07.34
Marathon: Josiah Thugwane (S. Africa)	2	12	36
3,000 *metres steeplechase:* Joseph Keter (Kenya)		8	07.12
110 *metres hurdles:* Allen Johnson (USA)			12.95
400 *metres hurdles:* Derrick Adkins (USA)			47.55
20 *km walk:* Jefferson Perez (Ecuador)	1	20	07
50 *km walk:* Robert Korzeniowski (Poland)	3	43	30
4 x 100 *metres relay:* Canada			37.69
4 x 400 *metres relay:* USA		2	55.99

	metres
High jump: Charles Austin (USA)	2.39
Pole vault: Jean Galfione (France)	5.92
Long jump: Carl Lewis (USA)	8.50
Triple jump: Kenny Harrison (USA)	18.09
Shot: Randy Barnes (USA)	21.62
Discus: Lars Riedel (Germany)	69.40
Hammer: Balazs Kiss (Hungary)	81.24
Javelin: Jan Zelezny (Czech Republic)	88.16
Decathlon: Dan O'Brien (USA)	8,824 points

ATHLETICS (WOMEN)

	hr.	min.	sec.
100 *metres:* Gail Devers (USA)			10.94
200 *metres:* Marie-José Pérec (France)			22.12
400 *metres:* Marie-José Pérec (France)			48.25
800 *metres:* Svetlana Masterkova (Russia)		1	57.73
1,500 *metres:* Svetlana Masterkova (Russia)		4	00.83
5,000 *metres:* Wang Junxia (China)		14	59.88
10,000 *metres:* Fernanda Ribeiro (Portugal)		31	01.63
Marathon: Fatuma Roba (Ethiopia)	2	26	05
100 *metres hurdles:* Lyudmila Engquist (Sweden)			12.58
400 *metres hurdles:* Deon Hemmings (Jamaica)			52.82
10 *km walk:* Yelena Nikolayeva (Russia)		41	49
4 x 100 *metres relay:* USA			41.95
4 x 400 *metres relay:* USA		3	20.91

	metres
High jump: Stefka Kostadinova (Bulgaria)	2.05
Long jump: Chioma Ajunwa (Nigeria)	7.12
Triple jump: Inessa Kravets (Ukraine)	15.33
Shot: Astrid Kumbernuss (Germany)	20.56
Discus: Ilke Wyludda (Germany)	69.66
Javelin: Heli Rantanen (Norway)	67.94
Heptathlon: Ghada Shouaa (Syria)	6,780 points

BADMINTON (MEN)
Singles: Poul-Erik Hoyer-Larsen (Denmark)
Doubles: Indonesia

BADMINTON (WOMEN)
Singles: Bang Soo-Hyun (S. Korea)
Doubles: China

BADMINTON (MIXED)
Doubles: S. Korea

BASEBALL
Team: Cuba

BASKETBALL
Men: USA
Women: USA

BEACH VOLLEYBALL
Men's Pairs: USA
Women's Pairs: Brazil

BOXING
Up to 48 kg: Daniel Petrov (Bulgaria)
Up to 51 kg: Maikro Romero (Cuba)
Up to 54 kg: Istvan Kovacs (Hungary)
Up to 57 kg: Somluck Kamsing (Thailand)
Up to 60 kg: Hocine Soltani (Algeria)
Up to 63.5 kg: Hector Vinent (Cuba)
Up to 67 kg: Oleg Saitov (Russia)
Up to 71 kg: David Reid (USA)
Up to 75 kg: Ariel Hernandez (Cuba)
Up to 81 kg: Vasili Jirov (Kazakhstan)
Up to 91 kg: Felix Savon (Cuba)
Over 91 kg: Vladimir Klichko (Ukraine)

CANOEING (MEN)
K1 500 metres: Antonio Rossi (Italy)
K1 1,000 metres: Knut Holmann (Norway)
K2 500 metres: Germany
K2 1,000 metres: Italy
K4 1,000 metres: Germany
C1 500 metres: Martin Doktor (Czech Republic)
C1 1,000 metres: Martin Doktor (Czech Republic)
C2 500 metres: Hungary
C2 1,000 metres: Germany
Slalom
K1: Oliver Fix (Germany)
C1: Michal Martikan (Slovakia)
C2: France

CANOEING (WOMEN)
K1 500 metres: Rita Koban (Hungary)
K2 500 metres: Sweden
K4 500 metres: Germany

Slalom
K1: Stepanka Hilgertova (Czech Republic)

CYCLING (MEN)

	hr.	min.	sec.
1 km time trial: Florian Rousseau (France)	1		02.712
Sprint: Jens Fiedler (Germany)			
4,000 metres individual pursuit: Andrea Collinelli (Italy)		4	20.893
4,000 metres team pursuit: France		4	05.930
Points race: Silvio Martinello (Italy)			
Individual road race: Pascal Richard (Switzerland)	4	53	56
Road time trial: Miguel Indurain (Spain)	1	04	05
Cross-country (mountain bike): Bart Brentjens (Netherlands)	2	17	38

CYCLING (WOMEN)

	hr.	min.	sec.
Sprint: Felicia Ballanger (France)			
3,000 metres individual pursuit: Antonella Bellutti (Italy)		3	33.595
Points race: Nathalie Lancien (France)			
Individual road race: Jeannie Longo-Ciprelli (France)	2	36	13
Individual time trial: Zulfia Zabirova (Russia)		36	40
Cross-country (mountain bike): Paola Pezzo (Italy)	1	50	51

DIVING (MEN)

Springboard: Ni Xiong (China), 701.46 points
Platform: Dimitri Sautin (Russia), 692.34 points

DIVING (WOMEN)

Springboard: Fu Mingxia (China), 547.68 points
Platform: Fu Mingxia (China), 521.58 points

EQUESTRIANISM

Three-Day Eventing
Individual: Blyth Tait (New Zealand) on Ready Teddy
Team: Australia
Dressage
Individual: Isabel Werth (Germany) on Gigolo
Team: Germany
Jumping
Individual: Ulrich Kirchhoff (Germany) on Jus de Pommes
Team: Germany

FENCING (MEN)

Foil
Individual: Alessandro Puccini (Italy)
Team: Russia
Sabre
Individual: Sergei Podnyakov (Russia)
Team: Russia
Epée
Individual: Alexander Beketov (Russia)
Team: Italy

FENCING (WOMEN)

Foil
Individual: Laura Badea (Romania)
Team: Italy
Epée
Individual: Laura Flessel (France)
Team: France

FOOTBALL

Men: Nigeria
Women: USA

GYMNASTICS (MEN)

Team: Russia
Individual all-round: Li Xiaoshuang (China)
Floor: Ioannis Melissanidis (Greece)
Pommel Horse: Lin Donghua (Switzerland)
Rings: Yuri Chechi (Italy)
Vault: Alexei Nemov (Russia)
Parallel Bars: Rustam Sharipov (Ukraine)
Horizontal Bar: Andreas Wecker (Germany)

GYMNASTICS (WOMEN)

Team: USA
Individual all-round: Lilia Podkopayeva (Ukraine)
Floor: Lilia Podkopayeva (Ukraine)
Beam: Shannon Miller (USA)
Vault: Simona Amanar (Romania)
Asymmetrical Bars: Svetlana Chorkina (Russia)
Rhythmic
Individual: Yekaterina Serebryanskaya (Ukraine)
Team: Spain

HANDBALL

Men: Croatia
Women: Denmark

HOCKEY

Men: Netherlands
Women: Australia

JUDO (MEN)

Up to 60 kg: Tadahiro Nomura (Japan)
Up to 65 kg: Udo Quellmalz (Germany)
Up to 71 kg: Kenzo Nakamura (Japan)
Up to 78 kg: Djamel Bouras (France)
Up to 86 kg: Jeon Ki-Young (S. Korea)
Up to 95 kg: Pawel Nastula (Poland)
Over 95 kg: David Douillet (France)

JUDO (WOMEN)

Up to 48 kg: Kye Sun (N. Korea)
Up to 52 kg: Marie-Claire Restoux (France)
Up to 56 kg: Driulis Gonzalez (Cuba)
Up to 61 kg: Yuko Emoto (Japan)
Up to 66 kg: Cho Min-Sun (S. Korea)
Up to 72 kg: Ulla Werbrouck (Hungary)
Over 72 kg: Sun Fu-Ming (China)

MODERN PENTATHLON

Individual: Alexander Parygin (Kazakhstan), 5,551 points

ROWING (MEN)

Single Sculls: Xeno Mueller (Switzerland)
Double Sculls: Italy
Quad Sculls: Germany
Coxless Pairs: Great Britain
Coxless Fours: Australia
Eights: Netherlands
Lightweight Double Sculls: Switzerland
Lightweight Coxless Fours: Denmark

ROWING (WOMEN)

Single Sculls: Yekaterina Khodotovich (Belarus)
Double Sculls: Canada
Quad Sculls: Germany
Coxless Pairs: Australia

Eights: Romania
Lightweight Double Sculls: Romania

SHOOTING (MEN)

Air Pistol: Roberto di Donna (Italy)
Rapid-Fire Pistol: Ralf Schumann (Germany)
Free Pistol: Boris Kokorev (Russia)
Small-Bore Rifle, 3 Positions: Jean-Pierre Amat (France)
Small-Bore Rifle, Prone: Christian Klees (Germany)
Air Rifle: Artem Khadzhibekov (Russia)
Running Target: Ling Yang (China)
Skeet: Ennio Falco (Italy)
Trap: Michael Diamond (Australia)
Double Trap: Russell Mark (Australia)

SHOOTING (WOMEN)

Air Pistol: Olga Klochneva (Russia)
Sport Pistol: Li Duihong (China)
Small-Bore Rifle, 3 Positions: Alexandra Ivosev (Yugoslavia)
Air Rifle: Renata Mauer (Poland)
Double Trap: Kim Rhode (USA)

SOFTBALL

Team: USA

SWIMMING (MEN)

	min.	sec.
50 *metres freestyle:* Aleksandr Popov (Russia)		22.13
100 *metres freestyle:* Aleksandr Popov (Russia)		48.74
200 *metres freestyle:* Danyon Loader (New Zealand)	1	47.63
400 *metres freestyle:* Danyon Loader (New Zealand)	3	47.97
1,500 *metres freestyle:* Kieren Perkins (Australia)	14	56.40
100 *metres backstroke:* Jeff Rouse (USA)		54.10
200 *metres backstroke:* Brad Bridgewater (USA)	1	58.54
100 *metres breaststroke:* Frederik Deburghgraeve (Belgium)	1	00.65
200 *metres breaststroke:* Norbert Rozsa (Hungary)	2	12.57
100 *metres butterfly:* Denis Pankratov (Russia)		52.27
200 *metres butterfly:* Denis Pankratov (Russia)	1	56.51
200 *metres individual medley:* Attila Czene (Hungary)	1	59.91
400 *metres individual medley:* Tom Dolan (USA)	4	14.90
4 x 100 *metres freestyle relay:* USA	3	15.41
4 x 200 *metres freestyle relay:* USA	7	14.84
4 x 100 *metres medley relay:* USA	3	34.84

SWIMMING (WOMEN)

	min.	sec.
50 *metres freestyle:* Amy van Dyken (USA)		24.87
100 *metres freestyle:* Le Jingyi (China)		54.50
200 *metres freestyle:* Claudia Poll (Costa Rica)	1	58.16
400 *metres freestyle:* Michelle Smith (Ireland)	4	07.25
800 *metres freestyle:* Brooke Bennett (USA)	8	27.89
100 *metres backstroke:* Beth Botsford (USA)	1	01.19
200 *metres backstroke:* Krysztina Egerszegi (Hungary)	2	07.83
100 *metres breaststroke:* Penelope Heyns (S. Africa)	1	07.73
200 *metres breaststroke:* Penelope Heyns (S. Africa)	2	25.41
100 *metres butterfly:* Amy van Dyken (USA)		59.10
200 *metres butterfly:* Susan O'Neill (Australia)	2	07.76
200 *metres individual medley:* Michelle Smith (Ireland)	2	13.93
400 *metres individual medley:* Michelle Smith (Ireland)	4	39.18
4 x 100 *metres freestyle relay:* USA	3	39.29
4 x 200 *metres freestyle relay:* USA	7	59.87
4 x 100 *metres medley relay:* USA	4	02.88

SYNCHRONIZED SWIMMING

Team: USA

TABLE TENNIS (MEN)

Singles: Liu Guoliang (China)
Doubles: China

TABLE TENNIS (WOMEN)

Singles: Deng Yaping (China)
Doubles: China

TENNIS (MEN)

Singles: Andre Agassi (USA)
Doubles: Australia

TENNIS (WOMEN)

Singles: Lindsay Davenport (USA)
Doubles: USA

VOLLEYBALL

Men: Netherlands
Women: Cuba

WATER POLO

Team: Spain

WEIGHTLIFTING

Up to 54 kg: Halil Mutlu (Turkey)
Up to 59 kg: Tang Ningsheng (China)
Up to 64 kg: Naim Suleymanoglu (Turkey)
Up to 70 kg: Zhang Xugang (China)
Up to 76 kg: Pablo Lara (Cuba)
Up to 83 kg: Pyrros Dimas (Greece)
Up to 91 kg: Alexei Petrov (Russia)
Under 99 kg: Akakidi Khakiashvilis (Greece)
Up to 108 kg: Timur Taimazov (Ukraine)
Over 108 kg: Andrei Chemerkin (Russia)

WRESTLING (FREESTYLE)

Up to 48 kg: Kim Il (N. Korea)
Up to 52 kg: Valentin Jordanov (Bulgaria)
Up to 57 kg: Kendall Cross (USA)
Up to 62 kg: Thomas Brands (USA)
Up to 68 kg: Vadim Bogiyev (Russia)
Up to 74 kg: Buvaisa Saityev (Russia)
Up to 82 kg: Khadshimurad Magomedov (Russia)
Up to 90 kg: Rasul Khadem Azghadi (Iran)
Up to 100 kg: Kurt Angle (USA)
Over 100 kg: Mahmut Demir (Turkey)

WRESTLING (GRECO-ROMAN)

Up to 48 kg: Sim Kwon-Ho (S. Korea)
Up to 52 kg: Arman Nazaryan (Armenia)
Up to 57 kg: Yovei Melnichenko (Kazakhstan)
Up to 62 kg: Wlodzimierz Zawadzki (Poland)
Up to 68 kg: Ryzsard Wolny (Poland)
Up to 74 kg: Feliberto Aguilera (Cuba)
Up to 82 kg: Hamza Yerlikaya (Turkey)
Up to 90 kg: Vyachetslav Oleynyk (Ukraine)
Up to 100 kg: Andreas Wronski (Poland)
Over 100 kg: Alexandr Karelin (Russia)

YACHTING (MEN)

Mistral Sailboard: Nikolas Kaklamanakis (Greece)
Finn: Mateusz Kusnierewicz (Poland)
470: Ukraine

YACHTING (WOMEN)

Mistral Sailboard: Lai-Shan Lee (Hong Kong)
Europe: Kristine Roug (Denmark)
470: Spain

YACHTING (MIXED)

Star: Brazil
Soling: Germany
Laser: Robert Scheidt (Brazil)
Tornado: Spain

MEDAL TABLE

	Gold	Silver	Bronze	Total
USA	44	32	25	101
Russia	26	21	16	63
Germany	20	18	27	65
China	16	22	12	50
France	15	7	15	37
Italy	13	10	12	35
Australia	9	9	23	41
Cuba	9	8	8	25
Ukraine	9	2	12	23
South Korea	7	15	5	27
Poland	7	5	5	17
Hungary	7	4	10	21
Spain	5	6	6	17
Romania	4	7	9	20
Netherlands	4	5	10	19
Greece	4	4	0	8
Czech Republic	4	3	4	11
Switzerland	4	3	0	7
Denmark	4	1	1	6
Turkey	4	1	1	6
Canada	3	11	8	22
Bulgaria	3	7	5	15
Japan	3	6	5	14
Kazakhstan	3	4	4	11
Brazil	3	3	9	15
New Zealand	3	2	1	6
South Africa	3	1	1	5
Ireland	3	0	1	4
Sweden	2	4	2	8
Norway	2	2	3	7
Belgium	2	2	2	6
Nigeria	2	1	3	6
North Korea	2	1	2	5
Algeria	2	0	1	3
Ethiopia	2	0	1	3
Great Britain	1	8	6	15
Belarus	1	6	8	15
Kenya	1	4	3	8
Jamaica	1	3	2	6
Finland	1	2	1	4
Indonesia	1	1	2	4
Yugoslavia	1	1	2	4
Iran	1	1	1	3
Slovakia	1	1	1	3
Armenia	1	1	0	2
Croatia	1	1	0	2
Portugal	1	0	1	2
Thailand	1	0	1	2
Burundi	1	0	0	1

	Gold	Silver	Bronze	Total
Costa Rica	1	0	0	1
Ecuador	1	0	0	1
Hong Kong	1	0	0	1
Syria	1	0	0	1
Argentina	0	2	1	3
Namibia	0	2	0	2
Slovenia	0	2	0	2
Austria	0	1	2	3
Malaysia	0	1	1	2
Moldova	0	1	1	2
Uzbekistan	0	1	1	2
Azerbaijan	0	1	0	1
Bahamas	0	1	0	1
Latvia	0	1	0	1
Philippines	0	1	0	1
Taiwan	0	1	0	1
Tonga	0	1	0	1
Zambia	0	1	0	1
Georgia	0	0	2	2
Morocco	0	0	2	2
Trinidad	0	0	2	2
India	0	0	1	1
Israel	0	0	1	1
Lithuania	0	0	1	1
Mexico	0	0	1	1
Mongolia	0	0	1	1
Mozambique	0	0	1	1
Puerto Rico	0	0	1	1
Tunisia	0	0	1	1
Uganda	0	0	1	1
	271	273	298	842

The Olympic Games

Venues of the modern Olympic Games

I	Athens, Greece	1896
II	Paris, France	1900
III	St Louis, USA	1904
*	Athens	1906
IV	London, Britain	1908
V	Stockholm, Sweden	1912
†VI	Berlin, Germany	1916
VII	Antwerp, Belgium	1920
VIII	Paris, France	1924
IX	Amsterdam, Netherlands	1928
X	Los Angeles, USA	1932
XI	Berlin, Germany	1936
†XII	Tokyo, Japan, then Helsinki, Finland	1940
†XIII	London, Britain	1944
XIV	London, Britain	1948
XV	Helsinki, Finland	1952
§XVI	Melbourne, Australia	1956
XVII	Rome, Italy	1960
XVIII	Tokyo, Japan	1964
XIX	Mexico City, Mexico	1968
XX	Munich, West Germany	1972
XXI	Montreal, Canada	1976
XXII	Moscow, USSR	1980
XXIII	Los Angeles, USA	1984
XXIV	Seoul, South Korea	1988
XXV	Barcelona, Spain	1992
XXVI	Atlanta, USA	1996
XXVII	Sydney, Australia	2000

WINTER OLYMPIC GAMES

I	Chamonix, France	1924
II	St Moritz, Switzerland	1928
III	Lake Placid, USA	1932
IV	Garmisch-Partenkirchen, Germany	1936
V	St Moritz, Switzerland	1948
VI	Oslo, Norway	1952
VII	Cortina d'Ampezzo, Italy	1956
VIII	Squaw Valley, USA	1960
IX	Innsbruck, Austria	1964
X	Grenoble, France	1968
XI	Sapporo, Japan	1972
XII	Innsbruck, Austria	1976
XIII	Lake Placid, USA	1980
XIV	Sarajevo, Yugoslavia	1984
XV	Calgary, Canada	1988
XVI	Albertville, France	1992
XVII	Lillehammer, Norway	1994
XVIII	Nagano, Japan	1998
XIX	Salt Lake City, USA	2002

* The 'Intercalated' Games
† These Games were scheduled but did not take place owing to World Wars
§ Equestrian events were held in Stockholm, Sweden

The Commonwealth Games

The Games were originally called the British Empire Games. From 1954 to 1966 the Games were known as the British Empire and Commonwealth Games, and from 1970 to 1974 as the British Commonwealth Games. Since 1978 the Games have been called the Commonwealth Games.

BRITISH EMPIRE GAMES

I	Hamilton, Canada	1930
II	London, England	1934
III	Sydney, Australia	1938
IV	Auckland, New Zealand	1950

BRITISH EMPIRE AND COMMONWEALTH GAMES

V	Vancouver, Canada	1954
VI	Cardiff, Wales	1958

VII	Perth, Australia	1962
VIII	Kingston, Jamaica	1966

BRITISH COMMONWEALTH GAMES

IX	Edinburgh, Scotland	1970
X	Christchurch, New Zealand	1974

COMMONWEALTH GAMES

XI	Edmonton, Canada	1978
XII	Brisbane, Australia	1982
XIII	Edinburgh, Scotland	1986
XIV	Auckland, New Zealand	1990
XV	Victoria, Canada	1994
XVI	Kuala Lumpur, Malaysia	1998
XVII	Manchester, England	2002

Sports Records

ATHLETICS WORLD RECORDS
AS AT 9 SEPTEMBER 1996

All the world records given below have been accepted by the International Amateur Athletic Federation except those marked with an asterisk* which are awaiting homologation. Fully automatic timing to 1/100th second is mandatory up to and including 400 metres. For distances up to and including 10,000 metres, records will be accepted to 1/100th second if timed automatically, and to 1/10th if hand timing is used.

MEN'S EVENTS

TRACK EVENTS	hr.	min.	sec.
100 metres			9.84
Donovan Bailey, Canada, 1996			
200 metres			19.32
Michael Johnson, USA, 1996			
400 metres			43.29
Butch Reynolds, USA, 1988			
800 metres		1	41.73
Sebastian Coe, GB, 1981			
1,000 metres		2	12.18
Sebastian Coe, GB, 1981			
1,500 metres		3	27.37
Noureddine Morceli, Algeria, 1995			
1 mile		3	44.39
Noureddine Morceli, Algeria, 1993			
2,000 metres		4	47.88
Noureddine Morceli, Algeria, 1995			
3,000 metres		7	20.67*
Daniel Komen, Kenya, 1996			
5,000 metres		12	44.39
Haile Gebrsilassie, Ethiopia, 1995			
10,000 metres		26	38.08*
Salah Hissou, Morocco, 1996			
20,000 metres		56	55.6
Arturo Barrios, Mexico, 1991			
21,101 metres (13 miles 196 yards 1 foot)	1	00	00.0
Arturo Barrios, Mexico, 1991			
25,000 metres	1	13	55.8
Toshihiko Seko, Japan, 1981			
30,000 metres	1	29	18.8
Toshihiko Seko, Japan, 1981			
110 metres hurdles (3 ft 6 in)			12.91
Colin Jackson, GB, 1993			
400 metres hurdles (3 ft 0 in)			46.78
Kevin Young, USA, 1992			
3,000 metres steeplechase		7	59.18
Moses Kiptanui, Kenya, 1995			

RELAYS		min.	sec.
4×100 metres			37.40
USA, 1992, 1993			
4×200 metres		1	19.11
Santa Monica TC, 1992			
4×400 metres		2	54.29
USA, 1993			
4×800 metres		7	03.89
GB, 1982			
4×1,500 metres		14	38.8
Federal Republic of Germany, 1977			

FIELD EVENTS	metres	ft	in
High jump	2.45	8	0½
Javier Sotomayor, Cuba, 1993			
Pole vault	6.14	20	1¾
Sergei Bubka, Ukraine, 1994			
Long jump	8.95	29	4½
Mike Powell, USA, 1991			
Triple jump	18.29	60	0¼
Jonathan Edwards, GB, 1995			
Shot	23.12	75	10¼
Randy Barnes, USA, 1990			
Discus	74.08	243	0
Jürgen Schult, GDR, 1986			
Hammer	86.74	284	7
Yuriy Sedykh, USSR, 1986			
Javelin	98.48	323	1
Jan Zelezny, Czech Rep., 1996			
Decathlon†	8,891 points		
Dan O'Brien, USA, 1992			

† Ten events comprising 100 m, long jump, shot, high jump, 400 m, 110 m hurdles, discus, pole vault, javelin, 1500 m

WALKING (TRACK)	hr.	min.	sec.
20,000 metres	1	18	35.2
Stefan Johansson, Sweden, 1992			
29,572 metres (18 miles 660 yards)	2	00	00.0
Maurizio Damilano, Italy, 1992			
30,000 metres	2	01	44.1
Maurizio Damilano, Italy, 1992			
50,000 metres	3	41	38.4
Raul Gonzalez, Mexico, 1979			

WOMEN'S EVENTS

TRACK EVENTS	min.	sec.
100 metres		10.49
Florence Griffith-Joyner, USA, 1988		
200 metres		21.34
Florence Griffith-Joyner, USA, 1988		
400 metres		47.60
Marita Koch, GDR, 1985		
800 metres	1	53.28
Jarmila Kratochvilova, Czechoslovakia, 1983		
1,500 metres	3	50.46
Qu Yunxia, China, 1993		
1 mile	4	12.56
Svetlana Masterkova, Russia, 1996		
3,000 metres	8	06.11
Wang Junxia, China, 1993		
5,000 metres	14	36.45
Fernanda Ribeiro, Portugal, 1995		
10,000 metres	29	31.78
Wang Junxia, China, 1993		
100 metres hurdles (2 ft 9 in)		12.21
Yordanka Donkova, Bulgaria, 1988		
400 metres hurdles (2 ft 6 in)		52.61
Kim Batten, USA, 1995		

RELAYS	min.	sec.
4×100 metres		41.37
GDR, 1985		
4×200 metres	1	28.15
GDR, 1980		
4×400 metres	3	15.17
USSR, 1988		
4×800 metres	7	50.17
USSR, 1984		

FIELD EVENTS	metres	ft	in
High jump	2.09	6	10¼
Stefka Kostadinova, Bulgaria, 1987			
Pole vault	4.45	14	7¼
Emma George, Australia, 1996			
Long jump	7.52	24	8¼
Galina Chistiakova, USSR, 1988			
Triple jump	15.50	50	10¼
Inessa Kravets, Ukraine, 1995			
Shot	22.63	74	3
Natalya Lisovskaya, USSR, 1987			
Discus	76.80	252	0
Gabriele Reinsch, GDR, 1988			
Hammer	69.42	227	9
Mihaela Melinte, Romania, 1996			
Javelin	80.00	262	5
Petra Felke, GDR, 1988			
Heptathlon†		7,291 points	
Jackie Joyner-Kersee, USA, 1988			

†Seven events comprising 100 m hurdles, shot, high jump, 200 m, long jump, javelin, 800 m

ATHLETICS NATIONAL (UK) RECORDS
AS AT 16 SEPTEMBER 1996

Records set anywhere by athletes eligible to represent Great Britain and Northern Ireland

MEN

TRACK EVENTS	hr.	min.	sec.
100 metres			9.87
Linford Christie, 1993			
200 metres			19.87
John Regis, 1994			
400 metres			44.37
Roger Black, 1996			
800 metres		1	41.73
Sebastian Coe, 1981			
1,000 metres		2	12.18
Sebastian Coe, 1981			
1,500 metres		3	29.67
Sebastian Coe, 1985			
1 mile		3	46.32
Steve Cram, 1985			
2,000 metres		4	51.39
Steve Cram, 1985			
3,000 metres		7	32.79
David Moorcroft, 1982			
5,000 metres		13	00.41
David Moorcroft, 1982			
10,000 metres		27	23.06
Eamonn Martin, 1988			
20,000 metres		57	28.7
Carl Thackery, 1990			
20,855 metres	1	00	00.0
Carl Thackery, 1990			
25,000 metres	1	15	22.6
Ron Hill, 1965			

	hr.	min.	sec.
30,000 metres	1	31	30.4
Jim Alder, 1970			
3,000 metres steeplechase		8	07.96
Mark Rowland, 1988			
110 metres hurdles			12.91
Colin Jackson, 1993			
400 metres hurdles			47.82
Kriss Akabusi, 1992			

RELAYS	min.	sec.
4×100 metres		37.77
GB team, 1993		
4×200 metres	1	21.29
GB team, 1989		
4×400 metres	2	56.60
GB team, 1996		
4×800 metres	7	03.89
GB team, 1982		

FIELD EVENTS	metres	ft	in
High jump	2.37	7	9¼
Steve Smith, 1992, 1993			
Pole vault	5.71	18	8¾
Nick Buckfield, 1996			
Long jump	8.23	27	0
Lynn Davies, 1968			
Triple jump	18.29	60	0¼
Jonathan Edwards, 1995			
Shot	21.68	71	1½
Geoff Capes, 1980			
Discus	64.32	211	0
William Tancred, 1974			
Hammer	77.54	254	5
Martin Girvan, 1984			
Javelin	91.46	300	1
Steve Backley, 1992			
Decathlon		8,847 points	
Daley Thompson, 1984			

WALKING (TRACK)	hr.	min.	sec.
20,000 metres	1	23	26.5
Ian McCombie, 1990			
30,000 metres	2	19	18
Christopher Maddocks, 1984			
50,000 metres	4	05	44.6
Paul Blagg, 1990			
26,037 metres (16 miles 315 yards)	2	00	00.0
Ron Wallwork, 1971			

WOMEN

TRACK EVENTS	min.	sec.
100 metres		11.10
Kathy Cook, 1981		
200 metres		22.10
Kathy Cook, 1984		
400 metres		49.43
Kathy Cook, 1984		
800 metres	1	56.21
Kelly Holmes, 1995		
1,500 metres	3	59.96
Zola Budd, 1985		
1 mile	4	17.57
Zola Budd, 1985		
3,000 metres	8	28.83
Zola Budd, 1985		
5,000 metres	14	46.76
Paula Radcliffe, 1996		

10,000 metres	30	57.07	
Liz McColgan, 1991			
100 metres hurdles		12.80	
Angela Thorp, 1996			
400 metres hurdles		52.74	
Sally Gunnell, 1993			
RELAYS	min.	sec.	
4×100 metres		42.43	
GB team, 1980			
4×200 metres	1	31.57	
GB team, 1977			
4×400 metres	3	22.01	
GB team, 1991			
4×800 metres	8	23.8	
GB team, 1971			

FIELD EVENTS	metres	ft	in
High jump	1.95	6	4¾
Diana Elliott, 1982			
Pole vault	4.00	13	1½
Janine Whitlock, 1996			
Long jump	6.90	22	7¾
Beverley Kinch, 1983			
Triple jump	14.78	48	6
Ashia Hansen, 1996			
Shot	19.36	63	6¼
Judy Oakes, 1988			
Discus	67.48	221	5
Margaret Ritchie, 1981			
Hammer	64.90	212	11
Lorraine Shaw, 1995			
Javelin	77.44	254	1
Fatima Whitbread, 1986			
Heptathlon		6,645 points	
Denise Lewis, 1996			

SWIMMING WORLD RECORDS
AS AT 9 SEPTEMBER 1996

MEN	min.	sec.
50 metres freestyle		21.81
Tom Jager, USA		
100 metres freestyle		48.21
Alexander Popov, Russia		
200 metres freestyle	1	46.69
Giorgio Lamberti, Italy		
400 metres freestyle	3	43.80
Kieren Perkins, Australia		
800 metres freestyle	7	46.00
Kieren Perkins, Australia		
1,500 metres freestyle	14	41.66
Kieren Perkins, Australia		
100 metres breaststroke	1	00.60
Fred Deburghgraeve, Belgium		
200 metres breaststroke	2	10.16
Mike Barrowman, USA		
100 metres butterfly		52.27
Denis Pankratov, Russia		
200 metres butterfly	1	55.22
Denis Pankratov, Russia		
100 metres backstroke		53.86
Jeff Rouse, USA		
200 metres backstroke	1	56.57
Martin Lopez-Zubero, Spain		
200 metres medley	1	58.16
Jani Sievinen, Finland		

400 metres medley	4	12.30
Tom Dolan, USA		
4×100 metres freestyle relay	3	15.11
USA		
4×200 metres freestyle relay	7	11.95
CIS		
4×100 metres medley relay	3	34.84
USA		

WOMEN	min.	sec.
50 metres freestyle		24.51
Jingyi Le, China		
100 metres freestyle		54.01
Jingyi Le, China		
200 metres freestyle	1	56.78
Franziska van Almsick, Germany		
400 metres freestyle	4	03.85
Janet Evans, USA		
800 metres freestyle	8	16.22
Janet Evans, USA		
1,500 metres freestyle	15	52.10
Janet Evans, USA		
100 metres breaststroke	1	07.02
Penny Heyns, South Africa		
200 metres breaststroke	2	24.76
Rebecca Brown, Australia		
100 metres butterfly		57.93
Mary Meagher, USA		
200 metres butterfly	2	05.96
Mary Meagher, USA		
100 metres backstroke	1	00.16
Cihong He, China		
200 metres backstroke	2	06.62
Krisztina Egerszegi, Hungary		
200 metres medley	2	11.65
Lin Li, China		
400 metres medley	4	36.10
Petra Schneider, GDR		
4×100 metres freestyle relay	3	37.91
USA		
4×200 metres freestyle relay	7	55.47
GDR		
4×100 metres medley relay	4	01.67
China		

Weights and Measures

SI UNITS

The Système International d'Unités (SI) is an international and coherent system of units devised to meet all known needs for measurement in science and technology. The system was adopted by the eleventh Conférence Générale des Poids et Mesures (CGPM) in 1960. A comprehensive description of the system is given in *SI The International System of Units*, HMSO. The British Standards describing the essential features of the International System of Units are *Specifications for SI units and recommendations for the use of their multiples and certain other units* (BS 5555:1993) and *Conversion Factors and Tables* (BS 350, Part 1:1974).

The system consists of seven base units and the derived units formed as products or quotients of various powers of the base units. Together the base units and the derived units make up the coherent system of units. In the UK the SI base units, and almost all important derived units, are realized at the National Physical Laboratory and disseminated through the National Measurement System.

Base Units

Metre (m) = unit of length
Kilogram (kg) = unit of mass
Second (s) = unit of time
Ampere (A) = unit of electric current
Kelvin (K) = unit of thermodynamic temperature
Mole (mol) = unit of amount of substance
Candela (cd) = unit of luminous intensity

Derived Units

For some of the derived SI units, special names and symbols exist; those approved by the CGPM are as follows:

Hertz (Hz) = unit of frequency
Newton (N) = unit of force
Pascal (Pa) = unit of pressure, stress
Joule (J) = unit of energy, work, quantity of heat
Watt (W) = unit of power, radiant flux
Coulomb (C) = unit of electric charge, quantity of electricity
Volt (V) = unit of electric potential, potential difference, electromotive force
Farad (F) = unit of electric capacitance
Ohm (Ω) = unit of electric resistance
Siemens (S) = unit of electric conductance
Weber (Wb) = unit of magnetic flux
Tesla (T) = unit of magnetic flux density
Henry (H) = unit of inductance
Degree Celsius (°C) = unit of Celsius temperature
Lumen (lm) = unit of luminous flux
Lux (lx) = unit of illuminance
Becquerel (Bq) = unit of activity (of a radionuclide)
Gray (Gy) = unit of absorbed dose, specific energy imparted, kerma, absorbed dose index
Sievert (Sv) = unit of dose equivalent, dose equivalent index

Supplementary Units

The derived units include, as a special case, the supplementary units which may be treated as dimensionless within the SI.

Radian (rad) = unit of plane angle
Steradian (sr) = unit of solid angle

Other derived units are expressed in terms of base units and/or supplementary units. Some of the more commonly-used derived units are the following:

Unit of area = square metre (m^2)
Unit of volume = cubic metre (m^3)
Unit of velocity = metre per second ($m\,s^{-1}$)
Unit of acceleration = metre per second squared ($m\,s^{-2}$)
Unit of density = kilogram per cubic metre ($kg\,m^{-3}$)
Unit of momentum = kilogram metre per second ($kg\,m\,s^{-1}$)
Unit of magnetic field strength = ampere per metre ($A\,m^{-1}$)
Unit of surface tension = newton per metre ($N\,m^{-1}$)
Unit of dynamic viscosity = pascal second (Pa s)
Unit of heat capacity = joule per kelvin ($J\,K^{-1}$)
Unit of specific heat capacity = joule per kilogram kelvin ($J\,kg^{-1}\,K^{-1}$)
Unit of heat flux density, irradiance = watt per square metre ($W\,m^{-2}$)
Unit of thermal conductivity = watt per metre kelvin ($W\,m^{-1}\,K^{-1}$)
Unit of electric field strength = volt per metre ($V\,m^{-1}$)
Unit of luminance = candela per square metre ($cd\,m^{-2}$)

SI Prefixes

Decimal multiples and submultiples of the SI units are indicated by SI prefixes. These are as follows:

multiples	submultiples
yotta (Y) $\times10^{24}$	deci (d) $\times10^{-1}$
zetta (Z) $\times10^{21}$	centi (c) $\times10^{-2}$
exa (E) $\times10^{18}$	milli (m) $\times10^{-3}$
peta (P) $\times10^{15}$	micro (µ) $\times10^{-6}$
tera (T) $\times10^{12}$	nano (n) $\times10^{-9}$
giga (G) $\times10^{9}$	pico (p) $\times10^{-12}$
mega (M) $\times10^{6}$	femto (f) $\times10^{-15}$
kilo (k) $\times10^{3}$	atto (a) $\times10^{-18}$
hecto (h) $\times10^{2}$	zepto (z) $\times10^{-21}$
deca (da) $\times10$	yocto (y) $\times10^{-24}$

METRIC UNITS

The metric primary standards are the metre as the unit of measurement of length, and the kilogram as the unit of measurement of mass. Other units of measurement are defined by reference to the primary standards.

Measurement of Length

Kilometre (km) = 1000 metres
Metre (m) is the length of the path travelled by light in vacuum during a time interval of 1/299 792 458 of a second
Decimetre (dm) = 1/10 metre
Centimetre (cm) = 1/100 metre
Millimetre (mm) = 1/1000 metre

Measurement of Area

Hectare (ha) = 100 ares
Decare = 10 ares

Are (a) = 100 square metres
Square metre = a superficial area equal to that of a square
    each side of which measures one metre
Square decimetre = 1/100 square metre
Square centimetre = 1/100 square decimetre
Square millimetre = 1/100 square centimetre

MEASUREMENT OF VOLUME

Cubic metre (m^3) = a volume equal to that of a cube each
    edge of which measures one metre
Cubic decimetre = 1/1000 cubic metre
Cubic centimetre (cc) = 1/1000 cubic decimetre
Hectolitre = 100 litres
Litre = a cubic decimetre
Decilitre = 1/10 litre
Centilitre = 1/100 litre
Millilitre = 1/1000 litre

MEASUREMENT OF CAPACITY

Hectolitre (hl) = 100 litres
Litre (l or L) = a cubic decimetre
Decilitre (dl) = 1/10 litre
Centilitre (cl) = 1/100 litre
Millilitre (ml) = 1/1000 litre

MEASUREMENT OF MASS OR WEIGHT

Tonne (t) = 1000 kilograms
Kilogram (kg) is equal to the mass of the international
    prototype of the kilogram
Hectogram (hg) = 1/10 kilogram
Gram (g) = 1/1000 kilogram
*Carat (metric) = 1/5 gram
Milligram (mg) = 1/1000 gram

*Used only for transactions in precious stones or pearls

METRICATION IN THE UK

The European Council Directive 80/181/EEC, as
amended by Council Directive 89/617/EEC, relates to
the use of units of measurement for economic, public
health, public safety or administrative purposes in the
member states of the European Union. The provisions of
the directives were incorporated into British law by the
Weights and Measures Act 1985 (Metrication) (Amendment) Order 1994 and the Units of Measurement Regulations 1994; these instruments amended the Weights and
Measures Act 1985. Parallel statutory rules amending
Northern Ireland weights and measures legislation were
made in May 1995.

    The general effect of the 1994 and 1995 legislation is to
end the use of imperial units of measurement for trade,
replacing them with metric units – *see* below for timetable
for UK metrication. Imperial units can, however, be used in
addition to metric units, as supplementary indications.

IMPERIAL UNITS

The imperial primary standards are the yard as the unit of
measurement of length and the pound as the unit of
measurement of mass. Other units of measurement are
defined by reference to the primary standards. Most of
these units are no longer authorized for use in trade in the
UK – *see* below.

MEASUREMENT OF LENGTH

*Mile = 1760 yards
Furlong = 220 yards
Chain = 22 yards

*Yard (yd) = 0.9144 metre
*Foot (ft) = 1/3 yard
*Inch (in) = 1/36 yard

MEASUREMENT OF AREA

Square mile = 640 acres
*Acre = 4840 square yards
Rood = 1210 square yards
Square yard (sq. yd) = a superficial area equal to that of a
    square each side of which measures one yard
Square foot (sq. ft) = 1/9 square yard
Square inch (sq. in) = 1/144 square foot

MEASUREMENT OF VOLUME

Cubic yard = a volume equal to that of a cube each edge of
    which measures one yard
Cubic foot = 1/27 cubic yard
Cubic inch = 1/1728 cubic foot

MEASUREMENT OF CAPACITY

Bushel = 8 gallons
Peck = 2 gallons
Gallon (gal) = 4.546 09 cubic decimetres
Quart (qt) = 1/4 gallon
*Pint (pt) = 1/2 quart
Gill = 1/4 pint
*Fluid ounce (fl oz) = 1/20 pint
Fluid drachm = 1/8 fluid ounce
Minim (min) = 1/60 fluid drachm

MEASUREMENT OF MASS OR WEIGHT

Ton = 2240 pounds
Hundredweight (cwt) = 112 pounds
Cental = 100 pounds
Quarter = 28 pounds
Stone = 14 pounds
*Pound (lb) = 0.453 592 37 kilogram
*Ounce (oz) = 1/16 pound
*†Ounce troy (oz tr) = 12/175 pound
Dram (dr) = 1/16 ounce
Grain (gr) = 1/7000 pound
Pennyweight (dwt) = 24 grains
Ounce apothecaries = 480 grains
Drachm (ℨ) = 1/8 ounce apothecaries
Scruple (℈) = 1/3 drachm

*Units of measurement still authorized for use in trade, etc., in the UK
†Used only for transactions in gold, silver or other precious metals, and
  articles made therefrom

PHASING-OUT OF IMPERIAL UNITS IN THE UK

The Weights and Measures Act 1985 enacted the legal
units for the United Kingdom. It was amended to
implement the provisions of European Council Directive
80/181/EEC, as amended by Directive 89/617/EEC, by
the Weights and Measures Act 1985 (Metrication)
(Amendment) Order 1994 and the Units of Measurement
Regulations 1994, and by parallel statutory rules in
Northern Ireland in May 1995.

    The effect of the amended legislation is to phase out the
use of imperial units for trade, replacing them with metric
units. With effect from 30 September 1995 imperial units
ceased to be authorized for use in the UK for economic,
public health, public safety and administrative purposes,
with the following exceptions:

Units of measurement authorized for use in specialized fields between 1 October 1995 and 31 December 1999

Unit	Field of application
fathom	Marine navigation
fluid ounce } pint	Beer, cider, water, lemonade, fruit juice in returnable containers
ounce } pound	Goods for sale loose from bulk
therm	Gas supply

Units of measurement authorized for use in specialized fields from 1 October 1995, without time limit

Unit	Field of application
inch foot yard mile	Road traffic signs, distance and speed measurement
pint	Dispense of draught beer or cider / Milk in returnable containers
acre	Land registration
troy ounce	Transactions in precious metals

MEASUREMENT OF ELECTRICITY

Units of measurement of electricity are defined by the Weights and Measures Act 1985 as follows:

Ampere (A) = that constant current which, if maintained in two straight parallel conductors of infinite length, of negligible circular cross-section and placed 1 metre apart in vacuum, would produce between these conductors a force equal to 2×10^{-7} newton per metre of length

Ohm (Ω) = the electric resistance between two points of a conductor when a constant potential difference of 1 volt, applied between the two points, produces in the conductor a current of 1 ampere, the conductor not being the seat of any electromotive force

Volt (V) = the difference of electric potential between two points of a conducting wire carrying a constant current of 1 ampere when the power dissipated between these points is equal to 1 watt

Watt (W) = the power which in one second gives rise to energy of 1 joule

Kilowatt (kW) = 1000 watts

Megawatt (MW) = one million watts

WATER AND LIQUOR MEASURES

1 cubic foot = 62.32 lb
1 gallon = 10 lb
1 cubic cm = 1 gram
1000 cubic cm = 1 litre; 1 kilogram
1 cubic metre = 1000 litres; 1000 kg; 1 tonne
An inch of rain on the surface of an acre (43560 sq. ft) = 3630 cubic ft = 100.992 tons
Cisterns: A cistern $4 \times 2\frac{1}{2}$ feet and 3 feet deep will hold brimful 186.963 gallons, weighing 1869.63 lb in addition to its own weight

WATER FOR SHIPS

Kilderkin = 18 gallons
Barrel = 36 gallons
Puncheon = 72 gallons
Butt = 110 gallons
Tun = 210 gallons

BOTTLES OF WINE

Traditional equivalents in standard champagne bottles:
Magnum = 2 bottles
Jeroboam = 4 bottles
Rehoboam = 6 bottles
Methuselah = 8 bottles
Salmanazar = 12 bottles
Balthazar = 16 bottles
Nebuchadnezzar = 20 bottles

A quarter of a bottle is known as a *nip*
An eighth of a bottle is known as a *baby*

ANGULAR AND CIRCULAR MEASURES

60 seconds (″) = 1 minute (′)
60 minutes = 1 degree (°)
90 degrees = 1 right angle or quadrant
Diameter of circle × 3.141 6 = circumference
Diameter squared × 0.7854 = area of circle
Diameter squared × 3.141 6 = surface of sphere
Diameter cubed × 0.523 = solidity of sphere
One degree of circumference × 57.3 = radius*
Diameter of cylinder × 3.141 6; product by length or height, gives the surface
Diameter squared × 0.7854; product by length or height, gives solid content

*Or, one radian (the angle subtended at the centre of a circle by an arc of the circumference equal in length to the radius) = 57.3 degrees

MILLION, BILLION, ETC.

Value in the UK
Million	thousand × thousand	10^6
*Billion	million × million	10^{12}
Trillion	million × billion	10^{18}
Quadrillion	million × trillion	10^{24}

Value in USA
Million	thousand × thousand	10^6
*Billion	thousand × million	10^9
Trillion	million × million	10^{12}
Quadrillion	million × billion US	10^{15}

*The American usage of billion (i.e. 10^9) is increasingly common, and is now universally used by statisticians

NAUTICAL MEASURES

DISTANCE

Distance at sea is measured in nautical miles. The British standard nautical mile was 6080 feet (the length of a minute of an arc of a great circle of the earth, rounded off to a mean value to allow for the length varying at different latitudes). This measure has been obsolete since 1970 when the international nautical mile of 1852 metres was adopted by the Hydrographic Department of the Ministry of Defence as a result of a recommendation by the International Hydrographic Bureau.

The cable (600 feet or 100 fathoms) was a measure approximately one-tenth of a nautical mile. Such distances are now expressed in decimal parts of a sea mile or in metres.

Soundings at sea were recorded in fathoms (6 feet). Depths are now expressed in metres on Admiralty charts.

SPEED

Speed is measured in nautical miles per hour, called knots. A ship moving at the rate of 30 nautical miles per hour is said to be doing 30 knots.

knots	m.p.h.	knots	m.p.h.
1	1.1515	9	10.3636
2	2.3030	10	11.5151
3	3.4545	15	17.2727
4	4.6060	20	23.0303
5	5.7575	25	28.7878
6	6.9090	30	34.5454
7	8.0606	35	40.3030
8	9.2121	40	46.0606

TONNAGE

The tonnage of a vessel is measured in tons of 100 cubic feet.

Gross tonnage = the total volume of all the enclosed spaces of a vessel

Net tonnage = gross tonnage less deductions for crew space, engine room, water ballast and other spaces not used for passengers or cargo

---

DISTANCE OF THE HORIZON

The limit of distance to which one can see varies with the height of the spectator. The greatest distance at which an object on the surface of the sea, or of a level plain, can be seen by a person whose eyes are at a height of five feet from the same level is nearly three miles. At a height of 20 feet the range is increased to nearly six miles, and an approximate rule for finding the range of vision for small heights is to increase the square root of the number of feet that the eye is above the level surface by a third of itself. The result is the distance of the horizon in miles, but is slightly in excess of that in the table below, which is computed by a more precise formula. The table may be used conversely to show the distance of an object of given height that is just visible from a point on the surface of the earth or sea. Refraction is taken into account both in the approximate rule and in the table.

Height in feet	range in miles
5	2.9
20	5.9
50	9.3
100	13.2
500	29.5
1,000	41.6
2,000	58.9
3,000	72.1
4,000	83.3
5,000	93.1
20,000	186.2

TEMPERATURE SCALES

The SI (International System) unit of temperature is the kelvin, which is defined as the fraction 1/273.16 of the temperature of the triple point of water (i.e. where ice, water and water vapour are in equilibrium). The zero of the Kelvin scale is the absolute zero of temperature. The freezing point of water is 273.15 K and the boiling point (as adopted in the International Temperature Scale of 1990) is 373.124 K.

The Celsius scale (formerly centigrade) is defined by subtracting 273.15 from the Kelvin temperature. The Fahrenheit scale is related to the Celsius scale by the relationships:

temperature °F = (temperature °C × 1.8) + 32
temperature °C = (temperature °F − 32) ÷ 1.8

It follows from these definitions that the freezing point of water is 0°C and 32°F. The boiling point is 99.974°C and 211.953°F.

The temperature of the human body varies from person to person and in the same person can be affected by a variety of factors. In most people body temperature varies between 36.5°C and 37.2°C (97.7–98.9°F).

Conversion between scales

°C	°F	°C	°F	°C	°F
100	212	60	140	20	68
99	210.2	59	138.2	19	66.2
98	208.4	58	136.4	18	64.4
97	206.6	57	134.6	17	62.6
96	204.8	56	132.8	16	60.8
95	203	55	131	15	59
94	201.2	54	129.2	14	57.2
93	199.4	53	127.4	13	55.4
92	197.6	52	125.6	12	53.6
91	195.8	51	123.8	11	51.8
90	194	50	122	10	50
89	192.2	49	120.2	9	48.2
88	190.4	48	118.4	8	46.4
87	188.6	47	116.6	7	44.6
86	186.8	46	114.8	6	42.8
85	185	45	113	5	41
84	183.2	44	111.2	4	39.2
83	181.4	43	109.4	3	37.4
82	179.6	42	107.6	2	35.6
81	177.8	41	105.8	1	33.8
80	176	40	104	zero	32
79	174.2	39	102.2	− 1	30.2
78	172.4	38	100.4	− 2	28.4
77	170.6	37	98.6	− 3	26.6
76	168.8	36	96.8	− 4	24.8
75	167	35	95	− 5	23
74	165.2	34	93.2	− 6	21.2
73	163.4	33	91.4	− 7	19.4
72	161.6	32	89.6	− 8	17.6
71	159.8	31	87.8	− 9	15.8
70	158	30	86	−10	14
69	156.2	29	84.2	−11	12.2
68	154.4	28	82.4	−12	10.4
67	152.6	27	80.6	−13	8.6
66	150.8	26	78.8	−14	6.8
65	149	25	77	−15	5
64	147.2	24	75.2	−16	3.2
63	145.4	23	73.4	−17	1.4
62	143.6	22	71.6	−18	0.4
61	141.8	21	69.8	−19	− 2.2

PAPER MEASURES

Printing Paper	*Writing Paper*
516 sheets = 1 ream	480 sheets = 1 ream
2 reams = 1 bundle	20 quires = 1 ream
5 bundles = 1 bale	24 sheets = 1 quire

Brown Papers

	inches		*inches*
Casing	46 × 36	Imperial Cap	29 × 22
Double Imperial	45 × 29	Haven Cap	26 × 21
Elephant	34 × 24	Bag Cap	24 × 19½
Double Four Pound	31 × 21	Kent Cap	21 × 18

Printing Papers

	inches		*inches*
Foolscap	17 × 13½	Double Large Post	33 × 21
Double Foolscap	27 × 17	Demy	22½ × 17½
Quad Foolscap	34 × 27	Double Demy	35 × 22½
Crown	20 × 15	Quad Demy	45 × 35
Double Crown	30 × 20	Music Demy	20 × 15½
Quad Crown	40 × 30	Medium	23 × 18
Double Quad Crown	60 × 40	Royal	25 × 20
Post	19¼ × 15½	Super Royal	27½ × 20½
Double Post	31½ × 19½	Elephant	28 × 23
		Imperial	30 × 22

Writing and Drawing Papers

	inches		*inches*
Emperor	72 × 48	Copy or Draft	20 × 16
Antiquarian	53 × 31	Demy	20 × 15½
Double Elephant	40 × 27	Post	19 × 15¼
Grand Eagle	42 × 28¾	Pinched Post	18½ × 14¾
Atlas	34 × 26	Foolscap	17 × 13½
Colombier	34½ × 23½	Double Foolscap	26½ × 16½
Imperial	30 × 22	Double Post	30½ × 19
Elephant	28 × 23	Double Large Post	33 × 21
Cartridge	26 × 21	Double Demy	31 × 20
Super Royal	27 × 19	Brief	16½ × 13¼
Royal	24 × 19	Pott	15 × 12½
Medium	22 × 17½		
Large Post	21 × 16½		

INTERNATIONAL PAPER SIZES

The basis of the international series of paper sizes is a rectangle having an area of one square metre, the sides of which are in the proportion of $1:\sqrt{2}$. The proportions $1:\sqrt{2}$ have a geometrical relationship, the side and diagonal of any square being in this proportion. The effect of this arrangement is that if the area of the sheet of paper is doubled or halved, the shorter side and the longer side of the new sheet are still in the same proportion $1:\sqrt{2}$. This feature is useful where photographic enlargement or reduction is used, as the proportions remain the same.

Description of the A series is by capital A followed by a figure. The basic size has the description A0 and the higher the figure following the letter, the greater is the number of sub-divisions and therefore the smaller the sheet. Half A0 is A1 and half A1 is A2. Where larger dimensions are required the A is preceded by a figure. Thus 2A means twice the size A0; 4A is four times the size of A0.

Subsidiary Series

B sizes are sizes intermediate between any two adjacent sizes of the A series. There is a series of C sizes which is used much less. A is for magazines and books, B for posters, wall charts and other large items, C for envelopes particularly where it is necessary for an envelope (in C series) to fit into another envelope. The size recommended for business correspondence is A4.

Long sizes (DL) are obtainable by dividing any appropriate sizes from the two series above into three, four or eight equal parts parallel with the shorter side in such a manner that the proportion of $1:\sqrt{2}$ is not maintained, the ratio between the longer and the shorter sides being greater than $\sqrt{2}:1$. In practice long sizes should be produced from the A series only.

It is an essential feature of these series that the dimensions are of the trimmed or finished size.

A Series

	mm		*mm*
A0	841 × 1189	A6	105 × 148
A1	594 × 841	A7	74 × 105
A2	420 × 594	A8	52 × 74
A3	297 × 420	A9	37 × 52
A4	210 × 297	A10	26 × 37
A5	148 × 210		

B Series

	mm		*mm*
B0	1000 × 1414	B6	125 × 176
B1	707 × 1000	B7	88 × 125
B2	500 × 707	B8	62 × 88
B3	353 × 500	B9	44 × 62
B4	250 × 353	B10	31 × 44
B5	176 × 250		

C Series		DL	
	mm		*mm*
C4	324 × 229	DL	110 × 220
C5	229 × 162		
C6	114 × 162		

BOUND BOOKS

The book sizes most commonly used are listed below. Approximate centimetre equivalents are also shown. International sizes are converted to their nearest imperial size, e.g. A4 = D4; A5 = D8.

		inches	*cm*
Crown 32mo	C32	2½ × 3¾	6 × 9
Crown 16mo	C16	3¾ × 5	9 × 13
Foolscap 8vo	F8	4¼ × 6¾	11 × 17
Demy 16mo	D16	4⅜ × 5⅝	11 × 14
Crown 8vo	C8	5 × 7½	13 × 19
Demy 8vo	D8	5⅝ × 8¾	14 × 22
Medium 8vo	M8	5¾ × 9	15 × 23
Royal 8vo	R8	6¼ × 10	16 × 25
Super Royal 8vo	suR8	6¾ × 10	17 × 25
Foolscap 4to	F4	6¾ × 8½	17 × 22
Crown 4to	C4	7½ × 10	19 × 25
Imperial 8vo	Imp8	7½ × 11	19 × 28
Demy 4to	D4	8¾ × 11¼	22 × 29
Royal 4to	R4	10 × 12½	25 × 31
Super Royal 4to	suR4	10 × 13½	25 × 34
Crown Folio	Cfol	10 × 15	25 × 38
Imperial Folio	Impfol	11 × 15	28 × 38

Folio = a sheet folded in half
Quarto (4to) = a sheet folded into four
Octavo (8vo) = a sheet folded into eight
Books are usually bound up in sheets of 16, 32 or 64 pages. Octavo books are generally printed 64 pages at a time, 32 pages on each side of a sheet of quad.

CONVERSION TABLES FOR WEIGHTS AND MEASURES

Bold figures equal units of either of the columns beside them; thus: 1 cm = 0.394 inches and 1 inch = 2.540 cm

LENGTH			AREA			VOLUME			WEIGHT (MASS)		
Centimetres		Inches	Square cm		Square in	Cubic cm		Cubic in	Kilograms		Pounds
2.540	1	0.394	6.452	1	0.155	16.387	1	0.061	0.454	1	2.205
5.080	2	0.787	12.903	2	0.310	32.774	2	0.122	0.907	2	4.409
7.620	3	1.181	19.355	3	0.465	49.161	3	0.183	1.361	3	6.614
10.160	4	1.575	25.806	4	0.620	65.548	4	0.244	1.814	4	8.819
12.700	5	1.969	32.258	5	0.775	81.936	5	0.305	2.268	5	11.023
15.240	6	2.362	38.710	6	0.930	98.323	6	0.366	2.722	6	13.228
17.780	7	2.756	45.161	7	1.085	114.710	7	0.427	3.175	7	15.432
20.320	8	3.150	51.613	8	1.240	131.097	8	0.488	3.629	8	17.637
22.860	9	3.543	58.064	9	1.395	147.484	9	0.549	4.082	9	19.842
25.400	10	3.937	64.516	10	1.550	163.871	10	0.610	4.536	10	22.046
50.800	20	7.874	129.032	20	3.100	327.742	20	1.220	9.072	20	44.092
76.200	30	11.811	193.548	30	4.650	491.613	30	1.831	13.608	30	66.139
101.600	40	15.748	258.064	40	6.200	655.484	40	2.441	18.144	40	88.185
127.000	50	19.685	322.580	50	7.750	819.355	50	3.051	22.680	50	110.231
152.400	60	23.622	387.096	60	9.300	983.226	60	3.661	27.216	60	132.277
177.800	70	27.559	451.612	70	10.850	1147.097	70	4.272	31.752	70	154.324
203.200	80	31.496	516.128	80	12.400	1310.968	80	4.882	36.287	80	176.370
228.600	90	35.433	580.644	90	13.950	1474.839	90	5.492	40.823	90	198.416
254.000	100	39.370	645.160	100	15.500	1638.710	100	6.102	45.359	100	220.464

Metres		Yards	Square m		Square yd	Cubic m		Cubic yd	Metric tonnes		Tons (UK)
0.914	1	1.094	0.836	1	1.196	0.765	1	1.308	1.016	1	0.984
1.829	2	2.187	1.672	2	2.392	1.529	2	2.616	2.032	2	1.968
2.743	3	3.281	2.508	3	3.588	2.294	3	3.924	3.048	3	2.953
3.658	4	4.374	3.345	4	4.784	3.058	4	5.232	4.064	4	3.937
4.572	5	5.468	4.181	5	5.980	3.823	5	6.540	5.080	5	4.921
5.486	6	6.562	5.017	6	7.176	4.587	6	7.848	6.096	6	5.905
6.401	7	7.655	5.853	7	8.372	5.352	7	9.156	7.112	7	6.889
7.315	8	8.749	6.689	8	9.568	6.116	8	10.464	8.128	8	7.874
8.230	9	9.843	7.525	9	10.764	6.881	9	11.772	9.144	9	8.858
9.144	10	10.936	8.361	10	11.960	7.646	10	13.080	10.161	10	9.842
18.288	20	21.872	16.723	20	23.920	15.291	20	26.159	20.321	20	19.684
27.432	30	32.808	25.084	30	35.880	22.937	30	39.239	30.481	30	29.526
36.576	40	43.745	33.445	40	47.840	30.582	40	52.318	40.642	40	39.368
45.720	50	54.681	41.806	50	59.799	38.228	50	65.398	50.802	50	49.210
54.864	60	65.617	50.168	60	71.759	45.873	60	78.477	60.963	60	59.052
64.008	70	76.553	58.529	70	83.719	53.519	70	91.557	71.123	70	68.894
73.152	80	87.489	66.890	80	95.679	61.164	80	104.636	81.284	80	78.737
82.296	90	98.425	75.251	90	107.639	68.810	90	117.716	91.444	90	88.579
91.440	100	109.361	83.613	100	119.599	76.455	100	130.795	101.605	100	98.421

Kilometres		Miles	Hectares		Acres	Litres		Gallons	Metric tonnes		Tons (US)
1.609	1	0.621	0.405	1	2.471	4.546	1	0.220	0.907	1	1.102
3.219	2	1.243	0.809	2	4.942	9.092	2	0.440	1.814	2	2.205
4.828	3	1.864	1.214	3	7.413	13.638	3	0.660	2.722	3	3.305
6.437	4	2.485	1.619	4	9.844	18.184	4	0.880	3.629	4	4.409
8.047	5	3.107	2.023	5	12.355	22.730	5	1.100	4.536	5	5.521
9.656	6	3.728	2.428	6	14.826	27.276	6	1.320	5.443	6	6.614
11.265	7	4.350	2.833	7	17.297	31.822	7	1.540	6.350	7	7.716
12.875	8	4.971	3.327	8	19.769	36.368	8	1.760	7.257	8	8.818
14.484	9	5.592	3.642	9	22.240	40.914	9	1.980	8.165	9	9.921
16.093	10	6.214	4.047	10	24.711	45.460	10	2.200	9.072	10	11.023
32.187	20	12.427	8.094	20	49.421	90.919	20	4.400	18.144	20	22.046
48.280	30	18.641	12.140	30	74.132	136.379	30	6.599	27.216	30	33.069
64.374	40	24.855	16.187	40	98.842	181.839	40	8.799	36.287	40	44.092
80.467	50	31.069	20.234	50	123.555	227.298	50	10.999	45.359	50	55.116
96.561	60	37.282	24.281	60	148.263	272.758	60	13.199	54.431	60	66.139
112.654	70	43.496	28.328	70	172.974	318.217	70	15.398	63.503	70	77.162
128.748	80	49.710	32.375	80	197.684	363.677	80	17.598	72.575	80	88.185
144.841	90	55.923	36.422	90	222.395	409.137	90	19.798	81.647	90	99.208
160.934	100	62.137	40.469	100	247.105	454.596	100	21.998	90.719	100	110.231

Abbreviations

A — Associate of
AA — Alcoholics Anonymous
Anti-Aircraft
Automobile Association
AAA — Amateur Athletic Association
AB — Able-bodied seaman
ABA — Amateur Boxing Association
abbr(ev) — abbreviation
ABM — Anti-ballistic missile
abr — abridged
ac — alternating current
a/c — account
AC — Aircraftman
(*Ante Christum*) Before Christ
Companion, Order of Australia
ACAS — Advisory, Conciliation and Arbitration Service
ACT — Australian Capital Territory
AD — (*Anno Domini*) In the year of our Lord
ADC — Aide-de-Camp
ADC(P) — Personal ADC to The Queen
adj — adjective
Adj — Adjutant
ad lib — (*ad libitum*) at pleasure
Adm — Admiral
Admission
adv — adverb
advocate
AE — Air Efficiency Award
AEA — Atomic Energy Authority
AEEU — Amalgamated Engineering and Electrical Union
AEM — Air Efficiency Medal
AERE — Atomic Energy Research Establishment
AFC — Air Force Cross
Association Football Club
AFM — Air Force Medal
AFRC — Agricultural and Food Research Council
AG — Adjutant-General
Attorney-General
AGM — air-to-ground missile
annual general meeting
AH — (*Anno Hegirae*) In the year of the Hegira
AI — Artificial intelligence
AIDS — Acquired immune deficiency syndrome
alt — altitude
am — (*ante meridiem*) before noon
AM — (*Anno mundi*) In the year of the world
amplitude modulation
amp — ampere
amplifier
ANC — African National Congress
anon — anonymous
ANZAC — Australian and New Zealand Army Corps
AO — Air Officer
Officer, Order of Australia
AOC — Air Officer Commanding
AONB — Area of Outstanding Natural Beauty
AS — Anglo-Saxon
ASA — Advertising Standards Authority
Amateur Swimming Association
asap — as soon as possible
ASB — Alternative Service Book

ASEAN — Association of South East Asian Nations
ASH — Action on Smoking and Health
ASLEF — Associated Society of Locomotive Engineers and Firemen
ASLIB — Association for Information Management
ATC — Air Training Corps
AUC — (*ab urbe condita*) In the year from the foundation of Rome
(*anno urbis conditae*) In the year of the founding of the city
AUT — Association of University Teachers
AV — Audio-visual
Authorized Version (*of Bible*)
AVR — Army Volunteer Reserve
AWOL — Absent without leave

b — born
bowled
BA — Bachelor of Arts
BAA — British Airports Authority
British Astronomical Association
BAF — British Athletics Federation
BAFTA — British Academy of Film and Television Arts
BAOR — British Army of the Rhine
Bart — Baronet
BAS — Bachelor in Agricultural Science
British Antarctic Survey
BB — Boys' Brigade
BBC — British Broadcasting Corporation
BBSRC — Biotechnology and Biological Sciences Research Council
BC — Before Christ
British Columbia
BCCI — Bank of Credit and Commerce International
B Ch (D) — Bachelor of (Dental) Surgery
BCL — Bachelor of Civil Law
B Com — Bachelor of Commerce
BD — Bachelor of Divinity
BDA — British Dental Association
BDS — Bachelor of Dental Surgery
B Ed — Bachelor of Education
BEM — British Empire Medal
B Eng — Bachelor of Engineering
BFI — British Film Institute
BFPO — British Forces Post Office
BL — British Library
B Litt — Bachelor of Letters *or* of Literature
BM — Bachelor of Medicine
British Museum
BMA — British Medical Association
B Mus — Bachelor of Music
BOTB — British Overseas Trade Board
Bp — Bishop
B Pharm — Bachelor of Pharmacy
B Phil — Bachelor of Philosophy
Br — Britain
British
BR — British Rail
Brig — Brigadier
Brit — Britain
British
BSc — Bachelor of Science

BSE — Bovine spongiform encephalopathy
BSI — British Standards Institution
BST — British Summer Time
Bt — Baronet
BTEC — Business and Technology Education Council
B Th — Bachelor of Theology
Btu — British thermal unit
BVM — (*Beata Virgo Maria*) Blessed Virgin Mary
BVMS — Bachelor of Veterinary Medicine and Surgery
BWB — British Waterways Board

c — (*circa*) about
C — Celsius
Centigrade
Conservative
CA — Chartered Accountant (*Scotland*)
CAA — Civil Aviation Authority
CAB — Citizens' Advice Bureau
Cantab — (of) Cambridge
Cantuar: — of Canterbury (*Archbishop*)
CAP — Common Agricultural Policy
Capt — Captain
Caricom — Caribbean Community and Common Market
Carliol: — of Carlisle (*Bishop*)
CB — Companion, Order of the Bath
CBE — Commander, Order of the British Empire
CBI — Confederation of British Industry
CC — Chamber of Commerce
Companion, Order of Canada
City Council
County Council
County Court
CCC — County Cricket Club
CCF — Combined Cadet Force
C Chem — Chartered Chemist
CD — Civil Defence
compact disc
Corps Diplomatique
Cdr — Commander
Cdre — Commodore
CDS — Chief of the Defence Staff
CE — Christian Era
Civil Engineer
C Eng — Chartered Engineer
Cento — Central Treaty Organization
Cestr: — of Chester (*Bishop*)
CET — Central European Time
Common External Tariff
cf — (*confer*) compare
CF — Chaplain to the Forces
CFC — Chlorofluorocarbon
CGC — Conspicuous Gallantry Cross
CGM — Conspicuous Gallantry Medal
CGS — Centimetre-gramme-second (*system*)
Chief of General Staff
CH — Companion of Honour
ChB/M — Bachelor/Master of Surgery
CI — Channel Islands
The Imperial Order of the Crown of India
CIA — Central Intelligence Agency
Cicestr: — of Chichester (*Bishop*)
CID — Criminal Investigation Department

CIE	Companion, Order of the Indian Empire	D Mus	Doctor of Music	*f*	(*forte*) loud
cif	cost, insurance and freight	DNA	deoxyribonucleic acid	F	Fahrenheit
C-in-C	Commander-in-Chief	DNB	*Dictionary of National Biography*		Fellow of
CIPFA	Chartered Institute of Public Finance and Accountancy	DNH	Department of National Heritage	FA	Football Association
		do	(*ditto*) the same	FANY	First Aid Nursing Yeomanry
CJD	Creutzfeld-Jakob disease	DoE	Department of the Environment	FAO	Food and Agriculture Organization (*UN*)
C Lit	Companion of Literature			FBA	Fellow, British Academy
CLJ	Commander, Order of St Lazarus of Jerusalem	DOS	Disk operating system (*computer*)	FBAA	Fellow, British Association of Accountants and Auditors
CM	(*Chirurgiae Magister*) Master of Surgery	DP	Data processing	FBI	Federal Bureau of Investigation
CMG	Companion, Order of St Michael and St George	D Ph *or* D Phil	Doctor of Philosophy	FBIM	Fellow, British Institute of Management
CND	Campaign for Nuclear Disarmament	DPP	Director of Public Prosecutions	FBS	Fellow, Botanical Society
c/o	care of	Dr	Doctor	FC	Football Club
CO	Commanding Officer	D Sc	Doctor of Science	FCA	Fellow, Institute of Chartered Accountants in England and Wales
	conscientious objector	DSC	Distinguished Service Cross		
COD	Cash on delivery	DSM	Distinguished Service Medal		
C of E	Church of England	DSO	Companion, Distinguished Service Order	FCCA	Fellow, Chartered Association of Certified Accountants
COHSE	Confederation of Health Service Employees	DSS	Department of Social Security	FCGI	Fellow, City and Guilds of London Institute
COI	Central Office of Information	DTI	Department of Trade and Industry	FCIA	Fellow, Corporation of Insurance Agents
Col	Colonel				
Con	Conservative	DTP	Desk-top publishing	FCIArb	Fellow, Chartered Institute of Arbitrators
Cpl	Corporal	Dunelm:	of Durham (*Bishop*)		
CPM	Colonial Police Medal	DV	(*Deo volente*) God willing	FCIB	Fellow, Chartered Institute of Bankers
CPRE	Council for the Protection of Rural England				Fellow, Corporation of Insurance Brokers
CPS	Crown Prosecution Service	E	East		
CPVE	Certificate of Pre-Vocational Education	Ebor:	of York (*Archbishop*)	FCIBSE	Fellow, Chartered Institution of Building Services Engineers
		EBRD	European Bank for Reconstruction and Development		
CRE	Commission for Racial Equality			FCII	Fellow, Chartered Insurance Institute
CSA	Child Support Agency	EC	European Community	FCIPS	Fellow, Chartered Institute of Purchasing and Supply
CSCE	Conference on Security and Co-operation in Europe	ECG	Electrocardiogram		
		ECGD	Export Credits Guarantee Department	FCIS	Fellow, Institute of Chartered Secretaries and Administrators
CSE	Certificate of Secondary Education				
		ECSC	European Coal and Steel Community	FCIT	Fellow, Chartered Institute of Transport
CSI	Companion, Order of the Star of India				
		ECU	European Currency Unit	FCMA	Fellow, Chartered Institute of Management Accountants
CVO	Commander, Royal Victorian Order	ED	Efficiency Decoration		
		EEC	European Economic Community	FCO	Foreign and Commonwealth Office
		EEG	Electroencephalogram	FCP	Fellow, College of Preceptors
d	(*denarius*) penny	EFA	European Fighter Aircraft	FD	(*Fidei Defensor*) Defender of the Faith
DBE	Dame Commander, Order of the British Empire	EFTA	European Free Trade Association		
				fec	(*fecit*) made this
dc	direct current	eg	(*exempli gratia*) for the sake of example	FEng	Fellow, Royal Academy of Engineering
DC	District Council				
	District of Columbia	EMS	European Monetary System	ff	(*fecerunt*) made this (*pl*)
DCB	Dame Commander, Order of the Bath	EMU	European Monetary Union	ff	(*fortissimo*) very loud
		ENEA	European Nuclear Energy Agency	FFA	Fellow, Faculty of Actuaries (*Scotland*)
D Ch	(*Doctor Chirurgiae*) Doctor of Surgery				Fellow, Institute of Financial Accountants
		EOC	Equal Opportunities Commission		
DCL	Doctor of Civil Law				
DCM	Distinguished Conduct Medal	EPSRC	Engineering and Physical Sciences Research Council	FFAS	Fellow, Faculty of Architects and Surveyors
DCMG	Dame Commander, Order of St Michael and St George	ER	(*Elizabetha Regina*) Queen Elizabeth	FFCM	Fellow, Faculty of Community Medicine
DCVO	Dame Commander, Royal Victorian Order			FFPHM	Fellow, Faculty of Public Health Medicine
		ERD	Emergency Reserve Decoration		
DD	Doctor of Divinity			FGS	Fellow, Geological Society
DDS	Doctor of Dental Surgery	ERM	Exchange Rate Mechanism	FHS	Fellow, Heraldry Society
DDT	dichlorodiphenyl-trichloroethane	ERNIE	Electronic random number indicator equipment	FHSM	Fellow, Institute of Health Service Management
		ESA	European Space Agency	FIA	Fellow, Institute of Actuaries
del	(*delineavit*) he/she drew it	ESP	Extra-sensory perception	FIBiol	Fellow, Institute of Biology
DFC	Distinguished Flying Cross	ESRC	Economic and Social Research Council	FICE	Fellow, Institution of Civil Engineers
DFEE	Department for Education and Employment				
		ETA	*Euzkadi ta Askatasuna* (Basque separatist organization)	FICS	Fellow, Institution of Chartered Shipbrokers
DFM	Distinguished Flying Medal				
DG	(*Dei gratia*) By the grace of God	et al	(*et alibi*) and elsewhere	FIEE	Fellow, Institution of Electrical Engineers
	Director-General		(*et alii*) and others		
DH	Department of Health	etc	(*et cetera*) and the other things/ and so forth	FIERE	Fellow, Institution of Electronic and Radio Engineers
DHA	District Health Authority				
Dip Ed	Diploma in Education	et seq	(*et sequentia*) and the following		
Dip H E	Diploma in Higher Education	EU	European Union	FIFA	International Association Football Federation
Dip Tech	Diploma in Technology	Euratom	European Atomic Energy Commission		
DJ	Disc jockey				
DL	Deputy Lieutenant	Exon:	of Exeter (*Bishop*)	FIM	Fellow, Institute of Metals
D Litt	Doctor of Letters *or* of Literature				

FIMM	Fellow, Institution of Mining and Metallurgy	FRMetS	Fellow, Royal Meteorological Society	HE	Her/His Excellency His Eminence
FInstF	Fellow, Institute of Fuel	FRMS	Fellow, Royal Microscopical Society	HGV	Heavy Goods Vehicle
FInstP	Fellow, Institute of Physics			HH	Her/His Highness
FIQS	Fellow, Institute of Quantity Surveyors	FRNS	Fellow, Royal Numismatic Society		Her/His Honour His Holiness
FIS	Fellow, Institute of Statisticians	FRPharmS	Fellow, Royal Pharmaceutical Society	HIM	Her/His Imperial Majesty
FJI	Fellow, Institute of Journalists	FRPS	Fellow, Royal Photographic Society	HIV	Human immunodeficiency virus
fl	(*floruit*) flourished			HJS	(*hic jacet sepultus*) here lies buried
FLA	Fellow, Library Association	FRS	Fellow, Royal Society		
FLS	Fellow, Linnaean Society	FRSA	Fellow, Royal Society of Arts	HM	Her/His Majesty('s)
FM	Field Marshal	FRSC	Fellow, Royal Society of Chemistry	HMAS	Her/His Majesty's Australian Ship
	frequency modulation			HMC	Headmasters' Conference
fo	folio	FRSE	Fellow, Royal Society of Edinburgh	HMI	Her/His Majesty's Inspector
FO	Flying Officer			HML	Her/His Majesty's Lieutenant
fob	free on board	FRSH	Fellow, Royal Society of Health	HMS	Her/His Majesty's Ship
FPA	Family Planning Association			HMSO	Her/His Majesty's Stationery Office
FPhS	Fellow, Philosophical Society	FRSL	Fellow, Royal Society of Literature		
FRAD	Fellow, Royal Academy of Dancing	FRTPI	Fellow, Royal Town Planning Institute	HNC	Higher National Certificate
				HND	Higher National Diploma
FRAeS	Fellow, Royal Aeronautical Society	FSA	Fellow, Society of Antiquaries	HOLMES	Home Office Large Major Enquiry System
FRAI	Fellow, Royal Anthropological Institute	FSS	Fellow, Royal Statistical Society	Hon	Honorary Honourable
FRAM	Fellow, Royal Academy of Music	FSVA	Fellow, Incorporated Society of Valuers and Auctioneers	hp	horse power
				HP	Hire purchase
FRAS	Fellow, Royal Asiatic Society	FT	*Financial Times*	HQ	Headquarters
	Fellow, Royal Astronomical Society	FTI	Fellow, Textile Institute	HRH	Her/His Royal Highness
		FTII	Fellow, Institute of Taxation	HSE	Health and Safety Executive
FRBS	Fellow, Royal Botanic Society	FZS	Fellow, Zoological Society		(*hic sepultus est*) here lies buried
	Fellow, Royal Society of British Sculptors			HSH	Her/His Serene Highness
FRCA	Fellow, Royal College of Anaesthetists	GATT	General Agreement on Tariffs and Trade	HTR	High temperature reactor
				HWM	High water mark
FRCGP	Fellow, Royal College of General Practitioners	GBE	Dame/Knight Grand Cross, Order of the British Empire		
FRCM	Fellow, Royal College of Music	GC	George Cross	I	Island
		GCB	Dame/Knight Grand Cross, Order of the Bath	IAAS	Incorporated Association of Architects and Surveyors
FRCO	Fellow, Royal College of Organists	GCE	General Certificate of Education	IAEA	International Atomic Energy Agency
FRCOG	Fellow, Royal College of Obstetricians and Gynaecologists	GCHQ	Government Communications Headquarters	IATA	International Air Transport Association
		GCIE	Knight Grand Commander, Order of the Indian Empire	ibid	(*ibidem*) in the same place
FRCP	Fellow, Royal College of Physicians, London			IBRD	International Bank for Reconstruction and Development
FRCPath	Fellow, Royal College of Pathologists	GCLJ	Knight Grand Cross, Order of St Lazarus of Jerusalem		
FRCPE *or*		GCMG	Dame/Knight Grand Cross, Order of St Michael and St George	ICAO	International Civil Aviation Organization
FRCPEd	Fellow, Royal College of Physicians, Edinburgh			ICBM	Inter-continental ballistic missile
FRCPI	Fellow, Royal College of Physicians, Ireland	GCSE	General Certificate of Secondary Education	ICFTU	International Confederation of Free Trade Unions
FRCPsych	Fellow, Royal College of Psychiatrists	GCSI	Knight Grand Commander, Order of the Star of India	ICJ	International Court of Justice
FRCR	Fellow, Royal College of Radiologists	GCVO	Dame/Knight Grand Cross, Royal Victorian Order	ICRC	International Committee of the Red Cross
FRCS	Fellow, Royal College of Surgeons of England	GDP	Gross domestic product	id	(*idem*) the same
FRCSE *or*		Gen	General	IDA	International Development Association
FRCSEd	Fellow, Royal College of Surgeons of Edinburgh	GHQ	General Headquarters	IDD	International direct dialling
		GM	George Medal	ie	(*id est*) that is
FRCSGlas	Fellow, Royal College of Physicians and Surgeons of Glasgow	GMB	General, Municipal, Boilermakers and Allied Trades Union	IEA	International Energy Agency
				IFAD	International Fund for Agricultural Development
FRCSI	Fellow, Royal College of Surgeons in Ireland	GMT	Greenwich Mean Time	IFC	International Finance Corporation
		GNP	Gross national product		
FRCVS	Fellow, Royal College of Veterinary Surgeons	GOC	General Officer Commanding	IHS	(*Iesus Hominum Salvator*) Jesus the Saviour of Mankind
		GP	General Practitioner		
FREconS	Fellow, Royal Economic Society	Gp Capt	Group Captain	ILO	International Labour Office/ Organization
		GSA	Girls' Schools Association		
FRGS	Fellow, Royal Geographical Society	GSO	General Staff Officer	ILR	Independent local radio
				IMF	International Monetary Fund
FRHistS	Fellow, Royal Historical Society			IMO	International Maritime Organization
FRHS	Fellow, Royal Horticultural Society	HAC	Honourable Artillery Company	Inc	Incorporated
				incog	(*incognito*) unknown, unrecognized
FRIBA	Fellow, Royal Institute of British Architects	HB	His Beatitude		
		HBM	Her/His Britannic Majesty('s)	INF	International Nuclear Force
FRICS	Fellow, Royal Institution of Chartered Surveyors	HCF	Highest common factor Honorary Chaplain to the Forces	INLA	Irish National Liberation Army
				in loc	(*in loco*) in its place

Inmarsat	International Maritime Satellite Organization	LHD	(*Literarum Humaniorum Doctor*) Doctor of Humane Letters/	MN	Merchant Navy	
INRI	(*Iesus Nazarenus Rex Iudaeorum*) Jesus of Nazareth, King of the Jews		Literature	MO	Medical Officer/Orderly	
		Lib	Liberal	MoD	Ministry of Defence	
		Lic	(*Licenciado*) lawyer (*Spanish*)	MoT	Ministry of Transport	
inst	(*instant*) current month	Lic Med	Licentiate in Medicine	MP	Member of Parliament	
Intelsat	International Telecommunications Satellite Organization	Lit	Literary		Military Police	
		Lit Hum	(*Literae Humaniores*) Faculty of classics and philosophy, Oxford	mph	miles per hour	
				MR	Master of the Rolls	
Interpol	International Criminal Police Commission	Litt D	Doctor of Letters	MRC	Medical Research Council	
		LJ	Lord Justice	MS	Master of Surgery	
IOC	International Olympic Committee	LLB	Bachelor of Laws		Manuscript (*pl* MSS)	
		LLD	Doctor of Laws		Multiple Sclerosis	
IOM	Isle of Man	LLM	Master of Laws	MSc	Master of Science	
IOU	I owe you	LM	Licentiate in Midwifery	MSF	Manufacturing, Science and Finance Union	
IOW	Isle of Wight	LMSSA	Licentiate in Medicine and Surgery, Society of Apothecaries			
IPLO	Irish People's Liberation Organization			MTh	Master of Theology	
				Mus B/D	Bachelor/Doctor of Music	
IQ	Intelligence quotient	loc cit	(*loco citato*) in the place cited	MV	Merchant Vessel Motor Vessel	
IRA	Irish Republican Army	log	logarithm			
IRC	International Red Cross	Londin:	of London (*Bishop*)	MVO	Member, Royal Victorian Order	
Is	Islands	Long	Longitude			
ISBN	International Standard Book Number	LS	(*loco sigilli*) place of the seal	MW	medium wave	
		LSA	Licentiate of Society of Apothecaries			
ISO	Imperial Service Order			N	North	
ITC	Independent Television Commission	Lsd	(*Librae, solidi, denarii*) £, shillings and pence	n/a	not applicable not available	
ITU	International Telecommunication Union	LSE	London School of Economics and Political Science	NAAFI	Navy, Army and Air Force Institutes	
ITV	Independent Television	Lt	Lieutenant	NALGO	National and Local Government Officers' Association	
		LTA	Lawn Tennis Association			
		Ltd	Limited (liability)			
JP	Justice of the Peace	LTh *or* L Theol	Licentiate in Theology	NASA	National Aeronautics and Space Administration	
		LVO	Lieutenant, Royal Victorian Order	NAS/UWT	National Association of Schoolmasters/Union of Women Teachers	
K	Köchel numeration (*of Mozart's works*)					
		LWM	Low water mark	NATO	North Atlantic Treaty Organization	
KBE	Knight Commander, Order of the British Empire			NB	New Brunswick (*nota bene*) note well	
KCB	Knight Commander, Order of the Bath	M	Member of Monsieur			
		MA	Master of Arts	NCC	Nature Conservancy Council	
KCIE	Knight Commander, Order of the Indian Empire	MAFF	Ministry of Agriculture, Fisheries and Food	NCIS	National Criminal Intelligence Service	
KCLJ	Knight Commander, Order of St Lazarus of Jerusalem	Maj	Major	NCO	Non-commissioned officer	
		max	maximum	NDPB	Non-departmental public body	
KCMG	Knight Commander, Order of St Michael and St George	MB	Bachelor of Medicine	NEB	New English Bible	
		MBA	Master of Business Administration	nem con	(*nemine contradicente*) no one contradicting	
KCSI	Knight Commander, Order of the Star of India	MBE	Member, Order of the British Empire	NERC	Natural Environment Research Council	
KCVO	Knight Commander, Royal Victorian Order					
		MC	Master of Ceremonies	nes	not elsewhere specified	
KG	Knight of the Garter		Military Cross	NFT	National Film Theatre	
KGB	(*Komitet Gosudarstvennoi Besopasnosti*) Committee of State Security (USSR)	MCC	Marylebone Cricket Club	NFU	National Farmers' Union	
		MCh(D)	Master of (Dental) Surgery	NHS	National Health Service	
		MD	Managing Director Doctor of Medicine	NI	National Insurance Northern Ireland	
KKK	Ku Klux Klan					
KLJ	Knight, Order of St Lazarus of Jerusalem	MDS	Master of Dental Surgery	NIV	New International Version (*of Bible*)	
ko	knock out (*boxing*)	ME	Middle English Myalgic Encephalomyelitis			
KP	Knight, Order of St Patrick			No	(*numero*) number	
KStJ	Knight, Order of St John of Jerusalem	MEC	Member of Executive Council	non seq	(*non sequitur*) it does not follow	
		MEd	Master of Education	Norvic:	of Norwich (*Bishop*)	
Kt	Knight	mega	one million times	NP	Notary Public	
KT	Knight of the Thistle	MEP	Member of the European Parliament	NRA	National Rifle Association National Rivers Authority	
kV	Kilovolt					
kW	Kilowatt	MFH	Master of Foxhounds	NS	New Style (*calendar*) Nova Scotia	
kWh	Kilowatt hour	Mgr	Monsignor			
		MI	Military Intelligence	NSPCC	National Society for the Prevention of Cruelty to Children	
		micro	one-millionth part			
L	Liberal	milli	one-thousandth part			
Lab	Labour	min	minimum	NSW	New South Wales	
Lat	Latitude	MIRAS	Mortgage Interest Relief at Source	NT	National Theatre National Trust New Testament	
lbw	leg before wicket					
lc	lower case (*printing*)	MLA	Member of Legislative Assembly			
LCJ	Lord Chief Justice			NUCPS	National Union of Civil and Public Servants	
LCM	Least/lowest common multiple	MLC	Member of Legislative Council			
		MLitt	Master of Letters	NUJ	National Union of Journalists	
LD	Liberal Democrat	Mlle	Mademoiselle	NUM	National Union of Mineworkers	
LDS	Licentiate in Dental Surgery	MLR	Minimum lending rate	NUPE	National Union of Public Employees	
LEA	Local Education Authority	MM	Military Medal			
		Mme	Madame	NUS	National Union of Students	

NUT	National Union of Teachers	
NVQ	National Vocational Qualification	
NWT	Northwest Territory	
NY	New York	
NZ	New Zealand	
OAPEC	Organization of Arab Petroleum Exporting Countries	
OAS	Organization of American States	
OAU	Organization of African Unity	
Ob *or* obit	died	
OBE	Officer, Order of the British Empire	
OC	Officer Commanding	
ODA	Overseas Development Administration	
OE	Old English omissions excepted	
OECD	Organization for Economic Co-operation and Development	
OED	*Oxford English Dictionary*	
Offer	Office of Electricity Regulation	
Ofgas	Office of Gas Supply	
OFM	Order of Friars Minor (*Franciscans*)	
Ofsted	Office for Standards in Education	
OFT	Office of Fair Trading	
Oftel	Office of Telecommunications	
Ofwat	Office of Water Services	
OHMS	On Her/His Majesty's Service	
OM	Order of Merit	
OND	Ordinary National Diploma	
op	(*opus*) work	
OP	Opposite prompt side (*of theatre*) Order of Preachers (*Dominicans*) out of print (*books*)	
op cit	(*opere citato*) in the work cited	
OPCS	Office of Population Censuses and Surveys	
OPEC	Organization of Petroleum Exporting Countries	
OPRAF	Office of Passenger Rail Franchising	
OPS	Office of Public Service	
ORR	Office of the Rail Regulator	
OS	Old Style (*calendar*) Ordnance Survey	
OSA	Order of St Augustine	
OSB	Order of St Benedict	
OST	Office of Science and Technology	
O StJ	Officer, Order of St John of Jerusalem	
OT	Old Testament	
OTC	Officers' Training Corps	
Oxon	(of) Oxford Oxfordshire	
p	page	
p	(*piano*) softly	
PA	Personal Assistant Press Association	
PAYE	Pay as You Earn	
pc	(*per centum*) in the hundred	
PC	personal computer Police Constable Privy Counsellor	
PCC	Press Complaints Commission	
PDSA	People's Dispensary for Sick Animals	
PE	Physical Education	
Petriburg:	of Peterborough (*Bishop*)	

PGA	Professional Golfers Association
PhD	Doctor of Philosophy
pinx(it)	he/she painted it
pl	plural
PLA	Port of London Authority
PLC	Public Limited Company
PLO	Palestine Liberation Organization
pm	(*post meridiem*) after noon
PM	Prime Minister
PMRAFNS	Princess Mary's Royal Air Force Nursing Service
PO	Petty Officer Pilot Officer Post Office postal order
POW	Prisoner of War
pp	pages (*per procurationem*) by proxy
PPARC	Particle Physics and Astronomy Research Council
PPS	Parliamentary Private Secretary
PR	Proportional representation Public relations
PRA	President of the Royal Academy
Pro tem	(*pro tempore*) for the time being
Prox	(*proximo*) next month
PRS	President of the Royal Society
PRSE	President of the Royal Society of Edinburgh
Ps	Psalm
PS	(*postscriptum*) postscript
PSBR	Public sector borrowing requirement
psc	passed Staff College
PSV	Public Service Vehicle
Pte	Private
PTO	Please turn over
QARANC	Queen Alexandra's Royal Army Nursing Corps
QARNNS	Queen Alexandra's Royal Naval Nursing Service
QB(D)	Queen's Bench (Division)
QC	Queen's Counsel
QED	(*quod erat demonstrandum*) which was to be proved
QGM	Queen's Gallantry Medal
QHC	Queen's Honorary Chaplain
QHDS	Queen's Honorary Dental Surgeon
QHNS	Queen's Honorary Nursing Sister
QHP	Queen's Honorary Physician
QHS	Queen's Honorary Surgeon
QMG	Quartermaster General
QPM	Queen's Police Medal
QS	Quarter Sessions
QSO	Quasi-stellar object (quasar) Queen's Service Order
quango	quasi-autonomous non-governmental organization
qv	(*quod vide*) which see
R	(*Regina*) Queen (*Rex*) King
RA	Royal Academy/Academician Royal Artillery
RAC	Royal Armoured Corps Royal Automobile Club
RADA	Royal Academy of Dramatic Art
RADC	Royal Army Dental Corps
RAE	Royal Aerospace Establishment

RAEC	Royal Army Educational Corps
RAeS	Royal Aeronautical Society
RAF	Royal Air Force
RAM	Random-access memory (*computer*) Royal Academy of Music
RAMC	Royal Army Medical Corps
RAN	Royal Australian Navy
RAOC	Royal Army Ordnance Corps
RAPC	Royal Army Pay Corps
RAVC	Royal Army Veterinary Corps
RBG	Royal Botanic Garden
RBS	Royal Society of British Sculptors
RC	Red Cross Roman Catholic
RCM	Royal College of Music
RCN	Royal Canadian Navy
RCT	Royal Corps of Transport
RD	Refer to drawer (*banking*) Royal Naval and Royal Marine Forces Reserve Decoration Rural Dean
RDI	Royal Designer for Industry
RE	Religious Education Royal Engineers
REME	Royal Electrical and Mechanical Engineers
Rep	Representative Republican
Rev(d)	Reverend
RFU	Rugby Football Union
RGN	Registered General Nurse
RGS	Royal Geographical Society
RHA	Regional Health Authority
RHS	Royal Horticultural Society Royal Humane Society
RI	Rhode Island Royal Institute of Painters in Watercolours Royal Institution
RIBA	Royal Institute of British Architects
RIP	(*Requiescat in pace*) May he/she rest in peace
RIR	Royal Irish Regiment
RL	Rugby League
RM	Registered Midwife Royal Marines
RMA	Royal Military Academy
RMN	Registered Mental Nurse
RMT	National Union of Rail, Maritime and Transport Workers
RN	Royal Navy
RNIB	Royal National Institute for the Blind
RNID	Royal National Institute for the Deaf
RNLI	Royal National Lifeboat Institution
RNR	Royal Naval Reserve
RNVR	Royal Naval Volunteer Reserve
RNXS	Royal Naval Auxiliary Service
RNZN	Royal New Zealand Navy
Ro	(*Recto*) on the right-hand page
ROC	Royal Observer Corps
Roffen:	of Rochester (*Bishop*)
ROI	Royal Institute of Oil Painters
ROM	Read-only memory (*computer*)
RoSPA	Royal Society for the Prevention of Accidents
RP	Royal Society of Portrait Painters
rpm	revolutions per minute
RRC	Lady of Royal Red Cross
RSA	Republic of South Africa Royal Scottish Academician Royal Society of Arts
RSC	Royal Shakespeare Company

RSCN	Registered Sick Children's Nurse	stet	let it stand (*printing*)	UTC	Co-ordinated Universal Time system
RSE	Royal Society of Edinburgh	stp	Standard temperature and pressure	UVF	Ulster Volunteer Force
RSM	Regimental Sergeant Major	STP	(*Sacrae Theologiae Professor*)		
RSPB	Royal Society for the Protection of Birds		Professor of Sacred Theology	v	(*versus*) against
RSPCA	Royal Society for the Prevention of Cruelty to Animals	Sub Lt	Sub-Lieutenant	VA	Vicar Apostolic
		SVQ	Scottish Vocational Qualification		Victoria and Albert Order
				VAD	Voluntary Aid Detachment
RSV	Revised Standard Version (*of Bible*)			VAT	Value added tax
		TA	Territorial Army	VC	Victoria Cross
RSVP	(*Répondez, s'il vous plaît*) Please reply	TB	Tuberculosis	VD	Venereal disease
		TCCB	Test and County Cricket Board		Volunteer Officers' Decoration
RSW	Royal Scottish Society of Painters in Watercolours	TCD	Trinity College, Dublin	VDU	Visual display unit
		TD	Territorial Efficiency Decoration	Ven	Venerable
RTPI	Royal Town Planning Institute			VHF	very high frequency
RU	Rugby Union			VIP	Very important person
RUC	Royal Ulster Constabulary	TEC	Training and Enterprise Council	Vo	(*Verso*) on the left-hand page
RV	Revised Version (*of Bible*)			VRD	Royal Naval Volunteer Reserve Officers' Decoration
RVM	Royal Victorian Medal	TEFL	Teaching English as a foreign language		
RWS	Royal Water Colour Society			VSO	Voluntary Service Overseas
RYS	Royal Yacht Squadron	temp	temperature	VTOL	Vertical take-off and landing (*aircraft*)
			temporary employee		
		TES	*Times Educational Supplement*		
s	second	TGWU	Transport and General Workers' Union	W	West
	(*solidus*) shilling			WCC	World Council of Churches
S	South	THES	*Times Higher Education Supplement*	WEA	Workers' Educational Association
SA	Salvation Army				
	South Africa	TLS	*Times Literary Supplement*	WEU	Western European Union
	South America	TNT	trinitrotoluene (*explosive*)	WFTU	World Federation of Trade Unions
	South Australia	trs	transpose (*printing*)		
SAE	stamped addressed envelope	TRH	Their Royal Highnesses	WHO	World Health Organization
Salop	Shropshire	TT	Teetotal	WI	West Indies
Sarum:	of Salisbury (*Bishop*)		Tourist Trophy (*motorcycle races*)		Women's Institute
SAS	Special Air Service Regiment			Winton:	of Winchester (*Bishop*)
SBS	Special Boat Squadron		Tuberculin tested	WIPO	World Intellectual Property Organization
SBN	Standard Book Number	TUC	Trades Union Congress		
ScD	Doctor of Science	TVEI	Technical and Vocational Education Initiative	WMO	World Meteorological Organization
SCM	State Certified Midwife				
SDLP	Social Democratic and Labour Party			WO	Warrant Officer
		U	Unionist	WRAC	Women's Royal Army Corps
SDP	Social Democratic Party	UAE	United Arab Emirates	WRAF	Women's Royal Air Force
SEAQ	Stock Exchange Automated Quotations system	uc	upper case (*printing*)	WRNS	Women's Royal Naval Service
		UCAS	Universities and Colleges Admissions Service	WRVS	Women's Royal Voluntary Service
SEN	State Enrolled Nurse				
SERPS	State Earnings Related Pension Scheme	UCATT	Union of Construction, Allied Trades and Technicians	WS	Writer to the Signet
SFO	Serious Fraud Office	UDA	Ulster Defence Association		
SHMIS	Society of Headmasters and Headmistresses of Independent Schools	UDI	Unilateral Declaration of Independence	YMCA	Young Men's Christian Association
		UDM	Union of Democratic Mineworkers	YWCA	Young Women's Christian Association
SI	(*Système International d'Unités*) International System of Units	UDR	Ulster Defence Regiment		
		UEFA	Union of European Football Associations	Ψ = seaport	
	Statutory Instrument				
sic	So written	UFF	Ulster Freedom Fighters		
Sig	Signature	UFO	Unidentified flying object		
	Signor	UHF	ultra-high frequency		
SJ	Society of Jesus (*Jesuits*)	UK	United Kingdom		
SLD	Social and Liberal Democrats	UKAEA	UK Atomic Energy Authority		
SMP	Statutory Maternity Pay	UN	United Nations		
SNP	Scottish National Party	UNESCO	United Nations Educational, Scientific and Cultural Organization		
SOE	Special Operations Executive				
SOS	Save Our Souls (*distress signal*)				
sp	(*sine prole*) without issue				
spgr	specific gravity	UNHCR	United Nations High Commissioner for Refugees		
SPQR	(*Senatus Populusque Romanus*) The Senate and People of Rome	UNICEF	United Nations Children's Fund		
		UNIDO	United Nations Industrial Development Organization		
SRN	State Registered Nurse				
SRO	Self Regulating Organizations	Unita	National Union for the Total Independence of Angola		
SS	Saints				
	Schutzstaffel (Nazi paramilitary organization)	UPU	Universal Postal Union		
		URC	United Reformed Church		
	Steamship	US(A)	United States (of America)		
SSC	Solicitor before Supreme Court (*Scotland*)	USDAW	Union of Shop, Distributive and Allied Workers		
SSF	Society of St Francis	USM	Unlisted Securities Market		
SSP	Statutory Sick Pay	USSR	Union of Soviet Socialist Republics		
SSSI	Site of special scientific interest				
STD	(*Sacrae Theologiae Doctor*) Doctor of Sacred Theology				
	Subscriber trunk dialling				

Index

SCOTTISH BORDERS LIBRARY SERVICE

Stop-press

CHANGES SINCE PAGES WENT TO PRESS

ROYAL HOUSEHOLDS
Aide-de-Camp General – Gen. Sir John Wilsey relinquishes appointment

PEERAGE
2nd Viscount Hanworth died
3rd Baron Daresbury died
Lord Amery of Lustleigh, PC, died
Marmaduke Hussey gazetted Baron Hussey of North Bradley
Field Marshal Sir Richard Vincent gazetted Baron Vincent of Coleshill

BARONETAGE AND KNIGHTAGE
Daniel Charles Williams, Governor-General of Grenada, appointed GCMG
Died: Sir Dennis Titchener-Barrett; Sir Charles Dorman; Sir Anthony Harris; Air Marshal Sir Rochford Hughes; Sir Peter Lloyd; Sir Reginald Pullen; Sir Jeremy Rowe

EUROPEAN PARLIAMENT
Kenneth Stewart, Labour MEP for Merseyside, died

GOVERNMENT DEPARTMENTS AND PUBLIC OFFICES
Home Office – 1,500 staff in the Prison Service made redundant in September 1996, including over 100 governors
British Library – major restructuring announced in September 1996
British Museum – Sir Martin Rees appointed a trustee
Department of National Heritage – A. Honnor appointed special adviser to Secretary of State

LAW COURTS AND OFFICES
Lords of Appeal in Ordinary – Lord Keith of Kinkel retired 30 September
Timothy Lloyd appointed to High Court (Chancery Division)
Timothy Walker appointed to High Court (Queen's Bench Division)
David E. Neuberger appointed to High Court (Chancery Division)
J. C. Warner appointed to Midland and Oxford circuit

POLICE SERVICE
Northamptonshire – C. Fox appointed chief constable

DEFENCE
Ministry of Defence – Richard Spring, MP, appointed parliamentary private secretary to Nicholas Soames and James Arbuthnot
Navy – Vice-Adm. Dunt to be Chief of Fleet Support in place of Vice-Adm. Sir Toby Frere; Cmdre B. Perowne to be promoted Rear-Admiral and to be Director-General, Fleet Support (Operations and Plans) in place of Rear-Adm. P. Spencer
Army – Maj.-Gen. R. Cordy-Simpson to be Deputy Force Commander Operations, Operation Joint Endeavour (in Bosnia), phase V, in acting rank of Lieutenant-General; Maj.-Gen. K. Drewienkiewicz to be Chief of Staff Headquarters Landcent, Operation Joint Endeavour, phase V; Maj.-Gen. M. D. Regan, OBE, retires
RAF – Air Vice-Marshal D. H. Hull retires

THE CHURCHES
Church of England
London – Ven. S. J. Oliver to be Canon Residentiary, St Paul's Cathedral
Winchester – Ven. J. M. Gledhill to be Suffragan Bishop of Southampton
St Edmundsbury and Ipswich – Rt. Revd Richard Lewis (Suffragan Bishop of Taunton, diocese of Bath and Wells) to be Bishop of St Edmundsbury and Ipswich
Worcester – Revd P. J. Marshall (Canon Residentiary, Ripon) to be Dean

Roman Catholic Church
Argyll and the Isles – Bishop Wright resigned
Burundi – Archbishop Ruhuna killed

LOCAL GOVERNMENT
Lord Mayor of London 1996–7: Alderman Roger Cork
Sheriffs of the City of London 1996–7: Clive Martin; Keith Knowles
Lord Lieutenant of Orkney, Brig. M. G. Dennison, died

MUSEUMS AND GALLERIES
Exeter Maritime Museum closed

THE MEDIA
Broadcasting Complaints Commission – Ms J. Leighton appointed chairman

TRADE UNIONS
Elizabeth Symons resigned as secretary-general of the Association of First Division Civil Servants

COUNTRIES OF THE WORLD
Afghanistan – Taliban rebels seized Kabul on 26–27 September, driving out government forces; a six-member interim ruling council was set up
Armenia – President Levon Ter-Petrosyan re-elected on 23 September; ballot followed by accusations of corruption and demonstrations
Bosnia – elections for a three-member presidency, national House of Representatives and assemblies for the Srpska Republika and Muslim-Croat Federation on 14 September; President Izetbegovic won most votes in presidential election, followed by Mladen Ivanic (Serb) and Kresimir Zubak (Croat)
Gambia – Col. Yayah Jammeh elected president on 27 September in first ballot since 1994 coup
Greece – general election on 22 September won by Pasok party; Costas Simitis reappointed Prime Minister
Grenada – Governor-General now Sir Daniel Williams, GCMG
Japan – Prime Minister Hashimoto dissolved the Diet on 27 September and called a general election for 20 October
Madagascar – President Zafy resigned on 5 September after his impeachment was confirmed; Prime Minister Ratsirahonana assumed presidential responsibilities
Thailand – Prime Minister Banharn Silpa-Archa resigned on 21 September and a general election was called

EVENTS – SEPTEMBER 1996

3–4. US aircraft and warships launched cruise missiles against Iraqi targets in southern Iraq. The air exclusion zone was extended from the 32nd to the 33rd parallel. **5.** The RFU reached an agreement with the other home rugby unions which saved the Five Nations Championship. **8.** Kurdish refugees fled to Iran following the capture of the towns of Degala and Koi Sanjak by the Iraqi government-backed Kurdistan Democratic Party (KDP). **9.** The KDP captured the city of Sulaimaniya. **16.** Roderick Wright resigned as the Roman Catholic bishop of Argyll and the Isles after going into hiding with a woman from his diocese; he was later revealed to be the father of a 15-year-old son by another woman. **19.** The Government abandoned plans to slaughter 147,000 cattle after the European Commission agreed to examine new scientific evidence which showed that BSE would die out naturally by 2001. **23.** Ten tons of explosives were found by police in a storage unit in Hornsey, north London. An IRA terrorist suspect was shot dead by police in a raid on a guesthouse in Hammersmith, west London, and five more suspects were detained in other raids in London. Four gunmen killed 21 people in a mosque in Pakistan in a wave of violence following the killing of Prime Minister Bhutto's estranged brother. **24.** China, France, Russia, the UK and the USA signed the Comprehensive Test Ban Treaty banning nuclear tests, although the treaty did not acquire legal status because of India's refusal to sign. **25–27.** Sixty-seven people died in clashes between Israeli security forces and Palestinians protesting against the opening of a tunnel near the Al Aqsa mosque in east Jerusalem. **28.** At Ascot, Frankie Dettori became the first jockey to win all seven races at a meeting.

OBITUARIES

September

3. Lord (Julian) Amery of Lustleigh, PC, former Conservative MP, junior minister and Minister of State, aged 77
   Robert (Bob) Brown, former Labour MP and junior minister, aged 75
5. Clem Thomas, rugby player and journalist, aged 67
13. Jane Baxter, film and stage actress, aged 87
14. Juliet Prowse, actress and dancer, aged 59
17. Spiro Agnew, vice-president of the USA 1969–73, aged 77
20. Paul Erdös, Hungarian-born mathematician, aged 83
21. Julius Silverman, former Labour MP, aged 90
23. Dorothy Lamour, American film actress, aged 81
23. Muhammad Najibullah, president of Afghanistan 1986–92, executed aged 49
28. Leslie Crowther, CBE, actor and comedian, aged 63